GB Rail Timetable

Sunday 11 December 2011 to Sund

Britain's national railway network and stations are owned by Network Ra
included in this Timetable, who work together closely to provide a co
opportunities. Details and identification codes are shown on the Train C

This Timetable contains rail services operated over the National Rai
Ireland, the Isle of Man, the Isle of Wight and the Channel Islands. Network Rail operates managed stations however the remainder are operated on their behalf by the Train Operating Companies. Details are shown in the Station Index. The Timetable Network Map shows the number of the individual table for each route.

Contents

YOUR FEEDBACK IS VALUABLE TO US

If you have any comments on the content of this book or feedback on how you feel it could be improved then please contact the Publications Manager by writing to;

Victoria Fox
Network Rail
Floor 4
Station House
Elder Gate
Milton Keynes
Buckinghamshire, MK9 1BB
Or e-mail: Victoria.Fox@NetworkRail.Co.Uk

Services on Public Holidays

Services will not operate on many parts of the rail network during Public Holidays and you are strongly advised to confirm your journey details if travelling around a holiday period. For more information visit www.nationalrail.co.uk/holidays

Engineering Work

It is sometimes necessary to carry out essential Engineering Work which means that services may be changed, particularly late at night or at weekends to allow this work to be carried out. Engineering Work is usually planned many weeks in advance and details of changes to train times can be obtained from the National Rail Enquiries website – www.nationalrail.co.uk/engineering

National Rail Conditions of Carriage

Details of the conditions against which all National Rail tickets are issued, including the conditions which apply to the carriage of luggage and cycles can be obtained from the National Rail Enquiries website – www.nationalrail.co.uk/nrcc

What's New?

Welcome to the GB Rail Timetable valid from Sunday 11 December 2011 to Sunday 13 May 2012.

Chiltern Railways

In September 2011 we launched our new Mainline service offering improved journey times - just 90 minutes between Birmingham Moor Street and London Marylebone. Our experience of running the new timetable means that we are making some further minor changes for December.

East Midlands Trains

On weekdays the 0610 St Pancras to Sheffield service will start at 0545 and run earlier throughout. The 0637 St Pancras to Sheffield service will call additionally at Wellingborough.

The following additional weekday services will run:

0656 Ambergate to Derby

1544 Lincoln to Newark North Gate

The following services will be extended:

1723 Lincoln to Grimsby will start at Newark North Gate at 1645

1825 Leicester to Nottingham will be extended to Lincoln

The 0645 Nottingham to S[illegible] at 0641 to provide a connection to the East Coast tra[illegible]

1725 Lincoln to Newark North Gate

1756 Newark to Lincoln

First Great Western

An additional direct service from Charlbury and Hanborough to London Paddington will operate on w[illegible]days as we s[illegible] maximise the customer benefits from the recent infrastructure upgrade on this route

[illegible] early morning weekday service will operate from Exeter St Davids to Par departing at 0628 calli[illegible] Dawlish, Teignmouth, Newton Abbot, Totnes, Ivybridge, Plymouth, Saltash, St Germans, Liskeard, Bodmin Parkway and Lostwithiel.

Sunday services will operate to Newquay with departures at the following times:

Departures from Par at 1018, 1331 and 1630

Departures from [illegible] 1510 and 1730

Connections have been improved at Liskeard between main line and Liskeard to Looe branch line services

National Express East Anglia

West Anglia

A new timetable will be introduced providing additional seating capacity on many routes.

Peak services between Cambridge and London will be speeded up by 8-9 minutes and certain services will be lengthened to 12 cars and formed of new Class 379 trains.

Peak services between London and Hertford East will run via Seven Sisters with limited stops.

Additional peak services will run between Broxbourne and London.

A new Stratford to Bishops Stortford local service will be introduced, increasing to a frequency of every 30 minutes during the course of this timetable, replacing the previous hourly Stratford to Stansted Airport service.

Great Eastern

Further additional capacity will be added to Great Eastern main line services. Some peak services will be lengthened from 8 to 12 cars and additional services will run from Ipswich (06.00) and Colchester Town (06.47) plus an additional off-peak service leaving Ipswich at 09.30 each running to London Liverpool Street. In the evening there will be a new service from London to Harwich International at 1932 which will form a convenient connection into the overnight Stena Line ship to the Hook of Holland.

The current gap in morning Sudbury branch line services will be filled by a new 0909 Marks Tey to Sudbury service and 0929 return.

Northern

Buckshaw Parkway station opened in October 2011. Located between Chorley and Leyland stations on the Manchester to Preston and Blackpool route (Table 82) it is served by three trains an hour in each direction, two Northern services and one First TransPennine Express.

From December 2011 the Preston – Ormskirk timetable (Table 99) will be revised to provide a more even, broadly 90 minute interval service and later last services in each direction.

Sherburn-in-Elmet, in the Vale of York, will be served by significantly more trains on the York – Selby /Hull route allowing later connections from York.

ScotRail

Due to the Olympic Games, ScotRail's timetable will run for one year, from 11 December 2011 – 8 December 2012. Additional services will include; two in each direction between Glasgow/Edinburgh – Inverness (on Sundays as well as every weekday); up to three services between Glasgow – Dundee; three more trains, each way, between Girvan – Ayr; and one peak Elgin – Inverness morning service. There will also be up to five more calls in each direction at Broughty Ferry.

Southern

Following infrastructure upgrades to enable longer trains to run, some trains will be extended up to 10 cars on the Sydenham to London Bridge route and extended up to 12 cars on the East Grinstead to London Bridge and Victoria route. Associated with this there are some minor changes to peak train services in the Metro area and on the Mainline

How to use this Timetable

Some tables are self-contained (such as Table 1 London–Shoeburyness) showing every train running between any two stations on the route. Train journey lengths vary from the under ¾ mile Stourbridge Town to Stourbridge Junction shuttle to the 773 mile Aberdeen to Penzance service. To show details of longer-distance services in a single table, short-distance services are omitted, these appearing in separate 'composite' tables.

WHICH TABLE?

General Layout of the Timetable

There are several ways of finding the correct table(s) for a journey. Tables start with the north bank of the Thames and radiate anti-clockwise around London as far as the south bank (Table 212, London-Faversham-Margate) with non-London tables (like the Cardiff Valleys) placed close to the appropriate London route. Internal Scottish routes follow from Table 216. Tables numbered 400-406 cover domestic Sleeper services. Once familiar with to this geographic layout, required tables can usually be found with relative ease, but there are more precise methods:

Using the Index

Look up your destination. If it appears in up to five tables, those tables are listed (for example Hilsea appears in Tables 156, 157, 158, 165 and 188). If it appears in six or more then there may be sub-divisions. If your destination is sub-divided in this way and your origin is NOT shown (for example Shipley is not shown under Lancaster) then look up the origin instead as it probably has fewer tables. Alongside the station name is shown a two character code indicating which operator is responsible for operating the facilities at that station (see also Train Operator pages).

Using the Timetable Network Map

If your journey is more complicated and involves several changes between tables, the Timetable Network Map will be very useful. For example, to plan a journey from North Berwick to Pontypridd one would not expect to find both in the same table. The map makes it clear that one has to change at Edinburgh and Cardiff and, as there is no through service between North Berwick and Pontypridd, allows one to look up possible routes, for example, via Crewe and Shrewsbury (Tables 65 and 131), Crewe and Birmingham (Tables 57 and 65) or York and Birmingham (Tables 51 and 57).

Using Route/Network Diagrams

For many tables a Route or Network Diagram is also provided. Route Diagrams are generally used for longer distance tables (for example Table 26) and show the route and stations served in diagrammatic form as well as the principal connecting links. Network Diagrams (for example Tables 152–154) are generally used where there is a dense network of shorter distance routes and show *all* stations and routes in the area concerned in diagrammatic form.

Using the Table

Having found the table you require make sure you look at the correct set of pages: Mondays to Fridays, Mondays to Saturdays, Saturdays, Sundays plus any relevant dates. Look for the station from which you will leave, read across until you find a suitable train, then read down to see when you will arrive at your destination.

↪ indicates the train is continued **in** a later column.

↩ indicates the train is continued **from** an earlier column.

Bold times denote through trains whilst light, *italic*, times are connections (Please read carefully the section on the "Connections" page). Check if there is a column-heading and if there is, refer to the foot of the table for an explanation.

Because of the large number of services that 'cross' Midnight, a Railway Timetable needs to be precise in the meaning of 'a day'. Trains starting their journeys before Midnight are shown towards the end of a table – but if you are looking for the 'last' train do not stop there, as there may be later ones at the start of the table!

A train crossing Midnight will be shown in full at the END of a table and any column heading denoting the day of the week applies to the day the train STARTS. For example a 2350 train headed 'SO' (see the general notes on inside front cover) commences 2350 Saturday and runs into Sunday. The train will also be shown at the front of the Sunday table with the times prior to Midnight shown with note 'p', e.g. 23p50, to indicate that they refer to the previous night.

Do not worry about the ambiguity as to which day Midnight itself belongs, for, to avoid this problem, all times skip from 2359 to 0001 and neither 0000 nor 2400 is ever used!

A two character code is shown at the head of each train column indicating which operator is providing the train service (see also Train Operator pages).

How to use this Timetable (continued)

Mileages between stations served (but not those shown for connecting purposes) are shown on the first page of each Timetable

Unique Timetable Number (as shown on the Insert Map and in the Index to Stations)

Stations served

Catering Information

Indicates the Operating Company of the train concerned

Indicates the days of the week (and in some cases dates) on which the Timetable operates

Principal stations on the route are shown in **bold**

For non-connecting stations only - indicates that additional services between these stations are included on other Timetables (see also below 'Route Diagrams')

Indicates the minimum interchange time (in minutes) that should be allowed when connecting between trains. Where no figure is shown, a minimum of 5 minutes should be allowed

Train runs on **S**aturdays **O**nly (see also page called 'References and Symbols used in this Timetable')

Seat Reservations symbols

Train time in ***italics*** indicate connecting times. The letter '**a**' alongside a connecting station indicates the arrival time at that station. Conversely, the letter '**d**' indicates the departure time

Table 97
Colne, Burnley, Accrington and Blackburn—Preston—Blackpool

Mondays to Saturdays

Miles	Miles		NT ◇ ⌶	NT ◇ ⌶	NT	NT	NT J		NT	NT ◇ ⌶	NT ◇ ⌶	NT	NT	NT ◇ ⌶	NT ◇ ⌶	NT SO ◇ K
0	—	**Colne** d			09 25							10 16				
2	—	Nelson d			09 31							10 22				
3½	—	Briefield d			09 34							10 25				
5½	—	**Burnley Central** 98 d			09 39							10 30				
6	—	Burnley Barracks 98 d										10 32				
—	—	Leeds 39 d	08 18							09 18				10 18		
—	—	Burnley Manchester Road 39 d	09 21							10 21				11 21		
7	—	Rose Grove d			09 44						10 36					
8½	—	Hapton d										10 39				
10	—	Huncoat d										10 42				
11½	—	Accrington d	09 31		09 51					10 31		10 46		11 31		
12½	—	Church & Oswaldtwistle d			09 54							10 49				
14½	—	Rishton d			09 58							10 52				
18	—	**Blackburn** a	09 39		10 03					10 39		10 57		11 39		
—	—	Manchester Victoria 94 a	*10 39*		*11 06*							*12 06*				
—	—	Clitheroe 94 d								*09 58*				*10 58*		
—	—	**Blackburn** d	09 39		10 03					10 39		10 59		11 39		
19½	—	Mill Hill (Lancashire) d			10 06							11 02				
20	—	Cherry Tree d			10 08							11 04				
21	—	Pleasington d										11 06				
26	—	Bamber Bridge d			10 16							11 13				
27½	—	Lostock Hall d			10 19							11 15				
30	—	**Preston 10** a	09 56		10 26					10 56		11 24		11 56		
—	—	London Euston 65 a	*12c 55*							*14c 75*				*14g 49*		
—	—	London Euston 65 d							*07f 40*			*08f 40*				
—	0	**Preston 10** d	09 58	10 02	10 27	10 32	10 38	.	10 50	10 58	11 02	11 26	11 45	11 58	12 02	12 21
35½	5½	Salwick d														
37½	7½	Kirkham & Wesham d			10 36				10 59			11 35	11 54			
41	—	Moss Side d										11 40				
43½	—	Lytham d			10 44							11 44				
44½	—	Ansdell & Fairhaven d			10 47							11 47				
46½	—	St Annes-on-the-Sea d			10 51							11 51				
48½	—	Squires Gate d			10 54							11 54				
49½	—	Blackpool Pleasure Beach d			10 57							11 57				
50	—	**Blackpool South** a			11 02							12 02				
—	14½	Poulton-le-Fylde d	10 14	10 18					11 07	11 14	11 18		12 02	12 14	12 18	
—	16½	Layton d							11 10				12 06			
—	17½	Blackpool North a	10 24	10 28		10 57	11 04		11 18	11 24	11 28		12 13	12 24	12 28	12 50

For general notes see front of timetable

J Mondays to Fridays until 1 November and from 31 March, also Saturdays until 2 November and from 1 March
K Until 2 November
c Saturdays arr. 10 minutes later
f Saturdays dep. 10 minutes earlier
g Saturdays arr. 1500

Intra-time letter indicating note at foot of page

For connecting stations only - indicates the Timetables on which the full service to and from the connecting station can be found (see also below under Route Diagrams)

A wavy line indicates that the train does not run on all dates included in the Timetable. In all such cases an additional headnote (in this case '**J**') will be used to provide full details

Train times indicate that the train stops at the station concerned. Arrival times are denoted by '**a**' against the station name and departure times by '**d**'. Where there is no time shown against a station then the train concerned does not serve that station

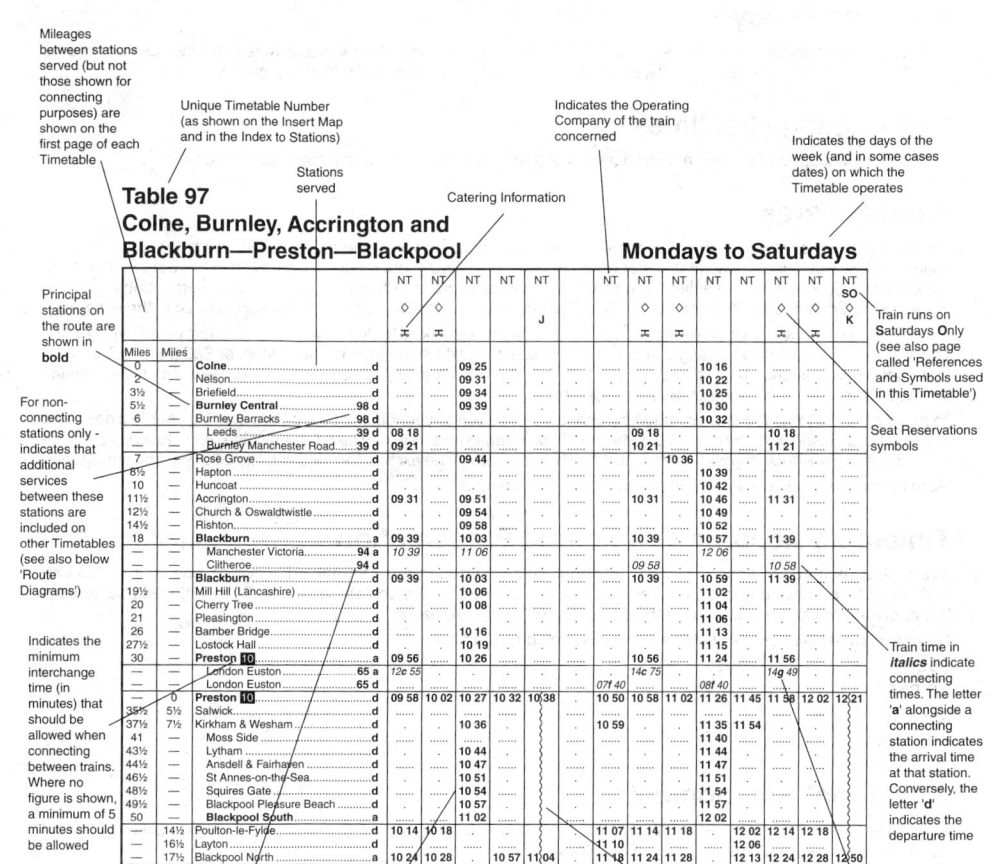

Route/Network Diagrams (see previous page): For many tables a Route/Network Diagram is also provided to show the routes and stations served in diagrammatic form. Where this is the case, a reference to the Route/Network Diagram will be provided at the top of each page of the Timetable concerned. Timetable numbers for connecting or alternative services will not be included within the Table itself; instead this will be indicated on the accompanying Route/Network Diagram

General Information

Smoking Policy

Smoking is not permitted on any National Rail service or in any station. In England and Wales, this includes all covered and uncovered concourses, ticket halls, platforms, footbridges and subways at station premises.

Left Luggage Facilities

Details of Left Luggage Facilities at individual stations are available at www.nationalrail.co.uk/stations

Penalty Fares

Penalty Fares are charged by Train Companies at some stations and on some trains. Where this is the case, warning notices will be displayed. Those stations at which Penalty Fares are in operation are indicated in the Station Index and the individual Table numbers section (see also Train Operator pages). Please be aware that at some stations where Penalty Fare Schemes are in place not all Train Operator services calling at that station are included in the scheme.

If you cannot produce a valid ticket for your entire journey when asked to do so, you may be charged a Penalty Fare. This will be either twice the full single fare to the next station at which the train is due to stop, or £20 (£50 on Transport for London services and stations, reducing to £25 if paid within 21 days), whichever is the greater. Any travel beyond the next station will be charged at the full single fare.

To avoid paying a Penalty Fare, you must purchase a valid ticket to your destination, before starting your journey. If the ticket office is closed and you cannot buy the ticket you need from a self service ticket machine, you must buy a Permit to Travel paying as much of your fare as possible. This permit must be exchanged for a valid ticket at the first opportunity.

More information is available at nationalrail.co.uk/penaltyfares.

Timetable Accuracy, Contents, Presentation

Every effort is made to ensure that the information contained in this Timetable is correct, however errors can still occur. If you have any questions or queries about the train services shown in this Timetable, please contact the appropriate operator shown in the Directory of Train Operators.

General comments about this publication should be addressed to:–

TSO,

PO Box 29,

Norwich,

NR3 1GN.

Additional Amendments

A facility Is available whereby details of any train service alterations introduced subsequent to the production of the GB Rail Timetable may be accessed through the Network Rail website

(see http:networkrail.co.uk). Follow the link to the "Timetables" on the home page. For up to date timetables, incorporating any changes to services please select the 'Route index / Timetable links' document link.

From time to time, further alterations may apply at short notice and details of these may be found at http://www.nationalrail.co.uk/service_disruptions/currentAndFuture.html.

Other National Rail Timetables

Regional and route specific Timetables are available from individual train companies. Please contact the relevant train company to request the latest version of the Timetable you require.

National Rail Enquiries offers an online 'Pocket Timetable' service which gives you the flexibility to create a customised Timetable based around your origin and destination, your own time requirements and the days of the week that you intend to travel. Visit www.nationalrail.co.uk/pockettimetables for more details.

Connections

Bold type times in vertical columns in the timetable show direct trains. In a few cases, where one train overtakes another, the times appear in more than one column and arrow symbols indicate where the train continues in the Timetable.

Many more journey opportunities are possible by changing trains. To help plan such journeys, times in light italic type are shown in some of the Timetables for departures (if the time is earlier than the bold type times for the station below in the column at which you should change trains) or arrivals (if they are later than the bold type times for the station above in the column at which you should change trains).

Where light type italic times are not shown you may have to refer to other tables in the book to work out your connecting services. In order to find the right table to reference, first look at the Route/Network Diagram that covers the table you are working from. This will show the principal connecting links and their table references, which may include the destination you are searching for. If your journey is not covered, follow the advice given on 'How to use this Timetable' under the headings 'Using the Timetable Network Map' and 'Using the Index'.

Connections between trains cannot be guaranteed. The nature of the integrated operation of railway passenger services means that to delay one train to await customers from a late running train arriving at a station may cause significant disruption to many other customers when they make connections at other stations along the route. Every endeavour is made to minimise the total disruption and particular attention is given to services operating infrequently and the last train services each day.

The aim of all Train Operating Companies is to run punctually; inevitably some disruption occurs from time to time. When planning a journey you may wish to consider the effects which any disruption could have and to allow some contingency margin when planning connections.

Minimum Interchange Times at Stations

Unless a connection is shown by times printed in light type, you should generally allow a minimum of five minutes between arrival and departure.

The exceptions to this rule are indicated by minimum interchange times (e.g. **15**) alongside the station name in the tables. In certain cases the minimum interchange time is different according to the Train Operators involved.

These are detailed below:-

STATION AND 'STANDARD' MINIMUM CONNECTIONAL ALLOWANCE (Minutes)		***EXCEPTIONS Showing the Train Operator(s) and minimum connectional allowance applicable***	
Barnham	5	*SN*	2
Bournemouth	5	*SW*	3
Brighton	10	*SN*	4
Cardiff Central	7	*AW*	3*
Clapham Junction	10	*SN*	5
Gatwick Airport	10	*SN*	5
Guildford	5	*GW*	4
Leatherhead	5	*SN*	3
London Blackfriars	3	SE	5
London Victoria	15	*SE, SN*	10
Luton	10	*FC*	4
Luton Airport Parkway	7	*FC*	4
Redhill	5	*SN*	3
St. Denys	5	*SW*	3
Southampton Central	5	*SN, SW*	4
Tulse Hill	3	FC	4
Wimbledon	6	*SN, FC*	5

Example

At Barnham a different minimum connectional allowance applies for Train Operator SN. This means that if your journey involves changing between two trains *both of which* are operated by SN, you need only allow 2 minutes. If, however, one or both trains are provided by any other Operator then the minimum of 5 minutes (as shown after the station name) applies.

* Applicable to Valley Lines services only (table 130).

Train Information

National Rail Enquiries

Timetable and Fares are available 24 hours a day at www.nationalrail.co.uk or, if you are on the move, at mobile.nationalrail.co.uk

National Rail Enquiries provides up-to-the-minute advice on all aspects of journey planning, fares and buying tickets, live train running updates and other useful information.

08457 48 49 50 24 Hours Daily

(calls may be recorded for training purposes)

0845 60 40 500 Welsh Language

0845 60 50 600 Textphone – 0600 - 2100 Daily

TrainTracker

For live train times for today and train Timetables for the next three months call TrainTracker™ on:

0871 200 49 50

Average calls to TrainTracker cost 10p a minute from a BT Landline. Charges from other operators may vary. Calls may be recorded for training purposes.

TrainTracker Text

For live departure and arrival times direct to your mobile text station name to TrainTracker™ Text on:

8 49 50

TrainTracker texts cost 25p for each successful response (plus usual text costs)

Train company numbers for disabled passengers requiring assistance:–

Company	Telephone	Textphone
Arriva Trains Wales	08453 003 005	0845 605 0600
c2c	01702 357640	08457 125 988
Chiltern Railways	08456 005 165	08457 078051
CrossCountry	0844 811 0125	0844 811 0126
East Coast	08457 225 225	18001 08457 225 225
East Midlands Trains	08457 125 678	18001 08457 125 678
Eurostar	08432 186 186	Not available
First Capital Connect	0800 058 2844	0800 975 1052
First Great Western	0800 197 1329/0845 600 5604	0800 294 9209
First Hull Trains	08450 710 222	08456 786 967
First TransPennine Express	0800 107 2149	0800 107 2061
Gatwick Express	0800 138 1016	0800 138 1018
Grand Central	0844 811 0072	0845 305 6815
Heathrow Connect	0845 678 6975	0800 294 9209
Heathrow Express	0845 600 1515	Not available
Island Line	0800 528 2100	0800 692 0792
London Midland	0800 0924260	0844 811 0134
London Overground	0845 601 4867	Not available
Merseyrail	0151 702 2071	0870 0552 681
National Express East Anglia	0800 028 28 78	0845 606 7245
Northern	0808 1561606	08456 045 608
ScotRail	0800 912 2 901	18001 0800 912 2 901
South West Trains	0800 52 82 100	0800 692 0792
Southeastern	0800 783 4524	0800 783 4548
Southern	0800 138 1016	0800 138 1018
Virgin Trains	08457 443366	08457 443367

Train Information (continued)

London Travel Information

0843 222 1234 | 24 hours (Daily) | www.tfl.gov.uk

Services to Europe on Eurostar via the Channel Tunnel

08432 186 186 | 0800-1900 (Daily) 0900-1700 (S+S) | www.eurostar.com

Ireland

NI Railways 028 90 66 6630 | 0700-2000 (M-F) 0800-1800 (S+S) | www.translink.co.uk
Iarnrod Eireann (IE) (Irish Rail) 00 353 183 66 222 | www.irishrail.ie

Transport Direct

Plan journeys by car, bus, train, tube, coach, plane at www.transportdirect.info. Transport Direct is the first door-to-door on-line journey planner for Great Britain.

It's free to use; simply enter your departure point, destination and time of travel and Transport Direct will offer a number of options by different modes of transport - both public and private. Journey plans are presented as step-by-step instructions supported by detailed maps including bus stops and other points of interest to travellers. Tickets for rail and coach journeys can be booked via retail web sites without the need to re-enter journey details. Transport Direct includes live travel news for rail and car users. The car journey planner gives route information that takes account of historical traffic level data, offering the user the choice to travel at a different time, or choose public transport. When travelling by public transport, users can adjust their expected walking speed to plan rail, coach and bus connections more efficiently. You can also access Transport Direct via mobile phone and PDA to find out when your next train is due or to check road conditions.

Bus Information in Great Britain

For details of buses within Greater London ring the Transport for London line: 0843 222 1234 (24-hours).

Bus information for the rest of Great Britain is available nationally from 'Traveline' which is run by local authorities and bus operators. There are regional call centres all of which share the same telephone number and any centre will switch calls pertaining to another part of the country through to the relevant centre. Alternatively codes for reaching the appropriate centre direct can be obtained from www.traveline.info/powercodes.html

The number is 0871 200 22 33 (calls from landlines cost 10p per minute) and centres are open at least between the hours of 0800 and 2000 daily (except Christmas Day and Boxing Day). Website: www.traveline.info

PlusBus

PlusBus is an easy-to-use add-on to your train ticket which gives unlimited bus travel on most bus services around the whole urban area of your origin or destination town or city. ***PlusBus*** is available to many towns and cities across Great Britain with season tickets also available for most ***PlusBus*** destinations. For more information visit www.plusbus.info

Traintaxi

Taxi symbols on the Station index pages

Where appears against any station that has sub-entries, there will be a taxi rank outside the station from which taxis should usually be available. This also applies to Basingstoke, Bournemouth, Chelmsford, Cheltenham, Colchester, Lincoln, Middlesbrough, Milton Keynes, Northampton, Sunderland and Swindon.

Where appears against any other station, there will be a taxi rank or a cab office within 100 metres of the station. However, you are advised to check availability before travelling, and to pre-book if necessary. Indication of a rank or office is no guarantee of cabs being available.

Visit **www.traintaxi.co.uk** for information on cab firms serving **all** train, tram, metro and underground stations in Great Britain, and all bus and ferry destinations listed in this *GB Rail Timetable*.

Rail Travel for Disabled Passengers

All train operators are able to carry disabled passengers and can provide additional assistance for boarding and alighting and information during train journeys.

If using a wheelchair, it is recommended that passengers book assistance in advance as space on trains for wheelchair users is limited.

National Rail produce a booklet called 'Rail Travel Made Easy' which details the provisions Train Companies make for disabled people. The booklet is available from major stations or can be obtained by writing to: Rail Travel Made Easy, PO Box 11631, Laurencekirk AB30 9AA. Alternatively, you can download a copy by visiting www.nationalrail.co.uk/passenger_services/disabled_passengers/

You can also see what facilities and services are available at stations throughout the UK, including stop-free routes by visiting www.nationalrail.co.uk

Seat Reservations, Luggage, Cycles and Animals

Seat Reservations

You can reserve seats on any train marked [R], [R], ◇ or ✗ at the top of the column in the timetable pages. Further detailed information is shown in the Directory of Train Operators.

Reservations can normally be made from about 12 weeks in advance of the day of travel, up to about 2 hours before the train departs from its start point, or, for early morning trains, up to 1600 hours the previous evening.

Where and How to Reserve

You can reserve either by visiting a station identified in the Index pages by ◇, or a rail appointed travel agent or by calling one of the telephone booking facilities listed on each Train Operator's page. Telephone reservations are only available when made in conjunction with purchasing a ticket. When reserving you will need to tell your station or agent:

1. Starting and finishing point of your journey.
2. Date of travel (Take care if your departure is soon after Midnight – see "How to use this Timetable").
3. Departure time of train.
4. Number of seats required.
5. You may be able to specify other preferences such as facing or back to direction of travel*, window seat, seat in Restaurant Car where available, seats round a table or airline style with fold down table where available.
   *Customers should note that some trains reverse their direction of travel during the journey.
6. First Class or Standard Accommodation (if you do not specify class of travel it will be assumed that you require Standard Accommodation).

Names on Seats

Your name can be included in your seat reservation label or on the electronic display above your seat, if you wish, when travelling First Class on some East Coast, East Midlands Trains and National Express East Anglia services or First and Standard Class on CrossCountry, First Great Western, First TransPennine Express, ScotRail and Virgin Trains services.

Connecting Reservations

If your journey involves changing between trains on which seats are reservable (including journeys crossing London or other major cities), through reservations on both services are available.

Children

Seats may be reserved for children, however, for a child under 5 years of age a seat may be reserved only if an appropriate child rail ticket is held.

Reservations Recommended

Trains shown [R] at the head of a column in the Timetable pages are expected to be very busy. Seat Reservations are therefore recommended for a comfortable journey and will consequently be provided free of charge to holders of valid travel tickets.

Seat Reservations, Luggage, Cycles and Animals (continued)

Reservations Compulsory

On trains shown 🅁 at the head of a column, Seat Reservations are compulsory and are available free of charge. Passengers may not be able to board the train if they do not have a reservation.

Trains For Weekends Away

Most long distance services after 1400 on Fridays and on Saturday mornings, also trains arriving in London on Sunday evenings and Monday mornings can be extremely busy.

Customers are advised to reserve seats in advance if planning to travel at these times.

Travelling at Peak Holiday Periods

Trains are usually extremely busy immediately before and after Bank Holidays and in some cases access to trains is only by reservation and/or boarding pass. Customers are advised to reserve seats as early as possible.

Cycles by Train

You can take your cycle on many National Rail services, however reservations may be required and restrictions may apply for peak services. Folded cycles can be carried on most train services. More information is shown in the Directory of Train Operators, the National Rail 'Cycling by Train' leaflet and online at www.nationalrail.co.uk/cycling. Cycle storage is also available at many stations.

Weekend First

Weekend First is available on many CrossCountry, East Coast*, East Midlands Trains, First Great Western*, First TransPennine Express*, Grand Central*, National Express East Anglia, ScotRail*, South West Trains* and Virgin Trains services on Saturdays, Sundays and Bank Holidays. If you hold a ticket for travel in Standard Class, you may be able to upgrade to the added comfort of First Class Accommodation on payment of an additional fare. On some services a 'Weekend First' ticket allows you to upgrade to First Class at weekends and Bank Holidays. Holders of Annual Gold Cards may also be able to upgrade on off-peak services for a small amount. Costs vary depending on the journey you are making.

*may only be purchased on trains at time of travel

More information can be found at www.nationalrail.co.uk/firstclass

Customers' Luggage and Animals

Customers may take up to 3 items of personal luggage free of charge; this includes 2 large items (such as suitcases or rucksacks) and 1 item of smaller hand luggage (such as a briefcase). Folded prams, non-folding prams and carrycots are also able to be carried. Full details of the free allowances are available at stations. Excess luggage and certain more bulky items (such as skis) may be carried, subject to available space, at an extra charge. On Gatwick Express services, bulky items such as skis are conveyed free in the luggage van. There is plenty of space on board for other luggage.

Passengers may take dogs, cats and other small animals (maximum two per passenger), free of charge and subject to certain conditions, provided they do not endanger or inconvenience other passengers or staff.

ScotRail allows dogs to accompany able-bodied passengers in Sleeper Services subject to a charge for cleaning of the compartment. The booking must be First Class, Standard Class with two people travelling together, or a Solo supplement is payable for exclusive use of a twin-berth cabin. First Great Western do **not** allow animals (except Guide Dogs) to travel in Sleeper Accommodation. There is no charge for Guide Dogs.

More information can be found at www.nationalrail.co.uk/luggageandanimals

Directory of Train Operators

The following pages contain details of the Train Operating Companies who operate trains included in this Timetable and indicate the services they provide.

Each operator is identified by a two character code listed below. The codes are displayed in the index alongside the station name indicating which operator is responsible for operating the facilities at that station. The code is also shown at the head of each train column in the timetable pages indicating which operator is providing the train service.

18 stations are the operating responsibility of Network Rail and are shown in the index by the code NR and information about Network Rail is shown at the end of the Train Operating Company pages.

Page No	Train Company Name	Code
13	Arriva Trains Wales	AW
14	c2c	CC
15	CrossCountry	XC
16	Chiltern Railways	CH
17	Devon & Cornwall Railway	DC
18	East Coast	GR
19	East Midlands Trains	EM
20	First Capital Connect	FC
21	First Great Western	GW
22	First Hull Trains	HT
23	First TransPennine Express	TP
24	Gatwick Express	GX
25	Grand Central	GC
26	Heathrow Connect	HC
27	Heathrow Express	HX
28	Island Line	IL
29	London Midland	LM
30	London Overground	LO
31	Merseyrail	ME
32	National Express East Anglia	LE
33	North Yorkshire Moors Railway	NY
34	Northern	NT
35	ScotRail	SR
36	South West Trains	SW
37	Southeastern	SE
38	Southern	SN
39	Virgin Trains	VT
40	West Coast Railway Co.	WR

Arriva Trains Wales

AW

ADDRESS	St Mary's House 47 Penarth Road Cardiff CF10 5DJ Telephone: 0845 6061 660 Website: www.arrivatrainswales.co.uk Email: customer.relations@arrivatrainswales.co.uk
MANAGING DIRECTOR	Tim Bell
RESERVATIONS AND TICKETS BY TELEPHONE AND ONLINE	Tickets may be booked in advance and seats reserved, by telephone, from the following numbers (0800–2000 daily): 0870 9000 773 for Great Britain, tickets and reservations. 0870 9000 767 for Group and 0845 300 3005 for Disabled travel arrangements. Textphone 0845 758 5469 Please allow 5 days for delivery.
RESERVATION DETAILS	All seat reservations are free to ticket holders.
CATERING ON TRAINS	At-seat catering service of cold snacks, sandwiches and hot and cold drinks on all services marked ⚻, for all or part of the journey. Complimentary meal service for first class and a counter service of hot and cold snacks for standard class on trains with ⊠. Train catering on Arriva Trains Wales services is provided by: At Seat Catering (2003) Ltd St Mary's House 47 Penarth Road Cardiff CF10 5DJ
CYCLES	See Cycling by Train leaflet, a guide to Arriva Trains Wales services for full details.
LOST PROPERTY	Contact Arriva Trains Wales Customer Relations on 0845 6061 660.
TRAIN SERVICE UPDATE	Please consult our website at www.arrivatrainswales.co.uk for real time service updates.
PENALTY FARES	Penalty Fares are not in force on Arriva Trains Wales services. Customers are reminded that they must have a valid ticket when boarding at a staffed station, if not it will be necessary to charge you the full single/return fare for the journey.
DISABLED PEOPLE'S PROTECTION POLICY	Address as above.
CODE OF PRACTICE FOR COMMENTS, COMPLAINTS AND SUGGESTIONS	Address as above.

ALCOHOL POLICY

Arriva Trains Wales have prohibited the consumption of alcohol on all services and stations between Caerphilly - Rhymney, and Pontypridd - Treherbert/Merthr Tydfil/Aberdare

c2c

A member of the National Express Group plc

ADDRESS	2nd Floor Cutlers Court 115 Houndsditch London EC3A 7BR Telephone: 0845 601 4873 Fax: 01603 214517 Website: www.c2c-online.co.uk
MANAGING DIRECTOR	Julian Drury
RESERVATIONS AND TICKETS BY TELEPHONE AND ONLINE	Tickets may be booked in advance by telephoning 08457 44 44 22 - 0800 to 2000 daily.
RESERVATION DETAILS	Reservations are not available.
CATERING ON TRAINS	Not available.
CYCLES	Cycles can be taken on off-peak trains free-of-charge when accompanied by a fare-paying passenger, subject to space availability. Bicycles are not permitted, Mondays to Fridays on services that arrive in London between 0715 and 0945, or those which leave London between 1630 and 1840. To comply with safety regulations, all cycles, with the exception of folding cycles which are completely enclosed in a container or case throughout the journey, must be conveyed in the designated area on trains. During engineering work, cycles cannot be accommodated on replacement bus services.
LOST PROPERTY	Telephone: 01702 357 699
TRAIN SERVICE UPDATE	Up to date train running information is available on the c2c website www.c2c-online.co.uk, the National Rail Enquiries website at nationalrail.co.uk or on BBC Ceefax page 433.
PENALTY FARES	If you travel without a valid ticket you may be charged a penalty fare of £20 or twice the full single fare, whichever is the greater.
DISABLED PEOPLE'S PROTECTION POLICY	Available from:- Customer Relations c2c FREEPOST ADM3968 Southend SS1 1ZS Telephone: 0845 601 4873 - 0830 to 1700 Monday to Friday
CODE OF PRACTICE FOR COMMENTS, COMPLAINTS AND SUGGESTIONS	Available from Customer Relations at above address or telephone 0845 601 4873.

CrossCountry

XC

ADDRESS	CrossCountry 5th Floor, Cannon House, 18 Priory Queensway, Birmingham B4 6BS Telephone: 08447 369 123 Textphone: 0121 200 6420 Fax: 0121 200 6005 Website: www.crosscountrytrains.co.uk Email: customer.relations@crosscountrytrains.co.uk
MANAGING DIRECTOR	Andy Cooper
RESERVATIONS AND TICKETS BY TELEPHONE AND ONLINE	On-line at crosscountrytrains.co.uk is the easiest way to purchase your tickets. If you prefer, you can also make telephone bookings on 0844 811 0124 between 0800 and 2200 daily. Parties of 10 or more should contact Group Travel on 0871 244 2388 between 0800 and 1800 weekdays
RESERVATION DETAILS	You are strongly advised to make a seat reservation in advance; especially when travelling on trains shown with the 🅁 symbol in timetables. Seat reservations are free of charge.
CATERING ON TRAINS	Catering is available on most CrossCountry trains. In First Class, on weekdays between 0630 and 1830 customers can enjoy complimentary light refreshments including hot and soft drinks, served at seat. In Standard Class we offer a range of quality snacks, sandwiches and hot drinks plus soft and alcoholic beverages between 0600 and 2000. For more information on the Nottingham - Cardiff and Birmingham - Stansted Airport routes please refer to our timetables.
CYCLES	We do not charge to carry your cycle. However, as space is very limited you will need to reserve in advance on nearly all our services. Please enquire before travelling. We are unable to accept powered cycles, tricycles, tandems or trailers on any of our services.
LOST PROPERTY	Contact Customer Relations on 08447 369 123 between 0800 and 2000 Monday to Saturday; or email lost.property@crosscountrytrains.co.uk
TRAIN SERVICE UPDATE	Details of major disruption to services and weekend engineering work are summarised on BBC Ceefax and BBCi on digital TV. Live travel updates are available on-line at crosscountrytrains.co.uk and details of all service disruptions can be found at nationalrail.co.uk/disruption/
PENALTY FARES	A Penalty Fares scheme is not currently in operation on CrossCountry trains. Visit crosscountrytrains.co.uk for the most up to date information. Should you board one of our trains without a valid ticket you will be charged the full Single or Return fare for your journey unless the ticket office is closed and a self-service ticket machine is not available.
DISABLED PEOPLE'S PROTECTION POLICY	We provide a Journey Care service for the disabled, elderly and infirm. By phoning our team on 0844 811 0125, textphone 0844 811 0126, beforehand we will, where possible, arrange help for your journey. Our Disabled People's Protection Policy is available on-line at crosscountrytrains.co.uk
CODE OF PRACTICE FOR COMMENTS, COMPLAINTS AND SUGGESTIONS	Copies of our Complaints Handling Procedure and Passenger's Charter are available on-line at crosscountrytrains.co.uk

Chiltern Railways

CH

ADDRESS	Customer Services Banbury ICC Merton Street Banbury Oxfordshire OX16 4RN Telephone: 08456 005 165 (Mondays to Fridays 0830-1730) Fax: 01926 729 914 Website: www.chilternrailways.co.uk
MANAGING DIRECTOR	Rob Brighouse
RESERVATIONS AND TICKETS BY TELEPHONE AND ONLINE	Telephone 08456 005 165 (0700-2000, 7 days a week)
RESERVATION DETAILS	Reservations can be made for travel in the Business Zone of our Mainline Silver trains. Reservations are not available on any other services.
CATERING ON TRAINS	Our Mainline Silver trains offer an on-board kitchen serving drinks and freshly cooked bacon-rolls and pastries on morning trains, Mondays to Fridays. An at-seat catering service is available on Mondays to Fridays on most other Mainline trains arriving in London before 1345 and leaving London between 0700 and 1445. If your train does not offer catering do not forget that our main stations offer excellent catering facilities. For more details check our website. Please allow enough time to purchase your refreshments before boarding your train.
CYCLES	Subject to space being available, and at the discretion of our staff, you can take your bike (except tandems) on any Chiltern Railways train on Saturdays, Sundays or Public Holidays. On Mondays to Fridays you can also use most of our trains. The only exceptions are our busiest peak hour services. For the safety and comfort of all our passengers bikes are not allowed at any point during the journey on any train: • Arriving London Marylebone or Birmingham Moor Street from 0745 to 1000 • Leaving London Marylebone or Birmingham Moor Street from 1630 to 1930 On our Mainline Silver trains you must put your bike in the special storage area at one end of the train. We are sorry, but bikes cannot be taken on rail replacement buses at any time. There are no restrictions on folding bikes at any time, provided they are fully folded. For information about cycle storage facilities at our stations see our website. Cycles can be hired from just outside London Marylebone station. For information visit www.tfl.gov.uk/barclayscyclehire.
LOST PROPERTY	If we find any item of lost property, we will always do our best to contact the owner if they can be identified. Items can be collected from London Marylebone up to 3 months after they have been handed in - we charge a collection fee to cover our administration costs. If you lose something on one of our trains or stations you can report it by: * Using the online form on our website * Using a Lost Property Form available at any Chiltern Railways ticket office, and returning it to a member of Chiltern Railways Staff. * By phone, fax or post using the contact details below: **Phone:** 08456 005 165 **Fax:** 020 7333 3002 **Write to:** Chiltern Railways Lost Property Marylebone Station London NW1 6JJ. Lost Property Office Operating Hours: Mondays to Fridays 1200 to 2000. Please allow up to 2 weeks for processing lost items. If you do not hear from us in that period, you should assume the item has not been found.
TRAIN SERVICE UPDATE	Visit our website www.chilternrailways.co.uk for current train running information and details of changes to train times because of engineering work or other special events.
PENALTY FARES	If you do not have a valid rail ticket for the journey you are making, you will have to pay a Penalty Fare of £20 or twice the single fare, whichever is the greater, for the journey you are making on Chiltern Railways services. For full details write to the above address, or see our website.
DISABLED PEOPLE'S PROTECTION POLICY	Copies of the Disabled People's Protection Policy can be obtained from the above address, or from our website.
CODE OF PRACTICE FOR COMMENTS, COMPLAINTS AND SUGGESTIONS	If you have any comments, complaints or suggestions regarding Chiltern Railways services, please write to the address shown above or telephone 08456 005 165 (0830-1730 Mondays to Fridays), Fax 01926 729 914. Alternatively you can use the 'Contact Us' option on our website.

Devon & Cornwall Railway

ADDRESS

MANAGING DIRECTOR

RESERVATIONS AND TICKETS BY TELEPHONE AND ONLINE

RESERVATION DETAILS

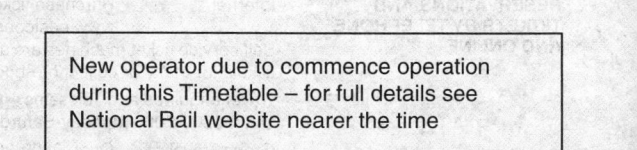

CATERING ON TRAINS

CYCLES

LOST PROPERTY

TRAIN SERVICE UPDATE

PENALTY FARES

DISABLED PEOPLE'S PROTECTION POLICY

CODE OF PRACTICE FOR COMMENTS, COMPLAINTS AND SUGGESTIONS

New operator due to commence operation during this Timetable – for full details see National Rail website nearer the time

East Coast

GR

ADDRESS	Freepost RSRJ-LJCX-GHST Plymouth PL4 6AB Telephone: 08457 225 333 Open 0700-2200 Monday to Sunday Fax: 0191 227 5986 Website: www.eastcoast.co.uk Email: customers@eastcoast.co.uk
MANAGING DIRECTOR	Karen Boswell
RESERVATIONS AND TICKETS BY TELEPHONE AND ONLINE	Internet — Purchase tickets via the internet 24 hours a day at www.eastcoast.co.uk Self service ticket machines are available at all East Coast stations. Purchase tickets for today or collect pre-booked tickets. Travel enquiries and Telesales 08457 225 225 Open 0800-2000 Monday-Saturday, 1000-2000 Sunday Group Travel — Open 0800-2000 Monday-Friday Discounts may be available for groups of 10 or more people. Assisted Travel — Open 0800-2000 Monday-Saturday, 1000-2000 Sunday Web support — 0800-2000 Monday to Saturday, 1000-2000 Sunday The minimum transaction is £10. Please allow 7 days from the time of booking for tickets to reach you through the post.
RESERVATION DETAILS	Seat Reservations can usually be made on any East Coast train up to ten weeks in advance. They are available to any ticket holder upon request, and are compulsory with some ticket types. Only one reservation can be made per single journey.
CATERING ON TRAINS	Passengers travelling in First Class will receive complimentary food and drink on board. For shorter journeys, you will be offered non-alcoholic drinks and snacks, while on longer trips you can look forward to something a little more substantial. Passengers in Standard Class can enjoy a wide range of refreshments from our caféBAR. An at-seat trolley service will also be available on selected services.
CYCLES	Bicycles are welcome on East Coast trains. A reservation must be made and bookings are subject to space being available. Reservations can be made by calling 08457 225 225 or at any East Coast ticket office.
LOST PROPERTY	If you lose something on a East Coast train or at a station please speak to a member of staff or contact us on 08457 225 333. Please note that charges are normally made for returning items of lost property and that we are unable to forward items of lost property on train services.
TRAIN SERVICE UPDATE	Visit www.eastcoast.co.uk or call National Rail Enquiries on 08457 48 49 50 (calls may be recorded for training purposes).
PENALTY FARES	East Coast does not operate a Penalty Fares scheme. However, you should always purchase a ticket valid for travel before you board any East Coast service as only full fare tickets are sold on our trains. The only exception being Disabled Railcard holders who will be sold appropriate discounted tickets on-board.
DISABLED PEOPLE'S PROTECTION POLICY	A copy of our DPPP can be obtained free of charge from the address at the top of this page. Our Assisted Travel Team can help you plan your journey and organise tickets, assistance and Seat Reservations. To ensure the best possible levels of assistance we recommend that you contact us no later than 1800 the day before you intend to travel. Telephone 08457 225 225 or textphone 18001 08457 225 225* (open 0800-2000 Monday-Saturday, 1000-2000 Sunday). * Please note that this number should only be used to contact the Assisted Travel Team. For all other enquiries please telephone 08457 225 225.
CODE OF PRACTICE FOR COMMENTS, COMPLAINTS AND SUGGESTIONS	Our Passenger's Charter is available from all East Coast stations or from our website www.eastcoast.co.uk. All correspondence should be sent using the address at the top of this page.

East Midlands Trains

EM

ADDRESS	East Midlands Trains Prospect Place Millennium Way Pride Park Derby DE24 8HG Telephone: 08457 125 678 Website: www.eastmidlandstrains.co.uk Email: getintouch@eastmidlandstrains.co.uk
MANAGING DIRECTOR	Tim Shoveller
RESERVATIONS AND TICKETS BY TELEPHONE AND ONLINE	Buy your tickets online at eastmidlandstrains.co.uk. You can buy tickets for all rail journeys (within Great Britain) with us. Alternatively call 08457 125 678 between 0800-2000 (7 days a week).
RESERVATION DETAILS	Seat Reservations on East Midlands Trains services are free. Just book in advance when you buy your ticket. We advise that you always make a reservation, as seats cannot be guaranteed without one. On our Local Services reservations are available on the Liverpool to Norwich services.
CATERING ON TRAINS	On our East Midlands London Services (to/from St Pancras International), we offer a range of delicious food options, plus snacks and hot and cold drinks. A trolley service is available on selected East Midlands Local Services (denoted by a symbol within the Timetable).
CYCLES	Two bicycles per train are accepted for free on all East Midlands Trains services; however reservations must be made in advance on reservable Services subject to availability.
LOST PROPERTY	Please allow a minimum of 24 hours for the items to be received at a lost property office. If your item is located you may be charged for the return of it and will be advised of this cost. To enquire about lost property, please call our Lost Property office, ideally between the hours of 1000 and 1600 Monday to Saturday on 0115 9576525.
TRAIN SERVICE UPDATE	Details of services and real time running information, including travel alerts by email are available through our website. Visit www.eastmidlandstrains.co.uk. Alternatively, call National Rail Enquiries on 08457 48 49 50 (calls may be recorded for training purposes).
PENALTY FARES	You should always buy a ticket in advance of boarding your train. Penalty Fares may be in operation on your service.
DISABLED PEOPLE'S PROTECTION POLICY	We aim to make travelling with us accessible to all our customers. If you require assistance in travelling, have special needs or mobility problems please call our team on 08457 125 678 option 3 to arrange help for your journey. A text direct service is also available on 18001 08457 125 678 (for people with hearing problems).
CODE OF PRACTICE FOR COMMENTS, COMPLAINTS AND SUGGESTIONS	Our Customer Relations team is available to receive your comments, complaints or suggestions. Please write to Customer Relations at the above address, or email getintouch@eastmidlandstrains.co.uk or call us on 08457 125 678 (option 5, 3 and 2)

First Capital Connect

FC

A member of the First Rail Division

ADDRESS

Freepost, RRBR-REEJ-KTKY
First Capital Connect
Customer Relations Department
PO Box 443
Plymouth PL4 6WP
Telephone: 0845 026 4700 (open 7 days a week 0700-2200 with the exception of Christmas Day)
Fax: 0845 676 9904
Website: www.firstcapitalconnect.co.uk
Email: customer.relations.fcc@firstgroup.com

MANAGING DIRECTOR

Neal Lawson

RESERVATIONS AND TICKETS BY TELEPHONE AND ONLINE

First Capital Connect does not offer telesales, however tickets can be booked at www.firstcapitalconnect.co.uk

RESERVATION DETAILS

Reservations are not available.

CATERING ON TRAINS

None.

CYCLES

We welcome passengers with bicycles on services where they can be safely accommodated, however restrictions apply, bicycles cannot be carried on:

- trains that are scheduled to arrive at a London terminal between 0700 and 1000;
- trains that are scheduled to depart from a London terminal between 1600 and 1900;
- trains running between Drayton Park and Moorgate;
- services between Royston and Ely that depart or arrive at Cambridge between 0745 and 0845, with the exception of the 0715 and 0745 departures from King's Cross;
- replacement bus services unless stated otherwise in any associated publicity; and
- any train where a member of our staff asks you to remove your bicycle.
- Bicycles cannot be conveyed within Travelcard Zone 1 in any direction between the hours of 0700-1000 and 1600-1900 Monday to Friday

Compact, folding bicycles can be carried on any service at any time.

LOST PROPERTY

In order to trace lost property please contact our Customer Relations department on 0845 026 4700, between 0700 - 2200 Monday to Sunday.

TRAIN SERVICE UPDATE

For current train information call National Rail enquiries on 08457 48 49 50 (calls may be recorded for training purposes) or check our website at: www.firstcapitalconnect.co.uk/live-info

PENALTY FARES

First Capital Connect operates a Penalty Fares System. If you do not have a valid ticket or permit to travel, you will be liable to pay a penalty fare. This is £20 or twice the appropriate single fare to the next station stop, whichever is greater. This does not apply for travel from Crews Hill.

If you do not buy a ticket, you could also be prosecuted and this can lead to a Criminal Conviction.

DISABLED PEOPLE'S PROTECTION POLICY

Our Disabled People's Protection Policy is available from Customer Relations, and is also available on our website and available at all staffed stations. First Capital Connect operates a dedicated telephone and textphone service for disabled or mobility impaired customers, the contact details are:

Telephone: 0800 058 2844

Textphone: 0800 975 1052

These are available 0700 - 2200, Monday to Sunday, with the exception of Christmas Day.

CODE OF PRACTICE FOR COMMENTS, COMPLAINTS AND SUGGESTIONS

Our Passenger's Charter details our code of practice and is available from all staffed stations and from our Customer Relations Department. The Customer Relations Department will be happy to assist with any comments, complaints or suggestions and can be contacted using the contact details above.

First Great Western

GW

A member of the First Rail Division

ADDRESS

Milford House
1 Milford Street
Swindon SN1 1HL
Telephone: 01793 499400
Fax: 01793 499460
Website: www.firstgreatwestern.co.uk. On our website you can create and print your own personalised timetables, download complete timetable booklets, find departure and arrival times for specific journeys, buy tickets, obtain live timetable updates specific to individual stations, check any late alterations to our services, view promotions and contact us with your comments.

MANAGING DIRECTOR

Mark Hopwood

RESERVATIONS AND TICKETS BY TELEPHONE AND ONLINE

Tickets may be booked in advance using credit and debit cards and seats reserved by ringing **08457 000 125** (open 0700-2200 Mondays to Fridays and 0700-2100 Saturdays and Sundays). Allow at least 5 working days for postal delivery. A next day delivery can be arranged at £5 per transaction. Arrangements can be made for tickets to be collected from Fast Ticket machines (the credit or debit card used for purchase will be needed at many stations). For Group Travel call **08457 000 125**.

RESERVATION DETAILS

A seat reservation, free of charge, can be made at the time of purchasing your ticket. Additional reservations, including those made by season ticket holders, are subject to a £5 fee.

CATERING ON TRAINS

Most First Great Western high speed services offer an Express Café service with freshly brewed coffee, hot baguettes and paninis and a wide range of drinks and snacks.

A Travelling Chef is available on many weekday services, preparing meals and snacks to order for both First and Standard Class customers. On a small number of weekday services, a Pullman restaurant provides à la carte dining to First and Standard Class customers, subject to availability.

First Class customers also enjoy additional complimentary services:

- An at-seat trolley service offering light refreshments (available on most Monday to Friday services between 0700-1900), including hot and cold drinks and light snacks appropriate to the time of day. The trolley also offers a range of items for sale from our Express Café.
- At the weekend and on weekdays after 1900, complimentary refreshments are available from the Express Cafe on production of valid travel tickets.

CYCLES

First Great Western welcomes customers with bicycles on services where they can be safely accommodated. However it is not possible to carry bicycles on some services particularly during peak periods. For full details of when bicycles cannot be carried or when reservations are required, please visit our website or pick up a leaflet at any of our staffed stations.

LOST PROPERTY

Customers who have left property on First Great Western services should contact our Customer Services team on **08457 000 125**.

TRAIN SERVICE UPDATE

For current train information including details of engineering work please visit our website: www.firstgreatwestern.co.uk

PENALTY FARES

These operate on most of our services. A penalty fare of £20 or twice the appropriate single fare to the next station stop (whichever is the greater) will be charged to anybody who is unable to produce a valid ticket or other authority when required to do so. For further information, pick up a leaflet about Penalty Fares from any staffed station.

DISABLED PEOPLE'S PROTECTION POLICY

Available from Customer Services Team
First Great Western
PO Box 313
Plymouth PL4 6YD
Tel: 08457 000 125
Email: fgwfeedback@firstgroup.com
Opening hours 0700-2200 daily

Customers requiring assistance should contact 0800 197 1329 (18001 0800 197 1329 textphone service), if possible giving 24 hours notice of travel plans.

CODE OF PRACTICE FOR COMMENTS, COMPLAINTS AND SUGGESTIONS

Your views leaflets and copies of the Passenger's Charter are available to download from our website www.firstgreatwestern.co.uk, at all staffed First Great Western stations or alternatively from the Customer Services Team at the address above.

First Hull Trains

ADDRESS	First Hull Trains Customer Services Freepost RLYY-XSTG-YXCK 4th Floor Europa House 184 Ferensway Hull HU1 3UT Telephone: 08456 76 99 05 Website: www.hulltrains.co.uk Email: customer.services@hulltrains.co.uk
MANAGING DIRECTOR	Cath Bellamy
RESERVATIONS AND TICKETS BY TELEPHONE AND ONLINE	First Hull Trains tickets can be booked in advance and seats reserved by ringing 08450 710 222 (0700 to 2200 Monday to Friday and 0800 to 1900 Saturday and Sunday). Please allow five working days for delivery. Tickets on departure are available.
RESERVATION DETAILS	Seat Reservations are free for First and Standard Class ticket holders. Season Ticket holders may reserve seats at a cost of £2 for First Class and £1 for Standard Class.
CATERING ON TRAINS	First Hull Trains provides a buffet on all services, and a comprehensive catering package for First Class passengers. Catering is subject to availability and may be limited when services are disrupted by engineering works or Bank Holidays.
CYCLES	Cycles and tandems are carried free of charge, however, a reservation is compulsory. Please telephone 08450 710 222
LOST PROPERTY	Please contact Customer Services.
TRAIN SERVICE UPDATE	Available at www.hulltrains.co.uk, or by telephone on 08450 710222.
PENALTY FARES	Penalty Fares are not in force on any Hull Trains Service
DISABLED PEOPLE'S PROTECTION POLICY	Available at: www.hulltrains.co.uk. Alternatively, a copy can be requested from Customer Services.
CODE OF PRACTICE FOR COMMENTS, COMPLAINTS AND SUGGESTIONS	First Hull Trains' Passenger's Charter is available at www.hulltrains.co.uk. Alternatively, any comments, complaints or suggestions can be sent to Customer Services

TP **First TransPennine Express** TP

A joint venture between First and Keolis

ADDRESS	7th Floor Bridgewater House 60 Whitworth Street Manchester M1 6LT Telephone: 08700 005151 Website: www.tpexpress.co.uk
MANAGING DIRECTOR	Vernon Barker
RESERVATIONS AND TICKETS BY TELEPHONE AND ONLINE	Reservations and tickets are available at www.tpexpress.co.uk and from all local staffed stations.
RESERVATION DETAILS	Seat Reservations are available at staffed stations. Seat Reservations for travel on First TransPennine Express services can be booked up until the day before travel. There is no charge for making a Seat Reservation if you have a rail ticket, or buy one at the same time.
CATERING ON TRAINS	Catering trolley services are available between 0700 and 1900 Monday to Friday on First TransPennine Express trains between Manchester Piccadilly and York, Manchester Piccadilly and Doncaster and Manchester Piccadilly and Preston. In addition to the above, all services between Manchester Airport, Manchester Piccadilly, Carlisle, Glasgow Central and Edinburgh convey a trolley service for the whole journey. This facility is also provided at weekends.
CYCLES	Customers may take their bicycle with them on First TransPennine Express trains at no extra cost. As space is limited to two bicycles per train, reservations for cycle space should be made at least 24 hours before the journey.
LOST PROPERTY	Customers who have left their property on First TransPennine Express trains or stations should contact 0845 600 1672.
TRAIN SERVICE UPDATE	For current train information call National Rail Enquiries on 0845 48 49 50 (calls may be recorded for monitoring purposes) or check our website at: www.tpexpress.co.uk/travelupdates
PENALTY FARES	Penalty Fares are not applicable on First TransPennine Express services. Customers are reminded that they must have a valid ticket when they travel. If not it will be necessary to charge the full Open Single or Return Fare for the journey.
DISABLED PEOPLE'S PROTECTION POLICY	Available online at www.tpexpress.co.uk and also from: Customer Relations First TransPennine Express ADMAIL 3878 Freepost Manchester M1 9YB Customers who have special needs and require customer assistance should contact us on 0800 107 2149. A textphone service is available on 0800 107 2061.
CODE OF PRACTICE FOR COMMENTS, COMPLAINTS AND SUGGESTIONS	Feedback leaflets and copies of the Passenger's Charter are available from all stations served by First TransPennine Express services or alternatively contact: Customer Relations, First TransPennine Express, ADMAIL 3878, Freepost, Manchester M1 9YB. Telephone: 0845 600 1671 Email: tpecustomer.relations@firstgroup.com

Gatwick Express

GX

ADDRESS	Southern Customer Services PO Box 3021 Bristol BS2 2BS Telephone: 0845 850 1530 Fax: 020 8929 8687 (Overseas: +44 208 9298687) Website: www.gatwickexpress.com Email: comments@southernrailway.com
MANAGING DIRECTOR	Chris Burchell
RESERVATIONS AND TICKETS BY TELEPHONE AND ONLINE	Reservations are not necessary on Gatwick Express services. For information and telesales please call 0845 850 1530. Tickets can also be purchased through our website at www.gatwickexpress.com
RESERVATION DETAILS	Reservations are not available.
CATERING ON TRAINS	An at-seat trolley service of drinks and light refreshments is available throughout the day.
CYCLES	Cycles and other bulky items such as skis are conveyed free in the luggage van of the Gatwick Expresss trains that do not run to/from Brighton. On the following trains, cycles are not permitted unless they are standard size folding cycles provided they are folded, Brighton depart 0632, 0640, 0656, 0715, 0730, 0744, Gatwick Airport depart 0705, 0720, 0735, 0750, 0805, 0820, London Victoria depart 1730, 1745, 1800, 1815, 1830, 1845.
LOST PROPERTY	Please call our Lost Property Office on 0845 850 15 30, select option 2.
TRAIN SERVICE UPDATE	Journey time is 30 minutes (35 minutes on Sundays). First Class and Express Class accommodation is available. From London Victoria at 0330, 0430, 0500 then every 15 minutes (15, 30, 45, 00 minutes past each hour) until 0001, 0030. From Gatwick Airport at 0435, 0520, 0550 then every 15 minutes (05, 20, 35, 50 minutes past each hour) until 0050, 0135. For current train information call 0845 850 15 30, select option 2.
PENALTY FARES	Penalty Fares will be applied for passengers without the correct ticket between Brighton and Gatwick Airport. The only passengers permitted to buy a ticket on the train are those travelling between Gatwick Airport and London Victoria in either direction.
DISABLED PEOPLE'S PROTECTION POLICY	Customers requiring assistance can book this prior to travel. Arrangements can be made by calling 0845 138 1016, textphone available 0800 138 1018. It is advisable to give 24 hours notice of travel plans, although customers will be given assistance if they arrive at the stations without notice but please allow a little extra time.
CODE OF PRACTICE FOR COMMENTS, COMPLAINTS AND SUGGESTIONS	Initially comments or issues requiring immediate attention should be addressed to any member of Gatwick Express staff on the train or platforms. Additionally Customer Comments forms and our Passenger's Charter are available at Gatwick Express ticket offices. Alternatively you may write to the address above.

Grand Central

GC

ADDRESS

Grand Central Railway Company Ltd
River House
17 Museum Street
York YO1 7DJ
Telephone: 0845 603 4852
Fax: 01904 466066
Website: www.grandcentralrail.com
Email: customer.services@grandcentralrail.com

MANAGING DIRECTOR

Tom Clift

RESERVATIONS AND TICKETS BY TELEPHONE AND ONLINE

Reservations are strongly advised on Friday afternoons, at weekends and Bank Holidays. Tickets and Seat Reservations are available in advance on our website www.grandcentralrail.com or over the phone by calling 0844 811 0071 (0800-2200 7 days a week). You can book tickets for all rail journeys within Great Britain with us. Tickets booked in advance can be sent by post (allow 5 working days), collected from self service ticket machines at certain stations or sent electronically by text message or email to print at home. Tickets can be purchased from the staff on the train at no extra cost. For group bookings, business travel and Carnet tickets please call 0845 603 4852

RESERVATION DETAILS

Complimentary Seat Reservations are available; these must be booked at least 24 hours in advance. To guarantee a seat we advise that you always make a reservation. Reservations are strongly advised on Friday afternoons, at weekends and Bank Holidays.

CATERING ON TRAINS

A buffet service is available on all services. In First Class customers enjoy complimentary light refreshments including hot and cold drinks, served at-seat. A complimentary light breakfast is served for customers travelling to or from London before 1000 Monday to Friday. Daily and weekend newspapers are provided. In Standard Class a buffet is available offering a selection of fair trade and locally sourced products, including hot, soft and alcoholic drinks, sandwiches, crisps and a large selection of other snacks. A standard class trolley service is provided on selected trains.

CYCLES

Normal sized cycles are conveyed free of charge subject to room being available, cycle reservations can be made by calling 0845 603 4852 or at any station ticket office. Passengers wishing to travel with larger sized cycles (Tandems etc) should call 0845 603 4852 in advance of travelling. During engineering work cycles cannot be accommodated on replacement bus services.

LOST PROPERTY

For trains travelling towards Sunderland or Bradford, please contact Northern Rail's Lost Property office on 0845 00 00 125. For trains travelling towards London, please contact King's Cross Lost Property Office on 0207 837 4334.

TRAIN SERVICE UPDATE

For live travel updates contact National Rail Enquiries on 08457 48 49 50, visit www.nationalrail.co.uk or call Train Tracker on 0871 200 4950. You can also text your station to 8 49 50 for live departures.

Details of weekend engineering work will be available on our website www.grandcentralrail.com or by calling 0845 603 4852.

PENALTY FARES

Grand Central does not operate a Penalty Fares System. Passengers can purchase tickets on the train at the same price as if purchased in advance or at stations.

DISABLED PEOPLE'S PROTECTION POLICY

Assisted travel can be booked by calling 0844 811 0072 (0800-2200 7 days a week) or using our text phone service on 0845 305 6815 please call at least 48 hours in advance. Our full Disabled People's Protection Policy is available on our website, by calling 0845 603 4852 or by writing to us at the address above. Copies are also available at staffed stations on our route.

CODE OF PRACTICE FOR COMMENTS, COMPLAINTS AND SUGGESTIONS

Copies of our Complaint Handling Guide, Passenger's Charter and comments forms are available from the above address or on our website. Customer Services can be contacted on 0845 603 4852.

Copies of comments forms are available at staffed stations on our route and from any member of Grand Central staff.

HC Heathrow Connect HC

A joint venture between First Rail Division and BAA (Heathrow Express)

ADDRESS	Freepost RLRZ-TZXE-BYKY Heathrow Connect 6th Floor, 50 Eastbourne Terrace London W2 6LX Telephone: 0845 678 6975 Fax: 020 8750 6615 Website: www.heathrowconnect.com Email: web_customer_correspondence@baa.com
MANAGING DIRECTORS	*Heathrow Connect is a joint venture between First Great Western and BAA (Heathrow Express).* Mark Hopwood (First Great Western) Richard Robinson (Heathrow Express)
RESERVATIONS AND TICKETS BY TELEPHONE AND ONLINE	Reservations are not necessary. Tickets can be booked by telephone on 0845 700 0125. Open 0700-2200 (0800-1900 Saturdays and Sundays). Allow 3 working days for delivery. A next day delivery can be arranged at £5 per transaction. Tickets may also be purchased through our website www.heathrowconnect.com
RESERVATION DETAILS	Reservations are not available.
CATERING ON TRAINS	Catering on trains is not available.
CYCLES	Cycles are carried free of charge, but are not allowed on trains timed to arrive at London Paddington between 0745-0945, or depart London Paddington between 1630-1830 Mondays to Fridays. In the interest of safety and customer comfort, we reserve the right to limit the number of cycles at other times.
LOST PROPERTY	Property lost at Paddington Station is collected by Network Rail, who can be contacted on 020 7313 1514. For items lost at Heathrow Airport call 020 8745 7727. For items lost on Heathrow Express trains, please ask our Customer Service Representatives, or alternatively email Heathrow Airport Lost Property at lrh.lostproperty@bagport.co.uk
TRAIN SERVICE UPDATE	For current train information call 0845 678 6975. Website: www.heathrowconnect.com
PENALTY FARES	Penalty Fares apply at stations between Hayes & Harlington and Paddington (incl). Customers are liable to a Penalty Fare of £20 to the next station stop.
DISABLED PEOPLE'S PROTECTION POLICY	This is available from Customer Relations at the above address and telephone number.
CODE OF PRACTICE FOR COMMENTS, COMPLAINTS AND SUGGESTIONS	It is our aim to try and resolve any issues or grievances on the spot. All our Customer Services Representative have a supply of comment forms and our Customer Care Line on 0845 604 15 15 can deal with any issues over the telephone or submit any comments to web_customer_correspondance@baa.com. If you wish to write with a suggestion or complain, please write to Customer Relations at the address at the top of this page, or through our website www.heathrowexpress.com

Heathrow Express

HX

ADDRESS

Heathrow Express
Customer Relations
FREEPOST
London W2 6LG
Telephone: 0845 604 1515 (call centre)
Fax: 020 8750 6615
Website: www.heathrowexpress.com
Email: web_customer_correspondence@baa.com

MANAGING DIRECTOR

Richard Robinson

RESERVATIONS AND TICKETS BY TELEPHONE AND ONLINE

Reservations are not necessary on Heathrow Express services. Tickets may be purchased online and from www.heathrowexpress.com as well as our ticket offices at Heathrow Airport, Paddington station and other appointed outlets. For details call our Customer Services team on 0845 600 1515 (24 hour service - local rate call) or visit www.heathrowexpress.com

RESERVATION DETAILS

Reservations are not available.

CATERING ON TRAINS

As the overall journey time is only 15 minutes, or 21 minutes to Terminal 5, there is currently no catering on Heathrow Express services.

CYCLES

Limited accommodation is available for cycles on Heathrow Express services, for passengers flying with their cycles from the airport. Heathrow Express reserve the right to limit the number of cycles conveyed on each train to no more than three at busy times. Cyclists not travelling onwards by air may use the service to and from Heathrow Terminals, subject to space being available for airline passengers.

LOST PROPERTY

Property lost at Paddington station is collected by Network Rail, who can be contacted on 020 7313 1514. For items lost at Heathrow Airport call 020 8745 7727. For items lost on Heathrow Express trains, please ask our Customer Service Representatives, or alternatively write to: Excess Baggage Co., Heathrow Airport, Middlesex UB3 5AP or email to heathrow.lostproperty@excess-baggage.com

TRAIN SERVICE UPDATE

For current information on train services please contact our customer care line on 0845 604 15 15, or through our website www.heathrowexpress.com

PENALTY FARES

Penalty Fares do not apply on Heathrow Express services, therefore customers may join the train without having first purchased a ticket or authority to travel. Customer Service Representatives on every train will accept cash, debit and credit cards, for ticket purchase. Please note however for tickets purchased on board there is a £5.00 premium to pay. Only full fare tickets are available to purchase on board the train. (However Disabled Railcard is accepted on board).

DISABLED PEOPLE'S PROTECTION POLICY

Heathrow Express trains have been specially designed with the needs of the disabled in mind. Platforms at all our stations give level access into the trains and there is space for wheelchairs on all trains. For further information on facilities for the disabled, call the Customer Care Line on 0845 604 15 15, or write to the Managing Director at the address at the top of this page.

CODE OF PRACTICE FOR COMMENTS, COMPLAINTS AND SUGGESTIONS

It is our aim to try and resolve any issues or grievances on the spot. All our Customer Service Representatives have a supply of comment forms and our Customer Care Line on 0845 604 15 15 can deal with any issues over the telephone or submit any comments at web_customer_correspondence@baa.com. If you wish to write with a suggestion or complaint, please write to the Managing Director at the address at the top of this page, or through our website www.heathrowexpress.com

Island Line Trains

ADDRESS	Friars Bridge Court 41–45 Blackfriars Road London SE1 8NZ Telephone: 08700 005151 Fax: 020 7620 5177 Website: www.southwesttrains.co.uk Email: customerrelations@swtrains.co.uk
MANAGING DIRECTOR	Andy Pitt
RESERVATIONS AND TICKETS BY TELEPHONE AND ONLINE	Reservations are not required on Island Line Trains services. Group travel information can be obtained by calling 023 8072 8162.
RESERVATION DETAILS	Reservations are not available.
CATERING ON TRAINS	There are no catering facilities on trains.
CYCLES	A maximum of 4 cycles may be carried in the Shanklin end of all trains at no extra charge. For the safety and comfort of our passengers, the guard may refuse to carry any further cycles on the train.
LOST PROPERTY	All items of lost property are retained at Ryde Esplanade Ticket Office. If you have lost an item please telephone the Ticket Office on 01983 562492 (0900-1700 Daily). A charge may be applicable on collection.
TRAIN SERVICE UPDATE	For current train information, please call our helpline on 0845 6000 650 or visit www.islandlinetrains.co.uk
PENALTY FARES	Penalty Fares are not in force on any Island Line Trains services.
DISABLED PEOPLE'S PROTECTION POLICY	Island Line Trains is committed to making travel easier for customers with disabilities including wheelchair users. For travel on the mainland, please call our Assisted Travel line on 0800 5282 100 (textphone 0800 692 0792), giving 24 hours notice before travelling. Please note that scooters cannot be conveyed on any Island Line Trains Service. For journeys wholly within Island Line Trains, please telephone 01983 812591 giving 24 hours notice if assistance is required.
CODE OF PRACTICE FOR COMMENTS, COMPLAINTS AND SUGGESTIONS	Feedback leaflets are available at Ryde Esplanade or Shanklin Ticket Offices. Copies of Island Line Trains' and South West Trains' Passenger's Charters are available from any staffed station or by writing to: Customer Service Centre South West Trains Overline House Southampton SO15 1GW Telephone 0845 6000 650 Fax 023 8072 8187 Email: customerrelations@swtrains.co.uk The Passenger's Charter is also featured on the website www.islandlinetrains.co.uk and www.southwesttrains.co.uk

London Midland

ADDRESS	PO Box 4323 Birmingham B2 4JB Telephone: 0844 811 0133 Website: www.londonmidland.com Email: comments@londonmidland.com
MANAGING DIRECTOR	Mike Hodson
RESERVATIONS AND TICKETS BY TELEPHONE AND ONLINE	Tickets can be booked in advance on-line at www.londonmidland.com or by ringing 0844 811 0133, 0800-2000 Monday to Sunday, please allow 5 days for delivery.
RESERVATION DETAILS	Seat reservations are not available. Group travel enquiries and bookings can be made on 0844 811 0133.
CATERING ON TRAINS	Catering is not available.
CYCLES	Cycles are carried free of charge on most off-peak services, however, advance reservations are required for our Birmingham–Liverpool, Birmingham-London and Crewe–London services. Cycles cannot be conveyed on trains arriving into London Euston between 0700 and 0959 and departing London Euston between 1600 and 1859 on Mondays to Fridays (excluding Bank Holidays). Folding cycles, completely folded down, are regarded as accompanied luggage and carried free.
LOST PROPERTY	Enquiries can be made at your nearest staffed station or by ringing Customer Relations on 0844 811 0133.
TRAIN SERVICE UPDATE	Available from National Rail Enquiries on 08457 48 49 50 (calls may be recorded for training purposes).
PENALTY FARES	A Penalty Fares System is in place across most of the London Midland network. If you board a service from a staffed station without a valid ticket or permit to travel, you will be liable to a £20 penalty fare or twice the standard single fare to the next station whichever is the greater. You can only purchase a ticket on-train when travelling from an unstaffed station. Details of the scheme are available at www.londonmidland.com or by writing to Customer Relations at the address below.
DISABLED PEOPLE'S PROTECTION POLICY	Available from Customer Relations London Midland PO Box 4323 Birmingham B2 4JB Telephone: 0844 811 0133
CODE OF PRACTICE FOR COMMENTS, COMPLAINTS AND SUGGESTIONS	Available from Customer Relations at the above address.

London Overground

LO

Operated by London Overground Rail Operations Ltd. (LOROL)
on behalf of Rail for London Ltd., a subsidiary of TfL

ADDRESS	125 Finchley Road London NW3 6HY Telephone: 0845 601 4867 Textphone 020 3031 9331 Website: www.tfl.gov.uk/overground Email: overgroundinfo@tfl.gov.uk
MANAGING DIRECTOR	Steve Murphy
RESERVATIONS AND TICKETS BY TELEPHONE AND ONLINE	Tickets may be booked in advance and seats reserved on many long distance national rail services from most London Overground ticket offices. Oyster tickets may be purchased online from https://oyster.tfl.gov.uk
RESERVATION DETAILS	Reservations are not available.
CATERING ON TRAINS	Catering is not provided on London Overground services.
CYCLES	London Overground allows folding bicycles free of charge on all trains at all times, provided it is safe to do so. Non-folding bicycles are also accepted free of charge but due to space constraints they are not permitted on the following routes between the times shown: • Willesden Junction (High Level) and Gospel Oak in both directions Mondays to Fridays (except Public Holidays) 0700-1000 and 1600-1900 • Gospel Oak and Blackhorse Road in both directions Mondays to Fridays (except Public Holidays) 0700-1000 and 1600-1900 • Watford Junction and Euston Mondays to Fridays (except Public Holidays) on services timed to arrive at Euston 0700-1000 or depart from Euston 1600-1900 • Highbury & Islington/Dalston Junction and New Cross/Crystal Palace/ West Croydon in both directions Mondays to Fridays (except Public Holidays) 0700-1000 and 1600-1900 Only one bicycle is allowed per customer within a limit of one bicycle per vestibule area. Tandems and three-wheeled vehicles cannot be accomodated on any London Overground train. Only folding bicycles can be carried on buses that replace trains due to engineering work.
LOST PROPERTY	Please contact the TfL Lost Property Office at Baker Street on 0845 330 9882 or our Customer Services Team on 0845 601 4867.
TRAIN SERVICE UPDATE	Information about London Overground services and fares can be obtained by telephoning either: • London Travel Information on 0843 222 1234 • National Rail Enquiries 08457 48 49 50 (calls may be recorded for training purposes). (Textphone 08456 050 600, 0800-2000 daily) A wide range of information about London Overground is also available from our website: www.tfl.gov.uk/overground
PENALTY FARES	London Overground operates a Penalty Fares Scheme. If you cannot produce, on request, a valid ticket for your entire journey or, when using Oyster to pay as you go, your Oyster card containing a record of the start of your Pay as you go journey, you will be liable to pay a Penalty Fare.
DISABLED PEOPLE'S PROTECTION POLICY	This can be obtained at any London Overground station or from our Customer Services Team at the above address.
CODE OF PRACTICE FOR COMMENTS, COMPLAINTS AND SUGGESTIONS	For a copy of the London Overground Customer Charter leaflet please ask at any London Overground station or contact our Customer Services Team at the above address.

Merseyrail

A Serco/Abellio company

ME

ADDRESS	Rail House Lord Nelson Street Liverpool L1 1JF Telephone: 0151 702 2071 2 Website: www.merseyrail.org
MANAGING DIRECTOR	Bart Schmeink
RESERVATIONS AND TICKETS BY TELEPHONE AND ONLINE	Tickets may be booked in advance and seats reserved from most Merseyrail stations for National Rail Services.
RESERVATION DETAILS	Reservations are not available.
CATERING ON TRAINS	Catering is not available.
CYCLES	Cycles carried free of charge at any time, subject to sufficient space being available.
LOST PROPERTY	Please contact:- Lost Property Office James Street Station James Street Liverpool L2 7PQ Phone: 0151 702 2951
TRAIN SERVICE UPDATE	For current train information please call 08457 48 49 50 (calls may be recorded for training purposes). ***For details of Bank Holiday services see also the boxed note immediately preceding Table 103.***
PENALTY FARES	Please refer to notices displayed at stations for details of the Penalty Fare Scheme in operation.
DISABLED PEOPLE'S PROTECTION POLICY	Available from:– Customer Relations Merseyrail Rail House Lord Nelson Street Liverpool L1 1JF Phone : 0151 702 2071 (Textphone 0870 0552 681) Fax : 0151 702 2413 or email: comment@merseyrail.org
CODE OF PRACTICE FOR COMMENTS, COMPLAINTS AND SUGGESTIONS	Available from above address

National Express East Anglia (NXEA)

LE

ADDRESS	Customer Relations National Express East Anglia Norwich Railway Station Station Approach Norwich NR1 1EF Telephone: 0845 600 7245 Fax: 01603 214567 Website: www.nationalexpresseastanglia.com Email: nxea.customerrelations@nationalexpress.com
MANAGING DIRECTOR	Andrew Chivers
RESERVATIONS AND TICKETS BY TELEPHONE AND ONLINE	Tickets may be booked in advance by telephoning 0845 600 7245 between 0800 and 2200 (Mondays to Fridays) and 0900 and 1800 (weekends and Bank Holidays). For Business Travel, please telephone 0845 850 9080
RESERVATION DETAILS	NXEA offers Seat Reservations on services between London Liverpool Street and Norwich at a charge of £2.50 per seat (£1 for season ticket holders).
CATERING ON TRAINS	Hot and cold drinks, sandwiches and light snacks are generally available on main line services between Norwich and London Liverpool Street and on Stansted Express services.
CYCLES	Accompanied bicycles are conveyed free of charge on most NXEA services, but are not permitted on Stansted Express services at any time or on weekday peak services to and from London. A similar restriction also applies at Cambridge. On main line and rural services, the number of bicycles per train is limited, so a free reservation is recommended. For further details, please call NXEA customer services on 0845 600 7245.
LOST PROPERTY	If you have lost an item of property on one of our trains or stations, please contact NXEA customer services on 0845 600 7245 or email us at nxea.lostproperty@nationalexpress.com
TRAIN SERVICE UPDATE	For current train service information, please contact NXEA customer services on 0845 600 7245 or call our recorded information line on 020 7247 5488.
PENALTY FARES	NXEA operates a Penalty Fares System on most of its network, except on designated 'paytrain' routes and from certain specified stations without ticket issuing facilities. Stations within the Penalty Fares area are identified by warning notices at each entrance. When travelling from these stations, you must have a valid ticket for your journey. For journeys where Oyster Pay as you Go (PAYG) is accepted, you must hold a valid Oyster card which has been touched in at the start of your journey. Oyster PAYG is not valid for travel outside the area where PAYG is accepted. If you cannot present a valid ticket for the journey you are making, you may be liable for a Penalty Fare (minimum £20).
DISABLED PEOPLE'S PROTECTION POLICY	Available from: Customer Relations, National Express East Anglia, Norwich Station, Station Approach, Norwich NR1 1EF. Customers who require assistance are recommended to book at least 24 hours in advance on 0800 028 28 78 or Textphone 0845 606 7245.
CODE OF PRACTICE FOR COMMENTS, COMPLAINTS AND SUGGESTIONS	Available from: Customer Relations, National Express East Anglia, Norwich Station, Station Approach, Norwich NR1 1EF. The NXEA Passenger's Charter is also available from the same address.

NY North Yorkshire Moors Railway NY

(Operators of steam and heritage services between Whitby, Grosmont, Goathland and Pickering)

ADDRESS	Pickering Station Pickering North Yorkshire YO18 7AJ Telephone: 01751-472508 (Customer Services and Information) Fax: 01751-476048 Website: www.nymr.co.uk Email: info@nymr.co.uk
GENERAL MANAGER	Philip Benham
RESERVATIONS AND TICKETS BY TELEPHONE AND ONLINE	Telephone: 01751-472508 Hours of operation: 31 March to 4 November and other operating dates: 0930-1630 (Monday - Friday), 1000-1430 (Saturday and Sunday); All other times: 1000-1430 (Monday - Friday). At least 7 days should be allowed for receipt of tickets purchased by telephone. National Rail tickets can be booked in advance from our office in Whitby – telephone 01947 605872.
RESERVATION DETAILS	Reservations are not available on normal services. They can be made for groups of 20 or more passengers and are required on North Yorkshire Moors Railways dining train services (between Pickering and Grosmont).
CATERING ON TRAINS	An at-seat trolley service of drinks and snacks is provided on most trains.
CYCLES	Cycles and dogs are carried for a charge of £2 (subject to space being available).
LOST PROPERTY	Enquiries about lost property should be made to Pickering Station at the above, or by telephone 01751-472508.
TRAIN SERVICE UPDATE	Updated train service information on all North Yorkshire Moors Railway is available on the website (see address above). A 'talking timetable' is also available giving current details of all North Yorkshire Moors Railway services by telephoning 01751-473535.
PENALTY FARES	Penalty Fares are not in force on any North Yorkshire Moors Railway service.
DISABLED PEOPLE'S PROTECTION POLICY	Available from the address above, or Pickering and Grosmont Stations.
CODE OF PRACTICE FOR COMMENTS, COMPLAINTS AND SUGGESTIONS	North Yorkshire Moors Railway welcomes comments from passengers. Comments/suggestion cards are available from stations and on-board staff, or alternatively please write to the General Manager. Details of the company's policy are available from the above address, or Pickering and Grosmont Stations.

Northern

A joint venture between Serco and Abellio

ADDRESS	Northern Rail Ltd Northern House 9 Rougier Street York YO1 6HZ Telephone: 08700 005151 Website: www.northernrail.org
MANAGING DIRECTOR	Ian Bevan
RESERVATIONS AND TICKETS BY TELEPHONE AND ONLINE	Reservations and tickets are available from all local staffed stations.
RESERVATION DETAILS	Tickets can be purchased in advance on-line at www.northernrail.org. Reservations and tickets are also available from all local staffed stations. For groups of 10 or more travelling on the Leeds-Settle-Carlisle line telephone 0800 9800 766, between 0900 and 1700 on Mondays to Fridays to make a booking. All accommodation on Northern trains is Standard Class.
CATERING ON TRAINS	On most Leeds-Settle-Carlisle services, food and drink can be purchased from the trolley which will pass through the train.
CYCLES	Up to two cycles can be carried on each service. This is subject to space being available, however, and cannot be booked in advance. For further details telephone 0845 000 0125.
LOST PROPERTY	Call 0845 000 0125, contact your nearest staffed station or write to Northern at the address below.
TRAIN SERVICE UPDATE	Information about Northern services and fares can be obtained by telephoning: **08457 48 49 50** (calls may be recorded for training purposes) or access the website on www.nationalrail.co.uk For more information on our services, please visit our website on www.northernrail.org The latest information on train running is available by phoning TrainTracker™ from National Rail Enquiries on 0871 200 4915 or by texting TrainTracker™. Text to 84950.
PENALTY FARES	Penalty Fares are not in force on any Northern service.
DISABLED PERSON'S PROTECTION POLICY	If you would like a copy of Northern's Policy or wish to arrange assistance for your journey, please phone: 0808 1561606. (Textphone 0845 604 5608) or by writing to Customer Relations, Northern, FREEPOST (RLSL-ABEC-BGUU), Leeds LS1 4DY or email: assistance@northernrail.org
CODE OF PRACTICE FOR COMMENTS, COMPLAINTS AND SUGGESTIONS	Please contact our Customer Helpline on 0845 000 0125, a textphone is available on 0845 604 5608. Alternatively you can write to us at: Customer Relations, Northern, FREEPOST (RLSL-ABEC-BGUU), Leeds LS1 4DY. If you would like a copy of the Northern Passenger's Charter, or Northern's Guide for Customers with Disabilities please contact our Customer Relations team.

ScotRail

A member of the First Rail Division

ADDRESS	1st Floor Atrium Court 50 Waterloo Street Glasgow G2 6HQ Telephone: 08700 00 51 51 Fax: 0141 335 4592 Website: www.scotrail.co.uk Email: scotrailcustomer.relations@firstgroup.com
MANAGING DIRECTOR	Steve Montgomery
RESERVATIONS AND TICKETS BY TELEPHONE AND ONLINE	Tickets may be purchased in advance and Sleepers or seats reserved, by telephone, using a debit/credit card from the following number: 08457 550033 (opening hours 0700-2200) Please allow 3 days for tickets by post, tickets on departure arrangements available at selected stations. Tickets can also be purchased through the website - www.scotrail.co.uk ScotRail customers can buy selected Caledonian Sleeper tickets online - and have the ticket confirmation sent to their mobile phone. Passengers simply turn up for their train, show the text message to train staff and hop on board. A confirmatory email is sent as a back-up. This free SMS service is available for 'Bargain Berth' tickets on the Caledonian Sleeper, which connects Scottish cities to Central London. Tickets can be booked up to 12 weeks in advance of travel - and right up until Midday on the day of travel, subject to availability. The berths start from just £19.
RESERVATION DETAILS	Seat Reservations are free and can be made from 12 weeks in advance up to approximately two hours prior to the departure of the train.
CATERING ON TRAINS	A Lounge Car is provided on all Caledonian Sleeper services offering a wide range of drinks, snacks and hot meals. A trolley service is available on many longer-distance services as indicated in the timetable.
CYCLES	Cycles are carried free on all ScotRail services subject to availability. Reservations are required on Caledonian Sleeper services and on longer distance routes. Tandems, tricycles, cycle trailers, motorcycles, mopeds or motorised cycles are not carried on any ScotRail service.
LOST PROPERTY	Please phone 0141 335 3276 (0700-1900 Mon-Sat)
TRAIN SERVICE UPDATE	Register with JourneyCheck/JourneyAlert on our website: www.scotrail.co.uk
PENALTY FARES	Penalty Fares are not in force on any ScotRail services.
DISABLED PEOPLE'S PROTECTION POLICY	Available from ScotRail Customer, PO Box 7031, Fort William PH33 6WW. Tel: 0800 912 2 901 or 18001 0800 912 2 901 Fax: 0141 335 4611 Travel arrangements may be made for disabled people by calling 0800 912 2 901*. A light travel scooter, length 104cm, width 56cm with a turning radius of 99cm and combined weight of 300kg can be conveyed. Details of station facilities and information on accessibility are available at www.nationalrail.co.uk or www.scotrail.co.uk. *For assisted travel, an advance notice of up to 24 hours notice is appreciated.
CODE OF PRACTICE FOR COMMENTS, COMPLAINTS AND SUGGESTIONS	ScotRail welcomes comments on the services we provide. A leaflet is available at all staffed ScotRail stations and also from the Customer Relations Manager at the address above. Tel: 0845 601 5929

South West Trains

SW

ADDRESS	Friars Bridge Court 41–45 Blackfriars Road London SE1 8NZ Telephone: 08700 005151 Fax: 020 7620 5177 Website: www.southwesttrains.co.uk Email: customerrelations@swtrains.co.uk
MANAGING DIRECTOR	Andy Pitt
RESERVATIONS AND TICKETS BY TELEPHONE AND ONLINE	Tickets may be booked in advance by telephone, on the following number: 0845 6000 650. Tickets may also be purchased via the South West Trains website (see above). When ordering, please allow 5 working days for ticket delivery.
RESERVATION DETAILS	Reservations are not available.
CATERING ON TRAINS	Catering on South West Trains is provided on those services marked with the symbol T for all or part of the journey. Catering may be provided from a buffet area, at seat trolley service or a combination of both according to the route and time of day. Comments on the service should be sent to the Customer Service Centre at the address below.
CYCLES	A limited number of cycles can be carried on most of our services except during the Monday to Friday peak periods. Restrictions apply on certain routes into and out of London Waterloo between 0715 and 1000 and between 1645 and 1900. At all times some services require advance reservations, as space is limited. To obtain full details of South West Trains Cycling Policy and full details of routes and times when cycles are not carried visit www.southwesttrains.co.uk, pick up a leaflet from stations served by South West Trains or contact our Customer Service Centre at the address shown. Cycles that can be folded to a size which allows them to be carried safely in the luggage racks on our services may be carried folded at all times. For reasons of safety and comfort of our passengers, if the available identified cycle spaces on the train are already taken, the guard has the right to refuse to carry any further cycles on that train.
LOST PROPERTY	A lost property helpline is available between 0730-1900 Mondays to Fridays by calling 020 7401 7861
TRAIN SERVICE UPDATE	For current train information, please call our helpline on 0845 6000 650 or visit www.southwesttrains.co.uk
PENALTY FARES	South West Trains has a duty to its fare paying passengers to ensure no-one travels for free. To this end South West Trains operates a Penalty Fares Scheme across its network, with the only exceptions being Dean, Mottisfont & Dunbridge and Romsey. Passengers travelling to and from stations within the penalty fares area without a valid ticket may be liable to a penalty of £20 or twice the single fare to the next station at which their train stops (whichever is the greater).
DISABLED PEOPLE'S PROTECTION POLICY	For a copy of this publication, please contact the Customer Service Centre at the address below. Assistance for mobility impaired passengers can be arranged by telephoning 0800 5282 100 between 0600 - 2200 daily. Please give at least 24 hours notice. A textphone facility is available on 0800 6920 792 (calls are charged at local rates).
CODE OF PRACTICE FOR COMMENTS, COMPLAINTS AND SUGGESTIONS	Copies of South West Trains Passenger's Charter are available from any staffed station or by writing to: Customer Service Centre, South West Trains, Overline House, Blechynden Terrace, Southampton SO15 1GW Telephone 0845 6000 650. Fax 023 8072 8187 Email: customerrelations@swtrains.co.uk The Passenger's Charter is also available on our website www.southwesttrains.co.uk

SE Southeastern SE

ADDRESS

Southeastern Customer Services
PO Box 63428
London SE1P 5FD
Telephone: 0845 000 2222
Assisted Travel: 0800 783 4524 (Textphone 0800 783 4548)
Fax: 0845 678 6976
Textphone: 0800 783 4548

Website: www.southeasternrailway.co.uk

Southeastern Customer Services is staffed 24 hours a day, seven days a week (closed Christmas Day). Comments and complaints are dealt with here by post, fax, and website as well as on the telephone.

MANAGING DIRECTOR

Charles Horton

RESERVATIONS AND TICKETS BY TELEPHONE AND ONLINE

Group travel (parties of 10 persons or more) on Southeastern services must be booked at least seven days in advance so that space can be allocated. To order, go to southeasternrailway.co.uk, select tickets, then group, then complete the online form.

Customers can renew their Season Tickets for one month or longer by completing the Season Ticket application form at their local ticket office.

For new monthly season ticket purchases, please complete an application form available at local stations or online at southeasternrailway.co.uk.

RESERVATIONS

Reservations are not available. Reservations are only needed on Southeastern services for Group Travel and mobility impaired customers who require assistance.

CATERING ON TRAINS

Catering is not available.

CYCLES

Cycles are not permitted on peak time services, which are those timed to arrive in London terminals between 0700 and 0959, and those timed to leave between 1600 and 1859. Folding cycles are permitted provided they are folded.

LOST PROPERTY

Customers who have lost property on a train or at a station should contact Southeastern Customer Services on 0845 000 2222.

TRAIN SERVICE UPDATE

For current train running information contact Southeastern Customer Services on 0845 000 2222

Information is also available from national and local radio station travel updates on Ceefax page 433, and from our website: southeasternrailway.co.uk, select journey.

PENALTY FARES

Southeastern operate a Penalty Fares Scheme on all routes. You must buy a valid ticket (or permit to travel) for your journey before boarding a train. If you do not have a valid ticket or permit to travel, you may have to pay a Penalty Fare of £20.00 or twice the single fare, whichever is the greater. Please pick up a Penalty Fare leaflet from a staffed station for your information.

DISABLED PEOPLE'S PROTECTION POLICY

Copies of the Disabled People's Protection Policy are available from Southeastern Customer Services.

If you have any special needs and would like help with planning your journey anywhere in Great Britain please call 0800 783 4524 or use the Textphone 0800 783 4548 - open 24 hours a day.

The Southeastern Assisted Travel team will offer advice and make any special arrangements you need. If at least 24 hours' notice can be given, this will be very much appreciated.

CODE OF PRACTICE FOR COMMENTS, COMPLAINTS AND SUGGESTIONS

Southeastern Passengers' Charter leaflets are available at any Southeastern sales point or Southeastern Customer Services at the address shown above.

Southern

SN

ADDRESS	Southern Customer Services PO Box 3021 Bristol BS2 2BS Telephone: 08451 27 29 20 (Customer Services) Fax: 08451 27 29 30 (Customer Services) Website: www.southernrailway.com Email: comments@southernrailway.com
MANAGING DIRECTOR	Chris Burchell
RESERVATIONS AND TICKETS BY TELEPHONE AND ONLINE	Discounted Advance Tickets are available from the Southern website.
RESERVATION DETAILS	Reservations are only required for Advance tickets. These reservations authorise the holder to travel on the specified train but do not identify individual seats.
CATERING ON TRAINS	A light refreshment of food and drinks is available on trains marked with ⊼ in the timetable.
CYCLES	Standard size folding cycles are welcome on all Southern trains (as long as they are folded) at any time. During peak periods, for non-folding cycles different restrictions apply at each station so please check with the station or our website before travelling.
LOST PROPERTY	Please call Southern Customer Services on 08451 27 29 20.
TRAIN SERVICE UPDATE	For current train information call Customer Services on 08451 27 29 20 or check our website at www.southernrailway.com
PENALTY FARES	Southern operate a Penalty Fares Scheme on all routes. You must buy a valid ticket (or permit to travel) for your journey before boarding a train. If you do not have a valid ticket or permit to travel, you may have to pay a Penalty Fare of £20.00 or twice the single fare, whichever is the greater. Please pick up a Penalty Fare leaflet from a staffed station for your information.
DISABLED PEOPLE'S PROTECTION POLICY	Available from Southern Customer Services at PO Box 3021 Bristol BS2 2BS. To get advice about accessible travel or to book assistance please call 0800 136 1016; Minicom/textphone – 0800 138 1018, Fax – 0800 138 1017
CODE OF PRACTICE FOR COMMENTS, COMPLAINTS AND SUGGESTIONS	Write to Southern Customer Services at the above address. Copies of Southern Passenger's charter are available from any staffed station. You can also obtain a copy by contacting Customer Services or from Southern's website.

VT Virgin Trains VT

The trading name of West Coast Trains Ltd

ADDRESS	Virgin Trains 85 Smallbrook Queensway Birmingham B5 4HA Telephone: 0845 000 8000 Textphone: 0121 654 7528 Website: www.virgintrains.com Email: customer.relations@virgintrains.co.uk
CHIEF EXECUTIVE	Tony Collins
MANAGING DIRECTOR	Chris Gibb
RESERVATIONS AND TICKETS BY TELEPHONE AND ONLINE	Buy tickets for Virgin Trains and any other train company in Great Britain on the internet at www.virgintrains.com or by calling 0871 977 4222 (calls to this number cost 10p a minute from a BT landline; calls from other operators may vary and cost more) - between 0800 and 2200 7 days a week. If you have a disability or have specific needs and wish to arrange assistance on your journey call the Virgin Trains JourneyCare service on 08457 44 33 66 (Textphone 08457 44 33 67) between 0800 and 2200 every day except Christmas Day or Boxing Day.
RESERVATION DETAILS	You are strongly advised to make a Seat Reservation in advance. Reservations can be made for the Quiet Zone carriage, where customers should refrain from using mobile phones or creating unnecessary noise. On routes to and from London, Standard Class Quiet Zone is in coach A and in coach H for First Class. On other routes, Quiet Zone is located in Standard Class, coach F. Seat reservations are free of charge.
CATERING ON TRAINS	In First Class on a Pendolino from Monday to Friday customers can enjoy a selection of snacks throughout the day, including a cooked breakfast on many morning peak services. In addition, Fairtrade tea, Fairtrade coffee, soft drinks and alcoholic drinks (alcohol is not offered with breakfast services) are served at seat throughout the day. A complimentary newspaper is also available. In First Class on Super Voyager from Monday to Friday customers can enjoy complimentary light refreshments, including Fairtrade tea, Fairtrade coffee, soft drinks and a newspaper with an at-seat service available, on most services. In Standard, we have a wide range of snacks and sandwiches, Fairtrade teas, fresh ground Fairtrade coffee, soft and alcoholic drinks and a selection of non-food items available at our onboard shop. The shop is generally open throughout. Pendolinos offer an at-seat trolley service to standard customers on Mondays to Fridays. For more information about our onboard service pick up a copy of Travelling with Virgin Trains.
CYCLES	Subject to availability of space cycles can be carried on all trains. Most trains can carry 3 cycles, and on journeys to and from London Euston, Pendolinos can carry tandems (however, tandems are not carried on Voyager services). An advance reservation is required for all journeys.
LOST PROPERTY	Call Customer Relations on 0845 000 8000 – 0830 to 1800 Mondays to Fridays, 0900 to 1600 Saturdays, answerphone available at all other times.
TRAIN SERVICE UPDATE	Details of any disruption to services or weekend engineering work are summarised on BBC Ceefax and on BBCi on digital TV. Details of Engineering work can also be found at www.virgintrains.com.
PENALTY FARES	Penalty Fares are not applicable on any Virgin Trains service.
DISABLED PEOPLE'S PROTECTION POLICY	Our Customer Relations Manager (at the address above) will be pleased to supply a free copy of the Disabled People's Protection Policy. It can also be downloaded at www.virgintrains.com. For information on station accessibility and to arrange special help please contact Virgin Trains JourneyCare (details above).
CODE OF PRACTICE FOR COMMENTS, COMPLAINTS AND SUGGESTIONS	We want you to tell us what you think of our service, good or bad. A copy of our Code of Practice for handling comments, complaints and suggestions together with Virgin Trains Passenger's Charter is available free on request from our Customer Relations Manager at the above address.

WR West Coast Railway Company WR

(Operators of the 'Jacobite' and 'Cambrian' Steam Services)

ADDRESS	Jesson Way Carnforth Lancashire LA5 9UR Telephone: 01524 737751/737753 Fax: 01524 735518 Website: www.westcoastrailways.co.uk Email: jacobite@wcrc.co.uk
GENERAL MANAGER	Mrs Pat Marshall
COMMERCIAL MANAGER	James Shuttleworth
RESERVATIONS AND TICKETS BY TELEPHONE AND ONLINE	Advance bookings are recommended and can be made on line, at www.westcoastrailways.co.uk, by post (enclose SAE) to the Carnforth Office (address above) or by telephone, on 01524 737751/737753, during normal office hours. Credit cards accepted. Tickets can also be purchased from the WCR Guard/Train Manager, on the train, on the day of travel (subject to availablility).
RESERVATION DETAILS	Phone 01524 737751/737753
CATERING ON TRAINS	A buffet service, serving hot and cold drinks and cold snacks, is available on all trains.
CYCLES	Cycles carried free of charge, subject to space.
LOST PROPERTY	Telephone: 01524 737751/737753
PENALTY FARES	Penalty Fares are not in force on any West Coast Railway Company service.
TRAIN SERVICE UPDATE	For current train information please phone 08457 48 49 50 (calls may be recorded for training purposes).
DISABLED PEOPLE'S PROTECTION POLICY	Available from the above address.
CODE OF PRACTICE FOR COMMENTS, COMPLAINTS AND SUGGESTIONS	West Coast Railway Company welcomes comments on services provided. Write to Carnforth office (address above).

Network Rail

NR

ADDRESS	King's Place York Way London N1 9AG Telephone: 020 7557 8000 Fax: 020 7557 9000 Website: www.networkrail.co.uk
CHIEF EXECUTIVE	David Higgins

Network Rail is responsible for operating 18 managed stations, indicated in the index by the code **NR**. Details of facilities provided, including the Disabled Peoples Protection Policy, are obtainable from the Network Rail Station Manager at the following station addresses:–

London Bridge	Network Rail Offices, Platform 14, London Bridge Station, Station Approach, London SE1 9SP
London Cannon Street	Cannon Street Station, Cannon Street, London EC4N 6AP
London Charing Cross	Network Rail Offices, Charing Cross Station, The Strand, London WC2 5HS
London Euston	Room 430, Stephenson Room, East Colonnade, Euston, London NW1 2RT
London Fenchurch Street	Network Rail Office, Fenchurch Place, London EC3M 4AJ
London King's Cross	Room 304, West Side Offices, King's Cross Station, London N1 9AP
London Liverpool Street	Network Rail Station Reception, Platform 10, Liverpool Street Station, London EC2M 7PY
London Paddington	Room B115, Tournament House, Paddington Station, London W2 1FT
London Victoria	3rd Floor, Kent Side Offices, Victoria Station, London SW1V 1JU
London Waterloo	CP2-4-G General Offices, Waterloo Station, London SE1 8SW
Birmingham New Street	Reception, Network Rail Offices, Station Forecourt, Birmingham New Street Station, Birmingham B2 4ND
Edinburgh	Room 255, North Block, Waverley Station, Edinburgh EH1 1BB
Gatwick Airport	Gatwick Airport Station, Gatwick Airport, Sussex RH6 0RD
Glasgow Central	Glasgow Central Station, Gordon Street, Glasgow G1 3SL
Leeds	Room 405, Administration Block, Leeds City Station, Leeds LS1 4DY
Manchester Piccadilly	9th Floor, Piccadilly Tower, Piccadilly Station, Manchester M60 7RA
Liverpool Lime Street	Station Manager, The Barrier Line Building, Liverpool Lime Street Station, Liverpool L1 1JF
London St Pancras International	Station Reception, St Pancras International Station, Pancras Road, London NW1 2QP

Staffed Left Luggage facilities, offering maximum security, are available at all Network Rail Stations.

If you wish to raise any issue concerning the rail infrastructure or the 18 managed stations operated by Network Rail (excluding matters concerning the running of trains or ticket purchase) please call the national 24 hour Helpline:- **08457 11 41 41**

Other Addresses

Department for Transport

Great Minster House, 76 Marsham Street, London SW1P 4DR

Telephone: 0300 330 3000

Email: rail@dft.gsi.gov.uk

Office of Rail Regulation

One Kemble Street, London WC2B 4AN

Telephone: 020 7282 2000

Fax: 020 7282 2040

Chair of the Board: Anna Walker
Chief Executive: Bill Emery

The main areas of the Regulator's statutory functions are:

- the issue, modification and enforcement of licences to operate trains, networks, stations and light maintenance depots;
- the approval of agreements for access by operators of railway assets to track, stations and light maintenance depots;
- the enforcement of domestic competition law; and consumer protection including a duty under the Railways Act 1993 in relation to the protection of the interests of users of railway services, including the disabled.

Publications are available from:

Sue MacSwan, The Library, ORR, 1 Waterhouse Square, 138–142 Holborn, London EC1N 2TQ

Telephone: 020 7282 2001

Email: rail.library@orr.gsi.gov.uk

Association of Train Operating Companies (ATOC)

3rd Floor, 40 Bernard Street, London WC1N 1BY

Telephone: 020 7841 8000

Chief Executive: Michael Roberts

ATOC represents the interests of most of the national and international passenger Train Operating Companies whose services are shown in this timetable. It manages a range of network services, products and responsibilities on behalf of these train operators including:

- the National Rail Conditions of Carriage (the passenger's contract with the train operators)
- the National Rail Enquiries Service
- the licensing of rail appointed travel agents
- National Railcards, the London Travelcard and Network Railcard.

London Underground Limited

Head Office

55 Broadway, London SW1H 0BD

Telephone: 020 7222 5600

Responsible for the operation of stations indicated in the Stations Index by the code **LT**

How to Cross London

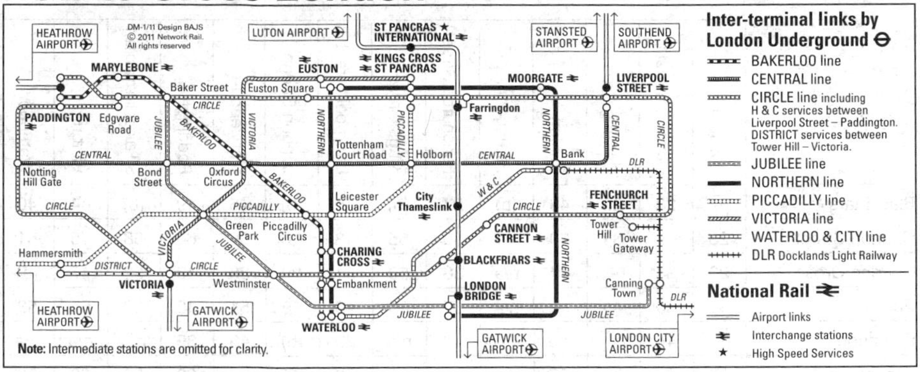

Note: Intermediate stations are omitted for clarity.

Introduction
The time taken to travel between London's stations will vary from journey to journey dependent on distance, mode of transport, time of day and the need to change en route. The quickest way to cross London is usually by the Underground network with frequent services operating between the following hours*:

- 0530 to 0015 on Monday to Friday
- 0630 to 0115 on Saturday
- 0700 to 0001 on Sunday

(* Times shown are approximate)

Buses also link many of London's main terminal stations including an extensive network of Night Bus services.

Ticket & Fares
Rail tickets for journeys routed via London are valid for transfer by London Underground or First Capital Connect services between London terminal stations, and other designated interchange stations* appropriate to the route of the through journey being made, at no extra cost. For example a Brighton to Leeds ticket is valid on London Underground services from Victoria to Kings Cross (Victoria Line), or alternatively on First Capital Connect services to St Pancras International. A Chelmsford to Southampton ticket is valid on London Underground services to Waterloo via either Liverpool Street (Circle Line) or Stratford (Jubilee Line).

(*NB. check on which cross London routes your ticket is valid before you travel. A break of journey is permitted at an intermediate Underground station, but a further ticket must be purchased in order to continue the journey)

London's Fare Zones – National Rail, Underground and Docklands Light Railway (DLR) stations within the Greater London area are in one of nine Fare Zones. Single and return tickets are available for through journeys to and from all Underground and DLR stations with prices determined by the number of zones crossed or travelled through.

A range of day and longer period Travelcards are also available and provide unlimited travel on National Rail, London Underground, London Overground, Docklands Light Railway and Tramlink services within the Fare Zones for which they are valid. All Travelcards, irrespective of the zones for which they are issued, can also be used on any London bus displaying this sign.

For information on ticket prices and availability contact your local staffed station, call National Rail Enquiries anytime on **08457 48 49 50*** (Textphone **0845 60 50 600**), or visit www.nationalrail.co.uk. * Calls may be recorded for training purposes.

More detailed information about London's Underground and Bus services, also Docklands Light Railway and London Tramlink is available anytime from London Travel Information on **0843 222 1234** (textphone **020 7918 3015**) or visit **www.tfl.gov.uk**.

First Capital Connect and Southeastern
First Capital Connect operates fast, direct services from Bedford, Luton and St Albans via Central London to East Croydon, Gatwick Airport and Brighton and stopping trains between Luton, St Albans, North London, the City, Streatham, Wimbledon and Sutton. There are nine Central London First Capital Connect stations with Underground connections. First Capital Connect connects with East Midlands Trains at Luton, Luton Airport Parkway, London St Pancras and Bedford – see Tables 52 and 53.

Southeastern, in partnership with First Capital Connect also operate trains between Kentish Town, the City and Sevenoaks and at peak times between Bedford, Luton, the City and various destinations in Kent.

London Overground
Direct trains run between:

- Richmond and Stratford
- Clapham Junction and Willesden Junction
- Watford Junction and Euston
- Gospel Oak and Barking
- Highbury & Islington to New Cross / Crystal Palace / West Croydon

Southern Services
Direct trains are provided between East Croydon, South London, Clapham Junction and stations to Watford Junction and Milton Keynes Central. These trains also stop at Imperial Wharf, West Brompton, Kensington (Olympia) and Shepherd's Bush. See table 176.

These trains provide connections to most of the Southern network at Clapham Junction.

Passengers requiring step free interchange for Southern main line trains to Gatwick Airport and the Sussex Coast should change at East Croydon, and step free interchange for Southern Metro trains is usually available at Balham.

Interchange for the West Midlands and North West is available at either Watford Junction or Milton Keynes.

Cross London Transfer Times (in minutes)

	Blackfriars **	Cannon Street	Charing Cross	Euston	Farringdon	Fenchurch Street*	Kings Cross	Liverpool Street	London Bridge	Marylebone	Paddington	St Pancras International †	Victoria	Waterloo
Blackfriars **	–	23	23	49	(b)	27	(b)	40	(b)	45	49	(b)	44	40
Cannon Street	23	–	34	60	44	30	55	43	(a)	56	60	58	55	51
Charing Cross	23	34	–	44	n/a	38	50	51	(a)	38	43	52	47	(a)
Euston	49	60	44	–	n/a	57	35	43	52	51	43	38	54	53
Farringdon	(b)	44	n/a	n/a	–	40	n/a	29	(b)	45	39	n/a	n/a	n/a
Fenchurch Street*	27	30	38	57	40	–	52	26	47	68	60	52	68	56
Kings Cross	(b)	55	50	35	n/a	52	–	41	50	50	45	30	56	55
Liverpool Street	40	43	51	43	29	26	41	–	49	56	55	41	126	62
London Bridge	(b)	(a)	(a)	52	(b)	47	50	49	–	58	62	60	n/a	(a)
Marylebone	45	56	38	51	45	68	50	56	58	–	32	53	58	47
Paddington	49	60	43	43	39	60	45	55	62	32	–	45	62	51
St Pancras International †	(b)	58	52	38	n/a	52	30	41	60	53	45	–	56	61
Victoria	44	55	47	54	n/a	68	56	126	n/a	58	62	56	–	124
Waterloo	40	51	(a)	53	n/a	56	55	62	(a)	47	51	61	124	–

All times are based on use of London Underground services and are shown as a guide only – extra time should be allowed during the early morning/late evening and on Sundays.

* Tower Hill Underground Station

† An additional 35 minutes should be allowed for Eurostar Connections

(a) Direct train services available (operated by Southeastern)

(b) Direct train services available (operated by First Capital Connect)

n/a Transfer not likely to be required as part of a through rail journey

** Blackfriars Underground Station is closed until 2011 to allow for major reconstruction work as part of the Thameslink improvement programme. During the period of closure, passengers are advised to use St Pancras, Farringdon or Elephant and Castle to connect with the Underground network. You should allow extra time for these connections

Some other useful transfers

If your journey requires a transfer between any of the following pairs of stations, you should allow a margin of at least the number of minutes shown when planning connections. All transfers are assumed to be by foot unless otherwise stated.

Ash Vale – North Camp	19
Bicester North – Town	30
Burnley Central – Manchester Rd	25
Burscough Bridge – Junction	20
Canterbury East – West	25
Catford – Bridge	10
Clock House – Kent House	15
Dorchester South – West	15
Dorking – Dorking Deepdene	9
East Croydon – West Croydon	25
Edenbridge – Edenbridge Town	20
Enfield Chase – Town	29
Falkirk High – Grahamston	44
Farnborough Main – North	24
Forest Gate – Wanstead Park	13
Gainsborough Central – Lea Rd	33
Hackney Central – Downs	14
Harringay – Green Lanes	14
Heath High Level – Low Level	10
Hertford North – East	34
Maidstone Barracks – East	16
New Mills Central – Newtown	25
Penge East – West	19
Purley Oaks – Sanderstead	10
Seven Sisters – South Tottenham	14
Southend Central – Victoria	17
Upper Warlingham – Whyteleafe	10
Walthamstow Central – Queen's Rd	14
West Hampstead – Thameslink	11
Windsor & Eton Central – Riverside	14
Yeovil Junction – Yeovil Pen Mill	15*

* This is a bus service which runs every 30 mins between 0700 and 1900 Mondays to Saturdays.

Airport Links

Aberdeen Airport

Aberdeen Airport is close to Dyce station, from where trains operate to Aberdeen, Elgin and Inverness. There are also some direct trains to Glasgow and Edinburgh. A shuttle bus runs between Dyce station and the airport, connecting with most trains during the day.

For full bus timetable information, call **0871 200 22 33**, or visit **www.travelinescotland.com**

Birmingham International Airport

Birmingham Airport is alongside Birmingham International station. The free Air-Rail Link transit system operates to the passenger terminals about every 2 minutes with a journey time of less than 2 minutes. Birmingham International station is served by direct trains from London Euston and Manchester Piccadilly. In addition a frequent service operates between Birmingham New Street and Birmingham International providing connections at Birmingham New Street to and from all parts of the country. (See Tables 65, 66, 68, 71, 74 and 116). Regular buses operated by National Express West Midlands (966) also run from Solihull station (see Tables 71 and 115) and through fares are available by purchasing a PlusBus ticket. The journey time is approximately 20 minutes and through ticketing is available. Solihull is served by Chiltern Railways services from London Marylebone, Gerrards Cross, Beaconsfield, High Wycombe, Princes Risborough, Haddenham & Thame Parkway, Bicester North, Banbury, Leamington Spa and Warwick and by London Midland local services.

Bournemouth (Hurn) International Airport

Bournemouth (Hurn) International Airport now has an hourly bus service to and from Bournemouth station. See www.bournemouth-airport-shuttle.co.uk or phone 01202 557007 for details.

Bristol International Airport

The Bristol Airport Flyer is the only express link between Bristol Temple Meads station, Bristol Bus Station, Clifton and Bristol Airport. The journey time to the city centre is approximately 30 minutes with services operating (every 10 minutes at Peak times) daily between 0230 and 0045.

Cardiff International Airport

The airport is served by a free bus link from Rhoose Cardiff International Rail Station to/from the airport operated by New Adventure Travel. Full details of the timetable and further information can be obtained from Traveline on **0871 200 22 33** or visit **www.traveline.info.**

The airport is also served by bus service X46 which is operated by EST Bus on Monday to Saturday with an hourly daytime frequency to/from Barry Rail Station, and bus service X5 which is operated by Watts Coaches on a Sunday with a two hourly frequency. In addition Cardiff Bus Service X91 also operates from Cardiff Central Bus Station (Stand F1) directly to the airport. Journey time is approximately 30 minutes and through ticketing is available from any rail station.

Coventry Airport

Coventry Airport is accessible from Coventry rail station by a scheduled bus service (No. 737). A combined discounted bus and rail ticket can be purchased for travel to the airport.

For bus times call **0871 200 22 33** or visit **www.traveline.info.**

Durham Tees Valley Airport

Durham Tees Valley Airport is located 7 miles east of Darlington Rail station. For information about Durham Tees Valley Airport visit www.durhamteesvalleyairport.com.

From Darlington - Arriva service 12 operates half-hourly throughout the day Mondays to Saturdays and hourly early mornings, evenings and Sundays, from Parkgate outside Darlington Station direct to the airport site. Journey time is approximately 25 minutes.

Please note that when the service is operating two buses an hour that one bus an hour serves the airport terminal directly whilst the other terminates at the hotel on the airport site. The hotel is a 10-minute walk from the terminal building.

For more information please telephone Traveline on **0871 200 22 33** or visit **www.traveline.info**

East Midlands Airport

The most convenient way to get to East Midlands Airport is via East Midlands Parkway Station, served by East Midlands Trains.

A taxi transfer service operates between East Midlands Parkway and the Airport. To guarantee a great price, book your taxi in advance at www.eastmidlandstrains.co.uk/taxi and fill out a booking form. Please ensure that you book at least 12 hours or more in advance of the taxi being required.

Edinburgh Airport

There are two ways to get to Edinburgh Airport by rail and bus:

- If you are travelling from Fife, Dundee and other areas north, you should catch a train to Inverkeithing – from here a frequent bus service operates to Edinburgh Airport
- If you are travelling from other parts of Scotland, including the Glasgow area, you should catch a train to Haymarket or Edinburgh Waverley – a frequent bus service operates to Edinburgh Airport from both these stations

For full bus timetable information, call **0871 200 22 33**, or visit **www.travelinescotland.com**

Exeter International Airport

Stagecoach operates an hourly daytime service (Service Number 56) from Exeter St. Davids station forecourt direct to Exeter Airport. For more information call Traveline on **0871 200 22 33** or visit **www.traveline.info.**

Airport Links (continued)

Glasgow Airport

There are three ways to get to Glasgow Airport by rail and bus:

- If you are travelling from Ayrshire or Inverclyde, you should catch a train to Paisley Gilmour Street – a frequent bus service operates from here to Glasgow Airport
- If you are travelling from north west Glasgow, Milngavie, Dumbarton, Helensburgh and the West Highlands, you should catch a train to Partick – from here a frequent bus service operates to Glasgow Airport
- If you are travelling from other parts of Scotland, including Edinburgh and the central belt, you should catch a train to Glasgow Central or Glasgow Queen Street – a frequent bus service operates to Glasgow Airport from both these stations

For full bus timetable information, call **0871 200 22 33**, or visit **www.travelinescotland.com**

Leeds Bradford International Airport

Leeds Bradford International Airport is located to the north of the cities of Bradford and Leeds, to the south of Harrogate and to the west of York. For more information on Leeds Bradford International Airport visit **www.leedsbradfordairport.co.uk**

From Leeds - Centrebus Airport Direct 757, operates half hourly throughout the day Mondays to Saturdays (hourly early mornings, evenings and Sundays) every day from Stand S7 from outside Leeds Rail Station (Leeds Station Interchange). The journey time is approximately 40 minutes. Through ticketing is available.

From Bradford - a half hourly combined service, provided by Centrebus Airport Direct services 737 and 747, operates throughout the day from Bradford Interchange rail station. Airport Direct 747 also operates close to Bradford Forster Square rail station (hourly). The journey time from Bradford is approximately 40 minutes. Through ticketing is available with a PlusBus ticket.

From Harrogate - Airport Direct 737, operates hourly, every day from Harrogate Bus Station to the airport. The journey time from Harrogate is approximately 35 minutes.

From York - There is no bus service between York and the airport. If you are travelling from the North East, please travel via Leeds, purchasing a combined rail and bus travel ticket.

Centrebus Airport Direct services 737, 747 and 757 run alongside other local bus services which link to Leeds Bradford International Airport.

For more information please telephone Traveline on **0871 200 22 33** or visit **www.traveline.info**

Liverpool John Lennon Airport

Regular bus services operate between Liverpool John Lennon Airport and the Liverpool South Parkway station; journey time is 10 minutes. Liverpool South Parkway is served by direct services from North, South and East Liverpool, Leeds, York, Sheffield, Nottingham, Manchester, Warrington, Southport, Crewe, Stafford, Wolverhampton and Birmingham.

The airport is located to the south of the city centre. A direct bus service operates between Lime Street, Moorfields and James Street stations to the airport seven days a week. Buses run every 30 minutes between 0600 & 0100 hours from the Liverpool City Centre Stations to the Airport, and between 0515 and 0015 from the Airport to the Liverpool City Centre Stations. Journey time is approximately 45 minutes.

For further information please contact **0871 200 22 33,** or visit **www.traveline.info**.

London City Airport

London City Airport is located in London's Docklands, to the east of the capital. There are no National Rail services direct to the airport.

Access to the airport is available via the Docklands Light Railway to and from London City Airport Station which is located next to the terminal building. Between Central London and the airport, passengers can travel on the London Underground Jubilee Line and change at Canning Town for the Docklands Light Railway. Connections between National Rail and the Docklands Light Railway are available at Greenwich, Lewisham, Limehouse, Stratford and Woolwich Arsenal.

For further information on London City Airport telephone **020 7646 0088** or visit **www.londoncityairport.com**.

London Gatwick Airport

Gatwick has its own railway station underneath the South Terminal. Access to the North Terminal is via a free transit.

Airport to/from London

Gatwick Express operate a dedicated non-stop service every 15 minutes throughout most of the day between London Victoria and Gatwick Airport (See Table 186).

Southern provides frequent trains throughout the day and hourly throughout the night between London Victoria and Gatwick Airport (See Table 186).

First Capital Connect operate direct services throughout the day between London St Pancras International, Farringdon, City Thameslink, London Blackfriars, London Bridge and Gatwick Airport (generally every 15 mins, See Table 52), a reduced frequency operates throughout the night. The most convenient connection option is Victoria. Overnight and at weekends it may be necessary to use London bus or Tube services to travel to/from stations north of London Bridge. Your rail ticket will be valid.

Airport to/from Reading

First Great Western operate a direct rail service between Reading and Gatwick – (See Table 148). Customers using this route should allow at least 7 minutes at Reading to make a connection.

Other direct services to/from Airport

Southern also operates direct services to/from Hastings, Southampton, Portsmouth and intermediate stations on the South Coast (See Tables 186, 187, 188, 189) Clapham Jn and East Croydon (SeeTable 186).

First Great Western operate services from Wokingham, North Camp and Guildford (See Table 148).

Airport Links (continued)

First Capital Connect provide regular direct services from Gatwick Airport to St. Albans, Luton, Bedford, East Croydon, Haywards Heath and Brighton (See Table 52). At Luton Airport Parkway, Luton and Bedford, they also offer convenient connections with East Midlands Trains to Leicester, Derby, Nottingham and Sheffield (See Table 53).

London Heathrow Airport

Airport to/from Central London

Heathrow Express operates a direct high-speed rail service from the Airport to London Paddington. Stations are located in all Heathrow terminals - Heathrow Central (Terminals 1, 2 & 3), Terminal 4 and Terminal 5. Journey time is 15 minutes between Paddington and Terminals 1, 2 and 3, with a further 6 minutes to Terminal 5. Trains run every 15 minutes. A free transfer service operates to Terminal 4 from Heathrow Central, departing every 15 minutes and arriving in 4 minutes.

- 0510 to 2325 from Paddington
- 0507 to 2342 from Heathrow Terminal 5 (0503 to 2348 on Sundays)
- 0512 to 2348 from Heathrow Terminal 1, 2 and 3 (0508 to 2353 on Sundays)

For further details see Table 118.

Through tickets can be purchased from any National Rail or London Underground Station to the airport via Heathrow Express.

For further information visit **www.heathrowexpress.com**.

Heathrow Connect operates a local rail service every 30 minutes between Heathrow Central and London Paddington, calling at Hayes & Harlington, Southall, Hanwell, West Ealing and Ealing Broadway. For details see Table 117.

Through tickets are available from most stations.

The London Underground Piccadilly Line connects central London with all five terminals (Terminal 1/2/3, Terminal 4 and Terminal 5).

Through single and return tickets can be issued to customers travelling via a Rail terminus in Zone 1. Sample journey time from Piccadilly Circus to the Airport is approximately one hour.

Airport to/from Reading

RailAir coaches leave from Reading railway station every 20 minutes during the daytime on Mondays to Fridays (every 30 minutes early weekday mornings and evenings, on weekends and public holidays). The luxury, air-conditioned coaches run non-stop to Terminals 1, 2 and 3 in 40-50 minutes. On the return journey from Heathrow Airport they only pick up passengers at Heathrow Central Bus Station (stands one and two) and not the terminals. Customers travelling to/from Terminal 4 should use Heathrow Connect from Terminal 1.

Follow the RailAir signs from your platform at Reading station. You can buy your ticket in the RailAir lounge, or combined rail and coach tickets are also available from many stations. You should allow 15 minutes at Reading to transfer between train and coach.

For further information telephone **0118 957 9425** or visit **www.RailAir.com.**

Airport to/from Woking

Coaches leave at half-hourly intervals throughout most of the day to/from Terminal 5 and Heathrow Central Bus Station (for Terminals 1, 2 and 3) (see Table 158A).

Customers travelling to Heathrow should exit on platform 5 and the coach leaves from outside the station.

On arrival at Woking customers should allow at least 10 minutes to transfer to your train after the arrival of the coach at the station. Combined rail and coach tickets are available from most National Rail stations and from the Railair sales points at the airport. Tickets may also be booked at **www.nationalexpress.com** or by calling **08717 818 181**. For through trains and coach times, telephone **08457 48 49 50.** (calls may be recorded for training purposes)

Airport to/from Feltham

London Buses operates frequent bus services from Feltham Station to Heathrow Airport. Route 285 operates to Hatton Cross and Heathrow Central Bus Station for Terminals 1, 2 and 3. Buses operate every 10 minutes during the day, 15 minutes in the evenings and on Sundays and 30 minutes throughout the night.

Route 490 operates to Hatton Cross and Terminals 4 and 5. Buses operate every 12 minutes during the day, 20 minutes in the evenings and on Sundays.

Customers should allow 10 minutes at Feltham to transfer between train and bus from the station forecourt adjoining platform 1.

Other direct services to/from Airport

A coach service, Green Line 724, runs throughout the day between Heathrow, West Drayton, Uxbridge, Rickmansworth, Watford, St. Albans, Hatfield, Welwyn Garden City, Hertford and Harlow. Tickets can only be purchased on the coach. A frequent bus service (route 140) runs 24 hours between Hayes & Harlington and Heathrow Airport (Central Bus Station).

For further information telephone **0870 608 7261** (Green Line Travel Information)

London Luton Airport

A frequent dedicated shuttle bus links Luton Airport with Luton Airport Parkway station – journey time 5 minutes. Luton Airport Parkway is served by frequent First Capital Connect services direct to Bedford, Central London, South London, Gatwick Airport and Brighton – see Table 52 for details. East Midlands Trains services link Luton Airport Parkway with St Pancras International and Leicester, Derby, Nottingham and Sheffield – see Table 53 for details.

In addition a coach link operates between the Airport, Luton railway station and town centre and Milton Keynes Central railway station and town centre (see Table 65B for details).

Airport Links (continued)

London Stansted Airport

Stansted Airport has its own railway station right in the heart of the airport terminal building.

The Stansted Express is a dedicated rail service operating between London Liverpool Street and Stansted Airport station (See Table 22). Trains run every 15 minutes throughout the day, seven days per week.

CrossCountry operates an hourly express service seven days a week between Birmingham and Stansted Airport calling at Leicester, Peterborough and Cambridge – see Table 49 – offering connections with services to Yorkshire and the North East. Customers should be advised to arrive at the airport 1 hour 45 minutes prior to their latest check-in time.

London Southend Airport

Southend Airport is served by its own brand new station adjacent to the airport, operated by Stobart Group. The station is served by trains on the London Liverpool Street to Southend Victoria line, generally every 20 minutes (every 10 minutes at peak times). Journey times to and from London are 52-54 minutes off-peak (55-56 minutes at peak times) and 62 minutes on Sundays.

Manchester Airport

The airport railway station is right in the heart of the airport complex, linked by covered travellators. The station is served by up to 8 trains per hour from Manchester Piccadilly and direct services operate between Middlesbrough, Newcastle, York, Leeds, Huddersfield, Cleethorpes, Doncaster, Sheffield, Edinburgh, Glasgow, Carlisle, Barrow-in-Furness, Windermere, Lancaster, Preston, Liverpool and the Airport. Additional regular services operate during the day, to/from many stations which can be found under the entry for Manchester Airport in the index in this timetable.

Newcastle Airport

Tyne & Wear Metro trains operate every 12 - 15 minutes most of the day between Newcastle Central Station and Newcastle Airport providing links with Northern, East Coast, First TransPennine Express and CrossCountry services. The journey time is about 25 minutes.

Tyne & Wear Metro services also run to Sunderland Rail station, a journey time of about an hour providing connections with Northern and Grand Central services.

Through ticketing is available to Newcastle Airport via the Tyne & Wear Metro.

For information please telephone Traveline on **0871 200 22 33** or visit **www.traveline.info**

Prestwick International Airport

Prestwick International Airport has its own rail station, served by fast and frequent trains from Glasgow, Paisley, Ayr and intermediate stations.

See Table 221 for details.

Robin Hood Airport

Doncaster Airport or Doncaster Sheffield

Robin Hood Airport is situated 7 miles south of Doncaster. For more information on Robin Hood Airport visit **www.robinhoodairport.com**

From Doncaster - First service 91 runs half hourly throughout the day Mondays to Saturdays, hourly early mornings, evenings and Sundays from Doncaster Frenchgate Interchange, which is adjacent to Doncaster Rail station, direct to the airport. Journey time is approximately 25 minutes.

Through ticketing is available to Robin Hood Airport via service 91.

Service 91 runs alongside other local bus services which link to Robin Hood Airport, including service X19 from Barnsley.

For more information please telephone Traveline on **0871 200 22 33** or visit **www.traveline.info**

Southampton Airport

Southampton Airport (Parkway) station is adjacent to Southampton Airport.

South West Trains operate up to 3 trains per hour between London Waterloo, Winchester and Southampton Airport (Parkway) with up to 2 direct services to Bournemouth, Poole, Wareham and Weymouth and most intermediate stations (See Table 158).

CrossCountry services link Southampton Airport Parkway with Bournemouth, Reading, Oxford, Newcastle and Manchester (see Table 51).

On Saturdays Southern operate trains every two hours between Brighton, Worthing, Chichester, Havant, Cosham, Fareham and Southampton Airport, at other times use Southern's regular trains to Southampton Central and connecting train to Southampton Airport.

Station index and table numbers

[10] Connection time
Ⓟ Station Car Park
🚲 Bicycle storage facility
◇ Seat reservations can be made at this station
⚠ Penalty Fare Schemes in operation on some or all services from this station
🚕 Taxi rank or cab office at station, or signposted and within 100 metres
Ⓤ Unstaffed station
[ ] Station Operator Code

A

Abbey Wood [SE] Ⓟ 🚲 ◇ ⚠ 🚕 200
Aber [AW] Ⓟ 130
Abercynon [AW] Ⓤ 130
Aberdare [AW] [3] Ⓟ ◇ 130
Aberdeen [SR] Ⓟ 🚲 ◇ 🚕
Birmingham 51, 65
Blackpool 65
Bournemouth 51
Bristol 51
Cambridge 26
Cardiff 51
Carlisle 65
Crewe 65, *Sleepers* 402
Darlington 26
Derby 51
Doncaster 26
Dundee 229
Dyce 240
Edinburgh 229
Elgin 240
Exeter 51
Glasgow 229
Grantham 26
Inverkeithing 229
Inverness 240
Inverurie 240
Kirkcaldy 229
Kyle of Lochalsh 239
Leeds 26
Liverpool 65
London 26, *Sleepers* 402
Manchester 65
Newcastle 26
Newport (South Wales) 51
Norwich 26
Oxenholme Lake District 65
Oxford 51
Paignton 51
Penzance 51
Perth 229
Peterborough 26
Plymouth 51
Preston 65, *Sleepers* 402
Reading 51
Sheffield 26
Southampton 51
Stirling 229
Thurso 239
Torquay 51
Watford 65
Wick 239
York 26
Aberdour [SR] Ⓟ 🚲 242
Aberdovey [AW] 🚲 Ⓤ 75
Abererch [AW] Ⓤ 75
Abergavenny [AW] Ⓟ 🚲 ◇ 🚕 131
Abergele & Pensarn [AW] Ⓟ Ⓤ 81
Aberystwyth [AW] Ⓟ ◇ 🚕 75
Accrington [NT] Ⓟ ◇ 🚕 41, 97
Achanalt [SR] Ⓟ 🚲 Ⓤ 239
Achnasheen [SR] Ⓟ 🚲 Ⓤ 239
Achnashellach [SR] Ⓟ 🚲 Ⓤ 239
Acklington [NT] Ⓟ 🚲 Ⓤ 48
Acle [LE] Ⓟ 🚲 Ⓤ 15
Acocks Green [LM] Ⓟ ⚠ 71
Acton Bridge [LM] Ⓟ Ⓤ 91
Acton Central [LO] 🚲 ⚠ 59
Acton Main Line [GW] ⚠ 117
Acton, South [LO] (see South Acton)
Adderley Park [LM] ◇ ⚠ 68
Addiewell [SR] Ⓟ 🚲 Ⓤ 225
Addlestone [SW] ⚠ 🚕 149
Adisham [SE] Ⓟ ⚠ Ⓤ 212
Adlington (Cheshire) [NT] Ⓟ Ⓤ 84
Adlington (Lancashire) [NT] Ⓟ 82
Adwick [NT] Ⓟ 🚲 Ⓤ 29, 31
Agbrigg [NT] (See Sandal & Agbrigg)
Aigburth [ME] Ⓟ ⚠ 103
Ainsdale [ME] Ⓟ ⚠ 103
Aintree [ME] Ⓟ ⚠ 103
Airbles [SR] Ⓟ 🚲 Ⓤ 226
Airdrie [SR] Ⓟ 🚲 ◇ 🚕 226
Albany Park [SE] ◇ ⚠ 200
Albrighton [LM] Ⓟ Ⓤ 74
Alderley Edge [NT] Ⓟ 🚲 84
Aldermaston [GW] Ⓟ Ⓤ 116
Aldershot [SW] Ⓟ 🚲 ◇ ⚠ 🚕 149, 155
Aldrington [SN] ⚠ Ⓤ 188
Alexandra Palace [FC] 🚲 ⚠ 🚕 24
Alexandra Parade [SR] 🚲 Ⓤ 226
Alexandria [SR] Ⓟ 🚲 226
Alfreton [EM] Ⓟ ◇ ⚠ 🚕 34, 49, 53
Allens West [NT] 🚲 Ⓤ 44
Alloa [SR] Ⓟ 🚲 Ⓤ 230
Alness [SR] Ⓟ 🚲 Ⓤ 239
Alnmouth for Alnwick [NT] Ⓟ 🚲 ◇ 26, 48, 51
Alresford [LE] 🚲 ⚠ 11
Alsager [EM] Ⓤ 50, 67
Althorne [LE] Ⓟ 🚲 Ⓤ 5
Althorpe [NT] Ⓤ 29
Altnabreac [SR] 🚲 Ⓤ 239
Alton [SW] Ⓟ 🚲 ◇ ⚠ 🚕 155
Altrincham [NT] Ⓟ 🚲 ◇ 🚕 88
Alvechurch [LM] Ⓟ ⚠ Ⓤ 69
Ambergate [EM] Ⓟ Ⓤ 56
Amberley [SN] 🚲 ⚠ Ⓤ 188
Amersham [LT] Ⓟ 🚲 ⚠ 🚕 114
Ammanford [AW] Ⓤ 129
Ancaster [EM] Ⓟ Ⓤ 19
Anderston [SR] 🚲 226
Andover [SW] Ⓟ 🚲 ⚠ ◇ 🚕 160
Anerley [LO] 🚲 ⚠ 178
Angel Road [LE] ⚠ Ⓤ 22
Angmering [SN] [3] Ⓟ 🚲 ◇ ⚠ 🚕 188
Annan [SR] Ⓟ 🚲 Ⓤ 216
Anniesland [SR] 🚲 🚕 226, 232
Ansdell & Fairhaven [NT] Ⓤ 97
Appleby [NT] Ⓟ ◇ 36
Appledore (Kent) [SN] Ⓤ 189
Appleford [GW] Ⓤ 116
Appley Bridge [NT] Ⓟ Ⓤ 82
Apsley [LM] Ⓟ 66
Arbroath [SR] Ⓟ 🚲 ◇ 🚕 26, 51, 229, *Sleepers* 402
Ardgay [SR] Ⓟ 🚲 Ⓤ 239
Ardlui [SR] 🚲 Ⓤ 227, *Sleepers* 404
Ardrossan Harbour [SR] Ⓟ 🚲 Ⓤ 221, *Ship* 221A
Ardrossan South Beach [SR] Ⓟ 🚲 221
Ardrossan Town [SR] 🚲 Ⓤ 221
Ardwick [NT] Ⓤ 78, 79
Argyle Street [SR] 226
Arisaig [SR] Ⓟ 🚲 Ⓤ 227
Arlesey [FC] Ⓟ 🚲 ⚠ 25
Armadale [SR] Ⓟ 🚲 Ⓤ 226
Armadale (Skye) *Ship* 227A
Armathwaite [NT] Ⓟ Ⓤ 36
Arnside [TP] Ⓤ 82
Arram [NT] Ⓤ 43
Arrochar & Tarbet [SR] Ⓟ 🚲 Ⓤ 227, *Sleepers* 404
Arundel [SN] Ⓟ 🚲 ◇ ⚠ 🚕 188
Ascot [SW] [3] Ⓟ 🚲 ◇ ⚠ 🚕 149
Ascott-under-Wychwood [GW] Ⓤ 126
Ash [SW] Ⓟ 🚲 ◇ ⚠ 148, 149
Ash Vale [SW] 🚲 ◇ ⚠ 149, 155
Ashburys [NT] Ⓤ 78, 79
Ashchurch for Tewkesbury [GW] Ⓟ 🚲 Ⓤ 57
Ashfield [SR] 🚲 Ⓤ 232
Ashford International [SE] Ⓟ 🚲 ◇ ⚠ 🚕 189, 194, 196, 207
Ashford (Surrey) [SW] Ⓟ 🚲 ◇ ⚠ 149
Ashley [NT] Ⓟ Ⓤ 88
Ashtead [SN] Ⓟ 🚲 ◇ ⚠ 152, 182
Ashton-under-Lyne [NT] Ⓟ 🚲 39
Ashurst [SN] Ⓟ ⚠ Ⓤ 184
Ashurst New Forest [SW] Ⓟ 🚲 ⚠ Ⓤ 158
Ashwell & Morden [FC] Ⓟ 🚲 ⚠ 25
Askam [NT] Ⓟ Ⓤ 100
Aslockton [EM] Ⓟ Ⓤ 19
Aspatria [NT] Ⓟ Ⓤ 100
Aspley Guise [LM] Ⓤ 64
Aston [LM] ⚠ 69, 70
Atherstone [LM] Ⓟ Ⓤ 67
Atherton [NT] Ⓟ 🚲 82
Attadale [SR] 🚲 Ⓤ 239
Attenborough [EM] ⚠ Ⓤ 56, 57

■10 Connection time
Ⓟ Station Car Park
🚲 Bicycle storage facility
◇ Seat reservations can be made at this station
⚠ Penalty Fare Schemes in operation on some or all services from this station
🚕 Taxi rank or cab office at station, or signposted and within 100 metres
Ⓤ Unstaffed station
[ ] Station Operator Code

Station index and table numbers

Attleborough [LE] Ⓟ Ⓤ 17
Auchinleck [SR] Ⓟ 🚲 Ⓤ 216
Audley End [LE] Ⓟ 🚲 ⚠ 🚕 22, 49
Aughton Park [ME] ⚠ 103
Aviemore [SR] Ⓟ 🚲 ◇ 🚕 229, *Sleepers* 403
Avoncliff [GW] Ⓤ 123
Avonmouth [GW] ■2 Ⓟ 🚲 Ⓤ 133
Axminster [SW] Ⓟ 🚲 ◇ 🚕 160
Aylesbury [CH] Ⓟ 🚲 ◇ ⚠ 🚕 114, 115
Aylesbury Vale Parkway [CH] Ⓟ 🚲 ◇ ⚠ 114
Aylesford [SE] ⚠ Ⓤ 208
Aylesham [SE] Ⓟ ◇ ⚠ 212
Ayr [SR] Ⓟ 🚲 ◇ 🚕 218, 221,221B

B

Bache [ME] Ⓤ 106
Backwell [GW] (see Nailsea)
Baglan [AW] Ⓟ 🚲 Ⓤ 128
Bagshot [SW] Ⓟ 🚲 ◇ ⚠ 149
Baildon [NT] Ⓟ Ⓤ 38
Baillieston [SR] 🚲 Ⓤ 220
Balcombe [SN] ◇ ⚠ 52, 186
Baldock [FC] Ⓟ ⚠ 25
Balham [SN] ■4 ◇ ⚠ 🚕 176, 177, 178, 182
Balloch [SR] 🚲 🚕 226
Balmossie [SR] 🚲 Ⓤ 229
Bamber Bridge [NT] Ⓟ Ⓤ 97
Bamford [NT] Ⓟ Ⓤ 78
Banavie [SR] Ⓟ 🚲 Ⓤ 227
Banbury [CH] Ⓟ 🚲 ◇ ⚠ 🚕 51, 71, 75, 115, 116
Bangor (Gwynedd) [AW] Ⓟ ◇ 🚕 65, 81, 131
Bank Hall [ME] ⚠ 103
Banstead [SN] ⚠ Ⓤ 182
Barassie [SR] Ⓟ 🚲 Ⓤ 221
Bardon Mill [NT] Ⓟ Ⓤ 48
Bare Lane [NT] Ⓟ Ⓤ 36, 98
Bargeddie [SR] Ⓟ 🚲 Ⓤ 220
Bargoed [AW] 🚕 130
Barking [CC] ◇ ⚠ 🚕 1, 62
Barlaston Orchard Place *Bus* 67
Barming [SE] Ⓟ ◇ ⚠ 196
Barmouth [AW] 🚲 75
Barnehurst [SE] ■4 Ⓟ ◇ ⚠ 🚕 200
Barnes [SW] 🚲 ◇ ⚠ 149
Barnes Bridge [SW] 🚲 ◇ ⚠ Ⓤ 149
Barnetby [TP] Ⓟ Ⓤ 27, 29, 30
Barnham [SN] Ⓟ 🚲 ◇ ⚠ 🚕 123, 188
Barnhill [SR] 🚲 Ⓤ 226
Barnsbury [LO] (see Caledonian Road)
Barnsley [NT] Ⓟ 🚲 ◇ 🚕 30, 34
Barnstaple [GW] Ⓟ 🚲 ◇ 🚕 136
Barnt Green [LM] Ⓟ ⚠ Ⓤ 69, 71
Barrhead [SR] Ⓟ 🚲 🚕 222
Barrhill [SR] Ⓟ 🚲 218
Barrow Haven [NT] Ⓤ 29
Barrow-in-Furness [TP] Ⓟ ◇ 🚕 65, 82, 100
Barrow Upon Soar [EM] ⚠ Ⓤ 53
Barry [AW] ■3 Ⓟ ◇ 🚕 130
Barry Docks [AW] Ⓤ 130
Barry Island [AW] Ⓤ 130
Barry Links [SR] 🚲 Ⓤ 229
Barton-on-Humber [NT] Ⓟ Ⓤ 29
Basildon [CC] 🚲 ◇ ⚠ 🚕 1
Basingstoke [SW] Ⓟ 🚲 ◇ ⚠ 🚕
- Aberdeen 51
- Bath 160
- Birmingham 51
- Bournemouth 158
- Bristol 160
- Brockenhurst 158
- Clapham Junction 155
- Coventry 51
- Crewe 51
- Derby 51
- Dorchester 158
- Dundee 51
- Eastleigh 158
- Edinburgh 51
- Exeter 160
- Fareham 158
- Farnborough 158
- Glasgow 51
- Leeds 51
- London 155
- Lymington 158
- Manchester 51
- Newcastle 51
- Oxford 51
- Poole 158
- Portsmouth 158
- Preston 51
- Reading 122
- Salisbury 160
- Sheffield 51
- Southampton 158
- Southampton Airport 158
- Stoke-on-Trent 51
- Surbiton 155
- Weymouth 158
- Weybridge 155
- Wimbledon 155
- Winchester 158
- Woking 155
- Wolverhampton 51
- Yeovil 160
- York 51

Bat & Ball [SE] Ⓟ ⚠ Ⓤ 52, 195
Bath Spa [GW] ■7 Ⓟ 🚲 ◇ ⚠ 🚕 123, 125, 132, 135, 160
Bathgate [SR] Ⓟ 🚲 ◇ 🚕 226
Batley [NT] Ⓟ 🚲 Ⓤ 39
Battersby [NT] Ⓤ 45
Battersea Park [SN] ■4 ◇ ⚠ 177, 178
Battle [SE] Ⓟ ◇ ⚠ 🚕 206
Battlesbridge [LE] Ⓟ 🚲 Ⓤ 5
Bayford [FC] Ⓟ ⚠ Ⓤ 24
Beaconsfield [CH] Ⓟ 🚲 ◇ ⚠ 🚕 115
Bearley [LM] Ⓟ ⚠ Ⓤ 115
Bearsden [SR] Ⓟ 🚲 🚕 226
Bearsted [SE] Ⓟ 🚲 ◇ ⚠ 196
Beasdale [SR] 🚲 Ⓤ 227
Beaulieu Road [SW] 🚲 ⚠ Ⓤ 158
Beauly [SR] Ⓟ 🚲 Ⓤ 239
Bebington [ME] Ⓟ ⚠ 🚕 106
Beccles [LE] Ⓟ 🚲 Ⓤ 13
Beckenham Hill [SE] 🚲 ◇ ⚠ 52, 195
Beckenham Junction [SE] ■4 Ⓟ 🚲 ◇ ⚠ 🚕 177, 195
Bedford [FC] ■7 Ⓟ 🚲 ◇ ⚠ 🚕
- Barnsley 53
- Bletchley 64
- Brighton 52, 186
- Chesterfield 53
- Derby 53
- Doncaster 53
- East Croydon 52
- Gatwick Airport 52, 186
- Haywards Heath 52, 186
- Herne Hill 52
- Hove 186
- Kettering 53
- Leeds 53
- Leicester 53
- London 52
- Luton 52
- Luton Airport Parkway 52
- Meadowhall 53
- Nottingham 53
- Redhill 52, 186
- St Albans 52
- Sheffield 53
- Sutton (Surrey) 52
- Wakefield 53
- Wellingborough 53
- Wimbledon 52
- York 53

Bedford St Johns [LM] Ⓤ 64
Bedhampton [SW] 🚲 ◇ ⚠ 156, 157, 188
Bedminster [GW] Ⓤ 134
Bedworth [LM] Ⓟ Ⓤ 67
Bedwyn [GW] Ⓟ 🚲 Ⓤ 116
Beeston [EM] Ⓟ 🚲 ◇ ⚠ 53, 56, 57
Bekesbourne [SE] Ⓟ ⚠ Ⓤ 212
Belfast
- Port of *Ship* (via Ayr/Cairnryan) 221B

Belle Vue [NT] Ⓤ 78
Bellgrove [SR] 🚲 Ⓤ 226
Bellingham [SE] 🚲 ◇ ⚠ 52, 195
Bellshill [SR] Ⓟ 🚲 225, 226

Station index and table numbers

10 Connection time
Ⓟ Station Car Park
🚲 Bicycle storage facility
◇ Seat reservations can be made at this station
⚠ Penalty Fare Schemes in operation on some or all services from this station
🚕 Taxi rank or cab office at station, or signposted and within 100 metres
Ⓤ Unstaffed station
[ ] Station Operator Code

Belmont [SN] ⚠ Ⓤ 182
Belper [EM] ⚠ Ⓤ 56
Beltring [SE] ⚠ Ⓤ 208
Belvedere [SE] ◇ ⚠ 200
Bempton [NT] Ⓤ 43
Ben Rhydding [NT] Ⓟ Ⓤ 38
Benfleet [CC] Ⓟ 🚲 ◇ ⚠ 🚕 1
Bentham [NT] Ⓟ Ⓤ 36
Bentley [SW] Ⓟ 🚲 ◇ ⚠ 155
Bentley (S. Yorks.) [NT] Ⓟ 🚲 Ⓤ 29, 31
Bere Alston [GW] Ⓟ Ⓤ 139
Bere Ferrers [GW] Ⓟ 🚲 Ⓤ 139
Berkhamsted [LM] Ⓟ 🚲 ◇ ⚠ 🚕 66, 176
Berkswell [LM] Ⓟ 🚲 ⚠ 68
Berney Arms [LE] 🚲 Ⓤ 15
Berry Brow [NT] Ⓤ 34
Berrylands [SW] Ⓟ 🚲 ◇ ⚠ 152
Berwick [SN] Ⓟ 🚲 ◇ ⚠ 189
Berwick-upon-Tweed [GR] Ⓟ 🚲 ◇ 🚕 26, 26K, 51
Bescar Lane [NT] Ⓤ 82
Bescot Stadium [LM] Ⓟ ◇ ⚠ 70
Betchworth [GW] Ⓤ 148
Bethnal Green [LE] 🚲 ⚠ Ⓤ 20, 21, 22
Betws-y-Coed [AW] Ⓤ 102
Beverley [NT] Ⓟ ◇ 🚕 43
Bexhill [SN] **4** ◇ ⚠ 🚕 189
Bexley [SE] Ⓟ ◇ ⚠ 🚕 200
Bexleyheath [SE] Ⓟ 🚲 ◇ ⚠ 🚕 200
Bicester North [CH] **3** Ⓟ 🚲 ◇ ⚠ 🚕 115
Bicester Town [CH] Ⓟ 🚲 Ⓤ 116
Bickley [SE] **4** Ⓟ ◇ ⚠ 52, 195
Bidston [ME] Ⓟ ⚠ 101, 106
Biggleswade [FC] Ⓟ 🚲 ⚠ 25
Bilbrook [LM] Ⓤ 74
Billericay [LE] Ⓟ 🚲 ⚠ 🚕 5
Billingham [NT] 🚲 🚕 Ⓤ 44
Billingshurst [SN] Ⓟ 🚲 ◇ ⚠ 🚕 188
Bingham [EM] Ⓟ Ⓤ 19
Bingley [NT] Ⓟ 🚲 ◇ 36
Birchgrove [AW] Ⓤ 130
Birchington-on-Sea [SE] Ⓟ 🚲 ◇ ⚠ 🚕 194, 212
Birchwood [TP] Ⓟ 🚲 🚕 39, 89
Birkbeck [SN] ⚠ Ⓤ 177
Birkdale [ME] Ⓟ ⚠ 103
Birkenhead Central [ME] ⚠ 106
Birkenhead North [ME] ⚠ 106
Birkenhead Park [ME] ⚠ 106
Birmingham International [VT] (for National Exhibition Centre and Airport) Ⓟ 🚲 ◇ ⚠ 🚕
Aberdeen 65
Aberystwyth 75
Banbury 71
Bangor (Gwynedd) 65, 81
Basingstoke 51
Birmingham 68
Blackpool 65
Bournemouth 51
Carlisle 65
Chester 65, 75, 81
Clapham Junction 66
Coventry 68
Crewe 65, 81
Derby 51
Dundee 65
East Croydon 66
Edinburgh 51, 65
Glasgow 51, 65
Holyhead 65, 75, 81
Inverness 65
Leamington Spa 71
Leeds 51
Liverpool 65
London 66, 116
Manchester 65
Manchester Airport 65
Milton Keynes Central 66
Newcastle 51
Northampton 66
Nottingham 51
Oxenholme Lake District 65
Oxford 51
Preston 65
Pwllheli 75
Reading 51
Rugby 66
Sheffield 51
Shrewsbury 75
Southampton 51
Stafford 68
Stoke-on-Trent 65
Watford 66
Wolverhampton 68
Wrexham 75
York 51
Birmingham
Moor Street [CH] ◇ ⚠ 🚕
New Street [NR] **12** 🚲 ◇ ⚠ 🚕
Snow Hill [LM] Ⓟ ◇ ⚠
Aberdeen 51, 65
Aberystwyth 75
Banbury 71
Bangor (Gwynedd) 65, 81
Barmouth 75
Barrow-in-Furness 65
Basingstoke 51
Birmingham International 68
Blackpool 65
Bournemouth 51
Bristol 57
Bromsgrove 71
Burton-on-Trent 57
Cambridge 49
Cardiff 57
Carlisle 65
Cheltenham Spa 57
Chester 75, 81
Clapham Junction 66
Coventry 68
Crewe 65
Darlington 51
Derby 57
Douglas (IOM) 98A
Dundee 51, 65
East Croydon 66
Edinburgh 51, 65
Ely 49
Exeter 51
Glasgow 51, 65
Gloucester 57
Hereford 71
Holyhead 65, 81
Inverness 65
Kidderminster 71
Leamington Spa 71
Leeds 51
Leicester 57
Lichfield 69
Liverpool 65, 91
Llandudno 81
London 66, 115, 116
Longbridge 69
Manchester 65, 84
Manchester Airport 65, 84
Milton Keynes Central 66
Newcastle 51
Newport (South Wales) 57
Northampton 66
Norwich 49
Nottingham 57
Nuneaton 57
Oxenholme Lake District 65
Oxford 116
Paignton 135
Penzance 135
Peterborough 49
Plymouth 135
Preston 65
Reading 116
Redditch 69
Rugby 66
Rugeley 70
Sheffield 51
Shrewsbury 74
Solihull 71
Southampton 51
Stafford 68
Stansted Airport 49
Stockport 65
Stoke-on-Trent 65
Stourbridge 71
Stratford-upon-Avon 71
Telford 74
Torquay 135
Walsall 70
Warrington 65
Warwick 71
Watford 66
Wigan 65
Wolverhampton 68
Worcester 71
Wrexham 75
York 51
Birnam [SR] (see Dunkeld)
Bishop Auckland [NT] Ⓟ 🚕 Ⓤ 44

Station index and table numbers

⑩ Connection time
Ⓟ Station Car Park
🚲 Bicycle storage facility
◇ Seat reservations can be made at this station
⚠ Penalty Fare Schemes in operation on some or all services from this station
🚕 Taxi rank or cab office at station, or signposted and within 100 metres
Ⓤ Unstaffed station
[ ] Station Operator Code

Bishopbriggs [SR] 🚲 228, 230
Bishops Lydeard Hithermead *Bus* 135E
Bishops Stortford [LE] Ⓟ 🚲 ◇ ⚠ 🚕 22
Bishopstone [SN] Ⓤ 189
Bishopton [SR] Ⓟ 🚲 219
Bitterne [SW] Ⓟ 🚲 ⚠ Ⓤ 165
Blackburn [NT] Ⓟ ◇ 🚕 41, 94, 97
Blackfriars [FC] (see London)
Blackheath [SE] ④ ◇ ⚠ 🚕 200
Blackhorse Road [LT] ⚠ 62
Blackpool
- **North [NT]** Ⓟ ◇ 🚕
- **Pleasure Beach [NT]** Ⓤ
- **South [NT]** 🚕 Ⓤ

Birmingham 65
Birmingham International 65
Blackburn 97
Bolton 82
Bradford 41
Burnley 97
Colne 97
Coventry 65
Crewe 65
Lancaster 65
Leeds 41
Liverpool 65, 90
London 65
Manchester 82
Manchester Airport 82
Milton Keynes Central 65
Preston 97
Rugby 65
St Helens 90
Stafford 65
Stockport 82
Warrington 65
Watford 65
Wigan 65
Wolverhampton 65
York 41

Blackridge [SR] Ⓟ 🚲 Ⓤ 226
Blackrod [NT] Ⓤ 82
Blackwater [GW] Ⓟ Ⓤ 148
Blaenau Ffestiniog [AW] Ⓤ 102
Blair Atholl [SR] Ⓟ 🚲 229, *Sleepers* 403
Blairhill [SR] Ⓟ 🚲 🚕 226
Blake Street [LM] Ⓟ ⚠ 69
Blakedown [LM] Ⓟ ⚠ Ⓤ 71
Blantyre [SR] Ⓟ 🚲 226
Blaydon [NT] Ⓤ 48
Bleasby [EM] Ⓤ 27
Bledlow, Village Hall *Bus* 115A
Bletchley [LM] Ⓟ 🚲 ◇ ⚠ 🚕 64, 66, 176
Bloxwich [LM] ⚠ Ⓤ 70
Bloxwich North [LM] ⚠ Ⓤ 70
Bluewater [SE] (see Greenhithe for Bluewater)
Blundellsands & Crosby [ME] Ⓟ ⚠ 103
Blythe Bridge [EM] Ⓟ Ⓤ 50
Bodmin Mount Folly *Bus* 135C
Bodmin Parkway [GW] Ⓟ 🚲 ◇ 🚕 51, 135, *Bus* 135C, *Sleepers* 406
Bodorgan [AW] Ⓟ Ⓤ 81
Bognor Regis [SN] Ⓟ 🚲 ◇ ⚠ 🚕 188
Bogston [SR] 🚲 Ⓤ 219
Bolton [NT] 🚲 ◇ 🚕 65, 82, 94
Bolton-upon-Dearne [NT] Ⓟ Ⓤ 31
Bookham [SW] Ⓟ 🚲 ◇ ⚠ 🚕 152, 182
Bootle [NT] Ⓤ 100
Bootle New Strand [ME] ⚠ 🚕 103
Bootle Oriel Road [ME] Ⓟ ⚠ 103
Bordesley [LM] ⚠ Ⓤ 71
Borehamwood [FC] (see Elstree)
Borough Green & Wrotham [SE] Ⓟ ◇ ⚠ 🚕 196
Borth [AW] Ⓟ Ⓤ 75
Bosham [SN] 🚲 ⚠ 188
Boston [EM] Ⓟ 🚲 ◇ 🚕 19
Botley [SW] Ⓟ 🚲 ⚠ Ⓤ 158
Bottesford [EM] Ⓟ Ⓤ 19
Bourne End [GW] ③ Ⓟ 🚲 ⚠ 120
Bournemouth [SW] Ⓟ 🚲 ◇ ⚠ 🚕 51, 158
Bournville [LM] ⚠ 69
Bow Brickhill [LM] Ⓤ 64
Bowes Park [FC] ⚠ 24
Bowling [SR] Ⓟ 🚲 Ⓤ 226
Box Hill & Westhumble [SN] Ⓟ ⚠ Ⓤ 152, 182
Bracknell [SW] Ⓟ 🚲 ◇ ⚠ 🚕 149
Bradford
- **Forster Square [NT]** Ⓟ 🚲 ◇ 🚕
- **Interchange [NT]** 🚲 ◇ 🚕

Blackpool 41
Blackburn 41
Brighouse 41
Cambridge 26
Carlisle 36
Grantham 26
Halifax 41
Huddersfield 41
Ilkley 38
Lancaster 36
Leeds 37
London 26
Manchester 41
Morecambe 36
Newark 26
Norwich 26
Peterborough 26
Preston 41
Retford 26
Rochdale 41
Selby 40
Settle 36
Shipley 37
Skipton 36
York 40

Bradford-on-Avon [GW] Ⓟ 🚲 ◇ 🚕 123, 160
Brading [IL] Ⓟ Ⓤ 167
Braintree [LE] Ⓟ 🚲 ⚠ 🚕 11
Braintree Freeport [LE] 🚲 ⚠ Ⓤ 11
Bramhall [NT] 84
Bramley (Hants) [GW] ⚠ 122
Bramley [NT] Ⓟ Ⓤ 37, 41
Brampton (Cumbria) [NT] Ⓟ Ⓤ 48
Brampton (Suffolk) [LE] Ⓤ 13
Branchton [SR] Ⓟ 🚲 Ⓤ 219
Brandon [LE] Ⓟ Ⓤ 17
Branksome [SW] Ⓟ 🚲 ◇ ⚠ 158
Braystones [NT] Ⓤ 100
Bredbury [NT] Ⓟ 🚲 78
Breich [SR] 🚲 Ⓤ 225
Brentford [SW] Ⓟ 🚲 ◇ 🚕 149
Brentwood [LE] Ⓟ 🚲 ⚠ 🚕 5
Bricket Wood [LM] Ⓤ 61
Bridge of Allan [SR] Ⓟ 🚲 Ⓤ 229,230
Bridge of Orchy [SR] Ⓟ 🚲 Ⓤ 227, *Sleepers* 404
Bridgend [AW] Ⓟ 🚲 ◇ 🚕 125, 128, 130
Bridgeton [SR] 🚲 🚕 226
Bridgwater [GW] Ⓟ ◇ 134, 135
Bridlington [NT] Ⓟ 🚲 ◇ 🚕 43
Brierfield [NT] Ⓟ Ⓤ 97
Brigg [NT] Ⓟ Ⓤ 30
Brighouse [NT] Ⓟ Ⓤ 26, 32, 41
Brighton [SN] ⑩ Ⓟ 🚲 ◇ ⚠ 🚕

Ashford International 189
Bath Spa 123
Bedford 52
Bognor Regis 188
Bristol 123
Cardiff 123
Chichester 188
Eastbourne 189
East Croydon 176, 186
Elstree & Borehamwood 52
Gatwick Airport 186
Hastings 189
Haywards Heath 186
Hove 188
Isle of Wight 167
Kensington (Olympia) 176
Lewes 189
Littlehampton 188
London 186
Luton 52
Luton Airport Parkway 52
Mill Hill Broadway 52
Milton Keynes Central 176
Portsmouth 188
Radlett 52
Redhill 186
St Albans 52
Salisbury 123
Seaford 189

Station index and table numbers

■10 Connection time
Ⓟ Station Car Park
🚲 Bicycle storage facility
◇ Seat reservations can be made at this station
⚠ Penalty Fare Schemes in operation on some or all services from this station
🚕 Taxi rank or cab office at station, or signposted and within 100 metres
Ⓤ Unstaffed station
[ ] Station Operator Code

Southampton Central 188
Watford Junction 176
West Hampstead Thameslink 52
Worthing 188
Brimsdown [LE] ⚠ 22
Brinnington [NT] 78
Bristol International Airport *Bus* 🚕 125B
Bristol
Parkway [GW] ■7 Ⓟ 🚲 ◇ ⚠ 🚕
Temple Meads [GW] ■10 Ⓟ 🚲 ◇ ⚠ 🚕
Aberdeen 51
Bath Spa 132
Birmingham 57
Brighton 123
Bristol International Airport *Bus* 125B
Cardiff 132
Carlisle 51
Cheltenham Spa 57
Crewe 51
Darlington 51
Derby 57
Dundee 51
Edinburgh 51
Exeter 135
Glasgow 51
Gloucester 134
Leeds 51
London 125, 160
Manchester 51
Newcastle 51
Newport (South Wales) 132
Nottingham 57
Paignton 135
Penzance 135
Plymouth 135
Portsmouth 123
Preston 51
Reading 125
Salisbury 123
Severn Beach 133
Sheffield 51
Slough 125
Southampton Central 123
Stoke-on-Trent 51
Swindon 125
Taunton 134
Temple Meads/Parkway 134
Torquay 135
Westbury 123
Weston-super-Mare 134
Weymouth 123
Wolverhampton 51
Worcester 57
York 51
Brithdir [AW] Ⓤ 130
British Steel Redcar [NT] Ⓤ 44
Briton Ferry [AW] Ⓟ Ⓤ 128
Brixton [SE] ◇ ⚠ 195
Broad Green [NT] 90
Broadbottom [NT] Ⓟ 79
Broadstairs [SE] Ⓟ 🚲 ◇ 🚕 194, 207, 212
Brockenhurst [SW] ■3 Ⓟ 🚲 ◇ ⚠ 🚕 51, 158
Brockholes [NT] Ⓤ 34
Brockley [LO] 🚲 ⚠ 178
Brodick *Ship* 221A
Bromborough [ME] Ⓟ 🚲 ⚠ 106
Bromborough Rake [ME] ⚠ 106
Bromley Cross [NT] Ⓟ 🚲 94
Bromley North [SE] Ⓟ ◇ ⚠ 🚕 204
Bromley South [SE] ■4 ◇ ⚠ 🚕 52, 195, 196, 212
Bromsgrove [LM] Ⓟ Ⓤ 69, 71
Brondesbury [LO] 🚲 ⚠ 59
Brondesbury Park [LO] 🚲 ⚠ 59
Brookmans Park [FC] Ⓟ 🚲 ⚠ 24
Brookwood [SW] ■3 Ⓟ 🚲 ◇ ⚠ 🚕 155
Broome [AW] Ⓤ 129
Broomfleet [NT] Ⓟ Ⓤ 29
Brora [SR] Ⓟ 🚲 Ⓤ 239
Brough [TP] Ⓟ 🚲 ◇ 🚕 29, 39
Broughty Ferry [SR] 🚲 Ⓤ 229
Broxbourne [LE] ■3 Ⓟ 🚲 ⚠ 🚕 22
Bruce Grove [LE] ⚠ 21
Brundall [LE] Ⓟ 🚲 15
Brundall Gardens [LE] 🚲 Ⓤ 15
Brunstane [SR] 🚲 Ⓤ 242
Brunswick [ME] Ⓟ 🚲 103
Bruton [GW] Ⓟ Ⓤ 123
Bryn [NT] Ⓤ 90
Buckenham [LE] 🚲 Ⓤ 15
Buckley [AW] Ⓟ Ⓤ 101
Bucknell [AW] Ⓤ 129
Buckshaw Parkway [NT] Ⓟ 82
Bude Strand *Bus* 135D
Bugle [GW] 🚲 Ⓤ 142
Builth Road [AW] Ⓤ 129
Bulwell [EM] Ⓟ Ⓤ 55
Bures [LE] 🚲 Ⓤ 10
Burgess Hill [SN] ■4 Ⓟ 🚲 ◇ ⚠ 🚕 52, 186, 188
Burley Park [NT] Ⓟ Ⓤ 35
Burley-in-Wharfedale [NT] Ⓟ 🚲 Ⓤ 38
Burnage [NT] 85
Burneside [TP] Ⓤ 83
Burnham [GW] Ⓟ 🚲 ⚠ 🚕 117
Burnham-on-Crouch [LE] Ⓟ 🚲 5
Burnham-on-Sea [GW] (see Highbridge)
Burnley Barracks [NT] Ⓤ 97
Burnley Central [NT] Ⓟ ◇ 97
Burnley Manchester Road [NT] Ⓟ Ⓤ 41, 97
Burnside [SR] 🚲 223
Burntisland [SR] Ⓟ 🚲 242
Burry Port [AW] (see Pembrey)
Burscough Bridge [NT] Ⓟ 82
Burscough Junction [NT] Ⓟ Ⓤ 99
Bursledon [SW] Ⓟ 🚲 ⚠ Ⓤ 165
Burton Joyce [EM] Ⓤ 27
Burton-on-Trent [EM] Ⓟ ◇ 🚕 51, 57
Bury St Edmunds [LE] Ⓟ 🚲 ◇ 🚕 14
Busby [SR] Ⓟ 🚲 Ⓤ 222
Bushey [LO] Ⓟ 🚲 ⚠ 🚕 60, 66
Bush Hill Park [LE] Ⓟ ⚠ 🚕 21
Butlers Lane [LM] ⚠ 69
Buxted [SN] Ⓟ 🚲 ⚠ 184
Buxton [NT] Ⓟ ◇ 82, 86
Byfleet & New Haw [SW] 🚲 ◇ ⚠ 🚕 149, 155
Bynea [AW] Ⓤ 129

C

Cadoxton [AW] Ⓟ ◇ 130
Caergwrle [AW] Ⓤ 101
Caerphilly [AW] ■3 Ⓟ 🚲 ◇ 🚕 130
Caersws [AW] Ⓟ Ⓤ 75
Caldercruix [SR] Ⓟ 🚲 Ⓤ 226
Caldicot [AW] Ⓤ 132
Caledonian Rd & Barnsbury [LO] ⚠ 59
Calstock [GW] Ⓟ 🚲 Ⓤ 139
Cam & Dursley [GW] Ⓟ 🚲 Ⓤ 134
Camberley [SW] Ⓟ 🚲 ◇ ⚠ 🚕 149
Camborne [GW] Ⓟ 🚲 ◇ 🚕 51, 135, *Sleepers* 406
Cambridge [LE] Ⓟ 🚲 ◇ ⚠ 🚕
Birmingham 49
Bishops Stortford 22
Broxbourne 22
Doncaster 26
Edinburgh 26
Ely 17
Finsbury Park 25
Grantham 26
Harlow 22
Harwich International 14
Hitchin 25
Ipswich 14
Kings Lynn 17
Leeds 26
Leicester 49
Liverpool 49
London
Kings Cross 17, 25
Liverpool St. 17, 22
Manchester 49
Newark 26
Newcastle 26
Norwich 17
Nottingham 49
Peterborough 17

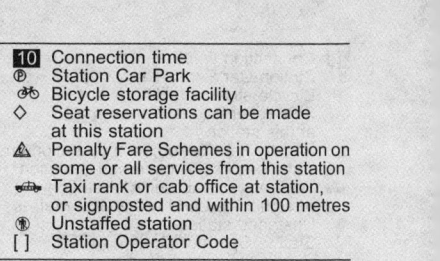

Station index and table numbers

10 Connection time
Ⓟ Station Car Park
🚲 Bicycle storage facility
◇ Seat reservations can be made at this station
⚠ Penalty Fare Schemes in operation on some or all services from this station
🚕 Taxi rank or cab office at station, or signposted and within 100 metres
Ⓤ Unstaffed station
[ ] Station Operator Code

Retford 26
Royston 25
Sheffield 49
Stansted Airport 22
Stevenage 25
Stockport 49
Tottenham Hale 22
Welwyn Garden City 25
York 26
Cambridge Heath [LE] ⚠ Ⓤ 21
Cambuslang [SR] 🚲 🚕 225, 226
Camden Road [LO] 🚲 ⚠ 59
Camelon [SR] Ⓟ 🚲 Ⓤ 224, 230
Canada Water [LT] 178
Canley [LM] Ⓟ 🚲 ⚠ 68
Canna *Ship* 227A
Cannock [LM] Ⓟ ⚠ Ⓤ 70
Cannon Street [NR] (see London)
Canonbury [LO] ⚠ 59,178
Canterbury East [SE] **4** Ⓟ 🚲 ◇ ⚠ 🚕 212
Canterbury West [SE] **4** Ⓟ 🚲 ◇ ⚠ 🚕 194, 207
Cantley [LE] Ⓟ 🚲 Ⓤ 15
Capenhurst [ME] Ⓟ Ⓤ 106
Carbis Bay [GW] Ⓟ Ⓤ 144
Cardenden [SR] Ⓟ 🚲 Ⓤ 242
Cardiff
Bay [AW] Ⓤ
Central [AW] **7** Ⓟ 🚲 ◇ 🚕
Queen Street [AW] **3** ◇
Aberdeen 51
Aberystwyth 75
Bangor (Gwynedd) 81, 131
Barry Island 130
Bath Spa 132
Birmingham 57
Bridgend 128, 130
Brighton 123
Bristol 132
Cheltenham Spa 57
Chester 75, 81, 131
Coryton 130
Crewe 131
Darlington 51
Derby 57
Dundee 51
Durham 51
Ebbw Vale Parkway 127
Edinburgh 51
Exeter 135
Fishguard Harbour 128
Gloucester 132
Hereford 131
Holyhead 81, 131
Leeds 51
Llandudno Junction 81, 131
London 125
Maesteg 128
Manchester 131
Merthyr Tydfil 130
Milford Haven 128
Newcastle 51
Newport (South Wales) 132
Nottingham 57
Paignton 135
Penzance 135
Plymouth 135
Pontypridd 130
Portsmouth 123
Reading 125
Rhoose 130
Rhymney 130
Rosslare Harbour 128
Sheffield 51
Shrewsbury 131
Slough 125
Southampton Central 123
Swansea 128
Swindon 125
Taunton 132, 134
Torquay 135
Treherbert 130
Weymouth 123
Worcester 57
Wrexham 75
York 51
Cardiff International Airport [AW] (see Rhoose)
Cardonald [SR] 🚲 219
Cardross [SR] Ⓟ 🚲 226
Carfin [SR] Ⓟ 🚲 Ⓤ 225
Cark [NT] Ⓟ Ⓤ 82
Carlisle [VT] **8** Ⓟ 🚲 ◇ 🚕
Aberdeen 65
Barrow-in-Furness 100
Birmingham 65
Blackpool 36, 65
Bolton 65
Bournemouth 51
Bradford 36
Bristol 51
Coventry 65
Crewe 65
Dumfries 216
Dundee 65
Exeter 51
Edinburgh 65
Glasgow 65, 216
Haymarket 65
Hexham 48
Inverness 65
Kilmarnock 216
Lancaster 65
Leeds 36
Liverpool 65
London 65, *Sleepers* 400, 401
Manchester 65
Manchester Airport 65
Milton Keynes Central 65
Motherwell 65
Newcastle 48
Oxenholme Lake District 65
Oxford 51
Penzance 51
Perth 65
Plymouth 51
Preston 65
Reading 51
Rugby 65
Settle 36
Skipton 36
Southampton 51
Stafford 65
Warrington 65
Watford 65, *Sleepers* 400, 401
Whitehaven 100
Wigan 65
Wolverhampton 65
Workington 100
Carlton [EM] Ⓟ Ⓤ 27
Carluke [SR] Ⓟ 🚲 226
Carmarthen [AW] Ⓟ 🚲 ◇ ⚠ 🚕 128
Carmyle [SR] 🚲 Ⓤ 220
Carnforth [TP] Ⓟ Ⓤ 36, 82
Carnoustie [SR] Ⓟ 🚲 🚕 Ⓤ 229, *Sleepers* 402
Carntyne [SR] 🚲 Ⓤ 226
Carpenders Park [LO] 🚲 ⚠ 🚕 60
Carrbridge [SR] Ⓟ 🚲 Ⓤ 229
Carshalton [SN] Ⓟ ◇ ⚠ 52, 179, 182
Carshalton Beeches [SN] ◇ ⚠ 182
Carstairs [SR] 🚲 65, 225, *Sleepers* 401
Cartsdyke [SR] 🚲 219
Castle Bar Park [GW] 117
Castle Cary [GW] Ⓟ ◇ 🚕 123, 135
Castlebay *Ship* 227C
Castleford [NT] Ⓟ 🚕 Ⓤ 32, 34
Castleton (Greater Manchester) **[NT]** Ⓟ Ⓤ 41
Castleton Moor [NT] Ⓟ Ⓤ 45
Caterham [SN] 🚲 ◇ ⚠ 🚕 181
Catford [SE] 🚲 ◇ ⚠ 52, 195
Catford Bridge [SE] 🚲 ◇ ⚠ 203
Cathays [AW] Ⓤ 130
Cathcart [SR] 🚲 223
Cattal [NT] 🚲 Ⓤ 35
Catterick Camp Centre *Bus* 26H
Catterick Garrison Kemmel *Bus* 26H
Catterick Garrison Tesco *Bus* 26H
Causeland [GW] Ⓤ 140
Cefn-y-Bedd [AW] Ⓟ 101
Chadwell Heath [LE] 🚲 ⚠ 5
Chafford Hundred [CC] Ⓟ 🚲 ◇ ⚠ 1
Chalfont & Latimer [LT] Ⓟ 🚲 ⚠ 🚕 114
Chalkwell [CC] 🚲 ◇ ⚠ 🚕 1
Chandlers Ford [SW] Ⓟ 🚲 ◇ ⚠ 158
Chapel-en-le-Frith [NT] Ⓟ Ⓤ 86
Chapelton [GW] Ⓟ Ⓤ 136
Chapeltown [NT] Ⓤ 34
Chappel & Wakes Colne [LE] 🚲 Ⓤ 10
Charing [SE] Ⓟ ◇ ⚠ 196

Station index and table numbers

(10) Connection time
Ⓟ Station Car Park
🚲 Bicycle storage facility
◇ Seat reservations can be made at this station
⚠ Penalty Fare Schemes in operation on some or all services from this station
🚕 Taxi rank or cab office at station, or signposted and within 100 metres
Ⓤ Unstaffed station
[ ] Station Operator Code

Charing Cross (Glasgow) **[SR]** 🚲 226
Charing Cross [NR] (see London)
Charlbury [GW] Ⓟ 🚲 126
Charlton [SE] (4) ◇ ⚠ 200
Chartham [SE] ⚠ Ⓤ 207
Chassen Road [NT] 89
Chatelherault [SR] 🚲 Ⓤ 226
Chatham [SE] (4) Ⓟ ◇ ⚠ 🚕 194, 200, 212
Chathill [NT] Ⓟ Ⓤ 48
Cheadle Hulme [NT] Ⓟ 🚲 84
Cheam [SN] Ⓟ 🚲 ◇ ⚠ 🚕 182
Cheddington [LM] Ⓟ 66
Chelford [NT] Ⓟ 🚲 Ⓤ 84
Chelmsford [LE] (3) Ⓟ 🚲 ◇ ⚠ 🚕 11
Chelsfield [SE] (3) Ⓟ ◇ ⚠ 🚕 204
Cheltenham Spa [GW] Ⓟ 🚲 ◇ 🚕 51, 57, 125
Chepstow [AW] Ⓟ 132
Cherry Tree [NT] Ⓟ Ⓤ 97
Chertsey [SW] Ⓟ 🚲 ◇ ⚠ 🚕 149
Cheshunt [LE] Ⓟ 🚲 ⚠ 🚕 21, 22
Chessington North [SW] Ⓟ 🚲 ◇ ⚠ 🚕 152
Chessington South [SW] Ⓟ 🚲 ◇ ⚠ 152
Chester [AW] Ⓟ ◇ 🚕
- Altrincham 88
- Bangor (Gwynedd) 81
- Birmingham 75, 81
- Cardiff 75, 81, 131
- Crewe 81
- Hereford 131
- Holyhead 81
- Liverpool 106
- Llandudno 81
- Llandudno Junction 81
- London 65
- Manchester 81, 88
- Newport (South Wales) 131
- Northwich 88
- Rhyl 81
- Runcorn East 81
- Shrewsbury 75, 131
- Stafford 65
- Stockport 88
- Warrington 81
- Wolverhampton 65, 75
- Wrexham 75

Chester Road [LM] Ⓟ ⚠ 69
Chesterfield [EM] Ⓟ 🚲 ◇ ⚠ 🚕 34, 49, 51, 53
Chester-le-Street [NT] Ⓟ 🚲 ◇ 🚕 Ⓤ 26, 39, 44, 51
Chestfield & Swalecliffe [SE] ◇ ⚠ 212
Chetnole [GW] Ⓤ 123
Chichester [SN] (4) Ⓟ 🚲 ◇ ⚠ 🚕 123, 165, 188
Chilham [SE] Ⓟ ⚠ Ⓤ 207
Chilworth [GW] Ⓤ 148
Chingford [LE] Ⓟ 🚲 ⚠ 🚕 20
Chinley [NT] Ⓟ Ⓤ 78
Chinnor, Estover Way *Bus* 115A
Chinnor, Lower Road *Bus* 115A
Chinnor, The Red Lion *Bus* 115A
Chinnor, The Wheatsheaf *Bus* 115A
Chippenham [GW] Ⓟ 🚲 ◇ ⚠ 🚕 123, 125
Chipping Norton West Street *Bus* 126A
Chipstead [SN] Ⓟ ⚠ 181
Chirk [AW] Ⓟ Ⓤ 75
Chislehurst [SE] Ⓟ ◇ ⚠ 🚕 204
Chiswick [SW] Ⓟ 🚲 Ⓤ 149
Cholsey [GW] Ⓟ 🚲 116
Chorley [NT] Ⓟ ◇ 82
Chorleywood [LT] Ⓟ 🚲 ⚠ 🚕 114
Christchurch [SW] Ⓟ 🚲 ◇ ⚠ 🚕 158
Christs Hospital [SN] Ⓟ 🚲 ◇ ⚠ 188
Church Fenton [NT] Ⓟ 🚲 Ⓤ 33, 40
Church & Oswaldtwistle [NT] Ⓤ 97
Church Stretton [AW] Ⓟ Ⓤ 129, 131
Cilmeri [AW] Ⓤ 129
City Thameslink [FC] (see London)
Clacton-on-Sea [LE] Ⓟ 🚲 ◇ ⚠ 🚕 11
Clandon [SW] Ⓟ 🚲 ◇ ⚠ 152
Clapham High Street [SN] 🚲 ⚠ Ⓤ 178
Clapham Junction [SW] (10) ◇ ⚠
- Alton 155
- Andover 160
- Ascot 149
- Basingstoke 155, 158
- Bexhill 189
- Birmingham 66
- Birmingham International 66
- Bognor Regis 188
- Bournemouth 158
- Brighton 186
- Bristol 160
- Chertsey 149
- Chessington 152
- Chichester 188
- Coventry 66
- Crystal Palace 177, 178
- Dorking 152, 182
- Eastbourne 189
- East Croydon 175, 176
- East Grinstead 184
- Effingham Junction 152
- Epsom 152, 182
- Epsom Downs 182
- Exeter 160
- Gatwick Airport 186
- Guildford 152, 156
- Hampton Court 152
- Hastings 189
- Haywards Heath 186
- Horsham 186
- Hounslow 149
- Hove 186
- Kensington (Olympia) 66, 176, 186
- Kingston 149, 152
- Lewes 189
- London
  - Victoria 175, 177
  - Waterloo 149, 152
- Milton Keynes Central 66, 176
- Northampton 66
- Oxted 184
- Portsmouth 156, 158, 188
- Purley 175
- Reading 149
- Redhill 186
- Rugby 66
- Salisbury 160
- Shepperton 152
- Southampton 158, 188
- Staines 149
- Surbiton 152
- Sutton (Surrey) 182
- Tattenham Corner 181
- Twickenham 149
- Uckfield 184
- Watford Junction 66, 176, 186
- West Croydon 177
- Weybridge 155
- Willesden Junction 176, 186
- Wimbledon 152
- Windsor 149
- Woking 155
- Worthing 188
- Yeovil Junction 160

Clapham (Nth Yorkshire) [NT] Ⓟ Ⓤ 36
Clapton [LE] ⚠ 20, 22
Clarbeston Road [AW] Ⓤ 128
Clarkston [SR] 🚲 222
Claverdon [LM] ⚠ Ⓤ 115
Claygate [SW] Ⓟ 🚲 ◇ ⚠ 🚕 152
Cleethorpes [TP] Ⓟ 🚲 ◇ 🚕 27, 29, 30
Cleland [SR] Ⓟ 🚲 Ⓤ 225
Clifton [NT] Ⓤ 82
Clifton Down [GW] Ⓟ Ⓤ 133
Clitheroe [NT] Ⓟ 94
Clock House [SE] 🚲 ◇ ⚠ 🚕 203
Clunderwen [AW] Ⓟ Ⓤ 128
Clydebank [SR] 🚲 🚕 226
Coatbridge Central [SR] Ⓟ 🚲 🚕 Ⓤ 224, 226
Coatbridge Sunnyside [SR] Ⓟ 🚲 226
Coatdyke [SR] Ⓟ 🚲 Ⓤ 226
Cobham & Stoke d'Abernon [SW] Ⓟ 🚲 ◇ ⚠ 🚕 152
Codsall [LM] Ⓟ Ⓤ 74
Cogan [AW] Ⓟ Ⓤ 130

10 Connection time
Ⓟ Station Car Park
🚲 Bicycle storage facility
◇ Seat reservations can be made at this station
⚠ Penalty Fare Schemes in operation on some or all services from this station
🚕 Taxi rank or cab office at station, or signposted and within 100 metres
Ⓤ Unstaffed station
[ ] Station Operator Code

Station index and table numbers

Colchester [LE] **4** Ⓟ 🚲 ◇ ⚠ 🚕 10, 11, 14
Colchester Town [LE] Ⓟ 🚲 ⚠ 11
Coleshill Parkway [LM] Ⓟ 🚲 ◇ 🚕 49, 57
Coll *Ship* 227B
Collingham [EM] Ⓤ 27
Collington [SN] ⚠ Ⓤ 189
Colne [NT] Ⓟ Ⓤ 97
Colonsay *Ship* 227B
Colwall [LM] Ⓟ ⚠ Ⓤ 71, 126
Colwyn Bay [AW] Ⓟ ◇ 🚕 81
Combe [GW] Ⓤ 126
Commondale [NT] Ⓤ 45
Congleton [NT] Ⓟ ◇ 51, 65, 84
Conisbrough [NT] Ⓟ Ⓤ 29
Connel Ferry [SR] Ⓟ 🚲 Ⓤ 227
Cononley [NT] Ⓟ Ⓤ 36
Conway Park [ME] 106
Conwy [AW] Ⓤ 81
Cooden Beach [SN] Ⓟ 🚲 ◇ ⚠ 189
Cookham [GW] Ⓟ 120
Cooksbridge [SN] Ⓟ ⚠ Ⓤ 189
Coombe Junction Halt [GW] Ⓤ 140
Copplestone [GW] Ⓟ Ⓤ 136
Corbridge [NT] Ⓟ Ⓤ 48
Corby [EM] ⚠ 53
Corby George Street *Bus* 26B
Corkerhill [SR] 🚲 Ⓤ 217
Corkickle [NT] Ⓤ 100
Corpach [SR] Ⓟ 🚲 Ⓤ 227
Corrour [SR] 🚲 Ⓤ 227, *Sleepers* 404
Coryton [AW] Ⓤ 130
Coseley [LM] Ⓟ ⚠ 68
Cosford [LM] Ⓟ Ⓤ 74, 75
Cosham [SW] Ⓟ 🚲 ◇ ⚠ 🚕 123, 158, 165, 188
Cottingham [NT] Ⓟ 🚕 Ⓤ 43
Cottingley [NT] Ⓤ 39
Coulsdon South [SN] Ⓟ ⚠ 🚕 186
Coulsdon Town [SN] Ⓟ ◇ 181
Coventry [VT] Ⓟ 🚲 ◇ ⚠ 🚕
Aberdeen 65
Barrow-in-Furness 65
Banbury 71
Basingstoke 51
Birmingham 68
Birmingham International 68
Blackpool 65
Bournemouth 51
Brighton 66
Carlisle 65
Clapham Junction 66
Crewe 65
Derby 51
Dundee 65
East Croydon 66
Edinburgh 51, 65
Gatwick Airport 66
Glasgow 51, 65
Holyhead 65
Inverness 65
Leamington Spa 71
Leeds 51
Liverpool 65
London 66
Manchester 65
Manchester Airport 65
Milton Keynes Central 66
Newcastle 51
Northampton 66
Nuneaton 67
Oxenholme Lake District 65
Oxford 51
Preston 65
Reading 51
Rugby 66
Sheffield 51
Southampton 51
Stafford 67, 68
Stoke-on-Trent 65
Watford 66
Wolverhampton 68
York 51
Cowden [SN] Ⓟ ⚠ Ⓤ 184
Cowdenbeath [SR] 🚲 ◇ 242
Cradley Heath [LM] Ⓟ 🚲 ◇ ⚠ 71, 115
Craigendoran [SR] Ⓟ 🚲 Ⓤ 226
Craignure *Ship* 227B
Cramlington [NT] Ⓟ 🚲 Ⓤ 48
Craven Arms [AW] Ⓟ Ⓤ 129, 131
Crawley [SN] Ⓟ 🚲 ◇ ⚠ 🚕 186, 188
Crayford [SE] Ⓟ ◇ ⚠ 200
Crediton [GW] Ⓟ 🚲 Ⓤ 136
Cressing [LE] 🚲 ⚠ Ⓤ 11
Cressington [ME] Ⓟ ⚠ 103
Creswell [EM] Ⓤ 55
Crewe [VT] **10** Ⓟ 🚲 ◇ 🚕
Aberdeen 65, *Sleepers* 402
Bangor (Gwynedd) 81
Barrow-in-Furness 65
Birmingham 65
Birmingham International 65
Blackpool 65
Bournemouth 51
Bristol 51
Cardiff 131
Carlisle 65
Cheltenham Spa 51
Chester 81
Coventry 65, 67
Derby 50
Douglas (IOM) 98A
Dundee 65, *Sleepers* 402
Edinburgh 65
Exeter 51
Fort William *Sleepers* 404
Glasgow 65
Hartford 91
Hereford 131
Holyhead 81
Inverkeithing *Sleepers* 402
Inverness 65, *Sleepers* 403
Kirkcaldy *Sleepers* 402
Lancaster 65
Liverpool 91
Liverpool South Parkway 91
Llandudno 81
London 65, 67
Manchester 84
Manchester Airport 84
Milton Keynes Central 65, 67
Newport (South Wales) 131
Northampton 67
Oxenholme Lake District 65
Oxford 51
Paignton 51
Penzance 51
Perth 65, *Sleepers* 403
Plymouth 51
Preston 65
Reading 51
Rugby 65, 67
Runcorn 91
Shrewsbury 131
Southampton 51
Stafford 65, 67
Stirling *Sleepers* 403
Stockport 84
Stoke-on-Trent 50
Torquay 51
Watford 65
Wilmslow 84
Wolverhampton 65
Crewkerne [SW] Ⓟ 🚲 ◇ ⚠ 160
Crews Hill [FC] ⚠ Ⓤ 24
Crianlarich [SR] Ⓟ 🚲 Ⓤ 227, *Sleepers* 404
Criccieth [AW] Ⓟ 🚲 Ⓤ 75
Cricklewood [FC] 🚲 ◇ ⚠ 52
Croftfoot [SR] 🚲 223
Crofton Park [SE] ◇ ⚠ 52, 195
Cromer [LE] Ⓟ 🚲 Ⓤ 16
Cromford [EM] Ⓟ Ⓤ 54, 56
Crompton [NT] (see Shaw)
Crookston [SR] 🚲 Ⓤ 217
Crosby [ME] (see Blundellsands)
Crossflatts [NT] Ⓟ 🚲 Ⓤ 36
Cross Gates [NT] Ⓟ 40
Cross Keys [AW] Ⓤ 127
Crosshill [SR] 223
Crossmyloof [SR] 🚲 Ⓤ 222
Croston [NT] Ⓟ Ⓤ 99
Crouch Hill [LO] ⚠ 62
Crowborough [SN] Ⓟ 🚲 ◇ ⚠ 184
Crowhurst [SE] Ⓟ ⚠ 206
Crowle [NT] Ⓤ 29
Crowthorne [GW] Ⓟ 🚲 148
Croy [SR] **3** Ⓟ 🚲 228, 230
Croydon
see East Croydon
see South Croydon
see West Croydon
Crystal Palace [LO] **4** Ⓟ ⚠ 🚕 177, 178
Cuddington [NT] Ⓟ Ⓤ 88
Cuffley [FC] Ⓟ 🚲 ⚠ 🚕 24

Station index and table numbers

[10] Connection time
Ⓟ Station Car Park
🚲 Bicycle storage facility
◇ Seat reservations can be made at this station
⚠ Penalty Fare Schemes in operation on some or all services from this station
🚕 Taxi rank or cab office at station, or signposted and within 100 metres
Ⓤ Unstaffed station
[ ] Station Operator Code

Culham [GW] Ⓟ 🚲 Ⓤ 116
Culrain [SR] 🚲 Ⓤ 239
Cumbernauld [SR] Ⓟ 🚲 🚕 224
Cupar [SR] Ⓟ 🚲 ◇ 51, 229
Curriehill [SR] Ⓟ 🚲 Ⓤ 225
Cuxton [SE] Ⓟ ⚠ Ⓤ 208
Cwmbach [AW] Ⓟ Ⓤ 130
Cwmbran [AW] Ⓟ 🚲 ◇ 🚕 131
Cynghordy [AW] Ⓤ 129

D

Dagenham Dock [CC] Ⓟ 🚲 ◇ ⚠ 1
Daisy Hill [NT] Ⓟ 🚲 82
Dalgety Bay [SR] Ⓟ 🚲 🚕 Ⓤ 242
Dalmally [SR] Ⓟ 🚲 Ⓤ 227
Dalmarnock [SR] 226
Dalmeny [SR] Ⓟ 🚲 242
Dalmuir [SR] Ⓟ 🚲 226, 227, *Sleepers* 404
Dalreoch [SR] Ⓟ 🚲 226
Dalry [SR] Ⓟ 🚲 Ⓤ 221
Dalston [NT] Ⓟ Ⓤ 100
Dalston Junction [LO] ⚠ 178
Dalston Kingsland [LO] ⚠ 59
Dalton [NT] Ⓟ Ⓤ 82
Dalwhinnie [SR] Ⓟ 🚲 Ⓤ 229, *Sleepers* 403
Danby [NT] Ⓟ Ⓤ 45
Danescourt [AW] Ⓤ 130
Danzey [LM] Ⓟ ⚠ Ⓤ 71
Darlington [GR] **[7]** Ⓟ 🚲 ◇ 🚕
Aberdeen 26
Birmingham 51
Bishop Auckland 44
Bournemouth 51
Bristol 51
Cambridge 26
Cardiff 51
Catterick Garrison *Bus* 26H
Derby 51
Doncaster 26
Durham 26
Dundee 26
Edinburgh 26
Exeter 51
Glasgow 26
Grantham 26
Huddersfield 39
Leeds 26
Liverpool 39
London 26
Manchester 39
Manchester Airport 39
Middlesbrough 44
Newark 26
Newcastle 26
Newport (South Wales) 51
Norwich 26
Northallerton 26
Oxford 51
Paignton 51
Penzance 51
Peterborough 26
Plymouth 51
Reading 51
Redcar 44
Retford 26
Richmond *Bus* 26H
Saltburn 44
Sheffield 26
Southampton 51
Stansted Airport 26
Sunderland 26, 44
Torquay 51
Whitby 45
York 26
Darnall [NT] Ⓤ 30
Darnley [SR] (see Priesthill)
Darsham [LE] Ⓟ 🚲 Ⓤ 13
Dartford [SE] **[4]** Ⓟ ◇ ⚠ 🚕 200, 212
Darton [NT] Ⓟ Ⓤ 34
Darwen [NT] Ⓤ 94
Datchet [SW] 🚲 ◇ ⚠ 149
Davenport [NT] Ⓟ 86
Dawlish [GW] Ⓟ ◇ 🚕 51, 135
Dawlish Warren [GW] Ⓟ 🚲 Ⓤ 135
Deal [SE] Ⓟ 🚲 ◇ ⚠ 🚕 194, 207
Dean [GW] 🚲 Ⓤ 158
Deansgate [NT] 82, 84, 85, 86, 89
Deganwy [AW] Ⓤ 81, 102
Deighton [NT] Ⓤ 39
Delamere [NT] Ⓟ Ⓤ 88
Denby Dale [NT] Ⓟ Ⓤ 34
Denham [CH] Ⓟ 🚲 ◇ ⚠ 🚕 115
Denham Golf Club [CH] ⚠ Ⓤ 115
Denmark Hill [SE] **[4]** ◇ ⚠ 52, 178, 195, 200
Dent [NT] Ⓟ Ⓤ 36
Denton [NT] Ⓤ 78
Deptford [SE] ◇ ⚠ 200
Derby [EM] **[6]** Ⓟ 🚲 ◇ ⚠ 🚕
Barnsley 53
Bedford 53
Belper 53, 56
Birmingham 57
Birmingham International 51
Bournemouth 51
Bristol 57
Burton-on-Trent 57
Cardiff 57
Chesterfield 53
Coventry 51
Crewe 50
Doncaster 53
Edinburgh 51
Exeter 51
Gloucester 57
Kettering 53
Leeds 53
Leicester 53
London 53
Long Eaton 56
Loughborough 53
Luton 53
Market Harborough 53
Matlock 56
Meadowhall 53
Newcastle 51
Newport (South Wales) 57
Nottingham 56
Oxford 51
Paignton 51
Penzance 51
Plymouth 51
Reading 51
Sheffield 53
Southampton 51
Stoke-on-Trent 50
Wakefield 53
Wellingborough 53
York 53
Derby Road [LE] 🚲 Ⓤ 13
Dereham 🚕 *Bus* 26A
Devonport [GW] Ⓟ 🚲 Ⓤ 135, 139
Dewsbury [TP] Ⓟ 🚲 ◇ 🚕 39, 41
Didcot Parkway [GW] Ⓟ 🚲 ◇ ⚠ 🚕 116, 125
Digby & Sowton [GW] Ⓟ Ⓤ 136
Dilton Marsh [GW] Ⓤ 123
Dinas Powys [AW] Ⓤ 130
Dinas Rhondda [AW] Ⓟ Ⓤ 130
Dingle Road [AW] Ⓤ 130
Dingwall [SR] Ⓟ 🚲 ◇ 🚕 239
Dinsdale [NT] Ⓤ 44
Dinting [NT] **[3]** Ⓟ 🚲 79
Disley [NT] Ⓟ 86
Diss [LE] Ⓟ 🚲 ◇ 🚕 11
Dockyard [GW] Ⓤ 135, 139
Dodworth [NT] Ⓟ Ⓤ 34
Dolau [AW] 🚲 Ⓤ 129
Doleham [SN] Ⓤ 189
Dolgarrog [AW] Ⓤ 102
Dolwyddelan [AW] Ⓟ Ⓤ 102
Doncaster [GR] **[7]** Ⓟ 🚲 ◇ 🚕
Aberdeen 26
Bedford 53
Birmingham 51
Bournemouth 51
Bristol 51
Cambridge 26
Cleethorpes 29
Darlington 26
Derby 53
Dundee 26
Durham 26
Edinburgh 26
Exeter 51
Gainsborough 18
Glasgow 26
Goole 29
Grantham 26
Grimsby 29
Hull 29

Station index and table numbers

10 Connection time
Ⓟ Station Car Park
🚲 Bicycle storage facility
◇ Seat reservations can be made at this station
⚠ Penalty Fare Schemes in operation on some or all services from this station
🚕 Taxi rank or cab office at station, or signposted and within 100 metres
Ⓤ Unstaffed station
[ ] Station Operator Code

Leeds 31
Leicester 53
Lincoln 18
London 26
Luton 53
Manchester 29
Manchester Airport 29
Middlesbrough 26
Newark 26
Newcastle 26
Norwich 26
Nottingham 53
Oxford 51
Paignton 51
Penzance 51
Peterborough 18, 26
Plymouth 51
Reading 51
Retford 26
Robin Hood Airport *Bus* 26F
Rotherham 29
Scunthorpe 29
Selby 29
Sheffield 29
Sleaford 18
Southampton 51
Spalding 18
Stansted Airport 26
Stevenage 26
Stockport 29
Sunderland 26
Torquay 51
Wakefield 31
York 26
Doncaster Interchange *Bus* 🚕 26F
Dorchester South [SW] Ⓟ 🚲 ◇ ⚠ 🚕 158
Dorchester West [GW] Ⓤ 123, 158
Dore & Totley [NT] Ⓟ Ⓤ 78
Dorking [SN] **4** Ⓟ 🚲 ◇ ⚠ 🚕 152, 182
Dorking Deepdene [GW] Ⓤ 148
Dorking West [GW] Ⓤ 148
Dormans [SN] ◇ ⚠ 184
Dorridge [LM] Ⓟ 🚲 ◇ ⚠ 71, 115
Douglas (IOM) *Ship* 98A
Dove Holes [NT] Ⓟ Ⓤ 86
Dovercourt [LE] Ⓟ 🚲 11
Dover Priory [SE] **4** Ⓟ 🚲 ◇ ⚠ 🚕 194, 207, 212
Dovey Junction [AW] **4** Ⓤ 75
Downham Market [FC] Ⓟ 🚲 ⚠ 🚕 17
Drayton Green [GW] Ⓤ 117
Drayton Park [FC] 🚲 ⚠ 24
Drem [SR] Ⓟ 🚲 Ⓤ 238
Driffield [NT] Ⓟ 🚲 🚕 43
Drigg [NT] Ⓤ 100
Droitwich Spa [LM] Ⓟ ◇ ⚠ 71
Dronfield [NT] Ⓟ Ⓤ 34
Drumchapel [SR] Ⓟ 🚲 🚕 226
Drumfrochar [SR] 🚲 Ⓤ 219
Drumgelloch [SR] Ⓟ 🚲 Ⓤ 226
Drumry [SR] Ⓟ 🚲 226
Dublin Ferryport *Ship* 81A
Duddeston [LM] ⚠ 69, 70
Dudley Port [LM] Ⓟ ⚠ 68
Duffield [EM] Ⓟ ⚠ Ⓤ 56
Duirinish [SR] Ⓟ 🚲 Ⓤ 239
Duke Street [SR] 🚲 Ⓤ 226
Dullingham [LE] Ⓟ 🚲 Ⓤ 14
Dumbarton Central [SR] 🚲 ◇ 🚕 226, 227
Dumbarton East [SR] 🚲 Ⓤ 226
Dumbreck [SR] 🚲 Ⓤ 217
Dumfries [SR] Ⓟ 🚲 ◇ 🚕 218
Dumpton Park [SE] ⚠ Ⓤ 212
Dun Laoghaire *Ship* 81A
Dunbar [GR] Ⓟ 🚲 ◇ 26, 51, 238
Dunblane [SR] Ⓟ 🚲 ◇ 229, 230, *Sleepers* 403
Duncraig [SR] 🚲 Ⓤ 239
Dundee [SR] Ⓟ 🚲 ◇ 🚕 26, 51, 65, 229, *Sleepers* 402
Dunfermline Queen Margaret [SR] Ⓟ 🚲 Ⓤ 242
Dunfermline Town [SR] Ⓟ 🚲 ◇ 🚕 242
Dunkeld & Birnam [SR] Ⓟ 🚲 Ⓤ 229, *Sleepers* 403
Dunlop [SR] 🚲 Ⓤ 222
Dunoon *Ship* 219A
Dunrobin Castle [SR] Ⓤ *Summer only* 239
Duns *Bus* 26K
Dunster Steep *Bus* 135E
Dunston [NT] Ⓤ 48
Dunton Green [SE] Ⓟ ⚠ Ⓤ 204
Durham [GR] Ⓟ 🚲 ◇ 🚕 26, 39, 44, 51
Durrington-on-Sea [SN] 🚲 ⚠ 188
Dursley [GW] (see Cam & Dursley)
Dyce [SR] Ⓟ 🚲 🚕 Ⓤ 229, 240
Dyffryn Ardudwy [AW] Ⓤ 75

E

Eaglescliffe [NT] Ⓟ 🚲 🚕 Ⓤ 26, 44
Ealing Broadway [GW] **3** ◇ ⚠ 🚕 116, 117
Earlestown [NT] **8** 81, 90
Earley [SW] Ⓟ 🚲 ⚠ 149
Earlsfield [SW] 🚲 ◇ ⚠ 152, 155
Earlston *Bus* 26K
Earlswood (Surrey) [SN] 🚲 ◇ ⚠ 186
Earlswood (West Midlands) [LM] Ⓟ ⚠ Ⓤ 71
East Croydon [SN] 🚲 ◇ ⚠ 🚕
Bedford 52
Bexhill 189
Birmingham 66
Birmingham International 66
Bognor Regis 188
Brighton 186
Caterham 181
Chichester 188
Clapham Junction 175, 176
Coventry 66
Eastbourne 189
East Grinstead 184
Gatwick Airport 186
Hastings 189
Haywards Heath 186
Horsham 186
Hove 186
Kensington (Olympia) 66, 176, 186
Lewes 189
Littlehampton 188
London 175
Luton 52
Luton Airport Parkway 52
Milton Keynes Central 66, 176
Northampton 66
Norwood Junction 177, 178
Oxted 184
Portsmouth 188
Purley 175
Redhill 186
Rugby 66
St Albans 52
St Pancras International 52
Seaford 189
Southampton Central 188
Tattenham Corner 181
Tonbridge 186
Uckfield 184
Watford Junction 66, 176, 186
West Hampstead Thameslink 52
Wolverhampton 66
Worthing 188
East Didsbury [NT] Ⓟ 85
East Dulwich [SN] ⚠ 177, 179
East Farleigh [SE] Ⓟ ⚠ Ⓤ 208
East Garforth [NT] Ⓤ 40
East Grinstead [SN] Ⓟ 🚲 ◇ ⚠ 🚕 184
East Kilbride [SR] Ⓟ 🚲 ◇ 🚕 222
East Malling [SE] ⚠ Ⓤ 196
East Midlands Parkway [EM] ⚠ 53
East Tilbury [CC] ◇ ⚠ 1
East Worthing [SN] ⚠ Ⓤ 188
Eastbourne [SN] **4** Ⓟ 🚲 ◇ ⚠ 🚕 189
Eastbrook [AW] Ⓟ Ⓤ 130
Easterhouse [SR] Ⓟ 🚲 226
Eastham Rake [ME] Ⓟ 🚲 ⚠ 106
Eastleigh [SW] **3** Ⓟ 🚲 ◇ ⚠ 🚕 158, 188
Eastrington [NT] Ⓤ 29
Ebbsfleet International [SE] ◇ ⚠ 🚕 194, 200, 207, 208, 212

Station index and table numbers

■10 Connection time
℗ Station Car Park
🚲 Bicycle storage facility
◇ Seat reservations can be made at this station
⚠ Penalty Fare Schemes in operation on some or all services from this station
🚕 Taxi rank or cab office at station, or signposted and within 100 metres
Ⓤ Unstaffed station
[ ] Station Operator Code

Ebbw Vale Parkway [AW] ℗ Ⓤ 127
Eccles [NT] ℗ 90
Eccles Road [LE] ℗ Ⓤ 17
Eccleston Park [NT] 90
Edale [NT] ℗ Ⓤ 78
Eden Camp *Bus* 26G
Eden Park [SE] ◇ ⚠ 203
Eden Project *Bus* 135B
Edenbridge [SN] ℗ ⚠ Ⓤ 186
Edenbridge Town [SN] ℗ 🚲 ◇ ⚠ 🚕 184
Edge Hill [NT] ℗ 89, 90, 91
Edinburgh [NR] ■10 ℗ 🚲 ◇ 🚕
Aberdeen 229
Airdrie 226
Bathgate 226
Birmingham New Street 51, 65
Birmingham International 51, 65
Blackpool 65
Bournemouth 51
Bristol 51
Cambridge 26
Cardiff 51
Carlisle 65
Carstairs 225
Cowdenbeath 242
Crewe 65
Croy 228
Dalmuir 226
Darlington 26
Derby 51
Doncaster 26
Dunbar 238
Dunblane 230
Dundee 229
Dunfermline 242
Dyce 229
Edinburgh Park 226, 230
Exeter 51
Falkirk 228, 230
Fort William 227
Glasgow 225, 226, 228
Glenrothes with Thornton 242
Grantham 26
Helensburgh 226
Inverkeithing 242
Inverness 229
Inverurie 229
Kirkcaldy 242
Lancaster 65
Larbert 230
Leeds 26
Linlithgow 230
Liverpool 65
Livingston 225, 226
London 26, *Sleepers* 400
Mallaig 227
Manchester 65
Manchester Airport 65
Markinch 229
Milngavie 226
Motherwell 225
Newcastle 26
Newcraighall 242
Newport (South Wales) 51
North Berwick 238
Oban 227
Oxenholme Lake District 65
Oxford 51
Paignton 51
Penzance 51
Perth 229
Peterborough 26
Plymouth 51
Polmont 230
Preston 65
Reading 51
Sheffield 26
Shotts 225
Southampton 51
Stafford 65
Stirling 230
Thurso 239
Torquay 51
Warrington 65
Watford 65, *Sleepers* 400
West Calder 225
Western Isles *Ship* 239B
Wigan 65
York 26
Edinburgh Park [SR] 🚲 Ⓤ 226, 230
Edmonton Green [LE] ⚠ 21
Effingham Junction [SW] ■6 ℗ 🚲 ◇ ⚠ 152, 182
Eggesford [GW] ℗ Ⓤ 136
Egham [SW] ℗ 🚲 ◇ ⚠ 🚕 149
Egton [NT] Ⓤ 45
Eigg *Ship* 227A
Elephant & Castle [FC] 🚲 ◇ ⚠
Ashford 196
Bromley South 195
Canterbury 212
Catford 195
Chatham 212
Dover 212
East Croydon 177
Faversham 212
London 52, 177
Luton 52
Maidstone 196
Margate 212
Ramsgate 212
Rochester 212
St Albans 52
St Pancras International 52, 177
Sevenoaks 195
Streatham 177
Sutton (Surrey) 179
Swanley 195
Wimbledon 179
Elgin [SR] ℗ 🚲 ◇ 🚕 240
Ellesmere Port [ME] 🚕 106, 109
Elmers End [SE] ■4 ℗ 🚲 ◇ ⚠ 203
Elmstead Woods [SE] ℗ ◇ ⚠ 🚕 204
Elmswell [LE] 🚲 Ⓤ 14
Elsecar [NT] Ⓤ 34
Elsenham [LE] 🚲 ⚠ 22
Elstree & Borehamwood [FC] ℗ 🚲 ◇ ⚠ 🚕 52
Eltham [SE] ℗ 🚲 ◇ ⚠ 🚕 200
Elton (Ches.) **[NT]** (see Ince & Elton)
Elton & Orston [EM] ℗ Ⓤ 19
Ely [LE] ■6 ℗ 🚲 ◇ ⚠ 🚕 14, 17, 49
Emerson Park [LE] 🚲 ⚠ Ⓤ 4
Emsworth [SN] ℗ 🚲 ◇ ⚠ 188
Enfield Chase [FC] ℗ 🚲 ⚠ 24
Enfield Lock [LE] 🚲 ⚠ 22
Enfield Town [LE] ⚠ 🚕 21
Entwistle [NT] Ⓤ 94
Epsom [SN] ■3 🚲 ◇ ⚠ 🚕 152, 182
Epsom Downs [SN] ⚠ Ⓤ 182
Erdington [LM] ⚠ 69
Eridge [SN] 🚲 ◇ ⚠ 184
Erith [SE] ◇ ⚠ 🚕 200
Esher [SW] ℗ 🚲 ◇ ⚠ 🚕 155
Eskdale [NT] (see Ravenglass)
Essex Road [FC] 🚲 ⚠ 24
Etchingham [SE] ℗ 🚲 ◇ ⚠ 206
Eton (see Windsor)
Euston [NR] (see London)
Euxton Balshaw Lane [NT] ℗ Ⓤ 90
Evesham [GW] ℗ 🚲 🚕 126
Ewell East [SN] ℗ 🚲 ◇ ⚠ 182
Ewell West [SW] ℗ 🚲 ◇ ⚠ 152
Exeter
Central [GW] ℗ 🚲 ◇
St Davids [GW] ■6 ℗ 🚲 ◇ ⚠ 🚕
St Thomas [GW] Ⓤ
Aberdeen 51
Andover 160
Barnstaple 136
Basingstoke 160
Birmingham 51
Bristol 135
Bude Strand *Bus* 135D
Cardiff 135
Carlisle 51
Clapham Junction 160
Crewe 51
Derby 51
Dundee 51
Edinburgh 51
Exmouth 136
Glasgow 51
Holsworthy *Bus* 135D
Leeds 51
London 135, 160, *Sleepers* 406
Manchester 51
Newcastle 51
Newport (South Wales) 135
Newquay 135
Newton Abbot 135
Nottingham 51
Okehampton *Summer only* 136
Okehampton West Street *Bus* 135D

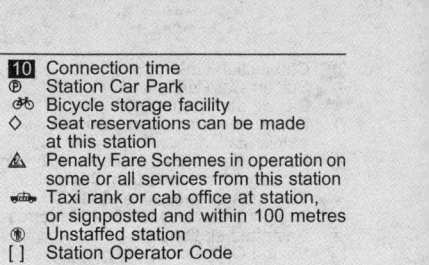

Station index and table numbers

[10] Connection time
Ⓟ Station Car Park
🚲 Bicycle storage facility
◇ Seat reservations can be made at this station
⚠ Penalty Fare Schemes in operation on some or all services from this station
🚕 Taxi rank or cab office at station, or signposted and within 100 metres
⊛ Unstaffed station
[ ] Station Operator Code

- Paignton 135
- Penzance 135
- Plymouth 135
- Preston 51
- Reading 135, *Sleepers* 406
- Salisbury 160
- Sheffield 51
- Taunton 135
- Torquay 135
- Truro 135
- Weston-super-Mare 135
- Wolverhampton 51
- York 51

Exhibition Centre [SR] 🚲 226
Exmouth [GW] Ⓟ 🚲 ◇ 135, 136
Exton [GW] Ⓟ 🚲 ⊛ 136
Eynsford [SE] Ⓟ ◇ ⚠ 52, 195

F

Fairbourne [AW] Ⓟ ⊛ 75
Fairfield [NT] ⊛ 78
Fairhaven [NT] (see Ansdell)
Fairlie [SR] Ⓟ 🚲 ⊛ 221
Fairwater [AW] ⊛ 130
Falconwood [SE] ◇ ⚠ 🚕 200
Falkirk Grahamston [SR] Ⓟ 🚲 ◇ 🚕 224, 230, *Sleepers* 403
Falkirk High [SR] Ⓟ 🚲 ◇ 🚕 228
Falls of Cruachan [SR] ⊛ *Summer only* 227
Falmer [SN] Ⓟ 🚲 ⚠ 189
Falmouth Docks [GW] Ⓟ ⊛ 143
Falmouth Town [GW] ⊛ 143
Fambridge [LE] (North Fambridge)
Fareham [SW] Ⓟ 🚲 ◇ ⚠ 🚕 123, 158, 165, 188
Farnborough (Main) [SW] Ⓟ 🚲 ◇ ⚠ 🚕 155,158
Farnborough North [GW] Ⓟ ⊛ 148
Farncombe [SW] Ⓟ 🚲 ◇ ⚠ 156
Farnham [SW] Ⓟ 🚲 ◇ ⚠ 🚕 155
Farningham Road [SE] Ⓟ ◇ ⚠ 212
Farnworth [NT] 82
Farringdon [LT] (see London)
Fauldhouse [SR] Ⓟ 🚲 ⊛ 225
Faversham [SE] [2] Ⓟ 🚲 ◇ ⚠ 🚕 194, 212
Faygate [SN] ⚠ ⊛ 186
Fazakerley [ME] ⚠ 103
Fearn [SR] Ⓟ 🚲 ⊛ 239
Featherstone [NT] ⊛ 32
Felixstowe [LE] 🚲 🚕 ⊛ 13
Feltham [SW] Ⓟ 🚲 ◇ ⚠ 149
Fenchurch Street [NR] (see London)
Feniton [SW] Ⓟ 🚲 ◇ ⚠ 160
Fenny Stratford [LM] ⊛ 64
Fernhill [AW] ⊛ 130
Ferriby [NT] Ⓟ 🚲 ⊛ 29
Ferryside [AW] ⊛ 128
Ffairfach [AW] ⊛ 129
Filey [NT] Ⓟ 🚕 ⊛ 43
Filton Abbey Wood [GW] Ⓟ 🚲 123, 132, 134, 135
Finchley Road & Frognal [LO] ⚠ 59
Finsbury Park [FC] ⚠ 🚕 24, 25
Finstock [GW] ⊛ 126
Fishbourne (Sussex) [SN] ⚠ ⊛ 188
Fishersgate [SN] ⚠ ⊛ 188
Fishguard Harbour [AW] ⊛ 128
Fiskerton [EM] Ⓟ ⊛ 27
Fitzwilliam [NT] Ⓟ ⊛ 31
Five Ways [LM] ⚠ 69
Flamingo Land *Bus* 26G
Fleet [SW] Ⓟ 🚲 ◇ ⚠ 🚕 155, 158
Flimby [NT] ⊛ 100
Flint [AW] Ⓟ ◇ 81
Flitwick [FC] Ⓟ 🚲 ◇ ⚠ 🚕 52
Flixton [NT] 🚲 89
Flowery Field [NT] ⊛ 79
Folkestone Central [SE] Ⓟ 🚲 ◇ ⚠ 🚕 194, 207
Folkestone West [SE] Ⓟ ◇ ⚠ 194, 207
Ford [SN] [4] 🚲 ◇ ⚠ 188
Forest Gate [LE] 🚲 ⚠ 5
Forest Hill [LO] [4] Ⓟ 🚲 ◇ ⚠ 🚕 178
Formby [ME] Ⓟ 🚲 ⚠ 103
Forres [SR] Ⓟ 🚲 ◇ 🚕 240
Forsinard [SR] Ⓟ 🚲 ⊛ 239
Fort Matilda [SR] Ⓟ 🚲 ⊛ 219
Fort William [SR] Ⓟ 🚲 ◇ 🚕 227, *Ship* 227A, *Sleepers* 404
Four Oaks [LM] Ⓟ ⚠ 69
Foxfield [NT] ⊛ 100
Foxton [FC] ⚠ ⊛ 25
Frant [SE] Ⓟ ◇ ⚠ 206
Fratton [SW] Ⓟ 🚲 ◇ ⚠ 🚕 123, 156, 157, 158, 165, 188
Freshfield [ME] Ⓟ 🚲 ⚠ 103
Freshford [GW] Ⓟ ⊛ 123
Frimley [SW] Ⓟ 🚲 ◇ ⚠ 149
Frinton-on-Sea [LE] Ⓟ 🚲 ⚠ 11
Frizinghall [NT] Ⓟ ⊛ 36, 37, 38
Frodsham [AW] Ⓟ ⊛ 81
Frognal [LO] (see Finchley Road)
Frome [GW] Ⓟ 🚲 🚕 123
Fulwell [SW] 🚲 ◇ ⚠ 149, 152
Furness Vale [NT] ⊛ 86
Furze Platt [GW] 120

G

Gainsborough Central [NT] Ⓟ ⊛ 30
Gainsborough Lea Road [EM] Ⓟ 🚲 ⊛ 18, 30
Galton Bridge (Smethwick) [LM] (see Smethwick Galton Bridge)
Garelochhead [SR] Ⓟ 🚲 ⊛ 227, *Sleepers* 404
Garforth [NT] Ⓟ 🚲 39, 40
Gargrave [NT] ⊛ 36
Garrowhill [SR] 🚲 226
Garscadden [SR] 🚲 226
Garsdale [NT] Ⓟ ⊛ 36
Garston (Hertfordshire) [LM] ⊛ 61
Garswood [NT] Ⓟ 90
Gartcosh [SR] Ⓟ 🚲 ⊛ 224
Garth (Powys) [AW] ⊛ 129
Garth (Mid Glamorgan) [AW] ⊛ 128
Garve [SR] Ⓟ 🚲 ⊛ 239
Gateshead [NT] (see Metrocentre)
Gathurst [NT] Ⓟ 🚲 ⊛ 82
Gatley [NT] Ⓟ 85
Gatwick Airport [NR] [10] ◇ ⚠ 🚕
- Bedford 52
- Bognor Regis 188
- Brighton 186
- Chichester 188
- City Thameslink 52, 186
- Clapham Junction 176, 186
- Eastbourne 189
- East Croydon 176, 186
- Elstree & Borehamwood 52
- Guildford 148
- Hastings 189
- Haywards Heath 186
- Hove 186
- Kensington (Olympia) 176
- Lewes 189
- London 186
- Luton 52, 186
- Luton Airport Parkway 52
- Mill Hill Broadway 52
- Milton Keynes Central 176
- Portsmouth 188
- Radlett 52
- Reading 148
- St Albans 52
- St Pancras International 52
- Southampton Central 188
- Watford Junction 176
- West Hampstead Thameslink 52
- Worthing 188
- York 53

Georgemas Junction [SR] [1] Ⓟ 🚲 ⊛ 239
Gerrards Cross [CH] [1] Ⓟ 🚲 ◇ ⚠ 🚕 115

Station index and table numbers

10	Connection time
Ⓟ	Station Car Park
🚲	Bicycle storage facility
◇	Seat reservations can be made at this station
⚠	Penalty Fare Schemes in operation on some or all services from this station
🚕	Taxi rank or cab office at station, or signposted and within 100 metres
Ⓤ	Unstaffed station
[ ]	Station Operator Code

■10 Connection time
Ⓟ Station Car Park
🚲 Bicycle storage facility
◇ Seat reservations can be made at this station
⚠ Penalty Fare Schemes in operation on some or all services from this station
🚕 Taxi rank or cab office at station, or signposted and within 100 metres
Ⓤ Unstaffed station
[ ] Station Operator Code

Station index and table numbers

Great Yarmouth [LE] Ⓟ 🚲 ◇ 🚕 15
Green Lane [ME] ⚠ 106
Green Road [NT] Ⓟ Ⓤ 100
Greenbank [NT] Ⓟ Ⓤ 88
Greenfaulds [SR] Ⓟ 🚲 Ⓤ 224
Greenfield [NT] 🚲 39
Greenford [LT] Ⓟ ⚠ 🚕 117
Greenhithe for Bluewater [SE] ◇ ⚠ 200, 212
Greenock Central [SR] Ⓟ 🚲 219
Greenock West [SR] 🚕 219
Greenwich [SE] ■4 ◇ ⚠ 200
Gretna Green [SR] Ⓟ 🚲 Ⓤ 216
Grimsby Docks [NT] Ⓤ 29
Grimsby Town [TP] Ⓟ 🚲 ◇ 🚕 26, 27, 29, 30
Grindleford [NT] Ⓤ 78
Grosmont [NT] [NY] Ⓟ Ⓤ 45
Grove Park [SE] ■4 ◇ ⚠ 🚕 204
Guide Bridge [NT] Ⓟ 78, 79
Guildford [SW] Ⓟ 🚲 ◇ ⚠ 🚕
Ascot 149
Birmingham 51
Clapham Junction 152, 155, 156
Gatwick Airport 148
London 152, 155, 156
Portsmouth 156
Reading 148
Surbiton 152
West Croydon 182
Guiseley [NT] Ⓟ 🚲 ◇ 38
Gunnersbury [LT] 59
Gunnislake [GW] Ⓟ 🚲 Ⓤ 139
Gunton [LE] Ⓟ 🚲 Ⓤ 16
Gwersyllt [AW] Ⓟ Ⓤ 101
Gypsy Lane [NT] 🚲 Ⓤ 45

H

Habrough [NT] Ⓟ Ⓤ 27, 29, 30
Hackbridge [SN] Ⓟ ◇ ⚠ 52, 179, 182
Hackney Central [LO] 🚲 ⚠ 🚕 59
Hackney Downs [LE] 🚲 ⚠ 20, 21, 22
Hackney Wick [LO] ⚠ 59
Haddenham & Thame Parkway [CH] Ⓟ 🚲 ◇ ⚠ 🚕 115
Haddiscoe [LE] Ⓟ 🚲 Ⓤ 15
Hadfield [NT] Ⓟ 🚲 79
Hadley Wood [FC] ⚠ 24
Hag Fold [NT] 82
Haggerston [LO] ⚠ 178
Hagley [LM] Ⓟ ⚠ 71
Hairmyres [SR] Ⓟ 🚲 Ⓤ 222
Hale [NT] Ⓟ 88
Halesworth [LE] Ⓟ 🚲 Ⓤ 13
Halewood [NT] 89
Halifax [NT] Ⓟ 🚲 ◇ 🚕 26, 32, 41
Hall Green [LM] Ⓟ ⚠ 71
Hall I' Th' Wood [NT] Ⓤ 94
Hall Road [ME] 🚲 ⚠ 103
Halling [SE] ⚠ Ⓤ 208
Haltwhistle [NT] Ⓟ 🚲 Ⓤ 48
Ham Street [SN] Ⓟ ◇ ⚠ 189
Hamble [SW] 🚲 ⚠ Ⓤ 165
Hamilton Central [SR] Ⓟ 🚲 ◇ 🚕 226
Hamilton Square [ME] ◇ ⚠ 🚕 106
Hamilton West [SR] Ⓟ 🚲 🚕 226
Hammerton [NT] Ⓟ Ⓤ 35
Hampden Park [SN] ■4 ◇ ⚠ 189
Hampstead Heath [LO] 🚲 ⚠ 59
Hampstead (South) [LO] (see South Hampstead)
Hampstead (West) (see West Hampstead) (see West Hampstead Thameslink)
Hampton [SW] 🚲 ⚠ 152
Hampton-in-Arden [LM] Ⓟ ⚠ 68
Hampton Court [SW] Ⓟ 🚲 ◇ ⚠ 152
Hampton Wick [SW] 🚲 ⚠ 149, 152
Hamstead [LM] ⚠ 70
Hamworthy [SW] 🚲 ◇ ⚠ 158
Hanborough [GW] Ⓟ 🚲 Ⓤ 126
Handforth [NT] 🚲 84
Hanley Bus Station *Bus* 67
Hanwell [GW] 🚲 ⚠ 117
Hapton [NT] Ⓤ 97
Harlech [AW] Ⓟ 🚲 Ⓤ 75
Harlesden [LT] 60
Harling Road [LE] Ⓟ 🚲 Ⓤ 17
Harlington (Beds.) **[FC]** Ⓟ 🚲 ◇ ⚠ 🚕 52
Harlington (Middx.) **[GW]** (see Hayes & Harlington)
Harlow Mill [LE] Ⓟ 🚲 ⚠ 22
Harlow Town [LE] Ⓟ 🚲 ◇ ⚠ 🚕 22
Harold Wood [LE] Ⓟ 🚲 ⚠ 🚕 5
Harpenden [FC] Ⓟ 🚲 ◇ ⚠ 🚕 52
Harrietsham [SE] Ⓟ ◇ ⚠ 196
Harringay [FC] ⚠ 24
Harringay Green Lanes [LO] ⚠ 62
Harrington [NT] Ⓟ Ⓤ 100
Harrogate [NT] Ⓟ 🚲 ◇ 🚕 26, 35
Harrow & Wealdstone [LT] Ⓟ ⚠ 🚕 60, 66, 176, 177
Harrow Road [CH] (see Sudbury & Harrow Road)
Harrow Sudbury Hill [CH] (see Sudbury Hill Harrow)
Harrow-on-the-Hill [LT] ■3 Ⓟ 🚲 ⚠ 🚕 114
Hartford [LM] Ⓟ ◇ 65, 91
Hartlebury [LM] Ⓟ ⚠ Ⓤ 71
Hartlepool [NT] Ⓟ 🚲 ◇ 🚕 26, 44
Hartwood [SR] Ⓟ 🚲 Ⓤ 225
Harwich International [LE] 🚲 ◇ 11, 14
Harwich Town [LE] 🚲 Ⓤ 11
Haslemere [SW] ■4 Ⓟ 🚲 ◇ ⚠ 🚕 156
Hassocks [SN] ■4 Ⓟ 🚲 ◇ ⚠ 🚕 52, 186
Hastings [SE] ■4 Ⓟ ◇ ⚠ 🚕 189, 206
Hatch End [LO] Ⓟ 🚲 ⚠ 🚕 60
Hatfield [FC] Ⓟ 🚲 ⚠ 🚕 24, 25
Hatfield & Stainforth [NT] Ⓟ 🚕 Ⓤ 29
Hatfield Peverel [LE] Ⓟ 🚲 ⚠ 11
Hathersage [NT] Ⓟ Ⓤ 78
Hattersley [NT] Ⓤ 79
Hatton (Derbyshire) **[EM]** (see Tutbury & Hatton)
Hatton (Warwickshire) **[CH]** Ⓟ ⚠ Ⓤ 71, 115
Havant [SW] Ⓟ 🚲 ◇ ⚠ 🚕 123, 156, 157, 165, 188
Havenhouse [EM] Ⓤ 19
Haverfordwest [AW] Ⓟ ◇ 🚕 128
Hawarden [AW] Ⓟ Ⓤ 101
Hawarden Bridge [AW] Ⓤ 101
Hawkhead [SR] 🚲 Ⓤ 217
Haydon Bridge [NT] Ⓟ 🚲 Ⓤ 48
Haydons Road [FC] Ⓟ ⚠ 52, 179
Hayes & Harlington [GW] ■3 Ⓟ 🚲 ◇ ⚠ 🚕 117
Hayes (Kent) [SE] Ⓟ 🚲 ◇ ⚠ 🚕 203
Hayle [GW] Ⓟ Ⓤ 51, 135, *Sleepers* 406
Haymarket (Edinburgh) **[SR]** Ⓟ 🚲 ◇ 🚕
Aberdeen 229
Bathgate 226
Birmingham 51, 65
Birmingham International 51, 65
Blackpool 65
Bournemouth 51
Bristol 51
Cambridge 26
Carlisle 65
Carstairs 225
Cowdenbeath 242
Crewe 65
Croy 228
Darlington 26
Derby 51
Doncaster 26
Dunblane 230
Dundee 229
Dunfermline 242
Edinburgh Park 226
Exeter 51
Glasgow 225, 226, 228
Inverness 229
Lancaster 65
Larbert 230

Station index and table numbers

❿ Connection time
Ⓟ Station Car Park
🚲 Bicycle storage facility
◇ Seat reservations can be made at this station
⚠ Penalty Fare Schemes in operation on some or all services from this station
🚕 Taxi rank or cab office at station, or signposted and within 100 metres
Ⓤ Unstaffed station
[ ] Station Operator Code

Station index and table numbers

[10] Connection time
Ⓟ Station Car Park
🚲 Bicycle storage facility
◇ Seat reservations can be made at this station
⚠ Penalty Fare Schemes in operation on some or all services from this station
🚕 Taxi rank or cab office at station, or signposted and within 100 metres
Ⓤ Unstaffed station
[ ] Station Operator Code

Station index and table numbers

■10 Connection time
Ⓟ Station Car Park
🚲 Bicycle storage facility
◇ Seat reservations can be made at this station
⚠ Penalty Fare Schemes in operation on some or all services from this station
🚕 Taxi rank or cab office at station, or signposted and within 100 metres
ⓤ Unstaffed station
[ ] Station Operator Code

Kildale [NT] Ⓟ ⓤ 45
Kildonan [SR] Ⓟ 🚲 ⓤ 239
Kilgetty [AW] ⓤ 128
Kilmarnock [SR] ■3 Ⓟ 🚲 ◇ 🚕 216, 218, 222
Kilmaurs [SR] Ⓟ 🚲 ⓤ 222
Kilpatrick [SR] Ⓟ 🚲 ⓤ 226
Kilwinning [SR] Ⓟ 🚲 🚕 218, 221
Kinbrace [SR] Ⓟ 🚲 ⓤ 239
Kingham [GW] Ⓟ 🚲 126, *Bus* 126A
Kinghorn [SR] 🚲 242
Kings Cross [NR] (see London)
Kings Langley [LM] Ⓟ 🚲 🚕 66
Kings Lynn [FC] Ⓟ 🚲 ◇ ⚠ 🚕 17, *Bus* 17A
Kings Lynn Bus Station 🚕 *Bus* 26A
Kings Norton [LM] Ⓟ ◇ ⚠ 69
Kings Nympton [GW] Ⓟ ⓤ 136
Kings Park [SR] 🚲 223
Kings Sutton [CH] ⚠ ⓤ 115, 116
Kingsknowe [SR] 🚲 ⓤ 225
Kingston [SW] ◇ ⚠ 🚕 149, 152
Kingswood [SN] Ⓟ ◇ ⚠ 181
Kingussie [SR] Ⓟ 🚲 229, *Sleepers* 403
Kintbury [GW] Ⓟ 🚲 ⓤ 116
Kirby Cross [LE] 🚲 ⚠ ⓤ 11
Kirkby [ME] Ⓟ ⚠ 🚕 82, 103
Kirkby in Ashfield [EM] Ⓟ ⓤ 55
Kirkby-in-Furness [NT] ⓤ 100
Kirkby Stephen [NT] Ⓟ ⓤ 36
Kirkcaldy [SR] Ⓟ 🚲 ◇ 🚕
Aberdeen 229
Birmingham 51
Bournemouth 51
Bristol 51
Carlisle 51
Crewe *Sleepers* 402
Derby 51
Dundee 229
Edinburgh 242
Inverness 229
London 26, *Sleepers* 402
Newcastle 26
Oxford 51
Penzance 51
Perth 229
Plymouth 51
Preston 51, *Sleepers* 402
Reading 51
Sheffield 51
Southampton 51
York 26
Kirkconnel [SR] Ⓟ 🚲 ⓤ 216
Kirkdale [ME] ⚠ 103
Kirkham & Wesham [NT] Ⓟ ◇ 82, 97
Kirk Sandall [NT] Ⓟ ⓤ 29
Kirkhill [SR] Ⓟ 🚲 ⓤ 223
Kirknewton [SR] Ⓟ 🚲 ⓤ 225
Kirkoswald [NT] (see Lazonby)
Kirkwood [SR] ⓤ 220
Kirton Lindsey [NT] Ⓟ ⓤ 30
Kiveton Bridge [NT] ⓤ 30
Kiveton Park [NT] Ⓟ 🚲 ⓤ 30
Knaresborough [NT] Ⓟ ⓤ 35
Knebworth [FC] Ⓟ 🚲 ⚠ 24, 25
Knighton [AW] ⓤ 129
Knockholt [SE] Ⓟ ◇ ⚠ 204
Knottingley [NT] Ⓟ ⓤ 32
Knucklas [AW] ⓤ 129
Knutsford [NT] Ⓟ 88
Kyle of Lochalsh [SR] Ⓟ 🚲 ◇ 239, *Ship* 239B

L

Ladybank [SR] Ⓟ 🚲 51, 229
Ladywell [SE] 🚲 ◇ ⚠ 203
Laindon [CC] Ⓟ 🚲 ◇ ⚠ 🚕 1
Lairg [SR] Ⓟ 🚲 ⓤ 239
Lake [IL] (IOW) ⓤ 167
Lake District [VT] (see Oxenholme)
Lakenheath [LE] ⓤ 17
Lamphey [AW] ⓤ 128
Lanark [SR] Ⓟ 🚲 🚕 226
Lancaster [VT] ■6 Ⓟ 🚲 ◇ 🚕
Aberdeen 65
Barrow-in-Furness 82
Birmingham 65
Blackpool 65
Bolton 82
Bournemouth 51
Bradford 36
Bristol 51
Carlisle 65
Chorley 82
Crewe 65
Douglas (IOM) 98A
Edinburgh 65
Exeter 51
Glasgow 65
Heysham Port 98
Leeds 36
Liverpool 65
London 65
Manchester 82
Manchester Airport 82
Millom 100
Milton Keynes Central 65
Morecambe 98
Oxenholme Lake District 65
Oxford 51
Paignton 51
Penzance 51
Plymouth 51
Preston 65
Reading 51
Skipton 36
Southampton 51
Stafford 65
Torquay 51
Warrington 65
Whitehaven 100
Wigan 65
Windermere 65
Workington 100
Lancing [SN] Ⓟ 🚲 ◇ ⚠ 🚕 188
Landywood [LM] Ⓟ ⚠ ⓤ 70
Langbank [SR] Ⓟ 🚲 ⓤ 219
Langho [NT] Ⓟ ⓤ 94
Langley [GW] Ⓟ 🚲 ⚠ 🚕 117
Langley Green [LM] Ⓟ ⚠ 71
Langley Mill [EM] ⓤ 34, 49, 53
Langside [SR] 🚲 ⓤ 223
Langwathby [NT] ⓤ 36
Langwith - Whaley Thorns [EM] ⓤ 55
Lapford [GW] ⓤ 136
Lapworth [CH] Ⓟ ⚠ ⓤ 71, 115
Larbert [SR] Ⓟ 🚲 ◇ 🚕 229, 230
Largs [SR] Ⓟ 🚲 🚕 221
Larkhall [SR] 🚲 ⓤ 226
Latimer [LT] (see Chalfont & Latimer)
Laurencekirk [SR] Ⓟ 🚲 ⓤ 229
Lawrence Hill [GW] ⓤ 133, 134
Layton [NT] Ⓟ ⓤ 82, 97
Lazonby & Kirkoswald [NT] ⓤ 36
Lea Green [NT] Ⓟ 🚲 90
Lea Hall [LM] Ⓟ ⚠ 68
Leagrave [FC] Ⓟ 🚲 ◇ ⚠ 🚕 52
Lealholm [NT] ⓤ 45
Leamington Spa [CH] ■8 Ⓟ 🚲 ◇ ⚠ 🚕 51, 71, 75, 115, 116
Leasowe [ME] Ⓟ ⚠ 106
Leatherhead [SN] Ⓟ 🚲 ◇ ⚠ 🚕 152, 182
Ledbury [LM] Ⓟ ⚠ ⓤ 71, 126
Lee [SE] Ⓟ ◇ ⚠ 200
Leeds [NR] ■10 Ⓟ 🚲 ◇ 🚕
Barnsley 34
Bedford 53
Birmingham 51
Birmingham International 51
Blackburn 41
Blackpool 41
Bournemouth 51
Bradford 37
Brighouse 41
Bristol 51
Burnley 41
Cambridge 26
Cardiff 51
Carlisle 36
Carnforth 36
Chesterfield 53
Darlington 26
Derby 53
Dewsbury 39
Doncaster 31
Edinburgh 26
Exeter 51
Glasgow 26
Goole 32
Grantham 26

Station index and table numbers

[10] Connection time
Ⓟ Station Car Park
🚲 Bicycle storage facility
◇ Seat reservations can be made at this station
⚠ Penalty Fare Schemes in operation on some or all services from this station
🚕 Taxi rank or cab office at station, or signposted and within 100 metres
Ⓤ Unstaffed station
[ ] Station Operator Code

Station index and table numbers

[10] Connection time
Ⓟ Station Car Park
🚲 Bicycle storage facility
◇ Seat reservations can be made at this station
⚠ Penalty Fare Schemes in operation on some or all services from this station
🚕 Taxi rank or cab office at station, or signposted and within 100 metres
Ⓤ Unstaffed station
[ ] Station Operator Code

Llandanwg [AW] Ⓤ 75
Llandecwyn [AW] Ⓤ 75
Llandeilo [AW] Ⓟ Ⓤ 129
Llandovery [AW] Ⓟ Ⓤ 129
Llandrindod [AW] Ⓟ ◇ 129
Llandudno [AW] ◇ 🚕 81, 102
Llandudno Junction [AW] Ⓟ ◇ 🚕 65, 81, 102, 131
Llandybie [AW] Ⓟ Ⓤ 129
Llanelli [AW] ◇ 128, 129
Llanfairfechan [AW] Ⓟ Ⓤ 81
Llanfairpwll [AW] Ⓟ Ⓤ 81
Llangadog [AW] Ⓤ 129
Llangammarch [AW] Ⓤ 129
Llangennech [AW] Ⓤ 129
Llangynllo [AW] Ⓤ 129
Llanharan [AW] Ⓟ Ⓤ 128
Llanhilleth [AW] Ⓟ Ⓤ 127
Llanishen [AW] Ⓟ Ⓤ 130
Llanrwst [AW] Ⓤ 102
Llansamlet [AW] Ⓟ Ⓤ 128
Llantwit Major [AW] Ⓟ 🚲 Ⓤ 130
Llanwrda [AW] Ⓤ 129
Llanwrtyd [AW] Ⓟ Ⓤ 129
Llwyngwril [AW] Ⓤ 75
Llwynypia [AW] Ⓟ Ⓤ 130
Loch Awe [SR] Ⓟ 🚲 Ⓤ 227
Loch Eil Outward Bound [SR] 🚲 Ⓤ 227
Lochailort [SR] Ⓟ 🚲 Ⓤ 227
Lochboisdale *Ship* 227C
Locheilside [SR] Ⓟ 🚲 Ⓤ 227
Lochgelly [SR] Ⓟ 🚲 Ⓤ 242
Lochluichart [SR] Ⓟ Ⓤ 239
Lochmaddy *Ship* 239B
Lochwinnoch [SR] Ⓟ 🚲 Ⓤ 221
Lockerbie [SR] Ⓟ 🚲 ◇ 🚕 51, 65
Lockwood [NT] Ⓟ Ⓤ 34
London
- **Blackfriars [FC]** [3] ◇ ⚠ 🚕
- **Cannon Street [NR]** [4] ◇ ⚠ 🚕
- **Charing Cross [NR]** [4] ◇ ⚠ 🚕
- **City Thameslink [FC]** [3] ◇ ⚠ 🚕
- **Euston [NR]** [15] Ⓟ 🚲 ◇ ⚠ 🚕
- **Farringdon [LT]** [3] ⚠
- **Fenchurch Street [NR]** [7] ◇ ⚠ 🚕
- **Kings Cross [NR]** [15] Ⓟ 🚲 ◇ ⚠ 🚕
- **Liverpool Street [NR]** [15] 🚲 ◇ ⚠ 🚕
- **London Bridge [NR]** [4] 🚲 ◇ ⚠ 🚕
- **Marylebone [CH]** [10] 🚲 ◇ ⚠ 🚕
- **Moorgate [LT]** ⚠
- **Paddington [NR]** [15] Ⓟ 🚲 ◇ ⚠ 🚕
- **St Pancras International [NR]** [15] Ⓟ ◇ ⚠ 🚕
- **Victoria [NR]** [15] Ⓟ 🚲 ◇ ⚠ 🚕
- **Waterloo [NR]** [15] Ⓟ 🚲 ◇ ⚠ 🚕
- **Waterloo East [SE]** [4] ⚠

Aberdeen 26, *Sleepers* 402
Aldershot 149, 155
Alexandra Palace 24
Alnmouth 26
Alton 155
Amersham 114
Arbroath 26, *Sleepers* 402
Ascot 149
Ashford International 196, 207
Aviemore *Sleepers* 403
Aylesbury 114, 115
Balham 177, 178
Banbury 115, 116
Bangor (Gwynedd) 65
Barking 1
Barnsley 53
Barrow-in-Furness 65
Basingstoke 155, 158
Bath Spa 125, 160
Beckenham Junction 177, 195
Bedford 52
Belper 53
Berwick-upon-Tweed 26
Bexhill 189
Bicester 115, 116
Birmingham 66, 115, 116
Birmingham International 66
Bishops Stortford 22
Blackburn 97
Blackpool 65
Bletchley 66
Bodmin Parkway 135, *Sleepers* 406
Bognor Regis 188
Bourne End 120
Bournemouth 158
Bradford 26
Braintree 11
Brighton 186
Bristol 125, 160
Bromley North 204
Bromley South 195
Broxbourne 22
Camborne 135, *Sleepers* 406
Cambridge 22, 25
Canterbury 207, 212
Cardiff 125
Carlisle 65, *Sleepers* 400, 401
Carstairs 65, *Sleepers* 401
Carmarthen 128
Caterham 181
Chatham 200, 212
Chelmsford 11
Cheltenham Spa 125
Chertsey 149
Chessington 152
Chester 65
Chesterfield 53
Chichester 188
Chingford 20
Clacton-on-Sea 11
Clapton 20, 22
Cleethorpes 29
Colchester 11
Coventry 66
Crewe 65
Cromer 16
Crystal Palace 177, 178
Darlington 26
Dartford 200
Derby 53
Didcot 116
Doncaster 26, 53
Dorking 152, 182
Douglas (IOM) 98A
Dover 207, 212
Dundee 26, *Sleepers* 402
Durham 26
Eaglescliffe 26
Eastbourne 189
East Croydon 175
East Grinstead 184
Edinburgh 26, *Sleepers* 400
Effingham Junction 152
Ely 17
Enfield Town 21
Epsom 152, 182
Epsom Downs 182
Exeter 135, 160, *Sleepers* 406
Fareham 158, 188
Felixstowe 13
Finsbury Park 24, 25
Folkestone 207
Fort William *Sleepers* 404
Gatwick Airport 186
Gillingham (Kent) 200, 212
Glasgow 26, 65, *Sleepers* 401
Gloucester 125
Grantham 26
Gravesend 200
Grays 1
Great Yarmouth 15
Greenford 117
Grove Park 204
Guildford 152, 155, 156
Halifax 26
Hampton Court 152
Harrogate 26
Harrow (Sudbury Hill) 115
Harrow & Wealdstone 60, 66
Harrow-on-the-Hill 114
Hartlepool 26
Harwich 11
Haslemere 156
Hastings 189, 206
Hatfield 24
Hayes (Kent) 203
Hayle *Sleepers* 406
Haywards Heath 186
Heathrow Airport 117, 118
Hedge End 158
Henley-on-Thames 121
Hereford 126
Herne Hill 195
Hertford East 22

10 Connection time
Ⓟ Station Car Park
🚲 Bicycle storage facility
◇ Seat reservations can be made at this station
⚠ Penalty Fare Schemes in operation on some or all services from this station
🚕 Taxi rank or cab office at station, or signposted and within 100 metres
Ⓤ Unstaffed station
[ ] Station Operator Code

Station index and table numbers

Hertford North 24
Heysham Port 98A
High Wycombe 115
Hitchin 24, 25
Holyhead 65
Horsham 182, 186
Hounslow 149
Hove 186, 188
Howden 29
Hull 26, 29
Huntingdon 25
Ilford 5
Inverkeithing 26, *Sleepers* 402
Inverness 26, 65, *Sleepers* 403
Ipswich 11
Ireland
  via Rosslare 128
Isle of Man 98A
Isle of Wight 158, 167
Keighley 26
Kettering 53
Kings Lynn 17
Kingston 149, 152
Kirkcaldy 26, *Sleepers* 402
Laindon 1
Lancaster 65
Leamington Spa 115, 116
Leeds 26, 53
Leicester 53
Lewes 186, 189
Lewisham 195, 199
Lichfield 67
Liskeard 135, *Sleepers* 406
Littlehampton 188
Liverpool 65
Llandudno 65
Llanelli 128
London City Airport 59
Lostwithiel 135, *Sleepers* 406
Lowestoft 13
Luton 52
Luton Airport Parkway 52
Macclesfield 65
Maidenhead 117
Maidstone 196, 208
Manchester 65
Manchester Airport 65
Margate 207, 212
Market Harborough 53
Marlow 120
Meadowhall 53
Middlesbrough 26
Milford Haven 128
Milton Keynes Central 66
Moreton-in-Marsh 126
Motherwell 26, 65, *Sleepers* 401
Newark 26
Newcastle 26
Newhaven 189
Newmarket 14
Newport (South Wales) 125
Newton Abbot 135, *Sleepers* 406
Northampton 66
Norwich 11
Nottingham 53
Nuneaton 67
Ore 189, 206
Orpington 195, 199
Oxenholme Lake District 65
Oxford 116
Oxted 184
Paignton 135
Par 135, *Sleepers* 406
Pembroke Dock 128
Penrith North Lakes 65
Penzance 135, *Sleepers* 406
Perth 26, 65, *Sleepers* 403
Peterborough 11, 25
Plymouth 135, *Sleepers* 406
Pontefract 26
Poole 158
Portsmouth 156, 158, 188
Preston 65
Purley 175
Ramsgate 207, 212
Reading
  via Paddington 116
  via Waterloo 149
Redhill 186
Redruth 135, *Sleepers* 406
Reigate 186
Retford 26
Richmond (Surrey) 149
Romford 5
Rugby 66
Runcorn 65
Ryde 167
Rye 189
St Albans 52
St Austell 135, *Sleepers* 406
St Erth 135, *Sleepers* 406
Salisbury 160
Seaford 189
Selby 26
Sevenoaks 195, 204
Shanklin (IOW) 167
Sheerness-on-Sea 212
Sheffield 53
Shenfield 5
Shepperton 152
Sheringham 16
Shipley 26
Shoeburyness 1
Shrewsbury 75
Skipton 26
Slough 117
Smitham (for Coulsdon) 181
Solihull 115
Southampton Airport Parkway 158
Southampton Central 158, 188
Southbury 21
Southend Central 1
Southend Victoria 5
Southminster 5
Stafford 65
Stansted Airport 22
Stevenage 24, 25
Stirling 26, *Sleepers* 403
Stockport 65
Stoke-on-Trent 65
Stratford (London) 5
Stratford-upon-Avon 115
Sunderland 26
Surbiton 152
Sutton (Surrey) 179, 182
Swanley 195
Swansea 125, 128
Swindon 125
Tamworth 67
Tattenham Corner 181
Taunton 135
Tilbury 1
Tonbridge 204
Torquay 135
Tottenham Hale 22
Truro 135, *Sleepers* 406
Tunbridge Wells 206
Uckfield 184
Upminster 1
Wakefield 26, 53
Walthamstow Central 20
Walton-on-the-Naze 11
Warrington 65
Warwick 71, 115
Watford 60, 66
Wellingborough 53
Welwyn Garden City 24
Wembley 60, 66, 115
Westbury (Wilts.) 135, 160
West Croydon 177, 178
Weston-super-Mare 125
Weybridge 149, 155
Weymouth 158
Wickford 5
Wigan 65
Willesden Junction 60
Wilmslow 65
Wimbledon 52, 152, 179
Winchester 158
Windsor & Eton 149
Witham 11
Woking 155, 156
Wolverhampton 66, 68
Woolwich Arsenal 200
Worcester 126
Worthing 188
Wrexham 65, 75
Yarmouth (IOW) 158
York 26, 53

London Bridge [NR] (see London)
London Fields [LE] ⚠ Ⓤ 21
London Gatwick Airport [NR] (see Gatwick Airport)
London Heathrow Airport [HX] (see Heathrow Airport)
London Southend Airport [LE] 5
London Road (Brighton) [SN] ◇ ⚠ 189
London Road (Guildford) [SW] Ⓟ 🚲 ◇ ⚠ 🚕 152
London Stansted Airport [LE] (see Stansted Airport)

Station index and table numbers

10 Connection time
Ⓟ Station Car Park
🚲 Bicycle storage facility
◇ Seat reservations can be made at this station
⚠ Penalty Fare Schemes in operation on some or all services from this station
🚕 Taxi rank or cab office at station, or signposted and within 100 metres
Ⓤ Unstaffed station
[ ] Station Operator Code

Long Buckby [LM] Ⓟ 68
Long Eaton [EM] Ⓟ 🚲 ◇ ⚠ 53, 56, 57
Long Preston [NT] Ⓟ Ⓤ 36
Longbeck [NT] 🚲 Ⓤ 44
Longbridge [LM] ◇ ⚠ 69
Longcross [SW] ⚠ Ⓤ 149
Longfield [SE] Ⓟ ◇ ⚠ 🚕 212
Longniddry [SR] Ⓟ 🚲 Ⓤ 238
Longport [EM] Ⓟ Ⓤ 50, 84
Longton [EM] Ⓟ Ⓤ 50
Looe [GW] Ⓟ 🚲 Ⓤ 140
Lostock [NT] Ⓟ 82
Lostock Gralam [NT] Ⓟ Ⓤ 88
Lostock Hall [NT] Ⓟ Ⓤ 97
Lostwithiel [GW] Ⓟ Ⓤ 51,135, *Sleepers* 406
Loughborough [EM] Ⓟ 🚲 ◇ ⚠ 🚕 53
Loughborough Junction [FC] 🚲 ◇ ⚠ 52, 177, 179, 195
Lowdham [EM] Ⓟ Ⓤ 27
Lower Sydenham [SE] 🚲 ◇ ⚠ 203
Lowestoft [LE] Ⓟ 🚲 ◇ 🚕 13, 15
Ludlow [AW] Ⓟ ◇ 131
Luton [FC] **10** Ⓟ 🚲 ◇ ⚠ 🚕 52, 53
Luton Airport (see London Luton Airport)
Luton Airport Parkway [FC] **7** Ⓟ 🚲 ◇ ⚠ 🚕 52, 53, 177, 179, 186
Luxulyan [GW] Ⓟ Ⓤ 142
Lydney [AW] Ⓟ Ⓤ 132
Lye [LM] Ⓟ ⚠ 71
Lymington Pier [SW] 🚲 ⚠ Ⓤ 158
Lymington Town [SW] Ⓟ 🚲 ◇ ⚠ 158
Lympstone Commando [GW] Ⓤ 136
Lympstone Village [GW] Ⓟ 🚲 Ⓤ 136
Lytham [NT] Ⓤ 97

M

Macclesfield [VT] Ⓟ 🚲 ◇ 🚕 51, 65, 84
Machynlleth [AW] **4** Ⓟ ◇ 75
Maesteg (Ewenny Road) [AW] Ⓤ 128
Maghull [ME] Ⓟ 🚲 ⚠ 🚕 103
Maidenhead [GW] **8** Ⓟ 🚲 ◇ ⚠ 🚕 116, 117, 120
Maiden Newton [GW] Ⓟ Ⓤ 123
Maidstone Barracks [SE] ⚠ Ⓤ 208
Maidstone East [SE] **4** Ⓟ ◇ ⚠ 🚕 196
Maidstone West [SE] **4** Ⓟ ◇ ⚠ 🚕 194, 200, 207, 208
Malden Manor [SW] Ⓟ 🚲 ◇ ⚠ 152
Mallaig [SR] 🚲 ◇ 227, *Ship* 227A
Malton [TP] Ⓟ 🚲 ◇ 🚕 39
Malvern Link [LM] Ⓟ ◇ ⚠ 71, 126
Manchester
  Oxford Road [NT] ◇ 🚕
  Piccadilly [NR] **10** Ⓟ 🚲 ◇ 🚕
  Victoria [NT] ◇ 🚕
 Aberdeen 65
 Altrincham 88
 Bangor (Gwynedd) 81
 Barrow-in-Furness 82
 Birmingham 65
 Birmingham International 65
 Blackpool 82
 Bolton 82
 Bournemouth 51
 Bradford 41
 Bristol 51
 Burnley 97
 Buxton 86
 Cambridge 49
 Cardiff 131
 Carlisle 65
 Carmarthen 128
 Cheadle Hulme 84
 Chester 81, 88
 Chinley 78
 Cleethorpes 29
 Clitheroe 94
 Coventry 65
 Crewe 84
 Darlington 39
 Doncaster 29
 Douglas (IOM) 98A
 Dundee 65
 Durham 39
 Edinburgh 65
 Exeter 51
 Glasgow 65
 Glossop 79
 Grimsby 29
 Guide Bridge 78
 Hadfield 79
 Heysham Port 98A
 Holyhead 81
 Huddersfield 39
 Hull 29, 39
 Inverness 65
 Kirkby 82
 Lancaster 82
 Leeds 39, 41
 Liverpool 89, 90
 Liverpool South Parkway 89
 Llandudno 81
 London 65
 Macclesfield 84
 Manchester Airport 85
 Marple 78
 Middlesbrough 39
 Milford Haven 128
 Milton Keynes Central 65
 Motherwell 65
 Newcastle 39
 New Mills 78, 86
 Newport (South Wales) 131
 Northwich 88
 Nottingham 49
 Oxenholme Lake District 65
 Oxford 51
 Paignton 51
 Penzance 51
 Peterborough 49
 Plymouth 51
 Preston 82
 Reading 51
 Rhyl 81
 Rochdale 41
 Rose Hill Marple 78
 Rugby 65
 St Helens 90
 Salford 82
 Scarborough 39
 Sheffield 78
 Shrewsbury 131
 Southampton 51
 Southport 82
 Stafford 84
 Stalybridge 39
 Stansted Airport 49
 Stockport 84
 Stoke-on-Trent 84
 Swansea 131
 Tenby 128
 Torquay 51
 Wakefield 39
 Warrington 89, 90
 Watford 65
 Wigan 82
 Wilmslow 84
 Windermere 82
 Wolverhampton 65
 York 39
Manchester Airport [TP] ◇
 Bangor (Gwynedd) 81
 Barrow-in-Furness 82
 Birmingham 65
 Birmingham International 65
 Blackburn 94
 Blackpool 82
 Bolton 82
 Carlisle 65
 Coventry 65
 Crewe 84
 Darlington 39
 Doncaster 29
 Durham 39
 Edinburgh 65
 Glasgow 65
 Huddersfield 39
 Hull 29, 39
 Holyhead 81
 Lancaster 82
 Leeds 39
 Liverpool 89

Station index and table numbers

[10] Connection time
Ⓟ Station Car Park
🚲 Bicycle storage facility
◇ Seat reservations can be made at this station
⚠ Penalty Fare Schemes in operation on some or all services from this station
🚕 Taxi rank or cab office at station, or signposted and within 100 metres
Ⓤ Unstaffed station
[ ] Station Operator Code

London 65
Manchester 85
Middlesbrough 39
Motherwell 65
Newcastle 39
Oxenholme Lake District 82
Penrith North Lakes 65
Preston 82
St Helens 90
Salford 82
Scarborough 39
Sheffield 78
Southport 82
Stafford 65, 84
Wakefield 39
Warrington 89
Watford 65
Wigan 82
Wilmslow 84
Windermere 82
Wolverhampton 65
York 39
Manea [LE] Ⓤ 14, 17
Manningtree [LE] **[2]** Ⓟ 🚲 ⚠ 🚕 11, 14
Manor Park [LE] 🚲 ⚠ 5
Manor Road [ME] 🚲 ⚠ 106
Manorbier [AW] Ⓤ 128
Manors [NT] Ⓤ 48
Mansfield [EM] Ⓟ 🚲 🚕 55
Mansfield Woodhouse [EM] Ⓟ Ⓤ 55
March [LE] Ⓟ ◇ 🚕 14, 17, 49
Marden [SE] Ⓟ ◇ ⚠ 207
Margate [SE] **[4]** Ⓟ 🚲 ◇ ⚠ 🚕 194, 207, 212
Market Harborough [EM] Ⓟ 🚲 ◇ ⚠ 🚕 53
Market Rasen [EM] Ⓟ 🚲 Ⓤ 27
Markinch [SR] Ⓟ 🚲 🚕 51, 229
Marks Tey [LE] **[2]** Ⓟ 🚲 ⚠ 10, 11
Marlow [GW] 🚲 Ⓤ 120
Marple [NT] Ⓟ 🚲 78
Marsden [NT] Ⓟ Ⓤ 39
Marske [NT] 🚲 Ⓤ 44
Marston Green [LM] Ⓟ ◇ ⚠ 68
Martin Mill [SE] Ⓟ ⚠ 207
Martins Heron [SW] Ⓟ 🚲 ◇ ⚠ 149
Marton [NT] Ⓟ 🚲 Ⓤ 45
Maryhill [SR] 🚲 Ⓤ 232
Maryland [LE] 🚲 ⚠ 🚕 5
Marylebone [CH] (see London)
Maryport [NT] Ⓟ Ⓤ 100
Matlock [EM] Ⓟ Ⓤ 56
Matlock Bath [EM] Ⓟ Ⓤ 56
Mauldeth Road [NT] 85
Maxwell Park [SR] 🚲 Ⓤ 223
Maybole [SR] Ⓟ 🚲 Ⓤ 218
Maze Hill [SE] ◇ ⚠ 200
Meadowhall [NT] Ⓟ 🚲 ◇
Barnsley 34
Castleford 34
Cleethorpes 29
Doncaster 29
Gainsborough 30
Grimsby 29
Huddersfield 34
Hull 29
Leeds 31
Lincoln 30
Manchester 29
Manchester Airport 29
Penistone 34
Pontefract 33
Retford 30
Rotherham 29
Scunthorpe 29
Sheffield 29
Wakefield 31
Worksop 30
York 29, 33
Meldreth [FC] Ⓟ 🚲 ⚠ 25
Melksham [GW] Ⓟ Ⓤ 123
Melrose *Bus* 26K
Melton [LE] Ⓟ 🚲 🚕 Ⓤ 13
Melton Mowbray [EM] Ⓟ 🚲 ◇ 🚕 49, 53
Menheniot [GW] Ⓟ Ⓤ 135
Menston [NT] Ⓟ 🚲 ◇ 38
Meols [ME] Ⓟ 🚲 ⚠ 🚕 106
Meols Cop [NT] Ⓤ 82
Meopham [SE] Ⓟ ◇ ⚠ 🚕 212
Merryton [SR] 🚲 Ⓤ 226
Merstham [SN] Ⓟ 🚲 ◇ ⚠ 🚕 186
Merthyr Tydfil [AW] Ⓟ ◇ 130
Merthyr Vale [AW] Ⓤ 130
Metheringham [EM] Ⓟ 🚲 Ⓤ 18
Metrocentre [NT] Ⓤ 44, 48
Mexborough [NT] Ⓟ 🚲 ◇ 29
Micheldever [SW] Ⓟ 🚲 ◇ ⚠ 158
Micklefield [NT] Ⓟ 🚲 Ⓤ 40
Middlesbrough [TP] Ⓟ 🚲 ◇ 🚕 26, 39, 44, 45
Middlewood [NT] Ⓤ 86
Midgham [GW] Ⓟ Ⓤ 116
Milford Haven [AW] Ⓟ 🚕 Ⓤ 128
Milford (Surrey) [SW] Ⓟ 🚲 ⚠ 156
Millbrook (Bedfordshire) [LM] Ⓤ 64
Millbrook (Hants.) [SW] 🚲 ⚠ Ⓤ 158
Mill Hill Broadway [FC] Ⓟ 🚲 ◇ ⚠ 52
Mill Hill (Lancashire) [NT] Ⓤ 97
Milliken Park [SR] 🚲 Ⓤ 221
Millom [NT] Ⓟ Ⓤ 100
Mills Hill [NT] Ⓟ Ⓤ 41
Milngavie [SR] Ⓟ 🚲 226
Milton Keynes Central [LM] Ⓟ 🚲 ◇ ⚠ 🚕
Birmingham International 66
Birmingham New Street 66
Blackpool 65
Bletchley 66
Brighton 66
Coventry 66, 67
Crewe 65, 67
Edinburgh 65
Gatwick Airport 66
Glasgow 65
Lancaster 65
Liverpool 65
London 67
Manchester 65
Northampton 66, 67
Oxenholme Lake District 65
Preston 65
Rugby 66, 67
Stafford 65, 67
Stockport 65
Stoke-on-Trent 65, 67
Tring 66
Warrington 65
Watford Junction 66, 176, 177
Wembley Central 66, 176, 177
Wigan 65
Wolverhampton 66
Minehead Bancks Street *Bus* 135E
Minehead Butlins *Bus* 135E
Minehead Parade *Bus* 135E
Minffordd [AW] Ⓤ 75
Minster [SE] **[4]** Ⓟ ⚠ Ⓤ 207
Mirfield [NT] Ⓟ 🚲 Ⓤ 39, 41
Mistley [LE] 🚲 Ⓤ 11
Mitcham Eastfields [SN] ◇ ⚠ 52, 179, 182
Mitcham Junction [SN] Ⓟ 🚲 ◇ ⚠ 52, 179, 182
Mobberley [NT] Ⓤ 88
Monifieth [SR] 🚲 Ⓤ 229
Monks Risborough [CH] ⚠ Ⓤ 115
Montpelier [GW] 🚲 Ⓤ 133
Montrose [SR] Ⓟ 🚲 ◇ 🚕 26, 51, 229, *Sleepers* 402
Moorfields [ME] (see Liverpool)
Moorgate [LT] ⚠ 24
Moorside [NT] 82
Moorthorpe [NT] Ⓟ Ⓤ 31, 33
Morar [SR] Ⓟ 🚲 Ⓤ 227
Morchard Road [GW] Ⓟ Ⓤ 136
Morden (Herts) **[FC]** (see Ashwell & Morden)
Morden South [FC] ⚠ Ⓤ 52, 179
Morecambe [NT] Ⓟ 🚲 ◇ 36, 98, 98A
Moreton (Dorset) [SW] Ⓟ 🚲 Ⓤ 158
Moreton (Merseyside) [ME] 🚲 ⚠ 🚕 106
Moreton-in-Marsh [GW] Ⓟ 🚲 ◇ 126
Morfa Mawddach [AW] Ⓤ 75
Morley [NT] Ⓟ Ⓤ 39
Morpeth [NT] Ⓟ 🚲 ◇ 🚕 26, 48, 51
Mortimer [GW] Ⓟ 122
Mortlake [SW] Ⓟ 🚲 ◇ ⚠ 149
Moses Gate [NT] Ⓤ 82
Moss Side [NT] Ⓤ 97

Station index and table numbers

10 Connection time
Ⓟ Station Car Park
🚲 Bicycle storage facility
◇ Seat reservations can be made at this station
⚠ Penalty Fare Schemes in operation on some or all services from this station
🚕 Taxi rank or cab office at station, or signposted and within 100 metres
Ⓤ Unstaffed station
[ ] Station Operator Code

Mossley (Greater Manchester) [NT] Ⓟ 🚲 39
Mossley Hill [NT] Ⓟ 89, 91
Mosspark [SR] 🚲 Ⓤ 217
Moston [NT] Ⓤ 41
Motherwell [SR] Ⓟ 🚲 ◇ 🚕
- Birmingham 51, 65
- Bournemouth 51
- Bristol 51
- Crewe 65
- Cumbernauld 224
- Darlington 26
- Doncaster 26
- Edinburgh 225
- Exeter 51
- Glasgow 225, 226
- Liverpool 65
- London 26, 65, *Sleepers* 401
- Manchester 65
- Manchester Airport 65
- Newcastle 26
- Oxenholme Lake District 65
- Oxford 51
- Paignton 51
- Penzance 51
- Peterborough 26
- Plymouth 51
- Reading 51
- Southampton 51
- Torquay 51
- Watford 65, *Sleepers* 401
- York 26

Motspur Park [SW] ◇ ⚠ 152
Mottingham [SE] Ⓟ ◇ ⚠ 200
Mottisfont & Dunbridge [GW] Ⓤ 158
Mouldsworth [NT] Ⓟ Ⓤ 88
Moulsecoomb [SN] ◇ ⚠ 189
Mount Florida [SR] 🚲 223
Mount Vernon [SR] 🚲 Ⓤ 220
Mountain Ash [AW] Ⓟ Ⓤ 130
Muck *Ship* 227A
Muir of Ord [SR] Ⓟ 🚲 Ⓤ 239
Muirend [SR] 🚲 223
Musselburgh [SR] Ⓟ 🚲 Ⓤ 238
Mytholmroyd [NT] Ⓤ 41

N

Nafferton [NT] Ⓤ 43
Nailsea & Backwell [GW] Ⓟ 🚲 134
Nairn [SR] Ⓟ 🚲 ◇ 🚕 240
Nantwich [AW] Ⓤ 131
Narberth [AW] Ⓤ 128
Narborough [EM] Ⓟ 57
National Exhibition Centre [VT] (see Birmingham International)
Navigation Road [NT] Ⓤ 88
Neath [AW] Ⓟ 🚲 ◇ 🚕 125, 128
Needham Market [LE] Ⓤ 11, 14
Neilston [SR] Ⓟ 🚲 🚕 223
Nelson [NT] Ⓟ 97
Neston [AW] Ⓟ Ⓤ 101
Netherfield [EM] Ⓤ 19
Nethertown [NT] Ⓟ Ⓤ 100
Netley [SW] Ⓟ 🚲 ◇ 165
New Barnet [FC] Ⓟ 🚲 ⚠ 24
New Beckenham [SE] **4** Ⓟ 🚲 ◇ ⚠ 203
New Brighton [ME] ⚠ 106
New Clee [NT] Ⓤ 29
New Cross [SE] **4** 🚲 ◇ ⚠ 178, 199, 200, 203, 204
New Cross Gate [LO] **4** 🚲 ⚠ 175, 178, 181, 182, 186
New Cumnock [SR] Ⓟ 🚲 Ⓤ 216
New Eltham [SE] Ⓟ ◇ ⚠ 200
New Haw [SW] (see Byfleet & New Haw)
New Holland [NT] 🚲 Ⓤ 29
New Hythe [SE] ⚠ Ⓤ 208
New Inn [AW] (see Pontypool and New Inn)
New Lane [NT] Ⓤ 82
New Malden [SW] **6** Ⓟ 🚲 ◇ ⚠ 🚕 152
New Mills Central [NT] 78
New Mills Newtown [NT] Ⓟ 🚲 86
New Milton [SW] Ⓟ 🚲 ◇ ⚠ 🚕 158
New Pudsey [NT] Ⓟ 🚲 ◇ 37, 41
New Southgate [FC] Ⓟ ⚠ 24
Newark Castle [EM] Ⓟ 🚲 Ⓤ 27
Newark North Gate [GR] **7** Ⓟ 🚲 ◇ 🚕 26, 27
Newbridge [AW] Ⓟ Ⓤ 127
Newbury [GW] Ⓟ 🚲 ◇ 🚕 116, 135
Newbury Racecourse [GW] Ⓤ 116
Newcastle [GR] **8** Ⓟ 🚲 ◇ 🚕
- Aberdeen 26
- Alnmouth 26
- Arbroath 26
- Berwick-upon-Tweed 26
- Birmingham 51
- Birmingham International 51
- Bournemouth 51
- Bradford 39
- Bristol 51
- Cambridge 26
- Cardiff 51
- Carlisle 48
- Chathill 48
- Darlington 26
- Derby 51
- Doncaster 26
- Dundee 26
- Edinburgh 26
- Exeter 51
- Glasgow 26, 216
- Grantham 26
- Haltwhistle 48
- Hartlepool 44
- Hexham 48
- Huddersfield 39
- Hull 26
- Leeds 26
- Liverpool 39
- London 26
- Manchester 39
- Manchester Airport 39
- MetroCentre 48
- Middlesbrough 44
- Morpeth 48
- Newark 26
- Newport (South Wales) 51
- Northallerton 26
- Norwich 26
- Oxford 51
- Paignton 51
- Penzance 51
- Peterborough 26
- Plymouth 51
- Preston 39
- Reading 51
- Retford 26
- Sheffield 26
- Southampton 51
- Stansted Airport 26
- Stockton 44
- Sunderland 44
- Torquay 51
- Whitby 45
- York 26

Newcraighall [SR] Ⓟ 🚲 Ⓤ 242
Newhaven Harbour [SN] ◇ Ⓤ 189
Newhaven Town [SN] 🚲 ⚠ 189
Newington [SE] Ⓟ ⚠ 212
Newmarket [LE] Ⓟ 🚲 Ⓤ 14
Newport (Essex) [LE] Ⓟ 🚲 ⚠ 22
Newport (S. Wales) [AW] Ⓟ 🚲 ◇ 🚕
- Aberdeen 51
- Bangor (Gwynedd) 131
- Bath Spa 132
- Birmingham 57
- Bristol 132
- Cardiff 132
- Cheltenham Spa 57
- Chester 131
- Crewe 131
- Darlington 51
- Derby 57
- Dundee 51
- Durham 51
- Edinburgh 51
- Exeter 135
- Gloucester 132
- Hereford 131
- Holyhead 131
- Leeds 51
- Llandudno Junction 131
- London 125
- Maesteg 128
- Manchester 131
- Milford Haven 128
- Newcastle 51

[10] Connection time
Ⓟ Station Car Park
🚲 Bicycle storage facility
◇ Seat reservations can be made at this station
⚠ Penalty Fare Schemes in operation on some or all services from this station
🚕 Taxi rank or cab office at station, or signposted and within 100 metres
🚶 Unstaffed station
[ ] Station Operator Code

Station index and table numbers

O

Station index and table numbers

10 Connection time
Ⓟ Station Car Park
🚲 Bicycle storage facility
◇ Seat reservations can be made at this station
⚠ Penalty Fare Schemes in operation on some or all services from this station
🚕 Taxi rank or cab office at station, or signposted and within 100 metres
Ⓤ Unstaffed station
[ ] Station Operator Code

Ormskirk [ME] Ⓟ 🚲 ◇ ⚠ 🚕 99, 103
Orpington [SE] **4** Ⓟ ◇ ⚠ 🚕 195, 199, 204, 206, 207
Orrell [NT] Ⓤ 82
Orrell Park [ME] ⚠ 103
Orston [EM] (see Elton & Orston)
Oswaldtwistle [NT] (see Church & Oswaldtwistle)
Otford [SE] **4** Ⓟ ◇ ⚠ 52, 195, 196
Oulton Broad North [LE] Ⓟ 🚲 Ⓤ 15
Oulton Broad South [LE] Ⓟ 🚲 Ⓤ 13
Oundle (Market Place) *Bus* 26B
Outwood [NT] Ⓟ 🚲 Ⓤ 31
Overpool [ME] Ⓤ 106
Overton [SW] Ⓟ 🚲 ◇ ⚠ 160
Oxenholme Lake District [VT] Ⓟ 🚲 ◇ 🚕 51, 65, 82, 83
Oxford [GW] Ⓟ 🚲 ◇ 🚕 51, 116, *Bus* 126
Oxshott [SW] Ⓟ 🚲 ◇ ⚠ 🚕 152
Oxted [SN] **3** Ⓟ 🚲 ◇ ⚠ 🚕 184

P

Paddington [NR] (see London)
Paddock Wood [SE] **4** Ⓟ 🚲 ◇ ⚠ 🚕 207, 208
Padgate [NT] Ⓟ Ⓤ 89
Padstow Old Rly Station *Bus* 135C
Paignton [GW] Ⓟ 🚲 ◇ 🚕 51, 135
Paisley Canal [SR] 🚲 Ⓤ 217
Paisley Gilmour Street [SR] Ⓟ 🚲 ◇ 🚕
- Ayr 221
- Ardrossan 221
- Belfast *Ship* 221B
- Clyde Coast *Ship* 219A, 219B, 221A
- Glasgow 219, 221
- Gourock 219
- Largs 221
- Stranraer 218
- Wemyss Bay 219

Paisley St James [SR] 🚲 Ⓤ 219
Palmers Green [FC] Ⓟ ⚠ 24
Pangbourne [GW] Ⓟ 🚲 116
Pannal [NT] Ⓟ 🚲 Ⓤ 35
Pantyffynnon [AW] Ⓤ 129
Par [GW] Ⓟ ◇ 51, 135, 142, *Sleepers* 406
Parbold [NT] 82
Park Street [LM] Ⓤ 61
Parkhouse [SR] (see Possilpark & Parkhouse)
Parkstone (Dorset) [SW] Ⓟ 🚲 ◇ 158
Parson Street [GW] Ⓤ 134
Partick [SR] 🚲 226
Parton [NT] Ⓟ Ⓤ 100
Patchway [GW] Ⓟ Ⓤ 132
Patricroft [NT] Ⓤ 90
Patterton [SR] Ⓟ 🚲 Ⓤ 223
Peartree [EM] Ⓤ 50
Peckham Rye [SN] **4** 🚲 ◇ ⚠ 52, 177, 178, 179, 195, 200
Pegswood [NT] Ⓤ 48
Pemberton [NT] Ⓤ 82
Pembrey & Burry Port [AW] Ⓟ Ⓤ 128
Pembroke [AW] Ⓟ Ⓤ 128
Pembroke Dock [AW] Ⓟ Ⓤ 128
Penally [AW] Ⓤ 128
Penarth [AW] Ⓟ ◇ 🚕 130
Pencoed [AW] Ⓤ 128
Pengam [AW] Ⓟ Ⓤ 130
Penge East [SE] Ⓟ 🚲 ◇ ⚠ 195
Penge West [LO] 🚲 ⚠ 178
Penhelig [AW] Ⓤ 75
Penistone [NT] Ⓟ 🚲 Ⓤ 34
Penketh [NT] (see Sankey for Penketh)
Penkridge [LM] Ⓟ Ⓤ 65, 68
Penmaenmawr [AW] Ⓤ 81
Penmere [GW] Ⓟ 🚲 Ⓤ 143
Penrhiwceiber [AW] Ⓤ 130
Penrhyndeudraeth [AW] Ⓟ 🚲 Ⓤ 75
Penrith North Lakes [VT] Ⓟ 🚲 ◇ 🚕 51, 65
Penryn [GW] 🚲 Ⓤ 143
Pensarn (Gwynedd) **[AW]** Ⓤ 75
Penshurst [SN] ⚠ Ⓤ 186
Pentre-bach [AW] Ⓤ 130
Pen-y-bont [AW] Ⓟ Ⓤ 129
Penychain [AW] Ⓤ 75
Penyffordd [AW] Ⓟ Ⓤ 101
Penzance [GW] Ⓟ 🚲 ◇ 🚕 51, 135, 144, *Sleepers* 406
Perranwell [GW] Ⓟ 🚲 Ⓤ 143
Perry Barr [LM] ◇ ⚠ 70
Pershore [GW] Ⓟ 🚲 Ⓤ 126
Perth [SR] Ⓟ 🚲 ◇ 🚕 26, 65, 229, *Sleepers* 403
Peterborough [GR] **8** Ⓟ 🚲 ◇ ⚠ 🚕
- Aberdeen 26
- Birmingham 49
- Bradford 26
- Cambridge 17
- Corby George Street *Bus* 26B
- Darlington 26
- Dereham *Bus* 26A
- Doncaster 26
- Dundee 26
- Edinburgh 26
- Ely 17
- Grantham 26
- Grimsby 26
- Hitchin 25
- Hull 26
- Huntingdon 25
- Ipswich 17
- Kettering Library *Bus* 26B
- Kings Lynn *Bus* 26A
- Leeds 26
- Leicester 49
- Lincoln 18, 26
- Liverpool 49
- London 14, 25
- Manchester 49
- March 17
- Newark 26
- Newcastle 26
- Norwich 17
- Nottingham 49
- Nuneaton 49
- Oundle (Market Place) *Bus* 26B
- Retford 26
- Sheffield 49
- Spalding 18
- Stansted Airport 49
- Stevenage 25
- Stockport 49
- Swaffham *Bus* 26A
- Wakefield 26
- York 26

Petersfield [SW] Ⓟ 🚲 ◇ ⚠ 🚕 156
Petts Wood [SE] **4** Ⓟ ◇ ⚠ 🚕 195, 199, 204
Pevensey & Westham [SN] Ⓟ 🚲 ⚠ 189
Pevensey Bay [SN] Ⓤ 189
Pewsey [GW] Ⓟ 🚲 ◇ ⚠ 135
Pickering [NY] Ⓟ 🚲 45
Pickering Eastgate *Bus* 26G
Pilning [GW] Ⓟ Ⓤ 132
Pinhoe [SW] ⚠ Ⓤ 160
Pitlochry [SR] Ⓟ 🚲 🚕 229, *Sleepers* 403
Pitsea [CC] Ⓟ 🚲 ◇ ⚠ 🚕 1
Pleasington [NT] Ⓟ Ⓤ 97
Pleasure Beach [NT] (see Blackpool)
Plockton [SR] Ⓟ 🚲 Ⓤ 239
Pluckley [SE] Ⓟ 🚲 ◇ ⚠ 207
Plumley [NT] Ⓟ Ⓤ 88
Plumpton [SN] Ⓟ ◇ ⚠ 189
Plumstead [SE] ◇ ⚠ 200
Plymouth [GW] Ⓟ 🚲 ◇ ⚠ 🚕
- Aberdeen 51
- Birmingham 51, 135
- Bristol 135
- Cardiff 135
- Carlisle 51
- Crewe 51
- Derby 51
- Dundee 51
- Edinburgh 51
- Exeter 135
- Glasgow 51
- Gunnislake 139
- Leeds 51
- London 135, *Sleepers* 406
- Manchester 51
- Newcastle 51

[10] Connection time
Ⓟ Station Car Park
🚲 Bicycle storage facility
◇ Seat reservations can be made at this station
⚠ Penalty Fare Schemes in operation on some or all services from this station
🚕 Taxi rank or cab office at station, or signposted and within 100 metres
Ⓤ Unstaffed station
[ ] Station Operator Code

Station index and table numbers

Newton Abbot 135
Nottingham 51
Paignton 135
Penzance 135
Preston 51
Reading 135, *Sleepers* 406
Sheffield 51
Taunton 135
Torquay 135
Wolverhampton 51
York 51
Pokesdown [SW] 🚲 ◇ ⚠ 158
Polegate [SN] Ⓟ 🚲 ◇ ⚠ 🚕 189
Polesworth [LM] Ⓟ Ⓤ 67
Pollokshaws East [SR] 🚲 Ⓤ 223
Pollokshaws West [SR] 🚲 Ⓤ 222
Pollokshields East [SR] 🚲 223
Pollokshields West [SR] 🚲 Ⓤ 223
Polmont [SR] [3] Ⓟ 🚲 ◇ 🚕 228, 230
Polsloe Bridge [GW] Ⓤ 136
Ponders End [LE] ⚠ 22
Pontarddulais [AW] Ⓟ Ⓤ 129
Pontefract Baghill [NT] Ⓟ Ⓤ 33
Pontefract Monkhill [NT] Ⓟ Ⓤ 26, 31, 32
Pontefract Tanshelf [NT] Ⓟ Ⓤ 32
Pontlottyn [AW] Ⓟ Ⓤ 130
Pont-y-Pant [AW] Ⓤ 102
Pontyclun [AW] Ⓟ Ⓤ 128
Pontypool & New Inn [AW] Ⓟ Ⓤ 131
Pontypridd [AW] [3] 🚲 ◇ 🚕 130
Poole [SW] [4] Ⓟ 🚲 ◇ ⚠ 🚕 158
Poppleton [NT] Ⓟ 🚲 Ⓤ 35
Portchester [SW] 🚲 ⚠ 158, 165, 188
Port Glasgow [SR] 🚲 🚕 219
Porth [AW] Ⓟ ◇ 130
Porthmadog [AW] Ⓤ 75
Portlethen [SR] Ⓟ 🚲 Ⓤ 229
Portslade [SN] Ⓟ 🚲 ◇ ⚠ 188
Portsmouth Arms [GW] Ⓟ Ⓤ 136
Portsmouth
Harbour [SW] 🚲 ◇ ⚠ 🚕
& Southsea [SW] Ⓟ 🚲 ◇ ⚠ 🚕
Bognor Regis 188
Brighton 188
Bristol 123
Cardiff 123
Chichester 188
Crawley 188
East Croydon 188
Exeter 160
Fareham 165
Gatwick Airport 188
Guildford 156
Haslemere 156
Havant 157
Horsham 188
Littlehampton 188
London 156, 158, 188
Reading
via Eastleigh 158
via Guildford 156
Redhill 188
Ryde 167
Salisbury 123
Sandown 167
Shanklin 167
Southampton Central 165
Winchester 158
Worthing 188
Port Sunlight [ME] 🚲 ⚠ 106
Port Talbot Parkway [AW] Ⓟ 🚲 ◇ 🚕 125, 128
Possilpark & Parkhouse [SR] 🚲 Ⓤ 232
Potters Bar [FC] Ⓟ ◇ ⚠ 🚕 24, 25
Poulton-le-Fylde [NT] Ⓟ ◇ 🚕 41, 82, 97
Poynton [NT] Ⓟ 84
Prees [AW] Ⓤ 131
Prescot [NT] Ⓟ 90
Prestatyn [AW] ◇ 🚕 Ⓤ 81
Prestbury [NT] Ⓟ Ⓤ 84
Preston [VT] [8] Ⓟ 🚲 ◇ 🚕
Aberdeen 65, *Sleepers* 402
Barrow-in-Furness 82
Birmingham 65
Birmingham International 65
Blackburn 97
Blackpool 97
Bolton 82
Bournemouth 51
Bradford 41
Bristol 51
Burnley 97
Carlisle 65
Chorley 82
Clitheroe 94, 97
Colne 97
Coventry 65
Crewe 65
Douglas (IOM) 98A
Dundee 65, *Sleepers* 402
Edinburgh 65
Exeter 51
Fort William *Sleepers* 404
Glasgow 65
Inverkeithing *Sleepers* 402
Inverness 65, *Sleepers* 403
Kirkcaldy *Sleepers* 402
Lancaster 65
Leeds 41
Liverpool 90
London 65
Manchester 82
Manchester Airport 82
Milton Keynes Central 65
Ormskirk 99
Oxenholme Lake District 65
Oxford 51
Paignton 51
Penzance 51
Perth 65, *Sleepers* 403
Plymouth 51
Reading 51
Rugby 65
Southampton 51
Stafford 65
Stirling *Sleepers* 403
Stockport 82
Torquay 51
Warrington 65
Watford 65
Wigan 65
Windermere 65
Wolverhampton 65
York 41
Preston Park [SN] ◇ ⚠ 52, 186, 188
Prestonpans [SR] Ⓟ 🚲 Ⓤ 238
Prestwick International Airport 🚕 Ⓤ 218, 221
Prestwick Town [SR] Ⓟ 🚲 🚕 218, 221
Priesthill & Darnley [SR] 🚲 Ⓤ 222
Princes Risborough [CH] [2] Ⓟ 🚲 ◇ ⚠ 🚕 115, 115A
Prittlewell [LE] Ⓟ 🚲 ⚠ 5
Prudhoe [NT] Ⓟ 🚲 Ⓤ 48
Pulborough [SN] Ⓟ 🚲 ◇ ⚠ 🚕 188
Purfleet [CC] Ⓟ 🚲 ◇ ⚠ 1
Purley [SN] [4] Ⓟ ◇ ⚠ 🚕 175, 181, 186
Purley Oaks [SN] Ⓟ ⚠ 175, 181
Putney [SW] 🚲 ◇ ⚠ 149
Pwllheli [AW] 🚲 🚕 75
Pyle [AW] Ⓟ 🚲 Ⓤ 128

Q

Quakers Yard [AW] Ⓤ 130
Queenborough [SE] Ⓟ ◇ ⚠ 212
Queens Park (Glasgow) **[SR]** 🚲 223
Queen s Park (London) **[LT]** 60
Queens Road, Peckham [SN] 🚲 ◇ ⚠ 177, 178, 179
Queen s Road, Walthamstow [LO] (see Walthamstow Queen s Road)
Queenstown Road (Battersea) [SW] ⚠ Ⓤ 149
Quintrell Downs [GW] Ⓤ 142

R

Radcliffe (Notts.) **[EM]** Ⓟ Ⓤ 19
Radlett [FC] Ⓟ 🚲 ◇ ⚠ 🚕 52
Radley [GW] Ⓟ Ⓤ 116

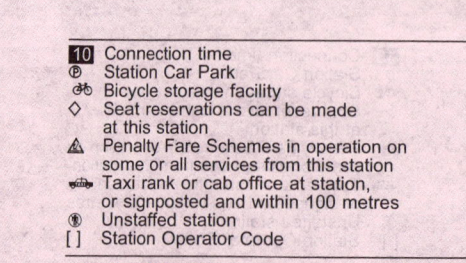

Station index and table numbers

■10 Connection time
Ⓟ Station Car Park
🚲 Bicycle storage facility
◇ Seat reservations can be made at this station
△ Penalty Fare Schemes in operation on some or all services from this station
🚕 Taxi rank or cab office at station, or signposted and within 100 metres
Ⓤ Unstaffed station
[ ] Station Operator Code

Radyr [AW] ■3 Ⓟ 🚲 ◇ 130
Rainford [NT] Ⓟ Ⓤ 82
Rainham (Essex) **[CC]** Ⓟ 🚲 ◇ △ 1
Rainham (Kent) [SE] Ⓟ ◇ △ 🚕 194, 212
Rainhill [NT] 90
Ramsgate [SE] ■4 Ⓟ 🚲 ◇ △ 🚕 194, 207, 212
Ramsgreave & Wilpshire [NT] Ⓟ Ⓤ 94
Rannoch [SR] Ⓟ 🚲 Ⓤ 227, *Sleepers* 404
Rauceby [EM] Ⓤ 19
Ravenglass for Eskdale [NT] Ⓤ 100
Ravensbourne [SE] ◇ △ 52, 195
Ravensthorpe [NT] Ⓤ 39
Rawcliffe [NT] Ⓤ 32
Rayleigh [LE] Ⓟ 🚲 △ 🚕 5
Raynes Park [SW] ■6 🚲 ◇ △ 🚕 152
Reading [GW] ■7 Ⓟ 🚲 ◇ △ 🚕
- Aberdeen 51
- Ascot 149
- Banbury 116
- Basingstoke 122
- Bath Spa 125
- Birmingham 116
- Bodmin Parkway 135, *Sleepers* 406
- Bournemouth 158
- Bristol 125
- Camborne 135, *Sleepers* 406
- Cardiff 125
- Carlisle 51
- Cheltenham Spa 125
- Clapham Junction 149
- Coventry 51
- Crewe 51
- Derby 51
- Didcot 116
- Dundee 51
- Edinburgh 51
- Exeter 135, *Sleepers* 406
- Gatwick Airport 148
- Glasgow 51
- Gloucester 125
- Guildford 148
- Hayle 135, *Sleepers* 406
- Heathrow Airport *Bus* 125A
- Henley-on-Thames 121
- Hereford 126
- Leamington Spa 116
- Leeds 51
- Liskeard 135, *Sleepers* 406
- London 116, 117, 149
- Lostwithiel 135, *Sleepers* 406
- Manchester 51
- Milford Haven 128
- Moreton-in-Marsh 126
- Newbury 116
- Newcastle 51
- Newport (South Wales) 125
- Newton Abbot 135, *Sleepers* 406
- Oxford 116
- Paignton 135
- Par 135, *Sleepers* 406
- Penzance 135, *Sleepers* 406
- Plymouth 135, *Sleepers* 406
- Poole 158
- Portsmouth
  - via Basingstoke 158
  - via Guildford 156
- Preston 51
- Redhill 148
- Redruth 135, *Sleepers* 406
- Rosslare Harbour 128
- Sheffield 51
- Slough 117
- Southampton 158
- St Austell 135, *Sleepers* 406
- St Erth 135, *Sleepers* 406
- Staines 149
- Swansea 125
- Swindon 125
- Taunton 135
- Torquay 135
- Truro 135, *Sleepers* 406
- Weston-super-Mare 125
- Weymouth 158
- Winchester 158
- Wolverhampton 51
- Worcester 126
- York 51

Reading West [GW] ■3 116, 122
Rectory Road [LE] △ 21
Redbridge [SW] Ⓟ △ Ⓤ 158
Redcar British Steel [NT] Ⓤ 44
Redcar Central [NT] Ⓟ 🚲 ◇ 🚕 44
Redcar East [NT] 🚲 Ⓤ 44
Reddish North [NT] Ⓟ 🚲 78
Reddish South [NT] Ⓤ 78
Redditch [LM] Ⓟ ◇ △ 69
Redhill [SN] Ⓟ 🚲 ◇ △ 🚕 148, 186, 188
Redland [GW] 🚲 Ⓤ 133
Redruth [GW] Ⓟ 🚲 ◇ 🚕 51, 135, *Sleepers* 406
Reedham (Norfolk) [LE] Ⓟ 🚲 Ⓤ 15
Reedham (Surrey) **[SN]** △ 181
Reigate [SN] Ⓟ 🚲 ◇ △ 148, 186
Renton [SR] 🚲 Ⓤ 226
Retford [GR] ■10 Ⓟ 🚲 ◇ 🚕 26, 30
Rhiwbina [AW] Ⓤ 130
Rhoose Cardiff Int. Airport [AW] Ⓟ 🚲 Ⓤ 130
Rhosneigr [AW] Ⓤ 81
Rhyl [AW] ◇ 🚕 81
Rhymney [AW] ■3 Ⓟ 🚕 Ⓤ 130
Ribblehead [NT] Ⓟ Ⓤ 36
Rice Lane [ME] △ 103
Richmond (Greater London) **[SW]** Ⓟ 🚲 ◇ △ 🚕 59, 149
Richmond (Market) 🚕 *Bus* 26H
Rickmansworth [LT] Ⓟ 🚲 △ 114
Riddlesdown [SN] 🚲 ◇ △ 184
Ridgmont [LM] Ⓤ 64
Riding Mill [NT] Ⓟ 🚲 Ⓤ 48
Risca & Pontymister [AW] Ⓟ Ⓤ 127
Rishton [NT] Ⓟ 🚲 Ⓤ 97
Robin Hood Airport 🚕 *Bus* 26F
Robertsbridge [SE] Ⓟ ◇ △ 206
Roby [NT] 90
Rochdale [NT] Ⓟ ◇ 🚕 41, 82
Roche [GW] Ⓤ 142
Rochester [SE] ■4 Ⓟ ◇ △ 🚕 194, 200, 212
Rochford [LE] Ⓟ 🚲 △ 🚕 5
Rock Ferry [ME] Ⓟ 🚲 ◇ △ 🚕 106
Rogart [SR] Ⓟ 🚲 Ⓤ 239
Rogerstone [AW] Ⓟ Ⓤ 127
Rolleston [EM] Ⓤ 27
Roman Bridge [AW] Ⓤ 102
Romford [LE] 🚲 ◇ △ 🚕 4, 5, 11
Romiley [NT] Ⓟ 🚲 78
Romsey [GW] Ⓟ 🚲 123, 158
Roose [NT] Ⓟ Ⓤ 82
Rose Grove [NT] Ⓤ 97
Rose Hill Marple [NT] Ⓟ 🚲 ◇ 78
Rosslare Harbour *Ship* 128
Rosyth [SR] Ⓟ Ⓤ 242
Rotherham Central [NT] Ⓟ ◇ 🚕 29, 31, 33
Rotherhithe [LO] △ 178
Rothesay *Ship* 219B
Roughton Road [LE] 🚲 Ⓤ 16
Rowlands Castle [SW] Ⓟ 🚲 ◇ △ 156
Rowley Regis [LM] Ⓟ ◇ △ 71, 115
Roy Bridge [SR] 🚲 Ⓤ 227, *Sleepers* 404
Roydon [LE] Ⓟ △ 22
Royston [FC] Ⓟ 🚲 ◇ △ 🚕 25
Ruabon [AW] Ⓟ Ⓤ 75
Rufford [NT] Ⓟ Ⓤ 99
Rugby [VT] Ⓟ 🚲 ◇ 🚕 65, 66, 67, 68
Rugeley Town [LM] Ⓟ Ⓤ 70
Rugeley Trent Valley [LM] Ⓤ 67, 70
Ruislip [CH] (see South and West Ruislip)
Rum *Ship* 227A
Runcorn [VT] Ⓟ 🚲 ◇ 🚕 65, 91
Runcorn East [AW] Ⓟ 81
Ruskington [EM] Ⓟ 🚲 Ⓤ 18
Ruswarp [NT] Ⓤ 45
Rutherglen [SR] 🚲 226
Ryde Esplanade [IL] ◇ 🚕 167
Ryde Pier Head [IL] Ⓟ 🚲 ◇ 167
Ryde St. Johns Road [IL] Ⓟ 🚲 Ⓤ 167
Ryder Brow [NT] Ⓤ 78
Rye [SN] Ⓟ △ 🚕 189

10 Connection time
Ⓟ Station Car Park
🚲 Bicycle storage facility
◇ Seat reservations can be made at this station
⚠ Penalty Fare Schemes in operation on some or all services from this station
🚕 Taxi rank or cab office at station, or signposted and within 100 metres
Ⓤ Unstaffed station
[ ] Station Operator Code

Station index and table numbers

Rye House [LE] ⚠ 22

S

St Albans [FC] Ⓟ 🚲 ◇ ⚠ 🚕 52, 186
St Albans Abbey [LM] Ⓟ Ⓤ 61
St Andrews Bus Station *Bus* 229, 229A
St Andrews Road [GW] Ⓟ 🚲 Ⓤ 133
St Annes-on-the-Sea [NT] Ⓟ ◇ 🚕 97
St Austell [GW] Ⓟ 🚲 ◇ 🚕 51, 135, *Bus* 135B, *Sleepers* 406
St Bees [NT] Ⓟ Ⓤ 100
St Budeaux Ferry Road [GW] Ⓤ 135, 139
St Budeaux Victoria Road [GW] Ⓤ 139
St Columb Road [GW] Ⓟ Ⓤ 142
St Denys [SW] Ⓟ 🚲 ◇ ⚠ 158, 165
St Erth [GW] Ⓟ ◇ 51, 135, 144, *Sleepers* 406
St Germans [GW] Ⓤ 135
St Helens Central [NT] Ⓟ ◇ 🚕 90
St Helens Junction [NT] Ⓟ 90
St Helier (Surrey) **[FC]** 🚲 ⚠ Ⓤ 52, 179
St Ives [GW] Ⓟ Ⓤ 144
St James' Park [GW] Ⓤ 136
St James Street [LE] 🚲 ⚠ 20
St Johns [SE] ◇ ⚠ 199, 200, 203, 204
St Keyne Wishing Well Halt [GW] Ⓤ 140
St Leonards Warrior Square [SE] **4** Ⓟ ◇ ⚠ 🚕 189, 206
St Margarets (Herts.) [LE] Ⓟ ⚠ 🚕 22
St Margarets (Greater London) **[SW]** 🚲 ◇ ⚠ 🚕 149
St Mary Cray [SE] Ⓟ ◇ ⚠ 52, 195, 196, 212
St Michaels [ME] Ⓟ ⚠ 103
St Neots [FC] Ⓟ 🚲 ⚠ 🚕 25
St Pancras International (see London)
Salford Central [NT] 82, 94
Salford Crescent [NT] 82, 94
Salfords [SN] ◇ ⚠ 186
Salhouse [LE] Ⓟ 🚲 Ⓤ 16
Salisbury [SW] Ⓟ 🚲 ◇ ⚠ 🚕 123, 158, 160
Saltaire [NT] Ⓤ 36
Saltash [GW] Ⓟ 🚲 Ⓤ 135
Saltburn [NT] Ⓤ 44
Saltcoats [SR] Ⓟ 🚲 🚕 221
Saltmarshe [NT] Ⓟ Ⓤ 29
Salwick [NT] Ⓤ 97
Sampford Courtenay Ⓤ 136
Sandal & Agbrigg [NT] Ⓟ 🚲 Ⓤ 31
Sandbach [NT] Ⓟ 🚲 84
Sanderstead [SN] Ⓟ ◇ ⚠ 🚕 184
Sandhills [ME] ⚠ 103
Sandhurst [GW] Ⓤ 148
Sandling [SE] Ⓟ ◇ ⚠ 207
Sandown [IL] Ⓟ 🚲 Ⓤ 167
Sandplace [GW] Ⓤ 140
Sandringham Norwich Gates *Bus* 17A
Sandringham Visitor Centre *Bus* 17A
Sandwell & Dudley [LM] Ⓟ 🚲 ◇ ⚠ 🚕 66, 68, 74
Sandwich [SE] Ⓟ ◇ ⚠ 194, 207
Sandy [FC] Ⓟ 🚲 ⚠ 25
Sankey for Penketh [NT] Ⓟ 89
Sanquhar [SR] Ⓟ 🚲 Ⓤ 216
Sarn [AW] Ⓟ Ⓤ 128
Saundersfoot [AW] Ⓤ 128
Saunderton [CH] Ⓟ 🚲 ⚠ Ⓤ 115
Sawbridgeworth [LE] Ⓟ ⚠ 22
Saxilby [EM] Ⓟ 🚲 Ⓤ 18, 30
Saxmundham [LE] Ⓟ 🚲 Ⓤ 13
Scarborough [TP] Ⓟ 🚲 ◇ 🚕 26, 39, 43
Scotscalder [SR] Ⓟ 🚲 Ⓤ 239
Scotstounhill [SR] Ⓟ 🚲 226
Scrabster *Ship* 239A
Scunthorpe [TP] Ⓟ ◇ 🚕 29
Sea Mills [GW] 🚲 Ⓤ 133
Seaford [SN] Ⓟ 🚲 ◇ ⚠ 🚕 189
Seaforth & Litherland [ME] ⚠ 🚕 103
Seaham [NT] Ⓟ Ⓤ 44
Seamer [TP] Ⓟ Ⓤ 39, 43
Seascale [NT] Ⓟ Ⓤ 100
Seaton Carew [NT] Ⓟ 🚲 Ⓤ 44
Seer Green [CH] Ⓟ 🚲 ⚠ 115
Selby [TP] Ⓟ 🚲 ◇ 🚕 26, 29, 39, 40, 41
Selhurst [SN] **4** 🚲 ◇ ⚠ 176, 177
Sellafield [NT] Ⓟ Ⓤ 100
Selling [SE] Ⓟ ⚠ Ⓤ 212
Selly Oak [LM] Ⓟ 🚲 ◇ ⚠ 69
Settle [NT] Ⓟ ◇ 36
Seven Kings [LE] 🚲 ⚠ 5
Seven Sisters [LE] ⚠ 21, 22
Sevenoaks [SE] **4** Ⓟ ◇ ⚠ 🚕 52, 195, 204, 206, 207
Severn Beach [GW] 🚲 Ⓤ 133
Severn Tunnel Junction [AW] Ⓟ 🚲 ◇ 123, 132
Shadwell [LO] ⚠ 178
Shalford [GW] Ⓟ Ⓤ 148
Shanklin [IL] Ⓟ 🚲 ◇ 🚕 167
Shawford [SW] Ⓟ 🚲 Ⓤ 158
Shawlands [SR] 🚲 Ⓤ 223
Sheerness-on-Sea [SE] 🚲 ◇ ⚠ 🚕 212
Sheffield [EM] **7** Ⓟ 🚲 ◇ ⚠ 🚕
Barnsley 34
Birmingham 51
Bournemouth 51
Bristol 51
Cambridge 49
Cardiff 51
Chesterfield 53
Cleethorpes 29
Darlington 26
Derby 53
Doncaster 29
Edinburgh 26
Exeter 51
Glasgow 26
Goole 29
Grimsby 29
Huddersfield 34
Hull 29
Leeds 31
Leicester 53
Lincoln 30
Liverpool 89
London 53
Luton 53
Manchester 78
Manchester Airport 78
Meadowhall 29, 35
Newcastle 26
New Mills 78
Newport (South Wales) 51
Norwich 49
Nottingham 53
Oxford 51
Paignton 51
Penistone 34
Penzance 51
Peterborough 49
Plymouth 51
Reading 51
Retford 30
Rotherham 29
Scunthorpe 29
Southampton 51
Stockport 78
Torquay 51
Wakefield 31
Warrington 89
York 29
Shelford [LE] ⚠ 22
Shenfield [LE] **3** Ⓟ 🚲 ◇ ⚠ 🚕 5, 11
Shenstone [LM] Ⓟ ⚠ 69
Shepherd s Bush [LO] ⚠ 66, 176, 177
Shepherds Well [SE] Ⓟ ⚠ 212
Shepley [NT] Ⓤ 34
Shepperton [SW] Ⓟ 🚲 ◇ ⚠ 🚕 152
Shepreth [FC] Ⓟ 🚲 ⚠ Ⓤ 25
Sherborne [SW] Ⓟ 🚲 ◇ ⚠ 🚕 160
Sherburn-in-Elmet [NT] Ⓤ 33
Sheringham [LE] Ⓟ 🚲 Ⓤ 16
Shettleston [SR] Ⓟ 🚲 🚕 226

Station index and table numbers

❿ Connection time
Ⓟ Station Car Park
🚲 Bicycle storage facility
◇ Seat reservations can be made at this station
⚠ Penalty Fare Schemes in operation on some or all services from this station
🚕 Taxi rank or cab office at station, or signposted and within 100 metres
Ⓤ Unstaffed station
[ ] Station Operator Code

Shieldmuir [SR] 🚲 Ⓤ 226
Shifnal [LM] Ⓟ Ⓤ 74
Shildon [NT] Ⓤ 44
Shiplake [GW] Ⓟ Ⓤ 121
Shipley [NT] Ⓟ 🚲 ◇ 26, 36, 37, 38
Shippea Hill [LE] Ⓟ Ⓤ 17
Shipton [GW] Ⓤ 126
Shirebrook [EM] Ⓤ 55
Shirehampton [GW] Ⓟ 🚲 Ⓤ 133
Shireoaks [NT] Ⓤ 30
Shirley [LM] Ⓟ 🚲 ◇ ⚠ 71
Shoeburyness [CC] Ⓟ 🚲 ◇ ⚠ 🚕 1
Sholing [SW] 🚲 ⚠ Ⓤ 165
Shoreditch High Street [LO] ⚠ 178
Shoreham (Kent) [SE] Ⓟ ⚠ Ⓤ 52, 195
Shoreham-by-Sea (Sussex) **[SN]** Ⓟ 🚲 ◇ ⚠ 🚕 188
Shortlands [SE] ❹ Ⓟ 🚲 ◇ ⚠ 52, 195
Shotton [AW] Ⓟ 🚕 81
Shotton High Level [AW] Ⓟ 🚕 101
Shotts [SR] Ⓟ 🚲 225
Shrewsbury [AW] Ⓟ ◇ 🚕
Aberystwyth 75
Bangor (Gwynedd) 131
Barmouth 75
Birmingham 74
Cardiff 131
Chester 75, 131
Crewe 131
Hereford 131
Holyhead 131
Llandudno Junction 131
Llandrindod 129
Llanelli 129
Machynlleth 75
Manchester 131
Newport (South Wales) 131
Pwllheli 75
Swansea 129
Telford Central 74
Whitchurch (Salop) 131
Wrexham 75
Wolverhampton 74
Sidcup [SE] ❹ Ⓟ ◇ ⚠ 🚕 200
Sileby [EM] ⚠ Ⓤ 53
Silecroft [NT] Ⓤ 100
Silsden [NT] (see Steeton & Silsden)
Silkstone Common [NT] Ⓟ Ⓤ 34
Silverdale [NT] Ⓤ 82
Silver Street [LE] ⚠ 21
Singer [SR] 🚲 🚕 226
Sittingbourne [SE] ❹ Ⓟ ◇ ⚠ 🚕 194, 212
Skegness [EM] 🚲 ◇ 🚕 19
Skewen [AW] Ⓟ Ⓤ 128
Skipton [NT] Ⓟ 🚲 ◇ 🚕 26, 36
Slade Green [SE] ❹ Ⓟ ◇ ⚠ 200
Slaithwaite [NT] Ⓟ Ⓤ 39
Slateford [SR] 🚲 Ⓤ 225
Sleaford [EM] Ⓟ 🚲 ◇ 🚕 18, 19
Sleights [NT] Ⓟ Ⓤ 45
Slough [GW] ❸ Ⓟ 🚲 ◇ ⚠ 🚕 116, 117, 119, 125, 135
Small Heath [LM] ⚠ 71
Smallbrook Junction [IL] Ⓤ 167
Smethwick Galton Bridge [LM] ❼ ◇ ⚠ 68, 71, 74, 75
Smethwick Rolfe Street [LM] ⚠ 68
Smithy Bridge [NT] Ⓟ Ⓤ 41
Snaith [NT] Ⓟ Ⓤ 32
Snodland [SE] Ⓟ ⚠ 🚕 Ⓤ 208
Snowdown [SE] ⚠ Ⓤ 212
Sole Street [SE] Ⓟ ◇ ⚠ 212
Solihull [LM] Ⓟ 🚲 ◇ ⚠ 71, 115
Somerleyton [LE] Ⓟ 🚲 Ⓤ 15
South Acton [LO] 🚲 ⚠ 59
South Bank [NT] 🚲 Ⓤ 44
South Bermondsey [SN] ◇ ⚠ 177, 178, 179
South Croydon [SN] ❹ Ⓟ ◇ ⚠ 175, 176, 181, 184
South Elmsall [NT] Ⓟ 🚲 Ⓤ 31
South Greenford [GW] Ⓤ 117
South Gyle [SR] Ⓟ 🚲 Ⓤ 242
South Hampstead [LO] ⚠ 60
South Kenton [LT] 60
South Merton [FC] ⚠ Ⓤ 52, 179
South Milford [NT] Ⓟ Ⓤ 39, 40
South Ruislip [CH] Ⓟ 🚲 ⚠ 🚕 115
South Tottenham [LO] ⚠ 62
South Wigston [EM] Ⓤ 57
South Woodham Ferrers [LE] Ⓟ 🚲 🚕 5
Southall [GW] ⚠ 117
Southampton Airport Parkway [SW] Ⓟ 🚲 ◇ ⚠ 🚕 51, 158, 188
Southampton Central [SW] Ⓟ 🚲 ◇ ⚠ 🚕
Aberdeen 51
Basingstoke 158
Bath Spa 123
Birmingham 51
Bognor Regis 188
Bournemouth 158
Brighton 188
Bristol 123
Brockenhurst 158
Cardiff 123
Carlisle 51
Chichester 188
Clapham Junction 158, 188
Crawley 188
Crewe 51
Derby 51
Dorchester 158
Dundee 51
East Croydon 188
Eastleigh 158
Edinburgh 51
Exeter 160
Fareham 165, 188
Gatwick Airport 188
Glasgow 51
Havant 165, 188
Horsham 188
Leeds 51
Littlehampton 188
London 158, 188
Lymington Pier 158
Manchester 51
Newcastle 51
Newport (South Wales) 123
Oxford 51
Poole 158
Portsmouth 165
Preston 51
Reading 158
Redhill 188
Romsey 123
Ryde 167
Salisbury 123
Shanklin 167
Sheffield 51
Swindon 123
Westbury (Wilts) 123
Weymouth 158
Winchester 158
Woking 158
Wolverhampton 51
Worthing 188
Yarmouth (IOW) 158
Yeovil 160
York 51
Southbourne [SN] ◇ ⚠ 188
Southbury [LE] ⚠ 21
Southease [SN] Ⓤ 189
Southend Airport [LE] ⚠ 🚕 5
Southend Central [CC] Ⓟ 🚲 ◇ ⚠ 🚕 1
Southend East [CC] Ⓟ 🚲 ◇ ⚠ 1
Southend Victoria [LE] 🚲 ◇ ⚠ 🚕 5
Southminster [LE] Ⓟ 🚲 Ⓤ 5
Southport [ME] 🚲 ◇ ⚠ 🚕 82, 103
Southsea [SW] (see Portsmouth & Southsea)
Southwick [SN] 🚲 ◇ ⚠ 188
Sowerby Bridge [NT] Ⓟ 🚲 Ⓤ 41
Sowton [GW] (see Digby & Sowton)
Spalding [EM] Ⓟ 🚲 🚕 18
Spean Bridge [SR] Ⓟ 🚲 Ⓤ 227, *Sleepers* 404
Spital [ME] 🚲 ⚠ 106
Spondon [EM] ⚠ Ⓤ 56
Spooner Row [LE] Ⓤ 17
Spring Road [LM] ⚠ 71
Springburn [SR] 🚲 224, 226
Springfield [SR] 🚲 Ⓤ 229
Squires Gate [NT] Ⓤ 97
Stafford [VT] Ⓟ 🚲 ◇ 🚕
Bangor (Gwynedd) 65
Birmingham 68

■10 Connection time
Ⓟ Station Car Park
🚲 Bicycle storage facility
◇ Seat reservations can be made at this station
⚠ Penalty Fare Schemes in operation on some or all services from this station
🚕 Taxi rank or cab office at station, or signposted and within 100 metres
ⓤ Unstaffed station
[ ] Station Operator Code

Station index and table numbers

Blackpool 65
Bournemouth 51
Bristol 51
Carlisle 65
Chester 65
Coventry 67, 68
Crewe 65
Edinburgh 65
Exeter 51
Glasgow 65
Holyhead 65
Lichfield 67
Liverpool 65
London 65
Manchester 84
Manchester Airport 84
Nuneaton 67
Oxenholme Lake District 65
Oxford 51
Paignton 51
Penzance 51
Plymouth 51
Preston 65
Reading 51
Rugby 65
Southampton 51
Stockport 84
Stoke-on-Trent 65, 68A
Tamworth 67
Torquay 51
Watford 65
Wolverhampton 68

Staines [SW] Ⓟ 🚲 ◇ ⚠ 🚕 149
Stainforth [NT] (see Hatfield & Stainforth)
Stallingborough [NT] ⓤ 29
Stalybridge [TP] Ⓟ 🚲 ◇ 39
Stamford [EM] Ⓟ ◇ 49
Stamford Hill [LE] ⚠ 21
Stanford-le-Hope [CC] Ⓟ 🚲 ◇ ⚠ 1
Stanlow & Thornton [NT] ⓤ 109
Stansted Airport [LE] 🚲 ◇ ⚠ 🚕 17, 22, 26, 49
Stansted Mountfitchet [LE] Ⓟ 🚲 ⚠ 🚕 22
Staplehurst [SE] Ⓟ 🚲 ◇ ⚠ 🚕 207
Stapleton Road [GW] 🚲 ⓤ 133, 134
Starbeck [NT] 🚲 ⓤ 35
Starcross [GW] 🚲 ⓤ 135
Staveley [TP] ⓤ 83
Stechford [LM] ⚠ 68
Steeton & Silsden [NT] Ⓟ 🚲 ⓤ 36
Stepps [SR] Ⓟ 🚲 ⓤ 224
Stevenage [FC] ■4 Ⓟ 🚲 ◇ ⚠ 🚕 24, 25, 26
Stevenston [SR] 🚲 ⓤ 221
Stewartby [LM] ⓤ 64
Stewarton [SR] Ⓟ 🚲 ⓤ 222
Stirling [SR] Ⓟ 🚲 ◇ 🚕 26, 229, 230, *Sleepers* 403

Stockport [VT] Ⓟ 🚲 ◇ 🚕
Altrincham 88
Birmingham 65
Birmingham International 65
Blackpool 82
Bolton 82
Bournemouth 51
Bristol 51
Buxton 86
Cambridge 49
Cardiff 131
Chester 88
Coventry 65
Crewe 84
Doncaster 29
Ely 49
Exeter 51
Hazel Grove 86
Hull 29
Liverpool 89
London 65
Macclesfield 84
Manchester 84
Newport (South Wales) 131
Northwich 88
Norwich 49
Nottingham 49
Oxford 51
Paignton 51
Penzance 51
Peterborough 49
Plymouth 51
Preston 82
Reading 51
Rugby 65
Salford Crescent 82
Sheffield 78
Southampton 51
Stafford 84
Stoke-on-Trent 84
Torquay 51
Watford 65
Wigan 82
Wolverhampton 65

Stocksfield [NT] Ⓟ 🚲 ⓤ 48
Stocksmoor [NT] Ⓟ 🚲 ⓤ 34
Stockton [NT] 🚲 🚕 ⓤ 44
Stoke d'Abernon [SW] (see Cobham)
Stoke Mandeville [CH] Ⓟ 🚲 ⚠ 114
Stoke Newington [LE] ⚠ 21
Stoke-on-Trent [VT] Ⓟ 🚲 ◇ 🚕 50, 51, 65, 67, 84
Stone [LM] 67
Stone Crown Street *Bus* 67
Stone Granville Square *Bus* 67
Stone Crossing [SE] ◇ ⚠ 200
Stonebridge Park [LT] 60
Stonegate [SE] Ⓟ 🚲 ◇ ⚠ 206
Stonehaven [SR] Ⓟ 🚲 ◇ 26, 51, 229, *Sleepers* 402
Stonehouse [GW] Ⓟ 125
Stoneleigh [SW] 🚲 ◇ ⚠ 152
Stornoway *Ship* 239B

Stourbridge Junction [LM] ■2 Ⓟ ◇ ⚠ 71, 72, 115
Stourbridge Town [LM] ⚠ 72
Stowmarket [LE] Ⓟ 🚲 ◇ 🚕 11, 14
Stranraer [SR] 🚲 ◇ 218
Stratford (London) **[LE]** ■7 ⚠ 🚕
Barking 1
Basildon 1
Bishops Stortford 22
Braintree 11
Broxbourne 22
Bury St. Edmunds 14
Cambridge 14
Chelsmford 11
Cheshunt 22
Clacton-on-Sea 11
Colchester 11
Ely 14
Gospel Oak 59, 176
Hackney 59
Harlow 22
Harwich 11
Hertford East 22
Highbury & Islington 59, 176
Ilford 5
Ipswich 11
London 5
Manningtree 11
Norwich 11
Peterborough 14
Richmond 59
Romford 5
Shenfield 5
Shoeburyness 1
Southend 1, 5
Southminster 5
Stansted Airport 22
Stowmarket 11
Tottenham Hale 22
Upminster 1
Walton-on-the-Naze 11
West Hampstead 59, 176
Wickford 5
Willesden Junction 59
Witham 11

Stratford International [SE] ⚠ 194, 200, 207, 208, 212
Stratford-upon-Avon [LM] Ⓟ 🚲 ◇ ⚠ 🚕 71, 115
Strathcarron [SR] Ⓟ 🚲 ⓤ 239
Strawberry Hill [SW] 🚲 ◇ ⚠ 149, 152
Streatham [SN] ■4 ◇ ⚠ 52, 177, 179
Streatham Common [SN] ■4 Ⓟ 🚲 ◇ ⚠ 176, 177
Streatham Hill [SN] ◇ ⚠ 🚕 177, 178
Streatley [GW] (see Goring & Streatley)
Streethouse [NT] Ⓟ ⓤ 32
Strines [NT] Ⓟ ⓤ 78
Stromeferry [SR] Ⓟ 🚲 ⓤ 239
Stromness 🚕 *Ship* 239A

Station index and table numbers

- ▪10 Connection time
- Ⓟ Station Car Park
- 🚲 Bicycle storage facility
- ◇ Seat reservations can be made at this station
- ⚠ Penalty Fare Schemes in operation on some or all services from this station
- 🚕 Taxi rank or cab office at station, or signposted and within 100 metres
- Ⓤ Unstaffed station
- [ ] Station Operator Code

Strood [SE] ▪4 Ⓟ 🚲 ◇ ⚠ 🚕 194, 200, 208, 212
Stroud [GW] Ⓟ 🚲 ◇ 🚕 125
Sturry [SE] ⚠ 207
Styal [NT] Ⓟ Ⓤ 84
Sudbury (Suffolk) **[LE]** 🚲 Ⓤ 10
Sudbury & Harrow Road [CH] ⚠ Ⓤ 115
Sudbury Hill Harrow [CH] ⚠ Ⓤ 115
Sugar Loaf [AW] Ⓤ 129
Summerston [SR] Ⓤ 232
Sunbury [SW] Ⓟ 🚲 ◇ ⚠ 152
Sunderland [NT] ◇ 🚕 26, 44, 48
Sundridge Park [SE] Ⓟ ◇ ⚠ 204
Sunningdale [SW] Ⓟ 🚲 ◇ ⚠ 🚕 149
Sunnymeads [SW] ⚠ Ⓤ 149
Surbiton [SW] ▪6 Ⓟ 🚲 ◇ ⚠ 🚕 152, 155
Surrey Quays [LO] ⚠ 178
Sutton Coldfield [LM] Ⓟ 🚲 ◇ ⚠ 69
Sutton Common [FC] ⚠ Ⓤ 52, 179
Sutton Parkway [EM] Ⓟ Ⓤ 55
Sutton (Surrey) [SN] ▪4 Ⓟ 🚲 ◇ ⚠ 🚕 52, 179, 182
Swaffham *Bus* 26A
Swale [SE] ⚠ Ⓤ 212
Swalecliffe [SE] (see Chestfield & Swalecliffe)
Swanley [SE] ▪4 Ⓟ ◇ ⚠ 🚕 52, 195, 196, 212
Swanscombe [SE] ◇ ⚠ 200
Swansea [AW] Ⓟ 🚲 ◇ 🚕
- Bristol 128
- Cardiff 128
- Camarthen 128
- Crewe 131
- Derby 57
- Fishguard Harbour 128
- Gloucester 57
- Hereford 131
- Llandrindod 129
- London 125, 128
- Manchester 128, 131
- Pembroke Dock 128
- Portsmouth 128
- Reading 125, 128
- Rosslare Harbour 128
- Shrewsbury 129
- Slough 125
- Tenby 128

Swanwick [SW] Ⓟ 🚲 ◇ ⚠ 🚕 165, 188
Sway [SW] Ⓟ 🚲 ◇ ⚠ 158
Swaythling [SW] Ⓟ 🚲 ◇ ⚠ 158
Swinderby [EM] Ⓤ 27
Swindon [GW] Ⓟ 🚲 ◇ ⚠ 🚕 123, 125
Swineshead [EM] Ⓤ 19
Swinton (Gtr. Manchester) **[NT]** 82
Swinton (S. Yorks.) [NT] Ⓟ 🚲 ◇ 29, 31, 33
Sydenham [LO] ◇ ⚠ 🚕 178
Sydenham Hill [SE] Ⓟ ⚠ 195
Syon Lane [SW] 🚲 ⚠ Ⓤ 149
Syston [EM] Ⓟ ⚠ Ⓤ 53

T

Tackley [GW] Ⓤ 116
Tadworth [SN] ◇ ⚠ 181
Taffs Well [AW] ▪3 Ⓟ Ⓤ 130
Tain [SR] Ⓟ Ⓤ 239
Talsarnau [AW] Ⓤ 75
Talybont [AW] Ⓤ 75
Tal-y-Cafn [AW] Ⓤ 102
Tame Bridge Parkway [LM] Ⓟ 🚲 ◇ ⚠ 70, 75
Tamworth [LM] Ⓟ ◇ 🚕 51, 57, 65, 67
Taplow [GW] Ⓟ 🚲 ⚠ 🚕 117
Tarbert *Ship* 239B
Tattenham Corner [SN] Ⓟ ◇ ⚠ 181
Taunton [GW] Ⓟ 🚲 ◇ ⚠ 🚕 51, 134, 135, *Bus* 135E
Taynuilt [SR] Ⓟ 🚲 Ⓤ 227
Teddington [SW] 🚲 ◇ ⚠ 149, 152
Tees-side Airport [NT] Ⓤ 44
Teignmouth [GW] Ⓟ 🚲 ◇ 🚕 51, 135
Telford Central [LM] Ⓟ ◇ 🚕 74, 75
Templecombe [SW] Ⓟ 🚲 ◇ ⚠ 160
Tenby [AW] Ⓟ Ⓤ 128
Tewkesbury [GW] (see Ashchurch)
Teynham [SE] Ⓟ ◇ ⚠ 212
Thame [CH] (see Haddenham & Thame Parkway)
Thames Ditton [SW] 🚲 ⚠ 152
Thatcham [GW] Ⓟ 🚲 116, 135
Thatto Heath [NT] Ⓟ 90
The Hawthorns [LM] Ⓟ ⚠ 71
The Lakes (Warwickshire) **[LM]** ⚠ Ⓤ 71
Theale [GW] Ⓟ 🚲 116, 135
Theobalds Grove [LE] ⚠ 21
Thetford [LE] Ⓟ ◇ 🚕 17, 49
Thirsk [TP] Ⓟ ◇ 26, 39
Thornaby [TP] Ⓟ 🚲 ◇ 🚕 39, 44
Thorne North [NT] Ⓟ 🚲 29
Thorne South [NT] Ⓟ Ⓤ 29
Thornford [GW] Ⓤ 123
Thornhill [AW] (see Lisvane)
Thornliebank [SR] 🚲 Ⓤ 222
Thornton (Ches.) **[NT]** (see Stanlow & Thornton)
Thornton (Fife) **[SR]** (see Glenrothes With Thornton)
Thornton Abbey [NT] Ⓤ 29
Thorntonhall [SR] 🚲 Ⓤ 222
Thornton Heath [SN] 🚲 ◇ ⚠ 🚕 176, 177
Thorpe Bay [CC] Ⓟ 🚲 ◇ ⚠ 🚕 1
Thorpe Culvert [EM] Ⓟ Ⓤ 19
Thorpe-le-Soken [LE] ▪1 Ⓟ 🚲 ⚠ 11
Three Bridges [SN] ▪4 Ⓟ 🚲 ◇ ⚠ 🚕 52, 186, 188
Three Oaks [SN] Ⓤ 189
Thurgarton [EM] Ⓤ 27
Thurnscoe [NT] Ⓟ Ⓤ 31
Thurso [SR] Ⓟ 🚲 ◇ 🚕 239, *Ship* 239A
Thurston [LE] Ⓟ 🚲 Ⓤ 14
Tilbury Riverside [CC] Ⓤ *Bus* 1A
Tilbury Town [CC] ▪3 🚲 ◇ ⚠ 1, *Bus* 1A
Tile Hill [LM] Ⓟ ⚠ 68
Tilehurst [GW] Ⓟ 🚲 116
Tipton [LM] Ⓟ ⚠ 68
Tiree *Ship* 227B
Tir-phil [AW] Ⓟ Ⓤ 130
Tisbury [SW] Ⓟ 🚲 ◇ ⚠ 160
Tiverton Parkway [GW] Ⓟ 🚲 ◇ ⚠ 🚕 51, 135
Todmorden [NT] Ⓟ 🚲 🚕 41
Tolworth [SW] Ⓟ 🚲 ◇ ⚠ 🚕 152
Tonbridge [SE] ▪4 Ⓟ 🚲 ◇ ⚠ 🚕 186, 204, 206, 207, 208
Ton Pentre [AW] Ⓤ 130
Tondu [AW] Ⓟ Ⓤ 128
Tonfanau [AW] Ⓤ 75
Tonypandy [AW] Ⓤ 130
Tooting [FC] ◇ ⚠ 52, 179
Topsham [GW] Ⓟ 🚲 Ⓤ 136
Torquay [GW] Ⓟ 🚲 ◇ 🚕 51, 135
Torre [GW] Ⓟ Ⓤ 135
Totley [NT] (see Dore & Totley)
Totnes [GW] Ⓟ 🚲 ◇ ⚠ 🚕 51, 135, *Sleepers* 406
Tottenham Hale [LE] ⚠ 🚕 22
Tottenham South [LO] (see South Tottenham)
Totton [SW] Ⓟ 🚲 ◇ ⚠ 158
Town Green [ME] Ⓟ ⚠ 103
Trafford Park [NT] 🚕 Ⓤ 89
Treforest [AW] Ⓟ ◇ 130
Treforest Estate [AW] Ⓤ 130
Trehafod [AW] Ⓟ Ⓤ 130
Treherbert [AW] Ⓤ 130
Treorchy [AW] Ⓟ Ⓤ 130
Trimley [LE] Ⓟ 🚲 Ⓤ 13
Tring [LM] Ⓟ 🚲 ⚠ 🚕 66, 176
Troed-y-rhiw [AW] Ⓤ 130
Troon [SR] Ⓟ 🚲 🚕 218, 221
Trowbridge [GW] Ⓟ 🚲 ◇ 🚕 123, 160

Station index and table numbers

■10 Connection time
Ⓟ Station Car Park
🚲 Bicycle storage facility
◇ Seat reservations can be made at this station
⚠ Penalty Fare Schemes in operation on some or all services from this station
🚕 Taxi rank or cab office at station, or signposted and within 100 metres
Ⓤ Unstaffed station
[ ] Station Operator Code

Truro [GW] Ⓟ 🚲 ◇ 🚕 51, 135, 143, *Sleepers* 406
Tulloch [SR] Ⓟ 🚲 Ⓤ 227, *Sleepers* 404
Tulse Hill [SN] ■3 ◇ ⚠ 52, 177, 179, 182
Tunbridge Wells [SE] ■4 Ⓟ 🚲 ◇ ⚠ 🚕 206
Turkey Street [LE] ⚠ 21
Tutbury & Hatton [EM] Ⓤ 50
Twickenham [SW] Ⓟ 🚲 ◇ ⚠ 149
Twyford [GW] ■3 Ⓟ 🚲 ⚠ 🚕 116, 117, 121
Ty Croes [AW] Ⓤ 81
Ty Glas [AW] Ⓤ 130
Tygwyn [AW] Ⓟ Ⓤ 75
Tyndrum Lower [SR] Ⓟ 🚲 Ⓤ 227
Tyndrum Upper [SR] (see Upper Tyndrum)
Tyseley [LM] ⚠ 71
Tywyn [AW] 🚲 Ⓤ 75

U

Uckfield [SN] Ⓟ 🚲 ◇ ⚠ 184
Uddingston [SR] Ⓟ 🚲 🚕 225, 226
Uig *Ship* 239B
Ulceby [NT] Ⓤ 29
Ullapool *Ship* 239B
Ulleskelf [NT] Ⓤ 33, 40
Ulverston [TP] ◇ 82
Umberleigh [GW] Ⓟ Ⓤ 136
University [LM] ◇ ⚠ 69, 71
Uphall [SR] Ⓟ 🚲 Ⓤ 226
Upholland [NT] Ⓤ 82
Upminster [CC] Ⓟ 🚲 ◇ ⚠ 🚕 1, 4
Upper Halliford [SW] ◇ ⚠ 152
Upper Holloway [LO] ⚠ 62
Upper Tyndrum [SR] Ⓟ 🚲 Ⓤ 227, *Sleepers* 404
Upper Warlingham [SN] Ⓟ 🚲 ◇ ⚠ 🚕 184
Upton [AW] Ⓤ 101
Upwey [SW] Ⓟ 🚲 ⚠ Ⓤ 123, 158
Urmston [NT] Ⓟ 🚲 89
Uttoxeter [EM] Ⓟ Ⓤ 50

V

Valley [AW] Ⓟ Ⓤ 81
Vauxhall (London) **[SW]** ◇ ⚠ 149, 152, 155
Victoria [NR] (see London)
Virginia Water [SW] Ⓟ 🚲 ◇ ⚠ 🚕 149

W

Waddon [SN] ◇ ⚠ 182
Wadebridge Bus Station *Bus* 135C
Wadhurst [SE] Ⓟ ◇ ⚠ 206
Wainfleet [EM] Ⓟ 🚲 Ⓤ 19
Wakefield
Kirkgate [NT] ■4 Ⓟ 🚲 Ⓤ
Westgate [GR] ■7 Ⓟ 🚲 ◇ 🚕
Barnsley 34
Bedford 53
Birmingham 51
Bournemouth 51
Bristol 51
Cambridge 26
Derby 53
Doncaster 31
Exeter 51
Huddersfield 39
Knottingley 32
Leeds 31
Leicester 53
Liverpool 39
London 26, 53
Luton 53
Manchester 39
Manchester Airport 39
Meadowhall 31
Newquay 51
Norwich 26
Nottingham 53
Paignton 51
Penzance 51
Plymouth 51
Pontefract 32
Sheffield 31
Southampton 51
Torquay 51
Wakes Colne [LE] (see Chappel & Wakes Colne)
Walkden [NT] 82
Wallasey Grove Road [ME] Ⓟ ⚠ 106
Wallasey Village [ME] ⚠ 106
Wallington [SN] Ⓟ ◇ ⚠ 🚕 182
Wallyford [SR] Ⓟ 🚲 Ⓤ 238
Walmer [SE] Ⓟ ◇ ⚠ 🚕 207
Walsall [LM] ◇ ⚠ 70
Walsden [NT] Ⓤ 41
Waltham Cross [LE] Ⓟ ⚠ 🚕 22
Walthamstow Central [LE] Ⓟ 🚲 ⚠ 🚕 20
Walthamstow Queen s Road [LO] 🚲 ⚠ 62
Walton (Merseyside) [ME] ⚠ 103
Walton-on-the-Naze [LE] 🚲 ⚠ 11
Walton-on-Thames [SW] Ⓟ 🚲 ◇ ⚠ 🚕 155
Wanborough [SW] ⚠ Ⓤ 148, 149
Wandsworth Common [SN] Ⓟ 🚲 ◇ ⚠ 🚕 176, 177, 178
Wandsworth Road [SN] ⚠ Ⓤ 176, 178
Wandsworth Town [SW] 🚲 ◇ ⚠ 149
Wanstead Park [LO] 🚲 ⚠ 62
Wapping [LO] ⚠ 178
Warblington [SN] ⚠ Ⓤ 188
Ware [LE] Ⓟ 🚲 ⚠ 🚕 22
Wareham [SW] Ⓟ 🚲 ◇ ⚠ 🚕 158
Wargrave [GW] Ⓟ 🚲 Ⓤ 121
Warminster [GW] Ⓟ 🚲 ◇ 🚕 123, 160
Warnham [SN] ⚠ Ⓤ 182
Warrington
Bank Quay [VT] Ⓟ ◇ 🚕
Central [TP] Ⓟ 🚲 ◇ 🚕
Aberdeen 65
Bangor (Gwynedd) 81
Birmingham 65
Bournemouth 51
Bristol 51
Cambridge 49
Carlisle 65
Chester 81
Crewe 65
Dundee 65
Edinburgh 65
Ellesmere Port 109
Exeter 51
Glasgow 65
Holyhead 81
Huddersfield 39
Hull 39
Inverness 65
Lancaster 65
Leeds 39
Liverpool 89, 90
Llandudno 81
London 65
Manchester 89, 90
Manchester Airport 89
Middlesbrough 39
Milton Keynes Central 65
Newcastle 39
Norwich 49
Nottingham 49
Oxenholme Lake District 65
Oxford 51
Paignton 51
Penzance 51
Peterborough 49
Plymouth 51
Preston 65
Reading 51
Rhyl 81
Runcorn East 81
St Helens 90
Scarborough 39
Sheffield 89
Southampton 51
Stafford 65
Stockport 89

Station index and table numbers

[10] Connection time
Ⓟ Station Car Park
🚲 Bicycle storage facility
◇ Seat reservations can be made at this station
⚠ Penalty Fare Schemes in operation on some or all services from this station
🚕 Taxi rank or cab office at station, or signposted and within 100 metres
Ⓤ Unstaffed station
[ ] Station Operator Code

Torquay 51
Widnes 89
Wigan 65
Wolverhampton 65
York 39
Warwick [CH] Ⓟ 🚲 ◇ ⚠ 🚕 71, 115
Warwick Parkway [CH] Ⓟ 🚲 ◇ ⚠ 🚕 71, 115
Watchet (West Somerset Ry) *Bus* 135E
Water Orton [LM] Ⓤ 57
Waterbeach [FC] Ⓟ 🚲 ⚠ Ⓤ 17
Wateringbury [SE] Ⓟ ⚠ Ⓤ 208
Waterloo (London) **[NR]** (see London)
Waterloo (Merseyside) [ME] ⚠ 103
Waterloo East [SE] (see London)
Watford High Street [LO] 🚲 ⚠ 60
Watford Junction [LM] Ⓟ 🚲 ◇ ⚠ 🚕
Aberdeen 65, *Sleepers* 402
Bangor (Gwynedd) 65
Birmingham 66
Birmingham International 66
Blackpool North 65
Bletchley 66
Brighton 66
Carlisle 65, *Sleepers* 400, 401
Clapham Junction 66
Coventry 66
Crewe 65
Dundee 65, *Sleepers* 402
East Croydon 66, 176, 177
Edinburgh 65, *Sleepers* 400
Fort William *Sleepers* 404
Gatwick Airport 66
Glasgow 65, *Sleepers* 401
Haywards Heath 66
Holyhead 65
Inverness 65, *Sleepers* 403
Kensington (Olympia) 66, 176, 177
Liverpool 65
London 60, 66, 67
Manchester 65
Manchester Airport 65
Milton Keynes Central 66, 176, 177
Motherwell 65, *Sleepers* 401
Northampton 66
Oxenholme Lake District 65
Perth 65, *Sleepers* 403
Preston 65
Rugby 66
St. Albans 61
Stafford 65
Stirling *Sleepers* 403
Stoke-on-Trent 65
Wolverhampton 66
Watford North [LM] Ⓤ 61
Watlington [FC] ⚠ Ⓤ 17
Watton-at-Stone [FC] ⚠ 24
Waun-gron Park [AW] Ⓤ 130
Wavertree Technology Park [NT] 🚲 90
Wealdstone [LT] (see Harrow & Wealdstone)
Wedgwood Old Road Bridge *Bus* 67
Weeley [LE] 🚲 ⚠ Ⓤ 11
Weeton [NT] Ⓟ Ⓤ 35
Welham Green [FC] Ⓟ ⚠ 24
Welling [SE] Ⓟ ◇ ⚠ 200
Wellingborough [EM] Ⓟ 🚲 ◇ ⚠ 🚕 53
Wellington (Shropshire) [LM] Ⓟ ◇ 🚕 75
Welshpool [AW] Ⓟ Ⓤ 75
Welwyn Garden City [FC] [4] ◇ ⚠ 🚕 24, 25
Welwyn North [FC] Ⓟ 🚲 ⚠ 🚕 24, 25
Wem [AW] Ⓟ Ⓤ 131
Wembley Central [LT] ⚠ 60, 66, 176, 177
Wembley Stadium [CH] ⚠ Ⓤ 115
Wembley (North) [LT] (see North Wembley)
Wemyss Bay [SR] Ⓟ 🚲 🚕 219, *Ship* 219B
Wendover [CH] Ⓟ 🚲 ◇ ⚠ 🚕 114
Wennington [NT] Ⓟ Ⓤ 36
Wesham [NT] (see Kirkham & Wesham)
West Allerton [NT] 89, 91
West Brompton [LT] ⚠ 66, 176, 177
West Byfleet [SW] Ⓟ 🚲 ◇ ⚠ 🚕 149, 155
West Calder [SR] Ⓟ 🚲 Ⓤ 225
West Croydon [LO] [4] ◇ ⚠ 🚕 177, 178, 182
West Drayton [GW] Ⓟ ⚠ 🚕 117
West Dulwich [SE] 🚲 ◇ ⚠ 195
West Ealing [GW] [3] ⚠ 117
West Ham [LT] ⚠ 1
West Hampstead [LO] ⚠ 59, 176
West Hampstead Thameslink [FC] ◇ ⚠ 52
West Horndon [CC] Ⓟ 🚲 ◇ ⚠ 🚕 1
West Kilbride [SR] Ⓟ 🚲 🚕 Ⓤ 221
West Kirby [ME] 🚲 ⚠ 🚕 106
West Malling [SE] Ⓟ 🚲 ◇ ⚠ 🚕 196
West Norwood [SN] [4] ◇ ⚠ 177, 178
West Ruislip [CH] [3] Ⓟ 🚲 ⚠ 115
West Runton [LE] 🚲 Ⓤ 16
West St Leonards [SE] Ⓟ ◇ ⚠ 206
West Sutton [FC] ⚠ Ⓤ 52, 179, 182
West Wickham [SE] Ⓟ 🚲 ◇ ⚠ 🚕 203
West Worthing [SN] Ⓟ 🚲 ◇ ⚠ 188
Westbury (Wilts.) **[GW]** Ⓟ 🚲 ◇ 🚕 123, 135, 160
Westcliff [CC] Ⓟ 🚲 ◇ ⚠ 🚕 1
Westcombe Park [SE] ◇ ⚠ 200
Westenhanger [SE] Ⓟ ⚠ Ⓤ 207
Wester Hailes [SR] Ⓟ 🚲 Ⓤ 225
Westerfield [LE] 🚲 Ⓤ 13
Westerton [SR] Ⓟ 🚲 226, 227, *Sleepers* 404
Westgate-on-Sea [SE] 🚲 ◇ ⚠ 212
Westham [SN] (see Pevensey & Westham)
Westhoughton [NT] Ⓤ 82
Westhumble [SN] (see Box Hill & Westhumble)
Weston Milton [GW] Ⓟ 🚲 Ⓤ 134
Weston-super-Mare [GW] Ⓟ 🚲 ◇ 🚕 51, 125, 134, 135
Wetheral [NT] Ⓟ Ⓤ 48
Weybridge [SW] Ⓟ 🚲 ◇ ⚠ 🚕 149, 155
Weymouth [SW] Ⓟ 🚲 ◇ ⚠ 🚕 123, 158
Whaley Bridge [NT] Ⓟ 86
Whalley [NT] Ⓟ Ⓤ 94
Whatstandwell [EM] Ⓟ Ⓤ 56
Whifflet [SR] Ⓟ 🚕 Ⓤ 220, 224, 226
Whimple [SW] Ⓟ 🚲 ⚠ Ⓤ 160
Whinhill [SR] 🚲 Ⓤ 219
Whiston [NT] Ⓟ 90
Whitby [NT] Ⓟ ◇ 🚕 45
Whitby Bus Station 🚕 *Bus* 26G
Whitchurch (Cardiff) [AW] Ⓤ 130
Whitchurch (Hants.) [SW] Ⓟ 🚲 ◇ ⚠ 160
Whitchurch (Shrops) [AW] Ⓟ Ⓤ 131
White Hart Lane [LE] ⚠ 21
White Notley [LE] 🚲 ⚠ Ⓤ 11
Whitechapel [LT] 178
Whitecraigs [SR] Ⓟ 🚲 223
Whitehaven [NT] Ⓟ ◇ 100
Whitland [AW] Ⓟ Ⓤ 128
Whitley Bridge [NT] Ⓟ Ⓤ 32
Whitlock's End [LM] ⚠ Ⓤ 71
Whitstable [SE] Ⓟ ◇ ⚠ 🚕 194, 212
Whittlesea [LE] Ⓟ Ⓤ 14, 17
Whittlesford Parkway [LE] Ⓟ 🚲 ⚠ 22
Whitton [SW] 🚲 ◇ ⚠ 149
Whitwell [EM] Ⓤ 55
Whyteleafe [SN] Ⓟ 🚲 ◇ ⚠ 181
Whyteleafe South [SN] Ⓟ 🚲 ◇ ⚠ 181
Wick [SR] Ⓟ 🚲 ◇ 🚕 239
Wickford [LE] [2] Ⓟ 🚲 ⚠ 🚕 5

Station index and table numbers

■10 Connection time
℗ Station Car Park
🚲 Bicycle storage facility
◇ Seat reservations can be made at this station
⚠ Penalty Fare Schemes in operation on some or all services from this station
🚕 Taxi rank or cab office at station, or signposted and within 100 metres
ⓤ Unstaffed station
[ ] Station Operator Code

Wickham Market [LE] ℗ 🚲 ⓤ 13
Widdrington [NT] ℗ 🚲 ⓤ 48
Widnes [NT] ℗ 🚕 49, 89
Widney Manor [LM] ℗ ⚠ 71
Wigan
- **North Western [VT]** ℗ ◇ 🚕
- **Wallgate [NT]** 🚲 🚕
- Barrow-in-Furness 65
- Birmingham 65
- Blackpool 90
- Bolton 82
- Bournemouth 51
- Bristol 51
- Carlisle 65
- Crewe 65
- Edinburgh 65
- Exeter 51
- Glasgow 65
- Kirkby 82
- Lancaster 65
- Liverpool 82, 90
- London 65
- Manchester 82
- Milton Keynes Central 65
- Manchester Airport 82
- Paignton 51
- Penzance 51
- Plymouth 51
- Preston 65
- Oxenholme Lake District 65
- Oxford 51
- Reading 51
- St Helens 90
- Southampton 51
- Southport 82
- Stafford 65
- Stockport 82
- Torquay 51
- Warrington 65
- Wolverhampton 65
- Windermere 65

Wigton [NT] ℗ 🚕 ⓤ 100
Wildmill [AW] ⓤ 128
Willesden Junction [LO] 🚲 ⚠ 59, 60, 176
Williamwood [SR] 🚲 223
Willington [EM] ⓤ 57
Wilmcote [LM] ⚠ ⓤ 71, 115
Wilmslow [NT] ℗ 🚲 ◇ 🚕 51, 65, 84, 85, 131
Wilnecote [LM] ⓤ 57
Wilpshire [NT] (see Ramsgreave and Wilpshire)
Wimbledon [SW] ■6 ℗ 🚲 ◇ ⚠ 🚕 52, 152, 155, 179, 182
Wimbledon Chase [FC] ⚠ ⓤ 52, 179
Winchelsea [SN] ⓤ 189
Winchester [SW] ℗ 🚲 ◇ ⚠ 🚕 51, 158
Winchfield [SW] ℗ 🚲 ◇ ⚠ 155
Winchmore Hill [FC] ⚠ 24
Windermere [TP] ℗ ◇ 🚕 65, 82, 83
Windsor & Eton Central [GW] ⚠ 🚕 119
Windsor & Eton Riverside [SW] ℗ 🚲 ◇ ⚠ 🚕 149
Winnersh [SW] 🚲 ◇ ⚠ 149
Winnersh Triangle [SW] ◇ ⚠ 149
Winsford [LM] ℗ ◇ 91
Wisbech *Bus* 🚕 26A
Wishaw [SR] ℗ 🚲 226
Witham [LE] ■2 ℗ 🚲 ◇ ⚠ 🚕 11
Witley [SW] ℗ 🚲 ⚠ 156
Witton [LM] ⚠ 70
Wivelsfield [SN] ■4 🚲 ◇ ⚠ 52, 186, 189
Wivenhoe [LE] ■3 ℗ 🚲 ⚠ 🚕 11
Woburn Sands [LM] ⓤ 64
Woking [SW] ℗ 🚲 ◇ ⚠ 🚕
- Aldershot 155
- Basingstoke 155
- Bournemouth 158
- Bristol 160
- Exeter 160
- Fareham 158
- Guildford 156
- Heathrow Airport *Bus* 158A
- London 149, 155, 156
- Portsmouth 156
- Salisbury 160
- Southampton 158
- Surbiton 155
- Weymouth 158

Wokingham [SW] ℗ 🚲 ◇ ⚠ 🚕 148, 149
Woldingham [SN] ℗ 🚲 ◇ ⚠ 184
Wolverhampton [VT] ■7 ℗ 🚲 ◇ ⚠ 🚕
- Bangor (Gwynedd) 65
- Birmingham 68
- Birmingham International 68
- Bournemouth 51
- Bristol 51
- Carlisle 65
- Chester 65, 75
- Coventry 68
- Crewe 65
- Edinburgh 65
- Exeter 51
- Glasgow 65
- Holyhead 65
- Liverpool 65
- London 66
- Macclesfield 84
- Manchester 65
- Manchester Airport 65
- Oxenholme Lake District 65
- Oxford 51
- Paignton 51
- Penzance 51
- Plymouth 51
- Preston 65
- Reading 51
- Rugby 66
- Shrewsbury 74
- Southampton 51
- Stafford 68
- Stockport 65
- Stoke-on-Trent 65
- Torquay 51
- Walsall 70
- Watford 66
- Wrexham 75

Wolverton [LM] ℗ 🚲 66
Wombwell [NT] ℗ ⓤ 34
Wood End [LM] ⚠ ⓤ 71
Wood Street [LE] ⚠ 20
Woodbridge [LE] ℗ 🚲 🚕 ⓤ 13
Woodgrange Park [LO] 🚲 ⚠ 62
Woodhall [SR] 🚲 219
Woodham Ferrers [LE] (South Woodham Ferrers)
Woodhouse [NT] ℗ ⓤ 30
Woodlesford [NT] ℗ 🚲 ⓤ 32, 34
Woodley [NT] ℗ ⓤ 78
Woodmansterne [SN] ⚠ 181
Woodsmoor [NT] 86
Wool [SW] ℗ 🚲 ◇ ⚠ 🚕 158
Woolston [SW] ℗ 🚲 ◇ ⚠ 165
Woolwich Arsenal [SE] ■4 ℗ ◇ ⚠ 🚕 200
Woolwich Dockyard [SE] ◇ ⚠ 200
Wootton Wawen [LM] ⚠ ⓤ 71
Worcester Foregate Street [LM] ■7 ◇ ⚠ 🚕 71, 126
Worcester Shrub Hill [LM] ■7 ℗ ◇ ⚠ 🚕 57, 71, 125, 126
Worcester Park [SW] ℗ 🚲 ◇ ⚠ 🚕 152
Workington [NT] ℗ ◇ 100
Worksop [NT] ℗ ◇ 30, 55
Worle [GW] ℗ 🚲 ⓤ 134
Worplesdon [SW] ℗ 🚲 ◇ ⚠ 155, 156
Worstead [LE] ℗ 🚲 ⓤ 16
Worthing [SN] ■4 ℗ 🚲 ◇ ⚠ 🚕 123, 188
Wrabness [LE] ℗ 🚲 ⓤ 11
Wraysbury [SW] ℗ ⚠ ⓤ 149
Wrenbury [AW] ℗ ⓤ 131
Wressle [NT] ⓤ 29
Wrexham Central [AW] ⓤ 101
Wrexham General [AW] ℗ ◇ 🚕 65, 75, 101
Wrotham [SE] (see Borough Green & Wrotham)
Wroxham [LE] (see Hoveton & Wroxham)
Wye [SE] ℗ ◇ ⚠ 207
Wylam [NT] ℗ 🚲 ⓤ 48
Wylde Green [LM] ℗ ⚠ 69
Wymondham [LE] ℗ 🚕 17
Wythall [LM] ⚠ 71

Station index and table numbers

[10] Connection time
Ⓟ Station Car Park
🚲 Bicycle storage facility
◇ Seat reservations can be mad…
at this station
⚠ Penalty Fare Schemes in operation o…
some or all services from this station
🚕 Taxi rank or cab office at station,
or signposted and within 100 metres
Ⓤ Unstaffed station
[ ] Station Operator Code

Y

Yalding [SE] Ⓟ ⚠ Ⓤ 208
Yardley Wood [LM] Ⓟ ⚠ 71
Yarm [TP] Ⓟ Ⓤ 39
Yarmouth (IOW) *Ship* 🚕 158
Yate [GW] Ⓟ 🚲 134
Yatton [GW] Ⓟ 🚲 134
Yeoford [GW] Ⓤ 136
Yeovil Bus Station *Bus* [SW] 123A,
Yeovil Junction [SW] Ⓟ 🚲 ◇ ⚠ 🚕 123A,160
Yeovil Pen Mill [GW] Ⓟ ◇ 123, 123A
Yetminster [GW] Ⓟ Ⓤ 123
Ynyswen [AW] Ⓤ 130
Yoker [SR] 🚲 Ⓤ 226
York [GR] [8] Ⓟ 🚲 ◇ 🚕
- Aberdeen 26
- Bedford 53
- Birmingham 51
- Birmingham International 51
- Blackpool 41
- Bournemouth 51
- Bradford 40
- Bristol 51
- Cambridge 26
- Cardiff 51
- Darlington 26
- Derby 53
- Doncaster 26
- Dundee 26
- Eden Camp *Bus* 26G
- Edinburgh 26
- Exeter 51
- Flamingo Land *Bus* 26G
- Glasgow 26
- Grantham 26
- Halifax 41
- Harrogate 35
- Hartlepool 26
- Huddersfield 39
- Hull 33
- Knaresborough 35
- Leeds 35, 40
- Leicester 53
- Liverpool 39
- London 26
- Luton 53
- Manchester 39
- Manchester Airport 39
- Middlesbrough 26
- Newark 26
- Newcastle 26
- Newport (South Wales) 51
- Newton Abbot 51
- Norwich 26
- Nottingham 53
- Oxford 51
- Paignton 51
- Penzance 51
- Peterborough 26
- Pickering Eastgate *Bus* 26G
- Plymouth 51
- Preston 41
- Reading 51
- Retford 26
- Scarborough 39
- Selby 33
- Sheffield 29
- Stansted Airport 26
- Southampton 51
- Sunderland 26
- Torquay 51
- Whitby *Bus* 26G

Yorton [AW] Ⓟ Ⓤ 131
Ystrad Mynach [AW] [3] Ⓟ ◇ 130
Ystrad Rhondda [AW] Ⓟ Ⓤ 130

Network Diagram for Tables 1, 4

DM-1/06
Design BAJS

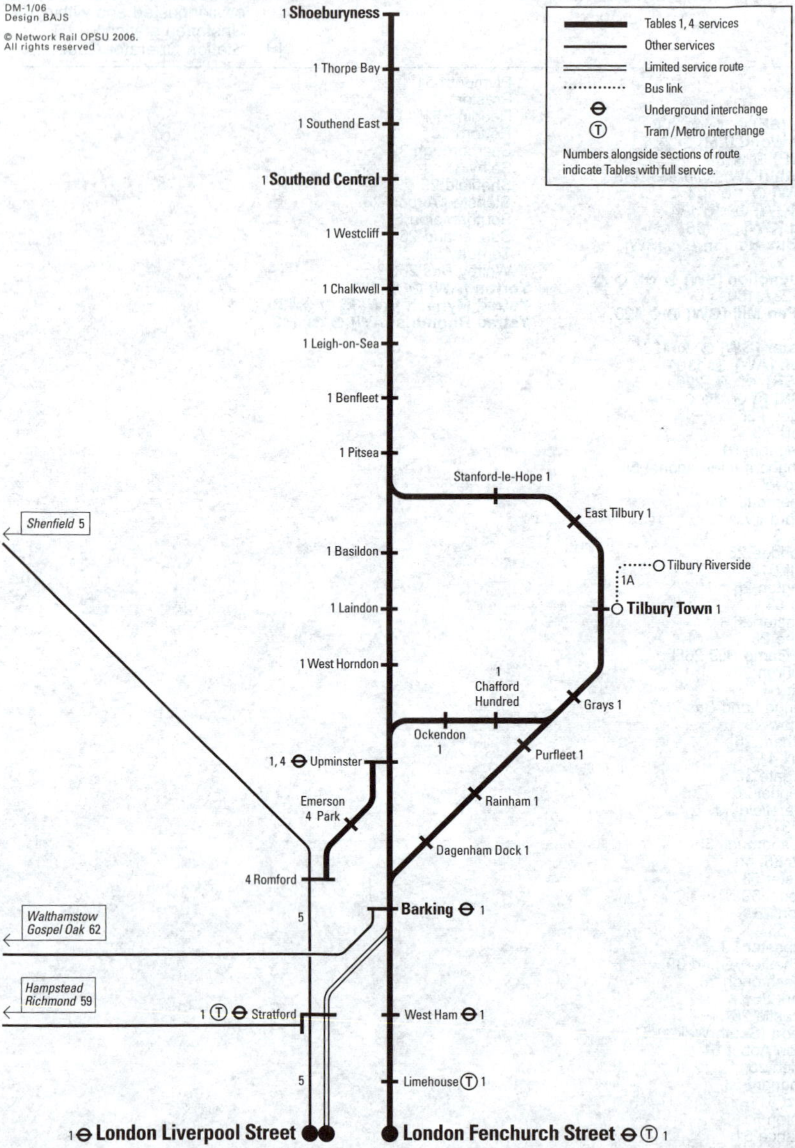

London - Southend Central and Shoeburyness

Network Diagram - see first page of Table I

Miles	Miles	Miles			CC MO	CC MX	CC MX	CC MO	CC MX	CC MX	CC MO	CC MX	CC MX		CC MX	CC MX	CC MO	CC MX	CC MX	CC MX	CC MX	CC MO	CC MX		CC MX
0	0	—	**London Fenchurch St** 7	Θ d	22p50	22p50	23p00			23p05	23p10	23p10			23p20	23p35	23p40	23p40	23p50	00 01		00 10	00 15		00 25
1¾	1¾	—	Limehouse	d	22p54	22p54				23p09	23p14	23p14			23p24	23p39	23p44	23p44	23p54			00 14	00 19		00 29
4¾	4¾	—	West Ham	Θ d	22p59	22p59	23p08			23p14	23p19	23p19			23p29	23p44	23p49	23p49	23p59	00 09		00 19	00 24		00 34
—	—	—	**London Liverpool St** 15	Θ d																					
—	—	—	Stratford 7	Θ d																					
7½	7½	—	Barking	Θ d	23p04	23p05	23p14			23p20	23p24	23p25			23p35	23p50	23p54	23p55	00 05	00 15		00 24	00 30		00 40
15¼	—	0	Upminster	Θ d	23p12	23p14	23p23				23p32	23p34			23p44		00 02	00 04	00 14	00 24		00 32			00 49
—	—	3	Ockendon	d	23p18	23p19									23p49				00 19						
—	—	5	Chafford Hundred	d	23p21	23p23									23p53				00 23						
19¼	—	—	West Horndon	d							23p37	23p39					00 07	00 09				00 37			00 54
22¾	—	—	Laindon	d			23p31				23p42	23p44					00 12	00 16		00 32		00 42			00 59
24½	—	—	Basildon	d			23p34				23p45	23p47					00 15	00 19		00 35		00 45			01 02
—	10½	—	Dagenham Dock	d						23p25						23p55							00 35		
—	12¾	—	Rainham	d						23p29						23p59							00 39		
—	16	—	Purfleet	d						23p34						00 04							00 44		
—	19¾	7½	Grays	d	23p25	23p27				23p42					23p57	00a10			00 27				00a50		
—	21½	—	**Tilbury Town** 3	d	23p28	23p30				23p45					00 01				00 30						
—	25¼	—	East Tilbury	d	23p34	23p36				23p51					00 06				00 36						
—	27¼	—	Stanford-le-Hope	d	23p37	23p40				23p55			←		00 10				00 40						
26½	32¼	—	Pitsea	d	23p45	23p48		←	←	00 06	23p49	23p52	00 06		00 18		00 19	00 22	00 48		←	00 49			01 06
29¼	35	—	Benfleet	d	23p49	23p52	23p41	23p49	23p52	→	23p52	23p56	00 10		00 22		00 22	00 26	00 52	00 42	00 52	00 52			01 10
32½	38¼	—	Leigh-on-Sea	d	→	→	23p45	23p53	23p56		23p57	23p59	00 15		00 27		00 27	00 31	→	00 46	00 56	00 57			01 14
34	39¾	—	Chalkwell	d			23p48	23p56	23p59		23p59	00 03	00 18		00 30		00 29	00 34		00 49	00 59	00 59			01 17
34¾	40½	—	Westcliff	d			23p51	23p58	00 02		00 02	00 06	00 20		00 32		00 32	00 36		00 52	01 02	01 02			01 20
35¾	41½	—	**Southend Central**	a			23p54	00 01	00 05		00 05	00 09	00 23		00 35		00 35	00 39		00 55	01 05	01 05			01 23
—	—	—		d			23p54	00 01	00 05		00 06	00 09	00 23		00 35		00 36	00 40		00 55	01 05	01 06			01 23
36½	42¼	—	Southend East	d			23p56	00 03	00 07		00 08	00 11	00 26		00 38		00 38	00 42		00 57	01 07	01 08			01 25
38	43¾	—	Thorpe Bay	d			23p59	00 06	00 11		00 10	00 15	00 29		00 41		00 40	00 46		01 01	01 11	01 11			01 29
39½	45¼	—	**Shoeburyness**	a			00 06	00 13	00 17		00 18	00 21	00 36		00 48		00 48	00 52		01 07	01 17	01 18			01 35

		CC	CC	CC	CC	CC	CC	CC	CC		CC	CC	CC	CC	CC	CC	CC	CC	CC		CC	CC	CC	CC	CC
London Fenchurch St 7	Θ d		05 10		05 40				06 10		06 20	06 40		06 44	06 48	07 00	07 09	07 13	07 15		07 30	07 40	07 43	07 48	07 50
Limehouse	d		05 14		05 44				06 14		06 24	06 44		06 48	06 52		07 13					07 44			07 54
West Ham	Θ d		05 19		05 49				06 19		06 29	06 49		06 53	06 57	07 08	07 18		07 23		07 38	07 49	07 53		07 59
London Liverpool St 15	Θ d																								
Stratford 7	Θ d																								
Barking	Θ d		05 25	05 39	05 55	05 45	06 05		06 25		06 35	06 55	06 50	07 00	07 03	07 14	07 25	07 26	07 29		07 44	07 55	07 58		08 05
Upminster	Θ d	05 28	05 34	05 48	06 04			06 31	06 34			07 04		07 10		07 23	07 34		07 38		07 53	08 04		08 09	08 15
Ockendon	d	05 33		05 56				06 36						07 15					07 45					08 16	
Chafford Hundred	d	05 37		06 00				06 40						07 19					07 49					08 20	
West Horndon	d		05 39		06 09				06 39			07 09					07 39					08 09			08 20
Laindon	d		05 44		06 14				06 45			07 14					07 44					08 14			08a26
Basildon	d		05 47		06 17				06 48			07 17				07 33	07 47				08 03	08 17			
Dagenham Dock	d					05 50	06 10				06 40		06 55		07 08			07 31					08 03		
Rainham	d					05 54	06 14				06 44		06 59		07 12			07 35					08 07		
Purfleet	d					05 59	06 19				06 49		07 04		07 17			07 40					08 13		
Grays	d	05a41		06a05		06 05	06 25	06a44			06 55		07 10	07a23	07 25			07 46	07 54				08 18	08 25	
Tilbury Town 3	d					06 08	06 28				06 58		07 13		07 28				07 58				08 22		
East Tilbury	d					06 14	06 34				07 04		07 19		07 34				08 04				08 28		
Stanford-le-Hope	d					06 18	06 38				07 08		07 23		07 38			07 56	08 08				08 32	08 35	
Pitsea	d		05 51		06 21	06 26	06a46		06 51		07 18	07 22	07a31		07a46		07 51	08a03	08a15			08 21	08 41	08a44	
Benfleet	d		05 55		06 25	06 31			06 55		07 22	07 26				07 39	07 55				08 09	08 25	→		
Leigh-on-Sea	d		06 00		06 30	06 35			07 00		07 27	07 30				07 44	07 59				08 14	08 30			
Chalkwell	d		06 03		06 33	06 38			07 03		07 30	07 33				07 47	08 02				08 17	08 33			
Westcliff	d		06 05		06 35	06 41			07 05		07 32	07 36				07 49	08 05				08 19	08 35			
Southend Central	a		06 08		06 38	06 43			07 08		07 35	07 38				07 52	08 07				08 22	08 38			
	d		06 08		06 38	06 43			07 08		07 35	07 38				07 52	08 07				08 22	08 38			
Southend East	d		06 10		06 40	06 45			07 10		07 37	07 40				07 54	08 09				08 24	08 40			
Thorpe Bay	d		06 14		06 44	06 49			07 14		07 40	07 44				07 58	08 13				08 28	08 44			
Shoeburyness	a		06 18		06 48	06 53			07 20		07 45	07 48				08 02	08 17				08 32	08 48			

		CC	CC	CC			CC	CC	CC	CC	CC	CC	CC	CC	CC		CC	CC	CC	CC	CC	CC	CC	CC	CC
London Fenchurch St 7	Θ d	08 00		08 03			08 09	08 14	08 20	08 30		08 40	08 50	08 54	09 00			09 10	09 16	09 20	09 30		09 35	09 40	
Limehouse	d			08 07			08 13		08 24			08 44	08 54					09 14	09 20	09 24			09 39	09 44	
West Ham	Θ d	08 08		08 12			08 18	08 23	08 29	08 38		08 49	08 59		09 08			09 19	09 25	09 29	09 38		09 44	09 49	
London Liverpool St 15	Θ d																								
Stratford 7	Θ d																								
Barking	Θ d	08 14		08 18			08 24	08 30	08 37	08 45		08 55	09 07	09 09	09 16			09 25	09 31	09 35	09 44		09 50	09 55	
Upminster	Θ d	08 23					08 33	08 41		08 54		09 04		09 18	09 25			09 34		09 45	09 53			10 04	
Ockendon	d							08 46						09 23						09 50					
Chafford Hundred	d							08 50						09 27						09 54					
West Horndon	d						08 38					09 09						09 39						10 09	
Laindon	d	08 31					08 44			09 03		09 14			09 34			09 44			10 01			10 14	
Basildon	d	08 34					08 47			09 06		09 17			09 37			09 47			10 04			10 17	
Dagenham Dock	d			08 23					08 42				09 12						09 36				09 55		
Rainham	d			08 27					08 46				09 16						09 40				09 59		
Purfleet	d			08 33					08 51				09 21						09 45				10 04		
Grays	d			08 38				08a54	08 57				09 27	09a31					09 51	09 58			10a10		
Tilbury Town 3	d			08 42					09 00				09 30						09 54	10 02					
East Tilbury	d			08 48					09 06				09 36						10 00	10 08					
Stanford-le-Hope	d		←	08 52					09 10		←		09 40						10 04	10 12					←
Pitsea	d	08 38	08 41	08a59			08 51		09 18	09 09	09 18	09 21	09 48				←	09 51	10 12	10 25		←		10 21	10 25
Benfleet	d	08 42	08 45				08 55		→	09 13	09 22	09 26	09 52		09 43		09 52	09 55	10 16	→	10 11	10 16		10 25	10 29
Leigh-on-Sea	d	08 46	08 50				08 59			09 18	09 27	09 30	→		09 48		09 57	10 00	→		10 15	10 20		10 30	10 34
Chalkwell	d	08 49	08 53				09 02			09 21	09 30	09 33			09 51		10 00	10 03			10 18	10 23		10 33	10 37
Westcliff	d	08 52	08 55				09 05			09 23	09 32	09 36			09 53		10 02	10 05			10 21	10 26		10 35	10 39
Southend Central	a	08 54	08 58				09 08			09 26	09 35	09 38			09 56		10 05	10 08			10 23	10 29		10 38	10 42
	d	08 55					09 08			09 26		09 38			09 56			10 08			10 23			10 38	
Southend East	d	08 57					09 10			09 28		09 40			09 58			10 10			10 25			10 40	
Thorpe Bay	d	09 00					09 14			09 32		09 44			10 02			10 14			10 29			10 44	
Shoeburyness	a	09 05					09 18			09 36		09 48			10 06			10 18			10 33			10 48	

London - Southend Central and Shoeburyness

Network Diagram - see first page of Table I

			CC	CC	CC	CC	CC	CC	CC	CC	CC		CC	CC	CC	CC	CC	CC	CC	CC	CC		CC	CC	CC
London Fenchurch St 7 ⊖	d		09 50	10 00		10 05	10 10	10 20	10 30		10 35		10 40	10 50	11 00		11 05	11 10	11 20	11 30			11 35	11 40	11 50
Limehouse	d		09 54			10 09	10 14	10 24			10 39		10 44	10 54			11 09	11 14	11 24				11 39	11 44	11 54
West Ham ⊖	d		09 59	10 08		10 14	10 19	10 29	10 38		10 44		10 49	10 59	11 08		11 14	11 19	11 29	11 38			11 44	11 49	11 59
London Liverpool St 15 ⊖	d																								
Stratford 7 ⊖	d																								
Barking ⊖	d		10 05	10 14		10 20	10 25	10 35	10 44		10 50		10 55	11 05	11 14		11 20	11 25	11 35	11 44			11 50	11 55	12 05
Upminster ⊖	d		10 14	10 23			10 34	10 44	10 53				11 04	11 14	11 23			11 34	11 44	11 53				12 04	12 14
Ockendon	d		10 19					10 49						11 19					11 49						12 19
Chafford Hundred	d		10 23					10 53						11 23					11 53						12 23
West Horndon	d						10 39						11 09					11 39						12 09	
Laindon	d			10 31			10 44		11 01				11 14		11 31			11 44		12 01				12 14	
Basildon	d			10 34			10 47		11 04				11 17		11 34			11 47		12 04				12 17	
Dagenham Dock	d					10 25					10 55						11 25						11 55		
Rainham	d					10 29					10 59						11 29						11 59		
Purfleet	d					10 34					11 04						11 34						12 04		
Grays	d		10 27			10a40		10 57			11a10			11 27			11a40		11 57				12a10		12 27
Tilbury Town 3	d		10 30					11 00						11 30					12 00						12 30
East Tilbury	d		10 36					11 06						11 36					12 06						12 36
Stanford-le-Hope	d		10 40					11 10						11 40					12 10						12 40
Pitsea	d		10 48		←		10 51	11 18		←			11 21	11 48		←		11 51	12 18		←			12 21	12 48
Benfleet	d		10 52	10 41	10 52		10 55	11 22	11 11	11 22			11 25	11 52	11 41	11 52		11 55	12 22	12 11	12 22			12 25	12 52
Leigh-on-Sea	d		→	10 45	10 56		11 00	→	11 15	11 26			11 30	→	11 45	11 57		12 00	→	12 15	12 26			12 30	→
Chalkwell	d			10 48	10 59		11 03		11 18	11 29			11 33		11 48	12 00		12 03		12 18	12 29			12 33	
Westcliff	d			10 51	11 02		11 05		11 21	11 32			11 35		11 51	12 02		12 05		12 21	12 32			12 35	
Southend Central	a			10 53	11 05		11 08		11 23	11 35			11 38		11 53	12 05		12 08		12 23	12 35			12 38	
	d			10 53			11 08		11 23				11 38		11 53			12 08		12 23				12 38	
Southend East	d			10 55			11 10		11 25				11 40		11 55			12 10		12 25				12 40	
Thorpe Bay	d			10 59			11 14		11 29				11 44		11 59			12 14		12 29				12 44	
Shoeburyness	a			11 03			11 18		11 33				11 48		12 03			12 18		12 33				12 48	

		CC	CC	CC	CC	CC	CC		CC	CC	CC	CC	CC	CC	CC	CC	CC		CC	CC	CC	CC	CC	CC	CC
London Fenchurch St 7 ⊖	d	12 00		12 05	12 10	12 20	12 30			12 35	12 40	12 50	13 00		13 05	13 10	13 20		13 30		13 35	13 40	13 50	14 00	
Limehouse	d			12 09	12 14	12 24				12 39	12 44	12 54			13 09	13 14	13 24				13 39	13 44	13 54		
West Ham ⊖	d	12 08		12 14	12 19	12 29	12 38			12 44	12 49	12 59	13 08		13 14	13 19	13 29		13 38		13 44	13 49	13 59	14 08	
London Liverpool St 15 ⊖	d																								
Stratford 7 ⊖	d																								
Barking ⊖	d	12 14		12 20	12 25	12 35	12 44			12 50	12 55	13 05	13 14		13 20	13 25	13 35		13 44		13 50	13 55	14 05	14 14	
Upminster ⊖	d	12 23			12 34	12 44	12 53				13 04	13 14	13 23			13 34	13 44		13 53			14 04	14 14	14 23	
Ockendon	d					12 49						13 19					13 49						14 19		
Chafford Hundred	d					12 53						13 23					13 53						14 23		
West Horndon	d				12 39						13 09					13 39						14 09			
Laindon	d	12 31			12 44		13 01				13 14		13 31			13 44			14 01			14 14		14 31	
Basildon	d	12 34			12 47		13 04				13 17		13 34			13 47			14 04			14 17		14 34	
Dagenham Dock	d			12 25						12 55					13 25						13 55				
Rainham	d			12 29						12 59					13 29						13 59				
Purfleet	d			12 34						13 04					13 34						14 04				
Grays	d			12a40		12 57				13a10		13 27			13a40		13 57				14a10		14 27		
Tilbury Town 3	d					13 00						13 30					14 00						14 30		
East Tilbury	d					13 06						13 36					14 06						14 36		
Stanford-le-Hope	d					13 10						13 40					14 10						14 40		
Pitsea	d		←		12 51	13 18			←		13 21	13 48		←		13 51	14 18			←		14 21	14 48		←
Benfleet	d	12 41	12 52		12 55	13 22	13 11		13 22		13 25	13 52	13 41	13 52		13 55	14 22		14 11	14 22		14 25	14 52	14 41	14 52
Leigh-on-Sea	d	12 45	12 57		13 00	→	13 15		13 27		13 30	→	13 45	13 57		14 00	→		14 15	14 26		14 30	→	14 45	14 56
Chalkwell	d	12 48	13 00		13 03		13 18		13 30		13 33		13 48	14 00		14 03			14 18	14 29		14 33		14 48	14 59
Westcliff	d	12 51	13 02		13 05		13 21		13 32		13 35		13 51	14 02		14 05			14 21	14 32		14 35		14 51	15 02
Southend Central	a	12 53	13 05		13 08		13 23		13 35		13 38		13 53	14 05		14 08			14 23	14 35		14 38		14 53	15 05
	d	12 53			13 08		13 23				13 38		13 53			14 08			14 23			14 38		14 53	
Southend East	d	12 55			13 10		13 25				13 40		13 55			14 10			14 25			14 40		14 55	
Thorpe Bay	d	12 59			13 14		13 29				13 44		13 59			14 14			14 29			14 44		14 59	
Shoeburyness	a	13 03			13 18		13 33				13 48		14 03			14 18			14 33			14 48		15 03	

		CC	CC		CC	CC	CC	CC	CC	CC	CC	CC	CC		CC	CC	CC	CC	CC	CC	CC	CC	CC		CC
London Fenchurch St 7 ⊖	d	14 05	14 10		14 20	14 30		14 35	14 40	14 50	15 00		15 05		15 10	15 20	15 25	15 30	15 35	15 40		15 50	15 55		16 00
Limehouse	d	14 09	14 14		14 24			14 39	14 44	14 54			15 09		15 14	15 24			15 39	15 44		15 54	15 59		
West Ham ⊖	d	14 14	14 19		14 29	14 38		14 44	14 49	14 59	15 08		15 14		15 19	15 29	15 33	15 38	15 44	15 49		15 59	16 04		16 08
London Liverpool St 15 ⊖	d																								
Stratford 7 ⊖	d																								
Barking ⊖	d	14 20	14 25		14 35	14 44		14 50	14 55	15 05	15 14		15 20		15 25	15 35	15 39	15 44	15 50	15 54		16 05	16 10		16 14
Upminster ⊖	d		14 34		14 44	14 53			15 04	15 14	15 23				15 34	15 44	15 48	15 53		16 02		16 14			16 23
Ockendon	d				14 49					15 19						15 49						16 19			
Chafford Hundred	d				14 53					15 23						15 53						16 23			
West Horndon	d		14 39						15 09						15 39					16 07					
Laindon	d		14 44			15 01			15 14		15 31				15 44		15 56	16 01		16 12					
Basildon	d		14 47			15 04			15 17		15 34				15 47		15 59	16 04		16 15					16 33
Dagenham Dock	d	14 25						14 55					15 25						15 55				16 15		
Rainham	d	14 29						14 59					15 29						15 59				16 19		
Purfleet	d	14 34						15 04					15 34						16 04				16 25		
Grays	d	14a40			14 57			15a10		15 27			15a40			15 57			16a10			16 27	16a33		
Tilbury Town 3	d				15 00					15 30						16 00						16 30			
East Tilbury	d				15 06					15 36						16 06						16 36			
Stanford-le-Hope	d				15 10					15 40						16 10					←	16 40			
Pitsea	d		14 51		15 18		←		15 21	15 48		←			15 51	16 22	16 03			16 19	16 22	16a48			
Benfleet	d		14 55		15 22	15 11	15 22		15 25	15 52	15 41	15 52			15 55	→	16 07	16 11		16 22	16 26				16 40
Leigh-on-Sea	d		15 00		→	15 15	15 26		15 30	→	15 45	15 56			16 00		16a12	16 15		16 27	16 30				16 45
Chalkwell	d		15 03			15 18	15 29		15 33		15 48	15 59			16 03			16 18		16 29	16 33				16 48
Westcliff	d		15 05			15 21	15 32		15 35		15 51	16 02			16 05			16 21		16 32	16 36				16 50
Southend Central	a		15 08			15 23	15 35		15 38		15 53	16 05			16 08			16 23		16 34	16 41				16 53
	d		15 08			15 23			15 38		15 53				16 08			16 23		16 35					16 53
Southend East	d		15 10			15 25			15 40		15 55				16 10			16 25		16 37					16 55
Thorpe Bay	d		15 14			15 29			15 44		15 59				16 14			16 29		16 39					16 59
Shoeburyness	a		15 18			15 33			15 48		16 03				16 20			16 33		16 44					17 05

Table I

Mondays to Fridays

London - Southend Central and Shoeburyness

Network Diagram - see first page of Table I

			CC	CC	CC	CC	CC	CC	CC	CC		CC	CC	CC	CC	CC	CC	CC	CC	CC		CC	CC	CC	CC	CC
London Fenchurch St 7	⊖	d	16 10	16 13	16 20	16 28	16 30	16 34	16 37	16 45		16 48	16 55	17 00	17 02	17 05	17 07	17 10	17 15	17 18		17 20	17 23	17 26	17 30	17 32
Limehouse		d	16 14	16 17	16 24		16 34	16 38	16 41	16 49		16 52	16 59			17 09	17 12	17 15	17 19			17 24	17 28	17 30		
West Ham	⊖	d	16 19	16 22	16 29	16 36	16 39	16 43	16 46			16 57	17 04				17 17	17 20		17 26		17 29	17 33	17 35		17 40
London Liverpool St 15	⊖	d																								
Stratford 7	⊖	d																								
Barking	⊖	d	16 25	16 28	16 35		16 45	16 49	16 52	16 59		17 03	17 10		17 15	17 19	17 22	17 26				17 35	17 39	17 42		17 46
Upminster	⊖	d	16 34		16 45		16 55		17 02	17 07		17 13			17 24		17 31		17 36	17 40			17 47			17 56
Ockendon		d			16 50				17 08						17 29											18 02
Chafford Hundred		d			16 54				17 12						17 34											18 06
West Horndon		d	16 39				17 00					17 18					17 36						17 52			
Laindon		d	16 44			16 56	17a08			17 16		17a26				17 35	17a43					17 51	17a59			
Basildon		d	16 47			16 59				17 19						17 39				17 50		17 55				
Dagenham Dock		d		16 33				16 54					17 15					17 31						17 47		
Rainham		d		16 37				16 58					17 19					17 35						17 51		
Purfleet		d		16 43				17 04					17 25					17 40						17 56		
Grays		d		16 49	16 59			17 10	17a18				17 31		17a40			17 46						18 02		18a13
Tilbury Town 3		d		16 52	17 02			17 13					17 34					17 50						18 06		
East Tilbury		d		16 58	17 08			17 19					17 40					17 56						18 12		
Stanford-le-Hope		d		17 02	17a15			17 23					17 44					18 00						18 16		
Pitsea		d	16 51	17a12				17a33		17 23			17a54			17 42		18a09		17 54		17 58		18a25		
Benfleet		d	16 55			17 06				17 27				17 33		17 46			17 52	17 58		18 03			18 08	
Leigh-on-Sea		d	17 00			17 11				17 32				17 38		17 51			17 56	18 02		18 07			18 12	
Chalkwell		d	17 03			17 14				17 34				17 41		17 53			17 59	18 05		18 10			18 15	
Westcliff		d	17 05			17 16				17 37				17 43		17 56			18 02	18 08		18 13			18 18	
Southend Central		a	17 08			17 19				17 39				17 46		17 58			18 04	18 13		18 15			18 20	
		d	17 08			17 19				17 39				17 46		17 58			18 04			18 15			18 20	
Southend East		d	17 10			17 21				17 41				17 48		18 00			18 06			18 17			18 22	
Thorpe Bay		d	17 14			17 24				17 44				17 50		18 03			18 10			18 21			18 26	
Shoeburyness		a	17 20			17 31				17 51				17 57		18 11			18 16			18 28			18 32	

			CC	CC	CC	CC		CC	CC	CC	CC	CC	CC	CC	CC	CC		CC	CC	CC	CC	CC	CC	CC	CC	CC
London Fenchurch St 7	⊖	d	17 35	17 37	17 41	17 45		17 47	17 51	17 53	17 56	18 00	18 02	18 06	18 09			18 12	18 21		18 23	18 27	18 31	18 35	18 42	18 46
Limehouse		d	17 39	17 42	17 45	17 49		17 52		17 57	18 00		18 06	18 10	18 13			18 16			18 27	18 31	18 35	18 39		18 51
West Ham	⊖	d	17 44	17 47	17 50			17 57	17 59		18 05	18 08	18 11		18 18			18 21			18 32	18 36	18 40		18 50	18 56
London Liverpool St 15	⊖	d																								
Stratford 7	⊖	d																								
Barking	⊖	d	17 50	17 53	17 56					18 08	18 11		18 17	18 20	18 24			18 28				18 42	18 46	18 49		19 01
Upminster	⊖	d		18 03				18 10	18 14				18 27		18 34						18 46	18 51		18 58		19 10
Ockendon		d						18 15					18 33								18 51			19 06		
Chafford Hundred		d						18 20					18 38								18 55			19 11		
West Horndon		d		18 08						18 21					18 39							18 56				19 15
Laindon		d	18 07	18a15						18 27				18 37	18 43				18 47			19 01				19 20
Basildon		d	18 10						18 24	18 31		18 35		18 41	18 47				18 51			19 04			19 12	19 23
Dagenham Dock		d			18 01						18 16							18 33					18 51			
Rainham		d			18 05						18 20							18 37					18 55			
Purfleet		d			18 11						18 25							18 42					19 01			
Grays		d			18 17			18a26			18 31		18 42					18 48			19 00		19 07	19a17		
Tilbury Town 3		d			18 20						18 35		18 46					18 52			19 03		19 10			
East Tilbury		d			18 26						18 41		18 52					18 58			19 09		19 16			
Stanford-le-Hope		d			18 30						18 45		18 56			←		19 02			19 13		19 20			
Pitsea		d	18 14		18a40				18 28	18 34	18 57	18 38	19a05	18 44	18 50	18 57		19a11		←	19a23	19 08	19a30			19 26
Benfleet		d	18 18			18 24			18 32	18 39	→	18 43		18 49	18 54	19 03			18 58	19 03		19 12			19 19	19 30
Leigh-on-Sea		d	18 23			18 28			18 37	18 43		18 47		18 53	18 59	→			19 03	19 07		19 16			19 24	19 35
Chalkwell		d	18 26			18 31			18 40	18 46		18 50		18 56	19 01				19 06	19 10		19 19			19 27	19 37
Westcliff		d	18 28			18 34			18 42	18 49		18 53		18 59	19 04				19 08	19 13		19 21			19 29	19 40
Southend Central		a	18 31			18 36			18 45	18 51		18 55		19 01	19 09				19 11	19 15		19 24			19 32	19 42
		d	18 31			18 36			18 45	18 51		18 55		19 01					19 11	19 15		19 24			19 32	19 42
Southend East		d	18 33			18 38			18 47	18 53		18 57		19 03					19 13	19 17		19 26			19 34	19 44
Thorpe Bay		d	18 36			18 42			18 50	18 57		19 01		19 07					19 16	19 21		19 28			19 37	19 47
Shoeburyness		a	18 43			18 48			18 58	19 03		19 07		19 13					19 23	19 28		19 35			19 44	19 53

				CC	CC	CC	CC	CC	CC	CC	CC	CC		CC	CC	CC	CC	CC	CC	CC	CC	CC		CC	CC	CC
London Fenchurch St 7	⊖	d		18 51	19 00	19 02	19 05		19 08	19 11	19 20	19 30			19 32	19 35	19 40	19 50	20 00		20 05	20 10		20 20	20 30	
Limehouse		d		18 55			19 09		19 12	19 15	19 24				19 36	19 39	19 44	19 54			20 09	20 14		20 24	20 34	
West Ham	⊖	d		19 00		19 10			19 17	19 20	19 29				19 41	19 44	19 49	19 59	20 08		20 14	20 19		20 29	20 39	
London Liverpool St 15	⊖	d																								
Stratford 7	⊖	d																								
Barking	⊖	d		19 06		19 16	19 19		19 23	19 26	19 35				19 47	19 50	19 55	20 05	20 14		20 20	20 25		20 35	20 45	
Upminster	⊖	d				19 26	19 30			19 35	19 44	19 50			19 56		20 04	20 14	20 23			20 34		20 44	20 54	
Ockendon		d				19 33					19 49							20 19						20 49		
Chafford Hundred		d				19 39					19 53							20 23						20 53		
West Horndon		d								19 40					20 01		20 09					20 39				
Laindon		d			19 26					19 45					20a07		20 14		20 31			20 44			21 02	
Basildon		d					19 40			19 48		20 00					20 17		20 34			20 47			21 05	
Dagenham Dock		d		19 11					19 28							19 55					20 25					
Rainham		d		19 15					19 32							19 59					20 29					
Purfleet		d		19 21					19 37							20 04					20 34					
Grays		d		19 27		19 46			19a43		19 57					20a10		20 27			20a40			20 57		
Tilbury Town 3		d		19 30		19 50					20 00							20 30						21 00		
East Tilbury		d		19 36		19 56					20 06							20 36						21 06		
Stanford-le-Hope		d		19 40		20 00		←			20 10							20 40						21 10		
Pitsea		d		19 48		20a07	19 44	19 48		19 52	20 18			←			20 21	20 48		←		20 51		21 18		←
Benfleet		d		→	19 33		19 48	19 52		19 56	20 22	20 06		20 22			20 26	20 52	20 41	20 52		20 55		21 22	21 12	21 22
Leigh-on-Sea		d			19 38		19 52	19 56		20 00	→	20 11		20 27			20 30	→	20 45	20 56		21 00		→	21 16	21 26
Chalkwell		d			19 41		19 55	19 59		20 03		20 14		20 30			20 33		20 48	20 59		21 03			21 19	21 29
Westcliff		d			19 43		19 58	20 02		20 06		20 16		20 32			20 36		20 51	21 02		21 05			21 22	21 32
Southend Central		a			19 46		20 00	20 07		20 08		20 19		20 35			20 38		20 53	21 05		21 08			21 24	21 35
		d			19 46		20 00			20 08		20 19					20 38		20 53			21 08			21 24	
Southend East		d			19 48		20 02			20 10		20 21					20 40		20 55			21 10			21 26	
Thorpe Bay		d			19 50		20 06			20 14		20 25					20 44		20 59			21 14			21 30	
Shoeburyness		a			19 57		20 10			20 18		20 29					20 48		21 03			21 18			21 34	

Table I

Mondays to Fridays

London - Southend Central and Shoeburyness

Network Diagram - see first page of Table I

		CC	CC	CC	CC	CC	CC		CC	CC	CC	CC	CC	CC	CC	CC	CC		CC	CC	CC	CC	CC	CC	CC
London Fenchurch St 7 ⊖	d		20 40	20 50	21 00		21 05		21 10	21 20	21 30			21 40	21 50	22 00			22 05	22 10	22 20	22 35	22 40	22 50	23 00
Limehouse	d		20 44	20 54			21 09		21 14	21 24	21 34			21 44	21 54				22 09	22 14	22 24	22 39	22 44	22 54	
West Ham ⊖	d		20 49	20 59	21 08		21 14		21 19	21 29	21 39			21 49	21 59	22 08			22 14	22 19	22 29	22 44	22 49	22 59	23 08
London Liverpool St 15 ⊖	d	20 35											21 35												
Stratford 7 ⊖	d	20 43											21 43												
Barking ⊖	d	20 50	20 55	21 05	21 14		21 20		21 25	21 35	21 45		21 50	21 55	22 05	22 14			22 20	22 25	22 35	22 50	22 55	23 05	23 14
Upminster ⊖	d		21 04	21 14	21 23				21 34	21 44	21 54			22 04	22 14	22 23				22 34	22 44		23 04	23 14	23 23
Ockendon	d			21 19						21 49					22 19						22 49			23 19	
Chafford Hundred	d			21 23						21 53					22 23						22 53			23 23	
West Horndon	d		21 09						21 39					22 09						22 39			23 09		
Laindon	d		21 14		21 31				21 44		22 02			22 14		22 31				22 44			23 14		23 31
Basildon	d		21 17		21 34				21 47		22 05			22 17		22 34				22 47			23 17		23 34
Dagenham Dock	d	20 55					21 25						21 55						22 25			22 55			
Rainham	d	20 59					21 29						21 59						22 29			22 59			
Purfleet	d	21 04					21 34						22 04						22 34			23 04			
Grays	d	21a12		21 27			21a40			21 57			22a12		22 27				22a40		22 57	23a10		23 27	
Tilbury Town 3	d			21 30						22 00					22 30						23 00			23 30	
East Tilbury	d			21 36						22 06					22 36						23 06			23 36	
Stanford-le-Hope	d			21 40						22 10					22 40						23 10			23 40	
Pitsea	d		21 21	21 48		←			21 51	22 18		←		22 21	22 48		←			22 51	23 18		23 22	23 48	
Benfleet	d		21 25	21 52	21 41	21 52			21 55	22 22	22 12	22 22		22 25	22 52	22 41	22 52			22 55	23 22		23 26	23 52	23 41
Leigh-on-Sea	d		21 30	→	21 45	21 56			22 00	→	22 16	22 26		22 30	→	22 45	22 56			23 00	23 26		23 30	→	23 45
Chalkwell	d		21 33		21 48	21 59			22 03		22 19	22 29		22 33		22 48	22 59			23 03	23 29		23 33		23 48
Westcliff	d		21 35		21 51	22 02			22 05		22 22	22 32		22 35		22 51	23 02			23 06	23 32		23 36		23 51
Southend Central	a		21 38		21 53	22 05			22 08		22 24	22 35		22 38		22 53	23 05			23 08	23 35		23 39		23 54
	d		21 38		21 53				22 08		22 24			22 38		22 53	23 05			23 08	23 35		23 39		23 54
Southend East	d		21 40		21 55				22 10		22 26			22 40		22 55	23 07			23 10	23 37		23 41		23 56
Thorpe Bay	d		21 44		21 59				22 14		22 30			22 44		22 59	23 10			23 14	23 41		23 45		23 59
Shoeburyness	a		21 48		22 03				22 18		22 34			22 48		23 03	23 15			23 18	23 47		23 51		00 06

		CC	CC		CC	CC	CC	CC	CC	CC
London Fenchurch St 7 ⊖	d		23 05		23 10		23 20	23 35	23 40	23 50
Limehouse	d		23 09		23 14		23 24	23 39	23 44	23 54
West Ham ⊖	d		23 14		23 19		23 29	23 44	23 49	23 59
London Liverpool St 15 ⊖	d									
Stratford 7 ⊖	d									
Barking ⊖	d		23 20		23 25		23 35	23 50	23 55	00 05
Upminster ⊖	d				23 34		23 44		00 04	00 14
Ockendon	d						23 49			00 19
Chafford Hundred	d						23 53			00 23
West Horndon	d				23 39				00 09	
Laindon	d				23 44				00 16	
Basildon	d				23 47				00 19	
Dagenham Dock	d		23 25					23 55		
Rainham	d		23 29					23 59		
Purfleet	d		23 34					00 04		
Grays	d		23 42				23 57	00a10		00 27
Tilbury Town 3	d		23 45				00 01			00 30
East Tilbury	d		23 51				00 06			00 36
Stanford-le-Hope	d		23 55			←	00 10			00 40
Pitsea	d	←	00 06		23 52	00 06	00 18		00 22	00 48
Benfleet	d	23 52	→		23 56	00 10	00 22		00 26	00 52
Leigh-on-Sea	d	23 56			23 59	00 15	00 27		00 31	00 56
Chalkwell	d	23 59			00 03	00 18	00 30		00 34	00 59
Westcliff	d	00 02			00 06	00 20	00 32		00 36	01 02
Southend Central	a	00 05			00 09	00 23	00 35		00 39	01 05
	d	00 05			00 09	00 23	00 35		00 40	01 05
Southend East	d	00 07			00 11	00 26	00 38		00 42	01 07
Thorpe Bay	d	00 11			00 15	00 29	00 41		00 46	01 11
Shoeburyness	a	00 17			00 21	00 36	00 48		00 52	01 17

Saturdays

		CC	CC	CC	CC	CC	CC	CC	CC	CC		CC	CC	CC	CC	CC	CC	CC	CC	CC		CC	CC	CC	CC
London Fenchurch St 7 ⊖	d	22p50	23p00		23p05	23p10		23p20	23p35	23p40		23p50	00 01		00 15	00 25			05 10	05 35		05 50	06 05	06 10	06 20
Limehouse	d	22p54			23p09	23p14		23p24	23p39	23p44		23p54			00 19	00 29			05 14	05 39		05 54	06 09	06 14	06 24
West Ham ⊖	d	22p59	23p08		23p14	23p19		23p29	23p44	23p49		23p59	00 09		00 24	00 34			05 19	05 44		05 59	06 14	06 19	06 29
London Liverpool St 15 ⊖	d																								
Stratford 7 ⊖	d																								
Barking ⊖	d	23p05	23p14		23p20	23p25		23p35	23p50	23p55		00 05	00 15		00 30	00 40			05 24	05 49		06 04	06 19	06 24	06 34
Upminster ⊖	d	23p14	23p23			23p34		23p44		00 04		00 14	00 24			00 49	05 05	05 27	05 32			06 12		06 32	06 42
Ockendon	d	23p19						23p49				00 19					05a12	05 32				06 18			06 48
Chafford Hundred	d	23p23						23p53				00 23						05 36				06 21			06 51
West Horndon	d					23p39				00 09						00 54			05 37					06 37	
Laindon	d		23p31			23p44				00 16			00 32			00 59			05 42					06 42	
Basildon	d		23p34			23p47				00 19			00 35			01 02			05 45					06 45	
Dagenham Dock	d				23p25				23p55						00 35					05 54			06 24		
Rainham	d				23p29				23p59						00 39					05 57			06 27		
Purfleet	d				23p34				00 04						00 44					06 03			06 33		
Grays	d	23p27			23p42			23p57	00a10			00 27			00a50			05a42		06a12		06 25	06a42		06 55
Tilbury Town 3	d	23p30			23p45			00 01				00 30										06 28			06 58
East Tilbury	d	23p36			23p51			00 06				00 36										06 34			07 04
Stanford-le-Hope	d	23p40			23p55		←	00 10				00 40										06 37			07 07
Pitsea	d	23p48		←	00 06	23p52	00 06	00 18		00 22		00 48		←		01 06			05 50			06 45		06 49	07 15
Benfleet	d	23p52	23p41	23p52	→	23p56	00 10	00 22		00 26		00 52	00 42	00 52		01 10			05 54			06 49		06 52	07 19
Leigh-on-Sea	d	→	23p45	23p56		23p59	00 15	00 27		00 31		→	00 46	00 56		01 14			05 58			06 53		06 57	07 23
Chalkwell	d		23p48	23p59		00 03	00 18	00 30		00 34			00 49	00 59		01 17			06 01			06 56		06 59	07 26
Westcliff	d		23p51	00 02		00 06	00 20	00 32		00 36			00 52	01 02		01 20			06 03			06 58		07 02	07 28
Southend Central	a		23p54	00 05		00 09	00 23	00 35		00 39			00 55	01 05		01 23			06 06			07 04		07 05	07 34
	d		23p54	00 05		00 09	00 23	00 35		00 40			00 55	01 05		01 23			06 07					07 06	
Southend East	d		23p56	00 07		00 11	00 26	00 38		00 42			00 57	01 07		01 25			06 09					07 08	
Thorpe Bay	d		23p59	00 11		00 15	00 29	00 41		00 46			01 01	01 11		01 29			06 12					07 10	
Shoeburyness	a		00 06	00 17		00 21	00 36	00 48		00 52			01 07	01 17		01 35			06 19					07 18	

Table I

Saturdays

London - Southend Central and Shoeburyness

Network Diagram - see first page of Table I

		CC	CC	CC	CC	CC		CC	CC	CC	CC	CC	CC	CC	CC	CC		CC	CC	CC	CC	CC	CC	CC	CC
London Fenchurch St 7	⊖ d	06 35	06 40	06 50	07 05	07 10		07 20	07 35	07 40	07 50	08 05	08 10	08 20	08 35	08 40		08 50	09 00		09 05	09 10	09 20	09 30	
Limehouse	d	06 39	06 44	06 54	07 09	07 14		07 24	07 39	07 44	07 54	08 09	08 14	08 24	08 39	08 44		08 54			09 09	09 14	09 24		
West Ham	⊖ d	06 44	06 49	06 59	07 14	07 19		07 29	07 44	07 49	07 59	08 14	08 19	08 29	08 44	08 49		08 59	09 08		09 14	09 19	09 29	09 38	
London Liverpool St 15	⊖ d																								
Stratford 7	⊖ d																								
Barking	⊖ d	06 49	06 54	07 04	07 19	07 24		07 34	07 49	07 54	08 04	08 19	08 24	08 34	08 49	08 54		09 04	09 13		09 19	09 24	09 34	09 43	
Upminster	⊖ d		07 02	07 12		07 32		07 42		08 02	08 12		08 32	08 42		09 02		09 12	09 21			09 32	09 42	09 51	
Ockendon	d			07 18				07 48			08 18			08 48				09 18					09 48		
Chafford Hundred	d			07 21				07 51			08 21			08 51				09 21					09 51		
West Horndon	d		07 07			07 37				08 07			08 37			09 07						09 37			
Laindon	d		07 12			07 42				08 12			08 42			09 12			09 29			09 42		09 59	
Basildon	d		07 15			07 45				08 15			08 45			09 15			09 32			09 45		10 02	
Dagenham Dock	d	06 54			07 24				07 54			08 24			08 54						09 24				
Rainham	d	06 57			07 27				07 57			08 27			08 57						09 27				
Purfleet	d	07 03			07 33				08 03			08 33			09 03						09 33				
Grays	d	07a12		07 25	07a42			07 55	08a12		08 25	08a42		08 55	09a12			09 25			09a42		09 55		
Tilbury Town 3	d			07 28				07 58			08 28			08 58				09 28					09 58		
East Tilbury	d			07 34				08 04			08 34			09 04				09 34					10 04		
Stanford-le-Hope	d			07 37				08 07			08 37			09 07				09 37					10 07		
Pitsea	d		07 19	07 45		07 49		08 15		08 19	08 45		08 49	09 15		09 19		09 45		←		09 49	10 15		←
Benfleet	d		07 22	07 49		07 52		08 19		08 22	08 49		08 52	09 19		09 22		09 49	09 38	09 49		09 52	10 19	10 08	10 19
Leigh-on-Sea	d		07 27	07 53		07 57		08 23		08 27	08 53		08 57	09 23		09 27		→	09 42	09 53		09 57	→	10 12	10 23
Chalkwell	d		07 29	07 56		07 59		08 26		08 29	08 56		08 59	09 26		09 29			09 45	09 56		09 59		10 15	10 26
Westcliff	d		07 32	07 58		08 02		08 28		08 32	08 58		09 02	09 28		09 32			09 47	09 58		10 02		10 17	10 28
Southend Central	a		07 35	08 04		08 05		08 34		08 35	09 04		09 05	09 34		09 35			09 50	10 04		10 05		10 20	10 34
	d		07 36			08 06				08 36			09 06			09 36			09 50			10 06		10 20	
Southend East	d		07 38			08 08				08 38			09 08			09 38			09 52			10 08		10 22	
Thorpe Bay	d		07 40			08 10				08 40			09 10			09 40			09 55			10 10		10 25	
Shoeburyness	a		07 48			08 18				08 48			09 18			09 48			10 02			10 18		10 32	

		CC		CC	CC	CC	CC	CC	CC	CC	CC	CC		CC	CC	CC	CC	CC	CC	CC	CC	CC		CC	CC
London Fenchurch St 7	⊖ d	09 35		09 40	09 50	10 00		10 05	10 10	10 20	10 30			10 35	10 40	10 50	11 00		11 05	11 10	11 20	11 30			11 35
Limehouse	d	09 39		09 44	09 54			10 09	10 14	10 24				10 39	10 44	10 54			11 09	11 14	11 24				11 39
West Ham	⊖ d	09 44		09 49	09 59	10 08		10 14	10 19	10 29	10 38			10 44	10 49	10 59	11 08		11 14	11 19	11 29	11 38			11 44
London Liverpool St 15	⊖ d																								
Stratford 7	⊖ d																								
Barking	⊖ d	09 49		09 54	10 04	10 13		10 19	10 24	10 34	10 43			10 49	10 54	11 04	11 13		11 19	11 24	11 34	11 43			11 49
Upminster	⊖ d			10 02	10 12	10 21			10 32	10 42	10 51				11 02	11 12	11 21			11 32	11 42	11 51			
Ockendon	d				10 18					10 48						11 18					11 48				
Chafford Hundred	d				10 21					10 51						11 21					11 51				
West Horndon	d			10 07					10 37						11 07					11 37					
Laindon	d			10 12		10 29			10 42		10 59				11 12		11 29			11 42		11 59			
Basildon	d			10 15		10 32			10 45		11 02				11 15		11 32			11 45		12 02			
Dagenham Dock	d	09 54						10 24						10 54					11 24						11 54
Rainham	d	09 57						10 27						10 57					11 27						11 57
Purfleet	d	10 03						10 33						11 03					11 33						12 03
Grays	d	10a12			10 25			10a42		10 55				11a12		11 25			11a42		11 55				12a12
Tilbury Town 3	d				10 28					10 58						11 28					11 58				
East Tilbury	d				10 34					11 04						11 34					12 04				
Stanford-le-Hope	d				10 37					11 07						11 37					12 08				
Pitsea	d			10 19	10 45		←		10 49	11 15		←			11 19	11 45		←		11 49	12 15			←	
Benfleet	d			10 22	10 49	10 38	10 49		10 52	11 19	11 08	11 19			11 22	11 49	11 38	11 49		11 52	12 19	12 08		12 19	
Leigh-on-Sea	d			10 27	→	10 42	10 53		10 57	→	11 12	11 23			11 27	→	11 42	11 53		11 57	→	12 12		12 23	
Chalkwell	d			10 29		10 45	10 56		10 59		11 15	11 26			11 29		11 45	11 56		11 59		12 15		12 26	
Westcliff	d			10 32		10 47	10 58		11 02		11 17	11 28			11 32		11 47	11 58		12 02		12 17		12 28	
Southend Central	a			10 35		10 50	11 04		11 05		11 20	11 34			11 35		11 50	12 04		12 05		12 20		12 34	
	d			10 36		10 50			11 06		11 20				11 36		11 50			12 06		12 20			
Southend East	d			10 38		10 52			11 08		11 22				11 38		11 52			12 08		12 22			
Thorpe Bay	d			10 40		10 55			11 10		11 25				11 40		11 55			12 10		12 25			
Shoeburyness	a			10 48		11 02			11 18		11 32				11 48		12 02			12 18		12 32			

		CC	CC	CC	CC	CC	CC	CC	and at the same minutes past each hour until	CC		CC	CC	CC	CC	CC	CC	CC	CC	CC		CC	CC	CC
London Fenchurch St 7	⊖ d	11 40	11 50	12 00		12 05	12 10	12 20		19 20		19 30		19 35	19 40	19 50	20 00		20 05	20 10		20 20	20 35	20 40
Limehouse	d	11 44	11 54			12 09	12 14	12 24		19 24				19 39	19 44	19 54			20 09	20 14		20 24	20 39	20 44
West Ham	⊖ d	11 49	11 59	12 08		12 14	12 19	12 29		19 29		19 38		19 44	19 49	19 59	20 08		20 14	20 19		20 29	20 44	20 49
London Liverpool St 15	⊖ d																							
Stratford 7	⊖ d																							
Barking	⊖ d	11 54	12 04	12 13		12 19	12 24	12 34		19 34		19 43		19 49	19 54	20 04	20 13		20 19	20 24		20 34	20 49	20 54
Upminster	⊖ d	12 02	12 12	12 21			12 32	12 42		19 42		19 51			20 02	20 12	20 21			20 32		20 42		21 02
Ockendon	d		12 18					12 48		19 48						20 18						20 48		
Chafford Hundred	d		12 21					12 51		19 51						20 21						20 51		
West Horndon	d	12 07					12 37								20 07					20 37				21 07
Laindon	d	12 12		12 29			12 42					19 59			20 12		20 29			20 42				21 12
Basildon	d	12 15		12 32			12 45					20 02			20 15		20 32			20 45				21 15
Dagenham Dock	d					12 24								19 54					20 24				20 54	
Rainham	d					12 27								19 57					20 27				20 57	
Purfleet	d					12 33								20 03					20 33				21 03	
Grays	d		12 25			12a42		12 55		19 55				20a12		20 25			20a42			20 55	21a12	
Tilbury Town 3	d		12 28					12 58		19 58						20 28						20 58		
East Tilbury	d		12 34					13 04		20 04						20 34						21 04		
Stanford-le-Hope	d		12 37					13 07		20 07						20 37						21 07		
Pitsea	d	12 19	12 45		←		12 49	13 15		20 15			←		20 19	20 45		←		20 49		21 15		21 19
Benfleet	d	12 22	12 49	12 38	12 49		12 52	13 19		20 19		20 08	20 19		20 22	20 49	20 38	20 49		20 52		21 19		21 22
Leigh-on-Sea	d	12 27	→	12 42	12 53		12 57	→		→		20 12	20 23		20 27	→	20 42	20 53		20 57		21 23		21 27
Chalkwell	d	12 29		12 45	12 56		12 59					20 15	20 26		20 29		20 45	20 56		20 59		21 26		21 29
Westcliff	d	12 32		12 47	12 58		13 02					20 17	20 28		20 32		20 47	20 58		21 02		21 28		21 32
Southend Central	a	12 35		12 50	13 04		13 05					20 20	20 34		20 35		20 50	21 04		21 05		21 34		21 35
	d	12 36		12 50			13 06					20 20			20 36		20 50			21 06				21 36
Southend East	d	12 38		12 52			13 08					20 22			20 38		20 52			21 08				21 38
Thorpe Bay	d	12 40		12 55			13 10					20 25			20 40		20 55			21 10				21 40
Shoeburyness	a	12 48		13 02			13 18					20 32			20 48		21 02			21 18				21 48

Table 1

Saturdays

London - Southend Central and Shoeburyness

Network Diagram - see first page of Table 1

			CC	CC	CC	CC	CC	CC		CC	CC	CC	CC	
London Fenchurch St 7	⊖	d	20 50	21 00		21 05	21 10	21 20		21 35	21 40	21 50	22 00	
Limehouse		d	20 54			21 09	21 14	21 24		21 39	21 44	21 54		
West Ham	⊖	d	20 59	21 08		21 14	21 19	21 29		21 44	21 49	21 59	22 08	
London Liverpool St 15	⊖	d												
Stratford 7	⊖	d												
Barking	⊖	d	21 04	21 13		21 19	21 24	21 34		21 49	21 54	22 04	22 13	
Upminster	⊖	d	21 12	21 21			21 32	21 42			22 02	22 12	22 21	
Ockendon		d	21 18					21 48				22 18		
Chafford Hundred		d	21 21					21 51				22 21		
West Horndon		d					21 37				22 07			
Laindon		d		21 29			21 42				22 12		22 29	
Basildon		d		21 32			21 45				22 15		22 32	
Dagenham Dock		d				21 24				21 54				
Rainham		d				21 27				21 57				
Purfleet		d				21 33				22 03				
Grays		d	21 25			21a42		21 55		22a12		22 25		
Tilbury Town 3		d	21 28					21 58				22 28		
East Tilbury		d	21 34					22 04				22 34		
Stanford-le-Hope		d	21 37					22 07				22 37		
Pitsea		d	21 45		←		21 49	22 15			22 19	22 45		←
Benfleet		d	21 49	21 38	21 49		21 52	22 19			22 22	22 49	22 38	22 49
Leigh-on-Sea		d	→	21 42	21 53		21 57	22 23			22 27	→	22 42	22 53
Chalkwell		d		21 45	21 56		21 59	22 26			22 29		22 45	22 56
Westcliff		d		21 47	21 58		22 02	22 28			22 32		22 47	22 58
Southend Central		a		21 50	22 04		22 05	22 34			22 35		22 50	23 04
		d		21 50			22 06				22 36		22 50	
Southend East		d		21 52			22 08				22 38		22 52	
Thorpe Bay		d		21 55			22 10				22 40		22 55	
Shoeburyness		a		22 02			22 18				22 48		23 02	

			CC	CC	CC	CC		CC	CC	CC	CC	CC	CC	CC
London Fenchurch St 7	⊖	d	22 05	22 10	22 20	22 35		22 40	22 50	23 05	23 10		23 20	23 35
Limehouse		d	22 09	22 14	22 24	22 39		22 44	22 54	23 09	23 14		23 24	23 39
West Ham	⊖	d	22 14	22 19	22 29	22 44		22 49	22 59	23 14	23 19		23 29	23 44
London Liverpool St 15	⊖	d												
Stratford 7	⊖	d												
Barking	⊖	d	22 19	22 24	22 34	22 49		22 54	23 04	23 19	23 24		23 34	23 49
Upminster	⊖	d		22 32	22 42			23 02	23 12		23 32		23 42	
Ockendon		d			22 48				23 18				23 48	
Chafford Hundred		d			22 51				23 21				23 51	
West Horndon		d		22 37				23 07			23 37			
Laindon		d		22 42				23 12			23 42			
Basildon		d		22 45				23 15			23 45			
Dagenham Dock		d	22 24			22 54				23 24				23 54
Rainham		d	22 27			22 57				23 27				23 57
Purfleet		d	22 33			23 03				23 33				00 03
Grays		d	22a42		22 55	23a12			23 25	23 38			23 55	00 08
Tilbury Town 3		d			22 58				23 28	23 41			23 58	00 11
East Tilbury		d			23 04				23 34	23 47			00 04	00 17
Stanford-le-Hope		d			23 07				23 37	23 50		←	00 07	00 20
Pitsea		d		22 49	23 15			23 19	23 45	23 58	23 49	23 58	00 15	00 28
Benfleet		d		22 52	23 19			23 22	23 49	→	23 52	00 01	00 19	→
Leigh-on-Sea		d		22 57	23 23			23 27	23 53		23 57	00 06	00 23	
Chalkwell		d		22 59	23 26			23 29	23 56		23 59	00 08	00 26	
Westcliff		d		23 02	23 28			23 32	23 58		00 02	00 11	00 28	
Southend Central		a		23 05	23 31			23 35	00 01		00 05	00 14	00 31	
		d		23 06	23 31			23 36	00 01		00 06	00 14	00 31	
Southend East		d		23 08	23 34			23 38	00 04		00 08	00 16	00 34	
Thorpe Bay		d		23 10	23 36			23 41	00 06		00 11	00 19	00 36	
Shoeburyness		a		23 18	23 43			23 48	00 13		00 18	00 26	00 43	

			CC	CC		CC
London Fenchurch St 7	⊖	d	23 40			23 50
Limehouse		d	23 44			23 54
West Ham	⊖	d	23 49			23 59
London Liverpool St 15	⊖	d				
Stratford 7	⊖	d				
Barking	⊖	d	23 54			00 04
Upminster	⊖	d	00 02			00 12
Ockendon		d				00 18
Chafford Hundred		d				00 21
West Horndon		d	00 07			
Laindon		d	00 12			
Basildon		d	00 15			
Dagenham Dock		d				
Rainham		d				
Purfleet		d				
Grays		d				00 25
Tilbury Town 3		d				00 28
East Tilbury		d				00 34
Stanford-le-Hope		d		←		00 37
Pitsea		d	00 19	00 28		00 45
Benfleet		d	00 22	00 31		00 49
Leigh-on-Sea		d	00 27	00 36		00 53
Chalkwell		d	00 29	00 38		00 56
Westcliff		d	00 32	00 41		00 58
Southend Central		a	00 35	00 44		01 01
		d	00 36	00 44		01 01
Southend East		d	00 38	00 46		01 04
Thorpe Bay		d	00 41	00 49		01 06
Shoeburyness		a	00 48	00 56		01 13

Table I

Sundays

London - Southend Central and Shoeburyness

Network Diagram - see first page of Table I

		CC A	CC A	CC A	CC A	CC A	CC A	CC A	CC A	CC A	CC	CC	CC	CC	CC	CC	CC	CC	CC		CC	CC	CC	CC
London Fenchurch St 7 ⊖	d	22p50	23p05	23p10		23p20	23p35	23p40		23p50	00 10	00 40	06 40		07 10	07 40	07 50	08 10				08 40	08 50	09 10
Limehouse	d	22p54	23p09	23p14		23p24	23p39	23p44		23p54	00 14	00 44	06 44		07 14	07 44	07 54	08 14				08 44	08 54	09 14
West Ham ⊖	d	22p59	23p14	23p19		23p29	23p44	23p49		23p59	00 19	00 49	06 49		07 19	07 49	07 59	08 19				08 49	08 59	09 19
London Liverpool St 15 ⊖	d																							
Stratford 7 ⊖	d																							
Barking ⊖	d	23p04	23p19	23p24		23p34	23p49	23p54		00 04	00 24	00 54	06 54	07 04	07 24	07 54	08 04	08 24	08 29		08 34	08 54	09 04	09 24
Upminster ⊖	d	23p12		23p32		23p42		00 02		00 12	00 32	01 02	07 02	07 12	07 32	08 02	08 12	08 32			08 42	09 02	09 12	09 32
Ockendon	d	23p18				23p48				00 18				07 18			08 18				08 48		09 18	
Chafford Hundred	d	23p21				23p51				00 21				07 21			08 21				08 51		09 21	
West Horndon	d			23p37				00 07			00 37	01 07	07 07		07 37	08 07		08 37				09 07		09 37
Laindon	d			23p42				00 12			00 42	01 12	07 12		07 42	08 12		08 42				09 12		09 42
Basildon	d			23p45				00 15			00 45	01 15	07 15		07 45	08 15		08 45				09 15		09 45
Dagenham Dock	d		23p24				23p54												08 33					
Rainham	d		23p27				23p57												08 37					
Purfleet	d		23p33				00 03												08 42					
Grays	d	23p25	23p38			23p55	00 08			00 25				07 25			08 25		08a50		08 55		09 25	
Tilbury Town 3	d	23p28	23p41			23p58	00 11			00 28				07 28			08 28				08 58		09 28	
East Tilbury	d	23p34	23p47			00 04	00 17			00 34				07 34			08 34				09 04		09 34	
Stanford-le-Hope	d	23p37	23p50		←	00 07	00 20		←	00 37				07 37			08 37				09 07		09 37	
Pitsea	d	23p45	23p58	23p49	23p58	00 15	00 28	00 19	00 28	00 45	00 49	01 19	07 19	07 45	07 49	08 19	08 45	08 49			09 15	09 19	09 45	09 49
Benfleet	d	23p49	→	23p52	00 01	00 19	→	00 22	00 31	00 49	00 52	01 22	07 22	07 49	07 52	08 22	08 49	08 52			09 19	09 22	09 49	09 52
Leigh-on-Sea	d	23p53		23p57	00 06	00 23		00 27	00 36	00 53	00 57	01 27	07 27	07 53	07 57	08 27	08 53	08 57			09 23	09 27	09 53	09 57
Chalkwell	d	23p56		23p59	00 08	00 26		00 29	00 38	00 56	00 59	01 29	07 29	07 56	07 59	08 29	08 56	08 59			09 26	09 29	09 56	09 59
Westcliff	d	23p58		00 02	00 11	00 28		00 32	00 41	00 58	01 02	01 32	07 32	07 58	08 02	08 32	08 58	09 02			09 28	09 32	09 58	10 02
Southend Central	a	00 01		00 05	00 14	00 31		00 35	00 44	01 01	01 05	01 35	07 34	08 04	08 05	08 34	09 04	09 05			09 34	09 35	10 04	10 05
	d	00 01		00 06	00 14	00 31		00 36	00 44	01 01	01 06	01 36	07 36		08 06	08 36		09 06				09 36		10 06
Southend East	d	00 04		00 08	00 16	00 34		00 38	00 46	01 04	01 08	01 38	07 38		08 08	08 38		09 08				09 38		10 08
Thorpe Bay	d	00 06		00 11	00 19	00 36		00 41	00 49	01 06	01 11	01 41	07 40		08 10	08 40		09 10				09 40		10 10
Shoeburyness	a	00 13		00 18	00 26	00 43		00 48	00 56	01 13	01 18	01 48	07 48		08 18	08 48		09 18				09 48		10 18

		CC	CC	CC	CC	CC		CC	CC	and at the same minutes past each hour until	CC	CC	CC	CC	CC		CC	CC	CC	CC	CC	CC	CC	CC
London Fenchurch St 7 ⊖	d			09 40	09 50	10 10			10 20		20 20	20 40	20 50	21 10			21 20	21 40	21 50	22 10	22 40	22 50	23 10	23 40
Limehouse	d			09 44	09 54	10 14			10 24		20 24	20 44	20 54	21 14			21 24	21 44	21 54	22 14	22 44	22 54	23 14	23 44
West Ham ⊖	d			09 49	09 59	10 19			10 29		20 29	20 49	20 59	21 19			21 29	21 49	21 59	22 19	22 49	22 59	23 19	23 49
London Liverpool St 15 ⊖	d																							
Stratford 7 ⊖	d																							
Barking ⊖	d	09 29	09 34	09 54	10 04	10 24		10 29	10 34		20 34	20 54	21 04	21 24	21 29		21 34	21 54	22 04	22 24	22 54	23 04	23 24	23 54
Upminster ⊖	d		09 42	10 02	10 12	10 32			10 42		20 42	21 02	21 12	21 32			21 42	22 02	22 12	22 32	23 02	23 12	23 32	00 02
Ockendon	d		09 48		10 18				10 48		20 48		21 18				21 48		22 18			23 18		
Chafford Hundred	d		09 51		10 21				10 51		20 51		21 21				21 51		22 21			23 21		
West Horndon	d			10 07		10 37						21 07		21 37				22 07		22 37	23 07		23 37	00 07
Laindon	d			10 12		10 42						21 12		21 42				22 12		22 42	23 12		23 42	00 12
Basildon	d			10 15		10 45						21 15		21 45				22 15		22 45	23 15		23 45	00 15
Dagenham Dock	d	09 33						10 33							21 33									
Rainham	d	09 37						10 37							21 37									
Purfleet	d	09 42						10 42							21 42									
Grays	d	09a50	09 55		10 25			10a50	10 55		20 55		21 25		21a50		21 55		22 25			23 25		
Tilbury Town 3	d		09 58		10 28				10 58		20 58		21 28				21 58		22 28			23 28		
East Tilbury	d		10 04		10 34				11 04		21 04		21 34				22 04		22 34			23 34		
Stanford-le-Hope	d		10 07		10 37				11 07		21 07		21 37				22 07		22 37			23 37		
Pitsea	d		10 15	10 19	10 45	10 49			11 15		21 15	21 19	21 45	21 49			22 15	22 19	22 45	22 49	23 19	23 45	23 49	00 19
Benfleet	d		10 19	10 22	10 49	10 52			11 19		21 19	21 22	21 49	21 52			22 19	22 22	22 49	22 52	23 22	23 49	23 52	00 22
Leigh-on-Sea	d		10 23	10 27	10 53	10 57			11 23		21 23	21 27	21 53	21 57			22 23	22 27	22 53	22 57	23 27	23 53	23 57	00 27
Chalkwell	d		10 26	10 29	10 56	10 59			11 26		21 26	21 29	21 56	21 59			22 26	22 29	22 56	22 59	23 29	23 56	23 59	00 29
Westcliff	d		10 28	10 32	10 58	11 02			11 28		21 28	21 32	21 58	22 02			22 28	22 32	22 58	23 02	23 32	23 58	00 02	00 32
Southend Central	a		10 34	10 35	11 04	11 05			11 34		21 34	21 35	22 04	22 05			22 31	22 35	23 01	23 05	23 35	00 01	00 05	00 35
	d			10 36		11 06						21 36		22 06			22 31	22 36	23 01	23 06	23 36	00 01	00 06	00 36
Southend East	d			10 38		11 08						21 38		22 08			22 33	22 38	23 03	23 08	23 38	00 03	00 08	00 38
Thorpe Bay	d			10 40		11 10						21 40		22 10			22 36	22 40	23 06	23 10	23 40	00 06	00 10	00 40
Shoeburyness	a			10 48		11 18						21 48		22 18			22 43	22 48	23 13	23 18	23 48	00 13	00 18	00 48

A not 11 December

Shoeburyness and Southend Central - London

Network Diagram - see first page of Table 1

Miles	Miles	Miles			CC MX	CC MX	CC MX	CC	CC	CC	CC	CC	CC		CC	CC	CC	CC	CC	CC	CC	CC	CC		CC
0	0	—	**Shoeburyness**	d			23p05		04 20		04 40	05 00			05 13	05 23			05 27		05 45				05 56
1½	1½	—	Thorpe Bay	d			23p09		04 24		04 44	05 04			05 17	05 27			05 31		05 49		05 56		06 00
3	3	—	Southend East	d			23p12		04 27		04 47	05 07			05 20	05 30			05 34		05 52		05 59		06 03
3¾	3¾	—	**Southend Central**	a			23p14		04 29		04 49	05 09			05 22	05 32			05 36		05 54		06 01		06 05
—	—	—		d	22p50		23p15		04 29		04 50	05 09			05 23	05 32			05 36	05 47	05 54		06 02		06 06
4¾	4¾	—	Westcliff	d	22p53		23p17		04 31		04 52	05 11			05 25	05 34			05 38	05 49	05 56		06 04		06 08
5½	5½	—	Chalkwell	d	22p55		23p19		04 34		04 54	05 14			05 27	05 37			05 41	05 51	05 59		06 06		06 10
7	7	—	Leigh-on-Sea	d	22p58		23p22		04 37		04 57	05 17			05 30	05 40			05 44	05 54	06 02		06 09		06 13
10¼	10¼	—	Benfleet	d	23p03		23p27		04 41		05 02	05 21			05 35	05 44			05 48	05 59	06 07		06 14		06 18
13	13	—	Pitsea	d	23p07		23p32		04 45		05 06	05 25			05 39	05 48			05 52	06 04	06 11		06 24		
—	18	—	Stanford-le-Hope	d	23p14			04 29			05 13				05 46				05 59	06 11			06 31		
—	20	—	East Tilbury	d	23p18			04 33			05 17				05 50				06 03	06 15			06 35		
—	23¾	—	**Tilbury Town 3**	d	23p24			04 39			05 23				05 56				06 09	06 21			06 41		
—	25½	0	Grays	d	23p27	23p33		04 42		05 09	05 26		05 48		06 00			06 11	06 13	06 25		06 29	06 45		
—	29¼	—	Purfleet	d		23p38					05 32				06 05				06 19			06 34	06 51		
—	32½	—	Rainham	d		23p43					05 37				06 10				06 24			06 40	06 56		
—	34¾	—	Dagenham Dock	d		23p47					05 40				06 14				06 27			06 43	07 00		
15	—	—	Basildon	d			23p36		04 49			05 29				05 52					06 15				06 25
16¾	—	—	Laindon	d			23p39		04 52			05 32				05 55					06 18				06 29
20¼	—	—	West Horndon	d			23p44		04 57			05 37				06 00					06 23				
—	—	2½	Chafford Hundred	d	23p31			04 46		05 13			05 52					06 15		06 30					
—	—	4½	Ockendon	d	23p35			04 50		05 17			05 56					06 19		06 37					
24¼	—	7½	Upminster	⊖ d	23p42		23p50	04 57	05 03	05a22		05 43	06 01			06 06	←	06a25		06 44	06 29				06 38
32	37¾	—	Barking	⊖ d	23p50	23p55	23p58	05 06	05 11		05 46	05 51	06 10		06 20	06 15	06 20		06 33	→	06 38	06 50	07 06		
—	—	—	Stratford 7	⊖ a		00 09		05 14							↪								↪		
—	—	—	**London Liverpool St 15**	⊖ a		00 20		05 27																	
35	40¾	—	West Ham	⊖ d	23p56		00 04		05 17		05 52	05 57	06 15			06 21	06 26		06 39		06 44	06 55			
37¾	43½	—	Limehouse	d	00 01		00 09		05 22		05 57	06 02	06 20			06 26	06 31		06 44		06 49	07 00			06 55
39½	45¼	—	**London Fenchurch St 7**	⊖ a	00 05		00 13		05 28		06 03	06 08	06 27			06 30	06 37		06 50		06 53	↪			07 01

		CC	CC	CC	CC	CC	CC	CC	CC		CC	CC	CC	CC	CC	CC	CC	CC	CC		CC	CC	CC	CC	CC
Shoeburyness	d			06 04			06 13		06 17			06 28			06 33	06 46								06 51	
Thorpe Bay	d			06 08		06 13	06 17		06 21			06 32			06 37	06 50								06 55	
Southend East	d			06 11		06 16	06 20		06 24			06 35			06 40	06 53								06 58	
Southend Central	a			06 13		06 18	06 22		06 26			06 37			06 42	06 55								07 00	
	d			06 13		06 18	06 23		06 26			06 38			06 42	06 55								07 00	
Westcliff	d			06 15		06 20	06 25		06 28			06 40			06 44	06 57								07 02	
Chalkwell	d			06 18		06 23	06 27		06 31			06 42			06 47	07 00								07 05	
Leigh-on-Sea	d			06 21		06 26	06 30		06 34			06 45			06 50	07 03								07 08	
Benfleet	d			06 26		06 31	06 35		06 39			06 50			06 55	07 08								07 13	
Pitsea	d			06 30		06 39			06 43					06 52	06 59				07 00				07 16	07 17	
Stanford-le-Hope	d					06 46								06 59					07 07				07 23		
East Tilbury	d					06 50								07 03					07 11				07 27		
Tilbury Town 3	d					06 56								07 09					07 18				07 33		
Grays	d				06 50	07 00								07 13					07 22		07 30		07 37		
Purfleet	d					07 05								07 18							07 35				
Rainham	d					07 11								07 24							07 41				
Dagenham Dock	d					07 14								07 27							07 44				
Basildon	d			06 34			06 42		06 47			06 57			07 03	07 15								07 21	
Laindon	d			06 37					06 50						07 07			07 20				07 37		07 25	
West Horndon	d			06 42					06 55						07 12			07 25				07 42			
Chafford Hundred	d				06 54														07 26				07 41		
Ockendon	d		←		06 58						←								07 30				07 46		
Upminster	⊖ d		06 44	06 48	07 05			←	07 01		07 05	07 10	←		07 18		←	07 30	07 37			07 47	07 54		←
Barking	⊖ d			06 57	→	07 21	07 01	07 06	07 10		07 14		07 21	07 34	07 27		07 34	07 39	07 46		07 51	07 56		07 42	07 46
Stratford 7	⊖ a					↪								↪					↪		↪	↪			
London Liverpool St 15	⊖ a																								
West Ham	⊖ d	←	06 58	07 03			07 07	07 12	07 16		07 20	07 23	07 26				07 39	07 44						07 47	07 52
Limehouse	d	07 00	07 03					07 17	07 21		07 25		07 32		07 36		07 44	07 49						07 52	
London Fenchurch St 7	⊖ a	07 07	07 09	07 13			07 17	07 23	07 27		07 31	07 34	07 38		07 42	07 45	07 51	07 56					08 17	07 59	08 02

		CC	CC	CC	CC		CC	CC	CC	CC	CC	CC	CC	CC	CC		CC	CC	CC	CC	CC	CC	CC	CC	CC
Shoeburyness	d		07 03					07 17					07 22		07 34								07 49		
Thorpe Bay	d		07 07				07 12	07 21					07 26		07 38						07 42		07 53		
Southend East	d		07 10				07 15	07 24					07 29		07 41						07 45		07 56		
Southend Central	a		07 12				07 17	07 26					07 31		07 43						07 47		07 58		
	d	07 08	07 13				07 18	07 27					07 32		07 43						07 48		07 59		
Westcliff	d	07 10	07 15				07 20	07 29					07 34		07 45						07 50		08 01		
Chalkwell	d	07 12	07 17				07 22	07 31					07 36		07 48						07 52		08 03		
Leigh-on-Sea	d	07 16	07 20				07 25	07 34					07 39		07 51						07 55		08 06		
Benfleet	d	07 20	07 25				07 30	07 39					07 44		07 56						08 00		08 11		
Pitsea	d	07 25					07 34					07 41	07 48						07 48	07 52	08 04				
Stanford-le-Hope	d	07 32									07 42	07 48							07 55	08 00					08 11
East Tilbury	d	07 36										07 52								08 04					08 15
Tilbury Town 3	d	07 42										07 58								08 10					08 21
Grays	d	07 46									07 52	08 02							08 06	08 14					08 25
Purfleet	d	07 51										08 07								08 19					
Rainham	d	07 57										08 13								08 25					
Dagenham Dock	d	08 00										08 16								08 28					
Basildon	d		07 32				07 39						07 53								08 09				
Laindon	d						07 42			07 50			07 56					08 07			08 12			08 22	
West Horndon	d									07 55								08 12						08 27	
Chafford Hundred	d										07 57								08 10						08 29
Ockendon	d										08 01								08 17						08 33
Upminster	⊖ d			←	←				←	08 02	08 09			←	08 13		←	08 17	08 24			←	08 28	08 32	08 40
Barking	⊖ d	08 07		07 51	07 56		07 59		08 07	08 10	08 18	08 23	08 13	08 18			08 23	08 26		08 35	08 29	08 35		08 42	08 50
Stratford 7	⊖ a	↪									↪	↪								↪					↪
London Liverpool St 15	⊖ a																								
West Ham	⊖ d			07 57	08 01				08 12	08 16			08 19	08 23			08 28	08 32	08 38		08 35			08 47	
Limehouse	d		07 59	08 02	08 06		08 08	08 13	08 17	08 21			08 24		08 30		08 33	08 37			08 40	08 45	08 48	08 52	
London Fenchurch St 7	⊖ a		08 05	08 08	08 12		08 15	08 19	08 24	08 27			08 31	08 34	08 37		08 40	08 43	08 48		08 46	08 51	08 55	08 58	

Table I

Mondays to Fridays

Shoeburyness and Southend Central - London

Network Diagram - see first page of Table I

			CC	CC	CC	CC	CC	CC	CC	CC	CC		CC	CC	CC	CC	CC	CC	CC	CC	CC		CC	CC	CC
Shoeburyness	d			07 54		08 05					08 11			08 25					08 40						09 05
Thorpe Bay	d			07 58		08 09					08 15			08 29					08 44						09 09
Southend East	d			08 01		08 12					08 18			08 32					08 47						09 12
Southend Central	a			08 03		08 14					08 20			08 34					08 49						09 14
	d			08 03		08 15					08 20			08 34					08 50				09 06		09 15
Westcliff	d			08 05		08 17					08 22			08 36					08 52				09 08		09 17
Chalkwell	d			08 08		08 19					08 25			08 39					08 54				09 10		09 19
Leigh-on-Sea	d			08 11		08 22					08 28			08 42					08 57				09 13		09 22
Benfleet	d			08 16		08 27					08 33			08 47					09 02				09 18		09 27
Pitsea	d		08 12	08 20						08 35	08 37			08 51				08 54	09 06					09 08	09 32
Stanford-le-Hope	d		08 19						08 33	08 42								09 01						09 16	
East Tilbury	d		08 23						08 37	08 46								09 05						09 20	
Tilbury Town 3	d		08 29						08 43	08 52								09 11						09 26	
Grays	d		08 33						08 47	08 56						09 03		09 15						09 29	
Purfleet	d		08 39						08 52							09 08		09 20							
Rainham	d		08 44						08 58							09 13		09 26							
Dagenham Dock	d		08 48						09 01							09 17		09 29							
Basildon	d			08 24							08 41			08 55					09 11				09 25		09 36
Laindon	d			08 28				08 38			08 45						09 04		09 14		09 17		09 28		09 39
West Horndon	d							08 43									09 10				09 22				09 44
Chafford Hundred	d									09 01														09 34	
Ockendon	d									09 05					←									09 38	
Upminster ⊖	d				←		←	08 49		09 12	08 54		←	09 06	09 12		09 16			←	09 28		09 38	09 45	09 50
Barking ⊖	d		08 54	08 45	08 50		08 54	08 58	09 08	→	09 03		09 08		09 21	09 23	09 25	09 35	09 30	09 35	09 37		09 46	09 53	09 58
Stratford 7 ⊖	a		→						→									→							
London Liverpool St 15 ⊖	a																								
West Ham ⊖	d			08 51	08 55		09 00	09 04			09 09				09 26	09 29	09 31				09 43		09 52	09 59	10 04
Limehouse	d			08 56			09 05	09 09			09 14		09 17	09 23	09 31	09 34	09 36			09 44	09 48		09 57	10 04	10 09
London Fenchurch St 7 ⊖	a			09 02	09 06	09 08	09 11	09 15			09 20		09 23	09 29	09 38	09 40	09 43		09 45	09 51	09 54		10 03	10 08	10 13

		CC	CC	CC	CC	CC	CC		CC	CC	CC		CC	CC	CC	CC		CC	CC	CC	CC	CC	CC	CC
Shoeburyness	d			09 20		09 35				09 50				15 05				15 20		15 35			15 50	
Thorpe Bay	d			09 24		09 39				09 54				15 09				15 24		15 39			15 54	
Southend East	d			09 27		09 42				09 57				15 12				15 27		15 42			15 57	
Southend Central	a			09 29		09 44				09 59				15 14				15 29		15 44			15 59	
	d		09 20	09 30		09 45			09 50	10 00				15 15		15 20		15 30		15 45		15 48	16 00	
Westcliff	d		09 23	09 32		09 47			09 53	10 02				15 17		15 23		15 32		15 47		15 50	16 02	
Chalkwell	d		09 25	09 34		09 49			09 55	10 04				15 19		15 25		15 34		15 49		15 53	16 04	
Leigh-on-Sea	d		09 28	09 37		09 52			09 58	10 07				15 22		15 28		15 37		15 52		15 56	16 07	
Benfleet	d		09 33	09 42		09 57			10 03	10 12				15 27		15 33		15 42		15 57		16 00	16 12	
Pitsea	d		09 37			10 02			10 07					15 32		15 37				16 02		16 04		
Stanford-le-Hope	d		09 44						10 14							15 44						16 11		
East Tilbury	d		09 48						10 18							15 48						16 15		
Tilbury Town 3	d		09 54						10 24			and at the same minutes past each hour until				15 54						16 21		
Grays	d	09 46	09 57				10 16		10 27						15 46	15 57					16 16	16 26		
Purfleet	d	09 51					10 21								15 51						16 21			
Rainham	d	09 56					10 26								15 56						16 26			
Dagenham Dock	d	10 00					10 30								16 00						16 30			
Basildon	d			09 49		10 06				10 19				15 36				15 49		16 06			16 19	
Laindon	d			09 52		10 09				10 22				15 39				15 52		16 09			16 22	
West Horndon	d					10 14								15 44						16 14				
Chafford Hundred	d		10 01						10 31							16 01						16 30		
Ockendon	d		10 05		←				10 35		←		←			16 05			←			16 34		←
Upminster ⊖	d		10 12	10 02	10 12	10 20			10 42	10 32	10 42		15 42	15 50		16 12		16 02	16 12	16 20		16 41	16 30	16 41
Barking ⊖	d	10 06	→	10 10	10 20	10 28	10 36		→	10 40	10 50		15 50	15 58	16 06	→		16 10	16 20	16 28	16 36	→	16 38	16 49
Stratford 7 ⊖	a																							
London Liverpool St 15 ⊖	a																							
West Ham ⊖	d	10 11		10 16	10 26	10 34	10 41			10 46	10 56		15 56	16 04	16 11			16 17	16 26	16 34			16 44	
Limehouse	d	10 16			10 31	10 39	10 46				11 01		16 01	16 09	16 16				16 31	16 39				
London Fenchurch St 7 ⊖	a	10 21		10 24	10 35	10 43	10 51			10 54	11 05		16 05	16 13	16 21			16 26	16 36	16 43	16 48		16 52	17 03

		CC	CC		CC	CC	CC	CC	CC	CC	CC	CC B	CC		CC	CC	CC	CC	CC	CC	CC	CC	CC		CC
Shoeburyness	d	16 05					16 15			16 28						16 50		16 56							17 10
Thorpe Bay	d	16 09					16 19			16 32						16 54		17 00							17 14
Southend East	d	16 12					16 22			16 35						16 57		17 03							17 17
Southend Central	a	16 14					16 24			16 37						16 59		17 05							17 19
	d	16 15				16 19	16 25	16 31		16 38					16 53	17 00		17 06							17 19
Westcliff	d	16 17				16 21	16 27	16 33		16 40					16 55	17 02		17 08							17 21
Chalkwell	d	16 19				16 23	16 29	16 35		16 42					16 58	17 04		17 10							17 24
Leigh-on-Sea	d	16 22				16 26	16 32	16 38		16 45					17 01	17 07		17 13							17 27
Benfleet	d	16 27				16 31	16 37	16 43		16 50					17 05	17 12		17 18							17 32
Pitsea	d	16 31				16 35		16 47		16 54			16 57		17 09	17 16		17 22					17 28		17 36
Stanford-le-Hope	d					16 42							17 04							17 19			17 35		
East Tilbury	d					16 46							17 08							17 23			17 39		
Tilbury Town 3	d					16 52							17 14							17 29			17 46		
Grays	d		16 39		16 52	16 57							17 18				17 22			17 32	17 46		17 51		
Purfleet	d		16 44		16 57												17 27			17 38	17 51				
Rainham	d		16 49		17 02												17 32			17 43	17 56				
Dagenham Dock	d		16 53		17 06												17 36			17 46	18 00				
Basildon	d	16 35					16 43	16 51		16 58					17 13	17 20		17 26							17 40
Laindon	d	16 38								17 01		17 13			17 17							17 49			17 44
West Horndon	d	16 43								17 06					17 22							17 54			
Chafford Hundred	d					17 01							17 23										17 55		
Ockendon	d					17 08					←		17 32						←				18 01		
Upminster ⊖	d	16 48				17 15	16 54		←	17 11	17 15	17 23	17 39		17 28	17 31			17 39			18 00	18 08		
Barking ⊖	d	16 57	17 00		17 16	→	17 03	17 09	17 16	17 20	17 25	17 32	→		17 36	17 40	17 42	17 44	17 47	17 52	18 06	18 08	18 16		
Stratford 7 ⊖	a				→																				
London Liverpool St 15 ⊖	a																								
West Ham ⊖	d	17 02					17 09		17 22		17 31							17 49		17 58	18 11	18 14			
Limehouse	d	17 08	17 10				17 14			17 29		17 42								18 03		18 19			
London Fenchurch St 7 ⊖	a	17 12	17 15				17 18	17 24	17 30	17 33	17 39	17 46			17 49	17 52	17 54	17 58	18 00	18 08	18 20	18 23	18 29		18 11

Shoeburyness and Southend Central - London

Network Diagram - see first page of Table 1

		CC	CC	CC	CC	CC	CC	CC	CC		CC	CC	CC	CC	CC	CC	CC	CC	CC		CC	CC	CC	CC	CC
Shoeburyness	d			17 30		17 46			18 05				18 20			18 35			18 50				19 05		
Thorpe Bay	d			17 34		17 50			18 09				18 24			18 39			18 54				19 09		
Southend East	d			17 37		17 53			18 12				18 27			18 42			18 57				19 12		
Southend Central	a			17 39		17 55			18 14				18 29			18 44			18 59				19 15		
	d			17 40		17 56			18 15			18 20	18 30			18 45		18 48	19 00				19 15		19 20
Westcliff	d			17 42		17 58			18 17			18 23	18 32			18 47		18 51	19 02				19 17		19 23
Chalkwell	d			17 44		18 00			18 19			18 25	18 34			18 49		18 53	19 04				19 19		19 25
Leigh-on-Sea	d			17 47		18 03			18 22			18 28	18 37			18 52		18 56	19 07				19 22		19 28
Benfleet	d			17 52		18 08			18 27			18 33	18 42			18 57		19 01	19 12				19 27		19 33
Pitsea	d		17 45	17 56	18 01	18 12		18 14	18 32			18 37				19 02		19 05					19 32		19 37
Stanford-le-Hope	d		17 52		18 08			18 21				18 44						19 12							19 44
East Tilbury	d		17 56		18 12			18 25				18 48						19 16							19 48
Tilbury Town 3	d		18 02		18 18			18 31				18 54						19 22							19 54
Grays	d		18 06		18 22			18 35			18 54	18 57					19 22	19 25						19 48	19 57
Purfleet	d		18 11					18 40			18 59						19 27							19 53	
Rainham	d		18 16					18 45			19 04						19 32							19 58	
Dagenham Dock	d		18 20					18 49			19 08						19 36							20 02	
Basildon	d			18 00		18 16			18 36				18 49			19 06			19 19				19 36		
Laindon	d	18 06		18 03		18 19			18 39				18 52			19 09			19 22				19 39		
West Horndon	d	18 11				18 24			18 44							19 14							19 44		
Chafford Hundred	d				18 27							19 02						19 29							20 01
Ockendon	d				18 33		←					19 07			←			19 34				←			20 05
Upminster ⊖	d	18 17			18 39	18 31	18 39		18 50			19 13	19 02	←	19 13	19 20		19 40	19 32		←	19 40	19 50		20 12
Barking ⊖	d	18 25	18 27		→	18 39		18 55	18 58		19 14	→	19 10	19 14	19 22	19 28	19 42	→	19 40		19 42	19 50	19 58	20 12	→
Stratford 7 ⊖	a										↪						↪							↪	
London Liverpool St 15 ⊖	a																								
West Ham ⊖	d	18 30	18 33	18 26		18 45		19 00	19 04				19 16	19 20	19 27	19 34			19 46		19 48	19 56	20 04		
Limehouse	d	18 35	18 38			18 50		19 05	19 09						19 32	19 39					19 53	20 01	20 09		
London Fenchurch St 7 ⊖	a	18 39	18 42	18 34		18 54	18 59	19 10	19 13				19 24	19 28	19 37	19 43			19 54		19 58	20 05	20 13		

		CC	CC	CC	CC		CC	CC	CC	CC	CC	CC	CC	CC		CC	CC	CC	CC	CC	CC	CC	CC	CC
Shoeburyness	d	19 20			19 35				19 50			20 05			20 20			20 35			21 05			21 20	
Thorpe Bay	d	19 24			19 39				19 54			20 09			20 24			20 39			21 09			21 24	
Southend East	d	19 27			19 42				19 57			20 12			20 27			20 42			21 12			21 27	
Southend Central	a	19 29			19 44				19 59			20 14			20 29			20 44			21 14			21 29	
	d	19 30			19 45			19 50	20 00			20 15		20 20	20 30			20 45		20 50	21 15		21 20	21 30	
Westcliff	d	19 32			19 47			19 53	20 02			20 17		20 23	20 32			20 47		20 53	21 17		21 23	21 32	
Chalkwell	d	19 34			19 49			19 55	20 04			20 19		20 25	20 34			20 49		20 55	21 19		21 25	21 34	
Leigh-on-Sea	d	19 37			19 52			19 58	20 07			20 22		20 28	20 37			20 52		20 58	21 22		21 28	21 37	
Benfleet	d	19 42			19 57			20 03	20 12			20 27		20 33	20 42			20 57		21 03	21 27		21 33	21 42	
Pitsea	d				20 02			20 07				20 32		20 37				21 02		21 07	21 32		21 37		
Stanford-le-Hope	d							20 14						20 44						21 14			21 44		
East Tilbury	d							20 18						20 48						21 18			21 48		
Tilbury Town 3	d							20 24						20 54						21 24			21 54		
Grays	d						20 16	20 27					20 46	20 57					21 16	21 27		21 46	21 57		
Purfleet	d						20 21						20 51						21 21			21 51			
Rainham	d						20 26						20 56						21 26			21 56			
Dagenham Dock	d						20 30						21 00						21 30			22 00			
Basildon	d	19 49			20 06				20 19			20 36			20 49			21 06			21 36			21 49	
Laindon	d	19 52			20 09				20 22			20 39			20 52			21 09			21 39			21 52	
West Horndon	d				20 14							20 44						21 14			21 44				
Chafford Hundred	d							20 31						21 01						21 31			22 01		
Ockendon	d			←				20 35		←				21 05			←			21 35			22 05		←
Upminster ⊖	d	20 02	←	20 12	20 20			20 42	20 32	20 42		20 50		21 12	21 02		21 12	21 20		21 42	21 50		22 12	22 02	22 12
Barking ⊖	d	20 10	20 12	20 20	20 28		20 36	→	20 40	20 50	20 51	20 58	21 06	→	21 10		21 20	21 28	21 36	21 50	21 58	22 06	→	22 10	22 20
Stratford 7 ⊖	a		20 21								21 00		21 15												
London Liverpool St 15 ⊖	a		20 33								21 12		21 26												
West Ham ⊖	d	20 16		20 26	20 34		20 41		20 46	20 56		21 04			21 16		21 26	21 34	21 41	21 56	22 04	22 11		22 16	22 26
Limehouse	d			20 31	20 39		20 46			21 01		21 09					21 31	21 39	21 46	22 01	22 09	22 16			22 31
London Fenchurch St 7 ⊖	a	20 25		20 35	20 43		20 51		20 54	21 05		21 13			21 24		21 35	21 43	21 52	22 05	22 13	22 21		22 24	22 35

			CC	CC	CC	CC	CC	CC	CC	CC	CC		CC
Shoeburyness	d		21 35			22 05			22 35				23 05
Thorpe Bay	d		21 39			22 09			22 39				23 09
Southend East	d		21 42			22 12			22 42				23 12
Southend Central	a		21 45			22 14			22 44				23 14
	d		21 45		21 50	22 15		22 20	22 45	22 50			23 15
Westcliff	d		21 47		21 53	22 17		22 23	22 47	22 53			23 17
Chalkwell	d		21 49		21 55	22 19		22 25	22 49	22 55			23 19
Leigh-on-Sea	d		21 52		21 58	22 22		22 28	22 52	22 58			23 22
Benfleet	d		21 57		22 03	22 27		22 33	22 57	23 03			23 27
Pitsea	d		22 02		22 07	22 32		22 37	23 02	23 07			23 32
Stanford-le-Hope	d				22 14			22 44		23 14			
East Tilbury	d				22 18			22 48		23 18			
Tilbury Town 3	d				22 24			22 54		23 24			
Grays	d			22 16	22 27		22 46	22 57		23 27	23 33		
Purfleet	d			22 21			22 51				23 38		
Rainham	d			22 26			22 56				23 43		
Dagenham Dock	d			22 30			23 00				23 47		
Basildon	d		22 06			22 36			23 06				23 36
Laindon	d		22 09			22 39			23 09				23 39
West Horndon	d		22 14			22 44			23 14				23 44
Chafford Hundred	d				22 31			23 01		23 31			
Ockendon	d				22 35			23 05		23 35			
Upminster ⊖	d		22 20		22 42	22 50		23 12	23 20	23 42			23 50
Barking ⊖	d		22 28	22 36	22 50	22 58	23 06	23 20	23 28	23 50	23 55		23 58
Stratford 7 ⊖	a										00 09		
London Liverpool St 15 ⊖	a										00 20		
West Ham ⊖	d		22 34	22 41	22 56	23 04	23 11	23 26	23 34	23 56			00 04
Limehouse	d		22 39	22 46	23 01	23 09	23 16	23 31	23 39	00 01			00 09
London Fenchurch St 7 ⊖	a		22 43	22 52	23 05	23 13	23 21	23 35	23 43	00 05			00 13

Table 1

Shoeburyness and Southend Central - London

Network Diagram - see first page of Table 1

		CC	CC	CC	CC	CC	CC	CC	CC	CC		CC	CC	CC	CC	CC	CC	CC	CC	CC		CC	CC	CC	CC
Shoeburyness	d			23p05		04 20		05 05				05 35			06 05			06 35				07 05			07 35
Thorpe Bay	d			23p09		04 23		05 08				05 38			06 08			06 38				07 08			07 38
Southend East	d			23p12		04 26		05 11				05 41			06 11			06 41				07 11			07 41
Southend Central	a			23p14		04 28		05 13				05 43			06 13			06 43				07 13			07 43
	d	22p50		23p15		04 29		05 14		05 20		05 44		05 50	06 14		06 20	06 44		06 50		07 14		07 20	07 44
Westcliff	d	22p53		23p17		04 31		05 16		05 23		05 46		05 53	06 16		06 23	06 46		06 53		07 16		07 23	07 46
Chalkwell	d	22p55		23p19		04 33		05 18		05 25		05 48		05 55	06 18		06 25	06 48		06 55		07 18		07 25	07 48
Leigh-on-Sea	d	22p58		23p22		04 36		05 21		05 28		05 51		05 58	06 21		06 28	06 51		06 58		07 21		07 28	07 51
Benfleet	d	23p03		23p27		04 40		05 25		05 32		05 55		06 02	06 25		06 32	06 55		07 02		07 25		07 32	07 55
Pitsea	d	23p07		23p32		04 44		05 29		05 36		05 59		06 06	06 29		06 36	06 59		07 06		07 29		07 36	07 59
Stanford-le-Hope	d	23p14			04 29					05 42				06 12			06 42			07 12				07 42	
East Tilbury	d	23p18			04 32					05 45				06 15			06 45			07 15				07 45	
Tilbury Town 3	d	23p24			04 38					05 51				06 21			06 51			07 21				07 51	
Grays	d	23p27	23p33		04 41				05 48	05 54			06 18	06 24		06 48	06 54		07 18	07 24			07 48	07 54	
Purfleet	d		23p38						05 53				06 23			06 53			07 23				07 53		
Rainham	d		23p43						05 58				06 28			06 58			07 28				07 58		
Dagenham Dock	d		23p47						06 02				06 32			07 02			07 32				08 02		
Basildon	d			23p36		04 47		05 32				06 02			06 32			07 02				07 32			08 02
Laindon	d			23p39		04 50		05 35				06 05			06 35			07 05				07 35			08 05
West Horndon	d			23p44		04 55		05 40				06 10			06 40			07 10				07 40			08 10
Chafford Hundred	d	23p31			04 45					05 59				06 29			06 59			07 29				07 59	
Ockendon	d	23p35			04 49		05 16			06 02				06 32			07 02			07 32				08 02	
Upminster ⊖	d	23p42		23p50	04a57	05 02	05a23	05 46		06 09		06 16		06 39	06 46		07 09	07 16		07 39		07 46		08 09	08 16
Barking ⊖	d	23p50	23p55	23p58		05 10		05 54	06 08	06 17		06 24	06 38	06 47	06 54	07 08	07 17	07 24	07 38	07 47		07 54	08 08	08 17	08 24
Stratford 7 ⊖	a		00 09																						
London Liverpool St 15 ⊖	a		00 20																						
West Ham ⊖	d	23p56		00 04		05 16		06 00	06 14	06 23		06 30	06 44	06 53	07 00	07 14	07 23	07 30	07 44	07 53		08 00	08 14	08 23	08 30
Limehouse	d	00 01		00 09		05 21		06 05	06 19	06 28		06 35	06 49	06 58	07 05	07 19	07 28	07 35	07 49	07 58		08 05	08 19	08 28	08 35
London Fenchurch St 7 ⊖	a	00 05		00 13		05 27		06 12	06 26	06 34		06 42	06 56	07 04	07 12	07 26	07 34	07 42	07 56	08 04		08 12	08 26	08 34	08 42

		CC	CC	CC	CC	CC		CC	CC	CC	CC	CC	CC	CC	CC	CC		CC	CC	CC	CC	CC	CC	CC	CC
Shoeburyness	d			07 50				08 05			08 20			08 35				08 50			09 05			09 20	
Thorpe Bay	d			07 53				08 08			08 23			08 38				08 53			09 08			09 23	
Southend East	d			07 56				08 11			08 26			08 41				08 56			09 11			09 26	
Southend Central	a			07 58				08 13			08 28			08 43				08 58			09 13			09 28	
	d		07 50	07 59				08 14		08 20	08 29			08 44		08 50		08 59			09 14		09 20	09 29	
Westcliff	d		07 53	08 01				08 16		08 23	08 31			08 46		08 53		09 01			09 16		09 23	09 31	
Chalkwell	d		07 55	08 03				08 18		08 25	08 33			08 48		08 55		09 03			09 18		09 25	09 33	
Leigh-on-Sea	d		07 58	08 06				08 21		08 28	08 36			08 51		08 58		09 06			09 21		09 28	09 36	
Benfleet	d		08 02	08 10				08 25		08 32	08 40			08 55		09 02		09 10			09 25		09 32	09 40	
Pitsea	d		08 06					08 29		08 36				08 59		09 06					09 29		09 36		
Stanford-le-Hope	d		08 12							08 42						09 12							09 42		
East Tilbury	d		08 15							08 45						09 15							09 45		
Tilbury Town 3	d		08 21							08 51						09 21							09 51		
Grays	d	08 18	08 24						08 48	08 54					09 18	09 24						09 48	09 54		
Purfleet	d	08 23							08 53						09 23							09 53			
Rainham	d	08 28							08 58						09 28							09 58			
Dagenham Dock	d	08 32							09 02						09 32							10 02			
Basildon	d			08 16				08 32			08 46			09 02				09 16			09 32			09 46	
Laindon	d			08 19				08 35			08 49			09 05				09 19			09 35			09 49	
West Horndon	d							08 40						09 10							09 40				
Chafford Hundred	d		08 29							08 59						09 29							09 59		
Ockendon	d		08 32			←				09 02			←			09 32				←			10 02		
Upminster ⊖	d		08 39	08 28	←	08 39		08 46		09 09	08 58	←	09 09	09 16		09 39		09 28	←	09 39	09 46		10 09	09 58	←
Barking ⊖	d	08 38	→	08 36	08 38	08 47		08 54	09 08	→	09 06	09 08	09 17	09 24	09 38	→		09 36	09 38	09 47	09 54	10 08	→	10 06	10 08
Stratford 7 ⊖	a	↪							↪						↪							↪			
London Liverpool St 15 ⊖	a																								
West Ham ⊖	d			08 42	08 44	08 53		09 00			09 12	09 14	09 23	09 30				09 42	09 44	09 53	10 00			10 12	10 14
Limehouse	d				08 49	08 58		09 05				09 19	09 28	09 35					09 49	09 58	10 05				10 19
London Fenchurch St 7 ⊖	a			08 53	08 56	09 04		09 12			09 23	09 26	09 34	09 42				09 53	09 56	10 04	10 12			10 23	10 26

		CC		CC	CC	CC	CC	CC	CC	CC	CC	CC		CC	CC	CC	CC	CC	CC	CC	CC	CC		CC	CC
Shoeburyness	d			09 35			09 50			10 05				10 20			10 35			10 50				11 05	
Thorpe Bay	d			09 38			09 53			10 08				10 23			10 38			10 53				11 08	
Southend East	d			09 41			09 56			10 11				10 26			10 41			10 56				11 11	
Southend Central	a			09 43			09 58			10 13				10 28			10 43			10 58				11 13	
	d			09 44		09 50	09 59			10 14		10 20		10 29			10 44		10 50	10 59				11 14	
Westcliff	d			09 46		09 53	10 01			10 16		10 23		10 31			10 46		10 53	11 01				11 16	
Chalkwell	d			09 48		09 55	10 03			10 18		10 25		10 33			10 48		10 55	11 03				11 18	
Leigh-on-Sea	d			09 51		09 58	10 06			10 21		10 28		10 36			10 51		10 58	11 06				11 21	
Benfleet	d			09 55		10 02	10 10			10 25		10 32		10 40			10 55		11 02	11 10				11 25	
Pitsea	d			09 59		10 06				10 29		10 36					10 59		11 06					11 29	
Stanford-le-Hope	d					10 12						10 42							11 12						
East Tilbury	d					10 15						10 45							11 15						
Tilbury Town 3	d					10 21						10 51							11 21						
Grays	d				10 18	10 24					10 48	10 54						11 18	11 24						11 48
Purfleet	d				10 23						10 53							11 23							11 53
Rainham	d				10 28						10 58							11 28							11 58
Dagenham Dock	d				10 32						11 02							11 32							12 02
Basildon	d			10 02			10 16			10 32				10 46			11 02			11 16				11 32	
Laindon	d			10 05			10 19			10 35				10 49			11 05			11 19				11 35	
West Horndon	d			10 10						10 40							11 10							11 40	
Chafford Hundred	d					10 29						10 59							11 29						
Ockendon	d	←				10 32			←			11 02				←			11 32			←			
Upminster ⊖	d	10 09		10 16		10 39	10 28	←	10 39	10 46		11 09		10 58	←	11 09	11 16		11 39	11 28	←	11 39		11 46	
Barking ⊖	d	10 17		10 24	10 38	→	10 36	10 38	10 47	10 54	11 08	→		11 06	11 08	11 17	11 24	11 38	→	11 36	11 38	11 47		11 54	12 08
Stratford 7 ⊖	a				↪						↪							↪							↪
London Liverpool St 15 ⊖	a																								
West Ham ⊖	d	10 23		10 30			10 42	10 44	10 53	11 00				11 12	11 14	11 23	11 30			11 42	11 44	11 53		12 00	
Limehouse	d	10 28		10 35				10 49	10 58	11 05					11 19	11 28	11 35				11 49	11 58		12 05	
London Fenchurch St 7 ⊖	a	10 34		10 42			10 53	10 56	11 04	11 12				11 23	11 26	11 34	11 42			11 53	11 56	12 04		12 12	

Table I

Saturdays

Shoeburyness and Southend Central - London

Network Diagram - see first page of Table I

		CC	CC	CC	CC	CC	CC	CC		CC	CC	CC	CC	CC	CC	CC	CC	CC		CC	CC	CC	CC	CC	CC
Shoeburyness	d		11 20			11 35				11 50			12 05			12 20				12 35			12 50		
Thorpe Bay	d		11 23			11 38				11 53			12 08			12 23				12 38			12 53		
Southend East	d		11 26			11 41				11 56			12 11			12 26				12 41			12 56		
Southend Central	a		11 28			11 43				11 58			12 13			12 28				12 43			12 58		
	d	11 20	11 29			11 44		11 50		11 59			12 14		12 20	12 29				12 44		12 50	12 59		
Westcliff	d	11 23	11 31			11 46		11 53		12 01			12 16		12 23	12 31				12 46		12 53	13 01		
Chalkwell	d	11 25	11 33			11 48		11 55		12 03			12 18		12 25	12 33				12 48		12 55	13 03		
Leigh-on-Sea	d	11 28	11 36			11 51		11 58		12 06			12 21		12 28	12 36				12 51		12 58	13 06		
Benfleet	d	11 32	11 40			11 55		12 02		12 10			12 25		12 32	12 40				12 55		13 02	13 10		
Pitsea	d	11 36				11 59		12 06					12 29		12 36					12 59		13 06			
Stanford-le-Hope	d	11 42						12 12							12 42							13 12			
East Tilbury	d	11 45						12 15							12 45							13 15			
Tilbury Town 3	d	11 51						12 21							12 51							13 21			
Grays	d	11 54					12 18	12 24						12 48	12 54						13 18	13 24			
Purfleet	d						12 23							12 53							13 23				
Rainham	d						12 28							12 58							13 28				
Dagenham Dock	d						12 32							13 02							13 32				
Basildon	d		11 46			12 02				12 16			12 32			12 46				13 02			13 16		
Laindon	d		11 49			12 05				12 19			12 35			12 49				13 05			13 19		
West Horndon	d					12 10							12 40							13 10					
Chafford Hundred	d	11 59						12 29							12 59							13 29			
Ockendon	d	12 02			←			12 32				←			13 02			←				13 32			←
Upminster ⊖	d	12 09	11 58	←	12 09	12 16		12 39		12 28	←	12 39	12 46		13 09	12 58	←	13 09		13 16		13 39	13 28	←	13 39
Barking ⊖	d	↪	12 06	12 08	12 17	12 24	12 38	↪		12 36	12 38	12 47	12 54	13 08	↪	13 06	13 08	13 17		13 24	13 38	↪	13 36	13 38	13 47
Stratford 7 ⊖	a						↪							↪							↪				
London Liverpool St 15 ⊖	a																								
West Ham ⊖	d		12 12	12 14	12 23	12 30				12 42	12 44	12 53	13 00			13 12	13 14	13 23		13 30			13 42	13 44	13 53
Limehouse	d			12 19	12 28	12 35					12 49	12 58	13 05				13 19	13 28		13 35				13 49	13 58
London Fenchurch St 7 ⊖	a		12 23	12 26	12 34	12 42				12 53	12 56	13 04	13 12			13 23	13 26	13 34		13 42			13 53	13 56	14 04

		CC	CC	CC		CC	CC	CC	CC	CC	CC	CC	CC	CC		CC	CC	CC	CC	CC	CC	CC	CC	CC	
Shoeburyness	d	13 05				13 20			13 35			13 50				14 05			14 20			14 35			
Thorpe Bay	d	13 08				13 23			13 38			13 53				14 08			14 23			14 38			
Southend East	d	13 11				13 26			13 41			13 56				14 11			14 26			14 41			
Southend Central	a	13 13				13 28			13 43			13 58				14 13			14 28			14 43			
	d	13 14		13 20		13 29			13 44		13 50	13 59				14 14		14 20	14 29			14 44		14 50	
Westcliff	d	13 16		13 23		13 31			13 46		13 53	14 01				14 16		14 23	14 31			14 46		14 53	
Chalkwell	d	13 18		13 25		13 33			13 48		13 55	14 03				14 18		14 25	14 33			14 48		14 55	
Leigh-on-Sea	d	13 21		13 28		13 36			13 51		13 58	14 06				14 21		14 28	14 36			14 51		14 58	
Benfleet	d	13 25		13 32		13 40			13 55		14 02	14 10				14 25		14 32	14 40			14 55		15 02	
Pitsea	d	13 29		13 36					13 59		14 06					14 29		14 36				14 59		15 06	
Stanford-le-Hope	d			13 42							14 12							14 42						15 12	
East Tilbury	d			13 45							14 15							14 45						15 15	
Tilbury Town 3	d			13 51							14 21							14 51						15 21	
Grays	d		13 48	13 54						14 18	14 24						14 48	14 54					15 18	15 24	
Purfleet	d		13 53							14 23							14 53						15 23		
Rainham	d		13 58							14 28							14 58						15 28		
Dagenham Dock	d		14 02							14 32							15 02						15 32		
Basildon	d	13 32				13 46			14 02			14 16				14 32			14 46			15 02			
Laindon	d	13 35				13 49			14 05			14 19				14 35			14 49			15 05			
West Horndon	d	13 40							14 10							14 40						15 10			
Chafford Hundred	d			13 59							14 29							14 59						15 29	
Ockendon	d			14 02				←			14 32			←				15 02			←			15 32	
Upminster ⊖	d	13 46		14 09		13 58	←	14 09	14 16		14 39	14 28	←	14 39		14 46		15 09	14 58	←	15 09	15 16		15 39	
Barking ⊖	d	13 54	14 08	↪		14 06	14 08	14 17	14 24	14 38	↪	14 36	14 38	14 47		14 54	15 08	↪	15 06	15 08	15 17	15 24	15 38	↪	
Stratford 7 ⊖	a		↪							↪							↪						↪		
London Liverpool St 15 ⊖	a																								
West Ham ⊖	d	14 00				14 12	14 14	14 23	14 30			14 42	14 44	14 53		15 00			15 12	15 14	15 23	15 30			
Limehouse	d	14 05					14 19	14 28	14 35				14 49	14 58		15 05				15 19	15 28	15 35			
London Fenchurch St 7 ⊖	a	14 12				14 23	14 26	14 34	14 42			14 53	14 56	15 04		15 12			15 23	15 26	15 34	15 42			

		CC	CC	CC	CC	CC	CC	CC	CC	CC		CC	CC	CC	CC	CC	CC	CC	CC	CC		CC	CC	CC	CC
Shoeburyness	d	14 50			15 05			15 20				15 35			15 50			16 05				16 20			16 35
Thorpe Bay	d	14 53			15 08			15 23				15 38			15 53			16 08				16 23			16 38
Southend East	d	14 56			15 11			15 26				15 41			15 56			16 11				16 26			16 41
Southend Central	a	14 58			15 13			15 28				15 43			15 58			16 13				16 28			16 43
	d	14 59			15 14		15 20	15 29				15 44		15 50	15 59			16 14		16 20		16 29			16 44
Westcliff	d	15 01			15 16		15 23	15 31				15 46		15 53	16 01			16 16		16 23		16 31			16 46
Chalkwell	d	15 03			15 18		15 25	15 33				15 48		15 55	16 03			16 18		16 25		16 33			16 48
Leigh-on-Sea	d	15 06			15 21		15 28	15 36				15 51		15 58	16 06			16 21		16 28		16 36			16 51
Benfleet	d	15 10			15 25		15 32	15 40				15 55		16 02	16 10			16 25		16 32		16 40			16 55
Pitsea	d				15 29		15 36					15 59		16 06				16 29		16 36					16 59
Stanford-le-Hope	d						15 42							16 12						16 42					
East Tilbury	d						15 45							16 15						16 45					
Tilbury Town 3	d						15 51							16 21						16 51					
Grays	d					15 48	15 54						16 18	16 24					16 48	16 54					
Purfleet	d					15 53							16 23						16 53						
Rainham	d					15 58							16 28						16 58						
Dagenham Dock	d					16 02							16 32						17 02						
Basildon	d	15 16			15 32			15 46				16 02			16 16			16 32				16 46			17 02
Laindon	d	15 19			15 35			15 49				16 05			16 19			16 35				16 49			17 05
West Horndon	d				15 40							16 10						16 40							17 10
Chafford Hundred	d						15 59							16 29						16 59					
Ockendon	d			←			16 02			←				16 32			←			17 02				←	
Upminster ⊖	d	15 28	←	15 39	15 46		16 09	15 58	←	16 09		16 16		16 39	16 28	←	16 39	16 46		17 09		16 58	←	17 09	17 16
Barking ⊖	d	15 36	15 38	15 47	15 54	16 08	↪	16 06	16 08	16 17		16 24	16 38	↪	16 36	16 38	16 47	16 54	17 08	↪		17 06	17 08	17 17	17 24
Stratford 7 ⊖	a					↪							↪						↪						
London Liverpool St 15 ⊖	a																								
West Ham ⊖	d	15 42	15 44	15 53	16 00			16 12	16 14	16 23		16 30			16 42	16 44	16 53	17 00				17 12	17 14	17 23	17 30
Limehouse	d		15 49	15 58	16 05				16 19	16 28		16 35				16 49	16 58	17 05					17 19	17 28	17 35
London Fenchurch St 7 ⊖	a	15 53	15 56	16 04	16 12			16 23	16 26	16 34		16 42			16 53	16 56	17 04	17 12				17 23	17 26	17 34	17 42

Shoeburyness and Southend Central - London

Network Diagram - see first page of Table I

		CC	CC	CC	CC	CC		CC	CC	CC	CC	CC	CC	CC	CC	CC		CC	CC	CC	CC	CC	CC	CC	CC
Shoeburyness	d			16 50				17 05			17 20			17 35				17 50			18 05			18 20	
Thorpe Bay	d			16 53				17 08			17 23			17 38				17 53			18 08			18 23	
Southend East	d			16 56				17 11			17 26			17 41				17 56			18 11			18 26	
Southend Central	a			16 58				17 13			17 28			17 43				17 58			18 13			18 28	
	d		16 50	16 59				17 14		17 20	17 29			17 44		17 50		17 59			18 14		18 20	18 29	
Westcliff	d		16 53	17 01				17 16		17 23	17 31			17 46		17 53		18 01			18 16		18 23	18 31	
Chalkwell	d		16 55	17 03				17 18		17 25	17 33			17 48		17 55		18 03			18 18		18 25	18 33	
Leigh-on-Sea	d		16 58	17 06				17 21		17 28	17 36			17 51		17 58		18 06			18 21		18 28	18 36	
Benfleet	d		17 02	17 10				17 25		17 32	17 40			17 55		18 02		18 10			18 25		18 32	18 40	
Pitsea	d		17 06					17 29		17 36				17 59		18 06					18 29		18 36		
Stanford-le-Hope	d		17 12							17 42						18 12							18 42		
East Tilbury	d		17 15							17 45						18 15							18 45		
Tilbury Town [3]	d		17 21							17 51						18 21							18 51		
Grays	d	17 18	17 24						17 48	17 54					18 18	18 24						18 48	18 54		
Purfleet	d	17 23							17 53						18 23							18 53			
Rainham	d	17 28							17 58						18 28							18 58			
Dagenham Dock	d	17 32							18 02						18 32							19 02			
Basildon	d			17 16				17 32			17 46			18 02				18 16			18 32			18 46	
Laindon	d			17 19				17 35			17 49			18 05				18 19			18 35			18 49	
West Horndon	d							17 40						18 10							18 40				
Chafford Hundred	d		17 29							17 59						18 29							18 59		
Ockendon	d		17 32			←				18 02			←			18 32				←			19 02		
Upminster ⊖	d		17 39	17 28	←	17 39		17 46		18 09	17 58	←	18 09	18 16		18 39		18 28	←	18 39	18 46		19 09	18 58	←
Barking ⊖	d	17 38	→	17 36	17 38	17 47		17 54	18 08	→	18 06	18 08	18 17	18 24	18 38	→		18 36	18 38	18 47	18 54	19 08	→	19 06	19 08
Stratford [7] ⊖	a	↪							↪						↪							↪			
London Liverpool St [15] ⊖	a																								
West Ham ⊖	d			17 42	17 44	17 53		18 00			18 12	18 14	18 23	18 30				18 42	18 44	18 53	19 00			19 12	19 14
Limehouse	d				17 49	17 58		18 05				18 19	18 28	18 35					18 49	18 58	19 05				19 19
London Fenchurch St [7] ⊖	a			17 53	17 56	18 04		18 12			18 23	18 26	18 34	18 42				18 53	18 56	19 04	19 12			19 23	19 26

		CC		CC	CC	CC	CC	CC	CC	CC	CC	CC		CC	CC	CC	CC	CC	CC	CC	CC	CC		CC	CC
Shoeburyness	d			18 35			18 50			19 05				19 20			19 35			19 50				20 05	
Thorpe Bay	d			18 38			18 53			19 08				19 23			19 38			19 53				20 08	
Southend East	d			18 41			18 56			19 11				19 26			19 41			19 56				20 11	
Southend Central	a			18 43			18 58			19 13				19 28			19 43			19 58				20 13	
	d			18 44		18 50	18 59			19 14		19 20		19 29			19 44		19 50	19 59				20 14	
Westcliff	d			18 46		18 53	19 01			19 16		19 23		19 31			19 46		19 53	20 01				20 16	
Chalkwell	d			18 48		18 55	19 03			19 18		19 25		19 33			19 48		19 55	20 03				20 18	
Leigh-on-Sea	d			18 51		18 58	19 06			19 21		19 28		19 36			19 51		19 58	20 06				20 21	
Benfleet	d			18 55		19 02	19 10			19 25		19 32		19 40			19 55		20 02	20 10				20 25	
Pitsea	d			18 59		19 06				19 29		19 36					19 59		20 06					20 29	
Stanford-le-Hope	d					19 12						19 42							20 12						
East Tilbury	d					19 15						19 45							20 15						
Tilbury Town [3]	d					19 21						19 51							20 21						
Grays	d				19 18	19 24					19 48	19 54						20 18	20 24						20 48
Purfleet	d				19 23						19 53							20 23							20 53
Rainham	d				19 28						19 58							20 28							20 58
Dagenham Dock	d				19 32						20 02							20 32							21 02
Basildon	d			19 02			19 16			19 32				19 46			20 02			20 16				20 32	
Laindon	d			19 05			19 19			19 35				19 49			20 05			20 19				20 35	
West Horndon	d			19 10						19 40							20 10							20 40	
Chafford Hundred	d					19 29						19 59							20 29						
Ockendon	d	←				19 32			←			20 02				←			20 32			←			
Upminster ⊖	d	19 09		19 16		19 39	19 28	←	19 39	19 46		20 09		19 58	←	20 09	20 16		20 39	20 28	←	20 39		20 46	
Barking ⊖	d	19 17		19 24	19 38	→	19 36	19 38	19 47	19 54	20 08	→		20 06	20 08	20 17	20 24	20 38	→	20 36	20 38	20 47		20 54	21 08
Stratford [7] ⊖	a				↪						↪							↪							
London Liverpool St [15] ⊖	a																								
West Ham ⊖	d	19 23		19 30			19 42	19 44	19 53	20 00				20 12	20 14	20 23	20 30			20 42	20 44	20 53		21 00	21 14
Limehouse	d	19 28		19 35				19 49	19 58	20 05					20 19	20 28	20 35				20 49	20 58		21 05	21 19
London Fenchurch St [7] ⊖	a	19 34		19 42			19 53	19 56	20 04	20 12				20 23	20 26	20 34	20 42			20 53	20 56	21 04		21 12	21 26

		CC	CC	CC	CC	CC	CC	CC		CC	CC	CC	CC	CC	CC	CC	CC	CC		CC	CC	CC	CC	CC	
Shoeburyness	d		20 35			20 50				21 05			21 35			22 05				22 35			23 05		
Thorpe Bay	d		20 38			20 53				21 08			21 38			22 08				22 38			23 08		
Southend East	d		20 41			20 56				21 11			21 41			22 11				22 41			23 11		
Southend Central	a		20 43			20 58				21 13			21 43			22 13				22 43			23 13		
	d	20 20	20 44		20 50	20 59				21 14		21 20	21 44		21 50	22 14		22 20		22 44		22 50	23 14	23 20	
Westcliff	d	20 23	20 46		20 53	21 01				21 16		21 23	21 46		21 53	22 16		22 23		22 46		22 53	23 16	23 23	
Chalkwell	d	20 25	20 48		20 55	21 03				21 18		21 25	21 48		21 55	22 18		22 25		22 48		22 55	23 18	23 25	
Leigh-on-Sea	d	20 28	20 51		20 58	21 06				21 21		21 28	21 51		21 58	22 21		22 28		22 51		22 58	23 21	23 28	
Benfleet	d	20 32	20 55		21 02	21 10				21 25		21 32	21 55		22 02	22 25		22 32		22 55		23 02	23 25	23 32	
Pitsea	d	20 36	20 59		21 06					21 29		21 36	21 59		22 06	22 29		22 36		22 59		23 06	23 29	23 36	
Stanford-le-Hope	d	20 42			21 12							21 42			22 12			22 42				23 12		23 42	
East Tilbury	d	20 45			21 15							21 45			22 15			22 45				23 15		23 45	
Tilbury Town [3]	d	20 51			21 21							21 51			22 21			22 51				23 21		23 51	
Grays	d	20 54		21 18	21 24						21 48	21 54		22 18	22 24		22 48	22 54			23 18	23 24		23 54	
Purfleet	d			21 23							21 53			22 23			22 53				23 23				
Rainham	d			21 28							21 58			22 28			22 58				23 28				
Dagenham Dock	d			21 32							22 02			22 32			23 02				23 32				
Basildon	d		21 02			21 16				21 32			22 02			22 32				23 02			23 32		
Laindon	d		21 05			21 19				21 35			22 05			22 35				23 05			23 35		
West Horndon	d		21 10							21 40			22 10			22 40				23 10			23 40		
Chafford Hundred	d	20 59			21 29							21 59			22 29			22 59				23 29		23 59	
Ockendon	d	21 02			21 32			←				22 02			22 32			23 02				23 32		00 02	
Upminster ⊖	d	21 09	21 16		21 39	21 28	←	21 39		21 46		22 09	22 16		22 39	22 46		23 09		23 16		23 39	23 46	00 08	
Barking ⊖	d	21 17	21 24	21 38	→	21 36	21 38	21 47		21 54	22 08	22 17	22 24	22 38	22 47	22 54	23 08	23 17		23 24	23a39	23 47	23 55	00a18	
Stratford [7] ⊖	a			↪																					
London Liverpool St [15] ⊖	a																								
West Ham ⊖	d	21 23	21 30			21 42	21 44	21 53		22 00	22 14	22 23	22 30	22 44	22 53	23 00	23 14	23 23		23 30		23 53	00 01		
Limehouse	d	21 28	21 35				21 49	21 58		22 05	22 19	22 28	22 35	22 49	22 58	23 05	23 19	23 28		23 35		23 58	00 06		
London Fenchurch St [7] ⊖	a	21 34	21 42			21 53	21 56	22 04		22 12	22 26	22 34	22 42	22 56	23 04	23 12	23 26	23 34		23 42		00 04	00 12		

Table 1

Sundays

Shoeburyness and Southend Central - London

Network Diagram - see first page of Table 1

		CC A	CC A	CC A	CC	CC	CC	CC	CC	CC		CC	CC	CC	CC	CC	CC		CC		CC	CC	CC	CC
Shoeburyness	d		23p05		05 35	06 05	06 11	06 35	07 05	07 11		07 35	08 05			08 35					21 05			21 35
Thorpe Bay	d		23p08		05 38	06 08	06 14	06 38	07 08	07 14		07 38	08 08			08 38					21 08			21 38
Southend East	d		23p11		05 41	06 11	06 17	06 41	07 11	07 17		07 41	08 11			08 41					21 11			21 41
Southend Central	a		23p13		05 43	06 13	06 19	06 43	07 13	07 19		07 43	08 13			08 43					21 13			21 43
	d	22p50	23p14	23p20	05 44	06 14	06 20	06 44	07 14	07 20		07 44	08 14	08 20		08 44	08 50		20 50		21 14	21 20		21 44
Westcliff	d	22p53	23p16	23p23	05 46	06 16	06 23	06 46	07 16	07 23		07 46	08 16	08 23		08 46	08 53		20 53		21 16	21 23		21 46
Chalkwell	d	22p55	23p18	23p25	05 48	06 18	06 25	06 48	07 18	07 25		07 48	08 18	08 25		08 48	08 55		20 55		21 18	21 25		21 48
Leigh-on-Sea	d	22p58	23p21	23p28	05 51	06 21	06 28	06 51	07 21	07 28		07 51	08 21	08 28		08 51	08 58		20 58		21 21	21 28		21 51
Benfleet	d	23p02	23p25	23p32	05 55	06 25	06 32	06 55	07 25	07 32		07 55	08 25	08 32		08 55	09 02		21 02		21 25	21 32		21 55
Pitsea	d	23p06	23p29	23p36	05 59	06 29	06 36	06 59	07 29	07 36		07 59	08 29	08 36		08 59	09 06		21 06		21 29	21 36		21 59
Stanford-le-Hope	d	23p12		23p42			06 42			07 42				08 42			09 12	and at the same minutes past each hour until	21 12			21 42		
East Tilbury	d	23p15		23p45			06 45			07 45				08 45			09 15		21 15			21 45		
Tilbury Town 3	d	23p21		23p51			06 51			07 51				08 51			09 21		21 21			21 51		
Grays	d	23p24		23p54			06 54			07 54				08 54	08 59		09 24		21 24			21 54	21 59	
Purfleet	d														09 04								22 04	
Rainham	d														09 09								22 09	
Dagenham Dock	d														09 13								22 13	
Basildon	d		23p32		06 02	06 32		07 02	07 32			08 02	08 32			09 02					21 32			22 02
Laindon	d		23p35		06 05	06 35		07 05	07 35			08 05	08 35			09 05					21 35			22 05
West Horndon	d		23p40		06 10	06 40		07 10	07 40			08 10	08 40			09 10					21 40			22 10
Chafford Hundred	d	23p29		23p59			06 59			07 59				08 59			09 29		21 29			21 59		
Ockendon	d	23p32		00 02			07 02			08 02				09 02			09 32		21 32			22 02		
Upminster	⊖ d	23p39	23p46	00 08	06 16	06 46	07 09	07 16	07 46	08 09		08 16	08 46	09 09		09 16	09 39		21 39		21 46	22 09		22 16
Barking	⊖ d	23p47	23p55	00a18	06 25	06 55	07 17	07 25	07 55	08 17		08 25	08 55	09 17	09a20	09 25	09 47		21 47		21 55	22 17	22a20	22 25
Stratford 7	⊖ a																							
London Liverpool St 15	⊖ a																							
West Ham	⊖ d	23p53	00 01		06 31	07 01	07 23	07 31	08 01	08 23		08 31	09 01	09 23		09 31	09 53		21 53		22 01	22 23		22 31
Limehouse	d	23p58	00 06		06 36	07 06	07 28	07 36	08 06	08 28		08 36	09 06	09 28		09 36	09 58		21 58		22 06	22 28		22 36
London Fenchurch St 7	⊖ a	00 04	00 12		06 42	07 12	07 34	07 42	08 12	08 34		08 42	09 12	09 34		09 42	10 04		22 04		22 12	22 34		22 42

		CC	CC	CC
Shoeburyness	d	22 05		22 35
Thorpe Bay	d	22 08		22 38
Southend East	d	22 11		22 41
Southend Central	a	22 13		22 43
	d	22 14	22 20	22 44
Westcliff	d	22 16	22 23	22 46
Chalkwell	d	22 18	22 25	22 48
Leigh-on-Sea	d	22 21	22 28	22 51
Benfleet	d	22 25	22 32	22 55
Pitsea	d	22 29	22 36	22 59
Stanford-le-Hope	d		22 42	
East Tilbury	d		22 45	
Tilbury Town 3	d		22 51	
Grays	d		22 54	
Purfleet	d			
Rainham	d			
Dagenham Dock	d			
Basildon	d	22 32		23 02
Laindon	d	22 35		23 05
West Horndon	d	22 40		23 10
Chafford Hundred	d		22 59	
Ockendon	d		23 02	
Upminster	⊖ d	22 46	23 09	23 16
Barking	⊖ d	22 55	23 17	23 25
Stratford 7	⊖ a			
London Liverpool St 15	⊖ a			
West Ham	⊖ d	23 01	23 23	23 31
Limehouse	d	23 06	23 28	23 36
London Fenchurch St 7	⊖ a	23 12	23 34	23 42

A not 11 December

Table 1A

Mondays to Fridays

Tilbury Town - Tilbury Riverside

Bus Service

Network Diagram - see first page of Table 1

		CC	CC	CC	CC	CC	CC	CC	CC	CC		CC	CC	CC	CC	CC	CC	CC	CC	CC		CC	CC	CC	CC
Tilbury Town 3	d	05 40	06 18	06 50	07 18	07 45	08 13	08 38	09 03	09 33		10 03	10 33	11 03	11 33	12 03	12 33	13 03	13 33	14 03		14 33	15 03	15 33	16 03
Tilbury Riverside	a	05 47	06 25	06 57	07 25	07 52	08 20	08 45	09 10	09 40		10 10	10 40	11 10	11 40	12 10	12 40	13 10	13 40	14 10		14 40	15 10	15 40	16 10

		CC	CC	CC	CC	CC		CC
Tilbury Town 3	d	16 33	17 03	17 33	18 00	18 30		19 00
Tilbury Riverside	a	16 40	17 10	17 40	18 07	18 37		19 07

Saturdays

		CC	CC	CC	CC	CC	CC	CC	CC	CC		CC	CC	CC	CC	CC	CC	CC	CC	CC		CC	CC	CC	CC
Tilbury Town 3	d	05 40	06 15	07 01	07 31	08 01	08 31	09 01	09 31	10 01		10 31	11 01	11 31	12 01	12 31	13 01	13 31	14 01	14 31		15 01	15 31	16 01	16 31
Tilbury Riverside	a	05 47	06 22	07 08	07 38	08 08	08 38	09 08	09 38	10 08		10 38	11 08	11 38	12 08	12 38	13 08	13 38	14 08	14 38		15 08	15 38	16 08	16 38

		CC	CC	CC	CC	CC
Tilbury Town 3	d	17 01	17 31	18 01	18 31	19 01
Tilbury Riverside	a	17 08	17 38	18 08	18 38	19 08

No Sunday Service

Table 1A

Mondays to Fridays

Tilbury Riverside - Tilbury Town

Bus Service

Network Diagram - see first page of Table 1

		CC	CC	CC	CC	CC	CC	CC	CC	CC		CC	CC	CC	CC	CC	CC	CC	CC	CC		CC	CC	CC	CC
Tilbury Riverside	d	05 50	06 30	07 00	07 30	07 55	08 23	08 50	09 12	09 42		10 12	10 42	11 12	11 42	12 12	12 42	13 12	13 42	14 12		14 42	15 12	15 42	16 12
Tilbury Town 3	a	05 57	06 37	07 07	07 37	08 02	08 30	08 57	09 19	09 49		10 19	10 49	11 19	11 49	12 19	12 49	13 19	13 49	14 19		14 49	15 19	15 49	16 19

		CC	CC	CC	CC	CC		CC
Tilbury Riverside	d	16 40	17 15	17 45	18 15	18 40		19 10
Tilbury Town 3	a	16 47	17 22	17 52	18 22	18 47		19 17

Saturdays

		CC	CC	CC	CC	CC	CC	CC	CC	CC		CC	CC	CC	CC	CC	CC	CC	CC	CC		CC	CC	CC	CC
Tilbury Riverside	d	05 50	06 30	07 10	07 50	08 09	08 39	09 09	09 39	10 09		10 39	11 09	11 39	12 09	12 39	13 09	13 39	14 09	14 39		15 09	15 39	16 09	16 39
Tilbury Town 3	a	05 57	06 37	07 17	07 57	08 16	08 46	09 16	09 46	10 16		10 46	11 16	11 46	12 16	12 46	13 16	13 46	14 16	14 46		15 16	15 46	16 16	16 46

		CC	CC	CC	CC	CC
Tilbury Riverside	d	17 09	17 39	18 09	18 39	19 09
Tilbury Town 3	a	17 16	17 46	18 16	18 46	19 16

No Sunday Service

Table 4

Mondays to Fridays

Romford - Upminster

Network Diagram - see first page of Table 1

Miles			LE	LE	LE	LE	LE	LE	LE	and every 30 minutes until	LE
0	**Romford**	d	06 12	06 42	07 06	07 30	07 54	08 18	08 42		19 42
2	Emerson Park	d	06 16	06 46	07 10	07 34	07 58	08 22	08 46		19 46
3½	**Upminster** ⊖	a	06 20	06 50	07 14	07 38	08 02	08 26	08 50		19 50

Saturdays

		LE	and every 30 minutes until	LE
Romford	d	06 12		19 42
Emerson Park	d	06 16		19 46
Upminster ⊖	a	06 20		19 50

No Sunday Service

Table 4

Mondays to Fridays

Upminster - Romford

Network Diagram - see first page of Table 1

Miles			LE	LE	LE	LE	LE	LE	LE	and every 30 minutes until	LE
0	**Upminster** ⊖	d	06 24	06 54	07 18	07 42	08 06	08 30	08 54		19 54
1½	Emerson Park	d	06 28	06 58	07 22	07 46	08 10	08 34	08 58		19 58
3½	**Romford**	a	06 32	07 02	07 26	07 50	08 14	08 38	09 02		20 02

Saturdays

		LE	and every 30 minutes until	LE
Upminster ⊖	d	06 24		19 54
Emerson Park	d	06 28		19 58
Romford	a	06 32		20 02

No Sunday Service

Network Diagram for Tables 5, 10, 11

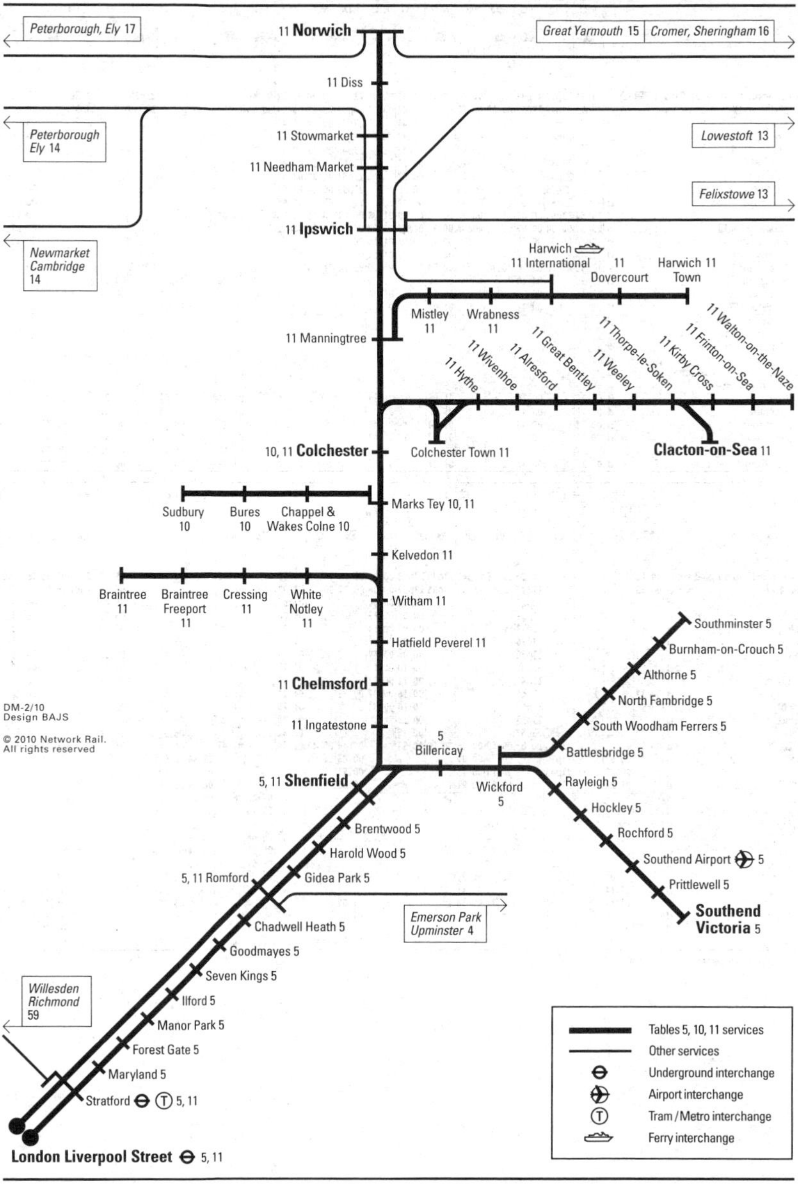

DM-2/10
Design BAJS

London - Shenfield, Southminster and Southend Victoria

Network Diagram - see first Page of Table 5

Miles	Miles			LE MO ■1	LE MO	LE MO ■1	LE MO ■1	LE MO	LE MO ■1	LE MO	LE MO	LE MX	LE MX	LE MX	LE MX ■1	LE MX ■1		LE TWThO ■1	LE TWThO ◇■1 🍵	LE TWThO ■1	LE TWThO ■1	LE TWThO ■1	LE TWThO	LE TWThO	LE TWThO
0	—	**London Liverpool Street** ■15 ⊖	d	23p15	23p35	23p45	00 02	00 05	00 15	00 35	00 45	23p35	00 20	00 32	00 46	00 50			23p30		23p50		23p55	00 01	←
4	—	Stratford ■7 ⊖	d	23p22	23p42	23p52	00 09	00 12	00 22	00 42	00 52	23p42	00 27	00 39	00 53	00 57			23b39		23p57		00 02	00 10	00 10
4½	—	Maryland	d		23p43			00 13		00 43		23p44	00 29	00 41									00 04	→	00 12
5¼	—	Forest Gate	d		23p45			00 15		00 45		23p46	00 31	00 43									00 06		00 14
6¼	—	Manor Park	d		23p47			00 17		00 47		23p48	00 33	00 45									00 08		00 16
7¼	—	Ilford ■2	d		23p50			00 20		00 50		23p51	00 36	00 48									00 11		00 19
8½	—	Seven Kings	d		23p53			00 23		00 53		23p53	00 38	00 50									00 13		00 21
9¼	—	Goodmayes	d		23p55			00 25		00 55		23p55	00 40	00 52									00 15		00 23
10	—	Chadwell Heath	d		23p57			00 27		00 57		23p57	00 42	00 54									00 17		00 25
12½	—	Romford	d	23p33	23p59	00 03		00 30	00 33	01 00	01 03	00 02	00 46	00 58		01 08							00 21		00 29
13½	—	Gidea Park ■2	d	23p37	00 04	00 07		00a36	00 37	01a06	01 07	00 05	00 50	01a02	01 07								00 25		00a32
15	—	Harold Wood	d	23p40	00 07	00 10			00 40		01 10	00 08	00 53										00 28		
18¼	—	Brentwood	d	23p44	00 11	00 14			00 44		01 14	00 12	00 57										00 32		
—	—	**Shenfield** ■3	a	23p50	00 18	00 20	00 30		00 50		01 20	00 18	01 03		01 17	01 20			00 02		00 20		00 38		
20¼	—	**Shenfield** ■3	d	23p50		00 20			00 50		01 20					01 20		23p43		00 05		00 23			
24¼	—	Billericay	d	23p56		00 26			00 56		01 26					01 26		23p49		00 11		00 29			
29	0	**Wickford** ■2	d	00 01		00 31			01 01		01 31					01 31		23p55		00 17		00 35			
—	2½	Battlesbridge	d																						
—	5	South Woodham Ferrers	d																						
—	8¼	North Fambridge	d																						
—	11¼	Althorne	d																						
—	14¼	Burnham-on-Crouch	d																						
—	16½	**Southminster**	a																						
33	—	Rayleigh	d	00 06		00 36			01 06		01 36					01 36		00 01		00 22		00 40			
36	—	Hockley	d	00 11		00 41			01 11		01 41					01 41		00 05		00 27		00 45			
38¾	—	Rochford	d	00 14		00 44			01 14		01 44					01 44		00 08		00 30		00 48			
39¾	—	Southend Airport ✈	d	00 17		00 47			01 17		01 47					01 47		00 11		00 33		00 51			
41	—	Prittlewell	d													01 50		00 14		00 36		00 54			
41½	—	**Southend Victoria**	a	00 27		00 57			01 27		01 57					01 58		00 18		00 40		00 58			

		LE TWThO ■1	LE TWThO ■1		LE FO ■1	LE FO	LE FO ■1	LE FO ■1	LE FO ■1	LE FO	LE FO	LE FO ■1	LE FO ■1	LE	LE ■1	LE ■1	LE ■1	LE		LE	LE ■1	LE ■1	LE	LE ■1	LE ■1
London Liverpool Street ■15 ⊖	d	00 18			23p15	23p20	23p45	23p45	23p48	23p50	00 01	00 15	00 18	00 55		05 23		05 28		05 37	05 52	05 55	06 00	06 02	
Stratford ■7 ⊖	d	00 25			23p22	23p27	23p52	23p52	23p55	23p57	00 08	00 22	00 25	01 02		05 30		05 35		05 44	06a01	06 02	06 07	06 09	
Maryland	d					23p29				23p59	00 10			01 04						05 46			06 09		
Forest Gate	d					23p31				00 01	00 12			01 06						05 48			06 11		
Manor Park	d					23p33				00 03	00 14			01 08						05 50			06 13		
Ilford ■2	d					23p36				00 06	00 17			01 11				05 40		05 53			06 16		
Seven Kings	d					23p38				00 08	00 19			01 13				05 42		05 55			06 18		
Goodmayes	d					23p40				00 10	00 21			01 15						05 57			06 20		
Chadwell Heath	d					23p42				00 12	00 23			01 17						05 59			06 22		
Romford	d	00 37				23p46				00 16	00 27	00 32		01 21		05 38		05 48		06 03			06 26		
Gidea Park ■2	d					23p50				00 20	00a31			01 25				05 51		06 07			06 30		
Harold Wood	d					23p53				00 23				01 28				05 54		06 10			06 33		
Brentwood	d					23p57				00 27				01 32				05 59		06 14			06 37		
Shenfield ■3	a	00 50			23p38	00 03	00 08	00 08	00 10	00 33		00 44	00 47	01 38		05 47		06 04		06 20		06 18	06 43	06 24	
Shenfield ■3	d		00 53		23p39		00 09	00 09				00 45					05 56	06 04				06 19			06 33
Billericay	d		00 59		23p45		00 15	00 15				00 51					06 02	06 10				06 25			06 39
Wickford ■2	d		01 04		23p51		00 21	00 21				00 56			05 16		06 09	06 16				06 31			06 46
Battlesbridge	d														05 20		06 13								06 50
South Woodham Ferrers	d														05 24		06 17								06 54
North Fambridge	d														05 41		06 24								07 03
Althorne	d														05 46		06 29								07 08
Burnham-on-Crouch	d														05 51		06 34								07 13
Southminster	a														05 57		06 40								07 19
Rayleigh	d		01 09		23p56		00 26	00 26				01 01						06 21				06 36			
Hockley	d		01 14		00 01		00 31	00 31				01 06						06 26				06 41			
Rochford	d		01 17		00 04		00 34	00 34				01 09						06 29				06 44			
Southend Airport ✈	d		01 20		00 07		00 37	00 37				01 12						06 32				06 47			
Prittlewell	d		01 23		00 10		00 40	00 40				01 15						06 35				06 50			
Southend Victoria	a		01 27		00 18		00 48	00 48				01 23						06 39				06 55			

b Previous night, stops to pick up only

London - Shenfield, Southminster and Southend Victoria

Network Diagram - see first Page of Table 5

Station		LE	LE	LE		LE	LE	LE	LE	LE	LE	LE	LE	LE		LE	LE	LE	LE	LE	LE	LE	LE	LE
			1	1				1	1		1		1			◇1	1	1		1	1	1		
London Liverpool Street 15 ⊖	d	06 10	06 12	06 15		06 20	06 30	06 35	06 38	06 40	06 48	06 50	06 55	07 00		07 00	07 02	07 08	07 10		07 13	07 18	07 20	07 30
Stratford 7 ⊖	d	06 17	06 19	06 22		06 27	06 37	06 42	06 45	06 47	06 55	06 57	07 02	07 07			07 09	07 15	07 17		07 20	07 25	07 27	07 37
Maryland	d	06 19				06 29	06 39			06 49		06 59		07 09					07 19				07 29	07 39
Forest Gate	d	06 21				06 31	06 41			06 51		07 01		07 11					07 21				07 31	07 41
Manor Park	d	06 23				06 33	06 43			06 53		07 03		07 13					07 23				07 33	07 43
Ilford 2	d	06 26				06 36	06 46			06 56		07 06		07 16					07 26				07 36	07 46
Seven Kings	d	06 28				06 38	06 48			06 58		07 08		07 18					07 28				07 38	07 48
Goodmayes	d	06 30				06 40	06 50			07 00		07 10		07 20					07 30				07 40	07 50
Chadwell Heath	d	06 32				06 42	06 52			07 02		07 12		07 22					07 32				07 42	07 52
Romford	d	06 36				06 46	06 56			07 06		07 16		07 26					07 36		07 28		07 46	07 56
Gidea Park 2	d	06 40				06 50	07 00			07 10		07 20		07 30					07 40				07 50	08 00
Harold Wood	d	06 43				06 53	07 03			07 13		07 23		07 33					07 43				07 53	08 03
Brentwood	d	06 47				06 57	07 07			07 17		07 27		07 37					07 47				07 57	08 07
Shenfield 3	a	06 53	06 35	06 38		07 03	07 13	06 58	07 00	07 23	07 11	07 33	07 18	07 43			07 24	07 30	07 53		07 38	07 40	08 03	08 13
Shenfield 3	d			06 39				06 59					07 19								07 39			
Billericay	d			06 45				07 05					07 25								07 45			
Wickford 2	d			06 51				07 11					07 31							07 36	07 51			
Battlesbridge	d																			07 40				
South Woodham Ferrers	d																			07 44				
North Fambridge	d																			07 53				
Althorne	d																			07 58				
Burnham-on-Crouch	d																			08 03				
Southminster	a																			08 09				
Rayleigh	d			06 56				07 16					07 36								07 56			
Hockley	d			07 01				07 21					07 41								08 01			
Rochford	d			07 04				07 24					07 44								08 04			
Southend Airport ✈	d			07 07				07 27					07 47								08 07			
Prittlewell	d			07 10				07 30					07 50								08 10			
Southend Victoria	a			07 14				07 34					07 54								08 14			

Station		LE	LE	LE	LE	LE	LE	LE	LE	LE		LE	LE	LE	LE	LE	LE	LE	LE	LE		LE	LE	LE	LE
		1	1		1		1	1		1		1		1	1			1	1	1			1		1
London Liverpool Street 15 ⊖	d	07 33	07 36	07 40	07 46	07 50		07 57	08 00	08 00		08 06	08 10	08 13	08 17	08 20	08 30		08 32	08 36		08 40	08 48	08 50	08 55
Stratford 7 ⊖	d	07 42	07 45	07 47	07 54	07 57		08 04	08 07	08 08		08 14	08 17	08 21	08 25	08 27	08 37		08 42	08 45		08 47	08 55	08 57	09 02
Maryland	d			07 49		07 59			08 09				08 19			08 29	08 39					08 49		08 59	
Forest Gate	d			07 51		08 01			08 11				08 21			08 31	08 41					08 51		09 01	
Manor Park	d			07 53		08 03			08 13				08 23			08 33	08 43					08 53		09 03	
Ilford 2	d			07 56		08 06			08 16				08 26			08 36	08 46					08 56		09 06	
Seven Kings	d			07 58		08 08			08 18				08 28			08 38	08 48					08 58		09 08	
Goodmayes	d			08 00		08 10			08 20				08 30			08 40	08 50					09 00		09 10	
Chadwell Heath	d			08 02		08 12			08 22				08 32			08 42	08 52					09 02		09 12	
Romford	d			08 06		08 16			08 26				08 36			08 46	08 56					09 06		09 16	
Gidea Park 2	d			08 10		08 20			08 30				08 40			08 50	09 00					09 10		09 20	
Harold Wood	d			08 13		08 23			08 33				08 43			08 53	09 03					09 13		09 23	
Brentwood	d			08 17		08 27			08 37				08 47			08 57	09 07					09 17		09 27	
Shenfield 3	a	07 59	08 01	08 25	08 10	08 35		08 21	08 43	08 25		08 30	08 53	08 38	08 41	09 03	09 13		08 59	09 01		09 23	09 11	09 33	09 18
Shenfield 3	d	07 59						08 21						08 39					08 59						09 19
Billericay	d	08 05						08 27						08 45					09 05						09 25
Wickford 2	d	08 11					08 16	08 33						08 51				08 56	09 11						09 31
Battlesbridge	d						08 20											09 00							
South Woodham Ferrers	d						08 24											09 04							
North Fambridge	d						08 31											09 11							
Althorne	d						08 36											09 16							
Burnham-on-Crouch	d						08 41											09 21							
Southminster	a						08 47											09 27							
Rayleigh	d	08 16						08 38						08 56					09 16						09 36
Hockley	d	08 21						08 43						09 01					09 21						09 41
Rochford	d	08 24						08 46						09 04					09 24						09 44
Southend Airport ✈	d	08 27						08 49						09 07					09 27						09 47
Prittlewell	d	08 30						08 52						09 10					09 30						09 50
Southend Victoria	a	08 34						08 56						09 14					09 34						09 54

London - Shenfield, Southminster and Southend Victoria

Network Diagram - see first Page of Table 5

		LE	LE 1	LE	LE 1	LE 1		LE 1	LE	LE	LE 1	LE 1	LE	LE 1	LE	LE 1		LE 1	LE	LE 1	LE	LE 1	LE 1	LE	LE
London Liverpool Street 15 ⊖	d	09 00	09 02	09 10		09 13		09 18	09 20	09 30	09 34	09 38	09 40	09 48	09 50			09 55	10 00	10 02	10 10	10 13	10 18	10 20	10 30
Stratford 7 ⊖	d	09 07	09 09	09 17		09 21		09 25	09 27	09 37	09 42	09 45	09 47	09 55	09 57			10 02	10 07	10 09	10 17	10 20	10 25	10 27	10 37
Maryland	d	09 09		09 19					09 29	09 39			09 49		09 59				10 09		10 19			10 29	10 39
Forest Gate	d	09 11		09 21					09 31	09 41			09 51		10 01				10 11		10 21			10 31	10 41
Manor Park	d	09 13		09 23					09 33	09 43			09 53		10 03				10 13		10 23			10 33	10 43
Ilford 2	d	09 16		09 26					09 36	09 46			09 56		10 06				10 16		10 26			10 36	10 46
Seven Kings	d	09 18		09 28					09 38	09 48			09 58		10 08				10 18		10 28			10 38	10 48
Goodmayes	d	09 20		09 30					09 40	09 50			10 00		10 10				10 20		10 30			10 40	10 50
Chadwell Heath	d	09 22		09 32					09 42	09 52			10 02		10 12				10 22		10 32			10 42	10 52
Romford	d	09 26		09 36					09 46	09 56		09 53	10 06		10 16				10 26		10 36	10 28		10 46	10 56
Gidea Park 2	d	09 30		09 40					09 50	10 00			10 10		10 20				10 30		10 40			10 50	11 00
Harold Wood	d	09 33		09 43					09 53	10 03			10 13		10 23				10 33		10 43			10 53	11 03
Brentwood	d	09 37		09 47					09 57	10 07			10 17		10 27				10 37		10 47			10 57	11 07
Shenfield 3	a	09 43	09 24	09 53		09 38		09 40	10 03	10 13	09 58	10 02	10 23	10 11	10 33			10 18	10 43	10 24	10 53	10 38	10 40	11 03	11 13
Shenfield 3	d					09 39					09 59							10 19				10 39			
Billericay	d					09 45					10 05							10 25				10 45			
Wickford 2	d				09 36	09 51					10 11					10 16		10 31				10 51			
Battlesbridge	d				09 40											10 20									
South Woodham Ferrers	d				09 44											10 24									
North Fambridge	d				09 51											10 31									
Althorne	d				09 56											10 36									
Burnham-on-Crouch	d				10 01											10 41									
Southminster	a				10 07											10 47									
Rayleigh	d					09 56					10 16							10 36				10 56			
Hockley	d					10 01					10 21							10 41				11 01			
Rochford	d					10 04					10 24							10 44				11 04			
Southend Airport ✈	d					10 07					10 27							10 47				11 07			
Prittlewell	d					10 10					10 30							10 50				11 10			
Southend Victoria	a					10 14					10 34							10 54				11 14			

		LE 1		LE 1	LE 1	LE	LE 1	LE	LE 1	LE	LE 1	LE		LE 1	LE 1	LE 1	LE	LE	LE 1	LE 1	LE	LE 1		LE	LE 1
London Liverpool Street 15 ⊖	d			10 35	10 38	10 40	10 48	10 50	10 55	11 00	11 02	11 10			11 13	11 18	11 20	11 30	11 35	11 38	11 40	11 48		11 50	
Stratford 7 ⊖	d			10 42	10 45	10 47	10 55	10 57	11 02	11 07	11 09	11 17			11 20	11 25	11 27	11 37	11 42	11 45	11 47	11 55		11 57	
Maryland	d					10 49		10 59		11 09		11 19					11 29	11 39			11 49			11 59	
Forest Gate	d					10 51		11 01		11 11		11 21					11 31	11 41			11 51			12 01	
Manor Park	d					10 53		11 03		11 13		11 23					11 33	11 43			11 53			12 03	
Ilford 2	d					10 56		11 06		11 16		11 26					11 36	11 46			11 56			12 06	
Seven Kings	d					10 58		11 08		11 18		11 28					11 38	11 48			11 58			12 08	
Goodmayes	d					11 00		11 10		11 20		11 30					11 40	11 50			12 00			12 10	
Chadwell Heath	d					11 02		11 12		11 22		11 32					11 42	11 52			12 02			12 12	
Romford	d				10 53	11 06		11 16		11 26		11 36			11 28		11 46	11 56		11 53	12 06			12 16	
Gidea Park 2	d					11 10		11 20		11 30		11 40					11 50	12 00			12 10			12 20	
Harold Wood	d					11 13		11 23		11 33		11 43					11 53	12 03			12 13			12 23	
Brentwood	d					11 17		11 27		11 37		11 47					11 57	12 07			12 17			12 27	
Shenfield 3	a			10 58	11 02	11 23	11 11	11 33	11 18	11 43	11 24	11 53			11 38	11 40	12 03	12 13	11 58	12 02	12 23	12 11		12 33	
Shenfield 3	d			10 59					11 19						11 39				11 59						
Billericay	d			11 05					11 25						11 45				12 05						
Wickford 2	d	10 56		11 11					11 31					11 36	11 51				12 11						12 16
Battlesbridge	d	11 00												11 40											12 20
South Woodham Ferrers	d	11 04												11 44											12 24
North Fambridge	d	11 11												11 51											12 31
Althorne	d	11 16												11 56											12 36
Burnham-on-Crouch	d	11 21												12 01											12 41
Southminster	a	11 27												12 07											12 47
Rayleigh	d			11 16					11 36						11 56				12 16						
Hockley	d			11 21					11 41						12 01				12 21						
Rochford	d			11 24					11 44						12 04				12 24						
Southend Airport ✈	d			11 27					11 47						12 07				12 27						
Prittlewell	d			11 30					11 50						12 10				12 30						
Southend Victoria	a			11 34					11 54						12 14				12 34						

London - Shenfield, Southminster and Southend Victoria

Network Diagram - see first Page of Table 5

		LE 1	LE	LE 1	LE	LE 1	LE 1	LE		LE	LE 1	LE 1	LE 1	LE	LE 1	LE	LE 1	LE		LE 1	LE	LE 1	LE 1	LE 1	LE
London Liverpool Street 15 ⊖	d	11 55	12 00	12 02	12 10	12 13	12 18	12 20		12 30		12 35	12 38	12 40	12 48	12 50	12 55	13 00		13 02	13 10		13 13	13 18	13 20
Stratford 7 ⊖	d	12 02	12 07	12 09	12 17	12 20	12 25	12 27		12 37		12 42	12 45	12 47	12 55	12 57	13 02	13 07		13 09	13 17		13 20	13 25	13 27
Maryland	d		12 09		12 19			12 29		12 39				12 49		12 59		13 09			13 19				13 29
Forest Gate	d		12 11		12 21			12 31		12 41				12 51		13 01		13 11			13 21				13 31
Manor Park	d		12 13		12 23			12 33		12 43				12 53		13 03		13 13			13 23				13 33
Ilford 2	d		12 16		12 26			12 36		12 46				12 56		13 06		13 16			13 26				13 36
Seven Kings	d		12 18		12 28			12 38		12 48				12 58		13 08		13 18			13 28				13 38
Goodmayes	d		12 20		12 30			12 40		12 50				13 00		13 10		13 20			13 30				13 40
Chadwell Heath	d		12 22		12 32			12 42		12 52				13 02		13 12		13 22			13 32				13 42
Romford	d		12 26		12 36	12 28		12 46		12 56			12 53	13 06		13 16		13 26			13 36		13 28		13 46
Gidea Park 2	d		12 30		12 40			12 50		13 00				13 10		13 20		13 30			13 40				13 50
Harold Wood	d		12 33		12 43			12 53		13 03				13 13		13 23		13 33			13 43				13 53
Brentwood	d		12 37		12 47			12 57		13 07				13 17		13 27		13 37			13 47				13 57
Shenfield 3	a	12 18	12 43	12 24	12 53	12 38	12 40	13 03		13 13		12 58	13 02	13 23	13 11	13 33	13 18	13 43		13 24	13 53		13 38	13 40	14 03
Shenfield 3	d	12 19				12 39						12 59					13 19						13 39		
Billericay	d	12 25				12 45						13 05					13 25						13 45		
Wickford 2	d	12 31				12 51					12 56	13 11					13 31					13 36	13 51		
Battlesbridge	d										13 00											13 40			
South Woodham Ferrers	d										13 04											13 44			
North Fambridge	d										13 11											13 51			
Althorne	d										13 16											13 56			
Burnham-on-Crouch	d										13 21											14 01			
Southminster	a										13 27											14 07			
Rayleigh	d	12 36				12 56						13 16					13 36						13 56		
Hockley	d	12 41				13 01						13 21					13 41						14 01		
Rochford	d	12 44				13 04						13 24					13 44						14 04		
Southend Airport ✈	d	12 47				13 07						13 27					13 47						14 07		
Prittlewell	d	12 50				13 10						13 30					13 50						14 10		
Southend Victoria	a	12 54				13 14						13 34					13 54						14 14		

		LE	LE 1	LE 1		LE	LE 1	LE	LE 1	LE 1	LE	LE 1	LE	LE 1		LE 1	LE	LE	LE 1	LE 1	LE 1	LE	LE 1	LE	
London Liverpool Street 15 ⊖	d	13 30	13 35	13 38		13 40	13 48	13 50		13 55	14 00	14 02	14 10	14 13		14 18	14 20	14 30		14 35	14 38	14 40	14 48	14 50	
Stratford 7 ⊖	d	13 37	13 42	13 45		13 47	13 55	13 57		14 02	14 07	14 09	14 17	14 20		14 25	14 27	14 37		14 42	14 45	14 47	14 55	14 57	
Maryland	d	13 39				13 49		13 59			14 09		14 19				14 29	14 39				14 49		14 59	
Forest Gate	d	13 41				13 51		14 01			14 11		14 21				14 31	14 41				14 51		15 01	
Manor Park	d	13 43				13 53		14 03			14 13		14 23				14 33	14 43				14 53		15 03	
Ilford 2	d	13 46				13 56		14 06			14 16		14 26				14 36	14 46				14 56		15 06	
Seven Kings	d	13 48				13 58		14 08			14 18		14 28				14 38	14 48				14 58		15 08	
Goodmayes	d	13 50				14 00		14 10			14 20		14 30				14 40	14 50				15 00		15 10	
Chadwell Heath	d	13 52				14 02		14 12			14 22		14 32				14 42	14 52				15 02		15 12	
Romford	d	13 56		13 53		14 06		14 16			14 26		14 36	14 28			14 46	14 56			14 53	15 06		15 16	
Gidea Park 2	d	14 00				14 10		14 20			14 30		14 40				14 50	15 00				15 10		15 20	
Harold Wood	d	14 03				14 13		14 23			14 33		14 43				14 53	15 03				15 13		15 23	
Brentwood	d	14 07				14 17		14 27			14 37		14 47				14 57	15 07				15 17		15 27	
Shenfield 3	a	14 13	13 58	14 02		14 23	14 11	14 33		14 18	14 43	14 24	14 53	14 38		14 40	15 03	15 13		14 58	15 02	15 23	15 11	15 33	
Shenfield 3	d		13 59							14 19				14 39						14 59					
Billericay	d		14 05							14 25				14 45						15 05					
Wickford 2	d		14 11						14 16	14 31				14 51					14 56	15 11					
Battlesbridge	d								14 20										15 00						
South Woodham Ferrers	d								14 24										15 04						
North Fambridge	d								14 31										15 11						
Althorne	d								14 36										15 16						
Burnham-on-Crouch	d								14 41										15 21						
Southminster	a								14 47										15 27						
Rayleigh	d		14 16							14 36				14 56						15 16					
Hockley	d		14 21							14 41				15 01						15 21					
Rochford	d		14 24							14 44				15 04						15 24					
Southend Airport ✈	d		14 27							14 47				15 07						15 27					
Prittlewell	d		14 30							14 50				15 10						15 30					
Southend Victoria	a		14 34							14 54				15 14						15 34					

London - Shenfield, Southminster and Southend Victoria

Network Diagram - see first Page of Table 5

		LE 1	LE	LE 1	LE	LE 1	LE 1	LE 1	LE	LE		LE 1	LE 1	LE	LE 1	LE	LE 1	LE 1	LE	LE 1		LE	LE 1	LE 1	LE 1
London Liverpool Street 15 ⊖	d	14 55	15 00	15 02	15 10		15 13	15 18	15 20	15 30		15 35	15 38	15 40	15 48	15 50		15 55	16 00	16 02		16 10	16 10	16 14	16 17
Stratford 7 ⊖	d	15 02	15 07	15 09	15 17		15 20	15 25	15 27	15 37		15 42	15 45	15 47	15 55	15 57		16 02	16 07	16 09		16 17	16 18	16 22	16 25
Maryland	d		15 09		15 19				15 29	15 39				15 49		15 59			16 09			16 19			
Forest Gate	d		15 11		15 21				15 31	15 41				15 51		16 01			16 11			16 21			
Manor Park	d		15 13		15 23				15 33	15 43				15 53		16 03			16 13			16 23			
Ilford 2	d		15 16		15 26				15 36	15 46				15 56		16 06			16 16			16 26			
Seven Kings	d		15 18		15 28				15 38	15 48				15 58		16 08			16 18			16 28			
Goodmayes	d		15 20		15 30				15 40	15 50				16 00		16 10			16 20			16 30			
Chadwell Heath	d		15 22		15 32				15 42	15 52				16 02		16 12			16 22			16 32			
Romford	d		15 26		15 36		15 28		15 46	15 56			15 53	16 06		16 16			16 26			16 36			
Gidea Park 2	d		15 30		15 40				15 50	16 00				16 10		16 20			16 30			16 40			
Harold Wood	d		15 33		15 43				15 53	16 03				16 13		16 23			16 33			16 43			
Brentwood	d		15 37		15 47				15 57	16 07				16 17		16 27			16 37			16 47			
Shenfield 3	a	15 18	15 43	15 24	15 53		15 38	15 40	16 03	16 13		15 58	16 02	16 23	16 11	16 33		16 18	16 43	16 24		16 53	16 34	16 38	16 41
Shenfield 3	d	15 19					15 39					15 59						16 19					16 34		
Billericay	d	15 25					15 45					16 05						16 25					16 41		
Wickford 2	d	15 31				15 36	15 51					16 11					16 14	16 31					16 48		
Battlesbridge	d					15 40											16 18								
South Woodham Ferrers	d					15 44											16 22								
North Fambridge	d					15 51											16 29								
Althorne	d					15 56											16 34								
Burnham-on-Crouch	d					16 01											16 39								
Southminster	a					16 07											16 45								
Rayleigh	d	15 36					15 56					16 16						16 36					16 53		
Hockley	d	15 41					16 01					16 21						16 41					16 57		
Rochford	d	15 44					16 04					16 24						16 44					17 01		
Southend Airport ✈	d	15 47					16 07					16 27						16 47					17 03		
Prittlewell	d	15 50					16 10					16 30						16 50					17 06		
Southend Victoria	a	15 54					16 14					16 34						16 54					17 15		

		LE	LE 1	LE	LE 1	LE 1		LE	LE	LE 1	LE 1	LE 1	LE	LE 1	LE	LE 1		LE	LE	LE ◇1	LE 1	LE	LE 1	LE	LE 1
London Liverpool Street 15 ⊖	d	16 20	16 24	16 28	16 32	16 34		16 36	16 40		16 40	16 44	16 47	16 47	16 50	16 54		16 57	17 00	17 02	17 04	17 07	17 08	17 10	17 12
Stratford 7 ⊖	d	16 27	16 32	16 35		16 42		16 43	16 47		16 48	16a52	16 54	16 55	16 57	17 02		17 04	17 07	17 10	17 13	17 14	17a16	17 17	17a20
Maryland	d	16 29		16 37					16 49						16 59				17 09					17 19	
Forest Gate	d	16 31		16 39					16 51						17 01				17 11					17 21	
Manor Park	d	16 33		16 41					16 53						17 03				17 13					17 23	
Ilford 2	d	16 36		16 44				16 50	16 56				17 00		17 06			17 10	17 16			17 20		17 26	
Seven Kings	d	16 38		16 47				16 52					17 02					17 12				17 22			
Goodmayes	d	16 40		16 49				16 54					17 04					17 14				17 24			
Chadwell Heath	d	16 42		16 51				16 56	17 00				17 06		17 10			17 16	17 20			17 26		17 30	
Romford	d	16 46		16 55				17 00	17 04				17 10		17 14			17 20	17 24			17 30		17 34	
Gidea Park 2	d	16 50		17a00				17 04	17a10				17 14		17a20			17 24	17a30			17 34		17a40	
Harold Wood	d	16 53						17 07					17 17					17 27				17 37			
Brentwood	d	16 57						17 11					17 21					17 31				17 41			
Shenfield 3	a	17 03	16 49		16 54	16 58		17 19			17 04		17 29	17 11		17 19		17 39			17 30	17 49			
Shenfield 3	d		16 49								17 04					17 19					17 30				
Billericay	d		16 56								17 11					17 26					17 37				
Wickford 2	d		17 03							17 06	17 18					17 33					17 44				
Battlesbridge	d									17 10															
South Woodham Ferrers	d									17 14															
North Fambridge	d									17 21															
Althorne	d									17 26															
Burnham-on-Crouch	d									17 31															
Southminster	a									17 37															
Rayleigh	d		17 08								17 23					17 38					17 49				
Hockley	d		17 12								17 27					17 42					17 53				
Rochford	d		17 16								17 31					17 46					17 57				
Southend Airport ✈	d		17 18								17 33					17 48					17 59				
Prittlewell	d		17 21								17 36					17 51					18 02				
Southend Victoria	a		17 27								17 42					17 57					18 08				

London - Shenfield, Southminster and Southend Victoria

Network Diagram - see first Page of Table 5

		LE		LE	LE	LE	LE	LE	LE	LE	LE	LE		LE	LE	LE	LE	LE	LE	LE	LE	LE		LE	LE
		1			1		1	1	1			1		1		1		1		1					1
							A	A										A							
London Liverpool Street 15 ⊖	d	17 15		17 17	17 18	17 20	17 20	17 22	17 25	17 27	17 30	17 32		17 34	17 36	17 38	17 39	17 40	17 42	17 45	17 46	17 49		17 52	17 52
Stratford 7 ⊖	d	17 23		17 24	17a26	17 27	17 29	17 31	17 34	17 34	17 37	17a40		17 43	17 43	17a47	17 46	17 49	17 49	17 53	17 53	17 56		17 59	18a01
Maryland	d					17 29					17 39				17 45						17 55				
Forest Gate	d					17 31					17 41								17 52					18 02	
Manor Park	d					17 33					17 43						17 50					18 00			
Ilford 2	d			17 30		17 36				17 40	17 46				17 50		17 53		17 56		18 00	18 03		18 06	
Seven Kings	d			17 32						17 42					17 52		17 56		17 59		18 02	18 06		18 09	
Goodmayes	d			17 34						17 44					17 54		17 58		18 01		18 04	18 08		18 11	
Chadwell Heath	d			17 36		17 40				17 46	17 50				17 56		18 00		18 03		18 06	18 10		18 13	
Romford	d			17 40		17 44				17 50	17 54				18 00		18 04		18 07		18 10	18 14		18 17	
Gidea Park 2	d			17 44		17a50				17 54	18a00				18 04		18a09		18a12		18 14	18 18		18a22	
Harold Wood	d			17 47						17 57					18 07						18 17	18 21			
Brentwood	d			17 51						18 01					18 11						18 21	18 25			
Shenfield 3	a	17 39		17 59			17 45		17 51	18 09				17 59	18 19			18 05		18 09	18 29	18 33			
Shenfield 3	d	17 39							17 52					17 59						18 09		18 36			
Billericay	d	17 46							17 58					18 06						18 16		→			
Wickford 2	d	17 53						18 00	18 05					18 13						18 23					
Battlesbridge	d							18 04																	
South Woodham Ferrers	d							18 08																	
North Fambridge	d							18 14																	
Althorne	d							18 19																	
Burnham-on-Crouch	d							18 24																	
Southminster	a							18 32																	
Rayleigh	d	17 58							18 10					18 18						18 28					
Hockley	d	18 02							18 15					18 22						18 32					
Rochford	d	18 06							18 18					18 26						18 36					
Southend Airport ✈	d	18 08							18 21					18 28						18 38					
Prittlewell	d	18 11							18 24					18 31						18 41					
Southend Victoria	a	18 17							18 30					18 37						18 47					

		LE	LE	LE	LE	LE	LE	LE		LE	LE	LE	LE	LE	LE	LE	LE	LE		LE	LE	LE	LE	LE	LE
		1		1		1		1		1				1	1		1			1	1			1	1
London Liverpool Street 15 ⊖	d	17 54	17 56	17 58	17 59	18 00	18 02	18 02		18 05		18 07	18 10	18 12	18 14	18 17	18 18	18 20		18 20	18 25	18 27	18 30	18 32	18 35
Stratford 7 ⊖	d	18 03	18 03	18a06	18 06	18 09	18 09	18 11		18 14		18 14	18 17	18a21	18 23	18 24	18a27	18 27		18 29	18 33	18 34	18 37	18a40	18 43
Maryland	d		18 05										18 19					18 29					18 39		
Forest Gate	d						18 12						18 21					18 31					18 41		
Manor Park	d				18 10								18 23					18 33					18 43		
Ilford 2	d		18 10		18 13		18 16					18 20	18 26			18 30		18 36				18 40	18 46		
Seven Kings	d		18 12		18 16		18 19					18 22				18 32						18 42			
Goodmayes	d		18 14		18 18		18 21					18 24				18 34						18 44			
Chadwell Heath	d		18 16		18 20		18 23					18 26	18 30			18 36		18 40				18 46	18 50		
Romford	d		18 20		18 24		18 27					18 30	18 34			18 40		18 44				18 50	18 54		
Gidea Park 2	d		18 24		18a29		18a32					18 34	18a40			18 44		18a50				18 54	19a00		
Harold Wood	d		18 27									18 37				18 47						18 57			
Brentwood	d		18 31								←	18 41				18 51						19 01			
Shenfield 3	a	18 19	18 39			18 25				18 31	18 33	18 49			18 40	18 59				18 45	18 50	19 09			18 59
Shenfield 3	d	18 19								18 31	18 36				18 41						18 50				18 59
Billericay	d	18 26								18 38	18 42				18 47						18 57				19 06
Wickford 2	d	18 33						18 40		18 45	18 49				18 54						19 04				19 13
Battlesbridge	d							18 44																	
South Woodham Ferrers	d							18 48																	
North Fambridge	d							18 54																	
Althorne	d							18 59																	
Burnham-on-Crouch	d							19 04																	
Southminster	a							19 12																	
Rayleigh	d	18 38								18 50	18 54				18 59						19 09				19 18
Hockley	d	18 42								18 55	18 59				19 04						19 13				19 22
Rochford	d	18 46								18 58	19 02				19 07						19 17				19 26
Southend Airport ✈	d	18 48								19 01	19 05				19 10						19 19				19 28
Prittlewell	d	18 51								19 04	19 08				19 13						19 22				19 31
Southend Victoria	a	18 58								19 10	19 14				19 19						19 28				19 37

A From Stratford from 27 February

London - Shenfield, Southminster and Southend Victoria

Network Diagram - see first Page of Table 5

		LE	LE 1	LE		LE 1	LE 1	LE	LE 1	LE	LE 1	LE	LE	LE 1		LE 1	LE	LE 1	LE 1	LE	LE	LE 1	LE 1	LE 1	
London Liverpool Street 15 ⊖	d	18 37	18 38	18 40		18 41	18 45	18 47	18 48	18 50	18 55	18 57	19 00	19 02		19 08	19 10	19 15	19 18	19 20	19 30	19 32	19 35	19 38	
Stratford 7 ⊖	d	18 44	18 46	18 47		18 49	18 53	18 54	18a56	18 57	19 03	19 04	19 07	19 09		19a15	19 17	19 22	19 25	19 27	19 37	19a39	19 42	19 45	
Maryland	d			18 49						18 59			19 09				19 19			19 29	19 39				
Forest Gate	d			18 51						19 01			19 11				19 21			19 31	19 41				
Manor Park	d			18 53						19 03			19 13				19 23			19 33	19 43				
Ilford 2	d	18 50		18 56				19 00		19 06		19 10	19 16				19 26			19 36	19 46				
Seven Kings	d	18 52						19 02				19 12	19 18				19 28			19 38	19 48				
Goodmayes	d	18 54						19 04				19 14	19 20				19 30			19 40	19 50				
Chadwell Heath	d	18 56		19 00				19 06		19 10		19 16	19 22				19 32			19 42	19 52				
Romford	d	19 00		19 04				19 10		19 14		19 20	19 26				19 36			19 46	19 56				
Gidea Park 2	d	19 04		19 08				19 14		19a20		19 24	19 30				19 40			19 50	20 00				
Harold Wood	d	19 07		19 11				19 17				19 27	19 33				19 43			19 53	20 03				
Brentwood	d	19 11		19 15				19 21				19 31	19 37				19 47			19 57	20 07				
Shenfield 3	a	19 19	19 02	19 23			19 10	19 29			19 20	19 39	19 43	19 24			19 53	19 38	19 40	20 03	20 13		19 58	20 00	
Shenfield 3	d						19 10				19 20							19 39					19 59		
Billericay	d						19 17				19 27							19 45					20 05		
Wickford 2	d					19 19	19 24				19 34							19 51					20 11		
Battlesbridge	d					19 23																			
South Woodham Ferrers	d					19 27																			
North Fambridge	d					19 34																			
Althorne	d					19 39																			
Burnham-on-Crouch	d					19 44																			
Southminster	a					19 52																			
Rayleigh	d						19 29				19 39							19 56					20 16		
Hockley	d						19 33				19 43							20 01					20 21		
Rochford	d						19 37				19 47							20 04					20 24		
Southend Airport ✈	d						19 39				19 49							20 07					20 27		
Prittlewell	d						19 42				19 52							20 10					20 30		
Southend Victoria	a						19 47				19 58							20 14					20 34		

		LE	LE 1	LE	LE 1	LE 1	LE	LE 1	LE	LE 1		LE 1	LE	LE	LE 1	LE 1	CC	LE 1	LE	LE 1		LE	LE 1	LE	LE 1
London Liverpool Street 15 ⊖	d	19 40	19 48	19 50		19 55	20 00	20 02	20 10	20 13		20 18	20 20	20 30		20 35	20 35	20 38	20 40	20 48		20 50	20 55	21 00	21 02
Stratford 7 ⊖	d	19 47	19 55	19 57		20 02	20 07	20 09	20 17	20 20		20 25	20 27	20 37		20 42	20a43	20 45	20 47	20 55		20 57	21 02	21 07	21 09
Maryland	d	19 49		19 59			20 09		20 19				20 29	20 39					20 49			20 59		21 09	
Forest Gate	d	19 51		20 01			20 11		20 21				20 31	20 41					20 51			21 01		21 11	
Manor Park	d	19 53		20 03			20 13		20 23				20 33	20 43					20 53			21 03		21 13	
Ilford 2	d	19 56		20 06			20 16		20 26				20 36	20 46					20 56			21 06		21 16	
Seven Kings	d	19 58		20 08			20 18		20 28				20 38	20 48					20 58			21 08		21 18	
Goodmayes	d	20 00		20 10			20 20		20 30				20 40	20 50					21 00			21 10		21 20	
Chadwell Heath	d	20 02		20 12			20 22		20 32				20 42	20 52					21 02			21 12		21 22	
Romford	d	20 06		20 16			20 26		20 36	20 28			20 46	20 56				20 53	21 06			21 16		21 26	
Gidea Park 2	d	20 10		20 20			20 30		20 40				20 50	21 00					21 10			21 20		21 30	
Harold Wood	d	20 13		20 23			20 33		20 43				20 53	21 03					21 13			21 23		21 33	
Brentwood	d	20 17		20 27			20 37		20 47				20 57	21 07					21 17			21 27		21 37	
Shenfield 3	a	20 23	20 11	20 33		20 18	20 43	20 24	20 53	20 38		20 40	21 03	21 13		20 58		21 02	21 23	21 11		21 33	21 18	21 43	21 24
Shenfield 3	d					20 19				20 39						20 59							21 19		
Billericay	d					20 25				20 45						21 05							21 25		
Wickford 2	d				20 16	20 31				20 51					20 56	21 11							21 31		
Battlesbridge	d				20 20										21 00										
South Woodham Ferrers	d				20 24										21 04										
North Fambridge	d				20 31										21 11										
Althorne	d				20 36										21 16										
Burnham-on-Crouch	d				20 41										21 21										
Southminster	a				20 47										21 27										
Rayleigh	d					20 36				20 56						21 16							21 36		
Hockley	d					20 41				21 01						21 21							21 41		
Rochford	d					20 44				21 04						21 24							21 44		
Southend Airport ✈	d					20 47				21 07						21 27							21 47		
Prittlewell	d					20 50				21 10						21 30							21 50		
Southend Victoria	a					20 54				21 14						21 34							21 54		

London - Shenfield, Southminster and Southend Victoria

Network Diagram - see first Page of Table 5

		LE	LE 1	LE 1	LE 1	LE		LE	LE 1	CC	LE 1	LE	LE 1	LE	LE 1	LE 1		LE 1	LE	LE 1	LE	LE		LE 1 MTWO	LE 1 MTWO
London Liverpool Street 15 ⊖	d	21 10		21 13	21 18	21 20		21 30	21 35	21 35	21 38	21 40	21 48	21 50		21 55		22 02	22 05	22 18	22 20	22 35		22 25	
Stratford 7 ⊖	d	21 17		21 20	21 25	21 27		21 37	21 42	21a43	21 45	21 47	21 55	21 57		22 02		22 09	22 12	22 25	22 27	22 42		22 32	
Maryland	d	21 19				21 29		21 39				21 49		21 59					22 14		22 29	22 44			
Forest Gate	d	21 21				21 31		21 41				21 51		22 01					22 16		22 31	22 46			
Manor Park	d	21 23				21 33		21 43				21 53		22 03					22 18		22 33	22 48			
Ilford 2	d	21 26				21 36		21 46				21 56		22 06					22 21		22 36	22 51			
Seven Kings	d	21 28				21 38		21 48				21 58		22 08					22 23		22 38	22 53			
Goodmayes	d	21 30				21 40		21 50				22 00		22 10					22 25		22 40	22 55			
Chadwell Heath	d	21 32				21 42		21 52				22 02		22 12					22 27		22 42	22 57			
Romford	d	21 36		21 28		21 46		21 56			21 53	22 06		22 16					22 31		22 46	23 01			
Gidea Park 2	d	21 40				21 50		22 00				22 10		22 20					22 35		22 50	23 05			
Harold Wood	d	21 43				21 53		22 03				22 13		22 23					22 38		22 53	23 08			
Brentwood	d	21 47				21 57		22 07				22 17		22 27					22 42		22 57	23 12			
Shenfield 3	a	21 53		21 38	21 40	22 03		22 13	21 58		22 02	22 23	22 11	22 33		22 18		22 24	22 48	22 40	23 03	23 18		22 48	
Shenfield 3	d			21 39					21 59							22 19								22 49	
Billericay	d			21 45					22 05							22 25								22 55	
Wickford 2	d		21 36	21 51					22 11						22 16	22 31								23 01	23 06
Battlesbridge	d		21 40												22 20										23 10
South Woodham Ferrers	d		21 44												22 24										23 14
North Fambridge	d		21 51												22 31										23 21
Althorne	d		21 56												22 36										23 26
Burnham-on-Crouch	d		22 01												22 41										23 31
Southminster	a		22 07												22 47										23 37
Rayleigh	d			21 56					22 16							22 36								23 06	
Hockley	d			22 01					22 21							22 41								23 11	
Rochford	d			22 04					22 24							22 44								23 14	
Southend Airport ✈	d			22 07					22 27							22 47								23 17	
Prittlewell	d			22 10					22 30							22 50								23 20	
Southend Victoria	a			22 14					22 34							22 54								23 24	

		LE MTWO	LE 1 MTWO	LE MTWO	LE 1 MTWO	LE ◇1 MTWO 🍴	LE 1 MTWO	LE MTWO		LE 1 ThFO	LE 1 ThFO	LE 1 ThFO	LE 1 ThFO	LE ThFO	LE 1 ThFO	LE ThFO		LE 1 ThFO	LE 1 ThFO	LE ThFO	LE	LE 1 ThFO	LE 1 ThFO	LE ThFO	
London Liverpool Street 15 ⊖	d	22 55	23 10	23 15		23 30	23 50	23 55		22 13		22 38	22 45	22 50	23 02	23 05		23 15	23 18	23 20	23 35	23 45	23 48	23 50	
Stratford 7 ⊖	d	23 02	23 17	23 22		23u39	23 57	00 02		22 20		22 45	22 52	22 57	23 09	23 12		23 22	23 25	23 27	23 42	23 52	23 55	23 57	
Maryland	d	23 04		23 24				00 04						22 59		23 14				23 29	23 44			23 59	
Forest Gate	d	23 06		23 26				00 06						23 01		23 16				23 31	23 46			00 01	
Manor Park	d	23 08		23 28				00 08						23 03		23 18				23 33	23 48			00 03	
Ilford 2	d	23 11		23 31				00 11						23 06		23 21				23 36	23 51			00 06	
Seven Kings	d	23 13		23 33				00 13						23 08		23 23				23 38	23 53			00 08	
Goodmayes	d	23 15		23 35				00 15						23 10		23 25				23 40	23 55			00 10	
Chadwell Heath	d	23 17		23 37				00 17						23 12		23 27				23 42	23 57			00 12	
Romford	d	23 21		23 41				00 21		22 28				23 16		23 31				23 46	00 02			00 16	
Gidea Park 2	d	23 25		23 45				00 25						23 20		23 35				23 50	00 05			00 20	
Harold Wood	d	23 28		23 48				00 28						23 23		23 38				23 53	00 08			00 23	
Brentwood	d	23 32		23 52				00 32						23 27		23 42				23 57	00 12			00 27	
Shenfield 3	a	23 38	23 40	23 58		00 02	00 20	00 38		22 38		23 00	23 08	23 33	23 24	23 48		23 38	23 40	00 03	00 18	00 08	00 10	00 33	
Shenfield 3	d				23 43					22 39			23 09					23 39				00 09			
Billericay	d				23 49					22 45			23 15					23 45				00 15			
Wickford 2	d				23 55					22 51	22 56		23 21					23 51				00 21			
Battlesbridge	d										23 00														
South Woodham Ferrers	d										23 04														
North Fambridge	d										23 11														
Althorne	d										23 16														
Burnham-on-Crouch	d										23 21														
Southminster	a										23 27														
Rayleigh	d				00 01					22 56			23 26					23 56				00 26			
Hockley	d				00 05					23 01			23 31					00 01				00 31			
Rochford	d				00 08					23 04			23 34					00 04				00 34			
Southend Airport ✈	d				00 11					23 07			23 37					00 07				00 37			
Prittlewell	d				00 14					23 10			23 40					00 10				00 40			
Southend Victoria	a				00 18					23 14			23 48					00 18				00 48			

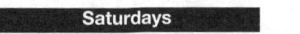

London - Shenfield, Southminster and Southend Victoria

Network Diagram - see first Page of Table 5

		LE 1	LE	LE	LE 1	LE 1	LE	LE	LE 1	LE 1		LE	LE	LE 1	LE 1	LE	LE 1	LE 1	LE 1	LE 1		LE 1	LE	LE 1	LE 1
London Liverpool Street 15 ⊖	d	23p15	23p20	23p35	23p45	23p48	23p50	00 01	00 15	00 18		00 20	00 32	00 46	00 50	00 55	05 21			05 28		05 34	05 40	05 51	06 02
Stratford 7 ⊖	d	23p22	23p27	23p42	23p52	23p55	23p57	00 08	00 22	00 25		00 27	00 39	00 53	00 57	01 02	05a30			05 35		05 41	05 47	06a00	06 09
Maryland	d		23p29	23p44			23p59	00 10				00 29	00 41			01 04							05 49		
Forest Gate	d		23p31	23p46			00 01	00 12				00 31	00 43			01 06							05 51		
Manor Park	d		23p33	23p48			00 03	00 14				00 33	00 45			01 08							05 53		
Ilford 2	d		23p36	23p51			00 06	00 17				00 36	00 48			01 11				05 40			05 56		
Seven Kings	d		23p38	23p53			00 08	00 19				00 38	00 50			01 13				05 42			05 58		
Goodmayes	d		23p40	23p55			00 10	00 21				00 40	00 52			01 15							06 00		
Chadwell Heath	d		23p42	23p57			00 12	00 23				00 42	00 54			01 17							06 02		
Romford	d		23p46	00 02			00 16	00 27	00 32			00 46	00 58		01 08	01 21				05 48		05 49	06 06		
Gidea Park 2	d		23p50	00 05			00 20	00a31				00 50	01a02	01 07		01 25				05 51			06 10		
Harold Wood	d		23p53	00 08			00 23					00 53				01 28				05 54			06 13		
Brentwood	d		23p57	00 12			00 27					00 57				01 32				05 59			06 17		
Shenfield 3	a	23p38	00 03	00 18	00 08	00 10	00 33		00 44	00 47		01 03		01 17	01 20	01 38				06 04		05 58	06 23		06 24
Shenfield 3	d	23p39			00 09				00 45						01 20					06 04					
Billericay	d	23p45			00 15				00 51						01 26					06 10					
Wickford 2	d	23p51			00 21				00 56						01 31			05 36	06 12	06 16					
Battlesbridge	d																	05 40	06 16						
South Woodham Ferrers	d																	05 44	06 20						
North Fambridge	d																	05 51	06 31						
Althorne	d																	05 56	06 36						
Burnham-on-Crouch	d																	06 01	06 41						
Southminster	a																	06 07	06 47						
Rayleigh	d	23p56			00 26				01 01						01 36					06 22					
Hockley	d	00 01			00 31				01 06						01 41					06 26					
Rochford	d	00 04			00 34				01 09						01 44					06 30					
Southend Airport ✈	d	00 07			00 37				01 12						01 47					06 32					
Prittlewell	d	00 10			00 40				01 15						01 50					06 35					
Southend Victoria	a	00 18			00 48				01 23						01 58					06 39					

		LE 1	LE	LE 1	LE 1	LE 1		LE 1	LE 1	LE	LE 1	LE 1	LE	LE 1	LE	LE 1		LE 1	LE 1	LE	LE	LE 1	LE 1	LE	LE 1
London Liverpool Street 15 ⊖	d	06 05	06 10	06 18	06 21			06 35	06 38	06 40	06 48	06 55	07 00	07 02	07 10			07 13	07 18	07 20	07 30	07 35	07 38	07 40	07 48
Stratford 7 ⊖	d	06 12	06 17	06 25	06a30			06 42	06 45	06 47	06 55	07 02	07 07	07 09	07 17			07 20	07 25	07 27	07 37	07 42	07 45	07 47	07 55
Maryland	d		06 19							06 49			07 09		07 19					07 29	07 39			07 49	
Forest Gate	d		06 21							06 51			07 11		07 21					07 31	07 41			07 51	
Manor Park	d		06 23							06 53			07 13		07 23					07 33	07 43			07 53	
Ilford 2	d		06 26							06 56			07 16		07 26					07 36	07 46			07 56	
Seven Kings	d		06 28							06 58			07 18		07 28					07 38	07 48			07 58	
Goodmayes	d		06 30							07 00			07 20		07 30					07 40	07 50			08 00	
Chadwell Heath	d		06 32							07 02			07 22		07 32					07 42	07 52			08 02	
Romford	d		06 36						06 53	07 06			07 26		07 36			07 28		07 46	07 56		07 53	08 06	
Gidea Park 2	d		06 40							07 10			07 30		07 40					07 50	08 00			08 10	
Harold Wood	d		06 43							07 13			07 33		07 43					07 53	08 03			08 13	
Brentwood	d		06 47							07 17			07 37		07 47					07 57	08 07			08 17	
Shenfield 3	a	06 30	06 53	06 40				06 58	07 02	07 23	07 11	07 18	07 43	07 24	07 53			07 38	07 40	08 03	08 13	07 58	08 02	08 23	08 11
Shenfield 3	d	06 30						06 59				07 19						07 39				07 59			
Billericay	d	06 36						07 05				07 25						07 45				08 05			
Wickford 2	d	06 43				06 56		07 11				07 31				07 36		07 51				08 11			
Battlesbridge	d					07 00										07 40									
South Woodham Ferrers	d					07 04										07 44									
North Fambridge	d					07 11										07 51									
Althorne	d					07 16										07 56									
Burnham-on-Crouch	d					07 21										08 01									
Southminster	a					07 27										08 07									
Rayleigh	d	06 48						07 16				07 36						07 56				08 16			
Hockley	d	06 53						07 21				07 41						08 01				08 21			
Rochford	d	06 56						07 24				07 44						08 04				08 24			
Southend Airport ✈	d	06 59						07 27				07 47						08 07				08 27			
Prittlewell	d	07 02						07 30				07 50						08 10				08 30			
Southend Victoria	a	07 05						07 34				07 54						08 14				08 34			

		LE		LE 1	LE 1	LE	LE 1	LE	LE 1	LE 1	LE	LE		LE 1	LE 1	LE 1	LE	LE 1	LE	LE 1	LE	LE 1		LE	LE 1
London Liverpool Street 15 ⊖	d	07 50			07 55	08 00	08 02	08 10	08 13	08 18	08 20	08 30			08 35	08 38	08 40	08 48	08 50	08 55	09 00	09 02		09 10	
Stratford 7 ⊖	d	07 57			08 02	08 07	08 09	08 17	08 20	08 25	08 27	08 37			08 42	08 45	08 47	08 55	08 57	09 02	09 07	09 09		09 17	
Maryland	d	07 59				08 09		08 19			08 29	08 39					08 49		08 59		09 09			09 19	
Forest Gate	d	08 01				08 11		08 21			08 31	08 41					08 51		09 01		09 11			09 21	
Manor Park	d	08 03				08 13		08 23			08 33	08 43					08 53		09 03		09 13			09 23	
Ilford 2	d	08 06				08 16		08 26			08 36	08 46					08 56		09 06		09 16			09 26	
Seven Kings	d	08 08				08 18		08 28			08 38	08 48					08 58		09 08		09 18			09 28	
Goodmayes	d	08 10				08 20		08 30			08 40	08 50					09 00		09 10		09 20			09 30	
Chadwell Heath	d	08 12				08 22		08 32			08 42	08 52					09 02		09 12		09 22			09 32	
Romford	d	08 16				08 26		08 36	08 28		08 46	08 56				08 53	09 06		09 16		09 26			09 36	
Gidea Park 2	d	08 20				08 30		08 40			08 50	09 00					09 10		09 20		09 30			09 40	
Harold Wood	d	08 23				08 33		08 43			08 53	09 03					09 13		09 23		09 33			09 43	
Brentwood	d	08 27				08 37		08 47			08 57	09 07					09 17		09 27		09 37			09 47	
Shenfield 3	a	08 33			08 18	08 43	08 24	08 53	08 38	08 40	09 03	09 13			08 58	09 02	09 23	09 11	09 33	09 18	09 43	09 24		09 53	
Shenfield 3	d				08 19				08 39						08 59					09 19					
Billericay	d				08 25				08 45						09 05					09 25					
Wickford 2	d			08 16	08 31				08 51					08 56	09 11					09 31					09 36
Battlesbridge	d			08 20										09 00											09 40
South Woodham Ferrers	d			08 24										09 04											09 44
North Fambridge	d			08 31										09 11											09 51
Althorne	d			08 36										09 16											09 56
Burnham-on-Crouch	d			08 41										09 21											10 01
Southminster	a			08 47										09 27											10 07
Rayleigh	d				08 36				08 56						09 16					09 36					
Hockley	d				08 41				09 01						09 21					09 41					
Rochford	d				08 44				09 04						09 24					09 44					
Southend Airport ✈	d				08 47				09 07						09 27					09 47					
Prittlewell	d				08 50				09 10						09 30					09 50					
Southend Victoria	a				08 54				09 14						09 34					09 54					

Table 5

Saturdays

London - Shenfield, Southminster and Southend Victoria

Network Diagram - see first Page of Table 5

		LE 1	LE 1	LE	LE	LE 1	LE 1	LE		LE 1	LE	LE 1	LE 1	LE	LE 1	LE	LE 1	LE 1		LE	LE	LE 1	LE 1	LE 1	LE
London Liverpool Street 15 ⊖	d	09 13	09 18	09 20	09 30	09 35	09 38	09 40		09 48	09 50		09 55	10 00	10 02	10 10	10 13	10 18		10 20	10 30		10 35	10 38	10 40
Stratford 7 ⊖	d	09 20	09 25	09 27	09 37	09 42	09 45	09 47		09 55	09 57		10 02	10 07	10 09	10 17	10 20	10 25		10 27	10 37		10 42	10 45	10 47
Maryland	d			09 29	09 39			09 49			09 59			10 09		10 19				10 29	10 39				10 49
Forest Gate	d			09 31	09 41			09 51			10 01			10 11		10 21				10 31	10 41				10 51
Manor Park	d			09 33	09 43			09 53			10 03			10 13		10 23				10 33	10 43				10 53
Ilford 2	d			09 36	09 46			09 56			10 06			10 16		10 26				10 36	10 46				10 56
Seven Kings	d			09 38	09 48			09 58			10 08			10 18		10 28				10 38	10 48				10 58
Goodmayes	d			09 40	09 50			10 00			10 10			10 20		10 30				10 40	10 50				11 00
Chadwell Heath	d			09 42	09 52			10 02			10 12			10 22		10 32				10 42	10 52				11 02
Romford	d	09 28		09 46	09 56		09 53	10 06			10 16			10 26		10 36	10 28			10 46	10 56			10 53	11 06
Gidea Park 2	d			09 50	10 00			10 10			10 20			10 30		10 40				10 50	11 00				11 10
Harold Wood	d			09 53	10 03			10 13			10 23			10 33		10 43				10 53	11 03				11 13
Brentwood	d			09 57	10 07			10 17			10 27			10 37		10 47				10 57	11 07				11 17
Shenfield 3	a	09 38	09 40	10 03	10 13	09 58	10 02	10 23		10 11	10 33		10 18	10 43	10 24	10 53	10 38	10 40		11 03	11 13		10 58	11 02	11 23
Shenfield 3	d	09 39				09 59							10 19				10 39						10 59		
Billericay	d	09 45				10 05							10 25				10 45						11 05		
Wickford 2	d	09 51				10 11						10 16	10 31				10 51					10 56	11 11		
Battlesbridge	d											10 20										11 00			
South Woodham Ferrers	d											10 24										11 04			
North Fambridge	d											10 31										11 11			
Althorne	d											10 36										11 16			
Burnham-on-Crouch	d											10 41										11 21			
Southminster	a											10 47										11 27			
Rayleigh	d	09 56				10 16							10 36				10 56						11 16		
Hockley	d	10 01				10 21							10 41				11 01						11 21		
Rochford	d	10 04				10 24							10 44				11 04						11 24		
Southend Airport ✈	d	10 07				10 27							10 47				11 07						11 27		
Prittlewell	d	10 10				10 30							10 50				11 10						11 30		
Southend Victoria	a	10 14				10 34							10 54				11 14						11 34		

		LE 1	LE	LE 1		LE	LE 1	LE	LE 1	LE 1	LE 1	LE	LE	LE 1		LE 1	LE	LE 1	LE	LE 1	LE 1	LE	LE 1	LE	
London Liverpool Street 15 ⊖	d	10 48	10 50	10 55		11 00	11 02	11 10		11 13	11 18	11 20	11 30	11 35		11 38	11 40	11 48	11 50		11 55	12 00	12 02	12 10	
Stratford 7 ⊖	d	10 55	10 57	11 02		11 07	11 09	11 17		11 20	11 25	11 27	11 37	11 42		11 45	11 47	11 55	11 57		12 02	12 07	12 09	12 17	
Maryland	d		10 59			11 09		11 19				11 29	11 39				11 49		11 59			12 09		12 19	
Forest Gate	d		11 01			11 11		11 21				11 31	11 41				11 51		12 01			12 11		12 21	
Manor Park	d		11 03			11 13		11 23				11 33	11 43				11 53		12 03			12 13		12 23	
Ilford 2	d		11 06			11 16		11 26				11 36	11 46				11 56		12 06			12 16		12 26	
Seven Kings	d		11 08			11 18		11 28				11 38	11 48				11 58		12 08			12 18		12 28	
Goodmayes	d		11 10			11 20		11 30				11 40	11 50				12 00		12 10			12 20		12 30	
Chadwell Heath	d		11 12			11 22		11 32				11 42	11 52				12 02		12 12			12 22		12 32	
Romford	d		11 16			11 26		11 36		11 28		11 46	11 56			11 53	12 06		12 16			12 26		12 36	
Gidea Park 2	d		11 20			11 30		11 40				11 50	12 00				12 10		12 20			12 30		12 40	
Harold Wood	d		11 23			11 33		11 43				11 53	12 03				12 13		12 23			12 33		12 43	
Brentwood	d		11 27			11 37		11 47				11 57	12 07				12 17		12 27			12 37		12 47	
Shenfield 3	a	11 11	11 33	11 18		11 43	11 24	11 53		11 38	11 40	12 03	12 13	11 58		12 02	12 23	12 11	12 33		12 18	12 43	12 24	12 53	
Shenfield 3	d			11 19						11 39				11 59							12 19				
Billericay	d			11 25						11 45				12 05							12 25				
Wickford 2	d			11 31					11 36	11 51				12 11						12 16	12 31				
Battlesbridge	d								11 40											12 20					
South Woodham Ferrers	d								11 44											12 24					
North Fambridge	d								11 51											12 31					
Althorne	d								11 56											12 36					
Burnham-on-Crouch	d								12 01											12 41					
Southminster	a								12 07											12 47					
Rayleigh	d			11 36						11 56				12 16							12 36				
Hockley	d			11 41						12 01				12 21							12 41				
Rochford	d			11 44						12 04				12 24							12 44				
Southend Airport ✈	d			11 47						12 07				12 27							12 47				
Prittlewell	d			11 50						12 10				12 30							12 50				
Southend Victoria	a			11 54						12 14				12 34							12 54				

Table 5

Saturdays

London - Shenfield, Southminster and Southend Victoria

Network Diagram - see first Page of Table 5

		LE	LE	LE	LE	LE	LE	LE	LE	LE		LE	LE	LE	LE	LE	LE	LE	LE	LE		LE	LE	LE	LE
		1	1			1	1	1		1			1		1		1	1	1				1	1	
London Liverpool Street 15 ⊖	d	12 13	12 18	12 20	12 30		12 35	12 38	12 40	12 48		12 50	12 55	13 00	13 02	13 10		13 13	13 18	13 20		13 30	13 35	13 38	13 40
Stratford 7 ⊖	d	12 20	12 25	12 27	12 37		12 42	12 45	12 47	12 55		12 57	13 02	13 07	13 09	13 17		13 20	13 25	13 27		13 37	13 42	13 45	13 47
Maryland	d			12 29	12 39				12 49			12 59		13 09		13 19				13 29		13 39			13 49
Forest Gate	d			12 31	12 41				12 51			13 01		13 11		13 21				13 31		13 41			13 51
Manor Park	d			12 33	12 43				12 53			13 03		13 13		13 23				13 33		13 43			13 53
Ilford 2	d			12 36	12 46				12 56			13 06		13 16		13 26				13 36		13 46			13 56
Seven Kings	d			12 38	12 48				12 58			13 08		13 18		13 28				13 38		13 48			13 58
Goodmayes	d			12 40	12 50				13 00			13 10		13 20		13 30				13 40		13 50			14 00
Chadwell Heath	d			12 42	12 52				13 02			13 12		13 22		13 32				13 42		13 52			14 02
Romford	d	12 28		12 46	12 56			12 53	13 06			13 16		13 26		13 36		13 28		13 46		13 56		13 53	14 06
Gidea Park 2	d			12 50	13 00				13 10			13 20		13 30		13 40				13 50		14 00			14 10
Harold Wood	d			12 53	13 03				13 13			13 23		13 33		13 43				13 53		14 03			14 13
Brentwood	d			12 57	13 07				13 17			13 27		13 37		13 47				13 57		14 07			14 17
Shenfield 3	a	12 38	12 40	13 03	13 13		12 58	13 02	13 23	13 11		13 33	13 18	13 43	13 24	13 53		13 38	13 40	14 03		14 13	13 58	14 02	14 23
Shenfield 3	d	12 39					12 59						13 19					13 39					13 59		
Billericay	d	12 45					13 05						13 25					13 45					14 05		
Wickford 2	d	12 51				12 56	13 11						13 31				13 36	13 51					14 11		
Battlesbridge	d					13 00											13 40								
South Woodham Ferrers	d					13 04											13 44								
North Fambridge	d					13 11											13 51								
Althorne	d					13 16											13 56								
Burnham-on-Crouch	d					13 21											14 01								
Southminster	a					13 27											14 07								
Rayleigh	d	12 56					13 16						13 36					13 56					14 16		
Hockley	d	13 01					13 21						13 41					14 01					14 21		
Rochford	d	13 04					13 24						13 44					14 04					14 24		
Southend Airport ✈	d	13 07					13 27						13 47					14 07					14 27		
Prittlewell	d	13 10					13 30						13 50					14 10					14 30		
Southend Victoria	a	13 14					13 34						13 54					14 14					14 34		

		LE	LE	LE	LE	LE		LE	LE	LE	LE	LE	LE	LE	LE	LE		LE	LE	LE	LE	LE	LE	LE	LE
		1		1	1			1		1	1			1	1	1			1		1		1		1
London Liverpool Street 15 ⊖	d	13 48	13 50		13 55	14 00		14 02	14 10	14 13	14 18	14 20	14 30		14 35	14 38		14 40	14 48	14 50	14 55	15 00	15 02	15 10	
Stratford 7 ⊖	d	13 55	13 57		14 02	14 07		14 09	14 17	14 20	14 25	14 27	14 37		14 42	14 45		14 47	14 55	14 57	15 02	15 07	15 09	15 17	
Maryland	d		13 59			14 09			14 19			14 29	14 39					14 49		14 59		15 09		15 19	
Forest Gate	d		14 01			14 11			14 21			14 31	14 41					14 51		15 01		15 11		15 21	
Manor Park	d		14 03			14 13			14 23			14 33	14 43					14 53		15 03		15 13		15 23	
Ilford 2	d		14 06			14 16			14 26			14 36	14 46					14 56		15 06		15 16		15 26	
Seven Kings	d		14 08			14 18			14 28			14 38	14 48					14 58		15 08		15 18		15 28	
Goodmayes	d		14 10			14 20			14 30			14 40	14 50					15 00		15 10		15 20		15 30	
Chadwell Heath	d		14 12			14 22			14 32			14 42	14 52					15 02		15 12		15 22		15 32	
Romford	d		14 16			14 26			14 36	14 28		14 46	14 56			14 53		15 06		15 16		15 26		15 36	
Gidea Park 2	d		14 20			14 30			14 40			14 50	15 00					15 10		15 20		15 30		15 40	
Harold Wood	d		14 23			14 33			14 43			14 53	15 03					15 13		15 23		15 33		15 43	
Brentwood	d		14 27			14 37			14 47			14 57	15 07					15 17		15 27		15 37		15 47	
Shenfield 3	a	14 11	14 33		14 18	14 43		14 24	14 53	14 38	14 40	15 03	15 13		14 58	15 02		15 23	15 11	15 33	15 18	15 43	15 24	15 53	
Shenfield 3	d				14 19					14 39					14 59						15 19				
Billericay	d				14 25					14 45					15 05						15 25				
Wickford 2	d			14 16	14 31					14 51				14 56	15 11						15 31				15 36
Battlesbridge	d			14 20										15 00											15 40
South Woodham Ferrers	d			14 24										15 04											15 44
North Fambridge	d			14 31										15 11											15 51
Althorne	d			14 36										15 16											15 56
Burnham-on-Crouch	d			14 41										15 21											16 01
Southminster	a			14 47										15 27											16 07
Rayleigh	d				14 36					14 56					15 16						15 36				
Hockley	d				14 41					15 01					15 21						15 41				
Rochford	d				14 44					15 04					15 24						15 44				
Southend Airport ✈	d				14 47					15 07					15 27						15 47				
Prittlewell	d				14 50					15 10					15 30						15 50				
Southend Victoria	a				14 54					15 14					15 34						15 54				

Table 5

Saturdays

London - Shenfield, Southminster and Southend Victoria

Network Diagram - see first Page of Table 5

		LE 1		LE 1	LE	LE	LE 1	LE 1	LE	LE 1	LE	LE 1		LE 1	LE	LE 1	LE	LE 1	LE 1	LE	LE	LE 1		LE 1	LE 1
London Liverpool Street 15 ⊖	d	15 13		15 18	15 20	15 30	15 35	15 38	15 40	15 48	15 50			15 55	16 00	16 02	16 10	16 13	16 18	16 20	16 30			16 35	16 38
Stratford 7 ⊖	d	15 20		15 25	15 27	15 37	15 42	15 45	15 47	15 55	15 57			16 02	16 07	16 09	16 17	16 20	16 25	16 27	16 37			16 42	16 45
Maryland	d				15 29	15 39			15 49		15 59				16 09		16 19			16 29	16 39				
Forest Gate	d				15 31	15 41			15 51		16 01				16 11		16 21			16 31	16 41				
Manor Park	d				15 33	15 43			15 53		16 03				16 13		16 23			16 33	16 43				
Ilford 2	d				15 36	15 46			15 56		16 06				16 16		16 26			16 36	16 46				
Seven Kings	d				15 38	15 48			15 58		16 08				16 18		16 28			16 38	16 48				
Goodmayes	d				15 40	15 50			16 00		16 10				16 20		16 30			16 40	16 50				
Chadwell Heath	d				15 42	15 52			16 02		16 12				16 22		16 32			16 42	16 52				
Romford	d	15 28			15 46	15 56		15 53	16 06		16 16				16 26		16 36	16 28		16 46	16 56				16 53
Gidea Park 2	d				15 50	16 00			16 10		16 20				16 30		16 40			16 50	17 00				
Harold Wood	d				15 53	16 03			16 13		16 23				16 33		16 43			16 53	17 03				
Brentwood	d				15 57	16 07			16 17		16 27				16 37		16 47			16 57	17 07				
Shenfield 3	a	15 38		15 40	16 03	16 13	15 58	16 02	16 23	16 11	16 33			16 18	16 43	16 24	16 53	16 38	16 40	17 03	17 13			16 58	17 02
Shenfield 3	d	15 39					15 59							16 19				16 39						16 59	
Billericay	d	15 45					16 05							16 25				16 45						17 05	
Wickford 2	d	15 51					16 11					16 16		16 31				16 51				16 56		17 11	
Battlesbridge	d											16 20										17 00			
South Woodham Ferrers	d											16 24										17 04			
North Fambridge	d											16 31										17 11			
Althorne	d											16 36										17 16			
Burnham-on-Crouch	d											16 41										17 21			
Southminster	a											16 47										17 27			
Rayleigh	d	15 56					16 16							16 36				16 56						17 16	
Hockley	d	16 01					16 21							16 41				17 01						17 21	
Rochford	d	16 04					16 24							16 44				17 04						17 24	
Southend Airport ✈	d	16 07					16 27							16 47				17 07						17 27	
Prittlewell	d	16 10					16 30							16 50				17 10						17 30	
Southend Victoria	a	16 14					16 34							16 54				17 14						17 34	

		LE	LE 1	LE	LE 1	LE	LE 1	LE		LE 1	LE 1	LE 1	LE	LE	LE 1	LE 1	LE	LE 1		LE	LE 1	LE 1	LE	LE 1	LE
London Liverpool Street 15 ⊖	d	16 40	16 48	16 50	16 55	17 00	17 02	17 10			17 13	17 18	17 20	17 30	17 35	17 38	17 40	17 48		17 50		17 55	18 00	18 02	18 10
Stratford 7 ⊖	d	16 47	16 55	16 57	17 02	17 07	17 09	17 17			17 20	17 25	17 27	17 37	17 42	17 45	17 47	17 55		17 57		18 02	18 07	18 09	18 17
Maryland	d	16 49		16 59		17 09		17 19					17 29	17 39			17 49			17 59			18 09		18 19
Forest Gate	d	16 51		17 01		17 11		17 21					17 31	17 41			17 51			18 01			18 11		18 21
Manor Park	d	16 53		17 03		17 13		17 23					17 33	17 43			17 53			18 03			18 13		18 23
Ilford 2	d	16 56		17 06		17 16		17 26					17 36	17 46			17 56			18 06			18 16		18 26
Seven Kings	d	16 58		17 08		17 18		17 28					17 38	17 48			17 58			18 08			18 18		18 28
Goodmayes	d	17 00		17 10		17 20		17 30					17 40	17 50			18 00			18 10			18 20		18 30
Chadwell Heath	d	17 02		17 12		17 22		17 32					17 42	17 52			18 02			18 12			18 22		18 32
Romford	d	17 06		17 16		17 26		17 36			17 28		17 46	17 56		17 53	18 06			18 16			18 26		18 36
Gidea Park 2	d	17 10		17 20		17 30		17 40					17 50	18 00			18 10			18 20			18 30		18 40
Harold Wood	d	17 13		17 23		17 33		17 43					17 53	18 03			18 13			18 23			18 33		18 43
Brentwood	d	17 17		17 27		17 37		17 47					17 57	18 07			18 17			18 27			18 37		18 47
Shenfield 3	a	17 23	17 11	17 33	17 18	17 43	17 24	17 53			17 38	17 40	18 03	18 13	17 58	18 02	18 23	18 11		18 33		18 18	18 43	18 24	18 53
Shenfield 3	d				17 19						17 39				17 59							18 19			
Billericay	d				17 25						17 45				18 05							18 25			
Wickford 2	d				17 31					17 36	17 51				18 11						18 16	18 31			
Battlesbridge	d									17 40											18 20				
South Woodham Ferrers	d									17 44											18 24				
North Fambridge	d									17 51											18 31				
Althorne	d									17 56											18 36				
Burnham-on-Crouch	d									18 01											18 41				
Southminster	a									18 07											18 47				
Rayleigh	d				17 36						17 56				18 16							18 36			
Hockley	d				17 41						18 01				18 21							18 41			
Rochford	d				17 44						18 04				18 24							18 44			
Southend Airport ✈	d				17 47						18 07				18 27							18 47			
Prittlewell	d				17 50						18 10				18 30							18 50			
Southend Victoria	a				17 54						18 14				18 34							18 54			

Table 5

London - Shenfield, Southminster and Southend Victoria

Network Diagram - see first Page of Table 5

		LE 1	LE 1	LE		LE	LE 1	LE 1	LE 1	LE	LE 1	LE	LE 1	LE		LE 1	LE	LE 1	LE 1	LE 1	LE	LE	LE 1	LE 1	
London Liverpool Street 15 ⊖	d	18 13	18 18	18 20		18 30		18 35	18 38	18 40	18 48	18 50	18 55	19 00		19 02	19 10		19 13	19 18	19 20	19 30	19 32	19 35	
Stratford 7 ⊖	d	18 20	18 25	18 27		18 37		18 42	18 45	18 47	18 55	18 57	19 02	19 07		19 09	19 17		19 20	19 25	19 27	19 37	19 39	19 43	
Maryland	d			18 29		18 39				18 49		18 59		19 09			19 19				19 29	19 39			
Forest Gate	d			18 31		18 41				18 51		19 01		19 11			19 21				19 31	19 41			
Manor Park	d			18 33		18 43				18 53		19 03		19 13			19 23				19 33	19 43			
Ilford 2	d			18 36		18 46				18 56		19 06		19 16			19 26				19 36	19 46			
Seven Kings	d			18 38		18 48				18 58		19 08		19 18			19 28				19 38	19 48			
Goodmayes	d			18 40		18 50				19 00		19 10		19 20			19 30				19 40	19 50			
Chadwell Heath	d			18 42		18 52				19 02		19 12		19 22			19 32				19 42	19 52			
Romford	d	18 28		18 46		18 56			18 53	19 06		19 16		19 26			19 36		19 28		19 46	19 56			
Gidea Park 2	d			18 50		19 00				19 10		19 20		19 30			19 40				19 50	20 00			
Harold Wood	d			18 53		19 03				19 13		19 23		19 33			19 43				19 53	20 03			
Brentwood	d			18 57		19 07				19 17		19 27		19 37			19 47				19 57	20 07			
Shenfield 3	a	18 38	18 40	19 03		19 13		18 58	19 02	19 23	19 11	19 33	19 18	19 43		19 24	19 53		19 38	19 40	20 03	20 13	19 56	19 59	
Shenfield 3	d	18 39						18 59					19 19						19 39					20 00	
Billericay	d	18 45						19 05					19 25						19 45					20 06	
Wickford 2	d	18 51					18 56	19 11					19 31					19 36	19 51					20 12	
Battlesbridge	d						19 00											19 40							
South Woodham Ferrers	d						19 04											19 44							
North Fambridge	d						19 11											19 51							
Althorne	d						19 16											19 56							
Burnham-on-Crouch	d						19 21											20 01							
Southminster	a						19 27											20 07							
Rayleigh	d	18 56						19 16					19 36						19 56					20 17	
Hockley	d	19 01						19 21					19 41						20 01					20 22	
Rochford	d	19 04						19 24					19 44						20 04					20 25	
Southend Airport ✈	d	19 07						19 27					19 47						20 07					20 28	
Prittlewell	d	19 10						19 30					19 50						20 10					20 31	
Southend Victoria	a	19 14						19 34					19 54						20 14					20 35	

		LE 1	LE	LE 1	LE	LE 1	LE 1	LE	LE 1	LE		LE 1	LE 1	LE	LE	LE 1	LE 1	LE 1	LE	LE 1		LE	LE 1	LE 1	LE
London Liverpool Street 15 ⊖	d	19 38	19 40	19 48	19 50		19 55	20 00	20 02	20 10		20 13	20 18	20 20	20 30		20 35	20 38	20 40	20 48		20 50	20 55	21 02	21 05
Stratford 7 ⊖	d	19 46	19 47	19 55	19 57		20 02	20 07	20 09	20 17		20 20	20 25	20 27	20 37		20 42	20 45	20 47	20 55		20 57	21 02	21 09	21 12
Maryland	d		19 49		19 59			20 09		20 19				20 29	20 39				20 49			20 59			21 14
Forest Gate	d		19 51		20 01			20 11		20 21				20 31	20 41				20 51			21 01			21 16
Manor Park	d		19 53		20 03			20 13		20 23				20 33	20 43				20 53			21 03			21 18
Ilford 2	d		19 56		20 06			20 16		20 26				20 36	20 46				20 56			21 06			21 21
Seven Kings	d		19 58		20 08			20 18		20 28				20 38	20 48				20 58			21 08			21 23
Goodmayes	d		20 00		20 10			20 20		20 30				20 40	20 50				21 00			21 10			21 25
Chadwell Heath	d		20 02		20 12			20 22		20 32				20 42	20 52				21 02			21 12			21 27
Romford	d	19 54	20 06		20 16			20 26		20 36		20 28		20 46	20 56			20 53	21 06			21 16			21 31
Gidea Park 2	d		20 10		20 20			20 30		20 40				20 50	21 00				21 10			21 20			21 35
Harold Wood	d		20 13		20 23			20 33		20 43				20 53	21 03				21 13			21 23			21 38
Brentwood	d		20 17		20 27			20 37		20 47				20 57	21 07				21 17			21 27			21 42
Shenfield 3	a	20 03	20 23	20 11	20 33		20 18	20 43	20 24	20 53		20 38	20 40	21 03	21 13		20 58	21 02	21 23	21 11		21 33	21 18	21 24	21 48
Shenfield 3	d						20 19					20 39					20 59						21 19		
Billericay	d						20 25					20 45					21 05						21 25		
Wickford 2	d					20 16	20 31					20 51				20 56	21 11						21 31		
Battlesbridge	d					20 20										21 00									
South Woodham Ferrers	d					20 24										21 04									
North Fambridge	d					20 31										21 11									
Althorne	d					20 36										21 16									
Burnham-on-Crouch	d					20 41										21 21									
Southminster	a					20 47										21 27									
Rayleigh	d						20 36					20 56					21 16						21 36		
Hockley	d						20 41					21 01					21 21						21 41		
Rochford	d						20 44					21 04					21 24						21 44		
Southend Airport ✈	d						20 47					21 07					21 27						21 47		
Prittlewell	d						20 50					21 10					21 30						21 50		
Southend Victoria	a						20 54					21 14					21 34						21 54		

Table 5

Saturdays

London - Shenfield, Southminster and Southend Victoria

Network Diagram - see first Page of Table 5

		LE 1	LE 1	LE 1	LE	LE 1		LE	LE 1	LE 1	LE	LE 1	LE 1	LE 1	LE	LE 1		LE 1	LE	LE	LE 1	LE 1	LE 1	LE	LE 1
London Liverpool Street 15 ⊖	d		21 13	21 18	21 20	21 35		21 35	21 38	21 48	21 50		21 55	22 02	22 05	22 13		22 18	22 20	22 35	22 38		22 45	22 50	23 02
Stratford 7 ⊖	d		21 20	21 25	21 27	21 42		21 42	21 45	21 55	21 57		22 02	22 09	22 12	22 20		22 25	22 27	22 42	22 45		22 52	22 57	23 09
Maryland	d				21 29			21 44			21 59				22 14				22 29	22 44				22 59	
Forest Gate	d				21 31			21 46			22 01				22 16				22 31	22 46				23 01	
Manor Park	d				21 33			21 48			22 03				22 18				22 33	22 48				23 03	
Ilford 2	d				21 36			21 51			22 06				22 21				22 36	22 51				23 06	
Seven Kings	d				21 38			21 53			22 08				22 23				22 38	22 53				23 08	
Goodmayes	d				21 40			21 55			22 10				22 25				22 40	22 55				23 10	
Chadwell Heath	d				21 42			21 57			22 12				22 27				22 42	22 57				23 12	
Romford	d		21 28		21 46			22 01	21 53		22 16				22 31	22 28			22 46	23 01	22 53			23 16	
Gidea Park 2	d				21 50			22 05			22 20				22 35				22 50	23 05				23 20	
Harold Wood	d				21 53			22 08			22 23				22 38				22 53	23 08				23 23	
Brentwood	d				21 57			22 12			22 27				22 42				22 57	23 12				23 27	
Shenfield 3	a		21 38	21 40	22 03	21 57		22 18	22 02	22 11	22 33		22 18	22 24	22 48	22 38		22 40	23 03	23 18	23 02		23 08	23 33	23 24
Shenfield 3	d		21 39			21 59							22 19			22 39							23 09		
Billericay	d		21 45			22 05							22 25			22 45							23 15		
Wickford 2	d	21 36	21 51			22 11						22 16	22 31			22 51						22 56	23 21		
Battlesbridge	d	21 40										22 20										23 00			
South Woodham Ferrers	d	21 44										22 24										23 04			
North Fambridge	d	21 51										22 31										23 11			
Althorne	d	21 56										22 36										23 16			
Burnham-on-Crouch	d	22 01										22 41										23 21			
Southminster	a	22 07										22 47										23 27			
Rayleigh	d		21 56			22 16							22 36			22 56							23 26		
Hockley	d		22 01			22 21							22 41			23 01							23 31		
Rochford	d		22 04			22 24							22 44			23 04							23 34		
Southend Airport ✈	d		22 07			22 27							22 47			23 07							23 37		
Prittlewell	d		22 10			22 30							22 50			23 10							23 40		
Southend Victoria	a		22 14			22 34							22 54			23 14							23 48		

		LE		LE 1	LE 1	LE	LE	LE 1	LE 1	LE
London Liverpool Street 15 ⊖	d	23 05		23 15	23 18	23 20	23 35	23 45	23 48	23 50
Stratford 7 ⊖	d	23 12		23 22	23 25	23 27	23 42	23 52	23 55	23 57
Maryland	d	23 14				23 29	23 44			23 59
Forest Gate	d	23 16				23 31	23 46			00 01
Manor Park	d	23 18				23 33	23 48			00 03
Ilford 2	d	23 21				23 36	23 51			00 06
Seven Kings	d	23 23				23 38	23 53			00 08
Goodmayes	d	23 25				23 40	23 55			00 10
Chadwell Heath	d	23 27				23 42	23 57			00 12
Romford	d	23 31				23 46	00 02			00 16
Gidea Park 2	d	23 35				23 50	00 05			00 20
Harold Wood	d	23 38				23 53	00 08			00 23
Brentwood	d	23 42				23 57	00 12			00 27
Shenfield 3	a	23 48		23 38	23 40	00 03	00 18	00 08	00 10	00 33
Shenfield 3	d			23 39				00 09		
Billericay	d			23 45				00 15		
Wickford 2	d			23 51				00 21		
Battlesbridge	d									
South Woodham Ferrers	d									
North Fambridge	d									
Althorne	d									
Burnham-on-Crouch	d									
Southminster	a									
Rayleigh	d			23 56				00 26		
Hockley	d			00 01				00 31		
Rochford	d			00 04				00 34		
Southend Airport ✈	d			00 07				00 37		
Prittlewell	d			00 10				00 40		
Southend Victoria	a			00 18				00 48		

Table 5

Sundays

London - Shenfield, Southminster and Southend Victoria

Network Diagram - see first Page of Table 5

		LE	LE	LE	LE	LE	LE	LE	LE	LE		LE	LE	LE	LE	LE	LE	LE	LE	LE		LE	LE	LE	LE
		1			1	1			1	1				1			1	1		1		1	1		1
		A	A	A	A	A	A									🚌			🚌						
London Liverpool Street 15 ⊖	d	23p15	23p20	23p35	23p45	23p48	23p50	00 01	00 15	00 18		00 20	00 32	00 50	00 55	06 05			06 35				07 55	08 05	08 15
Stratford 7 ⊖	d	23p22	23p27	23p42	23p52	23p55	23p57	00 08	00 22	00 25		00 27	00 39	00 57	01 02	06 25			06 55				08 02	08 12	08 22
Maryland	d		23p29	23p44			23p59	00 10				00 29	00 41		01 04									08 13	
Forest Gate	d		23p31	23p46			00 01	00 12				00 31	00 43		01 06									08 15	
Manor Park	d		23p33	23p48			00 03	00 14				00 33	00 45		01 08									08 17	
Ilford 2	d		23p36	23p51			00 06	00 17				00 36	00 48		01 11	06 40			07 10					08 20	
Seven Kings	d		23p38	23p53			00 08	00 19				00 38	00 50		01 13									08 23	
Goodmayes	d		23p40	23p55			00 10	00 21				00 40	00 52		01 15									08 25	
Chadwell Heath	d		23p42	23p57			00 12	00 23				00 42	00 54		01 17									08 27	
Romford	d		23p46	00 02			00 16	00 27	00 32			00 46	00 58	01 08	01 21	07 00			07 30					08 30	08 33
Gidea Park 2	d		23p50	00 05			00 20	00a31				00 50	01a02		01 25	07 07			07 37					08 34	08 37
Harold Wood	d		23p53	00 08			00 23					00 53			01 28	07 14			07 44					08 37	08 40
Brentwood	d		23p57	00 12			00 27					00 57			01 32	07 29			07 59					08 41	08 44
Shenfield 3	a	23p38	00 03	00 18	00 08	00 10	00 33		00 44	00 47		01 03		01 20	01 38	07 39			08 09				08 24	08 48	08 50
Shenfield 3	d	23p39			00 09				00 45					01 20				07 50				08 20			08 50
Billericay	d	23p45			00 15				00 51					01 26				07 56				08 26			08 56
Wickford 2	d	23p51			00 21				00 56					01 31			07 30	08 01		08 05		08 31			09 01
Battlesbridge	d																07 34			08 09					
South Woodham Ferrers	d																07 38			08 13					
North Fambridge	d																07 44			08 20					
Althorne	d																07 49			08 25					
Burnham-on-Crouch	d																07 54			08 30					
Southminster	a																08 00			08 36					
Rayleigh	d	23p56			00 26				01 01					01 36				08 06				08 36			09 06
Hockley	d	00 01			00 31				01 06					01 41				08 11				08 41			09 11
Rochford	d	00 04			00 34				01 09					01 44				08 14				08 44			09 14
Southend Airport ✈	d	00 07			00 37				01 12					01 47				08 17				08 47			09 17
Prittlewell	d	00 10			00 40				01 15					01 50											
Southend Victoria	a	00 18			00 48				01 23					01 58				08 25				08 55			09 25

		LE	LE	LE	LE	LE		LE	LE	LE	LE	LE	LE	LE	LE		LE		LE	LE	LE	LE	LE	LE
		◇1		1	1	1			1		1		1	1					1		1		1	
London Liverpool Street 15 ⊖	d	08 30	08 35		08 45	09 02		09 05	09 15	09 17	09 32	09 35		09 45	09 47		19 47		20 02	20 05	20 15	20 17	20 32	20 35
Stratford 7 ⊖	d		08 42		08 52	09 09		09 12	09 22	09 24	09 39	09 42		09 52	09 54		19 54		20 09	20 12	20 22	20 24	20 39	20 42
Maryland	d		08 43					09 13				09 43								20 13				20 43
Forest Gate	d		08 45					09 15		09 27		09 45			09 57		19 57			20 15		20 27		20 45
Manor Park	d		08 47					09 17		09 29		09 47			09 59		19 59			20 17		20 29		20 47
Ilford 2	d		08 50					09 20		09 32		09 50			10 02		20 02			20 20		20 32		20 50
Seven Kings	d		08 53					09 23		09 34		09 53			10 04		20 04			20 23		20 34		20 53
Goodmayes	d		08 55					09 25		09 36		09 55			10 06		20 06			20 25		20 36		20 55
Chadwell Heath	d		08 57					09 27		09 38		09 57			10 08		20 08			20 27		20 38		20 57
Romford	d		09 00		09 03			09 30	09 33	09 42		10 00		10 03	10 12		20 12			20 30	20 33	20 42		21 00
Gidea Park 2	d		09 04		09 07			09 34	09 37	09a47		10 04		10 07	10a17	and at the same minutes past each hour until	20a17			20 34	20 37	20a47		21 04
Harold Wood	d		09 07		09 10			09 37	09 40			10 07		10 10						20 37	20 40			21 07
Brentwood	d		09 11		09 14			09 41	09 44			10 11		10 14						20 41	20 44			21 11
Shenfield 3	a	08 57	09 18		09 20	09 30		09 48	09 50		10 00	10 18		10 20					20 30	20 48	20 50		21 00	21 18
Shenfield 3	d				09 20				09 50					10 20							20 50			
Billericay	d				09 26				09 56					10 26							20 56			
Wickford 2	d			09 05	09 31				10 01				10 05	10 31							21 01			
Battlesbridge	d			09 09									10 09											
South Woodham Ferrers	d			09 13									10 13											
North Fambridge	d			09 20									10 20											
Althorne	d			09 25									10 25											
Burnham-on-Crouch	d			09 30									10 30											
Southminster	a			09 36									10 36											
Rayleigh	d				09 36				10 06					10 36							21 06			
Hockley	d				09 41				10 11					10 41							21 11			
Rochford	d				09 44				10 14					10 44							21 14			
Southend Airport ✈	d				09 47				10 17					10 47							21 17			
Prittlewell	d																							
Southend Victoria	a				09 55				10 25					10 55							21 25			

A not 11 December

Table 5

Sundays

London - Shenfield, Southminster and Southend Victoria

Network Diagram - see first Page of Table 5

		LE 1	LE 1	LE	LE 1	LE	LE 1	LE	LE 1	LE	LE 1	LE 1
London Liverpool Street 15 ⊖	d		20 45	20 47	21 02	21 05	21 15	21 17	21 32	21 35		21 45
Stratford 7 ⊖	d		20 52	20 54	21 09	21 12	21 22	21 24	21 39	21 42		21 52
Maryland	d					21 13				21 43		
Forest Gate	d			20 57		21 15		21 27		21 45		
Manor Park	d			20 59		21 17		21 29		21 47		
Ilford 2	d			21 02		21 20		21 32		21 50		
Seven Kings	d			21 04		21 23		21 34		21 53		
Goodmayes	d			21 06		21 25		21 36		21 55		
Chadwell Heath	d			21 08		21 27		21 38		21 57		
Romford	d		21 03	21 12		21 30	21 33	21 42		22 00		22 03
Gidea Park 2	d		21 07	21a15		21 34	21 37	21a47		22 04		22 07
Harold Wood	d		21 10			21 37	21 40			22 07		22 10
Brentwood	d		21 14			21 41	21 44			22 11		22 14
Shenfield 3	a		21 20		21 30	21 48	21 50		22 00	22 18		22 20
Shenfield 3	d		21 20				21 50					22 20
Billericay	d		21 26				21 56					22 26
Wickford 2	d	21 05	21 31				22 01				22 05	22 31
Battlesbridge	d	21 09									22 09	
South Woodham Ferrers	d	21 13									22 13	
North Fambridge	d	21 20									22 20	
Althorne	d	21 25									22 25	
Burnham-on-Crouch	d	21 30									22 30	
Southminster	a	21 36									22 36	
Rayleigh	d		21 36				22 06					22 36
Hockley	d		21 41				22 11					22 41
Rochford	d		21 44				22 14					22 44
Southend Airport ✈	d		21 47				22 17					22 47
Prittlewell	d											
Southend Victoria	a		21 55				22 25					22 55

		LE	LE 1	LE	LE 1	LE	LE 1	LE	LE 1	LE 1	LE
London Liverpool Street 15 ⊖	d	21 47	22 02	22 05	22 15	22 17	22 32	22 35	22 45	23 02	23 05
Stratford 7 ⊖	d	21 54	22 09	22 12	22 22	22 24	22 39	22 42	22 52	23 09	23 12
Maryland	d			22 13				22 43			23 13
Forest Gate	d	21 57		22 15		22 27		22 45			23 15
Manor Park	d	21 59		22 17		22 29		22 47			23 17
Ilford 2	d	22 02		22 20		22 32		22 50			23 20
Seven Kings	d	22 04		22 23		22 34		22 53			23 23
Goodmayes	d	22 06		22 25		22 36		22 55			23 25
Chadwell Heath	d	22 08		22 27		22 38		22 57			23 27
Romford	d	22 12		22 30	22 33	22 42		23 00	23 03		23 30
Gidea Park 2	d	22a17		22 34	22 37	22a47		23 04	23 07		23 34
Harold Wood	d			22 37	22 40			23 07	23 10		23 37
Brentwood	d			22 41	22 44			23 11	23 14		23 41
Shenfield 3	a		22 30	22 48	22 50		23 00	23 18	23 20	23 30	23 48
Shenfield 3	d				22 50				23 20		
Billericay	d				22 56				23 26		
Wickford 2	d				23 01				23 31		
Battlesbridge	d										
South Woodham Ferrers	d										
North Fambridge	d										
Althorne	d										
Burnham-on-Crouch	d										
Southminster	a										
Rayleigh	d				23 06				23 36		
Hockley	d				23 11				23 41		
Rochford	d				23 14				23 44		
Southend Airport ✈	d				23 17				23 47		
Prittlewell	d										
Southend Victoria	a				23 27				23 57		

		LE 1	LE 1	LE	LE 1
London Liverpool Street 15 ⊖	d	23 15	23 32	23 35	23 45
Stratford 7 ⊖	d	23 22	23 39	23 42	23 52
Maryland	d			23 43	
Forest Gate	d			23 45	
Manor Park	d			23 47	
Ilford 2	d			23 50	
Seven Kings	d			23 53	
Goodmayes	d			23 55	
Chadwell Heath	d			23 57	
Romford	d	23 33		23 59	00 03
Gidea Park 2	d	23 37		00 04	00 07
Harold Wood	d	23 40		00 07	00 10
Brentwood	d	23 44		00 11	00 14
Shenfield 3	a	23 50	23 59	00 18	00 20
Shenfield 3	d	23 50			00 20
Billericay	d	23 56			00 26
Wickford 2	d	00 01			00 31
Battlesbridge	d				
South Woodham Ferrers	d				
North Fambridge	d				
Althorne	d				
Burnham-on-Crouch	d				
Southminster	a				
Rayleigh	d	00 06			00 36
Hockley	d	00 11			00 41
Rochford	d	00 14			00 44
Southend Airport ✈	d	00 17			00 47
Prittlewell	d				
Southend Victoria	a	00 27			00 57

Southend Victoria, Southminster and Shenfield - London

Network Diagram - see first Page of Table 5

Miles	Miles			LE MO ◇1	LE MO	CC MX	LE TWThO	LE TWThO ◇1	LE TWThO 1	LE FO ◇1	LE FO	LE FO 1	LE FO	LE	CC	LE	LE	LE 1	LE	LE	LE 1	LE
0	—	**Southend Victoria**	d											04 00			04 30				05 00	
0½	—	Prittlewell	d											04 02			04 32				05 02	
1¾	—	Southend Airport ✈	d											04 05			04 35				05 05	
2¾	—	Rochford	d											04 08			04 38				05 08	
5½	—	Hockley	d											04 12			04 42				05 11	
8¾	—	Rayleigh	d											04 16			04 46				05 16	
—	0	**Southminster**	d						23p06			22p56										
—	2¼	Burnham-on-Crouch	d						23p10			23p00										
—	5¼	Althorne	d						23p15			23p05										
—	8¼	North Fambridge	d						23p21			23p11										
—	11½	South Woodham Ferrers	d						23p26			23p16										
—	14	Battlesbridge	d						23p30			23p20										
12½	16½	**Wickford** 2	d						23p36			23p26		04 21			04 51				05 21	
17¼	—	Billericay	d						23p42			23p32		04 28			04 58				05 27	
—	—	**Shenfield** 3	a						23p49			23p39		04 39			05 09				05 35	
21¼	—	**Shenfield** 3	d		23p43		23p27	23p38	23p52		23p29	23p39	23p44	04 39			05 09	05 24		05 29	05 35	05 44
23¼	—	Brentwood	d		23p46		23p30				23p32		23p47	04 42			05 12			05 32		05 47
26½	—	Harold Wood	d		23p51		23p35				23p37		23p52	04 47			05 17			05 37		05 52
28	—	Gidea Park 2	d		23p55		23p39				23p41		23p56	04 51			05 21	05 31		05 41		05 56
29	—	Romford	d		23p57		23p41		00 03		23p43	23p47	23p58	04 53			05 23			05 43		05 58
31½	—	Chadwell Heath	d		00 01		23p45				23p47		00 02	04 57			05 27			05 47		06 02
32¼	—	Goodmayes	d		00 03		23p47				23p49		00 04	04 59			05 29			05 49		06 04
33	—	Seven Kings	d		00 05		23p49				23p51		00 06	05 01			05 31	05 36		05 51		06 06
34¼	—	Ilford 2	d		00 08		23p52				23p54		00 09	05 04		05 09	05 34		05 39	05 54		06 09
35¼	—	Manor Park	d		00 10		23p55				23p57		00 12			05 11			05 41	05 57		06 12
36¼	—	Forest Gate	d		00 12		23p57				23p59		00 14			05 14			05 44	05 59		06 14
37	—	Maryland	d		00 14		23p59				00 01		00 16			05 16			05 46	06 01		06 16
37½	—	Stratford 7 ⊖	d	23b57	00 16	00 09	00 02	00s04	00 13	23b52	00 04	23p56	00 19	05 10	05 14	05 18	05 40	05 42	05 48	06 04	05 49	06 19
41½	—	**London Liverpool Street** 15 ⊖	a	00 08	00 26	00 20	00 11	00 14	00 22	00 02	00 12	00 05	00 27	05 18	05 27	05 26	05 48	05 55	05 56	06 12	05 58	06 27

		LE 1	LE 1	LE 1	LE	LE	LE	LE 1	LE	LE 1	LE	LE 1	LE 1	LE	LE	LE 1	LE 1	LE 1	LE	LE
Southend Victoria	d		05 20					05 40				06 00				06 11				
Prittlewell	d		05 22					05 42				06 02				06 13				
Southend Airport ✈	d		05 25					05 45				06 05				06 16				
Rochford	d		05 28					05 48				06 08				06 19				
Hockley	d		05 31					05 51				06 11				06 22				
Rayleigh	d		05 36					05 56				06 16				06 27				
Southminster	d			05 26														06 09		
Burnham-on-Crouch	d			05 30														06 13		
Althorne	d			05 35														06 18		
North Fambridge	d			05 41														06 24		
South Woodham Ferrers	d			05 46														06 30		
Battlesbridge	d			05 50														06 34		
Wickford 2	d		05 41	05a56				06 01				06 21				06 32		06 40		
Billericay	d		05 47					06 07				06 27				06 39		06 46		
Shenfield 3	a		05 55					06 15				06 35				06 45		06 52		
Shenfield 3	d	05 53	05 55			06 04	06 14	06 15	06 24	06 25	06 34	06 35	06 41		06 44	06 45	06 50	06 53		06 54
Brentwood	d					06 07	06 17		06 27		06 37				06 47					06 57
Harold Wood	d					06 12	06 22		06 32		06 42				06 52					07 02
Gidea Park 2	d				06 06	06 16	06 26		06 36		06 45			06 49	06 55				06 59	07 05
Romford	d				06 08	06 18	06 28		06 38		06 48			06 51	06 58				07 01	07 08
Chadwell Heath	d				06 12	06 22	06 32		06 42		06 52			06 55	07 02				07 05	07 12
Goodmayes	d				06 14	06 24	06 34		06 44					06 57					07 07	
Seven Kings	d				06 16	06 26	06 36		06 46					06 59					07 09	
Ilford 2	d				06 19	06 29	06 39		06 49		06 57			07 02	07 07				07 12	07 17
Manor Park	d				06 22	06 32	06 42		06 52					07 05					07 15	
Forest Gate	d				06 24	06 34	06 44		06 54					07 07					07 17	
Maryland	d				06 26	06 36	06 46		06 56					07 09					07 19	
Stratford 7 ⊖	d	06 07	06 10		06 29	06 39	06 49	06 29	06 59	06 39	07 03	06 49	06s57	07 12	07 15	07s02	07s06	07s09	07 22	07 25
London Liverpool Street 15 ⊖	a	06 16	06 19		06 37	06 47	06 57	06 40	07 07	06 48	07 13	06 58	07 09	07 22	07 25	07 13	07 18	07 21	07 32	07 35

b Previous night, stops to set down only

Table 5

Mondays to Fridays

Southend Victoria, Southminster and Shenfield - London

Network Diagram - see first Page of Table 5

		LE	LE	LE		LE [1]		LE [1]	LE	LE	LE [1]		LE [1]	LE [1]		LE	LE	LE [1]	LE [1]	LE	LE	LE [1]	LE [1]		
Southend Victoria	d	06 26						06 40					06 50						07 03						
Prittlewell	d	06 28						06 42					06 52						07 05						
Southend Airport ✈	d	06 31						06 45					06 55						07 08						
Rochford	d	06 34						06 48					06 58						07 11						
Hockley	d	06 38						06 51					07 01						07 14						
Rayleigh	d	06 42						06 56					07 06						07 19						
Southminster	d																	06 48							
Burnham-on-Crouch	d																	06 52							
Althorne	d																	06 57							
North Fambridge	d																	07 04							
South Woodham Ferrers	d																	07 10							
Battlesbridge	d																	07 14							
Wickford [2]	d	06 47						07 01					07 11					07 19	07 24						
Billericay	d	06 54						07 08					07 18					07 26	07 31						
Shenfield [3]	a	07 01						07 14					07 24					07 32							
Shenfield [3]	d	07 01		07 04		07 08		07 14		07 14	07 19		07 24				07 24	07 32			07 34	07 38	07 41		
Brentwood	d			07 07						07 17							07 27				07 37				
Harold Wood	d			07 12						07 22							07 32				07 42				
Gidea Park [2]	d		07 09	07 15					07 19	07 25						07 29	07 35			07 39	07 45				
Romford	d		07 11	07 18					07 21	07 28						07 31	07 38			07 41	07 48				
Chadwell Heath	d		07 15	07 22					07 25	07 32						07 35	07 42			07 45	07 52				
Goodmayes	d		07 17						07 27	07 34						07 37	07 44			07 47	07 54				
Seven Kings	d		07 19						07 29	07 36						07 39	07 46			07 49	07 56				
Ilford [2]	d		07 22	07 27					07 32	07 39						07 42	07 49			07 52	07 59				
Manor Park	d		07 25						07 35							07 45				07 55					
Forest Gate	d		07 27						07 37							07 47				07 57					
Maryland	d		07 29						07 39							07 49				07 59					
Stratford [7] ⊖	d	07s19	07 32	07 35		07s23		07s31	07 42	07 45	07s35		07s41	07 44		07 52	07 55	07 50	07s52	08 02	08 05	07s55	07s58		
London Liverpool Street [15] ⊖	a	07 30	07 42	07 45		07 35		07 42	07 52	07 55	07 46		07 52	07 56		08 02	08 05	08 01	08 03	08 12	08 15	08 07	08 09		

		LE	LE	LE [1]	LE [1]		LE	LE	LE	LE		LE [1]	LE	LE [1]		LE [1]	LE [1]		LE	LE		LE	LE [1]	LE [1]	LE [1]
Southend Victoria	d			07 13						07 18		07 23				07 32							07 42		
Prittlewell	d			07 15						07 20		07 25				07 34							07 44		
Southend Airport ✈	d			07 18						07 23		07 28				07 37							07 47		
Rochford	d			07 21						07 26		07 31				07 40							07 50		
Hockley	d			07 24						07 30		07 34				07 43							07 53		
Rayleigh	d			07 29						07 34		07 39				07 48							07 58		
Southminster	d																							07 37	
Burnham-on-Crouch	d																							07 41	
Althorne	d																							07 46	
North Fambridge	d																							07 52	
South Woodham Ferrers	d																							07 59	
Battlesbridge	d																								
Wickford [2]	d			07 34						07 39		07 44				07 53							08 03	08 07	
Billericay	d			07 41						07 46		07 51				08 00							08 10	08 14	
Shenfield [3]	a			07 47						07 53		07 57				08 06							08 16		
Shenfield [3]	d		07 44	07 47	07 50			07 50		07 54		07 57	08 00	08 01		08 06	08 09					08 10	08 16		08 21
Brentwood	d		07 47					07 53		07 57			08 03									08 13			
Harold Wood	d		07 52					07 58		08 02			08 08									08 18			
Gidea Park [2]	d	07 49	07 55				07 59	08 02	08 05	08 09			08 12						08 15	08 19		08 22			
Romford	d	07 51	07 58				08 01	08 04	08 07	08 11			08 14						08 17	08 21		08 24			
Chadwell Heath	d	07 55	08 02				08 05	08 08	08 11	08 15			08 18						08 21	08 25		08 28			
Goodmayes	d	07 57	08 04				08 07	08 10	08 13	08 17			08 20						08 23	08 27		08 30			
Seven Kings	d	07 59	08 06				08 09	08 12	08 15	08 19			08 22						08 25	08 29		08 32			
Ilford [2]	d	08 02	08 09				08 12	08 15	08 18	08 22			08 25						08 28	08 32		08 35			
Manor Park	d	08 05							08 21										08 31						
Forest Gate	d	08 07							08 23										08 33						
Maryland	d	08 09							08 25										08 35						
Stratford [7] ⊖	d	08 12	08 15	08s04	08s07		08 18	08 21	08 28	08 31		08s15	08 34	08s18		08s23	08s25		08 38	08 41		08 44	08s33	08s35	08s38
London Liverpool Street [15] ⊖	a	08 22	08 25	08 15	08 19		08 28	08 31	08 38	08 41		08 26	08 43	08 30		08 36	08 38		08 48	08 51		08 53	08 46	08 48	08 50

Southend Victoria, Southminster and Shenfield - London

Network Diagram - see first Page of Table 5

		LE	LE	LE	LE	LE		LE			LE	LE	LE	LE	LE	LE		LE	LE	LE	LE	LE		LE	LE
					1	1		1						1	1					1	1			1	1
Southend Victoria	d					07 52								08 03						08 12					08 30
Prittlewell	d					07 54								08 05						08 14					08 32
Southend Airport ✈	d					07 57								08 08						08 17					08 35
Rochford	d					08 00								08 11						08 20					08 38
Hockley	d					08 03								08 14						08 23					08 41
Rayleigh	d					08 08								08 19						08 28					08 46
Southminster	d																							08 16	
Burnham-on-Crouch	d																							08 20	
Althorne	d																							08 25	
North Fambridge	d																							08 31	
South Woodham Ferrers	d																							08 37	
Battlesbridge	d																							08 41	
Wickford 2	d					08 13								08 24						08 33				08 46	08 51
Billericay	d					08 20								08 31						08 40				08 53	08 58
Shenfield 3	a					08 26								08 37						08 46				08 59	09 04
Shenfield 3	d			08 22	08 24	08 26		08 29					08 32	08 37	08 42				08 44	08 46	08 51	08 54		08 59	09 04
Brentwood	d			08 25									08 35						08 47			08 57			
Harold Wood	d			08 30									08 40						08 52			09 02			
Gidea Park 2	d		08 29	08 34								08 41	08 44					08 51	08 56			09 06			
Romford	d		08 31	08 36								08 43	08 46					08 53	08 58	08 55		09 08			
Chadwell Heath	d		08 35	08 40								08 47	08 50					08 57	09 02			09 12			
Goodmayes	d		08 37	08 42								08 49	08 52					08 59	09 04			09 14			
Seven Kings	d		08 39	08 44								08 51	08 54					09 01	09 06			09 16			
Ilford 2	d	08 38	08 42	08 47							08 50	08 54	08 57			09 00		09 04	09 09			09 19			
Manor Park	d	08 41									08 53					09 03			09 12			09 22			
Forest Gate	d	08 43									08 55					09 05			09 14			09 24			
Maryland	d	08 45									08 57					09 07			09 16			09 26			
Stratford 7 ⊖	d	08 48	08 51	08 54	08s41	08s43		08s45			09 00	09 03	09 06	08s56	08s59	09 10		09 13	09 19	09s05	09s08	09 29		09s16	09s22
London Liverpool Street 15 ⊖	a	08 58	09 01	09 03	08 54	08 56		08 58			09 10	09 13	09 14	09 08	09 11	09 20		09 23	09 27	09 16	09 19	09 37		09 29	09 33

					LE	LE	LE	LE	LE	LE	LE	LE		LE	LE	LE	LE	LE	LE	LE	LE	LE		LE	LE
							1		1	1	1			1		1	1			1	1	1			1
Southend Victoria	d									08 52						09 10				09 30					
Prittlewell	d									08 54						09 12				09 32					
Southend Airport ✈	d									08 57						09 15				09 35					
Rochford	d									09 00						09 18				09 38					
Hockley	d									09 03						09 21				09 41					
Rayleigh	d									09 08						09 26				09 46					
Southminster	d										08 56										09 36				
Burnham-on-Crouch	d										09 00										09 40				
Althorne	d										09 05										09 45				
North Fambridge	d										09 11										09 51				
South Woodham Ferrers	d										09 16										09 56				
Battlesbridge	d										09 20										10 00				
Wickford 2	d									09 13	09a26					09 31				09 51	10a06				
Billericay	d									09 20						09 37				09 57					
Shenfield 3	a									09 27						09 45				10 05					
Shenfield 3	d				09 04	09 14	09 21	09 24	09 25	09 27		09 34		09 38	09 44	09 45	09 51	09 54	10 04	10 05		10 08		10 14	10 18
Brentwood	d				09 07	09 17		09 27				09 37			09 47			09 57	10 07					10 17	
Harold Wood	d				09 12	09 22		09 32				09 42			09 52			10 02	10 12					10 22	
Gidea Park 2	d				09 16	09 26		09 36				09 46			09 56			10 06	10 16					10 26	
Romford	d				09 18	09 28		09 38				09 48			09 58	09 53		10 08	10 18					10 28	10 26
Chadwell Heath	d				09 22	09 32		09 42				09 52			10 02			10 12	10 22					10 32	
Goodmayes	d				09 24	09 34		09 44				09 54			10 04			10 14	10 24					10 34	
Seven Kings	d				09 26	09 36		09 46				09 56			10 06			10 16	10 26					10 36	
Ilford 2	d				09 29	09 39		09 49				09 59			10 09			10 19	10 29					10 39	
Manor Park	d				09 32	09 42		09 52				10 02			10 12			10 22	10 32					10 42	
Forest Gate	d				09 34	09 44		09 54				10 04			10 14			10 24	10 34					10 44	
Maryland	d				09 36	09 46		09 56				10 06			10 16			10 26	10 36					10 46	
Stratford 7 ⊖	d				09 39	09 49	09s37	09 59	09s41	09s43		10 09		09 52	10 19	10 01	10 05	10 29	10 39	10 19		10 22		10 49	10 34
London Liverpool Street 15 ⊖	a				09 47	09 58	09 49	10 07	09 53	09 55		10 17		10 01	10 27	10 10	10 14	10 37	10 47	10 28		10 31		10 57	10 43

Southend Victoria, Southminster and Shenfield - London

Network Diagram - see first Page of Table 5

		LE	LE 1		LE	LE 1	LE	LE 1		LE 1	LE 1	LE	LE	LE 1	LE 1	LE	LE 1	LE		LE 1	LE 1		LE	LE 1	LE
Southend Victoria	d		09 50					10 10						10 30						10 50					
Prittlewell	d		09 52					10 12						10 32						10 52					
Southend Airport ✈	d		09 55					10 15						10 35						10 55					
Rochford	d		09 58					10 18						10 38						10 58					
Hockley	d		10 01					10 21						10 41						11 01					
Rayleigh	d		10 06					10 26						10 46						11 06					
Southminster	d									10 16											10 56				
Burnham-on-Crouch	d									10 20											11 00				
Althorne	d									10 25											11 05				
North Fambridge	d									10 31											11 11				
South Woodham Ferrers	d									10 36											11 16				
Battlesbridge	d									10 40											11 20				
Wickford 2	d		10 11					10 31		10a46				10 51						11 11	11a26				
Billericay	d		10 17					10 37						10 57						11 17					
Shenfield 3	a		10 25					10 45						11 05						11 25					
Shenfield 3	d	10 24	10 25		10 34	10 38	10 44	10 45			10 51	10 54	11 04	11 05	11 08	11 14	11 20	11 24		11 25			11 34	11 38	11 44
Brentwood	d	10 27			10 37		10 47					10 57	11 07			11 17		11 27					11 37		11 47
Harold Wood	d	10 32			10 42		10 52					11 02	11 12			11 22		11 32					11 42		11 52
Gidea Park 2	d	10 36			10 46		10 56					11 06	11 16			11 26		11 36					11 46		11 56
Romford	d	10 38			10 48		10 58	10 53				11 08	11 18			11 28	11 28	11 38					11 48		11 58
Chadwell Heath	d	10 42			10 52		11 02					11 12	11 22			11 32		11 42					11 52		12 02
Goodmayes	d	10 44			10 54		11 04					11 14	11 24			11 34		11 44					11 54		12 04
Seven Kings	d	10 46			10 56		11 06					11 16	11 26			11 36		11 46					11 56		12 06
Ilford 2	d	10 49			10 59		11 09					11 19	11 29			11 39		11 49					11 59		12 09
Manor Park	d	10 52			11 02		11 12					11 22	11 32			11 42		11 52					12 02		12 12
Forest Gate	d	10 54			11 04		11 14					11 24	11 34			11 44		11 54					12 04		12 14
Maryland	d	10 56			11 06		11 16					11 26	11 36			11 46		11 56					12 06		12 16
Stratford 7 ⊖	d	10 59	10 39		11 09	10 52	11 19	11 01			11 05	11 29	11 39	11 19	11 22	11 49	11 36	11 59		11 39			12 09	11 52	12 19
London Liverpool Street 15 ⊖	a	11 07	10 48		11 17	11 01	11 27	11 10			11 14	11 37	11 47	11 28	11 31	11 57	11 45	12 07		11 48			12 17	12 01	12 27

		LE 1	LE 1	LE		LE	LE 1	LE 1	LE 1	LE	LE 1	LE	LE 1			LE	LE 1	LE	LE 1	LE 1	LE 1	LE	LE	LE 1	
Southend Victoria	d	11 10					11 30						11 50						12 10					12 30	
Prittlewell	d	11 12					11 32						11 52						12 12					12 32	
Southend Airport ✈	d	11 15					11 35						11 55						12 15					12 35	
Rochford	d	11 18					11 38						11 58						12 18					12 38	
Hockley	d	11 21					11 41						12 01						12 21					12 41	
Rayleigh	d	11 26					11 46						12 06						12 26					12 46	
Southminster	d							11 36												12 16					
Burnham-on-Crouch	d							11 40												12 20					
Althorne	d							11 45												12 25					
North Fambridge	d							11 51												12 31					
South Woodham Ferrers	d							11 56												12 36					
Battlesbridge	d							12 00												12 40					
Wickford 2	d	11 31					11 51	12a06					12 11						12 31	12a46				12 51	
Billericay	d	11 37					11 57						12 17						12 37					12 57	
Shenfield 3	a	11 45					12 05						12 25						12 45					13 05	
Shenfield 3	d	11 45	11 51	11 54		12 04	12 05		12 08	12 14	12 20	12 24	12 25			12 34	12 38	12 44	12 45		12 51	12 54	13 04	13 05	
Brentwood	d			11 57		12 07				12 17		12 27				12 37		12 47				12 57	13 07		
Harold Wood	d			12 02		12 12				12 22		12 32				12 42		12 52				13 02	13 12		
Gidea Park 2	d			12 06		12 16				12 26		12 36				12 46		12 56				13 06	13 16		
Romford	d	11 53		12 08		12 18				12 28	12 28	12 38				12 48		12 58	12 53			13 08	13 18		
Chadwell Heath	d			12 12		12 22				12 32		12 42				12 52		13 02				13 12	13 22		
Goodmayes	d			12 14		12 24				12 34		12 44				12 54		13 04				13 14	13 24		
Seven Kings	d			12 16		12 26				12 36		12 46				12 56		13 06				13 16	13 26		
Ilford 2	d			12 19		12 29				12 39		12 49				12 59		13 09				13 19	13 29		
Manor Park	d			12 22		12 32				12 42		12 52				13 02		13 12				13 22	13 32		
Forest Gate	d			12 24		12 34				12 44		12 54				13 04		13 14				13 24	13 34		
Maryland	d			12 26		12 36				12 46		12 56				13 06		13 16				13 26	13 36		
Stratford 7 ⊖	d	12 01	12 05	12 29		12 39	12 19		12 22	12 49	12 36	12 59	12 39			13 09	12 52	13 19	13 01		13 05	13 29	13 39	13 19	
London Liverpool Street 15 ⊖	a	12 10	12 14	12 37		12 47	12 28		12 31	12 57	12 45	13 07	12 48			13 17	13 01	13 27	13 10		13 14	13 37	13 47	13 28	

Southend Victoria, Southminster and Shenfield - London

Network Diagram - see first Page of Table 5

		LE 1	LE	LE 1	LE	LE 1	LE 1		LE	LE 1		LE	LE 1	LE 1	LE	LE	LE 1	LE 1	LE 1	LE		LE 1	LE	LE 1	
Southend Victoria	d					12 50							13 10				13 30							13 50	
Prittlewell	d					12 52							13 12				13 32							13 52	
Southend Airport ✈	d					12 55							13 15				13 35							13 55	
Rochford	d					12 58							13 18				13 38							13 58	
Hockley	d					13 01							13 21				13 41							14 01	
Rayleigh	d					13 06							13 26				13 46							14 06	
Southminster	d						12 56											13 36							
Burnham-on-Crouch	d						13 00											13 40							
Althorne	d						13 05											13 45							
North Fambridge	d						13 11											13 51							
South Woodham Ferrers	d						13 16											13 56							
Battlesbridge	d						13 20											14 00							
Wickford 2	d					13 11	13a26						13 31				13 51	14a06						14 11	
Billericay	d					13 17							13 37				13 57							14 17	
Shenfield 3	a					13 25							13 45				14 05							14 25	
Shenfield 3	d	13 08	13 14	13 20	13 24	13 25			13 34	13 38		13 44	13 45	13 51	13 54	14 04	14 05		14 08	14 14		14 20	14 24	14 25	
Brentwood	d		13 17		13 27				13 37			13 47			13 57	14 07				14 17			14 27		
Harold Wood	d		13 22		13 32				13 42			13 52			14 02	14 12				14 22			14 32		
Gidea Park 2	d		13 26		13 36				13 46			13 56			14 06	14 16				14 26			14 36		
Romford	d		13 28	13 28	13 38				13 48			13 58	13 53		14 08	14 18				14 28		14 28	14 38		
Chadwell Heath	d		13 32		13 42				13 52			14 02			14 12	14 22				14 32			14 42		
Goodmayes	d		13 34		13 44				13 54			14 04			14 14	14 24				14 34			14 44		
Seven Kings	d		13 36		13 46				13 56			14 06			14 16	14 26				14 36			14 46		
Ilford 2	d		13 39		13 49				13 59			14 09			14 19	14 29				14 39			14 49		
Manor Park	d		13 42		13 52				14 02			14 12			14 22	14 32				14 42			14 52		
Forest Gate	d		13 44		13 54				14 04			14 14			14 24	14 34				14 44			14 54		
Maryland	d		13 46		13 56				14 06			14 16			14 26	14 36				14 46			14 56		
Stratford 7 ⊖	d	13 22	13 49	13 36	13 59	13 39			14 09	13 52		14 19	14 01	14 05	14 29	14 39	14 19		14 22	14 49		14 36	14 59	14 39	
London Liverpool Street 15 ⊖	a	13 31	13 57	13 45	14 07	13 48			14 17	14 01		14 27	14 10	14 14	14 37	14 47	14 28		14 31	14 57		14 45	15 07	14 48	

		LE	LE 1	LE	LE 1	LE 1		LE 1	LE	LE	LE 1	LE 1	LE	LE 1	LE	LE 1		LE 1		LE	LE 1	LE	LE 1	LE 1	LE
Southend Victoria	d				14 10						14 30					14 50							15 10		
Prittlewell	d				14 12						14 32					14 52							15 12		
Southend Airport ✈	d				14 15						14 35					14 55							15 15		
Rochford	d				14 18						14 38					14 58							15 18		
Hockley	d				14 21						14 41					15 01							15 21		
Rayleigh	d				14 26						14 46					15 06							15 26		
Southminster	d					14 16												14 56							
Burnham-on-Crouch	d					14 20												15 00							
Althorne	d					14 25												15 05							
North Fambridge	d					14 31												15 11							
South Woodham Ferrers	d					14 36												15 16							
Battlesbridge	d					14 40												15 20							
Wickford 2	d				14 31	14a46					14 51					15 11		15a26					15 31		
Billericay	d				14 37						14 57					15 17							15 37		
Shenfield 3	a				14 45						15 05					15 25							15 45		
Shenfield 3	d	14 34	14 38	14 44	14 45			14 51	14 54	15 04	15 05	15 08	15 14	15 20	15 24	15 25				15 34	15 38	15 44	15 45	15 51	15 54
Brentwood	d	14 37		14 47					14 57	15 07			15 17		15 27					15 37		15 47			15 57
Harold Wood	d	14 42		14 52					15 02	15 12			15 22		15 32					15 42		15 52			16 02
Gidea Park 2	d	14 46		14 56					15 06	15 16			15 26		15 36					15 46		15 56			16 06
Romford	d	14 48		14 58	14 53				15 08	15 18			15 28	15 28	15 38					15 48		15 58	15 53		16 08
Chadwell Heath	d	14 52		15 02					15 12	15 22			15 32		15 42					15 52		16 02			16 12
Goodmayes	d	14 54		15 04					15 14	15 24			15 34		15 44					15 54		16 04			16 14
Seven Kings	d	14 56		15 06					15 16	15 26			15 36		15 46					15 56		16 06			16 16
Ilford 2	d	14 59		15 09					15 19	15 29			15 39		15 49					15 59		16 09			16 19
Manor Park	d	15 02		15 12					15 22	15 32			15 42		15 52					16 02		16 12			16 22
Forest Gate	d	15 04		15 14					15 24	15 34			15 44		15 54					16 04		16 14			16 24
Maryland	d	15 06		15 16					15 26	15 36			15 46		15 56					16 06		16 16			16 26
Stratford 7 ⊖	d	15 09	14 52	15 19	15 01			15 05	15 29	15 39	15 19	15 22	15 49	15 36	15 59	15 39				16 09	15 52	16 19	16 01	16 05	16 29
London Liverpool Street 15 ⊖	a	15 17	15 01	15 27	15 10			15 15	15 37	15 47	15 28	15 33	15 57	15 45	16 07	15 48				16 17	16 01	16 27	16 11	16 14	16 37

Southend Victoria, Southminster and Shenfield - London

Network Diagram - see first Page of Table 5

	LE		LE [1]	LE [1]	LE [1]	LE	LE [1]	LE	LE [1]		LE		LE [1]	LE	LE [1]	LE [1]	LE [1]	LE	LE	LE [1]	LE [1]		LE	LE [1]
Southend Victoria d			15 30						15 50						16 10					16 30				
Prittlewell d			15 32						15 52						16 12					16 32				
Southend Airport ✈ d			15 35						15 55						16 15					16 35				
Rochford d			15 38						15 58						16 18					16 38				
Hockley d			15 41						16 01						16 21					16 41				
Rayleigh d			15 46						16 06						16 26					16 46				
Southminster d				15 36												16 14								
Burnham-on-Crouch d				15 40												16 18								
Althorne d				15 45												16 23								
North Fambridge d				15 51												16 29								
South Woodham Ferrers d				15 56												16 34								
Battlesbridge d				16 00												16 38								
Wickford [2] d			15 51	16a06					16 11						16 31	16a44				16 51				
Billericay d			15 57						16 17						16 37					16 57				
Shenfield [3] a			16 05						16 25						16 45					17 05				
Shenfield [3] d	16 04		16 05		16 08	16 14	16 20	16 24	16 25		16 34		16 38	16 44	16 45		16 51	16 54	17 04	17 05	17 08		17 14	17 22
Brentwood d	16 07					16 17		16 27			16 37			16 47				16 57	17 07				17 17	
Harold Wood d	16 12					16 22		16 32			16 42			16 52				17 02	17 12				17 22	
Gidea Park [2] d	16 16					16 26		16 36			16 46			16 56				17 06	17 16				17 26	
Romford d	16 18					16 28		16 38			16 48			16 58				17 08	17 18				17 28	
Chadwell Heath d	16 22					16 32		16 42			16 52			17 02				17 12	17 22				17 32	
Goodmayes d	16 24					16 34		16 44			16 54			17 04				17 14	17 24				17 34	
Seven Kings d	16 26					16 36		16 46			16 56			17 06				17 16	17 26				17 36	
Ilford [2] d	16 29					16 39		16 49			16 59			17 09				17 19	17 29				17 39	
Manor Park d	16 32					16 42		16 52			17 02			17 12				17 22	17 32					
Forest Gate d	16 34					16 44		16 54			17 04			17 14				17 24	17 34					
Maryland d	16 36					16 46		16 56			17 06			17 16				17 26	17 36					
Stratford [7] ⊖ d	16 39		16 19		16 22	16 49	16 34	16 59	16 39		17 09		16 52	17 19	16 59		17 05	17 29	17 39	17 19	17 22		17 45	17 36
London Liverpool Street [15] ⊖ a	16 47		16 28		16 31	16 57	16 44	17 07	16 48		17 17		17 03	17 27	17 13		17 16	17 37	17 47	17 29	17 34		17 53	17 46

	LE	LE	LE [1]	LE [1]		LE	LE		LE [1]	LE	LE	LE [1]	LE [1]	LE [1]	LE	LE	LE [1]		LE	LE	LE [1]	LE [1]	LE	LE
Southend Victoria d			16 50									17 10					17 25					17 35		
Prittlewell d			16 52									17 12					17 27					17 37		
Southend Airport ✈ d			16 55									17 15					17 30					17 40		
Rochford d			16 58									17 18					17 33					17 43		
Hockley d			17 01									17 21					17 36					17 46		
Rayleigh d			17 06									17 26					17 41					17 51		
Southminster d													17 06											
Burnham-on-Crouch d													17 10											
Althorne d													17 15											
North Fambridge d													17 21											
South Woodham Ferrers d													17 26											
Battlesbridge d													17 30											
Wickford [2] d			17 11									17 31	17 37				17 46					17 56		
Billericay d			17 17									17 37					17 52					18 02		
Shenfield [3] a			17 25									17 45	17 48				18 00					18 10		
Shenfield [3] d		17 24	17 25	17 28			17 34		17 38		17 44	17 45	17 49	17 51		17 54	18 00			18 04	18 08	18 10		18 14
Brentwood d		17 27					17 37				17 47					17 57				18 07				18 17
Harold Wood d		17 32					17 42				17 52					18 02				18 12				18 22
Gidea Park [2] d	17 32	17 36				17 42	17 46			17 52	17 56				18 02	18 06			18 12	18 16			18 22	18 26
Romford d	17 34	17 38				17 44	17 48			17 54	17 58				18 04	18 08			18 14	18 18			18 24	18 28
Chadwell Heath d		17 42					17 52				18 02					18 12				18 22				18 32
Goodmayes d		17 44					17 54				18 04					18 14				18 24				18 34
Seven Kings d		17 46					17 56				18 06					18 16				18 26				18 36
Ilford [2] d	17 42	17 49				17 52	17 59			18 02	18 09				18 12	18 19			18 22	18 29			18 32	18 39
Manor Park d	17 45					17 55				18 05					18 15				18 25				18 35	
Forest Gate d	17 47					17 57				18 07					18 17				18 27				18 37	
Maryland d	17 49					17 59				18 09					18 19				18 29				18 39	
Stratford [7] ⊖ d	17 52	17 55	17 39	17 42		18 02	18 05		17 52	18 12	18 15	17 59	18 08	18 06	18 22	18 25	18 14		18 32	18 35	18 22	18 25	18 42	18 45
London Liverpool Street [15] ⊖ a	18 00	18 03	17 49	17 53		18 10	18 13		18 01	18 20	18 23	18 11	18 17	18 15	18 30	18 33	18 24		18 40	18 43	18 31	18 35	18 50	18 53

Southend Victoria, Southminster and Shenfield - London

Network Diagram - see first Page of Table 5

		LE 1	LE	LE		LE 1	LE 1		LE	LE 1	LE 1	LE 1	LE	LE 1		LE	LE 1	LE	LE 1	LE 1	LE 1	LE	LE 1	LE	
Southend Victoria	d					17 50					18 05						18 20		18 30						
Prittlewell	d					17 52					18 07						18 22		18 32						
Southend Airport ✈	d					17 55					18 10						18 25		18 35						
Rochford	d					17 58					18 13						18 28		18 38						
Hockley	d					18 01					18 16						18 31		18 41						
Rayleigh	d					18 06					18 21						18 36		18 46						
Southminster	d											17 56													
Burnham-on-Crouch	d											18 00													
Althorne	d											18 05													
North Fambridge	d											18 14													
South Woodham Ferrers	d											18 19													
Battlesbridge	d											18 23													
Wickford 2	d					18 11					18 26	18a29					18 41		18 51						
Billericay	d					18 17					18 32						18 47		18 57						
Shenfield 3	a					18 25					18 40						18 55		19 05						
Shenfield 3	d	18 20		18 24		18 25	18 27		18 34	18 38	18 40		18 44	18 51		18 54	18 57	19 04	19 05	19 08	19 13	19 14	19 20	19 24	
Brentwood	d			18 27					18 37				18 47			18 57		19 07				19 17		19 27	
Harold Wood	d			18 32					18 42				18 52			19 02		19 12				19 22		19 32	
Gidea Park 2	d		18 32	18 36					18 46				18 56			19 06		19 16				19 26		19 36	
Romford	d	18 28	18 34	18 38					18 48				18 58			19 08		19 18				19 28	19 28	19 38	
Chadwell Heath	d			18 42					18 52				19 02			19 12		19 22				19 32		19 42	
Goodmayes	d			18 44					18 54				19 04			19 14		19 24				19 34		19 44	
Seven Kings	d			18 46					18 56				19 06			19 16		19 26				19 36		19 46	
Ilford 2	d		18 42	18 49					18 59				19 09			19 19		19 29				19 39		19 49	
Manor Park	d		18 45	18 52					19 02				19 12			19 22		19 32				19 42		19 52	
Forest Gate	d		18 47	18 54					19 04				19 14			19 24		19 34				19 44		19 54	
Maryland	d		18 49	18 56					19 06				19 16			19 26		19 36				19 46		19 56	
Stratford 7 ⊖	d	18 36	18 52	18 59		18 39	18 42		19 09	18 52	18 55		19 19	19 05		19 29	19 11	19 39	19 19	19 22	19 27	19 49	19 36	19 59	
London Liverpool Street 15 ⊖	a	18 45	19 00	19 07		18 48	18 51		19 17	19 01	19 04		19 27	19 14		19 37	19 20	19 47	19 28	19 31	19 36	19 57	19 45	20 07	

		LE 1	LE 1		LE	LE 1	LE	LE 1	LE 1	LE 1		LE	LE	LE 1	LE 1	CC	LE 1	LE	LE 1	LE		LE 1		LE	LE 1
Southend Victoria	d	18 50						19 10						19 30								19 50			
Prittlewell	d	18 52						19 12						19 32								19 52			
Southend Airport ✈	d	18 55						19 15						19 35								19 55			
Rochford	d	18 58						19 18						19 38								19 58			
Hockley	d	19 01						19 21						19 41								20 01			
Rayleigh	d	19 06						19 26						19 46								20 06			
Southminster	d		18 36												19 17										
Burnham-on-Crouch	d		18 40												19 21										
Althorne	d		18 45												19 26										
North Fambridge	d		19 01												19 33										
South Woodham Ferrers	d		19 06												19 38										
Battlesbridge	d		19 10												19 42										
Wickford 2	d	19 11	19 17					19 31						19 51	19 55							20 11			
Billericay	d	19 17	19 23					19 37						19 57								20 17			
Shenfield 3	a	19 25	19 33					19 45						20 05	20 08							20 25			
Shenfield 3	d	19 25			19 34	19 38	19 44	19 45	19 51			19 54	20 04	20 05			20 08	20 14	20 20	20 24		20 25		20 34	20 38
Brentwood	d				19 37		19 47					19 57	20 07					20 17		20 27				20 37	
Harold Wood	d				19 42		19 52					20 02	20 12					20 22		20 32				20 42	
Gidea Park 2	d				19 46		19 56					20 06	20 16					20 26		20 36				20 46	
Romford	d				19 48		19 58	19 53				20 08	20 18					20 28	20 28	20 38				20 48	
Chadwell Heath	d				19 52		20 02					20 12	20 22					20 32		20 42				20 52	
Goodmayes	d				19 54		20 04					20 14	20 24					20 34		20 44				20 54	
Seven Kings	d				19 56		20 06					20 16	20 26					20 36		20 46				20 56	
Ilford 2	d				19 59		20 09					20 19	20 29					20 39		20 49				20 59	
Manor Park	d				20 02		20 12					20 22	20 32					20 42		20 52				21 02	
Forest Gate	d				20 04		20 14					20 24	20 34					20 44		20 54				21 04	
Maryland	d				20 06		20 16					20 26	20 36					20 46		20 56				21 06	
Stratford 7 ⊖	d	19 39			20 09	19 52	20 19	20 01	20 05	20 14		20 29	20 39	20 19		20 21	20 22	20 49	20 36	20 59		20 39		21 09	20 52
London Liverpool Street 15 ⊖	a	19 48			20 17	20 01	20 27	20 10	20 14	20 23		20 37	20 47	20 28		20 33	20 31	20 57	20 45	21 07		20 48		21 17	21 01

Southend Victoria, Southminster and Shenfield - London

Network Diagram - see first Page of Table 5

		CC	LE	LE [1]	LE [1]	LE [1]		LE [1]	CC	LE	LE	LE [1]	LE [1]	LE	LE	LE [1]		LE [1]	LE [1]	LE ◇[1] ☕	LE	LE [1]	LE	LE [1]	LE [1]
Southend Victoria	d			20 10								20 30				20 50								21 10	
Prittlewell	d			20 12								20 32				20 52								21 12	
Southend Airport ✈	d			20 15								20 35				20 55								21 15	
Rochford	d			20 18								20 38				20 58								21 18	
Hockley	d			20 21								20 41				21 01								21 21	
Rayleigh	d			20 26								20 46				21 06								21 26	
Southminster	d				20 16													20 56							
Burnham-on-Crouch	d				20 20													21 00							
Althorne	d				20 25													21 05							
North Fambridge	d				20 31													21 11							
South Woodham Ferrers	d				20 36													21 16							
Battlesbridge	d				20 40													21 20							
Wickford [2]	d			20 31	20a46							20 51				21 11		21a26						21 31	
Billericay	d			20 37								20 57				21 17								21 37	
Shenfield [3]	a			20 45								21 05				21 25								21 45	
Shenfield [3]	d		20 44	20 45		20 47		20 53		20 54	21 04	21 05	21 08	21 14	21 24	21 25			21 27		21 34	21 38	21 44	21 45	21 51
Brentwood	d		20 47							20 57	21 07			21 17	21 27						21 37		21 47		
Harold Wood	d		20 52							21 02	21 12			21 22	21 32						21 42		21 52		
Gidea Park [2]	d		20 56							21 06	21 16			21 26	21 36						21 46		21 56		
Romford	d		20 58	20 53						21 08	21 18			21 28	21 38						21 48		21 58	21 53	
Chadwell Heath	d		21 02							21 12	21 22			21 32	21 42						21 52		22 02		
Goodmayes	d		21 04							21 14	21 24			21 34	21 44						21 54		22 04		
Seven Kings	d		21 06							21 16	21 26			21 36	21 46						21 56		22 06		
Ilford [2]	d		21 09							21 19	21 29			21 39	21 49						21 59		22 09		
Manor Park	d		21 12							21 22	21 32			21 42	21 52						22 02		22 12		
Forest Gate	d		21 14							21 24	21 34			21 44	21 54						22 04		22 14		
Maryland	d		21 16							21 26	21 36			21 46	21 56						22 06		22 16		
Stratford [7] ⊖	d	21 00	21 19	21 01				21 07	21 15	21 29	21 39	21 19	21 22	21 49	21 59	21 39			21 42		22 09	21 52	22 19	22 01	22 05
London Liverpool Street [15] ⊖	a	21 12	21 27	21 10		21 12		21 16	21 26	21 37	21 47	21 28	21 31	21 57	22 07	21 48			21 51	21 55	22 17	22 01	22 27	22 10	22 14

		LE		LE [1] MTWO	LE [1] ThFO	LE [1]	LE [1]	LE	LE [1]	LE ◇[1] ThFO ☕	LE ThFO	LE MTWO		LE [1] MTWO	LE [1] ThFO	LE [1]	LE ◇[1] MTWO ☕	LE [1] ThFO	LE [1] MTWO	LE ThFO	LE [1] ThFO	LE [1]		LE [1] MTWO	LE MTWO
Southend Victoria	d			21 30	21 30									22 00	22 00										
Prittlewell	d			21 32	21 32									22 02	22 02										
Southend Airport ✈	d			21 35	21 35									22 05	22 05										
Rochford	d			21 38	21 38									22 08	22 08										
Hockley	d			21 41	21 41									22 11	22 11										
Rayleigh	d			21 46	21 46									22 16	22 16										
Southminster	d					21 36										22 16									
Burnham-on-Crouch	d					21 40										22 20									
Althorne	d					21 45										22 25									
North Fambridge	d					21 51										22 31									
South Woodham Ferrers	d					21 56										22 36									
Battlesbridge	d					22 00										22 40									
Wickford [2]	d			21 51	21 51	22a07								22 21	22 21	22a46									
Billericay	d			21 57	21 57									22 27	22 27										
Shenfield [3]	a			22 05	22 05									22 35	22 35										
Shenfield [3]	d	21 59			22 05		22 08	22 14	22 20		22 29	22 34			22 35			22 38	22 38	22 44	22 51			22 51	22 54
Brentwood	d	22 02						22 17			22 32	22 37								22 47					22 57
Harold Wood	d	22 07						22 22			22 37	22 42								22 52					23 02
Gidea Park [2]	d	22 11						22 26			22 41	22 46								22 56					23 06
Romford	d	22 13						22 28	22 28		22 43	22 48								22 58					23 08
Chadwell Heath	d	22 17						22 32			22 47	22 52								23 02					23 12
Goodmayes	d	22 19						22 34			22 49	22 54								23 04					23 14
Seven Kings	d	22 21						22 36			22 51	22 56								23 06					23 16
Ilford [2]	d	22 24						22 39			22 54	22 59								23 09					23 19
Manor Park	d	22 27						22 42			22 57	23 02								23 12					23 22
Forest Gate	d	22 29						22 44			22 59	23 04								23 14					23 24
Maryland	d	22 31						22 46			23 01	23 06								23 16					23 26
Stratford [7] ⊖	d	22 34			22 19		22 22	22 49	22 36		23 04	23 09			22 49			22 52	22 54	23 19	23 05	23 06		23 11	23 29
London Liverpool Street [15] ⊖	a	22 42			22 28		22 31	22 57	22 45	22 55	23 12	23 18			22 58		23 00	23 01	23 03	23 27	23 15	23 15		23 20	23 38

Southend Victoria, Southminster and Shenfield - London

Network Diagram - see first Page of Table 5

		LE	LE	LE	LE	LE	LE	LE		LE	LE	LE	LE	LE	LE	LE	LE	LE		LE
			1	1	1	1		1		1			1	1	◇1	1		1		
		ThFO	MTW O	ThFO	ThFO	MTW O	ThFO	ThFO		MTW O	MTW O	ThFO	MTW O	ThFO	MTW O	ThFO	ThFO	MTW O		MTW O
Southend Victoria	d		22 30	22 30									23 00	23 00						
Prittlewell	d		22 32	22 32									23 02	23 02						
Southend Airport ✈	d		22 35	22 35									23 05	23 05						
Rochford	d		22 38	22 38									23 08	23 08						
Hockley	d		22 41	22 41									23 11	23 11						
Rayleigh	d		22 46	22 46									23 16	23 16						
Southminster	d															22 56		23 06		
Burnham-on-Crouch	d															23 00		23 10		
Althorne	d															23 05		23 15		
North Fambridge	d															23 11		23 21		
South Woodham Ferrers	d															23 16		23 26		
Battlesbridge	d															23 20		23 30		
Wickford 2	d		22 51	22 51									23 21	23 21		23 26		23 36		
Billericay	d		22 57	22 57									23 27	23 27		23 32		23 42		
Shenfield 3	a		23 05	23 05									23 35	23 35		23 39		23 49		
Shenfield 3	d	22 59		23 05	23 08	23 08	23 14	23 20		23 20	23 27	23 29		23 35	23 38	23 39	23 44	23 52		23 54
Brentwood	d	23 02					23 17				23 30	23 32					23 47			23 57
Harold Wood	d	23 07					23 22				23 35	23 37					23 52			00 02
Gidea Park 2	d	23 11					23 26				23 39	23 41					23 56			00 06
Romford	d	23 13				23 19	23 28	23 28		23 31	23 41	23 43				23 47	23 58	00 03		00 08
Chadwell Heath	d	23 17					23 32				23 45	23 47					00 02			00 12
Goodmayes	d	23 19					23 34				23 47	23 49					00 04			00 14
Seven Kings	d	23 21					23 36				23 49	23 51					00 06			00 16
Ilford 2	d	23 24					23 39				23 52	23 54					00 09			00 19
Manor Park	d	23 27					23 42				23 55	23 57					00 12			00 22
Forest Gate	d	23 29					23 44				23 57	23 59					00 14			00 24
Maryland	d	23 31					23 46				23 59	00 01					00 16			00 26
Stratford 7 ⊖	d	23 34		23 19	23 22	23 31	23 49	23 36		23 41	00 02	00 04		23 49	00s04	23 56	00 19	00 13		00 29
London Liverpool Street 15 ⊖	a	23 42		23 28	23 31	23 40	23 57	23 45		23 50	00 11	00 12		23 58	00 14	00 05	00 27	00 22		00 38

Saturdays

		LE	LE	LE	CC	LE	LE	LE	LE	LE		LE	LE	LE	LE	LE	LE	LE	LE	LE			LE	LE	LE
		◇1		1			1		1	1			1	1		1	1			1				1	1
Southend Victoria	d						04 00		04 30				05 00				05 30							06 00	
Prittlewell	d						04 02		04 32				05 02				05 32							06 02	
Southend Airport ✈	d						04 05		04 35				05 05				05 35							06 05	
Rochford	d						04 08		04 38				05 08				05 38							06 08	
Hockley	d						04 12		04 42				05 11				05 41							06 11	
Rayleigh	d						04 16		04 46				05 16				05 46							06 16	
Southminster	d			22p56																					06 16
Burnham-on-Crouch	d			23p00																					06 20
Althorne	d			23p05																					06 25
North Fambridge	d			23p11																					06 31
South Woodham Ferrers	d			23p16																					06 36
Battlesbridge	d			23p20																					06 40
Wickford 2	d			23p26			04 21		04 51				05 21				05 51							06 21	06a46
Billericay	d			23p32			04 28		04 58				05 27				05 57							06 27	
Shenfield 3	a			23p39			04 39		05 09				05 35				06 05							06 35	
Shenfield 3	d		23p29	23p39		23p44	04 39		05 09	05 24			05 35		05 44	05 53	06 05		06 14	06 24				06 35	
Brentwood	d		23p32			23p47	04 42		05 12						05 47				06 17						
Harold Wood	d		23p37			23p52	04 47		05 17						05 52				06 22						
Gidea Park 2	d		23p41			23p56	04 51		05 21	05 31					05 56			06 16	06 26				06 36		
Romford	d		23p43	23p47		23p58	04 53		05 23				05 43		05 58			06 18	06 28				06 38	06 43	
Chadwell Heath	d		23p47			00 02	04 57		05 27						06 02			06 22	06 32				06 42		
Goodmayes	d		23p49			00 04	04 59		05 29						06 04			06 24	06 34				06 44		
Seven Kings	d		23p51			00 06	05 01		05 31	05 36					06 06			06 26	06 36				06 46		
Ilford 2	d		23p54			00 09	05 04	05 09	05 34			05 39			06 09			06 29	06 39				06 49		
Manor Park	d		23p57			00 12		05 11				05 41			06 12			06 32	06 42				06 52		
Forest Gate	d		23p59			00 14		05 14				05 44			06 14			06 34	06 44				06 54		
Maryland	d		00 01			00 16		05 16				05 46			06 16			06 36	06 46				06 56		
Stratford 7 ⊖	d	23b52	00 04	23p56	00 09	00 19	05 10	05 18	05 40	05 42		05 48	05 51	06 05	06 19	06 07	06 19	06 39	06 49	06 38			06 59	06 51	
London Liverpool Street 15 ⊖	a	00 02	00 12	00 05	00 20	00 27	05 18	05 26	05 48	05 55		05 56	06 00	06 14	06 27	06 16	06 28	06 47	06 57	06 47			07 07	07 00	

b Previous night, stops to set down only

Table 5

Saturdays

Southend Victoria, Southminster and Shenfield - London

Network Diagram - see first Page of Table 5

		LE	LE	LE 1	LE	LE		LE 1	LE 1	LE	LE 1	LE	LE 1	LE 1		LE		LE 1	LE	LE 1	LE 1	LE	LE	LE 1	LE 1
Southend Victoria	d							06 30					06 50							07 10				07 30	
Prittlewell	d							06 32					06 52							07 12				07 32	
Southend Airport ✈	d							06 35					06 55							07 15				07 35	
Rochford	d							06 38					06 58							07 18				07 38	
Hockley	d							06 41					07 01							07 21				07 41	
Rayleigh	d							06 46					07 06							07 26				07 46	
Southminster	d													06 56											07 36
Burnham-on-Crouch	d													07 00											07 40
Althorne	d													07 05											07 45
North Fambridge	d													07 11											07 51
South Woodham Ferrers	d													07 16											07 56
Battlesbridge	d													07 20											08 00
Wickford 2	d							06 51					07 11	07a26						07 31				07 51	08a06
Billericay	d							06 57					07 17							07 37				07 57	
Shenfield 3	a							07 05					07 25							07 45				08 05	
Shenfield 3	d		06 44	06 51		07 04		07 05	07 08	07 14	07 20	07 24	07 25			07 34		07 38	07 44	07 45	07 51	07 54	08 04	08 05	
Brentwood	d		06 47			07 07				07 17		07 27				07 37			07 47			07 57	08 07		
Harold Wood	d		06 52			07 12				07 22		07 32				07 42			07 52			08 02	08 12		
Gidea Park 2	d	06 46	06 56		07 06	07 16				07 26		07 36				07 46			07 56			08 06	08 16		
Romford	d	06 48	06 58		07 08	07 18				07 28	07 28	07 38				07 48			07 58	07 53		08 08	08 18		
Chadwell Heath	d	06 52	07 02		07 12	07 22				07 32		07 42				07 52			08 02			08 12	08 22		
Goodmayes	d	06 54	07 04		07 14	07 24				07 34		07 44				07 54			08 04			08 14	08 24		
Seven Kings	d	06 56	07 06		07 16	07 26				07 36		07 46				07 56			08 06			08 16	08 26		
Ilford 2	d	06 59	07 09		07 19	07 29				07 39		07 49				07 59			08 09			08 19	08 29		
Manor Park	d	07 02	07 12		07 22	07 32				07 42		07 52				08 02			08 12			08 22	08 32		
Forest Gate	d	07 04	07 14		07 24	07 34				07 44		07 54				08 04			08 14			08 24	08 34		
Maryland	d	07 06	07 16		07 26	07 36				07 46		07 56				08 06			08 16			08 26	08 36		
Stratford 7 ⊖	d	07 09	07 19	07 05	07 29	07 39		07 19	07 22	07 49	07 36	07 59	07 39			08 09		07 52	08 19	08 01	08 05	08 29	08 39	08 19	
London Liverpool Street 15 ⊖	a	07 17	07 27	07 14	07 37	07 47		07 28	07 31	07 57	07 45	08 07	07 48			08 17		08 01	08 27	08 10	08 14	08 37	08 47	08 28	

		LE 1		LE	LE 1	LE	LE 1	LE ◇1 🍴	LE	LE 1	LE	LE 1		LE 1	LE 1	LE	LE	LE 1	LE 1	LE	LE 1	LE		LE 1	LE 1
Southend Victoria	d						07 50					08 10						08 30						08 50	
Prittlewell	d						07 52					08 12						08 32						08 52	
Southend Airport ✈	d						07 55					08 15						08 35						08 55	
Rochford	d						07 58					08 18						08 38						08 58	
Hockley	d						08 01					08 21						08 41						09 01	
Rayleigh	d						08 06					08 26						08 46						09 06	
Southminster	d													08 16											08 56
Burnham-on-Crouch	d													08 20											09 00
Althorne	d													08 25											09 05
North Fambridge	d													08 31											09 11
South Woodham Ferrers	d													08 36											09 16
Battlesbridge	d													08 40											09 20
Wickford 2	d						08 11					08 31		08a46				08 51						09 11	09a26
Billericay	d						08 17					08 37						08 57						09 17	
Shenfield 3	a						08 25					08 45						09 05						09 25	
Shenfield 3	d	08 08		08 14	08 20	08 24	08 25		08 34	08 38	08 44	08 45			08 51	08 54	09 04	09 05	09 08	09 14	09 20	09 24		09 25	
Brentwood	d			08 17		08 27			08 37		08 47					08 57	09 07			09 17		09 27			
Harold Wood	d			08 22		08 32			08 42		08 52					09 02	09 12			09 22		09 32			
Gidea Park 2	d			08 26		08 36			08 46		08 56					09 06	09 16			09 26		09 36			
Romford	d			08 28	08 28	08 38			08 48		08 58	08 53				09 08	09 18			09 28	09 28	09 38			
Chadwell Heath	d			08 32		08 42			08 52		09 02					09 12	09 22			09 32		09 42			
Goodmayes	d			08 34		08 44			08 54		09 04					09 14	09 24			09 34		09 44			
Seven Kings	d			08 36		08 46			08 56		09 06					09 16	09 26			09 36		09 46			
Ilford 2	d			08 39		08 49			08 59		09 09					09 19	09 29			09 39		09 49			
Manor Park	d			08 42		08 52			09 02		09 12					09 22	09 32			09 42		09 52			
Forest Gate	d			08 44		08 54			09 04		09 14					09 24	09 34			09 44		09 54			
Maryland	d			08 46		08 56			09 06		09 16					09 26	09 36			09 46		09 56			
Stratford 7 ⊖	d	08 22		08 49	08 36	08 59	08 39		09 09	08 52	09 19	09 01			09 05	09 29	09 39	09 19	09 22	09 49	09 36	09 59		09 39	
London Liverpool Street 15 ⊖	a	08 31		08 57	08 45	09 07	08 48	08 55	09 17	09 01	09 27	09 10			09 14	09 37	09 47	09 28	09 31	09 57	09 45	10 07		09 48	

Southend Victoria, Southminster and Shenfield - London

Network Diagram - see first Page of Table 5

		LE	LE 1	LE	LE 1	LE 1	LE		LE	LE 1	LE 1	LE 1	LE	LE 1	LE	LE 1			LE	LE 1	LE	LE 1	LE 1	LE 1
Southend Victoria	d				09 10					09 30						09 50						10 10		
Prittlewell	d				09 12					09 32						09 52						10 12		
Southend Airport ✈	d				09 15					09 35						09 55						10 15		
Rochford	d				09 18					09 38						09 58						10 18		
Hockley	d				09 21					09 41						10 01						10 21		
Rayleigh	d				09 26					09 46						10 06						10 26		
Southminster	d										09 36												10 16	
Burnham-on-Crouch	d										09 40												10 20	
Althorne	d										09 45												10 25	
North Fambridge	d										09 51												10 31	
South Woodham Ferrers	d										09 56												10 36	
Battlesbridge	d										10 00												10 40	
Wickford 2	d				09 31					09 51	10a06					10 11						10 31	10a46	
Billericay	d				09 37					09 57						10 17						10 37		
Shenfield 3	a				09 45					10 05						10 25						10 45		
Shenfield 3	d		09 34	09 38	09 44	09 45	09 51	09 54		10 04	10 05		10 08	10 14	10 20	10 24	10 25			10 34	10 38	10 44	10 45		10 51
Brentwood	d		09 37		09 47			09 57		10 07				10 17		10 27				10 37		10 47			
Harold Wood	d		09 42		09 52			10 02		10 12				10 22		10 32				10 42		10 52			
Gidea Park 2	d		09 46		09 56			10 06		10 16				10 26		10 36				10 46		10 56			
Romford	d		09 48		09 58	09 53		10 08		10 18				10 28	10 28	10 38				10 48		10 58	10 53		
Chadwell Heath	d		09 52		10 02			10 12		10 22				10 32		10 42				10 52		11 02			
Goodmayes	d		09 54		10 04			10 14		10 24				10 34		10 44				10 54		11 04			
Seven Kings	d		09 56		10 06			10 16		10 26				10 36		10 46				10 56		11 06			
Ilford 2	d		09 59		10 09			10 19		10 29				10 39		10 49				10 59		11 09			
Manor Park	d		10 02		10 12			10 22		10 32				10 42		10 52				11 02		11 12			
Forest Gate	d		10 04		10 14			10 24		10 34				10 44		10 54				11 04		11 14			
Maryland	d		10 06		10 16			10 26		10 36				10 46		10 56				11 06		11 16			
Stratford 7 ⊖	d		10 09	09 52	10 19	10 01	10 05	10 29		10 39	10 19		10 22	10 49	10 36	10 59	10 39			11 09	10 52	11 19	11 01		11 05
London Liverpool Street 15 ⊖	a		10 17	10 01	10 27	10 10	10 14	10 37		10 47	10 28		10 31	10 57	10 45	11 07	10 48			11 17	11 01	11 27	11 10		11 14

		LE	LE	LE 1		LE 1	LE	LE 1	LE	LE 1	LE 1		LE	LE 1		LE	LE 1	LE 1	LE	LE	LE 1	LE 1	LE 1	LE	
Southend Victoria	d			10 30						10 50							11 10				11 30				
Prittlewell	d			10 32						10 52							11 12				11 32				
Southend Airport ✈	d			10 35						10 55							11 15				11 35				
Rochford	d			10 38						10 58							11 18				11 38				
Hockley	d			10 41						11 01							11 21				11 41				
Rayleigh	d			10 46						11 06							11 26				11 46				
Southminster	d										10 56											11 36			
Burnham-on-Crouch	d										11 00											11 40			
Althorne	d										11 05											11 45			
North Fambridge	d										11 11											11 51			
South Woodham Ferrers	d										11 16											11 56			
Battlesbridge	d										11 20											12 00			
Wickford 2	d			10 51						11 11	11a26						11 31				11 51	12a06			
Billericay	d			10 57						11 17							11 37				11 57				
Shenfield 3	a			11 05						11 25							11 45				12 05				
Shenfield 3	d	10 54	11 04	11 05		11 08	11 14	11 20	11 24	11 25			11 34	11 38		11 44	11 45	11 51	11 54	12 04	12 05		12 08	12 14	
Brentwood	d	10 57	11 07				11 17		11 27				11 37			11 47			11 57	12 07				12 17	
Harold Wood	d	11 02	11 12				11 22		11 32				11 42			11 52			12 02	12 12				12 22	
Gidea Park 2	d	11 06	11 16				11 26		11 36				11 46			11 56			12 06	12 16				12 26	
Romford	d	11 08	11 18				11 28	11 28	11 38				11 48			11 58	11 53		12 08	12 18				12 28	
Chadwell Heath	d	11 12	11 22				11 32		11 42				11 52			12 02			12 12	12 22				12 32	
Goodmayes	d	11 14	11 24				11 34		11 44				11 54			12 04			12 14	12 24				12 34	
Seven Kings	d	11 16	11 26				11 36		11 46				11 56			12 06			12 16	12 26				12 36	
Ilford 2	d	11 19	11 29				11 39		11 49				11 59			12 09			12 19	12 29				12 39	
Manor Park	d	11 22	11 32				11 42		11 52				12 02			12 12			12 22	12 32				12 42	
Forest Gate	d	11 24	11 34				11 44		11 54				12 04			12 14			12 24	12 34				12 44	
Maryland	d	11 26	11 36				11 46		11 56				12 06			12 16			12 26	12 36				12 46	
Stratford 7 ⊖	d	11 29	11 39	11 19		11 22	11 49	11 36	11 59	11 39			12 09	11 52		12 19	12 01	12 05	12 29	12 39	12 19		12 22	12 49	
London Liverpool Street 15 ⊖	a	11 37	11 47	11 28		11 31	11 57	11 45	12 07	11 48			12 17	12 01		12 27	12 10	12 14	12 37	12 47	12 28		12 31	12 57	

Table 5

Saturdays

Southend Victoria, Southminster and Shenfield - London

Network Diagram - see first Page of Table 5

		LE 1	LE	LE 1		LE	LE 1	LE	LE 1	LE 1		LE 1	LE	LE	LE 1	LE 1	LE	LE 1	LE	LE 1		LE 1		LE	LE 1
Southend Victoria	d			11 50					12 10						12 30					12 50					
Prittlewell	d			11 52					12 12						12 32					12 52					
Southend Airport ✈	d			11 55					12 15						12 35					12 55					
Rochford	d			11 58					12 18						12 38					12 58					
Hockley	d			12 01					12 21						12 41					13 01					
Rayleigh	d			12 06					12 26						12 46					13 06					
Southminster	d									12 16												12 56			
Burnham-on-Crouch	d									12 20												13 00			
Althorne	d									12 25												13 05			
North Fambridge	d									12 31												13 11			
South Woodham Ferrers	d									12 36												13 16			
Battlesbridge	d									12 40												13 20			
Wickford 2	d			12 11					12 31	12a46					12 51					13 11		13a26			
Billericay	d			12 17					12 37						12 57					13 17					
Shenfield 3	a			12 25					12 45						13 05					13 25					
Shenfield 3	d	12 20	12 24	12 25		12 34	12 38	12 44	12 45			12 51	12 54	13 04	13 05	13 08	13 14	13 20	13 24	13 25				13 34	13 38
Brentwood	d		12 27			12 37		12 47					12 57	13 07			13 17		13 27					13 37	
Harold Wood	d		12 32			12 42		12 52					13 02	13 12			13 22		13 32					13 42	
Gidea Park 2	d		12 36			12 46		12 56					13 06	13 16			13 26		13 36					13 46	
Romford	d	12 28	12 38			12 48		12 58	12 53				13 08	13 18			13 28	13 28	13 38					13 48	
Chadwell Heath	d		12 42			12 52		13 02					13 12	13 22			13 32		13 42					13 52	
Goodmayes	d		12 44			12 54		13 04					13 14	13 24			13 34		13 44					13 54	
Seven Kings	d		12 46			12 56		13 06					13 16	13 26			13 36		13 46					13 56	
Ilford 2	d		12 49			12 59		13 09					13 19	13 29			13 39		13 49					13 59	
Manor Park	d		12 52			13 02		13 12					13 22	13 32			13 42		13 52					14 02	
Forest Gate	d		12 54			13 04		13 14					13 24	13 34			13 44		13 54					14 04	
Maryland	d		12 56			13 06		13 16					13 26	13 36			13 46		13 56					14 06	
Stratford 7 ⊖	d	12 36	12 59	12 39		13 09	12 52	13 19	13 01			13 05	13 29	13 39	13 19	13 22	13 49	13 36	13 59	13 39				14 09	13 52
London Liverpool Street 15 ⊖	a	12 45	13 07	12 48		13 17	13 01	13 27	13 10			13 14	13 37	13 47	13 28	13 31	13 57	13 45	14 07	13 48				14 17	14 01

		LE	LE 1	LE 1	LE	LE		LE 1	LE 1	LE 1	LE	LE 1	LE	LE 1		LE		LE 1	LE	LE 1	LE 1	LE 1	LE	LE	LE 1
Southend Victoria	d		13 10					13 30						13 50						14 10					14 30
Prittlewell	d		13 12					13 32						13 52						14 12					14 32
Southend Airport ✈	d		13 15					13 35						13 55						14 15					14 35
Rochford	d		13 18					13 38						13 58						14 18					14 38
Hockley	d		13 21					13 41						14 01						14 21					14 41
Rayleigh	d		13 26					13 46						14 06						14 26					14 46
Southminster	d								13 36												14 16				
Burnham-on-Crouch	d								13 40												14 20				
Althorne	d								13 45												14 25				
North Fambridge	d								13 51												14 31				
South Woodham Ferrers	d								13 56												14 36				
Battlesbridge	d								14 00												14 40				
Wickford 2	d		13 31					13 51	14a06					14 11						14 31	14a46				14 51
Billericay	d		13 37					13 57						14 17						14 37					14 57
Shenfield 3	a		13 45					14 05						14 25						14 45					15 05
Shenfield 3	d	13 44	13 45	13 51	13 54	14 04		14 05		14 08	14 14	14 20	14 24	14 25		14 34		14 38	14 44	14 45		14 51	14 54	15 04	15 05
Brentwood	d	13 47			13 57	14 07					14 17		14 27			14 37			14 47				14 57	15 07	
Harold Wood	d	13 52			14 02	14 12					14 22		14 32			14 42			14 52				15 02	15 12	
Gidea Park 2	d	13 56			14 06	14 16					14 26		14 36			14 46			14 56				15 06	15 16	
Romford	d	13 58	13 53		14 08	14 18					14 28	14 28	14 38			14 48			14 58	14 53			15 08	15 18	
Chadwell Heath	d	14 02			14 12	14 22					14 32		14 42			14 52			15 02				15 12	15 22	
Goodmayes	d	14 04			14 14	14 24					14 34		14 44			14 54			15 04				15 14	15 24	
Seven Kings	d	14 06			14 16	14 26					14 36		14 46			14 56			15 06				15 16	15 26	
Ilford 2	d	14 09			14 19	14 29					14 39		14 49			14 59			15 09				15 19	15 29	
Manor Park	d	14 12			14 22	14 32					14 42		14 52			15 02			15 12				15 22	15 32	
Forest Gate	d	14 14			14 24	14 34					14 44		14 54			15 04			15 14				15 24	15 34	
Maryland	d	14 16			14 26	14 36					14 46		14 56			15 06			15 16				15 26	15 36	
Stratford 7 ⊖	d	14 19	14 01	14 05	14 29	14 39		14 19		14 22	14 49	14 36	14 59	14 39		15 09		14 52	15 19	15 01		15 05	15 29	15 39	15 19
London Liverpool Street 15 ⊖	a	14 27	14 10	14 14	14 37	14 47		14 28		14 31	14 57	14 45	15 07	14 48		15 17		15 01	15 27	15 10		15 14	15 37	15 47	15 28

Table 5

Saturdays

Southend Victoria, Southminster and Shenfield - London

Network Diagram - see first Page of Table 5

		LE 1		LE	LE 1	LE	LE 1	LE 1		LE	LE 1	LE		LE 1	LE 1	LE	LE	LE 1	LE 1	LE 1	LE	LE 1		LE	LE 1
Southend Victoria	d						14 50							15 10				15 30							15 50
Prittlewell	d						14 52							15 12				15 32							15 52
Southend Airport ✈	d						14 55							15 15				15 35							15 55
Rochford	d						14 58							15 18				15 38							15 58
Hockley	d						15 01							15 21				15 41							16 01
Rayleigh	d						15 06							15 26				15 46							16 06
Southminster	d							14 56											15 36						
Burnham-on-Crouch	d							15 00											15 40						
Althorne	d							15 05											15 45						
North Fambridge	d							15 11											15 51						
South Woodham Ferrers	d							15 16											15 56						
Battlesbridge	d							15 20											16 00						
Wickford 2	d						15 11	15a26						15 31				15 51	16a06						16 11
Billericay	d						15 17							15 37				15 57							16 17
Shenfield 3	a						15 25							15 45				16 05							16 25
Shenfield 3	d	15 08		15 14	15 20	15 24	15 25			15 34	15 38	15 44		15 45	15 51	15 54	16 04	16 05		16 08	16 14	16 20		16 24	16 25
Brentwood	d			15 17		15 27				15 37		15 47				15 57	16 07				16 17			16 27	
Harold Wood	d			15 22		15 32				15 42		15 52				16 02	16 12				16 22			16 32	
Gidea Park 2	d			15 26		15 36				15 46		15 56				16 06	16 16				16 26			16 36	
Romford	d			15 28	15 28	15 38				15 48		15 58		15 53		16 08	16 18				16 28	16 28		16 38	
Chadwell Heath	d			15 32		15 42				15 52		16 02				16 12	16 22				16 32			16 42	
Goodmayes	d			15 34		15 44				15 54		16 04				16 14	16 24				16 34			16 44	
Seven Kings	d			15 36		15 46				15 56		16 06				16 16	16 26				16 36			16 46	
Ilford 2	d			15 39		15 49				15 59		16 09				16 19	16 29				16 39			16 49	
Manor Park	d			15 42		15 52				16 02		16 12				16 22	16 32				16 42			16 52	
Forest Gate	d			15 44		15 54				16 04		16 14				16 24	16 34				16 44			16 54	
Maryland	d			15 46		15 56				16 06		16 16				16 26	16 36				16 46			16 56	
Stratford 7 ⊖	d	15 22		15 49	15 36	15 59	15 39			16 09	15 52	16 19		16 01	16 05	16 29	16 39	16 19		16 22	16 49	16 36		16 59	16 39
London Liverpool Street 15 ⊖	a	15 31		15 57	15 45	16 07	15 48			16 17	16 01	16 27		16 10	16 14	16 37	16 47	16 28		16 31	16 57	16 45		17 07	16 48

			LE	LE 1	LE	LE 1	LE 1	LE 1		LE	LE	LE 1	LE 1	LE	LE 1	LE	LE 1	LE 1			LE	LE 1	LE 1	LE	LE 1
Southend Victoria	d					16 10						16 30					16 50						17 10		
Prittlewell	d					16 12						16 32					16 52						17 12		
Southend Airport ✈	d					16 15						16 35					16 55						17 15		
Rochford	d					16 18						16 38					16 58						17 18		
Hockley	d					16 21						16 41					17 01						17 21		
Rayleigh	d					16 26						16 46					17 06						17 26		
Southminster	d						16 16											16 56							
Burnham-on-Crouch	d						16 20											17 00							
Althorne	d						16 25											17 05							
North Fambridge	d						16 31											17 11							
South Woodham Ferrers	d						16 36											17 16							
Battlesbridge	d						16 40											17 20							
Wickford 2	d					16 31	16a46					16 51					17 11	17a26					17 31		
Billericay	d					16 37						16 57					17 17						17 37		
Shenfield 3	a					16 45						17 05					17 25						17 44		
Shenfield 3	d		16 34	16 38	16 44	16 45		16 51		16 54	17 04	17 05	17 08	17 14	17 20	17 24	17 25				17 34	17 38	17 45	17 44	17 51
Brentwood	d		16 37		16 47					16 57	17 07			17 17		17 27					17 37			17 47	
Harold Wood	d		16 42		16 52					17 02	17 12			17 22		17 32					17 42			17 52	
Gidea Park 2	d		16 46		16 56					17 06	17 16			17 26		17 36					17 46			17 56	
Romford	d		16 48		16 58	16 53				17 08	17 18			17 28	17 28	17 38					17 48		17 53	17 58	
Chadwell Heath	d		16 52		17 02					17 12	17 22			17 32		17 42					17 52			18 02	
Goodmayes	d		16 54		17 04					17 14	17 24			17 34		17 44					17 54			18 04	
Seven Kings	d		16 56		17 06					17 16	17 26			17 36		17 46					17 56			18 06	
Ilford 2	d		16 59		17 09					17 19	17 29			17 39		17 49					17 59			18 09	
Manor Park	d		17 02		17 12					17 22	17 32			17 42		17 52					18 02			18 12	
Forest Gate	d		17 04		17 14					17 24	17 34			17 44		17 54					18 04			18 14	
Maryland	d		17 06		17 16					17 26	17 36			17 46		17 56					18 06			18 16	
Stratford 7 ⊖	d		17 09	16 52	17 19	17 01		17 05		17 29	17 39	17 19	17 22	17 49	17 36	17 59	17 39				18 09	17 52	18 01	18 19	18 05
London Liverpool Street 15 ⊖	a		17 17	17 01	17 27	17 10		17 14		17 37	17 47	17 28	17 31	17 57	17 45	18 07	17 48				18 17	18 01	18 10	18 27	18 14

Table 5

Saturdays

Southend Victoria, Southminster and Shenfield - London

Network Diagram - see first Page of Table 5

		LE	LE	LE 1		LE 1	LE 1	LE	LE 1	LE	LE 1		LE	LE 1		LE	LE 1	LE 1	LE 1	LE	LE	LE 1	LE 1	LE	
Southend Victoria	d			17 30							17 50						18 10					18 30			
Prittlewell	d			17 32							17 52						18 12					18 32			
Southend Airport ✈	d			17 35							17 55						18 15					18 35			
Rochford	d			17 38							17 58						18 18					18 38			
Hockley	d			17 41							18 01						18 21					18 41			
Rayleigh	d			17 46							18 06						18 26					18 46			
Southminster	d					17 36												18 16							
Burnham-on-Crouch	d					17 40												18 20							
Althorne	d					17 45												18 25							
North Fambridge	d					17 51												18 31							
South Woodham Ferrers	d					17 56												18 36							
Battlesbridge	d					18 00												18 40							
Wickford 2	d			17 51		18a06					18 11						18 31	18a46				18 51			
Billericay	d			17 57							18 17						18 37					18 57			
Shenfield 3	a			18 05							18 25						18 45					19 05			
Shenfield 3	d	17 54	18 04	18 05			18 08	18 14	18 20	18 24	18 25		18 34	18 38		18 44	18 45		18 51	18 54	19 04	19 05	19 08	19 14	
Brentwood	d	17 57	18 07					18 17		18 27			18 37			18 47				18 57	19 07			19 17	
Harold Wood	d	18 02	18 12					18 22		18 32			18 42			18 52				19 02	19 12			19 22	
Gidea Park 2	d	18 06	18 16					18 26		18 36			18 46			18 56				19 06	19 16			19 26	
Romford	d	18 08	18 18					18 28	18 28	18 38			18 48			18 58	18 53			19 08	19 18			19 28	
Chadwell Heath	d	18 12	18 22					18 32		18 42			18 52			19 02				19 12	19 22			19 32	
Goodmayes	d	18 14	18 24					18 34		18 44			18 54			19 04				19 14	19 24			19 34	
Seven Kings	d	18 16	18 26					18 36		18 46			18 56			19 06				19 16	19 26			19 36	
Ilford 2	d	18 19	18 29					18 39		18 49			18 59			19 09				19 19	19 29			19 39	
Manor Park	d	18 22	18 32					18 42		18 52			19 02			19 12				19 22	19 32			19 42	
Forest Gate	d	18 24	18 34					18 44		18 54			19 04			19 14				19 24	19 34			19 44	
Maryland	d	18 26	18 36					18 46		18 56			19 06			19 16				19 26	19 36			19 46	
Stratford 7 ⊖	d	18 29	18 39	18 19			18 22	18 49	18 36	18 59	18 39		19 09	18 52		19 19	19 01		19 05	19 29	19 39	19 19	19 22	19 49	
London Liverpool Street 15 ⊖	a	18 37	18 47	18 28			18 31	18 57	18 45	19 07	18 48		19 17	19 01		19 27	19 10		19 14	19 37	19 47	19 28	19 31	19 57	

		LE 1	LE	LE 1	LE 1		LE	LE 1	LE	LE 1		LE 1	LE	LE	LE 1	LE 1	LE 1	LE	LE 1	LE		LE 1		LE	LE 1
Southend Victoria	d			18 50						19 10					19 30							19 50			
Prittlewell	d			18 52						19 12					19 32							19 52			
Southend Airport ✈	d			18 55						19 15					19 35							19 55			
Rochford	d			18 58						19 18					19 38							19 58			
Hockley	d			19 01						19 21					19 41							20 01			
Rayleigh	d			19 06						19 26					19 46							20 06			
Southminster	d				18 56											19 36									
Burnham-on-Crouch	d				19 00											19 40									
Althorne	d				19 05											19 45									
North Fambridge	d				19 11											19 51									
South Woodham Ferrers	d				19 16											19 56									
Battlesbridge	d				19 20											20 00									
Wickford 2	d			19 11	19a26					19 31					19 51	20a06						20 11			
Billericay	d			19 17						19 37					19 57							20 17			
Shenfield 3	a			19 25						19 45					20 05							20 25			
Shenfield 3	d	19 20	19 24	19 25			19 34	19 38	19 44	19 45		19 51	19 54	20 04	20 05		20 08	20 14	20 20	20 24		20 25		20 34	20 38
Brentwood	d		19 27				19 37		19 47				19 57	20 07				20 17		20 27				20 37	
Harold Wood	d		19 32				19 42		19 52				20 02	20 12				20 22		20 32				20 42	
Gidea Park 2	d		19 36				19 46		19 56				20 06	20 16				20 26		20 36				20 46	
Romford	d	19 28	19 38				19 48		19 58	19 53			20 08	20 18				20 28	20 28	20 38				20 48	
Chadwell Heath	d		19 42				19 52		20 02				20 12	20 22				20 32		20 42				20 52	
Goodmayes	d		19 44				19 54		20 04				20 14	20 24				20 34		20 44				20 54	
Seven Kings	d		19 46				19 56		20 06				20 16	20 26				20 36		20 46				20 56	
Ilford 2	d		19 49				19 59		20 09				20 19	20 29				20 39		20 49				20 59	
Manor Park	d		19 52				20 02		20 12				20 22	20 32				20 42		20 52				21 02	
Forest Gate	d		19 54				20 04		20 14				20 24	20 34				20 44		20 54				21 04	
Maryland	d		19 56				20 06		20 16				20 26	20 36				20 46		20 56				21 06	
Stratford 7 ⊖	d	19 36	19 59	19 39			20 09	19 52	20 19	20 01		20 05	20 29	20 39	20s19		20 22	20 49	20 36	20 59		20 39		21 09	20 52
London Liverpool Street 15 ⊖	a	19 45	20 07	19 48			20 17	20 01	20 27	20 10		20 14	20 37	20 47	20 28		20 31	20 57	20 45	21 07		20 48		21 17	21 01

Table 5

Saturdays

Southend Victoria, Southminster and Shenfield - London

Network Diagram - see first Page of Table 5

	LE	LE ■1	LE ■1	LE ■1	LE		LE ■1	LE ■1	LE	LE ■1	LE ■1	LE ■1		LE	LE ■1		LE	LE ■1	LE ■1	LE	LE ■1	LE ■1	LE ■1	LE
Southend Victoria d		20 10					20 30				20 50							21 10			21 30			
Prittlewell d		20 12					20 32				20 52							21 12			21 32			
Southend Airport ✈ d		20 15					20 35				20 55							21 15			21 35			
Rochford d		20 18					20 38				20 58							21 18			21 38			
Hockley d		20 21					20 41				21 01							21 21			21 41			
Rayleigh d		20 26					20 46				21 06							21 26			21 46			
Southminster d			20 16									20 56										21 36		
Burnham-on-Crouch d			20 20									21 00										21 40		
Althorne d			20 25									21 05										21 45		
North Fambridge d			20 31									21 11										21 51		
South Woodham Ferrers d			20 36									21 16										21 56		
Battlesbridge d			20 40									21 20										22 00		
Wickford ■2 d		20 31	20a46				20 51				21 11	21a26						21 31			21 51	22a06		
Billericay d		20 37					20 57				21 17							21 37			21 57			
Shenfield ■3 a		20 45					21 05				21 25							21 45			22 05			
Shenfield ■3 d	20 44	20 45		20 51	20 59		21 05	21 08	21 14	21 20	21 25			21 29	21 38		21 44	21 45	21 51	21 59	22 05		22 08	22 14
Brentwood d	20 47				21 02				21 17					21 32			21 47			22 02				22 17
Harold Wood d	20 52				21 07				21 22					21 37			21 52			22 07				22 22
Gidea Park ■2 d	20 56				21 11				21 26					21 41			21 56			22 11				22 26
Romford d	20 58	20 53			21 13				21 28	21 28				21 43			21 58	21 53		22 13				22 28
Chadwell Heath d	21 02				21 17				21 32					21 47			22 02			22 17				22 32
Goodmayes d	21 04				21 19				21 34					21 49			22 04			22 19				22 34
Seven Kings d	21 06				21 21				21 36					21 51			22 06			22 21				22 36
Ilford ■2 d	21 09				21 24				21 39					21 54			22 09			22 24				22 39
Manor Park d	21 12				21 27				21 42					21 57			22 12			22 27				22 42
Forest Gate d	21 14				21 29				21 44					21 59			22 14			22 29				22 44
Maryland d	21 16				21 31				21 46					22 01			22 16			22 31				22 46
Stratford ■7 ⊖ d	21 19	21 01		21 05	21 34		21 19	21 22	21 49	21 36	21 39			22 04	21 52		22 19	22 01	22 05	22 34	22 19		22 22	22 49
London Liverpool Street ■15 ⊖ a	21 27	21 10		21 14	21 42		21 28	21 31	21 57	21 45	21 48			22 12	22 01		22 27	22 10	22 14	22 42	22 28		22 31	22 57

	LE ■1			LE	LE ■1	LE ■1	LE ■1	LE	LE ■1	LE ■1	LE		LE ■1	LE ■1	LE	LE ■1	LE	LE ■1	LE ■1	LE				
Southend Victoria d					22 00								22 30					23 00						
Prittlewell d					22 02								22 32					23 02						
Southend Airport ✈ d					22 05								22 35					23 05						
Rochford d					22 08								22 38					23 08						
Hockley d					22 11								22 41					23 11						
Rayleigh d					22 16								22 46					23 16						
Southminster d						22 16													22 56					
Burnham-on-Crouch d						22 20													23 00					
Althorne d						22 25													23 05					
North Fambridge d						22 31													23 11					
South Woodham Ferrers d						22 36													23 16					
Battlesbridge d						22 40													23 20					
Wickford ■2 d					22 21	22a46							22 51					23 21	23 26					
Billericay d					22 27								22 57					23 27	23 32					
Shenfield ■3 a					22 35								23 05					23 35	23 39					
Shenfield ■3 d	22 20			22 29	22 35		22 38	22 44	22 51		22 59		23 05	23 08	23 14	23 20	23 29	23 35	23 39	23 44				
Brentwood d				22 32				22 47			23 02				23 17		23 32			23 47				
Harold Wood d				22 37				22 52			23 07				23 22		23 37			23 52				
Gidea Park ■2 d				22 41				22 56			23 11				23 26		23 41			23 56				
Romford d	22 28			22 43				22 58			23 13				23 28	23 28	23 43		23 47	23 58				
Chadwell Heath d				22 47				23 02			23 17				23 32		23 47			00 02				
Goodmayes d				22 49				23 04			23 19				23 34		23 49			00 04				
Seven Kings d				22 51				23 06			23 21				23 36		23 51			00 06				
Ilford ■2 d				22 54				23 09			23 24				23 39		23 54			00 09				
Manor Park d				22 57				23 12			23 27				23 42		23 57			00 12				
Forest Gate d				22 59				23 14			23 29				23 44		23 59			00 14				
Maryland d				23 01				23 16			23 31				23 46		00 01			00 16				
Stratford ■7 ⊖ d	22 36			23 04	22 49		22 52	23 19	23 05	23 07	23 34		23 19	23 22	23 49	23 36	00 04	23 49	23 56	00 19				
London Liverpool Street ■15 ⊖ a	22 46			23 12	22 58		23 01	23 27	23 14	23 18	23 42		23 28	23 31	23 57	23 45	00 12	23 58	00 05	00 27				

Table 5

Sundays

Southend Victoria, Southminster and Shenfield - London

Network Diagram - see first Page of Table 5

		LE	LE	LE	LE	LE	LE	LE	LE	LE	LE	LE	LE	LE	LE	LE	LE	LE	LE	LE	LE	LE	LE
		◇1		1		1		1			1	1		1	1	1		1		1		1	
		A	A	A	A																		
							(bus)		(bus)	(bus)													
Southend Victoria	d					06 15		06 45			07 19				07 49					08 19			
Prittlewell	d																						
Southend Airport ✈	d					06 19		06 49			07 23				07 53					08 23			
Rochford	d					06 22		06 52			07 26				07 56					08 26			
Hockley	d					06 25		06 55			07 29				07 59					08 29			
Rayleigh	d					06 30		07 00			07 34				08 04					08 34			
Southminster	d			22p56												08 05							
Burnham-on-Crouch	d			23p00												08 09							
Althorne	d			23p05												08 14							
North Fambridge	d			23p11												08 20							
South Woodham Ferrers	d			23p16												08 25							
Battlesbridge	d			23p20												08 29							
Wickford 2	d			23p26		06 35		07 05			07 39				08 09	08a35				08 39			
Billericay	d			23p32		06 41		07 11			07 45				08 15					08 45			
Shenfield 3	a			23p39		06 53		07 22			07 53				08 23					08 52			
Shenfield 3	d		23p29	23p39	23p44		06 58		07 28	07 45		08 07	08 13	08 20	08 24			08 41	08 43	08 53		09 11	09 13
Brentwood	d		23p32	⌇	23p47		07 08		07 38				08 16		08 27				08 46	08 56			09 16
Harold Wood	d		23p37	⌇	23p52		07 23		07 53				08 21		08 32				08 51	09 01			09 21
Gidea Park 2	d		23p41	⌇	23p56		07 30		08 00				08 25		08 36		08 41		08 55	09 05	09 11		09 25
Romford	d		23p43	23p47	23p58		07 37		08 07				08 27		08 38		08 43		08 57	09 07	09 13		09 27
Chadwell Heath	d		23p47	⌇	00⌇02								08 31				08 47		09 01		09 17		09 31
Goodmayes	d		23p49	⌇	00⌇04								08 33				08 49		09 03		09 19		09 33
Seven Kings	d		23p51	⌇	00⌇06								08 35				08 51		09 05		09 21		09 35
Ilford 2	d		23p54	⌇	00⌇09		07 57		08 27				08 38				08 54		09 08		09 24		09 38
Manor Park	d		23p57	⌇	00⌇12								08 40				08 56		09 10		09 26		09 40
Forest Gate	d		23p59	⌇	00⌇14								08 42				08 58		09 12		09 28		09 42
Maryland	d		00⌇01	⌇	00⌇16								08 44						09 14				09 44
Stratford 7 ⊖	d	23b52	00⌇04	23p56	00⌇19		08 12		08a41			08s34	08 46	08s49	08 49		09 01	09s04	09 16	09 19	09 31	09s34	09 46
London Liverpool Street 15 ⊖	a	00⌇02	00⌇12	00⌇05	00⌇27		08 32			08 35		08 42	08 56	08 59	08 59		09 11	09 12	09 26	09 29	09 41	09 42	09 56

		LE	LE	LE	LE	LE	LE	LE	LE	LE	LE	LE	LE	LE	LE	LE		LE	LE	LE	LE	LE
		1	1		1		1		1		1	1		1		1		1		1		1
Southend Victoria	d	08 49					09 19				09 49					10 19		16 19				16 49
Prittlewell	d																					
Southend Airport ✈	d	08 53					09 23				09 53					10 23		16 23				16 53
Rochford	d	08 56					09 26				09 56					10 26		16 26				16 56
Hockley	d	08 59					09 29				09 59					10 29		16 29				16 59
Rayleigh	d	09 04					09 34				10 04					10 34		16 34				17 04
Southminster	d		09 05									10 05										
Burnham-on-Crouch	d		09 09									10 09										
Althorne	d		09 14									10 14										
North Fambridge	d		09 20									10 20										
South Woodham Ferrers	d		09 25									10 25					and at the same minutes past each hour until					
Battlesbridge	d		09 29									10 29										
Wickford 2	d	09 09	09a35				09 39				10 09	10a35				10 39		16 39				17 09
Billericay	d	09 15					09 45				10 15					10 45		16 45				17 15
Shenfield 3	a	09 22					09 52				10 22					10 52		16 52				17 22
Shenfield 3	d	09 23			09 41	09 43	09 53		10 11	10 13	10 23			10 41	10 43	10 53		16 53		17 11	17 13	17 23
Brentwood	d	09 26				09 46	09 56			10 16	10 26				10 46	10 56		16 56			17 16	17 26
Harold Wood	d	09 31				09 51	10 01			10 21	10 31				10 51	11 01		17 01			17 21	17 31
Gidea Park 2	d	09 35		09 41		09 55	10 05	10 11		10 25	10 35		10 41		10 55	11 05		17 05	17 11		17 25	17 35
Romford	d	09 37		09 43		09 57	10 07	10 13		10 27	10 37		10 43		10 57	11 07		17 07	17 13		17 27	17 37
Chadwell Heath	d			09 47		10 01		10 17		10 31			10 47		11 01				17 17		17 31	
Goodmayes	d			09 49		10 03		10 19		10 33			10 49		11 03				17 19		17 33	
Seven Kings	d			09 51		10 05		10 21		10 35			10 51		11 05				17 21		17 35	
Ilford 2	d			09 54		10 08		10 24		10 38			10 54		11 08				17 24		17 38	
Manor Park	d			09 56		10 10		10 26		10 40			10 56		11 10				17 26		17 40	
Forest Gate	d			09 58		10 12		10 28		10 42			10 58		11 12				17 28		17 42	
Maryland	d					10 14				10 44					11 14						17 44	
Stratford 7 ⊖	d	09 49		10 01	10s04	10 16	10 21	10 31	10s34	10 46	10 49		11 01	11s04	11 16	11 19		17 19	17 31	17s34	17 46	17 49
London Liverpool Street 15 ⊖	a	09 59		10 11	10 12	10 26	10 31	10 41	10 42	10 56	10 59		11 11	11 12	11 26	11 29		17 29	17 41	17 42	17 56	17 59

A not 11 December

b Previous night, stops to set down only

Table 5

Sundays

Southend Victoria, Southminster and Shenfield - London

Network Diagram - see first Page of Table 5

		LE 1		LE	LE 1	LE	LE 1	LE	LE 1	LE	LE 1	LE 1		LE	LE 1	LE	LE 1	LE	LE 1	LE	LE 1	LE 1		LE	LE 1
Southend Victoria	d						17 19				17 49						18 19				18 49				
Prittlewell	d																								
Southend Airport ✈	d						17 23				17 53						18 23				18 53				
Rochford	d						17 26				17 56						18 26				18 56				
Hockley	d						17 29				17 59						18 29				18 59				
Rayleigh	d						17 34				18 04						18 34				19 04				
Southminster	d	17 05										18 05										19 05			
Burnham-on-Crouch	d	17 09										18 09										19 09			
Althorne	d	17 14										18 14										19 14			
North Fambridge	d	17 20										18 20										19 20			
South Woodham Ferrers	d	17 25										18 25										19 25			
Battlesbridge	d	17 29										18 29										19 29			
Wickford 2	d	17a35					17 39				18 09	18a35					18 39				19 09	19a35			
Billericay	d						17 45				18 15						18 45				19 15				
Shenfield 3	a						17 52				18 22						18 52				19 22				
Shenfield 3	d				17 41	17 43	17 53		18 11	18 13	18 23				18 41	18 43	18 53		19 11	19 13	19 23				19 41
Brentwood	d					17 46	17 56			18 16	18 26					18 46	18 56			19 16	19 26				
Harold Wood	d					17 51	18 01			18 21	18 31					18 51	19 01			19 21	19 31				
Gidea Park 2	d			17 41		17 55	18 05	18 11		18 25	18 35			18 41		18 55	19 05	19 11		19 25	19 35			19 41	
Romford	d			17 43		17 57	18 07	18 13		18 27	18 37			18 43		18 57	19 07	19 13		19 27	19 37			19 43	
Chadwell Heath	d			17 47		18 01		18 17		18 31				18 47		19 01		19 17		19 31				19 47	
Goodmayes	d			17 49		18 03		18 19		18 33				18 49		19 03		19 19		19 33				19 49	
Seven Kings	d			17 51		18 05		18 21		18 35				18 51		19 05		19 21		19 35				19 51	
Ilford 2	d			17 54		18 08		18 24		18 38				18 54		19 08		19 24		19 38				19 54	
Manor Park	d			17 56		18 10		18 26		18 40				18 56		19 10		19 26		19 40				19 56	
Forest Gate	d			17 58		18 12		18 28		18 42				18 58		19 12		19 28		19 42				19 58	
Maryland	d					18 14				18 44						19 14				19 44					
Stratford 7 ⊖	d			18 01	18s04	18 16	18 19	18 31	18s34	18 46	18 49			19 01	19s04	19 16	19 19	19 31	19s34	19 46	19 49			20 01	20s04
London Liverpool Street 15 ⊖	a			18 11	18 12	18 26	18 31	18 41	18 42	18 56	18 59			19 11	19 12	19 26	19 29	19 41	19 42	19 56	19 59			20 11	20 12

		LE	LE 1	LE	LE 1	LE	LE 1	LE 1		LE	LE 1	LE	LE 1	LE	LE 1	LE	LE 1	LE 1		LE 1	LE 1	LE	LE 1	LE 1	LE
Southend Victoria	d		19 19				19 49						20 19				20 49						21 19		
Prittlewell	d																								
Southend Airport ✈	d		19 23				19 53						20 23				20 53						21 23		
Rochford	d		19 26				19 56						20 26				20 56						21 26		
Hockley	d		19 29				19 59						20 29				20 59						21 29		
Rayleigh	d		19 34				20 04						20 34				21 04						21 34		
Southminster	d							20 05										21 05							
Burnham-on-Crouch	d							20 09										21 09							
Althorne	d							20 14										21 14							
North Fambridge	d							20 20										21 20							
South Woodham Ferrers	d							20 25										21 25							
Battlesbridge	d							20 29										21 29							
Wickford 2	d		19 39				20 09	20a35					20 39				21 09	21a35					21 39		
Billericay	d		19 45				20 15						20 45				21 15						21 45		
Shenfield 3	a		19 52				20 22						20 52				21 22						21 52		
Shenfield 3	d	19 43	19 53		20 11	20 13	20 23				20 41	20 43	20 53		21 11	21 13	21 23			21 26	21 41	21 43	21 53	22 11	22 13
Brentwood	d	19 46	19 56			20 16	20 26					20 46	20 56			21 16	21 26					21 46	21 56		22 16
Harold Wood	d	19 51	20 01			20 21	20 31					20 51	21 01			21 21	21 31					21 51	22 01		22 21
Gidea Park 2	d	19 55	20 05	20 11		20 25	20 35			20 41		20 55	21 05	21 11		21 25	21 35					21 55	22 05		22 25
Romford	d	19 57	20 07	20 13		20 27	20 37			20 43		20 57	21 07	21 13		21 27	21 37					21 57	22 07		22 27
Chadwell Heath	d	20 01		20 17		20 31				20 47		21 01		21 17		21 31						22 01			22 31
Goodmayes	d	20 03		20 19		20 33				20 49		21 03		21 19		21 33						22 03			22 33
Seven Kings	d	20 05		20 21		20 35				20 51		21 05		21 21		21 35						22 05			22 35
Ilford 2	d	20 08		20 24		20 38				20 54		21 08		21 24		21 38						22 08			22 38
Manor Park	d	20 10		20 26		20 40				20 56		21 10		21 26		21 40						22 10			22 40
Forest Gate	d	20 12		20 28		20 42				20 58		21 12		21 28		21 42						22 12			22 42
Maryland	d	20 14				20 44						21 14				21 44						22 14			22 44
Stratford 7 ⊖	d	20 16	20 19	20 31	20s34	20 46	20 49			21 01	21s04	21 16	21 19	21 31	21s34	21 46	21 49			21s51	22s04	22 16	22 19	22s34	22 46
London Liverpool Street 15 ⊖	a	20 26	20 29	20 41	20 42	20 56	20 59			21 11	21 12	21 26	21 29	21 41	21 42	21 56	21 59			21 59	22 12	22 26	22 29	22 42	22 56

		LE 1	LE 1	LE 1		LE	LE 1	LE 1	LE	LE 1	LE 1	LE
Southend Victoria	d	21 49					22 19			22 49		
Prittlewell	d											
Southend Airport ✈	d	21 53					22 23			22 53		
Rochford	d	21 56					22 26			22 56		
Hockley	d	21 59					22 29			22 59		
Rayleigh	d	22 04					22 34			23 04		
Southminster	d		22 05								22 45	
Burnham-on-Crouch	d		22 09								22 49	
Althorne	d		22 14								22 54	
North Fambridge	d		22 20								23 00	
South Woodham Ferrers	d		22 25								23 05	
Battlesbridge	d		22 29								23 09	
Wickford 2	d	22 09	22a35				22 39			23 09	23 15	
Billericay	d	22 15					22 45			23 15		
Shenfield 3	a	22 22					22 52			23 22	23 26	
Shenfield 3	d	22 23		22 41		22 43	22 53	23 11	23 13	23 23		23 43
Brentwood	d	22 26				22 46	22 56		23 16	23 26		23 46
Harold Wood	d	22 31				22 51	23 01		23 21	23 31		23 51
Gidea Park 2	d	22 35				22 55	23 05		23 25	23 35		23 55
Romford	d	22 37				22 57	23 07		23 27	23 37		23 57
Chadwell Heath	d					23 01			23 31			00 01
Goodmayes	d					23 03			23 33			00 03
Seven Kings	d					23 05			23 35			00 05
Ilford 2	d					23 08			23 38			00 08
Manor Park	d					23 10			23 40			00 10
Forest Gate	d					23 12			23 42			00 12
Maryland	d					23 14			23 44			00 14
Stratford 7 ⊖	d	22 49		23s04		23 16	23 19	23s34	23 46	23 49		00 16
London Liverpool Street 15 ⊖	a	22 59		23 12		23 26	23 31	23 42	23 56	23 59		00 26

Table 10

Mondays to Fridays

Marks Tey - Sudbury

Miles			LE	LE	LE	LE	LE	LE	LE	LE	LE		LE	LE	LE	LE	LE	LE	LE	LE	LE		LE
0	**Colchester 4**	d																					
5	Marks Tey 2	d	06 01	06 52	07 39	08 22	09 09	10 01	11 01	12 01	13 01		14 01	15 01	16 01	17 07	18 05	19 11	20 05	21 01	22 01		23 01
8½	Chappel & Wakes Colne	d	06 07	06 58		08 28	09 15	10 07	11 07	12 07	13 07		14 07	15 07	16 07	17 13	18 11	19 17	20 11	21 07	22 07		23 07
11¾	Bures	d	06 13	07 04		08 34	09 21	10 13	11 13	12 13	13 13		14 13	15 13	16 13	17 19	18 17	19 23	20 17	21 13	22 13		23 13
16¾	**Sudbury**	a	06 21	07 12	07 55	08 42	09 29	10 21	11 21	12 21	13 21		14 21	15 21	16 21	17 27	18 25	19 31	20 25	21 21	22 21		23 21

Saturdays

		LE	LE	LE	LE	LE	LE	LE	LE	LE		LE	LE	LE	LE	LE	LE	LE	LE	LE
Colchester 4	d	05 50																		
Marks Tey 2	d	06 01	07 01	08 01	09 01	10 01	11 01	12 01	13 01	14 01		15 01	16 01	17 01	18 01	19 01	20 01	21 01	22 01	23 01
Chappel & Wakes Colne	d	06 07	07 07	08 07	09 07	10 07	11 07	12 07	13 07	14 07		15 07	16 07	17 07	18 07	19 07	20 07	21 07	22 07	23 07
Bures	d	06 13	07 13	08 13	09 13	10 13	11 13	12 13	13 13	14 13		15 13	16 13	17 13	18 13	19 13	20 13	21 13	22 13	23 13
Sudbury	a	06 21	07 21	08 21	09 21	10 21	11 21	12 21	13 21	14 21		15 21	16 21	17 21	18 21	19 21	20 21	21 21	22 21	23 21

Sundays

		LE	LE	LE	LE	LE	LE	LE	LE	LE		LE	LE	LE	LE	LE	LE
Colchester 4	d	07 07															
Marks Tey 2	d	07 15	08 15	09 15	10 15	11 15	12 15	13 15	14 15	15 15		16 15	17 15	18 15	19 15	20 15	21 15
Chappel & Wakes Colne	d	07 21	08 21	09 21	10 21	11 21	12 21	13 21	14 21	15 21		16 21	17 21	18 21	19 21	20 21	21 21
Bures	d	07 27	08 27	09 27	10 27	11 27	12 27	13 27	14 27	15 27		16 27	17 27	18 27	19 27	20 27	21 27
Sudbury	a	07 35	08 35	09 35	10 35	11 35	12 35	13 35	14 35	15 35		16 35	17 35	18 35	19 35	20 35	21 35

Table 10

Mondays to Fridays

Sudbury - Marks Tey

Miles			LE	LE	LE	LE	LE	LE	LE	LE	LE		LE	LE	LE	LE	LE	LE	LE	LE	LE		LE	LE
0	**Sudbury**	d	05 30	06 29	07 16	07 59	08 46	09 33	10 26	11 26	12 26		13 26	14 26	15 26	16 32	17 32	18 37	19 37	20 32	21 26		22 26	23 26
5	Bures	d	05 37	06 36	07 23	08 06	08 53	09 40	10 33	11 33	12 33		13 33	14 33	15 33	16 39	17 39	18 44	19 44	20 39	21 33		22 33	23 33
8¼	Chappel & Wakes Colne	d	05 43	06 42	07 29	08 12	08 59	09 46	10 39	11 39	12 39		13 39	14 39	15 39	16 45	17 45	18 50	19 50	20 45	21 39		22 39	23 39
11¾	Marks Tey 2	a	05 49	06 48	07 35	08 18	09 05	09 52	10 45	11 45	12 45		13 45	14 45	15 45	16 51	17 51	18 56	19 56	20 51	21 45		22 45	23 45
16¾	**Colchester 4**	a																						23 55

Saturdays

		LE	LE	LE	LE	LE	LE	LE	LE	LE		LE	LE	LE	LE	LE	LE	LE	LE	LE
Sudbury	d	06 26	07 26	08 26	09 26	10 26	11 26	12 26	13 26	14 26		15 26	16 26	17 26	18 26	19 26	20 26	21 26	22 26	23 26
Bures	d	06 33	07 33	08 33	09 33	10 33	11 33	12 33	13 33	14 33		15 33	16 33	17 33	18 33	19 33	20 33	21 33	22 33	23 33
Chappel & Wakes Colne	d	06 39	07 39	08 39	09 39	10 39	11 39	12 39	13 39	14 39		15 39	16 39	17 39	18 39	19 39	20 39	21 39	22 39	23 39
Marks Tey 2	a	06 45	07 45	08 45	09 45	10 45	11 45	12 45	13 45	14 45		15 45	16 45	17 45	18 45	19 45	20 45	21 45	22 45	23 45
Colchester 4	a																			23 59

Sundays

		LE	LE	LE	LE	LE	LE	LE	LE	LE		LE	LE	LE	LE	LE	LE
Sudbury	d	07 40	08 40	09 40	10 40	11 40	12 40	13 40	14 40	15 40		16 40	17 40	18 40	19 40	20 40	21 40
Bures	d	07 47	08 47	09 47	10 47	11 47	12 47	13 47	14 47	15 47		16 47	17 47	18 47	19 47	20 47	21 47
Chappel & Wakes Colne	d	07 53	08 53	09 53	10 53	11 53	12 53	13 53	14 53	15 53		16 53	17 53	18 53	19 53	20 53	21 53
Marks Tey 2	a	07 59	08 59	09 59	10 59	11 59	12 59	13 59	14 59	15 59		16 59	17 59	18 59	19 59	20 59	21 59
Colchester 4	a																22 08

London - Chelmsford, Colchester, Walton-on-Naze, Clacton, Harwich, Ipswich and Norwich

Network Diagram - see first Page of Table 5

Miles	Miles	Miles	Miles	Miles			LE MX ◇1 ☕	LE MO ◇1 ☕	LE MO 1	LE MO 1	LE MO 1	LE MO ◇1	LE MO 1	LE TWTh O 1	LE TWTh O 1	LE TWTh O 1	LE TWTh O ◇1 ☕	LE TWTh O ◇1 ☕	LE TWTh O 1	LE TWTh O 1	LE TWTh O 1	LE TWTh O 1
0	—	—	—	—	**London Liverpool Street** 15 ⊖	d	22p30	22p30	22p32	00 02	23p02	23p30	23p32	22p50		23p10	23p30			23p50	00 18	
4	—	—	—	—	Stratford 7 ⊖	d	22b38		22p39	00 09	23p09		23p39	22p57		23p17	23b39			23p57	00 25	
12¼	—	—	—	—	Romford	d															00 37	
20¼	—	—	—	—	Shenfield 3	d			23p01	00 31	23p31		00 01	23p21		23p41	00 02			00 21	00 51	
23½	—	—	—	—	Ingatestone	d				00 35	23p35			23p25						00 25	00 55	
29¾	—	—	—	—	**Chelmsford** 3	d	23p03		23p10	00 42	23p42		00 10	23p32		23p50	00 13			00 32	01 02	
36	—	—	—	—	Hatfield Peverel	d				00 48	23p48					23p56		←		00 38	01 08	
38½	0	—	—	—	**Witham** 2	d			23p21	00 55	23p55		00 21	23p43	23p45	00 03	00 24	00 24	00 26	00 45	01 15	
—	3	—	—	—	White Notley	d									23p52		↪		00 33			
—	4¼	—	—	—	Cressing	d									23p54				00 35			
—	5½	—	—	—	Braintree Freeport	d									23p57				00 38			
—	6¼	—	—	—	**Braintree**	a									00 01				00 42			
42¼	—	—	—	—	Kelvedon	d				00 59	23p59			23p47		00 07				00 49	01 19	
46¾	—	—	—	—	Marks Tey 2	d			23p28	01 05	00 05		00 28	23p53		00 13				00 55	01 25	
51¾	—	—	—	—	**Colchester** 4	a	23p22	23p23	23p36	01 18	00 12	00 27	00 39	00 05		00 20		00 36		01 07	01 45	
—	0	0	—	—	**Colchester** 4	d	23p23	23p23	23p36		00 12	00 27				00 20		00 37				00 41
—	—	2¼	—	—	Colchester Town	a																
—	—	—	—	—		d																
—	2¾	3¼	—	—	Hythe	d																
—	—	5¾	—	—	Wivenhoe 3	d			23p44													00 48
—	—	7½	—	—	Alresford (Essex)	d			23p47													00 52
—	—	9¾	—	—	Great Bentley	d			23p51													00 56
—	—	12½	—	—	Weeley	d																
—	—	14¾	0	—	Thorpe-le-Soken 1	a			23p58													01 03
—	—	—	—	—		d			23p58													01 03
—	—	—	4¾	—	**Clacton-on-Sea**	a			00 07													01 16
—	—	17¼	—	—	Kirby Cross	d																
—	—	18½	—	—	Frinton-on-Sea	d																
—	—	19¾	—	—	**Walton-on-the-Naze**	a																
59½	—	—	—	0	Manningtree 2	d	23p31	23p31			00 20	00 35				00 28		00 45				
—	—	—	—	1¾	Mistley	d																
—	—	—	—	5¾	Wrabness	d																
—	—	—	—	9½	Harwich International	d																
—	—	—	—	10¾	Dovercourt	d																
—	—	—	—	11¼	**Harwich Town**	a																
68¾	—	—	—	—	**Ipswich**	a	23p43	23p43			00 36	00 47				00 44		00 57				
—	—	—	—	—		d	23p44	23p44				00 48						00 58				
77	—	—	—	—	Needham Market	d																
80¾	—	—	—	—	Stowmarket	d	23p55	23p55				00 59						01 09				
—	—	—	—	—	**Peterborough** 8	a																
95	—	—	—	—	Diss	d	00 08	00 08				01 12						01 22				
115	—	—	—	—	**Norwich**	a	00 39	00 41				01 45						01 57				

b Previous night, stops to pick up only

London - Chelmsford, Colchester, Walton-on-Naze, Clacton, Harwich, Ipswich and Norwich

Network Diagram - see first Page of Table 5

		LE FO	LE FO	LE FO	LE FO	LE FO	LE FO	LE	LE	LE	LE	LE	LE	LE	LE	LE	LE	LE	LE	LE	LE		LE	LE	LE
		1	1	◇1	1	1	1		1	◇1	1	1	1	1	1	1	1	1	1	1	1		1	◇1	1
				☕																					
London Liverpool Street [15] ⊖	d	23p02	23p18	23p30		23p48	00 18											05 23						06 00	06 02
Stratford [7] ⊖	d	23p09	23p25	23b38		23p55	00 25											05 30							06 09
Romford	d																	05 38							
Shenfield [3]	d	23p25	23p41			00 11	00 47											05 48							06 25
Ingatestone	d		23p45			00 15	00 51											05 52							
Chelmsford [3]	d	23p34	23p52	00 03		00 22	00 58											05 59						06 30	06 34
Hatfield Peverel	d	23p40				00 28	01 04											06 05							
Witham [2]	d	23p47	00 03		00 05	00 35	01 11		05 21									06 12	06 16						06 45
White Notley	d				00 12				05 28										06 23						
Cressing	d				00 14				05 30										06 25						
Braintree Freeport	d				00 17				05 33										06 28						
Braintree	a				00 21				05 37										06 32						
Kelvedon	d	23p51				00 39	01 15											06 16							06 49
Marks Tey [2]	d	23p57				00 45	01 21											06 22							06 55
Colchester [4]	a	00 04	00 15	00 22		00 57	01 41											06 29						06 49	07 02
Colchester [4]	d	00 04	00 16	00 23						05 40			06 10		06 15	06 20		06 30						06 50	07 02
Colchester Town	a															06 27									
	d																								
Hythe	d																								07 07
Wivenhoe [3]	d		00 23															06 37							07 11
Alresford (Essex)	d		00 27																						07 14
Great Bentley	d		00 31																						07 18
Weeley	d																								07 22
Thorpe-le-Soken [1]	a		00 38															06 50							07 28
	d		00 38									06 03					06 31	06 50			06 56				07 28
Clacton-on-Sea	a		00 51															06 59							07 37
Kirby Cross	d											06 12					06 39				07 06				
Frinton-on-Sea	d											06 15					06 42				07 09				
Walton-on-the-Naze	a											06 19					06 46				07 13				
Manningtree [2]	d	00 12		00 31						05 49	05 56		06 18		06 23									06 58	
Mistley	d										06 00		06 22												
Wrabness	d										06 05		06 27												
Harwich International	d										06 13		06 35												
Dovercourt	d										06 16		06 38												
Harwich Town	a										06 18		06 40												
Ipswich	a	00 28		00 43						05 59					06 34									07 10	
	d			00 44				05 10		06 00				06 16						06 39			06 56	07 11	
Needham Market	d							05 20						06 25									07 05		
Stowmarket	d			00 55				05a26		06 12				06a30						06 51			07a10	07 22	
Peterborough [8]	a									07 38															
Diss	d			01 08																07 04				07 35	
Norwich	a			01 43																07 24				07 54	

		LE	LE	LE	LE	LE	LE		LE	LE	LE	LE	LE	LE	LE	LE	LE		LE	LE	LE	LE		LE	LE
		1	1	1	◇1	1	1		1	1	1	◇1	1	1	1	1	1		1	◇1	1	1		◇1	1
																				☕				☕	
London Liverpool Street [15] ⊖	d	06 12			06 25				06 38	06 48		07 00	07 02			07 08	07 18			07 30	07 36	07 46		07 55	
Stratford [7] ⊖	d	06 19			06u33				06 45	06 55			07 09			07 15	07 25			07u38	07 45	07 54			
Romford	d																								
Shenfield [3]	d	06 36							07 01	07 11		07u22	07 25			07 31	07 41				08 01	08 11			
Ingatestone	d	06 40								07 15							07 45				08 05				
Chelmsford [3]	d	06 47			06 58				07 10	07 22			07 34			07 40	07 52			08 03	08 12	08 20			
Hatfield Peverel	d	06 53											07 40												
Witham [2]	d	07 03			07 09				07 21	07 33			07 48			07 51	08 03				08 23	08 35	08 38		
White Notley	d	07 10											07 55									08 42			
Cressing	d	07 12											07 57									08 44			
Braintree Freeport	d	07 15											08 00									08 47			
Braintree	a	07 19											08 04									08 51			
Kelvedon	d								07 25							07 55					08 27				
Marks Tey [2]	d								07 31	07 40						08 01	08 11				08 33				
Colchester [4]	a				07 22				07 38	07 47		07 50				08 08	08 18			08 22	08 40		08 53	08 45	
Colchester [4]	d		07 10		07 23		07 26		07 43	07 48		07 51			07 56	08 08	08 19			08 23	08 41		08 56	08 47	
Colchester Town	a						07 34			07 56					08 03						08 49		09 03		
	d						07 38								08 07								09 07		
Hythe	d						07 42								08 11		08 23						09 11		
Wivenhoe [3]	d						07 46								08 15		08 27						09 15		
Alresford (Essex)	d														08 19								09 19		
Great Bentley	d														08 23								09 23		
Weeley	d														08 26				←				09 26		
Thorpe-le-Soken [1]	a						07 57								08 31		08 38		08 31				09 31		
	d					07 38	07 57								08 40		08 38		08 40				09 38		
Clacton-on-Sea	a						08 06								↪		08 47						↪		
Kirby Cross	d					07 47													08 45						
Frinton-on-Sea	d					07 50													08 48						
Walton-on-the-Naze	a					07 54													08 52						
Manningtree [2]	d		07 18	07 24	07 31				07 51			07 59				08 16				08 31				08 55	09 00
Mistley	d			07 28					07 55					08 02											09 04
Wrabness	d			07 33					08 01																09 09
Harwich International	d			07 41					08 10																09 17
Dovercourt	d			07 44					08 13																09 20
Harwich Town	a			07 46					08 15																09 22
Ipswich	a		07 30		07 42							08 11		08 17		08 29				08 43				09 07	
	d				07 44						08 03	08 12		08 19						08 44				09 08	
Needham Market	d													08 28											
Stowmarket	d				07 55						08 15	08 23		08a33						08 55					
Peterborough [8]	a										09 39														
Diss	d				08 08							08 36								09 08				09 29	
Norwich	a				08 27							08 55								09 27				09 48	

London - Chelmsford, Colchester, Walton-on-Naze, Clacton, Harwich, Ipswich and Norwich

Network Diagram - see first Page of Table 5

		LE 1	LE 1		LE 1	LE 1	LE 1	LE 1	LE ◇1 ☕	LE 1	LE 1	LE 1	LE ◇1 ☕		LE 1	LE 1	LE 1	LE 1	LE 1	LE 1	LE 1	LE ◇1 ☕	LE 1		LE 1
London Liverpool Street 15 ⊖	d		08 00		08 06	08 08	08 17		08 30	08 36	08 48		09 00					09 02	09 18			09 30	09 38		09 48
Stratford 7 ⊖	d		08 08		08 14		08 25		08u38	08 45	08 55							09 09	09 25			09u38	09 45		09 55
Romford	d																						09 53		
Shenfield 3	d		08 25		08 30		08 41			09 03	09 11							09 25	09 41				10 03		10 11
Ingatestone	d				08 34		08 45				09 15								09 45						10 15
Chelmsford 3	d		08 34		08 41		08 52		09 03	09 12	09 22							09 34	09 52			10 03	10 12		10 22
Hatfield Peverel	d				08 47													09 40							
Witham 2	d		08 45		08 54		09 03			09 23	09 35							09 47	10 03				10 23		10 34
White Notley	d										09 42														10 41
Cressing	d										09 44														10 43
Braintree Freeport	d										09 47														10 46
Braintree	a										09 51														10 50
Kelvedon	d		08 49							09 27								09 51					10 27		
Marks Tey 2	d		08 55				09 10			09 33								09 57					10 33		
Colchester 4	a		09 02		09 06	09 10	09 17		09 22	09 40			09 46					10 04	10 15			10 22	10 40		
Colchester 4	d		09 02		09 06	09 14	09 18		09 23	09 41			09 47				09 56	10 04	10 16		10 20	10 23	10 41		
Colchester Town	a					09 21				09 49							10 03				10 27		10 49		
	d																10 07								
Hythe	d																10 11								
Wivenhoe 3	d						09 25										10 15		10 23						
Alresford (Essex)	d																10 19								
Great Bentley	d																10 23								
Weeley	d							←									10 26			←					
Thorpe-le-Soken 1	a						09 36	09 31									10 31		10 35	10 31					
	d						09 36	09 38									10 37		10 35	10 37					
Clacton-on-Sea	a						09 45										→		10 44						
Kirby Cross	d							09 43												10 42					
Frinton-on-Sea	d							09 46												10 45					
Walton-on-the-Naze	a							09 50												10 49					
Manningtree 2	d				09 14				09 31				09 55		10 00			10 12				10 31			
Mistley	d														10 04										
Wrabness	d														10 09										
Harwich International	d														10 17										
Dovercourt	d														10 20										
Harwich Town	a														10 22										
Ipswich	a		09 20		09 26				09 43				10 07					10 25				10 43			
	d	09 19							09 44			10 00	10 08			10 19						10 44			
Needham Market	d	09 28														10 28									
Stowmarket	d	09a33							09 55			10 12				10a33						10 55			
Peterborough 8	a											11 37													
Diss	d								10 08				10 29									11 08			
Norwich	a								10 27				10 50									11 27			

		LE ◇1 ☕	LE 1	LE 1	LE 1	LE 1	LE 1	LE 1	LE 1		LE ◇1 ☕	LE 1	LE 1	LE 1	LE ◇1 ☕	LE 1	LE 1	LE 1	LE 1		LE 1	LE 1	LE 1	LE ◇1 ☕	LE 1
London Liverpool Street 15 ⊖	d	10 00				10 02	10 18				10 30	10 38	10 48		11 00				11 02		11 18			11 30	11 38
Stratford 7 ⊖	d					10 09	10 25				10u38	10 45	10 55						11 09		11 25			11u38	11 45
Romford	d											10 53													11 53
Shenfield 3	d					10 25	10 41					11 03	11 11						11 25		11 41				12 03
Ingatestone	d						10 45						11 15								11 45				
Chelmsford 3	d					10 34	10 52				11 03	11 12	11 22						11 34		11 52			12 03	12 12
Hatfield Peverel	d					10 40													11 40						
Witham 2	d					10 47	11 03					11 23	11 34						11 47		12 03				12 23
White Notley	d												11 41												
Cressing	d												11 43												
Braintree Freeport	d												11 46												
Braintree	a												11 50												
Kelvedon	d					10 51						11 27							11 51						12 27
Marks Tey 2	d					10 57						11 33							11 57						12 33
Colchester 4	a	10 46				11 04	11 15				11 22	11 40			11 46				12 04		12 15			12 22	12 40
Colchester 4	d	10 47			10 56	11 04	11 16		11 20		11 23	11 41			11 47			11 56	12 04		12 16		12 20	12 23	12 41
Colchester Town	a				11 03				11 27			11 49						12 03					12 27		12 49
	d				11 07													12 07							
Hythe	d				11 11													12 11							
Wivenhoe 3	d				11 15		11 23											12 15			12 23				
Alresford (Essex)	d				11 19													12 19							
Great Bentley	d				11 23													12 23							
Weeley	d				11 26			←										12 26				←			
Thorpe-le-Soken 1	a				11 31		11 35	11 31										12 31			12 35	12 31			
	d				11 37		11 35	11 37										12 37			12 35	12 37			
Clacton-on-Sea	a				→		11 44											→			12 44				
Kirby Cross	d							11 42														12 42			
Frinton-on-Sea	d							11 45														12 45			
Walton-on-the-Naze	a							11 49														12 49			
Manningtree 2	d	10 55	11 00			11 12					11 31				11 55	12 00			12 12					12 31	
Mistley	d		11 04													12 04									
Wrabness	d		11 09													12 09									
Harwich International	d		11 17													12 17									
Dovercourt	d		11 20													12 20									
Harwich Town	a		11 22													12 22									
Ipswich	a	11 07				11 25					11 43				12 07				12 25					12 43	
	d	11 08		11 19							11 44			12 00	12 08		12 19							12 44	
Needham Market	d			11 28													12 28								
Stowmarket	d			11a33							11 55			12 12			12a33							12 55	
Peterborough 8	a													13 37											
Diss	d	11 29									12 08				12 29									13 08	
Norwich	a	11 50									12 27				12 50									13 27	

London - Chelmsford, Colchester, Walton-on-Naze, Clacton, Harwich, Ipswich and Norwich

Network Diagram - see first Page of Table 5

		LE 1	LE ◇1 ⊏	LE 1	LE 1	LE 1	LE 1	LE 1	LE 1	LE 1	LE ◇1 ⊏	LE 1	LE 1	LE 1	LE ◇1 ⊏	LE 1	LE 1	LE 1	LE 1	LE 1	LE 1	LE 1	LE ◇1 ⊏
London Liverpool Street 15 ⊖	d	11 48	12 00				12 02	12 18			12 30	12 38	12 48		13 00				13 02	13 18			13 30
Stratford 7 ⊖	d	11 55					12 09	12 25			12u38	12 45	12 55						13 09	13 25			13u38
Romford	d											12 53											
Shenfield 3	d	12 11					12 25	12 41				13 03	13 11						13 25	13 41			
Ingatestone	d	12 15						12 45					13 15							13 45			
Chelmsford 3	d	12 22					12 34	12 52			13 03	13 12	13 22						13 34	13 52			14 03
Hatfield Peverel	d						12 40												13 40				
Witham 2	d	12 34					12 47	13 03				13 23	13 34						13 47	14 03			
White Notley	d	12 41											13 41										
Cressing	d	12 43											13 43										
Braintree Freeport	d	12 46											13 46										
Braintree	a	12 50											13 50										
Kelvedon	d						12 51					13 27							13 51				
Marks Tey 2	d						12 57					13 33							13 57				
Colchester 4	a		12 46				13 04	13 15			13 22	13 40			13 46				14 04	14 15			14 22
Colchester 4	d		12 47			12 56	13 04	13 16		13 20	13 23	13 41			13 47			13 56	14 04	14 16		14 20	14 23
Colchester Town	a					13 03				13 27		13 49						14 03				14 27	
	d					13 07												14 07					
Hythe	d					13 11												14 11					
Wivenhoe 3	d					13 15		13 23										14 15		14 23			
Alresford (Essex)	d					13 19												14 19					
Great Bentley	d					13 23												14 23					
Weeley	d					13 26			←									14 26			←		
Thorpe-le-Soken 1	a					13 31		13 35	13 31									14 31		14 35	14 31		
	d					13 37		13 35	13 37									14 37		14 35	14 37		
Clacton-on-Sea	a					↪		13 44										↪		14 44			
Kirby Cross	d								13 42												14 42		
Frinton-on-Sea	d								13 45												14 45		
Walton-on-the-Naze	a								13 49												14 49		
Manningtree 2	d		12 55	13 00			13 12				13 31				13 55	14 00			14 12				14 31
Mistley	d			13 04												14 04							
Wrabness	d			13 09												14 09							
Harwich International	d			13 17												14 17							
Dovercourt	d			13 20												14 20							
Harwich Town	a			13 22												14 22							
Ipswich	a		13 07				13 25				13 43				14 07				14 25				14 43
	d		13 08		13 19						13 44			14 00	14 08		14 19						14 44
Needham Market	d				13 28												14 28						
Stowmarket	d				13a33						13 55			14 12			14a33						14 55
Peterborough 8	a													15 37									
Diss	d		13 29								14 08				14 29								15 08
Norwich	a		13 50								14 27				14 50								15 27

		LE 1	LE 1	LE ◇1 ⊏	LE 1	LE 1	LE 1	LE 1	LE 1	LE 1	LE ◇1 ⊏	LE 1	LE 1	LE 1	LE ◇1 ⊏	LE 1	LE 1	LE 1	LE 1	LE 1	LE 1	LE 1
London Liverpool Street 15 ⊖	d	13 38	13 48	14 00				14 02		14 18	14 30	14 38	14 48		15 00				15 02		15 18	
Stratford 7 ⊖	d	13 45	13 55					14 09		14 25	14u38	14 45	14 55						15 09		15 25	
Romford	d	13 53										14 53										
Shenfield 3	d	14 03	14 11					14 25		14 41		15 03	15 11						15 25		15 41	
Ingatestone	d		14 15							14 45			15 15								15 45	
Chelmsford 3	d	14 12	14 22					14 34		14 52	15 03	15 12	15 22						15 34		15 52	
Hatfield Peverel	d							14 40											15 40			
Witham 2	d	14 23	14 34					14 47		15 03		15 23	15 35						15 47		16 03	
White Notley	d		14 41										15 42									
Cressing	d		14 43										15 44									
Braintree Freeport	d		14 46										15 47									
Braintree	a		14 50										15 51									
Kelvedon	d	14 27						14 51				15 27							15 51			
Marks Tey 2	d	14 33						14 57				15 33							15 57			
Colchester 4	a	14 40		14 46				15 04		15 15	15 22	15 40			15 46				16 04		16 15	
Colchester 4	d	14 41		14 47	14 56			15 04	15 20	15 16	15 23	15 41			15 47			15 56	16 04	16 14	16 16	
Colchester Town	a	14 49			15 03				15 27			15 49						16 03				
	d				15 07													16 07				
Hythe	d				15 11													16 11				
Wivenhoe 3	d				15 15					15 23								16 15			16 23	
Alresford (Essex)	d				15 19													16 19				
Great Bentley	d				15 23													16 23				
Weeley	d				15 26													16 26				←
Thorpe-le-Soken 1	a				15 31					15 35								16 31			16 35	16 31
	d				15 37					15 35								16 37			16 35	16 37
Clacton-on-Sea	a									15 44								↪			16 44	
Kirby Cross	d				15 42																	16 42
Frinton-on-Sea	d				15 45																	16 45
Walton-on-the-Naze	a				15 49																	16 49
Manningtree 2	d			14 55		15 00		15 12			15 31				15 55	16 00			16 12	16 23		
Mistley	d					15 04										16 04				16 27		
Wrabness	d					15 09										16 09				16 32		
Harwich International	d					15 17										16 17				16 41		
Dovercourt	d					15 20										16 20				16 44		
Harwich Town	a					15 22										16 22				16 46		
Ipswich	a			15 07				15 25			15 43				16 07				16 25			
	d			15 08			15 19				15 44			16 00	16 08		16 19					
Needham Market	d						15 28										16 28					
Stowmarket	d						15a33				15 55			16 12			16a33					
Peterborough 8	a													17 37								
Diss	d			15 29							16 08				16 29							
Norwich	a			15 48							16 27				16 50							

Table 11

Mondays to Fridays

London - Chelmsford, Colchester, Walton-on-Naze, Clacton, Harwich, Ipswich and Norwich

Network Diagram - see first Page of Table 5

		LE	LE	LE	LE	LE	LE	LE	LE	LE	LE	LE	LE	LE	LE	LE	LE	LE	LE	LE	LE	LE
			R				R									R						
		1	1	1	1	1	1	1	1	1	1	1	1	1	1	1	1	1	1	1	1	1
			☕				☕									☕						
London Liverpool Street 15 ⊖	d		15 30		15 38	15 48	16 00				16 02		16 14		16 17	16 30				16 32	16 34	
Stratford 7 ⊖	d				15 45	15 55					16 09		16 22		16 25						16 42	
Romford	d				15 53																	
Shenfield 3	d				16 03	16 11					16 25		16 38		16 41					16 54	16 58	
Ingatestone	d			16 00		16 15									16 46							
Chelmsford 3	d		16 00	16 07	16 12	16 22					16 34		16 48		16 53					17 04	17 08	
Hatfield Peverel	d			16 13							16 40										17 14	
Witham 2	d			16 20	16 24	16 35					16 47				17a06					17 14	17 21	
White Notley	d					16 42															17 28	
Cressing	d					16 44															17 30	
Braintree Freeport	d					16 47															17 33	
Braintree	a					16 51															17 39	
Kelvedon	d			16 24	16 28						16 51		16 59									
Marks Tey 2	d			16 30	16 34						16 57		17 05									
Colchester 4	a		16 21	16 38	16 41		16 46				17 04		17 12			17 16				17 26		
Colchester 4	d	16 20	16 21		16 42		16 47			16 56	17 04	17 09	17 16			17 17			17 24	17 27		
Colchester Town	a	16 27			16 50					17 03		17 16							17 33			
	d									17 07									17 37			
Hythe	d									17 11			17 20						17 41			
Wivenhoe 3	d									17 15			17 24						17 45			
Alresford (Essex)	d									17 19									17 49			
Great Bentley	d									17 23									17 53			
Weeley	d									17 26				←					17 56			←
Thorpe-le-Soken 1	a									17 31			17 35	17 31					18 01			18 01
	d									17 37			17 35	17 37					18 10			18 10
Clacton-on-Sea	a									↪			17 46						↪			
Kirby Cross	d													17 42								18 15
Frinton-on-Sea	d													17 45								18 18
Walton-on-the-Naze	a													17 49								18 22
Manningtree 2	d		16 29				16 55	17 00			17 12						17 24			17 35		
Mistley	d							17 04									17 28					
Wrabness	d							17 09									17 33					
Harwich International	d							17 17									17 41					
Dovercourt	d							17 20									17 44					
Harwich Town	a							17 22									17 46					
Ipswich	a		16 40				17 07				17 27					17 34				17 49		
	d		16 41				17 08		17 19							17 36		17 49				
Needham Market	d								17 28									17 58				
Stowmarket	d		16 52				17 19		17a33							17 47		18 04				
Peterborough 8	a																	19 38				
Diss	d		17 05				17 32									18 00						
Norwich	a		17 24				17 53									18 22						

London - Chelmsford, Colchester, Walton-on-Naze, Clacton, Harwich, Ipswich and Norwich

Network Diagram - see first Page of Table 5

		LE		LE	LE	LE	LE	LE	LE	LE	LE	LE	LE	LE	LE	LE	LE	LE	LE	LE	LE	LE
					R									R								R
		1		1	1	1	1	◇1	1	1	1	1	1	1	1	1	1	1	1	1	1	1
					A								B								B	
					☕									☕								☕
London Liverpool Street 15 ⊖	d	16 44		16 47	17 00			17 02	17 08		17 12	17 18	17 20	17 30		17 32		17 38			17 40	17 50
Stratford 7 ⊖	d	16 52		16 55				17 10	17 16		17 20	17 26	17 29			17 40		17 47			17 49	
Romford	d																					
Shenfield 3	d			17 11				17u26					17 45								18 05	
Ingatestone	d			17 16									17 49								18 09	
Chelmsford 3	d	17 15		17 23				17 36	17 40		17 44	17 50	17 57			18 05		18 12			18 17	
Hatfield Peverel	d										17 50					18 11						
Witham 2	d			17a36				17 46	17 50		17a59		18 10			18 17					18 31	
White Notley	d												18 17									
Cressing	d												18 19									
Braintree Freeport	d												18 22									
Braintree	a												18 28									
Kelvedon	d	17 27							17 55			18 02						18 25			18 37	
Marks Tey 2	d	17 32						17 54	18 00							18 25						
Colchester 4	a	17 40						18 01	18 08			18 12				18 32		18 36			18 48	18 42
Colchester 4	d	17 44	17 47				17 56	18 01	18 12			18 12			18 16	18 32		18 36		18 40	18 49	18 43
Colchester Town	a						18 03								18 26						18 59	
	d						18 07															
Hythe	d						18 11		18 16											18 44		
Wivenhoe 3	d	17 51					18 15		18 20							18 40				18 48		
Alresford (Essex)	d	17 55					18 19		18 24											18 52		
Great Bentley	d	17 59					18 23		18 28											18 56		
Weeley	d						18 26			←										18 59		
Thorpe-le-Soken 1	a	18 06					18 31		18 35	18 31						18 51				19 04		
	d	18 06					18 37		18 35	18 37						18 51			18 53	19 04		
Clacton-on-Sea	a	18 17					↪		18 46							19 02				19 13		
Kirby Cross	d									18 42									19 01			
Frinton-on-Sea	d									18 45									19 04			
Walton-on-the-Naze	a									18 49									19 08			
Manningtree 2	d		17 57					18 09				18 20		18 27			18 35	18 44				18 52
Mistley	d		18 01														18 39					
Wrabness	d		18 06														18 44					
Harwich International	d		18 15														18 52					
Dovercourt	d		18 18														18 55					
Harwich Town	a		18 22														18 57					
Ipswich	a				17 59			18 20				18 35		18 37				18 59				19 03
	d				18 00	18 16		18 24						18 39								19 04
Needham Market	d					18 25																
Stowmarket	d					18a30		18 35						18 50								19 16
Peterborough 8	a																					
Diss	d				18 21			18 47						19 03								19 29
Norwich	a				18 42			19 09						19 25								19 50

A The East Anglian

B From Stratford from 27 February

London - Chelmsford, Colchester, Walton-on-Naze, Clacton, Harwich, Ipswich and Norwich

Network Diagram - see first Page of Table 5

		LE	LE	LE	LE	LE	LE	LE	LE	LE		LE	LE	LE	LE	LE	LE	LE	LE	LE			LE	LE	LE
							R								R										
		1	1	1	1	1	1	1	1	1		1	1	1	1	1	1	1	1	1			1	1	1
							☕								☕										
London Liverpool Street 15 ⊖	d	17 52			17 58	18 00	18 10		18 12			18 18		18 20	18 30					18 32			18 38	18 48	
Stratford 7 ⊖	d	18 01			18 06	18 09			18 21			18 27		18 29						18 40			18 46	18 56	
Romford	d																								
Shenfield 3	d					18 25								18 45									19 02		
Ingatestone	d					18 29								18 49									19 07		
Chelmsford 3	d	18 25				18 37			18 46			18 52		18 57						19 05			19 14	19 20	
Hatfield Peverel	d	18 31							18 52	←										19 11					
Witham 2	d	18 37			18 41	19 01			18 58	19 01				19 11						19 17			19 24	19 30	
White Notley	d					↪				19 08															
Cressing	d									19 10															
Braintree Freeport	d									19 13															
Braintree	a									19 19															
Kelvedon	d				18 46							19 06		19 17						19 22					
Marks Tey 2	d	18 46							19 06					19 23									19 32		
Colchester 4	a	18 53			18 56		19 00		19 13			19 17		19 30	19 21					19 33			19 39	19 43	
Colchester 4	d	18 54			18 57		19 02	19 06	19 13			19 17	19 20	19 30	19 23					19 37	19 39		19 39	19 44	
Colchester Town	a							19 13					19 27				←				19 50				
	d							19 19																	
Hythe	d	18 58						19 23	19 18								19 23							19 48	
Wivenhoe 3	d	19 02						↪	19 22								19 27			19 44				19 52	
Alresford (Essex)	d																19 31			19 48					
Great Bentley	d																19 35			19 52					
Weeley	d																19 38			19 55					←
Thorpe-le-Soken 1	a	19 13							19 33								19 43			20 00				20 04	20 00
	d	19 13							19 33							19 35	19 43			20 08				20 04	20 08
Clacton-on-Sea	a	19 24							19 44								19 52			↪				20 15	
Kirby Cross	d															19 40									20 13
Frinton-on-Sea	d															19 43									20 16
Walton-on-the-Naze	a															19 47									20 22
Manningtree 2	d		19 00		19 05		19 11					19 25		19 40	19 32			19 38					19 47		
Mistley	d		19 04															19 42							
Wrabness	d		19 09															19 47							
Harwich International	d		19 17											20a01				19 55							
Dovercourt	d		19 20															19 58							
Harwich Town	a		19 22															20 00							
Ipswich	a				19 19		19 21					19 39			19 42								20 04		
	d			19 10			19 23								19 44				20 00						
Needham Market	d			19 19																					
Stowmarket	d			19a24			19 34								19 55				20 12						
Peterborough 8	a																		21 39						
Diss	d						19 47								20 08										
Norwich	a						20 09								20 30										

London - Chelmsford, Colchester, Walton-on-Naze, Clacton, Harwich, Ipswich and Norwich

Network Diagram - see first Page of Table 5

		LE R 1 ☕	LE 1	LE 1	LE 1	LE 1	LE 1		LE 1	LE 1	LE R 1 ☕	LE 1	LE 1	LE 1	LE 1	LE 1	LE ◇1 ☕		LE 1	LE 1	LE	LE 1	LE 1	LE 1	LE 1
London Liverpool Street 15 ⊖	d	19 00	19 02				19 08		19 18		19 30		19 32	19 38	19 48		20 00						20 02	20 18	
Stratford 7 ⊖	d		19 09				19 15		19 25				19 39	19 45	19 55								20 09	20 25	
Romford	d																								
Shenfield 3	d		19 25						19 41					20 01	20 11								20 25	20 41	
Ingatestone	d								19 45						20 15									20 45	
Chelmsford 3	d		19 34				19 38		19 52				20 02	20 10	20 22								20 34	20 52	
Hatfield Peverel	d		19 40											20 16									20 40		
Witham 2	d		19 49				19 50		20 03				20 13	20 23	20 34								20 47	21 03	
White Notley	d		19 56												20 41										
Cressing	d		19 58												20 43										
Braintree Freeport	d		20 01												20 46										
Braintree	a		20 05												20 50										
Kelvedon	d						19 55							20 27									20 51		
Marks Tey 2	d						20 00							20 33									20 57		
Colchester 4	a	19 47					20 07		20 15		20 19		20 25	20 40			20 46						21 04	21 15	
Colchester 4	d	19 47				19 56	20 08		20 16		20 20	20 20	20 25	20 41			20 47					20 56	21 04	21 16	
Colchester Town	a					20 03						20 27		20 49								21 03			
	d					20 07																21 07			
Hythe	d					20 11																21 11			
Wivenhoe 3	d					20 15			20 23													21 15		21 23	
Alresford (Essex)	d					20 19																21 19			
Great Bentley	d					20 23																21 23			
Weeley	d					20 26				←												21 26			←
Thorpe-le-Soken 1	a					20 31			20 35	20 31												21 31		21 35	21 31
	d					20 37			20 35	20 37									20 54			21 37		21 35	21 37
Clacton-on-Sea	a					↪			20 44										21 03			↪		21 44	
Kirby Cross	d									20 42															21 42
Frinton-on-Sea	d									20 45															21 45
Walton-on-the-Naze	a									20 49															21 49
Manningtree 2	d	19 55		20 00			20 16				20 28		20 34			20 38	20 55			21 00			21 12		
Mistley	d			20 04												20 42				21 04					
Wrabness	d			20 09												20 47				21 09					
Harwich International	d			20 17									20a54			20 55				21 17					
Dovercourt	d			20 20												20 58				21 20					
Harwich Town	a			20 22												21 00				21 22					
Ipswich	a	20 07					20 28				20 40						21 07						21 25		
	d	20 08			20 19						20 41						21 08				21 16				
Needham Market	d				20 28																21 26				
Stowmarket	d	20 19			20a33						20 52						21 19				21a32				
Peterborough 8	a																								
Diss	d	20 32									21 05						21 32								
Norwich	a	20 51									21 24						21 51								

		LE 1	LE ◇1 ☕		LE 1	LE 1	LE 1	LE ◇1 ☕	LE 1	LE	LE 1	LE 1	LE 1		LE 1	LE ◇1 ☕	LE 1	LE 1	LE 1	LE 1	LE 1	LE 1	LE 1		LE 1
London Liverpool Street 15 ⊖	d		20 30		20 38	20 48		21 00				21 02	21 18			21 30	21 38	21 48	22 00	22 02					22 18
Stratford 7 ⊖	d		20u38		20 45	20 55						21 09	21 25			21u38	21 45	21 55		22 09					22 25
Romford	d				20 53												21 53								
Shenfield 3	d				21 03	21 11						21 25	21 41				22 03	22 11		22 25					22 41
Ingatestone	d					21 15							21 45					22 15							22 45
Chelmsford 3	d		21 03		21 12	21 22						21 34	21 52			22 03	22 12	22 22	22 28	22 34					22 52
Hatfield Peverel	d											21 40								22 40					
Witham 2	d				21 23	21 34						21 47	22 03				22 23	22 34		22 47					23 03
White Notley	d					21 41												22 41							
Cressing	d					21 43												22 43							
Braintree Freeport	d					21 46												22 46							
Braintree	a					21 50												22 50							
Kelvedon	d				21 27							21 51					22 27			22 51					
Marks Tey 2	d				21 33							21 57					22 33			22 57					
Colchester 4	a		21 22		21 40			21 46				22 04	22 15			22 22	22 40		22 47	23 05					23 15
Colchester 4	d	21 20	21 23		21 41			21 47			21 56	22 04	22 16			22 23	22 41		22 47				22 56		23 16
Colchester Town	a	21 27			21 49						22 03						22 49						23 03		
	d										22 07												23 07		
Hythe	d										22 11												23 11		
Wivenhoe 3	d										22 15		22 23										23 15		23 23
Alresford (Essex)	d										22 19												23 19		
Great Bentley	d										22 23												23 23		
Weeley	d										22 26				←								23 26		
Thorpe-le-Soken 1	a										22 31		22 35		22 31								23 31		23 35
	d										22 37		22 35		22 37							23 16	23 37		23 35
Clacton-on-Sea	a										↪		22 44									23 25	↪		23 44
Kirby Cross	d														22 42										
Frinton-on-Sea	d														22 45										
Walton-on-the-Naze	a														22 49										
Manningtree 2	d		21 31					21 55	22 00			22 12				22 31			22 55		23 00				
Mistley	d								22 04												23 04				
Wrabness	d								22 09												23 09				
Harwich International	d						21 38		22 17			22a28									23 17				
Dovercourt	d								22 20												23 20				
Harwich Town	a								22 22												23 22				
Ipswich	a		21 43				22 03	22 07								22 43			23 08						
	d		21 44					22 08		22 16						22 44									
Needham Market	d									22 26															
Stowmarket	d		21 55					22 19		22a32						22 55									
Peterborough 8	a																								
Diss	d		22 08					22 32								23 08									
Norwich	a		22 27					22 51								23 27									

London - Chelmsford, Colchester, Walton-on-Naze, Clacton, Harwich, Ipswich and Norwich

Network Diagram - see first Page of Table 5

		LE 1	LE ◇1	LE 1	LE	LE 1	LE 1	LE ◇1	LE 1	LE 1	LE 1	LE 1	LE 1	LE ◇1	LE 1
						MTWO	MTWO	MTWO	MTWO	ThFO	ThFO	ThFO	ThFO	ThFO	ThFO
			ꟷP					ꟷP						ꟷP	
London Liverpool Street 15 ⊖	d		22 30			22 50	23 10	23 30	23 50	22 38		23 02	23 18	23 30	23 48
Stratford 7 ⊖	d		22u38			22 57	23 17	23u39	23 57	22 45		23 09	23 25	23u38	23 55
Romford	d														
Shenfield 3	d					23 20	23 41	00 02	00 21	23 01		23 25	23 41		00 11
Ingatestone	d					23 25			00 25	23 05			23 45		00 15
Chelmsford 3	d		23 03			23 32	23 50	00 13	00 32	23 12		23 34	23 52	00 03	00 22
Hatfield Peverel	d						23 56		00 38			23 40			00 28
Witham 2	d					23 42	00 03	00 24	00 45	23 23	23 25	23 47	00 03		00 35
White Notley	d										23 32				
Cressing	d										23 34				
Braintree Freeport	d										23 37				
Braintree	a										23 41				
Kelvedon	d					23 47	00 07		00 49	23 27		23 51			00 39
Marks Tey 2	d				23 46	23 53	00 13		00 55	23 33		23 57			00 45
Colchester 4	a		23 22		23 55	00 05	00 20	00 36	01 07	23 45		00 04	00 15	00 22	00 57
Colchester 4	d		23 23				00 20	00 37				00 04	00 16	00 23	
Colchester Town	a														
	d														
Hythe	d														
Wivenhoe 3	d												00 23		
Alresford (Essex)	d												00 27		
Great Bentley	d												00 31		
Weeley	d	←													
Thorpe-le-Soken 1	a	23 31											00 38		
	d	23 37											00 38		
Clacton-on-Sea	a												00 51		
Kirby Cross	d	23 42													
Frinton-on-Sea	d	23 45													
Walton-on-the-Naze	a	23 49													
Manningtree 2	d		23 31	23 36			00 28	00 45				00 12		00 31	
Mistley	d			23 40											
Wrabness	d			23 45											
Harwich International	d			23 53											
Dovercourt	d			23 56											
Harwich Town	a			23 58											
Ipswich	a		23 43				00 44	00 57				00 28		00 43	
	d		23 44					00 58						00 44	
Needham Market	d														
Stowmarket	d		23 55					01 09						00 55	
Peterborough 8	a														
Diss	d		00 08					01 22						01 08	
Norwich	a		00 39					01 57						01 43	

London - Chelmsford, Colchester, Walton-on-Naze, Clacton, Harwich, Ipswich and Norwich

Network Diagram - see first Page of Table 5

		LE ◇1 ☕	LE 1	LE 1	LE ◇1 ☕	LE 1	LE 1	LE 1	LE	LE 1		LE ◇1	LE 1	LE 1	LE 1	LE 1	LE 1	LE 1	LE 1	LE 1		LE ◇1 ☕	LE 1	LE 1	LE 1
London Liverpool Street 15 ⊖	d	22p30	23p02	23p18	23p30		23p48	00 18									05 34								06 02
Stratford 7 ⊖	d	22b38	23p09	23p25	23b38		23p55	00 25									05 41								06 09
Romford	d																05 49								
Shenfield 3	d		23p25	23p41			00 11	00 47									05 59								06 25
Ingatestone	d			23p45			00 15	00 51									06 03								
Chelmsford 3	d	23p03	23p34	23p52	00 03		00 22	00 58									06 10								06 34
Hatfield Peverel	d		23p40				00 28	01 04									06 16								06 40
Witham 2	d		23p47	00 03		00 05	00 35	01 11		05 34							06 23	06 34							06 47
White Notley	d					00 12				05 41								06 41							
Cressing	d					00 14				05 43								06 43							
Braintree Freeport	d					00 17				05 46								06 46							
Braintree	a					00 21				05 50								06 50							
Kelvedon	d		23p51				00 39	01 15									06 27								06 51
Marks Tey 2	d		23p57				00 45	01 21									06 33								06 57
Colchester 4	a	23p22	00 04	00 15	00 22		00 57	01 41									06 40								07 04
Colchester 4	d	23p23	00 04	00 16	00 23							05 40	05 52		06 20	06 24	06 40							06 56	07 04
Colchester Town	a														06 27									07 03	
	d																							07 07	
Hythe	d																							07 11	
Wivenhoe 3	d			00 23																				07 15	
Alresford (Essex)	d			00 27																				07 19	
Great Bentley	d			00 31																				07 23	
Weeley	d																							07 26	
Thorpe-le-Soken 1	a			00 38																				07 31	
	d			00 38															06 37					07 37	
Clacton-on-Sea	a			00 51																				→	
Kirby Cross	d																		06 42						
Frinton-on-Sea	d																		06 45						
Walton-on-the-Naze	a																		06 49						
Manningtree 2	d	23p31	00 12		00 31							05 49	06 00			06 32	06 48			07 00					07 12
Mistley	d												06 04							07 04					
Wrabness	d												06 09							07 09					
Harwich International	d												06 17							07 17					
Dovercourt	d												06 20							07 20					
Harwich Town	a												06 22							07 22					
Ipswich	a	23p43	00 28		00 43							05 59				06 44	07 00								07 25
	d	23p44			00 44				05 10			06 00		06 16								07 10	07 19		
Needham Market	d								05 20					06 25									07 28		
Stowmarket	d	23p55			00 55				05a26			06 12		06a30								07 21	07a33		
Peterborough 8	a											07 38													
Diss	d	00 08			01 08																	07 34			
Norwich	a	00 39			01 43																	07 53			

		LE 1	LE 1	LE ◇1 ☕	LE 1	LE 1		LE 1	LE 1	LE ◇1 ☕	LE 1	LE 1	LE 1	LE 1	LE 1	LE 1		LE 1	LE ◇1 ☕	LE 1	LE 1	LE ◇1 ☕	LE 1	LE 1	LE 1
London Liverpool Street 15 ⊖	d	06 18		06 30	06 38	06 48				07 00				07 02	07 18				07 30	07 38	07 48	08 00			
Stratford 7 ⊖	d	06 25		06u38	06 45	06 55								07 09	07 25				07u38	07 45	07 55				
Romford	d				06 53															07 53					
Shenfield 3	d	06 41			07 03	07 11								07 25	07 41					08 03	08 11				
Ingatestone	d	06 45				07 15									07 45						08 15				
Chelmsford 3	d	06 52		07 03	07 12	07 22								07 34	07 52				08 03	08 12	08 22				
Hatfield Peverel	d													07 40											
Witham 2	d	07 03			07 23	07 34								07 47	08 03					08 23	08 34				
White Notley	d					07 41															08 41				
Cressing	d					07 43															08 43				
Braintree Freeport	d					07 46															08 46				
Braintree	a					07 50															08 50				
Kelvedon	d				07 27									07 51						08 27					
Marks Tey 2	d				07 33									07 57						08 33					
Colchester 4	a	07 15		07 22	07 40					07 46				08 04	08 15				08 22	08 40		08 46			
Colchester 4	d	07 16		07 23	07 40			07 44		07 47			07 56	08 04	08 16			08 20	08 23	08 41		08 47			08 56
Colchester Town	a							07 51					08 03					08 27		08 49					09 03
	d												08 07												09 07
Hythe	d												08 11												09 11
Wivenhoe 3	d	07 23											08 15		08 23										09 15
Alresford (Essex)	d												08 19												09 19
Great Bentley	d												08 23												09 23
Weeley	d		←										08 26			←									09 26
Thorpe-le-Soken 1	a	07 35	07 31										08 31		08 35	08 31									09 31
	d	07 35	07 37										08 37		08 35	08 37									09 37
Clacton-on-Sea	a	07 44											→		08 44										→
Kirby Cross	d		07 42													08 42									
Frinton-on-Sea	d		07 45													08 45									
Walton-on-the-Naze	a		07 49													08 49									
Manningtree 2	d			07 31	07 48					07 55		08 00		08 12					08 31			08 55	09 00		
Mistley	d										08 02	08 04											09 04		
Wrabness	d											08 09											09 09		
Harwich International	d				08a09							08 17											09 17		
Dovercourt	d											08 20											09 20		
Harwich Town	a											08 22											09 22		
Ipswich	a			07 43						08 07	08 17			08 25					08 43			09 07			
	d			07 44					08 00	08 08	08 19								08 44			09 08		09 19	
Needham Market	d										08 28													09 28	
Stowmarket	d			07 55					08 12		08a33								08 55					09a33	
Peterborough 8	a								09 38																
Diss	d			08 08						08 29									09 08			09 29			
Norwich	a			08 27						08 50									09 27			09 50			

b Previous night, stops to pick up only

Table 11

Saturdays

London - Chelmsford, Colchester, Walton-on-Naze, Clacton, Harwich, Ipswich and Norwich

Network Diagram - see first Page of Table 5

		LE 1		LE 1	LE 1	LE 1	LE ◇1 ⊡	LE 1	LE 1	LE 1	LE ◇1 ⊡	LE 1		LE 1	LE 1	LE 1	LE 1	LE 1	LE 1	LE ◇1 ⊡	LE 1	LE 1		LE ◇1 ⊡	LE 1
London Liverpool Street 15 ⊖	d	08 02		08 18			08 30	08 38	08 48		09 00					09 02	09 18			09 30	09 38	09 48		10 00	
Stratford 7 ⊖	d	08 09		08 25			08u38	08 45	08 55							09 09	09 25			09u38	09 45	09 55			
Romford	d							08 53													09 53				
Shenfield 3	d	08 25		08 41				09 03	09 11							09 25	09 41				10 03	10 11			
Ingatestone	d			08 45					09 15								09 45					10 15			
Chelmsford 3	d	08 34		08 52			09 03	09 12	09 22							09 34	09 52			10 03	10 12	10 22			
Hatfield Peverel	d	08 40														09 40									
Witham 2	d	08 47		09 03				09 23	09 34							09 47	10 03				10 23	10 34			
White Notley	d								09 41													10 41			
Cressing	d								09 43													10 43			
Braintree Freeport	d								09 46													10 46			
Braintree	a								09 50													10 50			
Kelvedon	d	08 51						09 27								09 51					10 27				
Marks Tey 2	d	08 57						09 33								09 57					10 33				
Colchester 4	a	09 04		09 15			09 22	09 40			09 46					10 04	10 15			10 22	10 40			10 46	
Colchester 4	d	09 04		09 16		09 20	09 23	09 41			09 47				09 56	10 04	10 16		10 20	10 23	10 41			10 47	
Colchester Town	a					09 27		09 49							10 03				10 27		10 49				
	d														10 07										
Hythe	d														10 11										
Wivenhoe 3	d			09 23											10 15		10 23								
Alresford (Essex)	d														10 19										
Great Bentley	d														10 23										
Weeley	d				←										10 26			←							
Thorpe-le-Soken 1	a			09 35	09 31										10 31		10 35	10 31							
	d			09 35	09 37										10 37		10 35	10 37							
Clacton-on-Sea	a			09 44											→		10 44								
Kirby Cross	d				09 42													10 42							
Frinton-on-Sea	d				09 45													10 45							
Walton-on-the-Naze	a				09 49													10 49							
Manningtree 2	d	09 12					09 31				09 55	10 00				10 12				10 31				10 55	11 00
Mistley	d											10 04													11 04
Wrabness	d											10 09													11 09
Harwich International	d											10 17													11 17
Dovercourt	d											10 20													11 20
Harwich Town	a											10 22													11 22
Ipswich	a	09 25					09 43				10 07					10 25				10 43				11 07	
	d						09 44			10 00	10 08			10 19						10 44				11 08	
Needham Market	d													10 28											
Stowmarket	d						09 55			10 12				10a33						10 55					
Peterborough 8	a									11 37															
Diss	d						10 08				10 29									11 08				11 29	
Norwich	a						10 27				10 50									11 27				11 50	

		LE 1	LE 1	LE 1	LE 1	LE 1	LE 1	LE ◇1 ⊡		LE 1	LE 1	LE 1	LE ◇1 ⊡	LE 1	LE 1	LE 1	LE 1	LE 1		LE 1	LE 1	LE ◇1 ⊡	LE 1	LE 1	LE ◇1 ⊡
London Liverpool Street 15 ⊖	d			10 02	10 18			10 30		10 38	10 48		11 00				11 02	11 18				11 30	11 38	11 48	12 00
Stratford 7 ⊖	d			10 09	10 25			10u38		10 45	10 55						11 09	11 25				11u38	11 45	11 55	
Romford	d									10 53													11 53		
Shenfield 3	d			10 25	10 41					11 03	11 11						11 25	11 41					12 03	12 11	
Ingatestone	d				10 45						11 15							11 45						12 15	
Chelmsford 3	d			10 34	10 52			11 03		11 12	11 22						11 34	11 52				12 03	12 12	12 22	
Hatfield Peverel	d			10 40													11 40								
Witham 2	d			10 47	11 03					11 23	11 34						11 47	12 03					12 23	12 34	
White Notley	d										11 41													12 41	
Cressing	d										11 43													12 43	
Braintree Freeport	d										11 46													12 46	
Braintree	a										11 50													12 50	
Kelvedon	d			10 51						11 27							11 51						12 27		
Marks Tey 2	d			10 57						11 33							11 57						12 33		
Colchester 4	a			11 04	11 15			11 22		11 40			11 46				12 04	12 15				12 22	12 40		12 46
Colchester 4	d		10 56	11 04	11 16		11 20	11 23		11 41			11 47			11 56	12 04	12 16			12 20	12 23	12 41		12 47
Colchester Town	a		11 03				11 27			11 49						12 03					12 27		12 49		
	d		11 07													12 07									
Hythe	d		11 11													12 11									
Wivenhoe 3	d		11 15		11 23											12 15		12 23							
Alresford (Essex)	d		11 19													12 19									
Great Bentley	d		11 23													12 23									
Weeley	d		11 26			←										12 26				←					
Thorpe-le-Soken 1	a		11 31		11 35	11 31										12 31		12 35		12 31					
	d		11 37		11 35	11 37										12 37		12 35		12 37					
Clacton-on-Sea	a		→		11 44											→		12 44							
Kirby Cross	d					11 42														12 42					
Frinton-on-Sea	d					11 45														12 45					
Walton-on-the-Naze	a					11 49														12 49					
Manningtree 2	d			11 12				11 31					11 55	12 00			12 12					12 31			12 55
Mistley	d													12 04											
Wrabness	d													12 09											
Harwich International	d													12 17											
Dovercourt	d													12 20											
Harwich Town	a													12 22											
Ipswich	a			11 25				11 43					12 07				12 25					12 43			13 07
	d	11 19						11 44				12 00	12 08		12 19							12 44			13 08
Needham Market	d	11 28													12 28										
Stowmarket	d	11a33						11 55				12 12			12a33							12 55			
Peterborough 8	a											13 37													
Diss	d							12 08					12 29									13 08			13 29
Norwich	a							12 27					12 50									13 27			13 50

Table 11

Saturdays

London - Chelmsford, Colchester, Walton-on-Naze, Clacton, Harwich, Ipswich and Norwich

Network Diagram - see first Page of Table 5

		LE	LE	LE	LE	LE	LE	LE	LE	LE	LE	LE	LE	LE	LE	LE	LE	LE	LE	LE	LE	LE
		1	1	1	1	1	1	1	◇1	1	1	1	◇1	1	1	1	1	1	1	1	◇1	1
									☕				☕								☕	
London Liverpool Street [15] ⊖	d				12 02	12 18			12 30	12 38	12 48		13 00				13 02	13 18			13 30	13 38
Stratford [7] ⊖	d				12 09	12 25			12u38	12 45	12 55						13 09	13 25			13u38	13 45
Romford	d									12 53												13 53
Shenfield [3]	d				12 25	12 41				13 03	13 11						13 25	13 41				14 03
Ingatestone	d					12 45					13 15							13 45				
Chelmsford [3]	d				12 34	12 52			13 03	13 12	13 22						13 34	13 52			14 03	14 12
Hatfield Peverel	d				12 40												13 40					
Witham [2]	d				12 47	13 03				13 23	13 34						13 47	14 03				14 23
White Notley	d										13 41											
Cressing	d										13 43											
Braintree Freeport	d										13 46											
Braintree	a										13 50											
Kelvedon	d				12 51					13 27							13 51					14 27
Marks Tey [2]	d				12 57					13 33							13 57					14 33
Colchester [4]	a				13 04	13 15			13 22	13 40			13 46				14 04	14 15			14 22	14 40
Colchester [4]	d			12 56	13 04	13 16		13 20	13 23	13 41			13 47			13 56	14 04	14 16		14 20	14 23	14 41
Colchester Town	a			13 03				13 27		13 49						14 03				14 27		14 49
	d			13 07												14 07						
Hythe	d			13 11												14 11						
Wivenhoe [3]	d			13 15		13 23										14 15		14 23				
Alresford (Essex)	d			13 19												14 19						
Great Bentley	d			13 23												14 23						
Weeley	d			13 26			←									14 26			←			
Thorpe-le-Soken [1]	a			13 31		13 35	13 31									14 31		14 35	14 31			
	d			13 37		13 35	13 37									14 37		14 35	14 37			
Clacton-on-Sea	a			↪		13 44										↪		14 44				
Kirby Cross	d						13 42												14 42			
Frinton-on-Sea	d						13 45												14 45			
Walton-on-the-Naze	a						13 49												14 49			
Manningtree [2]	d	13 00			13 12				13 31				13 55	14 00			14 12				14 31	
Mistley	d	13 04												14 04								
Wrabness	d	13 09												14 09								
Harwich International	d	13 17												14 17								
Dovercourt	d	13 20												14 20								
Harwich Town	a	13 22												14 22								
Ipswich	a				13 25				13 43				14 07				14 25				14 43	
	d		13 19						13 44			14 00	14 08		14 19						14 44	
Needham Market	d		13 28												14 28							
Stowmarket	d		13a33						13 55			14 12			14a33						14 55	
Peterborough [8]	a											15 37										
Diss	d								14 08				14 29								15 08	
Norwich	a								14 27				14 50								15 27	

		LE	LE	LE	LE	LE	LE	LE	LE	LE	LE	LE	LE	LE	LE	LE	LE	LE	LE	LE	LE	LE	LE
		1	◇1	1	1	1	1	1	1	1	◇1	1	1	1	◇1	1	1	1	1	1	1	1	◇1
			☕								☕				☕								☕
London Liverpool Street [15] ⊖	d	13 48	14 00				14 02	14 18			14 30	14 38	14 48		15 00				15 02	15 18			15 30
Stratford [7] ⊖	d	13 55					14 09	14 25			14u38	14 45	14 55						15 09	15 25			15u38
Romford	d											14 53											
Shenfield [3]	d	14 11					14 25	14 41				15 03	15 11						15 25	15 41			
Ingatestone	d	14 15						14 45					15 15							15 45			
Chelmsford [3]	d	14 22					14 34	14 52			15 03	15 12	15 22						15 34	15 52			16 03
Hatfield Peverel	d						14 40												15 40				
Witham [2]	d	14 34					14 47	15 03				15 23	15 34						15 47	16 03			
White Notley	d	14 41											15 41										
Cressing	d	14 43											15 43										
Braintree Freeport	d	14 46											15 46										
Braintree	a	14 50											15 50										
Kelvedon	d						14 51					15 27							15 51				
Marks Tey [2]	d						14 57					15 33							15 57				
Colchester [4]	a		14 46				15 04	15 15			15 22	15 40			15 46				16 04	16 15			16 22
Colchester [4]	d		14 47			14 56	15 04	15 16		15 20	15 23	15 41			15 47			15 56	16 04	16 16		16 20	16 23
Colchester Town	a					15 03				15 27		15 49						16 03				16 27	
	d					15 07												16 07					
Hythe	d					15 11												16 11					
Wivenhoe [3]	d					15 15		15 23										16 15		16 23			
Alresford (Essex)	d					15 19												16 19					
Great Bentley	d					15 23												16 23					
Weeley	d					15 26			←									16 26			←		
Thorpe-le-Soken [1]	a					15 31		15 35	15 31									16 31		16 35	16 31		
	d					15 37		15 35	15 37									16 37		16 35	16 37		
Clacton-on-Sea	a					↪		15 44										↪		16 44			
Kirby Cross	d								15 42												16 42		
Frinton-on-Sea	d								15 45												16 45		
Walton-on-the-Naze	a								15 49												16 49		
Manningtree [2]	d		14 55	15 00			15 12				15 31				15 55	16 00			16 12				16 31
Mistley	d			15 04												16 04							
Wrabness	d			15 09												16 09							
Harwich International	d			15 17												16 17							
Dovercourt	d			15 20												16 20							
Harwich Town	a			15 22												16 22							
Ipswich	a		15 07				15 25				15 43				16 07				16 25				16 43
	d		15 08		15 19						15 44			16 00	16 08		16 19						16 44
Needham Market	d				15 28												16 28						
Stowmarket	d				15a33						15 55			16 12			16a33						16 55
Peterborough [8]	a													17 37									
Diss	d		15 29								16 08				16 29								17 08
Norwich	a		15 48								16 27				16 50								17 27

Table 11

Saturdays

London - Chelmsford, Colchester, Walton-on-Naze, Clacton, Harwich, Ipswich and Norwich

Network Diagram - see first Page of Table 5

		LE 1	LE 1	LE ◇1 ☕	LE 1	LE 1		LE 1	LE 1	LE 1	LE 1	LE 1	LE ◇1 ☕	LE 1	LE 1	LE 1		LE ◇1 ☕	LE 1	LE 1	LE 1	LE 1	LE 1	LE 1	LE 1
London Liverpool Street 15 ⊖	d	15 38	15 48	16 00					16 02	16 18			16 30	16 38	16 48			17 00				17 02	17 18		
Stratford 7 ⊖	d	15 45	15 55						16 09	16 25			16u38	16 45	16 55							17 09	17 25		
Romford	d	15 53												16 53											
Shenfield 3	d	16 03	16 11						16 25	16 41				17 03	17 11							17 25	17 41		
Ingatestone	d		16 15							16 45					17 15								17 45		
Chelmsford 3	d	16 12	16 22						16 34	16 52			17 03	17 12	17 22							17 34	17 52		
Hatfield Peverel	d								16 40													17 40			
Witham 2	d	16 23	16 34						16 47	17 03				17 23	17 34							17 47	18 03		
White Notley	d		16 41												17 41										
Cressing	d		16 43												17 43										
Braintree Freeport	d		16 46												17 46										
Braintree	a		16 50												17 50										
Kelvedon	d	16 27							16 51					17 27								17 51			
Marks Tey 2	d	16 33							16 57					17 33								17 57			
Colchester 4	a	16 40		16 46					17 04	17 15			17 22	17 40				17 46				18 04	18 15		
Colchester 4	d	16 41		16 47				16 56	17 04	17 16		17 20	17 23	17 41				17 47			17 56	18 04	18 16		18 20
Colchester Town	a	16 49						17 03				17 27		17 49							18 03				18 27
	d							17 07													18 07				
Hythe	d							17 11													18 11				
Wivenhoe 3	d							17 15		17 23											18 15		18 23		
Alresford (Essex)	d							17 19													18 19				
Great Bentley	d							17 23													18 23				
Weeley	d							17 26			←										18 26			←	
Thorpe-le-Soken 1	a							17 31		17 35	17 31										18 31		18 35	18 31	
	d							17 37		17 35	17 37										18 37		18 35	18 37	
Clacton-on-Sea	a							→		17 44											→		18 44		
Kirby Cross	d										17 42													18 42	
Frinton-on-Sea	d										17 45													18 45	
Walton-on-the-Naze	a										17 49													18 49	
Manningtree 2	d			16 55	17 00				17 12				17 31					17 55	18 00			18 12			
Mistley	d				17 04														18 04						
Wrabness	d				17 09														18 09						
Harwich International	d				17 17														18 17						
Dovercourt	d				17 20														18 20						
Harwich Town	a				17 22														18 22						
Ipswich	a			17 07					17 25				17 43					18 07				18 25			
	d			17 08		17 19							17 44			18 00		18 08		18 19					
Needham Market	d					17 28														18 28					
Stowmarket	d			17 19		17a33							17 55			18 12				18a33					
Peterborough 8	a															19 38									
Diss	d			17 32									18 08					18 29							
Norwich	a			17 51									18 27					18 50							

		LE ◇1 ☕		LE 1	LE 1	LE ◇1 ☕	LE 1	LE 1	LE 1	LE 1	LE 1	LE 1		LE 1	LE ◇1 ☕	LE 1	LE 1	LE 1	LE ◇1 ☕	LE 1	LE 1	LE 1		LE 1	LE 1
London Liverpool Street 15 ⊖	d	17 30		17 38	17 48	18 00				18 02	18 18				18 30	18 38	18 48		19 00					19 02	19 18
Stratford 7 ⊖	d	17u38		17 45	17 55					18 09	18 25				18u38	18 45	18 55							19 09	19 25
Romford	d			17 53												18 53									
Shenfield 3	d			18 03	18 11					18 25	18 41					19 03	19 11							19 25	19 41
Ingatestone	d				18 15						18 45						19 15								19 45
Chelmsford 3	d	18 03		18 12	18 22					18 34	18 52				19 03	19 12	19 22							19 34	19 52
Hatfield Peverel	d									18 40														19 40	
Witham 2	d			18 23	18 34					18 47	19 03					19 23	19 34							19 47	20 03
White Notley	d				18 41												19 41								
Cressing	d				18 43												19 43								
Braintree Freeport	d				18 46												19 46								
Braintree	a				18 50												19 50								
Kelvedon	d			18 27						18 51						19 27								19 51	
Marks Tey 2	d			18 33						18 57						19 33								19 57	
Colchester 4	a	18 22		18 40		18 46				19 04	19 15				19 22	19 40			19 46					20 04	20 15
Colchester 4	d	18 23		18 41		18 47			18 56	19 04	19 16			19 20	19 23	19 41			19 47			19 56		20 04	20 16
Colchester Town	a			18 49					19 03					19 27		19 49						20 03			
	d								19 07													20 07			
Hythe	d								19 11													20 11			
Wivenhoe 3	d								19 15		19 23											20 15			20 23
Alresford (Essex)	d								19 19													20 19			
Great Bentley	d								19 23													20 23			
Weeley	d								19 26			←										20 26			
Thorpe-le-Soken 1	a								19 31		19 35	19 31										20 31			20 35
	d								19 37		19 35	19 37										20 37			20 35
Clacton-on-Sea	a								→		19 44											→			20 44
Kirby Cross	d											19 42													
Frinton-on-Sea	d											19 45													
Walton-on-the-Naze	a											19 49													
Manningtree 2	d	18 31				18 55	19 00			19 12					19 31				19 55	20 00				20 12	
Mistley	d						19 04													20 04					
Wrabness	d						19 09													20 09					
Harwich International	d						19 17													20 17					
Dovercourt	d						19 20													20 20					
Harwich Town	a						19 22													20 22					
Ipswich	a	18 43				19 07				19 25					19 43				20 07					20 25	
	d	18 44				19 08		19 19							19 44			20 00	20 08		20 19				
Needham Market	d							19 28													20 28				
Stowmarket	d	18 55						19a33							19 55			20 12			20a33				
Peterborough 8	a																	21 37							
Diss	d	19 08				19 29									20 08				20 29						
Norwich	a	19 27				19 50									20 27				20 50						

Table 11

Saturdays

London - Chelmsford, Colchester, Walton-on-Naze, Clacton, Harwich, Ipswich and Norwich

Network Diagram - see first Page of Table 5

		LE 1	LE 1	LE ◇1 ☕	LE 1	LE 1	LE 1	LE ◇1 ☕		LE 1	LE	LE 1	LE 1	LE 1	LE 1	LE 1	LE ◇1 ☕	LE 1		LE 1	LE 1	LE 1	LE 1	LE	LE 1
London Liverpool Street 15 ⊖	d			19 30	19 32	19 38	19 48	20 00					20 02	20 18			20 30	20 38		20 48		21 00			
Stratford 7 ⊖	d			19u38	19 39	19 46	19 55						20 09	20 25			20u38	20 45		20 55					
Romford	d					19 54												20 53							
Shenfield 3	d				19 57	20 04	20 11						20 25	20 41				21 03		21 11					
Ingatestone	d						20 15							20 45						21 15					
Chelmsford 3	d			20 03	20 07	20 13	20 22						20 34	20 52			21 03	21 12		21 22					
Hatfield Peverel	d												20 40												
Witham 2	d				20 18	20 24	20 34						20 47	21 03				21 23		21 34					
White Notley	d						20 41													21 41					
Cressing	d						20 43													21 43					
Braintree Freeport	d						20 46													21 46					
Braintree	a						20 50													21 50					
Kelvedon	d					20 28							20 51					21 27							
Marks Tey 2	d					20 34							20 57					21 33							
Colchester 4	a			20 22	20 30	20 41		20 46					21 04	21 15			21 22	21 40				21 46			
Colchester 4	d		20 20	20 23	20 30	20 42		20 47				20 56	21 04	21 16		21 20	21 23	21 41				21 47			21 56
Colchester Town	a		20 27			20 50						21 03				21 27		21 49							22 03
	d											21 07													22 07
Hythe	d											21 11													22 11
Wivenhoe 3	d											21 15		21 23											22 15
Alresford (Essex)	d											21 19													22 19
Great Bentley	d											21 23													22 23
Weeley	d	←										21 26			←										22 26
Thorpe-le-Soken 1	a	20 31										21 31		21 35	21 31										22 31
	d	20 37										21 37		21 35	21 37										22 37
Clacton-on-Sea	a											→		21 44											→
Kirby Cross	d	20 42													21 42										
Frinton-on-Sea	d	20 45													21 45										
Walton-on-the-Naze	a	20 49													21 49										
Manningtree 2	d			20 31	20 39			20 55		21 00			21 12				21 31					21 55	22 00		
Mistley	d									21 04													22 04		
Wrabness	d									21 09													22 09		
Harwich International	d				20a54					21 17											21 38		22 17		
Dovercourt	d									21 20													22 20		
Harwich Town	a									21 22													22 22		
Ipswich	a			20 43				21 07					21 25				21 43				22 03	22 08			
	d			20 44				21 08			21 16						21 44							22 16	
Needham Market	d										21 26													22 26	
Stowmarket	d			20 55							21a32						21 55							22a32	
Peterborough 8	a																								
Diss	d			21 08				21 29									22 08								
Norwich	a			21 27				21 50									22 27								

		LE 1	LE 1	LE 1		LE ◇1 ☕	LE 1	LE 1	LE 1	LE 1	LE 1	LE 1	LE 1	LE 1		LE 1	LE ◇1 ☕	LE 1	LE 1	LE 1	LE	LE 1	LE 1	LE ◇1 ☕	
London Liverpool Street 15 ⊖	d	21 02	21 18			21 30	21 38	21 48	22 00	22 02				22 18			22 30	22 38				23 02	23 18	23 30	
Stratford 7 ⊖	d	21 09	21 25			21u38	21 45	21 55		22 09				22 25			22u38	22 45				23 09	23 25	23u38	
Romford	d						21 53											22 53							
Shenfield 3	d	21 25	21 41				22 03	22 11		22 25				22 41				23 03				23 25	23 41		
Ingatestone	d		21 45					22 15						22 45									23 45		
Chelmsford 3	d	21 34	21 52			22 03	22 12	22 22	22 28	22 34				22 52			23 03	23 12				23 34	23 52	00 03	
Hatfield Peverel	d	21 40								22 40												23 40			
Witham 2	d	21 47	22 03				22 23	22 34		22 47				23 03				23 23	23 25			23 47	00 03		
White Notley	d							22 41											23 32						
Cressing	d							22 43											23 34						
Braintree Freeport	d							22 46											23 37						
Braintree	a							22 50											23 41						
Kelvedon	d	21 51					22 27			22 51								23 27				23 51			
Marks Tey 2	d	21 57					22 33			22 57								23 33			23 46	23 57			
Colchester 4	a	22 04	22 15			22 22	22 40		22 47	23 05				23 15			23 22	23 45			23 59	00 04	00 15	00 22	
Colchester 4	d	22 04	22 16			22 23	22 41		22 48				22 56	23 16			23 23					00 04	00 16	00 23	
Colchester Town	a						22 49						23 03												
	d												23 07												
Hythe	d												23 11												
Wivenhoe 3	d		22 23										23 15	23 23									00 23		
Alresford (Essex)	d												23 19										00 27		
Great Bentley	d												23 23										00 31		
Weeley	d			←									23 26			←									
Thorpe-le-Soken 1	a		22 35	22 31									23 31	23 35		23 31							00 38		
	d		22 35	22 37								23 16	23 37	23 35		23 37							00 38		
Clacton-on-Sea	a		22 44									23 25	→	23 44									00 51		
Kirby Cross	d			22 42												23 42									
Frinton-on-Sea	d			22 45												23 45									
Walton-on-the-Naze	a			22 49												23 49									
Manningtree 2	d	22 12				22 31			22 56		23 00						23 31			23 36		00 12		00 31	
Mistley	d										23 04									23 40					
Wrabness	d										23 09									23 45					
Harwich International	d	22a28									23 17									23 53					
Dovercourt	d										23 20									23 56					
Harwich Town	a										23 22									23 58					
Ipswich	a					22 43			23 08								23 43					00 28		00 43	
	d					22 44											23 44							00 44	
Needham Market	d																								
Stowmarket	d					22 55											23 55							00 55	
Peterborough 8	a																								
Diss	d					23 08											00 08							01 08	
Norwich	a					23 27											00 27							01 31	

Table 11

Saturdays

London - Chelmsford, Colchester, Walton-on-Naze, Clacton, Harwich, Ipswich and Norwich

Network Diagram - see first Page of Table 5

		LE 1
London Liverpool Street 15 ⊖	d	23 48
Stratford 7 ⊖	d	23 55
Romford	d	
Shenfield 3	d	00 11
Ingatestone	d	00 15
Chelmsford 3	d	00 22
Hatfield Peverel	d	00 28
Witham 2	d	00 35
White Notley	d	
Cressing	d	
Braintree Freeport	d	
Braintree	a	
Kelvedon	d	00 39
Marks Tey 2	d	00 45
Colchester 4	a	00 57
Colchester 4	d	
Colchester Town	a	
	d	
Hythe	d	
Wivenhoe 3	d	
Alresford (Essex)	d	
Great Bentley	d	
Weeley	d	
Thorpe-le-Soken 1	a	
	d	
Clacton-on-Sea	a	
Kirby Cross	d	
Frinton-on-Sea	d	
Walton-on-the-Naze	a	
Manningtree 2	d	
Mistley	d	
Wrabness	d	
Harwich International	d	
Dovercourt	d	
Harwich Town	a	
Ipswich	a	
	d	
Needham Market	d	
Stowmarket	d	
Peterborough 8	a	
Diss	d	
Norwich	a	

Table 11

Sundays

London - Chelmsford, Colchester, Walton-on-Naze, Clacton, Harwich, Ipswich and Norwich

Network Diagram - see first Page of Table 5

		LE	LE	LE	LE	LE	LE	LE	LE	LE		LE	LE	LE	LE	LE	LE	LE	LE	LE		LE	LE	LE	LE
		◇1	1	1	◇1	1	1	1	1	1		1	1		1	1	1	1	1	1		1	◇1	◇1	1
		A	A	A	A		A																		
		☕			☕																				
London Liverpool Street 15 ⊖	d	22p30	23p02	23p18	23p30		23p48	00 18										07 55					08 30		
Stratford 7 ⊖	d	22b38	23p09	23p25	23b38		23p55	00 25										08 02							
Romford	d																								
Shenfield 3	d		23p25	23p41			00 11	00 47										08 24	08 31				08 58		09 01
Ingatestone	d			23p45			00 15	00 51											08 36						
Chelmsford 3	d	23p03	23p34	23p52	00 03		00 22	00 58										08 34	08 43						09 11
Hatfield Peverel	d		23p40				00 28	01 04											08 49						
Witham 2	d		23p47	00 03		00 05	00 35	01 11	07 34				08 24					08 44	08 55						09 21
White Notley	d					00 12			07 41				08 31												
Cressing	d					00 14			07 43				08 33												
Braintree Freeport	d					00 17			07 46				08 36												
Braintree	a					00 21			07 50				08 40												
Kelvedon	d		23p51				00 39	01 15											08 59						
Marks Tey 2	d		23p57				00 45	01 21											09 05						09 28
Colchester 4	a	23p22	00 04	00 15	00 22		00 57	01 32										08 56	09 12				09 24		09 36
Colchester 4	d	23p23	00 04	00 16	00 23					07 40		08 12				08 18	08 36	08 57	09 15				09 25	09 32	09 36
Colchester Town	a																								
	d																								
Hythe	d																								
Wivenhoe 3	d			00 23													08 44								09 44
Alresford (Essex)	d			00 27													08 47								09 47
Great Bentley	d			00 31													08 51								09 51
Weeley	d																								
Thorpe-le-Soken 1	a			00 38													08 58								09 58
	d			00 38													08 58			09 00					09 58
Clacton-on-Sea	a			00 51													09 07								10 07
Kirby Cross	d																			09 05					
Frinton-on-Sea	d																			09 08					
Walton-on-the-Naze	a																			09 12					
Manningtree 2	d	23p31	00 12		00 31					07 48		08 20				08 26		09 05	09 23			09 26	09 33	09 40	
Mistley	d															08 30						09 30			
Wrabness	d															08 35						09 35			
Harwich International	d														08 30	08 43		09a25				09 43			
Dovercourt	d															08 46						09 46			
Harwich Town	a															08 48						09 48			
Ipswich	a	23p43	00 28		00 43					08 00		08 32			08 53				09 35				09 45	09 51	
	d	23p44			00 44									08 45	09 02								09 46	09 55	
Needham Market	d														09 12										
Stowmarket	d	23p55			00 55									08a59	09a17								09 57	10 07	
Peterborough 8	a																							11 36	
Diss	d	00 08			01 08																		10 10		
Norwich	a	00 27			01 31																		10 31		

A not 11 December

b Previous night, stops to pick up only

Table 11

Sundays

London - Chelmsford, Colchester, Walton-on-Naze, Clacton, Harwich, Ipswich and Norwich

Network Diagram - see first Page of Table 5

		LE 1	LE 1	LE 1	LE 1	LE ◇1 ⊏P		LE 1	LE 1	LE 1	LE 1	LE 1	LE 1	LE ◇1 ⊏P	LE 1	LE 1		LE 1	LE 1	LE 1	LE 1	LE ◇1 ⊏P	LE 1	LE 1	LE 1
London Liverpool Street 15 ⊖	d		09 02			09 30		09 32				10 02		10 30	10 32				11 02			11 30	11 32		
Stratford 7 ⊖	d		09 09					09 39				10 09			10 39				11 09				11 39		
Romford	d																								
Shenfield 3	d		09 31					10 01				10 31			11 01				11 31				12 01		
Ingatestone	d		09 35									10 35							11 35						
Chelmsford 3	d		09 42					10 10				10 42			11 10				11 42				12 10		
Hatfield Peverel	d		09 48									10 48							11 48						
Witham 2	d	09 24	09 55					10 21	10 24			10 55			11 21	11 24			11 55				12 21	12 24	
White Notley	d	09 31							10 31							11 31								12 31	
Cressing	d	09 33							10 33							11 33								12 33	
Braintree Freeport	d	09 36							10 36							11 36								12 36	
Braintree	a	09 40							10 40							11 40								12 40	
Kelvedon	d		09 59									10 59							11 59						
Marks Tey 2	d		10 05					10 28				11 05			11 28				12 05				12 28		
Colchester 4	a		10 12			10 23		10 36				11 12		11 23	11 36				12 12			12 23	12 36		
Colchester 4	d		10 12			10 23		10 36				11 12		11 23	11 36				12 12			12 23	12 36		
Colchester Town	a																								
	d																								
Hythe	d																								
Wivenhoe 3	d							10 44							11 44								12 44		
Alresford (Essex)	d							10 47							11 47								12 47		
Great Bentley	d							10 51							11 51								12 51		
Weeley	d																								
Thorpe-le-Soken 1	a							10 58							11 58								12 58		
	d			10 00				10 58		11 00					11 58					12 00			12 58		13 00
Clacton-on-Sea	a							11 07							12 07								13 07		
Kirby Cross	d			10 05						11 05										12 05					13 05
Frinton-on-Sea	d			10 08						11 08										12 08					13 08
Walton-on-the-Naze	a			10 12						11 12										12 12					13 12
Manningtree 2	d		10 20		10 26	10 31						11 20	11 26	11 31					12 20		12 26	12 31			
Mistley	d				10 30								11 30								12 30				
Wrabness	d				10 35								11 35								12 35				
Harwich International	d				10 43								11 43								12 43				
Dovercourt	d				10 46								11 46								12 46				
Harwich Town	a				10 48								11 48								12 48				
Ipswich	a		10 32			10 43						11 32		11 43					12 32			12 43			
	d					10 44					11 02			11 44				11 55				12 44			
Needham Market	d										11 12														
Stowmarket	d					10 55					11a18			11 55				12 07				12 55			
Peterborough 8	a																	13 31							
Diss	d					11 08								12 08								13 08			
Norwich	a					11 29								12 29								13 29			

		LE 1		LE 1	LE 1	LE ◇1 ⊏P	LE 1	LE 1	LE 1	LE 1	LE 1	LE 1		LE ◇1 ⊏P	LE 1	LE 1	LE 1	LE 1	LE 1	LE 1	LE ◇1 ⊏P	LE 1		LE 1	LE 1
London Liverpool Street 15 ⊖	d			12 02		12 30	12 32			13 02				13 30	13 32				14 02		14 30	14 32			
Stratford 7 ⊖	d			12 09			12 39			13 09					13 39				14 09			14 39			
Romford	d																								
Shenfield 3	d			12 31			13 01			13 31					14 01				14 31			15 01			
Ingatestone	d			12 35						13 35									14 35						
Chelmsford 3	d			12 42			13 10			13 42					14 10				14 42			15 10			
Hatfield Peverel	d			12 48						13 48									14 48						
Witham 2	d			12 55			13 21	13 24		13 55					14 21	14 24			14 55			15 21		15 24	
White Notley	d							13 31								14 31								15 31	
Cressing	d							13 33								14 33								15 33	
Braintree Freeport	d							13 36								14 36								15 36	
Braintree	a							13 40								14 40								15 40	
Kelvedon	d			12 59						13 59									14 59						
Marks Tey 2	d			13 05			13 28			14 05					14 28				15 05			15 28			
Colchester 4	a			13 12		13 23	13 36			14 12				14 23	14 36				15 12		15 23	15 36			
Colchester 4	d			13 12		13 23	13 36			14 12				14 23	14 36				15 12		15 23	15 36			
Colchester Town	a																								
	d																								
Hythe	d																								
Wivenhoe 3	d						13 44								14 44							15 44			
Alresford (Essex)	d						13 47								14 47							15 47			
Great Bentley	d						13 51								14 51							15 51			
Weeley	d																								
Thorpe-le-Soken 1	a						13 58								14 58							15 58			
	d						13 58				14 00				14 58		15 00					15 58			
Clacton-on-Sea	a						14 07								15 07							16 07			
Kirby Cross	d										14 05						15 05								
Frinton-on-Sea	d										14 08						15 08								
Walton-on-the-Naze	a										14 12						15 12								
Manningtree 2	d			13 20	13 26	13 31				14 20		14 26		14 31					15 20	15 26	15 31				
Mistley	d				13 30							14 30								15 30					
Wrabness	d				13 35							14 35								15 35					
Harwich International	d				13 43							14 43								15 43					
Dovercourt	d				13 46							14 46								15 46					
Harwich Town	a				13 48							14 48								15 48					
Ipswich	a			13 32		13 43				14 32				14 43					15 32		15 43				
	d	13 02				13 44			13 55					14 44				15 02			15 44				15 55
Needham Market	d	13 12																15 12							
Stowmarket	d	13a18				13 55			14 07					14 55				15a18			15 55				16 07
Peterborough 8	a								15 31																17 31
Diss	d					14 08								15 08							16 08				
Norwich	a					14 29								15 29							16 29				

Table 11

Sundays

London - Chelmsford, Colchester, Walton-on-Naze, Clacton, Harwich, Ipswich and Norwich

Network Diagram - see first Page of Table 5

		LE 1	LE 1	LE 1	LE ◇1 ☕	LE 1	LE 1	LE 1		LE 1	LE 1	LE 1	LE ◇1 ☕	LE 1	LE 1	LE 1	LE 1	LE 1		LE 1	LE ◇1 ☕	LE 1	LE 1	LE 1	LE 1
London Liverpool Street 15 ⊖	d	15 02			15 30	15 32					16 02		16 30	16 32			17 02				17 30	17 32			
Stratford 7 ⊖	d	15 09				15 39					16 09			16 39			17 09					17 39			
Romford	d																								
Shenfield 3	d	15 31				16 01					16 31			17 01			17 31					18 01			
Ingatestone	d	15 35									16 35						17 35								
Chelmsford 3	d	15 42				16 10					16 42			17 10			17 42					18 10			
Hatfield Peverel	d	15 48									16 48						17 48								
Witham 2	d	15 55				16 21	16 24				16 55			17 21	17 24		17 55					18 21	18 24		
White Notley	d						16 31								17 31								18 31		
Cressing	d						16 33								17 33								18 33		
Braintree Freeport	d						16 36								17 36								18 36		
Braintree	a						16 40								17 40								18 40		
Kelvedon	d	15 59									16 59						17 59								
Marks Tey 2	d	16 05				16 28					17 05			17 28			18 05					18 28			
Colchester 4	a	16 12			16 23	16 36					17 12		17 23	17 36			18 12				18 23	18 36			
Colchester 4	d	16 12			16 23	16 36					17 12		17 23	17 36			18 12				18 23	18 36			
Colchester Town	a																								
	d																								
Hythe	d																								
Wivenhoe 3	d					16 44								17 44								18 44			
Alresford (Essex)	d					16 47								17 47								18 47			
Great Bentley	d					16 51								17 51								18 51			
Weeley	d																								
Thorpe-le-Soken 1	a					16 58								17 58								18 58			
	d		16 00			16 58		17 00						17 58				18 00				18 58		19 00	
Clacton-on-Sea	a					17 07								18 07								19 07			
Kirby Cross	d		16 05					17 05										18 05						19 05	
Frinton-on-Sea	d		16 08					17 08										18 08						19 08	
Walton-on-the-Naze	a		16 12					17 12										18 12						19 12	
Manningtree 2	d	16 20		16 26	16 31						17 20	17 26	17 31				18 20			18 26	18 31				
Mistley	d			16 30								17 30								18 30					
Wrabness	d			16 35								17 35								18 35					
Harwich International	d			16 43								17 43								18 43					
Dovercourt	d			16 46								17 46								18 46					
Harwich Town	a			16 48								17 48								18 48					
Ipswich	a	16 32			16 43						17 32		17 43				18 32				18 43				
	d				16 44					17 02			17 44			17 55					18 44				19 02
Needham Market	d									17 12															19 12
Stowmarket	d				16 55					17a18			17 55			18 07					18 55				19a18
Peterborough 8	a															19 32									
Diss	d				17 08								18 08								19 08				
Norwich	a				17 29								18 30								19 29				

		LE 1	LE 1	LE ◇1 ☕		LE 1	LE ◇1 ☕	LE 1	LE 1	LE 1	LE 1	LE ◇1 ☕	LE 1	LE 1		LE 1	LE	LE 1	LE 1	LE 1	LE 1	LE ◇1 ☕	LE 1	LE 1	
London Liverpool Street 15 ⊖	d	18 02		18 30		18 32	19 00		19 02			19 30	19 32					20 02				20 30	20 32		
Stratford 7 ⊖	d	18 09				18 39			19 09				19 39					20 09					20 39		
Romford	d																								
Shenfield 3	d	18 31				19 01			19 31				20 01					20 31					21 01		
Ingatestone	d	18 35							19 35									20 35							
Chelmsford 3	d	18 42				19 10	19 37		19 42				20 10					20 42					21 10		
Hatfield Peverel	d	18 48							19 48									20 48							
Witham 2	d	18 55				19 21		19 24	19 55				20 21	20 24				20 55					21 21	21 24	
White Notley	d							19 31						20 31										21 31	
Cressing	d							19 33						20 33										21 33	
Braintree Freeport	d							19 36						20 36										21 36	
Braintree	a							19 40						20 40										21 40	
Kelvedon	d	18 59							19 59									20 59							
Marks Tey 2	d	19 05				19 28			20 05				20 28					21 05					21 28		
Colchester 4	a	19 12		19 23		19 36	19 56		20 12			20 23	20 36					21 12				21 23	21 36		
Colchester 4	d	19 12		19 23		19 36	19 56		20 12			20 23	20 39			20 46		21 12				21 23	21 36		
Colchester Town	a																								
	d																								
Hythe	d																								
Wivenhoe 3	d					19 44							20 47										21 44		
Alresford (Essex)	d					19 47							20 50										21 47		
Great Bentley	d					19 51							20 54										21 51		
Weeley	d																								
Thorpe-le-Soken 1	a					19 58							21 01										21 58		
	d					19 58				20 00			21 01						21 03				21 58		
Clacton-on-Sea	a					20 07							21 10										22 07		
Kirby Cross	d									20 05									21 08						
Frinton-on-Sea	d									20 08									21 11						
Walton-on-the-Naze	a									20 12									21 15						
Manningtree 2	d	19 20	19 26	19 31			20 04		20 20		20 26	20 31				20 55		21 20			21 26	21 31			
Mistley	d		19 30								20 30										21 30				
Wrabness	d		19 35								20 35										21 35				
Harwich International	d		19 43								20 43					21a14				21 10	21 43				
Dovercourt	d		19 46								20 46										21 46				
Harwich Town	a		19 48								20 48										21 48				
Ipswich	a	19 32		19 43			20 16		20 32			20 43						21 32		21 36		21 43			
	d			19 44			20 17					20 44					21 02					21 44			
Needham Market	d																21 12								
Stowmarket	d			19 55			20 28					20 55					21a18					21 55			
Peterborough 8	a																								
Diss	d			20 08			20 41					21 08										22 08			
Norwich	a			20 29			21 02					21 29										22 29			

Table 11

Sundays

London - Chelmsford, Colchester, Walton-on-Naze, Clacton, Harwich, Ipswich and Norwich

Network Diagram - see first Page of Table 5

Station		LE	LE 1	LE 1	LE 1	LE ◇1 ⊡	LE 1	LE 1	LE 1	LE ◇1 ⊡	LE 1	LE 1	LE 1	LE 1	LE ◇1	LE 1
London Liverpool Street 15 ⊖	d		21 02			21 30	21 32		22 02	22 30		22 32		23 02	23 30	23 32
Stratford 7 ⊖	d		21 09				21 39		22 09			22 39		23 09		23 39
Romford	d															
Shenfield 3	d		21 31				22 01		22 31			23 01		23 31		00 01
Ingatestone	d		21 35						22 35					23 35		
Chelmsford 3	d		21 42				22 10		22 42			23 10		23 42		00 10
Hatfield Peverel	d		21 48						22 48					23 48		
Witham 2	d		21 55				22 21	22 24	22 55			23 21	23 24	23 55		00 21
White Notley	d							22 31					23 31			
Cressing	d							22 33					23 33			
Braintree Freeport	d							22 36					23 36			
Braintree	a							22 40					23 40			
Kelvedon	d		21 59						22 59					23 59		
Marks Tey 2	d	22 00	22 05				22 28		23 05			23 28		00 05		00 28
Colchester 4	a	22 08	22 12			22 23	22 36		23 12	23 23		23 36		00 12	00 27	00 39
Colchester 4	d		22 12			22 23	22 36		23 12	23 23		23 36		00 12	00 27	
Colchester Town	a															
	d															
Hythe	d															
Wivenhoe 3	d						22 44					23 44				
Alresford (Essex)	d						22 47					23 47				
Great Bentley	d						22 51					23 51				
Weeley	d															
Thorpe-le-Soken 1	a						22 58					23 58				
	d			22 00			22 58				23 00	23 58				
Clacton-on-Sea	a						23 07					00 07				
Kirby Cross	d			22 05							23 05					
Frinton-on-Sea	d			22 08							23 08					
Walton-on-the-Naze	a			22 12							23 12					
Manningtree 2	d		22 20		22 26	22 31			23 20	23 31				00 20	00 35	
Mistley	d				22 30											
Wrabness	d				22 35											
Harwich International	d				22 43											
Dovercourt	d				22 46											
Harwich Town	a				22 48											
Ipswich	a		22 32			22 43			23 32	23 43				00 36	00 47	
	d					22 44				23 44					00 48	
Needham Market	d															
Stowmarket	d					22 55				23 55					00 59	
Peterborough 8	a															
Diss	d					23 08				00 08					01 12	
Norwich	a					23 29				00 41					01 45	

Table 11

Mondays to Fridays

Norwich, Ipswich, Harwich, Clacton, Walton-on-Naze, Colchester and Chelmsford - London

Network Diagram - see first Page of Table 5

Miles	Miles	Miles	Miles	Miles			LE MO	LE MO	LE MX	LE TWThO	LE TWThO	LE TWThO	LE FO	LE FO	LE	LE	LE	LE	LE	LE	LE	LE	LE	LE
							◇1			◇1	1	1	◇1	1	1	◇1	1	1	1	◇1 ☕	1	1	1	1
0	—	—	—	—	**Norwich**	d	22p00			22p00			22p00							05 00				
20	—	—	—	—	Diss	d	22p17			22p17			22p17							05 18				
—	—	—	—	—	**Peterborough 8**	d																		
34¼	—	—	—	—	Stowmarket	d	22p29	00 06	23p47	22p29			22p29							05 30				
38	—	—	—	—	Needham Market	d		00 11	23p52															
46¼	—	—	—	—	**Ipswich**	a	22p41	00 23	00 05	22p41			22p41							05 42				
—	—	—	—	—		d	22p43			22p43			22p43			05 14				05 44				06 00
—	0	—	—	—	**Harwich Town**	d											05 24							
—	0½	—	—	—	Dovercourt	d											05 26							
—	1¾	—	—	—	Harwich International	d											05 29							
—	5½	—	—	—	Wrabness	d											05 35							
—	9½	—	—	—	Mistley	d											05 41							
55½	11¼	—	—	—	Manningtree 2	d	22p53			22p53			22p53			05 25	05a46			05 54				06 10
—	—	0	—	—	**Walton-on-the-Naze**	d															05 35			
—	—	1¼	—	—	Frinton-on-Sea	d															05 38			
—	—	2½	—	—	Kirby Cross	d															05 41			
—	—	—	0	—	**Clacton-on-Sea**	d													05 20				05 40	
—	—	5	4¾	—	Thorpe-le-Soken 1	a													05 28		05 47		05 48	
—	—	—	—	—		d													05 28				05 48	
—	—	7¼	—	—	Weeley	d																	05 52	
—	—	10	—	—	Great Bentley	d																	05 56	
—	—	12¼	—	—	Alresford (Essex)	d																	06 00	
—	—	14	—	—	Wivenhoe 3	d													05 38				06 04	
—	—	16½	—	—	Hythe	d																	06 08	
—	—	18	—	—	Colchester Town	a																		
—	—	—	—	—		d																		
63¼	—	—	—	—	**Colchester 4**	a	23p02			23p02			23p02			05 34			05 46	06 03			06 14	06 19
—	0	19¾	—	—	**Colchester 4**	d	23p03			23p03			23p03		05 12	05 35			05 47	06 05			06 15	06 20
68¼	—	—	—	—	Marks Tey 2	d									05 18				05 53					06 26
72¾	—	—	—	—	Kelvedon	d									05 23				05 59				06 25	06 32
—	—	—	—	0	**Braintree**	d					00 05	00 46		00 25				05 45						
—	—	—	—	0¾	Braintree Freeport	d					00 07	00 48		00 27				05 47						
—	—	—	—	2	Cressing	d					00 10	00 51		00 30				05 50						
—	—	—	—	3¼	White Notley	d					00 13	00 54		00 33				05 53						
76½	—	—	—	6¼	**Witham 2**	d	23p16			23p16	00a21	01a02	23p16	00a41	05 29	05 48		06a02	06 05			06 18	06 31	06 38
79	—	—	—	—	Hatfield Peverel	d									05 33							06 22		
85¼	—	—	—	—	**Chelmsford 3**	d	23p25			23p25			23p25		05 40	05 58			06 14			06 29	06 40	06 47
91½	—	—	—	—	Ingatestone	d									05 47							06 36		
94¾	—	—	—	—	Shenfield 3	a	23b36			23p36			23b36		05 52				06 24			06 41	06 50	
102¾	—	—	—	—	Romford	a																		
111¾	—	—	—	—	Stratford 7 ⊖	a	23b57			00s04			23b52		06 07	06s22			06 39	06s44		06s57	07s06	
115	—	—	—	—	**London Liverpool Street 15 ⊖**	a	00 08			00 14			00 02		06 16	06 34			06 48	06 54		07 09	07 18	07 24

b Previous night, stops to set down only

Norwich, Ipswich, Harwich, Clacton, Walton-on-Naze, Colchester and Chelmsford - London

Network Diagram - see first Page of Table 5

		LE	LE	LE	LE	LE	LE	LE	LE	LE	LE	LE	LE	LE	LE	LE	LE	LE	LE	LE	LE	LE
					R						R											R
		1	1	1	1	1	1	1	1	1	1	1	1	1	1	1	1	1		1	1	1
					☕						☕											☕
Norwich	d				05 30						06 00											06 25
Diss	d				05 48						06 18											06 43
Peterborough 8	d																					
Stowmarket	d	05 54			06 00						06 30								06 44			06 55
Needham Market	d	05 59																	06 49			
Ipswich	a	06 09			06 12						06 42								07 01			07 07
	d				06 14			06 29			06 44					06 52		06 59				07 09
Harwich Town	d								06 24								06 52					
Dovercourt	d								06 26								06 54					
Harwich International	d								06 29								06 57	07a28				
Wrabness	d								06 35								07 03					
Mistley	d								06 41								07 09					
Manningtree 2	d				06 24			06 39	06a46		06 54					07 02	07a14					07 19
Walton-on-the-Naze	d		06 05										06 32									
Frinton-on-Sea	d		06 08										06 35									
Kirby Cross	d		06 11										06 38									
Clacton-on-Sea	d					06 10						06 28			06 38						06 47	
Thorpe-le-Soken 1	a		06 17			06 18						06 36	06 44		06 46						06 55	
	d					06 18						06 36			06 46						06 55	
Weeley	d											06 40										
Great Bentley	d											06 43										
Alresford (Essex)	d											06 47										
Wivenhoe 3	d					06 29						06 51			06 57						07 06	
Hythe	d					06 33						06 55			07 01						07 10	
Colchester Town	a											06 59										
	d			06 19						06 47		07 03										
Colchester 4	a			06 26	06 33	06 39		06 48		06 54	07 03	07 13			07 07	07 12					07 16	07 28
Colchester 4	d			06 27	06 35	06 40		06 49		06 55	07 05				07 08	07 13					07 17	07 30
Marks Tey 2	d			06 33				06 55		07 01						07 19					07 23	
Kelvedon	d					06 50		07 00							07 18						07 29	
Braintree	d						06 40															
Braintree Freeport	d						06 42															
Cressing	d						06 45															
White Notley	d						06 48															
Witham 2	d			06 47			06 57	07 06		07 10				07 17						07 29	07 35	
Hatfield Peverel	d						07 02													07 33		
Chelmsford 3	d			06 56		07 03	07 09			07 19				07 27	07 31	07 35				07 40		
Ingatestone	d			07 03										07 33		07 42						
Shenfield 3	a			07 07			07 19							07 38	07 41					07 50		
Romford	a																					
Stratford 7 ⊖	a			07s23	07s15	07s27	07s35	07s38		07 44				07s55	07s58	08s01				08s07	08s09	
London Liverpool Street 15 ⊖	a			07 35	07 27	07 38	07 46	07 50		07 56	07 58			08 07	08 09	08 13				08 19	08 21	08 23

Norwich, Ipswich, Harwich, Clacton, Walton-on-Naze, Colchester and Chelmsford - London

Network Diagram - see first Page of Table 5

		LE	LE	LE	LE	LE	LE	LE	LE	LE	LE	LE	LE	LE	LE	LE	LE	LE	LE	LE	LE	LE
										R				R								R
		1	1	1	1	1	◇1	1	1	1	1	1	1	1		1	1	1	1	1	1	1
																						A
										☕				☕								☕
Norwich	d									06 50				07 05								07 40
Diss	d									07 08				07 23								07 58
Peterborough 8	d																					
Stowmarket	d						07 05			07 20				07 35	07 45							
Needham Market	d														07 50							
Ipswich	a						07 18			07 32				07 47	08 03							08 18
	d						07 18			07 34			07 38	07 49								08 20
Harwich Town	d										07 16											
Dovercourt	d										07 18											
Harwich International	d								07 15		07 21											
Wrabness	d										07 27											
Mistley	d										07 33											
Manningtree 2	d						07 28		07 32	07 44	07 38		07 49	07 59								
Walton-on-the-Naze	d		06 59															07 40				
Frinton-on-Sea	d		07 02															07 43				
Kirby Cross	d		07 05															07 46				
Clacton-on-Sea	d	06 51				07 05						07 16								07 45		
Thorpe-le-Soken 1	a	06 59	07 11			07 13						07 24						07 52		07 53		
	d	06 59				07 13						07 24						07 58		07 53		
Weeley	d	07 03										07 28						08 02				
Great Bentley	d	07 06										07 31						08 05				
Alresford (Essex)	d	07 10										07 35						08 09			←	
Wivenhoe 3	d	07 14				07 24						07 39						08 13		08 03	08 13	
Hythe	d	07 18										07 43						→			08 17	
Colchester Town	a	07 22																			08 21	
	d	07 27																	08 00		08 32	
Colchester 4	a	07 35				07 32	07 37		07 41		07 47	07 50	07 58	08 08					08 09	08 16	08 40	
Colchester 4	d					07 33	07 38		07 42		07 54		07 59	08 10					08 18		08 48	
Marks Tey 2	d						07 44		07 48				08 05						08 24		→	
Kelvedon	d					07 43	07 49				08 04		08 10						08 30			
Braintree	d				07 26												08 12					
Braintree Freeport	d				07 29												08 14					
Cressing	d				07 32												08 17					
White Notley	d				07 35												08 20					
Witham 2	d				07 44	07 50	07 55		08 03		08 10		08 16				08 28		08 36			
Hatfield Peverel	d				07 48				08 07								08 32					
Chelmsford 3	d			07 49	07 55	07 59		08 09	08 14		08 19					08 30	08 39		08 45			
Ingatestone	d			07 56				08 16								08 37	08 46					
Shenfield 3	a			08 01		08 09		08 21	08 23		08 29					08 42	08 51		08 55			
Romford	a																					
Stratford 7 ⊖	a			08s18	08s20	08s25	08s28	08s38	08s41		08s45		08s48	08s52		08s59	09s08					
London Liverpool Street 15 ⊖	a			08 30	08 32	08 38	08 40	08 50	08 54	08 42	08 58		09 01	09 04		09 11	09 19		09 21			09 24

A The East Anglian

Norwich, Ipswich, Harwich, Clacton, Walton-on-Naze, Colchester and Chelmsford - London

Network Diagram - see first Page of Table 5

		LE	LE	LE		LE	LE	LE	LE	LE	LE	LE	LE	LE		LE	LE	LE	LE	LE	LE	LE	LE	LE	
										R						R								R	
		1	1	◇1		1	1	1	1	1	1	1	1	1		1	1	1	1	1	1	1	1	1	
										☕						☕								☕	
Norwich	d									08 00						08 30								09 00	
Diss	d									08 17						08 47								09 17	
Peterborough 8	d																07 45								
Stowmarket	d			08 11						08 29		08 44					09 14							09 29	
Needham Market	d											08 49													
Ipswich	a			08 24						08 41		09 00				09 08	09 28							09 41	
	d			08 26						08 43			08 48			09 09					09 30			09 43	
Harwich Town	d	07 58				08 28																	09 28		
Dovercourt	d	08 00				08 30																	09 30		
Harwich International	d	08 03				08 33																	09 33		
Wrabness	d	08 09				08 39																	09 39		
Mistley	d	08 15				08 45																	09 45		
Manningtree 2	d	08 20		08 36		08a50				08 53			08 58			09 19					09 40		09a50	09 53	
Walton-on-the-Naze	d		08 00															09 00							
Frinton-on-Sea	d		08 03															09 03							
Kirby Cross	d		08 06															09 06							
Clacton-on-Sea	d								08 11										09 05						
Thorpe-le-Soken 1	a		08 11						08 19									09 12	09 13						
	d		08 12						08 19									09 17	09 13						
Weeley	d								08 23									09 21							
Great Bentley	d								08 26									09 24							
Alresford (Essex)	d								08 30									09 28				←			
Wivenhoe 3	d		08 22						08 34									09 32	09 23			09 32			
Hythe	d		08 26						08 38									→				09 36			
Colchester Town	a							←														09 40			
	d													08 58						09 35		09 44			
Colchester 4	a	08 29	08 35	08 45				08 40	08 46	09 02			09 08	09 05		09 28			09 31	09 42	09 49	09 52		10 02	
Colchester 4	d	08 37		08 45				08 48		09 03			09 12			09 30			09 33	09 43	09 50			10 03	
Marks Tey 2	d							08 54					09 18								09 56				
Kelvedon	d							09 00					09 23							09 52					
Braintree	d										09 00														
Braintree Freeport	d										09 02														
Cressing	d										09 05														
White Notley	d										09 08														
Witham 2	d	08 50					08 58	09 06			09 16		09 29						09 46	09 58	10 05				
Hatfield Peverel	d						09 02						09 33												
Chelmsford 3	d	08 59		09 04			09 09	09 15		09 21	09 26		09 40						09 56	10 07	10 14			10 21	
Ingatestone	d						09 16				09 32								10 02						
Shenfield 3	a						09 21	09 25			09 38		09 50						10 08	10 17					
Romford	a																			10 26					
Stratford 7 ⊖	a	09s23		09s28			09s37	09s41			09 52		10 05						10 22	10 34				10s45	
London Liverpool Street 15 ⊖	a	09 36		09 40			09 49	09 53		09 56	10 01		10 14			10 19			10 31	10 43	10 44			10 55	

		LE	LE	LE	LE	LE	LE	LE	LE	LE		LE	LE	LE	LE	LE	LE	LE	LE	LE		LE	LE	LE	LE
		1	1	1	1	◇1	1	1	1	1		1	◇1	1	1	1	1	◇1	1	1		1	1	1	1
						☕							☕					☕							
Norwich	d					09 30							10 00					10 30							
Diss	d					09 47							10 17					10 47							
Peterborough 8	d																		09 45						
Stowmarket	d				09 44								10 29				10 44		11 14						
Needham Market	d				09 49												10 49								
Ipswich	a				10 02	10 08							10 41				11 00	11 08	11 28						
	d			09 52		10 09							10 43			10 52		11 09							
Harwich Town	d						10 28													11 28					
Dovercourt	d						10 30													11 30					
Harwich International	d						10 33													11 33					
Wrabness	d						10 39													11 39					
Mistley	d						10 45													11 45					
Manningtree 2	d			10 02		10 19	10a50						10 53			11 02		11 19		11a50					
Walton-on-the-Naze	d							10 00														11 00			
Frinton-on-Sea	d							10 03														11 03			
Kirby Cross	d							10 06														11 06			
Clacton-on-Sea	d								10 05														11 05		
Thorpe-le-Soken 1	a							10 12	10 13													11 12	11 13		
	d							10 17	10 13													11 17	11 13		
Weeley	d							10 21														11 21			
Great Bentley	d							10 24														11 24			
Alresford (Essex)	d							10 28				←										11 28			←
Wivenhoe 3	d							10 32	10 23			10 32										11 32	11 23		11 32
Hythe	d							→				10 36										→			11 36
Colchester Town	a											10 40													11 40
	d	10 00								10 35		10 44		11 00										11 35	11 44
Colchester 4	a	10 07		10 11		10 28			10 31	10 42		10 52	11 02	11 07		11 11		11 28					11 31	11 42	11 52
Colchester 4	d			10 12		10 30			10 33	10 43			11 03			11 12		11 30					11 33	11 43	
Marks Tey 2	d			10 18						10 49						11 18								11 49	
Kelvedon	d			10 23						10 54						11 23								11 54	
Braintree	d		10 00												11 00										
Braintree Freeport	d		10 02												11 02										
Cressing	d		10 05												11 05										
White Notley	d		10 08												11 08										
Witham 2	d		10 16	10 29					10 46	11 00					11 16	11 29							11 46	12 00	
Hatfield Peverel	d			10 33												11 33									
Chelmsford 3	d		10 26	10 40					10 56	11 09			11 21		11 26	11 40							11 56	12 09	
Ingatestone	d		10 32						11 02						11 32								12 02		
Shenfield 3	a		10 38	10 50					11 08	11 19					11 38	11 50							12 08	12 19	
Romford	a									11 28														12 28	
Stratford 7 ⊖	a		10 52	11 05					11 22	11 36			11s45		11 52	12 05							12 22	12 36	
London Liverpool Street 15 ⊖	a		11 01	11 14		11 19			11 31	11 45			11 55		12 01	12 14		12 19					12 31	12 45	

Norwich, Ipswich, Harwich, Clacton, Walton-on-Naze, Colchester and Chelmsford - London

Network Diagram - see first Page of Table 5

		LE ◇1 ☕	LE 1	LE 1	LE 1	LE 1		LE ◇1 ☕	LE 1	LE 1	LE 1	LE 1	LE 1	LE ◇1 ☕	LE 1	LE 1		LE 1	LE 1	LE ◇1 ☕	LE 1	LE 1	LE 1	LE 1	LE 1
Norwich	d	11 00						11 30						12 00						12 30					
Diss	d	11 17						11 47						12 17						12 47					
Peterborough 8	d																				11 45				
Stowmarket	d	11 29				11 44								12 29					12 44		13 13				
Needham Market	d					11 49													12 49						
Ipswich	a	11 41				12 00		12 08						12 41					13 00	13 08	13 28				
	d	11 43			11 52			12 09						12 43				12 52		13 09					
Harwich Town	d								12 28													13 28			
Dovercourt	d								12 30													13 30			
Harwich International	d								12 33													13 33			
Wrabness	d								12 39													13 39			
Mistley	d								12 45													13 45			
Manningtree 2	d	11 53			12 02			12 19	12a50					12 53				13 02		13 19		13a50			
Walton-on-the-Naze	d									12 00													13 00		
Frinton-on-Sea	d									12 03													13 03		
Kirby Cross	d									12 06													13 06		
Clacton-on-Sea	d										12 05													13 05	
Thorpe-le-Soken 1	a									12 12	12 13												13 12	13 13	
	d									12 17	12 13												13 17	13 13	
Weeley	d									12 21													13 21		
Great Bentley	d									12 24													13 24		
Alresford (Essex)	d									12 28			←										13 28		
Wivenhoe 3	d									12 32	12 23		12 32										13 32	13 23	
Hythe	d									→			12 36										→		
Colchester Town	a												12 40												
	d		12 00									12 35	12 44		13 00										13 35
Colchester 4	a	12 02	12 07		12 11			12 28			12 31	12 42	12 52	13 02	13 07			13 11		13 28				13 31	13 42
Colchester 4	d	12 03			12 12			12 30			12 33	12 43		13 03				13 12		13 30				13 33	13 43
Marks Tey 2	d				12 18							12 49						13 18							13 49
Kelvedon	d				12 23							12 54						13 23							13 54
Braintree	d			12 00												13 00									
Braintree Freeport	d			12 02												13 02									
Cressing	d			12 05												13 05									
White Notley	d			12 08												13 08									
Witham 2	d			12 16	12 29						12 46	13 00				13 16		13 29						13 46	14 00
Hatfield Peverel	d				12 33													13 33							
Chelmsford 3	d	12 21		12 26	12 40						12 56	13 09		13 21		13 26		13 40						13 56	14 09
Ingatestone	d			12 32							13 02					13 32								14 02	
Shenfield 3	a			12 38	12 50						13 08	13 19				13 38		13 50						14 08	14 19
Romford	a											13 28													14 28
Stratford 7 ⊖	a	12s45		12 52	13 05						13 22	13 36		13s45		13 52		14 05						14 22	14 36
London Liverpool Street 15 ⊖	a	12 55		13 01	13 14			13 19			13 31	13 45		13 55		14 01		14 14		14 19				14 31	14 45

		LE 1		LE ◇1 ☕	LE 1	LE 1	LE 1	LE 1	LE ◇1 ☕	LE 1	LE 1	LE 1		LE 1	LE 1	LE ◇1 ☕	LE 1	LE 1	LE 1	LE 1	LE ◇1 ☕	LE 1		LE 1	LE 1
Norwich	d			13 00					13 30							14 00					14 30				
Diss	d			13 17					13 47							14 17					14 47				
Peterborough 8	d																					13 45			
Stowmarket	d			13 29				13 44								14 29				14 44		15 13			
Needham Market	d							13 49												14 49					
Ipswich	a			13 41				14 00	14 08							14 41				15 00	15 08	15 28			
	d			13 43			13 52		14 09							14 43			14 52		15 09				
Harwich Town	d									14 28														15 28	
Dovercourt	d									14 30														15 30	
Harwich International	d									14 33														15 33	
Wrabness	d									14 39														15 39	
Mistley	d									14 45														15 45	
Manningtree 2	d			13 53			14 02		14 19	14a50						14 53			15 02		15 19			15a50	
Walton-on-the-Naze	d										14 00														15 00
Frinton-on-Sea	d										14 03														15 03
Kirby Cross	d										14 06														15 06
Clacton-on-Sea	d											14 05													
Thorpe-le-Soken 1	a										14 12	14 13													15 12
	d										14 17	14 13													15 17
Weeley	d										14 21														15 21
Great Bentley	d										14 24														15 24
Alresford (Essex)	d	←									14 28				←										15 28
Wivenhoe 3	d	13 32									14 32	14 23			14 32										15 32
Hythe	d	13 36									→				14 36										→
Colchester Town	a	13 40													14 40										
	d	13 44			14 00									14 35	14 44		15 00								
Colchester 4	a	13 52		14 02	14 07		14 11		14 28			14 31		14 42	14 52	15 02	15 07		15 11		15 28				
Colchester 4	d			14 03			14 12		14 30			14 33		14 43		15 03			15 12		15 30				
Marks Tey 2	d						14 18							14 49					15 18						
Kelvedon	d						14 23							14 54					15 23						
Braintree	d					14 00												15 00							
Braintree Freeport	d					14 02												15 02							
Cressing	d					14 05												15 05							
White Notley	d					14 08												15 08							
Witham 2	d					14 16	14 29					14 46		15 00				15 16	15 29						
Hatfield Peverel	d						14 33												15 33						
Chelmsford 3	d			14 21		14 26	14 40					14 56		15 09		15 21		15 26	15 40						
Ingatestone	d					14 32						15 02						15 32							
Shenfield 3	a					14 38	14 50					15 08		15 19				15 38	15 50						
Romford	a													15 28											
Stratford 7 ⊖	a			14s45		14 52	15 05					15 22		15 36		15s45		15 52	16 05						
London Liverpool Street 15 ⊖	a			14 55		15 01	15 15		15 19			15 33		15 45		15 55		16 01	16 14		16 17				

Norwich, Ipswich, Harwich, Clacton, Walton-on-Naze, Colchester and Chelmsford - London

Network Diagram - see first Page of Table 5

		LE 1	LE 1	LE 1	LE ◇1 ☕	LE 1	LE 1	LE 1		LE 1	LE ◇1 ☕	LE 1	LE 1	LE 1	LE 1	LE 1	LE 1	LE ◇1 ☕		LE 1	LE 1	LE 1	LE 1	LE 1	LE ◇1 ☕
Norwich	d				15 00						15 30							16 00							16 30
Diss	d				15 17						15 47							16 17							16 47
Peterborough 8	d																								
Stowmarket	d				15 29					15 44								16 29					16 44		
Needham Market	d									15 49													16 49		
Ipswich	a				15 41					16 00	16 08							16 41					17 00		17 08
	d				15 43			15 52			16 09							16 43				16 52			17 09
Harwich Town	d											16 28												16 53	
Dovercourt	d											16 30												16 55	
Harwich International	d											16 33												16 58	
Wrabness	d											16 39												17 04	
Mistley	d											16 45												17 10	
Manningtree 2	d				15 53			16 02			16 19	16a50						16 53				17 02		17a15	17 19
Walton-on-the-Naze	d												16 00												
Frinton-on-Sea	d												16 03												
Kirby Cross	d												16 06												
Clacton-on-Sea	d	15 05												16 05											
Thorpe-le-Soken 1	a	15 13											16 12	16 13											
	d	15 13											16 17	16 13											
Weeley	d												16 21												
Great Bentley	d												16 24												
Alresford (Essex)	d			←									16 28				←								
Wivenhoe 3	d	15 23		15 32									16 32	16 23			16 32								
Hythe	d			15 36									→				16 36								
Colchester Town	a			15 40													16 40								
	d		15 35	15 44		16 00									16 35		16 44			16 56					
Colchester 4	a	15 31	15 42	15 52	16 02	16 07		16 11			16 28			16 31	16 42		16 54	17 02		17 05		17 11			17 28
Colchester 4	d	15 33	15 43		16 03			16 12			16 30			16 33	16 43	16 53		17 03				17 12			17 30
Marks Tey 2	d		15 49					16 18								16 59						17 18			
Kelvedon	d		15 54					16 23							16 52							17 23			
Braintree	d						16 00														17 00				
Braintree Freeport	d						16 02														17 02				
Cressing	d						16 05														17 05				
White Notley	d						16 08														17 08				
Witham 2	d	15 46	16 00				16 16	16 29						16 46	16 58	17 08					17 16	17 29			
Hatfield Peverel	d							16 33							17 02							17 33			
Chelmsford 3	d	15 56	16 09		16 21		16 26	16 40						16 56	17 09	17 17		17 21			17 26	17 40			
Ingatestone	d	16 02					16 32							17 02							17 32				
Shenfield 3	a	16 08	16 19				16 38	16 50						17 08	17 19	17 27					17 38	17 50			
Romford	a																								
Stratford 7 ⊖	a	16 22	16 34		16s45		16 52	17 05						17 22	17 36	17 42		17s45			17 52	18 06			
London Liverpool Street 15 ⊖	a	16 31	16 44		16 55		17 03	17 16			17 19			17 34	17 46	17 53		17 58			18 01	18 15			18 19

		LE 1	LE 1	LE 1		LE 1	LE 1	LE 1	LE 1	LE 1	LE ◇1 ☕	LE 1	LE 1	LE 1		LE 1	LE ◇1 ☕	LE 1	LE 1	LE 1	LE 1	LE 1	LE 1	LE 1	
Norwich	d										17 00						17 30								
Diss	d										17 17						17 47								
Peterborough 8	d	15 45																							
Stowmarket	d	17 13									17 29	17 45					17 59								
Needham Market	d											17 50													
Ipswich	a	17 28									17 41	18 04					18 11								
	d								17 33		17 43						18 13						18 22		
Harwich Town	d									17 28			18 00												
Dovercourt	d									17 30			18 02												
Harwich International	d									17 33			18 05												
Wrabness	d									17 39			18 11												
Mistley	d									17 45			18 17												
Manningtree 2	d								17 43	17a50	17 53		18a22										18 33		
Walton-on-the-Naze	d		17 00															17 57		18 33					
Frinton-on-Sea	d		17 03															18 00		18 36					
Kirby Cross	d		17 06															18 03		18 42					
Clacton-on-Sea	d			17 05															18 05						
Thorpe-le-Soken 1	a		17 12	17 13														18 09	18 13	18 48					
	d		17 17	17 13														18 17	18 13						
Weeley	d		17 21															18 21							
Great Bentley	d		17 24															18 24							
Alresford (Essex)	d		17 28					←										18 28						←	
Wivenhoe 3	d		17 32	17 23				17 32										18 32	18 23					18 32	
Hythe	d		→					17 36										→						18 36	
Colchester Town	a							17 40																18 40	
	d						17 30	17 44												18 32				18 44	
Colchester 4	a			17 31			17 37	17 52	17 52		18 02						18 28		18 33	18 39			18 42	18 52	
Colchester 4	d			17 33			17 48				18 03					18 12	18 30		18 33				18 43		
Marks Tey 2	d						17 54									18 18							18 49		
Kelvedon	d						17 59									18 23							18 54		
Braintree	d					17 44																18 33			
Braintree Freeport	d					17 46																18 36			
Cressing	d					17 49																18 39			
White Notley	d					17 52																18 42			
Witham 2	d			17 46		18 00	18 05							18 16		18 29			18 46			18 51	19 00		
Hatfield Peverel	d						18 09									18 33						18 55			
Chelmsford 3	d			17 56		18 09	18 16				18 21			18 26		18 40			18 56			19 02	19 09		
Ingatestone	d			18 02										18 32					19 02						
Shenfield 3	a			18 08		18 19	18 26							18 38		18 50			19 08			19 13	19 19		
Romford	a					18 28																	19 28		
Stratford 7 ⊖	a			18 22		18 36	18 42				18s45			18 52		19 05			19 22			19 27	19 36		
London Liverpool Street 15 ⊖	a			18 31		18 45	18 51				18 55			19 01		19 14	19 17		19 31			19 36	19 45		

Table 11

Mondays to Fridays

Norwich, Ipswich, Harwich, Clacton, Walton-on-Naze, Colchester and Chelmsford - London

Network Diagram - see first Page of Table 5

		LE 1	LE 1	LE 1	LE ◇1	LE 1	LE 1	LE 1	LE 1	LE ◇1	LE 1	LE 1	LE 1	LE 1	LE 1	LE 1	LE 1	LE 1	LE 1	LE 1	LE ◇1	LE 1	LE 1
Norwich	d				18 00					18 30											19 00		
Diss	d				18 17					18 47											19 17		
Peterborough 8	d																	17 45					
Stowmarket	d				18 29			18 45										19 13			19 29		
Needham Market	d							18 50															
Ipswich	a				18 41			19 02		19 08								19 28			19 41		
	d				18 43		18 47			19 09						19 23			19 35		19 43		
Harwich Town	d	18 26									19 05									19 28			
Dovercourt	d	18 28									19 07									19 30			
Harwich International	d	18 31									19 10									19 33			
Wrabness	d	18 37									19 16									19 39			
Mistley	d	18 43									19 22									19 45			
Manningtree 2	d	18a48			18 53		18 57			19 19	19a27					19 36			19 45	19a50	19 53		
Walton-on-the-Naze	d		18 54											19 15									
Frinton-on-Sea	d		18 57											19 18									
Kirby Cross	d		19 00											19 21									
Clacton-on-Sea	d												19 02										
Thorpe-le-Soken 1	a		19 08										19 10	19 27									
	d		19 17										19 10										
Weeley	d		19 21																				
Great Bentley	d		19 24																				
Alresford (Essex)	d		19 28														←						
Wivenhoe 3	d		19 32										19 23				19 32						
Hythe	d		→														19 36						
Colchester Town	a																19 40						
	d								19 08						19 35		19 44						20 00
Colchester 4	a				19 02		19 06		19 15	19 28			19 31		19 42	19 46	19 52		19 54		20 02		20 07
Colchester 4	d			18 55	19 03		19 12			19 30			19 33		19 43				19 55		20 03		
Marks Tey 2	d			19 01			19 18								19 49				20 01				
Kelvedon	d						19 23								19 54								
Braintree	d											19 24											
Braintree Freeport	d											19 27											
Cressing	d											19 30											
White Notley	d											19 33											
Witham 2	d			19 16			19 29					19 42	19 46		20 00				20 16				
Hatfield Peverel	d					←	19 33															←	
Chelmsford 3	d			19 26	19 21	19 26	19 40					19 51	19 56		20 09				20 26		20 21	20 26	
Ingatestone	d			→		19 32							20 02						→			20 32	
Shenfield 3	a					19 38	19 50						20 08		20 19							20 38	
Romford	a														20 28								
Stratford 7 ⊖	a				19s45	19 52	20 05					20 14	20 22		20 36						20s45	20 52	
London Liverpool Street 15 ⊖	a				19 55	20 01	20 14			20 19		20 23	20 31		20 45						20 55	21 01	

		LE 1	LE 1	LE 1	LE ◇1	LE 1	LE 1	LE 1	LE 1	LE 1	LE 1	LE 1	LE 1	LE ◇1	LE 1	LE 1	LE 1	LE 1	LE ◇1	LE 1	LE 1	LE 1	LE 1
Norwich	d				19 30									20 00					20 30				
Diss	d				19 47									20 17					20 47				
Peterborough 8	d																						
Stowmarket	d			19 44										20 29				20 44					
Needham Market	d			19 49														20 49					
Ipswich	a			20 00	20 09									20 41				21 00	21 08				
	d		19 52		20 09				20 20					20 43				21 00	21 09				
Harwich Town	d					20 05				20 28												21 05	
Dovercourt	d					20 07				20 30												21 07	
Harwich International	d					20 10				20 33							20 45	21a29				21 10	
Wrabness	d					20 16				20 39												21 16	
Mistley	d					20 22				20 45												21 22	
Manningtree 2	d		20 02		20 19	20a27			20 33	20a50				20 53			20 58		21 19			21 27	
Walton-on-the-Naze	d						19 55				20 33									21 00			
Frinton-on-Sea	d						19 58				20 36									21 03			
Kirby Cross	d						20 01				20 42									21 06			
Clacton-on-Sea	d							20 05													21 05		
Thorpe-le-Soken 1	a						20 07	20 13			20 48									21 12	21 13		
	d						20 17	20 13												21 17	21 13		
Weeley	d						20 21													21 21			
Great Bentley	d						20 24													21 24			
Alresford (Essex)	d						20 28						←							21 28			
Wivenhoe 3	d						20 32	20 23					20 32							21 32	21 23		
Hythe	d						→						20 36							→			
Colchester Town	a												20 40										
	d											20 35	20 44		21 00								21 35
Colchester 4	a		20 11		20 29			20 31	20 45			20 42	20 52	21 02	21 07		21 07		21 28		21 31	21 36	21 42
Colchester 4	d		20 12		20 30			20 33				20 50		21 03			21 12		21 30		21 33		21 43
Marks Tey 2	d		20 18									20 56					21 18						21 49
Kelvedon	d		20 23									21 01					21 23						21 54
Braintree	d	20 11														21 00							
Braintree Freeport	d	20 13														21 02							
Cressing	d	20 16														21 05							
White Notley	d	20 19														21 08							
Witham 2	d	20 27	20 31					20 46				21 07				21 16	21 29				21 46		22 00
Hatfield Peverel	d		20 35														21 33						
Chelmsford 3	d	20 36	20 42					20 56				21 16		21 21		21 26	21 40				21 56		22 09
Ingatestone	d							21 02								21 32					22 02		
Shenfield 3	a	20 46	20 52					21 08				21 26				21 38	21 50				22 08		22 19
Romford	a																						22 28
Stratford 7 ⊖	a		21 07					21 22				21 42		21s45		21 52	22 05				22 22		22 36
London Liverpool Street 15 ⊖	a	21 12	21 16		21 19			21 31				21 51		21 55		22 01	22 14		22 19		22 31		22 45

Norwich, Ipswich, Harwich, Clacton, Walton-on-Naze, Colchester and Chelmsford - London

Network Diagram - see first Page of Table 5

		LE ◇1 MTWO ☕	LE 1 MTWO	LE 1 MTWO	LE 1 MTWO	LE 1 MTWO	LE ◇1 MTWO	LE ◇1 ThFO ☕	LE 1 ThFO	LE 1 ThFO	LE 1 ThFO	LE 1 ThFO	LE 1 ThFO	LE ◇1 ThFO	LE 1 ThFO
Norwich	d	21 00					22 00	21 00						22 00	
Diss	d	21 17					22 17	21 17						22 17	
Peterborough 8	d														
Stowmarket	d	21 29					22 29	21 29						22 29	
Needham Market	d														
Ipswich	a	21 41					22 41	21 41						22 41	
	d	21 43				22 23	22 43	21 43				22 23		22 43	
Harwich Town	d														
Dovercourt	d														
Harwich International	d														
Wrabness	d														
Mistley	d														
Manningtree 2	d	21 53				22 33	22 53	21 53				22 33		22 53	
Walton-on-the-Naze	d														
Frinton-on-Sea	d														
Kirby Cross	d														
Clacton-on-Sea	d				22 05						22 05		22 05		
Thorpe-le-Soken 1	a				22 13						22 13		22 13		
	d				22 13						22 13		22 13		
Weeley	d														
Great Bentley	d														
Alresford (Essex)	d														
Wivenhoe 3	d				22 23						22 23		22 23		
Hythe	d														
Colchester Town	a														
	d			22 00						22 00					
Colchester 4	a	22 02		22 07	22 31	22 42	23 02	22 02		22 07	22 31	22 42	22 31	23 02	
Colchester 4	d	22 03		22 12	22 33	22 43	23 03	22 03		22 12	22 33	22 43	22 33	23 03	
Marks Tey 2	d			22 18		22 49				22 18		22 49			
Kelvedon	d			22 23		22 54				22 23		22 54			
Braintree	d		22 00						22 00						23 45
Braintree Freeport	d		22 02						22 02						23 47
Cressing	d		22 05						22 05						23 50
White Notley	d		22 08						22 08						23 53
Witham 2	d		22 16	22 29	22 46	23 00	23 16		22 16	22 29	22 46	23 00	22 46	23 16	00a01
Hatfield Peverel	d			22 33						22 33					
Chelmsford 3	d	22 21	22 26	22 40	22 56	23 09	23 25	22 21	22 26	22 40	22 56	23 09	22 56	23 25	
Ingatestone	d		22 32		23 02				22 32		23 02		23 02		
Shenfield 3	a		22 38	22 50	23 08	23 19	23 36		22 38	22 50	23 08	23 19	23 08	23s36	
Romford	a				23 19	23 31						23 28			
Stratford 7 ⊖	a	22s51	22 54	23 11	23 31	23 41	00s04	22s45	22 52	23 05	23 22	23 36	23 22	23s52	
London Liverpool Street 15 ⊖	a	23 00	23 03	23 20	23 40	23 50	00 14	22 55	23 01	23 15	23 31	23 45	23 31	00 02	

		LE ◇1	LE 1	LE 1	LE 1	LE 1	LE 1	LE 1	LE 1	LE 1
Norwich	d									
Diss	d									
Peterborough 8	d	19 45								
Stowmarket	d	21 09			21 44					22 44
Needham Market	d				21 49					22 49
Ipswich	a	21 23			22 00					23 00
	d	21 25								
Harwich Town	d			21 28				22 28		
Dovercourt	d			21 30				22 30		
Harwich International	d			21 33				22 33		
Wrabness	d			21 39				22 39		
Mistley	d			21 45				22 45		
Manningtree 2	d	21 35		21a50				22a50		
Walton-on-the-Naze	d					22 00				
Frinton-on-Sea	d					22 03				
Kirby Cross	d					22 06				
Clacton-on-Sea	d									
Thorpe-le-Soken 1	a					22 12				
	d					22 17				
Weeley	d					22 21				
Great Bentley	d					22 24				
Alresford (Essex)	d		←			22 28	←			
Wivenhoe 3	d		21 32			22 32	22 32			
Hythe	d		21 36			→	22 36			
Colchester Town	a		21 40				22 40			
	d		21 44				22 44			
Colchester 4	a	21 46	21 52				22 52			
Colchester 4	d									
Marks Tey 2	d									
Kelvedon	d									
Braintree	d								22 56	
Braintree Freeport	d								22 58	
Cressing	d								23 01	
White Notley	d								23 04	
Witham 2	d								23a12	
Hatfield Peverel	d									
Chelmsford 3	d									
Ingatestone	d									
Shenfield 3	a									
Romford	a									
Stratford 7 ⊖	a									
London Liverpool Street 15 ⊖	a									

		LE 1	LE 1	LE 1	LE ◇1	LE 1	LE 1		LE
Norwich	d					23 05			
Diss	d					23 22			
Peterborough 8	d				21 45				
Stowmarket	d				23 06	23 34			23 47
Needham Market	d								23 52
Ipswich	a				23 18	23 48			00 05
	d				23 19				
Harwich Town	d						23 28		
Dovercourt	d						23 30		
Harwich International	d						23 33		
Wrabness	d						23 39		
Mistley	d						23 45		
Manningtree 2	d				23 29		23 50		
Walton-on-the-Naze	d		23 00						
Frinton-on-Sea	d		23 03						
Kirby Cross	d		23 06						
Clacton-on-Sea	d			23 05					
Thorpe-le-Soken 1	a		23 12	23 13					
	d			23 13					
Weeley	d			23 17					
Great Bentley	d			23 20					
Alresford (Essex)	d			23 24					
Wivenhoe 3	d			23 28					
Hythe	d			23 32					
Colchester Town	a								
	d	23 00							
Colchester 4	a	23 07		23 38	23 40		23 59		
Colchester 4	d								
Marks Tey 2	d								
Kelvedon	d								
Braintree	d								
Braintree Freeport	d								
Cressing	d								
White Notley	d								
Witham 2	d								
Hatfield Peverel	d								
Chelmsford 3	d								
Ingatestone	d								
Shenfield 3	a								
Romford	a								
Stratford 7 ⊖	a								
London Liverpool Street 15 ⊖	a								

Table 11

Saturdays

Norwich, Ipswich, Harwich, Clacton, Walton-on-Naze, Colchester and Chelmsford - London

Network Diagram - see first Page of Table 5

		LE ◇[1]	LE	LE [1]	LE [1]	LE [1]	LE	LE [1]	LE ◇[1] ☕	LE [1]		LE [1]	LE ◇[1] ☕	LE [1]	LE [1]	LE [1]	LE [1]	LE [1]	LE [1]	LE ◇[1] ☕		LE [1]	LE [1]	LE [1]	LE
Norwich	d	22p00							05 00				05 30							06 00					
Diss	d	22p17							05 17				05 47							06 17					
Peterborough [8]	d																								
Stowmarket	d	22p29	23p47						05 29											06 29					06 44
Needham Market	d		23p52																						06 49
Ipswich	a	22p41	00 05						05 41				06 08							06 41					07 02
	d	22p43							05 43				06 09							06 43			06 52	06 59	
Harwich Town	d													06 28											
Dovercourt	d													06 30											
Harwich International	d													06 33										07a28	
Wrabness	d													06 39											
Mistley	d													06 45											
Manningtree [2]	d	22p53							05 53				06 19	06a50						06 53			07 02		
Walton-on-the-Naze	d														06 00										
Frinton-on-Sea	d														06 03										
Kirby Cross	d														06 06										
Clacton-on-Sea	d							05 30								06 05	06 24								
Thorpe-le-Soken [1]	a							05 38							06 12	06 13	06 32								
	d							05 38							06 17	06 13									
Weeley	d														06 21										
Great Bentley	d														06 24										
Alresford (Essex)	d														06 28				←						
Wivenhoe [3]	d							05 48							06 32	06 23			06 32						
Hythe	d														→				06 36						
Colchester Town	a																		06 40						
	d																	06 35	06 44						
Colchester [4]	a	23p02						05 57	06 02				06 28			06 31		06 42	06 52	07 02			07 11		
Colchester [4]	d	23p03			05 12	05 43	05 50		06 03			06 12	06 30			06 33		06 43		07 03			07 12		
Marks Tey [2]	d				05 18	05 49	05a57					06 18						06 49					07 18		
Kelvedon	d				05 23	05 54						06 23						06 54					07 23		
Braintree	d			00 25						06 00												07 00			
Braintree Freeport	d			00 27						06 02												07 02			
Cressing	d			00 30						06 05												07 05			
White Notley	d			00 33						06 08												07 08			
Witham [2]	d	23p16		00a41	05 29	06 00				06a16		06 29				06 46		07 00				07 16	07 29		
Hatfield Peverel	d				05 33	06 04						06 33											07 33		
Chelmsford [3]	d	23p25			05 40	06 11			06 21			06 40				06 56		07 09		07 21		07 26	07 40		
Ingatestone	d				05 47	06 18										07 02						07 32			
Shenfield [3]	a	23b36			05 52	06 23						06 50				07 08		07 19				07 38	07 50		
Romford	a																	07 28							
Stratford [7] ⊖	a	23b52			06 07	06 38			06s45			07 05				07 22		07 36		07s45		07 52	08 05		
London Liverpool Street [15] ⊖	a	00 02			06 16	06 47			06 55			07 14	07 19			07 31		07 45		07 55		08 01	08 14		

		LE ◇[1] ☕	LE [1]	LE [1]	LE [1]	LE [1]		LE [1]	LE ◇[1] ☕	LE [1]	LE [1]	LE [1]	LE	LE ◇[1] ☕	LE [1]	LE [1]		LE [1]	LE [1]	LE [1]	LE ◇[1] ☕	LE [1]	LE [1]	LE [1]	LE [1]
Norwich	d	06 30							07 00					07 30							08 00				
Diss	d	06 47							07 17					07 47							08 17				
Peterborough [8]	d																								
Stowmarket	d								07 29				07 45								08 29				08 44
Needham Market	d												07 50												08 49
Ipswich	a	07 08							07 41				08 03	08 08							08 41				09 00
	d	07 09							07 43			07 52		08 09							08 43			08 52	
Harwich Town	d							07 28							08 28										
Dovercourt	d							07 30							08 30										
Harwich International	d				07 20			07 33							08 33										
Wrabness	d							07 39							08 39										
Mistley	d							07 45							08 45										
Manningtree [2]	d	07 19			07 33			07a50	07 53			08 02		08 19	08a50						08 53			09 02	
Walton-on-the-Naze	d		07 00													08 00									
Frinton-on-Sea	d		07 03													08 03									
Kirby Cross	d		07 06													08 06									
Clacton-on-Sea	d			07 05														08 05							
Thorpe-le-Soken [1]	a		07 12	07 13												08 12		08 13							
	d		07 17	07 13												08 17		08 13							
Weeley	d		07 21													08 21									
Great Bentley	d		07 24													08 24									
Alresford (Essex)	d		07 28			←										08 28				←					
Wivenhoe [3]	d		07 32	07 23		07 32										08 32		08 23		08 32					
Hythe	d		→			07 36										→				08 36					
Colchester Town	a					07 40														08 40					
	d					07 44				08 00									08 35	08 44		09 00			
Colchester [4]	a	07 28		07 31	07 42	07 52			08 02	08 07		08 11		08 28				08 31	08 42	08 52	09 02	09 07		09 11	
Colchester [4]	d	07 30		07 33	07 43				08 03			08 12		08 30				08 33	08 43		09 03			09 12	
Marks Tey [2]	d				07 49							08 18							08 49					09 18	
Kelvedon	d				07 54							08 23							08 54					09 23	
Braintree	d										08 00												09 00		
Braintree Freeport	d										08 02												09 02		
Cressing	d										08 05												09 05		
White Notley	d										08 08												09 08		
Witham [2]	d			07 46	08 00						08 16	08 29						08 46	09 00				09 16	09 29	
Hatfield Peverel	d											08 33												09 33	
Chelmsford [3]	d			07 56	08 09				08 21		08 26	08 40						08 56	09 09		09 21		09 26	09 40	
Ingatestone	d			08 02							08 32							09 02					09 32		
Shenfield [3]	a			08 08	08 19						08 38	08 50						09 08	09 19				09 38	09 50	
Romford	a				08 28														09 28						
Stratford [7] ⊖	a			08 22	08 36				08s45		08 52	09 05						09 22	09 36		09s45		09 52	10 05	
London Liverpool Street [15] ⊖	a	08 19		08 31	08 45				08 55		09 01	09 14		09 19				09 31	09 45		09 55		10 01	10 14	

b Previous night, stops to set down only

Table 11

Saturdays

Norwich, Ipswich, Harwich, Clacton, Walton-on-Naze, Colchester and Chelmsford - London

Network Diagram - see first Page of Table 5

		LE ◇1 ☕		LE 1	LE 1	LE 1	LE 1	LE 1	LE 1	LE ◇1 ☕	LE 1	LE 1		LE 1	LE 1	LE ◇1 ☕	LE 1	LE 1	LE 1	LE 1	LE 1	LE ◇1 ☕		LE 1	LE 1
Norwich	d	08 30								09 00						09 30						10 00			
Diss	d	08 47								09 17						09 47						10 17			
Peterborough 8	d			07 45																					
Stowmarket	d			09 13						09 29					09 44							10 29			
Needham Market	d														09 49										
Ipswich	a	09 08		09 28						09 41					10 00	10 08						10 41			
	d	09 09								09 43				09 52		10 09						10 43			
Harwich Town	d				09 28												10 28								
Dovercourt	d				09 30												10 30								
Harwich International	d				09 33												10 33								
Wrabness	d				09 39												10 39								
Mistley	d				09 45												10 45								
Manningtree 2	d	09 19			09a50					09 53				10 02		10 19	10a50					10 53			
Walton-on-the-Naze	d					09 00												10 00							
Frinton-on-Sea	d					09 03												10 03							
Kirby Cross	d					09 06												10 06							
Clacton-on-Sea	d						09 05												10 05						
Thorpe-le-Soken 1	a					09 12	09 13											10 12	10 13						
	d					09 17	09 13											10 17	10 13						
Weeley	d					09 21												10 21							
Great Bentley	d					09 24												10 24							
Alresford (Essex)	d					09 28			←									10 28			←				
Wivenhoe 3	d					09 32	09 23		09 32									10 32	10 23		10 32				
Hythe	d					↪			09 36									↪			10 36				
Colchester Town	a								09 40												10 40				
	d							09 35	09 44		10 00									10 35	10 44			11 00	
Colchester 4	a	09 28					09 31	09 42	09 52	10 02	10 07			10 11		10 28			10 31	10 42	10 52	11 02		11 07	
Colchester 4	d	09 30					09 33	09 43		10 03				10 12		10 30			10 33	10 43		11 03			
Marks Tey 2	d							09 49						10 18						10 49					
Kelvedon	d							09 54						10 23						10 54					
Braintree	d											10 00													11 00
Braintree Freeport	d											10 02													11 02
Cressing	d											10 05													11 05
White Notley	d											10 08													11 08
Witham 2	d						09 46	10 00				10 16		10 29					10 46	11 00					11 16
Hatfield Peverel	d													10 33											
Chelmsford 3	d						09 56	10 09		10 21		10 26		10 40					10 56	11 09		11 21			11 26
Ingatestone	d						10 02					10 32							11 02						11 32
Shenfield 3	a						10 08	10 19				10 38		10 50					11 08	11 19					11 38
Romford	a							10 28												11 28					
Stratford 7 ⊖	a						10 22	10 36		10s45		10 52		11 05					11 22	11 36		11s45			11 52
London Liverpool Street 15 ⊖	a	10 19					10 31	10 45		10 55		11 01		11 14		11 19			11 31	11 45		11 55			12 01

		LE 1	LE 1	LE ◇1 ☕	LE 1	LE 1	LE 1	LE 1		LE 1	LE 1	LE ◇1 ☕	LE 1	LE 1	LE 1	LE 1	LE ◇1 ☕	LE 1		LE 1	LE 1	LE 1	LE 1	LE ◇1 ☕	LE 1
Norwich	d			10 30								11 00					11 30							12 00	
Diss	d			10 47								11 17					11 47							12 17	
Peterborough 8	d				09 47																				
Stowmarket	d		10 44		11 13							11 29				11 44								12 29	
Needham Market	d		10 49													11 49									
Ipswich	a		11 00	11 08	11 28							11 41				12 00	12 08							12 41	
	d	10 52		11 09								11 43			11 52		12 09							12 43	
Harwich Town	d					11 28												12 28							
Dovercourt	d					11 30												12 30							
Harwich International	d					11 33												12 33							
Wrabness	d					11 39												12 39							
Mistley	d					11 45												12 45							
Manningtree 2	d	11 02		11 19		11a50						11 53			12 02		12 19	12a50						12 53	
Walton-on-the-Naze	d						11 00													12 00					
Frinton-on-Sea	d						11 03													12 03					
Kirby Cross	d						11 06													12 06					
Clacton-on-Sea	d							11 05													12 05				
Thorpe-le-Soken 1	a						11 12	11 13												12 12	12 13				
	d						11 17	11 13												12 17	12 13				
Weeley	d						11 21													12 21					
Great Bentley	d						11 24													12 24					
Alresford (Essex)	d						11 28				←									12 28			←		
Wivenhoe 3	d						11 32	11 23			11 32									12 32	12 23		12 32		
Hythe	d						↪				11 36									↪			12 36		
Colchester Town	a										11 40												12 40		
	d									11 35	11 44		12 00									12 35	12 44		13 00
Colchester 4	a	11 11		11 28				11 31		11 42	11 52	12 02	12 07		12 11		12 28				12 31	12 42	12 52	13 02	13 07
Colchester 4	d	11 12		11 30				11 33		11 43		12 03			12 12		12 30				12 33	12 43		13 03	
Marks Tey 2	d	11 18								11 49					12 18							12 49			
Kelvedon	d	11 23								11 54					12 23							12 54			
Braintree	d													12 00											
Braintree Freeport	d													12 02											
Cressing	d													12 05											
White Notley	d													12 08											
Witham 2	d	11 29						11 46		12 00				12 16	12 29						12 46	13 00			
Hatfield Peverel	d	11 33													12 33										
Chelmsford 3	d	11 40						11 56		12 09		12 21		12 26	12 40						12 56	13 09		13 21	
Ingatestone	d							12 02						12 32							13 02				
Shenfield 3	a	11 50						12 08		12 19				12 38	12 50						13 08	13 19			
Romford	a									12 28												13 28			
Stratford 7 ⊖	a	12 05						12 22		12 36		12s45		12 52	13 05						13 22	13 36		13s45	
London Liverpool Street 15 ⊖	a	12 14		12 19				12 31		12 45		12 55		13 01	13 14		13 19				13 31	13 45		13 55	

Table 11

Saturdays

Norwich, Ipswich, Harwich, Clacton, Walton-on-Naze, Colchester and Chelmsford - London

Network Diagram - see first Page of Table 5

		LE 1	LE 1	LE 1		LE ◇1 ☕	LE 1	LE 1	LE 1	LE 1	LE 1	LE 1	LE ◇1 ☕	LE 1		LE 1	LE 1	LE 1	LE ◇1 ☕	LE 1	LE 1	LE 1	LE 1	LE 1	
Norwich	d					12 30							13 00						13 30						
Diss	d					12 47							13 17						13 47						
Peterborough 8	d						11 45																		
Stowmarket	d			12 44			13 13						13 29					13 44							
Needham Market	d			12 49														13 49							
Ipswich	a			13 00		13 08	13 28						13 41					14 00	14 08						
	d		12 52			13 09							13 43				13 52		14 09						
Harwich Town	d							13 28												14 28					
Dovercourt	d							13 30												14 30					
Harwich International	d							13 33												14 33					
Wrabness	d							13 39												14 39					
Mistley	d							13 45												14 45					
Manningtree 2	d		13 02			13 19		13a50					13 53				14 02		14 19	14a50					
Walton-on-the-Naze	d								13 00												14 00				
Frinton-on-Sea	d								13 03												14 03				
Kirby Cross	d								13 06												14 06				
Clacton-on-Sea	d									13 05												14 05			
Thorpe-le-Soken 1	a								13 12	13 13											14 12	14 13			
	d								13 17	13 13											14 17	14 13			
Weeley	d								13 21												14 21				
Great Bentley	d								13 24												14 24				
Alresford (Essex)	d								13 28			←									14 28			←	
Wivenhoe 3	d								13 32	13 23		13 32									14 32	14 23		14 32	
Hythe	d								→			13 36									→			14 36	
Colchester Town	a											13 40												14 40	
	d										13 35	13 44		14 00									14 35	14 44	
Colchester 4	a		13 11			13 28				13 31	13 42	13 52	14 02	14 07			14 11		14 28			14 31	14 42	14 52	
Colchester 4	d		13 12			13 30				13 33	13 43		14 03				14 12		14 30			14 33	14 43		
Marks Tey 2	d		13 18								13 49						14 18						14 49		
Kelvedon	d		13 23								13 54						14 23						14 54		
Braintree	d	13 00														14 00									
Braintree Freeport	d	13 02														14 02									
Cressing	d	13 05														14 05									
White Notley	d	13 08														14 08									
Witham 2	d	13 16	13 29							13 46	14 00					14 16	14 29					14 46	15 00		
Hatfield Peverel	d		13 33														14 33								
Chelmsford 3	d	13 26	13 40							13 56	14 09		14 21			14 26	14 40					14 56	15 09		
Ingatestone	d	13 32								14 02						14 32						15 02			
Shenfield 3	a	13 38	13 50							14 08	14 19					14 38	14 50					15 08	15 19		
Romford	a										14 28												15 28		
Stratford 7 ⊖	a	13 52	14 05							14 22	14 36		14s45			14 52	15 05					15 22	15 36		
London Liverpool Street 15 ⊖	a	14 01	14 14			14 19				14 31	14 45		14 55			15 01	15 14		15 19			15 31	15 45		

		LE ◇1 ☕	LE 1	LE 1	LE 1	LE 1	LE ◇1 ☕	LE 1	LE 1	LE 1		LE 1	LE 1	LE 1	LE ◇1 ☕	LE 1	LE 1	LE 1	LE 1	LE ◇1 ☕		LE 1	LE 1	LE 1	LE 1
Norwich	d	14 00					14 30								15 00					15 30					
Diss	d	14 17					14 47								15 17					15 47					
Peterborough 8	d							13 45																	
Stowmarket	d	14 29				14 44		15 13							15 29				15 44						
Needham Market	d					14 49													15 49						
Ipswich	a	14 41				15 00	15 08	15 28							15 41				16 00	16 08					
	d	14 43			14 52		15 09								15 43			15 52		16 09					
Harwich Town	d								15 28													16 28			
Dovercourt	d								15 30													16 30			
Harwich International	d								15 33													16 33			
Wrabness	d								15 39													16 39			
Mistley	d								15 45													16 45			
Manningtree 2	d	14 53			15 02		15 19		15a50						15 53			16 02		16 19		16a50			
Walton-on-the-Naze	d									15 00													16 00		
Frinton-on-Sea	d									15 03													16 03		
Kirby Cross	d									15 06													16 06		
Clacton-on-Sea	d											15 05												16 05	
Thorpe-le-Soken 1	a									15 12		15 13											16 12	16 13	
	d									15 17		15 13											16 17	16 13	
Weeley	d									15 21													16 21		
Great Bentley	d									15 24													16 24		
Alresford (Essex)	d									15 28				←									16 28		
Wivenhoe 3	d									15 32		15 23		15 32									16 32	16 23	
Hythe	d									→				15 36									→		
Colchester Town	a													15 40											
	d		15 00										15 35	15 44		16 00									16 35
Colchester 4	a	15 02	15 07		15 11		15 28					15 31	15 42	15 52	16 02	16 07		16 11		16 28				16 31	16 42
Colchester 4	d	15 03			15 12		15 30					15 33	15 43		16 03			16 12		16 30				16 33	16 43
Marks Tey 2	d				15 18								15 49					16 18							16 49
Kelvedon	d				15 23								15 54					16 23							16 54
Braintree	d			15 00													16 00								
Braintree Freeport	d			15 02													16 02								
Cressing	d			15 05													16 05								
White Notley	d			15 08													16 08								
Witham 2	d			15 16	15 29							15 46	16 00				16 16	16 29						16 46	17 00
Hatfield Peverel	d				15 33													16 33							
Chelmsford 3	d	15 21		15 26	15 40							15 56	16 09		16 21		16 26	16 40						16 56	17 09
Ingatestone	d			15 32								16 02					16 32							17 02	
Shenfield 3	a			15 38	15 50							16 08	16 19				16 38	16 50						17 08	17 19
Romford	a												16 28												17 28
Stratford 7 ⊖	a	15s45		15 52	16 05							16 22	16 36		16s45		16 52	17 05						17 22	17 36
London Liverpool Street 15 ⊖	a	15 55		16 01	16 14		16 19					16 31	16 45		16 55		17 01	17 14		17 19				17 31	17 45

Table 11

Saturdays

Norwich, Ipswich, Harwich, Clacton, Walton-on-Naze, Colchester and Chelmsford - London

Network Diagram - see first Page of Table 5

		LE 1	LE ◇1 🍴	LE 1	LE 1	LE 1		LE 1	LE ◇1 🍴	LE 1	LE 1	LE 1	LE 1	LE 1	LE 1	LE ◇1 🍴		LE 1	LE 1	LE 1	LE 1	LE ◇1 🍴	LE 1	LE 1	LE 1
Norwich	d		16 00						16 30							17 00						17 30			
Diss	d		16 17						16 47							17 17						17 47			
Peterborough 8	d									15 45															
Stowmarket	d		16 29					16 44		17 13						17 29					17 45	17 59			
Needham Market	d							16 49													17 50				
Ipswich	a		16 41					17 00	17 08	17 28						17 41					18 01	18 11			
	d		16 43			16 52			17 09							17 43				17 52		18 13			
Harwich Town	d										17 28												18 28		
Dovercourt	d										17 30												18 30		
Harwich International	d										17 33												18 33		
Wrabness	d										17 39												18 39		
Mistley	d										17 45												18 45		
Manningtree 2	d		16 53			17 02			17 19		17a50					17 53				18 02			18a50		
Walton-on-the-Naze	d											17 00												18 00	
Frinton-on-Sea	d											17 03												18 03	
Kirby Cross	d											17 06												18 06	
Clacton-on-Sea	d												17 05												18 05
Thorpe-le-Soken 1	a											17 12	17 13											18 12	18 13
	d											17 17	17 13											18 17	18 13
Weeley	d											17 21												18 21	
Great Bentley	d											17 24												18 24	
Alresford (Essex)	d	←										17 28			←									18 28	
Wivenhoe 3	d	16 32										17 32	17 23		17 32									18 32	18 23
Hythe	d	16 36										→			17 36									→	
Colchester Town	a	16 40													17 40										
	d	16 44		17 00										17 35	17 44			18 00							
Colchester 4	a	16 52	17 02	17 07		17 11			17 28				17 31	17 42	17 52	18 02		18 07		18 11		18 28			18 31
Colchester 4	d		17 03			17 12			17 30				17 33	17 43		18 03				18 12		18 30			18 33
Marks Tey 2	d					17 18								17 49						18 18					
Kelvedon	d					17 23								17 54						18 23					
Braintree	d				17 00														18 00						
Braintree Freeport	d				17 02														18 02						
Cressing	d				17 05														18 05						
White Notley	d				17 08														18 08						
Witham 2	d				17 16	17 29							17 46	18 00					18 16	18 29					18 46
Hatfield Peverel	d					17 33														18 33					
Chelmsford 3	d		17 21		17 26	17 40							17 56	18 09		18 21			18 26	18 40					18 56
Ingatestone	d				17 32								18 02						18 32						19 02
Shenfield 3	a				17 38	17 50							18 08	18 19					18 38	18 50					19 08
Romford	a													18 28											
Stratford 7 ⊖	a		17s45		17 52	18 05							18 22	18 36		18s45			18 52	19 05					19 22
London Liverpool Street 15 ⊖	a		17 55		18 01	18 14			18 19				18 31	18 45		18 55			19 01	19 14		19 19			19 31

		LE 1		LE 1	LE ◇1 🍴	LE 1	LE 1	LE 1	LE 1	LE ◇1 🍴	LE 1	LE 1		LE 1	LE 1	LE 1	LE 1	LE ◇1 🍴	LE 1	LE 1	LE 1	LE 1		LE 1	LE 1
Norwich	d				18 00					18 30								19 00							
Diss	d				18 17					18 47								19 17							
Peterborough 8	d										17 45														
Stowmarket	d				18 29				18 45		19 13							19 29				19 44			
Needham Market	d								18 50													19 49			
Ipswich	a				18 41				19 01	19 08	19 28							19 41				20 00			
	d				18 43			18 52		19 09								19 43			19 52			20 09	
Harwich Town	d											19 28													20 28
Dovercourt	d											19 30													20 30
Harwich International	d											19 33													20 33
Wrabness	d											19 39													20 39
Mistley	d											19 45													20 45
Manningtree 2	d				18 53			19 02		19 19		19a50						19 53			20 02			20 20	20a50
Walton-on-the-Naze	d													19 00											
Frinton-on-Sea	d													19 03											
Kirby Cross	d													19 06											
Clacton-on-Sea	d														19 05										
Thorpe-le-Soken 1	a													19 12	19 13										
	d													19 17	19 13										
Weeley	d													19 21											
Great Bentley	d													19 24											
Alresford (Essex)	d			←										19 28			←								
Wivenhoe 3	d			18 32										19 32	19 23		19 32								
Hythe	d			18 36										→			19 36								
Colchester Town	a			18 40													19 40								
	d	18 35		18 44		19 00										19 35	19 44		20 00						
Colchester 4	a	18 42		18 52	19 02	19 07		19 11		19 28					19 31	19 42	19 52	20 02	20 07		20 11			20 29	
Colchester 4	d	18 43			19 03			19 12		19 30					19 33	19 43		20 03			20 12			20 30	
Marks Tey 2	d	18 49						19 18								19 49					20 18				
Kelvedon	d	18 54						19 23								19 54					20 23				
Braintree	d						19 00													20 00					
Braintree Freeport	d						19 02													20 02					
Cressing	d						19 05													20 05					
White Notley	d						19 08													20 08					
Witham 2	d	19 00					19 16	19 29							19 46	20 00				20 16	20 29				
Hatfield Peverel	d							19 33													20 33				
Chelmsford 3	d	19 09			19 21		19 26	19 40							19 56	20 09		20 21		20 26	20 40				
Ingatestone	d						19 32								20 02					20 32					
Shenfield 3	a	19 19					19 38	19 50							20 08	20 19				20 38	20 50				
Romford	a	19 28														20 28									
Stratford 7 ⊖	a	19 36			19s45		19 52	20 05							20 22	20 36		20s45		20 52	21 05				
London Liverpool Street 15 ⊖	a	19 45			19 55		20 01	20 14		20 19					20 31	20 45		20 55		21 01	21 14			21 17	

Table 11

Saturdays

Norwich, Ipswich, Harwich, Clacton, Walton-on-Naze, Colchester and Chelmsford - London

Network Diagram - see first Page of Table 5

		LE 1	LE 1	LE 1	LE 1	LE ◇1	LE 1	LE 1		LE 1	LE 1	LE 1	LE 1	LE 1	LE 1	LE ◇1	LE 1	LE 1		LE ◇1	LE 1	LE 1	LE 1	LE 1	LE 1
Norwich	d					20 00														21 00					
Diss	d					20 17														21 17					
Peterborough 8	d															19 45									
Stowmarket	d					20 29					20 44					21 09				21 29				21 44	
Needham Market	d										20 49													21 49	
Ipswich	a					20 41					21 00					21 22				21 41				22 00	
	d					20 43					21 00	21 09				21 25				21 43			21 52		
Harwich Town	d																	21 28							
Dovercourt	d																	21 30							
Harwich International	d									20 45	21a29							21 33							
Wrabness	d																	21 39							
Mistley	d																	21 45							
Manningtree 2	d					20 53				20 58		21 19				21 35		21a50		21 53			22 02		
Walton-on-the-Naze	d	20 00											21 00												22 00
Frinton-on-Sea	d	20 03											21 03												22 03
Kirby Cross	d	20 06											21 06												22 06
Clacton-on-Sea	d		20 05											21 05											
Thorpe-le-Soken 1	a	20 12	20 13										21 12	21 13											22 12
	d	20 17	20 13										21 17	21 13											22 17
Weeley	d	20 21											21 21												22 21
Great Bentley	d	20 24											21 24												22 24
Alresford (Essex)	d	20 28			←								21 28				←								22 28
Wivenhoe 3	d	20 32	20 23		20 32								21 32	21 23			21 32								22 32
Hythe	d	→			20 36								→				21 36								→
Colchester Town	a				20 40												21 40								
	d			20 35	20 44		21 00								21 35		21 44				22 00				
Colchester 4	a		20 31	20 42	20 52	21 02	21 07			21 07		21 28		21 31	21 42	21 46	21 52			22 02	22 07		22 11		
Colchester 4	d		20 33	20 43		21 03				21 12		21 30		21 33	21 43					22 03			22 12		
Marks Tey 2	d			20 49						21 18					21 49								22 18		
Kelvedon	d			20 54						21 23					21 54								22 23		
Braintree	d							21 00														22 00			
Braintree Freeport	d							21 02														22 02			
Cressing	d							21 05														22 05			
White Notley	d							21 08														22 08			
Witham 2	d		20 46	21 00				21 16		21 29				21 46	22 00							22 16	22 29		
Hatfield Peverel	d									21 33													22 33		
Chelmsford 3	d		20 56	21 09		21 21		21 26		21 40				21 56	22 09					22 21		22 26	22 40		
Ingatestone	d		21 02					21 32						22 02								22 32			
Shenfield 3	a		21 08	21 19				21 38		21 50				22 08	22 19							22 38	22 50		
Romford	a			21 28											22 28										
Stratford 7 ⊖	a		21 22	21 36		21s45		21 52		22 05				22 22	22 36					22s45		22 52	23 05		
London Liverpool Street 15 ⊖	a		21 31	21 45		21 55		22 01		22 14		22 17		22 31	22 46					22 55		23 01	23 14		

		LE 1	LE 1	LE 1		LE 1	LE 1	LE ◇1	LE 1	LE 1	LE 1	LE 1	LE 1	LE ◇1		LE 1	LE 1	LE 1	LE						
Norwich	d							22 00								23 05									
Diss	d							22 17								23 22									
Peterborough 8	d													21 45											
Stowmarket	d							22 29	22 44					23 06		23 36			23 47						
Needham Market	d								22 49										23 52						
Ipswich	a							22 41	23 00					23 18		23 50			00 05						
	d		22 23					22 43				23 15		23 19											
Harwich Town	d					22 28											23 28								
Dovercourt	d					22 30											23 30								
Harwich International	d					22 33											23 33								
Wrabness	d					22 39											23 39								
Mistley	d					22 45											23 45								
Manningtree 2	d		22 33			22a50		22 53				23 25		23 29			23 50								
Walton-on-the-Naze	d										23 00														
Frinton-on-Sea	d										23 03														
Kirby Cross	d										23 06														
Clacton-on-Sea	d	22 05											23 05												
Thorpe-le-Soken 1	a	22 13									23 12		23 13												
	d	22 13											23 13												
Weeley	d												23 17												
Great Bentley	d												23 20												
Alresford (Essex)	d			←									23 24												
Wivenhoe 3	d	22 23		22 32									23 28												
Hythe	d			22 36									23 32												
Colchester Town	a			22 40																					
	d			22 44						23 00															
Colchester 4	a	22 31	22 42	22 52				23 02		23 07		23 35	23 38	23 40			23 59								
Colchester 4	d	22 33	22 43					23 03																	
Marks Tey 2	d		22 49																						
Kelvedon	d		22 54																						
Braintree	d						22 56											23 45							
Braintree Freeport	d						22 58											23 47							
Cressing	d						23 01											23 50							
White Notley	d						23 04											23 53							
Witham 2	d	22 46	23 00				23a12	23 16										00a01							
Hatfield Peverel	d																								
Chelmsford 3	d	22 56	23 09					23 25																	
Ingatestone	d	23 02																							
Shenfield 3	a	23 08	23 19					23s36																	
Romford	a		23 28																						
Stratford 7 ⊖	a	23 22	23 36					23s52																	
London Liverpool Street 15 ⊖	a	23 31	23 45					00 02																	

Table 11

Sundays

Norwich, Ipswich, Harwich, Clacton, Walton-on-Naze, Colchester and Chelmsford - London

Network Diagram - see first Page of Table 5

		LE	LE	LE	LE	LE	LE	LE	LE	LE	LE	LE	LE	LE	LE	LE	LE	LE	LE	LE	LE	LE	LE	LE	LE
		◇1		1	1				1	1	◇1	1	1	1	1	◇1	1	1	1	1	1	◇1	1	1	1
		A	A				🚌	🚌																	
											☕					☕						☕			
Norwich	d	22p00									07 00					08 00						09 00			
Diss	d	22p17									07 17					08 17						09 17			
Peterborough 8	d																								
Stowmarket	d	22p29	23p47								07 29					08 29						09 29			
Needham Market	d		23p52																						
Ipswich	a	22p41	00 05								07 41					08 41						09 41			
	d	22p43									07 43	07 46			08 09	08 43					09 09	09 43			
Harwich Town	d																	08 53						09 53	
Dovercourt	d																	08 55						09 55	
Harwich International	d									07 20		08a14						08 58						09 58	
Wrabness	d																	09 04						10 04	
Mistley	d																	09 10						10 10	
Manningtree 2	d	22p53								07 33	07 53				08 19	08 53		09a15			09 19	09 53		10a15	
Walton-on-the-Naze	d																08 30						09 30		
Frinton-on-Sea	d																08 33						09 33		
Kirby Cross	d																08 36						09 36		
Clacton-on-Sea	d													07 36						08 36					
Thorpe-le-Soken 1	a													07 44			08 42			08 44			09 42		
	d													07 44						08 44					
Weeley	d																								
Great Bentley	d													07 49						08 49					
Alresford (Essex)	d													07 53						08 53					
Wivenhoe 3	d													07 57						08 57					
Hythe	d																								
Colchester Town	a																								
	d																								
Colchester 4	a	23p02								07 42	08 02			08 05	08 29	09 02				09 05	09 29	10 02			
Colchester 4	d	23p03			06 56	07 07			07 26	07 43	08 03			08 06	08 30	09 03				09 06	09 30	10 03			
Marks Tey 2	d				07 02	07a14			07 32	07 49				08 12	08 36					09 12	09 36				
Kelvedon	d				07 07				07 37	07 54					08 41						09 41				
Braintree	d			00 25									08 00						09 00						10 00
Braintree Freeport	d			00 27									08 02						09 02						10 02
Cressing	d			00 30									08 05						09 05						10 05
White Notley	d			00 33									08 08						09 08						10 08
Witham 2	d	23p16		00a41	07 13				07 43	08 00			08a16	08 21	08 47				09a16	09 21	09 47				10a16
Hatfield Peverel	d				07 17				07 47						08 51						09 51				
Chelmsford 3	d	23p25			07 24				07 54	08 09				08 30	08 58					09 30	09 58				
Ingatestone	d				07 31				08 01						09 05						10 05				
Shenfield 3	a	23b36			07 36		06 58	07 45	08 06	08 19				08 40	09 10					09 40	10 10				
Romford	a																								
Stratford 7 ⊖	a	23b52					08 12		08s34	08s49				09s04	09s34					10s04	10s34				
London Liverpool Street 15 ⊖	a	00 02					08 32	08 35	08 42	08 59	09 03			09 12	09 42	10 01				10 12	10 42	11 01			

A not 11 December

b Previous night, stops to set down only

Table 11

Sundays

Norwich, Ipswich, Harwich, Clacton, Walton-on-Naze, Colchester and Chelmsford - London

Network Diagram - see first Page of Table 5

		LE 1	LE 1	LE	LE ◇1 ☕	LE 1		LE 1	LE 1	LE 1	LE 1	LE ◇1 ☕	LE 1	LE 1	LE 1	LE 1		LE 1	LE 1	LE ◇1 ☕	LE 1	LE 1	LE 1	LE 1	LE 1
Norwich	d				10 00							11 00								12 00					
Diss	d				10 17							11 17								12 17					
Peterborough 8	d																								
Stowmarket	d			10 18	10 29							11 29							12 18	12 29					
Needham Market	d			10 23															12 23						
Ipswich	a			10 35	10 41							11 41							12 35	12 41					
	d		10 09		10 43						11 09	11 43						12 09		12 43					13 09
Harwich Town	d							10 53						11 53								12 53			
Dovercourt	d							10 55						11 55								12 55			
Harwich International	d							10 58						11 58								12 58			
Wrabness	d							11 04						12 04								13 04			
Mistley	d							11 10						12 10								13 10			
Manningtree 2	d		10 19		10 53			11a15			11 19	11 53		12a15				12 19		12 53		13a15			13 19
Walton-on-the-Naze	d					10 30							11 30								12 30				
Frinton-on-Sea	d					10 33							11 33								12 33				
Kirby Cross	d					10 36							11 36								12 36				
Clacton-on-Sea	d	09 36								10 36						11 36								12 36	
Thorpe-le-Soken 1	a	09 44				10 42				10 44			11 42			11 44					12 42			12 44	
	d	09 44								10 44						11 44								12 44	
Weeley	d																								
Great Bentley	d	09 49								10 49						11 49								12 49	
Alresford (Essex)	d	09 53								10 53						11 53								12 53	
Wivenhoe 3	d	09 57								10 57						11 57								12 57	
Hythe	d																								
Colchester Town	a																								
	d																								
Colchester 4	a	10 05	10 29		11 02					11 05	11 29	12 02				12 05		12 29		13 02				13 05	13 29
Colchester 4	d	10 06	10 30		11 03					11 06	11 30	12 03				12 06		12 30		13 03				13 06	13 30
Marks Tey 2	d	10 12	10 36							11 12	11 36					12 12		12 36						13 12	13 36
Kelvedon	d		10 41								11 41							12 41							13 41
Braintree	d								11 00						12 00								13 00		
Braintree Freeport	d								11 02						12 02								13 02		
Cressing	d								11 05						12 05								13 05		
White Notley	d								11 08						12 08								13 08		
Witham 2	d	10 21	10 47						11a16	11 21	11 47				12a16	12 21		12 47					13a16	13 21	13 47
Hatfield Peverel	d		10 51								11 51							12 51							13 51
Chelmsford 3	d	10 30	10 58							11 30	11 58					12 30		12 58						13 30	13 58
Ingatestone	d		11 05								12 05							13 05							14 05
Shenfield 3	a	10 40	11 10							11 40	12 10					12 40		13 10						13 40	14 10
Romford	a																								
Stratford 7 ⊖	a	11s04	11s34							12s04	12s34					13s04		13s34						14s04	14s34
London Liverpool Street 15 ⊖	a	11 12	11 42		12 01					12 12	12 42	13 01				13 12		13 42		14 01				14 12	14 42

		LE 1		LE ◇1 ☕	LE 1	LE 1	LE 1	LE 1	LE 1	LE 1	LE ◇1 ☕	LE 1		LE 1	LE 1	LE 1	LE 1	LE 1	LE ◇1 ☕	LE 1	LE 1	LE 1		LE 1	LE 1
Norwich	d			13 00							14 00								15 00						
Diss	d			13 17							14 17								15 17						
Peterborough 8	d	11 46																13 46							
Stowmarket	d	13 13		13 29						14 18	14 29							15 13	15 29						
Needham Market	d									14 23															
Ipswich	a	13 28		13 41						14 35	14 41							15 28	15 41						
	d			13 43					14 09		14 43						15 09		15 43						16 09
Harwich Town	d					13 53								14 53							15 53				
Dovercourt	d					13 55								14 55							15 55				
Harwich International	d					13 58								14 58							15 58				
Wrabness	d					14 04								15 04							16 04				
Mistley	d					14 10								15 10							16 10				
Manningtree 2	d			13 53		14a15			14 19		14 53			15a15			15 19		15 53		16a15				16 19
Walton-on-the-Naze	d				13 30							14 30								15 30					
Frinton-on-Sea	d				13 33							14 33								15 33					
Kirby Cross	d				13 36							14 36								15 36					
Clacton-on-Sea	d							13 36								14 36								15 36	
Thorpe-le-Soken 1	a				13 42			13 44				14 42				14 44				15 42				15 44	
	d							13 44								14 44								15 44	
Weeley	d																								
Great Bentley	d							13 49								14 49								15 49	
Alresford (Essex)	d							13 53								14 53								15 53	
Wivenhoe 3	d							13 57								14 57								15 57	
Hythe	d																								
Colchester Town	a																								
	d																								
Colchester 4	a			14 02				14 05	14 29		15 02					15 05	15 29		16 02					16 05	16 29
Colchester 4	d			14 03				14 06	14 30		15 03					15 06	15 30		16 03					16 06	16 30
Marks Tey 2	d							14 12	14 36							15 12	15 36							16 12	16 36
Kelvedon	d								14 41								15 41								16 41
Braintree	d						14 00								15 00							16 00			
Braintree Freeport	d						14 02								15 02							16 02			
Cressing	d						14 05								15 05							16 05			
White Notley	d						14 08								15 08							16 08			
Witham 2	d						14a16	14 21	14 47						15a16	15 21	15 47					16a16		16 21	16 47
Hatfield Peverel	d								14 51								15 51								16 51
Chelmsford 3	d							14 30	14 58							15 30	15 58							16 30	16 58
Ingatestone	d								15 05								16 05								17 05
Shenfield 3	a							14 40	15 10							15 40	16 10							16 40	17 10
Romford	a																								
Stratford 7 ⊖	a							15s04	15s34							16s04	16s34							17s04	17s34
London Liverpool Street 15 ⊖	a			15 01				15 12	15 42		16 01					16 12	16 42		17 01					17 12	17 42

Table 11

Sundays

Norwich, Ipswich, Harwich, Clacton, Walton-on-Naze, Colchester and Chelmsford - London

Network Diagram - see first Page of Table 5

		LE	LE	LE	LE	LE	LE	LE	LE	LE	LE	LE	LE	LE	LE	LE	LE	LE	LE	LE	LE	LE	LE
			R																				
		1	1	1	1	1	1	◇1	1	1	◇1	1	1	1	1	1	1	◇1	1	1	1	1	1
			☕					☕			☕							☕					
Norwich	d		16 00					16 20			17 00							18 00					
Diss	d		16 17					16 37			17 17							18 17					
Peterborough 8	d									15 45													
Stowmarket	d	16 18	16 29					16 49		17 13	17 29						18 18	18 29					
Needham Market	d	16 23															18 23						
Ipswich	a	16 35	16 41					17 01		17 28	17 41						18 35	18 41					
	d		16 43					17 03	17 09		17 43					18 09		18 43					19 09
Harwich Town	d				16 53								17 53							18 53			
Dovercourt	d				16 55								17 55							18 55			
Harwich International	d				16 58								17 58							18 58			
Wrabness	d				17 04								18 04							19 04			
Mistley	d				17 10								18 10							19 10			
Manningtree 2	d		16 53		17a15				17 19		17 53		18a15			18 19		18 53		19a15			19 19
Walton-on-the-Naze	d			16 30								17 30							18 30				
Frinton-on-Sea	d			16 33								17 33							18 33				
Kirby Cross	d			16 36								17 36							18 36				
Clacton-on-Sea	d						16 36								17 36							18 36	
Thorpe-le-Soken 1	a			16 42			16 44					17 42			17 44				18 42			18 44	
	d						16 44								17 44							18 44	
Weeley	d																						
Great Bentley	d						16 49								17 49							18 49	
Alresford (Essex)	d						16 53								17 53							18 53	
Wivenhoe 3	d						16 57								17 57							18 57	
Hythe	d																						
Colchester Town	a																						
	d																						
Colchester 4	a		17 02				17 05	17 18	17 29		18 02				18 05	18 29		19 02				19 05	19 29
Colchester 4	d		17 03				17 06	17 21	17 30		18 03				18 06	18 30		19 03				19 06	19 30
Marks Tey 2	d						17 12		17 36						18 12	18 36						19 12	19 36
Kelvedon	d								17 41							18 41							19 41
Braintree	d					17 00								18 00							19 00		
Braintree Freeport	d					17 02								18 02							19 02		
Cressing	d					17 05								18 05							19 05		
White Notley	d					17 08								18 08							19 08		
Witham 2	d					17a16	17 21		17 47					18a16	18 21	18 47					19a16	19 21	19 47
Hatfield Peverel	d								17 51							18 51							19 51
Chelmsford 3	d						17 30		17 58						18 30	18 58						19 30	19 58
Ingatestone	d								18 05							19 05							20 05
Shenfield 3	a						17 40		18 10						18 40	19 10						19 40	20 10
Romford	a																						
Stratford 7 ⊖	a						18s04		18s34						19s04	19s34						20s04	20s34
London Liverpool Street 15 ⊖	a		18 01				18 12	18 28	18 42		19 01				19 12	19 42		20 01				20 12	20 42

		LE	LE	LE	LE	LE	LE	LE	LE	LE	LE	LE	LE	LE	LE	LE	LE	LE	LE	LE	LE	LE
		◇1	◇1	1	1	1	1	1	1	1	1	◇1	1	1	1	1	◇1	◇1	1	1	1	1
			☕									☕										
Norwich	d		19 00									20 00						21 00				
Diss	d		19 17									20 17						21 17				
Peterborough 8	d	17 45															19 45					
Stowmarket	d	19 13	19 29								20 18	20 29					21 06	21 29				
Needham Market	d										20 23											
Ipswich	a	19 28	19 41								20 35	20 41					21 18	21 41				
	d	19 28	19 43					20 09			20 35	20 43				21 09	21 19	21 43				
Harwich Town	d				19 53								20 53							21 53		
Dovercourt	d				19 55								20 55							21 55		
Harwich International	d				19 58					20 35	21a04		20 58							21 58		
Wrabness	d				20 04								21 04							22 04		
Mistley	d				20 10								21 10							22 10		
Manningtree 2	d	19 38	19 53		20a15			20 19		20 48		20 53	21a15			21 19	21 29	21 53		22a15		
Walton-on-the-Naze	d			19 30					20 30										21 30			
Frinton-on-Sea	d			19 33					20 33										21 33			
Kirby Cross	d			19 36					20 36										21 36			
Clacton-on-Sea	d						19 36								20 36							21 36
Thorpe-le-Soken 1	a			19 42			19 44		20 42						20 44				21 42			21 44
	d						19 44								20 44							21 44
Weeley	d																					
Great Bentley	d						19 49								20 49							21 49
Alresford (Essex)	d						19 53								20 53							21 53
Wivenhoe 3	d						19 57								20 57							21 57
Hythe	d																					
Colchester Town	a																					
	d																					
Colchester 4	a	19 49	20 02				20 05	20 29		20 57		21 02			21 05	21 29	21 40	22 02				22 05
Colchester 4	d		20 03				20 06	20 30		20 57		21 03			21 06	21 30		22 03				22 06
Marks Tey 2	d						20 12	20 36							21 12	21 36						22 12
Kelvedon	d							20 41								21 41						
Braintree	d					20 00								21 00							22 00	
Braintree Freeport	d					20 02								21 02							22 02	
Cressing	d					20 05								21 05							22 05	
White Notley	d					20 08								21 08							22 08	
Witham 2	d					20a16	20 21	20 47						21a16	21 21	21 47					22a16	22 21
Hatfield Peverel	d							20 51								21 51						
Chelmsford 3	d						20 30	20 58		21 15					21 30	21 58						22 30
Ingatestone	d							21 05								22 05						
Shenfield 3	a						20 40	21 10		21 25					21 40	22 10						22 40
Romford	a																					
Stratford 7 ⊖	a						21s04	21s34		21s51					22s04	22s34						23s04
London Liverpool Street 15 ⊖	a		21 01				21 12	21 42		21 59		22 01			22 12	22 42		23 01				23 12

Table 11

Sundays

Norwich, Ipswich, Harwich, Clacton, Walton-on-Naze, Colchester and Chelmsford - London

Network Diagram - see first Page of Table 5

		LE	LE	LE	LE	LE	LE	LE	LE
		1	1	1	1	1	◇1	1	1
Norwich	d						22 00		23 05
Diss	d						22 17		23 22
Peterborough 8	d								
Stowmarket	d			22 18			22 29		23 34
Needham Market	d			22 23					
Ipswich	a			22 35			22 41		23 48
	d	22 09					22 43		
Harwich Town	d							22 53	
Dovercourt	d							22 55	
Harwich International	d							22 58	
Wrabness	d							23 04	
Mistley	d							23 10	
Manningtree 2	d	22 19					22 53	23 15	
Walton-on-the-Naze	d		22 16						
Frinton-on-Sea	d		22 19						
Kirby Cross	d		22 22						
Clacton-on-Sea	d				22 22				
Thorpe-le-Soken 1	a		22 28		22 30				
	d				22 30				
Weeley	d								
Great Bentley	d								
Alresford (Essex)	d								
Wivenhoe 3	d				22 40				
Hythe	d								
Colchester Town	a								
	d								
Colchester 4	a	22 29			22 48		23 02	23 24	
Colchester 4	d	22 30					23 03		
Marks Tey 2	d	22 36							
Kelvedon	d	22 41							
Braintree	d					22 56			
Braintree Freeport	d					22 58			
Cressing	d					23 01			
White Notley	d					23 04			
Witham 2	d	22 47				23a12	23 16		
Hatfield Peverel	d	22 51							
Chelmsford 3	d	22 58					23 25		
Ingatestone	d	23 05							
Shenfield 3	a	23 10					23s36		
Romford	a								
Stratford 7 ⊖	a	23s34					23s57		
London Liverpool Street 15 ⊖	a	23 42					00 08		

Network Diagram for Tables 13, 14, 15, 16, 17

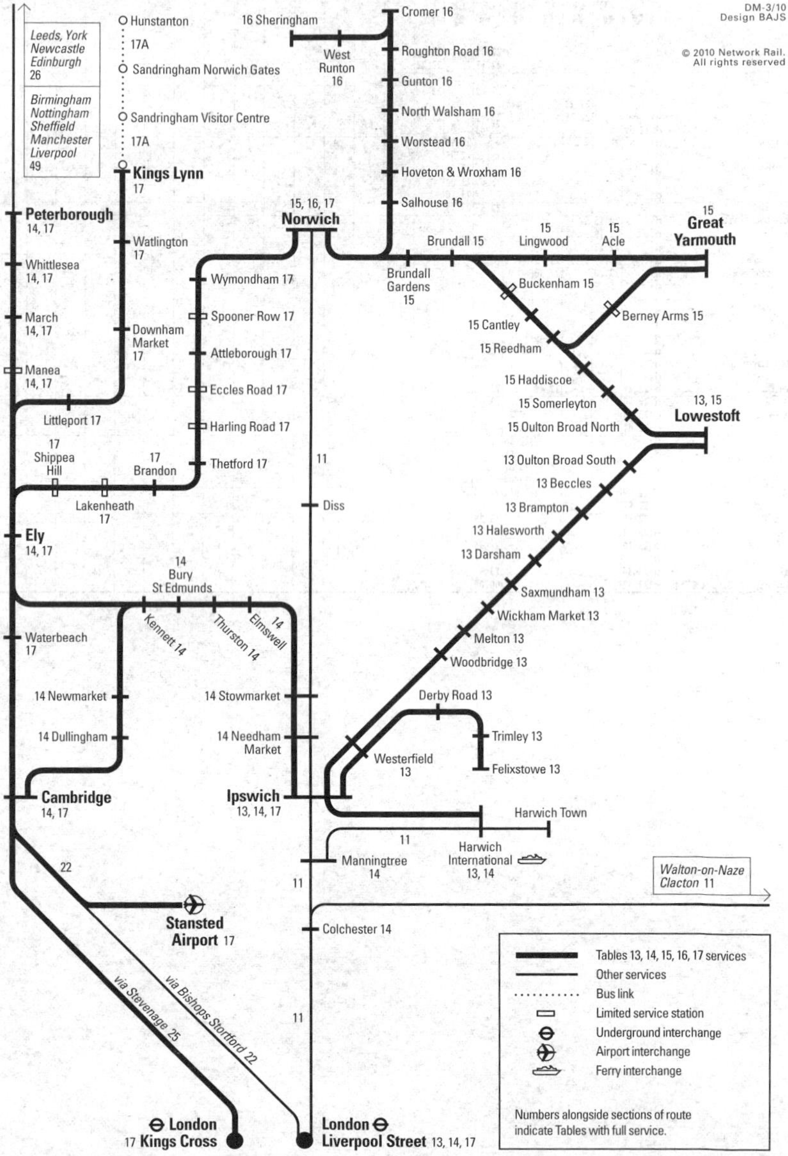

Ipswich - Felixstowe and Lowestoft

Network Diagram - see first Page of Table 13

Miles	Miles			LE	LE	LE		LE	LE	LE	LE 1	LE		LE	LE 1	LE	LE	LE	LE 1	LE	LE	LE		LE 1	LE
—	—	London Liverpool Street 15 ⊖	d																						
—	—	Harwich International	d								07 50														
0	—	**Ipswich**	d	05 04	06 04	06 20		07 14		07 35	08a17	08 25		08 58	09 13	09 58	10 13	10 58	11 13	11 58	12 13	12 58		13 13	13 58
3½	0	Westerfield	d	05 10	06 10	06 27		07 20		07 42		08 31		09 04	09 20	10 04	10 20	11 04	11 20	12 04	12 20	13 04		13 20	14 04
—	2½	Derby Road	d	05 15	06 15			07 25				08 36		09 09		10 09		11 09		12 09		13 09			14 09
—	10½	Trimley	d	05 24	06 24			07 34				08 45		09 18		10 18		11 18		12 18		13 18			14 18
—	12¼	**Felixstowe**	a	05 30	06 30			07 40				08 51		09 24		10 24		11 24		12 24		13 24			14 24
10¼	—	Woodbridge	d			06 39				07 54					09 32		10 32		11 32		12 32			13 32	
11½	—	Melton	d			06 43				07 58					09 36		10 36		11 36		12 36			13 36	
15¾	—	Wickham Market	d			06 49				08 04					09 42		10 42		11 42		12 42			13 42	
22½	—	Saxmundham	d			07a00			07 45	08 16					09 54		10a53		11 54		12a53			13 54	
26¾	—	Darsham	d						07 52	08 22					10 00				12 00					14 00	
32	—	Halesworth	d						08 02	08 32					10 10				12 10					14 10	
36	—	Brampton (Suffolk)	d						08 09	08 39					10 17				12 17					14 17	
40¼	—	Beccles	d						08 17	08 47					10 25				12 25					14 25	
46¾	—	Oulton Broad South	d						08 27	08 57					10 35				12 35					14 35	
49	—	**Lowestoft**	a						08 35	09 06					10 44				12 44					14 44	

		LE	LE	LE 1	LE	LE		LE		LE 1	LE	LE	LE	LE 1	LE	LE	LE	LE 1		LE 1	LE
London Liverpool Street 15 ⊖	d																				
Harwich International	d																			21 38	
Ipswich	d	14 13	14 58	15 13	15 54	15 58		16 58		17 13	17 58	18 13	18 58	19 13	19 58	20 13	20 58	21 13		22e13	22 28
Westerfield	d	14 20	15 04	15 20	16 01	16 04		17 04		17 20	18 04	18 20	19 04	19 20	20 04	20 20	21 04	21 20		22 20	22 37
Derby Road	d		15 09			16 09		17 09			18 09		19 09		20 09		21 09				22 42
Trimley	d		15 18			16 18		17 18			18 18		19 18		20 18		21 18				22 51
Felixstowe	a		15 24			16 24		17 24			18 24		19 24		20 24		21 24				22 57
Woodbridge	d	14 32		15 32	16 20					17 32		18 32		19 32		20 32		21 32		22 32	
Melton	d	14 36		15 36	16 24					17 36		18 36		19 36		20 36		21 36		22 36	
Wickham Market	d	14 42		15 42	16 30					17 42		18 42		19 42		20 42		21 42		22 42	
Saxmundham	d	14a53		15 54	16a41					17 54		18 54		19 54		20a53		21 54		22 54	
Darsham	d			16 00						18 00		19 00		20 00				22 00		23 00	
Halesworth	d			16 10						18 10		19 22		20 10				22 10		23 10	
Brampton (Suffolk)	d			16 17						18 17		19 29		20 17				22 17		23 17	
Beccles	d			16 25						18 25		19 37		20 25				22 25		23 25	
Oulton Broad South	d			16 35						18 35		19 47		20 35				22 35		23 35	
Lowestoft	a			16 44						18 44		19 56		20 44				22 44		23 44	

Saturdays

		LE	LE	LE	LE 1	LE	LE	LE	LE 1	LE		LE	LE	LE 1	LE	LE	LE	LE 1	LE	LE		LE	LE 1	LE	LE
London Liverpool Street 15 ⊖	d																								
Harwich International	d				07 50																				
Ipswich	d	05 58	06 58	07 13	08a17	07 58	08 13	08 58	09 13	09 58		10 13	10 58	11 13	11 58	12 13	12 58	13 13	13 58	14 13		14 58	15 13	15 58	16 13
Westerfield	d	06 04	07 04	07 20		08 04	08 20	09 04	09 20	10 04		10 20	11 04	11 20	12 04	12 20	13 04	13 20	14 04	14 20		15 04	15 20	16 04	16 20
Derby Road	d	06 09	07 09			08 09		09 09		10 09			11 09		12 09		13 09		14 09			15 09		16 09	
Trimley	d	06 18	07 18			08 18		09 18		10 18			11 18		12 18		13 18		14 18			15 18		16 18	
Felixstowe	a	06 24	07 24			08 24		09 24		10 24			11 24		12 24		13 24		14 24			15 24		16 24	
Woodbridge	d			07 32			08 32		09 32			10 32		11 32		12 32		13 32		14 32			15 32		16 32
Melton	d			07 36			08 36		09 36			10 36		11 36		12 36		13 36		14 36			15 36		16 36
Wickham Market	d			07 42			08 42		09 42			10 42		11 42		12 42		13 42		14 42			15 42		16 42
Saxmundham	d			07 54			08a53		09 54			10a53		11 54		12a53		13 54		14a53			15 54		16a53
Darsham	d			08 00					10 00					12 00				14 00					16 00		
Halesworth	d			08 10					10 10					12 10				14 10					16 10		
Brampton (Suffolk)	d			08 17					10 17					12 17				14 17					16 17		
Beccles	d			08 25					10 25					12 25				14 25					16 25		
Oulton Broad South	d			08 35					10 35					12 35				14 35					16 35		
Lowestoft	a			08 44					10 44					12 44				14 44					16 44		

		LE	LE 1	LE	LE	LE		LE 1	LE	LE	LE	LE 1	LE 1	LE
London Liverpool Street 15 ⊖	d													
Harwich International	d												21 38	
Ipswich	d	16 58	17 13	17 58	18 13	18 58		19 13	19 58	20 13	20 58	21 13	22 13	22 28
Westerfield	d	17 04	17 20	18 04	18 20	19 04		19 20	20 04	20 20	21 04	21 20	22 20	22 34
Derby Road	d	17 09		18 09		19 09			20 09		21 09			22 39
Trimley	d	17 18		18 18		19 18			20 18		21 18			22 48
Felixstowe	a	17 24		18 24		19 24			20 24		21 24			22 54
Woodbridge	d		17 32		18 32			19 32		20 32		21 32	22 32	
Melton	d		17 36		18 36			19 36		20 36		21 36	22 36	
Wickham Market	d		17 42		18 42			19 42		20 42		21 42	22 42	
Saxmundham	d		17 54		18a53			19 54		20a53		21 54	22 54	
Darsham	d		18 00					20 00				22 00	23 00	
Halesworth	d		18 10					20 10				22 10	23 10	
Brampton (Suffolk)	d		18 17					20 17				22 17	23 17	
Beccles	d		18 25					20 25				22 25	23 25	
Oulton Broad South	d		18 35					20 35				22 35	23 35	
Lowestoft	a		18 44					20 44				22 44	23 44	

Table 13

Sundays

Ipswich - Felixstowe and Lowestoft

Network Diagram - see first Page of Table 13

		LE ■1	LE ■1	LE	LE	LE ■1	LE	LE	LE	LE		LE	LE ■1	LE	LE	LE ■1	LE	LE	LE	LE ■1		LE ■1			
London Liverpool Street ■15 ⊖	d																								
Harwich International	d	08 30																		21 10					
Ipswich	d	08a53	10 00	10 55	11 55	12 00	12 55	13 55	14 00	14 55		15 55	16 00	16 55	17 55	18 00	18 55	19 55	20 00	21a36		22 00			
Westerfield	d		10 07	11 01	12 01	12 07	13 01	14 01	14 07	15 01		16 01	16 07	17 01	18 01	18 07	19 01	20 01	20 07			22 07			
Derby Road	d			11 06	12 06		13 06	14 06		15 06		16 06		17 06	18 06		19 06	20 06							
Trimley	d			11 15	12 15		13 15	14 15		15 15		16 15		17 15	18 15		19 15	20 15							
Felixstowe	a			11 21	12 21		13 21	14 21		15 21		16 21		17 21	18 21		19 21	20 21							
Woodbridge	d		10 19			12 19			14 19				16 19			18 19			20 19			22 19			
Melton	d		10 23			12 23			14 23				16 23			18 23			20 23			22 23			
Wickham Market	d		10 29			12 29			14 29				16 29			18 29			20 29			22 29			
Saxmundham	d		10 41			12 41			14 41				16 41			18 41			20 41			22 41			
Darsham	d		10 47			12 47			14 47				16 47			18 47			20 47			22 47			
Halesworth	d		10 57			12 57			14 57				16 57			18 57			20 57			22 57			
Brampton (Suffolk)	d		11 04			13 04			15 04				17 04			19 04			21 04			23 04			
Beccles	d		11 12			13 12			15 12				17 12			19 12			21 12			23 12			
Oulton Broad South	d		11 22			13 22			15 22				17 22			19 22			21 22			23 22			
Lowestoft	a		11 31			13 31			15 31				17 31			19 31			21 31			23 31			

Lowestoft and Felixstowe - Ipswich

Network Diagram - see first Page of Table 13

Miles	Miles		LE FO	LE MO	LE	LE	LE	LE	LE	LE	LE		LE	LE	LE	LE	LE	LE	LE	LE	LE		LE	LE
			◇1	◇1	◇1 TWThO	◇1		1	◇1	1	R 1 ☕		1		1	1	R 1 ☕	1	R 1 ☕	◇1	R 1 ☕		1	
0	—	**Lowestoft** d						05 25							06 11	06 42								
2¼	—	Oulton Broad South d						05 32							06 18	06 49								
8½	—	Beccles d						05 41							06 27	06 58								
13	—	Brampton (Suffolk) d						05 49							06 35	07 06								
17	—	Halesworth d						05 57							06 43	07 14								
22¼	—	Darsham d						06 05							06 51	07 22								
26½	—	Saxmundham d						06 14							07 05	07 31								
33¼	—	Wickham Market d						06 23							07 14	07 40								
37¼	—	Melton d						06 30							07 21	07 47								
38¾	—	Woodbridge d						06 35							07 26	07 52								
—	0	**Felixstowe** d					05 34							06 38										07 48
—	1¾	Trimley d					05 37							06 41										07 51
—	9¾	Derby Road d					05 47							06 51										08 01
45½	12¼	Westerfield d					05 52	06 46						06 56	07 37	08 03								08 07
49	—	**Ipswich** a					06 00	06 53						07 04	07 44	08 10								08 15
—	—	d	22p43	22p43	22p43	05 14		06 59	05 44	06 00	06 14		06 29				06 44	06 52	07 09	07 18	07 34		07 38	
—	—	Harwich International a						07 28																
—	—	London Liverpool Street 15 ⊖ a	00 02	00 08	00 14	06 34			06 54	07 24	07 27		07 50				07 58	08 13	08 23	08 40	08 42		09 01	

	LE	LE	LE	LE	LE	LE	LE		LE	LE	LE	LE	LE	LE	LE	LE	LE		LE	LE	LE	LE	LE	LE
		R 1 ☕	R 1 B ☕	◇1	R 1 ☕	1			R 1 ☕		1	1	R 1 ☕	1	◇1 ☕		◇1 ☕		1		◇1 ☕		1	◇1 ☕
Lowestoft d	07 27										09 08												11 08	
Oulton Broad South d	07 34										09 15												11 15	
Beccles d	07 43										09 24												11 24	
Brampton (Suffolk) d	07 51										09 32												11 32	
Halesworth d	07 59										09 40												11 40	
Darsham d	08 07										09 48												11 48	
Saxmundham d	08 18										09 57									10 57			11 57	
Wickham Market d	08 27										10 06									11 06			12 06	
Melton d	08 34										10 13									11 13			12 13	
Woodbridge d	08 39										10 18									11 18			12 18	
Felixstowe d							08 54			09 28						10 28						11 28		
Trimley d							08 57			09 31						10 31						11 31		
Derby Road d							09 10			09 41						10 41						11 41		
Westerfield d	08 50						09 15			09 46	10 29					10 46				11 29		11 46	12 29	
Ipswich a	08 57						09 25			09 54	10 36					10 54				11 36		11 54	12 36	
d		07 49	08 20	08 26	08 43	08 48			09 09			09 30	09 43	09 52	10 09		10 43		10 52		11 09			11 43
Harwich International a																								
London Liverpool Street 15 ⊖ a		09 04	09 24	09 40	09 56	10 14			10 19			10 44	10 55	11 14	11 19		11 55		12 14		12 19			12 55

	LE	LE	LE		LE	LE	LE	LE	LE	LE	LE	LE	LE		LE	LE	LE	LE	LE	LE	LE	LE	LE
	1	◇1 ☕			◇1 ☕	1		◇1 ☕		1	◇1 ☕	1	◇1 ☕			◇1 ☕	1		◇1 ☕		1	◇1 ☕	1
Lowestoft d										13 08											15 08		
Oulton Broad South d										13 15											15 15		
Beccles d										13 24											15 24		
Brampton (Suffolk) d										13 32											15 32		
Halesworth d										13 40											15 40		
Darsham d										13 48											15 48		
Saxmundham d							12 57			13 57								14 57			15 57		
Wickham Market d							13 06			14 06								15 06			16 06		
Melton d							13 13			14 13								15 13			16 13		
Woodbridge d							13 18			14 18								15 18			16 18		
Felixstowe d			12 28						13 28						14 28					15 28			
Trimley d			12 31						13 31						14 31					15 31			
Derby Road d			12 41						13 41						14 41					15 41			
Westerfield d			12 46				13 29		13 46	14 29					14 46			15 29		15 46	16 29		
Ipswich a			12 54				13 36		13 54	14 36					14 54			15 36		15 54	16 36		
d	11 52	12 09			12 43	12 52		13 09			13 43	13 52	14 09			14 43	14 52		15 09			15 43	15 52
Harwich International a																							
London Liverpool Street 15 ⊖ a	13 14	13 19			13 55	14 14		14 19			14 55	15 15	15 19			15 55	16 14		16 17			16 55	17 16

B The East Anglian

Lowestoft and Felixstowe - Ipswich

Network Diagram - see first Page of Table 13

		LE	LE	LE	LE	LE	LE	LE	LE	LE		LE	LE	LE	LE	LE	LE	LE	LE	LE		LE	LE	LE	LE
		◇1 ☕		◇1 ☕	1	◇1 ☕			1	◇1 ☕		◇1 ☕	1		◇1 ☕	1	◇1 ☕		1	◇1 ☕		1	1	◇1	
Lowestoft	d								17 08										18 49						
Oulton Broad South	d								17 15										18 56						
Beccles	d								17 24										19 05						
Brampton (Suffolk)	d								17 32										19 13						
Halesworth	d								17 40										19 21						
Darsham	d								17 48										19 29						
Saxmundham	d						17 09		17 57										19 57						
Wickham Market	d						17 18		18 06										20 06						
Melton	d						17 25		18 13										20 13						
Woodbridge	d						17 30		18 18										20 18						
Felixstowe	d		16 28					17 28						18 28				19 28							20 28
Trimley	d		16 31					17 31						18 31				19 31							20 31
Derby Road	d		16 41					17 41						18 41				19 41							20 41
Westerfield	d		16 46				17 41	17 46	18 29					18 46				19 46	20 29						20 46
Ipswich	a		16 54				17 49	17 54	18 36					18 54				19 54	20 37						20 54
	d	16 09		16 43	16 52	17 09				17 43		18 13	18 22		18 43	18 47	19 09			19 43		19 35	19 52	20 09	
Harwich International	a																								
London Liverpool Street 15 ⊖	a	17 19		17 58	18 15	18 19				18 55		19 17	19 45		19 55	20 14	20 19			20 55		21 01	21 16	21 19	

		LE	LE	LE	LE	LE		LE	LE	LE	LE	LE	LE	LE	LE
		◇1 ☕		1	◇1				◇1 ThFO ☕	◇1 MTWO ☕	1 ThFO	1 MTWO	◇1 ThFO	◇1 MTWO	
Lowestoft	d							21 08							
Oulton Broad South	d							21 15							
Beccles	d							21 24							
Brampton (Suffolk)	d							21 32							
Halesworth	d							21 40							
Darsham	d							21 48							
Saxmundham	d		20 57					21 57							
Wickham Market	d		21 06					22 06							
Melton	d		21 13					22 13							
Woodbridge	d		21 18					22 18							
Felixstowe	d					21 28									23 01
Trimley	d					21 31									23 04
Derby Road	d					21 41									23 14
Westerfield	d		21 29			21 46		22 29							23 19
Ipswich	a		21 36			21 54		22 36							23 27
	d	20 43		21 00	21 09				21 43	21 43	22 23	22 23	22 43	22 43	
Harwich International	a			21 29											
London Liverpool Street 15 ⊖	a	21 55			22 19				22 55	23 00	23 45	23 50	00 02	00 14	

Saturdays

		LE	LE	LE	LE	LE	LE	LE	LE	LE		LE	LE	LE	LE	LE	LE	LE	LE	LE		LE	LE	LE	LE
		◇1	◇1 ☕	◇1 ☕		1	◇1 ☕	1	1	◇1 ☕			1	◇1 ☕	1	◇1 ☕		◇1 ☕	1			◇1 ☕		1	◇1 ☕
Lowestoft	d					06 08							07 08											09 08	
Oulton Broad South	d					06 15							07 15											09 15	
Beccles	d					06 24							07 24											09 24	
Brampton (Suffolk)	d					06 32							07 32											09 32	
Halesworth	d					06 40							07 40											09 40	
Darsham	d					06 48							07 48											09 48	
Saxmundham	d					06 57							07 57							08 57				09 57	
Wickham Market	d					07 06							08 06							09 06				10 06	
Melton	d					07 13							08 13							09 13				10 13	
Woodbridge	d					07 18							08 18							09 18				10 18	
Felixstowe	d				06 28							07 28					08 28						09 28		
Trimley	d				06 31							07 31					08 31						09 31		
Derby Road	d				06 41							07 41					08 41						09 41		
Westerfield	d				06 46	07 29						07 46	08 29				08 46			09 29			09 46	10 29	
Ipswich	a				06 54	07 36						07 54	08 36				08 54			09 36			09 54	10 36	
	d	22p43	05 43	06 09			06 43	06 52	06 59	07 09				07 43	07 52	08 09		08 43	08 52			09 09			09 43
Harwich International	a								07 28																
London Liverpool Street 15 ⊖	a	00 02	06 55	07 19			07 55	08 14		08 19				08 55	09 14	09 19		09 55	10 14			10 19			10 55

		LE	LE	LE	LE	LE		LE	LE	LE	LE	LE	LE	LE	LE	LE		LE	LE	LE	LE	LE	LE	LE	LE
		1	◇1 ☕		◇1 ☕	1			◇1 ☕		1	◇1 ☕	1	◇1 ☕		◇1 ☕		1		◇1 ☕		1	◇1 ☕	1	◇1 ☕
Lowestoft	d										11 08											13 08			
Oulton Broad South	d										11 15											13 15			
Beccles	d										11 24											13 24			
Brampton (Suffolk)	d										11 32											13 32			
Halesworth	d										11 40											13 40			
Darsham	d										11 48											13 48			
Saxmundham	d							10 57			11 57								12 57			13 57			
Wickham Market	d							11 06			12 06								13 06			14 06			
Melton	d							11 13			12 13								13 13			14 13			
Woodbridge	d							11 18			12 18								13 18			14 18			
Felixstowe	d			10 28						11 28					12 28						13 28				
Trimley	d			10 31						11 31					12 31						13 31				
Derby Road	d			10 41						11 41					12 41						13 41				
Westerfield	d			10 46				11 29		11 46	12 29				12 46				13 29		13 46	14 29			
Ipswich	a			10 54				11 36		11 54	12 36				12 54				13 36		13 54	14 36			
	d	09 52	10 09		10 43	10 52			11 09			11 43	11 52	12 09		12 43		12 52		13 09			13 43	13 52	14 09
Harwich International	a																								
London Liverpool Street 15 ⊖	a	11 14	11 19		11 55	12 14			12 19			12 55	13 14	13 19		13 55		14 14		14 19			14 55	15 14	15 19

Table 13

Saturdays

Lowestoft and Felixstowe - Ipswich

Network Diagram - see first Page of Table 13

		LE		LE	LE	LE	LE	LE	LE	LE	LE	LE		LE	LE	LE	LE	LE	LE	LE	LE	LE		LE	LE
				◇1	1		◇1		1	◇1	1	◇1			◇1	1		◇1		1	◇1	1		◇1	
				⊡			⊡			⊡		⊡			⊡			⊡			⊡			⊡	
Lowestoft	d								15 08											17 08					
Oulton Broad South	d								15 15											17 15					
Beccles	d								15 24											17 24					
Brampton (Suffolk)	d								15 32											17 32					
Halesworth	d								15 40											17 40					
Darsham	d								15 48											17 48					
Saxmundham	d					14 57			15 57								16 57			17 57					
Wickham Market	d					15 06			16 06								17 06			18 06					
Melton	d					15 13			16 13								17 13			18 13					
Woodbridge	d					15 18			16 18								17 18			18 18					
Felixstowe	d	14 28						15 28						16 28					17 28						18 28
Trimley	d	14 31						15 31						16 31					17 31						18 31
Derby Road	d	14 41						15 41						16 41					17 41						18 41
Westerfield	d	14 46				15 29		15 46	16 29					16 46			17 29		17 46	18 29					18 46
Ipswich	a	14 54				15 36		15 54	16 36					16 54			17 36		17 54	18 36					18 54
	d			14 43	14 52		15 09			15 43	15 52	16 09			16 43	16 52		17 09			17 43	17 52		18 13	
Harwich International	a																								
London Liverpool Street 15 ⊖	a			15 55	16 14		16 19			16 55	17 14	17 19			17 55	18 14		18 19			18 55	19 14		19 19	

		LE	LE	LE	LE	LE	LE	LE		LE	LE	LE	LE	LE	LE	LE	LE	LE		LE	LE	LE	LE	LE	
		◇1	1		◇1		1	◇1		1	1		◇1		1	1				◇1	1	1	◇1		
		⊡			⊡			⊡					⊡							⊡					
Lowestoft	d						19 08											21 08							
Oulton Broad South	d						19 15											21 15							
Beccles	d						19 24											21 24							
Brampton (Suffolk)	d						19 32											21 32							
Halesworth	d						19 40											21 40							
Darsham	d						19 48											21 48							
Saxmundham	d			18 57			19 57							20 57				21 57							
Wickham Market	d			19 06			20 06							21 06				22 06							
Melton	d			19 13			20 13							21 13				22 13							
Woodbridge	d			19 18			20 18							21 18				22 18							
Felixstowe	d					19 28						20 28					21 28							22 58	
Trimley	d					19 31						20 31					21 31							23 01	
Derby Road	d					19 41						20 41					21 41							23 11	
Westerfield	d			19 29		19 46	20 29					20 46		21 29			21 46	22 29						23 16	
Ipswich	a			19 36		19 54	20 36					20 54		21 36			21 54	22 36						23 24	
	d	18 43	18 52		19 09			19 43		19 52	20 09		20 43		21 00	21 09				21 43	21 52	22 23	22 43		
Harwich International	a														21 29										
London Liverpool Street 15 ⊖	a	19 55	20 14		20 19			20 55		21 14	21 17		21 55			22 17				22 55	23 14	23 45	00 02		

Sundays

		LE	LE		LE	LE	LE	LE	LE		LE	LE	LE	LE	LE	LE		LE	LE	LE	LE	LE		LE
		◇1	◇1		1	1																		1
		A											1			1								
			⊡																					
Lowestoft	d				08 05	10 05			12 05				14 05			16 05				18 05				20 05
Oulton Broad South	d				08 12	10 12			12 12				14 12			16 12				18 12				20 12
Beccles	d				08 21	10 21			12 21				14 21			16 21				18 21				20 21
Brampton (Suffolk)	d				08 29	10 29			12 29				14 29			16 29				18 29				20 29
Halesworth	d				08 37	10 37			12 37				14 37			16 37				18 37				20 37
Darsham	d				08 45	10 45			12 45				14 45			16 45				18 45				20 45
Saxmundham	d				08 54	10 54			12 54				14 54			16 54				18 54				20 54
Wickham Market	d				09 03	11 03			13 03				15 03			17 03				19 03				21 03
Melton	d				09 10	11 10			13 10				15 10			17 10				19 10				21 10
Woodbridge	d				09 15	11 15			13 15				15 15			17 15				19 15				21 15
Felixstowe	d						11 25	12 25			13 25	14 25		15 25	16 25			17 25	18 25		19 25	20 25		
Trimley	d						11 28	12 28			13 28	14 28		15 28	16 28			17 28	18 28		19 28	20 28		
Derby Road	d						11 38	12 38			13 38	14 38		15 38	16 38			17 38	18 38		19 38	20 38		
Westerfield	d				09 26	11 26	11 43	12 43	13 26		13 43	14 43	15 26	15 43	16 43	17 26		17 43	18 43	19 26	19 43	20 43		21 26
Ipswich	a				09 33	11 33	11 50	12 50	13 33		13 50	14 50	15 33	15 50	16 50	17 33		17 50	18 50	19 33	19 50	20 50		21 33
	d	22p43	07 43																					
Harwich International	a																							
London Liverpool Street 15 ⊖	a	00 02	09 03																					

A not 11 December

Ipswich - Bury St. Edmunds, Cambridge, Ely and Peterborough

Network Diagram - see first Page of Table 13

Miles	Miles	Miles			LE		LE ◇1	LE 1	LE 1	LE 1	LE 1	LE 1	LE 1		LE 1	LE 1	LE 1	LE 1	LE 1	LE 1	LE 1	LE 1	LE 1		LE 1
—	—	—	London Liverpool Street 15 ⊖	d																					
—	—	—	Colchester	d			05 40																		
—	—	—	Manningtree	d			05 49																		
—	—	0	Harwich International	d							07 50														
0	—	18	**Ipswich**	d	05 10		06 00	06 16	06 56	08 03	08 19	09 19	10 00		10 19	11 19	12 00	12 19	13 19	14 00	14 19	15 19	16 00		16 19
8¼	—	—	Needham Market	d	05 20			06 25	07 05		08 28	09 28			10 28	11 28		12 28	13 28		14 28	15 28			16 28
12	—	—	Stowmarket	d	05 26		06 12	06 31	07 11	08 15	08 34	09 34	10 12		10 34	11 34	12 12	12 34	13 34	14 12	14 34	15 34	16 12		16 34
17¾	—	—	Elmswell	d	05 35			06 39	07 19		08 42	09 42			10 42	11 42		12 42	13 42		14 42	15 42			16 42
22¼	—	—	Thurston	d	05 41			06 45	07 25		08 48	09 48			10 48	11 48		12 48	13 48		14 48	15 48			16 48
—	—	—	**Bury St Edmunds**	a	05 48		06 28	06 51	07 31	08 31	08 54	09 54	10 28		10 54	11 54	12 28	12 54	13 54	14 28	14 54	15 54	16 28		16 54
26¼	—	—	**Bury St Edmunds**	d	05 49		06 29	06 53	07 32	08 31	08 56	09 56	10 29		10 56	11 56	12 29	12 56	13 56	14 29	14 56	15 56	16 29		16 56
36	0	—	Kennett	d	06 00			07 03	07 42			10 06				12 06			14 06			16 06			17 06
41	—	—	Newmarket	d	06 09			07 13	07 51		09 15	10 16			11 15	12 16		13 15	14 16		15 15	16 16			17 16
44¼	—	—	Dullingham	d	06 14			07 18	08 00		09 20				11 20			13 20			15 20				
55¼	—	—	**Cambridge**	a	06 36			07 39	08 19		09 39	10 39			11 39	12 39		13 39	14 39		15 39	16 39			17 39
70	14¾	—	**Ely 4**	a			06 59			09 00			10 58				12 58			14 58			16 58		
—	—	—		d			07 00			09 00			10 58				12 58			14 58			16 58		
79¾	—	—	Manea	d																					
85¼	—	—	March	d			07 16			09 17			11 15				13 15			15 15			17 15		
93¼	—	—	Whittlesea	d			07 27			09 28			11 26				13 26			15 26			17 26		
99¼	—	—	**Peterborough 8**	a			07 38			09 39			11 37				13 37			15 37			17 37		

		LE 1	LE 1	LE 1	LE 1	LE 1	LE 1	LE	LE
London Liverpool Street 15 ⊖	d								
Colchester	d								
Manningtree	d								
Harwich International	d								
Ipswich	d	17 19	17 49	18 16	19 10	20 00	20 19	21 16	22 16
Needham Market	d	17 28	17 58	18 25	19 19		20 28	21 26	22 26
Stowmarket	d	17 34	18 04	18 31	19 25	20 12	20 34	21 32	22 32
Elmswell	d	17 42	18 12	18 39	19 33		20 42	21 41	22 41
Thurston	d	17 48	18 18	18 45	19 39		20 48	21 47	22 47
Bury St Edmunds	a	17 54	18 24	18 51	19 45	20 28	20 54	21 54	22 54
Bury St Edmunds	d	17 56	18 25	18 56	19 56	20 29	20 56	21 55	
Kennett	d	18 06			20 06			22 06	
Newmarket	d	18 16		19 15	20 16		21 15	22 16	
Dullingham	d			19 20			21 20	22 22	
Cambridge	a	18 39		19 39	20 39		21 39	22 39	
Ely 4	a		18 52			21 00			
	d		19 00			21 00			
Manea	d								
March	d		19 16			21 17			
Whittlesea	d		19 28			21 28			
Peterborough 8	a		19 38			21 39			

Saturdays

		LE		LE ◇1	LE 1	LE 1	LE 1	LE 1	LE 1	LE 1		LE 1	LE 1	LE 1	LE 1	LE 1	LE 1	LE 1	LE 1	LE 1		LE 1	LE 1	LE 1	LE 1
London Liverpool Street 15 ⊖	d																								
Colchester	d			05 40																					
Manningtree	d			05 49																					
Harwich International	d							07 50																	
Ipswich	d	05 10		06 00	06 16	07 19	08 00	08 19	09 19	10 00		10 19	11 19	12 00	12 19	13 19	14 00	14 19	15 19	16 00		16 19	17 19	18 00	18 19
Needham Market	d	05 20			06 25	07 28		08 28	09 28			10 28	11 28		12 28	13 28		14 28	15 28			16 28	17 28		18 28
Stowmarket	d	05 26		06 12	06 31	07 34	08 12	08 34	09 34	10 12		10 34	11 34	12 12	12 34	13 34	14 12	14 34	15 34	16 12		16 34	17 34	18 12	18 34
Elmswell	d	05 35			06 39	07 42		08 42	09 42			10 42	11 42		12 42	13 42		14 42	15 42			16 42	17 42		18 42
Thurston	d	05 41			06 45	07 48		08 48	09 48			10 48	11 48		12 48	13 48		14 48	15 48			16 48	17 48		18 48
Bury St Edmunds	a	05 48		06 28	06 51	07 54	08 28	08 54	09 54	10 28		10 54	11 54	12 28	12 54	13 54	14 28	14 54	15 54	16 28		16 54	17 54	18 28	18 54
Bury St Edmunds	d	05 49		06 29	06 53	07 56	08 29	08 56	09 56	10 29		10 56	11 56	12 29	12 56	13 56	14 29	14 56	15 56	16 29		16 56	17 56	18 29	18 56
Kennett	d	06 00			07 03	08 06			10 06				12 06			14 06			16 06			17 06	18 06		
Newmarket	d	06 09			07 13	08 16		09 15	10 16			11 15	12 16		13 15	14 16		15 15	16 16			17 16	18 16		19 15
Dullingham	d	06 14			07 18	08 21		09 20				11 20			13 20			15 20							19 20
Cambridge	a	06 36			07 39	08 39		09 39	10 39			11 39	12 39		13 39	14 39		15 39	16 39			17 39	18 39		19 39
Ely 4	a			06 59			08 58			10 58				12 58			14 58			16 58				18 58	
	d			07 00			08 58			10 58				12 58			14 58			16 58				19 00	
Manea	d																								
March	d			07 16			09 15			11 15				13 15			15 15			17 15				19 16	
Whittlesea	d			07 27			09 26			11 26				13 26			15 26			17 26				19 28	
Peterborough 8	a			07 38			09 38			11 37				13 37			15 37			17 37				19 38	

Table 14

Saturdays

Ipswich - Bury St. Edmunds, Cambridge, Ely and Peterborough

Network Diagram - see first Page of Table 13

		LE [1]	LE [1]	LE [1]	LE	LE
London Liverpool Street [15] ⊖	d					
Colchester	d					
Manningtree	d					
Harwich International	d					
Ipswich	d	19 19	20 00	20 19	21 16	22 16
Needham Market	d	19 28		20 28	21 26	22 26
Stowmarket	d	19 34	20 12	20 34	21 32	22 32
Elmswell	d	19 42		20 42	21 41	22 41
Thurston	d	19 48		20 48	21 47	22 47
Bury St Edmunds	a	19 54	20 28	20 54	21 54	22 54
Bury St Edmunds	d	19 56	20 29	20 56	21 55	
Kennett	d	20 06			22 06	
Newmarket	d	20 16		21 15	22 16	
Dullingham	d			21 20	22 22	
Cambridge	a	20 39		21 39	22 39	
Ely [4]	a		20 58			
	d		20 59			
Manea	d					
March	d		21 15			
Whittlesea	d		21 27			
Peterborough [8]	a		21 37			

Sundays

		LE	LE [1]	LE ◇[1]	LE [1]	LE [1]	LE [1]	LE [1]	LE [1]	LE [1]	LE [1]	LE [1]	LE [1]	LE
London Liverpool Street [15] ⊖	d													
Colchester	d			09 32										
Manningtree	d			09 40										
Harwich International	d		08 30											
Ipswich	d	08 45	09b02	09 55	11 02	11 55	13 02	13 55	15 02	15 55	17 02	17 55	19 02	21 02
Needham Market	d		09 12		11 12		13 12		15 12		17 12		19 12	21 12
Stowmarket	d	08 59	09 18	10 07	11 18	12 07	13 18	14 07	15 18	16 07	17 18	18 07	19 18	21 18
Elmswell	d		09 27		11 27		13 27		15 27		17 27		19 27	21 27
Thurston	d		09 33		11 33		13 33		15 33		17 33		19 33	21 33
Bury St Edmunds	a	09 17	09 40	10 23	11 40	12 23	13 40	14 23	15 40	16 23	17 40	18 23	19 40	21 40
Bury St Edmunds	d		09 41	10 24	11 41	12 24	13 41	14 24	15 41	16 24	17 41	18 24	19 41	21 41
Kennett	d		09 52		11 52		13 52		15 52		17 52		19 52	21 52
Newmarket	d		10 01		12 01		14 01		16 01		18 01		20 01	22 01
Dullingham	d		10 06		12 06		14 06		16 06		18 06		20 06	22 06
Cambridge	a		10 24		12 24		14 25		16 25		18 25		20 24	22 24
Ely [4]	a			10 51		12 51		14 51		16 51		18 51		
	d			10 52		12 52		14 52		16 52		18 52		
Manea	d													
March	d			11 09		13 09		15 09		17 09		19 09		
Whittlesea	d			11 20		13 20		15 20		17 20		19 20		
Peterborough [8]	a			11 36		13 31		15 31		17 31		19 32		

b Arr. 0853

Peterborough, Ely, Cambridge and Bury St. Edmunds - Ipswich

Network Diagram - see first Page of Table 13

Miles	Miles	Miles			LE	LE	LE	LE	LE	LE	LE	LE	LE	LE	LE	LE	LE	LE	LE	LE	LE
					MX	MO	◇1	1	1	1		1	1	1		R 1 B ☕	1	1	R 1 ☕	1	1
0	—	—	**Peterborough 8**	d																07 45	
6	—	—	Whittlesea	d																07 53	
14	—	—	March	d																08 04	
19¼	—	—	Manea	d																	
29¼	0	—	**Ely 4**	a																08 31	
—	—	—		d																08 31	
45	—	—	**Cambridge**	d	22p43	23p00									06 41		07 43				
56	—	—	Dullingham	d	22p59	23p16											07 59				
58¼	—	—	Newmarket	d	23p05	23p22									07 01		08 04				
63¼	14¾	—	Kennett	d	23p13	23p30									07 09						
—	—	—	**Bury St Edmunds**	a	23p25	23p42									07 22		08 22			08 57	
73¼	—	—	**Bury St Edmunds**	d	23p26	23p43		05 33			06 23				07 23		08 23			08 58	
77¼	—	—	Thurston	d	23p32	23p49		05 39			06 29				07 29		08 29				
81¼	—	—	Elmswell	d	23p38	23p55		05 45			06 36				07 36		08 35				
87¼	—	—	Stowmarket	d	23p47	00 06		05 54			06 44				07 45		08 44			09 14	
90¾	—	—	Needham Market	d	23p52	00 11		05 59			06 49				07 50		08 49				
99¼	—	0	**Ipswich**	a	00 05	00 23		06 09			07 01				08 03	08 18	09 00		09 08	09 28	
—	—	—		d			05 14		06 00	06 29		06 52	06 59	07 38		08 20		08 48	09 09		09 30
—	—	18	Harwich International	a									07 28								
—	—	—	Manningtree	a			05 24		06 10	06 39		07 02		07 48				08 58	09 19		09 40
—	—	—	Colchester	a			05 34		06 19	06 48		07 12		07 58				09 08	09 28		09 49
—	—	—	London Liverpool Street 15 ⊖	a			06 34		07 24	07 50		08 13		09 01		09 24		10 14	10 19		10 44

		LE	LE	LE	LE	LE	LE	LE	LE	LE	LE	LE	LE	LE	LE	LE	LE	LE	LE	LE
		1	1	◇1 ☕	1	1	◇1 ☕	1	1	1	◇1 ☕	◇1 ☕	1	1	◇1 ☕	1	◇1 ☕	1	1	◇1 ☕
Peterborough 8	d							09 45								11 45				
Whittlesea	d							09 53								11 53				
March	d							10 04								12 04				
Manea	d																			
Ely 4	a							10 25								12 29				
	d							10 32								12 31				
Cambridge	d	08 43			09 43				10 43				11 43					12 43		
Dullingham	d				09 59								11 59							
Newmarket	d	09 03			10 04				11 03				12 04					13 03		
Kennett	d	09 11							11 11									13 11		
Bury St Edmunds	a	09 23			10 22			10 58	11 23				12 22			12 57		13 23		
Bury St Edmunds	d	09 23			10 23			10 58	11 23				12 23			12 57		13 23		
Thurston	d	09 29			10 29				11 29				12 29					13 29		
Elmswell	d	09 35			10 35				11 35				12 35					13 35		
Stowmarket	d	09 44			10 44			11 14	11 44			12 29	12 44			13 13	13 29	13 44		
Needham Market	d	09 49			10 49				11 49				12 49					13 49		
Ipswich	a	10 02		10 08	11 00		11 08	11 28	12 00		12 08	12 41	13 00		13 08	13 28	13 41	14 00		14 08
	d		09 52	10 09		10 52	11 09			11 52	12 09	12 43		12 52	13 09		13 43		13 52	14 09
Harwich International	a																			
Manningtree	a		10 02	10 19		11 02	11 19			12 02	12 19	12 52		13 02	13 19		13 52		14 02	14 19
Colchester	a		10 11	10 28		11 11	11 28			12 11	12 28	13 02		13 11	13 28		14 02		14 11	14 28
London Liverpool Street 15 ⊖	a		11 14	11 19		12 14	12 19			13 14	13 19	13 55		14 14	14 19		14 55		15 15	15 19

		LE	LE	LE	LE	LE	LE	LE	LE	LE	LE	LE	LE
		◇1 ☕	1	1	◇1 ☕	1	◇1 ☕	1	1	◇1 ☕	◇1 ☕	1	1
Peterborough 8	d					13 45							
Whittlesea	d					13 53							
March	d					14 04							
Manea	d												
Ely 4	a					14 29							
	d					14 31							
Cambridge	d		13 43					14 43				15 43	
Dullingham	d		13 59									15 59	
Newmarket	d		14 04					15 03				16 04	
Kennett	d							15 11					
Bury St Edmunds	a		14 22			14 57		15 23				16 22	
Bury St Edmunds	d		14 23			14 57		15 23				16 23	
Thurston	d		14 29					15 29				16 29	
Elmswell	d		14 35					15 35				16 35	
Stowmarket	d	14 29	14 44			15 13	15 29	15 44			16 29	16 44	
Needham Market	d		14 49					15 49				16 49	
Ipswich	a	14 41	15 00		15 08	15 28	15 41	16 00		16 08	16 41	17 00	
	d	14 43		14 52	15 09		15 43		15 52	16 09	16 43		16 52
Harwich International	a												
Manningtree	a	14 52		15 02	15 19		15 52		16 02	16 19	16 52		17 02
Colchester	a	15 02		15 11	15 28		16 02		16 11	16 28	17 02		17 11
London Liverpool Street 15 ⊖	a	15 55		16 14	16 17		16 55		17 16	17 19	17 58		18 15

B The East Anglian

Table 14

Mondays to Fridays

Peterborough, Ely, Cambridge and Bury St. Edmunds - Ipswich

Network Diagram - see first Page of Table 13

			LE ◇1 ⊡	LE 1	LE 1	LE ◇1 ⊡	LE 1	LE ◇1 ⊡	LE 1	LE ◇1 ⊡	LE 1		LE 1	LE ◇1 ⊡	LE 1	LE 1	LE 1	LE ◇1 ⊡	LE 1	LE 1	LE ◇1		LE 1	LE ◇1 ⊡	LE 1
Peterborough 8	d			15 45											17 45										
Whittlesea	d			15 53											17 53										
March	d			16 04											18 04										
Manea	d																								
Ely 4	a			16 28											18 28										
	d			16 31											18 31										
Cambridge	d						16 43				17 43								18 43						19 43
Dullingham	d						16 59				17 59														19 59
Newmarket	d						17 04				18 04								19 03						20 04
Kennett	d						17 12				18 12								19 11						
Bury St Edmunds	a			16 57			17 24				18 24				18 57				19 23						20 22
Bury St Edmunds	d			16 57			17 25				18 25				18 57				19 23						20 23
Thurston	d						17 31				18 31								19 29						20 29
Elmswell	d						17 37				18 37								19 35						20 35
Stowmarket	d			17 13		17 29	17 45	17 59		18 29	18 45				19 13			19 29	19 44					20 29	20 44
Needham Market	d						17 50				18 50								19 49						20 49
Ipswich	a		17 08	17 28		17 41	18 04	18 11		18 41	19 02			19 08	19 28			19 41	20 00		20 09			20 41	21 00
	d		17 09		17 33	17 43		18 13	18 22	18 43			18 47	19 09		19 23	19 35	19 43		19 52	20 09		20 20	20 43	21 00
Harwich International	a																								21 29
Manningtree	a		17 19		17 42	17 52			18 32	18 52			18 57	19 19		19 36	19 44	19 52		20 02	20 19		20 33	20 52	
Colchester	a		17 28		17 52	18 02		18 28	18 42	19 02			19 06	19 28		19 46	19 54	20 02		20 11	20 29		20 45	21 02	
London Liverpool Street 15 ⊖	a		18 19			18 55		19 17	19 45	19 55			20 14	20 19			21 01	20 55		21 16	21 19			21 55	

		LE ◇1	LE ◇1	LE ◇1 ThFO ⊡	LE ◇1 MTWO ⊡	LE 1	LE 1 ThFO		LE 1 MTWO	LE ◇1 ThFO	LE ◇1 MTWO	LE 1	LE ◇1	LE
Peterborough 8	d		19 45										21 45	
Whittlesea	d		19 53										21 53	
March	d		20 04										22 04	
Manea	d													
Ely 4	a		20 26										22 23	
	d		20 27										22 23	
Cambridge	d					20 43						21 43		22 43
Dullingham	d											21 59		22 59
Newmarket	d					21 03						22 04		23 05
Kennett	d					21 11								23 13
Bury St Edmunds	a		20 53			21 23						22 22	22 49	23 25
Bury St Edmunds	d		20 53			21 23						22 23	22 50	23 26
Thurston	d					21 29						22 29		23 32
Elmswell	d					21 35						22 35		23 38
Stowmarket	d		21 09	21 29	21 29	21 44				22 29	22 29	22 44	23 06	23 47
Needham Market	d					21 49						22 49		23 52
Ipswich	a	21 08	21 23	21 41	21 41	22 00				22 41	22 41	23 00	23 18	00 05
	d	21 09	21 25	21 43	21 43		22 23		22 23	22 43	22 43		23 19	
Harwich International	a													
Manningtree	a	21 19	21 35	21 52	21 52		22 33		22 33	22 52	22 52		23 29	
Colchester	a	21 28	21 46	22 02	22 02		22 42		22 42	23 02	23 02		23 40	
London Liverpool Street 15 ⊖	a	22 19		22 55	23 00		23 45		23 50	00 02	00 14			

Saturdays

		LE ◇1	LE	LE ◇1 ⊡	LE ◇1 ⊡	LE ◇1 ⊡	LE	LE 1	LE 1	LE ◇1 ⊡		LE ◇1 ⊡	LE	LE 1	LE ◇1 ⊡	LE ◇1 ⊡	LE 1	LE 1	LE ◇1 ⊡	LE 1		LE ◇1 ⊡	LE 1	LE 1	LE ◇1 ⊡
Peterborough 8	d																			07 45					
Whittlesea	d																			07 53					
March	d																			08 04					
Manea	d																								
Ely 4	a																			08 22					
	d																			08 31					
Cambridge	d		22p43										06 41				07 43						08 43		
Dullingham	d		22p59														07 59								
Newmarket	d		23p05										07 01				08 04						09 03		
Kennett	d		23p13										07 09										09 11		
Bury St Edmunds	a		23p25										07 22				08 22			08 57			09 23		
Bury St Edmunds	d		23p26				06 23						07 23				08 23			08 57			09 23		
Thurston	d		23p32				06 29						07 29				08 29						09 29		
Elmswell	d		23p38				06 36						07 36				08 35						09 35		
Stowmarket	d	22p29	23p47	05 29		06 29	06 44					07 29	07 45			08 29	08 44			09 13		09 29	09 44		
Needham Market	d		23p52				06 49						07 50				08 49						09 49		
Ipswich	a	22p41	00 05	05 41	06 08	06 41	07 02			07 08		07 41	08 03		08 08	08 41	09 00		09 08	09 28		09 41	10 00		10 08
	d	22p43		05 43	06 09	06 43		06 52	06 59	07 09		07 43		07 52	08 09	08 43		08 52	09 09			09 43		09 52	10 09
Harwich International	a								07 28																
Manningtree	a	22p52		05 52	06 19	06 52		07 02		07 19		07 52		08 02	08 19	08 52		09 02	09 19			09 52		10 02	10 19
Colchester	a	23p02		06 02	06 28	07 02		07 11		07 28		08 02		08 11	08 28	09 02		09 11	09 28			10 02		10 11	10 28
London Liverpool Street 15 ⊖	a	00 02		06 55	07 19	07 55		08 14		08 19		08 55		09 14	09 19	09 55		10 14	10 19			10 55		11 14	11 19

Table 14

Saturdays

Peterborough, Ely, Cambridge and Bury St. Edmunds - Ipswich

Network Diagram - see first Page of Table 13

		LE	LE	LE	LE	LE		LE	LE	LE	LE	LE	LE	LE	LE	LE		LE	LE	LE	LE	LE	LE	LE	LE
		◇1	1	1	◇1	1		◇1	1	1	◇1	◇1	1	1	◇1	1		◇1	1	1	◇1	◇1	1	1	◇1
		☕			☕			☕			☕	☕			☕			☕			☕	☕			☕
Peterborough 8	d					09 47										11 45									
Whittlesea	d					09 55										11 53									
March	d					10 06										12 04									
Manea	d																								
Ely 4	a					10 29										12 28									
	d					10 31										12 31									
Cambridge	d		09 43						10 43				11 43						12 43				13 43		
Dullingham	d		09 59										11 59										13 59		
Newmarket	d		10 04						11 03				12 04						13 03				14 04		
Kennett	d								11 11										13 11						
Bury St Edmunds	a		10 22			10 57			11 23				12 22			12 57			13 23				14 22		
Bury St Edmunds	d		10 23			10 57			11 23				12 23			12 57			13 23				14 23		
Thurston	d		10 29						11 29				12 29						13 29				14 29		
Elmswell	d		10 35						11 35				12 35						13 35				14 35		
Stowmarket	d	10 29	10 44			11 13		11 29	11 44			12 29	12 44			13 13		13 29	13 44			14 29	14 44		
Needham Market	d		10 49						11 49				12 49						13 49				14 49		
Ipswich	a	10 41	11 00		11 08	11 28		11 41	12 00		12 08	12 41	13 00		13 08	13 28		13 41	14 00		14 08	14 41	15 00		15 08
	d	10 43		10 52	11 09			11 43		11 52	12 09	12 43		12 52	13 09			13 43		13 52	14 09	14 43		14 52	15 09
Harwich International	a																								
Manningtree	a	10 52		11 02	11 19			11 52		12 02	12 19	12 52		13 02	13 19			13 52		14 02	14 19	14 52		15 02	15 19
Colchester	a	11 02		11 11	11 28			12 02		12 11	12 28	13 02		13 11	13 28			14 02		14 11	14 28	15 02		15 11	15 28
London Liverpool Street 15 ⊖	a	11 55		12 14	12 19			12 55		13 14	13 19	13 55		14 14	14 19			14 55		15 14	15 19	15 55		16 14	16 19

		LE		LE	LE	LE	LE	LE	LE	LE	LE	LE		LE	LE	LE	LE	LE	LE	LE	LE	LE		LE	LE
		1		◇1	1	1	◇1	◇1	1	1	◇1	1		◇1	1	1	◇1	◇1	1	1	◇1	1		◇1	1
				☕			☕	☕			☕			☕			☕	☕			☕			☕	
Peterborough 8	d	13 45										15 45										17 45			
Whittlesea	d	13 53										15 53										17 53			
March	d	14 04										16 04										18 04			
Manea	d																								
Ely 4	a	14 28										16 28										18 28			
	d	14 31										16 31										18 31			
Cambridge	d				14 43				15 43						16 43				17 43						18 43
Dullingham	d								15 59						16 59				17 59						
Newmarket	d				15 03				16 04						17 04				18 04						19 03
Kennett	d				15 11										17 12				18 12						19 11
Bury St Edmunds	a	14 57			15 23				16 22			16 57			17 24				18 24			18 57			19 23
Bury St Edmunds	d	14 57			15 23				16 23			16 57			17 25				18 25			18 57			19 23
Thurston	d				15 29				16 29						17 31				18 31						19 29
Elmswell	d				15 35				16 35						17 37				18 37						19 35
Stowmarket	d	15 13		15 29	15 44			16 29	16 44			17 13		17 29	17 45		17 59	18 29	18 45			19 13		19 29	19 44
Needham Market	d				15 49				16 49						17 50				18 50						19 49
Ipswich	a	15 28		15 41	16 00		16 08	16 41	17 00		17 08	17 28		17 41	18 01		18 11	18 41	19 01		19 08	19 28		19 41	20 00
	d			15 43		15 52	16 09	16 43		16 52	17 09			17 43		17 52	18 13	18 43		18 52	19 09			19 43	
Harwich International	a																								
Manningtree	a			15 52		16 02	16 19	16 52		17 02	17 19			17 52		18 02		18 52		19 02	19 19			19 52	
Colchester	a			16 02		16 11	16 28	17 02		17 11	17 28			18 02		18 11	18 28	19 02		19 11	19 28			20 02	
London Liverpool Street 15 ⊖	a			16 55		17 14	17 19	17 55		18 14	18 19			18 55		19 14	19 19	19 55		20 14	20 19			20 55	

		LE	LE	LE	LE	LE	LE	LE		LE	LE	LE	LE	LE	LE	LE	LE								
		1	1	◇1	1	1	◇1	◇1		1	1	1	◇1	1	1	◇1									
				☕				☕																	
Peterborough 8	d						19 45									21 45									
Whittlesea	d						19 53									21 53									
March	d						20 04									22 04									
Manea	d																								
Ely 4	a						20 26									22 23									
	d						20 27									22 23									
Cambridge	d				19 43					20 43				21 43			22 43								
Dullingham	d				19 59									21 59			22 59								
Newmarket	d				20 04					21 03				22 04			23 05								
Kennett	d									21 11							23 13								
Bury St Edmunds	a				20 22		20 53			21 23				22 22		22 49	23 25								
Bury St Edmunds	d				20 23		20 53			21 23				22 23		22 50	23 26								
Thurston	d				20 29					21 29				22 29			23 32								
Elmswell	d				20 35					21 35				22 35			23 38								
Stowmarket	d			20 29	20 44		21 09	21 29		21 44			22 29	22 44		23 06	23 47								
Needham Market	d				20 49					21 49				22 49			23 52								
Ipswich	a			20 41	21 00		21 22	21 41		22 00			22 41	23 00		23 18	00 05								
	d	19 52	20 09	20 43	21 00	21 09	21 25	21 43			21 52	22 23	22 43		23 15	23 19									
Harwich International	a				21 29																				
Manningtree	a	20 02	20 19	20 52		21 19	21 35	21 52			22 02	22 33	22 52		23 25	23 29									
Colchester	a	20 11	20 29	21 02		21 28	21 46	22 02			22 11	22 42	23 02		23 35	23 40									
London Liverpool Street 15 ⊖	a	21 14	21 17	21 55		22 17		22 55			23 14	23 45	00 02												

Table 14

Sundays

Peterborough, Ely, Cambridge and Bury St. Edmunds - Ipswich

Network Diagram - see first Page of Table 13

		LE	LE	LE	LE	LE	LE	LE	LE	LE		LE	LE	LE	LE	LE	LE	LE	LE	LE		LE	LE	LE	LE
		◇1		◇1	1	1	◇1	1	◇1			1	◇1	1	◇1	1	1	◇1	1	1		◇1	1	1	◇1
		A	A																						
				☕			☕		☕				☕		☕			☕				☕			☕
Peterborough 8	d																		11 46						
Whittlesea	d																		11 54						
March	d																		12 05						
Manea	d																								
Ely 4	a																		12 29						
	d																		12 31						
Cambridge	d		22p43													11 12							13 12		
Dullingham	d		22p59													11 28							13 28		
Newmarket	d		23p05													11 34							13 34		
Kennett	d		23p13													11 42							13 42		
Bury St Edmunds	a		23p25													11 54			12 57				13 54		
Bury St Edmunds	d		23p26							09 55						11 55			12 57				13 55		
Thurston	d		23p32							10 01						12 01							14 01		
Elmswell	d		23p38							10 07						12 07							14 07		
Stowmarket	d	22p29	23p47	07 29			08 29		09 29	10 18			10 29		11 29	12 18		12 29	13 13			13 29	14 18		14 29
Needham Market	d	⌇	23p52							10 23						12 23							14 23		
Ipswich	a	22p41	00⌇05	07 41			08 41		09 41	10 35			10 41		11 41	12 35		12 41	13 28			13 41	14 35		14 41
	d	22p43		07 43	07 46	08 09	08 43	09 09	09 43			10 09	10 43	11 09	11 43		12 09	12 43		13 09		13 43		14 09	14 43
Harwich International	a	⌇			08 14																				
Manningtree	a	22p52		07 52		08 19	08 52	09 19	09 52			10 19	10 52	11 19	11 52		12 19	12 52		13 19		13 52		14 19	14 52
Colchester	a	23p02		08 02		08 29	09 02	09 29	10 02			10 29	11 02	11 29	12 02		12 29	13 02		13 29		14 02		14 29	15 02
London Liverpool Street 15 ⊖	a	00⌇02		09 03		09 42	10 01	10 42	11 01			11 42	12 01	12 42	13 01		13 42	14 01		14 42		15 01		15 42	16 01

		LE	LE	LE	LE			LE	LE	LE	LE	LE	LE	LE		LE		LE	LE	LE	LE	LE		LE	LE
									R																
		1	1	◇1	1			1	1	◇1	1	1	◇1	1		1		◇1	1	◇1	◇1	1		1	◇1
				☕					☕	☕			☕					☕			☕				☕
Peterborough 8	d	13 46									15 45									17 45					
Whittlesea	d	13 55									15 53									17 53					
March	d	14 06									16 04									18 04					
Manea	d																								
Ely 4	a	14 29									16 23									18 23					
	d	14 31									16 31									18 31					
Cambridge	d				15 12									17 12								19 12			
Dullingham	d				15 28									17 28								19 28			
Newmarket	d				15 34									17 34								19 34			
Kennett	d				15 42									17 42								19 42			
Bury St Edmunds	a	14 57			15 54						16 57			17 54						18 57		19 54			
Bury St Edmunds	d	14 57			15 55						16 57			17 55						18 57		19 55			
Thurston	d				16 01									18 01								20 01			
Elmswell	d				16 07									18 07								20 07			
Stowmarket	d	15 13		15 29	16 18				16 29	16 49	17 13		17 29	18 18				18 29		19 13	19 29	20 18			20 29
Needham Market	d				16 23									18 23								20 23			
Ipswich	a	15 28		15 41	16 35				16 41	17 01	17 28		17 41	18 35				18 41		19 28	19 41	20 35			20 41
	d		15 09	15 43				16 09	16 43	17 03		17 09	17 43			18 09		18 43	19 09	19 28	19 43	20 35		20 09	20 43
Harwich International	a																					21 04			
Manningtree	a		15 19	15 52				16 19	16 52			17 19	17 52			18 19		18 52	19 19	19 38	19 52			20 19	20 52
Colchester	a		15 29	16 02				16 29	17 02	17 18		17 29	18 02			18 29		19 02	19 29	19 49	20 02			20 29	21 02
London Liverpool Street 15 ⊖	a		16 42	17 01				17 42	18 01	18 28		18 42	19 01			19 42		20 01	20 42		21 01			21 42	22 01

		LE		LE	LE	LE			LE	LE	LE
		1		◇1	◇1	1			1	◇1	
Peterborough 8	d			19 45							
Whittlesea	d			19 53							
March	d			20 04							
Manea	d										
Ely 4	a			20 23							
	d			20 23							
Cambridge	d					21 12					23 00
Dullingham	d					21 28					23 16
Newmarket	d					21 34					23 22
Kennett	d					21 42					23 30
Bury St Edmunds	a			20 49		21 54					23 42
Bury St Edmunds	d			20 50		21 55					23 43
Thurston	d					22 01					23 49
Elmswell	d					22 07					23 55
Stowmarket	d			21 06	21 29	22 18				22 29	00 06
Needham Market	d					22 23					00 11
Ipswich	a			21 18	21 41	22 35				22 41	00 23
	d	21 09		21 19	21 43				22 09	22 43	
Harwich International	a										
Manningtree	a	21 19		21 29	21 52				22 19	22 52	
Colchester	a	21 29		21 40	22 02				22 29	23 02	
London Liverpool Street 15 ⊖	a	22 42			23 01				23 42	00 08	

A not 11 December

Norwich - Great Yarmouth and Lowestoft

Network Diagram - see first Page of Table 13

Miles	Miles	Miles			LE	LE	LE	LE	LE	LE [1]	LE	LE	LE		LE	LE	LE	LE	LE	LE	LE	LE	LE		LE
—	—	—	London Liverpool Street [15] ⊖	d																					
0	0	0	**Norwich**	d	05 10	05 40	06 15	06 30	06 50	07 00	07 36		08 00		08 09	08 36	09 06	09 36	10 06	10 36	11 06	11 36	12 06		12 36
4¾	4¾	4¾	Brundall Gardens	d		05 47	06 22		06 57				08 07			08 43		09 43		10 43		11 43			12 43
5¾	5¾	5¾	Brundall	d	05 19	05 50	06 25	06 39	07 00	07 09	07 45		08 10			08 46		09 46	10 15	10 46		11 46	12 15		12 46
8	—	—	Lingwood	d			06 30		07 05						08 21	08 51		09 51		10 51					12 51
10½	—	—	Acle	d			06 38		07 13						08 28	08 58		09 56		10 56					12 56
—	7¾	7¾	Buckenham	d																					
—	10	10	Cantley	d		05 56				07 15	07 51		08 16						10 21			11 52	12 21		
—	12¼	12¼	Reedham (Norfolk)	d		06 00		06 47		07 19	07 55		08 21						10 25			11 57	12 25		
—	16	—	Berney Arms	d							08x01											12x03			
18¼	20½	—	**Great Yarmouth**	a	05 40		06 51		07 26		08 12				08 41	09 11		10 09		11 09		12 13			13 09
—	—	16¼	Haddiscoe	d		06 09				07 28			08 29						10 34				12 34		
—	—	18	Somerleyton	d		06 13				07 32			08 33						10 38				12 38		
—	—	22	Oulton Broad North	d		06 19		07 02		07 38			08 40				09 36		10 44		11 36		12 44		
—	—	23½	**Lowestoft**	a		06 26		07 09		07 45		08 35	08 46				09 43		10 51		11 43		12 51		

		LE	LE	LE	LE	LE	LE	LE	LE [1]		LE	LE	LE	LE	LE [1]	LE	LE	LE	LE		LE	LE	LE	LE	LE
London Liverpool Street [15] ⊖	d																								
Norwich	d	13 06	13 36	14 06	14 36	15 06	15 36	15 50	16 40		16 58	17 06	17 36	17 50	18 06	18 40	18 58	19 33	20 06		20 40	21 06	21 40	22 06	22 40
Brundall Gardens	d		13 43		14 43		15 43		16 47			17 13	17 43		18 13	18 47		19 40			20 47		21 47		
Brundall	d		13 46	14 15	14 46		15 46	15 59	16 50		17 07	17 16	17 46	17 59	18 16	18 50	19 07	19 43	20 15		20 50	21 15	21 50	22 15	22 49
Lingwood	d		13 51		14 51		15 51		16 55			17 21	17 51		18 21	18 55		19 48			20 55		21 55		
Acle	d		13 56		14 56		15 56		17 00			17 28	17 56		18 28	19 00		19 53			21 00		22 00		
Buckenham	d																								
Cantley	d			14 21		15 18		16 05			17 13			18 05			19 13		20 21			21 21		22 21	22 55
Reedham (Norfolk)	d			14 25		15 23		16 09			17 17			18 09			19 17		20 25			21 25		22 25	22 59
Berney Arms	d																								
Great Yarmouth	a		14 09		15 09		16 09		17 13			17 41	18 09		18 41	19 13		20 06			21 13		22 13		
Haddiscoe	d			14 34				16 18			17 26			18 18			19 26		20 34					22 34	23 08
Somerleyton	d			14 38				16 22			17 30			18 22			19 30		20 38					22 38	23 12
Oulton Broad North	d	13 36		14 44		15 38		16 28			17 36			18 28			19 36		20 44			21 40		22 44	23 18
Lowestoft	a	13 43		14 51		15 44		16 35			17 43			18 35			19 43		20 51			21 47		22 51	23 25

		LE
London Liverpool Street [15] ⊖	d	
Norwich	d	23 00
Brundall Gardens	d	
Brundall	d	23 09
Lingwood	d	23 14
Acle	d	23 18
Buckenham	d	
Cantley	d	
Reedham (Norfolk)	d	
Berney Arms	d	
Great Yarmouth	a	23 31
Haddiscoe	d	
Somerleyton	d	
Oulton Broad North	d	
Lowestoft	a	

Saturdays

		LE	LE	LE	LE	LE	LE	LE [1]	LE	LE		LE	LE	LE	LE	LE	LE	LE	LE	LE		LE	LE	LE	LE
London Liverpool Street [15] ⊖	d																								
Norwich	d	05 30	05 40	06 36	06 50	07 06	07 36	07 50	08 09	08 36		09 06	09 36	10 06	10 36	11 06	11 36	12 06	12 36	13 06		13 36	14 06	14 36	15 06
Brundall Gardens	d		05 47	06 43		07 13		07 57		08 43			09 43		10 43		11 43		12 43			13 43		14 43	
Brundall	d	05 39	05 50	06 46	06 59	07 16	07 45	08 00		08 46			09 46	10 15	10 46		11 46	12 15	12 46			13 46	14 15	14 46	
Lingwood	d			06 51		07 21			08 21	08 51			09 51		10 51				12 51			13 51		14 51	
Acle	d			06 56		07 28			08 28	08 58			09 56		10 56				12 56			13 56		14 56	
Buckenham	d													10x19											
Cantley	d		05 56		07 05		07 51	08 06						10 23			11 52	12 21					14 21		15 18
Reedham (Norfolk)	d	05 47	06 01		07 09		07 55	08 11						10 27			11 57	12 25					14 26		15 23
Berney Arms	d						08x01										12x03								
Great Yarmouth	a	06 02		07 09		07 41	08 12		08 41	09 11			10 09		11 09		12 13		13 09			14 09		15 09	
Haddiscoe	d		06 09		07 18			08 19						10 36				12 34					14 34		
Somerleyton	d		06 13		07 22			08 23						10 40				12 38					14 38		
Oulton Broad North	d		06 20		07 28			08 30				09 36		10 46		11 36		12 44		13 36			14 45		15 38
Lowestoft	a		06 26		07 35			08 36				09 43		10 53		11 43		12 51		13 43			14 51		15 44

		LE	LE	LE	LE	LE		LE	LE	LE	LE	LE	LE	LE	LE	LE		LE	LE	LE	LE
London Liverpool Street [15] ⊖	d																				
Norwich	d	15 36	15 50	16 40	16 58	17 06		17 36	17 50	18 06	18 40	18 58	19 33	20 06	20 40	21 06		21 40	22 06	22 40	23 00
Brundall Gardens	d	15 43		16 47		17 13		17 43		18 13	18 47		19 40		20 47			21 47			
Brundall	d	15 46	15 59	16 50	17 07	17 16		17 46	17 59	18 16	18 50	19 07	19 43	20 15	20 50	21 15		21 50	22 15	22 49	23 09
Lingwood	d	15 51		16 55		17 21		17 51		18 21	18 55		19 48		20 55			21 55			23 14
Acle	d	15 56		17 00		17 28		17 56		18 28	19 00		19 53		21 00			22 00			23 18
Buckenham	d																				
Cantley	d		16 05		17 13				18 05			19 13		20 21		21 21			22 21	22 55	
Reedham (Norfolk)	d		16 09		17 17				18 09			19 17		20 25		21 25			22 25	22 59	
Berney Arms	d																				
Great Yarmouth	a	16 09		17 13		17 41		18 09		18 41	19 13		20 06		21 13			22 13			23 31
Haddiscoe	d		16 18		17 26				18 18			19 26		20 34					22 34	23 08	
Somerleyton	d		16 22		17 30				18 22			19 30		20 38					22 38	23 12	
Oulton Broad North	d		16 28		17 36				18 28			19 36		20 44		21 40			22 44	23 18	
Lowestoft	a		16 35		17 43				18 35			19 43		20 51		21 47			22 51	23 25	

Table 15

Sundays

Norwich - Great Yarmouth and Lowestoft

Network Diagram - see first Page of Table 13

		LE 1	LE	LE	LE	LE	LE	LE	LE	LE	LE 1	LE
London Liverpool Street 15 ⊖	d											
Norwich	d	07 25	07 36	08 45	08 57	09 36	10 45	10 57	11 36	12 45	12 57	13 36
Brundall Gardens	d			08 52			10 52			12 52		
Brundall	d		07 45	08 55	09 06	09 45	10 55	11 06	11 45	12 55	13 06	13 45
Lingwood	d			09 00			11 00			13 00		
Acle	d			09 05			11 05			13 05		
Buckenham	d					09x49			11x49			
Cantley	d		07 51		09 12	09 53		11 12	11 53		13 12	13 51
Reedham (Norfolk)	d		07 55		09 16	09 57		11 16	11 57		13 16	13 55
Berney Arms	d		08x01			10x03			12x03			14x01
Great Yarmouth	a		08 12	09 18		10 14	11 18		12 14	13 18		14 12
Haddiscoe	d				09 25			11 25			13 25	
Somerleyton	d				09 29			11 29			13 29	
Oulton Broad North	d	07 53			09 35			11 35			13 35	
Lowestoft	a	08 00			09 42			11 42			13 42	

		LE	LE 1	LE A	LE B	LE	LE A	LE B	LE	LE	LE 1	LE
London Liverpool Street 15 ⊖	d											
Norwich	d	14 45	14 57	15 36	15 36	16 45	16 57	16 57	17 36	18 45	18 57	19 36
Brundall Gardens	d	14 52				16 52				18 52		
Brundall	d	14 55	15 06	15 45	15 45	16 55	17 06	17 06	17 45	18 55	19 06	19 45
Lingwood	d	15 00				17 00				19 00		
Acle	d	15 05				17 05				19 05		
Buckenham	d			15x49	15x49			17x10				
Cantley	d		15 12	15 53	15 53		17 14	17 14	17 51		19 12	19 51
Reedham (Norfolk)	d		15 16	15 57	15 57		17 18	17 18	17 55		19 16	19 55
Berney Arms	d			16x03								
Great Yarmouth	a	15 18		16 14	16 14	17 18			18 10	19 18		20 10
Haddiscoe	d		15 25				17 27	17 27			19 25	
Somerleyton	d		15 29				17 31	17 31			19 29	
Oulton Broad North	d		15 35				17 37	17 37			19 35	
Lowestoft	a		15 42				17 44	17 44			19 42	

		LE	LE 1	LE	LE
London Liverpool Street 15 ⊖	d				
Norwich	d	20 45	20 57	21 36	22 36
Brundall Gardens	d	20 52			22 43
Brundall	d	20 55	21 06	21 45	22 46
Lingwood	d	21 00			22 51
Acle	d	21 05			22 56
Buckenham	d				
Cantley	d		21 12	21 51	
Reedham (Norfolk)	d		21 16	21 55	
Berney Arms	d				
Great Yarmouth	a	21 18		22 10	23 09
Haddiscoe	d		21 25		
Somerleyton	d		21 29		
Oulton Broad North	d		21 35		
Lowestoft	a		21 42		

A from 25 March

B until 18 March

Lowestoft and Great Yarmouth - Norwich

Network Diagram - see first Page of Table 13

Miles	Miles	Miles			LE MX	LE MX	LE MO 1	LE	LE 1	LE	LE	LE	LE		LE 1	LE 1	LE	LE	LE	LE	LE	LE	LE		LE
0	—	—	**Lowestoft**	d		23p30	23p35		05 42		06 35				07 35	07 55			08 50		09 50		11 00		
1½	—	—	Oulton Broad North	d		23p34	23p39		05 46		06 39				07 39	07 59			08 54		09 54		11 04		
5½	—	—	Somerleyton	d					05 52		06 45				07 45				09 00		10 00				
7¼	—	—	Haddiscoe	d					05 56		06 49				07 49				09 04		10 04				
—	0	0	**Great Yarmouth**	d	23p34			05 47		06 27		07 02	07 35				08 17	08 47		09 17		10 17			11 17
—	—	4½	Berney Arms	d																					
11¼	—	8¼	Reedham (Norfolk)	d	23p47	23p52	23p54		06 05		06 58				07 58	08 14			09 13		10 13				
13½	—	10½	Cantley	d		23p56			06 09		07 02				08 02	08 19			09 17		10 17				
15¾	—	12¾	Buckenham	d																					
—	8	—	Acle	d				05 58		06 38		07 13	07 46				08 28	08 58		09 28		10 28			11 28
—	10½	—	Lingwood	d				06 03		06 43		07 18	07 51				08 33	09 03		09 33		10 33			11 33
17¾	12¾	14¾	Brundall	d	23p55	00 03	00 03	06 07	06 16	06 47	07 09	07 22	07 55		08 09		08 37		09 24	09 37	10 24	10 37			11 37
18¾	13¾	15¾	Brundall Gardens	d				06 10		06 50		07 25	07 58				08 40			09 40		10 40			11 40
23½	18½	20½	**Norwich**	a	00 07	00 14	00 13	06 20	06 27	07 00	07 20	07 35	08 08		08 20	08 34	08 50	09 17	09 35	09 50	10 35	10 50	11 35		11 50
—	—	—	London Liverpool Street 15 ⊖	a																					

		LE	LE	LE	LE	LE	LE	LE	LE		LE	LE	LE	LE 1	LE A	LE B	LE	LE	LE		LE	LE	LE	LE	LE 1
Lowestoft	d	11 50		13 00		13 50		15 00			15 50		16 50				17 50				18 55		19 55		21 00
Oulton Broad North	d	11 54		13 04		13 54		15 04			15 54		16 54				17 54				18 59		19 59		21 04
Somerleyton	d	12 00				14 00					16 00		17 00				18 00				19 05		20 05		
Haddiscoe	d	12 04				14 04					16 04		17 04				18 04				19 09		20 09		
Great Yarmouth	d		12 17		13 17		14 17		15 13			16 17		17 17	17 47	17 47		18 17	18 47			19 17		20 17	
Berney Arms	d								15x20						17x54										
Reedham (Norfolk)	d	12 13				14 13			15 28		16 13		17 13		18 01	18 01	18 13		19 01		19 18		20 18		
Cantley	d	12 17				14 17			15 32		16 17		17 17		18 05	18 05	18 17		19 05		19 22		20 22		
Buckenham	d																								
Acle	d		12 28		13 28		14 28					16 28		17 28				18 28				19 28		20 28	
Lingwood	d		12 33		13 33		14 33					16 33		17 33				18 33				19 33		20 33	
Brundall	d	12 24	12 37		13 37	14 24	14 37		15 38		16 24	16 37	17 24	17 37	18 12	18 12	18 24	18 37	19 12		19 29	19 37	20 29	20 37	
Brundall Gardens	d		12 40		13 40		14 40		15 41			16 40		17 40				18 40				19 40		20 40	
Norwich	a	12 35	12 50	13 35	13 50	14 35	14 50	15 35	15 50		16 35	16 50	17 35	17 50	18 23	18 23	18 35	18 50	19 23		19 40	19 50	20 40	20 50	21 35
London Liverpool Street 15 ⊖	a																								

		LE	LE	LE	LE 1		LE	LE
Lowestoft	d		21 50		22 50			23 30
Oulton Broad North	d		21 54		22 54			23 34
Somerleyton	d		22 00		23 00			
Haddiscoe	d		22 04		23 04			
Great Yarmouth	d	21 17		22 17			23 34	
Berney Arms	d							
Reedham (Norfolk)	d		22 13		23 13		23 47	23 52
Cantley	d		22 17		23 17			23 56
Buckenham	d							
Acle	d	21 28		22 28				
Lingwood	d	21 33		22 33				
Brundall	d	21 37	22 24	22 37	23 24		23 55	00 03
Brundall Gardens	d	21 40		22 40				
Norwich	a	21 50	22 35	22 50	23 35		00 07	00 14
London Liverpool Street 15 ⊖	a							

Saturdays

		LE	LE	LE	LE	LE	LE	LE	LE	LE		LE	LE	LE	LE	LE	LE	LE	LE	LE		LE	LE	LE	LE
Lowestoft	d		23p30		06 38			07 40				08 50		09 50		11 00		11 50		13 00			13 50		15 00
Oulton Broad North	d		23p34		06 42			07 44				08 54		09 54		11 04		11 54		13 04			13 54		15 04
Somerleyton	d				06 48			07 50				09 00		10 00				12 00					14 00		
Haddiscoe	d				06 52			07 54				09 04		10 04				12 04					14 04		
Great Yarmouth	d	23p34		06 17		07 17	07 45		08 17	08 47			09 17		10 17		11 17		12 17			13 17		14 17	
Berney Arms	d																								
Reedham (Norfolk)	d	23p47	23p52		07 01			08 03				09 13		10 13				12 13					14 13		
Cantley	d		23p56		07 05			08 07				09 17		10 17				12 17					14 17		
Buckenham	d																								
Acle	d			06 28		07 28	07 56		08 28	08 58			09 28		10 28		11 28		12 28			13 28		14 28	
Lingwood	d			06 33		07 33	08 01		08 33	09 03			09 33		10 33		11 33		12 33			13 33		14 33	
Brundall	d	23p55	00 03	06 37	07 12	07 37	08 05	08 14	08 37			09 24	09 37	10 24	10 37		11 37	12 24	12 37			13 37	14 24	14 37	
Brundall Gardens	d			06 40		07 40	08 08		08 40				09 40		10 40		11 40		12 40			13 40		14 40	
Norwich	a	00 07	00 14	06 50	07 24	07 50	08 18	08 25	08 50	09 17		09 35	09 50	10 35	10 52	11 35	11 50	12 35	12 50	13 35		13 52	14 35	14 50	15 35
London Liverpool Street 15 ⊖	a																								

A from 26 March

B until 23 March

Table 15

Saturdays

Lowestoft and Great Yarmouth - Norwich

Network Diagram - see first Page of Table 13

		LE	LE	LE	LE	LE		LE	LE	LE	LE	LE	LE	LE	LE	LE		LE	LE	LE	LE	LE	LE	LE	
																		1				1			
								A	B																
Lowestoft	d		15 50		16 50					17 50			18 55		19 55			21 00		21 50		22 50		23 30	
Oulton Broad North	d		15 54		16 54					17 54			18 59		19 59			21 04		21 54		22 54		23 34	
Somerleyton	d		16 00		17 00					18 00			19 05		20 05					22 00		23 00			
Haddiscoe	d		16 04		17 04					18 04			19 09		20 09					22 04		23 04			
Great Yarmouth	d	15 13		16 17		17 17		17 47	17 47		18 17	18 47		19 17		20 17			21 17		22 17		23 34		
Berney Arms	d	15x20						17x54																	
Reedham (Norfolk)	d	15 28	16 13		17 13			18 01	18 01	18 13		19 01	19 18		20 18					22 13		23 13	23 47	23 52	
Cantley	d	15 32	16 17		17 17			18 05	18 05	18 17		19 05	19 22		20 22					22 17		23 17		23 56	
Buckenham	d		16x21																						
Acle	d			16 28		17 28					18 28			19 28		20 28			21 28		22 28				
Lingwood	d			16 33		17 33					18 33			19 33		20 33			21 33		22 33				
Brundall	d	15 38	16 24	16 37	17 24	17 37		18 12	18 12	18 24	18 37	19 12	19 29	19 37	20 29	20 37			21 37	22 24	22 37	23 24	23 55	00 03	
Brundall Gardens	d	15 41		16 40		17 40					18 40			19 40		20 40			21 40		22 40				
Norwich	a	15 50	16 35	16 50	17 35	17 50		18 23	18 23	18 35	18 50	19 23	19 40	19 50	20 40	20 50		21 35	21 50	22 35	22 50	23 35	00 07	00 14	
London Liverpool Street 15 ⊖	a																								

Sundays

		LE	LE	LE	LE	LE	LE	LE	LE	LE		LE	LE	LE	LE	LE	LE	LE	LE	LE		LE	LE	LE	LE
									1				1							1				1	
		C	C														D	E							
Lowestoft	d		23p30			09 50			11 50				13 50			15 50				17 50				19 50	
Oulton Broad North	d		23p34			09 54			11 54				13 54			15 54				17 54				19 54	
Somerleyton	d					10 00			12 00				14 00			16 00				18 00				20 00	
Haddiscoe	d					10 04			12 04				14 04			16 04				18 04				20 04	
Great Yarmouth	d	23p34		08 20	09 22		10 18	11 22		12 18		13 22		14 20	15 22		16 18	16 18	17 22			18 18	19 22		20 20
Berney Arms	d			08x27			10x25			12x25				14x27			16x25								
Reedham (Norfolk)	d	23p47	23p52	08 34		10 13	10 32		12 13	12 32			14 13	14 34		16 13	16 32	16 32		18 13		18 31		20 13	20 33
Cantley	d		23p56	08 38		10 17	10 36		12 17	12 36			14 17	14 38		16 17	16 36	16 36		18 17		18 35		20 17	20 37
Buckenham	d					10x21	10x40			12x40															
Acle	d				09 33			11 33				13 33			15 33				17 33				19 33		
Lingwood	d				09 38			11 38				13 38			15 38				17 38				19 38		
Brundall	d	23p55	00 03	08 45	09 42	10 24	10 44	11 42	12 24	12 44		13 42	14 24	14 45	15 42	16 24	16 44	16 44	17 42	18 24		18 41	19 42	20 24	20 43
Brundall Gardens	d				09 45			11 45				13 45			15 45				17 45				19 45		
Norwich	a	00 07	00 14	08 55	09 55	10 35	10 55	11 55	12 35	12 55		13 55	14 35	14 55	15 55	16 35	16 55	16 55	17 55	18 35		18 52	19 55	20 35	20 55
London Liverpool Street 15 ⊖	a																								

		LE	LE	LE	LE	LE
			1			1
Lowestoft	d		21 50			23 35
Oulton Broad North	d		21 54			23 39
Somerleyton	d		22 00			
Haddiscoe	d		22 04			
Great Yarmouth	d	21 22		22 20	23 20	
Berney Arms	d					
Reedham (Norfolk)	d		22 13	22 33	23 33	23 54
Cantley	d		22 17	22 37	23 37	
Buckenham	d					
Acle	d	21 33				
Lingwood	d	21 38				
Brundall	d	21 42	22 24	22 43	23 43	00 03
Brundall Gardens	d	21 45			23 46	
Norwich	a	21 55	22 35	22 55	23 55	00 13
London Liverpool Street 15 ⊖	a					

A from 31 March
B until 24 March
C not 11 December
D from 25 March
E until 18 March

Table 16

Mondays to Saturdays

Norwich - Cromer and Sheringham

Network Diagram - see first Page of Table 13

Miles			LE SX	LE SO	LE SO	LE SX	LE	LE	LE	LE	LE	LE	LE	LE	LE	LE	LE	LE	LE	LE	LE
0	**Norwich**	d	05 15	05 20	05 45	05 45	07 15	08 21	09 45	10 45	11 45	12 45	13 45	14 45	15 45	16 45	17 45	18 51	19 55	21 15	22 45
6	Salhouse	d			05 55	05 55	07 25	08 31	09 55		11 55		13 55		15 55	16 55	17 55		20 05	21 25	22 55
8¾	Hoveton & Wroxham	d	05 29	05 34	06 00	06 00	07 30	08 36	10 00	10 59	12 00	12 59	14 00	14 59	16 00	17 00	18 00	19 05	20 10	21 30	23 00
13	Worstead	d			06 07	06 07	07 37	08 43		11 05		13 05		15 05	16 07	17 07	18 07	19 11	20 17	21 37	23 07
—	**North Walsham**	a	05 39	05 44	06 12	06 12	07 42	08 48	10 10	11 11	12 10	13 11	14 10	15 11	16 12	17 12	18 12	19 17	20 22	21 42	23 12
16	**North Walsham**	d	05 39	05 44	06 13	06 15	07 45	08 51	10 13	11 13	12 13	13 13	14 13	15 13	16 15	17 15	18 17	19 20	20 25	21 43	23 13
19¾	Gunton	d			06 19	06 21	07 51	08 57	10 19		12 19		14 19		16 21	17 21	18 23	19 26	20 31	21 49	23 19
23½	Roughton Road	d			06 25	06 28	07 57	09 04		11 24		13 24		15 24	16 27	17 27	18 30	19 33	20 38	21 55	23 25
—	**Cromer**	a	05 54	05 59	06 31	06 33	08 03	09 09	10 30	11 30	12 30	13 30	14 30	15 30	16 33	17 33	18 36	19 39	20 43	22 01	23 31
26½	**Cromer**	d	06 01	06 01	06 36	06 46	08 05	09 12	10 32	11 32	12 32	13 32	14 32	15 32	16 35	17 35	18 38	19 41	20 46	22 03	23 33
28¾	West Runton	d	06 05	06 06	06 40	06 50	08 10	09 16	10 37	11 37	12 37	13 37	14 37	15 37	16 40	17 40	18 43	19 46	20 50	22 08	23 38
30½	**Sheringham**	a	06 12	06 12	06 46	06 56	08 15	09 22	10 43	11 43	12 43	13 43	14 43	15 43	16 46	17 46	18 49	19 52	20 56	22 14	23 44

Sundays

		LE	LE	LE	LE	LE	LE	LE
Norwich	d	08 36	10 36	12 36	14 36	16 36	18 36	20 36
Salhouse	d	08 46	10 46	12 46	14 46	16 46	18 46	20 46
Hoveton & Wroxham	d	08 51	10 51	12 51	14 51	16 51	18 51	20 51
Worstead	d	08 58	10 58	12 58	14 58	16 58	18 58	20 58
North Walsham	a	09 03	11 03	13 03	15 03	17 03	19 03	21 03
North Walsham	d	09 04	11 06	13 06	15 06	17 06	19 06	21 06
Gunton	d	09 10	11 12	13 12	15 12	17 12	19 12	21 12
Roughton Road	d	09 16	11 19	13 19	15 19	17 19	19 19	21 19
Cromer	a	09 22	11 24	13 24	15 24	17 24	19 24	21 24
Cromer	d	09 25	11 27	13 27	15 27	17 27	19 27	21 27
West Runton	d	09 30	11 31	13 31	15 31	17 31	19 31	21 31
Sheringham	a	09 36	11 38	13 38	15 38	17 38	19 38	21 38

Table 16

Mondays to Saturdays

Sheringham and Cromer - Norwich

Network Diagram - see first Page of Table 13

Miles			LE MX	LE SX	LE SO	LE SX	LE	LE	LE	LE	LE	LE	LE	LE	LE	LE	LE	LE	LE	LE	LE	LE
0	**Sheringham**	d	23p47		06 22	06 32	07 16	08 23	09 46	10 46	11 46	12 46	13 46	14 46	15 46	16 49	17 49	18 55	19 57	21 10	22 17	23 47
1¾	West Runton	d	23p51		06 26	06 36	07 20	08 27	09 50	10 50	11 50	12 50	13 50	14 50	15 50	16 53	17 53	18 59	20 01	21 14	22 21	23 51
—	**Cromer**	a	23p55		06 30	06 40	07 24	08 31	09 54	10 54	11 54	12 54	13 54	14 54	15 54	16 57	17 57	19 03	20 05	21 18	22 25	23 55
4	**Cromer**	d	23p58	05 58	06 33	06 43	07 27	08 34	09 57	10 57	11 57	12 57	13 57	14 57	15 57	17 00	18 00	19 06	20 08	21 21	22 28	23 58
7	Roughton Road	d		06 04	06 39	06 49	07 33	08 40	10 03		12 03		14 03	15 03	16 03		18 06		20 14	21 27	22 34	
10¾	Gunton	d		06 10	06 45	06 55	07 39	08 46		11 08		13 08			16 09		18 12		20 20	21 33	22 40	
—	**North Walsham**	a	00 12	06 15	06 50	07 00	07 45	08 51	10 13	11 13	12 13	13 13	14 13	15 13	16 15	17 15	18 17	19 20	20 25	21 38	22 45	00 12
14½	**North Walsham**	d	00 13	06 16	06 51	07 01	07 45	08 52	10 13	11 14	12 13	13 14	14 13	15 14	16 15	17 15	18 18	19 21	20 26	21 43	22 46	00 13
17½	Worstead	d		06 21	06 56	07 06	07 50	08 57	10 18		12 18		14 18		16 20		18 23		20 31	21 48	22 51	
21¾	Hoveton & Wroxham	d	00 22	06 28	07 03	07 13	07 57	09 04	10 25	11 24	12 25	13 24	14 25	15 24	16 27	17 25	18 30	19 31	20 38	21 55	22 58	00 22
24½	Salhouse	d		06 32	07 07	07 17	08 02	09 08		11 28		13 28		15 28	16 32		18 34		20 42	21 59	23 02	
30½	**Norwich**	a	00 37	06 45	07 20	07 30	08 14	09 21	10 41	11 41	12 41	13 41	14 41	15 41	16 44	17 41	18 47	19 46	20 55	22 12	23 15	00 37

Sundays

		LE A	LE	LE	LE	LE	LE	LE	LE
Sheringham	d	23p47	09 42	11 42	13 42	15 42	17 42	19 42	21 42
West Runton	d	23p51	09 46	11 46	13 46	15 46	17 46	19 46	21 46
Cromer	a	23p55	09 50	11 50	13 50	15 50	17 50	19 50	21 50
Cromer	d	23p58	09 54	11 54	13 54	15 54	17 54	19 54	21 54
Roughton Road	d		10 00	12 00	14 00	16 00	18 00	20 00	22 00
Gunton	d		10 06	12 06	14 06	16 06	18 06	20 06	22 06
North Walsham	a	00 12	10 11	12 11	14 11	16 11	18 11	20 11	22 11
North Walsham	d	00 13	10 12	12 12	14 12	16 12	18 12	20 12	22 12
Worstead	d		10 17	12 17	14 17	16 17	18 17	20 17	22 17
Hoveton & Wroxham	d	00 22	10 24	12 24	14 24	16 24	18 24	20 24	22 24
Salhouse	d		10 28	12 28	14 28	16 28	18 28	20 28	22 28
Norwich	a	00 37	10 40	12 40	14 40	16 40	18 40	20 40	22 40

A not 11 December

For services to Great Yarmouth, please see Table 15

London and Cambridge - Ely, Kings Lynn, Peterborough and Norwich

Network Diagram - see first Page of Table 13

		LE MX 1	FC MO 1	FC MX 1	XC ◇1	XC ◇1	LE 1	FC 1	EM ◇	LE ◇1		FC 1	XC ◇1	EM ◇	LE 1	LE 1	FC 1	EM ◇	XC ◇1	FC 1		EM ◇	LE 1	FC 1	EM ◇
London Liverpool Street	d																								
London Kings Cross	d		23p15	23p15								05 45					06 45			07 15				07 45	
Ipswich	d									06 00															
Stansted Airport	d					05 16							06 06						07 21						
Cambridge	d	22p55	00 13	00 14	05 15	05 55	06 05	06 18				06 52	06 55		07 04	07 22	07 33		08 00	08 03			08 12	08 38	
Waterbeach	d		00 19	00 20				06 24				06 58					07 39			08 09				08 44	
Ely 4	a	23p09	00 29	00 30	05 29	06 09	06 19	06 33		06 59		07 07	07 10		07 18	07 38	07 48		08 14	08 20			08 26	08 53	
	d	23p10			05 30	06 10	06 20	06 33	06 51	07 00		07 08	07 12	07 05	07 19		07 48	07 45	08 15	08 21		08 15	08 29	08 54	08 50
Littleport	d							06 43				07 15					07 55			08 28				09 01	
Downham Market	d							06 54				07 24					08 04			08 37				09 10	
Watlington	d							07 00				07 31					08 10			08 43				09 16	
Kings Lynn	a							07 09				07 42					08 20			08 53				09 25	
Manea	d					06x20																			
March	d				05 46	06 28			07 07	07 16			07 28					08 01	08 31						09 07
Whittlesea	d				05 58	06 39				07 27			07 39					08 13							
Peterborough 8	a				06 08	06 50			07 25	07 38			07 51					08 24	08 50						09 25
Shippea Hill	d														07x28										
Lakenheath	d																								
Brandon	d	23p26					06 36							07 20	07 38								08 45		
Thetford	d	23p34					06 44							07 29	07 47							08 37	08 53		
Harling Road	d						06 53								07 55										
Eccles Road	d						06 58								08 00										
Attleborough	d	23p49					07 04							07 43	08 06							08 51	09 08		
Spooner Row	d														08x11										
Wymondham	d	23p57					07 11							07 50	08 16							08 58	09 16		
Norwich	a	00 11					07 27							08 13	08 30							09 13	09 30		

		LE 1	XC ◇1	LE 1	FC 1	EM ◇		EM ◇	XC ◇1	EM ◇	LE 1	FC 1	EM ◇	LE 1	XC ◇1	EM ◇		LE 1	FC 1	EM ◇	XC ◇1	EM ◇	LE 1	FC 1	EM ◇
London Liverpool Street	d																								
London Kings Cross	d				08 45							09 45							10 45					11 45	
Ipswich	d	08 03												10 00											
Stansted Airport	d		08 21						09 21						10 27						11 27				
Cambridge	d		09 00	09 12	09 38				10 00		10 12	10 37			11 00			11 12	11 35		12 00		12 12	12 33	
Waterbeach	d				09 44							10 43							11 41					12 39	
Ely 4	a	09 00	09 14	09 26	09 53				10 14		10 26	10 52		10 58	11 14			11 26	11 50		12 14		12 26	12 48	
	d	09 00	09 15	09 27	09 54	09 45		09 49	10 15	10 17	10 27	10 52	10 54	10 58	11 15	11 19		11 27	11 50	11 53	12 15	12 18	12 27	12 48	12 52
Littleport	d				10 01							10 59							11 57					12 55	
Downham Market	d				10 10							11 08							12 06					13 04	
Watlington	d				10 16							11 14							12 11					13 10	
Kings Lynn	a				10 25							11 22							12 20					13 20	
Manea	d																								
March	d	09 17	09 31						10 31					11 15	11 31						12 31				
Whittlesea	d	09 28												11 26											
Peterborough 8	a	09 39	09 50					10 26	10 50				11 27	11 37	11 50					12 24	12 50				13 25
Shippea Hill	d																								
Lakenheath	d																								
Brandon	d			09 43							10 43							11 43					12 43		
Thetford	d			09 51		10 06				10 41	10 51					11 41		11 51				12 39	12 51		
Harling Road	d																								
Eccles Road	d																								
Attleborough	d			10 06							11 06							12 06					13 06		
Spooner Row	d			10x11																					
Wymondham	d			10 16							11 14							12 14					13 14		
Norwich	a			10 30		10 44				11 14	11 30					12 13		12 30				13 13	13 30		

		LE 1		XC ◇1	EM ◇	LE 1	FC 1	EM ◇	XC ◇1	EM ◇	LE 1	FC 1		EM ◇	LE 1	XC ◇1	EM ◇	LE 1	FC 1	FC 1	EM ◇	XC ◇1		EM ◇	LE 1
London Liverpool Street	d																								
London Kings Cross	d						12 45					13 45								14 45					
Ipswich	d	12 00													14 00										
Stansted Airport	d			12 27					13 27							14 27						15 27			
Cambridge	d			13 00		13 12	13 34		14 00		14 12	14 35				15 00		15 12	15 24	15 35		16 00			16 12
Waterbeach	d						13 40					14 41							15 30	15 41					
Ely 4	a	12 58		13 14		13 26	13 49		14 14		14 26	14 50			14 58	15 14		15 26	15 40	15 50		16 14			16 26
	d	12 58		13 15	13 20	13 27	13 49	13 52	14 15	14 17	14 27	14 50		14 53	14 58	15 15	15 17	15 27		15 50	15 52	16 15		16 16	16 27
Littleport	d						13 57					14 57								15 57					
Downham Market	d						14 06					15 06								16 06					
Watlington	d						14 11					15 11								16 11					
Kings Lynn	a						14 21					15 20								16 20					
Manea	d																								
March	d	13 15		13 31					14 31						15 15	15 31						16 31			
Whittlesea	d	13 26													15 26										
Peterborough 8	a	13 37		13 50				14 25	14 50					15 27	15 37	15 50					16 27	16 50			
Shippea Hill	d																								
Lakenheath	d																								
Brandon	d					13 43					14 43							15 43							16 43
Thetford	d				13 41	13 51				14 38	14 51						15 38	15 51						16 37	16 51
Harling Road	d																								
Eccles Road	d																								
Attleborough	d					14 06					15 06							16 06							17 06
Spooner Row	d																								
Wymondham	d					14 14					15 14							16 14							17 14
Norwich	a				14 13	14 30				15 13	15 30						16 14	16 30						17 13	17 28

London and Cambridge - Ely, Kings Lynn, Peterborough and Norwich

Network Diagram - see first Page of Table 13

		FC 1	FC 1	EM ◇	LE 1	XC ◇1	EM ◇	LE 1		LE 1	FC 1	EM ◇	XC ◇1	FC 1	EM ◇	LE 1	LE 1 A	LE 1		EM ◇	LE 1	FC 1	XC ◇1	FC 1	LE 1
London Liverpool Street	d									15 58							17 07								18 07
London Kings Cross	d		15 44								16 44			17 14								17 44		18 14	
Ipswich	d				16 00																17 49				
Stansted Airport	d					16 27							17 27										18 21		
Cambridge	d	16 21	16 39			17 00		17 12		17 22	17 39		18 00	18 05		18 12	18 17	18 24				18 39	19 00	19 09	19 19
Waterbeach	d	16 27	16 45							17 28	17 45						18 23	18 30				18 45			19 25
Ely 4	a	16 36	16 55		16 58	17 14		17 26		17 38	17 55		18 14	18 19		18 26	18 32	18 40			18 52	18 55	19 14	19 23	19 34
	d	16 36	16 55	16 51	16 58	17 15	17 17	17 27			17 56	17 52	18 15		18 20	18 27	18 33			18 52	19 00	18 56	19 15	19 24	19 35
Littleport	d		17 02								18 03						18 40					19 03			19 42
Downham Market	d	16a50	17 11								18 12						18 50					19 12		19 39	19 52
Watlington	d		17 17								18 18						18 56					19 18			19 58
Kings Lynn	a		17 26								18 28						19 08					19 28		19 53	20 10
Manea	d												18x25												
March	d				17 15	17 31							18 33							19 08	19 16		19 31		
Whittlesea	d				17 26																19 28				
Peterborough 8	a			17 26	17 37	17 51						18 25	18 50							19 26	19 38		19 50		
Shippea Hill	d																								
Lakenheath	d																								
Brandon	d							17 43								18 43									
Thetford	d						17 38	17 51							18 41	18 51									
Harling Road	d																								
Eccles Road	d																								
Attleborough	d							18 06								19 06									
Spooner Row	d																								
Wymondham	d							18 14								19 14									
Norwich	a						18 18	18 28							19 15	19 28									

		EM ◇	LE 1	FC 1		EM ◇	XC ◇1	LE 1	EM ◇	LE 1	FC 1	LE 1	XC ◇1	FC 1		LE 1	FC 1	FC 1	FC 1	EM ◇	LE 1	FC 1		FC FX 1	FC FO 1
London Liverpool Street	d							19 07																	
London Kings Cross	d			18 44							19 45			20 15			20 45	21 15	21 45			22 15		23 15	23 15
Ipswich	d											20 00													
Stansted Airport	d						19 21						20 21												
Cambridge	d		19 25	19 39			20 00	20 15		20 20	20 40		21 00	21 10		21 15	21 38	22 08	22 38		22 55	23 08		00 14	00 14
Waterbeach	d			19 45				20 21			20 46			21 16			21 44	22 14	22 44			23 14		00 20	00 20
Ely 4	a		19 39	19 55			20 14	20 30		20 35	20 55	21 00	21 14	21 25		21 30	21 53	22 23	22 54		23 09	23 23		00 30	00 29
	d	19 27	19 40	19 56		19 52	20 15	20 31	20 16	20 37	20 55	21 00	21 15	21 25		21 30	21 53	22 23		22 15	23 10	23 23			00 29
Littleport	d			20 03				20 38			21 02			21 32			22 00	22 30				23 30			00 36
Downham Market	d			20 12				20 48			21 11			21 41			22 09	22 39				23 39			00 45
Watlington	d			20 18				20 54			21 17			21 47			22 15	22 45				23 45			00 51
Kings Lynn	a			20 28				21 05			21 26			21 56			22 24	22 54				23 54			01 00
Manea	d																								
March	d						20 31					21 17	21 31												
Whittlesea	d											21 28													
Peterborough 8	a					20 26	20 50					21 39	21 51												
Shippea Hill	d																								
Lakenheath	d																								
Brandon	d		19 56							20 53						21 46					23 26				
Thetford	d	19 50	20 04						20 37	21 01						21 55				22 36	23 34				
Harling Road	d																								
Eccles Road	d																								
Attleborough	d		20 19							21 16						22 10				22 50	23 49				
Spooner Row	d																								
Wymondham	d		20 27							21 24						22 17				22 57	23 57				
Norwich	a	20 22	20 41						21 14	21 38						22 31				23 18	00 11				

Saturdays

		LE 1	FC 1	XC ◇1	XC ◇1	LE 1	FC 1	EM ◇	LE ◇1	XC ◇1		EM ◇	LE 1	FC 1	EM ◇	XC ◇1	EM ◇	LE 1	FC 1	EM ◇		LE 1	XC ◇1	LE 1	FC 1
London Liverpool Street	d																								
London Kings Cross	d		23p15											06 45					07 45						08 45
Ipswich	d								06 00													08 00			
Stansted Airport	d				05 25					06 27						07 27							08 27		
Cambridge	d	22p55	00 14	05 15	05 55	06 08	06 32			06 57			07 00	07 35		08 00		08 12	08 35				09 00	09 12	09 35
Waterbeach	d		00 20				06 38							07 41					08 41						09 41
Ely 4	a	23p09	00 29	05 29	06 09	06 22	06 47		06 59	07 11			07 14	07 50		08 14		08 26	08 50			08 58	09 14	09 26	09 50
	d	23p10	00 29	05 30	06 10	06 23	06 47	06 51	07 00	07 12		07 06	07 15	07 50	07 53	08 15	08 14	08 27	08 50	08 54		08 58	09 15	09 27	09 50
Littleport	d		00 36				06 54							07 57					08 57						09 57
Downham Market	d		00 45				07 03							08 06					09 06						10 06
Watlington	d		00 51				07 09							08 11					09 11						10 11
Kings Lynn	a		01 00				07 20							08 20					09 20						10 20
Manea	d				06x20																				
March	d			05 46	06 28			07 07	07 16	07 29					08 08	08 31				09 11		09 15	09 31		
Whittlesea	d			05 58	06 39				07 27	07 40					08 19							09 26			
Peterborough 8	a			06 08	06 50			07 25	07 38	07 50					08 31	08 50				09 28		09 38	09 50		
Shippea Hill	d												07x24												
Lakenheath	d																								
Brandon	d	23p26				06 39						07 22	07 34					08 43						09 43	
Thetford	d	23p34				06 48						07 30	07 42				08 36	08 51						09 51	
Harling Road	d					06 56							07 51												
Eccles Road	d					07 01							07 56												
Attleborough	d	23p49				07 07						07 44	08 02				08 50	09 06						10 06	
Spooner Row	d												08x07												
Wymondham	d	23p57				07 15						07 51	08 12				08 57	09 14						10 14	
Norwich	a	00 11				07 29						08 13	08 30				09 15	09 30						10 30	

A The Fenman

London and Cambridge - Ely, Kings Lynn, Peterborough and Norwich

Network Diagram - see first Page of Table 13

		EM ◇	EM ◇	XC ◇1	EM ◇	LE 1		FC 1	EM ◇	LE 1	XC ◇1	EM ◇	LE 1	FC 1	EM ◇	XC ◇1		EM ◇	LE 1	FC 1	EM ◇	LE 1	XC ◇1	EM ◇	LE 1
London Liverpool Street	d																								
London Kings Cross	d							09 45						10 45						11 45					
Ipswich	d									10 00												12 00			
Stansted Airport	d			09 27							10 27					11 27							12 27		
Cambridge	d			10 00		10 12		10 35			11 00		11 12	11 35		12 00			12 12	12 35			13 00		13 12
Waterbeach	d							10 41						11 41						12 41					
Ely 4	a			10 14		10 26		10 50		10 58	11 14		11 26	11 50		12 14			12 26	12 50		12 58	13 14		13 26
	d	09 39	09 51	10 15	10 17	10 29		10 50	10 53	10 58	11 15	11 22	11 29	11 50	11 53	12 15		12 17	12 27	12 50	12 54	12 58	13 15	13 17	13 27
Littleport	d							10 57						11 57						12 57					
Downham Market	d							11 06						12 06						13 06					
Watlington	d							11 11						12 11						13 11					
Kings Lynn	a							11 20						12 20						13 20					
Manea	d																								
March	d			10 31						11 15	11 31					12 31						13 15	13 31		
Whittlesea	d									11 26												13 26			
Peterborough 8	a		10 25	10 50					11 24	11 37	11 50				12 24	12 50					13 26	13 37	13 50		
Shippea Hill	d																								
Lakenheath	d																								
Brandon	d					10 45							11 45						12 43						13 43
Thetford	d	10 04			10 40	10 54						11 44	11 54					12 39	12 51					13 39	13 51
Harling Road	d																								
Eccles Road	d																								
Attleborough	d					11 09							12 09						13 06						14 06
Spooner Row	d																								
Wymondham	d					11 16							12 16						13 14						14 14
Norwich	a	10 43			11 15	11 30						12 18	12 30					13 13	13 30					14 13	14 30

		FC 1		EM ◇	XC ◇1	EM ◇	LE 1	FC 1	EM ◇	LE 1	XC ◇1	EM ◇		LE 1	FC 1	EM ◇	XC ◇1	EM ◇	LE 1	FC 1	EM ◇	LE 1		XC ◇1	EM ◇
London Liverpool Street	d																								
London Kings Cross	d	12 45						13 45							14 45					15 45					
Ipswich	d									14 00												16 00			
Stansted Airport	d				13 27						14 27						15 27							16 27	
Cambridge	d	13 35			14 00		14 12	14 35			15 00			15 12	15 35		16 00		16 12	16 35				17 00	
Waterbeach	d	13 41						14 41							15 41					16 41					
Ely 4	a	13 50			14 14		14 26	14 50		14 58	15 14			15 26	15 50		16 14		16 26	16 50		16 58		17 14	
	d	13 50		13 53	14 15	14 17	14 27	14 50	14 53	14 58	15 15	15 17		15 27	15 50	15 52	16 15	16 17	16 27	16 50	16 52	16 58		17 15	17 17
Littleport	d	13 57						14 57							15 57					16 57					
Downham Market	d	14 06						15 06							16 06					17 06					
Watlington	d	14 11						15 11							16 11					17 11					
Kings Lynn	a	14 20						15 20							16 20					17 20					
Manea	d																								
March	d				14 31					15 15	15 31						16 31					17 15		17 31	
Whittlesea	d									15 26												17 26			
Peterborough 8	a			14 25	14 50				15 25	15 37	15 50					16 25	16 50				17 26	17 37		17 50	
Shippea Hill	d																								
Lakenheath	d													15x40											
Brandon	d						14 43							15 45					16 43						
Thetford	d					14 38	14 51					15 40		15 54				16 38	16 51						17 40
Harling Road	d																								
Eccles Road	d																								
Attleborough	d						15 06							16 09					17 06						
Spooner Row	d																								
Wymondham	d						15 14							16 16					17 14						
Norwich	a					15 13	15 30					16 15		16 30				17 13	17 30						18 18

		LE 1	FC 1	EM ◇	XC ◇1	EM ◇	LE 1	FC 1		EM ◇	LE 1	XC ◇1	FC 1	EM ◇	LE 1	FC 1	EM ◇	XC ◇1		EM ◇	LE 1	FC 1	LE 1	LE 1	FC 1
London Liverpool Street	d																								
London Kings Cross	d		16 45					17 45					18 15			18 45						19 45			20 45
Ipswich	d										18 00												20 00		
Stansted Airport	d				17 27							18 27						19 27							
Cambridge	d	17 12	17 35		18 00		18 12	18 35				19 00	19 04		19 12	19 40		20 00			20 12	20 40		21 12	21 40
Waterbeach	d		17 41					18 41								19 46						20 46			21 46
Ely 4	a	17 26	17 50		18 14		18 26	18 50			18 58	19 14	19 18		19 26	19 55		20 14			20 26	20 55	20 58	21 26	21 55
	d	17 27	17 50	17 52	18 15	18 15	18 27	18 50		18 53	19 00	19 15	19 19	19 23	19 29	19 55	19 51	20 15		20 16	20 27	20 55	20 59	21 27	21 55
Littleport	d		17 57					18 57								20 02						21 02			22 02
Downham Market	d		18 06					19 06					19 35			20 11						21 11			22 11
Watlington	d		18 11					19 11								20 17						21 17			22 17
Kings Lynn	a		18 20					19 20					19 52			20 25						21 25			22 25
Manea	d				18x25																				
March	d				18 33					19 09	19 16	19 31						20 31					21 15		
Whittlesea	d										19 28												21 27		
Peterborough 8	a			18 25	18 50					19 29	19 38	19 50					20 25	20 50					21 37		
Shippea Hill	d																								
Lakenheath	d																								
Brandon	d	17 43					18 43								19 45						20 43			21 43	
Thetford	d	17 51				18 37	18 51							19 44	19 54					20 37	20 51			21 51	
Harling Road	d																								
Eccles Road	d																								
Attleborough	d	18 06					19 06								20 09						21 06			22 06	
Spooner Row	d																								
Wymondham	d	18 14					19 14								20 16						21 14			22 14	
Norwich	a	18 30				19 19	19 30							20 18	20 30					21 14	21 30			22 30	

Table 17

Saturdays

London and Cambridge - Ely, Kings Lynn, Peterborough and Norwich

Network Diagram - see first Page of Table 13

		EM ◇	LE 1	FC 1		FC 1
London Liverpool Street	d					
London Kings Cross	d			22 15		23 15
Ipswich	d					
Stansted Airport	d					
Cambridge	d		22 30	23 11		00 14
Waterbeach	d			23 17		00 20
Ely 4	a		22 44	23 26		00 29
	d	22 16	22 45	23 26		00 29
Littleport	d			23 33		00 36
Downham Market	d			23 43		00 45
Watlington	d			23 48		00 51
Kings Lynn	a			23 58		01 00
Manea	d					
March	d					
Whittlesea	d					
Peterborough 8	a					
Shippea Hill	d					
Lakenheath	d					
Brandon	d		23 01			
Thetford	d	22 37	23 09			
Harling Road	d					
Eccles Road	d					
Attleborough	d	22 51	23 24			
Spooner Row	d					
Wymondham	d	22 58	23 32			
Norwich	a	23 20	23 46			

Sundays

until 1 January

		FC 1 A	LE 1	FC 1	FC 1	LE ◇1	LE 1	XC ◇1	FC 1	EM ◇		LE 1	XC ◇1	FC 1	LE 1	LE 1	XC ◇1	FC 1	LE 1	XC ◇1		FC 1	EM ◇	EM ◇	LE 1
London Liverpool Street	d																								
London Kings Cross	d	23p15		07 53	09 15				10 15					11 15				12 15				13 15			
Ipswich	d					09 55									11 55										13 55
Stansted Airport	d							10 25					11 25				12 25			13 25					
Cambridge	d	00 14	08 48	09 05	10 05		10 48	11 00	11 05			11 52	12 00	12 05		12 52	13 00	13 05	13 52	14 00		14 05			
Waterbeach	d	00 20		09 11	10 11				11 11					12 11				13 11				14 11			
Ely 4	a	00 29	09 02	09 20	10 20	10 51	11 02	11 14	11 20			12 06	12 15	12 20	12 51	13 06	13 15	13 20	14 06	14 14		14 20			14 51
	d	00 29	09 03	09 20	10 20	10 52	11 03	11 15	11 20	11 39		12 07	12 15	12 20	12 52	13 07	13 15	13 20	14 07	14 15		14 20	14 24	14 45	14 52
Littleport	d	00 36		09 27	10 27				11 27					12 27				13 27				14 27			
Downham Market	d	00 45		09 36	10 36				11 36					12 36				13 36				14 36			
Watlington	d	00 51		09 41	10 41				11 41					12 41				13 41				14 41			
Kings Lynn	a	01 00		09 50	10 50				11 50					12 50				13 50				14 50			
Manea	d																								
March	d					11 09		11 31					12 31		13 09		13 31			14 31					15 09
Whittlesea	d					11 20									13 20										15 20
Peterborough 8	a					11 36		11 50		12 16			12 50		13 31		13 50			14 50				15 24	15 31
Shippea Hill	d																								
Lakenheath	d		09x17				11x17									13x20									
Brandon	d		09 22				11 22					12 23				13 25			14 23				14 42		
Thetford	d		09 31				11 31					12 31				13 34			14 31				14 50		
Harling Road	d																								
Eccles Road	d																								
Attleborough	d		09 46				11 46					12 46				13 49			14 46				15 04		
Spooner Row	d																								
Wymondham	d		09 53				11 53					12 54				13 56			14 54				15 11		
Norwich	a		10 13				12 13					13 13				14 13			15 13				15 30		

		LE 1	XC ◇1	FC 1	EM ◇	EM ◇		LE 1	XC ◇1	FC 1	LE 1	EM ◇	LE 1	XC ◇1	FC 1	EM ◇		EM ◇	LE 1	XC ◇1	FC 1	EM ◇	EM ◇	LE 1	LE 1
London Liverpool Street	d																								
London Kings Cross	d			14 15						15 15					16 15						17 15				
Ipswich	d										15 55													17 55	
Stansted Airport	d		14 25						15 25					16 25						17 25					
Cambridge	d	14 52	15 00	15 05				15 52	16 00	16 05			16 52	17 00	17 05				17 52	18 00	18 05				18 52
Waterbeach	d			15 11						16 11					17 11						18 11				
Ely 4	a	15 06	15 14	15 20				16 06	16 15	16 20	16 51		17 06	17 15	17 20				18 06	18 15	18 20			18 51	19 06
	d	15 07	15 15	15 20	15 33	15 48		16 07	16 15	16 20	16 52	16 41	17 07	17 15	17 20	17 36		17 48	18 07	18 15	18 20	18 36	18 48	18 52	19 07
Littleport	d			15 27						16 27					17 27						18 27				
Downham Market	d			15 36						16 36					17 36						18 36				
Watlington	d			15 41						16 41					17 41						18 41				
Kings Lynn	a			15 50						16 50					17 50						18 50				
Manea	d																								
March	d		15 31						16 31		17 09			17 31						18 31				19 09	
Whittlesea	d										17 20													19 20	
Peterborough 8	a		15 50			16 22			16 50		17 31			17 50				18 23		18 50			19 24	19 32	
Shippea Hill	d																								
Lakenheath	d							16x20																	
Brandon	d	15 23						16 25					17 23						18 23						19 23
Thetford	d	15 31			15 54			16 34				17 02	17 31			17 57			18 31			18 57			19 31
Harling Road	d																								
Eccles Road	d																								
Attleborough	d	15 46						16 49					17 46						18 46						19 46
Spooner Row	d																								
Wymondham	d	15 54						16 56					17 54						18 54						19 54
Norwich	a	16 13			16 35			17 13				17 30	18 13			18 30			19 10			19 29			20 13

A not 11 December

Sundays
until 1 January

London and Cambridge - Ely, Kings Lynn, Peterborough and Norwich

Network Diagram - see first Page of Table 13

		XC ◇1		FC 1	EM ◇	EM ◇	LE 1	XC ◇1	FC 1	FC 1	EM ◇	EM ◇		LE 1	FC 1	FC 1	EM ◇	FC 1
London Liverpool Street	d																	
London Kings Cross	d			18 15					19 15	20 15					21 15	22 15		23 15
Ipswich	d																	
Stansted Airport	d	18 25						19 25										
Cambridge	d	19 00		19 05			19 52	20 00	20 05	21 05				21 52	22 05	23 05		00 13
Waterbeach	d			19 11					20 11	21 11					22 11	23 11		00 19
Ely 4	a	19 15		19 20			20 06	20 15	20 20	21 20				22 06	22 20	23 20		00 29
	d	19 15		19 20	19 26	19 48	20 07	20 15	20 20	21 20	20 35	21 44		22 07	22 20	23 20	22 32	
Littleport	d			19 27					20 27	21 27					22 27	23 27		
Downham Market	d			19 36					20 36	21 36					22 36	23 36		
Watlington	d								20 41	21 41					22 41	23 41		
Kings Lynn	a			19 50					20 50	21 50					22 50	23 50		
Manea	d																	
March	d	19 31						20 31										
Whittlesea	d																	
Peterborough 8	a	19 50				20 29		20 50				22 20						
Shippea Hill	d																	
Lakenheath	d																	
Brandon	d						20 23							22 23				
Thetford	d				19 50		20 31				20 56			22 31			22 53	
Harling Road	d																	
Eccles Road	d																	
Attleborough	d						20 46				21 10			22 46			23 07	
Spooner Row	d																	
Wymondham	d						20 54				21 17			22 54			23 14	
Norwich	a				20 29		21 10				21 35			23 13			23 28	

Sundays
8 January to 12 February

		FC 1	LE 1	FC 1	FC 1	LE ◇1	LE 1	XC ◇1	FC 1	EM ◇		LE 1	FC 1	LE 1	LE 1	XC ◇1	FC 1	LE 1	XC ◇1	FC 1		EM ◇	EM ◇	LE 1	LE 1
London Liverpool Street	d																								
London Kings Cross	d	23p15		07 53	09 15				10 15				11 15				12 15			13 15					
Ipswich	d					09 55								11 55										13 55	
Stansted Airport	d							10 25								12 25			13 25						
Cambridge	d	00 14	08 48	09 05	10 05		10 48	11 00	11 05			11 52	12 05		12 52	13 00	13 05	13 52	14 00	14 05					14 52
Waterbeach	d	00 20		09 11	10 11				11 11				12 11				13 11			14 11					
Ely 4	a	00 29	09 02	09 20	10 20	10 51	11 02	11 14	11 20			12 06	12 20	12 51	13 06	13 15	13 20	14 06	14 14	14 20				14 51	15 06
	d	00 29	09 03	09 20	10 20	10 52	11 03	11 15	11 20	11 39		12 07	12 20	12 52	13 07	13 15	13 20	14 07	14 15	14 20		14 24	14 45	14 52	15 07
Littleport	d	00 36		09 27	10 27				11 27				12 27				13 27			14 27					
Downham Market	d	00 45		09 36	10 36				11 36				12 36				13 36			14 36					
Watlington	d	00 51		09 41	10 41				11 41				12 41				13 41			14 41					
Kings Lynn	a	01 00		09 50	10 50				11 50				12 50				13 50			14 50					
Manea	d																								
March	d					11 09		11 31						13 09		13 31			14 31					15 09	
Whittlesea	d					11 20								13 20										15 20	
Peterborough 8	a					11 36		11 50		12 16				13 31		13 50			14 50				15 24	15 31	
Shippea Hill	d																								
Lakenheath	d		09x17				11x17								13x20										
Brandon	d		09 22				11 22					12 23			13 25			14 23				14 42			15 23
Thetford	d		09 31				11 31					12 31			13 34			14 31				14 50			15 31
Harling Road	d																								
Eccles Road	d																								
Attleborough	d		09 46				11 46					12 46			13 49			14 46				15 04			15 46
Spooner Row	d																								
Wymondham	d		09 53				11 53					12 54			13 56			14 54				15 11			15 54
Norwich	a		10 13				12 13					13 13			14 13			15 13				15 30			16 13

		FC 1	EM ◇	EM ◇	LE 1	XC ◇1		FC 1	LE 1	EM ◇	LE 1	XC ◇1	FC 1	EM ◇	EM ◇	LE 1		XC ◇1	FC 1	EM ◇	EM ◇	LE 1	LE 1	FC 1	EM ◇
London Liverpool Street	d																								
London Kings Cross	d	14 15						15 15					16 15						17 15					18 15	
Ipswich	d								15 55													17 55			
Stansted Airport	d					15 25						16 25						17 25							
Cambridge	d	15 05			15 52	16 00		16 05			16 52	17 00	17 05			17 52		18 00	18 05				18 52	19 05	
Waterbeach	d	15 11						16 11					17 11						18 11					19 11	
Ely 4	a	15 20			16 06	16 15		16 20	16 51		17 06	17 15	17 20			18 06		18 15	18 20			18 51	19 06	19 20	
	d	15 20	15 33	15 48	16 07	16 15		16 20	16 52	16 41	17 07	17 15	17 20	17 36	17 48	18 07		18 15	18 20	18 36	18 48	18 52	19 07	19 20	19 26
Littleport	d	15 27						16 27					17 27						18 27					19 27	
Downham Market	d	15 36						16 36					17 36						18 36					19 36	
Watlington	d	15 41						16 41					17 41						18 41					19 41	
Kings Lynn	a	15 50						16 50					17 50						18 50					19 50	
Manea	d																								
March	d					16 31			17 09			17 31						18 31				19 09			
Whittlesea	d								17 20													19 20			
Peterborough 8	a			16 22		16 49			17 31			17 50			18 23			18 51			19 24	19 32			
Shippea Hill	d																								
Lakenheath	d				16x20																				
Brandon	d				16 25						17 23					18 23							19 23		
Thetford	d		15 54		16 34					17 02	17 31			17 57		18 31				18 57			19 31		19 50
Harling Road	d																								
Eccles Road	d																								
Attleborough	d				16 49						17 46					18 46							19 46		
Spooner Row	d																								
Wymondham	d				16 56						17 54					18 54							19 54		
Norwich	a		16 35		17 13					17 35	18 13			18 30		19 10				19 29			20 13		20 29

Table 17

Sundays

8 January to 12 February

London and Cambridge - Ely, Kings Lynn, Peterborough and Norwich

Network Diagram - see first Page of Table 13

		EM ◇		LE 1	FC 1	FC 1	EM ◇	EM ◇	LE 1	FC 1	FC 1	EM ◇		FC 1
London Liverpool Street	d													
London Kings Cross	d				19 15	20 15				21 15	22 15			23 15
Ipswich	d													
Stansted Airport	d													
Cambridge	d			19 52	20 05	21 05			21 52	22 05	23 05			00 13
Waterbeach	d				20 11	21 11				22 11	23 11			00 19
Ely [4]	a			20 06	20 20	21 20			22 06	22 20	23 20			00 29
	d	19 48		20 07	20 20	21 20	20 35	21 44	22 07	22 20	23 20	22 32		
Littleport	d				20 27	21 27				22 27	23 27			
Downham Market	d				20 36	21 36				22 36	23 36			
Watlington	d				20 41	21 41				22 41	23 41			
Kings Lynn	a				20 50	21 50				22 50	23 50			
Manea	d													
March	d													
Whittlesea	d													
Peterborough [8]	a	20 29						22 20						
Shippea Hill	d													
Lakenheath	d													
Brandon	d			20 23					22 23					
Thetford	d			20 31			20 56		22 31			22 53		
Harling Road	d													
Eccles Road	d													
Attleborough	d			20 46			21 10		22 46			23 07		
Spooner Row	d													
Wymondham	d			20 54			21 17		22 54			23 14		
Norwich	a			21 10			21 35		23 13			23 28		

Sundays

from 19 February

		FC 1	LE 1	FC 1	FC 1	LE ◇1	LE 1	XC ◇1	FC 1	EM ◇		LE 1	XC ◇1	FC 1	LE 1	LE 1	XC ◇1	FC 1	LE 1	XC ◇1		FC 1	EM ◇	EM ◇	LE 1
London Liverpool Street	d																								
London Kings Cross	d	23p15		07 53	09 15				10 15					11 15				12 15				13 15			
Ipswich	d					09 55									11 55										13 55
Stansted Airport	d							10 25					11 25				12 25			13 25					
Cambridge	d	00 14	08 48	09 05	10 05		10 48	11 00	11 05			11 52	12 00	12 05		12 52	13 00	13 05	13 52	14 00		14 05			
Waterbeach	d	00 20		09 11	10 11				11 11					12 11				13 11				14 11			
Ely [4]	a	00 29	09 02	09 20	10 20	10 51	11 02	11 14	11 20			12 06	12 15	12 20	12 51	13 06	13 15	13 20	14 06	14 14		14 20			14 51
	d	00 29	09 03	09 20	10 20	10 52	11 03	11 15	11 20	11 39		12 07	12 15	12 20	12 52	13 07	13 15	13 20	14 07	14 15		14 20	14 24	14 45	14 52
Littleport	d	00 36		09 27	10 27				11 27					12 27				13 27				14 27			
Downham Market	d	00 45		09 36	10 36				11 36					12 36				13 36				14 36			
Watlington	d	00 51		09 41	10 41				11 41					12 41				13 41				14 41			
Kings Lynn	a	01 00		09 50	10 50				11 50					12 50				13 50				14 50			
Manea	d																								
March	d					11 09		11 31					12 31		13 09		13 31			14 31					15 09
Whittlesea	d					11 20									13 20										15 20
Peterborough [8]	a					11 36		11 50		12 16			12 50		13 31		13 50			14 50				15 24	15 31
Shippea Hill	d																								
Lakenheath	d		09x17				11x17									13x20									
Brandon	d		09 22				11 22					12 23				13 25			14 23				14 42		
Thetford	d		09 31				11 31					12 31				13 34			14 31				14 50		
Harling Road	d																								
Eccles Road	d																								
Attleborough	d		09 46				11 46					12 46				13 49			14 46				15 04		
Spooner Row	d																								
Wymondham	d		09 53				11 53					12 54				13 56			14 54				15 11		
Norwich	a		10 13				12 13					13 13				14 13			15 13				15 30		

		LE 1	XC ◇1	FC 1	EM ◇	EM ◇		LE 1	XC ◇1	FC 1	LE 1	EM ◇	LE 1	XC ◇1	FC 1	EM ◇		EM ◇	LE 1	XC ◇1	FC 1	EM ◇	EM ◇	LE 1	LE 1
London Liverpool Street	d																								
London Kings Cross	d			14 15						15 15					16 15						17 15				
Ipswich	d										15 55													17 55	
Stansted Airport	d		14 25						15 25					16 25						17 25					
Cambridge	d	14 52	15 00	15 05				15 52	16 00	16 05			16 52	17 00	17 05				17 52	18 00	18 05				18 52
Waterbeach	d			15 11						16 11					17 11						18 11				
Ely [4]	a	15 06	15 14	15 20				16 06	16 15	16 20	16 51		17 06	17 15	17 20				18 06	18 15	18 20			18 51	19 06
	d	15 07	15 15	15 20	15 33	15 48		16 07	16 15	16 20	16 52	16 41	17 07	17 15	17 20	17 36		17 48	18 07	18 15	18 20	18 36	18 48	18 52	19 07
Littleport	d			15 27						16 27					17 27						18 27				
Downham Market	d			15 36						16 36					17 36						18 36				
Watlington	d			15 41						16 41					17 41						18 41				
Kings Lynn	a			15 50						16 50					17 50						18 50				
Manea	d																								
March	d		15 31						16 31		17 09			17 31						18 31				19 09	
Whittlesea	d										17 20													19 20	
Peterborough [8]	a		15 50			16 22			16 50		17 31			17 50				18 23		18 50			19 24	19 32	
Shippea Hill	d																								
Lakenheath	d							16x20																	
Brandon	d	15 23						16 25					17 23						18 23						19 23
Thetford	d	15 31			15 54			16 34				17 02	17 31			17 57			18 31			18 57			19 31
Harling Road	d																								
Eccles Road	d																								
Attleborough	d	15 46						16 49					17 46						18 46						19 46
Spooner Row	d																								
Wymondham	d	15 54						16 56					17 54						18 54						19 54
Norwich	a	16 13			16 35			17 13				17 35	18 13			18 30			19 10			19 29			20 13

Table 17

Sundays

from 19 February

London and Cambridge - Ely, Kings Lynn, Peterborough and Norwich

Network Diagram - see first Page of Table 13

		XC ◇1		FC 1	EM ◇	EM ◇	LE 1	XC ◇1	FC 1	FC 1	EM ◇	EM ◇		LE 1	FC 1	FC 1	EM ◇	FC 1
London Liverpool Street	d																	
London Kings Cross	d			18 15					19 15	20 15					21 15	22 15		23 15
Ipswich	d																	
Stansted Airport	d	18 25						19 25										
Cambridge	d	19 00		19 05			19 52	20 00	20 05	21 05				21 52	22 05	23 05		00 13
Waterbeach	d			19 11					20 11	21 11					22 11	23 11		00 19
Ely 4	a	19 15		19 20			20 06	20 15	20 20	21 20				22 06	22 20	23 20		00 29
	d	19 15		19 20	19 26	19 48	20 07	20 15	20 20	21 20	20 35	21 44		22 07	22 20	23 20	22 32	
Littleport	d			19 27					20 27	21 27					22 27	23 27		
Downham Market	d			19 36					20 36	21 36					22 36	23 36		
Watlington	d			19 41					20 41	21 41					22 41	23 41		
Kings Lynn	a			19 50					20 50	21 50					22 50	23 50		
Manea	d																	
March	d	19 31						20 31										
Whittlesea	d																	
Peterborough 8	a	19 50				20 29		20 50				22 20						
Shippea Hill	d																	
Lakenheath	d																	
Brandon	d						20 23							22 23				
Thetford	d				19 50		20 31				20 56			22 31			22 53	
Harling Road	d																	
Eccles Road	d																	
Attleborough	d						20 46				21 10			22 46			23 07	
Spooner Row	d																	
Wymondham	d						20 54				21 17			22 54			23 14	
Norwich	a				20 29		21 10				21 35			23 13			23 28	

Norwich, Peterborough, Kings Lynn and Ely - Cambridge and London

Network Diagram - see first Page of Table 13

		FC MO	FC MX	FC	LE	FC	LE	EM	LE	EM		FC	LE	EM	FC	XC	FC	EM	FC	LE	LE	EM	XC	FC	FC
		1	1	1	1	1	1	◇	1 A	◇		1	1	◇	1	◇1	1	◇	1	1	1	◇	◇1	1	1
Norwich	d						05 33	05 50					06 33	06 52							07 37	07 57			
Wymondham	d						05 45	06 02					06 45								07 49				
Spooner Row	d																								
Attleborough	d						05 52	06 09					06 52								07 56				
Eccles Road	d																								
Harling Road	d																								
Thetford	d						06 06	06 23					07 06	07 20							08 10	08 24			
Brandon	d						06 14						07 14								08 18				
Lakenheath	d																								
Shippea Hill	d																								
Peterborough 8	d									06 27						07 12		07 35		07 45			08 18		
Whittlesea	d															07 20				07 53					
March	d									06 43						07 31		07 51		08 04			08 34		
Manea	d															07x38									
Kings Lynn	d	22p28	22p28	04 56	05 19	05 51			06 17			06 51					07 25		07 55					08 27	08 59
Watlington	d	22p35	22p35	05 03	05 26	05 58			06 24			06 58					07 32		08 02					08 34	09 06
Downham Market	d	22p41	22p41	05 09	05 33	06 04			06 31			07 04					07 38		08 08					08 40	09 12
Littleport	d	22p50	22p50	05 18	05 42	06 13			06 40			07 13					07 47		08 17					08 49	09 21
Ely 4	a	22p58	22p58	05 26	05 51	06 21	06 31	06 45	06 49	07 01		07 21	07 31	07 41		07 51	07 56	08 11	08 26	08 31	08 37	08 46	08 52	08 57	09 29
	d	22p58	22p58	05 26	05 52	06 21	06 32		06 50			07 21	07 33		07 48	07 52	07 56		08 26	08 31	08 39		08 52	08 57	09 29
Waterbeach	d	23p07	23p07	05 35	06 01	06 31			06 59			07 31			07 57				08 36					09 07	09 38
Cambridge	a	23p15	23p14	05 44	06 10	06 39	06 51		07 08			07 39	07 52		08 04	08 07	08 12		08 45		08 59		09 08	09 15	09 47
Stansted Airport	a															08 39							09 39		
Ipswich	a																			09 28					
London Kings Cross	a	00 39	00 40	06 38		07 39						08 39					09 09		09 44					10 14	10 46
London Liverpool Street	a				07 25				08 25																

		LE	EM	EM	XC	EM		LE	FC	LE	EM	XC	EM	FC	LE	EM		XC	EM	FC	LE	LE	EM	XC	EM
		1	◇	◇	◇1	◇		1	1	1	◇	◇1	◇	1	1	◇		◇1	◇	1	1	1	◇	◇1	◇
Norwich	d	08 40		08 57						09 40	09 57				10 40	10 57						11 40	11 57		
Wymondham	d	08 52								09 52					10 52							11 52			
Spooner Row	d																								
Attleborough	d	08 59								09 59					10 59							11 59			
Eccles Road	d																								
Harling Road	d																								
Thetford	d	09 13		09 24						10 13	10 24				11 13	11 24						12 13	12 24		
Brandon	d	09 21								10 21					11 21							12 21			
Lakenheath	d																								
Shippea Hill	d																								
Peterborough 8	d		08 59		09 18	09 40		09 45				10 18	10 44					11 17	11 41		11 45			12 18	12 43
Whittlesea	d							09 53													11 53				
March	d				09 34			10 04				10 34						11 34			12 04			12 34	
Manea	d																								
Kings Lynn	d								09 59					10 56						11 56					
Watlington	d								10 06					11 03						12 03					
Downham Market	d								10 12					11 09						12 09					
Littleport	d								10 21					11 18						12 18					
Ely 4	a	09 38	09 41	09 45	09 52	10 13		10 25	10 29	10 38	10 48	10 52	11 16	11 26	11 38	11 48		11 52	12 14	12 26	12 29	12 38	12 47	12 52	13 16
	d	09 39			09 53			10 32	10 29	10 39		10 52		11 26	11 39			11 52		12 26	12 31	12 39		12 52	
Waterbeach	d								10 38					11 35						12 35					
Cambridge	a	09 59			10 08				10 47	10 59		11 08		11 44	11 59			12 08		12 44		12 59		13 08	
Stansted Airport	a				10 40							11 40						12 40						13 40	
Ipswich	a							11 28													13 28				
London Kings Cross	a								11 44					12 35						13 35					
London Liverpool Street	a																								

		FC		LE	EM	XC	EM	FC	LE	LE	EM	XC	EM	FC	LE	EM	XC	FC	EM	FC	LE	LE		EM	XC
		1		1	◇	◇1	◇	1	1	1	◇	◇1	◇	1	1	◇	◇1	1	◇	1	1	1		◇	◇1
Norwich	d			12 40	12 57					13 40	13 57				14 40	14 57						15 40		15 52	
Wymondham	d			12 52						13 52					14 52							15 52			
Spooner Row	d																								
Attleborough	d			12 59						13 59					14 59							15 59		16 09	
Eccles Road	d																							16 14	
Harling Road	d																							16 18	
Thetford	d			13 13	13 24					14 13	14 24				15 13	15 24						16 13		16 27	
Brandon	d			13 21						14 21					15 21							16 21			
Lakenheath	d																								
Shippea Hill	d																								
Peterborough 8	d					13 18	13 41		13 45			14 18	14 41				15 18		15 40		15 45				16 18
Whittlesea	d								13 53												15 53				
March	d					13 34			14 04			14 34					15 34				16 04				16 34
Manea	d																								
Kings Lynn	d	12 56						13 56						14 56						15 55					
Watlington	d	13 03						14 03						15 03						16 02					
Downham Market	d	13 09						14 09						15 09						16 08					
Littleport	d	13 18						14 18						15 18						16 17					
Ely 4	a	13 26		13 38	13 49	13 52	14 14	14 26	14 29	14 38	14 47	14 52	15 14	15 26	15 38	15 47	15 52		16 13	16 24	16 28	16 38		16 48	16 52
	d	13 26		13 39		13 52		14 26	14 31	14 39		14 52		15 26	15 39		15 52	16 06		16 24	16 31	16 39			16 52
Waterbeach	d	13 35						14 35						15 35				16 16		16 33					
Cambridge	a	13 44		13 59		14 08		14 44		14 59		15 08		15 44	15 59		16 08	16 22		16 43		16 59			17 08
Stansted Airport	a					14 40						15 40													17 40
Ipswich	a								15 28												17 28				
London Kings Cross	a	14 34						15 34						16 34				17 32		17 35					
London Liverpool Street	a																								

A The Fenman

Norwich, Peterborough, Kings Lynn and Ely - Cambridge and London

Network Diagram - see first Page of Table 13

		FC [1]	EM ◇	FC [1]	LE [1]	EM ◇	XC ◇[1]	FC [1]	EM ◇	LE [1]	FC [1]	LE [1]	EM ◇	XC ◇[1]	FC [1]	EM ◇	XC ◇[1]	LE [1]		EM ◇	XC ◇[1]	FC [1]	EM ◇	LE ◇[1]	LE [1]
Norwich	d				16 38	16 57						17 35	17 54					18 40		18 57					19 40
Wymondham	d				16 50	17 09						17 47	18 06					18 52							19 52
Spooner Row	d				16x54																				
Attleborough	d				16 59							17 54	18 13					18 59							19 59
Eccles Road	d											17 59													
Harling Road	d											18 03													
Thetford	d				17 13	17 27						18 13	18 27					19 13		19 24					20 13
Brandon	d				17 21							18 21						19 21							20 21
Lakenheath	d																								
Shippea Hill	d																								
Peterborough [8]	d		16 41				17 18		17 42	17 45				18 18		18 45	18 59				19 18		19 40	19 45	
Whittlesea	d						17 26			17 53														19 53	
March	d						17 37			18 04				18 34		19 01	19 15				19 35			20 04	
Manea	d						17x44																		
Kings Lynn	d	16 37						17 37							18 37							19 37			
Watlington	d	16 44						17 44							18 44							19 44			
Downham Market	d	16 50		17 12				17 50							18 50							19 50			
Littleport	d	17 00						17 59							18 59							19 59			
Ely [4]	a	17 08	17 14	17 28	17 38	17 48	17 58	18 07	18 16	18 28		18 38	18 48	18 52	19 08	19 24	19 33	19 38		19 48	19 53	20 08	20 13	20 26	20 38
	d	17 08		17 28	17 39		17 59	18 08		18 31	18 28	18 39		18 52	19 08		19 33	19 39			19 53	20 08		20 27	20 39
Waterbeach	d	17 17						18 17							19 17							20 17			
Cambridge	a	17 24		17 44	17 59		18 16	18 24				18 59		19 08	19 24		19 50	19 59			20 08	20 26			20 56
Stansted Airport	a						18 54							19 39							20 39				
Ipswich	a									19 28														21 23	
London Kings Cross	a	18 32		18 38				19 36			19 38				20 33							21 32			
London Liverpool Street	a																								

		XC ◇[1]	FC [1]	XC ◇[1]		FC [1]	EM ◇	LE [1]	LE ◇[1]	XC ◇[1]	FC [1]	LE [1]
Norwich	d							21 15				22 40
Wymondham	d							21 27				22 52
Spooner Row	d											
Attleborough	d							21 34				22 59
Eccles Road	d											
Harling Road	d											
Thetford	d							21 48				23 13
Brandon	d							21 56				23 21
Lakenheath	d											
Shippea Hill	d											
Peterborough [8]	d	20 18		21 18			21 38		21 45	22 18		
Whittlesea	d								21 53			
March	d	20 35		21 34					22 04	22 35		
Manea	d											
Kings Lynn	d		20 37			21 37					22 28	
Watlington	d		20 44			21 44					22 35	
Downham Market	d		20 50			21 50					22 41	
Littleport	d		20 59			21 59					22 50	
Ely [4]	a	20 53	21 08	21 52		22 08	22 11	22 14	22 23	22 53	22 58	23 38
	d	20 53	21 08	21 52		22 08		22 15	22 23	22 53	22 58	23 39
Waterbeach	d		21 17			22 17					23 07	
Cambridge	a	21 08	21 26	22 08		22 24		22 34		23 10	23 14	23 56
Stansted Airport	a	21 40		22 52								
Ipswich	a								23 18			
London Kings Cross	a		22 32			23 32					00 40	
London Liverpool Street	a											

Saturdays

		FC [1]	FC [1]	LE [1]	EM ◇	EM ◇	FC [1]	LE [1]	EM ◇	XC ◇[1]		EM ◇	LE [1]	FC [1]	LE [1]	EM ◇	XC ◇[1]	FC [1]	EM ◇	LE [1]		EM ◇	XC ◇[1]	FC [1]	EM ◇
Norwich	d			05 37	05 52			06 40	06 53						07 40	07 57				08 40		08 57			
Wymondham	d			05 49	06 04			06 52							07 52					08 52					
Spooner Row	d																								
Attleborough	d			05 56	06 11			06 59							07 59					08 59					
Eccles Road	d																								
Harling Road	d																								
Thetford	d			06 10	06 25			07 13	07 22						08 13	08 24				09 13		09 24			
Brandon	d			06 18				07 21							08 21					09 21					
Lakenheath	d																								
Shippea Hill	d																								
Peterborough [8]	d					06 27				07 13		07 35	07 45				08 18		09 00				09 18		09 43
Whittlesea	d									07 21			07 53												
March	d					06 43				07 32		07 51	08 04				08 34						09 34		
Manea	d									07x39															
Kings Lynn	d	22p28	05 56				06 56							07 56				08 56						09 30	
Watlington	d	22p35	06 03				07 03							08 03				09 03							
Downham Market	d	22p41	06 09				07 09							08 09				09 09						09 41	
Littleport	d	22p50	06 18				07 18							08 18				09 18							
Ely [4]	a	22p58	06 26	06 35	06 46	07 01	07 26	07 38	07 45	07 52		08 11	08 22	08 26	08 38	08 47	08 52	09 26	09 35	09 38		09 48	09 52	09 58	10 14
	d	22p58	06 26	06 36			07 26	07 39		07 52			08 31	08 26	08 39		08 52	09 26		09 39			09 52	09 58	
Waterbeach	d	23p07	06 35				07 35							08 35				09 35							
Cambridge	a	23p14	06 44	06 56			07 44	07 59		08 08				08 44	08 59		09 07	09 44		09 59			10 07	10 13	
Stansted Airport	a									08 39							09 40						10 40		
Ipswich	a												09 28												
London Kings Cross	a	00 40	07 36				08 36							09 39				10 35						11 04	
London Liverpool Street	a																								

Norwich, Peterborough, Kings Lynn and Ely - Cambridge and London

Network Diagram - see first Page of Table 13

		FC 1	LE 1	LE 1	EM ◇	XC ◇1		EM ◇	FC 1	LE 1	EM ◇	XC ◇1	EM ◇	FC 1	LE 1	LE 1		EM ◇	XC ◇1	EM ◇	FC 1	LE 1	EM ◇	XC ◇1	EM ◇
Norwich	d			09 40	09 57					10 40	10 57					11 40		11 57				12 40	12 57		
Wymondham	d			09 52						10 52						11 52						12 52			
Spooner Row	d																								
Attleborough	d			09 59						10 59						11 59						12 59			
Eccles Road	d																								
Harling Road	d																								
Thetford	d			10 13	10 24					11 13	11 24					12 13		12 24				13 13	13 24		
Brandon	d			10 21						11 21						12 21						13 21			
Lakenheath	d			10x26																					
Shippea Hill	d																								
Peterborough 8	d		09 47			10 18		10 41				11 18	11 41		11 45				12 18	12 40				13 18	13 41
Whittlesea	d		09 55												11 53										
March	d		10 06			10 34						11 34			12 04				12 34					13 34	
Manea	d																								
Kings Lynn	d	09 56							10 56					11 56							12 56				
Watlington	d	10 03							11 03					12 03							13 03				
Downham Market	d	10 09							11 09					12 09							13 09				
Littleport	d	10 18							11 18					12 18							13 18				
Ely 4	a	10 26	10 29	10 39	10 47	10 52		11 17	11 26	11 38	11 48	11 52	12 14	12 26	12 28	12 38		12 47	12 52	13 13	13 26	13 38	13 47	13 52	14 14
	d	10 26	10 31	10 39		10 52			11 26	11 39		11 52		12 26	12 31	12 39			12 52		13 26	13 39		13 52	
Waterbeach	d	10 35							11 35					12 35							13 35				
Cambridge	a	10 44		10 59		11 07			11 44	11 59		12 07		12 44		12 59			13 07		13 44	13 59		14 07	
Stansted Airport	a					11 40						12 40							13 40					14 40	
Ipswich	a		11 28												13 28										
London Kings Cross	a	11 37							12 35					13 35							14 35				
London Liverpool Street	a																								

		FC 1		LE 1	LE 1	EM ◇	XC ◇1	EM ◇	FC 1	LE 1	EM ◇	XC ◇1		EM ◇	FC 1	LE 1	LE 1	EM ◇	XC ◇1	EM ◇	FC 1	LE 1		EM ◇	XC ◇1
Norwich	d				13 40	13 57				14 40	14 57						15 35	15 52				16 38		16 57	
Wymondham	d				13 52					14 52							15 47					16 50		17 09	
Spooner Row	d																					16x54			
Attleborough	d				13 59					14 59							15 54	16 09				16 59			
Eccles Road	d																15 59								
Harling Road	d																16 03								
Thetford	d				14 13	14 24				15 13	15 24						16 13	16 23				17 13		17 27	
Brandon	d				14 21					15 21							16 21					17 21			
Lakenheath	d																								
Shippea Hill	d																								
Peterborough 8	d			13 45			14 18	14 43				15 18		15 41		15 45			16 18	16 41					17 19
Whittlesea	d			13 53												15 53									17 27
March	d			14 04			14 34					15 34				16 04			16 34						17 38
Manea	d																								17x46
Kings Lynn	d	13 56							14 56						15 56						16 56				
Watlington	d	14 03							15 03						16 03						17 03				
Downham Market	d	14 09							15 09						16 09						17 09				
Littleport	d	14 18							15 18						16 18						17 18				
Ely 4	a	14 26		14 28	14 38	14 47	14 52	15 14	15 26	15 38	15 48	15 52		16 14	16 26	16 28	16 38	16 47	16 52	17 13	17 26	17 38		17 48	17 59
	d	14 26		14 31	14 39		14 52		15 26	15 39		15 52			16 26	16 31	16 39		16 52		17 26	17 39			18 00
Waterbeach	d	14 35							15 35						16 35						17 35				
Cambridge	a	14 44			14 59		15 07		15 44	15 59		16 07			16 44		16 59		17 07		17 44	17 59			18 17
Stansted Airport	a						15 40					16 40							17 40						18 53
Ipswich	a			15 28												17 28									
London Kings Cross	a	15 35							16 35						17 35						18 35				
London Liverpool Street	a																								

		EM ◇	FC 1	LE 1	LE 1	EM ◇	XC ◇1	FC 1		EM ◇	LE 1	EM ◇	XC ◇1	FC 1	EM ◇	LE ◇1	LE 1	XC ◇1		FC 1	LE 1	XC ◇1	FC 1	EM ◇	LE ◇1
Norwich	d				17 35	17 54					18 40	18 57					19 40				20 40				
Wymondham	d				17 47	18 06					18 52						19 52				20 52				
Spooner Row	d																								
Attleborough	d				17 54	18 13					18 59						19 59				20 59				
Eccles Road	d				17 59																				
Harling Road	d				18 03																				
Thetford	d				18 13	18 27					19 13	19 24					20 13				21 13				
Brandon	d				18 21						19 21						20 21				21 21				
Lakenheath	d																								
Shippea Hill	d										19x29														
Peterborough 8	d	17 39		17 45			18 18			18 44			19 18		19 41	19 45		20 18				21 18		21 38	21 45
Whittlesea	d			17 53												19 53									21 53
March	d			18 04			18 34			19 01			19 34			20 04		20 34				21 34			22 04
Manea	d																								
Kings Lynn	d		17 56					18 35						19 35						20 35			21 35		
Watlington	d		18 03					18 42						19 42						20 42			21 42		
Downham Market	d		18 09					18 48						19 48						20 48			21 48		
Littleport	d		18 18					18 57						19 57						20 57			21 57		
Ely 4	a	18 12	18 26	18 28	18 38	18 48	18 52	19 05		19 19	19 39	19 46	19 51	20 05	20 14	20 26	20 38	20 51		21 05	21 38	21 51	22 05	22 12	22 23
	d		18 26	18 31	18 39		18 53	19 05			19 39		19 52	20 05		20 27	20 39	20 51		21 05	21 39	21 51	22 05		22 23
Waterbeach	d		18 35					19 15						20 15						21 15			22 15		
Cambridge	a		18 44		18 59		19 09	19 21			19 59		20 08	20 21			20 59	21 07		21 21	21 59	22 07	22 21		
Stansted Airport	a						19 40						20 40					21 40				22 40			
Ipswich	a			19 28												21 22									23 18
London Kings Cross	a		19 35					20 30						21 32						22 31			23 31		
London Liverpool Street	a																								

Table 17

Saturdays

Norwich, Peterborough, Kings Lynn and Ely - Cambridge and London

Network Diagram - see first Page of Table 13

		XC ◇1	LE 1	FC 1
Norwich	d		22 40	
Wymondham	d		22 52	
Spooner Row	d			
Attleborough	d		22 59	
Eccles Road	d			
Harling Road	d			
Thetford	d		23 13	
Brandon	d		23 21	
Lakenheath	d			
Shippea Hill	d			
Peterborough 8	d	22 18		
Whittlesea	d			
March	d	22 34		
Manea	d			
Kings Lynn	d			23 10
Watlington	d			23 17
Downham Market	d			23 23
Littleport	d			23 32
Ely 4	a	22 53	23 38	23 41
	d	22 55	23 39	23 43
Waterbeach	d			23 52
Cambridge	a	23 10	23 59	23 59
Stansted Airport	a			
Ipswich	a			
London Kings Cross	a			
London Liverpool Street	a			

Sundays

until 1 January

		FC 1	FC 1	FC 1	LE 1	FC 1	LE 1	EM ◇	FC 1	LE 1	LE 1		FC 1	LE 1	XC ◇1	FC 1	LE 1	EM ◇	LE 1	EM ◇	XC ◇1		FC 1	LE 1	EM ◇	EM ◇
Norwich	d				09 03		10 03	10 47		11 03				12 03			13 03			13 49				14 03		14 49
Wymondham	d				09 15		10 15			11 15				12 15			13 15							14 15		
Spooner Row	d																									
Attleborough	d				09 22		10 22			11 22				12 22			13 22							14 22		
Eccles Road	d																									
Harling Road	d																									
Thetford	d				09 36		10 36	11 14		11 36				12 36			13 36			14 16				14 36		15 16
Brandon	d				09 44		10 44			11 44				12 44			13 44							14 44		
Lakenheath	d				09x49					11x49																
Shippea Hill	d																									
Peterborough 8	d										11 46				13 18			13 43	13 46		14 18				14 53	
Whittlesea	d										11 54								13 55							
March	d										12 05				13 34				14 06		14 34					
Manea	d																									
Kings Lynn	d		08 28	09 28		10 28			11 28				12 28			13 28							14 28			
Watlington	d		08 35	09 35		10 35			11 35				12 35			13 35							14 35			
Downham Market	d		08 41	09 41		10 41			11 41				12 41			13 41							14 41			
Littleport	d		08 50	09 50		10 50			11 50				12 50			13 50							14 50			
Ely 4	a		08 58	09 58	10 08	10 58	11 06	11 35	11 58	12 08	12 29		12 58	13 01	13 52	13 58	14 01	14 16	14 29	14 42	14 52		14 58	15 01	15 29	15 42
	d	05 26	08 58	09 58	10 09	10 58	11 07		11 58	12 09	12 31		12 58	13 04	13 52	13 58	14 04		14 31		14 52		14 58	15 04		
Waterbeach	d	05 35	09 07	10 07		11 07			12 07				13 07			14 07							15 07			
Cambridge	a	05 42	09 15	10 15	10 27	11 15	11 25		12 15	12 27			13 15	13 22	14 08	14 15	14 22				15 08		15 15	15 22		
Stansted Airport	a														14 45						15 45					
Ipswich	a										13 28								15 28							
London Kings Cross	a	06 39	10 09	11 08		12 08			13 08				14 08			15 08							16 08			
London Liverpool Street	a																									

		XC ◇1	FC 1	LE 1	LE 1	EM ◇		XC ◇1	EM ◇	FC 1	LE 1	EM ◇	EM ◇	XC ◇1	FC 1	LE 1		LE ◇1	FC 1	EM ◇	EM ◇	XC ◇1	FC 1	LE 1	EM ◇
Norwich	d			15 03					15 53		16 03		16 54			17 03					17 54			18 03	
Wymondham	d			15 15							16 15					17 15								18 15	
Spooner Row	d																								
Attleborough	d			15 22							16 22					17 22								18 22	
Eccles Road	d																								
Harling Road	d																								
Thetford	d			15 36					16 20		16 36		17 21			17 36					18 21			18 36	
Brandon	d			15 44							16 44					17 44								18 44	
Lakenheath	d			15x49																					
Shippea Hill	d																								
Peterborough 8	d	15 18			15 45	16 03		16 18	17a10			16 59		17 18				17 45		17 56		18 18			18 48
Whittlesea	d				15 53													17 53							
March	d	15 34			16 04			16 34						17 34				18 04		18 12		18 34			
Manea	d																								
Kings Lynn	d		15 28							16 28					17 28				17 58				18 28		
Watlington	d		15 35							16 35					17 35				18 05				18 35		
Downham Market	d		15 41							16 41					17 41				18 11				18 41		
Littleport	d		15 50							16 50					17 50				18 20				18 50		
Ely 4	a	15 52	15 58	16 03	16 23	16 38		16 52		16 58	17 01	17 32	17 45	17 52	17 58	18 01		18 23	18 28	18 32	18 44	18 52	18 58	19 01	19 21
	d	15 52	15 58	16 04	16 31			16 52		16 58	17 04			17 52	17 58	18 04		18 31	18 28			18 52	18 58	19 04	
Waterbeach	d		16 07							17 07					18 07				18 37				19 07		
Cambridge	a	16 08	16 15	16 22				17 07		17 15	17 22			18 07	18 15	18 22			18 45			19 07	19 15	19 22	
Stansted Airport	a	16 45						17 45						18 45								19 45			
Ipswich	a				17 28													19 28							
London Kings Cross	a		17 08							18 08					19 11				19 36				20 11		
London Liverpool Street	a																								

Table 17

Sundays

until 1 January

Norwich, Peterborough, Kings Lynn and Ely - Cambridge and London

Network Diagram - see first Page of Table 13

		EM ◇		XC ◇1	FC 1	LE ◇1	EM ◇	XC ◇1	FC 1	LE 1	EM ◇	XC ◇1		FC 1	EM ◇	XC ◇1	FC 1	LE 1							
Norwich	d	18 56								20 03	20 52							22 03							
Wymondham	d									20 15								22 15							
Spooner Row	d																								
Attleborough	d									20 22								22 22							
Eccles Road	d																								
Harling Road	d																								
Thetford	d	19 23								20 36	21 19							22 36							
Brandon	d									20 44								22 44							
Lakenheath	d																								
Shippea Hill	d																								
Peterborough 8	d			19 18		19 45	19 58	20 18				21 18			21 53	22 18									
Whittlesea	d					19 53																			
March	d			19 34		20 04		20 34				21 34				22 34									
Manea	d																								
Kings Lynn	d				19 28				20 28					21 28			22 28								
Watlington	d				19 35				20 35					21 35			22 35								
Downham Market	d				19 41				20 41					21 41			22 41								
Littleport	d				19 50				20 50					21 50			22 50								
Ely 4	a	19 44		19 52	19 58	20 23	20 31	20 52	20 58	21 01	21 40	21 52		21 58	22 28	22 52	22 58	23 01							
	d			19 52	19 58	20 23		20 52	20 58	21 04		21 52		21 58		22 52	22 58	23 04							
Waterbeach	d				20 07				21 07					22 07			23 07								
Cambridge	a			20 07	20 15			21 07	21 15	21 22		22 07		22 15		23 07	23 15	23 22							
Stansted Airport	a			20 45				21 45				22 45													
Ipswich	a					21 18																			
London Kings Cross	a				21 11				22 10					23 08			00 39								
London Liverpool Street	a																								

Sundays

8 January to 12 February

		FC 1	FC 1	LE 1	FC 1	LE 1	EM ◇	FC 1	LE 1	LE 1		FC 1	LE 1	FC 1	LE 1	EM ◇	LE 1	EM ◇	FC 1	LE 1		EM ◇	EM ◇	XC ◇1	FC 1
Norwich	d			09 03		10 03	10 47		11 03				12 03		13 03			13 49		14 03			14 49		
Wymondham	d			09 15		10 15			11 15				12 15		13 15					14 15					
Spooner Row	d																								
Attleborough	d			09 22		10 22			11 22				12 22		13 22					14 22					
Eccles Road	d																								
Harling Road	d																								
Thetford	d			09 36		10 36	11 14		11 36				12 36		13 36			14 16		14 36			15 16		
Brandon	d			09 44		10 44			11 44				12 44		13 44					14 44					
Lakenheath	d			09x49					11x49																
Shippea Hill	d																								
Peterborough 8	d									11 46						13 43	13 46					14 53		15 18	
Whittlesea	d									11 54							13 55								
March	d									12 05							14 06							15 34	
Manea	d																								
Kings Lynn	d	08 28	09 28		10 28			11 28				12 28		13 28					14 28						15 28
Watlington	d	08 35	09 35		10 35			11 35				12 35		13 35					14 35						15 35
Downham Market	d	08 41	09 41		10 41			11 41				12 41		13 41					14 41						15 41
Littleport	d	08 50	09 50		10 50			11 50				12 50		13 50					14 50						15 50
Ely 4	a	08 58	09 58	10 08	10 58	11 06	11 35	11 58	12 08	12 29		12 58	13 01	13 58	14 01	14 16	14 29	14 42	14 58	15 01		15 29	15 42	15 52	15 58
	d	08 58	09 58	10 09	10 58	11 07		11 58	12 09	12 31		12 58	13 04	13 58	14 04		14 31		14 58	15 04				15 52	15 58
Waterbeach	d	09 07	10 07		11 07			12 07				13 07		14 07					15 07						16 07
Cambridge	a	09 15	10 15	10 27	11 15	11 25		12 15	12 27			13 15	13 22	14 15	14 22				15 15	15 22				16 08	16 15
Stansted Airport	a																							16 45	
Ipswich	a									13 28							15 28								
London Kings Cross	a	10 09	11 08		12 08			13 08				14 08		15 08					16 08						17 08
London Liverpool Street	a																								

		LE 1	LE 1	EM ◇	EM ◇	FC 1		LE 1	EM ◇	EM ◇	XC ◇1	FC 1	LE 1	LE ◇1	FC 1	EM ◇		EM ◇	FC 1	LE 1	XC ◇1	EM ◇	EM ◇	FC 1	LE ◇1
Norwich	d	15 03			15 53			16 03		16 54			17 03					17 54		18 03			18 56		
Wymondham	d	15 15						16 15					17 15							18 15					
Spooner Row	d																								
Attleborough	d	15 22						16 22					17 22							18 22					
Eccles Road	d																								
Harling Road	d																								
Thetford	d	15 36			16 20			16 36		17 21			17 36					18 21		18 36			19 23		
Brandon	d	15 44						16 44					17 44							18 44					
Lakenheath	d	15x49																							
Shippea Hill	d																								
Peterborough 8	d		15 45	16 03	17a10				16 59		17 18			17 45		17 56					18 40	18 48			19 45
Whittlesea	d		15 53											17 53											19 53
March	d		16 04								17 34			18 04		18 12					18 56				20 04
Manea	d																								
Kings Lynn	d					16 28						17 28			17 58				18 28					19 28	
Watlington	d					16 35						17 35			18 05				18 35					19 35	
Downham Market	d					16 41						17 41			18 11				18 41					19 41	
Littleport	d					16 50						17 50			18 20				18 50					19 50	
Ely 4	a	16 03	16 23	16 38		16 58		17 01	17 32	17 45	17 52	17 58	18 01	18 23	18 28	18 32		18 44	18 58	19 01	19 15	19 21	19 44	19 58	20 23
	d	16 04	16 31			16 58		17 04			17 52	17 58	18 04	18 31	18 28				18 58	19 04	19 15			19 58	20 23
Waterbeach	d					17 07						18 07			18 37				19 07					20 07	
Cambridge	a	16 22				17 15		17 22			18 07	18 15	18 22		18 45				19 15	19 22	19 31			20 15	
Stansted Airport	a										18 45										20 08				
Ipswich	a		17 28											19 28											21 18
London Kings Cross	a					18 08						19 11			19 36				20 11					21 11	
London Liverpool Street	a																								

Table 17

Sundays

8 January to 12 February

Norwich, Peterborough, Kings Lynn and Ely - Cambridge and London

Network Diagram - see first Page of Table 13

		EM	FC	LE	XC	EM	FC	XC	FC	EM	XC	FC	LE
		◇	1	1	◇1	◇	1	◇1	1	◇	◇1	1	1
Norwich	d			20 03		20 52							22 03
Wymondham	d			20 15									22 15
Spooner Row	d												
Attleborough	d			20 22									22 22
Eccles Road	d												
Harling Road	d												
Thetford	d			20 36		21 19							22 36
Brandon	d			20 44									22 44
Lakenheath	d												
Shippea Hill	d												
Peterborough 8	d	19 58			20 25			21 25		21 53	22 18		
Whittlesea	d												
March	d				20 41			21 41			22 34		
Manea	d												
Kings Lynn	d		20 28				21 28					22 28	
Watlington	d		20 35				21 35					22 35	
Downham Market	d		20 41				21 41					22 41	
Littleport	d		20 50				21 50					22 50	
Ely 4	a	20 31	20 58	21 01	21 04	21 40	21 58	22 01		22 28	22 52	22 58	23 01
	d		20 58	21 04	21 07		21 58	22 01			22 52	22 58	23 04
Waterbeach	d		21 07				22 07		←			23 07	
Cambridge	a		21 15	21 22	21 22		22 15	22 16	22 15		23 07	23 15	23 22
Stansted Airport	a				21 59		→	22 45					
Ipswich	a												
London Kings Cross	a		22 10						23 08			00 39	
London Liverpool Street	a												

Sundays

from 19 February

		FC	FC	LE	FC	LE	EM	FC	LE	LE	FC	LE	XC	FC	LE	EM	LE	EM	XC	FC	LE	EM	EM
		1	1	1	1	1	◇	1	1	1	1	1	◇1	1	1	◇	1	◇	◇1	1	1	◇	◇
Norwich	d			09 03		10 03	10 47		11 03			12 03			13 03			13 49			14 03		14 49
Wymondham	d			09 15		10 15			11 15			12 15			13 15						14 15		
Spooner Row	d																						
Attleborough	d			09 22		10 22			11 22			12 22			13 22						14 22		
Eccles Road	d																						
Harling Road	d																						
Thetford	d			09 36		10 36	11 14		11 36			12 36			13 36			14 16			14 36		15 16
Brandon	d			09 44		10 44			11 44			12 44			13 44						14 44		
Lakenheath	d			09x49					11x49														
Shippea Hill	d																						
Peterborough 8	d									11 46			13 18			13 43	13 46		14 18			14 53	
Whittlesea	d									11 54							13 55						
March	d									12 05			13 34				14 06		14 34				
Manea	d																						
Kings Lynn	d	08 28	09 28		10 28			11 28			12 28			13 28						14 28			
Watlington	d	08 35	09 35		10 35			11 35			12 35			13 35						14 35			
Downham Market	d	08 41	09 41		10 41			11 41			12 41			13 41						14 41			
Littleport	d	08 50	09 50		10 50			11 50			12 50			13 50						14 50			
Ely 4	a	08 58	09 58	10 08	10 58	11 06	11 35	11 58	12 08	12 29	12 58	13 01	13 52	13 58	14 01	14 16	14 29	14 42	14 52	14 58	15 01	15 29	15 42
	d	08 58	09 58	10 09	10 58	11 07		11 58	12 09	12 31	12 58	13 04	13 52	13 58	14 04		14 31		14 52	14 58	15 04		
Waterbeach	d	09 07	10 07		11 07			12 07			13 07			14 07						15 07			
Cambridge	a	09 15	10 15	10 27	11 15	11 25		12 15	12 27		13 15	13 22	14 08	14 15	14 22				15 08	15 15	15 22		
Stansted Airport	a												14 45						15 45				
Ipswich	a									13 28							15 28						
London Kings Cross	a	10 09	11 08		12 08			13 08			14 08			15 08						16 08			
London Liverpool Street	a																						

		XC	FC	LE	LE	EM	XC	EM	FC	LE	EM	EM	XC	FC	LE	LE	FC	EM	EM	XC	FC	LE	EM
		◇1	1	1	1	◇	◇1	◇	1	1	◇	◇	◇1	1	1	◇1	1	◇	◇	◇1	1	1	◇
Norwich	d			15 03				15 53		16 03		16 54			17 03				17 54			18 03	
Wymondham	d			15 15						16 15					17 15							18 15	
Spooner Row	d																						
Attleborough	d			15 22						16 22					17 22							18 22	
Eccles Road	d																						
Harling Road	d																						
Thetford	d			15 36				16 20		16 36		17 21			17 36				18 21			18 36	
Brandon	d			15 44						16 44					17 44							18 44	
Lakenheath	d			15x49																			
Shippea Hill	d																						
Peterborough 8	d	15 18			15 45	16 03	16 18	17a10			16 59		17 18			17 45		17 56		18 18			18 48
Whittlesea	d				15 53											17 53							
March	d	15 34			16 04		16 34						17 34			18 04		18 12		18 34			
Manea	d																						
Kings Lynn	d		15 28						16 28					17 28			17 58				18 28		
Watlington	d		15 35						16 35					17 35			18 05				18 35		
Downham Market	d		15 41						16 41					17 41			18 11				18 41		
Littleport	d		15 50						16 50					17 50			18 20				18 50		
Ely 4	a	15 52	15 58	16 03	16 23	16 38	16 52		16 58	17 01	17 32	17 45	17 52	17 58	18 01	18 23	18 28	18 32	18 44	18 52	18 58	19 01	19 21
	d	15 52	15 58	16 04	16 31		16 52		16 58	17 04			17 52	17 58	18 04	18 31	18 28			18 52	18 58	19 04	
Waterbeach	d		16 07						17 07					18 07			18 37				19 07		
Cambridge	a	16 08	16 15	16 22			17 07		17 15	17 22			18 07	18 15	18 22		18 45			19 07	19 15	19 22	
Stansted Airport	a	16 45					17 45						18 45							19 45			
Ipswich	a				17 28											19 28							
London Kings Cross	a		17 08						18 08					19 11			19 36				20 11		
London Liverpool Street	a																						

Table 17

Sundays
from 19 February

Norwich, Peterborough, Kings Lynn and Ely - Cambridge and London

Network Diagram - see first Page of Table 13

		EM		XC	FC	LE	EM	XC	FC	LE	EM	XC		FC	EM	XC	FC	LE
		◇		◇ 1	1	◇ 1	◇	◇ 1	1	1	◇	◇ 1		1	◇	◇ 1	1	1
Norwich	d	18 56								20 03	20 52							22 03
Wymondham	d									20 15								22 15
Spooner Row	d																	
Attleborough	d									20 22								22 22
Eccles Road	d																	
Harling Road	d																	
Thetford	d	19 23								20 36	21 19							22 36
Brandon	d									20 44								22 44
Lakenheath	d																	
Shippea Hill	d																	
Peterborough 8	d			19 18		19 45	19 58	20 18				21 18			21 53	22 18		
Whittlesea	d					19 53												
March	d			19 34		20 04		20 34				21 34				22 34		
Manea	d																	
Kings Lynn	d				19 28				20 28					21 28			22 28	
Watlington	d				19 35				20 35					21 35			22 35	
Downham Market	d				19 41				20 41					21 41			22 41	
Littleport	d				19 50				20 50					21 50			22 50	
Ely 4	a	19 44		19 52	19 58	20 23	20 31	20 52	20 58	21 01	21 40	21 52		21 58	22 28	22 52	22 58	23 01
	d			19 52	19 58	20 23		20 52	20 58	21 04		21 52		21 58		22 52	22 58	23 04
Waterbeach	d				20 07				21 07					22 07			23 07	
Cambridge	a			20 07	20 15			21 07	21 15	21 22		22 07		22 15		23 07	23 15	23 22
Stansted Airport	a			20 45				21 45				22 45						
Ipswich	a					21 18												
London Kings Cross	a				21 11				22 10					23 08			00 39	
London Liverpool Street	a																	

Table 17A

Mondays to Fridays

Kings Lynn - Sandringham and Hunstanton

Bus Service

		FC	FC	FC		FC	FC	FC		FC		FC	FC		FC	FC	FC	FC	FC	FC		FC	FC	FC	FC
Kings Lynn	d	06 20	06 50	07 30		08 05	08 35	09 00		09 15		09 25	09 30		09 40	10 05	10 15	10 25	10 30	10 40		11 00	11 05	11 15	11 25
Sandringham Visitor Centre	a						09 03								10 06		10 39			11 06					
Sandringham Norwich Gates	a																								
Hunstanton Bus Station	a	07 07	07 37	08 22		08 51	09 36	09 39		10 07		10 18	10 00		10 38	10 59	11 08	11 18	11 04	11 38		11 33	11 59	12 07	12 18

		FC	FC	FC	FC	FC		FC	FC	FC	FC	FC	FC	FC	FC	FC		FC	FC	FC	FC	FC	FC	FC	FC
Kings Lynn	d	11 30	11 40	12 00	12 05	12 15		12 25	12 30	12 40	13 00	13 05	13 15	13 25	13 30	13 40		14 05	14 15	14 25	14 30	14 40	15 00	15 05	15 15
Sandringham Visitor Centre	a		12 06			12 39				13 06						14 06			14 39			15 06			
Sandringham Norwich Gates	a																								
Hunstanton Bus Station	a	12 04	12 38	12 33	12 59	13 08		13 18	13 04	13 38	13 33	13 59	14 07	14 18	14 04	14 38		14 59	15 08	15 18	15 04	15 38	15 33	16 04	16 07

		FC		FC	FC	FC		FC		FC	FC	FC			FC	FC	FC	FC	FC	FC	FC	FC		FC	
Kings Lynn	d	15 25		15 30	15 45	16 15		16 30		16 40	17 00	17 15			17 35	17 45	18 20	18 35	19 20	20 00	21 30	21 35		23 07	
Sandringham Visitor Centre	a				16 12	16 39				17 08															
Sandringham Norwich Gates	a																								
Hunstanton Bus Station	a	16 20		16 04	16 40	17 08		17 13		17 38	17 33	18 07			18 15	18 40	19 08	19 23	20 04	20 48	22 20	22 19		23 54	

Saturdays

		FC	FC	FC	FC	FC	FC	FC	FC	FC		FC	FC	FC	FC	FC	FC	FC	FC	FC		FC	FC	FC	FC
Kings Lynn	d	06 50	07 30	08 40	09 00	09 00	09 25	09 30	09 40	10 05		10 25	10 30	10 40	11 05	11 25	11 30	11 40	12 05	12 25		12 30	12 40	13 05	13 25
Sandringham Visitor Centre	a			09 06					10 06					11 06				12 06					13 06		
Sandringham Norwich Gates	a																								
Hunstanton Bus Station	a	07 37	08 22	09 38	09 39	09 56	10 18	10 04	10 38	10 59		11 18	11 04	11 38	11 59	12 18	12 04	12 38	12 59	13 18		13 04	13 38	13 59	14 18

		FC	FC	FC	FC	FC		FC	FC	FC	FC	FC	FC	FC	FC	FC		FC	FC	FC	FC	FC	FC		
Kings Lynn	d	13 30	13 40	14 05	14 25	14 30		14 40	15 05	15 25	15 30	15 40	16 15	16 30	16 40	17 15		17 35	17 45	18 35	20 00	21 30	23 07		
Sandringham Visitor Centre	a		14 06					15 06				16 06			17 06										
Sandringham Norwich Gates	a																								
Hunstanton Bus Station	a	14 04	14 38	14 59	15 18	15 04		15 38	15 59	16 18	16 04	16 37	17 10	17 13	17 37	18 10		18 15	18 38	19 23	20 48	22 20	23 54		

Sundays

		FC	FC	FC	FC	FC	FC	FC	FC	FC		FC	FC	FC	FC	FC	FC	FC	FC	FC		FC			
Kings Lynn	d	08 05	09 15	09 30	10 15	11 00	11 15	12 00	12 15	13 00		13 15	14 15	15 00	15 15	16 15	17 00	17 15	18 20	19 20		21 35			
Sandringham Visitor Centre	a				10 39				12 39				14 39			16 39									
Sandringham Norwich Gates	a																								
Hunstanton Bus Station	a	08 51	10 07	10 00	11 08	11 33	12 07	12 33	13 08	13 33		14 07	15 08	15 33	16 07	17 08	17 33	18 07	19 08	20 04		22 19			

Services are subject to variation on Bank Holidays

Table 17A

Hunstanton and Sandringham - Kings Lynn

Bus Service

		FC FO	FC	FC	FC	FC	FC	FC	FC	FC		FC	FC	FC	FC	FC	FC	FC	FC	FC		FC	FC	FC	FC
Hunstanton Bus Station	d	23p55	06 15	06 45	07 10	07 40	08 00	08 25	08 47	09 00		09 06	09 10	09 25	09 47	10 06	10 10	10 13	10 25	10 40		10 47	11 06	11 13	11 15
Sandringham Norwich Gates	d																								
Sandringham Visitor Centre	d							09 00						10 00				10 43	11 00						
Kings Lynn	a	00 41	07 08	07 34	08 07	08 41	08 42	09 23	09 40	09 50		10 00	09 41	10 23	10 40	11 00	10 41	11 07	11 23	11 10		11 40	12 00	12 07	11 46

		FC	FC	FC	FC	FC		FC	FC	FC	FC	FC	FC	FC	FC	FC		FC	FC	FC	FC	FC	FC	FC	FC
Hunstanton Bus Station	d	11 25	11 40	11 47	12 06	12 13		12 15	12 25	12 47	13 06	13 13	13 15	13 25	13 40	13 47		14 06	14 13	14 15	14 25	14 40	14 47	15 06	15 13
Sandringham Norwich Gates	d																								
Sandringham Visitor Centre	d	12 00				12 43			13 00					14 00					14 43		15 00				
Kings Lynn	a	12 23	12 10	12 40	13 00	13 07		12 46	13 23	13 40	14 00	14 07	13 46	14 23	14 10	14 40		15 00	15 07	14 46	15 23	15 10	15 40	16 00	16 07

		FC		FC		FC	FC	FC	FC	FC	FC	FC		FC	FC	FC	FC	FC	FC	FC	FC	FC		FC	FC
Hunstanton Bus Station	d	15 15		15 25		15 40	15 47	16 10	16 13	16 25	16 30	16 45		17 13	17 20	17 30	17 40	17 45	18 13	18 20	18 40	18 45		20 05	20 50
Sandringham Norwich Gates	d																								
Sandringham Visitor Centre	d			16 00					16 43	17 00															
Kings Lynn	a	15 52		16 23		16 10	16 42	17 06	17 07	17 28	17 00	17 44		18 07	18 13	18 00	18 07	18 40	19 01	19 10	19 08	19 33		20 49	21 36

		FC	FC	FC
Hunstanton Bus Station	d	22 20	22 23	23 55
Sandringham Norwich Gates	d			
Sandringham Visitor Centre	d			
Kings Lynn	a	23 01	23 07	00 41

Saturdays

		FC	FC	FC	FC	FC	FC	FC	FC	FC		FC	FC	FC	FC	FC	FC	FC	FC	FC		FC	FC	FC	FC
Hunstanton Bus Station	d	23p55	06 45	07 40	08 47	09 10	09 25	09 47	10 06	10 10		10 25	10 47	11 06	11 15	11 25	11 45	11 47	12 06	12 15		12 25	12 47	13 06	13 15
Sandringham Norwich Gates	d																								
Sandringham Visitor Centre	d						10 00					11 00				12 00						13 00			
Kings Lynn	a	00 41	07 34	08 31	09 40	09 41	10 23	10 40	11 00	10 41		11 23	11 40	12 00	11 46	12 23	12 16	12 40	13 00	12 46		13 23	13 40	14 00	13 46

		FC	FC	FC	FC	FC		FC	FC	FC	FC	FC	FC	FC	FC	FC		FC	FC	FC	FC	FC	FC	FC	FC
Hunstanton Bus Station	d	13 25	13 47	14 06	14 15	14 25		14 47	15 06	15 15	15 25	15 47	16 06	16 25	16 30	16 47		17 20	17 30	17 45	18 20	18 40	18 45	20 50	22 23
Sandringham Norwich Gates	d																								
Sandringham Visitor Centre	d	14 00				15 00					16 00			17 00											
Kings Lynn	a	14 23	14 40	15 00	14 46	15 23		15 40	16 00	15 52	16 23	16 40	17 00	17 23	17 00	17 40		18 13	18 00	18 40	19 10	19 08	19 33	21 36	23 07

		FC
Hunstanton Bus Station	d	23 55
Sandringham Norwich Gates	d	
Sandringham Visitor Centre	d	
Kings Lynn	a	00 41

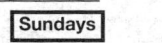

Sundays

		FC	FC	FC	FC	FC	FC	FC	FC	FC		FC	FC	FC	FC	FC	FC	FC	FC	FC		FC
Hunstanton Bus Station	d	23p55	09 00	10 13	10 40	11 13	11 40	12 13	13 13	13 40		14 13	14 40	15 13	15 40	16 13	17 13	17 40	18 13	20 05		2220
Sandringham Norwich Gates	d																					
Sandringham Visitor Centre	d			10 43				12 43				14 43				16 43						
Kings Lynn	a	00 41	09 50	11 07	11 10	12 07	12 10	13 07	14 07	14 10		15 07	15 10	16 07	16 10	17 07	18 07	18 07	19 01	20 49		2301

Services are subject to variation on Bank Holidays

Network Diagram for Tables 18, 19, 27, 29, 30

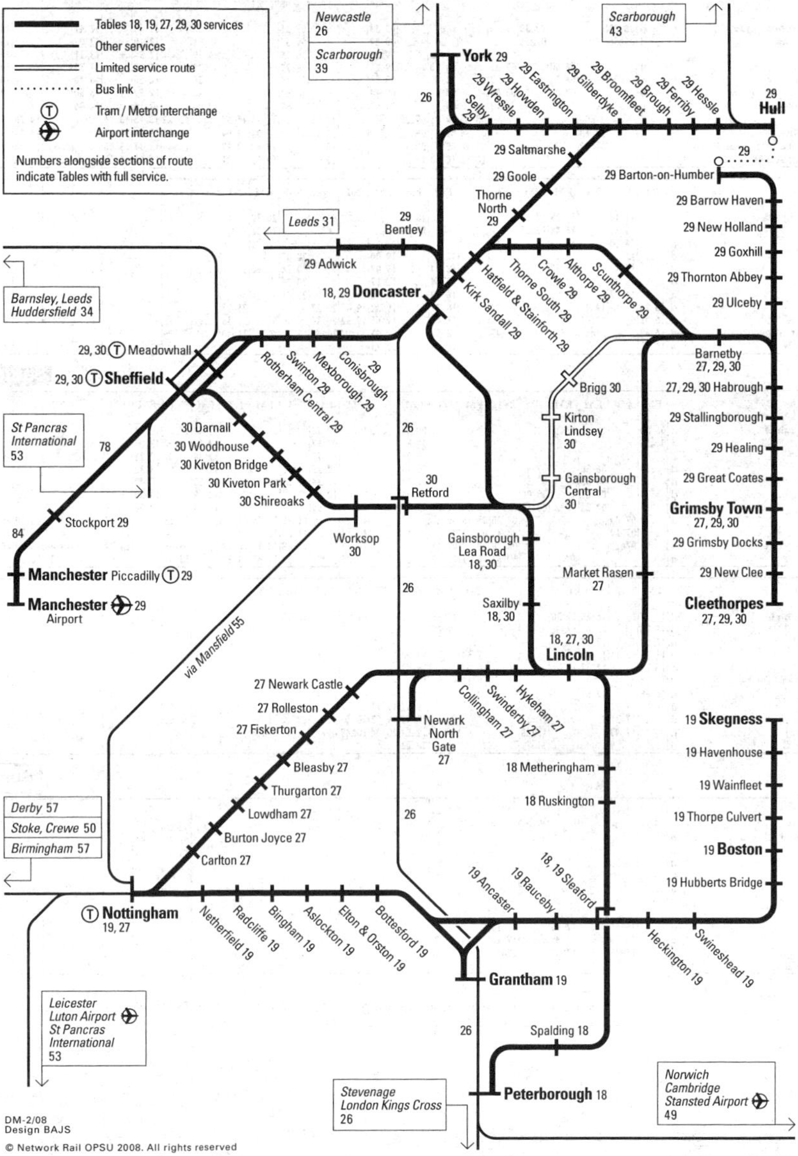

DM-2/08
Design BAJS

Peterborough - Sleaford, Lincoln and Doncaster

Network Diagram - see first Page of Table 18

Mondays to Fridays

Miles	Station		EM	NT	EM	EM	EM	NT	EM	NT	EM		NT	EM	NT	EM	EM	NT A	EM	NT	EM		NT	EM	NT
0	**Peterborough** 8	d	06 30			07 30					08 33			09 35			10 38		11 48		12 41			13 40	
16½	Spalding	d	06a56			07a56					08 57			09 57			11 01		12 10		13 03			14 02	
35½	Sleaford	a									09 25			10 25			11 29		12 38		13 31			14 30	
—		d			06 50		07 42		08 40		09 25			10 25			11 30		12 42		13 32			14 31	
40	Ruskington	d			06 58		07 50		08 48		09 34			10 34			11 38		12 50		13 40			14 39	
47½	Metheringham	d			07 09		08 00		08 59		09 44			10 44			11 48		12 59		13 50			14 49	
56¾	**Lincoln**	a			07 22		08 13		09 13		09 59			10 59			12 04		13 14		14 06			15 05	
—		d		07 00				08 25	09 15	09 25			10 25		11 25	11 54		12 27	13 15	13 26			14 25		15 24
62¾	Saxilby	d		07 10				08 34	09 24	09 34			10 34		11 34	12 04		12 36	13 24	13 35			14 34		15 33
72¼	Gainsborough Lea Road	d		07a22				08 48	09 37	09 48			10 48		11 48	12 17		12a48	13 37	13 48			14 48		15 48
93½	**Doncaster** 7	a						10 32	10 03	11 32			12 32		13 33	12 47			14 06	15 33			16 32		17 32

Station		NT	EM	NT	EM	EM	NT		EM	EM	EM	NT	NT	EM	EM	NT
Peterborough 8	d		15 10		16 25	17 32				18 36					20 30	
Spalding	d		15 32		16 48	17a58				19a02					20a56	
Sleaford	a		16 00		17 16											
	d		16 14		17 19				17 56		19 00			20 07		
Ruskington	d		16 22		17 27				18 04		19 07			20 14		
Metheringham	d		16 32		17 37				18 14		19 17			20 24		
Lincoln	a		16 47		17 51				18 29		19 32			20 41		
	d	16 25		17 22			18 24		18 31		19 32	19 43	20 27			21 27
Saxilby	d	16 35		17 31			18 33		18 42		19 41	19 52	20 36			21 36
Gainsborough Lea Road	d	16 48		17a43			18a45		18 57		19 53	20a04	20a48			21a48
Doncaster 7	a	18 35							19 25		20 23					

Saturdays

Station		EM	NT	EM	EM	EM	NT	EM	NT	EM		NT	EM	NT	EM	NT	EM	NT	EM	EM		NT	EM	NT	NT
Peterborough 8	d	06 30			07 30					08 33			09 33				11 48		12 41						
Spalding	d	06a56			07a56					08 57			09 57				12 10		13 03						
Sleaford	a									09 25			10 25				12 38		13 31						
	d			06 50		07 42				09 25			10 25				12 42		13 32						
Ruskington	d			06 58		07 50				09 34			10 34				12 50		13 40						
Metheringham	d			07 09		08 00				09 44			10 44				12 59		13 50						
Lincoln	a			07 22		08 13				09 59			10 59				13 14		14 06						
	d		07 00				08 25	09 15	09 25			10 25		11 25	11 54	12 27		13 25		14 10		14 25	15 10	15 24	16 25
Saxilby	d		07 10				08 34	09 24	09 34			10 34		11 34	12 04	12 36		13 34		14 19		14 34	15 20	15 33	16 35
Gainsborough Lea Road	d		07a22				08 48	09 37	09 48			10 48		11 48	12 17	12 49		13 48		14 32		14 48	15 32	15 48	16 48
Doncaster 7	a						10 32	10 11	11 32			12 33		13 32	12 47	14 32		15 34		15 01		16 32	16 01	17 32	18 38

Station		EM	NT	EM	EM	NT		EM	EM	EM	NT	NT	EM	EM	NT
Peterborough 8	d	15 11		16 25	17 30				18 36					20 28	
Spalding	d	15 33		16 48	17a56				19a02					20a54	
Sleaford	a	16 02		17 16											
	d	16 14		17 19				17 54		19 00			20 10		
Ruskington	d	16 22		17 27				18 02		19 07			20 17		
Metheringham	d	16 32		17 37				18 12		19 17			20 27		
Lincoln	a	16 48		17 51				18 27		19 32			20 40		
	d		17 22			18 24				19 32	19 43	20 27			21 27
Saxilby	d		17 31			18 33				19 41	19 52	20 36			21 36
Gainsborough Lea Road	d		17a43			18a45				19 54	20a04	20a48			21a48
Doncaster 7	a									20 23					

Sundays

Station			NT		NT		NT		NT
Peterborough 8	d								
Spalding	d								
Sleaford	a								
	d								
Ruskington	d								
Metheringham	d								
Lincoln	a								
	d		15 15		17 15		19 15		21 10
Saxilby	d		15 25		17 25		19 25		21 20
Gainsborough Lea Road	d		15a37		17a37		19a37		21a32
Doncaster 7	a								

For connections from London Kings Cross please refer to Table 25

Doncaster, Lincoln and Sleaford - Peterborough

Network Diagram - see first Page of Table 18

Mondays to Fridays

Miles			NT	EM	EM	EM	EM	NT	NT	EM	NT		EM	NT	EM	EM	NT	EM	NT	EM	EM		NT	EM	NT
0	**Doncaster** 7	d												09 01		10 24	10 04		11 04		13 05		12 03		13 02
21¼	Gainsborough Lea Road	d	06 25					07 38	08 24		09 38			10 38		10 52	11 38		12 38		13 31		13 39		14 38
30¾	Saxilby	d	06 37					07 51	08 37		09 51			10 51		11 05	11 51		12 51		13 44		13 52		14 51
36¾	**Lincoln**	a	06 53					08 06	08 52		10 06			11 06		11 17	12 06		13 06		13 55		14 06		15 06
—		d			07 05		08 00			09 10			10 15		11 10			12 10		13 30				14 41	
46¼	Metheringham	d			07 17		08 12			09 22			10 28		11 23			12 22		13 43				14 54	
53½	Ruskington	d			07 27		08 22			09 32			10 38		11 33			12 32		13 53				15 04	
58	Sleaford	a			07 36		08 31			09 41			10 50		11 42			12 41		14 02				15 13	
—		d					08 34			09 42			10 50		11 42			12 42		14 03				15 16	
77	Spalding	d		07 00		08 00	09 02			10 07			11 16		12 07			13 07		14 28				15 43	
93½	**Peterborough** 8	a		07 25		08 25	09 27			10 31			11 42		12 33			13 32		14 53				16 09	

		EM	EM	EM	NT	NT	EM		NT	EM	EM	NT	EM	NT	EM	EM	EM		NT	EM	EM				
Doncaster 7	d		14 27		14 03	15 04			16 03			17 01			19 34					20 33					
Gainsborough Lea Road	d		14 54		15 38	16 38			17 38			18 38		19 39	20 00				20 42	21 00					
Saxilby	d		15 07		15 51	16 51			17 51			18 51		19 52	20 13				20 55	21 14					
Lincoln	a		15 18		16 10	17 06			18 06			19 07		20 06	20 25				21 10	21 26					
	d	15 12		16 01			17 20				18 10		19 10				20 48								
Metheringham	d	15 25		16 14			17 33				18 23		19 22				21 01								
Ruskington	d	15 35		16 24			17 42				18 33		19 32				21 10								
Sleaford	a	15 44		16 34			17 51				18 42		19 41				21 19								
	d			16 34																					
Spalding	d			16 59						18 02						19 56					21 00				
Peterborough 8	a			17 25						18 28						20 21					21 26				

Saturdays

		NT	EM	EM	EM	EM	NT	NT	NT	EM		NT	EM	EM	NT	NT	EM	EM	NT	EM		NT	EM	EM	NT
Doncaster 7	d											09 03		10 24	10 04	11 04		13 05	12 03			13 04	15 07		14 01
Gainsborough Lea Road	d	06 25					07 38	08 24	09 38			10 38		10 52	11 38	12 38		13 31	13 37			14 36	15 33		15 40
Saxilby	d	06 37					07 51	08 37	09 51			10 51		11 05	11 51	12 51		13 44	13 50			14 49	15 46		15 53
Lincoln	a	06 53					08 06	08 52	10 06			11 06		11 16	12 06	13 06		13 55	14 07			15 06	15 57		16 10
	d			07 05		08 00				10 15			11 10				13 30			14 41				16 01	
Metheringham	d			07 17		08 12				10 28			11 23				13 43			14 54				16 14	
Ruskington	d			07 27		08 22				10 38			11 33				13 53			15 04				16 24	
Sleaford	a			07 36		08 31				10 50			11 42				14 02			15 13				16 34	
	d					08 34				10 50			11 42				14 03			15 16				16 34	
Spalding	d		07 00		08 00	09 02				11 16			12 07				14 28			15 41				16 59	
Peterborough 8	a		07 25		08 25	09 27				11 42			12 33				14 53			16 07				17 25	

		NT	EM	EM	NT	EM		EM	EM	NT	NT	EM	EM	NT	EM	EM									
Doncaster 7	d	15 04		16 27	16 01					17 00	18 02				20 33										
Gainsborough Lea Road	d	16 38		16 56	17 38					18 38	19 39			20 42	21 00										
Saxilby	d	16 51		17 09	17 51					18 51	19 52			20 55	21 14										
Lincoln	a	17 06		17 20	18 06					19 07	20 06			21 10	21 26										
	d		17 15					18 10	19 05				20 49												
Metheringham	d		17 28					18 23	19 17				21 02												
Ruskington	d		17 38					18 33	19 27				21 11												
Sleaford	a		17 47					18 42	19 36				21 20												
	d																								
Spalding	d					18 02						19 56				20 58									
Peterborough 8	a					18 28						20 21				21 23									

Sundays

			NT		NT		NT		NT																
Doncaster 7	d																								
Gainsborough Lea Road	d		14 26		16 35		18 35		20 24																
Saxilby	d		14 39		16 48		18 48		20 37																
Lincoln	a		14 54		17 02		19 03		20 51																
	d																								
Metheringham	d																								
Ruskington	d																								
Sleaford	a																								
	d																								
Spalding	d																								
Peterborough 8	a																								

For connections to London Kings Cross please refer to Table 25

Skegness - Grantham and Nottingham

Network Diagram - see first Page of Table 18

Mondays to Fridays

Miles	Miles			EM	EM		EM	EM	EM	EM	EM	EM		EM	EM	EM	EM	EM	EM	EM	EM	EM		EM	EM
							◇		◇		◇			◇		◇		◇		◇		◇			◇
0	—	**Skegness**	d					07 09		08 10		09 06			10 15		11 15		12 15		13 15			14 15	
3¼	—	Havenhouse	d					07 15																	
5	—	Wainfleet	d					07 19		08 18		09 14			10 23		11 23		12 23		13 23			14 23	
7	—	Thorpe Culvert	d					07 23																	
23¾	—	**Boston**	d		06 13			07 46		08 45		09 41			10 50		11 50		12 50		13 50			14 50	
27½	—	Hubberts Bridge	d					07 52																	
30¾	—	Swineshead	d					07 57																	
35¾	—	Heckington	d		06 27			08 02		08 59		09 55			11 04		12 04		13 04		14 04			15 04	
40¼	—	**Sleaford**	d		06 35			08 11		09 07		10 03			11 12		12 12		13 12		14 13			15 12	
42½	—	Rauceby	d		06 39			08 15																	
46¼	0	Ancaster	d		06 45			08 21							11 21										
57¾	—	**Grantham** [7]	a		07 04			08 42		09 35		10 31			11 41		12 41		13 41		14 42			15 41	
—	—		d	06 10	07 10		07 58	08 45	08 55	09 40	09 58	10 36		11 00	11 45	12 00	12 45	12 59	13 45	13 58	14 45	14 58		15 45	16 01
65¼	12¾	Bottesford	d	06 21	07 21		08 11			09 52					11 56				13 56					15 56	
67¾	—	Elton & Orston	d	06 25																					
69½	—	Aslockton	d	06 29	07 27		08 18	09 00				10 52					13 00				15 00				
71¾	—	Bingham	d	06 33	07 31		08 22	09 05		10 00		10 57			12 04		13 04		14 04		15 05			16 04	
75¼	—	Radcliffe (Notts)	d	06 39	07 37		08 28								12 09										
77	—	Netherfield	d		07 42		08 33																		
80¼	—	**Nottingham** [8]	a	06 54	07 54		08 40	09 20	09 36	10 18	10 36	11 14		11 35	12 23	12 36	13 23	13 36	14 23	14 36	15 23	15 36		16 22	16 36

		EM	EM	EM	EM	EM	EM	EM		EM	EM	EM	EM	EM
			◇		◇		◇			◇		◇		
Skegness	d	15 09		16 11		17 30		18 14			19 14		20 15	21 02
Havenhouse	d			16 17										
Wainfleet	d	15 17		16 21		17 38		18 22			19 22		20 23	21 10
Thorpe Culvert	d			16 25										
Boston	d	15 44		16 48		18 05		18 49			19 49		20 50	21 37
Hubberts Bridge	d	15 50												
Swineshead	d	15 55												
Heckington	d	16 01		17 04		18 19		19 04			20 05		21 04	21 51
Sleaford	d	16 10		17 13		18 27		19 13			20 13		21 12	22 00
Rauceby	d	16 14												
Ancaster	d	16 20												
Grantham [7]	a	16 41		17 42				19 41			20 40		21 43	
	d	16 45	17 00	17 45	17 58		18 56	19 45		19 59	20 44	20 59	21 47	
Bottesford	d			17 56				19 56					21 58	
Elton & Orston	d													
Aslockton	d			18 02				20 02					22 04	
Bingham	d	17 02		18 07		19 03	19 13	20 06			21 01		22 08	22 35
Radcliffe (Notts)	d							20 12						
Netherfield	d							20 16						
Nottingham [8]	a	17 20	17 36	18 22	18 36	19 22	19 36	20 25		20 31	21 21	21 35	22 25	22 54

Saturdays

		EM	EM	EM	EM	EM	EM	EM	EM	EM		EM	EM	EM	EM	EM	EM	EM	EM	EM		EM	EM	EM	EM
					◇		◇		◇			◇		◇		◇		◇		◇			◇		◇
Skegness	d					07 09		08 15		09 15			10 15		11 15		12 15		13 15			14 15		15 09	
Havenhouse	d					07 15																			
Wainfleet	d					07 19		08 23		09 23			10 23		11 23		12 23		13 23			14 23		15 17	
Thorpe Culvert	d					07 23																			
Boston	d		06 13			07 46		08 50		09 50			10 50		11 50		12 50		13 50			14 50		15 44	
Hubberts Bridge	d					07 52																		15 50	
Swineshead	d					07 57																		15 55	
Heckington	d		06 27			08 02		09 04		10 05			11 04		12 04		13 04		14 04			15 04		16 01	
Sleaford	d		06 35	06 50		08 11		09 12		10 14			11 12		12 12		13 12		14 13			15 12		16 10	
Rauceby	d		06 39			08 15																		16 14	
Ancaster	d		06 45			08 21							11 21											16 20	
Grantham [7]	a		07 07			08 42		09 41		10 43			11 41		12 41		13 41		14 42			15 41		16 41	
	d	06 10	07 10		07 58	08 45	09 09	09 45	09 58	10 46		10 58	11 45	11 58	12 45	12 58	13 45	13 58	14 45	14 58		15 45	15 58	16 45	16 56
Bottesford	d	06 21	07 21		08 11			09 56					11 56				13 56					15 56			
Elton & Orston	d	06 25																							
Aslockton	d	06 29	07 27		08 17	09 00				11 01					13 00				15 00						
Bingham	d	06 33	07 31		08 21	09 05		10 04		11 06			12 04		13 04		14 04		15 05			16 04		17 02	
Radcliffe (Notts)	d	06 39	07 37		08 27								12 09												
Netherfield	d		07 41		08 31																				
Nottingham [8]	a	06 54	07 53	08 30	08 39	09 20	09 40	10 22	10 40	11 24		11 35	12 23	12 36	13 23	13 36	14 23	14 36	15 23	15 36		16 22	16 36	17 20	17 36

		EM	EM	EM	EM	EM		EM	EM	EM	EM	EM	EM
			◇		◇			◇		◇			
Skegness	d	16 11		17 30		18 14			19 19		20 15		21 02
Havenhouse	d	16 17											
Wainfleet	d	16 21		17 38		18 22			19 27		20 23		21 10
Thorpe Culvert	d	16 25											
Boston	d	16 48		18 05		18 49			19 54		20 50		21 37
Hubberts Bridge	d												
Swineshead	d												
Heckington	d	17 04		18 19		19 04			20 10		21 04		21 51
Sleaford	d	17 13		18 27		19 13			20 18		21 12		22 00
Rauceby	d												
Ancaster	d												
Grantham [7]	a	17 42				19 41			20 45		21 43		
	d	17 45	18 03		18 58	19 45		20 03	20 48	20 58	21 47	22 02	
Bottesford	d	17 56				19 56					21 58		
Elton & Orston	d												
Aslockton	d	18 02				20 02					22 04		
Bingham	d	18 07		19 03	19 15	20 06			21 05		22 08		22 35
Radcliffe (Notts)	d					20 12							
Netherfield	d					20 16							
Nottingham [8]	a	18 22	18 36	19 23	19 36	20 25		20 37	21 24	21 32	22 25	22 32	22 54

For connections to London Kings Cross please refer to Table 26

Table 19

Sundays

Skegness - Grantham and Nottingham

Network Diagram - see first Page of Table 18

		EM	EM	EM	EM	EM	EM	EM	EM	EM		EM	EM	EM	EM	EM
		◇			◇	◇		◇	◇			◇		◇		◇
Skegness	d			14 10			16 17			18 07			19 15			
Havenhouse	d															
Wainfleet	d			14 18			16 25			18 15			19 23			
Thorpe Culvert	d															
Boston	d		12 13	14 45			16 52			18 42			19 50			
Hubberts Bridge	d															
Swineshead	d															
Heckington	d		12 27	14 59			17 06			18 56			20 04			
Sleaford	d		12 35	15 07			17 14			19 04			20 12		21 41	
Rauceby	d															
Ancaster	d															
Grantham 7	a		13 04	15 35			17 43			19 33			20 41		22 10	
	d	12 54		15 40	15 59	16 56	17 47	17 55	18 58	19 37		19 57	20 45	21 03	22 13	22 54
Bottesford	d	13 05														
Elton & Orston	d															
Aslockton	d	13 11														
Bingham	d	13 16		15 57			18 04	18 14		19 54			21 02		22 30	
Radcliffe (Notts)	d	13 21														
Netherfield	d	13 25														
Nottingham 8	a	13 33		16 17	16 28	17 25	18 23	18 29	19 33	20 12		20 31	21 21	21 35	22 49	23 28

For connections to London Kings Cross please refer to Table 26

Table 19

Nottingham and Grantham - Skegness

Network Diagram - see first Page of Table 18

Miles	Miles			EM	EM	EM	EM	EM	EM	EM	EM	EM	EM	EM	EM	EM	EM	EM	EM	EM	EM	EM
0	—	**Nottingham** 8	d	05 10		05 50	06 41	07 34	07 52	08 34	08 50	09 34	09 55	10 34	10 45	11 34	11 45	12 34	12 45	13 34	13 45	14 34
4½	—	Netherfield	d								08 56											
5	—	Radcliffe (Notts)	d								09 01								12 55			
8½	—	Bingham	d	05 24		06 04	06 55	07 48			09 07		10 09		10 59		11 59		13 01		13 59	
10¾	—	Aslockton	d	05 28				07 52			09 11				11 03						14 03	
14½	—	Elton & Orston	d																			
15	0	Bottesford	d	05 35		06 13	07 04	07 59			09 17				11 10				13 09			
22½	—	**Grantham** 7	a	05 49		06 27	07 18	08 12	08 23	09 07	09 31	10 06		11 07	11 23	12 07	12 19	13 07	13 23	14 05	14 23	15 07
—	—		d			06 31	07 24	08 16			09 36				11 27		12 25		13 27		14 27	
34	12¾	Ancaster	d					08 34											13 45			
37¾	—	Rauceby	d					08 40														
40	—	**Sleaford**	d			06 57	07 50	08 45			10 04		10 44		11 53		12 50		13 55		14 52	
44½	—	Heckington	d			07 04	07 57	08 52			10 11		10 51		12 00		12 57		14 02		14 59	
49½	—	Swineshead	d				08 03															
52¾	—	Hubberts Bridge	d				08 08															
56½	—	**Boston**	d		06 25	07 24	08 18	09 12			10 28		11 11		12 19		13 15		14 21		15 17	
73¼	—	Thorpe Culvert	d			07 46																
75¼	—	Wainfleet	d		06 49	07 51	08 43	09 36			10 52		11 35		12 44		13 40		14 46		15 42	
77	—	Havenhouse	d			07 54																
80¼	—	**Skegness**	a		07 03	08 05	08 56	09 49			11 05		11 50		12 58		13 54		15 00		15 56	

		EM	EM	EM	EM	EM	EM	EM	EM	EM	EM	EM	EM	EM
			◇			◇		◇		◇		◇		
Nottingham 8	d	14 45	15 34	15 45	16 14	16 34	16 45	17 34	17 45	18 37	18 45	20 34		20 51
Netherfield	d			15 51			16 51							
Radcliffe (Notts)	d			15 56			16 56		17 55					21 01
Bingham	d	14 59		16 02			17 02	17 48	18 01		18 59			21 07
Aslockton	d			16 06			17 06	17 52	18 05		19 03			21 11
Elton & Orston	d						17 10							
Bottesford	d	15 08		16 12			17 14		18 12		19 10			21 17
Grantham 7	a	15 22	16 08	16 25		17 08	17 28	18 09	18 25	19 08	19 23	21 07		21 32
	d	15 26		16 29			17 32		18 29		19 26			21 36
Ancaster	d						17 50				19 44			
Rauceby	d						17 56				19 50			
Sleaford	d	15 52		16 55	17a51		18 01		18 55		19 55		21 20	22 01
Heckington	d	15 59		17 02			18 08		19 02		20 02		21 28	22 08
Swineshead	d	16 05												
Hubberts Bridge	d	16 10											21 43	
Boston	d	16 20		17 21			18 26		19 21		20 19		21a53	22a29
Thorpe Culvert	d			17 43										
Wainfleet	d	16 45		17 48			18 51		19 46		20 43			
Havenhouse	d			17 51										
Skegness	a	16 59		18 00			19 05		20 00		20 57			

Saturdays

		EM	EM	EM	EM	EM	EM	EM	EM	EM	EM	EM	EM	EM	EM	EM	EM	EM	EM	EM	EM	EM	EM
								◇	◇		◇		◇		◇		◇		◇		◇		◇
Nottingham 8	d	05 10		05 50	06 41	06 55	07 28	07 45	08 32	08 45	09 34	09 55	10 34	10 45	11 34	11 45	12 34	12 45	13 34	13 45	14 34	14 45	15 34
Netherfield	d									08 51													
Radcliffe (Notts)	d									08 56								12 55					
Bingham	d	05 24		06 04	06 55		07 42			09 02		10 09		10 59		11 59		13 01		13 59		14 59	
Aslockton	d	05 28					07 46			09 06				11 03						14 03			
Elton & Orston	d																						
Bottesford	d	05 35		06 13	07 04		07 53			09 12				11 10				13 09				15 08	
Grantham 7	a	05 49		06 27	07 18		08 07	08 15	09 02	09 26	10 07		11 06	11 23	12 06	12 19	13 07	13 25	14 05	14 23	15 07	15 22	16 06
	d			06 31	07 24		08 16			09 30				11 27		12 25		13 29		14 27		15 26	
Ancaster	d						08 34																
Rauceby	d						08 40																
Sleaford	d			06 57	07 50	08a31	08 45			09 56		10 44		11 53		12 50		13 55		14 52		15 52	
Heckington	d			07 04	07 57		08 52			10 03		10 51		12 00		12 57		14 02		14 59		15 59	
Swineshead	d				08 03																	16 05	
Hubberts Bridge	d				08 08																	16 10	
Boston	d		06 25	07 24	08 18		09 11			10 22		11 11		12 19		13 15		14 21		15 17		16 20	
Thorpe Culvert	d			07 46																			
Wainfleet	d		06 49	07 51	08 43		09 35			10 47		11 35		12 44		13 40		14 46		15 42		16 45	
Havenhouse	d			07 54																			
Skegness	a		07 03	08 05	08 56		09 48			11 00		11 50		12 58		13 54		15 00		15 56		16 59	

		EM	EM	EM	EM	EM	EM	EM	EM	EM	EM
			◇		◇		◇		◇		
Nottingham 8	d	15 45	16 34	16 45	17 34	17 45	18 34	18 45	20 34		20 51
Netherfield	d	15 51		16 51							
Radcliffe (Notts)	d	15 56		16 56		17 55					21 01
Bingham	d	16 02		17 02	17 48	18 01		18 59			21 07
Aslockton	d	16 06		17 06	17 52	18 05		19 03			21 11
Elton & Orston	d			17 10							
Bottesford	d	16 12		17 14		18 12		19 10			21 17
Grantham 7	a	16 25	17 04	17 28	18 10	18 25	19 07	19 23	21 05		21 31
	d	16 29		17 32		18 29		19 26			21 36
Ancaster	d			17 50				19 44			
Rauceby	d			17 56				19 50			
Sleaford	d	16 55		18 01		18 55		19 55		21 21	22 01
Heckington	d	17 02		18 08		19 02		20 02		21 29	22 08
Swineshead	d										
Hubberts Bridge	d									21 43	
Boston	d	17 21		18 26		19 21		20 19		21a53	22a29
Thorpe Culvert	d	17 43									
Wainfleet	d	17 48		18 51		19 46		20 43			
Havenhouse	d	17 51									
Skegness	a	18 00		19 05		20 00		20 57			

For connections from London Kings Cross please refer to Table 26

Table 19

Sundays

Nottingham and Grantham - Skegness

Network Diagram - see first Page of Table 18

		EM	EM	EM	EM	EM	EM	EM	EM	EM		EM	EM	EM	EM	EM
			◇		◇	◇		◇		◇		◇		◇		◇
Nottingham 8 🚌	d	11 55	12 37		13 49	14 45	14 56	15 49	16 23	16 45		17 36	18 31	18 47	19 48	20 44
Netherfield	d								16 29			17 42				
Radcliffe (Notts)	d								16 34			17 46				
Bingham	d	12 11	12 51				15 10		16 40			17 52	18 45	19 01	20 02	20 58
Aslockton	d								16 44			17 56				
Elton & Orston	d															
Bottesford	d								16 50			18 03				
Grantham 7	a	12 29	13 11		14 20	15 18	15 31	16 20	17 03	17 15		18 16	19 08	19 21	20 22	21 18
	d	12 33		13 50			15 36		17 07				19 13		20 27	
Ancaster	d															
Rauceby	d															
Sleaford	d	12 59		14 16			16 04		17 36				19 41		20a55	
Heckington	d	13 06		14 23			16 11		17 43				19 48			
Swineshead	d															
Hubberts Bridge	d															
Boston	d	13 24		14 45			16 31		18 02				20a10			
Thorpe Culvert	d															
Wainfleet	d	13 49		15 09			16 55		18 27							
Havenhouse	d															
Skegness	a	14 00		15 24			17 10		18 38							

For connections from London Kings Cross please refer to Table 26

Network Diagram for Tables 20, 21, 22

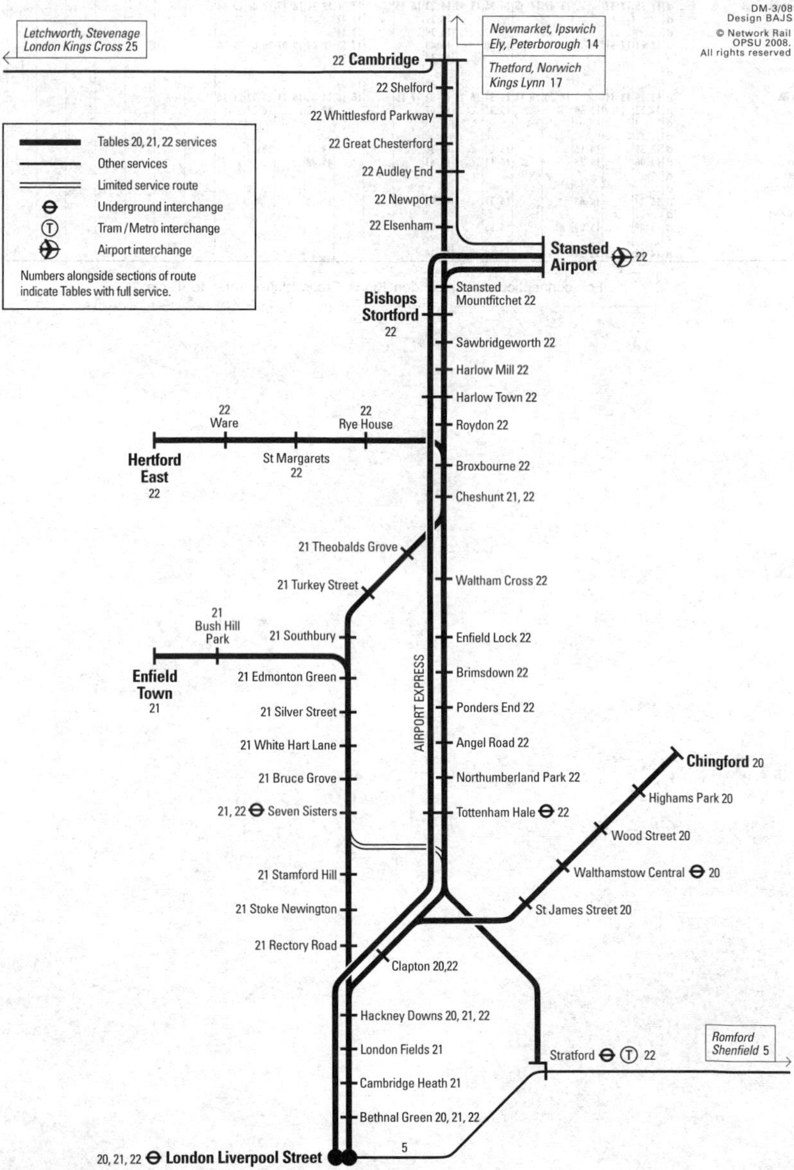

Table 20

Mondays to Fridays

London - Chingford

Network Diagram - see first Page of Table 20

Miles			LE	LE	LE	LE	LE MX	LE	LE	LE	LE	LE	LE	LE	LE	LE	LE	LE	LE		LE
0	**London Liverpool Street** 15 ⊖	d	23p48	00 03	00 18	00 33	00 48	01 03	06 03	06 33	06 48	07 03	07 18	07 33	07 48	08 05	08 18	08 35	08 48	and every 15 minutes until	15 48
1¼	Bethnal Green	d	23p51	00 06	00 21	00 36	.	.	06 06	06 36	06 51	07 06	07 21	07 36	07 51	.	08 21	.	08 51		15 51
3	Hackney Downs	d	23p55	00 10	00 25	00 40	00 55	01 10	06 10	06 40	06 55	07 10	07 25	07 40	07 55	08 12	08 25	08 42	08 55		15 55
4	Clapton	d	23p58	00 13	00 28	00 43	00 58	01 13	06 13	06 43	06 58	07 13	07 28	07 43	07 58	08 15	08 28	08 45	08 58		15 58
5¾	St James Street	d	00 01	00 16	00 32	00 47	01 02	01 17	06 16	06 46	07 01	07 17	07 32	07 47	08 02	08 18	08 31	08 48	09 01		16 01
6¼	Walthamstow Central ⊖	d	00 03	00 18	00 34	00 49	01 04	01 19	06 18	06 48	07 03	07 19	07 34	07 49	08 04	08 20	08 33	08 50	09 03		16 03
7	Wood Street	d	00 05	00 20	00 36	00 51	01 06	01 21	06 20	06 50	07 05	07 21	07 36	07 51	08 06	08 22	08 35	08 52	09 05		16 05
8½	Highams Park	d	00 08	00 23	00 39	00 54	01 09	01 24	06 23	06 53	07 08	07 24	07 39	07 54	08 09	08 25	08 38	08 55	09 08		16 08
10½	**Chingford**	a	00 14	00 29	00 44	00 59	01 14	01 29	06 29	06 59	07 17	07 29	07 44	08 02	08 14	08 32	08 44	09 01	09 14		16 14

		LE		LE	LE	LE	LE	LE	LE	LE	LE	LE	LE	LE		LE	LE	LE
London Liverpool Street 15 ⊖	d	16 03	and every 15 minutes until	16 48	17 03	17 18	17 33	17 48	18 03	18 18	18 33	18 48	19 03	19 18	and every 15 minutes until	23 18	23 33	23 48
Bethnal Green	d	16 06		16 51	.	17 21	.	17 51	.	18 21	.	18 51	.	19 21		23 21	.	23 51
Hackney Downs	d	16 10		16 55	17 10	17 25	17 40	17 55	18 10	18 25	18 40	18 55	19 10	19 25		23 25	.	23 55
Clapton	d	16 13		16 58	17 12	17 28	17 42	17 58	18 12	18 28	18 42	18 58	19 12	19 28		23 28	.	23 58
St James Street	d	16 16		17 01	17 16	17 31	17 46	18 01	18 16	18 31	18 46	19 01	19 16	19 31		23 31	.	00 01
Walthamstow Central ⊖	d	16 19		17 04	17 18	17 34	17 48	18 04	18 18	18 34	18 48	19 04	19 18	19 33		23 33	23 44	00 03
Wood Street	d	16 21		17 06	17 20	17 36	17 50	18 06	18 20	18 36	18 50	19 06	19 20	19 35		23 35	.	00 05
Highams Park	d	16 24		17 09	17 23	17 39	17 53	18 09	18 23	18 39	18 53	19 09	19 23	19 38		23 38	.	00 08
Chingford	a	16 31		17 16	17 31	17 46	18 01	18 16	18 31	18 46	19 01	19 16	19 29	19 44		23 44	23 54	00 14

Saturdays

		LE	LE	LE	LE	LE	LE	LE	LE		LE	LE	LE
London Liverpool Street 15 ⊖	d	23p48	00 03	00 18	00 33	00 48	01 03	06 03	06 33	and every 15 minutes until	23 18	23 33	23 48
Bethnal Green	d	23p51	00 06	00 21	00 36	.	.	06 06	06 36		23 21	.	23 51
Hackney Downs	d	23p55	00 10	00 25	00 40	00 55	01 10	06 10	06 40		23 25	.	23 55
Clapton	d	23p58	00 13	00 28	00 43	00 58	01 13	06 13	06 43		23 28	.	23 58
St James Street	d	00 01	00 16	00 32	00 47	01 02	01 17	06 16	06 46		23 31	.	00 01
Walthamstow Central ⊖	d	00 03	00 18	00 34	00 49	01 04	01 19	06 18	06 48		23 33	23 44	00 03
Wood Street	d	00 05	00 20	00 36	00 51	01 06	01 21	06 20	06 50		23 35	.	00 05
Highams Park	d	00 08	00 23	00 39	00 54	01 09	01 24	06 23	06 53		23 38	.	00 08
Chingford	a	00 14	00 29	00 44	00 59	01 14	01 29	06 29	06 59		23 44	23 54	00 14

Sundays

		LE A	LE	LE	LE	LE	LE	LE	LE	LE	LE	LE	LE		LE	LE
London Liverpool Street 15 ⊖	d	23p48	00 03	00 18	00 33	00 48	01 03	07 33	08 03	08 33	08 48	09 03	09 18	and every 15 minutes until	23 33	23 48
Bethnal Green	d	23p51	00 06	00 21	00 36	.	.	.	.	.	.	.	09 21		23 36	23 51
Hackney Downs	d	23p55	00 10	00 25	00 40	00 55	01 10	07 40	08 10	08 40	08 55	09 10	09 25		23 40	23 55
Clapton	d	23p58	00 13	00 28	00 43	00 58	01 13	07 43	08 13	08 43	08 58	09 13	09 28		23 43	23 58
St James Street	d	00 01	00 16	00 32	00 47	01 02	01 17	07 46	08 16	08 46	09 01	09 16	09 31		23 46	00 01
Walthamstow Central ⊖	d	00 03	00 18	00 34	00 49	01 04	01 19	07 48	08 18	08 48	09 03	09 18	09 33		23 48	00 03
Wood Street	d	00 05	00 20	00 36	00 51	01 06	01 21	07 50	08 20	08 50	09 05	09 20	09 35		23 50	00 05
Highams Park	d	00 08	00 23	00 39	00 54	01 09	01 24	07 53	08 23	08 53	09 08	09 23	09 38		23 53	00 08
Chingford	a	00 14	00 29	00 44	00 59	01 14	01 29	07 59	08 29	08 59	09 14	09 29	09 44		23 59	00 14

A not 11 December

Table 20

Mondays to Fridays

Chingford - London

Network Diagram - see first Page of Table 20

Miles			LE	LE	LE	LE	LE	LE	LE	LE	LE	LE	LE	LE	LE	LE	LE	LE	LE	LE	LE		LE
0	**Chingford**	d	05 10	05 25	05 40	05 55	06 10	06 29	06 44	06 59	07 14	07 29	07 44	07 59	08 14	08 29	08 44	08 57	09 12	09 27	09 40	and every 15 minutes until	17 25
2	Highams Park	d	05 14	05 29	05 44	05 59	06 14	06 33	06 48	07 03	07 18	07 33	07 48	08 03	08 18	08 33	08 48	09 01	09 16	09 31	09 44		17 29
3½	Wood Street	d	05 17	05 32	05 47	06 02	06 17	06 37	06 52	07 07	07 22	07 37	07 52	08 07	08 22	08 37	08 52	09 05	09 20	09 35	09 47		17 32
4¼	Walthamstow Central ⊖	d	05 19	05 34	05 49	06 04	06 19	06 39	06 54	07 09	07 24	07 39	07 54	08 09	08 24	08 39	08 54	09 07	09 22	09 37	09 49		17 34
4¾	St James Street	d	05 21	05 36	05 51	06 06	06 21	06 42	06 56	07 12	07 26	07 42	07 56	08 12	08 26	08 42	08 56	09 10	09 25	09 40	09 51		17 36
6½	Clapton	d	05 24	05 39	05 54	06 09	06 24	06 45	07 00	07 15	07 30	07 45	08 00	08 15	08 30	08 45	09 00	09 13	09 28	09 43	09 54		17 39
7½	Hackney Downs	d	05 28	05 43	05 58	06 13	06 28	06 49	07 03	07 19	07 33	07 49	08 03	08 19	08 33	08 49	09 03	09 17	09 32	09 47	09 58		17 43
9¼	Bethnal Green	d	05 32	05 47	06 02	06 17	06 32	06 53	07 07	.	07 37	.	08 07	.	08 37	.	09 07	09 21	09 36	09 51	10 02		17 47
10½	**London Liverpool Street** 15 ⊖	a	05 36	05 51	06 07	06 21	06 36	06 58	07 13	07 28	07 43	07 58	08 13	08 28	08 43	08 57	09 13	09 27	09 42	09 57	10 06		17 51

		LE	LE	LE	LE	LE	LE	LE	LE	LE	LE	LE	LE		LE
Chingford	d	17 40	17 55	18 10	18 25	18 40	18 55	19 10	19 25	19 40	19 55	20 10	20 25	and every 15 minutes until	23 25
Highams Park	d	17 44	17 59	18 14	18 29	18 44	18 59	19 14	19 29	19 44	19 59	20 14	20 29		23 29
Wood Street	d	17 47	18 02	18 17	18 32	18 47	19 02	19 17	19 32	19 47	20 02	20 17	20 32		23 32
Walthamstow Central ⊖	d	17 49	18 04	18 19	18 34	18 49	19 04	19 19	19 34	19 49	20 04	20 19	20 34		23 34
St James Street	d	17 51	18 06	18 21	18 36	18 51	19 06	19 21	19 36	19 51	20 06	20 21	20 36		23 36
Clapton	d	17 54	18 09	18 24	18 39	18 54	19 09	19 24	19 39	19 54	20 09	20 24	20 39		23 39
Hackney Downs	d	17 58	18 13	18 28	18 43	18 58	19 13	19 28	19 43	19 58	20 13	20 28	20 43		23 43
Bethnal Green	d	18 02	18 17	18 32	18 47	19 02	19 17	19 32	19 47	20 02	20 17	20 32	20 47		23 47
London Liverpool Street 15 ⊖	a	18 07	18 21	18 37	18 51	19 07	19 21	19 37	19 51	20 06	20 21	20 37	20 51		23 51

Saturdays

		LE		LE
Chingford	d	05 10	and every 15 minutes until	23 25
Highams Park	d	05 14		23 29
Wood Street	d	05 17		23 32
Walthamstow Central ⊖	d	05 19		23 34
St James Street	d	05 21		23 36
Clapton	d	05 24		23 39
Hackney Downs	d	05 28		23 43
Bethnal Green	d	05 32		23 47
London Liverpool Street 15 ⊖	a	05 36		23 51

Sundays

		LE		LE	LE		LE
Chingford	d	06 40	and every 15 minutes until	08 40	08 55	and every 15 minutes until	23 10
Highams Park	d	06 44		08 44	08 59		23 14
Wood Street	d	06 47		08 47	09 02		23 17
Walthamstow Central ⊖	d	06 49		08 49	09 04		23 19
St James Street	d	06 51		08 51	09 06		23 21
Clapton	d	06 54		08 54	09 09		23 24
Hackney Downs	d	06 58		08 58	09 13		23 28
Bethnal Green	d	.		.	09 17		23 32
London Liverpool Street 15 ⊖	a	07 06		09 06	09 21		23 36

Table 21

Mondays to Fridays

London - Cheshunt (via Seven Sisters) and Enfield Town

Network Diagram - see first Page of Table 20

Miles	Miles			LE	LE MX	LE MX	LE	LE	LE	LE	LE	LE		LE	LE	LE	LE	LE	LE	LE	LE	LE		LE	LE
0	0	**London Liverpool Street** [15] ⊖	d	23p30	23p45	00 01	05 45	06 00	06 15	06 21	06 36	06 45		06 51	07 06	07 15	07 21	07 36	07 45	07 51	08 00	08 07		08 15	08 30
1¼	1¼	Bethnal Green	d	23p33	23p48	00 03	05 48	06 03		06 24	06 39			06 54	07 09		07 24	07 39		07 54		08 10		08 18	08 33
1¾	1¾	Cambridge Heath	d	23p35	23p50	00 05	05 50	06 05		06 26	06 41			06 56	07 11		07 26	07 41		07 56		08 12		08 20	08 35
2½	2½	London Fields	d	23p37	23p52	00 07	05 52	06 07		06 28	06 43			06 58	07 13		07 28	07 43		07 58		08 14		08 22	08 37
3	3	Hackney Downs	d	23p39	23p54	00 09	05 54	06 09	06 22	06 30	06 45	06 52		07 00	07 15	07 22	07 30	07 45	07 52	08 00	08 07	08 16		08 24	08 39
3¾	3¾	Rectory Road	d	23p42	23p57	00 12	05 57	06 12		06 33	06 48	06 55		07 03	07 18	07 25	07 33	07 48	07 55	08 03		08 19		08 27	08 42
4¼	4¼	Stoke Newington	d	23p43	23p58	00 13	05 58	06 13		06 34	06 49	06 56		07 04	07 19	07 26	07 34	07 49	07 56	08 04		08 20		08 28	08 43
5	5	Stamford Hill	d	23p45	23p59	00 15	06 00	06 15		06 36	06 51	06 58		07 06	07 21	07 28	07 36	07 51	07 58	08 06		08 22		08 30	08 45
5½	5½	Seven Sisters ⊖	d	23p47	00 02	00 17	06 02	06 17	06 27	06 38	06 53	07 00		07 08	07 23	07 30	07 38	07 53	08 00	08 08	08 15	08 24		08 32	08 47
6¼	6¼	Bruce Grove	d	23p49	00 04	00 19	06 04	06 19		06 40	06 55	07 02		07 10	07 25	07 32	07 40	07 55	08 02	08 10		08 26		08 34	08 49
7¼	7¼	White Hart Lane	d	23p51	00 06	00 21	06 06	06 21		06 42	06 57	07 04		07 12	07 27	07 34	07 42	07 57	08 04	08 12		08 28		08 36	08 51
8	8	Silver Street	d	23p53	00 08	00 23	06 08	06 23		06 44	06 59	07 06		07 14	07 29	07 36	07 44	07 59	08 06	08 14		08 30		08 38	08 53
8½	8½	Edmonton Green	d	23p55	00 10	00 25	06 10	06 25	06 32	06 46	07 01	07 08		07 16	07 31	07 38	07 46	08 01	08 08	08 16	08 20	08 32		08 44	08 55
—	9¾	Bush Hill Park	d	23p58		00 28		06 28		06 49		07 11		07 19		07 41	07 49		08 11	08 19		08 35			08 58
—	10¾	**Enfield Town**	a	00 03		00 33		06 33		06 54		07 16		07 24		07 46	07 54		08 16	08 24		08 40			09 03
10½	—	Southbury	d		00 14		06 14		06 36		07 05				07 35			08 05			08 24			08 48	
12¼	—	Turkey Street	d		00 17		06 17		06 39		07 08				07 38			08 08			08 27			08 51	
13½	—	Theobalds Grove	d		00 19		06 19		06 41		07 10				07 40			08 10			08 29			08 53	
14½	—	**Cheshunt**	a		00 22		06 24		06 46		07 15				07 45			08 15			08 34			08 58	

		LE	LE	LE	LE	LE	LE		LE		LE	LE	LE	LE	LE	LE	LE	LE	LE		LE	LE	LE	LE
London Liverpool Street [15] ⊖	d	08 38	08 45	09 00	09 15	09 30	09 45		15 45		16 00	16 15	16 21	16 30	16 41	16 45	16 52	17 00	17 11		17 15	17 22	17 30	17 41
Bethnal Green	d		08 48	09 03	09 18	09 33	09 48		15 48		16 03	16 18	16 24	16 33		16 48		17 03			17 18		17 33	
Cambridge Heath	d	08 43	08 50	09 05	09 20	09 35	09 50		15 50		16 05	16 20	16 26	16 35		16 50	16 57	17 05			17 20	17 27	17 35	
London Fields	d	08 45	08 52	09 07	09 22	09 37	09 52		15 52		16 07	16 22	16 28	16 37		16 52	16 59	17 07			17 22	17 29	17 37	
Hackney Downs	d	08 47	08 54	09 09	09 24	09 39	09 54		15 54		16 09	16 24	16 30	16 39	16 48	16 54	17 01	17 09	17 18		17 24	17 31	17 39	17 48
Rectory Road	d	08 49	08 57	09 12	09 27	09 42	09 57	and at the same minutes past each hour until	15 57		16 12	16 27	16 33	16 42		16 57	17 03	17 12			17 27	17 33	17 42	
Stoke Newington	d	08 51	08 58	09 13	09 28	09 43	09 58		15 58		16 13	16 28	16 34	16 43		16 58	17 05	17 13			17 28	17 35	17 43	
Stamford Hill	d	08 53	09 00	09 15	09 30	09 45	10 00		16 00		16 15	16 30	16 36	16 45		17 00		17 15			17 30		17 45	
Seven Sisters ⊖	d	08 55	09 02	09 17	09 32	09 47	10 02		16 02		16 18	16 33	16 39	16 48	16 54	17 03	17 09	17 18	17 24		17 33	17 39	17 48	17 54
Bruce Grove	d	08 57	09 04	09 19	09 34	09 49	10 04		16 04		16 20	16 35	16 41	16 50		17 05	17 11	17 20			17 35	17 41	17 50	
White Hart Lane	d	08 59	09 06	09 21	09 36	09 51	10 06		16 06		16 22	16 37	16 43	16 52		17 07	17 13	17 22			17 37	17 43	17 52	
Silver Street	d	09 01	09 08	09 23	09 38	09 53	10 08		16 08		16 24	16 39	16 45	16 54		17 09	17 15	17 24			17 39	17 45	17 54	
Edmonton Green	d	09 03	09 10	09 25	09 40	09 55	10 10		16 10		16 26	16 41	16 47	16 56	17 00	17 11	17 17	17 26	17 30		17 41	17 47	17 56	18 00
Bush Hill Park	d		09 13	09 28		09 58					16 29		16 50	16 59		17 14		17 29			17 44		17 59	
Enfield Town	a		09 18	09 33		10 03					16 35		16 56	17 05		17 20		17 35			17 50		18 05	
Southbury	d	09 07			09 44		10 14		16 14			16 45					17 21					17 51		
Turkey Street	d	09 10			09 47		10 17		16 17			16 48					17 24					17 54		
Theobalds Grove	d	09 12			09 49		10 19		16 19			16 50					17 26					17 56		
Cheshunt	a	09 17			09 54		10 24		16 24			16 56			17 08		17 32		17 38			18 02		18 08

		LE	LE	LE	LE	LE		LE	LE	LE	LE	LE	LE	LE	LE	LE		LE	LE		LE	LE	LE	
London Liverpool Street [15] ⊖	d	17 45	17 52	18 00	18 11	18 15		18 22	18 30	18 41	18 45	19 00	19 15	19 22	19 30	19 45		20 00	20 15		23 15	23 30	23 45	
Bethnal Green	d	17 48		18 03		18 18			18 33		18 48	19 03	19 18		19 33	19 48		20 03	20 18		23 18	23 33	23 48	
Cambridge Heath	d	17 50	17 57	18 05		18 20		18 27	18 35		18 50	19 05	19 20		19 35	19 50		20 05	20 20		23 20	23 35	23 50	
London Fields	d	17 52	17 59	18 07		18 22		18 29	18 37		18 52	19 07	19 22	19 28	19 37	19 52		20 07	20 22		23 22	23 37	23 52	
Hackney Downs	d	17 54	18 01	18 09	18 18	18 24		18 31	18 39	18 48	18 54	19 09	19 24	19 30	19 39	19 54		20 09	20 24		23 24	23 39	23 54	
Rectory Road	d	17 57	18 03	18 12		18 27		18 33	18 42		18 57	19 12	19 27	19 32	19 42	19 57		20 12	20 27	and at the same minutes past each hour until	23 27	23 42	23 57	
Stoke Newington	d	17 58	18 05	18 13		18 28		18 35	18 43		18 58	19 13	19 28	19 34	19 43	19 58		20 13	20 28		23 28	23 43	23 58	
Stamford Hill	d	18 00		18 15		18 30			18 45		19 00	19 15	19 30		19 45	20 00		20 15	20 30		23 30	23 45	23 59	
Seven Sisters ⊖	d	18 03	18 09	18 18	18 24	18 33		18 39	18 48	18 54	19 03	19 17	19 32	19 37	19 47	20 02		20 17	20 32		23 32	23 47	00 02	
Bruce Grove	d	18 05	18 11	18 20		18 35		18 41	18 50		19 05	19 19	19 34	19 39	19 49	20 04		20 19	20 34		23 34	23 49	00 04	
White Hart Lane	d	18 07	18 13	18 22		18 37		18 43	18 52		19 07	19 21	19 36	19 41	19 51	20 06		20 21	20 36		23 36	23 51	00 06	
Silver Street	d	18 09	18 15	18 24		18 39		18 45	18 54		19 09	19 23	19 38	19 43	19 53	20 08		20 23	20 38		23 38	23 53	00 08	
Edmonton Green	d	18 11	18 17	18 26	18 30	18 41		18 47	18 56	19 00	19 11	19 25	19 40	19 45	19 55	20 10		20 25	20 40		23 40	23 55	00 10	
Bush Hill Park	d	18 14		18 29		18 44			18 59			19 28		19 48	19 58			20 28				23 58		
Enfield Town	a	18 20		18 35		18 50			19 05			19 33		19 53	20 03			20 33				00 03		
Southbury	d		18 21					18 51			19 15		19 44			20 14			20 44		23 44		00 14	
Turkey Street	d		18 24					18 54			19 18		19 47			20 17			20 47		23 47		00 17	
Theobalds Grove	d		18 26					18 56			19 21		19 50			20 19			20 49		23 49		00 19	
Cheshunt	a		18 32		18 38			19 02		19 08	19 26		19 54			20 24			20 54		23 54		00 22	

Saturdays

		LE	LE	LE	LE	LE	LE	LE	LE	LE		LE		LE
London Liverpool Street [15] ⊖	d	23p30	23p45	00 01	05 15	05 31	05 45	06 00	06 15	06 30		23 30		23 45
Bethnal Green	d	23p33	23p48	00 03	05 18		05 48	06 03	06 18	06 33		23 33		23 48
Cambridge Heath	d	23p35	23p50	00 05	05 20		05 50	06 05	06 20	06 35		23 35		23 50
London Fields	d	23p37	23p52	00 07	05 22		05 52	06 07	06 22	06 37		23 37		23 52
Hackney Downs	d	23p39	23p54	00 09	05 24	05 38	05 54	06 09	06 24	06 39		23 39		23 54
Rectory Road	d	23p42	23p57	00 12	05 27		05 57	06 12	06 27	06 42	and at the same minutes past each hour until	23 42		23 57
Stoke Newington	d	23p43	23p58	00 13	05 28		05 58	06 13	06 28	06 43		23 43		23 58
Stamford Hill	d	23p45	23p59	00 15	05 30		06 00	06 15	06 30	06 45		23 45		23 59
Seven Sisters ⊖	d	23p47	00 02	00 17	05 32	05 47	06 02	06 17	06 32	06 47		23 47		00 02
Bruce Grove	d	23p49	00 04	00 19	05 34	05 49	06 04	06 19	06 34	06 49		23 49		00 04
White Hart Lane	d	23p51	00 06	00 21	05 36	05 51	06 06	06 21	06 36	06 51		23 51		00 06
Silver Street	d	23p53	00 08	00 23	05 38	05 53	06 08	06 23	06 38	06 53		23 53		00 08
Edmonton Green	d	23p55	00 10	00 25	05 40	05 55	06 10	06 25	06 40	06 55		23 55		00 10
Bush Hill Park	d	23p58		00 28		05 58		06 28		06 58		23 58		
Enfield Town	a	00 03		00 33		06 03		06 33		07 03		00 03		
Southbury	d		00 14		05 44		06 14		06 44					00 14
Turkey Street	d		00 17		05 47		06 17		06 47					00 17
Theobalds Grove	d		00 19		05 49		06 19		06 49					00 19
Cheshunt	a		00 22		05 54		06 24		06 54					00 24

Table 21

Sundays

London - Cheshunt (via Seven Sisters) and Enfield Town

Network Diagram - see first Page of Table 20

		LE A	LE A	LE	LE	LE	LE	LE	LE	LE		LE	LE	LE	LE	LE		LE	LE		LE			
London Liverpool Street 15 ⊖	d	23p30	23p45	00 01	07 30	07 52	08 00	08 22	08 30	08 52		09 00	09 22	09 30	09 52	10 00		23 00	23 22		23 30			
Bethnal Green	d	23p33	23p48	00 03										09 33		10 03		23 03			23 33			
Cambridge Heath	d	23p35	23p50	00 05										09 35		10 05		23 05			23 35			
London Fields	d	23p37	23p52	00 07										09 37		10 07		23 07			23 37			
Hackney Downs	d	23p39	23p54	00 09	07 39	07 59	08 09	08 29	08 39	08 59		09 09	09 29	09 39	09 59	10 09		23 09	23 29		23 39			
Rectory Road	d	23p42	23p57	00 12	07 42		08 12		08 42			09 12		09 42		10 12	and at	23 12			23 42			
Stoke Newington	d	23p43	23p58	00 13	07 43		08 13		08 43			09 13		09 43		10 13	the same	23 13			23 43			
Stamford Hill	d	23p45	23p59	00 15	07 45		08 15		08 45			09 15		09 45		10 15	minutes	23 15			23 45			
Seven Sisters ⊖	d	23p47	00 02	00 17	07 47	08 04	08 17	08 34	08 47	09 04		09 17	09 34	09 47	10 04	10 17	past	23 17	23 34		23 47			
Bruce Grove	d	23p49	00 04	00 19	07 49		08 19		08 49			09 19		09 49		10 19	each	23 19			23 49			
White Hart Lane	d	23p51	00 06	00 21	07 51		08 21		08 51			09 21		09 51		10 21	hour until	23 21			23 51			
Silver Street	d	23p53	00 08	00 23	07 53		08 23		08 53			09 23		09 53		10 23		23 23			23 53			
Edmonton Green	d	23p55	00 10	00 25	07 55	08 08	08 25	08 38	08 55	09 08		09 25	09 38	09 55	10 08	10 25		23 25	23 38		23 55			
Bush Hill Park	d	23p58		00 28	07 58		08 28		08 58			09 28		09 58		10 28		23 28			23 58			
Enfield Town	a	00 03		00 33	08 03		08 33		09 03			09 33		10 03		10 33		23 33			00 03			
Southbury	d		00 14			08 12		08 42		09 12			09 42		10 12				23 42					
Turkey Street	d		00 17			08 15		08 45		09 15			09 45		10 15				23 45					
Theobalds Grove	d		00 19			08 17		08 47		09 17			09 47		10 17				23 47					
Cheshunt	a		00 24			08 20		08 52		09 20			09 52		10 20				23 50					

A not 11 December

Cheshunt (via Seven Sisters) and Enfield Town - London

Network Diagram - see first Page of Table 20

Miles	Miles			LE MX	LE MX 1	LE MX 1	LE	LE	LE	LE	LE	LE		LE	LE	LE	LE	LE	LE	LE	LE	LE		LE	LE
0	—	**Cheshunt**	d	23p31	23p52	23p58	05 16		06 01			06 33		06 48		06 52		07 18		07 22		07 48			07 52
1	—	Theobalds Grove	d	23p34			05 19		06 04			06 36				06 55				07 25					07 55
2¼	—	Turkey Street	d	23p36			05 21		06 06			06 38				06 57				07 27					07 57
4	—	Southbury	d	23p39			05 24		06 09			06 41				07 00				07 30					08 00
—	0	**Enfield Town**	d					05 52		06 18	06 33				06 54		07 09		07 24		07 39			07 54	
—	1	Bush Hill Park	d					05 55		06 21	06 36				06 57		07 12		07 27		07 42			07 57	
6	2¼	Edmonton Green	d	23p43			05 28	05 58	06 13	06 24	06 39	06 45		06 56	07 00	07 05	07 15	07 26	07 30	07 35	07 45	07 56		08 00	08 05
6½	2¾	Silver Street	d	23p45			05 30	06 00	06 15	06 26	06 41	06 47			07 02	07 07	07 17		07 32	07 37	07 47			08 02	08 07
7¼	3½	White Hart Lane	d	23p47			05 32	06 02	06 17	06 28	06 43	06 49			07 04	07 09	07 19		07 34	07 39	07 49			08 04	08 09
8¼	4½	Bruce Grove	d	23p49			05 34	06 04	06 19	06 30	06 45	06 51			07 06	07 11	07 21		07 36	07 41	07 51			08 06	08 11
9	5¼	Seven Sisters ⊖	d	23p51	00 04	00 11	05 36	06 06	06 21	06 33	06 48	06 54		07 02	07 09	07 14	07 24	07 32	07 39	07 44	07 54	08 02		08 09	08 14
9½	5¾	Stamford Hill	d	23p53			05 38	06 08	06 23	06 35	06 50	06 56			07 11		07 26		07 41		07 56			08 11	
10¼	6½	Stoke Newington	d	23p55			05 40	06 10	06 25	06 37	06 52	06 58			07 13	07 17	07 28		07 43	07 47	07 58			08 13	08 17
10¾	7	Rectory Road	d	23p56			05 41	06 11	06 26	06 39	06 54	07 00			07 15	07 18	07 30		07 45	07 48	08 00			08 15	08 18
11½	7¾	Hackney Downs	d	23p59		00 16	05 44	06 14	06 29	06 43	06 58	07 04		07 08	07 19	07 22	07 34	07 38	07 49	07 52	08 04	08 08		08 19	08 22
12	8¼	London Fields	d	00 01			05 46	06 16	06 31	06 45	07 00	07 06			07 21	07 24	07 36		07 51	07 54	08 06			08 21	08 24
12¾	9	Cambridge Heath	d	00 03			05 48	06 18	06 33	06 47	07 02	07 08			07 23		07 38		07 53		08 08			08 23	
13¼	9½	Bethnal Green	d	00 05			05 50	06 20	06 35	06 49		07 10			07 25		07 40		07 55		08 10			08 25	
14½	10¾	**London Liverpool Street** 15 ⊖	a	00 10	00 18	00 26	05 55	06 25	06 40	06 54	07 10	07 16		07 18	07 31	07 33	07 46	07 48	08 01	08 03	08 16	08 18		08 31	08 33

		LE	LE	LE	LE	LE	LE	LE		LE	LE	LE	LE	LE	LE	LE		LE		LE	LE	LE	LE	LE
Cheshunt	d		08 18		08 22		08 43				09 07		09 31		10 01					16 31			17 04	
Theobalds Grove	d				08 25		08 46				09 10		09 34		10 04					16 34			17 07	
Turkey Street	d				08 27		08 48				09 12		09 36		10 06					16 36			17 09	
Southbury	d				08 30		08 51				09 15		09 39		10 09					16 39			17 12	
Enfield Town	d	08 09		08 24		08 39		08 54		09 09		09 24		09 52		10 22		16 22			16 52	17 07		17 22
Bush Hill Park	d	08 12		08 27		08 42		08 57		09 12		09 27		09 55		10 25	and at the same minutes past each hour until	16 25			16 55	17 10		17 25
Edmonton Green	d	08 15	08 26	08 30	08 35	08 45	08 56	09 00		09 15	09 20	09 30	09 43	09 58	10 13	10 28		16 28		16 43	16 58	17 13	17 17	17 28
Silver Street	d	08 17		08 32	08 37	08 47		09 02		09 17	09 22	09 32	09 45	10 00	10 15	10 30		16 30		16 45	17 00	17 15	17 19	17 30
White Hart Lane	d	08 19		08 34	08 39	08 49		09 04		09 19	09 24	09 34	09 47	10 02	10 17	10 32		16 32		16 47	17 02	17 17	17 21	17 32
Bruce Grove	d	08 21		08 36	08 41	08 51		09 06		09 21	09 26	09 36	09 49	10 04	10 19	10 34		16 34		16 49	17 04	17 19	17 23	17 34
Seven Sisters ⊖	d	08 24	08 32	08 39	08 44	08 54	09 02	09 09		09 24	09 29	09 39	09 51	10 06	10 21	10 36		16 36		16 51	17 06	17 21	17 25	17 36
Stamford Hill	d	08 26		08 41		08 56		09 11		09 26		09 41	09 53	10 08	10 23	10 38		16 38		16 53	17 08	17 23	17 27	17 38
Stoke Newington	d	08 28		08 43	08 47	08 58		09 13		09 28	09 32	09 43	09 55	10 10	10 25	10 40		16 40		16 55	17 10	17 25	17 29	17 40
Rectory Road	d	08 30		08 45	08 48	09 00		09 15		09 30	09 33	09 45	09 56	10 11	10 26	10 41		16 41		16 56	17 11	17 26	17 30	17 41
Hackney Downs	d	08 34	08 38	08 49	08 52	09 04	09 08	09 19		09 34	09 37	09 49	09 59	10 14	10 29	10 44		16 44		16 59	17 14	17 29	17 35	17 44
London Fields	d	08 36		08 51	08 54	09 06		09 21		09 36	09 39	09 51	10 01	10 16	10 31	10 46		16 46		17 01	17 16	17 31		17 46
Cambridge Heath	d	08 38		08 53		09 08		09 23		09 38		09 53	10 03	10 18	10 33	10 48		16 48		17 03	17 18	17 33		17 48
Bethnal Green	d	08 40		08 55		09 10		09 25		09 40		09 55	10 05	10 20	10 35	10 50		16 50		17 05	17 20	17 35		17 50
London Liverpool Street 15 ⊖	a	08 46	08 48	08 59	09 03	09 16	09 18	09 31		09 46	09 48	10 01	10 10	10 25	10 40	10 55		16 55		17 10	17 25	17 40	17 44	17 55

		LE	LE	LE	LE		LE	LE	LE	LE	LE	LE	LE	LE	LE		LE	LE	LE	LE	LE	LE	LE	LE	LE
Cheshunt	d		17 39				18 09			18 39			19 09		19 31			20 01		20 31		21 01		21 31	
Theobalds Grove	d		17 42				18 12			18 42			19 12		19 34			20 04		20 34		21 04		21 34	
Turkey Street	d		17 44				18 14			18 44			19 14		19 36			20 06		20 36		21 06		21 36	
Southbury	d		17 47				18 17			18 47			19 17		19 39			20 09		20 39		21 09		21 39	
Enfield Town	d	17 37		17 52	18 07			18 22	18 37		18 52	19 07		19 22			19 52		20 22		20 52		21 22		21 52
Bush Hill Park	d	17 40		17 55	18 10			18 25	18 40		18 55	19 10		19 25			19 55		20 25		20 55		21 25		21 55
Edmonton Green	d	17 43	17 51	17 58	18 13		18 21	18 28	18 43	18 51	18 58	19 13	19 21	19 28	19 43		19 58	20 13	20 28	20 43	20 58	21 13	21 28	21 43	21 58
Silver Street	d	17 45		18 00	18 15			18 30	18 45		19 00	19 15		19 30	19 45		20 00	20 15	20 30	20 45	21 00	21 15	21 30	21 45	22 00
White Hart Lane	d	17 47		18 02	18 17			18 32	18 47		19 02	19 17		19 32	19 47		20 02	20 17	20 32	20 47	21 02	21 17	21 32	21 47	22 02
Bruce Grove	d	17 49		18 04	18 19			18 34	18 49		19 04	19 19		19 34	19 49		20 04	20 19	20 34	20 49	21 04	21 19	21 34	21 49	22 04
Seven Sisters ⊖	d	17 51	17 57	18 06	18 21		18 27	18 36	18 51	18 57	19 06	19 21	19 27	19 36	19 51		20 06	20 21	20 36	20 51	21 06	21 21	21 36	21 51	22 06
Stamford Hill	d	17 53		18 08	18 23			18 38	18 53		19 08	19 23		19 38	19 53		20 08	20 23	20 38	20 53	21 08	21 23	21 38	21 53	22 08
Stoke Newington	d	17 55	18 00	18 10	18 25		18 30	18 40	18 55	19 00	19 10	19 25	19 30	19 40	19 55		20 10	20 25	20 40	20 55	21 10	21 25	21 40	21 55	22 10
Rectory Road	d	17 56		18 11	18 26			18 41	18 56		19 11	19 26		19 41	19 56		20 11	20 26	20 41	20 56	21 11	21 26	21 41	21 56	22 11
Hackney Downs	d	17 59	18 03	18 14	18 29		18 33	18 44	18 59	19 03	19 14	19 29	19 33	19 44	19 59		20 14	20 29	20 44	20 59	21 14	21 29	21 44	21 59	22 14
London Fields	d	18 01		18 16	18 31			18 46	19 01		19 16	19 31		19 46	20 01		20 16	20 31	20 46	21 01	21 16	21 31	21 46	22 01	22 16
Cambridge Heath	d	18 03		18 18	18 33			18 48	19 03		19 18	19 33		19 48	20 03		20 18	20 33	20 48	21 03	21 18	21 33	21 48	22 03	22 18
Bethnal Green	d	18 05		18 20	18 35			18 50	19 05		19 20	19 35		19 50	20 05		20 20	20 35	20 50	21 05	21 20	21 35	21 50	22 05	22 20
London Liverpool Street 15 ⊖	a	18 10	18 12	18 25	18 40		18 42	18 55	19 10	19 12	19 25	19 40	19 43	19 55	20 09		20 25	20 40	20 55	21 10	21 25	21 40	21 55	22 10	22 25

			LE	LE	LE	LE	LE	LE	LE	LE 1	LE 1
Cheshunt	d		22 01		22 31		23 01		23 31	23 52	23 58
Theobalds Grove	d		22 04		22 34		23 04		23 34		
Turkey Street	d		22 06		22 36		23 06		23 36		
Southbury	d		22 09		22 39		23 09		23 39		
Enfield Town	d			22 22		22 52		23 22			
Bush Hill Park	d			22 25		22 55		23 25			
Edmonton Green	d		22 13	22 28	22 43	22 58	23 13	23 28	23 43		
Silver Street	d		22 15	22 30	22 45	23 00	23 15	23 30	23 45		
White Hart Lane	d		22 17	22 32	22 47	23 02	23 17	23 32	23 47		
Bruce Grove	d		22 19	22 34	22 49	23 04	23 19	23 34	23 49		
Seven Sisters ⊖	d		22 21	22 36	22 51	23 06	23 21	23 36	23 51	00 04	00 11
Stamford Hill	d		22 23	22 38	22 53	23 08	23 23	23 38	23 53		
Stoke Newington	d		22 25	22 40	22 55	23 10	23 25	23 40	23 55		
Rectory Road	d		22 26	22 41	22 56	23 11	23 26	23 41	23 56		
Hackney Downs	d		22 29	22 44	22 59	23 14	23 29	23 44	23 59		00 16
London Fields	d		22 31	22 46	23 01	23 16	23 31	23 46	00 01		
Cambridge Heath	d		22 33	22 48	23 03	23 18	23 33	23 48	00 03		
Bethnal Green	d		22 35	22 50	23 05	23 20	23 35	23 50	00 05		
London Liverpool Street 15 ⊖	a		22 40	22 55	23 10	23 25	23 40	23 55	00 10	00 18	00 26

Table 21

Saturdays

Cheshunt (via Seven Sisters) and Enfield Town - London

Network Diagram - see first Page of Table 20

		LE	LE 1	LE 1	LE 1	LE	LE	LE	LE		LE		LE	LE	LE	LE	LE	LE	LE	LE
Cheshunt	d	23p31	23p52	23p58	05 16	06 01		06 31		and at the same minutes past each hour until			22 01		22 31		23 01		23 31	
Theobalds Grove	d	23p34			05 19	06 04		06 34					22 04		22 34		23 04		23 34	
Turkey Street	d	23p36			05 21	06 06		06 36					22 06		22 36		23 06		23 36	
Southbury	d	23p39			05 24	06 09		06 39					22 09		22 39		23 09		23 39	
Enfield Town	d						06 22		06 52		21 52			22 22		22 52		23 22		23 52
Bush Hill Park	d						06 25		06 55		21 55			22 25		22 55		23 25		23 55
Edmonton Green	d	23p43			05 28	06 13	06 28	06 43	06 58		21 58		22 13	22 28	22 43	22 58	23 13	23 28	23 43	23 58
Silver Street	d	23p45			05 30	06 15	06 30	06 45	07 00		22 00		22 15	22 30	22 45	23 00	23 15	23 30	23 45	23 59
White Hart Lane	d	23p47			05 32	06 17	06 32	06 47	07 02		22 02		22 17	22 32	22 47	23 02	23 17	23 32	23 47	00 02
Bruce Grove	d	23p49			05 34	06 19	06 34	06 49	07 04		22 04		22 19	22 34	22 49	23 04	23 19	23 34	23 49	00 04
Seven Sisters ⊖	d	23p51	00 04	00 11	05 36	06 21	06 36	06 51	07 06		22 06		22 21	22 36	22 51	23 06	23 21	23 36	23 51	00 06
Stamford Hill	d	23p53			05 38	06 23	06 38	06 53	07 08		22 08		22 23	22 38	22 53	23 08	23 23	23 38	23 53	00 08
Stoke Newington	d	23p55			05 40	06 25	06 40	06 55	07 10		22 10		22 25	22 40	22 55	23 10	23 25	23 40	23 55	00 10
Rectory Road	d	23p56			05 41	06 26	06 41	06 56	07 11		22 11		22 26	22 41	22 56	23 11	23 26	23 41	23 56	00 11
Hackney Downs	d	23p59		00 16	05 45	06 29	06 44	06 59	07 14		22 14		22 29	22 44	22 59	23 14	23 29	23 44	23 59	00 14
London Fields	d	00 01				06 31	06 46	07 01	07 16		22 16		22 31	22 46	23 01	23 16	23 31	23 46	00 01	00 16
Cambridge Heath	d	00 03				06 33	06 48	07 03	07 18		22 18		22 33	22 48	23 03	23 18	23 33	23 48	00 03	00 18
Bethnal Green	d	00 05			05 49	06 35	06 50	07 05	07 20		22 20		22 35	22 50	23 05	23 20	23 35	23 50	00 05	00 20
London Liverpool Street 15 ⊖	a	00 10	00 18	00 26	05 54	06 40	06 55	07 10	07 25		22 25		22 40	22 55	23 10	23 24	23 40	23 55	00 10	00 25

Sundays

		LE A	LE A	LE	LE	LE	LE	LE	LE	LE		LE		LE	LE	LE	LE	LE
Cheshunt	d	23p31		07 45		08 15		08 45		09 15			and at the same minutes past each hour until		22 45		23 15	
Theobalds Grove	d	23p34		07 48		08 18		08 48		09 18					22 48		23 18	
Turkey Street	d	23p36		07 51		08 21		08 51		09 21					22 51		23 21	
Southbury	d	23p39		07 54		08 24		08 54		09 24					22 54		23 24	
Enfield Town	d		23p52		07 57		08 27		08 57			09 27		22 27		22 57		23 27
Bush Hill Park	d		23p55		08 00		08 30		09 00			09 30		22 30		23 00		23 30
Edmonton Green	d	23p43	23p58	07 57	08 03	08 27	08 33	08 57	09 03	09 27		09 33		22 33	22 57	23 03	23 27	23 33
Silver Street	d	23p45	23p59		08 05		08 35		09 05			09 35		22 35		23 05		23 35
White Hart Lane	d	23p47	00 02		08 07		08 37		09 07			09 37		22 37		23 07		23 37
Bruce Grove	d	23p49	00 04		08 09		08 39		09 09			09 39		22 39		23 09		23 39
Seven Sisters ⊖	d	23p51	00 06	08 03	08 11	08 33	08 41	09 03	09 11	09 33		09 41		22 41	23 03	23 11	23 33	23 41
Stamford Hill	d	23p53	00 08		08 13		08 43		09 13			09 43		22 43		23 13		23 43
Stoke Newington	d	23p55	00 10		08 15		08 45		09 15			09 45		22 45		23 15		23 45
Rectory Road	d	23p56	00 11		08 16		08 46		09 16			09 46		22 46		23 16		23 46
Hackney Downs	d	23p59	00 14	08 09	08 19	08 39	08 49	09 09	09 19	09 39		09 49		22 49	23 09	23 19	23 39	23 49
London Fields	d	00 01	00 16						09 21			09 51		22 51		23 21		23 51
Cambridge Heath	d	00 03	00 18						09 23			09 53		22 53		23 23		23 53
Bethnal Green	d	00 05	00 20						09 25			09 55		22 55		23 25		23 55
London Liverpool Street 15 ⊖	a	00 10	00 25	08 18	08 30	08 48	09 00	09 18	09 30	09 48		10 00		23 00	23 18	23 30	23 48	23 58

A not 11 December

London - Broxbourne, Hertford East, Bishops Stortford, Stansted Airport and Cambridge

Network Diagram - see first Page of Table 20

Miles	Miles			LE MO ■1	LE MO ■1	LE MO	LE MO ■1	LE MO	LE MO ■1	LE MO	LE MO ■1	LE MO ■1	LE MFO ■1	LE MThF O ■1	LE TWO ■1	LE MX ■1	LE MX ■1	LE MX ■1	LE MX ■1	LE MX ■1	LE ■1	XC ◇■1	LE ■1	LE ■1
0	—	**London Liverpool Street** ■15 ⊖	d			23p22	23p25		23p28			03 40	04 10	04 40	04 40	22p58	23p12	23p25	23p28	23p40	23p58		05 10	
1¼	—	Bethnal Green	d																					
3	—	Hackney Downs	d			23p29											23p18			23p46				
—	0	Stratford ■7 ⊖	d	22p45																				
4	—	Clapton	d																	23p49				
—	6¾	Seven Sisters ⊖	d			23p34																		
6	—	Tottenham Hale ⊖	d	22p55			23p37		23p40					04u52	04u59	23p10	23p25	23b37	23p40	23p53	00 10		05u22	
7	—	Northumberland Park	d																	23p55				
7¾	—	Angel Road	d																					
10	—	Ponders End	d	22p59					23p44								23p29			23p59				
10¾	—	Brimsdown	d	23p02					23p47								23p32			00 02				
11¾	—	Enfield Lock	d	23p04					23p49								23p34			00 04				
12¾	—	Waltham Cross	d	23p07				←	23p52								23p37			00 07				
14	—	Cheshunt	d	23p09		23p50		23p50	23p54	←				05 00	05 07	23p18	23p39		23p48	00 09	00 18			
17¼	—	**Broxbourne** ■3	a	23p14		→		23p55	23p59	23p55				05 04	05 11	23p22	23p44		23p52	00 14	00 22			
—	0	**Broxbourne** ■3	d	23p19				00 02	23p59	00 02				05 04	05 11	23p22	23p44		23p52	00 14	00 22			05 40
—	1¾	Rye House	d					→		00 06							23p47			00 17				05 43
—	3	St Margarets (Herts)	d							00 09							23p50			00 20				05 46
—	5	Ware	d							00 13							23p54			00 24				05 50
—	7	**Hertford East**	a							00 19							00 01			00 31				05 56
20	—	Roydon	d	23p24															23p56		00 26			
22¾	—	Harlow Town	d	23p28			23p52		00 05					05 10	05 17	23p28		23p54	23p59		00 30		05 37	
24½	—	Harlow Mill	d	23p31															00 03		00 33			
26¾	—	Sawbridgeworth	d	23p34	←				00 10		←								00 07		00 37		05 42	
30¼	—	**Bishops Stortford**	a	23p41	23p41		00 02		00 17		23p41			05 20	05 27	23p38		00 04	00 14		00 44		05 49	
—	—		d	23p42	23p42		00 03				23p42			05 20	05 27	23p39		00 04	00 14				05 50	
33¾	0	Stansted Mountfitchet	d	→	23p46						23p46			05 24	05 31				00 18					
—	—	**Stansted Airport**	a				00 12					04 30	05 00	05 39	05 39			00 13					05 59	
—	3¾	**Stansted Airport**	d																			05 16		
35½	8¼	Elsenham	d		23p50						23p50								00 22					
40	—	Newport (Essex)	d		23p55						23p55								00 27					
41¾	—	Audley End	d		23p58						23p58					23p51			00 30			05 37		
45¾	—	Great Chesterford	d		00 03						00 03								00 35					
49	—	Whittlesford Parkway	d		00 08						00 08					23p58			00 40					
52½	—	Shelford	d		00 12						00 12								00 44					
55¾	—	**Cambridge**	a		00 19						00 19					00 08			00 51			05 53		

		LE ■1	XC ◇■1	LE ■1	LE ■1	LE ■1	LE ■1	LE ■1		LE ■1	LE ■1	LE ■1	LE ■1	LE ■1	LE ■1	XC ◇■1	LE ■1	LE ■1		LE ■1	LE ■1	LE ■1	LE ■1	LE ■1	LE ■1
London Liverpool Street ■15 ⊖	d			05 25	05 28	05 40	05 42	05 52		05 55	05 58		06 10	06 12	06 25		06 28			06 40		06 42		06 55	06 58
Bethnal Green	d																								
Hackney Downs	d						05 48							06 18								06 48			
Stratford ■7 ⊖	d							06 03										06 35					06 50		
Clapton	d																								
Seven Sisters ⊖	d											←													
Tottenham Hale ⊖	d			05u37	05 40	05u52	05 55	06 15		06u07	06 10	06 15	06u22	06 25	06u37		06 40	06 45		06u52		06 55	07 00	07u07	07 10
Northumberland Park	d							→				06 17						06 48							
Angel Road	d											06 19													
Ponders End	d						05 59							06 29									07 04		
Brimsdown	d						06 02							06 32									07 07		
Enfield Lock	d						06 04					06 24		06 34								07 01			
Waltham Cross	d						06 07							06 37								07 04			
Cheshunt	d				05 48		06 09				06 18	06 28		06 39			06 48	06 55				07 06	07 11		07 18
Broxbourne ■3	a				05 52		06 14				06 22	06 32		06 44			06 52	06 59				07 11	07 16		07 22
Broxbourne ■3	d				05 52		06 14				06 24	06 36		06 44			06 52	06 59				07 14			07 22
Rye House	d						06 17					06 39		06 47								07 17			
St Margarets (Herts)	d						06 20					06 42		06 50								07 20			
Ware	d						06 24					06 46		06 54								07 24			
Hertford East	a						06 31					06 53		07 01								07 31			
Roydon	d				05 56						06 28						06 56								07 26
Harlow Town	d			05 52	06 00					06 26	06 32				06 54		07 09							07 24	07 30
Harlow Mill	d				06 03						06 35						07 13								07 33
Sawbridgeworth	d				06 07						06 38						07 16				←				07 37
Bishops Stortford	a			06 02	06 14	06 17					06 45		06 49				07 23	07 13		07 16	07 23				07 44
	d	05 55		06 02	06 14	06 18					06 45		06 49				07 26			07 17	07 26				07 44
Stansted Mountfitchet	d	05 59			06 18	06 23					06 50						→				07 30			07 35	07 48
Stansted Airport	a			06 15		06 29				06 44			06 59		07 12					07 30				07 43	
Stansted Airport	d		06 06													07 21									
Elsenham	d	06 03			06 22						06 53										07 34				07 52
Newport (Essex)	d	06 08			06 27						06 59										07 39				07 57
Audley End	d	06 11	06 23		06 30						07 02					07 37					07 42				08 00
Great Chesterford	d	06 16			06 35						07 07										07 47				08 05
Whittlesford Parkway	d	06 21			06 40						07 11										07 52				08 10
Shelford	d	06 25			06 44						07 16										07 56				08 14
Cambridge	a	06 32	06 38		06 56						07 26					07 58					08 07				08 23

b Previous night, stops to pick up only

London - Broxbourne, Hertford East, Bishops Stortford, Stansted Airport and Cambridge

Network Diagram - see first Page of Table 20

		LE	LE	LE	LE	LE	XC	LE	LE	LE	LE	LE	LE	LE	LE	LE	LE	LE	LE	XC	LE	LE
		1	1	1	1	1	◇1	1	1	1	1	1	1	1	1	1	1	1	1	◇1	1	1
		🚲		🚲				🚲		🚲				🚲		🚲					🚲	
London Liverpool Street 15 ⊖	d	07 10	07 12	07 25	07 28			07 40	07 42	07 55	07 58	08 03		08 10	08 12	08 25	08 28	08 33			08 40	08 42
Bethnal Green	d																					
Hackney Downs	d		07 18						07 48						08 18							08 48
Stratford 7 ⊖	d					07 34							08 04						08 34			
Clapton	d																					
Seven Sisters ⊖	d																					
Tottenham Hale ⊖	d	07u22	07 25	07u37	07 40	07 47		07u52	07 55	08u07	08 10	08 15	08 18	08u22	08 25	08u37	08 40	08 45	08 48		08u52	08 55
Northumberland Park	d					07 49							08 20						08 50			
Angel Road	d					07 51													08 52			
Ponders End	d		07 29						07 59						08 29							08 59
Brimsdown	d		07 32						08 02						08 32							09 02
Enfield Lock	d		07 34						08 04				08 26		08 34							09 04
Waltham Cross	d		07 37						08 07						08 37							09 07
Cheshunt	d		07 39		07 48	07 58			08 09		08 18		08 29		08 39		08 48		08 59			09 09
Broxbourne 3	a		07 44		07 52	08 04			08 14		08 22		08 34		08 44		08 52		09 04			09 14
Broxbourne 3	d		07 44		07 52	08 10			08 14		08 22		08 38		08 44		08 52		09 08			09 14
Rye House	d		07 47						08 17						08 47							09 17
St Margarets (Herts)	d		07 50						08 20						08 50							09 20
Ware	d		07 54						08 24						08 54							09 24
Hertford East	a		08 01						08 31						09 01							09 31
Roydon	d				07 56	08 15							08 42				08 56		09 12			
Harlow Town	d			07 55	08 00	08 19				08 25	08 33		08 46			08 54	09 04		09 16			
Harlow Mill	d				08 03						08 36		08 49						09 19			
Sawbridgeworth	d				08 07	08 24					08 40		08 53				09 10		09 23			
Bishops Stortford	a	07 47			08 14	08 32		08 19			08 47		09 02	08 50			09 17		09 32		09 20	
	d	07 48			08 14			08 20			08 47			08 51			09 17				09 21	
Stansted Mountfitchet	d				08 18					08 37	08 51						09 21					
Stansted Airport	a	07 59		08 13				08 30		08 45				09 00		09 14					09 30	
Stansted Airport	d						08 21													09 21		
Elsenham	d				08 22						08 55						09 25					
Newport (Essex)	d				08 27						09 00						09 30					
Audley End	d				08 30		08 37				09 03	08 52					09 33	09 22		09 39		
Great Chesterford	d				08 35						09 08						09 38					
Whittlesford Parkway	d				08 40						09 13						09 43					
Shelford	d				08 44						09 17						09 47					
Cambridge	a				08 52		08 58				09 25	09 07					09 54	09 41		09 58		

		LE	LE	LE	LE	LE	LE	LE	LE	LE	LE	XC	LE	LE	LE	LE	LE	LE	LE	LE	LE	LE	XC
		1	1	1	1	1	1	1	1	1	1	◇1	1	1	1	1	1	1	1	1	1	1	◇1
		🚲			🚲		🚲			🚲			🚲			🚲		🚲			🚲		
London Liverpool Street 15 ⊖	d	08 55	08 58		09 10	09 12	09 25	09 28		09 40	09 42		09 55	09 58		10 10	10 12	10 25	10 28		10 40	10 42	
Bethnal Green	d																						
Hackney Downs	d					09 18					09 48						10 18					10 48	
Stratford 7 ⊖	d			09 00					09 30						10 00					10 30			
Clapton	d																						
Seven Sisters ⊖	d																						
Tottenham Hale ⊖	d	09u07	09 10	09 13	09u22	09 25	09u37	09 40	09 43	09u52	09 55		10u07	10 10	10 13	10u22	10 25	10u37	10 40	10 43	10u52	10 55	
Northumberland Park	d			09 15					09 46						10 15								
Angel Road	d								09 48														
Ponders End	d					09 29					09 59						10 29					10 59	
Brimsdown	d					09 32					10 02						10 32					11 02	
Enfield Lock	d			09 21		09 34					10 04				10 21		10 34					11 04	
Waltham Cross	d					09 37			09 53		10 07						10 37			10 50		11 07	
Cheshunt	d		09 18	09 25		09 39		09 48	09 56		10 09			10 18	10 25		10 39		10 48	10 53		11 09	
Broxbourne 3	a		09 22	09 30		09 44		09 52	10 00		10 14			10 22	10 29		10 44		10 52	10 57		11 14	
Broxbourne 3	d		09 22	09 33		09 44		09 52	10 04		10 14			10 22	10 33		10 44		10 52	10 57		11 14	
Rye House	d					09 47					10 17						10 47					11 17	
St Margarets (Herts)	d					09 50					10 20						10 50					11 20	
Ware	d					09 54					10 24						10 54					11 24	
Hertford East	a					10 01					10 31						11 01					11 31	
Roydon	d			09 38				09 56							10 38				10 56				
Harlow Town	d	09 24	09 28	09 42			09 54	10 00	10 10				10 24	10 28	10 42			10 54	11 00	11 09			
Harlow Mill	d			09 45				10 03							10 45				11 03				
Sawbridgeworth	d			09 48				10 07	10 15						10 48				11 07	11 15			
Bishops Stortford	a		09 38	09 56	09 45			10 14	10 22	10 17				10 38	10 56	10 45			11 14	11 22	11 17		
	d		09 39		09 45			10 14		10 18				10 39		10 45			11 14		11 18		
Stansted Mountfitchet	d	09 37						10 18					10 35						11 18				
Stansted Airport	a	09 45			09 55		10 12			10 27			10 44			10 55		11 13			11 27		
Stansted Airport	d											10 27											11 27
Elsenham	d							10 22											11 22				
Newport (Essex)	d							10 27											11 27				
Audley End	d		09 51					10 30				10 40		10 51					11 30				11 40
Great Chesterford	d							10 35											11 35				
Whittlesford Parkway	d		09 58					10 40						10 58					11 40				
Shelford	d							10 44											11 44				
Cambridge	a		10 08					10 51				10 58		11 08					11 51				11 58

Table 22

Mondays to Fridays

London - Broxbourne, Hertford East, Bishops Stortford, Stansted Airport and Cambridge

Network Diagram - see first Page of Table 20

		LE 1 🚲	LE 1	LE 1	LE 1 🚲	LE 1		LE 1 🚲	LE 1	LE 1	LE 1 🚲	LE 1	XC ◇1	LE 1 🚲	LE 1	LE 1		LE 1 🚲	LE 1	LE 1 🚲	LE 1	LE 1	LE 1 🚲	LE 1	XC ◇1
London Liverpool Street 15 ⊖	d	10 55	10 58		11 10	11 12		11 25	11 28		11 40	11 42		11 55	11 58			12 10	12 12	12 25	12 28		12 40	12 42	
Bethnal Green	d																								
Hackney Downs	d					11 18						11 48							12 18					12 48	
Stratford 7 ⊖	d			11 00						11 30						12 00						12 30			
Clapton	d																								
Seven Sisters ⊖	d																								
Tottenham Hale ⊖	d	11u07	11 10	11 13	11u22	11 25		11u37	11 40	11 43	11u52	11 55		12u07	12 10	12 13		12u22	12 25	12u37	12 40	12 43	12u52	12 55	
Northumberland Park	d			11 15												12 15									
Angel Road	d																								
Ponders End	d					11 29						11 59							12 29					12 59	
Brimsdown	d					11 32						12 02							12 32					13 02	
Enfield Lock	d			11 21		11 34						12 04				12 21			12 34					13 04	
Waltham Cross	d					11 37				11 50		12 07							12 37			12 50		13 07	
Cheshunt	d		11 18	11 25		11 39			11 48	11 53		12 09			12 18	12 25			12 39		12 48	12 53		13 09	
Broxbourne 3	a		11 22	11 29		11 44			11 52	11 57		12 14			12 22	12 29			12 44		12 52	12 57		13 14	
Broxbourne 3	d		11 22	11 33		11 44			11 52	11 57		12 14			12 22	12 33			12 44		12 52	12 57		13 14	
Rye House	d					11 47						12 17							12 47					13 17	
St Margarets (Herts)	d					11 50						12 20							12 50					13 20	
Ware	d					11 54						12 24							12 54					13 24	
Hertford East	a					12 01						12 31							13 01					13 31	
Roydon	d			11 38					11 56							12 38					12 56				
Harlow Town	d	11 24	11 28	11 42				11 54	12 00	12 09				12 24	12 28	12 42				12 54	13 00	13 09			
Harlow Mill	d			11 45					12 03							12 45					13 03				
Sawbridgeworth	d			11 48					12 07	12 15						12 48					13 07	13 15			
Bishops Stortford	a		11 38	11 56	11 45				12 14	12 22	12 17				12 38	12 56		12 45			13 14	13 22	13 17		
	d		11 39		11 45				12 14		12 18				12 39			12 45			13 14		13 18		
Stansted Mountfitchet	d	11 35							12 18					12 35							13 18				
Stansted Airport	a	11 44			11 55			12 12			12 27			12 44				12 55		13 12			13 27		
Stansted Airport	d												12 27												13 27
Elsenham	d								12 22												13 22				
Newport (Essex)	d								12 27												13 27				
Audley End	d		11 51						12 30				12 40		12 51						13 30				13 40
Great Chesterford	d								12 35												13 35				
Whittlesford Parkway	d		11 58						12 40						12 58						13 40				
Shelford	d								12 44												13 44				
Cambridge	a		12 08						12 51				12 58		13 08						13 51				13 58

		LE 1 🚲		LE 1	LE 1	LE 1 🚲	LE 1	LE 1 🚲	LE 1	LE 1	LE 1 🚲	LE 1		XC ◇1	LE 1 🚲	LE 1	LE 1	LE 1 🚲	LE 1	LE 1 🚲	LE 1	LE 1		LE 1 🚲	LE 1
London Liverpool Street 15 ⊖	d	12 55		12 58		13 10	13 12	13 25	13 28		13 40	13 42			13 55	13 58		14 10	14 12	14 25	14 28			14 40	14 42
Bethnal Green	d																								
Hackney Downs	d						13 18					13 48							14 18						14 48
Stratford 7 ⊖	d				13 00					13 30							14 00					14 30			
Clapton	d																								
Seven Sisters ⊖	d																								
Tottenham Hale ⊖	d	13u07		13 10	13 13	13u22	13 25	13u37	13 40	13 43	13u52	13 55			14u07	14 10	14 13	14u22	14 25	14u37	14 40	14 43		14u52	14 55
Northumberland Park	d				13 15												14 15								
Angel Road	d																								
Ponders End	d						13 29					13 59							14 29						14 59
Brimsdown	d						13 32					14 02							14 32						15 02
Enfield Lock	d				13 21		13 34					14 04					14 21		14 34						15 04
Waltham Cross	d						13 37			13 50		14 07							14 37			14 50			15 07
Cheshunt	d			13 18	13 25		13 39		13 48	13 53		14 09				14 18	14 25		14 39		14 48	14 53			15 09
Broxbourne 3	a			13 22	13 29		13 44		13 52	13 57		14 14				14 22	14 29		14 44		14 52	14 57			15 14
Broxbourne 3	d			13 22	13 33		13 44		13 52	13 57		14 14				14 22	14 33		14 44		14 52	14 57			15 14
Rye House	d						13 47					14 17							14 47						15 17
St Margarets (Herts)	d						13 50					14 20							14 50						15 20
Ware	d						13 54					14 24							14 54						15 24
Hertford East	a						14 01					14 31							15 01						15 31
Roydon	d				13 38				13 56								14 38				14 56				
Harlow Town	d	13 24		13 28	13 42			13 54	14 00	14 09					14 24	14 28	14 42			14 54	15 00	15 09			
Harlow Mill	d				13 45				14 03								14 45				15 03				
Sawbridgeworth	d				13 48				14 07	14 15							14 48				15 07	15 15			
Bishops Stortford	a			13 38	13 56	13 45			14 14	14 22	14 17					14 38	14 56	14 45			15 14	15 22		15 17	
	d			13 39		13 45			14 14		14 18					14 39		14 45			15 14			15 18	
Stansted Mountfitchet	d	13 35							14 18						14 35						15 18				
Stansted Airport	a	13 44				13 55		14 12			14 27				14 44			14 55		15 13				15 27	
Stansted Airport	d													14 27											
Elsenham	d								14 22												15 22				
Newport (Essex)	d								14 27												15 27				
Audley End	d			13 51					14 30					14 40		14 51					15 30				
Great Chesterford	d								14 35												15 35				
Whittlesford Parkway	d			13 58					14 40							14 58					15 40				
Shelford	d								14 44												15 44				
Cambridge	a			14 08					14 51					14 58		15 09					15 51				

London - Broxbourne, Hertford East, Bishops Stortford, Stansted Airport and Cambridge

Network Diagram - see first Page of Table 20

		XC	LE	LE	LE	LE	LE	LE		LE	LE	LE	LE	XC	LE	LE	LE	LE		LE	LE	LE	LE	XC	LE
		◇1	1	1	1	1	1	1		1	1	1	1	◇1	1	1	1	1		1	1	1	1	◇1	1
			🚲			🚲		🚲				🚲			🚲			🚲			🚲				🚲
London Liverpool Street 15 ⊖	d		14 55	14 58		15 10	15 12	15 25		15 28		15 40	15 42		15 55	15 58		16 10		16 12	16 25	16 28			16 39
Bethnal Green	d																								
Hackney Downs	d						15 18						15 48							16 18					
Stratford 7 ⊖	d				15 00						15 30						16 00						16 30		
Clapton	d																								
Seven Sisters ⊖	d																								
Tottenham Hale ⊖	d		15u07	15 10	15 13	15u22	15 25	15u37		15 40	15 43	15u52	15 55		16u07	16 10	16 13	16u22		16 25	16u37	16 40	16 43		16u52
Northumberland Park	d				15 15												16 15								
Angel Road	d																16 17								
Ponders End	d						15 29						15 59							16 29			16 47		
Brimsdown	d						15 32						16 02							16 32			16 50		
Enfield Lock	d				15 21		15 34						16 04				16 22			16 34			16 52		
Waltham Cross	d						15 37				15 50		16 07							16 37			16 55		
Cheshunt	d			15 18	15 25		15 39			15 48	15 53		16 09			16 18	16 26			16 39			16 57		
Broxbourne 3	a			15 22	15 29		15 44			15 52	15 57		16 14			16 22	16 30			16 44		16 51	17 02		
Broxbourne 3	d			15 22	15 33		15 44			15 52	15 57		16 14			16 22	16 34			16 44		16 52	17 03		
Rye House	d						15 47						16 17							16 48					
St Margarets (Herts)	d						15 50						16 20							16 51					
Ware	d						15 54						16 24							16 55					
Hertford East	a						16 01						16 31							17 03					
Roydon	d				15 38					15 56						16 26	16 38								
Harlow Town	d		15 24	15 28	15 42			15 54		16 00	16 09				16 24	16 30	16 42				16 54	16 59	17 12		
Harlow Mill	d				15 45					16 03						16 33	16 45								
Sawbridgeworth	d				15 48					16 07	16 15					16 37	16 49					17 04			
Bishops Stortford	a			15 38	15 56	15 45				16 14	16 22	16 17				16 44	16 58	16 47				17 11	17 24		17 17
	d			15 41		15 45				16 14		16 18				16 44		16 48				17 11			17 18
Stansted Mountfitchet	d		15 35	15 45						16 18					16 35	16 48						17 15			
Stansted Airport	a		15 44			15 55		16 12				16 27			16 44			17 01			17 14				17 29
Stansted Airport	d	15 27												16 27										17 27	
Elsenham	d			15 49						16 22						16 52									
Newport (Essex)	d			15 55						16 27						16 57									
Audley End	d	15 40		15 59						16 30				16 40		17 00						17 25		17 40	
Great Chesterford	d			16 04						16 35						17 05									
Whittlesford Parkway	d			16 09						16 40						17 10						17 33			
Shelford	d			16 13						16 44						17 14									
Cambridge	a	15 58		16 20						16 51				16 58		17 21						17 44		17 58	

		LE	LE	LE		LE	LE	LE	LE	LE	LE	LE	LE	LE		LE	LE	LE	LE	XC	LE	LE	LE	LE	
			1			1	1		1	1	1		1			1	1		1	◇1	1		1		
									A																
							🚲			🚲							🚲				🚲				
London Liverpool Street 15 ⊖	d	16 41	16 43				16 54	16 56	17 07	17 09		17 11	17 13				17 24	17 26	17 37		17 39	17 41	17 43		
Bethnal Green	d																								
Hackney Downs	d	16 48						17 02				17 18						17 32				17 48			
Stratford 7 ⊖	d					16 47										17 17									
Clapton	d																								
Seven Sisters ⊖	d	16 54										17 24										17 54			
Tottenham Hale ⊖	d		16 55			16 58	17u06	17 09	17 19	17u22			17 25			17 28	17u36	17 39	17 49		17u52		17 55		
Northumberland Park	d					17 00										17 30									
Angel Road	d					17 02										17 32									
Ponders End	d							17 13										17 43							
Brimsdown	d							17 16										17 46							
Enfield Lock	d					17 07		17 18								17 37		17 48							
Waltham Cross	d			←		17 10		17 21						←		17 40		17 51						←	
Cheshunt	d	17 08	17 04	17 08		17 12		17 23				17 38	17 34	17 38		17 42		17 53				18 08	18 04	18 08	
Broxbourne 3	a	→	17 08	17 13		17 17		17 30				→	17 38	17 43		17 47		18 00				→	18 08	18 13	
Broxbourne 3	d		17 09	17 13		17 22							17 39	17 43		17 50							18 09	18 13	
Rye House	d			17 17										17 47		17 54								18 17	
St Margarets (Herts)	d			17 20										17 50		17 57								18 20	
Ware	d			17 24										17 54		18 01								18 24	
Hertford East	a			17 32										18 02		18 09								18 32	
Roydon	d		17 13			17 26					←		17 43										18 13		
Harlow Town	d		17 17			17 42	17 24			17 39	17 42		17 47				17 54				18 09		18 17		
Harlow Mill	d		17 20			→					17 45		17 50										18 20		
Sawbridgeworth	d		17 24								17 49		17 54								18 14		18 24		
Bishops Stortford	a		17 31				17 35		17 43		17 58		18 01				18 05		18 13				18 31		
	d		17 31				17 35		17 44				18 01				18 05		18 14				18 31		
Stansted Mountfitchet	d		17 36							17 52			18 06										18 36		
Stansted Airport	a						17 47			18 01							18 17				18 32				
Stansted Airport	d																			18 21					
Elsenham	d		17 39										18 09										18 39		
Newport (Essex)	d		17 45										18 15										18 45		
Audley End	d		17 48						17 56				18 18						18 26	18 38			18 48		
Great Chesterford	d		17 53										18 23										18 53		
Whittlesford Parkway	d		17 58						18 04				18 28						18 34				18 58		
Shelford	d		18 02										18 32										19 02		
Cambridge	a		18 11						18 15				18 41						18 45	18 58			19 14		

A The Fenman

Table 22

London - Broxbourne, Hertford East, Bishops Stortford, Stansted Airport and Cambridge

Network Diagram - see first Page of Table 20

		LE ■1	LE ■1 🚲	LE	LE ■1	LE ■1 🚲	LE ■1	LE	LE ■1	LE		LE ■1	LE ■1 🚲	LE	LE ■1	XC ◇■1	LE ■1 🚲	LE	LE ■1	LE		LE	LE ■1 🚲	LE	LE ■1
London Liverpool Street ■15 ⊖	d		17 54	17 56	18 07	18 09		18 11	18 13				18 24	18 26	18 37		18 39	18 41	18 43				18 54	18 56	19 07
Bethnal Green	d																								
Hackney Downs	d			18 02				18 18						18 32				18 48						19 02	
Stratford ■7 ⊖	d	17 47										18 17										18 47			
Clapton	d																								
Seven Sisters ⊖	d							18 24										18 54							
Tottenham Hale ⊖	d	17 58	18u06	18 09	18 19	18u22			18 25			18 28	18u36	18 39	18 49		18u52		18 55			18 58	19u06	19 09	19 19
Northumberland Park	d	18 00										18 30										19 00			
Angel Road	d	18 02										18 32										19 02			
Ponders End	d			18 13										18 43										19 13	
Brimsdown	d			18 16										18 46										19 16	
Enfield Lock	d	18 07		18 18								18 37		18 48								19 07		19 18	
Waltham Cross	d	18 10		18 21						←		18 40		18 51						←		19 10		19 21	
Cheshunt	d	18 12		18 23				18 38	18 34	18 38		18 42		18 53				19 08	19 04	19 08		19 12		19 23	
Broxbourne ■3	a	18 17		18 30				→	18 38	18 43		18 47		19 00				→	19 08	19 13		19 17		19 30	
Broxbourne ■3	d	18 22							18 39	18 43		18 50							19 09	19 13		19 22		19 35	
Rye House	d									18 47		18 54								19 17				19 38	
St Margarets (Herts)	d									18 50		18 57								19 20				19 41	
Ware	d									18 54		19 01								19 24				19 47	
Hertford East	a									19 02		19 09								19 32				19 55	
Roydon	d	18 26					←		18 43										19 13			19 26			
Harlow Town	d	18 42	18 24			18 39	18 42		18 47				18 54				19 09		19 17			19 42	19 24		
Harlow Mill	d	→					18 45		18 50										19 20			→			
Sawbridgeworth	d						18 49		18 54								19 14		19 24						
Bishops Stortford	a		18 35		18 43		18 58		19 01				19 05		19 13				19 31				19 35		19 43
	d		18 35		18 44				19 01				19 05		19 14				19 31				19 35		19 44
Stansted Mountfitchet	d					18 52			19 06										19 36						
Stansted Airport	a		18 47			19 01							19 17				19 32						19 47		
Stansted Airport	d															19 21									
Elsenham	d								19 09										19 39						
Newport (Essex)	d								19 15										19 45						
Audley End	d				18 56				19 18						19 26	19 38			19 48						19 56
Great Chesterford	d								19 23										19 53						
Whittlesford Parkway	d				19 04				19 28						19 34				19 58						20 04
Shelford	d								19 32										20 02						
Cambridge	a				19 17				19 43						19 46	19 58			20 12						20 13

		LE ■1 🚲	LE	LE ■1	LE ■1	LE ■1 🚲		LE ■1	LE ■1	XC ◇■1	LE ■1 🚲	LE ■1	LE ■1 🚲	LE ■1	LE ■1	LE ■1 🚲		LE ■1	LE ■1 🚲	LE ■1	LE ■1	LE ■1 🚲	LE ■1	XC ■1	LE ■1 🚲
London Liverpool Street ■15 ⊖	d	19 09		19 11	19 13	19 25		19 28			19 40	19 42	19 55	19 58		20 10		20 12	20 25	20 28		20 40	20 42		20 55
Bethnal Green	d																								
Hackney Downs	d				19 19							19 48						20 18					20 48		
Stratford ■7 ⊖	d								19 30						20 00						20 30				
Clapton	d																								
Seven Sisters ⊖	d																								
Tottenham Hale ⊖	d	19u22		19 25	19 28	19u37		19 40	19 43		19u52	19 55	20u07	20 10	20 13	20u22		20 25	20u37	20 40	20 43	20u52	20 55		21u07
Northumberland Park	d								19 45						20 15										
Angel Road	d								19 47																
Ponders End	d				19 32							19 59						20 29					20 59		
Brimsdown	d				19 35							20 02						20 32					21 02		
Enfield Lock	d				19 37							20 04			20 21			20 34					21 04		
Waltham Cross	d				19 40				19 53			20 07						20 37			20 50		21 07		
Cheshunt	d			19 34	19 42			19 49	19 55			20 09		20 18	20 25			20 39		20 48	20 53		21 09		
Broxbourne ■3	a			19 39	19 47			19 54	20 00			20 14		20 22	20 29			20 44		20 52	20 57		21 14		
Broxbourne ■3	d			19 39	19 47			19 54	20 03			20 14		20 22	20 33			20 44		20 52	20 57		21 14		
Rye House	d				19 50							20 17						20 47					21 17		
St Margarets (Herts)	d				19 53							20 20						20 50					21 20		
Ware	d				19 57							20 24						20 54					21 24		
Hertford East	a				20 04							20 31						21 01					21 31		
Roydon	d		←	19 43				19 59	20 08						20 38					20 56					
Harlow Town	d	19 39	19 42	19 47		19 57		20 03	20 12				20 24	20 28	20 42				20 54	21 00	21 09				21 24
Harlow Mill	d		19 45	19 50				20 06	20 15						20 45					21 03					
Sawbridgeworth	d		19 49	19 54				20 09	20 18						20 48					21 07	21 15				
Bishops Stortford	a		19 56	20 01				20 16	20 28		20 20			20 38	20 56	20 45				21 14	21 22	21 17			
	d			20 01				20 17			20 21			20 39		20 45				21 14		21 18			
Stansted Mountfitchet	d	19 52		20 06				20 21					20 36							21 18					21 35
Stansted Airport	a	19 59				20 15					20 30		20 43			20 55			21 12			21 27			21 44
Stansted Airport	d									20 21														21 27	
Elsenham	d			20 09				20 25												21 22					
Newport (Essex)	d			20 15				20 30												21 27					
Audley End	d			20 18				20 33		20 39				20 51						21 30				21 40	
Great Chesterford	d			20 23				20 38												21 35					
Whittlesford Parkway	d			20 28				20 43						20 58						21 40					
Shelford	d			20 32				20 47												21 44					
Cambridge	a			20 39				20 56		20 59				21 09						21 51				21 58	

London - Broxbourne, Hertford East, Bishops Stortford, Stansted Airport and Cambridge

Network Diagram - see first Page of Table 20

		LE 1		LE 1	LE 1 🚲	LE 1	LE 1 🚲	LE 1	LE 1	LE 1 🚲	LE 1	XC 1		LE 1 🚲	LE 1	LE 1	XC ◇1	LE 1 🚲	LE 1	XC 1	LE 1 🚲	LE 1		LE 1	LE 1 🚲
London Liverpool Street 15 ⊖	d	20 58			21 10	21 12	21 25	21 28		21 40	21 42			21 55	21 58			22 10	22 12		22 25	22 28			22 40
Bethnal Green	d																								
Hackney Downs	d					21 18					21 48								22 18						
Stratford 7 ⊖	d			21 00					21 30							22 00								22 30	
Clapton	d																								
Seven Sisters ⊖	d																								
Tottenham Hale ⊖	d	21 10		21 13	21u22	21 25	21u37	21 40	21 43	21u52	21 55			22u07	22 10	22 13		22u22	22 25		22u37	22 40		22 43	22u52
Northumberland Park	d			21 15												22 15									
Angel Road	d																								
Ponders End	d					21 29					21 59								22 29						
Brimsdown	d					21 32					22 02								22 32						
Enfield Lock	d			21 21		21 34					22 04					22 21			22 34						
Waltham Cross	d					21 37			21 50		22 07								22 37					22 50	
Cheshunt	d	21 18		21 25		21 39		21 48	21 53		22 09				22 18	22 25			22 39			22 48		22 53	
Broxbourne 3	a	21 22		21 29		21 44		21 52	21 57		22 14				22 22	22 29			22 44			22 52		22 57	
Broxbourne 3	d	21 22		21 33		21 44		21 52	21 57		22 14				22 22	22 33			22 44			22 52		22 57	
Rye House	d					21 47					22 17								22 47						
St Margarets (Herts)	d					21 50					22 20								22 50						
Ware	d					21 54					22 24								22 54						
Hertford East	a					22 01					22 31								23 01						
Roydon	d			21 38				21 56								22 38						22 56			
Harlow Town	d	21 28		21 42			21 54	22 00	22 09					22 24	22 28	22 42					22 54	23 00		23 09	
Harlow Mill	d			21 45				22 03								22 45						23 03			
Sawbridgeworth	d			21 48				22 07	22 15							22 48						23 07		23 15	
Bishops Stortford	a	21 38		21 56	21 45			22 14	22 22	22 17					22 38	22 56		22 45				23 14		23 22	23 17
	d	21 39			21 45			22 14		22 18					22 39			22 45				23 14			23 18
Stansted Mountfitchet	d							22 18						22 35			22 41					23 18			
Stansted Airport	a				21 55		22 12			22 27				22 44			22 52	22 57			23 12				23 30
Stansted Airport	d											22 27								22 57					
Elsenham	d							22 22														23 22			
Newport (Essex)	d							22 27														23 27			
Audley End	d	21 51						22 30				22 40			22 51					23 10		23 30			
Great Chesterford	d							22 35														23 35			
Whittlesford Parkway	d	21 58						22 40							22 58							23 40			
Shelford	d							22 44														23 44			
Cambridge	a	22 09						22 51				22 56			23 09					23 30		23 51			

		LE 1	LE 1 🚲	LE 1	LE 1	LE 1	LE 1	LE 1		LE 1	LE FX 1	LE FO 1
London Liverpool Street 15 ⊖	d	22 42	22 55	22 58		23 12	23 25	23 28		23 40	23 58	23 58
Bethnal Green	d											
Hackney Downs	d	22 48				23 18				23 46		
Stratford 7 ⊖	d				23 00							
Clapton	d									23 49		
Seven Sisters ⊖	d											
Tottenham Hale ⊖	d	22 55	23u07	23 10	23 13	23 25	23u37	23 40		23 53	00 10	00 10
Northumberland Park	d				23 15					23 55		
Angel Road	d											
Ponders End	d	22 59				23 29				23 59		
Brimsdown	d	23 02				23 32				00 02		
Enfield Lock	d	23 04			23 21	23 34				00 04		
Waltham Cross	d	23 07				23 37				00 07		
Cheshunt	d	23 09		23 18	23 25	23 39		23 48		00 09	00 18	00 18
Broxbourne 3	a	23 14		23 22	23 29	23 44		23 52		00 14	00 22	00 22
Broxbourne 3	d	23 14		23 22	23 29	23 44		23 52		00 14	00 22	00 22
Rye House	d	23 17				23 47				00 17		
St Margarets (Herts)	d	23 20				23 50				00 20		
Ware	d	23 24				23 54				00 24		
Hertford East	a	23 31				00 01				00 31		
Roydon	d				23 33			23 56			00 26	00 26
Harlow Town	d		23 24	23 28	23 37		23 54	23 59			00 30	00 30
Harlow Mill	d				23 40			00 03			00 33	00 33
Sawbridgeworth	d				23 44			00 07			00 37	00 37
Bishops Stortford	a			23 38	23 51		00 04	00 14			00 44	00 44
	d			23 39			00 04	00 14				00 44
Stansted Mountfitchet	d		23 35					00 18				00 48
Stansted Airport	a		23 43				00 13					
Stansted Airport	d											
Elsenham	d							00 22				00 52
Newport (Essex)	d							00 27				00 57
Audley End	d			23 51				00 30				01 00
Great Chesterford	d							00 35				01 05
Whittlesford Parkway	d			23 58				00 40				01 10
Shelford	d							00 44				
Cambridge	a			00 08				00 51				01 19

London - Broxbourne, Hertford East, Bishops Stortford, Stansted Airport and Cambridge

Network Diagram - see first Page of Table 20

		LE	LE	LE	LE	LE	LE	LE	XC	LE		LE	LE	LE	LE	LE	LE	XC	LE	LE		LE	LE	LE	LE
		[1]	[1]	[1]	[1]	[1]	[1]	[1]	◇[1]	[1]		[1]	[1]	[1]	[1]	[1]	[1]	◇[1]	[1]	[1]		[1]	[1]	[1]	[1]
London Liverpool Street [15] ⊖	d	22p58	23p12	23p25	23p28	23p40	23p58	04 10		04 40		05 10	05 21	05 25		05 40	05 42		05 51	05 55		05 58		06 10	06 12
Bethnal Green	d																								
Hackney Downs	d		23p18			23p46											05 48								06 18
Stratford [7] ⊖	d												05 30						06 00						
Clapton	d					23p49																			
Seven Sisters ⊖	d														←								←		
Tottenham Hale ⊖	d	23p10	23p25	23b37	23p40	23p53	00 10			04u52		05u22	05 40	05u37	05 40	05u52	05 55		06 13	06u07		06 10	06 13	06u22	06 25
Northumberland Park	d					23p55							↪						↪				06 15		
Angel Road	d																								
Ponders End	d		23p29			23p59											05 59								06 29
Brimsdown	d		23p32			00 02											06 02								06 32
Enfield Lock	d		23p34			00 04											06 04						06 21		06 34
Waltham Cross	d		23p37			00 07											06 07								06 37
Cheshunt	d	23p18	23p39		23p48	00 09	00 18			05 00					05 48		06 09					06 18	06 25		06 39
Broxbourne [3]	a	23p22	23p44		23p52	00 14	00 22			05 04					05 52		06 14					06 22	06 29		06 44
Broxbourne [3]	d	23p22	23p44		23p52	00 14	00 22			05 04					05 52		06 14					06 22	06 33		06 44
Rye House	d		23p47			00 17											06 17								06 47
St Margarets (Herts)	d		23p50			00 20											06 20								06 50
Ware	d		23p54			00 24											06 24								06 54
Hertford East	a		00 01			00 31											06 31								07 01
Roydon	d				23p56		00 26								05 56								06 38		
Harlow Town	d	23p28		23p54	23p59		00 30			05 10		05 37		05 52	06 00					06 24		06 28	06 42		
Harlow Mill	d				00 03		00 33								06 03								06 45		
Sawbridgeworth	d				00 07		00 37					05 42			06 07								06 48		
Bishops Stortford	a	23p38		00 04	00 14		00 44			05 20		05 49		06 02	06 14	06 17						06 38	06 56	06 45	
	d	23p39		00 04	00 14		00 44			05 20		05 50		06 02	06 14	06 18						06 39		06 45	
Stansted Mountfitchet	d				00 18		00 48			05 24				06 05	06 18					06 35					
Stansted Airport	a			00 13				05 00		05 39		05 59		06 13		06 27				06 44				06 57	
Stansted Airport	d								05 25									06 27							
Elsenham	d				00 22		00 52								06 22										
Newport (Essex)	d				00 27		00 57								06 27										
Audley End	d	23p51			00 30		01 00		05 37						06 30			06 40				06 51			
Great Chesterford	d				00 35		01 05								06 35										
Whittlesford Parkway	d	23p58			00 40		01 10								06 40							06 58			
Shelford	d				00 44										06 44										
Cambridge	a	00 08			00 51		01 19		05 54						06 51			06 56				07 08			

		LE	LE	LE	LE	LE		LE	XC	LE	LE	LE	LE	LE	LE	LE		LE	LE	LE	XC	LE	LE	LE	LE
		[1]	[1]	[1]	[1]	[1]		[1]	◇[1]	[1]	[1]	[1]	[1]	[1]	[1]	[1]		[1]	[1]	[1]	◇[1]	[1]	[1]	[1]	[1]
													cycle		cycle				cycle			cycle			cycle
London Liverpool Street [15] ⊖	d	06 21	06 25	06 28		06 40		06 42		06 55	06 58		07 10	07 12	07 25	07 28			07 40	07 42		07 55	07 58		08 10
Bethnal Green	d																								
Hackney Downs	d							06 48						07 18						07 48					
Stratford [7] ⊖	d	06 30										07 00						07 30						08 00	
Clapton	d																								
Seven Sisters ⊖	d				←																				
Tottenham Hale ⊖	d	06 43	06u37	06 40	06 43	06u52		06 55		07u07	07 10	07 13	07u22	07 25	07u37	07 40		07 43	07u52	07 55		08u07	08 10	08 13	08u22
Northumberland Park	d	↪										07 15												08 15	
Angel Road	d																								
Ponders End	d							06 59						07 29						07 59					
Brimsdown	d							07 02						07 32						08 02					
Enfield Lock	d							07 04				07 21		07 34						08 04				08 21	
Waltham Cross	d				06 50			07 07						07 37				07 50		08 07					
Cheshunt	d			06 48	06 53			07 09			07 18	07 25		07 39		07 48		07 53		08 09			08 18	08 25	
Broxbourne [3]	a			06 52	06 57			07 14			07 22	07 29		07 44		07 52		07 57		08 14			08 22	08 29	
Broxbourne [3]	d			06 52	06 57			07 14			07 22	07 33		07 44		07 52		07 57		08 14			08 22	08 33	
Rye House	d							07 17						07 47						08 17					
St Margarets (Herts)	d							07 20						07 50						08 20					
Ware	d							07 24						07 54						08 24					
Hertford East	a							07 31						08 01						08 31					
Roydon	d			06 56								07 38				07 56								08 38	
Harlow Town	d		06 54	07 00	07 09					07 24	07 28	07 42			07 54	08 00		08 09				08 24	08 28	08 42	
Harlow Mill	d			07 03								07 45				08 03								08 45	
Sawbridgeworth	d			07 07	07 15							07 48				08 07		08 15						08 48	
Bishops Stortford	a			07 14	07 22	07 17					07 38	07 56	07 45			08 14		08 22	08 17				08 38	08 56	08 45
	d			07 14		07 18					07 39		07 45			08 14			08 18				08 39		08 45
Stansted Mountfitchet	d			07 18						07 35						08 18						08 35			
Stansted Airport	a		07 12			07 27				07 44			07 57		08 12				08 27			08 44			08 57
Stansted Airport	d								07 27												08 27				
Elsenham	d			07 22												08 22									
Newport (Essex)	d			07 27												08 27									
Audley End	d			07 30					07 40		07 51					08 30					08 40		08 51		
Great Chesterford	d			07 35												08 35									
Whittlesford Parkway	d			07 40							07 58					08 40							08 58		
Shelford	d			07 44												08 44									
Cambridge	a			07 51					07 58		08 08					08 51					08 58		09 08		

b Previous night, stops to pick up only

Table 22

Saturdays

London - Broxbourne, Hertford East, Bishops Stortford, Stansted Airport and Cambridge

Network Diagram - see first Page of Table 20

		LE 1	LE 1 🚲	LE 1	LE 1	LE 1 🚲	LE 1	XC ◇1	LE 1 🚲	LE 1	LE 1	LE 1 🚲	LE 1	LE 1 🚲	LE 1	LE 1	LE 1 🚲	LE 1	XC ◇1	LE 1 🚲	LE 1	LE 1
London Liverpool Street 15 ⊖	d	08 12	08 25	08 28		08 40	08 42		08 55	08 58		09 10	09 12	09 25	09 28		09 40	09 42		09 55	09 58	
Bethnal Green	d																					
Hackney Downs	d	08 18					08 48						09 18					09 48				
Stratford 7 ⊖	d				08 30						09 00					09 30						10 00
Clapton	d																					
Seven Sisters ⊖	d																					
Tottenham Hale ⊖	d	08 25	08u37	08 40	08 43	08u52	08 55		09u07	09 10	09 13	09u22	09 25	09u37	09 40	09 43	09u52	09 55		10u07	10 10	10 13
Northumberland Park	d										09 15											10 15
Angel Road	d																					
Ponders End	d	08 29					08 59						09 29					09 59				
Brimsdown	d	08 32					09 02						09 32					10 02				
Enfield Lock	d	08 34					09 04				09 21		09 34					10 04				10 21
Waltham Cross	d	08 37			08 50		09 07						09 37			09 50		10 07				
Cheshunt	d	08 39		08 48	08 53		09 09			09 18	09 25		09 39		09 48	09 53		10 09			10 18	10 25
Broxbourne 3	a	08 44		08 52	08 57		09 14			09 22	09 29		09 44		09 52	09 57		10 14			10 22	10 29
Broxbourne 3	d	08 44		08 52	08 57		09 14			09 22	09 33		09 44		09 52	09 57		10 14			10 22	10 33
Rye House	d	08 47					09 17						09 47					10 17				
St Margarets (Herts)	d	08 50					09 20						09 50					10 20				
Ware	d	08 54					09 24						09 54					10 24				
Hertford East	a	09 01					09 31						10 01					10 31				
Roydon	d			08 56							09 38				09 56							10 38
Harlow Town	d		08 54	09 00	09 09				09 24	09 28	09 42			09 54	10 00	10 09				10 24	10 28	10 42
Harlow Mill	d			09 03							09 45				10 03							10 45
Sawbridgeworth	d			09 07	09 15						09 48				10 07	10 15						10 48
Bishops Stortford	a			09 14	09 22	09 17				09 38	09 56	09 45			10 14	10 22	10 17				10 38	10 56
	d			09 14		09 18				09 39		09 45			10 14		10 18				10 39	
Stansted Mountfitchet	d			09 18					09 35						10 18					10 35		
Stansted Airport	a		09 12			09 27			09 44			09 57		10 12			10 27			10 44		
Stansted Airport	d							09 27											10 27			
Elsenham	d			09 22											10 22							
Newport (Essex)	d			09 27											10 27							
Audley End	d			09 30				09 40		09 51					10 30				10 40		10 51	
Great Chesterford	d			09 35											10 35							
Whittlesford Parkway	d			09 40						09 58					10 40						10 58	
Shelford	d			09 44											10 44							
Cambridge	a			09 51				09 58		10 08					10 51				10 58		11 08	

		LE 1 🚲	LE 1	LE 1 🚲	LE 1	LE 1	LE 1 🚲	LE 1	XC ◇1	LE 1 🚲	LE 1	LE 1	LE 1 🚲	LE 1	LE 1 🚲	LE 1	LE 1	LE 1 🚲	LE 1	XC ◇1	LE 1 🚲	LE 1	LE 1
London Liverpool Street 15 ⊖	d	10 10	10 12	10 25	10 28		10 40	10 42		10 55	10 58		11 10	11 12	11 25	11 28		11 40	11 42		11 55	11 58	
Bethnal Green	d																						
Hackney Downs	d		10 18					10 48						11 18					11 48				
Stratford 7 ⊖	d					10 30						11 00					11 30						12 00
Clapton	d																						
Seven Sisters ⊖	d																						
Tottenham Hale ⊖	d	10u22	10 25	10u37	10 40	10 43	10u52	10 55		11u07	11 10	11 13	11u22	11 25	11u37	11 40	11 43	11u52	11 55		12u07	12 10	12 13
Northumberland Park	d											11 15											12 15
Angel Road	d																						
Ponders End	d		10 29					10 59						11 29					11 59				
Brimsdown	d		10 32					11 02						11 32					12 02				
Enfield Lock	d		10 34					11 04				11 21		11 34					12 04				12 21
Waltham Cross	d		10 37			10 50		11 07						11 37			11 50		12 07				
Cheshunt	d		10 39		10 48	10 53		11 09			11 18	11 25		11 39		11 48	11 53		12 09			12 18	12 25
Broxbourne 3	a		10 44		10 52	10 57		11 14			11 22	11 29		11 44		11 52	11 57		12 14			12 22	12 29
Broxbourne 3	d		10 44		10 52	10 57		11 14			11 22	11 33		11 44		11 52	11 57		12 14			12 22	12 33
Rye House	d		10 47					11 17						11 47					12 17				
St Margarets (Herts)	d		10 50					11 20						11 50					12 20				
Ware	d		10 54					11 24						11 54					12 24				
Hertford East	a		11 01					11 31						12 01					12 31				
Roydon	d				10 56							11 38				11 56							12 38
Harlow Town	d			10 54	11 00	11 09				11 24	11 28	11 42			11 54	12 00	12 09				12 24	12 28	12 42
Harlow Mill	d				11 03							11 45				12 03							12 45
Sawbridgeworth	d				11 07	11 15						11 48				12 07	12 15						12 48
Bishops Stortford	a	10 45			11 14	11 22	11 17				11 38	11 56	11 45			12 14	12 22	12 17				12 38	12 56
	d	10 45			11 14		11 18				11 39		11 45			12 14		12 18				12 39	
Stansted Mountfitchet	d				11 18					11 35						12 18					12 35		
Stansted Airport	a	10 57		11 13			11 27			11 44			11 57		12 12			12 27			12 44		
Stansted Airport	d								11 27											12 27			
Elsenham	d				11 22											12 22							
Newport (Essex)	d				11 27											12 27							
Audley End	d				11 30				11 40		11 51					12 30				12 40		12 51	
Great Chesterford	d				11 35											12 35							
Whittlesford Parkway	d				11 40						11 58					12 40						12 58	
Shelford	d				11 44											12 44							
Cambridge	a				11 51				11 58		12 08					12 51				12 58		13 08	

Table 22

Saturdays

London - Broxbourne, Hertford East, Bishops Stortford, Stansted Airport and Cambridge

Network Diagram - see first Page of Table 20

		LE 1 🛒	LE 1	LE 1 🛒		LE 1	LE 1	LE 1 🛒	LE 1	XC ◇1	LE 1 🛒	LE 1	LE 1	LE 1 🛒		LE 1	LE 1 🛒	LE 1	LE 1	LE 1 🛒	LE 1	XC ◇1	LE 1 🛒	LE 1	
London Liverpool Street 15 ⊖	d	12 10	12 12	12 25		12 28		12 40	12 42		12 55	12 58		13 10		13 12	13 25	13 28		13 40	13 42		13 55	13 58	
Bethnal Green	d																								
Hackney Downs	d		12 18						12 48							13 18					13 48				
Stratford 7 ⊖	d						12 30						13 00						13 30						
Clapton	d																								
Seven Sisters ⊖	d																								
Tottenham Hale ⊖	d	12u22	12 25	12u37		12 40	12 43	12u52	12 55		13u07	13 10	13 13	13u22		13 25	13u37	13 40	13 43	13u52	13 55		14u07	14 10	
Northumberland Park	d												13 15												
Angel Road	d																								
Ponders End	d		12 29						12 59							13 29					13 59				
Brimsdown	d		12 32						13 02							13 32					14 02				
Enfield Lock	d		12 34						13 04				13 21			13 34					14 04				
Waltham Cross	d		12 37				12 50		13 07							13 37			13 50		14 07				
Cheshunt	d		12 39			12 48	12 53		13 09			13 18	13 25			13 39		13 48	13 53		14 09			14 18	
Broxbourne 3	a		12 44			12 52	12 57		13 14			13 22	13 29			13 44		13 52	13 57		14 14			14 22	
Broxbourne 3	d		12 44			12 52	12 57		13 14			13 22	13 33			13 44		13 52	13 57		14 14			14 22	
Rye House	d		12 47						13 17							13 47					14 17				
St Margarets (Herts)	d		12 50						13 20							13 50					14 20				
Ware	d		12 54						13 24							13 54					14 24				
Hertford East	a		13 01						13 31							14 01					14 31				
Roydon	d					12 56							13 38					13 56							
Harlow Town	d			12 54		13 00	13 09				13 24	13 28	13 42				13 54	14 00	14 09				14 24	14 28	
Harlow Mill	d					13 03							13 45					14 03							
Sawbridgeworth	d					13 07	13 15						13 48					14 07	14 15						
Bishops Stortford	a	12 45				13 14	13 22	13 17				13 38	13 56	13 45				14 14	14 22	14 17				14 38	
	d	12 45				13 14		13 18				13 39		13 45				14 14		14 18				14 39	
Stansted Mountfitchet	d					13 18					13 35							14 18					14 35		
Stansted Airport	a	12 57		13 12				13 27			13 44			13 57			14 12			14 27			14 44		
Stansted Airport	d									13 27												14 27			
Elsenham	d					13 22												14 22							
Newport (Essex)	d					13 27												14 27							
Audley End	d					13 30				13 40		13 51						14 30				14 40		14 51	
Great Chesterford	d					13 35												14 35							
Whittlesford Parkway	d					13 40						13 58						14 40						14 58	
Shelford	d					13 44												14 44							
Cambridge	a					13 51				13 58		14 08						14 51				14 58		15 08	

		LE 1	LE 1 🛒	LE 1	LE 1 🛒	LE 1	LE 1	LE 1 🛒	LE 1	XC ◇1		LE 1 🛒	LE 1	LE 1	LE 1 🛒	LE 1	LE 1 🛒	LE 1	LE 1	LE 1 🛒		LE 1	XC ◇1	LE 1 🛒	LE 1
London Liverpool Street 15 ⊖	d		14 10	14 12	14 25	14 28		14 40	14 42			14 55	14 58		15 10	15 12	15 25	15 28		15 40		15 42		15 55	15 58
Bethnal Green	d																								
Hackney Downs	d			14 18					14 48							15 18						15 48			
Stratford 7 ⊖	d	14 00					14 30							15 00					15 30						
Clapton	d																								
Seven Sisters ⊖	d																								
Tottenham Hale ⊖	d	14 13	14u22	14 25	14u37	14 40	14 43	14u52	14 55			15u07	15 10	15 13	15u22	15 25	15u37	15 40	15 43	15u52		15 55		16u07	16 10
Northumberland Park	d	14 15												15 15											
Angel Road	d																								
Ponders End	d			14 29					14 59							15 29						15 59			
Brimsdown	d			14 32					15 02							15 32						16 02			
Enfield Lock	d	14 21		14 34					15 04					15 21		15 34						16 04			
Waltham Cross	d			14 37			14 50		15 07							15 37			15 50			16 07			
Cheshunt	d	14 25		14 39		14 48	14 53		15 09				15 18	15 25		15 39		15 48	15 53			16 09			16 18
Broxbourne 3	a	14 29		14 44		14 52	14 57		15 14				15 22	15 29		15 44		15 52	15 57			16 14			16 22
Broxbourne 3	d	14 33		14 44		14 52	14 57		15 14				15 22	15 33		15 44		15 52	15 57			16 14			16 22
Rye House	d			14 47					15 17							15 47						16 17			
St Margarets (Herts)	d			14 50					15 20							15 50						16 20			
Ware	d			14 54					15 24							15 54						16 24			
Hertford East	a			15 01					15 31							16 01						16 31			
Roydon	d	14 38				14 56								15 38				15 56							
Harlow Town	d	14 42			14 54	15 00	15 09					15 24	15 28	15 42			15 54	16 00	16 09					16 24	16 28
Harlow Mill	d	14 45				15 03								15 45				16 03							
Sawbridgeworth	d	14 48				15 07	15 15							15 48				16 07	16 15						
Bishops Stortford	a	14 56	14 45			15 14	15 22	15 17					15 38	15 56	15 45			16 14	16 22	16 17					16 38
	d		14 45			15 14		15 18					15 39		15 45			16 14		16 18					16 39
Stansted Mountfitchet	d					15 18						15 35						16 18						16 35	
Stansted Airport	a		14 57		15 12			15 27				15 44			15 57		16 12			16 27				16 44	
Stansted Airport	d									15 27													16 27		
Elsenham	d					15 22												16 22							
Newport (Essex)	d					15 27												16 27							
Audley End	d					15 30				15 40			15 51					16 30					16 40		16 51
Great Chesterford	d					15 35												16 35							
Whittlesford Parkway	d					15 40							15 58					16 40							16 58
Shelford	d					15 44												16 44							
Cambridge	a					15 51				15 58			16 08					16 51					16 58		17 08

Table 22

Saturdays

London - Broxbourne, Hertford East, Bishops Stortford, Stansted Airport and Cambridge

Network Diagram - see first Page of Table 20

		LE	LE	LE	LE	LE		LE	LE	LE	XC	LE	LE	LE	LE	LE		LE	LE	LE	LE	LE	XC	LE	LE
		1	1	1	1	1		1	1	1	◇1	1	1	1	1	1		1	1	1	1	1	◇1	1	1
			🚲		🚲				🚲			🚲			🚲			🚲			🚲			🚲	
London Liverpool Street 15 ⊖	d		16 10	16 12	16 25	16 28			16 40	16 42		16 55	16 58		17 10	17 12		17 25	17 28		17 40	17 42		17 55	17 58
Bethnal Green	d																								
Hackney Downs	d			16 18						16 48						17 18						17 48			
Stratford 7 ⊖	d	16 00						16 30						17 00						17 30					
Clapton	d																								
Seven Sisters ⊖	d																								
Tottenham Hale ⊖	d	16 13	16u22	16 25	16u37	16 40		16 43	16u52	16 55		17u07	17 10	17 13	17u22	17 25		17u37	17 40	17 43	17u52	17 55		18u07	18 10
Northumberland Park	d	16 15												17 15											
Angel Road	d																								
Ponders End	d			16 29						16 59						17 29						17 59			
Brimsdown	d			16 32						17 02						17 32						18 02			
Enfield Lock	d	16 21		16 34						17 04				17 21		17 34						18 04			
Waltham Cross	d			16 37				16 50		17 07						17 37				17 50		18 07			
Cheshunt	d	16 25		16 39		16 48		16 53		17 09			17 18	17 25		17 39			17 48	17 53		18 09			18 18
Broxbourne 3	a	16 29		16 44		16 52		16 57		17 14			17 22	17 29		17 44			17 52	17 57		18 14			18 22
Broxbourne 3	d	16 33		16 44		16 52		16 57		17 14			17 22	17 33		17 44			17 52	17 57		18 14			18 22
Rye House	d			16 47						17 17						17 47						18 17			
St Margarets (Herts)	d			16 50						17 20						17 50						18 20			
Ware	d			16 54						17 24						17 54						18 24			
Hertford East	a			17 01						17 31						18 01						18 31			
Roydon	d	16 38				16 56								17 38					17 56						
Harlow Town	d	16 42			16 54	17 00		17 09				17 24	17 28	17 42				17 54	18 00	18 09				18 24	18 28
Harlow Mill	d	16 45				17 03								17 45					18 03						
Sawbridgeworth	d	16 48				17 07		17 15						17 48					18 07	18 15					
Bishops Stortford	a	16 56	16 45			17 14		17 22	17 17				17 38	17 56	17 45				18 14	18 22	18 17				18 38
	d		16 45			17 14			17 18				17 39		17 45				18 14		18 18				18 39
Stansted Mountfitchet	d					17 18						17 35							18 18					18 35	
Stansted Airport	a		16 57		17 12				17 27			17 44			17 57			18 12			18 27			18 44	
Stansted Airport	d										17 27												18 27		
Elsenham	d					17 22													18 22						
Newport (Essex)	d					17 27													18 27						
Audley End	d					17 30					17 40		17 51						18 30				18 40		18 51
Great Chesterford	d					17 35													18 35						
Whittlesford Parkway	d					17 40							17 58						18 40						18 58
Shelford	d					17 44													18 44						
Cambridge	a					17 51					17 58		18 08						18 51				18 58		19 08

		LE		LE	LE	LE	LE	LE	LE	LE	XC	LE		LE	LE	LE	LE	LE	LE	LE	LE	LE		XC	LE
		1		1	1	1	1	1	1	1	◇1	1		1	1	1	1	1	1	1	1	1		1	1
				🚲		🚲			🚲			🚲				🚲		🚲			🚲				🚲
London Liverpool Street 15 ⊖	d			18 10	18 12	18 25	18 28		18 40	18 42		18 55		18 58		19 10	19 12	19 25	19 28		19 40	19 42			19 55
Bethnal Green	d																								
Hackney Downs	d				18 18					18 48							19 18					19 48			
Stratford 7 ⊖	d	18 00						18 30							19 00					19 30					
Clapton	d																								
Seven Sisters ⊖	d																								
Tottenham Hale ⊖	d	18 13		18u22	18 25	18u37	18 40	18 43	18u52	18 55		19u07		19 10	19 13	19u22	19 25	19u37	19 40	19 43	19u52	19 55			20u07
Northumberland Park	d	18 15													19 15										
Angel Road	d																								
Ponders End	d				18 29					18 59							19 29					19 59			
Brimsdown	d				18 32					19 02							19 32					20 02			
Enfield Lock	d	18 21			18 34					19 04					19 21		19 34					20 04			
Waltham Cross	d				18 37			18 50		19 07							19 37			19 50		20 07			
Cheshunt	d	18 25			18 39		18 48	18 53		19 09				19 18	19 25		19 39		19 48	19 53		20 09			
Broxbourne 3	a	18 29			18 44		18 52	18 57		19 14				19 22	19 29		19 44		19 52	19 57		20 14			
Broxbourne 3	d	18 33			18 44		18 52	18 57		19 14				19 22	19 33		19 44		19 52	19 57		20 14			
Rye House	d				18 47					19 17							19 47					20 17			
St Margarets (Herts)	d				18 50					19 20							19 50					20 20			
Ware	d				18 54					19 24							19 54					20 24			
Hertford East	a				19 01					19 31							20 01					20 31			
Roydon	d	18 38					18 56								19 38				19 56						
Harlow Town	d	18 42				18 54	19 00	19 09				19 24		19 28	19 42			19 54	20 00	20 09					20 24
Harlow Mill	d	18 45					19 03								19 45				20 03						
Sawbridgeworth	d	18 48					19 07	19 15							19 48				20 07	20 15					
Bishops Stortford	a	18 56		18 45			19 14	19 22	19 17					19 38	19 56	19 45			20 14	20 22	20 17				
	d			18 45			19 14		19 18					19 39		19 45			20 14		20 18				
Stansted Mountfitchet	d						19 18					19 35							20 18						20 35
Stansted Airport	a			18 57		19 12			19 27			19 44				19 57		20 12			20 27				20 44
Stansted Airport	d										19 27													20 27	
Elsenham	d						19 22												20 22						
Newport (Essex)	d						19 27												20 27						
Audley End	d						19 30				19 40			19 51					20 30					20 40	
Great Chesterford	d						19 35												20 35						
Whittlesford Parkway	d						19 40							19 58					20 40						
Shelford	d						19 44												20 44						
Cambridge	a						19 51				19 58			20 08					20 51					20 57	

London - Broxbourne, Hertford East, Bishops Stortford, Stansted Airport and Cambridge

Network Diagram - see first Page of Table 20

Station		LE 1	LE 1	LE 1 🛒	LE 1	LE 1 🛒	LE 1	LE 1		LE 1 🛒	LE 1	XC 1	LE 1 🛒	LE 1	LE 1	LE 1 🛒	LE 1	LE 1 🛒		LE 1	LE 1	LE 1 🛒	LE 1	XC 1	LE 1 🛒
London Liverpool Street 15 ⊖	d	19 58		20 10	20 12	20 25	20 28			20 40	20 42		20 55	20 58		21 10	21 12	21 25		21 28		21 40	21 42		21 55
Bethnal Green	d																								
Hackney Downs	d				20 18						20 48						21 18						21 48		
Stratford 7 ⊖	d		20 00					20 30							21 00						21 30				
Clapton	d																								
Seven Sisters ⊖	d																								
Tottenham Hale ⊖	d	20 10	20 13	20u22	20 25	20u37	20 40	20 43		20u52	20 55		21u07	21 10	21 13	21u22	21 25	21u37		21 40	21 43	21u52	21 55		22u07
Northumberland Park	d		20 15												21 15										
Angel Road	d																								
Ponders End	d				20 29						20 59						21 29						21 59		
Brimsdown	d				20 32						21 02						21 32						22 02		
Enfield Lock	d		20 21		20 34						21 04				21 21		21 34						22 04		
Waltham Cross	d				20 37			20 50			21 07						21 37				21 50		22 07		
Cheshunt	d	20 18	20 25		20 39		20 48	20 53			21 09			21 18	21 25		21 39			21 48	21 53		22 09		
Broxbourne 3	a	20 22	20 29		20 44		20 52	20 57			21 14			21 22	21 29		21 44			21 52	21 57		22 14		
Broxbourne 3	d	20 22	20 33		20 44		20 52	20 57			21 14			21 22	21 33		21 44			21 52	21 57		22 14		
Rye House	d				20 47						21 17						21 47						22 17		
St Margarets (Herts)	d				20 50						21 20						21 50						22 20		
Ware	d				20 54						21 24						21 54						22 24		
Hertford East	a				21 01						21 31						22 01						22 31		
Roydon	d		20 38				20 56								21 38					21 56					
Harlow Town	d	20 28	20 42			20 54	21 00	21 09					21 24	21 28	21 42			21 54		22 00	22 09				22 24
Harlow Mill	d		20 45				21 03								21 45					22 03					
Sawbridgeworth	d		20 48				21 07	21 15							21 48					22 07	22 15				
Bishops Stortford	a	20 38	20 56	20 45			21 14	21 22		21 17				21 38	21 56	21 45				22 14	22 22	22 17			
	d	20 39		20 45			21 14			21 18				21 39		21 45				22 14		22 18			
Stansted Mountfitchet	d						21 18						21 35							22 18					22 35
Stansted Airport	a			20 57		21 12				21 27			21 44			21 57		22 12				22 27			22 44
Stansted Airport	d											21 27												22 27	
Elsenham	d						21 22													22 22					
Newport (Essex)	d						21 27													22 27					
Audley End	d	20 51					21 30					21 40		21 51						22 30				22 40	
Great Chesterford	d						21 35													22 35					
Whittlesford Parkway	d	20 58					21 40							21 58						22 40					
Shelford	d						21 44													22 44					
Cambridge	a	21 08					21 51					22 01		22 08						22 51				23 01	

Station		LE 1	LE 1	LE 1 🛒		LE 1	LE 1 🛒	LE 1	LE 1	LE 1 🛒	LE 1	XC 1	LE 1 🛒	LE 1		LE 1	LE 1	LE 1	LE 1	LE 1	LE 1
London Liverpool Street 15 ⊖	d	21 58		22 10		22 12	22 25	22 28		22 40	22 42		22 55	22 58			23 12	23 25	23 28	23 40	23 58
Bethnal Green	d																				
Hackney Downs	d					22 18					22 48						23 18			23 46	
Stratford 7 ⊖	d		22 00						22 30							23 00					
Clapton	d																			23 49	
Seven Sisters ⊖	d																				
Tottenham Hale ⊖	d	22 10	22 13	22u22		22 25	22u37	22 40	22 43	22u52	22 55		23u07	23 10		23 13	23 25	23u37	23 40	23 53	00 10
Northumberland Park	d		22 15													23 15				23 55	
Angel Road	d																				
Ponders End	d					22 29					22 59						23 29			23 59	
Brimsdown	d					22 32					23 02						23 32			00 02	
Enfield Lock	d		22 21			22 34					23 04					23 21	23 34			00 04	
Waltham Cross	d					22 37			22 50		23 07						23 37			00 07	
Cheshunt	d	22 18	22 25			22 39		22 48	22 53		23 09			23 18		23 25	23 39		23 48	00 09	00 18
Broxbourne 3	a	22 22	22 29			22 44		22 52	22 57		23 14			23 22		23 29	23 44		23 52	00 14	00 22
Broxbourne 3	d	22 22	22 33			22 44		22 52	22 57		23 14			23 22		23 29	23 44		23 52	00 14	00 22
Rye House	d					22 47					23 17						23 47			00 17	
St Margarets (Herts)	d					22 50					23 20						23 50			00 20	
Ware	d					22 54					23 24						23 54			00 24	
Hertford East	a					23 01					23 31						00 01			00 31	
Roydon	d		22 38					22 56								23 33			23 56		00 26
Harlow Town	d	22 28	22 42				22 54	23 00	23 09				23 24	23 28		23 37		23 54	00 01		00 30
Harlow Mill	d		22 45					23 03								23 40			00 03		00 33
Sawbridgeworth	d		22 48					23 07	23 15							23 44			00 07		00 37
Bishops Stortford	a	22 38	22 56	22 45				23 14	23 22	23 17				23 38		23 51		00 04	00 14		00 44
	d	22 39		22 45				23 14		23 18				23 39				00 04	00 14		00 44
Stansted Mountfitchet	d							23 18					23 35						00 18		00 48
Stansted Airport	a			22 57			23 12			23 27			23 44					00 13			
Stansted Airport	d											23 27									
Elsenham	d							23 22											00 22		00 52
Newport (Essex)	d							23 27											00 27		00 57
Audley End	d	22 51						23 30				23 40		23 51					00 30		01 00
Great Chesterford	d							23 35											00 35		01 05
Whittlesford Parkway	d	22 58						23 40						23 58					00 40		01 10
Shelford	d							23 44											00 44		
Cambridge	a	23 09						23 51				23 55		00 08					00 51		01 19

Table 22

Sundays

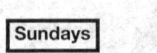

London - Broxbourne, Hertford East, Bishops Stortford, Stansted Airport and Cambridge

Network Diagram - see first Page of Table 20

		LE ■1 A	LE ■1 A	LE ■1 A	LE ■1 A	LE ■1 A	LE ■1 A	LE ■1	LE ■1	LE ■1		LE ■1	LE ■1	LE ■1	LE ■1	LE ■1	LE ■1 🚲	LE ■1 🚲	LE ■1 🚲	LE		LE ■1	LE	LE ■1 🚲	LE ■1
London Liverpool Street 15 ⊖	d	22p58	23p12	23p25	23p28	23p40	23p58	04 10	04 40	05 10		05 40	06 10	06 25	06 40	06 55	07 10	07 25	07 40			07 43	07 52	07 55	
Bethnal Green	d																								
Hackney Downs	d		23p18			23p46																	07 59		
Stratford 7 ⊖	d																								
Clapton	d					23p49																			
Seven Sisters ⊖	d																						08 04		
Tottenham Hale ⊖	d	23p10	23p25	23b37	23p40	23p53	00 10		04u52	05u22		05u52	06u22	06u37	06u52	07 07	07 22	07 37	07 52			07 55		08 07	
Northumberland Park	d					23p55																			
Angel Road	d																								
Ponders End	d		23p29			23p59																07 59			
Brimsdown	d		23p32			00 02																08 02			
Enfield Lock	d		23p34			00 04																08 04			
Waltham Cross	d		23p37			00 07																08 07			
Cheshunt	d	23p18	23p39		23p48	00 09	00 18					06 00										08 09	08 20		
Broxbourne 3	a	23p22	23p44		23p52	00 14	00 22					06 04										08 14	08 25		
Broxbourne 3	d	23p22	23p44		23p52	00 14	00 22					06 04								07 57		08 19	08 25		
Rye House	d		23p47			00 17														08 00			08 28		
St Margarets (Herts)	d		23p50			00 20														08 03			08 31		
Ware	d		23p54			00 24														08 07			08 35		
Hertford East	a		00 01			00 31														08 14			08 42		
Roydon	d				23p56		00 26															08 24			←
Harlow Town	d	23p28		23p54	00 01		00 30		05 07	05 37		06 10		06 52		07 22		07 52				08 28		08 22	08 28
Harlow Mill	d				00 03		00 33															→			08 31
Sawbridgeworth	d				00 07		00 37																		08 34
Bishops Stortford	a	23p38		00 04	00 14		00 44		05 17	05 47		06 20	06 45		07 15		07 45		08 15						08 41
	d	23p39		00 04	00 14		00 44		05 18	05 48		06 21	06 46		07 16		07 46		08 16						08 42
Stansted Mountfitchet	d				00 18		00 48		05 22					07 03				08 03							08 46
Stansted Airport	a			00 13				04 58	05 29	05 57		06 30	06 55	07 12	07 25	07 40	07 55	08 13	08 25					08 40	
Stansted Airport	d																								
Elsenham	d				00 22		00 52																		08 50
Newport (Essex)	d				00 27		00 57																		08 55
Audley End	d	23p51			00 30		01 00																		08 58
Great Chesterford	d				00 35		01 05																		09 03
Whittlesford Parkway	d	23p58			00 40		01 10																		09 08
Shelford	d				00 44																				09 12
Cambridge	a	00 08			00 51		01 19																		09 19

		LE ■1 🚲	LE	LE ■1 🚲	LE ■1	LE		LE ■1 🚲	LE ■1	LE	LE ■1 🚲	LE ■1	LE ■1 🚲	LE	LE ■1 🚲	LE ■1		LE	LE ■1 🚲	XC ◇■1	LE ■1	LE	LE ■1 🚲	LE ■1	LE ■1 🚲
London Liverpool Street 15 ⊖	d	08 10	08 22	08 25	08 28			08 40		08 52	08 55		09 10	09 22	09 25	09 28			09 40			09 52	09 55		10 10
Bethnal Green	d																								
Hackney Downs	d		08 29							08 59				09 29								09 59			
Stratford 7 ⊖	d								08 45												09 45				
Clapton	d																								
Seven Sisters ⊖	d		08 34							09 04				09 34								10 04			
Tottenham Hale ⊖	d	08 22		08 37	08 40			08 52	08 55		09 07		09 22		09 37	09 40			09 52		09 55		10 07		10 22
Northumberland Park	d																								
Angel Road	d																								
Ponders End	d								08 59												09 59				
Brimsdown	d								09 02												10 02				
Enfield Lock	d								09 04												10 04				
Waltham Cross	d					←			09 07									←			10 07				
Cheshunt	d		08 52		08 49	08 52			09 09	09 20				09 52		09 49		09 52			10 09	10 20			
Broxbourne 3	a		→		08 53	08 57			09 14	09 25				→		09 53		09 57			10 14	10 25			
Broxbourne 3	d				08 53	08 57			09 19	09 25						09 53		09 57			10 19	10 25			
Rye House	d					09 00				09 28								10 00				10 28			
St Margarets (Herts)	d					09 03				09 31								10 03				10 31			
Ware	d					09 07				09 35								10 07				10 35			
Hertford East	a					09 14				09 42								10 14				10 42			
Roydon	d								09 24			←									10 24			←	
Harlow Town	d			08 52	08 59				09 28		09 22	09 28			09 52	09 59					10 28		10 22	10 28	
Harlow Mill	d								→			09 31									→			10 31	
Sawbridgeworth	d				09 04							09 34				10 04								10 34	
Bishops Stortford	a	08 45			09 11			09 15				09 41	09 45			10 11			10 15					10 41	10 45
	d	08 46			09 12			09 16				09 42	09 46			10 12			10 16					10 42	10 46
Stansted Mountfitchet	d			09 03								09 46			10 03									10 46	
Stansted Airport	a	08 55		09 12				09 25			09 40		09 55		10 12				10 25				10 40		10 55
Stansted Airport	d																			10 25					
Elsenham	d											09 50												10 50	
Newport (Essex)	d											09 55												10 55	
Audley End	d				09 24							09 58				10 24				10 39				10 58	
Great Chesterford	d											10 03												11 03	
Whittlesford Parkway	d				09 31							10 08				10 31								11 08	
Shelford	d											10 12												11 12	
Cambridge	a				09 41							10 19				10 41				10 58				11 19	

A not 11 December

b Previous night, stops to pick up only

Table 22

Sundays

London - Broxbourne, Hertford East, Bishops Stortford, Stansted Airport and Cambridge

Network Diagram - see first Page of Table 20

		LE		LE	LE	LE	LE	XC	LE	LE	LE	LE		LE	LE	LE	LE	LE	LE	XC	LE	LE		LE	LE
				1 🚲	1		1 🚲	◇1	1		1 🚲	1		1 🚲		1 🚲	1		1 🚲	◇1	1			1 🚲	1
London Liverpool Street 15 ⊖	d	10 22		10 25	10 28		10 40			10 52	10 55			11 10	11 22	11 25	11 28		11 40			11 52		11 55	
Bethnal Green	d																								
Hackney Downs	d	10 29								10 59					11 29							11 59			
Stratford 7 ⊖	d								10 45												11 45				
Clapton	d																								
Seven Sisters ⊖	d	10 34								11 04					11 34							12 04			
Tottenham Hale ⊖	d			10 37	10 40		10 52		10 55		11 07			11 22		11 37	11 40		11 52		11 55			12 07	
Northumberland Park	d																								
Angel Road	d																								
Ponders End	d								10 59												11 59				
Brimsdown	d								11 02												12 02				
Enfield Lock	d								11 04												12 04				
Waltham Cross	d					←			11 07									←			12 07				
Cheshunt	d	10 52			10 49	10 52			11 09	11 20					11 52		11 49	11 52			12 09	12 20			
Broxbourne 3	a	↪			10 53	10 57			11 14	11 25					↪		11 53	11 57			12 14	12 25			
Broxbourne 3	d				10 53	10 57			11 19	11 25							11 53	11 57			12 19	12 25			
Rye House	d					11 00				11 28								12 00				12 28			
St Margarets (Herts)	d					11 03				11 31								12 03				12 31			
Ware	d					11 07				11 35								12 07				12 35			
Hertford East	a					11 14				11 42								12 14				12 42			
Roydon	d								11 24			←									12 24				←
Harlow Town	d			10 52	10 59				11 28		11 22	11 28				11 52	11 59				12 28			12 22	12 28
Harlow Mill	d								↪			11 31									↪				12 31
Sawbridgeworth	d				11 04							11 34					12 04								12 34
Bishops Stortford	a				11 11		11 15					11 41		11 45			12 11		12 15						12 41
	d				11 12		11 16					11 42		11 46			12 12		12 16						12 42
Stansted Mountfitchet	d			11 03								11 46				12 03									12 46
Stansted Airport	a			11 12			11 25				11 40			11 55		12 12			12 25					12 40	
Stansted Airport	d							11 25												12 25					
Elsenham	d											11 50													12 50
Newport (Essex)	d											11 55													12 55
Audley End	d				11 24			11 39				11 58					12 24			12 39					12 58
Great Chesterford	d											12 03													13 03
Whittlesford Parkway	d				11 31							12 08					12 31								13 08
Shelford	d											12 12													13 12
Cambridge	a				11 41			11 57				12 19					12 41			12 58					13 19

		LE	LE	LE	LE	LE	LE	XC		LE	LE	LE	LE	LE	LE	LE	LE	LE		LE	XC	LE	LE	LE	LE
		1 🚲		1 🚲	1		1 🚲	◇1		1		1 🚲	1	1 🚲		1 🚲	1			1 🚲	◇1	1		1 🚲	1
London Liverpool Street 15 ⊖	d	12 10	12 22	12 25	12 28		12 40				12 52	12 55		13 10	13 22	13 25	13 28			13 40			13 52	13 55	
Bethnal Green	d																								
Hackney Downs	d		12 29								12 59				13 29								13 59		
Stratford 7 ⊖	d									12 45												13 45			
Clapton	d																								
Seven Sisters ⊖	d		12 34								13 04				13 34								14 04		
Tottenham Hale ⊖	d	12 22		12 37	12 40		12 52			12 55		13 07		13 22		13 37	13 40			13 52		13 55		14 07	
Northumberland Park	d																								
Angel Road	d																								
Ponders End	d									12 59												13 59			
Brimsdown	d									13 02												14 02			
Enfield Lock	d									13 04												14 04			
Waltham Cross	d					←				13 07								←				14 07			
Cheshunt	d		12 52		12 49	12 52				13 09	13 20				13 52		13 49	13 52				14 09	14 20		
Broxbourne 3	a		↪		12 53	12 57				13 14	13 25				↪		13 53	13 57				14 14	14 25		
Broxbourne 3	d				12 53	12 57				13 19	13 25						13 53	13 57				14 19	14 25		
Rye House	d					13 00					13 28							14 00					14 28		
St Margarets (Herts)	d					13 03					13 31							14 03					14 31		
Ware	d					13 07					13 35							14 07					14 35		
Hertford East	a					13 14					13 42							14 14					14 42		
Roydon	d									13 24			←									14 24			←
Harlow Town	d			12 52	12 59					13 28		13 22	13 28			13 52	13 59					14 28		14 22	14 28
Harlow Mill	d									↪			13 31									↪			14 31
Sawbridgeworth	d				13 04								13 34				14 04								14 34
Bishops Stortford	a	12 45			13 11		13 15						13 41	13 45			14 11			14 15					14 41
	d	12 46			13 12		13 16						13 42	13 46			14 12			14 16					14 42
Stansted Mountfitchet	d			13 03									13 46			14 03									14 46
Stansted Airport	a	12 55		13 12			13 25					13 40		13 55		14 12				14 25				14 40	
Stansted Airport	d							13 25													14 25				
Elsenham	d												13 50												14 50
Newport (Essex)	d												13 55												14 55
Audley End	d				13 24			13 39					13 58				14 24				14 39				14 58
Great Chesterford	d												14 03												15 03
Whittlesford Parkway	d				13 31								14 08				14 31								15 08
Shelford	d												14 12												15 12
Cambridge	a				13 41			13 58					14 19				14 41				14 57				15 19

London - Broxbourne, Hertford East, Bishops Stortford, Stansted Airport and Cambridge

Network Diagram - see first Page of Table 20

		LE 1 🚲	LE	LE 1 🚲		LE 1	LE	LE 1 🚲	XC ◇1	LE 1	LE	LE 1 🚲	LE 1	LE 1 🚲		LE	LE 1 🚲	LE 1	LE	LE 1 🚲	XC ◇1	LE 1	LE	LE 1 🚲	
London Liverpool Street 15 ⊖	d	14 10	14 22	14 25		14 28		14 40			14 52	14 55		15 10		15 22	15 25	15 28		15 40			15 52	15 55	
Bethnal Green	d																								
Hackney Downs	d		14 29								14 59					15 29							15 59		
Stratford 7 ⊖	d									14 45												15 45			
Clapton	d																								
Seven Sisters ⊖	d		14 34								15 04					15 34							16 04		
Tottenham Hale ⊖	d	14 22		14 37		14 40		14 52		14 55		15 07		15 22			15 37	15 40		15 52		15 55		16 07	
Northumberland Park	d																								
Angel Road	d																								
Ponders End	d									14 59												15 59			
Brimsdown	d									15 02												16 02			
Enfield Lock	d									15 04												16 04			
Waltham Cross	d						←			15 07									←			16 07			
Cheshunt	d		14 52			14 49	14 52			15 09	15 20					15 52		15 49	15 52			16 09	16 20		
Broxbourne 3	a		→			14 53	14 57			15 14	15 25					→		15 53	15 57			16 14	16 25		
Broxbourne 3	d					14 53	14 57			15 19	15 25							15 53	15 57			16 19	16 25		
Rye House	d						15 00				15 28								16 00				16 28		
St Margarets (Herts)	d						15 03				15 31								16 03				16 31		
Ware	d						15 07				15 35								16 07				16 35		
Hertford East	a						15 14				15 42								16 14				16 42		
Roydon	d									15 24			←									16 24			
Harlow Town	d			14 52		14 59				15 28		15 22	15 28				15 52	15 59				16 28		16 22	
Harlow Mill	d									→			15 31									→			
Sawbridgeworth	d					15 04							15 34					16 04							
Bishops Stortford	a	14 45				15 11		15 15					15 41	15 45				16 11		16 15					
	d	14 46				15 12		15 16					15 42	15 46				16 12		16 16					
Stansted Mountfitchet	d			15 03									15 46				16 03								
Stansted Airport	a	14 55		15 12				15 25				15 40		15 55			16 12			16 25				16 40	
Stansted Airport	d								15 25												16 25				
Elsenham	d												15 50												
Newport (Essex)	d												15 55												
Audley End	d					15 24			15 39				15 58					16 24			16 39				
Great Chesterford	d												16 03												
Whittlesford Parkway	d					15 31							16 08					16 31							
Shelford	d												16 12												
Cambridge	a					15 41			15 58				16 19					16 41			16 58				

		LE 1	LE 1 🚲	LE	LE 1 🚲	LE 1	LE	LE 1 🚲	XC ◇1	LE 1		LE	LE 1 🚲	LE 1	LE 1 🚲	LE	LE 1 🚲	LE 1	LE	LE 1 🚲		XC ◇1 A	LE 1	LE	LE 1 🚲
London Liverpool Street 15 ⊖	d		16 10	16 22	16 25	16 28		16 40				16 52	16 55		17 10	17 22	17 25	17 28		17 40				17 52	17 55
Bethnal Green	d																								
Hackney Downs	d			16 29								16 59				17 29								17 59	
Stratford 7 ⊖	d									16 45													17 45		
Clapton	d																								
Seven Sisters ⊖	d			16 34								17 04				17 34								18 04	
Tottenham Hale ⊖	d		16 22		16 37	16 40		16 52		16 55			17 07		17 22		17 37	17 40		17 52			17 55		18 07
Northumberland Park	d																								
Angel Road	d																								
Ponders End	d									16 59													17 59		
Brimsdown	d									17 02													18 02		
Enfield Lock	d									17 04													18 04		
Waltham Cross	d						←			17 07									←				18 07		
Cheshunt	d			16 52		16 49	16 52			17 09		17 20				17 52		17 49	17 52				18 09	18 20	
Broxbourne 3	a			→		16 53	16 57			17 14		17 25				→		17 53	17 57				18 14	18 25	
Broxbourne 3	d					16 53	16 57			17 19		17 25						17 53	17 57				18 19	18 25	
Rye House	d						17 00					17 28							18 00					18 28	
St Margarets (Herts)	d						17 03					17 31							18 03					18 31	
Ware	d						17 07					17 35							18 07					18 35	
Hertford East	a						17 14					17 42							18 14					18 42	
Roydon	d	←								17 24				←									18 24		
Harlow Town	d	16 28			16 52	16 59				17 28			17 22	17 28			17 52	17 59					18 28		18 22
Harlow Mill	d	16 31								→				17 31									→		
Sawbridgeworth	d	16 34				17 04								17 34				18 04							
Bishops Stortford	a	16 41	16 45			17 11		17 15						17 41	17 45			18 11		18 15					
	d	16 42	16 46			17 12		17 16						17 42	17 46			18 12		18 16					
Stansted Mountfitchet	d	16 46			17 03									17 46			18 03								
Stansted Airport	a		16 55		17 12			17 25					17 40		17 55		18 12			18 25					18 40
Stansted Airport	d								17 25													18 25			
Elsenham	d	16 50												17 50											
Newport (Essex)	d	16 55												17 55											
Audley End	d	16 58				17 24			17 39					17 58				18 24				18 39			
Great Chesterford	d	17 03												18 03											
Whittlesford Parkway	d	17 08				17 31								18 08				18 31							
Shelford	d	17 12												18 12											
Cambridge	a	17 19				17 41			17 58					18 19				18 41				18 58			

A until 1 January, and then from 19 February

London - Broxbourne, Hertford East, Bishops Stortford, Stansted Airport and Cambridge

Network Diagram - see first Page of Table 20

		LE	LE	LE	LE	LE		LE	LE	XC	LE	LE	LE	LE	LE	LE		LE	LE	LE	LE	XC	LE	LE	LE
		1	1		1	1			1	◇1	1		1	1	1			1	1		1	1	1		1
			🚲		🚲				🚲				🚲		🚲			🚲			🚲				🚲
London Liverpool Street 15 ⊖	d		18 10	18 22	18 25	18 28			18 40			18 52	18 55		19 10	19 22		19 25	19 28		19 40			19 52	19 55
Bethnal Green	d																								
Hackney Downs	d			18 29								18 59				19 29								19 59	
Stratford 7 ⊖	d										18 45												19 45		
Clapton	d																								
Seven Sisters ⊖	d			18 34								19 04				19 34								20 04	
Tottenham Hale ⊖	d		18 22		18 37	18 40			18 52		18 55		19 07		19 22			19 37	19 40		19 52		19 55		20 07
Northumberland Park	d																								
Angel Road	d																								
Ponders End	d										18 59												19 59		
Brimsdown	d										19 02												20 02		
Enfield Lock	d										19 04												20 04		
Waltham Cross	d							←			19 07									←			20 07		
Cheshunt	d			18 52		18 49		18 52			19 09	19 20				19 52			19 49	19 52			20 09	20 20	
Broxbourne 3	a			↪		18 53		18 57			19 14	19 25				↪			19 53	19 57			20 14	20 25	
Broxbourne 3	d					18 53		18 57			19 19	19 25							19 53	19 57			20 19	20 25	
Rye House	d							19 00				19 28								20 00				20 28	
St Margarets (Herts)	d							19 03				19 31								20 03				20 31	
Ware	d							19 07				19 35								20 07				20 35	
Hertford East	a							19 14				19 42								20 14				20 42	
Roydon	d	←									19 24			←									20 24		
Harlow Town	d	18 28			18 52	18 59					19 28		19 22	19 28				19 52	19 59				20 28		20 22
Harlow Mill	d	18 31									↪			19 31									↪		
Sawbridgeworth	d	18 34				19 04								19 34					20 04						
Bishops Stortford	a	18 41	18 45			19 11			19 15					19 41	19 45				20 11		20 15				
	d	18 42	18 46			19 12			19 16					19 42	19 46				20 12		20 16				
Stansted Mountfitchet	d	18 46			19 03									19 46				20 03							
Stansted Airport	a		18 55		19 12				19 25				19 40		19 55			20 12			20 25				20 40
Stansted Airport	d									19 25												20 25			
Elsenham	d	18 50												19 50											
Newport (Essex)	d	18 55												19 55											
Audley End	d	18 58				19 24				19 39				19 58					20 24			20 39			
Great Chesterford	d	19 03												20 03											
Whittlesford Parkway	d	19 08				19 31								20 08					20 31						
Shelford	d	19 12												20 12											
Cambridge	a	19 19				19 41				19 58				20 19					20 41			20 57			

		LE		LE	LE	LE	LE	LE	XC	LE	LE	LE		LE	LE	LE	LE	LE	LE	LE	LE	XC		LE	LE
		1		1		1	1		1	1	1			1	1	1		1	1		1	1		1	
				🚲		🚲				🚲				🚲		🚲		🚲			🚲				
London Liverpool Street 15 ⊖	d			20 10	20 22	20 25	20 28			20 40		20 52		20 55		21 10	21 22	21 25	21 28		21 40				21 52
Bethnal Green	d																								
Hackney Downs	d				20 29							20 59					21 29								21 59
Stratford 7 ⊖	d										20 45													21 45	
Clapton	d																								
Seven Sisters ⊖	d				20 34							21 04					21 34								22 04
Tottenham Hale ⊖	d			20 22		20 37	20 40			20 52	20 55			21 07		21 22		21 37	21 40		21 52			21 55	
Northumberland Park	d																								
Angel Road	d																								
Ponders End	d										20 59													21 59	
Brimsdown	d										21 02													22 02	
Enfield Lock	d										21 04													22 04	
Waltham Cross	d							←			21 07									←				22 07	
Cheshunt	d				20 52		20 49	20 52			21 09	21 20					21 52		21 49	21 52				22 09	22 20
Broxbourne 3	a				↪		20 53	20 57			21 14	21 25					↪		21 53	21 57				22 14	22 25
Broxbourne 3	d						20 53	20 57			21 19	21 25							21 53	21 57				22 19	22 25
Rye House	d							21 00				21 28								22 00					22 28
St Margarets (Herts)	d							21 03				21 31								22 03					22 31
Ware	d							21 07				21 35								22 07					22 35
Hertford East	a							21 14				21 42								22 14					22 42
Roydon	d	←									21 24				←									22 24	
Harlow Town	d	20 28				20 52	20 59				21 28			21 22	21 28			21 52	21 59					22 28	
Harlow Mill	d	20 31									↪				21 31									↪	
Sawbridgeworth	d	20 34					21 04								21 34				22 04						
Bishops Stortford	a	20 41		20 45			21 11			21 15					21 41	21 45			22 11		22 15				
	d	20 42		20 46			21 12			21 16					21 42	21 46			22 12		22 16				
Stansted Mountfitchet	d	20 46				21 03									21 46			22 03							
Stansted Airport	a			20 55		21 12				21 27				21 40		21 55		22 12			22 25				
Stansted Airport	d								21 19													22 25			
Elsenham	d	20 50													21 50										
Newport (Essex)	d	20 55													21 55										
Audley End	d	20 58					21 24		21 33						21 58				22 24			22 40			
Great Chesterford	d	21 03													22 03										
Whittlesford Parkway	d	21 08					21 31								22 08				22 31						
Shelford	d	21 12													22 12										
Cambridge	a	21 19					21 41		21 47						22 19				22 41			22 57			

Table 22

Sundays

London - Broxbourne, Hertford East, Bishops Stortford, Stansted Airport and Cambridge

Network Diagram - see first Page of Table 20

		LE	LE	LE	XC	LE	LE	LE		LE	LE	LE	LE	LE	LE	LE	LE	LE		LE	LE	LE
		1	1	1	1		1	1			1	1		1	1			1		1		1
		🚲		🚲			🚲				🚲			🚲								
London Liverpool Street 15 ⊖	d	21 55		22 10		22 22	22 25	22 28			22 40		22 52	22 55			23 22	23 25		23 28		23 58
Bethnal Green	d																					
Hackney Downs	d					22 29							22 59				23 29					
Stratford 7 ⊖	d											22 45										
Clapton	d																					
Seven Sisters ⊖	d					22 34							23 04				23 34					
Tottenham Hale ⊖	d	22 07		22 22			22 37	22 40			22 52	22 55		23 07				23 37		23 40		00 10
Northumberland Park	d																					
Angel Road	d																					
Ponders End	d											22 59								23 44		
Brimsdown	d											23 02								23 47		
Enfield Lock	d											23 04								23 49		
Waltham Cross	d									←		23 07								23 52		
Cheshunt	d					22 52		22 49		22 52		23 09	23 20				23 50			23 54	←	00 18
Broxbourne 3	a					↪		22 53		22 57		23 14	23 25				23 55			23 59	23 55	00 22
Broxbourne 3	d							22 53		22 57		23 19	23 25				00 02			23 59	00 02	00 22
Rye House	d									23 00							↪				00 06	
St Margarets (Herts)	d									23 03											00 09	
Ware	d									23 07											00 13	
Hertford East	a									23 14											00 19	
Roydon	d		←									23 24			←	←						00 26
Harlow Town	d	22 22	22 28				22 52	22 59				23 28	23 32	23 22	23 28	23 32		23 52		00 05		00 30
Harlow Mill	d		22 31									↪	↪		23 31							00 33
Sawbridgeworth	d		22 34					23 04							23 34					00 10		00 37
Bishops Stortford	a		22 41	22 45				23 11			23 15				23 41	23 45		00 02		00 17		00 44
	d		22 42	22 46				23 12			23 16				23 42			00 03				
Stansted Mountfitchet	d		22 46				23 03								23 46							
Stansted Airport	a	22 40		22 55			23 12				23 25			23 40				00 12				
Stansted Airport	d				23 04																	
Elsenham	d		22 50												23 50							
Newport (Essex)	d		22 55												23 55							
Audley End	d		22 58		23 18			23 24							23 58							
Great Chesterford	d		23 03												00 03							
Whittlesford Parkway	d		23 08					23 31							00 08							
Shelford	d		23 12												00 12							
Cambridge	a		23 19		23 34			23 41							00 19							

Cambridge, Stansted Airport, Bishops Stortford, Hertford East and Broxbourne - London

Network Diagram - see first Page of Table 20

Miles	Miles			LE MO [1]	LE MO [1]	LE MO [1]	LE MFO [1]	LE MFO [1]	LE MFO [1]	LE TWThO [1]	LE MX [1]	LE MX [1]	LE MX [1]	LE MX [1]	LE MX [1]	LE MX [1]	LE [1]	LE [1]	XC [1]	LE [1]	LE [1]	LE [1]	XC [1]
0	—	**Cambridge**	d											22p51					04 44	04 48			05 17
3¼	—	Shelford	d											22p56									
6¾	—	Whittlesford Parkway	d											23p00						04 55			
10	—	Great Chesterford	d											23p04									
14	—	Audley End	d											23p10					04 58	05 03			05 35
15¾	—	Newport (Essex)	d											23p13									
20¼	0	Elsenham	d											23p19									
—	—	**Stansted Airport**	a																05 12				05 49
—	4½	**Stansted Airport**	d	23p15	23p30	23p45	01 00	01 30	05 30		23p45		23p15		23p30		23p59	00 30					
22½	8¼	Stansted Mountfitchet	d										23p21	23p24									
25½	—	**Bishops Stortford**	a		23p39				05 39					23p29	23p39		00 08	00 39		05 16			
—	—		d		23p39				05 39	05 39				23p29	23p39		00 08	00 39		05 16		05 30	
29	—	Sawbridgeworth	d											23p33						05 21		05 35	
31¼	—	Harlow Mill	d											23p37						05 24		05 38	
33	—	Harlow Town	d	23p30	23p47	23p59			05 47	05 47	23p59		23p32	23p40			00 16	00 47		05 27		05 41	
35¾	—	Roydon	d											23p44						05 31		05 45	
—	0	**Hertford East**	d									00 07				23p39					05 25		
—	2	Ware	d													23p43					05 29		
—	4	St Margarets (Herts)	d													23p47					05 33		
—	5¼	Rye House	d													23p50					05 36		
38½	—	**Broxbourne [3]**	a						05 53	05 53		00 19		23p48		23p54				05 36	05 40	05 50	
—	7	**Broxbourne [3]**	d						05 53	05 53		00 19		23p48		23p54				05 36	05 40	05 56	
41¾	—	Cheshunt	d						05 57	05 57				23p52		23p58				05 41	05 44	→	
43	—	Waltham Cross	d																		05 47		
44	—	Enfield Lock	d																		05 49		
45	—	Brimsdown	d																		05 52		
45¾	—	Ponders End	d																		05 54		
48	—	Angel Road	d																		05 57		
48¾	—	Northumberland Park	d																		05 59		
49¾	—	Tottenham Hale ⊖	d	23p46					06 07	06 07			23p48							05 49	06 03		
—	0	Seven Sisters ⊖	d		00 08	00 21					00 21			00 04	00 08	00 11							
51¾	—	Clapton	d																				
—	6¾	Stratford [7] ⊖	a																				
52¾	—	Hackney Downs	d									00 41				00 16					06 08		
54½	—	Bethnal Green	d																				
55¾	—	**London Liverpool Street [15]** ⊖	a	00 01	00 22	00 35	01 50	02 20	06 23	06 23	00 36	00 49	00 01	00 18	00 22	00 26	00 51	01 21		06 03	06 18		

		LE [1]	LE [1]	LE [1]	LE [1] 🚲	LE [1]	LE [1]	LE [1] 🚲	LE [1]	LE	LE [1]	LE	LE [1]	LE [1] 🚲	LE [1]	LE	LE [1] 🚲	LE [1]	LE	LE [1]	LE [1] 🚲	XC [1]	LE [1]
Cambridge	d		05 20	05 32			05 48				05 51				06 18					06 21		06 32	06 47
Shelford	d		05 25								05 56									06 26			
Whittlesford Parkway	d		05 29	05 39			05 55				06 00				06 25					06 30			06 55
Great Chesterford	d		05 33								06 04									06 34			
Audley End	d		05 39	05 48			06 04				06 10				06 34					06 40		06 46	07 04
Newport (Essex)	d		05 42								06 13									06 43			
Elsenham	d		05 48								06 19									06 49			
Stansted Airport	a																					07 09	
Stansted Airport	d				06 00			06 15						06 30			06 45				07 00		
Stansted Mountfitchet	d		05 51		06 06						06 22			06 36						06 52			
Bishops Stortford	a		05 57	06 01	06 10		06 17	06 24			06 28			06 40	06 47		06 54			06 58	07 09		07 17
	d		05 57	06 03	06 10		06 18	06 24			06 29		06 34	06 41	06 47		06 54			06 58	07 09		07 17
Sawbridgeworth	d		06 01	06 07							06 33		06 39							07 03	07 14		
Harlow Mill	d		06 05								06 37		06 42							07 06			
Harlow Town	d		06 08	06 13	06 18		06 27	06 33			06 40		06 56	06 50			07 03			07 10	07 20		
Roydon	d		06 12								06 44		07 00							07 14			
Hertford East	d					06 06				06 28									06 58				
Ware	d					06 10				06 32									07 02				
St Margarets (Herts)	d					06 14				06 36									07 06				
Rye House	d	←				06 17				06 39									07 09				
Broxbourne [3]	a	05 50	06 16	06 19		06 22	06 33			06 43	06 48		07 05						07 13	07 18			
Broxbourne [3]	d	05 56	06 16	06 20		06 26	06 34		06 40	06 44	06 49	07 00	07 10						07 14	07 18			
Cheshunt	d	06 01	06 20			06 30			06 44	06 48	06 53	07 04	07 14						07 18	07 23			
Waltham Cross	d	06 03				06 33			06 47			07 07	07 17				07 12						
Enfield Lock	d	06 06				06 35			06 49			07 09	07 19										
Brimsdown	d	06 08				06 38			06 52			07 12					07 17						
Ponders End	d	06 10				06 40						07 14											
Angel Road	d	06 14											07 24										
Northumberland Park	d	06 16							06 57				07 26			←		←					
Tottenham Hale ⊖	d	06 20	06 28	06 31	06 34	06 45	06 48	06 51	06 59		07 02	07 19	07 29	07 05	07 08	07 19	07 23	07 29		07 32	07 35		07 38
Seven Sisters ⊖	d									07 02		→	→						07 32				
Clapton	d																						
Stratford [7] ⊖	a	06 32		06 45					07 13									07 43					
Hackney Downs	d					06 52				07 08						07 26			07 38				
Bethnal Green	d																						
London Liverpool Street [15] ⊖	a		06 43		06 49	07 02	07 05	07 08		07 18	07 20			07 23	07 25	07 38	07 41		07 48	07 50	07 53		07 55

Table 22

Mondays to Fridays

Cambridge, Stansted Airport, Bishops Stortford, Hertford East and Broxbourne - London

Network Diagram - see first Page of Table 20

	LE	LE 1 ⊥	LE 1	LE	LE 1	LE	LE 1	LE 1 ⊥	LE 1 A	LE	LE 1 ⊥	LE 1	LE	LE 1	LE 1 ⊥	XC 1	LE 1	LE	LE 1 ⊥	LE 1	LE 1
Cambridge d					06 51				07 17					07 21		07 30	07 47				07 51
Shelford d					06 56									07 26							07 56
Whittlesford Parkway d					07 00				07 25					07 30			07 55				08 00
Great Chesterford d					07 04									07 34							08 04
Audley End d					07 10				07 34					07 40		07 44	08 04				08 10
Newport (Essex) d					07 13									07 43							08 13
Elsenham d					07 19									07 49							08 19
Stansted Airport a																08 09					
Stansted Airport d		07 15						07 30			07 43				08 00				08 15		
Stansted Mountfitchet d					07 22						07 49			07 52							08 22
Bishops Stortford a		07 24			07 28			07 39	07 47		07 53			07 58	08 09		08 17		08 24		08 28
d		07 24			07 28		07 34	07 41	07 47		07 54			07 58	08 09		08 17		08 24		08 28
Sawbridgeworth d					07 33		07 39							08 03	08 14						08 33
Harlow Mill d					07 36		07 42							08 06							08 36
Harlow Town d		07 33			07 40		07 56	07 50			08 03			08 10	08 20				08 33		08 40
Roydon d					07 44		08 00							08 14							08 44
Hertford East d			07 16	07 28									07 58							08 16	
Ware d			07 20	07 32									08 02							08 20	
St Margarets (Herts) d			07 24	07 36									08 06							08 24	
Rye House d			07 28	07 39									08 09							08 28	
Broxbourne 3 a			07 32	07 43	07 48		08 05						08 13	08 18						08 33	08 48
Broxbourne 3 d	07 30		07 40	07 44	07 48	08 00	08 10						08 14	08 18				08 30		08 40	08 48
Cheshunt d	07 34		07 44	07 48	07 53	08 04	08 14						08 18	08 23				08 34		08 44	08 53
Waltham Cross d	07 37		07 47			08 07	08 17				08 12							08 37		08 47	
Enfield Lock d	07 39	07 44	07 49			08 09	08 19											08 39		08 49	
Brimsdown d	07 42	07 47	07 52			08 12					08 17							08 42		08 52	
Ponders End d	07 44					08 14												08 44			
Angel Road d							08 24														
Northumberland Park d			07 57				08 26			←		←								08 57	
Tottenham Hale ⊖ d	07 49	07 53	07 59		08 02	08 19	08 29	08 05	08 08	08 19	08 23	08 29		08 32	08 35		08 38	08 49	08 52	08 59	09 02
Seven Sisters ⊖ d				08 02		↪	↪						08 32								
Clapton d																					
Stratford 7 ⊖ a			08 13									08 43								09 13	
Hackney Downs d	07 56			08 08						08 26			08 38					08 56			
Bethnal Green d																					
London Liverpool Street 15 ⊖ a	08 08	08 10		08 18	08 20			08 23	08 25	08 37	08 40		08 48	08 50	08 53		08 55	09 07	09 09		09 20

	LE 1 ⊥	XC ◇1	LE 1	LE	LE 1	LE 1 ⊥	LE	LE 1	LE 1 ⊥	LE 1	LE 1 ⊥	LE 1	LE 1	LE 1 ⊥	XC ◇1	LE 1	LE 1 ⊥	LE 1	LE 1	LE 1 ⊥	LE 1	LE 1 ⊥
Cambridge d		08 10			08 18			08 21					08 48		09 10				09 18			
Shelford d								08 26					08 53						09 23			
Whittlesford Parkway d					08 25			08 30					09 00						09 30			
Great Chesterford d								08 34					09 04						09 34			
Audley End d		08 25			08 34			08 40					09 10		09 24				09 40			
Newport (Essex) d								08 43					09 13						09 43			
Elsenham d								08 49					09 19						09 49			
Stansted Airport a		08 39													09 39							
Stansted Airport d	08 30					08 45			09 00		09 15			09 30			09 45			10 00		10 15
Stansted Mountfitchet d						08 51		08 53			09 21		09 24						09 52			10 21
Bishops Stortford a	08 39				08 48			08 58	09 09				09 29	09 39					09 58	10 09		
d	08 39			08 43	08 48			08 58	09 09			09 15	09 29	09 39				09 47	09 58	10 09		
Sawbridgeworth d				08 48				09 03				09 20	09 33					09 52	10 03			
Harlow Mill d								09 06				09 23	09 37						10 06			
Harlow Town d				08 53	08 57	09 02		09 10			09 32	09 26	09 40				10 00	10 05	10 09			10 32
Roydon d								09 14				09 30							10 13			
Hertford East d			08 39							09 09						09 39					10 09	
Ware d			08 43							09 13						09 43					10 13	
St Margarets (Herts) d			08 47							09 17						09 47					10 17	
Rye House d			08 50				←			09 20						09 50					10 20	
Broxbourne 3 a			08 55	09 00	09 03		09 00	09 18		09 25		09 35	09 46			09 54		10 11	10 17		10 24	
Broxbourne 3 d			08 55	09 09	09 04		09 09	09 18		09 25		09 39	09 46			09 54		10 12	10 17		10 24	
Cheshunt d			09 00	↪			09 14	09 23		09 30		09 43	09 50			09 58		10 16	10 21		10 28	
Waltham Cross d			09 02				09 16			09 32						10 01		10 19			10 31	
Enfield Lock d			09 05				09 19			09 35		09 47				10 03					10 33	
Brimsdown d			09 07							09 37						10 06					10 36	
Ponders End d			09 09							09 39						10 08					10 38	
Angel Road d							09 24					09 52										
Northumberland Park d							09 26					09 54										
Tottenham Hale ⊖ d	09 05		09 15		09 18	09 21	09 29	09 32	09 35	09 45	09 48	09 57	10 00	10 03		10 14	10 17	10 27	10 30	10 33	10 44	10 48
Seven Sisters ⊖ d																						
Clapton d																						
Stratford 7 ⊖ a							09 42					10 08						10 37				
Hackney Downs d			09 22							09 51						10 20					10 50	
Bethnal Green d																						
London Liverpool Street 15 ⊖ a	09 23		09 33		09 35	09 38		09 50	09 53	10 01	10 03		10 14	10 17		10 28	10 31		10 44	10 47	10 58	11 01

A The Fenman

Cambridge, Stansted Airport, Bishops Stortford, Hertford East and Broxbourne - London

Network Diagram - see first Page of Table 20

		LE	LE	LE	XC	LE		LE	LE	LE	LE	LE	LE	LE	LE	LE		XC	LE	LE	LE	LE	LE	LE	LE
		1	1	1	◇1	1		1	1	1	1	1	1	1	1	1		◇1	1	1	1	1	1	1	1
				🛒				🛒			🛒		🛒			🛒				🛒			🛒		🛒
Cambridge	d		10 04		10 10					10 21					11 04			11 10				11 21			
Shelford	d									10 26												11 26			
Whittlesford Parkway	d		10 11							10 30					11 11							11 30			
Great Chesterford	d									10 34												11 34			
Audley End	d		10 19		10 25					10 40					11 19			11 24				11 40			
Newport (Essex)	d									10 43												11 43			
Elsenham	d									10 49												11 49			
Stansted Airport	a				10 40													11 40							
Stansted Airport	d			10 30				10 45			11 00		11 15			11 30				11 45			12 00		12 15
Stansted Mountfitchet	d									10 52			11 21									11 52			12 21
Bishops Stortford	a		10 32	10 39						10 58	11 09				11 32	11 39						11 58	12 09		
	d	10 15	10 32	10 39					10 47	10 58	11 09			11 15	11 32	11 39					11 47	11 58	12 09		
Sawbridgeworth	d	10 20							10 52	11 03				11 20							11 52	12 03			
Harlow Mill	d	10 23								11 06				11 23								12 06			
Harlow Town	d	10 26	10 40					11 00	11 05	11 09			11 32	11 26	11 40					12 00	12 05	12 09			12 32
Roydon	d	10 30								11 13				11 30								12 13			
Hertford East	d					10 39						11 09							11 39					12 09	
Ware	d					10 43						11 13							11 43					12 13	
St Margarets (Herts)	d					10 47						11 17							11 47					12 17	
Rye House	d					10 50						11 20							11 50					12 20	
Broxbourne 3	a	10 35	10 46			10 54			11 11	11 17		11 24		11 35	11 46				11 54		12 11	12 17		12 24	
Broxbourne 3	d	10 39	10 46			10 54			11 12	11 17		11 24		11 39	11 46				11 54		12 12	12 17		12 24	
Cheshunt	d	10 43	10 50			10 58			11 16	11 21		11 28		11 43	11 50				11 58		12 16	12 21		12 28	
Waltham Cross	d					11 01			11 19			11 31							12 01		12 19			12 31	
Enfield Lock	d	10 47				11 03						11 33		11 47					12 03					12 33	
Brimsdown	d					11 06						11 36							12 06					12 36	
Ponders End	d					11 08						11 38							12 08					12 38	
Angel Road	d																								
Northumberland Park	d	10 52												11 52											
Tottenham Hale ⊖	d	10 56	11 00	11 03		11 14		11 17	11 27	11 30	11 33	11 44	11 48	11 56	12 00	12 03			12 14	12 17	12 27	12 30	12 33	12 44	12 48
Seven Sisters ⊖	d																								
Clapton	d																								
Stratford 7 ⊖	a	11 07							11 37					12 07							12 37				
Hackney Downs	d					11 20						11 50							12 20					12 50	
Bethnal Green	d																								
London Liverpool Street 15 ⊖	a		11 13	11 16		11 28		11 31		11 44	11 47	11 58	12 01		12 13	12 16			12 28	12 31		12 44	12 47	12 58	13 01

		LE		LE	LE	XC	LE	LE	LE	LE	LE	LE		LE	LE	LE	LE	XC	LE	LE	LE	LE		LE	LE
		1		1	1	◇1	1	1	1	1	1	1		1	1	1	1	◇1	1	1	1	1		1	1
					🛒			🛒			🛒			🛒			🛒			🛒				🛒	
Cambridge	d			12 04		12 10				12 21						13 04		13 10				13 21			
Shelford	d									12 26												13 26			
Whittlesford Parkway	d			12 11						12 30						13 11						13 30			
Great Chesterford	d									12 34												13 34			
Audley End	d			12 19		12 24				12 40						13 19		13 24				13 40			
Newport (Essex)	d									12 43												13 43			
Elsenham	d									12 49												13 49			
Stansted Airport	a					12 40												13 40							
Stansted Airport	d				12 30			12 45			13 00			13 15			13 30			13 45				14 00	
Stansted Mountfitchet	d									12 52				13 21								13 52			
Bishops Stortford	a			12 32	12 39					12 58	13 09					13 32	13 39					13 58		14 09	
	d	12 15		12 32	12 39				12 47	12 58	13 09				13 15	13 32	13 39				13 47	13 58		14 09	
Sawbridgeworth	d	12 20							12 52	13 03					13 20						13 52	14 03			
Harlow Mill	d	12 23								13 06					13 23							14 06			
Harlow Town	d	12 26		12 40				13 00	13 05	13 09				13 32	13 26	13 40				14 00	14 05	14 09			
Roydon	d	12 30								13 13					13 30							14 13			
Hertford East	d						12 39					13 09							13 39						14 09
Ware	d						12 43					13 13							13 43						14 13
St Margarets (Herts)	d						12 47					13 17							13 47						14 17
Rye House	d						12 50					13 20							13 50						14 20
Broxbourne 3	a	12 35		12 46			12 54		13 11	13 17		13 24			13 35	13 46			13 54		14 11	14 17			14 24
Broxbourne 3	d	12 39		12 46			12 54		13 12	13 17		13 24			13 39	13 46			13 54		14 12	14 17			14 24
Cheshunt	d	12 43		12 50			12 58		13 16	13 21		13 28			13 43	13 50			13 58		14 16	14 21			14 28
Waltham Cross	d						13 01		13 19			13 31							14 01		14 19				14 31
Enfield Lock	d	12 47					13 03					13 33			13 47				14 03						14 33
Brimsdown	d						13 06					13 36							14 06						14 36
Ponders End	d						13 08					13 38							14 08						14 38
Angel Road	d																								
Northumberland Park	d	12 52													13 52										
Tottenham Hale ⊖	d	12 56		13 00	13 03		13 14	13 17	13 27	13 30	13 33	13 44		13 48	13 56	14 00	14 03		14 14	14 17	14 27	14 30		14 33	14 44
Seven Sisters ⊖	d																								
Clapton	d																								
Stratford 7 ⊖	a	13 07							13 37						14 07						14 37				
Hackney Downs	d						13 20					13 50							14 20						14 50
Bethnal Green	d																								
London Liverpool Street 15 ⊖	a			13 13	13 16		13 28	13 31		13 44	13 47	13 58		14 01		14 13	14 16		14 28	14 31		14 44		14 47	14 58

Cambridge, Stansted Airport, Bishops Stortford, Hertford East and Broxbourne - London

Network Diagram - see first Page of Table 20

		LE 1 🚲	LE 1	LE 1	LE 1 🚲	XC ◇1	LE 1	LE 1 🚲		LE 1	LE 1	LE 1 🚲	LE 1	LE 1 🚲	LE 1	LE 1	LE 1 🚲	XC ◇1		LE 1	LE 1 🚲	LE 1	LE 1	LE 1 🚲	LE 1
Cambridge	d			14 04		14 10					14 21					15 04		15 10					15 21		
Shelford	d										14 26												15 26		
Whittlesford Parkway	d			14 11							14 30					15 11							15 30		
Great Chesterford	d										14 34												15 34		
Audley End	d			14 19		14 24					14 40					15 19		15 24					15 40		
Newport (Essex)	d										14 43												15 43		
Elsenham	d										14 49												15 49		
Stansted Airport	a					14 40												15 40							
Stansted Airport	d	14 15			14 30			14 45				15 00		15 15			15 30				15 45			16 00	
Stansted Mountfitchet	d	14 21									14 52			15 21									15 52		
Bishops Stortford	a			14 32	14 39						14 58	15 09				15 32	15 39						15 58	16 09	
	d		14 15	14 32	14 39					14 47	14 58	15 09			15 15	15 32	15 39					15 47	15 58	16 09	
Sawbridgeworth	d		14 20							14 52	15 03				15 20							15 52	16 03		
Harlow Mill	d		14 23								15 06				15 23								16 06		
Harlow Town	d	14 32	14 26	14 40				15 00		15 05	15 09			15 32	15 26	15 40					16 00	16 03	16 09		
Roydon	d		14 30								15 13				15 30								16 13		
Hertford East	d						14 39						15 09							15 39					16 09
Ware	d						14 43						15 13							15 43					16 13
St Margarets (Herts)	d						14 47						15 17							15 47					16 17
Rye House	d						14 50						15 20							15 50					16 20
Broxbourne 3	a		14 35	14 46			14 54			15 11	15 17		15 24		15 35	15 46				15 54		16 10	16 17		16 24
Broxbourne 3	d		14 39	14 46			14 54			15 12	15 17		15 24		15 39	15 46				15 54		16 10	16 17		16 24
Cheshunt	d		14 43	14 50			14 58			15 16	15 21		15 28		15 43	15 50				15 58		16 14	16 21		16 28
Waltham Cross	d						15 01			15 19			15 31							16 01		16 16			16 31
Enfield Lock	d		14 47				15 03						15 33		15 47					16 03					16 33
Brimsdown	d						15 06						15 36							16 06					16 36
Ponders End	d						15 08						15 38							16 08					16 38
Angel Road	d														15 52										
Northumberland Park	d		14 52												15 54							16 23			
Tottenham Hale ⊖	d	14 48	14 56	15 00	15 03		15 14	15 17		15 27	15 30	15 33	15 44	15 48	15 57	16 00	16 03			16 14	16 17	16 27	16 30	16 33	16 44
Seven Sisters ⊖	d																								
Clapton	d																								
Stratford 7 ⊖	a		15 07							15 37					16 08							16 37			
Hackney Downs	d						15 20						15 50							16 20					16 50
Bethnal Green	d																								
London Liverpool Street 15 ⊖	a	15 01		15 13	15 18		15 28	15 31			15 45	15 47	15 58	16 03		16 15	16 18			16 28	16 33		16 44	16 47	16 59

		LE 1 🚲	LE 1	LE 1		LE 1 🚲	XC ◇1	LE 1	LE 1 🚲	LE 1	LE 1	LE 1	LE 1 🚲	LE 1		LE 1 🚲	LE 1	LE 1	LE 1 🚲	XC ◇1	LE 1	LE 1 🚲	LE 1	LE 1	
Cambridge	d			15 51			16 10				16 21	16 40						16 51		17 10				17 21	
Shelford	d			15 56							16 26							16 56						17 26	
Whittlesford Parkway	d			16 00							16 30							17 00						17 30	
Great Chesterford	d			16 04							16 34							17 04						17 34	
Audley End	d			16 10			16 24				16 40	16 53						17 10		17 24				17 40	
Newport (Essex)	d			16 13							16 43							17 13						17 43	
Elsenham	d			16 19							16 49							17 19						17 49	
Stansted Airport	a						16 40													17 40					
Stansted Airport	d	16 15				16 30			16 45				17 00			17 15			17 30			17 45			
Stansted Mountfitchet	d	16 21		16 24							16 52					17 21		17 24						17 52	
Bishops Stortford	a			16 30		16 39					16 58		17 09					17 30	17 39					17 58	
	d		16 15	16 30		16 39				16 43	16 58		17 09				17 15	17 30	17 39				17 47	17 58	
Sawbridgeworth	d		16 20							16 48	17 03						17 20	17 35					17 52	18 03	
Harlow Mill	d		16 23							16 51							17 23							18 06	
Harlow Town	d	16 32	16 26	16 38					17 00	16 54	17 08					17 32	17 26	17 40				18 00	18 03	18 09	
Roydon	d		16 30							16 58							17 30							18 13	
Hertford East	d							16 39						17 09							17 39				
Ware	d							16 43						17 13							17 43				
St Margarets (Herts)	d							16 47						17 17							17 47				
Rye House	d							16 50						17 20							17 50				
Broxbourne 3	a		16 35	16 44				16 54		17 03	17 14			17 24			17 35	17 46			17 54		18 10	18 17	
Broxbourne 3	d		16 39	16 44				16 54		17 07	17 14			17 24			17 39	17 46			17 54		18 10	18 17	
Cheshunt	d		16 43	16 48				16 58		17 12	17 18			17 28			17 43	17 50			17 58		18 14	18 21	
Waltham Cross	d							17 01		17 14				17 31							18 01		18 17		
Enfield Lock	d		16 47					17 03						17 33			17 47				18 03				
Brimsdown	d							17 06						17 36							18 06				
Ponders End	d							17 08						17 38							18 08				
Angel Road	d		16 52														17 52								
Northumberland Park	d		16 54							17 21							17 54						18 23		
Tottenham Hale ⊖	d	16 48	16 57	17 00		17 03		17 14	17 18	17 24	17 27	17 30	17 33	17 44		17 49	17 57	18 00	18 03		18 14	18 19	18 27	18 30	
Seven Sisters ⊖	d																								
Clapton	d																								
Stratford 7 ⊖	a		17 08							17 35							18 08						18 38		
Hackney Downs	d							17 20						17 50							18 20				
Bethnal Green	d																								
London Liverpool Street 15 ⊖	a	17 01		17 16		17 18		17 30	17 32		17 42	17 46	17 48	17 59		18 03		18 16	18 18		18 28	18 33		18 44	

Cambridge, Stansted Airport, Bishops Stortford, Hertford East and Broxbourne - London

Network Diagram - see first Page of Table 20

		LE	LE	LE	LE	LE	LE	LE	LE	XC		LE	LE	LE	LE	LE	LE	LE	LE	XC		LE	LE	LE	LE
		1	1	1	1	1	1	1	1	◇1		1	1	1	1	1	1	1	1	◇1		1	1	1	1
		🚲		🚲			🚲		🚲					🚲		🚲			🚲				🚲		
Cambridge	d					17 51				18 18			18 21					18 51		19 10					19 21
Shelford	d					17 56							18 26					18 56							19 26
Whittlesford Parkway	d					18 00							18 30					19 00							19 30
Great Chesterford	d					18 04							18 34					19 04							19 34
Audley End	d					18 10				18 32			18 40					19 10		19 24					19 40
Newport (Essex)	d					18 13							18 43					19 13							19 43
Elsenham	d					18 19							18 49					19 19							19 49
Stansted Airport	a									18 54										19 39					
Stansted Airport	d	18 00		18 15			18 30		18 45					19 00		19 15			19 30				19 45		
Stansted Mountfitchet	d			18 21		18 24							18 52			19 21		19 24							19 52
Bishops Stortford	a	18 09				18 29	18 39						18 58	19 09				19 29	19 39						19 58
	d	18 09			18 15	18 30	18 39						18 58	19 09			19 15	19 30	19 39						19 58
Sawbridgeworth	d				18 20	18 35							19 03				19 20	19 35							20 03
Harlow Mill	d				18 23								19 06				19 23								20 06
Harlow Town	d			18 32	18 26	18 40			19 00				19 09			19 32	19 26	19 40					20 00		20 09
Roydon	d				18 30								19 13				19 30								20 13
Hertford East	d		18 09					18 39				18 25			19 09							19 39		19 25	
Ware	d		18 13					18 43				18 29			19 13							19 43		19 29	
St Margarets (Herts)	d		18 17					18 47				18 33			19 17							19 47		19 33	
Rye House	d		18 20					18 50				18 36			19 20							19 50		19 36	
Broxbourne 3	a		18 24		18 35	18 46		18 54				18 42	19 17		19 24		19 35	19 46				19 57		19 42	20 17
Broxbourne 3	d		18 24		18 39	18 46		18 54				19 10	19 17		19 24		19 39	19 46				19 57		20 12	20 17
Cheshunt	d		18 28		18 43	18 50		18 58				19 14	19 21		19 28		19 43	19 50				20 01		20 16	20 21
Waltham Cross	d		18 31					19 01				19 17			19 31							20 03		20 19	
Enfield Lock	d		18 33		18 47			19 03							19 33		19 47					20 06			
Brimsdown	d		18 36					19 06							19 36							20 08			
Ponders End	d		18 38					19 08							19 38							20 10			
Angel Road	d				18 52												19 52								
Northumberland Park	d				18 54							19 23					19 54								
Tottenham Hale ⊖	d	18 33	18 44	18 49	18 57	19 00	19 03	19 14	19 19			19 27	19 30	19 33	19 44	19 48	19 57	20 00	20 03			20 15	20 18	20 27	20 30
Seven Sisters ⊖	d																								
Clapton	d																								
Stratford 7 ⊖	a				19 08							19 38					20 08							20 37	
Hackney Downs	d		18 50					19 20							19 50							20 22			
Bethnal Green	d																								
London Liverpool Street 15 ⊖	a	18 47	18 58	19 03		19 16	19 18	19 28	19 33				19 45	19 48	19 58	20 01		20 14	20 17			20 31	20 33		20 45

		LE	LE	LE	LE	LE		LE	XC	LE	LE	LE	LE	LE	LE	LE		LE	LE	LE	XC	LE	LE	LE	LE
		1	1	1	1	1		1	◇1	1	1	1	1	1	1	1		1	1	1	◇1	1	1	1	1
		🚲		🚲				🚲			🚲			🚲		🚲				🚲			🚲		
Cambridge	d					20 04			20 10				20 21						21 04		21 10				21 21
Shelford	d												20 26												21 26
Whittlesford Parkway	d					20 11							20 30						21 11						21 30
Great Chesterford	d												20 34												21 34
Audley End	d					20 19			20 24				20 40						21 19		21 24				21 40
Newport (Essex)	d												20 43												21 43
Elsenham	d												20 49												21 49
Stansted Airport	a								20 39												21 40				
Stansted Airport	d	20 00		20 15				20 30			20 45			21 00		21 15				21 30			21 45		
Stansted Mountfitchet	d			20 21									20 52			21 21									21 52
Bishops Stortford	a	20 09				20 32		20 39					20 58	21 09					21 32	21 39					21 58
	d	20 09			20 15	20 32		20 39				20 47	20 58	21 09				21 15	21 32	21 39				21 47	21 58
Sawbridgeworth	d				20 20							20 52	21 03					21 20						21 52	22 03
Harlow Mill	d				20 23								21 06					21 23							22 06
Harlow Town	d			20 32	20 26	20 40					21 00	20 57	21 09			21 32		21 26	21 40				22 00	22 05	22 09
Roydon	d				20 30								21 13					21 30							22 13
Hertford East	d		20 10							20 39					21 09							21 39			
Ware	d		20 14							20 43					21 13							21 43			
St Margarets (Herts)	d		20 18							20 47					21 17							21 47			
Rye House	d		20 21							20 50					21 20							21 50			
Broxbourne 3	a		20 25		20 35	20 46				20 54		21 04	21 17		21 24			21 35	21 46			21 54		22 11	22 17
Broxbourne 3	d		20 25		20 39	20 46				20 54		21 07	21 17		21 24			21 39	21 46			21 54		22 12	22 17
Cheshunt	d		20 29		20 43	20 50				20 58		21 12	21 21		21 28			21 43	21 50			21 58		22 16	22 21
Waltham Cross	d		20 32							21 01		21 14			21 31							22 01		22 19	
Enfield Lock	d		20 34		20 47					21 03					21 33			21 47				22 03			
Brimsdown	d		20 37							21 06					21 36							22 06			
Ponders End	d		20 39							21 08					21 38							22 08			
Angel Road	d																								
Northumberland Park	d				20 52													21 52							
Tottenham Hale ⊖	d	20 33	20 44	20 48	20 56	21 00		21 03		21 14	21 17	21 23	21 30	21 33	21 44	21 48		21 56	22 00	22 03		22 14	22 17	22 27	22 30
Seven Sisters ⊖	d																								
Clapton	d																								
Stratford 7 ⊖	a				21 07							21 37						22 07						22 37	
Hackney Downs	d		20 50							21 20					21 50							22 20			
Bethnal Green	d																								
London Liverpool Street 15 ⊖	a	20 47	20 59	21 03		21 13		21 16		21 28	21 31		21 44	21 47	21 58	22 01			22 13	22 16		22 28	22 31		22 44

Cambridge, Stansted Airport, Bishops Stortford, Hertford East and Broxbourne - London

Network Diagram - see first Page of Table 20

		LE		LE	LE	LE	LE	XC	LE	LE	LE	LE		LE	LE	LE	LE	LE	LE	LE	LE
		1		1	1	1	1	◇1	1	1	1	1		1	1	1	1	1	1	1	1
Cambridge	d						22 04	22 10				22 21					22 51				
Shelford	d											22 26					22 56				
Whittlesford Parkway	d						22 11					22 30					23 00				
Great Chesterford	d											22 34					23 04				
Audley End	d						22 19	22 24				22 40					23 10				
Newport (Essex)	d											22 43					23 13				
Elsenham	d											22 49					23 19				
Stansted Airport	a																				
Stansted Airport	d	22 00			22 15				22 30		22 45			23 00		23 15		23 30		23 45	23 59
Stansted Mountfitchet	d				22 21			22a36				22 52				23 21	23 24				
Bishops Stortford	a	22 09					22 32		22 39			22 58		23 09			23 29	23 39			00 08
	d	22 09				22 15	22 32		22 39			22 58		23 09			23 29	23 39			00 08
Sawbridgeworth	d					22 20						23 03					23 33				
Harlow Mill	d					22 23						23 06					23 37				
Harlow Town	d				22 32	22 26	22 40				23 00	23 09				23 32	23 40			23 59	00 16
Roydon	d					22 30						23 13					23 44				
Hertford East	d			22 09						22 39					23 09				23 39		
Ware	d			22 13						22 43					23 13				23 43		
St Margarets (Herts)	d			22 17						22 47					23 17				23 47		
Rye House	d			22 20						22 50					23 20				23 50		
Broxbourne 3	a			22 24		22 35	22 46			22 54		23 17			23 24		23 48		23 54		
Broxbourne 3	d			22 24		22 39	22 46			22 54		23 17			23 24		23 48		23 54		
Cheshunt	d			22 28		22 43	22 50			22 58		23 21			23 28		23 52		23 58		
Waltham Cross	d			22 31						23 01					23 31						
Enfield Lock	d			22 33		22 47				23 03					23 33						
Brimsdown	d			22 36						23 06					23 36						
Ponders End	d			22 38						23 08					23 38						
Angel Road	d																				
Northumberland Park	d					22 52															
Tottenham Hale ⊖	d	22 33		22 44	22 48	22 56	23 00		23 03	23 14	23 17	23 30		23 33	23 44	23 48					
Seven Sisters ⊖	d																00 04	00 08	00 11	00 21	
Clapton	d																				
Stratford 7 ⊖	a					23 06															
Hackney Downs	d			22 50						23 20					23 50				00 16		
Bethnal Green	d																				
London Liverpool Street 15 ⊖	a	22 47		22 58	23 01	23 15	23 13		23 16	23 28	23 31	23 44		23 47	23 58	00 01	00 18	00 22	00 26	00 36	00 51

Saturdays

		LE	LE	LE	LE	LE	LE	LE	LE	LE		LE	XC	LE	LE	LE	LE	LE	LE	XC		LE	LE	LE	LE
		1	1	1	1	1	1	1	1	1		1	1	1	1	1	1	1	1 🚲	1		1	1 🚲	1	1
Cambridge	d		22p51										04 56					05 21		05 42					06 04
Shelford	d		22p56															05 26							
Whittlesford Parkway	d		23p00															05 30							06 11
Great Chesterford	d		23p04															05 34							
Audley End	d		23p10															05 40		05 56					06 19
Newport (Essex)	d		23p13															05 43							
Elsenham	d		23p19															05 49							
Stansted Airport	a												05 20							06 08					
Stansted Airport	d	23p15		23p30		23p45		23p59	00 30	01 00		01 30			05 30				06 00				06 15		
Stansted Mountfitchet	d	23p21	23p24															05 52					06 21		
Bishops Stortford	a		23p29	23p39				00 08	00 39						05 39			05 58	06 09						06 32
	d		23p29	23p39				00 08	00 39					05 15	05 39		05 47	05 58	06 09					06 15	06 32
Sawbridgeworth	d		23p33											05 20			05 52	06 03						06 20	
Harlow Mill	d		23p37											05 23				06 06						06 23	
Harlow Town	d	23p32	23p40			23p59		00 16	00 47					05 26			06 05	06 09					06 32	06 26	06 40
Roydon	d		23p44											05 30				06 13						06 30	
Hertford East	d				23p39		00 07															06 09			
Ware	d				23p43																	06 13			
St Margarets (Herts)	d				23p47																	06 17			
Rye House	d				23p50																	06 20			
Broxbourne 3	a		23p48		23p54		00 19							05 34			06 11	06 17				06 24		06 35	06 46
Broxbourne 3	d		23p48		23p54		00 19							05 34		05 54	06 12	06 17				06 24		06 39	06 46
Cheshunt	d		23p52		23p58									05 38		05 58	06 16	06 21				06 28		06 43	06 50
Waltham Cross	d													05 41		06 01	06 19					06 31			
Enfield Lock	d													05 43		06 03						06 33		06 47	
Brimsdown	d													05 46		06 06						06 36			
Ponders End	d													05 48		06 08						06 38			
Angel Road	d																								
Northumberland Park	d													05 52										06 52	
Tottenham Hale ⊖	d	23p48												05 55	06 01	06 14	06 27	06 30	06 33			06 44	06 48	06 56	07 00
Seven Sisters ⊖	d		00 04	00 08	00 11	00 21																			
Clapton	d																								
Stratford 7 ⊖	a													06 05			06 37							07 07	
Hackney Downs	d				00 16		00 41									06 20						06 50			
Bethnal Green	d																								
London Liverpool Street 15 ⊖	a	00 01	00 18	00 22	00 26	00 36	00 49	00 51	01 21	01 50		02 20		06 14	06 14	06 28		06 44	06 47			06 58	07 01		07 13

Table 22

Saturdays

Cambridge, Stansted Airport, Bishops Stortford, Hertford East and Broxbourne - London

Network Diagram - see first Page of Table 20

		LE 1 🚲	LE 1	LE 1 🚲	LE 1	LE 1		LE 1 🚲	XC 1	LE 1	LE 1 🚲	LE 1	LE 1	LE 1 🚲	LE 1	LE 1 🚲		LE 1	LE 1	LE 1 🚲	XC 1	LE 1	LE 1 🚲	LE 1	LE 1
Cambridge	d					06 21			06 40				07 04						07 21		07 40				08 04
Shelford	d					06 26													07 26						
Whittlesford Parkway	d					06 30							07 11						07 30						08 11
Great Chesterford	d					06 34													07 34						
Audley End	d					06 40			06 54				07 19						07 40		07 54				08 19
Newport (Essex)	d					06 43													07 43						
Elsenham	d					06 49													07 49						
Stansted Airport	a								07 09												08 08				
Stansted Airport	d	06 30		06 45				07 00			07 15			07 30		07 45				08 00			08 15		
Stansted Mountfitchet	d					06 52					07 21								07 52				08 21		
Bishops Stortford	a	06 39				06 58		07 09					07 32	07 39					07 58	08 09					08 32
	d	06 39			06 47	06 58		07 09				07 15	07 32	07 39				07 47	07 58	08 09				08 15	08 32
Sawbridgeworth	d				06 52	07 03						07 20						07 52	08 03					08 20	
Harlow Mill	d					07 06						07 23							08 06					08 23	
Harlow Town	d			07 00	07 05	07 09					07 32	07 26	07 40			08 00		08 05	08 09				08 32	08 26	08 40
Roydon	d					07 13						07 30							08 13					08 30	
Hertford East	d		06 39							07 09					07 39							08 09			
Ware	d		06 43							07 13					07 43							08 13			
St Margarets (Herts)	d		06 47							07 17					07 47							08 17			
Rye House	d		06 50							07 20					07 50							08 20			
Broxbourne 3	a		06 54		07 11	07 17				07 24		07 35	07 46		07 54			08 11	08 17			08 24		08 35	08 46
Broxbourne 3	d		06 54		07 12	07 17				07 24		07 39	07 46		07 54			08 12	08 17			08 24		08 39	08 46
Cheshunt	d		06 58		07 16	07 21				07 28		07 43	07 50		07 58			08 16	08 21			08 28		08 43	08 50
Waltham Cross	d		07 01		07 19					07 31					08 01			08 19				08 31			
Enfield Lock	d		07 03							07 33		07 47			08 03							08 33		08 47	
Brimsdown	d		07 06							07 36					08 06							08 36			
Ponders End	d		07 08							07 38					08 08							08 38			
Angel Road	d																								
Northumberland Park	d											07 52												08 52	
Tottenham Hale ⊖	d	07 03	07 14	07 17	07 27	07 30		07 33		07 44	07 48	07 56	08 00	08 03	08 14	08 17		08 27	08 30	08 33		08 44	08 48	08 56	09 00
Seven Sisters ⊖	d																								
Clapton	d																								
Stratford 7 ⊖	a				07 37							08 07						08 37						09 07	
Hackney Downs	d		07 20							07 50					08 20							08 50			
Bethnal Green	d																								
London Liverpool Street 15 ⊖	a	07 16	07 28	07 31		07 44		07 47		07 58	08 01		08 13	08 16	08 28	08 31			08 44	08 47		08 58	09 01		09 13

		LE 1 🚲		XC ◇1	LE 1	LE 1 🚲	LE 1	LE 1	LE 1 🚲	LE 1	LE 1 🚲	LE 1		LE 1	LE 1 🚲	XC ◇1	LE 1	LE 1 🚲	LE 1	LE 1	LE 1 🚲	LE 1		LE 1 🚲	LE 1
Cambridge	d			08 10				08 21						09 04		09 10				09 21					
Shelford	d							08 26												09 26					
Whittlesford Parkway	d							08 30						09 11						09 30					
Great Chesterford	d							08 34												09 34					
Audley End	d			08 24				08 40						09 19		09 24				09 40					
Newport (Essex)	d							08 43												09 43					
Elsenham	d							08 49												09 49					
Stansted Airport	a			08 39												09 40									
Stansted Airport	d	08 30				08 45			09 00		09 15				09 30			09 45			10 00			10 15	
Stansted Mountfitchet	d							08 52			09 21									09 52				10 21	
Bishops Stortford	a	08 39						08 58	09 09					09 32	09 39					09 58	10 09				
	d	08 39					08 47	08 58	09 09			09 15		09 32	09 39				09 47	09 58	10 09				10 15
Sawbridgeworth	d						08 52	09 03				09 20							09 52	10 03					10 20
Harlow Mill	d							09 06				09 23								10 06					10 23
Harlow Town	d					09 00	09 05	09 09			09 32	09 26		09 40				10 00	10 05	10 09				10 32	10 26
Roydon	d							09 13				09 30								10 13					10 30
Hertford East	d				08 39					09 09							09 39					10 09			
Ware	d				08 43					09 13							09 43					10 13			
St Margarets (Herts)	d				08 47					09 17							09 47					10 17			
Rye House	d				08 50					09 20							09 50					10 20			
Broxbourne 3	a				08 54		09 11	09 17		09 24		09 35		09 46			09 54		10 11	10 17		10 24			10 35
Broxbourne 3	d				08 54		09 12	09 17		09 24		09 39		09 46			09 54		10 12	10 17		10 24			10 39
Cheshunt	d				08 58		09 16	09 21		09 28		09 43		09 50			09 58		10 16	10 21		10 28			10 43
Waltham Cross	d				09 01		09 19			09 31							10 01		10 19			10 31			
Enfield Lock	d				09 03					09 33		09 47					10 03					10 33			10 47
Brimsdown	d				09 06					09 36							10 06					10 36			
Ponders End	d				09 08					09 38							10 08					10 38			
Angel Road	d																								
Northumberland Park	d											09 52													10 52
Tottenham Hale ⊖	d	09 03			09 14	09 17	09 27	09 30	09 33	09 44	09 48	09 56		10 00	10 03		10 14	10 17	10 27	10 30	10 33	10 44		10 48	10 56
Seven Sisters ⊖	d																								
Clapton	d																								
Stratford 7 ⊖	a						09 37					10 07							10 37						11 07
Hackney Downs	d				09 20					09 50							10 20					10 50			
Bethnal Green	d																								
London Liverpool Street 15 ⊖	a	09 16			09 28	09 31		09 44	09 47	09 58	10 01			10 13	10 16		10 28	10 31		10 44	10 47	10 58		11 01	

Cambridge, Stansted Airport, Bishops Stortford, Hertford East and Broxbourne - London

Network Diagram - see first Page of Table 20

		LE 1	LE 1 🛒	XC ◇1	LE 1	LE 1 🛒	LE 1	LE 1		LE 1 🛒	LE 1	LE 1 🛒	LE 1	LE 1	LE 1 🛒	XC ◇1	LE 1	LE 1 🛒		LE 1	LE 1	LE 1 🛒	LE 1	LE 1 🛒	LE 1
Cambridge	d	10 04		10 10				10 21						11 04		11 10					11 21				
Shelford	d							10 26													11 26				
Whittlesford Parkway	d	10 11						10 30						11 11							11 30				
Great Chesterford	d							10 34													11 34				
Audley End	d	10 19		10 24				10 40						11 19		11 24					11 40				
Newport (Essex)	d							10 43													11 43				
Elsenham	d							10 49													11 49				
Stansted Airport	a			10 40												11 40									
Stansted Airport	d		10 30			10 45				11 00		11 15			11 30			11 45				12 00		12 15	
Stansted Mountfitchet	d							10 52				11 21									11 52			12 21	
Bishops Stortford	a	10 32	10 39					10 58		11 09				11 32	11 39						11 58	12 09			
	d	10 32	10 39				10 47	10 58		11 09			11 15	11 32	11 39					11 47	11 58	12 09			12 15
Sawbridgeworth	d						10 52	11 03					11 20							11 52	12 03				12 20
Harlow Mill	d							11 06					11 23								12 06				12 23
Harlow Town	d	10 40				11 00	11 05	11 09				11 32	11 26	11 40				12 00		12 05	12 09			12 32	12 26
Roydon	d							11 13					11 30								12 13				12 30
Hertford East	d				10 39						11 09						11 39						12 09		
Ware	d				10 43						11 13						11 43						12 13		
St Margarets (Herts)	d				10 47						11 17						11 47						12 17		
Rye House	d				10 50						11 20						11 50						12 20		
Broxbourne 3	a	10 46			10 54		11 11	11 17			11 24		11 35	11 46			11 54			12 11	12 17		12 24		12 35
Broxbourne 3	d	10 46			10 54		11 12	11 17			11 24		11 39	11 46			11 54			12 12	12 17		12 24		12 39
Cheshunt	d	10 50			10 58		11 16	11 21			11 28		11 43	11 50			11 58			12 16	12 21		12 28		12 43
Waltham Cross	d				11 01		11 19				11 31						12 01			12 19			12 31		
Enfield Lock	d				11 03						11 33		11 47				12 03						12 33		12 47
Brimsdown	d				11 06						11 36						12 06						12 36		
Ponders End	d				11 08						11 38						12 08						12 38		
Angel Road	d																								
Northumberland Park	d												11 52												12 52
Tottenham Hale ⊖	d	11 00	11 03		11 14	11 17	11 27	11 30		11 33	11 44	11 48	11 56	12 00	12 03		12 14	12 17		12 27	12 30	12 33	12 44	12 48	12 56
Seven Sisters ⊖	d																								
Clapton	d																								
Stratford 7 ⊖	a						11 37						12 07							12 37					13 07
Hackney Downs	d				11 20						11 50						12 20						12 50		
Bethnal Green	d																								
London Liverpool Street 15 ⊖	a	11 13	11 16		11 28	11 31		11 44		11 47	11 58	12 01		12 13	12 16		12 28	12 31			12 44	12 47	12 58	13 01	

		LE 1	LE 1 🛒	XC ◇1		LE 1	LE 1 🛒	LE 1	LE 1	LE 1 🛒	LE 1	LE 1 🛒	LE 1	LE 1		LE 1 🛒	XC ◇1	LE 1	LE 1 🛒	LE 1	LE 1	LE 1 🛒	LE 1	LE 1 🛒	
Cambridge	d	12 04		12 10					12 21					13 04			13 10				13 21				
Shelford	d								12 26												13 26				
Whittlesford Parkway	d	12 11							12 30					13 11							13 30				
Great Chesterford	d								12 34												13 34				
Audley End	d	12 19		12 24					12 40					13 19			13 24				13 40				
Newport (Essex)	d								12 43												13 43				
Elsenham	d								12 49												13 49				
Stansted Airport	a			12 40													13 40								
Stansted Airport	d		12 30				12 45			13 00		13 15				13 30			13 45			14 00		14 15	
Stansted Mountfitchet	d								12 52			13 21									13 52			14 21	
Bishops Stortford	a	12 32	12 39						12 58	13 09				13 32		13 39					13 58	14 09			
	d	12 32	12 39					12 47	12 58	13 09			13 15	13 32		13 39				13 47	13 58	14 09			
Sawbridgeworth	d							12 52	13 03				13 20							13 52	14 03				
Harlow Mill	d								13 06				13 23								14 06				
Harlow Town	d	12 40					13 00	13 05	13 09			13 32	13 26	13 40					14 00	14 05	14 09			14 32	
Roydon	d								13 13				13 30								14 13				
Hertford East	d					12 39					13 09							13 39					14 09		
Ware	d					12 43					13 13							13 43					14 13		
St Margarets (Herts)	d					12 47					13 17							13 47					14 17		
Rye House	d					12 50					13 20							13 50					14 20		
Broxbourne 3	a	12 46				12 54		13 11	13 17		13 24		13 35	13 46				13 54		14 11	14 17		14 24		
Broxbourne 3	d	12 46				12 54		13 12	13 17		13 24		13 39	13 46				13 54		14 12	14 17		14 24		
Cheshunt	d	12 50				12 58		13 16	13 21		13 28		13 43	13 50				13 58		14 16	14 21		14 28		
Waltham Cross	d					13 01		13 19			13 31							14 01		14 19			14 31		
Enfield Lock	d					13 03					13 33		13 47					14 03					14 33		
Brimsdown	d					13 06					13 36							14 06					14 36		
Ponders End	d					13 08					13 38							14 08					14 38		
Angel Road	d																								
Northumberland Park	d												13 52												
Tottenham Hale ⊖	d	13 00	13 03			13 14	13 17	13 27	13 30	13 33	13 44	13 48	13 56	14 00		14 03		14 14	14 17	14 27	14 30	14 33	14 44	14 48	
Seven Sisters ⊖	d																								
Clapton	d																								
Stratford 7 ⊖	a							13 37					14 07							14 37					
Hackney Downs	d					13 20					13 50							14 20					14 50		
Bethnal Green	d																								
London Liverpool Street 15 ⊖	a	13 13	13 16			13 28	13 31		13 44	13 47	13 58	14 01		14 13		14 16		14 28	14 31		14 44	14 47	14 58	15 01	

Table 22

Saturdays

Cambridge, Stansted Airport, Bishops Stortford, Hertford East and Broxbourne - London

Network Diagram - see first Page of Table 20

		LE 1	LE 1	LE 1 🚲	XC ◇1	LE 1	LE 1 🚲	LE 1	LE 1	LE 1 🚲		LE 1	LE 1 🚲	LE 1	LE 1	LE 1 🚲	XC ◇1	LE 1	LE 1 🚲	LE 1		LE 1	LE 1 🚲	LE 1	LE 1 🚲
Cambridge	d		14 04		14 10				14 21						15 04		15 10					15 21			
Shelford	d								14 26													15 26			
Whittlesford Parkway	d		14 11						14 30						15 11							15 30			
Great Chesterford	d								14 34													15 34			
Audley End	d		14 19		14 24				14 40						15 19		15 24					15 40			
Newport (Essex)	d								14 43													15 43			
Elsenham	d								14 49													15 49			
Stansted Airport	a				14 40												15 40								
Stansted Airport	d			14 30			14 45			15 00			15 15			15 30			15 45				16 00		16 15
Stansted Mountfitchet	d								14 52				15 21									15 52			16 21
Bishops Stortford	a		14 32	14 39					14 58	15 09					15 32	15 39						15 58	16 09		
	d	14 15	14 32	14 39				14 47	14 58	15 09				15 15	15 32	15 39				15 47		15 58	16 09		
Sawbridgeworth	d	14 20						14 52	15 03					15 20						15 52		16 03			
Harlow Mill	d	14 23							15 06					15 23								16 06			
Harlow Town	d	14 26	14 40				15 00	15 05	15 09				15 32	15 26	15 40				16 00	16 05		16 09			16 32
Roydon	d	14 30							15 13					15 30								16 13			
Hertford East	d					14 39						15 09						15 39						16 09	
Ware	d					14 43						15 13						15 43						16 13	
St Margarets (Herts)	d					14 47						15 17						15 47						16 17	
Rye House	d					14 50						15 20						15 50						16 20	
Broxbourne 3	a	14 35	14 46			14 54		15 11	15 17			15 24		15 35	15 46			15 54		16 11		16 17		16 24	
Broxbourne 3	d	14 39	14 46			14 54		15 12	15 17			15 24		15 39	15 46			15 54		16 12		16 17		16 24	
Cheshunt	d	14 43	14 50			14 58		15 16	15 21			15 28		15 43	15 50			15 58		16 16		16 21		16 28	
Waltham Cross	d					15 01		15 19				15 31						16 01		16 19				16 31	
Enfield Lock	d	14 47				15 03						15 33		15 47				16 03						16 33	
Brimsdown	d					15 06						15 36						16 06						16 36	
Ponders End	d					15 08						15 38						16 08						16 38	
Angel Road	d																								
Northumberland Park	d	14 52												15 52											
Tottenham Hale ⊖	d	14 56	15 00	15 03		15 14	15 17	15 27	15 30	15 33		15 44	15 48	15 56	16 00	16 03		16 14	16 17	16 27		16 30	16 33	16 44	16 48
Seven Sisters ⊖	d																								
Clapton	d																								
Stratford 7 ⊖	a	15 07						15 37						16 07						16 37					
Hackney Downs	d					15 20						15 50						16 20						16 50	
Bethnal Green	d																								
London Liverpool Street 15 ⊖	a		15 13	15 16		15 28	15 31		15 44	15 47		15 58	16 01		16 13	16 16		16 28	16 31			16 44	16 47	16 58	17 01

		LE 1	LE 1	LE 1 🚲	XC ◇1	LE 1		LE 1 🚲	LE 1	LE 1	LE 1 🚲	LE 1	LE 1 🚲	LE 1	LE 1	LE 1 🚲		XC ◇1	LE 1	LE 1 🚲	LE 1	LE 1	LE 1 🚲	LE 1	LE 1 🚲
Cambridge	d		16 04		16 10					16 21					17 04			17 10				17 21			
Shelford	d									16 26												17 26			
Whittlesford Parkway	d		16 11							16 30					17 11							17 30			
Great Chesterford	d									16 34												17 34			
Audley End	d		16 19		16 24					16 40					17 19			17 24				17 40			
Newport (Essex)	d									16 43												17 43			
Elsenham	d									16 49												17 49			
Stansted Airport	a				16 40													17 40							
Stansted Airport	d			16 30				16 45			17 00		17 15			17 30				17 45			18 00		18 15
Stansted Mountfitchet	d									16 52			17 21									17 52			18 21
Bishops Stortford	a		16 32	16 39						16 58	17 09				17 32	17 39						17 58	18 09		
	d	16 15	16 32	16 39					16 47	16 58	17 09			17 15	17 32	17 39					17 47	17 58	18 09		
Sawbridgeworth	d	16 20							16 52	17 03				17 20							17 52	18 03			
Harlow Mill	d	16 23								17 06				17 23								18 06			
Harlow Town	d	16 26	16 40					17 00	17 05	17 09			17 32	17 26	17 40					18 00	18 05	18 09			18 32
Roydon	d	16 30								17 13				17 30								18 13			
Hertford East	d					16 39						17 09							17 39					18 09	
Ware	d					16 43						17 13							17 43					18 13	
St Margarets (Herts)	d					16 47						17 17							17 47					18 17	
Rye House	d					16 50						17 20							17 50					18 20	
Broxbourne 3	a	16 35	16 46			16 54			17 11	17 17		17 24		17 35	17 46				17 54		18 11	18 17		18 24	
Broxbourne 3	d	16 39	16 46			16 54			17 12	17 17		17 24		17 39	17 46				17 54		18 12	18 17		18 24	
Cheshunt	d	16 43	16 50			16 58			17 16	17 21		17 28		17 43	17 50				17 58		18 16	18 21		18 28	
Waltham Cross	d					17 01			17 19			17 31							18 01		18 19			18 31	
Enfield Lock	d	16 47				17 03						17 33		17 47					18 03					18 33	
Brimsdown	d					17 06						17 36							18 06					18 36	
Ponders End	d					17 08						17 38							18 08					18 38	
Angel Road	d																								
Northumberland Park	d	16 52												17 52											
Tottenham Hale ⊖	d	16 56	17 00	17 03		17 14		17 17	17 27	17 30	17 33	17 44	17 48	17 56	18 00	18 03			18 14	18 17	18 27	18 30	18 33	18 44	18 48
Seven Sisters ⊖	d																								
Clapton	d																								
Stratford 7 ⊖	a	17 07							17 37					18 07							18 37				
Hackney Downs	d					17 20						17 50							18 20					18 50	
Bethnal Green	d																								
London Liverpool Street 15 ⊖	a		17 13	17 16		17 28		17 31		17 44	17 47	17 58	18 01		18 13	18 16			18 28	18 31		18 44	18 47	18 58	19 01

Cambridge, Stansted Airport, Bishops Stortford, Hertford East and Broxbourne - London

Network Diagram - see first Page of Table 20

		LE		LE	LE	LE	LE	XC	LE	LE	LE	LE		LE	LE	LE	LE	XC	LE	LE	LE	LE		LE	LE
		1		1	1	1	1	◇1	1	1	1	1		1	1	1	1	◇1	1	1	1	1		1	1
					🛒		🛒				🛒			🛒			🛒			🛒				🛒	
Cambridge	d			18 04				18 18		18 21						19 04		19 10				19 21			
Shelford	d									18 26												19 26			
Whittlesford Parkway	d			18 11						18 30						19 11						19 30			
Great Chesterford	d									18 34												19 34			
Audley End	d			18 19				18 34		18 40						19 19		19 25				19 40			
Newport (Essex)	d									18 43												19 43			
Elsenham	d									18 49												19 49			
Stansted Airport	a							18 53										19 40							
Stansted Airport	d				18 30		18 45				19 00			19 15			19 30			19 45				20 00	
Stansted Mountfitchet	d									18 52				19 21								19 52			
Bishops Stortford	a			18 32	18 39					18 58	19 09					19 32	19 39					19 58		20 09	
	d	18 15		18 32	18 39				18 47	18 58	19 09				19 15	19 32	19 39				19 47	19 58		20 09	
Sawbridgeworth	d	18 20							18 52	19 03					19 20						19 52	20 03			
Harlow Mill	d	18 23								19 06					19 23							20 06			
Harlow Town	d	18 26		18 40			19 00		19 05	19 09				19 32	19 26	19 40				20 00	20 05	20 09			
Roydon	d	18 30								19 13					19 30							20 13			
Hertford East	d					18 39						19 09							19 39						20 09
Ware	d					18 43						19 13							19 43						20 13
St Margarets (Herts)	d					18 47						19 17							19 47						20 17
Rye House	d					18 50						19 20							19 50						20 20
Broxbourne 3	a	18 35		18 46		18 54			19 11	19 17		19 24			19 35	19 46			19 54		20 11	20 17			20 24
Broxbourne 3	d	18 39		18 46		18 54			19 12	19 17		19 24			19 39	19 46			19 54		20 12	20 17			20 24
Cheshunt	d	18 43		18 50		18 58			19 16	19 21		19 28			19 43	19 50			19 58		20 16	20 21			20 28
Waltham Cross	d					19 01			19 19			19 31							20 01		20 19				20 31
Enfield Lock	d	18 47				19 03						19 33			19 47				20 03						20 33
Brimsdown	d					19 06						19 36							20 06						20 36
Ponders End	d					19 08						19 38							20 08						20 38
Angel Road	d																								
Northumberland Park	d	18 52													19 52										
Tottenham Hale ⊖	d	18 56		19 00	19 03	19 14	19 17		19 27	19 30	19 33	19 44		19 48	19 56	20 00	20 03		20 14	20 17	20 27	20 30		20 33	20 44
Seven Sisters ⊖	d																								
Clapton	d																								
Stratford 7 ⊖	a	19 07							19 37						20 07						20 37				
Hackney Downs	d					19 20						19 50							20 20						20 50
Bethnal Green	d																								
London Liverpool Street 15 ⊖	a			19 13	19 16	19 28	19 31			19 44	19 47	19 58		20 01		20 13	20 16		20 28	20 31		20 44		20 47	20 58

		LE	LE	LE	LE	XC	LE	LE		LE	LE	LE	LE	LE	LE	LE	LE	XC		LE	LE	LE	LE	LE	LE
		1	1	1	1	◇1	1	1		1	1	1	1	1	1	1	1	◇1		1	1	1	1	1	1
		🛒			🛒			🛒				🛒		🛒			🛒				🛒				
Cambridge	d			20 04		20 10					20 21					21 04		21 10					21 21		
Shelford	d										20 26												21 26		
Whittlesford Parkway	d			20 11							20 30					21 11							21 30		
Great Chesterford	d										20 34												21 34		
Audley End	d			20 19		20 24					20 40					21 19		21 24					21 40		
Newport (Essex)	d										20 43												21 43		
Elsenham	d										20 49												21 49		
Stansted Airport	a					20 40												21 40							
Stansted Airport	d	20 15			20 30			20 45				21 00		21 15			21 30				21 45			22 00	
Stansted Mountfitchet	d	20 21									20 52			21 21									21 52		
Bishops Stortford	a			20 32	20 39						20 58	21 09				21 32	21 39						21 58	22 09	
	d		20 15	20 32	20 39					20 47	20 58	21 09			21 15	21 32	21 39					21 47	21 58	22 09	
Sawbridgeworth	d		20 20							20 52	21 03				21 20							21 52	22 03		
Harlow Mill	d		20 23								21 06				21 23								22 06		
Harlow Town	d	20 32	20 26	20 40				21 00		21 05	21 09			21 32	21 26	21 40					22 00	22 05	22 09		
Roydon	d		20 30								21 13				21 30								22 13		
Hertford East	d						20 39						21 09							21 39					22 09
Ware	d						20 43						21 13							21 43					22 13
St Margarets (Herts)	d						20 47						21 17							21 47					22 17
Rye House	d						20 50						21 20							21 50					22 20
Broxbourne 3	a		20 35	20 46			20 54			21 11	21 17		21 24		21 35	21 46				21 54		22 11	22 17		22 24
Broxbourne 3	d		20 39	20 46			20 54			21 12	21 17		21 24		21 39	21 46				21 54		22 12	22 17		22 24
Cheshunt	d		20 43	20 50			20 58			21 16	21 21		21 28		21 43	21 50				21 58		22 16	22 21		22 28
Waltham Cross	d						21 01			21 19			21 31							22 01		22 19			22 31
Enfield Lock	d		20 47				21 03						21 33		21 47					22 03					22 33
Brimsdown	d						21 06						21 36							22 06					22 36
Ponders End	d						21 08						21 38							22 08					22 38
Angel Road	d																								
Northumberland Park	d		20 52												21 52										
Tottenham Hale ⊖	d	20 48	20 56	21 00	21 03		21 14	21 17		21 27	21 30	21 33	21 44	21 48	21 56	22 00	22 03			22 14	22 17	22 27	22 30	22 33	22 44
Seven Sisters ⊖	d																								
Clapton	d																								
Stratford 7 ⊖	a		21 07							21 37					22 07							22 37			
Hackney Downs	d						21 20						21 50							22 20					22 50
Bethnal Green	d																								
London Liverpool Street 15 ⊖	a	21 01		21 13	21 16		21 28	21 31			21 44	21 47	21 58	22 01		22 13	22 16			22 28	22 31		22 44	22 47	22 58

Table 22

Saturdays

Cambridge, Stansted Airport, Bishops Stortford, Hertford East and Broxbourne - London

Network Diagram - see first Page of Table 20

		LE	LE	LE	LE	XC	LE	LE	LE	LE	LE	LE	LE	LE	LE	LE	LE
		[1]	[1]	[1]	[1]	◇[1]	[1]	[1]	[1]	[1]	[1]	[1]	[1]	[1]	[1]	[1]	[1]
Cambridge	d			22 04		22 10			22 21				22 51				
Shelford	d								22 26				22 56				
Whittlesford Parkway	d			22 11					22 30				23 00				
Great Chesterford	d								22 34				23 04				
Audley End	d			22 19		22 24			22 40				23 10				
Newport (Essex)	d								22 43				23 13				
Elsenham	d								22 49				23 19				
Stansted Airport	a					22 40											
Stansted Airport	d	22 15			22 30			22 45		23 00		23 15		23 30		23 45	23 59
Stansted Mountfitchet	d	22 21							22 52			23 21	23 22				
Bishops Stortford	a			22 32	22 39				22 58	23 09			23 28	23 39			00 08
	d		22 15	22 32	22 39				22 58	23 09			23 28	23 39			00 08
Sawbridgeworth	d		22 20						23 03				23 32				
Harlow Mill	d		22 23						23 06				23 36				
Harlow Town	d	22 32	22 26	22 40				23 00	23 09			23 32	23 39			23 59	00 16
Roydon	d		22 30						23 13				23 43				
Hertford East	d						22 39				23 09				23 39		
Ware	d						22 43				23 13				23 43		
St Margarets (Herts)	d						22 47				23 17				23 47		
Rye House	d						22 50				23 20				23 50		
Broxbourne [3]	a		22 35	22 46			22 54		23 17		23 24		23 47		23 54		
Broxbourne [3]	d		22 39	22 46			22 54		23 17		23 24		23 47		23 54		
Cheshunt	d		22 43	22 50			22 58		23 21		23 28		23 51		23 58		
Waltham Cross	d						23 01				23 31				00 01		
Enfield Lock	d		22 47				23 03				23 33				00 03		
Brimsdown	d						23 06				23 36				00 06		
Ponders End	d						23 08				23 38				00 08		
Angel Road	d																
Northumberland Park	d		22 52														
Tottenham Hale ⊖	d	22 48	22 56	23 00	23 03		23 14	23 17	23 30	23 33	23 44	23 48	23 59	00 03	00 14	00 17	
Seven Sisters ⊖	d																
Clapton	d																
Stratford [7] ⊖	a		23 07														
Hackney Downs	d						23 20				23 50				00 20		
Bethnal Green	d																
London Liverpool Street [15] ⊖	a	23 01	23 18	23 13	23 16		23 28	23 31	23 45	23 47	23 58	00 01	00 13	00 16	00 28	00 32	00 51

Sundays

		LE	LE	LE	LE	LE	LE	LE	LE	LE	LE	LE	LE	LE	LE	LE	LE	LE	LE	LE	LE	LE	LE
		[1]	[1]	[1]	[1]	[1]	[1]	[1]	[1]	[1]	[1]	[1]	[1]	[1]	[1]		[1]	[1]	[1]	[1]		[1]	[1]
		A	A	A	A	A	A																
											Bus	Bus		Bus	Bus			Bus		Bus			Bus
Cambridge	d		22p51																			07 32	
Shelford	d		22p56																				
Whittlesford Parkway	d		23p00																			07 39	
Great Chesterford	d		23p04																				
Audley End	d		23p10																			07 47	
Newport (Essex)	d		23p13																				
Elsenham	d		23p19																				
Stansted Airport	a																						
Stansted Airport	d	23p15		23p30		23p45	23p59		00 30	05 30	06 00	06 30		07 00	07 15			07 30		07 45			08 00
Stansted Mountfitchet	d	23p21	23p22																	07 51			
Bishops Stortford	a		23p28	23p39			00 08		00 39	05 39	06 09	06 39		07 09				07 39				08 00	08 09
	d		23p28	23p39			00 08		00 39	05 39	06 09	06 39	06 42	07 09			07 28	07 39				08 00	08 09
Sawbridgeworth	d		23p32										06 46				07 32					08 05	
Harlow Mill	d		23p36														07 36						
Harlow Town	d	23p32	23p39			23p59	00 16		00 47	05 47	06 17	06 47	06 51	07 17	07 30		07 39			08 02		08 10	
Roydon	d		23p43														07 43						
Hertford East	d				23p39			00 07													07 55		
Ware	d				23p43																07 59		
St Margarets (Herts)	d				23p47																08 03		
Rye House	d				23p50																08 06		
Broxbourne [3]	a		23p47		23p54			00 19		05 53			06 57				07 48				08 11	08 16	
Broxbourne [3]	d		23p47		23p54					05 53			06 57			07 41	07 52				08 11	08 16	
Cheshunt	d		23p51		23p58								07 01			07 45	07 57				08 15	08 20	
Waltham Cross	d				00 01								07 04				07 59						
Enfield Lock	d				00 03								07 06				08 02						
Brimsdown	d				00 06								07 09				08 04						
Ponders End	d				00 08								07 11				08 06						
Angel Road	d																						
Northumberland Park	d																		←				
Tottenham Hale ⊖	d	23p48	23p59	00 03	00 14	00 17				06 04	06 33	07 03	07 17	07 33	07 46		08 12	08 01	08 12	08 17		08 29	08 32
Seven Sisters ⊖	d															08 03	→				08 33		
Clapton	d																						
Stratford [7] ⊖	a																		08 23				
Hackney Downs	d				00 20											08 09					08 39		
Bethnal Green	d																						
London Liverpool Street [15] ⊖	a	00 01	00 13	00 16	00 28	00 32	00 51		01 21	06 18	06 46	07 16	07 30	07 46	08 01	08 18		08 15		08 31	08 48	08 43	08 46

A not 11 December

Cambridge, Stansted Airport, Bishops Stortford, Hertford East and Broxbourne - London

Network Diagram - see first Page of Table 20

Station		LE 1 🍴	LE	LE 1	LE 1 🍴	LE 1		LE 1 🍴	LE	LE 1	LE 1 🍴	LE 1 🍴	LE	LE 1 🍴	LE 1	LE 1		XC 1	LE 1 🍴	LE	LE 1	LE 1 🍴	LE 1 🍴	LE	LE 1
Cambridge	d			07 51						08 32				08 51				09 15			09 32				09 51
Shelford	d			07 56										08 56											09 56
Whittlesford Parkway	d			08 00						08 39				09 00							09 39				10 00
Great Chesterford	d			08 04										09 04											10 04
Audley End	d			08 10						08 47				09 10				09 28			09 47				10 10
Newport (Essex)	d			08 13										09 13											10 13
Elsenham	d			08 19										09 19											10 19
Stansted Airport	a																	09 45							
Stansted Airport	d	08 15			08 30			08 45			09 00	09 15			09 30				09 45			10 00	10 15		
Stansted Mountfitchet	d			08 22				08 51						09 22					09 51						10 22
Bishops Stortford	a			08 28	08 39					09 00	09 09			09 28	09 39						10 00	10 09			10 28
	d			08 28	08 39					09 00	09 09			09 28	09 39						10 00	10 09			10 28
Sawbridgeworth	d			08 32						09 05				09 32							10 05				10 32
Harlow Mill	d			08 36										09 36											10 36
Harlow Town	d	08 30		08 39				09 02		09 10		09 30		09 39					10 02		10 10		10 30		10 39
Roydon	d			08 43										09 43											10 43
Hertford East	d		08 25						08 55				09 25							09 55				10 25	
Ware	d		08 29						08 59				09 29							09 59				10 29	
St Margarets (Herts)	d		08 33						09 03				09 33							10 03				10 33	
Rye House	d		08 36						09 06				09 36							10 06				10 36	
Broxbourne 3	a		08 41	08 48					09 11	09 16			09 41	09 48						10 11	10 16			10 41	10 48
Broxbourne 3	d		08 41	08 52					09 11	09 16			09 41	09 52						10 11	10 16			10 41	10 52
Cheshunt	d		08 45	08 57					09 15	09 20			09 45	09 57						10 15	10 20			10 45	10 57
Waltham Cross	d			08 59										09 59											10 59
Enfield Lock	d			09 02										10 02											11 02
Brimsdown	d			09 04										10 04											11 04
Ponders End	d			09 06										10 06											11 06
Angel Road	d																								
Northumberland Park	d					←										←									
Tottenham Hale ⊖	d	08 46		09 12	09 01	09 12		09 17		09 29	09 32	09 46		10 12	10 01	10 12			10 17		10 29	10 32	10 46		11 12
Seven Sisters ⊖	d		09 03	→					09 33				10 03	→						10 33				11 03	→
Clapton	d																								
Stratford 7 ⊖	a					09 23										10 23									
Hackney Downs	d		09 09						09 39				10 09							10 39				11 09	
Bethnal Green	d																								
London Liverpool Street 15 ⊖	a	09 00	09 18		09 15			09 31	09 48	09 43	09 46	10 01	10 18		10 15				10 31	10 48	10 43	10 46	11 01	11 18	

Station		LE 1 🍴		LE 1	XC 1	LE 1 🍴	LE	LE 1	LE 1 🍴	LE 1 🍴	LE	LE 1		LE 1 🍴	LE 1	XC 1	LE 1 🍴	LE	LE 1	LE 1 🍴	LE 1 🍴	LE		LE 1	LE 1 🍴
Cambridge	d				10 15			10 32				10 51				11 15			11 32					11 51	
Shelford	d											10 56												11 56	
Whittlesford Parkway	d							10 39				11 00							11 39					12 00	
Great Chesterford	d											11 04												12 04	
Audley End	d				10 28			10 47				11 10				11 28			11 47					12 10	
Newport (Essex)	d											11 13												12 13	
Elsenham	d											11 19												12 19	
Stansted Airport	a				10 45											11 45									
Stansted Airport	d	10 30				10 45			11 00	11 15				11 30			11 45			12 00	12 15				12 30
Stansted Mountfitchet	d					10 51						11 22					11 51							12 22	
Bishops Stortford	a	10 39						11 00	11 09			11 28		11 39					12 00	12 09				12 28	12 39
	d	10 39						11 00	11 09			11 28		11 39					12 00	12 09				12 28	12 39
Sawbridgeworth	d							11 05				11 32							12 05					12 32	
Harlow Mill	d											11 36												12 36	
Harlow Town	d					11 02		11 10		11 30		11 39					12 02		12 10		12 30			12 39	
Roydon	d											11 43												12 43	
Hertford East	d						10 55				11 25							11 55				12 25			
Ware	d						10 59				11 29							11 59				12 29			
St Margarets (Herts)	d						11 03				11 33							12 03				12 33			
Rye House	d						11 06				11 36							12 06				12 36			
Broxbourne 3	a						11 11	11 16			11 41	11 48						12 11	12 16			12 41		12 48	
Broxbourne 3	d						11 11	11 16			11 41	11 52						12 11	12 16			12 41		12 52	
Cheshunt	d						11 15	11 20			11 45	11 57						12 15	12 20			12 45		12 57	
Waltham Cross	d											11 59												12 59	
Enfield Lock	d											12 02												13 02	
Brimsdown	d											12 04												13 04	
Ponders End	d											12 06												13 06	
Angel Road	d																								
Northumberland Park	d			←											←										
Tottenham Hale ⊖	d	11 01		11 12		11 17		11 29	11 32	11 46		12 12		12 01	12 12		12 17		12 29	12 32	12 46			13 12	13 01
Seven Sisters ⊖	d						11 33				12 03	→						12 33				13 03		→	
Clapton	d																								
Stratford 7 ⊖	a			11 23											12 23										
Hackney Downs	d						11 39				12 09							12 39				13 09			
Bethnal Green	d																								
London Liverpool Street 15 ⊖	a	11 15				11 31	11 48	11 43	11 46	12 01	12 18			12 15			12 31	12 48	12 43	12 46	13 01	13 18			13 15

Table 22

Sundays

Cambridge, Stansted Airport, Bishops Stortford, Hertford East and Broxbourne - London

Network Diagram - see first Page of Table 20

		LE	XC	LE	LE	LE	LE	LE		LE	LE	LE	LE	XC	LE	LE	LE	LE		LE	LE	LE	LE	LE	XC
		1	1	1 🚲		1	1 🚲	1 🚲			1	1 🚲	1	1	1 🚲		1	1 🚲		1 🚲		1	1 🚲	1	◇1 A 🚲
Cambridge	d		12 15			12 32					12 51			13 15			13 32					13 51			14 10
Shelford	d										12 56											13 56			
Whittlesford Parkway	d					12 39					13 00						13 39					14 00			
Great Chesterford	d										13 04											14 04			
Audley End	d		12 28			12 47					13 10			13 28			13 47					14 10			14 24
Newport (Essex)	d										13 13											14 13			
Elsenham	d										13 19											14 19			
Stansted Airport	a		12 45											13 45											14 45
Stansted Airport	d			12 45			13 00	13 15				13 30			13 45			14 00		14 15			14 30		
Stansted Mountfitchet	d			12 51							13 22				13 51							14 22			
Bishops Stortford	a					13 00	13 09				13 28	13 39					14 00	14 09				14 28	14 39		
	d					13 00	13 09				13 28	13 39					14 00	14 09				14 28	14 39		
Sawbridgeworth	d					13 05					13 32						14 05					14 32			
Harlow Mill	d										13 36											14 36			
Harlow Town	d			13 02		13 10		13 30			13 39				14 02		14 10			14 30		14 39			
Roydon	d										13 43											14 43			
Hertford East	d				12 55					13 25						13 55					14 25				
Ware	d				12 59					13 29						13 59					14 29				
St Margarets (Herts)	d				13 03					13 33						14 03					14 33				
Rye House	d				13 06					13 36						14 06					14 36				
Broxbourne 3	a				13 11	13 16				13 41	13 48					14 11	14 16				14 41	14 48			
Broxbourne 3	d				13 11	13 16				13 41	13 52					14 11	14 16				14 41	14 52			
Cheshunt	d				13 15	13 20				13 45	13 57					14 15	14 20				14 45	14 57			
Waltham Cross	d										13 59											14 59			
Enfield Lock	d										14 02											15 02			
Brimsdown	d										14 04											15 04			
Ponders End	d										14 06											15 06			
Angel Road	d																								
Northumberland Park	d	←											←											←	
Tottenham Hale ⊖	d	13 12		13 17		13 29	13 32	13 46			14 12	14 01	14 12		14 17		14 29	14 32		14 46		15 12	15 01	15 12	
Seven Sisters ⊖	d				13 33					14 03	→					14 33					15 03	→			
Clapton	d																								
Stratford 7 ⊖	a	13 23											14 23											15 23	
Hackney Downs	d				13 39					14 09						14 39					15 09				
Bethnal Green	d																								
London Liverpool Street 15 ⊖	a			13 31	13 48	13 43	13 46	14 01		14 18		14 15			14 31	14 48	14 43	14 46		15 01	15 18		15 15		

			LE	LE		LE	LE	LE	LE	LE	LE	LE	XC			LE	LE	LE	LE	LE	LE	LE	LE	LE	
			1 🚲			1	1 🚲	1 🚲		1	1 🚲	1	◇1 A 🚲			1 🚲		1	1 🚲	1 🚲		1	1 🚲	1	
Cambridge	d					14 32				14 51			15 10					15 32				15 51			
Shelford	d									14 56												15 56			
Whittlesford Parkway	d					14 39				15 00								15 39				16 00			
Great Chesterford	d									15 04												16 04			
Audley End	d					14 47				15 10			15 24					15 47				16 10			
Newport (Essex)	d									15 13												16 13			
Elsenham	d									15 19												16 19			
Stansted Airport	a												15 45												
Stansted Airport	d		14 45				15 00	15 15			15 30					15 45			16 00	16 15			16 30		
Stansted Mountfitchet	d		14 51							15 22						15 51						16 22			
Bishops Stortford	a					15 00	15 09			15 28	15 39							16 00	16 09			16 28	16 39		
	d					15 00	15 09			15 28	15 39							16 00	16 09			16 28	16 39		
Sawbridgeworth	d					15 05				15 32								16 05				16 32			
Harlow Mill	d									15 36												16 36			
Harlow Town	d		15 02			15 10		15 30		15 39						16 02		16 10		16 30		16 39			
Roydon	d									15 43												16 43			
Hertford East	d			14 55					15 25								15 55				16 25				
Ware	d			14 59					15 29								15 59				16 29				
St Margarets (Herts)	d			15 03					15 33								16 03				16 33				
Rye House	d			15 06					15 36								16 06				16 36				
Broxbourne 3	a			15 11		15 16			15 41	15 48							16 11	16 16			16 41	16 48			
Broxbourne 3	d			15 11		15 16			15 41	15 52							16 11	16 16			16 41	16 52			
Cheshunt	d			15 15		15 20			15 45	15 57							16 15	16 20			16 45	16 57			
Waltham Cross	d									15 59												16 59			
Enfield Lock	d									16 02												17 02			
Brimsdown	d									16 04												17 04			
Ponders End	d									16 06												17 06			
Angel Road	d																								
Northumberland Park	d											←												←	
Tottenham Hale ⊖	d		15 17			15 29	15 32	15 46		16 12	16 01	16 12				16 17		16 29	16 32	16 46		17 12	17 01	17 12	
Seven Sisters ⊖	d			15 33					16 03	→							16 33				17 03	→			
Clapton	d																								
Stratford 7 ⊖	a											16 23												17 23	
Hackney Downs	d			15 39					16 09								16 39				17 09				
Bethnal Green	d																								
London Liverpool Street 15 ⊖	a		15 31	15 48		15 43	15 46	16 01	16 18		16 15					16 31	16 48	16 43	16 46	17 01	17 18		17 15		

A until 1 January and then from 19 February

Table 22

Sundays

Cambridge, Stansted Airport, Bishops Stortford, Hertford East and Broxbourne - London

Network Diagram - see first Page of Table 20

		XC	LE	LE	LE	LE	LE	LE	LE	LE		LE	XC	LE	LE	LE	LE	LE	LE	LE		LE	LE	XC	LE
		◇1	1		1	1	1		1	1		1	◇1	1		1	1	1		1		1	1	◇1	1
			🚲			🚲	🚲			🚲				🚲			🚲	🚲				🚲			🚲
Cambridge	d	16 10			16 32				16 51				17 10			17 32				17 51				18 10	
Shelford	d								16 56											17 56					
Whittlesford Parkway	d				16 39				17 00							17 39				18 00					
Great Chesterford	d								17 04											18 04					
Audley End	d	16 23			16 47				17 10				17 24			17 47				18 10				18 24	
Newport (Essex)	d								17 13											18 13					
Elsenham	d								17 19											18 19					
Stansted Airport	a	16 45											17 45											18 45	
Stansted Airport	d		16 45			17 00	17 15			17 30				17 45			18 00	18 15				18 30			18 45
Stansted Mountfitchet	d		16 51						17 22					17 51						18 22					18 51
Bishops Stortford	a				17 00	17 09			17 28	17 39						18 00	18 09			18 28		18 39			
	d				17 00	17 09			17 28	17 39						18 00	18 09			18 28		18 39			
Sawbridgeworth	d				17 05				17 32							18 05				18 32					
Harlow Mill	d								17 36											18 36					
Harlow Town	d		17 02		17 10		17 30		17 39					18 02		18 10		18 30		18 39					19 02
Roydon	d								17 43											18 43					
Hertford East	d			16 55				17 25							17 55				18 25						
Ware	d			16 59				17 29							17 59				18 29						
St Margarets (Herts)	d			17 03				17 33							18 03				18 33						
Rye House	d			17 06				17 36							18 06				18 36						
Broxbourne 3	a			17 11	17 16			17 41	17 48						18 11	18 16			18 41	18 48					
Broxbourne 3	d			17 11	17 16			17 41	17 52						18 11	18 16			18 41	18 52					
Cheshunt	d			17 15	17 20			17 45	17 57						18 15	18 20			18 45	18 57					
Waltham Cross	d								17 59											18 59					
Enfield Lock	d								18 02											19 02					
Brimsdown	d								18 04											19 04					
Ponders End	d								18 06											19 06					
Angel Road	d																								
Northumberland Park	d											←											←		
Tottenham Hale ⊖	d		17 17		17 29	17 32	17 46		18 12	18 01		18 12		18 17		18 29	18 32	18 46		19 12		19 01	19 12		19 17
Seven Sisters ⊖	d			17 33				18 03	→						18 33				19 03	→					
Clapton	d																								
Stratford 7 ⊖	a											18 23											19 23		
Hackney Downs	d			17 39				18 09							18 39				19 09						
Bethnal Green	d																								
London Liverpool Street 15 ⊖	a		17 31	17 48	17 43	17 46	18 01	18 18		18 15				18 31	18 48	18 43	18 46	19 01	19 18			19 15			19 31

		LE	LE	LE	LE	LE		LE	LE	LE	XC	LE	LE	LE	LE	XC		LE	LE	LE	LE	LE	XC	LE	LE
			1	1	1			1	1	1	◇1	1		1	1	◇1		1		1	1	1	◇1	1	
											A					B									
				🚲	🚲				🚲			🚲			🚲			🚲			🚲			🚲	
Cambridge	d		18 32					18 51			19 10			19 32		19 36				19 51			20 10		
Shelford	d							18 56												19 56					
Whittlesford Parkway	d		18 39					19 00						19 39						20 00					
Great Chesterford	d							19 04												20 04					
Audley End	d		18 47					19 10			19 24			19 47		19 51				20 10			20 24		
Newport (Essex)	d							19 13												20 13					
Elsenham	d							19 19												20 19					
Stansted Airport	a										19 45					20 08							20 45		
Stansted Airport	d			19 00	19 15				19 30			19 45			20 00			20 15			20 30			20 45	
Stansted Mountfitchet	d							19 22				19 51								20 22				20 51	
Bishops Stortford	a		19 00	19 09				19 28	19 39					20 00	20 09					20 28	20 39				
	d		19 00	19 09				19 28	19 39					20 00	20 09					20 28	20 39				
Sawbridgeworth	d		19 05					19 32						20 05						20 32					
Harlow Mill	d							19 36												20 36					
Harlow Town	d		19 10		19 30			19 39				20 02		20 10				20 30		20 39				21 02	
Roydon	d							19 43												20 43					
Hertford East	d	18 55				19 25							19 55						20 25						20 55
Ware	d	18 59				19 29							19 59						20 29						20 59
St Margarets (Herts)	d	19 03				19 33							20 03						20 33						21 03
Rye House	d	19 06				19 36							20 06						20 36						21 06
Broxbourne 3	a	19 11	19 16			19 41		19 48					20 11	20 16					20 41	20 48					21 11
Broxbourne 3	d	19 11	19 16			19 41		19 52					20 11	20 16					20 41	20 52					21 11
Cheshunt	d	19 15	19 20			19 45		19 57					20 15	20 20					20 45	20 57					21 15
Waltham Cross	d							19 59												20 59					
Enfield Lock	d							20 02												21 02					
Brimsdown	d							20 04												21 04					
Ponders End	d							20 06												21 06					
Angel Road	d																								
Northumberland Park	d									←												←			
Tottenham Hale ⊖	d		19 29	19 32	19 46			20 12	20 01	20 12		20 17		20 29	20 32			20 46		21 12	21 01	21 12		21 17	
Seven Sisters ⊖	d	19 33				20 03		→					20 33						21 03	→					21 33
Clapton	d																								
Stratford 7 ⊖	a									20 23												21 23			
Hackney Downs	d	19 39				20 09							20 39						21 09						21 39
Bethnal Green	d																								
London Liverpool Street 15 ⊖	a	19 48	19 43	19 46	20 01	20 18			20 15			20 31	20 48	20 43	20 46			21 01	21 18		21 15			21 31	21 48

A until 1 January and then from 19 February

B from 8 January until 12 February

Table 22

Sundays

Cambridge, Stansted Airport, Bishops Stortford, Hertford East and Broxbourne - London

Network Diagram - see first Page of Table 20

		LE	LE	LE	LE	LE	LE	LE	XC	LE	XC
		[1]	[1]	[1]		[1]	[1]	[1]	◇[1]	[1]	◇[1]
									A		B
			🚲	🚲			🚲			🚲	
Cambridge	d	20 32				20 51			21 10		21 24
Shelford	d					20 56					
Whittlesford Parkway	d	20 39				21 00					
Great Chesterford	d					21 04					
Audley End	d	20 47				21 10			21 24		21 38
Newport (Essex)	d					21 13					
Elsenham	d					21 19					
Stansted Airport	a								21 45		21 59
Stansted Airport	d		21 00	21 15			21 30			21 45	
Stansted Mountfitchet	d					21 22				21 51	
Bishops Stortford	a	21 00	21 09			21 28	21 39				
	d	21 00	21 09			21 28	21 39				
Sawbridgeworth	d	21 05				21 32					
Harlow Mill	d					21 36					
Harlow Town	d	21 10		21 30		21 39				22 02	
Roydon	d					21 43					
Hertford East	d				21 25						
Ware	d				21 29						
St Margarets (Herts)	d				21 33						
Rye House	d				21 36						
Broxbourne [3]	a	21 16			21 41	21 48					
Broxbourne [3]	d	21 16			21 41	21 52					
Cheshunt	d	21 20			21 45	21 57					
Waltham Cross	d					21 59					
Enfield Lock	d					22 02					
Brimsdown	d					22 04					
Ponders End	d					22 06					
Angel Road	d										
Northumberland Park	d							←			
Tottenham Hale ⊖	d	21 29	21 32	21 46		22 12	22 01	22 12		22 17	
Seven Sisters ⊖	d				22 03	↪					
Clapton	d										
Stratford [7] ⊖	a							22 23			
Hackney Downs	d				22 09						
Bethnal Green	d										
London Liverpool Street [15] ⊖	a	21 43	21 46	22 01	22 18		22 15			22 31	

		LE	LE	LE	LE	LE	LE	LE	LE	XC	XC	LE
			[1]	[1]	[1]		[1]	[1]	[1]	◇[1]	◇[1]	[1]
										A	B	
Cambridge	d		21 32				21 51			22 10	22 17	
Shelford	d						21 56					
Whittlesford Parkway	d		21 39				22 00					
Great Chesterford	d						22 04					
Audley End	d		21 47				22 10			22 24	22 31	
Newport (Essex)	d						22 13					
Elsenham	d						22 19					
Stansted Airport	a									22 45	22 45	
Stansted Airport	d			22 00	22 15			22 30				22 45
Stansted Mountfitchet	d						22 22					22 51
Bishops Stortford	a		22 00	22 09			22 28	22 39				
	d		22 00	22 09			22 28	22 39				
Sawbridgeworth	d		22 05				22 32					
Harlow Mill	d						22 36					
Harlow Town	d		22 10		22 30		22 39					23 02
Roydon	d						22 43					
Hertford East	d	21 55				22 25						
Ware	d	21 59				22 29						
St Margarets (Herts)	d	22 03				22 33						
Rye House	d	22 06				22 36						
Broxbourne [3]	a	22 11	22 16			22 41	22 48					
Broxbourne [3]	d	22 11	22 16			22 41	22 52					
Cheshunt	d	22 15	22 20			22 45	22 57					
Waltham Cross	d						22 59					
Enfield Lock	d						23 02					
Brimsdown	d						23 04					
Ponders End	d						23 06					
Angel Road	d											
Northumberland Park	d								←			
Tottenham Hale ⊖	d		22 29	22 32	22 46		23 12	23 01	23 12			23 17
Seven Sisters ⊖	d	22 33				23 03	↪					
Clapton	d											
Stratford [7] ⊖	a								23 23			
Hackney Downs	d	22 39				23 09						
Bethnal Green	d											
London Liverpool Street [15] ⊖	a	22 48	22 43	22 46	23 01	23 18		23 15				23 31

		LE	LE	LE	LE	LE	LE	LE	LE
			[1]	[1]	[1]	[1]	[1]	[1]	[1]
Cambridge	d		22 32	22 51					
Shelford	d			22 56					
Whittlesford Parkway	d		22 39	23 00					
Great Chesterford	d			23 04					
Audley End	d		22 47	23 10					
Newport (Essex)	d			23 13					
Elsenham	d			23 19					
Stansted Airport	a								
Stansted Airport	d				23 00	23 15	23 30	23 45	23 59
Stansted Mountfitchet	d			23 22					
Bishops Stortford	a		23 00	23 28	23 09		23 39		00 08
	d		23 00		23 09		23 39		00 08
Sawbridgeworth	d		23 05						
Harlow Mill	d								
Harlow Town	d		23 10			23 30	23 47	23 59	00 16
Roydon	d								
Hertford East	d	22 55							
Ware	d	22 59							
St Margarets (Herts)	d	23 03							
Rye House	d	23 06							
Broxbourne [3]	a	23 11	23 16						
Broxbourne [3]	d	23 11	23 16						
Cheshunt	d	23 15	23 20						
Waltham Cross	d								
Enfield Lock	d								
Brimsdown	d								
Ponders End	d								
Angel Road	d								
Northumberland Park	d								
Tottenham Hale ⊖	d		23 29		23 32	23 46			
Seven Sisters ⊖	d	23 33					00 08	00 21	
Clapton	d								
Stratford [7] ⊖	a								
Hackney Downs	d	23 39							
Bethnal Green	d								
London Liverpool Street [15] ⊖	a	23 48	23 43		23 46	00 01	00 22	00 35	00 51

A until 1 January and then from 19 February

B from 8 January until 12 February

Network Diagram for Tables 24, 25

DM-2/11
Design BAJ3

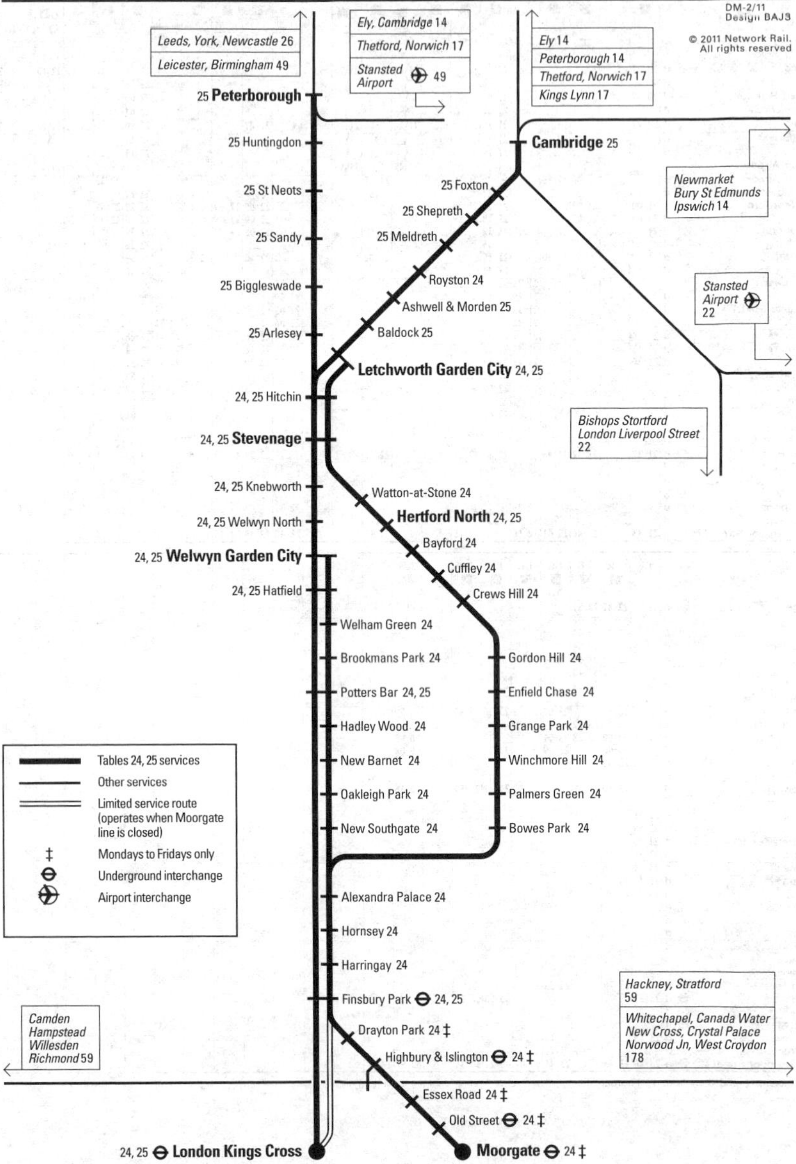

London - Welwyn Garden City, Hertford North and Letchworth Garden City

Network Diagram - see first Page of Table 24

Miles	Miles	Station		FC	FC	FC	FC	FC	FC	FC	FC	FC	FC	FC	FC	FC	FC	FC	FC	FC	FC	FC	FC
				MO	MX	MX	MX	MO	MX	MO	MX			MX	MO								
						1				1			1	1	1	1	1				1		
0	—	London Kings Cross 15 ⊖	d	23p26	23p26	23p36		23p41	23p41	00 07	00 06	00 11	00 36	01 06	01 06	01 36	05 23		05 26	05 56	06 06	06 11	06 26
—	0	**Moorgate** ⊖	d																				
—	0½	Old Street ⊖	d																				
—	1¾	Essex Road	d																				
—	2¼	Highbury & Islington ⊖	d																				
—	2¾	Drayton Park	d																				
2½	3½	Finsbury Park ⊖	d	23p32	23p32	23p41		23p47	23p47	00 12	00 12	00 17	00 41	01 11	01 11	01 41	05 28		05 32	06 02	06 11	06 17	06 32
3½	4½	Harringay	d	23p34	23p34			23p49	23p49		00 14	00 19							05 34	06 04		06 19	06 34
4	5	Hornsey	d	23p36	23p36			23p51	23p51		00 16	00 21							05 36	06 06		06 21	06 36
5	6	Alexandra Palace	d	23p38	23p38			23p53	23p53	00 17	00 18	00 23		01 16	01 16	01 45			05 38	06 08		06 23	06 38
6½	—	New Southgate	d					23p56	23p56			00 26				01 48						06 26	
8½	—	Oakleigh Park	d					23p59	23p59			00 29				01 51						06 29	
9¼	—	New Barnet	d					00 01	00 01			00 31				01 53						06 31	
10½	—	Hadley Wood	d					00 04	00 04			00 34				01 56						06 34	
12¾	—	Potters Bar	d			23p51		00 08	00 08			00 38	00 51			01 59	05 38				06 21	06 38	
14½	—	Brookmans Park	d					00 11	00 11			00 41										06 41	
15½	—	Welham Green	d					00 13	00 13			00 43										06 43	
17¾	—	Hatfield	d			23p57		00 16	00 16			00 46	00 57			02 05	05 44				06 27	06 46	
20¼	—	**Welwyn Garden City 4**	d			00 01		00 20	00a24			00a54	01 01			02 09	05 48				06 31	06a53	
22	—	Welwyn North	d			00 04		00 23					01s04			02s12	05 51				06 34		
25	—	Knebworth	d			00 08		00 28					01s08			02s16	05 55				06 38		
—	6¾	Bowes Park	d	23p41	23p41						00 21								05 41	06 11			06 41
—	7¾	Palmers Green	d	23p43	23p43					00 20	00 23			01 19	01 19				05 43	06 13			06 43
—	8¾	Winchmore Hill	d	23p45	23p45					00 22	00 25			01 21	01 21				05 45	06 15			06 45
—	9½	Grange Park	d	23p47	23p47						00 27								05 47	06 17			06 47
—	10¼	Enfield Chase	d	23p49	23p49					00 25	00 29			01 24	01 24				05 49	06 19			06 49
—	11	Gordon Hill	d	23p51	23p51					00 27	00 31			01 26	01 26				05 51	06 21			06 51
—	12½	Crews Hill	d	23p54	23p54						00 34								05 54	06 24			06 54
—	14¼	Cuffley	d	23p57	23p57					00 31	00 37			01 30	01 30				05 57	06 27			06 57
—	17¾	Bayford	d	00 02	00 02						00 42								06 02	06 32			07 02
—	20¾	**Hertford North**	d	00 07	00 07					00 39	00 47			01 38	01 38			05 50	06a10	06 40			07 10
—	25	Watton-at-Stone	d	00 13	00 13		←				00 53							05 55		06 45			07 15
27½	30	**Stevenage 4**	d	00a20	00 20	00 12	00 20	00 31		00 48	01 00		01 12	01 47	01 47	02 20	05 59	06a04		06a55	06 42		07a25
31¾	34¼	Hitchin 4	d		→	00 20	00 26	00 37		00 56	01 06		01a17	01 52	01 52	02a25	06a07				06 47		
34¾	37¼	**Letchworth Garden City**	a			00 29	00 36	00 52		01 00	01 15			02 01	02 06						06 51		

Station		FC	FC	FC	FC	FC	FC	FC	FC	FC	FC	FC	FC	FC	FC	FC	FC	FC	FC	FC	FC	FC	FC
		1			1			1				1								1			
London Kings Cross 15 ⊖	d	06 36			07 06			07 36				08 03								08 36			
Moorgate ⊖	d		06 35	06 50		07 05	07 20		07 33	07 38	07 48			07 58	08 03	08 08	08 18	08 23	08 28			08 33	08 38
Old Street ⊖	d		06 37	06 52		07 07	07 22		07 35	07 40	07 50			08 00	08 05	08 10	08 20	08 25	08 30			08 35	08 40
Essex Road	d		06 40	06 55		07 10	07 25		07 38	07 43	07 53			08 03	08 08	08 13	08 23	08 28	08 33			08 38	08 43
Highbury & Islington ⊖	d		06 42	06 57		07 12	07 27		07 40	07 45	07 55			08 05	08 10	08 15	08 25	08 30	08 35			08 40	08 45
Drayton Park	d		06 44	06 59		07 14	07 29		07 42	07 47	07 57			08 07	08 12	08 17	08 27	08 32	08 37			08 42	08 47
Finsbury Park ⊖	d	06 41	06 47	07 02	07 11	07 17	07 32	07 41	07 45	07 50	08 00	08 08		08 10	08 15	08 20	08 30	08 35	08 40	08 41		08 45	08 50
Harringay	d		06 49	07 04		07 19	07 34			07 52	08 02					08 22	08 32	08 37				08 47	08 52
Hornsey	d		06 51	07 06		07 21	07 36			07 54	08 04					08 24	08 34	08 39				08 49	08 54
Alexandra Palace	d		06 53	07 08		07 23	07 38		07 51	07 56	08 06			08 14	08 21	08 26	08 36	08 41	08 45			08 51	08 56
New Southgate	d		06 56			07 26				07 59						08 29		08 44					08 59
Oakleigh Park	d		06 59			07 29				08 02						08 32		08 47					09 02
New Barnet	d		07 01			07 31				08 04						08 34		08 49					09 04
Hadley Wood	d		07 04			07 34				08 07						08 37		08 52			←		09 07
Potters Bar	d	06 51	07 08		07 21	07 38		07 51		08 11		08 18				08 41		08 56		08 51	08 56		09 11
Brookmans Park	d		07 11			07 41				08 14						08 44		→			08 59		09 14
Welham Green	d		07 13			07 43				08 16						08 46					09 01		09 16
Hatfield	d	06 57	07 16		07 27	07 46		07 57		08 19		08 25				08 49				08 57	09 04		09 19
Welwyn Garden City 4	d	07 01	07a21		07 31	07a51		08 01		08a24		08 30				08a54				09 01	09a09		09a27
Welwyn North	d	07 04			07 34			08 04				08 33								09 04			
Knebworth	d	07 08			07 38			08 08				08 37								09 08			
Bowes Park	d			07 11			07 41				08 09			08 17			08 39		08 48				
Palmers Green	d			07 13			07 43		07 55		08 11			08 19	08 25		08 41		08 50			08 55	
Winchmore Hill	d			07 15			07 45		07 57		08 13			08 21	08 27		08 43		08 52			08 57	
Grange Park	d			07 17			07 47				08 15			08 23			08 45		08 54				
Enfield Chase	d			07 19			07 49		08 01		08 17			08 25	08 31		08 47		08 56			09 01	
Gordon Hill	d			07 21			07 51		08 03		08 19			08a29	08 33		08 49		08a59			09 03	
Crews Hill	d			07 24			07 54				08 22						08 52						
Cuffley	d			07 27			07 57		08 08		08 25				08 38		08 55					09 08	
Bayford	d			07 32			08 02				08 30						09 00						
Hertford North	d			07 40			08 10		08a16		08 37				08a46		09 07					09a16	
Watton-at-Stone	d			07 45			08 15				08 43		←				09 13						
Stevenage 4	d	07 12		07a55	07 42		08a25	08 12			08 51	08 41	08 51				09a22			09 12			
Hitchin 4	d	07a17			07 47			08a17			→	08 46	08 57							09a17			
Letchworth Garden City	a				07 51							08 50	09 03										

London - Welwyn Garden City, Hertford North and Letchworth Garden City

Network Diagram - see first Page of Table 24

	FC	FC	FC 1		FC	FC	FC	FC	FC 1	FC	FC	FC	FC		FC	FC 1	FC	FC	FC	FC	FC 1	FC	FC	
London Kings Cross 15 ⊖ d			09 06						09 36							10 06					10 36			
Moorgate ⊖ d	08 43	08 52				09 02	09 12	09 22				09 32	09 42		09 52			10 02	10 12	10 22			10 32	
Old Street ⊖ d	08 45	08 54				09 04	09 14	09 24				09 34	09 44		09 54			10 04	10 14	10 24			10 34	
Essex Road d	08 48	08 57				09 07	09 17	09 27				09 37	09 47		09 57			10 07	10 17	10 27			10 37	
Highbury & Islington ⊖ d	08 50	08 59				09 09	09 19	09 29				09 39	09 49		09 59			10 09	10 19	10 29			10 39	
Drayton Park d	08 52	09 01				09 11	09 21	09 31				09 41	09 51		10 01			10 11	10 21	10 31			10 41	
Finsbury Park ⊖ d	08 55	09 04	09 11			09 14	09 24	09 34	09 41			09 44	09 54		10 04	10 11		10 14	10 24	10 34	10 41		10 44	
Harringay d	08 57	09 06				09 16	09 26	09 36				09 46	09 56		10 06			10 16	10 26	10 36			10 46	
Hornsey d	08 59	09 08				09 18	09 28	09 38				09 48	09 58		10 08			10 18	10 28	10 38			10 48	
Alexandra Palace d	09 01	09 10				09 20	09 30	09 40				09 50	10 00		10 10			10 20	10 30	10 40			10 50	
New Southgate d						09 23		09 43					10 03					10 23		10 43				
Oakleigh Park d						09 26		09 46					10 06					10 26		10 46				
New Barnet d						09 28		09 48					10 08					10 28		10 48				
Hadley Wood d						09 31		09 51			←		10 11					10 31		10 51		←		
Potters Bar d			09 21			09 35		09 55	09 51		09 55		10 15			10 21		10 35		10 55	10 51	10 55		
Brookmans Park d						09 38		→			09 58		10 18					10 38		→		10 58		
Welham Green d						09 40					10 00		10 20					10 40				11 00		
Hatfield d			09 27			09 43			09 57		10 03		10 23			10 27		10 43			10 57	11 03		
Welwyn Garden City 4 d			09 31			09a49			10 01		10a09		10a29			10 31		10a49			11 01	11a09		
Welwyn North d			09 34						10 04							10 34					11 04			
Knebworth d			09 38						10 08							10 38					11 08			
Bowes Park d	09 04	09 13					09 33					09 53			10 13				10 33				10 53	
Palmers Green d	09 06	09 15					09 35					09 55			10 15				10 35				10 55	
Winchmore Hill d	09 08	09 17					09 37					09 57			10 17				10 37				10 57	
Grange Park d	09 10	09 19					09 39					09 59			10 19				10 39				10 59	
Enfield Chase d	09 12	09 21					09 41					10 01			10 21				10 41				11 01	
Gordon Hill d	09a16	09 23					09 43					10 03			10 23				10 43				11 03	
Crews Hill d		09 26					09 46					10 06			10 26				10 46				11 06	
Cuffley d		09 29					09 49					10 09			10 29				10 49				11 09	
Bayford d		09 34					09 54					10 14			10 34				10 54				11 14	
Hertford North d		09 39					10 09					10a20			10 39				11a00				11a20	
Watton-at-Stone d		09 45			←		10 15			←					10 45		←							
Stevenage 4 d		09 51	09 42		09 51		10 21		10 12	10 21					10 51	10 42	10 51				11 12			
Hitchin 4 d		→	09 47		09 57		→		10a17	10 27					→	10 47	10 57				11a17			
Letchworth Garden City a			09 51		10 03					10 33						10 51	11 03							

	FC	FC	FC 1	FC	FC	FC	FC	FC 1	FC		FC	FC	FC	FC 1	FC	FC	FC	FC	FC 1		FC	FC	FC	FC
London Kings Cross 15 ⊖ d			11 06					11 36						12 06					12 36					
Moorgate ⊖ d	10 42	10 52			11 02	11 12	11 22				11 32	11 42	11 52			12 02	12 12	12 22				12 32	12 42	12 52
Old Street ⊖ d	10 44	10 54			11 04	11 14	11 24				11 34	11 44	11 54			12 04	12 14	12 24				12 34	12 44	12 54
Essex Road d	10 47	10 57			11 07	11 17	11 27				11 37	11 47	11 57			12 07	12 17	12 27				12 37	12 47	12 57
Highbury & Islington ⊖ d	10 49	10 59			11 09	11 19	11 29				11 39	11 49	11 59			12 09	12 19	12 29				12 39	12 49	12 59
Drayton Park d	10 51	11 01			11 11	11 21	11 31				11 41	11 51	12 01			12 11	12 21	12 31				12 41	12 51	13 01
Finsbury Park ⊖ d	10 54	11 04	11 11		11 14	11 24	11 34	11 41			11 44	11 54	12 04	12 11		12 14	12 24	12 34	12 41			12 44	12 54	13 04
Harringay d	10 56	11 06			11 16	11 26	11 36				11 46	11 56	12 06			12 16	12 26	12 36				12 46	12 56	13 06
Hornsey d	10 58	11 08			11 18	11 28	11 38				11 48	11 58	12 08			12 18	12 28	12 38				12 48	12 58	13 08
Alexandra Palace d	11 00	11 10			11 20	11 30	11 40				11 50	12 00	12 10			12 20	12 30	12 40				12 50	13 00	13 10
New Southgate d	11 03				11 23		11 43					12 03				12 23		12 43					13 03	
Oakleigh Park d	11 06				11 26		11 46					12 06				12 26		12 46					13 06	
New Barnet d	11 08				11 28		11 48					12 08				12 28		12 48					13 08	
Hadley Wood d	11 11				11 31		11 51		←			12 11				12 31		12 51			←		13 11	
Potters Bar d	11 15		11 21		11 35		11 55	11 51	11 55			12 15		12 21		12 35		12 55	12 51		12 55		13 15	
Brookmans Park d	11 18				11 38		→		11 58			12 18				12 38		→			12 58		13 18	
Welham Green d	11 20				11 40				12 00			12 20				12 40					13 00		13 20	
Hatfield d	11 23		11 27		11 43			11 57	12 03			12 23		12 27		12 43			12 57		13 03		13 23	
Welwyn Garden City 4 d	11a29		11 31		11a49			12 01	12a09			12a29		12 31		12a49			13 01		13a09		13a29	
Welwyn North d			11 34					12 04						12 34					13 04					
Knebworth d			11 38					12 08						12 38					13 08					
Bowes Park d		11 13				11 33					11 53		12 13				12 33					12 53		13 13
Palmers Green d		11 15				11 35					11 55		12 15				12 35					12 55		13 15
Winchmore Hill d		11 17				11 37					11 57		12 17				12 37					12 57		13 17
Grange Park d		11 19				11 39					11 59		12 19				12 39					12 59		13 19
Enfield Chase d		11 21				11 41					12 01		12 21				12 41					13 01		13 21
Gordon Hill d		11 23				11 43					12 03		12 23				12 43					13 03		13 23
Crews Hill d		11 26				11 46					12 06		12 26				12 46					13 06		13 26
Cuffley d		11 29				11 49					12 09		12 29				12 49					13 09		13 29
Bayford d		11 34				11 54					12 14		12 34				12 54					13 14		13 34
Hertford North d		11 39				12a00					12a20		12 39				13a00					13a20		13 39
Watton-at-Stone d		11 45		←									12 45		←									13 45
Stevenage 4 d		11 51	11 42	11 51				12 12					12 51	12 42	12 51				13 12					13 51
Hitchin 4 d		→	11 47	11 57				12a17					→	12 47	12 57				13a17					→
Letchworth Garden City a			11 51	12 03										12 51	13 03									

Table 24

Mondays to Fridays

London - Welwyn Garden City, Hertford North and Letchworth Garden City

Network Diagram - see first Page of Table 24

		FC 1	FC	FC	FC	FC		FC 1	FC	FC	FC	FC	FC 1	FC	FC	FC		FC	FC 1	FC	FC	FC	FC	FC 1	FC
London Kings Cross 15 ⊖	d	13 06						13 36					14 06						14 36					15 06	
Moorgate ⊖	d			13 02	13 12	13 22				13 32	13 42	13 52			14 02	14 12		14 22			14 32	14 42	14 52		
Old Street ⊖	d			13 04	13 14	13 24				13 34	13 44	13 54			14 04	14 14		14 24			14 34	14 44	14 54		
Essex Road	d			13 07	13 17	13 27				13 37	13 47	13 57			14 07	14 17		14 27			14 37	14 47	14 57		
Highbury & Islington ⊖	d			13 09	13 19	13 29				13 39	13 49	13 59			14 09	14 19		14 29			14 39	14 49	14 59		
Drayton Park	d			13 11	13 21	13 31				13 41	13 51	14 01			14 11	14 21		14 31			14 41	14 51	15 01		
Finsbury Park ⊖	d	13 11		13 14	13 24	13 34		13 41		13 44	13 54	14 04	14 11		14 14	14 24		14 34	14 41		14 44	14 54	15 04	15 11	
Harringay	d			13 16	13 26	13 36				13 46	13 56	14 06			14 16	14 26		14 36			14 46	14 56	15 06		
Hornsey	d			13 18	13 28	13 38				13 48	13 58	14 08			14 18	14 28		14 38			14 48	14 58	15 08		
Alexandra Palace	d			13 20	13 30	13 40				13 50	14 00	14 10			14 20	14 30		14 40			14 50	15 00	15 10		
New Southgate	d			13 23		13 43					14 03				14 23			14 43				15 03			
Oakleigh Park	d			13 26		13 46					14 06				14 26			14 46				15 06			
New Barnet	d			13 28		13 48					14 08				14 28			14 48				15 08			
Hadley Wood	d			13 31		13 51			←		14 11				14 31			14 51		←		15 11			
Potters Bar	d	13 21		13 35		13 55		13 51	13 55		14 15		14 21		14 35			14 55	14 51	14 55		15 15		15 21	
Brookmans Park	d			13 38		↪			13 58		14 18				14 38			↪		14 58		15 18			
Welham Green	d			13 40					14 00		14 20				14 40					15 00		15 20			
Hatfield	d	13 27		13 43				13 57	14 03		14 23		14 27		14 43				14 57	15 03		15 23		15 27	
Welwyn Garden City 4	d	13 31		13a49				14 01	14a09		14a29		14 31		14a49				15 01	15a09		15a29		15 31	
Welwyn North	d	13 34						14 04					14 34						15 04					15 34	
Knebworth	d	13 38						14 08					14 38						15 08					15 38	
Bowes Park	d				13 33					13 53		14 13				14 33					14 53		15 13		
Palmers Green	d				13 35					13 55		14 15				14 35					14 55		15 15		
Winchmore Hill	d				13 37					13 57		14 17				14 37					14 57		15 17		
Grange Park	d				13 39					13 59		14 19				14 39					14 59		15 19		
Enfield Chase	d				13 41					14 01		14 21				14 41					15 01		15 21		
Gordon Hill	d				13 43					14 03		14 23				14 43					15 03		15 23		
Crews Hill	d				13 46					14 06		14 26				14 46					15 06		15 26		
Cuffley	d				13 49					14 09		14 29				14 49					15 09		15 29		
Bayford	d				13 54					14 14		14 34				14 54					15 14		15 34		
Hertford North	d				14a00					14a20		14 39				15a00					15a20		15 39		
Watton-at-Stone	d		←									14 45		←									15 45		←
Stevenage 4	d	13 42	13 51					14 12				14 51	14 42	14 51					15 12				15 51	15 42	15 51
Hitchin 4	d	13 47	13 57					14a17				↪	14 47	14 57					15a17				↪	15 47	15 57
Letchworth Garden City	a	13 51	14 03										14 51	15 03										15 51	16 03

		FC		FC	FC	FC 1	FC	FC	FC	FC	FC	FC 1		FC	FC	FC	FC	FC 1	FC	FC	FC	FC 1		FC	FC
London Kings Cross 15 ⊖	d					15 36			15 44			16 06						16 32				16 54		16 54	
Moorgate ⊖	d	15 02		15 12	15 22			15 32		15 42	15 52			16 02	16 08	16 18	16 23		16 28	16 33	16 38				16 48
Old Street ⊖	d	15 04		15 14	15 24			15 34		15 44	15 54			16 04	16 10	16 20	16 25		16 30	16 35	16 40				16 50
Essex Road	d	15 07		15 17	15 27			15 37		15 47	15 57			16 07	16 13	16 23	16 28		16 33	16 38	16 43				16 53
Highbury & Islington ⊖	d	15 09		15 19	15 29			15 39		15 49	15 59			16 09	16 16	16 26	16 31		16 36	16 41	16 46				16 56
Drayton Park	d	15 11		15 21	15 31			15 41		15 51	16 01			16 11	16 17	16 27	16 32		16 37	16 42	16 47				16 57
Finsbury Park ⊖	d	15 14		15 24	15 34	15 41		15 44	15 50	15 54	16 04	16 11		16 14	16 20	16 30	16 35	16 37	16 40	16 45	16 50	16 59		16 59	17 00
Harringay	d	15 16		15 26	15 36			15 46		15 56	16 06			16 16	16 23	16 33			16 43		16 53				
Hornsey	d	15 18		15 28	15 38			15 48		15 58	16 08			16 18	16 25	16 35			16 45		16 55				
Alexandra Palace	d	15 20		15 30	15 40			15 50		16 00	16 10			16 20	16 28	16 38	16 41		16 47	16 51	16 58				
New Southgate	d	15 23			15 43				15 55	16 03				16 23					16 50					17 04	
Oakleigh Park	d	15 26			15 46				15 58	16 06				16 26					16 54					17 08	
New Barnet	d	15 28			15 48				16 00	16 08				16 28					16 56					17 10	
Hadley Wood	d	15 31			15 51		←			16 11				16 31					16 59					17 12	
Potters Bar	d	15 35			15 55	15 51	15 55		16 05	16 15		16 21		16 35				16 47	17 03					17 16	
Brookmans Park	d	15 38			↪		15 58			16 18				16 38					17 06						
Welham Green	d	15 40					16 00			16 20				16 40					17 08						
Hatfield	d	15 43				15 58	16 03		16 11	16 23		16 28		16 43				16 54	17 11			17 15		17 22	
Welwyn Garden City 4	d	15a49				16 02	16a09		16a16	16a29		16 32		16a49				16 58	17a16			17 19		17a27	
Welwyn North	d					16 05						16 35						17 01				17 22			
Knebworth	d					16 09						16 39						17 06				17 26			
Bowes Park	d			15 33				15 53			16 13				16 30		16 44				17 00				17 07
Palmers Green	d			15 35				15 55			16 15				16 32	16 41	16 46			16 54	17 02				17 09
Winchmore Hill	d			15 37				15 57			16 17				16 35	16 44	16 49			16 57	17 05				17 12
Grange Park	d			15 39				15 59			16 19				16 37		16 51				17 07				17 14
Enfield Chase	d			15 41				16 01			16 21				16 39	16 47	16 53			17 01	17 09				17 16
Gordon Hill	d			15 43				16 03			16 23				16 41	16a51	16 55			17 03	17a12				17 18
Crews Hill	d			15 46				16 06			16 26				16 44					17 06					
Cuffley	d			15 49				16 09			16 29				16 47		17 00			17 09					17 23
Bayford	d			15 54				16 14			16 34				16 52					17 14					
Hertford North	d			16 09				16a20			16 39				16a58		17 09			17a20					17 33
Watton-at-Stone	d			16 15							16 45						17 15								17 38
Stevenage 4	d			16a23		16 12					16a53	16 45					17a23	17 10				17 36			17a46
Hitchin 4	d					16a17						16 50						17 17				17 42			
Letchworth Garden City	a											16 55						17 21				17 47			

London - Welwyn Garden City, Hertford North and Letchworth Garden City

Network Diagram - see first Page of Table 24

	FC	FC	FC	FC	FC	FC 1	FC		FC	FC	FC	FC	FC	FC	FC	FC 1	FC		FC	FC	FC	FC	FC	FC
London Kings Cross 15 ⊖ d						17 22				17 27						17 52				17 57				
Moorgate ⊖ d	16 53	16 58	17 03	17 08	17 13				17 18		17 23	17 28	17 33	17 38	17 43				17 48		17 53	17 58	18 03	18 08
Old Street ⊖ d	16 55	17 00	17 05	17 10	17 15				17 20		17 25	17 30	17 35	17 40	17 45				17 50		17 55	18 00	18 05	18 10
Essex Road d	16 58	17 03	17 08	17 13	17 18				17 23		17 28	17 33	17 38	17 43	17 48				17 53		17 58	18 03	18 08	18 13
Highbury & Islington ⊖ d	17 01	17 06	17 11	17 16	17 21				17 26		17 31	17 36	17 41	17 46	17 51				17 56		18 01	18 06	18 11	18 16
Drayton Park d	17 02	17 07	17 12	17 17	17 22				17 27		17 32	17 37	17 42	17 47	17 52				17 57		18 02	18 07	18 12	18 17
Finsbury Park ⊖ d	17 05	17 10	17 15	17 20	17 25	17 28			17 30	17 33	17 35	17 40	17 45	17 50	17 55	17 58			18 00	18 03	18 05	18 10	18 15	18 20
Harringay d	17 08		17 18	17 23							17 38		17 48	17 53							18 08		18 18	18 23
Hornsey d	17 10		17 20	17 25							17 40		17 50	17 55							18 10		18 20	18 25
Alexandra Palace d	17 12	17 16	17 23	17 27	17 31						17 42	17 46	17 53	17 57	18 01						18 12	18 16	18 23	18 27
New Southgate d	17 15			17 30						17 38	17 45			18 00						18 08	18 15			18 30
Oakleigh Park d	17 19			17 34						17 41	17 49			18 04						18 11	18 19			18 34
New Barnet d	17 21			17 36						17 43	17 51			18 06							18 21			18 36
Hadley Wood d	17 24			17 39							17 54			18 09						18 15	18 24			18 39
Potters Bar d	17 28			17 43						17 49	17 58			18 13						18 19	18 28			18 43
Brookmans Park d	17 31			17 46							18 01			18 16							18 31			18 46
Welham Green d	17 33			17 48			←				18 03			18 18			←				18 33			18 48
Hatfield d	17 36			17 51		17 44	17 51			17 55	18 06			18 21		18 14	18 21			18 25	18 36			18 51
Welwyn Garden City 4 d	17a41			→		17 48	17a56			18a00	18a11			→		18 18	18a26			18a30	18a41			→
Welwyn North d						17 52										18 22								
Knebworth d						17 56										18 26								
Bowes Park d			17 25						17 37				17 55						18 07				18 25	
Palmers Green d		17 19	17 27		17 34				17 39			17 49	17 57		18 04				18 09			18 19	18 27	
Winchmore Hill d		17 22	17 30		17 37				17 42			17 52	18 00		18 07				18 12			18 22	18 30	
Grange Park d			17 32						17 44				18 02						18 14				18 32	
Enfield Chase d		17 26	17 34		17 41				17 46			17 56	18 04		18 11				18 16			18 26	18 34	
Gordon Hill d		17a31	17 37		17a44				17 49			17 58	18 07		18a14				18 19			18 28	18 37	
Crews Hill d			17 40										18 10										18 40	
Cuffley d			17 43						17 53			18 03	18 13						18 23			18 33	18 43	
Bayford d			17 48										18 18										18 48	
Hertford North d			17a53						18 03			18a12	18a23						18 33			18a42	18a53	
Watton-at-Stone d									18 08										18 38					
Stevenage 4 d						18 04			18a16							18 34			18a46					
Hitchin 4 d						18 10										18 40								
Letchworth Garden City a						18 16										18 46								

	FC	FC 1	FC		FC	FC	FC	FC	FC	FC	FC 1	FC	FC		FC	FC	FC	FC 1	FC	FC	FC 1	FC	FC	
London Kings Cross 15 ⊖ d		18 22				18 27					18 52		18 57					19 18			19 34			
Moorgate ⊖ d	18 13				18 18		18 23	18 28	18 37	18 42					18 52	18 57	19 02		19 12	19 22				
Old Street ⊖ d	18 15				18 20		18 25	18 30	18 39	18 44					18 54	18 59	19 04		19 14	19 24				
Essex Road d	18 18				18 23		18 28	18 33	18 42	18 47					18 57	19 02	19 07		19 17	19 27				
Highbury & Islington ⊖ d	18 21				18 26		18 31	18 36	18 45	18 50					19 00	19 05	19 10		19 20	19 30				
Drayton Park d	18 22				18 27		18 32	18 37	18 46	18 51					19 01	19 06	19 11		19 21	19 31				
Finsbury Park ⊖ d	18 25	18 28			18 30	18 33	18 35	18 40	18 49	18 54	18 58		19 03		19 04	19 09	19 14	19 23	19 24	19 34	19 39			
Harringay d							18 38		18 52	18 57						19 12	19 17		19 27	19 37				
Hornsey d							18 40		18 54	18 59						19 14	19 19		19 29	19 39				
Alexandra Palace d	18 31						18 42	18 46	18 57	19 01						19 16	19 22		19 31	19 42				
New Southgate d						18 38	18 45			19 04			19 08			19 19			19 34					
Oakleigh Park d						18 41	18 49			19 08			19 11			19 23			19 38					
New Barnet d						18 43	18 51			19 10			19 13			19 25			19 40					
Hadley Wood d							18 54			19 13			19 16			19 28			19 43					
Potters Bar d						18 49	18 58			19 17			19 21			19 32		19 37	19 47					
Brookmans Park d							19 01			19 20						19 35			19 50					
Welham Green d			←				19 03			19 22		←				19 37			19 52			←		
Hatfield d		18 44	18 51			18 55	19 06			19 25	19 14	19 25	19 28			19 40		19 44	19 55		19 53	19 55		
Welwyn Garden City 4 d		18 49	18a56			19a00	19a11			→	19 19	19a30	19a33			19a45		19 49	→		20 00	20a00		
Welwyn North d		18 51									19 24							19 53			20 03			
Knebworth d		18 55									19 28							19 57			20 07			
Bowes Park d					18 37				18 59						19 11		19 24			19 44				
Palmers Green d	18 34				18 39			18 49	19 01						19 13		19 26			19 46				
Winchmore Hill d	18 37				18 42			18 52	19 04						19 16		19 29			19 49				
Grange Park d					18 44				19 06						19 18		19 31			19 51				
Enfield Chase d	18 41				18 46			18 56	19 08						19 20		19 33			19 53				
Gordon Hill d	18a44				18 49			18 58	19 11						19 23		19 36			19 56				
Crews Hill d									19 14								19 39							
Cuffley d					18 53			19 03	19 17						19 27		19 42			20 00				
Bayford d									19 22								19 47							
Hertford North d					19 03			19a12	19a27						19 37		19a52			20 09				
Watton-at-Stone d					19 08										19 42					20 15			←	
Stevenage 4 d		19 04			19 16						19 35				19a52			20 04		20 21	20 12		20 21	
Hitchin 4 d		19 10			19 22						19 42							20 13		→	20 17		20 27	
Letchworth Garden City a		19 16			19 27						19 46							20 17			20 23		20 32	

Table 24

Mondays to Fridays

London - Welwyn Garden City, Hertford North and Letchworth Garden City

Network Diagram - see first Page of Table 24

		FC	FC	FC	FC	FC	FC 1	FC	FC	FC 1		FC	FC	FC	FC	FC 1	FC	FC	FC 1	FC		FC	FC	FC	FC 1
London Kings Cross 15 ⊖	d		19 40				20 06			20 36						21 06			21 36						22 06
Moorgate ⊖	d	19 32		19 37	19 42	19 52		20 07	20 12				20 32	20 37	20 52		21 07	21 12				21 32	21 37	21 52	
Old Street ⊖	d	19 34		19 39	19 44	19 54		20 09	20 14				20 34	20 39	20 54		21 09	21 14				21 34	21 39	21 54	
Essex Road	d	19 37		19 42	19 47	19 57		20 12	20 17				20 37	20 42	20 57		21 12	21 17				21 37	21 42	21 57	
Highbury & Islington ⊖	d	19 40		19 45	19 50	19 59		20 14	20 19				20 39	20 44	20 59		21 14	21 19				21 39	21 44	21 59	
Drayton Park	d	19 41		19 46	19 51	20 01		20 16	20 21				20 41	20 46	21 01		21 16	21 21				21 41	21 46	22 01	
Finsbury Park ⊖	d	19 44	19 46	19 49	19 54	20 04	20 11	20 19	20 24	20 41			20 44	20 49	21 04	21 11	21 19	21 24	21 41			21 44	21 49	22 04	22 11
Harringay	d			19 52	19 57	20 06		20 21	20 26				20 46	20 51	21 06		21 21	21 26				21 46	21 51	22 06	
Hornsey	d			19 54	19 59	20 08		20 23	20 28				20 48	20 53	21 08		21 23	21 28				21 48	21 53	22 08	
Alexandra Palace	d			19 56	20 02	20 10		20 25	20 30				20 50	20 55	21 10		21 25	21 30				21 50	21 55	22 10	
New Southgate	d		19 51	19 59				20 28						20 58			21 28						21 58		
Oakleigh Park	d		19 54	20 03				20 31						21 01			21 31						22 01		
New Barnet	d		19 56	20 05				20 33						21 03			21 33						22 03		
Hadley Wood	d			20 08				20 36						21 06			21 36						22 06		
Potters Bar	d		20 02	20 12			20 21	20 40		20 51				21 10		21 21	21 40		21 51				22 10		22 21
Brookmans Park	d			20 15				20 43						21 13			21 43						22 13		
Welham Green	d			20 17				20 45						21 15			21 45						22 15		
Hatfield	d		20 08	20 20			20 27	20 48		20 57				21 18		21 27	21 48		21 57				22 18		22 27
Welwyn Garden City 4	d		20a13	20a25			20 31	20a54		21 01				21a24		21 31	21a54		22 01				22a24		22 31
Welwyn North	d						20 34			21 04						21 34			22 04						22 34
Knebworth	d						20 38			21 08						21 38			22 08						22 38
Bowes Park	d	19 51			20 04	20 13			20 33				20 53		21 13			21 33				21 53		22 13	
Palmers Green	d	19 53			20 06	20 15			20 35				20 55		21 15			21 35				21 55		22 15	
Winchmore Hill	d	19 56			20 09	20 17			20 37				20 57		21 17			21 37				21 57		22 17	
Grange Park	d	19 58			20 11	20 19			20 39				20 59		21 19			21 39				21 59		22 19	
Enfield Chase	d	20 00			20 13	20 21			20 41				21 01		21 21			21 41				22 01		22 21	
Gordon Hill	d	20 03			20 16	20 23			20 43				21 03		21 23			21 43				22 03		22 23	
Crews Hill	d	20 06				20 26			20 46				21 06		21 26			21 46				22 06		22 26	
Cuffley	d	20 09			20 20	20 29			20 49				21 09		21 29			21 49				22 09		22 29	
Bayford	d	20 14				20 34			20 54				21 14		21 34			21 54				22 14		22 34	
Hertford North	d	20a19			20a30	20 40			21 10				21a20		21a40			22 10				22a20		22a40	
Watton-at-Stone	d					20 45			21 15			←						22 15		←					
Stevenage 4	d					20a53	20 42		21 23	21 12		21 23				21 42		22 23	22 12	22 23					22 42
Hitchin 4	d						20 47		↪	21 17		21 28				21 47		↪	22 17	22 28					22 47
Letchworth Garden City	a						20 51			21 23		21 34				21 51			22 23	22 34					22 51

		FC	FC	FC 1	FC	FC		FC	FC 1	FC	FC	FC 1	FC	FC
London Kings Cross 15 ⊖	d	22 11	22 26	22 36		22 41		22 56	23 06	23 11	23 26	23 36		23 41
Moorgate ⊖	d													
Old Street ⊖	d													
Essex Road	d													
Highbury & Islington ⊖	d													
Drayton Park	d													
Finsbury Park ⊖	d	22 17	22 32	22 41		22 47		23 02	23 11	23 17	23 32	23 41		23 47
Harringay	d	22 19	22 34			22 49		23 04		23 19	23 34			23 49
Hornsey	d	22 21	22 36			22 51		23 06		23 21	23 36			23 51
Alexandra Palace	d	22 23	22 38			22 53		23 08		23 23	23 38			23 53
New Southgate	d	22 26				22 56				23 26				23 56
Oakleigh Park	d	22 29				22 59				23 29				23 59
New Barnet	d	22 31				23 01				23 31				00 01
Hadley Wood	d	22 34				23 04				23 34				00 04
Potters Bar	d	22 38		22 51		23 08			23 21	23 38		23 51		00 08
Brookmans Park	d	22 41				23 11				23 41				00 11
Welham Green	d	22 43				23 13				23 43				00 13
Hatfield	d	22 46		22 57		23 16			23 27	23 46		23 57		00 16
Welwyn Garden City 4	d	22a51		23 01		23a24			23 31	23a54		00 01		00a24
Welwyn North	d			23 04					23 34			00 04		
Knebworth	d			23 08					23 38			00 08		
Bowes Park	d		22 41					23 11			23 41			
Palmers Green	d		22 43					23 13			23 43			
Winchmore Hill	d		22 45					23 15			23 45			
Grange Park	d		22 47					23 17			23 47			
Enfield Chase	d		22 49					23 19			23 49			
Gordon Hill	d		22 51					23 21			23 51			
Crews Hill	d		22 54					23 24			23 54			
Cuffley	d		22 57					23 27			23 57			
Bayford	d		23 02					23 32			00 02			
Hertford North	d		23 07					23a38			00 07			
Watton-at-Stone	d		23 13		←						00 13		←	
Stevenage 4	d		23 21	23 12	23 21				23 42		00 20	00 12	00 20	
Hitchin 4	d		↪	23 17	23 30				23 50		↪	00 20	00 26	
Letchworth Garden City	a			23 26	23 36				23 54			00 29	00 36	

London - Welwyn Garden City, Hertford North and Letchworth Garden City

Network Diagram - see first Page of Table 24

		FC	FC 1	FC	FC	FC	FC	FC 1	FC 1	FC	FC 1	FC 1	FC	FC	FC 1	FC	FC	FC 1	FC	FC	FC 1	FC	FC
London Kings Cross 15 ⊖	d	23p26	23p36		23p41	00 06	00 11	00 36	01 06	01 11	01 36	05 23	05 26	05 56	06 06	06 11	06 26	06 36	06 41	06 56	07 06	07 11	07 26
Moorgate ⊖	d																						
Old Street ⊖	d																						
Essex Road	d																						
Highbury & Islington ⊖	d																						
Drayton Park	d																						
Finsbury Park ⊖	d	23p32	23p41		23p47	00 12	00 17	00 41	01 11	01 17	01 41	05 28	05 32	06 02	06 11	06 17	06 32	06 41	06 47	07 02	07 11	07 17	07 32
Harringay	d	23p34			23p49	00 14	00 19			01 19			05 34	06 04		06 19	06 34		06 49	07 04		07 19	07 34
Hornsey	d	23p36			23p51	00 16	00 21			01 21			05 36	06 06		06 21	06 36		06 51	07 06		07 21	07 36
Alexandra Palace	d	23p38			23p53	00 18	00 23		01 16	01 23	01 45		05 38	06 08		06 23	06 38		06 53	07 08		07 23	07 38
New Southgate	d				23p56		00 26			01 26	01 48					06 26			06 56			07 26	
Oakleigh Park	d				23p59		00 29			01 29	01 51					06 29			06 59			07 29	
New Barnet	d				00 01		00 31			01 31	01 53					06 31			07 01			07 31	
Hadley Wood	d				00 04		00 34			01 34	01 56					06 34			07 04			07 34	
Potters Bar	d		23p51		00 08		00 38	00 51		01 38	01 59	05 38			06 21	06 38		06 51	07 08		07 21	07 38	
Brookmans Park	d				00 11		00 41			01 41						06 41			07 11			07 41	
Welham Green	d				00 13		00 43			01 43						06 43			07 13			07 43	
Hatfield	d		23p57		00 16		00 46	00 57		01 46	02 05	05 44			06 27	06 46		06 57	07 16		07 27	07 46	
Welwyn Garden City 4	d		00 01		00a24		00a54	01 01		01a54	02 09	05 48			06 31	06a51		07 01	07a21		07 31	07a51	
Welwyn North	d		00 04					01s04			02s12	05 51			06 34			07 04			07 34		
Knebworth	d		00 08					01s08			02s16	05 55			06 38			07 08			07 38		
Bowes Park	d	23p41				00 21							05 41	06 11			06 41			07 11			07 41
Palmers Green	d	23p43				00 23			01 19				05 43	06 13			06 43			07 13			07 43
Winchmore Hill	d	23p45				00 25			01 21				05 45	06 15			06 45			07 15			07 45
Grange Park	d	23p47				00 27							05 47	06 17			06 47			07 17			07 47
Enfield Chase	d	23p49				00 29			01 24				05 49	06 19			06 49			07 19			07 49
Gordon Hill	d	23p51				00 31			01 26				05 51	06 21			06 51			07 21			07 51
Crews Hill	d	23p54				00 34							05 54	06 24			06 54			07 24			07 54
Cuffley	d	23p57				00 37			01 30				05 57	06 27			06 57			07 27			07 57
Bayford	d	00 02				00 42							06 02	06 32			07 02			07 32			08 02
Hertford North	d	00 07				00 47			01 38				06a07	06a37			07 07			07a37			08 07
Watton-at-Stone	d	00 13		←		00 53											07 13						08 13
Stevenage 4	d	00 20	00 12	00 20		01 00		01 12	01 47		02 20	05 59			06 41		07a20	07 12			07 42		08a20
Hitchin 4	d	→	00 20	00 26		01 06		01a17	01 52		02a25	06a07			06 47			07a17			07 47		
Letchworth Garden City	a		00 29	00 36		01 15			02 01						06 51						07 51		

		FC 1	FC	FC	FC 1	FC	FC	FC 1	FC	FC	FC 1	FC	FC	FC 1	FC	FC	FC 1	FC	FC	FC 1	FC	FC	FC 1
London Kings Cross 15 ⊖	d	07 36	07 41	07 56	08 06	08 11	08 26	08 36	08 41	08 56	09 06	09 11	09 26	09 36	09 41	09 56	10 06	10 11	10 26	10 36	10 41	10 56	11 06
Moorgate ⊖	d																						
Old Street ⊖	d																						
Essex Road	d																						
Highbury & Islington ⊖	d																						
Drayton Park	d																						
Finsbury Park ⊖	d	07 41	07 47	08 02	08 11	08 17	08 32	08 41	08 47	09 02	09 11	09 17	09 32	09 41	09 47	10 02	10 11	10 17	10 32	10 41	10 47	11 02	11 11
Harringay	d		07 49	08 04		08 19	08 34		08 49	09 04		09 19	09 34		09 49	10 04		10 19	10 34		10 49	11 04	
Hornsey	d		07 51	08 06		08 21	08 36		08 51	09 06		09 21	09 36		09 51	10 06		10 21	10 36		10 51	11 06	
Alexandra Palace	d		07 53	08 08		08 23	08 38		08 53	09 08		09 23	09 38		09 53	10 08		10 23	10 38		10 53	11 08	
New Southgate	d		07 56			08 26			08 56			09 26			09 56			10 26			10 56		
Oakleigh Park	d		07 59			08 29			08 59			09 29			09 59			10 29			10 59		
New Barnet	d		08 01			08 31			09 01			09 31			10 01			10 31			11 01		
Hadley Wood	d		08 04			08 34			09 04			09 34			10 04			10 34			11 04		
Potters Bar	d	07 51	08 08		08 21	08 38		08 51	09 08		09 21	09 38		09 51	10 08		10 21	10 38		10 51	11 08		11 21
Brookmans Park	d		08 11			08 41			09 11			09 41			10 11			10 41			11 11		
Welham Green	d		08 13			08 43			09 13			09 43			10 13			10 43			11 13		
Hatfield	d	07 57	08 16		08 27	08 46		08 57	09 16		09 27	09 46		09 57	10 16		10 27	10 46		10 57	11 16		11 27
Welwyn Garden City 4	d	08 01	08a21		08 31	08a51		09 01	09a21		09 31	09a51		10 01	10a21		10 31	10a51		11 01	11a21		11 31
Welwyn North	d	08 04			08 34			09 04			09 34			10 04			10 34			11 04			11 34
Knebworth	d	08 08			08 38			09 08			09 38			10 08			10 38			11 08			11 38
Bowes Park	d			08 11			08 41			09 11			09 41			10 11			10 41			11 11	
Palmers Green	d			08 13			08 43			09 13			09 43			10 13			10 43			11 13	
Winchmore Hill	d			08 15			08 45			09 15			09 45			10 15			10 45			11 15	
Grange Park	d			08 17			08 47			09 17			09 47			10 17			10 47			11 17	
Enfield Chase	d			08 19			08 49			09 19			09 49			10 19			10 49			11 19	
Gordon Hill	d			08 21			08 51			09 21			09 51			10 21			10 51			11 21	
Crews Hill	d			08 24			08 54			09 24			09 54			10 24			10 54			11 24	
Cuffley	d			08 27			08 57			09 27			09 57			10 27			10 57			11 27	
Bayford	d			08 32			09 02			09 32			10 02			10 32			11 02			11 32	
Hertford North	d			08a37			09 07			09a37			10 07			10a37			11 07			11a37	
Watton-at-Stone	d						09 13						10 13						11 13				
Stevenage 4	d	08 13			08 42		09a20	09 12			09 42		10a20	10 12			10 42		11a20	11 12			11 42
Hitchin 4	d	08a17			08 47			09a17			09 47			10a17			10 47			11a17			11 47
Letchworth Garden City	a				08 51						09 51						10 51						11 51

Table 24

Saturdays

London - Welwyn Garden City, Hertford North and Letchworth Garden City

Network Diagram - see first Page of Table 24

		FC		FC	FC 1	FC	FC	FC 1	FC	FC	FC 1	FC		FC	FC 1	FC	FC	FC 1	FC	FC	FC 1	FC		FC	FC 1
London Kings Cross 15 ⊖	d	11 11		11 26	11 36	11 41	11 56	12 06	12 11	12 26	12 36	12 41		12 56	13 06	13 11	13 26	13 36	13 41	13 56	14 06	14 11		14 26	14 36
Moorgate ⊖	d																								
Old Street ⊖	d																								
Essex Road	d																								
Highbury & Islington ⊖	d																								
Drayton Park	d																								
Finsbury Park ⊖	d	11 17		11 32	11 41	11 47	12 02	12 11	12 17	12 32	12 41	12 47		13 02	13 11	13 17	13 32	13 41	13 47	14 02	14 11	14 17		14 32	14 41
Harringay	d	11 19		11 34		11 49	12 04		12 19	12 34		12 49		13 04		13 19	13 34		13 49	14 04		14 19		14 34	
Hornsey	d	11 21		11 36		11 51	12 06		12 21	12 36		12 51		13 06		13 21	13 36		13 51	14 06		14 21		14 36	
Alexandra Palace	d	11 23		11 38		11 53	12 08		12 23	12 38		12 53		13 08		13 23	13 38		13 53	14 08		14 23		14 38	
New Southgate	d	11 26				11 56			12 26			12 56				13 26			13 56			14 26			
Oakleigh Park	d	11 29				11 59			12 29			12 59				13 29			13 59			14 29			
New Barnet	d	11 31				12 01			12 31			13 01				13 31			14 01			14 31			
Hadley Wood	d	11 34				12 04			12 34			13 04				13 34			14 04			14 34			
Potters Bar	d	11 38			11 51	12 08		12 21	12 38		12 51	13 08			13 21	13 38		13 51	14 08		14 21	14 38			14 51
Brookmans Park	d	11 41				12 11			12 41			13 11				13 41			14 11			14 41			
Welham Green	d	11 43				12 13			12 43			13 13				13 43			14 13			14 43			
Hatfield	d	11 46			11 57	12 16		12 27	12 46		12 57	13 16			13 27	13 46		13 57	14 16		14 27	14 46			14 57
Welwyn Garden City 4	d	11a51			12 01	12a21		12 31	12a51		13 01	13a21			13 31	13a51		14 01	14a21		14 31	14a51			15 01
Welwyn North	d				12 04			12 34			13 04				13 34			14 04			14 34				15 04
Knebworth	d				12 08			12 38			13 08				13 38			14 08			14 38				15 08
Bowes Park	d			11 41			12 11			12 41				13 11			13 41			14 11				14 41	
Palmers Green	d			11 43			12 13			12 43				13 13			13 43			14 13				14 43	
Winchmore Hill	d			11 45			12 15			12 45				13 15			13 45			14 15				14 45	
Grange Park	d			11 47			12 17			12 47				13 17			13 47			14 17				14 47	
Enfield Chase	d			11 49			12 19			12 49				13 19			13 49			14 19				14 49	
Gordon Hill	d			11 51			12 21			12 51				13 21			13 51			14 21				14 51	
Crews Hill	d			11 54			12 24			12 54				13 24			13 54			14 24				14 54	
Cuffley	d			11 57			12 27			12 57				13 27			13 57			14 27				14 57	
Bayford	d			12 02			12 32			13 02				13 32			14 02			14 32				15 02	
Hertford North	d			12 07			12a37			13 07				13a37			14 07			14a37				15 07	
Watton-at-Stone	d			12 13						13 13							14 13							15 13	
Stevenage 4	d			12a20	12 12			12 42		13a20	13 12				13 42		14a20	14 12			14 42			15a20	15 12
Hitchin 4	d				12a17			12 47			13a17				13 47			14a17			14 47				15a17
Letchworth Garden City	a							12 51							13 51						14 51				

		FC	FC	FC 1	FC	FC	FC 1	FC		FC	FC 1	FC	FC	FC 1	FC	FC	FC 1	FC		FC	FC 1	FC	FC	FC 1	FC
London Kings Cross 15 ⊖	d	14 41	14 56	15 06	15 11	15 26	15 36	15 41		15 56	16 06	16 11	16 26	16 36	16 41	16 56	17 06	17 11		17 26	17 36	17 41	17 56	18 06	18 11
Moorgate ⊖	d																								
Old Street ⊖	d																								
Essex Road	d																								
Highbury & Islington ⊖	d																								
Drayton Park	d																								
Finsbury Park ⊖	d	14 47	15 02	15 11	15 17	15 32	15 41	15 47		16 02	16 11	16 17	16 32	16 41	16 47	17 02	17 11	17 17		17 32	17 41	17 47	18 02	18 11	18 17
Harringay	d	14 49	15 04		15 19	15 34		15 49		16 04		16 19	16 34		16 49	17 04		17 19		17 34		17 49	18 04		18 19
Hornsey	d	14 51	15 06		15 21	15 36		15 51		16 06		16 21	16 36		16 51	17 06		17 21		17 36		17 51	18 06		18 21
Alexandra Palace	d	14 53	15 08		15 23	15 38		15 53		16 08		16 23	16 38		16 53	17 08		17 23		17 38		17 53	18 08		18 23
New Southgate	d	14 56			15 26			15 56				16 26			16 56			17 26				17 56			18 26
Oakleigh Park	d	14 59			15 29			15 59				16 29			16 59			17 29				17 59			18 29
New Barnet	d	15 01			15 31			16 01				16 31			17 01			17 31				18 01			18 31
Hadley Wood	d	15 04			15 34			16 04				16 34			17 04			17 34				18 04			18 34
Potters Bar	d	15 08		15 21	15 38		15 51	16 08			16 21	16 38		16 51	17 08		17 21	17 38			17 51	18 08		18 21	18 38
Brookmans Park	d	15 11			15 41			16 11				16 41			17 11			17 41				18 11			18 41
Welham Green	d	15 13			15 43			16 13				16 43			17 13			17 43				18 13			18 43
Hatfield	d	15 16		15 27	15 46		15 57	16 16			16 27	16 46		16 57	17 16		17 27	17 46			17 57	18 16		18 27	18 46
Welwyn Garden City 4	d	15a21		15 31	15a51		16 01	16a21			16 31	16a51		17 01	17a21		17 31	17a51			18 01	18a21		18 31	18a51
Welwyn North	d			15 34			16 04				16 34			17 04			17 34				18 04			18 34	
Knebworth	d			15 38			16 08				16 38			17 08			17 38				18 08			18 38	
Bowes Park	d		15 11			15 41				16 11			16 41			17 11				17 41			18 11		
Palmers Green	d		15 13			15 43				16 13			16 43			17 13				17 43			18 13		
Winchmore Hill	d		15 15			15 45				16 15			16 45			17 15				17 45			18 15		
Grange Park	d		15 17			15 47				16 17			16 47			17 17				17 47			18 17		
Enfield Chase	d		15 19			15 49				16 19			16 49			17 19				17 49			18 19		
Gordon Hill	d		15 21			15 51				16 21			16 51			17 21				17 51			18 21		
Crews Hill	d		15 24			15 54				16 24			16 54			17 24				17 54			18 24		
Cuffley	d		15 27			15 57				16 27			16 57			17 27				17 57			18 27		
Bayford	d		15 32			16 02				16 32			17 02			17 32				18 02			18 32		
Hertford North	d		15a37			16 07				16a37			17 07			17a37				18 07			18a37		
Watton-at-Stone	d					16 13							17 13							18 13					
Stevenage 4	d			15 42		16a20	16 12				16 42		17a20	17 12			17 42			18a20	18 12			18 42	
Hitchin 4	d			15 47			16a17				16 47			17a17			17 47				18a17			18 47	
Letchworth Garden City	a			15 51							16 51						17 51							18 51	

Table 24

Saturdays

London - Welwyn Garden City, Hertford North and Letchworth Garden City

Network Diagram - see first Page of Table 24

		FC	FC 1	FC		FC	FC 1	FC	FC	FC 1	FC	FC	FC 1	FC		FC	FC 1	FC	FC	FC 1	FC	FC	FC 1	FC
London Kings Cross 15 ⊖	d	18 26	18 36	18 41		18 56	19 06	19 11	19 26	19 36	19 41	19 56	20 06	20 11		20 26	20 36	20 41	20 56	21 06	21 11	21 26	21 36	21 41
Moorgate ⊖	d																							
Old Street ⊖	d																							
Essex Road	d																							
Highbury & Islington ⊖	d																							
Drayton Park	d																							
Finsbury Park ⊖	d	18 32	18 41	18 47		19 02	19 11	19 17	19 32	19 41	19 47	20 02	20 11	20 17		20 32	20 41	20 47	21 02	21 11	21 17	21 32	21 41	21 47
Harringay	d	18 34		18 49		19 04		19 19	19 34		19 49	20 04		20 19		20 34		20 49	21 04		21 19	21 34		21 49
Hornsey	d	18 36		18 51		19 06		19 21	19 36		19 51	20 06		20 21		20 36		20 51	21 06		21 21	21 36		21 51
Alexandra Palace	d	18 38		18 53		19 08		19 23	19 38		19 53	20 08		20 23		20 38		20 53	21 08		21 23	21 38		21 53
New Southgate	d			18 56				19 26			19 56			20 26				20 56			21 26			21 56
Oakleigh Park	d			18 59				19 29			19 59			20 29				20 59			21 29			21 59
New Barnet	d			19 01				19 31			20 01			20 31				21 01			21 31			22 01
Hadley Wood	d			19 04				19 34			20 04			20 34				21 04			21 34			22 04
Potters Bar	d		18 51	19 08			19 21	19 38		19 51	20 08		20 21	20 38			20 51	21 08		21 21	21 38		21 51	22 08
Brookmans Park	d			19 11				19 41			20 11			20 41				21 11			21 41			22 11
Welham Green	d			19 13				19 43			20 13			20 43				21 13			21 43			22 13
Hatfield	d		18 57	19 16			19 27	19 46		19 57	20 16		20 27	20 46			20 57	21 16		21 27	21 46		21 57	22 16
Welwyn Garden City 4	d		19 01	19a21			19 31	19a51		20 01	20a21		20 31	20a51			21 01	21a21		21 31	21a51		22 01	22a21
Welwyn North	d		19 04				19 34			20 04			20 34				21 04			21 34			22 04	
Knebworth	d		19 08				19 38			20 08			20 38				21 08			21 38			22 08	
Bowes Park	d	18 41				19 11			19 41			20 11				20 41			21 11			21 41		
Palmers Green	d	18 43				19 13			19 43			20 13				20 43			21 13			21 43		
Winchmore Hill	d	18 45				19 15			19 45			20 15				20 45			21 15			21 45		
Grange Park	d	18 47				19 17			19 47			20 17				20 47			21 17			21 47		
Enfield Chase	d	18 49				19 19			19 49			20 19				20 49			21 19			21 49		
Gordon Hill	d	18 51				19 21			19 51			20 21				20 51			21 21			21 51		
Crews Hill	d	18 54				19 24			19 54			20 24				20 54			21 24			21 54		
Cuffley	d	18 57				19 27			19 57			20 27				20 57			21 27			21 57		
Bayford	d	19 02				19 32			20 02			20 32				21 02			21 32			22 02		
Hertford North	d	19 07				19a37			20 07			20a37				21 07			21a37			22 07		
Watton-at-Stone	d	19 13							20 13							21 13						22 13		
Stevenage 4	d	19a20	19 12				19 42		20a20	20 12			20 42			21a20	21 12			21 42		22a20	22 12	
Hitchin 4	d		19a17				19 47			20a17			20 47				21a17			21 47			22a17	
Letchworth Garden City	a						19 51						20 51							21 51				

		FC	FC 1	FC	FC	FC 1	FC	FC	FC 1	FC		FC	FC 1	FC	FC	FC
London Kings Cross 15 ⊖	d	21 56	22 06	22 11	22 26	22 36	22 41	22 56	23 06	23 11		23 26	23 36		23 41	23 56
Moorgate ⊖	d															
Old Street ⊖	d															
Essex Road	d															
Highbury & Islington ⊖	d															
Drayton Park	d															
Finsbury Park ⊖	d	22 02	22 11	22 17	22 32	22 41	22 47	23 02	23 11	23 17		23 32	23 41		23 47	00 02
Harringay	d	22 04		22 19	22 34		22 49	23 04		23 19		23 34			23 49	00 04
Hornsey	d	22 06		22 21	22 36		22 51	23 06		23 21		23 36			23 51	00 06
Alexandra Palace	d	22 08		22 23	22 38		22 53	23 08		23 23		23 38			23 53	00 08
New Southgate	d			22 26			22 56			23 26					23 56	
Oakleigh Park	d			22 29			22 59			23 29					23 59	
New Barnet	d			22 31			23 01			23 31					00 01	
Hadley Wood	d			22 34			23 04			23 34					00 04	
Potters Bar	d		22 21	22 38		22 51	23 08		23 21	23 38			23 53		00 08	
Brookmans Park	d			22 41			23 11			23 41					00 11	
Welham Green	d			22 43			23 13			23 43					00 13	
Hatfield	d		22 27	22 46		22 57	23 16		23 27	23 46			23 59		00 16	
Welwyn Garden City 4	d		22 31	22a51		23 01	23a21		23 31	23a53			00 06		00a25	
Welwyn North	d		22 34			23 04			23 34				00 09			
Knebworth	d		22 38			23 08			23 38				00 13			
Bowes Park	d	22 11			22 41			23 11				23 41				00 11
Palmers Green	d	22 13			22 43			23 13				23 43				00 13
Winchmore Hill	d	22 15			22 45			23 15				23 45				00 15
Grange Park	d	22 17			22 47			23 17				23 47				00 17
Enfield Chase	d	22 19			22 49			23 19				23 49				00 19
Gordon Hill	d	22 21			22 51			23 21				23 51				00 21
Crews Hill	d	22 24			22 54			23 24				23 54				00 24
Cuffley	d	22 27			22 57			23 27				23 57				00 27
Bayford	d	22 32			23 02			23 32				00 02				00 32
Hertford North	d	22a37			23 07			23a37				00 07				00a39
Watton-at-Stone	d				23 13							00 13		←		
Stevenage 4	d		22 42		23a20	23 12			23 42			00 22	00 18	00 22		
Hitchin 4	d		22 47			23 20			23 50			↪	00 25	00 29		
Letchworth Garden City	a		22 51			23 26			23 54				00 30	00 37		

Table 24

Sundays

London - Welwyn Garden City, Hertford North and Letchworth Garden City

Network Diagram - see first Page of Table 24

		FC	FC	FC	FC	FC	FC	FC	FC	FC		FC	FC	FC	FC	FC	FC	FC	FC	FC		FC	FC	FC	FC
			1				1			1								1						1	
		A	A	A	A	A																			
London Kings Cross 15	⊖ d	23p26	23p36		23p41	23p56	00 06	00 26	00 32	00 53		00 56	01 11	05 56	06 26	06 41	06 56	07 06	07 11	07 26		07 41	07 56	08 06	08 11
Moorgate	⊖ d																								
Old Street	⊖ d																								
Essex Road	d																								
Highbury & Islington	⊖ d																								
Drayton Park	d																								
Finsbury Park	⊖ d	23p32	23p41		23p47	00 02	00 11	00 32	00 38	00 58		01 02	01 17	06 02	06 32	06 47	07 02	07 11	07 17	07 32		07 47	08 02	08 11	08 17
Harringay	d	23p34			23p49	00 04		00 34	00 40			01 04	01 19	06 04	06 34	06 49	07 04		07 19	07 34		07 49	08 04		08 19
Hornsey	d	23p36			23p51	00 06		00 36	00 42			01 06	01 21	06 06	06 36	06 51	07 06		07 21	07 36		07 51	08 06		08 21
Alexandra Palace	d	23p38			23p53	00 08		00 38	00 44			01 08	01 23	06 08	06 38	06 53	07 08		07 23	07 38		07 53	08 08		08 23
New Southgate	d				23p56				00 47				01 26			06 56			07 26			07 56			08 26
Oakleigh Park	d				23p59				00 50				01 29			06 59			07 29			07 59			08 29
New Barnet	d				00 01				00 52				01 31			07 01			07 31			08 01			08 31
Hadley Wood	d				00 04				00 55				01 34			07 04			07 34			08 04			08 34
Potters Bar	d		23p53		00 08		00 23		00 59	01 10			01 38			07 08		07 21	07 38			08 08		08 21	08 38
Brookmans Park	d				00 11				01 02				01 41			07 11			07 41			08 11			08 41
Welham Green	d				00 13				01 04				01 43			07 13			07 43			08 13			08 43
Hatfield	d		23p59		00 16		00 29		01 07	01 16			01 46			07 16		07 27	07 46			08 16		08 27	08 46
Welwyn Garden City 4	d		00 06		00a25		00 41		01a16	01 20			01a55			07a25		07 33	07a55			08a25		08 31	08a53
Welwyn North	d		00 09				00 44			01s24								07 36						08 34	
Knebworth	d		00 13				00 48			01s28								07 40						08 38	
Bowes Park	d	23p41				00 11		00 41				01 11		06 11	06 41		07 11			07 41			08 11		
Palmers Green	d	23p43				00 13		00 43				01 13		06 13	06 43		07 13			07 43			08 13		
Winchmore Hill	d	23p45				00 15		00 45				01 15		06 15	06 45		07 15			07 45			08 15		
Grange Park	d	23p47				00 17		00 47				01 17		06 17	06 47		07 17			07 47			08 17		
Enfield Chase	d	23p49				00 19		00 49				01 19		06 19	06 49		07 19			07 49			08 19		
Gordon Hill	d	23p51				00 21		00 51				01 21		06 21	06 51		07 21			07 51			08 21		
Crews Hill	d	23p54				00 24		00 54				01 24		06 24	06 54		07 24			07 54			08 24		
Cuffley	d	23p57				00 27		00 57				01 27		06 27	06 57		07 27			07 57			08 27		
Bayford	d	00 02				00 32		01 02				01 32		06 32	07 02		07 32			08 02			08 32		
Hertford North	d	00 07				00a39		01a09				01 37		06a39	07 07		07a39			08 07			08a37		
Watton-at-Stone	d	00 13		←								01 43			07 13					08 13					
Stevenage 4	d	00 22	00 18	00 22			00 53			01 32		01 51			07a22			07 45		08a23				08 42	
Hitchin 4	d	→	00 25	00 29			01 00			01a39		01 59						07 52						08 47	
Letchworth Garden City	a		00 30	00 37			01 04					02 05						07 56						08 51	

		FC	FC	FC	FC	FC		FC	FC	FC	FC	FC	FC	FC	FC	FC		FC	FC	FC	FC	FC	FC	FC	FC
					1						1					1						1			
London Kings Cross 15	⊖ d	08 26	08 41	08 56	09 06	09 11		09 26	09 41	09 56	10 06	10 11	10 26	10 41	10 56	11 06		11 11	11 26	11 41	11 56	12 06	12 11	12 26	12 41
Moorgate	⊖ d																								
Old Street	⊖ d																								
Essex Road	d																								
Highbury & Islington	⊖ d																								
Drayton Park	d																								
Finsbury Park	⊖ d	08 32	08 47	09 02	09 11	09 17		09 32	09 47	10 02	10 11	10 17	10 32	10 47	11 02	11 11		11 17	11 32	11 47	12 02	12 11	12 17	12 32	12 47
Harringay	d	08 34	08 49	09 04		09 19		09 34	09 49	10 04		10 19	10 34	10 49	11 04			11 19	11 34	11 49	12 04		12 19	12 34	12 49
Hornsey	d	08 36	08 51	09 06		09 21		09 36	09 51	10 06		10 21	10 36	10 51	11 06			11 21	11 36	11 51	12 06		12 21	12 36	12 51
Alexandra Palace	d	08 38	08 53	09 08		09 23		09 38	09 53	10 08		10 23	10 38	10 53	11 08			11 23	11 38	11 53	12 08		12 23	12 38	12 53
New Southgate	d		08 56			09 26			09 56			10 26		10 56				11 26		11 56			12 26		12 56
Oakleigh Park	d		08 59			09 29			09 59			10 29		10 59				11 29		11 59			12 29		12 59
New Barnet	d		09 01			09 31			10 01			10 31		11 01				11 31		12 01			12 31		13 01
Hadley Wood	d		09 04			09 34			10 04			10 34		11 04				11 34		12 04			12 34		13 04
Potters Bar	d		09 08		09 21	09 38			10 08		10 21	10 38		11 08		11 21		11 38		12 08		12 21	12 38		13 08
Brookmans Park	d		09 11			09 41			10 11			10 41		11 11				11 41		12 11			12 41		13 11
Welham Green	d		09 13			09 43			10 13			10 43		11 13				11 43		12 13			12 43		13 13
Hatfield	d		09 16		09 27	09 46			10 16		10 27	10 46		11 16		11 27		11 46		12 16		12 27	12 46		13 16
Welwyn Garden City 4	d		09a21		09 31	09a51			10a21		10 31	10a51		11a21		11 31		11a51		12a21		12 31	12a51		13a21
Welwyn North	d				09 34						10 34					11 34						12 34			
Knebworth	d				09 38						10 38					11 38						12 38			
Bowes Park	d	08 41		09 11				09 41		10 11			10 41		11 11				11 41		12 11			12 41	
Palmers Green	d	08 43		09 13				09 43		10 13			10 43		11 13				11 43		12 13			12 43	
Winchmore Hill	d	08 45		09 15				09 45		10 15			10 45		11 15				11 45		12 15			12 45	
Grange Park	d	08 47		09 17				09 47		10 17			10 47		11 17				11 47		12 17			12 47	
Enfield Chase	d	08 49		09 19				09 49		10 19			10 49		11 19				11 49		12 19			12 49	
Gordon Hill	d	08 51		09 21				09 51		10 21			10 51		11 21				11 51		12 21			12 51	
Crews Hill	d	08 54		09 24				09 54		10 24			10 54		11 24				11 54		12 24			12 54	
Cuffley	d	08 57		09 27				09 57		10 27			10 57		11 27				11 57		12 27			12 57	
Bayford	d	09 02		09 32				10 02		10 32			11 02		11 32				12 02		12 32			13 02	
Hertford North	d	09 07		09a37				10 07		10a37			11 07		11a37				12 07		12a37			13 07	
Watton-at-Stone	d	09 13						10 13					11 13						12 13					13 13	
Stevenage 4	d	09a20			09 42			10a20			10 42		11a20			11 42			12a20			12 42		13a20	
Hitchin 4	d				09 47						10 47					11 47						12 47			
Letchworth Garden City	a				09 51						10 51					11 51						12 51			

A not 11 December

Table 24

Sundays

London - Welwyn Garden City, Hertford North and Letchworth Garden City

Network Diagram - see first Page of Table 24

		FC	FC ■1	FC	FC	FC	FC	FC ■1	FC	FC	FC	FC	FC ■1	FC	FC	FC	FC	FC ■1	FC	FC	FC ■1	FC
London Kings Cross ■15 ⊖	d	12 56	13 06	13 11	13 26	13 41	13 56	14 06	14 11	14 26	14 41	14 56	15 06	15 11	15 26	15 41	15 56	16 06	16 11	16 26	16 36	16 41
Moorgate ⊖	d																					
Old Street ⊖	d																					
Essex Road	d																					
Highbury & Islington ⊖	d																					
Drayton Park	d																					
Finsbury Park ⊖	d	13 02	13 11	13 17	13 32	13 47	14 02	14 11	14 17	14 32	14 47	15 02	15 11	15 17	15 32	15 47	16 02	16 11	16 17	16 32	16 41	16 47
Harringay	d	13 04		13 19	13 34	13 49	14 04		14 19	14 34	14 49	15 04		15 19	15 34	15 49	16 04		16 19	16 34		16 49
Hornsey	d	13 06		13 21	13 36	13 51	14 06		14 21	14 36	14 51	15 06		15 21	15 36	15 51	16 06		16 21	16 36		16 51
Alexandra Palace	d	13 08		13 23	13 38	13 53	14 08		14 23	14 38	14 53	15 08		15 23	15 38	15 53	16 08		16 23	16 38		16 53
New Southgate	d			13 26		13 56			14 26		14 56			15 26		15 56			16 26			16 56
Oakleigh Park	d			13 29		13 59			14 29		14 59			15 29		15 59			16 29			16 59
New Barnet	d			13 31		14 01			14 31		15 01			15 31		16 01			16 31			17 01
Hadley Wood	d			13 34		14 04			14 34		15 04			15 34		16 04			16 34			17 04
Potters Bar	d		13 21	13 38		14 08		14 21	14 38		15 08		15 21	15 38		16 08		16 21	16 38		16 51	17 08
Brookmans Park	d			13 41		14 11			14 41		15 11			15 41		16 11			16 41			17 11
Welham Green	d			13 43		14 13			14 43		15 13			15 43		16 13			16 43			17 13
Hatfield	d		13 27	13 46		14 16		14 27	14 46		15 16		15 27	15 46		16 16		16 27	16 46		16 57	17 16
Welwyn Garden City ■4	d		13 31	13a51		14a21		14 31	14a51		15a21		15 31	15a51		16a21		16 31	16a51		17 01	17a21
Welwyn North	d		13 34					14 34					15 34					16 34			17 04	
Knebworth	d		13 38					14 38					15 38					16 38			17 08	
Bowes Park	d	13 11			13 41		14 11			14 41		15 11			15 41		16 11			16 41		
Palmers Green	d	13 13			13 43		14 13			14 43		15 13			15 43		16 13			16 43		
Winchmore Hill	d	13 15			13 45		14 15			14 45		15 15			15 45		16 15			16 45		
Grange Park	d	13 17			13 47		14 17			14 47		15 17			15 47		16 17			16 47		
Enfield Chase	d	13 19			13 49		14 19			14 49		15 19			15 49		16 19			16 49		
Gordon Hill	d	13 21			13 51		14 21			14 51		15 21			15 51		16 21			16 51		
Crews Hill	d	13 24			13 54		14 24			14 54		15 24			15 54		16 24			16 54		
Cuffley	d	13 27			13 57		14 27			14 57		15 27			15 57		16 27			16 57		
Bayford	d	13 32			14 02		14 32			15 02		15 32			16 02		16 32			17 02		
Hertford North	d	13a37			14 07		14a37			15 07		15a37			16 07		16a37			17 07		
Watton-at-Stone	d				14 13					15 13					16 13					17 13		
Stevenage ■4	d		13 42		14a20			14 42		15a20			15 42		16a20			16 42		17a20	17 12	
Hitchin ■4	d		13 47					14 47					15 47					16 47			17a17	
Letchworth Garden City	a		13 51					14 51					15 51					16 51				

		FC	FC ■1	FC	FC	FC ■1	FC	FC	FC ■1	FC	FC	FC ■1	FC	FC	FC ■1	FC	FC	FC	FC	FC ■1	FC	FC	FC
London Kings Cross ■15 ⊖	d	16 56	17 06	17 11	17 26	17 36	17 41	17 56	18 06	18 11	18 26	18 36	18 41	18 56	19 06	19 11	19 26	19 41	19 56	20 06	20 11	20 26	20 41
Moorgate ⊖	d																						
Old Street ⊖	d																						
Essex Road	d																						
Highbury & Islington ⊖	d																						
Drayton Park	d																						
Finsbury Park ⊖	d	17 02	17 11	17 17	17 32	17 41	17 47	18 02	18 11	18 17	18 32	18 41	18 47	19 02	19 11	19 17	19 32	19 47	20 02	20 11	20 17	20 32	20 47
Harringay	d	17 04		17 19	17 34		17 49	18 04		18 19	18 34		18 49	19 04		19 19	19 34	19 49	20 04		20 19	20 34	20 49
Hornsey	d	17 06		17 21	17 36		17 51	18 06		18 21	18 36		18 51	19 06		19 21	19 36	19 51	20 06		20 21	20 36	20 51
Alexandra Palace	d	17 08		17 23	17 38		17 53	18 08		18 23	18 38		18 53	19 08		19 23	19 38	19 53	20 08		20 23	20 38	20 53
New Southgate	d			17 26			17 56			18 26			18 56			19 26		19 56			20 26		20 56
Oakleigh Park	d			17 29			17 59			18 29			18 59			19 29		19 59			20 29		20 59
New Barnet	d			17 31			18 01			18 31			19 01			19 31		20 01			20 31		21 01
Hadley Wood	d			17 34			18 04			18 34			19 04			19 34		20 04			20 34		21 04
Potters Bar	d		17 21	17 38		17 51	18 08		18 21	18 38		18 51	19 08		19 21	19 38		20 08		20 21	20 38		21 08
Brookmans Park	d			17 41			18 11			18 41			19 11			19 41		20 11			20 41		21 11
Welham Green	d			17 43			18 13			18 43			19 13			19 43		20 13			20 43		21 13
Hatfield	d		17 27	17 46		17 57	18 16		18 27	18 46		18 57	19 16		19 27	19 46		20 16		20 27	20 46		21 16
Welwyn Garden City ■4	d		17 31	17a51		18 01	18a21		18 31	18a51		19 01	19a21		19 31	19a51		20a21		20 31	20a51		21a21
Welwyn North	d		17 34			18 04			18 34			19 04			19 34					20 34			
Knebworth	d		17 38			18 08			18 38			19 08			19 38					20 38			
Bowes Park	d	17 11			17 41			18 11			18 41			19 11			19 41		20 11			20 41	
Palmers Green	d	17 13			17 43			18 13			18 43			19 13			19 43		20 13			20 43	
Winchmore Hill	d	17 15			17 45			18 15			18 45			19 15			19 45		20 15			20 45	
Grange Park	d	17 17			17 47			18 17			18 47			19 17			19 47		20 17			20 47	
Enfield Chase	d	17 19			17 49			18 19			18 49			19 19			19 49		20 19			20 49	
Gordon Hill	d	17 21			17 51			18 21			18 51			19 21			19 51		20 21			20 51	
Crews Hill	d	17 24			17 54			18 24			18 54			19 24			19 54		20 24			20 54	
Cuffley	d	17 27			17 57			18 27			18 57			19 27			19 57		20 27			20 57	
Bayford	d	17 32			18 02			18 32			19 02			19 32			20 02		20 32			21 02	
Hertford North	d	17a37			18 07			18a37			19 07			19a37			20 07		20a37			21 07	
Watton-at-Stone	d				18 13						19 13						20 13					21 13	
Stevenage ■4	d		17 42		18a20	18 12			18 42		19a20	19 12			19 42		20a20			20 42		21a20	
Hitchin ■4	d		17 47			18a17			18 47			19 17			19 47					20 47			
Letchworth Garden City	a		17 51						18 51			19 21			19 51					20 51			

Sundays

London - Welwyn Garden City, Hertford North and Letchworth Garden City

Network Diagram - see first Page of Table 24

		FC	FC 1	FC		FC	FC	FC	FC 1	FC	FC	FC	FC	FC 1		FC	FC	FC
London Kings Cross 15 ⊖	d	20 56	21 06	21 11		21 26	21 41	21 56	22 06	22 11	22 26	22 41	22 56	23 06		23 11	23 26	23 41
Moorgate ⊖	d																	
Old Street ⊖	d																	
Essex Road	d																	
Highbury & Islington ⊖	d																	
Drayton Park	d																	
Finsbury Park ⊖	d	21 02	21 11	21 17		21 32	21 47	22 02	22 11	22 17	22 32	22 47	23 02	23 11		23 17	23 32	23 47
Harringay	d	21 04		21 19		21 34	21 49	22 04		22 19	22 34	22 49	23 04			23 19	23 34	23 49
Hornsey	d	21 06		21 21		21 36	21 51	22 06		22 21	22 36	22 51	23 06			23 21	23 36	23 51
Alexandra Palace	d	21 08		21 23		21 38	21 53	22 08		22 23	22 38	22 53	23 08			23 23	23 38	23 53
New Southgate	d			21 26			21 56			22 26		22 56				23 26		23 56
Oakleigh Park	d			21 29			21 59			22 29		22 59				23 29		23 59
New Barnet	d			21 31			22 01			22 31		23 01				23 31		00 01
Hadley Wood	d			21 34			22 04			22 34		23 04				23 34		00 04
Potters Bar	d		21 21	21 38			22 08		22 21	22 38		23 08		23 21		23 38		00 08
Brookmans Park	d			21 41			22 11			22 41		23 11				23 41		00 11
Welham Green	d			21 43			22 13			22 43		23 13				23 43		00 13
Hatfield	d		21 27	21 46			22 16		22 27	22 46		23 16		23 27		23 46		00 16
Welwyn Garden City 4	d		21 31	21a51			22a21		22 31	22a51		23a21		23 31		23a51		00 20
Welwyn North	d		21 34						22 34					23 34				00 23
Knebworth	d		21 38						22 38					23 38				00 28
Bowes Park	d	21 11				21 41		22 11			22 41		23 11				23 41	
Palmers Green	d	21 13				21 43		22 13			22 43		23 13				23 43	
Winchmore Hill	d	21 15				21 45		22 15			22 45		23 15				23 45	
Grange Park	d	21 17				21 47		22 17			22 47		23 17				23 47	
Enfield Chase	d	21 19				21 49		22 19			22 49		23 19				23 49	
Gordon Hill	d	21 21				21 51		22 21			22 51		23 21				23 51	
Crews Hill	d	21 24				21 54		22 24			22 54		23 24				23 54	
Cuffley	d	21 27				21 57		22 27			22 57		23 27				23 57	
Bayford	d	21 32				22 02		22 32			23 02		23 32				00 02	
Hertford North	d	21a37				22 07		22a37			23 07		23a37				00 07	
Watton-at-Stone	d					22 13					23 13						00 13	
Stevenage 4	d		21 42			22a20			22 42		23a20			23 42			00a20	00 31
Hitchin 4	d		21 47						22 47					23 47				00 37
Letchworth Garden City	a		21 51						22 51					23 51				00 52

Letchworth Garden City, Hertford North and Welwyn Garden City - London

Network Diagram - see first Page of Table 24

Miles	Miles			FC MX 1	FC MX	FC MO	FC MO 1	FC MX 1	FC	FC 1	FC	FC 1		FC	FC	FC	FC 1	FC	FC	FC	FC 1	FC		FC	FC 1
0	0	**Letchworth Garden City**	d		23p20		23p46	23p47			04 50					05 20	05 29			05 48	05 59				06 19
3	3	Hitchin 4	d	23p16	23p24		23p50	23p54		04 08	04 54	04 57				05 24	05 34			05 52	06 04				06 23
7¼	7¼	**Stevenage 4**	d	23p22	23p29	23p30	23p55	23p59		04 13	04 59	05 02				05 29	05 39			05 57	06 09			06 10	06 29
—	12¼	Watton-at-Stone	d		23p36	23p37					05 06					05 36				06 04				06 17	
—	16½	**Hertford North**	d		23p42	23p43				04 23	05 12					05 42				06 12				06 26	
—	19½	Bayford	d		23p46	23p47					05 16					05 46				06 16					
—	23	Cuffley	d		23p51	23p52				04 30	05 21					05 51				06 21				06 34	
—	24¾	Crews Hill	d		23p54	23p55					05 24					05 54				06 24					
—	26¼	Gordon Hill	d		23p57	23p58				04 34	05 27					05 57				06 27				06 38	
—	27	Enfield Chase	d		23p59	23p59				04 36	05 29					05 59				06 29				06 41	
—	27¾	Grange Park	d		00 01	00 02					05 31					06 01				06 31					
—	28½	Winchmore Hill	d		00 03	00 04				04 38	05 33					06 03				06 33				06 44	
—	29½	Palmers Green	d		00 05	00 06				04 40	05 35					06 05				06 35				06 46	
—	30½	Bowes Park	d		00 08	00 09					05 38					06 08				06 38					
9¾	—	Knebworth	d	23p25			23p58	00 02				05 06					05 43				06 13				06 33
12¾	—	Welwyn North	d	23p29			00 02	00 06				05 10					05 47				06 17				06 37
14½	—	**Welwyn Garden City 4**	d	23p32			00 05	00 09	04 10			05 13			05 33		05 50		05 58		06 20				06 40
17	—	Hatfield	d	23p35			00 08	00 12	04 14			05 16			05 37		05 54		06 02		06 24				06 44
19¼	—	Welham Green	d												05 41				06 06						
20¼	—	Brookmans Park	d						04 19						05 43				06 08						
22	—	Potters Bar	d	23p41			00 14	00 18	04 22			05 22			05 46		06 00		06 11		06 30				06 49
24¼	—	Hadley Wood	d						04 25						05 50				06 15						
25½	—	New Barnet	d						04 28			05 27			05 52				06 17						
26¼	—	Oakleigh Park	d						04 30			05 29			05 54				06 19						
28¼	—	New Southgate	d						04 33			05 32			05 57				06 22						
29¾	31¼	Alexandra Palace	d		00 10	00 11			04 36		05 41	05 35			06 00	06 10			06 25	06 40					
30¾	32¼	Hornsey	d		00 12	00 13			04 38	04u44	05 43				06 02	06 12			06 27	06 42					
31¼	32¾	Harringay	d		00 14	00 15			04 40		05 45			←	06 04	06 14		←	06 29	06 44		←			
32¼	33¾	Finsbury Park ⊖	d	23b51	00 17	00 18	00 27	00 29	04 42	04s47	05 47	05 39		05 47	06 07	06 17	06 09	06 17	06 32	06 47	06 39	06 47		06 54	06 58
—	34½	Drayton Park	d								↪					↪		06 19	06 34	↪		06 49		06 56	
—	35	Highbury & Islington ⊖	d															06 20	06 35			06 50		06 58	
—	35½	Essex Road	d															06 22	06 37			06 52		07 00	
—	36¾	Old Street ⊖	d															06 25	06 40			06 55		07 03	
—	37¼	**Moorgate** ⊖	a															06 30	06 45			07 01		07 08	
34¾	—	London Kings Cross 15 ⊖	a	00 01	00 26	00 27	00 39	00 40	04 51	05 00		05 48		05 55	06 15		06 18				06 48				07 07

		FC	FC	FC	FC	FC	FC	FC		FC	FC	FC	FC	FC 1	FC	FC	FC	FC		FC	FC	FC	FC	FC	FC
Letchworth Garden City	d				06 23					06 46				07 04						07 20					
Hitchin 4	d				06 27					06 50				07 08						07 24					
Stevenage 4	d				06 33					06 55		07 03		07 14						07 30		07 35			
Watton-at-Stone	d				06 40							07 10										07 42			
Hertford North	d			06 33	06 46						07 03	07 16				07 24	07 33				07 38	07 50		07 55	
Bayford	d			06 37							07 07					07 28					07 42				
Cuffley	d			06 42	06 54						07 12	07 24				07 33	07 41				07 47	07 57		08 02	
Crews Hill	d			06 45							07 15					07 36					07 50				
Gordon Hill	d			06 48	06 58		07 06				07 18	07 28			07 33	07 39	07 45				07 53	08 02		08 07	
Enfield Chase	d			06 51	07 01		07 08				07 21	07 31			07 35	07 42	07 48				07 56	08 04		08 09	
Grange Park	d			06 53			07 10				07 23				07 37	07 44					07 58			08 11	
Winchmore Hill	d			06 55	07 04		07 12				07 25	07 34			07 40	07 46	07 51				08 00			08 13	
Palmers Green	d			06 58	07 06		07 15				07 28	07 36			07 42	07 48	07 53				08 03			08 16	
Bowes Park	d			07 00			07 17				07 30				07 45	07 51					08 05	08 09		08 18	
Knebworth	d													07 18											
Welwyn North	d													07 24											
Welwyn Garden City 4	d	06 25	06 35			06 45		06 57		07 07			07 17	07 27				07 32		07 42			07 47		07 58
Hatfield	d	06 29	06 39			06 49		07 01		07 11			07 21	07 31				07 36		07 46			07 51		08 02
Welham Green	d	06 33				06 53		07 05					07 25					07 40					07 55		08 06
Brookmans Park	d	06 35				06 55		07 07					07 27					07 42					07 57		08 08
Potters Bar	d	06 38	06 46			06 58		07 10		07 18			07 30					07 45		07 52			08 00		08 11
Hadley Wood	d	06 42	06 49			07 02		07 14					07 34					07 49					08 04		08 15
New Barnet	d	06 45	06 52			07 05		07 17		07 23			07 37					07 52		07 57			08 07		08 18
Oakleigh Park	d	06 47	06 54			07 07		07 19		07 25			07 39					07 54		07 59			08 09		08 20
New Southgate	d	06 50	06 57			07 10		07 22		07 28			07 42					07 57		08 02			08 12		08 23
Alexandra Palace	d	06 53		07 03		07 13	07 20	07 25			07 33				07 47	07 53		08 00			08 08	08 11	08 15	08 21	
Hornsey	d	06 55		07 05		07 15	07 22	07 27			07 35				07 49			08 02			08 10	08 13	08 17	08 23	08 27
Harringay	d	06 57		07 07		07 17	07 24	07 29			07 37				07 51			08 04			08 12	08 15	08 19	08 25	08 29
Finsbury Park ⊖	d	07 00	07 03	07 09	07 14	07 20	07 27	07 32		07 35	07 39	07 44	07 48	07 47	07 54	07 58	08 02	08 06		08 10	08 14	08 18	08 22	08 28	08 32
Drayton Park	d	07 02		07 11	07 16	07 22	07 29	07 34			07 41	07 46	07 50		07 56	08 00	08 04	08 08			08 16	08 20	08 24	08 30	08 34
Highbury & Islington ⊖	d	07 04		07 13	07 18	07 24	07 31	07 36			07 43	07 48	07 52		07 58	08 02	08 06	08 10			08 18	08 22	08 26	08 32	08 36
Essex Road	d	07 06		07 15	07 20	07 26	07 33	07 38			07 45	07 50	07 54		08 00	08 04	08 08	08 12			08 20	08 24	08 28	08 34	08 38
Old Street ⊖	d	07 09		07 18	07 23	07 29	07 36	07 41			07 48	07 53	07 57		08 03	08 07	08 11	08 15			08 23	08 27	08 31	08 37	08 41
Moorgate ⊖	a	07 14		07 23	07 28	07 34	07 41	07 46			07 53	07 58	08 02		08 08	08 12	08 17	08 22			08 28	08 32	08 37	08 42	08 46
London Kings Cross 15 ⊖	a		07 10							07 43				07 57						08 17					

b Previous night, stops to set down only

Table 24

Mondays to Fridays

Letchworth Garden City, Hertford North and Welwyn Garden City - London

Network Diagram - see first Page of Table 24

		FC	FC	FC		FC	FC	FC	FC	FC	FC	FC	FC	FC 1		FC	FC	FC	FC	FC	FC 1	FC	FC	FC	
Letchworth Garden City	d																				08 59				
Hitchin 4	d													08 39							09 05				
Stevenage 4	d					08 05							08 34	08 45						09 04	09 11				
Watton-at-Stone	d					08 12							08 41							09 11					
Hertford North	d		08 05			08 20			08 30				08 50							09 17					
Bayford	d		08 09						08 34				08 54							09 21					
Cuffley	d		08 14			08 27			08 39				08 59							09 26					
Crews Hill	d		08 17						08 42				09 02							09 29					
Gordon Hill	d	08 15	08 20			08 32		08 37	08 45			08 55	09 05				09 12		09 27	09 32					
Enfield Chase	d	08 17	08 22			08 34		08 39	08 47			08 57	09 07				09 14		09 29	09 34					
Grange Park	d	08 19	08 24					08 41				08 59	09 09				09 16		09 31	09 36					
Winchmore Hill	d	08 21	08 26					08 43				09 01	09 11				09 18		09 33	09 38					
Palmers Green	d	08 24	08 29					08 46				09 04	09 14				09 21		09 36	09 41					
Bowes Park	d	08 26	08 31			08 38		08 48	08 52			09 06	09 16				09 23		09 38	09 43					
Knebworth	d													08 49							09 14				
Welwyn North	d													08 53							09 18				
Welwyn Garden City 4	d			08 14			08 18			08 32	08 42			08 58				09 04			09 21			09 24	
Hatfield	d			08 18			08 22			08 36	08 46			09 02				09 08			09 25			09 28	
Welham Green	d						08 26			08 40								09 12						09 32	
Brookmans Park	d						08 28			08 42								09 14						09 34	
Potters Bar	d			08 25			08 31			08 46	08 53							09 17			09 31			09 37	
Hadley Wood	d						08 35			08 49								09 21						09 41	
New Barnet	d			08 30			08 38			08 52	08 57							09 23						09 43	
Oakleigh Park	d			08 32			08 40			08 54	08 59							09 25						09 45	
New Southgate	d			08 35			08 43			08 57	09 02							09 28						09 48	
Alexandra Palace	d	08 29	08 34	08 38		08 41	08 46	08 51	08 55	09 00	09 05	09 09	09 19				09 26	09 31	09 42	09 46				09 51	
Hornsey	d	08 31				08 43	08 48		08 57	09 02		09 11	09 21				09 28	09 33		09 48				09 53	
Harringay	d	08 33				08 45	08 50		08 59	09 04		09 13	09 23			←	09 30	09 35		09 50		←	←	09 55	
Finsbury Park ⊖	d	08 36	08 40	08 43		08 48	08 53	08 57	09 02	09 07	09 10	09 16	09 26	09 19		09 26	09 33	09 38	09 46	09 53	09 40	09 46	09 53	09 58	
Drayton Park	d	08 38	08 42			08 50	08 55	08 59	09 04	09 09		09 18	↦			09 28	09 35	09 40	↦	↦		09 48	09 55	10 00	
Highbury & Islington ⊖	d	08 40	08 44			08 52	08 57	09 01	09 06	09 11		09 20				09 30	09 36	09 41				09 49	09 56	10 01	
Essex Road	d	08 42	08 46			08 54	08 59	09 03	09 08	09 13		09 22				09 32	09 38	09 43				09 51	09 58	10 03	
Old Street ⊖	d	08 45	08 49			08 57	09 02	09 06	09 11	09 16		09 25				09 35	09 41	09 46				09 54	10 01	10 06	
Moorgate ⊖	a	08 50	08 55			09 02	09 07	09 11	09 16	09 21		09 30				09 40	09 46	09 51				09 59	10 06	10 11	
London Kings Cross 15 ⊖	a			08 51							09 16			09 28							09 49				

		FC	FC	FC	FC	FC 1	FC	FC	FC	FC		FC 1	FC	FC	FC	FC 1	FC	FC	FC	FC		FC 1	FC	FC	FC
Letchworth Garden City	d					09 29				09 50		09 59				10 29				10 50					
Hitchin 4	d					09 34				09 54		10 04				10 34				10 54		11 04			
Stevenage 4	d				09 34	09 40				10 00		10 10				10 40				11 00		11 10			
Watton-at-Stone	d				09 41					10 06										11 06					
Hertford North	d		09 33		09 53					10 13					10 33			10 53		11 13					11 33
Bayford	d		09 37		09 57					10 17					10 37			10 57		11 17					11 37
Cuffley	d		09 42		10 02					10 22					10 42			11 02		11 22					11 42
Crews Hill	d		09 45		10 05					10 25					10 45			11 05		11 25					11 45
Gordon Hill	d		09 48		10 08					10 28					10 48			11 08		11 28					11 48
Enfield Chase	d		09 50		10 10					10 30					10 50			11 10		11 30					11 50
Grange Park	d		09 52		10 12					10 32					10 52			11 12		11 32					11 52
Winchmore Hill	d		09 54		10 14					10 34					10 54			11 14		11 34					11 54
Palmers Green	d		09 56		10 16					10 36					10 56			11 16		11 36					11 56
Bowes Park	d		09 59		10 19					10 39					10 59			11 19		11 39					11 59
Knebworth	d					09 44						10 14				10 44						11 14			
Welwyn North	d					09 48						10 18				10 48						11 18			
Welwyn Garden City 4	d	09 40		09 44		09 51			10 04			10 21		10 24		10 51	10 44		11 04			11 21		11 24	
Hatfield	d	09 43		09 48		09 55			10 08			10 25		10 28		10 55	10 48		11 08			11 25		11 28	
Welham Green	d			09 52					10 12					10 32			10 52		11 12					11 32	
Brookmans Park	d			09 54					10 14					10 34			10 54		11 14					11 34	
Potters Bar	d	09 49		09 57		10 01			10 17			10 31		10 37		11 01	10 57		11 17			11 31		11 37	
Hadley Wood	d			10 01					10 21					10 41			11 01		11 21					11 41	
New Barnet	d			10 03					10 23					10 43			11 03		11 23					11 43	
Oakleigh Park	d			10 05					10 25					10 45			11 05		11 25					11 45	
New Southgate	d			10 08					10 28					10 48			11 08		11 28					11 48	
Alexandra Palace	d		10 01	10 11	10 21				10 31	10 41				10 51	11 01		11 11	11 21	11 31	11 41				11 51	12 01
Hornsey	d		10 03	10 13	10 23				10 33	10 43				10 53	11 03		11 13	11 23	11 33	11 43				11 53	12 03
Harringay	d		10 05	10 15	10 25		←	←	10 35	10 45			←	10 55	11 05		11 15	11 25	11 35	11 45			←	11 55	12 05
Finsbury Park ⊖	d	10 01	10 08	10 18	10 28	10 10	10 18	10 28	10 38	10 48		10 40	10 48	10 58	11 08	11 10	11 18	11 28	11 38	11 48		11 40	11 48	11 58	12 08
Drayton Park	d		10 10	↦	↦		10 20	10 30	10 40	↦			10 50	11 00	11 10		11 20	11 30	11 40	↦			11 50	12 00	12 10
Highbury & Islington ⊖	d		10 11				10 21	10 31	10 41				10 51	11 01	11 11		11 21	11 31	11 41				11 51	12 01	12 11
Essex Road	d		10 13				10 23	10 33	10 43				10 53	11 03	11 13		11 23	11 33	11 43				11 53	12 03	12 13
Old Street ⊖	d		10 16				10 26	10 36	10 46				10 56	11 06	11 16		11 26	11 36	11 46				11 56	12 06	12 16
Moorgate ⊖	a		10 21				10 31	10 41	10 51				11 01	11 11	11 21		11 31	11 41	11 51				12 01	12 11	12 21
London Kings Cross 15 ⊖	a	10 08				10 19						10 49				11 19						11 49			

Letchworth Garden City, Hertford North and Welwyn Garden City - London

Network Diagram - see first Page of Table 24

		FC [1]	FC	FC	FC	FC		FC [1]	FC	FC	FC	FC [1]	FC	FC	FC	FC		FC [1]	FC	FC	FC	FC [1]	FC	FC	FC
Letchworth Garden City	d	11 29				11 50						12 29				12 50						13 29			
Hitchin [4]	d	11 34				11 54		12 04				12 34				12 54		13 04				13 34			
Stevenage [4]	d	11 40				12 00		12 10				12 40				13 00		13 10				13 40			
Watton-at-Stone	d					12 06										13 06									
Hertford North	d			11 53		12 13					12 33			12 53		13 13					13 33			13 53	
Bayford	d			11 57		12 17					12 37			12 57		13 17					13 37			13 57	
Cuffley	d			12 02		12 22					12 42			13 02		13 22					13 42			14 02	
Crews Hill	d			12 05		12 25					12 45			13 05		13 25					13 45			14 05	
Gordon Hill	d			12 08		12 28					12 48			13 08		13 28					13 48			14 08	
Enfield Chase	d			12 10		12 30					12 50			13 10		13 30					13 50			14 10	
Grange Park	d			12 12		12 32					12 52			13 12		13 32					13 52			14 12	
Winchmore Hill	d			12 14		12 34					12 54			13 14		13 34					13 54			14 14	
Palmers Green	d			12 16		12 36					12 56			13 16		13 36					13 56			14 16	
Bowes Park	d			12 19		12 39					12 59			13 19		13 39					13 59			14 19	
Knebworth	d	11 44						12 14				12 44						13 14				13 44			
Welwyn North	d	11 48						12 18				12 48						13 18				13 48			
Welwyn Garden City [4]	d	11 51	11 44		12 04			12 21		12 24		12 51	12 44		13 04			13 21		13 24		13 51	13 44		14 04
Hatfield	d	11 55	11 48		12 08			12 25		12 28		12 55	12 48		13 08			13 25		13 28		13 55	13 48		14 08
Welham Green	d		11 52		12 12					12 32			12 52		13 12					13 32			13 52		14 12
Brookmans Park	d		11 54		12 14					12 34			12 54		13 14					13 34			13 54		14 14
Potters Bar	d	12 01	11 57		12 17			12 31		12 37		13 01	12 57		13 17			13 31		13 37		14 01	13 57		14 17
Hadley Wood	d		12 01		12 21					12 41			13 01		13 21					13 41			14 01		14 21
New Barnet	d		12 03		12 23					12 43			13 03		13 23					13 43			14 03		14 23
Oakleigh Park	d		12 05		12 25					12 45			13 05		13 25					13 45			14 05		14 25
New Southgate	d		12 08		12 28					12 48			13 08		13 28					13 48			14 08		14 28
Alexandra Palace	d		12 11	12 21	12 31	12 41				12 51	13 01		13 11	13 21	13 31	13 41				13 51	14 01		14 11	14 21	14 31
Hornsey	d		12 13	12 23	12 33	12 43				12 53	13 03		13 13	13 23	13 33	13 43				13 53	14 03		14 13	14 23	14 33
Harringay	d		12 15	12 25	12 35	12 45			←	12 55	13 05		13 15	13 25	13 35	13 45			←	13 55	14 05		14 15	14 25	14 35
Finsbury Park ⊖	d	12 10	12 18	12 28	12 38	12 48		12 40	12 48	12 58	13 08	13 10	13 18	13 28	13 38	13 48		13 40	13 48	13 58	14 08	14 10	14 18	14 28	14 38
Drayton Park	d		12 20	12 30	12 40	→			12 50	13 00	13 10		13 20	13 30	13 40	→			13 50	14 00	14 10		14 20	14 30	14 40
Highbury & Islington ⊖	d		12 21	12 31	12 41				12 51	13 01	13 11		13 21	13 31	13 41				13 51	14 01	14 11		14 21	14 31	14 41
Essex Road	d		12 23	12 33	12 43				12 53	13 03	13 13		13 23	13 33	13 43				13 53	14 03	14 13		14 23	14 33	14 43
Old Street ⊖	d		12 26	12 36	12 46				12 56	13 06	13 16		13 26	13 36	13 46				13 56	14 06	14 16		14 26	14 36	14 46
Moorgate ⊖	a		12 31	12 41	12 51				13 01	13 11	13 21		13 31	13 41	13 51				14 01	14 11	14 21		14 31	14 41	14 51
London Kings Cross [15] ⊖	a	12 19						12 49				13 19						13 49				14 19			

		FC		FC [1]	FC	FC	FC	FC [1]	FC	FC	FC	FC		FC [1]	FC	FC	FC	FC	FC	FC [1]	FC	FC		FC	FC
Letchworth Garden City	d	13 50						14 29				14 50							15 20	15 29					15 50
Hitchin [4]	d	13 54		14 04				14 34				14 54		15 04					15 24	15 34					15 54
Stevenage [4]	d	14 00		14 10				14 40				15 00		15 10					15 30	15 40					16 00
Watton-at-Stone	d	14 06										15 06							15 36						16 06
Hertford North	d	14 13					14 33			14 53		15 13					15 33		15 53						16 13
Bayford	d	14 17					14 37			14 57		15 17					15 37		15 57						16 17
Cuffley	d	14 22					14 42			15 02		15 22					15 42		16 02						16 22
Crews Hill	d	14 25					14 45			15 05		15 25					15 45		16 05						16 25
Gordon Hill	d	14 28					14 48			15 08		15 28					15 48		16 08						16 28
Enfield Chase	d	14 30					14 50			15 10		15 30					15 50		16 10						16 30
Grange Park	d	14 32					14 52			15 12		15 32					15 52		16 12						16 32
Winchmore Hill	d	14 34					14 54			15 14		15 34					15 54		16 14						16 34
Palmers Green	d	14 36					14 56			15 16		15 36					15 56		16 16						16 36
Bowes Park	d	14 39					14 59			15 19		15 39					15 59		16 19						16 39
Knebworth	d			14 14				14 44						15 14						15 44					
Welwyn North	d			14 18				14 48						15 18						15 48					
Welwyn Garden City [4]	d			14 21		14 24		14 51	14 44		15 04			15 21		15 24		15 44		15 51				16 04	
Hatfield	d			14 25		14 28		14 55	14 48		15 08			15 25		15 28		15 48		15 55				16 08	
Welham Green	d					14 32			14 52		15 12					15 32		15 52						16 12	
Brookmans Park	d					14 34			14 54		15 14					15 34		15 54						16 14	
Potters Bar	d			14 31		14 37		15 01	14 57		15 17			15 31		15 37		15 57		16 01				16 17	
Hadley Wood	d					14 41			15 01		15 21					15 41		16 01						16 21	
New Barnet	d					14 43			15 03		15 23					15 43		16 03						16 23	
Oakleigh Park	d					14 45			15 05		15 25					15 45		16 05						16 25	
New Southgate	d					14 48			15 08		15 28					15 48		16 08						16 28	
Alexandra Palace	d	14 41				14 51	15 01		15 11	15 21	15 31	15 41				15 51	16 01	16 11	16 21					16 31	16 41
Hornsey	d	14 43				14 53	15 03		15 13	15 23	15 33	15 43				15 53	16 03	16 13	16 23					16 33	16 43
Harringay	d	14 45			←	14 55	15 05		15 15	15 25	15 35	15 45			←	15 55	16 05	16 15	16 25		←	←		16 35	16 45
Finsbury Park ⊖	d	14 48		14 40	14 48	14 58	15 08	15 10	15 18	15 28	15 38	15 48		15 40	15 48	15 58	16 08	16 18	16 28	16 10	16 18	16 28		16 38	16 48
Drayton Park	d	→			14 50	15 00	15 10		15 20	15 30	15 40	→			15 50	16 00	16 10	→	→		16 20	16 30		16 40	→
Highbury & Islington ⊖	d				14 51	15 01	15 11		15 21	15 31	15 41				15 51	16 01	16 11				16 21	16 31		16 41	
Essex Road	d				14 53	15 03	15 13		15 23	15 33	15 43				15 53	16 03	16 13				16 23	16 33		16 43	
Old Street ⊖	d				14 56	15 06	15 16		15 26	15 36	15 46				15 56	16 06	16 16				16 26	16 36		16 46	
Moorgate ⊖	a				15 01	15 11	15 21		15 31	15 41	15 51				16 01	16 11	16 21				16 31	16 41		16 51	
London Kings Cross [15] ⊖	a			14 49				15 19						15 49						16 19					

Table 24

Mondays to Fridays

Letchworth Garden City, Hertford North and Welwyn Garden City - London

Network Diagram - see first Page of Table 24

		FC 1	FC	FC	FC	FC	FC	FC 1		FC	FC	FC	FC	FC	FC	FC 1	FC	FC		FC	FC	FC	FC	FC 1	FC
Letchworth Garden City	d						16 20	16 29																17 29	
Hitchin 4	d	16 04					16 24	16 34								17 04								17 34	
Stevenage 4	d	16 10					16 30	16 40							16 59	17 10							17 29	17 40	
Watton-at-Stone	d						16 36								17 06								17 36		
Hertford North	d					16 33	16 43					16 53			17 13					17 36			17 43		
Bayford	d					16 37	16 47					16 57			17 17								17 47		
Cuffley	d					16 42	16 52					17 02			17 22					17 43			17 52		
Crews Hill	d					16 45	16 55					17 05			17 25								17 55		
Gordon Hill	d					16 48	16 58					17 08	17 18		17 28			17 38		17 48			17 58		
Enfield Chase	d					16 50	17 00					17 10	17 20		17 30			17 40		17 50			18 00		
Grange Park	d					16 52						17 12			17 32			17 42					18 02		
Winchmore Hill	d					16 54	17 02					17 14	17 22		17 34			17 44		17 52			18 04		
Palmers Green	d					16 56	17 05					17 16	17 25		17 36			17 46		17 55			18 06		
Bowes Park	d					16 59						17 19			17 39			17 49					18 09		
Knebworth	d	16 14						16 44								17 14								17 44	
Welwyn North	d	16 18						16 48								17 18								17 48	
Welwyn Garden City 4	d	16 21		16 24	16 40			16 51			16 44			17 04		17 21					17 34	17 46		17 51	
Hatfield	d	16 25		16 28	16 44			16 55			16 48			17 08		17 25					17 38	17 50		17 55	
Welham Green	d			16 32							16 52			17 12							17 42				
Brookmans Park	d			16 34							16 54			17 14							17 44				
Potters Bar	d	16 31		16 37	16 50			17 01			16 57			17 17		17 31					17 47	17 57		18 01	
Hadley Wood	d			16 41							17 01			17 21							17 51				
New Barnet	d			16 43							17 03			17 23							17 53				
Oakleigh Park	d			16 45							17 05			17 25							17 55				
New Southgate	d			16 48							17 08			17 28							17 58				
Alexandra Palace	d			16 51		17 01					17 11	17 21		17 31	17 41			17 51			18 01		18 11		
Hornsey	d			16 53		17 03					17 13	17 23		17 33	17 43			17 53			18 03		18 13		
Harringay	d		←	16 55		17 05				←	17 15	17 25		17 35	17 45		←	17 55			18 05		18 15		←
Finsbury Park	⊖ d	16 40	16 48	16 58	17 02	17 08	17 13	17 10		17 13	17 18	17 28	17 33	17 38	17 48	17 40	17 48	17 58		18 03	18 08	18 07	18 18	18 10	18 18
Drayton Park	d		16 50	17 00		17 10	→			17 15	17 20	17 30	17 35	17 40	→		17 50	18 00		18 05	18 10		→		18 20
Highbury & Islington	⊖ d		16 51	17 01		17 11				17 16	17 21	17 31	17 36	17 41			17 51	18 01		18 06	18 11				18 21
Essex Road	d		16 53	17 03		17 13				17 18	17 23	17 33	17 38	17 43			17 53	18 03		18 08	18 13				18 23
Old Street	⊖ d		16 56	17 06		17 16				17 21	17 26	17 36	17 41	17 46			17 56	18 06		18 11	18 16				18 26
Moorgate	⊖ a		17 01	17 11		17 21				17 26	17 31	17 41	17 46	17 51			18 01	18 11		18 16	18 21				18 31
London Kings Cross 15	⊖ a	16 49			17 10			17 19								17 49						18 17		18 19	

		FC	FC	FC		FC	FC 1	FC	FC	FC	FC 1	FC	FC	FC		FC	FC 1	FC	FC	FC	FC 1	FC	FC	FC	
Letchworth Garden City	d										18 29										19 29				
Hitchin 4	d						18 04				18 34						19 11				19 34				
Stevenage 4	d	17 53					18 10		18 23		18 40			18 53			19 17				19 40			19 59	
Watton-at-Stone	d	18 00							18 30					19 00										20 06	
Hertford North	d	18 06						18 18	18 36				18 48	19 06				19 18	19 36			19 48		20 12	
Bayford	d							18 22					18 52					19 22				19 52		20 16	
Cuffley	d	18 13						18 27	18 43				18 57	19 13				19 27	19 43			19 57		20 21	
Crews Hill	d							18 30					19 00					19 30				20 00		20 24	
Gordon Hill	d	18 18				18 23		18 33	18 48			18 53	19 03	19 18				19 33	19 48			20 03		20 27	
Enfield Chase	d	18 20				18 25		18 35	18 50			18 55	19 05	19 20				19 35	19 50			20 05		20 29	
Grange Park	d					18 27		18 37				18 57	19 07					19 37				20 07		20 31	
Winchmore Hill	d	18 22				18 29		18 39	18 52			18 59	19 09	19 22				19 39	19 52			20 09		20 33	
Palmers Green	d	18 25				18 31		18 41	18 55			19 01	19 11	19 25				19 41	19 55			20 11		20 35	
Bowes Park	d					18 34		18 44				19 04	19 14					19 44				20 14		20 38	
Knebworth	d						18 14				18 44						19 20				19 44				
Welwyn North	d						18 18				18 48						19 24				19 48				
Welwyn Garden City 4	d		18 04	18 16			18 28			18 34	18 51					19 04	19 28			19 34	19 51		19 58		
Hatfield	d		18 08	18 20			18 32			18 38	18 55					19 08	19 32			19 38	19 55		20 02		
Welham Green	d		18 12							18 42						19 12				19 42			20 06		
Brookmans Park	d		18 14							18 44						19 14				19 44			20 08		
Potters Bar	d		18 17	18 27			18 38			18 47	19 01					19 17	19 38			19 47	20 01		20 11		
Hadley Wood	d		18 21							18 51						19 21				19 51			20 15		
New Barnet	d		18 23							18 53						19 23				19 53			20 17		
Oakleigh Park	d		18 25							18 55						19 25				19 55			20 19		
New Southgate	d		18 28							18 58						19 28				19 58			20 22		
Alexandra Palace	d		18 31			18 36		18 46		19 01		19 06	19 16			19 31		19 46		20 01		20 16	20 25	20 40	
Hornsey	d		18 33			18 38		18 48		19 03		19 08	19 18			19 33		19 48		20 03		20 18	20 27	20 42	
Harringay	d		18 35			18 40		18 50		19 05		19 10	19 20			19 35		19 50		20 05		20 20	20 29	20 44	
Finsbury Park	⊖ d	18 32	18 38	18 38		18 43	18 47	18 53	19 02	19 08	19 10	19 13	19 23	19 32		19 38	19 47	19 53	20 02	20 08	20 10	20 23	20 32	20 47	
Drayton Park	d	18 34	18 40			18 45		18 55	19 04	19 10		19 15	19 25	19 34		19 40		19 55	20 04	20 10		20 25	20 34	→	
Highbury & Islington	⊖ d	18 35	18 41			18 46		18 56	19 05	19 11		19 16	19 26	19 35		19 41		19 56	20 05	20 11		20 26	20 35		
Essex Road	d	18 37	18 43			18 48		18 58	19 07	19 13		19 18	19 28	19 37		19 43		19 58	20 07	20 13		20 28	20 37		
Old Street	⊖ d	18 40	18 46			18 51		19 01	19 10	19 16		19 21	19 31	19 40		19 46		20 01	20 10	20 16		20 31	20 40		
Moorgate	⊖ a	18 45	18 51			18 56		19 06	19 15	19 21		19 26	19 36	19 45		19 51		20 06	20 15	20 21		20 36	20 45		
London Kings Cross 15	⊖ a			18 47			18 56				19 22						19 56				20 19				

Letchworth Garden City, Hertford North and Welwyn Garden City - London

Network Diagram - see first Page of Table 24

		FC 1	FC	FC	FC	FC 1	FC	FC	FC	FC 1		FC	FC	FC	FC 1	FC	FC	FC 1	FC	FC		FC	FC 1	FC	FC
Letchworth Garden City	d				20 20	20 29								21 20	21 29							22 20	22 29		
Hitchin 4	d	20 04			20 24	20 34				21 04				21 24	21 34			22 13				22 24	22 34		
Stevenage 4	d	20 10			20 29	20 40			20 59	21 10				21 29	21 40			22 18				22 29	22 40		
Watton-at-Stone	d				20 36				21 06					21 36								22 36			
Hertford North	d				20 42				21 12					21 42					22 12			22 42			
Bayford	d				20 46				21 16					21 46					22 16			22 46			
Cuffley	d				20 51				21 21					21 51					22 21			22 51			
Crews Hill	d				20 54				21 24					21 54					22 24			22 54			
Gordon Hill	d				20 57				21 27					21 57					22 27			22 57			
Enfield Chase	d				20 59				21 29					21 59					22 29			22 59			
Grange Park	d				21 01				21 31					22 01					22 31			23 01			
Winchmore Hill	d				21 03				21 33					22 03					22 33			23 03			
Palmers Green	d				21 05				21 35					22 05					22 35			23 05			
Bowes Park	d				21 08				21 38					22 08					22 38			23 08			
Knebworth	d	20 14				20 44				21 14					21 44			22 22					22 44		
Welwyn North	d	20 18				20 48				21 18					21 48			22 25					22 48		
Welwyn Garden City 4	d	20 21		20 28		20 51		20 58		21 21			21 28		21 51		21 58	22 28		22 30			22 51		23 00
Hatfield	d	20 25		20 32		20 55		21 02		21 25			21 32		21 55		22 02	22 32		22 34			22 55		23 04
Welham Green	d			20 36				21 06					21 36				22 06			22 38					23 08
Brookmans Park	d			20 38				21 08					21 38				22 08			22 40					23 10
Potters Bar	d	20 31		20 41		21 01		21 11		21 31			21 41		22 01		22 11	22 37		22 43			23 01		23 13
Hadley Wood	d			20 45				21 15					21 45				22 15			22 47					23 17
New Barnet	d			20 47				21 17					21 47				22 17			22 49					23 19
Oakleigh Park	d			20 49				21 19					21 49				22 19			22 51					23 21
New Southgate	d			20 52				21 22					21 52				22 22			22 54					23 24
Alexandra Palace	d			20 55	21 10			21 25	21 40				21 55	22 10			22 25		22 40	22 57		23 10			23 27
Hornsey	d			20 57	21 12			21 27	21 42				21 57	22 12			22 27		22 42	22 59		23 12			23 29
Harringay	d		←	20 59	21 14		←	21 29	21 44			←	21 59	22 14		←	22 29		22 44	23 01		23 14		←	23 31
Finsbury Park ⊖	d	20 40	20 47	21 02	21 17	21 10	21 17	21 32	21 47	21 40		21 47	22 02	22 17	22 10	22 17	22 32	22 46	22 47	23 04		23 17	23 10	23 17	23 34
Drayton Park	d		20 49	21 04	→		21 19	21 34	→			21 49		→								→			
Highbury & Islington ⊖	d		20 50	21 05			21 20	21 35				21 50													
Essex Road	d		20 52	21 07			21 22	21 37				21 52													
Old Street ⊖	d		20 55	21 10			21 25	21 40				21 55													
Moorgate ⊖	a		21 00	21 15			21 30	21 45				22 00													
London Kings Cross 15 ⊖	a	20 49				21 19				21 49			22 10		22 19	22 25	22 40	22 52	22 55	23 10			23 20	23 25	23 40

		FC	FC 1	FC	FC 1
Letchworth Garden City	d			23 20	23 47
Hitchin 4	d		23 16	23 24	23 54
Stevenage 4	d		23 22	23 29	23 59
Watton-at-Stone	d			23 36	
Hertford North	d	23 12		23 42	
Bayford	d	23 16		23 46	
Cuffley	d	23 21		23 51	
Crews Hill	d	23 24		23 54	
Gordon Hill	d	23 27		23 57	
Enfield Chase	d	23 29		23 59	
Grange Park	d	23 31		00 01	
Winchmore Hill	d	23 33		00 03	
Palmers Green	d	23 35		00 05	
Bowes Park	d	23 38		00 08	
Knebworth	d		23 25		00 02
Welwyn North	d		23 29		00 06
Welwyn Garden City 4	d		23 32		00 09
Hatfield	d		23 35		00 12
Welham Green	d				
Brookmans Park	d				
Potters Bar	d		23 41		00 18
Hadley Wood	d				
New Barnet	d				
Oakleigh Park	d				
New Southgate	d				
Alexandra Palace	d	23 40		00 10	
Hornsey	d	23 42		00 12	
Harringay	d	23 44		00 14	
Finsbury Park ⊖	d	23 47	23s51	00 17	00 29
Drayton Park	d				
Highbury & Islington ⊖	d				
Essex Road	d				
Old Street ⊖	d				
Moorgate ⊖	a				
London Kings Cross 15 ⊖	a	23 55	00 01	00 26	00 40

Table 24

Saturdays

Letchworth Garden City, Hertford North and Welwyn Garden City - London

Network Diagram - see first Page of Table 24

		FC 1	FC	FC 1	FC	FC 1	FC	FC 1	FC	FC		FC 1	FC	FC	FC 1	FC	FC	FC	FC 1	FC		FC	FC 1	FC	FC
Letchworth Garden City	d		23p20	23p47			04 50			05 20		05 29						06 20	06 29						
Hitchin 4	d	23p16	23p24	23p54		04 08	04 54	04 57		05 24		05 34			06 04			06 24	06 34				07 04		
Stevenage 4	d	23p22	23p29	23p59		04 13	04 59	05 02		05 30		05 40			06 10			06 30	06 40				07 10		
Watton-at-Stone	d		23p36				05 06			05 37								06 37							
Hertford North	d		23p42			04 23	05 12			05 43						06 13		06 43						07 13	
Bayford	d		23p46				05 16			05 47						06 17		06 47						07 17	
Cuffley	d		23p51			04 30	05 21			05 52						06 22		06 52						07 22	
Crews Hill	d		23p54				05 24			05 55						06 25		06 55						07 25	
Gordon Hill	d		23p57			04 34	05 27			05 58						06 28		06 58						07 28	
Enfield Chase	d		23p59			04 36	05 29			06 00						06 30		07 00						07 30	
Grange Park	d		00 01				05 31			06 02						06 32		07 02						07 32	
Winchmore Hill	d		00 03			04 38	05 33			06 04						06 34		07 04						07 34	
Palmers Green	d		00 05			04 40	05 35			06 06						06 36		07 06						07 36	
Bowes Park	d		00 08				05 38			06 09						06 39		07 09						07 39	
Knebworth	d	23p25		00 02				05 06				05 44			06 14				06 44				07 14		
Welwyn North	d	23p29		00 06				05 10				05 48			06 18				06 48				07 18		
Welwyn Garden City 4	d	23p32		00 09	04 10			05 13				05 51		05 58	06 21		06 28		06 51			06 58	07 21		07 28
Hatfield	d	23p35		00 12	04 14			05 16				05 55		06 02	06 25		06 32		06 55			07 02	07 25		07 32
Welham Green	d													06 06			06 36					07 06			07 36
Brookmans Park	d				04 19									06 08			06 38					07 08			07 38
Potters Bar	d	23p41		00 18	04 22			05 22				06 01		06 11	06 31		06 41		07 01			07 11	07 31		07 41
Hadley Wood	d				04 25									06 15			06 45					07 15			07 45
New Barnet	d				04 28			05 27						06 17			06 47					07 17			07 47
Oakleigh Park	d				04 30			05 29						06 19			06 49					07 19			07 49
New Southgate	d				04 33			05 32						06 22			06 52					07 22			07 52
Alexandra Palace	d		00 10		04 36		05 40	05 35		06 11				06 25		06 41	06 55	07 11				07 25		07 41	07 55
Hornsey	d		00 12		04 38	04u44	05 42			06 13				06 27		06 43	06 57	07 13				07 27		07 43	07 57
Harringay	d		00 14		04 40		05 44		←	06 15			←	06 29		06 45	06 59	07 15		←		07 29		07 45	07 59
Finsbury Park ⊖	d	23b51	00 17	00 29	04 42	04s47	05 47	05 39	05 47	06 18		06 10	06 18	06 32	06 40	06 48	07 02	07 18	07 10	07 18		07 32	07 40	07 48	08 02
Drayton Park	d						↪			↪								↪							
Highbury & Islington ⊖	d																								
Essex Road	d																								
Old Street ⊖	d																								
Moorgate ⊖	a																								
London Kings Cross 15 ⊖	a	00 01	00 26	00 40	04 51	05 00		05 48	05 55			06 20	06 25	06 40	06 47	06 55	07 10		07 19	07 25		07 40	07 49	07 55	08 10

		FC	FC 1	FC	FC	FC 1		FC	FC	FC	FC 1	FC	FC	FC 1	FC	FC		FC	FC 1	FC	FC	FC 1	FC	FC	FC
Letchworth Garden City	d		07 29								08 29								09 29						
Hitchin 4	d		07 34			08 04					08 34			09 04					09 34			10 04			
Stevenage 4	d	07 30	07 40			08 10				08 30	08 40			09 10				09 30	09 40			10 10			10 30
Watton-at-Stone	d	07 37								08 37								09 37							10 37
Hertford North	d	07 43						08 13		08 43					09 13			09 43					10 13		10 43
Bayford	d	07 47						08 17		08 47					09 17			09 47					10 17		10 47
Cuffley	d	07 52						08 22		08 52					09 22			09 52					10 22		10 52
Crews Hill	d	07 55						08 25		08 55					09 25			09 55					10 25		10 55
Gordon Hill	d	07 58						08 28		08 58					09 28			09 58					10 28		10 58
Enfield Chase	d	08 00						08 30		09 00					09 30			10 00					10 30		11 00
Grange Park	d	08 02						08 32		09 02					09 32			10 02					10 32		11 02
Winchmore Hill	d	08 04						08 34		09 04					09 34			10 04					10 34		11 04
Palmers Green	d	08 06						08 36		09 06					09 36			10 06					10 36		11 06
Bowes Park	d	08 09						08 39		09 09					09 39			10 09					10 39		11 09
Knebworth	d		07 44			08 14					08 44			09 14					09 44			10 14			
Welwyn North	d		07 48			08 18					08 48			09 18					09 48			10 18			
Welwyn Garden City 4	d		07 51		07 58	08 21			08 28		08 51		08 58	09 21		09 28			09 51		09 58	10 21		10 28	
Hatfield	d		07 55		08 02	08 25			08 32		08 55		09 02	09 25		09 32			09 55		10 02	10 25		10 32	
Welham Green	d				08 06				08 36				09 06			09 36					10 06			10 36	
Brookmans Park	d				08 08				08 38				09 08			09 38					10 08			10 38	
Potters Bar	d		08 01		08 11	08 31			08 41		09 01		09 11	09 31		09 41			10 01		10 11	10 31		10 41	
Hadley Wood	d				08 15				08 45				09 15			09 45					10 15			10 45	
New Barnet	d				08 17				08 47				09 17			09 47					10 17			10 47	
Oakleigh Park	d				08 19				08 49				09 19			09 49					10 19			10 49	
New Southgate	d				08 22				08 52				09 22			09 52					10 22			10 52	
Alexandra Palace	d	08 11			08 25			08 41	08 55	09 11			09 25		09 41	09 55		10 11			10 25		10 41	10 55	11 11
Hornsey	d	08 13			08 27			08 43	08 57	09 13			09 27		09 43	09 57		10 13			10 27		10 43	10 57	11 13
Harringay	d	08 15		←	08 29			08 45	08 59	09 15		←	09 29		09 45	09 59		10 15		←	10 29		10 45	10 59	11 15
Finsbury Park ⊖	d	08 18	08 10	08 18	08 32	08 40		08 48	09 02	09 18	09 10	09 18	09 32	09 40	09 48	10 02		10 18	10 10	10 18	10 32	10 40	10 48	11 02	11 18
Drayton Park	d	↪								↪								↪							↪
Highbury & Islington ⊖	d																								
Essex Road	d																								
Old Street ⊖	d																								
Moorgate ⊖	a																								
London Kings Cross 15 ⊖	a		08 19	08 25	08 40	08 49		08 55	09 10		09 20	09 25	09 40	09 49	09 55	10 10			10 20	10 25	10 40	10 49	10 55	11 10	

b Previous night, stops to set down only

Letchworth Garden City, Hertford North and Welwyn Garden City - London

Network Diagram - see first Page of Table 24

		FC 1		FC	FC	FC 1	FC	FC	FC	FC 1	FC	FC	
Letchworth Garden City	d	10 29								11 29			
Hitchin 4	d	10 34				11 04				11 34			
Stevenage 4	d	10 40				11 10			11 30	11 40			
Watton-at-Stone	d								11 37				
Hertford North	d						11 13		11 43				
Bayford	d						11 17		11 47				
Cuffley	d						11 22		11 52				
Crews Hill	d						11 25		11 55				
Gordon Hill	d						11 28		11 58				
Enfield Chase	d						11 30		12 00				
Grange Park	d						11 32		12 02				
Winchmore Hill	d						11 34		12 04				
Palmers Green	d						11 36		12 06				
Bowes Park	d						11 39		12 09				
Knebworth	d	10 44				11 14				11 44			
Welwyn North	d	10 48				11 18				11 48			
Welwyn Garden City 4	d	10 51			10 58	11 21		11 28		11 51		11 58	
Hatfield	d	10 55			11 02	11 25		11 32		11 55		12 02	
Welham Green	d				11 06			11 36				12 06	
Brookmans Park	d				11 08			11 38				12 08	
Potters Bar	d	11 01			11 11	11 31		11 41		12 01		12 11	
Hadley Wood	d				11 15			11 45				12 15	
New Barnet	d				11 17			11 47				12 17	
Oakleigh Park	d				11 19			11 49				12 19	
New Southgate	d				11 22			11 52				12 22	
Alexandra Palace	d				11 25		11 41	11 55	12 11			12 25	
Hornsey	d				11 27		11 43	11 57	12 13			12 27	
Harringay	d			←	11 29		11 45	11 59	12 15		←	12 29	
Finsbury Park ⊖	d	11 10		11 18	11 32	11 40	11 48	12 02	12 18	12 10	12 18	12 32	
Drayton Park	d								↦				
Highbury & Islington ⊖	d												
Essex Road	d												
Old Street ⊖	d												
Moorgate ⊖	a												
London Kings Cross 15 ⊖	a	11 20		11 25	11 40	11 49	11 55	12 10		12 19	12 25	12 42	

		FC 1	FC	FC	FC	FC 1	FC	FC	FC 1	FC		FC	FC
Letchworth Garden City	d					12 29							
Hitchin 4	d	12 04				12 34			13 04				
Stevenage 4	d	12 10			12 30	12 40			13 10				13 30
Watton-at-Stone	d				12 37								13 37
Hertford North	d		12 13		12 43					13 13			13 43
Bayford	d		12 17		12 47					13 17			13 47
Cuffley	d		12 22		12 52					13 22			13 52
Crews Hill	d		12 25		12 55					13 25			13 55
Gordon Hill	d		12 28		12 58					13 28			13 58
Enfield Chase	d		12 30		13 00					13 30			14 00
Grange Park	d		12 32		13 02					13 32			14 02
Winchmore Hill	d		12 34		13 04					13 34			14 04
Palmers Green	d		12 36		13 06					13 36			14 06
Bowes Park	d		12 39		13 09					13 39			14 09
Knebworth	d	12 14				12 44			13 14				
Welwyn North	d	12 18				12 48			13 18				
Welwyn Garden City 4	d	12 21		12 28		12 51		12 58	13 21			13 28	
Hatfield	d	12 25		12 32		12 55		13 02	13 25			13 32	
Welham Green	d			12 36				13 06				13 36	
Brookmans Park	d			12 38				13 08				13 38	
Potters Bar	d	12 31		12 41		13 01		13 11	13 31			13 41	
Hadley Wood	d			12 45				13 15				13 45	
New Barnet	d			12 47				13 17				13 47	
Oakleigh Park	d			12 49				13 19				13 49	
New Southgate	d			12 52				13 22				13 52	
Alexandra Palace	d		12 41	12 55	13 11			13 25		13 41		13 55	14 11
Hornsey	d		12 43	12 57	13 13			13 27		13 43		13 57	14 13
Harringay	d		12 45	12 59	13 15		←	13 29		13 45		13 59	14 15
Finsbury Park ⊖	d	12 40	12 48	13 02	13 18	13 10	13 18	13 32	13 40	13 48		14 02	14 18
Drayton Park	d				↦								↦
Highbury & Islington ⊖	d												
Essex Road	d												
Old Street ⊖	d												
Moorgate ⊖	a												
London Kings Cross 15 ⊖	a	12 49	12 55	13 10		13 19	13 25	13 40	13 49	13 55		14 10	

		FC 1	FC	FC	FC 1	FC	FC	FC		FC 1	FC	FC	FC 1
Letchworth Garden City	d	13 29								14 29			
Hitchin 4	d	13 34			14 04					14 34			15 04
Stevenage 4	d	13 40			14 10			14 30		14 40			15 10
Watton-at-Stone	d							14 37					
Hertford North	d					14 13		14 43					
Bayford	d					14 17		14 47					
Cuffley	d					14 22		14 52					
Crews Hill	d					14 25		14 55					
Gordon Hill	d					14 28		14 58					
Enfield Chase	d					14 30		15 00					
Grange Park	d					14 32		15 02					
Winchmore Hill	d					14 34		15 04					
Palmers Green	d					14 36		15 06					
Bowes Park	d					14 39		15 09					
Knebworth	d	13 44			14 14					14 44			15 14
Welwyn North	d	13 48			14 18					14 48			15 18
Welwyn Garden City 4	d	13 51		13 58	14 21		14 28			14 51		14 58	15 21
Hatfield	d	13 55		14 02	14 25		14 32			14 55		15 02	15 25
Welham Green	d			14 06			14 36					15 06	
Brookmans Park	d			14 08			14 38					15 08	
Potters Bar	d	14 01		14 11	14 31		14 41			15 01		15 11	15 31
Hadley Wood	d			14 15			14 45					15 15	
New Barnet	d			14 17			14 47					15 17	
Oakleigh Park	d			14 19			14 49					15 19	
New Southgate	d			14 22			14 52					15 22	
Alexandra Palace	d			14 25		14 41	14 55	15 11				15 25	
Hornsey	d			14 27		14 43	14 57	15 13				15 27	
Harringay	d		←	14 29		14 45	14 59	15 15			←	15 29	
Finsbury Park ⊖	d	14 10	14 18	14 32	14 40	14 48	15 02	15 18		15 10	15 18	15 32	15 40
Drayton Park	d							↦					
Highbury & Islington ⊖	d												
Essex Road	d												
Old Street ⊖	d												
Moorgate ⊖	a												
London Kings Cross 15 ⊖	a	14 19	14 25	14 40	14 49	14 55	15 10			15 19	15 25	15 40	15 49

		FC	FC	FC	FC 1	FC		FC	FC 1	FC	FC	FC	FC 1
Letchworth Garden City	d				15 29								16 29
Hitchin 4	d				15 34				16 04				16 34
Stevenage 4	d			15 30	15 40				16 10			16 30	16 40
Watton-at-Stone	d			15 37								16 37	
Hertford North	d	15 13		15 43						16 13		16 43	
Bayford	d	15 17		15 47						16 17		16 47	
Cuffley	d	15 22		15 52						16 22		16 52	
Crews Hill	d	15 25		15 55						16 25		16 55	
Gordon Hill	d	15 28		15 58						16 28		16 58	
Enfield Chase	d	15 30		16 00						16 30		17 00	
Grange Park	d	15 32		16 02						16 32		17 02	
Winchmore Hill	d	15 34		16 04						16 34		17 04	
Palmers Green	d	15 36		16 06						16 36		17 06	
Bowes Park	d	15 39		16 09						16 39		17 09	
Knebworth	d				15 44				16 14				16 44
Welwyn North	d				15 48				16 18				16 48
Welwyn Garden City 4	d		15 28		15 51			15 58	16 21		16 28		16 51
Hatfield	d		15 32		15 55			16 02	16 25		16 32		16 55
Welham Green	d		15 36					16 06			16 36		
Brookmans Park	d		15 38					16 08			16 38		
Potters Bar	d		15 41		16 01			16 11	16 31		16 41		17 01
Hadley Wood	d		15 45					16 15			16 45		
New Barnet	d		15 47					16 17			16 47		
Oakleigh Park	d		15 49					16 19			16 49		
New Southgate	d		15 52					16 22			16 52		
Alexandra Palace	d	15 41	15 55	16 11				16 25		16 41	16 55	17 11	
Hornsey	d	15 43	15 57	16 13				16 27		16 43	16 57	17 13	
Harringay	d	15 45	15 59	16 15		←		16 29		16 45	16 59	17 15	
Finsbury Park ⊖	d	15 48	16 02	16 18	16 10	16 18		16 32	16 40	16 48	17 02	17 18	17 10
Drayton Park	d			↦								↦	
Highbury & Islington ⊖	d												
Essex Road	d												
Old Street ⊖	d												
Moorgate ⊖	a												
London Kings Cross 15 ⊖	a	15 55	16 10		16 19	16 25		16 40	16 49	16 55	17 10		17 19

Table 24

Saturdays

Letchworth Garden City, Hertford North and Welwyn Garden City - London

Network Diagram - see first Page of Table 24

		FC	FC	FC		FC	FC	FC	FC	FC	FC	FC	FC	FC		FC	FC	FC	FC	FC	FC	FC	FC	FC	
				1					1			1					1			1				1	
Letchworth Garden City	d								17 29								18 29							19 29	
Hitchin [4]	d			17 04					17 34			18 04					18 34			19 04				19 34	
Stevenage [4]	d			17 10				17 30	17 40			18 10				18 30	18 40			19 10			19 30	19 40	
Watton-at-Stone	d							17 37								18 37							19 37		
Hertford North	d					17 13		17 43					18 13			18 43					19 13		19 43		
Bayford	d					17 17		17 47					18 17			18 47					19 17		19 47		
Cuffley	d					17 22		17 52					18 22			18 52					19 22		19 52		
Crews Hill	d					17 25		17 55					18 25			18 55					19 25		19 55		
Gordon Hill	d					17 28		17 58					18 28			18 58					19 28		19 58		
Enfield Chase	d					17 30		18 00					18 30			19 00					19 30		20 00		
Grange Park	d					17 32		18 02					18 32			19 02					19 32		20 02		
Winchmore Hill	d					17 34		18 04					18 34			19 04					19 34		20 04		
Palmers Green	d					17 36		18 06					18 36			19 06					19 36		20 06		
Bowes Park	d					17 39		18 09					18 39			19 09					19 39		20 09		
Knebworth	d			17 14					17 44			18 14					18 44			19 14				19 44	
Welwyn North	d			17 18					17 48			18 18					18 48			19 18				19 48	
Welwyn Garden City [4]	d		16 58	17 21			17 28		17 51		17 58	18 21		18 28			18 51		18 58	19 21		19 28		19 51	
Hatfield	d		17 02	17 25			17 32		17 55		18 02	18 25		18 32			18 55		19 02	19 25		19 32		19 55	
Welham Green	d		17 06				17 36				18 06			18 36					19 06			19 36			
Brookmans Park	d		17 08				17 38				18 08			18 38					19 08			19 38			
Potters Bar	d		17 11	17 31			17 41		18 01		18 11	18 31		18 41			19 01		19 11	19 31		19 41		20 01	
Hadley Wood	d		17 15				17 45				18 15			18 45					19 15			19 45			
New Barnet	d		17 17				17 47				18 17			18 47					19 17			19 47			
Oakleigh Park	d		17 19				17 49				18 19			18 49					19 19			19 49			
New Southgate	d		17 22				17 52				18 22			18 52					19 22			19 52			
Alexandra Palace	d		17 25			17 41	17 55	18 11			18 25		18 41	18 55		19 11			19 25		19 41	19 55	20 11		
Hornsey	d		17 27			17 43	17 57	18 13			18 27		18 43	18 57		19 13			19 27		19 43	19 57	20 13		
Harringay	d	←	17 29			17 45	17 59	18 15		←	18 29		18 45	18 59		19 15		←	19 29		19 45	19 59	20 15		
Finsbury Park ⊖	d	17 18	17 32	17 40		17 48	18 02	18 18	18 10	18 18	18 32	18 40	18 48	19 02		19 18	19 10	19 18	19 32	19 40	19 48	20 02	20 18	20 10	
Drayton Park	d							↪								↪							↪		
Highbury & Islington ⊖	d																								
Essex Road	d																								
Old Street ⊖	d																								
Moorgate ⊖	a																								
London Kings Cross [15] ⊖	a	17 25	17 40	17 49		17 55	18 10		18 19	18 25	18 40	18 49	18 55	19 10			19 19	19 25	19 40	19 49	19 55	20 10		20 19	

		FC	FC	FC	FC	FC	FC	FC	FC	FC		FC	FC	FC	FC	FC	FC	FC	FC	FC		FC	FC	FC	FC
				1				1				1				1			1					1	
Letchworth Garden City	d							20 29								21 29								22 29	
Hitchin [4]	d			20 04				20 34				21 04				21 34			22 04					22 34	
Stevenage [4]	d			20 10			20 30	20 40				21 10			21 30	21 40			22 10				22 30	22 40	
Watton-at-Stone	d						20 37								21 37								22 37		
Hertford North	d				20 13		20 43						21 13		21 43					22 13			22 43		
Bayford	d				20 17		20 47						21 17		21 47					22 17			22 47		
Cuffley	d				20 22		20 52						21 22		21 52					22 22			22 52		
Crews Hill	d				20 25		20 55						21 25		21 55					22 25			22 55		
Gordon Hill	d				20 28		20 58						21 28		21 58					22 28			22 58		
Enfield Chase	d				20 30		21 00						21 30		22 00					22 30			23 00		
Grange Park	d				20 32		21 02						21 32		22 02					22 32			23 02		
Winchmore Hill	d				20 34		21 04						21 34		22 04					22 34			23 04		
Palmers Green	d				20 36		21 06						21 36		22 06					22 36			23 06		
Bowes Park	d				20 39		21 09						21 39		22 09					22 39			23 09		
Knebworth	d			20 14				20 44				21 14				21 44			22 14					22 44	
Welwyn North	d			20 18				20 48				21 18				21 48			22 18					22 48	
Welwyn Garden City [4]	d		19 58	20 21		20 28		20 51		20 58		21 21		21 28		21 51		21 58	22 21			22 28		22 51	
Hatfield	d		20 02	20 25		20 32		20 55		21 02		21 25		21 32		21 55		22 02	22 25			22 32		22 55	
Welham Green	d		20 06			20 36				21 06				21 36				22 06				22 36			
Brookmans Park	d		20 08			20 38				21 08				21 38				22 08				22 38			
Potters Bar	d		20 11	20 31		20 41		21 01		21 11		21 31		21 41		22 01		22 11	22 31			22 41		23 01	
Hadley Wood	d		20 15			20 45				21 15				21 45				22 15				22 45			
New Barnet	d		20 17			20 47				21 17				21 47				22 17				22 47			
Oakleigh Park	d		20 19			20 49				21 19				21 49				22 19				22 49			
New Southgate	d		20 22			20 52				21 22				21 52				22 22				22 52			
Alexandra Palace	d		20 25		20 41	20 55	21 11			21 25			21 41	21 55	22 11			22 25		22 41		22 55	23 11		
Hornsey	d		20 27		20 43	20 57	21 13			21 27			21 43	21 57	22 13			22 27		22 43		22 57	23 13		
Harringay	d	←	20 29		20 45	20 59	21 15		←	21 29			21 45	21 59	22 15		←	22 29		22 45		22 59	23 15		←
Finsbury Park ⊖	d	20 18	20 32	20 40	20 48	21 02	21 18	21 10	21 18	21 32		21 40	21 48	22 02	22 18	22 10	22 18	22 32	22 40	22 48		23 02	23 18	23 10	23 18
Drayton Park	d						↪								↪								↪		
Highbury & Islington ⊖	d																								
Essex Road	d																								
Old Street ⊖	d																								
Moorgate ⊖	a																								
London Kings Cross [15] ⊖	a	20 25	20 40	20 49	20 55	21 10		21 19	21 25	21 40		21 49	21 55	22 10		22 19	22 25	22 40	22 49	22 55		23 10		23 19	23 25

Table 24

Saturdays

Letchworth Garden City, Hertford North and Welwyn Garden City - London

Network Diagram - see first Page of Table 24

		FC	FC ■1	FC	FC	FC ■1
Letchworth Garden City	d					23 46
Hitchin ■4	d		23 04			23 50
Stevenage ■4	d		23 10		23 30	23 55
Watton-at-Stone	d				23 37	
Hertford North	d			23 13	23 43	
Bayford	d			23 17	23 47	
Cuffley	d			23 22	23 52	
Crews Hill	d			23 25	23 55	
Gordon Hill	d			23 28	23 58	
Enfield Chase	d			23 30	23 59	
Grange Park	d			23 32	00 02	
Winchmore Hill	d			23 34	00 04	
Palmers Green	d			23 36	00 06	
Bowes Park	d			23 39	00 09	
Knebworth	d		23 14			23 59
Welwyn North	d		23 18			00 02
Welwyn Garden City ■4	d	22 58	23 21			00 06
Hatfield	d	23 02	23 25			00 10
Welham Green	d	23 06				
Brookmans Park	d	23 08				
Potters Bar	d	23 11	23 31			00 15
Hadley Wood	d	23 15				
New Barnet	d	23 17				
Oakleigh Park	d	23 19				
New Southgate	d	23 22				
Alexandra Palace	d	23 25		23 41	00 11	
Hornsey	d	23 27		23 43	00 13	
Harringay	d	23 29		23 45	00 15	
Finsbury Park ⊖	d	23 32	23 40	23 48	00 18	00s32
Drayton Park	d					
Highbury & Islington ⊖	d					
Essex Road	d					
Old Street ⊖	d					
Moorgate ⊖	a					
London Kings Cross ■15 ⊖	a	23 40	23 50	23 56	00 27	00 40

Sundays

		FC A	FC ■1 A	FC	FC	FC ■1	FC	FC	FC	FC		FC	FC ■1	FC	FC	FC	FC	FC	FC ■1	FC		FC	FC	FC	FC
Letchworth Garden City	d		23p46																08 29						
Hitchin ■4	d		23p50			06 33							07 33						08 34						
Stevenage ■4	d	23p30	23p55			06 39						07 30	07 39					08 30	08 39						09 30
Watton-at-Stone	d	23p37										07 37						08 37							09 37
Hertford North	d	23p43		06 13			06 43		07 13			07 43				08 13		08 43					09 13		09 43
Bayford	d	23p47		06 17			06 47		07 17			07 47				08 17		08 47					09 17		09 47
Cuffley	d	23p52		06 22			06 52		07 22			07 52				08 22		08 52					09 22		09 52
Crews Hill	d	23p55		06 25			06 55		07 25			07 55				08 25		08 55					09 25		09 55
Gordon Hill	d	23p58		06 28			06 58		07 28			07 58				08 28		08 58					09 28		09 58
Enfield Chase	d	23p59		06 30			07 00		07 30			08 00				08 30		09 00					09 30		10 00
Grange Park	d	00 02		06 32			07 02		07 32			08 02				08 32		09 02					09 32		10 02
Winchmore Hill	d	00 04		06 34			07 04		07 34			08 04				08 34		09 04					09 34		10 04
Palmers Green	d	00 06		06 36			07 06		07 36			08 06				08 36		09 06					09 36		10 06
Bowes Park	d	00 09		06 39			07 09		07 39			08 09				08 39		09 09					09 39		10 09
Knebworth	d		23p59			06 43							07 43						08 43						
Welwyn North	d		00 02			06 47							07 47						08 47						
Welwyn Garden City ■4	d		00 06		06 28	06 51		06 58		07 28			07 51		07 58		08 28		08 51			08 58		09 28	
Hatfield	d		00 10		06 32	06 54		07 02		07 32			07 54		08 02		08 32		08 54			09 02		09 32	
Welham Green	d				06 36			07 06		07 36					08 06		08 36					09 06		09 36	
Brookmans Park	d				06 38			07 08		07 38					08 08		08 38					09 08		09 38	
Potters Bar	d		00 15		06 41	07 00		07 11		07 41			08 00		08 11		08 41		09 00			09 11		09 41	
Hadley Wood	d				06 45			07 15		07 45					08 15		08 45					09 15		09 45	
New Barnet	d				06 47			07 17		07 47					08 17		08 47					09 17		09 47	
Oakleigh Park	d				06 49			07 19		07 49					08 19		08 49					09 19		09 49	
New Southgate	d				06 52			07 22		07 52					08 22		08 52					09 22		09 52	
Alexandra Palace	d	00 11		06 41	06 55		07 11	07 25	07 41	07 55		08 11			08 25	08 41	08 55	09 11				09 25	09 41	09 55	10 11
Hornsey	d	00 13		06 43	06 57		07 13	07 27	07 43	07 57		08 13			08 27	08 43	08 57	09 13				09 27	09 43	09 57	10 13
Harringay	d	00 15		06 45	06 59		07 15	07 29	07 45	07 59		08 15		←	08 29	08 45	08 59	09 15		←		09 29	09 45	09 59	10 15
Finsbury Park ⊖	d	00 18	00s32	06 48	07 02	07 10	07 18	07 32	07 48	08 02		08 18	08 10	08 18	08 32	08 48	09 02	09 18	09 10	09 18		09 32	09 48	10 02	10 18
Drayton Park	d											↪						↪							↪
Highbury & Islington ⊖	d																								
Essex Road	d																								
Old Street ⊖	d																								
Moorgate ⊖	a																								
London Kings Cross ■15 ⊖	a	00 26	00 40	06 56	07 13	07 20	07 27	07 45	07 56	08 15			08 20	08 26	08 40	08 55	09 10		09 19	09 25		09 40	09 55	10 10	

A not 11 December

Table 24

Sundays

Letchworth Garden City, Hertford North and Welwyn Garden City - London

Network Diagram - see first Page of Table 24

Station		FC [1]	FC	FC	FC [1]	FC		FC	FC	FC [1]	FC	FC	FC	FC	FC	FC [1]		FC	FC	FC	FC	FC	FC [1]	FC	FC
Letchworth Garden City	d	09 29			09 59					10 29						11 29							12 29		
Hitchin [4]	d	09 34			10 04					10 34						11 34							12 34		
Stevenage [4]	d	09 39			10 09				10 30	10 39					11 30	11 39						12 30	12 39		
Watton-at-Stone	d								10 37						11 37							12 37			
Hertford North	d					10 13			10 43				11 13		11 43					12 13		12 43			
Bayford	d					10 17			10 47				11 17		11 47					12 17		12 47			
Cuffley	d					10 22			10 52				11 22		11 52					12 22		12 52			
Crews Hill	d					10 25			10 55				11 25		11 55					12 25		12 55			
Gordon Hill	d					10 28			10 58				11 28		11 58					12 28		12 58			
Enfield Chase	d					10 30			11 00				11 30		12 00					12 30		13 00			
Grange Park	d					10 32			11 02				11 32		12 02					12 32		13 02			
Winchmore Hill	d					10 34			11 04				11 34		12 04					12 34		13 04			
Palmers Green	d					10 36			11 06				11 36		12 06					12 36		13 06			
Bowes Park	d					10 39			11 09				11 39		12 09					12 39		13 09			
Knebworth	d	09 43			10 13					10 43						11 43							12 43		
Welwyn North	d	09 47			10 17					10 47						11 47							12 47		
Welwyn Garden City [4]	d	09 51		09 58	10 21			10 28		10 51		10 58		11 28		11 51			11 58		12 28		12 51		12 58
Hatfield	d	09 54		10 02	10 24			10 32		10 54		11 02		11 32		11 54			12 02		12 32		12 54		13 02
Welham Green	d			10 06				10 36				11 06		11 36					12 06		12 36				13 06
Brookmans Park	d			10 08				10 38				11 08		11 38					12 08		12 38				13 08
Potters Bar	d	10 00		10 11	10 30			10 41		11 00		11 11		11 41		12 00			12 11		12 41		13 00		13 11
Hadley Wood	d			10 15				10 45				11 15		11 45					12 15		12 45				13 15
New Barnet	d			10 17				10 47				11 17		11 47					12 17		12 47				13 17
Oakleigh Park	d			10 19				10 49				11 19		11 49					12 19		12 49				13 19
New Southgate	d			10 22				10 52				11 22		11 52					12 22		12 52				13 22
Alexandra Palace	d			10 25		10 41		10 55	11 11			11 25	11 41	11 55	12 11				12 25	12 41	12 55	13 11			13 25
Hornsey	d			10 27		10 43		10 57	11 13			11 27	11 43	11 57	12 13				12 27	12 43	12 57	13 13			13 27
Harringay	d		←	10 29		10 45		10 59	11 15		←	11 29	11 45	11 59	12 15			←	12 29	12 45	12 59	13 15		←	13 29
Finsbury Park ⊖	d	10 10	10 18	10 32	10 40	10 48		11 02	11 18	11 10	11 18	11 32	11 48	12 02	12 18	12 10		12 18	12 32	12 48	13 02	13 18	13 10	13 18	13 32
Drayton Park	d								↪						↪							↪			
Highbury & Islington ⊖	d																								
Essex Road	d																								
Old Street ⊖	d																								
Moorgate ⊖	a																								
London Kings Cross [15] ⊖	a	10 19	10 25	10 40	10 49	10 55		11 10		11 19	11 25	11 40	11 55	12 10		12 19		12 25	12 40	12 55	13 10		13 19	13 25	13 40

Station		FC		FC	FC	FC [1]	FC	FC	FC	FC	FC	FC [1]		FC	FC	FC	FC	FC	FC [1]	FC	FC	FC		FC	FC
Letchworth Garden City	d					13 29						14 29							15 29						
Hitchin [4]	d					13 34						14 34							15 34						
Stevenage [4]	d				13 30	13 39					14 30	14 39						15 30	15 39						16 30
Watton-at-Stone	d				13 37						14 37							15 37							16 37
Hertford North	d	13 13			13 43				14 13		14 43					15 13		15 43				16 13			16 43
Bayford	d	13 17			13 47				14 17		14 47					15 17		15 47				16 17			16 47
Cuffley	d	13 22			13 52				14 22		14 52					15 22		15 52				16 22			16 52
Crews Hill	d	13 25			13 55				14 25		14 55					15 25		15 55				16 25			16 55
Gordon Hill	d	13 28			13 58				14 28		14 58					15 28		15 58				16 28			16 58
Enfield Chase	d	13 30			14 00				14 30		15 00					15 30		16 00				16 30			17 00
Grange Park	d	13 32			14 02				14 32		15 02					15 32		16 02				16 32			17 02
Winchmore Hill	d	13 34			14 04				14 34		15 04					15 34		16 04				16 34			17 04
Palmers Green	d	13 36			14 06				14 36		15 06					15 36		16 06				16 36			17 06
Bowes Park	d	13 39			14 09				14 39		15 09					15 39		16 09				16 39			17 09
Knebworth	d					13 43						14 43							15 43						
Welwyn North	d					13 47						14 47							15 47						
Welwyn Garden City [4]	d			13 28		13 51		13 58		14 28		14 51			14 58		15 28		15 51		15 58			16 28	
Hatfield	d			13 32		13 54		14 02		14 32		14 54			15 02		15 32		15 54		16 02			16 32	
Welham Green	d			13 36				14 06		14 36					15 06		15 36				16 06			16 36	
Brookmans Park	d			13 38				14 08		14 38					15 08		15 38				16 08			16 38	
Potters Bar	d			13 41		14 00		14 11		14 41		15 00			15 11		15 41		16 00		16 11			16 41	
Hadley Wood	d			13 45				14 15		14 45					15 15		15 45				16 15			16 45	
New Barnet	d			13 47				14 17		14 47					15 17		15 47				16 17			16 47	
Oakleigh Park	d			13 49				14 19		14 49					15 19		15 49				16 19			16 49	
New Southgate	d			13 52				14 22		14 52					15 22		15 52				16 22			16 52	
Alexandra Palace	d	13 41		13 55	14 11			14 25	14 41	14 55	15 11				15 25	15 41	15 55	16 11			16 25	16 41		16 55	17 11
Hornsey	d	13 43		13 57	14 13			14 27	14 43	14 57	15 13				15 27	15 43	15 57	16 13			16 27	16 43		16 57	17 13
Harringay	d	13 45		13 59	14 15		←	14 29	14 45	14 59	15 15			←	15 29	15 45	15 59	16 15		←	16 29	16 45		16 59	17 15
Finsbury Park ⊖	d	13 48		14 02	14 18	14 10	14 18	14 32	14 48	15 02	15 18	15 10		15 18	15 32	15 48	16 02	16 18	16 10	16 18	16 32	16 48		17 02	17 18
Drayton Park	d				↪						↪							↪							↪
Highbury & Islington ⊖	d																								
Essex Road	d																								
Old Street ⊖	d																								
Moorgate ⊖	a																								
London Kings Cross [15] ⊖	a	13 55		14 10		14 19	14 25	14 40	14 55	15 10		15 19		15 25	15 40	15 55	16 10		16 19	16 25	16 40	16 55		17 10	

Sundays

Letchworth Garden City, Hertford North and Welwyn Garden City - London

Network Diagram - see first Page of Table 24

		FC 1	FC	FC	FC	FC	FC 1	FC		FC	FC	FC	FC 1	FC	FC	FC	FC	FC		FC 1	FC	FC	FC	FC	FC
Letchworth Garden City	d	16 29					17 29						18 29							19 29					
Hitchin 4	d	16 34					17 34						18 34							19 34					
Stevenage 4	d	16 39					17 39					18 30	18 39					19 30		19 39					20 30
Watton-at-Stone	d											18 37						19 37							20 37
Hertford North	d				17 13					18 13		18 43				19 13		19 43					20 13		20 43
Bayford	d				17 17					18 17		18 47				19 17		19 47					20 17		20 47
Cuffley	d				17 22					18 22		18 52				19 22		19 52					20 22		20 52
Crews Hill	d				17 25					18 25		18 55				19 25		19 55					20 25		20 55
Gordon Hill	d				17 28					18 28		18 58				19 28		19 58					20 28		20 58
Enfield Chase	d				17 30					18 30		19 00				19 30		20 00					20 30		21 00
Grange Park	d				17 32					18 32		19 02				19 32		20 02					20 32		21 02
Winchmore Hill	d				17 34					18 34		19 04				19 34		20 04					20 34		21 04
Palmers Green	d				17 36					18 36		19 06				19 36		20 06					20 36		21 06
Bowes Park	d				17 39					18 39		19 09				19 39		20 09					20 39		21 09
Knebworth	d	16 43					17 43						18 43							19 43					
Welwyn North	d	16 47					17 47						18 47							19 47					
Welwyn Garden City 4	d	16 51		16 58		17 28	17 51	17 58			18 28		18 51		18 58		19 28			19 51		19 58		20 28	
Hatfield	d	16 54		17 02		17 32	17 54	18 02			18 32		18 54		19 02		19 32			19 54		20 02		20 32	
Welham Green	d			17 06		17 36		18 06			18 36				19 06		19 36					20 06		20 36	
Brookmans Park	d			17 08		17 38		18 08			18 38				19 08		19 38					20 08		20 38	
Potters Bar	d	17 00		17 11		17 41	18 00	18 11			18 41		19 00		19 11		19 41			20 00		20 11		20 41	
Hadley Wood	d			17 15		17 45		18 15			18 45				19 15		19 45					20 15		20 45	
New Barnet	d			17 17		17 47		18 17			18 47				19 17		19 47					20 17		20 47	
Oakleigh Park	d			17 19		17 49		18 19			18 49				19 19		19 49					20 19		20 49	
New Southgate	d			17 22		17 52		18 22			18 52				19 22		19 52					20 22		20 52	
Alexandra Palace	d			17 25	17 41	17 55		18 25		18 41	18 55	19 11			19 25	19 41	19 55	20 11				20 25	20 41	20 55	21 11
Hornsey	d			17 27	17 43	17 57		18 27		18 43	18 57	19 13			19 27	19 43	19 57	20 13				20 27	20 43	20 57	21 13
Harringay	d		←	17 29	17 45	17 59		18 29		18 45	18 59	19 15		←	19 29	19 45	19 59	20 15			←	20 29	20 45	20 59	21 15
Finsbury Park ⊖	d	17 10	17 18	17 32	17 48	18 02	18 10	18 32		18 48	19 02	19 18	19 10	19 18	19 32	19 48	20 02	20 18		20 10	20 18	20 32	20 48	21 02	21 18
Drayton Park	d											→						→							→
Highbury & Islington ⊖	d																								
Essex Road	d																								
Old Street ⊖	d																								
Moorgate ⊖	a																								
London Kings Cross 15 ⊖	a	17 19	17 25	17 40	17 55	18 10	18 19	18 40		18 55	19 10		19 19	19 25	19 40	19 55	20 10			20 19	20 25	20 40	20 55	21 10	

		FC 1	FC	FC		FC	FC	FC	FC 1	FC	FC	FC	FC	FC		FC 1	FC	FC	FC	FC	FC 1				
Letchworth Garden City	d	20 29							21 29							22 29					23 46				
Hitchin 4	d	20 34							21 34							22 34					23 50				
Stevenage 4	d	20 39						21 30	21 39					22 30		22 39				23 30	23 55				
Watton-at-Stone	d							21 37						22 37						23 37					
Hertford North	d					21 13		21 43				22 13		22 43					23 13	23 43					
Bayford	d					21 17		21 47				22 17		22 47					23 17	23 47					
Cuffley	d					21 22		21 52				22 22		22 52					23 22	23 52					
Crews Hill	d					21 25		21 55				22 25		22 55					23 25	23 55					
Gordon Hill	d					21 28		21 58				22 28		22 58					23 28	23 58					
Enfield Chase	d					21 30		22 00				22 30		23 00					23 30	23 59					
Grange Park	d					21 32		22 02				22 32		23 02					23 32	00 02					
Winchmore Hill	d					21 34		22 04				22 34		23 04					23 34	00 04					
Palmers Green	d					21 36		22 06				22 36		23 06					23 36	00 06					
Bowes Park	d					21 39		22 09				22 39		23 09					23 39	00 09					
Knebworth	d	20 43							21 43							22 43					23 58				
Welwyn North	d	20 47							21 47							22 47					00 02				
Welwyn Garden City 4	d	20 51		20 58			21 28		21 51		21 58		22 28			22 51		22 58			00 05				
Hatfield	d	20 54		21 02			21 32		21 54		22 02		22 32			22 54		23 02			00 08				
Welham Green	d			21 06			21 36				22 06		22 36					23 06							
Brookmans Park	d			21 08			21 38				22 08		22 38					23 08							
Potters Bar	d	21 00		21 11			21 41		22 00		22 11		22 41			23 00		23 11			00 14				
Hadley Wood	d			21 15			21 45				22 15		22 45					23 15							
New Barnet	d			21 17			21 47				22 17		22 47					23 17							
Oakleigh Park	d			21 19			21 49				22 19		22 49					23 19							
New Southgate	d			21 22			21 52				22 22		22 52					23 22							
Alexandra Palace	d			21 25		21 41	21 55	22 11			22 25	22 41	22 55	23 11				23 25	23 41	00 11					
Hornsey	d			21 27		21 43	21 57	22 13			22 27	22 43	22 57	23 13				23 27	23 43	00 13					
Harringay	d		←	21 29		21 45	21 59	22 15		←	22 29	22 45	22 59	23 15			←	23 29	23 45	00 15					
Finsbury Park ⊖	d	21 10	21 18	21 32		21 48	22 02	22 18	22 10	22 18	22 32	22 48	23 02	23 18		23 10	23 18	23 32	23 48	00 18	00 27				
Drayton Park	d							→						→											
Highbury & Islington ⊖	d																								
Essex Road	d																								
Old Street ⊖	d																								
Moorgate ⊖	a																								
London Kings Cross 15 ⊖	a	21 19	21 25	21 40		21 55	22 10		22 19	22 25	22 40	22 55	23 12			23 19	23 26	23 44	23 56	00 27	00 39				

London - Stevenage, Cambridge and Peterborough

Network Diagram - see first Page of Table 24

Miles	Miles			FC MX 1	FC MO 1	FC MX 1	FC 1	FC MO 1	FC MX 1	FC MO 1	FC MX 1	FC MO		FC MX	FC MX 1	FC MX	FC MO	FC MX 1	FC MX	FC MO 1	FC MX	FC MO 1		FC MX 1	FC 1
0	0	**London Kings Cross 15** ⊖	d	23p01	23p06	23p06	23p15			23p23	23p23	23p26		23p26	23p36		23p41	00 04	00 06	00 07		00 36		00 36	01 06
2½	2½	Finsbury Park ⊖	d		23p11	23p11				23p28	23p28	23p32		23p32	23p41		23p47	00 09	00 12	00 12		00 41		00 41	01 11
12¾	12¾	Potters Bar	d		23p21	23p21									23p51		00 08					00 51		00 51	
17¾	17¾	Hatfield	d		23p27	23p27									23p57		00 16					00 57		00 57	
20¼	20¼	Welwyn Garden City 4	d		23p31	23p31									00 01		00 20					01 01		01 01	
22	22	Welwyn North	d		23p34	23p34									00 04		00 23					01s04		01s04	
25	25	Knebworth	d		23p38	23p38									00 08		00 28					01s08		01s08	
—	—	Hertford North	d									00 07		00 07		←			00 47	00 39	←				01 38
27½	27½	**Stevenage 4**	d		23p42	23p42				23p47	23p47	00a20		00 20	00 12	00 20	00 31	00 31	01 00	00 48	01 00	01 12		01 12	01 47
31¾	31¾	Hitchin 4	d		23p47	23p50		←	←	23p52	23p53			→	00 20	00 26	00 37	00 39	→	00 56	01 06	01 17		01 17	01 52
34¾	—	Letchworth Garden City	d		23p51	23p54	23p44	23p51	23p54						00a29	00a36	00a52	00 43		01 00	01a15				02a06
36¾	—	Baldock	d		→	→		23p54	23p58									00 46		01 04					
41	—	Ashwell & Morden	d					23p59	00 03									00 51		01 09					
45	—	Royston	d				23p54	00 04	00 07									00 56		01 13					
48	—	Meldreth	d					00 08	00 11									00 59		01 17					
50	—	Shepreth	d					00 11	00 14									01 02		01 20					
51	—	Foxton	d					00 14	00 17									01 05		01 23					
58	—	**Cambridge**	a				00 10	00 29	00 29									01 22		01 39					
—	37	Arlesey	d							23p57	23p59											01s25		01s25	
—	41	Biggleswade	d	23p29						00 02	00 04											01s30		01s30	
—	44	Sandy	d							00 06	00 08											01s34		01s34	
—	51½	St Neots	d	23p38						00 13	00 15											01s42		01s42	
—	58¾	Huntingdon	d	23p45						00 21	00 23											01s52		01s52	
—	76¼	**Peterborough 8**	a	00 12						00 43	00 42											02 11		02 13	

		FC 1	FC 1	FC	FC 1	GR R 1 ⊏P	FC	FC 1		GR R 1 ⊏P	FC 1	FC 1	FC	GR R 1 ⊏P	FC 1	FC 1	FC 1	FC 1		GR R 1 ⊏PT	FC 1	FC 1	HT ◇1 ⊠	FC 1	GR R 1 ⊏PT
London Kings Cross 15 ⊖	d	01 36	05 23		05 45	05 50	05 56	06 06		06 15		06 23	06 26	06 30	06 36	06 45	06 53	07 06		07 08	07 15		07 20	07 23	07 35
Finsbury Park ⊖	d	01 41	05 28		05 50		06 02	06 11				06 28	06 32		06 41		06 58	07 11						07 28	
Potters Bar	d	01 59	05 38					06 21							06 51			07 21							
Hatfield	d	02 05	05 44					06 27							06 57			07 27							
Welwyn Garden City 4	d	02 09	05 48					06 31							07 01			07 31							
Welwyn North	d	02s12	05 51					06 34							07 04			07 34							
Knebworth	d	02s16	05 55					06 38							07 08			07 38							
Hertford North	d			05 50			06 40				←		07 10									←			
Stevenage 4	d	02 20	05 59	06a04	06 08	06 11	06a55	06 42		06 34	06 42	06 47	07a25	06 49	07 12		07 17	07 42		07 27		07 42	07a43	07 47	07a54
Hitchin 4	d	02 25	06 07		06 12			→			06 47	06 52			07 17		07 22	→				07 47		07 52	
Letchworth Garden City	d				06 16						06 51						07 26					07 51			
Baldock	d				06 19						06 55						07 29					07 55			
Ashwell & Morden	d				06 24						07 00						07 35					08 00			
Royston	d				06 29						07 06						07 39					08 06			
Meldreth	d				06 33						07 10						07 43					08 10			
Shepreth	d				06 36						07 13						07 46					08 13			
Foxton	d				06 38						07 16						07 49					08 16			
Cambridge	a				06 50						07 29					07 31	08 02				08 02	08 29			
Arlesey	d		06 13									06 57			07 23									07 57	
Biggleswade	d	02s37	06 18									07 02			07 28									08 02	
Sandy	d		06 22									07 06			07 32									08 06	
St Neots	d	02s47	06 29									07 13			07 39									08 13	
Huntingdon	d	02s57	06 37									07 21			07 47									08 21	
Peterborough 8	a	03 16	06 54			06 41				07 04		07 38		07 19	08 06					07 57				08 38	

		FC 1	FC 1	FC 1		FC 1	FC 1	FC 1	GR R 1 ⊏PT	FC 1	FC 1	FC 1	FC 1	GR R 1 ⊏P		FC 1	FC 1	FC 1	GR R 1 ⊏PT	FC 1	FC 1	FC 1	FC 1	GR R 1 ⊏PT	
London Kings Cross 15 ⊖	d	07 36	07 45	07 53		08 03	08 15	08 23	08 35	08 36	08 45	08 53	09 06	09 08		09 15		09 23	09 35	09 36	09 45	09 53	10 06	10 08	
Finsbury Park ⊖	d	07 41		07 58		08 08		08 28		08 41		08 58	09 11					09 28		09 41		09 58	10 11		
Potters Bar	d	07 51				08 18				08 51			09 21							09 51			10 21		
Hatfield	d	07 57				08 25				08 57			09 27							09 57			10 27		
Welwyn Garden City 4	d	08 01				08 30				09 01			09 31							10 01			10 31		
Welwyn North	d	08 04				08 33				09 04			09 34							10 04			10 34		
Knebworth	d	08 08				08 37				09 08			09 38							10 08			10 38		
Hertford North	d																←								
Stevenage 4	d	08 12		08 17		08 41		08 47	08a54	09 12		09 17	09 42	09 28			09 42	09 47	09a54	10 12		10 17	10 42	10 28	
Hitchin 4	d	08 17		08 22		08 46		08 52		09 17		09 22	→				09 47	09 52		10 17		10 22	→		
Letchworth Garden City	d			08 26		08 54						09 26					09 51					10 26			
Baldock	d			08 29		08 58						09 29					09 55					10 29			
Ashwell & Morden	d			08 35		09 03						09 35					10 00								
Royston	d			08 39		09 07						09 39					10 04					10 37			
Meldreth	d			08 43		09 11						09 43					10 08								
Shepreth	d			08 46		09 14						09 46					10 11								
Foxton	d			08 49		09 17						09 49					10 14								
Cambridge	a		08 32	09 02		09 29	09 03				09 31	10 02				10 03	10 27				10 31	10 54			
Arlesey	d	08 23						08 57		09 23								09 57		10 23					
Biggleswade	d	08 28						09 02		09 28								10 02		10 28					
Sandy	d	08 32						09 06		09 32								10 06		10 32					
St Neots	d	08 39						09 13		09 39								10 13		10 39					
Huntingdon	d	08 47						09 21		09 47								10 21		10 47					
Peterborough 8	a	09 06						09 38		10 06				10 00				10 38		11 06				10 59	

London - Stevenage, Cambridge and Peterborough

Network Diagram - see first Page of Table 24

		FC	FC	FC	GR	FC	FC	FC	FC	GR		FC	FC	FC	GR	FC	FC	FC	FC	GR		FC	FC	FC	GR
					R					R					R					R					R
		1	1	1	1	1	1	1	1	1		1	1	1	1	1	1	1	1	1		1	1	1	1
					⊏P⊥					⊏P					⊏P⊥					⊏P					⊏P⊥
London Kings Cross 15 ⊖	d	10 15		10 23	10 35	10 36	10 45	10 53	11 06	11 08		11 15		11 23	11 35	11 36	11 45	11 53	12 06	12 08		12 15		12 23	12 35
Finsbury Park ⊖	d			10 28		10 41		10 58	11 11					11 28		11 41		11 58	12 11					12 28	
Potters Bar	d					10 51			11 21							11 51			12 21						
Hatfield	d					10 57			11 27							11 57			12 27						
Welwyn Garden City 4	d					11 01			11 31							12 01			12 31						
Welwyn North	d					11 04			11 34							12 04			12 34						
Knebworth	d					11 08			11 38							12 08			12 38						
Hertford North	d		←										←										←		
Stevenage 4	d		10 42	10 47	10a54	11 12		11 17	11 42	11 27			11 42	11 47	11a54	12 12		12 17	12 42	12 28			12 42	12 47	12a54
Hitchin 4	d		10 47	10 52		11 17		11 22	→				11 47	11 52		12 17		12 22	→				12 47	12 52	
Letchworth Garden City	d		10 51					11 26					11 51					12 26					12 51		
Baldock	d		10 55					11 29					11 55					12 29					12 55		
Ashwell & Morden	d		11 00										12 00										13 00		
Royston	d		11 04					11 37					12 04					12 37					13 04		
Meldreth	d		11 08										12 08										13 08		
Shepreth	d		11 11										12 11										13 11		
Foxton	d		11 14										12 14										13 14		
Cambridge	a	11 01	11 27				11 30	11 54				12 01	12 27				12 31	12 54				13 01	13 27		
Arlesey	d			10 57		11 23								11 57		12 23								12 57	
Biggleswade	d			11 02		11 28								12 02		12 28								13 02	
Sandy	d			11 06		11 32								12 06		12 32								13 06	
St Neots	d			11 13		11 39								12 13		12 39								13 13	
Huntingdon	d			11 21		11 47								12 21		12 47								13 21	
Peterborough 8	a			11 38		12 06				11 57				12 38		13 06				12 59				13 38	

		FC	FC	FC	FC	GR		FC	FC	FC	GR	FC	FC	FC	FC	GR		FC	FC	FC	GR	FC	FC	FC	FC
						R					R					R					R				
		1	1	1	1	1		1	1	1	1	1	1	1	1	1		1	1	1	1	1	1	1	1
						⊏P					⊏P⊥					⊏P					⊏P⊥				
London Kings Cross 15 ⊖	d	12 36	12 45	12 53	13 06	13 08		13 15		13 23	13 35	13 36	13 45	13 53	14 06	14 08		14 15		14 23	14 35	14 36	14 45	14 53	15 06
Finsbury Park ⊖	d	12 41		12 58	13 11					13 28		13 41		13 58	14 11					14 28		14 41		14 58	15 11
Potters Bar	d	12 51			13 21							13 51			14 21							14 51			15 21
Hatfield	d	12 57			13 27							13 57			14 27							14 57			15 27
Welwyn Garden City 4	d	13 01			13 31							14 01			14 31							15 01			15 31
Welwyn North	d	13 04			13 34							14 04			14 34							15 04			15 34
Knebworth	d	13 08			13 38							14 08			14 38							15 08			15 38
Hertford North	d								←										←						
Stevenage 4	d	13 12		13 17	13 42	13 28			13 42	13 47	13a54	14 12		14 17	14 42	14 27			14 42	14 47	14a54	15 12		15 17	15 42
Hitchin 4	d	13 17		13 22	→				13 47	13 52		14 17		14 22	→				14 47	14 52		15 17		15 22	→
Letchworth Garden City	d			13 26					13 51					14 26					14 51					15 26	
Baldock	d			13 29					13 55					14 29					14 55					15 29	
Ashwell & Morden	d								14 00										15 00						
Royston	d			13 37					14 04					14 37					15 04					15 37	
Meldreth	d								14 08										15 08						
Shepreth	d								14 11										15 11						
Foxton	d								14 14										15 14						
Cambridge	a		13 30	13 54				14 01	14 27				14 30	14 54				15 01	15 27				15 30	15 54	
Arlesey	d	13 23								13 57		14 23								14 57		15 23			
Biggleswade	d	13 28								14 02		14 28								15 02		15 28			
Sandy	d	13 32								14 06		14 32								15 06		15 32			
St Neots	d	13 39								14 13		14 39								15 13		15 39			
Huntingdon	d	13 47								14 21		14 47								15 21		15 47			
Peterborough 8	a	14 06				13 59				14 38		15 06				14 58				15 38		16 06			

		GR		FC	FC	FC	GR	FC	FC	FC		FC		GR	FC	FC	FC	FC	FC	GR	FC	FC		FC	FC
		R					R							R						R					
		1		1	1	1	1	1	1	1		1		1	1	1	1	1	1	1	1	1		1	1
		⊏P					⊏P⊥							⊏P						⊏P⊥					
London Kings Cross 15 ⊖	d	15 08		15 15		15 23	15 35	15 36	15 44	15 53		16 06		16 08	16 14	16 17		16 22	16 32	16 33	16 40	16 44			16 50
Finsbury Park ⊖	d					15 28		15 41		15 58		16 11						16 27	16 37						16 55
Potters Bar	d							15 51				16 21							16 47						
Hatfield	d							15 58				16 28							16 54						
Welwyn Garden City 4	d							16 02				16 32							16 58						
Welwyn North	d							16 05				16 35							17 01						17 11
Knebworth	d							16 09				16 39						16 45	17 06						
Hertford North	d				←												←								
Stevenage 4	d	15 28			15 42	15 47	15a54	16 12		16 17		16 45		16 29		16 40	16 45	16 49	17 10	16a52					17 18
Hitchin 4	d				15 47	15 52		16 17		16 22		→					16 50	16 54	17 17					←	17 23
Letchworth Garden City	d				15 51				16 09	16 26						16 48	16 55		17 26			17 09		17 26	
Baldock	d				15 55					16 29						16 52	16 59		→					17 30	
Ashwell & Morden	d				16 00					16 34						16 57	17 04							17 35	
Royston	d				16 04				16 19	16 38						17a03	17 08					17 19		17 39	
Meldreth	d				16 08												17 12							17 43	
Shepreth	d				16 11												17 15							17 46	
Foxton	d				16 14												17 18							17 49	
Cambridge	a			16 03	16 28				16 34	16 54					17 01		17 30					17 34		18 02	
Arlesey	d					15 57		16 23										17 00							17 29
Biggleswade	d					16 02		16 28										17 05			17 07				17 34
Sandy	d					16 06		16 32										17 09							17 38
St Neots	d					16 13		16 39										17 22			17 17				17 45
Huntingdon	d					16 21		16 47										17a30			17 26				17 53
Peterborough 8	a	15 59				16 38		17 06						16 59							17 42				18 12

London - Stevenage, Cambridge and Peterborough

Network Diagram - see first Page of Table 24

Station		FC	FC	FC	FC	FC	FC	FC		GR	FC	FC	FC	FC	FC	FC	FC	FC		FC	FC	FC	FC	FC	GR
		1	1	1	1	1	1	1		R 1	1	1	1	1	1	1	1	1			1	1	1	1	R 1
London Kings Cross 15 ⊖	d	16 54	17 10	17 14		17 14	17 22	17 23		17 33	17 40	17 44		17 44	17 52	17 53	18 10	18 14				18 14	18 22	18 23	18 33
Finsbury Park ⊖	d	16 59				17 19	17 28							17 49	17 58							18 19	18 28		
Potters Bar	d																								
Hatfield	d	17 15					17 44								18 14								18 44		
Welwyn Garden City 4	d	17 19					17 48								18 18								18 49		
Welwyn North	d	17 22					17 52								18 22								18 51	18 41	
Knebworth	d	17 26				17 35	17 56								18 26								18 55		
Hertford North	d												←								←				
Stevenage 4	d	17 36			←	17 40	18 04	17 43		17a53			18 04	18 09	18 34	18 13					18 34	18 39	19 04		18a52
Hitchin 4	d	17 42	17 34		17 42	17 46	→				18 04		18 10	18 16	→		18 34				18 40	18 46	19 10	18 53	
Letchworth Garden City	d	→			17 47			17 52					18 16			18 22					18 48		→	18 57	
Baldock	d				17 51			17 55								18 26					18 52			19 01	
Ashwell & Morden	d				17 56			18 00								18 31					18 57			19 06	
Royston	d			17 48	18 01			18a07				18 18	18 30			18a37		18 52		18 56	19 02			19a13	
Meldreth	d				18 05								18 34							18 59					
Shepreth	d				18 08								18 37							19 02					
Foxton	d				18 10								18 39							19 05					
Cambridge	a			18 03	18 24							18 34	18 54					19 08		19 20	19 24				
Arlesey	d					17 51								18 21								18 51			
Biggleswade	d					17 56								18 26								18 56			
Sandy	d					18 00								18 30								19 00			
St Neots	d		17 51			18 08					18 21			18 38			18 51					19 08			
Huntingdon	d		17 59			18 16					18 29			18 46			18 59					19 16			
Peterborough 8	a		18 22			18 32					18 50			19 04			19 21					19 40			

Station		FC	FC	FC		FC	FC	FC	GR	FC	FC	FC	FC	FC		GR	FC	FC	FC	FC	FC	FC	FC	FC	
		1	1	1		1	1	1	R 1	1	1	1	1	1		R 1	1	1	1	1	1	1	1	1	
London Kings Cross 15 ⊖	d	18 40	18 44			18 44	18 52	18 53	19 06	19 10	19 15		19 18	19 23		19 33		19 34	19 45		19 53	20 06	20 10	20 15	
Finsbury Park ⊖	d					18 49	18 58						19 23	19 28				19 39			19 58	20 11			
Potters Bar	d												19 37									20 21			
Hatfield	d						19 14						19 44					19 53				20 27			
Welwyn Garden City 4	d						19 19						19 49					20 00				20 31			
Welwyn North	d						19 24						19 53					20 03				20 34			
Knebworth	d					19 05	19 28						19 57					20 07				20 38			
Hertford North	d											←					←								
Stevenage 4	d			←		19 10	19 35	19 13	19 26			19 35	20 04	19 47		19a52	20 04	20 12			20 17	20 42			
Hitchin 4	d			19 10		19 16	→			19 36		19 42	→	19 53			20 13	20 17		←	20 23	20 47			
Letchworth Garden City	d			19 16				19 22			19 40	19 52					20 17	20a23	20 10	20 17		20 51		20 40	
Baldock	d							19 26				19 55					→			20 21		→			
Ashwell & Morden	d							19 31				20 00								20 26					
Royston	d		19 18	19 31				19a38			19 50	20 05							20 20	20 31				20 50	
Meldreth	d			19 35								20 09								20 35					
Shepreth	d			19 38								20 12								20 38					
Foxton	d			19 41								20 15								20 40					
Cambridge	a		19 34	19 56							20 07	20 27							20 35	20 54				21 05	
Arlesey	d					19 21								19 59							20 29				
Biggleswade	d	19 07				19 26								20 04							20 34				
Sandy	d					19 30								20 08							20 38				
St Neots	d	19 17				19 38				19 54				20 15							20 45		20 45		
Huntingdon	d	19 26				19 46				20 02				20 23							20 58		20 53		
Peterborough 8	a	19 44				20 03			19 57	20 22				20 41							21 21		21 12		

Station		FC	FC	GR	FC	FC	FC	GR	FC	FC		FC	FC	FC	GR	FC	FC	FC	FC	FC		FC	FC	FC	FC
		1	1	R 1	1	1	1	R 1	1	1		1	1	1	R 1	1	1	1	1	1		1	1	1	
London Kings Cross 15 ⊖	d		20 23	20 35	20 36	20 45	20 53	21 00	21 06	21 07		21 15		21 23	21 35	21 36	21 45	21 53	22 06	22 07		22 15		22 23	22 26
Finsbury Park ⊖	d		20 28		20 41		20 58		21 11					21 28		21 41		21 58	22 11					22 28	22 32
Potters Bar	d				20 51				21 21							21 51			22 21						
Hatfield	d				20 57				21 27							21 57			22 27						
Welwyn Garden City 4	d				21 01				21 31							22 01			22 31						
Welwyn North	d				21 04				21 34							22 04			22 34						
Knebworth	d				21 08				21 38							22 08			22 38						
Hertford North	d																								23 07
Stevenage 4	d		20 47	20 54	21 12		21 17	21 20	21 42					21 47	21 55	22 12		22 17	22 42					22 47	23 21
Hitchin 4	d	←	20 53		21 17		21 22		21 47				←	21 53		22 17		22 22	22 47				←	22 53	→
Letchworth Garden City	d	20 51			21a23		21 29		21 51			21 40	21 51			22a23	22 10	22 29	22 51			22 40	22 51		
Baldock	d	20 55					21 32		→				21 55					22 32	→				22 55		
Ashwell & Morden	d	21 00					21 37						22 00					22 37					23 00		
Royston	d	21 04				21 19	21 42					21 50	22 04				22 20	22 42				22 50	23 04		
Meldreth	d	21 08					21 45						22 08					22 45					23 08		
Shepreth	d	21 11					21 48						22 11					22 48					23 11		
Foxton	d	21 14					21 51						22 14					22 51					23 14		
Cambridge	a	21 27				21 34	22 03					22 05	22 27				22 35	23 03				23 05	23 27		
Arlesey	d		20 59											21 59										22 59	
Biggleswade	d		21 04							21 35				22 04						22 35				23 04	
Sandy	d		21 08											22 08										23 08	
St Neots	d		21 15							21 44				22 15						22 44				23 15	
Huntingdon	d		21 23							21 51				22 23						22 51				23 23	
Peterborough 8	a		21 41	21 24				21 50		22 07				22 41	22 26					23 07				23 43	

London - Stevenage, Cambridge and Peterborough

Network Diagram - see first Page of Table 24

		FC 1	FC 1	FC	FC 1	FC 1		FC 1	FC 1	FC 1	FC	FC 1	FC
London Kings Cross 15 ⊖	d	22 36	22 53		23 01	23 06		23 15		23 23	23 26	23 36	
Finsbury Park ⊖	d	22 41	22 58			23 11				23 28	23 32	23 41	
Potters Bar	d	22 51				23 21						23 51	
Hatfield	d	22 57				23 27						23 57	
Welwyn Garden City 4	d	23 01				23 31						00 01	
Welwyn North	d	23 04				23 34						00 04	
Knebworth	d	23 08				23 38						00 08	
Hertford North	d			←							00 07		←
Stevenage 4	d	23 12	23 17	23 21		23 42				23 47	00 20	00 12	00 20
Hitchin 4	d	23 17	23 25	23 30		23 50			←	23 53	→	00 20	00 26
Letchworth Garden City	d	23a26	23 31	23a36		23 54		23 44	23 54			00a29	00a36
Baldock	d		23 34			→			23 58				
Ashwell & Morden	d		23 39						00 03				
Royston	d		23 44					23 54	00 07				
Meldreth	d								00 11				
Shepreth	d								00 14				
Foxton	d								00 17				
Cambridge	a		23 59					00 10	00 29				
Arlesey	d									23 59			
Biggleswade	d				23 29					00 04			
Sandy	d									00 08			
St Neots	d				23 38					00 15			
Huntingdon	d				23 45					00 23			
Peterborough 8	a				00 12					00 42			

Saturdays

		FC 1	FC 1	FC 1	FC 1	FC 1	FC	FC 1	FC	FC 1		FC 1	FC	FC 1	FC	FC 1	FC 1	FC 1	FC 1	FC 1		FC 1	GR R 1	FC 1	FC 1
London Kings Cross 15 ⊖	d	23p01	23p06	23p15		23p23	23p26	23p36		00 01		00 04	00 06	00 31		00 36	01 06	01 36	05 23	05 45		06 06	06 15		06 23
Finsbury Park ⊖	d		23p11			23p28	23p32	23p41				00 09	00 12			00 41	01 11	01 41	05 28	05 50		06 11			06 28
Potters Bar	d		23p21					23p51								00 51		01 59	05 38			06 21			
Hatfield	d		23p27					23p57								00 57		02 05	05 44			06 27			
Welwyn Garden City 4	d		23p31					00 01								01 01		02 09	05 48			06 31			
Welwyn North	d		23p34					00 04								01s04		02s12	05 51			06 34			
Knebworth	d		23p38					00 08								01s08		02s16	05 55			06 38			
Hertford North	d						00 07		←				00 47		←		01 38							←	
Stevenage 4	d		23p42			23p47	00 20	00 12	00 20	00s20		00 31	01 00	00s50	01 00	01 12	01 47	02 20	05 59	06 08		06 41	06 34	06 41	06 47
Hitchin 4	d		23p50		←	23p53	→	00 20	00 26	00s35		00 39	→	01s05	01 06	01 17	01 52	02 25	06 07	06 13		→		06 47	06 52
Letchworth Garden City	d		23p54	23p44	23p54			00a29	00a36			00 43		01s09	01a15		02a01			06 17				06 51	
Baldock	d		→		23p58							00 46		01s12						06 20				06 54	
Ashwell & Morden	d				00 03							00 51								06 25				06 59	
Royston	d			23p54	00 07							00 56		01s20						06 29				07 04	
Meldreth	d				00 11							00 59								06 33				07 08	
Shepreth	d				00 14							01 02								06 36				07 11	
Foxton	d				00 17							01 05								06 38				07 14	
Cambridge	a			00 10	00 29							01 22		01 35						06 53				07 27	
Arlesey	d					23p59										01s25			06 13						06 57
Biggleswade	d	23p29				00 04				00 43						01s30		02s37	06 18						07 02
Sandy	d					00 08										01s34			06 22						07 06
St Neots	d	23p38				00 15				00s53						01s42		02s47	06 29						07 13
Huntingdon	d	23p45				00 23				01s03						01s52		02s57	06 37						07 21
Peterborough 8	a	00 12				00 42				01 19						02 13		03 16	06 54				07 04		07 38

		FC	FC 1	FC 1	FC 1	GR R 1		FC 1	FC 1	FC	FC 1	FC 1	FC 1	FC 1	FC 1	FC 1		FC	FC 1	FC 1	FC 1	GR R 1	FC 1	FC 1	FC 1
London Kings Cross 15 ⊖	d	06 26	06 36	06 45	06 53	07 03		07 06	07 23	07 26	07 36	07 45	07 53	08 06	08 15	08 23		08 26	08 36	08 45	08 53	09 03	09 06	09 15	09 23
Finsbury Park ⊖	d	06 32	06 41		06 58			07 11	07 28	07 32	07 41		07 58	08 11		08 28		08 32	08 41		08 58		09 11		09 28
Potters Bar	d		06 51					07 21			07 51			08 21					08 51				09 21		
Hatfield	d		06 57					07 27			07 57			08 27					08 57				09 27		
Welwyn Garden City 4	d		07 01					07 31			08 01			08 31					09 01				09 31		
Welwyn North	d		07 04					07 34			08 04			08 34					09 04				09 34		
Knebworth	d		07 08					07 38			08 08			08 38					09 08				09 38		
Hertford North	d	07 07								08 07								09 07							
Stevenage 4	d	07a20	07 12		07 17	07 22		07 42	07 47	08a20	08 13		08 17	08 42		08 47		09a20	09 12		09 17	09 22	09 42		09 47
Hitchin 4	d		07 17		07 22			07 47	07 52		08 17		08 22	08 47		08 52			09 17		09 22		09 47		09 52
Letchworth Garden City	d				07 26			07 51					08 26	08 51							09 26		09 51		
Baldock	d				07 29			07 55					08 29	08 55							09 29		09 55		
Ashwell & Morden	d				07 34			08 00						09 00									10 00		
Royston	d				07 39			08 04					08 37	09 04							09 37		10 04		
Meldreth	d				07 42			08 08						09 08									10 08		
Shepreth	d				07 45			08 11						09 11									10 11		
Foxton	d				07 48			08 14						09 14									10 14		
Cambridge	a			07 30	08 00			08 27				08 30	08 54	09 27	09 01					09 30	09 54		10 27	10 01	
Arlesey	d		07 23						07 57		08 23					08 57			09 23						09 57
Biggleswade	d		07 28						08 02		08 28					09 02			09 28						10 02
Sandy	d		07 32						08 06		08 32					09 06			09 32						10 06
St Neots	d		07 39						08 13		08 39					09 13			09 39						10 13
Huntingdon	d		07 47						08 21		08 47					09 21			09 47						10 21
Peterborough 8	a		08 06			07 52			08 38		09 08					09 37			10 06			09 52			10 38

London - Stevenage, Cambridge and Peterborough

Network Diagram - see first Page of Table 24

		FC		FC	FC	FC	FC	FC	FC	FC	FC	FC		FC	GR	FC	FC	FC	FC	FC	FC	FC		FC	FC
				1	1	1	1	1	1		1	1		1	R 1	1	1	1		1	1	1		1	1
London Kings Cross 15 ⊖	d	09 26		09 36	09 45	09 53	10 06	10 15	10 23	10 26	10 36	10 45		10 53	11 03	11 06	11 15	11 23	11 26	11 36	11 45	11 53		12 06	12 15
Finsbury Park ⊖	d	09 32		09 41		09 58	10 11		10 28	10 32	10 41			10 58		11 11		11 28	11 32	11 41		11 58		12 11	
Potters Bar	d			09 51			10 21				10 51					11 21				11 51				12 21	
Hatfield	d			09 57			10 27				10 57					11 27				11 57				12 27	
Welwyn Garden City 4	d			10 01			10 31				11 01					11 31				12 01				12 31	
Welwyn North	d			10 04			10 34				11 04					11 34				12 04				12 34	
Knebworth	d			10 08			10 38				11 08					11 38				12 08				12 38	
Hertford North	d	10 07								11 07									12 07						
Stevenage 4	d	10a20		10 12		10 17	10 42		10 47	11a20	11 12			11 17	11 22	11 42		11 47	12a20	12 12		12 17		12 42	
Hitchin 4	d			10 17		10 22	10 47		10 52		11 17			11 22		11 47		11 52		12 17		12 22		12 47	
Letchworth Garden City	d					10 26	10 51							11 26		11 51						12 26		12 51	
Baldock	d					10 29	10 55							11 29		11 55						12 29		12 55	
Ashwell & Morden	d						11 00									12 00								13 00	
Royston	d					10 37	11 04							11 37		12 04						12 37		13 04	
Meldreth	d						11 08									12 08								13 08	
Shepreth	d						11 11									12 11								13 11	
Foxton	d						11 14									12 14								13 14	
Cambridge	a				10 30	10 54	11 27	11 01				11 30		11 54		12 27	12 01				12 30	12 54		13 27	13 01
Arlesey	d			10 23					10 57		11 23							11 57		12 23					
Biggleswade	d			10 28					11 02		11 28							12 02		12 28					
Sandy	d			10 32					11 06		11 32							12 06		12 32					
St Neots	d			10 39					11 13		11 39							12 13		12 39					
Huntingdon	d			10 47					11 21		11 47							12 21		12 47					
Peterborough 8	a			11 06					11 38		12 06				11 52			12 39		13 05					

		FC	FC	FC	FC	FC	GR	FC		FC	FC	FC	FC	FC	FC	FC	FC	FC		FC	FC	FC	FC	GR	FC
		1		1	1	1	R 1	1		1	1		1	1	1	1	1	1			1	1	1	R 1	1
London Kings Cross 15 ⊖	d	12 23	12 26	12 36	12 45	12 53	13 03	13 06		13 15	13 23	13 26	13 36	13 45	13 53	14 06	14 15	14 23		14 26	14 36	14 45	14 53	15 03	15 06
Finsbury Park ⊖	d	12 28	12 32	12 41		12 58		13 11			13 28	13 32	13 41		13 58	14 11		14 28		14 32	14 41		14 58		15 11
Potters Bar	d			12 51				13 21					13 51			14 21					14 51				15 21
Hatfield	d			12 57				13 27					13 57			14 27					14 57				15 27
Welwyn Garden City 4	d			13 01				13 31					14 01			14 31					15 01				15 31
Welwyn North	d			13 04				13 34					14 04			14 34					15 04				15 34
Knebworth	d			13 08				13 38					14 08			14 38					15 08				15 38
Hertford North	d		13 07									14 07								15 07					
Stevenage 4	d	12 47	13a20	13 12		13 17	13 22	13 42			13 47	14a20	14 12		14 17	14 42		14 47		15a20	15 12		15 17	15 22	15 42
Hitchin 4	d	12 52		13 17		13 22		13 47			13 52		14 17		14 22	14 47		14 52			15 17		15 22		15 47
Letchworth Garden City	d					13 26		13 51							14 26	14 51							15 26		15 51
Baldock	d					13 29		13 55							14 29	14 55							15 29		15 55
Ashwell & Morden	d							14 00								15 00									16 00
Royston	d					13 37		14 04							14 37	15 04							15 37		16 04
Meldreth	d							14 08								15 08									16 08
Shepreth	d							14 11								15 11									16 11
Foxton	d							14 14								15 14									16 14
Cambridge	a				13 30	13 54		14 27		14 01				14 30	14 54	15 27	15 01					15 30	15 54		16 27
Arlesey	d	12 57		13 23							13 57		14 23					14 57			15 23				
Biggleswade	d	13 02		13 28							14 02		14 28					15 02			15 28				
Sandy	d	13 06		13 32							14 06		14 32					15 06			15 32				
St Neots	d	13 13		13 39							14 13		14 39					15 13			15 39				
Huntingdon	d	13 21		13 47							14 21		14 47					15 21			15 47				
Peterborough 8	a	13 37		14 06			13 52				14 38		15 07					15 38			16 06			15 52	

		FC	FC	FC		FC	FC	FC	FC	FC	FC	FC	FC	FC		FC	FC	GR	FC	FC	FC	FC	FC	FC	
		1	1			1	1	1	1	1	1		1	1		1	1	R 1	1	1	1		1	1	
London Kings Cross 15 ⊖	d	15 15	15 23	15 26		15 36	15 45	15 53	16 06	16 15	16 23	16 26	16 36	16 40		16 45	16 53	17 03	17 06	17 15	17 23	17 26	17 36	17 40	
Finsbury Park ⊖	d		15 28	15 32		15 41		15 58	16 11		16 28	16 32	16 41				16 58		17 11		17 28	17 32	17 41		
Potters Bar	d					15 51			16 21				16 51						17 21				17 51		
Hatfield	d					15 57			16 27				16 57						17 27				17 57		
Welwyn Garden City 4	d					16 01			16 31				17 01						17 31				18 01		
Welwyn North	d					16 04			16 34				17 04						17 34				18 04		
Knebworth	d					16 08			16 38				17 08						17 38				18 08		
Hertford North	d			16 07								17 07										18 07			
Stevenage 4	d		15 47	16a20		16 12		16 17	16 42		16 47	17a20	17 12				17 17	17 22	17 42		17 47	18a20	18 12		
Hitchin 4	d		15 52			16 17		16 22	16 47		16 52		17 17				17 22		17 47		17 52		18 17		
Letchworth Garden City	d							16 26	16 51								17 26		17 51						
Baldock	d							16 29	16 55								17 29		17 55						
Ashwell & Morden	d								17 00										18 00						
Royston	d							16 37	17 04								17 37		18 04						
Meldreth	d								17 08										18 08						
Shepreth	d								17 11										18 11						
Foxton	d								17 14										18 14						
Cambridge	a	16 01					16 30	16 54	17 27	17 01						17 30	17 54		18 27	18 01					
Arlesey	d		15 57			16 23					16 57		17 23								17 57		18 23		
Biggleswade	d		16 02			16 28					17 02		17 28	17 08							18 02		18 28	18 08	
Sandy	d		16 06			16 32					17 06		17 32								18 06		18 32		
St Neots	d		16 13			16 39					17 13		17 39	17 18							18 13		18 39	18 18	
Huntingdon	d		16 21			16 47					17 21		17 47	17 26							18 21		18 47	18 26	
Peterborough 8	a		16 38			17 06					17 38		18 06	17 42				17 52			18 38		19 06	18 42	

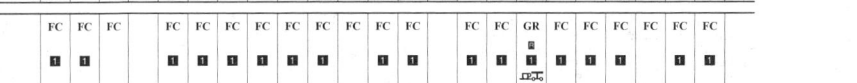

Table 25

Saturdays

London - Stevenage, Cambridge and Peterborough

Network Diagram - see first Page of Table 24

		FC	FC	FC	GR	FC	FC	FC	FC	FC		FC	FC	FC	FC	FC	FC	FC	GR	FC		FC	FC	FC	FC
		1	1	1	R 1	1	1	1		1		1	1	1	1	1	1		R 1	1		1	1	1	1
London Kings Cross 15 ⊖	d	17 45	17 53	18 06	18 08	18 15		18 23	18 26	18 36		18 40	18 45	18 53	19 06	19 15	19 23	19 26	19 30	19 36		19 45	19 53	20 06	20 23
Finsbury Park ⊖	d		17 58	18 11				18 28	18 32	18 41				18 58	19 11		19 28	19 32		19 41			19 58	20 11	20 28
Potters Bar	d			18 21						18 51					19 21					19 51				20 21	
Hatfield	d			18 27						18 57					19 27					19 57				20 27	
Welwyn Garden City 4	d			18 31						19 01					19 31					20 01				20 31	
Welwyn North	d			18 34						19 04					19 34					20 04				20 34	
Knebworth	d			18 38						19 08					19 38					20 08				20 38	
Hertford North	d						←		19 07									20 07							
Stevenage 4	d		18 17	18 42	18 28		18 42	18 47	19a20	19 12				19 17	19 42		19 47	20a20	19 49	20 12			20 17	20 42	20 47
Hitchin 4	d		18 22	→			18 47	18 52		19 17				19 22	19 47		19 52			20 17			20 22	20 47	20 52
Letchworth Garden City	d		18 26				18 51							19 26	19 51								20 26	20 51	
Baldock	d		18 29				18 55							19 29	19 55								20 29	20 55	
Ashwell & Morden	d						19 00								20 00									21 00	
Royston	d		18 37				19 04						19 19	19 37	20 04							20 19	20 37	21 04	
Meldreth	d						19 08								20 08									21 08	
Shepreth	d						19 11								20 11									21 11	
Foxton	d						19 14								20 14									21 14	
Cambridge	a	18 30	18 54			19 01	19 27						19 35	19 54	20 27	20 01						20 35	20 54	21 27	
Arlesey	d							18 57		19 23							19 57			20 23					20 57
Biggleswade	d							19 02		19 28		19 08					20 02			20 28					21 02
Sandy	d							19 06		19 32							20 06			20 32					21 06
St Neots	d							19 13		19 39		19 18					20 13			20 39					21 13
Huntingdon	d							19 21		19 47		19 26					20 21			20 47					21 21
Peterborough 8	a				18 58			19 38		20 06		19 44					20 39		20 19	21 06					21 37

		FC	FC	FC	FC	FC		FC	FC	FC	FC	FC	FC	FC	FC	FC		FC	FC	FC	FC	FC	FC	FC	FC
			1	1	1	1		1		1	1	1	1	1	1			1	1	1	1	1	1		1
London Kings Cross 15 ⊖	d	20 26	20 36	20 45	20 53	21 06		21 23	21 26	21 36	21 53	22 06	22 15		22 23	22 26		22 36	22 53	23 06	23 15		23 23	23 26	23 36
Finsbury Park ⊖	d	20 32	20 41		20 58	21 11		21 28	21 32	21 41	21 58	22 11			22 28	22 32		22 41	22 58	23 11			23 28	23 32	23 41
Potters Bar	d		20 51			21 21				21 51		22 21						22 51		23 21					23 53
Hatfield	d		20 57			21 27				21 57		22 27						22 57		23 27					23 59
Welwyn Garden City 4	d		21 01			21 31				22 01		22 31						23 01		23 31					00 06
Welwyn North	d		21 04			21 34				22 04		22 34						23 04		23 34					00 09
Knebworth	d		21 08			21 38				22 08		22 38						23 08		23 38					00 13
Hertford North	d	21 07							22 07							23 07								00 07	
Stevenage 4	d	21a20	21 12		21 17	21 42		21 47	22a20	22 12	22 17	22 42			22 47	23a20		23 12	23 17	23 42			23 47	00 22	00 18
Hitchin 4	d		21 17		21 22	21 47		21 52		22 17	22 22	22 47		←	22 54			23 20	23 24	23 50		←	23 54	→	00 25
Letchworth Garden City	d				21 26	21 51					22 26	22 51	22 40	22 51				23a26		23 54	23 43	23 54			00a30
Baldock	d				21 29	21 55					22 29	→		22 55						→		23 57			
Ashwell & Morden	d					22 00								23 00								00 02			
Royston	d			21 19	21 37	22 04					22 37		22 50	23 04							23 53	00 07			
Meldreth	d					22 08								23 08								00 11			
Shepreth	d					22 11								23 11								00 14			
Foxton	d					22 14								23 14								00 16			
Cambridge	a			21 35	21 54	22 27					22 54		23 05	23 27							00 10	00 29			
Arlesey	d		21 23					21 57		22 23					22 59				23 29				23 59		
Biggleswade	d		21 28					22 02		22 28					23 04				23 34				00 04		
Sandy	d		21 32					22 06		22 32					23 08				23 38				00 08		
St Neots	d		21 39					22 13		22 39					23 15				23 45				00 15		
Huntingdon	d		21 47					22 21		22 47					23 23				23 53				00 23		
Peterborough 8	a		22 06					22 37		23 06					23 43				00 13				00 43		

		FC		FC
				1
London Kings Cross 15 ⊖	d			23 53
Finsbury Park ⊖	d			23 58
Potters Bar	d			
Hatfield	d			
Welwyn Garden City 4	d			
Welwyn North	d			
Knebworth	d			
Hertford North	d	←		
Stevenage 4	d	00 22		00 29
Hitchin 4	d	00 29		00 36
Letchworth Garden City	d	00a37		
Baldock	d			
Ashwell & Morden	d			
Royston	d			
Meldreth	d			
Shepreth	d			
Foxton	d			
Cambridge	a			
Arlesey	d			00s43
Biggleswade	d			00s48
Sandy	d			00s51
St Neots	d			00s59
Huntingdon	d			01s06
Peterborough 8	a			01 25

Table 25

Sundays

London - Stevenage, Cambridge and Peterborough

Network Diagram - see first Page of Table 24

		FC	FC	FC	FC	FC	FC	FC	FC	FC		FC	FC	FC	FC	FC	FC	FC	FC	FC		FC	FC	FC	FC
		1	1	1	1	1		1		1		1	1	1	1	1			1	1		1		1	1
		A	A	A	A	A	A	A	A	A															
London Kings Cross 15 ⊖	d	22p53	23p06	23p15		23p23	23p26	23p36		23p53		00 06	00 15		00 23	00 53	00 56	06 26	06 53	07 06		07 23	07 26	07 53	08 06
Finsbury Park ⊖	d	22p58	23p11			23p28	23p32	23p41		23p58		00 11			00 28	00 58	01 02	06 32	06 58	07 11		07 28	07 32	07 58	08 11
Potters Bar	d		23p21					23p53				00 23				01 10				07 21					08 21
Hatfield	d		23p27					23p59				00 29				01 16				07 27					08 27
Welwyn Garden City 4	d		23p31					00 06				00 41				01 20				07 33					08 31
Welwyn North	d		23p34					00 09				00 44				01s24				07 36					08 34
Knebworth	d		23p38					00 13				00 48				01s28				07 40					08 38
Hertford North	d						00 07		←					←			01 37	07 07					08 07		
Stevenage 4	d	23p17	23p42			23p47	00 22	00 18	00 22	00 29		00 53	00 47	00 53	00 58	01 32	01 51	07a22	07 17	07 45		07 51	08a23	08 17	08 42
Hitchin 4	d	23p24	23p50		←	23p54	→	00 25	00 29	00 36		→	00 54	01 00	01 05	01 39	01 59		07 27	07 52		08 01		08 22	08 47
Letchworth Garden City	d		23p54	23p43	23p54			00a30	00a37				00 58	01 04			02a05		07 36	07 56				08 26	08 51
Baldock	d		→		23p57								01 01	01 08					07 39	07 59				08 29	08 55
Ashwell & Morden	d				00 02									01 13						08 04					09 00
Royston	d			23p53	00 07								01 09	01 17					07 47	08 09				08 37	09 04
Meldreth	d				00 11									01 21						08 13					09 08
Shepreth	d				00 14									01 24						08 16					09 11
Foxton	d				00 16									01 27						08 18					09 14
Cambridge	a			00 10	00 29								01 25	01 40					08 04	08 34				08 54	09 27
Arlesey	d	23p29				23p59				00s43					01s10	01s46						08 06			
Biggleswade	d	23p34				00 04				00s48					01s15	01s51						08 11			
Sandy	d	23p38				00 08				00s51					01s19	01s55						08 15			
St Neots	d	23p45				00 15				00s59					01s26	02s02						08 22			
Huntingdon	d	23p53				00 23				01s06					01s34	02s10						08 30			
Peterborough 8	a	00 13				00 43				01 25					01 54	02 30						08 51			

		FC	FC	FC	GR	FC		FC	FC	FC	FC	FC	FC	FC	FC	FC		GR	FC	FC	FC	FC	FC	FC	FC
					R													R							
		1		1	1	1		1	1		1	1	1	1		1		1	1	1	1		1	1	1
London Kings Cross 15 ⊖	d	08 23	08 26	08 53	09 03	09 06		09 15	09 23	09 26	09 53	10 06	10 15	10 23	10 26	10 53		11 03	11 06	11 15	11 23	11 26	11 53	12 06	12 15
Finsbury Park ⊖	d	08 28	08 32	08 58		09 11			09 28	09 32	09 58	10 11		10 28	10 32	10 58			11 11		11 28	11 32	11 58	12 11	
Potters Bar	d					09 21						10 21							11 21					12 21	
Hatfield	d					09 27						10 27							11 27					12 27	
Welwyn Garden City 4	d					09 31						10 31							11 31					12 31	
Welwyn North	d					09 34						10 34							11 34					12 34	
Knebworth	d					09 38						10 38							11 38					12 38	
Hertford North	d		09 07							10 07					11 07							12 07			
Stevenage 4	d	08 47	09a20	09 17	09 22	09 42			09 47	10a20	10 17	10 42		10 47	11a20	11 17		11 22	11 42		11 47	12a20	12 17	12 42	
Hitchin 4	d	08 52		09 22		09 47			09 52		10 22	10 47		10 52		11 22			11 47		11 52		12 22	12 47	
Letchworth Garden City	d			09 26		09 51					10 26	10 51				11 26			11 51				12 26	12 51	
Baldock	d			09 29		09 55					10 29	10 55				11 29			11 55				12 29	12 55	
Ashwell & Morden	d					10 00						11 00							12 00					13 00	
Royston	d			09 37		10 04					10 37	11 04				11 37			12 04				12 37	13 04	
Meldreth	d					10 08						11 08							12 08					13 08	
Shepreth	d					10 11						11 11							12 11					13 11	
Foxton	d					10 14						11 14							12 14					13 14	
Cambridge	a			09 54		10 27		10 00			10 54	11 27	11 00			11 54			12 27	12 00			12 54	13 27	13 00
Arlesey	d	08 57							09 57					10 57							11 57				
Biggleswade	d	09 02							10 02					11 02							12 02				
Sandy	d	09 06							10 06					11 06							12 06				
St Neots	d	09 13							10 13					11 13							12 13				
Huntingdon	d	09 21							10 21					11 21							12 21				
Peterborough 8	a	09 38			09 52				10 38					11 38				11 52			12 39				

		FC		FC	FC	GR	FC	FC	FC	FC	FC	FC		FC	FC	FC	FC	GR	FC	FC	FC	FC		FC	FC
						R												R							
		1			1	1	1	1	1		1	1		1	1		1	1	1	1	1			1	1
London Kings Cross 15 ⊖	d	12 23		12 26	12 53	13 03	13 06	13 15	13 23	13 26	13 53	14 06		14 15	14 23	14 26	14 53	15 03	15 06	15 15	15 23	15 26		15 53	16 06
Finsbury Park ⊖	d	12 28		12 32	12 58		13 11		13 28	13 32	13 58	14 11			14 28	14 32	14 58		15 11		15 28	15 32		15 58	16 11
Potters Bar	d						13 21					14 21							15 21						16 21
Hatfield	d						13 27					14 27							15 27						16 27
Welwyn Garden City 4	d						13 31					14 31							15 31						16 31
Welwyn North	d						13 34					14 34							15 34						16 34
Knebworth	d						13 38					14 38							15 38						16 38
Hertford North	d			13 07						14 07						15 07						16 07			
Stevenage 4	d	12 47		13a20	13 17	13 22	13 42		13 47	14a20	14 17	14 42			14 47	15a20	15 17	15 22	15 42		15 47	16a20		16 17	16 42
Hitchin 4	d	12 52			13 22		13 47		13 52		14 22	14 47			14 52		15 22		15 47		15 52			16 22	16 47
Letchworth Garden City	d				13 26		13 51				14 26	14 51					15 26		15 51					16 26	16 51
Baldock	d				13 29		13 55				14 29	14 55					15 29		15 55					16 29	16 55
Ashwell & Morden	d						14 00					15 00							16 00						17 00
Royston	d				13 37		14 04				14 37	15 04					15 37		16 04					16 37	17 04
Meldreth	d						14 08					15 08							16 08						17 08
Shepreth	d						14 11					15 11							16 11						17 11
Foxton	d						14 14					15 14							16 14						17 14
Cambridge	a				13 54		14 27	14 00			14 54	15 27		15 00			15 54		16 27	16 00				16 54	17 27
Arlesey	d	12 57							13 57						14 57						15 57				
Biggleswade	d	13 02							14 02						15 02						16 02				
Sandy	d	13 06							14 06						15 06						16 06				
St Neots	d	13 13							14 13						15 13						16 13				
Huntingdon	d	13 21							14 21						15 21						16 21				
Peterborough 8	a	13 38				13 52			14 38						15 38		15 52				16 38				

A not 11 December

Table 25

Sundays

London - Stevenage, Cambridge and Peterborough

Network Diagram - see first Page of Table 24

		FC	FC	FC	GR	FC	FC	FC		FC	FC	FC	GR	FC	FC	FC	FC	FC		FC	FC	GR	FC	FC	FC
		1	1		R 1	1	1	1		1	1		R 1	1	1	1	1	1		1		R 1	1	1	1
London Kings Cross 15 ⊖	d	16 15	16 23	16 26	16 35	16 36	16 53	17 06		17 15	17 23	17 26	17 35	17 36	17 53	18 06	18 10	18 15		18 23	18 26	18 35	18 36	18 53	19 06
Finsbury Park ⊖	d		16 28	16 32		16 41	16 58	17 11			17 28	17 32		17 41	17 58	18 11				18 28	18 32		18 41	18 58	19 11
Potters Bar	d					16 51		17 21						17 51		18 21							18 51		19 21
Hatfield	d					16 57		17 27						17 57		18 27							18 57		19 27
Welwyn Garden City 4	d					17 01		17 31						18 01		18 31							19 01		19 31
Welwyn North	d					17 04		17 34						18 04		18 34							19 04		19 34
Knebworth	d					17 08		17 38						18 08		18 38							19 08		19 38
Hertford North	d			17 07								18 07									19 07				
Stevenage 4	d		16 47	17a20	16a54	17 12	17 17	17 42			17 47	18a20	17a54	18 12	18 17	18 42				18 47	19a20	18a54	19 12	19 17	19 42
Hitchin 4	d		16 52			17 17	17 22	17 47			17 52			18 17	18 22	18 47				18 52			19 17	19 22	→
Letchworth Garden City	d						17 26	17 51							18 26	18 51							19 22	19 26	
Baldock	d						17 29	17 55							18 29	18 55								19 29	
Ashwell & Morden	d							18 00								19 00									
Royston	d						17 37	18 04							18 37	19 04							19a33	19 37	
Meldreth	d							18 08								19 08									
Shepreth	d							18 11								19 11									
Foxton	d							18 14								19 14									
Cambridge	a	17 00					17 54	18 27		18 00					18 54	19 27		19 00						19 54	
Arlesey	d		16 57			17 23					17 57			18 23						18 57					
Biggleswade	d		17 02			17 28					18 02			18 28			18 37			19 02					
Sandy	d		17 06			17 32					18 06			18 32						19 06					
St Neots	d		17 13			17 39					18 13			18 39			18 47			19 13					
Huntingdon	d		17 21			17 47					18 21			18 47			18 54			19 21					
Peterborough 8	a		17 39			18 06					18 38			19 05			19 12			19 39					

		GR	FC	FC		FC	FC	GR	HT	FC	FC	FC	FC	FC		GR	FC	FC	FC	FC	FC	GR	FC	FC	
			1	1		1		R 1	◇1 ⊠	1	1	1	1			R 1	1	1	1	1		R 1	1	1	
London Kings Cross 15 ⊖	d	19 08	19 15			19 23	19 26	19 35	19 45	19 53	20 06	20 15	20 23	20 26		20 35	20 53	21 06	21 15	21 23	21 26	21 35	21 53	22 06	
Finsbury Park ⊖	d					19 28	19 32			19 58	20 11		20 28	20 32			20 58	21 11		21 28	21 32		21 58	22 11	
Potters Bar	d										20 21							21 21						22 21	
Hatfield	d										20 27							21 27						22 27	
Welwyn Garden City 4	d										20 31							21 31						22 31	
Welwyn North	d										20 34							21 34						22 34	
Knebworth	d										20 38							21 38						22 38	
Hertford North	d			←			20 07							21 07							22 07				
Stevenage 4	d	19 28		19 42		19 47	20a20	19 54	20a04	20 17	20 42		20 47	21a20		20 54	21 17	21 42		21 47	22a20	21 55	22 17	22 42	
Hitchin 4	d			19 47		19 52				20 22	20 47		20 52				21 22	21 47		21 52			22 22	22 47	
Letchworth Garden City	d			19 51						20 26	20 51						21 26	21 51					22 26	22 51	
Baldock	d			19 55						20 29	20 55						21 29	21 55					22 29	22 55	
Ashwell & Morden	d			20 00							21 00							22 00						23 00	
Royston	d			20 04						20 37	21 04						21 37	22 04					22 37	23 04	
Meldreth	d			20 08							21 08							22 08						23 08	
Shepreth	d			20 11							21 11							22 11						23 11	
Foxton	d			20 14							21 14							22 14						23 14	
Cambridge	a		20 00	20 27						20 54	21 27	21 00					21 54	22 27	22 00				22 54	23 27	
Arlesey	d					19 57							20 57							21 57					
Biggleswade	d					20 02							21 02							22 02					
Sandy	d					20 06							21 06							22 06					
St Neots	d					20 13							21 13							22 13					
Huntingdon	d					20 21							21 21							22 21					
Peterborough 8	a	19 58				20 38		20 24					21 37			21 24				22 37		22 25			

		FC	FC	FC	FC	FC	FC	FC	FC	FC		FC
		1	1		1	1	1	1	1			
London Kings Cross 15 ⊖	d	22 15	22 23	22 26	22 53	23 06	23 15		23 23	23 26		23 41
Finsbury Park ⊖	d		22 28	22 32	22 58	23 11			23 28	23 32		23 47
Potters Bar	d					23 21						00 08
Hatfield	d					23 27						00 16
Welwyn Garden City 4	d					23 31						00 20
Welwyn North	d					23 34						00 23
Knebworth	d					23 38						00 28
Hertford North	d			23 07						00 07		
Stevenage 4	d		22 47	23a20	23 17	23 42			23 47	00a20		00 31
Hitchin 4	d		22 52		23 22	23 47		←	23 52			00 37
Letchworth Garden City	d				23 26	23 51	23 44	23 51				00a52
Baldock	d				23 29	→		23 54				
Ashwell & Morden	d							23 59				
Royston	d				23 37		23 54	00 04				
Meldreth	d							00 08				
Shepreth	d							00 11				
Foxton	d							00 14				
Cambridge	a	23 00			23 54		00 10	00 29				
Arlesey	d		22 57						23 57			
Biggleswade	d		23 02						00 02			
Sandy	d		23 06						00 06			
St Neots	d		23 13						00 13			
Huntingdon	d		23 21						00 21			
Peterborough 8	a		23 41						00 43			

Peterborough, Cambridge and Stevenage - London

Network Diagram - see first Page of Table 24

Miles	Miles			FC MX 1	FC MX	FC MO	FC MO 1	FC MO 1	FC MX 1	GR MX R 1	FC 1	FC		FC 1	FC 1	FC 1	FC 1	FC 1	FC 1	FC 1	FC 1	FC 1		FC	FC 1
0	—	**Peterborough 8**	d	22p30			23p01			23p40	03 25			04 10		05 10		05 40			05 50				06 17
17½	—	Huntingdon	d	22p44			23p15				03 39			04 24		05 24		05 55			06 05				06 32
24¾	—	St Neots	d	22p51			23p22				03 46			04 32		05 32		06 02			06 13				06 40
32¼	—	Sandy	d	22p59			23p30							04 39		05 39					06 21				
35¼	—	Biggleswade	d	23p02			23p33				03 56			04 43		05 43					06 25				
39¼	—	Arlesey	d	23p07			23p38							04 48		05 48					06 30				
—	0	**Cambridge**	d					23p15	23p15										05 35	05 45		06 15			
—	7	Foxton	d					23p24	23p25										05 44						
—	8	Shepreth	d					23p26	23p27										05 46						
—	10	Meldreth	d					23p29	23p30										05 49						
—	13	Royston	d					23p34	23p35						05 16		05 46		06 05	05 59		06 29			
—	17	Ashwell & Morden	d					23p38	23p39						05 21		05 51		06 10						
—	21¼	Baldock	d					23p43	23p44						05 26		05 56		06 15						
—	23¼	Letchworth Garden City	d		23p20			23p46	23p47			04 50			05 29		05 59		06 19	06 09		06 39		06 46	
44½	26	Hitchin 4	d	23p16	23p24		23p46	23p50	23p54		04 08	04 54		04 57	05 34	05 57	06 04	06 18	06 23		06 36	06 43		06 50	
48¾	30¼	**Stevenage 4**	d	23p22	23p29	23p30	23p51	23p55	23p59	00s21	04 13	04 59		05 02	05 39	06 02	06 09	06 24	06 29		06 42	06 48		06 55	06 59
—	—	Hertford North	a		23p42	23p43					04 23	05 12													
51¼	33	Knebworth	d	23p25				23p58	00 02					05 06	05 43		06 13		06 33		06 46				
54¼	36	Welwyn North	d	23p29				00 02	00 06					05 10	05 47		06 17		06 37		06 50				
56	37¾	Welwyn Garden City 4	d	23p32				00 05	00 09					05 13	05 50		06 20		06 40		06 54			07 07	
58½	40¼	Hatfield	d	23p35				00 08	00 12					05 16	05 54		06 24		06 44					07 11	
63½	45¼	Potters Bar	d	23p41				00 14	00 18					05 22	06 00		06 30		06 49					07 18	
73¾	55½	Finsbury Park ⊖	d	23b51	00 17	00 18	00s13	00 27	00 29		04s47	05 47		05 39	06 09	06 22	06 39	06 43	06 58		07 11	07 06		07 35	
76¼	58	**London Kings Cross 15** ⊖	a	00 01	00 26	00 27	00 24	00 39	00 40	00 57	05 00	05 55		05 48	06 18	06 29	06 48	06 50	07 07	06 38	07 19	07 15		07 43	07 24

		FC 1	FC 1	FC 1	FC 1	FC 1	FC	FC 1		FC 1	FC 1	FC 1	FC 1	FC 1	XC ◇1	FC 1	FC 1	FC 1		FC 1	FC 1	FC 1	FC 1	FC 1	FC 1
Peterborough 8	d					06 32		06 53						07 06	07 12	07 14		07 25					07 33	07 46	
Huntingdon	d		06 40			06 47		07 09						07 24		07 32		07 40					07 51	08 06	
St Neots	d		06 48			06 55		07 17						07 33		07 40		07 47					07 59	08 14	
Sandy	d		06 55			07 03								07 41									08 06		
Biggleswade	d		06 59			07 07								07 45				07 55					08 10		
Arlesey	d		07 04			07 12								07 50									08 15		
Cambridge	d			06 27	06 45						06 57	07 15			08a07						07 27	07 45			07 55
Foxton	d			06 37							07 07										07 37				08 05
Shepreth	d			06 40							07 10										07 40				08 07
Meldreth	d			06 43							07 13										07 43				08 10
Royston	d	06 43		06 50	06 59					07 13	07 21	07 29	07 34							07 43	07 51	07 59			08 15
Ashwell & Morden	d	06 48		06 55						07 18			07 38							07 48					08 19
Baldock	d	06 53		07 00						07 23			07 43							07 53					08 24
Letchworth Garden City	d	06 57		07 04	07 09		07 20			07 27	07 32		07 47							07 57	08 02				08 28
Hitchin 4	d	07 01		07 08		07 18	07 24			07 31	07 36		07 51	07 56			←			08 01	08 06		08 21		08 32
Stevenage 4	d	07 07		07 14		07 23	07 30	07 36		07 37	07 42			08 01		07 59	08 01			08 07	08 12		08 27	08 33	
Hertford North	a													↦											
Knebworth	d	07 11		07 18							07 46									08 11	08 16				
Welwyn North	d			07 24							07 50		07 59								08 20				
Welwyn Garden City 4	d			07 27			07 42				07 54										08 24				
Hatfield	d			07 31			07 46																		
Potters Bar	d						07 52																		
Finsbury Park ⊖	d	07 26		07 47		07 41	08 10			07 57	08 06						08 19				08 36		08 47		
London Kings Cross 15 ⊖	a	07 35	07 38	07 57	07 39	07 49	08 17	08 00		08 04	08 17	08 07	08 20			08 23	08 28	08 30		08 35	08 47	08 39	08 55	08 58	09 02

		FC 1	FC 1	FC 1		FC 1		GR R 1	GR R 1	FC 1	FC 1	FC 1	FC 1	FC 1		FC 1	FC 1		FC 1	GR R 1	FC 1	FC 1	FC 1	FC 1	
Peterborough 8	d					08 16		08 26					08 46				09 16					09 26		09 46	
Huntingdon	d					08 30							09 00				09 30					09 41		10 00	
St Neots	d					08 38							09 08				09 38					09 49		10 08	
Sandy	d					08 45							09 15									09 57		10 15	
Biggleswade	d					08 49							09 19				09 47					10 01		10 19	
Arlesey	d					08 54							09 24									10 06		10 24	
Cambridge	d	08 15									08 25	08 50		08 55		09 20			09 30				09 50		
Foxton	d										08 35			09 05											
Shepreth	d										08 37			09 07											
Meldreth	d										08 40			09 10											
Royston	d	08 29		08 34							08 45	09 04		09 15		09 34			09 44				10 04		
Ashwell & Morden	d			08 38							08 50			09 20											
Baldock	d			08 43							08 55			09 25					09 52						
Letchworth Garden City	d	08 39		08 47							08 59	09 14		09 29		09 44			09 55		09 59		10 14		
Hitchin 4	d		08 39	08 51		09 00				←	09 05		09 30	09 34					10 00		10 04	10 12		10 30	
Stevenage 4	d		08 45	08 56		09 07		08 58	09 00	09 07	09 11		09 36	09 40			09 58		10 06	10 09	10 10	10 18		10 36	
Hertford North	a					↦																			
Knebworth	d		08 49								09 14			09 44							10 14				
Welwyn North	d		08 53								09 18			09 48							10 18				
Welwyn Garden City 4	d		08 58								09 21			09 51							10 21				
Hatfield	d		09 02								09 25			09 55							10 25				
Potters Bar	d										09 31			10 01							10 31				
Finsbury Park ⊖	d		09 19	09 14						09 26	09 40		09 56	10 10					10 24		10 40			10 54	
London Kings Cross 15 ⊖	a	09 09	09 28	09 21				09 26	09 30	09 35	09 49	09 44	10 04	10 19		10 14	10 22		10 32	10 38	10 49	10 44	10 46	11 02	

b Previous night, stops to set down only

Peterborough, Cambridge and Stevenage - London

Network Diagram - see first Page of Table 24

		FC	FC	GR	FC	FC	FC		FC	FC		FC	FC		GR	GR	FC	FC	FC	FC		FC	FC	FC	
				R											R	R									
		1	1	1	1	1	1		1	1		1	1		1	1	1	1	1	1		1	1	1	
				⊡⚲											⊡⚲	⊡⚲									
Peterborough 8	d						10 16		10 46				11 16		11 27					11 46				12 16	
Huntingdon	d						10 34		11 00				11 34							12 00				12 34	
St Neots	d						10 41		11 08				11 41							12 08				12 41	
Sandy	d						10 49		11 15				11 49							12 15				12 49	
Biggleswade	d						10 53		11 19				11 53							12 19				12 53	
Arlesey	d						10 58		11 24				11 58							12 24				12 58	
Cambridge	d	09 55	10 15		10 30	10 50				10 55		11 15					11 30	11 45				11 55	12 15		
Foxton	d	10 05								11 05												12 05			
Shepreth	d	10 07								11 07												12 07			
Meldreth	d	10 10								11 10												12 10			
Royston	d	10 15			10 44	11 04				11 15							11 44					12 15			
Ashwell & Morden	d	10 20								11 20												12 20			
Baldock	d	10 25			10 52					11 25							11 52					12 25			
Letchworth Garden City	d	10 29			10 55	11 14				11 29							11 55					12 29			
Hitchin 4	d	10 34			11 00		11 04		11 30	11 34			12 04				12 00		←	12 30		12 34		13 04	
Stevenage 4	d	10 40		11 00	11 06		11 10		11 36	11 40			12 10		11 56	12 00	12 06		12 10	12 36		12 40		13 10	
Hertford North	a												↪											↪	
Knebworth	d	10 44					11 14			11 44									12 14			12 44			
Welwyn North	d	10 48					11 18			11 48									12 18			12 48			
Welwyn Garden City 4	d	10 51					11 21			11 51									12 21			12 51			
Hatfield	d	10 55					11 25			11 55									12 25			12 55			
Potters Bar	d	11 01					11 31			12 01									12 31			13 01			
Finsbury Park ⊖	d	11 10			11 24		11 40		11 54	12 10							12 24		12 40	12 54		13 10			
London Kings Cross 15 ⊖	a	11 19	11 05	11 29	11 32	11 44	11 49		12 02	12 19		12 04			12 24	12 29	12 32	12 35	12 49	13 03		13 19	13 04		

		GR	GR	FC	FC	FC		FC	FC	FC	FC		GR	GR	FC	FC		FC	FC	FC	FC	FC		GR	GR
		R	R										R	R										R	R
		1	1	1	1	1		1	1	1	1		1	1	1	1		1	1	1	1	1		1	1
		⊡	⊡⚲										⊡⚲	⊡⚲										⊡	⊡⚲
Peterborough 8	d	12 27						12 46			13 16		13 28						13 46			14 16		14 26	
Huntingdon	d							13 00			13 34								14 00			14 34			
St Neots	d							13 08			13 41								14 08			14 41			
Sandy	d							13 15			13 49								14 15			14 49			
Biggleswade	d							13 19			13 53								14 19			14 53			
Arlesey	d							13 24			13 58								14 24			14 58			
Cambridge	d			12 30	12 45				12 55	13 15					13 30	13 45				13 55	14 15				
Foxton	d								13 05											14 05					
Shepreth	d								13 07											14 07					
Meldreth	d								13 10											14 10					
Royston	d			12 44					13 15						13 44					14 15					
Ashwell & Morden	d								13 20											14 20					
Baldock	d			12 52					13 25						13 52					14 25					
Letchworth Garden City	d			12 55					13 29						13 55					14 29					
Hitchin 4	d			13 00		←		13 30	13 34		14 04				14 00			←	14 30	14 34		15 04			
Stevenage 4	d	12 57	13 02	13 06		13 10		13 36	13 40		14 10		13 58	14 02	14 06			14 10	14 36	14 40		15 10		14 56	15 00
Hertford North	a										↪											↪			
Knebworth	d					13 14			13 44									14 14		14 44					
Welwyn North	d					13 18			13 48									14 18		14 48					
Welwyn Garden City 4	d					13 21			13 51									14 21		14 51					
Hatfield	d					13 25			13 55									14 25		14 55					
Potters Bar	d					13 31			14 01									14 31		15 01					
Finsbury Park ⊖	d			13 24		13 40		13 54	14 10						14 24			14 40	14 54	15 10					
London Kings Cross 15 ⊖	a	13 26	13 30	13 33	13 35	13 49		14 02	14 19	14 04			14 26	14 30	14 32	14 34		14 49	15 03	15 19	15 05			15 25	15 29

		FC		FC	FC	FC	FC	FC	FC		GR	GR		FC	FC	FC	FC	FC	FC	FC		GR		GR	FC
											R	R										R		R	
		1		1	1	1	1	1	1		1	1		1	1	1	1	1	1	1		1		1	1
											⊡⚲	⊡⚲										⊡		⊡⚲	
Peterborough 8	d					14 46			15 16		15 27						15 46			16 16		16 25			
Huntingdon	d					15 00			15 34								16 00			16 34					
St Neots	d					15 08			15 41								16 08			16 41					
Sandy	d					15 15			15 49								16 15			16 49					
Biggleswade	d					15 19			15 53								16 19			16 53					
Arlesey	d					15 24			15 58								16 24			16 58					
Cambridge	d	14 30		14 45			14 55	15 15						15 30	15 45			15 55	16 15						16 25
Foxton	d						15 05											16 05							16 34
Shepreth	d						15 07											16 07							16 36
Meldreth	d						15 10											16 10							16 39
Royston	d	14 44					15 15							15 44				16 15							16 44
Ashwell & Morden	d						15 20											16 20							16 48
Baldock	d	14 52					15 25							15 52				16 25							16 53
Letchworth Garden City	d	14 55					15 29							15 55				16 29							16 56
Hitchin 4	d	15 00			←	15 30	15 34		16 04					16 00		←	16 30	16 34		17 04					17 00
Stevenage 4	d	15 06			15 10	15 36	15 40		16 10		15 57	16 02		16 06		16 10	16 36	16 40		17 10		16 54		17 00	17 06
Hertford North	a								↪											↪					
Knebworth	d				15 14		15 44									16 14		16 44							
Welwyn North	d				15 18		15 48									16 18		16 48							
Welwyn Garden City 4	d				15 21		15 51									16 21		16 51							
Hatfield	d				15 25		15 55									16 25		16 55							
Potters Bar	d				15 31		16 01									16 31		17 01							
Finsbury Park ⊖	d	15 24			15 40	15 54	16 10							16 24		16 40	16 54	17 10							17 24
London Kings Cross 15 ⊖	a	15 32		15 34	15 49	16 03	16 19	16 06			16 25	16 29		16 32	16 34	16 49	17 01	17 19	17 04			17 22		17 30	17 32

Peterborough, Cambridge and Stevenage - London

Network Diagram - see first Page of Table 24

		FC	FC	FC	FC	FC	FC			GR	GR	FC	FC	FC	FC	FC	FC	FC			FC	GR	GR	FC	FC
										R	R											R	R		
		1	1	1	1	1	1			1	1	1	1	1	1	1	1	1			1	1	1	1	1
										🍴	🍴											☕	🍴		
Peterborough 8	d			16 46			17 16			17 28								17 55			18 21	18 26			
Huntingdon	d			17 00			17 34								18 04			18 14			18 41				
St Neots	d			17 08			17 41								18 11			18 21			18 48				
Sandy	d			17 15			17 49											18 29			18 56				
Biggleswade	d			17 19			17 53											18 32			19 00				
Arlesey	d			17 24			17 58											18 37			19 05				
Cambridge	d	16 45			16 55	17 15						17 25	17 45			17 55	18 15							18 25	18 45
Foxton	d				17 05							17 34				18 05								18 34	
Shepreth	d				17 07							17 36				18 07								18 36	
Meldreth	d				17 10							17 39				18 10								18 39	
Royston	d				17 15							17 44				18 15								18 46	
Ashwell & Morden	d				17 20							17 48				18 20								18 51	
Baldock	d				17 25							17 53				18 25								18 56	
Letchworth Garden City	d				17 29							17 56				18 29								18 59	
Hitchin 4	d		←	17 30	17 34		18 04					18 00		←	18 29	18 34		18 43			19 11			19 03	
Stevenage 4	d		17 10	17 36	17 40		18 10			17 58	18 03	18 06		18 10	18 35	18 40		18 49			19 17	18 56	19 07	19 09	
Hertford North	a						↪														↪				
Knebworth	d		17 14		17 44									18 14		18 44									
Welwyn North	d		17 18		17 48									18 18		18 48									
Welwyn Garden City 4	d		17 21		17 51									18 28		18 51									
Hatfield	d		17 25		17 55									18 32		18 55									
Potters Bar	d		17 31		18 01									18 38		19 01									
Finsbury Park ⊖	d		17 40	17 54	18 10							18 24		18 47	18 54	19 10		19 07						19 29	
London Kings Cross 15 ⊖	a	17 35	17 49	18 02	18 19	18 05				18 27	18 31	18 32	18 38	18 56	19 02	19 22	19 08	19 14				19 25	19 36	19 36	19 38

		FC	FC	FC		FC	FC		GR	GR	FC	FC	FC	FC		GR	GR	FC	FC	GR	FC	FC	FC		
									R	R						R	R			R					
		1	1	1		1	1		1	1	1	1	1	1		1	1	1	1	1	1	1	1		
									☕	☕						🍴	🍴			🍴					
Peterborough 8	d		18 45				19 16		19 27					19 46		19 50							20 16		
Huntingdon	d		19 00				19 34							20 00									20 34		
St Neots	d		19 08				19 41							20 08									20 41		
Sandy	d		19 15				19 49							20 15									20 49		
Biggleswade	d		19 19				19 53							20 19									20 53		
Arlesey	d		19 24				19 58							20 24									20 58		
Cambridge	d			18 55		19 15					19 25	19 45							19 55		20 30	20 45			
Foxton	d			19 05							19 34								20 05						
Shepreth	d			19 07							19 36								20 07						
Meldreth	d			19 10							19 39								20 10						
Royston	d			19 15							19 44								20 15		20 44				
Ashwell & Morden	d			19 20							19 48								20 20						
Baldock	d			19 25							19 53								20 25		20 52				
Letchworth Garden City	d			19 29							19 56								20 29		20 55				
Hitchin 4	d	←	19 30	19 34			20 04				20 00		←	20 30				←	20 34		21 00		21 04		
Stevenage 4	d	19 17	19 36	19 40			20 10		19 56	20 01	20 06		20 10	20 36		20 21	20 23	20 36	20 40	20 59	21 06		21 10		
Hertford North	a						↪							↪											
Knebworth	d	19 20		19 44									20 14						20 44				21 14		
Welwyn North	d	19 24		19 48									20 18						20 48				21 18		
Welwyn Garden City 4	d	19 28		19 51									20 21						20 51				21 21		
Hatfield	d	19 32		19 55									20 25						20 55				21 25		
Potters Bar	d	19 38		20 01									20 31						21 01				21 31		
Finsbury Park ⊖	d	19 47	19 54	20 10							20 25		20 40					20 54	21 10		21 24		21 40		
London Kings Cross 15 ⊖	a	19 56	20 00	20 19		20 11			20 26	20 30	20 33	20 34	20 49			20 48	20 55	21 02	21 19	21 29	21 32	21 34	21 49		

		GR	FC	FC	FC	GR		FC	FC	FC		FC	FC	GR	FC	FC	GR	FC	FC	FC		GR			
		R				R								R			R					R			
		1		1	1	1		1	1	1			1	1	1	1	1	1		1		1			
		🍴				🍴								🍴			🍴					☕			
Peterborough 8	d	20 46			20 57	21 16				21 30				22 16		22 30	22 35					23 40			
Huntingdon	d				21 12					21 44						22 44									
St Neots	d				21 19					21 51						22 51									
Sandy	d				21 27					21 59						22 59									
Biggleswade	d				21 30					22 02						23 02									
Arlesey	d				21 35					22 07						23 07									
Cambridge	d			20 55				21 30	21 45				21 55		22 30					23 15					
Foxton	d			21 05									22 05							23 25					
Shepreth	d			21 07									22 07							23 27					
Meldreth	d			21 10									22 10							23 30					
Royston	d			21 15				21 44					22 15		22 44					23 35					
Ashwell & Morden	d			21 20									22 20							23 39					
Baldock	d			21 25				21 52					22 25		22 52					23 44					
Letchworth Garden City	d		21 20	21 29				21 55				22 20	22 29		22 55				23 20	23 47					
Hitchin 4	d		21 24	21 34	21 41			22 00		22 13		22 24	22 34		23 00	23 16		←	23 24	23 54					
Stevenage 4	d	21 15	21 29	21 40	21 47	21 48		22 06		22 18		22 29	22 40	22 47	23 06	23 22	23 05	23 22	23 29	23 59		00s21			
Hertford North	a		21 42									22 42				↪			23 42						
Knebworth	d			21 44						22 22			22 44					23 25		00 02					
Welwyn North	d			21 48						22 25			22 48					23 29		00 06					
Welwyn Garden City 4	d			21 51						22 28			22 51					23 32		00 09					
Hatfield	d			21 55						22 32			22 55					23 35		00 12					
Potters Bar	d			22 01						22 37			23 01					23 41		00 18					
Finsbury Park ⊖	d		22 17	22 10	22 05			22 24		22 46		23 17	23 10		23 24			23s51	00 17	00 29					
London Kings Cross 15 ⊖	a	21 45	22 25	22 19	22 11	22 19		22 32	22 34	22 52		23 25	23 20	23 14	23 32		23 36	00 01	00 26	00 40		00 57			

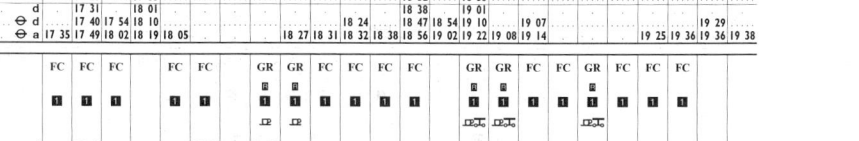

Table 25

Saturdays

Peterborough, Cambridge and Stevenage - London

Network Diagram - see first Page of Table 24

		FC	FC	FC	GR	FC	FC	FC	FC	FC		FC	FC	FC	FC	FC	FC	FC	FC	GR		FC	FC	FC	FC
		1		1	R 1	1		1		1		1	1		1	1	1	1	1	R 1		1		1	1
Peterborough 8	d	22p30			23p40	03 25		04 10					05 16		05 46				06 16	06 37				06 46	
Huntingdon	d	22p44				03 39		04 24					05 34		06 00				06 34					07 00	
St Neots	d	22p51				03 46		04 32					05 41		06 08				06 41					07 08	
Sandy	d	22p59						04 39					05 49		06 15				06 49					07 15	
Biggleswade	d	23p02				03 56		04 43					05 53		06 19				06 53					07 19	
Arlesey	d	23p07						04 48					05 58		06 24				06 58					07 24	
Cambridge	d			23p15								05 45				05 55	06 30	06 45							06 55
Foxton	d			23p25												06 05									07 05
Shepreth	d			23p27												06 07									07 07
Meldreth	d			23p30												06 10									07 10
Royston	d			23p35						05 15		06 00				06 15	06 44								07 15
Ashwell & Morden	d			23p39						05 20						06 20									07 20
Baldock	d			23p44						05 25						06 25	06 52								07 25
Letchworth Garden City	d		23p20	23p47			04 50		05 20	05 29		06 09		06 20		06 29	06 55								07 29
Hitchin 4	d	23p16	23p24	23p54		04 08	04 54	04 57	05 24	05 34			06 04	06 24	06 30	06 34	07 00		07 04			←		07 30	07 34
Stevenage 4	d	23p22	23p29	23p59	00s21	04 13	04 59	05 02	05 30	05 40			06 10	06 30	06 36	06 40	07 06		07 10	07 06		07 10	07 30	07 36	07 40
Hertford North	a		23p42			04 23	05 12		05 43					06 43					↪				07 43		
Knebworth	d	23p25		00 02				05 06		05 44			06 14			06 44						07 14			07 44
Welwyn North	d	23p29		00 06				05 10		05 48			06 18			06 48						07 18			07 48
Welwyn Garden City 4	d	23p32		00 09				05 13		05 51			06 21			06 51						07 21			07 51
Hatfield	d	23p35		00 12				05 16		05 55			06 25			06 55						07 25			07 55
Potters Bar	d	23p41		00 18				05 22		06 01			06 31			07 01						07 31			08 01
Finsbury Park ⊖	d	23b51	00 17	00 29		04s47	05 47	05 39	06 18	06 10			06 40	07 18	06 54	07 10	07 24					07 40	08 18	07 54	08 10
London Kings Cross 15 ⊖	a	00 01	00 26	00 40	00 57	05 00	05 55	05 48	06 25	06 20		06 39	06 47	07 25	07 01	07 19	07 31	07 36		07 37		07 49	08 25	08 01	08 19

			FC	FC	FC	GR		FC	FC	FC	FC	FC	FC		FC	GR		FC	FC	FC	FC	FC	FC	FC	FC
			1	1	1	R 1		1		1	1	1	1		1	R 1		1	1	1		1	1	1	1
Peterborough 8	d				07 18	07 37				07 46			08 09		08 18	08 32						08 46			09 09
Huntingdon	d				07 34					08 00			08 24		08 34							09 00			09 23
St Neots	d				07 41					08 08			08 33		08 41							09 08			09 31
Sandy	d				07 49					08 15					08 49							09 15			
Biggleswade	d				07 53					08 19			08 42		08 53							09 19			09 39
Arlesey	d				07 58					08 24					08 58							09 24			
Cambridge	d		07 30	07 45							07 55	08 15						08 30	08 45				08 55	09 15	
Foxton	d										08 05												09 05		
Shepreth	d										08 07												09 07		
Meldreth	d										08 10												09 10		
Royston	d		07 44								08 15							08 44					09 15		
Ashwell & Morden	d										08 20												09 20		
Baldock	d		07 52								08 25							08 52					09 25		
Letchworth Garden City	d		07 55								08 29							08 55					09 29		
Hitchin 4	d		08 00		08 04			←		08 30	08 34				09 04			09 00		←		09 30	09 34		
Stevenage 4	d		08 06		08 10	08 06		08 10	08 30	08 36	08 40				09 10	09 01		09 06		09 10	09 30	09 36	09 40		
Hertford North	a				↪				08 43						↪						09 43				
Knebworth	d							08 14			08 44									09 14			09 44		
Welwyn North	d							08 18			08 48									09 18			09 48		
Welwyn Garden City 4	d							08 21			08 51									09 21			09 51		
Hatfield	d							08 25			08 55									09 25			09 55		
Potters Bar	d							08 31			09 01									09 31			10 01		
Finsbury Park ⊖	d		08 24					08 40	09 18	08 54	09 10							09 24		09 40	10 18	09 54	10 10		
London Kings Cross 15 ⊖	a		08 31	08 36		08 37		08 49	09 25	09 01	09 20	09 04	09 13			09 30		09 31	09 39	09 49	10 25	10 01	10 20	10 04	10 11

		FC		FC	FC	XC	FC	FC	FC	FC	FC			FC	GR	FC	FC	GR	FC	FC	FC	FC		FC	
		1		1	1	◇1		1	1	1	1			1	R 1	1	1	R 1	1		1	1		1	
Peterborough 8	d				09 16	09 18		09 46			10 10			10 18	10 27			10 36			10 46				
Huntingdon	d				09 34			10 00			10 25			10 34							11 00				
St Neots	d				09 41			10 08			10 33			10 41							11 08				
Sandy	d				09 49			10 15						10 49							11 15				
Biggleswade	d				09 53			10 19			10 41			10 53							11 19				
Arlesey	d				09 58			10 24						10 58							11 24				
Cambridge	d	09 30		09 45		10a07			09 55	10 15						10 30	10 45					10 55		11 15	
Foxton	d								10 05													11 05			
Shepreth	d								10 07													11 07			
Meldreth	d								10 10													11 10			
Royston	d	09 44							10 15							10 44						11 15			
Ashwell & Morden	d								10 20													11 20			
Baldock	d	09 52							10 25							10 52						11 25			
Letchworth Garden City	d	09 55							10 29							10 55						11 29			
Hitchin 4	d	10 00			10 04			10 30	10 34					11 04		11 00			←		11 30	11 34			
Stevenage 4	d	10 06			10 10		10 30	10 36	10 40					11 10	10 59	11 06		11 07	11 10	11 30	11 36	11 40			
Hertford North	a						10 43							↪						11 43					
Knebworth	d				10 14				10 44										11 14			11 44			
Welwyn North	d				10 18				10 48										11 18			11 48			
Welwyn Garden City 4	d				10 21				10 51										11 21			11 51			
Hatfield	d				10 25				10 55										11 25			11 55			
Potters Bar	d				10 31				11 01										11 31			12 01			
Finsbury Park ⊖	d	10 24			10 40		11 18	10 54	11 10							11 24			11 40	12 18	11 54	12 10			
London Kings Cross 15 ⊖	a	10 31		10 35	10 49		11 25	11 01	11 20	11 04	11 14				11 27	11 31	11 37	11 38	11 49	12 25	12 01	12 19		12 04	

b Previous night, stops to set down only

Peterborough, Cambridge and Stevenage - London

Network Diagram - see first Page of Table 24

		FC	FC	FC	FC	FC	FC	FC			FC	GR	FC	FC	FC	FC	FC	FC		FC	FC	FC	FC		FC
												R													
		1	1	1		1	1	1			1	1	1	1	1		1	1		1	1	1	1		
Peterborough 8	d			11 18		11 46					12 19	12 33					12 46						13 16		
Huntingdon	d			11 34		12 00					12 34						13 00						13 34		
St Neots	d			11 41		12 08					12 41						13 08						13 41		
Sandy	d			11 49		12 15					12 49						13 15						13 49		
Biggleswade	d			11 53		12 19					12 53						13 19						13 53		
Arlesey	d			11 58		12 24					12 58						13 24						13 58		
Cambridge	d	11 30	11 45				11 55	12 15					12 30	12 45				12 55		13 15	13 30	13 45			
Foxton	d						12 05											13 05							
Shepreth	d						12 07											13 07							
Meldreth	d						12 10											13 10							
Royston	d	11 44					12 15						12 44					13 15			13 44				
Ashwell & Morden	d						12 20											13 20							
Baldock	d	11 52					12 25						12 52					13 25			13 52				
Letchworth Garden City	d	11 55					12 29						12 55					13 29			13 55				
Hitchin 4	d	12 00		12 04		12 30	12 34				13 04		13 00		←		13 30	13 34			14 00		14 04		
Stevenage 4	d	12 06		12 10	12 30	12 36	12 40				13 10	13 02	13 06		13 10	13 30	13 36	13 40			14 06		14 10		14 30
Hertford North	a				12 43						↪					13 43									14 43
Knebworth	d			12 14			12 44								13 14			13 44					14 14		
Welwyn North	d			12 18			12 48								13 18			13 48					14 18		
Welwyn Garden City 4	d			12 21			12 51								13 21			13 51					14 21		
Hatfield	d			12 25			12 55								13 25			13 55					14 25		
Potters Bar	d			12 31			13 01								13 31			14 01					14 31		
Finsbury Park ⊖	d	12 24		12 40	13 18	12 54	13 10						13 24		13 40	14 18	13 54	14 10			14 24		14 40		15 18
London Kings Cross 15 ⊖	a	12 32	12 35	12 49	13 25	13 01	13 19	13 04				13 31	13 31	13 35	13 49	14 25	14 01	14 19		14 04	14 31	14 35	14 49		15 25

		FC	FC	FC		FC		GR	FC	FC	FC	FC	FC	FC		FC		FC	FC	FC	FC	FC	FC	FC	
								R																	
		1	1	1		1		1	1	1	1		1	1		1		1	1	1		1	1	1	
Peterborough 8	d	13 46				14 16		14 32					14 46							15 19		15 46			
Huntingdon	d	14 00				14 34							15 00							15 34		16 00			
St Neots	d	14 08				14 41							15 08							15 41		16 08			
Sandy	d	14 15				14 49							15 15							15 49		16 15			
Biggleswade	d	14 19				14 53							15 19							15 53		16 19			
Arlesey	d	14 24				14 58							15 24							15 58		16 24			
Cambridge	d		13 55	14 15					14 30	14 45				14 55		15 15		15 30	15 45				15 55	16 15	
Foxton	d		14 05											15 05									16 05		
Shepreth	d		14 07											15 07									16 07		
Meldreth	d		14 10											15 10									16 10		
Royston	d		14 15						14 44					15 15				15 44					16 15		
Ashwell & Morden	d		14 20											15 20									16 20		
Baldock	d		14 25						14 52					15 25				15 52					16 25		
Letchworth Garden City	d		14 29						14 55					15 29				15 55					16 29		
Hitchin 4	d	14 30	14 34			15 04			15 00		←		15 30	15 34				16 00		16 04		16 30	16 34		
Stevenage 4	d	14 36	14 40			15 10		15 01	15 06		15 10	15 30	15 36	15 40				16 06		16 10	16 30	16 36	16 40		
Hertford North	a					↪						15 43									16 43				
Knebworth	d		14 44								15 14			15 44						16 14			16 44		
Welwyn North	d		14 48								15 18			15 48						16 18			16 48		
Welwyn Garden City 4	d		14 51								15 21			15 51						16 21			16 51		
Hatfield	d		14 55								15 25			15 55						16 25			16 55		
Potters Bar	d		15 01								15 31			16 01						16 31			17 01		
Finsbury Park ⊖	d	14 54	15 10						15 24		15 40	16 18	15 54	16 10				16 24		16 40	17 18	16 54	17 10		
London Kings Cross 15 ⊖	a	15 01	15 19	15 04				15 31	15 31	15 35	15 49	16 25	16 01	16 19		16 04		16 31	16 35	16 49	17 25	17 01	17 19	17 04	

		FC		GR	FC	FC	FC	FC	FC	FC		FC	FC	FC	FC		FC	FC	FC	FC		FC		GR	FC
				R																				R	
		1		1	1	1	1		1	1		1	1	1	1			1	1	1		1		1	1
Peterborough 8	d	16 16		16 33					16 46						17 18			17 46				18 16		18 32	
Huntingdon	d	16 34							17 00						17 34			18 00				18 34			
St Neots	d	16 41							17 08						17 41			18 08				18 41			
Sandy	d	16 49							17 15						17 49			18 15				18 49			
Biggleswade	d	16 53							17 19						17 53			18 19				18 53			
Arlesey	d	16 58							17 24						17 58			18 24				18 58			
Cambridge	d				16 30	16 45				16 55		17 15	17 30	17 45					17 55	18 15					18 30
Foxton	d									17 05									18 05						
Shepreth	d									17 07									18 07						
Meldreth	d									17 10									18 10						
Royston	d				16 44					17 15			17 44						18 15						18 44
Ashwell & Morden	d									17 20									18 20						
Baldock	d				16 52					17 25			17 52						18 25						18 52
Letchworth Garden City	d				16 55					17 29			17 55						18 29						18 55
Hitchin 4	d	17 04			17 00		←		17 30	17 34			18 00		18 04			18 30	18 34			19 04			19 00
Stevenage 4	d	17 10		17 03	17 06		17 10	17 30	17 36	17 40			18 06		18 10		18 30	18 36	18 40			19 10		19 01	19 06
Hertford North	a	↪						17 43									18 43					↪			
Knebworth	d						17 14			17 44					18 14				18 44						
Welwyn North	d						17 18			17 48					18 18				18 48						
Welwyn Garden City 4	d						17 21			17 51					18 21				18 51						
Hatfield	d						17 25			17 55					18 25				18 55						
Potters Bar	d						17 31			18 01					18 31				19 01						
Finsbury Park ⊖	d				17 24		17 40	18 18	17 54	18 10			18 24		18 40		19 18	18 54	19 10						19 24
London Kings Cross 15 ⊖	a			17 33	17 32	17 35	17 49	18 25	18 01	18 19		18 04	18 31	18 35	18 49		19 25	19 01	19 19	19 05				19 30	19 31

Table 25

Saturdays

Peterborough, Cambridge and Stevenage - London

Network Diagram - see first Page of Table 24

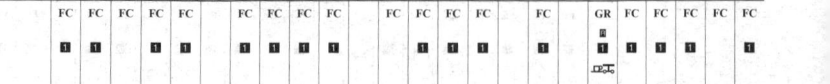

		FC	FC	FC	FC	FC		FC	FC	FC	FC		FC	FC	FC	FC		FC		GR	FC	FC	FC	FC	FC
																				R					
		1	1		1	1		1	1	1	1			1	1	1		1		1	1	1	1		1
Peterborough 8	d				18 46						19 16			19 46				20 16		20 33					20 46
Huntingdon	d				19 00						19 34			20 00				20 34							21 00
St Neots	d				19 08						19 41			20 08				20 41							21 08
Sandy	d				19 15						19 49			20 15				20 49							21 15
Biggleswade	d				19 19						19 53			20 19				20 53							21 19
Arlesey	d				19 24						19 58			20 24				20 58							21 24
Cambridge	d	18 45				18 55		19 15	19 30	19 45					19 55	20 15					20 30	20 45			
Foxton	d					19 05									20 05										
Shepreth	d					19 07									20 07										
Meldreth	d					19 10									20 10										
Royston	d					19 15			19 44						20 15						20 44				
Ashwell & Morden	d					19 20									20 20										
Baldock	d					19 25			19 52						20 25						20 52				
Letchworth Garden City	d					19 29			19 55						20 29						20 55				
Hitchin 4	d		←		19 30	19 34			20 00		20 04			20 30	20 34			21 04			21 00		←		21 30
Stevenage 4	d		19 10	19 30	19 36	19 40			20 06		20 10		20 30	20 36	20 40			21 10		21 02	21 06		21 10	21 30	21 36
Hertford North	a			19 43									20 43					→						21 43	
Knebworth	d		19 14			19 44					20 14				20 44								21 14		
Welwyn North	d		19 18			19 48					20 18				20 48								21 18		
Welwyn Garden City 4	d		19 21			19 51					20 21				20 51								21 21		
Hatfield	d		19 25			19 55					20 25				20 55								21 25		
Potters Bar	d		19 31			20 01					20 31				21 01								21 31		
Finsbury Park ⊖	d		19 40	20 18	19 54	20 10			20 24		20 40		21 18	20 54	21 10						21 24		21 40	22 18	21 54
London Kings Cross 15 ⊖	a	19 35	19 49	20 25	20 01	20 19		20 05	20 30	20 33	20 49		21 25	21 01	21 19	21 04				21 31	21 32	21 34	21 49	22 25	22 01

		FC		FC		GR	FC	FC	FC	FC	FC	FC		FC	FC	FC	FC	FC							
						R																			
		1		1		1	1	1	1		1	1		1	1		1	1							
Peterborough 8	d			21 16		21 21					21 46				22 16		22 46								
Huntingdon	d			21 34							22 00				22 34		23 00								
St Neots	d			21 41							22 08				22 41		23 08								
Sandy	d			21 49							22 15				22 49		23 15								
Biggleswade	d			21 53							22 19				22 53		23 19								
Arlesey	d			21 58							22 24				22 58		23 24								
Cambridge	d	20 55					21 30	21 45				21 55		22 30				23 15							
Foxton	d	21 05										22 05						23 24							
Shepreth	d	21 07										22 07						23 27							
Meldreth	d	21 10										22 10						23 30							
Royston	d	21 15					21 44					22 15		22 44				23 34							
Ashwell & Morden	d	21 20										22 20						23 39							
Baldock	d	21 25					21 52					22 25		22 52				23 43							
Letchworth Garden City	d	21 29					21 55					22 29		22 55				23 46							
Hitchin 4	d	21 34		22 04			22 00		←		22 30	22 34		23 00	23 04		23 30	23 50							
Stevenage 4	d	21 40		22 10		21 53	22 06		22 10	22 30	22 36	22 40		23 06	23 10	23 30	23 36	23 55							
Hertford North	a			→						22 43						23 43									
Knebworth	d	21 44							22 14			22 44			23 14			23 59							
Welwyn North	d	21 48							22 18			22 48			23 18			00 02							
Welwyn Garden City 4	d	21 51							22 21			22 51			23 21			00 06							
Hatfield	d	21 55							22 25			22 55			23 25			00 10							
Potters Bar	d	22 01							22 31			23 01			23 31			00 15							
Finsbury Park ⊖	d	22 10					22 24		22 40	23 18	22 54	23 10		23 24	23 40	00 18	00 04	00s32							
London Kings Cross 15 ⊖	a	22 19				22 24	22 31	22 34	22 49	23 25	23 01	23 19		23 31	23 50	00 26	00 12	00 40							

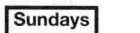

Sundays

		FC	FC	FC	FC	FC	FC	FC	FC	FC		FC	FC	FC	FC	FC	GR	FC	FC	FC		FC	FC	FC	FC
																	R								
			1	1	1	1		1	1			1	1	1		1	1	1	1	1		1	1		1
		A	A	A																					
Peterborough 8	d		22p46		05 46			06 46				07 46				08 46	09 09			09 15					09 46
Huntingdon	d		23p00		06 00			07 00				08 00				09 00				09 30					10 00
St Neots	d		23p08		06 08			07 08				08 08				09 08				09 37					10 08
Sandy	d		23p15		06 15			07 15				08 15				09 15									10 15
Biggleswade	d		23p19		06 19			07 19				08 19				09 19				09 45					10 19
Arlesey	d		23p24		06 24			07 24				08 24				09 24									10 24
Cambridge	d			23p15		06 28			07 28				07 55	08 28				08 55	09 20			09 28			
Foxton	d			23p24									08 05					09 05							
Shepreth	d			23p27									08 07					09 07							
Meldreth	d			23p30									08 10					09 10							
Royston	d			23p34		06 43			07 43				08 15	08 42				09 15				09 42			
Ashwell & Morden	d			23p39									08 20					09 20							
Baldock	d			23p43		06 51			07 51				08 25	08 50				09 25				09 50			
Letchworth Garden City	d			23p46		06 54			07 54				08 29	08 53				09 29				09 53	09 59		
Hitchin 4	d		23p30	23p50	06 33	06 58		07 33	07 59			08 30	08 34	08 57		09 30		09 34				09 57	10 04		10 30
Stevenage 4	d	23p30	23p36	23p55	06 39	07 04	07 30	07 39	08 04	08 30		08 36	08 39	09 03	09 30	09 36	09 38	09 39				10 03	10 09	10 30	10 36
Hertford North	a	23p43					07 43			08 43					09 43									10 43	
Knebworth	d			23p59	06 43			07 43					08 43					09 43					10 13		
Welwyn North	d			00 02	06 47			07 47					08 47					09 47					10 17		
Welwyn Garden City 4	d			00 06	06 51			07 51					08 51					09 51					10 21		
Hatfield	d			00 10	06 54			07 54					08 54					09 54					10 24		
Potters Bar	d			00 15	07 00			08 00					09 00					10 00					10 30		
Finsbury Park ⊖	d	00 18	00 04	00s32	07 10	07 32	08 18	08 10	08 22	09 18		08 54	09 10	09 21	10 18	09 54		10 10				10 21	10 40	11 18	10 54
London Kings Cross 15 ⊖	a	00 27	00 12	00 40	07 20	07 39	08 26	08 20	08 30	09 25		09 01	09 19	09 28	10 25	10 01	10 07	10 19	10 09	10 15		10 28	10 49	11 25	11 01

A not 11 December

Table 25

Sundays

Peterborough, Cambridge and Stevenage - London

Network Diagram - see first Page of Table 24

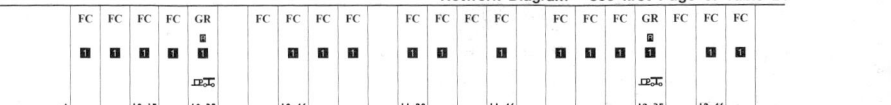

		FC	FC	FC	FC	GR		FC	FC	FC	FC		FC	FC	FC	FC		FC	FC	FC	GR	FC	FC	FC	
						R															R				
		1	1	1	1	1			1	1	1		1	1		1		1	1	1	1		1	1	
						🛒															🛒				
Peterborough 8	d			10 15		10 33			10 46				11 20			11 46					12 35		12 46		
Huntingdon	d			10 30					11 00				11 35			12 00							13 00		
St Neots	d			10 37					11 08				11 42			12 08							13 08		
Sandy	d								11 15							12 15							13 15		
Biggleswade	d			10 45					11 19				11 50			12 19							13 19		
Arlesey	d								11 24							12 24							13 24		
Cambridge	d	09 55	10 20		10 28					10 55	11 20			11 28				11 55	12 20	12 28				12 55	
Foxton	d	10 05								11 05								12 05						13 05	
Shepreth	d	10 07								11 07								12 07						13 07	
Meldreth	d	10 10								11 10								12 10						13 10	
Royston	d	10 15			10 42					11 15				11 42				12 15		12 42				13 15	
Ashwell & Morden	d	10 20								11 20								12 20						13 20	
Baldock	d	10 25			10 50					11 25				11 50				12 25		12 50				13 25	
Letchworth Garden City	d	10 29			10 53					11 29				11 53				12 29		12 53				13 29	
Hitchin 4	d	10 34			10 57				11 30	11 34				11 57		12 30		12 34		12 57			13 30	13 34	
Stevenage 4	d	10 39			11 03	11 04		11 30	11 36	11 39				12 03	12 30	12 36		12 39		13 03	13 05	13 30	13 36	13 39	
Hertford North	a							11 43							12 43							13 43			
Knebworth	d	10 43								11 43								12 43						13 43	
Welwyn North	d	10 47								11 47								12 47						13 47	
Welwyn Garden City 4	d	10 51								11 51								12 51						13 51	
Hatfield	d	10 54								11 54								12 54						13 54	
Potters Bar	d	11 00								12 00								13 00						14 00	
Finsbury Park ⊖	d	11 10			11 21			12 18	11 54	12 10				12 21	13 18	12 54		13 10		13 21		14 18	13 54	14 10	
London Kings Cross 15 ⊖	a	11 19	11 08	11 15	11 28	11 34		12 25	12 01	12 19	12 08		12 20	12 28	13 25	13 01		13 19	13 08	13 28	13 35	14 25	14 01	14 19	

		FC			FC	FC	FC	FC		FC	FC	GR		FC	FC	FC		FC	FC	FC	FC	FC			FC
												R													
		1			1		1	1		1	1	1			1	1		1	1		1	1			1
												🛒													
Peterborough 8	d						13 46					14 33			14 46						15 46				
Huntingdon	d						14 00								15 00						16 00				
St Neots	d						14 08								15 08						16 08				
Sandy	d						14 15								15 15						16 15				
Biggleswade	d						14 19								15 19						16 19				
Arlesey	d						14 24								15 24						16 24				
Cambridge	d	13 20			13 28			13 55		14 20	14 28					14 55		15 20	15 28			15 55			16 20
Foxton	d							14 05								15 05						16 05			
Shepreth	d							14 07								15 07						16 07			
Meldreth	d							14 10								15 10						16 10			
Royston	d				13 42			14 15			14 42					15 15			15 42			16 15			
Ashwell & Morden	d							14 20								15 20						16 20			
Baldock	d				13 50			14 25			14 50					15 25			15 50			16 25			
Letchworth Garden City	d				13 53			14 29			14 53					15 29			15 53			16 29			
Hitchin 4	d				13 57		14 30	14 34			14 57				15 30	15 34			15 57		16 30	16 34			
Stevenage 4	d				14 03	14 30	14 36	14 39			15 03	15 06		15 30	15 36	15 39			16 03	16 30	16 36	16 39			
Hertford North	a					14 43								15 43						16 43					
Knebworth	d							14 43								15 43						16 43			
Welwyn North	d							14 47								15 47						16 47			
Welwyn Garden City 4	d							14 51								15 51						16 51			
Hatfield	d							14 54								15 54						16 54			
Potters Bar	d							15 00								16 00						17 00			
Finsbury Park ⊖	d				14 21	15 18	14 54	15 10			15 21			16 18	15 54	16 10			16 21	17 18	16 54	17 10			
London Kings Cross 15 ⊖	a	14 08			14 28	15 25	15 01	15 19		15 08	15 28	15 34		16 25	16 01	16 19		16 08	16 28	17 25	17 01	17 19			17 08

			FC	GR	FC	FC		FC		FC	GR	FC	FC	FC		FC				FC	FC	GR	FC	FC	FC
				R							R											R			
			1	1	1	1		1		1	1		1	1		1				1	1	1		1	1
				🛒							🛒											🛒			
Peterborough 8	d			16 33	16 46								17 46											18 46	
Huntingdon	d				17 00								18 00											19 00	
St Neots	d				17 08								18 08											19 08	
Sandy	d				17 15								18 15											19 15	
Biggleswade	d				17 19								18 19											19 19	
Arlesey	d				17 24								18 24											19 24	
Cambridge	d		16 28			16 55		17 20		17 28				17 55		18 20				18 28	18 45				18 55
Foxton	d					17 05								18 05											19 05
Shepreth	d					17 07								18 07											19 07
Meldreth	d					17 10								18 10											19 10
Royston	d		16 42			17 15				17 42				18 15						18 42					19 15
Ashwell & Morden	d					17 20								18 20											19 20
Baldock	d		16 50			17 25				17 50				18 25						18 50					19 25
Letchworth Garden City	d		16 53			17 29				17 53				18 29						18 53					19 29
Hitchin 4	d		16 57		17 30	17 34				17 57			18 30	18 34						18 57				19 30	19 34
Stevenage 4	d		17 03	17 05	17 36	17 39				18 03	18 04	18 30	18 36	18 39						19 03		19 07	19 30	19 36	19 39
Hertford North	a											18 43											19 43		
Knebworth	d					17 43								18 43											19 43
Welwyn North	d					17 47								18 47											19 47
Welwyn Garden City 4	d					17 51								18 51											19 51
Hatfield	d					17 54								18 54											19 54
Potters Bar	d					18 00								19 00											20 00
Finsbury Park ⊖	d		17 21		17 54	18 10				18 21		19 18	18 54	19 10						19 21			20 18	19 54	20 10
London Kings Cross 15 ⊖	a		17 28	17 34	18 01	18 19		18 08		18 30	18 35	19 25	19 01	19 19		19 11				19 30	19 36	19 37	20 25	20 01	20 19

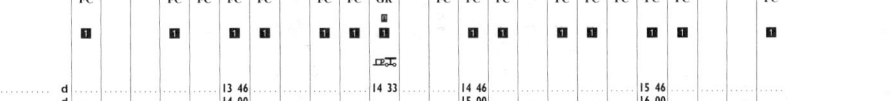

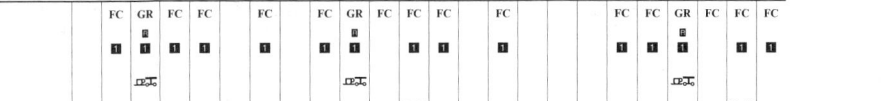

Table 25

Sundays

Peterborough, Cambridge and Stevenage - London

Network Diagram - see first Page of Table 24

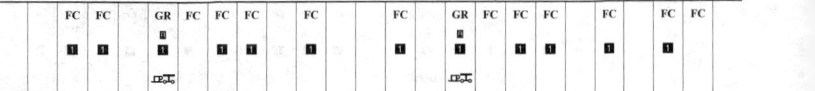

			FC	FC		GR	FC	FC	FC		FC			FC		GR	FC	FC	FC		FC		FC	FC	
						[R]										[R]									
			[1]	[1]		[1]		[1]	[1]		[1]			[1]		[1]		[1]	[1]		[1]		[1]		
						[trolley]										[trolley]									
Peterborough [8]	d							19 46										20 46							
Huntingdon	d							20 00										21 00							
St Neots	d							20 08										21 08							
Sandy	d							20 15										21 15							
Biggleswade	d							20 19										21 19							
Arlesey	d							20 24										21 24							
Cambridge	d		19 20	19 28					19 55		20 20			20 28					20 55		21 20		21 28		
Foxton	d								20 05										21 05						
Shepreth	d								20 07										21 07						
Meldreth	d								20 10										21 10						
Royston	d			19 42					20 15					20 42					21 15				21 42		
Ashwell & Morden	d								20 20										21 20						
Baldock	d			19 50					20 25					20 50					21 25				21 50		
Letchworth Garden City	d			19 53					20 29					20 53					21 29				21 53		
Hitchin [4]	d			19 57				20 30	20 34					20 57				21 30	21 34				21 57		
Stevenage [4]	d			20 03		20 07	20 30	20 36	20 39					21 03		21 08	21 30	21 36	21 39				22 03	22 30	
Hertford North	a						20 43										21 43							22 43	
Knebworth	d								20 43										21 43						
Welwyn North	d								20 47										21 47						
Welwyn Garden City [4]	d								20 51										21 51						
Hatfield	d								20 54										21 54						
Potters Bar	d								21 00										22 00						
Finsbury Park ⊖	d			20 21			21 18	20 54	21 10					21 21			22 18	21 54	22 10				22 21	23 18	
London Kings Cross [15] ⊖	a		20 11	20 28		20 35	21 25	21 01	21 19		21 11			21 28		21 35	22 25	22 03	22 19		22 10		22 28	23 26	

		FC	FC	FC	FC	GR	GR	FC	GR	FC		FC	FC
						[R]	[R]		[R]				
		[1]	[1]	[1]	[1]	[1]	[1]	[1]	[1]			[1]	[1]
				A	B								
						[trolley]	[trolley]		[trolley]				
Peterborough [8]	d	21 46				22 13	22 19		22 53			23 01	
Huntingdon	d	22 00										23 15	
St Neots	d	22 08										23 22	
Sandy	d	22 15										23 30	
Biggleswade	d	22 19										23 33	
Arlesey	d	22 24										23 38	
Cambridge	d		21 55	22 20	22 21			22 28					23 15
Foxton	d		22 05										23 24
Shepreth	d		22 07										23 26
Meldreth	d		22 10										23 29
Royston	d		22 15					22 42					23 34
Ashwell & Morden	d		22 20										23 38
Baldock	d		22 25					22 50					23 43
Letchworth Garden City	d		22 29					22 53					23 46
Hitchin [4]	d	22 30	22 34					22 57				23 46	23 50
Stevenage [4]	d	22 36	22 39			22 45	22 53	23 03	23s24	23 30		23 51	23 55
Hertford North	a									23 43			
Knebworth	d		22 43										23 58
Welwyn North	d		22 47										00 02
Welwyn Garden City [4]	d		22 51										00 05
Hatfield	d		22 54										00 08
Potters Bar	d		23 00										00 14
Finsbury Park ⊖	d	22 54	23 10					23 21		00 18		00s13	00 27
London Kings Cross [15] ⊖	a	23 01	23 19	23 08	23 08	23 16	23 21	23 28	23 53	00 27		00 24	00 39

A until 1 January, from 19 February

B from 8 January until 12 February

Route Diagram for Table 26

DM-4/10
Design BAJS

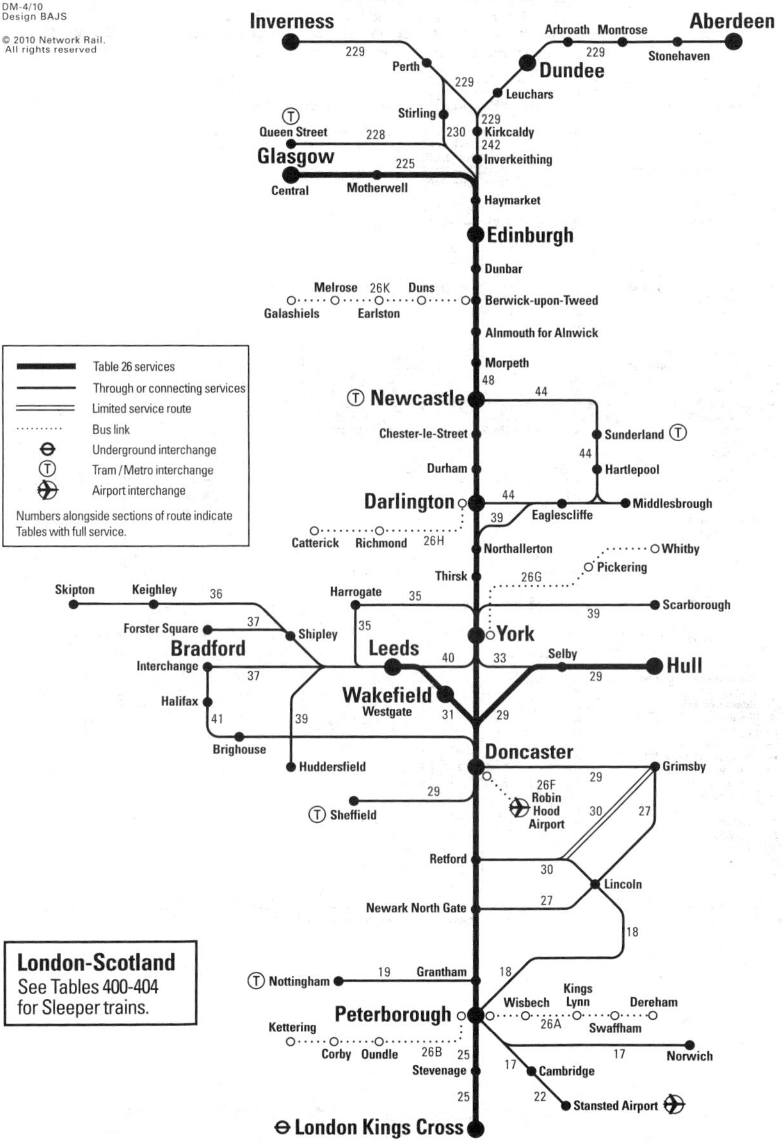

London - Humberside, Yorkshire, North East England and Scotland

Route Diagram - see first Page of Table 26

Miles	Miles	Miles			TP MO	GR MO	GR MX	GR MO	GR MX	TP MX	GR MO	GR MX	GR MO		GR MX	GR	TP	NT	NT	GR	XC	GR	NT		TP
						R	R	R	R		R	R	R		R	R				R		R			
					◇1	1	1	1	1	◇1	1	1	1		1	1	◇1			1	◇1	1			◇1
						🍴🛒	🍴🛒	🍴🛒	🍴		🍴🛒	🍴	🍴🛒		🍴	🍴				🍴	🛒	🍴			
0	—	—	**London Kings Cross [15]** ⊖	d		21p00	21p00	21p35	21p35		22p00	22p00	22p35		23p30	05 50									
27½	—	—	**Stevenage [4]**	d			21p20	21p55	21p55							06 11									
76¼	—	—	**Peterborough [8]**	a		21p45	21p50	22p25	22p26		22p45	22p46	23c25		00s24	06 41									
—	—	—	Norwich	d																					
—	—	—	**Peterborough [8]**	d		21p45	21p51	22p26	22p26		22p45	22p46				06 42									
105¼	—	—	**Grantham [7]**	a				22p47	22p47			23p07	23c48		00s46	07 02									
—	—	—		d				22p47	22p48			23p07				07 02									
120	—	—	**Newark North Gate [7]**	a			22p19	22p59	22p59			23p19	23c59		00s57	07 14									
—	—	—		d			22p19	22p59	23p00			23p19				07 14									
—	—	—	Lincoln	a																					
138½	—	—	**Retford [10]**	d				23p16	23p16							07 29									
156	0	—	**Doncaster [7]**	a			22p45	23p35	23p31		23p42	23p48	00s29		01s25	07 43									
—	—	—	Selby	a																					
—	—	—	Hull	a																					
—	—	—	Pontefract Monkhill	a																					
—	—	—	Wakefield Kirkgate [4]	a																					
—	19¾	—	**Wakefield Westgate [7]**	a				23p56	23p53							08 01									
—	29¾	—	**Leeds [10]**	a				00 15	00 12				01 37		02 38	08 21									
—	—	—	Brighouse	a																					
—	—	—	Halifax	a																					
—	—	—	Shipley	a																					
—	—	—	Bradford Forster Square	a																					
—	—	—	**Bradford Interchange**	a																					
—	—	—	Keighley	a																					
—	—	—	Skipton	a																					
—	—	—	Sheffield [7] 🚋	d																					
—	—	—	**Doncaster [7]**	d			22p45				23p43	23p49										06 15			
188½	—	—	**York [8]**	a		22p58	23p10				00 33	00 39										06 36			
—	—	—	Scarborough	a																					
—	—	—	Harrogate	a																					
—	—	—	Leeds [10]	d	22p12					22p42															06 35
—	—	—	**York [8]**	d	22p42	23p04	23p11			23b18	00 35	00 41					05 54					06 38			07 06
210¾	—	—	Thirsk	d	23p06					23p31							06 10								07 22
218½	—	—	Northallerton	d	23p16	23p39	23p40			23p49	01s07	01s11					06 18								07 30
232½	—	—	**Darlington [7]**	a	23p28	23p51	23p52			00 01	01s21	01s25					06 29					07 05			07 41
—	—	—	Eaglescliffe	a																					
—	—	—	Middlesbrough	a													07 03								
—	—	—	**Darlington [7]**	d	23p28	23p52	23p53			00 02									06 14			07 06	07 20		07 42
254½	—	—	**Durham**	d	23p45	00 09	00 11			00 20	01s39	01s43							06 35			07 23	07 41		07 59
260¼	—	—	Chester-le-Street	d															06 42				07 48		08 05
—	—	—	**Newcastle [8]** 🚋	a	00 15	00 43	00 45			00 51	02 12	02 18							06 54			07 39	08 05		08 16
—	—	—	Hartlepool	a																					
—	—	—	Sunderland 🚋	a																					
268½	—	—	**Newcastle [8]** 🚋	d														05 55		06 25	07 35	07 41			
285	—	—	Morpeth	d														06 15		06 40	07 48				
303¼	—	—	Alnmouth for Alnwick	d														06a32		06 54		08 07			
335½	—	—	**Berwick-upon-Tweed**	d																07 18	08 19	08 31			
363¾	—	—	Dunbar	d																07 42		08 54			
393	—	—	**Edinburgh [10]**	a																08 10	09 04	09 24			
—	—	0	**Edinburgh**	d																	09 11				
394¼	—	1¼	Haymarket	d																	09 16				
437¼	—	—	Motherwell	a																	10 04				
450¼	—	—	**Glasgow Central [15]**	a																	10 26				
—	—	—	Stirling	a																					
—	—	—	Perth	a																					
—	—	—	**Inverness**	a																					
—	—	13¼	Inverkeithing	a																					
—	—	26	Kirkcaldy	a																					
—	—	51	Leuchars [3]	a																					
—	—	59¼	**Dundee**	a																					
—	—	76¼	Arbroath	a																					
—	—	90	Montrose	a																					
—	—	114¼	Stonehaven	a																					
—	—	130½	**Aberdeen**	a																					

b Previous night, arr. 2307

c Previous night, stops to set down only

London - Humberside, Yorkshire, North East England and Scotland

Route Diagram - see first Page of Table 26

		XC	TP	NT	GR	NT	NT	TP	NT	NT	XC	NT	GR	GR	TP	XC	EM	TP	GR	GR	GR	HT	NT
					R								R	R					R	R	R		
		◇1	◇1		1			◇1			◇1		1	1	◇1	◇1	◇	◇1	1	1	1	◇1	
											A				B								
		☕			🍽☕			☕			☕		🍽	🍽	☕	☕		☕	🍽☕	🍽☕	🍽☕	⊠	
London Kings Cross [15] ⊖	d												06 15	06 30					07 00	07 05	07 08	07 20	
Stevenage [4]	d												06 34	06 49							07 27	07 44	
Peterborough [8]	a												07 04	07 19					07 45	07 50	07 57		
Norwich	d																05 50						
Peterborough [8]	d												07 05	07 20			07 27		07 45	07 50	07 58		
Grantham [7]	a												07 25	07 39			07 58				08 18	08 26	
	d												07 25	07 39							08 18	08 27	
Newark North Gate [7]	a												07 37								08 30		
	d												07 37								08 30		
Lincoln	a																						
Retford [10]	d												07 53								08 44	08 50	
Doncaster [7]	a												08 08	08 12						08 40	08 59	09 04	
Selby	a																					09 22	
Hull	a																					10 04	
Pontefract Monkhill	a																						
Wakefield Kirkgate [4]	a																						
Wakefield Westgate [7]	a													08 31						09 00			
Leeds [10]	a													08 50						09 19			
Brighouse	a																						
Halifax	a																						
Shipley	a																						
Bradford Forster Square	a																						
Bradford Interchange	a																						
Keighley	a																						
Skipton	a																						
Sheffield [7] 🚌	d	06 33									07 12					07 54							
Doncaster [7]	d	07 00											08 09			08 25					09 00		
York [8]	a	07 26											08 32			08 45			08 51		09 29		
Scarborough	a																						
Harrogate	a																						
Leeds [10]	d				07 10	07 29	07 41	07 50			07 57	07 13			08 12			08 28					07 43
York [8]	d	07 31	07 32		07 37	08a06	08a16	08 23			08 28	08a32	08 34		08 42	08 49		08a52	08 53				08a58
Thirsk	d		07 52					08 39															
Northallerton	d		08 00					08 49					08 53										
Darlington [7]	a	07 56			08 05						08 55		09 06		09 11	09 16			09 20				
Eaglescliffe	a																						
Middlesbrough	a		08 32					09 22															
Darlington [7]	d	07 58			08 05				08 22		08 57		09 06		09 12	09 17			09 21				
Durham	d	08 16			08 23				08 43		09 12		09 24		09 29	09 34							
Chester-le-Street	d								08 50														
Newcastle [8] 🚌	a	08 37			08 40				09 06		09 29		09 43		09 44	09 47			09 50				
Hartlepool	a																						
Sunderland 🚌	a																						
Newcastle [8] 🚌	d			07 58	08 41					09 15	09 35								09 53				
Morpeth	d			08a18	08 56					09a36													
Alnmouth for Alnwick	d										09 59												
Berwick-upon-Tweed	d				09 31						10 20								10 38				
Dunbar	d				09 56																		
Edinburgh [10]	a				10 20						11 05								11 25				
Edinburgh	d				10 27						11 11												
Haymarket	d				10 32						11 16												
Motherwell	a										11 52												
Glasgow Central [15]	a										12 14												
Stirling	a																						
Perth	a																						
Inverness	a																						
Inverkeithing	a				10 47																		
Kirkcaldy	a				11 04																		
Leuchars [3]	a				11 28																		
Dundee	a				11 43																		
Arbroath	a				12 00																		
Montrose	a				12 16																		
Stonehaven	a				12 39																		
Aberdeen	a				13 05																		

A ☕ to Edinburgh

B ☕ to York

London - Humberside, Yorkshire, North East England and Scotland

Route Diagram - see first Page of Table 26

		TP	NT	TP	NT		XC	GR	GR	NT	EM	XC	GC	GR	GR		TP	GC	NT	NT	TP	NT	XC	GR	GR
								R	R				R	R	R			R						R	R
		◇1		◇1			◇1	1	1			◇1	1	1	1		◇1	1			◇1		◇1	1	1
		🛒		🛒			🛒	🍴🛒	🍴🛒			🛒	🍴	🍴🛒	🍴🛒		🛒	🍴			🛒		🛒	🍴🛒	🍴🛒
London Kings Cross 15 ⊖	d							07 30	07 35				07 49	08 00	08 03									08 30	08 35
Stevenage 4	d								07 54																08 54
Peterborough 8	a							08 16							08 51									09 15	
Norwich	d																								
Peterborough 8	d							08 16			08 33				08 51									09 15	
Grantham 7	a								08 39																09 39
	d								08 39																09 39
Newark North Gate 7	a							08 44																09 43	
	d							08 44																09 43	
Lincoln	a										09 59														
Retford 10	d																								
Doncaster 7	a							09 09	09 12						09 39									10 08	10 12
Selby	a																								
Hull	a																								
Pontefract Monkhill	a																								
Wakefield Kirkgate 4	a																								
Wakefield Westgate 7	a								09 31						09 59										10 31
Leeds 10	a								09 50						10 19										10 50
Brighouse	a																								
Halifax	a																								
Shipley	a																								
Bradford Forster Square	a																								
Bradford Interchange	a																								
Keighley	a																								
Skipton	a																								
Sheffield 7 ⛴	d						08 21					08 48											09 21		
Doncaster 7	d							09 09				09 20												10 09	
York 8	a							09 33				09 44	09 47	09 50										10 32	
Scarborough	a																								
Harrogate	a																								
Leeds 10	d	08 28	08 41	08 57			09 05			08 29							09 28	←	09 33	09 41	09 57		10 05		
York 8	d	08 58	09a21	09 26			09 32	09 35		09a45		09 48	10 01	09 53			09 58	10 01	10a06	10a21	10 26		10 32	10 34	
Thirsk	d			09 46									→					10 18			10 46				
Northallerton	d	09 19		09 59													10 19	10 28			10 59			10 54	
Darlington 7	a	09 30					09 57	10 02				10 13		10 20			10 30						11 00	11 06	
Eaglescliffe	a																	10 46							
Middlesbrough	a			10 30																	11 30				
Darlington 7	d	09 31					09 59	10 03				10 15		10 21			10 31						11 02	11 07	
Durham	d	09 47					10 17	10 21				10 31					10 47						11 20	11 24	
Chester-le-Street	d	09 53																							
Newcastle 8 ⛴	a	10 07					10 30	10 39				10 44		10 50			11 05						11 34	11 43	
Hartlepool	a																	11 07							
Sunderland ⛴	a																	11 40							
Newcastle 8 ⛴	d				10 15		10 35	10 41						10 53								11 15	11 40		
Morpeth	d				10a36																	11a36			
Alnmouth for Alnwick	d							11 07																	
Berwick-upon-Tweed	d													11 38									12 22		
Dunbar	d						11 37																		
Edinburgh 10	a						12 03	12 15						12 25									13 06		
Edinburgh	d																						13 12		
Haymarket	d																						13 16		
Motherwell	a																						13 52		
Glasgow Central 15	a																						14 12		
Stirling	a																								
Perth	a																								
Inverness	a																								
Inverkeithing	a																								
Kirkcaldy	a																								
Leuchars 8	a																								
Dundee	a																								
Arbroath	a																								
Montrose	a																								
Stonehaven	a																								
Aberdeen	a																								

London - Humberside, Yorkshire, North East England and Scotland

Route Diagram - see first Page of Table 26

		XC	EM	EM	GR	GR	GR	TP	NT	TP	NT	XC	GR	GR	HT	NT	XC	GR	TP	NT	TP	NT
					R	R	R						R	R				R				
		◇1	◇		1	1	1	◇1		◇1		◇1	1	1	◇1		◇1	1	◇1		◇1	
																		A				
London Kings Cross 15 ⊖	d				09 00	09 03	09 08						09 30	09 35	09 48			10 00				
Stevenage 4	d						09 28							09 54								
Peterborough 8	a				09 45	09 51	10 00						10 15									
Norwich	d		07 57																			
Peterborough 8	d		09 27	09 35	09 45	09 51	10 00						10 15									
Grantham 7	a		09 57				10 20							10 40	10 49							
	d		09 58				10 20							10 40	10 50							
Newark North Gate 7	a						10 32						10 43									
	d						10 32						10 43									
Lincoln	a			10 59																		
Retford 10	d						10 48								11 11							
Doncaster 7	a					10 40	11 03						11 08	11 12	11 23							
Selby	a														11 39							
Hull	a														12 18							
Pontefract Monkhill	a																					
Wakefield Kirkgate 4	a																					
Wakefield Westgate 7	a					11 00								11 31								
Leeds 10	a					11 19								11 50								
Brighouse	a																					
Halifax	a																					
Shipley	a																					
Bradford Forster Square	a																					
Bradford Interchange	a																					
Keighley	a																					
Skipton	a																					
Sheffield 7	d	09 47	11a38									10 21					10 47					
Doncaster 7	d	10 19					11 03						11 10				11 19					
York 8	a	10 45			10 51		11 31						11 32				11 46	11 51				
Scarborough	a																					
Harrogate	a																					
Leeds 10	d							10 28	10 41	10 57		11 05				10 29			11 28	11 41	11 57	
York 8	d	10 48			10 53			10 58	11a19	11 26		11 32	11 35			11a44	11 48	11 53	11 58	12a21	12 26	
Thirsk	d									11 46											12 46	
Northallerton	d							11 19		11 59									12 19		12 59	
Darlington 7	a	11 13			11 20			11 30				11 57	12 03				12 13	12 21	12 30			
Eaglescliffe	a																					
Middlesbrough	a									12 30											13 30	
Darlington 7	d	11 15			11 21			11 31				12 00	12 05				12 15	12 21	12 31			
Durham	d	11 31						11 47				12 22	12 25				12 31		12 47			
Chester-le-Street	d							11 53														
Newcastle 8	a	11 45			11 50			12 06				12 34	12 41				12 44	12 51	13 03			
Hartlepool	a																					
Sunderland	a																					
Newcastle 8	d				11 52						12 15	12 38	12 44					12 52				13 15
Morpeth	d										12a36											13a36
Alnmouth for Alnwick	d												13 10									
Berwick-upon-Tweed	d				12 37													13 39				
Dunbar	d											13 41										
Edinburgh 10	a				13 25							14 10	14 15					14 22				
Edinburgh	d																	14 27				
Haymarket	d																	14 32				
Motherwell	a																					
Glasgow Central 15	a																					
Stirling	a																					
Perth	a																					
Inverness	a																					
Inverkeithing	a																	14 46				
Kirkcaldy	a																	15 03				
Leuchars 8	a																	15 28				
Dundee	a																	15 46				
Arbroath	a																	16 04				
Montrose	a																	16 20				
Stonehaven	a																	16 43				
Aberdeen	a																	17 09				

A The Northern Lights

London - Humberside, Yorkshire, North East England and Scotland

Route Diagram - see first Page of Table 26

		XC	EM	EM	GR	GR	GR	GR	GC	NT	XC	EM	GR	EM	GR	GR	TP	NT	GC	TP	NT	XC	GR
					R	R	R	R	R				R		R	R			R				R
		◇1	◇		1	1	1	1	1		◇1	◇	1		1	1	◇1		1	◇1		◇1	1
		A																					
		☕			🍽☕	🍽☕	🍽☕	🍽☕	🍽		☕		🍽☕		🍽☕	🍽	☕		🍽	☕		☕	🍽☕
London Kings Cross 15 ⊖	d				10 03	10 08	10 30	10 35	10 48				11 00		11 05	11 08			11 23				11 30
Stevenage 4	d					10 28		10 54								11 27							
Peterborough 8	a				10 50	10 59	11 15								11 51	11 57							12 15
Norwich	d		08 57									09 57											
Peterborough 8	d		10 28	10 38	10 50	10 59	11 15					11 28		11 48	11 51	11 58							12 15
Grantham 7	a		10 58			11 20		11 39				11 59				12 18							
	d		11 00			11 20		11 39				12 00				12 18							
Newark North Gate 7	a					11 36	11 43									12 30							12 43
	d						11 43									12 30							12 43
Lincoln	a			12 04										13 14									
Retford 10	d															12 44							
Doncaster 7	a				11 40		12 08	12 12	12 23					14 06	12 41	13 03							13 08
Selby	a																						
Hull	a																						
Pontefract Monkhill	a								12 47														
Wakefield Kirkgate 4	a								13 07														
Wakefield Westgate 7	a				12 00			12 31							13 00								
Leeds 10	a				12 19			12 50							13 19								
Brighouse	a								13 30														
Halifax	a								13 40														
Shipley	a																						
Bradford Forster Square	a																						
Bradford Interchange	a								13 55														
Keighley	a																						
Skipton	a																						
Sheffield 7 ⛴	d	11 21	12a38								11 47	13a38										12 21	
Doncaster 7	d						12 08				12 19					13 04							13 10
York 8	a						12 32				12 46		12 49			13 31			13 21				13 32
Scarborough	a																						
Harrogate	a																						
Leeds 10	d	12 05								11 29							12 28	12 41		12 57		13 05	
York 8	d	12 32					12 34			12a45	12 48		12 52				12 58	13a19	13 22	13 29		13 32	13 35
Thirsk	d																		13 39	13 49			
Northallerton	d						12 54										13 19		13 46	13 59			
Darlington 7	a	12 58					13 06				13 13		13 19				13 30					13 59	14 04
Eaglescliffe	a																		14 04				
Middlesbrough	a																			14 30			
Darlington 7	d	13 00					13 07				13 15		13 20				13 31					14 01	14 05
Durham	d	13 16					13 24				13 31						13 47					14 18	14 22
Chester-le-Street	d																13 53						
Newcastle 8 ⛴	a	13 29					13 43				13 45		13 49				14 06					14 30	14 39
Hartlepool	a																		14 23				
Sunderland ⛴	a																		14 50				
Newcastle 8 ⛴	d	13 38											13 51								14 15	14 36	14 43
Morpeth	d																				14a36	14 50	
Alnmouth for Alnwick	d	14 02																					15 09
Berwick-upon-Tweed	d	14 23											14 36										
Dunbar	d																					15 41	
Edinburgh 10	a	15 06											15 24									16 05	16 17
Edinburgh	d	15 11																					
Haymarket	d	15 16																					
Motherwell	a	15 52																					
Glasgow Central 15	a	16 23																					
Stirling	a																						
Perth	a																						
Inverness	a																						
Inverkeithing	a																						
Kirkcaldy	a																						
Leuchars 3	a																						
Dundee	a																						
Arbroath	a																						
Montrose	a																						
Stonehaven	a																						
Aberdeen	a																						

A ☕ to Edinburgh

Table 26

Mondays to Fridays

London - Humberside, Yorkshire, North East England and Scotland

Route Diagram - see first Page of Table 26

		GR	HT	XC	NT	GR	TP	NT	TP	NT	XC	EM	EM	GR	GR	GR	GR	NT	XC	EM	EM	GR
		R				R								R	R	R	R					R
		1	◇1	◇1		1	◇1		◇1		◇1	◇		1	1	1	1		◇1	◇		1
						A					B											
		🍽☕	⊠	☕		🍽☕	☕		☕		☕			🍽☕	🍽	🍽☕	🍽☕		☕			🍽☕
London Kings Cross [15] ⊖	d	11 35	11 48			12 00								12 05	12 08	12 30	12 35					13 00
Stevenage [4]	d	11 54													12 28		12 54					
Peterborough [8]	a													12 50	12 59	13 15						13 45
Norwich	d											10 57								11 57		
Peterborough [8]	d											12 26	12 41	12 50	12 59	13 15				13 27	13 40	13 45
Grantham [7]	a	12 39	12 48									12 58			13 20		13 39			13 56		
	d	12 39	12 49									12 59			13 21		13 39			13 58		
Newark North Gate [7]	a														13 36	13 43						
	d															13 43						
Lincoln	a												14 06								15 05	
Retford [10]	d		13 11																			
Doncaster [7]	a	13 12	13 23											13 39		14 08	14 12					
Selby	a		13 39																			
Hull	a		14 19																			
Pontefract Monkhill	a																					
Wakefield Kirkgate [4]	a																					
Wakefield Westgate [7]	a	13 31												13 59			14 31					
Leeds [10]	a	13 50												14 19			14 50					
Brighouse	a																					
Halifax	a																					
Shipley	a																					
Bradford Forster Square	a																					
Bradford Interchange	a																					
Keighley	a																					
Skipton	a																					
Sheffield [7]	d			12 47							13 21	14a38							13 47	15a38		
Doncaster [7]	d			13 19												14 08			14 19			
York [8]	a			13 40		13 53										14 32			14 44			14 50
Scarborough	a																					
Harrogate	a																					
Leeds [10]	d				12 29		13 28	13 42	13 57		14 05							13 29				
York [8]	d			13 43	13a44	13 54	13 58	14a22	14 26		14 32					14 34		14a44	14 48			14 52
Thirsk	d								14 46													
Northallerton	d						14 19		14 59							14 54						
Darlington [7]	a			14 12		14 22	14 30				14 58					15 06			15 13			15 19
Eaglescliffe	a																					
Middlesbrough	a								15 30													
Darlington [7]	d			14 13		14 23	14 31				15 00					15 07			15 15			15 20
Durham	d			14 30			14 47				15 16					15 24			15 31			
Chester-le-Street	d																					
Newcastle [8]	a			14 42		14 52	15 05				15 30					15 43			15 45			15 49
Hartlepool	a																					
Sunderland	a																					
Newcastle [8]	d					14 54				15 15	15 37											15 51
Morpeth	d									15a36												
Alnmouth for Alnwick	d										16 01											
Berwick-upon-Tweed	d					15 40					16 22											16 36
Dunbar	d																					
Edinburgh [10]	a					16 23					17 06											17 25
Edinburgh	d					16 33					17 11											
Haymarket	d					16 38					17 15											
Motherwell	a										17 52											
Glasgow Central [15]	a										18 16											
Stirling	a					17 19																
Perth	a					17 59																
Inverness	a					20 11																
Inverkeithing	a																					
Kirkcaldy	a																					
Leuchars [3]	a																					
Dundee	a																					
Arbroath	a																					
Montrose	a																					
Stonehaven	a																					
Aberdeen	a																					

A The Highland Chieftain

B ☕ to Edinburgh

London - Humberside, Yorkshire, North East England and Scotland

Route Diagram - see first Page of Table 26

		GR	GR	TP	TP	NT	XC	GR	GR	HT	NT	XC	GR	NT	TP	NT	XC	EM	GR	GR	EM	GR	GR
		R	R					R	R				R						R	R		R	R
		1	1	◇1	◇1		◇1	1	1	◇1		◇1	1		◇1		◇1	◇	1	1		1	1
							A										A						
		🍽🛒	🍽	🛒	🛒		🛒	🍽🛒	🍽🛒	⊠		🛒	🍽🛒		🛒		🛒		🍽🛒	🍽		🍽🛒	🍽🛒
London Kings Cross 15 ⊖	d	13 05	13 08					13 30	13 35	13 48			14 00						14 05	14 08		14 30	14 35
Stevenage 4	d		13 28						13 54											14 27			14 54
Peterborough 8	a	13 50	13 59					14 15											14 50	14 58		15 16	
Norwich	d																	12 57					
Peterborough 8	d	13 51	14 00					14 15										14 26	14 50	14 59	15 10	15 16	
Grantham 7	a		14 20						14 39	14 48								14 57		15 19			15 39
	d		14 20						14 39	14 49								14 58		15 19			15 39
Newark North Gate 7	a		14 32					14 43												15 35		15 43	
	d		14 32					14 43														15 43	
Lincoln	a																				16 47		
Retford 10	d		14 48							15 11													
Doncaster 7	a	14 39	15 02					15 08	15 12	15 23									15 39			16 08	16 12
Selby	a									15 39													
Hull	a									16 18													
Pontefract Monkhill	a																						
Wakefield Kirkgate 4	a																						
Wakefield Westgate 7	a	14 59							15 31										15 59				16 30
Leeds 10	a	15 19							15 50										16 19				16 52
Brighouse	a																						
Halifax	a																						
Shipley	a																						
Bradford Forster Square	a																						
Bradford Interchange	a																						
Keighley	a																						
Skipton	a																						
Sheffield 7 🚢	d						14 21					14 47					15 21	16a38					
Doncaster 7	d		15 03					15 09				15 19										16 08	
York 8	a		15 31					15 32				15 45	15 51									16 32	
Scarborough	a																						
Harrogate	a																						
Leeds 10	d			14 28	14 57		15 05				14 29			15 41	15 57		16 05						
York 8	d			14 58	15 26		15 32	15 34			15a46	15 48	15 53	16a21	16 26		16 32					16 34	
Thirsk	d				15 46										16 46								
Northallerton	d			15 19	15 59			15 54							16 59							16 54	
Darlington 7	a			15 30			15 58	16 06				16 13	16 21				16 58					17 06	
Eaglescliffe	a																						
Middlesbrough	a				16 30										17 30								
Darlington 7	d			15 31			16 00	16 07				16 15	16 21				17 00					17 07	
Durham	d			15 47			16 17	16 24				16 31					17 16					17 24	
Chester-le-Street	d			15 53																			
Newcastle 8 🚢	a			16 09			16 30	16 43				16 45	16 51				17 31					17 43	
Hartlepool	a																						
Sunderland 🚢	a																						
Newcastle 8 🚢	d					16 15	16 37						16 52			17 15	17 37						
Morpeth	d					16a36										17 36							
Alnmouth for Alnwick	d						17 02									18a20	18 02						
Berwick-upon-Tweed	d												17 39				18 23						
Dunbar	d						17 43																
Edinburgh 10	a						18 07						18 23				19 06						
Edinburgh	d						18 11						18 30				19 11						
Haymarket	d						18 15						18 34				19 16						
Motherwell	a																19 54						
Glasgow Central 15	a																20 15						
Stirling	a																						
Perth	a																						
Inverness	a																						
Inverkeithing	a						18 28						18 54										
Kirkcaldy	a						18 46						19 11										
Leuchars 3	a						19 22						19 39										
Dundee	a						19 35						19 53										
Arbroath	a						19 51						20 11										
Montrose	a						20 05						20 27										
Stonehaven	a						20 26						20 50										
Aberdeen	a						20 45						21 16										

A 🛒 to Edinburgh

London - Humberside, Yorkshire, North East England and Scotland

Route Diagram - see first Page of Table 26

		GC	NT	XC	NT		GR	TP	NT	NT	XC	EM	GR	GR	GR		GR	HT	EM	TP	XC	NT	GR	NT	NT
		R					R						R	R	R		R						R		
		1		◇1			1	◇1			◇1	◇	1	1	1		1	◇1		◇1	◇1		1		
											A														
London Kings Cross 15 ⊖	d	14 48					15 00						15 05	15 08	15 30		15 35	15 48					16 00		
Stevenage 4	d													15 28			15 54								
Peterborough 8	a												15 50	15 59	16 15										
Norwich	d											13 57													
Peterborough 8	d											15 28	15 50	15 59	16 15				16 25						
Grantham 7	a											15 59		16 20			16 40	16 48							
	d											16 01		16 20			16 40	16 49							
Newark North Gate 7	a													16 32	16 43										
	d													16 32	16 43										
Lincoln	a																		17 51						
Retford 10	d													16 48				17 11							
Doncaster 7	a	16 22											16 39	17 03	17 09		17 13	17 23							
Selby	a																	17 39							
Hull	a																	18 21							
Pontefract Monkhill	a	16 47																							
Wakefield Kirkgate 4	a	17 04																							
Wakefield Westgate 7	a												17 00				17 31								
Leeds 10	a												17 19				17 51								
Brighouse	a	17 29																							
Halifax	a	17 40																							
Shipley	a																								
Bradford Forster Square	a																								
Bradford Interchange	a	17 55																							
Keighley	a																								
Skipton	a																								
Sheffield 7	d			15 47							16 21	17a36									16 47				
Doncaster 7	d			16 19										17 04	17 10						17 19				
York 8	a			16 45			16 51							17 31	17 33						17 40		17 51		
Scarborough	a																								
Harrogate	a																								
Leeds 10	d		15 29					16 28	16 41		17 07									17 12		16 29		17 28	17 41
York 8	d		16a45	16 48			16 52	16 56	17a20		17 32				17 35					17 41	17 47	17a50	17 53	18a10	18a18
Thirsk	d							17 14												18 01					
Northallerton	d							17 22							17 55					18 09					
Darlington 7	a			17 13			17 20	17 33			17 58				18 07						18 13		18 21		
Eaglescliffe	a																								
Middlesbrough	a																			18 42					
Darlington 7	d			17 15			17 21	17 34			18 00				18 08						18 15		18 22		
Durham	d			17 31				17 51			18 16				18 25						18 32				
Chester-le-Street	d							17 57																	
Newcastle 8	a			17 45			17 50	18 09			18 33				18 41						18 46		18 51		
Hartlepool	a																								
Sunderland	a																								
Newcastle 8	d				17 38		17 52			18 25	18 39				18 43								18 53		
Morpeth	d				18a00					18a47															
Alnmouth for Alnwick	d														19 11										
Berwick-upon-Tweed	d						18 37				19 22												19 39		
Dunbar	d										19 45														
Edinburgh 10	a						19 26				20 09				20 14								20 22		
Edinburgh	d										20 14				20 16								20 29		
Haymarket	d										20 17				20 21								20 34		
Motherwell	a														21 03										
Glasgow Central 15	a														21 28										
Stirling	a																								
Perth	a																								
Inverness	a																								
Inverkeithing	a										20 30												20 51		
Kirkcaldy	a																						21 08		
Leuchars 3	a										21 25												21 37		
Dundee	a										21 41												21 52		
Arbroath	a																						22 09		
Montrose	a																						22 25		
Stonehaven	a																						22 48		
Aberdeen	a																						23 14		

A to Edinburgh

London - Humberside, Yorkshire, North East England and Scotland

Route Diagram - see first Page of Table 26

		TP	XC	EM	GR	GR	GR	GR	GC	NT	GR	TP FX	TP FO	XC	EM	GR	GR	NT	TP	GR	GR	XC
					R	R	R	R	R		R					R	R			R	R	
		◇1	◇1	◇	1	1	1	1	1		1	◇1	◇1	◇1	◇	1	1		◇1	1	1	◇1
			A														B					C
		⊼	⊼		⊏⊐⊼	⊏⊐	⊏⊐⊼	⊏⊐⊼	⊏⊐		⊏⊐⊼	⊼	⊼	⊼		⊏⊐⊼	⊏⊐⊼		⊼	⊏⊐⊼	⊏⊐⊼	⊼
London Kings Cross 15 ⊖	d				16 05	16 08	16 30	16 33	16 48		17 00					17 03	17 19			17 30	17 33	
Stevenage 4	d					16 29		16 52													17 53	
Peterborough 8	a				16 51	16 59	17 15									17 49	18 06			18 15		
Norwich	d			14 57											15 52							
Peterborough 8	d			16 28	16 51	17 00	17 15								17 27	17 50	18 06			18 16		
Grantham 7	a			16 59		17 20		17 39							17 58		18 27				18 41	
	d			17 00		17 20		17 39							17 58		18 27				18 41	
Newark North Gate 7	a					17 36	17 43										18 39			18 43		
	d						17 43										18 39			18 43		
Lincoln	a																					
Retford 10	d							18 02														
Doncaster 7	a				17 42		18 08									18 39	19 05				19 14	
Selby	a																19 22					
Hull	a																20 06					
Pontefract Monkhill	a																					
Wakefield Kirkgate 4	a																					
Wakefield Westgate 7	a				18 00			18 31								18 59					19 35	
Leeds 10	a				18 19			18 51								19 19					19 52	
Brighouse	a																					
Halifax	a																					
Shipley	a																					
Bradford Forster Square	a																					
Bradford Interchange	a																					
Keighley	a																					
Skipton	a																					
Sheffield 7	d		17 21	18a39										17 47	19a39							18 21
Doncaster 7	d						18 09															
York 8	a						18 33		18 39		18 49									19 26		
Scarborough	a																					
Harrogate	a																				20 28	
Leeds 10	d	17 57	18 06							17 29		18 28		18 35				18 41	18 57			19 06
York 8	d	18 25	18 33				18 35		18 44	18a46	18 51	18 57	18 57	19 04				19a21	19 26	19 28		19 35
Thirsk	d								19 00			19 14	19 14						19 46			
Northallerton	d	18 46					18 56		19 15			19 24	19 24						19 57			
Darlington 7	a	18 57	19 01				19 08				19 19			19 29						19 56		20 02
Eaglescliffe	a								19 33													
Middlesbrough	a											19 56	19 56						20 30			
Darlington 7	d	18 58	19 03				19 09				19 19			19 32						19 56		20 04
Durham	d	19 14	19 20				19 26							19 48						20 14		20 21
Chester-le-Street	d	19 20																				
Newcastle 8	a	19 34	19 35				19 42				19 49			20 03						20 33		20 34
Hartlepool	a								19 52													
Sunderland	a								20 21													
Newcastle 8	d		19 38				19 44				19 51			20 11								20 39
Morpeth	d						20 00															20 55
Alnmouth for Alnwick	d		20 06											20 35								
Berwick-upon-Tweed	d		20 27								20 39											21 26
Dunbar	d																					21 51
Edinburgh 10	a		21 11				21 20				21 27			21 35								22 16
Edinburgh	d		21 14																			
Haymarket	d		21 19																			
Motherwell	a		22 01																			
Glasgow Central 15	a		22 27																			
Stirling	a																					
Perth	a																					
Inverness	a																					
Inverkeithing	a																					
Kirkcaldy	a																					
Leuchars 3	a																					
Dundee	a																					
Arbroath	a																					
Montrose	a																					
Stonehaven	a																					
Aberdeen	a																					

A ⊼ to Edinburgh **B** The Hull Executive **C** ⊼ to Newcastle

London - Humberside, Yorkshire, North East England and Scotland

Route Diagram - see first Page of Table 26

		NT FX	XC	EM	GR	GR	GR	NT FX	GR	TP	XC	GR	GR	HT	EM	NT	XC	GR	GR	GR	TP	GC	GR FX
			◇1	◇	R 1	R 1	R 1		R 1	◇1	◇1 A	R 1	R 1	◇1	◇		◇1 B	R 1	R 1	R 1	◇1	R 1	R 1
			🍴		🍴	🍴	🍴		🍴		🍴	🍴	🍴	☒			🍴	🍴	🍴	🍴		🍴	🍴
London Kings Cross 15 ⊖	d				17 49	18 00	18 03		18 19			18 30	18 33	18 50				19 00	19 03	19 06		19 18	19 30
Stevenage 4	d												18 52							19 26			
Peterborough 8	a				18 36		18 54					19 17							19 50	19 57			20 15
Norwich	d			16 57											17 54								
Peterborough 8	d			18 26	18 40		18 55					19 18			19 26				19 51	19 57			20 16
Grantham 7	a			18 54	19 04				19 22				19 42	19 51	19 58					20 18			
	d			18 56	19 04				19 22				19 42	19 53						20 18			
Newark North Gate 7	a						19 22					19 45								20 31			20 43
	d						19 22					19 45								20 31			20 43
Lincoln	a																			21 01			
Retford 10	d				19 26								20 04	20 14									
Doncaster 7	a				19 41		19 47					20 10	20 20	20 27					20 39				21 08
Selby	a													20 48									
Hull	a													21 27									
Pontefract Monkhill	a																						
Wakefield Kirkgate 4	a																						
Wakefield Westgate 7	a				20 01		20 07						20 38						21 00				
Leeds 10	a				20 22		20 23						20 54						21 20				
Brighouse	a																						
Halifax	a																						
Shipley	a												21s12										
Bradford Forster Square	a												21 25										
Bradford Interchange	a																						
Keighley	a						20s55																
Skipton	a						21 15																
Sheffield 7 🚌	d		18 47	20a28							19 26						19 54						
Doncaster 7	d		19 16									20 10					20 17						21 09
York 8	a		19 38			19 48			20 12			20 33					20 46	20 50				21 17	21 31
Scarborough	a																						
Harrogate	a																						
Leeds 10	d	18 29						19 15		19 57	20 08					19 29					20 45		
York 8	d	19a43	19 45			19 49		19a53	20 14	20 29	20 33	20 36				20a45	20 48	20 52			21 14	21 19	21 33
Thirsk	d									20 49											21 31	21 36	
Northallerton	d								20 33	20 59											21 39	21 47	21 52
Darlington 7	a		20 10			20 17			20 46		20 58	21 04					21 14	21 19			21 51		22 05
Eaglescliffe	a																					22 04	
Middlesbrough	a									21 30													
Darlington 7	d		20 12			20 17			20 46		21 00	21 05					21 15	21 20			21 52		22 05
Durham	d		20 28						21 04		21 18	21 22					21 32				22 08		22 23
Chester-le-Street	d																				22 14		
Newcastle 8 🚌	a		20 42			20 47			21 23		21 31	21 38					21 44	21 50			22 28		22 41
Hartlepool	a																					22 24	
Sunderland 🚌	a																					22 51	
Newcastle 8 🚌	d					20 48					21 36	21 40						21 54					
Morpeth	d											21 56											
Alnmouth for Alnwick	d										22 02	22 12											
Berwick-upon-Tweed	d					21 33												22 39					
Dunbar	d					21 57																	
Edinburgh 10	a					22 25					23 04	23 20						23 34					
Edinburgh	d																						
Haymarket	d																						
Motherwell	a																						
Glasgow Central 15	a																						
Stirling	a																						
Perth	a																						
Inverness	a																						
Inverkeithing	a																						
Kirkcaldy	a																						
Leuchars 8	a																						
Dundee	a																						
Arbroath	a																						
Montrose	a																						
Stonehaven	a																						
Aberdeen	a																						

A 🍴 to Leeds

B 🍴 to Doncaster

London - Humberside, Yorkshire, North East England and Scotland

Route Diagram - see first Page of Table 26

		NT	GR	GR	EM	GC	NT	XC	XC	GR	GR	HT	HT	GR	XC	GR	GR	TP	GR	GR
			FO			A						B	C							
London Kings Cross 15 ⊖	d		19 30	19 33		19 48				20 00	20 05	20 30	20 30	20 35		21 00	21 35		22 00	23 30
Stevenage 4	d			19 52										20 54		21 20	21 55			
Peterborough 8	a		20 15								20 50			21 24		21 50	22 26		22 46	00s24
Norwich	d				18 57															
Peterborough 8	d		20 16		20 28						20 50			21 25		21 51	22 26		22 46	
Grantham 7	a			20 40	20 58							21 31	21 31	21 46			22 47		23 07	00s46
	d			20 40								21 32	21 32	21 46			22 48		23 07	
Newark North Gate 7	a		20 43								21 18			21 58		22 19	22 59		23 19	00s57
	d		20 43								21 18			21 58		22 19	23 00		23 19	
Lincoln	a																			
Retford 10	d											21 52	21 52				23 16			
Doncaster 7	a		21 08	21 13		21 22					21 43	22 06	22 06	22 22		22 45	23 31		23 48	01s25
Selby	a											22 21	22 21							
Hull	a											23 06	23 10							
Pontefract Monkhill	a																			
Wakefield Kirkgate 4	a																			
Wakefield Westgate 7	a			21 31							22 06			22 40			23 53			
Leeds 10	a			21 51							22 25			23 00			00 12			02 38
Brighouse	a					22 23														
Halifax	a					22 33														
Shipley	a																			
Bradford Forster Square	a																			
Bradford Interchange	a					22 48														
Keighley	a																			
Skipton	a																			
Sheffield 7	d							20 21	20 53						21 54					
Doncaster 7	d		21 09						21 20						22 31	22 45			23 49	
York 8	a		21 31						21 45	21 50					22 53	23 10			00 39	
Scarborough	a																			
Harrogate	a																			
Leeds 10	d						20 29	21a05										22 42		
York 8	d		21 33				21a47		21 49	21 52						23 11		23 18	00 41	
Thirsk	d																	23 31		
Northallerton	d		21 52													23 40		23 49	01s11	
Darlington 7	a		22 05						22 15	22 20						23 52		00 01	01s25	
Eaglescliffe	a																			
Middlesbrough	a																			
Darlington 7	d		22 05						22 16	22 20						23 53		00 02		
Durham	d		22 23						22 34	22 38						00 11		00 20	01s43	
Chester-le-Street	d																			
Newcastle 8	a		22 41						22 50	22 57						00 45		00 51	02 18	
Hartlepool	a																			
Sunderland	a																			
Newcastle 8	d	22 00	22 42																	
Morpeth	d	22a21	22 56																	
Alnmouth for Alnwick	d		23 12																	
Berwick-upon-Tweed	d		23 38																	
Dunbar	d																			
Edinburgh 10	a		00 31																	
Edinburgh	d																			
Haymarket	d																			
Motherwell	a																			
Glasgow Central 15	a																			
Stirling	a																			
Perth	a																			
Inverness	a																			
Inverkeithing	a																			
Kirkcaldy	a																			
Leuchars 8	a																			
Dundee	a																			
Arbroath	a																			
Montrose	a																			
Stonehaven	a																			
Aberdeen	a																			

A ⊡ to Doncaster ☒ from Doncaster
◇ from Doncaster R to Doncaster

B until 23 March

C from 26 March

Table 26

Saturdays

London - Humberside, Yorkshire, North East England and Scotland

Route Diagram - see first Page of Table 26

		GR	GR	GR	TP	GR	GR	TP	NT	GR		XC	GR	NT	TP	NT	TP	NT	GR	NT		XC	NT	TP	NT
		R	R	R		R	R			R			R						R						
		1	1	1	◇1	1	1	◇1		1		◇1	1		◇1		◇1		1			◇1		◇1	
		🍴🛒	🍴🛒	🍴		🍴	🍴			🍴🛒		🛒	🍴🛒						🍴🛒			🛒		🛒	
London Kings Cross 15 ⊖	d	19p30	21p00	21p35		22p00	23p30																		
Stevenage 4	d		21p20	21p55																					
Peterborough 8	a	20p15	21p50	22p26		22p46	00s24																		
Norwich	d																								
Peterborough 8	d	20p16	21p51	22p26		22p46																			
Grantham 7	a			22p47		23p07	00s46																		
	d			22p48		23p07																			
Newark North Gate 7	a	20p43	22p19	22p59		23p19	00s57																		
	d	20p43	22p19	23p00		23p19																			
Lincoln	a																								
Retford 10	d			23p16																					
Doncaster 7	a	21p08	22p45	23p31		23p48	01s25																		
Selby	a																								
Hull	a																								
Pontefract Monkhill	a																								
Wakefield Kirkgate 4	a																								
Wakefield Westgate 7	a			23p53																					
Leeds 10	a			00 12			02 38																		
Brighouse	a																								
Halifax	a																								
Shipley	a																								
Bradford Forster Square	a																								
Bradford Interchange	a																								
Keighley	a																								
Skipton	a																								
Sheffield 7 ⛴	d																					06 49			
Doncaster 7	d	21p09	22p45			23p49							06 10									07 17			
York 8	a	21p31	23p10			00 39							06 30									07 43			
Scarborough	a																								
Harrogate	a																								
Leeds 10	d				22p42										06 35	06 38			07 10	06 36			07 41	07 50	07 13
York 8	d	21p33	23p11		23b18	00 41		05 54					06 32		07 06	07a15	07 32		07 35	07a46		07 48	08a20	08 23	08a26
Thirsk	d				23p31			06 10							07 22		07 52							08 39	
Northallerton	d	21p52	23p40		23p49	01s11		06 18					06 51		07 30		08 00							08 49	
Darlington 7	a	22p05	23p52		00 01	01s25		06 29					07 05		07 41				08 04			08 13			
Eaglescliffe	a																								
Middlesbrough	a							07 03									08 32							09 22	
Darlington 7	d	22p05	23p53		00 02								07 05	07 21	07 42				08 05			08 15			
Durham	d	22p23	00 11		00 20	01s43							07 23	07 42	07 59				08 23			08 31			
Chester-le-Street	d													07 49	08 05										
Newcastle 8 ⛴	a	22p41	00 45		00 51	02 18							07 39	08 05	08 16				08 39			08 44			
Hartlepool	a																								
Sunderland ⛴	a																								
Newcastle 8 ⛴	d	22p42							05 55	06 30		07 38	07 42					07 58	08 41						
Morpeth	d	22p56							06 17	06 43		07 51						08a19	08 56						
Alnmouth for Alnwick	d	23p12							06a34	06 57			08 08												
Berwick-upon-Tweed	d	23p38								07 21		08 24	08 32						09 31						
Dunbar	d									07 48			08 55						09 56						
Edinburgh 10	a	00 31								08 17		09 07	09 24						10 24						
Edinburgh	d											09 11							10 27						
Haymarket	d											09 16							10 32						
Motherwell	a											10 05													
Glasgow Central 15	a											10 25													
Stirling	a																								
Perth	a																								
Inverness	a																								
Inverkeithing	a																		10 47						
Kirkcaldy	a																		11 04						
Leuchars 3	a																		11 28						
Dundee	a																		11 43						
Arbroath	a																		12 00						
Montrose	a																		12 16						
Stonehaven	a																		12 39						
Aberdeen	a																		13 05						

b Previous night, arr. 2307

Table 26

Saturdays

London - Humberside, Yorkshire, North East England and Scotland

Route Diagram - see first Page of Table 26

		NT	NT	XC	GR	TP		XC	GR	TP	NT	TP	NT	TP	NT	XC		EM	GR	GR	GC	EM	XC	GR	GR
				◇1 A	R 1	◇1 B		◇1	R 1	◇1				◇1		◇1		◇	R 1	R 1	R 1		◇1	R 1	R 1
London Kings Cross 15 ⊖	d				06 15				07 00										07 03	07 30	07 48			08 00	08 03
Stevenage 4	d				06 34														07 22						
Peterborough 8	a				07 04														07 52	08 15					08 50
Norwich	d																	05 52							
Peterborough 8	d				07 05													07 27	07 53	08 15		08 33			08 50
Grantham 7	a				07 25													07 55	08 13						09 12
	d				07 25													07 58	08 13						09 12
Newark North Gate 7	a				07 37														08 25						09 24
	d				07 37														08 25						09 24
Lincoln	a																					09 59			
Retford 10	d				07 53															08 54					
Doncaster 7	a				08 08														08 49	09 09					09 49
Selby	a																								
Hull	a																								
Pontefract Monkhill	a																								
Wakefield Kirkgate 4	a																								
Wakefield Westgate 7	a																		09 08						10 07
Leeds 10	a																		09 26						10 27
Brighouse	a																								
Halifax	a																								
Shipley	a																								
Bradford Forster Square	a																								
Bradford Interchange	a																								
Keighley	a																								
Skipton	a																								
Sheffield 7	d			07 12				07 54								08 21		09a38					08 48		
Doncaster 7	d				08 08			08 25												09 11			09 20		
York 8	a				08 31			08 48	08 52											09 33	09 39		09 44	09 49	
Scarborough	a																								
Harrogate	a																								
Leeds 10	d			07 57		08 12				08 28	07 39	08 28	08 41	08 57		09 05									
York 8	d			08 27	08 35	08 42		08 50	08 53	08 58	08a59	09a03	09a21	09 26		09 33				09 36	09 44		09 49	09 52	
Thirsk	d													09 46							10 00				
Northallerton	d				08 54					09 19				09 59							10 16				
Darlington 7	a			08 56	09 07	09 11		09 16	09 21	09 30						09 58				10 03			10 15	10 20	
Eaglescliffe	a																				10 37				
Middlesbrough	a													10 30											
Darlington 7	d	08 22		08 57	09 07	09 12		09 18	09 22	09 31						10 00				10 04			10 16	10 21	
Durham	d	08 43		09 14	09 25	09 29		09 35		09 47						10 16				10 21			10 33		
Chester-le-Street	d	08 50								09 53															
Newcastle 8	a	09 01		09 26	09 41	09 46		09 47	09 52	10 07						10 31				10 37			10 45	10 50	
Hartlepool	a																				11 07				
Sunderland	a																				11 40				
Newcastle 8	d		09 15	09 35	09 44				09 54						10 15	10 36				10 39				10 54	
Morpeth	d		09a36												10a35										
Alnmouth for Alnwick	d			09 59																11 05					
Berwick-upon-Tweed	d			10 20					10 39															11 39	
Dunbar	d															11 38									
Edinburgh 10	a			11 05	11 13				11 31							12 07				12 15				12 31	
Edinburgh	d			11 11																					
Haymarket	d			11 16																					
Motherwell	a			11 52																					
Glasgow Central 15	a			12 13																					
Stirling	a																								
Perth	a																								
Inverness	a																								
Inverkeithing	a																								
Kirkcaldy	a																								
Leuchars 3	a																								
Dundee	a																								
Arbroath	a																								
Montrose	a																								
Stonehaven	a																								
Aberdeen	a																								

A to Edinburgh

B to York

Table 26

Saturdays

London - Humberside, Yorkshire, North East England and Scotland

Route Diagram - see first Page of Table 26

		EM		TP	NT	TP	NT	XC	GR	NT	XC	GR		TP	NT	TP	NT	XC	EM	EM	GR	GR		HT	NT
									R			R									R	R			
		◇1		◇1		◇1		◇1	1		◇1	1		◇1		◇1		◇1	◇		1	1		◇1	
		🍴		🛒		🛒		🛒	🍴🛒		🛒	🍴🛒		🛒		🛒		🛒			🍴🛒	🍴🛒		☒	
London Kings Cross 15 ⊖	d								08 30			09 00									09 03	09 30		09 48	
Stevenage 4	d																				09 22				
Peterborough 8	a								09 15												09 52	10 15			
Norwich	d																		07 57						
Peterborough 8	d								09 15										09 30	09 33	09 53	10 15			
Grantham 7	a																		09 58		10 14			10 48	
	d																		09 58		10 14			10 49	
Newark North Gate 7	a								09 43												10 26				
	d								09 43												10 26				
Lincoln	a																			10 59					
Retford 10	d																					10 53		11 10	
Doncaster 7	a								10 08												10 50	11 08		11 24	
Selby	a																							11 40	
Hull	a																							12 20	
Pontefract Monkhill	a																								
Wakefield Kirkgate 4	a																								
Wakefield Westgate 7	a																				11 07				
Leeds 10	a																				11 27				
Brighouse	a																								
Halifax	a																								
Shipley	a																								
Bradford Forster Square	a																								
Bradford Interchange	a																								
Keighley	a																								
Skipton	a																								
Sheffield 7 ⛴	d	09 21						09 21			09 47							10 21	11a38						
Doncaster 7	d	09 55							10 09		10 19											11 09			
York 8	a	10 16							10 33		10 40	10 52										11 32			
Scarborough	a																								
Harrogate	a																								
Leeds 10	d			09 28	09 41	09 57		10 05		09 29				10 28	10 41	10 57		11 05							10 29
York 8	d			09 58	10a21	10 26		10 32	10 35	10a45	10 48	10 53		10 58	11a18	11 26		11 32				11 35			11a45
Thirsk	d					10 46										11 46									
Northallerton	d			10 19		10 59			10 54					11 19		11 59									
Darlington 7	a			10 30				10 58	11 07		11 13	11 21		11 30				11 57				12 03			
Eaglescliffe	a																								
Middlesbrough	a					11 30										12 30									
Darlington 7	d			10 31				11 00	11 07		11 15	11 22		11 31				12 00				12 04			
Durham	d			10 47				11 16	11 25		11 31			11 47				12 16				12 21			
Chester-le-Street	d													11 53											
Newcastle 8 ⛴	a			11 05				11 29	11 41		11 46	11 51		12 06				12 31				12 37			
Hartlepool	a																								
Sunderland ⛴	a																								
Newcastle 8 ⛴	d						11 15	11 36	11 44			11 54					12 15	12 36				12 40			
Morpeth	d						11a36										12a35								
Alnmouth for Alnwick	d																					13 06			
Berwick-upon-Tweed	d							12 20				12 39													
Dunbar	d																	13 38							
Edinburgh 10	a							13 04	13 13			13 31						14 07				14 15			
Edinburgh	d							13 11																	
Haymarket	d							13 16																	
Motherwell	a							13 52																	
Glasgow Central 15	a							14 13																	
Stirling	a																								
Perth	a																								
Inverness	a																								
Inverkeithing	a																								
Kirkcaldy	a																								
Leuchars 3	a																								
Dundee	a																								
Arbroath	a																								
Montrose	a																								
Stonehaven	a																								
Aberdeen	a																								

London - Humberside, Yorkshire, North East England and Scotland

Route Diagram - see first Page of Table 26

		XC	GR	TP	NT	TP	NT	XC	EM	GR	GR	GC	XC	EM	GR	EM	GR	TP	GC	NT	TP	NT	XC
			■R							■R	■R	■R			■R		■R		■R				
		◇■1	■1	◇■1		◇■1		◇■1	◇	■1	■1	■1	◇■1	◇	■1		■1	◇■1	■1		◇■1		◇■1
			A					B				C											
		☕	🍴☕			☕		☕		🍴☕	🍴☕	🍴	☕		🍴☕		🍴☕	☕	🍴		☕		☕
London Kings Cross 15 ⊖	d		10 00							10 03	10 30	10 48			11 00		11 03		11 20				
Stevenage 4	d																11 22						
Peterborough 8	a									10 50	11 15						11 52						
Norwich	d								08 57					09 57									
Peterborough 8	d								10 26	10 51	11 15			11 25		11 48	11 53						
Grantham 7	a								10 57	11 10				11 57			12 13						
	d								10 58	11 10				11 58			12 13						
Newark North Gate 7	a									11 23	11 43						12 25						
	d									11 23	11 43						12 25						
Lincoln	a															13 14							
Retford 10	d																						
Doncaster 7	a									11 50	12 08	12 18					12 50						
Selby	a																						
Hull	a																						
Pontefract Monkhill	a																						
Wakefield Kirkgate 4	a											12 42											
Wakefield Westgate 7	a									12 07							13 07						
Leeds 10	a									12 27							13 27						
Brighouse	a											13 05											
Halifax	a											13 21											
Shipley	a																						
Bradford Forster Square	a																						
Bradford Interchange	a											13 38											
Keighley	a																						
Skipton	a																						
Sheffield 7 ⛴	d	10 47						11 21	12a38				11 47	13a38									12 21
Doncaster 7	d	11 19									12 08		12 17										
York 8	a	11 40	11 51								12 33		12 39		12 48				13 14				
Scarborough	a																						
Harrogate	a																						
Leeds 10	d			11 28	11 41	11 57		12 05										12 28		12 41	12 57		13 05
York 8	d	11 48	11 53	11 58	12a21	12 26		12 32			12 34		12 48		12 53			12 58	13 16	13a19	13 26		13 32
Thirsk	d					12 46													13 33		13 46		
Northallerton	d			12 19		12 59					12 54							13 19	13 40		13 59		
Darlington 7	a	12 13	12 21	12 30				12 58			13 06		13 13		13 20			13 30					13 57
Eaglescliffe	a																		13 58				
Middlesbrough	a					13 30															14 30		
Darlington 7	d	12 15	12 22	12 31				13 00			13 07		13 15		13 21			13 31					13 59
Durham	d	12 31		12 47				13 16			13 24		13 31					13 47					14 16
Chester-le-Street	d																	13 53					
Newcastle 8 ⛴	a	12 45	12 51	13 03				13 29			13 40		13 44		13 50			14 06					14 28
Hartlepool	a																		14 20				
Sunderland ⛴	a																		14 50				
Newcastle 8 ⛴	d		12 54				13 15	13 35			13 44				13 54							14 15	14 35
Morpeth	d						13a37															14a37	14 48
Alnmouth for Alnwick	d							14 00															
Berwick-upon-Tweed	d		13 40					14 20							14 39								
Dunbar	d																						15 40
Edinburgh 10	a		14 24					15 07			15 15				15 31								16 04
Edinburgh	d		14 27					15 11															
Haymarket	d		14 32					15 16															
Motherwell	a							15 52															
Glasgow Central 15	a							16 23															
Stirling	a																						
Perth	a																						
Inverness	a																						
Inverkeithing	a		14 46																				
Kirkcaldy	a		15 03																				
Leuchars 3	a		15 28																				
Dundee	a		15 46																				
Arbroath	a		16 04																				
Montrose	a		16 20																				
Stonehaven	a		16 43																				
Aberdeen	a		17 09																				

A The Northern Lights
B ☕ to Edinburgh
C ■1 to Doncaster 🍴 to Doncaster ■R to Doncaster

Table 26

Saturdays

London - Humberside, Yorkshire, North East England and Scotland

Route Diagram - see first Page of Table 26

		GR	GR	HT	XC	NT	GR	TP	NT	TP	NT	XC	EM	EM	GR	GR	NT	XC	EM	GR	GR	TP
		R 1	R 1	◇1	◇1		R 1	◇1		◇1		◇1	◇		R 1	R 1		◇1	◇	R 1	R 1	◇1
							A					B										
London Kings Cross 15 ⊖	d	11 30	11 35	11 48			12 00								12 03	12 30				13 00	13 03	
Stevenage 4	d																				13 22	
Peterborough 8	a	12 15	12 21												12 51	13 15					13 52	
Norwich	d												10 57						11 57			
Peterborough 8	d	12 15	12 22										12 25	12 41	12 51	13 15			13 28		13 53	
Grantham 7	a			12 48									12 58		13 14				13 56	14 00	14 13	
	d			12 49									12 58		13 15				13 58	14 00	14 13	
Newark North Gate 7	a														13 26	13 43					14 25	
	d														13 27	13 43					14 25	
Lincoln	a													14 06								
Retford 10	d	12 53		13 10																		
Doncaster 7	a	13 09	13 12	13 24											13 52	14 09					14 50	
Selby	a			13 40																		
Hull	a			14 22																		
Pontefract Monkhill	a																					
Wakefield Kirkgate 4	a																					
Wakefield Westgate 7	a		13 30												14 11						15 07	
Leeds 10	a		13 50												14 31						15 27	
Brighouse	a																					
Halifax	a																					
Shipley	a																					
Bradford Forster Square	a																					
Bradford Interchange	a																					
Keighley	a																					
Skipton	a																					
Sheffield 7	d				12 47							13 21	14a38					13 47	15a38			
Doncaster 7	d	13 10			13 19											14 10		14 19				
York 8	a	13 33			13 40		13 52									14 33		14 40		14 51		
Scarborough	a																					
Harrogate	a																					
Leeds 10	d					12 29		13 28	13 42	13 57		14 05					13 29					14 28
York 8	d	13 35			13 43	13a48	13 53	13 58	14a22	14 26		14 32				14 35	14a44	14 48		14 53		14 58
Thirsk	d									14 46												
Northallerton	d							14 19		14 59						14 54						15 19
Darlington 7	a	14 03			14 12		14 21	14 30				14 58				15 07		15 13		15 20		15 30
Eaglescliffe	a																					
Middlesbrough	a									15 30												
Darlington 7	d	14 04			14 13		14 22	14 31				15 00				15 07		15 15		15 21		15 31
Durham	d	14 21			14 30			14 47				15 16				15 25		15 31				15 47
Chester-le-Street	d																					15 53
Newcastle 8	a	14 38			14 42		14 51	15 05				15 29				15 41		15 45		15 50		16 09
Hartlepool	a																					
Sunderland	a																					
Newcastle 8	d	14 40					14 53				15 15	15 34				15 44				15 54		
Morpeth	d										15a35											
Alnmouth for Alnwick	d	15 06										15 59										
Berwick-upon-Tweed	d						15 40					16 19								16 39		
Dunbar	d																					
Edinburgh 10	a	16 15					16 26					17 07				17 15				17 31		
Edinburgh	d						16 32					17 11										
Haymarket	d						16 38					17 16										
Motherwell	a											17 52										
Glasgow Central 15	a											18 11										
Stirling	a						17 18															
Perth	a						17 59															
Inverness	a						20 11															
Inverkeithing	a																					
Kirkcaldy	a																					
Leuchars 3	a																					
Dundee	a																					
Arbroath	a																					
Montrose	a																					
Stonehaven	a																					
Aberdeen	a																					

A The Highland Chieftain

B to Edinburgh

Table 26

Saturdays

London - Humberside, Yorkshire, North East England and Scotland

Route Diagram - see first Page of Table 26

		NT	TP	NT	XC	GR	XC	GR	NT	TP		NT	NT	XC	EM	GR	EM	GR	HT	NT		XC	GR	TP	NT
						R		R								R		R					R		
			◇1		◇1	1	◇1	1		◇1				◇1	◇	1		1	◇1			◇1	1	◇1	
					A									A											
			trolley		trolley	restaurant	trolley	restaurant						trolley		restaurant		restaurant	⊠			trolley	restaurant	trolley	
London Kings Cross 15 ⊖	d					13 30		14 00								14 03		14 30	14 48				15 00		
Stevenage 4	d																								
Peterborough 8	a					14 15										14 50		15 15							
Norwich	d														12 57										
Peterborough 8	d					14 15									14 26	14 50	15 11	15 15							
Grantham 7	a														14 57	15 09			15 48						
	d														14 58	15 09			15 49						
Newark North Gate 7	a															15 22		15 43							
	d															15 22		15 43							
Lincoln	a																16 48								
Retford 10	d					14 54													16 10						
Doncaster 7	a					15 11										15 47		16 08	16 24						
Selby	a																		16 41						
Hull	a																		17 27						
Pontefract Monkhill	a																								
Wakefield Kirkgate 4	a																								
Wakefield Westgate 7	a															16 07									
Leeds 10	a															16 27									
Brighouse	a																								
Halifax	a																								
Shipley	a																								
Bradford Forster Square	a																								
Bradford Interchange	a																								
Keighley	a																								
Skipton	a																								
Sheffield 7 🚋	d				14 21		14 47							15 21	16a38							15 47			
Doncaster 7	d					15 12	15 19											16 08				16 19			
York 8	a					15 33	15 40	15 49										16 32				16 41	16 52		
Scarborough	a																								
Harrogate	a																								
Leeds 10	d	14 41	14 57		15 05				15 41	15 57				16 05						15 29				16 28	16 41
York 8	d	15a17	15 26		15 32	15 36	15 48	15 51	16a21	16 26				16 32				16 35		16a44		16 48	16 53	16 58	17a21
Thirsk	d		15 46							16 46														17 15	
Northallerton	d		15 59							16 59								16 54						17 23	
Darlington 7	a				15 58	16 03	16 13	16 19						16 58				17 07				17 13	17 21	17 34	
Eaglescliffe	a																								
Middlesbrough	a		16 30							17 30															
Darlington 7	d				16 00	16 04	16 15	16 20						17 00				17 07				17 15	17 22	17 35	
Durham	d				16 16	16 21	16 31							17 16				17 25				17 31		17 52	
Chester-le-Street	d																							17 58	
Newcastle 8 🚋	a				16 29	16 39	16 45	16 49						17 29				17 41				17 45	17 51	18 10	
Hartlepool	a																								
Sunderland 🚋	a																								
Newcastle 8 🚋	d			16 15	16 35	16 44		16 52				17 00	17 22	17 37				17 44					17 54		
Morpeth	d			16a36								17 22	17a42												
Alnmouth for Alnwick	d				17 00							17a45		18 01											
Berwick-upon-Tweed	d							17 40						18 21									18 40		
Dunbar	d				17 39																				
Edinburgh 10	a				18 05	18 13		18 27						19 08				19 15					19 31		
Edinburgh	d				18 11			18 30						19 11											
Haymarket	d				18 15			18 35						19 16											
Motherwell	a													19 52											
Glasgow Central 15	a													20 11											
Stirling	a																								
Perth	a																								
Inverness	a																								
Inverkeithing	a				18 28			18 54																	
Kirkcaldy	a				18 46			19 11																	
Leuchars 3	a				19 17			19 38																	
Dundee	a				19 32			19 52																	
Arbroath	a				19 49			20 10																	
Montrose	a				20 03			20 26																	
Stonehaven	a				20 23			20 49																	
Aberdeen	a				20 43			21 15																	

A trolley to Edinburgh

London - Humberside, Yorkshire, North East England and Scotland

Route Diagram - see first Page of Table 26

		TP	NT	XC	EM	GR		GR	GC	EM	XC	NT	GR	NT	TP	XC		EM	GR	GR	GC	GR	TP	XC	NT
						R		R	R				R						R	R	R	R			
		◇1		◇1	◇	1		1	1		◇1		1		◇1	◇1		◇	1	1	1	1	◇1	◇1	
				A					B							A									
		[trolley]		[trolley]		[restaurant][trolley]		[restaurant]	[restaurant]		[trolley]		[restaurant][trolley]			[trolley]			[restaurant][trolley]	[restaurant][trolley]	[restaurant]	[restaurant][trolley]		[trolley]	
London Kings Cross 15 ⊖	d					15 03		15 30	15 48				16 00						16 03	16 30	16 48	17 00			
Stevenage 4	d					15 22																			
Peterborough 8	a					15 52		16 15											16 50	17 15					
Norwich	d				13 57													14 57							
Peterborough 8	d				15 25	15 53		16 15		16 25								16 27	16 51	17 15					
Grantham 7	a				15 57	16 13												16 55	17 11						
	d				15 58	16 13												16 56	17 11						
Newark North Gate 7	a					16 25													17 23	17 43					
	d					16 25													17 23	17 43					
Lincoln	a									17 51															
Retford 10	d							16 53																	
Doncaster 7	a					16 50		17 08	17 20										17 49	18 08					
Selby	a																								
Hull	a																								
Pontefract Monkhill	a																								
Wakefield Kirkgate 4	a								17 44																
Wakefield Westgate 7	a					17 07													18 07						
Leeds 10	a					17 27													18 27						
Brighouse	a								18 06																
Halifax	a								18 23																
Shipley	a																								
Bradford Forster Square	a																								
Bradford Interchange	a								18 39																
Keighley	a																								
Skipton	a																								
Sheffield 7 [tram]	d			16 21	17a34						16 47					17 21		18a39						17 47	
Doncaster 7	d							17 09			17 19									18 08					
York 8	a							17 33			17 37		17 49							18 32	18 39	18 50			
Scarborough	a																								
Harrogate	a																								
Leeds 10	d	16 57		17 05								16 29		17 41	17 57	18 06							18 28	18 35	18 41
York 8	d	17 26		17 31				17 35			17 47	17a52	17 53	18a24	18 26	18 32				18 35	18 43	18 53	18 58	19 05	19a21
Thirsk	d	17 46													18 46						18 59				
Northallerton	d	17 58													18 59					18 55	19 10		19 19		
Darlington 7	a			17 56				18 02			18 12		18 21			18 59				19 07		19 23	19 30	19 35	
Eaglescliffe	a																				19 28				
Middlesbrough	a	18 30													19 31										
Darlington 7	d			17 58				18 03			18 14		18 22			19 00				19 08		19 24	19 31	19 37	
Durham	d			18 14				18 20			18 30					19 18				19 25			19 47	19 53	
Chester-le-Street	d																						19 53		
Newcastle 8 [tram]	a			18 29				18 39			18 44		18 51			19 31				19 41		19 53	20 07	20 08	
Hartlepool	a																				19 47				
Sunderland [tram]	a																				20 21				
Newcastle 8 [tram]	d		18 19	18 36				18 41					18 53			19 37				19 45		19 57			
Morpeth	d		18a40																	20 00					
Alnmouth for Alnwick	d							19 08								20 04									
Berwick-upon-Tweed	d			19 18									19 39			20 25						20 43			
Dunbar	d			19 41																					
Edinburgh 10	a			20 06				20 16					20 27			21 09				21 19		21 33			
Edinburgh	d			20 14												21 13									
Haymarket	d			20 18												21 18									
Motherwell	a															22 00									
Glasgow Central 15	a															22 22									
Stirling	a																								
Perth	a																								
Inverness	a																								
Inverkeithing	a			20 33																					
Kirkcaldy	a			20 50																					
Leuchars 3	a			21 25																					
Dundee	a			21 43																					
Arbroath	a																								
Montrose	a																								
Stonehaven	a																								
Aberdeen	a																								

A [trolley] to Edinburgh

B 1 to Doncaster [restaurant] to Doncaster R to Doncaster

London - Humberside, Yorkshire, North East England and Scotland

Route Diagram - see first Page of Table 26

		TP		NT	XC	EM	GR	GR	GR	GR	HT	XC		NT	GR	TP	XC	EM	GR	GR	GR	GR		EM	XC
		◇1			◇1	◇	R 1	R 1	R 1	R 1	◇1	◇1			R 1	◇1	◇1	◇	R 1	R 1	R 1	R 1		◇	◇1
London Kings Cross 15 ⊖	d						17 03	17 10	17 30	17 35	17 48				18 00				18 03	18 08	18 30	18 35			
Stevenage 4	d						17 22													18 28					
Peterborough 8	a						17 52	17 58	18 16	18 22									18 51	18 58	19 15	19 21			
Norwich	d					15 52												16 57						17 54	
Peterborough 8	d					17 27	17 53	17 59	18 16	18 22								18 26	18 52	18 59	19 15	19 22		19 30	
Grantham 7	a					17 58	18 13	18 20			18 48							18 55		19 19				19 59	
	d					18 03	18 13	18 20			18 49							18 58		19 20					
Newark North Gate 7	a						18 25		18 45										19 18	19 33	19 43				
	d						18 25		18 45										19 18	19 33	19 43				
Lincoln	a																			20 03					
Retford 10	d										19 12								19 34						
Doncaster 7	a						18 49	18 53	19 09	19 14	19 26								19 49		20 08	20 12			
Selby	a							19 09			19 42														
Hull	a							19 54			20 24														
Pontefract Monkhill	a																								
Wakefield Kirkgate 4	a																								
Wakefield Westgate 7	a						19 07			19 32									20 07			20 32			
Leeds 10	a						19 26			19 48									20 26			20 47			
Brighouse	a																								
Halifax	a																								
Shipley	a																								
Bradford Forster Square	a																								
Bradford Interchange	a																								
Keighley	a																					21s13			
Skipton	a																					21 29			
Sheffield 7	d				18 21	19a39						18 47					19 22	20a27							19 54
Doncaster 7	d								19 10			19 18									20 08				20 19
York 8	a								19 33			19 39			19 53						20 32				20 40
Scarborough	a																								
Harrogate	a									20 28															
Leeds 10	d	18 57			19 05									18 29		19 57	20 08								
York 8	d	19 26			19 32				19 36			19 44		19a45	19 55	20 29	20 33				20 35				20 48
Thirsk	d	19 46														20 49									
Northallerton	d	19 57														20 59					20 55				
Darlington 7	a				19 57				20 04			20 11			20 22		20 58				21 07				21 13
Eaglescliffe	a																								
Middlesbrough	a	20 30														21 30									
Darlington 7	d				19 59				20 04			20 13			20 23		21 00				21 08				21 15
Durham	d				20 15				20 22			20 30					21 17				21 25				21 31
Chester-le-Street	d																								
Newcastle 8	a				20 28				20 41			20 42			20 52		21 29				21 44				21 44
Hartlepool	a																								
Sunderland	a																								
Newcastle 8	d			20 20	20 38										20 54		21 38								
Morpeth	d			20a41	20 53										21 09										
Alnmouth for Alnwick	d														21 25		22 02								
Berwick-upon-Tweed	d				21 24										21 49										
Dunbar	d				21 50										22 13										
Edinburgh 10	a				22 14										22 41		23 10								
Edinburgh	d																								
Haymarket	d																								
Motherwell	a																								
Glasgow Central 15	a																								
Stirling	a																								
Perth	a																								
Inverness	a																								
Inverkeithing	a																								
Kirkcaldy	a																								
Leuchars 3	a																								
Dundee	a																								
Arbroath	a																								
Montrose	a																								
Stonehaven	a																								
Aberdeen	a																								

Table 26

Saturdays

London - Humberside, Yorkshire, North East England and Scotland

Route Diagram - see first Page of Table 26

		GR	GC	GC	GR	HT	EM	TP		NT	XC	XC	GR	GR	EM		GR	XC		EM	GR	XC	EM	XC	
		R	R	R	R								R	R			R				R				
		1	1	1	1	◇1	◇	◇1			◇1	◇1	1	1			1	◇1		◇1	1	◇1	◇1	◇1	
				A						B															
		bar trolley	bar	bar	bar trolley	⊠						trolley	bar trolley	bar trolley			bar trolley			bar	bar trolley		bar		
London Kings Cross 15 ⊖	d	19 00	19 07	19 20	19 30	19 48							20 00	20 30			21 00				22 00				
Stevenage 4	d				19 49																				
Peterborough 8	a				20 19								20 46	21 15			21 45				22 46				
Norwich	d						18 57																		
Peterborough 8	d				20 20		20 27						20 47	21 15	21 27		21 46				22 47				
Grantham 7	a				20 40	20 49	20 58							21 35	22 00						23 06				
	d				20 40	20 50								21 35							23 06				
Newark North Gate 7	a				20 52								21 14	21 47							23 18				
	d				20 52								21 14	21 47							23 18				
Lincoln	a																								
Retford 10	d					21 14								22 02							23 33				
Doncaster 7	a			20 51	21 16	21 28							21 39	22 17							23 48				
Selby	a					21 44																			
Hull	a					22 26																			
Pontefract Monkhill	a			21 15																					
Wakefield Kirkgate 4	a																								
Wakefield Westgate 7	a				21 34									22 35							00 05				
Leeds 10	a				21 50									22 55							00 25				
Brighouse	a			21 57																					
Halifax	a			22 08																					
Shipley	a				22s11																				
Bradford Forster Square	a				22 24																				
Bradford Interchange	a			22 24																					
Keighley	a																								
Skipton	a																								
Sheffield 7	d										20 53	20 24						21 21		21 25		22 09	22 19	22 27	
Doncaster 7	d										21 23		21 40									22 34		22 53	
York 8	a	20 49	20 54								21 44		22 02				22 51					22 57			
Scarborough	a																								
Harrogate	a																								
Leeds 10	d							20 45		20§48		21b15						22a02		22a19			23a04	23a27	
York 8	d	20 52	20 58					21 14		21a30	21 48	21a57	22 05				22 52								
Thirsk	d		21 15					21 31																	
Northallerton	d		21 22					21 39									23 13								
Darlington 7	a	21 19						21 51			22 13		22 33				23 26								
Eaglescliffe	a		21 40																						
Middlesbrough	a																								
Darlington 7	d	21 20						21 52			22 15		22 34				23 26								
Durham	d							22 08			22 31		22 52				23 44								
Chester-le-Street	d							22 14																	
Newcastle 8	a	21 52						22 28			22 47		23 11				00 04								
Hartlepool	a		21 59																						
Sunderland	a		22 36																						
Newcastle 8	d																								
Morpeth	d																								
Alnmouth for Alnwick	d																								
Berwick-upon-Tweed	d																								
Dunbar	d																								
Edinburgh 10	a																								
Edinburgh	d																								
Haymarket	d																								
Motherwell	a																								
Glasgow Central 15	a																								
Stirling	a																								
Perth	a																								
Inverness	a																								
Inverkeithing	a																								
Kirkcaldy	a																								
Leuchars 8	a																								
Dundee	a																								
Arbroath	a																								
Montrose	a																								
Stonehaven	a																								
Aberdeen	a																								

A 1 to Doncaster bar to Doncaster R to Doncaster

B from 31 March

Table 26

Sundays

until 12 February

London - Humberside, Yorkshire, North East England and Scotland

Route Diagram - see first Page of Table 26

		GR	GR	TP	XC	GR	TP	XC	GR	NT	GR	TP	XC	TP	GR	GR	TP	XC	GR	GC		GR	GR	TP	XC
		R	R			R			R		R				R	R			R	R		R	R		
		1	1	◇1	◇1	1	◇1	◇1	1		1	◇1	◇1	◇1	1	1	◇1	◇1	1	1		1	1	◇1	◇1
		A	A					B					B									C			B
London Kings Cross 15 ⊖	d	21p00	22p00												09 00	09 03			09 30	09 48		10 00	10 03		
Stevenage 4	d															09 22									
Peterborough 8	a	21p45	22p46													09 52			10 15				10 50		
Norwich	d																								
Peterborough 8	d	21p46	22p47													09 53			10 15				10 50		
Grantham 7	a		23p06													10 13							11 10		
	d		23p06													10 13							11 10		
Newark North Gate 7	a		23p18													10 25							11 22		
	d		23p18													10 25							11 22		
Lincoln	a																								
Retford 10	d		23p33																10 54						
Doncaster 7	a		23p48													10 50			11 09				11 47		
Selby	a																								
Hull	a																								
Pontefract Monkhill	a																								
Wakefield Kirkgate 4	a																								
Wakefield Westgate 7	a		00 05													11 08							12 06		
Leeds 10	a		00 25													11 30							12 29		
Brighouse	a																								
Halifax	a																								
Shipley	a																								
Bradford Forster Square	a																								
Bradford Interchange	a																								
Keighley	a																								
Skipton	a																								
Sheffield 7	d												09 21					10 21							11 21
Doncaster 7	d										09 37								11 09						
York 8	a	22p51									09 58				10 46				11 33	11 36		11 49			
Scarborough	a																								
Harrogate	a																								
Leeds 10	d			07 40			08 40	09 08				09 40	10 08				10 40	11 08						11 40	12 08
York 8	d	22p52		08 21		09 00	09 10	09 37			10 00	10 13	10 33	10 42	10 53		11 10	11 32	11 35	11 41		11 51		12 08	12 32
Thirsk	d			08 37										10 59						11 58					
Northallerton	d	23p13		08 45		09 18	09 31					10 35		11 07			11 31			12 06				12 29	
Darlington 7	a	23p26		08 56		09 31	09 42	10 02			10 27	10 46	10 58		11 20		11 42	11 57	12 02			12 19		12 40	12 57
Eaglescliffe	a																			12 23					
Middlesbrough	a			09 25										11 39											
Darlington 7	d	23p26				09 31	09 43	10 04		10 20	10 28	10 47	11 00		11 21		11 43	11 59	12 03			12 20		12 41	12 59
Durham	d	23p44				09 49	09 59	10 21			10 45	11 08	11 17				11 59	12 16	12 20					12 57	13 15
Chester-le-Street	d																								
Newcastle 8	a	00 04				10 05	10 18	10 34			11 01	11 24	11 29		11 50		12 15	12 29	12 36			12 49		13 12	13 32
Hartlepool	a									10 59										12 50					
Sunderland	a									11 26										13 21					
Newcastle 8	d				09 45	10 13		10 38		11a48	11 03		11 38		11 52			12 38	12 44			12 54			13 36
Morpeth	d				09 58	10 29																			
Alnmouth for Alnwick	d				10 12	10 45													13 10						14 00
Berwick-upon-Tweed	d					11 09		11 20			11 48		12 20		12 37							13 41			14 21
Dunbar	d					11 33												13 40	13 54						
Edinburgh 10	a				11 13	12 01		12 03			12 35		13 03		13 24			14 07	14 22			14 24			15 05
Edinburgh	d							12 17	09 10				13 10									14 33			15 10
Haymarket	d							12 21	09 14				13 15									14 38			15 15
Motherwell	a							12 55					13 50												15 51
Glasgow Central 15	a							13 12					14 14												16 13
Stirling	a																								
Perth	a																								
Inverness	a																								
Inverkeithing	a								09 31													14 56			
Kirkcaldy	a								09 48													15 13			
Leuchars 3	a								10 13													15 37			
Dundee	a								10 27													15 52			
Arbroath	a								10 45													16 09			
Montrose	a								11 01													16 25			
Stonehaven	a								11 24													16 48			
Aberdeen	a								11 52													17 14			

A not 11 December

B to Edinburgh

C The Northern Lights

Table 26

Sundays
until 12 February

London - Humberside, Yorkshire, North East England and Scotland

Route Diagram - see first Page of Table 26

		EM	GR	HT	TP	GR	GR	TP	XC	GR	EM	GC	GR	GR	TP	GR	XC	GR	HT	XC	TP	GR	GR
			R			R	R			R		R	R	R		R		R				R	R
		◇1	1	◇1	◇1	1	1	◇1	◇1	1	◇	1	1	1	◇1	1	◇1	1	◇1	◇1	◇1	1	1
												A	B				C						
		☕	☕🍴	⊠		☕🍴	☕🍴		🍴	☕🍴		☕	☕🍴	☕🍴		☕🍴	🍴	☕🍴	⊠	🍴		☕🍴	☕🍴
London Kings Cross 15 ⊖	d		10 30	10 45		11 00	11 03			11 30		11 48	12 00	12 03		12 20		12 30	12 45			13 00	13 03
Stevenage 4	d			11u05			11 22												13u05				13 22
Peterborough 8	a		11 15				11 52			12 15				12 50		13 08		13 15					13 52
Norwich	d										10 47												
Peterborough 8	d		11 15				11 53			12 15	12 18			12 50		13 08		13 15					13 53
Grantham 7	a			11 48			12 13				12 53			13 10					13 48				14 13
	d			11 49			12 13				12 54			13 10					13 49				14 13
Newark North Gate 7	a		11 43				12 25							13 22				13 43					14 25
	d		11 43				12 25							13 22				13 43					14 25
Lincoln	a																						
Retford 10	d			12 10						12 54									14 10				
Doncaster 7	a		12 08	12 23			12 50			13 09		13 16		13 47		13 56		14 09	14 23				14 50
Selby	a			12 43															14 39				
Hull	a			13 25															15 21				
Pontefract Monkhill	a																						
Wakefield Kirkgate 4	a											13 45											
Wakefield Westgate 7	a						13 08							14 06									15 08
Leeds 10	a						13 30							14 29									15 30
Brighouse	a											14 08											
Halifax	a											14 19											
Shipley	a																						
Bradford Forster Square	a																						
Bradford Interchange	a											14 37											
Keighley	a																						
Skipton	a																						
Sheffield 7 🚋	d	11 31							12 21		14a35						13 21			13 51			
Doncaster 7	d	11 53	12 08							13 09						13 57		14 09		14 15			
York 8	a	12 15	12 31			12 46				13 33			13 49			14 19		14 32		14 40		14 50	
Scarborough	a																						
Harrogate	a																						
Leeds 10	d				12 12			12 40	13 08						13 40		14 08				14 12		
York 8	d		12 35		12 42	12 53		13 10	13 32	13 35			13 51		14 10	14 22	14 32	14 35		14 46	14 50	14 52	
Thirsk	d				13 00																15 13		
Northallerton	d		12 55		13 08			13 31							14 31			14 54			15 21		
Darlington 7	a		13 07			13 21		13 42	13 57	14 02			14 19		14 42	14 49	14 57	15 07		15 13		15 19	
Eaglescliffe	a																						
Middlesbrough	a				13 40																15 52		
Darlington 7	d		13 08			13 22		13 43	13 59	14 03			14 19		14 43	14 50	14 59	15 07		15 14		15 20	
Durham	d		13 25					13 59	14 15	14 20					14 59	15 07	15 15	15 25		15 31			
Chester-le-Street	d							14 05															
Newcastle 8 🚋	a		13 41			13 51		14 17	14 28	14 36			14 49		15 15	15 26	15 28	15 41		15 44		15 49	
Hartlepool	a																						
Sunderland 🚋	a																						
Newcastle 8 🚋	d		13 45			13 54			14 36	14 42			14 52				15 37	15 45				15 54	
Morpeth	d								14 49														
Alnmouth for Alnwick	d									15 08							16 02						
Berwick-upon-Tweed	d					14 39							15 39				16 22					16 39	
Dunbar	d								15 41														
Edinburgh 10	a		15 18			15 26			16 06	16 16			16 22				17 06	17 15				17 27	
Edinburgh	d												16 30				17 11						
Haymarket	d												16 35				17 15						
Motherwell	a																17 52						
Glasgow Central 15	a																18 12						
Stirling	a												17 17										
Perth	a												17 53										
Inverness	a												20 19										
Inverkeithing	a																						
Kirkcaldy	a																						
Leuchars 3	a																						
Dundee	a																						
Arbroath	a																						
Montrose	a																						
Stonehaven	a																						
Aberdeen	a																						

A 1 to Doncaster
B The Highland Chieftain
C 🍴 to Edinburgh

Table 26

Sundays

until 12 February

London - Humberside, Yorkshire, North East England and Scotland

Route Diagram - see first Page of Table 26

		TP		XC	GR	NT	GC	XC	GR	GR	TP	XC		GR	HT	TP	XC	GR	TP	XC	EM	GR		GR	GC
					[R]		[R]		[R]	[R]				[R]				[R]				[R]		[R]	[R]
		◇1		◇1	1		1	◇1	1	1	◇1	◇1		1	◇1	◇1	◇1	1	◇1	◇1	◇	1		1	1
				A								A													B
				[trolley]	[restaurant/trolley]		[restaurant]	[trolley]	[restaurant/trolley]	[restaurant/trolley]		[trolley]		[restaurant/trolley]	[⊠]		[trolley]	[restaurant/trolley]		[trolley]		[restaurant/trolley]		[restaurant/trolley]	[restaurant]
London Kings Cross 15 ⊖	d				13 30		13 48		14 00	14 03				14 30	14 45			15 00				15 03		15 30	15 48
Stevenage 4	d														15u05							15 22			
Peterborough 8	a				14 15					14 51				15 16								15 52		16 16	
Norwich	d																				13 49				
Peterborough 8	d				14 15					14 52				15 16							15 26	15 53		16 16	
Grantham 7	a									15 12					15 48						15 56	16 13		16 37	
	d									15 12					15 49						15 59	16 13		16 37	
Newark North Gate 7	a									15 24				15 45								16 25			
	d									15 24				15 45								16 25			
Lincoln	a																								
Retford 10	d				14 54										16 10							16 40			
Doncaster 7	a				15 09					15 49				16 10	16 23							16 57		17 10	17 19
Selby	a														16 44										
Hull	a														17 26										
Pontefract Monkhill	a																								
Wakefield Kirkgate 4	a																								17 47
Wakefield Westgate 7	a									16 08												17 17			
Leeds 10	a									16 29												17 39			
Brighouse	a																								18 10
Halifax	a																								18 20
Shipley	a																								
Bradford Forster Square	a																								
Bradford Interchange	a																								18 37
Keighley	a																								
Skipton	a																								
Sheffield 7 ⛴	d			14 21				14 51				15 21					15 51			16 21	17a40				
Doncaster 7	d				15 09			15 19						16 10			16 17							17 10	
York 8	a				15 32		15 40	15 43	15 49					16 34			16 40	16 47						17 35	
Scarborough	a																								
Harrogate	a																								
Leeds 10	d	14 40		15 08							15 40	16 08				16 12			16 40	17 08					
York 8	d	15 10		15 32	15 35		15 44	15 47	15 51		16 10	16 32		16 35		16 42	16 47	16 52	17 10	17 32				17 37	
Thirsk	d						16 08									17 04									
Northallerton	d	15 31					16 15				16 31			16 57		17 16			17 31						
Darlington 7	a	15 42		15 57	16 02			16 13	16 19		16 42	16 57		17 09			17 15	17 20	17 42	17 57				18 05	
Eaglescliffe	a						16 33																		
Middlesbrough	a															17 50									
Darlington 7	d	15 44		15 59	16 03	16 12		16 14	16 19		16 43	16 59		17 10			17 17	17 21	17 43	17 59				18 06	
Durham	d	16 00		16 15	16 20			16 31			16 59	17 15		17 28			17 34		17 59	18 15				18 24	
Chester-le-Street	d	16 06																	18 05						
Newcastle 8 ⛴	a	16 18		16 28	16 39			16 44	16 49		17 14	17 30		17 44			17 47	17 51	18 18	18 28				18 40	
Hartlepool	a					16 50	16 58																		
Sunderland ⛴	a					17 22	17 27																		
Newcastle 8 ⛴	d			16 34	16 42	17a48			16 53			17 38		17 47				17 54		18 36				18 42	
Morpeth	d																								
Alnmouth for Alnwick	d			16 59	17 09							18 02												19 10	
Berwick-upon-Tweed	d								17 40			18 23						18 39		19 18					
Dunbar	d			17 40																19 41					
Edinburgh 10	a			18 07	18 18				18 23			19 06		19 18				19 26		20 05				20 18	
Edinburgh	d			18 13					18 42			19 18													
Haymarket	d			18 16					18 47			19 23													
Motherwell	a											20 00													
Glasgow Central 15	a											20 20													
Stirling	a																								
Perth	a																								
Inverness	a																								
Inverkeithing	a			18 28					19 01																
Kirkcaldy	a			18 44					19 18																
Leuchars 3	a			19 14					19 43																
Dundee	a			19 29					19 57																
Arbroath	a			19 46					20 15																
Montrose	a			20 00					20 31																
Stonehaven	a			20 23					20 54																
Aberdeen	a			20 43					21 20																

A [trolley] to Edinburgh

B 1 to Doncaster

Table 26

Sundays

until 12 February

London - Humberside, Yorkshire, North East England and Scotland

Route Diagram - see first Page of Table 26

		XC	GR	TP	XC	EM	GR	EM	GR	GR	TP	GC	GR	GR	GR	TP	XC	XC	GR	GR	HT	XC
			R				R		R	R			R	R	R				R	R		
		◇1	1	◇1	◇1	◇	1	◇	1	1	◇1	1	1	1	1	◇1	◇1	◇1	1	1	◇1	◇1
					A																	
London Kings Cross 15 ⊖	d		16 00				16 05		16 30	16 35		16 48	17 00	17 05	17 20				17 30	17 35	17 45	
Stevenage 4	d									16 54										17 54	18u05	
Peterborough 8	a						16 50		17 15					17 50					18 15			
Norwich	d					14 49		15 53														
Peterborough 8	d					16 24	16 50	17 11	17 15					17 50					18 15			
Grantham 7	a					16 54	17 10	17 45		17 39					18 23				18 35	18 41	18 48	
	d					16 56	17 10	17 55		17 39					18 23				18 35	18 41	18 49	
Newark North Gate 7	a						17 22		17 43					18 18	18 36							
	d						17 22		17 43					18 18	18 36							
Lincoln	a																					
Retford 10	d									18 02											19 10	
Doncaster 7	a						17 48		18 08	18 17				18 48	19 03				19 09	19 14	19 23	
Selby	a														19 23						19 45	
Hull	a														20 03						20 26	
Pontefract Monkhill	a																					
Wakefield Kirkgate 4	a																					
Wakefield Westgate 7	a						18 12			18 38				19 07						19 32		
Leeds 10	a						18 31			18 58				19 28						19 53		
Brighouse	a																					
Halifax	a																					
Shipley	a																					
Bradford Forster Square	a																					
Bradford Interchange	a																					
Keighley	a																					
Skipton	a																					
Sheffield 7	d	16 51			17 21	18a34		19a31									17 51	18 21				18 51
Doncaster 7	d	17 17							18 09								18 15		19 11			19 17
York 8	a	17 42	17 46						18 31			18 40	18 46						19 35			19 43
Scarborough	a																					
Harrogate	a																					
Leeds 10	d			17 40	18 08						18 12					18 40	18 57	19 08				
York 8	d	17 46	17 51	18 10	18 32				18 35		18 42	18 47	18 52			19 10	19 21	19 32	19 37			19 46
Thirsk	d										19 00	19 04										
Northallerton	d			18 31					18 55		19 08	19 18				19 31						
Darlington 7	a	18 11	18 18	18 42	18 57				19 07				19 21			19 42	19 46	19 59	20 04			20 11
Eaglescliffe	a											19 35										
Middlesbrough	a										19 40											
Darlington 7	d	18 13	18 19	18 43	18 59				19 08				19 22			19 43	19 48	20 00	20 05			20 13
Durham	d	18 30		18 59	19 15				19 25							19 59	20 04	20 18	20 22			20 29
Chester-le-Street	d															20 05						
Newcastle 8	a	18 43	18 48	19 16	19 30				19 41				19 51			20 18	20 19	20 31	20 38			20 42
Hartlepool	a											20 06										
Sunderland	a											20 39										
Newcastle 8	d		18 54		19 40				19 44				19 53					20 38	20 43			20 51
Morpeth	d								19 59									20 53	20 59			
Alnmouth for Alnwick	d				20 05														21 15			
Berwick-upon-Tweed	d		19 39		20 25								20 39					21 26				
Dunbar	d								20 54									21 51				
Edinburgh 10	a		20 26		21 08				21 17				21 26					22 16	22 22			22 23
Edinburgh	d				21 12				21 21													
Haymarket	d				21 16				21 26													
Motherwell	a				21 53				22 06													
Glasgow Central 15	a				22 14				22 29													
Stirling	a																					
Perth	a																					
Inverness	a																					
Inverkeithing	a																					
Kirkcaldy	a																					
Leuchars 3	a																					
Dundee	a																					
Arbroath	a																					
Montrose	a																					
Stonehaven	a																					
Aberdeen	a																					

A to Edinburgh

Table 26

Sundays

until 12 February

London - Humberside, Yorkshire, North East England and Scotland

Route Diagram - see first Page of Table 26

		EM	GR	GR	TP	GC	XC	GR	GR	EM	XC	GR	GR	GR	GC	TP	XC	GR	GR	HT	EM	XC
			Ⓡ	Ⓡ		Ⓡ		Ⓡ	Ⓡ			Ⓡ	Ⓡ		Ⓡ			Ⓡ	Ⓡ			
		◇	[1]	[1]	◇[1]	[1]	◇[1]	[1]	[1]	◇	◇[1]	[1]	[1]		[1]	◇[1]	◇[1]	[1]	[1]	◇[1]	◇	◇[1]
							A								B							
			🍴🛒	🍴🛒		🍴	🛒	🍴🛒	🍴🛒		🛒	🍴🛒	🍴🛒	🍴🛒	🍴		🛒	🍴🛒	🍴🛒	⊠		
London Kings Cross [15] ⊖	d		18 00	18 05		18 23		18 30	18 35			19 00	19 05	19 08	19 23			19 30	19 35	19 45		
Stevenage [4]	d								18 54					19 28					19 54	20 05		
Peterborough [8]	a			18 53				19 16					19 50	19 58				20 17	20 24			
Norwich	d	16 54								17 54											18 56	
Peterborough [8]	d	18 26		18 53				19 17		19 26			19 51	19 59				20 17	20 25		20 31	
Grantham [7]	a	18 56							19 40	19 56				20 20					20 45	20 50	21 01	
	d	18 58							19 40					20 20					20 45	20 51		
Newark North Gate [7]	a			19 22				19 44					20 18	20 33				20 46				
	d			19 22				19 44					20 18	20 34				20 46				
Lincoln	a													21 03								
Retford [10]	d								20 03											21 11		
Doncaster [7]	a			19 50				20 09	20 19				20 47		20 58			21 13	21 17	21 25		
Selby	a																			21 43		
Hull	a																			22 26		
Pontefract Monkhill	a																					
Wakefield Kirkgate [4]	a														21 22							
Wakefield Westgate [7]	a			20 09					20 38				21 05						21 36			
Leeds [10]	a			20 25					20 55				21 29						21 57			
Brighouse	a														21 46							
Halifax	a														21 57							
Shipley	a																					
Bradford Forster Square	a																					
Bradford Interchange	a														22 11							
Keighley	a								21s22													
Skipton	a								21 42													
Sheffield [7] 🚊	d	20a31					19 21				19 51						20 21					20 51
Doncaster [7]	d							20 10			20 18							21 14				21 23
York [8]	a		19 46			20 14		20 32			20 45	20 49						21 36				21 44
Scarborough	a																					
Harrogate	a			21 06																		
Leeds [10]	d				19 40		20 08									20 40	21 08					
York [8]	d		19 51		20 10	20 20	20 32	20 35			20 47	20 51				21 08	21a31	21 40				21 47
Thirsk	d				20 26	20 36										21 26						
Northallerton	d				20 36	20 44		20 55								21 34						
Darlington [7]	a		20 18				20 59	21 07			21 12	21 19				21 45		22 17				22 22
Eaglescliffe	a					21 01																
Middlesbrough	a				21 07																	
Darlington [7]	d		20 19				21 00	21 08			21 14	21 20				21 46		22 18				22 24
Durham	d						21 18	21 25			21 32					22 03		22 36				22 41
Chester-le-Street	d																					
Newcastle [8] 🚊	a		20 48				21 31	21 43			21 44	21 49				22 17		23 09				23 10
Hartlepool	a					21 21																
Sunderland 🚊	a					21 51																
Newcastle [8] 🚊	d		21 00				21 38					21 51										
Morpeth	d											22 07										
Alnmouth for Alnwick	d						22 06					22 23										
Berwick-upon-Tweed	d		21 49									22 47										
Dunbar	d											23 12										
Edinburgh [10]	a		22 36				23 08					23 41										
Edinburgh	d																					
Haymarket	d																					
Motherwell	a																					
Glasgow Central [15]	a																					
Stirling	a																					
Perth	a																					
Inverness	a																					
Inverkeithing	a																					
Kirkcaldy	a																					
Leuchars [3]	a																					
Dundee	a																					
Arbroath	a																					
Montrose	a																					
Stonehaven	a																					
Aberdeen	a																					

A 🛒 to Leeds

B [1] to Doncaster 🍴 to Doncaster Ⓡ to Doncaster

Table 26

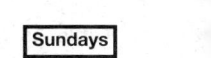

Sundays
until 12 February

London - Humberside, Yorkshire, North East England and Scotland

Route Diagram - see first Page of Table 26

		GR	GR	GR			TP	GR	EM	GR		GR		GR
		R	R	R				R		R		R		R
		1	1	1			◇1	1	◇	1		1		1
		🍴	🍴	🍴				🍴		🍴		🍴		🍴
London Kings Cross 15 ⊖	d	20 00	20 05	20 35				21 00		21 35		22 00		22 35
Stevenage 4	d			20 54						21 55				
Peterborough 8	a	20 45	20 50	21 24				21 45		22 25		22 45		23s25
Norwich	d								20 52					
Peterborough 8	d	20 45	20 51	21 25				21 45	22 22	22 26		22 45		
Grantham 7	a			21 45					22 52	22 47				23s48
	d			21 45						22 47				
Newark North Gate 7	a			21 57						22 59				23s59
	d			21 57						22 59				
Lincoln	a													
Retford 10	d		21 29							23 16				
Doncaster 7	a		21 47	22 22						23 35		23 42		00s29
Selby	a													
Hull	a													
Pontefract Monkhill	a													
Wakefield Kirkgate 4	a													
Wakefield Westgate 7	a		22 06	22 40						23 56				
Leeds 10	a		22 26	23 00						00 15				01 37
Brighouse	a													
Halifax	a													
Shipley	a													
Bradford Forster Square	a													
Bradford Interchange	a													
Keighley	a													
Skipton	a													
Sheffield 7 ⛴	d													
Doncaster 7	d											23 43		
York 8	a	21 52						22 58				00 33		
Scarborough	a													
Harrogate	a													
Leeds 10	d						22 12							
York 8	d	21 58					22 42	23 04				00 35		
Thirsk	d						23 06							
Northallerton	d						23 16	23 39				01s07		
Darlington 7	a	22 38					23 28	23 51				01s21		
Eaglescliffe	a													
Middlesbrough	a													
Darlington 7	d	22 39					23 28	23 52						
Durham	d	22 56					23 45	00 09				01s39		
Chester-le-Street	d													
Newcastle 8 ⛴	a	23 30					00 15	00 43				02 12		
Hartlepool	a													
Sunderland ⛴	a													
Newcastle 8 ⛴	d													
Morpeth	d													
Alnmouth for Alnwick	d													
Berwick-upon-Tweed	d													
Dunbar	d													
Edinburgh 10	a													
Edinburgh	d													
Haymarket	d													
Motherwell	a													
Glasgow Central 15	a													
Stirling	a													
Perth	a													
Inverness	a													
Inverkeithing	a													
Kirkcaldy	a													
Leuchars 8	a													
Dundee	a													
Arbroath	a													
Montrose	a													
Stonehaven	a													
Aberdeen	a													

Table 26

Sundays

19 February to 25 March

London - Humberside, Yorkshire, North East England and Scotland

Route Diagram - see first Page of Table 26

		GR	GR	TP	XC	GR	TP	XC	GR	GR	TP	XC	TP	GR	GR	TP	XC	GR	GC	GR	GR	TP	XC	EM
		R	R			R			R	R				R	R			R	R	R	R			
		1	1	◇1	◇1	1	◇1	◇1	1	1	◇1	◇1	◇1	1	1	◇1	◇1	1	1	1	1	◇1	◇1	◇1
								A				A								B			A	
		⊡⌶	⊡⌶		⌶	⊡⌶		⌶	⊡⌶	⊡⌶		⌶		⊡⌶	⊡⌶		⌶	⊡⌶	⊡	⊡⌶	⊡⌶		⌶	⊡
London Kings Cross 15 ⊖	d	21p00	22p00											09 00	09 03			09 30	09 48	10 00	10 03			
Stevenage 4	d														09 22									
Peterborough 8	a	21p45	22p46												09 52			10 15			10 50			
Norwich	d																							
Peterborough 8	d	21p46	22p47												09 53			10 15			10 50			
Grantham 7	a		23p06												10 13						11 10			
	d		23p06												10 13						11 10			
Newark North Gate 7	a		23p18												10 25						11 22			
	d		23p18												10 25						11 22			
Lincoln	a																							
Retford 10	d		23p33															10 54						
Doncaster 7	a		23p48												10 50			11 09			11 47			
Selby	a																							
Hull	a																							
Pontefract Monkhill	a																							
Wakefield Kirkgate 4	a																							
Wakefield Westgate 7	a		00 05												11 08						12 06			
Leeds 10	a		00 25												11 30						12 29			
Brighouse	a																							
Halifax	a																							
Shipley	a																							
Bradford Forster Square	a																							
Bradford Interchange	a																							
Keighley	a																							
Skipton	a																							
Sheffield 7 ⇌	d											09 21					10 21						11 21	11 31
Doncaster 7	d									09 37								11 09						11 53
York 8	a	22p51								09 58				10 46				11 33	11 36	11 49				12 15
Scarborough	a																							
Harrogate	a																							
Leeds 10	d			07 40			08 40	09 08			09 40	10 08				10 40	11 08					11 40	12 08	
York 8	d	22p52		08 24		09 00	09 10	09 37		10 00	10b13	10 33	10 42	10 53		11 10	11 32	11 35	11 41	11 51		12 08	12 32	
Thirsk	d			08 40									10 59						11 58					
Northallerton	d	23p13		08 48		09 18	09 31				10 35		11 07			11 31			12 06			12 29		
Darlington 7	a	23p26		08 59		09 31	09 42	10 02		10 27	10 46	10 58		11 20		11 42	11 57	12 02		12 19		12 40	12 57	
Eaglescliffe	a																		12 23					
Middlesbrough	a			09 28									11 39											
Darlington 7	d	23p26				09 31	09 43	10 04		10 28	10 47	11 00		11 21		11 43	11 59	12 03		12 20		12 41	12 59	
Durham	d	23p44				09 49	09 59	10 21		10 45	11 08	11 17				11 59	12 16	12 20				12 57	13 15	
Chester-le-Street	d																							
Newcastle 8 ⇌	a	00 04				10 05	10 18	10 34		11 01	11 24	11 29		11 50		12 15	12 29	12 36		12 49		13 12	13 32	
Hartlepool	a																		12 50					
Sunderland ⇌	a																		13 21					
Newcastle 8 ⇌	d				09 45	10 13		10 38		11 03		11 38		11 52			12 38	12 44		12 54			13 36	
Morpeth	d				09 58	10 29																		
Alnmouth for Alnwick	d				10 12	10 45												13 10					14 00	
Berwick-upon-Tweed	d					11 09		11 20		11 48		12 20		12 37						13 41			14 21	
Dunbar	d					11 33											13 40	13 54						
Edinburgh 10	a				11 13	12 01		12 03		12 35		13 03		13 24			14 07	14 22		14 24			15 05	
Edinburgh	d							12 17	09 10			13 10								14 33			15 10	
Haymarket	d							12 21	09 14			13 15								14 38			15 15	
Motherwell	a							12 55				13 50											15 51	
Glasgow Central 15	a							13 12				14 14											16 13	
Stirling	a																							
Perth	a																							
Inverness	a																							
Inverkeithing	a								09 31											14 56				
Kirkcaldy	a								09 48											15 13				
Leuchars 3	a								10 13											15 37				
Dundee	a								10 27											15 52				
Arbroath	a								10 45											16 09				
Montrose	a								11 01											16 25				
Stonehaven	a								11 24											16 48				
Aberdeen	a								11 52											17 14				

A ⌶ to Edinburgh

B The Northern Lights

Table 26

Sundays

19 February to 25 March

London - Humberside, Yorkshire, North East England and Scotland

Route Diagram - see first Page of Table 26

		GR	HT	TP	GR	GR		TP	XC	GR	EM	GC	GR	GR	TP	GR		XC	GR	HT	XC	TP	GR	GR	TP
		R			R	R				R		R	R	R		R			R				R	R	
		1	◇1	◇1	1	1		◇1	◇1	1	◇	1	1	1	◇1	1		◇1	1	◇1	◇1	◇1	1	1	◇1
												A	B					C							
		RT	⊠		RT	RT			T	RT		R	RT	RT		RT		T	RT	⊠	T		RT	RT	
London Kings Cross 15 ⊖	d	10 30	10 45		11 00	11 03				11 30		11 48	12 00	12 03		12 20			12 30	12 45			13 00	13 03	
Stevenage 4	d		11u05			11 22														13u05				13 22	
Peterborough 8	a	11 15				11 52				12 15				12 50		13 08			13 15					13 52	
Norwich	d										10 47														
Peterborough 8	d	11 15				11 53				12 15	12 18			12 50		13 08			13 15					13 53	
Grantham 7	a		11 48			12 13					12 53			13 10						13 48				14 13	
	d		11 49			12 13					12 54			13 10						13 49				14 13	
Newark North Gate 7	a	11 43				12 25								13 22					13 43					14 25	
	d	11 43				12 25								13 22					13 43					14 25	
Lincoln	a																								
Retford 10	d		12 10							12 54										14 10					
Doncaster 7	a	12 08	12 23			12 50				13 09		13 16		13 47		13 56			14 09	14 23				14 50	
Selby	a		12 43																	14 39					
Hull	a		13 25																	15 21					
Pontefract Monkhill	a																								
Wakefield Kirkgate 4	a											13 45													
Wakefield Westgate 7	a					13 08								14 06										15 08	
Leeds 10	a					13 30								14 29										15 30	
Brighouse	a											14 08													
Halifax	a											14 19													
Shipley	a																								
Bradford Forster Square	a																								
Bradford Interchange	a											14 37													
Keighley	a																								
Skipton	a																								
Sheffield 7 ⛴	d								12 21		14a35							13 21			13 51				
Doncaster 7	d	12 08								13 09						13 57			14 09		14 15				
York 8	a	12 31			12 46					13 33			13 49			14 19			14 32		14 40		14 50		
Scarborough	a																								
Harrogate	a																								
Leeds 10	d			12 12				12 40	13 08						13 40			14 08				14 12			14 40
York 8	d	12 35		12 42	12 53			13 10	13 32	13 35			13 51		14 10	14 22		14 32	14 35		14 46	14 50	14 52		15 10
Thirsk	d			13 00																		15 13			
Northallerton	d	12 55		13 08				13 31							14 31				14 54			15 21			15 31
Darlington 7	a	13 07			13 21			13 42	13 57	14 02			14 19		14 42	14 49		14 57	15 07		15 13		15 19		15 42
Eaglescliffe	a																								
Middlesbrough	a			13 40																		15 52			
Darlington 7	d	13 08			13 22			13 43	13 59	14 03			14 19		14 43	14 50		14 59	15 07		15 14		15 20		15 44
Durham	d	13 25						13 59	14 15	14 20					14 59	15 07		15 15	15 25		15 31				16 00
Chester-le-Street	d							14 05																	16 06
Newcastle 8 ⛴	a	13 41			13 51			14 17	14 28	14 36			14 49		15 15	15 26		15 28	15 41		15 44		15 49		16 18
Hartlepool	a																								
Sunderland ⛴	a																								
Newcastle 8 ⛴	d	13 45			13 54				14 36	14 42			14 52					15 37	15 45				15 54		
Morpeth	d								14 49																
Alnmouth for Alnwick	d									15 08								16 02							
Berwick-upon-Tweed	d				14 39								15 39					16 22					16 39		
Dunbar	d								15 41																
Edinburgh 10	a	15 18			15 26				16 06	16 16			16 22					17 06	17 15				17 27		
Edinburgh	d												16 30					17 11							
Haymarket	d												16 35					17 15							
Motherwell	a																	17 52							
Glasgow Central 15	a																	18 12							
Stirling	a												17 17												
Perth	a												17 53												
Inverness	a												20 19												
Inverkeithing	a																								
Kirkcaldy	a																								
Leuchars 3	a																								
Dundee	a																								
Arbroath	a																								
Montrose	a																								
Stonehaven	a																								
Aberdeen	a																								

A 1 to Doncaster
B The Highland Chieftain
C T to Edinburgh

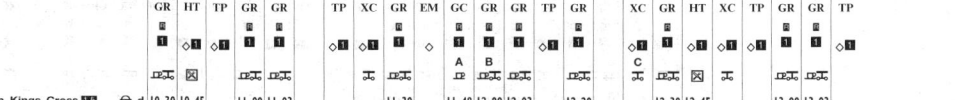

Table 26

Sundays

19 February to 25 March

London - Humberside, Yorkshire, North East England and Scotland

Route Diagram - see first Page of Table 26

		XC	GR	GC	XC	GR	GR	TP	XC	GR	HT	TP	XC	GR	TP	XC	EM	GR	GR	GC	XC	GR
			R	R		R	R			R				R				R	R	R		R
		◇1	1	1	◇1	1	1	◇1	◇1	1	◇1	◇1	◇1	1	◇1	◇1	◇	1	1	1	◇1	1
		A							A											B		
		trolley	DP trolley	DP	trolley	DP trolley	DP trolley		trolley	DP trolley	☒		trolley	DP trolley		trolley		DP trolley	DP trolley	DP	trolley	DP trolley
London Kings Cross 15 ⊖	d		13 30	13 48		14 00	14 03			14 30	14 45			15 00				15 03	15 30	15 48		16 00
Stevenage 4	d										15u05							15 22				
Peterborough 8	a		14 15				14 51			15 16								15 52	16 16			
Norwich	d																13 49					
Peterborough 8	d		14 15				14 52			15 16							15 26	15 53	16 16			
Grantham 7	a						15 12				15 48						15 56	16 13	16 37			
	d						15 12				15 49						15 59	16 13	16 37			
Newark North Gate 7	a						15 24			15 45								16 25				
	d						15 24			15 45								16 25				
Lincoln	a																					
Retford 10	d		14 54								16 10							16 40				
Doncaster 7	a		15 09				15 49			16 10	16 23							16 57	17 10	17 19		
Selby	a										16 44											
Hull	a										17 26											
Pontefract Monkhill	a																					
Wakefield Kirkgate 4	a																			17 47		
Wakefield Westgate 7	a						16 08											17 17				
Leeds 10	a						16 29											17 39				
Brighouse	a																			18 10		
Halifax	a																			18 20		
Shipley	a																					
Bradford Forster Square	a																					
Bradford Interchange	a																			18 37		
Keighley	a																					
Skipton	a																					
Sheffield 7 ⛴	d	14 21			14 51				15 21				15 51			16 21	17a40				16 51	
Doncaster 7	d		15 09		15 19					16 10			16 17						17 10		17 17	
York 8	a		15 32	15 40	15 43	15 49				16 34			16 40	16 47					17 35		17 42	17 46
Scarborough	a																					
Harrogate	a																					
Leeds 10	d	15 08						15 40	16 08			16 12			16 40	17 08						
York 8	d	15 32	15 35	15 44	15 47	15 51		16 10	16 32	16 35		16 42	16 47	16 52	17 10	17 32			17 37		17 46	17 51
Thirsk	d			16 08								17 04										
Northallerton	d			16 15				16 31		16 57		17 16			17 31							
Darlington 7	a	15 57	16 02		16 13	16 19		16 42	16 57	17 09			17 15	17 20	17 42	17 57			18 05		18 11	18 18
Eaglescliffe	a			16 33																		
Middlesbrough	a											17 50										
Darlington 7	d	15 59	16 03		16 14	16 19		16 43	16 59	17 10			17 17	17 21	17 43	17 59			18 06		18 13	18 19
Durham	d	16 15	16 20		16 31			16 59	17 15	17 28			17 34		17 59	18 15			18 24		18 30	
Chester-le-Street	d														18 05							
Newcastle 8 ⛴	a	16 28	16 39		16 44	16 49		17 14	17 30	17 44			17 47	17 51	18 18	18 28			18 40		18 43	18 48
Hartlepool	a			16 58																		
Sunderland ⛴	a			17 27																		
Newcastle 8 ⛴	d	16 34	16 42			16 53			17 38	17 47				17 54		18 36			18 42			18 54
Morpeth	d																					
Alnmouth for Alnwick	d	16 59	17 09						18 02										19 10			
Berwick-upon-Tweed	d					17 40			18 23					18 39		19 18						19 39
Dunbar	d	17 40														19 41						
Edinburgh 10	a	18 07	18 18			18 23			19 06	19 18				19 26		20 05			20 18			20 26
Edinburgh	d	18 13				18 42			19 18													
Haymarket	d	18 17				18 47			19 23													
Motherwell	a								20 00													
Glasgow Central 15	a								20 20													
Stirling	a																					
Perth	a																					
Inverness	a																					
Inverkeithing	a	18 28				19 01																
Kirkcaldy	a	18 44				19 18																
Leuchars 3	a	19 14				19 43																
Dundee	a	19 29				19 57																
Arbroath	a	19 46				20 15																
Montrose	a	20 00				20 31																
Stonehaven	a	20 23				20 54																
Aberdeen	a	20 43				21 20																

A trolley to Edinburgh

B 1 to Doncaster

Table 26

Sundays

19 February to 25 March

London - Humberside, Yorkshire, North East England and Scotland

Route Diagram - see first Page of Table 26

		TP	XC	EM	GR	EM	GR	GR	TP	GC	GR	GR	GR	TP	XC	XC	GR	GR	HT	XC	EM	GR
					R		R	R			R	R	R				R	R				R
		◇1	◇1	◇	1	◇	1	1	◇1	1	1	1	1	◇1	◇1	◇1	1	1	◇1	◇1	◇	1
			A																			
London Kings Cross 15 ⊖	d				16 05		16 30	16 35		16 48	17 00	17 05	17 20				17 30	17 35	17 45			18 00
Stevenage 4	d							16 54										17 54	18u05			
Peterborough 8	a				16 50		17 15					17 50					18 15					
Norwich	d			14 49		15 53															16 54	
Peterborough 8	d			16 24	16 50	17 11	17 15					17 50					18 15				18 26	
Grantham 7	a			16 54	17 10	17 45		17 39					18 23				18 35	18 41	18 48		18 56	
	d			16 56	17 10	17 55		17 39					18 23				18 35	18 41	18 49		18 58	
Newark North Gate 7	a				17 22		17 43					18 18	18 36									
	d				17 22		17 43					18 18	18 36									
Lincoln	a																					
Retford 10	d							18 02											19 10			
Doncaster 7	a				17 48		18 08	18 17				18 48	19 03				19 09	19 14	19 23			
Selby	a												19 23						19 45			
Hull	a												20 03						20 26			
Pontefract Monkhill	a																					
Wakefield Kirkgate 4	a																					
Wakefield Westgate 7	a				18 12			18 38				19 07						19 32				
Leeds 10	a				18 31			18 58				19 28						19 53				
Brighouse	a																					
Halifax	a																					
Shipley	a																					
Bradford Forster Square	a																					
Bradford Interchange	a																					
Keighley	a																					
Skipton	a																					
Sheffield 7	d		17 21	18a34		19a31									17 51	18 21				18 51	20a31	
Doncaster 7	d						18 09								18 15		19 11			19 17		
York 8	a						18 31			18 40	18 46						19 35			19 43		19 46
Scarborough	a																					
Harrogate	a																					
Leeds 10	d	17 40	18b08						18 12					18 40	18c57	19 08						
York 8	d	18 10	18 32				18 35		18 42	18 47	18 52			19 10	19 21	19 32	19 37			19 46		19 51
Thirsk	d								19 00	19 04												
Northallerton	d	18 31					18 55		19 08	19 18				19 31								
Darlington 7	a	18 42	18 57				19 07				19 21			19 42	19 46	19 59	20 04			20 11		20 18
Eaglescliffe	a									19 35												
Middlesbrough	a								19 40													
Darlington 7	d	18 43	18 59				19 08				19 22			19 43	19 48	20 00	20 05			20 13		20 19
Durham	d	18 59	19 15				19 25							19 59	20 04	20 18	20 22			20 29		
Chester-le-Street	d													20 05								
Newcastle 8	a	19 16	19 30				19 41				19 51			20 18	20 19	20 31	20 38			20 42		20 48
Hartlepool	a									20 04												
Sunderland	a									20 37												
Newcastle 8	d		19 40				19 44				19 53					20 38	20 43			20 51		21 00
Morpeth	d						19 59									20 53	20 59					
Alnmouth for Alnwick	d		20 05														21 15					
Berwick-upon-Tweed	d		20 25								20 39					21 26						21 49
Dunbar	d						20 54									21 51						
Edinburgh 10	a		21 08				21 17				21 26					22 16	22 22			22 23		22 36
Edinburgh	d		21 12				21 21															
Haymarket	d		21 16				21 26															
Motherwell	a		21 53				22 06															
Glasgow Central 15	a		22 14				22 29															
Stirling	a																					
Perth	a																					
Inverness	a																					
Inverkeithing	a																					
Kirkcaldy	a																					
Leuchars 3	a																					
Dundee	a																					
Arbroath	a																					
Montrose	a																					
Stonehaven	a																					
Aberdeen	a																					

A to Edinburgh

Table 26

Sundays

19 February to 25 March

London - Humberside, Yorkshire, North East England and Scotland

Route Diagram - see first Page of Table 26

		GR	TP	GC	XC	GR	GR	EM	XC	GR	GR	GR	GC	TP	XC	GR	GR	HT	EM	XC	GR	GR
		R		R		R	R			R	R		R			R	R				R	R
		1	◇1	1	◇1	1	1	◇	◇1	1	1		1	◇1	◇1	1	1	◇1	◇	◇1	1	1
					A								B									
		Restaurant, trolley		Restaurant	trolley	Restaurant, trolley	Restaurant, trolley		trolley	Restaurant, trolley	Restaurant, trolley	Restaurant, trolley	Restaurant		trolley	Restaurant, trolley	Restaurant, trolley	⊠			Restaurant, trolley	Restaurant, trolley
London Kings Cross 15 ⊖	d	18 05		18 23		18 30	18 35			19 00	19 05	19 08	19 23			19 30	19 35	19 45			20 00	20 05
Stevenage 4	d						18 54					19 28					19 54	20 05				
Peterborough 8	a	18 53				19 16					19 50	19 58				20 17	20 24				20 45	20 50
Norwich	d							17 54											18 56			
Peterborough 8	d	18 53				19 17		19 26			19 51	19 59				20 17	20 25		20 31		20 45	20 51
Grantham 7	a						19 40	19 56				20 20					20 45	20 50	21 01			
	d						19 40					20 20					20 45	20 51				
Newark North Gate 7	a	19 22				19 44					20 18	20 33				20 46						
	d	19 22				19 44					20 18	20 34				20 46						
Lincoln	a											21 03										
Retford 10	d						20 03											21 11				21 29
Doncaster 7	a	19 50				20 09	20 19				20 47		20 58			21 13	21 17	21 25				21 47
Selby	a																	21 43				
Hull	a																	22 26				
Pontefract Monkhill	a																					
Wakefield Kirkgate 4	a												21 22									
Wakefield Westgate 7	a	20 09					20 38				21 05						21 36					22 06
Leeds 10	a	20 25					20 55				21 29						21 57					22 26
Brighouse	a												21 46									
Halifax	a												21 57									
Shipley	a																					
Bradford Forster Square	a																					
Bradford Interchange	a												22 11									
Keighley	a						21s22															
Skipton	a						21 42															
Sheffield 7	d				19 21				19 51						20 21					20 51		
Doncaster 7	d					20 10			20 18							21 14				21 23		
York 8	a			20 14		20 32			20 45	20 49						21 36				21 44	21 52	
Scarborough	a																					
Harrogate	a	21 06																				
Leeds 10	d		19 40		20 08									20 40	21 08							
York 8	d		20 10	20 20	20 32	20 35			20 47	20 51				21 08	21a31	21 40				21 47	21 58	
Thirsk	d		20 26	20 36										21 26								
Northallerton	d		20 36	20 44		20 55								21 34								
Darlington 7	a				20 59	21 07			21 12	21 19				21 45		22 17				22 22	22 38	
Eaglescliffe	a			21 01																		
Middlesbrough	a		21 07																			
Darlington 7	d				21 00	21 08			21 14	21 20				21 46		22 18				22 24	22 39	
Durham	d				21 18	21 25			21 32					22 03		22 36				22 41	22 56	
Chester-le-Street	d																					
Newcastle 8	a				21 31	21 43			21 44	21 49				22 17		23 09				23 10	23 30	
Hartlepool	a			21 21																		
Sunderland	a			21 51																		
Newcastle 8	d				21 38					21 51												
Morpeth	d									22 07												
Alnmouth for Alnwick	d				22 06					22 23												
Berwick-upon-Tweed	d									22 47												
Dunbar	d									23 12												
Edinburgh 10	a				23 08					23 41												
Edinburgh	d																					
Haymarket	d																					
Motherwell	a																					
Glasgow Central 15	a																					
Stirling	a																					
Perth	a																					
Inverness	a																					
Inverkeithing	a																					
Kirkcaldy	a																					
Leuchars 3	a																					
Dundee	a																					
Arbroath	a																					
Montrose	a																					
Stonehaven	a																					
Aberdeen	a																					

A trolley to Leeds

B 1 to Doncaster, Restaurant to Doncaster, R to Doncaster

Table 26

Sundays

19 February to 25 March

London - Humberside, Yorkshire, North East England and Scotland

Route Diagram - see first Page of Table 26

		GR			TP	GR	EM	GR	GR			GR
		R				R		R	R			R
		1			◇1	1	◇	1	1			1
		🍴				🍴		🍴	🍴			🍴
London Kings Cross 15 ⊖	d	20 35				21 00		21 35	22 00			22 35
Stevenage 4	d	20 54						21 55				
Peterborough 8	a	21 24				21 45		22 25	22 45			23s25
Norwich	d						20 52					
Peterborough 8	d	21 25				21 45	22 22	22 26	22 45			
Grantham 7	a	21 45					22 52	22 47				23s48
	d	21 45						22 47				
Newark North Gate 7	a	21 57						22 59				23s59
	d	21 57						22 59				
Lincoln	a											
Retford 10	d							23 16				
Doncaster 7	a	22 22						23 35	23 42			00s29
Selby	a											
Hull	a											
Pontefract Monkhill	a											
Wakefield Kirkgate 4	a											
Wakefield Westgate 7	a	22 40						23 56				
Leeds 10	a	23 00						00 15				01 37
Brighouse	a											
Halifax	a											
Shipley	a											
Bradford Forster Square	a											
Bradford Interchange	a											
Keighley	a											
Skipton	a											
Sheffield 7 🚌	d											
Doncaster 7	d								23 43			
York 8	a					22 58			00 33			
Scarborough	a											
Harrogate	a											
Leeds 10	d				22 12							
York 8	d				22 42	23 04			00 35			
Thirsk	d				23 06							
Northallerton	d				23 16	23 39			01s07			
Darlington 7	a				23 28	23 51			01s21			
Eaglescliffe	a											
Middlesbrough	a											
Darlington 7	d				23 28	23 52						
Durham	d				23 45	00 09			01s39			
Chester-le-Street	d											
Newcastle 8 🚌	a				00 15	00 43			02 12			
Hartlepool	a											
Sunderland 🚌	a											
Newcastle 8 🚌	d											
Morpeth	d											
Alnmouth for Alnwick	d											
Berwick-upon-Tweed	d											
Dunbar	d											
Edinburgh 10	a											
Edinburgh	d											
Haymarket	d											
Motherwell	a											
Glasgow Central 15	a											
Stirling	a											
Perth	a											
Inverness	a											
Inverkeithing	a											
Kirkcaldy	a											
Leuchars 3	a											
Dundee	a											
Arbroath	a											
Montrose	a											
Stonehaven	a											
Aberdeen	a											

Table 26

Sundays

from 1 April

London - Humberside, Yorkshire, North East England and Scotland

Route Diagram - see first Page of Table 26

		GR	GR	TP	XC	GR	TP	XC	GR	NT	GR	TP	XC	TP	TP	GR	GR	TP	XC	GR		GC	GR	GR	TP
		R	R			R			R		R					R	R			R		R	R	R	
		1	1	◇1	◇1	1	◇1	◇1	1		1	◇1	◇1	◇1	◇1	1	1	◇1	◇1	1		1	1	1	◇1
								A					A										B		
		🍴🛒	🍴🛒		🛒	🍴🛒		🛒	🍴🛒		🍴🛒		🛒			🍴🛒	🍴🛒		🛒	🍴🛒		🍴	🍴🛒	🍴🛒	
London Kings Cross 15 ⊖	d	21p00	22p00													09 00	09 03			09 30		09 48	10 00	10 03	
Stevenage 4	d																09 22								
Peterborough 8	a	21p45	22p46														09 52			10 15				10 50	
Norwich	d																								
Peterborough 8	d	21p46	22p47														09 53			10 15				10 50	
Grantham 7	a		23p06														10 13							11 10	
	d		23p06														10 13							11 10	
Newark North Gate 7	a		23p18														10 25							11 22	
	d		23p18														10 25							11 22	
Lincoln	a																								
Retford 10	d		23p33																	10 54					
Doncaster 7	a		23p48														10 50			11 09				11 47	
Selby	a																								
Hull	a																								
Pontefract Monkhill	a																								
Wakefield Kirkgate 4	a																								
Wakefield Westgate 7	a		00 05														11 08							12 06	
Leeds 10	a		00 25														11 30							12 29	
Brighouse	a																								
Halifax	a																								
Shipley	a																								
Bradford Forster Square	a																								
Bradford Interchange	a																								
Keighley	a																								
Skipton	a																								
Sheffield 7	d												09 21						10 21						
Doncaster 7	d										09 37									11 09					
York 8	a	22p51									09 58					10 46				11 33		11 36	11 49		
Scarborough	a																								
Harrogate	a																								
Leeds 10	d						08 40	09 08				09 40	10 08	10 17				10 40	11 08						11 40
York 8	d	22p52		08 21		09 00	09 10	09 37			10 00	10 06	10 33	10 42	10 42	10 53		11 10	11 32	11 35		11 41	11 51		12 08
Thirsk	d			08 37										10 59	10 59							11 58			
Northallerton	d	23p13		08 45		09 18	09 31					10 29		11 07	11 07			11 31				12 06			12 29
Darlington 7	a	23p26		08 56		09 31	09 42	10 02			10 27	10 40	10 58			11 20		11 42	11 57	12 02			12 19		12 40
Eaglescliffe	a																					12 23			
Middlesbrough	a			09 25										11 38	11 39										
Darlington 7	d	23p26				09 31	09 43	10 04		10 20	10 28	10 41	11 00			11 21		11 43	11 59	12 03			12 20		12 41
Durham	d	23p44				09 49	09 59	10 21			10 45	11 00	11 17					11 59	12 16	12 20					12 57
Chester-le-Street	d																								
Newcastle 8	a	00 04				10 05	10 18	10 34			11 01	11 17	11 29			11 50		12 15	12 29	12 36			12 49		13 12
Hartlepool	a									10 59												12 50			
Sunderland	a									11 26												13 21			
Newcastle 8	d				09 45	10 13		10 38		11a48	11 03		11 38			11 52			12 38	12 44			12 54		
Morpeth	d				09 58	10 29																			
Alnmouth for Alnwick	d				10 12	10 45														13 10					
Berwick-upon-Tweed	d					11 09		11 20			11 48		12 20			12 37							13 41		
Dunbar	d					11 33													13 40	13 54					
Edinburgh 10	a				11 13	12 01		12 03			12 35		13 03			13 24			14 07	14 22			14 24		
Edinburgh	d							12 17	09 10				13 10										14 33		
Haymarket	d							12 21	09 14				13 15										14 38		
Motherwell	a							12 55					13 50												
Glasgow Central 15	a							13 12					14 14												
Stirling	a																								
Perth	a																								
Inverness	a																								
Inverkeithing	a								09 31														14 56		
Kirkcaldy	a								09 48														15 13		
Leuchars 3	a								10 13														15 37		
Dundee	a								10 27														15 52		
Arbroath	a								10 45														16 09		
Montrose	a								11 01														16 25		
Stonehaven	a								11 24														16 48		
Aberdeen	a								11 52														17 14		

A 🛒 to Edinburgh

B The Northern Lights

Table 26

Sundays
from 1 April

London - Humberside, Yorkshire, North East England and Scotland

Route Diagram - see first Page of Table 26

		XC	EM	GR	HT	TP	GR	GR	TP	XC	GR	EM	GC	GR	GR	TP	GR	XC	GR	HT	XC	TP	GR
				R			R	R			R		R	R	R		R		R				R
		◇1	◇1	1	◇1	◇1	1	1	◇1	◇1	1	◇	1	1	1	◇1	1	◇1	1	◇1	◇1	◇1	1
		A											B	C				A					
					⊠															⊠			
London Kings Cross 15 ⊖	d			10 30	10 45		11 00	11 03			11 30		11 48	12 00	12 03		12 20		12 30	12 45			13 00
Stevenage 4	d				11u05			11 22												13u05			
Peterborough 8	a			11 15				11 52			12 15				12 50		13 08		13 15				
Norwich	d											10 47											
Peterborough 8	d			11 15				11 53			12 15	12 18			12 50		13 08		13 15				
Grantham 7	a				11 48			12 13				12 53			13 10					13 48			
	d				11 49			12 13				12 54			13 10					13 49			
Newark North Gate 7	a			11 43				12 25							13 22				13 43				
	d			11 43				12 25							13 22				13 43				
Lincoln	a																						
Retford 10	d				12 10						12 54									14 10			
Doncaster 7	a			12 08	12 23			12 50			13 09		13 16		13 47		13 56		14 09	14 23			
Selby	a				12 43															14 39			
Hull	a				13 25															15 21			
Pontefract Monkhill	a																						
Wakefield Kirkgate 4	a												13 45										
Wakefield Westgate 7	a							13 08							14 06								
Leeds 10	a							13 30							14 29								
Brighouse	a												14 08										
Halifax	a												14 19										
Shipley	a																						
Bradford Forster Square	a																						
Bradford Interchange	a												14 37										
Keighley	a																						
Skipton	a																						
Sheffield 7	d	11 21	11 31							12 21		14a35						13 21			13 51		
Doncaster 7	d		11 53	12 08							13 09						13 57		14 09		14 15		
York 8	a		12 15	12 31			12 46				13 33			13 49			14 19		14 32		14 40		14 50
Scarborough	a																						
Harrogate	a																						
Leeds 10	d	12 08				12 12			12 40	13 08						13 40		14 08				14 12	
York 8	d	12 32		12 35		12 42	12 53		13 10	13 32	13 35			13 51		14 10	14 22	14 32	14 35		14 46	14 50	14 52
Thirsk	d					13 00																15 13	
Northallerton	d			12 55		13 08			13 31							14 31			14 54			15 21	
Darlington 7	a	12 57		13 07			13 21		13 42	13 57	14 02			14 19		14 42	14 49	14 57	15 07		15 13		15 19
Eaglescliffe	a																						
Middlesbrough	a					13 40																15 52	
Darlington 7	d	12 59		13 08			13 22		13 43	13 59	14 03			14 19		14 43	14 50	14 59	15 07		15 14		15 20
Durham	d	13 15		13 25					13 59	14 15	14 20					14 59	15 07	15 15	15 25		15 31		
Chester-le-Street	d								14 05														
Newcastle 8	a	13 32		13 41			13 51		14 17	14 28	14 36			14 49		15 15	15 26	15 28	15 41		15 44		15 49
Hartlepool	a																						
Sunderland	a																						
Newcastle 8	d	13 36		13 45			13 54			14 36	14 42			14 52				15 37	15 45				15 54
Morpeth	d									14 49													
Alnmouth for Alnwick	d	14 00									15 08							16 02					
Berwick-upon-Tweed	d	14 21					14 39							15 39				16 22					16 39
Dunbar	d									15 41													
Edinburgh 10	a	15 05		15 18			15 26			16 06	16 16			16 22				17 06	17 15				17 27
Edinburgh	d	15 10												16 30				17 11					
Haymarket	d	15 15												16 35				17 15					
Motherwell	a	15 51																17 52					
Glasgow Central 15	a	16 13																18 12					
Stirling	a													17 17									
Perth	a													17 53									
Inverness	a													20 19									
Inverkeithing	a																						
Kirkcaldy	a																						
Leuchars 3	a																						
Dundee	a																						
Arbroath	a																						
Montrose	a																						
Stonehaven	a																						
Aberdeen	a																						

A to Edinburgh

B 1 to Doncaster

C The Highland Chieftain

Table 26

Sundays

from 1 April

London - Humberside, Yorkshire, North East England and Scotland

Route Diagram - see first Page of Table 26

		GR		TP	XC	GR	NT	GC	XC	GR	GR	TP		XC	GR	HT	TP	XC	GR	TP	XC	EM		GR	GR
		R 1		◇1	◇1	R 1		R 1	◇1	R 1	R 1	◇1		◇1	R 1	◇1	◇1	◇1	R 1	◇1	◇1	◇		R 1	R 1
					A									A											
London Kings Cross 15 ⊖	d	13 03				13 30		13 48		14 00	14 03				14 30	14 45			15 00					15 03	15 30
Stevenage 4	d	13 22														15u05								15 22	
Peterborough 8	a	13 52				14 15					14 51				15 16									15 52	16 16
Norwich	d																					13 49			
Peterborough 8	d	13 53				14 15					14 52				15 16							15 26		15 53	16 16
Grantham 7	a	14 13									15 12					15 48						15 56		16 13	16 37
	d	14 13									15 12					15 49						15 59		16 13	16 37
Newark North Gate 7	a	14 25									15 24				15 45									16 25	
	d	14 25									15 24				15 45									16 25	
Lincoln	a																								
Retford 10	d					14 54										16 10								16 40	
Doncaster 7	a	14 50				15 09					15 49				16 10	16 23								16 57	17 10
Selby	a															16 44									
Hull	a															17 26									
Pontefract Monkhill	a																								
Wakefield Kirkgate 4	a																								
Wakefield Westgate 7	a	15 08									16 08													17 17	
Leeds 10	a	15 30									16 29													17 39	
Brighouse	a																								
Halifax	a																								
Shipley	a																								
Bradford Forster Square	a																								
Bradford Interchange	a																								
Keighley	a																								
Skipton	a																								
Sheffield 7	d				14 21				14 51					15 21				15 51			16 21	17a40			
Doncaster 7	d					15 09			15 19						16 10			16 17							17 10
York 8	a					15 32		15 40	15 43	15 49					16 34			16 40	16 47						17 35
Scarborough	a																								
Harrogate	a																								
Leeds 10	d			14 40	15 08							15 40		16 08			16 12			16 40	17 08				
York 8	d			15 10	15 32	15 35		15 44	15 47	15 51		16 10		16 32	16 35		16 42	16 47	16 52	17 10	17 32				17 37
Thirsk	d							16 08									17 04								
Northallerton	d			15 31				16 15				16 31			16 57		17 16			17 31					
Darlington 7	a			15 42	15 57	16 02			16 13	16 19		16 42		16 57	17 09			17 15	17 20	17 42	17 57				18 05
Eaglescliffe	a							16 33																	
Middlesbrough	a																17 50								
Darlington 7	d			15 44	15 59	16 03	16 12		16 14	16 19		16 43		16 59	17 10			17 17	17 21	17 43	17 59				18 06
Durham	d			16 00	16 15	16 20			16 31			16 59		17 15	17 28			17 34		17 59	18 15				18 24
Chester-le-Street	d			16 06																18 05					
Newcastle 8	a			16 19	16 28	16 39			16 44	16 49		17 14		17 30	17 44			17 47	17 51	18 18	18 28				18 40
Hartlepool	a						16 50	16 58																	
Sunderland	a						17 20	17 27																	
Newcastle 8	d				16 34	16 42	17a48			16 53				17 38	17 47				17 54		18 36				18 42
Morpeth	d																								
Alnmouth for Alnwick	d				16 59	17 09								18 02											19 10
Berwick-upon-Tweed	d									17 40				18 23					18 39		19 18				
Dunbar	d				17 40																19 41				
Edinburgh 10	a				18 07	18 18				18 23				19 06	19 18				19 26		20 05				20 18
Edinburgh	d				18 13					18 42				19 18											
Haymarket	d				18 16					18 47				19 23											
Motherwell	a													20 00											
Glasgow Central 15	a													20 20											
Stirling	a																								
Perth	a																								
Inverness	a																								
Inverkeithing	a				18 28					19 01															
Kirkcaldy	a				18 44					19 18															
Leuchars 8	a				19 14					19 43															
Dundee	a				19 29					19 57															
Arbroath	a				19 46					20 15															
Montrose	a				20 00					20 31															
Stonehaven	a				20 23					20 54															
Aberdeen	a				20 43					21 20															

A — to Edinburgh

Sundays
from 1 April

London - Humberside, Yorkshire, North East England and Scotland

Route Diagram - see first Page of Table 26

		GC	XC	GR	TP	XC	EM	GR	EM	GR	GR	TP	GC	GR	GR	GR	TP	XC	XC	GR	GR	HT
		R		R				R		R				R	R	R				R	R	
		1	◇1	1	◇1	◇1	◇	1	◇	1	1	◇1	1	1	1	1	◇1	◇1	◇1	1	1	◇1
		A				B																
		🍽	🛒	🍽🛒		🛒		🍽🛒		🍽🛒	🍽🛒		🍽	🍽🛒	🍽🛒	🍽🛒		🛒	🛒	🍽🛒	🍽🛒	⊠
London Kings Cross [15] ⊖	d	15 48		16 00				16 05		16 30	16 35		16 48	17 00	17 05	17 20				17 30	17 35	17 45
Stevenage [4]	d										16 54										17 54	18u05
Peterborough [8]	a							16 50		17 15					17 50					18 15		
Norwich	d						14 49		15 53													
Peterborough [8]	d						16 24	16 50	17 11	17 15					17 50					18 15		
Grantham [7]	a						16 54	17 10	17 45		17 39					18 23				18 35	18 41	18 48
	d						16 56	17 10	17 55		17 39					18 23				18 35	18 41	18 49
Newark North Gate [7]	a							17 22		17 43					18 18	18 36						
	d							17 22		17 43					18 18	18 36						
Lincoln	a																					
Retford [10]	d										18 02											19 10
Doncaster [7]	a	17 19						17 48		18 08	18 17				18 48	19 03				19 09	19 14	19 23
Selby	a															19 23						19 45
Hull	a															20 03						20 26
Pontefract Monkhill	a																					
Wakefield Kirkgate [4]	a	17 47																				
Wakefield Westgate [7]	a							18 12			18 38				19 07						19 32	
Leeds [10]	a							18 31			18 58				19 28						19 53	
Brighouse	a	18 10																				
Halifax	a	18 20																				
Shipley	a																					
Bradford Forster Square	a																					
Bradford Interchange	a	18 37																				
Keighley	a																					
Skipton	a																					
Sheffield [7] 🚊	d		16 51			17 21	18a34		19a31									17 51	18 21			
Doncaster [7]	d		17 17							18 09								18 15		19 11		
York [8]	a		17 42	17 46						18 31			18 40	18 46						19 35		
Scarborough	a																					
Harrogate	a																					
Leeds [10]	d				17 40	18 08						18 12					18 40	18 57	19 08			
York [8]	d		17 46	17 51	18 10	18 32				18 35		18 42	18 47	18 52			19 10	19 21	19 32	19 37		
Thirsk	d											18 59	19 04									
Northallerton	d				18 31					18 55		19 08	19 18				19 31					
Darlington [7]	a		18 11	18 18	18 42	18 57				19 07				19 21			19 42	19 46	19 59	20 04		
Eaglescliffe	a												19 35									
Middlesbrough	a											19 40										
Darlington [7]	d		18 13	18 19	18 43	18 59				19 08				19 22			19 43	19 48	20 00	20 05		
Durham	d		18 30		18 59	19 15				19 25							19 59	20 04	20 18	20 22		
Chester-le-Street	d																20 05					
Newcastle [8] 🚊	a		18 43	18 48	19 16	19 30				19 41				19 51			20 18	20 19	20 31	20 38		
Hartlepool	a												20 06									
Sunderland 🚊	a												20 39									
Newcastle [8] 🚊	d			18 54		19 40				19 44				19 53					20 38	20 43		
Morpeth	d									19 59									20 53	20 59		
Alnmouth for Alnwick	d					20 05														21 15		
Berwick-upon-Tweed	d			19 39		20 25								20 39					21 26			
Dunbar	d									20 54									21 51			
Edinburgh [10]	a			20 26		21 08				21 17				21 26					22 16	22 22		
Edinburgh	d					21 12				21 21												
Haymarket	d					21 16				21 26												
Motherwell	a					21 53				22 06												
Glasgow Central [15]	a					22 14				22 29												
Stirling	a																					
Perth	a																					
Inverness	a																					
Inverkeithing	a																					
Kirkcaldy	a																					
Leuchars [3]	a																					
Dundee	a																					
Arbroath	a																					
Montrose	a																					
Stonehaven	a																					
Aberdeen	a																					

A [1] to Doncaster

B 🛒 to Edinburgh

Table 26

Sundays

from 1 April

London - Humberside, Yorkshire, North East England and Scotland

Route Diagram - see first Page of Table 26

		XC	EM	GR	GR	TP	GC	XC	GR	GR	EM	XC	GR	GR	GR	GC	TP	XC	GR	GR	HT	EM
		◇1	◇	R 1	R 1	◇1	R 1	◇1	R 1	R 1	◇	◇1	R 1	R 1		R 1	◇1	◇1	R 1	R 1	◇1	◇
								A								B						
London Kings Cross 15 ⊖	d			18 00	18 05		18 23		18 30	18 35			19 00	19 05	19 08	19 23			19 30	19 35	19 45	
Stevenage 4	d									18 54					19 28					19 54	20 05	
Peterborough 8	a				18 53				19 16					19 50	19 58				20 17	20 24		
Norwich	d		16 54								17 54											18 56
Peterborough 8	d		18 26		18 53				19 17		19 26			19 51	19 59				20 17	20 25		20 31
Grantham 7	a		18 56							19 40	19 56				20 20					20 45	20 50	21 01
	d		18 58							19 40					20 20					20 45	20 51	
Newark North Gate 7	a				19 22				19 44					20 18	20 33				20 46			
	d				19 22				19 44					20 18	20 34				20 46			
Lincoln	a														21 03							
Retford 10	d									20 03											21 11	
Doncaster 7	a				19 50				20 09	20 19				20 47		20 58			21 13	21 17	21 25	
Selby	a																				21 43	
Hull	a																				22 26	
Pontefract Monkhill	a																					
Wakefield Kirkgate 4	a															21 22						
Wakefield Westgate 7	a				20 09					20 38				21 05						21 36		
Leeds 10	a				20 25					20 55				21 29						21 57		
Brighouse	a															21 46						
Halifax	a															21 57						
Shipley	a																					
Bradford Forster Square	a																					
Bradford Interchange	a															22 11						
Keighley	a									21s22												
Skipton	a									21 42												
Sheffield 7	d	18 51	20a31					19 21				19 51						20 21				
Doncaster 7	d	19 17							20 10			20 18							21 14			
York 8	a	19 43		19 46			20 14		20 32			20 45	20 49						21 36			
Scarborough	a																					
Harrogate	a				21 06																	
Leeds 10	d					19 40		20 08									20 40	21 08				
York 8	d	19 46		19 51		20 10	20 20	20 32	20 35			20 47	20 51				21 08	21a31	21 40			
Thirsk	d					20 26	20 36										21 26					
Northallerton	d					20 36	20 44		20 55								21 34					
Darlington 7	a	20 11		20 18				20 59	21 07			21 12	21 19				21 45		22 17			
Eaglescliffe	a						21 01															
Middlesbrough	a					21 07																
Darlington 7	d	20 13		20 19				21 00	21 08			21 14	21 20				21 46		22 18			
Durham	d	20 29						21 18	21 25			21 32					22 03		22 36			
Chester-le-Street	d																					
Newcastle 8	a	20 42		20 48				21 31	21 43			21 44	21 49				22 17		23 09			
Hartlepool	a						21 21															
Sunderland	a						21 51															
Newcastle 8	d	20 51		21 00				21 38					21 51									
Morpeth	d												22 07									
Alnmouth for Alnwick	d							22 06					22 23									
Berwick-upon-Tweed	d			21 49									22 47									
Dunbar	d												23 12									
Edinburgh 10	a	22 23		22 36				23 08					23 41									
Edinburgh	d																					
Haymarket	d																					
Motherwell	a																					
Glasgow Central 15	a																					
Stirling	a																					
Perth	a																					
Inverness	a																					
Inverkeithing	a																					
Kirkcaldy	a																					
Leuchars 3	a																					
Dundee	a																					
Arbroath	a																					
Montrose	a																					
Stonehaven	a																					
Aberdeen	a																					

A to Leeds

B 1 to Doncaster to Doncaster R to Doncaster

Table 26

Sundays
from 1 April

London - Humberside, Yorkshire, North East England and Scotland

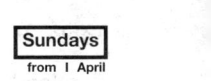

Route Diagram - see first Page of Table 26

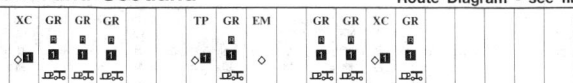

		XC	GR	GR	GR	TP	GR	EM	GR	GR	XC	GR
		◇1	R 1	R 1	R 1	◇1	R 1	◇	R 1	R 1	◇1	R 1
London Kings Cross 15 ⊖	d		20 00	20 05	20 35		21 00		21 35	22 00		22 35
Stevenage 4	d				20 54				21 55			
Peterborough 8	a		20 45	20 50	21 24		21 45		22 25	22 45		23s25
Norwich	d							20 52				
Peterborough 8	d		20 45	20 51	21 25		21 45	22 22	22 26	22 45		
Grantham 7	a				21 45			22 52	22 47			23s48
	d				21 45				22 47			
Newark North Gate 7	a				21 57				22 59			23s59
	d				21 57				22 59			
Lincoln	a											
Retford 10	d			21 29					23 16			
Doncaster 7	a			21 47	22 22				23 35	23 42		00s29
Selby	a											
Hull	a											
Pontefract Monkhill	a											
Wakefield Kirkgate 4	a											
Wakefield Westgate 7	a			22 06	22 40				23 56			
Leeds 10	a			22 26	23 00				00 15			01 37
Brighouse	a											
Halifax	a											
Shipley	a											
Bradford Forster Square	a											
Bradford Interchange	a											
Keighley	a											
Skipton	a											
Sheffield 7	d	20 51									22 21	
Doncaster 7	d	21 23								23 43		
York 8	a	21 44	21 52				22 58			00 33		
Scarborough	a											
Harrogate	a											
Leeds 10	d					22 12					23a01	
York 8	d	21 47	21 58			22 42	23 04			00 35		
Thirsk	d					23 06						
Northallerton	d					23 16	23 39			01s07		
Darlington 7	a	22 22	22 38			23 28	23 51			01s21		
Eaglescliffe	a											
Middlesbrough	a											
Darlington 7	d	22 24	22 39			23 28	23 52					
Durham	d	22 41	22 56			23 45	00 09			01s39		
Chester-le-Street	d											
Newcastle 8	a	23 10	23 30			00 15	00 43			02 12		
Hartlepool	a											
Sunderland	a											
Newcastle 8	d											
Morpeth	d											
Alnmouth for Alnwick	d											
Berwick-upon-Tweed	d											
Dunbar	d											
Edinburgh 10	a											
Edinburgh	d											
Haymarket	d											
Motherwell	a											
Glasgow Central 15	a											
Stirling	a											
Perth	a											
Inverness	a											
Inverkeithing	a											
Kirkcaldy	a											
Leuchars 3	a											
Dundee	a											
Arbroath	a											
Montrose	a											
Stonehaven	a											
Aberdeen	a											

Scotland, North East England, Yorkshire and Humberside - London

Route Diagram - see first Page of Table 26

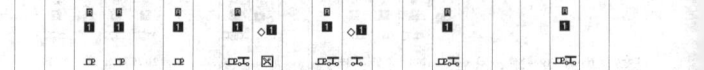

Miles	Miles	Miles			GR MX	GR MX	EM	GR	GR	EM	GR	XC	GR	NT	GR
					R 1	R 1		R 1	R 1	◇1	R 1	◇1	R 1		R 1
—	—	0	**Aberdeen**	d		18p16									
—	—	16¼	Stonehaven	d		18p33									
—	—	40½	Montrose	d		18p56									
—	—	54¼	Arbroath	d		19p12									
—	—	71¼	**Dundee**	d		19p30									
—	—	79½	Leuchars 3	d		19p44									
—	—	104½	Kirkcaldy	d		20p08									
—	—	117¼	Inverkeithing	d		20p24									
—	—	—	**Inverness**	d											
—	—	—	Perth	d											
—	—	—	Stirling	d											
0	—	—	**Glasgow Central** 15	d											
12¾	—	—	Motherwell	d											
56	—	129¼	Haymarket	d		20p43									
57¼	—	130½	**Edinburgh** 10	a		20p48									
—	—	—	**Edinburgh**	d		21p00									
86½	—	—	Dunbar	d		21p21									
114¾	—	—	**Berwick-upon-Tweed**	d		21p47									
147	—	—	Alnmouth for Alnwick	d		22p10									
165¼	—	—	Morpeth	d		22p26									
181¾	—	—	**Newcastle** 8	a		22p43									
—	—	—	Sunderland	d											
—	—	—	Hartlepool	d										07 03	
—	—	—	**Newcastle** 8	d	21p15	22p44							04 45	07a51	
190	—	—	Chester-le-Street	d											
195¾	—	—	**Durham**	d	21p27	22p58							04 59		
217¾	—	—	**Darlington** 7	a	21p45	23p19							05 16		
—	—	—	Middlesbrough	d											
—	—	—	Eaglescliffe	d											
—	—	—	**Darlington** 7	d	21p46	23p19							05 17		
231¾	—	—	Northallerton	d	21p57	23c46							05 29		
239½	—	—	Thirsk	d											
261¾	—	—	**York** 8	a	22p17	00 13							05 57		
—	—	—	Leeds 10	a		00 50									
—	—	—	Harrogate	d											
—	—	—	Scarborough	d											
—	—	—	**York** 8	d	22p19								06 00		
294¼	—	—	**Doncaster** 7	a	22p42								06 21		
—	—	—	Skipton	d											
—	—	—	Keighley	d											
—	—	—	**Bradford Interchange**	d											
—	—	—	Bradford Forster Square	d											
—	—	—	Shipley	d											
—	—	—	Halifax	d											
—	—	—	Brighouse	d											
—	0	—	**Leeds** 10	d					05 05	05 25	05 30	06 00			06 05
—	10	—	**Wakefield Westgate** 7	d					05 16	05 37	05 42	06 12			06 17
—	—	—	Wakefield Kirkgate 4	d											
—	—	—	Pontefract Monkhill	d											
—	—	—	Sheffield 7	a								06 41			
—	—	—	Hull	d											
—	—	—	Selby	d											
—	29¾	—	**Doncaster** 7	d	22p42				05 35	05a55	06 02		06 22		06 35
311¾	—	—	**Retford** 10	d					05 50						06 50
—	—	—	Lincoln	d											
330¼	—	—	**Newark North Gate** 7	a	23p06				06 05		06 27		06 46		07 05
—	—	—		d	23p06				06 05		06 27		06 46		07 05
344¾	—	—	**Grantham** 7	a	23p18				06 17		06 40		06 59		07 17
—	—	—		d	23p18		05 51		06 17		06 40		06 59		07 18
374	—	—	**Peterborough** 8	a	23p39		06 25		06 38		07 00		07 20		07 38
—	—	—	Norwich	a											
—	—	—	**Peterborough** 8	d	23p40			06 10	06 40		07 00		07 20		07 40
422¾	—	—	**Stevenage** 4	a	00s21										
450¼	—	—	**London Kings Cross** 15 ⊖	a	00 57			07 01	07 33		07 54		08 14		08 36

b Previous night, stops to pick up only

c Previous night, stops to set down only

Table 26

Mondays to Fridays

Scotland, North East England, Yorkshire and Humberside - London

Route Diagram - see first Page of Table 26

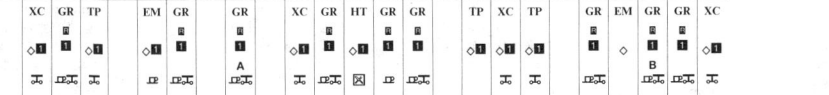

		XC	GR	TP	EM	GR	GR	XC	GR	HT	GR	GR	TP	XC	TP	GR	EM	GR	GR	XC
			R			R	R		R		R	R				R		R	R	
		◇1	1	◇1	◇1	1	1	◇1	1	◇1	1	1	◇1	◇1	◇1	1	◇	1	1	◇1
							A											B		
Aberdeen	d																			
Stonehaven	d																			
Montrose	d																			
Arbroath	d																			
Dundee	d																			
Leuchars 8	d																			
Kirkcaldy	d																			
Inverkeithing	d																			
Inverness	d																			
Perth	d																			
Stirling	d																			
Glasgow Central 15	d																			
Motherwell	d																			
Haymarket	d																			
Edinburgh 10	a																			
Edinburgh	d																			
Dunbar	d																			
Berwick-upon-Tweed	d																			
Alnmouth for Alnwick	d																			
Morpeth	d																			
Newcastle 8	a																			
Sunderland	d																			
Hartlepool	d																			
Newcastle 8	d		05 25						05 56				06 11	06 25		06 30				06 44
Chester-le-Street	d												06 21							
Durham	d		05 38						06 09				06 28	06 37		06 42				06 56
Darlington 7	a		05 56						06 27				06 44	06 53		07 00				07 12
Middlesbrough	d			05 55																
Eaglescliffe	d																			
Darlington 7	d		05 57						06 28				06 45	06 54		07 00				07 14
Northallerton	d		06 08	06 23									06 56			07 13				
Thirsk	d			06 31									07 04		←					
York 8	a		06 28	06 49					06 56				07 30	07 20	07 30	07 33				07 40
Leeds 10	a			07 20									→		08 04					08 08
Harrogate	d																			
Scarborough	d																			
York 8	d		06 30					06 32	06 58					07 23		07 35				
Doncaster 7	a		06 52											07 48						
Skipton	d																		06 55	
Keighley	d																		07u06	
Bradford Interchange	d																			
Bradford Forster Square	d						06 30													
Shipley	d						06u35												07u14	
Halifax	d																			
Brighouse	d																			
Leeds 10	d	06 15			06 34	06 40	07 00	07 05				07 15							07 40	08 11
Wakefield Westgate 7	d	06 27			06 46	06 51	07 12	07 18				07 26							07 51	08 23
Wakefield Kirkgate 4	d																			
Pontefract Monkhill	d																			
Sheffield 7	a				07 25			07 50						08 18						08 51
Hull	d									06 25								07 00		
Selby	d									07 00								07 34		
Doncaster 7	d	06a43	06 53			07 09				07 18		07 45						07 55	08 10	
Retford 10	d									07 40										
Lincoln	d										07 20									
Newark North Gate 7	a					07 35					07 49							08 20	08 37	
	d					07 35					07 55							08 21	08 37	
Grantham 7	a		07 25							08 01		08 16						08 33		
	d		07 25							08 02		08 16					08 27	08 34		
Peterborough 8	a		07 46						08 09		08 26					08 41	08 57	09 01	09 06	
Norwich	a																10 44			
Peterborough 8	d		07 50						08 11		08 26					08 41		09 02	09 06	
Stevenage 4	a										08 57	09 00								
London Kings Cross 15 ⊖	a		08 44			08 53	08 59		09 08	09 18	09 26	09 30				09 39		09 56	10 02	

A West Riding Limited
B The Hull Executive

Table 26

Mondays to Fridays

Scotland, North East England, Yorkshire and Humberside - London

Route Diagram - see first Page of Table 26

		GR	GR	GC	TP		EM		GC	XC	GR	GR					GR	NT	TP	XC	TP	GR	NT	HT	EM
		■R	■R	■R					■R		■R	■R					■R					■R			
		■1	■1	■1	◇■1		◇		■1	◇■1	■1	■1					■1		◇■1	◇■1	◇■1	■1		◇■1	◇
		🍴🛒	🍴🛒	🍴	🛒				🍴	🛒	🍴🛒	🍴🛒					🍴🛒		🛒	🛒	🛒	🍴🛒		⊠	
Aberdeen	d																								
Stonehaven	d																								
Montrose	d																								
Arbroath	d																								
Dundee	d																								
Leuchars ■3	d																								
Kirkcaldy	d																								
Inverkeithing	d																								
Inverness	d																								
Perth	d																								
Stirling	d																								
Glasgow Central ■15	d																								
Motherwell	d																								
Haymarket	d																								
Edinburgh ■10	a																								
Edinburgh	d		05 40									05 48								06 06		06 25			
Dunbar	d											06 08													
Berwick-upon-Tweed	d	06 00										06 33								06 46		07 06			
Alnmouth for Alnwick	d	06 19										06 53								07 08			07 20		
Morpeth	d	06 35										07 09											07 54		
Newcastle ■8 ⛴	a	06 52	07 02									07 26								07 38		07 53	08 19		
Sunderland ⛴	d								06 45																
Hartlepool	d								07 09									09 01							
Newcastle ■8 ⛴	d	06 55	07 03							07 25		07 28						09a51	07 33	07 41		07 55			
Chester-le-Street	d																		07 42						
Durham	d	07 07								07 37		07 41							07 49	07 55					
Darlington ■7	a	07 25								07 53		07 58							08 05	08 10		08 23			
Middlesbrough	d				07 12																				
Eaglescliffe	d								07 30																
Darlington ■7	d	07 31								07 54		07 59							08 06	08 12		08 24			
Northallerton	d				07 43				07 50										08 17						
Thirsk	d				07 51				07 59										08 25		←				
York ■8	a	07 59			08 11				08 16	08 21		08 27							08 47	08 41	08 47	08 53			
Leeds ■10	a				08 52														→	09 08	09 22				
Harrogate	d										07 28														
Scarborough	d																								
York ■8	d	08 00							08 20	08 24		08 29										08 55			
Doncaster ■7	a									08 48		08 52													
Skipton	d																								
Keighley	d																								
Bradford Interchange	d			06 51																					
Bradford Forster Square	d																								
Shipley	d																								
Halifax	d			07 07																					
Brighouse	d			07 18																					
Leeds ■10	d										08 15						08 45			09 11					
Wakefield Westgate ■7	d										08 27						08 56			09 24					
Wakefield Kirkgate ■4	d			07 42																					
Pontefract Monkhill	d			08 01																					
Sheffield ■7 🚋	a									09 17										09 51					
Hull	d																							08 25	
Selby	d																							08 58	
Doncaster ■7	d			08 31							08 45	08 53					09 16							09 24	
Retford ■10	d	08 33																						09 39	
Lincoln	d																								
Newark North Gate ■7	a											09 16													
	d											09 16													
Grantham ■7	a										09 18													10 00	
	d						09 10				09 19													10 01	10 11
Peterborough ■8	a						09 39					09 47					10 08								10 40
Norwich	a						11 14																		12 13
Peterborough ■8	d											09 48					10 08								
Stevenage ■4	a										10 08														
London Kings Cross ■15 ⊖	a	10 04	09 40	10 13					10 25		10 38	10 45					11 02					10 54		11 09	

Scotland, North East England, Yorkshire and Humberside - London

Route Diagram - see first Page of Table 26

		GR	GR	XC	GR	XC	XC	GR	NT	TP	GR	GC	TP	NT	EM	NT	EM	GR	GR	XC
		R	R		R			R			R	R						R	R	
		1	1	◇1	1	◇1	◇1	1		◇1	1	1	◇1				◇	1	1	◇1
						A	B													
Aberdeen	d																			
Stonehaven	d																			
Montrose	d																			
Arbroath	d																			
Dundee	d																			
Leuchars	d																			
Kirkcaldy	d																			
Inverkeithing	d																			
Inverness	d																			
Perth	d																			
Stirling	d																			
Glasgow Central	d					06 01	06 01												06 50	
Motherwell	d					06 16	06 16												07 04	
Haymarket	d					06 57	06 57												07 45	
Edinburgh	a					07 02	07 02												07 52	
Edinburgh	d		06 55	07 00		07 07	07 07	07 30											08 00	
Dunbar	d					07 27	07 27													
Berwick-upon-Tweed	d			07 39				08 11												
Alnmouth for Alnwick	d			07 59															08 58	
Morpeth	d			08 13					08 49											
Newcastle	a		08 22	08 30		08 38	08 38	08 56	09 14										09 27	
Sunderland	d											08 42								
Hartlepool	d											09 07		10 02		11 02				
Newcastle	d		08 25	08 35		08 43	08 43	08 58					09 15	10a51		11a51			09 28	09 35
Chester-le-Street	d												09 24							
Durham	d		08 37	08 47		08 56	08 56						09 31						09 41	09 47
Darlington	a		08 55	09 03		09 11	09 11	09 25					09 47						09 59	10 04
Middlesbrough	d									08 50										
Eaglescliffe	d											09 27								
Darlington	d		08 56	09 04		09 13	09 13	09 26					09 48						09 59	10 05
Northallerton	d		09 07							09 18		09 46	09 59							
Thirsk	d									09 28		09 57								
York	a		09 27	09 31		09 41	09 41	09 53		09 47		10 16	10 21						10 28	10 32
Leeds	a					10 08	10 08			10 22			10 52							
Harrogate	d																			
Scarborough	d																			
York	d		09 29	09 35				09 55			10 01	10 25							10 29	10 34
Doncaster	a		09 52	09 57							10 24								10 53	10 57
Skipton	d																			
Keighley	d																			
Bradford Interchange	d																			
Bradford Forster Square	d																			
Shipley	d																			
Halifax	d																			
Brighouse	d																			
Leeds	d	09 15			09 45	10 11	10 11											10 15		
Wakefield Westgate	d	09 27			09 56	10 23	10 23											10 27		
Wakefield Kirkgate	d																			
Pontefract Monkhill	d																			
Sheffield	a			10 20		10 51	10 51													11 20
Hull	d																			
Selby	d																			
Doncaster	d	09 45	09 53		10 16						10 24				10 24			10 45	10 53	
Retford	d										10 39									
Lincoln	d														11a17					
Newark North Gate	a		10 16								10 54								11 17	
	d		10 16								10 54								11 17	
Grantham	a	10 17									11 06							11 17		
	d	10 17									11 06						11 10	11 17		
Peterborough	a		10 47		11 06						11 26						11 39		11 47	
Norwich	a																13 13			
Peterborough	d		10 48		11 06						11 27								11 49	
Stevenage	a	11 00									11 56							12 00		
London Kings Cross	a	11 29	11 46		12 00			11 55			12 24	12 29						12 29	12 46	

A until 10 February. from Edinburgh

B from 13 February

Scotland, North East England, Yorkshire and Humberside - London

Route Diagram - see first Page of Table 26

		GR	XC	GR	NT	TP	TP		HT	GR	NT	EM	GR	GR	GC	XC			GR	XC	GR	NT	TP	TP	GR
		R		R						R			R	R	R				R		R				R
		1	◇1	1		◇1	◇1		◇1	1		◇	1	1	1	◇1			1	◇1	1		◇1	◇1	1
			A																	A					
Aberdeen	d																								
Stonehaven	d																								
Montrose	d																								
Arbroath	d																								
Dundee	d		06 32																						
Leuchars 3	d		06 46																						
Kirkcaldy	d		07 21																						
Inverkeithing	d		07 43																						
Inverness	d																								
Perth	d																								
Stirling	d																								
Glasgow Central 15	d																			07 50					
Motherwell	d																			08 05					
Haymarket	d		08 01																	08 50					
Edinburgh 10	a		08 06																	08 55					
Edinburgh	d		08 10	08 30																09 08	09 30				
Dunbar	d																			09 28					
Berwick-upon-Tweed	d		08 50																	09 51	10 11				
Alnmouth for Alnwick	d																								
Morpeth	d				09 49																	10 49			
Newcastle 8	a		09 39	09 55	10 14															10 38	10 56	11 14			
Sunderland	d																								
Hartlepool	d										12 02														
Newcastle 8	d		09 41	09 56			10 17				12a52			10 25		10 35				10 44	10 58			11 15	
Chester-le-Street	d																							11 24	
Durham	d		09 55				10 31							10 37		10 47				10 56				11 31	
Darlington 7	a		10 10	10 25			10 46							10 55		11 03				11 12	11 25			11 46	
Middlesbrough	d					09 50																	10 50		
Eaglescliffe	d																								
Darlington 7	d		10 12	10 25			10 48							10 56		11 04				11 13	11 26			11 48	
Northallerton	d					10 18	10 59							11 07									11 18	11 59	
Thirsk	d					10 28																	11 28		
York 8	a		10 41	10 53		10 47	11 23							11 27		11 31				11 41	11 53		11 47	12 21	
Leeds 10	a		11 07			11 22	11 52													12 08			12 22	12 52	
Harrogate	d																								
Scarborough	d																								
York 8	d			10 55										11 29		11 34					11 55				12 01
Doncaster 7	a													11 52		11 57									12 24
Skipton	d																								
Keighley	d																								
Bradford Interchange	d														10 22										
Bradford Forster Square	d																								
Shipley	d																								
Halifax	d														10 37										
Brighouse	d														10 48										
Leeds 10	d	10 45	11 11										11 15						11 45	12 12					
Wakefield Westgate 7	d	10 56	11 24										11 27						11 56	12 24					
Wakefield Kirkgate 4	d														11 11										
Pontefract Monkhill	d														11 34										
Sheffield 7	a		11 51													12 20				12 51					
Hull	d								10 30																
Selby	d								11 03																
Doncaster 7	d	11 16							11 24				11 45	11 53	12 08				12 16						12 24
Retford 10	d								11 39																12 39
Lincoln	d																								
Newark North Gate 7	a													12 16											12 54
	d									11 54				12 16											12 55
Grantham 7	a								12 00	12 05			12 16												13 07
	d								12 01	12 05		12 11	12 16												13 07
Peterborough 8	a	12 07								12 27		12 40		12 48					13 06						13 27
Norwich	a											14 13													
Peterborough 8	d	12 08								12 27				12 49					13 07						13 28
Stevenage 4	a									12 57			13 02												13 58
London Kings Cross 15 ⊖	a	13 02		12 54					13 10	13 26			13 30	13 43	13 45				14 00		13 55				14 26

A from Edinburgh

Scotland, North East England, Yorkshire and Humberside - London

Route Diagram - see first Page of Table 26

		EM	GR		GR	XC	NT	EM	GR	XC		GR	NT		TP	TP	HT	GR	EM	GR	GR	XC			GR
			R		R				R			R						R		R	R				R
		◇	1		1	◇1			1	◇1		1			◇1	◇1	◇1	1	◇	1	1	◇1			1
										A															
			🍴☕		🍴☕	☕			🍴☕	☕		🍴☕			☕	☕	⊠	🍴		🍴☕	🍴☕	☕			🍴☕
Aberdeen	d											07 52													
Stonehaven	d											08 09													
Montrose	d											08 32													
Arbroath	d											08 48													
Dundee	d											09 06													
Leuchars 3	d											09 20													
Kirkcaldy	d											09 44													
Inverkeithing	d											10 01													
Inverness	d																								
Perth	d																								
Stirling	d																								
Glasgow Central 15	d									09 00															
Motherwell	d									09 15															
Haymarket	d									09 58		10 17													
Edinburgh 10	a									10 02		10 25													
Edinburgh	d				10 00					10 10		10 30													
Dunbar	d																								
Berwick-upon-Tweed	d									10 49															
Alnmouth for Alnwick	d				10 58																				
Morpeth	d									11 21			11 49												
Newcastle 8 ⛴	a				11 27					11 39		11 55	12 13												
Sunderland ⛴	d																								
Hartlepool	d																								
Newcastle 8 ⛴	d				11 28	11 35				11 44		11 57				12 17					12 25	12 35			
Chester-le-Street	d																								
Durham	d				11 41	11 47				11 56						12 29					12 37	12 47			
Darlington 7	a				11 59	12 04				12 12		12 25				12 45					12 55	13 04			
Middlesbrough	d														11 50										
Eaglescliffe	d																								
Darlington 7	d				11 59	12 05				12 13		12 26				12 46					12 56	13 04			
Northallerton	d														12 18	12 58					13 07				
Thirsk	d														12 28										
York 8	a				12 28	12 31				12 41		12 54			12 47	13 21					13 27	13 31			
Leeds 10	a									13 07					13 22	13 52									
Harrogate	d																								
Scarborough	d																								
York 8	d				12 29	12 34						12 55									13 29	13 34			
Doncaster 7	a				12 53	12 57															13 52	13 57			
Skipton	d																								
Keighley	d																								
Bradford Interchange	d																								
Bradford Forster Square	d																								
Shipley	d																								
Halifax	d																								
Brighouse	d																								
Leeds 10	d		12 15						12 45	13 11										13 15					13 45
Wakefield Westgate 7	d		12 27				12 39		12 56	13 23										13 27					13 57
Wakefield Kirkgate 4	d						12a42																		
Pontefract Monkhill	d																								
Sheffield 7 ⛴	a					13 20				13 51												14 20			
Hull	d																12 30								
Selby	d																13 03								
Doncaster 7	d		12 45		12 53			13 05	13 16								13 24			13 45	13 53				14 16
Retford 10	d																13 39								
Lincoln	d							13a55																	
Newark North Gate 7	a				13 17																14 16				
	d				13 17													13 54			14 16				
Grantham 7	a		13 17														14 00	14 05		14 16					
	d	13 09	13 17														14 01	14 05	14 10	14 16					
Peterborough 8	a	13 39			13 47				14 07									14 26	14 39		14 51				15 07
Norwich	a	15 13																	16 14						
Peterborough 8	d				13 49				14 07									14 26			14 52				15 08
Stevenage 4	a		14 02															14 56		15 00					
London Kings Cross 15 ⊖	a		14 30		14 46				15 03			14 53					15 10	15 25		15 29	15 45				16 03

A ☕ from Edinburgh

Scotland, North East England, Yorkshire and Humberside - London

Route Diagram - see first Page of Table 26

		XC	GR	NT	TP	GR	GC	NT	TP		NT	EM	NT	EM	GR	GR	XC	NT	GR		XC		GR	NT	TP
			R			R	R								R	R			R				R		
		◇1	1		◇1	1	1		◇1					◇	1	1	◇1		1		◇1		1		◇1
		A	B																				C		
		✕	🍽✕		✕	🍽✕	🍽		✕						🍽✕	🍽✕	✕		🍽✕		✕		🍽✕		✕
Aberdeen	d	08 20																					09 52		
Stonehaven	d	08 38																					10 09		
Montrose	d	08 59																					10 32		
Arbroath	d	09 15																					10 49		
Dundee	d	09 32																					11 06		
Leuchars 3	d	09 47																					11 20		
Kirkcaldy	d	10 17																					11 44		
Inverkeithing	d	10 32																					12 01		
Inverness	d		07 55																						
Perth	d		09 56																						
Stirling	d		10 30																						
Glasgow Central 15	d																				10 59				
Motherwell	d																				11 14				
Haymarket	d	10 54	11 11																		11 57		12 17		
Edinburgh 10	a	10 58	11 17																		12 02		12 25		
Edinburgh	d	11 05	11 30													12 00					12 08		12 30		
Dunbar	d	11 25																							
Berwick-upon-Tweed	d	11 48														12 41					12 47				
Alnmouth for Alnwick	d	12 08																							
Morpeth	d			12 49																				13 49	
Newcastle 8 ⛴	a	12 38	12 55	13 13												13 26					13 34		13 55	14 13	
Sunderland ⛴	d						12 28																		
Hartlepool	d						12 52	13 02			14 02		15 02												
Newcastle 8 ⛴	d	12 41	12 56					13a51	13 15		14a51		15a51			13 28	13 35				13 42		13 56		
Chester-le-Street	d								13 24																
Durham	d	12 53							13 31							13 41	13 47				13 54				
Darlington 7	a	13 10	13 25						13 46							13 59	14 04				14 10		14 25		
Middlesbrough	d				12 50																				13 50
Eaglescliffe	d						13 12																		
Darlington 7	d	13 11	13 25						13 48							13 59	14 05				14 11		14 25		
Northallerton	d				13 18		13 31		13 58																14 18
Thirsk	d				13 28		13 42																		14 28
York 8	a	13 41	13 53		13 47		14 00		14 23							14 28	14 31				14 41		14 53		14 47
Leeds 10	a	14 07			14 22				14 52												15 07				15 23
Harrogate	d																								
Scarborough	d																								
York 8	d		13 55			14 01	14 05									14 29	14 34						14 55		
Doncaster 7	a					14 22										14 53	14 57								
Skipton	d																								
Keighley	d																								
Bradford Interchange	d																								
Bradford Forster Square	d																								
Shipley	d																								
Halifax	d																								
Brighouse	d																								
Leeds 10	d	14 11													14 15				14 45		15 11				
Wakefield Westgate 7	d	14 23													14 27			14 39	14 56		15 23				
Wakefield Kirkgate 4	d																	14a42							
Pontefract Monkhill	d																								
Sheffield 7 ⛴	a	14 51															15 20				15 51				
Hull	d																								
Selby	d																								
Doncaster 7	d					14 23						14 27			14 45	14 53			15 16						
Retford 10	d					14 39																			
Lincoln	d											15a18													
Newark North Gate 7	a					14 54										15 17									
	d					14 54										15 18									
Grantham 7	a					15 06									15 16										
	d					15 06								15 11	15 16										
Peterborough 8	a					15 26								15 38		15 47			16 05						
Norwich	a													17 13											
Peterborough 8	d					15 27										15 49			16 06						
Stevenage 4	a					15 57									16 02										
London Kings Cross 15 ⊖	a		15 54			16 25	16 09								16 29	16 46			17 00				16 54		

A ✕ from Edinburgh

B The Highland Chieftain

C The Northern Lights

Scotland, North East England, Yorkshire and Humberside - London

Route Diagram - see first Page of Table 26

		TP	GR	NT	EM		GR	GR	XC	HT	NT	GR	XC	GR	NT		TP FX	GR	NT	EM	GR		XC	TP FO	TP
		◇1	R 1		◇		R 1	R 1	◇1	◇1		R 1	◇1	R 1			◇1	R 1		◇	R 1		◇1	◇1 A	◇1
Aberdeen	d																								
Stonehaven	d																								
Montrose	d																								
Arbroath	d																								
Dundee	d																								
Leuchars 3	d																								
Kirkcaldy	d																								
Inverkeithing	d																								
Inverness	d																								
Perth	d																								
Stirling	d																								
Glasgow Central 15	d																								
Motherwell	d																								
Haymarket	d																								
Edinburgh 10	a																								
Edinburgh	d												13 06	13 30											
Dunbar	d												13 28												
Berwick-upon-Tweed	d													14 11											
Alnmouth for Alnwick	d												14 08												
Morpeth	d														14 49										
Newcastle 8	a												14 38	14 56	15 14										
Sunderland	d																								
Hartlepool	d			16 02															17 03						
Newcastle 8	d	14 18		16a51				14 25	14 35				14 42	14 58					17a51				15 03		15 15
Chester-le-Street	d																								15 24
Durham	d	14 31						14 38	14 47				14 55										15 16		15 31
Darlington 7	a	14 46						14 55	15 03				15 10	15 24									15 32		15 46
Middlesbrough	d																14 50							14 50	
Eaglescliffe	d																								
Darlington 7	d	14 48						14 56	15 04				15 12	15 25									15 33		15 48
Northallerton	d	14 59						15 07									15 18							15 18	15 59
Thirsk	d																15 28							15 28	
York 8	a	15 22						15 27	15 31				15 41	15 53			15 47						16 01	15 47	16 21
Leeds 10	a	15 52											16 07				16 22						16 32	16 59	16 52
Harrogate	d																								
Scarborough	d																								
York 8	d							15 29	15 34					15 55				16 01							
Doncaster 7	a							15 52	15 57									16 24							
Skipton	d																								
Keighley	d																								
Bradford Interchange	d																								
Bradford Forster Square	d																								
Shipley	d																								
Halifax	d																								
Brighouse	d																								
Leeds 10	d						15 15					15 45	16 11								16 15		16 40		
Wakefield Westgate 7	d						15 27				15 39	15 56	16 23								16 27		16 52		
Wakefield Kirkgate 4	d										15a42														
Pontefract Monkhill	d																								
Sheffield 7	a								16 20				16 51										17 20		
Hull	d									15 10															
Selby	d									15 45															
Doncaster 7	d						15 45	15 53		16 04		16 16						16 24			16 45				
Retford 10	d									16 19								16 39							
Lincoln	d																								
Newark North Gate 7	a							16 18										16 54							
	d		15 52					16 18										16 54							
Grantham 7	a		16 03				16 17			16 39								17 07			17 16				
	d		16 03		16 10		16 17			16 40								17 07		17 11	17 16				
Peterborough 8	a		16 24		16 39			16 48				17 06						17 27		17 40					
Norwich	a				18 18															19 15					
Peterborough 8	d		16 25					16 49				17 07						17 28							
Stevenage 4	a		16 54				17 00											17 58			18 03				
London Kings Cross 15 ⊖	a		17 22				17 30	17 42		17 46		18 01		17 56				18 27			18 31				

A 1 to York ◇ to York

Scotland, North East England, Yorkshire and Humberside - London

Route Diagram - see first Page of Table 26

		GR	GR	GC	NT	XC	GR	NT	TP	TP	GR	EM	GR	GR	XC	HT	GR	XC	GR	NT
		R	R	R			R				R		R	R			R		R	
		1	1	1		◇1	1		◇1	◇1	1	◇	1	1	◇1	◇1	1	◇1	1	
						A														
Aberdeen	d																			
Stonehaven	d																			
Montrose	d																			
Arbroath	d																			
Dundee	d																			
Leuchars 3	d																			
Kirkcaldy	d																			
Inverkeithing	d																			
Inverness	d																			
Perth	d																			
Stirling	d																			
Glasgow Central 15	d					12 51														
Motherwell	d					13 06														
Haymarket	d																			
Edinburgh 10	a					13 54														
Edinburgh	d	14 00				14 08	14 30											15 08	15 30	
Dunbar	d																	15 28		
Berwick-upon-Tweed	d					14 49	15 11												16 11	
Alnmouth for Alnwick	d	14 58																		
Morpeth	d							15 49												16 49
Newcastle 8	a	15 27				15 34	15 56	16 14										16 35	16 56	17 15
Sunderland	d																			
Hartlepool	d																			
Newcastle 8	d	15 28				15 41	15 58			16 15				16 25	16 35			16 42	16 58	
Chester-le-Street	d									16 24										
Durham	d	15 41				15 53				16 31				16 37	16 47			16 52		
Darlington 7	a	16 00				16 09	16 25			16 46				16 55	17 03			17 10	17 25	
Middlesbrough	d								15 50											
Eaglescliffe	d																			
Darlington 7	d	16 00				16 10	16 26			16 48				16 56	17 04			17 10	17 26	
Northallerton	d								16 18	16 59				17 07						
Thirsk	d								16 28											
York 8	a	16 28				16 41	16 53		16 47	17 23				17 28	17 31			17 40	17 53	
Leeds 10	a					17 06			17 22	17 52								18 07		
Harrogate	d																			
Scarborough	d																			
York 8	d	16 29					16 55							17 30	17 34				17 56	
Doncaster 7	a	16 52												17 52	17 57					
Skipton	d																			
Keighley	d																			
Bradford Interchange	d			15 37																
Bradford Forster Square	d																			
Shipley	d																			
Halifax	d			15 52																
Brighouse	d			16 05																
Leeds 10	d		16 45		16 57	17 11							17 15				17 45	18 11		
Wakefield Westgate 7	d		16 56		17 09	17 23							17 27				17 56	18 23		
Wakefield Kirkgate 4	d			16 40																
Pontefract Monkhill	d			16 56																
Sheffield 7	a					17 51									18 20			18 51		
Hull	d															17 10				
Selby	d															17 43				
Doncaster 7	d	16 52	17 16	17 25	17a45								17 45	17 54		18 02	18 16			
Retford 10	d												17 59			18 17				
Lincoln	d																			
Newark North Gate 7	a	17 19												18 17						
	d	17 19									17 54			18 17						
Grantham 7	a										18 05		18 22			18 38				
	d										18 05	18 11	18 22			18 39				
Peterborough 8	a	17 49	18 06								18 26	18 38		18 48			19 06			
Norwich	a											20 22								
Peterborough 8	d	17 50	18 07								18 26			18 50			19 07			
Stevenage 4	a										18 56		19 07							
London Kings Cross 15 ⊖	a	18 45	19 02	19 05			18 54				19 25		19 36	19 45		19 47	20 00		19 53	

A from Edinburgh

Scotland, North East England, Yorkshire and Humberside - London

Route Diagram - see first Page of Table 26

		TP	TP	GR	EM	GR	NT	GR	XC	GR	XC	TP FO	GR	TP FX	GC	NT	NT	EM	GR	GR	XC
		◇1	◇1	R 1	◇	R 1		R 1	◇1	R 1	◇1 A	◇1	R 1	◇1	R 1				R 1	R 1	◇1
Aberdeen	d																				
Stonehaven	d																				
Montrose	d																				
Arbroath	d																				
Dundee	d																				
Leuchars 3	d																				
Kirkcaldy	d																				
Inverkeithing	d																				
Inverness	d																				
Perth	d																				
Stirling	d																				
Glasgow Central 15	d										15 00										
Motherwell	d										15 14										
Haymarket	d										15 56										
Edinburgh 10	a										16 01										
Edinburgh	d										16 05		16 30							17 00	
Dunbar	d																				
Berwick-upon-Tweed	d												17 11								
Alnmouth for Alnwick	d										17 01									17 58	
Morpeth	d										17 16										
Newcastle 8	a										17 34		17 56							18 27	
Sunderland	d														17 31	18 42					
Hartlepool	d														17 55		19 02				
Newcastle 8	d		17 02					17 25	17 32		17 41		17 58			19a05	19a51			18 28	18 35
Chester-le-Street	d		17 11						17 41												
Durham	d		17 18					17 37	17 48		17 53									18 41	18 47
Darlington 7	a		17 35					17 55	18 03		18 09		18 24							19 00	19 04
Middlesbrough	d	16 50										17 50		17 50							
Eaglescliffe	d														18 20						
Darlington 7	d		17 36					17 56	18 05		18 10		18 25							19 00	19 05
Northallerton	d	17 18	17 47					18 07				18 18		18 18	18 40						
Thirsk	d	17 28										18 28		18 28	18 49						
York 8	a	17 47	18 09					18 27	18 31		18 41	18 47	18 53	18 47	19 07					19 28	19 31
Leeds 10	a	18 22	18 37								19 08			19 37							
Harrogate	d																				
Scarborough	d						16 23														
York 8	d			18 01				18 29	18 34				18 55		19 10					19 29	19 34
Doncaster 7	a			18 22				18 52	18 57											19 53	19 57
Skipton	d																				
Keighley	d																				
Bradford Interchange	d																				
Bradford Forster Square	d																				
Shipley	d																				
Halifax	d																				
Brighouse	d																				
Leeds 10	d					18 15				18 45	19 11								19 15		
Wakefield Westgate 7	d					18 27				18 56	19 23								19 27		
Wakefield Kirkgate 4	d																				
Pontefract Monkhill	d																				
Sheffield 7	a								19 20		19 51										20 20
Hull	d						17 52														
Selby	d						18 26														
Doncaster 7	d			18 23		18 45	18a47	18 53		19 15								19 34	19 45	19 54	
Retford 10	d			18 38																	
Lincoln	d																	20a25			
Newark North Gate 7	a			18 53				19 17												20 17	
	d			18 53				19 17												20 17	
Grantham 7	a			19 05		19 16													20 16		
	d			19 05	19 08	19 16													20 16		
Peterborough 8	a			19 27	19 38			19 50		20 05										20 46	
Norwich	a				21 14																
Peterborough 8	d			19 27				19 50		20 06										20 46	
Stevenage 4	a			19 56		20 01		20 20					20 23						20 59	21 15	
London Kings Cross 15 ⊖	a			20 26		20 30		20 48		21 01			20 55		21 05				21 29	21 45	

A from Edinburgh

Scotland, North East England, Yorkshire and Humberside - London

Route Diagram - see first Page of Table 26

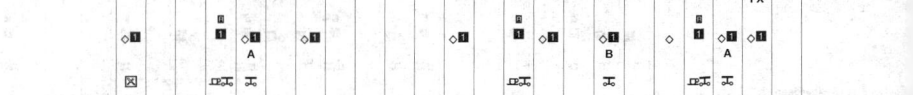

		HT			GR	XC	NT	TP	NT			NT	TP		GR	TP	NT	XC	EM	EM	GR	XC	TP FX		NT
		◇1			R 1	◇1 A		◇1					◇1		R 1	◇1		◇1 B		◇	R 1	◇1 A	◇1		
		⊠			🍴	☕									🍴			☕			🍴	☕			
Aberdeen	d														14 50										
Stonehaven	d														15 07										
Montrose	d														15 30										
Arbroath	d														15 46										
Dundee	d														16 04										
Leuchars 3	d														16 18										
Kirkcaldy	d														16 45										
Inverkeithing	d														17 03										
Inverness	d																								
Perth	d																								
Stirling	d																								
Glasgow Central 15	d																					16 52			
Motherwell	d																					17 14			
Haymarket	d														17 19							17 54			
Edinburgh 10	a														17 27							17 59			
Edinburgh	d					17 08									17 30							18 04			
Dunbar	d					17 28									17 51							18 25			
Berwick-upon-Tweed	d					17 51									18 16							18 48			
Alnmouth for Alnwick	d																					19 08			19 22
Morpeth	d						18 26										19 01								19 47
Newcastle 8 ⛴	a					18 38	18 49								19 03		19 25					19 38			20 07
Sunderland ⛴	d											21 58													
Hartlepool	d								20 10																
Newcastle 8 ⛴	d					18 41			21a02			22a19	18 52		19 04			19 33				19 40			
Chester-le-Street	d												19 01												
Durham	d					18 53							19 08					19 48				19 53			
Darlington 7	a					19 09							19 24		19 33			20 03				20 08			
Middlesbrough	d							18 50															18 50		
Eaglescliffe	d																								
Darlington 7	d					19 10							19 25		19 33			20 05				20 10			
Northallerton	d							19 18					19 36										19 18		
Thirsk	d							19 26								←							19 26		
York 8	a					19 39		19 50					20 07		20 01	20 07		20 31				20 41	19 50		
Leeds 10	a					20 08							↪			20 35						21 08	21 37		
Harrogate	d																								
Scarborough	d																								
York 8	d														20 03			20 34							
Doncaster 7	a														20 26			21 00							
Skipton	d																								
Keighley	d																								
Bradford Interchange	d																								
Bradford Forster Square	d																								
Shipley	d																								
Halifax	d																								
Brighouse	d																								
Leeds 10	d				19 45	20 11															20 45	21 11			
Wakefield Westgate 7	d				19 56	20 23															20 56	21 23			
Wakefield Kirkgate 4	d																								
Pontefract Monkhill	d																								
Sheffield 7 ⛴	a					20 51												21 26				21 51			
Hull	d	19 10																							
Selby	d	19 43																							
Doncaster 7	d	20 02			20 16										20 27				20 33		21 16				
Retford 10	d	20 17																			21 33				
Lincoln	d																		21a26						
Newark North Gate 7	a																								
	d																								
Grantham 7	a	20 37																			21 55				
	d	20 38																		21 10	21 55				
Peterborough 8	a				21 03										21 16					21 37	22 15				
Norwich	a																			23 18					
Peterborough 8	d				21 04										21 16						22 16				
Stevenage 4	a														21 47						22 47				
London Kings Cross 15 ⊖	a	21 46			21 58										22 19						23 14				

A ☕ to Leeds

B ☕ to York

Scotland, North East England, Yorkshire and Humberside - London

Route Diagram - see first Page of Table 26

		TP	GR	XC	GR		TP	TP	NT		NT	GR		NT
			R		R							R		
		◇1	1	◇1	1		◇1	◇1				1		
Aberdeen	d											18 16		
Stonehaven	d											18 33		
Montrose	d											18 56		
Arbroath	d											19 12		
Dundee	d											19 30		
Leuchars 3	d											19 44		
Kirkcaldy	d											20 08		
Inverkeithing	d											20 24		
Inverness	d													
Perth	d													
Stirling	d													
Glasgow Central 15	d			18 59										
Motherwell	d			19 15										
Haymarket	d			19 53								20 43		
Edinburgh 10	a			19 58								20 48		
Edinburgh	d		18 30	20 05								21 00		
Dunbar	d		18 51	20 25								21 21		
Berwick-upon-Tweed	d		19 14	20 48								21 47		
Alnmouth for Alnwick	d		19 36	21 08								22 10		
Morpeth	d		19 53									22 26		22 45
Newcastle 8	a		20 12	21 38								22 43		23 07
Sunderland	d													
Hartlepool	d													
Newcastle 8	d		20 14		21 15			21 54			22 21	22 44		
Chester-le-Street	d										22 30			
Durham	d		20 27		21 27			22 08			22 39	22 58		
Darlington 7	a		20 45		21 45			22 24			22 59	23 19		
Middlesbrough	d	20 04					21 50							
Eaglescliffe	d													
Darlington 7	d	20 35	20 46		21 46		22 19	22 25				23 19		
Northallerton	d	20 46			21 57		22 30	22 36				23s46		
Thirsk	d	21 00					22 38							
York 8	a	21 24	21 14		22 17		22 56	23 00				00 13		
Leeds 10	a							23 33				00 50		
Harrogate	d													
Scarborough	d													
York 8	d		21 16		22 19									
Doncaster 7	a		21 38		22 42									
Skipton	d													
Keighley	d													
Bradford Interchange	d													
Bradford Forster Square	d													
Shipley	d													
Halifax	d													
Brighouse	d													
Leeds 10	d													
Wakefield Westgate 7	d								21 57					
Wakefield Kirkgate 4	d								22 00					
Pontefract Monkhill	d								22a18					
Sheffield 7	a													
Hull	d													
Selby	d													
Doncaster 7	d		21 39		22 42									
Retford 10	d													
Lincoln	d													
Newark North Gate 7	a		22 02		23 06									
	d		22 02		23 06									
Grantham 7	a		22 15		23 18									
	d		22 15		23 18									
Peterborough 8	a		22 35		23 39									
Norwich	a													
Peterborough 8	d		22 35		23 40									
Stevenage 4	a		23 05		00s21									
London Kings Cross 15 ⊖	a		23 36		00 57									

Scotland, North East England, Yorkshire and Humberside - London

Route Diagram - see first Page of Table 26

		GR	GR	EM	GR	GR	TP	XC	GR	XC	EM	NT	GR	XC	GR	GR	GR	TP
		R	R		R	R			R				R		R	R	R	
		1	1		1	1	◇1	◇1	1	◇1	◇1		1	◇1	1	1	1	◇1
		☕	☕		☕🍴	☕🍴		🍴	☕🍴	🍴	☕		☕🍴	🍴	☕🍴	☕🍴	☕🍴	🍴
Aberdeen	d		18p16															
Stonehaven	d		18p33															
Montrose	d		18p56															
Arbroath	d		19p12															
Dundee	d		19p30															
Leuchars [3]	d		19p44															
Kirkcaldy	d		20p08															
Inverkeithing	d		20p24															
Inverness	d																	
Perth	d																	
Stirling	d																	
Glasgow Central [15]	d																	
Motherwell	d																	
Haymarket	d		20p43															
Edinburgh [10]	a		20p48															
Edinburgh	d		21p00															
Dunbar	d		21p21															
Berwick-upon-Tweed	d		21p47															
Alnmouth for Alnwick	d		22p10															
Morpeth	d		22p26															
Newcastle [8]	a		22p43															
Sunderland	d																	
Hartlepool	d											07 03						
Newcastle [8]	d	21p15	22p44			04 45						07a51			06 00			06 11
Chester-le-Street	d																	06 21
Durham	d	21p27	22p58			04 59									06 12			06 28
Darlington [7]	a	21p45	23p19			05 16									06 30			06 44
Middlesbrough	d						05 55											
Eaglescliffe	d																	
Darlington [7]	d	21p46	23p19			05 17									06 30			06 45
Northallerton	d	21p57	23c46			05 29	06 23											06 56
Thirsk	d						06 31											07 04
York [8]	a	22p17	00 13			05 57	06 49								06 58			07 30
Leeds [10]	a		00 50				07 20											→
Harrogate	d																	
Scarborough	d																	
York [8]	d	22p19				06 00								06 17	07 00			
Doncaster [7]	a	22p42				06 22									07 23			
Skipton	d																	
Keighley	d																	
Bradford Interchange	d																	
Bradford Forster Square	d																	
Shipley	d																	
Halifax	d																	
Brighouse	d																	
Leeds [10]	d				05 05			06 00	06 05	06 15	06 34		07 05	07 10				
Wakefield Westgate [7]	d				05 16			06 12	06 17	06 29	06 46		07 16	07 23				
Wakefield Kirkgate [4]	d																	
Pontefract Monkhill	d																	
Sheffield [7]	a							06 45			07 22			07 51				
Hull	d																06 50	
Selby	d															←	07 24	
Doncaster [7]	d	22p42			05 35	06 23			06 35	06a46			07 35		07 24	07 35	07 43	
Retford [10]	d				05 49				06 49				→					
Lincoln	d																	
Newark North Gate [7]	a	23p06			06 04				07 04							07 59		
	d	23p06			06 04				07 04							07 59		
Grantham [7]	a	23p18			06 17				07 17							08 11	08 16	
	d	23p18		05 51	06 17				07 17							08 11	08 16	
Peterborough [8]	a	23p39		06 25	06 37	07 11			07 37						08 13	08 31	08 38	
Norwich	a																	
Peterborough [8]	d	23p40			06 37	07 13			07 37						08 14	08 32	08 39	
Stevenage [4]	a	00s21			07 06				08 06							09 01		
London Kings Cross [15]	a	00 57			07 37	08 08			08 37						09 10	09 30	09 36	

b Previous night, stops to pick up only

c Previous night, stops to set down only

Table 26

Saturdays

Scotland, North East England, Yorkshire and Humberside - London

Route Diagram - see first Page of Table 26

		XC	TP	GR	EM	EM		GR	GR	XC	GR	GC	TP			GC		GR	NT	NT	EM	GR	XC	GR	HT
				R				R	R		R	R				R		R				R		R	
		◇1	◇1	1	◇1	◇		1	1	◇1	1	1	◇1			1		1			◇	1	◇1	1	◇1
												A													
		T	T	☕T	☕			☕T	☕T	T	☕T	✕☕	T			☕		☕T				☕T	T	☕T	⊠
Aberdeen	d																								
Stonehaven	d																								
Montrose	d																								
Arbroath	d																								
Dundee	d																								
Leuchars 3	d																								
Kirkcaldy	d																								
Inverkeithing	d																								
Inverness	d																								
Perth	d																								
Stirling	d																								
Glasgow Central 15	d																								
Motherwell	d																								
Haymarket	d																								
Edinburgh 10	a																								
Edinburgh	d																								
Dunbar	d																								
Berwick-upon-Tweed	d																								
Alnmouth for Alnwick	d																								
Morpeth	d																								
Newcastle 8 ⛴	a																								
Sunderland ⛴	d															06 43			07 55	08 30					
Hartlepool	d															07 09									
Newcastle 8 ⛴	d	06 22		06 30						06 45	06 55								08a18	08a52		07 22	07 35		
Chester-le-Street	d																								
Durham	d	06 37		06 42						06 57	07 07											07 35	07 47		
Darlington 7	a	06 52		07 00						07 13	07 25											07 52	08 03		
Middlesbrough	d												07 12												
Eaglescliffe	d															07 30									
Darlington 7	d	06 54		07 01						07 14	07 26											07 53	08 04		
Northallerton	d			07 12									07 43			07 48						08 06			
Thirsk	d		←										07 51			07 57									
York 8	a	07 21	07 30	07 32						07 40	07 53		08 11			08 14						08 27	08 30		
Leeds 10	a		08 04							08 08			08 52												
Harrogate	d																								
Scarborough	d																								
York 8	d	07 24		07 34							07 55					08 16						08 28	08 34		
Doncaster 7	a	07 49		07 56							08 17											08 53	08 57		
Skipton	d							06 55																	
Keighley	d							07u08																	
Bradford Interchange	d											06 51													
Bradford Forster Square	d								07 33																
Shipley	d							07u18	07u39																
Halifax	d											07 03													
Brighouse	d											07 14													
Leeds 10	d				07 34			07 35	08 05	08 12														08 40	
Wakefield Westgate 7	d				07 46				08 16	08 24														08 51	
Wakefield Kirkgate 4	d											07 38													
Pontefract Monkhill	d											07 58													
Sheffield 7 ⛴	a	08 18			08 21					08 51													09 20		
Hull	d																								08 25
Selby	d																	←							09 00
Doncaster 7	d			07 57				08 09	08 35		08 18	08 31						08 35				08 53		09 12	09 23
Retford 10	d								→									08 52							09 38
Lincoln	d																								
Newark North Gate 7	a			08 21														09 08				09 19			
	d			08 21														09 08				09 19			
Grantham 7	a							08 41														09 32			09 59
	d					08 20		08 42													09 03	09 32			09 59
Peterborough 8	a			08 51		08 58												09 36			09 41			10 00	
Norwich	a					10 43															11 15				
Peterborough 8	d			08 51														09 37						10 00	
Stevenage 4	a																								
London Kings Cross 15 ⊖	a			09 46				09 52			09 54	10 09				10 15		10 31				10 44		10 55	11 09

A ☕ to Doncaster ✕ from Doncaster

Table 26

Saturdays

Scotland, North East England, Yorkshire and Humberside - London

Route Diagram - see first Page of Table 26

		GR		EM	GR	XC	TP	GR	NT			GR		XC	EM	EM	GR	XC	GR	NT	TP	GC		NT	TP
		R			R			R				R					R		R			R			
		1		◇	1	◇1	◇1	1				1		◇1		◇	1	◇1	1		◇1	1			◇1
																		A							
		🛏🍴			🛏🍴	🍴	🍴	🛏🍴				🛏🍴		🍴			🛏🍴	🍴	🛏🍴		🍴	🛏			🍴
Aberdeen	d																								
Stonehaven	d																								
Montrose	d																								
Arbroath	d																								
Dundee	d																								
Leuchars 3	d																								
Kirkcaldy	d																								
Inverkeithing	d																								
Inverness	d																								
Perth	d																								
Stirling	d																								
Glasgow Central 15	d																	06 01							
Motherwell	d																	06 16							
Haymarket	d																	06 57							
Edinburgh 10	a																	07 02							
Edinburgh	d					06 06		06 20				06 55		07 00				07 07	07 30						
Dunbar	d							06 40										07 27							
Berwick-upon-Tweed	d					06 48		07 05						07 40					08 12						
Alnmouth for Alnwick	d					07 08		07 25	07 22					08 00											
Morpeth	d							07 41	07 55					08 14						08 49					
Newcastle 8 ⛴	a					07 38		07 58	08 20			08 22		08 32				08 37	08 57	09 14					
Sunderland ⛴	d																					08 30			
Hartlepool	d																					08 54		09 02	
Newcastle 8 ⛴	d					07 40	07 43	07 59				08 24		08 36				08 43	08 59					09a51	09 15
Chester-le-Street	d																								09 24
Durham	d					07 52	07 57					08 37		08 48				08 56							09 31
Darlington 7	a					08 08	08 13	08 27				08 55		09 04				09 12	09 25						09 47
Middlesbrough	d																				08 50				
Eaglescliffe	d																					09 17			
Darlington 7	d					08 10	08 14	08 27				08 56		09 05				09 13	09 26						09 48
Northallerton	d						08 26					09 07									09 18	09 40			09 59
Thirsk	d						08 34														09 28	09 49			
York 8	a					08 41	08 52	08 55				09 27		09 32				09 43	09 54		09 47	10 06			10 21
Leeds 10	a					09 07	09 22											10 09			10 22				10 52
Harrogate	d				08 13																				
Scarborough	d																								
York 8	d							08 56				09 29		09 35					09 56			10 09			
Doncaster 7	a											09 52		09 57											
Skipton	d																								
Keighley	d																								
Bradford Interchange	d																								
Bradford Forster Square	d																								
Shipley	d																								
Halifax	d																								
Brighouse	d																								
Leeds 10	d				09 05	09 11											10 05	10 12							
Wakefield Westgate 7	d				09 17	09 24											10 16	10 24							
Wakefield Kirkgate 4	d																								
Pontefract Monkhill	d																								
Sheffield 7 ⛴	a					09 52								10 20				10 51							
Hull	d																								
Selby	d																								
Doncaster 7	d				09 35							09 52			10 24		10 35								
Retford 10	d											10 07													
Lincoln	d	09 30													11a16										
Newark North Gate 7	a	09 52			09 59												10 59								
	d	09 52			09 59												10 59								
Grantham 7	a	10 06			10 12							10 29					11 11								
	d	10 06		10 09	10 12							10 29				11 10	11 13								
Peterborough 8	a	10 26		10 38	10 36			10 05				10 50				11 39	11 36								
Norwich	a			12 18												13 13									
Peterborough 8	d	10 27			10 36			10 06				10 51					11 36								
Stevenage 4	a	10 59			11 06																				
London Kings Cross 15 ⊖	a	11 27			11 38			11 02				11 46					12 31		11 56			12 07			

A 🍴 from Edinburgh

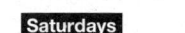

Scotland, North East England, Yorkshire and Humberside - London

Route Diagram - see first Page of Table 26

		GR	XC	NT	NT	HT	NT	NT		EM	GR	XC	GR	NT	TP	TP	GR	GC		XC		EM	GR	XC	GR
		R 1	◇1			◇1				◇	R 1	◇1	R 1		◇1	◇1	R 1	R 1		◇1		◇	R 1	◇1	R 1
Aberdeen	d																								
Stonehaven	d																								
Montrose	d																								
Arbroath	d																								
Dundee	d											06 32													
Leuchars 3	d											06 46													
Kirkcaldy	d											07 21													
Inverkeithing	d											07 38													
Inverness	d																								
Perth	d																								
Stirling	d																								
Glasgow Central 15	d	06 50																						07 50	
Motherwell	d	07 04																						08 05	
Haymarket	d	07 46										07 56												08 50	
Edinburgh 10	a	07 52										08 01												08 54	
Edinburgh	d	08 00										08 05	08 30				09 00							09 06	09 30
Dunbar	d																							09 26	
Berwick-upon-Tweed	d											08 46	09 11											09 49	10 11
Alnmouth for Alnwick	d	08 58										09 08													
Morpeth	d													09 49											
Newcastle 8	a	09 27										09 39	09 58	10 14			10 23							10 38	10 57
Sunderland	d																								
Hartlepool	d			10 02			11 02	12 02																	
Newcastle 8	d	09 28	09 35	10a51			11a51	12a52				09 41	09 59			10 15	10 25			10 35				10 44	10 59
Chester-le-Street	d															10 24									
Durham	d	09 41	09 47									09 55				10 31	10 38			10 47				10 56	
Darlington 7	a	09 59	10 04									10 10	10 28			10 47	10 55			11 03				11 12	11 27
Middlesbrough	d														09 50										
Eaglescliffe	d																								
Darlington 7	d	09 59	10 05									10 12	10 28			10 48	10 56			11 04				11 13	11 28
Northallerton	d														10 18	10 59	11 07								
Thirsk	d														10 28										
York 8	a	10 28	10 31									10 41	10 56		10 47	11 22	11 28			11 31				11 41	11 56
Leeds 10	a											11 08			11 22	11 53								12 07	
Harrogate	d																								
Scarborough	d																								
York 8	d	10 29	10 34										10 58				11 30			11 34					11 57
Doncaster 7	a	10 52	10 57														11 52			11 57					
Skipton	d																								
Keighley	d																								
Bradford Interchange	d																	10 22							
Bradford Forster Square	d																								
Shipley	d																								
Halifax	d																	10 38							
Brighouse	d																	10 48							
Leeds 10	d										11 05	11 11											12 05	12 11	
Wakefield Westgate 7	d				10 29						11 16	11 23											12 16	12 24	
Wakefield Kirkgate 4	d				10a32													11 11							
Pontefract Monkhill	d																	11 35							
Sheffield 7	a		11 20									11 51								12 20				12 51	
Hull	d					10 30																			
Selby	d					11 05																			
Doncaster 7	d	10 52				11 25					11 35						11 53	12 05					12 35		
Retford 10	d					11 40											12 08								
Lincoln	d																								
Newark North Gate 7	a	11 18									11 59												13 02		
	d	11 18									11 59												13 02		
Grantham 7	a					12 00					12 11												13 14		
	d					12 00				12 07	12 11											13 09	13 14		
Peterborough 8	a	11 48								12 38	12 32						12 48					13 38	13 35		
Norwich	a									14 13												15 13			
Peterborough 8	d	11 49									12 33						12 50						13 37		
Stevenage 4	a										13 01														
London Kings Cross 15 ⊖	a	12 46				13 09					13 31		12 55				13 45	13 46					14 31		13 55

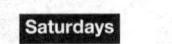

Scotland, North East England, Yorkshire and Humberside - London

Route Diagram - see first Page of Table 26

		NT	TP	TP	GR	XC	EM	EM	GR	XC	GR	NT	TP	TP	GR	XC	HT	EM	GR	XC
					R				R		R				R				R	
			◇1	◇1	1	◇1		◇	1	◇1	1		◇1	◇1	1	◇1	◇1	◇	1	◇1
										A										A
			[trolley]	[trolley]	[FP trolley]	[trolley]			[FP trolley]	[trolley]	[FP trolley]		[trolley]	[trolley]	[FP trolley]	[trolley]	⊠		[FP trolley]	[trolley]
Aberdeen	d										07 52									08 20
Stonehaven	d										08 09									08 38
Montrose	d										08 32									08 59
Arbroath	d										08 48									09 15
Dundee	d										09 06									09 32
Leuchars [3]	d										09 20									09 47
Kirkcaldy	d										09 44									10 17
Inverkeithing	d										10 01									10 32
Inverness	d																			
Perth	d																			
Stirling	d																			
Glasgow Central [15]	d									09 00										
Motherwell	d									09 15										
Haymarket	d									09 57	10 19									10 52
Edinburgh [10]	a									10 02	10 26									10 58
Edinburgh	d				10 00					10 05	10 30				11 00					11 05
Dunbar	d																			11 25
Berwick-upon-Tweed	d									10 48	11 11									11 48
Alnmouth for Alnwick	d				10 58															12 08
Morpeth	d	10 49								11 19		11 49								
Newcastle [8] ⛴	a	11 13			11 27					11 38	11 58	12 13			12 23					12 38
Sunderland ⛴	d																			
Hartlepool	d																			
Newcastle [8] ⛴	d			11 15	11 28	11 35				11 42	11 59			12 17	12 25	12 35				12 44
Chester-le-Street	d			11 24																
Durham	d			11 31	11 41	11 47				11 55				12 29	12 38	12 47				12 56
Darlington [7]	a			11 46	11 59	12 04				12 11	12 28			12 45	12 55	13 03				13 12
Middlesbrough	d		10 50										11 50							
Eaglescliffe	d																			
Darlington [7]	d			11 48	11 59	12 05				12 12	12 28			12 46	12 56	13 04				13 13
Northallerton	d		11 18	11 59									12 18	12 58	13 07					
Thirsk	d		11 28										12 28							
York [8]	a		11 47	12 21	12 28	12 31				12 42	12 56		12 47	13 21	13 27	13 31				13 41
Leeds [10]	a		12 22	12 52						13 08			13 22	13 52						14 08
Harrogate	d																			
Scarborough	d																			
York [8]	d				12 29	12 34					12 58				13 29	13 34				
Doncaster [7]	a				12 52	12 57									13 51	13 57				
Skipton	d																			
Keighley	d																			
Bradford Interchange	d																			
Bradford Forster Square	d																			
Shipley	d																			
Halifax	d																			
Brighouse	d																			
Leeds [10]	d								13 05	13 11									14 05	14 11
Wakefield Westgate [7]	d								13 16	13 23									14 16	14 24
Wakefield Kirkgate [4]	d																			
Pontefract Monkhill	d																			
Sheffield [7] ⛴	a					13 20				13 51						14 20				14 51
Hull	d																13 30			
Selby	d																14 06			
Doncaster [7]	d				12 52		13 05		13 35						13 52		14 25		14 35	
Retford [10]	d														14 07		14 40			
Lincoln	d						13a55													
Newark North Gate [7]	a				13 17				13 59										15 03	
	d				13 17				13 59										15 03	
Grantham [7]	a								14 12								15 01		15 16	
	d							14 07	14 12								15 01	15 10	15 16	
Peterborough [8]	a				13 46			14 41	14 32						14 47			15 39	15 36	
Norwich	a							16 15										17 13		
Peterborough [8]	d				13 49				14 32						14 49				15 36	
Stevenage [4]	a								15 01											
London Kings Cross [15] ⊖	a				14 45				15 31		14 55				15 45		16 10		16 31	

A [trolley] from Edinburgh

Scotland, North East England, Yorkshire and Humberside - London

Route Diagram - see first Page of Table 26

		TP	GC	GR	NT	NT	TP	GR	XC	NT			NT	EM	GR	NT	EM	GR	XC	GR		NT	TP	TP	GR
			R	R				R							R			R		R					R
		◇1	1	1			◇1	1	◇1						1		◇	1	◇1	1			◇1	◇1	1
				A																B					
		⊼	⊡	⊡⊼			⊼	⊡⊼	⊼						⊡⊼			⊡⊼	⊼	⊡⊼			⊼	⊼	⊡⊼
Aberdeen	d																			09 52					
Stonehaven	d																			10 09					
Montrose	d																			10 32					
Arbroath	d																			10 49					
Dundee	d																			11 06					
Leuchars 3	d																			11 20					
Kirkcaldy	d																			11 44					
Inverkeithing	d																			12 01					
Inverness	d			07 55																					
Perth	d			09 56																					
Stirling	d			10 30																					
Glasgow Central 15	d																		10 59						
Motherwell	d																		11 14						
Haymarket	d			11 11															11 56	12 17					
Edinburgh 10	a			11 17															12 02	12 25					
Edinburgh	d			11 30				12 00											12 09	12 30					13 00
Dunbar	d																								
Berwick-upon-Tweed	d			12 11															12 48	13 11					
Alnmouth for Alnwick	d							12 58																	
Morpeth	d				12 49																	13 49			
Newcastle 8	a			12 58	13 13			13 27											13 35	13 58		14 15			14 23
Sunderland	d		12 18																						
Hartlepool	d		12 43			13 02				14 02			15 02			16 02									
Newcastle 8	d			12 59		13a51	13 15	13 28	13 35	14a51			15a51			16a51			13 44	13 59				14 18	14 25
Chester-le-Street	d						13 24																		
Durham	d						13 31	13 41	13 47										13 56					14 31	14 38
Darlington 7	a			13 28			13 46	13 59	14 04										14 12	14 28				14 46	14 55
Middlesbrough	d	12 50																					13 50		
Eaglescliffe	d		13 05																						
Darlington 7	d			13 28			13 48	13 59	14 05										14 13	14 28				14 48	14 56
Northallerton	d	13 18	13 27				13 58																14 18	14 59	15 07
Thirsk	d	13 28	13 36																				14 28		
York 8	a	13 47	13 53	13 56			14 23	14 28	14 31										14 41	14 56			14 47	15 22	15 28
Leeds 10	a	14 22					14 52												15 06				15 22	15 53	
Harrogate	d																								
Scarborough	d																								
York 8	d		13 55	13 58				14 29	14 34											14 58					15 30
Doncaster 7	a							14 53	14 57																15 52
Skipton	d																								
Keighley	d																								
Bradford Interchange	d																								
Bradford Forster Square	d																								
Shipley	d																								
Halifax	d																								
Brighouse	d																								
Leeds 10	d														14 40			15 05	15 12						
Wakefield Westgate 7	d														14 52			15 17	15 24						
Wakefield Kirkgate 4	d																								
Pontefract Monkhill	d																								
Sheffield 7	a								15 20										15 51						
Hull	d																								
Selby	d																								
Doncaster 7	d							14 53						15 07	15 11			15 35							15 53
Retford 10	d																								16 07
Lincoln	d													15a57											
Newark North Gate 7	a							15 17										15 59							
	d							15 18										15 59							
Grantham 7	a																	16 12							
	d																16 07	16 12							
Peterborough 8	a							15 47							15 59		16 40	16 33							16 47
Norwich	a																18 18								
Peterborough 8	d							15 49							16 00			16 33							16 49
Stevenage 4	a																	17 03							
London Kings Cross 15 ⊖	a		15 49	15 57				16 45							16 56			17 33		17 00					17 46

A The Highland Chieftain

B The Northern Lights

Table 26

Saturdays

Scotland, North East England, Yorkshire and Humberside - London

Route Diagram - see first Page of Table 26

		XC		HT	EM	NT		EM	GR	XC	GR	NT	TP		XC	TP		GR	GC	GR	XC	GR	NT	TP	TP
									R		R							R	R	R		R			
		◇1		◇1				◇	1	◇1	1		◇1		◇1	◇1		1	1	1	◇1	1		◇1	◇1
																					A				
		[trolley]		⊠					[restaurant][trolley]	[trolley]	[restaurant][trolley]		[trolley]		[trolley]	[trolley]		[restaurant][trolley]	[restaurant]	[restaurant][trolley]	[trolley]	[restaurant][trolley]		[trolley]	[trolley]
Aberdeen	d																								
Stonehaven	d																								
Montrose	d																								
Arbroath	d																								
Dundee	d																								
Leuchars 3	d																								
Kirkcaldy	d																								
Inverkeithing	d																								
Inverness	d																								
Perth	d																								
Stirling	d																								
Glasgow Central 15	d																				12 51				
Motherwell	d																				13 06				
Haymarket	d																								
Edinburgh 10	a																				13 54				
Edinburgh	d									13 08	13 30							14 00			14 08	14 30			
Dunbar	d									13 29															
Berwick-upon-Tweed	d										14 11										14 49	15 11			
Alnmouth for Alnwick	d									14 09								14 58							
Morpeth	d											14 49											15 49		
Newcastle 8 ⛴	a									14 39	14 56	15 14						15 27			15 35	15 56	16 15		
Sunderland ⛴	d																								
Hartlepool	d					17 02																			
Newcastle 8 ⛴	d	14 35				17a51				14 44	14 58				15 07	15 15		15 28			15 41	15 58			16 15
Chester-le-Street	d															15 24									16 24
Durham	d	14 47								14 56					15 19	15 31		15 41			15 53				16 31
Darlington 7	a	15 03								15 12	15 25				15 35	15 46		15 59			16 10	16 25			16 46
Middlesbrough	d												14 50											15 50	
Eaglescliffe	d																								
Darlington 7	d	15 04								15 13	15 26				15 36	15 48		15 59			16 11	16 26			16 48
Northallerton	d												15 18			15 59								16 18	16 59
Thirsk	d												15 28											16 28	
York 8	a	15 31								15 41	15 53		15 47		16 03	16 21		16 28			16 41	16 53		16 47	17 23
Leeds 10	a									16 07			16 22		16 32	16 52					17 07			17 22	17 52
Harrogate	d																								
Scarborough	d																								
York 8	d	15 34									15 55							16 29				16 55			
Doncaster 7	a	15 57																16 55							
Skipton	d																								
Keighley	d																								
Bradford Interchange	d																		15 22						
Bradford Forster Square	d																								
Shipley	d																								
Halifax	d																		15 35						
Brighouse	d																		15 46						
Leeds 10	d								16 05	16 12					16 40					17 05	17 11				
Wakefield Westgate 7	d								16 17	16 24					16 52					17 17	17 23				
Wakefield Kirkgate 4	d																		16 11						
Pontefract Monkhill	d																		16 29						
Sheffield 7 ⛴	a	16 20								16 51					17 20						17 51				
Hull	d			15 30																					
Selby	d			16 05																					
Doncaster 7	d			16 23	16 27				16 35									16 56	17 03	17 35					
Retford 10	d			16 38																					
Lincoln	d				17a20																				
Newark North Gate 7	a								16 59									17 19		17 59					
	d								16 59									17 19		17 59					
Grantham 7	a			16 59					17 11											18 11					
	d			16 59				17 06	17 11											18 11					
Peterborough 8	a							17 37	17 31									17 49		18 31					
Norwich	a							19 19																	
Peterborough 8	d								17 32									17 49		18 32					
Stevenage 4	a																			19 01					
London Kings Cross 15 ⊖	a			18 08					18 27		17 55							18 44	18 45	19 30		18 55			

A [trolley] from Edinburgh

Scotland, North East England, Yorkshire and Humberside - London

Route Diagram - see first Page of Table 26

Station		EM	GR	XC	EM	EM	GR	XC	GR	NT	NT	TP	TP	GR	XC	HT	GR	XC	GR	TP
		◇	R 1	◇1	◇1	◇	R 1	◇1	R 1			◇1	◇1	R 1	◇1	◇1	R 1	◇1	R 1	◇1
Aberdeen	d																			
Stonehaven	d																			
Montrose	d																			
Arbroath	d																			
Dundee	d																			
Leuchars 3	d																			
Kirkcaldy	d																			
Inverkeithing	d																			
Inverness	d																			
Perth	d																			
Stirling	d																			
Glasgow Central 15	d																	15 00		
Motherwell	d																	15 14		
Haymarket	d																	15 56		
Edinburgh 10	a																	16 01		
Edinburgh	d		15 00					15 08	15 30					16 00				16 05	16 30	
Dunbar	d							15 28												
Berwick-upon-Tweed	d								16 11										17 11	
Alnmouth for Alnwick	d																	17 03		
Morpeth	d										16 49							17 17		
Newcastle 8	a		16 23					16 35	16 56		17 13			17 23				17 35	17 56	
Sunderland	d																			
Hartlepool	d																			
Newcastle 8	d		16 25	16 35				16 41	16 58				17 02	17 25	17 32			17 44	17 58	
Chester-le-Street	d												17 11		17 41					
Durham	d		16 38	16 47				16 52					17 18	17 38	17 48			17 56		
Darlington 7	a		16 55	17 03				17 09	17 25				17 34	17 55	18 03			18 12	18 25	
Middlesbrough	d											16 50								17 50
Eaglescliffe	d																			
Darlington 7	d		16 56	17 04				17 10	17 26				17 35	17 56	18 05			18 13	18 26	
Northallerton	d		17 07									17 18	17 46	18 07						18 18
Thirsk	d											17 28								18 28
York 8	a		17 27	17 31				17 41	17 53			17 47	18 09	18 27	18 31			18 41	18 53	18 47
Leeds 10	a							18 08				18 22	18 37					19 08		19 35
Harrogate	d																			
Scarborough	d									16 23										
York 8	d		17 29	17 34	17 50				17 55					18 29	18 34				18 55	
Doncaster 7	a		17 52	17 57	18 11									18 52	18 57					
Skipton	d																			
Keighley	d																			
Bradford Interchange	d																			
Bradford Forster Square	d																			
Shipley	d																			
Halifax	d																			
Brighouse	d																			
Leeds 10	d						18 05	18 11									19 05	19 11		
Wakefield Westgate 7	d						18 16	18 23									19 16	19 24		
Wakefield Kirkgate 4	d																			
Pontefract Monkhill	d																			
Sheffield 7	a			18 20	18 44			18 51							19 21			19 51		
Hull	d									17 52						18 30				
Selby	d									18 26						19 05				
Doncaster 7	d		17 53				18 39			18a47				18 53		19 27	19 36			
Retford 10	d		18 07																	
Lincoln	d																			
Newark North Gate 7	a						19 02							19 17			20 00			
	d						19 02							19 17			20 00			
Grantham 7	a						19 15									19 57	20 12			
	d	18 15				19 08	19 15									19 57	20 12			
Peterborough 8	a	18 42	18 47			19 39	19 35							19 47			20 32			
Norwich	a	20 18				21 14														
Peterborough 8	d		18 50				19 36							19 49			20 33			
Stevenage 4	a																21 02			
London Kings Cross 15 ⊖	a		19 45				20 31		19 55					20 45		21 09	21 31		20 55	

Table 26

Saturdays

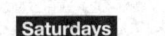

Scotland, North East England, Yorkshire and Humberside - London

Route Diagram - see first Page of Table 26

		GC	NT	GR	XC	NT	NT	NT	NT	GR	XC	TP	TP	GR	TP	NT	NT	XC	XC	GR	TP
		R		R						R				R						R	
		1		1	◇1					1	◇1	◇1	◇1	1	◇1			◇1	◇1	1	◇1
											A							B	C		
		⊡		⊡⊼	⊼					⊡⊼	⊼			⊡⊼				⊼	⊼	⊡⊼	
Aberdeen	d													14 50							
Stonehaven	d													15 07							
Montrose	d													15 30							
Arbroath	d													15 46							
Dundee	d													16 04							
Leuchars 3	d													16 18							
Kirkcaldy	d													16 45							
Inverkeithing	d													17 01							
Inverness	d																				
Perth	d																				
Stirling	d																				
Glasgow Central 15	d																		16 52		
Motherwell	d																		17 14		
Haymarket	d													17 18					17 56		
Edinburgh 10	a													17 26					18 01		
Edinburgh	d			17 00							17 08			17 30					18 05	18 30	
Dunbar	d										17 28			17 50					18 25		
Berwick-upon-Tweed	d										17 51			18 15					18 48	19 11	
Alnmouth for Alnwick	d			17 58													18 48		19 08		
Morpeth	d		17 52													18 50	19 13				
Newcastle 8	a		18 15	18 27							18 38			19 01		19 13	19 34		19 41	20 01	
Sunderland	d	17 29				18 42		20 38	21 43												
Hartlepool	d	17 53					19 02														
Newcastle 8	d			18 28	18 35	19a04	19a51	21a04	22a04		18 44		18 52	19 03				19 35	19 44		
Chester-le-Street	d												19 01								
Durham	d			18 41	18 48						18 56		19 08					19 49	19 56		
Darlington 7	a			18 59	19 04						19 12		19 24	19 31				20 05	20 12		
Middlesbrough	d											18 50									20 10
Eaglescliffe	d	18 12																			
Darlington 7	d			18 59	19 05						19 13		19 25	19 32				20 06	20 13		
Northallerton	d	18 31										19 18	19 36								20 39
Thirsk	d	18 41										19 26			←						20 47
York 8	a	18 58		19 28	19 31						19 41	19 50	20 07	20 00	20 07			20 31	20 42		21 06
Leeds 10	a										20 08		↪		20 35				21 07		21 37
Harrogate	d																				
Scarborough	d																				
York 8	d	19 01		19 29	19 34									20 01				20 34			
Doncaster 7	a			19 54	19 57									20 25				20 55			
Skipton	d																				
Keighley	d																				
Bradford Interchange	d																				
Bradford Forster Square	d																				
Shipley	d																				
Halifax	d																				
Brighouse	d																				
Leeds 10	d									20 05	20 11								21 11		
Wakefield Westgate 7	d									20 16	20 23								21 23		
Wakefield Kirkgate 4	d																				
Pontefract Monkhill	d																				
Sheffield 7	a				20 20						20 52							21 20	21 51		
Hull	d																				
Selby	d																				
Doncaster 7	d			19 55						20 35				20 25							
Retford 10	d									↪											
Lincoln	d																				
Newark North Gate 7	a																				
	d																				
Grantham 7	a			20 26										20 57							
	d			20 26										20 58							
Peterborough 8	a			20 48										21 19							
Norwich	a																				
Peterborough 8	d			20 49										21 21							
Stevenage 4	a													21 52							
London Kings Cross 15 ⊖	a	20 57		21 46										22 24							

A ⊼ to Leeds

B ⊼ to York

C ⊼ from Edinburgh to Leeds

Table 26

Saturdays

Scotland, North East England, Yorkshire and Humberside - London

Route Diagram - see first Page of Table 26

		GR	EM	GR		EM	NT		TP	NT
		R 1		R 1		◇			◇1	
Aberdeen	d									
Stonehaven	d									
Montrose	d									
Arbroath	d									
Dundee	d									
Leuchars 3	d									
Kirkcaldy	d									
Inverkeithing	d									
Inverness	d									
Perth	d									
Stirling	d									
Glasgow Central 15	d									
Motherwell	d									
Haymarket	d									
Edinburgh 10	a									
Edinburgh	d	19 00								
Dunbar	d	19 20								
Berwick-upon-Tweed	d	19 45								
Alnmouth for Alnwick	d	20 07								
Morpeth	d	20 24					21 15			
Newcastle 8	a	20 41					21 39			
Sunderland	d									
Hartlepool	d									
Newcastle 8	d	20 42								21 50
Chester-le-Street	d									21 59
Durham	d	20 55								22 08
Darlington 7	a	21 14								22 29
Middlesbrough	d								21 50	
Eaglescliffe	d									22a48
Darlington 7	d	21 14							22 19	
Northallerton	d	21 26							22 30	
Thirsk	d								22 38	
York 8	a	21 46							22 57	
Leeds 10	a								23 33	
Harrogate	d									
Scarborough	d									
York 8	d	21 48								
Doncaster 7	a	22 16								
Skipton	d									
Keighley	d									
Bradford Interchange	d									
Bradford Forster Square	d									
Shipley	d									
Halifax	d									
Brighouse	d									
Leeds 10	d									
Wakefield Westgate 7	d									
Wakefield Kirkgate 4	d									
Pontefract Monkhill	d									
Sheffield 7	a									
Hull	d									
Selby	d			←						
Doncaster 7	d		20 33	20 35						
Retford 10	d			20 50						
Lincoln	d		21a26							
Newark North Gate 7	a			21 05						
	d			21 05						
Grantham 7	a									
	d					21 07				
Peterborough 8	a			21 34		21 36				
Norwich	a					23 20				
Peterborough 8	d			21 35						
Stevenage 4	a									
London Kings Cross 15 ⊖	a			22 30						

Table 26

Sundays

until 12 February

Scotland, North East England, Yorkshire and Humberside - London

Route Diagram - see first Page of Table 26

		GR		GR	GC	GR	TP	XC	XC			GR	HT	EM	XC	GR		GR	EM	XC		GR	TP	GC	NT
		R 1		R 1	R ◇1	R 1	◇1	◇1	◇1			R 1	◇1	◇1	◇1	R 1		R 1	◇1	◇1		R 1	◇1	R 1	
					A																				
Aberdeen	d																								
Stonehaven	d																								
Montrose	d																								
Arbroath	d																								
Dundee	d																								
Leuchars 3	d																								
Kirkcaldy	d																								
Inverkeithing	d																								
Inverness	d																								
Perth	d																								
Stirling	d																								
Glasgow Central 15	d																								
Motherwell	d																								
Haymarket	d																								
Edinburgh 10	a																								
Edinburgh	d																								
Dunbar	d																								
Berwick-upon-Tweed	d																								
Alnmouth for Alnwick	d																								
Morpeth	d																								
Newcastle 8	a																								
Sunderland	d																							09 12	09 28
Hartlepool	d																							09 36	
Newcastle 8	d					07 55	08 00									08 55				09 20		09 25	09 31		09a50
Chester-le-Street	d																						09 40		
Durham	d					08 08	08 13									09 07				09 33		09 37	09 47		
Darlington 7	a					08 25	08 31									09 25				09 48		09 55	10 03		
Middlesbrough	d																								
Eaglescliffe	d																							09 59	
Darlington 7	d					08 26	08 31									09 26				09 50		09 56	10 04		
Northallerton	d						08 43															10 07	10 15	10 20	
Thirsk	d						08 51																	10 29	
York 8	a					08 55	09 11									09 53				10 18		10 27	10 41	10 45	
Leeds 10	a						09 38													10 51			11 08		
Harrogate	d																								
Scarborough	d																								
York 8	d	08 00				08 56									09 28	09 56						10 29		10 50	
Doncaster 7	a	08 21																				10 51			
Skipton	d																								
Keighley	d																								
Bradford Interchange	d				07 55																				
Bradford Forster Square	d																								
Shipley	d																								
Halifax	d				08 07																				
Brighouse	d				08 18																				
Leeds 10	d			08 05				08 10	09 00			09 05		09 44	10 00			10 05	10 15	11 00					
Wakefield Westgate 7	d			08 16				08 23	09 11			09 17		09 58	10 12			10 17	10 27	11 12					
Wakefield Kirkgate 4	d				08 43																				
Pontefract Monkhill	d																								
Sheffield 7	a							08 51						10 25					10 57						
Hull	d												09 30												
Selby	d												10 05												
Doncaster 7	d	08 22		08 35	09 06				09a31			09 35	10 24		10a28			10 35		11a28		10 52			
Retford 10	d			08 49									10 38					10 51							
Lincoln	d																								
Newark North Gate 7	a			09 04								09 59						11 06				11 15			
	d			09 04								09 59						11 06				11 15			
Grantham 7	a			09 17								10 11	10 59					11 19							
	d			09 17								10 11	10 59					11 19							
Peterborough 8	a	09 09		09 38		10 03						10 32				11 01		11 41				11 47			
Norwich	a																								
Peterborough 8	d	09 09		09 38		10 04						10 33				11 02		11 41				11 50			
Stevenage 4	a	09 38										11 04	11s48												
London Kings Cross 15 ⊖	a	10 07		10 34	10 40	10 58						11 34	12 14			11 59		12 37				12 43		12 44	

A ◇ from Doncaster R to Doncaster

Table 26

Sundays
until 12 February

Scotland, North East England, Yorkshire and Humberside - London

Route Diagram - see first Page of Table 26

		GR	NT	TP	NT	GR		XC	GR	GR	TP	HT	NT	EM	GR	XC		GR	GC	GR	TP	GR	GR	EM	EM
		R				R			R	R					R			R	R	R		R	R		
		1		◇1		1		◇1	1	1	◇1	◇1		◇	1	◇1		1	1	1	◇1	1	1	◇1	◇
		🍴				🍴		🛒	🍴	🍴		⊠			🍴	🛒		🍴	🍴	🍴		🍴	🍴	🍴	
Aberdeen	d																								
Stonehaven	d																								
Montrose	d																								
Arbroath	d																								
Dundee	d																								
Leuchars 3	d																								
Kirkcaldy	d																								
Inverkeithing	d																								
Inverness	d																								
Perth	d																								
Stirling	d																								
Glasgow Central 15	d																								
Motherwell	d																								
Haymarket	d																								
Edinburgh 10	a																								
Edinburgh	d							08 50	09 00	09 30						09 50		10 00		10 30			10 55		
Dunbar	d																								
Berwick-upon-Tweed	d							09 33		10 11										11 11					
Alnmouth for Alnwick	d															10 49		10 58							
Morpeth	d															11 04							12 06		
Newcastle 8 ⛴	a							10 19	10 25	10 57						11 19		11 27		11 56			12 23		
Sunderland ⛴	d																								
Hartlepool	d		10 01		11 00								12 01												
Newcastle 8 ⛴	d	10 00	10a48		11a48			10 24	10 28	10 59	11 08		12a48			11 25		11 28		11 58	12 10		12 25		
Chester-le-Street	d																								
Durham	d							10 37	10 42		11 20					11 37		11 41			12 22		12 38		
Darlington 7	a	10 26						10 53	11 00	11 26	11 36					11 54		12 00		12 25	12 38		12 55		
Middlesbrough	d			10 15																					
Eaglescliffe	d																								
Darlington 7	d	10 27						10 54	11 01	11 27	11 37					11 55		12 00		12 26	12 39		12 56		
Northallerton	d			10 43					11 14		11 49												13 07		
Thirsk	d			10 51																					
York 8	a	10 54		11 10				11 23	11 34	11 54	12 12					12 22		12 28		12 53	13 11		13 28		
Leeds 10	a			11 38				11 51			12 38					12 51					13 38				
Harrogate	d																								
Scarborough	d																								
York 8	d	10 56							11 36	11 56								12 30		12 55			13 30		
Doncaster 7	a								11 59									12 53					13 53		
Skipton	d																								
Keighley	d																								
Bradford Interchange	d																		12 04						
Bradford Forster Square	d																								
Shipley	d																								
Halifax	d																		12 15						
Brighouse	d																		12 26						
Leeds 10	d					11 05		12 00							12 05	13 00						13 05		13 59	
Wakefield Westgate 7	d					11 17		12 12							12 17	13 12						13 16		14 12	
Wakefield Kirkgate 4	d																		12 51						
Pontefract Monkhill	d																								
Sheffield 7 ⛴	a																							14 44	
Hull	d											11 30													
Selby	d											12 05													
Doncaster 7	d					11 35		12a28	12 00			12 26			12 37	13a28		12 54	13 23			13 35	13 54		
Retford 10	d								12 15			12 40											14 08		
Lincoln	d																								
Newark North Gate 7	a					11 59									13 00			13 17				13 59			
	d					12 00									13 00			13 17				13 59			
Grantham 7	a					12 12						13 01			13 13							14 11			
	d					12 13						13 01		13 12	13 15							14 11			14 22
Peterborough 8	a	12 01				12 34			12 56					13 41	13 38			13 47				14 32	14 48		14 51
Norwich	a													15 30											16 35
Peterborough 8	d	12 01				12 35			12 56						13 40			13 50				14 33	14 49		
Stevenage 4	a					13 05						13s46										15 06			
London Kings Cross 15 ⊖	a	12 54				13 35			13 53	13 56		14 14			14 34			14 45	14 55	14 57		15 34	15 43		

Table 26

Sundays
until 12 February

Scotland, North East England, Yorkshire and Humberside - London

Route Diagram - see first Page of Table 26

		GR		XC	TP	GC	GR	TP	GR	GR	NT	XC		NT	EM	EM	HT	GR	XC	GR	TP	GR		GR	XC
		R				R	R		R	R								R		R		R		R	
		■1		◇■1	◇■1	■1	■1	◇■1	■1	■1		◇■1			◇	◇	◇■1	■1	◇■1	■1	◇■1	■1		■1	◇■1
															A	B				C					
		⊡🛒		🛒		⊡	⊡🛒		⊡🛒	⊡🛒		🛒					⊠	⊡🛒	🛒	⊡🛒		⊡🛒		⊡🛒	🛒
Aberdeen	d																			09 47					
Stonehaven	d																			10 04					
Montrose	d																			10 27					
Arbroath	d																			10 43					
Dundee	d																			11 02					
Leuchars ■3	d																			11 16					
Kirkcaldy	d																			11 40					
Inverkeithing	d																			11 56					
Inverness	d																								
Perth	d																								
Stirling	d																								
Glasgow Central ■15	d																		10 55						
Motherwell	d																		11 10						
Haymarket	d																		11 51	12 16					
Edinburgh ■10	a																		11 55	12 23					
Edinburgh	d			11 05			11 30			12 00									12 08	12 30				13 00	
Dunbar	d			11 25																					
Berwick-upon-Tweed	d			11 50			12 11												12 49	13 11					
Alnmouth for Alnwick	d			12 10						12 58															
Morpeth	d																								
Newcastle ■8 ⛴	a			12 37			12 57			13 27									13 34	13 58				14 23	
Sunderland ⛴	d					12 11					13 28														
Hartlepool	d					12 36								14 01											
Newcastle ■8 ⛴	d			12 40			12 59	13 04	13 12	13 28	13a49	13 35		14a48					13 40	13 59	14 08	14 12		14 25	14 35
Chester-le-Street	d							13 13																	
Durham	d			12 52				13 20	13 24	13 41		13 47							13 52		14 20	14 25		14 38	14 47
Darlington ■7	a			13 08			13 27	13 36	13 41	13 59		14 04							14 09	14 28	14 36	14 42		14 56	15 03
Middlesbrough	d				12 45																				
Eaglescliffe	d					13 02																			
Darlington ■7	d			13 09			13 28	13 37	13 42	13 59		14 05							14 10	14 28	14 37	14 43		14 57	15 04
Northallerton	d				13 13	13 23			13 55												14 49	14 57			
Thirsk	d				13 23	13 32																			
York ■8	a			13 36	13 43	13 48	13 56	14 10	14 15	14 28		14 31							14 37	14 56	15 12	15 18		15 24	15 31
Leeds ■10	a			14 03	14 08			14 38											15 05		15 38				
Harrogate	d																								
Scarborough	d																								
York ■8	d					13 52	13 57		14 16	14 29		14 34								14 58		15 19		15 29	15 34
Doncaster ■7	a								14 44	14 53		14 57										15 43		15 52	15 57
Skipton	d																								
Keighley	d																								
Bradford Interchange	d																								
Bradford Forster Square	d																								
Shipley	d																								
Halifax	d																								
Brighouse	d																								
Leeds ■10	d	14 05		14 10														15 05	15 10						
Wakefield Westgate ■7	d	14 17		14 23														15 16	15 23						
Wakefield Kirkgate ■4	d																								
Pontefract Monkhill	d																								
Sheffield ■7 ⛴	a			14 52								15 21							15 51						16 21
Hull	d																14 30								
Selby	d																15 05								
Doncaster ■7	d	14 35							14 44	14 53							15 26	15 35				15 43		15 54	
Retford ■10	d																15 40							16 08	
Lincoln	d																								
Newark North Gate ■7	a	14 59								15 17								15 59				16 07			
	d	14 59								15 17								15 59				16 08			
Grantham ■7	a	15 11															16 01	16 11							
	d	15 11													15 20	15 20	16 01	16 11							
Peterborough ■8	a	15 32							15 38	15 46					15 58	15 58		16 32				16 38		16 49	
Norwich	a														17 30	17 35									
Peterborough ■8	d	15 33							15 39	15 49								16 33				16 38		16 50	
Stevenage ■4	a																16s46	17 05							
London Kings Cross ■15 ⊖	a	16 27				15 46	15 55		16 33	16 45							17 15	17 34		16 55		17 37		17 44	

A until 1 January

B from 8 January until 12 February

C The Northern Lights

Table 26

Sundays
until 12 February

Scotland, North East England, Yorkshire and Humberside - London

Route Diagram - see first Page of Table 26

		XC	TP	GC	GR	TP	XC	NT		NT	EM	GR	GR	GC	NT	EM	GR	XC		GR	TP	HT	GR	EM	GR
				R	R							R	R	R			R			R			R		R
		◇1	◇1	1	1	◇1	◇1				◇	1	1	1		◇	1	◇1		1	◇1	◇1	1	◇	1
		A			B													A							
Aberdeen	d																	11 12		11 47					
Stonehaven	d																	11 29		12 04					
Montrose	d																	11 50		12 27					
Arbroath	d																	12 06		12 43					
Dundee	d																	12 25		13 01					
Leuchars 3	d																	12 38		13 15					
Kirkcaldy	d																	13 03		13 39					
Inverkeithing	d																	13 18		13 58					
Inverness	d				09 40																				
Perth	d				11 58																				
Stirling	d				12 34																				
Glasgow Central 15	d	11 51																							
Motherwell	d	12 07																							
Haymarket	d	12 49			13 14													13 37		14 18					
Edinburgh 10	a	12 54			13 19													13 42		14 25					
Edinburgh	d	13 06			13 30		13 50						14 00					14 08		14 30					
Dunbar	d	13 25																							
Berwick-upon-Tweed	d				14 12		14 33											14 49		15 11					
Alnmouth for Alnwick	d	14 08											14 58												
Morpeth	d																								
Newcastle 8	a	14 35			14 59		15 18						15 27					15 34		15 57					
Sunderland	d			14 12				15 28																	
Hartlepool	d			14 36						16 01					16 51										
Newcastle 8	d	14 40			15 00	15 07	15 23	15a48		16a48			15 28		17a48			15 40		15 59	16 08		16 12		
Chester-le-Street	d					15 16																			
Durham	d	14 52				15 23	15 36						15 41					15 52			16 20		16 24		
Darlington 7	a	15 08			15 29	15 39	15 52						16 00					16 08		16 27	16 36		16 41		
Middlesbrough	d		14 42																						
Eaglescliffe	d			14 59																					
Darlington 7	d	15 09			15 29	15 40	15 53						16 00					16 09		16 28	16 37		16 42		
Northallerton	d		15 10	15 22																	16 49		16 54		
Thirsk	d		15 18	15 31																					
York 8	a	15 37	15 42	15 46	15 57	16 12	16 19						16 28					16 37		16 56	17 12		17 16		
Leeds 10	a	16 03	16 08			16 38												17 06			17 38				
Harrogate	d																								
Scarborough	d																								
York 8	d			15 50	15 59		16 23						16 29							16 57			17 17		
Doncaster 7	a						16 48						16 53												
Skipton	d																								
Keighley	d																								
Bradford Interchange	d													15 42											
Bradford Forster Square	d																								
Shipley	d																								
Halifax	d													15 54											
Brighouse	d													16 05											
Leeds 10	d	16 10										16 15					16 45	17 10							17 15
Wakefield Westgate 7	d	16 22										16 27					16 56	17 22							17 27
Wakefield Kirkgate 4	d													16 30											
Pontefract Monkhill	d																								
Sheffield 7	a	16 51					17 19											17 51							
Hull	d																					16 30			
Selby	d																					17 05			
Doncaster 7	d											16 46	16 53	17 12			17 17					17 26			17 46
Retford 10	d																					17 40			18 00
Lincoln	d																								
Newark North Gate 7	a												17 17				17 44						17 59		
	d												17 17				17 44						17 59		
Grantham 7	a											17 17										18 01			18 23
	d										16 22	17 17				17 21						18 01		18 17	18 23
Peterborough 8	a										16 55		17 46			17 50	18 14						18 28	18 46	
Norwich	a										18 30					19 29								20 29	
Peterborough 8	d												17 49				18 14						18 29		
Stevenage 4	a											18 04										18s49			19 07
London Kings Cross 15 ⊖	a			17 45	17 57							18 35	18 45	18 50			19 12			18 56		19 18	19 22		19 37

A from Edinburgh

B The Highland Chieftain

Table 26

Sundays
until 12 February

Scotland, North East England, Yorkshire and Humberside - London

Route Diagram - see first Page of Table 26

		GR	XC	GR	EM	XC	TP	GR	TP	GR	GR	XC	EM	GR	XC	TP	GR	TP	XC	HT	GR
		R		R				R		R	R			R			R				R
		1	◇1	1	◇1	◇1	◇1	1	◇1	1	1	◇1	◇	1	◇1	◇1	1	◇1	◇1	◇1	1
						A									A						
		🍽🍴	🍴	🍽🍴	🍽	🍴		🍽🍴		🍽🍴	🍽🍴	🍴		🍽🍴	🍴		🍽🍴		🍴	☒	🍽🍴
Aberdeen	d																13 50				
Stonehaven	d																14 07				
Montrose	d																14 30				
Arbroath	d																14 46				
Dundee	d																15 04				
Leuchars 3	d																15 18				
Kirkcaldy	d																15 42				
Inverkeithing	d																15 58				
Inverness	d																				
Perth	d																				
Stirling	d																				
Glasgow Central 15	d					13 49									14 55						
Motherwell	d					14 04									15 11						
Haymarket	d					14 42									15 51		16 18				
Edinburgh 10	a					14 47									15 56		16 25				
Edinburgh	d	15 00				15 07		15 30			16 00				16 05		16 30				
Dunbar	d					15 27															
Berwick-upon-Tweed	d							16 11									17 11				
Alnmouth for Alnwick	d										16 58				17 07						
Morpeth	d														17 22						
Newcastle 8	a	16 23				16 34		16 56			17 27				17 37		17 57				
Sunderland	d																				
Hartlepool	d																				
Newcastle 8	d	16 25	16 35			16 40		16 58	17 05		17 28	17 35			17 40	17 52	17 59		18 20		
Chester-le-Street	d								17 14												
Durham	d	16 38	16 47			16 52			17 21		17 41	17 47			17 52	18 04			18 32		
Darlington 7	a	16 56	17 03			17 08		17 25	17 37		18 00	18 04			18 08	18 20	18 26		18 49		
Middlesbrough	d						16 42														
Eaglescliffe	d																				
Darlington 7	d	16 57	17 04			17 09		17 26	17 38		18 00	18 05			18 09	18 21	18 27		18 51		
Northallerton	d						17 10		17 49							18 33					
Thirsk	d						17 18											←			
York 8	a	17 24	17 30			17 37	17 42	17 53	18 12		18 28	18 31			18 36	19 03	18 56	19 03	19 17		
Leeds 10	a					18 04	18 08		18 38						19 03	→		19 38			
Harrogate	d			17 05																	
Scarborough	d																				
York 8	d	17 29	17 34		17 40			17 55			18 29	18 34					18 57		19 24		
Doncaster 7	a	17 52	17 57		18 05						18 53	18 57							19 47		
Skipton	d																				
Keighley	d																				
Bradford Interchange	d																				
Bradford Forster Square	d																				
Shipley	d																				
Halifax	d																				
Brighouse	d																				
Leeds 10	d			17 45		18 10				18 15				18 45	19 10						19 15
Wakefield Westgate 7	d			17 57		18 22				18 27				18 56	19 22						19 26
Wakefield Kirkgate 4	d																				
Pontefract Monkhill	d																				
Sheffield 7	a		18 23		18 39	18 51						19 21			19 50				20 16		
Hull	d																			18 30	
Selby	d																			19 05	
Doncaster 7	d	17 54		18 17						18 46	18 53			19 17						19 26	19 45
Retford 10	d																			19 40	19 59
Lincoln	d																				
Newark North Gate 7	a			18 42							19 17			19 44							
	d			18 43							19 17			19 44							
Grantham 7	a	18 27								19 17										20 01	20 22
	d	18 27								19 17			19 27							20 01	20 22
Peterborough 8	a	18 50		19 13							19 47		19 56	20 14							
Norwich	a												21 35								
Peterborough 8	d	18 50		19 13							19 50			20 15							
Stevenage 4	a									20 07										20s50	21 08
London Kings Cross 15 ⊖	a	19 45		20 12				19 53		20 35	20 46			21 12			20 56			21 18	21 35

A 🍴 from Edinburgh

Table 26

Sundays

until 12 February

Scotland, North East England, Yorkshire and Humberside - London

Route Diagram - see first Page of Table 26

		GR	GR	XC	TP	GC	GR	NT	TP	XC	GR	NT	NT	EM	GR	XC	GR	TP	TP	GR	NT	GR	XC
		R	R			R	R				R				R		R			R		R	
		1	1	◇1	◇1	1	1		◇1	◇1	1			◇	1	◇1	1	◇1	◇1	1		1	◇1
				A												A							
Aberdeen	d																						
Stonehaven	d																						
Montrose	d																						
Arbroath	d																						
Dundee	d																						
Leuchars 3	d																						
Kirkcaldy	d																						
Inverkeithing	d																						
Inverness	d																						
Perth	d																						
Stirling	d																						
Glasgow Central 15	d															16 55							18 57
Motherwell	d															17 11							19 11
Haymarket	d															17 51							19 51
Edinburgh 10	a															17 56							19 56
Edinburgh	d	17 00		17 07			17 30				18 00					18 07	18 30			19 00		20 00	20 05
Dunbar	d			17 27			17 50									18 26				19 20		20 21	20 29
Berwick-upon-Tweed	d			17 52			18 15									18 52	19 11			19 45		20 46	20 55
Alnmouth for Alnwick	d										18 58											21 09	
Morpeth	d																					21 26	
Newcastle 8	a	18 23		18 36			19 00				19 27					19 36	19 56			20 30		21 42	21 48
Sunderland	d					18 12		18 43				19 28	20 28										
Hartlepool	d					18 36																	
Newcastle 8	d	18 25		18 39			19 02	19a05	19 10	19 25	19 28	19a52	20a47			19 40	19 58		20 08	20 32	21 06	21 44	
Chester-le-Street	d																				21 15		
Durham	d	18 38		18 51					19 22	19 37	19 41					19 52			20 20	20 45	21 24	21 58	
Darlington 7	a	18 55		19 07			19 29		19 38	19 53	20 00					20 08	20 24		20 36	21 03	21 44	22 16	
Middlesbrough	d				18 45													20 06					
Eaglescliffe	d					18 59															22a00		
Darlington 7	d	18 56		19 08			19 30		19 39	19 54	20 00					20 09	20 25		20 37	21 04		22 17	
Northallerton	d	19 07			19 13	19 21												20 38	20 49			22 30	
Thirsk	d				19 21	19 30												20 46					
York 8	a	19 28		19 35	19 42	19 47	19 57		20 11	20 21	20 28					20 36	20 53	21 06	21 12	21 31		23 02	
Leeds 10	a			20 05	20 08				20 38							21 02			21 38			23 34	
Harrogate	d																						
Scarborough	d																						
York 8	d	19 30				19 51	19 59			20 24	20 29						20 55			21 33			
Doncaster 7	a	19 53								20 47	20 53						21 18			21 55			
Skipton	d																						
Keighley	d																						
Bradford Interchange	d																						
Bradford Forster Square	d																						
Shipley	d																						
Halifax	d																						
Brighouse	d																						
Leeds 10	d		19 45	20 10											20 45	21 10							
Wakefield Westgate 7	d		19 56	20 22											20 56	21 22							
Wakefield Kirkgate 4	d																						
Pontefract Monkhill	d																						
Sheffield 7	a			20 51						21 17						21 50							
Hull	d																						
Selby	d																						
Doncaster 7	d	19 54	20 19								20 53				21 15		21 19			21 56			
Retford 10	d														21 29								
Lincoln	d																						
Newark North Gate 7	a	20 17	20 43								21 17						21 47			22 19			
	d	20 17	20 43								21 17						21 47			22 19			
Grantham 7	a						20 47								21 52		22 00			22 32			
	d						20 48							21 19	21 52		22 00			22 32			
Peterborough 8	a	20 48	21 13				21 08				21 46			21 52	22 13		22 19			22 53			
Norwich	a													23 28									
Peterborough 8	d	20 50	21 13				21 08				21 48				22 13		22 19			22 53			
Stevenage 4	a														22 45		22 52			23s24			
London Kings Cross 15 ⊖	a	21 44	22 10			21 45	22 03				22 46				23 16		23 21			23 53			

A to Leeds

Table 26

Sundays
until 12 February

Scotland, North East England, Yorkshire and Humberside - London

Route Diagram - see first Page of Table 26

		GR	TP
		R	
		1	◇1
Aberdeen	d		
Stonehaven	d		
Montrose	d		
Arbroath	d		
Dundee	d		
Leuchars [8]	d		
Kirkcaldy	d		
Inverkeithing	d		
Inverness	d		
Perth	d		
Stirling	d		
Glasgow Central [15]	d		
Motherwell	d		
Haymarket	d		
Edinburgh [10]	a		
Edinburgh	d	21 00	
Dunbar	d	21 21	
Berwick-upon-Tweed	d	21 46	
Alnmouth for Alnwick	d	22 08	
Morpeth	d		
Newcastle [8]	a	22 42	
Sunderland	d		
Hartlepool	d		
Newcastle [8]	d		
Chester-le-Street	d		
Durham	d		
Darlington [7]	a		
Middlesbrough	d		22 06
Eaglescliffe	d		
Darlington [7]	d		
Northallerton	d		22 35
Thirsk	d		22 43
York [8]	a		23 09
Leeds [10]	a		23 38
Harrogate	d		
Scarborough	d		
York [8]	d		
Doncaster [7]	a		
Skipton	d		
Keighley	d		
Bradford Interchange	d		
Bradford Forster Square	d		
Shipley	d		
Halifax	d		
Brighouse	d		
Leeds [10]	d		
Wakefield Westgate [7]	d		
Wakefield Kirkgate [4]	d		
Pontefract Monkhill	d		
Sheffield [7]	a		
Hull	d		
Selby	d		
Doncaster [7]	d		
Retford [10]	d		
Lincoln	d		
Newark North Gate [7]	a		
	d		
Grantham [7]	a		
	d		
Peterborough [8]	a		
Norwich	a		
Peterborough [8]	d		
Stevenage [4]	a		
London Kings Cross [15] ⊖	a		

Table 26

Sundays

19 February to 25 March

Scotland, North East England, Yorkshire and Humberside - London

Route Diagram - see first Page of Table 26

		GR	GR	GC	GR	TP	XC	XC	GR	HT	EM	XC	GR	GR	EM	XC	GR	TP	GC	GR
		R 1	R 1	R ◇1	R 1	◇1	◇1	◇1	R 1	◇1	◇1	◇1	R 1	R 1	◇1	◇1	R 1	◇1	R 1	R 1
				A																
Aberdeen	d																			
Stonehaven	d																			
Montrose	d																			
Arbroath	d																			
Dundee	d																			
Leuchars 3	d																			
Kirkcaldy	d																			
Inverkeithing	d																			
Inverness	d																			
Perth	d																			
Stirling	d																			
Glasgow Central 15	d																			
Motherwell	d																			
Haymarket	d																			
Edinburgh 10	a																			
Edinburgh	d																			
Dunbar	d																			
Berwick-upon-Tweed	d																			
Alnmouth for Alnwick	d																			
Morpeth	d																			
Newcastle 8	a																			
Sunderland	d																		09 12	
Hartlepool	d																		09 36	
Newcastle 8	d				07 55	08 00							08 55			09 20	09 25	09 31		10 00
Chester-le-Street	d																	09 40		
Durham	d				08 08	08 13							09 07			09 33	09 37	09 47		
Darlington 7	a				08 25	08 31							09 25			09 48	09 55	10 03		10 26
Middlesbrough	d																			
Eaglescliffe	d																		09 59	
Darlington 7	d				08 26	08 31							09 26			09 50	09 56	10 04		10 27
Northallerton	d					08 43											10 07	10 15	10 20	
Thirsk	d					08 51													10 29	
York 8	a				08 55	09 11							09 53			10 18	10 27	10 41	10 45	10 54
Leeds 10	a					09 38										10 51		11 08		
Harrogate	d																			
Scarborough	d																			
York 8	d	08 00			08 56							09 28	09 56				10 29		10 50	10 56
Doncaster 7	a	08 21															10 51			
Skipton	d																			
Keighley	d																			
Bradford Interchange	d			07 55																
Bradford Forster Square	d																			
Shipley	d																			
Halifax	d			08 07																
Brighouse	d			08 18																
Leeds 10	d		08 05				08 10	09 00	09 05		09 44	10 00		10 05	10 15	11 00				
Wakefield Westgate 7	d		08 16				08 23	09 11	09 17		09 58	10 12		10 17	10 27	11 12				
Wakefield Kirkgate 4	d			08 43																
Pontefract Monkhill	d																			
Sheffield 7	a						08 51				10 25				10 57					
Hull	d									09 30										
Selby	d									10 05										
Doncaster 7	d	08 22	08 35	09 06				09a31	09 35	10 24		10a28		10 35		11a28	10 52			
Retford 10	d		08 49							10 38				10 51						
Lincoln	d																			
Newark North Gate 7	a		09 04						09 59					11 06			11 15			
	d		09 04						09 59					11 06			11 15			
Grantham 7	a		09 17						10 11	10 59				11 19						
	d		09 17						10 11	10 59				11 19						
Peterborough 8	a	09 09	09 38		10 03				10 32				11 01	11 41			11 47			12 01
Norwich	a																			
Peterborough 8	d	09 09	09 38		10 04				10 33				11 02	11 41			11 50			12 01
Stevenage 4	a	09 38							11 04	11s48										
London Kings Cross 15 ⊖	a	10 07	10 34	10 40	10 58				11 34	12 14			11 59	12 37			12 43		12 44	12 54

A ◇ from Doncaster R to Doncaster

Table 26

Sundays

19 February to 25 March

Scotland, North East England, Yorkshire and Humberside - London

Route Diagram - see first Page of Table 26

		TP	GR	XC	GR	GR	TP	HT	EM	GR	XC	GR	GC	GR	TP	GR	GR	EM	EM	GR	XC	TP	GC
			R		R	R				R		R	R	R		R	R			R			R
		◇1	1	◇1	1	1	◇1	◇1	◇	1	◇1	1	1	1	◇1	1	1	◇1	◇	1	◇1	◇1	1
			R🍴	🍴	R🍴	R🍴		⊠		R🍴	🍴	R🍴	R	R🍴		R🍴	R🍴	R		R🍴	🍴		R
Aberdeen	d																						
Stonehaven	d																						
Montrose	d																						
Arbroath	d																						
Dundee	d																						
Leuchars 3	d																						
Kirkcaldy	d																						
Inverkeithing	d																						
Inverness	d																						
Perth	d																						
Stirling	d																						
Glasgow Central 15	d																						
Motherwell	d																						
Haymarket	d																						
Edinburgh 10	a																						
Edinburgh	d			08 50	09 00	09 30					09 50	10 00		10 30			10 55				11 05		
Dunbar	d																				11 25		
Berwick-upon-Tweed	d			09 33		10 11								11 11							11 50		
Alnmouth for Alnwick	d										10 49	10 58									12 10		
Morpeth	d										11 04						12 06						
Newcastle 8	a			10 19	10 25	10 57					11 19	11 27		11 56			12 23				12 37		
Sunderland	d																						12 11
Hartlepool	d																						12 36
Newcastle 8	d			10 24	10 28	10 59	11 08				11 25	11 28		11 58	12 10		12 25				12 40		
Chester-le-Street	d																						
Durham	d			10 37	10 42		11 20				11 37	11 41			12 22		12 38				12 52		
Darlington 7	a			10 53	11 00	11 26	11 36				11 54	12 00		12 25	12 38		12 55				13 08		
Middlesbrough	d	10 15																				12 45	
Eaglescliffe	d																						13 02
Darlington 7	d			10 54	11 01	11 27	11 37				11 55	12 00		12 26	12 39		12 56				13 09		
Northallerton	d	10 43			11 14		11 49										13 07					13 13	13 23
Thirsk	d	10 51																				13 23	13 32
York 8	a	11 10		11 23	11 34	11 54	12 12				12 22	12 28		12 53	13 11		13 28				13 36	13 43	13 48
Leeds 10	a	11 38		11 51			12 38				12 51				13 38						14 03	14 08	
Harrogate	d																						
Scarborough	d																						
York 8	d				11 36	11 56						12 30		12 55			13 30						13 52
Doncaster 7	a				11 59							12 53					13 53						
Skipton	d																						
Keighley	d																						
Bradford Interchange	d												12 04										
Bradford Forster Square	d																						
Shipley	d																						
Halifax	d												12 15										
Brighouse	d												12 26										
Leeds 10	d		11 05	12 00						12 05	13 00					13 05		13 59		14 05	14 10		
Wakefield Westgate 7	d		11 17	12 12						12 17	13 12					13 16		14 12		14 17	14 23		
Wakefield Kirkgate 4	d												12 51										
Pontefract Monkhill	d																						
Sheffield 7	a																	14 44			14 52		
Hull	d							11 30															
Selby	d							12 05															
Doncaster 7	d		11 35	12a28	12 00			12 26		12 37	13a28	12 54	13 23			13 35	13 54			14 35			
Retford 10	d				12 15			12 40									14 08						
Lincoln	d																						
Newark North Gate 7	a		11 59							13 00		13 17				13 59				14 59			
	d		12 00							13 00		13 17				13 59				14 59			
Grantham 7	a		12 12					13 01		13 13						14 11				15 11			
	d		12 13					13 01	13 12	13 15						14 11			14 22	15 11			
Peterborough 8	a		12 34		12 56				13 41	13 38		13 47				14 32	14 48		14 51	15 32			
Norwich	a								15 30										16 35				
Peterborough 8	d		12 35		12 56					13 40		13 50				14 33	14 49			15 33			
Stevenage 4	a		13 05					13s46								15 06							
London Kings Cross 15 ⊖	a		13 35		13 53	13 56		14 14		14 34		14 45	14 55	14 57		15 34	15 43			16 27			15 46

Table 26

Sundays

19 February to 25 March

Scotland, North East England, Yorkshire and Humberside - London

Route Diagram - see first Page of Table 26

		GR		TP	GR	GR	XC	EM	HT	GR	XC	GR		TP	GR	GR	XC	XC	TP	GC	GR	TP		XC	EM
		R 1		◇1	R 1	R 1	◇1	◇	◇1	R 1	◇1	R 1		◇1	R 1	R 1	◇1	◇1	◇1	R 1	R 1	◇1		◇1	◇
												A						B			C				
Aberdeen	d											09 47													
Stonehaven	d											10 04													
Montrose	d											10 27													
Arbroath	d											10 43													
Dundee	d											11 02													
Leuchars 3	d											11 16													
Kirkcaldy	d											11 40													
Inverkeithing	d											11 56													
Inverness	d																				09 40				
Perth	d																				11 58				
Stirling	d																				12 34				
Glasgow Central 15	d										10 55							11 51							
Motherwell	d										11 10							12 07							
Haymarket	d										11 51	12 16						12 49			13 14				
Edinburgh 10	a										11 55	12 23						12 54			13 19				
Edinburgh	d	11 30				12 00					12 08	12 30				13 00		13 06			13 30			13 50	
Dunbar	d																	13 25							
Berwick-upon-Tweed	d	12 11									12 49	13 11									14 12			14 33	
Alnmouth for Alnwick	d					12 58												14 08							
Morpeth	d																								
Newcastle 8	a	12 57				13 27					13 34	13 58				14 23		14 35			14 59			15 18	
Sunderland	d																			14 12					
Hartlepool	d																			14 36					
Newcastle 8	d	12 59		13 04	13 12	13 28	13 35				13 40	13 59		14 08	14 12	14 25	14 35	14 40			15 00	15 07		15 23	
Chester-le-Street	d			13 13																		15 16			
Durham	d			13 20	13 24	13 41	13 47				13 52			14 20	14 25	14 38	14 47	14 52				15 23		15 36	
Darlington 7	a	13 27		13 36	13 41	13 59	14 04				14 09	14 28		14 36	14 42	14 56	15 03	15 08			15 29	15 39		15 52	
Middlesbrough	d																		14 42						
Eaglescliffe	d																			14 59					
Darlington 7	d	13 28		13 37	13 42	13 59	14 05				14 10	14 28		14 37	14 43	14 57	15 04	15 09			15 29	15 40		15 53	
Northallerton	d				13 55									14 49	14 57				15 10	15 22					
Thirsk	d																		15 18	15 31					
York 8	a	13 56		14 10	14 15	14 28	14 31				14 37	14 56		15 12	15 18	15 24	15 31	15 37	15 42	15 46	15 57	16 12		16 19	
Leeds 10	a			14 38							15 05			15 38				16 03	16 08			16 38			
Harrogate	d																								
Scarborough	d																								
York 8	d	13 57			14 16	14 29	14 34					14 58			15 19	15 29	15 34			15 50	15 59			16 23	
Doncaster 7	a				14 44	14 53	14 57								15 43	15 52	15 57							16 48	
Skipton	d																								
Keighley	d																								
Bradford Interchange	d																								
Bradford Forster Square	d																								
Shipley	d																								
Halifax	d																								
Brighouse	d																								
Leeds 10	d									15 05	15 10							16 10							
Wakefield Westgate 7	d									15 16	15 23							16 22							
Wakefield Kirkgate 4	d																								
Pontefract Monkhill	d																								
Sheffield 7	a						15 21				15 51						16 21	16 51						17 19	
Hull	d								14 30																
Selby	d								15 05																
Doncaster 7	d				14 44	14 53			15 26	15 35					15 43	15 54									
Retford 10	d								15 40							16 08									
Lincoln	d																								
Newark North Gate 7	a					15 17				15 59					16 07										
	d					15 17				15 59					16 08										
Grantham 7	a								16 01	16 11															
	d							15 20	16 01	16 11															16 22
Peterborough 8	a				15 38	15 46		15 58		16 32					16 38	16 49									16 55
Norwich	a							17 35																	18 30
Peterborough 8	d				15 39	15 49				16 33					16 38	16 50									
Stevenage 4	a								16s46	17 05															
London Kings Cross 15 ⊖	a	15 55			16 33	16 45			17 15	17 34		16 55			17 37	17 44				17 45	17 57				

A The Northern Lights

B from Edinburgh

C The Highland Chieftain

Table 26

Sundays

19 February to 25 March

Scotland, North East England, Yorkshire and Humberside - London

Route Diagram - see first Page of Table 26

		GR	GR	GC	EM	GR	XC	GR	TP	HT	GR	EM	GR	GR	XC	GR	EM	XC	TP	GR	TP	GR	GR
		R	R	R		R		R			R		R	R		R				R		R	R
		1	1	1	◇	1	◇1	1	◇1	◇1	1	◇	1	1	◇1	1	◇1	◇1	◇1	1	◇1	1	1
							A											A					
Aberdeen	d						11 12	11 47															
Stonehaven	d						11 29	12 04															
Montrose	d						11 50	12 27															
Arbroath	d						12 06	12 43															
Dundee	d						12 25	13 01															
Leuchars 3	d						12 38	13 15															
Kirkcaldy	d						13 03	13 39															
Inverkeithing	d						13 18	13 58															
Inverness	d																						
Perth	d																						
Stirling	d																						
Glasgow Central 15	d																	13 49					
Motherwell	d																	14 04					
Haymarket	d						13 37	14 18										14 42					
Edinburgh 10	a						13 42	14 25										14 47					
Edinburgh	d		14 00				14 08	14 30						15 00				15 07		15 30			16 00
Dunbar	d																	15 27					
Berwick-upon-Tweed	d						14 49	15 11												16 11			
Alnmouth for Alnwick	d		14 58																				16 58
Morpeth	d																						
Newcastle 8	a		15 27				15 34	15 57						16 23				16 34		16 56			17 27
Sunderland	d																						
Hartlepool	d																						
Newcastle 8	d		15 28				15 40	15 59	16 08		16 12			16 25	16 35			16 40		16 58	17 05		17 28
Chester-le-Street	d																				17 14		
Durham	d		15 41				15 52		16 20		16 24			16 38	16 47			16 52			17 21		17 41
Darlington 7	a		16 00				16 08	16 27	16 36		16 41			16 56	17 03			17 08		17 25	17 37		18 00
Middlesbrough	d																		16 42				
Eaglescliffe	d																						
Darlington 7	d		16 00				16 09	16 28	16 37		16 42			16 57	17 04			17 09		17 26	17 38		18 00
Northallerton	d								16 49		16 54								17 10		17 49		
Thirsk	d																		17 18				
York 8	a		16 28				16 37	16 56	17 12		17 16			17 24	17 30			17 37	17 42	17 53	18 12		18 28
Leeds 10	a						17 06		17 38									18 04	18 08		18 38		
Harrogate	d															17 05							
Scarborough	d																						
York 8	d		16 29					16 57			17 17			17 29	17 34		17 40			17 55			18 29
Doncaster 7	a		16 53											17 52	17 57		18 05						18 53
Skipton	d																						
Keighley	d																						
Bradford Interchange	d			15 42																			
Bradford Forster Square	d																						
Shipley	d																						
Halifax	d			15 54																			
Brighouse	d			16 05																			
Leeds 10	d	16 15				16 45	17 10						17 15			17 45		18 10				18 15	
Wakefield Westgate 7	d	16 27				16 56	17 22						17 27			17 57		18 22				18 27	
Wakefield Kirkgate 4	d			16 30																			
Pontefract Monkhill	d																						
Sheffield 7	a						17 51								18 23		18 39	18 51					
Hull	d									16 30													
Selby	d									17 05													
Doncaster 7	d	16 46	16 53	17 12		17 17				17 26			17 46	17 54		18 17						18 46	18 53
Retford 10	d									17 40			18 00										
Lincoln	d																						
Newark North Gate 7	a		17 17			17 44					17 59					18 42							19 17
	d		17 17			17 44					17 59					18 43							19 17
Grantham 7	a	17 17								18 01			18 23	18 27								19 17	
	d	17 17			17 21					18 01		18 17	18 23	18 27								19 17	
Peterborough 8	a		17 46		17 50	18 14					18 28	18 46		18 50		19 13							19 47
Norwich	a				19 29							20 29											
Peterborough 8	d		17 49			18 14					18 29			18 50		19 13							19 50
Stevenage 4	a	18 04								18s49			19 07									20 07	
London Kings Cross 15 ⊖	a	18 35	18 45	18 50		19 12		18 56		19 18	19 22		19 37	19 45		20 12				19 53		20 35	20 46

A from Edinburgh

Table 26

Sundays

19 February to 25 March

Scotland, North East England, Yorkshire and Humberside - London

Route Diagram - see first Page of Table 26

		XC	EM	GR		XC		TP	GR	TP	XC	HT	GR	GR		GR	XC	TP	GC	GR	TP	XC	GR	EM	
				R					R				R	R		R			R	R			R		
		◇1	◇	1		◇1		◇1	1	◇1	◇1	◇1	1	1		1	◇1	◇1	1	1	◇1	◇1	1	◇	
						A											B								
		⊼		⊡⊼		⊼			⊡⊼		⊼	⊠	⊡⊼	⊡⊼		⊡⊼	⊼		⊡	⊡⊼		⊼	⊡⊼		
Aberdeen	d								13 50																
Stonehaven	d								14 07																
Montrose	d								14 30																
Arbroath	d								14 46																
Dundee	d								15 04																
Leuchars 3	d								15 18																
Kirkcaldy	d								15 42																
Inverkeithing	d								15 58																
Inverness	d																								
Perth	d																								
Stirling	d																								
Glasgow Central 15	d					14 55																			
Motherwell	d					15 11																			
Haymarket	d					15 51			16 18																
Edinburgh 10	a					15 56			16 25																
Edinburgh	d					16 05			16 30					17 00			17 07			17 30			18 00		
Dunbar	d																17 27			17 50					
Berwick-upon-Tweed	d								17 11								17 52			18 15					
Alnmouth for Alnwick	d					17 07																	18 58		
Morpeth	d					17 22																			
Newcastle 8 ⛴	a					17 37			17 57					18 23			18 36			19 00			19 27		
Sunderland ⛴	d																		18 12						
Hartlepool	d																		18 36						
Newcastle 8 ⛴	d	17 35				17 40		17 52	17 59		18 20			18 25			18 39			19 02	19 10	19 25	19 28		
Chester-le-Street	d																								
Durham	d	17 47				17 52		18 04			18 32			18 38			18 51				19 22	19 37	19 41		
Darlington 7	a	18 04				18 08		18 20	18 26		18 49			18 55			19 07			19 29	19 38	19 53	20 00		
Middlesbrough	d																	18 45							
Eaglescliffe	d																		18 59						
Darlington 7	d	18 05				18 09		18 21	18 27		18 51			18 56			19 08			19 30	19 39	19 54	20 00		
Northallerton	d							18 33						19 07				19 13	19 21						
Thirsk	d									←								19 21	19 30						
York 8	a	18 31				18 36		19 03	18 56	19 03	19 17			19 28			19 35	19 42	19 47	19 57	20 11	20 21	20 28		
Leeds 10	a					19 03		→		19 38							20 05	20 08			20 38				
Harrogate	d																								
Scarborough	d																								
York 8	d	18 34							18 57		19 24			19 30					19 51	19 59		20 24	20 29		
Doncaster 7	a	18 57									19 47			19 53								20 47	20 53		
Skipton	d																								
Keighley	d																								
Bradford Interchange	d																								
Bradford Forster Square	d																								
Shipley	d																								
Halifax	d																								
Brighouse	d																								
Leeds 10	d			18 45		19 10							19 15			19 45	20 10								
Wakefield Westgate 7	d			18 56		19 22							19 26			19 56	20 22								
Wakefield Kirkgate 4	d																								
Pontefract Monkhill	d																								
Sheffield 7 ⛴	a	19 21				19 50					20 16						20 51					21 17			
Hull	d											18 30													
Selby	d											19 05													
Doncaster 7	d			19 17								19 26	19 45	19 54		20 19							20 53		
Retford 10	d											19 40	19 59												
Lincoln	d																								
Newark North Gate 7	a			19 44										20 17		20 43							21 17		
	d			19 44										20 17		20 43							21 17		
Grantham 7	a											20 01	20 22							20 47					
	d		19 27									20 01	20 22							20 48				21 19	
Peterborough 8	a		19 56	20 14										20 48		21 13				21 08			21 46	21 52	
Norwich	a		21 35																					23 28	
Peterborough 8	d			20 15										20 50		21 13				21 08			21 48		
Stevenage 4	a											20s50	21 08												
London Kings Cross 15 ⊖	a			21 12					20 56			21 18	21 35	21 44		22 10			21 45	22 03			22 46		

A ⊼ from Edinburgh

B ⊼ to Leeds

Table 26

Sundays

19 February to 25 March

Scotland, North East England, Yorkshire and Humberside - London

Route Diagram - see first Page of Table 26

		GR	XC	GR	TP	TP	GR	NT	GR	XC		GR	TP
		R		R			R		R			R	
		1	◇1	1	◇1	◇1	1		1	◇1		1	◇1
			A										
		(restaurant)	(trolley)	(restaurant)			(restaurant)		(restaurant)			(restaurant)	
Aberdeen	d												
Stonehaven	d												
Montrose	d												
Arbroath	d												
Dundee	d												
Leuchars 3	d												
Kirkcaldy	d												
Inverkeithing	d												
Inverness	d												
Perth	d												
Stirling	d												
Glasgow Central 15	d		16 55							18 57			
Motherwell	d		17 11							19 11			
Haymarket	d		17 51							19 51			
Edinburgh 10	a		17 56							19 56			
Edinburgh	d		18 07	18 30			19 00		20 00	20 05		21 00	
Dunbar	d		18 26				19 20		20 21	20 29		21 21	
Berwick-upon-Tweed	d		18 52	19 11			19 45		20 46	20 55		21 46	
Alnmouth for Alnwick	d								21 09			22 08	
Morpeth	d								21 26				
Newcastle 8 ⛴	a		19 36	19 56			20 30		21 42	21 48		22 42	
Sunderland ⛴	d												
Hartlepool	d												
Newcastle 8 ⛴	d		19 40	19 58		20 08	20 32	21 06	21 44				
Chester-le-Street	d							21 15					
Durham	d		19 52			20 20	20 45	21 24	21 58				
Darlington 7	a		20 08	20 24		20 36	21 03	21 44	22 16				
Middlesbrough	d				20 06								22 06
Eaglescliffe	d							22a00					
Darlington 7	d		20 09	20 25		20 37	21 04		22 17				
Northallerton	d				20 38	20 49			22 30				22 35
Thirsk	d				20 46								22 43
York 8	a		20 36	20 53	21 06	21 12	21 31		23 02				23 09
Leeds 10	a		21 02			21 38			23 34				23 38
Harrogate	d												
Scarborough	d												
York 8	d			20 55			21 33						
Doncaster 7	a			21 18			21 55						
Skipton	d												
Keighley	d												
Bradford Interchange	d												
Bradford Forster Square	d												
Shipley	d												
Halifax	d												
Brighouse	d												
Leeds 10	d	20 45	21 10										
Wakefield Westgate 7	d	20 56	21 22										
Wakefield Kirkgate 4	d												
Pontefract Monkhill	d												
Sheffield 7 ⛴	a		21 50										
Hull	d												
Selby	d												
Doncaster 7	d	21 15		21 19			21 56						
Retford 10	d	21 29											
Lincoln	d												
Newark North Gate 7	a			21 47			22 19						
	d			21 47			22 19						
Grantham 7	a	21 52		22 00			22 32						
	d	21 52		22 00			22 32						
Peterborough 8	a	22 13		22 19			22 53						
Norwich	a												
Peterborough 8	d	22 13		22 19			22 53						
Stevenage 4	a	22 45		22 52			23s24						
London Kings Cross 15 ⊖	a	23 16		23 21			23 53						

A (trolley) to Leeds

Table 26

Sundays

from 1 April

Scotland, North East England, Yorkshire and Humberside - London

Route Diagram - see first Page of Table 26

		GR		GR	GC	GR	TP	XC	XC			GR	HT	EM	XC	GR		GR	EM	XC		GR	TP	GC	NT
		R 1		R 1	R ◇1 A	R 1	◇1	◇1	◇1			R 1	◇1	◇1	◇1	R 1		R 1	◇1	◇1		R 1	◇1	R 1	
Aberdeen	d																								
Stonehaven	d																								
Montrose	d																								
Arbroath	d																								
Dundee	d																								
Leuchars 3	d																								
Kirkcaldy	d																								
Inverkeithing	d																								
Inverness	d																								
Perth	d																								
Stirling	d																								
Glasgow Central 15	d																								
Motherwell	d																								
Haymarket	d																								
Edinburgh 10	a																								
Edinburgh	d																								
Dunbar	d																								
Berwick-upon-Tweed	d																								
Alnmouth for Alnwick	d																								
Morpeth	d																								
Newcastle 8	a																								
Sunderland	d																							09 12	09 28
Hartlepool	d																							09 36	
Newcastle 8	d					07 55	08 00									08 55				09 20		09 25	09 31		09a50
Chester-le-Street	d																						09 40		
Durham	d					08 08	08 13									09 07				09 33		09 37	09 47		
Darlington 7	a					08 25	08 31									09 25				09 48		09 55	10 03		
Middlesbrough	d																								
Eaglescliffe	d																							09 59	
Darlington 7	d					08 26	08 31									09 26				09 50		09 56	10 04		
Northallerton	d						08 43															10 07	10 15	10 20	
Thirsk	d						08 51																	10 29	
York 8	a					08 55	09 11									09 53				10 18		10 27	10 41	10 45	
Leeds 10	a						09 38													10 51			11 08		
Harrogate	d																								
Scarborough	d																								
York 8	d	08 00				08 56									09 28	09 56						10 29		10 50	
Doncaster 7	a	08 21																				10 51			
Skipton	d																								
Keighley	d																								
Bradford Interchange	d				08 05																				
Bradford Forster Square	d																								
Shipley	d																								
Halifax	d																								
Brighouse	d																								
Leeds 10	d			08 05				08 10	09 00			09 05		09 32	10 00			10 05	10 15	11 00					
Wakefield Westgate 7	d			08 16				08 23	09 11			09 17		09 46	10 12			10 17	10 27	11 12					
Wakefield Kirkgate 4	d				08 43																				
Pontefract Monkhill	d																								
Sheffield 7	a							08 51						10 13					10 57						
Hull	d												09 30												
Selby	d												10 05												
Doncaster 7	d	08 22		08 35	09 06				09a31			09 35	10 24		10a28			10 35		11a28		10 52			
Retford 10	d			08 49									10 38					10 51							
Lincoln	d																								
Newark North Gate 7	a			09 04								09 59						11 06				11 15			
	d			09 04								09 59						11 06				11 15			
Grantham 7	a			09 17								10 11	10 59					11 19							
	d			09 17								10 11	10 59					11 19							
Peterborough 8	a	09 09		09 38		10 03						10 32				11 01		11 41				11 47			
Norwich	a																								
Peterborough 8	d	09 09		09 38		10 04						10 33				11 02		11 41				11 50			
Stevenage 4	a	09 38										11 04	11s48												
London Kings Cross 15 ⊖	a	10 07		10 34	10 40	10 58						11 34	12 14			11 59		12 37				12 43		12 44	

A ◇ from Doncaster R to Doncaster

Table 26

Sundays

from 1 April

Scotland, North East England, Yorkshire and Humberside - London

Route Diagram - see first Page of Table 26

		GR	NT	TP	NT	GR		XC	GR	GR	TP	HT	NT	EM	GR	XC		GR	GC	GR	TP	GR	GR	EM	EM
		R				R			R	R					R			R	R	R		R	R		
		1		◇1		1		◇1	1	1	◇1	◇1		◇	1	◇1		1	1	1	◇1	1	1	◇1	◇
		🍽🛒				🍽🛒		🛒	🍽🛒	🍽🛒		⊠			🍽🛒	🛒		🍽🛒	🍽	🍽🛒		🍽🛒	🍽🛒	🍽	
Aberdeen	d																								
Stonehaven	d																								
Montrose	d																								
Arbroath	d																								
Dundee	d																								
Leuchars 3	d																								
Kirkcaldy	d																								
Inverkeithing	d																								
Inverness	d																								
Perth	d																								
Stirling	d																								
Glasgow Central 15	d																								
Motherwell	d																								
Haymarket	d																								
Edinburgh 10	a																								
Edinburgh	d							08 50	09 00	09 30						09 50		10 00		10 30			10 55		
Dunbar	d																								
Berwick-upon-Tweed	d							09 33		10 11										11 11					
Alnmouth for Alnwick	d															10 49		10 58							
Morpeth	d															11 04							12 06		
Newcastle 8 🚢	a							10 19	10 25	10 57						11 19		11 27		11 56			12 23		
Sunderland 🚢	d																								
Hartlepool	d		10 01		11 00								12 01												
Newcastle 8 🚢	d	10 00	10a48		11a48			10 24	10 28	10 59	11 08		12a48			11 25		11 28		11 58	12 10		12 25		
Chester-le-Street	d																								
Durham	d							10 37	10 42		11 20					11 37		11 41			12 22		12 38		
Darlington 7	a	10 26						10 53	11 00	11 26	11 36					11 54		12 00		12 25	12 38		12 55		
Middlesbrough	d			10 15																					
Eaglescliffe	d																								
Darlington 7	d	10 27						10 54	11 01	11 27	11 37					11 55		12 00		12 26	12 39		12 56		
Northallerton	d			10 43					11 14		11 49												13 07		
Thirsk	d			10 51																					
York 8	a	10 54		11 10				11 23	11 34	11 54	12 12					12 22		12 28		12 53	13 11		13 28		
Leeds 10	a			11 38				11 51			12 38					12 51					13 37				
Harrogate	d																								
Scarborough	d																								
York 8	d	10 56							11 36	11 56								12 30		12 55			13 30		
Doncaster 7	a								11 59									12 53					13 53		
Skipton	d																								
Keighley	d																								
Bradford Interchange	d																		12 04						
Bradford Forster Square	d																								
Shipley	d																								
Halifax	d																		12 15						
Brighouse	d																		12 26						
Leeds 10	d					11 05		12 00							12 05	13 00						13 05		13 59	
Wakefield Westgate 7	d					11 17		12 12							12 17	13 12						13 16		14 12	
Wakefield Kirkgate 4	d																		12 51						
Pontefract Monkhill	d																								
Sheffield 7 🚢	a																							14 44	
Hull	d											11 30													
Selby	d											12 05													
Doncaster 7	d					11 35		12a28	12 00			12 26			12 37	13a28		12 54	13 23			13 35	13 54		
Retford 10	d								12 15			12 40											14 08		
Lincoln	d																								
Newark North Gate 7	a					11 59									13 00			13 17				13 59			
	d					12 00									13 00			13 17				13 59			
Grantham 7	a					12 12						13 01			13 13							14 11			
	d					12 13						13 01		13 12	13 15							14 11			14 22
Peterborough 8	a	12 01				12 34			12 56					13 41	13 38			13 47				14 32	14 48		14 51
Norwich	a													15 30											16 35
Peterborough 8	d	12 01				12 35			12 56						13 40			13 50				14 33	14 49		
Stevenage 4	a					13 05						13s46										15 06			
London Kings Cross 15 ⊖	a	12 54				13 35			13 53	13 56		14 14			14 34			14 45	14 55	14 57		15 34	15 43		

Table 26

Sundays
from 1 April

Scotland, North East England, Yorkshire and Humberside - London

Route Diagram - see first Page of Table 26

		GR	XC	TP	GC	GR	TP	GR	GR	NT	XC	NT	EM	HT	GR	XC	GR	TP	GR	GR	XC	XC
		R			R	R		R	R						R		R		R	R		
		1	◇1	◇1	1	1	◇1	1	1		◇1		◇	◇1	1	◇1	1	◇1	1	1	◇1	◇1
																	A					B
		Restaurant, Trolley	Trolley		Restaurant	Restaurant, Trolley		Restaurant, Trolley	Restaurant, Trolley		Trolley			⊠	Restaurant, Trolley	Trolley	Restaurant, Trolley		Restaurant, Trolley	Restaurant, Trolley	Trolley	Trolley
Aberdeen	d																09 47					
Stonehaven	d																10 04					
Montrose	d																10 27					
Arbroath	d																10 43					
Dundee	d																11 02					
Leuchars 3	d																11 16					
Kirkcaldy	d																11 40					
Inverkeithing	d																11 56					
Inverness	d																					
Perth	d																					
Stirling	d																					
Glasgow Central 15	d															10 55						11 51
Motherwell	d															11 10						12 07
Haymarket	d															11 51	12 16					12 49
Edinburgh 10	a															11 55	12 23					12 54
Edinburgh	d		11 05			11 30			12 00							12 08	12 30			13 00		13 06
Dunbar	d		11 25																			13 25
Berwick-upon-Tweed	d		11 50			12 11										12 49	13 11					
Alnmouth for Alnwick	d		12 10						12 58													14 08
Morpeth	d																					
Newcastle 8	a		12 37			12 57			13 27							13 34	13 58			14 23		14 35
Sunderland	d				12 11					13 28												
Hartlepool	d				12 36							14 01										
Newcastle 8	d		12 40			12 59	13 04	13 12	13 28	13a49	13 35	14a48				13 40	13 59	14 08	14 12	14 25	14 35	14 40
Chester-le-Street	d						13 13															
Durham	d		12 52				13 20	13 24	13 41		13 47					13 52		14 20	14 25	14 38	14 47	14 52
Darlington 7	a		13 08			13 27	13 36	13 41	13 59		14 04					14 09	14 28	14 36	14 42	14 56	15 03	15 08
Middlesbrough	d			12 45																		
Eaglescliffe	d				13 02																	
Darlington 7	d		13 09			13 28	13 37	13 42	13 59		14 05					14 10	14 28	14 37	14 43	14 57	15 04	15 09
Northallerton	d			13 13	13 23			13 55										14 49	14 57			
Thirsk	d			13 23	13 32																	
York 8	a		13 36	13 43	13 48	13 56	14 10	14 15	14 28		14 31					14 37	14 56	15 12	15 18	15 24	15 31	15 37
Leeds 10	a		14 03	14 08			14 38									15 05		15 38				16 03
Harrogate	d																					
Scarborough	d																					
York 8	d				13 52	13 57		14 16	14 29		14 34						14 58		15 19	15 29	15 34	
Doncaster 7	a							14 44	14 53		14 57								15 43	15 52	15 57	
Skipton	d																					
Keighley	d																					
Bradford Interchange	d																					
Bradford Forster Square	d																					
Shipley	d																					
Halifax	d																					
Brighouse	d																					
Leeds 10	d	14 05	14 10												15 05	15 10						16 10
Wakefield Westgate 7	d	14 17	14 23												15 16	15 23						16 22
Wakefield Kirkgate 4	d																					
Pontefract Monkhill	d																					
Sheffield 7	a		14 52								15 21					15 51					16 21	16 51
Hull	d													14 30								
Selby	d													15 05								
Doncaster 7	d	14 35						14 44	14 53					15 26	15 35				15 43	15 54		
Retford 10	d													15 40						16 08		
Lincoln	d																					
Newark North Gate 7	a	14 59							15 17						15 59				16 07			
	d	14 59							15 17						15 59				16 08			
Grantham 7	a	15 11												16 01	16 11							
	d	15 11											15 20	16 01	16 11							
Peterborough 8	a	15 32						15 38	15 46				15 58		16 32				16 38	16 49		
Norwich	a												17 35									
Peterborough 8	d	15 33						15 39	15 49						16 33				16 38	16 50		
Stevenage 4	a													16s46	17 05							
London Kings Cross 15 ⊖	a	16 27			15 46	15 55		16 33	16 45					17 15	17 34		16 55		17 37	17 44		

A The Northern Lights

B Trolley from Edinburgh

Table 26

Sundays

from 1 April

Scotland, North East England, Yorkshire and Humberside - London

Route Diagram - see first Page of Table 26

		TP	GC	GR	TP	XC	NT	NT	EM	GR	GR	GC	NT	EM	GR	XC	GR	TP	HT	GR	EM	GR	GR
			■R	■R						■R	■R	■R			■R		■R			■R		■R	■R
		◇■1	■1	■1	◇■1	◇■1			◇	■1	■1	■1		◇	■1	◇■1	■1	◇■1	◇■1	■1	◇	■1	■1
				A												B							
			⊏	⊏⊥		⊥				⊏⊥	⊏⊥	⊏			⊏⊥	⊥	⊏⊥		☒	⊏⊥		⊏⊥	⊏⊥
Aberdeen	d															11 12	11 47						
Stonehaven	d															11 29	12 04						
Montrose	d															11 50	12 27						
Arbroath	d															12 06	12 43						
Dundee	d															12 25	13 01						
Leuchars ■3	d															12 38	13 15						
Kirkcaldy	d															13 03	13 39						
Inverkeithing	d															13 18	13 58						
Inverness	d			09 40																			
Perth	d			11 58																			
Stirling	d			12 34																			
Glasgow Central ■15	d																						
Motherwell	d																						
Haymarket	d			13 14												13 37	14 18						
Edinburgh ■10	a			13 19												13 42	14 25						
Edinburgh	d			13 30		13 50					14 00					14 08	14 30						15 00
Dunbar	d																						
Berwick-upon-Tweed	d			14 12		14 33										14 49	15 11						
Alnmouth for Alnwick	d										14 58												
Morpeth	d																						
Newcastle ■8 ⛴	a			14 59		15 18					15 27					15 34	15 57						16 23
Sunderland ⛴	d		14 12				15 28																
Hartlepool	d		14 36					16 01					16 51										
Newcastle ■8 ⛴	d			15 00	15 07	15 23	15a48	16a48			15 28		17a48			15 40	15 59	16 08		16 12			16 25
Chester-le-Street	d				15 16																		
Durham	d				15 23	15 36					15 41					15 52		16 20		16 24			16 38
Darlington ■7	a			15 29	15 39	15 52					16 00					16 08	16 27	16 36		16 41			16 56
Middlesbrough	d	14 42																					
Eaglescliffe	d		14 59																				
Darlington ■7	d			15 29	15 40	15 53					16 00					16 09	16 28	16 37		16 42			16 57
Northallerton	d	15 10	15 22															16 49		16 54			
Thirsk	d	15 18	15 31																				
York ■8	a	15 42	15 46	15 57	16 12	16 19					16 28					16 37	16 56	17 12		17 16			17 24
Leeds ■10	a	16 08			16 38											17 06		17 38					
Harrogate	d																						
Scarborough	d																						
York ■8	d		15 50	15 59		16 23					16 29						16 57			17 17			17 29
Doncaster ■7	a					16 48					16 53												17 52
Skipton	d																						
Keighley	d																						
Bradford Interchange	d											15 42											
Bradford Forster Square	d																						
Shipley	d																						
Halifax	d											15 54											
Brighouse	d											16 05											
Leeds ■10	d									16 15					16 45	17 10						17 15	
Wakefield Westgate ■7	d									16 27					16 56	17 22						17 27	
Wakefield Kirkgate ■4	d											16 30											
Pontefract Monkhill	d																						
Sheffield ■7 ⛴	a					17 19										17 51							
Hull	d																		16 30				
Selby	d																		17 05				
Doncaster ■7	d									16 46	16 53	17 12			17 17				17 26			17 46	17 54
Retford ■10	d																		17 40			18 00	
Lincoln	d																						
Newark North Gate ■7	a										17 17				17 44					17 59			
	d										17 17				17 44					17 59			
Grantham ■7	a									17 17									18 01			18 23	18 27
	d								16 22	17 17				17 21					18 01		18 17	18 23	18 27
Peterborough ■8	a								16 55		17 46			17 50	18 14					18 28	18 46		18 50
Norwich	a								18 30					19 29							20 29		
Peterborough ■8	d										17 49				18 14					18 29			18 50
Stevenage ■4	a									18 04									18s49			19 07	
London Kings Cross ■15 ⊖	a		17 45	17 57						18 35	18 45	18 50			19 12		18 56		19 18	19 22		19 37	19 45

A The Highland Chieftain

B ⊥ from Edinburgh

Table 26

Sundays
from 1 April

Scotland, North East England, Yorkshire and Humberside - London

Route Diagram - see first Page of Table 26

		XC	GR	EM	XC	TP	GR	TP	GR	GR	XC	EM	GR	XC	TP	GR	TP	XC	HT	GR	GR
			R				R		R	R			R			R				R	R
		◇1	1	◇1	◇1	◇1	1	◇1	1	1	◇1	◇	1	◇1	◇1	1	◇1	◇1	◇1	1	1
					A									A							
		⚒	🍽⚒	🍽	⚒		🍽⚒		🍽⚒	🍽⚒	⚒		🍽⚒	⚒		🍽⚒		⚒	☒	🍽⚒	🍽⚒
Aberdeen	d															13 50					
Stonehaven	d															14 07					
Montrose	d															14 30					
Arbroath	d															14 46					
Dundee	d															15 04					
Leuchars 3	d															15 18					
Kirkcaldy	d															15 42					
Inverkeithing	d															15 58					
Inverness	d																				
Perth	d																				
Stirling	d																				
Glasgow Central 15	d				13 49									14 55							
Motherwell	d				14 04									15 11							
Haymarket	d				14 42									15 51		16 18					
Edinburgh 10	a				14 47									15 56		16 25					
Edinburgh	d				15 07		15 30			16 00				16 05		16 30					17 00
Dunbar	d				15 27																
Berwick-upon-Tweed	d						16 11									17 11					
Alnmouth for Alnwick	d									16 58				17 07							
Morpeth	d													17 22							
Newcastle 8 ⛴	a				16 34		16 56			17 27				17 37		17 57					18 23
Sunderland ⛴	d																				
Hartlepool	d																				
Newcastle 8 ⛴	d	16 35			16 40		16 58	17 05		17 28	17 35			17 40	17 52	17 59		18 20			18 25
Chester-le-Street	d							17 14													
Durham	d	16 47			16 52			17 21		17 41	17 47			17 52	18 04			18 32			18 38
Darlington 7	a	17 03			17 08		17 25	17 37		18 00	18 04			18 08	18 20	18 26		18 49			18 55
Middlesbrough	d					16 42															
Eaglescliffe	d																				
Darlington 7	d	17 04			17 09		17 26	17 38		18 00	18 05			18 09	18 21	18 27		18 51			18 56
Northallerton	d					17 10		17 49							18 33						19 07
Thirsk	d					17 18											←				
York 8	a	17 30			17 37	17 42	17 53	18 12		18 28	18 31			18 36	19 03	18 56	19 03	19 17			19 28
Leeds 10	a				18 04	18 08		18 38						19 03	→		19 38				
Harrogate	d		17 05																		
Scarborough	d																				
York 8	d	17 34		17 40			17 55			18 29	18 34					18 57		19 24			19 30
Doncaster 7	a	17 57		18 05						18 53	18 57							19 47			19 53
Skipton	d																				
Keighley	d																				
Bradford Interchange	d																				
Bradford Forster Square	d																				
Shipley	d																				
Halifax	d																				
Brighouse	d																				
Leeds 10	d		17 45		18 10				18 15				18 45	19 10						19 15	
Wakefield Westgate 7	d		17 57		18 22				18 27				18 56	19 22						19 26	
Wakefield Kirkgate 4	d																				
Pontefract Monkhill	d																				
Sheffield 7 ⛴	a	18 23		18 28	18 51						19 21			19 50				20 16			
Hull	d																		18 30		
Selby	d																		19 05		
Doncaster 7	d		18 17						18 46	18 53			19 17						19 26	19 45	19 54
Retford 10	d																		19 40	19 59	
Lincoln	d																				
Newark North Gate 7	a		18 42							19 17			19 44								20 17
	d		18 43							19 17			19 44								20 17
Grantham 7	a								19 17										20 01	20 22	
	d								19 17			19 27							20 01	20 22	
Peterborough 8	a		19 13							19 47		19 56	20 14								20 48
Norwich	a											21 35									
Peterborough 8	d		19 13							19 50			20 15								20 50
Stevenage 4	a								20 07										20s50	21 08	
London Kings Cross 15 ⊖	a		20 12				19 53		20 35	20 46			21 12			20 56			21 18	21 35	21 44

A ⚒ from Edinburgh

Table 26

Sundays

from 1 April

Scotland, North East England, Yorkshire and Humberside - London

Route Diagram - see first Page of Table 26

		GR	XC	TP	GC	GR	NT	TP	XC	GR		NT	NT	EM	GR	XC	GR	TP	TP	GR	NT	GR	XC	GR	TP
		R 1	◇1	◇1	R 1	R 1		◇1	◇1	R 1				◇	R 1	◇1	R 1	◇1	◇1	R 1		R 1	◇1	R 1	◇1
			A													A									
Aberdeen	d																								
Stonehaven	d																								
Montrose	d																								
Arbroath	d																								
Dundee	d																								
Leuchars 3	d																								
Kirkcaldy	d																								
Inverkeithing	d																								
Inverness	d																								
Perth	d																								
Stirling	d																								
Glasgow Central 15	d															16 55							18 57		
Motherwell	d															17 11							19 11		
Haymarket	d															17 51							19 51		
Edinburgh 10	a															17 56							19 56		
Edinburgh	d		17 07			17 30				18 00						18 07	18 30			19 00		20 00	20 05	21 00	
Dunbar	d		17 27			17 50										18 26				19 20		20 21	20 29	21 21	
Berwick-upon-Tweed	d		17 52			18 15										18 52	19 11			19 45		20 46	20 55	21 46	
Alnmouth for Alnwick	d									18 58												21 09		22 08	
Morpeth	d																					21 26			
Newcastle 8	a		18 36			19 00				19 27						19 36	19 56			20 30		21 42	21 48	22 42	
Sunderland	d				18 12		18 43					19 28	20 29												
Hartlepool	d				18 36																				
Newcastle 8	d		18 39			19 02	19a05	19 10	19 25	19 28		19a52	20a47			19 40	19 58		20 08	20 32	21 06	21 44			
Chester-le-Street	d																				21 15				
Durham	d		18 51					19 22	19 37	19 41						19 52			20 20	20 45	21 24	21 58			
Darlington 7	a		19 07			19 29		19 38	19 53	20 00						20 08	20 24		20 36	21 03	21 44	22 16			
Middlesbrough	d			18 45														20 06							22 06
Eaglescliffe	d				18 59																22a00				
Darlington 7	d		19 08			19 30		19 39	19 54	20 00						20 09	20 25		20 37	21 04		22 17			
Northallerton	d			19 13	19 21													20 38	20 49			22 30			22 34
Thirsk	d			19 21	19 30													20 46							22 42
York 8	a		19 35	19 42	19 47	19 57		20 11	20 21	20 28						20 36	20 53	21 06	21 12	21 31		23 02			23 09
Leeds 10	a		20 05	20 08				20 38								21 02			21 38			23 34			23 38
Harrogate	d																								
Scarborough	d																								
York 8	d				19 51	19 59			20 24	20 29							20 55			21 33					
Doncaster 7	a								20 47	20 53							21 18			21 55					
Skipton	d																								
Keighley	d																								
Bradford Interchange	d																								
Bradford Forster Square	d																								
Shipley	d																								
Halifax	d																								
Brighouse	d																								
Leeds 10	d	19 45	20 10												20 45	21 10									
Wakefield Westgate 7	d	19 56	20 22												20 56	21 22									
Wakefield Kirkgate 4	d																								
Pontefract Monkhill	d																								
Sheffield 7	a		20 51						21 17							21 50									
Hull	d																								
Selby	d																								
Doncaster 7	d	20 19								20 53					21 15		21 19			21 56					
Retford 10	d														21 29										
Lincoln	d																								
Newark North Gate 7	a	20 43								21 17							21 47			22 19					
	d	20 43								21 17							21 47			22 19					
Grantham 7	a					20 47									21 52		22 00			22 32					
	d					20 48								21 19	21 52		22 00			22 32					
Peterborough 8	a	21 13				21 08				21 46				21 52	22 13		22 19			22 53					
Norwich	a													23 28											
Peterborough 8	d	21 13				21 08				21 48					22 13		22 19			22 53					
Stevenage 4	a														22 45		22 52			23s24					
London Kings Cross 15 ⊖	a	22 10			21 45	22 03				22 46					23 16		23 21			23 53					

A to Leeds

Table 26A

Mondays to Saturdays

Peterborough - Wisbech, Kings Lynn, Swaffham and Dereham

Bus Service

		GR SX	GR SX	GR SO	GR	GR	GR	GR	GR	GR	GR	GR	GR	GR	GR	GR	GR	GR	GR	GR	GR	GR	GR
Peterborough	d	07 00	07 30	07 35	08 05	08 35	09 05	09 35	10 05	10 35	11 05	11 35	12 05	12 35	13 05	13 35	14 05	14 35	15 05	15 35	16 05	16 35	17 10
Wisbech Bus Station	d	07 51	08 21	08 26	08 56	09 26	09 56	10 26	10 56	11 26	11 56	12 26	12 56	13 26	13 56	14 26	14 56	15 26	15 56	16 26	16 56	17 26	18 00
Kings Lynn Bus Station	d	08 32	09 02	09 02	09 32	10 02	10 32	11 02	11 32	12 02	12 32	13 02	13 32	14 02	14 32	15 02	15 32	16 02	16 32	17 02	17 32	18 02	18 35
Swaffham Market Place	d	09 04	09 34	09 34	10 04	10 34	11 04	11 34	12 04	12 34	13 04	13 34	14 04	14 34	15 04	15 34	16 04	16 34	17 04	17 34	18 04	18 34	19 06
Dereham Market Place	a	09 37	10 07	10 07	10 37	11 07	11 37	12 07	12 37	13 07	13 37	14 07	14 37	15 07	15 37	16 07	16 37	17 07	17 37	18 07	18 37	19 07	19 37

		GR	GR	GR	GR	GR	GR	GR
Peterborough	d	17 40	18 10	18 40	19 10	20 10	21 10	22 10
Wisbech Bus Station	d	18 30	19 00	19 30	20 00	21 00	22 00	23 00
Kings Lynn Bus Station	d	18a58	19 35	19a58	20 35	21 35	22a28	23a28
Swaffham Market Place	d		20 06		21 06	22 06		
Dereham Market Place	a		20 37		21 37	22 37		

Sundays

		GR	GR	GR	GR	GR	GR	GR	GR	GR	GR	GR	GR	GR	GR	GR
Peterborough	d	08 10	09 10	10 10	11 10	12 10	13 10	14 10	15 10	16 10	17 10	18 10	19 10	20 10	21 10	22 10
Wisbech Bus Station	d	09 00	10 00	11 00	12 00	13 00	14 00	15 00	16 00	17 00	18 00	19 00	20 00	21 00	22 00	23 00
Kings Lynn Bus Station	d	09 35	10 35	11 35	12 35	13 35	14 35	15 35	16 35	17 35	18 35	19 35	20 35	21 35	22a28	23a28
Swaffham Market Place	d	10 06	11 06	12 06	13 06	14 06	15 06	16 06	17 06	18 06	19 06	20 06	21 06	22 06		
Dereham Market Place	a	10 37	11 37	12 37	13 37	14 37	15 37	16 37	17 37	18 37	19 37	20 37	21 37	22 37		

Mondays to Saturdays

Dereham, Swaffham, Kings Lynn and Wisbech - Peterborough

Bus Service

		GR SX	GR SX	GR	GR	GR	GR SX	GR SO	GR SX	GR SO	GR SX	GR SO	GR SX	GR SO	GR	GR	GR	GR	GR	GR	GR	GR	GR
Dereham Market Place	d						07 05	07 09	07 30	07 39	08 00	08 09	08 35	08 36	09 05	09 35	10 05	10 35	11 05	11 35	12 05	12 35	13 05
Swaffham Market Place	d						07 35	07 39	08 02	08 09	08 32	08 39	09 07	09 07	09 37	10 07	10 37	11 07	11 35	12 07	12 37	13 07	13 37
Kings Lynn Bus Station	d	05 40	06 10	06 45	07 15	07 45	08 15	08 15	08 45	08 45	09 15	09 15	09 45	09 45	10 15	10 45	11 15	11 45	12 15	12 45	13 15	13 45	14 15
Wisbech Bus Station	d	06 13	06 43	07 18	07 48	08 18	08 48	08 48	09 18	09 18	09 48	09 48	10 18	10 18	10 48	11 18	11 48	12 18	12 48	13 18	13 48	14 18	14 48
Peterborough	a	06 54	07 24	07 59	08 29	08 59	09 29	09 29	09 59	09 59	10 29	10 29	10 59	10 59	11 29	11 59	12 29	12 59	13 29	13 59	14 29	14 59	15 29

		GR	GR	GR	GR	GR	GR	GR	GR SO	GR SX	GR SO	GR SX	GR	GR
Dereham Market Place	d	13 35	14 05	14 35	15 05	15 35	16 05	16 35	17 40	17 44	18 40	18 44	19 44	20 44
Swaffham Market Place	d	14 07	14 37	15 07	15 37	16 07	16 37	17 07	18 12	18 14	19 12	19 14	20 14	21 14
Kings Lynn Bus Station	d	14 45	15 15	15 45	16 15	16 45	17 15	17 45	18 50	18 50	19 50	19 50	20 50	21 50
Wisbech Bus Station	d	15 18	15 48	16 18	16 48	17 18	17 48	18 18	19 22	19 22	20 22	20 22	21 22	22 22
Peterborough	a	15 59	16 29	16 59	17 29	17 59	18 29	18 59	20 01	20 01	21 01	21 01	22 01	23 01

Sundays

		GR	GR	GR	GR	GR	GR	GR	GR	GR	GR	GR	GR	GR	GR	GR	GR
Dereham Market Place	d				08 44	09 44	10 44	11 44	12 44	13 44	14 44	15 44	16 44	17 44	18 44	19 44	20 44
Swaffham Market Place	d				09 14	10 14	11 14	12 14	13 14	14 14	15 14	16 14	17 14	18 14	19 14	20 14	21 14
Kings Lynn Bus Station	d	06 50	07 50	08 50	09 50	10 50	11 50	12 50	13 50	14 50	15 50	16 50	17 50	18 50	19 50	20 50	21 50
Wisbech Bus Station	d	07 22	08 22	09 22	10 22	11 22	12 22	13 22	14 22	15 22	16 22	17 22	18 22	19 22	20 22	21 22	22 22
Peterborough	a	08 01	09 01	10 01	11 01	12 01	13 01	14 01	15 01	16 01	17 01	18 01	19 01	20 01	21 01	22 01	23 01

Sunday service operates on Bank Holiday Monday

Mondays to Saturdays

Peterborough - Oundle, Corby and Kettering

Bus Service

		GR	GR	GR	GR	GR	GR	GR	GR	GR	GR	GR	GR	GR	GR
		Bus	Bus	Bus	Bus	Bus	Bus	Bus	Bus	Bus	Bus	Bus	Bus	Bus	Bus
Peterborough Queensgate	d	07 05	07 40	09 10	10 10	11 10	12 10	13 10	14 10	15 10	16 10	17 10	18 30	19 30	20 30
Oundle Market Place	a	07 27	08 22	09 32	10 32	11 32	12 32	13 32	14 32	15 32	16 32	17 32	18 57	19 57	20 57
Corby George Street	a	08 05	09 05	10 05	11 05	12 05	13 05	14 05	15 05	16 05	17 05	18 05	19 25	20 25	21 25
Kettering Library	a	08 35	09 35	10 35	11 35	12 35	13 35	14 35	15 35	16 35	17 35	18 35	19 55	20 55	21 55

Sundays

		GR	GR	GR	GR	GR	GR
		Bus	Bus	Bus	Bus	Bus	Bus
Peterborough Queensgate	d	10 10	12 10	14 10	16 10	18 10	20 10
Oundle Market Place	a	10 37	12 37	14 37	16 37	18 37	20 37
Corby George Street	a	11 05	13 05	15 05	17 05	19 05	21 05
Kettering Library	a	11 35	13 35	15 35	17 35	19 35	21 33

Mondays to Saturdays

Kettering and Corby, Oundle - Peterborough

Bus Service

		GR	GR	GR	GR	GR	GR	GR	GR	GR	GR	GR	GR	GR	GR	GR
		Bus	Bus	Bus	Bus	Bus	Bus	Bus	Bus	Bus	Bus	Bus	Bus	Bus	Bus	Bus
Kettering Library	d	05 30	06 00	07 05		08 45	09 45	10 45	11 45	12 45	13 45	14 45	15 45	16 50	17 55	18 55
Corby George Street	d	05 55	06 25	07 30		09 10	10 10	11 10	12 10	13 10	14 10	15 10	16 10	17 15	18 20	19 20
Oundle Market Place	d	06 23	06 53	07 58	08 38	09 38	10 38	11 38	12 38	13 38	14 38	15 38	16 38	17 43	18 48	19 48
Peterborough Queensgate	a	06 40	07 25	08 30	09 00	10 00	11 00	12 00	13 00	14 00	15 00	16 00	17 00	18 05	19 10	20 20

Sundays

		GR	GR	GR	GR	GR	GR
		Bus	Bus	Bus	Bus	Bus	Bus
Kettering Library	d	08 15	10 15	12 15	14 15	16 15	18 15
Corby George Street	d	08 40	10 40	12 40	14 40	16 40	18 40
Oundle Market Place	d	09 08	11 08	13 08	15 08	17 08	19 08
Peterborough Queensgate	a	09 40	11 40	13 40	15 40	17 40	19 40

Table 26F

Mondays to Saturdays

Doncaster - Robin Hood Airport

Bus Service

		GR	GR	GR	GR	GR	GR	GR	GR	GR
Doncaster Interchange	d	05 35	06 35	07 35	08 35	09 35	10 35	11 35	12 35	13 35
Robin Hood Airport	a	05 59	06 59	07 59	08 59	09 59	10 59	11 59	12 59	13 59

		GR	GR	GR	GR	GR	GR	GR	GR	GR
Doncaster Interchange	d	14 35	15 35	16 35	17 35	18 35	19 35	20 35	21 35	22 35
Robin Hood Airport	a	14 59	15 59	16 59	17 59	18 59	19 59	20 59	21 59	22 59

Sundays

		GR	GR	GR	GR	GR	GR	GR	GR	GR
Doncaster Interchange	d	08 35	09 35	10 35	11 35	12 35	13 35	15 35	16 35	17 35
Robin Hood Airport	a	08 59	09 59	10 59	11 59	12 59	13 59	15 59	16 59	17 59

Mondays to Saturdays

Robin Hood Airport - Doncaster

Bus Service

		GR	GR	GR	GR	GR	GR	GR	GR	GR
Robin Hood Airport	d	06 05	07 05	08 05	09 05	10 05	11 05	12 05	13 05	14 05
Doncaster Interchange	a	06 30	07 30	08 30	09 30	10 30	11 30	12 30	13 30	14 30

		GR	GR	GR	GR	GR	GR	GR	GR	GR
Robin Hood Airport	d	15 05	16 05	17 05	18 05	19 05	20 05	21 05	22 05	23 05
Doncaster Interchange	a	15 30	16 30	17 30	18 30	19 30	20 30	21 30	22 30	23 30

Sundays

		GR	GR	GR	GR	GR	GR	GR	GR	GR	GR
Robin Hood Airport	d	09 05	10 05	11 05	12 05	13 05	14 05	15 05	16 05	17 05	18 05
Doncaster Interchange	a	09 30	10 30	11 30	12 30	13 30	14 30	15 30	16 30	17 30	18 30

Table 26G

Mondays to Fridays

York - Pickering and Whitby

Bus Service

		GR	GR	GR	GR	GR	GR	GR	GR	GR	GR
York	d	08 38	09 42	10 42	11 42	12 42	13 42	14 42	15 44	16 19	18 09
Eden Camp	a	09 42	10 42	11 42	12 42	13 42	14 42	15 42	16 52	17 27	19 07
Flamingo Land	a										
Pickering Eastgate	a	09 58	10 58	11 58	12 58	13 58	14 58	15 58	17 08	17 43	19 23
Whitby Bus Station	a	11 02		13 02				17 02			

Saturdays

		GR	GR	GR	GR	GR	GR	GR	GR
York	d	08 42	10 42	11 42	13 42	14 42	15 42	16 42	17 42
Eden Camp	a	09 42	11 42	12 42	14 42	15 42	16 42	17 42	18 42
Flamingo Land	a								
Pickering Eastgate	a	09 58	11 58	12 58	14 58	15 58	16 58	17 58	18 58
Whitby Bus Station	a	11 02	13 02			17 02			

Sundays

		GR	GR
York	d	12 52	14 52
Eden Camp	a	13 58	15 52
Flamingo Land	a		
Pickering Eastgate	a	14 14	16 08
Whitby Bus Station	a		

Mondays to Fridays

Whitby and Pickering - York

Bus Service

		GR	GR	GR	GR	GR	GR	GR	GR	GR	GR	GR
Whitby Bus Station	d					11 14		13 14			17 50	
Pickering Eastgate	d	06 47	08 47	09 17	11 17	12 17	13 17	14 17	15 37	17 25	18 53	19 35
Flamingo Land	d											
Eden Camp	d	07 03	09 03	09 33	11 33	12 33	13 27	14 33	16 09	17 41	19 09	19 45
York	a	08 10	10 05	10 35	12 35	13 35	14 35	15 35	17 37	19 08	20 08	20 50

Saturdays

		GR	GR	GR	GR	GR	GR	GR	GR
Whitby Bus Station	d				11 14		13 14	17 50	
Pickering Eastgate	d	07 07	09 17	11 17	12 17	13 17	14 17	18 53	19 13
Flamingo Land	d								
Eden Camp	d	07 23	09 33	11 33	12 33	13 27	14 33	19 09	19 29
York	a	08 25	10 35	12 35	13 35	14 35	15 35	20 08	20 50

Sundays

		GR	GR	GR
Whitby Bus Station	d			
Pickering Eastgate	d	08 52	14 27	16 27
Flamingo Land	d			
Eden Camp	d	09 08	14 43	16 43
York	a	10 25	15 45	18 05

Table 26H

Mondays to Saturdays

Darlington - Richmond and Catterick

Bus Service

		GR SX	GR SX	GR	GR	GR	GR	GR	GR	GR	GR	GR	GR	GR	GR	GR	GR	GR	GR	GR	GR	GR	GR
Darlington	d	06 23	06 53	07 33	08 03	08 33	09 03	09 33	10 03	10 33	11 03	11 33	12 03	12 33	13 03	13 33	14 03	14 33	15 03	15 33	16 03	16 33	17 03
Richmond (Market)	a	06 54	07 24	08 04	08 34	09 04	09 34	10 04	10 34	11 04	11 34	12 04	12 34	13 04	13 34	14 04	14 34	15 04	15 34	16 04	16 34	17 04	17 34
Catterick Garrison Tesco	a	07 05	07 35	08 15	08 45	09 15	09 45	10 15	10 45	11 15	11 45	12 15	12 45	13 15	13 45	14 15	14 45	15 15	15 45	16 15	16 45	17 15	17 45
Catterick Camp Centre	a	07 07	07 37	08 17	08 47	09 17	09 47	10 17	10 47	11 17	11 47	12 17	12 47	13 17	13 47	14 17	14 47	15 17	15 47	16 17	16 47	17 17	17 47
Catterick Garrison Kemmel	a	07 15	07 45	08 25	08 55	09 25	09 55	10 25	10 55	11 25	11 55	12 25	12 55	13 25	13 55	14 25	14 55	15 25	15 55	16 25	16 55	17 25	17 55

		GR	GR	GR	GR	GR
Darlington	d	17 33	18 03	19 03	20 03	21 03
Richmond (Market)	a	18 04	18 36	19 36	20 36	21 36
Catterick Garrison Tesco	a	18 15	18 47	19 47	20 47	21 47
Catterick Camp Centre	a	18 17	18 49	19 49	20 49	21 49
Catterick Garrison Kemmel	a	18 25	18 57	19 57	20 57	21 57

Sundays

		GR	GR	GR	GR	GR	GR	GR	GR	GR	GR	GR	GR	GR	GR	GR	GR	GR
Darlington	d	09 03	10 03	11 03	12 03	13 03	14 03	15 03	16 03	17 03	18 03	18 33	19 03	19 33	20 03	21 03	22 03	23 03
Richmond (Market)	a	09 34	10 34	11 34	12 34	13 34	14 34	15 34	16 34	17 34	18 36	19 06	19 36	20 06	20 36	21 36	22 36	23 36
Catterick Garrison Tesco	a	09 45	10 45	11 45	12 45	13 45	14 45	15 45	16 45	17 45	18 47	19 17	19 47	20 17	20 47	21 47	22 47	23 47
Catterick Camp Centre	a	09 47	10 47	11 47	12 47	13 47	14 47	15 47	16 47	17 47	18 49	19 19	19 49	20 19	20 49	21 49	22 49	23 49
Catterick Garrison Kemmel	a	09 55	10 55	11 55	12 55	13 55	14 55	15 55	16 55	17 55	18 57	19 27	19 57	20 27	20 57	21 57	22 57	23 57

Mondays to Saturdays

Catterick and Richmond - Darlington

Bus Service

		GR SX	GR SX	GR SO	GR SX	GR SO	GR	GR	GR	GR	GR	GR	GR	GR	GR	GR	GR	GR	GR	GR	GR	GR	GR
Catterick Garrison Kemmel	d	06 22	07 22	07 27	07 52	07 57	08 32	09 02	09 32	10 02	10 32	11 02	11 32	12 02	12 32	13 02	13 32	14 02	14 32	15 02	15 32	16 02	16 32
Catterick Camp Centre	d	06 30	07 30	07 35	08 00	08 05	08 40	09 10	09 40	10 10	10 40	11 10	11 40	12 10	12 40	13 10	13 40	14 10	14 40	15 10	15 40	16 10	16 40
Catterick Garrison Tesco	d	06 32	07 32	07 37	08 02	08 07	08 42	09 12	09 42	10 12	10 42	11 12	11 42	12 12	12 42	13 12	13 42	14 12	14 42	15 12	15 42	16 12	16 42
Richmond (Market)	d	06 44	07 44	07 49	08 14	08 19	08 54	09 24	09 54	10 24	10 54	11 24	11 54	12 24	12 54	13 24	13 54	14 24	14 54	15 24	15 54	16 24	16 54
Darlington	a	07 15	08 20	08 20	08 45	08 50	09 25	09 55	10 25	10 55	11 25	11 55	12 25	12 55	13 25	13 55	14 25	14 55	15 25	15 55	16 25	16 55	17 25

		GR	GR	GR	GR	GR		GR	GR	GR
Catterick Garrison Kemmel	d	17 02	17 32	18 02	18 32	19 02		20 02	21 02	22 02
Catterick Camp Centre	d	17 10	17 40	18 10	18 40	19 10		20 10	21 10	22 10
Catterick Garrison Tesco	d	17 12	17 42	18 12	18 42	19 12		20 12	21 12	22 12
Richmond (Market)	d	17 24	17 54	18 24	18 54	19 24		20 24	21 24	22 24
Darlington	a	17 55	18 25	18 55	19 25	19 57		20 57	21 57	22 57

Sundays

		GR	GR	GR	GR	GR	GR	GR	GR	GR	GR	GR	GR	GR	GR
Catterick Garrison Kemmel	d	09 02	10 02	11 02	12 02	13 02	14 02	15 02	16 02	17 02	18 02	19 02	20 02	21 02	22 02
Catterick Camp Centre	d	09 10	10 10	11 10	12 10	13 10	14 10	15 10	16 10	17 10	18 10	19 10	20 10	21 10	22 10
Catterick Garrison Tesco	d	09 12	10 12	11 12	12 12	13 12	14 12	15 12	16 12	17 12	18 12	19 12	20 12	21 12	22 12
Richmond (Market)	d	09 24	10 24	11 24	12 24	13 24	14 24	15 24	16 24	17 24	18 24	19 24	20 24	21 24	22 24
Darlington	a	09 55	10 55	11 55	12 55	13 55	14 55	15 55	16 55	17 55	18 55	19 57	20 57	21 57	22 57

Table 26K

Berwick-upon-Tweed - Scottish Border Towns

Bus Service

Mondays to Fridays

This service is operated by First Lowland under contract to Scottish Borders Council. Telephone 01835 824000

		XC	XC	XC	XC	XC	XC	XC	XC	XC
Berwick-upon-Tweed	d	06 57	08 12	09 52	10 52	12 52	15 07	17 47	18 47	20 22
Duns	a	07 30	08 45	10 25	11 25	13 25	15 40	18 20	19 20	20 55
Earlston	a	08 08	09 33	11 03	12 03	14 03	16 28	18 58	19 58	21 33
Melrose	a	08 22	09 47	11 15	12 15	14 15	16 40	19 10	20 10	21 45
Galashiels Bus Station	a	08 40	10 02	11 30	12 30	14 30	16 55	19 25	20 25	22 00

Saturdays

		XC	XC	XC	XC	XC	XC
Berwick-upon-Tweed	d	08 22	10 52	12 52	15 17	17 17	19 17
Duns	a	08 55	11 25	13 25	15 50	17 50	19 50
Earlston	a	09 33	12 03	14 03	16 28	18 28	20 28
Melrose	a	09 47	12 15	14 15	16 40	18 40	20 40
Galashiels Bus Station	a	10 02	12 30	14 30	16 55	18 55	20 55

Sundays

		XC	XC	XC	XC	XC	XC
Berwick-upon-Tweed	d	10 52	12 52	15 17	17 42	19 07	20 37
Duns	a	11 25	13 40	15 50	18 30	19 55	21 10
Earlston	a	12 03	14 18	16 28	19 08	20 33	21 48
Melrose	a	12 15	14 30	16 40	19 20	20 45	22 00
Galashiels Bus Station	a	12 30	14 45	16 55	19 35	21 00	22 15

Scottish Border Towns - Berwick-upon-Tweed

Bus Service

Mondays to Fridays

This service is operated by First Lowland under contract to Scottish Borders Council. Telephone 01835 824000

		XC	XC	XC	XC	XC	XC	XC	XC
Galashiels Bus Station	d	06 25	07 40	08 10	10 50	12 50	14 40	16 32	17 20
Melrose	d	06 40	07 55	08 28	11 05	13 05	14 55	16 50	17 35
Earlston	d	06 52	08 07	08 40	11 17	13 17	15 07	17 02	17 47
Duns	d	07 30	08 50	09 20	11 55	13 55	15 55	17 40	18 30
Berwick-upon-Tweed	a	08 01	09 26	09 56	12 26	14 26	16 26	18 11	19 01

Saturdays

		XC	XC	XC	XC	XC	XC
Galashiels Bus Station	d	06 35	08 20	10 50	12 50	14 50	17 20
Melrose	d	06 50	08 35	11 05	13 05	15 05	17 35
Earlston	d	07 02	08 47	11 17	13 17	15 17	17 52
Duns	d	07 40	09 25	11 55	13 55	15 55	18 30
Berwick-upon-Tweed	a	08 11	09 56	12 26	14 26	16 26	19 01

Sundays

		XC	XC	XC	XC	XC	XC
Galashiels Bus Station	d	08 50	10 50	12 35	14 50	16 35	18 35
Melrose	d	09 05	11 05	12 50	15 05	16 50	18 50
Earlston	d	09 17	11 17	13 02	15 17	17 02	19 02
Duns	d	09 55	11 55	13 40	15 55	17 40	19 40
Berwick-upon-Tweed	a	10 26	12 26	14 26	16 26	18 26	20 26

Table 27

Mondays to Fridays

Cleethorpes - Lincoln - Newark - Nottingham

Network Diagram - see first Page of Table 18

Miles	Miles			EM	EM	EM	GR	EM	EM	EM	EM	EM		EM	EM	EM	EM	EM	EM	EM	EM	EM		EM	EM
						◇1 A ☕	R 1 B ☕	C		D		D			D		D		D	D	D			D	
0	—	**Cleethorpes**	d		05 49																				
3¼	—	**Grimsby Town**	d		05 56				07 03					09 20				11 28				13 49			
11¼	—	Habrough	d		06 06				07 13					09 30				11 38				13 59			
17¾	—	Barnetby	d		06 15				07 22					09 39				11 47				14 08			
32¼	—	Market Rasen	d		06 32				07 39					09 55				12 03				14 24			
47	—	**Lincoln**	a		06 51				07 57					10 14				12 22				14 44			
—	—		d	05 26	06 53	07 04	07 20	07 26	07 59	08 35	09 11	09 32		10 15	10 36	11 35	11 42	12 23	12 30	13 40	14 33	14 46		15 30	15 45
51	—	Hykeham	d	05 34	07 01			07 34		08 43					10 44				12 38					15 37	
55¾	—	Swinderby	d	05 40	07 07			07 40		08 49					10 50				12 44					15 43	
58½	0	Collingham	d	05 45	07 12	07 19		07 45	08 15	08 54	09 26			10 32	10 55			12 40	12 48			15 02		15 48	
—	5	**Newark North Gate** 7	a	05 56	07 22		07 49		08 25		09 35			10 44		12 01		12 52				15 11			16 11
—	—		d	05 59																					
63½	—	**Newark Castle**	d	06 10		07 29		07 56		09 04		09 56			11 05		12 05		12 57	14 05	14 59			15 58	
67	—	Rolleston	d	06 16				08 02				10 02							13 04					16 04	
68	—	Fiskerton	d	06 18				08 04				10 04							13 06					16 06	
69¾	—	Bleasby	d	06 22				08 08				10 08							13 09					16 10	
70¾	—	Thurgarton	d	06 25				08 10				10 11							13 12					16 12	
71½	—	Lowdham	d	06 29		07 42		08 14		09 18		10 15			11 18		12 18		13 17	14 17	15 12			16 16	
75¾	—	Burton Joyce	d	06 34				08 18				10 19									15 16				
77¾	—	Carlton	d	06 38				08 22				10 23							13 23		15 20			16 23	
80¾	—	**Nottingham** 8	a	06 47		07 57		08 30		09 30		10 30			11 30		12 30		13 30	14 30	15 29			16 30	

		EM	EM	EM	EM	EM	EM	EM		EM	EM	EM
		D		D		D						
Cleethorpes	d										21 15	
Grimsby Town	d		15 45				18 29				21 22	
Habrough	d		15 55				18 39				21 33	
Barnetby	d		16 04				18 48				21 42	
Market Rasen	d		16 19				19 03				21 57	
Lincoln	a		16 38				19 22				22 15	
	d	16 34	16 44	17 28	18 18	18 35	19 25	20 45		21 42		22 27
Hykeham	d	16 42		17 36			19 33					22 35
Swinderby	d	16 48		17 42			19 39					22 41
Collingham	d	16 53	16 59	17 47	18 34		19 44	21 00				22 46
Newark North Gate 7	a		17 12		18 44		19 54					
	d											
Newark Castle	d	17 04		17 58		19 03		21 13		22 09		22 57
Rolleston	d			18 04								
Fiskerton	d			18 06								23 04
Bleasby	d			18 10								23 07
Thurgarton	d			18 13								
Lowdham	d	17 16		18 17		19 16		21 26		22 22		23 12
Burton Joyce	d			18 21								23 16
Carlton	d	17 22		18 24								23 20
Nottingham 8	a	17 30		18 32		19 29		21 42		22 34		23 32

Saturdays

		EM	EM	EM	EM	EM	EM	EM	GR	EM		EM	EM	EM	EM	EM	EM	EM	EM	EM		EM	EM	EM	EM
			◇1 A ☕	C		D		D	R 1 B ☕			D		D		D	D	D		D		D		D	D
Cleethorpes	d																								
Grimsby Town	d				06 50					09 20					11 28				13 49				16 00		
Habrough	d				07 00					09 30					11 38				13 59				16 09		
Barnetby	d				07 09					09 39					11 47				14 08				16 18		
Market Rasen	d				07 26					09 55					12 03				14 24				16 33		
Lincoln	a				07 44					10 14					12 22				14 44				16 52		
	d	05 26	07 04	07 26	07 46	08 35	09 01	09 19	09 30	10 15		10 36	11 35	11 42	12 23	12 30	13 40	14 35	14 45	15 27		16 34	16 54	17 26	18 34
Hykeham	d	05 34		07 34		08 43						10 44				12 38				15 34		16 42		17 34	
Swinderby	d	05 40		07 40		08 49						10 50				12 44				15 40		16 48		17 40	
Collingham	d	05 45	07 19	07 45	08 02	08 54	09 16			10 32		10 55			12 40	12 48			15 01	15 45		16 53	17 09	17 45	
Newark North Gate 7	a	05 56			08 12		09 25		09 52	10 44			12 01		12 52				15 11				17 22		
	d	05 59																							
Newark Castle	d	06 10	07 29	07 55		09 04		09 48				11 04		12 05		12 57	14 05	15 01		15 58		17 03		17 57	19 02
Rolleston	d	06 16		08 02				09 55								13 04				16 04				18 03	
Fiskerton	d	06 18		08 04				09 57								13 06				16 06				18 05	
Bleasby	d	06 22		08 07				10 01								13 09				16 10				18 09	
Thurgarton	d	06 25		08 10				10 04								13 12				16 12				18 12	
Lowdham	d	06 29	07 42	08 14		09 18		10 08				11 17		12 18		13 17	14 17	15 14		16 16		17 16		18 16	19 16
Burton Joyce	d	06 34		08 18				10 13										15 19						18 20	
Carlton	d	06 38		08 22				10 17								13 23		15 23		16 23		17 22		18 23	
Nottingham 8	a	06 47	07 58	08 30		09 30		10 25				11 29		12 30		13 30	14 30	15 30		16 30		17 30		18 31	19 29

A To St Pancras International
B To London Kings Cross
C From Sleaford to Leicester
D To Leicester

For connections to London Kings Cross please refer to Table 26

Table 27

Saturdays

Cleethorpes - Lincoln - Newark - Nottingham

Network Diagram - see first Page of Table 18

		EM	EM	EM	EM
Cleethorpes	d				
Grimsby Town	d	18 26		19 45	
Habrough	d	18 36		19 54	
Barnetby	d	18 47		20 03	
Market Rasen	d	19 02		20 18	
Lincoln	a	19 21		20 37	
	d	19 23	19 35		20 45
Hykeham	d	19 31			
Swinderby	d	19 37			
Collingham	d	19 42			21 00
Newark North Gate 7	a	19 52			
	d				
Newark Castle	d		20 03		21 10
Rolleston	d				
Fiskerton	d				
Bleasby	d				
Thurgarton	d				
Lowdham	d		20 16		21 23
Burton Joyce	d				
Carlton	d				
Nottingham 8	a		20 30		21 39

Sundays

		EM	EM	EM	EM	EM	EM	EM	EM	EM		EM
Cleethorpes	d											
Grimsby Town	d											
Habrough	d											
Barnetby	d											
Market Rasen	d											
Lincoln	a											
	d	11 05	13 00	15 00	17 25	18 05	19 03	20 05	21 00	21 26		22 10
Hykeham	d			15 08		18 13	19 11	20 13	21 08	21 34		22 18
Swinderby	d			15 14		18 19	19 17	20 19	21 14	21 40		22 24
Collingham	d	11 20	13 15	15 18		18 23	19 22	20 23	21 18	21 45		22 28
Newark North Gate 7	a	11 30	13 25	15 28	17 49				21 27	21 55		
	d			15 32					21 31			
Newark Castle	d			15 42		18 34	19 33	20 35	21 40			22 39
Rolleston	d					18 40						22 45
Fiskerton	d					18 42						22 47
Bleasby	d					18 46						22 50
Thurgarton	d					18 49						22 53
Lowdham	d			15 55		18 53	19 45	20 47	21 53			22 58
Burton Joyce	d					18 57						23 02
Carlton	d					19 01						23 05
Nottingham 8	a			16 11		19 11	20 03	21 03	22 09			23 17

For connections to London Kings Cross please refer to Table 26

Nottingham - Newark - Lincoln - Cleethorpes

Network Diagram - see first Page of Table 18

Miles	Miles			EM	EM	EM A	EM	EM	EM B	EM C	EM	EM		EM C	EM C	EM	EM C	EM A	EM C	EM	EM C	EM A		EM C	EM D
0	—	**Nottingham** 8 (tram)	d		05 55	06 53			08 05	09 21				10 29	11 17		12 27		13 17		14 29			15 27	16 14
3	—	Carlton	d		06 01	06 59			08 12	09 28					11 23				13 23					15 33	16 20
5	—	Burton Joyce	d		06 05	07 03			08 16						11 27				13 27						16 24
9¼	—	Lowdham	d		06 10	07 08			08 20	09 34				10 40	11 32		12 38		13 32		14 40			15 40	16 29
10	—	Thurgarton	d		06 14	07 12			08 24						11 36				13 36						16 33
11	—	Bleasby	d		06 17	07 15			08 27						11 39				13 39						16 36
12¾	—	Fiskerton	d		06 20	07 18			08 30						11 42				13 42						16 39
13¾	—	Rolleston	d		06 22	07 20			08 33						11 45				13 44						16 42
17¼	—	**Newark Castle**	d		06 30	07 28			08 40	09 51				10 59	11 52		12 54		13 53		14 53			15 54	16 54
—	0	**Newark North Gate** 7	a																						
—	—		d				07 40	08 31			09 57	10 50				12 06		13 02				15 28			
22¼	5	Collingham	d		06 40	07 36	07 49	08 40			10 05			11 09	12 01	12 15		13 11	14 01			15 37		16 03	17 03
25	—	Swinderby	d		06 44		07 54	08 45						11 13		12 19			14 05					16 07	
29¾	—	Hykeham	d		06 50		08 00	08 51						11 19		12 26			14 11					16 13	
33¾	—	**Lincoln**	a		07 04	07 56	08 10	09 02	09 07	10 17	10 23	11 14		11 31	12 21	12 36	13 20	13 30	14 23		15 22	15 55		16 25	17 18
—	—		d	05 57			08 14				10 25					12 37				14 37					
48½	—	Market Rasen	d	06 13			08 31				10 42					12 54				14 53					
63½	—	Barnetby	a	06 30			08 48				10 59					13 10				15 10					
69½	—	Habrough	a	06 41			09 01				11 08					13 19				15 19					
77½	—	**Grimsby Town**	a	06 56			09 15				11 23					13 35				15 34					
80¾	—	**Cleethorpes**	a																						

		EM	EM	EM C	EM	EM C	EM	EM C		EM	GR R 1 E (catering)	EM ◇1 F (catering)	EM
Nottingham 8 (tram)	d			17 17	17 50	18 15		19 20				20 29	22 25
Carlton	d			17 23		18 21		19 26					22 31
Burton Joyce	d			17 27		18 25		19 30					22 35
Lowdham	d			17 32	18 01	18 30		19 35				20 40	22 40
Thurgarton	d			17 36		18 34							
Bleasby	d			17 39		18 37		19 40					22 45
Fiskerton	d			17 42		18 40		19 43					22 48
Rolleston	d			17 45		18 43		19 46					
Newark Castle	d			17 53	18 18	18 53		19 55				20 54	22 57
Newark North Gate 7	a												23 06
	d	16 45	17 28				19 34			20 03	20 31		23 09
Collingham	d		17 36	18 02	18 27	19 02	19 43			20 12		21 03	23 18
Swinderby	d			18 07	18 31	19 06							23 23
Hykeham	d			18 13	18 37	19 12							23 29
Lincoln	a	17 13	18 00	18 26	18 50	19 23	20 01	20 17		20 27	21 01	21 22	23 41
	d	17 23					20 02						
Market Rasen	d	17 39					20 19						
Barnetby	a	17 54					20 35						
Habrough	a	18 03					20 44						
Grimsby Town	a	18 15					20 56						
Cleethorpes	a						21 03						

Saturdays

		EM	EM	EM A	EM	EM	EM	EM	EM C	EM		EM C	EM C	EM	EM C	EM A	EM C	EM	EM C	EM A		EM C	EM C	EM	EM C
Nottingham 8 (tram)	d		05 55	06 55			08 01		09 23			10 29	11 17		12 27		13 17		14 29			15 23	16 14		17 13
Carlton	d		06 01	07 01			08 08		09 29				11 23				13 23					15 29	16 20		17 19
Burton Joyce	d		06 05	07 05			08 12						11 27				13 27						16 24		17 23
Lowdham	d		06 10	07 10			08 17		09 36			10 40	11 32		12 38		13 32		14 40			15 36	16 29		17 28
Thurgarton	d		06 14	07 14			08 21						11 36				13 36						16 33		17 32
Bleasby	d		06 17	07 17			08 24						11 39				13 39						16 36		17 35
Fiskerton	d		06 20	07 20			08 27						11 42				13 42						16 39		17 38
Rolleston	d		06 22	07 22			08 30						11 45				13 44						16 42		17 41
Newark Castle	d		06 30	07 29			08 37		09 50			10 58	11 55		12 51		13 51		14 55			15 50	16 51		17 49
Newark North Gate 7	a																								
	d					08 20		09 35		10 52				12 06		13 02				15 29					
Collingham	d		06 40	07 39		08 29		09 43				11 08	12 08	12 15		13 11	14 00			15 38		15 59	17 00		17 58
Swinderby	d		06 44			08 34						11 12		12 19			14 05					16 03			18 03
Hykeham	d		06 50			08 41						11 18		12 26			14 11					16 09			18 09
Lincoln	a		07 02	07 58		08 55	09 09	09 59	10 17	11 20		11 30	12 27	12 36	13 18	13 30	14 23		15 22	15 56		16 21	17 16		18 22
	d	05 38			08 12			10 07						12 37				14 52						17 21	
Market Rasen	d	05 54			08 30			10 24						12 54				15 07						17 37	
Barnetby	a	06 11			08 47			10 40						13 10				15 23						17 53	
Habrough	a	06 22			09 01			10 50						13 20				15 33						18 02	
Grimsby Town	a	06 37			09 15			11 08						13 36				15 48						18 17	
Cleethorpes	a																								

A To Peterborough
B From Worksop
C From Leicester
D From Leicester to Sleaford
E From London Kings Cross
F From St Pancras International

For connections from London Kings Cross please refer to Table 26

Table 27

Saturdays

Nottingham - Newark - Lincoln - Cleethorpes

Network Diagram - see first Page of Table 18

		EM	EM	GR	EM	EM		EM	EM
				1	◇1				
			A	B	C			A	A
Nottingham 8	d		18 15		19 29			20 29	21 25
Carlton	d		18 21						
Burton Joyce	d		18 25						21 33
Lowdham	d		18 30		19 40			20 40	21 37
Thurgarton	d		18 34						
Bleasby	d		18 37						21 42
Fiskerton	d		18 40						21 46
Rolleston	d		18 43						
Newark Castle	d		18 53		19 53			20 56	21 57
Newark North Gate 7	a								22 06
	d	18 07		19 33		20 32			22 09
Collingham	d	18 16	19 02		20 08	20 41		21 04	22 18
Swinderby	d		19 07						22 22
Hykeham	d		19 13						22 28
Lincoln	a	18 35	19 25	20 03	20 26	20 56		21 23	22 40
	d	18 35				20 58			
Market Rasen	d	18 51				21a15			
Barnetby	a	19 07							
Habrough	a	19 16							
Grimsby Town	a	19 31							
Cleethorpes	a								

Sundays

		EM	EM	EM	EM	EM	EM	EM	GR	EM		EM	EM
									B				
Nottingham 8	d			16 33		17 26	18 42	19 33		20 37			22 28
Carlton	d					17 32							22 34
Burton Joyce	d					17 35							22 37
Lowdham	d			16 44		17 39	18 52	19 43		20 47			22 42
Thurgarton	d					17 43							22 46
Bleasby	d					17 46							22 49
Fiskerton	d					17 50							22 52
Rolleston	d					17 52							22 54
Newark Castle	d			16 59		18 00	19 07	19 58		21 03			23 03
Newark North Gate 7	a						19 17						23 13
	d	11 35	13 35		17 56		19 22		20 34			22 10	23 17
Collingham	d	11 43	13 43	17 08		18 09	19 30	20 07		21 12		22 19	23 25
Swinderby	d			17 12		18 14	19 35	20 12		21 17			23 30
Hykeham	d			17 18		18 20	19 41	20 18		21 23			23 36
Lincoln	a	12 02	14 02	17 31	18 20	18 33	19 53	20 30	21 03	21 35		22 37	23 48
	d												
Market Rasen	d												
Barnetby	a												
Habrough	a												
Grimsby Town	a												
Cleethorpes	a												

A From Leicester **B** From London Kings Cross **C** From St Pancras International

For connections from London Kings Cross please refer to Table 26

Hull and Cleethorpes - Doncaster - Meadowhall, Sheffield, Manchester and Manchester Airport, Cleethorpes - Barton-on-Humber

Network Diagram - see first Page of Table 18

Miles	Miles	Miles	Miles	Miles			NT MX	NT MX	TP MX	TP MO	TP	TP	EM	TP	NT	NT	NT MO	NT MO	NT MX	TP	TP	EM	TP	NT	NT
									◇1	◇1	◇1	◇1	◇1	◇1						◇1	◇1		◇1		
							A	B					C			B	D	D	E			F	G		
													⊠							🛒	🛒		🛒		🚌
0	0	—	—	—	**Hull**	d	22p20										05 20						06 00		
4¾	4¾	—	—	—	Hessle	d	22p27																		
7½	7½	—	—	—	Ferriby	d	22p32																		
10½	10½	—	—	—	Brough	d	22p37										05 32						06 12		
14½	14½	—	—	—	Broomfleet	d																			
17	17	—	—	—	Gilberdyke	d																	06 19		
—	19¼	—	—	—	Eastrington	d																			
—	22¼	—	—	—	Howden	d																	06 26		
—	25	—	—	—	Wressle	d																			
—	31	—	—	—	**Selby**	a																	06 36		
—	—	—	—	—		d												06 18					06 36		
—	—	—	—	—	York 8 33	a																			
20¾	—	—	—	—	Saltmarshe	d																			
23¾	—	—	—	—	Goole	d	22p51										05 46								
31	—	—	—	—	Thorne North	d	23p00										05 55								
—	—	0	0	—	**Cleethorpes**	d															05 18	05 49		06 00	
—	—	1½	1½	—	New Clee	d																			
—	—	2¼	2¼	—	Grimsby Docks	d																			
—	—	3¼	3¼	—	**Grimsby Town**	a															05 25	05 55		06 08	
—	—	—	—	—		d															05 26	05 56		06 08	
—	—	5¼	5¼	—	Great Coates	d																			
—	—	6¼	6¼	—	Healing	d																		06 15	
—	—	7½	7½	—	Stallingborough	d																		06 18	
—	—	11¼	11¼	—	Habrough	d															05 36	06 06		06 24	
—	—	—	13	—	Ulceby	d																		06 28	
—	—	—	15¾	—	Thornton Abbey	d																			
—	—	—	17¼	—	Goxhill	d																		06 35	
—	—	—	19¼	—	New Holland	d																		06 40	
—	—	—	20¾	—	Barrow Haven	d																		06 43	
—	—	—	22¾	—	**Barton-on-Humber**	a																		06 48	
—	—	—	—	—	Barton-on-Humber	d																			06 53
—	—	—	—	—	Hull Paragon Interchange	a																			07 20
—	—	17¾	—	—	Barnetby	d															05 45	06a15			
—	—	29	—	—	**Scunthorpe**	a															06 00				
—	—	—	—	—		d															06 00				
—	—	32½	—	—	Althorpe	d															06 05				
—	—	36¼	—	—	Crowle	d															06 11				
—	—	42¼	—	—	Thorne South	d															06 20				
34¼	—	45¼	—	—	Hatfield & Stainforth	d	23p06										06 01				06 25				
37	—	48	—	—	Kirk Sandall	d	23p10										06 06								
—	—	—	—	0	Adwick 31	d																			
—	—	—	—	2¼	Bentley (S.Yorks) 31	d																			
41	49¼	52	—	4	**Doncaster 7** 31	a	23p21										06 15	06 38			06 38				
—	—	—	—	—	London Kings Cross 15 ⊖26	a																			
—	—	—	—	—	York 8 26	d			04 00	04 23	05 26			05 57						06 28					
—	—	—	—	—	**Doncaster 7**	d	23p22					05 40	05 57		06 00		06 25		06 25		06 40				
45¾	—	—	—	—	Conisbrough	d	23p29								06 07		06 32		06 32						
48	—	—	—	—	Mexborough	d	23p33								06 11		06 36		06 36						
49¼	—	—	—	—	Swinton (S.Yorks)	d	23p36	23p56							06 14	06 23	06 39		06 39						
53¾	—	—	—	—	Rotherham Central	d	23p45	00 03							06 22	06 31	06 46		06 46						
56½	—	—	—	—	**Meadowhall** 🚊	d	23p54	00 09				05 58			06 27	06 38	06 52		06 52		06 58				
60	—	—	—	—	**Sheffield 7** 🚊	a	00 04	00 23				06 08	06 18		06 38	06 47	07 05		07 05		07 06				
—	—	—	—	—		d						06 11									07 09				
96¾	—	—	—	—	Stockport 78	a						06 53									07 53				
102¾	—	—	—	—	**Manchester Piccadilly 10** 🚊	a			06 02	06 02	06 50	07 02		07 19						07 51	08 02		08 05		
112½	—	—	—	—	**Manchester Airport** 85 ✈	a			06 24	06 24	07 12	07 29		07 42						08 12	08 26				

A until 23 March
B From Leeds
C From Leeds to St Pancras International
D until 26 March and from 2 April
E from 27 March
F To Newark North Gate
G To Liverpool Lime Street

Table 29

Hull and Cleethorpes - Doncaster - Meadowhall, Sheffield, Manchester and Manchester Airport, Cleethorpes - Barton-on-Humber

Network Diagram - see first Page of Table 18

		NT	HT	TP	XC		NT	XC	NT	TP		EM	NT	NT	NT	XC	NT	GR	NT	NT	TP	XC		NT
			◇1	◇1	◇1			◇1		◇1						◇1		1			◇1	◇1		
					A		B	C	D			E				F		G	H	I		J		D
Hull	d	06 03	06 25	06 37													06 40	07 00	07 07		07 37			
Hessle	d	06 10															06 47							
Ferriby	d	06 15															06 52							
Brough	d	06 20	06 37	06 49													06 57	07 12	07 19		07 49			
Broomfleet	d																							
Gilberdyke	d	06 27															07 04		07 26					
Eastrington	d																		07 31					
Howden	d		06 49																07 35		08 01			
Wressle	d																		07 40					
Selby	a		06 59	07 08														07 33	07 48		08 10			
	d		07 00	07 08														07 34	07 48		08 11			
York 8 33	a																		08 21					
Saltmarshe	d	06 33															07 10							
Goole	d	06 38															07 15							
Thorne North	d	06 47															07 24							
Cleethorpes	d									06 18			07 00											
New Clee	d																							
Grimsby Docks	d												07 05											
Grimsby Town	a									06 25			07 08											
	d									06 26		07 03	07 08											
Great Coates	d												07 12											
Healing	d												07 15											
Stallingborough	d												07 18											
Habrough	d									06 36		07 13	07 24											
Ulceby	d												07 28											
Thornton Abbey	d												07 32											
Goxhill	d												07 35											
New Holland	d												07 40											
Barrow Haven	d												07 43											
Barton-on-Humber	a												07 48											
Barton-on-Humber	d														08 10									
Hull Paragon Interchange	a														08 37									
Barnetby	d									06 45		07a22												
Scunthorpe	a									07 00														
	d									07 00										07 22				
Althorpe	d																			07 27				
Crowle	d																			07 33				
Thorne South	d																			07 41				
Hatfield & Stainforth	d	06 53															07 30			07 47				
Kirk Sandall	d	06 57															07 34			07 51				
Adwick 31	d													07 29										
Bentley (S.Yorks) 31	d													07 33										
Doncaster 7 31	a	07 08	07 17							07 33				07 37			07 46	07 52		08 04				
London Kings Cross 15 ⊖26	a		09 18															09 56						
York 8 26	d							06 32								07 23						07 44		
Doncaster 7	d				06 45		07 02			07 35				07 39		07 55	07 48							
Conisbrough	d						07 09							07 46			07 55							
Mexborough	d						07 13							07 50			07 59							
Swinton (S.Yorks)	d						07 16		07 30					07 53			08 02							08 34
Rotherham Central	d						07 27		07 39					08 00			08 12							08 43
Meadowhall	d						07 33		07 45	07 53				08 06			08 23							08 51
Sheffield 7	a				07 11		07 40	07 50	07 56	08 00				08 18		08 18	08 33					08 51		08 59
	d									08 05														
Stockport 78	a									08 53														
Manchester Piccadilly 10	a			08 36						09 02											09 36			
Manchester Airport 85	a									09 33														

A From Leeds to Southampton Central
B To Worksop
C To Plymouth
D From Leeds
E To Newark North Gate
F From Newcastle to Reading
G **The Hull Executive**
H From Beverley to Hull
I To Adwick
J From Newcastle to Plymouth

Hull and Cleethorpes - Doncaster - Meadowhall, Sheffield, Manchester and Manchester Airport, Cleethorpes - Barton-on-Humber

Network Diagram - see first Page of Table 18

		NT	TP	XC	NT	NT	NT	NT	HT	XC	NT	NT	NT	TP	TP	TP	NT	NT	NT	NT	EM	XC	NT	XC
			◇1	◇1					◇1	◇1				◇1	◇1	◇1						◇1		◇1
				A		B	B	C		D	E		F		G				B		H	I	C	J
			🚲	🚲					⊠	🚲				🚲	🚲	🚲		🚌				🚲		🚲
Hull	d					07 40	08 03		08 25				08 28	08 40					08 56	09 02				
Hessle	d					07 47							08 35											
Ferriby	d					07 52							08 40											
Brough	d					07 57	08 15		08 37				08 45	08 52					09 08	09 14				
Broomfleet	d					08 02																		
Gilberdyke	d					08 07							08 52							09 21				
Eastrington	d																							
Howden	d								08 49											09 28				
Wressle	d																							
Selby	a								08 58					09 11						09 38				
	d								08 58					09 11						09 38				
York 8 33	a																			10 10				
Saltmarshe	d					08 12																		
Goole	d					08 17	08 29						09 01						09 23					
Thorne North	d					08 26							09 09											
Cleethorpes	d		07 26													08 26	08 55							
New Clee	d																08x58							
Grimsby Docks	d																09 00							
Grimsby Town	a		07 33													08 33	09 03							
	d		07 34													08 34	09 03				09 20			
Great Coates	d																09 07							
Healing	d																09 10							
Stallingborough	d																09 13							
Habrough	d		07 44													08 44	09 19				09 30			
Ulceby	d																09 23							
Thornton Abbey	d																09 27							
Goxhill	d																09 30							
New Holland	d																09 35							
Barrow Haven	d																09 38							
Barton-on-Humber	a																09 43							
Barton-on-Humber	d																	10 00						
Hull Paragon Interchange	a																	10 27						
Barnetby	d		07 53													08 53					09a39			
Scunthorpe	a		08 08													09 08								
	d		08 08					08 19								09 08							09 19	
Althorpe	d							08 24															09 24	
Crowle	d							08 30															09 30	
Thorne South	d							08 39															09 39	
Hatfield & Stainforth	d					08 33		08 45					09 16										09 44	
Kirk Sandall	d					08 36		08 50					09 20										09 49	
Adwick 31	d	08 15			08 33							09 15												
Bentley (S.Yorks) 31	d	08 18			08 37							09 19												
Doncaster 7 31	a	08 23	08 38		08 41	08 46	08 54	09 01	09 24			09 24	09 31			09 38			09 49				10 01	
London Kings Cross 15 ⊖26	a								11 09															
York 8 26	d			08 24						08 44					09 28							09 35		09 45
Doncaster 7	d	08 25	08 41	08 50			08 56	09 01				09 26				09 42			09 50			09 58	10 04	
Conisbrough	d	08 32						09 08				09 33											10 11	
Mexborough	d	08 36						09 12				09 35											10 15	
Swinton (S.Yorks)	d	08 42						09 16			09 35	09 42											10 18	
Rotherham Central	d	08 50						09 27			09 44	09 50											10 27	
Meadowhall 🚊	d	08 57	09 01				09 16	09 33			09 50	09 55				10 01			10 08				10 33	
Sheffield 7 🚊	a	09 05	09 08	09 17			09 26	09 41		09 51	10 00	10 05				10 08			10 19			10 20	10 41	10 51
	d		09 11													10 11								
Stockport 78	a		09 53													10 53								
Manchester Piccadilly 10 🚊	a		10 02											10 36	10 49	11 02								
Manchester Airport 85 ✈	a		10 26												11 12	11 26								

A From Newcastle to Southampton Central
B From Bridlington
C To Lincoln
D From Edinburgh to Plymouth
E From Leeds
F From Scarborough
G From Manchester Airport
H To Newark North Gate
I From Edinburgh to Reading
J From Glasgow Central to Plymouth

Hull and Cleethorpes - Doncaster - Meadowhall, Sheffield, Manchester and Manchester Airport, Cleethorpes - Barton-on-Humber

Network Diagram - see first Page of Table 18

		NT	NT	NT	TP	TP	NT	NT	XC	NT	XC	NT	NT	NT	HT	TP	TP	NT	NT	NT	EM	XC
					◇1	◇1			◇1		◇1				◇1	◇1	◇1					◇1
		A		B			C	D	E	F	G	A								C	H	I
					🛒	🛒			🛒		🛒				⊠	🛒	🛒		🚌			🛒
Hull	d			09 25	09 40		09 56	10 08						10 18	10 30	10 40				10 57		
Hessle	d			09 32										10 25								
Ferriby	d			09 37										10 30								
Brough	d			09 42	09 52		10 08	10 20						10 35	10 42	10 52				11 09		
Broomfleet	d																					
Gilberdyke	d			09 49				10 26						10 42								
Eastrington	d																					
Howden	d							10 34							10 54							
Wressle	d																					
Selby	a				10 11			10 47							11 03	11 11						
	d				10 11			10 47							11 03	11 11						
York 8 33	a							11 18														
Saltmarshe	d																					
Goole	d			10 01			10 22							11 01						11 23		
Thorne North	d			10 09										11 08								
Cleethorpes	d					09 26											10 26	10 55				
New Clee	d																	10x58				
Grimsby Docks	d																	11 00				
Grimsby Town	a					09 33											10 33	11 03				
	d					09 34											10 34	11 03			11 28	
Great Coates	d																	11 07				
Healing	d																	11 10				
Stallingborough	d																	11 13				
Habrough	d																10 44	11 19			11 38	
Ulceby	d																	11 23				
Thornton Abbey	d																	11 27				
Goxhill	d																	11 30				
New Holland	d																	11 35				
Barrow Haven	d																	11 38				
Barton-on-Humber	a																	11 43				
Barton-on-Humber	d																		12 00			
Hull Paragon Interchange	a																		12 27			
Barnetby	d					09 53											10 53				11a47	
Scunthorpe	a					10 08											11 08					
	d					10 08				10 19							11 08					
Althorpe	d									10 24												
Crowle	d									10 30												
Thorne South	d									10 39												
Hatfield & Stainforth	d			10 15						10 44				11 14								
Kirk Sandall	d			10 20						10 49				11 19								
Adwick 31	d		10 15										11 15									
Bentley (S.Yorks) 31	d		10 19										11 19									
Doncaster 7 31	a		10 24	10 30		10 38	10 47			11 00			11 24	11 29	11 24		11 38			11 48		
London Kings Cross 15 ⊖26	a														13 10							
York 8 26	d								10 34		10 44											11 34
Doncaster 7	d		10 26			10 42	10 49		10 58	11 04			11 26				11 42			11 48		11 58
Conisbrough	d		10 33							11 11			11 33									
Mexborough	d		10 37							11 15			11 37									
Swinton (S.Yorks)	d	10 35	10 43							11 18		11 35	11 43									
Rotherham Central	d	10 44	10 52							11 27		11 44	11 52									
Meadowhall 🚊	d	10 50	10 58			11 01	11 08			11 33		11 51	11 56				12 01			12 08		
Sheffield 7 🚊	a	11 01	11 05			11 08	11 20		11 20	11 41	11 51	12 01	12 05				12 08			12 19		12 20
	d					11 11											12 11					
Stockport 78	a					11 53											12 53					
Manchester Piccadilly 10 🚊	a				11 36	12 02										12 36	13 02					
Manchester Airport 85 ✈	a					12 26											13 26					

A From Leeds
B From Beverley
C From Bridlington
D To Hull
E From Newcastle to Southampton Central
F To Lincoln
G From Dundee to Plymouth
H To Newark North Gate
I From Newcastle to Reading

Table 29

Mondays to Fridays

Hull and Cleethorpes - Doncaster - Meadowhall, Sheffield, Manchester and Manchester Airport, Cleethorpes - Barton-on-Humber

Network Diagram - see first Page of Table 18

	NT	NT	XC	NT	NT	NT	TP	TP	NT	NT	XC	NT	NT	HT	TP	XC	NT	NT	TP	NT	NT	NT
			◇1				◇1	◇1			◇1			◇1	◇1	◇1			◇1			
		A	B	C					D	E	F	A				G	C					H
			🛒				🛒	🛒			🛒			⊠	🛒	🛒			🛒		🚌	
Hull d						11 23	11 40		11 55	12 03			12 18	12 30	12 40							12 57
Hessle d						11 30							12 25									
Ferriby d						11 35							12 30									
Brough d						11 40	11 52		12 07	12 15			12 35	12 42	12 52							13 09
Broomfleet d						11 45																
Gilberdyke d						11 50							12 43									
Eastrington d																						
Howden d										12 27				12 55								
Wressle d																						
Selby a							12 11			12 37				13 03	13 11							
d							12 11			12 38				13 03	13 11							
York 8 33 a										13 04												
Saltmarshe d													12 49									
Goole d						12 01			12 22				13 01									13 23
Thorne North d						12 09							13 09									
Cleethorpes d								11 26											12 26	12 55		
New Clee d																				12x58		
Grimsby Docks d																				13 00		
Grimsby Town a								11 33											12 33	13 03		
d								11 34											12 34	13 03		
Great Coates d																				13 07		
Healing d																				13 10		
Stallingborough d																				13 13		
Habrough d																				13 19		
Ulceby d																				13 23		
Thornton Abbey d																				13 27		
Goxhill d																				13 30		
New Holland d																				13 35		
Barrow Haven d																				13 38		
Barton-on-Humber a																				13 43		
Barton-on-Humber d																					14 00	
Hull Paragon Interchange a																					14 27	
Barnetby d								11 53											12 53			
Scunthorpe a								12 08											13 08			
d		11 19						12 08				12 19							13 08			
Althorpe d		11 24										12 24										
Crowle d		11 30										12 30										
Thorne South d		11 39										12 39										
Hatfield & Stainforth d		11 44				12 15						12 44	13 13									
Kirk Sandall d		11 49				12 20						12 49	13 18									
Adwick 31 d					12 15													13 14				
Bentley (S.Yorks) 31 d					12 19													13 18				
Doncaster 7 31 a		12 00			12 25	12 30		12 38	12 47			13 01	13 30	13 24				13 26	13 38			13 47
London Kings Cross 15 ⊖26 a														15 10								
York 8 26 d	11 05		11 45								12 34					12 44						
Doncaster 7 d		12 03			12 26			12 42	12 48		12 59	13 02						13 26	13 42			13 48
Conisbrough d		12 11			12 33							13 11						13 33				
Mexborough d		12 15			12 37							13 15						13 37				
Swinton (S.Yorks) d	12 10	12 18		12 35	12 43							13 18					13 35	13 42				
Rotherham Central d	12 19	12 27		12 44	12 52							13 27					13 44	13 52				
Meadowhall 🚊 d	12 24	12 33		12 51	12 56			13 01	13 07			13 33					13 51	13 56	14 01			14 05
Sheffield 7 🚊 a	12 36	12 41	12 51	13 01	13 05			13 08	13 20		13 20	13 41				13 51	14 01	14 05	14 08			14 20
d								13 11											14 11			
Stockport 78 a								13 53											14 53			
Manchester Piccadilly 10 🚊 a							13 36	14 02							14 36				15 02			
Manchester Airport 85 ✈ a								14 26											15 26			

A To Lincoln
B From Glasgow Central to Plymouth
C From Leeds
D From Bridlington
E To Hull
F From Newcastle to Southampton Central
G From Glasgow Central to Penzance
H From Scarborough

Hull and Cleethorpes - Doncaster - Meadowhall, Sheffield, Manchester and Manchester Airport, Cleethorpes - Barton-on-Humber

Network Diagram - see first Page of Table 18

			NT	XC	NT	XC	NT	NT	NT	TP	TP	EM	NT	NT	XC	NT	XC	NT	NT	NT	TP	TP	NT
				◇1		◇1				◇1	◇1				◇1		◇1				◇1	◇1	
			A	B	C	D	E					F	G	A	H	C	I	E					
				🍴		🍴				🍴	🍴				🍴		🍴				🍴	🍴	
Hull		d	13 12						13 25	13 40			13 57	14 18						14 25	14 40		
Hessle		d							13 32											14 32			
Ferriby		d							13 37											14 37			
Brough		d	13 24						13 42	13 52			14 09	14 30						14 42	14 52		
Broomfleet		d																					
Gilberdyke		d	13 32						13 49											14 49			
Eastrington		d	13 36																				
Howden		d	13 41											14 42									
Wressle		d	13 47																				
Selby		a	13 54							14 11				14 53							15 11		
		d	13 55							14 11				14 53							15 11		
York [8]	33	a	14 27											15 25									
Saltmarshe		d																					
Goole		d							14 01				14 23							15 01			
Thorne North		d							14 09											15 09			
Cleethorpes		d									13 26											14 26	14 55
New Clee		d																					14x58
Grimsby Docks		d																					15 00
Grimsby Town		a									13 33											14 33	15 03
		d									13 34	13 49										14 34	15 03
Great Coates		d																					15 07
Healing		d																					15 10
Stallingborough		d																					15 13
Habrough		d										13 59										14 44	15 19
Ulceby		d																					15 23
Thornton Abbey		d																					15 27
Goxhill		d																					15 30
New Holland		d																					15 35
Barrow Haven		d																					15 38
Barton-on-Humber		a																					15 43
Barton-on-Humber		d																					
Hull Paragon Interchange		a																					
Barnetby		d									13 53	14a08										14 53	
Scunthorpe		a									14 08											15 08	
		d			13 19						14 08					14 19						15 08	
Althorpe		d			13 24											14 24							
Crowle		d			13 30											14 30							
Thorne South		d			13 39											14 39							
Hatfield & Stainforth		d			13 44				14 15							14 44				15 15			
Kirk Sandall		d			13 49				14 20							14 49				15 20			
Adwick	31	d						14 15											15 15				
Bentley (S.Yorks)	31	d						14 19											15 19				
Doncaster [7]	31	a			13 59			14 24	14 31		14 38		14 46			14 59			15 24	15 30		15 38	
London Kings Cross [15]	⊖26	a																					
York [8]	26	d		13 34		13 44									14 34		14 44						
Doncaster [7]		d		13 58	14 03			14 26			14 42		14 48		14 58	15 04			15 25			15 42	
Conisbrough		d			14 12			14 31								15 11			15 32				
Mexborough		d			14 16			14 35								15 15			15 37				
Swinton (S.Yorks)		d			14 18		14 35	14 42								15 18		15 35	15 42				
Rotherham Central		d			14 29		14 44	14 52								15 27		15 44	15 50				
Meadowhall 🚊		d			14 34		14 50	14 56			15 01		15 07			15 33		15 50	15 57			16 01	
Sheffield [7] 🚊		a		14 20	14 42	14 51	15 01	15 05			15 08		15 19		15 20	15 41	15 51	16 01	16 05			16 08	
		d									15 11											16 11	
Stockport	78	a									15 53											16 53	
Manchester Piccadilly [10] 🚊		a								15 36	16 02										16 36	17 02	
Manchester Airport	85 ✈	a									16 26											17 32	

A To Hull
B From Newcastle to Reading
C To Lincoln
D From Aberdeen to Penzance
E From Leeds
F To Newark North Gate
G From Bridlington
H From Newcastle to Eastleigh
I From Glasgow Central to Penzance

Table 29

Mondays to Fridays

Hull and Cleethorpes - Doncaster - Meadowhall, Sheffield, Manchester and Manchester Airport, Cleethorpes - Barton-on-Humber

Network Diagram - see first Page of Table 18

		NT	NT	NT	XC	NT	NT	HT	XC	TP			NT	NT	NT	TP	TP	EM	NT	XC	NT		NT	NT	TP
										FO															
					◇1			◇1	◇1	◇1						◇1	◇1			◇1					◇1
			A		B	C	D		E				F	G				H	I	B	J		D	A	
		🚌																							
					⊼			⊠	⊼	⊼						⊼	⊼			⊼					⊼
Hull	d		14 57	15 02				15 10							15 24	15 40			15 57		16 10			16 26	16 40
Hessle	d														15 31									16 33	
Ferriby	d														15 36									16 38	
Brough	d		15 09	15 14				15 22							15 41	15 52			16 09		16 22			16 43	16 52
Broomfleet	d																							16 49	
Gilberdyke	d														15 49						16 29			16 53	
Eastrington	d																								
Howden	d			15 26				15 36													16 36				
Wressle	d																								
Selby	a			15 36				15 45								16 11					16 46				17 11
	d			15 38				15 45								16 11					16 47				17 11
York 8 33	a			16 06																	17 13				
Saltmarshe	d																							16 59	
Goole	d		15 23												16 00				16 23					17 04	
Thorne North	d														16 09									17 12	
Cleethorpes	d																15 26								
New Clee	d																								
Grimsby Docks	d																								
Grimsby Town	a																15 33								
	d																15 34	15 45							
Great Coates	d																								
Healing	d																								
Stallingborough	d																								
Habrough	d																	15 55							
Ulceby	d																								
Thornton Abbey	d																								
Goxhill	d																								
New Holland	d																								
Barrow Haven	d																								
Barton-on-Humber	a																								
Barton-on-Humber	d	16 00																							
Hull Paragon Interchange	a	16 27																							
Barnetby	d																15 53	16a03							
Scunthorpe	a																16 08								
	d						15 19										16 08						16 19		
Althorpe	d						15 24																16 24		
Crowle	d						15 30																16 30		
Thorne South	d						15 39																16 39		
Hatfield & Stainforth	d						15 44								16 14								16 44	17 18	
Kirk Sandall	d						15 49								16 19								16 49	17 22	
Adwick 31	d													16 15											
Bentley (S.Yorks) 31	d													16 19											
Doncaster 7 31	a		15 47				15 59	16 03						16 24	16 30		16 38		16 47				16 59	17 34	
London Kings Cross 15 ⊖26	a							17 46																	
York 8 26	d				15 34	15 01			15 44	15 57										16 04					
Doncaster 7	d		15 48		15 58		16 03							16 26			16 42		16 48				17 01		
Conisbrough	d						16 11							16 33									17 08		
Mexborough	d						16 15							16 37									17 12		
Swinton (S.Yorks)	d					16 01	16 16						16 35	16 42									17 16		
Rotherham Central	d					16 09	16 27						16 44	16 50									17 27		
Meadowhall 🚊	d		16 07			16 18	16 33						16 50	16 55			17 01		17 09				17 33		
Sheffield 7 🚊	a		16 20		16 20	16 27	16 41		16 51				17 00	17 05			17 08		17 20	17 20			17 41		
	d																17 11								
Stockport 78	a																17 53								
Manchester Piccadilly 10 🚊	a									17 21						17 36	18 02								18 37
Manchester Airport 85 ✈	a																18 26								

A From Scarborough
B From Newcastle to Reading
C From Sheffield
D To Lincoln
E From Edinburgh to Plymouth
F From Leeds
G To Retford
H To Newark North Gate
I From Bridlington
J To Hull

Hull and Cleethorpes - Doncaster - Meadowhall, Sheffield, Manchester and Manchester Airport, Cleethorpes - Barton-on-Humber

Network Diagram - see first Page of Table 18

		XC	NT	NT	TP	NT	NT	NT	TP	XC	NT	HT	NT	XC		NT	NT		NT	TP	EM			NT	NT
		◇1 A	B		◇1	C			◇1 D	◇1 E		◇1	F	◇1 G		H	B			◇1	I			J	K
Hull	d					16 54			17 01			17 10	17 18											17 42	17 52
Hessle	d												17 25											17 49	
Ferriby	d												17 30											17 54	
Brough	d					17 06			17 13			17 22	17 35											17 59	18 04
Broomfleet	d												17 40												
Gilberdyke	d					17 13							17 45											18 06	
Eastrington	d												17 49												
Howden	d											17 34	17 54												
Wressle	d												17 59												
Selby	a								17 31			17 42	18 06												18 25
	d											17 43	18 07												18 26
York 8 33	a												18 33												
Saltmarshe	d																							18 12	
Goole	d					17 22																		18 19	
Thorne North	d																							18 28	
Cleethorpes	d				16 26		16 55													17 26					
New Clee	d																								
Grimsby Docks	d						17 00																		
Grimsby Town	a				16 33		17 03													17 33					
	d				16 34		17 04													17 34	18 29				
Great Coates	d						17 08																		
Healing	d						17 11																		
Stallingborough	d						17 14																		
Habrough	d				16 44		17 20													17 44	18 39				
Ulceby	d						17 23																		
Thornton Abbey	d						17 28																		
Goxhill	d						17 31																		
New Holland	d						17 35																		
Barrow Haven	d						17 38																		
Barton-on-Humber	a						17 44																		
Barton-on-Humber	d							18 00																	
Hull Paragon Interchange	a							18 27																	
Barnetby	d				16 53															17 53	18a47				
Scunthorpe	a				17 08															18 08					
	d				17 08						17 19									18 08					
Althorpe	d										17 24														
Crowle	d										17 30														
Thorne South	d										17 39														
Hatfield & Stainforth	d										17 44													18 34	
Kirk Sandall	d										17 49													18 39	
Adwick 31	d															18 14									
Bentley (S.Yorks) 31	d															18 18									
Doncaster 7 31	a				17 38	17 46					17 58	18 02				18 25				18 38				18 51	18 47
London Kings Cross 15 ⊖26	a											19 47												→	
York 8 26	d	16 44								17 34				17 44											
Doncaster 7	d			17 24	17 42	17 47				17 59	18 02								18 26	18 42					18 49
Conisbrough	d			17 31							18 09								18 33						
Mexborough	d			17 35							18 13								18 37						
Swinton (S.Yorks)	d		17 35	17 42							18 16						18 35		18 42						
Rotherham Central	d		17 44	17 50							18 27						18 45		18 49						
Meadowhall	d		17 50	17 57	18 01	18 07					18 32						18 50		18 57	19 01					19 06
Sheffield 7	a	17 51	18 01	18 04	18 08	18 19				18 20	18 42			18 51			19 00		19 06	19 08					19 17
	d				18 11															19 11					
Stockport 78	a				18 53															19 53					
Manchester Piccadilly 10	a				19 02															20 02					
Manchester Airport 85	a				19 28															20 39					

A From Glasgow Central to Plymouth
B From Leeds
C From Bridlington
D To Huddersfield
E From Newcastle to Reading
F To Leeds
G From Edinburgh to Plymouth
H To Scunthorpe
I To Newark North Gate
J To Sheffield
K From Scarborough

Table 29

Mondays to Fridays

Hull and Cleethorpes - Doncaster - Meadowhall, Sheffield, Manchester and Manchester Airport, Cleethorpes - Barton-on-Humber

Network Diagram - see first Page of Table 18

		TP	XC		NT	NT	NT	XC	TP	NT	NT	TP	TP		NT	TP	NT	NT	NT	HT	NT	NT	XC	NT	XC
									FO			ThFO	MT WO												
		◇1	◇1					◇1	◇1			◇1	◇1			◇1				◇1			◇1		◇1
			A		B		C	D		E		F	G			H							I	J	K
		⚲	⚲					⚲										🚌		⊠			⚲		
Hull	d	17 58					18 23								18 53	18 59				19 10	19 15	19 25			
Hessle	d						18 30															19 32			
Ferriby	d						18 35															19 37			
Brough	d	18 10					18 40								19 05	19 11				19 22	19 28	19 42			
Broomfleet	d																								
Gilberdyke	d						18 47														19 36	19 49			
Eastrington	d																								
Howden	d																			19 34	19 43				
Wressle	d																								
Selby	a	18 29														19 29				19 42	19 53				
	d	18 29																		19 43	19 53				
York 8 33	a																				20 21				
Saltmarshe	d																								
Goole	d						18 59								19 19							20 01			
Thorne North	d						19 08															20 09			
Cleethorpes	d											18 26	18 26				19 00								
New Clee	d																								
Grimsby Docks	d																19 05								
Grimsby Town	a											18 33	18 33				19 08								
	d											18 34	18 34				19 09								
Great Coates	d																19 13								
Healing	d																19 16								
Stallingborough	d																19 19								
Habrough	d																19 25								
Ulceby	d																19 28								
Thornton Abbey	d																19 33								
Goxhill	d																19 36								
New Holland	d																19 40								
Barrow Haven	d																19 43								
Barton-on-Humber	a																19 49								
Barton-on-Humber	d																	19 53							
Hull Paragon Interchange	a																	20 20							
Barnetby	d											18 53	18 53												
Scunthorpe	a											19 08	19 08												
	d					18 19						19 08	19 08						19 15						
Althorpe	d					18 24													19 20						
Crowle	d					18 30													19 26						
Thorne South	d					18 39													19 35						
Hatfield & Stainforth	d					18 46	19 15												19 40			20 15			
Kirk Sandall	d					18 50	19 19												19 45			20 20			
Adwick 31	d																								
Bentley (S.Yorks) 31	d				←																				
Doncaster 7 31	a				18 51	19 01	19 31					19 38	19 38		19 48				19 57	20 01		20 33			
London Kings Cross 15 ⊖26	a																			21 46					
York 8 26	d		18 34					18 45	19 08														19 34		19 44
Doncaster 7	d		18 58		19 01						19 28	19 42	19 42		19 49								19 58	20 03	
Conisbrough	d				19 08						19 35													20 10	
Mexborough	d				19 12						19 39													20 14	
Swinton (S.Yorks)	d				19 15					19 35	19 43													20 17	
Rotherham Central	d				19 23					19 45	19 50													20 28	
Meadowhall 🚊	d				19 28					19 51	19 57	20 01	20 01		20 08									20 33	
Sheffield 7 🚊	a		19 20		19 37			19 51		19 59	20 05	20 08	20 08		20 18								20 20	20 41	20 51
	d											20 11	20 11												
Stockport 78	a											20 53	20 56												
Manchester Piccadilly 10 🚊	a	19 57							20 33			21 02	21 05												
Manchester Airport 85 ✈	a								20 57			21 36	21 38												

A From Newcastle to Guildford
B From Hull
C From Bridlington
D From Glasgow Central to Bristol Temple Meads
E From Leeds
H To Leeds
I From Newcastle to BirminghamNew Street
J To Worksop
K From Edinburgh to Bristol Temple Meads

Hull and Cleethorpes - Doncaster - Meadowhall, Sheffield, Manchester and Manchester Airport, Cleethorpes - Barton-on-Humber

Network Diagram - see first Page of Table 18

		NT	TP	NT	XC	NT	TP	XC	TP	TP	NT	NT	TP	NT	NT	NT	EM	TP	NT	NT	NT	NT	NT	NT	NT
							FO		FX	FX															
			◇1		◇1		◇1	◇1	◇1	◇1			◇1			🚌		◇1						🚌	
		A			B	C		D	E		A						F					A	G	H	A
Hull	d					20 03	20 35		20 45					20 56				21 33					22 20	22 20	
Hessle	d					20 10																	22 27	22 35	
Ferriby	d					20 15																	22 32	22 45	
Brough	d					20 20	20 47		20 57					21 08				21 45					22 37	22 54	
Broomfleet	d																								
Gilberdyke	d					20 27												21 52						23 19	
Eastrington	d																								
Howden	d																								
Wressle	d																								
Selby	a						21 06		21 16									22 07							
	d						21 06											22 07							
York 8 33	a																								
Saltmarshe	d																								
Goole	d					20 36								21 22					21 35				22 51	23 49	
Thorne North	d					20 44													21 44				23 00	00 04	
Cleethorpes	d		19 26										20 26		21 03		21 15								
New Clee	d																								
Grimsby Docks	d														21 08										
Grimsby Town	a		19 33										20 33		21 11		21 21								
	d		19 34										20 34		21 11		21 22								
Great Coates	d														21 15										
Healing	d														21 18										
Stallingborough	d														21 21										
Habrough	d		19 44												21 27		21 33								
Ulceby	d														21 31										
Thornton Abbey	d														21 35										
Goxhill	d														21 38										
New Holland	d														21 43										
Barrow Haven	d														21 46										
Barton-on-Humber	a														21 51										
Barton-on-Humber	d															21 56									
Hull Paragon Interchange	a															22 23									
Barnetby	d		19 53										20 53				21a42								
Scunthorpe	a		20 08										21 08												
	d		20 08	20 21									21 08							21 31	22 21				
Althorpe	d			20 26																21 36	22 26				
Crowle	d			20 32																21 42	22 32				
Thorne South	d			20 41																21 51	22 41				
Hatfield & Stainforth	d			20 46		20 51													21 50	21 56	22 46		23 06	00 14	
Kirk Sandall	d			20 51		20 56													21 54	22 01	22 51		23 10	00 24	
Adwick 31	d																								
Bentley (S.Yorks) 31	d																								
Doncaster 7 31	a		20 40	21 01		21 05							21 40	21 47					22 08	22 11	23 03		23 21	00 38	
London Kings Cross 15 ⊖26	a																								
York 8 26	d				20 34			20 44		21 14															
Doncaster 7	d		20 42		21 02	21 07						21 30	21 42	21 48						22 13			23 22	00 38	
Conisbrough	d		20 50			21 14						21 37								22 20			23 29	00 58	
Mexborough	d		20 54			21 17						21 41								22 24			23 33	01 13	
Swinton (S.Yorks)	d	20 35	20 57			21 20					21 35	21 44								22 29		22 35	23 36	01 18	23 56
Rotherham Central	d	20 45	21 03			21 28					21 44	21 55								22 38		22 46	23 45	01 38	00 03
Meadowhall 🚊	d	20 51	21 09			21 34					21 52	22 03	21 59	22 07						22 44		22 53	23 54	01 48	00 09
Sheffield 7 🚊	a	21 02	21 19		21 26	21 46		21 51			22 04	22 11	22 08	22 21						22 54		23 02	00 04	02 08	00 23
	d												22 11												
Stockport 78	a												22 53												
Manchester Piccadilly 10 🚊	a						22 33			22 33			23 02					23 37							
Manchester Airport 85 ✈	a						22 57			22 57			23 26												

A From Leeds
B From Newcastle to Birmingham New Street
C From Bridlington
D From Glasgow Central to Birmingham New Street
E To Leeds
F To Lincoln
G until 23 March
H from 26 March

Table 29

Saturdays

Hull and Cleethorpes - Doncaster - Meadowhall, Sheffield, Manchester and Manchester Airport, Cleethorpes - Barton-on-Humber

Network Diagram - see first Page of Table 18

		NT	NT	TP	TP	TP	TP	NT	NT	NT		TP	NT	NT	NT	XC	NT	XC	TP	TP	NT	TP	NT
				◇1	◇1	◇1	◇1					◇1				◇1		◇1	◇1	◇1		◇1	
		A	B						A	C						D		E		F			B
														bus									
												trolley				trolley		trolley		trolley			
Hull	d	22p20							05 20											06 00	06 06	06 37	
Hessle	d	22p27																			06 13		
Ferriby	d	22p32																			06 18		
Brough	d	22p37							05 32											06 12	06 23	06 49	
Broomfleet	d																						
Gilberdyke	d																			06 19	06 31		
Eastrington	d																						
Howden	d																			06 26			
Wressle	d																						
Selby	a																			06 36		07 08	
	d														06 18					06 36		07 08	
York 8	33 a																						
Saltmarshe	d																				06 37		
Goole	d	22p51							05 46												06 42		
Thorne North	d	23p00							05 55												06 50		
Cleethorpes	d											05 18	06 00										
New Clee	d																						
Grimsby Docks	d																						
Grimsby Town	a											05 25	06 08										
	d											05 26	06 08										
Great Coates	d																						
Healing	d												06 15										
Stallingborough	d												06 18										
Habrough	d											05 36	06 24										
Ulceby	d												06 28										
Thornton Abbey	d																						
Goxhill	d												06 35										
New Holland	d												06 40										
Barrow Haven	d												06 43										
Barton-on-Humber	a												06 48										
Barton-on-Humber	d													06 53									
Hull Paragon Interchange	a													07 20									
Barnetby	d											05 45											
Scunthorpe	a											06 00											
	d											06 00											
Althorpe	d											06 05											
Crowle	d											06 11											
Thorne South	d											06 20											
Hatfield & Stainforth	d	23p06							06 01			06 25									06 56		
Kirk Sandall	d	23p10							06 06												07 01		
Adwick	31 d																						
Bentley (S.Yorks)	31 d																						
Doncaster 7	31 a	23p21							06 15			06 38			06 39						07 11		
London Kings Cross 15 ⊖	26 a																						
York 8	26 d			03 52	05 26		05 57											06 17	06 28				
Doncaster 7	d	23p22				05 40		06 00	06 23	06 23		06 40				06 47	07 02						
Conisbrough	d	23p29						06 07	06 30	06 30							07 09						
Mexborough	d	23p33						06 11	06 34	06 34							07 13						
Swinton (S.Yorks)	d	23p36	23p56					06 14	06 37	06 37							07 16						07 30
Rotherham Central	d	23p45	00 03					06 25	06 49	06 49							07 26						07 38
Meadowhall	d	23p54	00 09			05 58		06 30	06 52	06 52		06 58					07 32						07 47
Sheffield 7	a	00 04	00 23			06 08		06 38	07 05	07 05		07 06				07 15	07 40	07 51					07 54
	d					06 11						07 09											
Stockport	78 a					06 53						07 53											
Manchester Piccadilly 10	a			06 02	06 50	07 02	07 19					08 02							07 51	08 05		08 36	
Manchester Airport	85 ✈ a			06 24	07 12	07 29	07 42					08 26							08 12				

A until 24 March
B From Leeds
C from 31 March
D From Leeds to Southampton Central
E To Plymouth
F To Liverpool Lime Street

Hull and Cleethorpes - Doncaster - Meadowhall, Sheffield, Manchester and Manchester Airport, Cleethorpes - Barton-on-Humber

Network Diagram - see first Page of Table 18

		NT	NT	TP			NT	EM	GR	NT			NT	NT	NT	XC				NT	TP	XC	NT	NT	TP
				◇1					R 1							◇1					◇1	◇1			◇1
		A	A				B	C		D					E	F				G		H	I		
				⊼					⊼					bus		⊼					⊼	⊼			⊼
Hull	d	06 40							06 50						07 07						07 37				
Hessle	d	06 47																							
Ferriby	d	06 52																							
Brough	d	06 57							07 02						07 19						07 49				
Broomfleet	d																								
Gilberdyke	d	07 04													07 26										
Eastrington	d														07 31										
Howden	d														07 35						08 01				
Wressle	d														07 40										
Selby	a								07 23						07 48						08 10				
	d								07 24						07 48						08 11				
York 8 33	a														08 21										
Saltmarshe	d	07 10																							
Goole	d	07 15																							
Thorne North	d	07 24																							
Cleethorpes	d			06 18									07 00												07 26
New Clee	d																								
Grimsby Docks	d												07 05												
Grimsby Town	a			06 25									07 08												07 33
	d			06 26				06 50					07 08												07 34
Great Coates	d												07 12												
Healing	d												07 15												
Stallingborough	d												07 18												
Habrough	d			06 36				07 00					07 24												07 44
Ulceby	d												07 28												
Thornton Abbey	d												07 32												
Goxhill	d												07 35												
New Holland	d												07 40												
Barrow Haven	d												07 43												
Barton-on-Humber	a												07 48												
Barton-on-Humber	d													08 20											
Hull Paragon Interchange	a													08 52											
Barnetby	d			06 45				07a09																	07 53
Scunthorpe	a			07 00																					08 08
	d			07 00																07 30					08 08
Althorpe	d																			07 35					
Crowle	d																			07 42					
Thorne South	d																			07 51					
Hatfield & Stainforth	d	07 30																		07 56					
Kirk Sandall	d	07 34																		08 01					
Adwick 31	d		07 23																					08 15	
Bentley (S.Yorks) 31	d		07 27																					08 19	
Doncaster 7 31	a	07 46	07 31	07 33					07 43	← 07 46										08 12				08 23	08 38
London Kings Cross 15 ⊖26	a	↪							09 36																
York 8 26	d						←									07 24						07 44			
Doncaster 7	d		07 39	07 35			07 39			07 48						07 52								08 26	08 41
Conisbrough	d		↪				07 46			07 55														08 33	
Mexborough	d						07 50			07 59														08 37	
Swinton (S.Yorks)	d						07 53			08 02													08 35	08 43	
Rotherham Central	d						08 01			08 14													08 44	08 50	
Meadowhall	d			07 53			08 07			08 25													08 51	08 56	09 01
Sheffield 7	a			08 00			08 18			08 32						08 18						08 51	08 59	09 05	09 08
	d			08 05																					09 11
Stockport 78	a			08 53																					09 53
Manchester Piccadilly 10	a			09 02																	09 36				10 02
Manchester Airport 85	a			09 26																					10 26

A To Sheffield
B From Adwick
C To Newark North Gate
D From Hull
E From Beverley to Hull
F From Newcastle to Reading
G To Adwick
H From Newcastle to Plymouth
I From Leeds

Hull and Cleethorpes - Doncaster - Meadowhall, Sheffield, Manchester and Manchester Airport, Cleethorpes - Barton-on-Humber

Network Diagram - see first Page of Table 18

		NT		NT	XC	NT	NT	HT	XC	NT	NT	NT		TP	TP	TP	NT	NT	NT	NT	EM	XC	NT	XC	NT
					◇1			◇1	◇1					◇1	◇1	◇1						◇1		◇1	
					A	B	C		D	E		F			E		B				G	H	C	I	E
					🛒			⊠	🛒					🛒	🛒	🛒			🚌			🛒		🛒	
Hull	d			07 40		08 03		08 25				08 29		08 40			08 56			09 02					
Hessle	d			07 47								08 36													
Ferriby	d			07 52								08 41													
Brough	d			07 57		08 15		08 37				08 46		08 52			09 08			09 14					
Broomfleet	d			08 02																					
Gilberdyke	d			08 07								08 53								09 21					
Eastrington	d																								
Howden	d							08 49												09 28					
Wressle	d																								
Selby	a							08 59						09 11						09 38					
	d							09 00						09 11						09 38					
York 8 33	a																			10 14					
Saltmarshe	d			08 12																					
Goole	d			08 17		08 29						09 02					09 23								
Thorne North	d			08 26								09 10													
Cleethorpes	d															08 26		09 00							
New Clee	d																	09x03							
Grimsby Docks	d																	09 05							
Grimsby Town	a															08 33		09 08							
	d															08 34		09 08			09 20				
Great Coates	d																	09 12							
Healing	d																	09 15							
Stallingborough	d																	09 18							
Habrough	d															08 44		09 24			09 30				
Ulceby	d																	09 28							
Thornton Abbey	d																	09 32							
Goxhill	d																	09 35							
New Holland	d																	09 40							
Barrow Haven	d																	09 43							
Barton-on-Humber	a																	09 48							
Barton-on-Humber	d																		10 00						
Hull Paragon Interchange	a																		10 27						
Barnetby	d															08 53					09a39				
Scunthorpe	a															09 08									
	d						08 19									09 08							09 19		
Althorpe	d						08 24																09 24		
Crowle	d						08 30																09 30		
Thorne South	d						08 39																09 39		
Hatfield & Stainforth	d			08 33			08 46					09 17											09 44		
Kirk Sandall	d			08 37			08 50					09 21											09 49		
Adwick 31	d	08 33									09 15														
Bentley (S.Yorks) 31	d	08 37									09 19														
Doncaster 7 31	a	08 42		08 50		08 58	09 02	09 23			09 24	09 32				09 38	09 48						10 01		
London Kings Cross 15 ⊖26	a							11 08																	
York 8 26	d				08 34				08 44						09 25							09 35		09 46	
Doncaster 7	d				08 58	09 01	09 03				09 26					09 42	09 49					09 58	10 04		
Conisbrough	d						09 11				09 33												10 11		
Mexborough	d						09 15				09 37												10 15		
Swinton (S.Yorks)	d						09 18			09 35	09 42												10 18		10 35
Rotherham Central	d						09 27			09 46	09 51												10 27		10 44
Meadowhall 🚊	d					09 24	09 33			09 50	09 55					10 01	10 08						10 33		10 50
Sheffield 7 🚊	a				09 20	09 33	09 41		09 52	10 00	10 05					10 08	10 19					10 20	10 41	10 51	11 00
	d															10 11									
Stockport 78	a															10 53									
Manchester Piccadilly 10 🚊	a													10 36	10 49	11 02									
Manchester Airport 85 ✈	a														11 12	11 26									

- **A** From Newcastle to Southampton Central
- **B** From Bridlington
- **C** To Lincoln
- **D** From Edinburgh to Plymouth
- **E** From Leeds
- **F** From Scarborough
- **G** To Newark North Gate
- **H** From Edinburgh to Reading
- **I** From Glasgow Central to Plymouth

Table 29

Saturdays

Hull and Cleethorpes - Doncaster - Meadowhall, Sheffield, Manchester and Manchester Airport, Cleethorpes - Barton-on-Humber

Network Diagram - see first Page of Table 18

Station		NT	NT	TP	TP	NT	NT	XC		NT	XC	NT	NT	NT	HT	TP	TP	NT	NT	NT	NT	XC	NT	NT	XC
				◇1	◇1			◇1			◇1				◇1	◇1	◇1					◇1			◇1
			A			B	C	D		E	F	G								B	C	H		E	I
					🛒			🛒			🛒				⊠		🛒					🛒			🛒
																			🚌						
Hull	d		09 25	09 40		09 56	10 08							10 18	10 30	10 40				10 57	11 05				
Hessle	d		09 32											10 25											
Ferriby	d		09 37											10 30											
Brough	d		09 42	09 52		10 08	10 20							10 35	10 42	10 52				11 09	11 17				
Broomfleet	d																								
Gilberdyke	d		09 49				10 27							10 43											
Eastrington	d																								
Howden	d						10 34								10 54						11 29				
Wressle	d																								
Selby	a			10 11			10 47								11 04	11 11					11 39				
	d			10 11			10 47								11 05	11 11					11 41				
York 8 33	a						11 18														12 08				
Saltmarshe	d																								
Goole	d		09 58			10 22								10 58						11 23					
Thorne North	d		10 06											11 06											
Cleethorpes	d				09 26												10 26	10 55							
New Clee	d																	10x58							
Grimsby Docks	d																	11 00							
Grimsby Town	a				09 33												10 33	11 03							
	d				09 34												10 34	11 03							
Great Coates	d																	11 07							
Healing	d																	11 10							
Stallingborough	d																	11 13							
Habrough	d																10 44	11 19							
Ulceby	d																	11 23							
Thornton Abbey	d																	11 27							
Goxhill	d																	11 30							
New Holland	d																	11 35							
Barrow Haven	d																	11 38							
Barton-on-Humber	a																	11 43							
Barton-on-Humber	d																		12 00						
Hull Paragon Interchange	a																		12 27						
Barnetby	d				09 53												10 53								
Scunthorpe	a				10 08												11 08								
	d				10 08					10 19							11 08							11 18	
Althorpe	d									10 24														11 23	
Crowle	d									10 30														11 29	
Thorne South	d									10 39														11 38	
Hatfield & Stainforth	d		10 12							10 44				11 11										11 43	
Kirk Sandall	d		10 17							10 49				11 17										11 48	
Adwick 31	d	10 15											11 15												
Bentley (S.Yorks) 31	d	10 19											11 19												
Doncaster 7 31	a	10 24	10 27		10 38	10 47				11 01			11 24	11 27	11 24		11 38			11 47				11 58	
London Kings Cross 15 ⊖26	a														13 08										
York 8 26	d							10 34			10 45											11 34	11 05		11 45
Doncaster 7	d	10 26			10 42	10 49		10 58		11 04			11 26				11 42			11 49		11 58		12 03	
Conisbrough	d	10 33								11 11			11 33											12 11	
Mexborough	d	10 37								11 15			11 37											12 15	
Swinton (S.Yorks)	d	10 43								11 18		11 35	11 43										12 10	12 18	
Rotherham Central	d	10 52								11 27		11 44	11 52										12 19	12 27	
Meadowhall 🚊	d	10 58			11 01	11 08				11 33		11 50	11 58				12 01			12 08			12 24	12 33	
Sheffield 7 🚊	a	11 06			11 08	11 20		11 20		11 41	11 51	12 00	12 05				12 08			12 20		12 20	12 36	12 41	12 51
	d				11 11												12 11								
Stockport 78	a				11 53												12 53								
Manchester Piccadilly 10 🚊	a			11 36	12 02											12 36	13 02								
Manchester Airport 85 ✈	a				12 26												13 26								

A From Beverley
B From Bridlington
C To Hull
D From Newcastle to Southampton Central
E To Lincoln
F From Dundee to Plymouth
G From Leeds
H From Newcastle to Reading
I From Glasgow Central to Plymouth

Table 29

Saturdays

Hull and Cleethorpes - Doncaster - Meadowhall, Sheffield, Manchester and Manchester Airport, Cleethorpes - Barton-on-Humber

Network Diagram - see first Page of Table 18

		NT	NT	NT		NT	EM	TP	TP	NT	NT	XC	NT	XC		NT	NT	NT	TP	TP	NT	NT	NT	NT	XC
								◇1	◇1			◇1		◇1					◇1	◇1					◇1
		A					B			C		D	E	F		A							G	H	I
								⚲	⚲			⚲		⚲					⚲	⚲		🚌			⚲
Hull	d					11 23		11 40		11 55	12 03							12 18	12 40				12 57	13 12	
Hessle	d					11 30												12 25							
Ferriby	d					11 35												12 30							
Brough	d					11 40		11 52		12 07	12 15							12 35	12 52				13 09	13 24	
Broomfleet	d					11 45																			
Gilberdyke	d					11 50												12 42						13 32	
Eastrington	d																							13 36	
Howden	d										12 27													13 42	
Wressle	d																							13 47	
Selby	a							12 11			12 37								13 11					13 54	
	d							12 11			12 38								13 11					13 55	
York 8 33	a										13 04													14 27	
Saltmarshe	d																	12 48							
Goole	d					11 58				12 22								12 58					13 23		
Thorne North	d					12 07												13 06							
Cleethorpes	d			11 10					11 26											12 26	12 55				
New Clee	d																				12x58				
Grimsby Docks	d																				13 00				
Grimsby Town	a			11 16					11 33											12 33	13 03				
	d			11 17			11 28		11 34											12 34	13 03				
Great Coates	d																				13 07				
Healing	d																				13 10				
Stallingborough	d																				13 13				
Habrough	d			11 28			11 38														13 19				
Ulceby	d																				13 23				
Thornton Abbey	d																				13 27				
Goxhill	d																				13 30				
New Holland	d																				13 35				
Barrow Haven	d																				13 38				
Barton-on-Humber	a																				13 43				
Barton-on-Humber	d																					14 00			
Hull Paragon Interchange	a																					14 27			
Barnetby	d			11 38			11a47		11 53											12 53					
Scunthorpe	a								12 08											13 08					
	d								12 08				12 18							13 08					
Althorpe	d												12 23												
Crowle	d												12 29												
Thorne South	d												12 38												
Hatfield & Stainforth	d					12 13							12 43					13 12							
Kirk Sandall	d					12 17							12 48					13 17							
Adwick 31	d		12 14														13 15								
Bentley (S.Yorks) 31	d		12 18														13 19								
Doncaster 7 31	a		12 24			12 28			12 38	12 48			12 59				13 24	13 27		13 38			13 46		
London Kings Cross 15 ⊖26	a																								
York 8 26	d											12 34		12 45											13 34
Doncaster 7	d		12 26						12 42	12 49		12 58	13 04				13 24			13 42			13 48		13 58
Conisbrough	d		12 33										13 11				13 32								
Mexborough	d		12 37										13 15				13 36								
Swinton (S.Yorks)	d	12 35	12 43										13 18			13 35	13 42								
Rotherham Central	d	12 44	12 52										13 27			13 44	13 52								
Meadowhall 🚊	d	12 50	12 58						13 01	13 08			13 33			13 50	13 58			14 01			14 08		
Sheffield 7 🚊	a	13 00	13 05	13 23					13 08	13 20		13 20	13 41	13 51		14 00	14 05			14 08			14 20		14 20
	d								13 11											14 11					
Stockport 78	a								13 53											14 53					
Manchester Piccadilly 10 🚊	a							13 36	14 02										14 36	15 02					
Manchester Airport 85 ✈	a								14 26											15 26					

A From Leeds
B To Newark North Gate
C From Bridlington
D From Newcastle to Southampton Central
E To Lincoln
F From Glasgow Central to Penzance
G From Scarborough
H To Hull
I From Newcastle to Reading

Table 29

Saturdays

Hull and Cleethorpes - Doncaster - Meadowhall, Sheffield, Manchester and Manchester Airport, Cleethorpes - Barton-on-Humber

Network Diagram - see first Page of Table 18

		NT	XC	NT	NT	NT	HT	TP	TP	EM		NT	NT	XC	NT	XC	NT	NT	NT	TP	TP	NT	NT	NT	NT
			◇1				◇1	◇1	◇1					◇1		◇1				◇1	◇1				
		A	B	C						D		E	F	G	A	H	C					I			
			🛒				⊠		🛒					🛒		🛒					🛒			🚌	
Hull	d					13 18	13 30	13 40				13 57	14 18						14 25	14 40		14 56			15 02
Hessle	d					13 25													14 32						
Ferriby	d					13 30													14 37						
Brough	d					13 35	13 42	13 52				14 09	14 30						14 42	14 52		15 08			15 14
Broomfleet	d																								
Gilberdyke	d					13 43													14 49						
Eastrington	d																								
Howden	d						13 56						14 42												15 26
Wressle	d																								
Selby	a						14 05	14 11					14 53							15 11					15 36
	d						14 06	14 11					14 53							15 11					15 38
York 8 33	a												15 25												16 06
Saltmarshe	d																								
Goole	d					13 58						14 23							14 58			15 23			
Thorne North	d					14 07													15 06						
Cleethorpes	d								13 26												14 26		15 00		
New Clee	d																						15x03		
Grimsby Docks	d																						15 05		
Grimsby Town	a								13 33												14 33		15 08		
	d								13 34	13 49											14 34		15 08		
Great Coates	d																						15 12		
Healing	d																						15 15		
Stallingborough	d																						15 18		
Habrough	d									13 59											14 44		15 24		
Ulceby	d																						15 28		
Thornton Abbey	d																						15 32		
Goxhill	d																						15 35		
New Holland	d																						15 40		
Barrow Haven	d																						15 43		
Barton-on-Humber	a																						15 48		
Barton-on-Humber	d																							16 00	
Hull Paragon Interchange	a																							16 27	
Barnetby	d								13 53	14a08											14 53				
Scunthorpe	a								14 08												15 08				
	d	13 19							14 08						14 19						15 08				
Althorpe	d	13 24													14 24										
Crowle	d	13 30													14 30										
Thorne South	d	13 39													14 39										
Hatfield & Stainforth	d	13 44				14 13									14 44				15 12						
Kirk Sandall	d	13 49				14 17									14 49				15 17						
Adwick 31	d				14 15													15 15							
Bentley (S.Yorks) 31	d				14 19													15 19							
Doncaster 7 31	a	13 57			14 24	14 30	14 25		14 38			14 47			14 59			15 24	15 27		15 38	15 47			
London Kings Cross 15 ⊖26	a						16 09																		
York 8 26	d		13 44											14 34		14 44									
Doncaster 7	d	14 01			14 26				14 42			14 48		14 58	15 04			15 26			15 42	15 49			
Conisbrough	d	14 11			14 33										15 11			15 33							
Mexborough	d	14 15			14 37										15 15			15 37							
Swinton (S.Yorks)	d	14 18		14 35	14 43										15 18		15 35	15 42							
Rotherham Central	d	14 27		14 44	14 52										15 27		15 44	15 50							
Meadowhall 🚋	d	14 33		14 50	14 58				15 01			15 07			15 33		15 50	15 57			16 01	16 07			
Sheffield 7 🚋	a	14 40	14 51	15 00	15 05				15 08			15 20		15 20	15 41	15 51	16 00	16 05			16 08	16 22			
	d								15 11												16 11				
Stockport 78	a								15 53												16 53				
Manchester Piccadilly 10 🚋	a							15 36	16 02											16 36	17 02				
Manchester Airport 85 ✈	a								16 26												17 32				

A To Lincoln
B From Aberdeen to Penzance
C From Leeds
D To Newark North Gate
E From Bridlington
F To Hull
G From Newcastle to Southampton Central
H From Glasgow Central to Penzance
I From Scarborough

Table 29

Saturdays

Hull and Cleethorpes - Doncaster - Meadowhall, Sheffield, Manchester and Manchester Airport, Cleethorpes - Barton-on-Humber

Network Diagram - see first Page of Table 18

		XC	NT	NT	NT	HT	TP	XC	NT	NT	NT	TP	NT	EM	XC	NT	NT	NT	TP	XC	NT	NT	TP
		◇[1]				◇[1]	◇[1]	◇[1]				◇[1]			◇[1]				◇[1]	◇[1]			◇[1]
		A		B				C	D	E			F	G	A	H	B			I	D		
		🛒				⊠	🛒	🛒				🛒			🛒					🛒			🛒
Hull	d				15 18	15 30	15 40						15 57			16 10		16 27	16 40				
Hessle	d				15 25													16 34					
Ferriby	d				15 30													16 39					
Brough	d				15 35	15 42	15 52						16 09			16 22		16 44	16 52				
Broomfleet	d																	16 49					
Gilberdyke	d				15 42											16 29		16 54					
Eastrington	d																						
Howden	d					15 54										16 36							
Wressle	d																						
Selby	a					16 04	16 11									16 46			17 11				
	d					16 05	16 11									16 47			17 11				
York [8] 33	a															17 13							
Saltmarshe	d																	16 59					
Goole	d				15 58								16 23					17 04					
Thorne North	d				16 06													17 13					
Cleethorpes	d										15 20	15 26											16 26
New Clee	d																						
Grimsby Docks	d																						
Grimsby Town	a										15 26	15 33											16 33
	d										15 27	15 34		16 00									16 34
Great Coates	d																						
Healing	d																						
Stallingborough	d																						
Habrough	d										15 37			16 09									
Ulceby	d																						
Thornton Abbey	d																						
Goxhill	d																						
New Holland	d																						
Barrow Haven	d																						
Barton-on-Humber	a																						
Barton-on-Humber	d																						
Hull Paragon Interchange	a																						
Barnetby	d										15 48	15 53		16a18									16 53
Scunthorpe	a											16 08											17 08
	d			15 18								16 08					16 19						17 08
Althorpe	d			15 23													16 24						
Crowle	d			15 29													16 30						
Thorne South	d			15 38													16 39						
Hatfield & Stainforth	d			15 43	16 12												16 44	17 19					
Kirk Sandall	d			15 48	16 17												16 49	17 23					
Adwick 31	d									16 15													
Bentley (S.Yorks) 31	d									16 18													
Doncaster [7] 31	a			15 58	16 27	16 23				16 25		16 38	16 47				16 57	17 35					17 38
London Kings Cross [15] ⊖26	a					18 08																	
York [8] 26	d	15 34	15 01					15 45							16 06					16 44			
Doncaster [7]	d	15 58		16 01						16 26		16 42	16 48				17 00					17 24	17 42
Conisbrough	d			16 11						16 33							17 08					17 31	
Mexborough	d			16 15						16 37							17 12					17 35	
Swinton (S.Yorks)	d		16 01	16 18					16 35	16 41							17 16				17 35	17 42	
Rotherham Central	d		16 09	16 27					16 44	16 50							17 27				17 44	17 50	
Meadowhall 🚊	d		16 18	16 33					16 50	16 55		17 01	17 08				17 33				17 50	17 57	18 01
Sheffield [7] 🚊	a	16 20	16 27	16 41				16 51	17 00	17 05	17 23	17 08	17 19		17 20		17 41			17 51	18 00	18 05	18 08
	d											17 11											18 11
Stockport 78	a											17 53											18 53
Manchester Piccadilly [10] 🚊	a						17 36					18 02							18 37				19 02
Manchester Airport 85 ✈	a											18 26											19 28

A From Newcastle to Reading
B To Lincoln
C From Edinburgh to Plymouth
D From Leeds
E To Retford
F From Bridlington
G To Newark North Gate
H To Hull
I From Glasgow Central to Plymouth

Table 29

Saturdays

Hull and Cleethorpes - Doncaster - Meadowhall, Sheffield, Manchester and Manchester Airport, Cleethorpes - Barton-on-Humber

Network Diagram - see first Page of Table 18

		NT	NT	NT	TP	NT	XC	NT	EM	XC	NT	NT	NT	TP	EM	NT	NT	TP	XC	NT	NT	HT	NT
					◇1		◇1		◇1	◇1				◇1				◇1	◇1			◇1	
		A			B	B	C	D	E	F	G	H			I	J	K		L	M			A
				🚌			🛒		☕	🛒				🛒					🛒			⊠	
Hull	d	16 54			17 01	17 18										17 42	17 52	17 58				18 30	18 32
Hessle	d					17 25										17 49							18 39
Ferriby	d					17 30										17 54							18 44
Brough	d	17 06			17 13	17 35										17 59	18 03	18 10				18 43	18 49
Broomfleet	d					17 40																	
Gilberdyke	d	17 13				17 45										18 06							18 56
Eastrington	d					17 49																	
Howden	d					17 54																18 55	
Wressle	d					17 59																	
Selby	a				17 32	18 06											18 26	18 29				19 04	
	d					18 07											18 26	18 29				19 05	
York 8 33	a					18 33																	
Saltmarshe	d															18 12							
Goole	d	17 22														18 19							19 05
Thorne North	d															18 28							19 14
Cleethorpes	d		17 00											17 26									
New Clee	d																						
Grimsby Docks	d		17 05																				
Grimsby Town	a		17 08											17 33									
	d		17 09											17 34	18 26								
Great Coates	d		17 13																				
Healing	d		17 16																				
Stallingborough	d		17 19																				
Habrough	d		17 25											17 44	18 36								
Ulceby	d		17 28																				
Thornton Abbey	d		17 33																				
Goxhill	d		17 36																				
New Holland	d		17 40																				
Barrow Haven	d		17 43																				
Barton-on-Humber	a		17 49																				
Barton-on-Humber	d			18 00																			
Hull Paragon Interchange	a			18 27																			
Barnetby	d													17 53	18a44								
Scunthorpe	a													18 08									
	d							17 18						18 08							18 19		
Althorpe	d							17 23													18 24		
Crowle	d							17 29													18 30		
Thorne South	d							17 38													18 39		
Hatfield & Stainforth	d							17 43								18 34					18 46		19 21
Kirk Sandall	d							17 48								18 39					18 50		19 25
Adwick 31	d										18 16												
Bentley (S.Yorks) 31	d										18 20									←			
Doncaster 7 31	a	17 48						17 58			18 27			18 38		18 50	18 47			18 50	19 01	19 26	19 36
London Kings Cross 15 ⊖26	a															→						21 09	
York 8 26	d						17 34		17 50	17 44									18 34				
Doncaster 7	d	17 49					17 58	18 02	18 18				18 26	18 42			18 48		18 58	19 01			
Conisbrough	d							18 09					18 33							19 08			
Mexborough	d							18 13					18 37							19 12			
Swinton (S.Yorks)	d							18 16				18 35	18 42							19 15			
Rotherham Central	d							18 27				18 44	18 49							19 23			
Meadowhall 🚊	d	18 08						18 33				18 50	18 56	19 01			19 08			19 28			
Sheffield 7 🚊	a	18 21					18 20	18 41	18 44	18 51		19 00	19 06	19 08			19 19		19 21	19 37			
	d													19 11									
Stockport 78	a													19 53									
Manchester Piccadilly 10 🚊	a													20 02				19 57					
Manchester Airport 85 ✈	a													20 36									

A From Bridlington
B To Leeds
C From Newcastle to Reading
D To Lincoln
E To St Pancras International
F From Edinburgh to Exeter St Davids
G To Scunthorpe
H From Leeds
I To Newark North Gate
J To Sheffield
K From Scarborough
L From Newcastle to Birmingham New Street
M From Hull

Table 29

Saturdays

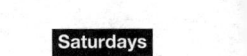

Hull and Cleethorpes - Doncaster - Meadowhall, Sheffield, Manchester and Manchester Airport, Cleethorpes - Barton-on-Humber

Network Diagram - see first Page of Table 18

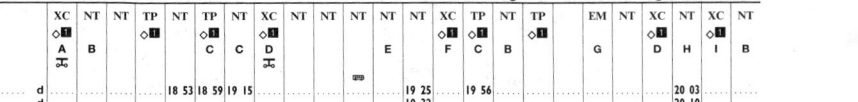

		XC	NT	NT	TP	NT	TP	NT	XC	NT	NT	NT	NT	NT	XC	TP	NT	TP		EM	NT	XC	NT	XC	NT
		◇1			◇1		◇1		◇1						◇1	◇1		◇1				◇1		◇1	
		A	B				C	C	D				E		F	C	B			G		D	H	I	B
		trolley							trolley			bus													
Hull	d					18 53	18 59	19 15						19 25		19 56							20 03		
Hessle	d													19 32									20 10		
Ferriby	d													19 37									20 15		
Brough	d					19 05	19 11	19 28						19 42		20 08							20 20		
Broomfleet	d																								
Gilberdyke	d							19 36						19 50									20 27		
Eastrington	d																								
Howden	d							19 43																	
Wressle	d																								
Selby	a						19 29	19 52								20 26									
	d							19 53																	
York 8 33	a							20 21																	
Saltmarshe	d																								
Goole	d					19 19								19 58									20 36		
Thorne North	d													20 07									20 44		
Cleethorpes	d				18 26					18 36	19 00							19 26							
New Clee	d																								
Grimsby Docks	d										19 05														
Grimsby Town	a				18 33					18 42	19 08							19 33							
	d				18 34					18 43	19 09							19 34		19 45					
Great Coates	d										19 13														
Healing	d										19 16														
Stallingborough	d										19 19														
Habrough	d									18 53	19 25							19 44		19 54					
Ulceby	d										19 29														
Thornton Abbey	d										19 34														
Goxhill	d										19 37														
New Holland	d										19 41														
Barrow Haven	d										19 44														
Barton-on-Humber	a										19 50														
Barton-on-Humber	d											19 53													
Hull Paragon Interchange	a											20 20													
Barnetby	d				18 53					19 02								19 53		20a03					
Scunthorpe	a				19 08													20 08							
	d				19 08								19 19					20 08			20 21				
Althorpe	d												19 24								20 26				
Crowle	d												19 30								20 32				
Thorne South	d												19 39								20 41				
Hatfield & Stainforth	d												19 44	20 16							20 46		20 51		
Kirk Sandall	d												19 49	20 20							20 51		20 56		
Adwick 31	d																								
Bentley (S.Yorks) 31	d																								
Doncaster 7 31	a				19 38	19 47							19 59	20 31				20 40			21 03		21 05		
London Kings Cross 15 ⊖26	a																								
York 8 26	d	18 44							19 34						19 44							20 34		20 45	
Doncaster 7	d			19 28	19 42	19 50			19 58				20 03					20 42				21 00	21 07		
Conisbrough	d			19 35									20 10					20 50					21 14		
Mexborough	d			19 39									20 14					20 54					21 18		
Swinton (S.Yorks)	d		19 35	19 43									20 17				20 35	20 57					21 21		21 34
Rotherham Central	d		19 44	19 51									20 28				20 45	21 03					21 28		21 42
Meadowhall	d		19 51	19 57	20 01	20 08							20 33				20 51	21 09					21 35		21 50
Sheffield 7	a	19 51	20 00	20 06	20 08	20 18			20 20	20 34			20 41		20 52		21 00	21 19				21 20	21 46	21 51	22 02
	d				20 11																				
Stockport 78	a				20 53																				
Manchester Piccadilly 10	a				21 02																				
Manchester Airport 85	a				21 36																				

A From Glasgow Central to Bristol Temple Meads
B From Leeds
C To Leeds
D From Newcastle to Birmingham New Street
E To Worksop
F From Edinburgh to Birmingham New Street
G To Lincoln
H From Bridlington
I From Glasgow Central to Birmingham New Street

Table 29

Saturdays

Hull and Cleethorpes - Doncaster - Meadowhall, Sheffield, Manchester and Manchester Airport, Cleethorpes - Barton-on-Humber

Network Diagram - see first Page of Table 18

		NT	TP	NT	NT	NT	NT	TP	NT	NT	NT	NT	NT	NT
			◇1					◇1						
												A	A	B
							🚌							
Hull	d			20 55	21 01			21 33						22 17
Hessle	d													22 24
Ferriby	d													22 29
Brough	d			21 07	21 13			21 45						22 34
Broomfleet	d													
Gilberdyke	d							21 52						
Eastrington	d													
Howden	d				21 25									
Wressle	d													
Selby	a				21 35			22 07						
	d				21 35			22 07						
York 8 33	a				21 57									
Saltmarshe	d													
Goole	d			21 21					21 35					22 48
Thorne North	d								21 44					22 57
Cleethorpes	d		20 26			21 03								
New Clee	d													
Grimsby Docks	d					21 08								
Grimsby Town	a		20 33			21 11								
	d		20 34			21 11								
Great Coates	d					21 15								
Healing	d					21 18								
Stallingborough	d					21 21								
Habrough	d					21 27								
Ulceby	d					21 31								
Thornton Abbey	d					21 35								
Goxhill	d					21 38								
New Holland	d					21 43								
Barrow Haven	d					21 46								
Barton-on-Humber	a					21 51								
Barton-on-Humber	d						21 53							
Hull Paragon Interchange	a						20 20							
Barnetby	d		20 53											
Scunthorpe	a		21 08											
	d		21 08							21 31	22 21			
Althorpe	d									21 36	22 26			
Crowle	d									21 42	22 32			
Thorne South	d									21 51	22 41			
Hatfield & Stainforth	d								21 50	21 56	22 46			23 03
Kirk Sandall	d								21 54	22 01	22 51			23 07
Adwick 31	d													
Bentley (S.Yorks) 31	d													
Doncaster 7 31	a		21 40	21 45					22 08	22 11	23 02			23 18
London Kings Cross 15 ⊖26	a													
York 8 26	d													
Doncaster 7	d	21 30	21 42	21 47						22 13				23 19
Conisbrough	d	21 37								22 20				23 26
Mexborough	d	21 41								22 24				23 30
Swinton (S.Yorks)	d	21 44								22 29		22 37	23 30	23 33
Rotherham Central	d	21 55								22 37		22 46	23 38	23 43
Meadowhall 🚊	d	22 03	21 59	22 12						22 43		22 53	23 44	23 49
Sheffield 7 🚊	a	22 13	22 10	22 22						22 54		23 03	23 58	23 59
	d													
Stockport 78	a													
Manchester Piccadilly 10 🚊	a							23 37						
Manchester Airport 85 ✈	a													

A From Leeds

B From Bridlington

Table 29

Sundays
until 1 January

Hull and Cleethorpes - Doncaster - Meadowhall, Sheffield, Manchester and Manchester Airport, Cleethorpes - Barton-on-Humber

Network Diagram - see first Page of Table 18

		TP	TP	TP	TP	TP	NT			NT		XC	NT	NT	NT	TP	NT	XC	HT	NT		TP	NT	XC	TP
		◇1	◇1	◇1	◇1	◇1						◇1				◇1		◇1	◇1			◇1		◇1	◇1
												B	C					D						E	
												⚭						⚭	☒					⚭	
Hull	d													08 40	08 54	09 00			09 30	09 33					
Hessle	d																			09 40					
Ferriby	d																			09 45					
Brough	d													08 52	09 06	09 12			09 42	09 50					
Broomfleet	d																								
Gilberdyke	d													08 59						09 57					
Eastrington	d																								
Howden	d														09 18				09 54						
Wressle	d																								
Selby	a														09 27	09 32			10 04						
	d														09 28	09 33			10 05						
York 8 33	a														09 52										
Saltmarshe	d																								
Goole	d													09 09			09 43			10 06					
Thorne North	d																09 51			10 14					
Cleethorpes	d																					09 26			10 26
New Clee	d																								
Grimsby Docks	d																								
Grimsby Town	a																					09 33			10 33
	d																					09 34			10 34
Great Coates	d																								
Healing	d																								
Stallingborough	d																								
Habrough	d																					09 44			10 44
Ulceby	d																								
Thornton Abbey	d																								
Goxhill	d																								
New Holland	d																								
Barrow Haven	d																								
Barton-on-Humber	a																								
Barton-on-Humber	d																								
Hull Paragon Interchange	a																								
Barnetby	d																					09 53			10 53
Scunthorpe	a																					10 08			11 08
	d																					10 08			11 08
Althorpe	d																								
Crowle	d																								
Thorne South	d																								
Hatfield & Stainforth	d																09 57			10 20					
Kirk Sandall	d																10 02			10 25					
Adwick 31	d																								
Bentley (S.Yorks) 31	d																								
Doncaster 7 31	a													09 29			10 11		10 23	10 35		10 40			11 38
London Kings Cross 15 ⊖26	a																		12 14						
York 8 26	d	02 44	03 59	05 12	06 12	07 12												09 28						10 28	
Doncaster 7	d						08 03			09 13		09 32		09 39			10 13	10 30				10 42	11 13	11 30	11 42
Conisbrough	d						08 10			09 20							10 20						11 20		
Mexborough	d						08 14			09 24							10 24						11 24		
Swinton (S.Yorks)	d						08 17			09 28			09 35				10 27						11 27		
Rotherham Central	d						08 25			09 35			09 48				10 35						11 35		
Meadowhall 🚋	d						08 30			09 41			09 54	10 00			10 40					11 00	11 40		12 00
Sheffield 7 🚋	a						08 41			09 51		09 55	10 03	10 08			10 52	10 54				11 07	11 51	11 53	12 07
	d																					11 10			12 10
Stockport 78	a																					11 53			12 50
Manchester Piccadilly 10 🚋	a	04 02	05 17	06 34	07 34	08 34										11 03						12 06			13 05
Manchester Airport 85 ✈	a					08 55																12 27			13 29

B From Leeds to Plymouth
C From Leeds
D To Plymouth
E From Newcastle to Plymouth

Table 29

Sundays

until 1 January

Hull and Cleethorpes - Doncaster - Meadowhall, Sheffield, Manchester and Manchester Airport, Cleethorpes - Barton-on-Humber

Network Diagram - see first Page of Table 18

		NT	TP	NT	NT	XC		HT	TP	NT	NT	TP	NT	XC	NT	TP		TP	NT	TP	NT	XC	NT	NT	TP
			◇■			◇■		◇■	◇■			◇■		◇■		◇■		◇■		◇■		◇■			◇■
		A		B		C								D	E	F					B	C		E	F
						✠		⊠						✠								✠			
Hull	d	10 50	10 58					11 30		11 46	11 53	12 00			12 46			12 58	13 29					13 35	
Hessle	d																							13 42	
Ferriby	d																							13 47	
Brough	d	11 02	11 10					11 42		11 58	12 05	12 12			12 58			13 10	13 41					13 52	
Broomfleet	d																								
Gilberdyke	d	11 09									12 12				13 05									14 00	
Eastrington	d																								
Howden	d							11 54		12 10									13 53						
Wressle	d																								
Selby	a		11 28					12 04		12 19		12 32						13 28	14 02						
	d		11 29					12 05		12 20		12 32						13 29	14 03						
York ■ 33	a									12 44									14 30						
Saltmarshe	d																								
Goole	d	11 18			11 43						12 21				13 14								13 43	14 08	
Thorne North	d	11 26			11 51						12 29												13 51		
Cleethorpes	d								11 26																
New Clee	d																								
Grimsby Docks	d																								
Grimsby Town	a								11 33																
	d								11 34																
Great Coates	d																								
Healing	d																								
Stallingborough	d																								
Habrough	d																								
Ulceby	d																								
Thornton Abbey	d																								
Goxhill	d																								
New Holland	d																								
Barrow Haven	d																								
Barton-on-Humber	a																								
Barton-on-Humber	d																								
Hull Paragon Interchange	a																								
Barnetby	d								11 53																
Scunthorpe	a								12 08																
	d								12 08																
Althorpe	d																								
Crowle	d																								
Thorne South	d																								
Hatfield & Stainforth	d				11 57																		13 57		
Kirk Sandall	d				12 02																		14 02		
Adwick 31	d																								
Bentley (S.Yorks) 31	d																								
Doncaster ■ 31	a	11 46			12 11			12 25	12 40		12 47				13 37								14 11	14 31	
London Kings Cross ■ ⊖26	a							14 14																	
York ■ 26	d					11 28								12 28		13 15						13 40			14 15
Doncaster ■	d	11 48			12 13	12 30			12 42				13 13	13 30	13 38					13 42			14 13	14 33	
Conisbrough	d				12 20								13 20										14 20		
Mexborough	d				12 24								13 24										14 24		
Swinton (S.Yorks)	d			12 05	12 27								13 27								14 06		14 30		
Rotherham Central	d			12 13	12 38								13 36								14 14		14 42		
Meadowhall 🚌	d	12 08		12 21	12 43				13 00				13 44		13 56					14 00	14 21		14 48	14 52	
Sheffield ■ 🚌	a	12 18		12 32	12 55	12 54			13 07				13 52	13 54	14 06					14 07	14 32	14 52	14 55	15 03	
	d								13 10											14 11					
Stockport 78	a								13 53											14 53					
Manchester Piccadilly ■ 🚌	a		12 54						14 06			13 54				14 34		14 54		15 06					15 34
Manchester Airport 85 ✈	a								14 27							14 55				15 28					15 55

A From Bridlington
B From Leeds
C From Edinburgh to Plymouth
D From Edinburgh to Penzance
E From Scarborough
F From Newcastle

Table 29

Sundays
until 1 January

Hull and Cleethorpes - Doncaster - Meadowhall, Sheffield, Manchester and Manchester Airport, Cleethorpes - Barton-on-Humber

Network Diagram - see first Page of Table 18

		NT			TP	HT	XC	XC	NT	NT	TP	TP		XC	NT	XC	NT	NT	NT		TP	XC		HT	
					◇1	◇1	◇1	◇1			◇1	◇1		◇1		◇1					◇1	◇1		◇1	
							A	B		C				A	D	E		F				H			
						⊠	⚲	⚲						⚲		⚲						⚲		⊠	
Hull	d	14 23				14 30				14 41	14 58							15 41	16 00					16 30	
Hessle	d																								
Ferriby	d																								
Brough	d	14 35				14 42				14 53	15 10							15 53	16 12					16 42	
Broomfleet	d																								
Gilberdyke	d									15 00								16 00							
Eastrington	d																								
Howden	d	14 47				14 54													16 24					16 54	
Wressle	d																								
Selby	a	14 56				15 04					15 28								16 33					17 04	
	d	14 57				15 05					15 29								16 34					17 05	
York 8 33	a	15 25																	16 59						
Saltmarshe	d																								
Goole	d									15 09							15 43	16 09							
Thorne North	d																15 51								
Cleethorpes	d				13 26							14 26									15 26				
New Clee	d																								
Grimsby Docks	d																								
Grimsby Town	a				13 33							14 33									15 33				
	d				13 34							14 34									15 34				
Great Coates	d																								
Healing	d																								
Stallingborough	d																								
Habrough	d											14 44													
Ulceby	d																								
Thornton Abbey	d																								
Goxhill	d																								
New Holland	d																								
Barrow Haven	d																								
Barton-on-Humber	a																								
Barton-on-Humber	d																								
Hull Paragon Interchange	a																								
Barnetby	d				13 53							14 53									15 53				
Scunthorpe	a				14 08							15 08									16 08				
	d				14 08							15 08									16 08				
Althorpe	d																								
Crowle	d																								
Thorne South	d																								
Hatfield & Stainforth	d																15 57								
Kirk Sandall	d																16 02								
Adwick 31	d																								
Bentley (S.Yorks) 31	d																								
Doncaster 7 31	a				14 37	15 25				15 32		15 39					16 11	16 32			16 39			17 25	
London Kings Cross 15 ⊖26	a					17 15																		19 18	
York 8 26	d						14 34	14 40						15 34		15 40						16 23			
Doncaster 7	d				14 42		14 59		15 13	15 33		15 42		15 59			16 13	16 33			16 42	16 51			
Conisbrough	d								15 20								16 20								
Mexborough	d								15 24								16 24								
Swinton (S.Yorks)	d								15 30						16 05		16 29								
Rotherham Central	d								15 41						16 13		16 41								
Meadowhall 🚋	d				15 00				15 48	15 52		16 00			16 19		16 47	16 53			17 00				
Sheffield 7 🚋	a				15 07		15 21	15 51	15 55	16 01		16 07		16 21	16 31	16 51	16 55	17 04			17 07	17 19			
	d				15 11							16 11									17 11				
Stockport 78	a				15 53							16 53									17 53				
Manchester Piccadilly 10 🚋	a				16 06						16 54	17 06									18 06				
Manchester Airport 85 ✈	a				16 27							17 27									18 27				

A From Newcastle to Reading
B From Glasgow Central to Penzance
C From Bridlington
D From Leeds
E From Glasgow Central to Plymouth
F From Scarborough
G From Newcastle
H From Edinburgh to Reading

Table 29

Sundays
until 1 January

Hull and Cleethorpes - Doncaster - Meadowhall, Sheffield, Manchester and Manchester Airport, Cleethorpes - Barton-on-Humber

Network Diagram - see first Page of Table 18

Station		XC	NT	NT	TP	TP	NT	XC		NT	NT	EM	XC	NT	NT	TP	HT	XC		NT	TP	XC	NT	NT	TP
		◇1			◇1	◇1		◇1				◇1	◇1			◇1	◇1	◇1			◇1	◇1			◇1
		A		B				C			D	E	F		G			H				I		B	
		🍴						🍴				🍽	🍴				⊠	🍴				🍴			
Hull	d			16 41	16 58		17 23								17 41		18 30							18 38	18 58
Hessle	d																								
Ferriby	d																								
Brough	d			16 53	17 10		17 35								17 53		18 42							18 50	19 10
Broomfleet	d																								
Gilberdyke	d			17 00											18 00									18 57	
Eastrington	d																								
Howden	d						17 47										18 54								
Wressle	d																								
Selby	a				17 28		17 56										19 04								19 28
	d				17 29		17 57										19 05								19 29
York 8 33	a						18 25																		
Saltmarshe	d																								
Goole	d			17 09						17 42					18 09									19 06	
Thorne North	d									17 50														19 14	
Cleethorpes	d					16 26										17 26									
New Clee	d																								
Grimsby Docks	d																								
Grimsby Town	a					16 33										17 33									
	d					16 34										17 34									
Great Coates	d																								
Healing	d																								
Stallingborough	d																								
Habrough	d															17 44									
Ulceby	d																								
Thornton Abbey	d																								
Goxhill	d																								
New Holland	d																								
Barrow Haven	d																								
Barton-on-Humber	a																								
Barton-on-Humber	d																								
Hull Paragon Interchange	a																								
Barnetby	d					16 53										17 53									
Scunthorpe	a					17 08										18 08									
	d					17 08										18 08									
Althorpe	d																								
Crowle	d																								
Thorne South	d																								
Hatfield & Stainforth	d									17 56														19 20	
Kirk Sandall	d									18 01														19 25	
Adwick 31	d																								
Bentley (S.Yorks) 31	d																								
Doncaster 7 31	a			17 31		17 38				18 09					18 33	18 38	19 25							19 35	
London Kings Cross 15 ⊖26	a																21 18								
York 8 26	d	16 40						17 34				17 40	17 40					18 34		18 10	18 33	18 40			
Doncaster 7	d		17 13	17 32		17 42		17 59				18 08		18 19	18 34	18 42		18 59					19 18	19 37	
Conisbrough	d		17 21											18 26									19 25		
Mexborough	d		17 25											18 30									19 29		
Swinton (S.Yorks)	d		17 30								18 10			18 33						19 01			19 33		
Rotherham Central	d		17 41								18 19			18 42						19 13			19 41		
Meadowhall 🚋	d		17 48	17 53		18 00					18 25			18 47	18 53	19 00				19 18			19 47	19 57	
Sheffield 7 🚋	a	17 51	17 55	18 01		18 07		18 23			18 36	18 39	18 51	18 57	19 03	19 07		19 21		19 27		19 50	19 55	20 06	
	d					18 11										19 11									
Stockport 78	a					18 53										19 53									
Manchester Piccadilly 10 🚋	a				18 54	19 06										20 09					19 54				20 54
Manchester Airport 85 ✈	a					19 27										20 30									

A From Aberdeen to Plymouth
B From Bridlington
C From Newcastle to Reading
D From Leeds
E To St Pancras International
F From Glasgow Central to Plymouth
G From Scarborough
H From Newcastle to Guildford
I From Glasgow Central to Bristol Temple Meads

Table 29

Sundays
until 1 January

Hull and Cleethorpes - Doncaster - Meadowhall, Sheffield, Manchester and Manchester Airport, Cleethorpes - Barton-on-Humber

Network Diagram - see first Page of Table 18

		TP	XC	NT	NT	XC	NT	TP	XC	NT	NT	XC	NT	TP	TP	NT	NT
		◇■	◇■			◇■		◇■	◇■			◇■		◇■	◇■		
			A		B	C			A	E		F			G	B	
			⚲						⚲								
Hull	d			19 24						20 01	20 29				21 00		21 35
Hessle	d									20 08							
Ferriby	d									20 13							
Brough	d			19 36						20 18	20 41				21 12		21 47
Broomfleet	d																
Gilberdyke	d									20 25							21 54
Eastrington	d																
Howden	d			19 48							20 53						
Wressle	d																
Selby	a			19 57							21 02				21 30		
	d			19 58							21 03						
York ■ 33	a			20 25							21 30						
Saltmarshe	d																
Goole	d									20 34							22 03
Thorne North	d									20 42							22 11
Cleethorpes	d	18 26						19 26						20 26			
New Clee	d																
Grimsby Docks	d																
Grimsby Town	a	18 33						19 33						20 33			
	d	18 34						19 34						20 34			
Great Coates	d																
Healing	d																
Stallingborough	d																
Habrough	d													20 44			
Ulceby	d																
Thornton Abbey	d																
Goxhill	d																
New Holland	d																
Barrow Haven	d																
Barton-on-Humber	a																
Barton-on-Humber	d																
Hull Paragon Interchange	a																
Barnetby	d	18 53						19 53						20 53			
Scunthorpe	a	19 08						20 08						21 08			
	d	19 08						20 08						21 08			
Althorpe	d																
Crowle	d																
Thorne South	d																
Hatfield & Stainforth	d																22 15
Kirk Sandall	d																22 20
Adwick 31	d																
Bentley (S.Yorks) 31	d																
Doncaster ■ 31	a	19 38						20 40		20 59				21 40			22 32
London Kings Cross ■ ⊖26	a																
York ■ 26	d		19 24			19 40			20 24			20 40	20 50				
Doncaster ■	d	19 42	19 50				20 14	20 42	20 50	21 01				21 42			22 40
Conisbrough	d						20 21			21 08							22 47
Mexborough	d						20 25			21 12							22 51
Swinton (S.Yorks)	d				20 09		20 29			21 15			21 45	21 52		22 32	22 53
Rotherham Central	d				20 17		20 41			21 22			21 52	21 58		22 40	22 58
Meadowhall	d	20 00			20 23		20 47	21 00		21 28			21 58	22 04		22 45	23 04
Sheffield ■	a	20 07	20 16		20 34	20 51	20 55	21 07	21 17	21 38		21 50	22 09	22 13		22 54	23 15
	d	20 11						21 11									
Stockport 78	a	20 53						21 53									
Manchester Piccadilly ■	a	21 06						22 06									
Manchester Airport 85 ✈	a	21 27						22 27									

A From Newcastle to Birmingham New Street
B From Leeds
C From Edinburgh to Bristol Temple Meads
E From Scarborough
F From Glasgow Central to Birmingham New Street
G To Leeds

Table 29

Sundays

8 January to 12 February

Hull and Cleethorpes - Doncaster - Meadowhall, Sheffield, Manchester and Manchester Airport, Cleethorpes - Barton-on-Humber

Network Diagram - see first Page of Table 18

			NT	NT	XC	NT	NT	NT	TP	TP	NT	XC	HT	NT	TP	NT	XC
					◇1				◇1			◇1	◇1				◇1
					B	C						D					E
										bus					bus		
					trolley							trolley	⊠				trolley
Hull		d					08 40	08 54	09 00				09 30	09 33			
Hessle		d												09 40			
Ferriby		d												09 45			
Brough		d					08 52	09 06	09 12				09 42	09 50			
Broomfleet		d															
Gilberdyke		d					08 59							09 57			
Eastrington		d															
Howden		d						09 18					09 54				
Wressle		d															
Selby		a						09 27	09 32				10 04				
		d						09 28	09 33				10 05				
York 8	33	a						09 52									
Saltmarshe		d															
Goole		d					09 09				09 43			10 06			
Thorne North		d									09 51			10 14			
Cleethorpes		d													08 55		
New Clee		d															
Grimsby Docks		d															
Grimsby Town		a													09 15		
		d													09 15		
Great Coates		d															
Healing		d															
Stallingborough		d															
Habrough		d													09 40		
Ulceby		d															
Thornton Abbey		d															
Goxhill		d															
New Holland		d															
Barrow Haven		d															
Barton-on-Humber		a															
Barton-on-Humber		d															
Hull Paragon Interchange		a															
Barnetby		d													09 55		
Scunthorpe		a													10 20		
		d													10 20		
Althorpe		d															
Crowle		d															
Thorne South		d															
Hatfield & Stainforth		d									09 57			10 20			
Kirk Sandall		d									10 02			10 25			
Adwick	31	d															
Bentley (S.Yorks)	31	d															
Doncaster 7	31	a					09 29				10 11		10 23	10 35	11 10		
London Kings Cross 15	⊖26	a											12 14				
York 8	26	d										09 28					10 28
Doncaster 7		d	08 03	09 13	09 32		09 39			10 10	10 13	10 30			11 10	11 13	11 30
Conisbrough		d	08 10	09 20							10 20					11 20	
Mexborough		d	08 14	09 24							10 24					11 24	
Swinton (S.Yorks)		d	08 17	09 28		09 35					10 27					11 27	
Rotherham Central		d	08 25	09 35		09 48					10 35					11 35	
Meadowhall	tram	d	08 30	09 41		09 54	10 00			10 40	10 40				11 40	11 40	
Sheffield 7	tram	a	08 41	09 51	09 55	10 03	10 08			11 00	10 52	10 54			12 00	11 51	11 53
		d															
Stockport	78	a															
Manchester Piccadilly 10	tram	a							11 03								
Manchester Airport	85 ✈	a															

B From Leeds to Plymouth
C From Leeds
D To Plymouth
E From Newcastle to Plymouth

Table 29

Sundays

8 January to 12 February

Hull and Cleethorpes - Doncaster - Meadowhall, Sheffield, Manchester and Manchester Airport, Cleethorpes - Barton-on-Humber

Network Diagram - see first Page of Table 18

		NT	TP	NT	TP	NT	XC	HT	NT	NT	TP	TP	NT	XC	NT	TP	TP	NT	NT	XC	TP	NT	NT
			◇1				◇1	◇1				◇1		◇1		◇1	◇1			◇1			
		A		B			C							D	E	F			B	C			E
					Bus		Trolley	⊠			Bus			Trolley						Trolley	Bus		
Hull	d	10 50	10 58					11 30	11 46	11 53		12 00			12 46		12 58	13 29					13 35
Hessle	d																						13 42
Ferriby	d																						13 47
Brough	d	11 02	11 10					11 42	11 58	12 05		12 12			12 58		13 10	13 41					13 52
Broomfleet	d																						
Gilberdyke	d	11 09								12 12					13 05								14 00
Eastrington	d																						
Howden	d							11 54	12 10									13 53					
Wressle	d																						
Selby	a		11 28					12 04	12 19			12 32					13 28	14 02					
	d		11 29					12 05	12 20			12 32					13 29	14 03					
York 8 33	a								12 44									14 30					
Saltmarshe	d																						
Goole	d	11 18				11 43				12 21					13 14							13 43	14 08
Thorne North	d	11 26				11 51				12 29												13 51	
Cleethorpes	d				10 05						11 05												
New Clee	d																						
Grimsby Docks	d																						
Grimsby Town	a				10 25						11 25												
	d				10 25						11 25												
Great Coates	d																						
Healing	d																						
Stallingborough	d																						
Habrough	d																						
Ulceby	d																						
Thornton Abbey	d																						
Goxhill	d																						
New Holland	d																						
Barrow Haven	d																						
Barton-on-Humber	a																						
Barton-on-Humber	d																						
Hull Paragon Interchange	a																						
Barnetby	d				10 55						11 55												
Scunthorpe	a				11 20						12 20												
	d				11 20						12 20												
Althorpe	d																						
Crowle	d																						
Thorne South	d																						
Hatfield & Stainforth	d					11 57																13 57	
Kirk Sandall	d					12 02																14 02	
Adwick 31	d																						
Bentley (S.Yorks) 31	d																						
Doncaster 7 31	a	11 46			12 10	12 11		12 25		12 47	13 10				13 37							14 11	14 31
London Kings Cross 15 ⊖26	a							14 14															
York 8 26	d						11 28							12 28		13 15				13 40			
Doncaster 7	d	11 48			12 10	12 13	12 30				13 10		13 13	13 30	13 38						14 12	14 13	14 33
Conisbrough	d					12 20							13 20									14 20	
Mexborough	d					12 24							13 24									14 24	
Swinton (S.Yorks)	d			12 05		12 27							13 27						14 06			14 30	
Rotherham Central	d			12 13		12 38							13 36						14 14			14 42	
Meadowhall	d	12 08		12 21	12 40	12 43					13 40		13 44		13 56				14 21		14 42	14 48	14 52
Sheffield 7	a	12 18		12 32	13 00	12 55	12 54				14 00		13 52	13 54	14 06				14 32	14 52	15 02	14 55	15 03
	d																						
Stockport 78	a																						
Manchester Piccadilly 10	a		12 54									13 54				14 34	14 54						
Manchester Airport 85	a															14 55							

A From Bridlington
B From Leeds
C From Edinburgh to Plymouth
D From Edinburgh to Penzance
E From Scarborough
F From Newcastle

Table 29

Sundays

8 January to 12 February

Hull and Cleethorpes - Doncaster - Meadowhall, Sheffield, Manchester and Manchester Airport, Cleethorpes - Barton-on-Humber

Network Diagram - see first Page of Table 18

			NT		XC ◇1 B 🍴	XC ◇1 C 🍴	TP 🚌	HT ◇1 ☒	NT	NT D	TP ◇1		XC ◇1 B 🍴	NT E	XC ◇1 F 🍴	TP 🚌	NT	NT G	NT		XC ◇1 H 🍴			XC ◇1 I 🍴
Hull d			14 23					14 30		14 41	14 58							15 41	16 00					
Hessle d																								
Ferriby d																								
Brough d			14 35					14 42		14 53	15 10							15 53	16 12					
Broomfleet d																								
Gilberdyke d										15 00								16 00						
Eastrington d																								
Howden d			14 47					14 54											16 24					
Wressle d																								
Selby a			14 56					15 04			15 28								16 33					
d			14 57					15 05			15 29								16 34					
York 8 33 a			15 25																16 59					
Saltmarshe d																								
Goole d										15 09							15 43	16 09						
Thorne North d																	15 51							
Cleethorpes d							13 05									14 05								
New Clee d																								
Grimsby Docks d																								
Grimsby Town a							13 25									14 25								
d							13 25									14 25								
Great Coates d																								
Healing d																								
Stallingborough d																								
Habrough d																								
Ulceby d																								
Thornton Abbey d																								
Goxhill d																								
New Holland d																								
Barrow Haven d																								
Barton-on-Humber a																								
Barton-on-Humber d																								
Hull Paragon Interchange a																								
Barnetby d							13 55									14 55								
Scunthorpe a							14 20									15 20								
d							14 20									15 20								
Althorpe d																								
Crowle d																								
Thorne South d																								
Hatfield & Stainforth d																	15 57							
Kirk Sandall d																	16 02							
Adwick 31 d																								
Bentley (S.Yorks) 31 d																								
Doncaster 7 31 a							15 10	15 25		15 32						16 10	16 11	16 32						
London Kings Cross 15 ⊖26 a								17 15																
York 8 26 d					14 34	14 40							15 34		15 40						16 23			16 40
Doncaster 7 d					14 59		15 10		15 13	15 33			15 59			16 10	16 13	16 33			16 51			
Conisbrough d									15 20								16 20							
Mexborough d									15 24								16 24							
Swinton (S.Yorks) d									15 30					16 05			16 29							
Rotherham Central d									15 41					16 13			16 41							
Meadowhall 🚊 d							15 40		15 48	15 52				16 19		16 40	16 47	16 53						
Sheffield 7 🚊 a					15 21	15 51	16 00		15 55	16 01			16 21	16 31	16 51	17 00	16 55	17 04			17 19			17 51
d																								
Stockport 78 a																								
Manchester Piccadilly 10 🚊 a											16 54													
Manchester Airport 85 ✈ a																								

B From Newcastle to Reading
C From Glasgow Central to Penzance
D From Bridlington
E From Leeds
F From Glasgow Central to Plymouth
G From Scarborough
H From Edinburgh to Reading
I From Aberdeen to Plymouth

Table 29

Sundays

8 January to 12 February

Hull and Cleethorpes - Doncaster - Meadowhall, Sheffield, Manchester and Manchester Airport, Cleethorpes - Barton-on-Humber

Network Diagram - see first Page of Table 18

		TP	HT	NT	NT	TP	NT	XC		NT	NT	EM	XC	TP	NT	NT	XC	NT			XC	TP	HT	NT	NT
			◇1			◇1		◇1				◇1	◇1				◇1				◇1		◇1		
					A			B			C	D	E			F	G				H				A
		🚌	☒					✈				🍴	✈	🚌			✈				✈	🚌	☒		
Hull	d		16 30		16 41	16 58	17 23									17 41							18 30		18 38
Hessle	d																								
Ferriby	d																								
Brough	d		16 42		16 53	17 10	17 35									17 53							18 42		18 50
Broomfleet	d																								
Gilberdyke	d				17 00											18 00									18 57
Eastrington	d																								
Howden	d		16 54				17 47																18 54		
Wressle	d																								
Selby	a		17 04			17 28	17 56																19 04		
	d		17 05			17 29	17 57																19 05		
York 8 33	a						18 25																		
Saltmarshe	d																								
Goole	d				17 09					17 42						18 09									19 06
Thorne North	d									17 50															19 14
Cleethorpes	d	15 05												16 05								17 05			
New Clee	d																								
Grimsby Docks	d																								
Grimsby Town	a	15 25												16 25								17 25			
	d	15 25												16 25								17 25			
Great Coates	d																								
Healing	d																								
Stallingborough	d																								
Habrough	d																								
Ulceby	d																								
Thornton Abbey	d																								
Goxhill	d																								
New Holland	d																								
Barrow Haven	d																								
Barton-on-Humber	a																								
Barton-on-Humber	d																								
Hull Paragon Interchange	a																								
Barnetby	d	15 55												16 55								17 55			
Scunthorpe	a	16 20												17 20								18 20			
	d	16 20												17 20								18 20			
Althorpe	d																								
Crowle	d																								
Thorne South	d																								
Hatfield & Stainforth	d									17 56															19 20
Kirk Sandall	d									18 01															19 25
Adwick 31	d																								
Bentley (S.Yorks) 31	d																								
Doncaster 7 31	a	17 10	17 25		17 31					18 09				18 10		18 33						19 10	19 25		19 35
London Kings Cross 15 ⊖26	a		19 18																				21 18		
York 8 26	d							17 34				17 40	17 40				18 34	18 10			18 40				
Doncaster 7	d	17 10		17 13	17 32			17 59				18 08		18 10	18 19	18 34	18 59					19 10		19 18	19 37
Conisbrough	d			17 21											18 26									19 25	
Mexborough	d			17 25											18 30									19 29	
Swinton (S.Yorks)	d			17 30							18 10				18 33			19 01						19 33	
Rotherham Central	d			17 41							18 19				18 42			19 13						19 41	
Meadowhall 🚊	d	17 40		17 48	17 53						18 25			18 40	18 47	18 53		19 18				19 40		19 47	19 57
Sheffield 7 🚊	a	18 00		17 55	18 01			18 23			18 36	18 39	18 51	19 00	18 57	19 03	19 21	19 27			19 50	20 00		19 55	20 06
	d																								
Stockport 78	a																								
Manchester Piccadilly 10 🚊	a					18 54																			
Manchester Airport 85 ✈	a																								

A From Bridlington
B From Newcastle to Reading
C From Leeds
D To St Pancras International
E From Glasgow Central to Plymouth
F From Scarborough
G From Newcastle to Guildford
H From Glasgow Central to Bristol Temple Meads

Table 29

Hull and Cleethorpes - Doncaster - Meadowhall, Sheffield, Manchester and Manchester Airport, Cleethorpes - Barton-on-Humber

Sundays

8 January to 12 February

Network Diagram - see first Page of Table 18

		TP	XC	NT	NT	XC	TP	NT	XC	NT	NT	XC	TP	NT	TP	TP	NT	NT
		◇1	◇1			◇1			◇1			◇1				◇1		
			A		B	C			A	E		F				G	B	
							bus						bus		bus			
			trolley						trolley									
Hull	d	18 58		19 24						20 01	20 29					21 00		21 35
Hessle	d									20 08								
Ferriby	d									20 13								
Brough	d	19 10		19 36						20 18	20 41					21 12		21 47
Broomfleet	d																	
Gilberdyke	d									20 25								21 54
Eastrington	d																	
Howden	d			19 48							20 53							
Wressle	d																	
Selby	a	19 28		19 57							21 02					21 30		
	d	19 29		19 58							21 03							
York 8 33	a			20 25							21 30							
Saltmarshe	d																	
Goole	d									20 34								22 03
Thorne North	d									20 42								22 11
Cleethorpes	d						18 05						19 05		20 05			
New Clee	d																	
Grimsby Docks	d																	
Grimsby Town	a						18 25						19 25		20 25			
	d						18 25						19 25		20 25			
Great Coates	d																	
Healing	d																	
Stallingborough	d																	
Habrough	d																	
Ulceby	d																	
Thornton Abbey	d																	
Goxhill	d																	
New Holland	d																	
Barrow Haven	d																	
Barton-on-Humber	a																	
Barton-on-Humber	d																	
Hull Paragon Interchange	a																	
Barnetby	d						18 55						19 55		20 55			
Scunthorpe	a						19 20						20 20		21 20			
	d						19 20						20 20		21 20			
Althorpe	d																	
Crowle	d																	
Thorne South	d																	
Hatfield & Stainforth	d																	22 15
Kirk Sandall	d																	22 20
Adwick 31	d																	
Bentley (S.Yorks) 31	d																	
Doncaster 7 31	a						20 10			20 59			21 10		22 10			22 32
London Kings Cross 15 ⊖26	a																	
York 8 26	d		19 24			19 40			20 24			20 40		20 50				
Doncaster 7	d		19 50				20 10	20 14	20 50	21 01			21 10		22 10			22 40
Conisbrough	d							20 21		21 08								22 47
Mexborough	d							20 25		21 12								22 51
Swinton (S.Yorks)	d				20 09			20 29		21 15				21 45	22 30		22 32	22 53
Rotherham Central	d				20 17			20 41		21 22				21 52	22 50		22 40	22 58
Meadowhall ⇌	d				20 23		20 40	20 47		21 28			21 40	21 58	23 00		22 45	23 04
Sheffield 7 ⇌	a		20 16		20 34	20 51	21 00	20 55	21 17	21 38		21 50	22 00	22 09	23 20		22 54	23 15
	d																	
Stockport 78	a																	
Manchester Piccadilly 10 ⇌	a	20 54																
Manchester Airport 85 ✈	a																	

A From Newcastle to Birmingham New Street
B From Leeds
C From Edinburgh to Bristol Temple Meads
E From Scarborough
F From Glasgow Central to Birmingham New Street
G To Leeds

Table 29

Sundays

19 February to 25 March

Hull and Cleethorpes - Doncaster - Meadowhall, Sheffield, Manchester and Manchester Airport, Cleethorpes - Barton-on-Humber

Network Diagram - see first Page of Table 18

		TP	TP	TP	TP	TP	NT			NT		XC	NT	NT	NT	TP	NT	XC	HT	NT		TP	NT	XC	TP
		◇1	◇1	◇1	◇1	◇1						◇1				◇1		◇1	◇1			◇1		◇1	◇1
												B	C					D						E	
												⚯						⚯	☒					⚯	
Hull	d													08 40	08 54	09 00			09 30	09 33					
Hessle	d																			09 40					
Ferriby	d																			09 45					
Brough	d													08 52	09 06	09 12			09 42	09 50					
Broomfleet	d																								
Gilberdyke	d													08 59						09 57					
Eastrington	d																								
Howden	d														09 18				09 54						
Wressle	d																								
Selby	a														09 27	09 32			10 04						
	d														09 28	09 33			10 05						
York 8 33	a														09 52										
Saltmarshe	d																								
Goole	d													09 09			09 43			10 06					
Thorne North	d																09 51			10 14					
Cleethorpes	d																					09 26			10 26
New Clee	d																								
Grimsby Docks	d																								
Grimsby Town	a																					09 33			10 33
	d																					09 34			10 34
Great Coates	d																								
Healing	d																								
Stallingborough	d																								
Habrough	d																					09 44			10 44
Ulceby	d																								
Thornton Abbey	d																								
Goxhill	d																								
New Holland	d																								
Barrow Haven	d																								
Barton-on-Humber	a																								
Barton-on-Humber	d																								
Hull Paragon Interchange	a																								
Barnetby	d																					09 53			10 53
Scunthorpe	a																					10 08			11 08
	d																					10 08			11 08
Althorpe	d																								
Crowle	d																								
Thorne South	d																								
Hatfield & Stainforth	d																09 57			10 20					
Kirk Sandall	d																10 02			10 25					
Adwick 31	d																								
Bentley (S.Yorks) 31	d																								
Doncaster 7 31	a													09 29			10 11		10 23	10 35		10 40			11 38
London Kings Cross 15 ⊖26	a																		12 14						
York 8 26	d	02 29	03 44	04 58	05 55	06 55												09 28						10 28	
Doncaster 7	d						08 03			09 13		09 32		09 39			10 13	10 30				10 42	11 13	11 30	11 42
Conisbrough	d						08 10			09 20							10 20						11 20		
Mexborough	d						08 14			09 24							10 24						11 24		
Swinton (S.Yorks)	d						08 17			09 28			09 35				10 27						11 27		
Rotherham Central	d						08 25			09 35			09 48				10 35						11 35		
Meadowhall 🚋	d						08 30			09 41			09 54	10 00			10 40					11 00	11 40		12 00
Sheffield 7 🚋	a						08 41			09 51		09 55	10 03	10 08			10 52	10 54				11 07	11 51	11 53	12 07
	d																					11 10			12 10
Stockport 78	a																					11 53			12 50
Manchester Piccadilly 10 🚋	a	04 02	05 17	06 34	07 34	08 34										11 03						12 06			13 05
Manchester Airport 85 ✈	a	04 23	05 38	06 55	07 55	08 55																12 27			13 29

B From Leeds to Newton Abbot
C From Leeds
D To Newton Abbot
E From Newcastle to Newton Abbot

Table 29

Sundays

19 February to 25 March

Hull and Cleethorpes - Doncaster - Meadowhall, Sheffield, Manchester and Manchester Airport, Cleethorpes - Barton-on-Humber

Network Diagram - see first Page of Table 18

		NT	TP	NT	NT	XC		HT	TP	NT	NT	TP	NT	XC	NT	TP		TP	NT	TP	NT	XC	NT	NT
			◇■1			◇■1		◇■1	◇■1			◇■1		◇■1		◇■1		◇■1		◇■1		◇■1		
		A		B		C								C	D	E					B	C		D
						🛒		⊠						🛒								🛒		
Hull	d	10 50	10 58					11 30		11 46	11 53	12 00			12 46			12 58	13 29					13 35
Hessle	d																							13 42
Ferriby	d																							13 47
Brough	d	11 02	11 10					11 42		11 58	12 05	12 12			12 58			13 10	13 41					13 52
Broomfleet	d																							
Gilberdyke	d	11 09									12 12				13 05									14 00
Eastrington	d																							
Howden	d							11 54		12 10									13 53					
Wressle	d																							
Selby	a		11 28					12 04		12 19		12 32						13 28	14 02					
	d		11 29					12 05		12 20		12 32						13 29	14 03					
York ■8 33	a									12 44									14 30					
Saltmarshe	d																							
Goole	d	11 18			11 43						12 21				13 14								13 43	14 08
Thorne North	d	11 26			11 51						12 29												13 51	
Cleethorpes	d								11 26															
New Clee	d																							
Grimsby Docks	d																							
Grimsby Town	a								11 33															
	d								11 34															
Great Coates	d																							
Healing	d																							
Stallingborough	d																							
Habrough	d																							
Ulceby	d																							
Thornton Abbey	d																							
Goxhill	d																							
New Holland	d																							
Barrow Haven	d																							
Barton-on-Humber	a																							
Barton-on-Humber	d																							
Hull Paragon Interchange	a																							
Barnetby	d								11 53															
Scunthorpe	a								12 08															
	d								12 08															
Althorpe	d																							
Crowle	d																							
Thorne South	d																							
Hatfield & Stainforth	d				11 57																		13 57	
Kirk Sandall	d				12 02																		14 02	
Adwick 31	d																							
Bentley (S.Yorks) 31	d																							
Doncaster ■7 31	a	11 46			12 11			12 25	12 40		12 47				13 37								14 11	14 31
London Kings Cross ■15 ⊖26	a							14 14																
York ■8 26	d					11 28								12 28		13 15						13 40		
Doncaster ■7	d	11 48			12 13	12 30			12 42				13 13	13 30	13 38					13 42			14 13	14 33
Conisbrough	d				12 20								13 20										14 20	
Mexborough	d				12 24								13 24										14 24	
Swinton (S.Yorks)	d			12 05	12 27								13 27								14 06		14 30	
Rotherham Central	d			12 13	12 38								13 36								14 14		14 42	
Meadowhall 🚊	d	12 08		12 21	12 43				13 00				13 44		13 56					14 00	14 21		14 48	14 52
Sheffield ■7 🚊	a	12 18		12 32	12 55	12 54			13 07				13 52	13 54	14 06					14 07	14 32	14 52	14 55	15 03
	d								13 10											14 11				
Stockport 78	a								13 53											14 53				
Manchester Piccadilly ■10 🚊	a		12 54						14 06			13 54				14 34		14 54		15 06				
Manchester Airport 85 ✈	a								14 27							14 55				15 28				

A From Bridlington
B From Leeds
C From Edinburgh to Newton Abbot
D From Scarborough

Table 29

Sundays

19 February to 25 March

Hull and Cleethorpes - Doncaster - Meadowhall, Sheffield, Manchester and Manchester Airport, Cleethorpes - Barton-on-Humber

Network Diagram - see first Page of Table 18

	NT			TP	HT	XC	XC	NT	NT	TP	TP		XC	NT	XC	NT	NT	NT		TP	XC		HT	
				◇1	◇1	◇1	◇1			◇1	◇1		◇1		◇1					◇1	◇1		◇1	
						A	B		C				A	D	B		E				G			
					⊠	🍴	🍴						🍴		🍴						🍴		⊠	
Hull d	14 23				14 30				14 41	14 58							15 41	16 00					16 30	
Hessle d																								
Ferriby d																								
Brough d	14 35				14 42				14 53	15 10							15 53	16 12					16 42	
Broomfleet d																								
Gilberdyke d									15 00								16 00							
Eastrington d																								
Howden d	14 47				14 54													16 24					16 54	
Wressle d																								
Selby a	14 56				15 04					15 28								16 33					17 04	
d	14 57				15 05					15 29								16 34					17 05	
York 8 33 a	15 25																	16 59						
Saltmarshe d																								
Goole d									15 09							15 43	16 09							
Thorne North d																15 51								
Cleethorpes d				13 26							14 26									15 26				
New Clee d																								
Grimsby Docks d																								
Grimsby Town a				13 33							14 33									15 33				
d				13 34							14 34									15 34				
Great Coates d																								
Healing d																								
Stallingborough d																								
Habrough d											14 44													
Ulceby d																								
Thornton Abbey d																								
Goxhill d																								
New Holland d																								
Barrow Haven d																								
Barton-on-Humber a																								
Barton-on-Humber d																								
Hull Paragon Interchange a																								
Barnetby d				13 53							14 53									15 53				
Scunthorpe a				14 08							15 08									16 08				
d				14 08							15 08									16 08				
Althorpe d																								
Crowle d																								
Thorne South d																								
Hatfield & Stainforth d																15 57								
Kirk Sandall d																16 02								
Adwick 31 d																								
Bentley (S.Yorks) 31 d																								
Doncaster 7 31 a				14 37	15 25				15 32		15 39					16 11	16 32			16 39			17 25	
London Kings Cross 15 ⊖26 a					17 15																		19 18	
York 8 26 d						14 34	14 40						15 34		15 40						16 23			
Doncaster 7 d				14 42		14 59		15 13	15 33		15 42		15 59			16 13	16 33			16 42	16 51			
Conisbrough d								15 20								16 20								
Mexborough d								15 24								16 24								
Swinton (S.Yorks) d								15 30						16 05		16 29								
Rotherham Central d								15 41						16 13		16 41								
Meadowhall 🚋 d				15 00				15 48	15 52		16 00			16 19		16 47	16 53			17 00				
Sheffield 7 🚋 a				15 07		15 21	15 51	15 55	16 01		16 07		16 21	16 31	16 51	16 55	17 04			17 07	17 19			
d				15 11							16 11									17 11				
Stockport 78 a				15 53							16 53									17 53				
Manchester Piccadilly 10 🚋 a				16 06						16 54	17 06									18 06				
Manchester Airport 85 ✈ a				16 34							17 27									18 27				

A From Newcastle to Reading
B From Glasgow Central to Exeter St Davids
C From Bridlington
D From Leeds
E From Scarborough
G From Edinburgh to Reading

Table 29

Sundays

19 February to 25 March

Hull and Cleethorpes - Doncaster - Meadowhall, Sheffield, Manchester and Manchester Airport, Cleethorpes - Barton-on-Humber

Network Diagram - see first Page of Table 18

		XC	NT	NT	TP	TP	NT	XC		NT	NT	EM	XC	NT	NT	TP	HT	XC		NT		XC	NT	NT	TP
		◇1			◇1	◇1		◇1				◇1	◇1			◇1	◇1	◇1				◇1			◇1
		A		B				C			D	E	F		G			H				I		B	
Hull	d			16 41	16 58		17 23								17 41		18 30							18 38	18 58
Hessle	d																								
Ferriby	d																								
Brough	d			16 53	17 10		17 35								17 53		18 42							18 50	19 10
Broomfleet	d																								
Gilberdyke	d			17 00											18 00									18 57	
Eastrington	d																								
Howden	d						17 47										18 54								
Wressle	d																								
Selby	a				17 28		17 56										19 04								19 28
	d				17 29		17 57										19 05								19 29
York 8 33	a						18 25																		
Saltmarshe	d																								
Goole	d			17 09						17 42					18 09									19 06	
Thorne North	d									17 50														19 14	
Cleethorpes	d					16 26										17 26									
New Clee	d																								
Grimsby Docks	d																								
Grimsby Town	a					16 33										17 33									
	d					16 34										17 34									
Great Coates	d																								
Healing	d																								
Stallingborough	d																								
Habrough	d															17 44									
Ulceby	d																								
Thornton Abbey	d																								
Goxhill	d																								
New Holland	d																								
Barrow Haven	d																								
Barton-on-Humber	a																								
Barton-on-Humber	d																								
Hull Paragon Interchange	a																								
Barnetby	d					16 53										17 53									
Scunthorpe	a					17 08										18 08									
	d					17 08										18 08									
Althorpe	d																								
Crowle	d																								
Thorne South	d																								
Hatfield & Stainforth	d									17 56														19 20	
Kirk Sandall	d									18 01														19 25	
Adwick 31	d																								
Bentley (S.Yorks) 31	d																								
Doncaster 7 31	a			17 31		17 38				18 09					18 33	18 38	19 25							19 35	
London Kings Cross 15 ⊖26	a																21 18								
York 8 26	d	16 40						17 34				17 40	17 40					18 34		18 10		18 40			
Doncaster 7	d		17 13	17 32		17 42		17 59				18 08		18 19	18 34	18 42		18 59					19 18	19 37	
Conisbrough	d		17 21											18 26									19 25		
Mexborough	d		17 25											18 30									19 29		
Swinton (S.Yorks)	d		17 30								18 10			18 33						19 01			19 33		
Rotherham Central	d		17 41								18 19			18 42						19 13			19 41		
Meadowhall	d		17 48	17 53		18 00					18 25			18 47	18 53	19 00				19 18			19 47	19 57	
Sheffield 7	a	17 51	17 55	18 01		18 07		18 23			18 36	18 39	18 51	18 57	19 03	19 07		19 21		19 27		19 50	19 55	20 06	
	d					18 11										19 11									
Stockport 78	a					18 53										19 53									
Manchester Piccadilly 10	a				18 54	19 06										20 09									20 54
Manchester Airport 85	a					19 27										20 30									

A From Aberdeen to Exeter St Davids
B From Bridlington
C From Newcastle to Reading
D From Leeds
E To St Pancras International
F From Glasgow Central to Exeter St Davids
G From Scarborough
H From Newcastle to Guildford
I From Glasgow Central to Bristol Temple Meads

Table 29

Sundays

19 February to 25 March

Hull and Cleethorpes - Doncaster - Meadowhall, Sheffield, Manchester and Manchester Airport, Cleethorpes - Barton-on-Humber

Network Diagram - see first Page of Table 18

		TP	XC	NT	NT	XC	NT	TP	XC	NT	NT	XC	NT	TP	TP	NT	NT
		◇1	◇1			◇1		◇1	◇1			◇1		◇1	◇1		
			A		B	C			A	E		F			G	B	
Hull	d			19 24						20 01	20 29				21 00		21 35
Hessle	d									20 08							
Ferriby	d									20 13							
Brough	d			19 36						20 18	20 41				21 12		21 47
Broomfleet	d																
Gilberdyke	d									20 25							21 54
Eastrington	d																
Howden	d			19 48							20 53						
Wressle	d																
Selby	a			19 57							21 02				21 30		
	d			19 58							21 03						
York 8 33	a			20 25							21 30						
Saltmarshe	d																
Goole	d									20 34							22 03
Thorne North	d									20 42							22 11
Cleethorpes	d	18 26						19 26						20 26			
New Clee	d																
Grimsby Docks	d																
Grimsby Town	a	18 33						19 33						20 33			
	d	18 34						19 34						20 34			
Great Coates	d																
Healing	d																
Stallingborough	d																
Habrough	d													20 44			
Ulceby	d																
Thornton Abbey	d																
Goxhill	d																
New Holland	d																
Barrow Haven	d																
Barton-on-Humber	a																
Barton-on-Humber	d																
Hull Paragon Interchange	a																
Barnetby	d	18 53						19 53						20 53			
Scunthorpe	a	19 08						20 08						21 08			
	d	19 08						20 08						21 08			
Althorpe	d																
Crowle	d																
Thorne South	d																
Hatfield & Stainforth	d																22 15
Kirk Sandall	d																22 20
Adwick 31	d																
Bentley (S.Yorks) 31	d																
Doncaster 7 31	a	19 38						20 40		20 59				21 40			22 32
London Kings Cross 15 26	a																
York 8 26	d		19 24			19 40			20 24			20 40	20 50				
Doncaster 7	d	19 42	19 50				20 14	20 42	20 50	21 01				21 42			22 40
Conisbrough	d						20 21			21 08							22 47
Mexborough	d						20 25			21 12							22 51
Swinton (S.Yorks)	d				20 09		20 29			21 15			21 45	21 52		22 32	22 53
Rotherham Central	d				20 17		20 41			21 22			21 52	21 58		22 40	22 58
Meadowhall	d	20 00			20 23		20 47	21 00		21 28			21 58	22 04		22 45	23 04
Sheffield 7	a	20 07	20 16		20 34	20 51	20 55	21 07	21 17	21 38		21 50	22 09	22 13		22 54	23 15
	d	20 11						21 11									
Stockport 78	a	20 53						21 53									
Manchester Piccadilly 10	a	21 06						22 06									
Manchester Airport 85	a	21 27						22 27									

A From Newcastle to Birmingham New Street
B From Leeds
C From Edinburgh to Bristol Temple Meads
E From Scarborough
F From Glasgow Central to Birmingham New Street
G To Leeds

Table 29

Sundays

from 1 April

Hull and Cleethorpes - Doncaster - Meadowhall, Sheffield, Manchester and Manchester Airport, Cleethorpes - Barton-on-Humber

Network Diagram - see first Page of Table 18

	TP	TP	TP	TP	NT	TP	NT	XC	NT	NT	NT	TP	NT	XC	HT	NT	TP	NT	XC	TP	NT	TP
						◇1		◇1				◇1		◇1	◇1		◇1		◇1	◇1		◇1
								A	B			C		D					E		F	G
Hull d										08 40	08 54	09 00			09 30	09 33					10 50	10 58
Hessle d																09 40						
Ferriby d																09 45						
Brough d										08 52	09 06	09 12			09 42	09 50					11 02	11 10
Broomfleet d																						
Gilberdyke d										08 59						09 57					11 09	
Eastrington d																						
Howden d											09 18				09 54							
Wressle d																						
Selby a											09 27	09 32			10 04							11 28
d											09 28				10 05							
York 8 33 a											09 52											
Saltmarshe d																						
Goole d										09 09			09 43			10 06					11 18	
Thorne North d													09 51			10 14					11 26	
Cleethorpes d																	09 26			10 26		
New Clee d																						
Grimsby Docks d																						
Grimsby Town a																	09 33			10 33		
d																	09 34			10 34		
Great Coates d																						
Healing d																						
Stallingborough d																						
Habrough d																	09 44			10 44		
Ulceby d																						
Thornton Abbey d																						
Goxhill d																						
New Holland d																						
Barrow Haven d																						
Barton-on-Humber a																						
Barton-on-Humber d																						
Hull Paragon Interchange a																						
Barnetby d																	09 53			10 53		
Scunthorpe a																	10 08			11 08		
d																	10 08			11 08		
Althorpe d																						
Crowle d																						
Thorne South d																						
Hatfield & Stainforth d													09 57			10 20						
Kirk Sandall d													10 02			10 25						
Adwick 31 d																						
Bentley (S.Yorks) 31 d																						
Doncaster 7 31 a										09 29			10 11		10 23	10 35	10 40			11 38	11 46	
London Kings Cross 15 ⊖26 a															12 14							
York 8 26 d	01 30	03 30	04 55	05 55		08 30								09 28					10 28			
Doncaster 7 d					08 03		09 13	09 32		09 39			10 13	10 30			10 42	11 13	11 30	11 42	11 48	
Conisbrough d					08 10		09 20						10 20					11 20				
Mexborough d					08 14		09 24						10 24					11 24				
Swinton (S.Yorks) d					08 17		09 28		09 35				10 27					11 27				
Rotherham Central d					08 25		09 35		09 48				10 35					11 35				
Meadowhall d					08 30		09 41		09 54	10 00			10 40				11 00	11 40		12 00	12 08	
Sheffield 7 a					08 41		09 51	09 55	10 03	10 08			10 52	10 54			11 07	11 51	11 53	12 07	12 18	
d																	11 10			12 10		
Stockport 78 a																	11 53			12 53		
Manchester Piccadilly 10 a	03 55	05 55	07 40	08 40		10 33											12 06			13 06		
Manchester Airport 85 a	04 20	06 20	08 05	09 05		10 55											12 27			13 27		

A From Leeds to Plymouth
B From Leeds
C To Leeds
D To Plymouth
E From Newcastle to Plymouth
F From Bridlington
G To Huddersfield

Table 29

Sundays
from 1 April

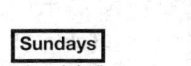

Hull and Cleethorpes - Doncaster - Meadowhall, Sheffield, Manchester and Manchester Airport, Cleethorpes - Barton-on-Humber

Network Diagram - see first Page of Table 18

	NT	NT	XC	HT	TP	NT	NT	TP	NT	XC	NT	TP	TP	NT	TP	NT	XC	NT	NT	TP	TP	NT
			◇1	◇1	◇1			◇1		◇1		◇1	◇1		◇1		◇1			◇1	◇1	
	A		B					C		D	E	C	F			A	B		E	F		
			⚲	⊠						⚲							⚲					
Hull d				11 30		11 46	11 53	12 00			12 46	12 58		13 29					13 35			14 23
Hessle d																			13 42			
Ferriby d																			13 47			
Brough d				11 42		11 58	12 05	12 12			12 58	13 10		13 41					13 52			14 35
Broomfleet d																						
Gilberdyke d							12 12				13 05								14 00			
Eastrington d																						
Howden d				11 54		12 10								13 53								14 47
Wressle d																						
Selby a				12 04		12 19		12 32				13 28		14 02								14 56
d				12 05		12 20								14 03								14 57
York 8 33 a						12 44								14 30								15 25
Saltmarshe d																						
Goole d		11 43					12 21				13 14							13 43	14 08			
Thorne North d		11 51					12 29											13 51				
Cleethorpes d					11 26																13 26	
New Clee d																						
Grimsby Docks d																						
Grimsby Town a					11 33																13 33	
d					11 34																13 34	
Great Coates d																						
Healing d																						
Stallingborough d																						
Habrough d																						
Ulceby d																						
Thornton Abbey d																						
Goxhill d																						
New Holland d																						
Barrow Haven d																						
Barton-on-Humber a																						
Barton-on-Humber d																						
Hull Paragon Interchange a																						
Barnetby d					11 53																13 53	
Scunthorpe a					12 08																14 08	
d					12 08																14 08	
Althorpe d																						
Crowle d																						
Thorne South d																						
Hatfield & Stainforth d		11 57																13 57				
Kirk Sandall d		12 02																14 02				
Adwick 31 d																						
Bentley (S.Yorks) 31 d																						
Doncaster 7 31 a		12 11		12 25	12 40		12 47				13 37							14 11	14 31		14 37	
London Kings Cross 15 ⊖26 a				14 14																		
York 8 26 d			11 28							12 28			13 15				13 40			14 15		
Doncaster 7 d		12 13	12 30		12 42				13 13	13 30	13 38				13 42			14 13	14 33		14 42	
Conisbrough d		12 20							13 20									14 20				
Mexborough d		12 24							13 24									14 24				
Swinton (S.Yorks) d	12 05	12 27							13 27							14 06		14 30				
Rotherham Central d	12 13	12 38							13 36							14 14		14 42				
Meadowhall ⇌ d	12 21	12 43			13 00				13 44		13 56				14 00	14 21		14 48	14 52		15 00	
Sheffield 7 ⇌ a	12 32	12 55	12 54		13 07				13 52	13 54	14 06				14 07	14 32	14 52	14 55	15 03		15 07	
d					13 10										14 11						15 11	
Stockport 78 a					13 53										14 53						15 53	
Manchester Piccadilly 10 ⇌ a					14 06								15 08		15 06					16 08	16 06	
Manchester Airport 85 ✈ a					14 27								15 24		15 28					16 24	16 34	

A From Leeds
B From Edinburgh to Plymouth
C To Huddersfield
D From Edinburgh to Penzance
E From Scarborough
F From Newcastle

Table 29

Sundays
from 1 April

Hull and Cleethorpes - Doncaster - Meadowhall, Sheffield, Manchester and Manchester Airport, Cleethorpes - Barton-on-Humber

Network Diagram - see first Page of Table 18

	HT		XC	XC	NT	NT	TP	TP	XC	NT	XC		NT	NT	NT	TP	TP	XC	HT	XC	NT		NT	TP
	◇1		◇1	◇1			◇1	◇1	◇1		◇1					◇1	◇1	◇1	◇1	◇1				◇1
			A	B		C		D	A	E	F			G		H		I		J			C	
	⊠		⊥	⊥					⊥		⊥							⊥	⊠	⊥				
Hull d	14 30					14 41		14 58						15 41	16 00				16 30				16 41	
Hessle d																								
Ferriby d																								
Brough d	14 42					14 53		15 10						15 53	16 12				16 42				16 53	
Broomfleet d																								
Gilberdyke d						15 00								16 00									17 00	
Eastrington d																								
Howden d	14 54														16 24				16 54					
Wressle d																								
Selby a	15 04							15 28							16 33				17 04					
d	15 05														16 34				17 05					
York 8 33 a															16 59									
Saltmarshe d																								
Goole d						15 09							15 43	16 09									17 09	
Thorne North d													15 51											
Cleethorpes d							14 26										15 26							16 26
New Clee d																								
Grimsby Docks d																								
Grimsby Town a							14 33										15 33							16 33
d							14 34										15 34							16 34
Great Coates d																								
Healing d																								
Stallingborough d																								
Habrough d							14 44																	
Ulceby d																								
Thornton Abbey d																								
Goxhill d																								
New Holland d																								
Barrow Haven d																								
Barton-on-Humber a																								
Barton-on-Humber d																								
Hull Paragon Interchange a																								
Barnetby d							14 53										15 53							16 53
Scunthorpe a							15 08										16 08							17 08
d							15 08										16 08							17 08
Althorpe d																								
Crowle d																								
Thorne South d																								
Hatfield & Stainforth d													15 57											
Kirk Sandall d													16 02											
Adwick 31 d																								
Bentley (S.Yorks) 31 d																								
Doncaster 7 31 a	15 25					15 32	15 39						16 11	16 32			16 39		17 25				17 31	17 38
London Kings Cross 15 ⊖26 a	17 15																		19 18					
York 8 26 d			14 34	14 40					15 34		15 40					16 15		16 23		16 40				
Doncaster 7 d			14 59		15 13	15 33	15 42		15 59				16 13	16 33			16 42	16 51			17 13		17 32	17 42
Conisbrough d					15 20								16 20								17 21			
Mexborough d					15 24								16 24								17 25			
Swinton (S.Yorks) d					15 30					16 05			16 29								17 30			
Rotherham Central d					15 41					16 13			16 41								17 41			
Meadowhall ⇌ d					15 48	15 52	16 00			16 19			16 47	16 53			17 00				17 48		17 53	18 00
Sheffield 7 ⇌ a			15 21	15 51	15 55	16 01	16 07		16 21	16 31	16 51		16 55	17 04			17 07	17 19		17 51	17 55		18 01	18 08
d							16 11										17 11							18 11
Stockport 78 a							16 53										17 53							18 53
Manchester Piccadilly 10 ⇌ a							17 06									18 08	18 06							19 06
Manchester Airport 85 ✈ a							17 27									18 24	18 27							19 27

A From Newcastle to Reading
B From Glasgow Central to Penzance
C From Bridlington
D To Huddersfield
E From Leeds
F From Glasgow Central to Plymouth
G From Scarborough
H From Newcastle
I From Edinburgh to Reading
J From Aberdeen to Plymouth

Table 29

Sundays
from 1 April

Hull and Cleethorpes - Doncaster - Meadowhall, Sheffield, Manchester and Manchester Airport, Cleethorpes - Barton-on-Humber

Network Diagram - see first Page of Table 18

Station		TP ◇1 A	NT	XC ◇1 B	EM ◇1 C	NT	NT D	XC ◇1 E		NT	NT F	TP ◇1	HT ◇1	XC ◇1 G	NT	XC ◇1 H	NT	NT I		TP ◇1	TP ◇1 A	XC ◇1 J	NT	NT D	XC ◇1 K
Hull	d	16 58	17 23								17 41		18 30					18 38			18 58		19 24		
Hessle	d																								
Ferriby	d																								
Brough	d	17 10	17 35								17 53		18 42					18 50			19 10		19 36		
Broomfleet	d																								
Gilberdyke	d										18 00							18 57							
Eastrington	d																								
Howden	d		17 47										18 54										19 48		
Wressle	d																								
Selby	a	17 28	17 56										19 04								19 28		19 57		
	d		17 57										19 05										19 58		
York 8 33	a		18 25																				20 25		
Saltmarshe	d																								
Goole	d					17 42					18 09							19 06							
Thorne North	d					17 50												19 14							
Cleethorpes	d											17 26								18 26					
New Clee	d																								
Grimsby Docks	d																								
Grimsby Town	a											17 33								18 33					
	d											17 34								18 34					
Great Coates	d																								
Healing	d																								
Stallingborough	d																								
Habrough	d											17 44													
Ulceby	d																								
Thornton Abbey	d																								
Goxhill	d																								
New Holland	d																								
Barrow Haven	d																								
Barton-on-Humber	a																								
Barton-on-Humber	d																								
Hull Paragon Interchange	a																								
Barnetby	d											17 53								18 53					
Scunthorpe	a											18 08								19 08					
	d											18 08								19 08					
Althorpe	d																								
Crowle	d																								
Thorne South	d																								
Hatfield & Stainforth	d					17 56												19 20							
Kirk Sandall	d					18 01												19 25							
Adwick 31	d																								
Bentley (S.Yorks) 31	d																								
Doncaster 7 31	a					18 09					18 33	18 38	19 25					19 35		19 38					
London Kings Cross 15 ⊖26	a												21 18												
York 8 26	d			17 34	17 40			17 40						18 34	18 10	18 40						19 24			19 40
Doncaster 7	d			17 59	18 06					18 19	18 34	18 42		18 59			19 18	19 37		19 42		19 50			
Conisbrough	d									18 26							19 25								
Mexborough	d									18 30							19 29								
Swinton (S.Yorks)	d						18 10			18 33					19 01		19 33							20 09	
Rotherham Central	d						18 19			18 42					19 13		19 41							20 17	
Meadowhall	d						18 25			18 47	18 53	19 00			19 18		19 47	19 57		20 00				20 23	
Sheffield 7	a			18 23	18 28		18 36	18 51		18 57	19 03	19 07		19 21	19 27	19 50	19 55	20 06		20 07		20 16		20 34	20 51
	d											19 11								20 11					
Stockport 78	a											19 53								20 53					
Manchester Piccadilly 10	a											20 09								21 06					
Manchester Airport 85	a											20 30								21 27					

A To Huddersfield
B From Newcastle to Reading
C To St Pancras International
D From Leeds
E From Glasgow Central to Plymouth
F From Scarborough
G From Newcastle to Guildford
H From Glasgow Central to Bristol Temple Meads
I From Bridlington
J From Newcastle to Birmingham New Street
K From Edinburgh to Bristol Temple Meads

Table 29

Sundays
from 1 April

Hull and Cleethorpes - Doncaster - Meadowhall, Sheffield, Manchester and Manchester Airport, Cleethorpes - Barton-on-Humber

Network Diagram - see first Page of Table 18

		NT	TP			XC	NT	NT	XC	NT	TP	TP	NT	NT
			◇1			◇1			◇1		◇1	◇1		
						B	C		D			E	F	
						⚲								
Hull	d						20 01	20 29				21 00		21 35
Hessle	d						20 08							
Ferriby	d						20 13							
Brough	d						20 18	20 41				21 12		21 47
Broomfleet	d													
Gilberdyke	d						20 25							21 54
Eastrington	d													
Howden	d							20 53						
Wressle	d													
Selby	a							21 02				21 30		
	d							21 03						
York 8 33	a							21 30						
Saltmarshe	d													
Goole	d						20 34							22 03
Thorne North	d						20 42							22 11
Cleethorpes	d		19 26								20 26			
New Clee	d													
Grimsby Docks	d													
Grimsby Town	a		19 33								20 33			
	d		19 34								20 34			
Great Coates	d													
Healing	d													
Stallingborough	d													
Habrough	d										20 44			
Ulceby	d													
Thornton Abbey	d													
Goxhill	d													
New Holland	d													
Barrow Haven	d													
Barton-on-Humber	a													
Barton-on-Humber	d													
Hull Paragon Interchange	a													
Barnetby	d		19 53								20 53			
Scunthorpe	a		20 08								21 08			
	d		20 08								21 08			
Althorpe	d													
Crowle	d													
Thorne South	d													
Hatfield & Stainforth	d													22 15
Kirk Sandall	d													22 20
Adwick 31	d													
Bentley (S.Yorks) 31	d													
Doncaster 7 31	a		20 40				20 59				21 40			22 32
London Kings Cross 15 ⊖26	a													
York 8 26	d					20 24			20 40	20 50				
Doncaster 7	d	20 14	20 42			20 50	21 01				21 42			22 40
Conisbrough	d	20 21					21 08							22 47
Mexborough	d	20 25					21 12							22 51
Swinton (S.Yorks)	d	20 29					21 15			21 45	21 52		22 32	22 53
Rotherham Central	d	20 41					21 22			21 52	21 58		22 40	22 58
Meadowhall 🚊	d	20 47	21 00				21 28			21 58	22 04		22 45	23 04
Sheffield 7 🚊	a	20 55	21 07			21 17	21 38		21 50	22 09	22 13		22 54	23 15
	d		21 11											
Stockport 78	a		21 53											
Manchester Piccadilly 10 🚊	a		22 06											
Manchester Airport 85 ✈	a		22 27											

B From Newcastle to Birmingham New Street
C From Scarborough
D From Glasgow Central to Birmingham New Street
E To Leeds
F From Leeds

Manchester Airport, Manchester, Sheffield and Meadowhall-Doncaster-Cleethorpes and Hull Barton-on-Humber - Cleethorpes

Network Diagram - see first Page of Table 18

Miles	Miles	Miles	Miles	Miles			TP MX ◇1	TP MO ◇1 A			NT MX	NT MO	NT C	NT MO D	NT E	GR 1 F		NT C	EM G	NT	NT	NT C	XC ◇1 H	NT	NT
0	—	—	—	—	**Manchester Airport** 85	d	20p47																		
9¾	—	—	—	—	**Manchester Piccadilly** 10	d	21b20																		
15¾	—	—	—	—	Stockport 78	d	21p28																		
52½	—	—	—	—	**Sheffield** 7	a	22p08																		
—	—	—	—	—		d	22p11	22p30			23p27	23p34	05 22		05 29						06 18	06 28	06 33		
56	—	—	—	—	**Meadowhall**	d	22p16	22p35			23p33	23p40	05 28		05 35						06 24	06 34			
58¾	—	—	—	—	Rotherham Central	d					23p39	23p47	05 34		05 41						06 30	06 40			
63¼	—	—	—	—	Swinton (S.Yorks)	d					23p48	23p55	05a42		05 49						06 38	06a51			
64½	—	—	—	—	Mexborough	d					23p51	23p58			05 52						06 41				
66¾	—	—	—	—	Conisbrough	d					23p55	00 02			05 56						06 45				
—	—	—	—	—	London Kings Cross	d																			
71½	—	—	—	—	**Doncaster** 7	a	22p42	22p56			00 07	00 13			06 06						06 56		06 57		
—	—	—	—	—	York 8 26	a																	07 26		
—	0	0	—	0	**Doncaster** 31	d	22p44	22p58						05 52	06 12	06 15		06 26		06 39	06 59				
—	—	—	—	1¾	Bentley (S.Yorks) 31	a												06 29			07 02				
—	—	—	—	4	Adwick 31	a												06 33			07 08				
75½	—	4	—	—	Kirk Sandall	d	22p49								06 18					06 45					
78¼	—	6¾	—	—	Hatfield & Stainforth	d	22p54								06 23					06 50					
—	—	9¾	—	—	Thorne South	d	22p58													06 55					
—	—	15¾	—	—	Crowle	d	23p07													07 04					
—	—	19½	—	—	Althorpe	d	23p12													07 10					
—	—	23	—	—	**Scunthorpe**	a	23p17	23p23												07 18					
—	—	—	—	—		d	23p18	23p24																	
—	—	34½	—	—	Barnetby	d	23p32	23p38											06 31						
—	—	—	—	—	Hull Paragon Interchange	d																		06 20	
—	—	—	—	—	Barton-on-Humber	a																		06 52	
—	—	—	0	—	**Barton-on-Humber**	d																			06 58
—	—	—	2	—	Barrow Haven	d																			07 03
—	—	—	3½	—	New Holland	d																			07 07
—	—	—	5½	—	Goxhill	d																			07 11
—	—	—	7	—	Thornton Abbey	d																			
—	—	—	9¾	—	Ulceby	d																			07 19
—	—	40¾	11½	—	Habrough	d	23p42												06 41						07 23
—	—	44½	15¼	—	Stallingborough	d																			07 28
—	—	45½	16¼	—	Healing	d																			07 31
—	—	46½	17¼	—	Great Coates	d																			
—	—	48¾	19½	—	**Grimsby Town**	a	23p55	23p57											06 56						07 38
—	—	—	—	—		d	23p56	23p58																	07 39
—	—	49¾	20½	—	Grimsby Docks	d																			
—	—	50½	21¼	—	New Clee	d																			
—	—	52	22¾	—	**Cleethorpes**	a	00 09	00 09																	07 51
81¼	—	—	—	—	Thorne North	d									06 28										
88¾	—	—	—	—	Goole	d									06 37										
92¼	—	—	—	—	Saltmarshe	d									06 42										
—	—	—	—	—	York 8 33	d										06a36									
—	18¾	—	—	—	**Selby**	a								06 14											
—	24½	—	—	—	Wressle	d																			
—	27	—	—	—	Howden	d																			
—	30	—	—	—	Eastrington	d																			
95½	32¼	—	—	—	Gilberdyke	d									06 51										
98	34¾	—	—	—	Broomfleet	d									06 55										
102	38¾	—	—	—	Brough	d									07 01										
105	41¾	—	—	—	Ferriby	d									07 05										
107¾	44½	—	—	—	Hessle	d									07 10										
112	49¾	—	—	—	**Hull**	a									07 21										

A until 2 January and from 20 February
C To Leeds
D until 26 March and from 2 April
E To Beverley
F To Edinburgh
G From Lincoln
H From Derby to Newcastle
b Previous night, arr. 2113

Table 29

Mondays to Fridays

Manchester Airport, Manchester, Sheffield and Meadowhall-Doncaster-Cleethorpes and Hull Barton-on-Humber - Cleethorpes

Network Diagram - see first Page of Table 18

Station		NT	NT	NT	TP	XC	NT	NT	NT	TP	NT	NT	NT	NT	NT	NT	NT	XC	NT	EM	TP
			A		◇1	◇1 B	A	A	C	◇1	D		A			F	G	◇1 H	A	I	◇1
Manchester Airport 85	d				05 15																06 55
Manchester Piccadilly 10	d				05 44					06 21											07 20
Stockport 78	d				05 52																07 28
Sheffield 7	a				06 49																08 10
	d			06 52	06 55	07 12	07 14							07 24			07 41	07 54			08 11
Meadowhall	d			06 58	07 01		07 21							07 30			07 47				08 16
Rotherham Central	d			07 04			07 27							07 36			07 55				
Swinton (S.Yorks)	d			07 14			07a35							07 44			08 03				
Mexborough	d			07 17										07 47			08 06				
Conisbrough	d			07 21										07 51			08 10				
London Kings Cross	d																				
Doncaster 7	a			07 32	07 22									08 01			08 19	08 24			08 38
York 8 26	a					08 22												08 45			
Doncaster 31	d		07 08	07 34	07 24			07 26			07 28		07 56	08 03		08 16	08 21		08 26		08 41
Bentley (S.Yorks) 31	a		07 11	07 37				07 29					07 59			08 18			08 29		
Adwick 31	a		07 15	07 43				07 33					08 03			08 24			08 33		
Kirk Sandall	d										07 34			08 09							
Hatfield & Stainforth	d										07 39			08 14							
Thorne South	d													08 18							
Crowle	d													08 27							
Althorpe	d													08 33							
Scunthorpe	a				07 49									08 44							09 06
	d				07 50																09 07
Barnetby	d				08 04															08 49	09 21
Hull Paragon Interchange	d	06 55																			
Barton-on-Humber	a	07 30																			
Barton-on-Humber	d														07 58						
Barrow Haven	d														08 03						
New Holland	d														08 06						
Goxhill	d														08 11						
Thornton Abbey	d														08 14						
Ulceby	d														08 18						
Habrough	d				08 12										08 23					09 01	09 29
Stallingborough	d														08 28						
Healing	d														08 31						
Great Coates	d														08 34						
Grimsby Town	a				08 26										08 39					09 15	09 43
	d				08 33										08 39						09 44
Grimsby Docks	d														08 42						
New Clee	d														08x44						
Cleethorpes	a				08 44										08 49						09 55
Thorne North	d										07 44										
Goole	d										07 53						08 43				
Saltmarshe	d										07 58										
York 8 33	d											07 29									
Selby	a									07 43		07 50									
Wressle	d											07 58									
Howden	d									07 52		08 03									
Eastrington	d											08 08									
Gilberdyke	d								07 39		08 04	08 12									
Broomfleet	d								07 43			08 16									
Brough	d								07 49	08 04	08 12	08 22					08 57				
Ferriby	d								07 53		08 16	08 27									
Hessle	d								07 58		08 21	08 31									
Hull	a								08 11	08 20	08 34	08 46					09 13				

A To Leeds
B From Birmingham New Street to Glasgow Central
C To Scarborough
D To Beverley
F From Scunthorpe
G To Bridlington
H From Birmingham New Street to Newcastle
I From Newark North Gate

Manchester Airport, Manchester, Sheffield and Meadowhall-Doncaster-Cleethorpes and Hull Barton-on-Humber - Cleethorpes

Network Diagram - see first Page of Table 18

		TP	NT	XC	GR	NT	NT	NT	HT	NT	NT	XC	NT	NT	NT	NT	TP	TP	NT	XC	NT	NT
		◇1		◇1	R 1				◇1			◇1					◇1	◇1		◇1		
			A	B	C	D					F	G	A	H					A	I		
		🛒		🛒	🍴🛒				⊠			🛒			🚌		🛒	🛒		🛒		
Manchester Airport 85 ✈	d																07 53					
Manchester Piccadilly 10 🚊	d	07 36															08 20	08 42				
Stockport 78	d																08 28					
Sheffield 7 🚊	a																09 08					
	d		08 14	08 21						08 24	08 41	08 48		08 53			09 11		09 14	09 21		09 24
Meadowhall 🚊	d		08 21							08 31	08 47			09 00			09 16		09 21			09 30
Rotherham Central	d		08 28							08 37				09 06					09 27			09 37
Swinton (S.Yorks)	d		08a37							08 48				09 16					09a36			09 48
Mexborough	d									08 51				09 19								09 51
Conisbrough	d									08 55				09 23								09 55
London Kings Cross	d				07 08				07 20													
Doncaster 7	a				08 59				09 04	09 06	09 15	09 18		09 31			09 35					10 05
York 8 26	a			09 26	09 29							09 44								10 26		
Doncaster 31	d				10a24		08 49	08 55	09 05	09 06	09 18		09 26	09 34			09 37				09 51	10 07
Bentley (S.Yorks) 31	a						08 52						09 29	09 37								
Adwick 31	a						08 58						09 33	09 43								
Kirk Sandall	d							09 01		09 14											09 57	10 13
Hatfield & Stainforth	d							09 06		09 19											10 02	10 18
Thorne South	d									09 24												10 23
Crowle	d									09 32												10 32
Althorpe	d									09 38												10 38
Scunthorpe	a									09 46							10 02					10 46
	d																10 03					
Barnetby	d																10 17					
Hull Paragon Interchange	d														09 05							
Barton-on-Humber	a														09 40							
Barton-on-Humber	d															09 52						
Barrow Haven	d															09 57						
New Holland	d															10 00						
Goxhill	d															10 05						
Thornton Abbey	d															10 08						
Ulceby	d															10 12						
Habrough	d															10 17						
Stallingborough	d															10 22						
Healing	d															10 25						
Great Coates	d															10 28						
Grimsby Town	a															10 33	10 39					
	d															10 33	10 40					
Grimsby Docks	d															10 36						
New Clee	d															10x38						
Cleethorpes	a															10 43	10 51					
Thorne North	d							09 11													10 07	
Goole	d							09 19			09 35										10 16	
Saltmarshe	d																					
York 8 33	d					08 43																
Selby	a	08 57				09 06			09 22									09 57				
Wressle	d																					
Howden	d					09 16			09 33													
Eastrington	d																					
Gilberdyke	d							09 28													10 24	
Broomfleet	d																					
Brough	d					09 28		09 35	09 45		09 52							10 16			10 32	
Ferriby	d							09 40													10 37	
Hessle	d							09 45													10 41	
Hull	a	09 31				09 47		09 58	10 04		10 09							10 35			10 54	

A To Leeds
B From Birmingham New Street to Edinburgh
C To London Kings Cross
D From Beverley
F To Bridlington
G From Birmingham New Street to Newcastle
H From Worksop
I From Bath Spa to Glasgow Central

Manchester Airport, Manchester, Sheffield and Meadowhall-Doncaster-Cleethorpes and Hull Barton-on-Humber - Cleethorpes

Network Diagram - see first Page of Table 18

		NT		NT	XC	NT	NT	NT	EM	TP	TP	NT		XC	GR	NT	NT		NT	XC	HT			NT
					◇1					◇1	◇1			◇1	■ 1					◇1	◇1			
				B	C	D	E	F	G			E		H	I				K	L				E
					🍴					🍴	🍴			🍴	🍽🍴					🍴	⊠			
Manchester Airport 85 ✈ d										08 55														
Manchester Piccadilly 10 🚌 d										09 20	09 42													
Stockport 78 d										09 28														
Sheffield 7 🚌 a										10 08														
d		09 29		09 41	09 47			09 53		10 11		10 14		10 21			10 24		10 41	10 47				
Meadowhall 🚌 d		09 35		09 47				09 59		10 16		10 21					10 30		10 47					
Rotherham Central d		09 42						10 06				10 27					10 36							
Swinton (S.Yorks) d		09 51						10 15				10a36					10 44							
Mexborough d								10 18									10 47							
Conisbrough d								10 22									10 51							
London Kings Cross d															09 08						09 48			
Doncaster 7 a				10 15	10 18			10 32		10 35					11 03		11 04		11 14	11 18	11 23			
York 8 26 a		10 56			10 45									11 26	11 31					11 46				
Doncaster 31 d				10 19			10 26	10 34		10 37					12a24	10 51	11 08		11 19		11 24			11 26
Bentley (S.Yorks) 31 a							10 29	10 37																11 29
Adwick 31 a							10 33	10 43																11 33
Kirk Sandall d																10 57	11 14							
Hatfield & Stainforth d																11 02	11 19							
Thorne South d																	11 24							
Crowle d																	11 32							
Althorpe d																	11 38							
Scunthorpe a										11 02							11 46							
d										11 03														
Barnetby d									10 59	11 17														
Hull Paragon Interchange d																								
Barton-on-Humber a																								
Barton-on-Humber d																								
Barrow Haven d																								
New Holland d																								
Goxhill d																								
Thornton Abbey d																								
Ulceby d																								
Habrough d									11 08															
Stallingborough d																								
Healing d																								
Great Coates d																								
Grimsby Town a									11 23	11 37														
d										11 38														
Grimsby Docks d																								
New Clee d																								
Cleethorpes a										11 50														
Thorne North d																11 07								
Goole d				10 38												11 16			11 37					
Saltmarshe d																								
York 8 33 d						10 20																		
Selby a						10 40					10 57										11 39			
Wressle d																								
Howden d						10 50															11 50			
Eastrington d																								
Gilberdyke d						10 57										11 25								
Broomfleet d																11 30								
Brough d				10 51		11 05					11 16					11 36			11 51		12 02			
Ferriby d																11 40								
Hessle d																11 45								
Hull a				11 09		11 23					11 35					12 01			12 09		12 18			

B To Scarborough
C From Guildford to Newcastle
D From Leeds
E To Leeds
F From Lincoln
G From Newark North Gate
H From Plymouth to Edinburgh
I To London Kings Cross. 🍴 from York
K To Bridlington
L From Reading to Newcastle

Manchester Airport, Manchester, Sheffield and Meadowhall-Doncaster-Cleethorpes and Hull Barton-on-Humber - Cleethorpes

Network Diagram - see first Page of Table 18

	NT	NT	NT	TP	TP	NT	XC	NT	NT	NT	NT	XC	NT	NT	EM	TP	TP	NT	XC	GR	NT
				◇1	◇1		◇1					◇1				◇1	◇1		◇1	R 1	
	A					B	C	D			F	G	B	A	H			B	I	J	K
		🚌		🛒	🛒		🛒					🛒				🛒	🛒		🛒	R🛒	
Manchester Airport 85 ✈ d				09 55												10 55					
Manchester Piccadilly 10 🚇 d				10 20	10 42											11 20	11 42				
Stockport 78 d				10 28												11 28					
Sheffield 7 🚇 a				11 08												12 08					
d	10 53			11 11		11 14	11 21			11 24	11 41	11 47		11 53		12 11		12 14	12 21		
Meadowhall 🚇 d	10 59			11 16		11 21				11 30	11 47			11 59		12 16		12 21			
Rotherham Central d	11 05					11 27				11 37				12 05				12 27			
Swinton (S.Yorks) d	11 16					11a36				11 48				12 16				12a36			
Mexborough d	11 19									11 51				12 19							
Conisbrough d	11 23									11 55				12 23							
London Kings Cross d																				11 08	
Doncaster 7 a	11 32			11 35						12 04	12 15	12 18		12 32		12 35				13 03	
York 8 26 a							12 26					12 46							13 26	13 31	
Doncaster 31 d	11 34			11 37					11 51	12 08	12 19		12 26	12 34		12 37				14a22	
Bentley (S.Yorks) 31 a	11 37												12 29	12 38							
Adwick 31 a	11 43												12 33	12 43							
Kirk Sandall d									11 57	12 14											
Hatfield & Stainforth d									12 02	12 19											
Thorne South d										12 24											
Crowle d										12 32											
Althorpe d										12 38											
Scunthorpe a				12 02						12 46						13 02					
d				12 03												13 03					
Barnetby d				12 17											13 10	13 17					
Hull Paragon Interchange d		11 05																			
Barton-on-Humber a		11 40																			
Barton-on-Humber d			11 52																		
Barrow Haven d			11 57																		
New Holland d			12 00																		
Goxhill d			12 05																		
Thornton Abbey d			12 08																		
Ulceby d			12 12																		
Habrough d			12 17	12 26											13 19						
Stallingborough d			12 22																		
Healing d			12 25																		
Great Coates d			12 28																		
Grimsby Town a			12 33	12 39											13 35	13 37					
d			12 33	12 40												13 38					
Grimsby Docks d			12 36																		
New Clee d			12x38																		
Cleethorpes a			12 43	12 52												13 50					
Thorne North d									12 07												
Goole d									12 16		12 35										
Saltmarshe d																					
York 8 33 d								11 45													12 47
Selby a					11 57			12 04									12 57				13 06
Wressle d																					
Howden d								12 14													13 16
Eastrington d																					
Gilberdyke d								12 21	12 27												
Broomfleet d																					
Brough d					12 16			12 29	12 35		12 49						13 16				13 28
Ferriby d									12 40												
Hessle d									12 44												
Hull a					12 36			12 49	12 58		13 09						13 35				13 48

A From Lincoln
B To Leeds
C From Plymouth to Glasgow Central
D From Hull
F To Scarborough
G From Winchester to Newcastle
H From Newark North Gate
I From Plymouth to Edinburgh
J To London Kings Cross. 🛒 from York
K From Selby

Manchester Airport, Manchester, Sheffield and Meadowhall-Doncaster-Cleethorpes and Hull Barton-on-Humber - Cleethorpes

Network Diagram - see first Page of Table 18

	NT	NT		NT	XC	HT	NT	NT	NT	NT	TP	TP	NT	XC		NT	NT	NT		NT	NT	XC	NT	NT
					◇1	◇1					◇1	◇1		◇1								◇1		
				B	C		D	E					D	F		G				I	B	J	D	
					[trolley]	[restaurant]			[bus]		[trolley]	[trolley]		[trolley]								[trolley]		
Manchester Airport 85 ✈ d											11 55													
Manchester Piccadilly 10 🚉 d											12 20	12 42												
Stockport 78 d											12 28													
Sheffield 7 🚉 a											13 08													
d		12 24		12 41	12 47			12 53			13 11		13 14	13 21				13 24		13 28	13 41	13 47		13 53
Meadowhall 🚉 d		12 30		12 47				12 59			13 16		13 21					13 30		13 35	13 46			13 59
Rotherham Central d		12 37						13 05					13 27					13 37		13 41				14 05
Swinton (S.Yorks) d		12 48						13 16					13a36					13 47		13 50				14 17
Mexborough d		12 51						13 19										13 50						14 20
Conisbrough d		12 55						13 23										13 54						14 24
London Kings Cross d						11 48																		
Doncaster 7 a		13 04		13 15	13 18	13 23		13 33			13 35							14 04			14 15	14 18		14 32
York 8 26 a					13 40									14 26						14 55		14 44		
Doncaster 31 d	12 51	13 08		13 19		13 24	13 26	13 34			13 37						13 50	14 08			14 19		14 26	14 34
Bentley (S.Yorks) 31 a							13 29	13 37															14 29	14 37
Adwick 31 a							13 33	13 43															14 33	14 43
Kirk Sandall d	12 57	13 14															13 56	14 14						
Hatfield & Stainforth d	13 02	13 19															14 01	14 19						
Thorne South d		13 24																14 26						
Crowle d		13 33																14 34						
Althorpe d		13 39																14 40						
Scunthorpe a		13 46									14 02							14 48						
d											14 03													
Barnetby d											14 17													
Hull Paragon Interchange d									13 05															
Barton-on-Humber a									13 40															
Barton-on-Humber d										13 52														
Barrow Haven d										13 57														
New Holland d										14 00														
Goxhill d										14 05														
Thornton Abbey d										14 08														
Ulceby d										14 12														
Habrough d										14 17	14 26													
Stallingborough d										14 22														
Healing d										14 25														
Great Coates d										14 28														
Grimsby Town a										14 33	14 39													
d										14 33	14 40													
Grimsby Docks d										14 36														
New Clee d										14x38														
Cleethorpes a										14 43	14 52													
Thorne North d	13 07																14 06							
Goole d	13 16			13 38													14 16				14 37			
Saltmarshe d																	14 21							
York 8 33 d																13 44								
Selby a						13 39						13 57				14 07								
Wressle d																								
Howden d						13 50										14 17								
Eastrington d																								
Gilberdyke d	13 27																14 27							
Broomfleet d																								
Brough d	13 35			13 52		14 02						14 16				14 30	14 36				14 54			
Ferriby d	13 40																14 40							
Hessle d	13 44																14 45							
Hull a	14 00			14 09		14 19						14 35				14 52	14 56				15 12			

B To Bridlington
C From Reading to Newcastle
D To Leeds
E From Lincoln
F From Penzance to Glasgow Central
G From Hull
I To Sheffield
J From Southampton Central to Newcastle

Manchester Airport, Manchester, Sheffield and Meadowhall-Doncaster-Cleethorpes and Hull Barton-on-Humber - Cleethorpes

Network Diagram - see first Page of Table 18

Station		EM	TP	TP	NT	XC	NT	NT	NT	NT	XC	HT	NT	NT	NT	NT	TP	TP	NT	XC
			◇1	◇1		◇1					◇1	◇1					◇1	◇1		◇1
		A			B	C	D	E		G	H		B	A	Bus				B	I
Manchester Airport 85	d		12 55														13 55			
Manchester Piccadilly 10	d		13 20	13 42													14 20	14 42		
Stockport 78	d		13 28														14 28			
Sheffield 7	a		14 08														15 08			
	d		14 11		14 14	14 21			14 24	14 41	14 47			14 53			15 11		15 14	15 21
Meadowhall	d		14 16		14 21				14 30	14 47				14 59			15 16		15 20	
Rotherham Central	d				14 27				14 37					15 05					15 26	
Swinton (S.Yorks)	d				14a35				14 48					15 16					15a34	
Mexborough	d								14 51					15 19						
Conisbrough	d								14 55					15 23						
London Kings Cross	d											13 48								
Doncaster 7	a		14 35						15 04	15 17	15 18	15 23		15 33			15 35			
York 8 26	a					15 26					15 45									16 28
Doncaster 31	d		14 37					14 50	15 07	15 19		15 24	15 26	15 34			15 37			
Bentley (S.Yorks) 31	a												15 29	15 37						
Adwick 31	a												15 33	15 42						
Kirk Sandall	d							14 57	15 14											
Hatfield & Stainforth	d							15 02	15 19											
Thorne South	d								15 24											
Crowle	d								15 32											
Althorpe	d								15 38											
Scunthorpe	a		15 02						15 47								16 02			
	d		15 03														16 03			
Barnetby	d	15 11	15 17														16 17			
Hull Paragon Interchange	d														15 05					
Barton-on-Humber	a														15 40					
Barton-on-Humber	d															15 52				
Barrow Haven	d															15 57				
New Holland	d															16 00				
Goxhill	d															16 05				
Thornton Abbey	d															16 08				
Ulceby	d															16 12				
Habrough	d	15 19														16 17	16 26			
Stallingborough	d															16 22				
Healing	d															16 25				
Great Coates	d															16 28				
Grimsby Town	a	15 34	15 37													16 33	16 39			
	d		15 38													16 33	16 40			
Grimsby Docks	d															16 36				
New Clee	d																			
Cleethorpes	a		15 50													16 42	16 52			
Thorne North	d							15 07												
Goole	d							15 16		15 37										
Saltmarshe	d																			
York 8 33	d						14 47													
Selby	a			14 57			15 06					15 39						15 57		
Wressle	d																			
Howden	d						15 16					15 50								
Eastrington	d																			
Gilberdyke	d							15 27												
Broomfleet	d																			
Brough	d			15 16			15 28	15 35		15 51		16 02						16 16		
Ferriby	d							15 40												
Hessle	d							15 44												
Hull	a			15 35			15 48	15 55		16 08		16 18						16 35		

A From Lincoln
B To Leeds
C From Plymouth to Aberdeen
D From Hull
E To Beverley
G To Scarborough
H From Reading to Newcastle
I From Penzance to Glasgow Central

Table 29

Manchester Airport, Manchester, Sheffield and Meadowhall-Doncaster-Cleethorpes and Hull Barton-on-Humber - Cleethorpes

Network Diagram - see first Page of Table 18

		NT	NT		NT	NT	XC		NT	TP	NT	TP	NT	XC		GR	NT			NT	NT	XC		NT	HT
							◇1			◇1		◇1		◇1		1						◇1			◇1
					B	C	D		E		F		B	G		H				J	C	K			
Manchester Airport 85	d									14 55															
Manchester Piccadilly	d									15 20		15 42													
Stockport 78	d									15 28															
Sheffield	a									16 08															
	d		15 24			15 41	15 47		15 53	16 11			16 14	16 21			16 23				16 41	16 47			
Meadowhall	d		15 30			15 47			15 59	16 16			16 20				16 29				16 47				
Rotherham Central	d		15 37						16 05				16 26				16 37								
Swinton (S.Yorks)	d		15 48						16 16				16a36				16 47								
Mexborough	d		15 51						16 19								16 50								
Conisbrough	d		15 55						16 23								16 54								
London Kings Cross	d															15 08									15 48
Doncaster	a		16 04			16 15	16 18		16 32	16 35						17 03	17 07				17 16	17 18			17 23
York 26	a						16 45							17 28		17 31						17 40			
Doncaster 31	d	15 51	16 08		16 16	16 19			16 34	16 37						18a22				16 51	17 19			17 22	17 24
Bentley (S.Yorks) 31	a				16 19				16 37																
Adwick 31	a				16 23				16 43																
Kirk Sandall	d	15 57	16 14																	16 57				17 28	
Hatfield & Stainforth	d	16 02	16 19																	17 02				17 33	
Thorne South	d		16 24																					17 39	
Crowle	d		16 33																					17 48	
Althorpe	d		16 39																					17 54	
Scunthorpe	a		16 46							17 02														18 01	
	d									17 03															
Barnetby	d									17 17															
Hull Paragon Interchange	d																								
Barton-on-Humber	a																								
Barton-on-Humber	d																								
Barrow Haven	d																								
New Holland	d																								
Goxhill	d																								
Thornton Abbey	d																								
Ulceby	d																								
Habrough	d																								
Stallingborough	d																								
Healing	d																								
Great Coates	d																								
Grimsby Town	a									17 37															
	d									17 38															
Grimsby Docks	d																								
New Clee	d																								
Cleethorpes	a									17 50															
Thorne North	d	16 07																		17 07	17 33				
Goole	d	16 16				16 38														17 16	17 42				
Saltmarshe	d	16 21																							
York 33	d										16 12														
Selby	a										16 36	17 00													17 39
Wressle	d										16 44														
Howden	d										16 49														17 50
Eastrington	d																								
Gilberdyke	d	16 27									16 55									17 24					
Broomfleet	d																								
Brough	d	16 35				16 52					17 03	17 18								17 32	17 55				18 02
Ferriby	d	16 39									17 08									17 37					
Hessle	d	16 44									17 12									17 41					
Hull	a	16 57				17 06					17 27	17 37								17 54	18 13				18 21

B To Leeds
C To Bridlington
D From Southampton Central to Newcastle
E From Lincoln
F From Hull
G From Plymouth to Dundee
H To London Kings Cross
J To Beverley
K From Reading to Newcastle

Manchester Airport, Manchester, Sheffield and Meadowhall-Doncaster-Cleethorpes and Hull Barton-on-Humber - Cleethorpes

Network Diagram - see first Page of Table 18

	NT	NT	NT	EM	NT	NT	TP	TP	NT	XC	NT			NT	NT	GC	XC	NT	TP	NT	NT	NT		NT
							◇1	◇1		◇1						R 1	◇1		◇1					
	A	B	C	D	🚌		🍴	🍴	B	E 🍴					G	H 🛏	I 🍴	J	🍴	B	K	C		B
Manchester Airport 85 ✈ d							15 55																	
Manchester Piccadilly 10 ⛴ d							16 20	16 42											17 42					
Stockport 78 d							16 28																	
Sheffield 7 ⛴ a							17 08																	
d			16 53				17 11		17 13	17 21	17 27				17 41		17 47					17 53		18 13
Meadowhall ⛴ d			16 59				17 16		17 20		17 33				17 47							17 59		18 20
Rotherham Central d			17 05						17 26		17 39											18 05		18 26
Swinton (S.Yorks) d			17 16						17a36		17 48											18 16		18a36
Mexborough d			17 19								17 51											18 20		
Conisbrough d			17 23								17 55											18 24		
London Kings Cross d																16 48								
Doncaster 7 a			17 32				17 35				18 07				18 12	18 20						18 35		
York 8 26 a										18 29						18 44	19 01							
Doncaster 31 d		17 26	17 34				17 47							17 56	18 16					18 26	18 29	18 39		
Bentley (S.Yorks) 31 a		17 29	17 37																	18 29				
Adwick 31 a		17 33	17 43																	18 33				
Kirk Sandall d														18 02							18 37	18 45		
Hatfield & Stainforth d														18 07							18 42	18 50		
Thorne South d																					18 47			
Crowle d																					18 55			
Althorpe d																					19 01			
Scunthorpe a							18 12														19 10			
d							18 13																	
Barnetby d				17 55			18 27																	
Hull Paragon Interchange d					17 10																			
Barton-on-Humber a					17 45																			
Barton-on-Humber d						17 55																		
Barrow Haven d						18 00																		
New Holland d						18 03																		
Goxhill d						18 08																		
Thornton Abbey d						18 11																		
Ulceby d						18 15																		
Habrough d				18 03		18 20	18 36																	
Stallingborough d						18 25																		
Healing d						18 28																		
Great Coates d						18 31																		
Grimsby Town a				18 15		18 36	18 49																	
d						18 36	18 50																	
Grimsby Docks d						18 39																		
New Clee d																								
Cleethorpes a						18 45	19 01																	
Thorne North d														18 12								18 55		
Goole d														18 21	18 36							19 12		
Saltmarshe d														18 26										
York 8 33 d	17 19																	18 18						
Selby a	17 45							17 59										18 42	19 00					
Wressle d																		18 50						
Howden d	17 56							18 08										18 54						
Eastrington d																		18 59						
Gilberdyke d	18 03													18 37				19 03				19 21		
Broomfleet d														18 41										
Brough d	18 11							18 20						18 47	18 53			19 10	19 19			19 29		
Ferriby d														18 51								19 34		
Hessle d														18 56								19 38		
Hull a	18 30							18 39						19 06	19 09			19 29	19 38			19 50		

A From Hull
B To Leeds
C From Lincoln
D From Newark North Gate
E From Plymouth to Glasgow Central
G To Scarborough
H To Sunderland
I From Southampton Central to Edinburgh
J From Leeds
K From Adwick

Table 29

Mondays to Fridays

Manchester Airport, Manchester, Sheffield and Meadowhall-Doncaster-Cleethorpes and Hull Barton-on-Humber - Cleethorpes

Network Diagram - see first Page of Table 18

		XC	TP	GR	NT	NT	XC	NT	NT		NT	NT	NT	TP	TP	NT	XC	NT			NT	NT	XC	NT	NT
		◇1	◇1	R 1			◇1							◇1	◇1		◇1						◇1		
		A		B		C	D	E	F							F	A					H	I		F
Manchester Airport 85	d		16 55											17 55											
Manchester Piccadilly 10	d		17 20											18 20	18 42										
Stockport 78	d		17 28											18 28											
Sheffield 7	a		18 10											19 09											
	d	18 21	18 24		18 29	18 41	18 47	19 00						19 11		19 18	19 26	19 30				19 44	19 54		
Meadowhall	d		18 29		18 35	18 47		19 06						19 16		19 25		19 36				19 50			
Rotherham Central	d				18 42			19 12								19 31		19 42							
Swinton (S.Yorks)	d				18 50			19 20								19a40		19 51							
Mexborough	d				18 53			19 23										19 55							
Conisbrough	d				18 57			19 27										19 59							
London Kings Cross	d			17 19																					
Doncaster 7	a		18 53	19 05	19 09	19 12	19 14	19 36						19 41				20 08				20 12	20 15		
York 8 26	a	19 29					19 38										20 30						20 46		
Doncaster 31	d		18 55	19 07		19 16			19 20		19 21			19 48							19 53	20 17		20 25	20 26
Bentley (S.Yorks) 31	a								19 23																20 29
Adwick 31	a								19 27																20 33
Kirk Sandall	d										19 27										19 59			20 31	
Hatfield & Stainforth	d										19 32										20 04			20 36	
Thorne South	d										19 36													20 41	
Crowle	d										19 45													20 50	
Althorpe	d										19 51													20 56	
Scunthorpe	a		19 23								19 59			20 14										21 04	
	d		19 23											20 14											
Barnetby	d		19 37											20 28											
Hull Paragon Interchange	d											19 25													
Barton-on-Humber	a											19 52													
Barton-on-Humber	d												19 58												
Barrow Haven	d												20 03												
New Holland	d												20 06												
Goxhill	d												20 11												
Thornton Abbey	d												20 14												
Ulceby	d												20 18												
Habrough	d												20 23												
Stallingborough	d												20 28												
Healing	d												20 31												
Great Coates	d												20 34												
Grimsby Town	a		19 57										20 39	20 47											
	d		19 58										20 39	20 48											
Grimsby Docks	d												20 42												
New Clee	d																								
Cleethorpes	a		20 10										20 48	21 00											
Thorne North	d																				20 09				
Goole	d					19 37															20 18	20 36			
Saltmarshe	d																								
York 8 33	d																								
Selby	a			19 22											20 00										
Wressle	d																								
Howden	d														20 10										
Eastrington	d																								
Gilberdyke	d																				20 26				
Broomfleet	d																								
Brough	d			19 45		19 54									20 22						20 34	20 50			
Ferriby	d																				20 39				
Hessle	d																				20 43				
Hull	a			20 06		20 10									20 43						20 56	21 07			

A From Plymouth to Edinburgh
B **The Hull Executive**
C To Bridlington
D From Reading to Newcastle
E From Retford
F To Leeds
H To Beverley
I From Southampton Central to Newcastle. to Doncaster

Manchester Airport, Manchester, Sheffield and Meadowhall-Doncaster-Cleethorpes and Hull
Barton-on-Humber - Cleethorpes

Network Diagram - see first Page of Table 18

		HT ◇1 ☒	NT A	EM B	TP ◇1	TP FX ◇1 C	TP FO ◇1 D	TP FX ◇1 E	TP FO ◇1 F	NT	GC R 1 G	NT I	NT	XC ◇1 J	NT I	NT (bus)	NT	TP FO ◇1	NT K	NT L	NT I	TP FX ◇1
Manchester Airport 85	d				18 55													19 55				
Manchester Piccadilly 10	d				19 18	20 11	20 11	20 11	20 11									20 20				
Stockport 78	d				19 26													20 28				
Sheffield 7	a				20 08													21 11				
	d		19 58		20 11					20 15		20 27	20 38	20 53				21 11	21 15	21 15	21 30	21 34
Meadowhall	d		20 04		20 16					20 21		20 35	20 45					21 16	21 21	21 21	21 36	21 40
Rotherham Central	d		20 11							20 27		20 41	20 52						21 27	21 27	21 42	
Swinton (S.Yorks)	d		20 22							20 36		20a50	21 00						21 36	21 36	21a50	
Mexborough	d		20 25							20 39			21 03						21 39	21 39		
Conisbrough	d		20 29							20 43			21 07						21 43	21 43		
London Kings Cross	d	18 50									19 18											
Doncaster 7	a	20 27	20 37		20 44					20 55	20 58		21 18	21 19				21 40	21 54	21 54		22 02
York 8 26	a										21 21			21 45								
Doncaster 31	d	20 33	20 44		20 45					20 56			21 18		21 22			21 42	21 56	21 56		22 05
Bentley (S.Yorks) 31	a														21 25							
Adwick 31	a														21 29							
Kirk Sandall	d									21 03			21 26						22 02	22 02		
Hatfield & Stainforth	d									21 08			21 31						22 07	22 07		
Thorne South	d												21 38									
Crowle	d												21 46									
Althorpe	d												21 52									
Scunthorpe	a				21 11								22 01					22 07				22 30
	d				21 12													22 08				22 31
Barnetby	d			20 35	21 26													22 22				22 46
Hull Paragon Interchange	d															21 25						
Barton-on-Humber	a															21 52						
Barton-on-Humber	d																21 58					
Barrow Haven	d																22 03					
New Holland	d																22 06					
Goxhill	d																22 11					
Thornton Abbey	d																22 14					
Ulceby	d																22 18					
Habrough	d			20 44	21 35												22 23	22 31				22 54
Stallingborough	d																22 28					
Healing	d																22 31					
Great Coates	d																22 34					
Grimsby Town	a			20 56	21 48												22 39	22 44				23 09
	d			20 56	21 49												22 39	22 45				23 10
Grimsby Docks	d																22 42					
New Clee	d																					
Cleethorpes	a			21 03	22 00												22 48	22 57				23 20
Thorne North	d									21 14									22 13	22 13		
Goole	d									21a23									22 22	22 22		
Saltmarshe	d																		22 26	22 26		
York 8 33	d																					
Selby	a	20 48	21 01			21 34	21 33	21 33	21 34													
Wressle	d																					
Howden	d	20 59				21 43	21 43	21 43	21 43													
Eastrington	d																					
Gilberdyke	d		21 15																22 32	22 32		
Broomfleet	d																					
Brough	d	21 11	21 23			21 55	21 55	21 55	21 55										22 39	22 39		
Ferriby	d		21 28																			
Hessle	d		21 32																			
Hull	a	21 27	21 45			22 15	22 15	22 17	22 17										22 58	23 02		

A To Bridlington
B From Newark North Gate
C until 22 March. From Liverpool Lime Street
D until 23 March. From Liverpool Lime Street
E from 26 March. From Liverpool Lime Street
F from 30 March. From Liverpool Lime Street
G To Sunderland
I To Leeds
J From Reading to Newcastle
K until 23 March. To Beverley
L from 26 March. To Beverley

Manchester Airport, Manchester, Sheffield and Meadowhall-Doncaster-Cleethorpes and Hull Barton-on-Humber - Cleethorpes

Network Diagram - see first Page of Table 18

		HT	HT	XC	NT	NT	TP	HT	HT	NT	TP	NT	NT	NT	NT
		◇1	◇1	◇1			◇1	◇1	◇1		◇1				
		A	B	C	D	E	F	A	B	G		G		G	
		⊠	⊠					⊠	⊠						
Manchester Airport 85 ✈	d										20 47				
Manchester Piccadilly 10	d										21 20				
Stockport 78	d										21 28				
Sheffield 7	a										22 08				
	d			21 54							22 11	22 24	22 34	23 15	23 27
Meadowhall	d										22 16	22 30	22 40	23 21	23 33
Rotherham Central	d											22 36	22 46	23 27	23 39
Swinton (S.Yorks)	d											22a45	22 54	23a36	23 48
Mexborough	d												22 57		23 51
Conisbrough	d												23 01		23 55
London Kings Cross	d	20 30	20 30												
Doncaster 7	a	22 06	22 06	22 29							22 42		23 12		00 07
York 8 26	a			22 53											
Doncaster 31	d	22 06	22 06					22 20	22 20	22 26	22 44		23 15		
Bentley (S.Yorks) 31	a									22 29					
Adwick 31	a									22 33					
Kirk Sandall	d										22 49		23 21		
Hatfield & Stainforth	d										22 54		23 26		
Thorne South	d										22 58				
Crowle	d										23 07				
Althorpe	d										23 12				
Scunthorpe	a										23 17				
	d										23 18				
Barnetby	d										23 32				
Hull Paragon Interchange	d														
Barton-on-Humber	a														
Barton-on-Humber	d														
Barrow Haven	d														
New Holland	d														
Goxhill	d														
Thornton Abbey	d														
Ulceby	d														
Habrough	d										23 42				
Stallingborough	d														
Healing	d														
Great Coates	d														
Grimsby Town	a										23 55				
	d										23 56				
Grimsby Docks	d														
New Clee	d														
Cleethorpes	a										00 09				
Thorne North	d												23 32		
Goole	d												23a43		
Saltmarshe	d														
York 8 33	d				22 13	22 13									
Selby	a	22 21	22 21		22 32	22 32		22 50	22 50						
Wressle	d														
Howden	d	22 32	22 32		22 41	22 41		23 03	23 03						
Eastrington	d														
Gilberdyke	d				22 48	22 48									
Broomfleet	d														
Brough	d	22 47	22 47		22 55	22 55	23 06	23 15	23 15						
Ferriby	d				23 00	23 00									
Hessle	d				23 05	23 09									
Hull	a	23 06	23 10		23 18	23 22	23 25	23 34	23 35						

A until 23 March
B from 26 March
C From Southampton Central to Leeds
D until 23 March. From Hull
E from 26 March
F From Leeds
G To Leeds

Manchester Airport, Manchester, Sheffield and Meadowhall-Doncaster-Cleethorpes and Hull Barton-on-Humber - Cleethorpes

Network Diagram - see first Page of Table 18

		TP		NT	NT	GR	NT	EM	NT	NT		NT	NT	XC	NT	NT	TP		XC	NT		NT	NT	TP	NT
		◇1				1								◇1			◇1		◇1					◇1	
						B	C	D	E				E	F					G	E		E	H		C
Manchester Airport 85	d	20p47															05 20								
Manchester Piccadilly 10	d	21b20															05 44							06 21	
Stockport 78	d	21p28															05 52								
Sheffield 7	a	22p08															06 49								
	d	22p11		23p27			05 29					06 12	06 28	06 49	06 52		06 55		07 12	07 14					
Meadowhall	d	22p16		23p33			05 35					06 18	06 34		06 58		07 01			07 21					
Rotherham Central	d			23p39			05 41					06 24	06 40		07 04					07 27					
Swinton (S.Yorks)	d			23p48			05 49					06 35	06a51		07 15					07a33					
Mexborough	d			23p51			05 52					06 38			07 18										
Conisbrough	d			23p55			05 56					06 42			07 22										
London Kings Cross	d																								
Doncaster 7	a	22p42		00 07			06 06					06 53		07 16	07 33		07 22								
York 8 26	a													07 43					08 23						
Doncaster 31	d	22p44			05 52	06 10	06 12		06 26	06 47		06 55			07 34		07 24					07 26			07 28
Bentley (S.Yorks) 31	a								06 29			06 58			07 37							07 29			
Adwick 31	a								06 33			07 05			07 43							07 33			
Kirk Sandall	d	22p49					06 18			06 53															07 34
Hatfield & Stainforth	d	22p54					06 23			06 58															07 39
Thorne South	d	22p58								07 03															
Crowle	d	23p07								07 11															
Althorpe	d	23p12								07 17															
Scunthorpe	a	23p17								07 27							07 49								
	d	23p18															07 50								
Barnetby	d	23p32						06 12									08 04								
Hull Paragon Interchange	d																								
Barton-on-Humber	a																								
Barton-on-Humber	d															06 58									
Barrow Haven	d															07 03									
New Holland	d															07 07									
Goxhill	d															07 11									
Thornton Abbey	d																								
Ulceby	d															07 19									
Habrough	d	23p42						06 22								07 23									
Stallingborough	d															07 28									
Healing	d															07 31									
Great Coates	d																								
Grimsby Town	a	23p55						06 37								07 38	08 24								
	d	23p56														07 39	08 33								
Grimsby Docks	d																								
New Clee	d																								
Cleethorpes	a	00 09														07 51	08 44								
Thorne North	d						06 28																		07 44
Goole	d						06 37																		07 53
Saltmarshe	d						06 42																		07 58
York 8 33	d					06a30																			
Selby	a				06 11																			07 43	
Wressle	d																								
Howden	d																							07 52	
Eastrington	d																								
Gilberdyke	d						06 51																07 39		08 04
Broomfleet	d						06 55																07 43		
Brough	d						07 01																07 49	08 04	08 12
Ferriby	d						07 05																07 53		08 16
Hessle	d						07 10																07 58		08 21
Hull	a						07 22																08 11	08 20	08 37

B To Edinburgh
C To Beverley
D From Lincoln
E To Leeds
F From Derby to Newcastle
G From Birmingham New Street to Glasgow Central
H To Scarborough
b Previous night, arr. 2113

Table 29

Saturdays

Manchester Airport, Manchester, Sheffield and Meadowhall-Doncaster-Cleethorpes and Hull Barton-on-Humber - Cleethorpes

Network Diagram - see first Page of Table 18

Station		NT		NT	NT	NT	NT	NT	XC	NT	EM	NT	TP	TP	NT	XC		NT	NT	NT	NT		NT	XC	
									◇1				◇1	◇1		◇1								◇1	
							B	C	D	E	F				E	G		H					C	D	
					🚌																				
									🛒				🛒	🛒		🛒								🛒	
Manchester Airport 85 ✈	d												06 55												
Manchester Piccadilly 10 🚇	d												07 20	07 36											
Stockport 78	d												07 28												
Sheffield 7 🚇	a												08 10												
	d	07 24						07 41	07 54			08 03	08 11		08 14	08 21					08 25		08 41	08 48	
Meadowhall 🚇	d	07 30						07 47					08 16		08 22						08 31		08 47		
Rotherham Central	d	07 36						07 55							08 28						08 35				
Swinton (S.Yorks)	d	07 46						08 03							08a37						08 47				
Mexborough	d	07 49						08 06													08 51				
Conisbrough	d	07 53						08 10													08 55				
London Kings Cross	d																								
Doncaster 7	a	08 01						08 19	08 23				08 38								09 05		09 14	09 18	
York 8 26	a								08 48							09 27								09 44	
Doncaster 31	d	08 03					08 16	08 21		08 26			08 41						08 53	08 54	09 07		09 18		
Bentley (S.Yorks) 31	a						08 19			08 29										08 57					
Adwick 31	a						08 23			08 33										09 04					
Kirk Sandall	d	08 09																	09 00		09 14				
Hatfield & Stainforth	d	08 14																	09 05		09 19				
Thorne South	d	08 18																			09 24				
Crowle	d	08 27																			09 32				
Althorpe	d	08 33																			09 38				
Scunthorpe	a	08 44											09 06								09 47				
	d												09 07												
Barnetby	d										08 52	09 39	09 21												
Hull Paragon Interchange	d				06 55																				
Barton-on-Humber	a				07 30																				
Barton-on-Humber	d					08 00																			
Barrow Haven	d					08 05																			
New Holland	d					08 08																			
Goxhill	d					08 13																			
Thornton Abbey	d					08 16																			
Ulceby	d					08 20																			
Habrough	d					08 25					09 01	09 48	09 29												
Stallingborough	d					08 30																			
Healing	d					08 33																			
Great Coates	d					08 36																			
Grimsby Town	a					08 41					09 15	10 00	09 43												
	d					08 43						10 01	09 44												
Grimsby Docks	d					08 45																			
New Clee	d					08x48																			
Cleethorpes	a					08 52						10 13	09 55												
Thorne North	d																		09 10						
Goole	d							08 43											09 19				09 38		
Saltmarshe	d																								
York 8 33	d			07 38														08 43							
Selby	a			07 57										08 57				09 06							
Wressle	d			08 05																					
Howden	d			08 10														09 16							
Eastrington	d			08 15																					
Gilberdyke	d			08 17															09 28						
Broomfleet	d			08 21																					
Brough	d			08 27				08 57										09 28	09 36				09 55		
Ferriby	d			08 32															09 40						
Hessle	d			08 36															09 45						
Hull	a			08 50				09 13						09 31				09 48	09 58				10 12		

B From Scunthorpe
C To Bridlington
D From Birmingham New Street to Newcastle
E To Leeds
F From Lincoln
G From Birmingham New Street to Edinburgh
H From Beverley

Table 29

Saturdays

Manchester Airport, Manchester, Sheffield and Meadowhall-Doncaster-Cleethorpes and Hull Barton-on-Humber - Cleethorpes

Network Diagram - see first Page of Table 18

		NT	NT	NT	NT	TP	TP	NT	EM	XC	NT	NT			NT	NT	NT	XC	NT	NT	EM	TP		TP	NT
						◇1	◇1		◇1	◇1								◇1				◇1		◇1	
		A						A	B	C						E	F	G	A	H	I				A
				🚌		🛒			🍽	🛒								🛒				🛒		🛒	
Manchester Airport 85 ✈	d					07 53																08 55			
Manchester Piccadilly 10 ⇌	d					08 20	08 42															09 20		09 42	
Stockport 78	d					08 28																09 28			
Sheffield 7 ⇌	a					09 08																10 08			
	d		08 53			09 11		09 14	09 21	09 21		09 25			09 31		09 41	09 47		09 53		10 11			10 14
Meadowhall ⇌	d		09 00			09 16		09 21				09 34			09 38		09 47			09 59		10 16			10 21
Rotherham Central	d		09 06					09 27				09 41			09 45					10 05					10 27
Swinton (S.Yorks)	d		09 16					09a36				09 49			09 53					10 15					10a36
Mexborough	d		09 19									09 52								10 18					
Conisbrough	d		09 23									09 56								10 22					
London Kings Cross	d																								
Doncaster 7	a		09 33			09 35			09 53			10 07					10 14	10 17		10 32		10 35			
York 8 26	a								10 16	10 26					10 56			10 40							
Doncaster 31	d	09 26	09 34			09 37					09 41	10 08					10 19		10 26	10 34		10 37			
Bentley (S.Yorks) 31	a	09 29	09 37																10 29	10 37					
Adwick 31	a	09 33	09 43																10 33	10 43					
Kirk Sandall	d										09 48	10 15													
Hatfield & Stainforth	d										09 53	10 20													
Thorne South	d											10 25													
Crowle	d											10 33													
Althorpe	d											10 39													
Scunthorpe	a					10 02						10 48										11 02			
	d					10 03																11 03			
Barnetby	d					10 17															10 41	11 17			
Hull Paragon Interchange	d			09 05																					
Barton-on-Humber	a			09 40																					
Barton-on-Humber	d				09 52																				
Barrow Haven	d				09 57																				
New Holland	d				10 00																				
Goxhill	d				10 05																				
Thornton Abbey	d				10 08																				
Ulceby	d				10 12																				
Habrough	d				10 17																10 50				
Stallingborough	d				10 22																				
Healing	d				10 25																				
Great Coates	d				10 28																				
Grimsby Town	a				10 33	10 39															11 08	11 37			
	d				10 33	10 40																11 38			
Grimsby Docks	d				10 36																				
New Clee	d				10x38																				
Cleethorpes	a				10 43	10 51																11 50			
Thorne North	d										09 58														
Goole	d										10 07						10 38								
Saltmarshe	d																								
York 8 33	d															09 50									
Selby	a						09 57									10 09								10 57	
Wressle	d																								
Howden	d															10 19									
Eastrington	d																								
Gilberdyke	d										10 15					10 26									
Broomfleet	d																								
Brough	d						10 16				10 23					10 34	10 51							11 16	
Ferriby	d										10 28														
Hessle	d										10 32														
Hull	a						10 35				10 45					10 53	11 09							11 35	

A To Leeds
B From St Pancras International
C From Bristol Temple Meads to Glasgow Central
D To Edinburgh
E From Beverley
F To Scarborough
G From Guildford to Newcastle
H From Lincoln
I From Newark North Gate

Table 29

Saturdays

Manchester Airport, Manchester, Sheffield and Meadowhall-Doncaster-Cleethorpes and Hull Barton-on-Humber - Cleethorpes

Network Diagram - see first Page of Table 18

		XC	NT	NT		NT	NT	XC	HT		NT	NT	NT	NT	TP	TP	NT	XC		NT	NT		NT	NT	XC
		◇1						◇1	◇1						◇1	◇1		◇1							◇1
		A					C	D			E	F					E	G					H	I	J
		🛒						🛒	⊠				🚌		🛒	🛒		🛒							🛒
Manchester Airport 85 ✈	d														09 55										
Manchester Piccadilly 10	d														10 20	10 42									
Stockport 78	d														10 28										
Sheffield 7	a														11 08										
	d	10 21		10 24			10 41	10 47				10 53			11 11		11 14	11 21			11 24			11 41	11 47
Meadowhall	d			10 30			10 47					10 59			11 16		11 21				11 30			11 47	
Rotherham Central	d			10 36								11 05					11 27				11 37				
Swinton (S.Yorks)	d			10 44								11 16					11a36				11 47				
Mexborough	d			10 50								11 19									11 50				
Conisbrough	d			10 54								11 23									11 54				
London Kings Cross	d								09 48																
Doncaster 7	a			11 04			11 13	11 15	11 24			11 32			11 35						12 04			12 14	12 15
York 8 26	a	11 26						11 40										12 26							12 39
Doncaster 31	d		10 41	11 08			11 18		11 26		11 26	11 34			11 37					11 41	12 08			12 17	
Bentley (S.Yorks) 31	a										11 29	11 37													
Adwick 31	a										11 33	11 43													
Kirk Sandall	d		10 47	11 14																11 47	12 14				
Hatfield & Stainforth	d		10 52	11 19																11 52	12 19				
Thorne South	d			11 24																	12 24				
Crowle	d			11 32																	12 32				
Althorpe	d			11 38																	12 38				
Scunthorpe	a			11 46											12 02						12 46				
	d														12 03										
Barnetby	d														12 17										
Hull Paragon Interchange	d												11 05												
Barton-on-Humber	a												11 40												
Barton-on-Humber	d													11 52											
Barrow Haven	d													11 57											
New Holland	d													12 00											
Goxhill	d													12 05											
Thornton Abbey	d													12 08											
Ulceby	d													12 12											
Habrough	d													12 17	12 26										
Stallingborough	d													12 22											
Healing	d													12 25											
Great Coates	d													12 28											
Grimsby Town	a													12 33	12 39										
	d													12 33	12 40										
Grimsby Docks	d													12 36											
New Clee	d													12x38											
Cleethorpes	a													12 43	12 52										
Thorne North	d		10 57																	11 57					
Goole	d		11 07				11 38													12 07				12 38	
Saltmarshe	d																								
York 8 33	d					10 43																	11 45		
Selby	a					11 03			11 40							11 57							12 04		
Wressle	d																								
Howden	d					11 15			11 51														12 14		
Eastrington	d																								
Gilberdyke	d		11 17			11 21														12 16			12 21		
Broomfleet	d		11 21																						
Brough	d		11 27			11 31	11 52		12 03							12 16				12 24			12 29	12 51	
Ferriby	d		11 32																	12 29					
Hessle	d		11 36																	12 33					
Hull	a		11 51			11 51	12 10		12 20							12 36				12 45			12 49	13 11	

A From Plymouth to Edinburgh
C To Bridlington
D From Bournemouth to Newcastle
E To Leeds
F From Lincoln
G From Plymouth to Glasgow Central
H From Hull
I To Scarborough
J From Southampton Central to Newcastle

Table 29

Saturdays

Manchester Airport, Manchester, Sheffield and Meadowhall-Doncaster-Cleethorpes and Hull Barton-on-Humber - Cleethorpes

Network Diagram - see first Page of Table 18

Station		NT	NT			EM	NT	TP	TP	NT	XC	NT	NT			NT	NT	XC	HT	NT	NT	NT	NT	TP	TP
								◇1	◇1		◇1							◇1	◇1					◇1	◇1
		A	B			C				A	D					F	G	H		A	B				
								🛒			🛒							🛒	⊠			🚌		🛒	
Manchester Airport 85 ✈	d							10 55																11 55	
Manchester Piccadilly 10	d							11 20	11 42															12 20	12 42
Stockport 78	d							11 28																12 28	
Sheffield 7	a							12 08																13 08	
	d		11 53				12 00	12 11		12 14	12 21		12 24				12 41	12 47			12 53			13 11	
Meadowhall	d		11 59					12 16		12 21			12 30				12 47				12 59			13 16	
Rotherham Central	d		12 05							12 27			12 37								13 05				
Swinton (S.Yorks)	d		12 16							12a36			12 47								13 16				
Mexborough	d		12 19										12 50								13 19				
Conisbrough	d		12 23										12 54								13 23				
London Kings Cross	d																		11 48						
Doncaster 7	a		12 33					12 35					13 04				13 14	13 17	13 24		13 32			13 35	
York 8 26	a										13 26							13 40							
Doncaster 31	d	12 26	12 34					12 37				12 42	13 08				13 17		13 26	13 26	13 34			13 37	
Bentley (S.Yorks) 31	a	12 29	12 37																	13 29	13 37				
Adwick 31	a	12 33	12 43																	13 33	13 43				
Kirk Sandall	d											12 48	13 14												
Hatfield & Stainforth	d											12 53	13 19												
Thorne South	d												13 24												
Crowle	d												13 33												
Althorpe	d												13 39												
Scunthorpe	a							13 02					13 46											14 02	
	d							13 03																14 03	
Barnetby	d					13 11	13 38	13 17																14 18	
Hull Paragon Interchange	d																					13 05			
Barton-on-Humber	a																					13 40			
Barton-on-Humber	d																						13 52		
Barrow Haven	d																						13 57		
New Holland	d																						14 00		
Goxhill	d																						14 05		
Thornton Abbey	d																						14 08		
Ulceby	d																						14 12		
Habrough	d					13 20	13 47																14 17	14 26	
Stallingborough	d																						14 22		
Healing	d																						14 25		
Great Coates	d																						14 28		
Grimsby Town	a					13 36	14 00	13 37															14 33	14 39	
	d						14 00	13 38															14 33	14 40	
Grimsby Docks	d																						14 36		
New Clee	d																						14x38		
Cleethorpes	a						14 11	13 50															14 43	14 52	
Thorne North	d											12 58													
Goole	d											13 07					13 37								
Saltmarshe	d																								
York 8 33	d															12 47									
Selby	a								12 57							13 06			13 40						13 57
Wressle	d																								
Howden	d															13 16			13 51						
Eastrington	d																								
Gilberdyke	d											13 15													
Broomfleet	d																								
Brough	d								13 16			13 23				13 28	13 51		14 03						14 16
Ferriby	d											13 28													
Hessle	d											13 32													
Hull	a								13 35			13 45				13 48	14 08		14 22						14 35

A To Leeds
B From Lincoln
C From Newark North Gate
D From Plymouth to Edinburgh
F From Hull
G To Bridlington
H From Reading to Newcastle

Table 29

Saturdays

Manchester Airport, Manchester, Sheffield and Meadowhall-Doncaster-Cleethorpes and Hull Barton-on-Humber - Cleethorpes

Network Diagram - see first Page of Table 18

		NT	XC	NT	NT	NT	NT	NT	XC	NT	NT	TP	TP	NT	XC	NT	NT	NT	NT	XC
			◇■1						◇■1			◇■1	◇■1		◇■1					◇■1
		A	B					D	E	A	F			A	G			H	I	J
			🍴						🍴			🍴	🍴		🍴					🍴
Manchester Airport 85 ✈	d											12 55								
Manchester Piccadilly ■10 🚢	d											13 20	13 42							
Stockport 78	d											13 28								
Sheffield ■7 🚢	a											14 08								
	d	13 14	13 21		13 24	13 28		13 41	13 47		13 53	14 11		14 14	14 21		14 24		14 41	14 47
Meadowhall 🚢	d	13 21			13 30	13 35		13 47			13 59	14 16		14 21			14 30		14 47	
Rotherham Central	d	13 27			13 37	13 42					14 05			14 27			14 37			
Swinton (S.Yorks)	d	13a36			13 47	13 51					14 17			14a36			14 48			
Mexborough	d				13 50						14 20						14 51			
Conisbrough	d				13 54						14 24						14 55			
London Kings Cross	d																			
Doncaster ■7	a				14 03			14 16	14 18		14 32	14 35					15 04		15 16	15 17
York ■8 26	a		14 26			14 56			14 40						15 28					15 40
Doncaster 31	d			13 41	14 07			14 17		14 26	14 34	14 37				14 40	15 07		15 17	
Bentley (S.Yorks) 31	a									14 29	14 37									
Adwick 31	a									14 33	14 43									
Kirk Sandall	d			13 47	14 13											14 46	15 13			
Hatfield & Stainforth	d			13 52	14 18											14 51	15 18			
Thorne South	d				14 25												15 23			
Crowle	d				14 33												15 31			
Althorpe	d				14 39												15 37			
Scunthorpe	a				14 48							15 02					15 46			
	d											15 03								
Barnetby	d											15 17								
Hull Paragon Interchange	d																			
Barton-on-Humber	a																			
Barton-on-Humber	d																			
Barrow Haven	d																			
New Holland	d																			
Goxhill	d																			
Thornton Abbey	d																			
Ulceby	d																			
Habrough	d																			
Stallingborough	d																			
Healing	d																			
Great Coates	d																			
Grimsby Town	a											15 37								
	d											15 38								
Grimsby Docks	d																			
New Clee	d																			
Cleethorpes	a											15 50								
Thorne North	d			13 57												14 56				
Goole	d			14 07				14 38								15 07			15 37	
Saltmarshe	d			14 12																
York ■8 33	d						13 44											14 47		
Selby	a						14 07						14 57					15 06		
Wressle	d																			
Howden	d						14 17											15 16		
Eastrington	d																			
Gilberdyke	d			14 16												15 15				
Broomfleet	d																			
Brough	d			14 24			14 30	14 52					15 16			15 23		15 28	15 51	
Ferriby	d			14 29												15 28				
Hessle	d			14 33												15 32				
Hull	a			14 48			14 52	15 09					15 35			15 45		15 48	16 08	

A To Leeds
B From Penzance to Glasgow Central
D To Bridlington
E From Southampton Central to Newcastle
F From Lincoln
G From Plymouth to Aberdeen
H From Hull
I To Scarborough
J From Reading to Newcastle

Table 29

Saturdays

Manchester Airport, Manchester, Sheffield and Meadowhall-Doncaster-Cleethorpes and Hull Barton-on-Humber - Cleethorpes

Network Diagram - see first Page of Table 18

	EM	NT	NT	NT	NT	TP	TP	NT	XC	NT	NT		NT	XC	NT		NT	HT	NT	NT	TP	TP	NT	XC
						◇1	◇1		◇1					◇1				◇1			◇1	◇1		◇1
	A	B	A					B	C				E	F	G		B		A				B	H
				(bus)		(trolley)			(trolley)					(trolley)				(restaurant)			(trolley)			(trolley)
Manchester Airport 85 ✈ d						13 55															14 55			
Manchester Piccadilly 10 d						14 20	14 42														15 20	15 42		
Stockport 78 d						14 28															15 28			
Sheffield 7 a						15 08															16 08			
d			14 53			15 11		15 14	15 21		15 24		15 41	15 47					15 53	16 00	16 11		16 14	16 21
Meadowhall d			14 59			15 16		15 21			15 30		15 47						15 59		16 16		16 21	
Rotherham Central d			15 05					15 27			15 36								16 05				16 27	
Swinton (S.Yorks) d			15 17					15a36			15 47								16 16				16a36	
Mexborough d			15 20								15 50								16 19					
Conisbrough d			15 24								15 54								16 23					
London Kings Cross d																		14 48						
Doncaster 7 a			15 34			15 35					16 04		16 14	16 18				16 24	16 32		16 35			
York 8 26 a									16 26					16 41										17 26
Doncaster 31 d		15 26	15 34			15 37				15 41	16 08		16 19				16 25	16 26	16 34		16 37			
Bentley (S.Yorks) 31 a		15 29	15 37														16 28		16 37					
Adwick 31 a		15 33	15 43														16 32		16 43					
Kirk Sandall d										15 47	16 14													
Hatfield & Stainforth d										15 52	16 19													
Thorne South d											16 24													
Crowle d											16 33													
Althorpe d											16 39													
Scunthorpe a						16 02					16 46										17 02			
d						16 03															17 03			
Barnetby d	15 25					16 17														17 38	17 17			
Hull Paragon Interchange d				15 05																				
Barton-on-Humber a				15 40																				
Barton-on-Humber d					15 54																			
Barrow Haven d					15 59																			
New Holland d					16 02																			
Goxhill d					16 07																			
Thornton Abbey d					16 10																			
Ulceby d					16 14																			
Habrough d	15 33				16 19	16 26														17 47				
Stallingborough d					16 24																			
Healing d					16 27																			
Great Coates d					16 30																			
Grimsby Town a	15 48				16 35	16 39														18 01	17 37			
d					16 35	16 40														18 02	17 38			
Grimsby Docks d					16 38																			
New Clee d																								
Cleethorpes a					16 44	16 52														18 11	17 50			
Thorne North d										15 57														
Goole d										16 07			16 38											
Saltmarshe d																								
York 8 33 d															16 12									
Selby a							15 57								16 36			16 41				17 00		
Wressle d															16 44									
Howden d															16 49			16 54						
Eastrington d																								
Gilberdyke d										16 18					16 55									
Broomfleet d																								
Brough d							16 16			16 26			16 52		17 03			17 10				17 18		
Ferriby d										16 30					17 08									
Hessle d										16 35					17 12									
Hull a							16 35			16 48			17 06		17 27			17 27				17 37		

A From Lincoln
B To Leeds
C From Penzance to Glasgow Central
E To Bridlington
F From Southampton Central to Newcastle
G From Hull
H From Plymouth to Dundee

Table 29

Saturdays

Manchester Airport, Manchester, Sheffield and Meadowhall-Doncaster-Cleethorpes and Hull Barton-on-Humber - Cleethorpes

Network Diagram - see first Page of Table 18

		NT			NT	NT	XC		NT	NT	NT	NT	EM	NT	NT	TP	TP	NT	XC		NT	NT		NT	XC
							◇1									◇1	◇1		◇1						◇1
					B	C	D		E		F	G	G					F	H					I	J
														🚌											
							🍴									🍴			🍴						🍴
Manchester Airport 85 ✈	d															15 55									
Manchester Piccadilly 10 🚇	d															16 20	16 42								
Stockport 78	d															16 28									
Sheffield 7 🚇	a															17 08									
	d	16 24				16 41	16 47					16 53				17 11		17 14	17 21		17 25			17 41	17 47
Meadowhall 🚇	d	16 30				16 47						16 59				17 16		17 21			17 31			17 47	
Rotherham Central	d	16 37										17 05						17 27			17 37				
Swinton (S.Yorks)	d	16 46										17 16						17a37			17 45				
Mexborough	d	16 49										17 19									17 48				
Conisbrough	d	16 53										17 23									17 52				
London Kings Cross	d																								
Doncaster 7	a	17 06				17 12	17 16					17 32				17 35					18 11			18 13	
York 8 26	a						17 37												18 28						18 58
Doncaster 31	d				16 42	17 19				17 22	17 26	17 34				17 43						17 47		18 16	
Bentley (S.Yorks) 31	a										17 29	17 37													
Adwick 31	a										17 33	17 43													
Kirk Sandall	d				16 48					17 29												17 53			
Hatfield & Stainforth	d				16 53					17 34												17 58			
Thorne South	d									17 39															
Crowle	d									17 48															
Althorpe	d									17 54															
Scunthorpe	a									18 02						18 08									
	d															18 09									
Barnetby	d												17 54			18 23									
Hull Paragon Interchange	d													17 10											
Barton-on-Humber	a													17 45											
Barton-on-Humber	d														17 55										
Barrow Haven	d														18 00										
New Holland	d														18 03										
Goxhill	d														18 08										
Thornton Abbey	d														18 11										
Ulceby	d														18 15										
Habrough	d												18 02		18 20	18 32									
Stallingborough	d														18 25										
Healing	d														18 28										
Great Coates	d														18 31										
Grimsby Town	a												18 17		18 36	18 45									
	d														18 36	18 46									
Grimsby Docks	d														18 43										
New Clee	d																								
Cleethorpes	a														18 50	18 58									
Thorne North	d				16 58	17 31																18 03			
Goole	d				17 07	17 40																18 12		18 36	
Saltmarshe	d																					18 17			
York 8 33	d								17 19																
Selby	a								17 45								17 59								
Wressle	d																								
Howden	d								17 56								18 08								
Eastrington	d																								
Gilberdyke	d				17 14				18 03													18 23			
Broomfleet	d																					18 27			
Brough	d				17 22	17 52			18 11								18 20					18 33		18 53	
Ferriby	d				17 27																	18 38			
Hessle	d				17 31																	18 42			
Hull	a				17 47	18 13			18 30								18 39					18 55		19 09	

B To Beverley
C To Bridlington
D From Reading to Newcastle
E From Hull
F To Leeds
G From Lincoln
H From Plymouth to Glasgow Central
I To Scarborough
J From Southampton Central to Newcastle

Table 29

Saturdays

Manchester Airport, Manchester, Sheffield and Meadowhall-Doncaster-Cleethorpes and Hull Barton-on-Humber - Cleethorpes

Network Diagram - see first Page of Table 18

		NT	TP	NT	NT	NT	GR	NT	XC	EM	TP	NT	NT	XC	NT	NT	HT	NT	NT	NT	TP	TP
			◇1				R 1		◇1		◇1			◇1			◇1				◇1	◇1
				A	B	C		A	D	E			G	H		A		I				
Manchester Airport 85 ✈	d										16 55										17 55	
Manchester Piccadilly 10	d		17 42								17 20										18 20	18 42
Stockport 78	d										17 28										18 28	
Sheffield 7	a										18 10										19 09	
	d					17 53		18 13	18 21		18 24	18 29	18 41	18 47				19 00			19 11	
Meadowhall	d					17 58		18 21			18 30	18 35	18 47					19 06			19 16	
Rotherham Central	d					18 05		18 27				18 42						19 12				
Swinton (S.Yorks)	d					18 16		18a37				18 50						19 18				
Mexborough	d					18 20						18 53						19 23				
Conisbrough	d					18 24						18 57						19 25				
London Kings Cross	d						17 10										17 48					
Doncaster 7	a					18 38	18 53				18 58	19 08	19 13	19 16			19 26	19 39			19 41	
York 8 26	a								19 26					19 39								
Doncaster 31	d			18 26	18 29	18 40	18 53				19 00		19 16		19 20	19 22	19 28				19 48	
Bentley (S.Yorks) 31	a			18 29												19 25						
Adwick 31	a			18 33												19 29						
Kirk Sandall	d				18 36	18 47									19 27							
Hatfield & Stainforth	d				18 41	18 52									19 32							
Thorne South	d				18 46										19 37							
Crowle	d				18 54										19 46							
Althorpe	d				19 00										19 52							
Scunthorpe	a				19 10						19 25				20 01						20 14	
	d										19 26										20 14	
Barnetby	d									19 08	19 40										20 28	
Hull Paragon Interchange	d																		19 25			
Barton-on-Humber	a																		19 52			
Barton-on-Humber	d																			19 58		
Barrow Haven	d																			20 03		
New Holland	d																			20 06		
Goxhill	d																			20 11		
Thornton Abbey	d																			20 14		
Ulceby	d																			20 18		
Habrough	d									19 16										20 23		
Stallingborough	d																			20 28		
Healing	d																			20 31		
Great Coates	d																			20 34		
Grimsby Town	a									19 31	20 00									20 39	20 47	
	d										20 01									20 39	20 48	
Grimsby Docks	d																			20 42		
New Clee	d																					
Cleethorpes	a										20 12									20 48	21 00	
Thorne North	d					18 57																
Goole	d					19 12							19 37									
Saltmarshe	d																					
York 8 33	d	18 18																				
Selby	a	18 42	19 00				19 09										19 42					20 00
Wressle	d	18 50																				
Howden	d	18 54															19 53					20 10
Eastrington	d	18 59																				
Gilberdyke	d	19 03				19 21																
Broomfleet	d																					
Brough	d	19 10	19 19			19 29	19 36						19 54				20 05					20 22
Ferriby	d					19 34																
Hessle	d					19 38																
Hull	a	19 29	19 38			19 50	19 54						20 10				20 24					20 43

A To Leeds
B From Adwick
C From Lincoln
D From Plymouth to Edinburgh
E From Newark North Gate
G To Bridlington
H From Reading to Newcastle
I From Retford

Table 29

Saturdays

Manchester Airport, Manchester, Sheffield and Meadowhall-Doncaster-Cleethorpes and Hull Barton-on-Humber - Cleethorpes

Network Diagram - see first Page of Table 18

		NT	XC	NT	NT	NT	NT	XC	NT	NT	TP	NT	XC	NT	NT	XC	NT	TP	HT
			◇1					◇1			◇1		◇1			◇1		◇1	◇1
		A	B	C			E	F	A	G			H	A		I	A	J	
																			⊠
Manchester Airport 85	d										18 55								
Manchester Piccadilly 10	d										19 18								
Stockport 78	d										19 26								
Sheffield 7	a										20 08								
	d	19 18	19 22			19 25	19 44	19 54		19 58	20 11	20 15	20 24	20 27	20 38	20 53			
Meadowhall	d	19 25				19 31	19 50			20 04	20 16	20 21		20 35	20 45				
Rotherham Central	d	19 31				19 37				20 11		20 27		20 41	20 53				
Swinton (S.Yorks)	d	19a40				19 47				20 21		20 40		20a50	21 01				
Mexborough	d					19 50				20 24		20 43			21 04				
Conisbrough	d					19 54				20 28		20 47			21 08				
London Kings Cross	d																		19 48
Doncaster 7	a					20 02	20 14	20 17		20 36	20 44	20 55			21 18	21 21			21 28
York 8 26	a		20 29					20 40					21 57			21 44			
Doncaster 31	d				19 55	20 07	20 16		20 26	20 43	20 45	20 56			21 20		21 22		21 30
Bentley (S.Yorks) 31	a								20 29								21 25		
Adwick 31	a								20 33								21 29		
Kirk Sandall	d				20 01	20 13						21 03			21 26				
Hatfield & Stainforth	d				20 06	20 18						21 08			21 31				
Thorne South	d					20 22									21 38				
Crowle	d					20 31									21 46				
Althorpe	d					20 37									21 52				
Scunthorpe	a					20 45					21 11				22 01				
	d										21 12								
Barnetby	d										21 26								
Hull Paragon Interchange	d																		
Barton-on-Humber	a																		
Barton-on-Humber	d																		
Barrow Haven	d																		
New Holland	d																		
Goxhill	d																		
Thornton Abbey	d																		
Ulceby	d																		
Habrough	d										21 35								
Stallingborough	d																		
Healing	d																		
Great Coates	d																		
Grimsby Town	a										21 48								
	d										21 49								
Grimsby Docks	d																		
New Clee	d																		
Cleethorpes	a										22 00								
Thorne North	d				20 11							21 14							
Goole	d				20 20		20 36					21a23							
Saltmarshe	d																		
York 8 33	d			19 47															
Selby	a			20 06						21 01									21 44
Wressle	d																		
Howden	d			20 16														21 39	21 55
Eastrington	d																		
Gilberdyke	d				20 28					21 15									
Broomfleet	d																		
Brough	d			20 30	20 36		20 49			21 23								21 51	22 07
Ferriby	d				20 41					21 28									
Hessle	d				20 45					21 32									
Hull	a			20 48	21 00		21 07			21 47								22 10	22 26

A To Leeds
B From Plymouth to Edinburgh
C From Blackpool North
E To Beverley
F From Southampton Central to Newcastle
G To Bridlington
H From Plymouth
I From Reading to Newcastle
J From Leeds

Table 29

Saturdays

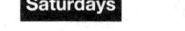

Manchester Airport, Manchester, Sheffield and Meadowhall-Doncaster-Cleethorpes and Hull Barton-on-Humber - Cleethorpes

Network Diagram - see first Page of Table 18

		NT	NT	NT	NT	TP	XC	NT	NT	TP	NT		XC	NT	TP	NT
						◇1	◇1			◇1			◇1		◇1	
		A	B			C	D	E	B		B		F		G	
				🚌												
Manchester Airport 85 ✈	d									20 47						
Manchester Piccadilly 10 🚇	d									21 20						
Stockport 78	d									21 28						
Sheffield 7 🚇	a									22 08						
	d	21 14	21 30			21 34	22 09			22 11	22 24		22 27	22 30		23 27
Meadowhall 🚇	d	21 21	21 36			21 40				22 16	22 30			22 36		23 33
Rotherham Central	d	21 27	21 42								22 36			22 45		23 39
Swinton (S.Yorks)	d	21 32	21a50								22a45			22 53		23 48
Mexborough	d	21 35												22 56		23 51
Conisbrough	d	21 39												23 00		23 55
London Kings Cross	d															
Doncaster 7	a	21 54				22 03	22 30			22 36			22 51	23 09		00 08
York 8 26	a						22 57									
Doncaster 31	d	21 56				22 05			22 26	22 37				23 10		
Bentley (S.Yorks) 31	a								22 29							
Adwick 31	a								22 33							
Kirk Sandall	d	22 02								22 43				23 17		
Hatfield & Stainforth	d	22 07								22 47				23 22		
Thorne South	d									22 52						
Crowle	d									23 00						
Althorpe	d									23 06						
Scunthorpe	a					22 30				23 11						
	d					22 31				23 11						
Barnetby	d					22 46				23 26						
Hull Paragon Interchange	d			21 25												
Barton-on-Humber	a			21 52												
Barton-on-Humber	d				21 58											
Barrow Haven	d				22 03											
New Holland	d				22 06											
Goxhill	d				22 11											
Thornton Abbey	d				22 14											
Ulceby	d				22 18											
Habrough	d				22 23	22 54				23 34						
Stallingborough	d				22 28											
Healing	d				22 31											
Great Coates	d				22 34											
Grimsby Town	a				22 39	23 09				23 47						
	d				22 39	23 10				23 48						
Grimsby Docks	d				22 42											
New Clee	d															
Cleethorpes	a				22 48	23 20				23 59						
Thorne North	d	22 13												23 27		
Goole	d	22 22												23a38		
Saltmarshe	d	22 26														
York 8 33	d							22 11								
Selby	a							22 29								
Wressle	d															
Howden	d							22 39								
Eastrington	d															
Gilberdyke	d	22 32						22 45								
Broomfleet	d															
Brough	d	22 40						22 53							23 06	
Ferriby	d							22 58								
Hessle	d							23 02								
Hull	a	22 58						23 14							23 25	

A To Beverley
B To Leeds
C from 18 February
D From Southampton Central
E From Hull
F From Plymouth to Leeds
G From Leeds

Table 29

Sundays
until 1 January

Manchester Airport, Manchester, Sheffield and Meadowhall-Doncaster-Cleethorpes and Hull Barton-on-Humber - Cleethorpes

Network Diagram - see first Page of Table 18

	NT	NT	NT	NT	NT	XC	NT	GR	NT		TP	TP	XC	NT	NT		NT	NT	NT		XC	EM		NT
	A			B	C	◇1 D	B	R 1 E	F		◇1 G	◇1	◇1 H		C				B		◇1 I	◇1 J		B
Manchester Airport 85 d																								
Manchester Piccadilly 10 d											09 11													
Stockport 78 d																								
Sheffield 7 a																								
d	23p27	08 00			08 45	09 21	09 36					09 52	10 21		10 26		11 05				11 21	11 31		11 36
Meadowhall d	23p33	08 06			08 51		09 42					09 57			10 32		11 11							11 42
Rotherham Central d	23p39	08 12			08 57		09 48					10 03					11 17							11 49
Swinton (S.Yorks) d	23p48	08 20			09 05		09a58					10 09					11 25							12a00
Mexborough d	23p51	08 23			09 08							10 13					11 28							
Conisbrough d	23p55	08 27			09 12							10 17					11 32							
London Kings Cross d																								
Doncaster 7 a	00 08	08 38			09 22							10 26			10 51		11 43					11 52		
York 8 26 a						10 29							11 29								12 29	12 15		
Doncaster 31 d			09 07	09 12	09 26			09 37	10 19			10 28			10 55			11 07	11 12					
Bentley (S.Yorks) 31 a				09 15															11 15					
Adwick 31 a				09 19															11 19					
Kirk Sandall d			09 13															11 13						
Hatfield & Stainforth d			09 18															11 18						
Thorne South d																								
Crowle d																								
Althorpe d																								
Scunthorpe a												10 54												
d												10 55												
Barnetby d												11 09												
Hull Paragon Interchange d																								
Barton-on-Humber a																								
Barton-on-Humber d																								
Barrow Haven d																								
New Holland d																								
Goxhill d																								
Thornton Abbey d																								
Ulceby d																								
Habrough d																								
Stallingborough d																								
Healing d																								
Great Coates d																								
Grimsby Town a												11 29												
d												11 33												
Grimsby Docks d																								
New Clee d																								
Cleethorpes a												11 40												
Thorne North d			09 24		09 38				10 31									11 25						
Goole d			09a35		09 47				10 40						11 14			11a36						
Saltmarshe d																								
York 8 33 d								09a58						10 40										
Selby a											10 44			10 58										
Wressle d																								
Howden d														11 08										
Eastrington d																								
Gilberdyke d					09 55				10 48						11 24									
Broomfleet d																								
Brough d					10 03				10 56		11 04			11 19	11 32									
Ferriby d									11 00															
Hessle d									11 05															
Hull a					10 21				11 17		11 18			11 41	11 47									

A not 11 December
B To Leeds
C To Scarborough
D To Glasgow Central
E To Edinburgh
F To Bridlington
G From Liverpool Lime Street
H From Birmingham New Street to Edinburgh
I From Birmingham New Street to Glasgow Central
J From Leicester

Table 29

Sundays
until 1 January

Manchester Airport, Manchester, Sheffield and Meadowhall-Doncaster-Cleethorpes and Hull Barton-on-Humber - Cleethorpes

Network Diagram - see first Page of Table 18

		NT	HT	TP	XC	NT		NT		TP	TP		EM	NT	XC	NT		NT		NT	XC	HT	TP	XC	NT
			◇1	◇1	◇1					◇1	◇1		◇		◇1						◇1	◇1	◇1	◇1	
					A			B					E	F	G			H		F	I			J	
			⊠		🛒										🛒						🛒	⊠		🛒	
Manchester Airport 85 ✈	d			10 44																			12 55		
Manchester Piccadilly 10 🚌	d			11 18						12 01	12 18		12 44										13 20		
Stockport 78	d			11 27							12 28		12 55										13 28		
Sheffield 7 🚌	a			12 09							13 08		13 37										14 08		
	d			12 11	12 21	12 24		12 28			13 11				13 21			13 24		13 36	13 51		14 11	14 21	14 22
Meadowhall 🚌	d			12 16		12 30		12 34			13 16							13 30		13 42			14 16		14 28
Rotherham Central	d					12 36												13 36		13 49					14 35
Swinton (S.Yorks)	d					12 49												13 47		13a57					14 46
Mexborough	d					12 52												13 50							14 49
Conisbrough	d					12 56												13 54							14 53
London Kings Cross	d		10 45																			12 45			
Doncaster 7	a		12 23	12 35		13 04		12 56			13 34							14 02			14 13	14 23	14 35		15 03
York 8 26	a				13 29										14 29						14 40			15 29	
Doncaster 31	d		12 29	12 37		13 05		12 58						13 12				14 05				14 25	14 37		15 05
Bentley (S.Yorks) 31	a													13 15											
Adwick 31	a													13 19											
Kirk Sandall	d					13 11																			15 11
Hatfield & Stainforth	d					13 16																			15 16
Thorne South	d																								
Crowle	d																								
Althorpe	d																								
Scunthorpe	a			13 06																			15 02		
	d			13 06																			15 03		
Barnetby	d			13 21																			15 17		
Hull Paragon Interchange	d																								
Barton-on-Humber	a																								
Barton-on-Humber	d																								
Barrow Haven	d																								
New Holland	d																								
Goxhill	d																								
Thornton Abbey	d																								
Ulceby	d																								
Habrough	d			13 29																					
Stallingborough	d																								
Healing	d																								
Great Coates	d																								
Grimsby Town	a			13 42																			15 37		
	d			13 43																			15 38		
Grimsby Docks	d																								
New Clee	d																								
Cleethorpes	a			13 53																			15 49		
Thorne North	d					13 22																			15 24
Goole	d					13a32		13 17										14 25							15a33
Saltmarshe	d																								
York 8 33	d	12 05														13 40									
Selby	a	12 24	12 43							13 23						13 59						14 39			
Wressle	d																								
Howden	d	12 34	12 54													14 09						14 50			
Eastrington	d																								
Gilberdyke	d							13 25										14 33							
Broomfleet	d																								
Brough	d	12 46	13 07					13 33		13 41						14 21		14 41				15 03			
Ferriby	d							13 38																	
Hessle	d							13 42																	
Hull	a	13 06	13 25					13 57		13 59						14 40		15 01				15 21			

A From Bristol Temple Meads to Edinburgh
B To Scarborough
C To Edinburgh
D To Newcastle
E To Norwich
F To Leeds
G From Bristol Temple Meads to Glasgow Central
H To Bridlington
I From Birmingham New Street to Newcastle
J From Plymouth to Aberdeen

Table 29

Sundays
until 1 January

Manchester Airport, Manchester, Sheffield and Meadowhall-Doncaster-Cleethorpes and Hull Barton-on-Humber - Cleethorpes

Network Diagram - see first Page of Table 18

	NT		NT		TP	XC	NT	TP	XC	NT	NT			NT	XC	NT	HT	TP	XC	NT	NT			TP
					◇1	◇1		◇1	◇1						◇1		◇1	◇1	◇1					◇1
			A			C	D		E		F			D	G				H		A			
						ꝏ			ꝏ						ꝏ		☒		ꝏ					
Manchester Airport 85 ✈ d								13 55										14 55						
Manchester Piccadilly 10 ⇌ d					14 02			14 20										15 20						16 02
Stockport 78 d								14 28										15 28						
Sheffield 7 ⇌ a								15 08										16 09						
d			14 28			14 51		15 11	15 21	15 24	15 28			15 36	15 51			16 11	16 21	16 24	16 28			
Meadowhall ⇌ d			14 34					15 16		15 30	15 34			15 42				16 16		16 30	16 34			
Rotherham Central d										15 37				15 50						16 37				
Swinton (S.Yorks) d										15 47				15a58						16 47				
Mexborough d										15 50										16 50				
Conisbrough d										15 54										16 54				
London Kings Cross d																	14 45							
Doncaster 7 a			14 56			15 13		15 35		16 04	15 56				16 15		16 23	16 35		17 03	16 56			
York 8 26 a						15 43			16 29						16 40				17 29					
Doncaster 31 d			14 59				15 12	15 37			15 56						16 30	16 37		17 04	16 58			
Bentley (S.Yorks) 31 a							15 15																	
Adwick 31 a							15 19																	
Kirk Sandall d																				17 10				
Hatfield & Stainforth d																				17 15				
Thorne South d																								
Crowle d																								
Althorpe d																								
Scunthorpe a								16 02										17 02						
d								16 03										17 03						
Barnetby d								16 17										17 17						
Hull Paragon Interchange d																								
Barton-on-Humber a																								
Barton-on-Humber d																								
Barrow Haven d																								
New Holland d																								
Goxhill d																								
Thornton Abbey d																								
Ulceby d																								
Habrough d								16 26																
Stallingborough d																								
Healing d																								
Great Coates d																								
Grimsby Town a								16 39										17 37						
d								16 40										17 38						
Grimsby Docks d																								
New Clee d																								
Cleethorpes a								16 50										17 48						
Thorne North d											16 10									17 24				
Goole d			15 19								16 19									17a33	17 17			
Saltmarshe d																								
York 8 33 d	14 49															16 06								
Selby a	15 08				15 23											16 24	16 44							17 23
Wressle d																								
Howden d	15 18															16 34	16 55							
Eastrington d																								
Gilberdyke d			15 29								16 27										17 25			
Broomfleet d																								
Brough d	15 30		15 37		15 41						16 35					16 46	17 07				17 33			17 41
Ferriby d																								
Hessle d																								
Hull a	15 49		15 56		15 59						16 53					17 07	17 26				17 51			17 59

A To Scarborough
C From Birmingham New Street to Newcastle
D To Leeds
E From Plymouth to Glasgow Central
F To Bridlington
G From Guildford to Newcastle
H From Penzance to Edinburgh

Table 29

Sundays

until 1 January

Manchester Airport, Manchester, Sheffield and Meadowhall-Doncaster-Cleethorpes and Hull Barton-on-Humber - Cleethorpes

Network Diagram - see first Page of Table 18

		NT	XC	NT	NT	TP	XC	NT		NT		NT	XC	TP	XC	NT	NT	GR			TP	XC	NT	NT	NT
			◇■1			◇■1	◇■1						◇■1	◇■1	◇■1			■ 1			◇■1	◇■1			
			A		B		C			D		B	A		F		G					I			B
			🛒				🛒						🛒		🛒			🍴🛒				🛒			
Manchester Airport 85 ⇌	d					15 55								16 55											
Manchester Piccadilly 10	d					16 20								17 20							18 02				
Stockport 78	d					16 28								17 28											
Sheffield 7	a					17 08								18 08											
	d	16 36	16 51			17 11	17 21	17 25		17 28		17 36	17 51	18 11	18 21	18 25	18 28					18 51	18 57		
Meadowhall	d	16 42				17 16		17 31		17 34		17 44		18 16		18 31	18 35						19 05		
Rotherham Central	d	16 49						17 37				17 50				18 37							19 11		
Swinton (S.Yorks)	d	16 58						17 47				17a58				18 48							19 19		
Mexborough	d							17 50								18 51									
Conisbrough	d							17 54								18 55									
London Kings Cross	d																	17 20							
Doncaster 7	a		17 13			17 35		18 05		17 55			18 13	18 35		19 06	18 54	19 03				19 15			
York 8 26	a	17 59	17 42				18 29						19 18		19 29							19 43	20 18		
Doncaster 31	d				17 14	17 37				17 57				18 37			18 55	19 04							19 27
Bentley (S.Yorks) 31	a				17 17																				19 30
Adwick 31	a				17 21																				19 34
Kirk Sandall	d																19 01								
Hatfield & Stainforth	d																19 06								
Thorne South	d																								
Crowle	d																								
Althorpe	d																								
Scunthorpe	a					18 02								19 02											
	d					18 03								19 03											
Barnetby	d					18 17								19 17											
Hull Paragon Interchange	d																								
Barton-on-Humber	a																								
Barton-on-Humber	d																								
Barrow Haven	d																								
New Holland	d																								
Goxhill	d																								
Thornton Abbey	d																								
Ulceby	d																								
Habrough	d													19 26											
Stallingborough	d																								
Healing	d																								
Great Coates	d																								
Grimsby Town	a					18 37								19 39											
	d					18 38								19 40											
Grimsby Docks	d																								
New Clee	d																								
Cleethorpes	a					18 48								19 48											
Thorne North	d																19 12								
Goole	d									18 16							19 21								
Saltmarshe	d																								
York 8 33	d			17 11																				19 10	
Selby	a			17 30														19 23			19 28			19 35	
Wressle	d																								
Howden	d			17 41																				19 46	
Eastrington	d																								
Gilberdyke	d									18 24							19 29								
Broomfleet	d																								
Brough	d			17 53						18 32							19 37	19 45			19 48			19 58	
Ferriby	d																								
Hessle	d																								
Hull	a			18 12						18 48							19 55	20 03			20 05			20 17	

A From Reading to Newcastle
B To Leeds
C From Plymouth to Glasgow Central
D To Bridlington
F From Plymouth to Edinburgh
G To Beverley
I From Reading to Edinburgh

Table 29

Sundays
until 1 January

Manchester Airport, Manchester, Sheffield and Meadowhall-Doncaster-Cleethorpes and Hull Barton-on-Humber - Cleethorpes

Network Diagram - see first Page of Table 18

	HT	TP	TP		XC	NT		NT	XC	NT	TP	TP	XC		NT		XC	HT	TP	NT	NT	NT	NT
	◇1	◇1	◇1		◇1				◇1		◇1	◇1	◇1				◇1	◇1	◇1				
					A			C	D				E				D				C		C
	⊠								⚲				⚲					⊠					
Manchester Airport 85 ✈ d		17 55									18 55								19 55				
Manchester Piccadilly 10 ⇌ d		18 20	19 02								19 20	20 06							20 18				
Stockport 78 d		18 28									19 28								20 27				
Sheffield 7 ⇌ a		19 08									20 08								21 08				
d		19 11			19 21	19 29		19 36	19 51	20 02	20 11		20 21		20 28		20 51		21 11			21 24	21 36
Meadowhall ⇌ d		19 16				19 35		19 42		20 09	20 16				20 34				21 16			21 30	21 42
Rotherham Central d						19 41		19 49							20 40							21 37	21 48
Swinton (S.Yorks) d						19 49		19a57							20 48							21 47	21a56
Mexborough d						19 52									20 51							21 50	
Conisbrough d						19 56									20 55							21 54	
London Kings Cross d	17 45																	19 45					
Doncaster 7 a	19 23	19 35				20 07			20 16	20 30	20 35				21 05		21 19	21 25	21 35			22 03	
York 8 26 a					20 29				20 45				21 31				21 44						
Doncaster 31 d	19 30	19 37								20 30	20 37				21 07			21 27	21 37		21 52	22 04	
Bentley (S.Yorks) 31 a																					21 55		
Adwick 31 a																					21 59		
Kirk Sandall d															21 13								
Hatfield & Stainforth d															21 18								
Thorne South d																							
Crowle d																							
Althorpe d																							
Scunthorpe a		20 02									21 02								22 02				
d		20 03									21 03								22 03				
Barnetby d		20 17									21 17								22 17				
Hull Paragon Interchange d																							
Barton-on-Humber a																							
Barton-on-Humber d																							
Barrow Haven d																							
New Holland d																							
Goxhill d																							
Thornton Abbey d																							
Ulceby d																							
Habrough d											21 26								22 26				
Stallingborough d																							
Healing d																							
Great Coates d																							
Grimsby Town a		20 37									21 39								22 39				
d		20 38									21 40								22 40				
Grimsby Docks d																							
New Clee d																							
Cleethorpes a		20 48									21 50								22 50				
Thorne North d															21 24								
Goole d										20 49					21a34							22 23	
Saltmarshe d																							
York 8 33 d																				21 41			
Selby a	19 45		20 17									21 38						21 43		22 00			
Wressle d																							
Howden d	19 56																	21 55		22 10			
Eastrington d																							
Gilberdyke d										20 57												22 31	
Broomfleet d																							
Brough d	20 08		20 36							21 05		21 58						22 07		22 22		22 39	
Ferriby d																							
Hessle d																							
Hull a	20 26		20 54							21 23		22 12						22 26		22 36		22 56	

A From Plymouth to Edinburgh
C To Leeds
D From Reading to Newcastle
E From Plymouth

Table 29

Sundays
until 1 January

Manchester Airport, Manchester, Sheffield and Meadowhall-Doncaster-Cleethorpes and Hull Barton-on-Humber - Cleethorpes

Network Diagram - see first Page of Table 18

Station		TP	NT	NT	TP	NT
		◇1 A			◇1	
Manchester Airport 85 ✈	d					
Manchester Piccadilly 10 ⇌	d					
Stockport 78	d					
Sheffield 7 ⇌	a					
	d		22 13	22 26	22 30	23 34
Meadowhall ⇌	d		22 19	22 32	22 35	23 40
Rotherham Central	d			22 38		23 47
Swinton (S.Yorks)	d			22 48		23 55
Mexborough	d			22 51		23 58
Conisbrough	d			22 55		00 02
London Kings Cross	d					
Doncaster 7	a		22 38	23 05	22 56	00 13
York 8 26	a					
Doncaster 31	d		22 41		22 58	
Bentley (S.Yorks) 31	a					
Adwick 31	a					
Kirk Sandall	d					
Hatfield & Stainforth	d					
Thorne South	d					
Crowle	d					
Althorpe	d					
Scunthorpe	a				23 23	
	d				23 24	
Barnetby	d				23 38	
Hull Paragon Interchange	d					
Barton-on-Humber	a					
Barton-on-Humber	d					
Barrow Haven	d					
New Holland	d					
Goxhill	d					
Thornton Abbey	d					
Ulceby	d					
Habrough	d					
Stallingborough	d					
Healing	d					
Great Coates	d					
Grimsby Town	a				23 57	
	d				23 58	
Grimsby Docks	d					
New Clee	d					
Cleethorpes	a				00 09	
Thorne North	d		22 53			
Goole	d		23 02			
Saltmarshe	d					
York 8 33	d					
Selby	a					
Wressle	d					
Howden	d					
Eastrington	d					
Gilberdyke	d		23 10			
Broomfleet	d					
Brough	d	23 02	23 18			
Ferriby	d					
Hessle	d					
Hull	a	23 19	23 39			

A From Leeds

Table 29

Sundays

8 January to 12 February

Manchester Airport, Manchester, Sheffield and Meadowhall-Doncaster-Cleethorpes and Hull Barton-on-Humber - Cleethorpes

Network Diagram - see first Page of Table 18

		NT	NT	NT	NT	NT	TP	XC	NT	GR	NT	TP	TP	XC	NT	NT	NT	NT	NT	XC	EM	GR
								◇1		1		◇1		◇1						◇1	◇1	1
					A	B		C	A	D	E	F		G		B			A	H	I	D
							🚌	🛒		🍴🛒			🚌	🛒						🛒	🍴	🍴🛒
Manchester Airport 85 ✈	d																					
Manchester Piccadilly 10	d											09 11										
Stockport 78	d																					
Sheffield 7	a																					
	d	23p27	08 00			08 45	09 00	09 21	09 36				09 55	10 21		10 26	11 05			11 21	11 31	
Meadowhall	d	23p33	08 06			08 51	09 20		09 42				10 15			10 32	11 11					
Rotherham Central	d	23p39	08 12			08 57	09 30		09 48								11 17					
Swinton (S.Yorks)	d	23p48	08 20			09 05	09 42		09a58								11 25					
Mexborough	d	23p51	08 23			09 08	09 47										11 28					
Conisbrough	d	23p55	08 27			09 12	10 02										11 32					
London Kings Cross	d																					10 30
Doncaster 7	a	00 08	08 38			09 22	10 22						10 45			10 51	11 43				11 52	12 08
York 8 26	a							10 29						11 29						12 29	12 15	12 31
Doncaster 31	d			09 07	09 12	09 26				09 37	10 19		10 45			10 55		11 07	11 12			
Bentley (S.Yorks) 31	a				09 15														11 15			
Adwick 31	a				09 19														11 19			
Kirk Sandall	d			09 13														11 13				
Hatfield & Stainforth	d			09 18														11 18				
Thorne South	d																					
Crowle	d																					
Althorpe	d																					
Scunthorpe	a												11 35									
	d												11 35									
Barnetby	d												12 00									
Hull Paragon Interchange	d																					
Barton-on-Humber	a																					
Barton-on-Humber	d																					
Barrow Haven	d																					
New Holland	d																					
Goxhill	d																					
Thornton Abbey	d																					
Ulceby	d																					
Habrough	d																					
Stallingborough	d																					
Healing	d																					
Great Coates	d																					
Grimsby Town	a												12 30									
	d												12 30									
Grimsby Docks	d																					
New Clee	d																					
Cleethorpes	a												12 50									
Thorne North	d			09 24		09 38					10 31							11 25				
Goole	d			09a35		09 47					10 40					11 14		11a36				
Saltmarshe	d																					
York 8 33	d									09a58					10 40							
Selby	a											10 44			10 58							
Wressle	d																					
Howden	d														11 08							
Eastrington	d																					
Gilberdyke	d					09 55					10 48					11 24						
Broomfleet	d																					
Brough	d					10 03					10 56	11 04			11 19	11 32						
Ferriby	d										11 00											
Hessle	d										11 05											
Hull	a					10 21					11 17	11 18			11 41	11 47						

A To Leeds
B To Scarborough
C To Glasgow Central
D To Edinburgh
E To Bridlington
F From Liverpool Lime Street
G From Birmingham New Street to Edinburgh
H From Birmingham New Street to Glasgow Central
I From Leicester

Table 29

Sundays

8 January to 12 February

Manchester Airport, Manchester, Sheffield and Meadowhall-Doncaster-Cleethorpes and Hull Barton-on-Humber - Cleethorpes

Network Diagram - see first Page of Table 18

		NT	NT	HT	TP	XC	NT	NT	TP	EM	NT	TP	XC	NT	NT	NT	XC	HT	TP	XC
				◇1		◇1			◇1	◇			◇1				◇1	◇1		◇1
		A				B		C		F	A		G		H	A	I			J
Manchester Airport 85 ✈	d																			
Manchester Piccadilly 10	d								12 01	12 44										
Stockport 78	d									12 55										
Sheffield 7	a									13 37										
	d	11 36			12 20	12 21	12 24	12 28				13 15	13 21		13 24	13 36	13 51		14 20	14 21
Meadowhall	d	11 42			12 40		12 30	12 34				13 35			13 30	13 42			14 40	
Rotherham Central	d	11 49					12 36								13 36	13 49				
Swinton (S.Yorks)	d	12a00					12 49								13 47	13a57				
Mexborough	d						12 52								13 50					
Conisbrough	d						12 56								13 54					
London Kings Cross	d			10 45														12 45		
Doncaster 7	a			12 23	13 10		13 04	12 56				14 05			14 02		14 13	14 23	15 10	
York 8 26	a					13 29							14 29				14 40			15 29
Doncaster 31	d			12 29	13 10		13 05	12 58			13 12				14 05			14 25	15 10	
Bentley (S.Yorks) 31	a										13 15									
Adwick 31	a										13 19									
Kirk Sandall	d						13 11													
Hatfield & Stainforth	d						13 16													
Thorne South	d																			
Crowle	d																			
Althorpe	d																			
Scunthorpe	a				14 00														16 00	
	d				14 00														16 00	
Barnetby	d				14 25														16 25	
Hull Paragon Interchange	d																			
Barton-on-Humber	a																			
Barton-on-Humber	d																			
Barrow Haven	d																			
New Holland	d																			
Goxhill	d																			
Thornton Abbey	d																			
Ulceby	d																			
Habrough	d																			
Stallingborough	d																			
Healing	d																			
Great Coates	d																			
Grimsby Town	a				14 55														16 55	
	d				14 55														16 55	
Grimsby Docks	d																			
New Clee	d																			
Cleethorpes	a				15 15														17 15	
Thorne North	d						13 22													
Goole	d						13a32	13 17							14 25					
Saltmarshe	d																			
York 8 33	d		12 05											13 40						
Selby	a		12 24	12 43					13 23					13 59				14 39		
Wressle	d																			
Howden	d		12 34	12 54										14 09				14 50		
Eastrington	d																			
Gilberdyke	d							13 25							14 33					
Broomfleet	d																			
Brough	d		12 46	13 07				13 33	13 41					14 21	14 41			15 03		
Ferriby	d							13 38												
Hessle	d							13 42												
Hull	a		13 06	13 25				13 57	13 59					14 40	15 01			15 21		

A To Leeds
B From Bristol Temple Meads to Edinburgh
C To Scarborough
F To Norwich
G From Bristol Temple Meads to Glasgow Central
H To Bridlington
I From Birmingham New Street to Newcastle
J From Plymouth to Aberdeen

Table 29

Sundays

8 January to 12 February

Manchester Airport, Manchester, Sheffield and Meadowhall-Doncaster-Cleethorpes and Hull Barton-on-Humber - Cleethorpes

Network Diagram - see first Page of Table 18

	NT		NT	NT		TP	XC	NT	TP	XC	NT		NT		NT	XC	NT	HT	TP	XC	NT		NT	
						◇1	◇1			◇1						◇1		◇1		◇1				
				A			C	D		E			F		D	C				G			A	
							⊤		▭	⊤						⊤		⊠	▭	⊤				
Manchester Airport 85 d																								
Manchester Piccadilly 10 d						14 02																		
Stockport 78 d																								
Sheffield 7 a																								
d	14 22			14 28			14 51		15 20	15 21	15 24		15 28		15 36	15 51			16 20	16 21	16 24		16 28	
Meadowhall d	14 28			14 34					15 40		15 30		15 34		15 42				16 40		16 30		16 34	
Rotherham Central d	14 35										15 37				15 50						16 37			
Swinton (S.Yorks) d	14 46										15 47				15a58						16 47			
Mexborough d	14 49										15 50										16 50			
Conisbrough d	14 53										15 54										16 54			
London Kings Cross d																		14 45						
Doncaster 7 a	15 03			14 56			15 13		16 10		16 04		15 56			16 15		16 23	17 10		17 03		16 56	
York 8 26 a							15 43			16 29						16 40				17 29				
Doncaster 31 d	15 05			14 59				15 12	16 10				15 56					16 30	17 10		17 04		16 58	
Bentley (S.Yorks) 31 a								15 15																
Adwick 31 a								15 19																
Kirk Sandall d	15 11																				17 10			
Hatfield & Stainforth d	15 16																				17 15			
Thorne South d																								
Crowle d																								
Althorpe d																								
Scunthorpe a									17 00										18 00					
d									17 00										18 00					
Barnetby d									17 25										18 25					
Hull Paragon Interchange d																								
Barton-on-Humber a																								
Barton-on-Humber d																								
Barrow Haven d																								
New Holland d																								
Goxhill d																								
Thornton Abbey d																								
Ulceby d																								
Habrough d																								
Stallingborough d																								
Healing d																								
Great Coates d																								
Grimsby Town a									17 55										18 55					
d									17 55										18 55					
Grimsby Docks d																								
New Clee d																								
Cleethorpes a									18 15										19 15					
Thorne North d	15 24												16 10								17 24			
Goole d	15a33			15 19									16 19								17a33		17 17	
Saltmarshe d																								
York 8 33 d			14 49														16 06							
Selby a			15 08			15 23											16 24	16 44						
Wressle d																								
Howden d			15 18														16 34	16 55						
Eastrington d																								
Gilberdyke d				15 29									16 27										17 25	
Broomfleet d																								
Brough d			15 30	15 37		15 41							16 35				16 46	17 07					17 33	
Ferriby d																								
Hessle d																								
Hull a			15 49	15 56		15 59							16 53				17 07	17 26					17 51	

A To Scarborough
C From Birmingham New Street to Newcastle
D To Leeds
E From Plymouth to Glasgow Central
F To Bridlington
G From Penzance to Edinburgh

Table 29

Sundays

8 January to 12 February

Manchester Airport, Manchester, Sheffield and Meadowhall-Doncaster-Cleethorpes and Hull Barton-on-Humber - Cleethorpes

Network Diagram - see first Page of Table 18

		TP	NT	XC	NT	NT	TP	XC		NT	NT		NT	XC	TP	XC	NT	NT		GR		TP	XC	NT	NT
																				R					
		◇1		◇1				◇1						◇1		◇1				1		◇1	◇1		
				A		B		C			D		B	F		G		H					J		
Manchester Airport 85	d																								
Manchester Piccadilly 10	d	16 02																				18 02			
Stockport 78	d																								
Sheffield 7	a																								
	d		16 36	16 51			17 20	17 21		17 25	17 28		17 36	17 51	18 20	18 21	18 25	18 28					18 51	18 57	
Meadowhall	d		16 42				17 40			17 31	17 34		17 44		18 40		18 31	18 35						19 05	
Rotherham Central	d		16 49							17 37			17 50				18 37							19 11	
Swinton (S.Yorks)	d		16 58							17 47			17a58				18 48							19 19	
Mexborough	d									17 50							18 51								
Conisbrough	d									17 54							18 55								
London Kings Cross	d																			17 20					
Doncaster 7	a			17 13			18 10			18 05	17 55			18 13	19 10		19 06	18 54		19 03			19 15		
York 8 26	a		17 59	17 42				18 29						19 18		19 29							19 43	20 18	
Doncaster 31	d					17 14	18 10				17 57				19 10			18 55		19 04					
Bentley (S.Yorks) 31	a					17 17																			
Adwick 31	a					17 21																			
Kirk Sandall	d																	19 01							
Hatfield & Stainforth	d																	19 06							
Thorne South	d																								
Crowle	d																								
Althorpe	d																								
Scunthorpe	a						19 00								20 00										
	d						19 00								20 00										
Barnetby	d						19 25								20 25										
Hull Paragon Interchange	d																								
Barton-on-Humber	a																								
Barton-on-Humber	d																								
Barrow Haven	d																								
New Holland	d																								
Goxhill	d																								
Thornton Abbey	d																								
Ulceby	d																								
Habrough	d																								
Stallingborough	d																								
Healing	d																								
Great Coates	d																								
Grimsby Town	a						19 55								20 55										
	d						19 55								20 55										
Grimsby Docks	d																								
New Clee	d																								
Cleethorpes	a						20 15								21 15										
Thorne North	d																	19 12							
Goole	d										18 16							19 21							
Saltmarshe	d																								
York 8 33	d				17 11																				19 10
Selby	a	17 23			17 30															19 23		19 28			19 35
Wressle	d																								
Howden	d				17 41																				19 46
Eastrington	d																								
Gilberdyke	d										18 24							19 29							
Broomfleet	d																								
Brough	d	17 41			17 53						18 32							19 37		19 45		19 48			19 58
Ferriby	d																								
Hessle	d																								
Hull	a	17 59			18 12						18 48							19 55		20 03		20 05			20 17

A From Birmingham New Street to Newcastle
B To Leeds
C From Plymouth to Glasgow Central
D To Bridlington
F From Reading to Newcastle
G From Plymouth to Edinburgh
H To Beverley
J From Reading to Edinburgh

Table 29

Sundays

8 January to 12 February

Manchester Airport, Manchester, Sheffield and Meadowhall-Doncaster-Cleethorpes and Hull Barton-on-Humber - Cleethorpes

Network Diagram - see first Page of Table 18

		NT	HT	TP	TP	XC	NT	NT	XC	NT	TP	TP	XC	NT	XC	HT	NT	NT	TP	NT
			◇1	◇1		◇1			◇1		◇1		◇1		◇1	◇1				
		A				B		A	D				E		D			A		
			⊠		bus				trolley			bus	trolley			⊠			bus	
Manchester Airport 85 ✈	d																			
Manchester Piccadilly 10	d			19 02							20 06									
Stockport 78	d																			
Sheffield 7	a																			
	d				19 20	19 21	19 29	19 36	19 51	20 02		20 20	20 21	20 28	20 51				21 20	21 24
Meadowhall	d				19 40		19 35	19 42		20 09		20 40		20 34					21 40	21 30
Rotherham Central	d						19 41	19 49						20 40						21 37
Swinton (S.Yorks)	d						19 49	19a57						20 48						21 47
Mexborough	d						19 52							20 51						21 50
Conisbrough	d						19 56							20 55						21 54
London Kings Cross	d		17 45													19 45				
Doncaster 7	a		19 23		20 10		20 07		20 16	20 30		21 10		21 05	21 19	21 25			22 10	22 03
York 8 26	a					20 29			20 45				21 31		21 44					
Doncaster 31	d	19 27	19 30		20 10					20 30		21 10		21 07		21 27		21 52	22 10	22 04
Bentley (S.Yorks) 31	a	19 30																21 55		
Adwick 31	a	19 34																21 59		
Kirk Sandall	d													21 13						
Hatfield & Stainforth	d													21 18						
Thorne South	d																			
Crowle	d																			
Althorpe	d																			
Scunthorpe	a				21 00							22 00							23 00	
	d				21 00							22 00							23 00	
Barnetby	d				21 25							22 25							23 25	
Hull Paragon Interchange	d																			
Barton-on-Humber	a																			
Barton-on-Humber	d																			
Barrow Haven	d																			
New Holland	d																			
Goxhill	d																			
Thornton Abbey	d																			
Ulceby	d																			
Habrough	d											22 40								
Stallingborough	d																			
Healing	d																			
Great Coates	d																			
Grimsby Town	a				21 55							23 05							23 55	
	d				21 55							23 05							23 55	
Grimsby Docks	d																			
New Clee	d																			
Cleethorpes	a				22 15							23 25							00 15	
Thorne North	d													21 24						
Goole	d									20 49				21a34						22 23
Saltmarshe	d																			
York 8 33	d																21 41			
Selby	a		19 45	20 17							21 38					21 43	22 00			
Wressle	d																			
Howden	d		19 56													21 55	22 10			
Eastrington	d																			
Gilberdyke	d									20 57										22 31
Broomfleet	d																			
Brough	d		20 08	20 36						21 05	21 58					22 07	22 22			22 39
Ferriby	d																			
Hessle	d																			
Hull	a		20 26	20 54						21 23	22 12					22 26	22 36			22 56

A To Leeds
B From Plymouth to Edinburgh
D From Reading to Newcastle
E From Plymouth

Table 29

Sundays

8 January to 12 February

Manchester Airport, Manchester, Sheffield and Meadowhall-Doncaster-Cleethorpes and Hull Barton-on-Humber - Cleethorpes

Network Diagram - see first Page of Table 18

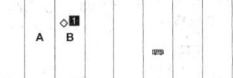

		NT	TP	NT	NT	TP	NT
			◇1				
		A	B				
Manchester Airport 85	d						
Manchester Piccadilly 10	d						
Stockport 78	d						
Sheffield 7	a						
	d	21 36		22 13	22 26	22 30	23 34
Meadowhall	d	21 42		22 19	22 32	22 50	23 40
Rotherham Central	d	21 48			22 38		23 47
Swinton (S.Yorks)	d	21a56			22 48		23 55
Mexborough	d				22 51		23 58
Conisbrough	d				22 55		00 02
London Kings Cross	d						
Doncaster 7	a			22 38	23 05	23 20	00 13
York 8 26	a						
Doncaster 31	d			22 41		23 20	
Bentley (S.Yorks) 31	a						
Adwick 31	a						
Kirk Sandall	d						
Hatfield & Stainforth	d						
Thorne South	d						
Crowle	d						
Althorpe	d						
Scunthorpe	a					00 10	
	d					00 10	
Barnetby	d					00 35	
Hull Paragon Interchange	d						
Barton-on-Humber	a						
Barton-on-Humber	d						
Barrow Haven	d						
New Holland	d						
Goxhill	d						
Thornton Abbey	d						
Ulceby	d						
Habrough	d						
Stallingborough	d						
Healing	d						
Great Coates	d						
Grimsby Town	a					01 05	
	d					01 05	
Grimsby Docks	d						
New Clee	d						
Cleethorpes	a					01 25	
Thorne North	d			22 53			
Goole	d			23 02			
Saltmarshe	d						
York 8 33	d						
Selby	a						
Wressle	d						
Howden	d						
Eastrington	d						
Gilberdyke	d			23 10			
Broomfleet	d						
Brough	d		23 02	23 18			
Ferriby	d						
Hessle	d						
Hull	a		23 19	23 39			

A To Leeds

B From Leeds

Table 29

Sundays

19 February to 25 March

Manchester Airport, Manchester, Sheffield and Meadowhall-Doncaster-Cleethorpes and Hull Barton-on-Humber - Cleethorpes

Network Diagram - see first Page of Table 18

		NT	NT	NT	NT	NT	XC	NT	GR	NT	TP	TP	XC	NT	NT	NT	NT	NT	XC	EM	NT
							◇1		R 1		◇1	◇1	◇1						◇1	◇1	
					A	B	C	A	D	E	F		G		B			A	H	I	A
Manchester Airport 85 ✈	d																				
Manchester Piccadilly 10	d										09 11										
Stockport 78	d																				
Sheffield 7	a																				
	d	23p27	08 00			08 45	09 21	09 36				09 52	10 21		10 26	11 05			11 21	11 31	11 36
Meadowhall	d	23p33	08 06			08 51		09 42				09 57			10 32	11 11					11 42
Rotherham Central	d	23p39	08 12			08 57		09 48				10 03				11 17					11 49
Swinton (S.Yorks)	d	23p48	08 20			09 05		09a58				10 09				11 25					12a00
Mexborough	d	23p51	08 23			09 08						10 13				11 28					
Conisbrough	d	23p55	08 27			09 12						10 17				11 32					
London Kings Cross	d																				
Doncaster 7	a	00 08	08 38			09 22						10 26			10 51	11 43				11 52	
York 8 26	a						10 29						11 29						12 29	12 15	
Doncaster 31	d			09 07	09 12	09 26			09 37	10 19		10 28			10 55		11 07	11 12			
Bentley (S.Yorks) 31	a				09 15													11 15			
Adwick 31	a				09 19													11 19			
Kirk Sandall	d			09 13													11 13				
Hatfield & Stainforth	d			09 18													11 18				
Thorne South	d																				
Crowle	d																				
Althorpe	d																				
Scunthorpe	a											10 54									
	d											10 55									
Barnetby	d											11 09									
Hull Paragon Interchange	d																				
Barton-on-Humber	a																				
Barton-on-Humber	d																				
Barrow Haven	d																				
New Holland	d																				
Goxhill	d																				
Thornton Abbey	d																				
Ulceby	d																				
Habrough	d																				
Stallingborough	d																				
Healing	d																				
Great Coates	d																				
Grimsby Town	a											11 29									
	d											11 33									
Grimsby Docks	d																				
New Clee	d																				
Cleethorpes	a											11 40									
Thorne North	d			09 24		09 38				10 31							11 25				
Goole	d			09a35		09 47				10 40					11 14		11a36				
Saltmarshe	d																				
York 8 33	d								09a58					10 40							
Selby	a										10 44			10 58							
Wressle	d																				
Howden	d													11 08							
Eastrington	d																				
Gilberdyke	d					09 55				10 48					11 24						
Broomfleet	d																				
Brough	d					10 03				10 56	11 04			11 19	11 32						
Ferriby	d									11 00											
Hessle	d									11 05											
Hull	a					10 21				11 17	11 18			11 41	11 47						

A To Leeds
B To Scarborough
C To Glasgow Central
E To Bridlington
F From Liverpool Lime Street
G From Birmingham New Street to Edinburgh
H From Birmingham New Street to Glasgow Central
I From Leicester

Table 29

Sundays

19 February to 25 March

Manchester Airport, Manchester, Sheffield and Meadowhall-Doncaster-Cleethorpes and Hull Barton-on-Humber - Cleethorpes

Network Diagram - see first Page of Table 18

		NT	HT	TP	XC	NT	NT	TP	TP	EM	NT	XC	NT	NT	NT	XC	HT	TP	XC	NT
			◇1	◇1	◇1			◇1	◇1	◇		◇1				◇1	◇1	◇1	◇1	
					A		B			E	F	G		H	F	I			J	
			⊠		⚲							⚲				⚲	⊠		⚲	
Manchester Airport 85 ✈	d			10 44														12 55		
Manchester Piccadilly 10 🚌	d			11 18				12 01	12 18	12 44								13 20		
Stockport 78	d			11 27					12 28	12 55								13 28		
Sheffield 7 🚌	a			12 09					13 08	13 37								14 08		
	d			12 11	12 21	12 24	12 28		13 11			13 21		13 24	13 36	13 51		14 11	14 21	14 22
Meadowhall 🚌	d			12 16		12 30	12 34		13 16					13 30	13 42			14 16		14 28
Rotherham Central	d					12 36								13 36	13 49					14 35
Swinton (S.Yorks)	d					12 49								13 47	13a57					14 46
Mexborough	d					12 52								13 50						14 49
Conisbrough	d					12 56								13 54						14 53
London Kings Cross	d		10 45														12 45			
Doncaster 7	a		12 23	12 35		13 04	12 56		13 34					14 02		14 13	14 23	14 35		15 03
York 8 26	a				13 29							14 29				14 40			15 29	
Doncaster 31	d		12 29	12 37		13 05	12 58				13 12			14 05			14 25	14 37		15 05
Bentley (S.Yorks) 31	a										13 15									
Adwick 31	a										13 19									
Kirk Sandall	d					13 11														15 11
Hatfield & Stainforth	d					13 16														15 16
Thorne South	d																			
Crowle	d																			
Althorpe	d																			
Scunthorpe	a			13 06														15 02		
	d			13 06														15 03		
Barnetby	d			13 21														15 17		
Hull Paragon Interchange	d																			
Barton-on-Humber	a																			
Barton-on-Humber	d																			
Barrow Haven	d																			
New Holland	d																			
Goxhill	d																			
Thornton Abbey	d																			
Ulceby	d																			
Habrough	d			13 29																
Stallingborough	d																			
Healing	d																			
Great Coates	d																			
Grimsby Town	a			13 42														15 37		
	d			13 43														15 38		
Grimsby Docks	d																			
New Clee	d																			
Cleethorpes	a			13 53														15 49		
Thorne North	d					13 22														15 24
Goole	d					13a32	13 17							14 25						15a33
Saltmarshe	d																			
York 8 33	d	12 05											13 40							
Selby	a	12 24	12 43					13 23					13 59				14 39			
Wressle	d																			
Howden	d	12 34	12 54										14 09				14 50			
Eastrington	d																			
Gilberdyke	d						13 25							14 33						
Broomfleet	d																			
Brough	d	12 46	13 07				13 33	13 41					14 21	14 41			15 03			
Ferriby	d						13 38													
Hessle	d						13 42													
Hull	a	13 06	13 25				13 57	13 59					14 40	15 01			15 21			

A From Bristol Temple Meads to Edinburgh
B To Scarborough
D To Newcastle
E To Norwich
F To Leeds
G From Bristol Temple Meads to Glasgow Central
H To Bridlington
I From Birmingham New Street to Newcastle
J From Bristol Temple Meads to Aberdeen

Table 29

Sundays

19 February to 25 March

Manchester Airport, Manchester, Sheffield and Meadowhall-Doncaster-Cleethorpes and Hull Barton-on-Humber - Cleethorpes

Network Diagram - see first Page of Table 18

		NT		NT		TP	XC	NT	TP	XC	NT	NT		GR	NT	XC	NT	HT	TP	XC	NT	NT			TP
						◇1	◇1		◇1	◇1				1		◇1		◇1	◇1	◇1					◇1
				A			C	D		E		F		B	D	C				G		A			
Manchester Airport 85	d								13 55										14 55						
Manchester Piccadilly 10	d					14 02			14 20										15 20						16 02
Stockport 78	d								14 28										15 28						
Sheffield 7	a								15 08										16 09						
	d			14 28			14 51		15 11	15 21	15 24	15 28			15 36	15 51			16 11	16 21	16 24	16 28			
Meadowhall	d			14 34					15 16		15 30	15 34			15 42				16 16		16 30	16 34			
Rotherham Central	d										15 37				15 50						16 37				
Swinton (S.Yorks)	d										15 47				15a58						16 47				
Mexborough	d										15 50										16 50				
Conisbrough	d										15 54										16 54				
London Kings Cross	d													14 30				14 45							
Doncaster 7	a			14 56			15 13		15 35		16 04	15 56		16 10		16 15		16 23	16 35		17 03	16 56			
York 8 26	a						15 43			16 29				16 34		16 40				17 29					
Doncaster 31	d			14 59				15 12	15 37			15 56						16 30	16 37		17 04	16 58			
Bentley (S.Yorks) 31	a							15 15																	
Adwick 31	a							15 19																	
Kirk Sandall	d																				17 10				
Hatfield & Stainforth	d																				17 15				
Thorne South	d																								
Crowle	d																								
Althorpe	d																								
Scunthorpe	a								16 02										17 02						
	d								16 03										17 03						
Barnetby	d								16 17										17 17						
Hull Paragon Interchange	d																								
Barton-on-Humber	a																								
Barton-on-Humber	d																								
Barrow Haven	d																								
New Holland	d																								
Goxhill	d																								
Thornton Abbey	d																								
Ulceby	d																								
Habrough	d								16 26																
Stallingborough	d																								
Healing	d																								
Great Coates	d																								
Grimsby Town	a								16 39										17 37						
	d								16 40										17 38						
Grimsby Docks	d																								
New Clee	d																								
Cleethorpes	a								16 50										17 48						
Thorne North	d											16 10									17 24				
Goole	d			15 19								16 19									17a33	17 17			
Saltmarshe	d																								
York 8 33	d	14 49															16 06								
Selby	a	15 08				15 23											16 24	16 44							17 23
Wressle	d																								
Howden	d	15 18															16 34	16 55							
Eastrington	d																								
Gilberdyke	d			15 29								16 27										17 25			
Broomfleet	d																								
Brough	d	15 30		15 37		15 41						16 35					16 46	17 07				17 33			17 41
Ferriby	d																								
Hessle	d																								
Hull	a	15 49		15 56		15 59						16 53					17 07	17 26				17 51			17 59

A To Scarborough
C From Birmingham New Street to Newcastle
D To Leeds
E From Bristol Temple Meads to Glasgow Central
F To Bridlington
G From Newton Abbot to Edinburgh

Table 29

Sundays

19 February to 25 March

Manchester Airport, Manchester, Sheffield and Meadowhall-Doncaster-Cleethorpes and Hull Barton-on-Humber - Cleethorpes

Network Diagram - see first Page of Table 18

		NT	XC	NT	NT	TP	XC	NT		NT		NT	XC	TP	XC	NT	NT	GR		GR	TP	XC	NT	NT	NT
																		🅱		🅱					
			◇1			◇1	◇1						◇1	◇1	◇1			1		1	◇1	◇1			
			A		B		C			D		B	F		G		H			I		J			B
			⚲				⚲						⚲		⚲			⚲		⚲		⚲			
Manchester Airport 85 ✈	d					15 55								16 55											
Manchester Piccadilly 10	d					16 20								17 20							18 02				
Stockport 78	d					16 28								17 28											
Sheffield 7	a					17 08								18 08											
	d	16 36	16 51			17 11	17 21	17 25		17 28		17 36	17 51	18 11	18 21	18 25	18 28					18 51	18 57		
Meadowhall	d	16 42				17 16		17 31		17 34		17 44		18 16		18 31	18 35						19 05		
Rotherham Central	d	16 49						17 37				17 50				18 37							19 11		
Swinton (S.Yorks)	d	16 58						17 47				17a58				18 48							19 19		
Mexborough	d							17 50								18 51									
Conisbrough	d							17 54								18 55									
London Kings Cross	d																	17 20		17 30					
Doncaster 7	a		17 13			17 35		18 05		17 55			18 13	18 35		19 06	18 54	19 03		19 09		19 15			
York 8 26	a	17 59	17 42				18 29						19 18		19 29					19 35		19 43	20 18		
Doncaster 31	d				17 14	17 37				17 57				18 37			18 55	19 04							19 27
Bentley (S.Yorks) 31	a				17 17																				19 30
Adwick 31	a				17 21																				19 34
Kirk Sandall	d																19 01								
Hatfield & Stainforth	d																19 06								
Thorne South	d																								
Crowle	d																								
Althorpe	d																								
Scunthorpe	a					18 02								19 02											
	d					18 03								19 03											
Barnetby	d					18 17								19 17											
Hull Paragon Interchange	d																								
Barton-on-Humber	a																								
Barton-on-Humber	d																								
Barrow Haven	d																								
New Holland	d																								
Goxhill	d																								
Thornton Abbey	d																								
Ulceby	d																								
Habrough	d													19 26											
Stallingborough	d																								
Healing	d																								
Great Coates	d																								
Grimsby Town	a					18 37								19 39											
	d					18 38								19 40											
Grimsby Docks	d																								
New Clee	d																								
Cleethorpes	a					18 48								19 48											
Thorne North	d																19 12								
Goole	d									18 16							19 21								
Saltmarshe	d																								
York 8 33	d			17 11																				19 10	
Selby	a			17 30														19 23			19 28			19 35	
Wressle	d																								
Howden	d			17 41																				19 46	
Eastrington	d																								
Gilberdyke	d									18 24							19 29								
Broomfleet	d																								
Brough	d			17 53						18 32							19 37	19 45			19 48			19 58	
Ferriby	d																								
Hessle	d																								
Hull	a			18 12						18 48							19 55	20 03			20 05			20 17	

A From Birmingham New Street to Newcastle
B To Leeds
C From Newton Abbot to Glasgow Central
D To Bridlington
F From Reading to Newcastle
G From Newton Abbot to Edinburgh
H To Beverley
I To Edinburgh
J From Reading to Edinburgh

Table 29

Sundays

19 February to 25 March

Manchester Airport, Manchester, Sheffield and Meadowhall-Doncaster-Cleethorpes and Hull Barton-on-Humber - Cleethorpes

Network Diagram - see first Page of Table 18

		HT	TP	TP	XC	NT	NT	XC	NT	TP	TP	XC	NT	XC	HT	TP	NT	NT	NT	NT
		◇■	◇■	◇■	◇■			◇■		◇■	◇■	◇■		◇■	◇■	◇■				
					A		C	D				E		D				C		C
		⊠						⚲				⚲			⊠					
Manchester Airport 85 ✈	d		17 55							18 55						19 55				
Manchester Piccadilly 10 ⇌	d		18 20	19 02						19 20	20 06					20 18				
Stockport 78	d		18 28							19 28						20 27				
Sheffield 7 ⇌	a		19 08							20 08						21 08				
	d		19 11		19 21	19 29	19 36	19 51	20 02	20 11		20 21	20 28	20 51		21 11			21 24	21 36
Meadowhall ⇌	d		19 16			19 35	19 42		20 09	20 16			20 34			21 16			21 30	21 42
Rotherham Central	d					19 41	19 49						20 40						21 37	21 48
Swinton (S.Yorks)	d					19 49	19a57						20 48						21 47	21a56
Mexborough	d					19 52							20 51						21 50	
Conisbrough	d					19 56							20 55						21 54	
London Kings Cross	d	17 45													19 45					
Doncaster 7	a	19 23	19 35			20 07		20 16	20 30	20 35			21 05	21 19	21 25	21 35			22 03	
York 8 26	a				20 29			20 45				21 31		21 44						
Doncaster 31	d	19 30	19 37						20 30	20 37			21 07		21 27	21 37		21 52	22 04	
Bentley (S.Yorks) 31	a																	21 55		
Adwick 31	a																	21 59		
Kirk Sandall	d												21 13							
Hatfield & Stainforth	d												21 18							
Thorne South	d																			
Crowle	d																			
Althorpe	d																			
Scunthorpe	a		20 02							21 02						22 02				
	d		20 03							21 03						22 03				
Barnetby	d		20 17							21 17						22 17				
Hull Paragon Interchange	d																			
Barton-on-Humber	a																			
Barton-on-Humber	d																			
Barrow Haven	d																			
New Holland	d																			
Goxhill	d																			
Thornton Abbey	d																			
Ulceby	d																			
Habrough	d									21 26						22 26				
Stallingborough	d																			
Healing	d																			
Great Coates	d																			
Grimsby Town	a		20 37							21 39						22 39				
	d		20 38							21 40						22 40				
Grimsby Docks	d																			
New Clee	d																			
Cleethorpes	a		20 48							21 50						22 50				
Thorne North	d												21 24							
Goole	d								20 49				21a34						22 23	
Saltmarshe	d																			
York 8 33	d																21 41			
Selby	a	19 45		20 17							21 38				21 43		22 00			
Wressle	d																			
Howden	d	19 56													21 55		22 10			
Eastrington	d																			
Gilberdyke	d								20 57										22 31	
Broomfleet	d																			
Brough	d	20 08		20 36					21 05		21 58				22 07		22 22		22 39	
Ferriby	d																			
Hessle	d																			
Hull	a	20 26		20 54					21 23		22 12				22 26		22 36		22 56	

A From Newton Abbot to Edinburgh
C To Leeds
D From Reading to Newcastle
E From Newton Abbot

Table 29

Sundays
19 February to 25 March

Manchester Airport, Manchester, Sheffield and Meadowhall-Doncaster-Cleethorpes and Hull Barton-on-Humber - Cleethorpes

Network Diagram - see first Page of Table 18

		TP	NT	NT	TP		NT
		◇1			◇1		
		A					
Manchester Airport 85 ✈	d						
Manchester Piccadilly 10 🚌	d						
Stockport 78	d						
Sheffield 7 🚌	a						
	d		22 13	22 26	22 30		23 34
Meadowhall 🚌	d		22 19	22 32	22 35		23 40
Rotherham Central	d			22 38			23 47
Swinton (S.Yorks)	d			22 48			23 55
Mexborough	d			22 51			23 58
Conisbrough	d			22 55			00 02
London Kings Cross	d						
Doncaster 7	a		22 38	23 05	22 56		00 13
York 8 26	a						
Doncaster 31	d		22 41		22 58		
Bentley (S.Yorks) 31	a						
Adwick 31	a						
Kirk Sandall	d						
Hatfield & Stainforth	d						
Thorne South	d						
Crowle	d						
Althorpe	d						
Scunthorpe	a				23 23		
	d				23 24		
Barnetby	d				23 38		
Hull Paragon Interchange	d						
Barton-on-Humber	a						
Barton-on-Humber	d						
Barrow Haven	d						
New Holland	d						
Goxhill	d						
Thornton Abbey	d						
Ulceby	d						
Habrough	d						
Stallingborough	d						
Healing	d						
Great Coates	d						
Grimsby Town	a				23 57		
	d				23 58		
Grimsby Docks	d						
New Clee	d						
Cleethorpes	a				00 09		
Thorne North	d		22 53				
Goole	d		23 02				
Saltmarshe	d						
York 8 33	d						
Selby	a						
Wressle	d						
Howden	d						
Eastrington	d						
Gilberdyke	d		23 10				
Broomfleet	d						
Brough	d	23 02	23 18				
Ferriby	d						
Hessle	d						
Hull	a	23 19	23 39				

A From Leeds

Table 29

Sundays
from 1 April

Manchester Airport, Manchester, Sheffield and Meadowhall-Doncaster-Cleethorpes and Hull Barton-on-Humber - Cleethorpes

Network Diagram - see first Page of Table 18

Station		NT	NT	NT	NT	NT	XC	NT	GR	NT		TP	XC	TP	NT	NT		NT	NT	NT		XC	EM		NT
							◇1		1			◇1	◇1	◇1								◇1	◇1		
					A	B	C	A	D	E			F	G		B				A		H	I		A
Manchester Airport 85	d																								
Manchester Piccadilly 10	d																								
Stockport 78	d																								
Sheffield 7	a																								
	d	23p27	08 00			08 45	09 21	09 36				09 52	10 21			10 26		11 05				11 21	11 31		11 36
Meadowhall	d	23p33	08 06			08 51		09 42				09 57				10 32		11 11							11 42
Rotherham Central	d	23p39	08 12			08 57		09 48				10 03						11 17							11 49
Swinton (S.Yorks)	d	23p48	08 20			09 05		09a58				10 09						11 25							12a00
Mexborough	d	23p51	08 23			09 08						10 13						11 28							
Conisbrough	d	23p55	08 27			09 12						10 17						11 32							
London Kings Cross	d																								
Doncaster 7	a	00 08	08 38			09 22						10 26				10 51		11 43					11 52		
York 8 26	a						10 29						11 29									12 29	12 15		
Doncaster 31	d			09 07	09 12	09 26			09 37	10 19		10 28				10 55			11 07	11 12					
Bentley (S.Yorks) 31	a				09 15															11 15					
Adwick 31	a				09 19															11 19					
Kirk Sandall	d			09 13															11 13						
Hatfield & Stainforth	d			09 18															11 18						
Thorne South	d																								
Crowle	d																								
Althorpe	d																								
Scunthorpe	a											10 54													
	d											10 55													
Barnetby	d											11 09													
Hull Paragon Interchange	d																								
Barton-on-Humber	a																								
Barton-on-Humber	d																								
Barrow Haven	d																								
New Holland	d																								
Goxhill	d																								
Thornton Abbey	d																								
Ulceby	d																								
Habrough	d																								
Stallingborough	d																								
Healing	d																								
Great Coates	d																								
Grimsby Town	a											11 29													
	d											11 33													
Grimsby Docks	d																								
New Clee	d																								
Cleethorpes	a											11 40													
Thorne North	d			09 24		09 38				10 31									11 25						
Goole	d			09a35		09 47				10 40						11 14			11a36						
Saltmarshe	d																								
York 8 33	d								09a58						10 40										
Selby	a														10 58										
Wressle	d																								
Howden	d														11 08										
Eastrington	d																								
Gilberdyke	d					09 55				10 48						11 24									
Broomfleet	d																								
Brough	d					10 03				10 56				11 04	11 19	11 32									
Ferriby	d									11 00															
Hessle	d									11 05															
Hull	a					10 21				11 17				11 21	11 41	11 47									

A To Leeds
B To Scarborough
C To Glasgow Central
D To Edinburgh
E To Bridlington
F From Birmingham New Street to Edinburgh
G From Leeds
H From Birmingham New Street to Glasgow Central
I From Leicester

Table 29

Sundays

from 1 April

Manchester Airport, Manchester, Sheffield and Meadowhall-Doncaster-Cleethorpes and Hull Barton-on-Humber - Cleethorpes

Network Diagram - see first Page of Table 18

		NT	HT	TP	XC	NT	NT	TP	EM	NT	XC	TP	NT	NT	NT	XC	HT	TP	XC	NT
			◇1	◇1	◇1			◇1	◇		◇1	◇1				◇1	◇1	◇1	◇1	
					A		B		E	F	G	H		I	F	J			K	
			⊠		🍴						🍴					🍴	⊠		🍴	
Manchester Airport 85 ✈	d			10 44														12 55		
Manchester Piccadilly 10	d			11 18				12 20	12 44									13 20		
Stockport 78	d			11 27				12 28	12 55									13 29		
Sheffield 7	a			12 09				13 08	13 37									14 08		
	d			12 11	12 21	12 24	12 28	13 11			13 21			13 24	13 36	13 51		14 10	14 21	14 22
Meadowhall	d			12 16		12 30	12 34	13 16						13 30	13 42			14 16		14 28
Rotherham Central	d					12 36								13 36	13 49					14 35
Swinton (S.Yorks)	d					12 49								13 47	13a57					14 46
Mexborough	d					12 52								13 50						14 49
Conisbrough	d					12 56								13 54						14 53
London Kings Cross	d		10 45														12 45			
Doncaster 7	a		12 23	12 35		13 04	12 56	13 34						14 02		14 13	14 23	14 35		15 03
York 8 26	a				13 29						14 29					14 40			15 29	
Doncaster 31	d		12 29	12 37		13 05	12 58			13 12				14 05			14 25	14 37		15 05
Bentley (S.Yorks) 31	a									13 15										
Adwick 31	a									13 19										
Kirk Sandall	d					13 11														15 11
Hatfield & Stainforth	d					13 16														15 16
Thorne South	d																			
Crowle	d																			
Althorpe	d																			
Scunthorpe	a			13 06														15 02		
	d			13 06														15 03		
Barnetby	d			13 21														15 17		
Hull Paragon Interchange	d																			
Barton-on-Humber	a																			
Barton-on-Humber	d																			
Barrow Haven	d																			
New Holland	d																			
Goxhill	d																			
Thornton Abbey	d																			
Ulceby	d																			
Habrough	d			13 29																
Stallingborough	d																			
Healing	d																			
Great Coates	d																			
Grimsby Town	a			13 42														15 37		
	d			13 43														15 38		
Grimsby Docks	d																			
New Clee	d																			
Cleethorpes	a			13 53														15 49		
Thorne North	d					13 22														15 24
Goole	d					13a32	13 17							14 25						15a33
Saltmarshe	d																			
York 8 33	d	12 05											13 40							
Selby	a	12 24	12 43										13 59				14 39			
Wressle	d																			
Howden	d	12 34	12 54										14 09				14 50			
Eastrington	d																			
Gilberdyke	d						13 25							14 33						
Broomfleet	d																			
Brough	d	12 46	13 07				13 33					13 41	14 21	14 41			15 03			
Ferriby	d						13 38													
Hessle	d						13 42													
Hull	a	13 06	13 25				13 57					13 59	14 40	15 01			15 21			

A From Bristol Temple Meads to Edinburgh
B To Scarborough
E To Norwich
F To Leeds
G From Bristol Temple Meads to Glasgow Central
H From Huddersfield
I To Bridlington
J From Birmingham New Street to Newcastle
K From Plymouth to Aberdeen

Table 29

Sundays

from 1 April

Manchester Airport, Manchester, Sheffield and Meadowhall-Doncaster-Cleethorpes and Hull Barton-on-Humber - Cleethorpes

Network Diagram - see first Page of Table 18

	NT		NT		XC	NT	TP	XC	NT	TP	NT		GR	NT	XC	NT	HT	TP	XC	NT	NT			NT
					◇1		◇1	◇1		◇1			1		◇1		◇1	◇1	◇1					
			A		C	D		E		F	G		B	D	H				I		A			
					⊤			⊤					⊏⊤		⊤		☒		⊤					
Manchester Airport 85 ✈ d							13 55											14 55						
Manchester Piccadilly 10 d							14 20											15 20						
Stockport 78 d							14 28											15 28						
Sheffield 7 a							15 08											16 09						
d			14 28		14 51		15 11	15 21	15 24		15 28			15 36	15 51			16 11	16 21	16 24	16 28			16 36
Meadowhall d			14 34				15 16		15 30		15 34			15 42				16 16		16 30	16 34			16 42
Rotherham Central d									15 37					15 50						16 37				16 49
Swinton (S.Yorks) d									15 47					15a58						16 47				16 58
Mexborough d									15 50											16 50				
Conisbrough d									15 54											16 54				
London Kings Cross d													14 30				14 45							
Doncaster 7 a			14 56		15 13		15 35		16 04		15 56		16 10		16 15		16 23	16 35		17 03	16 56			
York 8 26 a					15 43			16 29					16 34		16 40				17 29					17 59
Doncaster 31 d			14 59			15 12	15 37				15 56						16 30	16 37		17 04	16 58			
Bentley (S.Yorks) 31 a						15 15																		
Adwick 31 a						15 19																		
Kirk Sandall d																				17 10				
Hatfield & Stainforth d																				17 15				
Thorne South d																								
Crowle d																								
Althorpe d																								
Scunthorpe a							16 02											17 02						
d							16 03											17 03						
Barnetby d							16 17											17 17						
Hull Paragon Interchange d																								
Barton-on-Humber a																								
Barton-on-Humber d																								
Barrow Haven d																								
New Holland d																								
Goxhill d																								
Thornton Abbey d																								
Ulceby d																								
Habrough d							16 26																	
Stallingborough d																								
Healing d																								
Great Coates d																								
Grimsby Town a							16 39											17 37						
d							16 40											17 38						
Grimsby Docks d																								
New Clee d																								
Cleethorpes a							16 50											17 48						
Thorne North d											16 10									17 24				
Goole d			15 19								16 19									17a33	17 17			
Saltmarshe d																								
York 8 33 d	14 49															16 06								
Selby a	15 08															16 24	16 44							
Wressle d																								
Howden d	15 18															16 34	16 55							
Eastrington d																								
Gilberdyke d			15 29								16 27										17 25			
Broomfleet d																								
Brough d	15 30		15 37							15 41	16 35					16 46	17 07				17 33			
Ferriby d																								
Hessle d																								
Hull a	15 49		15 56							15 59	16 53					17 07	17 26				17 51			

A To Scarborough
B To Edinburgh
C From Birmingham New Street to Newcastle
D To Leeds
E From Plymouth to Glasgow Central
F From Huddersfield
G To Bridlington
H From Guildford to Newcastle
I From Penzance to Edinburgh

Table 29

Sundays
from 1 April

Manchester Airport, Manchester, Sheffield and Meadowhall-Doncaster-Cleethorpes and Hull Barton-on-Humber - Cleethorpes

Network Diagram - see first Page of Table 18

	XC	NT	TP	XC	NT	TP	NT		NT		NT	XC	TP	XC	NT	NT	GR			XC	NT	NT	TP	NT
	◇1 A	B	◇1	◇1 C		◇1 D			E		B	◇1 A	◇1	◇1 G		H	R 1			◇1 J		B	◇1 D	
Manchester Airport 85 ✈ d			15 55										16 55											
Manchester Piccadilly 10 d			16 20										17 20											
Stockport 78 d			16 28										17 28											
Sheffield 7 a			17 08										18 08											
d	16 51		17 11	17 21	17 25				17 28		17 36	17 51	18 11	18 21	18 25	18 28				18 51	18 57			
Meadowhall d			17 16		17 31				17 34		17 44		18 16		18 31	18 35					19 05			
Rotherham Central d					17 37						17 50				18 37						19 11			
Swinton (S.Yorks) d					17 47						17a58				18 48						19 19			
Mexborough d					17 50										18 51									
Conisbrough d					17 54										18 55									
London Kings Cross d																	17 20							
Doncaster 7 a	17 13		17 35		18 05				17 55			18 13	18 35		19 06	18 54	19 03			19 15				
York 8 26 a	17 42			18 29								19 18		19 29						19 43	20 18			
Doncaster 31 d		17 14	17 37						17 57				18 37			18 55	19 04					19 27		
Bentley (S.Yorks) 31 a		17 17																				19 30		
Adwick 31 a		17 21																				19 34		
Kirk Sandall d																19 01								
Hatfield & Stainforth d																19 06								
Thorne South d																								
Crowle d																								
Althorpe d																								
Scunthorpe a			18 02										19 02											
d			18 03										19 03											
Barnetby d			18 17										19 17											
Hull Paragon Interchange d																								
Barton-on-Humber a																								
Barton-on-Humber d																								
Barrow Haven d																								
New Holland d																								
Goxhill d																								
Thornton Abbey d																								
Ulceby d																								
Habrough d													19 26											
Stallingborough d																								
Healing d																								
Great Coates d																								
Grimsby Town a			18 37										19 39											
d			18 38										19 40											
Grimsby Docks d																								
New Clee d																								
Cleethorpes a			18 48										19 48											
Thorne North d																19 12								
Goole d									18 16							19 21								
Saltmarshe d																								
York 8 33 d							17 11																	19 10
Selby a							17 30										19 23							19 35
Wressle d																								
Howden d							17 41																	19 46
Eastrington d																								
Gilberdyke d									18 24							19 29								
Broomfleet d																								
Brough d						17 41	17 53		18 32							19 37	19 45						19 51	19 58
Ferriby d																								
Hessle d																								
Hull a						17 59	18 12		18 48							19 55	20 03						20 05	20 17

A From Reading to Newcastle
B To Leeds
C From Plymouth to Glasgow Central
D From Huddersfield
E To Bridlington
G From Plymouth to Edinburgh
H To Beverley
J From Reading to Edinburgh

Table 29

Sundays
from 1 April

Manchester Airport, Manchester, Sheffield and Meadowhall-Doncaster-Cleethorpes and Hull Barton-on-Humber - Cleethorpes

Network Diagram - see first Page of Table 18

		HT	TP	XC		NT		NT	XC	TP	NT	TP	XC	NT			XC	TP	HT	TP	NT	NT	NT	NT	
		◇1	◇1	◇1					◇1	◇1		◇1	◇1				◇1	◇1	◇1	◇1					
				A				C	D	E			F				D	E				C		C	
		☒							⚯				⚯						☒						
Manchester Airport 85 ✈	d		17 55									18 55								19 55					
Manchester Piccadilly 10 ⛴	d		18 20									19 20								20 18					
Stockport 78	d		18 28									19 28								20 27					
Sheffield 7 ⛴	a		19 08									20 08								21 08					
	d		19 11	19 21		19 29		19 36	19 51		20 02	20 11	20 21	20 28			20 51			21 11			21 24	21 36	
Meadowhall ⛴	d		19 16			19 35		19 42			20 09	20 16		20 34						21 16			21 30	21 42	
Rotherham Central	d					19 41		19 49						20 40									21 37	21 48	
Swinton (S.Yorks)	d					19 49		19a57						20 48									21 47	21a56	
Mexborough	d					19 52								20 51									21 50		
Conisbrough	d					19 56								20 55									21 54		
London Kings Cross	d	17 45																	19 45						
Doncaster 7	a	19 23	19 35			20 07			20 16		20 30	20 35		21 05			21 19		21 25	21 35			22 03		
York 8 26	a			20 29					20 45				21 31				21 44								
Doncaster 31	d	19 30	19 37								20 30	20 37		21 07					21 27	21 37		21 52	22 04		
Bentley (S.Yorks) 31	a																					21 55			
Adwick 31	a																					21 59			
Kirk Sandall	d													21 13											
Hatfield & Stainforth	d													21 18											
Thorne South	d																								
Crowle	d																								
Althorpe	d																								
Scunthorpe	a		20 02									21 02								22 02					
	d		20 03									21 03								22 03					
Barnetby	d		20 17									21 17								22 17					
Hull Paragon Interchange	d																								
Barton-on-Humber	a																								
Barton-on-Humber	d																								
Barrow Haven	d																								
New Holland	d																								
Goxhill	d																								
Thornton Abbey	d																								
Ulceby	d																								
Habrough	d											21 26								22 26					
Stallingborough	d																								
Healing	d																								
Great Coates	d																								
Grimsby Town	a		20 37									21 39								22 39					
	d		20 38									21 40								22 40					
Grimsby Docks	d																								
New Clee	d																								
Cleethorpes	a		20 48									21 50								22 50					
Thorne North	d													21 24											
Goole	d										20 49			21a34									22 23		
Saltmarshe	d																								
York 8 33	d																				21 41				
Selby	a	19 45																	21 43		22 00				
Wressle	d																								
Howden	d	19 56																	21 55		22 10				
Eastrington	d																								
Gilberdyke	d										20 57												22 31		
Broomfleet	d																								
Brough	d	20 08								20 36	21 05							21 58	22 07		22 22		22 39		
Ferriby	d																								
Hessle	d																								
Hull	a	20 26								20 54	21 23							22 12	22 26		22 36		22 56		

A From Plymouth to Edinburgh
C To Leeds
D From Reading to Newcastle
E From Huddersfield
F From Plymouth

Table 29

Sundays
from 1 April

Manchester Airport, Manchester, Sheffield and Meadowhall-Doncaster-Cleethorpes and Hull Barton-on-Humber - Cleethorpes

Network Diagram - see first Page of Table 18

		TP	NT	NT	TP		NT
		◇1 A			◇1		
Manchester Airport 85 ✈	d						
Manchester Piccadilly 10 🚌	d						
Stockport 78	d						
Sheffield 7 🚌	a						
	d		22 13	22 26	22 30		23 34
Meadowhall 🚌	d		22 19	22 32	22 35		23 40
Rotherham Central	d			22 38			23 47
Swinton (S.Yorks)	d			22 48			23 55
Mexborough	d			22 51			23 58
Conisbrough	d			22 55			00 02
London Kings Cross	d						
Doncaster 7	a		22 38	23 05	22 56		00 13
York 8 26	a						
Doncaster 31	d		22 41		22 58		
Bentley (S.Yorks) 31	a						
Adwick 31	a						
Kirk Sandall	d						
Hatfield & Stainforth	d						
Thorne South	d						
Crowle	d						
Althorpe	d						
Scunthorpe	a				23 23		
	d				23 24		
Barnetby	d				23 38		
Hull Paragon Interchange	d						
Barton-on-Humber	a						
Barton-on-Humber	d						
Barrow Haven	d						
New Holland	d						
Goxhill	d						
Thornton Abbey	d						
Ulceby	d						
Habrough	d						
Stallingborough	d						
Healing	d						
Great Coates	d						
Grimsby Town	a				23 57		
	d				23 58		
Grimsby Docks	d						
New Clee	d						
Cleethorpes	a				00 09		
Thorne North	d		22 53				
Goole	d		23 02				
Saltmarshe	d						
York 8 33	d						
Selby	a						
Wressle	d						
Howden	d						
Eastrington	d						
Gilberdyke	d		23 10				
Broomfleet	d						
Brough	d	23 02	23 18				
Ferriby	d						
Hessle	d						
Hull	a	23 19	23 39				

A From Leeds

Sheffield - Retford and Lincoln

Network Diagram - see first Page of Table 18

Miles		NT	NT	NT	NT	NT	NT	NT	NT
						B		C	C
—	Huddersfield 34 d								
—	Barnsley 34 d								
—	Meadowhall 34 d					07 33		09 33	10 33
0	**Sheffield** 7 d	05 39	05 46	06 43	07 30	07 44	08 44	09 44	10 44
2¼	Darnall d		05 51	06 48	07 35		08 49	09 49	10 49
5¼	Woodhouse d		05 56	06 53	07 40		08 54	09 54	10 54
9½	Kiveton Bridge d		06 03	07 00	07 47		09 01	10 01	11 01
10¾	Kiveton Park d	05 54	06 06	07 03	07 50	07 59	09 04	10 04	11 04
13¾	Shireoaks d		06 11	07 08	07 55		09 09	10 09	11 09
15¾	Worksop d	06 01	06 23	07 14	07 59	08a10	09 13	10 13	11 13
23½	**Retford** 10 a	06 10	06 37	07 23	08 09		09 23	10 23	11 23
—	d	06 10		07 24	08 09		09 23	10 24	11 23
33	Gainsborough Lea Road 18 d	06 25		07 38	08 24		09 38	10 38	11 38
42½	Saxilby 18 d	06 37		07 51	08 37		09 51	10 51	11 51
48½	**Lincoln** 18 a	06 53		08 06	08 52		10 06	11 06	12 06

Miles		NT	NT	NT	NT	NT	NT	NT	NT	NT	NT	NT	NT	NT
		C	C	C	C	C	C	D	C			B		
—	Huddersfield 34 d												20 18	
—	Barnsley 34 d												21 12	
—	Meadowhall 34 d	11 33	12 33	13 33	14 34	15 33	16 33	16 55	17 33			20 33	21 30	
0	**Sheffield** 7 d	11 44	12 44	13 44	14 44	15 44	16 44	17 24	17 44	18 45	19 48	20 44	21 44	22 44
2¼	Darnall d	11 49	12 49	13 49	14 50	15 49	16 49	17 29	17 49	18 50	19 53	20 49	21 49	22 49
5¼	Woodhouse d	11 54	12 54	13 54	14 55	15 54	16 54	17 34	17 54	18 55	19 58	20 54	21 54	22 54
9½	Kiveton Bridge d	12 01	13 01	14 01	15 02	16 01	17 01	17 41	18 01	19 02	20 05	21 01	22 01	23 01
10¾	Kiveton Park d	12 04	13 04	14 04	15 05	16 04	17 04	17 44	18 04	19 05	20 08	21 04	22 04	23 04
13¾	Shireoaks d	12 09	13 09	14 09	15 09	16 09	17 09	17 48	18 09	19 10	20 13	21 09	22 07	23 09
15¾	Worksop d	12 13	13 13	14 13	15 14	16 13	17 13	17 52	18 13	19 14	20 17	21a21	22 14	23a22
23½	**Retford** 10 a	12 23	13 23	14 23	15 23	16 23	17 23	18 06	18 23	19 24	20 27		22 28	
—	d	12 23	13 23	14 23	15 24	16 23	17 23		18 23	19 24	20 27			
33	Gainsborough Lea Road 18 d	12 38	13 39	14 38	15 38	16 38	17 38		18 38	19 39	20 42			
42½	Saxilby 18 d	12 51	13 52	14 51	15 51	16 51	17 51		18 51	19 52	20 55			
48½	**Lincoln** 18 a	13 06	14 06	15 06	16 10	17 06	18 06		19 07	20 06	21 10			

Sundays

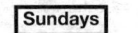

	NT	NT	NT	NT	NT	NT
Huddersfield 34 d						
Barnsley 34 d						
Meadowhall 34 d						
Sheffield 7 d	13 42	13 57	15 43	17 43	19 32	21 06
Darnall d		14 03	15 48	17 48	19 37	21 11
Woodhouse d		14 08	15 53	17 53	19 42	21 16
Kiveton Bridge d		14 14	16 00	18 00	19 49	21 23
Kiveton Park d		14 17	16 03	18 03	19 52	21 26
Shireoaks d		14 22	16 07	18 07	19 56	21 30
Worksop d	14 02	14 26	16 11	18 11	20 00	21 39
Retford 10 a	14 11	14 39	16 20	18 20	20 09	21 48
d	14 12		16 21	18 21	20 10	
Gainsborough Lea Road 18 d	14 26		16 35	18 35	20 24	
Saxilby 18 d	14 39		16 48	18 48	20 37	
Lincoln 18 a	14 54		17 02	19 03	20 51	

B From Doncaster
C From Scunthorpe
D From Adwick

For connections to London Kings Cross please refer to Table 26

Table 30

Saturdays

Sheffield - Retford and Lincoln

Network Diagram - see first Page of Table 18

	NT	NT	NT A	NT	NT	NT	NT	NT B	NT B		NT B	NT	NT B	NT B	NT B	NT B	NT	NT B	NT C		NT B	NT B	NT	NT B
Huddersfield 34 d																								
Barnsley 34 d			06 21																					
Meadowhall 34 d			06 42					09 33	10 33		11 33		12 33	13 33	14 33	15 33		16 33	16 55		17 33	18 33		20 33
Sheffield 7 d	05 39	05 46	06a55	06 43	07 30	08 03	08 44	09 44	10 44		11 44	12 00	12 44	13 44	14 44	15 44	16 00	16 44	17 23		17 44	18 45	19 48	20 44
Darnall d		05 51		06 48	07 35	08 08	08 49	09 49	10 49		11 49	12 05	12 49	13 49	14 49	15 49	16 05	16 49	17 29		17 49	18 50	19 53	20 48
Woodhouse d		05 56		06 53	07 40	08 13	08 54	09 54	10 54		11 54	12 10	12 54	13 54	14 54	15 54	16 10	16 54	17 34		17 54	18 55	19 58	20 54
Kiveton Bridge d		06 03		07 00	07 47	08 20	09 01	10 01	11 01		12 01	12 17	13 01	14 01	15 01	16 01	16 17	17 01	17 40		18 01	19 02	20 05	21 00
Kiveton Park d	05 54	06 06		07 03	07 50	08 23	09 04	10 04	11 04		12 04	12 20	13 04	14 04	15 04	16 04	16 20	17 04	17 43		18 04	19 05	20 08	21 04
Shireoaks d		06 11		07 08	07 55	08 28	09 09	10 09	11 09		12 09	12 25	13 09	14 09	15 09	16 09	16 25	17 09	17 48		18 09	19 10	20 13	21 09
Worksop d	06 01	06 23		07 14	07 59	08 32	09 13	10 13	11 13		12 13	12 35	13 13	14 13	15 13	16 13	16 36	17 13	17 52		18 13	19 14	20 17	21a24
Retford 10 a	06 10	06 38		07 23	08 09	08 42	09 23	10 23	11 23		12 23	12 44	13 23	14 23	15 23	16 23	16 46	17 23	18 06		18 23	19 24	20 27	
d	06 10			07 24	08 09	08 42	09 23	10 23	11 23		12 23	12 45	13 23	14 23	15 23	16 23	16 46	17 23			18 24	19 24	20 27	
Gainsborough Lea Road 18 d	06 25			07 38	08 24		09 38	10 38	11 38		12 38		13 37	14 36	15 40	16 38		17 38			18 38	19 39	20 42	
Saxilby 18 d	06 37			07 51	08 37		09 51	10 51	11 51		12 51		13 50	14 49	15 53	16 51		17 51			18 51	19 52	20 55	
Lincoln 18 a	06 53			08 06	08 52		10 06	11 06	12 06		13 06		14 07	15 06	16 10	17 06		18 06			19 07	20 06	21 10	
Gainsborough Central d						08 57						13 00					17 01							
Kirton Lindsey d						09 11						13 13					17 15							
Brigg d						09 24						13 22					17 27							
Barnetby 29 a						09 38						13 37					17 37							
Habrough 29 a						09 48						13 47					17 47							
Grimsby Town 29 a						10 00						14 00					18 01							
Cleethorpes 29 a						10 13						14 11					18 11							

		NT	NT
Huddersfield 34 d		20 18	
Barnsley 34 d		21 12	
Meadowhall 34 d		21 29	
Sheffield 7 d		21 44	22 44
Darnall d		21 49	22 49
Woodhouse d		21 54	22 54
Kiveton Bridge d		22 01	23 01
Kiveton Park d		22 04	23 04
Shireoaks d		22 08	23 09
Worksop d		22 14	23a22
Retford 10 a		22 28	
d			
Gainsborough Lea Road 18 d			
Saxilby 18 d			
Lincoln 18 a			
Gainsborough Central d			
Kirton Lindsey d			
Brigg d			
Barnetby 29 a			
Habrough 29 a			
Grimsby Town 29 a			
Cleethorpes 29 a			

A To Nottingham
B From Scunthorpe
C From Adwick

For connections to London Kings Cross please refer to Table 26

Table 30

Mondays to Fridays

Lincoln and Retford - Sheffield

Network Diagram - see first Page of Table 18

Miles			NT MX	NT	NT A	NT A	NT A	NT A	NT A	NT	NT A
0	**Lincoln**	18 d		07 00		08 25	09 25	10 25	11 25	12 27	13 26
6	Saxilby	18 d		07 10		08 34	09 34	10 34	11 34	12 36	13 35
15½	Gainsborough Lea Road	18 d		07 22		08 48	09 48	10 48	11 48	12 49	13 48
25	**Retford** 10	a		07 36		09 02	10 02	11 02	12 02	13 03	14 02
—		d		07 40		09 02	10 02	11 02	12 02	13 03	14 02
32¾	Worksop	d	23p28	07 52	08 14	09 14	10 14	11 14	12 14	13 15	14 14
34¾	Shireoaks	d	23p32	07 55	08 19	09 18	10 18	11 18	12 18	13 19	14 18
37¾	Kiveton Park	d	23p38	08 01	08 25	09 24	10 24	11 24	12 24	13 25	14 24
39	Kiveton Bridge	d	23p41	08 04	08 28	09 27	10 27	11 27	12 27	13 28	14 27
43¼	Woodhouse	d	23p52	08 10	08 34	09 33	10 33	11 33	12 33	13 34	14 33
46¼	Darnall	d	23p57	08 15	08 39	09 38	10 38	11 38	12 38	13 39	14 38
48½	**Sheffield** 7	a	00 04	08 26	08 48	09 47	10 47	11 47	12 48	13 48	14 48
—	Meadowhall	34 a			08 59	09 58	10 58	11 58	12 58		14 58
—	Barnsley	34 a									
—	Huddersfield	34 a									

Miles			NT A	NT A	NT C	NT	NT D	NT	NT	NT	NT	NT	NT	NT
0	**Lincoln**	18 d	14 25	15 24	16 25	17 22		18 24	19 43	20 27		21 27		
6	Saxilby	18 d	14 34	15 33	16 35	17 31		18 33	19 52	20 36		21 36		
15½	Gainsborough Lea Road	18 d	14 48	15 48	16 48	17 44		18 46	20 05	20 49		21 49		
25	**Retford** 10	a	15 02	16 02	17 02	17 58		19 04	20 18	21 03		22 03		
—		d	15 02	16 02	17 02	17 58	18 14	19 04	20 19	21 03		22 03	22 45	
32¾	Worksop	d	15 14	16 14	17 14	18 10	18 25	19 16	20 31	21 15	21 26	22 15	22 58	23 28
34¾	Shireoaks	d	15 18	16 18	17 18		18 29	19 20	20 35		21 30	22 19	23 02	23 32
37¾	Kiveton Park	d	15 24	16 24	17 24		18 34	19 26	20 41	21 23	21 36	22 25	23 08	23 38
39	Kiveton Bridge	d	15 27	16 27	17 27		18 37	19 29	20 44		21 39	22 28	23 11	23 41
43¼	Woodhouse	d	15 33	16 33	17 33		18 43	19 35	20 50		21 46	22 34	23 17	23 52
46¼	Darnall	d	15 38	16 38	17 38		18 48	19 40	20 55		21 51	22 39	23 22	23 57
48½	**Sheffield** 7	a	15 48	16 48	17 49	18 35	18 57	19 54	21 05	21 44	22 03	22 50	23 33	00 04
—	Meadowhall	34 a	15 58	16 58	17 58		19 06							
—	Barnsley	34 a												
—	Huddersfield	34 a												

Sundays

		NT E	NT	NT	NT	NT	NT
Lincoln	18 d			17 15	19 15	21 10	
Saxilby	18 d			17 25	19 25	21 20	
Gainsborough Lea Road	18 d			17 37	19 37	21 32	
Retford 10	a			17 51	19 51	21 46	
	d		14 50	17 51	19 51	21 46	22 24
Worksop	d	23p28	15 01	18 03	20 03	21 58	22 35
Shireoaks	d	23p32	15 05	18 06	20 06	22 01	22 39
Kiveton Park	d	23p38	15 10	18 12	20 12	22 07	22 44
Kiveton Bridge	d	23p41	15 13	18 15	20 15	22 10	22 47
Woodhouse	d	23p47	15 19	18 21	20 21	22 16	22 53
Darnall	d	23p52	15 24	18 26	20 26	22 21	22 58
Sheffield 7	a	00§01	15 33	18 35	20 35	22 29	23 07
Meadowhall	34 a		15 42				
Barnsley	34 a		16 03				
Huddersfield	34 a		16 53				

A To Adwick
C To Hull
D To Doncaster
E not 11 December

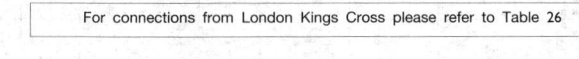

For connections from London Kings Cross please refer to Table 26

Table 30

Saturdays

Lincoln and Retford - Sheffield

Network Diagram - see first Page of Table 18

		NT	NT	NT	NT A	NT A	NT A	NT A	NT	NT A		NT A	NT A	NT A	NT	NT B	NT	NT C	NT	NT		NT	NT	NT	NT
Cleethorpes	29 d								11 10						15 20					18 36					
Grimsby Town	29 d								11 17						15 27					18 43					
Habrough	29 d								11 28						15 37					18 53					
Barnetby	29 d								11 38						15 48					19 02					
Brigg	d								11 44						15 53					19 08					
Kirton Lindsey	d								11 53						16 02					19 17					
Gainsborough Central	d								12 20						16 20					19 35					
Lincoln	18 d			07 00	08 25	09 25	10 25	11 25		12 27		13 25	14 25	15 24		16 25	17 22		18 24			19 43	20 27		21 27
Saxilby	18 d			07 10	08 34	09 34	10 34	11 34		12 36		13 34	14 34	15 33		16 35	17 31		18 33			19 52	20 36		21 36
Gainsborough Lea Road	18 d			07 22	08 48	09 48	10 48	11 48		12 49		13 48	14 48	15 48		16 48	17 44		18 46			20 05	20 49		21 49
Retford 10	a			07 36	09 02	10 02	11 02	12 02	12 35	13 03		14 02	15 02	16 02	16 35	17 02	17 58		19 04	19 49		20 16	21 03		22 03
	d			07 40	09 02	10 02	11 02	12 02	12 35	13 03		14 02	15 02	16 02	16 35	17 02	17 58	18 14	19 04	19 50		20 18	21 03		22 03
Worksop	d	23p28	06 30	07 52	09 14	10 14	11 14	12 14	12 47	13 15		14 14	15 14	16 14	16 47	17 14	18 10	18 25	19 16	20 01		20 31	21 15	21 26	22 15
Shireoaks	d	23p32	06 33	07 55	09 18	10 18	11 18	12 18	12 51	13 19		14 18	15 18	16 18	16 51	17 18		18 29	19 20	20 05		20 35		21 30	22 19
Kiveton Park	d	23p38	06 39	08 01	09 24	10 24	11 24	12 24	12 57	13 25		14 24	15 24	16 24	16 57	17 24		18 34	19 26	20 09		20 41	21 23	21 36	22 25
Kiveton Bridge	d	23p41	06 42	08 04	09 27	10 27	11 27	12 27	13 00	13 28		14 27	15 27	16 27	17 00	17 27		18 37	19 29	20 14		20 44		21 39	22 28
Woodhouse	d	23p52	06 48	08 10	09 33	10 33	11 33	12 33	13 06	13 34		14 33	15 33	16 33	17 06	17 33		18 43	19 35	20 21		20 50		21 44	22 34
Darnall	d	23p57	06 53	08 15	09 38	10 38	11 38	12 38	13 11	13 39		14 38	15 38	16 38	17 11	17 38		18 48	19 40	20 26		20 55		21 49	22 39
Sheffield 7	a	00 04	07 02	08 26	09 48	10 48	11 48	12 48	13 23	13 48		14 48	15 48	16 48	17 23	17 49	18 35	18 57	19 54	20 34		21 05	21 46	22 00	22 50
Meadowhall	34 a				09 58	10 58	11 58	12 58		13 58		14 58	15 58	16 58		17 57		19 06							
Barnsley	34 a																								
Huddersfield	34 a																								

		NT	NT
Cleethorpes	29 d		
Grimsby Town	29 d		
Habrough	29 d		
Barnetby	29 d		
Brigg	d		
Kirton Lindsey	d		
Gainsborough Central	d		
Lincoln	18 d		
Saxilby	18 d		
Gainsborough Lea Road	18 d		
Retford 10	a		
	d	22 45	
Worksop	d	22 58	23 28
Shireoaks	d	23 02	23 32
Kiveton Park	d	23 08	23 38
Kiveton Bridge	d	23 11	23 41
Woodhouse	d	23 17	23 47
Darnall	d	23 22	23 52
Sheffield 7	a	23 32	00 01
Meadowhall	34 a		
Barnsley	34 a		
Huddersfield	34 a		

A To Adwick

B To Hull

C To Doncaster

For connections from London Kings Cross please refer to Table 26

Network Diagram for Tables 31, 32, 33, 34

DM-5/10
Design BAJS

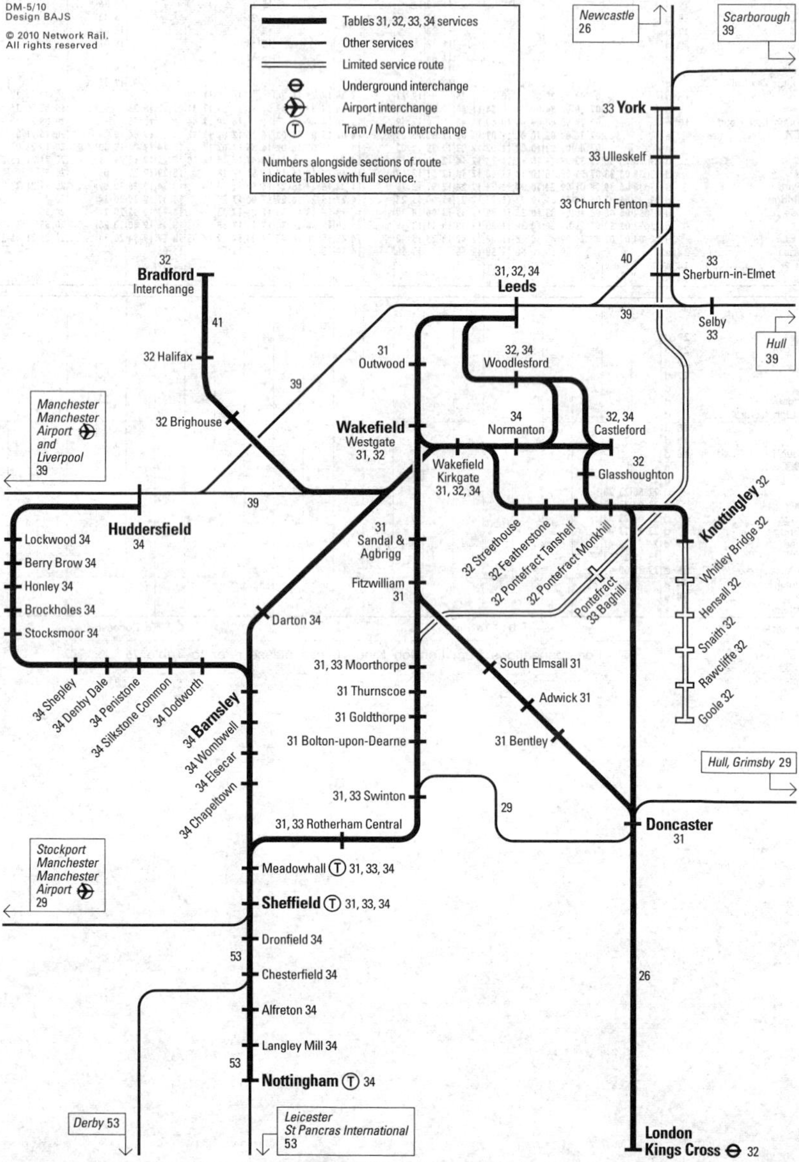

Sheffield, Doncaster and Wakefield - Leeds

Network Diagram - see first page of Table 31

Miles	Miles				NT MO	NT MX	EM MO	NT MX	GR MX	GR MO	EM MO	NT MX	NT		NT	NT	NT	NT	NT	NT	NT	NT	NT		NT	NT
							◇1 A		R 1	R 1	◇1 B															
—	0	**Sheffield 7**	29	d	22p39	23p15	23p16	23p24			23p30		05 22		05 50			06 06	06 18	06 28	06 49				06 52	07 06
—	3½	Meadowhall	29	d	22p45	23p21		23p30					05 28		05 56			06 12	06 24	06 34	06 55				06 58	07 12
—	6¼	Rotherham Central	29	d		23p27							05 34						06 30	06 40					07 04	
—	10¾	Swinton (S.Yorks)	29	d		23p36							05 42						06 38	06 51					07 14	
—	13	Bolton-upon-Dearne		d		23p41							05 46							06 56						
—	14¼	Goldthorpe		d		23p44							05 49							06 58						
—	15	Thurnscoe		d		23p47							05 52							07 01						
—	18½	Moorthorpe		d		23p52							05 57							07 06						
0	—	**Doncaster 7**		d					23p32	23p36							06 26		06 59			07 08	07 26		07 34	
1¾	—	Bentley (S.Yorks)		d													06 29		07 02			07 11	07 29		07 37	
4	—	Adwick		a													06 33		07 08			07 15	07 33		07 43	
—	—			d													06 33					07 15	07 33			
8¾	—	South Elmsall		d													06 39					07 21	07 39			
13¼	22¼	Fitzwilliam		d									06 02				06 44			07 12		07 34	07 44			
18	27	Sandal & Agbrigg		d								←	06 08				06 50			07 18		07 40	07 50			
19¾	28¾	**Wakefield Westgate 7**	32,39	a		00 09	23p40		23p53	23p56	00 01	00 09	06 12				06 54			07 22		07 44	07 54			
—	—			d		00 10	23p41		23p53	23p56	00 02	00 10	06 13			06 24	06 54			07 23		07 44	07 54			
—	—	Pontefract Monkhill	32	d		↪																↪	↪			
—	—	Wakefield Kirkgate 4	32,34,39	a	23p26			00s10							06 27	06 29		06 49			07 27					07 49
—	—			d	23p27										06 28			06 50			07 28					07 50
22¼	31¼	Outwood		d									06 18				06 59			07 28						
29¾	38¾	**Leeds 10**	32,34	a	00 05		00 01		00 12	00 15	00 18	00 29	06 33		06 50		07 14	07 28		07 44	07 51					08 25

			XC	NT	NT	GR	NT	NT	NT		NT	GR	NT	NT	NT	NT	XC	NT	GR		NT	NT	NT	GR	NT	NT
			◇1			R 1						R 1					◇1		R 1					R 1		
Sheffield 7	29	d	07 12				07 14	07 20			07 51		08 06		08 14	08 18	08 21						08 51			08 53
Meadowhall	29	d					07 21	07 26			07 57		08 12		08 21	08 25							08 57			09 00
Rotherham Central	29	d					07 27								08 28											09 06
Swinton (S.Yorks)	29	d					07 35								08 37											09 16
Bolton-upon-Dearne		d					07 39								08 41											
Goldthorpe		d					07 42								08 44											
Thurnscoe		d					07 45								08 47											
Moorthorpe		d					07 54								08 52											
Doncaster 7		d				07 44			07 56			08 12		08 16				08 26	08 41			08 49		09 12	09 26	09 34
Bentley (S.Yorks)		d							07 59					08 18				08 29				08 52			09 29	09 37
Adwick		a							08 03					08 24				08 33				08 58			09 33	09 43
		d							08 03									08 33							09 33	
South Elmsall		d							08 09									08 39							09 39	
Fitzwilliam		d					08 00		08 14						08 58			08 45							09 44	
Sandal & Agbrigg		d		←	←		08 06		08 20						09 04			08 50			←				09 50	
Wakefield Westgate 7	32,39	a	07 36	07 44	07 54	08 01	08 10		08 24			08 31			09 08		08 46	08 54	09 00		09 08			09 31	09 54	
		d	07 37	07 44	07 54	08 01	08 11		08 25			08 31			09 08		08 47	08 55	09 00		09 08			09 31	09 54	
Pontefract Monkhill	32	d													↪										↪	
Wakefield Kirkgate 4	32,34,39	a						07 57			08 27		08 49			08 57							09 27			
		d						07 58			08 28		08 50			08 58							09 28			
Outwood		d		07 49	07 59		08 16		08 29									08 59			09 13					
Leeds 10	32,34	a	07 52	08 02	08 13	08 21	08 36	08 21	08 42		08 49	08 50	09 25			09 20	09 03	09 14	09 19		09 31		09 49	09 50		

			NT	NT	NT		XC	NT	NT	GR	NT	NT	GR	NT	NT		NT	NT	NT	XC	NT	GR	NT	NT	GR	
							◇1			R 1			R 1							◇1		R 1			R 1	
Sheffield 7	29	d	09 06	09 14	09 18		09 21		09 29			09 50			09 53		10 06	10 14	10 18	10 21				10 50		
Meadowhall	29	d	09 12	09 21	09 24				09 35			09 56			09 59		10 12	10 21	10 24					10 56		
Rotherham Central	29	d		09 27					09 42						10 06			10 27								
Swinton (S.Yorks)	29	d		09 36					09 51						10 15			10 36								
Bolton-upon-Dearne		d		09 41														10 41								
Goldthorpe		d		09 43														10 43								
Thurnscoe		d		09 46														10 46								
Moorthorpe		d		09 51					10a01									10 53								
Doncaster 7		d								09 41			10 12	10 26	10 34							10 42			11 13	
Bentley (S.Yorks)		d												10 29	10 37											
Adwick		a												10 33	10 43											
		d												10 33												
South Elmsall		d												10 39												
Fitzwilliam		d		09 56										10 44				10 59								
Sandal & Agbrigg		d		10 02				←			←			10 50				11 05			←		←			
Wakefield Westgate 7	32,39	a		10 06			09 46	09 54		09 59	10 06		10 31	10 54				11 09		10 46	10 54	11 00	11 09		11 31	
		d		10 06			09 47	09 54		09 59	10 06		10 31	10 54				11 09		10 47	10 54	11 00	11 09		11 31	
Pontefract Monkhill	32	d		↪										↪				↪								
Wakefield Kirkgate 4	32,34,39	a	09 49		09 57							10 27					10 49		10 57					11 27		
		d	09 50		09 58							10 28					10 50		10 58					11 28		
Outwood		d						09 59			10 11										10 59		11 14			
Leeds 10	32,34	a	10 25		10 18		10 02	10 14		10 19	10 31	10 48	10 50				11 25		11 18	11 02	11 15	11 19	11 31	11 48	11 50	

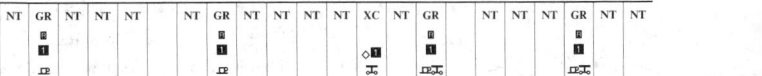

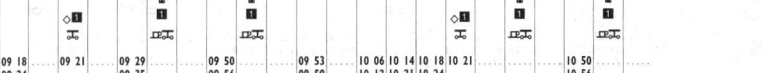

A until 26 March

B from 2 April

Sheffield, Doncaster and Wakefield - Leeds

Network Diagram - see first page of Table 31

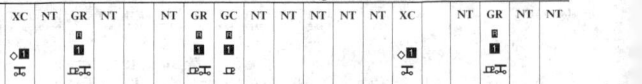

Station	Table		NT	NT	NT	NT	NT	XC	NT	GR	NT		NT	GR	GC	NT	NT	NT	NT	NT	XC		NT	GR	NT	NT
										R				R	R									R		
								◇1		1				1	1						◇1			1		
Sheffield 7	29	d		10 53	11 06	11 14	11 18	11 21					11 50				11 53	12 06	12 14	12 18	12 21					12 50
Meadowhall	29	d		10 59	11 12	11 21	11 24						11 56				11 59	12 12	12 21	12 24						12 56
Rotherham Central	29	d		11 05		11 27											12 05		12 27							
Swinton (S.Yorks)	29	d		11 16		11 36											12 16		12 36							
Bolton-upon-Dearne		d				11 41													12 41							
Goldthorpe		d				11 43													12 43							
Thurnscoe		d				11 46													12 46							
Moorthorpe		d				11 53													12 52							
Doncaster 7		d	11 26	11 34						11 41				12 12	12 24	12 26	12 34							12 41		
Bentley (S.Yorks)		d	11 29	11 37												12 29	12 38									
Adwick		a	11 33	11 43												12 33	12 43									
		d	11 33													12 33										
South Elmsall		d	11 39													12 39										
Fitzwilliam		d	11 45			11 59										12 44			12 58							
Sandal & Agbrigg		d	11 50			12 05			←		←					12 49			13 05				←		←	
Wakefield Westgate 7	32,39	a	11 54			12 09		11 46	11 54	12 00	12 09			12 31		12 51			13 09		12 46		12 51	13 00	13 09	
		d	11 55			12 09		11 47	11 55	12 01	12 09			12 31		12 52			13 09		12 47		12 52	13 01	13 09	
Pontefract Monkhill	32	d	→			→									12 49	→			→							
Wakefield Kirkgate 4	32,34,39	a			11 49		11 57						12 27		13 07			12 49		12 57						13 27
		d			11 50		11 58						12 28					12 50		12 58						13 28
Outwood		d							11 59		12 14												12 56		13 14	
Leeds 10	32,34	a			12 25		12 18	12 01	12 15	12 19	12 31		12 48	12 50				13 25		13 18	13 03		13 13	13 19	13 29	13 49

Station	Table		GR	NT	NT	NT	NT		NT	XC	NT	NT	GR	NT	NT	GR	NT		NT	NT	NT	NT	XC	NT	GR	NT
			R										R			R									R	
			1							◇1			1			1							◇1		1	
Sheffield 7	29	d			12 53	13 06	13 14		13 18	13 21		13 29			13 50				13 53	14 06	14 14	14 18	14 21			
Meadowhall	29	d			12 59	13 12	13 21		13 24			13 35			13 56				13 59	14 12	14 21	14 24				
Rotherham Central	29	d			13 05		13 27					13 41							14 05		14 27					
Swinton (S.Yorks)	29	d			13 16		13 36					13 50							14 17		14 35					
Bolton-upon-Dearne		d					13 41														14 40					
Goldthorpe		d					13 43														14 42					
Thurnscoe		d					13 46														14 45					
Moorthorpe		d					13 53					14a01									14 52					
Doncaster 7		d	13 12	13 26	13 34								13 41			14 12	14 26		14 34						14 41	
Bentley (S.Yorks)		d		13 29	13 37												14 29		14 37							
Adwick		a		13 33	13 43												14 33		14 43							
		d		13 33													14 33									
South Elmsall		d		13 39													14 39									
Fitzwilliam		d		13 45			13 59										14 45				14 58					
Sandal & Agbrigg		d		13 50			14 05				←			←			14 50				15 04			←		←
Wakefield Westgate 7	32,39	a	13 31	13 54			14 09			13 46	13 54		13 59	14 09		14 31	14 54				15 08		14 46	14 54	14 59	15 08
		d	13 31	13 55			14 09			13 47	13 55		13 59	14 09		14 31	14 55				15 08		14 47	14 55	14 59	15 08
Pontefract Monkhill	32	d		→			→										→				→					
Wakefield Kirkgate 4	32,34,39	a				13 50			13 57						14 27					14 49		14 57				
		d				13 50			13 58						14 28					14 50		14 58				
Outwood		d									13 59			14 14										14 59		15 13
Leeds 10	32,34	a	13 50			14 25			14 18	14 02	14 14		14 19	14 31	14 48	14 50				15 25		15 18	15 01	15 13	15 19	15 31

Station	Table		NT		GR	NT	NT	NT	NT	NT	XC	NT	GR		NT	NT	GR	NT	GC	NT	NT	NT	NT		XC	GR
					R								R				R		R							R
					1						◇1		1				1		1						◇1	1
Sheffield 7	29	d	14 50				14 53	15 06	15 14	15 18	15 21					15 50				15 53	16 06	16 14	16 18		16 21	
Meadowhall	29	d	14 56				14 59	15 12	15 20	15 24						15 56				15 59	16 12	16 20	16 24			
Rotherham Central	29	d					15 05		15 26											16 05		16 26				
Swinton (S.Yorks)	29	d					15 16		15 34											16 16		16 36				
Bolton-upon-Dearne		d							15 39													16 40				
Goldthorpe		d							15 41													16 43				
Thurnscoe		d							15 44													16 46				
Moorthorpe		d							15 51													16 53				
Doncaster 7		d			15 12	15 26	15 34						15 41				16 12	16 16	16 24	16 34						16 41
Bentley (S.Yorks)		d				15 29	15 37											16 19		16 37						
Adwick		a				15 33	15 42											16 23		16 43						
		d				15 33												16 23								
South Elmsall		d				15 39												16 29								
Fitzwilliam		d				15 44			15 57									16 33				16 59				
Sandal & Agbrigg		d				15 50			16 03			←			←			16 39				17 05				
Wakefield Westgate 7	32,39	a			15 31	15 54			16 08		15 46	15 54	15 59		16 08		16 30	16 43				17 09			16 49	17 00
		d			15 31	15 54			16 08		15 47	15 54	15 59		16 08		16 30	16 43				17 09			16 50	17 00
Pontefract Monkhill	32	d				→			→										16 48			→				
Wakefield Kirkgate 4	32,34,39	a	15 27					15 49		15 57						16 27			17 04		16 49		16 57			
		d	15 28					15 50		15 58						16 28					16 50		16 58			
Outwood		d										15 59			16 13			16 49								
Leeds 10	32,34	a	15 49		15 50			16 25		16 18	16 02	16 14	16 19		16 31	16 49	16 52	17 03			17 25		17 18		17 04	17 19

Sheffield, Doncaster and Wakefield - Leeds

Network Diagram - see first page of Table 31

Station			NT	NT	GR	NT	NT	NT	NT		NT	XC	NT	GR	NT	XC	NT	GR	NT		NT	NT	XC	NT	GR	NT
					R 1 ☕🛒							◇1 🛒		R 1 ☕🛒		◇1 🛒		R 1 ☕🛒					◇1 🛒		R 1 ☕🛒	
Sheffield 7	29 🚋	d		16 50			16 53	17 06	17 13		17 18	17 21				17 47	17 50		18 06		18 13	18 18	18 21			
Meadowhall	29 🚋	d		16 56			16 59	17 12	17 20		17 24						17 56		18 12		18 20	18 24				
Rotherham Central	29	d					17 05		17 26												18 26					
Swinton (S.Yorks)	29	d					17 16		17 36												18 36					
Bolton-upon-Dearne		d							17 40												18 41					
Goldthorpe		d							17 43												18 43					
Thurnscoe		d							17 46												18 46					
Moorthorpe		d							17 52												18 53					
Doncaster 7		d			17 13	17 26	17 34							17 42										18 26	18 40	
Bentley (S.Yorks)		d				17 29	17 37																	18 29		
Adwick		a				17 33	17 43																	18 33		
		d				17 33																		18 33		
South Elmsall		d				17 39																		18 39		
Fitzwilliam		d				17 45			17 58												18 59			18 45		
Sandal & Agbrigg		d	←			17 51			18 05				←		←						19 05			18 50		←
Wakefield Westgate 7	32,39	a	17 09		17 31	17 55			18 09			17 47	17 55	18 00	18 09	18 13					19 10		18 47	18 54	18 59	19 10
		d	17 09		17 31	17 55			18 09			17 48	17 55	18 00	18 09	18 14		18 31			19 10		18 48	18 55	18 59	19 10
Pontefract Monkhill	32	d				↪			↪												↪					
Wakefield Kirkgate 4	32,34,39	a		17 28				17 49			17 57						18 28		18 50			18 59				
		d		17 28				17 50			17 58						18 32		18 50			18 59				
Outwood		d	17 14										18 00		18 14									18 59		19 15
Leeds 10	32,34	a	17 31	17 48	17 51			18 25			18 18	18 03	18 14	18 19	18 32	18 31	18 51	18 51	19 27			19 23	19 03	19 14	19 19	19 31

Station			GR	NT	NT		NT	NT	XC	NT	GR	GR	NT	NT	GR		NT	NT	XC	NT	GR	NT	GR	NT	XC	
			R 1 ☕🛒						◇1 🛒		R 1 ☕🛒	R 1 ☕🛒			R 1 ☕🛒				◇1 🛒		R 1 ☕🛒		R 1 ☕🛒		◇1	
Sheffield 7	29 🚋	d		18 50	19 06		19 18	19 22	19 26					19 51			20 06	20 18	20 21			20 27		21 09	21 21	
Meadowhall	29 🚋	d		18 56	19 12		19 25	19 28						19 57			20 12	20 24				20 35		21 15		
Rotherham Central	29	d					19 31															20 41				
Swinton (S.Yorks)	29	d					19 40															20 50				
Bolton-upon-Dearne		d					19 44															20 55				
Goldthorpe		d					19 47															20 57				
Thurnscoe		d					19 50															21 00				
Moorthorpe		d					20 00															21 05				
Doncaster 7		d	19 17							19 20	19 42	19 49			20 20					20 26	20 40		21 13			
Bentley (S.Yorks)		d								19 23										20 29						
Adwick		a								19 27										20 33						
		d								19 27										20 33						
South Elmsall		d								19 33										20 39						
Fitzwilliam		d					20 05			19 46										20 45		21 11				
Sandal & Agbrigg		d					20 11			19 51			←							20 51		21 17				
Wakefield Westgate 7	32,39	a	19 35				20 15		19 50	19 55	20 01	20 07	20 15		20 38				20 46	20 55	21 00	21 22	21 31		21 46	
		d	19 35				20 16		19 51	19 56	20 01	20 07	20 16		20 38				20 47	20 55	21 00	21 22	21 31		21 47	
Pontefract Monkhill	32	d					↪																			
Wakefield Kirkgate 4	32,34,39	a		19 29	19 50			19 58						20 28			20 49	20 57						21 52		
		d		19 32	19 50			19 58						20 28			20 50	20 58						21 52		
Outwood		d								20 00			20 21							21 00		21 27				
Leeds 10	32,34	a	19 52	19 55	20 26			20 19	20 05	20 17	20 22	20 23	20 34	20 48	20 54		21 26	21 20	21 05	21 14	21 20	21 47	21 51	22 29	22 02	

Station			NT FX	NT FO	NT	EM	GR	NT	GR	NT FX	EM		NT	NT	XC	NT FO	NT	NT	EM	GR	NT FX		NT FO	NT FX		
						◇1 ☕	R 1 ☕🛒		R 1 ☕		◇1 ☕				◇1				◇1 ☕	R 1 ☕						
Sheffield 7	29 🚋	d				21 25		21 30		22 06	22 19			22 24	22 30				22 53		23 15		23 15	23 24		
Meadowhall	29 🚋	d						21 36		22 12				22 30							23 21		23 21	23 30		
Rotherham Central	29	d						21 42						22 36							23 27		23 27			
Swinton (S.Yorks)	29	d						21 50						22 45							23 36		23 36			
Bolton-upon-Dearne		d						21 55						22 49							23 41		23 41			
Goldthorpe		d						21 57						22 52							23 44		23 44			
Thurnscoe		d						22 00						22 55							23 47		23 47			
Moorthorpe		d						22 05						23 00							23 52		23 52			
Doncaster 7		d	21 22	21 22			21 43		22 22				22 26							23 32						
Bentley (S.Yorks)		d	21 25	21 25									22 29													
Adwick		a	21 29	21 29									22 33													
		d	21 29	21 29									22 33													
South Elmsall		d	21 35	21 35									22 39													
Fitzwilliam		d	21 45	21 46				22 11					22 45	23 07												
Sandal & Agbrigg		d	21 51	21 52				22 17					22 51	23 13				←								
Wakefield Westgate 7	32,39	a	21 56	21 56		21 59	22 06	22 21	22 40		22 46		22 55	23 17	22 59			23 17	23 21	23 53	00 09					
		d	21 56	21 57	21 57	22 00	22 06	22 21	22 40		22 47		22 55	23 18	23 00		23 04	23 18	23 22	23 53	00 10					
Pontefract Monkhill	32	d												↪												
Wakefield Kirkgate 4	32,34,39	a			22 00					22 51							23 07							00s10		
		d								22 51						22 51										
Outwood		d	22 01	22 02				22 26					23 00					23 23								
Leeds 10	32,34	a	22 15	22 15		22 19	22 25	22 46	23 00	23 30	23 04		23 14		23 15	23 30		23 41	23 41	00 12	00 29		00 30			

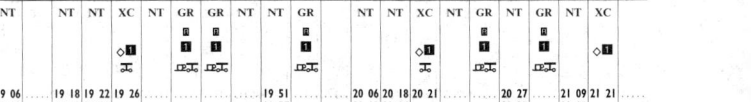

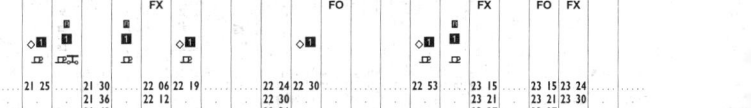

Table 31

Saturdays

Sheffield, Doncaster and Wakefield - Leeds

Network Diagram - see first page of Table 31

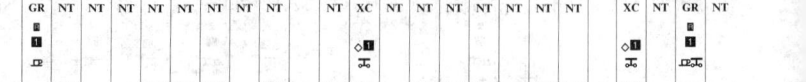

			GR	NT	NT	NT	NT	NT	NT	NT	NT		NT	XC	NT	NT	NT	NT	NT	NT	NT		XC	NT	GR	NT
			R 1											◇1									◇1		R 1	
Sheffield 7	29	d		23p15			06 06	06 12	06 28		06 52		07 06	07 12		07 14	07 51	08 06		08 14	08 18		08 21			
Meadowhall	29	d		23p21			06 12	06 18	06 34		06 58		07 12			07 21	07 57	08 12		08 22	08 25					
Rotherham Central	29	d		23p27				06 24	06 40		07 04					07 27				08 28						
Swinton (S.Yorks)	29	d		23p36				06 35	06 51		07 15					07 33				08 37						
Bolton-upon-Dearne		d		23p41					06 56							07 38				08 42						
Goldthorpe		d		23p44					06 58							07 40				08 44						
Thurnscoe		d		23p47					07 01							07 43				08 47						
Moorthorpe		d		23p52					07 06							07 52				08 53						
Doncaster 7		d	23p32			06 26		06 55		07 26	07 34								08 16					08 26	08 50	
Bentley (S.Yorks)		d				06 29		06 58		07 29	07 37								08 19					08 29		
Adwick		a				06 33		07 05		07 33	07 43								08 23					08 33		
		d				06 33				07 33														08 33		
South Elmsall		d				06 39				07 39														08 39		
Fitzwilliam		d				06 44			07 12	07 44						07 58				09 09				08 45		
Sandal & Agbrigg		d				06 50			07 18	07 50					←	08 04				09 15				08 49		←
Wakefield Westgate 7	32,39	a	23p53			06 54			07 22	07 54				07 36	07 54	08 10				09 19			08 45	08 54	09 08	09 19
		d	23p53		06 24	06 54			07 23	07 54				07 37	07 54	08 11				09 19			08 46	08 55	09 08	09 19
Pontefract Monkhill	32	d								↪										↪						
Wakefield Kirkgate 4	32,34,39	a			06 29		06 49						07 49				08 27	08 49			08 57					
		d					06 50						07 50				08 28	08 50			08 58					
Outwood		d				06 59			07 28						07 59	08 16								08 58		09 24
Leeds 10	32,34	a	00 12	00 30		07 13	07 28		07 44				08 25	07 52	08 14	08 32	08 49	09 25			09 20		09 03	09 14	09 26	09 40

			NT	NT	NT	NT	NT		NT	NT	XC	NT	NT	GR	NT	NT	NT		NT	NT	NT	NT	XC	NT	GR	NT
											◇1			R 1									◇1		R 1	
Sheffield 7	29	d	08 51			08 53	09 06		09 14	09 18	09 21		09 29			09 50			09 53	10 06	10 14	10 18	10 21			
Meadowhall	29	d	08 57			09 00	09 12		09 21	09 24			09 35			09 56			09 59	10 12	10 21	10 24				
Rotherham Central	29	d				09 06			09 27				09 42						10 05		10 27					
Swinton (S.Yorks)	29	d				09 16			09 36				09 51						10 15		10 36					
Bolton-upon-Dearne		d							09 41												10 41					
Goldthorpe		d							09 43												10 43					
Thurnscoe		d							09 46												10 46					
Moorthorpe		d							09 53				10a02								10 53					
Doncaster 7		d		08 54	09 26	09 34								09 50			10 26		10 34						10 50	
Bentley (S.Yorks)		d		08 57	09 29	09 37											10 29		10 37							
Adwick		a		09 04	09 33	09 43											10 33		10 43							
		d			09 33												10 33									
South Elmsall		d			09 39												10 39									
Fitzwilliam		d			09 45				10 09								10 45				11 09					
Sandal & Agbrigg		d			09 49				10 15			←			←		10 49				11 15			←		←
Wakefield Westgate 7	32,39	a			09 54				10 19		09 46	09 54		10 07	10 19		10 54				11 19		10 46	10 54	11 07	11 19
		d			09 55				10 19		09 47	09 55		10 07	10 19		10 55				11 19		10 47	10 55	11 07	11 19
Pontefract Monkhill	32	d			↪				↪								↪				↪					
Wakefield Kirkgate 4	32,34,39	a	09 27				09 49			09 57						10 27				10 49		10 57				
		d	09 28				09 50			09 58						10 28				10 50		10 58				
Outwood		d										09 58			10 24									10 58		11 24
Leeds 10	32,34	a	09 49				10 25			10 18	10 02	10 14		10 27	10 40	10 48				11 25		11 18	11 02	11 14	11 27	11 40

			NT		NT	NT	NT	NT	NT	XC	NT	GR	NT		NT	GC	NT	NT	NT	NT	NT	XC	NT		GR	NT
										◇1		R 1				R 1						◇1			R 1	
Sheffield 7	29	d	10 50			10 53	11 06	11 14	11 18	11 21					11 50			11 53	12 06	12 14	12 18	12 21				
Meadowhall	29	d	10 56			10 59	11 12	11 21	11 24						11 56			11 59	12 12	12 21	12 24					
Rotherham Central	29	d				11 05		11 27										12 05		12 27						
Swinton (S.Yorks)	29	d				11 16		11 36										12 16		12 36						
Bolton-upon-Dearne		d						11 41												12 41						
Goldthorpe		d						11 43												12 43						
Thurnscoe		d						11 46												12 46						
Moorthorpe		d						11 53												12 53						
Doncaster 7		d			11 26	11 34						11 50				12 20	12 26	12 34							12 50	
Bentley (S.Yorks)		d			11 29	11 37											12 29	12 37								
Adwick		a			11 33	11 43											12 33	12 43								
		d			11 33												12 33									
South Elmsall		d			11 39												12 39									
Fitzwilliam		d			11 45			12 09									12 45			13 09						
Sandal & Agbrigg		d			11 49			12 15			←		←				12 49			13 15			←			←
Wakefield Westgate 7	32,39	a			11 54			12 19		11 46	11 54	12 07	12 19				12 54			13 19		12 46	12 54		13 07	13 19
		d			11 55			12 19		11 47	11 55	12 07	12 19				12 55			13 19		12 47	12 55		13 07	13 19
Pontefract Monkhill	32	d			↪			↪									↪			↪						
Wakefield Kirkgate 4	32,34,39	a	11 27				11 49		11 57						12 27	12 42			12 49		12 57					
		d	11 28				11 50		11 58						12 28				12 50		12 58					
Outwood		d									11 58		12 24										12 58			13 24
Leeds 10	32,34	a	11 48				12 25		12 18	12 02	12 14	12 27	12 40		12 48				13 25		13 18	13 02	13 13		13 27	13 43

Table 31

Saturdays

Sheffield, Doncaster and Wakefield - Leeds

Network Diagram - see first page of Table 31

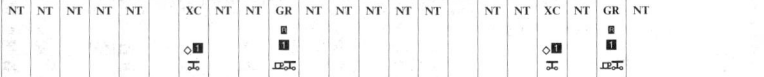

Station			NT	GR	NT	NT	NT	NT	NT		XC	NT	NT	GR	NT	NT	NT	NT	NT		NT	NT	XC	NT	GR	NT
				R 1							◇1			R 1									◇1		R 1	
Sheffield 7	29	d	12 50			12 53	13 06	13 14	13 18		13 21		13 29			13 50		13 53	14 06		14 14	14 18	14 21			
Meadowhall	29	d	12 56			12 59	13 12	13 21	13 24				13 35			13 56		13 59	14 12		14 21	14 24				
Rotherham Central	29	d				13 05		13 27					13 41					14 05			14 27					
Swinton (S.Yorks)	29	d				13 16		13 36					13 50					14 17			14 36					
Bolton-upon-Dearne		d						13 41													14 41					
Goldthorpe		d						13 43													14 43					
Thurnscoe		d						13 46													14 46					
Moorthorpe		d						13 53					14a01								14 53					
Doncaster 7		d		13 13	13 26	13 34								13 53			14 26	14 34							14 50	
Bentley (S.Yorks)		d			13 29	13 37											14 29	14 37								
Adwick		a			13 33	13 43											14 33	14 43								
		d			13 33												14 33									
South Elmsall		d			13 39												14 39									
Fitzwilliam		d			13 45			14 09									14 45				15 09					
Sandal & Agbrigg		d			13 49			14 15				←			←		14 49				15 15			←		←
Wakefield Westgate 7	32,39	a		13 30	13 54			14 19			13 46	13 54		14 11	14 19		14 54				15 19		14 46	14 54	15 07	15 19
		d		13 31	13 55			14 19			13 47	13 55		14 12	14 19		14 55				15 19		14 47	14 55	15 07	15 19
Pontefract Monkhill	32	d			↪			↪									↪				↪					
Wakefield Kirkgate 4	32,34,39	a	13 27				13 50		13 57							14 27			14 49			14 57				
		d	13 28				13 50		13 58							14 28			14 50			14 58				
Outwood		d										13 58			14 24									14 58		15 24
Leeds 10	32,34	a	13 49	13 50			14 25		14 18		14 02	14 14		14 31	14 40	14 48			15 25			15 18	15 02	15 14	15 27	15 40

Station			NT	NT	NT		NT	NT	NT	XC	NT	GR	NT	NT	NT		NT	NT	NT	NT	XC	NT	GR	NT	NT	
										◇1		R 1									◇1		R 1			
Sheffield 7	29	d	14 50		14 53		15 06	15 14	15 18	15 21				15 50			15 53	16 06	16 14	16 18	16 21				16 50	
Meadowhall	29	d	14 56		14 59		15 12	15 21	15 24					15 56			15 59	16 12	16 21	16 24					16 56	
Rotherham Central	29	d			15 05			15 27									16 05		16 27							
Swinton (S.Yorks)	29	d			15 17			15 36									16 16		16 36							
Bolton-upon-Dearne		d						15 41											16 41							
Goldthorpe		d						15 43											16 43							
Thurnscoe		d						15 46											16 46							
Moorthorpe		d						15 53											16 53							
Doncaster 7		d		15 26	15 34							15 50			16 25		16 34						16 50			
Bentley (S.Yorks)		d		15 29	15 37										16 28		16 37									
Adwick		a		15 33	15 43										16 32		16 43									
		d		15 33											16 32											
South Elmsall		d		15 39											16 38											
Fitzwilliam		d		15 45				16 09							16 42				17 09							
Sandal & Agbrigg		d		15 49				16 15			←		←		16 48				17 15			←		←		
Wakefield Westgate 7	32,39	a		15 54				16 19		15 46	15 54	16 07	16 19		16 52				17 19		16 46	16 52	17 07	17 19		
		d		15 55				16 19		15 47	15 55	16 07	16 19		16 52				17 19		16 47	16 52	17 07	17 19		
Pontefract Monkhill	32	d		↪				↪							↪				↪							
Wakefield Kirkgate 4	32,34,39	a	15 27				15 49		15 57					16 27				16 49		16 57					17 28	
		d	15 28				15 50		15 58					16 28				16 50		16 58					17 28	
Outwood		d									15 58		16 24									16 59		17 24		
Leeds 10	32,34	a	15 49				16 25		16 18	16 02	16 13	16 27	16 40	16 49				17 25		17 18	17 02	17 13	17 27	17 41	17 48	

Station			GC	NT	NT	NT	NT	NT	XC	NT	GR		XC	NT	NT	NT	NT	NT	XC	NT	GR		NT	GR	NT	NT
			R 1						◇1		R 1		◇1						◇1		R 1			R 1		
Sheffield 7	29	d			16 53	17 06	17 14	17 18	17 21				17 47		17 50	18 06	18 13	18 18	18 21						18 50	19 06
Meadowhall	29	d			16 59	17 12	17 21	17 24							17 56	18 12	18 21	18 24							18 56	19 12
Rotherham Central	29	d			17 05		17 27										18 27									
Swinton (S.Yorks)	29	d			17 16		17 37										18 37									
Bolton-upon-Dearne		d					17 41										18 41									
Goldthorpe		d					17 44										18 44									
Thurnscoe		d					17 47										18 47									
Moorthorpe		d					17 52										18 53									
Doncaster 7		d	17 21	17 26	17 34						17 50									18 26	18 50			19 14		
Bentley (S.Yorks)		d		17 29	17 37															18 29						
Adwick		a		17 33	17 43															18 33						
		d		17 33																18 33						
South Elmsall		d		17 39																18 39						
Fitzwilliam		d		17 45			18 13										19 09			18 44						
Sandal & Agbrigg		d		17 51			18 19			←				←			19 15			18 50			←			
Wakefield Westgate 7	32,39	a		17 55			18 23		17 47	17 55	18 07		18 12	18 23			19 19		18 46	18 53	19 07		19 19	19 32		
		d		17 55			18 23		17 47	17 55	18 07		18 13	18 23			19 19		18 47	18 54	19 07		19 19	19 33		
Pontefract Monkhill	32	d		↪			↪										↪									
Wakefield Kirkgate 4	32,34,39	a	17 44			17 49		17 57							18 28	18 50		18 59							19 29	19 50
		d				17 50		17 58							18 32	18 50		18 59							19 32	19 50
Outwood		d								18 00				18 28						18 57			19 24			
Leeds 10	32,34	a				18 25		18 18	18 02	18 14	18 27		18 31	18 44	18 51	19 27		19 23	19 01	19 14	19 26		19 43	19 48	19 55	20 26

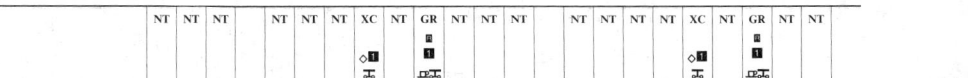

Table 31

Saturdays

Sheffield, Doncaster and Wakefield - Leeds

Network Diagram - see first page of Table 31

			NT	NT	XC	NT	GR		NT	GR	NT	NT	NT	XC	NT	NT	GC	GR	NT	XC	NT	NT	EM	NT	GR	EM
					◇1		R 1			R 1				◇1			R 1	R 1		◇1			◇1		R 1	◇1
Sheffield 7	29	d	19 16	19 18	19 22						19 51	20 06	20 18	20 24		20 27			21 06	21 21			21 25	21 30		22 19
Meadowhall	29	d	19 22	19 25							19 57	20 12	20 24			20 35			21 12					21 36		
Rotherham Central	29	d		19 31												20 41								21 42		
Swinton (S.Yorks)	29	d		19 40												20 50								21 50		
Bolton-upon-Dearne		d		19 44												20 55								21 54		
Goldthorpe		d		19 47												20 57								21 57		
Thurnscoe		d		19 50												21 00								22 00		
Moorthorpe		d		20 01												21 05								22 05		
Doncaster 7		d				19 22	19 50			20 12					20 26		20 53	21 17			21 22				22 18	
Bentley (S.Yorks)		d				19 25									20 29						21 25					
Adwick		a				19 29									20 33						21 29					
		d				19 29									20 33						21 29					
South Elmsall		d				19 35									20 39						21 35					
Fitzwilliam		d		20 07		19 48									20 44	21 11					21 42			22 11		
Sandal & Agbrigg		d		20 13		19 53			←						20 50	21 17					21 48			22 17		
Wakefield Westgate 7	32,39	a		20 17	19 49	19 57	20 07		20 17	20 32				20 48	20 54	21 22		21 34		21 48	21 52		21 59	22 21	22 35	22 44
		d		20 17	19 50	19 58	20 07		20 17	20 33				20 49	20 54	21 22		21 34		21 49	21 53	21 57	22 00	22 21	22 35	22 45
Pontefract Monkhill	32	d		→													21 16									
Wakefield Kirkgate 4	32,34,39	a	19 58								20 28	20 49	20 57						21 52			22 00				
		d	19 58								20 28	20 50	20 58						21 52							
Outwood		d				20 02			20 22						20 59	21 27					21 58			22 26		
Leeds 10	32,34	a	20 20		20 05	20 16	20 26		20 38	20 47	20 48	21 26	21 20	21 03	21 18	21 47		21 50	22 29	22 02	22 17		22 19	22 45	22 55	23 04

			NT		NT	NT	XC	NT	NT	GR
							◇1			R 1
Sheffield 7	29	d				22 24	22 27			
Meadowhall	29	d				22 30				
Rotherham Central	29	d				22 36				
Swinton (S.Yorks)	29	d				22 45				
Bolton-upon-Dearne		d				22 49				
Goldthorpe		d				22 52				
Thurnscoe		d				22 55				
Moorthorpe		d				23 00				
Doncaster 7		d	22 26				22 53			23 48
Bentley (S.Yorks)		d	22 29							
Adwick		a	22 33							
		d	22 33							
South Elmsall		d	22 39							
Fitzwilliam		d	22 44			23 07				
Sandal & Agbrigg		d	22 50			23 13			←	
Wakefield Westgate 7	32,39	a	22 54			23 18	23 10		23 18	00 05
		d	22 54		23 04	23 18	23 11		23 18	00 05
Pontefract Monkhill	32	d				→				
Wakefield Kirkgate 4	32,34,39	a			23 07					
		d						22 51		
Outwood		d	22 59						23 23	
Leeds 10	32,34	a	23 14				23 27	23 30	23 40	00 25

Sundays

until 5 February

			GR	NT	NT	NT	XC	NT	XC	GR	NT		NT	NT	XC	GR	NT	NT	XC	GR	NT		NT	GC	NT	XC
			R 1 A			◇	◇1		◇1	R 1					◇1	R 1			◇1	R 1				R 1		◇1
Sheffield 7	29	d			08 39	09 17	09 21	09 36	10 21				10 39	11 17	11 21		11 36	12 16	12 21				12 39		13 17	13 21
Meadowhall	29	d			08 45	09 23		09 42					10 45	11 23			11 42	12 23					12 45		13 23	
Rotherham Central	29	d						09 48									11 49									
Swinton (S.Yorks)	29	d						09 58									12 00									
Bolton-upon-Dearne		d						10 03									12 04									
Goldthorpe		d						10 05									12 07									
Thurnscoe		d						10 08									12 10									
Moorthorpe		d						10 13									12 15									
Doncaster 7		d	23p48	09 12						10 50	11 12					11 48				12 50	13 12			13 17		
Bentley (S.Yorks)		d		09 15							11 15										13 15					
Adwick		a		09 19							11 19										13 19					
		d		09 19							11 19										13 19					
South Elmsall		d		09 25							11 25										13 25					
Fitzwilliam		d		09 30				10 19			11 30						12 21				13 30					
Sandal & Agbrigg		d		09 36				10 25			11 36						12 27				13 36					
Wakefield Westgate 7	32,39	a	00 05	09 40			09 44	10 29	10 44	11 08	11 40				11 44	12 06	12 31		12 44	13 08	13 40					13 45
		d	00 05	09 40			09 45	10 30	10 45	11 08	11 40				11 45	12 06	12 31		12 45	13 08	13 40					13 46
Pontefract Monkhill	32	d																								
Wakefield Kirkgate 4	32,34,39	a			09 29	09 55							11 29	11 52				12 52					13 29	13 45	13 52	
		d			09 30	09 55							11 30	11 53				12 53					13 30		13 53	
Outwood		d		09 45				10 35			11 45						12 36				13 45					
Leeds 10	32,34	a	00 25	09 59	10 04	10 15	10 02	10 52	11 02	11 30	11 59		12 05	12 18	12 01	12 29	12 53	13 18	13 02	13 30	13 59		14 04		14 18	14 02

A not 11 December

Table 31

Sundays

until 5 February

Sheffield, Doncaster and Wakefield - Leeds

Network Diagram - see first page of Table 31

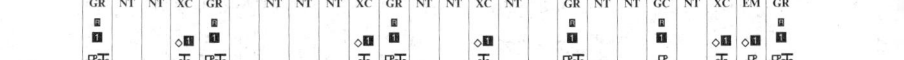

		GR	NT	NT	XC	GR		NT	NT	NT	XC	GR	NT	NT	XC	NT		GR	NT	NT	GC	NT	XC	EM	GR
		R				R						R						R			R				R
		1			◇1	1					◇1	1			◇1			1			1		◇1	◇1	1
Sheffield 7	29 d		13 36	14 17	14 21				14 39	15 17	15 21		15 36	16 17	16 21	16 36				16 39		17 17	17 21	17 34	
Meadowhall	29 d		13 42	14 23					14 45	15 23			15 42	16 23		16 42				16 45		17 23			
Rotherham Central	29 d		13 49										15 50			16 49									
Swinton (S.Yorks)	29 d		13 57										15 58			16 58									
Bolton-upon-Dearne	d		14 01										16 02			17 02									
Goldthorpe	d		14 04										16 05			17 05									
Thurnscoe	d		14 07										16 08			17 08									
Moorthorpe	d		14 12										16 13			17a13									
Doncaster 7	d	13 48				14 50		15 12				15 50						16 59	17 14		17 20				17 49
Bentley (S.Yorks)	d							15 15											17 17						
Adwick	a							15 19											17 21						
	d							15 19											17 21						
South Elmsall	d							15 25											17 27						
Fitzwilliam	d		14 17					15 30					16 19						17 32						
Sandal & Agbrigg	d		14 23					15 36					16 25						17 38						
Wakefield Westgate 7	32,39 a	14 06	14 27		14 44	15 08		15 40			15 44	16 08	16 29		16 44			17 17	17 42				17 47	18 06	18 12
	d	14 06	14 28		14 45	15 08		15 40			15 45	16 08	16 29		16 45			17 17	17 42				17 47	18 07	18 12
Pontefract Monkhill	32 d																								
Wakefield Kirkgate 4	32,34,39 a			14 52					15 29	15 52				16 52						17 29	17 47	17 52			
	d			14 53					15 30	15 53				16 53						17 30		17 53			
Outwood	d		14 33					15 45					16 34						17 47						
Leeds 10	32,34 a	14 29	14 47	15 18	15 02	15 30		15 59	16 04	16 18	16 02	16 29	16 54	17 18	17 02			17 39	18 01	18 05		18 18	18 02	18 24	18 31

		NT		XC	GR	NT	XC	GR	GR	NT	NT	NT		XC	NT	GR	NT	GR	NT	XC	GR	GC		NT	EM
					R			R	R							R		R			R	R			
				◇1	1		◇1	1	1					◇1		1		1		◇1	1	1			◇1
Sheffield 7	29 d	17 36		17 51		18 17	18 21			18 39	18 57	19 16		19 21			19 36		20 17	20 21				20 39	21 03
Meadowhall	29 d	17 44				18 23				18 45	19 05	19 23					19 42		20 23					20 45	
Rotherham Central	29 d	17 50									19 11						19 49								
Swinton (S.Yorks)	29 d	17 58									19 19						19 57								
Bolton-upon-Dearne	d	18 03															20 02								
Goldthorpe	d	18 05															20 04								
Thurnscoe	d	18 08															20 07								
Moorthorpe	d	18 13									19a29						20 12								
Doncaster 7	d			18 15	18 19			18 49	19 14						19 27	19 50		20 19			20 47	21 01			
Bentley (S.Yorks)	d														19 30										
Adwick	a														19 34										
	d														19 34										
South Elmsall	d														19 41										
Fitzwilliam	d	18 19													19 47		20 18								
Sandal & Agbrigg	d	18 25													19 53		20 24								
Wakefield Westgate 7	32,39 a	18 29		18 33	18 38		18 47	19 07	19 32					19 48	19 57	20 09	20 28	20 38		20 46	21 05				21 27
	d	18 30		18 34	18 38		18 48	19 07	19 32					19 49	19 57	20 09	20 28	20 38		20 47	21 05				21 28
Pontefract Monkhill	32 d																								
Wakefield Kirkgate 4	32,34,39 a					18 52				19 29		19 52							20 52			21 22		21 29	
	d					18 53				19 30		19 53							20 53					21 30	
Outwood	d	18 35													20 02		20 33								
Leeds 10	32,34 a	18 50		18 51	18 58	19 18	19 04	19 28	19 53	20 05		20 18		20 05	20 16	20 25	20 52	20 55	21 16	21 03	21 29			22 04	21 44

		GR	XC	GR	NT	NT	GR	XC		NT	EM	GR
		R		R			R					R
		1	◇1	1			1	◇1			◇1	1
Sheffield 7	29 d		21 21			21 36		22 21		22 39	23 16	
Meadowhall	29 d					21 42				22 45		
Rotherham Central	29 d					21 48						
Swinton (S.Yorks)	29 d					21 56						
Bolton-upon-Dearne	d					22 00						
Goldthorpe	d					22 03						
Thurnscoe	d					22 06						
Moorthorpe	d					22 11						
Doncaster 7	d	21 18		21 48	21 52		22 23					23 36
Bentley (S.Yorks)	d				21 55							
Adwick	a				21 59							
	d				21 59							
South Elmsall	d				22 05							
Fitzwilliam	d				22 12	22 17						
Sandal & Agbrigg	d				22 18	22 23						
Wakefield Westgate 7	32,39 a	21 36	21 47	22 06	22 22	22 27	22 40	22 43			23 40	23 56
	d	21 36	21 48	22 06	22 23	22 28	22 40	22 43			23 41	23 56
Pontefract Monkhill	32 d											
Wakefield Kirkgate 4	32,34,39 a									23 26		
	d									23 27		
Outwood	d				22 28	22 33						
Leeds 10	32,34 a	21 57	22 04	22 26	22 41	22 52	23 00	23 01		00 05	00 01	00 15

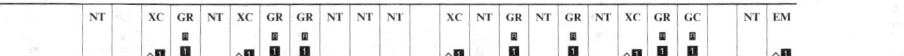

Sheffield, Doncaster and Wakefield - Leeds

Network Diagram - see first page of Table 31

			GR	NT	NT	NT	XC	NT	XC	GR	NT		NT	NT	XC	GR	NT	NT	XC	GR	NT		NT	GC	NT	XC
			R 1			◇	◇1		◇1	R 1					◇1	R 1			◇1	R 1				R 1		◇1
Sheffield 7	29	d			08 39	09 17	09 21	09 36	10 21				10 39	11 17	11 21		11 36	12 16	12 21				12 39		13 17	13 21
Meadowhall	29	d			08 45	09 23		09 42					10 45	11 23			11 42	12 23					12 45		13 23	
Rotherham Central	29	d						09 48									11 49									
Swinton (S.Yorks)	29	d						09 58									12 00									
Bolton-upon-Dearne		d						10 03									12 04									
Goldthorpe		d						10 05									12 07									
Thurnscoe		d						10 08									12 10									
Moorthorpe		d						10 13									12 15									
Doncaster 7		d	23p48	09 12						10 50	11 12					11 48				12 50	13 12			13 17		
Bentley (S.Yorks)		d		09 15							11 15										13 15					
Adwick		a		09 19							11 19										13 19					
		d		09 19							11 19										13 19					
South Elmsall		d		09 25							11 25										13 25					
Fitzwilliam		d		09 30				10 19			11 30						12 21				13 30					
Sandal & Agbrigg		d		09 36				10 25			11 36						12 27				13 36					
Wakefield Westgate 7	32,39	a	00 05	09 40			09 44	10 29	10 44	11 08	11 40				11 44	12 06	12 31		12 44	13 08	13 40					13 45
		d	00 05	09 40			09 45	10 30	10 45	11 08	11 40				11 45	12 06	12 31		12 45	13 08	13 40					13 46
Pontefract Monkhill	32	d																								
Wakefield Kirkgate 4	32,34,39	a			09 29	09 55							11 29	11 52				12 52					13 29	13 45	13 52	
		d			09 30	09 55							11 30	11 53				12 53					13 30		13 53	
Outwood		d		09 45				10 35			11 45						12 36				13 45					
Leeds 10	32,34	a	00 25	09 59	10 04	10 15	10 02	10 52	11 02	11 30	11 59		12 05	12 18	12 01	12 29	12 53	13 18	13 02	13 30	13 59		14 04		14 18	14 02

			GR	NT	NT	XC	GR		NT	NT	NT	XC	GR	NT	NT	XC	NT		GR	NT	NT	GC	NT	XC		EM
			R 1			◇1	R 1					◇1	R 1			◇1			R 1			R 1		◇1 A		◇1
Sheffield 7	29	d		13 36	14 17	14 21				14 39	15 17	15 21		15 36	16 17	16 21	16 36				16 39		17 17	17 21		17 34
Meadowhall	29	d		13 42	14 23					14 45	15 23			15 42	16 23		16 42				16 45		17 23			
Rotherham Central	29	d		13 49										15 50			16 49									
Swinton (S.Yorks)	29	d		13 57										15 58			16 58									
Bolton-upon-Dearne		d		14 01										16 02			17 02									
Goldthorpe		d		14 04										16 05			17 05									
Thurnscoe		d		14 07										16 08			17 08									
Moorthorpe		d		14 12										16 13			17a13									
Doncaster 7		d	13 48				14 50		15 12				15 50						16 59	17 14		17 20				
Bentley (S.Yorks)		d							15 15											17 17						
Adwick		a							15 19											17 21						
		d							15 19											17 21						
South Elmsall		d							15 25											17 27						
Fitzwilliam		d		14 17					15 30					16 19						17 32						
Sandal & Agbrigg		d		14 23					15 36					16 25						17 38						
Wakefield Westgate 7	32,39	a	14 06	14 27		14 44	15 08		15 40			15 44	16 08	16 29		16 44			17 17	17 42				17 47		18 06
		d	14 06	14 28		14 45	15 08		15 40			15 45	16 08	16 29		16 45			17 17	17 42				17 47		18 07
Pontefract Monkhill	32	d																								
Wakefield Kirkgate 4	32,34,39	a			14 52					15 29	15 52				16 52						17 29	17 47	17 52			
		d			14 53					15 30	15 53				16 53						17 30		17 53			
Outwood		d		14 33					15 45					16 34						17 47						
Leeds 10	32,34	a	14 29	14 47	15 18	15 02	15 30		15 59	16 04	16 18	16 02	16 29	16 54	17 18	17 02			17 39	18 01	18 05		18 18	18 02		18 24

			GR		NT	XC	GR	NT	XC	GR	GR	NT	NT		NT	XC	NT	GR	NT	GR	NT	XC	GR		GC	NT
			R 1			◇1	R 1		◇1	R 1	R 1					◇1		R 1		R 1		◇1	R 1		R 1	
Sheffield 7	29	d			17 36	17 51		18 17	18 21			18 39	18 57		19 16	19 21			19 36		20 17	20 21				20 39
Meadowhall	29	d			17 44			18 23				18 45	19 05		19 23				19 42		20 23					20 45
Rotherham Central	29	d			17 50								19 11						19 49							
Swinton (S.Yorks)	29	d			17 58								19 19						19 57							
Bolton-upon-Dearne		d			18 03														20 02							
Goldthorpe		d			18 05														20 04							
Thurnscoe		d			18 08														20 07							
Moorthorpe		d			18 13								19a29						20 12							
Doncaster 7		d	17 49			18 15	18 19			18 49	19 14						19 27	19 50		20 19			20 47		21 01	
Bentley (S.Yorks)		d															19 30									
Adwick		a															19 34									
		d															19 34									
South Elmsall		d															19 41									
Fitzwilliam		d			18 19												19 47		20 18							
Sandal & Agbrigg		d			18 25												19 53		20 24							
Wakefield Westgate 7	32,39	a	18 12		18 29	18 33	18 38		18 47	19 07	19 32					19 48	19 57	20 09	20 28	20 38		20 46	21 05			
		d	18 12		18 30	18 34	18 38		18 48	19 07	19 32					19 49	19 57	20 09	20 28	20 38		20 47	21 05			
Pontefract Monkhill	32	d																								
Wakefield Kirkgate 4	32,34,39	a						18 52				19 29			19 52						20 52				21 22	21 29
		d						18 53				19 30			19 53						20 53					21 30
Outwood		d			18 35												20 02		20 33							
Leeds 10	32,34	a	18 31		18 50	18 51	18 58	19 18	19 04	19 28	19 53	20 05			20 18	20 05	20 16	20 25	20 52	20 55	21 16	21 03	21 29			22 04

A not 12 February

Sundays

12 February to 25 March

Sheffield, Doncaster and Wakefield - Leeds

Network Diagram - see first page of Table 31

			EM	GR	XC	GR	NT	NT	GR		XC	NT	EM	GR
			◇1	R 1	◇1	R 1			R 1		◇1		◇1	R 1
Sheffield [7]	29	d	21 03		21 21			21 36			22 21	22 39	23 16	
Meadowhall	29	d						21 42				22 45		
Rotherham Central	29	d						21 48						
Swinton (S.Yorks)	29	d						21 56						
Bolton-upon-Dearne		d						22 00						
Goldthorpe		d						22 03						
Thurnscoe		d						22 06						
Moorthorpe		d						22 11						
Doncaster [7]		d		21 18		21 48	21 52		22 23					23 36
Bentley (S.Yorks)		d					21 55							
Adwick		a					21 59							
		d					21 59							
South Elmsall		d					22 05							
Fitzwilliam		d					22 12	22 17						
Sandal & Agbrigg		d					22 18	22 23						
Wakefield Westgate [7]	32,39	a	21 27	21 36	21 47	22 06	22 22	22 27	22 40		22 43		23 40	23 56
		d	21 28	21 36	21 48	22 06	22 23	22 28	22 40		22 43		23 41	23 56
Pontefract Monkhill	32	d												
Wakefield Kirkgate [4]	32,34,39	a										23 26		
		d										23 27		
Outwood		d					22 28	22 33						
Leeds [10]	32,34	a	21 44	21 57	22 04	22 26	22 41	22 52	23 00		23 01	00 05	00 01	00 15

Sundays

from 1 April

			GR	NT	NT	NT	XC	NT	XC	GR	NT		NT	NT	XC	GR	NT	NT	XC	GR	NT		NT	GC	NT	XC
			R 1			◇	◇1		◇1	R 1					◇1	R 1			◇1	R 1				R 1		◇1
Sheffield [7]	29	d			08 39	09 17	09 21	09 36	10 21				10 39	11 17	11 21		11 36	12 16	12 21				12 39		13 17	13 21
Meadowhall	29	d			08 45	09 23		09 42					10 45	11 23			11 42	12 23					12 45		13 23	
Rotherham Central	29	d						09 48									11 49									
Swinton (S.Yorks)	29	d						09 58									12 00									
Bolton-upon-Dearne		d						10 03									12 04									
Goldthorpe		d						10 05									12 07									
Thurnscoe		d						10 08									12 10									
Moorthorpe		d						10 13									12 15									
Doncaster [7]		d	23p48	09 12						10 50	11 12					11 48				12 50	13 12			13 17		
Bentley (S.Yorks)		d		09 15							11 15										13 15					
Adwick		a		09 19							11 19										13 19					
		d		09 19							11 19										13 19					
South Elmsall		d		09 25							11 25										13 25					
Fitzwilliam		d		09 30				10 19			11 30						12 21				13 30					
Sandal & Agbrigg		d		09 36				10 25			11 36						12 27				13 36					
Wakefield Westgate [7]	32,39	a	00 05	09 40			09 44	10 29	10 44	11 08	11 40				11 44	12 06	12 31		12 44	13 08	13 40					13 45
		d	00 05	09 40			09 45	10 30	10 45	11 08	11 40				11 45	12 06	12 31		12 45	13 08	13 40					13 46
Pontefract Monkhill	32	d																								
Wakefield Kirkgate [4]	32,34,39	a			09 29	09 55							11 29	11 52				12 52					13 29	13 45	13 52	
		d			09 30	09 55							11 30	11 53				12 53					13 30		13 53	
Outwood		d		09 45				10 35			11 45						12 36				13 45					
Leeds [10]	32,34	a	00 25	09 59	10 04	10 15	10 02	10 52	11 02	11 30	11 59		12 05	12 18	12 01	12 29	12 53	13 18	13 02	13 30	13 59		14 04		14 18	14 02

			GR	NT	NT	XC	GR		NT	NT	NT	XC	GR	NT	NT	XC	NT		GR	NT	NT	GC	NT	XC	GR	NT
			R 1			◇1	R 1					◇1	R 1			◇1			R 1			R 1		◇1	R 1	
Sheffield [7]	29	d		13 36	14 17	14 21				14 39	15 17	15 21		15 36	16 17	16 21	16 36				16 39		17 17	17 21		17 36
Meadowhall	29	d		13 42	14 23					14 45	15 23			15 42	16 23		16 42				16 45		17 23			17 44
Rotherham Central	29	d		13 49										15 50			16 49									17 50
Swinton (S.Yorks)	29	d		13 57										15 58			16 58									17 58
Bolton-upon-Dearne		d		14 01										16 02			17 02									18 03
Goldthorpe		d		14 04										16 05			17 05									18 05
Thurnscoe		d		14 07										16 08			17 08									18 08
Moorthorpe		d		14 12										16 13			17a13									18 13
Doncaster [7]		d	13 48				14 50		15 12				15 50						16 59	17 14		17 20			17 49	
Bentley (S.Yorks)		d							15 15											17 17						
Adwick		a							15 19											17 21						
		d							15 19											17 21						
South Elmsall		d							15 25											17 27						
Fitzwilliam		d		14 17					15 30					16 19						17 32						18 19
Sandal & Agbrigg		d		14 23					15 36					16 25						17 38						18 25
Wakefield Westgate [7]	32,39	a	14 06	14 27		14 44	15 08		15 40			15 44	16 08	16 29		16 44			17 17	17 42				17 47	18 12	18 29
		d	14 06	14 28		14 45	15 08		15 40			15 45	16 08	16 29		16 45			17 17	17 42				17 47	18 12	18 30
Pontefract Monkhill	32	d																								↪
Wakefield Kirkgate [4]	32,34,39	a			14 52					15 29	15 52				16 52						17 29	17 47	17 52			
		d			14 53					15 30	15 53				16 53						17 30		17 53			
Outwood		d		14 33					15 45					16 34						17 47						
Leeds [10]	32,34	a	14 29	14 47	15 18	15 02	15 30		15 59	16 04	16 18	16 02	16 29	16 54	17 18	17 02			17 39	18 01	18 05		18 18	18 02	18 31	

Table 31

Sundays

from 1 April

Sheffield, Doncaster and Wakefield - Leeds

Network Diagram - see first page of Table 31

			EM		NT	XC	GR	NT	XC	GR	GR	NT	NT		NT	XC	NT	GR	NT	GR	NT	XC	GR		GC	GR
							R			R	R							R		R			R		R	R
			◇1			◇1	1		◇1	1	1					◇1		1		1		◇1	1		1	1
Sheffield 7	29 ⛴	d	17 45			17 51		18 17	18 21			18 39	18 57		19 16	19 21			19 36		20 17	20 21				
Meadowhall	29 ⛴	d						18 23				18 45	19 05		19 23				19 42		20 23					
Rotherham Central	29	d											19 11						19 49							
Swinton (S.Yorks)	29	d											19 19						19 57							
Bolton-upon-Dearne		d																	20 02							
Goldthorpe		d																	20 04							
Thurnscoe		d																	20 07							
Moorthorpe		d											19a29						20 12							
Doncaster 7		d				18 15	18 19			18 49	19 14						19 27	19 50		20 19			20 47		21 01	21 18
Bentley (S.Yorks)		d															19 30									
Adwick		a															19 34									
		d															19 34									
South Elmsall		d															19 41									
Fitzwilliam		d															19 47		20 18							
Sandal & Agbrigg		d			←												19 53		20 24							
Wakefield Westgate 7	32,39	a	18 17		18 29	18 33	18 38		18 47	19 07	19 32					19 40	19 57	20 09	20 28	20 38		20 46	21 05			21 36
		d	18 18		18 30	18 34	18 38		18 48	19 07	19 32					19 49	19 57	20 09	20 28	20 38		20 47	21 05			21 36
Pontefract Monkhill	32	d																								
Wakefield Kirkgate 4	32,34,39	a						18 52				19 29			19 52						20 52				21 22	
		d						18 53				19 30			19 53						20 53					
Outwood		d			18 35												20 02		20 33							
Leeds 10	32,34	a	18 30		18 50	18 51	18 58	19 18	19 04	19 28	19 53	20 05			20 18	20 05	20 16	20 25	20 52	20 55	21 16	21 03	21 29			21 57

			NT	EM	XC	GR	NT	NT	GR		XC	NT	GR	EM
						R			R				R	
				◇1	◇1	1			1		◇1		1	◇1
Sheffield 7	29 ⛴	d	20 39	21 13	21 21			21 36			22 21	22 39		23 30
Meadowhall	29 ⛴	d	20 45					21 42				22 45		
Rotherham Central	29	d						21 48						
Swinton (S.Yorks)	29	d						21 56						
Bolton-upon-Dearne		d						22 00						
Goldthorpe		d						22 03						
Thurnscoe		d						22 06						
Moorthorpe		d						22 11						
Doncaster 7		d				21 48	21 52		22 23				23 36	
Bentley (S.Yorks)		d					21 55							
Adwick		a					21 59							
		d					21 59							
South Elmsall		d					22 05							
Fitzwilliam		d					22 12	22 17						
Sandal & Agbrigg		d					22 18	22 23						
Wakefield Westgate 7	32,39	a		21 39	21 47	22 06	22 22	22 27	22 40		22 43		23 56	00 01
		d		21 40	21 48	22 06	22 23	22 28	22 40		22 43		23 56	00 02
Pontefract Monkhill	32	d												
Wakefield Kirkgate 4	32,34,39	a	21 29									23 26		
		d	21 30									23 27		
Outwood		d					22 28	22 33						
Leeds 10	32,34	a	22 04	21 57	22 04	22 26	22 41	22 52	23 00		23 01	00 05	00 15	00 18

Leeds - Wakefield, Doncaster and Sheffield

Network Diagram - see first page of Table 31

Miles	Miles			NT MX	NT MX	NT MX	GR	EM	GR	NT	XC	NT		NT	GR	XC	NT	EM	NT	GR	NT	GR		XC	NT
							R 1	◇1 ⊠	R 1		◇1				R 1	◇1		◇1		R 1		R 1 A		◇1	
0	0	**Leeds** 10 32,34	d	22p37	23p09		05 05	05 25	05 30	05 33	06 00			06 05	06 05	06 15	06 19	06 34	06 38	06 40	06 43	07 00		07 05	
7½	7½	Outwood	d		23p20					05 44							06 28				06 54				
—	—	Wakefield Kirkgate 4 32,34,39	a	23p10										06 21					07 07						
—	—		d	23p10								06 04		06 21					07 08						
—	—	Pontefract Monkhill	d																						
10	10	**Wakefield Westgate** 7 32,39	a		23p24	00 17	05 16	05 36	05 42	05 49	06 11				06 16	06 26	06 32	06 45		06 51	06 58	07 12		07 17	
—	—		d		23p24		05 16	05 37	05 42	05 49	06 12				06 17	06 27	06 33	06 46		06 51	06 58			07 18	
11¾	11¾	Sandal & Agbrigg	d		23p28					05 53							06 36				07 02				
16½	16½	Fitzwilliam	d		23p35					06 00							06 43				07 09				
21	—	South Elmsall	d														06 48								
25¾	—	Adwick	a														06 53								
—	—		d														06 54								
28	—	Bentley (S.Yorks)	d														06 58								
29¾	—	**Doncaster** 7	a				05 35	05 55	06 01						06 34	06 43	07 08			07 09					
—	20¼	Moorthorpe	d		23p41					06 06											07 15				
—	23¾	Thurnscoe	d		23p47					06 12											07 21				
—	24½	Goldthorpe	d		23p49					06 15											07 23				
—	25¾	Bolton-upon-Dearne	d		23p52					06 18											07 26				
—	28	Swinton (S.Yorks) 29	a		23p56					06 23											07 30				
—	32½	Rotherham Central 29	a		00 03					06 31											07 37				←
—	35¼	Meadowhall 29	a	23p51	00 08					06 37		06 41		06 49					07 48		07 44				07 48
—	38¾	**Sheffield** 7 29	a	00 02	00 23			06 18		06 47	06 41	06 55		07 00		07 11		07 25	→		07 56			07 50	07 58

		NT	NT	GR	NT	GC	NT	NT		NT	GR	NT	NT	XC	NT	NT	GR	NT		NT	NT	NT	GR	NT	NT
				R 1		R 1					R 1			◇1			R 1						R 1		
Leeds 10 32,34	d	07 05		07 15	07 18		07 29	07 35			07 40	07 48	08 02	08 11			08 15	08 19		08 32	08 37		08 45	08 48	09 05
Outwood	d				07 28					←		07 59						08 28				←		08 59	
Wakefield Kirkgate 4 32,34,39	a	07 25					08 00	07 54		08 00			08 23							09 03	08 54	09 03			09 23
	d	07 25				07 42	08 04	07 55		08 04			08 23							09 05	08 55	09 05			09 23
Pontefract Monkhill	d					08 01	→													→					
Wakefield Westgate 7 32,39	a			07 26	07 34						07 51	08 03		08 22			08 27	08 31					08 56	09 03	
	d			07 26	07 34						07 51	08 03		08 23			08 27	08 32					08 56	09 03	
Sandal & Agbrigg	d				07 36							08 07						08 36						09 07	
Fitzwilliam	d				07 43							08 14						08 41						09 14	
South Elmsall	d				07 49													08 46							
Adwick	a				07 52													08 52							
	d		07 29		07 52										08 15	08 33		08 52							
Bentley (S.Yorks)	d		07 33		07 56										08 18	08 37		08 56							
Doncaster 7	a		07 37	07 45	08 07	08 29					08 09				08 23	08 41	08 45	09 06					09 15		
Moorthorpe	d											08 20												09 20	
Thurnscoe	d											08 26												09 26	
Goldthorpe	d											08 28												09 28	
Bolton-upon-Dearne	d											08 31												09 31	
Swinton (S.Yorks) 29	a		07 53									08 34			08 42									09 35	
Rotherham Central 29	a		08 00									08 43			08 50									09 44	
Meadowhall 29	a	07 53	08 05					08 31		08 45		08 50	08 52		08 56						09 27	09 46		09 50	09 52
Sheffield 7 29	a	08 05	08 18					08 39		08 56		08 59	09 02	08 51	09 05						09 37	09 56		10 00	10 02

		XC	NT	GR		NT	NT	NT	NT	GR	NT	NT	XC	NT		GR	NT	NT	NT	NT	GR	NT	GC	NT	
		◇1		R 1						R 1			◇1			R 1					R 1		R 1		
Leeds 10 32,34	d	09 11		09 15		09 20	09 32	09 37		09 45	09 48	10 05	10 11			10 15	10 20	10 32	10 37		10 45	10 48		11 05	
Outwood	d					09 29			←		09 59						10 29			←		10 59			
Wakefield Kirkgate 4 32,34,39	a						10 01	09 55	10 01			10 23						11 01	10 54	11 01				11 23	
	d						10 04	09 56	10 04			10 23						11 04	10 55	11 04			11 11	11 23	
Pontefract Monkhill	d						→											→					11 34		
Wakefield Westgate 7 32,39	a	09 23		09 27		09 33				09 56	10 03		10 22			10 27	10 33				10 56	11 03			
	d	09 24		09 27		09 33				09 56	10 03		10 23			10 27	10 33				10 56	11 03			
Sandal & Agbrigg	d					09 35					10 07						10 36					11 07			
Fitzwilliam	d					09 44					10 14						10 44					11 14			
South Elmsall	d					09 47											10 49								
Adwick	a					09 52											10 54								
	d		09 15			09 53								10 15			10 55								
Bentley (S.Yorks)	d		09 19			09 57								10 19			10 59								
Doncaster 7	a		09 24	09 45		10 08				10 15				10 24		10 44	11 09				11 15		12 07		
Moorthorpe	d										10 20											11 20			
Thurnscoe	d										10 26											11 26			
Goldthorpe	d										10 28											11 28			
Bolton-upon-Dearne	d										10 31											11 31			
Swinton (S.Yorks) 29	a		09 42								10 35			10 42								11 35			
Rotherham Central 29	a		09 50								10 44			10 52								11 44			
Meadowhall 29	a		09 55					10 27	10 46		10 50	10 52		10 57					11 27	11 46		11 51		11 52	
Sheffield 7 29	a	09 51	10 05					10 37	10 56		11 01	11 02	10 51	11 05					11 37	11 57		12 01		12 02	

A West Riding Limited

Leeds - Wakefield, Doncaster and Sheffield

Network Diagram - see first page of Table 31

			XC	NT	GR	NT	NT	NT	NT	NT	GR		NT	NT	XC	NT	GR	NT	NT	NT	NT		GR	NT	NT	XC
			◇1		R 1						R 1				◇1		R 1						R 1			◇1
Leeds 10	32,34	d	11 11		11 15	11 20		11 32	11 37		11 45		11 48	12 05	12 12		12 15	12 20	12 32	12 37			12 45	12 48	13 05	13 11
Outwood		d				11 29				←			11 59					12 29			←			12 59		
Wakefield Kirkgate 4	32,34,39	a						12 01	11 54	12 01				12 23					13 02	12 54	13 02				13 23	
		d						12 04	11 55	12 04				12 23					13 04	12 55	13 04				13 23	
Pontefract Monkhill		d						→											→							
Wakefield Westgate 7	32,39	a	11 23		11 27	11 33					11 56		12 03		12 23		12 27	12 33					12 56	13 03		13 22
		d	11 24		11 27	11 33					11 56		12 03		12 24		12 27	12 33					12 56	13 03		13 23
Sandal & Agbrigg		d				11 36							12 07					12 36						13 07		
Fitzwilliam		d				11 44							12 14					12 44						13 14		
South Elmsall		d				11 49												12 49								
Adwick		a				11 54												12 52								
		d		11 15		11 55										12 15		12 53								
Bentley (S.Yorks)		d		11 19		11 59										12 19		12 57								
Doncaster 7		a		11 24	11 45	12 08					12 15					12 25	12 45	13 07					13 15			
Moorthorpe		d					11 59						12 20											13 20		
Thurnscoe		d											12 26											13 26		
Goldthorpe		d											12 28											13 28		
Bolton-upon-Dearne		d											12 31											13 31		
Swinton (S.Yorks)	29	a		11 43			12 08						12 35			12 42								13 35		
Rotherham Central	29	a		11 52			12 18						12 44			12 52								13 44		
Meadowhall	29 🚋	a		11 55			12 24		12 27	12 46			12 51	12 52		12 55				13 27	13 46			13 51	13 52	
Sheffield 7	29 🚋	a	11 51	12 05			12 36		12 37	12 56			13 01	13 02	12 51	13 05				13 37	13 56			14 01	14 02	13 51

			NT	GR	NT	NT	NT		NT	GR	NT	NT	XC	NT	GR	NT	NT		NT	NT	GR	NT	NT	XC	NT	GR
				R 1						R 1			◇1		R 1						R 1			◇1		R 1
Leeds 10	32,34	d		13 15	13 20	13 32	13 37			13 45	13 48	14 05	14 11		14 15	14 20	14 32		14 37		14 45	14 48	15 05	15 11		15 15
Outwood		d			13 29				←		13 59					14 29				←		14 59				
Wakefield Kirkgate 4	32,34,39	a				14 01	13 54		14 01			14 23					15 01		14 54	15 01			15 23			
		d				14 04	13 55		14 04			14 23					15 04		14 55	15 04			15 23			
Pontefract Monkhill		d				→											→									
Wakefield Westgate 7	32,39	a		13 27	13 33					13 56	14 03		14 22		14 27	14 33					14 56	15 03		15 22		15 27
		d		13 27	13 33					13 57	14 03		14 23		14 27	14 33					14 56	15 03		15 23		15 27
Sandal & Agbrigg		d			13 36						14 07					14 36						15 07				
Fitzwilliam		d			13 44						14 14					14 44						15 14				
South Elmsall		d			13 49											14 49										
Adwick		a			13 54											14 52										
		d	13 14		13 55									14 15		14 53									15 15	
Bentley (S.Yorks)		d	13 18		13 59									14 19		14 57									15 19	
Doncaster 7		a	13 26	13 44	14 08					14 15				14 24	14 44	15 08					15 15				15 24	15 44
Moorthorpe		d									14 20											15 20				
Thurnscoe		d									14 26											15 26				
Goldthorpe		d									14 28											15 28				
Bolton-upon-Dearne		d									14 31											15 31				
Swinton (S.Yorks)	29	a	13 42								14 35			14 41								15 35			15 42	
Rotherham Central	29	a	13 51								14 44			14 52								15 44			15 50	
Meadowhall	29 🚋	a	13 55				14 27		14 46		14 50	14 52		14 55					15 27	15 46		15 50	15 51		15 55	
Sheffield 7	29 🚋	a	14 05				14 37		14 56		15 01	15 02	14 51	15 05					15 37	15 56		16 01	16 03	15 51	16 05	

			NT		NT	NT	NT	NT	GR	NT	NT	XC	NT		GR	NT	GC	NT	NT	XC	NT	GR	NT		NT	NT
									R 1			◇1			R 1		R 1			◇1		R 1				
Leeds 10	32,34	d	15 20			15 32	15 37		15 45	15 48	16 05	16 11			16 15	16 20		16 32	16 37	16 40		16 45	16 48		16 57	17 05
Outwood		d	15 29					←		15 59						16 29					←		16 59			
Wakefield Kirkgate 4	32,34,39	a				16 01	15 54	16 01			16 23							17 01	16 54		17 01					17 22
		d				16 04	15 55	16 04			16 23						16 40	17 04	16 55		17 04					17 23
Pontefract Monkhill		d				→											16 56	→								
Wakefield Westgate 7	32,39	a	15 33						15 56	16 03		16 22			16 27	16 32				16 51		16 56	17 03		17 08	
		d	15 33						15 56	16 03		16 23			16 27	16 32				16 52		16 56	17 03		17 09	
Sandal & Agbrigg		d	15 36							16 07						16 35							17 07			
Fitzwilliam		d	15 44							16 14						16 43							17 14		17 18	
South Elmsall		d	15 49													16 48									17 25	
Adwick		a	15 54													16 53									17 29	
		d	15 55										16 15			16 54									17 30	
Bentley (S.Yorks)		d	15 59										16 19			16 58									17 35	
Doncaster 7		a	16 08						16 15				16 24		16 45	17 07	17 24					17 16			17 45	
Moorthorpe		d			15 50					16 20													17 20			
Thurnscoe		d								16 26													17 26			
Goldthorpe		d								16 28													17 28			
Bolton-upon-Dearne		d								16 31													17 31			
Swinton (S.Yorks)	29	a			16 00					16 35			16 42										17 35			
Rotherham Central	29	a			16 09					16 44			16 50										17 44			
Meadowhall	29 🚋	a			16 17		16 27	16 46		16 50	16 52		16 55						17 27		17 46		17 50			17 51
Sheffield 7	29 🚋	a			16 27		16 37	16 56		17 00	17 02	16 51	17 05						17 37	17 20	17 56		18 01			18 03

Leeds - Wakefield, Doncaster and Sheffield

Network Diagram - see first page of Table 31

Mondays to Fridays

		XC	GR	NT	NT	NT	NT	GR		NT	NT	XC	NT	GR	NT	NT	NT	NT		GR	NT	NT	XC	GR	NT
		◇1	R 1					R 1				◇1		R 1						R 1			◇1	R 1	
Leeds 10 32,34	d	17 11	17 15	17 20	17 32	17 37		17 45		17 46	18 05	18 11		18 15	18 20	18 32	18 43			18 45	18 48	19 05	19 11	19 15	19 19
Outwood	d			17 29			←			17 57					18 29			←			18 59				19 28
Wakefield Kirkgate 4 32,34,39	a				18 01	17 54	18 01				18 23					19 04	18 59	19 04				19 24			
	d				18 04	17 55	18 04				18 23					19 05	18 59	19 05				19 24			
Pontefract Monkhill	d				→											→									
Wakefield Westgate 7 32,39	a	17 22	17 27	17 33				17 56		18 01		18 22		18 27	18 33					18 56	19 03		19 22	19 27	19 32
	d	17 23	17 27	17 33				17 56		18 01		18 23		18 27	18 33					18 56	19 03		19 23	19 27	19 32
Sandal & Agbrigg	d			17 36						18 07					18 36						19 07				19 35
Fitzwilliam	d			17 44						18 14					18 44						19 14				19 42
South Elmsall	d			17 49											18 50										19 47
Adwick	a			17 54											18 55										19 52
	d			17 55									18 14		18 56										19 53
Bentley (S.Yorks)	d			17 59									18 18		19 00										19 59
Doncaster 7	a		17 44	18 08				18 15					18 25	18 44	19 08					19 13				19 44	20 07
Moorthorpe	d									18 20											19 20				
Thurnscoe	d									18 26											19 26				
Goldthorpe	d									18 28											19 28				
Bolton-upon-Dearne	d									18 31											19 31				
Swinton (S.Yorks) 29	a									18 35											19 35				
Rotherham Central 29	a									18 44											19 45				
Meadowhall 29	a					18 27	18 46			18 50	18 52						19 33	19 47			19 50	19 52			
Sheffield 7 29	a	17 51				18 38	18 56			19 00	19 04	18 51					19 43	19 56			19 59	20 04	19 51		

		NT	NT	NT		GR	NT	XC	NT	NT	NT	GR	NT	XC		NT	NT	NT	NT	NT	NT	NT	NT		
						R 1		◇1				R 1		◇1											
Leeds 10 32,34	d	19 37	19 43			19 45	19 48	20 11	20 20	20 30	20 37	20 45	20 48	21 11		21 21		21 37	21 48		22 37	22 40	23 09		
Outwood	d			←			19 59		20 29				20 59			21 30			21 59			22 49	23 20		
Wakefield Kirkgate 4 32,34,39	a	20 06	19 59	20 06						20 46	21 06							22 06			23 10				
	d	20 07	20 00	20 07						20 46	21 07						21 47	22 07		22 55	23 10				
Pontefract Monkhill	d	→																							
Wakefield Westgate 7 32,39	a					19 56	20 03	20 22	20 33			20 56	21 03	21 22		21 34	21 53		22 03	23 01		22 53	23 24		
	d					19 56	20 03	20 23	20 33			20 56	21 03	21 23		21 34			22 03			22 53	23 24		
Sandal & Agbrigg	d						20 07		20 36				21 07			21 37			22 07			22 56	23 28		
Fitzwilliam	d						20 14		20 44				21 13			21 44			22 14			23 03	23 35		
South Elmsall	d								20 49							21 49						23 08			
Adwick	a								20 54							21 54						23 13			
	d								20 55							21 55						23 14			
Bentley (S.Yorks)	d								20 59							21 59						23 18			
Doncaster 7	a					20 16			21 10			21 15				22 08						23 28			
Moorthorpe	d						20 20						21 20						22 20				23 41		
Thurnscoe	d						20 26						21 27						22 26				23 47		
Goldthorpe	d						20 28						21 29						22 28				23 49		
Bolton-upon-Dearne	d						20 31						21 32						22 31				23 52		
Swinton (S.Yorks) 29	a						20 35						21 35						22 35				23 56		
Rotherham Central 29	a						20 44						21 44						22 46				00 03		
Meadowhall 29	a		20 33	20 45			20 51			21 18	21 45		21 51					22 47	22 52		23 51		00 08		
Sheffield 7 29	a		20 44	20 58			21 02	20 51		21 30	21 57		22 04	21 51				22 58	23 02		00 02		00 23		

Saturdays

		NT	NT	GR	XC	GR	XC	NT	EM	NT		NT	NT	NT	GR	XC	NT	NT	GC	NT		EM	NT	NT	NT
				R 1	◇1	R 1	◇1		◇1						R 1	◇1			R 1			◇1			
Leeds 10 32,34	d	22p37	23p09	05 05	06 00	06 05	06 15	06 20	06 34	06 38		06 43		07 05	07 05	07 10		07 20		07 29		07 34	07 35		07 48
Outwood	d		23p20					06 29				06 54						07 29						←	07 59
Wakefield Kirkgate 4 32,34,39	a	23p10								07 07				07 25						08 00			07 54	08 00	
	d	23p10								07 08				07 25					07 38	08 04			07 55	08 04	
Pontefract Monkhill	d																		07 58	→					
Wakefield Westgate 7 32,39	a		23p24	05 16	06 11	06 17	06 28	06 33	06 45			06 58			07 16	07 22		07 34				07 45			08 03
	d		23p24	05 16	06 12	06 17	06 29	06 33	06 46			06 58			07 16	07 23		07 34				07 46			08 03
Sandal & Agbrigg	d		23p28					06 36				07 02						07 37							08 07
Fitzwilliam	d		23p35					06 44				07 09						07 44							08 14
South Elmsall	d							06 49										07 49							
Adwick	a							06 54										07 54							
	d							06 55									07 23	07 55							
Bentley (S.Yorks)	d							06 59									07 27	07 59							
Doncaster 7	a			05 34		06 34	06 46	07 07							07 35		07 31	08 07	08 27						
Moorthorpe	d		23p41									07 15													08 20
Thurnscoe	d		23p47									07 21													08 26
Goldthorpe	d		23p49									07 23													08 28
Bolton-upon-Dearne	d		23p52									07 26													08 31
Swinton (S.Yorks) 29	a		23p56									07 30					07 53								08 35
Rotherham Central 29	a		00 03									07 37	←				08 01								08 44
Meadowhall 29	a	23p51	00 08							07 48		07 46	07 48	07 53			08 06						08 31	08 45	08 49
Sheffield 7 29	a	00 02	00 23		06 45		07 15		07 22	→		07 54	07 58	08 05		07 51	08 18					08 21	08 39	08 56	08 59

Table 31

Leeds - Wakefield, Doncaster and Sheffield

Network Diagram - see first page of Table 31

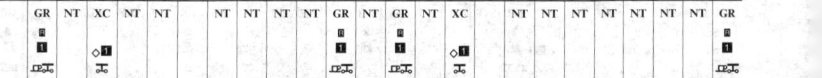

	GR	NT	XC	NT	NT		NT	NT	NT	NT	GR	NT	GR	NT	XC		NT	NT	NT	NT	NT	NT	NT	GR
	R 1 ✠		◇1 ✠								R 1 ✠		R 1 ✠		◇1 ✠									R 1 ✠
Leeds 10 32,34 d	08 05	08 05	08 12				08 20	08 32	08 37		08 40	08 48	09 05	09 05	09 11			09 20	09 32	09 37		09 48	10 05	10 05
Outwood d							08 29			↤		08 59						09 29			↤	09 59		
Wakefield Kirkgate 4 32,34,39 a		08 23						09 03	08 54	09 03				09 23					10 01	09 55	10 01		10 23	
d		08 23						09 05	08 55	09 05				09 23					10 04	09 56	10 04		10 23	
Pontefract Monkhill d								↦											↦					
Wakefield Westgate 7 32,39 a	08 16		08 23				08 33				08 51	09 03	09 17		09 23			09 33				10 03		10 16
d	08 16		08 24				08 33				08 51	09 03	09 17		09 24			09 33				10 03		10 16
Sandal & Agbrigg d							08 36					09 07						09 35				10 07		
Fitzwilliam d							08 44					09 14						09 44				10 14		
South Elmsall d							08 49											09 47						
Adwick a							08 54											09 53						
d				08 15	08 33		08 55										09 15	09 53						
Bentley (S.Yorks) d				08 19	08 37		08 59										09 19	09 57						
Doncaster 7 a	08 34			08 23	08 42		09 07				09 12		09 34				09 24	10 08						10 35
Moorthorpe d												09 20										10 20		
Thurnscoe d												09 26										10 26		
Goldthorpe d												09 28										10 28		
Bolton-upon-Dearne d												09 31										10 31		
Swinton (S.Yorks) 29 a				08 43								09 35					09 42					10 35		
Rotherham Central 29 a				08 50								09 45					09 50					10 44		
Meadowhall 29 🚋 a		08 52		08 56					09 27	09 46		09 50		09 52			09 54			10 27	10 46	10 50	10 52	
Sheffield 7 29 🚋 a		09 02	08 51	09 05					09 37	09 56		10 00		10 02	09 52		10 05			10 37	10 56	11 00	11 02	

	XC		NT	NT	NT	NT	NT	NT	GR	GC	NT		XC	NT	NT	NT	NT	NT	NT	NT	NT		GR	XC
	◇1 ✠								R 1 ✠	R 1			◇1 ✠										R 1 ✠	◇1 ✠
Leeds 10 32,34 d	10 12			10 20	10 32	10 37		10 48	11 05		11 05		11 11		11 20		11 32	11 37		11 48	12 05		12 05	12 11
Outwood d				10 29			↤	10 59							11 29				↤	11 59				
Wakefield Kirkgate 4 32,34,39 a					11 01	10 54	11 01				11 23						12 01	11 54	12 01		12 23			
d					11 04	10 55	11 04			11 11	11 23						12 04	11 55	12 04		12 23			
Pontefract Monkhill d					↦					11 35							↦							
Wakefield Westgate 7 32,39 a	10 23			10 33				11 03	11 16				11 22		11 33					12 03			12 16	12 23
d	10 24			10 33				11 03	11 16				11 23		11 33					12 03			12 16	12 24
Sandal & Agbrigg d				10 36				11 07							11 36					12 07				
Fitzwilliam d				10 44				11 14							11 44					12 14				
South Elmsall d				10 49											11 49									
Adwick a				10 54											11 54									
d			10 15	10 55										11 15	11 55									
Bentley (S.Yorks) d			10 19	10 59										11 19	11 59									
Doncaster 7 a			10 24	11 07					11 35	12 03				11 24	12 07								12 35	
Moorthorpe d								11 20								11 59				12 20				
Thurnscoe d								11 26												12 26				
Goldthorpe d								11 28												12 28				
Bolton-upon-Dearne d								11 31												12 31				
Swinton (S.Yorks) 29 a			10 42					11 35						11 42		12 08				12 35				
Rotherham Central 29 a			10 52					11 44						11 52		12 18				12 43				
Meadowhall 29 🚋 a			10 57			11 27	11 46	11 50			11 52			11 57		12 24		12 27	12 46	12 49	12 52			
Sheffield 7 29 🚋 a	10 51		11 06			11 37	11 57	12 00			12 02		11 51	12 05		12 36		12 37	12 56	13 00	13 02			12 51

	NT	NT	NT	NT	NT	NT	NT		GR	XC	NT	NT	NT	NT	NT	NT	NT		GR	XC	NT	NT	NT	NT
									R 1 ✠	◇1 ✠									R 1 ✠	◇1 ✠				
Leeds 10 32,34 d		12 20	12 32	12 37		12 48	13 05		13 05	13 11		13 20	13 32	13 37		13 48	14 05		14 05	14 11		14 20	14 32	14 37
Outwood d		12 29			↤	12 59						13 29			↤	13 59						14 29		
Wakefield Kirkgate 4 32,34,39 a			13 02	12 54	13 02		13 23						14 01	13 54	14 01		14 23						15 01	14 54
d			13 04	12 55	13 04		13 23						14 04	13 55	14 04		14 23						15 04	14 55
Pontefract Monkhill d			↦										↦										↦	
Wakefield Westgate 7 32,39 a		12 33				13 03			13 16	13 22		13 33				14 03			14 16	14 23		14 33		
d		12 33				13 03			13 16	13 23		13 33				14 03			14 16	14 24		14 33		
Sandal & Agbrigg d		12 36				13 07						13 36				14 07						14 36		
Fitzwilliam d		12 44				13 14						13 44				14 14						14 44		
South Elmsall d		12 49										13 49										14 49		
Adwick a		12 54										13 54										14 54		
d	12 14	12 55									13 15	13 55									14 15	14 55		
Bentley (S.Yorks) d	12 18	12 59									13 19	13 59									14 19	14 59		
Doncaster 7 a	12 24	13 07							13 35		13 24	14 07							14 35		14 24	15 07		
Moorthorpe d						13 20										14 20								
Thurnscoe d						13 26										14 26								
Goldthorpe d						13 28										14 28								
Bolton-upon-Dearne d						13 31										14 31								
Swinton (S.Yorks) 29 a	12 42					13 35					13 42					14 35					14 43			
Rotherham Central 29 a	12 52					13 43					13 52					14 43					14 52			
Meadowhall 29 🚋 a	12 57			13 27	13 46	13 49	13 52				13 57			14 27	14 46	14 49	14 52				14 57			15 27
Sheffield 7 29 🚋 a	13 05			13 37	13 56	14 00	14 02			13 51	14 05			14 37	14 56	15 00	15 02			14 51	15 05			15 37

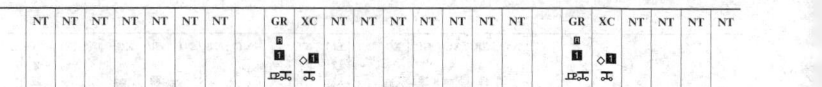

Table 31

Saturdays

Leeds - Wakefield, Doncaster and Sheffield

Network Diagram - see first page of Table 31

	NT	GR	NT	NT	GR	XC	NT	NT	NT	NT	NT	NT	NT	GR	GC	NT	XC	NT	NT	NT	NT
		R 1			R 1	◇1								R 1	R 1		◇1				
Leeds 10 32,34 d		14 40	14 48	15 05	15 05	15 12		15 20		15 32	15 37		15 48	16 05		16 05	16 12		16 20	16 32	16 37
Outwood d	←		14 59					15 29				←	15 59						16 29		
Wakefield Kirkgate 4 32,34,39 a	15 01			15 23						16 01	15 54	16 01				16 23				17 01	16 54
d	15 04			15 23						16 04	15 55	16 04			16 11	16 23				17 04	16 55
Pontefract Monkhill d										↳					16 29					↳	
Wakefield Westgate 7 32,39 a		14 52	15 03		15 16	15 23		15 33					16 03	16 17			16 23		16 33		
d		14 52	15 03		15 17	15 24		15 33					16 03	16 17			16 24		16 33		
Sandal & Agbrigg d			15 07					15 36					16 07						16 36		
Fitzwilliam d			15 14					15 44					16 14						16 44		
South Elmsall d								15 49											16 49		
Adwick a								15 54											16 54		
d							15 15	15 55										16 15	16 55		
Bentley (S.Yorks) d							15 19	15 59										16 18	16 59		
Doncaster 7 a		15 10			15 34		15 24	16 07						16 35	17 02			16 25	17 07		
Moorthorpe d			15 20						15 50				16 20								
Thurnscoe d			15 26										16 26								
Goldthorpe d			15 28										16 28								
Bolton-upon-Dearne d			15 31										16 31								
Swinton (S.Yorks) 29 a			15 35				15 42		16 01				16 35					16 41			
Rotherham Central 29 a			15 43				15 50		16 09				16 43					16 50			
Meadowhall 29 a	15 46		15 49	15 51			15 56		16 17		16 27	16 46	16 49			16 52		16 55			17 27
Sheffield 7 29 a	15 56		16 00	16 03		15 51	16 05		16 27		16 37	16 56	17 00			17 02	16 51	17 05			17 37

	XC	NT	NT	NT	GR	XC	NT	NT	NT	NT	NT	NT	NT	GR	XC	NT	NT	NT	NT	NT	NT	GR
	◇1				R 1	◇1								R 1	◇1							R 1
Leeds 10 32,34 d	16 40		16 48	17 05	17 05	17 11	17 20		17 32	17 37		17 48	18 05	18 05	18 11	18 20	18 32	18 37		18 48	19 05	19 05
Outwood d		←	16 59				17 29				←	17 59				18 29			←	18 59		
Wakefield Kirkgate 4 32,34,39 a		17 01		17 22					18 01	17 54	18 01		18 23				19 04	18 54	19 04		19 24	
d		17 04		17 23					18 04	17 55	18 04		18 23				19 05	18 55	19 05		19 24	
Pontefract Monkhill d									↳								↳					
Wakefield Westgate 7 32,39 a	16 51		17 03		17 17	17 22	17 33					18 03		18 16	18 22	18 33				19 03		19 16
d	16 52		17 03		17 17	17 23	17 33					18 03		18 16	18 23	18 33				19 03		19 16
Sandal & Agbrigg d			17 07				17 36					18 07				18 36				19 07		
Fitzwilliam d			17 14				17 44					18 14				18 44				19 14		
South Elmsall d							17 49									18 49						
Adwick a							17 54									18 54						
d							17 55	18 16								18 55						
Bentley (S.Yorks) d							17 59	18 20								18 59						
Doncaster 7 a					17 35		18 07	18 27						18 35		19 07						19 36
Moorthorpe d			17 20									18 20								19 20		
Thurnscoe d			17 26									18 26								19 26		
Goldthorpe d			17 28									18 28								19 28		
Bolton-upon-Dearne d			17 31									18 31								19 31		
Swinton (S.Yorks) 29 a			17 35									18 35								19 35		
Rotherham Central 29 a			17 43									18 44								19 44		
Meadowhall 29 a		17 46	17 49	17 51						18 27	18 46	18 50	18 52					19 28	19 47	19 50	19 52	
Sheffield 7 29 a	17 20	17 56	18 00	18 03		17 51				18 38	18 56	19 00	19 03		18 51			19 39	19 56	20 00	20 04	

	XC	NT	NT	NT	NT	NT	GR	XC	NT	NT	NT	NT	XC	NT	NT	NT	NT	NT	NT	NT	NT	NT
	◇1						R 1	◇1					◇1									
Leeds 10 32,34 d	19 11	19 20	19 37	19 43		19 48	20 05	20 11	20 20	20 30	20 37	20 48	21 11	21 20		21 37	21 48	22 16			22 37	22 44
Outwood d		19 29			←	19 59			20 29			20 59		21 29			21 59	22 25				22 55
Wakefield Kirkgate 4 32,34,39 a			20 06	19 59	20 06					20 46	21 06					22 06					23 10	
d			20 07	20 00	20 07					20 46	21 07				21 48	22 07			22 55	23 07		
Pontefract Monkhill d			↳																	23a29		
Wakefield Westgate 7 32,39 a	19 23	19 33				20 03	20 16	20 22	20 33			21 03	21 22	21 33	21 53		22 03	22 29	23 01			22 59
d	19 24	19 33				20 03	20 16	20 23	20 33			21 03	21 23	21 33			22 03	22 30				22 59
Sandal & Agbrigg d		19 36				20 07			20 36			21 07		21 36			22 07	22 33				23 03
Fitzwilliam d		19 44				20 14			20 44			21 13		21 44			22 14	22 39				23 10
South Elmsall d		19 49							20 49					21 49				22 44				
Adwick a		19 54							20 54					21 54				22 50				
d		19 55							20 55					21 55				22 50				
Bentley (S.Yorks) d		19 59							20 59					21 59				22 54				
Doncaster 7 a		20 07					20 35		21 07					22 07				23 04				
Moorthorpe d						20 20						21 19					22 20					23 15
Thurnscoe d						20 26						21 25					22 26					23 21
Goldthorpe d						20 28						21 27					22 28					23 23
Bolton-upon-Dearne d						20 31						21 30					22 31					23 26
Swinton (S.Yorks) 29 a						20 35						21 34					22 37					23 30
Rotherham Central 29 a						20 45						21 41					22 44					23 37
Meadowhall 29 a				20 33	20 45	20 50				21 19	21 45	21 49				22 47	22 52					23 43
Sheffield 7 29 a	19 51			20 44	20 58	21 00		20 52		21 30	21 57	22 02	21 51			22 58	23 03					23 58

Table 31

Sundays
until 5 February

Leeds - Wakefield, Doncaster and Sheffield

Network Diagram - see first page of Table 31

			GR	XC	GC	NT	NT	XC	NT	GR	EM		XC	NT	GR	EM	NT	NT	NT	XC	GR		NT	NT	NT	XC
Leeds 10	32,34	d	08 05	08 10		08 34	08 48	09 00	09 05	09 05	09 44		10 00	10 02	10 05	10 15	10 17	10 18	10 57	11 00	11 05		11 18	11 29		12 00
Outwood		d					08 59											10 27					11 29			
Wakefield Kirkgate 4	32,34,39	a				09 03			09 21					10 18			10 46		11 13					11 46		
		d			08 43	09 03			09 21					10 18			10 46		11 13					11 46		
Pontefract Monkhill		d																								
Wakefield Westgate 7	32,39	a	08 16	08 22			09 03	09 11		09 17	09 57		10 11		10 16	10 26		10 32		11 11	11 16		11 33			12 11
		d	08 16	08 23			09 03	09 11		09 17	09 58		10 12		10 17	10 27		10 32		11 12	11 17		11 33			12 12
Sandal & Agbrigg		d					09 07											10 35					11 37			
Fitzwilliam		d					09 14											10 42					11 44			
South Elmsall		d																10 47								
Adwick		a																10 52								
		d																10 53								
Bentley (S.Yorks)		d																10 57								
Doncaster 7		a	08 34		09 04			09 31		09 35			10 28		10 35			11 05		11 28	11 35					12 28
Moorthorpe		d					09 20																11 50			
Thurnscoe		d					09 26																11 56			
Goldthorpe		d					09 28																11 58			
Bolton-upon-Dearne		d					09 31																12 01			
Swinton (S.Yorks)	29	a					09 35																12 05			
Rotherham Central	29	a					09 44																12 12		←	
Meadowhall	29	a				09 44	09 53		09 57					10 51			11 32		11 46				12 20	12 17	12 20	
Sheffield 7	29	a		08 51		09 55	10 03	09 55	10 04		10 25		10 54	11 02		10 57	11 44		11 56	11 53			→	12 29	12 32	12 54

			GR	NT	NT	GC	NT		XC	GR	NT	EM	NT	GR	XC	NT	NT		GR	NT	XC	NT	NT	XC	GR	GC
Leeds 10	32,34	d	12 05	12 18	12 29		12 34		13 00	13 05	13 18	13 59	14 05	14 05	14 10	14 17	14 18		15 05	15 05	15 10	15 18	16 04	16 10	16 15	
Outwood		d		12 27							13 29						14 27					15 29				
Wakefield Kirkgate 4	32,34,39	a			12 46		13 04						14 21			14 46				15 22			16 21			
		d			12 46	12 51	13 04						14 21			14 46				15 22			16 22			16 30
Pontefract Monkhill		d																								
Wakefield Westgate 7	32,39	a	12 17	12 31					13 11	13 16	13 33	14 11		14 17	14 22		14 31		15 16		15 22	15 33		16 21	16 27	
		d	12 17	12 32					13 12	13 16	13 33	14 12		14 17	14 23		14 32		15 16		15 23	15 33		16 22	16 27	
Sandal & Agbrigg		d		12 35							13 37						14 35					15 37				
Fitzwilliam		d		12 41							13 45						14 41					15 44				
South Elmsall		d		12 46													14 46									
Adwick		a		12 52													14 52									
		d		12 52													14 52									
Bentley (S.Yorks)		d		12 56													14 56									
Doncaster 7		a	12 36	13 04		13 22			13 28	13 35				14 35			15 05		15 35						16 45	17 10
Moorthorpe		d									13 51											15 50				
Thurnscoe		d									13 57											15 56				
Goldthorpe		d									13 59											15 58				
Bolton-upon-Dearne		d									14 02											16 01				
Swinton (S.Yorks)	29	a									14 06											16 05				
Rotherham Central	29	a									14 13											16 12				
Meadowhall	29	a			13 18		13 48				14 20		14 54			15 35				15 55		16 19	16 56			
Sheffield 7	29	a			13 29		13 58		13 54		14 32	14 44	15 06		14 52	15 44				16 05	15 51	16 31	17 05	16 51		

			NT		NT	GR	NT	XC	GR	NT	GR	NT	XC		GR	NT	NT	NT	GR	NT	XC	GR	NT		GR	XC
Leeds 10	32,34	d	16 17		16 18	16 45	17 05	17 10	17 15	17 18	17 45	18 05	18 10		18 15		18 17	18 18	18 45	19 04	19 10	19 15	19 18		19 45	20 10
Outwood		d			16 27					17 29								18 27					19 29			
Wakefield Kirkgate 4	32,34,39	a	16 46				17 21					18 21					18 45			19 21						
		d	16 46				17 21					18 22					18 45			19 21						
Pontefract Monkhill		d																								
Wakefield Westgate 7	32,39	a			16 32	16 56		17 21	17 27	17 33	17 56		18 21		18 27			18 32	18 56		19 21	19 26	19 33		19 56	20 21
		d			16 32	16 56		17 22	17 27	17 33	17 57		18 22		18 27			18 32	18 56		19 22	19 26	19 33		19 56	20 22
Sandal & Agbrigg		d			16 35					17 37								18 35					19 37			
Fitzwilliam		d			16 42					17 47								18 42					19 44			
South Elmsall		d			16 47													18 47								
Adwick		a			16 52													18 52								
		d			16 53													18 53								
Bentley (S.Yorks)		d			16 57													18 57								
Doncaster 7		a			17 06	17 17			17 45		18 16				18 45			19 06	19 17			19 44			20 16	
Moorthorpe		d								17 54						18 52							19 50			
Thurnscoe		d								18 00													19 56			
Goldthorpe		d								18 02													19 58			
Bolton-upon-Dearne		d								18 05													20 01			
Swinton (S.Yorks)	29	a								18 10						19 01							20 09			
Rotherham Central	29	a								18 17						19 12							20 16			
Meadowhall	29	a	17 34				17 55			18 25		18 56				19 18	19 32			19 54			20 22			
Sheffield 7	29	a	17 44				18 05	17 51		18 36		19 05	18 51			19 27	19 43			20 04	19 50		20 34			20 51

Table 31

Leeds - Wakefield, Doncaster and Sheffield

Sundays
until 5 February

Network Diagram - see first page of Table 31

			NT	NT	GR	XC	NT	NT	NT		NT
					R 1	◇1					
Leeds 10	32,34	d	20 17	20 18	20 45	21 10	21 18		21 40		22 17
Outwood		d		20 27			21 27		21 51		
Wakefield Kirkgate 4	32,34,39	a	20 46								22 46
		d	20 46								22 46
Pontefract Monkhill		d									
Wakefield Westgate 7	32,39	a		20 31	20 56	21 21	21 31		21 55		
		d		20 32	20 56	21 22	21 31		21 55		
Sandal & Agbrigg		d		20 35			21 34		21 59		
Fitzwilliam		d		20 41			21 41		22 06		
South Elmsall		d		20 46			21 46				
Adwick		a		20 52			21 51				
		d		20 52			21 52				
Bentley (S.Yorks)		d		20 56			21 56				
Doncaster 7		a		21 05	21 14		22 05				
Moorthorpe		d						21 36	22 13		
Thurnscoe		d							22 19		
Goldthorpe		d							22 21		
Bolton-upon-Dearne		d							22 24		
Swinton (S.Yorks)	29	a						21 45	22 32		
Rotherham Central	29	a						21 52	22 39		
Meadowhall	29	a	21 33					21 57	22 45		23 30
Sheffield 7	29	a	21 42			21 50		22 09	22 54		23 43

Sundays
12 February to 25 March

			GR	XC	GC	NT	NT	XC	NT	GR	EM		XC	NT	GR	EM	NT	NT	NT	XC	GR		NT	NT	NT	XC
			R 1	◇1	R 1			◇1		R 1	◇1		◇1		R 1	◇1				◇1	R 1					◇1
Leeds 10	32,34	d	08 05	08 10		08 34	08 48	09 00	09 05	09 05	09 44		10 00	10 02	10 05	10 15	10 17	10 18	10 57	11 00	11 05		11 18	11 29		12 00
Outwood		d					08 59											10 27					11 29			
Wakefield Kirkgate 4	32,34,39	a				09 03			09 21					10 18			10 46		11 13					11 46		
		d			08 43	09 03			09 21					10 18			10 46		11 13					11 46		
Pontefract Monkhill		d																								
Wakefield Westgate 7	32,39	a	08 16	08 22			09 03	09 11		09 17	09 57		10 11		10 16	10 26		10 32		11 11	11 16		11 33			12 11
		d	08 16	08 23			09 03	09 11		09 17	09 58		10 12		10 17	10 27		10 32		11 12	11 17		11 33			12 12
Sandal & Agbrigg		d					09 07											10 35					11 37			
Fitzwilliam		d					09 14											10 42					11 44			
South Elmsall		d																10 47								
Adwick		a																10 52								
		d																10 53								
Bentley (S.Yorks)		d																10 57								
Doncaster 7		a	08 34		09 04			09 31		09 35			10 28		10 35			11 05		11 28	11 35					12 28
Moorthorpe		d					09 20																11 50			
Thurnscoe		d					09 26																11 56			
Goldthorpe		d					09 28																11 58			
Bolton-upon-Dearne		d					09 31																12 01			
Swinton (S.Yorks)	29	a					09 35																12 05			
Rotherham Central	29	a					09 44																12 12		←	
Meadowhall	29	a				09 44	09 53		09 57					10 51			11 32		11 46				12 20	12 17	12 20	
Sheffield 7	29	a		08 51		09 55	10 03	09 55	10 04		10 25		10 54	11 02		10 57	11 44		11 56	11 53			→	12 29	12 32	12 54

			GR	NT	NT	GC	NT		XC	GR	NT	EM	NT	GR	XC	NT	NT		GR	NT	XC	NT	NT	XC	GR	GC
			R 1			R 1			◇1	R 1		◇1		R 1	◇1				R 1		◇1			◇1	R 1	R 1
Leeds 10	32,34	d	12 05	12 18	12 29		12 34		13 00	13 05	13 18	13 59	14 05	14 05	14 10	14 17	14 18		15 05	15 05	15 10	15 18	16 04	16 10	16 15	
Outwood		d		12 27							13 29						14 27					15 29				
Wakefield Kirkgate 4	32,34,39	a			12 46		13 04						14 21			14 46				15 22			16 21			
		d			12 46	12 51	13 04						14 21			14 46				15 22			16 22			16 30
Pontefract Monkhill		d																								
Wakefield Westgate 7	32,39	a	12 17	12 31					13 11	13 16	13 33	14 11		14 17	14 22		14 31		15 16		15 22	15 33		16 21	16 27	
		d	12 17	12 32					13 12	13 16	13 33	14 12		14 17	14 23		14 32		15 16		15 23	15 33		16 22	16 27	
Sandal & Agbrigg		d		12 35							13 37						14 35					15 37				
Fitzwilliam		d		12 41							13 45						14 41					15 44				
South Elmsall		d		12 46													14 46									
Adwick		a		12 52													14 52									
		d		12 52													14 52									
Bentley (S.Yorks)		d		12 56													14 56									
Doncaster 7		a	12 36	13 04		13 22			13 28	13 35				14 35			15 05		15 35						16 45	17 10
Moorthorpe		d									13 51											15 50				
Thurnscoe		d									13 57											15 56				
Goldthorpe		d									13 59											15 58				
Bolton-upon-Dearne		d									14 02											16 01				
Swinton (S.Yorks)	29	a									14 06											16 05				
Rotherham Central	29	a									14 13											16 12				
Meadowhall	29	a			13 18		13 48				14 20		14 54			15 35				15 55		16 19	16 56			
Sheffield 7	29	a			13 29		13 58		13 54		14 32	14 44	15 06		14 52	15 44				16 05	15 51	16 31	17 05	16 51		

Sundays
12 February to 25 March

Leeds - Wakefield, Doncaster and Sheffield

Network Diagram - see first page of Table 31

Station			NT		NT	GR	NT	XC	GR	NT	GR	NT	XC		GR	NT	NT	NT	GR	NT	XC	GR	NT		GR	XC
						R 1		◇1	R 1		R 1		◇1		R 1				R 1		◇1	R 1			R 1	◇1
Leeds 10	32,34	d	16 17		16 18	16 45	17 05	17 10	17 15	17 18	17 45	18 05	18 10		18 15		18 17	18 18	18 45	19 04	19 10	19 15	19 18		19 45	20 10
Outwood		d			16 27					17 29								18 27					19 29			
Wakefield Kirkgate 4	32,34,39	a	16 46				17 21					18 21					18 45			19 21						
		d	16 46				17 21					18 22					18 45			19 21						
Pontefract Monkhill		d																								
Wakefield Westgate 7	32,39	a			16 32	16 56		17 21	17 27	17 33	17 56		18 21		18 27			18 32	18 56		19 21	19 26	19 33		19 56	20 21
		d			16 32	16 56		17 22	17 27	17 33	17 57		18 22		18 27			18 32	18 56		19 22	19 26	19 33		19 56	20 22
Sandal & Agbrigg		d			16 35					17 37								18 35					19 37			
Fitzwilliam		d			16 42					17 47								18 42					19 44			
South Elmsall		d			16 47													18 47								
Adwick		a			16 52													18 52								
		d			16 53													18 53								
Bentley (S.Yorks)		d			16 57													18 57								
Doncaster 7		a			17 06	17 17			17 45		18 16				18 45			19 06	19 17			19 44			20 16	
Moorthorpe		d								17 54						18 52							19 50			
Thurnscoe		d								18 00													19 56			
Goldthorpe		d								18 02													19 58			
Bolton-upon-Dearne		d								18 05													20 01			
Swinton (S.Yorks)	29	a								18 10						19 01							20 09			
Rotherham Central	29	a								18 17						19 12							20 16			
Meadowhall	29	a	17 34				17 55			18 25		18 56				19 18	19 32			19 54			20 22			
Sheffield 7	29	a	17 44				18 05	17 51		18 36		19 05	18 51			19 27	19 43			20 04	19 50		20 34			20 51

Station			NT	NT	GR	XC	NT	NT	NT		NT
					R 1	◇1					
Leeds 10	32,34	d	20 17	20 18	20 45	21 10	21 18		21 40		22 17
Outwood		d		20 27			21 27		21 51		
Wakefield Kirkgate 4	32,34,39	a	20 46								22 46
		d	20 46								22 46
Pontefract Monkhill		d									
Wakefield Westgate 7	32,39	a		20 31	20 56	21 21	21 31		21 55		
		d		20 32	20 56	21 22	21 31		21 55		
Sandal & Agbrigg		d		20 35			21 34		21 59		
Fitzwilliam		d		20 41			21 41		22 06		
South Elmsall		d		20 46			21 46				
Adwick		a		20 52			21 51				
		d		20 52			21 52				
Bentley (S.Yorks)		d		20 56			21 56				
Doncaster 7		a		21 05	21 14		22 05				
Moorthorpe		d						21 36	22 13		
Thurnscoe		d							22 19		
Goldthorpe		d							22 21		
Bolton-upon-Dearne		d							22 24		
Swinton (S.Yorks)	29	a						21 45	22 32		
Rotherham Central	29	a						21 52	22 39		
Meadowhall	29	a	21 33					21 57	22 45		23 30
Sheffield 7	29	a	21 42			21 50		22 09	22 54		23 43

Sundays
from 1 April

Station			GR	XC	GC	NT	NT	XC	NT	GR	EM		XC	NT	GR	EM	NT	NT	NT	XC	GR		NT	NT	NT	XC
			R 1	◇1	R 1			◇1		R 1	◇1		◇1		R 1	◇1				◇1	R 1					◇1
Leeds 10	32,34	d	08 05	08 10		08 34	08 48	09 00	09 05	09 05	09 32		10 00	10 02	10 05	10 15	10 17	10 18	10 57	11 00	11 05		11 18	11 29		12 00
Outwood		d					08 59											10 27					11 29			
Wakefield Kirkgate 4	32,34,39	a				09 03			09 21					10 18			10 46		11 13					11 46		
		d			08 43	09 03			09 21					10 18			10 46		11 13					11 46		
Pontefract Monkhill		d																								
Wakefield Westgate 7	32,39	a	08 16	08 22			09 03	09 11		09 17	09 45		10 11		10 16	10 26		10 32		11 11	11 16		11 33			12 11
		d	08 16	08 23			09 03	09 11		09 17	09 46		10 12		10 17	10 27		10 32		11 12	11 17		11 33			12 12
Sandal & Agbrigg		d					09 07											10 35					11 37			
Fitzwilliam		d					09 14											10 42					11 44			
South Elmsall		d																10 47								
Adwick		a																10 52								
		d																10 53								
Bentley (S.Yorks)		d																10 57								
Doncaster 7		a	08 34		09 04			09 31		09 35			10 28		10 35			11 05		11 28	11 35					12 28
Moorthorpe		d					09 20																11 50			
Thurnscoe		d					09 26																11 56			
Goldthorpe		d					09 28																11 58			
Bolton-upon-Dearne		d					09 31																12 01			
Swinton (S.Yorks)	29	a					09 35																12 05			
Rotherham Central	29	a					09 44																12 12		←	
Meadowhall	29	a				09 44	09 53		09 57					10 51			11 32		11 46				12 20	12 17	12 20	
Sheffield 7	29	a		08 51		09 55	10 03	09 55	10 04		10 13		10 54	11 02		10 57	11 44		11 56	11 53			→	12 29	12 32	12 54

Table 31

Sundays

from 1 April

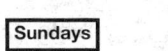

Leeds - Wakefield, Doncaster and Sheffield

Network Diagram - see first page of Table 31

Station			GR	NT	NT	GC	NT		XC	GR	NT	EM	NT	GR	XC	NT	NT		GR	NT	XC	NT	NT	XC	GR	GC
			R 1			R 1			◇1	R 1		◇1		R 1	◇1				R 1		◇1			◇1	R 1	R 1
Leeds 10	32,34	d	12 05	12 18	12 29		12 34		13 00	13 05	13 18	13 59	14 05	14 05	14 10	14 17	14 18		15 05	15 05	15 10	15 18	16 04	16 10	16 15	
Outwood		d		12 27							13 29						14 27					15 29				
Wakefield Kirkgate 4	32,34,39	a			12 46		13 04						14 21			14 46				15 22			16 21			
		d			12 46	12 51	13 04						14 21			14 46				15 22			16 22			16 30
Pontefract Monkhill		d																								
Wakefield Westgate 7	32,39	a	12 17	12 31					13 11	13 16	13 33	14 11		14 17	14 22		14 31		15 16		15 22	15 33		16 21	16 27	
		d	12 17	12 32					13 12	13 16	13 33	14 12		14 17	14 23		14 32		15 16		15 23	15 33		16 22	16 27	
Sandal & Agbrigg		d		12 35							13 37						14 35					15 37				
Fitzwilliam		d		12 41							13 45						14 41					15 44				
South Elmsall		d		12 46													14 46									
Adwick		a		12 52													14 52									
		d		12 52													14 52									
Bentley (S.Yorks)		d		12 56													14 56									
Doncaster 7		a	12 36	13 04		13 22			13 28	13 35				14 35			15 05		15 35						16 45	17 10
Moorthorpe		d									13 51											15 50				
Thurnscoe		d									13 57											15 56				
Goldthorpe		d									13 59											15 58				
Bolton-upon-Dearne		d									14 02											16 01				
Swinton (S.Yorks)	29	a									14 06											16 05				
Rotherham Central	29	a									14 13											16 12				
Meadowhall	29	a			13 18		13 48				14 20		14 54			15 35				15 55		16 19	16 56			
Sheffield 7	29	a			13 29		13 58		13 54		14 32	14 44	15 06		14 52	15 44				16 05	15 51	16 31	17 05	16 51		

Station			NT		NT	GR	NT	XC	GR	NT	GR	NT	XC		GR	NT	NT	NT	GR	NT	XC	GR	NT		GR	XC
						R 1		◇1	R 1		R 1		◇1		R 1				R 1		◇1	R 1			R 1	◇1
Leeds 10	32,34	d	16 17		16 18	16 45	17 05	17 10	17 15	17 18	17 45	18 05	18 10		18 15		18 17	18 18	18 45	19 04	19 10	19 15	19 18		19 45	20 10
Outwood		d			16 27					17 29								18 27					19 29			
Wakefield Kirkgate 4	32,34,39	a	16 46				17 21					18 21					18 45			19 21						
		d	16 46				17 21					18 22					18 45			19 21						
Pontefract Monkhill		d																								
Wakefield Westgate 7	32,39	a			16 32	16 56		17 21	17 27	17 33	17 56		18 21		18 27			18 32	18 56		19 21	19 26	19 33		19 56	20 21
		d			16 32	16 56		17 22	17 27	17 33	17 57		18 22		18 27			18 32	18 56		19 22	19 26	19 33		19 56	20 22
Sandal & Agbrigg		d			16 35					17 37								18 35					19 37			
Fitzwilliam		d			16 42					17 47								18 42					19 44			
South Elmsall		d			16 47													18 47								
Adwick		a			16 52													18 52								
		d			16 53													18 53								
Bentley (S.Yorks)		d			16 57													18 57								
Doncaster 7		a			17 06	17 17			17 45		18 16				18 45			19 06	19 17			19 44			20 16	
Moorthorpe		d								17 54						18 52							19 50			
Thurnscoe		d								18 00													19 56			
Goldthorpe		d								18 02													19 58			
Bolton-upon-Dearne		d								18 05													20 01			
Swinton (S.Yorks)	29	a								18 10						19 01							20 09			
Rotherham Central	29	a								18 17						19 12							20 16			
Meadowhall	29	a	17 34				17 55			18 25		18 56				19 18	19 32			19 54			20 22			
Sheffield 7	29	a	17 44				18 05	17 51		18 36		19 05	18 51			19 27	19 43			20 04	19 50		20 34			20 51

Station			NT	NT	GR	XC	NT	NT	NT		NT
					R 1	◇1					
Leeds 10	32,34	d	20 17	20 18	20 45	21 10	21 18		21 40		22 17
Outwood		d		20 27			21 27		21 51		
Wakefield Kirkgate 4	32,34,39	a	20 46								22 46
		d	20 46								22 46
Pontefract Monkhill		d									
Wakefield Westgate 7	32,39	a		20 31	20 56	21 21	21 31		21 55		
		d		20 32	20 56	21 22	21 31		21 55		
Sandal & Agbrigg		d		20 35			21 34		21 59		
Fitzwilliam		d		20 41			21 41		22 06		
South Elmsall		d		20 46			21 46				
Adwick		a		20 52			21 51				
		d		20 52			21 52				
Bentley (S.Yorks)		d		20 56			21 56				
Doncaster 7		a		21 05	21 14		22 05				
Moorthorpe		d						21 36	22 13		
Thurnscoe		d							22 19		
Goldthorpe		d							22 21		
Bolton-upon-Dearne		d							22 24		
Swinton (S.Yorks)	29	a						21 45	22 32		
Rotherham Central	29	a						21 52	22 39		
Meadowhall	29	a	21 33					21 57	22 45		23 30
Sheffield 7	29	a	21 42			21 50		22 09	22 54		23 43

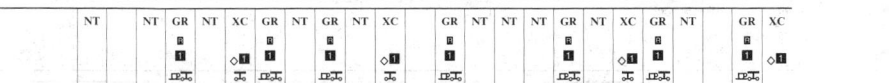

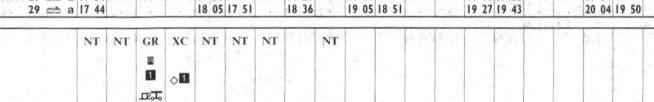

Table 32

Mondays to Saturdays

Bradford, Leeds and Wakefield - Pontefract, Knottingley and Goole

Network Diagram - see first page of Table 31

Miles	Miles	Station		NT SX	NT	NT	NT SO	NT SX	NT	GC SO	GC SX	NT		NT SO	NT SX	NT	NT	NT	NT	NT	NT SO	NT SX		NT	NT
										R 1 A ☕	R 1 ☕														
—	—	Bradford Interchange 41	d							06 51	06 51														
—	—	Halifax 41	d							07 03	07 07														
—	—	Brighouse 41	d							07 14	07 18														
0	—	**Leeds** 10 31,34	d	05 46		06 38	07 00	07 00				07 29		08 00	08 05		08 32	09 00		09 32	10 00	10 00			10 32
6	—	Woodlesford 34	d	05 54		06 46	07 08	07 08				07 37		08 08	08 15		08 40	09 08		09 40	10 08	10 08			10 40
10¾	—	Castleford 34	a	06 03		06 54	07 19	07 17				07 45		08 17	08 24		08 48	09 17		09 48	10 17	10 17			10 48
—	—		d	06 05		06 57	07 19	07 19				07 48		08 19	08 26		08 51	09 19		09 51	10 18	10 19			10 51
12¼	—	Glasshoughton	d	06 09			07 24	07 24						08 24	08 31			09 24			10 24	10 24			
—	0	**Wakefield Westgate** 7 31,39	d		06 24																				
—	1	Wakefield Kirkgate 4 31,34,39	a		06 29	07 07				07 36	07 40	08 00					09 03			10 01					11 01
—	—		d		06 29				07 31	07 38	07 42					08 31			09 31					10 31	
—	5¼	Streethouse	d		06 36				07 39							08 39			09 39					10 39	
—	7	Featherstone	d		06 40				07 43							08 43			09 43					10 43	
—	9	Pontefract Tanshelf	d		06 44				07 46							08 46			09 46					10 46	
14	9¾	Pontefract Monkhill	a	06 14	06 46		07 28	07 28	07 50	07 56	07 58			08 28	08 35	08 49		09 28	09 49		10 28	10 28		10 49	
—	—		d	06 14	06 47		07 28	07 28	07 50	07 58	08 01			08 28	08 35	08 49		09 28	09 49		10 28	10 28		10 49	
—	—	London Kings Cross 15 ⊖26	a							10 09	10 13														
16	—	**Knottingley**	a	06 20	06 55		07 36	07 36	07 56					08 36	08 44	08 56		09 37	09 56		10 36	10 36		10 56	
—	—		d																						
20¼	—	Whitley Bridge	d																						
22	—	Hensall	d																						
25¾	—	Snaith	d																						
28½	—	Rawcliffe	d																						
32½	—	**Goole**	a																						

Station		NT	GC SX	GC SO	NT	NT	NT	NT		NT	NT	NT	NT	NT	NT	NT	NT SO	NT SX		NT	NT	GC SO	NT	NT	GC SX
			R 1 ☕	R 1 ☕																		R 1 ☕			R 1 ☕
Bradford Interchange 41	d		10 22	10 22																		15 22			15 37
Halifax 41	d		10 37	10 38																		15 35			15 52
Brighouse 41	d		10 48	10 48																		15 46			16 05
Leeds 10 31,34	d	11 00				11 32	12 00			12 32	13 00		13 32	14 00		14 32	15 00	15 00			15 32		16 00		
Woodlesford 34	d	11 08				11 40	12 08			12 40	13 08		13 40	14 08		14 40	15 08	15 08			15 40		16 08		
Castleford 34	a	11 17				11 48	12 17			12 48	13 17		13 48	14 17		14 48	15 17	15 17			15 48		16 17		
	d	11 19				11 51	12 19			12 51	13 19		13 51	14 19		14 51	15 19	15 19			15 51		16 19		
Glasshoughton	d	11 24					12 24				13 24			14 24			15 24	15 24					16 24		
Wakefield Westgate 7 31,39	d																								
Wakefield Kirkgate 4 31,34,39	a		11 10	11 11		12 01				13 02			14 01			15 01					16 01	16 09			16 36
	d		11 11	11 11	11 31			12 31				13 31			14 31					15 31		16 11		16 31	16 40
Streethouse	d				11 39			12 39				13 39			14 39					15 39				16 39	
Featherstone	d				11 43			12 43				13 43			14 43					15 43				16 43	
Pontefract Tanshelf	d				11 46			12 46				13 46			14 46					15 46				16 46	
Pontefract Monkhill	a	11 29	11 33	11 34	11 49		12 28	12 49			13 28	13 49		14 28	14 49		15 28	15 28		15 49		16 27	16 28	16 49	16 55
	d	11 29	11 34	11 35	11 49		12 28	12 49			13 28	13 49		14 28	14 49		15 28	15 28		15 49		16 29	16 28	16 49	16 56
London Kings Cross 15 ⊖26	a		13 45	13 46																		18 45			19 05
Knottingley	a	11 35			11 56		12 35	12 56			13 35	13 56		14 35	14 56		15 34	15 36		15 56			16 36	16 56	
	d																								
Whitley Bridge	d																								
Hensall	d																								
Snaith	d																								
Rawcliffe	d																								
Goole	a																								

Station		NT	NT SO	NT SX		NT	NT	NT	NT	NT	NT SO	NT SX	NT	NT		NT	NT	NT	NT	NT	NT	NT	NT SX	NT SO	NT
Bradford Interchange 41	d																								
Halifax 41	d																								
Brighouse 41	d																								
Leeds 10 31,34	d	16 32	17 16	17 16			17 32	18 00		18 32	18 59	18 59		19 37		20 05		20 37	21 05		21 37	22 08			22 37
Woodlesford 34	d	16 40	17 24	17 24			17 40	18 08		18 40	19 08	19 08		19 45		20 13		20 45	21 13		21 45	22 16			22 45
Castleford 34	a	16 48	17 33	17 34			17 48	18 17		18 48	19 17	19 18		19 53		20 22		20 53	21 22		21 53	22 27			22 53
	d	16 51	17 36	17 36			17 51	18 19		18 51	19 19	19 19		19 56		20 24		20 56	21 24		21 56	22 27			22 56
Glasshoughton	d		17 40	17 40				18 24			19 24	19 24				20 29			21 29			22 32			
Wakefield Westgate 7 31,39	d																			21 57			23 04	23 04	
Wakefield Kirkgate 4 31,34,39	a	17 01					18 01			19 04				20 06				21 06		22 00	22 06		23 07	23 07	23 10
	d					17 31			18 33				19 33				20 54			22 00			23 07	23 07	
Streethouse	d					17 39			18 41				19 41				21 02			22 08			23 15	23 15	
Featherstone	d					17 43			18 45				19 45				21 06			22 12			23 19	23 19	
Pontefract Tanshelf	d					17 46			18 48				19 48				21 09			22 16			23 23	23 23	
Pontefract Monkhill	a		17 44	17 44		17 49		18 28	18 51		19 28	19 28	19 51			20 33	21 12		21 33	22 18		22 36	23 25	23 29	
	d		17 44	17 44		17 49		18 28	18 51		19 28	19 28	19 51			20 33	21 12		21 33	22 19		22 36	23 26		
London Kings Cross 15 ⊖26	a																								
Knottingley	a		17 51	17 51		17 57		18 35	18 58		19 35	19 35	19 58			20 40	21 19		21 40	22 25		22 44	23 32		
	d		17 53	17 53																					
Whitley Bridge	d		17 59	17 59																					
Hensall	d		18 03	18 03																					
Snaith	d		18 10	18 10																					
Rawcliffe	d		18 15	18 15																					
Goole	a		18 30	18 30																					

A ☕ to Pontefract Monkhill

Table 32

Sundays

Bradford, Leeds and Wakefield - Pontefract, Knottingley and Goole

Network Diagram - see first page of Table 31

		GC	GC	GC	NT	NT	NT	NT	GC	NT	NT	NT	NT	GC	NT	NT	NT	NT	NT	NT	NT
			◇1	◇1					◇1					◇1							
		B	A	B																	
		🚌	☕	☕					☕					☕							
Bradford Interchange 41	d		07 55	08 05					12 04					15 42							
Halifax 41	d	07 30	08 07						12 15					15 54							
Brighouse 41	d	07 50	08 18						12 26					16 05							
Leeds 10 31,34	d				08 34	09 34	10 17	11 17		12 34	13 17	14 17	15 17		16 17	17 17	18 17	19 17	20 17	21 17	22 17
Woodlesford 34	d				08 42	09 42	10 25	11 25		12 42	13 25	14 25	15 25		16 25	17 25	18 25	19 25	20 25	21 25	22 25
Castleford 34	a				08 50	09 50	10 33	11 33		12 50	13 33	14 33	15 33		16 33	17 33	18 33	19 35	20 33	21 33	22 33
	d				08 53	09 53	10 36	11 36		12 53	13 36	14 36	15 36		16 36	17 36	18 36	19 36	20 36	21 36	22 36
Glasshoughton	d					09 57		11 40			13 40		15 40			17 40		19 40		21 40	
Wakefield Westgate 7 31,39	d	08 31																			
Wakefield Kirkgate 4 31,34,39	a		08 42	08 42	09 03		10 46		12 48	13 04		14 46		16 27	16 46		18 45		20 46		22 46
	d																				
Streethouse	d																				
Featherstone	d																				
Pontefract Tanshelf	d																				
Pontefract Monkhill	a					10 02		11 45			13 45		15 45			17 45		19 45		21 45	
	d					10 02		11 45			13 45		15 45			17 45		19 45		21 45	
London Kings Cross 15 ⊖26	a		10 40	10 40					14 56					18 50							
Knottingley	a					10 08		11 52			13 52		15 52			17 52		19 52		21 52	
	d																				
Whitley Bridge	d																				
Hensall	d																				
Snaith	d																				
Rawcliffe	d																				
Goole	a																				

B from 01 April to 13 May

A from 11 Dec to 25 March

Table 32

Mondays to Saturdays

Goole, Knottingley and Pontefract - Wakefield and Leeds, Bradford

Network Diagram - see first page of Table 31

Miles	Miles			NT SX	NT SO	NT SX	NT	NT SX	NT SX	NT SO	NT	NT		NT	NT	NT	NT	NT	NT	NT	NT	NT		NT	NT
0	—	**Goole**	d						07 04	07 04															
4	—	Rawcliffe	d						07 11	07 11															
6¾	—	Snaith	d						07 16	07 16															
10½	—	Hensall	d						07 23	07 23															
12¼	—	Whitley Bridge	d						07 30	07 30															
16½	—	**Knottingley**	a						07 38	07 37															
—	—		d	06 25			06 56		07 38	07 38		07 53		08 16		08 53	09 16		09 53	10 16		10 53		11 16	
—	—	London Kings Cross 15 ⊖26	d																						
18½	0	Pontefract Monkhill	a	06 29			07 00		07 42	07 42		07 57		08 20		08 57	09 20		09 57	10 20		10 57		11 20	
—	—		d	06 29			07 00		07 42	07 42		07 57		08 20		08 57	09 20		09 57	10 20		10 57		11 20	
—	0¾	Pontefract Tanshelf	d				07 03					08 00				09 00			10 00			11 00			
—	2¾	Featherstone	d				07 06					08 03				09 03			10 03			11 03			
—	4½	Streethouse	d				07 10					08 07				09 07			10 07			11 07			
—	8¾	Wakefield Kirkgate 4 31,34,39	a				07 21					08 18				09 18			10 20			11 18			
—	—		d		06 50	06 50					07 50				08 50			09 50			10 50				11 50
—	9¾	**Wakefield Westgate** 7 31,39	a																						
20	—	Glasshoughton 34	d	06 34					07 48	07 48				08 25			09 25			10 25				11 25	
21½	—	Castleford	a	06 38	07 00	06 59			07 52	07 52	07 59			08 30	09 00		09 29	10 00		10 29	11 00			11 29	12 00
—	—		d	06 41	07 02	07 02		07 38	07 55	07 55	08 01			08 32	09 02		09 32	10 02		10 32	11 02			11 32	12 02
26½	—	Woodlesford 34	d	06 50	07 12	07 12		07 47	08 04	08 04	08 11			08 41	09 12		09 41	10 12		10 41	11 12			11 41	12 12
32½	—	**Leeds** 10 31,34	a	07 04	07 28	07 28		08 01	08 18	08 18	08 25			08 54	09 25		09 53	10 25		10 55	11 25			11 54	12 25
—	—	Brighouse 41	a																						
—	—	Halifax 41	a																						
—	—	Bradford Interchange 41	a																						

		NT	NT	NT	GC SX R 1 ☕	NT	NT	NT		NT	NT SO	NT SX	NT	NT	NT	NT	NT	NT		NT	GC SX R 1 ☕	NT	NT	NT	NT
Goole	d																								
Rawcliffe	d																								
Snaith	d																								
Hensall	d																								
Whitley Bridge	d																								
Knottingley	a																								
	d	11 53	12 16			12 53	13 16			13 53	14 16	14 16		14 53	15 16		15 53	16 16				16 53	17 15		18 02
London Kings Cross 15 ⊖26	d				10 48																14 48				
Pontefract Monkhill	a	11 57	12 20		12 47	12 57	13 20			13 57	14 20	14 20		14 57	15 20		15 57	16 20			16 47	16 57	17 19		18 06
	d	11 57	12 20		12 49	12 57	13 20			13 57	14 20	14 20		14 57	15 20		15 57	16 20			16 48	16 57	17 19		18 06
Pontefract Tanshelf	d	12 00				13 00				14 00				15 00			16 00					17 00			18 09
Featherstone	d	12 03				13 03				14 03				15 03			16 03					17 03			18 12
Streethouse	d	12 07				13 07				14 07				15 07			16 07					17 07			18 16
Wakefield Kirkgate 4 31,34,39	a	12 18			13 07	13 18				14 18				15 18			16 19				17 04	17 18			18 27
	d			12 50	13 09			13 50					14 50			15 50				16 50	17 08			17 50	
Wakefield Westgate 7 31,39	a																								
Glasshoughton 34	d		12 25				13 25				14 25	14 25			15 25			16 25					17 24		
Castleford	a		12 29	13 00			13 29	14 00			14 28	14 29	15 00		15 29	16 00		16 29		17 00			17 28	18 00	
	d		12 32	13 02			13 32	14 02			14 32	14 32	15 02		15 32	16 02		16 32		17 02			17 31	18 02	
Woodlesford 34	d		12 41	13 12			13 41	14 12			14 41	14 41	15 12		15 41	16 12		16 41		17 12			17 41	18 12	
Leeds 10 31,34	a		12 54	13 25			13 53	14 25			14 53	14 53	15 25		15 54	16 25		16 54		17 25			17 54	18 25	
Brighouse 41	a				13 30																17 29				
Halifax 41	a				13 40																17 40				
Bradford Interchange 41	a				13 55																17 55				

		NT	NT	NT		NT	NT	NT	NT	GC SO R 1 ☕	NT	NT	NT SX	NT SO		NT	NT	NT SX	NT SO	NT	NT
Goole	d					18 49															
Rawcliffe	d					18 56															
Snaith	d					19 01															
Hensall	d					19 08															
Whitley Bridge	d					19 12															
Knottingley	a					19 20															
	d	18 39		19 02		19 21		19 55	20 16			21 16	21 23	21 23			22 16			22 30	23 05
London Kings Cross 15 ⊖26	d									19 20											
Pontefract Monkhill	a	18 43		19 06		19 25		19 59	20 20	21 15		21 20	21 27	21 27			22 22			22 34	23 09
	d	18 43		19 06		19 25		19 59	20 20	21 16		21 20	21 27	21 27			22 22			22 34	23 09
Pontefract Tanshelf	d			19 09				20 02					21 30	21 30						22 37	
Featherstone	d			19 12				20 05					21 33	21 33						22 40	
Streethouse	d			19 16				20 09					21 37	21 37						22 44	
Wakefield Kirkgate 4 31,34,39	a			19 28				20 20					21 47	21 47						22 55	
	d		18 50				19 50				20 50		21 47	21 48		21 52		22 51	22 51	22 55	
Wakefield Westgate 7 31,39	a												21 53	21 53						23 01	
Glasshoughton 34	d	18 48				19 30			20 25			21 25					22 27				23 14
Castleford	a	18 54	19 00			19 34	20 00		20 29		21 00	21 29				22 04	22 31	23 01	23 02		23 18
	d	18 57	19 03			19 37	20 02		20 32		21 02	21 32				22 05	22 34	23 04	23 04		23 21
Woodlesford 34	d	19 06	19 13			19 46	20 12		20 44		21 12	21 41				22 15	22 43	23 14	23 14		23 30
Leeds 10 31,34	a	19 20	19 27			20 00	20 26		20 57		21 26	21 53				22 29	22 57	23 30	23 30		23 44
Brighouse 41	a									21 57											
Halifax 41	a									22 08											
Bradford Interchange 41	a									22 24											

Table 32

Sundays

Goole, Knottingley and Pontefract - Wakefield and Leeds, Bradford

Network Diagram - see first page of Table 31

		NT	NT	NT	GC	NT	NT	NT	NT	GC	NT	NT		NT	GC	NT	NT	NT	NT
					◇1					◇1					◇1				
					⌨					⌨					⌨				
Goole	d																		
Rawcliffe	d																		
Snaith	d																		
Hensall	d																		
Whitley Bridge	d																		
Knottingley	a																		
	d		10 26			12 26		14 26			16 26			18 26			20 26		22 26
London Kings Cross 15 ⊖26	d				11 48					15 48					19 23				
Pontefract Monkhill	a		10 30			12 30		14 30			16 30			18 30			20 30		22 30
	d		10 30			12 30		14 30			16 30			18 30			20 30		22 30
Pontefract Tanshelf	d																		
Featherstone	d																		
Streethouse	d																		
Wakefield Kirkgate 4 31,34,39	a				13 45					17 47					21 22				
	d	09 30		11 30	13 46		13 30		15 30	17 48		17 30			21 23	19 30		21 30	
Wakefield Westgate 7 31,39	a																		
Glasshoughton 34	d		10 35			12 35		14 35			16 35			18 35			20 35		22 35
Castleford	a	09 40	10 39	11 40		12 39	13 40	14 39	15 40		16 39	17 40		18 39		19 41	20 39	21 40	22 39
	d	09 42	10 42	11 41		12 42	13 42	14 42	15 41		16 42	17 42		18 42		19 44	20 42	21 42	22 42
Woodlesford 34	d	09 52	10 51	11 51		12 52	13 51	14 51	15 51		16 51	17 51		18 51		19 53	20 51	21 51	22 51
Leeds 10 31,34	a	10 04	11 04	12 05		13 05	14 04	15 04	16 04		17 04	18 05		19 04		20 05	21 03	22 04	23 04
Brighouse 41	a				14 08					18 10					21 46				
Halifax 41	a				14 19					18 20					21 57				
Bradford Interchange 41	a				14 37					18 37					22 11				

Sheffield and Selby - York

Local services only

Network Diagram - see first page of Table 31

Mondays to Fridays

Miles	Miles			NT	NT	NT	NT	NT	NT	NT	NT	NT	NT	NT	NT	NT	NT	NT	NT	NT	NT	NT	NT
					H	B	H		H		C		H	C	H	C	D	C		H	C	L	F
0	—	**Sheffield** 7	29,31 d							09 29							13 29						
3½	—	Meadowhall	29,31 d							09 35							13 35						
6¼	—	Rotherham Central	29,31 d							09 42							13 41						
10¾	—	Swinton (S.Yorks)	29,31 d							09 51							13 50						
18½	—	Moorthorpe	31 d							10 01							14 01						
25½	—	Pontefract Baghill	d							10 10							14 10						
—	—	Hull	29 d			07 07		09 02			10 08			12 03		13 12		14 18	15 02		16 10		17 18
—	0	**Selby**	d	06 48		07 48		09 38			10 47	11 40		12 38		13 55		14 53	15 38		16 47		18 07
33¾	8¼	Sherburn-in-Elmet	d	07 00		08 03		09 53		10 27	11 00	11 52				14 09	14 28	15 05					
36	10½	Church Fenton	d	07 04	08 00		09 05		10 05	10 32			12 05		14 06		14 32			16 05		17 53	
38	12½	Ulleskelf	d			08 09				10 36							14 36					17 58	
46¾	21	**York** 8	29 a	07 20	08 16	08 21	09 21	10 10	10 21	10 56	11 18	12 14	12 21	13 04	14 22	14 27	14 55	15 25	16 06	16 21	17 13	18 10	18 33

		TP ◇1	NT	NT	NT	NT	NT
		F	H		H		H
Sheffield 7	29,31 d						
Meadowhall	29,31 d						
Rotherham Central	29,31 d						
Swinton (S.Yorks)	29,31 d						
Moorthorpe	31 d						
Pontefract Baghill	d						
Hull	29 d	18 59		19 15			
Selby	d	19a29		19 53		21 21	
Sherburn-in-Elmet	d						
Church Fenton	d		19 05		21 12		23 27
Ulleskelf	d				21 16		
York 8	29 a		19 21	20 21	21 30	21 43	23 44

Saturdays

		NT	NT	NT	NT	NT	NT	NT	NT	NT	NT	NT	NT	NT	NT	NT	NT	NT	NT	TP ◇1	NT	NT	TP ◇1
		C	H	B	H		H		C	C	H		H	C		C		H	C	F	H	F	F
Sheffield 7	29,31 d							09 29							13 29								
Meadowhall	29,31 d							09 35							13 35								
Rotherham Central	29,31 d							09 42							13 41								
Swinton (S.Yorks)	29,31 d							09 51							13 50								
Moorthorpe	31 d							10 02							14 01								
Pontefract Baghill	d							10 10							14 10								
Hull	29 d			07 07		09 02			10 08	11 05		12 03		13 12		14 18	15 02		16 10	17 01		17 18	18 59
Selby	d	06 48		07 48		09 38			10 47	11 40		12 38		13 55		14 53	15 38		16 47	17a32		18 07	19a29
Sherburn-in-Elmet	d	07 00		08 03		09 53		10 27	11 00					14 09	14 28	15 05							
Church Fenton	d	07 04	08 05		09 05		10 05	10 32			12 05		14 06		14 32			16 05			18 05		
Ulleskelf	d			08 09				10 36							14 36						18 10		
York 8	29 a	07 20	08 20	08 21	09 21	10 14	10 21	10 55	11 18	12 08	12 21	13 04	14 22	14 27	14 55	15 25	16 06	16 21	17 13		18 24	18 33	

		NT	NT	NT	NT	NT
		H	F	H		H
Sheffield 7	29,31 d					
Meadowhall	29,31 d					
Rotherham Central	29,31 d					
Swinton (S.Yorks)	29,31 d					
Moorthorpe	31 d					
Pontefract Baghill	d					
Hull	29 d		19 15		21 01	
Selby	d		19 53		21 35	
Sherburn-in-Elmet	d					
Church Fenton	d	19 05		21 12		23 21
Ulleskelf	d			21 16		
York 8	29 a	19 21	20 21	21 30	21 57	23 38

Sundays

		NT	NT	NT	NT	NT	NT	NT	NT	NT	NT	NT	NT	NT	NT	NT	NT	NT	NT
		J		K		H		H			H			H			H		L
Sheffield 7	29,31 d											16 36			18 57				
Meadowhall	29,31 d											16 42			19 05				
Rotherham Central	29,31 d											16 49			19 11				
Swinton (S.Yorks)	29,31 d											16 58			19 19				
Moorthorpe	31 d											17 13			19 29				
Pontefract Baghill	d											17 21			19 38				
Hull	29 d		08 54		11 46		13 29		14 23	16 00			17 23			19 24		20 29	
Selby	d		09 28		12 20		14 03		14 57	16 34			17 57			19 58		21 03	
Sherburn-in-Elmet	d											17 38			19 56				
Church Fenton	d	09 18		10 52		12 49		14 49			16 49	17 43		18 47	20 00		20 49		23 07
Ulleskelf	d																		
York 8	29 a	09 34	09 52	11 08	12 44	13 02	14 30	15 02	15 25	16 59	17 02	17 59	18 25	19 01	20 18	20 25	21 03	21 30	23 23

B From Beverley
C To Hull
D To Sheffield
F To Leeds
H From Blackpool North
J From Bradford Interchange
K From Huddersfield
L From Leeds

Table 33

Mondays to Fridays

York - Selby and Sheffield

Local services only

Network Diagram - see first page of Table 31

Miles	Miles				NT	NT A	NT	NT B	NT C	NT K	NT E	NT	NT	NT K	NT F	NT G	NT K	NT F	NT F	NT H	NT K	NT A	NT F	TP FO I
0	0	**York 8**	29	d	05 44	07 06	07 29	07 48	08 43	09 11	10 20	11 00	11 05	11 09	11 45	12 47	13 09	13 44	14 47	15 01	15 08	16 08	16 12	16 13
8¾	8¾	Ulleskelf		d		07 15							11 15							15 11				
10¾	10¾	Church Fenton		a		07 20		08 00		09 22			11 19	11 20			13 20			15 15	15 20	16 20		16 25
—	—			d									11 19							15 15				
12¾	12¾	Sherburn-in-Elmet		d					08 55			11 12	11 23					13 56		15 19			16 25	
—	21	**Selby**		a	06 08		07 50		09 06		10 40	11 24			12 04	13 06		14 07	15 06				16 36	
—	—	Hull	29	a			08 46		09 47		11 23				12 49	13 48		14 52	15 48				17 27	
21¼	—	Pontefract Baghill		d									11 43							15 38				
28¼	—	Moorthorpe	31	a									11 59							15 50				
36	—	Swinton (S.Yorks)	29,31	a									12 08							16 00				
40½	—	Rotherham Central	29,31	a									12 18							16 09				
43¼	—	Meadowhall	29,31	a									12 24							16 17				
46¾	—	**Sheffield 7**	29,31	a									12 36							16 27				

			NT F	NT D	NT E	NT F	NT K	NT B	NT L	NT M	NT B
York 8	29	d	17 19	18 05	18 18	19 04	20 17	21 22	22 13	22 13	23 13
Ulleskelf		d		18 15				21 31			
Church Fenton		a	17 30	18 21		19 17		21 33			23 28
		d	17 30								
Sherburn-in-Elmet		d	17 34		18 31		20 29				
Selby		a	17 45		18 42		20 42		22 32	22 32	
Hull	29	a	18 30		19 29				23 18	23 22	
Pontefract Baghill		d									
Moorthorpe	31	a									
Swinton (S.Yorks)	29,31	a									
Rotherham Central	29,31	a									
Meadowhall	29,31	a									
Sheffield 7	29,31	a									

Saturdays

			NT	NT A	NT	NT E	NT C	NT K	NT C	NT	NT	NT K	NT F	NT F	NT K	NT	NT F	NT	NT K	NT K	NT F	NT F	NT K	NT
York 8	29	d	06 09	07 06	07 38	08 09	08 43	09 11	09 50	10 43	11 05	11 09	11 45	12 47	13 09	13 44	14 47	15 01	15 09	16 08	16 12	17 19	18 05	18 18
Ulleskelf		d		07 15							11 15							15 11					18 15	
Church Fenton		a		07 20		08 20		09 22			11 19	11 20			13 20			15 15	15 21	16 20		17 30	18 21	
		d									11 19							15 15				17 30		
Sherburn-in-Elmet		d					08 55				11 23					13 56		15 19			16 25	17 34		18 31
Selby		a	06 30		07 57		09 06		10 09	11 03			12 04	13 06		14 07	15 06				16 36	17 45		18 42
Hull	29	a			08 50		09 47		10 53	11 51			12 49	13 48		14 52	15 48				17 27	18 30		19 29
Pontefract Baghill		d									11 43							15 38						
Moorthorpe	31	a									11 59							15 50						
Swinton (S.Yorks)	29,31	a									12 08							16 01						
Rotherham Central	29,31	a									12 18							16 09						
Meadowhall	29,31	a									12 24							16 17						
Sheffield 7	29,31	a									12 36							16 27						

			NT F	NT K	NT F	NT F	NT E
York 8	29	d	19 04	19 47	21 18	22 11	23 13
Ulleskelf		d			21 27		
Church Fenton		a	19 17		21 33		23 28
		d					
Sherburn-in-Elmet		d					
Selby		a		20 06		22 29	
Hull	29	a		20 48		23 14	
Pontefract Baghill		d					
Moorthorpe	31	a					
Swinton (S.Yorks)	29,31	a					
Rotherham Central	29,31	a					
Meadowhall	29,31	a					
Sheffield 7	29,31	a					

Sundays

			NT A	NT A	NT	NT A	NT	NT	NT A	NT	NT A	NT	NT	NT A	NT	NT	NT A	NT	NT	NT B
York 8	29	d	08 50	09 52	10 40	11 52	12 05	13 40	13 52	14 49	15 52	16 06	17 11	17 52	18 10	19 10	19 52	20 50	21 41	21 52
Ulleskelf		d																		
Church Fenton		a	09 01	10 03		12 03			14 03		16 03			18 03	18 21		20 03	21 01		22 04
		d													18 21			21 01		
Sherburn-in-Elmet		d													18 25			21 05		
Selby		a			10 58		12 24	13 59		15 08		16 24	17 30			19 35			22 00	
Hull	29	a			11 41		13 06	14 40		15 49		17 07	18 12			20 17			22 36	
Pontefract Baghill		d													18 40			21 20		
Moorthorpe	31	a													18 51			21 35		
Swinton (S.Yorks)	29,31	a													19 01			21 45		
Rotherham Central	29,31	a													19 12			21 52		
Meadowhall	29,31	a													19 18			21 57		
Sheffield 7	29,31	a													19 27			22 09		

A To Blackpool North
B To Leeds
C From Beverley
E From Leeds
F From Hull
G From Selby
H From Sheffield
I From Middlesbrough
K From Blackpool North
L until 23 March
M from 26 March

Nottingham, Sheffield - Barnsley - Huddersfield and Leeds

Network Diagram - see first page of Table 31

Miles	Miles			NT MO	NT MX	NT MX	NT	NT	NT	NT	NT	NT		NT	NT	NT	NT	NT	TP	NT	NT	NT		NT	EM
																			◇1						◇
						A			B					C				C	D	E				F	G
0	—	**Nottingham 8**	d	21p30																		06 23			06 40
12	—	Langley Mill	d	21p52																		06 38			
18¼	—	Alfreton	d	22p00																		06 46			07 02
28¼	—	Chesterfield	d	22p13													06 26					06 58			07 13
33½	—	Dronfield	d	22p20													06 33					07 05			07 20
40½	—	**Sheffield 7** 29,31	a	22p36													06 46					07 18			07 31
—	—		d	22p39	23p15	23p24	05 16	05 22	05 29	05 36	05 50	06 06		06 18	06 28	06 36	06 49	06 52	06 55	07 06	07 14	07 20		07 24	
44	3½	**Meadowhall 4** 29,31	a	22p44	23p20	23p29	05 22	05 27	05 34	05 41	05 55	06 11		06 23	06 33	06 41	06 54	06 57	07 00	07 11	07 20	07 25		07 30	
—	—		d	22p45	23p21	23p30	05 22	05 28		05 42	05 56	06 12			06 34	06 42	06 55			07 12	07 21	07 26			
47¾	7¼	Chapeltown	d	22p51		23p36	05 28			05 48		06 18				06 48				07 18					
51	10½	Elsecar	d	22p56		23p41	05 33					06 23								07 23					
52½	12	Wombwell	d	23p00		23p45	05 37			05 55		06 27				06 55				07 27					
56½	16	**Barnsley**	a	23p05		23p50	05 44			06 00	06 10	06 32				07 00	07 09			07 32		07 41			
—	—		d	23p10		23p51				06 01	06 10	06 33				07 01	07 12			07 33		07 42			
—	19	Dodworth	d							06 07						07 07									
—	20¼	Silkstone Common	d							06 11						07 11									
—	23½	Penistone	d							06 18						07 18									
—	27½	Denby Dale	d							06 24						07 24									
—	29¾	Shepley	d							06 29						07 29									
—	30¾	Stocksmoor	d							06 32						07 32									
—	32¾	Brockholes	d							06 36						07 36									
—	33¾	Honley	d							06 38						07 38									
—	34¾	Berry Brow	d							06 41						07 41									
—	35¾	Lockwood	d							06 44						07 44									
—	37	**Huddersfield**	a							06 50						07 49									
60	—	Darton	d	23p15		23p56						06 38								07 38					
67½	—	**Wakefield Kirkgate 4** 31	a	23p26		00s10					06 27	06 49					07 27			07 49		07 57			
—	—		d	23p27							06 28	06 50					07 28			07 50		07 58			
70½	—	Normanton	d	23p34							06 33	06 54					07 33			07 54					
74	—	Castleford	a	23p40								06 59								07 59					
78¾	—	Woodlesford	a	23p53								07 12								08 11					
84¾	—	**Leeds 10** 31	a	00 05	00 29			06 33			06 50	07 28			07 44		07 51			08 25	08 36	08 21			

			NT	NT	NT	EM	NT	TP	NT		NT	NT	NT	EM	NT	NT	NT	NT	TP		NT	NT	NT	NT	NT	NT
						◇1		◇1						◇					◇1							
				H	I	J		D				F		G	H		K		D				F	L		M
Nottingham 8		d									07 13			07 45								08 11				
Langley Mill		d									07 29											08 31				
Alfreton		d									07 37			08 07								08 39				
Chesterfield		d				07 42					07 50			08 18								08 51				
Dronfield		d				07 49								08 25								08 58				
Sheffield 7	29,31	a				08 00					08 08			08 38								09 16				
		d	07 36	07 41	07 51		08 06	08 11	08 14		08 18	08 24	08 36		08 41	08 51	08 53	09 06	09 11		09 14	09 18	09 24	09 29	09 36	09 41
Meadowhall 4	29,31	a	07 41	07 46	07 57		08 11	08 16	08 21		08 24	08 30	08 41		08 46	08 56	08 59	09 11	09 16		09 20	09 23	09 29	09 34	09 41	09 46
		d	07 42		07 57		08 12		08 21		08 25		08 42			08 57		09 12			09 21	09 24			09 42	
Chapeltown		d	07 48				08 18						08 48					09 18							09 48	
Elsecar		d					08 23											09 23								
Wombwell		d	07 55				08 27						08 55					09 27							09 55	
Barnsley		a	08 00		08 11		08 32				08 40		09 00			09 11		09 32				09 40			10 00	
		d	08 01		08 12		08 33				08 42		09 01			09 12		09 33				09 42			10 01	
Dodworth		d	08 07										09 07												10 07	
Silkstone Common		d	08 11										09 11												10 11	
Penistone		d	08 18										09 18												10 18	
Denby Dale		d	08 24										09 24												10 24	
Shepley		d	08 29										09 29												10 29	
Stocksmoor		d	08 32										09 32												10 32	
Brockholes		d	08 36										09 36												10 36	
Honley		d	08 38										09 38												10 38	
Berry Brow		d	08 41										09 41												10 41	
Lockwood		d	08 44										09 44												10 44	
Huddersfield		a	08 49										09 49												10 49	
Darton		d					08 38											09 38								
Wakefield Kirkgate 4	31	a			08 27		08 49				08 57					09 27		09 49				09 57				
		d			08 28		08 50				08 58					09 28		09 50				09 58				
Normanton		d					08 54											09 54								
Castleford		a					09 00											10 00								
Woodlesford		a					09 12											10 12								
Leeds 10	31	a			08 49		09 25		09 31		09 20					09 49		10 25			10 31	10 18				

A To Wakefield Westgate
B To Beverley
C To Adwick
D From Manchester Airport to Cleethorpes
E From Worksop
F To Scunthorpe
G To Liverpool Lime Street
H To Bridlington
I From Retford
J From Derby
K From Worksop to Adwick
L To York
M To Scarborough

Nottingham, Sheffield - Barnsley - Huddersfield and Leeds

Network Diagram - see first page of Table 31

		NT	NT	NT	TP	NT	NT	NT	NT	NT	NT	NT	NT	TP	NT	NT	NT	NT	NT	NT	NT	NT
					◇1									◇1								
			A		B			C		D		A		B			C		E		A	
Nottingham 8	d						09 15									10 15						
Langley Mill	d						09 32									10 32						
Alfreton	d						09 40									10 40						
Chesterfield	d						09 52									10 52						
Dronfield	d						09 59									10 59						
Sheffield 7 29,31	a						10 16									11 17						
	d	09 50	09 53	10 06	10 11	10 14	10 18	10 24	10 36	10 41	10 50	10 53	11 06	11 11	11 14	11 18	11 24	11 36	11 41	11 50	11 53	12 06
Meadowhall 4 29,31	a	09 55	09 58	10 11	10 16	10 20	10 23	10 29	10 41	10 46	10 55	10 58	11 11	11 16	11 20	11 23	11 29	11 41	11 46	11 55	11 58	12 11
	d	09 56		10 12		10 21	10 24		10 42		10 56		11 12		11 21	11 24		11 42		11 56		12 12
Chapeltown	d			10 18					10 48				11 18					11 48				12 18
Elsecar	d			10 23									11 23									12 23
Wombwell	d			10 27					10 55				11 27					11 55				12 27
Barnsley	a	10 11		10 32			10 40		11 00		11 11		11 32			11 40		12 00		12 10		12 32
	d	10 12		10 33			10 42		11 01		11 12		11 33			11 41		12 01		12 11		12 33
Dodworth	d								11 07									12 07				
Silkstone Common	d								11 11									12 11				
Penistone	d								11 18									12 18				
Denby Dale	d								11 24									12 24				
Shepley	d								11 29									12 29				
Stocksmoor	d								11 32									12 32				
Brockholes	d								11 36									12 36				
Honley	d								11 38									12 38				
Berry Brow	d								11 41									12 41				
Lockwood	d								11 44									12 44				
Huddersfield	a								11 49									12 49				
Darton	d			10 38									11 38									12 38
Wakefield Kirkgate 4 31	a	10 27		10 49			10 57				11 27		11 49			11 57				12 27		12 49
	d	10 28		10 50			10 58				11 28		11 50			11 58				12 28		12 50
Normanton	d			10 54									11 54									12 54
Castleford	a			11 00									12 00									13 00
Woodlesford	a			11 12									12 12									13 12
Leeds 10 31	a	10 48		11 25		11 31	11 18				11 48		12 25		12 31	12 18				12 48		13 25

		TP	NT	NT	NT	NT	NT	NT	NT	NT	TP	NT	NT	NT	NT	NT	NT	NT	NT	NT	TP	NT	NT
		◇1									◇1										◇1		
		B			C		D		A		B			C	F		D		G		B		
Nottingham 8	d			11 15									12 15										13 15
Langley Mill	d			11 31									12 32										13 32
Alfreton	d			11 39									12 40										13 40
Chesterfield	d			11 52									12 52										13 52
Dronfield	d			11 59									12 59										13 59
Sheffield 7 29,31	a			12 16									13 16										14 16
	d	12 11	12 14	12 18	12 24	12 36	12 41	12 50	12 53	13 06	13 11	13 14	13 18	13 24	13 29	13 36	13 41	13 50	13 53	14 06	14 11	14 14	14 18
Meadowhall 4 29,31	a	12 16	12 20	12 23	12 29	12 41	12 46	12 55	12 58	13 11	13 16	13 20	13 23	13 29	13 34	13 41	13 46	13 55	13 58	14 11	14 16	14 20	14 23
	d		12 21	12 24		12 42		12 56		13 12		13 21	13 24			13 42		13 56		14 12		14 21	14 24
Chapeltown	d					12 48				13 18						13 48				14 18			
Elsecar	d									13 23										14 23			
Wombwell	d					12 55				13 27						13 55				14 27			
Barnsley	a			12 40		13 00		13 11		13 32			13 40			14 00		14 11		14 32			14 40
	d			12 42		13 01		13 12		13 33			13 42			14 01		14 12		14 33			14 42
Dodworth	d					13 07										14 07							
Silkstone Common	d					13 11										14 11							
Penistone	d					13 18										14 18							
Denby Dale	d					13 24										14 24							
Shepley	d					13 29										14 29							
Stocksmoor	d					13 32										14 32							
Brockholes	d					13 36										14 36							
Honley	d					13 38										14 38							
Berry Brow	d					13 41										14 41							
Lockwood	d					13 44										14 44							
Huddersfield	a					13 49										14 49							
Darton	d									13 38										14 38			
Wakefield Kirkgate 4 31	a			12 57				13 27		13 50			13 57					14 27		14 49			14 57
	d			12 58				13 28		13 50			13 58					14 28		14 50			14 58
Normanton	d									13 54										14 54			
Castleford	a									14 00										15 00			
Woodlesford	a									14 12										15 12			
Leeds 10 31	a		13 29	13 18				13 49		14 25		14 31	14 18					14 48		15 25		15 31	15 18

A From Lincoln to Adwick
B From Manchester Airport to Cleethorpes
C To Scunthorpe
D To Bridlington
E To Scarborough
F To Sheffield
G To Adwick

Nottingham, Sheffield - Barnsley - Huddersfield and Leeds

Network Diagram - see first page of Table 31

			NT	NT	NT	NT	NT		NT	TP	NT	NT	NT	NT	NT	NT	NT		NT	TP	NT	NT	NT	NT	NT	NT
										◇1										◇1						
			A		B		C			D			A		E		C			D			F		E	
Nottingham 8		d										14 15										15 15				
Langley Mill		d										14 30										15 32				
Alfreton		d										14 38										15 40				
Chesterfield		d										14 52										15 53				
Dronfield		d										14 59										16 00				
Sheffield 7	29,31	a										15 16										16 16				
		d	14 24	14 36	14 41	14 50	14 53		15 06	15 11	15 14	15 18	15 24	15 36	15 41	15 50	15 53		16 06	16 11	16 14	16 18	16 23	16 36	16 41	16 50
Meadowhall 4	29,31	a	14 29	14 41	14 46	14 55	14 58		15 11	15 16	15 20	15 23	15 29	15 41	15 46	15 55	15 58		16 11	16 16	16 20	16 23	16 29	16 41	16 46	16 55
		d		14 42		14 56			15 12		15 20	15 24		15 42		15 56			16 12		16 20	16 24		16 42		16 56
Chapeltown		d		14 48					15 18					15 48					16 18					16 48		
Elsecar		d							15 23										16 23					16 53		
Wombwell		d		14 55					15 27					15 55					16 27					16 57		
Barnsley		a		15 00		15 11			15 32			15 40		16 00		16 11			16 32			16 40		17 02		17 11
		d		15 01		15 12			15 33			15 42		16 01		16 12			16 33			16 42		17 03		17 12
Dodworth		d		15 07										16 07										17 09		
Silkstone Common		d		15 11										16 11										17 13		
Penistone		d		15 18										16 18										17 20		
Denby Dale		d		15 24										16 24										17 26		
Shepley		d		15 29										16 29										17 31		
Stocksmoor		d		15 32										16 32										17 34		
Brockholes		d		15 36										16 36										17 38		
Honley		d		15 38										16 38										17 40		
Berry Brow		d		15 41										16 41										17 43		
Lockwood		d		15 44										16 44										17 46		
Huddersfield		a		15 49										16 49										17 50		
Darton		d							15 38										16 38							
Wakefield Kirkgate 4	31	a				15 27			15 49			15 57				16 27			16 49			16 57				17 28
		d				15 28			15 50			15 58				16 28			16 50			16 58				17 28
Normanton		d							15 54										16 54							
Castleford		a							16 00										17 00							
Woodlesford		a							16 12										17 12							
Leeds 10	31	a				15 49			16 25		16 31	16 18				16 49			17 25		17 31	17 18				17 48

			NT		NT	TP	NT	NT	NT	NT	NT	NT	NT		NT	NT	NT	TP	NT	NT	NT	NT	NT		NT	TP
						◇1												◇1								◇1
			C			D			F		B		G					D	F		E		H			D
Nottingham 8		d						16 15									17 15									
Langley Mill		d						16 32									17 32									
Alfreton		d						16 40									17 40									
Chesterfield		d						16 55									17 52									
Dronfield		d						17 02									17 59									
Sheffield 7	29,31	a						17 17									18 14									
		d	16 53		17 06	17 11	17 13	17 18	17 27	17 36	17 41	17 50	17 53		18 06	18 13	18 18	18 24	18 29	18 36	18 41	18 50	19 00		19 06	19 11
Meadowhall 4	29,31	a	16 58		17 11	17 16	17 20	17 23	17 32	17 41	17 46	17 55	17 58		18 12	18 20	18 23	18 29	18 34	18 41	18 46	18 55	19 06		19 12	19 16
		d			17 12		17 20	17 24		17 42		17 56			18 12	18 20	18 24			18 42		18 56			19 12	
Chapeltown		d			17 18					17 48					18 18					18 48					19 18	
Elsecar		d			17 23					17 53					18 23					18 53					19 23	
Wombwell		d			17 27					17 57					18 27					18 57					19 27	
Barnsley		a			17 32			17 40		18 02		18 11			18 33		18 42			19 02		19 14			19 33	
		d			17 33			17 42		18 03		18 12			18 33		18 42			19 08		19 14			19 33	
Dodworth		d								18 09										19 14						
Silkstone Common		d								18 13										19 18						
Penistone		d								18 27										19 25						
Denby Dale		d								18 33										19 31						
Shepley		d								18 38										19 36						
Stocksmoor		d								18 41										19 39						
Brockholes		d								18 45										19 43						
Honley		d								18 47										19 45						
Berry Brow		d								18 50										19 48						
Lockwood		d								18 53										19 51						
Huddersfield		a								18 57										19 56						
Darton		d			17 38										18 38										19 38	
Wakefield Kirkgate 4	31	a			17 49			17 57				18 28			18 50		18 59					19 29			19 50	
		d			17 50			17 58				18 32			18 50		18 59					19 32			19 50	
Normanton		d			17 54										18 54										19 54	
Castleford		a			18 00										19 00										20 00	
Woodlesford		a			18 12										19 13										20 12	
Leeds 10	31	a			18 25		18 32	18 18				18 51			19 27	19 31	19 23					19 55			20 26	

A To Scunthorpe
B To Scarborough
C From Lincoln to Adwick
D From Manchester Airport to Cleethorpes
E To Bridlington
F To Doncaster
G From Lincoln to Hull
H From Retford to Doncaster

Table 34

Mondays to Fridays

Nottingham, Sheffield - Barnsley - Huddersfield and Leeds

Network Diagram - see first page of Table 31

	NT	NT	NT	NT	NT	NT	NT		NT	TP	NT	NT	NT	NT	NT	NT	TP FO		NT	NT	TP FX	NT	NT FO	NT FX
										◇1							◇1				◇1			
			A		B		C			D	E			F			D		B		G			
Nottingham 8 ⇌ d		18 15										19 15												
Langley Mill d		18 32										19 32												
Alfreton d		18 40										19 40												
Chesterfield d		18 52										19 52												
Dronfield d		18 59										19 59												
Sheffield 7 29,31 ⇌ a		19 17										20 15												
d	19 18	19 22	19 30	19 36	19 44	19 51	19 58		20 06	20 11	20 15	20 18	20 27	20 38	20 41	21 09	21 11		21 15	21 30	21 34	21 41	22 06	22 06
Meadowhall 4 29,31 ⇌ a	19 24	19 27	19 35	19 41	19 49	19 56	20 03		20 11	20 16	20 20	20 24	20 34	20 44	20 47	21 14	21 16		21 21	21 35	21 39	21 46	22 11	22 11
d	19 25	19 28		19 42		19 57			20 12			20 24	20 35		20 47	21 15				21 36		21 47	22 12	22 12
Chapeltown d				19 48					20 18						20 53	21 21						21 53	22 18	22 18
Elsecar d				19 53					20 23							21 26							22 23	22 23
Wombwell d				19 57					20 27						21 00	21 30						22 00	22 27	22 27
Barnsley a		19 42		20 02		20 12			20 32			20 40			21 07	21 35						22 05	22 32	22 32
d		19 42		20 08		20 12			20 33			20 42			21 08	21 36						22 08		22 33
Dodworth d				20 14											21 14							22 14		
Silkstone Common d				20 18											21 18							22 18		
Penistone d				20 25											21 25							22 25		
Denby Dale d				20 31											21 31							22 31		
Shepley d				20 36											21 36							22 36		
Stocksmoor d				20 39											21 39							22 39		
Brockholes d				20 43											21 43							22 43		
Honley d				20 45											21 45							22 45		
Berry Brow d				20 48											21 48							22 48		
Lockwood d				20 51											21 51							22 51		
Huddersfield a				20 55											21 56							22 57		
Darton d									20 38							21 41								22 38
Wakefield Kirkgate 4 31 a		19 58				20 28			20 49			20 57				21 52								22 51
d		19 58				20 28			20 50			20 58				21 52								22 51
Normanton d									20 54							21 57								22 56
Castleford a									21 00							22 04								23 01
Woodlesford a									21 12							22 14								23 14
Leeds 10 31 a	20 34	20 19				20 48			21 26			21 20	21 47			22 29				22 46				23 30

	TP	NT	NT FO		NT	NT	NT	NT FX	NT FO	NT FX	NT
	◇1										
	D					E				H	A
Nottingham 8 ⇌ d		21 11									
Langley Mill d		21 38									
Alfreton d		21 46									
Chesterfield d		22 00									
Dronfield d		22 07									
Sheffield 7 29,31 ⇌ a		22 19									
d	22 11				22 24	22 34	22 41	23 15	23 15	23 24	23 27
Meadowhall 4 29,31 ⇌ a	22 16				22 30	22 39	22 46	23 20	23 20	23 29	23 32
d					22 30		22 47	23 21	23 21	23 30	
Chapeltown d							22 53			23 36	
Elsecar d							22 58			23 41	
Wombwell d							23 02			23 45	
Barnsley a							23 07			23 50	
d							23 08			23 51	
Dodworth d							23 14				
Silkstone Common d							23 18				
Penistone d							23 25				
Denby Dale d							23 31				
Shepley d							23 36				
Stocksmoor d							23 39				
Brockholes d							23 43				
Honley d							23 45				
Berry Brow d							23 48				
Lockwood d							23 51				
Huddersfield a							23 55				
Darton d										23 56	
Wakefield Kirkgate 4 31 a										00s10	
d			22 51								
Normanton d			22 56								
Castleford a			23 01								
Woodlesford a			23 14								
Leeds 10 31 a			23 30		23 41			00 29	00 30		

A To Doncaster
B To Beverley
C To Bridlington
D From Manchester Airport to Cleethorpes
E To Goole
F To Scunthorpe
G To Cleethorpes
H To Wakefield Westgate

Nottingham, Sheffield - Barnsley - Huddersfield and Leeds

Network Diagram - see first page of Table 31

			NT	NT	NT	NT	NT	NT	NT	NT	NT		TP	NT	NT	NT	EM	NT	NT	NT	EM		NT	TP	NT	NT
					A			B			B		◇1 C			D	◇ E		F	G	◇1 H			◇1 C		
Nottingham 8		d															06 40									07 11
Langley Mill		d																								07 27
Alfreton		d															07 02									07 35
Chesterfield		d															07 13				07 42					07 50
Dronfield		d															07 20				07 49					
Sheffield 7	29,31	a															07 31				07 59					08 08
		d	23p15	05 15	05 29	05 43	06 06	06 12	06 28	06 36	06 52		06 55	07 06	07 14	07 24		07 36	07 41	07 51			08 06	08 11	08 14	08 18
Meadowhall 4	29,31	a	23p20	05 20	05 34	05 48	06 11	06 17	06 33	06 41	06 57		07 00	07 11	07 20	07 29		07 41	07 46	07 57			08 11	08 16	08 21	08 25
		d	23p21	05 21		05 49	06 12		06 34	06 42				07 12	07 21			07 42		07 57			08 12		08 22	08 25
Chapeltown		d		05 27		05 55	06 18			06 48				07 18				07 48					08 18			
Elsecar		d		05 32		06 01	06 23							07 23									08 23			
Wombwell		d		05 36		06 05	06 27			06 55				07 27				07 55					08 27			
Barnsley		a		05 43		06 11	06 32			07 00				07 32				08 00		08 11			08 32			08 40
		d					06 33			07 01				07 33				08 01		08 12			08 33			08 42
Dodworth		d								07 07								08 07								
Silkstone Common		d								07 11								08 11								
Penistone		d								07 18								08 18								
Denby Dale		d								07 24								08 24								
Shepley		d								07 29								08 29								
Stocksmoor		d								07 32								08 32								
Brockholes		d								07 36								08 36								
Honley		d								07 38								08 38								
Berry Brow		d								07 41								08 41								
Lockwood		d								07 44								08 44								
Huddersfield		a								07 49								08 49								
Darton		d					06 38							07 38									08 38			
Wakefield Kirkgate 4	31	a					06 49							07 49						08 27			08 49			08 57
		d					06 50							07 50						08 28			08 50			08 58
Normanton		d					06 54							07 54									08 54			
Castleford		a					07 00							07 59									09 00			
Woodlesford		a					07 12							08 11									09 12			
Leeds 10	31	a	00 30				07 28		07 44					08 25	08 32					08 49			09 25		09 40	09 20

			NT	NT	EM	NT	NT		NT	NT	TP	NT	NT	NT	NT	NT	NT		NT	NT	NT	TP	NT	NT	NT	NT
			D		◇ E	F			B		◇1 C			D	I		J			K		◇1 C			D	
Nottingham 8		d			07 45								08 11											09 15		
Langley Mill		d											08 31											09 32		
Alfreton		d			08 07								08 39											09 40		
Chesterfield		d			08 18								08 51											09 52		
Dronfield		d			08 25								08 58											09 59		
Sheffield 7	29,31	a			08 38								09 16											10 15		
		d	08 25	08 36		08 41	08 51		08 53	09 06	09 11	09 14	09 18	09 25	09 29	09 36	09 41		09 50	09 53	10 06	10 11	10 14	10 18	10 24	10 36
Meadowhall 4	29,31	a	08 30	08 41		08 46	08 56		08 59	09 11	09 15	09 20	09 23	09 33	09 35	09 41	09 46		09 55	09 58	10 11	10 16	10 20	10 23	10 29	10 41
		d		08 42			08 57			09 12		09 21	09 24			09 42			09 56		10 12		10 21	10 24		10 42
Chapeltown		d		08 48						09 18						09 48					10 18					10 48
Elsecar		d								09 23											10 23					
Wombwell		d		08 55						09 27						09 55					10 27					10 55
Barnsley		a		09 00			09 11			09 32			09 40			10 00			10 11		10 32			10 40		11 00
		d		09 01			09 12			09 33			09 42			10 01			10 12		10 33			10 42		11 01
Dodworth		d		09 07												10 07										11 07
Silkstone Common		d		09 11												10 11										11 11
Penistone		d		09 18												10 18										11 18
Denby Dale		d		09 24												10 24										11 24
Shepley		d		09 29												10 29										11 29
Stocksmoor		d		09 32												10 32										11 32
Brockholes		d		09 36												10 36										11 36
Honley		d		09 38												10 38										11 38
Berry Brow		d		09 41												10 41										11 41
Lockwood		d		09 44												10 44										11 44
Huddersfield		a		09 49												10 49										11 49
Darton		d								09 38											10 38					
Wakefield Kirkgate 4	31	a					09 27			09 49			09 57						10 27		10 49			10 57		
		d					09 28			09 50			09 58						10 28		10 50			10 58		
Normanton		d								09 54											10 54					
Castleford		a								10 00											11 00					
Woodlesford		a								10 12											11 12					
Leeds 10	31	a					09 49			10 25		10 40	10 18						10 48		11 25		11 40	11 18		

A To Beverley
B To Adwick
C From Manchester Airport to Cleethorpes
D To Scunthorpe
E To Liverpool Lime Street
F To Bridlington
G From Retford
H From Derby
I To York
J To Scarborough
K From Lincoln to Adwick

Table 34

Saturdays

Nottingham, Sheffield - Barnsley - Huddersfield and Leeds

Network Diagram - see first page of Table 31

Station			NT		NT	NT	NT	TP	NT	NT	NT	NT	NT		NT	NT	NT	TP	NT	NT	NT	NT	NT		NT	NT
								◇1										◇1								
			A			B		C			D		E			B		C			D		A			B
Nottingham 8		d								10 15										11 15						
Langley Mill		d								10 32										11 31						
Alfreton		d								10 40										11 39						
Chesterfield		d								10 52										11 52						
Dronfield		d								10 59																
Sheffield 7	29,31	a								11 15										12 16						
		d	10 41		10 50	10 53	11 06	11 11	11 14	11 18	11 24	11 36	11 41		11 50	11 53	12 06	12 11	12 14	12 18	12 24	12 36	12 41		12 50	12 53
Meadowhall 4	29,31	a	10 46		10 55	10 58	11 11	11 16	11 20	11 23	11 29	11 41	11 46		11 55	11 58	12 11	12 16	12 20	12 23	12 29	12 41	12 46		12 55	12 58
		d			10 56		11 12		11 21	11 24		11 42			11 56		12 12		12 21	12 24		12 42			12 56	
Chapeltown		d					11 18					11 48					12 18					12 48				
Elsecar		d					11 23										12 23									
Wombwell		d					11 27					11 55					12 27					12 55				
Barnsley		a			11 11		11 32			11 40		12 00			12 10		12 32			12 40		13 00			13 11	
		d			11 12		11 33			11 41		12 01			12 11		12 33			12 42		13 01			13 12	
Dodworth		d										12 07										13 07				
Silkstone Common		d										12 11										13 11				
Penistone		d										12 18										13 18				
Denby Dale		d										12 24										13 24				
Shepley		d										12 29										13 29				
Stocksmoor		d										12 32										13 32				
Brockholes		d										12 36										13 36				
Honley		d										12 38										13 38				
Berry Brow		d										12 41										13 41				
Lockwood		d										12 44										13 44				
Huddersfield		a										12 49										13 49				
Darton		d					11 38										12 38									
Wakefield Kirkgate 4	31	a			11 27		11 49			11 57					12 27		12 49			12 57					13 27	
		d			11 28		11 50			11 58					12 28		12 50			12 58					13 28	
Normanton		d					11 54										12 54									
Castleford		a					12 00										13 00									
Woodlesford		a					12 12										13 12									
Leeds 10	31	a			11 48		12 25		12 40	12 18					12 48		13 25		13 43	13 18					13 49	

Station			NT	TP	NT	NT	NT	NT	NT		NT	NT	NT	NT	TP	NT	NT	NT	NT		NT	NT	NT	NT	TP	NT
				◇1											◇1										◇1	
				C			D	F			A		B		C			D			E		B		C	
Nottingham 8		d				12 15											13 15									
Langley Mill		d				12 32											13 32									
Alfreton		d				12 40											13 40									
Chesterfield		d				12 52											13 52									
Dronfield		d				12 59											13 59									
Sheffield 7	29,31	a				13 15											14 15									
		d	13 06	13 11	13 14	13 18	13 24	13 29	13 36		13 41	13 50	13 53	14 06	14 11	14 14	14 18	14 24	14 36		14 41	14 50	14 53	15 06	15 11	15 14
Meadowhall 4	29,31	a	13 11	13 16	13 20	13 23	13 29	13 34	13 41		13 46	13 55	13 58	14 11	14 16	14 20	14 23	14 29	14 41		14 46	14 55	14 58	15 11	15 16	15 20
		d	13 12		13 21	13 24			13 42			13 56		14 12		14 21	14 24		14 42			14 56		15 12		15 21
Chapeltown		d	13 18						13 48					14 18					14 48					15 18		
Elsecar		d	13 23											14 23										15 23		
Wombwell		d	13 27						13 55					14 27					14 55					15 27		
Barnsley		a	13 32			13 40			14 00			14 11		14 32			14 40		15 00			15 11		15 32		
		d	13 33			13 42			14 01			14 12		14 33			14 42		15 01			15 12		15 33		
Dodworth		d							14 07										15 07							
Silkstone Common		d							14 11										15 11							
Penistone		d							14 18										15 18							
Denby Dale		d							14 24										15 24							
Shepley		d							14 29										15 29							
Stocksmoor		d							14 32										15 32							
Brockholes		d							14 36										15 36							
Honley		d							14 38										15 38							
Berry Brow		d							14 41										15 41							
Lockwood		d							14 44										15 44							
Huddersfield		a							14 49										15 49							
Darton		d	13 38											14 38										15 38		
Wakefield Kirkgate 4	31	a	13 50			13 57						14 27		14 49			14 57					15 27		15 49		
		d	13 50			13 58						14 28		14 50			14 58					15 28		15 50		
Normanton		d	13 54											14 54										15 54		
Castleford		a	14 00											15 00										16 00		
Woodlesford		a	14 12											15 12										16 12		
Leeds 10	31	a	14 25		14 40	14 18						14 48		15 25		15 40	15 18					15 49		16 25		16 40

A To Bridlington
B From Lincoln to Adwick
C From Manchester Airport to Cleethorpes
D To Scunthorpe
E To Scarborough
F To York

Table 34

Saturdays

Nottingham, Sheffield - Barnsley - Huddersfield and Leeds

Network Diagram - see first page of Table 31

		NT	NT	NT	NT	NT	NT	NT	TP	NT	NT	NT	NT	NT	NT	NT	NT	TP	NT	NT	NT	NT
									◇1									◇1				
			A		B		C		D			E		B		C		D			E	
Nottingham 8	d	14 15									15 15									16 15		
Langley Mill	d	14 30									15 32									16 32		
Alfreton	d	14 38									15 40									16 40		
Chesterfield	d	14 52									15 53									16 55		
Dronfield	d	14 59									16 00									17 02		
Sheffield 7 29,31	a	15 15									16 14									17 17		
	d	15 18	15 24	15 36	15 41	15 50	15 53	16 06	16 11	16 14	16 18	16 24	16 36	16 41	16 50	16 53	17 06	17 11	17 14	17 18	17 25	17 36
Meadowhall 4 29,31	a	15 23	15 29	15 41	15 46	15 55	15 58	16 11	16 16	16 20	16 23	16 29	16 41	16 46	16 55	16 58	17 11	17 16	17 21	17 23	17 30	17 41
	d	15 24		15 42		15 56		16 12		16 21	16 24		16 42		16 56		17 12		17 21	17 24		17 42
Chapeltown	d			15 48				16 18					16 48				17 18					17 48
Elsecar	d							16 23					16 53				17 23					17 53
Wombwell	d			15 55				16 27					16 57				17 27					17 57
Barnsley	a	15 40		16 00		16 11		16 32			16 40		17 02		17 11		17 32			17 40		18 02
	d	15 42		16 01		16 12		16 33			16 42		17 03		17 12		17 33			17 42		18 03
Dodworth	d			16 07									17 09									18 09
Silkstone Common	d			16 11									17 13									18 13
Penistone	d			16 18									17 20									18 20
Denby Dale	d			16 24									17 26									18 26
Shepley	d			16 29									17 31									18 31
Stocksmoor	d			16 32									17 34									18 34
Brockholes	d			16 36									17 38									18 38
Honley	d			16 38									17 40									18 40
Berry Brow	d			16 41									17 43									18 43
Lockwood	d			16 44									17 46									18 46
Huddersfield	a			16 49									17 50									18 51
Darton	d							16 38									17 38					
Wakefield Kirkgate 4 31	a	15 57				16 27		16 49			16 57				17 28		17 49			17 57		
	d	15 58				16 28		16 50			16 58				17 28		17 50			17 58		
Normanton	d							16 54									17 54					
Castleford	a							17 00									18 00					
Woodlesford	a							17 12									18 12					
Leeds 10 31	a	16 18				16 49		17 25		17 41	17 18				17 48		18 25		18 44	18 18		

		NT	NT	NT	NT	NT	NT	TP	NT	NT	NT	NT	NT	NT	TP	NT	NT	NT	NT	NT	NT	NT	NT
								◇1							◇1								
		F		G				D	E		B		H		D			A		I		B	
Nottingham 8	d						17 15									18 15							
Langley Mill	d						17 32									18 32							
Alfreton	d						17 40									18 40							
Chesterfield	d						17 52									18 55							
Dronfield	d						17 59									19 02							
Sheffield 7 29,31	a						18 14									19 15							
	d	17 41	17 50	17 53	18 06	18 13	18 18	18 24	18 29	18 36	18 41	18 50	19 00	19 06	19 11	19 16	19 18	19 25	19 36	19 44	19 51	19 58	20 06
Meadowhall 4 29,31	a	17 46	17 55	17 57	18 12	18 20	18 23	18 29	18 34	18 41	18 46	18 55	19 06	19 11	19 16	19 22	19 24	19 30	19 41	19 49	19 56	20 03	20 11
	d		17 56		18 12	18 21	18 24			18 42		18 56		19 12		19 22	19 25		19 42		19 57		20 12
Chapeltown	d				18 18					18 48				19 18					19 48				20 18
Elsecar	d				18 23					18 53				19 23					19 53				20 23
Wombwell	d				18 27					18 57				19 27					19 57				20 27
Barnsley	a		18 11		18 33		18 42			19 02		19 14		19 33		19 40			20 02		20 12		20 32
	d		18 12		18 33		18 42			19 03		19 14		19 33		19 42			20 08		20 12		20 33
Dodworth	d									19 09									20 14				
Silkstone Common	d									19 13									20 18				
Penistone	d									19 20									20 25				
Denby Dale	d									19 26									20 31				
Shepley	d									19 31									20 36				
Stocksmoor	d									19 34									20 39				
Brockholes	d									19 38									20 43				
Honley	d									19 41									20 45				
Berry Brow	d									19 44									20 48				
Lockwood	d									19 46									20 51				
Huddersfield	a									19 51									20 55				
Darton	d				18 38									19 38									20 38
Wakefield Kirkgate 4 31	a		18 28		18 50		18 59					19 29		19 50		19 58					20 28		20 49
	d		18 32		18 50		18 59					19 32		19 50		19 58					20 28		20 50
Normanton	d				18 54									19 54									20 54
Castleford	a				19 00									20 00									21 00
Woodlesford	a				19 13									20 12									21 12
Leeds 10 31	a		18 51		19 27	19 43	19 23					19 55		20 26		20 20	20 38				20 48		21 26

A To Scunthorpe
B To Bridlington
C From Lincoln to Adwick
D From Manchester Airport to Cleethorpes
E To Doncaster
F To Scarborough
G From Lincoln to Hull
H From Retford to Doncaster
I To Beverley

Table 34

Saturdays

Nottingham, Sheffield - Barnsley - Huddersfield and Leeds

Network Diagram - see first page of Table 31

		TP ◇1 A	NT B	NT	NT	NT C		NT	NT	NT D	NT	TP ◇1 E	NT	NT	TP ◇1 A	NT		NT	NT	NT B	NT	NT F			
Nottingham 8	d			19 15												21 15									
Langley Mill	d			19 32												21 31									
Alfreton	d			19 40												21 39									
Chesterfield	d			19 52												21 50									
Dronfield	d			19 59												21 57									
Sheffield 7 29,31	a			20 15												22 13									
	d	20 11	20 15	20 18	20 27	20 38		20 41	21 06	21 14	21 30	21 34	21 41	22 06	22 11				22 24	22 30	22 41	23 27			
Meadowhall 4 29,31	a	20 16	20 20	20 24	20 34	20 44		20 47	21 11	21 21	21 36	21 39	21 46	22 11	22 16				22 30	22 35	22 46	23 32			
	d			20 24	20 35			20 47	21 12		21 36		21 47	22 12					22 30		22 47				
Chapeltown	d							20 53	21 18				21 53	22 18							22 53				
Elsecar	d								21 23					22 23							22 58				
Wombwell	d							21 00	21 27				22 00	22 27							23 02				
Barnsley	a			20 40				21 07	21 33				22 05	22 32							23 07				
	d			20 42				21 08	21 33				22 08								23 08				
Dodworth	d							21 14					22 14								23 14				
Silkstone Common	d							21 18					22 18								23 18				
Penistone	d							21 25					22 25								23 25				
Denby Dale	d							21 31					22 31								23 31				
Shepley	d							21 36					22 36								23 36				
Stocksmoor	d							21 39					22 39								23 39				
Brockholes	d							21 43					22 43								23 43				
Honley	d							21 45					22 45								23 45				
Berry Brow	d							21 48					22 48								23 48				
Lockwood	d							21 51					22 51								23 51				
Huddersfield	a							21 56					22 56								23 59				
Darton	d								21 38																
Wakefield Kirkgate 4 31	a			20 57					21 52																
	d			20 58					21 52									22 51							
Normanton	d								21 57									22 56							
Castleford	a								22 04									23 02							
Woodlesford	a								22 14									23 14							
Leeds 10 31	a			21 20	21 47				22 29		22 45							23 30	23 40						

Sundays

		NT F	NT	NT G	TP H (bus)	NT ◇	NT	NT	TP ◇1 I	TP J (bus)		NT G	EM ◇ K	NT	NT F	NT	NT	NT	TP ◇1 L	NT		TP J (bus)	NT B	NT G	NT
Nottingham 8	d												09 31			10 06				11 15					
Langley Mill	d															10 27				11 31					
Alfreton	d												09 53			10 35				11 39					
Chesterfield	d												10 08			10 54				11 51					
Dronfield	d												10 15			11 01				11 58					
Sheffield 7 29,31	a												10 33			11 15				12 15					
	d	08 00	08 39	08 45	09 00	09 17	09 36	09 39	09 52	09 55		10 26		10 39	11 05	11 17	11 36	11 49	12 11	12 16		12 20	12 24	12 28	12 35
Meadowhall 4 29,31	a	08 05	08 44	08 50	09 20	09 22	09 41	09 44	09 57	10 15		10 31		10 44	11 10	11 22	11 41	11 54	12 16	12 22		12 40	12 29	12 33	12 40
	d		08 45			09 23	09 42	09 45						10 45		11 23	11 42	11 55		12 23					12 41
Chapeltown	d		08 51					09 51						10 51				12 01							
Elsecar	d		08 56					09 56						10 56				12 06							
Wombwell	d		09 00					10 00						11 00				12 10							
Barnsley	a		09 05			09 37		10 05						11 05		11 37		12 15		12 37					12 55
	d		09 10			09 37		10 06						11 10		11 37		12 16		12 37					13 06
Dodworth	d							10 12										12 22							13 12
Silkstone Common	d							10 16										12 26							13 16
Penistone	d							10 23										12 33							13 23
Denby Dale	d							10 29										12 39							13 29
Shepley	d							10 34										12 44							13 34
Stocksmoor	d							10 37										12 47							13 37
Brockholes	d							10 41										12 51							13 41
Honley	d							10 43										12 53							13 43
Berry Brow	d							10 46										12 56							13 46
Lockwood	d							10 49										12 59							13 49
Huddersfield	a							10 53										13 08							13 53
Darton	d		09 15											11 15											
Wakefield Kirkgate 4 31	a		09 29			09 55								11 29		11 52				12 52					
	d		09 30			09 55								11 30		11 53				12 53					
Normanton	d		09 34											11 34											
Castleford	a		09 40											11 40											
Woodlesford	a		09 52											11 51											
Leeds 10 31	a		10 04			10 15	10 52							12 05		12 18	12 53			13 18					

- **A** From Manchester Airport to Cleethorpes
- **B** To Goole
- **C** To Scunthorpe
- **D** To Beverley
- **E** 17 December until 31 December and from 18 February. To Cleethorpes
- **F** To Doncaster
- **G** To Scarborough
- **H** from 8 January until 12 February. To Doncaster
- **I** until 1 January and from 19 February. To Cleethorpes
- **J** from 8 January until 12 February. To Cleethorpes
- **K** To Liverpool Lime Street
- **L** until 1 January and from 19 February. From Manchester Airport to Cleethorpes

Table 34

Sundays

Nottingham, Sheffield - Barnsley - Huddersfield and Leeds

Network Diagram - see first page of Table 31

			NT	TP	TP	NT	NT		NT	NT	TP	TP	NT	TP	NT	NT	NT		TP	NT	TP	NT	NT	NT	NT	TP
				◇1							◇1	◇1							◇1							◇1
				A	B		C				D	E		F	G	H			I		F	J	C		K	I
					🚌									🚌							🚌					
Nottingham 8		d				12 19							13 09							14 19						
Langley Mill		d				12 35							13 27							14 35						
Alfreton		d				12 43							13 35							14 43						
Chesterfield		d				12 54							13 46							14 54						
Dronfield		d				13 01							13 53							15 01						
Sheffield 7	29,31	a				13 16							14 07							15 15						
		d	12 39	13 11	13 15	13 17	13 24		13 36	13 39	14 10	14 11	14 17	14 20	14 22	14 28	14 39		15 11	15 17	15 20	15 24	15 28	15 36	15 39	16 11
Meadowhall 4	29,31	a	12 44	13 16	13 35	13 22	13 29		13 41	13 44	14 15	14 16	14 22	14 40	14 27	14 33	14 44		15 16	15 22	15 40	15 29	15 33	15 41	15 42	16 16
		d	12 45			13 23			13 42	13 45			14 23				14 45			15 23				15 42	15 43	
Chapeltown		d	12 55							13 51							14 51								15 49	
Elsecar		d	13 00							13 56							14 56								15 54	
Wombwell		d	13 04							14 00							15 00								15 58	
Barnsley		a	13 09			13 37				14 05			14 37				15 05			15 37					16 03	
		d	13 10			13 37				14 06			14 37				15 10			15 37					16 04	
Dodworth		d								14 12															16 10	
Silkstone Common		d								14 16															16 14	
Penistone		d								14 23															16 21	
Denby Dale		d								14 29															16 27	
Shepley		d								14 34															16 32	
Stocksmoor		d								14 37															16 35	
Brockholes		d								14 41															16 39	
Honley		d								14 43															16 41	
Berry Brow		d								14 46															16 44	
Lockwood		d								14 49															16 47	
Huddersfield		a								14 53															16 53	
Darton		d	13 15														15 15									
Wakefield Kirkgate 4	31	a	13 29			13 52							14 52				15 29			15 52						
		d	13 30			13 53							14 53				15 30			15 53						
Normanton		d	13 34														15 34									
Castleford		a	13 40														15 40									
Woodlesford		a	13 51														15 51									
Leeds 10	31	a	14 04			14 18			14 47				15 18				16 04			16 18				16 54		

			NT		TP	NT	NT	NT	NT	NT	TP	NT	TP		NT	NT	NT	NT	TP	NT	TP	NT	NT		NT	NT
											◇1								◇1							
					F	G	H	L	M		I		F		J	C			I		F	J	N			L
					🚌								🚌								🚌					
Nottingham 8		d	15 12									16 14								17 14						
Langley Mill		d	15 34									16 30								17 30						
Alfreton		d	15 44									16 38								17 38						
Chesterfield		d	15 53									16 50								17 51						
Dronfield		d	16 00									16 57								17 58						
Sheffield 7	29,31	a	16 15									17 15								18 14						
		d	16 17		16 20	16 24	16 28	16 36	16 39	16 54	17 11	17 17	17 20		17 25	17 28	17 36	17 39	18 11	18 17	18 20	18 25	18 28		18 39	18 57
Meadowhall 4	29,31	a	16 22		16 40	16 29	16 33	16 41	16 44	16 59	17 16	17 22	17 40		17 30	17 33	17 44	17 46	18 16	18 22	18 40	18 30	18 34		18 44	19 04
		d	16 23						16 45	17 00		17 23					17 44	17 46		18 23					18 45	
Chapeltown		d							16 51									17 52							18 51	
Elsecar		d							16 56									17 58							18 56	
Wombwell		d							17 00									18 01							19 00	
Barnsley		a	16 37						17 05	17 14		17 37						18 08		18 37					19 05	
		d	16 37						17 10	17 15		17 37						18 10		18 37					19 10	
Dodworth		d								17 21								18 16								
Silkstone Common		d								17 25								18 20								
Penistone		d								17 32								18 27								
Denby Dale		d								17 38								18 34								
Shepley		d								17 43								18 39								
Stocksmoor		d								17 46								18 41								
Brockholes		d								17 50								18 45								
Honley		d								17 52								18 48								
Berry Brow		d								17 55								18 51								
Lockwood		d								17 58								18 53								
Huddersfield		a								18 05								18 58								
Darton		d							17 15																19 15	
Wakefield Kirkgate 4	31	a	16 52						17 29			17 52								18 52					19 29	
		d	16 53						17 30			17 53								18 53					19 30	
Normanton		d							17 34																19 34	
Castleford		a							17 40																19 41	
Woodlesford		a							17 51																19 53	
Leeds 10	31	a	17 18						18 05			18 18					18 50			19 18					20 05	

A until 1 January, from 19 February. From Manchester Piccadilly to Doncaster
B from 8 January until 12 February. To Doncaster
C To Bridlington
D from 1 April. From Manchester Airport to Cleethorpes
E until 1 January, from 19 February until 25 March. From Manchester Airport to Cleethorpes
F from 8 January until 12 February. To Cleethorpes
G To Goole
H To Scarborough
I until 1 January and from 19 February. From Manchester Airport to Cleethorpes
J To Doncaster
K From Retford
L To York
M From Lincoln
N To Beverley

Table 34

Sundays

Nottingham, Sheffield - Barnsley - Huddersfield and Leeds

Network Diagram - see first page of Table 31

		TP	NT	TP	NT	NT	NT	NT	TP	NT	TP	NT	NT	NT	TP	TP	NT	NT	NT	NT	NT	TP	TP	NT	NT
		◇1							◇1						◇1							◇1			
		A		B	C			D	A		B	E			A	B	D			D	C	F	B		C
				🚌							🚌					🚌							🚌		
Nottingham 8 🚌	d		18 14							19 19				20 13										21 30	
Langley Mill	d		18 30							19 35				20 29										21 52	
Alfreton	d		18 38							19 43				20 37										22 00	
Chesterfield	d		18 52							19 54				20 48										22 13	
Dronfield	d		18 58							20 01														22 20	
Sheffield 7 29,31 🚌	a		19 16							20 15				21 14										22 36	
	d	19 11	19 16	19 20	19 29	19 36	19 39	20 02	20 11	20 17	20 20	20 28	20 39		21 11	21 20	21 24	21 36	21 43	22 13	22 26	22 30	22 30	22 39	23 34
Meadowhall 4 29,31 🚌	a	19 16	19 22	19 40	19 34	19 41	19 44	20 08	20 16	20 22	20 40	20 33	20 44		21 16	21 40	21 29	21 41	21 48	22 18	22 31	22 35	22 50	22 44	23 39
	d		19 23			19 42	19 45			20 23			20 45					21 42	21 49					22 45	
Chapeltown	d						19 51						20 51						21 55					22 51	
Elsecar	d						19 56						20 56						22 00					22 56	
Wombwell	d						20 00						21 00						22 04					23 00	
Barnsley	a		19 37				20 05			20 37			21 06						22 09					23 05	
	d		19 37				20 06			20 37			21 10											23 10	
Dodworth	d						20 12																		
Silkstone Common	d						20 16																		
Penistone	d						20 23																		
Denby Dale	d						20 29																		
Shepley	d						20 34																		
Stocksmoor	d						20 37																		
Brockholes	d						20 41																		
Honley	d						20 43																		
Berry Brow	d						20 46																		
Lockwood	d						20 49																		
Huddersfield	a						20 53																		
Darton	d												21 15											23 15	
Wakefield Kirkgate 4 31	a		19 52							20 52			21 29											23 26	
	d		19 53							20 53			21 30											23 27	
Normanton	d												21 34											23 34	
Castleford	a												21 40											23 40	
Woodlesford	a												21 51											23 53	
Leeds 10 31	a		20 18			20 52				21 16			22 04					22 52						00 05	

A until 1 January, from 19 February. From Manchester Airport to Cleethorpes

B from 8 January until 12 February. To Cleethorpes

C To Doncaster

D To Hull

E To Goole

F until 1 January and from 19 February. To Cleethorpes

Leeds and Huddersfield - Barnsley - Sheffield, Nottingham

Network Diagram - see first page of Table 31

Miles	Miles		NT MX	NT MX A	NT MX	NT	NT	TP ◇1 B	NT	NT C	NT		NT	NT	NT D	TP ◇1 E	NT	NT F	NT	NT	TP ◇1 E		NT	NT G
0	—	**Leeds** 10 31 d	22p37		23p09						05 33			06 05					06 38	06 43			07 05	
6	—	Woodlesford d	22p45																06 46					
10¾	—	Castleford d	22p56																06 57					
14¼	—	Normanton d	23p01																07 03					
17¼	—	Wakefield Kirkgate 4 31 a	23p10											06 21					07 07				07 25	
—	—	d	23p10										06 04	06 21					07 08				07 25	
24¾	—	Darton d	23p24										06 15						07 19					
—	0	**Huddersfield** d															06 10							
—	1¼	Lockwood d															06 13							
—	2¼	Berry Brow d															06 16							
—	3¼	Honley d															06 19							
—	4¼	Brockholes d															06 22							
—	6¼	Stocksmoor d															06 26							
—	7¼	Shepley d															06 28							
—	9½	Denby Dale d															06 34							
—	13½	Penistone d															06 42							
—	16¾	Silkstone Common d															06 47							
—	18	Dodworth d															06 51							
28¼	21	**Barnsley** a	23p31										06 20	06 37			06 57		07 25				07 40	
—	—	d	23p31			05 23			05 50				06 21	06 38			06 58		07 25				07 40	
32¼	25	Wombwell d	23p36			05 28			05 55				06 26				07 03		07 30					
33¾	26½	Elsecar d	23p40			05 32			05 59				06 30				07 07		07 34					
37	29¾	Chapeltown d	23p45			05 37			06 04				06 35				07 12		07 39					
40¾	33½	**Meadowhall** 29,31 ⇌ a	23p51		00 08	05 43			06 15		06 37		06 41	06 49			07 21		07 48	07 44			07 53	
—	—	d	23p51	23p54	00 09	05 43		05 58	06 15	06 27	06 38		06 42	06 49	06 52	06 58	07 21	07 33	07 49	07 45	07 53		07 54	08 06
44¼	37	**Sheffield** 7 29,31 ⇌ a	00 02	00 04	00 23	05 54		06 08	06 25	06 38	06 47		06 55	07 00	07 05	07 06	07 29	07 40	07 58	07 56	08 00		08 05	08 18
—	—	d					06 00							07 03									08 05	
51¼	—	Dronfield d					06 10							07 13									08 15	
56½	—	Chesterfield d					06 16							07 20									08 24	
66½	—	Alfreton d					06 30							07 33									08 35	
72¾	—	Langley Mill d					06 37							07 40									08 42	
84¾	—	**Nottingham** a					07 06							08 02									09 02	

	NT	NT D	NT H	NT	NT I	NT	NT		NT G	TP ◇1 E	NT J	NT	NT H	NT	NT K	NT I	NT		NT	NT G	TP ◇1 E	NT J	NT	NT H
Leeds 10 31 d			07 29	07 35		07 48	08 02						08 32	08 37			08 48		09 05					09 32
Woodlesford d			07 37										08 40											09 40
Castleford d			07 48										08 51											09 51
Normanton d			07 54		←								08 57			←								09 57
Wakefield Kirkgate 4 31 a			08 00	07 54	08 00		08 23						09 03	08 54		09 03			09 23					10 01
d			08 04	07 55	08 04		08 23						09 05	08 55		09 05			09 23					10 04
Darton d			→		08 15								→			09 17								→
Huddersfield d	07 10											08 10											09 13	
Lockwood d	07 13											08 13											09 16	
Berry Brow d	07 16											08 16											09 19	
Honley d	07 19											08 19											09 22	
Brockholes d	07 22											08 22											09 25	
Stocksmoor d	07 26											08 26											09 29	
Shepley d	07 28											08 28											09 31	
Denby Dale d	07 34											08 34											09 36	
Penistone d	07 42											08 42											09 44	
Silkstone Common d	07 47											08 47											09 49	
Dodworth d	07 51											08 51											09 53	
Barnsley a	07 57			08 11	08 21		08 39					08 57		09 11		09 23			09 39				10 00	
d	07 58			08 14	08 24		08 40					08 58		09 14		09 24			09 40				10 01	
Wombwell d	08 03				08 29							09 03				09 29							10 06	
Elsecar d	08 07				08 33							09 07				09 33								
Chapeltown d	08 12				08 38							09 12				09 38							10 13	
Meadowhall 29,31 ⇌ a	08 20			08 31	08 45	08 50	08 52					09 20		09 27		09 46	09 50		09 52				10 20	
d	08 21	08 23		08 31	08 45	08 51	08 52		08 57	09 01	09 16	09 21		09 28	09 33	09 46	09 50		09 52	09 55	10 01	10 08	10 21	
Sheffield 7 29,31 ⇌ a	08 29	08 33		08 39	08 56	08 59	09 02		09 05	09 08	09 26	09 28		09 37	09 41	09 56	10 00		10 02	10 05	10 08	10 19	10 30	
d							09 05												10 05					
Dronfield d							09 15												10 15					
Chesterfield d							09 22												10 22					
Alfreton d							09 32												10 33					
Langley Mill d							09 40												10 40					
Nottingham a							10 00												11 00					

A until 23 March. From Hull
B From Doncaster to Manchester Airport
C From Doncaster
D From Hull
E From Cleethorpes to Manchester Airport
F From Doncaster to Worksop
G From Adwick
H To Sheffield
I From Leeds
J From Bridlington
K From Scunthorpe to Lincoln

Leeds and Huddersfield - Barnsley - Sheffield, Nottingham

Network Diagram - see first page of Table 31

			NT	NT	NT		NT	NT	NT	TP	NT	NT	NT	NT	NT		NT	NT	NT	NT	TP	NT	NT	NT	NT	
				A	B				C	◇1 D ✠	E		F		A		B			C	◇1 D ✠	E		G	F	
Leeds 10	31	d	09 37				09 48	10 05					10 32	10 37				10 48	11 05						11 32	
Woodlesford		d											10 40												11 40	
Castleford		d											10 51												11 51	
Normanton		d			←								10 57				←								11 57	
Wakefield Kirkgate 4	31	a	09 55		10 01			10 23					11 01	10 54			11 01		11 23						12 01	
		d	09 56		10 04			10 23					11 04	10 55			11 04		11 23						12 04	
Darton		d			10 15								→				11 15								→	
Huddersfield		d										10 13											11 13			
Lockwood		d										10 16											11 16			
Berry Brow		d										10 19											11 19			
Honley		d										10 22											11 22			
Brockholes		d										10 25											11 25			
Stocksmoor		d										10 29											11 29			
Shepley		d										10 31											11 31			
Denby Dale		d										10 36											11 36			
Penistone		d										10 44											11 44			
Silkstone Common		d										10 49											11 49			
Dodworth		d										10 53											11 53			
Barnsley		a	10 12		10 21			10 39				11 00		11 11			11 21		11 39				12 00			
		d	10 14		10 24			10 40				11 01		11 14			11 24		11 40				12 01			
Wombwell		d			10 29							11 06					11 29						12 06			
Elsecar		d			10 33												11 33									
Chapeltown		d			10 38							11 13					11 38						12 13			
Meadowhall	29,31 🚌	a	10 27		10 46		10 50	10 52				11 20		11 27			11 46	11 51	11 52				12 20			
		d	10 28	10 33	10 47		10 50	10 52	10 58	11 01	11 08	11 21		11 28	11 33		11 46	11 51	11 52	11 56	12 01	12 08	12 21	12 24		
Sheffield 7	29,31 🚌	a	10 37	10 41	10 56		11 01	11 02	11 05	11 08	11 20	11 30		11 37	11 41		11 57	12 01	12 02	12 05	12 08	12 19	12 30	12 36		
		d						11 05											12 05							
Dronfield		d						11 15											12 15							
Chesterfield		d						11 22											12 22							
Alfreton		d						11 33											12 33							
Langley Mill		d						11 40											12 40							
Nottingham		a						12 00											13 01							

			NT	NT	NT	NT	NT	NT	TP	NT	NT		NT	NT	NT	NT	NT	NT	NT	TP	NT		NT	NT	NT	NT
				A	B			C	◇1 D ✠	E			F		A	B			C	◇1 D ✠	H			F		A
Leeds 10	31	d	11 37			11 48	12 05						12 32	12 37			12 48	13 05						13 32	13 37	
Woodlesford		d											12 40											13 40		
Castleford		d											12 51											13 51		
Normanton		d			←								12 57			←								13 57		
Wakefield Kirkgate 4	31	a	11 54		12 01		12 23						13 02	12 54		13 02		13 23						14 01	13 54	
		d	11 55		12 04		12 23						13 04	12 55		13 04		13 23						14 04	13 55	
Darton		d			12 15								→			13 17								→		
Huddersfield		d									12 13												13 13			
Lockwood		d									12 16												13 16			
Berry Brow		d									12 19												13 19			
Honley		d									12 22												13 22			
Brockholes		d									12 25												13 25			
Stocksmoor		d									12 29												13 29			
Shepley		d									12 31												13 31			
Denby Dale		d									12 36												13 36			
Penistone		d									12 44												13 44			
Silkstone Common		d									12 49												13 49			
Dodworth		d									12 53												13 53			
Barnsley		a	12 11		12 21		12 39				13 00			13 11		13 22		13 39					14 00		14 11	
		d	12 14		12 24		12 40				13 01			13 14		13 24		13 40					14 01		14 14	
Wombwell		d			12 29						13 06					13 29							14 06			
Elsecar		d			12 33											13 33										
Chapeltown		d			12 38						13 13					13 38							14 13			
Meadowhall	29,31 🚌	a	12 27		12 46	12 51	12 52				13 20			13 27		13 46	13 51	13 52					14 20		14 27	
		d	12 28	12 33	12 46	12 51	12 52	12 56	13 01	13 07	13 21			13 28	13 33	13 46	13 51	13 52	13 56	14 01	14 05		14 21		14 28	14 34
Sheffield 7	29,31 🚌	a	12 37	12 41	12 56	13 01	13 02	13 05	13 08	13 20	13 29			13 37	13 41	13 56	14 01	14 02	14 05	14 08	14 20		14 29		14 37	14 42
		d					13 05											14 05								
Dronfield		d					13 15											14 15								
Chesterfield		d					13 22											14 22								
Alfreton		d					13 33											14 33								
Langley Mill		d					13 40											14 40								
Nottingham		a					14 00											15 00								

A From Scunthorpe to Lincoln
B From Leeds
C From Adwick
D From Cleethorpes to Manchester Airport
E From Bridlington
F To Sheffield
G From York
H From Scarborough

Leeds and Huddersfield - Barnsley - Sheffield, Nottingham

Network Diagram - see first page of Table 31

Station	Table	a/d	NT A	NT	NT	NT B	TP ◇1 C		NT D	NT	NT E	NT	NT F	NT A	NT	NT	NT B		TP ◇1 C	NT G	NT H	NT	NT E	NT	EM ◇ I	NT F
Leeds 10	31	d		13 48	14 05						14 32	14 37			14 48	15 05							15 32	15 37		
Woodlesford		d									14 40												15 40			
Castleford		d									14 51												15 51			
Normanton		d	←								14 57			←									15 57			
Wakefield Kirkgate 4	31	a	14 01		14 23						15 01	14 54		15 01		15 23							16 01	15 54		
		d	14 04		14 23						15 04	14 55		15 04		15 23							16 04	15 55		
Darton		d	14 15								↪			15 15									↪			
Huddersfield		d								14 13												15 13				
Lockwood		d								14 16												15 16				
Berry Brow		d								14 19												15 19				
Honley		d								14 22												15 22				
Brockholes		d								14 25												15 25				
Stocksmoor		d								14 29												15 29				
Shepley		d								14 31												15 31				
Denby Dale		d								14 36												15 36				
Penistone		d								14 44												15 44				
Silkstone Common		d								14 49												15 49				
Dodworth		d								14 53												15 53				
Barnsley		a	14 21		14 39					15 00		15 13		15 21		15 39						16 00		16 11		
		d	14 24		14 40					15 01		15 14		15 24		15 40						16 01		16 14		
Wombwell		d	14 29							15 06				15 29								16 06				
Elsecar		d	14 33											15 33												
Chapeltown		d	14 38							15 13				15 38								16 13				
Meadowhall	29,31	a	14 46	14 50	14 52					15 20		15 27		15 46	15 50	15 51						16 20		16 27		
		d	14 46	14 50	14 52	14 56	15 01		15 07	15 21		15 28	15 33	15 46	15 50	15 52	15 57		16 01	16 07	16 18	16 21		16 28		16 33
Sheffield 7	29,31	a	14 56	15 01	15 02	15 05	15 08		15 19	15 29		15 37	15 41	15 56	16 01	16 03	16 05		16 08	16 20	16 27	16 29		16 37		16 41
		d			15 05											16 04									16 38	
Dronfield		d			15 15											16 14									16 48	
Chesterfield		d			15 22											16 21									16 56	
Alfreton		d			15 33											16 32									17 07	
Langley Mill		d			15 40											16 40										
Nottingham		a			16 00											17 00									17 31	

Station	Table	a/d	NT A		NT	NT	NT J	TP ◇1 C	NT D	NT	NT E	NT	NT F		EM ◇ I	NT A	NT	NT	NT K	TP ◇1 C	NT D	NT	NT E		NT	NT L
Leeds 10	31	d			15 48	16 05					16 32	16 37					16 48	17 05					17 32		17 37	
Woodlesford		d									16 40												17 40			
Castleford		d									16 51												17 51			
Normanton		d	←								16 57					←		17 18					17 57			
Wakefield Kirkgate 4	31	a	16 01			16 23					17 01	16 54				17 01		17 22					18 01		17 54	
		d	16 04			16 23					17 04	16 55				17 04		17 23					18 04		17 55	
Darton		d	16 15								↪					17 15							↪			
Huddersfield		d								16 13												17 13				
Lockwood		d								16 16												17 16				
Berry Brow		d								16 19												17 19				
Honley		d								16 22												17 22				
Brockholes		d								16 25												17 25				
Stocksmoor		d								16 29												17 29				
Shepley		d								16 31												17 31				
Denby Dale		d								16 36												17 36				
Penistone		d								16 44												17 44				
Silkstone Common		d								16 49												17 49				
Dodworth		d								16 53												17 53				
Barnsley		a	16 21			16 39				17 00		17 11				17 21		17 39				18 00			18 11	
		d	16 24			16 40				17 01		17 14				17 24		17 40				18 01			18 14	
Wombwell		d	16 29							17 06						17 29						18 06				
Elsecar		d	16 33													17 33										
Chapeltown		d	16 38							17 13						17 38						18 13				
Meadowhall	29,31	a	16 46		16 50	16 52				17 20		17 27				17 46	17 50	17 51				18 20			18 27	
		d	16 46		16 50	16 52	16 55	17 01	17 09	17 21		17 28	17 33			17 46	17 50	17 52	17 57	18 01	18 07	18 21			18 28	18 32
Sheffield 7	29,31	a	16 56		17 00	17 02	17 05	17 08	17 20	17 32		17 37	17 41			17 56	18 01	18 03	18 04	18 08	18 19	18 29			18 38	18 42
		d				17 05									17 44			18 05								
Dronfield		d				17 15									17 56			18 15								
Chesterfield		d				17 22									18 02			18 22								
Alfreton		d				17 33									18 12			18 33								
Langley Mill		d				17 40												18 40								
Nottingham		a				18 00									18 34			19 00								

A From Leeds
B From Adwick
C From Cleethorpes to Manchester Airport
D From Bridlington
E To Sheffield
F From Scunthorpe to Lincoln
G From Scarborough
H From Sheffield
I From Liverpool Lime Street to Norwich
J From Adwick to Retford
K From Doncaster
L From Scunthorpe

Leeds and Huddersfield - Barnsley - Sheffield, Nottingham

Network Diagram - see first page of Table 31

		NT	NT	NT	NT	NT	NT	TP		NT	NT	NT	NT	NT	NT	NT	NT	NT		NT	TP	NT	NT	NT	NT
								◇1													◇1				
		A	B	B			C	D		E	F	G	A	B		A				C	D	G		H	B
								⚮																	
Leeds 10	31 d			17 43	17 46	18 05								18 32	18 43		18 48	19 05							19 37
Woodlesford	d													18 40											19 45
Castleford	d													18 51											19 56
Normanton	d	←												19 00		←									20 02
Wakefield Kirkgate 4	31 a	18 01				18 23								19 04	18 59	19 04		19 24							20 06
	d	18 04				18 23								19 05	18 59	19 05		19 24							20 07
Darton	d	18 15												↪		19 19									↪
Huddersfield	d		17 56	18 22																			19 18		
Lockwood	d		17 59	18 25																			19 21		
Berry Brow	d		18 02	18 28																			19 24		
Honley	d		18 05	18 31																			19 27		
Brockholes	d		18 08	18 34																			19 30		
Stocksmoor	d		18 12	18 38																			19 34		
Shepley	d		18 14	18 40																			19 36		
Denby Dale	d		18 19	18 45																			19 43		
Penistone	d		18 31	18 53																			19 49		
Silkstone Common	d		18 36	18 58																			19 54		
Dodworth	d		18 40	19 02							←		←										19 58		
Barnsley	a	18 21	18 47	19 08		18 39					18 47		19 08		19 15	19 26		19 40					20 05		
	d	18 24	18 55	19 10		18 40					18 55		19 10		19 18	19 26		19 40					20 06		
Wombwell	d	18 29	↪	↪							19 00		19 15			19 31							20 11		
Elsecar	d	18 33									19 04					19 35									
Chapeltown	d	18 38									19 09		19 22			19 38							20 18		
Meadowhall 29,31 🚌	a	18 46			18 50	18 52					19 17		19 27		19 33	19 47	19 50	19 52					20 24		
	d	18 46			18 50	18 52	18 57	19 01		19 06	19 17	19 28	19 30		19 34	19 47	19 51	19 52		19 57	20 01	20 08	20 26	20 33	
Sheffield 7 29,31 🚌	a	18 56			19 00	19 04	19 06	19 08		19 17	19 27	19 37	19 42		19 43	19 56	19 59	20 04		20 05	20 08	20 18	20 36	20 41	
	d					19 05												20 05							
Dronfield	d					19 15												20 15							
Chesterfield	d					19 22												20 22							
Alfreton	d					19 33												20 33							
Langley Mill	d					19 40												20 40							
Nottingham	a					20 00												21 00							

		NT	NT	NT		TP	NT	EM	NT	NT	NT	NT	TP	NT		NT	NT	NT	NT	NT	NT	NT	NT	NT	
						◇1		◇					◇1												
			A			I		J	K	L			D	C		G		M					N		
Leeds 10	31 d	19 43		19 48			20 30				20 37	20 48							21 37	21 48		22 37		23 09	
Woodlesford	d										20 45								21 45			22 45			
Castleford	d										20 56								21 56			22 56			
Normanton	d		←								21 02								22 02			23 01			
Wakefield Kirkgate 4	31 a	19 59	20 06				20 46				21 06								22 06			23 10			
	d	20 00	20 07				20 46				21 07								22 07			23 10			
Darton	d		20 19								21 18								22 21			23 24			
Huddersfield	d								20 18								21 18				22 18				
Lockwood	d								20 21								21 21				22 21				
Berry Brow	d								20 24								21 24				22 24				
Honley	d								20 27								21 27				22 27				
Brockholes	d								20 30								21 30				22 30				
Stocksmoor	d								20 34								21 34				22 34				
Shepley	d								20 36								21 36				22 36				
Denby Dale	d								20 41								21 41				22 41				
Penistone	d								20 49								21 49				22 49				
Silkstone Common	d								20 54								21 54				22 54				
Dodworth	d								20 58								21 58				22 58				
Barnsley	a	20 16	20 24				21 02		21 08		21 24						22 05		22 27		23 05	23 31			
	d	20 16	20 24				21 03		21 12		21 24						22 06		22 28		23 06	23 31			
Wombwell	d		20 29						21 17		21 29						22 11		22 33		23 11	23 36			
Elsecar	d		20 33								21 33								22 37		23 15	23 40			
Chapeltown	d		20 38						21 24		21 38						22 18		22 42		23 20	23 45			
Meadowhall 29,31 🚌	a	20 33	20 45	20 51			21 18		21 28		21 45	21 51					22 24		22 47	22 52	23 25	23 51		00 08	
	d	20 35	20 46	20 51		21 09	21 20		21 30	21 34	21 46	21 52	21 59	22 03		22 07	22 25	22 44	22 47	22 53	23 26	23 51	23{54	00 09	
Sheffield 7 29,31 🚌	a	20 44	20 58	21 02		21 19	21 30		21 40	21 46	21 57	22 04	22 08	22 11		22 21	22 36	22 54	22 58	23 02	23 36	00 02	00}04	00 23	
	d							21 39																	
Dronfield	d							21 49																	
Chesterfield	d							21 55																	
Alfreton	d							22 05																	
Langley Mill	d							22 12																	
Nottingham	a							22 38																	

A From Leeds
B To Sheffield
C From Doncaster
D From Cleethorpes to Manchester Airport
E From Scarborough
F From Huddersfield
G From Hull
H From Doncaster to Worksop
I From Cleethorpes
J From Liverpool Lime Street
K To Retford
L From Bridlington
M From Scunthorpe
N until 23 March. From Hull

Leeds and Huddersfield - Barnsley - Sheffield, Nottingham

Network Diagram - see first page of Table 31

Station	Table		NT	NT A	NT	NT	TP ◇1 B	NT	NT C	NT	NT D		TP ◇1 E 🛒	NT	NT C	NT	NT	TP ◇1 E 🛒	NT	NT F	NT		NT D	NT G	NT	NT H
Leeds 10	31	d	22p37		23p09											06 38	06 43		07 05					07 29	07 35	
Woodlesford		d	22p45													06 46								07 37		
Castleford		d	22p56													06 57								07 48		
Normanton		d	23p01													07 03								07 54		←
Wakefield Kirkgate 4	31	a	23p10													07 07			07 25					08 00	07 54	08 00
		d	23p10													07 08			07 25					08 04	07 55	08 04
Darton		d	23p24													07 19								→		08 15
Huddersfield		d												06 10							07 10					
Lockwood		d												06 13							07 13					
Berry Brow		d												06 16							07 16					
Honley		d												06 19							07 19					
Brockholes		d												06 22							07 22					
Stocksmoor		d												06 26							07 26					
Shepley		d												06 28							07 28					
Denby Dale		d												06 34							07 34					
Penistone		d												06 42							07 42					
Silkstone Common		d												06 47							07 47					
Dodworth		d												06 51							07 51					
Barnsley		a	23p31											06 57		07 25			07 40		07 57				08 11	08 21
		d	23p31			05 23		05 50		06 21				06 58		07 25			07 40		07 58				08 14	08 24
Wombwell		d	23p36			05 28		05 55		06 26				07 03		07 30					08 03					08 29
Elsecar		d	23p40			05 32		05 59		06 30				07 07		07 34					08 07					08 33
Chapeltown		d	23p45			05 37		06 04		06 35				07 12		07 39					08 12					08 38
Meadowhall	29,31 🚊	a	23p51		00 08	05 43		06 10		06 41				07 21		07 48	07 46		07 53		08 20				08 31	08 45
		d	23p51	23p54	00 09	05 43	05 58	06 10	06 30	06 42	06 52		06 58	07 21	07 32	07 49	07 47	07 53	07 54	08 07	08 21		08 25		08 31	08 46
Sheffield 7	29,31 🚊	a	00 02	00 04	00 23	05 54	06 08	06 25	06 38	06 55	07 05		07 06	07 29	07 40	07 58	07 54	08 00	08 05	08 18	08 29		08 32		08 39	08 56
		d								07 03									08 05							
Dronfield		d								07 13									08 15							
Chesterfield		d								07 20									08 24							
Alfreton		d								07 33									08 35							
Langley Mill		d								07 40									08 42							
Nottingham		a								08 02									09 02							

Station	Table		NT	NT	NT F	TP ◇1 E 🛒	NT		NT I	NT G	NT	NT J	NT H	NT	NT	NT F	TP ◇1 E 🛒		NT I	NT	NT G	NT	NT J	NT H	NT	NT
Leeds 10	31	d	07 48	08 05						08 32	08 37			08 48	09 05						09 32	09 37			09 48	10 05
Woodlesford		d								08 40											09 40					
Castleford		d								08 51											09 51					
Normanton		d								08 57			←								09 57			←		
Wakefield Kirkgate 4	31	a		08 23						09 03	08 54		09 03		09 23						10 01	09 55		10 01		10 23
		d		08 23						09 05	08 55		09 05		09 23						10 04	09 56		10 04		10 23
Darton		d								→			09 17								→			10 15		
Huddersfield		d					08 10													09 13						
Lockwood		d					08 13													09 16						
Berry Brow		d					08 16													09 19						
Honley		d					08 19													09 22						
Brockholes		d					08 22													09 25						
Stocksmoor		d					08 26													09 29						
Shepley		d					08 28													09 31						
Denby Dale		d					08 34													09 36						
Penistone		d					08 42													09 44						
Silkstone Common		d					08 47													09 49						
Dodworth		d					08 51													09 53						
Barnsley		a		08 39			08 57				09 11		09 23		09 39					10 00		10 12		10 21		10 39
		d		08 40			08 58				09 14		09 24		09 40					10 01		10 14		10 24		10 40
Wombwell		d					09 03						09 29							10 06				10 29		
Elsecar		d					09 07						09 33											10 33		
Chapeltown		d					09 12						09 38							10 13				10 38		
Meadowhall	29,31 🚊	a	08 49	08 52			09 19				09 27		09 46	09 50	09 52					10 20		10 27		10 46	10 50	10 52
		d	08 51	08 52	08 56	09 01	09 20		09 24		09 29	09 33	09 46	09 50	09 52	09 55	10 01		10 08	10 21		10 28	10 33	10 47	10 50	10 52
Sheffield 7	29,31 🚊	a	08 59	09 02	09 05	09 08	09 28		09 33		09 37	09 41	09 56	10 00	10 02	10 05	10 08		10 19	10 30		10 37	10 41	10 56	11 00	11 02
		d		09 05											10 04											11 05
Dronfield		d		09 16											10 14											11 15
Chesterfield		d		09 23											10 21											11 22
Alfreton		d		09 32											10 32											11 35
Langley Mill		d		09 41											10 40											11 40
Nottingham		a		10 00											11 00											12 00

A until 24 March. From Hull
B From Doncaster to Manchester Airport
C From Doncaster
D From Hull
E From Cleethorpes to Manchester Airport
F From Adwick
G To Sheffield
H From Leeds
I From Bridlington
J From Scunthorpe to Lincoln

Table 34

Saturdays

Leeds and Huddersfield - Barnsley - Sheffield, Nottingham

Network Diagram - see first page of Table 31

			NT		TP	NT	NT	NT	NT	NT	NT	NT	NT		NT	TP	NT	NT	NT	NT	NT	NT	NT		NT	NT
					◇1											◇1										
			A		B	C		D		E	F				A	B	C		G	D		E	F			
Leeds 10	31	d						10 32	10 37			10 48	11 05							11 32	11 37				11 48	12 05
Woodlesford		d						10 40												11 40						
Castleford		d						10 51												11 51						
Normanton		d						10 57			←									11 57			←			
Wakefield Kirkgate 4	31	a						11 01	10 54		11 01		11 23							12 01	11 54		12 01			12 23
		d						11 04	10 55		11 04		11 23							12 04	11 55		12 04			12 23
Darton		d						↪			11 15									↪			12 15			
Huddersfield		d					10 13											11 13								
Lockwood		d					10 16											11 16								
Berry Brow		d					10 19											11 19								
Honley		d					10 22											11 22								
Brockholes		d					10 25											11 25								
Stocksmoor		d					10 29											11 29								
Shepley		d					10 31											11 31								
Denby Dale		d					10 36											11 36								
Penistone		d					10 44											11 44								
Silkstone Common		d					10 49											11 49								
Dodworth		d					10 53											11 53								
Barnsley		a					11 00		11 11		11 21		11 39					12 00			12 11		12 21			12 39
		d					11 01		11 14		11 24		11 40					12 01			12 14		12 24			12 40
Wombwell		d					11 06				11 29							12 06					12 29			
Elsecar		d									11 33												12 33			
Chapeltown		d					11 13				11 38							12 13					12 38			
Meadowhall	29,31	a					11 20		11 27		11 46	11 50	11 52					12 20			12 27		12 46		12 49	12 52
		d	10 58		11 01	11 08	11 21		11 28	11 33	11 46	11 50	11 52		11 58	12 01	12 08	12 21	12 24		12 28	12 33	12 46		12 50	12 52
Sheffield 7	29,31	a	11 06		11 08	11 20	11 30		11 37	11 41	11 57	12 00	12 02		12 05	12 08	12 20	12 30	12 36		12 37	12 41	12 56		13 00	13 02
		d											12 05													13 05
Dronfield		d											12 15													13 15
Chesterfield		d											12 22													13 22
Alfreton		d											12 33													13 33
Langley Mill		d											12 40													13 40
Nottingham		a											13 01													14 00

			NT	TP	NT	NT	NT	NT	NT		NT	NT	NT	NT	TP	NT	NT	NT	NT		NT	NT	NT	NT	NT	TP
				◇1											◇1											◇1
			A	B	C		D		E		F			A	B	H		D			E	F			A	B
Leeds 10	31	d					12 32	12 37				12 48	13 05					13 32	13 37				13 48	14 05		
Woodlesford		d					12 40											13 40								
Castleford		d					12 51											13 51								
Normanton		d					12 57				←							13 57				←				
Wakefield Kirkgate 4	31	a					13 02	12 54			13 02		13 23					14 01	13 54			14 01		14 23		
		d					13 04	12 55			13 04		13 23					14 04	13 55			14 04		14 23		
Darton		d					↪				13 17							↪				14 15				
Huddersfield		d				12 08											13 13									
Lockwood		d				12 11											13 16									
Berry Brow		d				12 14											13 19									
Honley		d				12 17											13 22									
Brockholes		d				12 20											13 25									
Stocksmoor		d				12 24											13 29									
Shepley		d				12 26											13 31									
Denby Dale		d				12 36											13 36									
Penistone		d				12 44											13 44									
Silkstone Common		d				12 49											13 49									
Dodworth		d				12 53											13 53									
Barnsley		a				13 00		13 11			13 22		13 38				14 00		14 11			14 21		14 39		
		d				13 01		13 14			13 24		13 40				14 01		14 14			14 24		14 40		
Wombwell		d				13 06					13 29						14 06					14 29				
Elsecar		d									13 33											14 33				
Chapeltown		d				13 13					13 38						14 13					14 38				
Meadowhall	29,31	a				13 20		13 27			13 46	13 49	13 52				14 20		14 27			14 46	14 49	14 52		
		d	12 58	13 01	13 08	13 21		13 28	13 33		13 46	13 50	13 52	13 58	14 01	14 08	14 21		14 28		14 33	14 46	14 50	14 52	14 58	15 01
Sheffield 7	29,31	a	13 05	13 08	13 20	13 29		13 37	13 41		13 56	14 00	14 02	14 05	14 08	14 20	14 29		14 37		14 40	14 56	15 00	15 02	15 05	15 08
		d											14 05											15 05		
Dronfield		d											14 15											15 15		
Chesterfield		d											14 22											15 22		
Alfreton		d											14 33											15 33		
Langley Mill		d											14 40											15 40		
Nottingham		a											15 00											16 00		

A From Adwick
B From Cleethorpes to Manchester Airport
C From Bridlington
D To Sheffield
E From Scunthorpe to Lincoln
F From Leeds
G From York
H From Scarborough

Table 34

Saturdays

Leeds and Huddersfield - Barnsley - Sheffield, Nottingham

Network Diagram - see first page of Table 31

Station	Table		NT	NT	NT		NT	NT	NT	NT	NT	NT	TP	NT	NT		NT	NT	NT	EM	NT	NT	NT	NT	NT	
													◇■1							◇						
			A		B			C	D			E	F	G	H			B		I	C	D			J	
													[trolley]													
Leeds ■10	31	d			14 32		14 37			14 48	15 05							15 32	15 37				15 48	16 05		
Woodlesford		d			14 40													15 40								
Castleford		d			14 51													15 51								
Normanton		d			14 57				←									15 57				←				
Wakefield Kirkgate ■4	31	a			15 01		14 54		15 01		15 23							16 01	15 54			16 01		16 23		
		d			15 04		14 55		15 04		15 23							16 04	15 55			16 04		16 23		
Darton		d			→				15 15									→				16 15				
Huddersfield		d		14 13													15 13									
Lockwood		d		14 16													15 16									
Berry Brow		d		14 19													15 19									
Honley		d		14 22													15 22									
Brockholes		d		14 25													15 25									
Stocksmoor		d		14 29													15 29									
Shepley		d		14 31													15 31									
Denby Dale		d		14 36													15 36									
Penistone		d		14 44													15 44									
Silkstone Common		d		14 49													15 49									
Dodworth		d		14 53													15 53									
Barnsley		a		15 00			15 13		15 21		15 39						16 00		16 11			16 21		16 39		
		d		15 01			15 14		15 24		15 40						16 01		16 14			16 24		16 40		
Wombwell		d		15 06					15 29								16 06					16 29				
Elsecar		d							15 33													16 33				
Chapeltown		d		15 13					15 38								16 13					16 38				
Meadowhall	29,31	a		15 20			15 27		15 46	15 49	15 51						16 20		16 27			16 46	16 49	16 52		
		d	15 07	15 21			15 28	15 33	15 46	15 50	15 52	15 57	16 01	16 07	16 18		16 21		16 28		16 33	16 46	16 50	16 52	16 55	
Sheffield ■7	29,31	a	15 20	15 29			15 37	15 41	15 56	16 00	16 03	16 05	16 08	16 22	16 27		16 29		16 37		16 41	16 56	17 00	17 02	17 05	
		d									16 04									16 38				17 05		
Dronfield		d									16 14									16 48				17 15		
Chesterfield		d									16 21									16 53				17 22		
Alfreton		d									16 32									17 04				17 33		
Langley Mill		d									16 40													17 40		
Nottingham		a									17 00									17 29				18 00		

Station	Table		TP	NT	NT	NT	NT	NT	EM	NT	NT		NT	NT	TP	NT	NT	NT	NT	NT	NT		NT	NT	NT	TP
			◇■1						◇						◇■1											◇■1
			F	A		B		C	I	D				K	F	A		B		C	D				K	F
			[trolley]												[trolley]											[trolley]
Leeds ■10	31	d				16 32	16 37				16 48		17 05					17 32	17 37				17 48	18 05		
Woodlesford		d				16 40												17 40								
Castleford		d				16 51												17 51								
Normanton		d				16 57				←			17 18					17 57			←					
Wakefield Kirkgate ■4	31	a				17 01	16 54			17 01			17 22					18 01	17 54		18 01			18 23		
		d				17 04	16 55			17 04			17 23					18 04	17 55		18 04			18 23		
Darton		d				→				17 15								→			18 15					
Huddersfield		d			16 13												17 13									
Lockwood		d			16 16												17 16									
Berry Brow		d			16 19												17 19									
Honley		d			16 22												17 22									
Brockholes		d			16 25												17 25									
Stocksmoor		d			16 29												17 29									
Shepley		d			16 31												17 31									
Denby Dale		d			16 36												17 36									
Penistone		d			16 44												17 44									
Silkstone Common		d			16 49												17 49									
Dodworth		d			16 53												17 53									
Barnsley		a			17 00		17 11			17 21			17 39				18 00		18 11		18 21			18 39		
		d			17 01		17 14			17 24			17 40				18 01		18 14		18 24			18 40		
Wombwell		d			17 06					17 29							18 06				18 29					
Elsecar		d								17 33											18 33					
Chapeltown		d			17 13					17 38							18 13				18 38					
Meadowhall	29,31	a			17 20		17 27			17 46	17 49		17 51				18 20		18 27		18 46		18 50	18 52		
		d	17 01	17 08	17 21		17 28	17 33		17 46	17 50		17 52	17 57	18 01	18 08	18 21		18 28	18 33	18 46		18 50	18 52	18 56	19 01
Sheffield ■7	29,31	a	17 08	17 19	17 32		17 37	17 41		17 56	18 00		18 03	18 05	18 08	18 21	18 29		18 38	18 41	18 56		19 00	19 03	19 06	19 08
		d							17 44				18 06											19 05		
Dronfield		d							17 55				18 15											19 15		
Chesterfield		d							18 01				18 22											19 22		
Alfreton		d							18 11				18 33											19 33		
Langley Mill		d											18 40											19 40		
Nottingham		a							18 33				19 00											20 00		

A From Bridlington
B To Sheffield
C From Scunthorpe to Lincoln
D From Leeds
E From Adwick
F From Cleethorpes to Manchester Airport
G From Scarborough
H From York
I From Liverpool Lime Street to Norwich
J From Adwick to Retford
K From Doncaster

Table 34

Saturdays

Leeds and Huddersfield - Barnsley - Sheffield, Nottingham

Network Diagram - see first page of Table 31

			NT	NT	NT	NT	NT		NT	NT	NT	NT	TP	NT	NT	NT	NT		NT	NT	NT	TP	NT	EM	NT	NT
													◇1									◇1		◇		
			A		B	C			D			E	F	B		G	C			D		H		I	J	K
Leeds 10	31	d				18 32	18 37			18 48	19 05						19 37		19 43		19 48		20 30			
Woodlesford		d				18 40											19 45									
Castleford		d				18 51											19 56									
Normanton		d				19 00			←								20 02			←						
Wakefield Kirkgate 4	31	a				19 04	18 54		19 04		19 24						20 06		19 59	20 06			20 46			
		d				19 05	18 55		19 05		19 24						20 07		20 00	20 07			20 46			
Darton		d				→			19 19								→			20 19						
Huddersfield		d		18 13											19 18										20 18	
Lockwood		d		18 16											19 21										20 21	
Berry Brow		d		18 19											19 24										20 24	
Honley		d		18 22											19 27										20 27	
Brockholes		d		18 25											19 30										20 30	
Stocksmoor		d		18 29											19 34										20 34	
Shepley		d		18 31											19 36										20 36	
Denby Dale		d		18 36											19 41										20 41	
Penistone		d		18 44											19 49										20 52	
Silkstone Common		d		18 49											19 54										20 57	
Dodworth		d		18 53											19 58										21 01	
Barnsley		a		19 01			19 11		19 26		19 40				20 05				20 16	20 24			21 02		21 09	
		d		19 01			19 14		19 26		19 40				20 06				20 16	20 24			21 03		21 12	
Wombwell		d		19 06					19 31						20 11					20 29					21 17	
Elsecar		d							19 35											20 33						
Chapeltown		d		19 13					19 40						20 18					20 38					21 24	
Meadowhall	29,31 🚌	a		19 20			19 28		19 47	19 50	19 52				20 24				20 33	20 45	20 50		21 19		21 28	
		d	19 08	19 20	19 28		19 30		19 47	19 51	19 52	19 57	20 01	20 08	20 24	20 33			20 35	20 46	20 51	21 09	21 20		21 29	21 35
Sheffield 7	29,31 🚌	a	19 19	19 30	19 37		19 39		19 56	20 00	20 04	20 06	20 08	20 18	20 36	20 41			20 44	20 58	21 00	21 19	21 30		21 41	21 46
		d									20 05													21 38		
Dronfield		d									20 15													21 48		
Chesterfield		d									20 22													21 54		
Alfreton		d									20 33													22 05		
Langley Mill		d									20 40													22 12		
Nottingham		a									21 00													22 33		

			NT		NT	TP	NT	NT	NT	NT	NT	NT	NT		NT	NT
						◇1										
						H	E	B		L						K
Leeds 10	31	d	20 37		20 48						21 37	21 48			22 44	
Woodlesford		d	20 45								21 45					
Castleford		d	20 56								21 56					
Normanton		d	21 02								22 02					
Wakefield Kirkgate 4	31	a	21 06								22 06					
		d	21 07								22 07					
Darton		d	21 18								22 21					
Huddersfield		d							21 18				22 18			
Lockwood		d							21 21				22 21			
Berry Brow		d							21 24				22 24			
Honley		d							21 27				22 27			
Brockholes		d							21 30				22 30			
Stocksmoor		d							21 34				22 34			
Shepley		d							21 36				22 36			
Denby Dale		d							21 41				22 41			
Penistone		d							21 49				22 49			
Silkstone Common		d							21 54				22 54			
Dodworth		d							21 58				22 58			
Barnsley		a	21 24						22 05		22 27		23 05			
		d	21 24						22 06		22 28		23 06			
Wombwell		d	21 29						22 11		22 33		23 11			
Elsecar		d	21 33								22 37		23 15			
Chapeltown		d	21 38						22 18		22 42		23 20			
Meadowhall	29,31 🚌	a	21 45		21 49				22 24		22 47	22 52	23 25		23 43	
		d	21 46		21 50	21 59	22 03	22 12	22 25	22 43	22 48	22 53	23 26		23 44	23 49
Sheffield 7	29,31 🚌	a	21 57		22 02	22 10	22 13	22 22	22 36	22 54	22 58	23 03	23 36		23 58	23 59
		d														
Dronfield		d														
Chesterfield		d														
Alfreton		d														
Langley Mill		d														
Nottingham		a														

A From Scarborough
B From Hull
C To Sheffield
D From Leeds
E From Doncaster
F From Cleethorpes to Manchester Airport
G From Scunthorpe to Worksop
H From Cleethorpes
I From Liverpool Lime Street
J To Retford
K From Bridlington
L From Scunthorpe

Table 34

Sundays

Leeds and Huddersfield - Barnsley - Sheffield, Nottingham

Network Diagram - see first page of Table 31

		NT	NT	TP	NT	NT	NT	NT	NT	NT		NT	TP	NT	TP	NT	NT	NT	TP	NT		TP	NT	NT	NT
				◇1											◇1							◇1			
		A		B	A				C			D	E 🚌		F			A	G 🚌			F	H		
Leeds 10 31	d					08 34	08 48	09 05						10 02			10 17			10 57				11 18	11 29
Woodlesford	d					08 42											10 25								
Castleford	d					08 53											10 36								
Normanton	d					08 58											10 41								
Wakefield Kirkgate 4 31	a					09 03		09 21						10 18			10 46			11 13					11 46
	d					09 03		09 21						10 18			10 46			11 13					11 46
Darton	d					09 17											11 00								
Huddersfield	d									09 19						10 15									
Lockwood	d									09 22						10 18									
Berry Brow	d									09 25						10 21									
Honley	d									09 28						10 24									
Brockholes	d									09 31						10 27									
Stocksmoor	d									09 35						10 31									
Shepley	d									09 37						10 33									
Denby Dale	d									09 42						10 39									
Penistone	d									09 50						10 46									
Silkstone Common	d									09 55						10 52									
Dodworth	d									09 59						10 55									
Barnsley	a					09 24		09 40		10 06				10 37		11 03	11 08			11 32					12 05
	d					09 24		09 41		10 12				10 38		11 03	11 12			11 33					12 06
Wombwell	d					09 29				10 17							11 17								
Elsecar	d					09 33				10 21							11 21								
Chapeltown	d					09 38				10 26							11 26								
Meadowhall 29,31 🚋	a					09 44	09 53	09 57		10 32				10 51		11 20	11 32			11 46				12 20	12 17
	d	08 30		09 00	09 41	09 44	09 54	09 57	10 00	10 33		10 40	10∫40	10 51	11∫00	11 20	11 35	11 40	11∫40	11 46		12∫00	12 08	12 21	12 17
Sheffield 7 29,31 🚋	a	08 41		09 07	09 51	09 55	10 03	10 04	10 08	10 43		10 52	11∫00	11 02	11∫07	11 28	11 44	11 51	12∫00	11 56		12∫07	12 18	12 32	12 29
	d		09 00					10 07						11 03						12 00					12 31
Dronfield	d		09 10					10 17						11 13						12 10					12 42
Chesterfield	d		09 17					10 23						11 20						12 18					12 49
Alfreton	d		09 28					10 33						11 30						12 28					12 59
Langley Mill	d		09 35					10 41						11 38						12 36					13 07
Nottingham	a		09 53					10 57						11 53						12 52					13 24

		NT	TP	NT	TP	NT		TP	NT	NT	NT	TP	NT	NT	TP	NT		NT	NT	TP	NT	NT	TP	NT	NT
					◇1							◇1								◇1					
			G 🚌	D	F			G 🚌	A		I	J			E 🚌	D		I		F			G 🚌	A	H
Leeds 10 31	d					12 29				12 34			13 18						14 05			14 17			
Woodlesford	d									12 42												14 25			
Castleford	d									12 53												14 36			
Normanton	d									12 58												14 41			
Wakefield Kirkgate 4 31	a					12 46				13 04									14 21			14 46			
	d					12 46				13 04									14 21			14 46			
Darton	d									13 18												15 00			
Huddersfield	d	11 29												13 19							14 15				
Lockwood	d	11 32												13 22							14 18				
Berry Brow	d	11 35												13 25							14 21				
Honley	d	11 38												13 28							14 24				
Brockholes	d	11 41												13 31							14 27				
Stocksmoor	d	11 45												13 35							14 31				
Shepley	d	11 47												13 37							14 33				
Denby Dale	d	11 52												13 42							14 39				
Penistone	d	12 00												13 50							14 46				
Silkstone Common	d	12 05												13 55							14 52				
Dodworth	d	12 09												13 59							14 55				
Barnsley	a	12 16				13 05				13 24				14 06					14 40		15 03	15 07			
	d	12 17				13 06				13 24				14 12					14 41		15 03	15 12			
Wombwell	d	12 22								13 29				14 17								15 17			
Elsecar	d	12 26								13 33				14 21								15 21			
Chapeltown	d	12 31								13 38				14 26								15 26			
Meadowhall 29,31 🚋	a	12 34				13 18				13 48			14 20	14 32					14 54		15 20	15 35			
	d	12 35	12∫40	12 43	13∫00	13 18		13∫40	13 44	13 51	13 56	14∫00	14 21	14 33	14∫42	14 48		14 52	14 56	15∫00	15 21	15 35	15∫40	15 48	15 52
Sheffield 7 29,31 🚋	a	12 47	13∫00	12 55	13∫07	13 29		14∫00	13 52	13 58	14 06	14∫07	14 32	14 48	15∫02	14 55		15 03	15 06	15∫07	15 28	15 44	16∫00	15 55	16 01
	d					13 31													15 07						
Dronfield	d					13 42													15 17						
Chesterfield	d					13 48													15 24						
Alfreton	d					13 59													15 34						
Langley Mill	d					14 06													15 42						
Nottingham	a					14 22													15 59						

A From Doncaster
B To Manchester Piccadilly
C From Hull
D From Goole
E from 8 January until 12 February. From Doncaster
F until 1 January, from 19 February. From Cleethorpes to Manchester Airport
G from 8 January until 12 February. From Cleethorpes
H From Bridlington
I From Scarborough
J until 1 January and from 19 February. From Doncaster to Manchester Airport

Leeds and Huddersfield - Barnsley - Sheffield, Nottingham

Network Diagram - see first page of Table 31

		NT	TP	NT	NT	TP	NT	NT	NT	TP	NT	TP	NT	NT	NT	TP	TP	NT	NT	TP	NT	NT
			◇1							◇1						◇1	◇1					
			A			B	C	D		A		B	E	F		G	H			B	E	D
						🚌						🚌								🚌		
Leeds 10	31 d	15 05		15 18					16 04		16 17				17 05			17 18				
Woodlesford	d										16 25											
Castleford	d										16 36											
Normanton	d										16 41											
Wakefield Kirkgate 4	31 a	15 22							16 21		16 46				17 21							
	d	15 22							16 22		16 46				17 21							
Darton	d										17 00											
Huddersfield	d				15 19														17 19			
Lockwood	d				15 22														17 22			
Berry Brow	d				15 25														17 25			
Honley	d				15 28														17 28			
Brockholes	d				15 31														17 31			
Stocksmoor	d				15 35														17 35			
Shepley	d				15 37														17 37			
Denby Dale	d				15 42														17 47			
Penistone	d				15 50														17 54			
Silkstone Common	d				15 55														18 00			
Dodworth	d				15 59														18 03			
Barnsley	a	15 41			16 06				16 41		17 07				17 40				18 11			
	d	15 42			16 12				16 42		17 12				17 41				18 12			
Wombwell	d				16 17						17 17								18 17			
Elsecar	d				16 21						17 21								18 21			
Chapeltown	d				16 26						17 26								18 26			
Meadowhall 29,31 🚊	a	15 55		16 19	16 32				16 56		17 34				17 55			18 25	18 32			
	d	15 56	16⌇00	16 19	16 34	16⌇40	16 47	16 53	16 56	17⌇00	17 35	17⌇40	17 48	17 53	17 56	18⌇00	18⌇00	18 25	18 33	18⌇40	18 47	18 53
Sheffield 7 29,31 🚊	a	16 05	16⌇07	16 31	16 44	17⌇00	16 55	17 04	17 05	17⌇07	17 44	18⌇00	17 55	18 01	18 05	18⌇07	18⌇08	18 36	18 44	19⌇00	18 57	19 03
	d	16 07							17 07						18 07							
Dronfield	d	16 17							17 17						18 17							
Chesterfield	d	16 23							17 23						18 25							
Alfreton	d	16 33							17 33						18 36							
Langley Mill	d	16 41							17 41						18 43							
Nottingham	a	16 56							17 58						19 00							

		NT	TP	NT	NT	TP	NT	NT	NT	TP	NT	NT	TP	NT	TP	NT	EM	NT	TP	NT	TP	NT	NT
			◇1							◇1					◇1		◇				◇1		
			A	I		B	E		F	A			B	E	A	D	J		B	I	K		
						🚌							🚌						🚌				
Leeds 10	31 d	18 05			18 17			19 04			19 18							20 17					21 40
Woodlesford	d				18 25													20 25					
Castleford	d				18 36													20 36					
Normanton	d				18 40													20 41					
Wakefield Kirkgate 4	31 a	18 21			18 45			19 21										20 46					
	d	18 22			18 45			19 21										20 46					
Darton	d				18 59													21 00					
Huddersfield	d											19 19											
Lockwood	d											19 22											
Berry Brow	d											19 25											
Honley	d											19 28											
Brockholes	d											19 31											
Stocksmoor	d											19 35											
Shepley	d											19 37											
Denby Dale	d											19 42											
Penistone	d											19 50											
Silkstone Common	d											19 55											
Dodworth	d											19 59											
Barnsley	a	18 41			19 05			19 40				20 06						21 07					
	d	18 42			19 11			19 40				20 12						21 12				22 21	
Wombwell	d				19 17							20 17						21 17				22 26	
Elsecar	d				19 21							20 21						21 21				22 30	
Chapeltown	d				19 26							20 26						21 26				22 35	
Meadowhall 29,31 🚊	a	18 56			19 32			19 54			20 22	20 34						21 33				22 40	22 45
	d	18 56	19⌇00	19 18	19 33	19⌇40	19 47	19 54	19 57	20⌇00	20 23	20 34	20⌇40	20 47	21⌇00	21 28		21 33	21⌇40	21 58	22⌇04	22 41	22 45
Sheffield 7 29,31 🚊	a	19 05	19⌇07	19 27	19 43	20⌇00	19 55	20 04	20 06	20⌇07	20 34	20 43	21⌇00	20 55	21⌇07	21 38		21 42	22⌇00	22 09	22⌇13	22 51	22 54
	d	19 07						20 06									21 40						
Dronfield	d	19 17						20 16									21 50						
Chesterfield	d	19 25						20 23									21 56						
Alfreton	d	19 36						20 34									22 07						
Langley Mill	d	19 43						20 41									22 14						
Nottingham	a	19 59						20 57									22 35						

A until 1 January, from 19 February. From Cleethorpes to Manchester Airport
B from 8 January until 12 February. From Cleethorpes
C From Goole
D From Scarborough
E From Doncaster
F From Bridlington
G until 1 January, from 19 February until 25 March. From Cleethorpes to Manchester Airport
H from 1 April. From Cleethorpes to Manchester Airport
I From York
J From Liverpool Lime Street
K until 1 January, from 19 February. From Cleethorpes

Table 34

Sundays

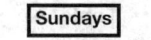

Leeds and Huddersfield - Barnsley - Sheffield, Nottingham

Network Diagram - see first page of Table 31

			TP A	NT B	NT
Leeds 10	31	d			22 17
Woodlesford		d			22 25
Castleford		d			22 36
Normanton		d			22 41
Wakefield Kirkgate 4	31	a			22 46
		d			22 46
Darton		d			23 00
Huddersfield		d			
Lockwood		d			
Berry Brow		d			
Honley		d			
Brockholes		d			
Stocksmoor		d			
Shepley		d			
Denby Dale		d			
Penistone		d			
Silkstone Common		d			
Dodworth		d			
Barnsley		a			23 07
		d			23 12
Wombwell		d			23 17
Elsecar		d			23 21
Chapeltown		d			23 26
Meadowhall	29,31	a			23 30
		d	23 00	23 04	23 32
Sheffield 7	29,31	a	23 20	23 15	23 43
		d			
Dronfield		d			
Chesterfield		d			
Alfreton		d			
Langley Mill		d			
Nottingham		a			

A from 8 January until 12 February. From Cleethorpes **B** From Hull

Network Diagram for Tables 35, 36, 37, 38

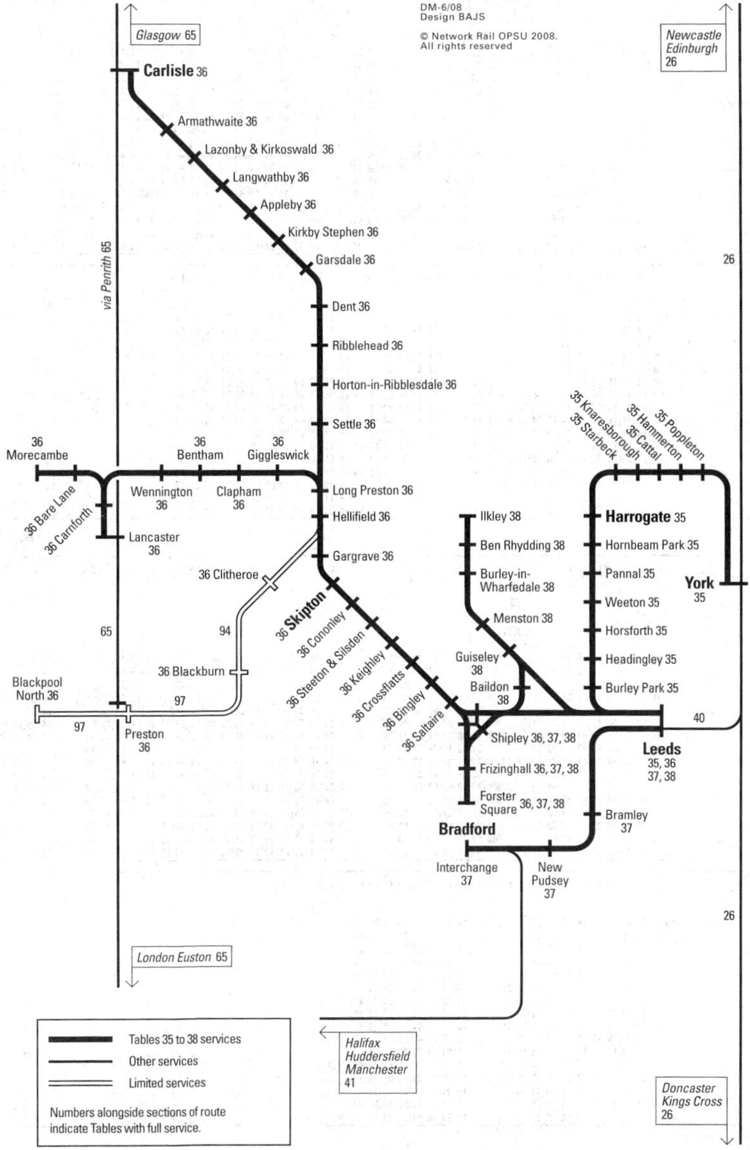

York - Harrogate - Leeds

Network Diagram - see first page of Table 35

Miles			NT	NT	NT	GR	NT	NT	NT	NT	NT		NT	NT	NT	NT	NT	NT	NT	NT	NT		NT	NT	NT
						R 1 A (buffet)																			
0	**York** [8]	40 d					06 52				07 57			08 45	09 10		10 11		11 11		12 11			13 11	
3	Poppleton	d					06 56				08 01			08 50	09 14		10 15		11 15		12 15			13 15	
8¾	Hammerton	d					07 04				08 09			08 58	09 22		10 23		11 23		12 23			13 23	
10¼	Cattal	d					07 07				08 12			09 01	09 26		10 26		11 26		12 26			13 26	
16¾	**Knaresborough**	a					07 15				08 21			09 09	09 34		10 34		11 34		12 34			13 34	
—		d			07 00		07 24	07 42	07 56		08 21		08 55	09 10	09 35	10 05	10 35	11 05	11 35	12 05	12 35		13 05	13 35	14 05
18¼	Starbeck	d			07 03		07 27	07 45	07 59		08 24		08 58	09 13	09 38	10 08	10 38	11 08	11 38	12 08	12 38		13 08	13 38	14 08
20½	**Harrogate**	a			07 08		07 32	07 50	08 04		08 29		09 03	09 18	09 43	10 13	10 43	11 13	11 43	12 13	12 43		13 13	13 43	14 13
—		d	06 05	06 28	07 11	07 28	07 40	07 51	08 06	08 14	08 30		09 04	09 19	09 44	10 14	10 44	11 14	11 44	12 14	12 44		13 14	13 44	14 14
21½	Hornbeam Park	d	06 08	06 30	07 14		07 42	07 54		08 17	08 33		09 07	09 22	09 47	10 17	10 47	11 17	11 47	12 17	12 47		13 17	13 47	14 17
23¾	Pannal	d	06 13	06 35	07 19		07 47	07 59		08 22	08 38			09 27	09 52	10 22	10 52	11 22	11 52	12 22	12 52		13 22	13 52	14 22
27	Weeton	d	06 18	06 40	07 23		07 51	08 03		08 26	08 42			09 31	09 56	10 26	10 56	11 26	11 56	12 26	12 56		13 26	13 56	14 26
33	Horsforth	d	06 27	06 48	07 32	07u45	08 00	08 12	08 23	08 35	08 51		09 22	09 40	10 05	10 35	11 05	11 35	12 05	12 35	13 05		13 35	14 05	14 35
35¾	Headingley	d	06 31	06 52	07 36		08 04	08 16	08 27	08 39	08 55		09 26	09 44	10 09	10 39	11 09	11 39	12 09	12 39	13 09		13 39	14 09	14 39
36½	Burley Park	d	06 34	06 54	07 38		08 06	08 18	08 29	08 41	08 57		09 27	09 47	10 11	10 41	11 11	11 41	12 11	12 41	13 11		13 41	14 11	14 41
38¾	**Leeds** [10]	40 a	06 44	07 06	07 49	07 57	08 16	08 32	08 40	08 52	09 08		09 37	09 56	10 22	10 52	11 22	11 52	12 22	12 52	13 22		13 52	14 22	14 52

		NT	NT	NT	NT	NT	NT		NT	NT	NT	NT	NT	NT	NT	NT	NT
York [8]	40 d	14 11		15 11		16 11			17 09	17 29		18 11		19 11	20 11	21 11	22 11
Poppleton	d	14 15		15 15		16 15			17 13	17 35		18 15		19 15	20 15	21 16	22 15
Hammerton	d	14 23		15 23		16 23			17 21	17 43		18 23		19 23	20 23	21 23	22 23
Cattal	d	14 26		15 26		16 26			17 25	17 46		18 26		19 26	20 26	21 27	22 27
Knaresborough	a	14 34		15 34		16 34			17 33	17 54		18 34		19 34	20 34	21 34	22 35
	d	14 35	15 05	15 35	16 05	16 35	17 05		17 33	17 55	18 05	18 35	19 05	19 35	20 35	21 35	22 36
Starbeck	d	14 38	15 08	15 38	16 08	16 38	17 08		17 37	17 58	18 12	18 38	19 08	19 38	20 38	21 39	22 40
Harrogate	a	14 43	15 13	15 43	16 13	16 43	17 13		17 41	18 03	18 17	18 43	19 13	19 43	20 43	21 43	22 45
	d	14 44	15 14	15 44	16 14	16 44	17 14		17 43	18 04	18 18	18 44	19 14	19 44	20 44	21 45	22 47
Hornbeam Park	d	14 47	15 17	15 47	16 17	16 47	17 17		17 45	18 07	18 21	18 47	19 17	19 47	20 47	21 48	22 49
Pannal	d	14 52	15 22	15 52	16 22	16 52	17 22		17 50	18 12	18 26	18 52	19 22	19 52	20 52	21 53	22 54
Weeton	d	14 56	15 26	15 56	16 26	16 56	17 26		17 55	18 16	18 30	18 56	19 26	19 56	20 56	21 58	22 59
Horsforth	d	15 05	15 35	16 05	16 35	17 05	17 38		18 03	18 25	18 39	19 05	19 35	20 05	21 05	22 06	23 08
Headingley	d	15 09	15 39	16 09	16 39	17 09	17 42		18 07	18 29	18 43	19 09	19 39	20 09	21 09	22 10	23 12
Burley Park	d	15 11	15 41	16 11	16 41	17 11	17 44		18 09	18 31	18 45	19 11	19 41	20 11	21 11	22 13	23 15
Leeds [10]	40 a	15 22	15 52	16 22	16 52	17 22	17 55		18 20	18 43	18 55	19 24	19 52	20 22	21 23	22 23	23 24

Saturdays

		NT	NT	NT	NT	GR	NT	NT	NT	NT		NT	NT	NT	NT	NT	NT	NT	NT	NT		NT	NT	NT	NT
						R 1 A (buffet)																			
York [8]	40 d			06 53			07 57		08 45	09 10			10 11		11 11		12 11		13 11			14 11		15 11	
Poppleton	d			06 57			08 01		08 49	09 14			10 15		11 15		12 15		13 15			14 15		15 15	
Hammerton	d			07 05			08 09		08 57	09 22			10 23		11 23		12 23		13 23			14 23		15 23	
Cattal	d			07 08			08 12		09 00	09 26			10 26		11 26		12 26		13 26			14 26		15 26	
Knaresborough	a			07 16			08 20		09 08	09 34			10 34		11 34		12 34		13 34			14 34		15 34	
	d		06 47	07 21	07 51		08 21	08 51	09 09	09 35		10 05	10 35	11 05	11 35	12 05	12 35	13 05	13 35	14 05		14 35	15 05	15 35	16 05
Starbeck	d		06 50	07 24	07 54		08 24	08 54	09 12	09 38		10 08	10 38	11 08	11 38	12 08	12 38	13 08	13 38	14 08		14 38	15 08	15 38	16 08
Harrogate	a		06 55	07 29	07 59		08 29	08 59	09 17	09 43		10 13	10 43	11 13	11 43	12 13	12 43	13 13	13 43	14 13		14 43	15 13	15 43	16 13
	d	06 06	06 56	07 31	08 00	08 13	08 30	09 00	09 18	09 44		10 14	10 44	11 14	11 44	12 14	12 44	13 14	13 44	14 14		14 44	15 14	15 44	16 14
Hornbeam Park	d	06 08	06 59	07 33	08 03		08 33	09 03	09 21	09 47		10 17	10 47	11 17	11 47	12 17	12 47	13 17	13 47	14 17		14 47	15 17	15 47	16 17
Pannal	d	06 13	07 04	07 38	08 08		08 38	09 08	09 26	09 52		10 22	10 52	11 22	11 52	12 22	12 52	13 22	13 52	14 22		14 52	15 22	15 52	16 22
Weeton	d	06 18	07 08	07 42	08 12		08 42	09 12	09 30	09 56		10 26	10 56	11 26	11 56	12 26	12 56	13 26	13 56	14 26		14 56	15 26	15 56	16 26
Horsforth	d	06 28	07 17	07 51	08 21		08 51	09 21	09 39	10 05		10 35	11 05	11 35	12 05	12 35	13 05	13 35	14 05	14 35		15 05	15 35	16 05	16 35
Headingley	d	06 32	07 21	07 55	08 25		08 55	09 25	09 43	10 09		10 39	11 09	11 39	12 09	12 39	13 09	13 39	14 09	14 39		15 09	15 39	16 09	16 39
Burley Park	d	06 34	07 23	07 57	08 27		08 57	09 27	09 47	10 11		10 41	11 11	11 41	12 11	12 41	13 11	13 41	14 11	14 41		15 11	15 41	16 11	16 41
Leeds [10]	40 a	06 45	07 34	08 08	08 38	08 45	09 08	09 37	09 55	10 22		10 52	11 22	11 52	12 22	12 52	13 20	13 52	14 22	14 52		15 22	15 52	16 22	16 52

		NT	NT	NT	NT	NT		NT	NT	NT	NT
York [8]	40 d	16 11		16 51	17 20			18 11	19 11	20 11	21 57
Poppleton	d	16 15		16 55	17 24			18 15	19 15	20 15	22 01
Hammerton	d	16 23		17 03	17 32			18 23	19 23	20 23	22 09
Cattal	d	16 26		17 06	17 35			18 26	19 26	20 26	22 12
Knaresborough	a	16 34		17 14	17 43			18 34	19 34	20 34	22 20
	d	16 35	17 05	17 15	17 44	18 05		18 35	19 35	20 36	22 21
Starbeck	d	16 38	17 08	17 18	17 47	18 12		18 38	19 38	20 39	22 24
Harrogate	a	16 43	17 13	17 23	17 52	18 17		18 43	19 43	20 44	22 29
	d	16 44	17 14	17 37	17 59	18 18		18 44	19 44	20 45	22 37
Hornbeam Park	d	16 47	17 17	17 39	18 01	18 21		18 47	19 47	20 48	22 39
Pannal	d	16 52	17 22	17 44	18 06	18 26		18 52	19 52	20 53	22 44
Weeton	d	16 56	17 26	17 49	18 11	18 30		18 56	19 56	20 57	22 49
Horsforth	d	17 05	17 38	17 57	18 19	18 39		19 05	20 05	21 06	22 57
Headingley	d	17 09	17 42	18 01	18 23	18 43		19 09	20 09	21 10	23 01
Burley Park	d	17 11	17 44	18 04	18 26	18 45		19 11	20 11	21 12	23 04
Leeds [10]	40 a	17 22	17 55	18 16	18 39	18 55		19 22	20 22	21 23	23 14

A To London Kings Cross

Table 35

Sundays

York - Harrogate - Leeds

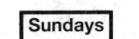

Network Diagram - see first page of Table 35

			NT	NT	NT	NT	NT	NT	GR R 1 A	NT	NT		NT	NT	NT	NT
York 8	40	d				12 18	14 20	16 18		17 17	18 17		19 17	20 17	21 26	
Poppleton		d				12 22	14 24	16 22		17 21	18 21		19 21	20 21	21 30	
Hammerton		d				12 30	14 32	16 30		17 29	18 29		19 29	20 29	21 38	
Cattal		d				12 33	14 35	16 33		17 32	18 32		19 32	20 32	21 41	
Knaresborough		a				12 41	14 43	16 41		17 40	18 40		19 40	20 40	21 49	
		d			11 42	12 42	14 44	16 42		17 42	18 42		19 42	20 42	21 50	
Starbeck		d			11 45	12 45	14 47	16 45		17 45	18 45		19 45	20 45	21 53	
Harrogate		a			11 50	12 50	14 52	16 50		17 50	18 50		19 50	20 50	21 58	
		d	09 53	10 53	11 53	12 53	14 53	16 53	17 05	17 53	18 53		19 53	20 53	22 02	23 12
Hornbeam Park		d	09 56	10 56	11 56	12 56	14 56	16 56		17 56	18 56		19 56	20 56	22 04	23 15
Pannal		d	10 01	11 01	12 01	13 01	15 01	17 01		18 01	19 01		20 01	21 01	22 09	23 20
Weeton		d	10 05	11 05	12 05	13 05	15 05	17 05		18 05	19 05		20 05	21 05	22 14	23 24
Horsforth		d	10 14	11 14	12 14	13 14	15 14	17 14		18 14	19 14		20 14	21 14	22 23	23 33
Headingley		d	10 18	11 18	12 18	13 18	15 18	17 18		18 18	19 18		20 18	21 18	22 27	23 37
Burley Park		d	10 20	11 20	12 20	13 20	15 20	17 20		18 20	19 20		20 20	21 20	22 30	23 39
Leeds 10	40	a	10 30	11 30	12 30	13 30	15 30	17 30	17 32	18 30	19 30		20 30	21 30	22 38	23 54

A To London Kings Cross

Leeds - Harrogate - York

Network Diagram - see first page of Table 35

Mondays to Fridays

Miles				NT MX	NT	NT	NT	NT	NT	NT	NT	NT		NT	NT	NT	NT	NT	NT	NT	NT	NT		NT	NT	NT
0	**Leeds** 10	40	d	23p29	06 09	06 29	07 13	07 43	07 59	08 29	08 59	09 29		09 59	10 29	10 59	11 29	11 59	12 29	12 59	13 29	13 59		14 29	14 59	15 29
2¼	Burley Park		d	23p33	06 13	06 33	07 17	07 47	08 03	08 33	09 03	09 33		10 03	10 33	11 03	11 33	12 03	12 33	13 03	13 33	14 03		14 33	15 03	15 33
3	Headingley		d	23p36	06 16	06 36	07 20	07 50	08 06	08 36	09 06	09 36		10 06	10 36	11 06	11 36	12 06	12 36	13 06	13 36	14 06		14 36	15 06	15 36
5¾	Horsforth		d	23p41	06 21	06 41	07 25	07 55	08 11	08 41	09 11	09 41		10 11	10 41	11 11	11 41	12 11	12 41	13 11	13 41	14 11		14 41	15 11	15 41
11¾	Weeton		d	23p49	06 29	06 49	07 33		08 19	08 49	09 19	09 49		10 19	10 49	11 19	11 49	12 19	12 49	13 19	13 49	14 19		14 49	15 19	15 49
15	Pannal		d	23p55	06 35	06 55	07 39		08 25	08 55	09 25	09 55		10 25	10 55	11 25	11 55	12 25	12 55	13 25	13 55	14 25		14 55	15 25	15 55
17¼	Hornbeam Park		d	23p58	06 40	07 00	07 44	08 10	08 30	09 00	09 30	10 00		10 30	11 00	11 30	12 00	12 30	13 00	13 30	14 00	14 30		15 00	15 30	16 00
18¼	**Harrogate**		a	00 06	06 43	07 05	07 49	08 13	08 33	09 03	09 33	10 03		10 33	11 03	11 33	12 03	12 33	13 05	13 33	14 03	14 33		15 03	15 33	16 03
—			d		06 45	07 05	07 49	08 16	08 34	09 05	09 35	10 05		10 35	11 05	11 35	12 05	12 35	13 07	13 35	14 05	14 35		15 05	15 35	16 05
20½	Starbeck		d		06 49	07 08	07 52	08 19	08 38	09 08	09 38	10 08		10 38	11 08	11 38	12 08	12 38	13 10	13 38	14 08	14 38		15 08	15 38	16 08
22	**Knaresborough**		a		06 54	07 16	07 59	08 25	08 45	09 14	09 45	10 14		10 45	11 14	11 45	12 14	12 45	13 16	13 45	14 14	14 45		15 14	15 45	16 14
—			d		06 55	07 19	07 59	08 28		09 15		10 14			11 14		12 14		13 16		14 14			15 14		16 14
28½	Cattal		d		07 03	07 27	08 07	08 36		09 23		10 22			11 22		12 22		13 24		14 22			15 22		16 22
30	Hammerton		d		07 06	07 30	08 11	08 39		09 27		10 26			11 26		12 26		13 28		14 26			15 26		16 26
35¾	Poppleton		d		07 13	07 37	08 18	08 46		09 34		10 33			11 33		12 33		13 35		14 33			15 33		16 33
38¾	**York** 8	40	a		07 21	07 48	08 32	08 58		09 45		10 45			11 44		12 45		13 44		14 44			15 46		16 45

			NT	NT	NT	NT	NT	NT		NT	NT	NT	NT	NT	GR R 1 B	NT	NT	NT		NT
Leeds 10	40	d	15 59	16 29	16 42	16 59	17 13	17 29		17 44	17 59	18 29	18 59	19 29	19 59	20 29	21 29	22 31		23 29
Burley Park		d	16 03	16 33	16 46	17 03	17 17	17 33		17 48	18 03	18 33	19 03	19 33		20 33	21 33	22 35		23 33
Headingley		d	16 06	16 36	16 49	17 06	17 20	17 36		17 51	18 06	18 36	19 06	19 36		20 36	21 36	22 38		23 36
Horsforth		d	16 11	16 41	16a55	17 11	17 25	17 41		17 56	18 11	18 41	19 11	19 41		20 41	21 41	22 43		23 41
Weeton		d	16 19	16 49		17 19	17 33	17 49			18 19	18 49	19 19	19 49		20 49	21 49	22 52		23 49
Pannal		d	16 25	16 55		17 25	17 39	17 55			18 25	18 55	19 25	19 55		20 55	21 55	22 57		23 55
Hornbeam Park		d	16 30	17 00		17 30	17 44	18 00			18 30	19 00	19 30	20 00		21 00	22 00	23 03		23 58
Harrogate		a	16 33	17 03		17 33	17 47	18 03		18 15	18 33	19 03	19 33	20 03	20 28	21 03	22 03	23 09		00 06
		d	16 35	17 05		17 35	17 49	18 05		18 16	18 35	19 05	19 35	20 05		21 05	22 05			
Starbeck		d	16 38	17 08		17 38	17 52	18 08		18 20	18 39	19 08	19 38	20 08		21 08	22 08			
Knaresborough		a	16 45	17 13		17 45	18 01	18 14		18 26	18 45	19 14	19 45	20 14		21 14	22 16			
		d		17 13				18 14				19 14		20 14		21 14				
Cattal		d		17 21				18 22				19 22		20 22		21 22				
Hammerton		d		17 25				18 26				19 26		20 26		21 26				
Poppleton		d		17 32				18 33				19 33		20 33		21 33				
York 8	40	a		17 50				18 46				19 43		20 45		21 47				

Saturdays

			NT	NT	NT	NT	NT	NT	NT	NT	NT		NT	NT	NT	NT	NT	NT	NT	NT	NT		NT	NT	NT	NT
Leeds 10	40	d	23p29	06 09	06 36	07 13	07 39	07 54	08 29	08 59	09 29		09 59	10 29	10 59	11 29	11 59	12 29	12 59	13 29	13 59		14 29	14 59	15 29	15 59
Burley Park		d	23p33	06 13	06 40	07 17	07 43	07 58	08 33	09 03	09 33		10 03	10 33	11 03	11 33	12 03	12 33	13 03	13 33	14 03		14 33	15 03	15 33	16 03
Headingley		d	23p36	06 16	06 43	07 20	07 46	08 01	08 36	09 06	09 36		10 06	10 36	11 06	11 36	12 06	12 36	13 06	13 36	14 06		14 36	15 06	15 36	16 06
Horsforth		d	23p41	06 21	06 48	07 25	07 51	08 06	08 41	09 11	09 41		10 11	10 41	11 11	11 41	12 11	12 41	13 11	13 41	14 11		14 41	15 11	15 41	16 11
Weeton		d	23p49	06 29	06 56	07 33	07 59	08 14	08 49	09 19	09 49		10 19	10 49	11 19	11 49	12 19	12 49	13 19	13 49	14 19		14 49	15 19	15 49	16 19
Pannal		d	23p55	06 35	07 02	07 39	08 09	08 22	08 55	09 25	09 55		10 25	10 55	11 25	11 55	12 25	12 55	13 25	13 55	14 25		14 55	15 25	15 55	16 25
Hornbeam Park		d	23p58	06 40	07 07	07 44	08 14	08 28	09 00	09 30	10 00		10 30	11 00	11 30	12 00	12 30	13 00	13 30	14 00	14 30		15 00	15 30	16 00	16 30
Harrogate		a	00 06	06 43	07 10	07 47	08 17	08 31	09 03	09 33	10 03		10 33	11 03	11 33	12 03	12 33	13 03	13 33	14 03	14 33		15 03	15 33	16 03	16 33
		d		06 45	07 12	07 49	08 19	08 31	09 05	09 35	10 05		10 35	11 05	11 35	12 05	12 35	13 05	13 35	14 05	14 35		15 05	15 35	16 05	16 35
Starbeck		d		06 49	07 15	07 52	08 22	08 36	09 08	09 38	10 08		10 38	11 08	11 38	12 08	12 38	13 08	13 38	14 08	14 38		15 08	15 38	16 08	16 38
Knaresborough		a		06 54	07 21	07 59	08 28	08 42	09 14	09 45	10 14		10 45	11 14	11 45	12 14	12 45	13 14	13 45	14 14	14 45		15 14	15 45	16 14	16 45
		d		06 55	07 21	07 59	08 28		09 15		10 14			11 14		12 14		13 14		14 14			15 14		16 14	
Cattal		d		07 03	07 29	08 07	08 36		09 23		10 22			11 22		12 22		13 22		14 22			15 22		16 22	
Hammerton		d		07 06	07 33	08 11	08 40		09 27		10 26			11 26		12 26		13 26		14 26			15 26		16 26	
Poppleton		d		07 13	07 40	08 19	08 47		09 34		10 33			11 33		12 33		13 33		14 33			15 33		16 33	
York 8	40	a		07 21	07 46	08 26	08 59		09 45		10 45			11 45		12 45		13 48		14 44			15 46		16 44	

			NT	NT	NT	NT	NT		NT	NT	GR R 1 B	NT	NT	NT	NT
Leeds 10	40	d	16 29	16 59	17 13	17 29	17 59		18 29	19 29	19 59	20 33	21 20	22 33	23 21
Burley Park		d	16 33	17 03	17 17	17 33	18 03		18 33	19 33		20 37	21 24	22 37	23 25
Headingley		d	16 36	17 06	17 20	17 36	18 06		18 36	19 36		20 40	21 27	22 40	23 28
Horsforth		d	16 41	17 11	17 25	17 41	18 11		18 41	19 41		20 45	21 32	22 45	23 33
Weeton		d	16 49	17 19	17 33	17 49	18 19		18 49	19 49		20 53	21 40	22 53	23 41
Pannal		d	16 55	17 25	17 39	17 55	18 25		18 55	19 55		20 59	21 46	22 59	23 47
Hornbeam Park		d	17 00	17 30	17 44	18 00	18 30		19 00	20 00		21 04	21 51	23 04	23 52
Harrogate		a	17 03	17 33	17 47	18 03	18 33		19 03	20 04	20 28	21 07	21 54	23 10	23 58
		d	17 08	17 35	17 49	18 05	18 35		19 05	20 04		21 09	21 56		
Starbeck		d	17 11	17 38	17 52	18 08	18 38		19 08	20 08		21 12	21 59		
Knaresborough		a	17 17	17 45	18 00	18 14	18 45		19 14	20 14		21 18	22 06		
		d	17 21			18 14			19 14	20 14		21 18			
Cattal		d	17 29			18 22			19 22	20 22		21 26			
Hammerton		d	17 34			18 26			19 26	20 26		21 31			
Poppleton		d	17 41			18 33			19 33	20 33		21 38			
York 8	40	a	17 52			18 44			19 45	20 47		21 48			

B From London Kings Cross

Table 35

Sundays

Leeds - Harrogate - York

Network Diagram - see first page of Table 35

			NT	NT	NT	NT	NT	NT	NT	NT	NT		GR R 1 A	NT	NT	NT
Leeds 10	40	d	09 54	10 54	12 54	14 54	15 54	16 54	17 54	18 54	19 54		20 37	21 16	22 26	23 23
Burley Park		d	09 59	10 59	12 59	14 59	15 59	16 59	17 59	18 59	19 59			21 21	22 31	23 28
Headingley		d	10 01	11 01	13 01	15 01	16 01	17 01	18 01	19 01	20 01			21 23	22 33	23 30
Horsforth		d	10 07	11 07	13 07	15 07	16 07	17 07	18 07	19 07	20 07			21 29	22 39	23 36
Weeton		d	10 14	11 14	13 14	15 14	16 14	17 14	18 14	19 14	20 14			21 37	22 46	23 43
Pannal		d	10 20	11 20	13 20	15 20	16 20	17 20	18 20	19 20	20 20			21 43	22 52	23 49
Hornbeam Park		d	10 25	11 25	13 25	15 25	16 25	17 25	18 25	19 25	20 25			21 48	22 57	23 54
Harrogate		a	10 31	11 28	13 28	15 28	16 28	17 28	18 28	19 28	20 28		21 06	21 51	23 03	23 59
		d		11 30	13 30	15 30	16 30	17 33	18 30	19 30	20 30			21 53		
Starbeck		d		11 34	13 34	15 34	16 34	17 36	18 34	19 34	20 34			21 57		
Knaresborough		a		11 39	13 39	15 39	16 39	17 42	18 39	19 39	20 39			22 03		
		d		11 40	13 40	15 40	16 45	17 44	18 44	19 44	20 45					
Cattal		d		11 48	13 48	15 48	16 53	17 52	18 52	19 52	20 53					
Hammerton		d		11 51	13 51	15 51	16 56	17 55	18 55	19 55	20 56					
Poppleton		d		11 58	13 58	15 58	17 03	18 02	19 02	20 02	21 03					
York 8	40	a		12 07	14 08	16 06	17 10	18 10	19 12	20 11	21 15					

A From London Kings Cross

Leeds and Bradford - Skipton, Lancaster, Morecambe and Carlisle

Network Diagram - see first page of Table 35

Miles	Miles	Miles		NT MX	NT	NT	NT	NT	NT	NT	NT	NT		NT	NT	NT	NT	NT	NT	NT	NT	NT		NT
—	—	—	London Kings Cross 15 . ⊖26 d																					
0	0	—	**Leeds 10** 37 d	23p18		05 29		06 16		06 56		07 25			07 51		08 19	08 25		08 49	08 56			09 26
—	—	0	**Bradford Forster Square** 37 d				06 04		06 39		07 15			07 42		08 09			08 41			09 11		
—	—	1¾	Frizinghall 37 d				06 07		06 43		07 18			07 45		08 12			08 44			09 14		
10¾	10¾	2¾	Shipley 37 a	23p31		05 41	06 11	06 27	06 47	07 08	07 22	07 36		07 49	08 02	08 16	08 31	08 37	08 48	09 01	09 07	09 18		09 37
—	—	—	d	23p32		05 42	06 12	06 28	06 48	07 08	07 23	07 37		07 50	08 03	08 17	08 32	08 37	08 49	09 02	09 09	09 19		09 38
11½	11½	—	Saltaire d	23p34		05 44	06 14	06 30	06 50	07 10	07 25	07 39		07 52	08 05	08 20		08 40	08 52		09 11	09 22		09 40
13¾	13¾	—	Bingley d	23p38		05 49	06 18	06 34	06 54	07 14	07 29	07 43		07 56	08 09	08 24	08 37	08 44	08 56	09 06	09 14	09 26		09 44
14½	14½	—	Crossflatts d	23p40		05 51	06 20	06 36	06 56	07 17	07 31	07 46		07 58	08 11	08 26		08 46	08 58		09 17	09 28		09 47
17	17	—	Keighley d	23p44		05 56	06 25	06 41	07 01	07 21	07 36	07 50		08 03	08 15	08 31	08 43	08 50	09 03	09 12	09 21	09 33		09 51
20	20	—	Steeton & Silsden d	23p48		06 00	06 29	06 45	07 05	07 26	07 40	07 55		08 07	08 19	08 35		08 54	09 07		09 26	09 37		09 56
23¼	23¼	—	Cononley d	23p52		06 05	06 33	06 49	07 09	07 30	07 44	07 59		08 11	08 23	08 40		08 59	09 12		09 30	09 42		10 00
26¼	26¼	—	**Skipton** a	00 02		06 12	06 42	06 59	07 18	07 39	07 52	08 08		08 20	08 32	08 48	08 55	09 09	09 20	09 24	09 40	09 50		10 11
—	—	—	d		05 40	06 15											09 00			09 26				
30	30	—	Gargrave d		05 45												09 05			09 32				
—	—	—	Blackpool North 94 d																					
—	—	—	Preston d																					
—	—	—	Blackburn 97 d																					
—	—	—	Clitheroe 94 d																					
36¼	36¼	—	Hellifield d		05 54	06 26											09 14			09 40				
37½	37½	—	Long Preston d		05 57												09 17			09 43				
—	41¼	—	Giggleswick d		06 07												09 24							
—	48	—	Clapham (Nth Yorkshire) d		06 15												09 33							
—	51¼	—	Bentham d		06 21												09 39							
—	54½	—	Wennington d		06 26												09 44							
—	64	—	Carnforth 82 a		06 42												10 00							
—	70¼	—	**Lancaster 6** 65,82,98 a		06 52												10 12							
—	72¾	—	Bare Lane 98 a														10 26							
—	75½	—	**Morecambe** 98 a														10 33							
41¼	—	—	Settle d			06 34														09 50				
47½	—	—	Horton-in-Ribblesdale d																	09 58				
52¼	—	—	Ribblehead d			06 49														10 06				
58¼	—	—	Dent d																	10 16				
61¾	—	—	Garsdale d			07 04														10 21				
71½	—	—	Kirkby Stephen d			07 16														10 34				
82¼	—	—	Appleby d			07 30														10 47				
93¼	—	—	Langwathby d			07 44														11 01				
97½	—	—	Lazonby & Kirkoswald d			07 49														11 07				
103	—	—	Armathwaite d			07 57														11 15				
113	—	—	**Carlisle 8** 65 a			08 17														11 34				

	NT	NT	NT	NT	NT A	NT	NT	NT		NT	NT	NT	NT	NT	NT	NT	NT	NT		NT	NT	NT	NT	NT
London Kings Cross 15 . ⊖26 d																								
Leeds 10 37 d		09 47	09 56		10 19	10 26		10 49		10 56		11 26		11 56		12 26		12 49		12 56		13 26		13 49
Bradford Forster Square 37 d	09 41			10 11			10 41				11 11		11 41		12 11		12 41				13 11		13 41	
Frizinghall 37 d	09 44			10 14			10 44				11 14		11 44		12 14		12 44				13 14		13 44	
Shipley 37 a	09 48	10 01	10 07	10 18	10 31	10 37	10 48	11 01		11 07	11 18	11 38	11 48	12 07	12 18	12 37	12 48	13 01		13 07	13 18	13 37	13 48	14 03
d	09 49	10 02	10 08	10 19	10 32	10 38	10 49	11 02		11 08	11 19	11 39	11 49	12 08	12 19	12 38	12 49	13 02		13 08	13 19	13 38	13 49	14 03
Saltaire d	09 52		10 10	10 22		10 40	10 52			11 10	11 21	11 40	11 51	12 10	12 22	12 40	12 52			13 10	13 22	13 40	13 52	
Bingley d	09 56	10 06	10 14	10 26	10 37	10 44	10 56	11 06		11 14	11 25	11 44	11 55	12 14	12 26	12 44	12 56	13 06		13 14	13 26	13 44	13 56	14 08
Crossflatts d	09 58		10 17	10 28		10 47	10 58			11 17	11 27	11 47	11 57	12 17	12 28	12 47	12 58			13 17	13 28	13 47	13 58	
Keighley d	10 03	10 12	10 21	10 33	10 42	10 51	11 03	11 12		11 21	11 32	11 51	12 02	12 21	12 33	12 51	13 03	13 12		13 21	13 33	13 51	14 03	14 14
Steeton & Silsden d	10 07		10 26	10 37		10 56	11 07			11 26	11 36	11 56	12 06	12 26	12 37	12 56	13 07			13 26	13 37	13 56	14 07	
Cononley d	10 12		10 30	10 42		11 00	11 12			11 30	11 40	12 00	12 10	12 30	12 42	13 00	13 12			13 30	13 42	14 00	14 11	
Skipton a	10 20	10 24	10 39	10 50	10 55	11 11	11 20	11 24		11 40	11 50	12 11	12 20	12 40	12 50	13 10	13 20	13 24		13 38	13 50	14 10	14 20	14 26
d		10 26			11 00			11 26										13 26						14 34
Gargrave d					11 05													13 31						14 39
Blackpool North 94 d																								
Preston d																								
Blackburn 97 d																								
Clitheroe 94 d																								
Hellifield d					11 14			11 37										13 40						14 48
Long Preston d					11 17													13 42						14 51
Giggleswick d					11 24																			14 58
Clapham (Nth Yorkshire) d					11 33																			15 07
Bentham d					11 39																			15 13
Wennington d					11 44																			15 18
Carnforth 82 a					12 00																			15 34
Lancaster 6 65,82,98 a					12 11																			15 47
Bare Lane 98 a					12 34																			16 09
Morecambe 98 a					12 39																			16 13
Settle d		10 44						11 46										13 48						
Horton-in-Ribblesdale d								11 54										13 57						
Ribblehead d								12 02										14 05						
Dent d								12 12										14 14						
Garsdale d								12 17										14 20						
Kirkby Stephen d		11 22						12 30										14 32						
Appleby d		11 36						12 43										14 45						
Langwathby d								12 57										14 59						
Lazonby & Kirkoswald d								13 03										15 04						
Armathwaite d								13 11										15 12						
Carlisle 8 65 a		12 17						13 29										15 32						

A To Heysham Port

Leeds and Bradford - Skipton, Lancaster, Morecambe and Carlisle

Network Diagram - see first page of Table 35

Station		NT	NT	NT	NT		NT	NT	NT	NT	NT	NT	NT	NT	NT		NT	NT	NT	NT	NT	NT	NT	NT	NT
London Kings Cross 15	⊖26 d																								
Leeds 10	37 d	13 56		14 26			14 49	14 56		15 26		15 56		16 26			16 39	16 56		17 26		17 39	17 56	18 06	
Bradford Forster Square	37 d		14 11		14 41				15 11		15 41		16 11		16 40				17 11		17 38				18 16
Frizinghall	37 d		14 14		14 44				15 14		15 44		16 14		16 43				17 14		17 41				18 19
Shipley	37 a	14 07	14 18	14 37	14 48		15 01	15 07	15 18	15 37	15 48	16 07	16 18	16 37	16 48		16 53	17 07	17 18	17 37	17 45	17 53	18 07	18 18	18 23
	d	14 08	14 19	14 38	14 49		15 02	15 08	15 19	15 38	15 49	16 08	16 19	16 38	16 49		16 55	17 08	17 19	17 38	17 46	17 54	18 08	18 18	18 23
Saltaire	d	14 10	14 22	14 40	14 52			15 10	15 22	15 40	15 52	16 10	16 22	16 40	16 52			17 10	17 22	17 40	17 49	17 56	18 10		18 27
Bingley	d	14 14	14 26	14 44	14 56		15 06	15 14	15 26	15 44	15 56	16 14	16 26	16 44	16 56		17 03	17 14	17 26	17 44	17 53	18 00	18 14	18 24	18 31
Crossflatts	d	14 17	14 28	14 47	14 58			15 17	15 28	15 47	15 58	16 17	16 28	16 47	16 58			17 17	17 28	17 47	17 55	18 03	18 17		18 33
Keighley	d	14 21	14 33	14 51	15 03		15 12	15 21	15 33	15 51	16 03	16 21	16 33	16 51	17 03		17 10	17 21	17 33	17 51	18 00	18 07	18 21	18 29	18 38
Steeton & Silsden	d	14 26	14 37	14 56	15 07			15 26	15 37	15 56	16 07	16 26	16 37	16 56	17 07			17 26	17 37	17 56	18 04	18 12	18 26	18 34	18 42
Cononley	d	14 30	14 41	15 00	15 12			15 30	15 42	16 00	16 11	16 30	16 41	17 00	17 11			17 30	17 42	18 00	18 09	18 16	18 30		18 47
Skipton	a	14 40	14 50	15 10	15 20		15 24	15 40	15 50	16 10	16 20	16 40	16 50	17 10	17 19		17 24	17 40	17 50	18 10	18 17	18 24	18 40	18 45	18 55
	d						15 26										17 24							18 46	
Gargrave	d																17 30							18 51	
Blackpool North	94 d																								
Preston	d																								
Blackburn	97 d																								
Clitheroe	94 d																								
Hellifield	d						15 37										17 39							19 00	
Long Preston	d																17 42							19 02	
Giggleswick	d																17 49								
Clapham (Nth Yorkshire)	d																17 57								
Bentham	d																18 04								
Wennington	d																18 09								
Carnforth	82 a																18 29								
Lancaster 6	65,82,98 a																18 42								
Bare Lane	98 a																18 55								
Morecambe	98 a																19 01								
Settle	d						15 45																	19 08	
Horton-in-Ribblesdale	d						15 53																	19 17	
Ribblehead	d						16 01																	19 25	
Dent	d						16 11																	19 34	
Garsdale	d						16 16																	19 40	
Kirkby Stephen	d						16 29																	19 52	
Appleby	d						16 41																	20 05	
Langwathby	d						16 55																	20 19	
Lazonby & Kirkoswald	d						17 01																	20 24	
Armathwaite	d						17 09																	20 32	
Carlisle 8	65 a						17 28																	20 52	

Station			NT	NT	NT	NT	NT	NT	NT	NT	NT		NT	GR R 1	NT	NT	NT	NT	NT	NT	NT		NT	NT	
London Kings Cross 15	⊖26 d													18 03											
Leeds 10	37 d		18 26		18 54		19 19	19 26		19 56			20 26	20 33	20 56		21 26	21 56		22 26	22 56			23 18	
Bradford Forster Square	37 d			18 41		19 07			19 36		20 07					21 05			22 05				23 09		
Frizinghall	37 d			18 44		19 10			19 39		20 10					21 08			22 08				23 12		
Shipley	37 a		18 38	18 48	19 05	19 14	19 31	19 37	19 43	20 07	20 15		20 37		21 07	21 12	21 38	22 07	22 12	22 37	23 08		23 16	23 31	
	d		18 38	18 49	19 06	19 15	19 32	19 38	19 44	20 08	20 15		20 38		21 08	21 14	21 38	22 08	22 14	22 38	23 09		23 17	23 32	
Saltaire	d		18 40	18 51	19 08	19 18		19 40	19 47	20 10	20 17		20 40		21 10	21 17	21 40	22 10	22 16	22 40	23 11		23 20	23 34	
Bingley	d		18 44	18 55	19 12	19 22	19 36	19 44	19 51	20 14	20 21		20 44		21 14	21 21	21 44	22 14	22 20	22 44	23 16		23 24	23 38	
Crossflatts	d		18 47	18 57	19 15	19 24		19 47	19 53	20 17	20 23		20 47		21 17	21 23	21 47	22 17	22 22	22 47	23 18		23 26	23 40	
Keighley	d		18 51	19 02	19 19	19 29	19 42	19 51	19 58	20 21	20 28		20 51	20s55	21 21	21 28	21 51	22 21	22 27	22 51	23 23		23 31	23 44	
Steeton & Silsden	d		18 56	19 06	19 24	19 33		19 56	20 02	20 26	20 32		20 56		21 26	21 32	21 56	22 26	22 31	22 56	23 27		23 35	23 48	
Cononley	d		19 00	19 10	19 28	19 38		20 00	20 07	20 30	20 36		21 00		21 30	21 37	22 00	22 30	22 35	23 00	23 32		23 40	23 52	
Skipton	a		19 10	19 19	19 35	19 46	19 57	20 10	20 15	20 37	20 47		21 10	21 15	21 40	21 44	22 10	22 40	22 42	23 11	23 38		23 48	00 02	
	d						20 00																		
Gargrave	d						20 06																		
Blackpool North	94 d																								
Preston	d																								
Blackburn	97 d																								
Clitheroe	94 d																								
Hellifield	d						20 15																		
Long Preston	d						20 18																		
Giggleswick	d																								
Clapham (Nth Yorkshire)	d																								
Bentham	d																								
Wennington	d																								
Carnforth	82 a																								
Lancaster 6	65,82,98 a																								
Bare Lane	98 a																								
Morecambe	98 a																								
Settle	d						20 24																		
Horton-in-Ribblesdale	d						20 32																		
Ribblehead	d						20a42																		
Dent	d																								
Garsdale	d																								
Kirkby Stephen	d																								
Appleby	d																								
Langwathby	d																								
Lazonby & Kirkoswald	d																								
Armathwaite	d																								
Carlisle 8	65 a																								

Leeds and Bradford - Skipton, Lancaster, Morecambe and Carlisle

Network Diagram - see first page of Table 35

	NT	NT	NT	NT	NT	NT	NT	NT	NT		NT	NT	NT	NT	NT	NT	NT	NT	NT		NT	NT B	NT	NT
London Kings Cross 15 ⊖26 d																								
Leeds 10 37 d	23p18	05 55		06 19	06 56		07 56		08 19		08 25		08 49	08 56		09 26		09 47	09 56			10 19	10 26	
Bradford Forster Square 37 d			06 10			07 11		08 11				08 41			09 11		09 41				10 11			10 41
Frizinghall 37 d			06 13			07 14		08 14				08 44			09 14		09 44				10 14			10 44
Shipley 37 a	23p31	06 07	06 17	06 31	07 08	07 18	08 08	08 18	08 31		08 37	08 48	09 01	09 07	09 18	09 37	09 48	10 01	10 07		10 18	10 31	10 37	10 48
d	23p32	06 08	06 19	06 32	07 08	07 19	08 08	08 19	08 32		08 37	08 49	09 02	09 09	09 19	09 38	09 49	10 02	10 08		10 19	10 32	10 38	10 49
Saltaire d	23p34	06 10	06 22		07 10	07 22	08 10	08 22			08 40	08 52		09 11	09 22	09 40	09 52		10 10		10 22		10 40	10 52
Bingley d	23p38	06 15	06 26	06 36	07 14	07 26	08 14	08 26	08 37		08 44	08 56	09 06	09 14	09 26	09 44	09 56	10 06	10 14		10 26	10 37	10 44	10 56
Crossflatts d	23p40	06 17	06 28		07 17	07 28	08 16	08 28			08 46	08 58		09 17	09 28	09 47	09 58		10 17		10 28		10 47	10 58
Keighley d	23p44	06 22	06 33	06 42	07 21	07 33	08 20	08 33	08 43		08 50	09 03	09 12	09 21	09 33	09 51	10 03	10 12	10 21		10 33	10 42	10 51	11 03
Steeton & Silsden d	23p48	06 26	06 37		07 26	07 37	08 24	08 37			08 54	09 07		09 26	09 37	09 56	10 07		10 26		10 37		10 56	11 07
Cononley d	23p52	06 31	06 42		07 30	07 42	08 28	08 42			08 59	09 12		09 30	09 42	10 00	10 12		10 30		10 42		11 00	11 12
Skipton a	00 02	06 38	06 49	06 55	07 39	07 50	08 39	08 50	08 55		09 09	09 20	09 24	09 40	09 50	10 11	10 20	10 24	10 39		10 50	10 55	11 11	11 20
d		06 40		06 56					09 00				09 26					10 26				11 00		
Gargrave d		06 45							09 05				09 32									11 05		
Blackpool North 94 d																								
Preston d																								
Blackburn 97 d																								
Clitheroe 94 d																								
Hellifield d		06 54		07 08					09 14				09 40									11 14		
Long Preston d		06 57							09 17				09 43									11 17		
Giggleswick d		07 07							09 24													11 25		
Clapham (Nth Yorkshire) d		07 15							09 33													11 33		
Bentham d		07 21							09 39													11 39		
Wennington d		07 26							09 44													11 44		
Carnforth 82 a		07 42							10 00													12 00		
Lancaster 6 65,82,98 a		07 52							10 12													12 11		
Bare Lane 98 a									10 25													12 31		
Morecambe 98 a									10 32													12 36		
Settle d				07 15									09 50					10 44						
Horton-in-Ribblesdale d				07 24									09 58											
Ribblehead d				07 32									10 06											
Dent d				07 41									10 16											
Garsdale d				07 47									10 21											
Kirkby Stephen d				07 59									10 34					11 22						
Appleby d				08 12									10 47					11 36						
Langwathby d				08 26									11 01											
Lazonby & Kirkoswald d				08 31									11 07											
Armathwaite d				08 39									11 15											
Carlisle 8 65 a				08 58									11 34					12 17						

	NT	NT	NT	NT	NT		NT	NT	NT	NT	NT	NT	NT	NT	NT		NT	NT	NT	NT	NT	NT	NT	NT
London Kings Cross 15 ⊖26 d																								
Leeds 10 37 d	10 49	10 56		11 26			11 56		12 26		12 49	12 56		13 26			13 49	13 56		14 26		14 49	14 56	
Bradford Forster Square 37 d			11 11		11 41			12 11		12 41			13 11		13 41				14 11		14 41			15 11
Frizinghall 37 d			11 14		11 44			12 14		12 44			13 14		13 44				14 14		14 44			15 14
Shipley 37 a	11 01	11 07	11 18	11 38	11 48		12 07	12 18	12 37	12 48	13 01	13 07	13 18	13 37	13 48		14 03	14 07	14 18	14 37	14 48	15 01	15 07	15 18
d	11 02	11 08	11 19	11 38	11 49		12 08	12 19	12 38	12 49	13 02	13 08	13 19	13 38	13 49		14 03	14 08	14 19	14 38	14 49	15 02	15 08	15 19
Saltaire d		11 10	11 21	11 40	11 51		12 10	12 22	12 40	12 52		13 10	13 22	13 40	13 52			14 10	14 22	14 40	14 52		15 10	15 22
Bingley d	11 06	11 14	11 25	11 44	11 55		12 14	12 26	12 44	12 56	13 06	13 14	13 26	13 44	13 56		14 08	14 14	14 26	14 44	14 56	15 06	15 14	15 26
Crossflatts d		11 17	11 27	11 47	11 57		12 17	12 28	12 47	12 58		13 17	13 28	13 47	13 58			14 17	14 28	14 47	14 58		15 17	15 28
Keighley d	11 12	11 21	11 32	11 51	12 02		12 21	12 33	12 51	13 03	13 12	13 21	13 33	13 51	14 03		14 14	14 21	14 33	14 51	15 03	15 12	15 21	15 33
Steeton & Silsden d		11 26	11 36	11 56	12 06		12 26	12 37	12 56	13 07		13 26	13 37	13 56	14 07			14 26	14 37	14 56	15 07		15 26	15 37
Cononley d		11 30	11 40	12 00	12 10		12 30	12 42	13 00	13 12		13 30	13 42	14 00	14 11			14 30	14 41	15 00	15 12		15 30	15 42
Skipton a	11 24	11 40	11 50	12 11	12 20		12 40	12 50	13 10	13 20	13 24	13 38	13 50	14 10	14 20		14 26	14 40	14 50	15 10	15 20	15 24	15 40	15 50
d	11 26										13 26						14 34					15 26		
Gargrave d											13 31						14 39							
Blackpool North 94 d																								
Preston d																								
Blackburn 97 d																								
Clitheroe 94 d																								
Hellifield d	11 37										13 40						14 48					15 37		
Long Preston d											13 42						14 51							
Giggleswick d																	14 59							
Clapham (Nth Yorkshire) d																	15 07							
Bentham d																	15 13							
Wennington d																	15 18							
Carnforth 82 a																	15 34							
Lancaster 6 65,82,98 a																	15 45							
Bare Lane 98 a																	15 55							
Morecambe 98 a																	16 02							
Settle d	11 46										13 48											15 45		
Horton-in-Ribblesdale d	11 54										13 57											15 53		
Ribblehead d	12 02										14 05											16 01		
Dent d	12 12										14 14											16 11		
Garsdale d	12 17										14 20											16 16		
Kirkby Stephen d	12 30										14 32											16 29		
Appleby d	12 43										14 45											16 41		
Langwathby d	12 57										14 59											16 55		
Lazonby & Kirkoswald d	13 03										15 04											17 01		
Armathwaite d	13 11										15 12											17 09		
Carlisle 8 65 a	13 29										15 27											17 28		

B To Heysham Port

Table 36

Saturdays

Leeds and Bradford - Skipton, Lancaster, Morecambe and Carlisle

Network Diagram - see first page of Table 35

	NT		NT	NT	NT	NT	NT	NT	NT	NT	NT		NT	NT	NT	NT	NT	NT	NT	NT	NT		NT	NT
London Kings Cross 15 ⊖26 d																								
Leeds 10 37 d	15 26			15 56		16 26		16 39	16 56		17 26			17 50	17 56		18 26		18 56		19 19		19 26	
Bradford Forster Square 37 d			15 41		16 11		16 40			17 11			17 41			18 11		18 41		19 07				19 36
Frizinghall 37 d			15 44		16 14		16 43			17 14			17 44			18 14		18 44		19 10				19 39
Shipley 37 a	15 37		15 48	16 07	16 18	16 37	16 48	16 53	17 07	17 18	17 37		17 48	18 02	18 07	18 18	18 38	18 48	19 07	19 14	19 31		19 37	19 43
d	15 38		15 49	16 08	16 19	16 38	16 49	16 55	17 08	17 19	17 38		17 49	18 03	18 08	18 19	18 38	18 49	19 08	19 15	19 32		19 38	19 44
Saltaire d	15 40		15 52	16 10	16 22	16 40	16 52		17 10	17 22	17 40		17 51		18 10	18 22	18 40	18 51	19 10	19 18			19 40	19 47
Bingley d	15 44		15 56	16 14	16 26	16 44	16 56	17 03	17 14	17 26	17 44		17 55	18 08	18 14	18 26	18 44	18 55	19 14	19 22	19 36		19 44	19 51
Crossflatts d	15 47		15 58	16 17	16 28	16 47	16 58		17 17	17 28	17 47		17 57		18 17	18 28	18 47	18 57	19 17	19 24			19 47	19 53
Keighley d	15 51		16 03	16 21	16 33	16 51	17 03	17 10	17 21	17 33	17 51		18 02	18 14	18 21	18 33	18 51	19 02	19 21	19 29	19 42		19 51	19 58
Steeton & Silsden d	15 56		16 07	16 26	16 37	16 56	17 07		17 26	17 37	17 56		18 06	18 19	18 26	18 37	18 56	19 06	19 26	19 33			19 56	20 02
Cononley d	16 00		16 11	16 30	16 41	17 00	17 11		17 30	17 42	18 00		18 10		18 30	18 42	19 00	19 10	19 30	19 38			20 00	20 07
Skipton a	16 10		16 20	16 40	16 50	17 10	17 19	17 24	17 40	17 50	18 10		18 17	18 29	18 40	18 50	19 10	19 19	19 40	19 46	19 57		20 10	20 15
d								17 24						18 35							20 00			
Gargrave d								17 30						18 40							20 06			
Blackpool North 94 d																								
Preston d																								
Blackburn 97 d																								
Clitheroe 94 d																								
Hellifield d								17 39						18 49							20 15			
Long Preston d								17 42						18 51							20 18			
Giggleswick d								17 49																
Clapham (Nth Yorkshire) d								17 57																
Bentham d								18 04																
Wennington d								18 09																
Carnforth 82 a								18 26																
Lancaster 6 65,82,98 a								18 38																
Bare Lane 98 a								18 53																
Morecambe 98 a								18 59																
Settle d														18 57							20 24			
Horton-in-Ribblesdale d														19 06							20 32			
Ribblehead d														19 14							20a42			
Dent d														19 23										
Garsdale d														19 29										
Kirkby Stephen d														19 41										
Appleby d														19 54										
Langwathby d														20 08										
Lazonby & Kirkoswald d														20 13										
Armathwaite d														20 21										
Carlisle 8 65 a														20 41										

	NT	NT	NT	GR ◇ 1 ✕	NT	NT	NT		NT	NT	NT	NT	NT	NT
London Kings Cross 15 ⊖26 d				18 35										
Leeds 10 37 d	19 56		20 26	20 54	20 56		21 26			22 03	22 26	22 56		23 18
Bradford Forster Square 37 d		20 07				21 05			22 01				23 05	
Frizinghall 37 d		20 10				21 08			22 04				23 08	
Shipley 37 a	20 07	20 15	20 37		21 07	21 12	21 38		22 08	22 15	22 37	23 08	23 12	23 31
d	20 08	20 15	20 38		21 08	21 17	21 38		22 09	22 16	22 38	23 09	23 14	23 32
Saltaire d	20 10	20 17	20 40		21 10	21 20	21 40		22 12	22 18	22 40	23 11	23 17	23 34
Bingley d	20 14	20 21	20 44		21 14	21 24	21 44		22 16	22 22	22 44	23 15	23 21	23 38
Crossflatts d	20 17	20 23	20 47		21 17	21 26	21 47		22 18	22 25	22 47	23 18	23 23	23 40
Keighley d	20 21	20 28	20 51	21s13	21 21	21 31	21 51		22 23	22 29	22 51	23 22	23 28	23 44
Steeton & Silsden d	20 26	20 32	20 56		21 26	21 35	21 56		22 27	22 34	22 56	23 27	23 32	23 48
Cononley d	20 30	20 36	21 00		21 30	21 40	22 00		22 31	22 38	23 00	23 31	23 37	23 52
Skipton a	20 37	20 47	21 10	21 29	21 40	21 47	22 10		22 39	22 47	23 11	23 40	23 44	00 02
d														
Gargrave d														
Blackpool North 94 d														
Preston d														
Blackburn 97 d														
Clitheroe 94 d														
Hellifield d														
Long Preston d														
Giggleswick d														
Clapham (Nth Yorkshire) d														
Bentham d														
Wennington d														
Carnforth 82 a														
Lancaster 6 65,82,98 a														
Bare Lane 98 a														
Morecambe 98 a														
Settle d														
Horton-in-Ribblesdale d														
Ribblehead d														
Dent d														
Garsdale d														
Kirkby Stephen d														
Appleby d														
Langwathby d														
Lazonby & Kirkoswald d														
Armathwaite d														
Carlisle 8 65 a														

Table 36

Sundays

until 1 January

Leeds and Bradford - Skipton, Lancaster, Morecambe and Carlisle

Network Diagram - see first page of Table 35

			NT A	NT	NT	NT	NT	NT	NT	NT	NT		NT	NT	NT	NT	NT	NT	NT	NT	NT		NT	NT	NT	NT
London Kings Cross 15	⊖26	d																								
Leeds 10	37	d	23p18	08 40	09 00	10 08		10 51	11 08	12 08			13 08	13 15	14 08		14 57	15 08	16 08		17 08		17 21	17 33	18 08	
Bradford Forster Square	37	d					10 48				12 48					14 48				16 48						18 48
Frizinghall	37	d					10 51				12 51					14 51				16 51						18 51
Shipley	37	a	23p31	08 52	09 15	10 19	10 54	11 03	11 19	12 19	12 54		13 19	13 28	14 19	14 54	15 09	15 19	16 19	16 54	17 19		17 33	17 45	18 19	18 54
		d	23p32	08 53	09 16	10 20	10 55	11 04	11 20	12 20	12 55		13 20	13 29	14 20	14 55	15 10	15 20	16 20	16 55	17 20		17 34	17 46	18 20	18 55
Saltaire		d	23p34	08 55	09 18	10 22	10 57		11 22	12 22	12 57		13 22		14 22	14 57		15 22	16 22	16 57	17 22				18 22	18 57
Bingley		d	23p38	09 00	09 23	10 26	11 01	11 09	11 26	12 26	13 01		13 26	13 34	14 26	15 01	15 15	15 26	16 26	17 01	17 26		17 39	17 50	18 26	19 01
Crossflatts		d	23p40	09 02	09 25	10 28	11 03		11 28	12 28	13 03		13 28		14 28	15 03		15 28	16 28	17 03	17 28				18 28	19 03
Keighley		d	23p44	09 07	09 30	10 32	11 08	11 15	11 32	12 32	13 08		13 32	13 39	14 32	15 08	15 20	15 32	16 32	17 08	17 32		17 44	17 56	18 32	19 08
Steeton & Silsden		d	23p48	09 11	09 34	10 36	11 12		11 36	12 36	13 12		13 36		14 36	15 12		15 36	16 36	17 12	17 36				18 36	19 12
Cononley		d	23p52	09 16	09 39	10 40	11 16		11 40	12 40	13 16		13 40		14 40	15 16		15 40	16 40	17 16	17 40				18 40	19 16
Skipton		a	00 02	09 23	09 46	10 48	11 23	11 28	11 48	12 48	13 23		13 48	13 53	14 48	15 23	15 33	15 48	16 48	17 23	17 48		17 57	18 08	18 48	19 23
		d		09 26	09 48			11 30						13 54			15 36						18 00	18 11		
Gargrave		d		09 31	09 53			11 35						14 00			15 41						18 05			
Blackpool North	94	d																								
Preston		d																								
Blackburn	97	d																								
Clitheroe	94	d																								
Hellifield		d		09 40	10 02			11 44						14 08			15 50						18 14	18 22		
Long Preston		d		09 43				11 46						14 11			15 53						18 18			
Giggleswick		d		09 52				11 54									16 00						18 25			
Clapham (Nth Yorkshire)		d		10 00				12 02									16 08						18 33			
Bentham		d		10 06				12 08									16 15						18 39			
Wennington		d		10 11				12 13									16 20						18 44			
Carnforth	82	a		10 28				12 30									16 36						19 05			
Lancaster 6	65,82,98	a		10 40				12 44									16 46						19 25			
Bare Lane	98	a		10 51				13 07									16 56						19 31			
Morecambe	98	a		10 57				13 13									17 03						19 39			
Settle		d			10 10									14 17										18 30		
Horton-in-Ribblesdale		d			10 19									14 26										18 39		
Ribblehead		d			10 27									14 34										18 47		
Dent		d			10 37									14 44										18 57		
Garsdale		d			10 43									14 50										19 02		
Kirkby Stephen		d			10 56									15 03										19 15		
Appleby		d			11 09									15 15										19 28		
Langwathby		d			11 23									15 29										19 42		
Lazonby & Kirkoswald		d			11 29									15 35										19 48		
Armathwaite		d			11 37									15 43										19 56		
Carlisle 8	65	a			11 56									16 00										20 13		

			NT	NT	NT	GR R 1 (trolley symbol)	NT		NT	NT	NT
London Kings Cross 15	⊖26	d				18 35					
Leeds 10	37	d	19 08	20 08		21 03	21 08		22 08		23 20
Bradford Forster Square	37	d			20 48					22 48	
Frizinghall	37	d			20 51					22 51	
Shipley	37	a	19 19	20 19	20 54		21 19		22 19	22 54	23 31
		d	19 20	20 20	20 55		21 20		22 20	22 55	23 32
Saltaire		d	19 22	20 22	20 57		21 22		22 22	22 57	23 34
Bingley		d	19 26	20 26	21 01		21 26		22 26	23 01	23 38
Crossflatts		d	19 28	20 28	21 03		21 28		22 28	23 03	23 40
Keighley		d	19 32	20 32	21 08	21s22	21 32		22 32	23 08	23 44
Steeton & Silsden		d	19 36	20 36	21 12		21 36		22 36	23 12	23 48
Cononley		d	19 40	20 40	21 16		21 40		22 40	23 16	23 52
Skipton		a	19 48	20 48	21 23	21 42	21 48		22 48	23 23	23 59
		d									
Gargrave		d									
Blackpool North	94	d									
Preston		d									
Blackburn	97	d									
Clitheroe	94	d									
Hellifield		d									
Long Preston		d									
Giggleswick		d									
Clapham (Nth Yorkshire)		d									
Bentham		d									
Wennington		d									
Carnforth	82	a									
Lancaster 6	65,82,98	a									
Bare Lane	98	a									
Morecambe	98	a									
Settle		d									
Horton-in-Ribblesdale		d									
Ribblehead		d									
Dent		d									
Garsdale		d									
Kirkby Stephen		d									
Appleby		d									
Langwathby		d									
Lazonby & Kirkoswald		d									
Armathwaite		d									
Carlisle 8	65	a									

A not 11 December

Table 36

Sundays

8 January to 12 February

Leeds and Bradford - Skipton, Lancaster, Morecambe and Carlisle

Network Diagram - see first page of Table 35

		NT	NT	NT	NT	NT	NT	NT	NT	NT
London Kings Cross 15 ⊖26	d									
Leeds 10 37	d	23p18	09 00	10 08		10 51	11 08	12 08		13 08
Bradford Forster Square 37	d				10 48				12 48	
Frizinghall 37	d				10 51				12 51	
Shipley 37	a	23p31	09 15	10 19	10 54	11 03	11 19	12 19	12 54	13 19
	d	23p32	09 16	10 20	10 55	11 04	11 20	12 20	12 55	13 20
Saltaire	d	23p34	09 18	10 22	10 57		11 22	12 22	12 57	13 22
Bingley	d	23p38	09 23	10 26	11 01	11 09	11 26	12 26	13 01	13 26
Crossflatts	d	23p40	09 25	10 28	11 03		11 28	12 28	13 03	13 28
Keighley	d	23p44	09 30	10 32	11 08	11 15	11 32	12 32	13 08	13 32
Steeton & Silsden	d	23p48	09 34	10 36	11 12		11 36	12 36	13 12	13 36
Cononley	d	23p52	09 39	10 40	11 16		11 40	12 40	13 16	13 40
Skipton	a	00 02	09 46	10 48	11 23	11 28	11 48	12 48	13 23	13 48
	d		09 48			11 30				
Gargrave	d		09 53			11 35				
Blackpool North 94	d									
Preston	d									
Blackburn 97	d									
Clitheroe 94	d									
Hellifield	d		10 02			11 44				
Long Preston	d					11 46				
Giggleswick	d					11 54				
Clapham (Nth Yorkshire)	d					12 02				
Bentham	d					12 08				
Wennington	d					12 13				
Carnforth 82	a					12 30				
Lancaster 6 65,82,98	a					12 44				
Bare Lane 98	a					13 07				
Morecambe 98	a					13 13				
Settle	d		10 10							
Horton-in-Ribblesdale	d		10 19							
Ribblehead	d		10 27							
Dent	d		10 37							
Garsdale	d		10 43							
Kirkby Stephen	d		10 56							
Appleby	d		11 09							
Langwathby	d		11 23							
Lazonby & Kirkoswald	d		11 29							
Armathwaite	d		11 37							
Carlisle 8 65	a		11 56							

		NT	NT	NT	NT	NT	NT	NT	NT	NT	NT	NT	NT	NT
London Kings Cross 15 ⊖26	d													
Leeds 10 37	d	13 15	14 08		14 57	15 08	16 08		17 08	17 21	17 33	18 08		19 08
Bradford Forster Square 37	d			14 48				16 48					18 48	
Frizinghall 37	d			14 51				16 51					18 51	
Shipley 37	a	13 28	14 19	14 54	15 09	15 19	16 19	16 54	17 19	17 33	17 45	18 19	18 54	19 19
	d	13 29	14 20	14 55	15 10	15 20	16 20	16 55	17 20	17 34	17 46	18 20	18 55	19 20
Saltaire	d		14 22	14 57		15 22	16 22	16 57	17 22			18 22	18 57	19 22
Bingley	d	13 34	14 26	15 01	15 15	15 26	16 26	17 01	17 26	17 39	17 50	18 26	19 01	19 26
Crossflatts	d		14 28	15 03		15 28	16 28	17 03	17 28			18 28	19 03	19 28
Keighley	d	13 39	14 32	15 08	15 20	15 32	16 32	17 08	17 32	17 44	17 56	18 32	19 08	19 32
Steeton & Silsden	d		14 36	15 12		15 36	16 36	17 12	17 36			18 36	19 12	19 36
Cononley	d		14 40	15 16		15 40	16 40	17 16	17 40			18 40	19 16	19 40
Skipton	a	13 53	14 48	15 23	15 33	15 48	16 48	17 23	17 48	17 57	18 08	18 48	19 23	19 48
	d	13 54			15 36					18 00	18 11			
Gargrave	d	14 00			15 41					18 05				
Blackpool North 94	d													
Preston	d													
Blackburn 97	d													
Clitheroe 94	d													
Hellifield	d	14 08			15 50					18 14	18 22			
Long Preston	d	14 11			15 53					18 18				
Giggleswick	d				16 00					18 25				
Clapham (Nth Yorkshire)	d				16 08					18 33				
Bentham	d				16 15					18 39				
Wennington	d				16 20					18 44				
Carnforth 82	a				16 36					19 00				
Lancaster 6 65,82,98	a				16 46					19 13				
Bare Lane 98	a				16 56					19 25				
Morecambe 98	a				17 03					19 31				
Settle	d	14 17									18 30			
Horton-in-Ribblesdale	d	14 26									18 39			
Ribblehead	d	14 34									18 47			
Dent	d	14 44									18 57			
Garsdale	d	14 50									19 02			
Kirkby Stephen	d	15 03									19 15			
Appleby	d	15 15									19 28			
Langwathby	d	15 29									19 42			
Lazonby & Kirkoswald	d	15 35									19 48			
Armathwaite	d	15 43									19 56			
Carlisle 8 65	a	16 00									20 13			

		NT	NT	GR ■ 1 🍴	NT	NT	NT	NT
London Kings Cross 15 ⊖26	d			18 35				
Leeds 10 37	d	20 08		21 03	21 08	22 08		23 20
Bradford Forster Square 37	d		20 48				22 48	
Frizinghall 37	d		20 51				22 51	
Shipley 37	a	20 19	20 54		21 19	22 19	22 54	23 31
	d	20 20	20 55		21 20	22 20	22 55	23 32
Saltaire	d	20 22	20 57		21 22	22 22	22 57	23 34
Bingley	d	20 26	21 01		21 26	22 26	23 01	23 38
Crossflatts	d	20 28	21 03		21 28	22 28	23 03	23 40
Keighley	d	20 32	21 08	21s22	21 32	22 32	23 08	23 44
Steeton & Silsden	d	20 36	21 12		21 36	22 36	23 12	23 48
Cononley	d	20 40	21 16		21 40	22 40	23 16	23 52
Skipton	a	20 48	21 23	21 42	21 48	22 48	23 23	23 59
	d							
Gargrave	d							
Blackpool North 94	d							
Preston	d							
Blackburn 97	d							
Clitheroe 94	d							
Hellifield	d							
Long Preston	d							
Giggleswick	d							
Clapham (Nth Yorkshire)	d							
Bentham	d							
Wennington	d							
Carnforth 82	a							
Lancaster 6 65,82,98	a							
Bare Lane 98	a							
Morecambe 98	a							
Settle	d							
Horton-in-Ribblesdale	d							
Ribblehead	d							
Dent	d							
Garsdale	d							
Kirkby Stephen	d							
Appleby	d							
Langwathby	d							
Lazonby & Kirkoswald	d							
Armathwaite	d							
Carlisle 8 65	a							

Table 36

Sundays

19 February to 25 March

Leeds and Bradford - Skipton, Lancaster, Morecambe and Carlisle

Network Diagram - see first page of Table 35

Station		NT	NT	NT	NT	NT	NT	NT	NT	NT	NT	NT	NT	NT	NT	NT	NT	NT	NT	NT	NT	NT	NT
London Kings Cross 15 ⊖26	d																						
Leeds 10 37	d	23p18	09 00	10 08		10 51	11 08	12 08		13 08	13 15	14 08		14 57	15 08	16 08		17 08	17 21	17 33	18 08		19 08
Bradford Forster Square 37	d				10 48				12 48				14 48				16 48					18 48	
Frizinghall 37	d				10 51				12 51				14 51				16 51					18 51	
Shipley 37	a	23p31	09 15	10 19	10 54	11 03	11 19	12 19	12 54	13 19	13 28	14 19	14 54	15 09	15 19	16 19	16 54	17 19	17 33	17 45	18 19	18 54	19 19
	d	23p32	09 16	10 20	10 55	11 04	11 20	12 20	12 55	13 20	13 29	14 20	14 55	15 10	15 20	16 20	16 55	17 20	17 34	17 46	18 20	18 55	19 20
Saltaire	d	23p34	09 18	10 22	10 57		11 22	12 22	12 57	13 22		14 22	14 57		15 22	16 22	16 57	17 22			18 22	18 57	19 22
Bingley	d	23p38	09 23	10 26	11 01	11 09	11 26	12 26	13 01	13 26	13 34	14 26	15 01	15 15	15 26	16 26	17 01	17 26	17 39	17 50	18 26	19 01	19 26
Crossflatts	d	23p40	09 25	10 28	11 03		11 28	12 28	13 03	13 28		14 28	15 03		15 28	16 28	17 03	17 28			18 28	19 03	19 28
Keighley	d	23p44	09 30	10 32	11 08	11 15	11 32	12 32	13 08	13 32	13 39	14 32	15 08	15 20	15 32	16 32	17 08	17 32	17 44	17 56	18 32	19 08	19 32
Steeton & Silsden	d	23p48	09 34	10 36	11 12		11 36	12 36	13 12	13 36		14 36	15 12		15 36	16 36	17 12	17 36			18 36	19 12	19 36
Cononley	d	23p52	09 39	10 40	11 16		11 40	12 40	13 16	13 40		14 40	15 16		15 40	16 40	17 16	17 40			18 40	19 16	19 40
Skipton	a	00 02	09 46	10 48	11 23	11 28	11 48	12 48	13 23	13 48	13 53	14 48	15 23	15 33	15 48	16 48	17 23	17 48	17 57	18 08	18 48	19 23	19 48
	d		09 48			11 30					13 54			15 36					18 00	18 11			
Gargrave	d		09 53			11 35					14 00			15 41					18 05				
Blackpool North 94	d																						
Preston	d																						
Blackburn 97	d																						
Clitheroe 94	d																						
Hellifield	d		10 02			11 44					14 08			15 50					18 14	18 22			
Long Preston	d					11 46					14 11			15 53					18 18				
Giggleswick	d					11 54								16 00					18 25				
Clapham (Nth Yorkshire)	d					12 02								16 08					18 33				
Bentham	d					12 08								16 15					18 39				
Wennington	d					12 13								16 20					18 44				
Carnforth 82	a					12 30								16 36					19 00				
Lancaster 6 65,82,98	a					12 44								16 46					19 13				
Bare Lane 98	a					13 07								16 56					19 29				
Morecambe 98	a					13 13								17 03					19 35				
Settle	d		10 10								14 17									18 30			
Horton-in-Ribblesdale	d		10 19								14 26									18 39			
Ribblehead	d		10 27								14 34									18 47			
Dent	d		10 37								14 44									18 57			
Garsdale	d		10 43								14 50									19 02			
Kirkby Stephen	d		10 56								15 03									19 15			
Appleby	d		11 09								15 15									19 28			
Langwathby	d		11 23								15 29									19 42			
Lazonby & Kirkoswald	d		11 29								15 35									19 48			
Armathwaite	d		11 37								15 43									19 56			
Carlisle 8 65	a		11 56								16 00									20 13			

Station		NT	NT	GR R 1	NT	NT	NT	NT
London Kings Cross 15 ⊖26	d			18 35				
Leeds 10 37	d	20 08		21 03	21 08	22 08		23 20
Bradford Forster Square 37	d		20 48				22 48	
Frizinghall 37	d		20 51				22 51	
Shipley 37	a	20 19	20 54		21 19	22 19	22 54	23 31
	d	20 20	20 55		21 20	22 20	22 55	23 32
Saltaire	d	20 22	20 57		21 22	22 22	22 57	23 34
Bingley	d	20 26	21 01		21 26	22 26	23 01	23 38
Crossflatts	d	20 28	21 03		21 28	22 28	23 03	23 40
Keighley	d	20 32	21 08	21s22	21 32	22 32	23 08	23 44
Steeton & Silsden	d	20 36	21 12		21 36	22 36	23 12	23 48
Cononley	d	20 40	21 16		21 40	22 40	23 16	23 52
Skipton	a	20 48	21 23	21 42	21 48	22 48	23 23	23 59
	d							
Gargrave	d							
Blackpool North 94	d							
Preston	d							
Blackburn 97	d							
Clitheroe 94	d							
Hellifield	d							
Long Preston	d							
Giggleswick	d							
Clapham (Nth Yorkshire)	d							
Bentham	d							
Wennington	d							
Carnforth 82	a							
Lancaster 6 65,82,98	a							
Bare Lane 98	a							
Morecambe 98	a							
Settle	d							
Horton-in-Ribblesdale	d							
Ribblehead	d							
Dent	d							
Garsdale	d							
Kirkby Stephen	d							
Appleby	d							
Langwathby	d							
Lazonby & Kirkoswald	d							
Armathwaite	d							
Carlisle 8 65	a							

Table 36

Sundays
from 1 April

Leeds and Bradford - Skipton, Lancaster, Morecambe and Carlisle

Network Diagram - see first page of Table 35

			NT	NT	NT	NT	NT	NT	NT	NT	NT	NT	NT	NT	NT	NT	NT	NT	NT	NT	NT	NT	NT	NT
London Kings Cross 15	⊖26	d																						
Leeds 10	37	d	23p18	08 40	09 00		10 08		10 51	11 08	12 08		13 08	13 15	14 08		14 57	15 08	16 08		17 08	17 21	17 33	18 08
Bradford Forster Square	37	d						10 48				12 48				14 48				16 48				
Frizinghall	37	d						10 51				12 51				14 51				16 51				
Shipley	37	a	23p31	08 52	09 15		10 19	10 54	11 03	11 19	12 19	12 54	13 19	13 28	14 19	14 54	15 09	15 19	16 19	16 54	17 19	17 33	17 45	18 19
		d	23p32	08 53	09 16		10 20	10 55	11 04	11 20	12 20	12 55	13 20	13 29	14 20	14 55	15 10	15 20	16 20	16 55	17 20	17 34	17 46	18 20
Saltaire		d	23p34	08 55	09 18		10 22	10 57		11 22	12 22	12 57	13 22		14 22	14 57		15 22	16 22	16 57	17 22			18 22
Bingley		d	23p38	09 00	09 23		10 26	11 01	11 09	11 26	12 26	13 01	13 26	13 34	14 26	15 01	15 15	15 26	16 26	17 01	17 26	17 39	17 50	18 26
Crossflatts		d	23p40	09 02	09 25		10 28	11 03		11 28	12 28	13 03	13 28		14 28	15 03		15 28	16 28	17 03	17 28			18 28
Keighley		d	23p44	09 07	09 30		10 32	11 08	11 15	11 32	12 32	13 08	13 32	13 39	14 32	15 08	15 20	15 32	16 32	17 08	17 32	17 44	17 56	18 32
Steeton & Silsden		d	23p48	09 11	09 34		10 36	11 12		11 36	12 36	13 12	13 36		14 36	15 12		15 36	16 36	17 12	17 36			18 36
Cononley		d	23p52	09 16	09 39		10 40	11 16		11 40	12 40	13 16	13 40		14 40	15 16		15 40	16 40	17 16	17 40			18 40
Skipton		a	00 02	09 23	09 46		10 48	11 23	11 28	11 48	12 48	13 23	13 48	13 53	14 48	15 23	15 33	15 48	16 48	17 23	17 48	17 57	18 08	18 48
		d		09 26	09 48				11 30					13 54			15 36					18 00	18 11	
Gargrave		d		09 31	09 53				11 35					14 00			15 41					18 05		
Blackpool North	94	d				08 36																		
Preston		d				09 05																		
Blackburn	97	d				09 27																		
Clitheroe	94	d				09 51																		
Hellifield		d		09 40	10 02	10 15			11 44					14 08			15 50					18 14	18 22	
Long Preston		d		09 43					11 46					14 11			15 53					18 18		
Giggleswick		d		09 52					11 54								16 00					18 25		
Clapham (Nth Yorkshire)		d		10 00					12 02								16 08					18 33		
Bentham		d		10 06					12 08								16 15					18 39		
Wennington		d		10 11					12 13								16 20					18 44		
Carnforth	82	a		10 28					12 30								16 36					19 00		
Lancaster 6	65,82,98	a							12 44								16 46					19 13		
Bare Lane	98	a							13 07								16 56					19 29		
Morecambe	98	a							13 13								17 03					19 35		
Settle		d			10 10	10 35								14 17									18 30	
Horton-in-Ribblesdale		d			10 19	10 44								14 26									18 39	
Ribblehead		d			10 27	10 52								14 34									18 47	
Dent		d			10 37	11 02								14 44									18 57	
Garsdale		d			10 43	11 07								14 50									19 02	
Kirkby Stephen		d			10 56	11 20								15 03									19 15	
Appleby		d			11 09	11 34								15 15									19 28	
Langwathby		d			11 23	11 48								15 29									19 42	
Lazonby & Kirkoswald		d			11 29	11 54								15 35									19 48	
Armathwaite		d			11 37	12 02								15 43									19 56	
Carlisle 8	65	a			11 56	12 17								16 00									20 13	

			NT	NT	NT	NT	GR	NT	NT	NT	NT
London Kings Cross 15	⊖26	d					18 35				
Leeds 10	37	d		19 08	20 08		21 03	21 08	22 08		23 20
Bradford Forster Square	37	d	18 48			20 48				22 48	
Frizinghall	37	d	18 51			20 51				22 51	
Shipley	37	a	18 54	19 19	20 19	20 54		21 19	22 19	22 54	23 31
		d	18 55	19 20	20 20	20 55		21 20	22 20	22 55	23 32
Saltaire		d	18 57	19 22	20 22	20 57		21 22	22 22	22 57	23 34
Bingley		d	19 01	19 26	20 26	21 01		21 26	22 26	23 01	23 38
Crossflatts		d	19 03	19 28	20 28	21 03		21 28	22 28	23 03	23 40
Keighley		d	19 08	19 32	20 32	21 08	21s22	21 32	22 32	23 08	23 44
Steeton & Silsden		d	19 12	19 36	20 36	21 12		21 36	22 36	23 12	23 48
Cononley		d	19 16	19 40	20 40	21 16		21 40	22 40	23 16	23 52
Skipton		a	19 23	19 48	20 48	21 23	21 42	21 48	22 48	23 23	23 59
		d									
Gargrave		d									
Blackpool North	94	d									
Preston		d									
Blackburn	97	d									
Clitheroe	94	d									
Hellifield		d									
Long Preston		d									
Giggleswick		d									
Clapham (Nth Yorkshire)		d									
Bentham		d									
Wennington		d									
Carnforth	82	a									
Lancaster 6	65,82,98	a									
Bare Lane	98	a									
Morecambe	98	a									
Settle		d									
Horton-in-Ribblesdale		d									
Ribblehead		d									
Dent		d									
Garsdale		d									
Kirkby Stephen		d									
Appleby		d									
Langwathby		d									
Lazonby & Kirkoswald		d									
Armathwaite		d									
Carlisle 8	65	a									

Carlisle, Morecambe, Lancaster and Skipton - Bradford and Leeds

Network Diagram - see first page of Table 35

Miles	Miles	Miles			NT	NT	NT	NT	NT	GR [8] [1]	NT	NT	NT		NT	NT	NT	NT	NT	NT	NT	NT	NT		NT
0	—	—	**Carlisle** [8]	65 d														05 53							
10	—	—	Armathwaite	d														06 07							
15½	—	—	Lazonby & Kirkoswald	d														06 14							
19¾	—	—	Langwathby	d														06 20							
30¾	—	—	Appleby	d														06 35							
41½	—	—	Kirkby Stephen	d														06 48							
51¼	—	—	Garsdale	d																					
54¾	—	—	Dent	d																					
60¾	—	—	Ribblehead	d														07 16							
65½	—	—	Horton-in-Ribblesdale	d														07 22							
71¾	—	—	Settle	d														07 30							
—	0	—	**Morecambe**	98 d																					
—	1¾	—	Bare Lane	98 d																					
—	4¼	—	**Lancaster** [6]	65,82,98 d																	07 10				
—	11½	—	Carnforth	82 d																	07 20				
—	21	—	Wennington	d																	07 33				
—	24¼	—	Bentham	d																	07 39				
—	27½	—	Clapham (Nth Yorkshire)	d																	07 45				
—	34¼	—	Giggleswick	d																	07 54				
75½	38	—	Long Preston	d														07 36			08 02				
76¾	39¼	—	Hellifield	d														07 39			08 06				
—	—	—	Clitheroe	94 a																					
—	—	—	Blackburn	94,97 a																					
—	—	—	Preston [8]	97 a																					
—	—	—	Blackpool North	97 a																					
83	45½	—	Gargrave	d														07 47			08 14				
86¾	49¼	—	**Skipton**	a														07 55			08 23				
—	—	—		d	05 48	06 02	06 16	06 27	06 42	06 55	07 01	07 08	07 24		07 30	07 39	07 47	07 57	08 01	08 15	08 27	08 32	08 43		09 02
89¾	52¼	—	Cononley	d	05 52	06 06	06 20	06 31	06 46		07 05	07 12	07 28		07 34		07 51		08 05	08 19		08 36	08 47		09 06
93	55½	—	Steeton & Silsden	d	05 56	06 10	06 25	06 35	06 51		07 10	07 17	07 33		07 39	07 47	07 56	08 04	08 10	08 24		08 40	08 51		09 10
96	58½	—	Keighley	d	06 01	06 15	06 29	06 40	06 56	07u06	07 15	07 21	07 37		07 43	07 51	08 00	08 09	08 14	08 28	08 37	08 45	08 56		09 15
98½	61	—	Crossflatts	d	06 04	06 18	06 33	06 43	07 00		07 19	07 26	07 41		07 47		08 04		08 18	08 32		08 48	08 59		09 18
99¼	61¾	—	Bingley	d	06 07	06 21	06 35	06 46	07 02		07 22	07 28	07 44		07 50	07 56	08 07	08 14	08 21	08 35	08 42	08 51	09 02		09 21
101½	64	—	Saltaire	d	06 10	06 24	06 39	06 49	07 06		07 25	07 32	07 48		07 54		08 11		08 25	08 39		08 54	09 05		09 24
102¼	64¾	0	Shipley	a	06 12	06 27	06 41	06 53	07 08		07 28	07 34	07 50		07 56	08 01	08 13	08 19	08 27	08 41	08 46	08 57	09 07		09 27
—	—	—		d	06 13	06 28	06 42	06 53	07 09	07u14	07 28	07 35	07 50		08 00	08 01	08 13	08 19	08 28	08 41	08 47	08 58	09 08		09 28
—	—	1	Frizinghall	37 a		06 32		06 57			07 32				08 03				08 31			09 02			09 32
—	—	2¾	**Bradford Forster Square**	37 a		06 38		07 03			07 39				08 09				08 38			09 09			09 38
113	75½	—	**Leeds** [10]	37 a	06 27		06 57		07 23	07 29		07 49	08 05			08 18	08 28	08 37		08 56	09 04		09 22		
—	—	—	London Kings Cross [15]	⊖26 a						10 02															

		NT	NT	NT	NT	NT	NT	NT	NT		NT	NT	NT	NT	NT	NT	NT	NT	NT		NT	NT	NT	NT	NT
Carlisle [8]	65 d								08 53																11 55
Armathwaite	d								09 07																12 09
Lazonby & Kirkoswald	d								09 14																12 16
Langwathby	d								09 20																12 22
Appleby	d								09 35																12 37
Kirkby Stephen	d								09 48																12 50
Garsdale	d								10 02																13 03
Dent	d								10 07																13 08
Ribblehead	d								10 17																13 18
Horton-in-Ribblesdale	d								10 24																13 24
Settle	d								10 32																13 32
Morecambe	98 d															10 34									
Bare Lane	98 d															10 38									
Lancaster [6]	65,82,98 d															10 49									
Carnforth	82 d															11 09									
Wennington	d															11 23									
Bentham	d															11 29									
Clapham (Nth Yorkshire)	d															11 35									
Giggleswick	d															11 44									
Long Preston	d															11 52									13 38
Hellifield	d								10 39							11 56									13 41
Clitheroe	94 a																								
Blackburn	94,97 a																								
Preston [8]	97 a																								
Blackpool North	97 a																								
Gargrave	d															12 04									13 49
Skipton	a								10 54							12 13									13 57
	d	09 18	09 32	09 48	10 02	10 18	10 32	10 48	10 59		11 02	11 18	11 33	11 48	12 02	12 13	12 18	12 32	12 48		13 02	13 18	13 32	13 48	13 58
Cononley	d	09 22	09 36	09 52	10 06	10 22	10 36	10 52			11 06	11 22	11 37	11 52	12 06		12 22	12 36	12 52		13 06	13 22	13 36	13 52	
Steeton & Silsden	d	09 26	09 40	09 56	10 10	10 26	10 40	10 56			11 10	11 26	11 41	11 56	12 10		12 26	12 40	12 56		13 10	13 26	13 40	13 56	
Keighley	d	09 31	09 45	10 01	10 15	10 31	10 45	11 01	11 09		11 15	11 31	11 46	12 01	12 15	12 23	12 31	12 45	13 01		13 15	13 31	13 45	14 01	14 09
Crossflatts	d	09 34	09 48	10 04	10 18	10 34	10 48	11 04			11 18	11 34	11 49	12 04	12 18		12 34	12 48	13 04		13 18	13 34	13 48	14 04	
Bingley	d	09 37	09 51	10 07	10 21	10 37	10 51	11 07	11 13		11 21	11 37	11 52	12 07	12 21		12 37	12 51	13 07		13 21	13 37	13 51	14 07	14 13
Saltaire	d	09 40	09 54	10 10	10 24	10 40	10 54	11 10			11 24	11 40	11 55	12 10	12 24		12 40	12 54	13 10		13 24	13 40	13 54	14 10	
Shipley	a	09 43	09 58	10 12	10 27	10 42	10 57	11 12	11 18		11 27	11 43	11 58	12 14	12 27	12 33	12 42	12 57	13 12		13 27	13 42	13 57	14 12	14 18
	d	09 44	09 58	10 14	10 28	10 44	10 58	11 14	11 18		11 28	11 44	11 58	12 14	12 28	12 33	12 44	12 58	13 14		13 28	13 44	13 58	14 14	14 18
Frizinghall	37 a		10 02		10 32		11 02				11 32		12 02		12 32			13 02			13 32		14 02		
Bradford Forster Square	37 a		10 08		10 38		11 08				11 38		12 10		12 38			13 08			13 38		14 08		
Leeds [10]	37 a	09 59		10 28		10 58		11 28	11 36			11 58		12 29		12 55	12 58		13 28			13 58		14 28	14 37
London Kings Cross [15]	⊖26 a																								

Carlisle, Morecambe, Lancaster and Skipton - Bradford and Leeds

Network Diagram - see first page of Table 35

Station			NT	NT	NT	NT	NT	NT A	NT	NT	NT	NT	NT	NT	NT	NT	NT	NT	NT	NT	NT	NT	NT	NT
Carlisle 8	65	d											14 04				15 05							
Armathwaite		d											14 18											
Lazonby & Kirkoswald		d											14 25											
Langwathby		d											14 31											
Appleby		d											14 47				15 42							
Kirkby Stephen		d											15 00				15 55							
Garsdale		d											15 13											
Dent		d											15 18											
Ribblehead		d											15 27											
Horton-in-Ribblesdale		d											15 34											
Settle		d											15 43				16 35							
Morecambe	98	d						13 29													16 19			
Bare Lane	98	d						13 36													16 23			
Lancaster 6	65,82,98	d						13 48																
Carnforth	82	d						13 58													16 32			
Wennington		d						14 12													16 46			
Bentham		d						14 18													16 52			
Clapham (Nth Yorkshire)		d						14 24													16 59			
Giggleswick		d						14 33													17 10			
Long Preston		d						14 40													17 18			
Hellifield		d						14 44					15 50								17 22			
Clitheroe	94	a																						
Blackburn	94,97	a																						
Preston 8	97	a																						
Blackpool North	97	a																						
Gargrave		d						14 52													17 30			
Skipton		a						15 03					16 05				16 55				17 39			
		d	14 02	14 18	14 32	14 48	15 00	15 10	15 18	15 32	15 48	16 02	16 10	16 18	16 36	16 49	16 58	17 02	17 19	17 28	17 40	17 49	18 02	18 16
Cononley		d	14 06	14 22	14 36	14 52	15 04		15 22	15 36	15 52	16 06		16 22	16 40	16 53		17 06	17 23	17 32		17 53	18 06	18 20
Steeton & Silsden		d	14 10	14 27	14 40	14 56	15 08		15 26	15 40	15 56	16 10		16 26	16 44	16 57		17 10	17 27	17 36		17 57	18 10	18 25
Keighley		d	14 15	14 31	14 45	15 01	15 13	15 20	15 31	15 45	16 01	16 15	16 21	16 31	16 49	17 02	17 08	17 15	17 32	17 41	17 50	18 02	18 15	18 29
Crossflatts		d	14 18	14 35	14 48	15 04	15 16		15 34	15 48	16 04	16 18		16 34	16 52	17 05		17 18	17 35	17 44		18 05	18 18	18 33
Bingley		d	14 21	14 38	14 51	15 07	15 19	15 25	15 37	15 51	16 07	16 21	16 26	16 37	16 55	17 08	17 15	17 21	17 38	17 47		18 08	18 21	18 35
Saltaire		d	14 24	14 42	14 54	15 10	15 22		15 40	15 54	16 10	16 24		16 40	16 58	17 11		17 24	17 41	17 50		18 11	18 24	18 39
Shipley		a	14 28	14 44	14 57	15 12	15 26	15 30	15 43	15 57	16 12	16 27	16 31	16 42	17 02	17 13	17 20	17 27	17 43	17 55	17 58	18 13	18 28	18 42
		d	14 28	14 45	14 58	15 14	15 28	15 30	15 44	15 58	16 14	16 28	16 31	16 44	17 02	17 15	17 23	17 28	17 45	17 56	17 58	18 14	18 28	18 44
Frizinghall	37	a	14 32		15 02		15 32			16 02		16 31			17 06			17 32		17 59			18 32	
Bradford Forster Square	37	a	14 38		15 08		15 38			16 08		16 38			17 12			17 38		18 05			18 38	
Leeds 10	37	a		15 00		15 28		15 47	15 58		16 28		16 51	16 58		17 29	17 40		18 00		18 15	18 29		18 59
London Kings Cross 15	⊖26	a																						

Station			NT	NT	NT	NT	NT	NT	NT	NT	NT	NT	NT	NT	NT	NT	NT	NT	NT
Carlisle 8	65	d	16 18								18 18								
Armathwaite		d	16 32								18 32								
Lazonby & Kirkoswald		d	16 39								18 39								
Langwathby		d	16 45								18 45								
Appleby		d	17 01								19 00								
Kirkby Stephen		d	17 14								19 13								
Garsdale		d	17 27								19 26								
Dent		d	17 32								19 31								
Ribblehead		d	17 42								19 41						21 00		
Horton-in-Ribblesdale		d	17 48								19 47						21 06		
Settle		d	17 57								19 55						21 14		
Morecambe	98	d											19 08						
Bare Lane	98	d											19 12						
Lancaster 6	65,82,98	d											19 24						
Carnforth	82	d											19 34						
Wennington		d											19 48						
Bentham		d											19 54						
Clapham (Nth Yorkshire)		d											20 00						
Giggleswick		d											20 09						
Long Preston		d	18 03										20 17				21 20		
Hellifield		d	18 06								20 03		20 21				21 23		
Clitheroe	94	a																	
Blackburn	94,97	a																	
Preston 8	97	a																	
Blackpool North	97	a																	
Gargrave		d	18 14										20 29				21 31		
Skipton		a	18 23								20 18		20 38				21 38		
		d	18 28	18 32	18 48	19 00	19 18	19 32	19 48	19 54	20 20	20 23	20 42	20 48	20 54	21 18	21 48	21 54	22 18
Cononley		d		18 36	18 52	19 04	19 22	19 36	19 52	19 58		20 29		20 52	20 58	21 22	21 52	21 58	22 22
Steeton & Silsden		d		18 40	18 56	19 08	19 26	19 40	19 56	20 02		20 33		20 56	21 02	21 26	21 56	22 02	22 26
Keighley		d	18 38	18 45	19 01	19 13	19 31	19 45	20 01	20 07	20 30	20 38	20 52	21 01	21 07	21 31	22 01	22 07	22 31
Crossflatts		d		18 48	19 04	19 16	19 34	19 48	20 04	20 10		20 41		21 04	21 10	21 34	22 04	22 10	22 34
Bingley		d	18 42	18 51	19 07	19 19	19 37	19 51	20 07	20 13	20 34	20 44		21 07	21 13	21 37	22 07	22 13	22 37
Saltaire		d		18 54	19 10	19 22	19 40	19 54	20 10	20 17		20 47		21 10	21 16	21 40	22 10	22 16	22 40
Shipley		a	18 48	18 58	19 12	19 25	19 42	19 58	20 12	20 19	20 39	20 49	20 59	21 12	21 19	21 42	22 13	22 21	22 42
		d	18 48	18 58	19 14	19 26	19 44	19 58	20 14	20 20	20 41	20 50	20 59	21 14	21 19	21 43	22 14	22 21	22 43
Frizinghall	37	a		19 02		19 29		20 01		20 24					21 23			22 24	
Bradford Forster Square	37	a		19 08		19 35		20 08		20 32					21 29			22 31	
Leeds 10	37	a	19 07		19 31		19 59		20 28		21 01	21 05	21 17	21 30		21 59	22 33		23 01
London Kings Cross 15	⊖26	a																	

A From Heysham Port

Table 36

Saturdays

Carlisle, Morecambe, Lancaster and Skipton - Bradford and Leeds

Network Diagram - see first page of Table 35

			NT	NT	NT	NT	GR	NT	NT	NT	NT		NT	NT	NT	NT	NT	NT	NT	NT	NT		NT	NT	NT	NT
				A	B		■ 1																			
Carlisle 8	65	d																					07 52			
Armathwaite		d																					08 06			
Lazonby & Kirkoswald		d																					08 13			
Langwathby		d																					08 19			
Appleby		d																					08 34			
Kirkby Stephen		d																					08 47			
Garsdale		d																					09 00			
Dent		d																					09 05			
Ribblehead		d									07 16												09 15			
Horton-in-Ribblesdale		d									07 22												09 21			
Settle		d									07 30												09 29			
Morecambe	98	d																								
Bare Lane	98	d																								
Lancaster 6	65,82,98	d																		08 24						
Carnforth	82	d																		08 34						
Wennington		d																		08 48						
Bentham		d																		08 53						
Clapham (Nth Yorkshire)		d																		09 00						
Giggleswick		d																		09 08						
Long Preston		d									07 36									09 16						
Hellifield		d									07 39									09 20			09 37			
Clitheroe	94	a																								
Blackburn	94,97	a																								
Preston 8	97	a																								
Blackpool North	97	a																								
Gargrave		d									07 47									09 28						
Skipton		a									07 55									09 37			09 53			
		d	05 48	06 02	06 10	06 47	06 55	07 05	07 30	07 47	07 57		08 01	08 18	08 32	08 48	09 02	09 18	09 32	09 42	09 48		09 57	10 02	10 18	10 32
Cononley		d	05 52	06 06	06 14	06 51		07 09	07 34	07 51			08 05	08 22	08 36	08 52	09 06	09 22	09 36		09 52			10 06	10 22	10 36
Steeton & Silsden		d	05 56	06 10	06 18	06 56		07 14	07 39	07 56	08 04		08 10	08 27	08 40	08 56	09 10	09 26	09 40		09 56			10 10	10 26	10 40
Keighley		d	06 01	06 15	06 23	07 00	07u08	07 19	07 43	08 00	08 09		08 14	08 31	08 45	09 01	09 15	09 31	09 45	09 52	10 01		10 08	10 15	10 31	10 45
Crossflatts		d	06 04	06 18	06 26	07 04		07 23	07 47	08 04			08 18	08 35	08 48	09 04	09 18	09 34	09 48		10 04			10 18	10 34	10 48
Bingley		d	06 07	06 21	06 29	07 07		07 26	07 50	08 07	08 14		08 21	08 38	08 51	09 07	09 21	09 37	09 51	09 58	10 07		10 12	10 21	10 37	10 51
Saltaire		d	06 10	06 24	06 32	07 11		07 29	07 54	08 11			08 25	08 42	08 54	09 10	09 24	09 40	09 54		10 10			10 24	10 40	10 54
Shipley		a	06 12	06 27	06 37	07 13		07 32	07 56	08 13	08 19		08 27	08 44	08 57	09 12	09 27	09 43	09 58	10 02	10 12		10 19	10 27	10 42	10 57
		d	06 13	06 28	06 37	07 13	07u18	07 32	08 00	08 13	08 19		08 28	08 44	08 58	09 14	09 28	09 44	09 58	10 02	10 14		10 19	10 28	10 44	10 58
Frizinghall	37	a		06 32	06 41			07 36	08 03				08 31		09 02		09 32		10 02					10 32		11 02
Bradford Forster Square	37	a		06 38	06 47			07 42	08 09				08 38		09 09		09 38		10 08					10 38		11 08
Leeds 10	37	a	06 27			07 27	07 33			08 28	08 37			08 58		09 28		09 59		10 20	10 28		10 34		10 58	
London Kings Cross 15	⊖26	a					09 52																			

			NT	NT	NT	NT	NT		NT	NT	NT	NT	NT	NT	NT	NT	NT		NT	NT	NT	NT	NT	NT	NT	NT
																										C
Carlisle 8	65	d				09 26														11 51						
Armathwaite		d				09 40														12 05						
Lazonby & Kirkoswald		d				09 47														12 12						
Langwathby		d				09 53														12 18						
Appleby		d				10 08														12 33						
Kirkby Stephen		d				10 21														12 46						
Garsdale		d				10 35														12 59						
Dent		d				10 40														13 04						
Ribblehead		d				10 49														13 14						
Horton-in-Ribblesdale		d				10 56														13 20						
Settle		d				11 04														13 28						
Morecambe	98	d									10 34															13 29
Bare Lane	98	d									10 38															13 36
Lancaster 6	65,82,98	d									10 49															13 48
Carnforth	82	d									11 09															13 58
Wennington		d									11 23															14 12
Bentham		d									11 29															14 18
Clapham (Nth Yorkshire)		d									11 36															14 25
Giggleswick		d									11 44															14 33
Long Preston		d									11 52									13 34						14 40
Hellifield		d				11 11					11 56									13 37						14 44
Clitheroe	94	a																								
Blackburn	94,97	a																								
Preston 8	97	a																								
Blackpool North	97	a																								
Gargrave		d									12 04									13 45						14 52
Skipton		a				11 26					12 13									13 55						15 03
		d	10 48	11 02	11 18	11 28	11 33		11 48	12 02	12 13	12 18	12 32	12 48	13 02	13 18	13 32		13 48	13 58	14 02	14 18	14 32	14 48	15 00	15 10
Cononley		d	10 52	11 06	11 22		11 37		11 52	12 06		12 22	12 36	12 52	13 06	13 22	13 36		13 52		14 06	14 22	14 36	14 52	15 04	
Steeton & Silsden		d	10 56	11 10	11 26		11 41		11 56	12 10		12 26	12 40	12 56	13 10	13 26	13 40		13 56		14 10	14 27	14 40	14 56	15 08	
Keighley		d	11 01	11 15	11 31	11 38	11 46		12 01	12 15	12 23	12 31	12 45	13 01	13 15	13 31	13 45		14 01	14 09	14 15	14 31	14 45	15 01	15 13	15 20
Crossflatts		d	11 04	11 18	11 34		11 49		12 04	12 18		12 34	12 48	13 04	13 18	13 34	13 48		14 04		14 18	14 35	14 48	15 04	15 16	
Bingley		d	11 07	11 21	11 37	11 42	11 52		12 07	12 21		12 37	12 51	13 07	13 21	13 37	13 51		14 07	14 13	14 21	14 38	14 51	15 07	15 19	15 25
Saltaire		d	11 10	11 24	11 40		11 55		12 10	12 24		12 40	12 54	13 10	13 24	13 40	13 54		14 10		14 24	14 42	14 54	15 10	15 22	
Shipley		a	11 12	11 27	11 43	11 49	11 58		12 14	12 27	12 33	12 42	12 57	13 12	13 27	13 42	13 57		14 12	14 18	14 28	14 44	14 57	15 12	15 26	15 30
		d	11 14	11 28	11 44	11 49	11 58		12 14	12 28	12 33	12 44	12 58	13 14	13 28	13 44	13 58		14 14	14 18	14 28	14 45	14 58	15 14	15 28	15 30
Frizinghall	37	a		11 32			12 02			12 32			13 02		13 32		14 02				14 32		15 02		15 32	
Bradford Forster Square	37	a		11 38			12 10			12 38			13 08		13 38		14 08				14 38		15 08		15 38	
Leeds 10	37	a	11 28		11 58	12 07			12 29		12 55	12 58		13 28		13 58			14 28	14 37		15 00		15 28		15 47
London Kings Cross 15	⊖26	a																								

A from 31 March

B until 24 March

C From Heysham Port

Table 36

Saturdays

Carlisle, Morecambe, Lancaster and Skipton - Bradford and Leeds

Network Diagram - see first page of Table 35

	NT		NT	NT	NT	NT	NT	NT	NT	NT	NT		NT	NT	NT	NT	NT	NT	NT	NT	NT		NT	NT
Carlisle 8 65 d							14 26							15 49					16 18					
Armathwaite d							14 40												16 32					
Lazonby & Kirkoswald d							14 47												16 39					
Langwathby d							14 53												16 45					
Appleby d							15 09							16 26					17 01					
Kirkby Stephen d							15 22							16 39					17 14					
Garsdale d							15 35												17 27					
Dent d							15 40												17 32					
Ribblehead d							15 49												17 42					
Horton-in-Ribblesdale d							15 56												17 48					
Settle d							16 04							17 16					17 57					
Morecambe 98 d																16 19								
Bare Lane 98 d																16 24								
Lancaster 6 65,82,98 d																16 40								
Carnforth 82 d																16 50								
Wennington d																17 04								
Bentham d																17 09								
Clapham (Nth Yorkshire) d																17 16								
Giggleswick d																17 25								
Long Preston d																17 33			18 03					
Hellifield d							16 11									17 36			18 06					
Clitheroe 94 a																								
Blackburn 94,97 a																								
Preston 8 97 a																								
Blackpool North 97 a																								
Gargrave d																17 44			18 14					
Skipton a							16 26							17 38		17 54			18 23					
d	15 18		15 32	15 48	16 02	16 18	16 28	16 33	16 49	17 02	17 19		17 28	17 41	17 49	17 58	18 02	18 16	18 28	18 32	18 48		19 00	19 18
Cononley d	15 22		15 36	15 52	16 06	16 22		16 37	16 53	17 06	17 23		17 32		17 53		18 06	18 20		18 36	18 52		19 04	19 22
Steeton & Silsden d	15 26		15 40	15 56	16 10	16 26		16 41	16 57	17 10	17 27		17 36		17 57		18 10	18 25		18 40	18 56		19 08	19 26
Keighley d	15 31		15 45	16 01	16 15	16 31	16 38	16 46	17 02	17 15	17 32		17 41	17 51	18 02	18 08	18 15	18 29	18 38	18 45	19 01		19 13	19 31
Crossflatts d	15 34		15 48	16 04	16 18	16 34		16 49	17 05	17 18	17 35		17 44		18 05		18 18	18 33		18 48	19 04		19 16	19 34
Bingley d	15 37		15 51	16 07	16 21	16 37	16 42	16 52	17 08	17 21	17 38		17 47	17 55	18 08	18 14	18 21	18 35	18 42	18 51	19 07		19 19	19 37
Saltaire d	15 40		15 54	16 10	16 24	16 40		16 55	17 11	17 24	17 41		17 50		18 11		18 24	18 39		18 54	19 10		19 22	19 40
Shipley a	15 43		15 57	16 12	16 27	16 42	16 49	16 59	17 13	17 27	17 43		17 55	18 00	18 13	18 19	18 28	18 42	18 48	18 58	19 12		19 25	19 42
d	15 44		15 58	16 14	16 28	16 44	16 49	16 59	17 15	17 28	17 45		17 56	18 00	18 14	18 19	18 28	18 44	18 48	18 58	19 14		19 26	19 44
Frizinghall 37 a			16 02		16 31			17 03		17 32			17 59				18 32			19 02			19 29	
Bradford Forster Square 37 a			16 08		16 38			17 08		17 38			18 05				18 38			19 08			19 35	
Leeds 10 37 a	15 58			16 28		16 58	17 07		17 29		18 00			18 17	18 29	18 42		18 59	19 07		19 29			19 59
London Kings Cross 15 ⊖26 a																								

	NT	NT	NT	NT	NT	NT	NT		NT	NT	NT	NT	NT	NT
Carlisle 8 65 d				18 07										
Armathwaite d				18 21										
Lazonby & Kirkoswald d				18 28										
Langwathby d				18 34										
Appleby d				18 49										
Kirkby Stephen d				19 02										
Garsdale d				19 15										
Dent d				19 20										
Ribblehead d				19 30							21 00			
Horton-in-Ribblesdale d				19 36							21 06			
Settle d				19 44							21 14			
Morecambe 98 d						19 09								
Bare Lane 98 d						19 13								
Lancaster 6 65,82,98 d						19 24								
Carnforth 82 d						19 35								
Wennington d						19 49								
Bentham d						19 54								
Clapham (Nth Yorkshire) d						20 01								
Giggleswick d						20 10								
Long Preston d						20 18					21 20			
Hellifield d				19 52		20 21					21 23			
Clitheroe 94 a														
Blackburn 94,97 a														
Preston 8 97 a														
Blackpool North 97 a														
Gargrave d						20 29					21 31			
Skipton a				20 07		20 38					21 38			
d	19 32	19 48	19 54	20 07	20 18	20 38	20 48		20 54	21 18		21 48	21 54	22 18
Cononley d	19 36	19 52	19 58		20 22		20 52		20 58	21 22		21 52	21 58	22 22
Steeton & Silsden d	19 40	19 56	20 02		20 26		20 56		21 02	21 26		21 56	22 02	22 26
Keighley d	19 45	20 01	20 07	20 17	20 31	20 48	21 01		21 07	21 31		22 01	22 07	22 31
Crossflatts d	19 48	20 04	20 10		20 33		21 04		21 10	21 34		22 04	22 10	22 34
Bingley d	19 51	20 07	20 13	20 22	20 37	20 53	21 07		21 13	21 37		22 07	22 13	22 37
Saltaire d	19 54	20 10	20 17		20 39		21 10		21 16	21 40		22 10	22 16	22 40
Shipley a	19 57	20 12	20 20	20 27	20 42	20 57	21 12		21 22	21 42		22 13	22 20	22 42
d	19 58	20 14	20 20	20 28	20 43	20 57	21 14		21 22	21 43		22 14	22 21	22 43
Frizinghall 37 a	20 01		20 24						21 26				22 24	
Bradford Forster Square 37 a	20 08		20 32						21 32				22 31	
Leeds 10 37 a		20 28		20 46	21 00	21 16	21 30			21 59		22 33		23 01
London Kings Cross 15 ⊖26 a														

Table 36

Sundays
until 1 January

Carlisle, Morecambe, Lancaster and Skipton - Bradford and Leeds

Network Diagram - see first page of Table 35

Station	Table		NT	NT	NT	NT	NT	NT	NT	NT	NT	NT	NT	NT	NT	NT	NT	NT A	NT	NT	NT	NT	NT	NT
Carlisle 8	65	d						09 25									13 51						16 37	
Armathwaite		d						09 39									14 05						16 51	
Lazonby & Kirkoswald		d						09 46									14 12						16 58	
Langwathby		d						09 53									14 19						17 05	
Appleby		d						10 07									14 33						17 20	
Kirkby Stephen		d						10 21									14 47						17 34	
Garsdale		d						10 34									15 00						17 47	
Dent		d						10 40									15 06						17 53	
Ribblehead		d						10 49									15 15						18 02	
Horton-in-Ribblesdale		d						10 56									15 22						18 09	
Settle		d						11 04									15 30						18 19	
Morecambe	98	d											12 20					14 46						17 45
Bare Lane	98	d											12 24					14 50						17 49
Lancaster 6	65,82,98	d											12 48											18 04
Carnforth	82	d											12 58					15 00						18 14
Wennington		d											13 12					15 14						18 28
Bentham		d											13 17					15 20						18 33
Clapham (Nth Yorkshire)		d											13 24					15 26						18 40
Giggleswick		d											13 32					15 35						18 49
Long Preston		d						11 10					13 40				15 36	15 45						18 57
Hellifield		d						11 13					13 44				15 39	15 49					18 26	19 00
Clitheroe	94	a																						
Blackburn	94,97	a																						
Preston 8	97	a																						
Blackpool North	97	a																						
Gargrave		d						11 21					13 52				15 47	15 57						19 09
Skipton		a						11 30					14 01				15 54	16 06					18 41	19 17
		d	08 35	09 15	09 36	10 15	11 15	11 30	11 37	12 15	13 15	13 37	14 02	14 15	15 15	15 37	15 57	16 08	16 15	17 15	17 37	18 15	18 43	19 18
Cononley		d	08 39	09 19	09 40	10 19	11 19		11 41	12 19	13 19	13 41		14 19	15 19	15 41			16 19	17 19	17 41	18 19		
Steeton & Silsden		d	08 44	09 23	09 44	10 23	11 23		11 45	12 23	13 23	13 45		14 23	15 23	15 45			16 23	17 23	17 45	18 23		
Keighley		d	08 48	09 28	09 49	10 28	11 28	11 40	11 50	12 28	13 28	13 50	14 12	14 28	15 28	15 50	16 07	16 18	16 28	17 28	17 50	18 28	18 53	19 28
Crossflatts		d	08 52	09 31	09 52	10 31	11 31		11 53	12 31	13 31	13 53		14 31	15 31	15 53			16 31	17 31	17 53	18 31		
Bingley		d	08 54	09 34	09 55	10 34	11 34	11 44	11 56	12 34	13 34	13 56	14 16	14 34	15 34	15 56	16 11	16 23	16 34	17 34	17 56	18 34	18 57	19 32
Saltaire		d	08 58	09 37	09 58	10 37	11 37		11 59	12 37	13 37	13 59		14 37	15 37	15 59			16 37	17 37	17 59	18 37		
Shipley		a	09 00	09 39	10 01	10 39	11 39	11 49	12 02	12 39	13 39	14 02	14 21	14 39	15 39	16 02	16 16	16 27	16 39	17 39	18 02	18 39	19 02	19 37
		d	09 00	09 40	10 01	10 40	11 40	11 49	12 02	12 40	13 40	14 02	14 21	14 40	15 40	16 02	16 16	16 29	16 40	17 40	18 02	18 40	19 03	19 38
Frizinghall	37	a			10 05				12 06			14 06				16 06					18 06			
Bradford Forster Square	37	a			10 12				12 12			14 12				16 12					18 12			
Leeds 10	37	a	09 14	09 54		10 54	11 54	12 06		12 54	13 54		14 39	14 54	15 54		16 34	16 47	16 54	17 54		18 54	19 21	19 56
London Kings Cross 15	⊖26	a																						

Station	Table		NT	NT	NT	NT	NT	NT	NT	NT
Carlisle 8	65	d								
Armathwaite		d								
Lazonby & Kirkoswald		d								
Langwathby		d								
Appleby		d								
Kirkby Stephen		d								
Garsdale		d								
Dent		d								
Ribblehead		d								
Horton-in-Ribblesdale		d								
Settle		d								
Morecambe	98	d					20 00			
Bare Lane	98	d					20 04			
Lancaster 6	65,82,98	d					20 18			
Carnforth	82	d					20 28			
Wennington		d					20 42			
Bentham		d					20 47			
Clapham (Nth Yorkshire)		d					20 54			
Giggleswick		d					21 03			
Long Preston		d					21 11			
Hellifield		d					21 14			
Clitheroe	94	a								
Blackburn	94,97	a								
Preston 8	97	a								
Blackpool North	97	a								
Gargrave		d					21 22			
Skipton		a					21 31			
		d	19 24	19 37	20 15	21 15	21 33	21 39	22 15	23 15
Cononley		d	19 28	19 41	20 19	21 19		21 43	22 19	23 19
Steeton & Silsden		d	19 32	19 45	20 23	21 23		21 47	22 23	23 23
Keighley		d	19 37	19 50	20 28	21 28	21 43	21 52	22 28	23 29
Crossflatts		d	19 40	19 53	20 31	21 31		21 55	22 31	23 31
Bingley		d	19 43	19 56	20 34	21 34	21 48	21 58	22 34	23 34
Saltaire		d	19 46	19 59	20 37	21 37		22 01	22 37	23 37
Shipley		a	19 48	20 02	20 39	21 39	21 53	22 04	22 39	23 41
		d	19 49	20 02	20 40	21 40	21 54	22 04	22 40	23 41
Frizinghall	37	a		20 06				22 08		
Bradford Forster Square	37	a		20 12				22 14		
Leeds 10	37	a	20 03		20 54	21 54	22 10		22 54	23 58
London Kings Cross 15	⊖26	a								

A From Lancaster

Table 36

Sundays

8 January to 12 February

Carlisle, Morecambe, Lancaster and Skipton - Bradford and Leeds

Network Diagram - see first page of Table 35

			NT	NT	NT	NT	NT	NT	NT	NT	NT	NT	NT	NT	NT	NT	NT	NT	NT	NT	NT	NT	NT	NT
																		A						
Carlisle 8	65	d						09 25									13 51						16 37	
Armathwaite		d						09 39									14 05						16 51	
Lazonby & Kirkoswald		d						09 46									14 12						16 58	
Langwathby		d						09 53									14 19						17 05	
Appleby		d						10 07									14 33						17 20	
Kirkby Stephen		d						10 21									14 47						17 34	
Garsdale		d						10 34									15 00						17 47	
Dent		d						10 40									15 06						17 53	
Ribblehead		d						10 49									15 15						18 02	
Horton-in-Ribblesdale		d						10 56									15 22						18 09	
Settle		d						11 04									15 30						18 19	
Morecambe	98	d											12 20					14 46						17 45
Bare Lane	98	d											12 24					14 50						17 49
Lancaster 6	65,82,98	d											12 48											18 04
Carnforth	82	d											12 58					15 00						18 14
Wennington		d											13 12					15 14						18 28
Bentham		d											13 17					15 20						18 33
Clapham (Nth Yorkshire)		d											13 24					15 26						18 40
Giggleswick		d											13 32					15 35						18 49
Long Preston		d						11 10					13 40				15 36	15 45						18 57
Hellifield		d						11 13					13 44				15 39	15 49					18 26	19 00
Clitheroe	94	a																						
Blackburn	94,97	a																						
Preston 8	97	a																						
Blackpool North	97	a																						
Gargrave		d						11 21					13 52				15 47	15 57						19 09
Skipton		a						11 30					14 01				15 54	16 06					18 41	19 17
		d	08 35	09 15	09 36	10 15	11 15	11 30	11 37	12 15	13 15	13 37	14 02	14 15	15 15	15 37	15 57	16 08	16 15	17 15	17 37	18 15	18 43	19 18
Cononley		d	08 39	09 19	09 40	10 19	11 19		11 41	12 19	13 19	13 41		14 19	15 19	15 41			16 19	17 19	17 41	18 19		
Steeton & Silsden		d	08 44	09 23	09 44	10 23	11 23		11 45	12 23	13 23	13 45		14 23	15 23	15 45			16 23	17 23	17 45	18 23		
Keighley		d	08 48	09 28	09 49	10 28	11 28	11 40	11 50	12 28	13 28	13 50	14 12	14 28	15 28	15 50	16 07	16 18	16 28	17 28	17 50	18 28	18 53	19 28
Crossflatts		d	08 52	09 31	09 52	10 31	11 31		11 53	12 31	13 31	13 53		14 31	15 31	15 53			16 31	17 31	17 53	18 31		
Bingley		d	08 54	09 34	09 55	10 34	11 34	11 44	11 56	12 34	13 34	13 56	14 16	14 34	15 34	15 56	16 11	16 23	16 34	17 34	17 56	18 34	18 57	19 32
Saltaire		d	08 58	09 37	09 58	10 37	11 37		11 59	12 37	13 37	13 59		14 37	15 37	15 59			16 37	17 37	17 59	18 37		
Shipley		a	09 00	09 39	10 01	10 39	11 39	11 49	12 02	12 39	13 39	14 02	14 21	14 39	15 39	16 02	16 16	16 27	16 39	17 39	18 02	18 39	19 02	19 37
		d	09 00	09 40	10 01	10 40	11 40	11 49	12 02	12 40	13 40	14 02	14 21	14 40	15 40	16 02	16 16	16 29	16 40	17 40	18 02	18 40	19 03	19 38
Frizinghall	37	a			10 05				12 06			14 06				16 06					18 06			
Bradford Forster Square	37	a			10 12				12 12			14 12				16 12					18 12			
Leeds 10	37	a	09 14	09 54		10 54	11 54	12 06		12 54	13 54		14 39	14 54	15 54		16 34	16 47	16 54	17 54		18 54	19 21	19 56
London Kings Cross 15	⊖26	a																						

			NT	NT	NT	NT	NT	NT	NT	NT
Carlisle 8	65	d								
Armathwaite		d								
Lazonby & Kirkoswald		d								
Langwathby		d								
Appleby		d								
Kirkby Stephen		d								
Garsdale		d								
Dent		d								
Ribblehead		d								
Horton-in-Ribblesdale		d								
Settle		d								
Morecambe	98	d					20 00			
Bare Lane	98	d					20 04			
Lancaster 6	65,82,98	d					20 20			
Carnforth	82	d					20 30			
Wennington		d					20 44			
Bentham		d					20 49			
Clapham (Nth Yorkshire)		d					20 56			
Giggleswick		d					21 05			
Long Preston		d					21 13			
Hellifield		d					21 16			
Clitheroe	94	a								
Blackburn	94,97	a								
Preston 8	97	a								
Blackpool North	97	a								
Gargrave		d					21 24			
Skipton		a					21 33			
		d	19 24	19 37	20 15	21 15	21 33	21 39	22 15	23 15
Cononley		d	19 28	19 41	20 19	21 19		21 43	22 19	23 19
Steeton & Silsden		d	19 32	19 45	20 23	21 23		21 47	22 23	23 23
Keighley		d	19 37	19 50	20 28	21 28	21 43	21 52	22 28	23 29
Crossflatts		d	19 40	19 53	20 31	21 31		21 55	22 31	23 31
Bingley		d	19 43	19 56	20 34	21 34	21 48	21 58	22 34	23 34
Saltaire		d	19 46	19 59	20 37	21 37		22 01	22 37	23 37
Shipley		a	19 48	20 02	20 39	21 39	21 53	22 04	22 39	23 41
		d	19 49	20 02	20 40	21 40	21 54	22 04	22 40	23 41
Frizinghall	37	a		20 06				22 08		
Bradford Forster Square	37	a		20 12				22 14		
Leeds 10	37	a	20 03		20 54	21 54	22 10		22 54	23 58
London Kings Cross 15	⊖26	a								

A From Lancaster

Table 36

Sundays

19 February to 25 March

Carlisle, Morecambe, Lancaster and Skipton - Bradford and Leeds

Network Diagram - see first page of Table 35

		NT	NT	NT	NT	NT	NT	NT	NT	NT	NT	NT	NT	NT	NT	NT	NT A	NT	NT	NT	NT	NT	NT
Carlisle 8	65 d						09 25									13 51						16 37	
Armathwaite	d						09 39									14 05						16 51	
Lazonby & Kirkoswald	d						09 46									14 12						16 58	
Langwathby	d						09 53									14 19						17 05	
Appleby	d						10 07									14 33						17 20	
Kirkby Stephen	d						10 21									14 47						17 34	
Garsdale	d						10 34									15 00						17 47	
Dent	d						10 40									15 06						17 53	
Ribblehead	d						10 49									15 15						18 02	
Horton-in-Ribblesdale	d						10 56									15 22						18 09	
Settle	d						11 04									15 30						18 19	
Morecambe	98 d											12 20					14 46						17 45
Bare Lane	98 d											12 24					14 50						17 49
Lancaster 6	65,82,98 d											12 48											18 04
Carnforth	82 d											12 58					15 00						18 14
Wennington	d											13 12					15 14						18 28
Bentham	d											13 17					15 20						18 33
Clapham (Nth Yorkshire)	d											13 24					15 26						18 40
Giggleswick	d											13 32					15 35						18 49
Long Preston	d						11 10					13 40				15 36	15 45						18 57
Hellifield	d						11 13					13 44				15 39	15 49					18 26	19 00
Clitheroe	94 a																						
Blackburn	94,97 a																						
Preston 8	97 a																						
Blackpool North	97 a																						
Gargrave	d						11 21					13 52				15 47	15 57						19 09
Skipton	a						11 30					14 01				15 54	16 06					18 41	19 17
	d	08 35	09 15	09 36	10 15	11 15	11 30	11 37	12 15	13 15	13 37	14 02	14 15	15 15	15 37	15 57	16 08	16 15	17 15	17 37	18 15	18 43	19 18
Cononley	d	08 39	09 19	09 40	10 19	11 19		11 41	12 19	13 19	13 41		14 19	15 19	15 41			16 19	17 19	17 41	18 19		
Steeton & Silsden	d	08 44	09 23	09 44	10 23	11 23		11 45	12 23	13 23	13 45		14 23	15 23	15 45			16 23	17 23	17 45	18 23		
Keighley	d	08 48	09 28	09 49	10 28	11 28	11 40	11 50	12 28	13 28	13 50	14 12	14 28	15 28	15 50	16 07	16 18	16 28	17 28	17 50	18 28	18 53	19 28
Crossflatts	d	08 52	09 31	09 52	10 31	11 31		11 53	12 31	13 31	13 53		14 31	15 31	15 53			16 31	17 31	17 53	18 31		
Bingley	d	08 54	09 34	09 55	10 34	11 34	11 44	11 56	12 34	13 34	13 56	14 16	14 34	15 34	15 56	16 11	16 23	16 34	17 34	17 56	18 34	18 57	19 32
Saltaire	d	08 58	09 37	09 58	10 37	11 37		11 59	12 37	13 37	13 59		14 37	15 37	15 59			16 37	17 37	17 59	18 37		
Shipley	a	09 00	09 39	10 01	10 39	11 39	11 49	12 02	12 39	13 39	14 02	14 21	14 39	15 39	16 02	16 16	16 27	16 39	17 39	18 02	18 39	19 02	19 37
	d	09 00	09 40	10 01	10 40	11 40	11 49	12 02	12 40	13 40	14 02	14 21	14 40	15 40	16 02	16 16	16 29	16 40	17 40	18 02	18 40	19 03	19 38
Frizinghall	37 a			10 05				12 06			14 06				16 06					18 06			
Bradford Forster Square	37 a			10 12				12 12			14 12				16 12					18 12			
Leeds 10	37 a	09 14	09 54		10 54	11 54	12 06		12 54	13 54		14 39	14 54	15 54		16 34	16 47	16 54	17 54		18 54	19 21	19 56
London Kings Cross 15	⊖26 a																						

		NT	NT	NT	NT	NT	NT	NT	NT
Carlisle 8	65 d								
Armathwaite	d								
Lazonby & Kirkoswald	d								
Langwathby	d								
Appleby	d								
Kirkby Stephen	d								
Garsdale	d								
Dent	d								
Ribblehead	d								
Horton-in-Ribblesdale	d								
Settle	d								
Morecambe	98 d					20 00			
Bare Lane	98 d					20 04			
Lancaster 6	65,82,98 d					20 20			
Carnforth	82 d					20 30			
Wennington	d					20 44			
Bentham	d					20 49			
Clapham (Nth Yorkshire)	d					20 56			
Giggleswick	d					21 05			
Long Preston	d					21 13			
Hellifield	d					21 16			
Clitheroe	94 a								
Blackburn	94,97 a								
Preston 8	97 a								
Blackpool North	97 a								
Gargrave	d					21 24			
Skipton	a					21 33			
	d	19 24	19 37	20 15	21 15	21 33	21 39	22 15	23 15
Cononley	d	19 28	19 41	20 19	21 19		21 43	22 19	23 19
Steeton & Silsden	d	19 32	19 45	20 23	21 23		21 47	22 23	23 23
Keighley	d	19 37	19 50	20 28	21 28	21 43	21 52	22 28	23 29
Crossflatts	d	19 40	19 53	20 31	21 31		21 55	22 31	23 31
Bingley	d	19 43	19 56	20 34	21 34	21 48	21 58	22 34	23 34
Saltaire	d	19 46	19 59	20 37	21 37		22 01	22 37	23 37
Shipley	a	19 48	20 02	20 39	21 39	21 53	22 04	22 39	23 41
	d	19 49	20 02	20 40	21 40	21 54	22 04	22 40	23 41
Frizinghall	37 a		20 06				22 08		
Bradford Forster Square	37 a		20 12				22 14		
Leeds 10	37 a	20 03		20 54	21 54	22 10		22 54	23 58
London Kings Cross 15	⊖26 a								

A From Lancaster

Table 36

Sundays
from 1 April

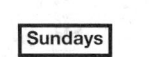

Carlisle, Morecambe, Lancaster and Skipton - Bradford and Leeds

Network Diagram - see first page of Table 35

		NT	NT	NT	NT	NT	NT	NT	NT	NT		NT	NT	NT	NT	NT	NT	NT	NT	NT		NT	NT	NT	NT
																		A							
Carlisle 8 65	d						09 25										13 51							16 37	
Armathwaite	d						09 39										14 05							16 51	
Lazonby & Kirkoswald	d						09 46										14 12							16 58	
Langwathby	d						09 53										14 19							17 05	
Appleby	d						10 07										14 33							17 20	
Kirkby Stephen	d						10 21										14 47							17 34	
Garsdale	d						10 34										15 00							17 47	
Dent	d						10 40										15 06							17 53	
Ribblehead	d						10 49										15 15							18 02	
Horton-in-Ribblesdale	d						10 56										15 22							18 09	
Settle	d						11 04										15 30							18 19	
Morecambe 98	d												12 31					14 46							17 45
Bare Lane 98	d												12 35					14 50							17 49
Lancaster 6 65,82,98	d												12 48												18 04
Carnforth 82	d												12 58					15 00							18 14
Wennington	d												13 12					15 14							18 28
Bentham	d												13 17					15 20							18 33
Clapham (Nth Yorkshire)	d												13 24					15 26							18 40
Giggleswick	d												13 32					15 35							18 49
Long Preston	d						11 10						13 40				15 36	15 45							18 57
Hellifield	d						11 13						13 44				15 39	15 49						18 26	19 00
Clitheroe 94	a																								
Blackburn 94,97	a																								
Preston 8 97	a																								
Blackpool North 97	a																								
Gargrave	d						11 21						13 52				15 47	15 57							19 09
Skipton	a						11 30						14 01				15 54	16 06						18 41	19 17
	d	08 35	09 15	09 36	10 15	11 15	11 30	11 37	12 15	13 15		13 37	14 02	14 15	15 15	15 37	15 57	16 08	16 15	17 15		17 37	18 15	18 43	19 18
Cononley	d	08 39	09 19	09 40	10 19	11 19		11 41	12 19	13 19		13 41		14 19	15 19	15 41			16 19	17 19		17 41	18 19		
Steeton & Silsden	d	08 44	09 23	09 44	10 23	11 23		11 45	12 23	13 23		13 45		14 23	15 23	15 45			16 23	17 23		17 45	18 23		
Keighley	d	08 48	09 28	09 49	10 28	11 28	11 40	11 50	12 28	13 28		13 50	14 12	14 28	15 28	15 50	16 07	16 18	16 28	17 28		17 50	18 28	18 53	19 28
Crossflatts	d	08 52	09 31	09 52	10 31	11 31		11 53	12 31	13 31		13 53		14 31	15 31	15 53			16 31	17 31		17 53	18 31		
Bingley	d	08 54	09 34	09 55	10 34	11 34	11 44	11 56	12 34	13 34		13 56	14 16	14 34	15 34	15 56	16 11	16 23	16 34	17 34		17 56	18 34	18 57	19 32
Saltaire	d	08 58	09 37	09 58	10 37	11 37		11 59	12 37	13 37		13 59		14 37	15 37	15 59			16 37	17 37		17 59	18 37		
Shipley	a	09 00	09 39	10 01	10 39	11 39	11 49	12 02	12 39	13 39		14 02	14 21	14 39	15 39	16 02	16 16	16 27	16 39	17 39		18 02	18 39	19 02	19 37
	d	09 00	09 40	10 01	10 40	11 40	11 49	12 02	12 40	13 40		14 02	14 21	14 40	15 40	16 02	16 16	16 29	16 40	17 40		18 02	18 40	19 03	19 38
Frizinghall 37	a			10 05				12 06				14 06				16 06						18 06			
Bradford Forster Square 37	a			10 12				12 12				14 12				16 12						18 12			
Leeds 10 37	a	09 14	09 54		10 54	11 54	12 06		12 54	13 54			14 39	14 54	15 54		16 34	16 47	16 54	17 54			18 54	19 21	19 56
London Kings Cross 15 ⊖26	a																								

		NT	NT	NT	NT	NT		NT	NT	NT	NT
		🚲									
Carlisle 8 65	d	17 41									
Armathwaite	d	17 55									
Lazonby & Kirkoswald	d	18 03									
Langwathby	d	18 09									
Appleby	d	18 25									
Kirkby Stephen	d	18 38									
Garsdale	d	18 52									
Dent	d	18 57									
Ribblehead	d	19 07									
Horton-in-Ribblesdale	d	19 14									
Settle	d	19 22									
Morecambe 98	d							20 00			
Bare Lane 98	d							20 04			
Lancaster 6 65,82,98	d							20 20			
Carnforth 82	d							20 30			
Wennington	d							20 44			
Bentham	d							20 49			
Clapham (Nth Yorkshire)	d							20 56			
Giggleswick	d							21 05			
Long Preston	d							21 13			
Hellifield	d	19 32						21 16			
Clitheroe 94	a	19 56									
Blackburn 94,97	a	20 22									
Preston 8 97	a	20 47									
Blackpool North 97	a	21 16									
Gargrave	d							21 24			
Skipton	a							21 33			
	d		19 24	19 37	20 15	21 15		21 33	21 39	22 15	23 15
Cononley	d		19 28	19 41	20 19	21 19			21 43	22 19	23 19
Steeton & Silsden	d		19 32	19 45	20 23	21 23			21 47	22 23	23 23
Keighley	d		19 37	19 50	20 28	21 28		21 43	21 52	22 28	23 29
Crossflatts	d		19 40	19 53	20 31	21 31			21 55	22 31	23 31
Bingley	d		19 43	19 56	20 34	21 34		21 48	21 58	22 34	23 34
Saltaire	d		19 46	19 59	20 37	21 37			22 01	22 37	23 37
Shipley	a		19 48	20 02	20 39	21 39		21 53	22 04	22 39	23 41
	d		19 49	20 02	20 40	21 40		21 54	22 04	22 40	23 41
Frizinghall 37	a			20 06					22 08		
Bradford Forster Square 37	a			20 12					22 14		
Leeds 10 37	a		20 03		20 54	21 54		22 10		22 54	23 58
London Kings Cross 15 ⊖26	a										

A From Lancaster

Table 37

Mondays to Fridays

Leeds - Shipley and Bradford

Network Diagram - see first page of Table 35

Miles	Miles			NT	NT	NT	NT	NT	NT	NT	NT	NT		NT	NT	NT	NT	NT	NT	NT	NT	NT		NT	NT
0	0	**Leeds** 10	d	05 08	05 29	05 51	06 03	06 16	06 22		06 37				06 49	06 51	06 56	07 08		07 23		07 25		07 37	
10¾	—	**Shipley**	a		05 41			06 27							07 01		07 08					07 36			
—	—		d							06 28		06 41		06 53	07 02				07 15		07 28				07 47
11¾	—	Frizinghall	d							06 32		06 44		06 57	07 04				07 17		07 32				07 49
—	4	Bramley	d	05 15		05 58			06 29		06 44							07 15		07 30				07 44	
—	5¾	New Pudsey	d	05 20		06 02	06 13		06 34		06 49					07 01		07 20		07 35				07 49	
—	9½	**Bradford Interchange**	a	05 28		06 13	06 21		06 42		06 57					07 11		07 28		07 43				07 57	
13½	—	**Bradford Forster Square**	a							06 38		06 50		07 03	07 10				07 22		07 39				07 56

		NT	NT	NT	NT	NT	NT	NT		NT	NT	NT	NT	NT	NT	NT	NT	NT		NT	NT	NT	NT	NT	NT
Leeds 10	d	07 39	07 51		07 51	08 08		08 10			08 19	08 23	08 25	08 37		08 40		08 49		08 51	08 56	09 07		09 10	09 23
Shipley	a	07 50			08 02			08 22			08 31		08 37			08 51		09 01			09 07			09 21	
	d	07 51		08 00			08 13	08 23		08 28					08 48	08 52	08 58						09 18	09 22	
Frizinghall	d	07 53		08 03			08 16	08 25		08 31					08 50	08 54	09 02						09 21	09 24	
Bramley	d					08 15						08 30		08 44								09 14			09 30
New Pudsey	d		08 01			08 20						08 35		08 49						09 00		09 19			09 35
Bradford Interchange	a		08 09			08 28						08 43		08 57						09 12		09 28			09 43
Bradford Forster Square	a	07 59		08 09			08 22	08 31		08 38					08 56	09 00	09 09						09 27	09 31	

		NT	NT	NT		NT	NT	NT	NT	NT	NT	NT	NT	NT		NT	NT	NT	NT	NT	NT	NT	NT	NT	
Leeds 10	d		09 26	09 37			09 40		09 47	09 53	09 56	10 07		10 10			10 19	10 23	10 26	10 37		10 40		10 49	
Shipley	a		09 37				09 52		10 01		10 07			10 21			10 31		10 37			10 51		11 01	
	d	09 28				09 44	09 52	09 58					10 14	10 22		10 28					10 44	10 52	10 58		
Frizinghall	d	09 32				09 47	09 54	10 02					10 17	10 24		10 32					10 47	10 54	11 02		
Bramley	d			09 44								10 14						10 30		10 44					
New Pudsey	d			09 49						10 02		10 20						10 35		10 49					
Bradford Interchange	a			09 57						10 12		10 28						10 43		10 57					
Bradford Forster Square	a	09 38				09 53	10 02	10 08					10 23	10 30		10 38					10 53	11 00	11 08		

		NT	NT	NT	NT	NT	NT	NT	NT	NT		NT	NT	NT	NT	NT	NT	NT	NT	NT		NT	NT	NT	NT
Leeds 10	d	10 53	10 56	11 07		11 10	11 23		11 26	11 37			11 40	11 53		11 56	12 07		12 10	12 23			12 26	12 37	
Shipley	a		11 07			11 21			11 38				11 51			12 07			12 21				12 37		
	d				11 14	11 22		11 28				11 44	11 52		11 58			12 14	12 22			12 28			12 44
Frizinghall	d				11 17	11 24		11 32				11 47	11 54		12 02			12 17	12 24			12 32			12 47
Bramley	d			11 14			11 30			11 44							12 14			12 30				12 44	
New Pudsey	d	11 02		11 19			11 35			11 49				12 02			12 19			12 35				12 49	
Bradford Interchange	a	11 11		11 28			11 43			11 57				12 11			12 28			12 43				12 57	
Bradford Forster Square	a				11 23	11 30		11 38				11 53	12 00		12 10			12 24	12 31			12 38			12 53

		NT	NT	NT	NT	NT		NT	NT	NT	NT	NT	NT	NT	NT	NT		NT	NT	NT	NT	NT	NT	NT	NT
Leeds 10	d	12 40		12 49	12 53	12 56		13 07		13 10	13 23		13 26	13 37		13 40			13 49	13 53	13 56	14 07		14 10	14 23
Shipley	a	12 51		13 01		13 07				13 21			13 37			13 51			14 03		14 07			14 21	
	d	12 52	12 58						13 14	13 22		13 28			13 44	13 52		13 58					14 14	14 22	
Frizinghall	d	12 54	13 02						13 17	13 24		13 32			13 47	13 54		14 02					14 17	14 24	
Bramley	d							13 14			13 30			13 44								14 14			14 30
New Pudsey	d				13 02			13 19			13 35			13 49						14 02		14 19			14 35
Bradford Interchange	a				13 12			13 28			13 43			13 58						14 12		14 28			14 43
Bradford Forster Square	a	13 00	13 08						13 23	13 30		13 38			13 53	14 00		14 08					14 23	14 30	

		NT		NT	NT	NT	NT	NT	NT	NT	NT	NT		NT	NT	NT	NT	NT	NT	NT	NT	NT		NT	NT
Leeds 10	d			14 26	14 37		14 40		14 49	14 53	14 56	15 07			15 10	15 23		15 26	15 37		15 40	15 52			15 56
Shipley	a			14 37			14 51		15 01		15 07				15 21			15 37			15 52				16 07
	d	14 28				14 44	14 52	14 58						15 14	15 22		15 28			15 44	15 52			15 58	
Frizinghall	d	14 32				14 47	14 54	15 02						15 17	15 24		15 32			15 47	15 55			16 02	
Bramley	d				14 44							15 14				15 30			15 44						
New Pudsey	d				14 49					15 02		15 19				15 35			15 49			16 01			
Bradford Interchange	a				14 57					15 12		15 28				15 43			15 57			16 10			
Bradford Forster Square	a	14 38				14 53	15 00	15 08						15 23	15 30		15 38			15 53	16 01			16 08	

		NT	NT	NT	NT	NT	NT	NT		NT	NT	NT	NT	NT	NT	NT	NT	NT		NT	NT	NT	NT	NT	NT
Leeds 10	d	16 07		16 10	16 23		16 26			16 35	16 37	16 39	16 51		16 56	17 07		17 10		17 23		17 26		17 36	17 37
Shipley	a			16 21			16 37			16 49		16 53			17 07			17 21				17 37		17 49	
	d		16 14	16 22		16 28		16 44		16 49				17 02			17 15	17 22			17 28		17 44	17 50	
Frizinghall	d		16 17	16 24		16 31		16 47		16 52				17 06			17 17	17 24			17 32		17 46	17 52	
Bramley	d	16 14			16 30						16 44					17 14				17 30					17 44
New Pudsey	d	16 19			16 35						16 49		17 00			17 19				17 35					17 49
Bradford Interchange	a	16 28			16 43						16 57		17 10			17 28				17 43					17 57
Bradford Forster Square	a		16 23	16 30		16 38		16 53		16 58				17 12			17 23	17 30			17 38		17 53	17 58	

		NT	NT	NT		NT	NT	NT	NT	NT	NT	NT	NT	NT		NT	NT	NT	NT	NT	NT	NT	NT	NT	
Leeds 10	d	17 39	17 51			17 56		18 06	18 08	18 10	18 23		18 26	18 37			18 40	18 51		18 54	19 08		19 10		
Shipley	a	17 53				18 07		18 18		18 22			18 38				18 52			19 05			19 21		
	d			17 56			18 14			18 22		18 28				18 44	18 52		18 58			19 14	19 22	19 26	
Frizinghall	d			17 59			18 17			18 24		18 32				18 46	18 55		19 02			19 17	19 24	19 29	
Bramley	d								18 15		18 30			18 44							19 15				
New Pudsey	d		18 01						18 20		18 35			18 49				19 01			19 20				
Bradford Interchange	a		18 10						18 28		18 43			18 58				19 10			19 28				
Bradford Forster Square	a			18 05			18 23			18 31		18 38				18 52	19 01		19 08			19 23	19 30	19 35	

Table 37

Leeds - Shipley and Bradford

Network Diagram - see first page of Table 35

		NT	NT	NT	NT	NT	NT	NT	NT	NT		NT	NT	NT	NT	NT	NT	NT	GR	NT		NT	NT	NT	NT
																			R 1						
Leeds 10	d	19 19	19 23	19 26	19 37			19 56	20 08				20 26	20 37		20 51		20 56	21 00	21 08			21 26	21 37	
Shipley	a	19 31		19 37				20 07					20 37					21 07	21s12				21 38		
	d					19 44	19 58			20 20		20 28			20 48		21 03					21 19			21 48
Frizinghall	d					19 47	20 01			20 24		20 30			20 51		21 05					21 23			21 51
Bramley	d		19 30		19 44				20 15					20 44						21 15				21 44	
New Pudsey	d		19 35		19 49				20 20					20 49		21 01				21 20				21 49	
Bradford Interchange	a		19 44		19 57				20 28					20 57		21 10				21 28				21 57	
Bradford Forster Square	a					19 53	20 08			20 32		20 36			20 57		21 12		21 25			21 29			21 57

		NT	NT	NT	NT	NT		NT	NT	NT	NT	NT	NT
Leeds 10	d		21 56	22 08		22 26		22 37			22 56	23 08	23 18
Shipley	a		22 07			22 37					23 08		23 31
	d	22 03			22 21				22 48	23 03			
Frizinghall	d	22 05			22 24				22 51	23 05			
Bramley	d			22 15				22 44				23 15	
New Pudsey	d			22 20				22 49				23 20	
Bradford Interchange	a			22 28				22 57				23 29	
Bradford Forster Square	a	22 11			22 31				22 57	23 13			

Saturdays

		NT	NT	NT	NT	NT A	NT	NT B	NT	NT		NT	NT	NT	NT	NT	NT	NT	NT	NT		NT	NT	NT	NT
Leeds 10	d	05 37	05 51	05 55	06 16		06 19		06 37			06 51	06 56	07 08	07 10	07 23		07 37		07 51			07 56	08 08	08 10
Shipley	a			06 07			06 31						07 08		07 21								08 08		08 22
	d					06 28		06 37		06 44					07 22		07 32		07 47			08 00			08 23
Frizinghall	d					06 32		06 41		06 47					07 24		07 36		07 49			08 03			08 25
Bramley	d	05 44	05 58		06 23				06 44					07 15		07 30		07 44						08 15	
New Pudsey	d	05 49	06 02		06 28				06 49			07 01		07 20		07 35		07 49		08 01				08 20	
Bradford Interchange	a	05 57	06 13		06 36				06 57			07 11		07 28		07 43		07 57		08 09				08 28	
Bradford Forster Square	a					06 38		06 47		06 55					07 30		07 42		07 56			08 09			08 31

		NT	NT	NT	NT	NT		NT	NT	NT	NT	NT	NT	NT	NT	NT		NT	NT	NT	NT	NT	NT	NT	NT
Leeds 10	d		08 19	08 23	08 25	08 37			08 40		08 49	08 51	08 56	09 07		09 10		09 23		09 26	09 37		09 40		09 47
Shipley	a		08 31		08 37				08 51		09 01		09 07			09 21				09 37			09 52		10 01
	d	08 28						08 44	08 52	08 58					09 14	09 22			09 28			09 44	09 52	09 58	
Frizinghall	d	08 31						08 46	08 54	09 02					09 17	09 24			09 32			09 47	09 54	10 02	
Bramley	d			08 30		08 44								09 14				09 30			09 44				
New Pudsey	d			08 35		08 49						09 00		09 19				09 35			09 49				
Bradford Interchange	a			08 43		08 57						09 12		09 28				09 43			09 57				
Bradford Forster Square	a	08 38						08 53	09 00	09 09					09 24	09 31			09 38			09 53	10 02	10 08	

		NT		NT	NT	NT	NT	NT	NT	NT	NT	NT		NT	NT	NT	NT	NT	NT	NT	NT	NT		NT	NT
Leeds 10	d	09 53		09 56	10 07		10 10		10 19	10 23	10 26	10 37			10 40		10 49	10 53	10 56	11 07		11 10		11 23	
Shipley	a			10 07			10 21		10 31		10 37				10 51		11 01		11 07			11 21			
	d					10 14	10 22	10 28						10 44	10 52	10 58					11 14	11 22			11 28
Frizinghall	d					10 17	10 24	10 32						10 47	10 54	11 02					11 17	11 24			11 32
Bramley	d				10 14					10 30		10 44								11 14				11 30	
New Pudsey	d	10 02			10 19					10 35		10 49						11 02		11 19				11 35	
Bradford Interchange	a	10 11			10 28					10 43		10 57						11 12		11 28				11 43	
Bradford Forster Square	a					10 23	10 30	10 38						10 53	11 00	11 08					11 23	11 30			11 38

		NT	NT	NT	NT	NT	NT	NT		NT	NT	NT	NT	NT	NT	NT	NT	NT		NT	NT	NT	NT	NT	NT
Leeds 10	d	11 26	11 37		11 40	11 53		11 56		12 07		12 10	12 23		12 26	12 37		12 40			12 49	12 53	12 56	13 07	
Shipley	a	11 38			11 51			12 07				12 21			12 37			12 51			13 01		13 07		
	d			11 44	11 52		11 58				12 14	12 22		12 28			12 44	12 52		12 58					13 14
Frizinghall	d			11 47	11 54		12 02				12 17	12 24		12 32			12 47	12 54		13 02					13 17
Bramley	d		11 44							12 14			12 30			12 44								13 14	
New Pudsey	d		11 49			12 02				12 19			12 35			12 49						13 02		13 19	
Bradford Interchange	a		11 57			12 12				12 28			12 43			12 57						13 12		13 28	
Bradford Forster Square	a			11 53	12 00		12 10				12 24	12 31		12 38			12 53	13 00		13 08					13 23

		NT	NT	NT		NT	NT	NT	NT	NT	NT	NT	NT	NT		NT	NT	NT	NT	NT	NT	NT	NT	NT	
Leeds 10	d	13 10	13 23			13 26	13 37		13 40		13 49	13 53	13 56	14 07			14 10	14 23		14 26	14 37		14 40		
Shipley	a	13 21				13 37			13 51		14 03		14 07				14 21			14 37			14 51		
	d	13 22		13 28				13 44	13 52	13 58						14 14	14 22		14 28			14 44	14 52	14 58	
Frizinghall	d	13 24		13 32				13 47	13 54	14 02						14 17	14 24		14 32			14 47	14 54	15 02	
Bramley	d		13 30				13 44							14 14				14 30			14 44				
New Pudsey	d		13 35				13 49					14 02		14 19				14 35			14 49				
Bradford Interchange	a		13 43				13 58					14 12		14 28				14 43			14 58				
Bradford Forster Square	a	13 30		13 38				13 53	14 00	14 08						14 23	14 30		14 38			14 53	15 00	15 08	

		NT	NT	NT	NT	NT	NT	NT	NT	NT		NT	NT	NT	NT	NT	NT	NT	NT	NT		NT	NT	NT	NT
Leeds 10	d	14 49	14 53	14 56	15 07		15 10	15 23		15 26		15 37		15 40	15 52		15 56	16 07		16 10		16 23		16 26	
Shipley	a	15 01		15 07			15 21			15 37				15 52			16 07			16 21				16 37	
	d					15 14	15 22		15 28				15 44	15 52		15 58			16 14	16 22			16 28		16 44
Frizinghall	d					15 17	15 24		15 32				15 47	15 55		16 02			16 17	16 24			16 31		16 47
Bramley	d				15 14			15 30				15 44						16 14				16 30			
New Pudsey	d		15 02		15 19			15 35				15 49			16 01			16 19				16 35			
Bradford Interchange	a		15 12		15 28			15 43				15 57			16 10			16 28				16 43			
Bradford Forster Square	a					15 23	15 30		15 38				15 53	16 01		16 08			16 23	16 30			16 38		16 53

A from 31 March

B until 24 March

Saturdays

Leeds - Shipley and Bradford

Network Diagram - see first page of Table 35

		NT	NT	NT	NT	NT		NT	NT	NT	NT	NT	NT	NT	NT	NT		NT	NT	NT	NT	NT	NT	NT	NT
Leeds 10	d	16 35	16 37	16 39	16 51			16 56	17 07		17 10	17 23		17 26	17 37			17 40		17 50	17 51	17 56	18 08		18 10
Shipley	a	16 49		16 53				17 07			17 21			17 37				17 51		18 02		18 07			18 22
	d	16 49				16 59				17 15	17 22		17 28			17 44		17 52	17 56					18 14	18 22
Frizinghall	d	16 52				17 03				17 17	17 24		17 32			17 46		17 54	17 59					18 17	18 24
Bramley	d		16 44						17 14			17 30			17 44								18 15		
New Pudsey	d		16 49		17 00				17 19			17 35			17 49						18 01		18 20		
Bradford Interchange	a		16 57		17 10				17 28			17 43			17 57						18 09		18 28		
Bradford Forster Square	a	16 58				17 08				17 23	17 30		17 38			17 53		18 00	18 05					18 23	18 31

		NT		NT	NT	NT	NT	NT	NT	NT	NT	NT		NT	NT	NT	NT	NT	NT	NT	NT	NT		NT	NT
Leeds 10	d	18 23			18 26	18 37		18 40	18 51		18 56	19 08			19 10		19 19	19 23	19 26	19 37				19 56	20 08
Shipley	a				18 38			18 52			19 07				19 21		19 31		19 37					20 07	
	d			18 28			18 44	18 52		18 58				19 14	19 22	19 26					19 44	19 58			
Frizinghall	d			18 32			18 46	18 55		19 02				19 17	19 24	19 29					19 47	20 01			
Bramley	d	18 30				18 44						19 15						19 30		19 44					20 15
New Pudsey	d	18 35				18 49			19 01			19 20						19 35		19 49					20 20
Bradford Interchange	a	18 43				18 58			19 10			19 28						19 44		19 57					20 28
Bradford Forster Square	a			18 38			18 52	19 01		19 08				19 23	19 30	19 35					19 53	20 08			

		NT	NT	NT	NT	NT	NT	NT		NT	NT	NT	NT	NT	NT	NT	GR	NT		NT	NT	NT	NT	NT	NT
																	R 1								
Leeds 10	d			20 26	20 37		20 51			20 56	21 08		21 26	21 37			21 59	22 03		22 08		22 26	22 37		
Shipley	a			20 37						21 07			21 38				22s11	22 15				22 37			
	d	20 20	20 28			20 48		21 03				21 22			21 48	22 03					22 21			22 48	23 03
Frizinghall	d	20 24	20 30			20 51		21 05				21 26			21 51	22 05					22 24			22 51	23 05
Bramley	d				20 44						21 15			21 44						22 15			22 44		
New Pudsey	d				20 49		21 01				21 20			21 49						22 20			22 49		
Bradford Interchange	a				20 57		21 10				21 28			21 57						22 28			22 57		
Bradford Forster Square	a	20 32	20 36			20 57		21 12				21 32			21 57	22 11	22 24				22 31			22 57	23 13

		NT	NT	NT
Leeds 10	d	22 56	23 00	23 18
Shipley	a	23 08		23 31
	d			
Frizinghall	d			
Bramley	d		23 07	
New Pudsey	d		23 12	
Bradford Interchange	a		23 21	
Bradford Forster Square	a			

Sundays

		NT	NT	NT	NT A	NT	NT	NT	NT	NT		NT	NT	NT	NT	NT	NT	NT	NT	NT		NT	NT	NT	NT
Leeds 10	d	08 02	08 21	08 34	08 40	08 45	09 00	09 02	09 18	09 34		09 35	09 54			10 08	10 12	10 34	10 35	10 51		10 54	11 08	11 12	11 34
Shipley	a			08 45	08 52		09 15			09 45						10 19		10 45		11 03			11 19		11 45
	d			08 46						09 46				10 01	10 15			10 46							11 46
Frizinghall	d			08 48						09 48				10 05	10 18			10 48							11 48
Bramley	d	08 09	08 28					09 09	09 25				10 01				10 19					11 01		11 19	
New Pudsey	d	08 14	08 33			08 54		09 14	09 30			09 44	10 06				10 24		10 44			11 06		11 24	
Bradford Interchange	a	08 22	08 41			09 03		09 22	09 38			09 53	10 14				10 32		10 53			11 14		11 32	
Bradford Forster Square	a			08 54						09 54				10 12	10 24			10 54							11 54

		NT	NT	NT	NT	NT		NT	NT	NT	NT	NT	NT	NT	NT	NT		NT	NT	NT	NT	NT	NT	NT	NT
Leeds 10	d	11 35	11 54			12 08		12 12	12 34	12 35	12 54	13 08	13 12	13 15	13 34	13 35		13 54			14 08	14 12	14 34	14 35	14 54
Shipley	a					12 19			12 45			13 19		13 28	13 45						14 19		14 45		
	d			12 02	12 15				12 46						13 46				14 02	14 15			14 46		
Frizinghall	d			12 06	12 18				12 48						13 48				14 06	14 18			14 48		
Bramley	d		12 01					12 19			13 01		13 19					14 01				14 19			15 01
New Pudsey	d	11 44	12 06					12 24		12 44	13 06		13 24			13 44		14 06				14 24		14 44	15 06
Bradford Interchange	a	11 53	12 14					12 32		12 53	13 14		13 32			13 53		14 14				14 32		14 53	15 14
Bradford Forster Square	a			12 12	12 24				12 54						13 54				14 12	14 24			14 54		

		NT		NT	NT	NT	NT	NT	NT	NT	NT	NT		NT	NT	NT	NT	NT	NT	NT	NT	NT		NT	NT
Leeds 10	d	14 57		15 08	15 12	15 34	15 35	15 54			16 08	16 13		16 35	16 35	16 54	17 08	17 12	17 21	17 33	17 35	17 37		17 54	
Shipley	a	15 09		15 19		15 45					16 19				16 46		17 19		17 33	17 45		17 48			
	d					15 46			16 02	16 15					16 46							17 49			18 02
Frizinghall	d					15 48			16 06	16 18					16 48							17 51			18 06
Bramley	d				15 19			16 01				16 20				17 01		17 19						18 01	
New Pudsey	d				15 24		15 44	16 06				16 25		16 44		17 06		17 24			17 44			18 06	
Bradford Interchange	a				15 32		15 53	16 14				16 33		16 53		17 14		17 32			17 53			18 14	
Bradford Forster Square	a					15 54			16 12	16 24					16 55							17 58			18 12

		NT	NT	NT	NT	NT	NT	NT		NT	NT	NT	NT	NT	NT	NT	NT	NT		NT	NT	NT	NT	NT	NT
Leeds 10	d		18 08	18 13	18 34	18 35	19 03	19 08		19 34	19 35	19 54			20 08	20 12	20 34	20 35		21 04	21 08	21 34	21 35		22 05
Shipley	a		18 19		18 45			19 19		19 45					20 19		20 45				21 19	21 45			
	d	18 15			18 46					19 46			20 02	20 15			20 46					21 46		22 04	
Frizinghall	d	18 18			18 48					19 48			20 06	20 18			20 48					21 48		22 08	
Bramley	d			18 20			19 10					20 01				20 19				21 12			21 43		22 12
New Pudsey	d			18 25		18 44	19 15				19 44	20 06				20 24		20 44		21 17			21 47		22 17
Bradford Interchange	a			18 33		18 53	19 24				19 53	20 14				20 34		20 53		21 25			21 56		22 27
Bradford Forster Square	a	18 24			18 54					19 54			20 12	20 24			20 54					21 54		22 14	

A until 1 January and from 1 April

Table 37

Sundays

Leeds - Shipley and Bradford

Network Diagram - see first page of Table 35

		NT	NT	NT		NT	NT	NT
Leeds 10	d		22 08	22 34		22 38	23 20	23 22
Shipley	a		22 19	22 46			23 31	
	d	22 15		22 47				
Frizinghall	d	22 18		22 49				
Bramley	d					22 45		23 29
New Pudsey	d					22 50		23 34
Bradford Interchange	a					22 58		23 43
Bradford Forster Square	a	22 24		22 55				

Table 37

Mondays to Fridays

Bradford and Shipley - Leeds

Network Diagram - see first page of Table 35

Miles	Miles			NT MX	NT MO	NT MX	NT	NT	NT	NT	NT	GR R 1 A		NT	NT	NT	NT	NT	NT	NT	NT	GR R 1		NT	NT
0	—	**Bradford Forster Square**	d				05 59	06 04		06 15		06 30		06 39		06 44		06 55			07 11			07 15	
—	0	**Bradford Interchange**	d	23p46	23p47	00 37					06 18						06 48			07 02					07 20
—	3½	New Pudsey	d	23p54	23p55						06 27						06 57			07 11					07 28
—	5½	Bramley	d	23p58	23p59						06 31						07 01			07 15					
1¾	—	Frizinghall	d				06 02	06 07		06 18				06 43		06 47		06 58			07 14			07 18	
2¾	—	**Shipley**	a				06 06	06 11		06 22				06 47		06 51		07 02			07 18			07 22	
—	—		d				06 07		06 13			06u35			06 42			07 02	07 09			07u14			
13½	9½	**Leeds** 10	a	00 08	00 08	00 55	06 22		06 27		06 41	06 52			06 57		07 09	07 16	07 23	07 27		07 29			07 39

		NT	NT	NT	NT	NT	NT	NT		NT	NT	NT	NT	NT	NT	NT	NT	NT		NT	NT	NT	NT	NT	NT
Bradford Forster Square	d			07 42	07 46					07 59	08 09			08 16			08 26				08 41	08 46			
Bradford Interchange	d		07 34				07 50						08 05			08 20				08 34				08 50	
New Pudsey	d		07 42				07 58						08 13			08 28				08 42				08 58	
Bramley	d		07 46				08 02						08 18							08 46				09 02	
Frizinghall	d			07 45	07 49					08 02	08 12			08 19			08 29				08 44	08 49			
Shipley	a			07 49	07 53					08 06	08 16			08 23			08 33				08 48	08 53			
	d	07 35				07 50		08 01		08 07		08 13			08 19		08 33	08 41					08 47		09 08
Leeds 10	a	07 49	07 57			08 05	08 12	08 18		08 24		08 28	08 29		08 37	08 39	08 49	08 56		08 57			09 04	09 12	09 22

		NT	NT	NT		NT	NT	NT	NT	NT	NT	NT	NT	NT		NT	NT	NT	NT	NT	NT	NT	NT	NT	
Bradford Forster Square	d	09 01		09 11		09 16		09 31		09 41		09 46		10 01			10 11		10 16		10 31	10 41			
Bradford Interchange	d		09 04				09 20		09 34				09 50			10 05				10 18				10 34	
New Pudsey	d		09 12				09 27		09 42				09 58			10 13				10 28				10 42	
Bramley	d		09 16						09 46				10 02			10 17								10 46	
Frizinghall	d	09 04		09 14		09 19		09 34		09 44		09 49		10 04			10 14		10 19		10 34	10 44			
Shipley	a	09 08		09 18		09 23		09 38		09 48		09 53		10 08			10 18		10 23		10 38	10 48			
	d	09 09						09 39			09 44			10 09				10 14			10 39		10 44		
Leeds 10	a	09 25	09 27				09 39	09 53	09 57		09 59		10 12	10 25		10 27		10 28		10 38	10 53		10 58	10 59	

		NT	NT	NT	NT	NT	NT	NT	NT	NT		NT	NT	NT	NT	NT	NT	NT	NT	NT		NT	NT	NT	NT
Bradford Forster Square	d	10 46		11 01		11 11		11 16				11 31	11 41			11 46		12 01		12 11			12 16		
Bradford Interchange	d		10 50		11 05					11 20					11 34		11 50		12 05					12 19	
New Pudsey	d		10 58		11 13					11 28					11 42		11 58		12 13					12 28	
Bramley	d		11 02		11 17										11 46		12 02		12 17						
Frizinghall	d	10 49		11 04		11 14		11 19				11 34	11 44			11 49		12 04		12 14			12 19		
Shipley	a	10 53		11 08		11 18		11 23				11 38	11 48			11 53		12 08		12 18			12 23		
	d			11 09			11 14		11 18			11 39		11 44				12 09				12 14			12 33
Leeds 10	a		11 13	11 24	11 27		11 28		11 36	11 39		11 55		11 58	12 00		12 12	12 24	12 27			12 29		12 39	12 55

		NT	NT	NT	NT	NT		NT	NT	NT	NT	NT	NT	NT	NT	NT		NT	NT	NT	NT	NT	NT	NT	NT
Bradford Forster Square	d	12 31	12 41			12 46			13 01		13 11		13 16		13 31	13 41				13 46		14 01		14 11	
Bradford Interchange	d				12 34			12 50		13 05				13 19					13 34		13 50		14 05		
New Pudsey	d				12 42			12 58		13 13				13 28					13 42		13 58		14 13		
Bramley	d				12 46			13 02		13 17									13 46		14 02		14 17		
Frizinghall	d	12 34	12 44			12 49			13 04		13 14		13 19		13 34	13 44				13 49		14 04		14 14	
Shipley	a	12 38	12 48			12 53			13 08		13 18		13 23		13 38	13 48				13 53		14 08		14 18	
	d	12 39		12 44					13 09			13 14			13 39			13 44				14 09			14 14
Leeds 10	a	12 55		12 58	12 59			13 12	13 24	13 27		13 28		13 40	13 54			13 58	14 00		14 13	14 24	14 27		14 28

		NT		NT	NT	NT	NT	NT	NT	NT	NT	NT		NT	NT	NT	NT	NT	NT	NT	NT	NT		NT	NT
Bradford Forster Square	d	14 16				14 31		14 41		14 46		15 01			15 11		15 16			15 31	15 41				15 46
Bradford Interchange	d				14 19		14 34				14 50			15 05				15 19						15 34	
New Pudsey	d				14 28		14 42				14 58			15 13				15 28						15 42	
Bramley	d						14 46				15 02			15 17										15 46	
Frizinghall	d	14 19				14 34		14 44		14 49		15 04			15 14		15 19			15 34	15 44				15 49
Shipley	a	14 23				14 38		14 48		14 53		15 08			15 18		15 23			15 38	15 48				15 53
	d			14 18		14 39			14 45			15 09				15 14			15 30	15 39		15 44			
Leeds 10	a			14 37	14 39	14 52	15 00		15 00		15 12	15 24		15 27		15 28		15 39	15 47	15 54		15 58		16 00	

		NT	NT	NT	NT	NT	NT	NT		NT	NT	NT	NT	NT	NT	NT	NT	NT		NT	NT	NT	NT	NT	NT
Bradford Forster Square	d		16 01		16 11		16 16				16 31		16 40		16 44		17 01			17 11		17 16			17 31
Bradford Interchange	d	15 50		16 05				16 19				16 34				16 50		17 04					17 19		
New Pudsey	d	15 58		16 13				16 28				16 42				16 58		17 13					17 28		
Bramley	d	16 02		16 17								16 46				17 02		17 17							
Frizinghall	d		16 04		16 14		16 19				16 34		16 43		16 48		17 04			17 14		17 19			17 34
Shipley	a		16 08		16 18		16 23				16 38		16 48		16 52		17 08			17 18		17 23			17 38
	d		16 09			16 14				16 31	16 39			16 44			17 09				17 15			17 23	17 39
Leeds 10	a	16 12	16 24	16 27		16 28		16 39		16 51	16 53	16 58		16 58		17 12	17 24	17 27			17 29		17 39	17 40	17 55

		NT	NT	NT		NT	NT	NT	NT	NT	NT	NT	NT	NT		NT	NT	NT	NT	NT	NT	NT	NT	NT	
Bradford Forster Square	d		17 38			17 46			18 01		18 11		18 16			18 27		18 41		18 46			19 01		
Bradford Interchange	d	17 34					17 50			18 04				18 19			18 34					18 52		19 05	
New Pudsey	d	17 42					17 58			18 13				18 28			18 40					19 00		19 13	
Bramley	d	17 46					18 02			18 17							18 45					19 04		19 17	
Frizinghall	d		17 41			17 49			18 04		18 14		18 19			18 30		18 44		18 49			19 04		
Shipley	a		17 45			17 53			18 08		18 18		18 23			18 34		18 48		18 53			19 08		
	d			17 45				17 58	18 09			18 14				18 34			18 44		18 48		19 09		
Leeds 10	a	17 57		18 00			18 12	18 15	18 24	18 29		18 29		18 39		18 48	18 56		18 59		19 07	19 13	19 26	19 28	

A West Riding Limited

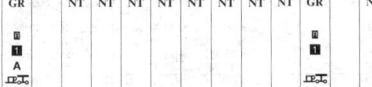

Bradford and Shipley - Leeds

Network Diagram - see first page of Table 35

		NT	NT	NT	NT	NT	NT	NT	NT	NT		NT	NT	NT	NT	NT	NT	NT	NT	NT		NT	NT	NT	NT
Bradford Forster Square	d	19 07			19 31		19 36	19 41				20 07				20 25		20 38						21 05	
Bradford Interchange	d			19 19		19 34				19 50				20 04	20 19		20 37						21 04		
New Pudsey	d			19 27		19 42				19 59				20 13	20 28		20 46						21 13		
Bramley	d					19 46				20 03				20 17			20 50						21 17		
Frizinghall	d	19 10			19 34		19 39	19 44				20 10				20 28		20 41						21 08	
Shipley	a	19 14			19 38		19 43	19 48				20 15				20 32		20 45						21 12	
	d		19 14		19 39				19 44				20 14						20 41	20 50		20 59			21 14
Leeds 10	a		19 31	19 39	19 55	19 56			19 59	20 13			20 28	20 29	20 38		20 59		21 01	21 05		21 17	21 25		21 30

		NT	NT	NT	NT	NT		NT	NT	NT	NT	NT	NT	NT	NT FX	NT FO		NT	NT	NT					
Bradford Forster Square	d	21 25	21 38					22 05			22 25		22 38					23 09	23 20						
Bradford Interchange	d				21 37	22 04				22 19		22 37			23 04	23 04				23 46					
New Pudsey	d				21 46	22 13				22 28		22 46			23 13	23 13				23 54					
Bramley	d				21 50	22 17						22 50			23 17	23 17				23 58					
Frizinghall	d	21 28	21 41					22 08			22 28		22 41					23 12	23 23						
Shipley	a	21 32	21 45					22 12			22 32		22 45					23 16	23 27						
	d			21 43					22 14					22 43											
Leeds 10	a			21 59	22 01	22 25			22 33	22 41		23 00		23 01	23 26	23 27				00 08					

Saturdays

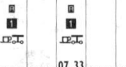

		NT	NT	NT	NT	NT	NT	NT	NT	NT		NT	NT	NT	GR R 1	NT	GR R 1	NT	NT	NT		NT	NT	NT	NT
Bradford Forster Square	d			06 01	06 10		06 15		07 01			07 11		07 15			07 33			07 59		08 11			08 16
Bradford Interchange	d	23p46	00 37					06 26		07 05						07 20		07 34	07 50					08 05	
New Pudsey	d	23p54						06 35		07 14						07 28		07 42	07 58					08 14	
Bramley	d	23p58						06 39		07 18								07 46	08 02					08 18	
Frizinghall	d			06 04	06 13		06 18		07 04			07 14		07 18						08 02		08 14			08 19
Shipley	a			06 08	06 17		06 22		07 08			07 18		07 23						08 06		08 18			08 23
	d			06 08		06 13			07 09				07 13		07u18		07u39			08 07			08 13		
Leeds 10	a	00 08	00 55	06 22		06 27		06 49	07 23	07 27			07 27		07 33	07 39	07 54	07 57	08 11	08 24			08 28	08 30	

		NT	NT	NT	NT	NT		NT	NT	NT	NT	NT	NT	NT	NT	NT		NT	NT	NT	NT	NT	NT	NT	NT
Bradford Forster Square	d			08 31		08 41			08 46		09 01		09 11		09 16			09 31		09 41		09 46			10 01
Bradford Interchange	d		08 20		08 34					08 50		09 04				09 20			09 34				09 50		
New Pudsey	d		08 28		08 42					08 58		09 12				09 27			09 42				09 58		
Bramley	d				08 46					09 02		09 16							09 46				10 02		
Frizinghall	d			08 34		08 44			08 49		09 04		09 14		09 19			09 34		09 44		09 49			10 04
Shipley	a			08 38		08 48			08 53		09 08		09 18		09 23			09 38		09 48		09 53			10 08
	d	08 19		08 38				08 44			09 09			09 14				09 39			09 44			10 02	10 09
Leeds 10	a	08 37	08 39	08 54	08 56			08 58		09 12	09 25	09 27		09 28		09 39		09 53	09 58		09 59		10 12	10 20	10 25

		NT		NT	NT	NT	NT	NT	NT	NT	NT	NT		NT	NT	NT	NT	NT	NT	NT	NT	NT		NT	NT
Bradford Forster Square	d			10 11		10 16			10 31	10 41				10 46		11 01		11 11		11 16		11 31		11 41	
Bradford Interchange	d	10 05						10 18				10 34			10 50		11 05				11 20				
New Pudsey	d	10 13						10 28				10 42			10 58		11 13				11 28				
Bramley	d	10 17										10 46			11 02		11 17								
Frizinghall	d			10 14		10 19			10 34	10 44				10 49		11 04		11 14		11 19		11 34		11 44	
Shipley	a			10 18		10 23			10 38	10 48				10 53		11 08		11 18		11 23		11 38		11 48	
	d				10 14		10 19		10 39		10 44					11 09			11 14			11 39			11 44
Leeds 10	a	10 27			10 28		10 34	10 38	10 53		10 58	11 00			11 13	11 24	11 27		11 28		11 39	11 55			11 58

		NT	NT	NT	NT	NT	NT	NT		NT	NT	NT	NT	NT	NT	NT	NT	NT		NT	NT	NT	NT	NT	NT
Bradford Forster Square	d		11 46			12 01		12 11			12 16			12 31		12 41		12 46			13 01		13 11		13 16
Bradford Interchange	d	11 34			11 50		12 05					12 19			12 34					12 50		13 05			
New Pudsey	d	11 42			11 58		12 13					12 28			12 42					12 58		13 13			
Bramley	d	11 46			12 02		12 17								12 46					13 02		13 17			
Frizinghall	d		11 49			12 04		12 14			12 19			12 34		12 44		12 49			13 04		13 14		13 19
Shipley	a		11 53			12 08		12 18			12 23			12 38		12 48		12 53			13 08		13 18		13 23
	d			11 49		12 09				12 14			12 33	12 39			12 44				13 09			13 14	
Leeds 10	a	12 00		12 07	12 12	12 24	12 27			12 29		12 39	12 55	12 55	12 58		12 58			13 12	13 24	13 27		13 28	

		NT	NT	NT		NT	NT	NT	NT	NT	NT	NT	NT	NT		NT	NT	NT	NT	NT	NT	NT	NT	NT	
Bradford Forster Square	d		13 31			13 41		13 46		14 01		14 11		14 16				14 31		14 41		14 46		15 01	
Bradford Interchange	d	13 19		13 34					13 50		14 05						14 19		14 34				14 50		
New Pudsey	d	13 28		13 42					13 58		14 13						14 28		14 42				14 58		
Bramley	d			13 46					14 02		14 17								14 46				15 02		
Frizinghall	d		13 34			13 44		13 49		14 04		14 14		14 19				14 34		14 44		14 49		15 04	
Shipley	a		13 38			13 48		13 53		14 08		14 18		14 23				14 38		14 48		14 53		15 08	
	d		13 39				13 44			14 09			14 14			14 18		14 39			14 45			15 09	
Leeds 10	a	13 39	13 54	13 58			13 58		14 14	14 24	14 27		14 28			14 37	14 39	14 53	14 58		15 00		15 10	15 24	

		NT	NT	NT	NT	NT	NT	NT	NT	NT		NT	NT	NT	NT	NT	NT	NT	NT	NT		NT	NT	NT	NT
Bradford Forster Square	d		15 11		15 16			15 31	15 41				15 46		16 01		16 11		16 16			16 31	16 40		
Bradford Interchange	d	15 05				15 19						15 34		15 50		16 05				16 19					16 34
New Pudsey	d	15 13				15 28						15 42		15 58		16 13				16 28					16 42
Bramley	d	15 17										15 46		16 02		16 17									16 46
Frizinghall	d		15 14		15 19			15 34	15 44				15 49		16 04		16 14		16 19			16 34	16 43		
Shipley	a		15 18		15 23			15 38	15 48				15 53		16 08		16 18		16 23			16 38	16 48		
	d			15 14			15 30	15 39		15 44					16 09			16 14				16 39		16 44	
Leeds 10	a	15 27		15 28		15 39	15 47	15 54		15 58		16 00		16 12	16 24	16 27		16 28		16 39		16 53		16 58	16 59

Table 37

Saturdays

Bradford and Shipley - Leeds

Network Diagram - see first page of Table 35

		NT	NT	NT	NT	NT		NT	NT	NT	NT	NT	NT	NT	NT	NT		NT	NT	NT	NT	NT	NT	NT	NT
Bradford Forster Square	d	16 44			17 01			17 11		17 16		17 31		17 41		17 46				18 01		18 11		18 16	
Bradford Interchange	d			16 50		17 04					17 19		17 34					17 50			18 04				18 19
New Pudsey	d			16 58		17 13					17 28		17 42					17 58			18 13				18 28
Bramley	d			17 02		17 17							17 46					18 02			18 17				
Frizinghall	d	16 48			17 04			17 14		17 19		17 34		17 44		17 49				18 04		18 14		18 19	
Shipley	a	16 52			17 08			17 18		17 23		17 38		17 48		17 53				18 08		18 18		18 23	
	d		16 49		17 09				17 15			17 39			17 45				18 00	18 09			18 14		
Leeds 10	a		17 07	17 12	17 24	17 27			17 29		17 39	17 55	17 57		18 00			18 12	18 17	18 24	18 29		18 29		18 39

		NT		NT	NT	NT	NT	NT	NT	NT	NT	NT		NT	NT	NT	NT	NT	NT	NT	NT	NT		NT	NT
Bradford Forster Square	d			18 31		18 41		18 46			19 01			19 07			19 31		19 36	19 41				20 07	
Bradford Interchange	d				18 34					18 52		19 05				19 18		19 34				19 50			
New Pudsey	d				18 43					19 00		19 13				19 28		19 42				19 58			
Bramley	d				18 47					19 04		19 17						19 46				20 02			
Frizinghall	d			18 34		18 44		18 49			19 04			19 10			19 34		19 39	19 44				20 10	
Shipley	a			18 38		18 48		18 53			19 08			19 14			19 38		19 43	19 48				20 15	
	d	18 19		18 38			18 44		18 48		19 09				19 14		19 39				19 44				20 14
Leeds 10	a	18 42		18 52	18 56		18 59		19 07	19 13	19 26	19 28			19 29	19 39	19 55	19 58			19 59	20 12			20 28

		NT	NT	NT	NT	NT	NT	NT		NT	NT	NT	NT	NT	NT	NT	NT	NT		NT	NT	NT	NT	NT	NT
Bradford Forster Square	d			20 25			20 38					21 05		21 25		21 38		22 01					22 25		22 38
Bradford Interchange	d	20 04	20 19			20 37					21 04				21 37					22 04		22 19		22 37	
New Pudsey	d	20 13	20 28			20 46					21 13				21 46					22 13		22 28		22 46	
Bramley	d	20 17				20 50					21 17				21 50					22 17				22 50	
Frizinghall	d			20 28			20 41					21 08		21 28		21 41		22 04					22 28		22 41
Shipley	a			20 32			20 45					21 12		21 32		21 45		22 08					22 32		22 45
	d				20 28			20 43		20 57			21 14				21 43				22 14				
Leeds 10	a	20 30	20 38		20 46	20 59		21 00		21 16	21 25		21 30		21 59		21 59			22 24	22 33	22 37		23 01	

		NT	NT	NT		NT																			
Bradford Forster Square	d			23 05		23 20																			
Bradford Interchange	d		23 04																						
New Pudsey	d		23 13																						
Bramley	d		23 17																						
Frizinghall	d			23 08		23 23																			
Shipley	a			23 12		23 27																			
	d	22 43																							
Leeds 10	a	23 01	23 26																						

Sundays

		NT A	NT	NT	NT	NT	NT	NT	NT	NT		NT	NT	NT	NT	NT	NT	NT	NT	NT		NT	NT	NT	NT
Bradford Forster Square	d				09 02			10 02				10 38		10 48		11 02							12 02		12 38
Bradford Interchange	d	00 04	08 31			09 20			10 04	10 25					11 02		11 25		11 44			12 02		12 25	
New Pudsey	d	00 12	08 39			09 29			10 12	10 33					11 10		11 33		11 53			12 10		12 33	
Bramley	d	00 16	08 43			09 33			10 16	10 37							11 37		11 57					12 37	
Frizinghall	d				09 05			10 05				10 41		10 51		11 05							12 05		12 41
Shipley	a				09 08			10 08				10 44		10 54		11 09							12 08		12 44
	d			09 00	09 10		09 40	10 08					10 40			11 10		11 40		11 49			12 08		
Leeds 10	a	00 27	08 51	09 14	09 24	09 42	09 54	10 22	10 25	10 46			10 54		11 21	11 24	11 48	11 54	12 05	12 06		12 22	12 22	12 46	

		NT	NT	NT	NT	NT		NT	NT	NT	NT	NT	NT	NT	NT	NT		NT	NT	NT	NT	NT	NT	NT	NT
Bradford Forster Square	d			12 48		13 02						14 02			14 38				14 48		15 02				16 02
Bradford Interchange	d		12 44		13 02			13 25		13 44	14 02			14 25				14 44		15 02		15 25		15 44	
New Pudsey	d		12 53		13 10			13 33		13 53	14 11			14 33				14 53		15 10		15 33		15 53	
Bramley	d		12 57					13 37		13 57				14 37				14 57				15 37		15 57	
Frizinghall	d			12 51		13 05						14 05			14 41				14 51		15 05				16 05
Shipley	a			12 54		13 08						14 08			14 44				14 54		15 08				16 08
	d	12 40				13 08			13 40			14 08	14 21			14 40					15 08		15 40		16 08
Leeds 10	a	12 54	13 06		13 22	13 22		13 46	13 54	14 06	14 22	14 22	14 39	14 48		14 54		15 06		15 22	15 24	15 46	15 54	16 06	16 22

		NT		NT	NT	NT	NT	NT	NT	NT	NT	NT		NT	NT	NT	NT	NT	NT	NT	NT	NT		NT	NT
Bradford Forster Square	d						16 38			16 48		17 02						18 02		18 38				18 48	
Bradford Interchange	d	16 03			16 25				16 44		17 02			17 25		17 44	18 02		18 25			18 44			
New Pudsey	d	16 11			16 33				16 53		17 10			17 33		17 53	18 10		18 33			18 53			
Bramley	d				16 37				16 57					17 37		17 57			18 37			18 57			
Frizinghall	d						16 41			16 51		17 05						18 05		18 41				18 51	
Shipley	a						16 44			16 54		17 08						18 08		18 44				18 54	
	d			16 16		16 29		16 40				17 09			17 40			18 08			18 40				19 03
Leeds 10	a	16 22		16 34	16 46	16 47		16 54	17 05		17 21	17 23		17 46	17 54	18 05	18 21	18 23	18 46		18 54	19 07			19 21

		NT	NT	NT	NT	NT	NT	NT		NT	NT	NT	NT	NT	NT	NT	NT	NT		NT	NT	NT	NT	NT	NT
Bradford Forster Square	d		19 02							20 02		20 38		20 48		21 02							22 02		22 38
Bradford Interchange	d	19 02		19 25			19 44	20 02			20 25				21 02		21 26			21 44		22 02		22 26	
New Pudsey	d	19 10		19 33			19 53	20 10			20 33				21 10		21 34			21 53		22 10		22 35	
Bramley	d			19 37			19 57				20 37						21 38			21 57				22 39	
Frizinghall	d		19 05							20 05		20 41		20 51		21 05							22 05		22 41
Shipley	a		19 08							20 08		20 44		20 54		21 08							22 09		22 44
	d		19 08		19 38	19 49				20 08			20 40			21 08		21 40			21 54		22 09		
Leeds 10	a	19 22	19 22	19 47	19 56	20 03	20 08	20 22		20 22	20 47		20 54		21 22	21 24	21 48	21 54		22 05	22 10	22 21	22 23	22 47	

A not 11 December

Table 37

Sundays

Bradford and Shipley - Leeds

Network Diagram - see first page of Table 35

		NT	NT	NT		NT	NT	NT	NT
Bradford Forster Square	d		22 48			23 05			
Bradford Interchange	d			23 04			23 25		23 47
New Pudsey	d			23 12			23 33		23 55
Bramley	d						23 37		23 59
Frizinghall	d		22 51			23 08			
Shipley	a		22 54			23 11			
	d	22 40				23 11		23 41	
Leeds 10	a	22 54		23 23		23 28	23 46	23 58	00 08

Leeds and Bradford - Ilkley

Network Diagram - see first page of Table 35

Miles	Miles			NT	NT	NT SX	NT SX	NT SO	NT SX	NT SX	NT SO	NT SX		NT SX	NT SX	NT	NT	NT SO	NT SX	NT	NT	NT		NT	NT
0	—	**Leeds 10**	d	06 02		06 34		07 02	07 03			07 29		07 35		08 02		08 32	08 35		09 02			09 32	
—	0	**Bradford Forster Square** 37	d		06 15		06 44			07 11	07 15				07 46		08 16			08 46		09 16			09 46
—	1¾	Frizinghall 37	d		06 18		06 47			07 14	07 18				07 49		08 19			08 49		09 19			09 49
—	2¾	Shipley 37	d		06 22		06 51			07 18	07 23				07 53		08 23			08 53		09 23			09 53
—	4¼	Baildon	d		06 25		06 54			07 21	07 26				07 56		08 26			08 56		09 26			09 56
10¼	7½	Guiseley	d	06 14	06 31	06 48	07 00	07 14	07 15	07 27	07 32	07 42		07 50	08 02	08 14	08 32	08 44	08 48	09 02	09 14	09 32		09 45	10 02
11½	8¾	Menston	d	06 17	06 34	06 51	07 03	07 17	07 18	07 30	07 35	07 45		07 53	08 05	08 17	08 35	08 47	08 51	09 05	09 17	09 35		09 48	10 05
13	10¼	Burley-in-Wharfedale	d	06 20	06 37	06 54	07 06	07 20	07 21	07 33	07 38	07 48		07 56	08 09	08 20	08 38	08 50	08 54	09 08	09 20	09 38		09 52	10 08
15¼	12½	Ben Rhydding	d	06 23	06 40	06 57	07 09	07 24	07 24	07 36	07 41	07 52		07 59	08 12	08 23	08 41	08 53	08 57	09 11	09 24	09 41		09 55	10 11
16¼	13½	**Ilkley**	a	06 29	06 46	07 03	07 15	07 29	07 30	07 41	07 47	07 57		08 05	08 18	08 29	08 49	09 02	09 03	09 17	09 33	09 47		10 01	10 17

		NT	NT	NT	NT	NT	NT	NT		NT	NT	NT	NT	NT	NT	NT SO	NT SX	NT		NT	NT	NT	NT	NT	NT
Leeds 10	d	10 02		10 32		11 02		11 32			12 02		12 32		13 02			13 32			14 02		14 32		15 02
Bradford Forster Square 37	d		10 16		10 46		11 16			11 46		12 16		12 46		13 16	13 16			13 46		14 16		14 46	
Frizinghall 37	d		10 19		10 49		11 19			11 49		12 19		12 49		13 19	13 19			13 49		14 19		14 49	
Shipley 37	d		10 23		10 53		11 23			11 53		12 23		12 53		13 23	13 23			13 53		14 23		14 53	
Baildon	d		10 26		10 56		11 26			11 56		12 26		12 56		13 26	13 26			13 56		14 26		14 56	
Guiseley	d	10 14	10 32	10 44	11 02	11 14	11 32	11 44		12 02	12 14	12 32	12 44	13 02	13 14	13 32	13 32	13 44		14 02	14 14	14 32	14 44	15 02	15 14
Menston	d	10 17	10 35	10 47	11 05	11 17	11 35	11 47		12 05	12 17	12 35	12 47	13 05	13 17	13 35	13 35	13 47		14 05	14 17	14 35	14 47	15 05	15 17
Burley-in-Wharfedale	d	10 20	10 38	10 50	11 08	11 20	11 38	11 50		12 08	12 20	12 38	12 50	13 08	13 20	13 38	13 38	13 50		14 08	14 20	14 38	14 50	15 08	15 20
Ben Rhydding	d	10 23	10 41	10 53	11 11	11 23	11 41	11 53		12 11	12 23	12 41	12 53	13 11	13 23	13 41	13 42	13 53		14 11	14 23	14 41	14 53	15 11	15 23
Ilkley	a	10 30	10 47	10 59	11 17	11 29	11 47	12 00		12 17	12 29	12 47	13 01	13 17	13 29	13 47	13 47	13 59		14 17	14 29	14 47	14 59	15 17	15 31

		NT	NT	NT		NT	NT	NT	NT	NT	NT SX	NT SO	NT SX	NT		NT SX	NT SO	NT SX	NT SO	NT SX	NT SX	NT SO	NT	NT	
Leeds 10	d		15 32			16 02		16 32		17 02	17 15			17 32		17 47			18 02	18 02			18 32		
Bradford Forster Square 37	d	15 16		15 46			16 16		16 44			17 16	17 16				17 46	17 46			18 11	18 16		18 46	
Frizinghall 37	d	15 19		15 49			16 19		16 48			17 19	17 19				17 49	17 49			18 14	18 19		18 49	
Shipley 37	d	15 23		15 53			16 23		16 52			17 23	17 25				17 53	17 53			18 19	18 23		18 53	
Baildon	d	15 26		15 56			16 26		16 55			17 26	17 28				17 57	17 57			18 22	18 26		18 56	
Guiseley	d	15 32	15 44	16 02		16 14	16 32	16 44	17 01	17 14	17 28	17 32	17 35	17 44		17 59	18 02	18 07	18 14	18 19	18 27	18 32	18 44	19 02	
Menston	d	15 35	15 47	16 05		16 17	16 35	16 47	17 04	17 17	17 31	17 35	17 38	17 47		18 02	18 05	18 10	18 17	18 22	18 30	18 35	18 47	19 05	
Burley-in-Wharfedale	d	15 38	15 50	16 08		16 20	16 38	16 50	17 07	17 20	17 34	17 38	17 42	17 51		18 05	18 08	18 17	18 20	18 26	18 35	18 38	18 50	19 08	
Ben Rhydding	d	15 41	15 53	16 11		16 23	16 41	16 53	17 10	17 23	17 37	17 41	17 46	17 54		18 09	18 12	18 20	18 23	18 29	18 39	18 41	18 53	19 11	
Ilkley	a	15 47	15 59	16 17		16 29	16 47	17 00	17 17	17 29	17 43	17 47	17 51	18 00		18 16	18 17	18 26	18 30	18 35	18 44	18 47	19 01	19 17	

		NT	NT	NT	NT	NT	NT	NT	NT	NT		NT	NT
Leeds 10	d	19 02	19 32		20 02		21 06		22 06			23 15	
Bradford Forster Square 37	d			19 41		20 38		21 38		22 38			23 20
Frizinghall 37	d			19 44		20 41		21 41		22 41			23 23
Shipley 37	d			19 48		20 46		21 45		22 45			23 27
Baildon	d			19 51		20 49		21 48		22 48			23 30
Guiseley	d	19 14	19 44	19 56	20 14	20 54	21 18	21 54	22 18	22 54		23 27	23 36
Menston	d	19 17	19 47	19 59	20 17	20 57	21 21	21 57	22 21	22 57		23 30	23 39
Burley-in-Wharfedale	d	19 20	19 50	20 02	20 20	21 00	21 24	22 00	22 24	23 00		23 33	23 42
Ben Rhydding	d	19 24	19 53	20 06	20 23	21 04	21 27	22 03	22 27	23 03		23 36	23 45
Ilkley	a	19 29	20 00	20 12	20 30	21 10	21 33	22 09	22 34	23 09		23 42	23 51

Sundays

		NT	NT	NT	NT	NT	NT	NT	NT	NT		NT	NT	NT	NT	NT	NT	NT	NT	NT		NT	NT	NT	NT
Leeds 10	d	09 12	10 12		11 12	12 12		13 12	14 12			15 12	16 12		17 12	18 12		19 12	20 12			21 12	22 12		23 16
Bradford Forster Square 37	d			10 38			12 38			14 38				16 38			18 38			20 38				22 38	
Frizinghall 37	d			10 41			12 41			14 41				16 41			18 41			20 41				22 41	
Shipley 37	d			10 44			12 44			14 44				16 44			18 44			20 44				22 44	
Baildon	d			10 47			12 47			14 47				16 47			18 47			20 47				22 47	
Guiseley	d	09 23	10 23	10 52	11 23	12 23	12 52	13 23	14 23	14 52		15 23	16 23	16 52	17 23	18 23	18 52	19 23	20 23	20 52		21 23	22 23	22 52	23 27
Menston	d	09 26	10 26	10 55	11 26	12 26	12 55	13 26	14 26	14 55		15 26	16 26	16 55	17 26	18 26	18 55	19 26	20 26	20 55		21 26	22 26	22 55	23 30
Burley-in-Wharfedale	d	09 29	10 29	10 58	11 29	12 29	12 58	13 29	14 29	14 58		15 29	16 29	16 58	17 29	18 29	18 58	19 29	20 29	20 58		21 29	22 29	22 58	23 33
Ben Rhydding	d	09 33	10 33	11 02	11 33	12 33	13 02	13 33	14 33	15 02		15 33	16 33	17 02	17 33	18 33	19 02	19 33	20 33	21 02		21 33	22 33	23 02	23 37
Ilkley	a	09 38	10 38	11 07	11 38	12 38	13 07	13 38	14 38	15 07		15 38	16 38	17 07	17 38	18 38	19 07	19 38	20 38	21 07		21 38	22 38	23 07	23 42

Table 38

Mondays to Saturdays

Ilkley - Bradford and Leeds

Network Diagram - see first page of Table 35

Miles	Miles			NT SX	NT SO	NT SX	NT SO	NT SX	NT SX	NT	NT	NT SX		NT SX	NT SX	NT SX	NT SO	NT SX	NT SO	NT SX	NT	NT SO		NT SX	NT
0	0	**Ilkley**	d	06 04	06 09	06 17	06 19	06 34	06 50	07 10	07 22	07 39		07 50	07 57	08 05	08 10	08 17	08 21	08 24	08 40	08 51		08 54	09 10
1	1	Ben Rhydding	d	06 06	06 11	06 19	06 21	06 36	06 52	07 12	07 24	07 42		07 52	07 59	08 07	08 12	08 19	08 23	08 26	08 42	08 53		08 56	09 12
3¼	3¼	Burley-in-Wharfedale	d	06 12	06 17	06 25	06 27	06 42	06 58	07 18	07 30	07 48		07 58	08 04	08 13	08 18	08 25	08 29	08 32	08 48	08 59		09 02	09 18
4¾	4¾	Menston	d	06 15	06 20	06 28	06 30	06 45	07 01	07 21	07 33	07 51		08 01	08 07	08 16	08 21	08 28	08 32	08 35	08 51	09 02		09 05	09 21
6	6	Guiseley	d	06 18	06 23	06 31	06 34	06 48	07 04	07 24	07 36	07 54		08 04	08 11	08 19	08 24	08 31	08 35	08 39	08 54	09 05		09 08	09 24
—	9¼	Baildon	d			06 36	06 39		07 09		07 41			08 09					08 40	08 44		09 10		09 13	
—	10¾	Shipley	37 a			06 41	06 43		07 14		07 47			08 12					08 43	08 47		09 14		09 18	
—	11¾	Frizinghall	37 a			06 44	06 47		07 17		07 49			08 16					08 46	08 50		09 17		09 21	
—	13½	**Bradford Forster Square**	37 a			06 50	06 55		07 22		07 56			08 22					08 53	08 56		09 24		09 27	
16¼	—	**Leeds** 10	a	06 32	06 39			07 02		07 38		08 09			08 25	08 35	08 39	08 46			09 11				09 39

		NT	NT	NT	NT	NT	NT	NT		NT	NT	NT	NT	NT	NT	NT	NT	NT		NT	NT	NT	NT	NT	NT
Ilkley	d	09 21	09 40	09 51	10 10	10 21	10 40	10 51		11 10	11 21	11 40	11 51	12 10	12 21	12 40	12 51	13 10		13 21	13 40	13 51	14 10	14 21	14 40
Ben Rhydding	d	09 23	09 42	09 53	10 12	10 23	10 42	10 53		11 12	11 23	11 42	11 53	12 12	12 23	12 42	12 53	13 12		13 23	13 42	13 53	14 12	14 23	14 42
Burley-in-Wharfedale	d	09 29	09 48	09 59	10 18	10 29	10 48	10 59		11 18	11 29	11 48	11 59	12 18	12 29	12 48	12 59	13 18		13 29	13 48	13 58	14 18	14 29	14 48
Menston	d	09 32	09 51	10 02	10 21	10 32	10 51	11 02		11 21	11 32	11 51	12 02	12 21	12 32	12 51	13 02	13 21		13 32	13 51	14 01	14 21	14 32	14 51
Guiseley	d	09 35	09 54	10 05	10 25	10 35	10 54	11 05		11 24	11 35	11 54	12 05	12 24	12 35	12 54	13 05	13 24		13 35	13 54	14 05	14 24	14 35	14 54
Baildon	d	09 40		10 10		10 40		11 10			11 40		12 10		12 40		13 10			13 40		14 10		14 40	
Shipley	37 a	09 44		10 14		10 44		11 14			11 44		12 14		12 44		13 14			13 44		14 14		14 44	
Frizinghall	37 a	09 47		10 17		10 47		11 17			11 47		12 17		12 47		13 17			13 47		14 17		14 47	
Bradford Forster Square	37 a	09 53		10 23		10 53		11 23			11 53		12 24		12 53		13 23			13 53		14 23		14 53	
Leeds 10	a		10 11		10 41		11 08			11 39		12 08		12 39		13 08		13 38			14 09		14 39		15 10

		NT	NT	NT		NT	NT	NT SO	NT SX	NT	NT	NT	NT SO	NT SX		NT	NT SO	NT SX	NT	NT SX	NT SO	NT SX	NT	NT	
Ilkley	d	14 51	15 10	15 21		15 40	15 51	16 10	16 12	16 21	16 40	16 51	17 10	17 14		17 21	17 40	17 42	17 51	18 04	18 10	18 10	18 21	18 40	
Ben Rhydding	d	14 53	15 12	15 23		15 42	15 53	16 12	16 14	16 23	16 42	16 53	17 12	17 16		17 23	17 42	17 44	17 53	18 06	18 12	18 12	18 23	18 42	
Burley-in-Wharfedale	d	14 59	15 18	15 29		15 48	15 59	16 18	16 20	16 29	16 48	16 59	17 18	17 22		17 29	17 48	17 50	17 59	18 12	18 18	18 18	18 29	18 48	
Menston	d	15 02	15 21	15 32		15 51	16 02	16 21	16 23	16 32	16 51	17 02	17 21	17 25		17 32	17 51	17 53	18 02	18 15	18 21	18 21	18 32	18 51	
Guiseley	d	15 05	15 24	15 35		15 54	16 05	16 24	16 27	16 35	16 54	17 05	17 24	17 29		17 35	17 54	17 56	18 05	18 18	18 24	18 24	18 35	18 54	
Baildon	d	15 10		15 40			16 10			16 40		17 10				17 40			18 10				18 40		
Shipley	37 a	15 14		15 44			16 14			16 44		17 14				17 43			18 14				18 43		
Frizinghall	37 a	15 17		15 47			16 17			16 47		17 17				17 46			18 17				18 46		
Bradford Forster Square	37 a	15 23		15 53			16 23			16 53		17 23				17 53			18 23				18 52		
Leeds 10	a		15 40			16 10		16 38	16 46		17 09		17 38	17 44			18 09	18 16		18 35	18 40	18 45		19 09	

		NT	NT	NT	NT	NT	NT	NT	NT	NT		NT	NT	NT											
Ilkley	d	18 51	19 10	19 21	19 41	20 05	20 21	20 40	21 21	21 40		22 21	22 40	23 20											
Ben Rhydding	d	18 53	19 12	19 23	19 43	20 07	20 23	20 42	21 23	21 42		22 23	22 42	23 23											
Burley-in-Wharfedale	d	18 59	19 18	19 29	19 49	20 13	20 29	20 48	21 29	21 48		22 29	22 48	23 28											
Menston	d	19 02	19 21	19 32	19 52	20 16	20 32	20 51	21 32	21 51		22 32	22 51	23 31											
Guiseley	d	19 05	19 24	19 35	19 55	20 19	20 35	20 54	21 35	21 54		22 35	22 54	23 35											
Baildon	d	19 10		19 40		20 24		20 59		21 59			22 59												
Shipley	37 a	19 14		19 44		20 27		21 03		22 02			23 02												
Frizinghall	37 a	19 17		19 47		20 30		21 05		22 05			23 05												
Bradford Forster Square	37 a	19 23		19 53		20 36		21 12		22 11			23 13												
Leeds 10	a		19 40		20 12		20 53		21 49			22 49		23 49											

Sundays

		NT	NT	NT	NT	NT	NT	NT	NT	NT		NT	NT	NT	NT	NT	NT	NT	NT	NT		NT	NT	NT	NT
Ilkley	d	09 21	09 53	10 21	11 21	11 53	12 21	13 21	13 53	14 21		15 21	15 53	16 21	17 21	17 53	18 21	19 21	19 53	20 21		21 21	21 53	22 21	23 21
Ben Rhydding	d	09 23	09 55	10 23	11 23	11 55	12 23	13 23	13 55	14 23		15 23	15 55	16 23	17 23	17 55	18 23	19 23	19 55	20 23		21 23	21 55	22 23	23 23
Burley-in-Wharfedale	d	09 29	10 01	10 29	11 29	12 01	12 29	13 29	14 01	14 29		15 29	16 01	16 29	17 29	18 01	18 29	19 29	20 01	20 29		21 29	22 01	22 29	23 29
Menston	d	09 32	10 04	10 32	11 32	12 04	12 32	13 32	14 04	14 32		15 32	16 04	16 32	17 32	18 04	18 32	19 32	20 04	20 32		21 32	22 04	22 32	23 32
Guiseley	d	09 35	10 07	10 35	11 35	12 07	12 35	13 35	14 07	14 35		15 35	16 07	16 35	17 35	18 07	18 35	19 35	20 07	20 35		21 35	22 07	22 35	23 35
Baildon	d		10 12			12 12			14 12				16 12			18 12			20 12				22 12		
Shipley	37 a		10 15			12 15			14 15				16 15			18 15			20 15				22 15		
Frizinghall	37 a		10 18			12 18			14 18				16 18			18 18			20 18				22 18		
Bradford Forster Square	37 a		10 24			12 24			14 24				16 24			18 24			20 24				22 24		
Leeds 10	a	09 50		10 49	11 49		12 49	13 49		14 49		15 49		16 49	17 49		18 49	19 49		20 49		21 49		22 49	23 50

Network Diagram for Tables 39, 40, 41, 43

DM-6/10
Design BAJS

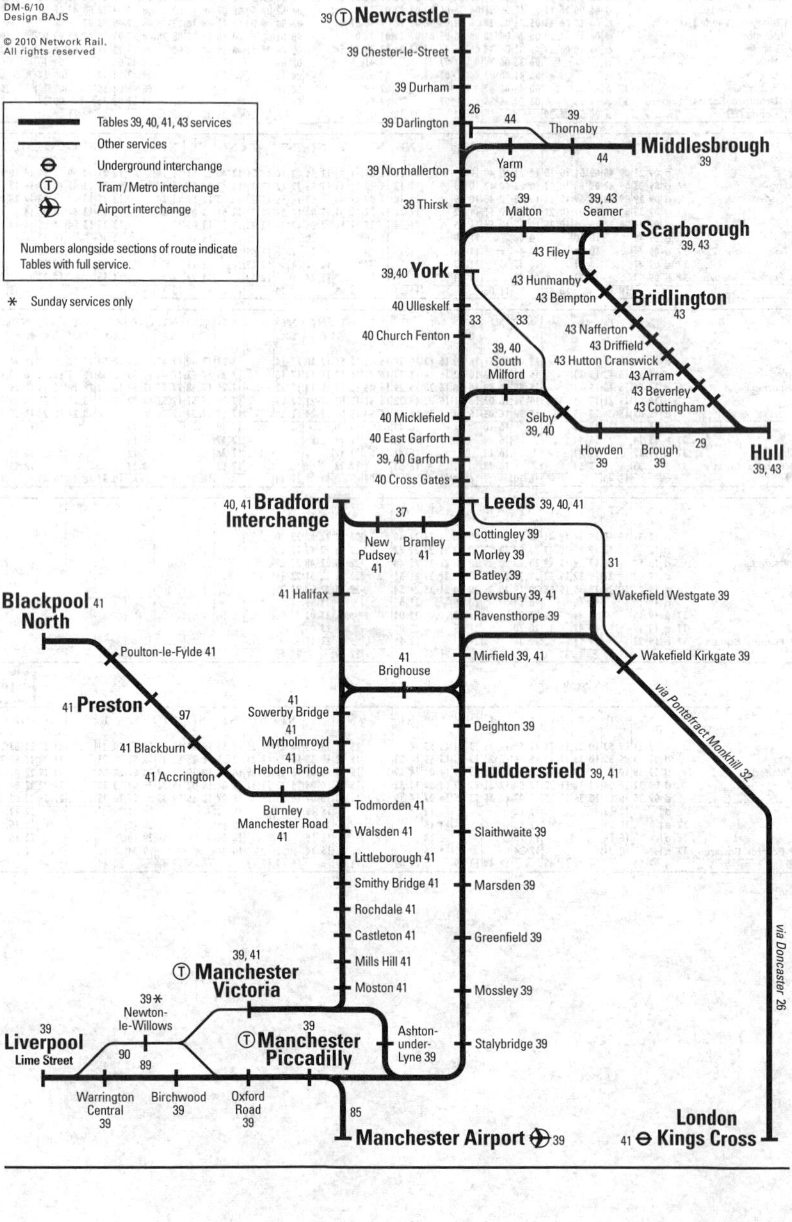

Newcastle, Middlesbrough, Scarborough, York, Hull, Leeds and Wakefield - Huddersfield - Manchester, Manchester Airport and Liverpool

Network Diagram - see first Page of Table 39

Miles	Miles	Miles	Miles	Miles	Station		TP	TP	TP	TP	TP	TP	TP	TP	TP		TP	TP	NT	NT	TP	NT	NT	NT	TP
								MX	MO	MO	MO	MX	MO	MX	MX		MO								
							◇1	◇1	◇1	◇1	◇1	◇1	◇1	◇1	◇1		◇1	◇1			◇1				◇1
							A		B	A															
0	—	—	—	—	**Newcastle** 8	d		21p54																	
8¼	—	—	—	—	Chester-le-Street	d																			
14	—	—	—	—	Durham	d		22p08																	
—	—	0	—	—	**Middlesbrough**	d			22p06	22p06															
—	—	3¼	—	—	Thornaby	d			22p11	22p11															
—	—	8½	—	—	Yarm	d			22p19	22p19															
36	—	—	—	—	**Darlington** 7	d		22p25																	
50	—	20¾	—	—	Northallerton	d		22p36	22p35	22p34															
57¾	—	28½	—	—	Thirsk	d			22p43	22p42															
—	—	—	0	—	**Scarborough**	d	21p20																		
—	—	—	2¾	—	Seamer	d	21p25																		
—	—	—	21	—	Malton	d	21p43																		
80	—	50¾	42	—	**York** 8	a	22p09	23p00	23p09	23p09															
—	—	—	—	—		d	22p12	23p06	23p12	23p12	01 38	01 38	02 47	02 52	04 00		04 23	05 26			05 57				06 28
—	—	—	—	0	**Wakefield Westgate**	d																	06 41		
—	—	—	—	1	Wakefield Kirkgate	d																	06 46		
—	0	—	—	—	**Hull**	d																			
—	10½	—	—	—	Brough	d																			
—	22¼	—	—	—	Howden	d																			
—	31	—	—	—	Selby	d																			
—	38¾	—	—	—	South Milford	d																			
98¼	44½	—	60¼	—	Garforth	d															06 12				
105½	51¾	—	67½	—	**Leeds** 10	a	22p36	23p33	23p38	23p38	02 04	02 19	03 13	03 33	04 42		04 49	05 52			06 22				06 52
—	—	—	—	—		d	22p40	23p35	23p40	23p40	02 05	02 20	03 15	03 35	04 50		04 50	05 55		06 13	06 25			06 43	06 55
108½	—	—	—	—	Cottingley	d																		06 48	
110	—	—	—	—	Morley	d														06 21				06 52	
113½	—	—	—	—	Batley	d														06 26				06 57	
114¾	—	—	—	—	**Dewsbury**	a	22p50	23p45	23p51	23p51								06 06		06 29	06 36			07 00	07 06
—	—	—	—	—		d	22p51	23p46	23p51	23p51								06 06		06 29	06 36			07 01	07 06
116	—	—	—	—	Ravensthorpe	d																		07 04	
117¾	—	—	—	10½	Mirfield	d														06 35			06 59	07 08	
120¾	—	—	—	13½	Deighton	d																	07 06	07 16	
122¾	—	—	—	15½	**Huddersfield**	a	23p02	23p54	23p59	00 02	02 42	02 42	03 56	03 56	05 27		05 27	06 14			06 44		07 12	07 20	07 15
—	—	—	—	—		d	23p04	23p55	00 01	00 04	02 45	02 45	03 59	03 59	05 28		05 28	06 15	06 29		06 45	06 57			07 16
127¼	—	—	—	20	Slaithwaite	d													06 36			07 04			
129¾	—	—	—	22½	Marsden	d													06 42			07 12			
135¾	—	—	—	28½	Greenfield	d													06 50			07 20			
138	—	—	—	30¾	Mossley (Grtr Manchester)	d													06 54			07 24			
140¾	—	—	—	33½	**Stalybridge**	a												06 33	06 59		07 03	07 29			07 34
—	—	—	—	—		d												06 33	07 00		07 04	07 30			07 34
—	—	—	—	34¾	Ashton-under-Lyne	d													07 04			07 34			
—	—	—	—	41¼	**Manchester Victoria**	a	23b53			00s53									07 17	07 53		07 47			
148¼	—	—	—	—	**Manchester Piccadilly** 10	a	00 08	00 53	00 43	01 08	03 44	03 44	04 58	04 58	06 02		06 02	06 50			07 19				07 51
—	—	—	—	—		d		00 54	00 44	01 10	03 44	03 44	05 00	05 00	06 08		06 08	06 54			07 23				07 54
—	—	—	—	—	**Manchester Airport**	a		01 10	00 57	01 23	04 00	04 00	05 19	05 19	06 24		06 24	07 12			07 42				08 12
148¾	—	—	—	—	Manchester Oxford Road	a																			
161¼	—	—	—	—	Birchwood	a																			
164½	—	—	—	—	Warrington Central	a																			
177½	—	—	—	—	Liverpool South Parkway 7	a																			
183	—	—	—	—	**Liverpool Lime Street** 10	a																			

A From 2 April

B Until 26 March

b Previous night, stops to set down only

Newcastle, Middlesbrough, Scarborough, York, Hull, Leeds and Wakefield - Huddersfield - Manchester, Manchester Airport and Liverpool

Network Diagram - see first Page of Table 39

		TP ◇1 🛒	NT	NT	TP ◇1 🛒	NT	TP ◇1 🛒	NT	NT	NT A	NT	NT	NT	TP ◇1 🛒	NT B	TP ◇1 C 🛒	NT	NT A	NT	TP ◇1 🛒	TP ◇1 🛒	NT
Newcastle 8	d															06 11						
Chester-le-Street	d															06 21						
Durham	d															06 28						
Middlesbrough	d				05 55			06 51														
Thornaby	d				06 00			06a56														
Yarm	d				06 08																	
Darlington 7	d															06 45						
Northallerton	d				06 23											06 56						
Thirsk	d				06 31											07 04						
Scarborough	d													06 30						07 00		
Seamer	d													06 35						07 05		
Malton	d													06 53						07 23		
York 8	a				06 49									07 23		07 30				07 50		
	d				06 55									07 26		07 40				07 55		
Wakefield Westgate	d											07 41										08 39
Wakefield Kirkgate	d											07 46										08 45
Hull	d	06 00					06 37		07 07												07 37	
Brough	d	06 12					06 49		07 19												07 49	
Howden	d	06 26							07 35												08 01	
Selby	d	06 36					07 08		07a48												08 11	
South Milford	d																					
Garforth	d				07 10		07 24													08 12		
Leeds 10	a	07 00			07 20		07 35							07 52		08 04				08 22	08 36	
	d	07 08	07 13		07 23		07 38						07 43	07 55		08 08			08 13	08 25	08 40	
Cottingley	d												07 48						08 18			
Morley	d		07 21										07 52						08 22			
Batley	d		07 26										07 57						08 27			
Dewsbury	a		07 29		07 34								08 00	08 06					08 30	08 36		
	d		07 29		07 34								08 01	08 06					08 31	08 36		
Ravensthorpe	d												08 04						08 34			
Mirfield	d		07 36									07 59	08 08						08 38			08 58
Deighton	d											08 04	08 13									09 05
Huddersfield	a	07 25			07 43		07 56					08 11	08 20	08 15		08 25				08 44	08 58	09 11
	d	07 26		07 33	07 44		07 57				08 02			08 16		08 26	08 30			08 45	08 59	
Slaithwaite	d			07 40							08 09						08 37					
Marsden	d			07 55							08 15						08 43					
Greenfield	d			08 03							08 23						08 51					
Mossley (Grtr Manchester)	d			08 07		←					08 27						08 55					
Stalybridge	a	07 43		08 12	08 01	08 12	08 17				08 32					08 44	09 00					
	d	07 46		08 13	08 02	08 13	08 17			08 22	08 33				08 40	08 46	09 01	09 22				
Ashton-under-Lyne	d			→		08 17				08 26	08 37				08 44		09 05	09 26				
Manchester Victoria	a		08 53			08 31				08 36	08 52				08 54		09 20	09 37	09 53			
Manchester Piccadilly 10	a	08 05			08 19		08 36							08 51		09 05				09 19	09 36	
	d	08 07			08 24									08 54		09 07				09 24		
Manchester Airport ✈	a				08 42									09 12						09 42		
Manchester Oxford Road	a	08 09														09 09						
Birchwood	a	08 25														09 25						
Warrington Central	a	08 30														09 30						
Liverpool South Parkway 7 ✈	a	08 47														09 47						
Liverpool Lime Street 10	a	08 58								09 43						09 58		10 43				

A until 23 March **B** from 26 March **C** 🛒 from York

Newcastle, Middlesbrough, Scarborough, York, Hull, Leeds and Wakefield - Huddersfield - Manchester, Manchester Airport and Liverpool

Network Diagram - see first Page of Table 39

		NT	TP ◇1 🛒	NT	NT	NT A	TP ◇1 🛒		NT	NT B	NT	TP ◇1 🛒	TP ◇1 🛒	NT	NT	NT	TP ◇1 🛒		NT A	TP ◇1 🛒	NT	NT B	NT	TP ◇1 🛒	NT
Newcastle 8 ⛴	d											07 33													
Chester-le-Street	d											07 42													
Durham	d											07 49													
Middlesbrough	d		07 12	07 32	08 32																			08 50	09 32
Thornaby	d		07 17	07a37	08a37																			08 55	09a37
Yarm	d		07 27																					09 03	
Darlington 7	d											08 06													
Northallerton	d		07 43									08 17												09 18	
Thirsk	d		07 51									08 25												09 28	
Scarborough	d						07 40													08 48					
Seamer	d						07 45													08 53					
Malton	d						08 03													09 11					
York 8	a		08 11				08 30					08 47								09 38				09 47	
	d		08 25				08 40					08 57					09 28			09 40				09 57	
Wakefield Westgate	d														09 39										
Wakefield Kirkgate	d														09 45										
Hull	d												08 40	09 02											
Brough	d												08 52	09 14											
Howden	d													09 28											
Selby	d												09 11	09a38											
South Milford	d																								
Garforth	d		08 40									09 12												10 12	
Leeds 10	a		08 52				09 04					09 22	09 36				09 52			10 04				10 22	
	d	08 43	08 55				09 08				09 13	09 25	09 40			09 43	09 55			10 08			10 13	10 25	
Cottingley	d	08 48									09 18					09 48									
Morley	d	08 52									09 22					09 52							10 21		
Batley	d	08 57									09 27					09 57							10 26		
Dewsbury	a	09 00	09 06								09 30	09 36				10 00	10 06						10 29	10 36	
	d	09 01	09 06								09 31	09 36				10 01	10 06						10 29	10 36	
Ravensthorpe	d	09 04														10 04									
Mirfield	d	09 08									09 37				09 58	10 08							10 35		
Deighton	d	09 16													10 05	10 14									
Huddersfield	a	09 20	09 15				09 25					09 45	09 58		10 11	10 21	10 15			10 25				10 45	
	d		09 16				09 26		09 30			09 46	09 59				10 16			10 26	10 30			10 46	
Slaithwaite	d								09 37												10 37				
Marsden	d								09 43												10 43				
Greenfield	d								09 51												10 51				
Mossley (Grtr Manchester)	d								09 55												10 55				
Stalybridge	a						09 43		10 00											10 43	11 00				
	d					09 40	09 46		10 01	10 22									10 40	10 46	11 01	11 22			
Ashton-under-Lyne	d					09 44			10 05	10 26									10 44		11 05	11 26			
Manchester Victoria ⛴	a					09 55			10 20	10 36	10 53								10 55		11 20	11 35	11 53		
Manchester Piccadilly 10 ⛴	a		09 49				10 05					10 19	10 36				10 49			11 05				11 19	
	d		09 54				10 07					10 24					10 54			11 07				11 24	
Manchester Airport ✈	a		10 12									10 42					11 12							11 45	
Manchester Oxford Road	a						10 09													11 09					
Birchwood	a						10 25													11 25					
Warrington Central	a						10 30													11 30					
Liverpool South Parkway 7 ✈	a						10 47													11 47					
Liverpool Lime Street 10	a						10 58			11 43										11 58		12 43			

A from 26 March

B until 23 March

Newcastle, Middlesbrough, Scarborough, York, Hull, Leeds and Wakefield - Huddersfield - Manchester, Manchester Airport and Liverpool

Network Diagram - see first Page of Table 39

		TP	NT		NT	NT	TP	TP	NT	NT	NT	TP	NT		TP	NT	NT	TP	TP	NT	TP	NT	NT		NT
																		FO	FX						
		◇1					◇1	◇1				◇1			◇1			◇1	◇1		◇1				
										A										B			A		
Newcastle 8	d						09 15											10 17	10 17						
Chester-le-Street	d						09 24																		
Durham	d						09 31											10 31	10 31						
Middlesbrough	d											09 50	10 32												
Thornaby	d											09 55	10a37												
Yarm	d											10 03													
Darlington 7	d						09 48											10 48	10 48						
Northallerton	d						09 59					10 18						10 59	10 59						
Thirsk	d											10 28													
Scarborough	d							09 48													10 48				
Seamer	d							09 53													10 53				
Malton	d							10 11													11 11				
York 8	a						10 21	10 38				10 47						11 23	11 23		11 38				
	d						10 27	10 40				10 57						11 26	11 26		11 40				
Wakefield Westgate	d				10 39											11 39									
Wakefield Kirkgate	d				10 45											11 45									
Hull	d	09 40	10 08												10 40										
Brough	d	09 52	10 20												10 52										
Howden	d		10 34																						
Selby	d	10 11	10a47												11 11										
South Milford	d																								
Garforth	d											11 12													
Leeds 10	a	10 36					10 52	11 04				11 22			11 36			11 52	11 52		12 04				
	d	10 40				10 43	10 55	11 08			11 13	11 25			11 40		11 43	11 55	11 55		12 08				12 13
Cottingley	d					10 48											11 48								
Morley	d					10 52					11 21						11 52								12 21
Batley	d					10 57					11 26						11 57								12 26
Dewsbury	a					11 00	11 06				11 29	11 36					12 00	12 06	12 06						12 29
	d					11 01	11 06				11 29	11 36					12 01	12 06	12 06						12 29
Ravensthorpe	d					11 04											12 04								
Mirfield	d				10 58	11 08					11 35					11 58	12 08								12 35
Deighton	d				11 05	11 14										12 05	12 17								
Huddersfield	a	10 58			11 11	11 22	11 15	11 25				11 45			11 58	12 11	12 21	12 15	12 15		12 25				
	d	10 59					11 16	11 26	11 30			11 46			11 59			12 16	12 16		12 26	12 30			
Slaithwaite	d								11 37													12 37			
Marsden	d								11 43													12 43			
Greenfield	d								11 51													12 51			
Mossley (Grtr Manchester)	d								11 55													12 55			
Stalybridge	a							11 43	12 00												12 43	13 00			
	d							11 46	12 01	12 22										12 40	12 46	13 01	13 22		
Ashton-under-Lyne	d								12 05	12 26										12 44		13 05	13 26		
Manchester Victoria	a								12 20	12 35	12 53									12 55		13 20	13 35		13 53
Manchester Piccadilly 10	a	11 36					11 49	12 05				12 19			12 36			12 49	12 49		13 05				
	d						11 54	12 07				12 24						12 54	12 54		13 07				
Manchester Airport	a						12 12					12 42						13 11	13 12						
Manchester Oxford Road	a							12 09													13 09				
Birchwood	a							12 25													13 25				
Warrington Central	a							12 30													13 30				
Liverpool South Parkway 7	a							12 47													13 47				
Liverpool Lime Street 10	a							12 58		13 43											13 58		14 43		

A until 23 March

B from 26 March

Newcastle, Middlesbrough, Scarborough, York, Hull, Leeds and Wakefield - Huddersfield - Manchester, Manchester Airport and Liverpool

Network Diagram - see first Page of Table 39

		TP ◇1	NT	TP ◇1	NT	NT	NT	TP ◇1	NT A		TP ◇1	NT	NT B	NT	TP ◇1	NT	TP ◇1	NT	NT		NT	TP ◇1	NT A	TP ◇1	NT
Newcastle 8	d							11 15														12 17			
Chester-le-Street	d							11 24																	
Durham	d							11 31														12 29			
Middlesbrough	d	10 50	11 31												11 50	12 32									
Thornaby	d	10 55	11a36												11 55	12a37									
Yarm	d	11 03													12 03										
Darlington 7	d							11 48														12 46			
Northallerton	d	11 18						11 59							12 18							12 58			
Thirsk	d	11 28													12 28										
Scarborough	d										11 48													12 48	
Seamer	d										11 53													12 53	
Malton	d										12 11													13 11	
York 8	a	11 47						12 21			12 38				12 47							13 21		13 38	
	d	11 57						12 26			12 40				12 57							13 24		13 40	
Wakefield Westgate	d					12 39													13 39						
Wakefield Kirkgate	d					12 45													13 45						
Hull	d			11 40	12 03												12 40	13 12							
Brough	d			11 52	12 15												12 52	13 24							
Howden	d				12 27													13 41							
Selby	d			12 11	12a37												13 11	13a54							
South Milford	d																								
Garforth	d	12 12													13 12										
Leeds 10	a	12 22		12 36				12 52			13 04				13 22		13 35					13 52		14 04	
	d	12 25		12 40			12 43	12 55			13 08			13 13	13 25		13 40				13 43	13 55		14 08	
Cottingley	d						12 48														13 48				
Morley	d						12 52							13 21							13 52				
Batley	d						12 57							13 26							13 57				
Dewsbury	a	12 36					13 00	13 06						13 29	13 36						14 00	14 06			
	d	12 36					13 01	13 06						13 29	13 36						14 01	14 06			
Ravensthorpe	d						13 04														14 04				
Mirfield	d					12 58	13 08							13 35					13 58		14 08				
Deighton	d					13 05	13 14												14 05		14 14				
Huddersfield	a	12 45		12 58		13 11	13 21	13 15			13 25				13 45		13 58		14 11		14 21	14 15		14 25	
	d	12 46		12 59				13 16			13 26	13 30			13 46		13 59					14 16		14 26	14 30
Slaithwaite	d											13 37													14 37
Marsden	d											13 43													14 43
Greenfield	d											13 51													14 51
Mossley (Grtr Manchester)	d											13 55													14 55
Stalybridge	a										13 43	14 00												14 43	15 00
	d								13 40		13 46	14 01	14 22										14 40	14 46	15 01
Ashton-under-Lyne	d								13 44			14 05	14 26										14 44		15 05
Manchester Victoria	a								13 55			14 20	14 35	14 52									14 58		15 20
Manchester Piccadilly 10	a	13 19		13 36				13 49			14 05				14 19		14 36					14 49		15 05	
	d	13 24						13 54			14 07				14 24							14 54		15 07	
Manchester Airport	a	13 42						14 12							14 42							15 12			
Manchester Oxford Road	a										14 09													15 09	
Birchwood	a										14 25													15 25	
Warrington Central	a										14 30													15 30	
Liverpool South Parkway 7	a										14 47													15 47	
Liverpool Lime Street 10	a										14 58		15 43											15 58	

A from 26 March

B until 23 March

Newcastle, Middlesbrough, Scarborough, York, Hull, Leeds and Wakefield - Huddersfield - Manchester, Manchester Airport and Liverpool

Network Diagram - see first Page of Table 39

		NT	NT	TP	NT		TP	NT	NT	NT	TP	NT	TP	NT	NT		NT	TP	NT	TP	NT	NT	NT	TP	NT
				◇1			◇1				◇1		◇1					◇1		◇1				◇1	
		A										B			A										
Newcastle 8	d										13 15													14 18	
Chester-le-Street	d										13 24														
Durham	d										13 31													14 31	
Middlesbrough	d			12 50	13 32													13 50	14 32						
Thornaby	d			12 55	13a37													13 55	14a37						
Yarm	d			13 03														14 03							
Darlington 7	d										13 48													14 48	
Northallerton	d			13 18							13 58							14 18						14 59	
Thirsk	d			13 28														14 28							
Scarborough	d												13 48												
Seamer	d												13 53												
Malton	d												14 11												
York 8	a			13 47							14 23		14 38					14 47						15 22	
	d			13 57							14 26		14 40					14 57						15 26	
Wakefield Westgate	d								14 39													15 39			
Wakefield Kirkgate	d								14 45													15 45			
Hull	d						13 40	14 18												14 40	15 02				
Brough	d						13 52	14 30												14 52	15 14				
Howden	d							14 42													15 26				
Selby	d						14 11	14a53												15 11	15a36				
South Milford	d																								
Garforth	d			14 12														15 12							
Leeds 10	a			14 22			14 36				14 52		15 04					15 23		15 36				15 52	
	d		14 13	14 25			14 40			14 43	14 55		15 08				15 13	15 25		15 40			15 43	15 55	
Cottingley	d									14 48													15 48		
Morley	d		14 21							14 52							15 21						15 52		
Batley	d		14 26							14 57							15 26						15 57		
Dewsbury	a		14 29	14 36						15 00	15 06						15 29	15 36					16 00	16 06	
	d		14 29	14 36						15 01	15 06						15 29	15 36					16 01	16 06	
Ravensthorpe	d									15 04													16 04		
Mirfield	d		14 35						14 58	15 08							15 35					15 58	16 08		
Deighton	d								15 05	15 16												16 05	16 14		
Huddersfield	a			14 45			14 58		15 11	15 21	15 15		15 25					15 45		15 58		16 11	16 21	16 15	
	d			14 46			14 59				15 16		15 26	15 30				15 46		15 59				16 16	
Slaithwaite	d													15 37											
Marsden	d													15 43											
Greenfield	d													15 51											
Mossley (Grtr Manchester)	d													15 55											
Stalybridge	a												15 43	16 00											
	d	15 22										15 40	15 46	16 01	16 22										16 42
Ashton-under-Lyne	d	15 26										15 44		16 05	16 26										16 46
Manchester Victoria	a	15 35	15 53									15 55		16 21	16 35		16 52								16 58
Manchester Piccadilly 10	a			15 19			15 36				15 49		16 05					16 19		16 36				16 49	
	d			15 24							15 54		16 07					16 24						16 54	
Manchester Airport	a			15 42							16 12							16 42						17 12	
Manchester Oxford Road	a												16 09												
Birchwood	a												16 25												
Warrington Central	a												16 30												
Liverpool South Parkway 7	a												16 47												
Liverpool Lime Street 10	a	16 43											16 58		17 43										

A until 23 March

B from 26 March

Table 39

Mondays to Fridays

Newcastle, Middlesbrough, Scarborough, York, Hull, Leeds and Wakefield - Huddersfield - Manchester, Manchester Airport and Liverpool

Network Diagram - see first Page of Table 39

		TP	NT	NT	TP FX	TP FO	TP FO	TP FX	NT	NT	NT	TP	TP FO	NT	TP	GC	NT	NT	TP FO	TP FX	NT	TP
		◇1			◇1	◇1	◇1	◇1				◇1	◇1		◇1	R 1			◇1	◇1		◇1
		🍴			🍴	🍴	🍴	🍴				🍴			🍴	🍴			🍴	🍴		🍴
Newcastle 8 ⛴	d											15 15										
Chester-le-Street	d											15 24										
Durham	d											15 31										
Middlesbrough	d				14 50								14 50	15 32					15 50	15 50	16 32	
Thornaby	d				14 55								14 55	15a37					15 55	15 55	16a37	
Yarm	d				15 03								15 03						16 03	16 03		
Darlington 7	d											15 48										
Northallerton	d				15 18							15 59	15 18						16 18	16 18		
Thirsk	d				15 28								15 28						16 28	16 28		
Scarborough	d	14 48													15 48							
Seamer	d	14 53													15 53							
Malton	d	15 11													16 11							
York 8	a	15 38			15 47							16 21	15 47		16 38				16 47	16 47		
	d	15 40			15 57	15 57						16 26	16 13		16 40				16 57	16 57		
Wakefield Westgate	d									16 39												
Wakefield Kirkgate	d									16 45						17 08						
Hull	d						15 40	15 40	16 10													16 40
Brough	d						15 52	15 52	16 22													16 52
Howden	d								16 36													
Selby	d						16 11	16 11	16a46													17 11
South Milford	d																					
Garforth	d				16 12		16 22												17 12	17 12		
Leeds 10	a	16 04			16 22	16 22	16 36	16 36				16 52	16 59		17 04				17 22	17 22		17 36
	d	16 08		16 13	16 25	16 25	16 40	16 40			16 43	16 55			17 08			17 13	17 26	17 26		17 40
Cottingley	d			16 18							16 48							17 18				
Morley	d			16 22							16 52							17 22				
Batley	d			16 27							16 57							17 27				
Dewsbury	a			16 30	16 36	16 36					17 00	17 06						17 30	17 37	17 37		
	d			16 31	16 36	16 36					17 01	17 06						17 31	17 37	17 37		
Ravensthorpe	d			16 34							17 04							17 34				
Mirfield	d			16 38						16 58	17 08					17a20		17 38				
Deighton	d									17 05	17 14											
Huddersfield	a	16 25			16 45	16 45	16 58	16 58		17 11	17 21	17 15			17 25				17 46	17 46		17 58
	d	16 26	16 30		16 46	16 46	16 59	16 59				17 16			17 26		17 30		17 46	17 46		17 59
Slaithwaite	d		16 37														17 37					
Marsden	d		16 43														17 43					
Greenfield	d		16 51														17 51					
Mossley (Grtr Manchester)	d		16 55														17 55					
Stalybridge	a	16 43	17 00				17 18	17 18							17 43		18 00					18 18
	d	16 46	17 01				17 18	17 18							17 46		18 01					18 18
Ashton-under-Lyne	d		17 05														18 05					
Manchester Victoria ⛴	a		17 24	17 53													18 20	18 54				
Manchester Piccadilly 10 ⛴	a	17 05			17 25	17 21	17 36	17 36				17 49			18 05				18 19	18 19		18 37
	d	17 07										17 54			18 07					18 24		
Manchester Airport ✈	a											18 12								18 42		
Manchester Oxford Road	a	17 09													18 09							
Birchwood	a	17 25													18 25							
Warrington Central	a	17 30													18 30							
Liverpool South Parkway 7 ✈	a	17 47													18 47							
Liverpool Lime Street 10	a	18 01													19 01							

Newcastle, Middlesbrough, Scarborough, York, Hull, Leeds and Wakefield - Huddersfield - Manchester, Manchester Airport and Liverpool

Network Diagram - see first Page of Table 39

		NT	NT	NT	TP	TP	TP		NT	NT	TP	TP	NT	NT	NT	TP	TP		TP	NT	NT	TP	NT	NT	TP
																			FO			FX			FO
					◇1	◇1	◇1				◇1	◇1				◇1	◇1		◇1			◇1			◇1
					🛒		🛒				🛒	🛒				🛒									
Newcastle 8	d				16 15							17 02													
Chester-le-Street	d				16 24							17 11													
Durham	d				16 31							17 18													
Middlesbrough	d										16 50		17 39						17 50			17 50	18 32	18 45	
Thornaby	d										16 55		17a44						17 55			17 55	18a37	18 50	
Yarm	d										17 03								18 03			18 03			
Darlington 7	d				16 48							17 36												19a12	
Northallerton	d				16 59						17 18	17 47							18 18			18 18			
Thirsk	d										17 28								18 28			18 28			
Scarborough	d						16 48										17 48								
Seamer	d						16 53										17 53								
Malton	d						17 11										18 11								
York 8	a				17 23		17 38				17 47	18 09					18 38		18 47			18 47			
	d				17 26		17 40				17 57	18 12					18 40					19 08			19 08
Wakefield Westgate	d		17 39											18 39											
Wakefield Kirkgate	d		17 45											18 45											
Hull	d					17 01										17 58									
Brough	d					17 13										18 10									
Howden	d																								
Selby	d					17 32										18 29									
South Milford	d																								
Garforth	d										18 12											19 22			19 22
Leeds 10	a				17 52	17 58	18 04				18 22	18 37				18 52	19 04					19 37			19 37
	d			17 43	17 55	18 02	18 08			18 13	18 25	18 40			18 43	18 55	19 08				19 13	19 40			19 40
Cottingley	d			17 48						18 18					18 48						19 18				
Morley	d			17 52						18 22					18 52						19 22				
Batley	d			17 57						18 27					18 57						19 27				
Dewsbury	a			18 00	18 06	18 13				18 30	18 36				19 00	19 06					19 30	19 51			19 51
	d			18 01	18 06	18 13				18 31	18 36				19 01	19 06					19 31	19 51			19 51
Ravensthorpe	d			18 04						18 34					19 04						19 34				
Mirfield	d		17 58	18 08						18 38				18 58	19 08						19 38				
Deighton	d		18 05	18 13										19 05	19 13						19 45				
Huddersfield	a		18 11	18 20	18 15	18 23	18 25				18 45	19 00		19 11	19 20	19 15	19 25				19 49	19 59			19 59
	d	18 04			18 16		18 26		18 30		18 46	19 01				19 16	19 26			19 30		20 00			20 00
Slaithwaite	d	18 11							18 37											19 37					
Marsden	d	18 17							18 43											19 43					
Greenfield	d								18 51											19 51					
Mossley (Grtr Manchester)	d								18 55											19 55					
Stalybridge	a	18 30					18 43		19 01								19 43			20 00					
	d	18 31					18 46		19 01								19 46			20 01					
Ashton-under-Lyne	d	18 35							19 05											20 05					
Manchester Victoria 🚢	a	18 48							19 20	19 54										20 20					
Manchester Piccadilly 10 🚢	a				18 49		19 05				19 21	19 32				19 57	20 05					20 33			20 33
	d				18 54		19 07					19 40					20 07					20 40			20 40
Manchester Airport ✈	a				19 13							19 59										20 57			20 57
Manchester Oxford Road	a						19 09										20 09								
Birchwood	a						19 25										20 25								
Warrington Central	a						19 30										20 30								
Liverpool South Parkway 7 ✈	a						19 47										20 47								
Liverpool Lime Street 10	a						20 01										21 01								

Newcastle, Middlesbrough, Scarborough, York, Hull, Leeds and Wakefield - Huddersfield - Manchester, Manchester Airport and Liverpool

Network Diagram - see first Page of Table 39

		TP	NT		NT	TP	TP	NT	NT	TP	NT	TP	NT		NT	TP	NT	TP	TP	TP	TP	TP	NT		TP
																FX		FO	FX		FX				
		◇1				◇1	◇1			◇1		◇1				◇1		◇1	◇1	◇1	◇1	◇1			◇1
Newcastle 8 ⛴	d									18 52															
Chester-le-Street	d									19 01															
Durham	d									19 08															
Middlesbrough	d						18 50									18 50	19 40			20 04					20 50
Thornaby	d						18 55									18 55	19a45			20 09					20 55
Yarm	d						19 03									19 03									21 03
Darlington 7	d									19 25										20 35					
Northallerton	d						19 18			19 36						19 18				20 46					21 18
Thirsk	d						19 26									19 26				21 00					
Scarborough	d					18 48						19 48										20 48			
Seamer	d					18 53						19 53										20 53			
Malton	d					19 11						20 11										21 11			
York 8	a					19 38	19 50			20 07		20 38				19 50				21 24		21 38			21 43
	d					19 40				20 10		20 40				21 14			21 14						21 46
Wakefield Westgate	d				19 42						20 50												21 41		
Wakefield Kirkgate	d				19 45						20 56												21 50		
Hull	d	18 59	19 15															20 35			20 45				
Brough	d	19 11	19 28															20 47			20 57				
Howden	d		19 43																						
Selby	d	19 30	19a53															21 06			21 16				
South Milford	d																	21 16			21 26				
Garforth	d																								
Leeds 10	a	19 56				20 04				20 35		21 04				21 37		21 35	21 37		21 44				22 07
	d					20 08			20 13	20 40		21 08			21 13	21 40		21 40	21 40						22 10
Cottingley	d								20 18						21 18										
Morley	d								20 22						21 22										
Batley	d								20 27						21 27										
Dewsbury	a								20 30	20 51					21 30	21 51		21 51	21 51						
	d								20 31	20 51					21 31	21 51		21 51	21 51						
Ravensthorpe	d								20 34						21 34										
Mirfield	d				19 59				20 37		21 09				21 38								22 03		
Deighton	d				20 08				20 44		21 16				21 45								22 10		
Huddersfield	a				20 13	20 25			20 51	20 59	21 21	21 25			21 49	21 59		21 59	21 59				22 14		22 27
	d					20 26		20 30		21 00		21 26	21 30			22 00		22 00	22 00						22 28
Slaithwaite	d							20 37					21 37												
Marsden	d							20 43					21 43												
Greenfield	d							20 51					21 51												
Mossley (Grtr Manchester)	d							20 55					21 55												
Stalybridge	a					20 43		21 00				21 43	22 00												22 45
	d					20 46		21 01				21 46	22 01												22 46
Ashton-under-Lyne	d							21 05					22 05												
Manchester Victoria ⛴	a							21 20					22 20												
Manchester Piccadilly 10 ⛴	a					21 05				21 33		22 05				22 33		22 33	22 33						23 05
	d					21 07				21 40		22 07				22 40		22 40	22 40						
Manchester Airport ✈	a									21 57						22 57		22 57	22 57						
Manchester Oxford Road	a					21 09						22 09													
Birchwood	a					21 25						22 25													
Warrington Central	a					21 30						22 30													
Liverpool South Parkway 7 ✈	a					21 47						22 47													
Liverpool Lime Street 10	a					22 01						23 01													

Newcastle, Middlesbrough, Scarborough, York, Hull, Leeds and Wakefield - Huddersfield - Manchester, Manchester Airport and Liverpool

Network Diagram - see first Page of Table 39

		NT	TP	TP	NT	NT	TP	NT	NT		NT	TP	NT
			◇1	◇1			◇1					◇1	
Newcastle 8	d											21 54	22 21
Chester-le-Street	d												22 30
Durham	d											22 08	22 39
Middlesbrough	d	21 01		21 50									
Thornaby	d	21a06		21 55									
Yarm	d												
Darlington 7	d			22 19								22 25	22a59
Northallerton	d			22 30								22 36	
Thirsk	d			22 38									
Scarborough	d		22 03										
Seamer	d		22 08										
Malton	d		22 26										
York 8	a		22 55	22 56								23 00	
	d											23 06	
Wakefield Westgate	d								22 48				
Wakefield Kirkgate	d								22 53				
Hull	d						21 33						
Brough	d						21 45						
Howden	d												
Selby	d						22 07						
South Milford	d						22 16						
Garforth	d												
Leeds 10	a						22 35					23 33	
	d					22 18	22 40				23 13	23 35	
Cottingley	d					22 23					23 18		
Morley	d					22 27					23 22		
Batley	d					22 32					23 27		
Dewsbury	a					22 35	22 51				23 30	23 45	
	d					22 36	22 51				23 31	23 46	
Ravensthorpe	d					22 39					23 34		
Mirfield	d					22 44			23 06		23 38		
Deighton	d					22 49			23 14		23 45		
Huddersfield	a					22 54	22 59		23 21		23 49	23 54	
	d				22 34		23 00	23 05				23 55	
Slaithwaite	d				22 41			23 12					
Marsden	d				22 47			23 18					
Greenfield	d				22 55			23 26					
Mossley (Grtr Manchester)	d				22 59			23 30					
Stalybridge	a				23 04			23 35					
	d				23 05			23 36					
Ashton-under-Lyne	d				23 09			23 40					
Manchester Victoria	a				23 24			23 53					
Manchester Piccadilly 10	a						23 37					00 53	
	d											00 54	
Manchester Airport ✈	a											01 10	
Manchester Oxford Road	a												
Birchwood	a												
Warrington Central	a												
Liverpool South Parkway 7 ✈	a												
Liverpool Lime Street 10	a												

Newcastle, Middlesbrough, Scarborough, York, Hull, Leeds and Wakefield - Huddersfield - Manchester, Manchester Airport and Liverpool

Network Diagram - see first Page of Table 39

		TP	TP	TP	TP	TP	TP	TP	TP	NT		NT	TP	NT	TP	NT	NT	NT	NT	NT	NT	NT	TP	NT	NT
		◇1	◇1	◇1	◇1	◇1	◇1	◇1	◇1				◇1		◇1								◇1		
																		A	B					C	C
Newcastle 8	d	21p54																							
Chester-le-Street	d																								
Durham	d	22p08																							
Middlesbrough	d												05 55			06 51									
Thornaby	d												06 00			06a56									
Yarm	d												06 08												
Darlington 7	d	22p25																							
Northallerton	d	22p36											06 23												
Thirsk	d												06 31												
Scarborough	d																						06 30		
Seamer	d																						06 35		
Malton	d																						06 53		
York 8	a	23p00											06 49										07 23		
	d	23p06	01 52	02 40	03 52	05 26	05 57	06 28					06 55										07 26		
Wakefield Westgate	d																				07 29				
Wakefield Kirkgate	d																				07 35				
Hull	d								06 00						06 37		07 07								
Brough	d								06 12						06 49		07 19								
Howden	d								06 26								07 35								
Selby	d								06 36						07 08		07a48								
South Milford	d																								
Garforth	d						06 12						07 10		07 24										
Leeds 10	a	23p33	02 18	03 06	04 34	05 52	06 22	06 52	07 00				07 20		07 35								07 52		
	d	23p35	02 20	03 10	04 45	05 55	06 25	06 55	07 08	07 13			07 23		07 38							07 43	07 55		
Cottingley	d																					07 48			
Morley	d									07 21												07 52			
Batley	d									07 26												07 57			
Dewsbury	a	23p45				06 06	06 36	07 06		07 29			07 34									08 00	08 06		
	d	23p46				06 06	06 36	07 06		07 29			07 34									08 01	08 06		
Ravensthorpe	d																					08 04			
Mirfield	d									07 35											07 50	08 08			
Deighton	d																				07 56	08 13			
Huddersfield	a	23p54	02 56	03 49	05 27	06 14	06 44	07 15	07 25				07 43		07 56						08 03	08 20	08 15		
	d	23p55	02 56	03 59	05 28	06 15	06 45	07 16	07 26			07 33	07 44		07 57					08 02			08 16		
Slaithwaite	d											07 40								08 09					
Marsden	d											07 55								08 15					
Greenfield	d											08 03								08 23					
Mossley (Grtr Manchester)	d											08 07		←						08 27					
Stalybridge	a					06 33	07 03	07 34	07 43			08 12	08 01	08 12	08 17					08 32					
	d					06 33	07 04	07 34	07 46			08 13	08 02	08 13	08 17			08 22	08 22	08 33				08 40	
Ashton-under-Lyne	d											→		08 17				08 26	08 26	08 37				08 44	
Manchester Victoria	a									08 53				08 31				08 35	08 35	08 52				08 55	09d39
Manchester Piccadilly 10	a	00 53	03 44	04 52	06 02	06 50	07 19	07 51	08 05				08 19		08 36								08 51		
	d	00 54	03 44	04 54	06 08	06 54	07 23	07 54	08 07				08 24										08 54		
Manchester Airport	a	01 10	04 00	05 10	06 24	07 12	07 42	08 12					08 42										09 12		
Manchester Oxford Road	a								08 09																
Birchwood	a								08 25																
Warrington Central	a								08 30																
Liverpool South Parkway 7	a								08 47																
Liverpool Lime Street 10	a								08 58										09 43						10 43

A from 18 February until 24 March

B until 11 February

C from 31 March

Newcastle, Middlesbrough, Scarborough, York, Hull, Leeds and Wakefield - Huddersfield - Manchester, Manchester Airport and Liverpool

Network Diagram - see first Page of Table 39

		TP	NT	NT	NT	NT	TP	TP	NT	NT	TP	NT	NT	NT	NT	TP	NT	NT	NT	NT	TP	TP	NT	NT
		◇1					◇1	◇1			◇1					◇1					◇1	◇1		
				A	B									C	C			A	B					
		🍴					🍴	🍴			🍴					🍴					🍴	🍴		
Newcastle 8	d	06 11																			07 43			
Chester-le-Street	d	06 21																						
Durham	d	06 28																			07 57			
Middlesbrough	d										07 12	07 32	08 32											
Thornaby	d										07 17	07a37	08a37											
Yarm	d										07 27													
Darlington 7	d	06 45																			08 14			
Northallerton	d	06 56									07 43										08 26			
Thirsk	d	07 04									07 51										08 34			
Scarborough	d						06 58									07 48								
Seamer	d						07 03									07 53								
Malton	d						07 21									08 11								
York 8	a	07 30					07 47				08 11					08 38					08 52			
	d	07 40					07 53				08 25					08 40					08 57			
Wakefield Westgate	d								08 29															09 29
Wakefield Kirkgate	d								08 35															09 35
Hull	d							07 37														08 40	09 02	
Brough	d							07 49														08 52	09 14	
Howden	d							08 01															09 28	
Selby	d							08 11														09 11	09a38	
South Milford	d																							
Garforth	d						08 12				08 40										09 12			
Leeds 10	a	08 04					08 22	08 36			08 52					09 04					09 22	09 36		
	d	08 08				08 13	08 25	08 40		08 43	08 55					09 08				09 13	09 25	09 40		
Cottingley	d					08 18				08 48										09 18				
Morley	d					08 22				08 52										09 22				
Batley	d					08 27				08 57										09 27				
Dewsbury	a					08 30	08 36			09 00	09 06									09 30	09 36			
	d					08 31	08 36			09 01	09 06									09 31	09 36			
Ravensthorpe	d					08 34				09 04														
Mirfield	d					08 38			08 51	09 08										09 37				09 51
Deighton	d								08 58	09 17														09 58
Huddersfield	a	08 25					08 44	08 58	09 05	09 21	09 15					09 25					09 45	09 58		10 05
	d	08 26	08 30				08 45	08 59			09 16					09 26	09 30				09 46	09 59		
Slaithwaite	d		08 37														09 37							
Marsden	d		08 43														09 43							
Greenfield	d		08 51														09 51							
Mossley (Grtr Manchester)	d		08 55														09 55							
Stalybridge	a	08 44	09 00													09 43	10 00							
	d	08 46	09 01	09 22	09 22									09 40		09 46	10 01	10 22	10 22					
Ashton-under-Lyne	d		09 05	09 26	09 26									09 44			10 05	10 26	10 26					
Manchester Victoria 🚢	a		09 20	09 35	09 35	09 53								09 55	10d39		10 20	10 35	10 35	10 53				
Manchester Piccadilly 10 🚢	a	09 05					09 19	09 36			09 49					10 05					10 19	10 36		
	d	09 07					09 24				09 54					10 07					10 24			
Manchester Airport ✈	a						09 42				10 12										10 42			
Manchester Oxford Road	a	09 09														10 09								
Birchwood	a	09 25														10 25								
Warrington Central	a	09 30														10 30								
Liverpool South Parkway 7 ✈	a	09 47														10 47								
Liverpool Lime Street 10	a	09 58			10 43										11 43	10 58			11 43					

A from 18 February until 24 March

B until 11 February

C from 31 March

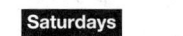

Newcastle, Middlesbrough, Scarborough, York, Hull, Leeds and Wakefield - Huddersfield - Manchester, Manchester Airport and Liverpool

Network Diagram - see first Page of Table 39

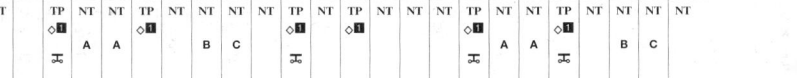

		NT		TP	NT	NT	TP	NT	NT	NT	NT	TP	NT	TP	NT	NT	NT	TP	NT	NT	TP	NT	NT	NT	NT
				◇1			◇1					◇1		◇1				◇1			◇1				
					A	A			B	C									A	A			B	C	
				🛒								🛒						🛒			🛒				
Newcastle 8	d																	09 15							
Chester-le-Street	d																	09 24							
Durham	d																	09 31							
Middlesbrough	d											08 50	09 32												
Thornaby	d											08 55	09a37												
Yarm	d											09 03													
Darlington 7	d																	09 48							
Northallerton	d											09 18						09 59							
Thirsk	d											09 28													
Scarborough	d						08 48														09 48				
Seamer	d						08 53														09 53				
Malton	d						09 11														10 11				
York 8	a						09 38					09 47						10 21			10 38				
	d			09 25			09 40					09 57						10 27			10 40				
Wakefield Westgate	d															10 29									
Wakefield Kirkgate	d															10 35									
Hull	d													09 40	10 08										
Brough	d													09 52	10 20										
Howden	d														10 34										
Selby	d													10 11	10a47										
South Milford	d																								
Garforth	d											10 12													
Leeds 10	a			09 53			10 04					10 22		10 36				10 52			11 04				
	d	09 43		09 55			10 08				10 13	10 25		10 40			10 43	10 55			11 08				11 13
Cottingley	d	09 48															10 48								
Morley	d	09 52									10 21						10 52								11 21
Batley	d	09 57									10 26						10 57								11 26
Dewsbury	a	10 00		10 06							10 29	10 36					11 00	11 06							11 29
	d	10 01		10 06							10 29	10 36					11 01	11 06							11 29
Ravensthorpe	d	10 04															11 04								
Mirfield	d	10 08									10 35					10 51	11 08								11 35
Deighton	d	10 14														10 58	11 14								
Huddersfield	a	10 21		10 15			10 25					10 45		10 58		11 05	11 21	11 15			11 25				
	d			10 16			10 26	10 30				10 46		10 59				11 16			11 26	11 30			
Slaithwaite	d							10 37														11 37			
Marsden	d							10 43														11 43			
Greenfield	d							10 51														11 51			
Mossley (Grtr Manchester)	d							10 55														11 55			
Stalybridge	a						10 43	11 00													11 43	12 00			
	d				10 40		10 46	11 01	11 22	11 22									11 40		11 46	12 01	12 22	12 22	
Ashton-under-Lyne	d				10 44			11 05	11 26	11 26									11 44			12 05	12 26	12 26	
Manchester Victoria	a				10 55	11d39		11 20	11 35	11 35	11 53								11 55	12d39		12 20	12 36	12 36	12 53
Manchester Piccadilly 10	a			10 49			11 05					11 19		11 36				11 49			12 05				
	d			10 54			11 07					11 24						11 54			12 07				
Manchester Airport	a			11 12								11 42						12 12							
Manchester Oxford Road	a						11 09														12 09				
Birchwood	a						11 25														12 25				
Warrington Central	a						11 30														12 30				
Liverpool South Parkway 7	a						11 47														12 47				
Liverpool Lime Street 10	a					12 43	11 58			12 43										13 43	12 58			13 43	

A from 31 March

B from 18 February until 24 March

C until 11 February

Table 39

Saturdays

Newcastle, Middlesbrough, Scarborough, York, Hull, Leeds and Wakefield - Huddersfield - Manchester, Manchester Airport and Liverpool

Network Diagram - see first Page of Table 39

		TP	NT	TP	NT	NT	NT	TP	NT	NT	TP	NT	NT	NT	NT	TP	NT	TP	NT	NT	GC	NT	TP	NT	NT
		◇1		◇1				◇1			◇1					◇1		◇1					◇1		
									A	A			B	C										A	A
		⊼						⊼			⊼					⊼		⊼					⊼		
Newcastle 8 ⛴	d							10 15															11 15		
Chester-le-Street	d							10 24															11 24		
Durham	d							10 31															11 31		
Middlesbrough	d	09 50	10 32													10 50	11 32								
Thornaby	d	09 55	10a37													10 55	11a36								
Yarm	d	10 03														11 03									
Darlington 7	d							10 48															11 48		
Northallerton	d	10 18						10 59								11 18							11 59		
Thirsk	d	10 28														11 28									
Scarborough	d										10 48														
Seamer	d										10 53														
Malton	d										11 11														
York 8	a	10 47						11 22			11 38					11 47							12 21		
	d	10 57						11 26			11 40					11 57							12 26		
Wakefield Westgate	d					11 29														12 29					
Wakefield Kirkgate	d					11 35														12 35	12 43				
Hull	d			10 40	11 05													11 40	12 03						
Brough	d			10 52	11 17													11 52	12 15						
Howden	d				11 29														12 27						
Selby	d			11 11	11a40													12 11	12a37						
South Milford	d																								
Garforth	d	11 12														12 12									
Leeds 10	a	11 22		11 36				11 53			12 04					12 22		12 36					12 52		
	d	11 25		11 40			11 43	11 55			12 08				12 13	12 25		12 40				12 43	12 55		
Cottingley	d						11 48															12 48			
Morley	d						11 52								12 21							12 52			
Batley	d						11 57								12 26							12 57			
Dewsbury	a	11 36					12 00	12 06							12 29	12 36						13 00	13 06		
	d	11 36					12 01	12 06							12 29	12 36						13 01	13 06		
Ravensthorpe	d						12 04															13 04			
Mirfield	d					11 49	12 08								12 35					12 49	12a55	13 08			
Deighton	d					11 58	12 14													12 58		13 14			
Huddersfield	a	11 45		11 58		12 05	12 21	12 15			12 25					12 45		12 58		13 05		13 21	13 15		
	d	11 46		11 59				12 16			12 26	12 30				12 46		12 59					13 16		
Slaithwaite	d											12 37													
Marsden	d											12 43													
Greenfield	d											12 51													
Mossley (Grtr Manchester)	d											12 55													
Stalybridge	a										12 43	13 00													
	d								12 40		12 46	13 01	13 22	13 22										13 40	
Ashton-under-Lyne	d								12 44			13 05	13 26	13 26										13 44	
Manchester Victoria ⛴	a								12 53	13d39		13 20	13 35	13 35	13 53									13 55	14d39
Manchester Piccadilly 10 ⛴	a	12 19		12 36				12 49			13 05					13 19		13 36					13 49		
	d	12 24						12 54			13 07					13 24							13 54		
Manchester Airport ✈	a	12 42						13 12								13 42							14 12		
Manchester Oxford Road	a										13 09														
Birchwood	a										13 25														
Warrington Central	a										13 30														
Liverpool South Parkway 7 ✈	a										13 47														
Liverpool Lime Street 10	a									14 43	13 58			14 43											15 43

A from 31 March **B** from 18 February until 24 March **C** until 11 February

Table 39 **Saturdays**

Newcastle, Middlesbrough, Scarborough, York, Hull, Leeds and Wakefield - Huddersfield - Manchester, Manchester Airport and Liverpool

Network Diagram - see first Page of Table 39

		TP	NT	NT		NT	NT	TP	NT	TP	NT	NT	NT	TP	NT		TP	NT	NT	NT	NT	TP	NT	TP
		◇[1]						◇[1]		◇[1]				◇[1]			◇[1]					◇[1]		◇[1]
				A		B									C				A	B				
								🛒		🛒				🛒			🛒					🛒		
Newcastle [8]	d													12 17										
Chester-le-Street	d																							
Durham	d													12 29										
Middlesbrough	d							11 50	12 32													12 50	13 32	
Thornaby	d							11 55	12a37													12 55	13a37	
Yarm	d							12 03														13 03		
Darlington [7]	d													12 46										
Northallerton	d							12 18						12 58								13 18		
Thirsk	d							12 28														13 28		
Scarborough	d	11 48															12 48							
Seamer	d	11 53															12 53							
Malton	d	12 11															13 11							
York [8]	a	12 38						12 47						13 21			13 38					13 47		
	d	12 40						12 57						13 24			13 40					13 57		
Wakefield Westgate	d											13 39												
Wakefield Kirkgate	d											13 45												
Hull	d									12 40	13 12													13 40
Brough	d									12 52	13 24													13 52
Howden	d										13 42													
Selby	d									13 11	13a54													14 11
South Milford	d																							
Garforth	d							13 12														14 12		
Leeds [10]	a	13 04						13 22		13 36				13 52			14 04					14 22		14 35
	d	13 08					13 13	13 25		13 40			13 43	13 55			14 08				14 13	14 25		14 37
Cottingley	d												13 48											
Morley	d						13 21						13 52								14 21			
Batley	d						13 26						13 57								14 26			
Dewsbury	a						13 29	13 36					14 00	14 06							14 29	14 36		
	d						13 29	13 36					14 01	14 06							14 29	14 36		
Ravensthorpe	d												14 04											
Mirfield	d						13 35					13 58	14 08								14 35			
Deighton	d											14 05	14 14											
Huddersfield	a	13 25						13 45		13 58		14 11	14 21	14 15			14 25					14 45		14 55
	d	13 26	13 30					13 46		13 59				14 16			14 26	14 30				14 46		14 56
Slaithwaite	d		13 37															14 37						
Marsden	d		13 43															14 43						
Greenfield	d		13 51															14 51						
Mossley (Grtr Manchester)	d		13 55															14 55						
Stalybridge	a	13 43	14 00														14 43	15 00						
	d	13 46	14 01	14 22		14 22									14 40		14 46	15 01	15 22	15 22				
Ashton-under-Lyne	d		14 05	14 26		14 26									14 44			15 05	15 26	15 26				
Manchester Victoria	a		14 20	14 35		14 35	14 53								14 55	15d39		15 20	15 35	15 35	15 53			
Manchester Piccadilly [10]	a	14 05						14 19		14 36				14 49			15 05					15 19		15 36
	d	14 07						14 24						14 54			15 07					15 24		
Manchester Airport	a							14 42						15 12								15 42		
Manchester Oxford Road	a	14 09															15 09							
Birchwood	a	14 25															15 25							
Warrington Central	a	14 30															15 30							
Liverpool South Parkway [7]	a	14 47															15 47							
Liverpool Lime Street [10]	a	14 58				15 43										16 43	15 58			16 43				

A from 18 February until 24 March **B** until 11 February **C** from 31 March

Newcastle, Middlesbrough, Scarborough, York, Hull, Leeds and Wakefield - Huddersfield - Manchester, Manchester Airport and Liverpool

Network Diagram - see first Page of Table 39

Station		NT	NT	NT	TP	NT	NT	TP	NT	NT	NT	NT	TP	NT	TP	NT	NT	NT	TP	NT	NT	TP	NT	NT	TP
					◇1			◇1					◇1		◇1				◇1			◇1			◇1
						A	A			B	C									A	A				
					🚲			🚲					🚲						🚲			🚲			🚲
Newcastle 8	d				13 15														14 18						
Chester-le-Street	d				13 24																				
Durham	d				13 31														14 31						
Middlesbrough	d												13 50	14 32											14 50
Thornaby	d												13 55	14a37											14 55
Yarm	d												14 03												15 03
Darlington 7	d				13 48														14 48						
Northallerton	d				13 58								14 18						14 59						15 18
Thirsk	d												14 28												15 28
Scarborough	d							13 48														14 48			
Seamer	d							13 53														14 53			
Malton	d							14 11														15 11			
York 8	a				14 23			14 38					14 47						15 22			15 38			15 47
	d				14 26			14 40					14 57						15 26			15 40			15 57
Wakefield Westgate	d		14 39														15 29								
Wakefield Kirkgate	d		14 45														15 35								
Hull	d	14 18													14 40	15 02									
Brough	d	14 30													14 52	15 14									
Howden	d	14 42														15 26									
Selby	d	14a53													15 11	15a36									
South Milford	d																								
Garforth	d												15 12												16 12
Leeds 10	a				14 52			15 04					15 22		15 36				15 53			16 04			16 22
	d			14 43	14 55			15 08				15 13	15 25		15 40			15 43	15 55			16 08		16 13	16 25
Cottingley	d			14 48														15 48						16 18	
Morley	d			14 52								15 21						15 52						16 22	
Batley	d			14 57								15 26						15 57						16 27	
Dewsbury	a			15 00	15 06							15 29	15 36					16 00	16 06					16 30	16 36
	d			15 01	15 06							15 29	15 36					16 01	16 06					16 31	16 36
Ravensthorpe	d			15 04														16 04						16 34	
Mirfield	d		14 58	15 08								15 35					15 51	16 08						16 38	
Deighton	d		15 05	15 14													15 58	16 15							
Huddersfield	a		15 11	15 21	15 15			15 25					15 45		15 58		16 05	16 21	16 15			16 25			16 45
	d				15 16			15 26	15 30				15 46		15 59				16 16			16 26	16 30		16 46
Slaithwaite	d								15 37														16 37		
Marsden	d								15 43														16 43		
Greenfield	d								15 51														16 51		
Mossley (Grtr Manchester)	d								15 55														16 55		
Stalybridge	a							15 43	16 00													16 43	17 00		
	d					15 40		15 46	16 01	16 22	16 22									16 40		16 46	17 01		
Ashton-under-Lyne	d					15 44			16 05	16 26	16 26									16 44			17 05		
Manchester Victoria	a					15 55	16d39		16 20	16 35	16 35	16 53								16 55	17d39		17 20	17 53	
Manchester Piccadilly 10	a				15 49			16 05					16 19		16 36				16 49			17 05			17 21
	d				15 54			16 07					16 24						16 54			17 07			
Manchester Airport	a				16 12								16 42						17 12						
Manchester Oxford Road	a							16 09														17 09			
Birchwood	a							16 25														17 25			
Warrington Central	a							16 30														17 30			
Liverpool South Parkway 7	a							16 47														17 47			
Liverpool Lime Street 10	a						17 43	16 58			17 43										18 43	18 01			

A from 31 March

B from 18 February until 24 March

C until 11 February

Newcastle, Middlesbrough, Scarborough, York, Hull, Leeds and Wakefield - Huddersfield - Manchester, Manchester Airport and Liverpool

Network Diagram - see first Page of Table 39

Station		NT	TP	NT	NT	NT	NT	TP	NT	NT	NT	NT	TP	NT	NT	TP		NT	TP	NT	GC	NT	TP	TP	NT
			◇1					◇1	A	B	C	C	◇1			◇1			◇1				◇1	◇1	A
Newcastle 8	d							15 15															16 15		
Chester-le-Street	d							15 24															16 24		
Durham	d							15 31															16 31		
Middlesbrough	d	15 32														15 50		16 32							
Thornaby	d	15a37														15 55		16a37							
Yarm	d															16 03									
Darlington 7	d							15 48															16 48		
Northallerton	d							15 59								16 18							16 59		
Thirsk	d															16 28									
Scarborough	d												15 48												
Seamer	d												15 53												
Malton	d												16 11												
York 8	a							16 21					16 38			16 47							17 23		
	d							16 26					16 40			16 57							17 26		
Wakefield Westgate	d					16 29														17 29					
Wakefield Kirkgate	d					16 35														17 35	17 45				
Hull	d		15 40	16 10															16 40					17 01	
Brough	d		15 52	16 22															16 52					17 13	
Howden	d			16 36																					
Selby	d		16 11	16a46															17 11					17 32	
South Milford	d																								
Garforth	d															17 12									
Leeds 10	a		16 36					16 52					17 04			17 22			17 36				17 52	17 58	
	d		16 40				16 43	16 55					17 08		17 13	17 26			17 40			17 43	17 55		
Cottingley	d						16 48								17 18							17 48			
Morley	d						16 52								17 22							17 52			
Batley	d						16 57								17 27							17 57			
Dewsbury	a						17 00	17 06							17 30	17 37						18 00	18 06		
	d						17 01	17 06							17 31	17 37						18 01	18 06		
Ravensthorpe	d						17 04								17 34							18 04			
Mirfield	d					16 51	17 08								17 38					17 51	17a57	18 08			
Deighton	d					16 58	17 14													17 58		18 13			
Huddersfield	a		16 58			17 05	17 21	17 15					17 25			17 46			17 58	18 05		18 21	18 15		
	d		16 59		17 04			17 16					17 26	17 30		17 46			17 59				18 16		
Slaithwaite	d				17 11									17 37											
Marsden	d				17a17									17 43											
Greenfield	d													17 51											
Mossley (Grtr Manchester)	d													17 55											
Stalybridge	a		17 18										17 43	18 00					18 18						
	d		17 18						17 22	17 22	17 40		17 46	18 01					18 18						18 22
Ashton-under-Lyne	d								17 26	17 26	17 44			18 05											18 26
Manchester Victoria	a								17 35	17 35	17 56	18d39		18 20	18 54										18 35
Manchester Piccadilly 10	a		17 36					17 49					18 05			18 19			18 37				18 49		
	d							17 54					18 07			18 24							18 54		
Manchester Airport	a							18 12								18 42							19 13		
Manchester Oxford Road	a												18 09												
Birchwood	a												18 25												
Warrington Central	a												18 30												
Liverpool South Parkway 7	a												18 47												
Liverpool Lime Street 10	a									18 43		19 43	19 01												

A from 18 February until 24 March

B until 11 February

C from 31 March

Table 39

Saturdays

Newcastle, Middlesbrough, Scarborough, York, Hull, Leeds and Wakefield - Huddersfield - Manchester, Manchester Airport and Liverpool

Network Diagram - see first Page of Table 39

		NT		TP	NT	NT	TP	TP	NT	NT	NT	TP		TP	NT	NT	TP	NT	TP	NT	NT	TP		TP	NT
				◇1			◇1	◇1				◇1		◇1			◇1		◇1			◇1		◇1	
		A																							
Newcastle 8	d							17 02																	
Chester-le-Street	d							17 11																	
Durham	d							17 18																	
Middlesbrough	d						16 50		17 39								17 50	18 32						18 50	19 40
Thornaby	d						16 55		17a44								17 55	18a37						18 55	19a45
Yarm	d						17 03										18 03							19 03	
Darlington 7	d							17 35																	
Northallerton	d						17 18	17 46									18 18							19 18	
Thirsk	d						17 28										18 28							19 26	
Scarborough	d			16 48										17 48								18 48			
Seamer	d			16 53										17 53								18 53			
Malton	d			17 11										18 11								19 11			
York 8	a			17 38			17 47	18 09						18 38			18 47					19 38		19 50	
	d			17 40			17 57	18 12						18 40			19 08					19 40			
Wakefield Westgate	d									18 29											19 41				
Wakefield Kirkgate	d									18 37											19 45				
Hull	d											17 58							18 59	19 15					
Brough	d											18 10							19 11	19 28					
Howden	d																			19 43					
Selby	d											18 29							19 30	19a53					
South Milford	d																								
Garforth	d						18 12										19 22								
Leeds 10	a			18 04			18 22	18 37				18 52		19 04			19 35		19 56			20 04			
	d			18 08		18 13	18 25	18 40			18 43	18 55		19 08		19 13	19 40					20 08			
Cottingley	d					18 18					18 48					19 18									
Morley	d					18 22					18 52					19 22									
Batley	d					18 27					18 57					19 27									
Dewsbury	a					18 30	18 36				19 00	19 06				19 30	19 51								
	d					18 31	18 36				19 01	19 06				19 31	19 51								
Ravensthorpe	d					18 34					19 04					19 34									
Mirfield	d					18 38				18 51	19 08					19 38					19 59				
Deighton	d									19 00	19 13					19 45					20 08				
Huddersfield	a			18 25			18 45	18 58		19 06	19 20	19 15		19 25		19 49	19 59				20 13	20 25			
	d			18 26	18 30		18 46	18 59				19 16		19 26	19 30		20 00					20 26			
Slaithwaite	d				18 37										19 37										
Marsden	d				18 43										19 43										
Greenfield	d				18 51										19 51										
Mossley (Grtr Manchester)	d				18 55										19 55										
Stalybridge	a			18 43	19 00									19 43	20 00							20 43			
	d	18 22		18 46	19 01									19 46	20 01							20 46			
Ashton-under-Lyne	d	18 26			19 05										20 05										
Manchester Victoria	a	18 35			19 20	19 54									20 20										
Manchester Piccadilly 10	a			19 05			19 21	19 32				19 57		20 05			20 33					21 05			
	d			19 07				19 40						20 07			20 40					21 07			
Manchester Airport	a							19 59									20 57								
Manchester Oxford Road	a			19 09										20 09								21 09			
Birchwood	a			19 25										20 25								21 25			
Warrington Central	a			19 30										20 30								21 30			
Liverpool South Parkway 7	a			19 47										20 47								21 47			
Liverpool Lime Street 10	a	19 43		20 01										21 01								22 01			

A until 11 February

Table 39

Saturdays

Newcastle, Middlesbrough, Scarborough, York, Hull, Leeds and Wakefield - Huddersfield - Manchester, Manchester Airport and Liverpool

Network Diagram - see first Page of Table 39

		NT	NT	TP ◇1	TP ◇1	NT	TP ◇1	NT		NT	NT	TP ◇1	NT	NT	TP ◇1	TP ◇1	NT	NT	TP ◇1	NT	NT	NT	TP ◇1 A	TP ◇1 B	NT
Newcastle 8	d			18 52																					21 50
Chester-le-Street	d			19 01																					21 59
Durham	d			19 08																					22 08
Middlesbrough	d											20 10	20 45		20 50								21 50	21 50	
Thornaby	d											20 15	20a50		20 55								21 55	21 55	
Yarm	d											20 23			21 03										
Darlington 7	d			19 25																			22 19	22 19	22a29
Northallerton	d			19 36								20 39			21 18								22 30	22 30	
Thirsk	d											20 47											22 38	22 38	
Scarborough	d						19 48									22 03									
Seamer	d						19 53									22 08									
Malton	d						20 11									22 26									
York 8	a			20 07			20 38					21 06			21 44	22 55							22 57	22 57	
	d			20 10			20 40					21 14			21 46								23 07	23 07	
Wakefield Westgate	d					20 50								21 41							22 42				
Wakefield Kirkgate	d					20 56								21 50							22 47				
Hull	d				19 56			21 01											21 33						
Brough	d				20 08			21 13											21 45						
Howden	d							21 25																	
Selby	d				20 27			21a35											22 07						
South Milford	d				20 36														22 16						
Garforth	d																								
Leeds 10	a			20 35	20 56		21 04					21 37			22 07				22 35				23 33	23 33	
	d		20 13	20 40			21 08				21 13	21 40			22 10			22 17	22 40			23 05	23 35	23 35	
Cottingley	d		20 18								21 18							22 22				23 10			
Morley	d		20 22								21 22							22 26				23 14			
Batley	d		20 27								21 27							22 31				23 19			
Dewsbury	a		20 30	20 51							21 30	21 51						22 34	22 51			23 22	23 46	23 46	
	d		20 31	20 51							21 31	21 51						22 35	22 51			23 23	23 46	23 46	
Ravensthorpe	d		20 34								21 34							22 38				23 26			
Mirfield	d		20 38			21 09					21 38			22 03				22 42			23 00	23 30			
Deighton	d		20 44			21 16					21 45			22 10				22 48			23 08	23 37			
Huddersfield	a		20 48	20 59		21 21	21 25				21 49	21 59		22 14	22 27			22 53	22 59		23 15	23 41	23 55	23 55	
	d	20 30	20 48	21 00			21 26			21 30		22 00			22 28		22 34		23 00	23 05			23 56	23 56	
Slaithwaite	d	20 37	20 55							21 37							22 41			23 12					
Marsden	d	20 43	21a02							21 43							22 47			23 18					
Greenfield	d	20 51								21 51							22 55			23 26					
Mossley (Grtr Manchester)	d	20 55								21 55							22 59			23 30					
Stalybridge	a	21 00					21 43			22 01					22 45		23 04			23 35					
	d	21 01					21 46			22 01					22 46		23 05			23 36					
Ashton-under-Lyne	d	21 05								22 06							23 09			23 40					
Manchester Victoria	a	21 20								22 20							23 24			23 53					
Manchester Piccadilly 10	a			21 33			22 05					22 33			23 05				23 37				00 27	00 27	
	d			21 40			22 07					22 40												00 31	
Manchester Airport	a			21 57								22 57												00 46	
Manchester Oxford Road	a						22 09																		
Birchwood	a						22 25																		
Warrington Central	a						22 30																		
Liverpool South Parkway 7	a						22 47																		
Liverpool Lime Street 10	a						23 01																		

A until 11 February, from 31 March

B from 18 February until 24 March

Newcastle, Middlesbrough, Scarborough, York, Hull and Leeds - Huddersfield - Manchester, Manchester Airport and Liverpool

Network Diagram - see first Page of Table 39

		TP	TP	TP	TP	TP	TP	NT	TP	TP	NT		TP	TP	NT	NT	TP	TP	TP	NT	NT	TP		TP	TP
		◇1	◇1	◇1	◇1	◇1	◇1		◇1	◇1			◇1	◇1			◇1	◇1	◇1			◇1		◇1	◇1
		A																							
Newcastle 8	d													08 00								09 31			
Chester-le-Street	d																					09 40			
Durham	d													08 13								09 47			
Middlesbrough	d	21p50													09 31									10 15	
Thornaby	d	21p55													09a36									10 20	
Yarm	d																							10 28	
Darlington 7	d	22p19												08 31								10 04			
Northallerton	d	22p30												08 43								10 15		10 43	
Thirsk	d	22p38												08 51										10 51	
Scarborough	d																		09 20						
Seamer	d																		09 25						
Malton	d																		09 43						
York 8	a	22p57												09 11					10 09			10 41		11 10	
	d	23p07	02 44	03 59	05 12	06 12	07 12			08 10			08 45	09 15					10 15			10 45		11 15	
Hull	d							08 54									09 00								10 58
Brough	d							09 06									09 12								11 10
Howden	d							09 18																	
Selby	d							09a27									09 33								11 29
South Milford	d																09 42								11 38
Garforth	d																								
Leeds 10	a	23p33	03 10	04 25	05 38	06 38	07 38			08 37			09 08	09 38			10 00		10 38			11 08		11 38	11 56
	d	23p35	03 10	04 25	05 40	06 40	07 40			08 40	08 47		09 15	09 40			10 08		10 40	10 44		11 10		11 40	11 59
Cottingley	d										08 52									10 49					
Morley	d										08 56									10 53					
Batley	d										09 01									10 58					
Dewsbury	a	23p46			05 51	06 51	07 51			08 51	09 04			09 51					10 51	11 01				11 51	
	d	23p46			05 51	06 51	07 51			08 51	09 05			09 51					10 51	11 02				11 51	
Ravensthorpe	d										09 08									11 05					
Mirfield	d										09 12									11 09					
Deighton	d										09 19									11 15					
Huddersfield	a	23p55	03 29	04 44	06 00	07 00	08 00			09 00	09 23		09 33	10 00			10 25		11 00	11 20		11 27		12 00	12 16
	d	23p56	03 30	04 45	06 01	07 01	08 01			09 01			09 34	10 01			10 26		11 01			11 28		12 01	12 17
Slaithwaite	d																								
Marsden	d																								
Greenfield	d																								
Mossley (Grtr Manchester)	d																								
Stalybridge	a					07 18	08 18			09 18			09 52				10 45					11 45			
	d					07 19	08 19			09 19			09 53			10 18	10 46				11 18	11 46			
Ashton-under-Lyne	d															10 22					11 22				
Manchester Victoria	a															10 36					11 36				
	d																								
Manchester Piccadilly 10	a	00 27	04 02	05 17	06 34	07 34	08 34			09 34			10 10	10 34			11 03		11 34			12 05		12 34	12 54
	d						08 38		09 07	09 38			10 12	10 38				11 07	11 38			12 07		12 38	
Manchester Airport	a						08 55			09 55				10 55					11 55					12 55	
Manchester Oxford Road	a								09 09				10 14					11 09				12 09			
Newton-le-Willows	a																								
Birchwood	a								09 25				10 28					11 25				12 25			
Warrington Central	a								09 30				10 33					11 30				12 30			
Liverpool South Parkway 7	a								09 47				10 49					11 47				12 47			
Liverpool Lime Street 10	a								10 00				11 00					11 59				12 58			

A not 11 December

Table 39

Sundays

until 1 January

Newcastle, Middlesbrough, Scarborough, York, Hull and Leeds - Huddersfield - Manchester, Manchester Airport and Liverpool

Network Diagram - see first Page of Table 39

		NT	NT	NT	TP	TP	NT	TP	NT		TP	TP	TP	NT	NT	TP	TP	NT	NT	NT		TP	NT	TP	TP
					◇1	◇1		◇1			◇1	◇1	◇1			◇1	◇1					◇1		◇1	◇1
Newcastle 8	d					11 08						12 10					13 04								14 08
Chester-le-Street	d																13 13								
Durham	d					11 20						12 22					13 20								14 20
Middlesbrough	d	11 31														12 45		13 31							
Thornaby	d	11a36														12 50		13a36							
Yarm	d															12 58									
Darlington 7	d					11 37						12 39					13 37								14 37
Northallerton	d					11 49										13 13									14 49
Thirsk	d															13 23									
Scarborough	d				10 51						11 51													13 51	
Seamer	d				10 56						11 56													13 56	
Malton	d				11 14						12 14													14 14	
York 8	a				11 40	12 12					12 40	13 11				13 43	14 10							14 40	15 12
	d				11 45	12 15					12 45	13 15				13 45	14 15					14 33		14 45	15 15
Hull	d		11 46					12 00					12 58	13 29					14 23						
Brough	d		11 58					12 12					13 10	13 41					14 35						
Howden	d		12 10											13 53					14 47						
Selby	d		12a19					12 32					13 29	14a02					14a56						
South Milford	d												13 38												
Garforth	d																								
Leeds 10	a				12 09	12 38		12 56			13 08	13 38	13 56			14 08	14 38					14 56		15 08	15 38
	d				12 10	12 40	12 44	12 59			13 10	13 40	13 59			14 10	14 40			14 44		14 59		15 10	15 40
Cottingley	d						12 49													14 49					
Morley	d						12 53													14 53					
Batley	d						12 58													14 58					
Dewsbury	a					12 51	13 01					13 51					14 51			15 01					15 51
	d					12 51	13 02					13 51					14 51			15 02					15 51
Ravensthorpe	d						13 05													15 05					
Mirfield	d						13 09													15 09					
Deighton	d						13 20													15 20					
Huddersfield	a				12 27	13 00	13 24	13 16			13 27	14 00	14 16			14 27	15 00			15 24		15 16		15 27	16 00
	d				12 28	13 01		13 17			13 28	14 01	14 17			14 28	15 01					15 17		15 28	16 01
Slaithwaite	d																								
Marsden	d																								
Greenfield	d																								
Mossley (Grtr Manchester)	d																								
Stalybridge	a				12 45						13 45					14 45								15 45	
	d			12 18	12 46				13 18		13 46				14 18	14 46							15 18	15 46	
Ashton-under-Lyne	d			12 22					13 22						14 22								15 22		
Manchester Victoria	a			12 36					13 36						14 36								15 36		
	d																								
Manchester Piccadilly 10	a				13 05	13 34		13 54			14 05	14 34	14 54			15 05	15 34					15 54		16 05	16 34
	d				13 07	13 38					14 07	14 38				15 07	15 38							16 07	16 38
Manchester Airport	a					13 55						14 55					15 55								16 55
Manchester Oxford Road	a				13 09						14 09					15 09								16 09	
Newton-le-Willows	a																								
Birchwood	a				13 25						14 25					15 25								16 25	
Warrington Central	a				13 30						14 30					15 30								16 30	
Liverpool South Parkway 7	a				13 47						14 47					15 47								16 47	
Liverpool Lime Street 10	a				13 58						14 58					15 58								16 58	

Table 39

Sundays
until 1 January

Newcastle, Middlesbrough, Scarborough, York, Hull and Leeds - Huddersfield - Manchester, Manchester Airport and Liverpool

Network Diagram - see first Page of Table 39

		TP	NT	NT	TP	TP	NT		NT	TP	NT	TP	TP	TP	NT	NT	TP	TP		NT	NT	TP	NT	TP	TP
		◇1			◇1	◇1				◇1		◇1	◇1	◇1			◇1	◇1				◇1		◇1	◇1
Newcastle 8	d					15 07							16 08					17 05							17 52
Chester-le-Street	d					15 16												17 14							
Durham	d					15 23							16 20					17 21							18 04
Middlesbrough	d				14 42		15 31										16 42			17 45					
Thornaby	d				14 47		15a36										16 47			17a50					
Yarm	d				14 55												16 55								
Darlington 7	d					15 40							16 37					17 38							18 21
Northallerton	d				15 10								16 49				17 10	17 49							18 33
Thirsk	d				15 18												17 18								
Scarborough	d											15 51												17 51	
Seamer	d											15 56												17 56	
Malton	d											16 14												18 14	
York 8	a				15 42	16 12						16 40	17 12				17 42	18 12						18 40	19 03
	d				15 45	16 15				16 33		16 45	17 15				17 45	18 15				18 33		18 45	19 15
Hull	d	14 58	16 00											16 58	17 23										
Brough	d	15 10	16 12											17 10	17 35										
Howden	d		16 24												17 47										
Selby	d	15 29	16a33											17 29	17a56										
South Milford	d	15 38												17 38											
Garforth	d																								
Leeds 10	a	15 56			16 08	16 38				16 56		17 08	17 38	17 56			18 08	18 38				18 57		19 08	19 38
	d	15 59			16 10	16 40			16 44	16 59		17 10	17 40	17 59			18 10	18 40			18 44	18 59		19 10	19 40
Cottingley	d								16 49												18 49				
Morley	d								16 53												18 53				
Batley	d								16 58												18 58				
Dewsbury	a					16 51			17 01				17 51					18 51			19 01				19 51
	d					16 51			17 02				17 51					18 51			19 02				19 51
Ravensthorpe	d								17 05												19 05				
Mirfield	d								17 09												19 09				
Deighton	d								17 20												19 20				
Huddersfield	a	16 16			16 27	17 00			17 24	17 16		17 27	18 00	18 16			18 27	19 00			19 24	19 16		19 27	20 00
	d	16 17			16 28	17 01				17 17		17 28	18 01	18 17			18 28	19 01				19 17		19 28	20 01
Slaithwaite	d																								
Marsden	d																								
Greenfield	d																								
Mossley (Grtr Manchester)	d																								
Stalybridge	a				16 45							17 45					18 45							19 45	
	d			16 18	16 46						17 18	17 46				18 18	18 46						19 18	19 46	
Ashton-under-Lyne	d			16 22							17 22					18 22							19 22		
Manchester Victoria	a			16 36							17 36					18 35							19 36		
	d																								
Manchester Piccadilly 10	a	16 54			17 05	17 34				17 54		18 05	18 34	18 54			19 05	19 34				19 54		20 05	20 34
	d				17 07	17 38						18 07	18 38				19 07	19 38						20 07	20 38
Manchester Airport	a					17 55							18 55					19 55							20 55
Manchester Oxford Road	a				17 09							18 09					19 09							20 09	
Newton-le-Willows	a																								
Birchwood	a				17 25							18 25					19 25							20 25	
Warrington Central	a				17 30							18 30					19 30							20 30	
Liverpool South Parkway 7	a				17 47							18 47					19 47							20 47	
Liverpool Lime Street 10	a				17 58							18 58					19 58							20 58	

Table 39

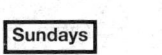

Sundays
until 1 January

Newcastle, Middlesbrough, Scarborough, York, Hull and Leeds - Huddersfield - Manchester, Manchester Airport and Liverpool

Network Diagram - see first Page of Table 39

		TP	NT	NT	TP		TP	NT	NT	NT	TP	TP	NT	TP	TP	NT		NT	TP	NT	TP				
		◇1			◇1		◇1				◇1	◇1		◇1	◇1				◇1		◇1				
Newcastle 8 ⛴	d						19 10							20 08		21 06									
Chester-le-Street	d															21 15									
Durham	d						19 22							20 20		21 24									
Middlesbrough	d				18 45			19 31				20 06									22 06				
Thornaby	d				18 50			19a36				20 11									22 11				
Yarm	d				18 58							20 19									22 19				
Darlington 7	d						19 39							20 37		21a44									
Northallerton	d				19 13							20 38		20 49							22 35				
Thirsk	d				19 21							20 46									22 43				
Scarborough	d										19 51								21 20						
Seamer	d										19 56								21 25						
Malton	d										20 14								21 43						
York 8	a				19 42		20 11				20 40	21 06		21 12					22 09		23 09				
	d				19 45		20 15				20 45			21 15					22 12		23 12				
Hull	d	18 58	19 24						20 29						21 00										
Brough	d	19 10	19 36						20 41						21 12										
Howden	d		19 48						20 53																
Selby	d	19 29	19a57						21a02						21 31										
South Milford	d	19 38													21 40										
Garforth	d																								
Leeds 10	a	19 54			20 08		20 38				21 08			21 38	21 59				22 36		23 38				
	d	19 59			20 10		20 40			20 44	21 10			21 40					22 40	22 44	23 40				
Cottingley	d									20 49										22 49					
Morley	d									20 53										22 53					
Batley	d									20 58										22 58					
Dewsbury	a						20 50			21 01				21 51						23 01	23 51				
	d						20 51			21 02				21 51						23 02	23 51				
Ravensthorpe	d									21 05										23 05					
Mirfield	d									21 09										23 09					
Deighton	d									21 15										23 16					
Huddersfield	a	20 16			20 27		21 00			21 19	21 27			22 00					22 57	23 20	23 59				
	d	20 17			20 28		21 01			21 19	21 28			22 01					22 58		00 01				
Slaithwaite	d									21 26															
Marsden	d									21a33															
Greenfield	d																								
Mossley (Grtr Manchester)	d																								
Stalybridge	a				20 45		21 18							22 18					23 18						
	d			20 18	20 46		21 19						21 18	22 19				22 18	23 19						
Ashton-under-Lyne	d			20 22									21 22					22 22							
Manchester Victoria ⛴	a			20 36									21 36					22 36							
	d																								
Manchester Piccadilly 10 ⛴	a	20 54			21 05		21 36				22 05			22 36					23 36		00 43				
	d				21 07						22 07			22 38							00 44				
Manchester Airport ✈	a													22 55							00 57				
Manchester Oxford Road	a				21 09						22 09														
Newton-le-Willows	a																								
Birchwood	a				21 25						22 25														
Warrington Central	a				21 30						22 30														
Liverpool South Parkway 7 ✈	a				21 47						22 47														
Liverpool Lime Street 10	a				21 58						22 58														

Table 39

Sundays

8 January to 12 February

Newcastle, Middlesbrough, Scarborough, York, Hull and Leeds - Huddersfield - Manchester, Manchester Airport and Liverpool

Network Diagram - see first Page of Table 39

		TP	TP	TP	TP	TP	TP	NT	TP	TP	NT	TP	TP	NT	NT	TP	TP	TP	NT	NT	TP	TP	TP
		◇1	◇1	◇1	◇1	◇1	◇1		◇1	◇1		◇1	◇1			◇1	◇1	◇1			◇1	◇1	◇1
Newcastle 8	d												08 00								09 31		
Chester-le-Street	d																				09 40		
Durham	d												08 13								09 47		
Middlesbrough	d	21p50												09 31								10 15	
Thornaby	d	21p55												09a36								10 20	
Yarm	d																					10 28	
Darlington 7	d	22p19											08 31								10 04		
Northallerton	d	22p30											08 43								10 15	10 43	
Thirsk	d	22p38											08 51									10 51	
Scarborough	d																	09 20					
Seamer	d																	09 25					
Malton	d																	09 43					
York 8	a	22p57											09 11					10 09			10 41	11 10	
	d	23p07	02 44	03 59	05 12	06 12	07 12			08 10		08 45	09 15					10 15			10 45	11 15	
Hull	d							08 54								09 00							10 58
Brough	d							09 06								09 12							11 10
Howden	d							09 18															
Selby	d							09a27								09 33							11 29
South Milford	d															09 42							11 38
Garforth	d																						
Leeds 10	a	23p33	03 10	04 25	05 38	06 38	07 38			08 37		09 08	09 38			10 00		10 38			11 08	11 38	11 56
	d	23p35	03 10	04 25	05 40	06 40	07 40			08 40	08 47	09 15	09 40			10 08		10 40	10 44		11 10	11 40	11 59
Cottingley	d										08 52								10 49				
Morley	d										08 56								10 53				
Batley	d										09 01								10 58				
Dewsbury	a	23p46			05 51	06 51	07 51			08 51	09 04		09 51					10 51	11 01			11 51	
	d	23p46			05 51	06 51	07 51			08 51	09 05		09 51					10 51	11 02			11 51	
Ravensthorpe	d										09 08								11 05				
Mirfield	d										09 12								11 09				
Deighton	d										09 19								11 15				
Huddersfield	a	23p55	03 29	04 44	06 00	07 00	08 00			09 00	09 23	09 33	10 00			10 25		11 00	11 20		11 27	12 00	12 16
	d	23p56	03 30	04 45	06 01	07 01	08 01			09 01		09 34	10 01			10 26		11 01			11 28	12 01	12 17
Slaithwaite	d																						
Marsden	d																						
Greenfield	d																						
Mossley (Grtr Manchester)	d																						
Stalybridge	a					07 18	08 18			09 18		09 52				10 45					11 45		
	d					07 19	08 19			09 19		09 53			10 18	10 46				11 18	11 46		
Ashton-under-Lyne	d														10 22					11 22			
Manchester Victoria	a														10 36					11 36			
	d																						
Manchester Piccadilly 10	a	00 27	04 02	05 17	06 34	07 34	08 34			09 34		10 10	10 34			11 03		11 34			12 05	12 34	12 54
	d						08 38		09 07	09 38		10 12	10 38				11 07	11 38			12 07	12 38	
Manchester Airport	a						08 55			09 55			10 55					11 55				12 55	
Manchester Oxford Road	a								09 09			10 14					11 09				12 09		
Newton-le-Willows	a																						
Birchwood	a								09 25			10 28					11 25				12 25		
Warrington Central	a								09 30			10 33					11 30				12 30		
Liverpool South Parkway 7	a								09 47			10 49					11 47				12 47		
Liverpool Lime Street 10	a								10 00			11 00					11 59				12 58		

Table 39

Sundays

8 January to 12 February

Newcastle, Middlesbrough, Scarborough, York, Hull and Leeds - Huddersfield - Manchester, Manchester Airport and Liverpool

Network Diagram - see first Page of Table 39

		NT	NT	NT	TP	TP	NT	TP	NT		TP	TP	TP	NT	NT	TP	TP	NT	NT	NT		TP	NT	TP	TP
					◇1	◇1		◇1			◇1	◇1	◇1			◇1	◇1					◇1		◇1	◇1
Newcastle 8	d					11 08						12 10					13 04								14 08
Chester-le-Street	d																13 13								
Durham	d					11 20						12 22					13 20								14 20
Middlesbrough	d	11 31														12 45		13 31							
Thornaby	d	11a36														12 50		13a36							
Yarm	d															12 58									
Darlington 7	d					11 37						12 39					13 37								14 37
Northallerton	d					11 49										13 13									14 49
Thirsk	d															13 23									
Scarborough	d				10 51						11 51													13 51	
Seamer	d				10 56						11 56													13 56	
Malton	d				11 14						12 14													14 14	
York 8	a				11 40	12 12					12 40	13 11				13 43	14 10							14 40	15 12
	d				11 45	12 15					12 45	13 15				13 45	14 15					14 33		14 45	15 15
Hull	d		11 46					12 00					12 58	13 29					14 23						
Brough	d		11 58					12 12					13 10	13 41					14 35						
Howden	d		12 10											13 53					14 47						
Selby	d		12a19					12 32					13 29	14a02					14a56						
South Milford	d												13 38												
Garforth	d																								
Leeds 10	a				12 09	12 38		12 56			13 08	13 38	13 56			14 08	14 38					14 56		15 08	15 38
	d				12 10	12 40	12 44	12 59			13 10	13 40	13 59			14 10	14 40			14 44		14 59		15 10	15 40
Cottingley	d						12 49													14 49					
Morley	d						12 53													14 53					
Batley	d						12 58													14 58					
Dewsbury	a					12 51	13 01					13 51					14 51			15 01					15 51
	d					12 51	13 02					13 51					14 51			15 02					15 51
Ravensthorpe	d						13 05													15 05					
Mirfield	d						13 09													15 09					
Deighton	d						13 20													15 20					
Huddersfield	a				12 27	13 00	13 24	13 16			13 27	14 00	14 16			14 27	15 00			15 24		15 16		15 27	16 00
	d				12 28	13 01		13 17			13 28	14 01	14 17			14 28	15 01					15 17		15 28	16 01
Slaithwaite	d																								
Marsden	d																								
Greenfield	d																								
Mossley (Grtr Manchester)	d																								
Stalybridge	a				12 45						13 45					14 45								15 45	
	d			12 18	12 46				13 18		13 46				14 18	14 46							15 18	15 46	
Ashton-under-Lyne	d			12 22					13 22						14 22								15 22		
Manchester Victoria	a			12 36					13 36						14 36								15 36		
	d																								
Manchester Piccadilly 10	a				13 05	13 34		13 54			14 05	14 34	14 54			15 05	15 34					15 54		16 05	16 34
	d				13 07	13 38					14 07	14 38				15 07	15 38							16 07	16 38
Manchester Airport	a					13 55						14 55					15 55								16 55
Manchester Oxford Road	a				13 09						14 09					15 09								16 09	
Newton-le-Willows	a																								
Birchwood	a				13 25						14 25					15 25								16 25	
Warrington Central	a				13 30						14 30					15 30								16 30	
Liverpool South Parkway 7	a				13 47						14 47					15 47								16 47	
Liverpool Lime Street 10	a				13 58						14 58					15 58								16 58	

Table 39

Sundays

8 January to 12 February

Newcastle, Middlesbrough, Scarborough, York, Hull and Leeds - Huddersfield - Manchester, Manchester Airport and Liverpool

Network Diagram - see first Page of Table 39

		TP	NT	NT	TP	TP	NT		NT	TP	NT	TP	TP	TP	NT	NT	TP	TP		NT	NT	TP	NT	TP	TP
		◇1			◇1	◇1				◇1		◇1	◇1	◇1			◇1	◇1				◇1		◇1	◇1
Newcastle 8 ⛴	d					15 07							16 08					17 05							17 52
Chester-le-Street	d					15 16												17 14							
Durham	d					15 23							16 20					17 21							18 04
Middlesbrough	d				14 42		15 31										16 42			17 45					
Thornaby	d				14 47		15a36										16 47			17a50					
Yarm	d				14 55												16 55								
Darlington 7	d					15 40							16 37					17 38							18 21
Northallerton	d				15 10								16 49				17 10	17 49							18 33
Thirsk	d				15 18												17 18								
Scarborough	d											15 51												17 51	
Seamer	d											15 56												17 56	
Malton	d											16 14												18 14	
York 8	a				15 42	16 12						16 40	17 12				17 42	18 12						18 40	19 03
	d				15 45	16 15				16 33		16 45	17 15				17 45	18 15				18 33		18 45	19 15
Hull	d	14 58	16 00											16 58	17 23										
Brough	d	15 10	16 12											17 10	17 35										
Howden	d		16 24												17 47										
Selby	d	15 29	16a33											17 29	17a56										
South Milford	d	15 38												17 38											
Garforth	d																								
Leeds 10	a	15 56			16 08	16 38				16 56		17 08	17 38	17 56			18 08	18 38				18 57		19 08	19 38
	d	15 59			16 10	16 40			16 44	16 59		17 10	17 40	17 59			18 10	18 40			18 44	18 59		19 10	19 40
Cottingley	d								16 49												18 49				
Morley	d								16 53												18 53				
Batley	d								16 58												18 58				
Dewsbury	a					16 51			17 01				17 51					18 51			19 01				19 51
	d					16 51			17 02				17 51					18 51			19 02				19 51
Ravensthorpe	d								17 05												19 05				
Mirfield	d								17 09												19 09				
Deighton	d								17 20												19 20				
Huddersfield	a	16 16			16 27	17 00			17 24	17 16		17 27	18 00	18 16			18 27	19 00			19 24	19 16		19 27	20 00
	d	16 17			16 28	17 01				17 17		17 28	18 01	18 17			18 28	19 01				19 17		19 28	20 01
Slaithwaite	d																								
Marsden	d																								
Greenfield	d																								
Mossley (Grtr Manchester)	d																								
Stalybridge	a				16 45							17 45					18 45							19 45	
	d			16 18	16 46						17 18	17 46				18 18	18 46						19 18	19 46	
Ashton-under-Lyne	d			16 22							17 22					18 22							19 22		
Manchester Victoria ⛴	a			16 36							17 36					18 35							19 36		
	d																								
Manchester Piccadilly 10 ⛴	a	16 54			17 05	17 34				17 54		18 05	18 34	18 54			19 05	19 34				19 54		20 05	20 34
	d				17 07	17 38						18 07	18 38				19 07	19 38						20 07	20 38
Manchester Airport ✈	a					17 55							18 55					19 55							20 55
Manchester Oxford Road	a				17 09							18 09					19 09							20 09	
Newton-le-Willows	a																								
Birchwood	a				17 25							18 25					19 25							20 25	
Warrington Central	a				17 30							18 30					19 30							20 30	
Liverpool South Parkway 7 ✈	a				17 47							18 47					19 47							20 47	
Liverpool Lime Street 10	a				17 58							18 58					19 58							20 58	

Table 39

Sundays

8 January to 12 February

Newcastle, Middlesbrough, Scarborough, York, Hull and Leeds - Huddersfield - Manchester, Manchester Airport and Liverpool

Network Diagram - see first Page of Table 39

		TP	NT	NT	TP	TP	NT	NT	NT	TP	TP	NT	TP	TP	NT	NT	TP	NT	TP
		◇1			◇1	◇1				◇1	◇1		◇1	◇1			◇1		◇1
Newcastle 8	d					19 10							20 08		21 06				
Chester-le-Street	d														21 15				
Durham	d					19 22							20 20		21 24				
Middlesbrough	d				18 45		19 31				20 06								22 06
Thornaby	d				18 50		19a36				20 11								22 11
Yarm	d				18 58						20 19								22 19
Darlington 7	d					19 39							20 37		21a44				
Northallerton	d				19 13						20 38		20 49						22 35
Thirsk	d				19 21						20 46								22 43
Scarborough	d									19 51							21 20		
Seamer	d									19 56							21 25		
Malton	d									20 14							21 43		
York 8	a				19 42	20 11				20 40	21 06		21 12				22 09		23 09
	d				19 45	20 15				20 45			21 15				22 12		23 12
Hull	d	18 58	19 24					20 29						21 00					
Brough	d	19 10	19 36					20 41						21 12					
Howden	d		19 48					20 53											
Selby	d	19 29	19a57					21a02						21 31					
South Milford	d	19 38												21 40					
Garforth	d																		
Leeds 10	a	19 54			20 08	20 38				21 08			21 38	21 59			22 36		23 38
	d	19 59			20 10	20 40			20 44	21 10			21 40				22 40	22 44	23 40
Cottingley	d								20 49									22 49	
Morley	d								20 53									22 53	
Batley	d								20 58									22 58	
Dewsbury	a					20 50			21 01				21 51					23 01	23 51
	d					20 51			21 02				21 51					23 02	23 51
Ravensthorpe	d								21 05									23 05	
Mirfield	d								21 09									23 09	
Deighton	d								21 15									23 16	
Huddersfield	a	20 16			20 27	21 00			21 19	21 27			22 00				22 57	23 20	23 59
	d	20 17			20 28	21 01			21 19	21 28			22 01				22 58		00 01
Slaithwaite	d								21 26										
Marsden	d								21a33										
Greenfield	d																		
Mossley (Grtr Manchester)	d																		
Stalybridge	a				20 45	21 18							22 18				23 18		
	d			20 18	20 46	21 19						21 18	22 19			22 18	23 19		
Ashton-under-Lyne	d			20 22								21 22				22 22			
Manchester Victoria	a			20 36								21 36				22 36			
	d																		
Manchester Piccadilly 10	a	20 54			21 05	21 36				22 05			22 36				23 36		00 43
	d				21 07					22 07			22 38						00 44
Manchester Airport ✈	a												22 55						00 57
Manchester Oxford Road	a				21 09					22 09									
Newton-le-Willows	a																		
Birchwood	a				21 25					22 25									
Warrington Central	a				21 30					22 30									
Liverpool South Parkway 7 ✈	a				21 47					22 47									
Liverpool Lime Street 10	a				21 58					22 58									

Table 39

Sundays

19 February to 25 March

Newcastle, Middlesbrough, Scarborough, York, Hull and Leeds - Huddersfield - Manchester, Manchester Airport and Liverpool

Network Diagram - see first Page of Table 39

		TP	TP	TP	TP	TP	TP	NT	TP	TP	NT		TP	NT	NT	NT	TP	TP	TP	NT	TP	NT		NT	TP
		◇1	◇1	◇1	◇1	◇1	◇1		◇1	◇1			◇1				◇1	◇1	◇1		◇1				◇1
Newcastle 8	d																08 00								09 31
Chester-le-Street	d																								09 40
Durham	d																08 13								09 47
Middlesbrough	d	21p50												09 21											
Thornaby	d	21p55												09a26											
Yarm	d																								
Darlington 7	d	22p19															08 31								10 04
Northallerton	d	22p30															08 43								10 15
Thirsk	d	22p38															08 51								
Scarborough	d																				09 20				
Seamer	d																				09 25				
Malton	d																				09 43				
York 8	a	22p57															09 11				10 09				10 41
	d	23p07	02 29	03 44	04 58	05 55	06 55			08 10			08 45				09 15				10 15				10 45
Hull	d							08 54										09 00							
Brough	d							09 06										09 12							
Howden	d							09 18																	
Selby	d							09a27										09 33							
South Milford	d																	09 42							
Garforth	d																								
Leeds 10	a	23p33	03 10	04 25	05 38	06 38	07 36			08 37			09 08				09 38	10 00			10 38				11 08
	d	23p35	03 10	04 25	05 40	06 40	07 40			08 40	08 47		09 15				09 40	10 08			10 40	10 44			11 10
Cottingley	d										08 52											10 49			
Morley	d										08 56											10 53			
Batley	d										09 01											10 58			
Dewsbury	a	23p46			05 51	06 51	07 51			08 51	09 04						09 51				10 51	11 01			
	d	23p46			05 51	06 51	07 51			08 51	09 05						09 51				10 51	11 02			
Ravensthorpe	d										09 08											11 05			
Mirfield	d										09 12											11 09			
Deighton	d										09 19											11 15			
Huddersfield	a	23p55	03 29	04 44	06 00	07 00	08 00			09 00	09 23		09 33				10 00	10 25			11 00	11 20			11 27
	d	23p56	03 30	04 45	06 01	07 01	08 01			09 01			09 34				10 01	10 26			11 01				11 28
Slaithwaite	d																								
Marsden	d																								
Greenfield	d																								
Mossley (Grtr Manchester)	d																								
Stalybridge	a					07 18	08 18			09 18			09 52					10 45							11 45
	d					07 19	08 19			09 19			09 53		10 18			10 46						11 18	11 46
Ashton-under-Lyne	d														10 22									11 22	
Manchester Victoria	a														10 36									11 36	
	d																								
Manchester Piccadilly 10	a	00 27	04 02	05 17	06 34	07 34	08 34			09 34			10 10				10 34	11 03			11 34				12 05
	d	00 31	04 06	05 21	06 38	07 38	08 38		09 07	09 38			10 12			10 31	10 38		11 07	11 12	11 38				12 07
Manchester Airport	a	00 46	04 23	05 38	06 55	07 55	08 55			09 55							10 55				11 55				
Manchester Oxford Road	a								09 09				10 14			10 34			11 09	11 14					12 09
Newton-le-Willows	a																								
Birchwood	a								09 25				10 28						11 25						12 25
Warrington Central	a								09 30				10 33						11 30						12 30
Liverpool South Parkway 7	a								09 47				10 49						11 47						12 47
Liverpool Lime Street 10	a								10 00				11 00			11 16			11 59	12 02					12 58

Table 39

Sundays

19 February to 25 March

Newcastle, Middlesbrough, Scarborough, York, Hull and Leeds - Huddersfield - Manchester, Manchester Airport and Liverpool

Network Diagram - see first Page of Table 39

		NT	TP	TP	NT	NT	NT	TP	NT		TP	NT	TP	NT	TP	NT	NT	TP	TP	TP		NT	NT	NT	NT
			◇1	◇1				◇1			◇1		◇1		◇1			◇1	◇1	◇1					
Newcastle 8	d										11 08							12 10							
Chester-le-Street	d																								
Durham	d										11 20							12 22							
Middlesbrough	d		10 15		11 22															12 45		13 22			
Thornaby	d		10 20		11a27															12 50		13a27			
Yarm	d		10 28																	12 58					
Darlington 7	d										11 37							12 39							
Northallerton	d		10 43								11 49									13 13					
Thirsk	d		10 51																	13 23					
Scarborough	d							10 51							11 51										
Seamer	d							10 56							11 56										
Malton	d							11 14							12 14										
York 8	a		11 10					11 40			12 12				12 40			13 11		13 43					
	d		11 15					11 45			12 15				12 45			13 15		13 45					
Hull	d			10 58		11 46							12 00						12 58				13 29	14 23	
Brough	d			11 10		11 58							12 12						13 10				13 41	14 35	
Howden	d					12 10																	13 53	14 47	
Selby	d			11 29		12a19							12 32						13 29				14a02	14a56	
South Milford	d			11 38															13 38						
Garforth	d																								
Leeds 10	a		11 38	11 56				12 09			12 38		12 56		13 08			13 38	13 56	14 08					
	d		11 40	11 59				12 10			12 40	12 44	12 59		13 10			13 40	13 59	14 10					
Cottingley	d											12 49													
Morley	d											12 53													
Batley	d											12 58													
Dewsbury	a		11 51								12 51	13 01						13 51							
	d		11 51								12 51	13 02						13 51							
Ravensthorpe	d											13 05													
Mirfield	d											13 09													
Deighton	d											13 20													
Huddersfield	a		12 00	12 16				12 27			13 00	13 24	13 16		13 27			14 00	14 16	14 27					
	d		12 01	12 17				12 28			13 01		13 17		13 28			14 01	14 17	14 28					
Slaithwaite	d																								
Marsden	d																								
Greenfield	d																								
Mossley (Grtr Manchester)	d																								
Stalybridge	a							12 45							13 45					14 45					
	d						12 18	12 46						13 18	13 46	14 18				14 46					
Ashton-under-Lyne	d						12 22							13 22		14 22									
Manchester Victoria	a						12 36							13 36		14 36									
	d																								
Manchester Piccadilly 10	a		12 34	12 54				13 05			13 34		13 54		14 05			14 34	14 54	15 05					
	d	12 11	12 38					13 07	13 12		13 38				14 07		14 20	14 38		15 07					15 12
Manchester Airport ✈	a		12 55								13 55							14 55							
Manchester Oxford Road	a	12 13						13 09	13 14						14 09		14 22			15 09					15 14
Newton-le-Willows	a																								
Birchwood	a							13 25							14 25					15 25					
Warrington Central	a							13 30							14 30					15 30					
Liverpool South Parkway 7 ✈	a							13 47							14 47					15 47					
Liverpool Lime Street 10	a	13 02						13 58	14 02						14 58		15 04			15 58					16 02

Table 39

Sundays

19 February to 25 March

Newcastle, Middlesbrough, Scarborough, York, Hull and Leeds - Huddersfield - Manchester, Manchester Airport and Liverpool

Network Diagram - see first Page of Table 39

		TP	NT	TP	NT	TP	NT		TP	TP	NT	NT	TP	NT	NT	TP	NT	TP		NT	TP	NT	TP	TP	NT
		◇1		◇1		◇1			◇1	◇1			◇1			◇1		◇1			◇1		◇1	◇1	
Newcastle 8	d	13 04							14 08							15 07							16 08		
Chester-le-Street	d	13 13														15 16									
Durham	d	13 20							14 20							15 23							16 20		
Middlesbrough	d												14 42	15 22											
Thornaby	d												14 47	15a27											
Yarm	d												14 55												
Darlington 7	d	13 37							14 37							15 40							16 37		
Northallerton	d								14 49				15 10										16 49		
Thirsk	d												15 18												
Scarborough	d					13 51															15 51				
Seamer	d					13 56															15 56				
Malton	d					14 14															16 14				
York 8	a	14 10				14 40			15 12				15 42			16 12					16 40		17 12		
	d	14 15		14 33		14 45			15 15				15 45			16 15		16 33			16 45		17 15		
Hull	d									14 58	16 00													16 58	17 23
Brough	d									15 10	16 12													17 10	17 35
Howden	d										16 24														17 47
Selby	d									15 29	16a33													17 29	17a56
South Milford	d									15 38														17 38	
Garforth	d																								
Leeds 10	a	14 38		14 56		15 08			15 38	15 56			16 08			16 38		16 56			17 08		17 38	17 56	
	d	14 40	14 44	14 59		15 10			15 40	15 59			16 10			16 40	16 44	16 59			17 10		17 40	17 59	
Cottingley	d		14 49														16 49								
Morley	d		14 53														16 53								
Batley	d		14 58														16 58								
Dewsbury	a	14 51	15 01						15 51							16 51	17 01						17 51		
	d	14 51	15 02						15 51							16 51	17 02						17 51		
Ravensthorpe	d		15 05														17 05								
Mirfield	d		15 09														17 09								
Deighton	d		15 20														17 20								
Huddersfield	a	15 00	15 24	15 16		15 27			16 00	16 16			16 27			17 00	17 24	17 16			17 27		18 00	18 16	
	d	15 01		15 17		15 28			16 01	16 17			16 28			17 01		17 17			17 28		18 01	18 17	
Slaithwaite	d																								
Marsden	d																								
Greenfield	d																								
Mossley (Grtr Manchester)	d																								
Stalybridge	a					15 45							16 45								17 45				
	d				15 18	15 46						16 18	16 46							17 18	17 46				
Ashton-under-Lyne	d				15 22							16 22								17 22					
Manchester Victoria	a				15 36							16 36								17 36					
	d																								
Manchester Piccadilly 10	a	15 34		15 54		16 05			16 34	16 54			17 05			17 34		17 54			18 05		18 34	18 54	
	d	15 38				16 07	16 12		16 38				17 07		17 12	17 38					18 07	18 12	18 38		
Manchester Airport	a	15 55							16 55							17 55							18 55		
Manchester Oxford Road	a					16 09	16 14						17 09		17 14						18 09	18 14			
Newton-le-Willows	a																								
Birchwood	a					16 25							17 25								18 25				
Warrington Central	a					16 30							17 30								18 30				
Liverpool South Parkway 7	a					16 47							17 47								18 47				
Liverpool Lime Street 10	a					16 58	17 02						17 58		18 02						18 58	19 02			

Table 39

Sundays

19 February to 25 March

Newcastle, Middlesbrough, Scarborough, York, Hull and Leeds - Huddersfield - Manchester, Manchester Airport and Liverpool

Network Diagram - see first Page of Table 39

		NT	TP	NT	NT	TP	NT	TP	NT	TP	NT	TP	TP	NT	NT	TP	TP	NT	NT	NT	NT	TP	TP
			◇1			◇1		◇1		◇1		◇1	◇1			◇1	◇1					◇1	◇1
Newcastle 8	d					17 05						17 52					19 10						
Chester-le-Street	d					17 14																	
Durham	d					17 21						18 04					19 22						
Middlesbrough	d		16 42	17 37												18 45		19 21					20 06
Thornaby	d		16 47	17a42												18 50		19a26					20 11
Yarm	d		16 55													18 58							20 19
Darlington 7	d					17 38						18 21					19 39						
Northallerton	d		17 10			17 49						18 33				19 13							20 38
Thirsk	d		17 18													19 21							20 46
Scarborough	d									17 51												19 51	
Seamer	d									17 56												19 56	
Malton	d									18 14												20 14	
York 8	a		17 42			18 12				18 40		19 03				19 42	20 11					20 40	21 06
	d		17 45			18 15		18 33		18 45		19 15				19 45	20 15					20 45	
Hull	d												18 58	19 24					20 29				
Brough	d												19 10	19 36					20 41				
Howden	d													19 48					20 53				
Selby	d												19 29	19a57					21a02				
South Milford	d												19 38										
Garforth	d																						
Leeds 10	a		18 08			18 38		18 57		19 08		19 38	19 54			20 08	20 38					21 08	
	d		18 10			18 40	18 44	18 59		19 10		19 40	19 59			20 10	20 40			20 44		21 10	
Cottingley	d						18 49													20 49			
Morley	d						18 53													20 53			
Batley	d						18 58													20 58			
Dewsbury	a					18 51	19 01					19 51					20 50			21 01			
	d					18 51	19 02					19 51					20 51			21 02			
Ravensthorpe	d						19 05													21 05			
Mirfield	d						19 09													21 09			
Deighton	d						19 20													21 15			
Huddersfield	a		18 27			19 00	19 24	19 16		19 27		20 00	20 16			20 27	21 00			21 19		21 27	
	d		18 28			19 01		19 17		19 28		20 01	20 17			20 28	21 01			21 19		21 28	
Slaithwaite	d																			21 26			
Marsden	d																			21a33			
Greenfield	d																						
Mossley (Grtr Manchester)	d																						
Stalybridge	a		18 45							19 45						20 45	21 18						
	d	18 18	18 46						19 18	19 46					20 18	20 46	21 19						
Ashton-under-Lyne	d	18 22							19 22						20 22								
Manchester Victoria	a	18 35							19 36						20 36								
	d																						
Manchester Piccadilly 10	a		19 05			19 34		19 54		20 05		20 34	20 54			21 05	21 36					22 05	
	d		19 07		19 12	19 38				20 07	20 12	20 38				21 07					21 12	22 07	
Manchester Airport	a					19 55						20 55											
Manchester Oxford Road	a		19 09		19 14					20 09	20 14					21 09					21 14	22 09	
Newton-le-Willows	a																						
Birchwood	a		19 25							20 25						21 25						22 25	
Warrington Central	a		19 30							20 30						21 30						22 30	
Liverpool South Parkway 7	a		19 47							20 47						21 47						22 47	
Liverpool Lime Street 10	a		19 58		20 02					20 58	21 02					21 58					22 02	22 58	

Table 39

Sundays

19 February to 25 March

Newcastle, Middlesbrough, Scarborough, York, Hull and Leeds - Huddersfield - Manchester, Manchester Airport and Liverpool

Network Diagram - see first Page of Table 39

		NT	TP		TP	NT	NT	TP	NT	TP
			◇1		◇1			◇1		◇1
Newcastle 8	d		20 08			21 06				
Chester-le-Street	d					21 15				
Durham	d		20 20			21 24				
Middlesbrough	d									22 06
Thornaby	d									22 11
Yarm	d									22 19
Darlington 7	d		20 37			21a44				
Northallerton	d		20 49							22 35
Thirsk	d									22 43
Scarborough	d							21 20		
Seamer	d							21 25		
Malton	d							21 43		
York 8	a		21 12					22 09		23 09
	d		21 15					22 12		23 12
Hull	d				21 00					
Brough	d				21 12					
Howden	d									
Selby	d				21 31					
South Milford	d				21 40					
Garforth	d									
Leeds 10	a		21 38		21 59			22 36		23 38
	d		21 40					22 40	22 44	23 40
Cottingley	d								22 49	
Morley	d								22 53	
Batley	d								22 58	
Dewsbury	a		21 51						23 01	23 51
	d		21 51						23 02	23 51
Ravensthorpe	d								23 05	
Mirfield	d								23 09	
Deighton	d								23 16	
Huddersfield	a		22 00					22 57	23 20	23 59
	d		22 01					22 58		00 01
Slaithwaite	d									
Marsden	d									
Greenfield	d									
Mossley (Grtr Manchester)	d									
Stalybridge	a		22 18					23 18		
	d	21 18	22 19				22 18	23 19		
Ashton-under-Lyne	d	21 22					22 22			
Manchester Victoria ⛴	a	21 36					22 36			
	d									
Manchester Piccadilly 10 ⛴	a		22 36					23 36		00 43
	d		22 38							00 44
Manchester Airport ✈	a		22 55							00 57
Manchester Oxford Road	a									
Newton-le-Willows	a									
Birchwood	a									
Warrington Central	a									
Liverpool South Parkway 7 ✈	a									
Liverpool Lime Street 10	a									

Table 39

Sundays
from 1 April

Newcastle, Middlesbrough, Scarborough, York, Hull and Leeds - Huddersfield - Manchester, Manchester Airport and Liverpool

Network Diagram - see first Page of Table 39

		TP	TP	TP	TP	TP	NT	TP	NT	NT	NT	NT	TP		NT	TP	TP	TP	NT	TP	NT	NT	TP
		◇1						◇1					◇1			◇1	◇1	◇1		◇1			◇1
			🚌	🚌	🚌	🚌				🚌	🚌	🚌			🚌				🚌		🚌		
Newcastle 8	d															08 00							09 31
Chester-le-Street	d																						09 40
Durham	d															08 13							09 47
Middlesbrough	d	21p50							09 31														
Thornaby	d	21p55							09a36														
Yarm	d																						
Darlington 7	d	22p19														08 31							10 04
Northallerton	d	22p30														08 43							10 15
Thirsk	d	22p38														08 51							
Scarborough	d																			09 20			
Seamer	d																			09 25			
Malton	d																			09 43			
York 8	a	22p57														09 11				10 09			10 41
	d	23p07	01 30	03 30	04 55	05 55							08 30			09 15		09 45		10 15			10 45
Hull	d						08 54										09 00						
Brough	d						09 06										09 12						
Howden	d						09 18																
Selby	d						09a27										09 33						
South Milford	d																09 42						
Garforth	d																						
Leeds 10	a	23p33	02 20	04 20	05 45	06 45							08 53			09 38	10 00	10 08		10 38			11 08
	d	23p35	02 20	04 20	05 45	06 45						08 45	08 58			09 40		10 10		10 40		10 44	11 10
Cottingley	d											09 00										10 49	
Morley	d											09 10										10 53	
Batley	d											09 20			←							10 58	
Dewsbury	a	23p46			06 10	07 10						09 28	09 09		09 28	09 51				10 51		11 01	
	d	23p46			06 10	07 10						09 28	09 09		09 28	09 51				10 51		11 02	
Ravensthorpe	d											→			09 35							11 05	
Mirfield	d														09 40							11 09	
Deighton	d														09 50							11 15	
Huddersfield	a	23p55	02 55	04 55	06 35	07 35							09 18		09 59	10 02				11 02		11 20	
	d	23p56	02 55	04 55	06 35	07 35					09 10		09 24			10 03			10 10	11 04	11 10		
Slaithwaite	d										09 26								10 26		11 26		
Marsden	d										09 31								10 31		11 31		
Greenfield	d										09 51								10 51		11 51		
Mossley (Grtr Manchester)	d										09 57								10 57		11 57		
Stalybridge	a				07 20	08 20					10 05								11 05		12 05		
	d				07 20	08 20				10 02	10 05								11 05		12 05		
Ashton-under-Lyne	d									10 02	10 15								11 15		12 15		
Manchester Victoria	a									10 26	10 39		10 10			10 53		11 04	11 39	11 53	12 39		12 04
	d							09 15					10 18	10 15		10 54		11 09		11 54			12 09
Manchester Piccadilly 10	a	00 27	03 55	05 55	07 40	08 40							10 33			11 08				12 08			
	d		03 55	05 55	07 40	08 40							10 38			11 10				12 10			
Manchester Airport ✈	a		04 20	06 20	08 05	09 05							10 55			11 24				12 24			
Manchester Oxford Road	a																						
Newton-le-Willows	a							09 33						10 33				11 26					12 26
Birchwood	a																						
Warrington Central	a																						
Liverpool South Parkway 7 ✈	a																						
Liverpool Lime Street 10	a							09 56						10 57				11 56					12 56

Newcastle, Middlesbrough, Scarborough, York, Hull and Leeds - Huddersfield - Manchester, Manchester Airport and Liverpool

Network Diagram - see first Page of Table 39

Station		TP	NT	NT	TP	TP	TP	NT	NT		NT	TP	TP
		◇1			◇1	◇1	◇1					◇1	◇1
				bus					bus				
Newcastle 8	d						11 08						
Chester-le-Street	d												
Durham	d						11 20						
Middlesbrough	d	10 15	11 31										
Thornaby	d	10 20	11a36										
Yarm	d	10 28											
Darlington 7	d						11 37						
Northallerton	d	10 43					11 49						
Thirsk	d	10 51											
Scarborough	d					10 51							11 51
Seamer	d					10 56							11 56
Malton	d					11 14							12 14
York 8	a	11 10				11 40	12 12						12 40
	d	11 15				11 45	12 15						12 45
Hull	d				10 58			11 46				12 00	
Brough	d				11 10			11 58				12 12	
Howden	d							12 10					
Selby	d				11 29			12a19				12 32	
South Milford	d				11 38								
Garforth	d												
Leeds 10	a	11 38			11 56	12 09	12 38					12 56	13 08
	d	11 40			11 59	12 10	12 40				12 44	12 59	13 10
Cottingley	d										12 49		
Morley	d										12 53		
Batley	d										12 58		
Dewsbury	a	11 51			12 10		12 51				13 01	13 10	
	d	11 51			12 10		12 51				13 02	13 10	
Ravensthorpe	d										13 05		
Mirfield	d										13 09		
Deighton	d										13 20		
Huddersfield	a	12 02			12 24		13 02				13 24	13 20	
	d	12 04		12 10			13 04		13 10				
Slaithwaite	d			12 26					13 26				
Marsden	d			12 31					13 31				
Greenfield	d			12 51					13 51				
Mossley (Grtr Manchester)	d			12 57					13 57				
Stalybridge	a			13 05					14 05				
	d			13 05					14 05				
Ashton-under-Lyne	d			13 15					14 15				
Manchester Victoria	a	12 53		13 39		13 04	13 53		14 39				14 04
	d	12 54				13 09	13 54						14 09
Manchester Piccadilly 10	a	13 08					14 08						
	d	13 10					14 10						
Manchester Airport ✈	a	13 24					14 24						
Manchester Oxford Road	a												
Newton-le-Willows	a					13 26							14 26
Birchwood	a												
Warrington Central	a												
Liverpool South Parkway 7 ✈	a												
Liverpool Lime Street 10	a					13 56							14 56

Station		TP	NT	TP	TP	TP	NT	NT		NT	NT	NT	TP
		◇1		◇1	◇1	◇1							◇1
			bus								bus		
Newcastle 8	d	12 10				13 04							
Chester-le-Street	d					13 13							
Durham	d	12 22				13 20							
Middlesbrough	d				12 45			13 31					
Thornaby	d				12 50			13a36					
Yarm	d				12 58								
Darlington 7	d	12 39				13 37							
Northallerton	d				13 13								
Thirsk	d				13 23								
Scarborough	d												
Seamer	d												
Malton	d												
York 8	a	13 11			13 43	14 10							
	d	13 15			13 45	14 15							14 33
Hull	d			12 58			13 29			14 23			
Brough	d			13 10			13 41			14 35			
Howden	d						13 53			14 47			
Selby	d			13 29			14a02			14a56			
South Milford	d			13 38									
Garforth	d												
Leeds 10	a	13 37		13 56	14 08	14 38							14 56
	d	13 40		13 59	14 10	14 40						14 44	14 59
Cottingley	d											14 49	
Morley	d											14 53	
Batley	d											14 58	
Dewsbury	a	13 51		14 10		14 51						15 01	15 10
	d	13 51		14 10		14 51						15 02	15 10
Ravensthorpe	d											15 05	
Mirfield	d											15 09	
Deighton	d											15 20	
Huddersfield	a	14 02		14 20		15 02						15 24	15 20
	d	14 04	14 10			15 04					15 10		
Slaithwaite	d		14 26								15 26		
Marsden	d		14 31								15 31		
Greenfield	d		14 51								15 51		
Mossley (Grtr Manchester)	d		14 57								15 56		
Stalybridge	a		15 05								16 05		
	d		15 05								16 05		
Ashton-under-Lyne	d		15 15								16 15		
Manchester Victoria	a	14 53	15 39		15 09	15 53					16 39		
	d	14 53			15 09	15 54							
Manchester Piccadilly 10	a	15 08				16 08							
	d	15 10				16 10							
Manchester Airport ✈	a	15 24				16 24							
Manchester Oxford Road	a												
Newton-le-Willows	a				15 26								
Birchwood	a												
Warrington Central	a												
Liverpool South Parkway 7 ✈	a												
Liverpool Lime Street 10	a				15 56								

Table 39

Sundays

from 1 April

Newcastle, Middlesbrough, Scarborough, York, Hull and Leeds - Huddersfield - Manchester, Manchester Airport and Liverpool

Network Diagram - see first Page of Table 39

		TP	TP	NT	TP	TP	TP	NT	NT	NT	NT	TP	TP	TP	NT	TP	TP	TP	NT	NT	NT	NT	TP
		◇1	◇1		◇1	◇1	◇1					◇1	◇1	◇1		◇1	◇1	◇1					◇1
				🚌						🚌					🚌						🚌		
Newcastle [8]	d		14 08				15 07							16 08				17 05					
Chester-le-Street	d						15 16											17 14					
Durham	d		14 20				15 23							16 20				17 21					
Middlesbrough	d					14 42		15 31									16 42			17 45			
Thornaby	d					14 47		15a36									16 47			17a50			
Yarm	d					14 55											16 55						
Darlington [7]	d		14 37				15 40							16 37				17 38					
Northallerton	d		14 49			15 10								16 49			17 10	17 49					
Thirsk	d					15 18											17 18						
Scarborough	d	13 51											15 51										
Seamer	d	13 56											15 56										
Malton	d	14 14											16 14										
York [8]	a	14 40	15 12			15 42	16 12						16 40	17 12			17 42	18 12					
	d	14 45	15 15			15 45	16 15					16 33	16 45	17 15			17 45	18 15					18 33
Hull	d				14 58				16 00							16 58			17 23				
Brough	d				15 10				16 12							17 10			17 35				
Howden	d								16 24										17 47				
Selby	d				15 29				16a33							17 29			17a56				
South Milford	d				15 38											17 38							
Garforth	d																						
Leeds [10]	a	15 07	15 38		15 56	16 08	16 38					16 56	17 08	17 38		17 56	18 08	18 38					18 57
	d	15 10	15 40		15 59	16 10	16 40				16 44	16 59	17 10	17 40		17 59	18 10	18 40				18 44	18 59
Cottingley	d										16 49											18 49	
Morley	d										16 53											18 53	
Batley	d										16 58											18 58	
Dewsbury	a		15 51		16 10		16 51				17 01	17 10		17 51		18 10		18 51				19 01	19 10
	d		15 51		16 10		16 51				17 02	17 10		17 51		18 10		18 51				19 02	19 10
Ravensthorpe	d										17 05											19 05	
Mirfield	d										17 09											19 09	
Deighton	d										17 20											19 20	
Huddersfield	a		16 02		16 22		17 02				17 24	17 20		18 02		18 20		19 02				19 24	19 20
	d		16 04	16 10			17 04			17 10				18 04	18 10			19 04			19 10		
Slaithwaite	d			16 26						17 26					18 26						19 26		
Marsden	d			16 31						17 31					18 31						19 31		
Greenfield	d			16 51						17 51					18 51						19 51		
Mossley (Grtr Manchester)	d			16 57						17 57					18 57						19 57		
Stalybridge	a			17 05						18 05					19 05						20 05		
	d			17 05						18 05					19 05						20 05		
Ashton-under-Lyne	d			17 15						18 15					19 15						20 15		
Manchester Victoria	a	16 05	16 53	17 39		17 04	17 53			18 39			18 04	18 54	19 39		19 09	19 53			20 39		
	d	16 09	16 54			17 09	17 54						18 09	18 54			19 09	19 54					
Manchester Piccadilly [10]	a		17 08				18 08							19 10				20 08					
	d		17 10				18 10							19 10				20 10					
Manchester Airport	a		17 24				18 24							19 26				20 24					
Manchester Oxford Road	a																						
Newton-le-Willows	a	16 26				17 26							18 26				19 26						
Birchwood	a																						
Warrington Central	a																						
Liverpool South Parkway [7]	a																						
Liverpool Lime Street [10]	a	16 56				17 56							18 56				19 56						

Table 39

Sundays
from 1 April

Newcastle, Middlesbrough, Scarborough, York, Hull and Leeds - Huddersfield - Manchester, Manchester Airport and Liverpool

Network Diagram - see first Page of Table 39

		TP	TP	NT	TP		TP	TP	NT	NT	NT	NT	TP	TP	TP	TP		NT	NT	TP	NT	TP			
		◇1	◇1	🚌	◇1		◇1	◇1					◇1	◇1	◇1	◇1			🚌	◇1		◇1			
Newcastle 8	d		17 52					19 10							20 08			21 06							
Chester-le-Street	d																	21 15							
Durham	d		18 04					19 22							20 20			21 24							
Middlesbrough	d						18 45			19 31				20 06								22 06			
Thornaby	d						18 50			19a36				20 11								22 11			
Yarm	d						18 58							20 19								22 19			
Darlington 7	d		18 21					19 39							20 37			21a44							
Northallerton	d		18 33				19 13							20 38	20 49							22 34			
Thirsk	d						19 21							20 46								22 42			
Scarborough	d	17 51											19 51							21 20					
Seamer	d	17 56											19 56							21 25					
Malton	d	18 14											20 14							21 43					
York 8	a	18 40	19 03				19 42	20 11					20 40	21 06	21 12					22 09		23 09			
	d	18 45	19 15				19 45	20 15					20 45		21 15					22 12		23 12			
Hull	d				18 58				19 24		20 29					21 00									
Brough	d				19 10				19 36		20 41					21 12									
Howden	d								19 48		20 53														
Selby	d				19 29				19a57		21a02					21 31									
South Milford	d				19 38											21 40									
Garforth	d																								
Leeds 10	a	19 08	19 38		19 56		20 08	20 38					21 08		21 38	21 59				22 36		23 38			
	d	19 10	19 40		19 59		20 10	20 40				20 44	21 10		21 40					22 40	22 44	23 40			
Cottingley	d											20 49									22 49				
Morley	d											20 53									22 53				
Batley	d											20 58									22 58				
Dewsbury	a		19 51		20 10			20 51				21 01			21 51					22 50	23 01	23 51			
	d		19 51		20 10			20 51				21 02			21 51					22 51	23 02	23 51			
Ravensthorpe	d											21 05									23 05				
Mirfield	d											21 09									23 09				
Deighton	d											21 15									23 16				
Huddersfield	a		20 02		20 20			21 02				21 19			22 02					23 02	23 20	00 02			
	d		20 04	20 10				21 04				21 19			22 04					23 04		00 04			
Slaithwaite	d			20 26								21 26													
Marsden	d			20 31								21a33													
Greenfield	d			20 51																					
Mossley (Grtr Manchester)	d			20 57																					
Stalybridge	a			21 05																					
	d			21 05															22 52						
Ashton-under-Lyne	d			21 15															23 02						
Manchester Victoria	a	20 04	20 53	21 39			21 04	21 52					22 04		22 52				23 26	23s53		00s53			
	d	20 09	20 54				21 09	21 54					22 09		22 53										
Manchester Piccadilly 10	a		21 08					22 13							23 07					00 08		01 08			
	d		21 09												23 09							01 10			
Manchester Airport ✈	a		21 24												23 24							01 23			
Manchester Oxford Road	a																								
Newton-le-Willows	a	20 26					21 26						22 26												
Birchwood	a																								
Warrington Central	a																								
Liverpool South Parkway 7 ✈	a																								
Liverpool Lime Street 10	a	20 56					21 56						22 56												

Table 39

Mondays to Fridays

Liverpool, Manchester Airport and Manchester - Huddersfield - Wakefield, Leeds, Hull, York, Scarborough, Middlesbrough and Newcastle

Network Diagram - see first Page of Table 39

Miles	Miles	Miles	Miles	Miles			TP	TP	TP	TP	TP	TP	TP	TP	TP		TP	TP	TP	NT	TP	TP	TP	NT	NT
									MX	MO	MX		MX	MX	MO			MX	MO						
							◇1	◇1	◇1	◇1	◇1	◇1	◇1	◇1	◇1		◇1	◇1	◇1		◇1	◇1	◇1		
							A	B		A		B			B		A								
0	—	—	—	—	**Liverpool Lime Street** 10	d	20p22	20p22		21p52		21p52	22p30												
5½	—	—	—	—	Liverpool South Parkway 7 ✈	d	20p32			22p02			22p40												
18½	—	—	—	—	Warrington Central	d	20p45			22p15			22p53												
21¾	—	—	—	—	Birchwood	d	20p50			22p20			22p58												
34¼	—	—	—	—	Manchester Oxford Road	d	21p07			22p37			23p17												
—	—	—	—	—	**Manchester Airport** ✈	d			21p20		22p22			23p18	23p22		23p20	00 38	00 48			04 12			
34¾	—	—	—	—	**Manchester Piccadilly** 10	a	21p09		21p36	22p39	22p36		23p19	23p34	23p35		23p37	00 51	01 01			04 27			
—	—	—	—	—		d	21p11		21p42	22p42	22p42		23p21	23p38	23p39		23p42	00 53	01 03			04 30	05 39		
—	—	—	—	0	**Manchester Victoria**	d		21p05				22b38		23p56	23p55										
—	—	—	—	6½	Ashton-under-Lyne	d																			
42¼	—	—	—	7¾	**Stalybridge**	a	21p24		21p55	22p54	22p55		23p34										05 52		
—	—	—	—	—		d	21p24		21p55	22p54	22p55		23p34										05 52		
45	—	—	—	10½	Mossley (Grtr Manchester)	d																			
47½	—	—	—	12¾	Greenfield	d																			
53¼	—	—	—	18¾	Marsden	d																			
55¾	—	—	—	21¼	Slaithwaite	d																			
60¼	—	—	—	25¾	**Huddersfield**	a	21p42		22p15	23p12	23p15	23p23	23p52	00 25	00 40		00 11					05 31	06 10		
—	—	—	—	—		d	21p43		22p16	23p12	23p16	23p26	23p53	00 26	00 43		00 12			05 32		05 38	06 11		
62¼	—	—	—	27¾	Deighton	d														05 36					
65¼	—	—	—	30¾	Mirfield	d														05 41					
66¾	—	—	—	—	Ravensthorpe	d																			
68¼	—	—	—	—	**Dewsbury**	a		21p58	22p25	23p22	23p25	23p35		00s35											
—	—	—	—	—		d		21p59	22p26	23p22	23p26	23p35													
69¾	—	—	—	—	Batley	d																			
73	—	—	—	—	Morley	d																			
74½	—	—	—	—	Cottingley	d																			
77½	0	—	0	—	**Leeds** 10	a	22p04	22p12	22p41	23p39	23p41	23p50	00 30	00 50	01 04		00 51	02 01	02 32			06 01	06 32		
—	—	—	—	—		d	22p12	22p12	22p42	23p42	23p42	23p53	00 32	00 54	01 06		00 54	02 08	02 34			06 04	06 35	06 38	06 48
84¾	7¼	—	7¼	—	Garforth	d																		06 50	06 58
—	12¾	—	—	—	South Milford	a																			
—	20¾	—	—	—	Selby	a																			07 20
—	29½	—	—	—	Howden	a																			
—	41¼	—	—	—	Brough	a																			
—	51¾	—	—	—	**Hull**	a																			
—	—	—	—	—	Wakefield Kirkgate	a														05 57					
—	—	—	—	—	**Wakefield Westgate**	a														06 05					
103	—	0	25½	—	**York** 8	a	22p40	22p40	23p07	00 26	00 09	00 22	01 16	01 43	01 34		01 22	02 45	03 04			06 28	07 01	07 15	
—	—	—	—	—		d	22p42	22p42	23p18												05 54	06 40	07 06		
—	—	—	46½	—	Malton	d																07 04			
—	—	—	64¾	—	Seamer	a																07 21			
—	—	—	67½	—	**Scarborough**	a																07 30			
125½	—	22¼	—	—	Thirsk	a	23p06	23p05	23p31												06 10		07 22		
133	—	30½	—	—	Northallerton	a	23p16	23p15	23p49												06 18		07 30		
147	—	—	—	—	**Darlington** 7	a	23p28	23p28	00 01												06 29		07 41		
—	—	42¼	—	—	Yarm	d																			
—	—	47½	—	—	Thornaby	a															06 53				
—	—	50¾	—	—	**Middlesbrough**	a															07 03				
169	—	—	—	—	Durham	a	23p45	23p45	00 19														07 58		
174¾	—	—	—	—	Chester-le-Street	a																	08 04		
183	—	—	—	—	**Newcastle** 8	a	00 15	00 15	00 51														08 16		

A Until 26 March

B From 2 April

b Previous night, arr. 2229

Liverpool, Manchester Airport and Manchester - Huddersfield - Wakefield, Leeds, Hull, York, Scarborough, Middlesbrough and Newcastle

Network Diagram - see first Page of Table 39

		TP	NT	NT	NT	TP	NT	NT	NT	TP	TP	NT	NT	NT	NT	TP		NT	NT	TP	TP	NT
		◇1				◇1				◇1	◇1					◇1				◇1	◇1	
						trolley					trolley					trolley				trolley	trolley	
Liverpool Lime Street 10	d															06 15						
Liverpool South Parkway 7 ✈	d															06 25						
Warrington Central	d															06 38						
Birchwood	d															06 43						
Manchester Oxford Road	d															07 07						
Manchester Airport ✈	d	05 37									06 23									07 05	07 05	
Manchester Piccadilly 10	a	05 51									06 39					07 09				07 22	07 22	
	d	05 57				06 21					06 54					07 11				07 27	07 27	
Manchester Victoria	d						05 51						06 17	06 55				06 43				06 58
Ashton-under-Lyne	d													07 05								
Stalybridge	a										07 07			07 10		07 23						
	d								06 41		07 07			07 11		07 23						
Mossley (Grtr Manchester)	d								06 45					07 15								
Greenfield	d								06 49					07 19								
Marsden	d							06 48	06 58					07 28								
Slaithwaite	d							06 52	07 02					07 32								
Huddersfield	a	06 26				06 54		07 00	07 10		07 25			07 41		07 44				07 56	07 56	
	d	06 27		06 31	06 41	06 56		07 00			07 26				07 29	07 45			07 49	07 57	07 57	
Deighton	d			06 34	06 45			07 03											07 53			
Mirfield	d			06 39	06 50			07 08				07 20							07 58			08 06
Ravensthorpe	d			06 42				07 11				07 23										
Dewsbury	a	06 36		06 46		07 05		07 15				07 27				07 54				08 06	08 06	08 11
	d	06 37		06 46		07 06		07 15				07 35				07 55				08 07	08 07	08 12
Batley	d			06 49				07 18				07 38										08 15
Morley	d			06 55				07 24				07 44										08 21
Cottingley	d			06 59				07 28				07 47										08 24
Leeds 10	a	06 52		07 09		07 19	07 27	07 38			07 47	07 56	07 57		08 29	08 10		08 12		08 24	08 24	08 33
	d	06 55	06 58			07 23	07 29				07 50		08 00			08 12		08 15		08 28	08 28	
Garforth	d		07 10				07 41				08 00		08 12					08 27				
South Milford	a		07 20										08 22					08 38				
Selby	a		07 31			07 43							08 36					08 53				
Howden	a					07 52																
Brough	a					08 04																
Hull	a					08 20																
Wakefield Kirkgate	a				07 03														08 13			
Wakefield Westgate	a				07 10														08 20			
York 8	a	07 22					08 06				08 21					08 35				08 52	08 52	
	d	07 25								07 32	08 23					08 40	08 42			08 58		
Malton	d	07 49														09 04						
Seamer	a	08 06														09 21						
Scarborough	a	08 15														09 30						
Thirsk	a									07 52	08 39											
Northallerton	a									08 00	08 49									09 18		
Darlington 7	a																09 11			09 30		
Yarm	d									08 14	09 03											
Thornaby	a									08 24	09 11											
Middlesbrough	a									08 32	09 22											
Durham	a																09 28			09 47		
Chester-le-Street	a																			09 53		
Newcastle 8	a																09 44			10 07		

Liverpool, Manchester Airport and Manchester - Huddersfield - Wakefield, Leeds, Hull, York, Scarborough, Middlesbrough and Newcastle

Network Diagram - see first Page of Table 39

		TP	NT	NT	NT	TP	NT		NT	TP	NT	TP	NT	NT	NT	NT	TP		NT	TP	NT	NT	TP	NT	NT
		◇1 🛒				◇1 🛒				◇1 🛒		◇1 🛒					◇1 🛒			◇1 🛒			◇1 🛒		
Liverpool Lime Street 10	d									07 15					07 16								08 22		
Liverpool South Parkway 7 ✈	d									07 25													08 32		
Warrington Central	d									07 40													08 45		
Birchwood	d									07 45													08 50		
Manchester Oxford Road	d									08 06													09 07		
Manchester Airport ✈	d					07 35						08 05								08 35					
Manchester Piccadilly 10 ⛴	a					07 49				08 08		08 22								08 49			09 09		
	d	07 36				07 56				08 10		08 26					08 42			08 55			09 11		
Manchester Victoria ⛴	d		07 40								07 48		08 00	08 02	08 27									08 48	08 57
Ashton-under-Lyne	d		07 49											08 12	08 37										09 07
Stalybridge	a	07 49	07 54			08 09				08 26				08 18	08 41								09 26		09 13
	d	07 49	07 54			08 09				08 26					08 42								09 26		
Mossley (Grtr Manchester)	d		07 59												08 46										
Greenfield	d		08 03												08 50										
Marsden	d		08 11												08 59										
Slaithwaite	d		08 16												09 03										
Huddersfield	a	08 09	08 24			08 28				08 44		08 56			09 13		09 15			09 26			09 44		
	d	08 10		08 13	08 21	08 30	08 33		08 37	08 45		08 57					09 16		09 23	09 27	09 31	09 35	09 45		
Deighton	d			08 16			08 36		08 40												09 34	09 38			
Mirfield	d			08 21			08 41		08 45				09 07								09 39	09 43			
Ravensthorpe	d			08 24			08 44														09 42				
Dewsbury	a	08 19		08 27		08 39	08 48					09 06	09 12							09 36	09 46				
	d	08 20		08 27		08 39	08 53					09 07	09 12							09 37	09 46				
Batley	d			08 30			08 56						09 15								09 49				
Morley	d			08 36			09 02						09 21								09 55				
Cottingley	d			08 39			09 06														09 59				
Leeds 10	a	08 36		08 52	09 27	08 54	09 17			09 09	09 12	09 22	09 32				09 36		10 27	09 52	10 07		10 09	10 12	
	d	08 38				08 57				09 12	09 15	09 28				09 33	09 38			09 57			10 12	10 15	
Garforth	d					09 05					09 27									10 05				10 27	
South Milford	a										09 38													10 38	
Selby	a	08 57									09 53					10 40	09 57							10 53	
Howden	a															10 50									
Brough	a															11 04	10 15								
Hull	a	09 31														11 23	10 35								
Wakefield Kirkgate	a								09 02													10 02			
Wakefield Westgate	a								09 08													10 10			
York 8	a					09 23				09 36		09 52								10 23			10 36		
	d					09 26				09 41		09 58								10 26			10 41		
Malton	d									10 04													11 04		
Seamer	a									10 21													11 21		
Scarborough	a									10 30													11 30		
Thirsk	a					09 45														10 45					
Northallerton	a					09 58						10 18								10 58					
Darlington 7	a											10 30													
Yarm	d					10 13														11 13					
Thornaby	a					10 21														11 21					
Middlesbrough	a					10 30														11 30					
Durham	a											10 47													
Chester-le-Street	a																								
Newcastle 8 ⛴	a											11 05													

Liverpool, Manchester Airport and Manchester - Huddersfield - Wakefield, Leeds, Hull, York, Scarborough, Middlesbrough and Newcastle

Network Diagram - see first Page of Table 39

		TP	NT		NT	NT	TP	NT	NT	TP	NT	NT	TP		NT	TP	NT	NT	NT	TP	NT	TP	NT		NT
		◇1					◇1			◇1			◇1			◇1				◇1		◇1			
																			A						
Liverpool Lime Street 10	d					08 44							09 22						09 46						
Liverpool South Parkway 7	d												09 32												
Warrington Central	d												09 45												
Birchwood	d												09 50												
Manchester Oxford Road	d												10 07												
Manchester Airport	d	09 05								09 35						10 05						10 35			
Manchester Piccadilly 10	a	09 22								09 52			10 09			10 22						10 52			
	d	09 27					09 42			09 57			10 11			10 27				10 42		10 57			
Manchester Victoria	d		09 00		09 27	09 57									09 48		10 00	10 27	10 57						
Ashton-under-Lyne	d				09 37	10 07												10 37	11 07						
Stalybridge	a				09 42	10 13							10 26					10 42	11 13						
	d				09 42								10 26					10 42							
Mossley (Grtr Manchester)	d				09 47													10 47							
Greenfield	d				09 51													10 51							
Marsden	d				09 59													10 59							
Slaithwaite	d				10 04													11 04							
Huddersfield	a	09 56			10 12		10 15			10 26			10 44			10 56		11 12		11 15		11 26			
	d	09 57					10 16		10 23	10 27	10 31	10 35	10 45			10 57				11 16	11 23	11 27	11 31		11 35
Deighton	d										10 34	10 38											11 34		11 38
Mirfield	d		10 07								10 39	10 43					11 07						11 39		11 43
Ravensthorpe	d										10 42												11 42		
Dewsbury	a	10 06	10 12							10 36	10 46					11 06	11 12					11 36	11 46		
	d	10 07	10 12							10 37	10 46					11 07	11 12					11 37	11 46		
Batley	d		10 15								10 49						11 15						11 49		
Morley	d		10 21								10 55						11 21						11 55		
Cottingley	d										10 59												11 59		
Leeds 10	a	10 22	10 32				10 36		11 27	10 52	11 07		11 09		11 13	11 22	11 33			11 36	12 27	11 52	12 07		
	d	10 28					10 38	10 41		10 57			11 12		11 15	11 28				11 38		11 57			
Garforth	d							10 53		11 05					11 27							12 05			
South Milford	a														11 38										
Selby	a						10 57								11 54					11 57					
Howden	a																								
Brough	a						11 15													12 15					
Hull	a						11 35													12 36					
Wakefield Kirkgate	a											11 02													12 02
Wakefield Westgate	a											11 08													12 08
York 8	a	10 52						11 19		11 23			11 36			11 52						12 23			
	d	10 58								11 26			11 41			11 58						12 26			
Malton	d												12 04												
Seamer	a												12 21												
Scarborough	a												12 30												
Thirsk	a									11 45												12 45			
Northallerton	a	11 18								11 58						12 18						12 58			
Darlington 7	a	11 30														12 30									
Yarm	d									12 13												13 14			
Thornaby	a									12 21												13 22			
Middlesbrough	a									12 30												13 30			
Durham	a	11 47														12 47									
Chester-le-Street	a	11 53																							
Newcastle 8	a	12 06														13 03									

A until 23 March

Liverpool, Manchester Airport and Manchester - Huddersfield - Wakefield, Leeds, Hull, York, Scarborough, Middlesbrough and Newcastle

Network Diagram - see first Page of Table 39

		TP	NT	TP	NT	NT	NT	TP	NT		NT	TP	NT	NT	TP	NT	TP	NT	NT		NT	TP	NT	TP	NT
		◇1		◇1				◇1				◇1			◇1		◇1					◇1		◇1	
		🛒		🛒				🛒				🛒			🛒		🛒					🛒		🛒	
Liverpool Lime Street 10	d	10 22					10 46								11 22						11 46				
Liverpool South Parkway 7 ✈	d	10 32													11 32										
Warrington Central	d	10 45													11 45										
Birchwood	d	10 50													11 50										
Manchester Oxford Road	d	11 07													12 07										
Manchester Airport ✈	d			11 05								11 35					12 05							12 35	
Manchester Piccadilly 10 ⛴	a	11 09		11 22								11 52			12 09		12 22							12 52	
	d	11 11		11 27				11 42				11 57			12 11		12 27					12 42		12 57	
Manchester Victoria ⛴	d		10 48		11 00	11 27	11 57									11 48		12 00	12 27		12 57				
Ashton-under-Lyne	d					11 37	12 07												12 37		13 07				
Stalybridge	a	11 26				11 42	12 13								12 26				12 42		13 13				
	d	11 26				11 42									12 26				12 42						
Mossley (Grtr Manchester)	d					11 47													12 47						
Greenfield	d					11 51													12 51						
Marsden	d					11 59													12 59						
Slaithwaite	d					12 04													13 04						
Huddersfield	a	11 44		11 56		12 12		12 15				12 26			12 44		12 56		13 12			13 15		13 26	
	d	11 45		11 57				12 16			12 23	12 27	12 31	12 35	12 45		12 57					13 16	13 23	13 27	13 31
Deighton	d												12 34	12 38											13 34
Mirfield	d				12 07								12 39	12 43				13 07							13 39
Ravensthorpe	d												12 42												13 42
Dewsbury	a			12 06	12 12							12 36	12 46				13 06	13 12						13 36	13 46
	d			12 07	12 12							12 37	12 46				13 07	13 12						13 37	13 46
Batley	d				12 15								12 49					13 15							13 49
Morley	d				12 21								12 55					13 21							13 55
Cottingley	d												12 59												13 59
Leeds 10	a	12 09	12 12	12 22	12 31			12 36			13 27	12 52	13 07		13 09	13 12	13 22	13 32				13 36	14 27	13 51	14 07
	d	12 12	12 15	12 28				12 38	12 41			12 57			13 12	13 15	13 28					13 38		13 57	
Garforth	d		12 27						12 53			13 05				13 27								14 05	
South Milford	a		12 38													13 38									
Selby	a		12 50					12 57								13 51						13 57			
Howden	a																								
Brough	a							13 15														14 15			
Hull	a							13 35														14 35			
Wakefield Kirkgate	a													13 02											
Wakefield Westgate	a													13 08											
York 8	a	12 36		12 52					13 19			13 23			13 36		13 52							14 23	
	d	12 41		12 58								13 29			13 41		13 58							14 26	
Malton	d	13 04													14 04										
Seamer	a	13 21													14 21										
Scarborough	a	13 31													14 30										
Thirsk	a											13 48												14 45	
Northallerton	a			13 18								13 58					14 18							14 58	
Darlington 7	a			13 30													14 30								
Yarm	d											14 13												15 13	
Thornaby	a											14 21												15 21	
Middlesbrough	a											14 30												15 30	
Durham	a			13 47													14 47								
Chester-le-Street	a			13 53																					
Newcastle 8 ⛴	a			14 06													15 05								

Liverpool, Manchester Airport and Manchester - Huddersfield - Wakefield, Leeds, Hull, York, Scarborough, Middlesbrough and Newcastle

Network Diagram - see first Page of Table 39

Station		NT	TP	NT	TP	NT	NT	NT	TP	NT	NT	TP	NT	NT	TP	NT	TP FX	TP FO	NT	NT	NT	TP	NT
			◇1		◇1				◇1			◇1			◇1		◇1	◇1				◇1	
Liverpool Lime Street 10	d		12 22					12 46							13 22						13 46		
Liverpool South Parkway 7 ✈	d		12 32												13 32								
Warrington Central	d		12 45												13 45								
Birchwood	d		12 50												13 50								
Manchester Oxford Road	d		13 07												14 07								
Manchester Airport ✈	d				13 05							13 35					14 05	14 05					
Manchester Piccadilly 10	a		13 09		13 22							13 52			14 09		14 22	14 22					
	d		13 11		13 27				13 42			13 57			14 11		14 27	14 27				14 42	
Manchester Victoria	d			12 48		13 00	13 27	13 57								13 48			14 00	14 27	14 57		
Ashton-under-Lyne	d						13 37	14 07												14 37	15 07		
Stalybridge	a		13 26				13 42	14 13							14 26					14 42	15 13		
	d		13 26				13 42								14 26					14 42			
Mossley (Grtr Manchester)	d						13 47													14 47			
Greenfield	d						13 51													14 51			
Marsden	d						13 59													14 59			
Slaithwaite	d						14 04													15 04			
Huddersfield	a		13 44		13 56		14 12		14 15			14 26			14 44		14 56	14 56		15 12		15 15	
	d	13 35	13 45		13 57				14 16		14 23	14 27	14 31	14 35	14 45		14 57	14 57				15 16	15 23
Deighton	d	13 38											14 34	14 38									
Mirfield	d	13 43				14 07							14 39	14 43					15 07				
Ravensthorpe	d												14 42										
Dewsbury	a				14 06	14 12						14 36	14 46				15 06	15 06	15 12				
	d				14 07	14 12						14 37	14 46				15 07	15 07	15 12				
Batley	d					14 15							14 49						15 15				
Morley	d					14 21							14 55						15 21				
Cottingley	d												14 59										
Leeds 10	a		14 09	14 13	14 22	14 32			14 36		15 27	14 52	15 07		15 09	15 12	15 22	15 22	15 32			15 36	16 27
	d		14 12	14 15	14 28				14 38	14 41		14 57			15 12	15 15	15 28	15 28				15 38	
Garforth	d			14 27						14 53		15 05				15 27							
South Milford	a			14 38												15 38							
Selby	a			14 51					14 57							15 53						15 57	
Howden	a																						
Brough	a								15 15													16 15	
Hull	a								15 35													16 35	
Wakefield Kirkgate	a	14 02												15 02									
Wakefield Westgate	a	14 08												15 08									
York 8	a		14 36		14 52					15 18		15 23			15 36		15 49	15 52					
	d		14 41		14 58							15 26			15 41								
Malton	d		15 04												16 04								
Seamer	a		15 21												16 21								
Scarborough	a		15 30												16 30								
Thirsk	a											15 45											
Northallerton	a				15 18							15 58											
Darlington 7	a				15 30																		
Yarm	d											16 13											
Thornaby	a											16 21											
Middlesbrough	a											16 30											
Durham	a				15 47																		
Chester-le-Street	a				15 53																		
Newcastle 8	a				16 09																		

Liverpool, Manchester Airport and Manchester - Huddersfield - Wakefield, Leeds, Hull, York, Scarborough, Middlesbrough and Newcastle

Network Diagram - see first Page of Table 39

		TP	NT	NT	TP	NT	TP	NT	NT	NT	TP	NT	NT	TP	NT	NT	TP	NT	TP	NT	NT	NT
		◇1			◇1		◇1				◇1			◇1			◇1		◇1			
		🛒			🛒		🛒				🛒			🛒			🛒		🛒			
Liverpool Lime Street 10	d				14 22					14 46							15 22					
Liverpool South Parkway 7 ✈	d				14 32												15 32					
Warrington Central	d				14 45												15 45					
Birchwood	d				14 50												15 50					
Manchester Oxford Road	d				15 07												16 07					
Manchester Airport ✈	d	14 35					15 05							15 35					16 05			
Manchester Piccadilly 10 ⛴	a	14 52			15 09		15 22							15 52			16 09		16 22			
	d	14 57			15 11		15 27				15 42			15 57			16 11		16 27			
Manchester Victoria ⛴	d					14 48		15 00	15 27	15 57								15 48		16 00	16 17	16 27
Ashton-under-Lyne	d								15 37	16 07											16 27	16 37
Stalybridge	a				15 26				15 42	16 13							16 26				16 33	16 42
	d				15 26				15 42								16 26					16 42
Mossley (Grtr Manchester)	d								15 47													16 47
Greenfield	d								15 51													16 51
Marsden	d								15 59													16 59
Slaithwaite	d								16 04													17 04
Huddersfield	a	15 26			15 44		15 56		16 12		16 15			16 26			16 44		16 56			17 12
	d	15 27	15 31	15 35	15 45		15 57				16 16		16 23	16 27	16 31	16 35	16 45		16 57			
Deighton	d		15 34	15 38											16 34	16 38						
Mirfield	d		15 39	15 43				16 07							16 39	16 43				17 07		
Ravensthorpe	d		15 42												16 42							
Dewsbury	a	15 36	15 46				16 06	16 12						16 36	16 46				17 06	17 12		
	d	15 37	15 46				16 07	16 12						16 37	16 46				17 07	17 12		
Batley	d		15 49					16 15							16 49					17 15		
Morley	d		15 55					16 21							16 55					17 21		
Cottingley	d		15 59												16 59							
Leeds 10	a	15 52	16 07		16 09	16 12	16 22	16 32			16 36		17 27	16 52	17 07		17 09	17 12	17 22	17 31		
	d	15 57			16 12	16 15	16 28				16 38	16 57		16 57			17 12	17 15	17 24			
Garforth	d	16 05				16 27								17 05				17 28	17 34			
South Milford	a					16 39												17 39				
Selby	a					16 54					17 00							17 51				
Howden	a																					
Brough	a										17 18											
Hull	a										17 37											
Wakefield Kirkgate	a			16 02												17 02						
Wakefield Westgate	a			16 08								17 08				17 12						
York 8	a	16 23			16 36		16 52							17 21			17 37		17 55			
	d	16 26			16 41		16 56							17 24			17 41		18 00			
Malton	d				17 04									17 47					18 24			
Seamer	a				17 21									18 04					18 41			
Scarborough	a				17 30									18 15					18 50			
Thirsk	a	16 45					17 14										18 00					
Northallerton	a	16 58					17 22										18 08					
Darlington 7	a						17 33															
Yarm	d	17 13															18 23					
Thornaby	a	17 21															18 32					
Middlesbrough	a	17 30															18 42					
Durham	a						17 50															
Chester-le-Street	a						17 56															
Newcastle 8 ⛴	a						18 09															

Liverpool, Manchester Airport and Manchester - Huddersfield - Wakefield, Leeds, Hull, York, Scarborough, Middlesbrough and Newcastle

Network Diagram - see first Page of Table 39

		TP	NT	NT	NT	TP	NT		NT	NT	TP	NT	NT	TP	TP	NT	NT		TP	NT	TP	TP	NT	NT	NT
														FX	FO						FO				
		◇1				◇1					◇1			◇1	◇1				◇1		◇1	◇1			
Liverpool Lime Street 10	d						15 46				16 22												16 46		
Liverpool South Parkway 7	d										16 32														
Warrington Central	d										16 45														
Birchwood	d										16 50														
Manchester Oxford Road	d										17 07														
Manchester Airport	d					16 35								17 05								17 35			
Manchester Piccadilly 10	a					16 52					17 09			17 22								17 52			
	d	16 42				16 56					17 11			17 26	17 26				17 42			17 56			
Manchester Victoria	d						16 57					16 48	17 15			17 00	17 27						17 57		
Ashton-under-Lyne	d						17 07						17 24				17 38						18 07		
Stalybridge	a					17 08	17 12				17 26		17 29	17 38	17 38		17 43					18 08	18 12		
	d					17 08	17 12				17 26		17 29	17 38	17 38		17 43					18 08	18 12		
Mossley (Grtr Manchester)	d						17 17						17 34				17 48						18 17		
Greenfield	d						17 21						17 38				17 52						18 21		
Marsden	d						17 29										18 01						18 29		
Slaithwaite	d						17 34																18 34		
Huddersfield	a	17 15				17 26	17 42				17 44		17 54	17 56	17 57		18 12		18 15			18 26	18 43		
	d	17 16			17 23	17 27			17 31	17 35	17 45			17 57	17 57				18 16	18 23		18 27		18 36	18 40
Deighton	d								17 34	17 38														18 39	18 43
Mirfield	d								17 39	17 43						18 07								18 44	18 48
Ravensthorpe	d								17 42															18 47	
Dewsbury	a					17 36			17 46					18 06	18 07	18 13						18 36		18 51	
	d					17 37			17 46					18 07	18 07	18 13						18 37		18 56	
Batley	d								17 49							18 16								18 59	
Morley	d								17 55							18 22								19 05	
Cottingley	d								17 59															19 09	
Leeds 10	a	17 36			18 29	17 52			18 06		18 09	18 12		18 22	18 22	18 34			18 36	19 28		18 52		19 19	
	d	17 38	17 41	17 46		17 57					18 12	18 15		18 28	18 28				18 38			18 57			
Garforth	d		17 53	17 57		18 05						18 27										19 05			
South Milford	a			18 09								18 38							18 51						
Selby	a	17 59		18 21								18 49							19 00						
Howden	a	18 08																							
Brough	a	18 20																	19 18						
Hull	a	18 39																	19 38						
Wakefield Kirkgate	a									18 02															19 02
Wakefield Westgate	a									18 08															19 08
York 8	a		18 18			18 23					18 36			18 53	18 53							19 23			
	d					18 25					18 41			18 57							18 57	19 26			
Malton	d										19 04														
Seamer	a										19 21														
Scarborough	a										19 30														
Thirsk	a													19 13							19 13	19 45			
Northallerton	a					18 45								19 24							19 24	19 57			
Darlington 7	a					18 57																			
Yarm	d													19 38							19 38	20 11			
Thornaby	a													19 46							19 46	20 21			
Middlesbrough	a													19 56							19 56	20 30			
Durham	a					19 14																			
Chester-le-Street	a					19 20																			
Newcastle 8	a					19 34																			

Liverpool, Manchester Airport and Manchester - Huddersfield - Wakefield, Leeds, Hull, York, Scarborough, Middlesbrough and Newcastle

Network Diagram - see first Page of Table 39

		TP	NT		TP	NT	NT	TP	TP	NT	NT	TP	NT		NT	TP	NT	TP	NT	NT	NT	NT	TP		TP
								FO	FX														FX		FX
		◇1			◇1			◇1	◇1			◇1				◇1		◇1					◇1		◇1
																							A		B
		⚲			⚲			⚲	⚲																
Liverpool Lime Street 10	d	17 22														18 22							19 22		19 22
Liverpool South Parkway 7 ✈	d	17 32														18 32							19 32		19 32
Warrington Central	d	17 45														18 45							19 45		19 45
Birchwood	d	17 50														18 50							19 50		19 50
Manchester Oxford Road	d	18 07														19 07							20 07		20 07
Manchester Airport ✈	d											18 35						19 20							
Manchester Piccadilly 10	a	18 09										18 52				19 09		19 36					20 09		20 09
	d	18 11			18 27			18 42	18 42			18 57				19 11		19 42					20 11		20 11
Manchester Victoria	d		17 43			18 00	18 27										19 00		19 27						
Ashton-under-Lyne	d						18 37												19 37						
Stalybridge	a	18 26					18 42									19 26			19 42				20 26		20 26
	d	18 26					18 42									19 26			19 42				20 26		20 26
Mossley (Grtr Manchester)	d						18 47												19 47						
Greenfield	d						18 51												19 51						
Marsden	d						18 59												19 59						
Slaithwaite	d						19 04												20 04						
Huddersfield	a	18 44			18 56		19 12	19 15	19 15			19 26				19 44		20 15	20 12				20 44		20 44
	d	18 45			18 57			19 16	19 16		19 23	19 27	19 31		19 35	19 45		20 16		20 25	20 31	20 35	20 45		20 45
Deighton	d												19 34		19 38						20 34	20 38			
Mirfield	d					19 08							19 39		19 43		20 07				20 39	20 43			
Ravensthorpe	d												19 42								20 42				
Dewsbury	a				19 06	19 13						19 36	19 46				20 12	20 25			20 46				
	d				19 07	19 13						19 37	19 46				20 12	20 26			20 46				
Batley	d					19 16							19 49				20 15				20 49				
Morley	d					19 22							19 55				20 21				20 55				
Cottingley	d												19 59								20 59				
Leeds 10	a	19 09	19 13		19 23	19 33		19 36	19 36		20 29	19 52	20 07			20 09	20 34	20 41		21 25	21 07		21 09		21 09
	d	19 12	19 15		19 28			19 38	19 38	19 41		19 57				20 12		20 45					21 12		21 12
Garforth	d		19 27							19 53		20 05													
South Milford	a							19 51	19 50														21 23		21 23
Selby	a							20 00	20 00														21 33		21 34
Howden	a							20 09	20 09														21 42		21 42
Brough	a							20 21	20 21														21 54		21 54
Hull	a							20 43	20 43														22 17		22 15
Wakefield Kirkgate	a														20 02							21 02			
Wakefield Westgate	a														20 09							21 09			
York 8	a	19 36	19 53		19 53					20 22		20 23				20 36		21 09							
	d	19 41										20 29				20 41		21 14							
Malton	d	20 04														21 04									
Seamer	a	20 21														21 21									
Scarborough	a	20 30														21 30									
Thirsk	a											20 48						21 30							
Northallerton	a											20 58						21 38							
Darlington 7	a																	21 51							
Yarm	d											21 13													
Thornaby	a											21 21													
Middlesbrough	a											21 30													
Durham	a																	22 08							
Chester-le-Street	a																	22 14							
Newcastle 8	a																	22 28							

A From 26 March **B** Until 22 March

Liverpool, Manchester Airport and Manchester - Huddersfield - Wakefield, Leeds, Hull, York, Scarborough, Middlesbrough and Newcastle

Network Diagram - see first Page of Table 39

		TP	TP	TP	NT	NT	NT	NT	NT		TP	NT	TP	TP	NT	NT	NT	NT	TP		NT	TP	TP	TP	TP
		FO	FO													FX	FO					FX	FO	FO	FX
		◇1	◇1	◇1							◇1		◇1	◇1					◇1			◇1	◇1	◇1	◇1
		A	B																						
Liverpool Lime Street 10	d	19 22	19 22								20 22											22 30	22 30		
Liverpool South Parkway 7 ✈	d	19 32	19 32								20 32											22 40	22 40		
Warrington Central	d	19 45	19 45								20 45											22 53	22 53		
Birchwood	d	19 50	19 50								20 50											22 58	22 58		
Manchester Oxford Road	d	20 07	20 07								21 07											23 17	23 17		
Manchester Airport ✈	d			20 20										21 20					22 22					23 18	23 18
Manchester Piccadilly 10	a	20 09	20 09	20 36							21 09			21 36					22 36			23 19	23 19	23 34	23 34
	d	20 11	20 11	20 42							21 11			21 42					22 42			23 21	23 21	23 38	23 38
Manchester Victoria	d				20 27							21 27			22 08						23 00				23 56
Ashton-under-Lyne	d				20 37							21 37			22 18						23 10				
Stalybridge	a	20 26	20 26		20 42						21 26	21 42		21 55	22 22				22 55		23 14	23 34	23 34		
	d	20 26	20 26		20 42						21 26	21 42		21 55	22 23				22 55		23 15	23 34	23 34		
Mossley (Grtr Manchester)	d				20 47							21 47			22 27						23 19				
Greenfield	d				20 51							21 51			22 31						23 23				
Marsden	d				20 59							21 59			22 40						23 32				
Slaithwaite	d				21 04							22 04			22 44						23 36				
Huddersfield	a	20 44	20 44	21 15	21 12						21 44	22 12		22 15	22 53				23 15		23 44	23 52	23 52	00 09	00 25
	d	20 45	20 45	21 16			21 27	21 31	21 35		21 45			22 16		22 25	22 25	22 31	23 16			23 53	23 53	00 09	00 26
Deighton	d							21 34	21 38									22 34							
Mirfield	d							21 39	21 43									22 39							
Ravensthorpe	d							21 42										22 42							
Dewsbury	a			21 25				21 46						22 25				22 46	23 25					00s18	00s35
	d			21 26				21 46						22 26				22 46	23 26						
Batley	d							21 49										22 49							
Morley	d							21 55										22 55							
Cottingley	d							21 59										22 59							
Leeds 10	a	21 09	21 09	21 41			22 25	22 08			22 09			22 41		23 26	23 27	23 07	23 41			00 30	00 31	00 35	00 50
	d	21 12	21 12	21 42		21 55					22 12		22 22	22 42					23 42			00 32	00 34	00 37	00 54
Garforth	d					22 07																			
South Milford	a	21 24	21 24										22 36												
Selby	a	21 34	21 34										22 46												
Howden	a	21 43	21 43																						
Brough	a	21 55	21 55										23 05												
Hull	a	22 15	22 17										23 25												
Wakefield Kirkgate	a								22 02																
Wakefield Westgate	a								22 10																
York 8	a			22 06		22 32					22 38			23 07					00 09			01 16	01 16	01 20	01 43
	d			22 09										23 18											
Malton	d			22 32																					
Seamer	a			22 49																					
Scarborough	a			22 58																					
Thirsk	a													23 31											
Northallerton	a													23 49											
Darlington 7	a													00 01											
Yarm	d																								
Thornaby	a																								
Middlesbrough	a																								
Durham	a													00 19											
Chester-le-Street	a																								
Newcastle 8	a													00 51											

A Until 23 March

B From 30 March

Table 39

Saturdays

Liverpool, Manchester Airport and Manchester - Huddersfield - Wakefield, Leeds, Hull, York, Scarborough, Middlesbrough and Newcastle

Network Diagram - see first Page of Table 39

		TP	TP	TP	TP	TP	TP	TP	TP	TP		TP	NT	NT	NT	NT	TP	TP	TP	NT		NT	NT	NT	NT
		◇1	◇1	◇1	◇1	◇1	◇1	◇1	◇1	◇1		◇1					◇1	◇1	◇1						
Liverpool Lime Street 10	d			22p30																					
Liverpool South Parkway 7 ✈	d			22p40																					
Warrington Central	d			22p53																					
Birchwood	d			22p58																					
Manchester Oxford Road	d			23p17																					
Manchester Airport ✈	d	21p20	22p22		23p18	00 38	04 15		04 15			05 37							06 23						
Manchester Piccadilly 10	a	21p36	22p36	23p19	23p34	00 51	04 29		04 29			05 51							06 39						
	d	21p42	22p42	23p21	23p38	00 53	04 30		04 30	05 39		05 57					06 21		06 54						
Manchester Victoria	d																			06 17		06 55			
Ashton-under-Lyne	d																					07 05			
Stalybridge	a	21p55	22p55	23p34						05 52									07 07			07 10			
	d	21p55	22p55	23p34						05 52									07 07			07 11			
Mossley (Grtr Manchester)	d																					07 15			
Greenfield	d																					07 19			
Marsden	d														07 00							07 28			
Slaithwaite	d														07 04							07 32			
Huddersfield	a	22p15	23p15	23p52	00 09	01 34	05 10		05 10	06 10		06 26			07 12		06 54		07 25			07 41			
	d	22p16	23p16	23p53	00 09	01 35	05 11		05 11	06 11		06 27	06 31	06 41			06 56		07 26					07 29	07 32
Deighton	d												06 34	06 45											07 36
Mirfield	d												06 39	06 50											07 41
Ravensthorpe	d												06 42												
Dewsbury	a	22p25	23p25		00s18							06 36	06 46				07 05								
	d	22p26	23p26									06 37	06 46				07 06								
Batley	d												06 49												
Morley	d												06 55												
Cottingley	d												06 59												
Leeds 10	a	22p41	23p41	00 31	00 35	02 13	05 32		05 32	06 32		06 52	07 07				07 19		07 48	07 57				08 30	
	d	22p42	23p42	00 34	00 37	02 16	05 34		05 34	06 35		06 55				07 14	07 23		07 50	08 00			08 12		
Garforth	d																		08 00	08 12			08 24		
South Milford	a																			08 22			08 36		
Selby	a															07 37	07 43			08 36			08 54		
Howden	a																07 52								
Brough	a																08 04								
Hull	a																08 20								
Wakefield Kirkgate	a													07 03											07 57
Wakefield Westgate	a													07 10											08 08
York 8	a	23p07	00 09	01 16	01 20	02 45	06 00		06 00	07 01		07 22							08 21						
	d	23p18						05 54	06 40	07 06		07 25						07 32	08 23						
Malton	d								07 04			07 49													
Seamer	a								07 21			08 06													
Scarborough	a								07 30			08 15													
Thirsk	a	23p31						06 10		07 22								07 52	08 39						
Northallerton	a	23p49						06 18		07 30								08 00	08 49						
Darlington 7	a	00 01						06 29		07 41															
Yarm	d																	08 14	09 03						
Thornaby	a							06 53										08 24	09 11						
Middlesbrough	a							07 03										08 32	09 22						
Durham	a	00 19								07 58															
Chester-le-Street	a									08 04															
Newcastle 8	a	00 51								08 16															

Liverpool, Manchester Airport and Manchester - Huddersfield - Wakefield, Leeds, Hull, York, Scarborough, Middlesbrough and Newcastle

Network Diagram - see first Page of Table 39

		TP		TP	TP	NT		TP	NT	NT	NT	NT	TP	NT	NT	TP		NT	TP	NT	NT	NT	TP	NT	TP
		◇1		◇1				◇1					◇1			◇1			◇1				◇1		◇1
										A											A	B			
		🛒		🛒				🛒					🛒			🛒			🛒						🛒
Liverpool Lime Street 10	d	06 15								06 46						07 15					07 16				
Liverpool South Parkway 7 ✈	d	06 25														07 25									
Warrington Central	d	06 38														07 40									
Birchwood	d	06 43														07 45									
Manchester Oxford Road	d	07 07														08 06									
Manchester Airport ✈	d			07 05									07 33						08 05						08 35
Manchester Piccadilly 10	a	07 09		07 22									07 48			08 08			08 22						08 49
	d	07 11		07 27				07 36					07 56			08 10			08 26				08 42		08 57
Manchester Victoria	d					06 58			07 40	07 57								07 48		08 00	08 27	08 27			
Ashton-under-Lyne	d								07 49	08 07											08 37	08 37			
Stalybridge	a	07 23						07 49	07 54	08 13			08 09			08 26					08 41	08 41			
	d	07 23						07 49	07 54				08 09			08 26					08 42	08 42			
Mossley (Grtr Manchester)	d								07 59												08 46	08 46			
Greenfield	d								08 03												08 50	08 50			
Marsden	d								08 11												08 59	08 59			
Slaithwaite	d								08 16												09 03	09 03			
Huddersfield	a	07 44		07 56				08 09	08 24				08 28			08 44			08 56		09 12	09 12	09 15		09 26
	d	07 45		07 57				08 10			08 14	08 21	08 30	08 33	08 37	08 45			08 57				09 16	09 23	09 27
Deighton	d										08 17			08 36	08 40										
Mirfield	d					08 06					08 22			08 41	08 45					09 07					
Ravensthorpe	d										08 25			08 44											
Dewsbury	a	07 54		08 06		08 11		08 19			08 29		08 39	08 48					09 06	09 12					09 36
	d	07 55		08 07		08 12		08 20			08 29		08 39	08 53					09 07	09 12					09 37
Batley	d					08 15					08 32			08 56						09 15					
Morley	d					08 21					08 38			09 02						09 21					
Cottingley	d					08 24					08 42			09 06											
Leeds 10	a	08 10		08 24		08 31		08 36			08 52	09 27	08 54	09 16		09 09		09 12	09 22	09 32			09 36	10 27	09 52
	d	08 12		08 28	08 28			08 38					08 57			09 12		09 15	09 28				09 38		09 57
Garforth	d												09 05					09 27							10 05
South Milford	a																	09 38							
Selby	a							08 57										09 53					09 57		
Howden	a																								
Brough	a																						10 15		
Hull	a							09 31															10 35		
Wakefield Kirkgate	a														09 02										
Wakefield Westgate	a														09 08										
York 8	a	08 35		08 52	09 03								09 23			09 36			09 52						10 23
	d	08 40	08 42	08 58									09 26			09 41			09 58						10 26
Malton	d	09 04														10 04									
Seamer	a	09 21														10 21									
Scarborough	a	09 30														10 30									
Thirsk	a												09 45												10 45
Northallerton	a			09 18									09 58						10 18						10 58
Darlington 7	a		09 11	09 30															10 30						
Yarm	d												10 13												11 13
Thornaby	a												10 21												11 21
Middlesbrough	a												10 30												11 30
Durham	a		09 27	09 47															10 47						
Chester-le-Street	a			09 53																					
Newcastle 8	a		09 46	10 07															11 05						

A until 11 February, from 31 March

B from 18 February until 24 March

Table 39

Saturdays

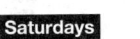

Liverpool, Manchester Airport and Manchester - Huddersfield - Wakefield, Leeds, Hull, York, Scarborough, Middlesbrough and Newcastle

Network Diagram - see first Page of Table 39

		NT		NT	TP	NT	NT	TP	NT	NT	NT	TP		NT	NT	TP	NT	NT	TP	NT	NT	TP		NT	NT
					◇1			◇1				◇1				◇1			◇1			◇1			
											A										B				
					⚲			⚲				⚲				⚲			⚲						
Liverpool Lime Street 10	d				08 22						08 44								09 22						
Liverpool South Parkway 7 ✈	d				08 32														09 32						
Warrington Central	d				08 45														09 45						
Birchwood	d				08 50														09 50						
Manchester Oxford Road	d				09 07														10 07						
Manchester Airport ✈	d							09 05								09 35						10 05			
Manchester Piccadilly 10 ⛴	a				09 09			09 22								09 52			10 09			10 22			
	d				09 11			09 27				09 42				09 57			10 11			10 27			
Manchester Victoria ⛴	d					08 48	08 57		09 00	09 27	09 57									09 48	09 57			10 00	10 27
Ashton-under-Lyne	d						09 07			09 37	10 07										10 07				10 37
Stalybridge	a				09 26		09 13			09 42	10 13								10 26		10 13				10 42
	d				09 26					09 42									10 26						10 42
Mossley (Grtr Manchester)	d									09 47															10 47
Greenfield	d									09 51															10 51
Marsden	d									09 59															10 59
Slaithwaite	d									10 04															11 04
Huddersfield	a				09 44			09 56		10 12		10 15				10 26			10 44			10 56			11 12
	d	09 31		09 35	09 45			09 57				10 16			10 23	10 27	10 31	10 35	10 45			10 57			
Deighton	d	09 34		09 38													10 34	10 38							
Mirfield	d	09 39		09 43					10 07								10 39	10 43						11 07	
Ravensthorpe	d	09 42															10 42								
Dewsbury	a	09 46						10 06	10 12							10 36	10 46					11 06		11 12	
	d	09 46						10 07	10 12							10 37	10 46					11 07		11 12	
Batley	d	09 49							10 15								10 49							11 15	
Morley	d	09 55							10 21								10 55							11 21	
Cottingley	d	09 59															10 59								
Leeds 10	a	10 07			10 09	10 12		10 22	10 32			10 36			11 27	10 52	11 07		11 09	11 13		11 22		11 35	
	d				10 12	10 15		10 28				10 38		10 41		10 57			11 12	11 15		11 28			
Garforth	d					10 27								10 53		11 05				11 27					
South Milford	a					10 38														11 38					
Selby	a					10 53						10 57								11 55					
Howden	a																								
Brough	a											11 15													
Hull	a											11 35													
Wakefield Kirkgate	a			10 02														11 02							
Wakefield Westgate	a			10 10														11 08							
York 8	a				10 36			10 52						11 18		11 23			11 36			11 52			
	d				10 41			10 58								11 26			11 41			11 58			
Malton	d				11 04														12 04						
Seamer	a				11 21														12 21						
Scarborough	a				11 30														12 30						
Thirsk	a															11 45									
Northallerton	a							11 18								11 58						12 18			
Darlington 7	a							11 30														12 30			
Yarm	d															12 13									
Thornaby	a															12 21									
Middlesbrough	a															12 30									
Durham	a							11 47														12 47			
Chester-le-Street	a							11 53																	
Newcastle 8 ⛴	a							12 06														13 03			

A until 11 February and from 31 March

B from 18 February until 24 March

Table 39

Saturdays

Liverpool, Manchester Airport and Manchester - Huddersfield - Wakefield, Leeds, Hull, York, Scarborough, Middlesbrough and Newcastle

Network Diagram - see first Page of Table 39

		NT	TP	NT	TP	NT	NT	TP	NT	NT	TP	NT	NT	NT	TP	NT	NT	TP	NT	NT	TP	NT	NT
			◇1		◇1			◇1			◇1				◇1			◇1			◇1		
		A								B				A									B
			🚲		🚲			🚲			🚲							🚲			🚲		
Liverpool Lime Street 10	d	09 46						10 22						10 46							11 22		
Liverpool South Parkway 7 ✈	d							10 32													11 32		
Warrington Central	d							10 45													11 45		
Birchwood	d							10 50													11 50		
Manchester Oxford Road	d							11 07													12 07		
Manchester Airport ✈	d				10 35						11 05							11 35					
Manchester Piccadilly 10 🚢	a				10 52			11 09			11 22							11 52			12 09		
	d		10 42		10 57			11 11			11 27				11 42			11 57			12 11		
Manchester Victoria 🚢	d	10 57							10 48	10 57		11 00	11 27	11 57								11 48	11 57
Ashton-under-Lyne	d	11 07								11 07			11 37	12 07									12 07
Stalybridge	a	11 13						11 26		11 13			11 42	12 13							12 26		12 13
	d							11 26					11 42								12 26		
Mossley (Grtr Manchester)	d												11 47										
Greenfield	d												11 51										
Marsden	d												11 59										
Slaithwaite	d												12 04										
Huddersfield	a		11 15		11 26			11 44			11 56		12 12		12 15			12 26			12 44		
	d		11 16	11 23	11 27	11 31	11 35	11 45			11 57				12 16		12 23	12 27	12 31	12 35	12 45		
Deighton	d					11 34	11 38												12 34	12 38			
Mirfield	d					11 39	11 43					12 07							12 39	12 43			
Ravensthorpe	d					11 42													12 42				
Dewsbury	a				11 36	11 46					12 06	12 12						12 36	12 46				
	d				11 37	11 46					12 07	12 12						12 37	12 46				
Batley	d					11 49						12 15							12 49				
Morley	d					11 55						12 21							12 55				
Cottingley	d					11 59													12 59				
Leeds 10	a		11 36	12 27	11 52	12 07		12 09	12 12		12 22	12 32			12 36		13 27	12 52	13 07		13 09	13 12	
	d		11 38		11 57			12 12	12 15		12 28				12 38	12 41		12 57			13 12	13 15	
Garforth	d				12 05				12 27							12 53		13 05				13 27	
South Milford	a								12 38													13 38	
Selby	a		11 57						12 50						12 57							13 52	
Howden	a																						
Brough	a		12 15												13 15								
Hull	a		12 36												13 35								
Wakefield Kirkgate	a						12 02													13 02			
Wakefield Westgate	a						12 08													13 08			
York 8	a				12 23			12 36			12 52					13 19		13 23			13 36		
	d				12 26			12 41			12 58							13 26			13 41		
Malton	d							13 04													14 04		
Seamer	a							13 21													14 21		
Scarborough	a							13 30													14 30		
Thirsk	a				12 45													13 45					
Northallerton	a				12 59						13 18							13 58					
Darlington 7	a										13 30												
Yarm	d				13 14													14 13					
Thornaby	a				13 22													14 21					
Middlesbrough	a				13 30													14 30					
Durham	a										13 47												
Chester-le-Street	a										13 53												
Newcastle 8 🚢	a										14 06												

A until 11 February, from 31 March

B from 18 February until 24 March

Table 39

Saturdays

Liverpool, Manchester Airport and Manchester - Huddersfield - Wakefield, Leeds, Hull, York, Scarborough, Middlesbrough and Newcastle

Network Diagram - see first Page of Table 39

		TP	NT	NT	NT	TP	NT	TP	NT	NT	TP	NT	NT	TP	NT	NT	NT	TP	NT	NT	TP	NT
		◇1				◇1		◇1			◇1			◇1				◇1			◇1	
					A								B				A					
Liverpool Lime Street 10	d				11 46						12 22						12 46					
Liverpool South Parkway 7	d										12 32											
Warrington Central	d										12 45											
Birchwood	d										12 50											
Manchester Oxford Road	d										13 07											
Manchester Airport	d	12 05						12 35						13 05							13 35	
Manchester Piccadilly 10	a	12 22						12 52			13 09			13 22							13 52	
	d	12 27				12 42		12 57			13 11			13 27				13 42			13 57	
Manchester Victoria	d		12 00	12 27	12 57							12 48	12 57		13 00	13 27	13 57					
Ashton-under-Lyne	d			12 37	13 07								13 07			13 37	14 07					
Stalybridge	a			12 42	13 13						13 26		13 13			13 42	14 13					
	d			12 42							13 26					13 42						
Mossley (Grtr Manchester)	d			12 47												13 47						
Greenfield	d			12 51												13 51						
Marsden	d			12 59												13 59						
Slaithwaite	d			13 04												14 04						
Huddersfield	a	12 56		13 12		13 15		13 26			13 44			13 56		14 12		14 15			14 26	
	d	12 57				13 16	13 23	13 27	13 31	13 35	13 45			13 57				14 16		14 23	14 27	14 31
Deighton	d								13 34	13 38												14 34
Mirfield	d		13 07						13 39	13 43					14 07							14 39
Ravensthorpe	d								13 42													14 42
Dewsbury	a	13 06	13 12					13 36	13 46					14 06	14 12						14 36	14 46
	d	13 07	13 12					13 37	13 46					14 07	14 12						14 37	14 46
Batley	d		13 15						13 49						14 15							14 49
Morley	d		13 21						13 55						14 21							14 55
Cottingley	d								13 59													14 59
Leeds 10	a	13 22	13 32			13 36	14 27	13 52	14 07		14 09	14 14		14 22	14 32			14 36		15 27	14 52	15 07
	d	13 28				13 38		13 57			14 12	14 15		14 28				14 38	14 41		14 57	
Garforth	d							14 05				14 27							14 53		15 05	
South Milford	a											14 38										
Selby	a					13 57						14 51						14 57				
Howden	a																					
Brough	a					14 15												15 15				
Hull	a					14 35												15 35				
Wakefield Kirkgate	a									14 02												
Wakefield Westgate	a									14 08												
York 8	a	13 52						14 23			14 36			14 52					15 17		15 23	
	d	13 58						14 26			14 41			14 58							15 26	
Malton	d										15 04											
Seamer	a										15 21											
Scarborough	a										15 30											
Thirsk	a							14 45													15 45	
Northallerton	a	14 18						14 58						15 18							15 58	
Darlington 7	a	14 30												15 30								
Yarm	d							15 13													16 13	
Thornaby	a							15 21													16 21	
Middlesbrough	a							15 30													16 30	
Durham	a	14 47												15 47								
Chester-le-Street	a													15 53								
Newcastle 8	a	15 05												16 09								

A until 11 February, from 31 March

B from 18 February until 24 March

Liverpool, Manchester Airport and Manchester - Huddersfield - Wakefield, Leeds, Hull, York, Scarborough, Middlesbrough and Newcastle

Network Diagram - see first Page of Table 39

		NT	TP	NT	NT	TP	NT	NT	NT	TP	NT	TP	NT	NT	TP	NT	NT	TP	NT	NT	NT	TP	NT
			◇1			◇1				◇1		◇1			◇1			◇1				◇1	
					A				B								A				B		
Liverpool Lime Street 10	d		13 22						13 46						14 22						14 46		
Liverpool South Parkway 7	d		13 32												14 32								
Warrington Central	d		13 45												14 45								
Birchwood	d		13 50												14 50								
Manchester Oxford Road	d		14 07												15 07								
Manchester Airport	d					14 05						14 35						15 05					
Manchester Piccadilly 10	a		14 09			14 22						14 52			15 09			15 22					
	d		14 11			14 27				14 42		14 57			15 11			15 27				15 42	
Manchester Victoria	d			13 48	13 57		14 00	14 27	14 57							14 48	14 57		15 00	15 27	15 57		
Ashton-under-Lyne	d				14 07			14 37	15 07								15 07			15 37	16 07		
Stalybridge	a		14 26		14 13			14 42	15 13						15 26		15 13			15 42	16 13		
	d		14 26					14 42							15 26					15 42			
Mossley (Grtr Manchester)	d							14 47												15 47			
Greenfield	d							14 51												15 51			
Marsden	d							14 59												15 59			
Slaithwaite	d							15 04												16 04			
Huddersfield	a		14 44			14 56		15 12		15 15		15 26			15 44			15 56		16 12		16 15	
	d	14 35	14 45			14 57				15 16	15 23	15 27	15 31	15 35	15 45			15 57				16 16	16 23
Deighton	d	14 38											15 34	15 38									
Mirfield	d	14 43					15 07						15 39	15 43					16 07				
Ravensthorpe	d												15 42										
Dewsbury	a					15 06	15 12					15 36	15 46					16 06	16 12				
	d					15 07	15 12					15 37	15 46					16 07	16 12				
Batley	d						15 15						15 49						16 15				
Morley	d						15 21						15 55						16 21				
Cottingley	d												15 59										
Leeds 10	a		15 09	15 10		15 22	15 32			15 36	16 27	15 52	16 08		16 09	16 12		16 22	16 31			16 36	17 27
	d		15 12	15 15		15 28				15 38		15 57			16 12	16 15		16 28				16 38	
Garforth	d			15 27								16 05				16 27							
South Milford	a			15 38												16 39							
Selby	a			15 53						15 57						16 54						17 00	
Howden	a																						
Brough	a									16 15												17 18	
Hull	a									16 35												17 37	
Wakefield Kirkgate	a	15 02												16 02									
Wakefield Westgate	a	15 08												16 08									
York 8	a		15 36			15 52						16 23			16 36			16 52					
	d		15 41									16 26			16 41			16 58					
Malton	d		16 04												17 04								
Seamer	a		16 21												17 21								
Scarborough	a		16 30												17 30								
Thirsk	a											16 45						17 15					
Northallerton	a											16 58						17 23					
Darlington 7	a																	17 34					
Yarm	d											17 13											
Thornaby	a											17 21											
Middlesbrough	a											17 30											
Durham	a																	17 51					
Chester-le-Street	a																	17 57					
Newcastle 8	a																	18 10					

A from 18 February until 24 March

B until 11 February, from 31 March

Table 39

Saturdays

Liverpool, Manchester Airport and Manchester - Huddersfield - Wakefield, Leeds, Hull, York, Scarborough, Middlesbrough and Newcastle

Network Diagram - see first Page of Table 39

		TP ◇1	NT	NT	TP ◇1	NT		NT A	TP ◇1	NT	NT	NT B	TP ◇1	NT	TP ◇1	NT		NT	NT	TP ◇1	NT	NT A	TP ◇1	NT	NT
Liverpool Lime Street 10	d				15 22							15 46								16 22					
Liverpool South Parkway 7	d				15 32															16 32					
Warrington Central	d				15 45															16 45					
Birchwood	d				15 50															16 50					
Manchester Oxford Road	d				16 07															17 07					
Manchester Airport	d	15 35							16 05						16 35								17 05		
Manchester Piccadilly 10	a	15 52			16 09				16 22						16 52					17 09			17 22		
	d	15 57			16 11				16 27				16 42		16 56					17 11			17 26		
Manchester Victoria	d					15 48		15 57		16 00	16 27	16 57									16 48	16 57		17 00	17 27
Ashton-under-Lyne	d							16 07			16 37	17 07										17 07			17 37
Stalybridge	a				16 26			16 13			16 42	17 13			17 08					17 26		17 13	17 38		17 42
	d				16 26						16 42				17 08					17 26			17 38		17 42
Mossley (Grtr Manchester)	d										16 47														17 47
Greenfield	d										16 51														17 51
Marsden	d										16 59					17 29									17 59
Slaithwaite	d										17 04					17 33									18 04
Huddersfield	a	16 26			16 44				16 56		17 12		17 15		17 26	17 41				17 44			17 56		18 12
	d	16 27	16 31	16 35	16 45				16 57				17 16	17 23	17 27			17 31	17 35	17 45			17 57		
Deighton	d		16 34	16 38														17 34	17 38						
Mirfield	d		16 39	16 43						17 07								17 39	17 43					18 07	
Ravensthorpe	d		16 42															17 42							
Dewsbury	a	16 36	16 46						17 06	17 12					17 36			17 46					18 06	18 12	
	d	16 37	16 46						17 07	17 12					17 37			17 46					18 07	18 13	
Batley	d		16 49							17 15								17 49						18 16	
Morley	d		16 55							17 21								17 55						18 22	
Cottingley	d		16 59															17 59							
Leeds 10	a	16 52	17 08		17 09	17 12			17 22	17 31			17 36	18 29	17 52			18 06		18 09	18 12		18 21	18 31	
	d	16 57			17 12	17 15			17 24				17 38		17 57					18 12	18 15		18 28		
Garforth	d	17 05				17 30			17 34						18 05						18 27				
South Milford	a					17 41															18 38				
Selby	a					17 55							17 59								18 50				
Howden	a												18 08												
Brough	a												18 20												
Hull	a												18 39												
Wakefield Kirkgate	a			17 02															18 02						
Wakefield Westgate	a			17 12															18 08						
York 8	a	17 23			17 36				17 55						18 22					18 36			18 52		
	d	17 26			17 41										18 26					18 41			18 58		
Malton	d				18 04															19 04					
Seamer	a				18 21															19 21					
Scarborough	a				18 30															19 30					
Thirsk	a	17 45													18 45										
Northallerton	a	17 58													18 58								19 17		
Darlington 7	a																						19 30		
Yarm	d	18 13													19 13										
Thornaby	a	18 21													19 21										
Middlesbrough	a	18 30													19 31										
Durham	a																						19 47		
Chester-le-Street	a																						19 53		
Newcastle 8	a																						20 07		

A from 18 February until 24 March

B until 11 February, from 31 March

Table 39

Saturdays

Liverpool, Manchester Airport and Manchester - Huddersfield - Wakefield, Leeds, Hull, York, Scarborough, Middlesbrough and Newcastle

Network Diagram - see first Page of Table 39

		NT	XC	TP	NT	TP	NT	NT	TP	NT	NT	NT	NT	TP	NT	NT	TP	NT	NT	TP	NT	TP
			◇1	◇1		◇1			◇1					◇1			◇1			◇1		◇1
		A									B											
			⚲																			
Liverpool Lime Street 10	d	16 46							17 22											18 22		
Liverpool South Parkway 7 ✈	d								17 32											18 32		
Warrington Central	d								17 45											18 45		
Birchwood	d								17 50											18 50		
Manchester Oxford Road	d								18 07											19 07		
Manchester Airport ✈	d					17 35											18 35					19 20
Manchester Piccadilly 10 🚋	a					17 52			18 09								18 52			19 09		19 36
	d			17 42		17 56			18 11					18 42			18 57			19 11		19 42
Manchester Victoria 🚋	d	17 57								17 43	17 57	18 00	18 27								19 00	
Ashton-under-Lyne	d	18 07									18 07		18 37									
Stalybridge	a	18 13				18 08			18 26		18 13		18 42							19 26		
	d					18 08			18 26				18 42							19 26		
Mossley (Grtr Manchester)	d												18 47									
Greenfield	d												18 51									
Marsden	d												18 59									
Slaithwaite	d												19 04									
Huddersfield	a			18 15		18 26			18 44				19 12	19 15			19 26			19 44		20 15
	d			18 16	18 23	18 27	18 31	18 35	18 45					19 16		19 23	19 27	19 31	19 35	19 45		20 16
Deighton	d						18 34	18 39										19 34	19 38			
Mirfield	d						18 39	18 44				19 08						19 39	19 43		20 07	
Ravensthorpe	d						18 42											19 42				
Dewsbury	a					18 36	18 46		18 55			19 13					19 36	19 46			20 12	20 25
	d					18 37	18 46		18 55			19 13					19 37	19 46			20 12	20 26
Batley	d						18 49					19 16						19 49			20 15	
Morley	d						18 55					19 22						19 55			20 21	
Cottingley	d						18 59											19 59				
Leeds 10	a			18 36	19 28	18 52	19 07		19 10	19 13		19 33		19 36		20 30	19 52	20 07		20 09	20 33	20 41
	d		18 35	18 38		18 57			19 12	19 16				19 38	19 41		19 57			20 12		20 45
Garforth	d					19 05				19 28					19 53		20 05					
South Milford	a			18 51										19 51								
Selby	a			19 00										20 00								
Howden	a													20 09								
Brough	a			19 18										20 21								
Hull	a			19 38										20 43								
Wakefield Kirkgate	a							19 02											20 02			
Wakefield Westgate	a							19 08											20 09			
York 8	a		18 58			19 23			19 36	19 53					20 18		20 23			20 36		21 09
	d		19 05			19 26			19 41								20 29			20 41		21 14
Malton	d								20 04											21 04		
Seamer	a								20 21											21 21		
Scarborough	a								20 30											21 30		
Thirsk	a					19 45											20 48					21 30
Northallerton	a					19 57											20 58					21 38
Darlington 7	a		19 35																			21 51
Yarm	d					20 11											21 13					
Thornaby	a					20 21											21 21					
Middlesbrough	a					20 30											21 30					
Durham	a		19 52																			22 08
Chester-le-Street	a																					22 14
Newcastle 8 🚋	a		20 08																			22 28

A until 11 February

B from 18 February until 24 March

Table 39

Saturdays

Liverpool, Manchester Airport and Manchester - Huddersfield - Wakefield, Leeds, Hull, York, Scarborough, Middlesbrough and Newcastle

Network Diagram - see first Page of Table 39

		NT	NT	NT	NT	TP	TP	NT		XC	TP	NT	NT	NT	NT	TP	NT	TP		NT	TP	NT	NT	NT	TP
						◇1	◇1			◇1	◇1					◇1		◇1			◇1				◇1
										🚲															
Liverpool Lime Street 10	d						19 22									20 22									
Liverpool South Parkway 7 ✈	d						19 32									20 32									
Warrington Central	d						19 45									20 45									
Birchwood	d						19 50									20 50									
Manchester Oxford Road	d						20 07									21 07									
Manchester Airport ✈	d										20 20										21 20				22 22
Manchester Piccadilly 10 ⛴	a						20 09				20 36					21 09					21 36				22 36
	d						20 11				20 42					21 11					21 42				22 42
Manchester Victoria ⛴	d	19 27						20 27									21 27					22 08			
Ashton-under-Lyne	d	19 37						20 37									21 37					22 18			
Stalybridge	a	19 42					20 26	20 42								21 26	21 41				21 55	22 22			22 55
	d	19 42					20 26	20 42								21 26	21 42				21 55	22 23			22 55
Mossley (Grtr Manchester)	d	19 47						20 47									21 46					22 27			
Greenfield	d	19 51						20 51									21 50					22 31			
Marsden	d	19 59						20 59						21 19			21 59					22 40			
Slaithwaite	d	20 04						21 04						21 23			22 03					22 44			
Huddersfield	a	20 12					20 44	21 12			21 15			21 30		21 44	22 12				22 15	22 53			23 15
	d		20 25	20 31	20 35		20 45				21 16		21 27	21 31	21 35	21 45					22 16		22 20	22 25	23 16
Deighton	d			20 34	20 38									21 34	21 38								22 23		
Mirfield	d			20 39	20 43									21 39	21 43								22 28		
Ravensthorpe	d			20 42										21 42									22 31		
Dewsbury	a			20 46							21 25			21 46							22 25		22 35		23 25
	d			20 46							21 26			21 46							22 26		22 35		23 26
Batley	d			20 49										21 49									22 38		
Morley	d			20 55										21 55									22 44		
Cottingley	d			20 59										21 59									22 48		
Leeds 10	a		21 25	21 07			21 09				21 41		22 24	22 07		22 09					22 41		22 56	23 26	23 41
	d					21 08	21 12			21 15	21 42	22 00				22 12		22 22		22 37	22 42				23 42
Garforth	d											22 12													
South Milford	a					21 20												22 36							
Selby	a					21 30												22 46							
Howden	a					21 39																			
Brough	a					21 51												23 05							
Hull	a					22 10												23 25							
Wakefield Kirkgate	a				21 02										22 02					23 10					
Wakefield Westgate	a				21 09										22 10										
York 8	a						21 41			21 57	22 06	22 36				22 38					23 07				00 09
	d										22 14														
Malton	d										22 37														
Seamer	a										22 54														
Scarborough	a										23 03														
Thirsk	a																								
Northallerton	a																								
Darlington 7	a																								
Yarm	d																								
Thornaby	a																								
Middlesbrough	a																								
Durham	a																								
Chester-le-Street	a																								
Newcastle 8 ⛴	a																								

Table 39

Saturdays

Liverpool, Manchester Airport and Manchester - Huddersfield - Wakefield, Leeds, Hull, York, Scarborough, Middlesbrough and Newcastle

Network Diagram - see first Page of Table 39

		NT	TP	TP	TP	TP	TP
			◇1	◇1	◇1	◇1	
			A	B	C	D	B
Liverpool Lime Street 10	d		22 30	22 30			
Liverpool South Parkway 7 ✈	d		22 40	22 40			
Warrington Central	d		22 53	22 53			
Birchwood	d		22 58	22 58			
Manchester Oxford Road	d		23 17	23 17			
Manchester Airport ✈	d				23 24	23 24	23 25
Manchester Piccadilly 10	a		23 19	23 19	23 39	23 39	23 50
	d		23 21	23 21	23 41	23 41	23 50
Manchester Victoria	d	23 00			23 56	23 56	
Ashton-under-Lyne	d	23 10					
Stalybridge	a	23 14	23 34	23 34			
	d	23 15	23 34	23 34			
Mossley (Grtr Manchester)	d	23 19					
Greenfield	d	23 23					
Marsden	d	23 32					
Slaithwaite	d	23 36					
Huddersfield	a	23 43	23 52	23 52	00 25	00 25	00 50
	d		23 53		00 26	00 26	00 50
Deighton	d						
Mirfield	d						
Ravensthorpe	d						
Dewsbury	a				00s35	00s35	
	d						
Batley	d						
Morley	d						
Cottingley	d						
Leeds 10	a		00 14		00 50	00 50	01 25
	d		00 15		00 54	00 54	01 25
Garforth	d						
South Milford	a						
Selby	a						
Howden	a						
Brough	a						
Hull	a						
Wakefield Kirkgate	a						
Wakefield Westgate	a						
York 8	a		00 42		01 22	01 32	02 15
	d						
Malton	d						
Seamer	a						
Scarborough	a						
Thirsk	a						
Northallerton	a						
Darlington 7	a						
Yarm	d						
Thornaby	a						
Middlesbrough	a						
Durham	a						
Chester-le-Street	a						
Newcastle 8	a						

A until 24 March
B from 31 March
C until 11 February
D from 18 February until 24 March

Table 39

Sundays
until 1 January

Liverpool, Manchester Airport and Manchester - Huddersfield, Leeds, Hull, York, Scarborough, Middlesbrough and Newcastle

Network Diagram - see first Page of Table 39

		TP	TP	TP	TP	TP	TP	NT	NT	TP	NT	TP	TP	TP	NT	NT	TP	TP	TP	TP	TP	NT	NT
		◇1	◇1	◇1	◇1	◇1	◇1			◇1		◇1	◇1	◇1			◇1	◇1	◇1	◇1	◇1		
		A	A	A				B															
Liverpool Lime Street 10	d		22p30											08 22					09 22		10 22		
Liverpool South Parkway 7	d		22p40											08 32					09 32		10 32		
Warrington Central	d		22p53											08 45					09 45		10 45		
Birchwood	d		22p58											08 50					09 50		10 50		
Newton-le-Willows	d																						
Manchester Oxford Road	d		23p17											09 10					10 07		11 07		
Manchester Airport	d	22p22		23p24														09 03		10 20			
Manchester Piccadilly 10	a	22p36	23p19	23p39										09 11				09 17	10 09	10 37	11 09		
	d	22p42	23p21	23p41	01 42	05 02	06 42			07 42			08 30	09 11				09 27	10 11	10 42	11 11		
Manchester Victoria	a			23p55																			
	d			23p56							08 43				09 43							10 43	11 43
Ashton-under-Lyne	d										08 53				09 53							10 53	11 53
Stalybridge	a	22p55	23p34				06 53			07 54	08 58		08 42	09 24	09 59				10 24		11 24	10 59	11 59
	d	22p55	23p34				06 54			07 54			08 42	09 24					10 24		11 24		
Mossley (Grtr Manchester)	d																						
Greenfield	d																						
Marsden	d																						
Slaithwaite	d																						
Huddersfield	a	23p15	23p52	00 25	02 11	05 31	07 11			08 11			09 00	09 42				09 55	10 42	11 11	11 42		
	d	23p16	23p53	00 26	02 12	05 32	07 12	07 23	07 51	08 12			09 02	09 43		09 51		10 12	10 43	11 12	11 43		
Deighton	d							07 32	07 54							09 54							
Mirfield	d							07 42	07 59							09 59							
Ravensthorpe	d							07 47	08 02							10 02							
Dewsbury	a	23p25		00s35			07 21	07 55	08 06	08 21			09 11			10 06		10 22		11 21			
	d	23p26					07 22	07 55	08 06	08 22			09 11			10 06		10 22		11 22			
Batley	d							08 03	08 09							10 09							
Morley	d							08 15	08 15							10 15							
Cottingley	d							08 25	08 19							10 19							
Leeds 10	a	23p41	00 14	00 50	02 33	05 53	07 37	08 40	08 27	08 37			09 27	10 07		10 27		10 37	11 04	11 37	12 04		
	d	23p42	00 15	00 54	02 35	05 55	07 40			08 40		09 12	09 40	10 22				10 40	11 12	11 40	12 12		
Garforth	d																						
South Milford	a													10 34									
Selby	a													10 44									
Howden	a																						
Brough	a													11 03									
Hull	a													11 18									
York 8	a	00 09	00 42	01 22	03 03	06 23	08 08			09 07		09 37	10 07					11 07	11 39	12 05	12 39		
	d						08 21			09 10		09 40	10 13				10 42	11 10	11 44	12 08	12 42		
Malton	d											10 04							12 08				
Seamer	a											10 20							12 25				
Scarborough	a											10 30							12 34				
Thirsk	a						08 37										10 59				12 59		
Northallerton	a						08 45			09 30			10 35				11 07	11 30		12 28	13 07		
Darlington 7	a						08 56			09 42			10 46					11 42		12 40			
Yarm	d																11 21				13 22		
Thornaby	a						09 16										11 29				13 30		
Middlesbrough	a						09 25										11 39				13 40		
Durham	a									09 59			11 08					11 59		12 57			
Chester-le-Street	a																						
Newcastle 8	a									10 18			11 24					12 15		13 12			

A not 11 December

B not until 18 December

Table 39

Sundays
until 1 January

Liverpool, Manchester Airport and Manchester - Huddersfield, Leeds, Hull, York, Scarborough, Middlesbrough and Newcastle

Network Diagram - see first Page of Table 39

		NT	TP	TP	TP	TP	NT	TP	TP		NT	NT	TP	TP	TP	TP	NT	TP	TP	NT		NT	TP	TP	TP
			◇1	◇1	◇1	◇1		◇1	◇1				◇1	◇1	◇1	◇1		◇1	◇1				◇1	◇1	◇1
Liverpool Lime Street 10	d				11 22				12 22						13 22				14 22						15 22
Liverpool South Parkway 7 ✈	d				11 32				12 32						13 32				14 32						15 32
Warrington Central	d				11 45				12 45						13 45				14 45						15 45
Birchwood	d				11 50				12 50						13 50				14 50						15 50
Newton-le-Willows	d																								
Manchester Oxford Road	d				12 07				13 07						14 07				15 07						16 07
Manchester Airport ✈	d		11 20			12 19							13 20			14 20							15 20		
Manchester Piccadilly 10	a		11 35		12 09	12 38			13 09				13 37		14 09	14 37			15 09				15 37		16 09
	d		11 42	12 01	12 11	12 42		13 02	13 11				13 42	14 02	14 11	14 42		15 02	15 11				15 42	16 02	16 11
Manchester Victoria	a																								
	d						12 43				13 43						14 43			15 43					
Ashton-under-Lyne	d						12 53				13 53						14 53			15 53					
Stalybridge	a				12 24		12 59		13 24		13 59				14 24		14 59		15 24	15 59					16 24
	d				12 24				13 24						14 24				15 24						16 24
Mossley (Grtr Manchester)	d																								
Greenfield	d																								
Marsden	d																								
Slaithwaite	d																								
Huddersfield	a		12 11	12 32	12 42	13 11		13 32	13 42				14 11	14 32	14 42	15 11		15 32	15 42				16 11	16 32	16 42
	d	11 58	12 12	12 33	12 43	13 12		13 33	13 43			13 58	14 12	14 33	14 43	15 12		15 33	15 43			15 58	16 12	16 33	16 43
Deighton	d	12 01										14 01										16 01			
Mirfield	d	12 06										14 06										16 06			
Ravensthorpe	d	12 09										14 09										16 09			
Dewsbury	a	12 13	12 21			13 21						14 13	14 21			15 21						16 13	16 22		
	d	12 13	12 22			13 22						14 13	14 22			15 22						16 13	16 22		
Batley	d	12 16										14 16										16 16			
Morley	d	12 22										14 22										16 22			
Cottingley	d	12 26										14 26										16 26			
Leeds 10	a	12 34	12 37	12 54	13 04	13 37		13 54	14 04			14 34	14 37	14 53	15 04	15 37		15 54	16 04			16 34	16 37	16 54	17 04
	d		12 40	13 01	13 12	13 40		13 57	14 12				14 40	15 01	15 12	15 40		15 57	16 12				16 40	17 01	17 12
Garforth	d																								
South Milford	a			13 13										15 14										17 14	
Selby	a			13 23										15 23										17 23	
Howden	a																								
Brough	a			13 41										15 41										17 41	
Hull	a			13 59										15 59										17 59	
York 8	a		13 07		13 39	14 05		14 24	14 38				15 07		15 35	16 05		16 22	16 38				17 07		17 39
	d		13 10		13 43	14 10			14 50				15 10		15 43	16 10			16 42				17 10		17 43
Malton	d				14 07										16 07										18 07
Seamer	a				14 24										16 24										18 24
Scarborough	a				14 33										16 33										18 33
Thirsk	a								15 12										17 04						
Northallerton	a		13 30			14 30			15 20				15 30			16 30			17 16				17 30		
Darlington 7	a		13 42			14 42							15 42			16 42							17 42		
Yarm	d								15 35										17 32						
Thornaby	a								15 44										17 41						
Middlesbrough	a								15 52										17 50						
Durham	a		13 59			14 59							16 00			16 59							17 59		
Chester-le-Street	a		14 05										16 06										18 05		
Newcastle 8	a		14 17			15 15							16 18			17 14							18 18		

Table 39

Sundays

until 1 January

Liverpool, Manchester Airport and Manchester - Huddersfield, Leeds, Hull, York, Scarborough, Middlesbrough and Newcastle

Network Diagram - see first Page of Table 39

Station		TP ◇1	NT	TP ◇1	TP ◇1	NT	NT		TP ◇1	TP ◇1	TP ◇1	TP ◇1	NT	TP ◇1	TP ◇1	NT	NT	TP ◇1		TP ◇1	TP ◇1	TP ◇1	TP ◇1	NT	NT
Liverpool Lime Street 10	d				16 22						17 22				18 22						19 22		20 22		
Liverpool South Parkway 7 ✈	d				16 32						17 32				18 32						19 32		20 32		
Warrington Central	d				16 45						17 45				18 45						19 45		20 45		
Birchwood	d				16 50						17 50				18 50						19 50		20 50		
Newton-le-Willows	d																								
Manchester Oxford Road	d				17 07						18 07				19 07						20 07		21 07		
Manchester Airport ✈	d	16 20							17 20			18 20						19 20				20 20			
Manchester Piccadilly 10	a	16 37			17 09				17 37		18 09	18 37			19 09			19 37			20 09	20 37	21 09		
	d	16 42		17 02	17 11				17 42	18 02	18 11	18 42		19 02	19 11			19 42		20 06	20 11	20 42	21 11		
Manchester Victoria	a																								
	d		16 43			17 43							18 43			19 43								20 43	21 43
Ashton-under-Lyne	d		16 53			17 53							18 53			19 53								20 53	21 53
Stalybridge	a		16 59		17 24	17 59					18 24		18 59		19 24	19 59					20 24		21 24	20 59	21 57
	d				17 24						18 24				19 24						20 24		21 24		
Mossley (Grtr Manchester)	d																								
Greenfield	d																								
Marsden	d																								
Slaithwaite	d																								
Huddersfield	a	17 11		17 32	17 42				18 11	18 32	18 42	19 11		19 32	19 42			20 11		20 36	20 42	21 11	21 42		
	d	17 12		17 33	17 43		17 58		18 12	18 33	18 43	19 12		19 33	19 43		19 58	20 12		20 37	20 43	21 12	21 43		
Deighton	d						18 01										20 01								
Mirfield	d						18 06										20 06								
Ravensthorpe	d						18 09										20 09								
Dewsbury	a	17 21					18 13		18 21			19 21					20 13	20 21				21 21			
	d	17 22					18 13		18 22			19 22					20 13	20 22				21 22			
Batley	d						18 16										20 16								
Morley	d						18 22										20 22								
Cottingley	d						18 26										20 26								
Leeds 10	a	17 37		17 54	18 04		18 34		18 37	18 54	19 04	19 37		19 54	20 04		20 34	20 37		20 58	21 04	21 37	22 04		
	d	17 40		17 57	18 12				18 40	19 01	19 12	19 40		19 57	20 12			20 40		21 04	21 12	21 40	22 12		
Garforth	d																								
South Milford	a									19 16															
Selby	a									19 28				20 17						21 38					
Howden	a																								
Brough	a									19 48				20 36						21 58					
Hull	a									20 05				20 54						22 12					
York 8	a	18 07		18 23	18 38				19 05		19 38	20 04			20 38			21 05			21 38	22 08	22 40		
	d	18 10			18 42				19 10		19 46	20 10			20 44			21 08				22 10	22 42		
Malton	d										20 10				21 08							22 35			
Seamer	a										20 27				21 25							22 51			
Scarborough	a										20 36				21 34							22 59			
Thirsk	a				18 59							20 26						21 26					23 06		
Northallerton	a	18 30			19 07				19 30			20 34						21 34					23 16		
Darlington 7	a	18 42							19 42									21 45					23 28		
Yarm	d				19 22							20 50													
Thornaby	a				19 30							20 58													
Middlesbrough	a				19 40							21 07													
Durham	a	18 59							19 59									22 02					23 45		
Chester-le-Street	a								20 05																
Newcastle 8	a	19 16							20 18									22 17					00 15		

Table 39

Sundays
until 1 January

Liverpool, Manchester Airport and Manchester - Huddersfield, Leeds, Hull, York, Scarborough, Middlesbrough and Newcastle

Network Diagram - see first Page of Table 39

		TP	NT	TP	TP		TP
		◇1		◇1	◇1		◇1
Liverpool Lime Street 10	d				21 52		
Liverpool South Parkway 7	d				22 02		
Warrington Central	d				22 15		
Birchwood	d				22 20		
Newton-le-Willows	d						
Manchester Oxford Road	d				22 37		
Manchester Airport	d			21 20			23 20
Manchester Piccadilly 10	a			21 37	22 39		23 37
	d			21 42	22 42		23 42
Manchester Victoria	a						
	d						
Ashton-under-Lyne	d						
Stalybridge	a				22 54		
	d				22 54		
Mossley (Grtr Manchester)	d						
Greenfield	d						
Marsden	d		21 47				
Slaithwaite	d		21 51				
Huddersfield	a		21 57	22 11	23 12		00 11
	d		21 57	22 12	23 12		00 12
Deighton	d		22 01				
Mirfield	d		22 06				
Ravensthorpe	d		22 09				
Dewsbury	a		22 13	22 21	23 22		
	d		22 13	22 22	23 22		
Batley	d		22 16				
Morley	d		22 22				
Cottingley	d		22 26				
Leeds 10	a		22 34	22 37	23 39		00 51
	d	22 22		22 40	23 42		00 54
Garforth	d						
South Milford	a	22 34					
Selby	a	22 44					
Howden	a						
Brough	a	23 02					
Hull	a	23 19					
York 8	a			23 11	00 26		01 22
	d						
Malton	d						
Seamer	a						
Scarborough	a						
Thirsk	a						
Northallerton	a						
Darlington 7	a						
Yarm	d						
Thornaby	a						
Middlesbrough	a						
Durham	a						
Chester-le-Street	a						
Newcastle 8	a						

Table 39

Sundays

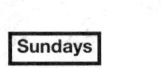

8 January to 12 February

Liverpool, Manchester Airport and Manchester - Huddersfield, Leeds, Hull, York, Scarborough, Middlesbrough and Newcastle

Network Diagram - see first Page of Table 39

		TP	TP	TP	TP	TP	TP	NT	NT	TP	NT	TP	TP	TP	NT	NT	TP	TP	TP	TP	TP	NT	NT
		◇1	◇1	◇1	◇1	◇1	◇1	🚌		◇1		◇1	◇1	◇1			◇1	◇1	◇1	◇1	◇1		
Liverpool Lime Street 10	d		22p30											08 22					09 22		10 22		
Liverpool South Parkway 7 ✈	d		22p40											08 32					09 32		10 32		
Warrington Central	d		22p53											08 45					09 45		10 45		
Birchwood	d		22p58											08 50					09 50		10 50		
Newton-le-Willows	d																						
Manchester Oxford Road	d		23p17											09 10					10 07		11 07		
Manchester Airport ✈	d	22p22		23p24														09 03		10 20			
Manchester Piccadilly 10	a	22p36	23p19	23p39										09 11				09 17	10 09	10 37	11 09		
	d	22p42	23p21	23p41	01 42	05 02	06 42			07 42			08 28	09 11				09 27	10 11	10 42	11 11		
Manchester Victoria	a			23p55																			
	d			23p56							08 43				09 43							10 43	11 43
Ashton-under-Lyne	d										08 53				09 53							10 53	11 53
Stalybridge	a	22p55	23p34				06 53			07 54	08 58		08 41	09 24	09 59				10 24		11 24	10 59	11 59
	d	22p55	23p34				06 54			07 54			08 41	09 24					10 24		11 24		
Mossley (Grtr Manchester)	d																						
Greenfield	d																						
Marsden	d																						
Slaithwaite	d																						
Huddersfield	a	23p15	23p52	00 25	02 11	05 31	07 11			08 11			08 59	09 42				09 55	10 42	11 11	11 42		
	d	23p16	23p53	00 26	02 12	05 32	07 12	07 23	07 51	08 12			09 02	09 43		09 51		10 12	10 43	11 12	11 43		
Deighton	d							07 32	07 54							09 54							
Mirfield	d							07 42	07 59							09 59							
Ravensthorpe	d							07 47	08 02							10 02							
Dewsbury	a	23p25		00s35			07 21	07 55	08 06	08 21			09 11			10 06		10 22		11 21			
	d	23p26					07 22	07 55	08 06	08 22			09 11			10 06		10 22		11 22			
Batley	d							08 03	08 09							10 09							
Morley	d							08 15	08 15							10 15							
Cottingley	d							08 25	08 19							10 19							
Leeds 10	a	23p41	00 14	00 50	02 33	05 53	07 37	08 40	08 27	08 37			09 27	10 07		10 27		10 37	11 04	11 37	12 04		
	d	23p42	00 15	00 54	02 35	05 55	07 40			08 40		09 12	09 40	10 22				10 40	11 12	11 40	12 12		
Garforth	d																						
South Milford	a													10 34									
Selby	a													10 44									
Howden	a																						
Brough	a													11 03									
Hull	a													11 18									
York 8	a	00 09	00 42	01 22	03 03	06 23	08 08			09 07		09 37	10 07					11 07	11 39	12 05	12 39		
	d						08 21			09 10		09 40	10 13				10 42	11 10	11 44	12 08	12 42		
Malton	d											10 04							12 08				
Seamer	a											10 20							12 25				
Scarborough	a											10 30							12 34				
Thirsk	a						08 37										10 59				12 59		
Northallerton	a						08 45			09 30			10 35				11 07	11 30		12 28	13 07		
Darlington 7	a						08 56			09 42			10 46					11 42		12 40			
Yarm	d																11 21				13 22		
Thornaby	a						09 16										11 29				13 30		
Middlesbrough	a						09 25										11 39				13 40		
Durham	a									09 59			11 08					11 59		12 57			
Chester-le-Street	a																						
Newcastle 8	a									10 18			11 24					12 15		13 12			

Table 39

Sundays

8 January to 12 February

Liverpool, Manchester Airport and Manchester - Huddersfield, Leeds, Hull, York, Scarborough, Middlesbrough and Newcastle

Network Diagram - see first Page of Table 39

		NT	TP	TP	TP	TP	NT	TP	TP		NT	NT	TP	TP	TP	TP	NT	TP	TP	NT		NT	TP	TP	TP
			◇1	◇1	◇1	◇1		◇1	◇1				◇1	◇1	◇1	◇1		◇1	◇1				◇1	◇1	◇1
Liverpool Lime Street 10	d				11 22				12 22						13 22				14 22						15 22
Liverpool South Parkway 7 ✈	d				11 32				12 32						13 32				14 32						15 32
Warrington Central	d				11 45				12 45						13 45				14 45						15 45
Birchwood	d				11 50				12 50						13 50				14 50						15 50
Newton-le-Willows	d																								
Manchester Oxford Road	d				12 07				13 07						14 07				15 07						16 07
Manchester Airport ✈	d		11 20			12 19							13 20			14 20							15 20		
Manchester Piccadilly 10 ⛴	a		11 35		12 09	12 38			13 09				13 37		14 09	14 37			15 09				15 37		16 09
	d		11 42	12 01	12 11	12 42		13 02	13 11				13 42	14 02	14 11	14 42		15 02	15 11				15 42	16 02	16 11
Manchester Victoria ⛴	a																								
	d						12 43				13 43						14 43			15 43					
Ashton-under-Lyne	d						12 53				13 53						14 53			15 53					
Stalybridge	a				12 24		12 59		13 24		13 59				14 24		14 59		15 24	15 59					16 24
	d				12 24				13 24						14 24				15 24						16 24
Mossley (Grtr Manchester)	d																								
Greenfield	d																								
Marsden	d																								
Slaithwaite	d																								
Huddersfield	a		12 11	12 32	12 42	13 11		13 32	13 42				14 11	14 32	14 42	15 11		15 32	15 42				16 11	16 32	16 42
	d	11 58	12 12	12 33	12 43	13 12		13 33	13 43			13 58	14 12	14 33	14 43	15 12		15 33	15 43			15 58	16 12	16 33	16 43
Deighton	d	12 01										14 01										16 01			
Mirfield	d	12 06										14 06										16 06			
Ravensthorpe	d	12 09										14 09										16 09			
Dewsbury	a	12 13	12 21			13 21						14 13	14 21			15 21						16 13	16 22		
	d	12 13	12 22			13 22						14 13	14 22			15 22						16 13	16 22		
Batley	d	12 16										14 16										16 16			
Morley	d	12 22										14 22										16 22			
Cottingley	d	12 26										14 26										16 26			
Leeds 10	a	12 34	12 37	12 54	13 04	13 37		13 54	14 04			14 34	14 37	14 53	15 04	15 37		15 54	16 04			16 34	16 37	16 54	17 04
	d		12 40	13 01	13 12	13 40		13 57	14 12				14 40	15 01	15 12	15 40		15 57	16 12				16 40	17 01	17 12
Garforth	d																								
South Milford	a			13 13										15 14										17 14	
Selby	a			13 23										15 23										17 23	
Howden	a																								
Brough	a			13 41										15 41										17 41	
Hull	a			13 59										15 59										17 59	
York 8	a		13 07		13 39	14 05		14 24	14 38				15 07		15 35	16 05		16 22	16 38				17 07		17 39
	d		13 10		13 43	14 10			14 50				15 10		15 43	16 10			16 42				17 10		17 43
Malton	d				14 07										16 07										18 07
Seamer	a				14 24										16 24										18 24
Scarborough	a				14 33										16 33										18 33
Thirsk	a								15 12										17 04						
Northallerton	a		13 30			14 30			15 20				15 30			16 30			17 16				17 30		
Darlington 7	a		13 42			14 42							15 42			16 42							17 42		
Yarm	d								15 35										17 32						
Thornaby	a								15 44										17 41						
Middlesbrough	a								15 52										17 50						
Durham	a		13 59			14 59							16 00			16 59							17 59		
Chester-le-Street	a		14 05										16 06										18 05		
Newcastle 8 ⛴	a		14 17			15 15							16 18			17 14							18 18		

Sundays

8 January to 12 February

Liverpool, Manchester Airport and Manchester - Huddersfield, Leeds, Hull, York, Scarborough, Middlesbrough and Newcastle

Network Diagram - see first Page of Table 39

		TP	NT	TP	TP	NT	NT		TP	TP	TP	TP	NT	TP	TP	NT	NT	TP		TP	TP	TP	TP	NT	NT
		◇1		◇1	◇1				◇1	◇1	◇1	◇1		◇1	◇1			◇1		◇1	◇1	◇1	◇1		
Liverpool Lime Street 10	d				16 22						17 22				18 22						19 22		20 22		
Liverpool South Parkway 7 ✈	d				16 32						17 32				18 32						19 32		20 32		
Warrington Central	d				16 45						17 45				18 45						19 45		20 45		
Birchwood	d				16 50						17 50				18 50						19 50		20 50		
Newton-le-Willows	d																								
Manchester Oxford Road	d				17 07						18 07				19 07						20 07		21 07		
Manchester Airport ✈	d	16 20							17 20			18 20						19 20				20 20			
Manchester Piccadilly 10 🚢	a	16 37			17 09				17 37		18 09	18 37			19 09			19 37			20 09	20 37	21 09		
	d	16 42		17 02	17 11				17 42	18 02	18 11	18 42		19 02	19 11			19 42		20 06	20 11	20 42	21 11		
Manchester Victoria 🚢	a																								
	d		16 43			17 43							18 43			19 43								20 43	21 43
Ashton-under-Lyne	d		16 53			17 53							18 53			19 53								20 53	21 53
Stalybridge	a		16 59		17 24	17 59					18 24		18 59		19 24	19 59					20 24		21 24	20 59	21 57
	d				17 24						18 24				19 24						20 24		21 24		
Mossley (Grtr Manchester)	d																								
Greenfield	d																								
Marsden	d																								
Slaithwaite	d																								
Huddersfield	a	17 11		17 32	17 42				18 11	18 32	18 42	19 11		19 32	19 42			20 11		20 36	20 42	21 11	21 42		
	d	17 12		17 33	17 43		17 58		18 12	18 33	18 43	19 12		19 33	19 43		19 58	20 12		20 37	20 43	21 12	21 43		
Deighton	d						18 01										20 01								
Mirfield	d						18 06										20 06								
Ravensthorpe	d						18 09										20 09								
Dewsbury	a	17 21					18 13		18 21			19 21					20 13	20 21				21 21			
	d	17 22					18 13		18 22			19 22					20 13	20 22				21 22			
Batley	d						18 16										20 16								
Morley	d						18 22										20 22								
Cottingley	d						18 26										20 26								
Leeds 10	a	17 37		17 54	18 04		18 34		18 37	18 54	19 04	19 37		19 54	20 04		20 34	20 37		20 58	21 04	21 37	22 04		
	d	17 40		17 57	18 12				18 40	19 01	19 12	19 40		19 57	20 12			20 40		21 04	21 12	21 40	22 12		
Garforth	d																								
South Milford	a									19 16															
Selby	a									19 28				20 17						21 38					
Howden	a																								
Brough	a									19 48				20 36						21 58					
Hull	a									20 05				20 54						22 12					
York 8	a	18 07		18 23	18 38				19 05		19 38	20 04			20 38			21 05			21 38	22 08	22 40		
	d	18 10			18 42				19 10		19 46	20 10			20 44			21 08				22 10	22 42		
Malton	d										20 10				21 08							22 35			
Seamer	a										20 27				21 25							22 51			
Scarborough	a										20 36				21 34							22 59			
Thirsk	a				18 59							20 26						21 26					23 06		
Northallerton	a	18 30			19 07				19 30			20 34						21 34					23 16		
Darlington 7	a	18 42							19 42									21 45					23 28		
Yarm	d				19 22							20 50													
Thornaby	a				19 30							20 58													
Middlesbrough	a				19 40							21 07													
Durham	a	18 59							19 59									22 02					23 45		
Chester-le-Street	a								20 05																
Newcastle 8 🚢	a	19 16							20 18									22 17					00 15		

Table 39

Sundays

8 January to 12 February

Liverpool, Manchester Airport and Manchester - Huddersfield, Leeds, Hull, York, Scarborough, Middlesbrough and Newcastle

Network Diagram - see first Page of Table 39

		TP	NT	TP	TP		TP
		◇1		◇1	◇1		◇1
Liverpool Lime Street 10	d				21 52		
Liverpool South Parkway 7 ✈	d				22 02		
Warrington Central	d				22 15		
Birchwood	d				22 20		
Newton-le-Willows	d						
Manchester Oxford Road	d				22 37		
Manchester Airport ✈	d			21 20			23 20
Manchester Piccadilly 10 ⛴	a			21 37	22 39		23 37
	d			21 42	22 42		23 42
Manchester Victoria ⛴	a						
	d						
Ashton-under-Lyne	d						
Stalybridge	a				22 54		
	d				22 54		
Mossley (Grtr Manchester)	d						
Greenfield	d						
Marsden	d		21 47				
Slaithwaite	d		21 51				
Huddersfield	a		21 57	22 11	23 12		00 11
	d		21 57	22 12	23 12		00 12
Deighton	d		22 01				
Mirfield	d		22 06				
Ravensthorpe	d		22 09				
Dewsbury	a		22 13	22 21	23 22		
	d		22 13	22 22	23 22		
Batley	d		22 16				
Morley	d		22 22				
Cottingley	d		22 26				
Leeds 10	a		22 34	22 37	23 39		00 51
	d	22 22		22 40	23 42		00 54
Garforth	d						
South Milford	a	22 34					
Selby	a	22 44					
Howden	a						
Brough	a	23 02					
Hull	a	23 19					
York 8	a			23 11	00 26		01 22
	d						
Malton	d						
Seamer	a						
Scarborough	a						
Thirsk	a						
Northallerton	a						
Darlington 7	a						
Yarm	d						
Thornaby	a						
Middlesbrough	a						
Durham	a						
Chester-le-Street	a						
Newcastle 8 ⛴	a						

Table 39

Sundays

19 February to 25 March

Liverpool, Manchester Airport and Manchester - Huddersfield, Leeds, Hull, York, Scarborough, Middlesbrough and Newcastle

Network Diagram - see first Page of Table 39

		TP	TP	TP	TP	TP	TP	NT	NT	TP	NT		TP	TP	TP	NT	NT	TP	TP	TP	TP	TP		NT	NT
		◇1	◇1	◇1	◇1	◇1	◇1	🚌		◇1			◇1	◇1	◇1			◇1	◇1	◇1	◇1	◇1			
Liverpool Lime Street 10	d		22p30												08 22					09 22		10 22			
Liverpool South Parkway 7 ✈	d		22p40												08 32					09 32		10 32			
Warrington Central	d		22p53												08 45					09 45		10 45			
Birchwood	d		22p58												08 50					09 50		10 50			
Newton-le-Willows	d																								
Manchester Oxford Road	d		23p17												09 10					10 07		11 07			
Manchester Airport ✈	d	22p22		23p24	01 22	04 43	06 24			07 24				07 50					09 03		10 20				
Manchester Piccadilly 10 🚢	a	22p36	23p19	23p39	01 36	04 57	06 38			07 37				08 04	09 11				09 17	10 09	10 37	11 09			
	d	22p42	23p21	23p41	01 42	05 02	06 42			07 42				08 28	09 11				09 27	10 11	10 42	11 11			
Manchester Victoria 🚢	a			23p55																					
	d			23p56							08 43					09 43								10 43	11 43
Ashton-under-Lyne	d										08 53					09 53								10 53	11 53
Stalybridge	a	22p55	23p34				06 53			07 54	08 58			08 41	09 24	09 59				10 24		11 24		10 59	11 59
	d	22p55	23p34				06 54			07 54				08 41	09 24					10 24		11 24			
Mossley (Grtr Manchester)	d																								
Greenfield	d																								
Marsden	d																								
Slaithwaite	d																								
Huddersfield	a	23p15	23p52	00 25	02 11	05 31	07 11			08 11				08 59	09 42				09 55	10 42	11 11	11 42			
	d	23p16	23p53	00 26	02 12	05 32	07 12	07 23	07 51	08 12				09 02	09 43		09 51		10 12	10 43	11 12	11 43			
Deighton	d							07 32	07 54								09 54								
Mirfield	d							07 42	07 59								09 59								
Ravensthorpe	d							07 47	08 02								10 02								
Dewsbury	a	23p25		00s35			07 21	07 55	08 06	08 21				09 11			10 06		10 22		11 21				
	d	23p26					07 22	07 55	08 06	08 22				09 11			10 06		10 22		11 22				
Batley	d							08 03	08 09								10 09								
Morley	d							08 15	08 15								10 15								
Cottingley	d							08 25	08 19								10 19								
Leeds 10	a	23p41	00 14	00 50	02 33	05 53	07 36	08 40	08 27	08 37				09 27	10 07		10 27		10 37	11 04	11 37	12 04			
	d	23p42	00 15	00 54	02 35	05 55	07 40			08 40			09 12	09 40	10 22				10 40	11 12	11 40	12 12			
Garforth	d																								
South Milford	a														10 34										
Selby	a														10 44										
Howden	a																								
Brough	a														11 03										
Hull	a														11 18										
York 8	a	00 09	00 42	01 32	03 14	06 34	08 20			09 07			09 37	10 07					11 07	11 39	12 05	12 39			
	d						08 24			09 10			09 40	10 13				10 42	11 10	11 44	12 08	12 42			
Malton	d												10 04							12 08					
Seamer	a												10 20							12 25					
Scarborough	a												10 30							12 34					
Thirsk	a						08 40											10 59				12 59			
Northallerton	a						08 48			09 30				10 35				11 07	11 30		12 28	13 07			
Darlington 7	a						08 59			09 42				10 46					11 42		12 40				
Yarm	d																	11 21				13 22			
Thornaby	a						09 19											11 29				13 30			
Middlesbrough	a						09 28											11 39				13 40			
Durham	a									09 59				11 08					11 59		12 57				
Chester-le-Street	a																								
Newcastle 8 🚢	a									10 18				11 24					12 15		13 12				

Table 39

Sundays

19 February to 25 March

Liverpool, Manchester Airport and Manchester - Huddersfield, Leeds, Hull, York, Scarborough, Middlesbrough and Newcastle

Network Diagram - see first Page of Table 39

		NT	TP	TP	TP	TP	NT	TP	TP		NT	NT	TP	TP	TP	TP	NT	TP	TP	NT		NT	TP	TP	TP
			◇1	◇1	◇1	◇1		◇1	◇1				◇1	◇1	◇1	◇1		◇1	◇1				◇1	◇1	◇1
Liverpool Lime Street 10	d				11 22				12 22						13 22				14 22						15 22
Liverpool South Parkway 7 ✈	d				11 32				12 32						13 32				14 32						15 32
Warrington Central	d				11 45				12 45						13 45				14 45						15 45
Birchwood	d				11 50				12 50						13 50				14 50						15 50
Newton-le-Willows	d																								
Manchester Oxford Road	d				12 07				13 07						14 07				15 07						16 07
Manchester Airport ✈	d		11 20			12 19							13 20			14 20							15 20		
Manchester Piccadilly 10	a		11 35		12 09	12 38			13 09				13 37		14 09	14 37			15 09				15 37		16 09
	d		11 42	12 01	12 11	12 42		13 02	13 11				13 42	14 02	14 11	14 42		15 02	15 11				15 42	16 02	16 11
Manchester Victoria	a																								
	d						12 43				13 43						14 43			15 43					
Ashton-under-Lyne	d						12 53				13 53						14 53			15 53					
Stalybridge	a				12 24		12 59		13 24		13 59				14 24		14 59		15 24	15 59					16 24
	d				12 24				13 24						14 24				15 24						16 24
Mossley (Grtr Manchester)	d																								
Greenfield	d																								
Marsden	d																								
Slaithwaite	d																								
Huddersfield	a		12 11	12 32	12 42	13 11		13 32	13 42				14 11	14 32	14 42	15 11		15 32	15 42				16 11	16 32	16 42
	d	11 58	12 12	12 33	12 43	13 12		13 33	13 43			13 58	14 12	14 33	14 43	15 12		15 33	15 43			15 58	16 12	16 33	16 43
Deighton	d	12 01										14 01										16 01			
Mirfield	d	12 06										14 06										16 06			
Ravensthorpe	d	12 09										14 09										16 09			
Dewsbury	a	12 13	12 21			13 21						14 13	14 21			15 21						16 13	16 22		
	d	12 13	12 22			13 22						14 13	14 22			15 22						16 13	16 22		
Batley	d	12 16										14 16										16 16			
Morley	d	12 22										14 22										16 22			
Cottingley	d	12 26										14 26										16 26			
Leeds 10	a	12 34	12 37	12 54	13 04	13 37		13 54	14 04			14 34	14 37	14 53	15 04	15 37		15 54	16 04			16 34	16 37	16 54	17 04
	d		12 40	13 01	13 12	13 40		13 57	14 12				14 40	15 01	15 12	15 40		15 57	16 12				16 40	17 01	17 12
Garforth	d																								
South Milford	a			13 13										15 14										17 14	
Selby	a			13 23										15 23										17 23	
Howden	a																								
Brough	a			13 41										15 41										17 41	
Hull	a			13 59										15 59										17 59	
York 8	a		13 07		13 39	14 05		14 24	14 38				15 07		15 35	16 05		16 22	16 38				17 07		17 39
	d		13 10		13 43	14 10			14 50				15 10		15 43	16 10			16 42				17 10		17 43
Malton	d				14 07										16 07										18 07
Seamer	a				14 24										16 24										18 24
Scarborough	a				14 33										16 33										18 33
Thirsk	a								15 12										17 04						
Northallerton	a		13 30			14 30			15 20				15 30			16 30			17 16				17 30		
Darlington 7	a		13 42			14 42							15 42			16 42							17 42		
Yarm	d								15 35										17 32						
Thornaby	a								15 44										17 41						
Middlesbrough	a								15 52										17 50						
Durham	a		13 59			14 59							16 00			16 59							17 59		
Chester-le-Street	a		14 05										16 06										18 05		
Newcastle 8	a		14 17			15 15							16 18			17 14							18 18		

Table 39

Sundays

19 February to 25 March

Liverpool, Manchester Airport and Manchester - Huddersfield, Leeds, Hull, York, Scarborough, Middlesbrough and Newcastle

Network Diagram - see first Page of Table 39

		TP	NT	TP	TP	NT	NT	TP	TP	TP	TP	NT	TP	TP	NT	NT	TP	TP	TP	TP	TP	NT	NT
		◇1		◇1	◇1			◇1	◇1	◇1	◇1		◇1	◇1			◇1	◇1	◇1	◇1	◇1		
Liverpool Lime Street 10	d				16 22					17 22				18 22					19 22		20 22		
Liverpool South Parkway 7 ✈	d				16 32					17 32				18 32					19 32		20 32		
Warrington Central	d				16 45					17 45				18 45					19 45		20 45		
Birchwood	d				16 50					17 50				18 50					19 50		20 50		
Newton-le-Willows	d																						
Manchester Oxford Road	d				17 07					18 07				19 07					20 07		21 07		
Manchester Airport ✈	d	16 20						17 20			18 20						19 20			20 20			
Manchester Piccadilly 10	a	16 37			17 09			17 37		18 09	18 37			19 09			19 37		20 09	20 37	21 09		
	d	16 42		17 02	17 11			17 42	18 02	18 11	18 42		19 02	19 11			19 42	20 06	20 11	20 42	21 11		
Manchester Victoria	a																						
	d		16 43			17 43						18 43			19 43							20 43	21 43
Ashton-under-Lyne	d		16 53			17 53						18 53			19 53							20 53	21 53
Stalybridge	a		16 59		17 24	17 59				18 24		18 59		19 24	19 59				20 24		21 24	20 59	21 57
	d				17 24					18 24				19 24					20 24		21 24		
Mossley (Grtr Manchester)	d																						
Greenfield	d																						
Marsden	d																						
Slaithwaite	d																						
Huddersfield	a	17 11		17 32	17 42			18 11	18 32	18 42	19 11		19 32	19 42			20 11	20 36	20 42	21 11	21 42		
	d	17 12		17 33	17 43		17 58	18 12	18 33	18 43	19 12		19 33	19 43		19 58	20 12	20 37	20 43	21 12	21 43		
Deighton	d						18 01									20 01							
Mirfield	d						18 06									20 06							
Ravensthorpe	d						18 09									20 09							
Dewsbury	a	17 21					18 13	18 21			19 21					20 13	20 21			21 21			
	d	17 22					18 13	18 22			19 22					20 13	20 22			21 22			
Batley	d						18 16									20 16							
Morley	d						18 22									20 22							
Cottingley	d						18 26									20 26							
Leeds 10	a	17 37		17 54	18 04		18 34	18 37	18 54	19 04	19 37		19 54	20 04		20 34	20 37	20 58	21 04	21 37	22 04		
	d	17 40		17 57	18 12			18 40	19 01	19 12	19 40		19 57	20 12			20 40	21 04	21 12	21 40	22 12		
Garforth	d																						
South Milford	a								19 16														
Selby	a								19 28				20 17					21 38					
Howden	a																						
Brough	a								19 48				20 36					21 58					
Hull	a								20 05				20 54					22 12					
York 8	a	18 07		18 23	18 38			19 05		19 38	20 04			20 38			21 05		21 38	22 08	22 40		
	d	18 10			18 42			19 10		19 46	20 10			20 44			21 08			22 10	22 42		
Malton	d									20 10				21 08						22 35			
Seamer	a									20 27				21 25						22 51			
Scarborough	a									20 36				21 34						22 59			
Thirsk	a				18 59						20 26						21 26				23 06		
Northallerton	a	18 30			19 07			19 30			20 34						21 34				23 16		
Darlington 7	a	18 42						19 42									21 45				23 28		
Yarm	d				19 22						20 50												
Thornaby	a				19 30						20 58												
Middlesbrough	a				19 40						21 07												
Durham	a	18 59						19 59									22 02				23 45		
Chester-le-Street	a							20 05															
Newcastle 8	a	19 16						20 18									22 17				00 15		

Table 39

Sundays

19 February to 25 March

Liverpool, Manchester Airport and Manchester - Huddersfield, Leeds, Hull, York, Scarborough, Middlesbrough and Newcastle

Network Diagram - see first Page of Table 39

		TP	NT	TP	TP		TP
		◇1		◇1	◇1		◇1
Liverpool Lime Street 10	d				21 52		
Liverpool South Parkway 7 ✈	d				22 02		
Warrington Central	d				22 15		
Birchwood	d				22 20		
Newton-le-Willows	d						
Manchester Oxford Road	d				22 37		
Manchester Airport ✈	d			21 20			23 20
Manchester Piccadilly 10	a			21 37	22 39		23 37
	d			21 42	22 42		23 42
Manchester Victoria	a						
	d						
Ashton-under-Lyne	d						
Stalybridge	a				22 54		
	d				22 54		
Mossley (Grtr Manchester)	d						
Greenfield	d						
Marsden	d		21 47				
Slaithwaite	d		21 51				
Huddersfield	a		21 57	22 11	23 12		00 11
	d		21 57	22 12	23 12		00 12
Deighton	d		22 01				
Mirfield	d		22 06				
Ravensthorpe	d		22 09				
Dewsbury	a		22 13	22 21	23 22		
	d		22 13	22 22	23 22		
Batley	d		22 16				
Morley	d		22 22				
Cottingley	d		22 26				
Leeds 10	a		22 34	22 37	23 39		00 51
	d	22 22		22 40	23 42		00 54
Garforth	d						
South Milford	a	22 34					
Selby	a	22 44					
Howden	a						
Brough	a	23 02					
Hull	a	23 19					
York 8	a			23 11	00 26		01 22
	d						
Malton	d						
Seamer	a						
Scarborough	a						
Thirsk	a						
Northallerton	a						
Darlington 7	a						
Yarm	d						
Thornaby	a						
Middlesbrough	a						
Durham	a						
Chester-le-Street	a						
Newcastle 8	a						

Table 39

Sundays
from 1 April

Liverpool, Manchester Airport and Manchester - Huddersfield, Leeds, Hull, York, Scarborough, Middlesbrough and Newcastle

Network Diagram - see first Page of Table 39

		TP	TP	TP	TP	NT	TP	NT	TP	TP	TP		TP	NT	NT	TP	TP	TP	TP	NT	TP	TP		NT	TP
		◇1							◇1	◇1	◇1		◇1			◇1	◇1	◇1	◇1		◇1	◇1			◇1
			🚌	🚌	🚌	🚌	🚌	🚌						🚌						🚌				🚌	
Liverpool Lime Street 10	d															08 22					09 22				10 22
Liverpool South Parkway 7 ✈	d																								
Warrington Central	d																								
Birchwood	d																								
Newton-le-Willows	d															08 41					09 40				10 41
Manchester Oxford Road	d																								
Manchester Airport ✈	d	22p22	23p25	01 20	05 05		06 05						07 50						09 03			10 03			
Manchester Piccadilly 10	a	22p36	23p50	01 45	05 30		06 30						08 03						09 19			10 18			
	d	22p42	23p50	01 45	05 30		06 30						08 05						09 20			10 21			
Manchester Victoria	a												08 20			09 03			09 35		10 03	10 35			11 03
	d							07 43					08 23	08 43		09 05			09 38	09 43	10 05	10 38		10 43	11 05
Ashton-under-Lyne	d							08 07						09 07						10 07				11 07	
Stalybridge	a	22p55					06 55	08 17						09 17						10 17				11 17	
	d	22p55					06 55							09 17						10 17				11 17	
Mossley (Grtr Manchester)	d													09 25						10 25				11 25	
Greenfield	d													09 31						10 31				11 31	
Marsden	d													09 51						10 51				11 51	
Slaithwaite	d													09 56						10 56				11 56	
Huddersfield	a	23p15	00 50	02 45	06 30		07 40						09 10	10 12		09 51				11 12	10 54			12 12	
	d	23p16	00 50	02 45	06 30	07 23	07 40						09 12		09 44	09 53					10 56				
Deighton	d					07 32									09 47										
Mirfield	d					07 42									09 52										
Ravensthorpe	d					07 47									09 55										
Dewsbury	a	23p25			06 55	07 55	08 05						09 22		09 59				10 21			11 21			11 58
	d	23p26			06 55	07 55	08 05						09 22		10 03				10 23			11 22			11 59
Batley	d					08 03									10 06										
Morley	d					08 15									10 12										
Cottingley	d					08 25									10 15										
Leeds 10	a	23p41	01 25	03 20	07 20	08 40	08 30						09 37		10 23	10 14			10 38		11 15	11 37			12 12
	d	23p42	01 25	03 20	07 20					08 40	09 12		09 40			10 17	10 24		10 40		11 18	11 40			12 12
Garforth	d																								
South Milford	a																10 36								
Selby	a																10 46								
Howden	a																								
Brough	a																11 04								
Hull	a																11 21								
York 8	a	00 09	02 15	04 10	08 10					09 08	09 37		10 04			10 41			11 08		11 39	12 05			12 39
	d								08 21	09 10	09 40		10 06			10 42		10 42	11 10		11 44	12 08			12 42
Malton	d										10 04										12 08				
Seamer	a										10 20										12 25				
Scarborough	a										10 30										12 34				
Thirsk	a								08 37							10 59		10 59							12 59
Northallerton	a								08 45	09 30			10 28			11 07		11 07	11 30			12 28			13 07
Darlington 7	a								08 56	09 42			10 40						11 42			12 40			
Yarm	d															11 21		11 21							13 22
Thornaby	a								09 16							11 29		11 29							13 30
Middlesbrough	a								09 25							11 38		11 39							13 40
Durham	a									09 59			11 00						11 59			12 57			
Chester-le-Street	a																								
Newcastle 8	a									10 18			11 17						12 15			13 12			

Table 39

Sundays

from 1 April

Liverpool, Manchester Airport and Manchester - Huddersfield, Leeds, Hull, York, Scarborough, Middlesbrough and Newcastle

Network Diagram - see first Page of Table 39

		NT	TP	NT	TP	TP	TP	NT	TP		TP	NT	TP	NT	TP	TP	TP	NT	TP	TP		NT	TP	NT	TP
			◇1		◇1	◇1	◇1		◇1		◇1		◇1		◇1	◇1	◇1		◇1	◇1			◇1		◇1
				🚌				🚌						🚌				🚌						🚌	
Liverpool Lime Street 10	d					11 22					12 22					13 22				14 22					
Liverpool South Parkway 7 ✈	d																								
Warrington Central	d																								
Birchwood	d																								
Newton-le-Willows	d					11 40					12 41					13 40				14 41					
Manchester Oxford Road	d																								
Manchester Airport ✈	d		11 03				12 03						13 03				14 03						15 03		
Manchester Piccadilly 10	a		11 18				12 18						13 18				14 18						15 18		
	d		11 21				12 21						13 21				14 21						15 21		
Manchester Victoria	a		11 35			12 03	12 35				13 03		13 35			14 03	14 35			15 03			15 35		
	d		11 38	11 43		12 05	12 38	12 43			13 05		13 38	13 43		14 05	14 38	14 43		15 05			15 38	15 43	
Ashton-under-Lyne	d			12 07				13 07						14 07				15 07						16 07	
Stalybridge	a			12 17				13 17						14 17				15 17						16 17	
	d			12 17				13 17						14 17				15 17						16 17	
Mossley (Grtr Manchester)	d			12 25				13 25						14 25				15 25						16 25	
Greenfield	d			12 31				13 31						14 31				15 31						16 31	
Marsden	d			12 51				13 51						14 51				15 51						16 51	
Slaithwaite	d			12 56				13 56						14 56				15 56						16 56	
Huddersfield	a			13 12				14 12						15 12				16 12						17 12	
	d	11 58			12 30				13 30			13 58			14 30				15 30			15 58			16 30
Deighton	d	12 01										14 01										16 01			
Mirfield	d	12 06										14 06										16 06			
Ravensthorpe	d	12 09										14 09										16 09			
Dewsbury	a	12 13	12 21		12 42	12 58	13 21		13 39		13 58	14 13	14 21		14 39	14 58	15 21		15 39	15 58		16 13	16 21		16 39
	d	12 13	12 22		12 43	12 59	13 22		13 40		13 59	14 13	14 22		14 40	14 59	15 22		15 40	15 59		16 13	16 22		16 40
Batley	d	12 16										14 16										16 16			
Morley	d	12 22										14 22										16 22			
Cottingley	d	12 26										14 26										16 26			
Leeds 10	a	12 34	12 37		12 57	13 12	13 37		13 54		14 11	14 34	14 37		14 54	15 12	15 37		15 54	16 12		16 34	16 37		16 55
	d		12 40		13 01	13 12	13 40		13 57		14 12		14 40		15 01	15 12	15 40		15 57	16 12			16 40		17 01
Garforth	d																								
South Milford	a				13 13										15 13										17 14
Selby	a				13 23										15 23										17 23
Howden	a																								
Brough	a				13 41										15 41										17 41
Hull	a				13 59										15 59										17 59
York 8	a		13 07			13 39	14 04		14 24		14 38		15 07			15 37	16 05		16 24	16 38			17 07		
	d		13 10			13 43	14 10				14 50		15 10			15 43	16 10			16 42			17 10		
Malton	d					14 07										16 07									
Seamer	a					14 24										16 24									
Scarborough	a					14 33										16 33									
Thirsk	a										15 12									17 04					
Northallerton	a		13 30				14 30				15 20		15 30				16 30			17 16			17 30		
Darlington 7	a		13 42				14 42						15 42				16 42						17 42		
Yarm	d										15 35									17 32					
Thornaby	a										15 44									17 40					
Middlesbrough	a										15 52									17 50					
Durham	a		13 59				14 59						16 00				16 59						17 59		
Chester-le-Street	a		14 05										16 06										18 05		
Newcastle 8	a		14 17				15 15						16 19				17 14						18 18		

Table 39

Sundays
from 1 April

Liverpool, Manchester Airport and Manchester - Huddersfield, Leeds, Hull, York, Scarborough, Middlesbrough and Newcastle

Network Diagram - see first Page of Table 39

		TP	TP	NT	TP	TP	NT		TP	NT	TP	TP	TP	NT	TP	TP	NT	TP		NT	TP	TP	TP	NT	TP
		◇1	◇1		◇1	◇1			◇1		◇1	◇1	◇1		◇1	◇1		◇1			◇1	◇1	◇1		◇1
				bus						bus				bus						bus				bus	
Liverpool Lime Street 10	d	15 22				16 22						17 22				18 22						19 22			20 22
Liverpool South Parkway 7 ✈	d																								
Warrington Central	d																								
Birchwood	d																								
Newton-le-Willows	d	15 40				16 41						17 41				18 40						19 40			20 40
Manchester Oxford Road	d																								
Manchester Airport ✈	d		16 03						17 03				18 03					19 03					20 03		
Manchester Piccadilly 10	a		16 18						17 18				18 18					19 18					20 18		
	d		16 21						17 21				18 21					19 21					20 21		
Manchester Victoria	a	16 03	16 35			17 03			17 35			18 03	18 35			19 03		19 35				20 03	20 35		21 03
	d	16 05	16 38	16 43		17 05			17 38	17 43		18 05	18 38	18 43		19 05		19 38		19 43		20 05	20 38	20 43	21 05
Ashton-under-Lyne	d			17 07						18 07				19 07						20 07				21 07	
Stalybridge	a			17 17						18 17				19 17						20 17				21 17	
	d			17 17						18 17				19 17						20 17				21 17	
Mossley (Grtr Manchester)	d			17 25						18 25				19 25						20 25				21 25	
Greenfield	d			17 31						18 31				19 31						20 31				21 31	
Marsden	d			17 51						18 51				19 51						20 51				21 51	
Slaithwaite	d			17 56						18 56				19 56						20 56				21 56	
Huddersfield	a			18 12						19 12				20 12						21 12				22 12	
	d				17 30		17 58				18 30				19 30		19 58				20 33				
Deighton	d						18 01										20 01								
Mirfield	d						18 06										20 06								
Ravensthorpe	d						18 09										20 09								
Dewsbury	a	16 58	17 21		17 39	17 58	18 13		18 21		18 39	18 58	19 21		19 39	19 58	20 13	20 21			20 42	20 56	21 22		21 58
	d	16 59	17 22		17 40	17 59	18 13		18 22		18 40	18 59	19 22		19 40	19 59	20 13	20 22			20 43	20 57	21 22		21 59
Batley	d						18 16										20 16								
Morley	d						18 22										20 22								
Cottingley	d						18 26										20 26								
Leeds 10	a	17 12	17 37		17 54	18 12	18 34		18 37		18 55	19 12	19 37		19 55	20 12	20 34	20 37			20 58	21 12	21 37		22 12
	d	17 12	17 40		17 57	18 12			18 40		19 01	19 12	19 40		19 57	20 12		20 40			21 04	21 12	21 40		22 12
Garforth	d																								
South Milford	a										19 16														
Selby	a										19 29				20 17						21 38				
Howden	a																								
Brough	a										19 51				20 36						21 58				
Hull	a										20 05				20 54						22 12				
York 8	a	17 40	18 07		18 24	18 38			19 05			19 36	20 04			20 38		21 05				21 38	22 08		22 40
	d	17 43	18 10			18 42			19 10			19 46	20 10			20 44		21 08					22 10		22 42
Malton	d	18 07										20 10				21 08							22 35		
Seamer	a	18 24										20 27				21 25							22 51		
Scarborough	a	18 33										20 36				21 34							22 59		
Thirsk	a					18 58							20 26					21 26							23 05
Northallerton	a		18 30			19 07			19 30				20 34					21 34							23 15
Darlington 7	a		18 42						19 42									21 45							23 28
Yarm	d					19 22							20 50												
Thornaby	a					19 30							20 58												
Middlesbrough	a					19 40							21 07												
Durham	a		18 59						19 59									22 02							23 45
Chester-le-Street	a								20 05																
Newcastle 8	a		19 16						20 18									22 17							00 15

Table 39

Sundays
from 1 April

Liverpool, Manchester Airport and Manchester - Huddersfield, Leeds, Hull, York, Scarborough, Middlesbrough and Newcastle

Network Diagram - see first Page of Table 39

		TP	NT	TP	NT		TP	TP
		◇1		◇1			◇1	◇1
					🚌			
Liverpool Lime Street 10	d						21 52	
Liverpool South Parkway 7 ✈	d							
Warrington Central	d							
Birchwood	d							
Newton-le-Willows	d						22 09	
Manchester Oxford Road	d							
Manchester Airport ✈	d			21 03				23 22
Manchester Piccadilly 10 ⛴	a			21 18				23 35
	d			21 21				23 39
Manchester Victoria ⛴	a			21 35			22 29	23 52
	d			21 38	21 43		22 38	23 55
Ashton-under-Lyne	d				22 07			
Stalybridge	a				22 17			
	d							
Mossley (Grtr Manchester)	d							
Greenfield	d							
Marsden	d		21 47					
Slaithwaite	d		21 51					
Huddersfield	a		21 57	22 23			23 23	00 40
	d		21 57	22 26			23 26	00 43
Deighton	d		22 01					
Mirfield	d		22 06					
Ravensthorpe	d		22 09					
Dewsbury	a		22 13	22 35			23 35	
	d		22 13	22 35			23 35	
Batley	d		22 16					
Morley	d		22 22					
Cottingley	d		22 26					
Leeds 10	a		22 34	22 50			23 50	01 04
	d	22 22		22 53			23 53	01 06
Garforth	d							
South Milford	a	22 34						
Selby	a	22 44						
Howden	a							
Brough	a	23 02						
Hull	a	23 19						
York 8	a			23 28			00 22	01 34
	d							
Malton	d							
Seamer	a							
Scarborough	a							
Thirsk	a							
Northallerton	a							
Darlington 7	a							
Yarm	d							
Thornaby	a							
Middlesbrough	a							
Durham	a							
Chester-le-Street	a							
Newcastle 8 ⛴	a							

Table 40

Mondays to Fridays

York and Selby - Leeds

Miles	Miles			GR MX R 1 ⊐P	TP MO ◇1	TP MX ◇1	TP MO ◇1	TP MX ◇1	TP MX ◇1	TP MO ◇1	TP ◇1	NT			TP ◇1	NT	TP ◇1 ⊥	XC ◇1 ⊥	TP ◇1 ⊥	NT	TP ◇1 ⊥	TP ◇1 ⊥		NT	TP ◇1 ⊥
0	—	**York 8**	33 d	00 17	01 38	01 38	02 47	02 52	04 00	04 23	05 26	05 40			05 57	06 13	06 28	06 32			06 55			07 06	07 26
8¾	—	Ulleskelf	33 d																					07 15	
10¾	—	Church Fenton	33 d																					07 21	
—	0	**Selby**	d																06 36	06 42		07 08			
—	7¾	South Milford	d																	06 51					
15¾	11	Micklefield	d									05 59				06 28				06 58				07 28	
17½	12¾	East Garforth	d									06 03				06 32				07 02				07 32	
18	13¼	Garforth	d									06 05			06 12	06 35				07 04	07 10	07 24		07 35	
21	16¼	Cross Gates	d									06 10				06 40				07 09				07 40	07 44
25½	20¾	**Leeds 10**	a	00 50	02 04	02 19	03 13	03 33	04 42	04 49	05 52	06 21			06 22	06 49	06 52	06 55	07 00	07 19	07 20	07 35		07 49	07 52
—	—	Bradford Interchange	37 a													07 11				07 43				08 09	

		NT		TP ◇1 ⊥	XC ◇1 ⊥	NT	NT	TP ◇1 ⊥		TP ◇1 ⊥	NT	TP ◇1 ⊥	NT	TP ◇1 ⊥		XC ◇1 ⊥	NT	TP ◇1 ⊥		TP ◇1 ⊥	NT	TP ◇1 ⊥	TP ◇1 ⊥	XC ◇1 ⊥	NT
York 8	33 d			07 40	07 44		07 48	07 55			08 12	08 25		08 40		08 44		08 57			09 11	09 28	09 40	09 45	
Ulleskelf	33 d																								
Church Fenton	33 d						08 05														09 23				
Selby	d	07 26				07 43				08 11			08 24				08 43			09 11					09 43
South Milford	d	07 35				07 52							08 34				08 53								09 52
Micklefield	d	07 41				07 57	08 13				08 27		08 41				08 56				09 30				09 58
East Garforth	d	07 46				08 01	08 17				08 31		08 45				09 01				09 34				10 02
Garforth	d	07 48				08 04	08 20	08 12			08 33	08 40	08 48				09 04	09 12			09 37				10 05
Cross Gates	d	07 53				08 10	08 25				08 38		08 52				09 08				09 42				10 10
Leeds 10	a	08 02		08 04	08 08	08 19	08 35	08 22		08 36	08 49	08 52	09 02	09 04		09 08	09 19	09 22		09 36	09 51	09 52	10 04	10 08	10 19
Bradford Interchange	37 a	08 28				08 43					09 12						09 43				10 12				10 43

		TP ◇1 ⊥	TP ◇1 ⊥	NT			TP ◇1 ⊥	TP ◇1 ⊥	XC ◇1 ⊥	NT	TP ◇1 ⊥		NT	TP ◇1 ⊥		NT	TP ◇1 ⊥	TP ◇1 ⊥	XC ◇1 ⊥	NT		TP ◇1 ⊥	TP ◇1 ⊥	NT	
York 8	33 d	09 57		10 11			10 27	10 40	10 44		10 57		11 05			11 09	11 26	11 40	11 45			11 57		12 13	
Ulleskelf	33 d												11 15												
Church Fenton	33 d												11a19			11 21									
Selby	d		10 11							10 42				11 11						11 43			12 11		
South Milford	d									10 52										11 52					
Micklefield	d			10 29						10 57						11 29				11 57				12 28	
East Garforth	d			10 33						11 02						11 33				12 02				12 32	
Garforth	d	10 12		10 35						11 05	11 12					11 35				12 05		12 12		12 35	
Cross Gates	d			10 40						11 09						11 40				12 09				12 40	
Leeds 10	a	10 22	10 36	10 49			10 52	11 04	11 07	11 19	11 22			11 36		11 49	11 52	12 04	12 08	12 19		12 22	12 36	12 49	
Bradford Interchange	37 a			11 11						11 43						12 11				12 43				13 12	

		TP ◇1 ⊥	TP ◇1 ⊥	XC ◇1 ⊥	NT		TP ◇1 ⊥	TP ◇1 ⊥	NT	TP ◇1 ⊥		TP ◇1 ⊥	XC ◇1 ⊥	NT		TP ◇1 ⊥	TP ◇1 ⊥	NT	TP ◇1 ⊥	TP ◇1 ⊥		XC ◇1 ⊥	NT		TP ◇1 ⊥
York 8	33 d	12 26	12 40	12 44			12 57		13 09	13 24		13 40	13 44			13 57		14 13	14 26	14 40		14 44			14 57
Ulleskelf	33 d																								
Church Fenton	33 d								13 21																
Selby	d				12 43			13 11						13 43			14 11						14 43		
South Milford	d				12 53									13 52									14 52		
Micklefield	d				12 58				13 29					13 57				14 29					14 56		
East Garforth	d				13 02				13 33					14 02				14 33					15 00		
Garforth	d				13 05		13 12		13 35					14 05		14 12		14 35					15 03		15 12
Cross Gates	d				13 10				13 40					14 09				14 40					15 08		
Leeds 10	a	12 52	13 04	13 07	13 19		13 22	13 35	13 49	13 52		14 04	14 07	14 20		14 22	14 36	14 49	14 52	15 04		15 07	15 19		15 23
Bradford Interchange	37 a				13 43				14 12					14 43				15 12					15 43		

		NT	TP ◇1 ⊥	NT	TP ◇1 ⊥	TP ◇1 ⊥		XC ◇1 ⊥	NT	TP FX ◇1 ⊥	TP FO ◇1 ⊥	XC ◇1 ⊥	TP FO ◇1 ⊥	TP FX ◇1 ⊥	NT			TP FO	TP ◇1 ⊥	TP ◇1 ⊥	XC ◇1 ⊥	NT	TP ◇1 ⊥	TP ◇1 ⊥	NT
York 8	33 d	15 01		15 08	15 26	15 40		15 44		15 57	15 57	16 04			16 08			16 13	16 26	16 40	16 44		16 57		17 13
Ulleskelf	33 d	15 11																							
Church Fenton	33 d	15a15		15 20											16 20			16 38							
Selby	d		15 11						15 41				16 11	16 11								16 43		17 11	
South Milford	d								15 52													16 53			
Micklefield	d			15 29					15 55						16 28							16 58			17 28
East Garforth	d			15 33					15 59						16 32							17 02			17 32
Garforth	d			15 35					16 02	16 12			16 22		16 35							17 05	17 12		17 35
Cross Gates	d			15 40					16 07						16 40							17 10			17 40
Leeds 10	a		15 36	15 49	15 52	16 04		16 07	16 19	16 22	16 22	16 32	16 36	16 36	16 49			16 59	16 52	17 04	17 06	17 19	17 22	17 36	17 49
Bradford Interchange	37 a			16 10					16 43						17 10										18 10

York and Selby - Leeds

		NT		TP	TP	TP	XC	NT		TP	NT	NT		TP	TP	TP	XC	NT	NT	NT	TP	TP		TP	XC
				◇1 ⚲	◇1	◇1 ⚲	◇1 ⚲			◇1 ⚲				◇1 ⚲	◇1 ⚲	◇1	◇1 ⚲				◇1	◇1		◇1	◇1 ⚲
York 8	33 d	17 19		17 26		17 40	17 44			17 57		18 05		18 12		18 40	18 45			19 04	19 08			19 40	19 44
Ulleskelf	33 d											18 15													
Church Fenton	33 d	17 30										18 22								19 20					
Selby	d	17a45			17 32			17 38			18 00				18 29			18 46	19 00			19 30			
South Milford	d							17 49										18 52							
Micklefield	d							17 56				18 30						18 58		19 28					
East Garforth	d							18 01				18 34						19 02		19 32					
Garforth	d							18 03		18 12	18 18	18 36						19 04	19 15	19 34	19 22				
Cross Gates	d							18 08				18 41						19 10		19 39					
Leeds 10	a			17 52	17 58	18 04	18 07	18 19		18 22	18 32	18 49		18 37	18 52	19 04	19 08	19 20	19 27	19 48	19 37	19 56		20 04	20 08
Bradford Interchange	37 a							18 43			18 58	19 10						19 44							

		TP	NT		TP	XC	TP	TP		TP	NT	TP	TP	NT	NT	TP	NT								
							FO	FX		FX					FO										
		◇1			◇1	◇1 ⚲	◇1	◇1		◇1		◇1	◇1			◇1									
															A										
York 8	33 d	20 10	20 13		20 40	20 44		21 14			21 22	21 46		22 14	22 14	23 06	23 13								
Ulleskelf	33 d										21 31														
Church Fenton	33 d										21 33						23 28								
Selby	d						21 06			21 16			22 07												
South Milford	d						21 16			21 26			22 16												
Micklefield	d		20 27								21 41			22 29	22 28		23 35								
East Garforth	d		20 31								21 45			22 34	22 32		23 39								
Garforth	d		20 34								21 47			22 36	22 34		23 42								
Cross Gates	d		20 39								21 52			22 40	22 39		23 47								
Leeds 10	a	20 35	20 48		21 04	21 08	21 35	21 37		21 44	22 01	22 07	22 35	22 52	22 56	23 33	23 56								
Bradford Interchange	37 a		21 10																						

Saturdays

		GR	TP	TP	TP	TP	TP		NT	XC		TP	TP	NT	TP		TP	NT	TP			TP	XC	NT	TP
		1 ⊓P	◇1	◇1	◇1	◇1	◇1			◇1 ⚲		◇1	◇1 ⚲		◇1		◇1		◇1			◇1 ⚲	◇1 ⚲		◇1 ⚲
York 8	33 d	00 17	01 52	02 40	03 52	05 26	05 57		06 13	06 17		06 28			06 55			07 06	07 26			07 40	07 44		07 53
Ulleskelf	33 d																	07 15							
Church Fenton	33 d																	07 21							
Selby	d												06 36	06 42			07 08							07 42	
South Milford	d													06 51										07 52	
Micklefield	d								06 28					06 58				07 28						07 57	
East Garforth	d								06 32					07 02				07 32						08 02	
Garforth	d						06 12		06 35					07 04	07 10		07 24	07 35						08 07	08 12
Cross Gates	d								06 40					07 09				07 40	07 44					08 10	
Leeds 10	a	00 50	02 18	03 06	04 34	05 52	06 22		06 49	06 57		06 52	07 00	07 19	07 20		07 35	07 49	07 52			08 04	08 08	08 19	08 22
Bradford Interchange	37 a								07 11					07 43				08 09						08 43	

		TP	NT	TP	TP			XC	NT	TP	TP	NT	TP	TP	XC	NT			TP	TP	NT	TP	TP		XC
		◇1 ⚲		◇1 ⚲	◇1 ⚲			◇1 ⚲		◇1 ⚲	◇1 ⚲		◇1 ⚲	◇1	◇1 ⚲				◇1 ⚲	◇1		◇1 ⚲	◇1 ⚲		◇1 ⚲
York 8	33 d		08 09	08 25	08 40			08 44		08 57		09 11	09 25	09 40	09 46				09 57		10 11	10 27	10 40		10 45
Ulleskelf	33 d																								
Church Fenton	33 d		08 21									09 23													
Selby	d	08 11							08 43		09 11					09 43				10 11					
South Milford	d								08 53							09 53									
Micklefield	d		08 26						08 58			09 30				09 58					10 29				
East Garforth	d		08 30						09 02			09 34				10 02					10 33				
Garforth	d		08 34	08 40					09 05	09 12		09 37				10 05			10 12		10 35				
Cross Gates	d		08 39						09 10			09 42				10 10					10 41				
Leeds 10	a	08 36	08 49	08 52	09 04			09 07	09 19	09 22	09 36	09 51	09 53	10 04	10 09	10 19			10 22	10 36	10 49	10 52	11 04		11 08
Bradford Interchange	37 a		09 12						09 43			10 11				10 43					11 12				

		NT		TP	NT	TP	NT	TP	TP	XC	NT			TP	TP	NT	TP	TP	XC	NT		TP		TP	NT
				◇1 ⚲		◇1		◇1 ⚲	◇1 ⚲	◇1 ⚲				◇1 ⚲	◇1 ⚲		◇1 ⚲	◇1	◇1 ⚲			◇1 ⚲		◇1 ⚲	
York 8	33 d			10 57	11 05		11 09	11 26	11 40	11 45				11 57		12 13	12 26	12 40	12 45			12 57			13 09
Ulleskelf	33 d				11 15																				
Church Fenton	33 d				11a19		11 21																		13 21
Selby	d	10 42				11 11					11 43				12 11					12 44				13 11	
South Milford	d	10 52									11 53									12 56					
Micklefield	d	10 56					11 29				11 58					12 28				12 58					13 29
East Garforth	d	11 00					11 33				12 02					12 32				13 03					13 33
Garforth	d	11 03		11 12			11 35				12 05			12 12		12 35				13 06		13 12			13 35
Cross Gates	d	11 08					11 40				12 10					12 40				13 10					13 40
Leeds 10	a	11 19		11 22		11 36	11 49	11 53	12 04	12 07	12 19			12 22	12 36	12 49	12 52	13 04	13 08	13 20		13 22		13 36	13 49
Bradford Interchange	37 a	11 43					12 12				12 43					13 12				13 43					14 12

A from 16 Dec

Table 40

Saturdays

York and Selby - Leeds

		TP	TP	XC	NT		TP	TP		NT	TP	TP	XC	NT		TP	NT	TP		NT	TP	TP	XC	NT	TP
		◇1 🚲	◇1 🚲	◇1 🚲			◇1 🚲	◇1			◇1 🚲	◇1 🚲	◇1 🚲			◇1 🚲		◇1			◇1 🚲	◇1 🚲	◇1 🚲		◇1 🚲
York 8	33 d	13 24	13 40	13 44			13 57			14 13	14 26	14 40	14 44			14 57	15 01			15 09	15 26	15 40	15 45		15 57
Ulleskelf	33 d																15 11								
Church Fenton	33 d																15a15			15 21					
Selby	d				13 43			14 11						14 43				15 11						15 41	
South Milford	d				13 53									14 54										15 52	
Micklefield	d				13 58					14 29				14 57						15 29				15 56	
East Garforth	d				14 02					14 33				15 02						15 33				16 01	
Garforth	d				14 05		14 12			14 35				15 05		15 12				15 35				16 03	16 12
Cross Gates	d				14 10					14 40				15 09						15 40				16 08	
Leeds 10	a	13 52	14 04	14 08	14 19		14 22	14 35		14 49	14 52	15 04	15 06	15 19		15 22		15 36		15 49	15 53	16 04	16 07	16 18	16 22
Bradford Interchange	37 a				14 43					15 12				15 43						16 10				16 43	

		XC	TP	NT			TP	TP	XC	NT	TP	TP	NT	NT		TP	TP	TP	XC	NT	TP	NT	TP		
		◇1 🚲	◇1 🚲				◇1 🚲	◇1 🚲	◇1 🚲		◇1 🚲	◇1				◇1 🚲	◇1	◇1	◇1 🚲		◇1		◇1		
York 8	33 d	16 06		16 08			16 26	16 40	16 44		16 57		17 12	17 19		17 26		17 40	17 44		17 57	18 05	18 12		
Ulleskelf	33 d																					18 15			
Church Fenton	33 d			16 20										17 30								18 22			
Selby	d		16 11							16 43		17 11		17a45			17 32			17 39					
South Milford	d									16 53										17 49					
Micklefield	d			16 28						16 58			17 29							17 56		18 30			
East Garforth	d			16 32						17 02			17 33							18 01		18 34			
Garforth	d			16 35						17 05	17 12		17 36							18 04	18 12	18 36			
Cross Gates	d			16 40						17 10			17 41							18 08		18 41			
Leeds 10	a	16 32	16 36	16 49			16 52	17 04	17 07	17 19	17 22	17 36	17 49			17 52	17 58	18 04	18 08	18 18	18 22	18 49	18 37		
Bradford Interchange	37 a			17 10						17 43			18 09							18 43		19 10			

		TP	TP	XC	NT	NT	NT	TP	TP	TP		XC		TP	NT	TP	TP	XC	TP	NT		NT	TP	TP	
		◇1	◇1	◇1 🚲				◇1	◇1	◇1		◇1 🚲		◇1		◇1	◇1	◇1 🚲	◇1	A		B	◇1	◇1	
York 8	33 d		18 40	18 44			19 04	19 08		19 40		19 44		20 10	20 13		20 40	20 45	21 14	21 18		21 18	21 46		
Ulleskelf	33 d																			21 27		21 27			
Church Fenton	33 d						19 20													21 33		21 33			
Selby	d	18 29			18 46	18 55			19 30							20 27								22 07	
South Milford	d				18 55											20 36								22 16	
Micklefield	d				18 58		19 28								20 27					21 41		21 41			
East Garforth	d				19 02		19 32								20 31					21 45		21 45			
Garforth	d				19 05	19 12	19 34	19 22							20 34					21 47		21 47			
Cross Gates	d				19 10		19 39								20 39					21 52		21 52			
Leeds 10	a	18 52	19 04	19 08	19 21	19 25	19 48	19 35	19 56	20 04		20 08		20 35	20 48	20 56	21 04	21 07	21 37	21 57		22 01	22 07	22 35	
Bradford Interchange	37 a				19 44										21 10										

		NT	TP	NT
			◇1	
York 8	33 d	22 13	23 07	23 13
Ulleskelf	33 d			
Church Fenton	33 d			23 28
Selby	d			
South Milford	d			
Micklefield	d	22 28		23 35
East Garforth	d	22 32		23 39
Garforth	d	22 34		23 42
Cross Gates	d	22 39		23 47
Leeds 10	a	22 50	23 33	23 56
Bradford Interchange	37 a			

Sundays

until 12 February

		TP	TP	TP	TP	TP	TP	TP	NT	TP		XC	TP	NT	TP	XC		TP	NT	TP		XC	TP	TP	NT
		◇1	◇1	◇1	◇1	◇1	◇1	◇1		◇1		◇1 🚲	◇1		◇1	◇1 🚲		◇1		◇1		◇1 🚲	◇1	◇1	
York 8	33 d	02 44	03 59	05 12	06 12	07 12	08 10	08 45	08 50	09 15		09 28		09 52	10 15	10 28		10 45	10 57	11 15		11 28		11 45	11 52
Ulleskelf	33 d																								
Church Fenton	33 d								09 02					10 04											12 04
Selby	d												09 33										11 29		
South Milford	d												09 42										11 38		
Micklefield	d								09 09					10 12					11 12						12 11
East Garforth	d								09 13					10 16					11 16						12 15
Garforth	d								09 16					10 18					11 18						12 18
Cross Gates	d								09 21					10 23					11 23						12 23
Leeds 10	a	03 10	04 25	05 38	06 38	07 38	08 37	09 08	09 30	09 38		09 54	10 00	10 32	10 38	10 51		11 08	11 32	11 38		11 51	11 56	12 09	12 32
Bradford Interchange	37 a								09 53					10 53					11 53						12 53

A from 31 March

B until 24 March

Table 40

Sundays
until 12 February

York and Selby - Leeds

		TP ◇1	XC ◇1 ⊼	TP ◇1	TP ◇1		NT	TP ◇1	TP ◇1	XC ◇1 ⊼		TP ◇1	NT	TP ◇1	TP ◇1		XC ◇1 ⊼	TP ◇1		NT	TP ◇1	TP ◇1	XC ◇1 ⊼	TP ◇1
York 8 33 d		12 15	12 28		12 45		12 52	13 15		13 40		13 45	13 52	14 15	14 33		14 40	14 45		14 52	15 15		15 40	15 45
Ulleskelf 33 d																								
Church Fenton 33 d													14 04											
Selby d				12 32					13 29													15 29		
South Milford d									13 38													15 38		
Micklefield d							13 07						14 11							15 07				
East Garforth d							13 11						14 15							15 11				
Garforth d							13 13						14 18							15 13				
Cross Gates d							13 18						14 23							15 18				
Leeds 10 a		12 38	12 51	12 56	13 08		13 27	13 38	13 56	14 03		14 08	14 32	14 38	14 56		15 05	15 08		15 27	15 38	15 56	16 03	16 08
Bradford Interchange 37 a							13 53						14 53							15 53				

	NT			TP ◇1	TP ◇1	XC ◇1 ⊼	TP ◇1	NT		TP ◇1	TP ◇1		XC ◇1 ⊼	TP ◇1	NT	NT	TP ◇1	TP ◇1	XC ◇1 ⊼	TP ◇1	NT			TP ◇1
York 8 33 d	15 52			16 15	16 33	16 40	16 45	16 52		17 15			17 40	17 45	17 52	18 10	18 15	18 33	18 40	18 45	18 52			19 15
Ulleskelf 33 d																								
Church Fenton 33 d	16 04														18 04	18a21								
Selby d											17 29													
South Milford d											17 38													
Micklefield d	16 11							17 07							18 11						19 07			
East Garforth d	16 15							17 11							18 15						19 11			
Garforth d	16 18							17 13							18 18						19 13			
Cross Gates d	16 23							17 18							18 23						19 18			
Leeds 10 a	16 32			16 38	16 56	17 06	17 08	17 27		17 38	17 56		18 04	18 08	18 32		18 38	18 57	19 03	19 08	19 27			19 38
Bradford Interchange 37 a	16 53							17 53							18 53						19 53			

	TP ◇1	XC ◇1 ⊼	TP ◇1	NT	TP ◇1	XC ◇1 ⊼	TP ◇1			NT	TP ◇1	TP ◇1		NT	TP ◇1	GR 1 ⊼	TP ◇1							
York 8 33 d		19 40	19 45	19 52	20 15	20 40	20 45			20 57	21 15			21 52	22 12	23 03	23 12							
Ulleskelf 33 d																								
Church Fenton 33 d				20 04										22 04										
Selby d	19 29											21 31												
South Milford d	19 38											21 40												
Micklefield d				20 12						21 12				22 12										
East Garforth d				20 16						21 17				22 16										
Garforth d				20 18						21 19				22 19										
Cross Gates d				20 23						21 24				22 23										
Leeds 10 a	19 54	20 05	20 08	20 32	20 38	21 02	21 08			21 33	21 38	21 59		22 32	22 36	23 34	23 38							
Bradford Interchange 37 a				20 53						21 56														

Sundays
19 February to 25 March

	TP ◇1	TP ◇1	TP ◇1	TP ◇1	TP ◇1	TP ◇1	TP ◇1	NT	TP ◇1		XC ◇1 ⊼	TP ◇1	NT	TP ◇1	XC ◇1 ⊼		TP ◇1	NT	TP ◇1		XC ◇1 ⊼	TP ◇1	TP ◇1	NT
York 8 33 d	02 29	03 44	04 58	05 55	06 55	08 10	08 45	08 50	09 15		09 28		09 52	10 15	10 28		10 45	10 57	11 15		11 28		11 45	11 52
Ulleskelf 33 d																								
Church Fenton 33 d								09 02					10 04											12 04
Selby d												09 33										11 29		
South Milford d												09 42										11 38		
Micklefield d								09 09					10 12					11 12						12 11
East Garforth d								09 13					10 16					11 16						12 15
Garforth d								09 16					10 18					11 18						12 18
Cross Gates d								09 21					10 23					11 23						12 23
Leeds 10 a	03 10	04 25	05 38	06 38	07 36	08 37	09 08	09 30	09 38		09 54	10 00	10 32	10 38	10 51		11 08	11 32	11 38		11 51	11 56	12 09	12 32
Bradford Interchange 37 a								09 53					10 53					11 53						12 53

		TP ◇1	XC ◇1 ⊼	TP ◇1	TP ◇1		NT	TP ◇1	TP ◇1	XC ◇1 ⊼		TP ◇1	NT	TP ◇1	TP ◇1		XC ◇1 ⊼	TP ◇1		NT	TP ◇1	TP ◇1	XC ◇1 ⊼	TP ◇1
York 8 33 d		12 15	12 28		12 45		12 52	13 15		13 40		13 45	13 52	14 15	14 33		14 40	14 45		14 52	15 15		15 40	15 45
Ulleskelf 33 d																								
Church Fenton 33 d													14 04											
Selby d				12 32					13 29													15 29		
South Milford d									13 38													15 38		
Micklefield d							13 07						14 11							15 07				
East Garforth d							13 11						14 15							15 11				
Garforth d							13 13						14 18							15 13				
Cross Gates d							13 18						14 23							15 18				
Leeds 10 a		12 38	12 51	12 56	13 08		13 27	13 38	13 56	14 03		14 08	14 32	14 38	14 56		15 05	15 08		15 27	15 38	15 56	16 03	16 08
Bradford Interchange 37 a							13 53						14 53							15 53				

Table 40

Sundays
19 February to 25 March

York and Selby - Leeds

			NT			TP	TP	XC	TP	NT		TP	TP		XC	TP	NT	NT	TP	TP	XC	TP	NT			TP
						◇1	◇1	◇1	◇1			◇1	◇1		◇1	◇1			◇1	◇1	◇1	◇1				◇1
								🛒							🛒						🛒					
York 8	33	d	15 52			16 15	16 33	16 40	16 45	16 52		17 15			17 40	17 45	17 52	18 10	18 15	18 33	18 40	18 45	18 52			19 15
Ulleskelf	33	d																								
Church Fenton	33	d	16 04														18 04	18a21								
Selby		d											17 29													
South Milford		d											17 38													
Micklefield		d	16 11							17 07							18 11						19 07			
East Garforth		d	16 15							17 11							18 15						19 11			
Garforth		d	16 18							17 13							18 18						19 13			
Cross Gates		d	16 23							17 18							18 23						19 18			
Leeds 10		a	16 32			16 38	16 56	17 06	17 08	17 27		17 38	17 56		18 04	18 08	18 32		18 38	18 57	19 03	19 08	19 27			19 38
Bradford Interchange	37	a	16 53							17 53							18 53						19 53			

			TP	XC	TP	NT	TP	XC	TP			NT	TP	TP		NT	TP	GR	TP							
																		R								
			◇1	◇1	◇1		◇1	◇1	◇1				◇1	◇1			◇1	1	◇1							
				🛒				🛒										🍴								
York 8	33	d		19 40	19 45	19 52	20 15	20 40	20 45			20 57	21 15			21 52	22 12	23 03	23 12							
Ulleskelf	33	d																								
Church Fenton	33	d				20 04										22 04										
Selby		d	19 29											21 31												
South Milford		d	19 38											21 40												
Micklefield		d				20 12						21 12				22 12										
East Garforth		d				20 16						21 17				22 16										
Garforth		d				20 18						21 19				22 19										
Cross Gates		d				20 23						21 24				22 23										
Leeds 10		a	19 54	20 05	20 08	20 32	20 38	21 02	21 08			21 33	21 38	21 59		22 32	22 36	23 34	23 38							
Bradford Interchange	37	a				20 53						21 56														

Sundays
from 1 April

			TP	TP	TP	TP	TP	TP	NT	TP	XC		TP	TP	NT	TP	XC		TP	NT	TP		XC	TP	TP	NT
							◇1	◇1		◇1	◇1		◇1	◇1		◇1	◇1		◇1		◇1		◇1	◇1	◇1	
			🚌	🚌	🚌	🚌																				
											🛒						🛒						🛒			
York 8	33	d	01 30	03 30	04 55	05 55	08 10	08 30	08 50	09 15	09 28			09 45	09 52	10 15	10 28		10 45	10 57	11 15		11 28		11 45	11 52
Ulleskelf	33	d																								
Church Fenton	33	d							09 02						10 04											12 04
Selby		d											09 33											11 29		
South Milford		d											09 42											11 38		
Micklefield		d							09 09						10 12					11 12						12 11
East Garforth		d							09 13						10 16					11 16						12 15
Garforth		d							09 16						10 18					11 18						12 18
Cross Gates		d							09 21						10 23					11 23						12 23
Leeds 10		a	02 20	04 20	05 45	06 45	08 37	08 53	09 30	09 38	09 54		10 00	10 08	10 32	10 38	10 51		11 08	11 32	11 38		11 51	11 56	12 09	12 32
Bradford Interchange	37	a							09 53						10 53					11 53						12 53

				TP	XC	TP	TP		NT	TP	TP	XC		TP	NT	TP	TP		XC	TP		NT	TP	TP	XC	TP
				◇1	◇1	◇1	◇1			◇1	◇1	◇1		◇1		◇1	◇1		◇1	◇1			◇1	◇1	◇1	◇1
					🛒							🛒							🛒						🛒	
York 8	33	d		12 15	12 28		12 45		12 52	13 15		13 40		13 45	13 52	14 15	14 33		14 40	14 45		14 52	15 15		15 40	15 45
Ulleskelf	33	d																								
Church Fenton	33	d													14 04											
Selby		d				12 32					13 29													15 29		
South Milford		d									13 38													15 38		
Micklefield		d							13 07						14 11							15 07				
East Garforth		d							13 11						14 15							15 11				
Garforth		d							13 13						14 18							15 13				
Cross Gates		d							13 18						14 23							15 18				
Leeds 10		a		12 38	12 51	12 56	13 08		13 27	13 37	13 56	14 03		14 08	14 32	14 38	14 56		15 05	15 07		15 27	15 38	15 56	16 03	16 08
Bradford Interchange	37	a							13 53						14 53							15 53				

			NT			TP	TP	XC	TP	NT		TP	TP		XC	TP	NT	NT	TP	TP	XC	TP	NT			TP
						◇1	◇1	◇1	◇1			◇1	◇1		◇1	◇1			◇1	◇1	◇1	◇1				◇1
								🛒							🛒						🛒					
York 8	33	d	15 52			16 15	16 33	16 40	16 45	16 52		17 15			17 40	17 45	17 52	18 10	18 15	18 33	18 40	18 45	18 52			19 15
Ulleskelf	33	d																								
Church Fenton	33	d	16 04														18 04	18a21								
Selby		d											17 29													
South Milford		d											17 38													
Micklefield		d	16 11							17 07							18 11						19 07			
East Garforth		d	16 15							17 11							18 15						19 11			
Garforth		d	16 18							17 13							18 18						19 13			
Cross Gates		d	16 23							17 18							18 23						19 18			
Leeds 10		a	16 32			16 38	16 56	17 06	17 08	17 27		17 38	17 56		18 04	18 08	18 32		18 38	18 57	19 03	19 08	19 27			19 38
Bradford Interchange	37	a	16 53							17 53							18 53						19 53			

Table 40

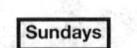

York and Selby - Leeds

			TP	XC	TP	NT	TP	XC	TP		NT	NT	TP	TP		NT	TP	GR	TP
																		R	
			◇1	◇1	◇1		◇1	◇1	◇1				◇1	◇1			◇1	1	◇1
				✠				✠										✠	
York 8	33	d		19 40	19 45	19 52	20 15	20 40	20 45		20 50	20 57	21 15			21 52	22 12	23 03	23 12
Ulleskelf	33	d																	
Church Fenton	33	d				20 04					21a01					22 04			
Selby		d	19 29											21 31					
South Milford		d	19 38											21 40					
Micklefield		d				20 12						21 12				22 12			
East Garforth		d				20 16						21 17				22 16			
Garforth		d				20 18						21 19				22 19			
Cross Gates		d				20 23						21 24				22 23			
Leeds 10		a	19 56	20 05	20 08	20 32	20 38	21 02	21 08			21 33	21 38	21 59		22 32	22 36	23 34	23 38
Bradford Interchange	37	a				20 53						21 56							

Leeds - Selby and York

Miles	Miles			TP MX	TP MO	TP MO	TP MX	TP MO	TP MX	TP MO	TP MX	TP MO		TP	TP	NT	NT	TP	NT	GR	TP	NT		NT	TP
				◇1	◇1	◇1	◇1	◇1	◇1	◇1	◇1	◇1		◇1	◇1			◇1		R 1	◇1				◇1
					A	B		A		B															
																				🍴🛒	🛒				🛒
—	—	Bradford Interchange	37 d																			07 02		07 20	
0	0	**Leeds 10**	d	23p42	23p42	23p53	00 32	00 54	00 54	01 06	02 08	02 34		06 04	06 35	06 38	06 48	06 55	06 58	07 10	07 23	07 29		07 41	07 50
4¼	4¼	Cross Gates	d													06 44			07 05			07 36			
7¼	7¼	Garforth	d													06 50	06 58		07 10			07 41		07 51	08 00
8	8	East Garforth	d													06 52			07 12			07 43			
9	9	Micklefield	d													06 56			07 16			07 47			
—	12¾	South Milford	d																07 20						
—	20¾	**Selby**	a														07 20		07 31		07 43				
14¾	—	Church Fenton	33 a																					07 59	
16½	—	Ulleskelf	33 a																						
25½	—	**York 8**	33 a	00 09	00 26	00 22	01 14	01 22	01 43	01 34	02 45	03 04		06 28	07 01	07 15		07 22		07 34		08 06		08 16	08 21

		XC	NT	TP	NT	TP	TP	NT		TP	XC	TP	NT	TP	NT	TP	NT	TP		XC	TP	NT	TP	TP	NT
		◇1		◇1		◇1	◇1			◇1	◇1	◇1		◇1		◇1		◇1		◇1	◇1		◇1	◇1	
		🛒		🛒		🛒	🛒			🛒	🛒	🛒		🛒		🛒		🛒		🛒	🛒		🛒	🛒	
Bradford Interchange	37 d		07 34		07 50			08 20					08 50				09 20					09 50			10 18
Leeds 10	d	07 57	08 00	08 12	08 15	08 28	08 38	08 41		08 57	09 05	09 12	09 15	09 28	09 33	09 38	09 41	09 57		10 05	10 12	10 15	10 28	10 38	10 41
Cross Gates	d		08 06		08 22			08 48					09 22				09 48					10 22			10 48
Garforth	d		08 12		08 27			08 53		09 05			09 27				09 53	10 05				10 27			10 53
East Garforth	d		08 14		08 29			08 56					09 29				09 56					10 29			10 56
Micklefield	d		08 18		08 33			08 59					09 33				09 59					10 33			10 59
South Milford	d		08 22		08 38								09 38									10 38			
Selby	a		08 36		08 53		08 57						09 53			09 57						10 53		10 57	
Church Fenton	33 a							09 05									10 05								
Ulleskelf	33 a																								
York 8	33 a	08 22		08 35		08 52		09 21		09 23	09 26	09 36		09 52	10 06		10 21	10 23		10 26	10 36		10 52		11 19

		TP	XC	TP		NT	TP	TP	NT	TP	XC	TP	NT	TP		TP	NT	TP	XC	TP	NT	TP	TP	NT	
		◇1	◇1	◇1			◇1	◇1		◇1	◇1	◇1		◇1		◇1		◇1	◇1	◇1		◇1	◇1		
		🛒	🛒	🛒			🛒	🛒		🛒	🛒	🛒		🛒		🛒		🛒	🛒	🛒		🛒	🛒		
Bradford Interchange	37 d					10 50			11 20				11 50				12 19				12 50			13 19	
Leeds 10	d	10 57	11 05	11 12		11 15	11 28	11 38	11 41	11 57	12 05	12 12	12 15	12 28		12 38	12 41	12 57	13 05	13 12	13 15	13 28	13 38	13 42	
Cross Gates	d					11 22			11 48				12 22				12 48				13 22			13 49	
Garforth	d	11 05				11 27			11 53	12 05			12 27				12 53	13 05			13 27			13 54	
East Garforth	d					11 29			11 56				12 29				12 56				13 29			13 57	
Micklefield	d					11 33			11 59				12 33				12 59				13 33			14 00	
South Milford	d					11 38							12 38								13 38				
Selby	a					11 54		11 57					12 50			12 57					13 51		13 57		
Church Fenton	33 a								12 05															14 06	
Ulleskelf	33 a																								
York 8	33 a	11 23	11 26	11 36			11 52		12 21	12 23	12 26	12 36		12 52			13 19	13 23	13 26	13 36		13 52		14 22	

		TP	XC	TP	NT	TP	TP	NT	TP	XC		TP	NT	TP FX	TP FO	TP	NT	TP	XC	TP		NT	TP	TP	NT
		◇1	◇1	◇1		◇1	◇1		◇1	◇1		◇1		◇1	◇1	◇1		◇1	◇1	◇1			◇1	◇1	
		🛒	🛒	🛒		🛒	🛒		🛒	🛒		🛒		🛒	🛒	🛒		🛒	🛒	🛒			🛒	🛒	
Bradford Interchange	37 d				13 50			14 19					14 50				15 19					15 50			16 19
Leeds 10	d	13 57	14 05	14 12	14 15	14 28	14 38	14 41	14 57	15 05		15 12	15 15	15 28	15 28	15 38	15 41	15 57	16 05	16 12		16 15	16 28	16 38	16 41
Cross Gates	d				14 22			14 48					15 22				15 48					16 22			16 48
Garforth	d	14 05			14 27			14 53	15 05				15 27				15 53	16 05				16 27			16 53
East Garforth	d				14 29			14 56					15 29				15 56					16 30			16 56
Micklefield	d				14 33			14 59					15 33				15 59					16 34			16 59
South Milford	d				14 38								15 38									16 39			
Selby	a				14 51		14 57						15 53			15 57						16 54		17 00	
Church Fenton	33 a																16 05								
Ulleskelf	33 a																								
York 8	33 a	14 23	14 26	14 36		14 52		15 18	15 23	15 26		15 36		15 49	15 52		16 21	16 23	16 28	16 36			16 52		17 20

		TP	XC	TP	NT	TP		NT	TP	NT	NT	TP	XC	TP	NT	TP		XC	TP	NT	TP	XC	TP	NT	TP
		◇1	◇1	◇1		◇1			◇1			◇1	◇1	◇1		◇1		◇1	◇1		◇1	◇1	◇1		◇1
		🛒	🛒	🛒		🛒			🛒			🛒	🛒	🛒		🛒		🛒	🛒		🛒	🛒	🛒		🛒
Bradford Interchange	37 d				16 50					17 19					17 50					18 19				18 52	
Leeds 10	d	16 57	17 07	17 12	17 15	17 24		17 28	17 38	17 41	17 46	17 57	18 06	18 12	18 15	18 28		18 35	18 38	18 41	18 57	19 06	19 12	19 15	19 28
Cross Gates	d			17 18	17 22			17 35		17 48	17 52				18 22					18 48				19 22	
Garforth	d	17 05			17 28	17 34		17 40		17 53	17 57	18 05			18 27					18 53	19 05			19 27	
East Garforth	d				17 30			17 42		17 56	18 00				18 29					18 56				19 29	
Micklefield	d				17 34			17 46		17 59	18 04				18 33					18 59				19 33	
South Milford	d				17 39						18 09				18 38				18 51						
Selby	a				17 51				17 59		18 21				18 49				19 00						
Church Fenton	33 a							17 51												19 05					
Ulleskelf	33 a							17 57																	
York 8	33 a	17 21	17 28	17 37		17 55		18 10		18 18		18 23	18 29	18 36		18 53		19 01		19 21	19 23	19 29	19 36	19 53	19 53

A until 26 March

B from 2 April

Table 40 **Mondays to Fridays**

Leeds - Selby and York

		TP		NT	TP	XC	TP	TP	NT	TP	TP	TP		NT	TP	TP	TP	NT	TP						
		◇1			◇1	◇1	◇1	◇1		◇1	◇1	◇1			◇1	◇1	◇1		◇1						
										FX A	B														
		🛒																							
Bradford Interchange	37 d			19 19					20 19									22 19							
Leeds 10	d	19 38		19 41	19 57	20 08	20 12	20 45	20 48	21 12	21 12	21 42		21 55	22 12	22 22	22 42	23 02	23 42						
Cross Gates	d			19 48					20 55					22 02				23 09							
Garforth	d			19 53	20 05				21 00					22 07				23 14							
East Garforth	d			19 55					21 02					22 10				23 17							
Micklefield	d			19 59					21 06					22 14				23 21							
South Milford	d	19 51								21 24	21 24					22 36									
Selby	a	20 00								21 33	21 34					22 46									
Church Fenton	33 a								21 11									23 27							
Ulleskelf	33 a								21 15																
York 8	33 a			20 22	20 23	20 30	20 36	21 09	21 30			22 06		22 32	22 38		23 07	23 44	00 09						

Saturdays

		TP	TP	TP	TP	TP	TP	NT	TP	GR		NT	TP	NT	TP	XC	NT	TP	NT	TP		TP	TP	NT	TP
										R															
		◇1	◇1	◇1	◇1	◇1	◇1		◇1	1			◇1		◇1	◇1		◇1		◇1			◇1		◇1
										🍴					🛒	🛒		🛒		🛒			🛒		🛒
Bradford Interchange	37 d													07 20			07 34							08 20	
Leeds 10	d	23p42	00 34	00 37	02 16	05 34	06 35	06 38	06 55	07 10		07 14	07 23	07 41	07 50	07 57	08 00	08 12	08 12	08 28		08 28	08 38	08 41	08 57
Cross Gates	d							06 44						07 48			08 06		08 20					08 48	
Garforth	d							06 50						07 53	08 00		08 12		08 24					08 53	09 05
East Garforth	d							06 52						07 56			08 14		08 26					08 56	
Micklefield	d							06 56						07 59			08 18		08 30					08 59	
South Milford	d																08 22		08 36						
Selby	a											07 37	07 43				08 36		08 54				08 57		
Church Fenton	33 a													08 05										09 05	
Ulleskelf	33 a																								
York 8	33 a	00 09	01 16	01 20	02 45	06 00	07 01	07 15	07 22	07 34				08 20	08 21	08 23		08 35		08 52		09 03		09 21	09 23

		XC	TP	NT	TP	TP		NT	TP	XC	TP	NT	TP	TP	NT	TP		XC	TP	NT	TP	TP	NT	TP	XC
		◇1	◇1		◇1	◇1			◇1	◇1	◇1		◇1	◇1		◇1		◇1	◇1		◇1	◇1		◇1	◇1
		🛒	🛒		🛒				🛒	🛒	🛒		🛒	🛒		🛒		🛒	🛒			🛒		🛒	🛒
Bradford Interchange	37 d			08 50				09 20				09 50			10 18					10 50			11 20		
Leeds 10	d	09 05	09 12	09 15	09 28	09 38		09 41	09 57	10 05	10 12	10 15	10 28	10 38	10 41	10 57		11 05	11 12	11 15	11 28	11 38	11 41	11 57	12 05
Cross Gates	d			09 22				09 48				10 22			10 48					11 22			11 48		
Garforth	d			09 27				09 53	10 05			10 27			10 53	11 05				11 27			11 53	12 05	
East Garforth	d			09 29				09 56				10 29			10 56					11 29			11 56		
Micklefield	d			09 33				09 59				10 33			10 59					11 33			11 59		
South Milford	d			09 38								10 38								11 38					
Selby	a			09 53		09 57						10 53		10 57						11 55		11 57			
Church Fenton	33 a							10 05															12 05		
Ulleskelf	33 a																								
York 8	33 a	09 27	09 36		09 52			10 21	10 23	10 26	10 36		10 52		11 18	11 23		11 26	11 36		11 52		12 21	12 23	12 26

		TP		NT	TP	TP	NT	TP	XC	TP	NT	TP		TP	NT	TP	XC	TP	NT	TP	TP	NT		TP	XC
		◇1			◇1	◇1		◇1	◇1	◇1		◇1		◇1		◇1	◇1	◇1		◇1	◇1			◇1	◇1
		🛒			🛒			🛒	🛒	🛒		🛒				🛒	🛒	🛒		🛒	🛒			🛒	🛒
Bradford Interchange	37 d			11 50			12 19				12 50				13 19				13 50			14 19			
Leeds 10	d	12 12		12 15	12 28	12 38	12 41	12 57	13 05	13 12	13 15	13 28		13 38	13 42	13 57	14 05	14 12	14 15	14 28	14 38	14 41		14 57	15 05
Cross Gates	d			12 22			12 48				13 22				13 49				14 22			14 48			
Garforth	d			12 27			12 53	13 05			13 27				13 54	14 05			14 27			14 53		15 05	
East Garforth	d			12 29			12 56				13 29				13 57				14 29			14 56			
Micklefield	d			12 33			12 59				13 33				14 00				14 33			14 59			
South Milford	d			12 38							13 38								14 38						
Selby	a			12 50		12 57					13 52			13 57					14 51		14 57				
Church Fenton	33 a														14 06										
Ulleskelf	33 a																								
York 8	33 a	12 36			12 52		13 19	13 23	13 26	13 36		13 52			14 22	14 23	14 26	14 36		14 52		15 17		15 23	15 28

		TP	NT	TP	TP	NT	TP	XC		TP	NT	TP	TP	NT	TP	XC	TP	NT		TP	TP	NT	TP	XC	TP
		◇1		◇1	◇1		◇1	◇1		◇1		◇1	◇1		◇1	◇1	◇1			◇1	◇1		◇1	◇1	◇1
		🛒		🛒				🛒		🛒		🛒			🛒	🛒								🛒	
Bradford Interchange	37 d		14 50			15 19					15 50			16 19				16 50				17 19			
Leeds 10	d	15 12	15 15	15 28	15 38	15 41	15 57	16 05		16 12	16 15	16 28	16 38	16 41	16 57	17 05	17 12	17 15		17 24	17 38	17 41	17 57	18 06	18 12
Cross Gates	d		15 22			15 48					16 22			16 48				17 23				17 48			
Garforth	d		15 27			15 53	16 05				16 27			16 53	17 05			17 30		17 34		17 53	18 05		
East Garforth	d		15 29			15 56					16 30			16 56				17 32				17 56			
Micklefield	d		15 33			15 59					16 34			16 59				17 36				17 59			
South Milford	d		15 38								16 39							17 41							
Selby	a		15 53		15 57						16 54		17 00					17 55			17 59				
Church Fenton	33 a					16 05																18 05			
Ulleskelf	33 a																					18 09			
York 8	33 a	15 36		15 52		16 21	16 23	16 26		16 36		16 52		17 21	17 23	17 26	17 36			17 55		18 24	18 22	18 28	18 36

A from 26 March

B until 23 March, FO from 30 March

Table 40

Saturdays

Leeds - Selby and York

			NT	TP ◇1	XC ◇1 🛒		TP ◇1	NT	TP ◇1	XC ◇1 🛒	TP ◇1	NT	TP ◇1	NT	TP ◇1		XC ◇1 🛒	TP ◇1	TP ◇1	NT	TP ◇1	TP ◇1	XC ◇1 🛒	TP ◇1	NT
Bradford Interchange	37	d	17 50					18 19				18 52		19 18						20 19					
Leeds 10		d	18 15	18 28	18 35		18 38	18 41	18 57	19 05	19 12	19 16	19 38	19 41	19 57		20 08	20 12	20 45	20 48	21 08	21 12	21 15	21 42	22 00
Cross Gates		d	18 22					18 48				19 22		19 48						20 55					22 07
Garforth		d	18 27					18 53	19 05			19 28		19 53	20 05					21 00					22 12
East Garforth		d	18 29					18 56				19 30		19 56						21 02					22 14
Micklefield		d	18 33					18 59				19 34		19 59						21 06					22 18
South Milford		d	18 38				18 51						19 51								21 21				
Selby		a	18 50				19 00						20 00								21 30				
Church Fenton	33	a						19 05												21 11					
Ulleskelf	33	a																		21 16					
York 8	33	a		18 52	18 58			19 21	19 23	19 26	19 36	19 53		20 18	20 23		20 29	20 36	21 09	21 30		21 41	21 57	22 06	22 36

			TP ◇1	TP ◇1	TP ◇1	NT	TP ◇1
Bradford Interchange	37	d				22 19	
Leeds 10		d	22 12	22 22	22 42	22 56	23 42
Cross Gates		d				23 03	
Garforth		d				23 08	
East Garforth		d				23 11	
Micklefield		d				23 15	
South Milford		d		22 36			
Selby		a		22 46			
Church Fenton	33	a				23 21	
Ulleskelf	33	a					
York 8	33	a	22 38		23 07	23 38	00 09

Sundays

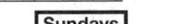

until 12 February

			TP ◇1 A	TP ◇1 A	TP ◇1 A	TP ◇1	TP ◇1	TP ◇1	TP ◇1	NT	XC ◇1 🛒		TP ◇1	TP ◇1	NT	XC ◇1 🛒	TP ◇1	NT	TP ◇1	XC ◇1 🛒	TP ◇1		NT	TP ◇1	XC ◇1 🛒	TP ◇1
Bradford Interchange	37	d								08 31					09 20			10 04					11 02			
Leeds 10		d	23p42	00 15	00 54	02 35	05 55	07 40	08 40	08 54	09 08		09 12	09 40	09 50	10 08	10 22	10 28	10 40	11 08	11 12		11 25	11 40	12 08	12 12
Cross Gates		d								09 00					09 56			10 34					11 32			
Garforth		d								09 06					10 02			10 40					11 37			
East Garforth		d								09 08					10 04			10 42					11 39			
Micklefield		d								09 12					10 08			10 46					11 43			
South Milford		d															10 35									
Selby		a															10 44									
Church Fenton	33	a								09 18								10 52								
Ulleskelf	33	a																								
York 8	33	a	00 09	00 42	01 22	03 03	06 23	08 08	09 07	09 34	09 34		09 37	10 07	10 28	10 29		11 08	11 07	11 29	11 39		11 59	12 05	12 29	12 39

			NT	TP ◇1	TP ◇1	XC ◇1 🛒	TP ◇1		NT	TP ◇1	TP ◇1	XC ◇1 🛒	TP ◇1	NT	TP ◇1	TP ◇1	XC ◇1 🛒		TP ◇1	NT	TP ◇1	TP ◇1	XC ◇1 🛒	TP ◇1	NT	TP ◇1
Bradford Interchange	37	d	12 02						13 02					14 02						15 02					16 03	
Leeds 10		d	12 25	12 40	13 01	13 08	13 12		13 25	13 40	13 57	14 08	14 12	14 25	14 40	15 01	15 08		15 12	15 25	15 40	15 57	16 08	16 12	16 25	16 40
Cross Gates		d	12 32						13 32					14 32						15 32					16 32	
Garforth		d	12 37						13 37					14 37						15 37					16 37	
East Garforth		d	12 39						13 39					14 39						15 39					16 39	
Micklefield		d	12 43						13 43					14 43						15 43					16 43	
South Milford		d			13 14											15 14										
Selby		a			13 23											15 23										
Church Fenton	33	a	12 48											14 48											16 48	
Ulleskelf	33	a																								
York 8	33	a	13 02	13 07		13 29	13 39		13 59	14 05	14 24	14 29	14 38	15 02	15 07		15 29		15 35	15 59	16 05	16 22	16 29	16 38	17 02	17 07

			TP ◇1		XC ◇1 🛒	TP ◇1	NT	TP ◇1	TP ◇1	XC ◇1 🛒	TP ◇1	NT	TP ◇1		XC ◇1 🛒	TP ◇1	XC ◇1 🛒	TP ◇1	NT	TP ◇1	TP ◇1	XC ◇1	TP ◇1		NT	TP ◇1
Bradford Interchange	37	d					17 02					18 02							19 02						20 02	
Leeds 10		d	17 01		17 08	17 12	17 25	17 40	17 57	18 08	18 12	18 23	18 40		18 57	19 01	19 08	19 12	19 25	19 40	19 57	20 08	20 12		20 25	20 40
Cross Gates		d					17 32					18 30							19 32						20 32	
Garforth		d					17 37					18 35							19 37						20 37	
East Garforth		d					17 39					18 38							19 39						20 39	
Micklefield		d					17 43					18 41							19 43						20 43	
South Milford		d	17 14													19 16										
Selby		a	17 23													19 28					20 17					
Church Fenton	33	a										18 47													20 48	
Ulleskelf	33	a																								
York 8	33	a			17 29	17 39	18 02	18 07	18 23	18 29	18 38	19 01	19 05		19 18		19 29	19 38	19 59	20 04		20 29	20 38		21 03	21 05

A not 11 December

Table 40

Sundays
until 12 February

Leeds - Selby and York

Station			TP	XC	TP	NT	TP	TP	TP		TP	NT	TP
			◇1	◇1 ⚲	◇1		◇1	◇1	◇1		◇1		◇1
Bradford Interchange	37	d				21 02							
Leeds 10		d	21 04	21 08	21 12	21 26	21 40	22 12	22 22		22 40	22 43	23 42
Cross Gates		d				21 33						22 49	
Garforth		d				21 38						22 55	
East Garforth		d				21 40						22 57	
Micklefield		d				21 44						23 01	
South Milford		d							22 35				
Selby		a	21 38						22 44				
Church Fenton	33	a										23 07	
Ulleskelf	33	a											
York 8	33	a		21 31	21 38	22 00	22 08	22 40			23 11	23 23	00 26

Sundays
19 February to 25 March

Station			TP	TP	TP	TP	TP	TP	TP	NT	XC		TP	TP	NT	XC	TP	NT	TP	XC	TP		NT	TP	XC	TP
			◇1	◇1	◇1	◇1	◇1	◇1	◇1		◇1 ⚲		◇1	◇1		◇1 ⚲	◇1		◇1	◇1 ⚲	◇1			◇1	◇1 ⚲	◇1
Bradford Interchange	37	d								08 31					09 20			10 04					11 02			
Leeds 10		d	23p42	00 15	00 54	02 35	05 55	07 40	08 40	08 54	09 08		09 12	09 40	09 50	10 08	10 22	10 28	10 40	11 08	11 12		11 25	11 40	12 08	12 12
Cross Gates		d								09 00					09 56			10 34					11 32			
Garforth		d								09 06					10 02			10 40					11 37			
East Garforth		d								09 08					10 04			10 42					11 39			
Micklefield		d								09 12					10 08			10 46					11 43			
South Milford		d															10 35									
Selby		a															10 44									
Church Fenton	33	a								09 18								10 52								
Ulleskelf	33	a																								
York 8	33	a	00 09	00 42	01 32	03 14	06 34	08 20	09 07	09 34	09 34		09 37	10 07	10 28	10 29		11 08	11 07	11 29	11 39		11 59	12 05	12 29	12 39

Station			NT	TP	TP	XC	TP		NT	TP	TP	XC	TP	NT	TP	TP	XC		TP	NT	TP	TP	XC	TP	NT	TP
				◇1	◇1	◇1 ⚲	◇1			◇1	◇1	◇1 ⚲	◇1		◇1	◇1	◇1 ⚲		◇1		◇1	◇1	◇1 ⚲	◇1		◇1
Bradford Interchange	37	d	12 02						13 02					14 02						15 02					16 03	
Leeds 10		d	12 25	12 40	13 01	13 08	13 12		13 25	13 40	13 57	14 08	14 12	14 25	14 40	15 01	15 08		15 12	15 25	15 40	15 57	16 08	16 12	16 25	16 40
Cross Gates		d	12 32						13 32					14 32						15 32					16 32	
Garforth		d	12 37						13 37					14 37						15 37					16 37	
East Garforth		d	12 39						13 39					14 39						15 39					16 39	
Micklefield		d	12 43						13 43					14 43						15 43					16 43	
South Milford		d			13 14											15 14										
Selby		a			13 23											15 23										
Church Fenton	33	a	12 48											14 48											16 48	
Ulleskelf	33	a																								
York 8	33	a	13 02	13 07		13 29	13 39		13 59	14 05	14 24	14 29	14 38	15 02	15 07		15 29		15 35	15 59	16 05	16 22	16 29	16 38	17 02	17 07

Station			TP		XC	TP	NT	TP	TP	XC	TP	NT	TP		XC	TP	XC	TP	NT	TP	TP	XC	TP		NT	TP
			◇1		◇1 ⚲	◇1		◇1	◇1	◇1 ⚲	◇1		◇1		◇1 ⚲	◇1	◇1 ⚲	◇1		◇1	◇1	◇1	◇1			◇1
Bradford Interchange	37	d					17 02					18 02							19 02						20 02	
Leeds 10		d	17 01		17 08	17 12	17 25	17 40	17 57	18 08	18 12	18 23	18 40		18 57	19 01	19 08	19 12	19 25	19 40	19 57	20 08	20 12		20 25	20 40
Cross Gates		d					17 32					18 30							19 32						20 32	
Garforth		d					17 37					18 35							19 37						20 37	
East Garforth		d					17 39					18 38							19 39						20 39	
Micklefield		d					17 43					18 41							19 43						20 43	
South Milford		d	17 14													19 16										
Selby		a	17 23													19 28					20 17					
Church Fenton	33	a										18 47													20 48	
Ulleskelf	33	a																								
York 8	33	a			17 29	17 39	18 02	18 07	18 23	18 29	18 38	19 01	19 05		19 18		19 29	19 38	19 59	20 04		20 29	20 38		21 03	21 05

Station			TP	XC	TP	NT	TP	TP	TP		TP	NT	TP
			◇1	◇1 ⚲	◇1		◇1	◇1	◇1		◇1		◇1
Bradford Interchange	37	d				21 02							
Leeds 10		d	21 04	21 08	21 12	21 26	21 40	22 12	22 22		22 40	22 43	23 42
Cross Gates		d				21 33						22 49	
Garforth		d				21 38						22 55	
East Garforth		d				21 40						22 57	
Micklefield		d				21 44						23 01	
South Milford		d							22 35				
Selby		a	21 38						22 44				
Church Fenton	33	a										23 07	
Ulleskelf	33	a											
York 8	33	a		21 31	21 38	22 00	22 08	22 40			23 11	23 23	00 26

Table 40

Sundays
from 1 April

Leeds - Selby and York

		TP ◇1	TP 🚌	TP 🚌	TP 🚌	TP ◇1	NT	XC ◇1 🛒	TP ◇1	TP ◇1		NT	XC ◇1 🛒	TP ◇1	TP ◇1	NT	TP ◇1	XC ◇1 🛒	TP ◇1	NT		TP ◇1	XC ◇1 🛒	TP ◇1	NT
Bradford Interchange	37 d						08 31					09 20				10 04				11 02					12 02
Leeds 10	d	23p42	01 25	03 20	07 20	08 40	08 54	09 08	09 12	09 40		09 50	10 08	10 17	10 24	10 28	10 40	11 08	11 18	11 25		11 40	12 08	12 12	12 25
Cross Gates	d						09 00					09 56				10 34				11 32					12 32
Garforth	d						09 06					10 02				10 40				11 37					12 37
East Garforth	d						09 08					10 04				10 42				11 39					12 39
Micklefield	d						09 12					10 08				10 46				11 43					12 43
South Milford	d														10 37										
Selby	a														10 46										
Church Fenton	33 a						09 18									10 52									12 48
Ulleskelf	33 a																								
York 8	33 a	00 09	02 15	04 10	08 10	09 08	09 34	09 34	09 37	10 04		10 28	10 29	10 41		11 08	11 08	11 29	11 39	11 59		12 05	12 29	12 39	13 02

		TP ◇1	TP ◇1	XC ◇1 🛒	TP ◇1	NT		TP ◇1	TP ◇1	XC ◇1 🛒	TP ◇1	NT	TP ◇1	TP ◇1	XC ◇1 🛒	TP ◇1		NT	TP ◇1	TP ◇1	XC ◇1 🛒	TP ◇1	NT	TP ◇1	TP ◇1
Bradford Interchange	37 d					13 02						14 02						15 02					16 03		
Leeds 10	d	12 40	13 01	13 08	13 12	13 25		13 40	13 57	14 08	14 12	14 25	14 40	15 01	15 08	15 12		15 25	15 40	15 57	16 08	16 12	16 25	16 40	17 01
Cross Gates	d					13 32						14 32						15 32					16 32		
Garforth	d					13 37						14 37						15 37					16 37		
East Garforth	d					13 39						14 39						15 39					16 39		
Micklefield	d					13 43						14 43						15 43					16 43		
South Milford	d		13 14											15 14											17 14
Selby	a		13 23											15 23											17 23
Church Fenton	33 a											14 48											16 48		
Ulleskelf	33 a																								
York 8	33 a	13 07		13 29	13 39	13 59		14 04	14 24	14 29	14 38	15 02	15 07		15 29	15 37		15 59	16 05	16 24	16 29	16 38	17 02	17 07	

		XC ◇1 🛒		TP ◇1	NT	TP ◇1	TP ◇1	XC ◇1 🛒	TP ◇1	NT	TP ◇1	XC ◇1 🛒		TP ◇1	XC ◇1 🛒	TP ◇1	NT	TP ◇1	TP ◇1	XC ◇1	TP ◇1	NT		TP ◇1	TP ◇1
Bradford Interchange	37 d				17 02					18 02							19 02					20 02			
Leeds 10	d	17 08		17 12	17 25	17 40	17 57	18 08	18 12	18 23	18 40	18 57		19 01	19 08	19 12	19 25	19 40	19 57	20 08	20 12	20 25		20 40	21 04
Cross Gates	d				17 32					18 30							19 32					20 32			
Garforth	d				17 37					18 35							19 37					20 37			
East Garforth	d				17 39					18 38							19 39					20 39			
Micklefield	d				17 43					18 41							19 43					20 43			
South Milford	d													19 16											
Selby	a													19 29					20 17						21 38
Church Fenton	33 a									18 47												20 48			
Ulleskelf	33 a																								
York 8	33 a	17 29		17 40	18 02	18 07	18 24	18 29	18 38	19 01	19 05	19 18			19 29	19 36	19 59	20 04		20 29	20 38	21 03		21 05	

		XC ◇1 🛒	TP ◇1	NT	TP ◇1	TP ◇1	TP ◇1	NT		TP ◇1	TP ◇1
Bradford Interchange	37 d			21 02							
Leeds 10	d	21 08	21 12	21 26	21 40	22 12	22 22	22 43		22 53	23 53
Cross Gates	d			21 33				22 49			
Garforth	d			21 38				22 55			
East Garforth	d			21 40				22 57			
Micklefield	d			21 44				23 01			
South Milford	d						22 35				
Selby	a						22 44				
Church Fenton	33 a							23 07			
Ulleskelf	33 a										
York 8	33 a	21 31	21 38	22 00	22 08	22 40		23 23		23 28	00 22

Leeds and Bradford - Huddersfield, Blackpool North, Rochdale and Manchester Victoria via Halifax and Brighouse

Network Diagram - see first Page of Table 39

Miles	Miles	Miles	Miles	Miles				NT	NT	NT	NT	NT	NT	NT	GC	NT		NT	NT	NT	NT	NT	NT	NT	NT	NT
								MX	MX																	
															R 1											
														A					B			C			B	
—	—	—	—	—	York 8	40	d											06 13						07 06		
—	—	—	—	—	Selby	40	d															06 42				07 26
0	0	—	—	0	**Leeds 10**	37,39	d	22p37	23p08	05 08	05 51	06 03	06 13			06 37		06 51		07 08	07 13	07 23	07 37	07 51		08 08
4	4	—	—	—	Bramley	37	d	22p44	23p15	05 15	05 58					06 44				07 15		07 30	07 44			08 15
5¾	5¾	—	—	—	New Pudsey	37	d	22p49	23p20	05 20	06 02	06 13				06 49		07 01		07 20		07 35	07 49	08 01		08 20
9½	9½	—	—	—	**Bradford Interchange**	37	a	22p57	23p29	05 28	06 13	06 21				06 57		07 11		07 28		07 43	07 57	08 09		08 28
—	—	—	—	—			d	23p00	23p31	05 32	06 14	06 24			06 51	07 00		07 14		07 31		07 46	08 00	08 12		08 32
17½	17½	0	—	—	**Halifax**		a	23p12	23p44	05 44	06 25	06 36			07 06	07 12		07 25		07 43		07 59	08 12	08 23		08 44
—	—	—	—	—			d	23p12	23p44	05 44	06 26	06 36		07 02	07 07	07 12		07 26		07 44		08 06	08 12	08 24		08 44
—	—	—	9¼	—	Dewsbury	39	d						06 29								07 29					
—	—	—	12¼	—	Mirfield	39	d						06 35								07 36					
—	—	5¼	16¼	—	Brighouse		d		23p55				06 49	07a12	07 18						07 49	08 16				
—	—	—	—	—	London Kings Cross 15 ⊖	26	a								10 13											
—	—	10½	—	—	**Huddersfield**	39	a		00 08													08 30				
21	21	—	22	—	Sowerby Bridge		d	23p19		05 51		06 43	06 59			07 19					07 59		08 19			
25	25	—	26	—	Mytholmroyd		d	23p25		05 57		06 49	07 05			07 25					08 05		08 25			
26¼	26¼	—	27¼	—	**Hebden Bridge**		a	23p28		06 00	06 37	06 52	07 08			07 28		07 37		07 55	08 08		08 28	08 35		08 56
—	—	—	—	—			d	23p28		06 00	06 38	06 52	07 08			07 28		07 38		07 56	08 08		08 28	08 36		08 56
—	39	—	—	—	Burnley Manchester Road	97	a				06 57							07 57						08 57		
—	45¼	—	—	—	Accrington	97	a				07 06							08 06						09 06		
—	51½	—	—	—	Blackburn	97	a				07 16							08 14						09 14		
—	63½	—	—	—	**Preston 8**	97	a				07 36							08 38						09 32		
—	78	—	—	—	Poulton-le-Fylde	97	a				07 54							08 56						09 50		
—	81	—	—	—	**Blackpool North**	97	a				08 05							09 05						10 01		
30½	—	—	—	—	Todmorden		d	23p36		06 08		06 59	07 15			07 36			07 44	08 04	08 15		08 36			09 04
32	—	—	—	—	Walsden		d	23p39		06 11		07 02				07 39			07 47				08 39			
36	—	—	—	—	Littleborough		d	23p45		06 17		07 09	07 23			07 45			07 53		08 23		08 45			
37	—	—	—	—	Smithy Bridge		d	23p48		06 20		07 11	07 25			07 48			07 56		08 25		08 48			
39¼	—	—	—	—	**Rochdale**		a	23p52		06 24		07 15	07 29			07 51			08 00	08 14	08 29		08 51			09 14
—	—	—	—	—			d	23p52		06 24		07 16	07 30			07 51			08 00	08 14	08 30		08 51		09 04	09 14
41	—	—	—	—	Castleton		d			06 27		07 19	07 33			07 54			08 03	08 17	08 33				09 07	
43¾	—	—	—	—	Mills Hill		d			06 32		07 24	07 38			07 59			08 08	08 22	08 37				09 12	
45¾	—	—	—	—	Moston		d			06 35		07 27	07 41			08 02			08 11	08 25	08 40				09 15	
49¾	—	—	—	—	**Manchester Victoria**		a	00 10		06 48		07 39	07 53			08 14			08 22	08 37	08 53		09 08		09 26	09 30

			NT	NT	NT	NT	NT	NT	NT	NT	NT		NT	GC	NT	NT	NT	NT	NT	NT	NT		NT	NT	NT
														R 1											
				C		D	B			C			E		B			C		E	B				C
York 8	40	d				08 12							09 11							10 11					
Selby	40	d		07 43						08 43								09 43							10 42
Leeds 10	37,39	d	08 13	08 23	08 37	08 51		09 07	09 13	09 23	09 37		09 53			10 07	10 13	10 23	10 37	10 53			11 07	11 13	11 23
Bramley	37	d		08 30	08 44			09 14		09 30	09 44					10 14		10 30	10 44				11 14		11 30
New Pudsey	37	d		08 35	08 49	09 00		09 19		09 35	09 49		10 02			10 20		10 35	10 49	11 02			11 19		11 35
Bradford Interchange	37	a		08 43	08 57	09 12		09 28		09 43	09 57		10 12			10 28		10 43	10 57	11 11			11 28		11 43
		d		08 46	09 00	09 13		09 32		09 46	10 00		10 14	10 22		10 32		10 46	11 00	11 12			11 31		11 46
Halifax		a		08 59	09 12	09 25		09 44		09 59	10 12		10 25	10 33		10 44		10 59	11 12	11 25			11 43		11 59
		d		09 06	09 12	09 25		09 44		10 06	10 12		10 26	10 37		10 44		11 06	11 12	11 25			11 44		12 06
Dewsbury	39	d	08 31						09 31								10 29							11 29	
Mirfield	39	d	08 38						09 37								10 35							11 35	
Brighouse		d	08 49	09 16					09 49	10 16				10 48			10 49	11 16						11 49	12 16
London Kings Cross 15 ⊖	26	a												13 45											
Huddersfield	39	a		09 29						10 29								11 30							12 30
Sowerby Bridge		d	08 59		09 19				09 59		10 19						10 59		11 19					11 59	
Mytholmroyd		d	09 05		09 25				10 05		10 25						11 05		11 25					12 05	
Hebden Bridge		a	09 08		09 28	09 37		09 56	10 08		10 28		10 37			10 56	11 08		11 28	11 37			11 55	12 08	
		d	09 08		09 28	09 37		09 56	10 08		10 28		10 38			10 56	11 08		11 28	11 38			11 56	12 08	
Burnley Manchester Road	97	a				09 56							10 57							11 57					
Accrington	97	a				10 06							11 06							12 06					
Blackburn	97	a				10 14							11 14							12 14					
Preston 8	97	a				10 32							11 32							12 32					
Poulton-le-Fylde	97	a				10 50							11 50							12 50					
Blackpool North	97	a				11 01							12 00							13 00					
Todmorden		d	09 15		09 36			10 04	10 15		10 36					11 04	11 15		11 36				12 03	12 15	
Walsden		d			09 39						10 39								11 39						
Littleborough		d	09 23		09 45				10 23		10 45						11 23		11 45					12 23	
Smithy Bridge		d	09 25		09 48				10 25		10 48						11 25		11 48					12 25	
Rochdale		a	09 29		09 51			10 14	10 29		10 51					11 14	11 29		11 51				12 13	12 29	
		d	09 30		09 51		10 05	10 14	10 30		10 51				11 04	11 14	11 30		11 51		12 04		12 14	12 30	
Castleton		d	09 33				10 08		10 33						11 07		11 33				12 07			12 33	
Mills Hill		d	09 37				10 13		10 38						11 12		11 38				12 12			12 38	
Moston		d	09 40				10 16		10 41						11 15		11 41				12 15			12 41	
Manchester Victoria		a	09 53		10 08		10 25	10 32	10 53		11 08				11 26	11 32	11 53		12 08		12 25		12 30	12 53	

A To Leeds
B To Wigan Wallgate
C To Wakefield Westgate
D From Manchester Victoria
E From Blackpool North

For connections to Liverpool Lime Street please refer to Table 90

Leeds and Bradford - Huddersfield, Blackpool North, Rochdale and Manchester Victoria via Halifax and Brighouse

Network Diagram - see first Page of Table 39

	NT	NT A	NT B	NT	NT	NT C		NT	NT A	NT B	NT	NT	NT C	NT	NT A	NT B		NT	NT	NT C	NT	NT A	NT B	NT
York 8 40 d		11 09							12 13						13 09							14 13		
Selby 40 d						11 43							12 43							13 43				
Leeds 10 37,39 d	11 37	11 53		12 07	12 13	12 23		12 37	12 53		13 07	13 13	13 23	13 37	13 53			14 07	14 13	14 23	14 37	14 53		15 07
Bramley 37 d	11 44			12 14		12 30		12 44			13 14		13 30	13 44				14 14		14 30	14 44			15 14
New Pudsey 37 d	11 49	12 02		12 19		12 35		12 49	13 02		13 19		13 35	13 49	14 02			14 19		14 35	14 49	15 02		15 19
Bradford Interchange 37 a	11 57	12 11		12 28		12 43		12 57	13 12		13 28		13 43	13 58	14 12			14 28		14 43	14 57	15 12		15 28
d	12 00	12 14		12 32		12 46		13 00	13 14		13 32		13 46	14 00	14 14			14 32		14 46	15 00	15 14		15 32
Halifax a	12 12	12 25		12 44		12 59		13 12	13 25		13 44		13 59	14 12	14 25			14 44		14 59	15 12	15 25		15 44
d	12 12	12 26		12 44		13 06		13 12	13 26		13 44		14 06	14 13	14 26			14 44		15 06	15 12	15 26		15 44
Dewsbury 39 d					12 29							13 29							14 29					
Mirfield 39 d					12 35							13 35							14 35					
Brighouse d					12 49	13 16						13 49	14 16						14 49	15 16				
London Kings Cross 15 ⊖26 a																								
Huddersfield 39 a						13 29							14 29							15 29				
Sowerby Bridge d	12 19				12 59			13 19				13 59		14 19					14 59		15 19			
Mytholmroyd d	12 25				13 05			13 25				14 05		14 25					15 05		15 25			
Hebden Bridge a	12 28	12 37		12 56	13 08			13 28	13 37		13 56	14 08		14 28	14 37			14 56	15 08		15 28	15 37		15 56
d	12 28	12 38		12 56	13 08			13 28	13 38		13 56	14 08		14 29	14 38			14 56	15 08		15 28	15 38		15 56
Burnley Manchester Road 97 a		12 57							13 57						14 57							15 57		
Accrington 97 a		13 06							14 06						15 06							16 06		
Blackburn 97 a		13 14							14 14						15 14							16 14		
Preston 8 97 a		13 32							14 32						15 32							16 32		
Poulton-le-Fylde 97 a		13 50							14 50						15 50							16 50		
Blackpool North 97 a		14 00							15 00						16 00							17 00		
Todmorden d	12 36			13 04	13 15			13 36			14 04	14 15		14 36				15 04	15 15		15 36			16 04
Walsden d	12 39							13 39						14 39							15 39			
Littleborough d	12 45				13 23			13 45				14 23		14 46					15 23		15 45			
Smithy Bridge d	12 48				13 25			13 48				14 25		14 48					15 25		15 48			
Rochdale a	12 51			13 14	13 29			13 51			14 14	14 29		14 51				15 14	15 29		15 51			16 14
d	12 51		13 04	13 14	13 30			13 51		14 04	14 14	14 30		14 52		15 04		15 14	15 30		15 51		16 04	16 14
Castleton d			13 07		13 33					14 07		14 33				15 07			15 33				16 07	
Mills Hill d			13 12		13 38					14 12		14 38				15 12			15 38				16 12	
Moston d			13 15		13 41					14 15		14 41				15 15			15 41				16 15	
Manchester Victoria ⇌ a	13 08		13 25	13 32	13 53			14 08		14 25	14 32	14 52		15 08		15 25		15 31	15 53		16 08		16 27	16 32

	NT	GC R 1 ☕		NT C	NT	NT A	NT D	NT	NT	NT C	NT	NT		NT D	NT	NT	NT C	NT	NT A	NT	NT	NT		NT C
York 8 40 d						15 08						16 08							17 13					
Selby 40 d				14 43						15 41														17 38
Leeds 10 37,39 d	15 13			15 23	15 37	15 52		16 07	16 13	16 23	16 37	16 51			17 07	17 13	17 23	17 37	17 51		18 08	18 13		18 23
Bramley 37 d				15 30	15 44			16 14		16 30	16 44				17 14		17 30	17 44			18 15			18 30
New Pudsey 37 d				15 35	15 49	16 01		16 19		16 35	16 49	17 00			17 19		17 35	17 49	18 01		18 20			18 35
Bradford Interchange 37 a				15 43	15 57	16 10		16 28		16 43	16 57	17 10			17 28		17 43	17 57	18 10		18 28			18 43
d		15 37		15 46	16 00	16 13		16 32		16 46	17 00	17 12			17 31		17 46	18 00	18 12		18 32			18 46
Halifax a		15 50		15 59	16 12	16 24		16 44		16 59	17 12	17 23			17 43		17 59	18 12	18 24		18 44			18 59
d		15 52		16 06	16 12	16 25		16 44		17 06	17 12	17 24			17 44		18 06	18 12	18 24		18 44			19 06
Dewsbury 39 d	15 29								16 31							17 31						18 31		
Mirfield 39 d	15 35								16 38							17 38						18 38		
Brighouse d	15 49	16 05		16 16					16 49	17 16						17 49	18 16					18 49		19 16
London Kings Cross 15 ⊖26 a		19 05																						
Huddersfield 39 a				16 29						17 29							18 30							19 29
Sowerby Bridge d	15 59				16 19	16 32			16 59		17 19	17 31				17 59		18 19	18 31			18 59		
Mytholmroyd d	16 05				16 25				17 05		17 25					18 05		18 25				19 05		
Hebden Bridge a	16 08				16 28	16 38		16 56	17 08		17 28	17 37			17 56	18 08		18 28	18 37		18 56	19 08		
d	16 08				16 28	16 39		16 56	17 08		17 28	17 38			17 56	18 08		18 28	18 38		18 56	19 08		
Burnley Manchester Road 97 a						16 57						17 57							18 57					
Accrington 97 a						17 06						18 06							19 06					
Blackburn 97 a						17 14						18 14							19 14					
Preston 8 97 a						17 32						18 33							19 32					
Poulton-le-Fylde 97 a						17 56						18 50							19 50					
Blackpool North 97 a						18 06						18 58							20 00					
Todmorden d	16 15				16 36			17 04	17 15		17 36				18 04	18 15		18 36			19 04	19 15		
Walsden d					16 39						17 39					18 19		18 39				19 19		
Littleborough d	16 23				16 45				17 23		17 45					18 25		18 45				19 25		
Smithy Bridge d	16 25				16 48				17 25		17 48					18 28		18 48				19 28		
Rochdale a	16 29				16 51			17 14	17 29		17 51				18 14	18 32		18 51			19 15	19 32		
d	16 30				16 51		17 03	17 14	17 30		17 51			18 02	18 14	18 32		18 51		19 00	19 15	19 32		
Castleton d	16 33						17 06		17 33					18 05		18 35				19 03		19 35		
Mills Hill d	16 38						17 11		17 38					18 10		18 40				19 08		19 40		
Moston d	16 41						17 14		17 41					18 13		18 43				19 11		19 43		
Manchester Victoria ⇌ a	16 52				17 08		17 23	17 32	17 53		18 08			18 21	18 32	18 54		19 09		19 21	19 32	19 54		

A From Blackpool North
B To Wigan Wallgate
C To Wakefield Westgate
D To Blackburn

For connections to Liverpool Lime Street please refer to Table 90

Leeds and Bradford - Huddersfield, Blackpool North, Rochdale and Manchester Victoria via Halifax and Brighouse

Network Diagram - see first Page of Table 39

			NT	NT A	NT	NT B	NT	NT	NT	NT		NT	NT A	NT	NT	NT	NT	NT
York [8]	40	d		18 05									20 13					
Selby	40	d	18 00			18 46												
Leeds [10]	37,39	d	18 37	18 51	19 08	19 23		19 37	20 08			20 37	20 51	21 08	21 37	22 08	22 37	23 08
Bramley	37	d	18 44		19 15	19 30		19 44	20 15			20 44		21 15	21 44	22 15	22 44	23 15
New Pudsey	37	d	18 49	19 01	19 20	19 35		19 49	20 20			20 49	21 01	21 20	21 49	22 20	22 49	23 20
Bradford Interchange	37	a	18 58	19 10	19 28	19 44		19 57	20 28			20 57	21 10	21 28	21 57	22 28	22 57	23 29
		d	19 00	19 12	19 32	19 46		20 00	20 31			21 00	21 13	21 31	22 00	22 31	23 00	23 31
Halifax		a	19 12	19 24	19 44	19 59		20 12	20 44			21 12	21 24	21 44	22 12	22 44	23 12	23 44
		d	19 12	19 24	19 44	20 06		20 12	20 44			21 12	21 25	21 44	22 12	22 44	23 12	23 44
Dewsbury	39	d																
Mirfield	39	d																
Brighouse		d				20 16			20 55					21 55		22 55		23 55
London Kings Cross [15] ⊖26		a																
Huddersfield	39	a				20 29			21 08					22 08		23 08		00 08
Sowerby Bridge		d	19 19					20 19				21 19			22 19		23 19	
Mytholmroyd		d	19 25					20 25				21 25			22 25		23 25	
Hebden Bridge		a	19 28	19 36	19 56			20 28				21 28	21 36		22 28		23 28	
		d	19 28	19 36	19 56			20 28				21 28	21 37		22 28		23 28	
Burnley Manchester Road	97	a		19 56									21 56					
Accrington	97	a		20 05									22 05					
Blackburn	97	a		20 14									22 13					
Preston [8]	97	a		20 32									22 31					
Poulton-le-Fylde	97	a		20 50									22 49					
Blackpool North	97	a		21 00									22 59					
Todmorden		d	19 36		20 04			20 36				21 36			22 36		23 36	
Walsden		d	19 39					20 39				21 39			22 39		23 39	
Littleborough		d	19 45					20 45				21 45			22 45		23 45	
Smithy Bridge		d	19 48					20 48				21 48			22 48		23 48	
Rochdale		a	19 52		20 14			20 52				21 52			22 52		23 52	
		d	19 52		20 14		20 25	20 52		21 25		21 52			22 52		23 52	
Castleton		d	19 55				20 28	20 55		21 28		21 55			22 55			
Mills Hill		d	20 00				20 33	21 00		21 33		22 00			23 00			
Moston		d	20 03				20 36	21 03		21 36		22 03			23 03			
Manchester Victoria		a	20 15		20 32		20 46	21 13		21 46		22 15			23 15		00 10	

Saturdays

			NT	NT	NT	NT	NT	GC R 1 C	NT	NT D	NT		NT	NT	NT B	NT	NT	NT D	NT	NT	NT B		NT	NT E	NT D	NT
York [8]	40	d									06 13						07 06							08 09		
Selby	40	d													06 42						07 42					
Leeds [10]	37,39	d	22p37	23p08	05 37	05 51	06 16		06 37		06 51		07 08	07 13	07 23	07 37	07 51		08 08	08 13	08 23		08 37	08 51		09 07
Bramley	37	d	22p44	23p15	05 44	05 58	06 23		06 44				07 15		07 30	07 44			08 15		08 30		08 44			09 14
New Pudsey	37	d	22p49	23p20	05 49	06 02	06 28		06 49		07 01		07 20		07 35	07 49	08 01		08 20		08 35		08 49	09 00		09 19
Bradford Interchange	37	a	22p57	23p29	05 57	06 13	06 36		06 57		07 11		07 28		07 43	07 57	08 09		08 28		08 43		08 57	09 12		09 28
		d	23p00	23p31	06 00	06 14	06 40	06 51	07 00		07 14		07 31		07 46	08 00	08 12		08 32		08 46		09 00	09 13		09 32
Halifax		a	23p12	23p44	06 12	06 25	06 52	07 02	07 12		07 25		07 43		07 59	08 12	08 23		08 44		08 59		09 12	09 24		09 44
		d	23p12	23p44	06 12	06 26	06 52	07 03	07 12		07 26		07 44		08 06	08 12	08 24		08 44		09 06		09 12	09 24		09 44
Dewsbury	39	d												07 29						08 31						
Mirfield	39	d												07 35						08 38						
Brighouse		d		23p55				07 14						07 49	08 16					08 49	09 16					
London Kings Cross [15] ⊖26		a						10 09																		
Huddersfield	39	a		00 08											08 30						09 29					
Sowerby Bridge		d	23p19		06 19		06 59		07 19					07 59		08 19				08 59			09 19			
Mytholmroyd		d	23p25		06 25		07 05		07 25					08 05		08 25				09 05			09 25			
Hebden Bridge		a	23p28		06 28	06 37	07 08		07 28		07 37		07 55	08 08		08 28	08 35		08 56	09 08			09 28	09 37		09 56
		d	23p28		06 28	06 38	07 08		07 28	07 33	07 38		07 56	08 08		08 28	08 36		08 56	09 08			09 28	09 37		09 56
Burnley Manchester Road	97	a				06 57					07 57						08 57							09 56		
Accrington	97	a				07 06					08 06						09 06							10 06		
Blackburn	97	a				07 16					08 14						09 14							10 14		
Preston [8]	97	a				07 36					08 38						09 32							10 32		
Poulton-le-Fylde	97	a				07 54					08 56						09 50							10 50		
Blackpool North	97	a				08 05					09 05						10 01							11 01		
Todmorden		d	23p36		06 35		07 15		07 36	07 44			08 04	08 15		08 36			09 04	09 15			09 36			10 04
Walsden		d	23p39		06 38				07 39	07 47						08 39							09 39			
Littleborough		d	23p45		06 45		07 23		07 45	07 53				08 23		08 45				09 23			09 45			
Smithy Bridge		d	23p48		06 47		07 25		07 48	07 56				08 25		08 48				09 25			09 48			
Rochdale		a	23p52		06 54		07 29		07 52	08 00			08 14	08 29		08 51			09 14	09 29			09 51			10 14
		d	23p52		06 55		07 30		07 52	08 00			08 14	08 30		08 51		09 04	09 14	09 30			09 51		10 05	10 14
Castleton		d			06 58		07 33		07 55	08 03			08 17	08 33				09 07		09 33					10 08	
Mills Hill		d			07 03		07 38		08 00	08 08			08 22	08 37				09 12		09 37					10 13	
Moston		d			07 06		07 41		08 03	08 11			08 25	08 40				09 15		09 40					10 16	
Manchester Victoria		a	00 10		07 17		07 53		08 14	08 21			08 37	08 53		09 08		09 25	09 32	09 53			10 07		10 25	10 32

A From Blackpool North
B To Wakefield Westgate
C to Brighouse
D To Wigan Wallgate
E From Leeds

For connections to Liverpool Lime Street please refer to Table 90

Table 41

Saturdays

Leeds and Bradford - Huddersfield, Blackpool North, Rochdale and Manchester Victoria via Halifax and Brighouse

Network Diagram - see first Page of Table 39

Station	Table		NT	NT	NT	NT	GC		NT	NT	NT	NT	NT	NT	NT	NT	NT		NT	NT	NT	NT	NT	NT	NT	NT
							R 1																			
				A		B			C			A		B	C				A		B	C			A	
York 8	40	d				09 11								10 11							11 09					
Selby	40	d		08 43								09 43							10 42						11 43	
Leeds 10	37,39	d	09 13	09 23	09 37	09 53				10 07	10 13	10 23	10 37	10 53		11 07	11 13		11 23	11 37	11 53		12 07	12 13	12 23	12 37
Bramley	37	d		09 30	09 44					10 14		10 30	10 44			11 14			11 30	11 44			12 14		12 30	12 44
New Pudsey	37	d		09 35	09 49	10 02				10 19		10 35	10 49	11 02		11 19			11 35	11 49	12 02		12 19		12 35	12 49
Bradford Interchange	37	a		09 43	09 57	10 11				10 28		10 43	10 57	11 12		11 28			11 43	11 57	12 12		12 28		12 43	12 57
		d		09 46	10 00	10 14	10 22			10 32		10 46	11 00	11 14		11 31			11 46	12 00	12 14		12 32		12 46	13 00
Halifax		a		10 01	10 12	10 25	10 34			10 44		10 59	11 12	11 24		11 43			11 59	12 12	12 25		12 44		12 59	13 12
		d		10 06	10 12	10 26	10 38			10 44		11 06	11 12	11 26		11 44			12 06	12 12	12 26		12 44		13 06	13 12
Dewsbury	39	d	09 31								10 29						11 29							12 29		
Mirfield	39	d	09 37								10 35						11 35							12 35		
Brighouse		d	09 49	10 16			10 48				10 49	11 16					11 49		12 16					12 49	13 16	
London Kings Cross 15 ⊖26		a					13 46																			
Huddersfield	39	a		10 29								11 30							12 30						13 29	
Sowerby Bridge		d	09 59		10 19						10 59		11 19				11 59			12 19				12 59		13 19
Mytholmroyd		d	10 05		10 25						11 05		11 25				12 05			12 25				13 05		13 25
Hebden Bridge		a	10 08		10 28	10 37				10 56	11 08		11 28	11 36		11 55	12 08			12 28	12 37		12 56	13 08		13 28
		d	10 08		10 28	10 38				10 56	11 08		11 28	11 38		11 56	12 08			12 28	12 38		12 56	13 08		13 28
Burnley Manchester Road	97	a				10 57								11 57							12 57					
Accrington	97	a				11 06								12 06							13 06					
Blackburn	97	a				11 14								12 14							13 14					
Preston 8	97	a				11 32								12 32							13 32					
Poulton-le-Fylde	97	a				11 50								12 50							13 50					
Blackpool North	97	a				12 00								13 00							14 00					
Todmorden		d	10 15		10 36					11 04	11 15		11 36			12 03	12 15			12 36			13 04	13 15		13 36
Walsden		d			10 39								11 39							12 39						13 39
Littleborough		d	10 23		10 45						11 23		11 45				12 23			12 45				13 23		13 45
Smithy Bridge		d	10 25		10 48						11 25		11 48				12 25			12 48				13 25		13 48
Rochdale		a	10 29		10 51					11 14	11 29		11 51			12 13	12 29			12 51			13 14	13 29		13 51
		d	10 30		10 51				11 04	11 14	11 30		11 51		12 04	12 14	12 30			12 51		13 04	13 14	13 30		13 51
Castleton		d	10 33						11 07		11 33				12 07		12 33					13 07		13 33		
Mills Hill		d	10 38						11 12		11 38				12 12		12 38					13 12		13 38		
Moston		d	10 41						11 15		11 41				12 15		12 41					13 15		13 41		
Manchester Victoria	⛴	a	10 53		11 07				11 26	11 32	11 53		12 07		12 25	12 32	12 53			13 07		13 25	13 32	13 53		14 07

Station	Table		NT		NT	NT	NT	NT	NT	NT	NT	NT	NT		NT	NT	NT	GC	NT	NT	NT	NT	NT		NT	NT
																		R 1								
			B		C			A		B	C				A		B		C			A			B	D
York 8	40	d	12 13							13 09							14 13								15 09	
Selby	40	d						12 44							13 43							14 43				
Leeds 10	37,39	d	12 53			13 07	13 13	13 23	13 37	13 53		14 07	14 13		14 23	14 37	14 53			15 07	15 13	15 23	15 37		15 52	
Bramley	37	d				13 14		13 30	13 44			14 14			14 30	14 44				15 14		15 30	15 44			
New Pudsey	37	d	13 02			13 19		13 35	13 49	14 02		14 19			14 35	14 49	15 02			15 19		15 35	15 49		16 01	
Bradford Interchange	37	a	13 12			13 28		13 43	13 58	14 12		14 28			14 43	14 58	15 12			15 28		15 43	15 57		16 10	
		d	13 14			13 32		13 46	14 00	14 14		14 32			14 46	15 01	15 14	15 22		15 32		15 46	16 00		16 13	
Halifax		a	13 25			13 44		13 59	14 12	14 25		14 44			14 59	15 13	15 25	15 33		15 44		15 59	16 12		16 24	
		d	13 26			13 44		14 06	14 13	14 26		14 44			15 06	15 13	15 26	15 35		15 44		16 06	16 12		16 25	
Dewsbury	39	d					13 29						14 29								15 29					
Mirfield	39	d					13 35						14 35								15 35					
Brighouse		d					13 49	14 16					14 49		15 16			15 46			15 49	16 16				
London Kings Cross 15 ⊖26		a																18 45								
Huddersfield	39	a						14 29							15 29							16 29				
Sowerby Bridge		d					13 59		14 19				14 59			15 20					15 59		16 19		16 31	
Mytholmroyd		d					14 05		14 25				15 05			15 26					16 05		16 25			
Hebden Bridge		a	13 37			13 56	14 08		14 28	14 37		14 56	15 08			15 29	15 37			15 56	16 08		16 28		16 37	
		d	13 38			13 56	14 08		14 29	14 38		14 56	15 08			15 29	15 38			15 56	16 08		16 28		16 38	
Burnley Manchester Road	97	a	13 57							14 57							15 57								16 57	
Accrington	97	a	14 06							15 06							16 06								17 06	
Blackburn	97	a	14 14							15 14							16 14								17 14	
Preston 8	97	a	14 32							15 32							16 32								17 32	
Poulton-le-Fylde	97	a	14 50							15 50							16 50								17 56	
Blackpool North	97	a	15 00							16 00							17 00								18 06	
Todmorden		d				14 04	14 15		14 36			15 04	15 15			15 37				16 04	16 15		16 36			
Walsden		d							14 39							15 40							16 39			
Littleborough		d					14 23		14 46				15 23			15 46					16 23		16 45			
Smithy Bridge		d					14 25		14 48				15 25			15 49					16 25		16 48			
Rochdale		a				14 14	14 29		14 51			15 14	15 29			15 52				16 14	16 29		16 51			
		d			14 04	14 14	14 30		14 52		15 04	15 14	15 30			15 52			16 04	16 14	16 30		16 51			17 03
Castleton		d			14 07		14 33				15 07		15 33						16 07		16 33					17 06
Mills Hill		d			14 12		14 38				15 12		15 38						16 12		16 38					17 11
Moston		d			14 15		14 41				15 15		15 41						16 15		16 41					17 14
Manchester Victoria	⛴	a			14 25	14 32	14 53		15 08		15 25	15 32	15 53			16 08			16 26	16 32	16 53		17 07			17 23

A To Wakefield Westgate
B From Blackpool North
C To Wigan Wallgate
D To Blackburn

For connections to Liverpool Lime Street please refer to Table 90

Table 41

Saturdays

Leeds and Bradford - Huddersfield, Blackpool North, Rochdale and Manchester Victoria via Halifax and Brighouse

Network Diagram - see first Page of Table 39

Station			NT	NT	NT A	NT	NT B	NT C	NT		NT	NT A	NT	NT B
York 8	40	d					16 08							17 12
Selby	40	d			15 41							16 43		
Leeds 10	37,39	d	16 07	16 13	16 23	16 37	16 51		17 07		17 13	17 23	17 37	17 51
Bramley	37	d	16 14		16 30	16 44			17 14			17 30	17 44	
New Pudsey	37	d	16 19		16 35	16 49	17 00		17 19			17 35	17 49	18 01
Bradford Interchange	37	a	16 28		16 43	16 57	17 10		17 28			17 43	17 57	18 09
		d	16 32		16 46	17 00	17 12		17 32			17 46	18 00	18 12
Halifax		a	16 44		16 59	17 12	17 23		17 44			17 59	18 12	18 23
		d	16 44		17 06	17 12	17 24		17 44			18 06	18 12	18 24
Dewsbury	39	d		16 31							17 31			
Mirfield	39	d		16 38							17 38			
Brighouse		d		16 49	17 16						17 49	18 16		
London Kings Cross 15 ⊖	26	a												
Huddersfield	39	a			17 29							18 30		
Sowerby Bridge		d		16 59		17 19	17 31				17 59		18 19	18 31
Mytholmroyd		d		17 05		17 25					18 05		18 25	
Hebden Bridge		a	16 56	17 08		17 28	17 37		17 56		18 08		18 28	18 37
		d	16 56	17 08		17 28	17 38		17 56		18 08		18 28	18 38
Burnley Manchester Road	97	a					17 57							18 57
Accrington	97	a					18 06							19 06
Blackburn	97	a					18 14							19 14
Preston 8	97	a					18 33							19 32
Poulton-le-Fylde	97	a					18 50							19 50
Blackpool North	97	a					19 00							20 00
Todmorden		d	17 04	17 15		17 36			18 04		18 15		18 36	
Walsden		d				17 39					18 19		18 39	
Littleborough		d		17 23		17 45					18 25		18 45	
Smithy Bridge		d		17 25		17 48					18 28		18 48	
Rochdale		a	17 14	17 29		17 51			18 14		18 32		18 51	
		d	17 14	17 30		17 51		18 02	18 14		18 32		18 51	
Castleton		d		17 33				18 05			18 35			
Mills Hill		d		17 38				18 10			18 40			
Moston		d		17 41				18 13			18 43			
Manchester Victoria		a	17 33	17 53		18 07		18 22	18 32		18 54		19 10	

Station			NT	NT	NT	NT A	NT		NT B	NT	NT A	NT	NT	NT
York 8	40	d							18 05					
Selby	40	d				17 39					18 46			
Leeds 10	37,39	d		18 08	18 13	18 23	18 37		18 51	19 08	19 23	19 37	20 08	20 37
Bramley	37	d		18 15		18 30	18 44			19 15	19 30	19 44	20 15	20 44
New Pudsey	37	d		18 20		18 35	18 49		19 01	19 20	19 35	19 49	20 20	20 49
Bradford Interchange	37	a		18 28		18 43	18 58		19 10	19 28	19 44	19 57	20 28	20 57
		d		18 32		18 46	19 00		19 12	19 32	19 46	20 00	20 31	21 00
Halifax		a		18 44		18 59	19 12		19 24	19 44	19 59	20 12	20 44	21 12
		d		18 44		19 06	19 13		19 24	19 44	20 06	20 12	20 44	21 12
Dewsbury	39	d			18 31									
Mirfield	39	d			18 38									
Brighouse		d			18 49	19 16					20 16		20 55	
London Kings Cross 15 ⊖	26	a												
Huddersfield	39	a				19 29					20 29		21 08	
Sowerby Bridge		d			18 59		19 19					20 19		21 19
Mytholmroyd		d			19 05		19 25					20 25		21 25
Hebden Bridge		a		18 56	19 08		19 28		19 36	19 56		20 28		21 28
		d		18 56	19 08		19 28		19 36	19 56		20 28		21 28
Burnley Manchester Road	97	a							19 56					
Accrington	97	a							20 05					
Blackburn	97	a							20 14					
Preston 8	97	a							20 32					
Poulton-le-Fylde	97	a							20 50					
Blackpool North	97	a							21 00					
Todmorden		d		19 04	19 15		19 36			20 04		20 36		21 36
Walsden		d			19 19		19 39					20 39		21 39
Littleborough		d			19 25		19 45					20 45		21 45
Smithy Bridge		d			19 28		19 48					20 48		21 48
Rochdale		a		19 15	19 32		19 52			20 14		20 52		21 52
		d	19 02	19 15	19 32		19 52			20 14		20 52		21 52
Castleton		d	19 05		19 35		19 55					20 55		21 55
Mills Hill		d	19 10		19 40		20 00					21 00		22 00
Moston		d	19 13		19 43		20 03					21 03		22 03
Manchester Victoria		a	19 22	19 32	19 54		20 15			20 32		21 14		22 14

Station			NT B	NT	NT		NT	NT	NT	NT
York 8	40	d	20 13							
Selby	40	d								
Leeds 10	37,39	d	20 51	21 08	21 37		22 08		22 37	23 00
Bramley	37	d		21 15	21 44		22 15		22 44	23 07
New Pudsey	37	d	21 01	21 20	21 49		22 20		22 49	23 12
Bradford Interchange	37	a	21 10	21 28	21 57		22 28		22 57	23 21
		d	21 13	21 31	22 00		22 31		23 00	23 23
Halifax		a	21 24	21 44	22 12		22 44		23 12	23 36
		d	21 25	21 44	22 12		22 44		23 12	23 36
Dewsbury	39	d								
Mirfield	39	d								
Brighouse		d		21 55			22 55			23 47
London Kings Cross 15 ⊖	26	a								
Huddersfield	39	a		22 08			23 08			23 59
Sowerby Bridge		d			22 19				23 19	
Mytholmroyd		d			22 25				23 25	
Hebden Bridge		a	21 36		22 28				23 28	
		d	21 37		22 28				23 28	
Burnley Manchester Road	97	a	21 56							
Accrington	97	a	22 05							
Blackburn	97	a	22 13							
Preston 8	97	a	22 31							
Poulton-le-Fylde	97	a	22 49							
Blackpool North	97	a	22 59							
Todmorden		d			22 36				23 36	
Walsden		d			22 39				23 39	
Littleborough		d			22 45				23 45	
Smithy Bridge		d			22 48				23 48	
Rochdale		a			22 52				23 52	
		d			22 52			23 04	23 52	
Castleton		d			22 55			23 07		
Mills Hill		d			23 00			23 12		
Moston		d			23 03			23 15		
Manchester Victoria		a			23 14			23 27	00 08	

A To Wakefield Westgate
B From Blackpool North
C To Blackburn

For connections to Liverpool Lime Street please refer to Table 90

Table 41

Sundays

Leeds and Bradford - Huddersfield, Blackpool North, Rochdale and Manchester Victoria via Halifax and Brighouse

Network Diagram - see first Page of Table 39

			NT	GC	NT	NT	NT	NT	NT	NT	NT	NT	NT	NT	NT	GC	NT	NT	NT	NT	NT	NT	NT	NT
			A	R 1 B ☕												R 1 ☕								
York 8	40	d								08 50			09 52		10 57				11 52		12 52			13 52
Selby	40	d																						
Leeds 10	37,39	d	22p37			08 21	08 45	09 02	09 18	09 35	09 54	10 12	10 35	10 54	11 35		11 54	12 12	12 35	12 54	13 35	13 54	14 12	14 35
Bramley	37	d	22p44			08 28		09 09	09 25		10 01	10 19		11 01			12 01	12 19		13 01		14 01	14 19	
New Pudsey	37	d	22p49			08 33	08 54	09 14	09 30	09 44	10 06	10 24	10 44	11 06	11 44		12 06	12 24	12 44	13 06	13 44	14 06	14 24	14 44
Bradford Interchange	37	a	22p57			08 41	09 03	09 22	09 38	09 53	10 14	10 32	10 53	11 14	11 53		12 14	12 32	12 53	13 14	13 53	14 14	14 32	14 53
		d	23p00	07 55		08 45	09 05	09 25	09 44	09 55	10 17	10 35	10 55	11 17	11 55	12 04	12 17	12 35	12 55	13 17	13 55	14 17	14 35	14 55
Halifax		a	23p12	08 06		08 57	09 17	09 37	09 57	10 07	10 29	10 48	11 07	11 29	12 07	12 15	12 29	12 48	13 07	13 29	14 07	14 29	14 48	15 07
		d	23p12	08 07		09 01	09 17	09 37	09 59	10 07	10 29	10 48	11 07	11 29	12 07	12 15	12 29	12 48	13 07	13 29	14 07	14 29	14 48	15 07
Dewsbury	39	d																						
Mirfield	39	d																						
Brighouse		d		08 18					10 09			10 58				12 26		12 58					14 58	
London Kings Cross 15 ⊖26		a		10 40												14 55								
Huddersfield	39	a							10 22			11 12						13 12					15 12	
Sowerby Bridge		d	23p19			09 06		09 44			10 36			11 36			12 36			13 36		14 40		
Mytholmroyd		d	23p25			09 12		09 50			10 42			11 42			12 42			13 42		14 46		
Hebden Bridge		a	23p28			09 17	09 29	09 53		10 19	10 45		11 19	11 45	12 19		12 45		13 19	13 45	14 19	14 49		15 19
		d	23p28			09 17	09 29	09 53		10 19	10 45		11 19	11 45	12 19		12 45		13 19	13 45	14 19	14 49		15 19
Burnley Manchester Road	97	a					09 50			10 38			11 38		12 38				13 38		14 38			15 38
Accrington	97	a					09 59			10 47			11 47		12 47				13 47		14 47			15 47
Blackburn	97	a					10 07			10 56			11 55		12 55				13 55		14 55			15 55
Preston 8	97	a					10 27			11 13			12 13		13 13				14 13		15 13			16 13
Poulton-le-Fylde	97	a					10 45			11 31			12 31		13 31				14 30		15 32			16 31
Blackpool North	97	a					10 53			11 39			12 38		13 38				14 38		15 39			16 38
Todmorden		d	23p36			09 24		10 00			10 52			11 52			12 52			13 52		14 57		
Walsden		d	23p39			09 27		10 03			10 55			11 55			12 55			13 55		15 00		
Littleborough		d	23p45			09 34		10 10			11 02			12 02			13 02			14 02		15 06		
Smithy Bridge		d	23p48			09 36		10 12			11 04			12 04			13 04			14 04		15 09		
Rochdale		a	23p52			09 41		10 16			11 08			12 08			13 08			14 08		15 13		
		d	23p52		08 58	09 41		10 17			11 09			12 09			13 09			14 09		15 13		
Castleton		d			09 01	09 44		10 20			11 12			12 12			13 12			14 12		15 16		
Mills Hill		d			09 06	09 49		10 25			11 17			12 17			13 17			14 17		15 21		
Moston		d			09 09	09 52		10 28			11 20			12 20			13 20			14 20		15 24		
Manchester Victoria ⛴		a	00 08		09 19	10 02		10 38			11 30			12 30			13 30			14 30		15 37		

			NT	GC	NT	NT	NT	NT	NT	NT	NT	NT	NT	NT	NT	NT	NT	NT	NT	NT	NT	NT	NT
				R 1 ☕																C	D		
York 8	40	d			14 52			15 52		16 52			17 52		18 52			19 52		20 57	20 57		
Selby	40	d																					
Leeds 10	37,39	d	14 54		15 35	15 54	16 13	16 35	16 54	17 35	17 54	18 13	18 35	19 03	19 35	19 54	20 12	20 35	21 04	21 35	21 35	22 05	22 38
Bramley	37	d	15 01			16 01	16 20		17 01		18 01	18 20		19 10		20 01	20 19		21 12	21 43	21 43	22 12	22 45
New Pudsey	37	d	15 06		15 44	16 06	16 25	16 44	17 06	17 44	18 06	18 25	18 44	19 15	19 44	20 06	20 24	20 44	21 17	21 47	21 47	22 17	22 50
Bradford Interchange	37	a	15 14		15 53	16 14	16 33	16 53	17 14	17 53	18 14	18 33	18 53	19 24	19 53	20 14	20 34	20 53	21 25	21 56	21 56	22 27	22 58
		d	15 17	15 42	15 55	16 17	16 36	16 55	17 17	17 55	18 17	18 36	18 55	19 27	19 55	20 19	20 35	20 55	21 28	22 00	22 00	22 29	23 01
Halifax		a	15 29	15 54	16 07	16 29	16 49	17 07	17 29	18 07	18 29	18 49	19 07	19 39	20 07	20 31	20 47	21 07	21 40	22 12	22 12	22 42	23 14
		d	15 29	15 54	16 07	16 29	16 49	17 07	17 29	18 07	18 29	18 49	19 07	19 39	20 07	20 31	20 48	21 07	21 40	22 12	22 17	22 42	23 14
Dewsbury	39	d																					
Mirfield	39	d																					
Brighouse		d		16 05			16 59					18 59					20 58					22 52	23a25
London Kings Cross 15 ⊖26		a		18 50																			
Huddersfield	39	a					17 12					19 12					21 12					23 04	
Sowerby Bridge		d	15 36			16 36			17 36		18 40			19 46		20 38			21 47	22 19	22 24		
Mytholmroyd		d	15 42			16 42			17 42		18 46			19 52		20 44			21 53	22 25	22 30		
Hebden Bridge		a	15 45		16 19	16 45		17 19	17 45	18 19	18 49		19 19	19 55	20 19	20 47		21 19	21 57	22 28	22 33		
		d	15 45		16 19	16 45		17 19	17 45	18 19	18 49		19 19	19 55	20 19	20 47		21 19		22 28	22 33		
Burnley Manchester Road	97	a			16 38			17 38		18 38			19 38		20 38			21 38					
Accrington	97	a			16 47			17 47		18 47			19 47		20 47			21 47					
Blackburn	97	a			16 55			17 55		18 55			19 56		20 55			21 55					
Preston 8	97	a			17 13			18 13		19 13			20 14		21 13			22 13					
Poulton-le-Fylde	97	a			17 31			18 31		19 31			20 32		21 31			22 31					
Blackpool North	97	a			17 38			18 38		19 38			20 39		21 38			22 38					
Todmorden		d	15 52			16 52			17 52		18 57			20 02		20 54				22 35	22 40		
Walsden		d	15 55			16 55			17 55		19 00			20 05		20 57				22 38	22 43		
Littleborough		d	16 02			17 02			18 02		19 06			20 11		21 03				22 45	22 50		
Smithy Bridge		d	16 04			17 04			18 04		19 09			20 14		21 06				22 47	22 52		
Rochdale		a	16 08			17 08			18 08		19 13			20 18		21 10				22 51	22 56		
		d	16 09			17 09			18 09		19 13			20 19		21 11				22 52	22 57		
Castleton		d	16 12			17 12			18 12		19 16			20 22		21 14				22 55	23 00		
Mills Hill		d	16 17			17 17			18 17		19 21			20 27		21 19				23 00	23 05		
Moston		d	16 20			17 20			18 20		19 24			20 30		21 22				23 03	23 08		
Manchester Victoria ⛴		a	16 30			17 30			18 30		19 37			20 41		21 33				23 12	23 17		

A not 11 December

B until 25 March. R to Brighouse

C until 25 March

D from 1 April

For connections to Liverpool Lime Street please refer to Table 90

Manchester Victoria, Rochdale, Blackpool North and Huddersfield - Bradford and Leeds via Brighouse and Halifax

Network Diagram - see first Page of Table 39

Miles	Miles	Miles	Miles		NT MX	NT MX	NT	NT	NT A	NT	NT A	NT	NT	NT	NT	NT A	NT	NT	NT B	NT	NT A	NT
0	—	—	—	**Manchester Victoria** ⛴ d	22p28	23p20			05 51			06 17	06 43		06 58		07 17	07 48		08 00		08 22
4	—	—	—	Moston d	22p34	23p27						06 23			07 04		07 23			08 06		
6	—	—	—	Mills Hill d	22p39	23p32						06 28			07 09		07 28			08 11		
8¾	—	—	—	Castleton d	22p44	23p37						06 33			07 14		07 33			08 16		
10½	—	—	—	**Rochdale** a	22p47	23p40			06 05			06 36	06 56		07 17		07 36	08 01		08 19		08 34
—	—	—	—	d	22p48	23p41			06 05			06 37	06 56		07 18		07 37	08 01		08 20		08 35
12¾	—	—	—	Smithy Bridge d	22p52	23p45			06 09			06 41			07 22		07 41			08 24		08 39
13¾	—	—	—	Littleborough d	22p55	23p48			06 13			06 44			07 25		07 44			08 27		08 42
17¾	—	—	—	Walsden d	23p01	23p54			06 19			06 50			07 31		07 50					08 48
19¼	—	—	—	Todmorden d	23p05	23p58			06 22			06 54	07 08		07 35		07 54	08 13		08 34		08 52
—	0	—	—	**Blackpool North** 97 d							05 29					06 28					07 29	
—	3	—	—	Poulton-le-Fylde 97 d							05 35					06 34					07 35	
—	17½	—	—	**Preston** 8 97 d							05 54					06 54					07 54	
—	29½	—	—	Blackburn 97 d							06 10					07 10					08 10	
—	35¾	—	—	Accrington 97 d							06 17					07 17					08 17	
—	42	—	—	Burnley Manchester Road 97 d							06 26					07 26					08 26	
23½	54¾	—	0	**Hebden Bridge** a	23p11	00 04			06 29		06 49	07 00	07 14		07 41	07 49	08 00	08 19		08 41	08 49	08 58
—	—	—	—	d	23p11	00 04	05 47	06 17	06 29		06 50	07 00	07 16		07 41	07 50	08 00	08 21		08 41	08 50	09 00
24¾	56	—	1¼	Mytholmroyd d	23p15	00 08	05 50	06 20	06 32			07 03	07 19		07 45		08 04			08 44		09 03
28¾	60	—	5¼	Sowerby Bridge d	23p20	00 13	05 56	06 26	06 38		06 57	07 09	07 25		07 50	07 57	08 09			08 50	08 57	09 09
—	—	0	—	**Huddersfield** 39 d										07 29					08 21			
—	—	—	—	London Kings Cross 15 ⊖26 d																		
—	—	5¼	11	Brighouse d										07 39	07 59				08 33	08 58		
—	—	—	15	Mirfield 39 a											08 06					09 06		
—	—	—	18	Dewsbury 39 a											08 11					09 12		
32¼	63½	10½	—	**Halifax** a	23p29	00 20	06 02	06 32	06 45		07 03	07 16	07 32	07 50		08 03	08 16	08 33	08 43		09 03	09 15
—	—	—	—	d	23p29	00 20	06 03	06 33	06 45	07 02	07 03	07 16	07 33	07 50		08 03	08 16	08 33	08 48		09 03	09 16
40¼	71½	—	—	**Bradford Interchange** a	23p43	00 34	06 16	06 46	07 00		07 17	07 31	07 47	08 03		08 17	08 31	08 47	09 02		09 17	09 31
—	—	—	—	d	23p46	00 37	06 18	06 48	07 02		07 20	07 34	07 50	08 05		08 20	08 34	08 50	09 04		09 20	09 34
43¾	75	—	—	New Pudsey 37 a	23p54		06 27	06 57	07 11		07 28	07 42	07 58	08 13		08 28	08 42	08 58	09 12		09 27	09 42
45¾	77	—	—	Bramley 37 a	23p58		06 30	07 00	07 14			07 46	08 02	08 18			08 46	09 02	09 16			09 46
49¾	81	—	27¼	**Leeds** 10 37,39 a	00 08	00 55	06 41	07 09	07 27	07 56	07 39	07 57	08 12	08 29	08 33	08 39	08 57	09 12	09 27	09 32	09 39	09 57
—	—	—	—	Selby 40 a								08 36	08 53					09 53				
—	—	—	—	York 8 40 a					08 06		08 16					09 21					10 21	

	NT C	NT	NT B	NT	NT A	NT	NT	NT	NT B	NT	NT A	NT	NT D	NT	NT B	NT	NT A	NT	NT D	NT	NT B	NT
Manchester Victoria ⛴ d	08 30	08 48		09 00		09 22	09 33	09 48		10 00		10 21	10 30	10 48		11 00		11 21	11 30	11 48		12 00
Moston d	08 36			09 06			09 39			10 06			10 36			11 06			11 36			12 06
Mills Hill d	08 40			09 11			09 44			10 11			10 40			11 11			11 40			12 11
Castleton d	08 45			09 16			09 49			10 16			10 45			11 16			11 45			12 16
Rochdale a	08 51	09 02		09 19		09 35	09 54	10 02		10 19		10 34	10 51	11 02		11 19		11 34	11 51	12 02		12 19
d		09 02		09 20		09 36		10 02		10 20		10 35		11 02		11 20		11 35		12 02		12 20
Smithy Bridge d				09 24		09 40				10 24		10 39				11 24		11 39				12 24
Littleborough d				09 27		09 43				10 27		10 42				11 27		11 42				12 27
Walsden d						09 49						10 48						11 48				
Todmorden d		09 14		09 34		09 53		10 14		10 34		10 52		11 14		11 34		11 52		12 14		12 34
Blackpool North 97 d					08 29						09 29						10 29					
Poulton-le-Fylde 97 d					08 35						09 35						10 35					
Preston 8 97 d					08 54						09 54						10 54					
Blackburn 97 d					09 10						10 10						11 10					
Accrington 97 d					09 17						10 17						11 17					
Burnley Manchester Road 97 d					09 26						10 26						11 28					
Hebden Bridge a		09 20		09 41	09 49	09 59		10 20		10 41	10 49	10 58		11 20		11 41	11 49	11 58		12 20		12 41
d		09 21		09 41	09 50	10 00		10 21		10 41	10 50	11 00		11 21		11 41	11 50	12 00		12 21		12 41
Mytholmroyd d				09 44		10 03				10 44		11 03				11 44		12 03				12 44
Sowerby Bridge d				09 50		10 09				10 50		11 09				11 50		12 09				12 50
Huddersfield 39 d			09 23						10 23						11 23						12 23	
London Kings Cross 15 ⊖26 d																						
Brighouse d			09 33	09 58					10 33	10 58					11 33	11 58					12 33	12 58
Mirfield 39 a				10 06						11 06						12 06						13 06
Dewsbury 39 a				10 12						11 12						12 12						13 12
Halifax a		09 33	09 44		10 02	10 15		10 33	10 43		11 02	11 15		11 33	11 43		12 02	12 15		12 33	12 43	
d		09 33	09 49		10 03	10 16		10 33	10 49		11 03	11 16		11 33	11 49		12 03	12 16		12 33	12 49	
Bradford Interchange a		09 47	10 02		10 17	10 31		10 47	11 02		11 17	11 31		11 47	12 02		12 17	12 31		12 47	13 02	
d		09 50	10 05		10 18	10 34		10 50	11 05		11 20	11 34		11 50	12 05		12 19	12 34		12 50	13 05	
New Pudsey 37 a		09 58	10 13		10 27	10 42		10 58	11 13		11 28	11 42		11 58	12 13		12 27	12 42		12 58	13 13	
Bramley 37 a		10 02	10 17			10 46		11 02	11 17			11 46		12 02	12 17			12 46		13 02	13 17	
Leeds 10 37,39 a		10 12	10 27	10 32	10 38	10 59		11 13	11 27	11 33	11 39	12 00		12 12	12 27	12 31	12 39	12 59		13 12	13 27	13 32
Selby 40 a		10 53						11 54						12 50						13 51		
York 8 40 a					11 19						12 21						13 19					

A To Blackpool North
B From Wakefield Westgate
C From Kirkby
D From Wigan Wallgate

For connections from Liverpool Lime Street please refer to Table 90

Table 41

Mondays to Fridays

Manchester Victoria, Rochdale, Blackpool North and Huddersfield - Bradford and Leeds via Brighouse and Halifax

Network Diagram - see first Page of Table 39

	NT	NT	NT	NT	GC		NT	NT	NT	NT	NT	NT	NT	NT	NT		NT	NT	NT	NT	NT	NT	NT	NT
					R 1																			
	A		B				C				B		C		A			B		C		A		B
					☕																			
Manchester Victoria ⛴ d		12 21	12 30	12 48				13 00		13 21	13 30	13 48		14 00			14 21	14 30	14 48		15 00		15 21	15 30
Moston d			12 36					13 06			13 36			14 06				14 36			15 06			15 36
Mills Hill d			12 40					13 11			13 40			14 11				14 40			15 11			15 40
Castleton d			12 45					13 16			13 45			14 16				14 45			15 16			15 45
Rochdale a		12 34	12 51	13 02				13 19		13 34	13 51	14 02		14 19			14 34	14 51	15 02		15 19		15 34	15 51
d		12 35		13 02				13 20		13 35		14 02		14 20			14 35		15 02		15 20		15 35	
Smithy Bridge d		12 39						13 24		13 39				14 24			14 39				15 24		15 39	
Littleborough d		12 42						13 27		13 42				14 27			14 42				15 27		15 42	
Walsden d		12 48								13 48							14 48						15 48	
Todmorden d		12 52		13 14				13 34		13 52		14 14		14 34			14 52		15 14		15 34		15 52	
Blackpool North 97 d	11 29								12 29						13 29							14 29		
Poulton-le-Fylde 97 d	11 35								12 35						13 35							14 35		
Preston 8 97 d	11 54								12 54						13 54							14 54		
Blackburn 97 d	12 10								13 10						14 10							15 10		
Accrington 97 d	12 17								13 17						14 17							15 17		
Burnley Manchester Road 97 d	12 26								13 26						14 26							15 26		
Hebden Bridge a	12 49	12 58		13 20				13 41	13 49	13 58		14 20		14 41	14 49		14 58		15 20		15 41	15 49	16 00	
d	12 50	13 00		13 21				13 41	13 50	14 00		14 21		14 41	14 50		15 00		15 21		15 41	15 50	16 01	
Mytholmroyd d		13 03						13 44		14 03				14 44			15 03				15 44		16 04	
Sowerby Bridge d		13 09						13 50		14 09				14 50			15 09				15 50		16 10	
Huddersfield 39 d							13 23						14 23							15 23				
London Kings Cross 15 ⊖26 d					10 48																			
Brighouse d					13 31		13 33	13 58					14 33	14 58						15 33	15 58			
Mirfield 39 a								14 06						15 06							16 06			
Dewsbury 39 a								14 12						15 12							16 12			
Halifax a	13 02	13 15		13 33	13 40		13 45		14 02	14 15		14 33	14 43		15 02		15 15		15 33	15 43		16 02	16 16	
d	13 03	13 16		13 33	13 42		13 49		14 03	14 16		14 33	14 49		15 03		15 16		15 33	15 49		16 03	16 17	
Bradford Interchange a	13 17	13 31		13 47	13 55		14 02		14 17	14 31		14 47	15 02		15 17		15 31		15 47	16 02		16 17	16 31	
d	13 19	13 34		13 50			14 05		14 19	14 34		14 50	15 05		15 19		15 34		15 50	16 05		16 19	16 34	
New Pudsey 37 a	13 27	13 42		13 58			14 13		14 28	14 42		14 58	15 13		15 27		15 42		15 58	16 13		16 27	16 42	
Bramley 37 a		13 46		14 02			14 17			14 46		15 02	15 17				15 46		16 02	16 17			16 46	
Leeds 10 37,39 a	13 40	14 00		14 13			14 27	14 32	14 39	15 00		15 12	15 27	15 32	15 39		16 00		16 12	16 27	16 32	16 39	16 58	
Selby 40 a				14 51								15 53							16 54					
York 8 40 a	14 22								15 18						16 21							17 20		

	NT		NT	NT	NT	NT	NT	NT	GC		NT		NT	NT	NT	NT	NT		NT	NT	NT		NT	NT
									R 1															
			C		A		B				C					B			C					D
									☕															
Manchester Victoria ⛴ d	15 48			16 00		16 24	16 30	16 48					17 00		17 17	17 30	17 43			18 00			18 21	18 26
Moston d				16 06			16 36						17 06		17 24	17 36	17 49							18 32
Mills Hill d				16 11			16 40						17 11		17 28	17 40	17 54			18 09				18 36
Castleton d				16 16			16 45						17 16		17 33	17 45	17 59			18 14				18 41
Rochdale a	16 02			16 19		16 37	16 51	17 02					17 19		17 37	17 51	18 02			18 18			18 35	18 47
d	16 02			16 20		16 37		17 02					17 20		17 38		18 03			18 18			18 36	
Smithy Bridge d				16 24		16 41							17 24		17 42					18 22			18 40	
Littleborough d				16 27		16 45							17 27		17 45		18 08			18 26			18 43	
Walsden d						16 51									17 51					18 32			18 49	
Todmorden d	16 14			16 34		16 54		17 14					17 34		17 55		18 16			18 35			18 53	
Blackpool North 97 d					15 29									16 29							17 14			
Poulton-le-Fylde 97 d					15 35									16 35							17 20			
Preston 8 97 d					15 54									16 54							17 44			
Blackburn 97 d					16 10									17 10							18 11			
Accrington 97 d					16 17									17 17							18 19			
Burnley Manchester Road 97 d					16 26									17 26							18 28			
Hebden Bridge a	16 20			16 41	16 49	17 01		17 20					17 41	17 49	17 59		18 22			18 42	18 49		18 59	
d	16 21			16 41	16 50	17 01		17 21					17 41	17 50	17 59		18 23			18 42	18 50		19 00	
Mytholmroyd d				16 44		17 04							17 44		18 05					18 45			19 03	
Sowerby Bridge d				16 50		17 10							17 50		18 10					18 51			19 09	
Huddersfield 39 d			16 23								17 23								18 23					
London Kings Cross 15 ⊖26 d									14 48															
Brighouse d			16 33	16 58					17 30		17 33		17 58						18 33	18 59				
Mirfield 39 a				17 06									18 07							19 07				
Dewsbury 39 a				17 12									18 13							19 13				
Halifax a	16 33		16 46		17 02	17 17		17 33	17 40		17 49			18 02	18 15		18 35		18 46		19 03		19 15	
d	16 33		16 49		17 03	17 17		17 33	17 41		17 49			18 03	18 15		18 35		18 49		19 03		19 16	
Bradford Interchange a	16 47		17 02		17 17	17 31		17 47	17 55		18 04			18 17	18 31		18 49		19 02		19 17		19 31	
d	16 50		17 04		17 19	17 34		17 50			18 04			18 19	18 34		18 52		19 05		19 19		19 34	
New Pudsey 37 a	16 58		17 13		17 28	17 42		17 58			18 13			18 28	18 40		19 00		19 13		19 27		19 42	
Bramley 37 a	17 02		17 17			17 46		18 02			18 17				18 45		19 04		19 17				19 46	
Leeds 10 37,39 a	17 12		17 27	17 31	17 39	17 57		18 12			18 29		18 34	18 39	18 56		19 13		19 28	19 33	19 39		19 56	
Selby 40 a	17 51							18 49						20 42										
York 8 40 a					18 18												19 53				20 22			

A To Blackpool North
B From Wigan Wallgate
C From Wakefield Westgate
D From Clitheroe

For connections from Liverpool Lime Street please refer to Table 90

Table 41

Manchester Victoria, Rochdale, Blackpool North and Huddersfield - Bradford and Leeds via Brighouse and Halifax

Network Diagram - see first Page of Table 39

Station		NT	NT	NT	NT	NT	NT	NT		NT	NT	NT	NT	NT		GC	NT	NT		NT		NT			
																◇■ A ☒	FX	FO							
Manchester Victoria ⛴	d	18 48		19 00		19 21	19 55			20 21	20 55			21 21						22 28		23 20			
Moston	d			19 06		19 27	20 01			20 27	21 01			21 27						22 34		23 27			
Mills Hill	d			19 11		19 32	20 05			20 32	21 06			21 32						22 39		23 32			
Castleton	d			19 16		19 37	20 10			20 37	21 11			21 37						22 44		23 37			
Rochdale	a	19 01		19 19		19 40	20 14			20 40	21 16			21 40						22 47		23 40			
	d	19 01		19 19		19 41				20 41				21 41						22 48		23 41			
Smithy Bridge	d			19 23		19 45				20 45				21 45						22 52		23 45			
Littleborough	d			19 27		19 48				20 48				21 48						22 55		23 48			
Walsden	d					19 54				20 54				21 54						23 01		23 54			
Todmorden	d	19 13		19 34		19 58				20 58				21 58						23 05		23 58			
Blackpool North 97	d				18 29								20 29												
Poulton-le-Fylde 97	d				18 35								20 35												
Preston 8 97	d				18 54								20 54												
Blackburn 97	d				19 10								21 10												
Accrington 97	d				19 17								21 17												
Burnley Manchester Road 97	d				19 26								21 28												
Hebden Bridge	a	19 20		19 41	19 49	20 04				21 04			21 50	22 04						23 11		00 04			
	d	19 20		19 41	19 50	20 05				21 05			21 51	22 05						23 11		00 04			
Mytholmroyd	d			19 44		20 08				21 08				22 08						23 15		00 08			
Sowerby Bridge	d			19 50		20 14				21 14				22 14						23 20		00 13			
Huddersfield 39	d		19 23					20 25				21 27					22 25	22 25							
London Kings Cross 15 ⊖26	d															19 48									
Brighouse	d		19 33	19 58				20 35				21 37				22 24	22 35	22 35							
Mirfield 39	a			20 07																					
Dewsbury 39	a			20 12																					
Halifax	a	19 32	19 43		20 03	20 20		20 45		21 20		21 47	22 03	22 20		22 33	22 45	22 45		23 29		00 20			
	d	19 32	19 49		20 03	20 21		20 49		21 21		21 49	22 03	22 21		22 34	22 49	22 49		23 29		00 20			
Bradford Interchange	a	19 48	20 02		20 17	20 35		21 02		21 35		22 02	22 17	22 35		22 48	23 02	23 02		23 43		00 34			
	d	19 50	20 04		20 19	20 37		21 04		21 37		22 04	22 19	22 37			23 04	23 04		23 46		00 37			
New Pudsey 37	a	19 59	20 13		20 28	20 46		21 13		21 46		22 13	22 28	22 46			23 13	23 13		23 54					
Bramley 37	a	20 03	20 16			20 49		21 16		21 49		22 16		22 49			23 16	23 16		23 58					
Leeds 10 37,39	a	20 13	20 29	20 34	20 38	20 59		21 25		22 01		22 25	22 41	23 00			23 26	23 27		00 08		00 55			
Selby 40	a																								
York 8 40	a				21 30								23 44												

Saturdays

Station		NT	NT	NT	NT	NT	NT	NT	NT	NT		NT	NT	NT	NT	NT	NT	NT	NT	NT		NT	NT	NT	NT
						B						B			C		B		D			C		B	
Manchester Victoria ⛴	d	22p28	23p20		05 54		06 17	06 43		06 58			07 17	07 48		08 00		08 22	08 30	08 48			09 00		09 22
Moston	d	22p34	23p27				06 23			07 04			07 23			08 06			08 36				09 06		
Mills Hill	d	22p39	23p32				06 28			07 09			07 28			08 11			08 40				09 11		
Castleton	d	22p44	23p37				06 33			07 14			07 33			08 16			08 45				09 16		
Rochdale	a	22p47	23p40		06 08		06 36	06 56		07 17			07 36	08 01		08 19		08 35	08 51	09 02			09 19		09 35
	d	22p48	23p41		06 09		06 37	06 56		07 18			07 37	08 01		08 20		08 35		09 02			09 20		09 36
Smithy Bridge	d	22p52	23p45		06 13		06 41			07 22			07 41			08 24		08 39					09 24		09 40
Littleborough	d	22p55	23p48		06 16		06 44			07 25			07 44			08 27		08 42					09 27		09 43
Walsden	d	23p01	23p54		06 22		06 50			07 31			07 50					08 48							09 49
Todmorden	d	23p05	23p58		06 26		06 54	07 08		07 35			07 54	08 13		08 34		08 52		09 14			09 34		09 53
Blackpool North 97	d					05 29						06 28					07 29							08 29	
Poulton-le-Fylde 97	d					05 35						06 34					07 35							08 35	
Preston 8 97	d					05 54						06 54					07 54							08 54	
Blackburn 97	d					06 10						07 10					08 10							09 10	
Accrington 97	d					06 17						07 17					08 17							09 17	
Burnley Manchester Road 97	d					06 26						07 26					08 26							09 26	
Hebden Bridge	a	23p11	00 04		06 32	06 49	07 00	07 14		07 41		07 49	08 00	08 19		08 41	08 49	09 00		09 20			09 41	09 49	09 59
	d	23p11	00 04	05 55	06 33	06 50	07 00	07 16		07 41		07 50	08 00	08 21		08 41	08 50	09 00		09 21			09 41	09 50	10 00
Mytholmroyd	d	23p15	00 08	05 58	06 36		07 04	07 19		07 45			08 04			08 44		09 03					09 44		10 03
Sowerby Bridge	d	23p20	00 13	06 04	06 42	06 57	07 09	07 25		07 50		07 57	08 09			08 50	08 57	09 09					09 50		10 09
Huddersfield 39	d								07 29						08 21							09 23			
London Kings Cross 15 ⊖26	d																								
Brighouse	d								07 39	07 59					08 33	08 58						09 33	09 58		
Mirfield 39	a									08 06						09 06							10 06		
Dewsbury 39	a									08 11						09 12							10 12		
Halifax	a	23p29	00 20	06 10	06 48	07 03	07 16	07 32	07 50			08 03	08 16	08 33	08 43		09 03	09 16		09 33		09 44		10 02	10 15
	d	23p29	00 20	06 11	06 49	07 03	07 16	07 33	07 50			08 03	08 16	08 33	08 48		09 03	09 16		09 33		09 49		10 03	10 16
Bradford Interchange	a	23p43	00 34	06 24	07 03	07 17	07 31	07 47	08 03			08 17	08 31	08 47	09 02		09 17	09 31		09 47		10 02		10 17	10 31
	d	23p46	00 37	06 26	07 05	07 20	07 34	07 50	08 05			08 20	08 34	08 50	09 04		09 20	09 34		09 50		10 05		10 18	10 34
New Pudsey 37	a	23p54		06 35	07 14	07 28	07 42	07 58	08 14			08 28	08 42	08 58	09 12		09 27	09 42		09 58		10 13		10 27	10 42
Bramley 37	a	23p58		06 38	07 17		07 46	08 02	08 18				08 46	09 02	09 16			09 46		10 02		10 17			10 46
Leeds 10 37,39	a	00 08	00 55	06 49	07 27	07 39	07 57	08 11	08 30	08 31		08 39	08 56	09 12	09 27	09 32	09 39	09 58		10 12		10 27	10 32	10 38	11 00
Selby 40	a						08 36							09 53						10 53					
York 8 40	a					08 20						09 21					10 21							11 18	

A ☒ from Brighouse ◇ from Brighouse

B To Blackpool North

C From Wakefield Westgate

D From Kirkby

For connections from Liverpool Lime Street please refer to Table 90

Manchester Victoria, Rochdale, Blackpool North and Huddersfield - Bradford and Leeds via Brighouse and Halifax

Network Diagram - see first Page of Table 39

		NT A	NT	NT B	NT	NT C		NT	NT D	NT	NT B	NT	NT C	NT	NT D	NT		NT B	NT	NT C	NT	GC	NT D	NT	NT B
Manchester Victoria	d	09 33	09 48		10 00			10 21	10 30	10 48		11 00		11 21	11 30	11 48			12 00		12 21		12 30	12 48	
Moston	d	09 39			10 06				10 36			11 06			11 36				12 06				12 36		
Mills Hill	d	09 44			10 11				10 40			11 11			11 40				12 11				12 40		
Castleton	d	09 49			10 16				10 45			11 16			11 45				12 16				12 45		
Rochdale	a	09 54	10 02		10 19			10 34	10 51	11 02		11 19		11 34	11 51	12 02			12 19		12 34		12 51	13 02	
	d		10 02		10 20			10 35		11 02		11 20		11 35		12 02			12 20		12 35			13 02	
Smithy Bridge	d				10 24			10 39				11 24		11 39					12 24		12 39				
Littleborough	d				10 27			10 42				11 27		11 42					12 27		12 42				
Walsden	d							10 48						11 48							12 48				
Todmorden	d		10 14		10 34			10 52		11 14		11 34		11 52		12 14			12 34		12 52			13 14	
Blackpool North	97 d					09 29							10 29							11 29					
Poulton-le-Fylde	97 d					09 35							10 35							11 35					
Preston 8	97 d					09 54							10 54							11 54					
Blackburn	97 d					10 10							11 10							12 10					
Accrington	97 d					10 18							11 17							12 17					
Burnley Manchester Road	97 d					10 26							11 28							12 26					
Hebden Bridge	a		10 20		10 41	10 50		10 58		11 20		11 41	11 49	11 58		12 20			12 41	12 49	12 58			13 20	
	d		10 21		10 41	10 50		11 00		11 21		11 41	11 50	12 00		12 21			12 41	12 50	13 00			13 21	
Mytholmroyd	d				10 44			11 03				11 44		12 03					12 44		13 03				
Sowerby Bridge	d				10 50			11 09				11 50		12 09					12 50		13 09				
Huddersfield	39 d			10 23							11 23							12 23							13 23
London Kings Cross 15 ⊖26	d																					10 48			
Brighouse	d			10 33	10 58						11 33	11 58						12 33	12 58			13 06			13 33
Mirfield	39 a				11 06							12 06							13 06						
Dewsbury	39 a				11 12							12 12							13 12						
Halifax	a		10 33	10 43		11 02		11 15		11 33	11 43		12 02	12 15		12 33		12 43		13 02	13 15	13 21		13 33	13 45
	d		10 33	10 49		11 03		11 16		11 33	11 49		12 03	12 16		12 33		12 49		13 03	13 16	13 22		13 33	13 49
Bradford Interchange	a		10 47	11 02		11 17		11 31		11 47	12 02		12 17	12 31		12 47		13 02		13 17	13 31	13 38		13 47	14 02
	d		10 50	11 05		11 20		11 34		11 50	12 05		12 19	12 34		12 50		13 05		13 19	13 34			13 50	14 05
New Pudsey	37 a		10 58	11 13		11 28		11 42		11 58	12 13		12 27	12 42		12 58		13 13		13 27	13 42			13 58	14 13
Bramley	37 a		11 02	11 17				11 46		12 02	12 17			12 46		13 02		13 17			13 46			14 02	14 17
Leeds 10	37,39 a		11 13	11 27	11 35	11 39		12 00		12 12	12 27	12 32	12 39	12 58		13 12		13 27	13 32	13 39	13 58			14 14	14 27
Selby	40 a		11 55							12 50						13 52								14 51	
York 8	40 a					12 21							13 19							14 22					

		NT		NT	NT	NT D	NT	NT B	NT	NT C	NT	NT D		NT	NT B	NT	NT C	NT	NT D	NT	NT B	NT		NT C	NT
Manchester Victoria	d	13 00			13 21	13 30	13 48		14 00		14 21	14 30		14 48		15 00		15 21	15 30	15 48		16 00			16 24
Moston	d	13 06				13 36			14 06			14 36				15 06			15 36			16 06			
Mills Hill	d	13 11				13 40			14 11			14 40				15 11			15 40			16 11			
Castleton	d	13 16				13 45			14 16			14 45				15 16			15 45			16 16			
Rochdale	a	13 19			13 34	13 51	14 02		14 19		14 34	14 51		15 02		15 19		15 34	15 51	16 02		16 19			16 37
	d	13 20			13 35		14 02		14 20		14 35			15 02		15 20		15 35		16 02		16 20			16 37
Smithy Bridge	d	13 24			13 39				14 24		14 39					15 24		15 39				16 24			16 41
Littleborough	d	13 27			13 42				14 27		14 42					15 27		15 42				16 27			16 45
Walsden	d				13 48						14 48							15 48							16 51
Todmorden	d	13 34			13 52		14 14		14 34		14 52			15 14		15 34		15 52		16 14		16 34			16 54
Blackpool North	97 d			12 29						13 29							14 29							15 29	
Poulton-le-Fylde	97 d			12 35						13 35							14 35							15 35	
Preston 8	97 d			12 53						13 54							14 54							15 54	
Blackburn	97 d			13 09						14 10							15 10							16 10	
Accrington	97 d			13 16						14 17							15 17							16 17	
Burnley Manchester Road	97 d			13 25						14 26							15 26							16 26	
Hebden Bridge	a	13 41		13 49	13 58		14 20		14 41	14 49	14 58			15 20		15 41	15 49	16 00		16 20		16 41		16 49	17 01
	d	13 41		13 50	14 00		14 21		14 41	14 50	15 00			15 21		15 41	15 50	16 01		16 21		16 41		16 50	17 01
Mytholmroyd	d	13 44			14 03				14 44		15 03					15 44		16 04				16 44			17 04
Sowerby Bridge	d	13 50			14 09				14 50		15 09					15 50		16 10				16 50			17 10
Huddersfield	39 d							14 23							15 23						16 23				
London Kings Cross 15 ⊖26	d																								
Brighouse	d	13 58						14 33	14 58						15 33	15 58					16 33	16 58			
Mirfield	39 a	14 06							15 06							16 06						17 06			
Dewsbury	39 a	14 12							15 12							16 12						17 12			
Halifax	a			14 02	14 15		14 33	14 43		15 02	15 15			15 33	15 43		16 02	16 16		16 33	16 46			17 02	17 17
	d			14 03	14 16		14 33	14 49		15 03	15 16			15 33	15 49		16 03	16 17		16 33	16 49			17 03	17 17
Bradford Interchange	a			14 17	14 31		14 47	15 02		15 17	15 31			15 47	16 02		16 17	16 31		16 47	17 02			17 17	17 31
	d			14 19	14 34		14 50	15 05		15 19	15 34			15 50	16 05		16 19	16 34		16 50	17 04			17 19	17 34
New Pudsey	37 a			14 28	14 42		14 58	15 13		15 27	15 42			15 58	16 13		16 27	16 42		16 58	17 13			17 28	17 42
Bramley	37 a				14 46		15 02	15 17			15 46			16 02	16 17			16 46		17 02	17 17				17 46
Leeds 10	37,39 a	14 32		14 39	14 58		15 10	15 27	15 32	15 39	16 00			16 12	16 27	16 31	16 39	16 59		17 12	17 27	17 31		17 39	17 57
Selby	40 a						15 53							16 54						17 55					
York 8	40 a			15 17						16 21							17 21							18 24	

A From Blackburn
B From Wakefield Westgate
C To Blackpool North
D From Wigan Wallgate

For connections from Liverpool Lime Street please refer to Table 90

Manchester Victoria, Rochdale, Blackpool North and Huddersfield - Bradford and Leeds via Brighouse and Halifax

Network Diagram - see first Page of Table 39

		NT A	NT	NT	NT B	NT	NT C	NT		GC	NT A	NT	NT	NT B	NT	NT	NT	NT D		NT	NT	NT	NT E	NT	NT
Manchester Victoria	d	16 30	16 48			17 00		17 18			17 30	17 43			18 00		18 21	18 28		18 48		19 00		19 21	
Moston	d	16 36				17 06		17 24			17 36	17 49						18 34				19 06		19 27	
Mills Hill	d	16 40				17 11		17 29			17 40	17 54			18 09			18 39				19 10		19 32	
Castleton	d	16 45				17 16		17 34			17 45	17 59			18 14			18 44				19 15		19 37	
Rochdale	a	16 51	17 02			17 19		17 37			17 51	18 02			18 18		18 35	18 47		19 01		19 19		19 40	
	d		17 02	17 03		17 20		17 38				18 03	18 02		18 18		18 36			19 01		19 19		19 41	
Smithy Bridge	d					17 24		17 42							18 22		18 40					19 23		19 45	
Littleborough	d					17 27		17 46				18 08			18 26		18 43					19 27		19 48	
Walsden	d							17 52							18 32		18 49							19 54	
Todmorden	d		17 14			17 34		17 55				18 16			18 35		18 53			19 13		19 34		19 58	
Blackpool North 97	d						16 29									17 14							18 29		
Poulton-le-Fylde 97	d						16 35									17 20							18 35		
Preston 8 97	d						16 54									17 44							18 54		
Blackburn 97	d			18a21			17 10						19a21			18 11							19 10		
Accrington 97	d						17 17									18 19							19 17		
Burnley Manchester Road 97	d						17 26									18 28							19 26		
Hebden Bridge	a		17 20			17 41	17 49	18 02				18 22			18 42	18 49	18 59			19 19		19 41	19 49	20 04	
	d		17 21			17 41	17 50	18 02				18 23			18 42	18 50	19 00			19 20		19 41	19 50	20 05	
Mytholmroyd	d					17 44		18 05							18 45		19 03					19 44		20 08	
Sowerby Bridge	d					17 50		18 11							18 51		19 09					19 50		20 14	
Huddersfield 39	d				17 23									18 23							19 23				20 25
London Kings Cross 15 ⊖26	d									15 48															
Brighouse	d				17 33	17 58				18 07				18 33	18 59						19 33	19 58			20 35
Mirfield 39	a					18 07									19 07							20 07			
Dewsbury 39	a					18 12									19 13							20 12			
Halifax	a		17 33		17 49		18 02	18 17		18 23		18 35		18 46		19 02	19 15			19 32	19 43		20 03	20 20	20 45
	d		17 33		17 49		18 03	18 18		18 24		18 35		18 49		19 03	19 16			19 32	19 49		20 03	20 21	20 49
Bradford Interchange	a		17 47		18 04		18 17	18 32		18 39		18 49		19 02		19 17	19 31			19 48	20 02		20 17	20 35	21 02
	d		17 50		18 04		18 19	18 34				18 52		19 05		19 18	19 34			19 50	20 04		20 19	20 37	21 04
New Pudsey 37	a		17 58		18 13		18 28	18 43				19 00		19 13		19 27	19 42			19 58	20 13		20 28	20 46	21 13
Bramley 37	a		18 02		18 17			18 46				19 04		19 17			19 46			20 02	20 16			20 49	21 16
Leeds 10 37,39	a		18 12		18 29	18 31	18 39	18 56				19 13		19 28	19 33	19 39	19 58			20 12	20 30	20 33	20 38	20 59	21 25
Selby 40	a		18 50				20 06																		
York 8 40	a											19 53				20 18							21 30		

		NT	NT	NT		GC	NT	NT	NT	NT	NT
Manchester Victoria	d	20 21					21 21	22 21		22 54	23 20
Moston	d	20 27					21 27	22 27			23 26
Mills Hill	d	20 32					21 32	22 32			23 31
Castleton	d	20 37					21 37	22 37			23 36
Rochdale	a	20 40					21 40	22 42		23 07	23 41
	d	20 41					21 41			23 07	
Smithy Bridge	d	20 45					21 45			23 11	
Littleborough	d	20 48					21 48			23 15	
Walsden	d	20 54					21 54			23 21	
Todmorden	d	20 58					21 58			23 24	
Blackpool North 97	d			20 29							
Poulton-le-Fylde 97	d			20 35							
Preston 8 97	d			20 54							
Blackburn 97	d			21 10							
Accrington 97	d			21 17							
Burnley Manchester Road 97	d			21 28							
Hebden Bridge	a	21 04		21 50			22 04			23 31	
	d	21 05		21 51			22 05			23 31	
Mytholmroyd	d	21 08					22 08			23 34	
Sowerby Bridge	d	21 14					22 14			23 40	
Huddersfield 39	d		21 27						22 25		
London Kings Cross 15 ⊖26	d					19 20					
Brighouse	d		21 38			21 59			22 35		
Mirfield 39	a										
Dewsbury 39	a										
Halifax	a	21 20	21 47	22 03		22 08	22 20		22 45	23 46	
	d	21 21	21 48	22 03		22 10	22 21		22 49	23 47	
Bradford Interchange	a	21 35	22 02	22 17		22 24	22 35		23 02	00 02	
	d	21 37	22 04	22 19			22 37		23 04	00 04	
New Pudsey 37	a	21 46	22 13	22 28			22 46		23 13	00 12	
Bramley 37	a	21 49	22 16				22 49		23 16	00 15	
Leeds 10 37,39	a	21 59	22 24	22 37			23 01		23 26	00 27	
Selby 40	a										
York 8 40	a			23 38							

A From Wigan Wallgate
B From Wakefield Westgate
C To Hull
D From Clitheroe

For connections from Liverpool Lime Street please refer to Table 90

Table 41

Sundays

Manchester Victoria, Rochdale, Blackpool North and Huddersfield - Bradford and Leeds via Brighouse and Halifax

Network Diagram - see first Page of Table 39

			NT	NT	NT	NT	NT	NT	NT	NT	NT		NT	NT	NT	NT	NT	NT	NT	GC	NT		NT	NT	NT	NT
			A																	■ ☕						
Manchester Victoria	⛴	d	22p54	08 32			09 08		10 08				11 08			12 08			13 08					14 08		
Moston		d					09 15		10 15				11 15			12 15			13 15					14 15		
Mills Hill		d					09 19		10 19				11 19			12 19			13 19					14 19		
Castleton		d					09 24		10 24				11 24			12 24			13 24					14 24		
Rochdale		a	23p07	08 48			09 28		10 28				11 28			12 28			13 28					14 28		
		d	23p07				09 28		10 28				11 28			12 28			13 28					14 28		
Smithy Bridge		d	23p11				09 32		10 32				11 32			12 32			13 32					14 32		
Littleborough		d	23p15				09 36		10 36				11 36			12 36			13 36					14 36		
Walsden		d	23p21				09 42		10 42				11 42			12 42			13 42					14 42		
Todmorden		d	23p24				09 45		10 45				11 45			12 45			13 45					14 45		
Blackpool North	97	d						09 01			10 11				11 13			12 11					13 13			14 11
Poulton-le-Fylde	97	d						09 07			10 17				11 19			12 17					13 19			14 17
Preston [8]	97	d						09 27			10 37				11 37			12 37					13 37			14 37
Blackburn	97	d						09 44			10 54				11 54			12 54					13 54			14 54
Accrington	97	d						09 51			11 01				12 01			13 01					14 01			15 01
Burnley Manchester Road	97	d						10 00			11 10				12 10			13 10					14 10			15 10
Hebden Bridge		a	23p31				09 52	10 22	10 52		11 32		11 52		12 32	12 52		13 32	13 52				14 32	14 52		15 32
		d	23p31				09 52	10 22	10 52		11 32		11 52		12 32	12 52		13 32	13 52				14 32	14 52		15 32
Mytholmroyd		d	23p34				09 55		10 55				11 55			12 55			13 55					14 55		
Sowerby Bridge		d	23p40				10 01		11 01				12 01			13 01			14 01					15 01		
Huddersfield	39	d				09 27				11 08							13 08								15 08	
London Kings Cross [15] ⊖	26	d																		11 48						
Brighouse		d				09 37				11 18							13 18			14 09					15 18	
Mirfield	39	a																								
Dewsbury	39	a																								
Halifax		a	23p46			09 48	10 08	10 34	11 08	11 28	11 44		12 08		12 44	13 08	13 28	13 44	14 08	14 19			14 44	15 08	15 28	15 44
		d	23p47		09 05	09 48	10 08	10 45	11 08	11 29	11 45		12 08	12 29	12 45	13 08	13 29	13 46	14 08	14 20	14 29		14 45	15 08	15 29	15 46
Bradford Interchange		a	00 02		09 18	10 01	10 22	11 00	11 22	11 42	11 59		12 22	12 42	12 59	13 22	13 42	14 00	14 22	14 37	14 42		14 59	15 22	15 42	16 00
		d	00 04		09 20	10 04	10 25	11 02	11 25	11 44	12 02		12 25	12 44	13 02	13 25	13 44	14 02	14 25		14 44		15 02	15 25	15 44	16 03
New Pudsey	37	a	00 12		09 29	10 12	10 33	11 10	11 33	11 53	12 10		12 33	12 53	13 10	13 33	13 53	14 10	14 33		14 53		15 10	15 33	15 53	16 11
Bramley	37	a	00 15		09 32	10 16	10 37		11 37	11 56			12 37	12 56		13 37	13 56		14 37		14 56			15 37	15 56	
Leeds [10]	37,39	a	00 27		09 42	10 25	10 46	11 21	11 48	12 05	12 22		12 46	13 06	13 22	13 46	14 06	14 22	14 48		15 06		15 22	15 46	16 06	16 22
Selby	40	a																								
York [8]	40	a			10 28	11 08		11 59			13 02				13 59			15 02					15 59			17 02

			NT	NT	NT	NT	NT		NT	NT	GC	NT	NT	NT	NT	NT	NT		NT	NT	NT	NT	GC	NT	NT	NT
											■ ☕															
Manchester Victoria	⛴	d	15 08			16 08				17 08				18 08			19 08			20 08				21 08		22 08
Moston		d	15 15			16 15				17 15				18 15			19 15			20 15				21 15		22 15
Mills Hill		d	15 19			16 19				17 19				18 19			19 19			20 19				21 19		22 19
Castleton		d	15 24			16 24				17 24				18 24			19 24			20 24				21 24		22 24
Rochdale		a	15 28			16 28				17 28				18 28			19 28			20 28				21 28		22 28
		d	15 28			16 28				17 28				18 28			19 28			20 28				21 28		22 28
Smithy Bridge		d	15 32			16 32				17 32				18 32			19 32			20 32				21 32		22 32
Littleborough		d	15 36			16 36				17 36				18 36			19 36			20 36				21 36		22 36
Walsden		d	15 42			16 42				17 42				18 42			19 42			20 42				21 42		22 42
Todmorden		d	15 45			16 45				17 45				18 45			19 45			20 45				21 45		22 45
Blackpool North	97	d			15 13				16 11				17 11			18 11			19 13			20 11			21 13	
Poulton-le-Fylde	97	d			15 19				16 17				17 17			18 17			19 19			20 17			21 19	
Preston [8]	97	d			15 37				16 37				17 37			18 37			19 37			20 37			21 39	
Blackburn	97	d			15 54				16 54				17 54			18 54			19 54			20 54			21 55	
Accrington	97	d			16 01				17 01				18 01			19 01			20 01			21 01			22 02	
Burnley Manchester Road	97	d			16 10				17 10				18 10			19 10			20 10			21 10			22 12	
Hebden Bridge		a	15 52		16 32	16 52			17 32	17 52			18 32	18 52		19 32	19 52		20 32	20 52		21 32		21 52	22 34	22 52
		d	15 52		16 32	16 52			17 32	17 52			18 32	18 52		19 32	19 52		20 32	20 52		21 32		21 52	22 34	22 52
Mytholmroyd		d	15 55			16 55				17 55				18 55			19 55			20 55				21 55		22 55
Sowerby Bridge		d	16 01			17 01				18 01				19 01			20 01			21 01				22 01		23 01
Huddersfield	39	d					17 08								19 08						21 08					
London Kings Cross [15] ⊖	26	d									15 48												19 23			
Brighouse		d					17 17				18 11				19 18						21 18		21 47			
Mirfield	39	a																								
Dewsbury	39	a																								
Halifax		a	16 08		16 44	17 08	17 27		17 44	18 08	18 20		18 44	19 08	19 28	19 44	20 08		20 44	21 08	21 28	21 44	21 57	22 08	22 46	23 08
		d	16 08	16 29	16 45	17 08	17 29		17 45	18 08	18 21	18 29	18 45	19 08	19 29	19 45	20 08		20 45	21 08	21 30	21 45	21 58	22 09	22 47	23 08
Bradford Interchange		a	16 22	16 42	16 59	17 22	17 42		17 59	18 22	18 36	18 42	18 59	19 22	19 42	19 59	20 22		20 59	21 22	21 42	21 59	22 11	22 23	23 01	23 22
		d	16 25	16 44	17 02	17 25	17 44		18 02	18 25		18 44	19 02	19 25	19 44	20 02	20 25		21 02	21 26	21 44	22 02		22 26	23 04	23 25
New Pudsey	37	a	16 33	16 53	17 10	17 33	17 53		18 10	18 33		18 53	19 10	19 33	19 53	20 10	20 33		21 10	21 34	21 53	22 10		22 34	23 12	23 33
Bramley	37	a	16 37	16 56		17 37	17 56			18 37		18 56		19 37	19 56		20 37			21 38	21 56			22 38		23 37
Leeds [10]	37,39	a	16 46	17 05	17 21	17 46	18 05		18 21	18 46		19 07	19 22	19 47	20 08	20 22	20 47		21 22	21 48	22 05	22 21		22 47	23 23	23 46
Selby	40	a																								
York [8]	40	a			18 02				19 01				19 59			21 03			22 00							

A not 11 December

For connections from Liverpool Lime Street please refer to Table 90

Table 43

Mondays to Saturdays

Hull - Beverley, Bridlington and Scarborough

Network Diagram - see first Page of Table 39

Miles			NT	TP	TP	NT	NT	NT	NT	TP	NT		NT	NT	TP	NT	NT	NT	NT	TP	TP		NT	NT	NT
																SX	SO						SX	SO	
				◇1	◇1					◇1 🛒					◇1 🛒					◇1 🛒	◇1 🛒				
0	**Hull**	d	06 23			06 54	07 14	07 36	07 52		08 14		08 37	09 17		09 47	09 47	10 14	10 44				11 14	11 14	11 44
4	Cottingham	d	06 30			07 01	07 21	07 43	07 59		08 21		08 44	09 24		09 54	09 54	10 21	10 51				11 21	11 21	11 51
8¼	**Beverley**	d	06 36			07 07	07 27	07a51	08 05		08 27		08a52	09 30		10 00	10 01	10 27	10 57				11 28	11 28	11 57
11¼	Arram	d				07 12			08 10																
16¼	Hutton Cranswick	d				07 19	07 36		08 17		08 36			09 39		10 09	10 10		11 06						12 06
19½	Driffield	d	06 48			07 24	07 42		08 22		08 42			09 45		10 15	10 15	10 39	11 12				11 40	11 40	12 12
21½	Nafferton	d				07 28	07 46		08 26		08 46			09 49		10 19	10 19		11 16						12 16
31	**Bridlington**	a	07 06			07 40	07 59		08 40		08 57			10 02		10 31	10 32	10 56	11 29				11 55	11 55	12 29
—		d				07 49					09 00					10 37	10 36						12 05	12 05	
34½	Bempton	d				07 56					09 07					10 44	10 43						12 12	12 12	
41¾	Hunmanby	d				08 06					09 17					10 54	10 53						12 22	12 22	
44½	Filey	d				08 11					09 22					10 59	10 58						12 27	12 27	
51	Seamer	d		07 21	08 06	08 22				09 21	09 34				10 21	11 10	11 10			11 21	12 21		12 38	12 39	
53¾	**Scarborough**	a		07 30	08 15	08 30				09 30	09 41				10 30	11 17	11 17			11 30	12 30		12 44	12 45	

		NT	NT	TP	TP	TP	NT		NT	NT	NT	TP	NT	NT	NT	NT	TP		TP	NT	NT	NT	NT	NT	TP
				SO	SX					SO	SX					SX				SO	SX		SX	SO	SX
				◇1 🛒	◇1 🛒	◇1 🛒						◇1 🛒					◇1 🛒		◇1 🛒						◇1 🛒
Hull	d	12 14	12 44				13 14		13 44	14 14	14 14		14 44	15 14	15 44	16 00				16 14	16 19	16 44	17 14	17 14	
Cottingham	d	12 21	12 51				13 21		13 51	14 21	14 21		14 51	15 21	15 51	16 07				16 21	16 26	16 51	17 21	17 21	
Beverley	d	12 27	12 57				13 28		13 57	14 27	14 27		14 57	15 27	15 57	16a14				16 27	16 32	16 57	17 27	17 27	
Arram	d		13 02												16 02										
Hutton Cranswick	d		13 09						14 06				15 06		16 09					16 36	16 41		17 36	17 36	
Driffield	d	12 39	13 14				13 40		14 12	14 39	14 39		15 12	15 39	16 14					16 41	16 46	17 09	17 42	17 42	
Nafferton	d		13 18						14 16				15 16		16 18					16 45	16 50		17 46	17 46	
Bridlington	a	12 56	13 33				13 55		14 29	14 55	14 56		15 27	15 56	16 33					16 56	17 01	17 26	17 59	18 00	
	d						14 05						15 31							17 04	17 04				
Bempton	d						14 12						15 38							17 10	17 10				
Hunmanby	d						14 22						15 48							17 20	17 20				
Filey	d						14 27						15 53							17 25	17 25				
Seamer	d			13 21	13 21	14 21	14 38					15 21	16 05				16 21		17 21	17 36	17 36				18 04
Scarborough	a			13 30	13 31	14 30	14 45					15 30	16 10				16 30		17 30	17 43	17 43				18 15

		TP	TP		NT	NT	NT	NT	NT	TP	TP	TP	TP		NT	NT	NT	NT	NT	TP	NT	TP	TP	NT	NT
		SO	SX				SX	SO		SO	SX	SO	SX		SX	SO	SO	SX				SX	SO		SX
		◇1	◇1 🛒							◇1	◇1 🛒	◇1	◇1 🛒							◇1		◇1	◇1	A	B
Hull	d				17 38	17 57	18 14	18 15	18 44						19 17	19 20	20 14	20 14	21 10		21 48			23 00	23 04
Cottingham	d				17 45	18 04	18 21	18 22	18 51						19 24	19 27	20 21	20 21	21 17		21 55			23 07	23 11
Beverley	d				17 51	18a12	18 27	18 29	18a58						19 30	19 33	20 27	20 27	21a25		22 01			23a15	23a19
Arram	d				17 56												20 32	20 32							
Hutton Cranswick	d				18 03		18 36	18 38							19 39	19 42	20 39	20 39			22 10				
Driffield	d				18 08		18 42	18 43							19 44	19 47	20 44	20 44			22 16				
Nafferton	d				18 12		18 46	18 47							19 49	19 52	20 48	20 48			22 20				
Bridlington	a				18 24		19 02	19 01							20 00	20 03	21 02	21 04			22 33				
	d				18 30										20 03	20 20									
Bempton	d				18 37										20 10	20 27									
Hunmanby	d				18 47										20 20	20 37									
Filey	d				18 52										20 25	20 42									
Seamer	d	18 21	18 41		19 03					19 21	19 21	20 21	20 21		20 36	20 54				21 21		22 49	22 54		
Scarborough	a	18 30	18 50		19 09					19 30	19 30	20 30	20 30		20 45	21 04				21 30		22 58	23 03		

A until 24 March, SO from 31 March

B from 26 March

Sundays

Hull - Beverley, Bridlington and Scarborough

Network Diagram - see first Page of Table 39

		NT	TP	NT	NT	NT	TP	NT	NT	TP		NT	NT	TP	NT	NT	NT	TP	NT	NT		NT	TP	TP	TP
			◇1				◇1			◇1				◇1				◇1					◇1	◇1	◇1
Hull	d	09 00		09 25	10 25	11 25		12 00	13 00			14 05	15 05		16 05	16 55	17 15		18 00	19 00		20 00			
Cottingham	d	09 07		09 32	10 32	11 32		12 07	13 07			14 12	15 12		16 12	17 02	17 22		18 07	19 07		20 06			
Beverley	d	09 13		09 38	10 38	11 38		12 13	13 13			14 18	15 18		16 18	17 08	17 28		18 13	19 13		20a13			
Arram	d			09 43																					
Hutton Cranswick	d			09 50	10 47			12 22				14 27			16 27		17 37			19 22					
Driffield	d	09 25		09 55	10 53	11 50		12 28	13 25			14 33	15 30		16 33	17 20	17 43		18 25	19 28					
Nafferton	d			09 59	10 57			12 32				14 37			16 37		17 47			19 32					
Bridlington	a	09 41		10 11	11 08	12 06		12 43	13 42			14 48	15 46		16 48	17 37	18 00		18 39	19 45					
	d			10 13	11 11			12 46				14 51			16 53				18 45						
Bempton	d			10 20	11 18			12 53				14 58			17 00				18 52						
Hunmanby	d			10 30	11 28			13 03				15 08			17 10				19 02						
Filey	d			10 35	11 33			13 08				15 13			17 15				19 07						
Seamer	d		10 20	10 46	11 44		12 25	13 20		14 24		15 24		16 24	17 26			18 24	19 19				20 27	21 25	22 51
Scarborough	a		10 30	10 54	11 50		12 34	13 25		14 33		15 30		16 33	17 32			18 33	19 24				20 36	21 34	22 59

Scarborough, Bridlington and Beverley - Hull

Network Diagram - see first Page of Table 39

Miles			TP SX ◇1 🛒	TP SO ◇1	NT SO	NT SX	NT SX	NT	NT	NT	NT		TP SO ◇1 🛒	TP SX ◇1 🛒	TP SX ◇1 🛒	TP SO ◇1 🛒	NT	TP SX ◇1 🛒	TP SO ◇1	NT	NT		NT	TP ◇1 🛒	NT
0	**Scarborough**	d	06 30	06 30							06 50		06 58	07 00	07 40	07 48		08 48	08 48				09 02	09 48	
2¾	Seamer	d	06a35	06a35							06 55		07a03	07a05	07a45	07a53		08a53	08a53				09 07	09a53	
9¼	Filey	d									07 04												09 16		
12	Hunmanby	d									07 09												09 21		
19¼	Bempton	d									07 19												09 31		
22¾	**Bridlington**	a									07 25												09 38		
—		d						06 46	07 14		07 32						08 08				09 05		09 41		10 11
32¼	Nafferton	d						06 56	07 24		07 43						08 19				09 16		09 52		
24¼	Driffield	d						07 01	07 29		07 47						08 23				09 20		09 56		10 24
37½	Hutton Cranswick	d						07 05	07 33		07 52						08 28				09 25		10 01		
42½	Arram	d									07 59										09 32				
45½	**Beverley**	d			06 30	06 38	06 58	07 15	07 43	07 57	08 06						08 38			09 00	09 37		10 11		10 37
49¾	Cottingham	d			06 36	06 44	07 03	07 21	07 49	08 03	08 12						08 44			09 06	09 43		10 17		10 43
53¾	**Hull**	a			06 44	06 53	07 13	07 33	07 59	08 13	08 23						08 54			09 15	09 53		10 27		10 53

		NT	TP ◇1 🛒	NT SX	NT SO	NT	NT SX		NT SO	TP SX ◇1 🛒	TP SO ◇1	NT	TP ◇1 🛒	NT	NT	NT	TP ◇1 🛒		NT	TP ◇1 🛒	NT SX	NT SO	NT SX	NT SO	TP ◇1 🛒
Scarborough	d	10 00	10 48				11 28		11 28	11 48	11 48		12 48			13 28	13 48			14 48			14 54	14 54	15 48
Seamer	d	10 05	10a53				11 33		11 33	11a53	11a53		12a53			13 33	13a53			14a53			14 59	14 59	15a53
Filey	d	10 14					11 42		11 42							13 42							15 08	15 08	
Hunmanby	d	10 19					11 47		11 47							13 47							15 13	15 12	
Bempton	d	10 29					11 57		11 57							13 57							15 23	15 22	
Bridlington	a	10 36					12 04		12 04							14 04							15 30	15 30	
	d	10 41		11 11	11 11	11 41	12 09		12 10			12 41		13 11	13 41	14 11			14 41		15 11	15 11	15 36	15 38	
Nafferton	d	10 52				11 52						12 52			13 52				14 52				15 47	15 49	
Driffield	d	10 56		11 24	11 24	11 56	12 22		12 23			12 56		13 24	13 56	14 24			14 56		15 24	15 24	15 51	15 53	
Hutton Cranswick	d	11 01				12 01						13 01			14 01				15 01				15 56	15 58	
Arram	d					12 08																			
Beverley	d	11 11		11 37	11 37	12 13	12 36		12 37			13 11		13 37	14 11	14 37			15 11		15 37	15 38	16 06	16 08	
Cottingham	d	11 17		11 43	11 43	12 19	12 42		12 43			13 17		13 43	14 17	14 43			15 17		15 43	15 44	16 12	16 14	
Hull	a	11 27		11 53	11 54	12 29	12 54		12 54			13 27		13 53	14 27	14 53			15 30		15 53	15 53	16 24	16 25	

		NT SO	NT SX		NT	NT SO	NT SX	TP SO ◇1	TP SX ◇1 🛒	NT SO	NT SX	TP ◇1	NT SX		NT SO	NT	NT	TP ◇1	NT	NT SO	TP ◇1	NT SX	TP SX ◇1		NT
Scarborough	d					16 23	16 23	16 48	16 48			17 48					17 53	18 48		19 40	19 48	20 03	20 48		
Seamer	d					16 28	16 28	16a53	16a53			17a53					17 58	18a53		19 45	19a53	20 08	20a53		
Filey	d					16 37	16 37										18 07			19 54		20 17			
Hunmanby	d					16 42	16 42										18 12			19 59		20 25			
Bempton	d					16 52	16 52										18 22			20 09		20 34			
Bridlington	a					16 59	16 59										18 29			20 17		20 42			
	d	16 09	16 09		16 41	17 04	17 04			17 34	17 34					18 15	18 41		19 10	20 27		20 44			
Nafferton	d				16 52					17 45	17 45						18 52		19 21	20 38		20 55			
Driffield	d	16 22	16 22		16 56	17 17	17 16			17 49	17 49					18 28	18 56		19 25	20 42		21 00			
Hutton Cranswick	d				17 01					17 54	17 54						19 01		19 30	20 47		21 05			
Arram	d				17 08																				
Beverley	d	16 35	16 35		17 13	17 30	17 30			18 04	18 04		18 20		18 21	18 41	19 11		19 40	20 57		21 14			21 40
Cottingham	d	16 41	16 41		17 19	17 36	17 36			18 10	18 10		18 26		18 26	18 47	19 17		19 46	21 03		21 20			21 46
Hull	a	16 50	16 51		17 30	17 48	17 49			18 20	18 21		18 36		18 36	18 58	19 27		19 58	21 15		21 30			21 57

		NT SO	NT SX	TP ◇1	NT
Scarborough	d			22 03	
Seamer	d			22a08	
Filey	d				
Hunmanby	d				
Bempton	d				
Bridlington	a				
	d	21 28	21 28		22 42
Nafferton	d	21 39	21 39		22 53
Driffield	d	21 43	21 43		22 58
Hutton Cranswick	d	21 48	21 48		23 03
Arram	d				
Beverley	d	21 58	21 59		23 13
Cottingham	d	22 04	22 05		23 19
Hull	a	22 14	22 14		23 28

Table 43

Sundays

Scarborough, Bridlington and Beverley - Hull

Network Diagram - see first Page of Table 39

		TP ◇1	NT	TP ◇1	NT	TP ◇1	NT	NT	TP ◇1	NT
Scarborough	d	09 20		10 51	11 12	11 51	12 08		13 51	14 08
Seamer	d	09a25		10a56	11 17	11a56	12 13		13a56	14 13
Filey	d				11 26		12 22			14 22
Hunmanby	d				11 30		12 27			14 27
Bempton	d				11 40		12 37			14 37
Bridlington	a				11 48		12 44			14 44
	d		09 51		11 51		12 51	13 51		14 51
Nafferton	d		10 02		12 01			14 02		
Driffield	d		10 06		12 06		13 04	14 06		15 04
Hutton Cranswick	d		10 11		12 10			14 11		
Arram	d									
Beverley	d		10 21		12 20		13 17	14 21		15 17
Cottingham	d		10 27		12 25		13 23	14 27		15 23
Hull	a		10 37		12 35		13 33	14 37		15 33

			NT	TP ◇1	NT	NT	NT	TP ◇1	NT	NT	NT		NT	TP ◇1	TP ◇1	
Scarborough	d			15 51	16 08			17 51		18 08			19 40	19 51	21 20	
Seamer	d			15a56	16 13			17a56		18 13			19 45	19a56	21a25	
Filey	d				16 22					18 22			19 54			
Hunmanby	d				16 27					18 27			19 59			
Bempton	d				16 37					18 37			20 09			
Bridlington	a				16 44					18 44			20 16			
	d		15 51		16 51	17 21	17 51		18 11	18 57	19 57		20 19			
Nafferton	d		16 02			17 32				19 08	20 08					
Driffield	d		16 06		17 04	17 36	18 04		18 24	19 12	20 12		20 32			
Hutton Cranswick	d		16 11			17 41				19 17	20 17					
Arram	d									19 24						
Beverley	d		16 21		17 17	17 51	18 17		18 37	19 29	20 27		20 45			
Cottingham	d		16 27		17 23	17 57	18 23		18 43	19 35	20 33		20 51			
Hull	a		16 37		17 34	18 07	18 33		18 53	19 45	20 43		21 00			

Network Diagram for Tables 44, 45, 48

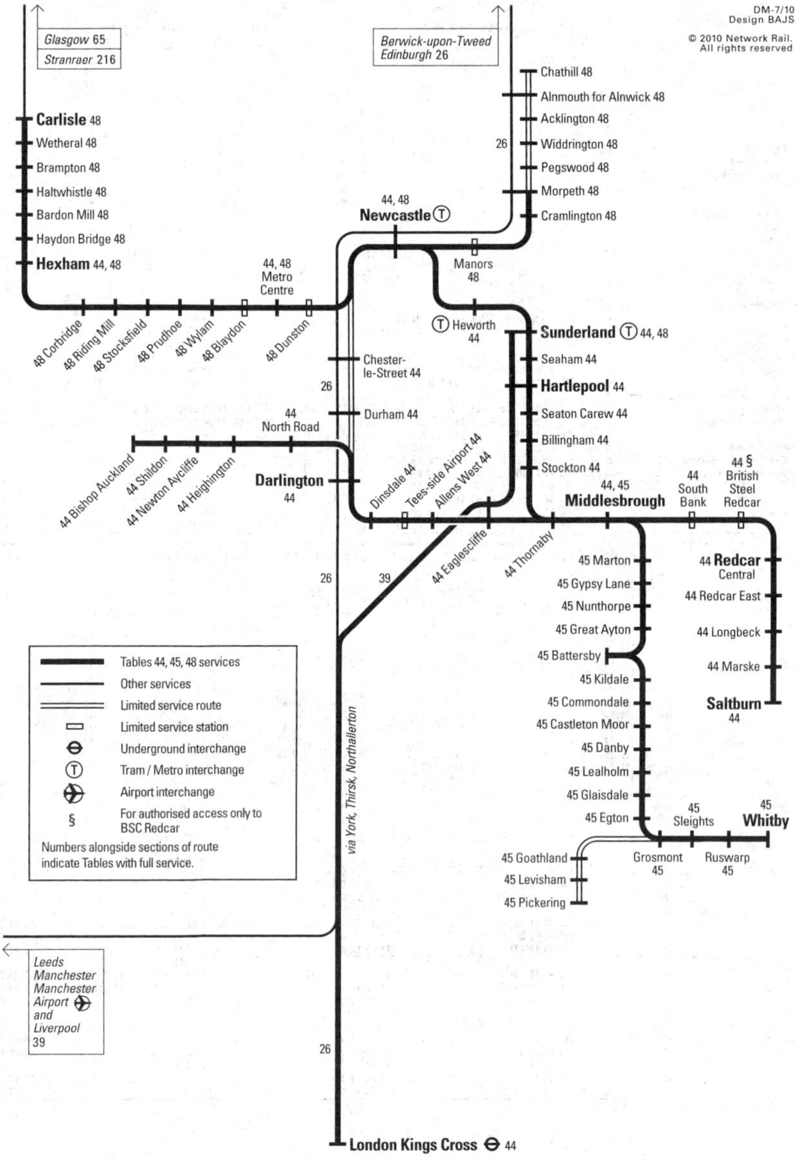

Newcastle, Sunderland, Bishop Auckland and Darlington - Middlesbrough and Saltburn

Network Diagram - see first Page of Table 44

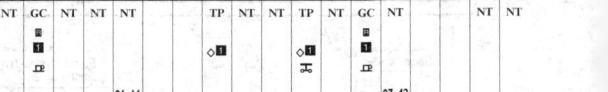

Miles	Miles		NT	NT	NT	TP	NT	GC	NT	NT	NT			TP	NT	NT	TP	NT	GC	NT			NT	NT
						◇1		R 1						◇1			◇1		R 1					
—	—	Hexham 48 d									06 16									07 42				
—	—	Metrocentre 48 d																		08 16				
—	0	**Newcastle** 8 26 d	06 00								07 00				07 30					08 30				
—	2¾	Heworth d	06 07								07 07				07 37					08 37				
—	12	**Sunderland** a	06 19								07 18				07 49					08 50				
—	—	d	06 20					06 45			07 19				07 50				08 42	08 51				
—	17¼	Seaham d	06 28								07 27				07 58					08 58				
—	30	**Hartlepool** d	06a46					07 09			07 45				08 15				09 07	09 15				
—	32¼	Seaton Carew d									07 49				08 19					09 19				
—	37¼	Billingham d									07 56				08 26					09 26				
—	41¾	Stockton d									08 04				08 33					09 34				
0	—	**Bishop Auckland** d								07 20								08 21						09 26
2¾	—	Shildon d								07 25								08 26						09 31
5	—	Newton Aycliffe d								07 30								08 31						09 36
6¼	—	Heighington d								07 33								08 34						09 39
10¾	—	North Road d								07 42								08 43						09 48
—	—	Chester-le-Street 26 d																						
—	—	Durham 26 d																						
12	—	**Darlington** 7 26 a								07 46								08 47						09 51
—	—	d			06 30	06 36	06 58		07 25	07 48						08 30		08 59					09 30	09 53
15¾	—	Dinsdale d			06 37		07 03		07 30	07 53						08 35		09 04						09 59
17½	—	Tees-side Airport d																						
20	—	Allens West d			06 43		07 10		07 37	08 00						08 42		09 11					09 40	10 05
20¾	—	Eaglescliffe a			06 45		07 12	07 29	07 39	08 02						08 44		09 13	09 26				09 42	10 07
—	—	d			06 46		07 12	07 30	07 39	08 02						08 44		09 13	09 27				09 43	10 08
—	—	London Kings Cross 15 ⊖26 a						10 25											12 29					
23¾	44	Thornaby d			06 51	06 54	07 17		07 46	08 08	08 12			08 24	08 39	08 50	09 12	09 20		09 39			09 48	10 13
27	47¼	**Middlesbrough** a			06 57	07 03	07 23		07 52	08 14	08 22			08 32	08 47	08 56	09 22	09 26		09 50			09 58	10 19
—	—	d		06 34	06 59		07 24		07 54							08 57		09 27					09 58	10 20
29½	—	South Bank d							07 58							09 01								
32¾	—	British Steel Redcar § d							08 04															
34½	—	**Redcar Central** d		06 44	07 09		07 34		08 07							09 09		09 37					10 09	10 31
35½	—	Redcar East d		06 47			07 37		08 10							09 11		09 40					10 11	10 33
37	—	Longbeck d		06 51			07 41		08 14							09 15		09 44					10 15	10 37
37½	—	Marske d		06 52			07 42		08 15							09 17		09 45					10 17	10 39
39½	—	**Saltburn** a		07 01	07 21		07 50		08 23							09 26		09 53					10 25	10 51

	TP	NT		NT	NT	TP	NT			NT	NT	TP	NT		NT	NT	GC		TP	NT		NT	NT	TP
	◇1					◇1						◇1					R 1		◇1					◇1
Hexham 48 d		08 45					09 45						10 44							11 43				
Metrocentre 48 d		09 16					10 16						11 16							12 16				
Newcastle 8 26 d		09 30					10 30						11 30							12 30				
Heworth d		09 37					10 37						11 37							12 37				
Sunderland a		09 49					10 49						11 49							12 49				
d		09 50					10 50						11 50				12 28			12 50				
Seaham d		09 58					10 58						11 58							12 58				
Hartlepool d		10 15					11 16						12 15				12 52			13 15				
Seaton Carew d		10 19					11 20						12 19							13 19				
Billingham d		10 26					11 27						12 26							13 26				
Stockton d		10 33					11 34						12 33							13 33				
Bishop Auckland d											11 25												13 25	
Shildon d											11 30												13 30	
Newton Aycliffe d											11 35												13 35	
Heighington d											11 38												13 38	
North Road d											11 47												13 47	
Chester-le-Street 26 d																								
Durham 26 d																								
Darlington 7 26 a											11 51												13 51	
d				10 30	10 53					11 30	11 53				12 30	12 53						13 30	13 53	
Dinsdale d					10 58						11 59					12 58							13 58	
Tees-side Airport d																								
Allens West d				10 40	11 05					11 40	12 05				12 40	13 05						13 40	14 05	
Eaglescliffe a				10 42	11 07					11 42	12 07				12 42	13 07	13 11					13 42	14 09	
d				10 43	11 07					11 43	12 08				12 43	13 07	13 12					13 43	14 09	
London Kings Cross 15 ⊖26 a																	16 09							
Thornaby d	10 22	10 39		10 49	11 13	11 22	11 40			11 48	12 13	12 22	12 39		12 48	13 13			13 23	13 39		13 48	14 14	14 22
Middlesbrough a	10 30	10 48		10 55	11 19	11 30	11 50			11 56	12 19	12 30	12 50		12 54	13 19			13 30	13 48		13 54	14 20	14 30
d				10 56	11 20					11 56	12 20				12 56	13 20						13 56	14 21	
South Bank d																								
British Steel Redcar § d																								
Redcar Central d				11 06	11 31					12 06	12 31				13 06	13 31						14 06	14 31	
Redcar East d				11 09	11 33					12 09	12 33				13 09	13 33						14 09	14 34	
Longbeck d				11 13	11 37					12 13	12 37				13 13	13 37						14 13	14 38	
Marske d				11 14	11 39					12 14	12 39				13 14	13 39						14 14	14 39	
Saltburn a				11 23	11 49					12 24	12 47				13 23	13 49						14 24	14 50	

§ For authorised access only to BSC Redcar

Newcastle, Sunderland, Bishop Auckland and Darlington - Middlesbrough and Saltburn

Network Diagram - see first Page of Table 44

	NT		NT		NT	TP	NT		NT	NT	TP	NT			NT	NT	TP	NT	NT	NT	NT	GC	TP	
						◇1					◇1						◇1					R 1	◇1	
Hexham 48 d	12 45						13 45					14 43						15 42		16 14				
Metrocentre 48 d	13 16						14 14					15 16						16 16		16 38				
Newcastle 8 26 d	13 30						14 30					15 30						16 30		16 53				
Heworth d	13 37						14 37					15 37						16 37		17 00				
Sunderland a	13 49						14 49					15 49						16 49		17 14				
d	13 50						14 50					15 50						16 50		17 15		17 31		
Seaham d	13 58						14 58					15 58						16 58		17 22				
Hartlepool d	14 15						15 15					16 15						17 15		17 39		17 55		
Seaton Carew d	14 19						15 19					16 19						17 19		17 43				
Billingham d	14 26						15 26					16 26						17 26		17 50				
Stockton d	14 33						15 33					16 33						17 33		17 57				
Bishop Auckland d										15 25						16 24								
Shildon d										15 30						16 29								
Newton Aycliffe d										15 35						16 34								
Heighington d										15 38						16 37								
North Road d										15 47						16 46								
Chester-le-Street 26 d																								
Durham 26 d																								
Darlington 7 26 a										15 51						16 50								
d			14 30		14 53				15 30	15 53					16 29	16 53			17 30		18 00			
Dinsdale d					14 58					15 58					16 35	16 58			17 35		18 06			
Tees-side Airport d																								
Allens West d			14 40		15 05				15 40	16 05					16 42	17 05			17 42		18 12			
Eaglescliffe a			14 42		15 07				15 42	16 07					16 44	17 07			17 44		18 14	18 17		
d			14 43		15 07				15 43	16 07					16 44	17 07			17 44		18 15	18 20		
London Kings Cross 15 ⊖26 a																						21 05		
Thornaby d	14 37		14 49		15 13	15 22	15 39		15 48	16 13	16 22	16 39			16 50	17 13	17 22	17 39	17 52	18 03	18 21		18 32	
Middlesbrough a	14 44		14 54		15 19	15 30	15 48		15 54	16 19	16 30	16 47			16 56	17 19	17 30	17 48	17 56	18 15	18 26		18 42	
d			14 56		15 20				15 56	16 20					16 58	17 20			17 58		18 27			
South Bank d										16 25											18 32			
British Steel Redcar § d																								
Redcar Central d			15 06		15 31				16 06	16 32					17 08	17 31			18 08		18 39			
Redcar East d			15 09		15 33				16 09	16 35					17 11	17 33			18 11		18 42			
Longbeck d			15 13		15 37				16 13	16 39					17 15	17 37			18 15		18 46			
Marske d			15 14		15 39				16 14	16 40					17 16	17 39			18 16		18 47			
Saltburn a			15 23		15 49				16 23	16 49					17 25	17 49			18 25		18 56			

	NT		NT	NT		TP	NT	NT	TP		NT			NT		TP	NT	NT	NT			NT		
						◇1			◇1							◇1								
Hexham 48 d	16 43			17 45							18 45													
Metrocentre 48 d	17 16			18 16							19 18													
Newcastle 8 26 d	17 30			18 30							19 30						20 30		21 18					
Heworth d	17 37			18 37							19 37						20 37		21 25					
Sunderland a	17 50			18 49							19 50						20 49		21 37					
d	17 50			18 50							19 50						20 50		21 38					
Seaham d	17 58			18 58							19 58						20 58		21 46					
Hartlepool d	18 15			19 15							20 15						21 15		22 03					
Seaton Carew d	18 19			19 19							20 19						21 19		22 07					
Billingham d	18 26			19 26							20 26						21 26		22 14					
Stockton d	18 33			19 33							20 33						21 33		22 21					
Bishop Auckland d			18 02					19 25										21 10						
Shildon d			18 07					19 30										21 15						
Newton Aycliffe d			18 12					19 35										21 20						
Heighington d			18 15					19 38										21 23						
North Road d			18 24					19 47										21 32						
Chester-le-Street 26 d																								
Durham 26 d																								
Darlington 7 26 a			18 28					19 51										21 36						
d			18 30				19 30	19 53						20 32				21 38				22 38		
Dinsdale d			18 35				19 35	19 59						20 35				21 43				22 43		
Tees-side Airport d																								
Allens West d			18 42				19 42	20 05						20 42				21 50				22 50		
Eaglescliffe a			18 44				19 44	20 07						20 45				21 52				22 52		
d			18 44				19 44	20 08						20 45				21 52				22 52		
London Kings Cross 15 ⊖26 a																								
Thornaby d	18 39		18 50	19 36		19 47	19 54	20 14	20 22		20 38			20 50		21 22	21 40	21 58	22 30			22 58		
Middlesbrough a	18 48		18 56	19 47		19 56	20 00	20 21	20 30		20 48			20 58		21 30	21 48	22 05	22 36			23 04		
d			18 58				20 00							20 59				22 06						
South Bank d																								
British Steel Redcar § d																								
Redcar Central d			19 08				20 11							21 08				22 17						
Redcar East d			19 11				20 14							21 11				22 19						
Longbeck d			19 15				20 18							21 15				22 23						
Marske d			19 16				20 19							21 16				22 25						
Saltburn a			19 25				20 28							21 25				22 34						

§ For authorised access only to BSC Redcar

Newcastle, Sunderland, Bishop Auckland and Darlington - Middlesbrough and Saltburn

Network Diagram - see first Page of Table 44

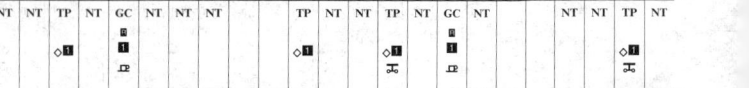

	NT	NT	NT	TP	NT	GC	NT	NT	NT			TP	NT	NT	TP	NT	GC	NT			NT	NT	TP	NT
				◇1		R 1 ⊐						◇1			◇1 ⊤		R 1 ⊐						◇1 ⊤	
Hexham 48 d									06 16									07 42						08 43
Metrocentre 48 d																		08 16						09 16
Newcastle 8 26 ⛴ d	06 00								07 00				07 30					08 30						09 30
Heworth ⛴ d	06 07								07 07				07 37					08 37						09 37
Sunderland ⛴ a	06 27								07 20				07 49					08 50						09 49
d	06 28					06 43			07 21				07 50				08 30	08 51						09 50
Seaham d	06 35								07 29				07 58					08 58						09 58
Hartlepool d	06a54					07 09			07 45				08 15				08 54	09 15						10 15
Seaton Carew d									07 49				08 19					09 19						10 19
Billingham d									07 56				08 26					09 26						10 26
Stockton d									08 04				08 33					09 34						10 33
Bishop Auckland d								07 20								08 21						09 26		
Shildon d								07 25								08 26						09 31		
Newton Aycliffe d								07 30								08 31						09 36		
Heighington d								07 33								08 34						09 40		
North Road d								07 42								08 43						09 48		
Chester-le-Street 26 d																								
Durham 26 d																								
Darlington 7 26 a								07 46								08 47						09 54		
d			06 28	06 36	06 58		07 30	07 48						08 23		08 59					09 30	09 55		
Dinsdale d			06 34		07 03		07 35	07 53						08 28		09 04						09 59		
Tees-side Airport d																								
Allens West d			06 40		07 10		07 42	08 00						08 35		09 11					09 40	10 05		
Eaglescliffe a			06 42		07 12	07 29	07 43	08 02						08 37		09 13	09 15				09 42	10 07		
d			06 43		07 12	07 30	07 43	08 02						08 37		09 13	09 17				09 43	10 08		
London Kings Cross 15 ⊖26 a						10 15											12 07							
Thornaby d			06 48	06 53	07 17		07 49	08 08	08 13			08 24	08 39	08 45	09 12	09 19		09 39			09 48	10 13	10 22	10 39
Middlesbrough a			06 54	07 03	07 23		07 55	08 14	08 23			08 32	08 47	08 51	09 22	09 26		09 50			09 54	10 17	10 30	10 48
d		06 34	06 59		07 25		07 56							08 53		09 27					09 56	10 20		
South Bank d							08 00							08 57										
British Steel Redcar § d																								
Redcar Central d		06 44	07 09		07 35		08 08							09 05		09 38					10 06	10 31		
Redcar East d		06 47			07 38		08 10							09 07		09 40					10 09	10 33		
Longbeck d		06 51			07 42		08 14							09 11		09 44					10 13	10 37		
Marske d		06 52			07 43		08 16							09 13		09 46					10 14	10 39		
Saltburn a		07 00	07 21		07 51		08 24							09 23		09 55					10 23	10 49		

		NT	NT	TP	NT			NT	NT	TP	NT		NT	GC	NT		TP	NT		NT	NT	TP	NT	
				◇1 ⊤						◇1 ⊤				R 1 ⊐			◇1 ⊤					◇1 ⊤		
Hexham 48 d					09 46						10 44							11 45					12 45	
Metrocentre 48 d					10 17						11 16							12 16					13 16	
Newcastle 8 26 ⛴ d					10 30						11 30							12 30					13 30	
Heworth ⛴ d					10 37						11 37							12 37					13 37	
Sunderland ⛴ a					10 49						11 49							12 49					13 49	
d					10 50						11 50			12 18				12 50					13 50	
Seaham d					10 58						11 58							12 58					13 58	
Hartlepool d					11 16						12 15			12 43				13 15					14 15	
Seaton Carew d					11 20						12 19							13 19					14 19	
Billingham d					11 27						12 26							13 26					14 26	
Stockton d					11 34						12 33							13 33					14 33	
Bishop Auckland d									11 25												13 25			
Shildon d									11 30												13 30			
Newton Aycliffe d									11 35												13 35			
Heighington d									11 38												13 38			
North Road d									11 47												13 47			
Chester-le-Street 26 d																								
Durham 26 d																								
Darlington 7 26 a									11 51												13 51			
d		10 30	10 53					11 32	11 53				12 32		12 53					13 30	13 53			
Dinsdale d			10 58						11 59						12 58						13 58			
Tees-side Airport d																								
Allens West d		10 40	11 05					11 42	12 05				12 42		13 05					13 40	14 05			
Eaglescliffe a		10 42	11 07					11 44	12 07				12 44	13 04	13 07					13 42	14 07			
d		10 43	11 07					11 45	12 08				12 45	13 05	13 07					13 43	14 07			
London Kings Cross 15 ⊖26 a														15 49										
Thornaby d		10 48	11 13	11 22	11 40			11 50	12 13	12 22	12 39		12 50		13 13		13 23	13 39		13 48	14 13	14 22	14 39	
Middlesbrough a		10 54	11 19	11 30	11 50			11 56	12 19	12 30	12 49		12 56		13 19		13 30	13 48		13 55	14 19	14 30	14 46	
d		10 56	11 20					11 56	12 20				12 56		13 20					13 56	14 20			
South Bank d																								
British Steel Redcar § d																								
Redcar Central d		11 06	11 31					12 06	12 31				13 07		13 31					14 06	14 31			
Redcar East d		11 09	11 33					12 08	12 33				13 09		13 33					14 09	14 33			
Longbeck d		11 13	11 37					12 12	12 37				13 13		13 37					14 13	14 37			
Marske d		11 14	11 39					12 14	12 39				13 15		13 39					14 14	14 39			
Saltburn a		11 23	11 49					12 24	12 48				13 23		13 49					14 23	14 50			

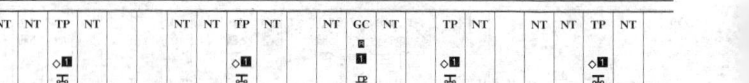

§ For authorised access only to BSC Redcar

Table 44

Saturdays

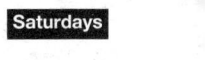

Newcastle, Sunderland, Bishop Auckland and Darlington - Middlesbrough and Saltburn

Network Diagram - see first Page of Table 44

	NT		NT	TP	NT		NT	NT	TP	NT			NT	NT	TP	NT	NT	NT	GC	NT	TP		NT	
				◇1 🛒					◇1 🛒						◇1				R 1 🍴		◇1 🛒			
Hexham 48 d					13 43					14 43						15 45		16 14					16 45	
Metrocentre 48 d					14 16					15 16						16 16		16 38					17 16	
Newcastle 8 26 🚇 d					14 30					15 30						16 30		16 53					17 30	
Heworth 🚇 d					14 37					15 37						16 37		17 00					17 37	
Sunderland 🚇 a					14 49					15 49						16 49		17 14					17 50	
d					14 50					15 50						16 50		17 15	17 29				17 50	
Seaham d					14 58					15 58						16 58		17 22					17 58	
Hartlepool d					15 15					16 15						17 15		17 39	17 53				18 15	
Seaton Carew d					15 19					16 19						17 19		17 43					18 19	
Billingham d					15 26					16 26						17 26		17 50					18 26	
Stockton d					15 33					16 33						17 33		17 57					18 33	
Bishop Auckland d								15 25						16 23										
Shildon d								15 30						16 28										
Newton Aycliffe d								15 35						16 33										
Heighington d								15 38						16 36										
North Road d								15 47						16 45										
Chester-le-Street 26 d																								
Durham 26 d																								
Darlington 7 26 a								15 51						16 49										
d	14 30		14 53				15 30	15 53					16 29	16 53			17 30			18 00				
Dinsdale d			14 58					15 58					16 35	16 58			17 35			18 06				
Tees-side Airport d																								
Allens West d	14 40		15 05				15 40	16 05					16 42	17 05			17 42			18 12				
Eaglescliffe a	14 42		15 07				15 42	16 07					16 44	17 07			17 44		18 11	18 14				
d	14 43		15 07				15 43	16 07					16 44	17 07			17 44		18 12	18 15				
London Kings Cross 15 ⊖26 a																			20 57					
Thornaby d	14 49		15 13	15 22	15 39		15 48	16 13	16 22	16 39			16 50	17 13	17 22	17 39	17 52	18 04		18 20	18 22		18 39	
Middlesbrough a	14 54		15 19	15 30	15 48		15 54	16 19	16 30	16 47			16 56	17 19	17 30	17 49	17 56	18 15		18 26	18 30		18 48	
d	14 56		15 20				15 56	16 20					16 58	17 20			17 58			18 27				
South Bank d								16 25												18 32				
British Steel Redcar § d																								
Redcar Central d	15 06		15 31				16 06	16 32					17 08	17 31			18 08			18 39				
Redcar East d	15 09		15 33				16 09	16 35					17 11	17 33			18 11			18 42				
Longbeck d	15 13		15 37				16 13	16 39					17 15	17 37			18 15			18 46				
Marske d	15 14		15 39				16 14	16 40					17 16	17 39			18 16			18 47				
Saltburn a	15 23		15 49				16 23	16 49					17 25	17 48			18 25			18 56				

	NT	TP	NT		NT	NT	TP		NT		NT	TP	NT	NT			NT
		◇1					◇1					◇1					
Hexham 48 d			17 43						18 45								
Metrocentre 48 d			18 16						19 18					20 47			
Newcastle 8 26 🚇 d			18 30						19 30					21 00			21 50
Heworth 🚇 d			18 37						19 37					21 08			
Sunderland 🚇 a			18 49						19 50					21 20			
d			18 50						19 50					21 20			
Seaham d			18 58						19 58					21 28			
Hartlepool d			19 15						20 15					21 45			
Seaton Carew d			19 19						20 19					21 49			
Billingham d			19 26						20 26					21 56			
Stockton d			19 33						20 33					22 03			
Bishop Auckland d	18 02					19 25							21 10				
Shildon d	18 07					19 30							21 15				
Newton Aycliffe d	18 12					19 35							21 20				
Heighington d	18 15					19 38							21 23				
North Road d	18 24					19 47							21 32				
Chester-le-Street 26 d																	21 59
Durham 26 d																	22 08
Darlington 7 26 a	18 28					19 51							21 36				22 29
d	18 30				19 36	19 53					20 30		21 38				22 34
Dinsdale d	18 35				19 41	19 59					20 35		21 43				22 39
Tees-side Airport d																	
Allens West d	18 42				19 48	20 05					20 42		21 50				22 46
Eaglescliffe a	18 44				19 50	20 07					20 44		21 52				22 48
d	18 44				19 50	20 08					20 44		21 52				22 48
London Kings Cross 15 ⊖26 a																	
Thornaby d	18 50	19 22	19 39		19 56	20 13	20 21		20 38		20 50	21 22	21 59	22 10			22 54
Middlesbrough a	18 56	19 31	19 48		20 02	20 20	20 30		20 48		20 57	21 30	22 06	22 18			23 02
d	18 58				20 02						20 58		22 06				
South Bank d																	
British Steel Redcar § d																	
Redcar Central d	19 08				20 13						21 08		22 17				
Redcar East d	19 11				20 15						21 11		22 19				
Longbeck d	19 15				20 19						21 15		22 23				
Marske d	19 16				20 21						21 16		22 25				
Saltburn a	19 25				20 30						21 25		22 34				

§ For authorised access only to BSC Redcar

Table 44

Sundays until 12 February

Newcastle, Sunderland, Bishop Auckland and Darlington - Middlesbrough and Saltburn

Network Diagram - see first Page of Table 44

		NT	TP	GC	NT	NT	NT		NT	TP		NT	NT		GC	NT	NT		NT			TP	NT	GC	NT
			◇1	R 1 ☕						◇1					R 1 ☕							◇1		R 1 ☕	
Hexham	48 d																								
Metrocentre	48 d												10 48				11 48		12 48						
Newcastle 8	26 ⛴ d				09 00		09 45						11 00				12 00		13 00						
Heworth	⛴ d				09 07		09 52						11 06				12 06		13 06						
Sunderland	⛴ a				09 22		10 05						11 22				12 21		13 22						
	d			09 12			10 06						11 22		12 11		12 21							14 12	
Seaham	d						10 14						11 30				12 29								
Hartlepool	d			09 36			10 31						11 46		12 36		12 45							14 36	
Seaton Carew	d						10 35						11 51				12 50								
Billingham	d						10 42						11 58				12 57								
Stockton	d						10 49						12 05				13 04								
Bishop Auckland	d								10 17							12 17									
Shildon	d								10 22							12 22									
Newton Aycliffe	d								10 27							12 27									
Heighington	d								10 30							12 30									
North Road	d								10 39							12 39									
Chester-le-Street	26 d																								
Durham	26 d																								
Darlington 7	26 a								10 43							12 44									
	d	08 45	09 00			09 45			10 45			11 45				12 46							13 45		14 45
Dinsdale	d	08 50				09 50			10 50			11 50				12 51							13 50		14 50
Tees-side Airport	d																								
Allens West	d	08 57				09 57			10 57			11 57				12 58							13 57		14 57
Eaglescliffe	a	08 59		09 58		09 59			10 59			11 59	12 11		12 59	13 00							13 59	14 58	14 59
	d	08 59		09 59		09 59			10 59			11 59			13 02	13 00							13 59	14 59	14 59
London Kings Cross 15 ⊖	26 a			12 44											15 46									17 45	
Thornaby	d	09 05	09 16			10 05	10 55		11 05	11 30		12 05				13 06	13 10					13 30	14 05		15 05
Middlesbrough	a	09 10	09 25			10 10	11 05		11 13	11 39		12 10				13 11	13 20					13 40	14 11		15 11
	d	09 12				10 12			11 14			12 12				13 13							14 12		15 12
South Bank	d																								
British Steel Redcar §	d																								
Redcar Central	d	09 22				10 22			11 23			12 22				13 23							14 22		15 22
Redcar East	d	09 25				10 25			11 26			12 25				13 26							14 25		15 25
Longbeck	d	09 29				10 29			11 30			12 29				13 30							14 29		15 29
Marske	d	09 30				10 30			11 31			12 30				13 31							14 30		15 30
Saltburn	a	09 37				10 37			11 39			12 37				13 38							14 37		15 37

		NT	NT	TP	NT	NT	NT		TP	NT	NT	GC		NT	NT	NT	TP	NT	NT	TP		NT		NT	NT
				◇1					◇1			R 1 ☕					◇1			◇1					
Hexham	48 d																								
Metrocentre	48 d	13 48	14 48				15 48				16 48				17 48	18 48									
Newcastle 8	26 ⛴ d	14 00	15 00				16 00				17 00				18 00	19 00						20 00		21 06	
Heworth	⛴ d	14 06	15 06				16 06				17 06				18 07	19 06						20 07			
Sunderland	⛴ a	14 21	15 22				16 21				17 21				18 21	19 22						20 21			
	d	14 21					16 21				17 21	18 12			18 21							20 21			
Seaham	d	14 29					16 29				17 29				18 29							20 29			
Hartlepool	d	14 45					16 45				17 46	18 36			18 45							20 45			
Seaton Carew	d	14 50					16 50				17 51				18 50							20 50			
Billingham	d	14 57					16 57				17 58				18 57							20 57			
Stockton	d	15 04					17 04				18 05				19 04							21 04			
Bishop Auckland	d				15 17					17 16								19 17							
Shildon	d				15 22					17 21								19 22							
Newton Aycliffe	d				15 27					17 26								19 27							
Heighington	d				15 30					17 29								19 30							
North Road	d				15 39					17 38								19 39							
Chester-le-Street	26 d																							21 15	
Durham	26 d																							21 24	
Darlington 7	26 a				15 43					17 42								19 43						21 44	
	d				15 45	16 45				17 45				18 45				19 45	20 32					21 45	22 45
Dinsdale	d				15 50	16 50				17 50				18 50				19 50	20 37					21 51	
Tees-side Airport	d																								
Allens West	d				15 57	16 57				17 57				18 57				19 57	20 44					21 58	
Eaglescliffe	a				15 59	16 59				17 59	18 11	18 58		18 59				19 59	20 46					22 00	22 56
	d				15 59	16 59				17 59		18 59		18 59				19 59	20 46					22 00	22 56
London Kings Cross 15 ⊖	26 a											21 45													
Thornaby	d	15 10		15 45	16 05	17 05	17 09		17 41	18 05				19 05	19 09		19 30	20 05	20 52	20 58		21 08		22 05	23 02
Middlesbrough	a	15 18		15 52	16 10	17 11	17 18		17 50	18 10				19 10	19 18		19 40	20 10	20 57	21 07		21 20		22 10	23 10
	d				16 12	17 12				18 12				19 12				20 12	20 58					22 11	
South Bank	d																								
British Steel Redcar §	d																								
Redcar Central	d				16 22	17 22				18 22				19 22				20 22	21 08					22 21	
Redcar East	d				16 25	17 25				18 25				19 25				20 25	21 11					22 24	
Longbeck	d				16 29	17 29				18 29				19 29				20 29	21 15					22 28	
Marske	d				16 30	17 30				18 30				19 30				20 30	21 16					22 29	
Saltburn	a				16 37	17 37				18 37				19 37				20 37	21 24					22 37	

§ For authorised access only to BSC Redcar

Table 44

Sundays

19 February to 25 March

Newcastle, Sunderland, Bishop Auckland and Darlington - Middlesbrough and Saltburn

Network Diagram - see first Page of Table 44

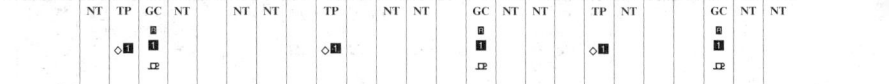

	NT	TP	GC	NT		NT	NT		TP		NT	NT		GC	NT	NT		TP	NT			GC	NT	NT
		◇1	R 1 ☕						◇1					R 1 ☕				◇1				R 1 ☕		
Hexham 48 d																								
Metrocentre 48 d																								
Newcastle 8 26 ⛴ d																								
Heworth ⛴ d																								
Sunderland ⛴ a																								
d			09 12				10 27					11 27		12 11		12 27						14 12		14 27
Seaham d							10 36					11 36				12 35								14 35
Hartlepool d			09 36				10 55					11 55		12 36		12 57						14 36		14 51
Seaton Carew d							11 01					12 01				13 01								14 55
Billingham d							11 08					12 08				13 08								15 02
Stockton d							11 15					12 15				13 15								15 09
Bishop Auckland d						10 17									12 17									
Shildon d						10 22									12 22									
Newton Aycliffe d						10 27									12 27									
Heighington d						10 30									12 30									
North Road d						10 39									12 39									
Chester-le-Street 26 d																								
Durham 26 d																								
Darlington 7 26 a						10 43									12 44									
d	08 45	09 03		09 45		10 45					11 45				12 46				13 45				14 45	
Dinsdale d	08 50			09 50		10 50					11 50				12 51				13 50				14 50	
Tees-side Airport d																								
Allens West d	08 57			09 57		10 57					11 57				12 58				13 57				14 57	
Eaglescliffe a	08 59		09 58	09 59		10 59					11 59	12 24		12 59	13 00				13 59			14 58	14 59	
d	08 59		09 59	09 59		10 59					11 59			13 02	13 00				13 59			14 59	14 59	
London Kings Cross 15 ⊖26 a			12 44											15 46								17 45		
Thornaby d	09 05	09 19		10 05		11 05	11 21		11 30		12 05				13 06	13 21		13 30	14 05				15 05	15 15
Middlesbrough a	09 10	09 28		10 10		11 13	11 30		11 39		12 10				13 11	13 31		13 40	14 11				15 11	15 25
d	09 12			10 12		11 14					12 12				13 13				14 12				15 12	
South Bank d																								
British Steel Redcar § d																								
Redcar Central d	09 22			10 22		11 23					12 22				13 23				14 22				15 22	
Redcar East d	09 25			10 25		11 26					12 25				13 26				14 25				15 25	
Longbeck d	09 29			10 29		11 30					12 29				13 30				14 29				15 29	
Marske d	09 30			10 30		11 31					12 30				13 31				14 30				15 30	
Saltburn a	09 37			10 37		11 39					12 37				13 38				14 37				15 37	

		TP	NT		NT		NT		TP	NT	NT		GC	NT			TP	NT	NT	NT	TP	NT	NT	NT
		◇1							◇1				R 1 ☕				◇1				◇1			
Hexham 48 d																								
Metrocentre 48 d																								
Newcastle 8 26 ⛴ d																							21 06	
Heworth ⛴ d																								
Sunderland ⛴ a																								
d							16 27				17 27		18 12					18 43				20 28		
Seaham d							16 36				17 35							18 51				20 36		
Hartlepool d							16 52				17 51		18 36					19 07				20 52		
Seaton Carew d							16 57				17 55							19 11				20 56		
Billingham d							17 04				18 02							19 18				21 03		
Stockton d							17 11				18 09							19 25				21 10		
Bishop Auckland d			15 17							17 16									19 17					
Shildon d			15 22							17 21									19 22					
Newton Aycliffe d			15 27							17 26									19 27					
Heighington d			15 30							17 29									19 30					
North Road d			15 39							17 38									19 39					
Chester-le-Street 26 d																							21 15	
Durham 26 d																							21 24	
Darlington 7 26 a			15 43							17 42									19 43				21 44	
d			15 45		16 45					17 45				18 45					19 45	20 32			21 45	22 45
Dinsdale d			15 50		16 50					17 50				18 50					19 50	20 37			21 51	
Tees-side Airport d																								
Allens West d			15 57		16 57					17 57				18 57					19 57	20 44			21 58	
Eaglescliffe a			15 59		16 59					17 59	18 14		18 58	18 59					19 59	20 46			22 00	22 56
d			15 59		16 59					17 59			18 59	18 59					19 59	20 46			22 00	22 56
London Kings Cross 15 ⊖26 a													21 45											
Thornaby d		15 45	16 05		17 05		17 16		17 41	18 05				19 05			19 30	19 40	20 05	20 52	20 58	21 16	22 05	23 02
Middlesbrough a		15 52	16 10		17 11		17 25		17 50	18 10				19 10			19 40	19 50	20 10	20 57	21 07	21 26	22 10	23 10
d			16 12		17 12					18 12				19 12					20 12	20 58			22 11	
South Bank d																								
British Steel Redcar § d																								
Redcar Central d			16 22		17 22					18 22				19 22					20 22	21 08			22 21	
Redcar East d			16 25		17 25					18 25				19 25					20 25	21 11			22 24	
Longbeck d			16 29		17 29					18 29				19 29					20 29	21 15			22 28	
Marske d			16 30		17 30					18 30				19 30					20 30	21 16			22 29	
Saltburn a			16 37		17 37					18 37				19 37					20 37	21 24			22 37	

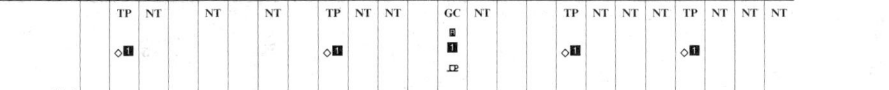

§ For authorised access only to BSC Redcar

Table 44

Sundays
from 1 April

Newcastle, Sunderland, Bishop Auckland and Darlington - Middlesbrough and Saltburn

Network Diagram - see first Page of Table 44

	NT	TP	GC	NT	NT	NT	NT	TP	TP	NT	NT	GC	NT	NT	NT	TP	NT	GC
		◇1	R 1 ☕					◇1	◇1			R 1 ☕				◇1		R 1 ☕
Hexham 48 d																		
Metrocentre 48 d											10 48			11 48	12 48			
Newcastle 8 26 ⛴ d				09 00		09 45					11 00			12 00	13 00			
Heworth ⛴ d				09 07		09 52					11 06			12 06	13 06			
Sunderland ⛴ a				09 22		10 05					11 22			12 21	13 22			
d			09 12			10 06					11 22	12 11		12 21				14 12
Seaham d						10 14					11 30			12 29				
Hartlepool d			09 36			10 31					11 46	12 36		12 45				14 36
Seaton Carew d						10 35					11 51			12 50				
Billingham d						10 42					11 58			12 57				
Stockton d						10 49					12 05			13 04				
Bishop Auckland d							10 17						12 17					
Shildon d							10 22						12 22					
Newton Aycliffe d							10 27						12 27					
Heighington d							10 30						12 30					
North Road d							10 39						12 39					
Chester-le-Street 26 d																		
Durham 26 d																		
Darlington 7 26 a							10 43						12 44					
d	08 45	09 00			09 45		10 45			11 45			12 46				13 45	
Dinsdale d	08 50				09 50		10 50			11 50			12 51				13 50	
Tees-side Airport d																		
Allens West d	08 57				09 57		10 57			11 57			12 58				13 57	
Eaglescliffe a	08 59		09 58		09 59		10 59			11 59	12 11	12 59	13 00				13 59	14 58
d	08 59		09 59		09 59		10 59			11 59		13 02	13 00				13 59	14 59
London Kings Cross 15 ⊖26 a			12 44									15 46						17 45
Thornaby d	09 05	09 16			10 05	10 55	11 05	11 30	11 30	12 05			13 06	13 11		13 30	14 05	
Middlesbrough a	09 10	09 25			10 10	11 05	11 13	11 38	11 39	12 10			13 11	13 20		13 40	14 11	
d	09 12				10 12		11 14			12 12			13 13				14 12	
South Bank d																		
British Steel Redcar § d																		
Redcar Central d	09 22				10 22		11 23			12 22			13 23				14 22	
Redcar East d	09 25				10 25		11 26			12 25			13 26				14 25	
Longbeck d	09 29				10 29		11 30			12 29			13 30				14 29	
Marske d	09 30				10 30		11 31			12 30			13 31				14 30	
Saltburn a	09 37				10 37		11 39			12 37			13 38				14 37	

	NT	NT	NT	TP	NT	NT	NT	TP	NT	NT	GC	NT	NT	NT	TP	NT	NT	TP	NT	NT	NT
				◇1				◇1			R 1 ☕				◇1			◇1			
Hexham 48 d																					
Metrocentre 48 d		13 48	14 48				15 48			16 48			17 48	18 48							
Newcastle 8 26 ⛴ d		14 00	15 00				16 00			17 00			18 00	19 00					20 00	21 06	
Heworth ⛴ d		14 06	15 06				16 06			17 06			18 07	19 06					20 07		
Sunderland ⛴ a		14 21	15 22				16 21			17 22			18 21	19 22					20 21		
d		14 21					16 21			17 22	18 12		18 21						20 21		
Seaham d		14 29					16 29			17 30			18 29						20 29		
Hartlepool d		14 45					16 45			17 46	18 36		18 45						20 45		
Seaton Carew d		14 50					16 50			17 51			18 50						20 50		
Billingham d		14 57					16 57			17 58			18 57						20 57		
Stockton d		15 04					17 04			18 05			19 04						21 04		
Bishop Auckland d					15 17				17 16							19 17					
Shildon d					15 22				17 21							19 22					
Newton Aycliffe d					15 27				17 26							19 27					
Heighington d					15 30				17 29							19 30					
North Road d					15 39				17 38							19 39					
Chester-le-Street 26 d																				21 15	
Durham 26 d																				21 24	
Darlington 7 26 a					15 43				17 42							19 43				21 44	
d	14 45				15 45	16 45			17 45			18 45				19 45	20 32			21 45	22 45
Dinsdale d	14 50				15 50	16 50			17 50			18 50				19 50	20 37			21 51	
Tees-side Airport d																					
Allens West d	14 57				15 57	16 57			17 57			18 57				19 57	20 44			21 58	
Eaglescliffe a	14 59				15 59	16 59			17 59	18 11	18 58	18 59				19 59	20 46			22 00	22 56
d	14 59				15 59	16 59			17 59		18 59	18 59				19 59	20 46			22 00	22 56
London Kings Cross 15 ⊖26 a											21 45										
Thornaby d	15 05	15 10		15 45	16 05	17 05	17 10	17 41	18 05			19 05	19 09		19 30	20 05	20 52	20 58	21 08	22 05	23 02
Middlesbrough a	15 11	15 18		15 52	16 10	17 11	17 18	17 50	18 10			19 10	19 18		19 40	20 10	20 57	21 07	21 20	22 10	23 10
d	15 12				16 12	17 12			18 12			19 12				20 12	20 58			22 11	
South Bank d																					
British Steel Redcar § d																					
Redcar Central d	15 22				16 22	17 22			18 22			19 22				20 22	21 08			22 21	
Redcar East d	15 25				16 25	17 25			18 25			19 25				20 25	21 11			22 24	
Longbeck d	15 29				16 29	17 29			18 29			19 29				20 29	21 15			22 28	
Marske d	15 30				16 30	17 30			18 30			19 30				20 30	21 16			22 29	
Saltburn a	15 37				16 37	17 37			18 37			19 37				20 37	21 24			22 37	

§ For authorised access only to BSC Redcar

Saltburn and Middlesbrough - Darlington, Bishop Auckland, Sunderland and Newcastle

Network Diagram - see first Page of Table 44

Miles	Miles			NT	TP ◇1	NT	NT	NT	NT	TP ◇1	NT	NT	NT	NT	NT	NT	NT	TP ◇1	NT	NT	TP ◇1	NT	NT
0	—	**Saltburn**	d					06 22					07 12	07 25	07 54				08 31			09 31	09 58
2	—	Marske	d					06 26					07 16	07 29	07 58				08 35			09 35	10 02
2½	—	Longbeck	d					06 29					07 19	07 32	08 01				08 38			09 38	10 05
4	—	Redcar East	d					06 32					07 22	07 35	08 04				08 41			09 41	10 08
5	—	**Redcar Central**	d					06 35					07 25	07 38	08 07				08 44			09 44	10 11
6¾	—	British Steel Redcar §	d																				
10	—	South Bank	d																08 51				
12½	0	**Middlesbrough**	a					06 45					07 36	07 49	08 19				08 56			09 55	10 22
—	—		d	05 45	05 55			06 47	06 51	07 12	07 32		07 37	07 49	08 20	08 32	08 44	08 50	09 08	09 32	09 50	09 56	10 22
15¾	3¼	Thornaby	d	05 50	06a00			06 52	06 56	07a17	07 37		07 42	07 54	08 25	08 37	08 50	08a55	09 13	09 37	09a55	10 01	10 27
—	—	London Kings Cross 15 ⊖26	d																				
18¾	—	Eaglescliffe	a	05 55				06 57					07 47	07 59	08 30		08 55		09 18			10 06	10 32
—	—		d	05 55				06 57					07 47	08 00	08 31		08 55		09 18			10 07	10 33
19½	—	Allens West	d	05 58				07 00					07 50	08 02	08 33		08 58		09 21			10 09	10 35
22	—	Tees-side Airport	d																				
23¾	—	Dinsdale	d	06 04				07 06					07 56	08 09	08 40		09 04		09 27				10 42
27½	—	**Darlington** 7	26 a	06 14				07 19					08 07	08 19	08 50		09 13		09 39			10 23	10 52
—	—		d	06 14		06 47		07 20				07 48		08 22	08 52								10 54
28¾	—	North Road	d			06 50						07 51			08 55								10 57
33¼	—	Heighington	d			06 58						07 59			09 03								11 05
34½	—	Newton Aycliffe	d			07 02						08 03			09 07								11 08
36¾	—	Shildon	d			07 06						08 07			09 11								11 13
39½	—	**Bishop Auckland**	a			07 14						08 15			09 18								11 20
—	5½	Stockton	d						07 02		07 43					08 43				09 43			
—	10	Billingham	d						07 09		07 50					08 50				09 50			
—	15	Seaton Carew	d						07 15		07 56					08 56				09 56			
—	17¼	**Hartlepool**	d				07 03		07 21		08 02					09 01				10 02			
—	30	Seaham	d				07 18		07 36		08 17					09 15				10 17			
—	35¼	**Sunderland**	a				07 28		07 50		08 28					09 27				10 28			
—	—		d				07 30		07 55		08 30					09 30				10 30			
—	44½	Heworth	d				07 41		08 07		08 42					09 42				10 42			
—	47¼	**Newcastle** 8	26 a	06 54			07 51	08 05	08 16		08 52			09 06		09 51				10 51			
—	—	Metrocentre	48 a				08 00									10 02				11 01			
—	—	Hexham	48 a				08 39									10 36				11 38			

		NT	GC R 1 ☕	TP ◇1	NT	NT	NT	TP ◇1	NT	NT	NT	TP ◇1	NT	NT	NT	GC R 1 ☕	TP ◇1	NT	NT	NT	TP FO ◇1	TP FX ◇1	NT
Saltburn	d				10 31	10 58			11 31	11 57			12 30	12 58				13 31	13 57				14 31
Marske	d				10 35	11 02			11 35	12 01			12 34	13 02				13 35	14 02				14 35
Longbeck	d				10 38	11 05			11 38	12 04			12 37	13 05				13 38	14 05				14 38
Redcar East	d				10 41	11 08			11 41	12 07			12 40	13 08				13 41	14 08				14 41
Redcar Central	d				10 44	11 11			11 45	12 10			12 43	13 11				13 44	14 11				14 44
British Steel Redcar §	d																						
South Bank	d																						
Middlesbrough	a				10 54	11 21			11 55	12 21			12 54	13 21				13 54	14 21				14 54
	d	10 32		10 50	10 55	11 22	11 31	11 50	11 56	12 22	12 32	12 50	12 55	13 22	13 32		13 50	13 55	14 22	14 32	14 50	14 50	14 55
Thornaby	d	10 37		10a55	11 00	11 27	11 36	11a55	12 01	12 27	12 37	12a55	13 00	13 27	13 37		13a55	14 00	14 27	14 37	14a55	14a55	15 00
London Kings Cross 15 ⊖26	d		07 49													11 23							
Eaglescliffe	a		10 46		11 05	11 32			12 06	12 32			13 05	13 32		14 04		14 05	14 32				15 05
	d		10 47		11 06	11 33			12 06	12 33			13 06	13 33		14 05		14 06	14 33				15 06
Allens West	d				11 08	11 35			12 09	12 35			13 08	13 35				14 08	14 35				15 08
Tees-side Airport	d																						
Dinsdale	d					11 42				12 42				13 42					14 42				
Darlington 7	26 a				11 23	11 52			12 24	12 54			13 23	13 52				14 23	14 52				15 23
	d									12 54									14 54				
North Road	d									12 57									14 57				
Heighington	d									13 05									15 05				
Newton Aycliffe	d									13 08									15 08				
Shildon	d									13 13									15 13				
Bishop Auckland	a									13 20									15 20				
Stockton	d	10 43					11 42				12 42				13 43					14 43			
Billingham	d	10 50					11 50				12 50				13 50					14 50			
Seaton Carew	d	10 56					11 56				12 56				13 56					14 56			
Hartlepool	d	11 02	11 13				12 02				13 02				14 02	14 24				15 02			
Seaham	d	11 17					12 17				13 17				14 17					15 17			
Sunderland	a	11 27	11 40				12 27				13 28				14 27	14 50				15 27			
	d	11 30					12 30				13 30				14 30					15 30			
Heworth	d	11 42					12 42				13 42				14 42					15 42			
Newcastle 8	26 a	11 51					12 52				13 51				14 51					15 51			
Metrocentre	48 a	12 01					13 01				14 01				15 01					16 01			
Hexham	48 a	12 38					13 38				14 38				15 39					16 38			

§ For authorised access only to BSC Redcar

Saltburn and Middlesbrough - Darlington, Bishop Auckland, Sunderland and Newcastle

Network Diagram - see first Page of Table 44

		NT	NT	TP	NT	NT	NT	TP	NT	NT	NT	TP	NT	NT	NT	NT	TP	NT	NT	GC	NT	NT
				◇1				◇1				◇1					◇1			R 1		
Saltburn	d	14 58			15 31	15 58			16 27	16 58			17 31	17 58				18 31	18 58			19 31
Marske	d	15 02			15 35	16 02			16 31	17 02			17 35	18 02				18 35	19 02			19 35
Longbeck	d	15 05			15 38	16 05			16 34	17 05			17 38	18 05				18 38	19 05			19 38
Redcar East	d	15 08			15 41	16 08			16 37	17 08			17 41	18 08				18 41	19 08			19 41
Redcar Central	d	15 11			15 44	16 11			16 40	17 11			17 44	18 11				18 44	19 11			19 44
British Steel Redcar §	d								16 43													
South Bank	d								16 49	17 18												
Middlesbrough	a	15 21			15 54	16 21			16 54	17 23			17 54	18 21				18 54	19 21			19 54
	d	15 22	15 32	15 50	15 55	16 22	16 32	16 50	16 55	17 24	17 39	17 50	17 55	18 22	18 32	18 45	18 50	18 55	19 22		19 40	19 55
Thornaby	d	15 27	15 37	15a55	16 00	16 28	16 37	16a55	17 00	17 29	17 44	17a55	18 00	18 27	18 37	18 50	18a55	19 00	19 27		19 45	20 00
London Kings Cross 15 ⊖26	d																			16 48		
Eaglescliffe	a	15 32			16 05	16 35			17 05	17 34			18 05	18 32				19 05	19 32	19 33		20 05
	d	15 33			16 06	16 35			17 06	17 35			18 06	18 33				19 06	19 33	19 34		20 06
Allens West	d	15 35			16 08	16 38			17 08	17 37			18 08	18 35				19 08	19 35			20 08
Tees-side Airport	d																					
Dinsdale	d	15 42			16 15	16 44			17 15	17 44			18 15					19 15				20 15
Darlington 7 26	a	15 54			16 23	16 52			17 24	17 53			18 23	18 50		19 12		19 23	19 50			20 23
	d	15 54							17 26					18 54								20 32
North Road	d	15 57							17 29					18 57								20 35
Heighington	d	16 05							17 37					19 05								20 43
Newton Aycliffe	d	16 08							17 40					19 08								20 46
Shildon	d	16 13							17 45					19 13								20 51
Bishop Auckland	a	16 20							17 52					19 20								20 58
Stockton	d		15 43				16 44				17 50				18 43						19 51	
Billingham	d		15 50				16 51				17 57				18 50						19 58	
Seaton Carew	d		15 56				16 57				18 03				18 56						20 04	
Hartlepool	d		16 02				17 03				18 09				19 02					19 53	20 10	
Seaham	d		16 17				17 18				18 24				19 17						20 27	
Sunderland	a		16 27				17 28				18 38				19 27					20 21	20 37	
	d		16 30				17 30				18 42				19 29						20 38	
Heworth	d		16 42				17 42				18 55				19 42						20 53	
Newcastle 8 26	a		16 51				17 51				19 05				19 51						21 02	
Metrocentre 48	a		17 01				18 01								20 01						21 11	
Hexham 48	a		17 38				18 32															

		TP	TP	NT	NT	GC	TP	NT	NT
		◇1	◇1			R 1	◇1		
Saltburn	d			20 32				21 30	22 36
Marske	d			20 36				21 34	22 40
Longbeck	d			20 39				21 37	22 43
Redcar East	d			20 42				21 40	22 46
Redcar Central	d			20 45				21 43	22 49
British Steel Redcar §	d								
South Bank	d								
Middlesbrough	a			20 55				21 53	22 59
	d	20 04	20 50	20 56	21 01		21 50	21 54	23 00
Thornaby	d	20 09	20a55	21 01	21 06		21 55	21 59	23 05
London Kings Cross 15 ⊖26	d					19 18			
Eaglescliffe	a			21 06		22 04		22 04	23 10
	d			21 07		22 05		22 05	23 11
Allens West	d			21 09				22 07	23 13
Tees-side Airport	d								
Dinsdale	d			21 16				22 14	23 20
Darlington 7 26	a	20 29		21 24			22 15	22 25	23 30
	d								
North Road	d								
Heighington	d								
Newton Aycliffe	d								
Shildon	d								
Bishop Auckland	a								
Stockton	d				21 12				
Billingham	d				21 19				
Seaton Carew	d				21 25				
Hartlepool	d				21 31	22 25			
Seaham	d				21 46				
Sunderland	a				21 57	22 51			
	d				21 58				
Heworth	d				22 09				
Newcastle 8 26	a				22 19				
Metrocentre 48	a								
Hexham 48	a								

§ For authorised access only to BSC Redcar

Table 44

Saturdays

Saltburn and Middlesbrough - Darlington, Bishop Auckland, Sunderland and Newcastle

Network Diagram - see first Page of Table 44

		NT	TP	NT	NT	NT	NT	TP	NT	NT	NT	NT	NT	NT	NT	TP	NT	NT	TP	NT	NT	NT	GC
			◇1					◇1								◇1			◇1				R 1
Saltburn	d					06 22					07 12	07 26	07 55				08 31			09 31	09 58		
Marske	d					06 26					07 16	07 30	07 59				08 35			09 35	10 02		
Longbeck	d					06 29					07 19	07 33	08 02				08 38			09 38	10 05		
Redcar East	d					06 32					07 22	07 36	08 05				08 41			09 41	10 08		
Redcar Central	d					06 35					07 25	07 39	08 08				08 44			09 44	10 11		
British Steel Redcar §	d																						
South Bank	d											07 46					08 51						
Middlesbrough	a					06 45					07 36	07 51	08 18				08 56			09 55	10 22		
	d	05 45	05 55			06 47	06 51	07 12	07 32		07 37	07 52	08 19	08 32	08 44	08 50	09 08	09 32	09 50	09 56	10 22	10 32	
Thornaby	d	05 50	06a00			06 52	06 56	07a17	07 37		07 42	07 57	08 24	08 37	08 50	08a55	09 13	09 37	09a55	10 01	10 27	10 37	
London Kings Cross 15 ⊖26	d																						07 48
Eaglescliffe	a	05 55				06 57					07 47	08 02	08 29		08 55		09 21			10 06	10 32		10 37
	d	05 55				06 57					07 47	08 03	08 30		08 55		09 21			10 07	10 33		10 38
Allens West	d	05 58				07 00					07 50	08 05	08 32		08 58		09 24			10 09	10 35		
Tees-side Airport	d																						
Dinsdale	d	06 04				07 06					07 56	08 12	08 39		09 04		09 30				10 42		
Darlington 7	26 a	06 13				07 20					08 05	08 22	08 50		09 13		09 42			10 23	10 52		
	d			06 47		07 21				07 48		08 22	08 52								10 54		
North Road	d			06 50						07 51			08 55								10 57		
Heighington	d			06 58						07 59			09 03								11 05		
Newton Aycliffe	d			07 01						08 03			09 07								11 08		
Shildon	d			07 06						08 07			09 11								11 13		
Bishop Auckland	a			07 14						08 15			09 18								11 20		
Stockton	d						07 02		07 43					08 43				09 43				10 43	
Billingham	d						07 09		07 50					08 50				09 50				10 50	
Seaton Carew	d						07 15		07 56					08 56				09 56				10 56	
Hartlepool	d				07 03		07 21		08 02					09 02				10 02				11 02	11 14
Seaham	d				07 18		07 36		08 17					09 16				10 17				11 17	
Sunderland	a				07 28		07 50		08 28					09 27				10 28				11 27	11 40
	d				07 30		07 55		08 30					09 30				10 30				11 30	
Heworth	d				07 41		08 07		08 42					09 42				10 42				11 42	
Newcastle 8	26 a				07 51	08 05	08 18		08 52			09 01		09 51				10 51				11 51	
Metrocentre	48 a				08 00									10 02				11 01				12 01	
Hexham	48 a				08 40									10 37				11 38				12 38	

		TP	NT	NT	NT	TP	NT	NT	NT	TP	NT	NT	NT	GC	TP	NT	NT	NT	TP	NT	NT	NT	TP
		◇1				◇1				◇1				R 1	◇1				◇1				◇1
Saltburn	d		10 31	10 58			11 31	11 57			12 30	12 58				13 31	13 57			14 31	14 58		
Marske	d		10 35	11 02			11 35	12 01			12 34	13 02				13 35	14 02			14 35	15 02		
Longbeck	d		10 38	11 05			11 38	12 04			12 37	13 05				13 38	14 05			14 38	15 05		
Redcar East	d		10 41	11 08			11 41	12 07			12 40	13 08				13 41	14 08			14 41	15 08		
Redcar Central	d		10 44	11 11			11 44	12 10			12 43	13 11				13 44	14 11			14 44	15 11		
British Steel Redcar §	d																						
South Bank	d																						
Middlesbrough	a		10 54	11 21			11 54	12 21			12 54	13 21				13 54	14 21			14 54	15 21		
	d	10 50	10 55	11 22	11 32	11 50	11 55	12 22	12 32	12 50	12 55	13 22	13 32		13 50	13 55	14 22	14 32	14 50	14 55	15 22	15 32	15 50
Thornaby	d	10a55	11 00	11 27	11 36	11a55	12 00	12 27	12 37	12a55	13 00	13 27	13 37		13a55	14 00	14 27	14 37	14a55	15 00	15 27	15 37	15a55
London Kings Cross 15 ⊖26	d													11 20									
Eaglescliffe	a		11 05	11 32			12 05	12 32			13 08	13 32		13 58		14 05	14 32			15 05	15 32		
	d		11 06	11 33			12 06	12 33			13 09	13 33		13 59		14 06	14 33			15 06	15 33		
Allens West	d		11 08	11 35			12 08	12 35			13 11	13 35				14 08	14 35			15 08	15 35		
Tees-side Airport	d																						
Dinsdale	d			11 42				12 42				13 42					14 42				15 42		
Darlington 7	26 a		11 23	11 52			12 23	12 54			13 26	13 52				14 23	14 52			15 23	15 54		
	d							12 54									14 54				15 54		
North Road	d							12 57									14 57				15 57		
Heighington	d							13 05									15 05				16 05		
Newton Aycliffe	d							13 08									15 08				16 08		
Shildon	d							13 13									15 13				16 13		
Bishop Auckland	a							13 20									15 20				16 20		
Stockton	d				11 42				12 42				13 43					14 43				15 43	
Billingham	d				11 50				12 50				13 50					14 50				15 50	
Seaton Carew	d				11 56				12 56				13 56					14 56				15 56	
Hartlepool	d				12 02				13 02				14 02	14 22				15 02				16 02	
Seaham	d				12 17				13 17				14 17					15 17				16 17	
Sunderland	a				12 27				13 28				14 27	14 50				15 27				16 27	
	d				12 30				13 30				14 30					15 30				16 30	
Heworth	d				12 42				13 42				14 42					15 42				16 42	
Newcastle 8	26 a				12 52				13 51				14 51					15 51				16 51	
Metrocentre	48 a				13 01				14 01				15 02					16 01				17 01	
Hexham	48 a				13 38				14 38				15 37					16 38				17 39	

§ For authorised access only to BSC Redcar

Table 44

Saturdays

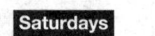

Saltburn and Middlesbrough - Darlington, Bishop Auckland, Sunderland and Newcastle

Network Diagram - see first Page of Table 44

			NT		NT	NT	TP	NT	NT	NT	TP	NT	NT		NT	TP	NT	GC	NT	NT	NT	TP	NT		TP	NT
							◇1				◇1					◇1		R 1				◇1			◇1	
Saltburn		d	15 31		15 58			16 27	16 58			17 31	17 58				18 31		18 58		19 31					20 32
Marske		d	15 35		16 02			16 31	17 02			17 35	18 02				18 35		19 02		19 35					20 36
Longbeck		d	15 38		16 05			16 34	17 05			17 38	18 05				18 38		19 05		19 38					20 39
Redcar East		d	15 41		16 08			16 37	17 08			17 41	18 08				18 41		19 08		19 41					20 42
Redcar Central		d	15 44		16 11			16 40	17 11			17 44	18 11				18 44		19 11		19 44					20 45
British Steel Redcar §		d						16 43																		
South Bank		d						16 49	17 18																	
Middlesbrough		a	15 54		16 21			16 54	17 23			17 54	18 21				18 54		19 21		19 54					20 55
		d	15 55		16 22	16 32	16 50	16 55	17 24	17 39	17 50	17 55	18 22		18 32	18 50	18 55		19 22	19 40	19 55	20 10	20 45		20 50	20 56
Thornaby		d	16 00		16 27	16 37	16a55	17 00	17 29	17 44	17a55	18 00	18 27		18 37	18a55	19 00		19 27	19 45	20 00	20a15	20 50		20a55	21 01
London Kings Cross 15 ⊖26		d																16 48								
Eaglescliffe		a	16 05		16 32			17 05	17 34			18 05	18 32				19 05	19 28	19 32		20 05					21 06
		d	16 06		16 33			17 06	17 35			18 06	18 33				19 06	19 29	19 33		20 06					21 07
Allens West		d	16 08		16 35			17 08	17 37			18 08	18 35				19 08		19 35		20 08					21 09
Tees-side Airport		d																								
Dinsdale		d	16 15		16 42			17 15	17 44			18 15					19 15				20 15					21 16
Darlington 7	26	a	16 23		16 52			17 24	17 53			18 24	18 50				19 23		19 52		20 26					21 24
		d						17 26					18 54								20 32					
North Road		d						17 29					18 57								20 35					
Heighington		d						17 37					19 05								20 43					
Newton Aycliffe		d						17 40					19 08								20 46					
Shildon		d						17 45					19 13								20 51					
Bishop Auckland		a						17 52					19 21								20 58					
Stockton		d				16 43				17 50					18 43					19 51			20 56			
Billingham		d				16 50				17 57					18 50					19 58			21 03			
Seaton Carew		d				16 56				18 03					18 56					20 04			21 09			
Hartlepool		d				17 02				18 09					19 02			19 49		20 10			21 15			
Seaham		d				17 17				18 24					19 17					20 27			21 30			
Sunderland	⇌	a				17 27				18 38					19 27			20 21		20 37			21 40			
		d				17 30				18 42					19 30					20 38			21 43			
Heworth	⇌	d				17 42				18 55					19 42					20 53			21 54			
Newcastle 8	26 ⇌	a				17 51				19 04					19 51					21 04			22 04			
Metrocentre	48	a				18 01									20 01											
Hexham	48	a				18 32																				

			GC	TP	NT	NT
			R 1	◇1		
Saltburn		d			21 30	22 36
Marske		d			21 34	22 40
Longbeck		d			21 37	22 43
Redcar East		d			21 40	22 46
Redcar Central		d			21 43	22 49
British Steel Redcar §		d				
South Bank		d				
Middlesbrough		a			21 53	22 59
		d		21 50	21 54	23 00
Thornaby		d		21 55	21 59	23 05
London Kings Cross 15 ⊖26		d	19 07			
Eaglescliffe		a	21 40		22 04	23 10
		d	21 41		22 05	23 11
Allens West		d			22 07	23 13
Tees-side Airport		d				
Dinsdale		d			22 14	23 20
Darlington 7	26	a		22 15	22 24	23 30
		d				
North Road		d				
Heighington		d				
Newton Aycliffe		d				
Shildon		d				
Bishop Auckland		a				
Stockton		d				
Billingham		d				
Seaton Carew		d				
Hartlepool		d	22 01			
Seaham		d				
Sunderland	⇌	a	22 36			
		d				
Heworth	⇌	d				
Newcastle 8	26 ⇌	a				
Metrocentre	48	a				
Hexham	48	a				

§ For authorised access only to BSC Redcar

Table 44

Sundays until 12 February

Saltburn and Middlesbrough - Darlington, Bishop Auckland, Sunderland and Newcastle

Network Diagram - see first Page of Table 44

		NT	NT	NT	NT	NT	TP	NT	NT	NT		NT	GC	TP	NT	NT	NT	NT	TP	NT		NT	NT	NT	NT
							◇■1						R ■1 ☕	◇■1					◇■1						
Saltburn	d					09 44			10 44			11 44			12 44			13 44		14 44				15 44	
Marske	d					09 48			10 48			11 48			12 48			13 48		14 48				15 48	
Longbeck	d					09 51			10 51			11 51			12 51			13 51		14 51				15 51	
Redcar East	d					09 54			10 54			11 54			12 54			13 54		14 54				15 54	
Redcar Central	d					09 57			10 57			11 57			12 57			13 57		14 57				15 57	
British Steel Redcar §	d																								
South Bank	d																								
Middlesbrough	a					10 07			11 07			12 07			13 07			14 07		15 07				16 07	
	d	08 38	09 08		09 31	10 08	10 15		11 08	11 31		12 08		12 45	13 08		13 31	14 08	14 42	15 08			15 31	16 08	
Thornaby	d	08 43	09 13		09 36	10 13	10a20		11 13	11 36		12 13		12a50	13 13		13 36	14 13	14a47	15 13			15 36	16 13	
London Kings Cross 15 ⊖26	d												09 48												
Eaglescliffe	a	08 48	09 18			10 18			11 18			12 18	12 23		13 18			14 18		15 18				16 18	
	d	08 49	09 19			10 19		10 36	11 19			12 19	12 25		13 19			14 19		15 19				16 19	16 26
Allens West	d	08 51	09 21			10 21			11 21			12 21			13 21			14 21		15 21				16 21	
Tees-side Airport	d																								
Dinsdale	d	08 58	09 28			10 28			11 28			12 28			13 28			14 28		15 28				16 28	
Darlington 7 26	a	09 07	09 37			10 37			11 37			12 36			13 37			14 37		15 39				16 37	
	d		09 38						11 38									14 38						16 38	
North Road	d		09 41						11 41									14 41						16 41	
Heighington	d		09 49						11 49									14 49						16 49	
Newton Aycliffe	d		09 52						11 52									14 52						16 52	
Shildon	d		09 57						11 57									14 57						16 57	
Bishop Auckland	a		10 02						12 02									15 04						17 02	
Stockton	d				09 42			10 41		11 42							13 42						15 42		16 32
Billingham	d				09 49			10 49		11 49							13 49						15 49		16 39
Seaton Carew	d				09 55			10 55		11 55							13 55						15 55		16 45
Hartlepool	d				10 01			11 00		12 01			12 52				14 01						16 01		16 51
Seaham	d				10 16			11 16		12 16							14 16						16 16		17 07
Sunderland	a				10 26			11 26		12 26			13 21				14 26						16 26		17 22
	d			09 28	10 28			11 28		12 28						13 28	14 28					15 28	16 28		17 28
Heworth	d			09 39	10 38			11 38		12 38						13 39	14 39					15 39	16 39		17 39
Newcastle 8 26	a			09 50	10 48			11 48		12 48						13 49	14 48					15 48	16 48		17 48
Metrocentre 48	a			10 01	10 59			11 57		12 59						13 59	14 59					15 59	16 57		17 59
Hexham 48	a																								

		GC	TP	NT	NT	NT		TP	NT	NT	NT	GC	TP	NT	GC	NT		NT	TP	NT					
		R ■1 ☕	◇■1					◇■1				■1 ☕	◇■1		R ■1 ☕				◇■1						
Saltburn	d			16 44		17 44			18 44					19 44		20 44		21 37		22 44					
Marske	d			16 48		17 48			18 48					19 48		20 48		21 41		22 48					
Longbeck	d			16 51		17 51			18 51					19 51		20 51		21 44		22 51					
Redcar East	d			16 54		17 54			18 54					19 54		20 54		21 47		22 54					
Redcar Central	d			16 57		17 57			18 57					19 57		20 57		21 50		22 57					
British Steel Redcar §	d																								
South Bank	d																								
Middlesbrough	a			17 07		18 07			19 07					20 11		21 07		22 00		23 07					
	d		16 42	17 08	17 45	18 08		18 45	19 08		19 31		20 06	20 12		21 08		22 02	22 06	23 08					
Thornaby	d		16a47	17 13	17 50	18 13		18a50	19 13		19 36		20a11	20 17		21 13		22 07	22a11	23 13					
London Kings Cross 15 ⊖26	d	13 48										16 48			18 23										
Eaglescliffe	a	16 33		17 18		18 18			19 18			19 35		20 22	21 01	21 18		22 12		23 18					
	d	16 34		17 19		18 19			19 19			19 39		20 22	21 03	21 19		22 12		23 18					
Allens West	d			17 21		18 21			19 21					20 25		21 21		22 15		23 21					
Tees-side Airport	d																								
Dinsdale	d			17 28		18 28			19 28					20 31		21 28		22 21		23 27					
Darlington 7 26	a			17 37		18 37			19 37					20 43		21 38		22 32		23 38					
	d					18 38																			
North Road	d					18 41																			
Heighington	d					18 49																			
Newton Aycliffe	d					18 52																			
Shildon	d					18 57																			
Bishop Auckland	a					19 02																			
Stockton	d				17 56						19 42														
Billingham	d				18 03						19 49														
Seaton Carew	d				18 09						19 55														
Hartlepool	d	17 01			18 15						20 01	20 13			21 23										
Seaham	d				18 30						20 16														
Sunderland	a	17 27			18 41						20 25	20 39			21 51										
	d				18 43					19 28	20 28														
Heworth	d				18 54					19 39	20 40														
Newcastle 8 26	a				19 05					19 52	20 47														
Metrocentre 48	a																								
Hexham 48	a																								

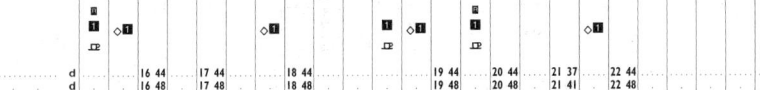

§ For authorised access only to BSC Redcar

Table 44

Sundays

19 February to 25 March

Saltburn and Middlesbrough - Darlington, Bishop Auckland, Sunderland and Newcastle

Network Diagram - see first Page of Table 44

Station			NT	NT	NT	NT	TP	NT	NT	NT	NT		GC	TP	NT	NT	NT	TP	NT	NT	NT		NT	GC	TP	NT
							◇1						R 1 ☕	◇1				◇1						R 1 ☕	◇1	
Saltburn		d				09 44			10 44		11 44				12 44		13 44		14 44		15 44					16 44
Marske		d				09 48			10 48		11 48				12 48		13 48		14 48		15 48					16 48
Longbeck		d				09 51			10 51		11 51				12 51		13 51		14 51		15 51					16 51
Redcar East		d				09 54			10 54		11 54				12 54		13 54		14 54		15 54					16 54
Redcar Central		d				09 57			10 57		11 57				12 57		13 57		14 57		15 57					16 57
British Steel Redcar §		d																								
South Bank		d																								
Middlesbrough		a				10 07			11 07		12 07				13 07		14 07		15 07		16 07					17 07
		d	08 38	09 08	09 21	10 08	10 15		11 08	11 22	12 08			12 45	13 08	13 22	14 08	14 42	15 08	15 22	16 08				16 42	17 08
Thornaby		d	08 43	09 13	09 26	10 13	10a20		11 13	11 27	12 13			12a50	13 13	13 27	14 13	14a47	15 13	15 27	16 13				16a47	17 13
London Kings Cross 15	⊖26	d											09 48											13 48		
Eaglescliffe		a	08 48	09 18		10 18			11 18		12 18		12 23		13 18		14 18		15 18		16 18			16 33		17 18
		d	08 49	09 19		10 19		10 27	11 19		12 19		12 25		13 19		14 19		15 19		16 19		16 26	16 34		17 19
Allens West		d	08 51	09 21		10 21			11 21		12 21				13 21		14 21		15 21		16 21					17 21
Tees-side Airport		d																								
Dinsdale		d	08 58	09 28		10 28			11 28		12 28				13 28		14 28		15 28		16 28					17 28
Darlington 7	26	a	09 07	09 37		10 37			11 37		12 36				13 37		14 37		15 39		16 37					17 37
		d		09 38					11 38								14 38				16 38					
North Road		d		09 41					11 41								14 41				16 41					
Heighington		d		09 49					11 49								14 49				16 49					
Newton Aycliffe		d		09 52					11 52								14 52				16 52					
Shildon		d		09 57					11 57								14 57				16 57					
Bishop Auckland		a		10 02					12 02								15 04				17 02					
Stockton		d			09 32			10 33		11 33						13 33				15 33			16 32			
Billingham		d			09 40			10 40		11 40						13 40				15 40			16 39			
Seaton Carew		d			09 46			10 46		11 46						13 46				15 46			16 45			
Hartlepool		d			09 52			10 52		11 52			12 52			13 52				15 52			16 50	17 01		
Seaham		d			10 07			11 07		12 07						14 07				16 07			17 07			
Sunderland	⛴	a			10 21			11 21		12 21			13 21			14 21				16 21			17 21	17 27		
		d																								
Heworth	⛴	d																								
Newcastle 8	26 ⛴	a																								
Metrocentre	48	a																								
Hexham	48	a																								

Station			NT	NT	TP	NT	NT		GC	TP	NT	GC	NT	NT	TP	NT
					◇1				1 ☕	◇1		R 1 ☕			◇1	
Saltburn		d		17 44		18 44					19 44		20 44	21 37		22 44
Marske		d		17 48		18 48					19 48		20 48	21 41		22 48
Longbeck		d		17 51		18 51					19 51		20 51	21 44		22 51
Redcar East		d		17 54		18 54					19 54		20 54	21 47		22 54
Redcar Central		d		17 57		18 57					19 57		20 57	21 50		22 57
British Steel Redcar §		d														
South Bank		d														
Middlesbrough		a		18 07		19 07					20 11		21 07	22 00		23 07
		d	17 37	18 08	18 45	19 08	19 21			20 06	20 12		21 08	22 02	22 06	23 08
Thornaby		d	17 42	18 13	18a50	19 13	19 26			20a11	20 17		21 13	22 07	22a11	23 13
London Kings Cross 15	⊖26	d							16 48			18 23				
Eaglescliffe		a		18 18		19 18			19 35		20 22	21 01	21 18	22 12		23 18
		d		18 19		19 19			19 39		20 22	21 03	21 19	22 12		23 18
Allens West		d		18 21		19 21					20 25		21 21	22 15		23 21
Tees-side Airport		d														
Dinsdale		d		18 28		19 28					20 31		21 28	22 21		23 27
Darlington 7	26	a		18 37		19 37					20 43		21 38	22 32		23 38
		d		18 38												
North Road		d		18 41												
Heighington		d		18 49												
Newton Aycliffe		d		18 52												
Shildon		d		18 57												
Bishop Auckland		a		19 02												
Stockton		d	17 48				19 32									
Billingham		d	17 55				19 40									
Seaton Carew		d	18 01				19 46									
Hartlepool		d	18 07				19 52		20 11			21 23				
Seaham		d	18 22				20 07									
Sunderland	⛴	a	18 36				20 22		20 37			21 51				
		d														
Heworth	⛴	d														
Newcastle 8	26 ⛴	a														
Metrocentre	48	a														
Hexham	48	a														

§ For authorised access only to BSC Redcar

Table 44

Sundays
from 1 April

Saltburn and Middlesbrough - Darlington, Bishop Auckland, Sunderland and Newcastle

Network Diagram - see first Page of Table 44

	NT	NT	NT	NT	NT	TP	NT	NT	NT		NT	GC	TP	NT	NT	NT	NT	TP	NT		NT	NT	NT	NT
						◇1						R 1 ☕	◇1					◇1						
Saltburn d					09 44			10 44			11 44			12 44			13 44		14 44				15 44	
Marske d					09 48			10 48			11 48			12 48			13 48		14 48				15 48	
Longbeck d					09 51			10 51			11 51			12 51			13 51		14 51				15 51	
Redcar East d					09 54			10 54			11 54			12 54			13 54		14 54				15 54	
Redcar Central d					09 57			10 57			11 57			12 57			13 57		14 57				15 57	
British Steel Redcar § d																								
South Bank d																								
Middlesbrough a					10 07			11 07			12 07			13 07			14 07		15 07				16 07	
d	08 38	09 08		09 31	10 08	10 15		11 08	11 31		12 08		12 45	13 08		13 31	14 08	14 42	15 08			15 31	16 08	
Thornaby d	08 43	09 13		09 36	10 13	10a20		11 13	11 36		12 13		12a50	13 13		13 36	14 13	14a47	15 13			15 36	16 13	
London Kings Cross 15 ⊖26 d												09 48												
Eaglescliffe a	08 48	09 18			10 18			11 18			12 18	12 23		13 18			14 18		15 18				16 18	
d	08 49	09 19			10 19		10 36	11 19			12 19	12 25		13 19			14 19		15 19				16 19	16 26
Allens West d	08 51	09 21			10 21			11 21			12 21			13 21			14 21		15 21				16 21	
Tees-side Airport d																								
Dinsdale d	08 58	09 28			10 28			11 28			12 28			13 28			14 28		15 28				16 28	
Darlington 7 26 a	09 07	09 37			10 37			11 37			12 36			13 37			14 37		15 39				16 37	
d		09 38						11 38									14 38						16 38	
North Road d		09 41						11 41									14 41						16 41	
Heighington d		09 49						11 49									14 49						16 49	
Newton Aycliffe d		09 52						11 52									14 52						16 52	
Shildon d		09 57						11 57									14 57						16 57	
Bishop Auckland a		10 02						12 02									15 04						17 02	
Stockton d				09 42			10 41		11 42							13 42						15 42		16 32
Billingham d				09 49			10 49		11 49							13 49						15 49		16 39
Seaton Carew d				09 55			10 55		11 55							13 55						15 55		16 45
Hartlepool d				10 01			11 00		12 01			12 52				14 01						16 01		16 51
Seaham d				10 16			11 16		12 16							14 16						16 16		17 07
Sunderland ⛴ a				10 26			11 26		12 26			13 21				14 26						16 26		17 20
d			09 28	10 28			11 28		12 28						13 28	14 28					15 28	16 28		17 26
Heworth ⛴ d			09 39	10 38			11 38		12 38						13 39	14 39					15 39	16 39		17 39
Newcastle 8 26 ⛴ a			09 50	10 48			11 48		12 48						13 49	14 48					15 48	16 48		17 48
Metrocentre 48 a			10 01	10 59			11 57		12 59						13 59	14 59					15 59	16 57		17 59
Hexham 48 a																								

	GC	TP	NT	NT	NT		TP	NT	NT	NT	GC	TP	NT	GC	NT		NT	TP	NT
	R 1 ☕	◇1					◇1				1 ☕	◇1		R 1 ☕				◇1	
Saltburn d			16 44		17 44			18 44					19 44		20 44		21 37		22 44
Marske d			16 48		17 48			18 48					19 48		20 48		21 41		22 48
Longbeck d			16 51		17 51			18 51					19 51		20 51		21 44		22 51
Redcar East d			16 54		17 54			18 54					19 54		20 54		21 47		22 54
Redcar Central d			16 57		17 57			18 57					19 57		20 57		21 50		22 57
British Steel Redcar § d																			
South Bank d																			
Middlesbrough a			17 07		18 07			19 07					20 11		21 07		22 00		23 07
d		16 42	17 08	17 45	18 08		18 45	19 08		19 31		20 06	20 12		21 08		22 02	22 06	23 08
Thornaby d		16a47	17 13	17 50	18 13		18a50	19 13		19 36		20a11	20 17		21 13		22 07	22a11	23 13
London Kings Cross 15 ⊖26 d	13 48										16 48			18 23					
Eaglescliffe a	16 33		17 18		18 18			19 18			19 35		20 22	21 01	21 18		22 12		23 18
d	16 34		17 19		18 19			19 19			19 39		20 22	21 03	21 19		22 12		23 18
Allens West d			17 21		18 21			19 21					20 25		21 21		22 15		23 21
Tees-side Airport d																			
Dinsdale d			17 28		18 28			19 28					20 31		21 28		22 21		23 27
Darlington 7 26 a			17 37		18 37			19 37					20 43		21 38		22 32		23 38
d					18 38														
North Road d					18 41														
Heighington d					18 49														
Newton Aycliffe d					18 52														
Shildon d					18 57														
Bishop Auckland a					19 02														
Stockton d				17 56						19 42									
Billingham d				18 03						19 49									
Seaton Carew d				18 09						19 55									
Hartlepool d	17 01			18 15						20 01	20 13			21 23					
Seaham d				18 30						20 16									
Sunderland ⛴ a	17 27			18 41						20 26	20 39			21 51					
d				18 43					19 28	20 29									
Heworth ⛴ d				18 54					19 39	20 40									
Newcastle 8 26 ⛴ a				19 05					19 52	20 47									
Metrocentre 48 a																			
Hexham 48 a																			

§ For authorised access only to BSC Redcar

Table 45

Mondays to Fridays

Middlesbrough and Pickering - Whitby

Network Diagram - see first Page of Table 44

Miles			NT	NT	NT	NY A 🛏	NT	NT	NY A 🛏	NT	NT	NT	NY B 🛏	NY C 🛏	NT	NT	NT
—	Newcastle 8	44 ⛴ d			07 30			10 30			13 30	15 30				16 30	18 30
0	**Middlesbrough**	d	07 04	08 14	08 47		10 38	11 50		14 16	14 46	16 47			17 40	17 54	19 49
3	Marton	d	07 09	08 19	08 52		10 43	11 56		14 21	14 52	16 52			17 45	17 59	19 54
4	Gypsy Lane	d	07 12	08 23	08 55		10 46	12 00		14 24	14 55	16 55			17 48	18 02	19 57
4½	Nunthorpe	d	07 17	08a29	09a01		10 49	12a04		14 27	15a00	17a00			17 51	18a07	20a03
8½	Great Ayton	d	07 23				10 55			14 33					17 57		
11	Battersby	a	07 29				11 01			14 39					18 03		
—		d	07 36				11 05			14 43					18 07		
12¾	Kildale	d	07 41				11 10			14 48					18 12		
16¼	Commondale	d	07 48				11 17			14 55					18 19		
18½	Castleton Moor	d	07 52				11 20			14 58					18 22		
20	Danby	d	07 55				11 23			15 01					18 25		
23½	Lealholm	d	08 02				11 30			15 08					18 32		
25½	Glaisdale	a	08 07				11 34			15 12					18 36		
—		d	08 09				11 37			15 15					18 39		
27¼	Egton	d	08 13				11 40			15 18					18 42		
—	**Pickering** §	d															
—	Levisham §	d															
—	Goathland §	d															
28¾	Grosmont	d	08 17			10 10	11 44		13 10	15 22			16 35	17 10	18 46		
32	Sleights	d	08 26			10 24	11 53		13 24	15 31			16 49	17 24	18 55		
33½	Ruswarp	d	08 31				11 58			15 36					19 00		
35	**Whitby**	a	08 38			10 35	12 05		13 35	15 43			17 00	17 35	19 07		

Saturdays

		NT	NT	NT	NY D 🛏	NT	NT	NY D 🛏	NT	NT	NT	NY E 🛏	NY F 🛏	NT	NT	NT
Newcastle 8	44 ⛴ d			07 30			10 30			13 30	15 30				16 30	18 30
Middlesbrough	d	07 04	08 14	08 47		10 38	11 50		14 16	14 46	16 47			17 40	17 54	19 49
Marton	d	07 09	08 19	08 52		10 43	11 56		14 21	14 52	16 52			17 45	17 59	19 54
Gypsy Lane	d	07 12	08 23	08 55		10 46	12 00		14 24	14 55	16 55			17 48	18 02	19 57
Nunthorpe	d	07 17	08a27	08a59		10 49	12a04		14 27	15a00	16a59			17 51	18a05	20a03
Great Ayton	d	07 23				10 55			14 33					17 57		
Battersby	a	07 29				11 01			14 39					18 03		
	d	07 36				11 05			14 43					18 07		
Kildale	d	07 41				11 10			14 48					18 12		
Commondale	d	07 48				11 17			14 55					18 19		
Castleton Moor	d	07 52				11 20			14 58					18 22		
Danby	d	07 55				11 23			15 01					18 25		
Lealholm	d	08 02				11 30			15 08					18 32		
Glaisdale	a	08 07				11 34			15 12					18 36		
	d	08 09				11 37			15 15					18 39		
Egton	d	08 13				11 40			15 18					18 42		
Pickering §	d															
Levisham §	d															
Goathland §	d															
Grosmont	d	08 17			10 10	11 44		13 10	15 22			16 35	17 10	18 46		
Sleights	d	08 26			10 24	11 53		13 24	15 31			16 49	17 24	18 55		
Ruswarp	d	08 31				11 58			15 36					19 00		
Whitby	a	08 38			10 35	12 05		13 35	15 43			17 00	17 35	19 07		

Sundays

until 18 March

		NT
Newcastle 8	44 ⛴ d	21 06
Middlesbrough	d	22a10
Marton	d	
Gypsy Lane	d	
Nunthorpe	d	
Great Ayton	d	
Battersby	a	
	d	
Kildale	d	
Commondale	d	
Castleton Moor	d	
Danby	d	
Lealholm	d	
Glaisdale	a	
	d	
Egton	d	
Pickering §	d	
Levisham §	d	
Goathland §	d	
Grosmont	d	
Sleights	d	
Ruswarp	d	
Whitby	a	

§ North Yorkshire Moors Railway. For full service between Grosmont and Pickering please refer to separate publicity

A from 2 April

B from 2 April until 05 April

C Runs only on 6 April, 9 April and 7 May

D from 24 March

E from 24 March until 21 April and then from 12 May

F Runs only on 28 April and 5 May

No Sunday Service operated by Northern Rail

For connections to Darlington please refer to Table 44

Table 45

Sundays
from 25 March

Middlesbrough and Pickering - Whitby

Network Diagram - see first Page of Table 44

		NY	NY	NY A	NY B	NT
Newcastle ■ 44	d	.	.	.	.	21 06
Middlesbrough	d	.	.	.	.	22a10
Marton	d	.	.	.	.	.
Gypsy Lane	d	.	.	.	.	.
Nunthorpe	d	.	.	.	.	.
Great Ayton	d	.	.	.	.	.
Battersby	a	.	.	.	.	.
	d	.	.	.	.	.
Kildale	d	.	.	.	.	.
Commondale	d	.	.	.	.	.
Castleton Moor	d	.	.	.	.	.
Danby	d	.	.	.	.	.
Lealholm	d	.	.	.	.	.
Glaisdale	a	.	.	.	.	.
	d	.	.	.	.	.
Egton	d	.	.	.	.	.
Pickering §	d	.	.	.	.	.
Levisham §	d	.	.	.	.	.
Goathland §	d	.	.	.	.	.
Grosmont	d	10 10	13 10	16 35	17 10	.
Sleights	d	10 24	13 24	16 49	17 24	.
Ruswarp	d	.	.	.	.	.
Whitby	a	10 35	13 35	17 00	17 35	.

§ North Yorkshire Moors Railway. For full service between Grosmont and Pickering please refer to separate publicity

A Does not runs on 8 April, 29 April and 6 May

B Runs only on 8 April, 29 April and 6 May

No Sunday Service operated by Northern Rail

For connections to Darlington please refer to Table 44

Table 45

Mondays to Fridays

Whitby - Pickering and Middlesbrough

Network Diagram - see first Page of Table 44

Miles			NT	NT	NT	NT	NY A	NT	NT	NY A	NT		NT	NT	NY B	NY G	NT	NT
0	**Whitby**	d				08 50	11 00		12 41	14 00				16 00	17 28	18 00		19 15
1½	Ruswarp	d				08 54	11 08		12 45	14 08				16 04	17 36	18 08		19 19
3	Sleights	d				08 59	~		12 50	~				16 09	~	~		19 24
6¼	Grosmont	d				09 07	11a20		12 58	14a20				16 17	17a48	18a20		19 32
—	Goathland §	a																
—	Levisham §	a																
—	**Pickering** §	a																
7¾	Egton	d				09 10			13 01					16 21				19 35
9½	Glaisdale	a				09 14			13 05					16 25				19 39
—		d				09 17			13 08					16 28				19 42
11½	Lealholm	d				09 22			13 13					16 33				19 47
15	Danby	d				09 28			13 19					16 40				19 53
16½	Castleton Moor	d				09 31			13 22					16 44				19 56
18¼	Commondale	d				09 35			13 26					16 47				20 00
22¼	Kildale	d				09 42			13 33					16 54				20 07
24	Battersby	a				09 47			13 38					16 59				20 12
—		d				09 51			13 42					17 04				20 16
26½	Great Ayton	d				09 56			13 47					17 09				20 21
30½	Nunthorpe	d	07 21	08 31	09 16	10 03		12 16	13 54		15 16		17 02	17 16			18 24	20 28
31	Gypsy Lane	d	07 23	08 33	09 18	10 05		12 18	13 56		15 18		17 04	17 18			18 26	20 30
32	Marton	d	07 25	08 36	09 21	10 08		12 21	13 59		15 21		17 06	17 20			18 29	20 33
35	**Middlesbrough**	a	07 31	08 43	09 29	10 17		12 28	14 07		15 28		17 15	17 30			18 35	20 41
—	Newcastle 8 44	a	08 52		10 51			13 51			16 51							

Saturdays

		NT	NT	NT	NT	NY D	NT	NT	NY D	NT		NT	NT	NY E	NY F	NT	NT
Whitby	d				08 50	11 00		12 41	14 00				16 00	17 30	18 02		19 15
Ruswarp	d				08 54	11 08		12 45	14 08				16 04	17 36	18 08		19 19
Sleights	d				08 59	~		12 50	~				16 09	~	~		19 24
Grosmont	d				09 07	11a20		12 58	14a20				16 17	17a50	18a22		19 32
Goathland §	a																
Levisham §	a																
Pickering §	a																
Egton	d				09 10			13 01					16 21				19 35
Glaisdale	a				09 14			13 05					16 25				19 39
	d				09 17			13 08					16 28				19 42
Lealholm	d				09 22			13 13					16 33				19 47
Danby	d				09 28			13 19					16 40				19 53
Castleton Moor	d				09 31			13 22					16 44				19 56
Commondale	d				09 35			13 26					16 47				20 00
Kildale	d				09 42			13 33					16 54				20 07
Battersby	a				09 47			13 38					16 59				20 12
	d				09 51			13 42					17 04				20 16
Great Ayton	d				09 56			13 47					17 09				20 21
Nunthorpe	d	07 21	08 31	09 16	10 03		12 16	13 54		15 16		17 02	17 16			18 24	20 28
Gypsy Lane	d	07 23	08 33	09 18	10 05		12 18	13 56		15 18		17 04	17 18			18 26	20 30
Marton	d	07 25	08 36	09 21	10 08		12 21	13 59		15 21		17 06	17 20			18 29	20 33
Middlesbrough	a	07 31	08 43	09 29	10 17		12 27	14 07		15 28		17 15	17 30			18 35	20 41
Newcastle 8 44	a	08 52		10 51			13 51			16 51							22 04

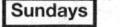

Sundays

from 25 March

		NY	NY	NY C	NY H
Whitby	d	11 00	14 00	17 30	18 02
Ruswarp	d	11 08	14 08	17 36	18 08
Sleights	d			~	~
Grosmont	d	11a20	14a20	17a50	18a22
Goathland §	a				
Levisham §	a				
Pickering §	a				
Egton	d				
Glaisdale	a				
	d				
Lealholm	d				
Danby	d				
Castleton Moor	d				
Commondale	d				
Kildale	d				
Battersby	a				
	d				
Great Ayton	d				
Nunthorpe	d				
Gypsy Lane	d				
Marton	d				
Middlesbrough	a				
Newcastle 8 44	a				

§ North Yorkshire Moors Railway. For full service between Grosmont and Pickering please refer to separate publicity

A from 2 April

B from 2 April until 05 April

C Does not run on 8 April, 29 April and 6 May

D from 24 March

E from 24 March until 21 April and then from 12 May

F 28 April and 5 May

G Runs only on 6 April, 9 April and 7 May

H Runs only on 8 April, 29 April and 6 May

No Sunday Services prior to 25 March
No Sunday Service operated by Northern Rail
For connections to Darlington please refer to Table 44

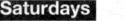

Chathill and Morpeth - Newcastle - Metrocentre, Hexham and Carlisle

Network Diagram - see first Page of Table 44

Miles	Miles			GR	NT	NT	GR	XC	NT	NT		XC		NT		NT	NT	GR	NT	NT	NT	NT		NT	NT
				■R ■1 🍴			■R ■1 🍴	◇■1 🍴				◇■1 🍴						■R ■1a 🍴							
0	—	**Chathill**	d						07 08																
11¼	—	Alnmouth for Alnwick 26	d	06 19			06 53	07 08	07 20			07 59						08 58							
17½	—	Acklington	d						07 36																
22¾	—	Widdrington	d						07 44																
27½	—	Pegswood	d						07 50																
39½	—	**Morpeth** 26	d	06 35			07 09		07 54			08 13				08 49						09 49			
36¼	—	Cramlington	d						08 02							08 57						09 57			
45½	—	Manors	d						08 15							09 10						10 10			
46	—	**Newcastle ■8** 26 ⛴	a	06 52			07 26	07 38	08 19			08 30				09 14		09 27				10 14			
—	—	Sunderland 26,44 ⛴	d							07 30											09 30				
—	—	**Newcastle ■8** ⛴	d		06 30	06 47				07 53				08 24			08 54		09 26	09 44	09 54	10 15		10 22	10 44
48¼	2¼	Dunston	d																		09 59				
49½	3½	**Metrocentre**	a							08 00				08 31			09 01		09 33	09 52	10 02	10 22		10 29	10 52
—	—		d							08 01				08 32			09 02		09 33		10 02			10 32	
—	5½	Blaydon	d							08 05							09 06								
—	9¾	Wylam	d		06 44					08 11				08 40			09 12				10 10				
—	12	Prudhoe	d		06 48	07 03				08 15				08 44			09 16		09 43		10 14			10 42	
—	14½	Stocksfield	d		06 53					08 20				08 48			09 21				10 18				
—	16¾	Riding Mill	d		06 57					08 24							09 25				10 23				
—	19¼	Corbridge	d		07 01					08 28							09 29				10 26				
—	22¼	**Hexham**	a		07 10	07 16				08 39				08 58			09 39		09 56		10 36			10 55	
—	—		d			07 16								08 59					09 56					10 55	
—	30	Haydon Bridge	d			07 25								09 08										11 04	
—	33¾	Bardon Mill	d			07 32								09 14										11 11	
—	38½	Haltwhistle	d			07 39								09 21					10 15					11 18	
—	50¾	Brampton (Cumbria)	d			07 54								09 37										11 33	
—	57½	Wetheral	d			08 03								09 46										11 42	
—	61¾	**Carlisle ■8**	a			08 13								09 57					10 48					11 57	

		NT	NT	GR	XC	NT	NT	NT		NT	XC	NT	NT	NT	NT	NT	NT	NT		NT	XC	NT	NT	NT	NT
				■R ■1 🍴	◇■1 🍴						◇■1 🍴										◇■1 🍴				
Chathill	d																								
Alnmouth for Alnwick 26	d			10 58							12 08										14 08				
Acklington	d																								
Widdrington	d																								
Pegswood	d																								
Morpeth 26	d		10 49		11 21					11 49					12 49					13 49					14 49
Cramlington	d		10 57							11 57					12 57					13 57					14 57
Manors	d		11 10							12 10					13 10					14 10					15 10
Newcastle ■8 26 ⛴	a		11 14	11 27	11 39					12 13	12 38				13 13					14 13	14 38				15 14
Sunderland 26,44 ⛴	d	10 30						11 30						12 30				13 30						14 30	
Newcastle ■8 ⛴	d	10 54	11 15			11 22	11 42	11 54		12 14		12 22	12 43	12 54	13 15	13 22	13 44	13 54		14 15		14 24	14 44	14 54	15 15
Dunston	d																								
Metrocentre	a	11 01	11 22			11 31	11 51	12 01		12 22		12 31	12 52	13 01	13 22	13 31	13 51	14 01		14 22		14 31	14 51	15 01	15 22
	d	11 02				11 32		12 02				12 32		13 02		13 32		14 02				14 32		15 02	
Blaydon	d																								
Wylam	d	11 10						12 10						13 10				14 10						15 10	
Prudhoe	d	11 14				11 42		12 14				12 42		13 14		13 43		14 14				14 42		15 16	
Stocksfield	d	11 18						12 18						13 18				14 18						15 18	
Riding Mill	d	11 23						12 23						13 23				14 23						15 23	
Corbridge	d	11 26						12 26						13 26				14 26						15 26	
Hexham	a	11 38				11 55		12 38				12 55		13 38		13 55		14 38				14 55		15 39	
	d					11 55						12 55				13 56						14 55			
Haydon Bridge	d											13 04										15 04			
Bardon Mill	d											13 11										15 11			
Haltwhistle	d					12 14						13 18				14 15						15 18			
Brampton (Cumbria)	d											13 33										15 33			
Wetheral	d											13 42										15 42			
Carlisle ■8	a					12 47						13 54				14 49						15 57			

For connections from London Kings Cross please refer to Table 26

Chathill and Morpeth - Newcastle - Metrocentre, Hexham and Carlisle

Network Diagram - see first Page of Table 44

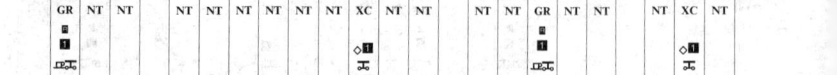

			GR	NT	NT	NT	NT	NT	NT	NT	NT	XC	NT	NT	NT	NT	GR	NT	NT	NT	XC	NT
			R 1									◇1					R 1				◇1	
Chathill		d																				19 10
Alnmouth for Alnwick	26	d	14 58									17 01					17 58				19 08	19 22
Acklington		d																				19 30
Widdrington		d																				19 37
Pegswood		d																				19 43
Morpeth	26	d					15 49				16 49	17 16							18 26	19 01		19 47
Cramlington		d					15 57				16 57								18 34	19 09		19 56
Manors		d					16 10				17 10											
Newcastle 8	26	a	15 27				16 14				17 15	17 34					18 27		18 49	19 25	19 38	20 07
Sunderland	26,44	d				15 30				16 30						17 30						
Newcastle 8		d		15 24	15 44	15 54	16 15	16 22	16 44	16 54			17 16	17 24	17 44	17 54		18 24				
Dunston		d													17 50							
Metrocentre		a		15 31	15 51	16 01	16 22	16 33	16 53	17 01			17 23	17 31	17 53	18 01		18 31				
		d		15 32		16 02		16 33		17 02			17 24	17 32		18 02		18 32				
Blaydon		d												17 36								
Wylam		d				16 10		16 41		17 10			17 32	17 42		18 10		18 40				
Prudhoe		d		15 42		16 14		16 45		17 14			17 36	17 46		18 14		18 44				
Stocksfield		d				16 18		16 50		17 18				17 51		18 18		18 48				
Riding Mill		d				16 23		16 54		17 23				17 55		18 23		18 53				
Corbridge		d				16 26		16 58		17 26				17 59		18 26		18 56				
Hexham		a		15 56		16 38		17 03		17 38			17 51	18 09		18 32		19 02				
		d		15 56				17 03					17 52			18 33		19 03				
Haydon Bridge		d		16 05				17 12					18 01			18 42						
Bardon Mill		d						17 19					18 07			18 48						
Haltwhistle		d		16 18				17 26					18 14			18 55		19 22				
Brampton (Cumbria)		d						17 41					18 30			19 11						
Wetheral		d						17 50					18 39			19 20						
Carlisle 8		a		16 51				17 59					18 54			19 35		19 55				

			NT	NT	GR	NT	NT	XC	NT	NT	GR	NT	NT
					R 1			◇1			R 1		
Chathill		d											
Alnmouth for Alnwick	26	d			19 36			21 08			22 10		
Acklington		d											
Widdrington		d											
Pegswood		d											
Morpeth	26	d			19 53						22 26		22 45
Cramlington		d											22 53
Manors		d											
Newcastle 8	26	a			20 12			21 38			22 43		23 07
Sunderland	26,44	d		19 29			20 38						
Newcastle 8		d	19 24	19 54		20 15	21 04		21 18	21 52		22 35	
Dunston		d											
Metrocentre		a	19 28	20 01		20 22	21 11		21 25	22 01		22 42	
		d	19 32			20 23			21 26			22 43	
Blaydon		d											
Wylam		d	19 40			20 31			21 34			22 51	
Prudhoe		d	19 44			20 35			21 38			22 55	
Stocksfield		d	19 48			20 39			21 42			22 59	
Riding Mill		d	19 53			20 44			21 47			23 04	
Corbridge		d	19 56			20 47			21 50			23 07	
Hexham		a	19 59			20 57			21 56			23 18	
		d	20 03						21 57				
Haydon Bridge		d	20 12						22 06				
Bardon Mill		d	20 18						22 12				
Haltwhistle		d	20 25						22 19				
Brampton (Cumbria)		d	20 41						22 35				
Wetheral		d	20 50						22 43				
Carlisle 8		a	21 04						22 59				

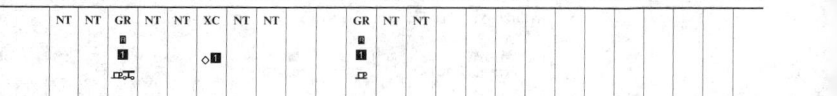

For connections from London Kings Cross please refer to Table 26

Table 48

Saturdays

Chathill and Morpeth - Newcastle - Metrocentre, Hexham and Carlisle

Network Diagram - see first Page of Table 44

			NT	XC	NT	GR	NT		XC	NT			NT	NT	GR	XC	NT	NT	NT	NT	NT		NT	NT	NT	GR
				◇1		R 1			◇1						R 1	◇1										R 1
Chathill		d			07 10																					
Alnmouth for Alnwick	26	d		07 08	07 22	07 25			08 00						08 58	09 08										10 58
Acklington		d			07 37																					
Widdrington		d			07 45																					
Pegswood		d			07 51																					
Morpeth	26	d			07 55	07 41			08 14				08 49							09 49					10 49	
Cramlington		d			08 03								08 57							09 57					10 57	
Manors		d			08 16								09 10							10 10					11 10	
Newcastle 8	26 ⛴	a		07 38	08 20	07 58			08 32				09 14		09 27	09 39				10 14					11 13	11 27
Sunderland	26,44 ⛴	d					07 30												09 30					10 30		
Newcastle 8	⛴	d	06 30				07 53			08 24				08 54			09 26	09 44	09 54	10 15	10 22		10 45	10 54	11 15	
Dunston		d																	09 59							
Metrocentre		a					08 00			08 31				09 01			09 33	09 52	10 02	10 22	10 29		10 54	11 01	11 22	
		d					08 01			08 32				09 02			09 34		10 02		10 32			11 02		
Blaydon		d					08 05							09 06												
Wylam		d	06 44				08 11			08 40				09 12					10 10					11 10		
Prudhoe		d	06 48				08 15			08 44				09 16			09 43		10 14		10 42			11 14		
Stocksfield		d	06 53				08 20			08 48				09 21					10 18					11 18		
Riding Mill		d	06 57				08 24							09 25					10 23					11 23		
Corbridge		d	07 01				08 28							09 29					10 26					11 26		
Hexham		a	07 07				08 40			08 58				09 39			09 57		10 37		10 55			11 38		
		d	07 07							08 59							09 57				10 55					
Haydon Bridge		d	07 16							09 08											11 04					
Bardon Mill		d	07 23							09 14											11 11					
Haltwhistle		d	07 30							09 21							10 15				11 18					
Brampton (Cumbria)		d	07 45							09 37											11 33					
Wetheral		d	07 54							09 46											11 42					
Carlisle 8		a	08 04							09 57							10 48				11 57					

			XC	NT	NT	NT	NT		XC	NT	NT	NT	NT	GR	NT	NT	NT		NT	XC	NT	NT	NT	NT	GR	NT
			◇1						◇1					R 1						◇1					R 1	
Chathill		d																								
Alnmouth for Alnwick	26	d							12 08					12 58						14 09					14 58	
Acklington		d																								
Widdrington		d																								
Pegswood		d																								
Morpeth	26	d	11 19				11 49						12 49						13 49					14 49		
Cramlington		d					11 57						12 57						13 57					14 57		
Manors		d					12 11						13 10						14 10					15 11		
Newcastle 8	26 ⛴	a	11 38				12 13		12 38				13 13	13 27					14 15	14 39				15 14	15 27	
Sunderland	26,44 ⛴	d				11 30						12 30					13 30						14 30			
Newcastle 8	⛴	d		11 22	11 44	11 54	12 15			12 22	12 44	12 54	13 14		13 22	13 44	13 54		14 15		14 24	14 44	14 56	15 15		15 24
Dunston		d																								
Metrocentre		a		11 31	11 52	12 01	12 23			12 31	12 52	13 01	13 22		13 31	13 51	14 01		14 23		14 31	14 51	15 02	15 22		15 31
		d		11 32		12 02				12 32		13 02			13 32		14 02				14 32		15 02			15 32
Blaydon		d																								
Wylam		d				12 10						13 10					14 10						15 10			
Prudhoe		d		11 42		12 14				12 43		13 14			13 43		14 14				14 42		15 16			15 42
Stocksfield		d				12 18						13 18					14 18						15 18			
Riding Mill		d				12 23						13 23					14 23						15 23			
Corbridge		d				12 26						13 26					14 26						15 26			
Hexham		a		11 55		12 38				12 55		13 38			13 55		14 38				14 55		15 37			15 56
		d		11 55						12 56					13 56						14 55					15 56
Haydon Bridge		d								13 05											15 04					16 05
Bardon Mill		d								13 11											15 11					
Haltwhistle		d		12 14						13 18					14 15						15 18					16 18
Brampton (Cumbria)		d								13 33											15 33					
Wetheral		d								13 42											15 42					
Carlisle 8		a		12 47						13 54					14 49						15 57					16 53

For connections from London Kings Cross please refer to Table 26

Chathill and Morpeth - Newcastle - Metrocentre, Hexham and Carlisle

Network Diagram - see first Page of Table 44

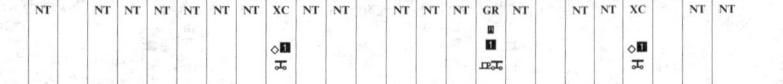

Station			NT		NT	NT	NT	NT	NT	NT	XC	NT	NT		NT	NT	NT	GR	NT		NT	NT	XC		NT	NT
											◇1							R 1					◇1			
Chathill		d																				18 36				
Alnmouth for Alnwick	26	d									17 03							17 58				18 48	19 08			
Acklington		d																				18 56				
Widdrington		d																				19 03				
Pegswood		d																				19 09				
Morpeth	26	d				15 49				16 49	17 17						17 52				18 50	19 13				
Cramlington		d				15 57				16 57							18 00				18 58	19 22				
Manors		d				16 11				17 10																
Newcastle 8	26 ⛴	a				16 15				17 13	17 35						18 15	18 27			19 13	19 34	19 41			
Sunderland	26,44 ⛴	d			15 30				16 30							17 30										19 30
Newcastle 8	⛴	d	15 44		15 54	16 15	16 22	16 46	16 54			17 16	17 24		17 43	17 54			18 24						19 25	19 54
Dunston		d													17 50											
Metrocentre		a	15 51		16 01	16 22	16 31	16 53	17 01			17 23	17 31		17 53	18 01			18 31						19 31	20 01
		d			16 02		16 31		17 02			17 24	17 32			18 02			18 32						19 32	
Blaydon		d											17 36													
Wylam		d			16 10		16 40		17 10			17 32	17 42			18 10			18 40						19 42	
Prudhoe		d			16 14		16 44		17 14			17 36	17 46			18 14			18 44						19 46	
Stocksfield		d			16 18		16 48		17 18				17 51			18 18			18 48						19 50	
Riding Mill		d			16 23		16 53		17 23				17 55			18 23			18 53						19 55	
Corbridge		d			16 26		16 56		17 26				17 59			18 26			18 56						19 58	
Hexham		a			16 38		17 02		17 39			17 51	18 12			18 32			19 02						20 04	
		d					17 03					17 52				18 33			19 03						20 05	
Haydon Bridge		d					17 12					18 01				18 42									20 14	
Bardon Mill		d					17 18					18 07				18 48									20 20	
Haltwhistle		d					17 25					18 14				18 55			19 22						20 27	
Brampton (Cumbria)		d					17 41					18 30				19 11									20 43	
Wetheral		d					17 50					18 39				19 20									20 52	
Carlisle 8		a					18 03					18 54				19 35			19 53						21 03	

Station			GR	NT	NT		NT	NT			NT
			R 1								
Chathill		d									
Alnmouth for Alnwick	26	d	20 07								
Acklington		d									
Widdrington		d									
Pegswood		d									
Morpeth	26	d	20 24				21 15				
Cramlington		d					21 23				
Manors		d									
Newcastle 8	26 ⛴	a	20 41				21 39				
Sunderland	26,44 ⛴	d									
Newcastle 8	⛴	d		20 15	20 30			21 18			21 52
Dunston		d									
Metrocentre		a		20 22	20 39			21 25			22 01
		d		20 23				21 26			22 02
Blaydon		d									
Wylam		d		20 31				21 34			22 10
Prudhoe		d		20 35				21 38			22a13
Stocksfield		d		20 39				21 42			
Riding Mill		d		20 44				21 47			
Corbridge		d		20 47				21 50			
Hexham		a		20 59				21 56			
		d						21 57			
Haydon Bridge		d						22 06			
Bardon Mill		d						22 12			
Haltwhistle		d						22 19			
Brampton (Cumbria)		d						22 35			
Wetheral		d						22 43			
Carlisle 8		a						22 59			

For connections from London Kings Cross please refer to Table 26

Table 48

Sundays
until 12 February

Chathill and Morpeth - Newcastle - Metrocentre, Hexham and Carlisle

Network Diagram - see first Page of Table 44

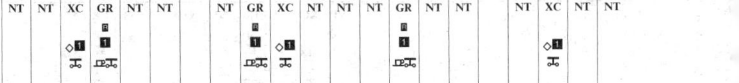

		NT	NT	NT	NT	NT	XC	GR	NT	NT		NT	GR	XC	NT	NT	NT	GR	NT	NT		NT	XC	NT	NT
							◇1 ✕	R 1 ✕					R 1 ✕	◇1 ✕				R 1 ✕					◇1 ✕		
Chathill	d																								
Alnmouth for Alnwick 26	d						10 49	10 58						12 10				12 58					14 08		
Acklington	d																								
Widdrington	d																								
Pegswood	d																								
Morpeth 26	d						11 04						12 06												
Cramlington	d																								
Manors	d																								
Newcastle 8 26 ⛴	a						11 19	11 27					12 23	12 37				13 27					14 35		
Sunderland 26,44 ⛴	d		09 28			10 28						11 28					12 28					13 28			
Newcastle 8 ⛴	d	09 10	09 53	10 10	10 30	10 50			11 10	11 30		11 50			12 10	12 30	12 50		13 10	13 30		13 50		14 10	14 30
Dunston	d																								
Metrocentre	a	09 17	10 01	10 17	10 37	10 59			11 17	11 37		11 57			12 17	12 37	12 59		13 17	13 37		13 59		14 17	14 37
	d	09 18		10 18					11 18						12 18				13 18					14 18	
Blaydon	d																								
Wylam	d	09 26		10 26					11 26						12 26				13 26					14 26	
Prudhoe	d	09 30		10 30					11 30						12 30				13 30					14 30	
Stocksfield	d	09 34		10 34					11 34						12 34				13 34					14 34	
Riding Mill	d	09 39		10 39					11 39						12 39				13 39					14 39	
Corbridge	d	09 42		10 42					11 42						12 42				13 42					14 42	
Hexham	a	09 48		10 48					11 48						12 48				13 48					14 48	
	d	09 49		10 49					11 49						12 49				13 49					14 49	
Haydon Bridge	d	09 58		10 58											12 58										
Bardon Mill	d	10 04		11 04											13 04										
Haltwhistle	d	10 11		11 11					12 08						13 11				14 08					15 08	
Brampton (Cumbria)	d	10 27		11 27											13 27										
Wetheral	d	10 35		11 35											13 35										
Carlisle 8	a	10 44		11 49					12 38						13 45				14 38					15 40	

		NT	GR	NT	NT	NT		NT	NT	NT	GR	XC	NT	NT	NT	NT		NT		NT	GR		NT	GR	GR
			R 1 ✕								R 1 ✕	◇1 ✕									R 1 ✕			R 1 ✕	R 1 ✕
Chathill	d																								
Alnmouth for Alnwick 26	d		14 58								16 58	17 07									18 58			21 09	22 08
Acklington	d																								
Widdrington	d																								
Pegswood	d																								
Morpeth 26	d											17 22												21 26	
Cramlington	d																								
Manors	d																								
Newcastle 8 26 ⛴	a		15 27								17 27	17 37									19 27			21 42	22 42
Sunderland 26,44 ⛴	d	14 28				15 28				16 28					17 28										
Newcastle 8 ⛴	d	14 50		15 10	15 30	15 50		16 10	16 30	16 50			17 10	17 30	17 50	18 10		18 30		18 50			20 15		
Dunston	d																								
Metrocentre	a	14 59		15 17	15 37	15 59		16 19	16 37	16 57			17 17	17 37	17 59	18 17		18 37		18 59			20 22		
	d			15 18				16 20					17 18			18 18							20 23		
Blaydon	d																								
Wylam	d			15 26				16 28					17 26			18 26							20 31		
Prudhoe	d			15 30				16 32					17 30			18 30							20 35		
Stocksfield	d			15 34				16 37					17 34			18 34							20 39		
Riding Mill	d			15 39				16 41					17 39			18 39							20 44		
Corbridge	d			15 42				16 45					17 42			18 42							20 47		
Hexham	a			15 48				16 51					17 48			18 48							20 53		
	d			15 49				16 51					17 49			18 49							20 54		
Haydon Bridge	d			15 58												18 58							21 03		
Bardon Mill	d			16 04												19 04							21 09		
Haltwhistle	d			16 11				17 10					18 08			19 11							21 16		
Brampton (Cumbria)	d			16 27												19 27							21 32		
Wetheral	d			16 35												19 35							21 40		
Carlisle 8	a			16 45				17 44					18 38			19 45							21 51		

For connections from London Kings Cross please refer to Table 26

Table 48

Sundays

19 February to 25 March

Chathill and Morpeth - Newcastle - Metrocentre, Hexham and Carlisle

Network Diagram - see first Page of Table 44

	NT	NT	NT	NT	XC	NT	GR	NT	NT		NT	GR	XC	NT	NT	NT	GR	NT	NT		NT	XC	NT	NT
					◇1		R 1					R 1	◇1				R 1					◇1		
Chathill d																								
Alnmouth for Alnwick 26 d					10 49		10 58						12 10				12 58					14 08		
Acklington d																								
Widdrington d																								
Pegswood d																								
Morpeth 26 d					11 04							12 06												
Cramlington d																								
Manors d																								
Newcastle 8 26 a					11 19		11 27					12 23	12 37				13 27					14 35		
Sunderland 26,44 d																								
Newcastle 8 d	09 10	09 53	10 10	10 30		10 50		11 10	11 30		11 50			12 10	12 30	12 50		13 10	13 30		13 50		14 10	14 30
Dunston d																								
Metrocentre a	09 17	10 01	10 17	10 37		10 59		11 17	11 37		11 57			12 17	12 37	12 59		13 17	13 37		13 59		14 17	14 37
d	09 18		10 18					11 18						12 18				13 18					14 18	
Blaydon d																								
Wylam d	09 26		10 26					11 26						12 26				13 26					14 26	
Prudhoe d	09 30		10 30					11 30						12 30				13 30					14 30	
Stocksfield d	09 34		10 34					11 34						12 34				13 34					14 34	
Riding Mill d	09 39		10 39					11 39						12 39				13 39					14 39	
Corbridge d	09 42		10 42					11 42						12 42				13 42					14 42	
Hexham a	09 48		10 48					11 48						12 48				13 48					14 48	
d	09 49		10 49					11 49						12 49				13 49					14 49	
Haydon Bridge d	09 58		10 58											12 58										
Bardon Mill d	10 04		11 04											13 04										
Haltwhistle d	10 11		11 11					12 08						13 11				14 08					15 08	
Brampton (Cumbria) d	10 27		11 27											13 27										
Wetheral d	10 35		11 35											13 35										
Carlisle 8 a	10 44		11 49					12 38						13 45				14 38					15 40	

	NT	GR	NT	NT	NT		NT	NT	NT	GR	XC	NT	NT	NT	NT		NT	NT	GR	NT	GR	GR		
		R 1								R 1	◇1								R 1		R 1	R 1		
Chathill d																								
Alnmouth for Alnwick 26 d		14 58								16 58	17 07								18 58		21 09	22 08		
Acklington d																								
Widdrington d																								
Pegswood d																								
Morpeth 26 d											17 22										21 26			
Cramlington d																								
Manors d																								
Newcastle 8 26 a		15 27								17 27	17 37								19 27		21 42	22 42		
Sunderland 26,44 d																								
Newcastle 8 d	14 50		15 10	15 30	15 50		16 10	16 30	16 50			17 10	17 30	17 50	18 10		18 30	18 50		20 15				
Dunston d																								
Metrocentre a	14 59		15 17	15 37	15 59		16 19	16 37	16 57			17 17	17 37	17 59	18 17		18 37	18 59		20 22				
d			15 18				16 20					17 18			18 18					20 23				
Blaydon d																								
Wylam d			15 26				16 28					17 26			18 26					20 31				
Prudhoe d			15 30				16 32					17 30			18 30					20 35				
Stocksfield d			15 34				16 37					17 34			18 34					20 39				
Riding Mill d			15 39				16 41					17 39			18 39					20 44				
Corbridge d			15 42				16 45					17 42			18 42					20 47				
Hexham a			15 48				16 51					17 48			18 48					20 53				
d			15 49				16 51					17 49			18 49					20 54				
Haydon Bridge d			15 58												18 58					21 03				
Bardon Mill d			16 04												19 04					21 09				
Haltwhistle d			16 11				17 10					18 08			19 11					21 16				
Brampton (Cumbria) d			16 27												19 27					21 32				
Wetheral d			16 35												19 35					21 40				
Carlisle 8 a			16 45				17 44					18 38			19 45					21 51				

For connections from London Kings Cross please refer to Table 26

Table 48

Sundays
from 1 April

Chathill and Morpeth - Newcastle - Metrocentre, Hexham and Carlisle

Network Diagram - see first Page of Table 44

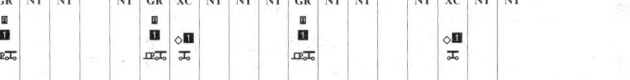

			NT	NT	NT	NT	NT	XC	GR	NT	NT		NT	GR	XC	NT	NT	NT	GR	NT	NT		NT	XC	NT	NT
									R					R					R							
								◇1	1					1	◇1				1					◇1		
								trolley	restaurant					restaurant	trolley				restaurant					trolley		
Chathill		d																								
Alnmouth for Alnwick	26	d						10 49	10 58						12 10				12 58					14 08		
Acklington		d																								
Widdrington		d																								
Pegswood		d																								
Morpeth	26	d						11 04						12 06												
Cramlington		d																								
Manors		d																								
Newcastle 8	26 ⛴	a						11 19	11 27					12 23	12 37				13 27					14 35		
Sunderland	26,44 ⛴	d		09 28			10 28						11 28					12 28					13 28			
Newcastle 8	⛴	d	09 10	09 53	10 10	10 30	10 50			11 10	11 30		11 50			12 10	12 30	12 50		13 10	13 30		13 50		14 10	14 30
Dunston		d																								
Metrocentre		a	09 17	10 01	10 17	10 37	10 59			11 17	11 37		11 57			12 17	12 37	12 59		13 17	13 37		13 59		14 17	14 37
		d	09 18		10 18					11 18						12 18				13 18					14 18	
Blaydon		d																								
Wylam		d	09 26		10 26					11 26						12 26				13 26					14 26	
Prudhoe		d	09 30		10 30					11 30						12 30				13 30					14 30	
Stocksfield		d	09 34		10 34					11 34						12 34				13 34					14 34	
Riding Mill		d	09 39		10 39					11 39						12 39				13 39					14 39	
Corbridge		d	09 42		10 42					11 42						12 42				13 42					14 42	
Hexham		a	09 48		10 48					11 48						12 48				13 48					14 48	
		d	09 49		10 49					11 49						12 49				13 49					14 49	
Haydon Bridge		d	09 58		10 58											12 58										
Bardon Mill		d	10 04		11 04											13 04										
Haltwhistle		d	10 11		11 11					12 08						13 11				14 08					15 08	
Brampton (Cumbria)		d	10 27		11 27											13 27										
Wetheral		d	10 35		11 35											13 35										
Carlisle 8		a	10 44		11 49					12 38						13 45				14 38					15 40	

			NT	GR	NT	NT	NT		NT	NT	NT	GR	XC	NT	NT	NT	NT		NT		NT	GR		NT	GR	GR
				R								R										R			R	R
				1								1	◇1									1			1	1
				restaurant								restaurant	trolley									restaurant			restaurant	restaurant
Chathill		d																								
Alnmouth for Alnwick	26	d		14 58								16 58	17 07									18 58			21 09	22 08
Acklington		d																								
Widdrington		d																								
Pegswood		d																								
Morpeth	26	d											17 22												21 26	
Cramlington		d																								
Manors		d																								
Newcastle 8	26 ⛴	a		15 27								17 27	17 37									19 27			21 42	22 42
Sunderland	26,44 ⛴	d	14 28				15 28				16 28					17 26										
Newcastle 8	⛴	d	14 50		15 10	15 30	15 50		16 10	16 30	16 50			17 10	17 30	17 50	18 10		18 30		18 50			20 15		
Dunston		d																								
Metrocentre		a	14 59		15 17	15 37	15 59		16 19	16 37	16 57			17 17	17 37	17 59	18 17		18 37		18 59			20 22		
		d			15 18				16 20					17 18			18 18							20 23		
Blaydon		d																								
Wylam		d			15 26				16 28					17 26			18 26							20 31		
Prudhoe		d			15 30				16 32					17 30			18 30							20 35		
Stocksfield		d			15 34				16 37					17 34			18 34							20 39		
Riding Mill		d			15 39				16 41					17 39			18 39							20 44		
Corbridge		d			15 42				16 45					17 42			18 42							20 47		
Hexham		a			15 48				16 51					17 48			18 48							20 53		
		d			15 49				16 51					17 49			18 49							20 54		
Haydon Bridge		d			15 58												18 58							21 03		
Bardon Mill		d			16 04												19 04							21 09		
Haltwhistle		d			16 11				17 10					18 08			19 11							21 16		
Brampton (Cumbria)		d			16 27												19 27							21 32		
Wetheral		d			16 35												19 35							21 40		
Carlisle 8		a			16 45				17 44					18 38			19 45							21 51		

For connections from London Kings Cross please refer to Table 26

Carlisle, Hexham and Metrocentre - Newcastle - Morpeth and Chathill

Network Diagram - see first Page of Table 44

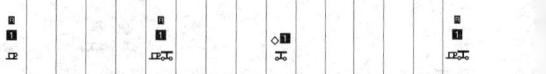

Miles	Miles			NT MX	NT	NT	NT	GR	XC	GR	NT	NT		NT	GR	NT	NT	NT	XC	NT	NT	NT		NT	GR
								R 1	◇1	R 1					R 1				◇1						R 1
0	—	**Carlisle** 8	d				06 25					07 17					08 28							09 37	
4¼	—	Wetheral	d				06 33					07 25					08 36								
11	—	Brampton (Cumbria)	d				06 43					07 35					08 46								
23¼	—	Haltwhistle	d				06 57					07 49					09 00							10 08	
28	—	Bardon Mill	d				07 05					07 57					09 08								
31¾	—	Haydon Bridge	d				07 10					08 02					09 13								
39½	—	**Hexham**	a				07 19					08 11					09 22							10 26	
—	—		d	23p20		06 16	07 19				07 42	08 11				08 45	09 22				09 45			10 26	
42½	—	Corbridge	d	23p24		06 20	07 24				07 46	08 16				08 49					09 49				
45	—	Riding Mill	d	23p29		06 25	07 27				07 51	08 20				08 54					09 54				
47¼	—	Stocksfield	d	23p33		06 29	07 31				07 55	08 24				08 58					09 58				
49¾	—	Prudhoe	d	23p37		06 33	07 37				07 59	08 29				09 02	09 34				10 02			10 38	
52	—	Wylam	d	23p41		06 37	07 41				08 03	08 33				09 06					10 06				
56¼	—	Blaydon	d								08 09	08 39													
58¼	—	**Metrocentre**	a	23p50			07 49				08 14	08 44				09 15	09 45				10 16			10 49	
—	—		d	23p50			07 50				08 16	08 44				09 16	09 46			10 01	10 16	10 31		10 50	
59½	1¼	Dunston	d									08 47													
61¾	3½	**Newcastle** 8 ⛴	a	00 05		06 55	08 04				08 27	08 57				09 26	10 00			10 10	10 27	10 39		11 07	
—	—	Sunderland 26,44 ⛴	a			07 18					08 50					09 49					10 49				
—	—	**Newcastle** 8 26 ⛴	d		05 55			06 25	07 35	07 41				07 58	08 41			09 15	09 35	10 15					10 41
—	4	Manors	d															09 17		10 17					
—	13¼	Cramlington	d		06 07									08 07				09 28		10 28					
—	20	**Morpeth** 26	d		06 15			06 40	07a47					08a18	08a56			09a36		10a36					
—	22	Pegswood	d																						
—	26¾	Widdrington	d																						
—	32	Acklington	d																						
—	38¼	Alnmouth for Alnwick 26	d		06 32			06a54		08a07									09a58						11a07
—	49½	**Chathill**	a		06 46																				

		NT	NT	NT	NT	NT	NT	NT		NT	GR	NT	NT	NT	NT	XC	NT	NT		NT	NT	XC	GR	NT	NT
											R 1					◇1						◇1	R 1		
Carlisle 8	d				10 28					11 34					12 28						13 28				
Wetheral	d				10 36										12 36						13 36				
Brampton (Cumbria)	d				10 46										12 46						13 46				
Haltwhistle	d				11 00					12 03					13 00						14 00				
Bardon Mill	d				11 08										13 08						14 09				
Haydon Bridge	d				11 13										13 13						14 15				
Hexham	a				11 22					12 21					13 22						14 24				
	d		10 44		11 22		11 43			12 22			12 45		13 22			13 45			14 24				14 43
Corbridge	d		10 48				11 47						12 49					13 49							14 47
Riding Mill	d		10 53				11 52						12 54					13 54							14 52
Stocksfield	d		10 57				11 56						12 58					13 58							14 56
Prudhoe	d		11 01		11 33		12 00			12 33			13 02		13 34			14 02			14 33				15 00
Wylam	d		11 05				12 04						13 06					14 06							15 04
Blaydon	d																								
Metrocentre	a		11 15		11 45		12 15			12 44			13 15		13 45			14 13			14 45				15 15
	d	11 00	11 16	11 31	11 46	12 01	12 16	12 31		12 45		13 00	13 16	13 31	13 46		14 01	14 14		14 30	14 46			15 01	15 16
Dunston	d																								
Newcastle 8 ⛴	a	11 11	11 26	11 39	11 59	12 10	12 27	12 39		12 57		13 10	13 26	13 39	14 00		14 10	14 27		14 39	15 03			15 10	15 27
Sunderland 26,44 ⛴	a		11 49				12 49						13 49					14 49							15 49
Newcastle 8 26 ⛴	d	11 15				12 15					12 44	13 15				13 38	14 15					14 36	14 43	15 15	
Manors	d	11 17				12 17						13 17					14 17							15 17	
Cramlington	d	11 28				12 28						13 28					14 28							15 28	
Morpeth 26	d	11a36				12a36						13a36					14a36					14a49		15a36	
Pegswood	d																								
Widdrington	d																								
Acklington	d																								
Alnmouth for Alnwick 26	d										13a10					14a01							15a09		
Chathill	a																								

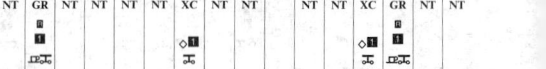

For connections to London Kings Cross please refer to Table 26

Carlisle, Hexham and Metrocentre - Newcastle - Morpeth and Chathill

Network Diagram - see first Page of Table 44

		NT	NT	XC		NT	NT	NT	NT	XC	NT	NT	XC	NT		NT	NT	NT	NT	GR	NT	NT	XC	GR
																				R				R
				◇1						◇1			◇1							1			◇1	1
Carlisle 8	d		14 33						15 26							16 28			17 28			18 37		
Wetheral	d															16 36			17 36			18 45		
Brampton (Cumbria)	d															16 46			17 46			18 54		
Haltwhistle	d		15 03						15 55							17 00			18 01			19 09		
Bardon Mill	d															17 08			18 08			19 16		
Haydon Bridge	d															17 13			18 13			19 21		
Hexham	a		15 21						16 13							17 22			18 27			19 30		
	d		15 21				15 42		16 14			16 43				17 22		17 45	18 28		18 45	19 31		
Corbridge	d						15 46					16 47						17 49	18 32		18 49	19 35		
Riding Mill	d						15 51					16 52						17 54	18 37		18 54	19 40		
Stocksfield	d						15 55					16 56						17 58	18 41		18 58	19 44		
Prudhoe	d		15 32				16 00		16 25			17 00				17 34		18 02	18 45		19 02	19 48		
Wylam	d						16 04					17 04						18 06	18 49		19 06	19 52		
Blaydon	d																				19 12			
Metrocentre	a		15 44				16 15		16 38			17 15				17 45		18 15	19 00		19 17	20 00		
	d	15 31	15 45			16 01	16 16	16 31	16 38		17 01	17 16		17 29		17 46	18 06	18 16	19 00		19 18	20 01		
Dunston	d																18 08							
Newcastle 8 ⛴	a	15 39	15 54			16 11	16 26	16 39	16 48		17 09	17 27		17 37		17 59	18 14	18 28	19 12		19 28	20 15		
Sunderland 26,44 ⛴	a						16 49		17 14			17 50						18 49			19 50			
Newcastle 8 26 ⛴	d			15 37		16 15				16 37	17 15		17 37	17 38			18 25			18 43			19 38	19 44
Manors	d					16 17					17 17			17 41			18 27							
Cramlington	d					16 28					17 28			17 52			18 38							
Morpeth 26	d					16a36					17 36			18a00			18a47							19a58
Pegswood	d										17 40													
Widdrington	d										17 46													
Acklington	d										18 02													
Alnmouth for Alnwick 26	d			16a00						17a00	18 21		18a01							19a09			20a04	
Chathill	a										18 35													

		XC	NT	NT	XC	NT	NT	XC	GR	NT		NT	NT	GR FO	NT
									R					R	
		◇1			◇1			◇1	1					1	
Carlisle 8	d			19 41									21 28		
Wetheral	d												21 36		
Brampton (Cumbria)	d												21 46		
Haltwhistle	d			20 10									22 01		
Bardon Mill	d												22 08		
Haydon Bridge	d												22 13		
Hexham	a			20 28									22 22		
	d			20 28			21 12						22 23		23 20
Corbridge	d			20 33			21 16						22 27		23 24
Riding Mill	d			20 37			21 21						22 32		23 29
Stocksfield	d			20 41			21 25						22 36		23 33
Prudhoe	d			20 46			21 29						22 40		23 37
Wylam	d			20 49			21 33						22 44		23 41
Blaydon	d														
Metrocentre	a			20 58			21 44						22 53		23 50
	d		20 31	20 59		21 22	21 45					22 15	22 53		23 50
Dunston	d														
Newcastle 8 ⛴	a		20 39	21 10		21 30	21 55					22 25	23 07		00 05
Sunderland 26,44 ⛴	a														
Newcastle 8 26 ⛴	d	20 11			20 39			21 36	21 40	22 00				22 42	
Manors	d														
Cramlington	d									22 12					
Morpeth 26	d				20a54				21 56	22a21				22 56	
Pegswood	d														
Widdrington	d														
Acklington	d														
Alnmouth for Alnwick 26	d	20a34						21a59	22a10					23a11	
Chathill	a														

For connections to London Kings Cross please refer to Table 26

Table 48

Saturdays

Carlisle, Hexham and Metrocentre - Newcastle - Morpeth and Chathill

Network Diagram - see first Page of Table 44

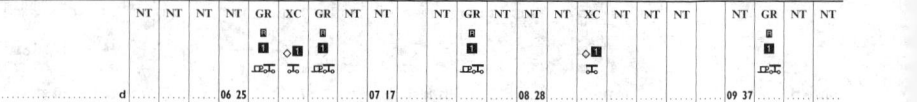

		NT	NT	NT	NT	GR	XC	GR	NT	NT	NT	GR	NT	NT	NT	XC	NT	NT	NT	NT	GR	NT	NT
						R 1	◇1	R 1				R 1				◇1					R 1		
Carlisle 8	d				06 25					07 17				08 28						09 37			
Wetheral	d				06 33					07 25				08 36									
Brampton (Cumbria)	d				06 43					07 35				08 46									
Haltwhistle	d				06 57					07 49				09 00						10 08			
Bardon Mill	d				07 05					07 57				09 08									
Haydon Bridge	d				07 10					08 02				09 13									
Hexham	a				07 19					08 11				09 22						10 26			
	d	23p20		06 16	07 19				07 42	08 11			08 43	09 22				09 46		10 26			10 44
Corbridge	d	23p24		06 20	07 24				07 46	08 16			08 47					09 50					10 48
Riding Mill	d	23p29		06 25	07 28				07 51	08 20			08 52					09 55					10 53
Stocksfield	d	23p33		06 29	07 32				07 55	08 24			08 56					09 59					10 57
Prudhoe	d	23p37		06 33	07 37				07 59	08 29			09 00	09 34				10 03		10 38			11 01
Wylam	d	23p41		06 37	07 41				08 03	08 33			09 04					10 07					11 05
Blaydon	d								08 09	08 39													
Metrocentre	a	23p50			07 50				08 14	08 44			09 15	09 45				10 16		10 49			11 15
	d	23p50			07 51				08 16	08 44			09 16	09 46			10 01	10 17	10 31	10 50		10 59	11 16
Dunston	d									08 47													
Newcastle 8	a	00 05		06 56	08 08				08 27	08 57			09 26	10 03			10 10	10 27	10 39	11 07		11 10	11 26
Sunderland 26,44	a			07 20					08 50				09 49					10 49					11 49
Newcastle 8 26	d		05 55			06 30	07 38	07 42			07 58	08 41			09 15	09 35	10 15				10 39	11 15	
Manors	d														09 17		10 17					11 17	
Cramlington	d		06 07								08 09				09 28		10 28					11 28	
Morpeth 26	d		06 17			06 43	07a50				08a19	08a55			09a36		10a35					11a36	
Pegswood	d																						
Widdrington	d																						
Acklington	d																						
Alnmouth for Alnwick 26	d		06 35			06a57		08a08								09a58					11a05		
Chathill	a		06 50																				

		NT	NT	NT	NT	NT	NT	GR	NT	NT	NT	NT	XC	NT	NT	NT	NT	XC	GR	NT	NT	NT	NT
								R 1					◇1					◇1	R 1				
Carlisle 8	d		10 28				11 34					12 28					13 29						14 33
Wetheral	d		10 36									12 36					13 38						
Brampton (Cumbria)	d		10 46									12 46					13 48						
Haltwhistle	d		11 00				12 03					13 00					14 02						15 03
Bardon Mill	d		11 08									13 08					14 10						
Haydon Bridge	d		11 13									13 13					14 15						
Hexham	a		11 22				12 21					13 22					14 23						15 21
	d		11 22		11 45		12 22			12 45		13 22			13 43		14 24				14 43		15 21
Corbridge	d				11 49					12 49					13 47						14 47		
Riding Mill	d				11 54					12 54					13 52						14 52		
Stocksfield	d				11 58					12 58					13 56						14 56		
Prudhoe	d		11 33		12 02		12 33			13 02		13 34			14 00		14 36				15 00		15 32
Wylam	d				12 06					13 06					14 04						15 04		
Blaydon	d																						
Metrocentre	a		11 45		12 15		12 45			13 15		13 45			14 15		14 46				15 15		15 44
	d	11 31	11 46	12 01	12 16	12 31	12 45		13 01	13 16	13 30	13 46		14 01	14 16	14 31	14 48			15 00	15 16	15 31	15 45
Dunston	d																						
Newcastle 8	a	11 39	11 59	12 10	12 27	12 39	12 57		13 10	13 26	13 39	13 59		14 10	14 27	14 39	15 00			15 11	15 27	15 39	15 54
Sunderland 26,44	a				12 49					13 49					14 49						15 49		
Newcastle 8 26	d			12 15				12 40	13 15				13 35	14 15				14 35	14 40	15 15			
Manors	d			12 17					13 17					14 17						15 17			
Cramlington	d			12 28					13 28					14 28						15 28			
Morpeth 26	d			12a35					13a37					14a37				14a47		15a35			
Pegswood	d																						
Widdrington	d																						
Acklington	d																						
Alnmouth for Alnwick 26	d							13a06					13a59						15a06				
Chathill	a																						

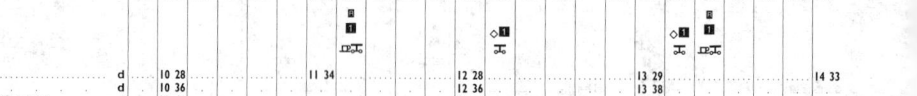

For connections to London Kings Cross please refer to Table 26

Table 48

Saturdays

Carlisle, Hexham and Metrocentre - Newcastle - Morpeth and Chathill

Network Diagram - see first Page of Table 44

		XC		NT	NT	NT	NT	XC	NT	NT	NT	NT		XC	NT	NT	NT	GR	NT	NT	XC	GR		NT	NT
		◇1 🛒						◇1 🛒						◇1 🛒				R 1 🍽			◇1 🛒	R 1 🍽🛒			
Carlisle 8	d						15 26					16 28					17 28			18 37					
Wetheral	d											16 36					17 36			18 45					
Brampton (Cumbria)	d											16 46					17 46			18 54					
Haltwhistle	d						15 55					17 00					18 01			19 09					
Bardon Mill	d											17 08					18 08			19 16					
Haydon Bridge	d											17 13					18 13			19 21					
Hexham	a						16 13					17 22					18 22			19 30					
	d				15 45		16 14				16 45	17 22				17 43	18 23		18 45	19 31					
Corbridge	d				15 49						16 49					17 47	18 27		18 49	19 35					
Riding Mill	d				15 54						16 54					17 52	18 32		18 54	19 40					
Stocksfield	d				15 58						16 58					17 56	18 36		18 58	19 44					
Prudhoe	d				16 02		16 25				17 02	17 34				18 00	18 40		19 02	19 48					
Wylam	d				16 06						17 06					18 04	18 44		19 06	19 52					
Blaydon	d																		19 12						
Metrocentre	a				16 15		16 38				17 15	17 44				18 15	18 54		19 17	20 00					
	d			16 01	16 16	16 30	16 38		16 50	17 07	17 16	17 45			18 06	18 16	18 54		19 18	20 01				20 15	
Dunston	d														18 08										
Newcastle 8 ⛴	a			16 10	16 26	16 38	16 48		16 58	17 15	17 27	17 59			18 14	18 26	19 07		19 28	20 15				20 23	
Sunderland 26,44 ⛴	a				16 49		17 14				17 50					18 49			19 50						
Newcastle 8 26 ⛴	d	15 34		16 15				16 35	17 00	17 22				17 37	18 19			18 41			19 37	19 45			20 20
Manors	d			16 17					17 03	17 24					18 21										
Cramlington	d			16 28					17 14	17 35					18 32										20 32
Morpeth 26	d			16a36					17 22	17a42					18a40							19a59			20a41
Pegswood	d								17 25																
Widdrington	d								17 31																
Acklington	d								17 38																
Alnmouth for Alnwick 26	d	15a58						16a58	17 46					18a00				19a07			20a03				
Chathill	a								17 59																

		XC	NT	NT	GR	NT	XC	NT		NT
		◇1 🛒			R 1 🍽🛒		◇1 🛒			
Carlisle 8	d			19 41						21 20
Wetheral	d									21 27
Brampton (Cumbria)	d									21 37
Haltwhistle	d			20 10						21 52
Bardon Mill	d									21 59
Haydon Bridge	d									22 04
Hexham	a			20 28						22 13
	d			20 28		21 14				22 14
Corbridge	d			20 33		21 18				22 18
Riding Mill	d			20 37		21 23				22 23
Stocksfield	d			20 41		21 27				22 27
Prudhoe	d			20 46		21 31				22 31
Wylam	d			20 49		21 35				22 35
Blaydon	d									
Metrocentre	a			20 58		21 44				22 44
	d		20 47	20 59		21 45		22 30		22 45
Dunston	d									
Newcastle 8 ⛴	a		20 55	21 11		21 57		22 39		23 00
Sunderland 26,44 ⛴	a		21 20							
Newcastle 8 26 ⛴	d	20 38			20 54		21 38			
Manors	d									
Cramlington	d									
Morpeth 26	d	20a50			21 09					
Pegswood	d									
Widdrington	d									
Acklington	d									
Alnmouth for Alnwick 26	d				21a24		22a01			
Chathill	a									

For connections to London Kings Cross please refer to Table 26

Table 48

Sundays

until 12 February

Carlisle, Hexham and Metrocentre - Newcastle - Morpeth and Chathill

Network Diagram - see first Page of Table 44

		XC	NT	NT	GR	NT	NT	NT	NT	NT	NT	GR	NT	NT	NT	XC	NT	NT	NT	XC	GR	NT	NT
		◇1			R 1							R 1				◇1				◇1	R 1		
Carlisle 8	d			09 05				10 05			11 12				12 05				13 12				
Wetheral	d			09 12				10 12							12 12								
Brampton (Cumbria)	d			09 22				10 22							12 22								
Haltwhistle	d			09 36				10 36			11 40				12 36				13 40				
Bardon Mill	d			09 44				10 44							12 44								
Haydon Bridge	d			09 49				10 49							12 49								
Hexham	a			09 58				10 58			11 58				12 58				13 58				
	d			09 59				10 59			11 59				12 59				13 59				
Corbridge	d			10 03				11 03			12 03				13 03				14 03				
Riding Mill	d			10 08				11 08			12 08				13 08				14 08				
Stocksfield	d			10 12				11 12			12 12				13 12				14 12				
Prudhoe	d			10 16				11 16			12 16				13 16				14 16				
Wylam	d			10 20				11 20			12 20				13 20				14 20				
Blaydon	d																						
Metrocentre	a			10 29				11 29			12 29				13 29				14 29				
	d		10 10	10 30		10 48	11 10	11 30	11 48	12 10	12 30		12 48	13 15	13 30		13 48	14 10	14 30			14 48	15 10
Dunston	d																						
Newcastle 8	a		10 18	10 40		10 56	11 18	11 40	11 56	12 18	12 40		12 56	13 23	13 40		13 56	14 18	14 40			14 56	15 18
Sunderland 26,44	a					11 22			12 21				13 22				14 21					15 22	
Newcastle 8 26	d	09 45			10 13							12 44				13 36				14 36	14 42		
Manors	d																						
Cramlington	d																						
Morpeth 26	d	09 58			10 29															14a48			
Pegswood	d																						
Widdrington	d																						
Acklington	d																						
Alnmouth for Alnwick 26	d	10a11			10a43							13a10				13a59					15a08		
Chathill	a																						

		NT	XC	NT	NT	NT	XC	GR	NT	NT	NT	XC	NT	NT	NT	GR	NT	NT	NT	XC	GR	NT	XC
			◇1				◇1	R 1				◇1				R 1				◇1	R 1		◇1
Carlisle 8	d	14 12				15 05					16 12				17 12				18 05			20 15	
Wetheral	d					15 12													18 12				
Brampton (Cumbria)	d					15 22													18 22				
Haltwhistle	d	14 40				15 36					16 40				17 40				18 36			20 43	
Bardon Mill	d					15 44													18 44				
Haydon Bridge	d					15 49													18 49				
Hexham	a	14 58				15 58					16 58				17 58				18 58			21 01	
	d	14 59				15 59					16 59				17 59				18 59			21 01	
Corbridge	d	15 03				16 03					17 03				18 03				19 03			21 05	
Riding Mill	d	15 08				16 08					17 08				18 08				19 08			21 10	
Stocksfield	d	15 12				16 12					17 12				18 12				19 12			21 14	
Prudhoe	d	15 16				16 16					17 16				18 16				19 16			21 18	
Wylam	d	15 20				16 20					17 20				18 20				19 20			21 22	
Blaydon	d																						
Metrocentre	a	15 29				16 29					17 29				18 29				19 29			21 31	
	d	15 30		15 48	16 10	16 30			16 48	17 10	17 30		17 48	18 10	18 30		18 48	19 10	19 30			21 31	
Dunston	d																						
Newcastle 8	a	15 40		15 58	16 18	16 40			16 56	17 18	17 40		17 58	18 18	18 40		18 56	19 18	19 40			21 43	
Sunderland 26,44	a			16 21					17 21				18 21				19 22						
Newcastle 8 26	d		15 37				16 34	16 42				17 38				18 42				19 40	19 44		20 38
Manors	d																						
Cramlington	d																						
Morpeth 26	d																				19a58		20a52
Pegswood	d																						
Widdrington	d																						
Acklington	d																						
Alnmouth for Alnwick 26	d		16a01				16a58	17a08				18a01				19a08				20a04			
Chathill	a																						

For connections to London Kings Cross please refer to Table 26

Table 48

Sundays
until 12 February

Carlisle, Hexham and Metrocentre - Newcastle - Morpeth and Chathill

Network Diagram - see first Page of Table 44

		GR R 1		XC ◇1	GR R 1
Carlisle 8	d				
Wetheral	d				
Brampton (Cumbria)	d				
Haltwhistle	d				
Bardon Mill	d				
Haydon Bridge	d				
Hexham	a				
	d				
Corbridge	d				
Riding Mill	d				
Stocksfield	d				
Prudhoe	d				
Wylam	d				
Blaydon	d				
Metrocentre	a				
	d				
Dunston	d				
Newcastle 8	a				
Sunderland 26,44	a				
Newcastle 8 26	d	20 43		21 38	21 51
Manors	d				
Cramlington	d				
Morpeth 26	d	20 59			22 07
Pegswood	d				
Widdrington	d				
Acklington	d				
Alnmouth for Alnwick 26	d	21a13		22a04	22a22
Chathill	a				

Sundays
19 February to 25 March

		XC ◇1	NT	NT	GR R 1	NT	NT	NT	NT	NT		NT	GR R 1	NT	NT	NT	XC ◇1	NT	NT	NT		XC ◇1	GR R 1	NT	NT
Carlisle 8	d			09 05				10 05				11 12				12 05				13 12					
Wetheral	d			09 12				10 12								12 12									
Brampton (Cumbria)	d			09 22				10 22								12 22									
Haltwhistle	d			09 36				10 36				11 40				12 36				13 40					
Bardon Mill	d			09 44				10 44								12 44									
Haydon Bridge	d			09 49				10 49								12 49									
Hexham	a			09 58				10 58				11 58				12 58				13 58					
	d			09 59				10 59				11 59				12 59				13 59					
Corbridge	d			10 03				11 03				12 03				13 03				14 03					
Riding Mill	d			10 08				11 08				12 08				13 08				14 08					
Stocksfield	d			10 12				11 12				12 12				13 12				14 12					
Prudhoe	d			10 16				11 16				12 16				13 16				14 16					
Wylam	d			10 20				11 20				12 20				13 20				14 20					
Blaydon	d																								
Metrocentre	a			10 29				11 29				12 29				13 29				14 29					
	d		10 10	10 30		10 48	11 10	11 30	11 48	12 10		12 30		12 48	13 15	13 30		13 48	14 10	14 30				14 48	15 10
Dunston	d																								
Newcastle 8	a		10 18	10 40		10 56	11 18	11 40	11 56	12 18		12 40		12 56	13 23	13 40		13 56	14 18	14 40				14 56	15 18
Sunderland 26,44	a																								
Newcastle 8 26	d	09 45			10 13								12 44				13 36					14 36	14 42		
Manors	d																								
Cramlington	d																								
Morpeth 26	d	09 58			10 29																	14a48			
Pegswood	d																								
Widdrington	d																								
Acklington	d																								
Alnmouth for Alnwick 26	d	10a11			10a43								13a10				13a59						15a08		
Chathill	a																								

For connections to London Kings Cross please refer to Table 26

Table 48

Sundays

19 February to 25 March

Carlisle, Hexham and Metrocentre - Newcastle - Morpeth and Chathill

Network Diagram - see first Page of Table 44

		NT	XC	NT	NT	NT		XC	GR	NT	NT	NT	XC	NT	NT	NT		GR	NT	NT	NT	XC	GR	NT	XC
									R									R					R		
			◇1					◇1	1				◇1					1				◇1	1		◇1
Carlisle 8	d	14 12				15 05						16 12				17 12					18 05			20 15	
Wetheral	d					15 12															18 12				
Brampton (Cumbria)	d					15 22															18 22				
Haltwhistle	d	14 40				15 36						16 40				17 40					18 36			20 43	
Bardon Mill	d					15 44															18 44				
Haydon Bridge	d					15 49															18 49				
Hexham	a	14 58				15 58						16 58				17 58					18 58			21 01	
	d	14 59				15 59						16 59				17 59					18 59			21 01	
Corbridge	d	15 03				16 03						17 03				18 03					19 03			21 05	
Riding Mill	d	15 08				16 08						17 08				18 08					19 08			21 10	
Stocksfield	d	15 12				16 12						17 12				18 12					19 12			21 14	
Prudhoe	d	15 16				16 16						17 16				18 16					19 16			21 18	
Wylam	d	15 20				16 20						17 20				18 20					19 20			21 22	
Blaydon	d																								
Metrocentre	a	15 29				16 29						17 29				18 29					19 29			21 31	
	d	15 30		15 48	16 10	16 30				16 48	17 10	17 30		17 48	18 10	18 30			18 48	19 10	19 30			21 31	
Dunston	d																								
Newcastle 8	a	15 40		15 58	16 18	16 40				16 56	17 18	17 40		17 58	18 18	18 40			18 56	19 18	19 40			21 43	
Sunderland 26,44	a																								
Newcastle 8 26	d		15 37					16 34	16 42				17 38					18 42				19 40	19 44		20 38
Manors	d																								
Cramlington	d																								
Morpeth 26	d																						19a58		20a52
Pegswood	d																								
Widdrington	d																								
Acklington	d																								
Alnmouth for Alnwick 26	d		16a01					16a58	17a08				18a01					19a08				20a04			
Chathill	a																								

		GR		XC	GR
		R			R
		1		◇1	1
Carlisle 8	d				
Wetheral	d				
Brampton (Cumbria)	d				
Haltwhistle	d				
Bardon Mill	d				
Haydon Bridge	d				
Hexham	a				
	d				
Corbridge	d				
Riding Mill	d				
Stocksfield	d				
Prudhoe	d				
Wylam	d				
Blaydon	d				
Metrocentre	a				
	d				
Dunston	d				
Newcastle 8	a				
Sunderland 26,44	a				
Newcastle 8 26	d	20 43		21 38	21 51
Manors	d				
Cramlington	d				
Morpeth 26	d	20 59			22 07
Pegswood	d				
Widdrington	d				
Acklington	d				
Alnmouth for Alnwick 26	d	21a13		22a04	22a22
Chathill	a				

For connections to London Kings Cross please refer to Table 26

Table 48

Sundays
from 1 April

Carlisle, Hexham and Metrocentre - Newcastle - Morpeth and Chathill

Network Diagram - see first Page of Table 44

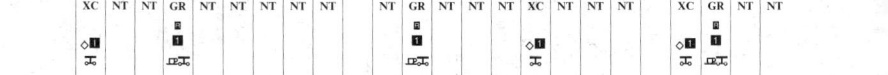

		XC	NT	NT	GR	NT	NT	NT	NT	NT		NT	GR	NT	NT	NT	XC	NT	NT	NT		XC	GR	NT	NT
		◇1			R 1								R 1				◇1					◇1	R 1		
Carlisle 8	d			09 05				10 05				11 12				12 05				13 12					
Wetheral	d			09 12				10 12								12 12									
Brampton (Cumbria)	d			09 22				10 22								12 22									
Haltwhistle	d			09 36				10 36				11 40				12 36				13 40					
Bardon Mill	d			09 44				10 44								12 44									
Haydon Bridge	d			09 49				10 49								12 49									
Hexham	a			09 58				10 58				11 58				12 58				13 58					
	d			09 59				10 59				11 59				12 59				13 59					
Corbridge	d			10 03				11 03				12 03				13 03				14 03					
Riding Mill	d			10 08				11 08				12 08				13 08				14 08					
Stocksfield	d			10 12				11 12				12 12				13 12				14 12					
Prudhoe	d			10 16				11 16				12 16				13 16				14 16					
Wylam	d			10 20				11 20				12 20				13 20				14 20					
Blaydon	d																								
Metrocentre	a			10 29				11 29				12 29				13 29				14 29					
	d		10 10	10 30		10 48	11 10	11 30	11 48	12 10		12 30		12 48	13 15	13 30		13 48	14 10	14 30				14 48	15 10
Dunston	d																								
Newcastle 8 ⛴	a		10 18	10 40		10 56	11 18	11 40	11 56	12 18		12 40		12 56	13 23	13 40		13 56	14 18	14 40				14 56	15 18
Sunderland 26,44 ⛴	a					11 22			12 21					13 22				14 21						15 22	
Newcastle 8 26 ⛴	d	09 45			10 13								12 44				13 36					14 36	14 42		
Manors	d																								
Cramlington	d																								
Morpeth 26	d	09 58			10 29																	14a48			
Pegswood	d																								
Widdrington	d																								
Acklington	d																								
Alnmouth for Alnwick 26	d	10a11			10a43								13a10				13a59						15a08		
Chathill	a																								

		NT	XC	NT	NT	NT		XC	GR	NT	NT	NT	XC	NT	NT	NT		GR	NT	NT	NT	XC	GR	NT	XC
			◇1					◇1	R 1				◇1					R 1				◇1	R 1		◇1
Carlisle 8	d	14 12				15 05						16 12				17 12					18 05			20 15	
Wetheral	d					15 12															18 12				
Brampton (Cumbria)	d					15 22															18 22				
Haltwhistle	d	14 40				15 36						16 40				17 40					18 36			20 43	
Bardon Mill	d					15 44															18 44				
Haydon Bridge	d					15 49															18 49				
Hexham	a	14 58				15 58						16 58				17 58					18 58			21 01	
	d	14 59				15 59						16 59				17 59					18 59			21 01	
Corbridge	d	15 03				16 03						17 03				18 03					19 03			21 05	
Riding Mill	d	15 08				16 08						17 08				18 08					19 08			21 10	
Stocksfield	d	15 12				16 12						17 12				18 12					19 12			21 14	
Prudhoe	d	15 16				16 16						17 16				18 16					19 16			21 18	
Wylam	d	15 20				16 20						17 20				18 20					19 20			21 22	
Blaydon	d																								
Metrocentre	a	15 29				16 29						17 29				18 29					19 29			21 31	
	d	15 30		15 48	16 10	16 30				16 48	17 10	17 30		17 48	18 10	18 30			18 48	19 10	19 30			21 31	
Dunston	d																								
Newcastle 8 ⛴	a	15 40		15 58	16 18	16 40				16 56	17 18	17 40		17 58	18 18	18 40			18 56	19 18	19 40			21 43	
Sunderland 26,44 ⛴	a			16 21						17 22				18 21					19 22						
Newcastle 8 26 ⛴	d		15 37					16 34	16 42				17 38					18 42				19 40	19 44		20 38
Manors	d																								
Cramlington	d																								
Morpeth 26	d																						19a58		20a52
Pegswood	d																								
Widdrington	d																								
Acklington	d																								
Alnmouth for Alnwick 26	d		16a01					16a58	17a08				18a01					19a08				20a04			
Chathill	a																								

For connections to London Kings Cross please refer to Table 26

Table 48

Sundays
from 1 April

Carlisle, Hexham and Metrocentre - Newcastle - Morpeth and Chathill

Network Diagram - see first Page of Table 44

			GR	XC	GR
			R		R
			1	◇1	1
			☕		☕
Carlisle 8		d			
Wetheral		d			
Brampton (Cumbria)		d			
Haltwhistle		d			
Bardon Mill		d			
Haydon Bridge		d			
Hexham		a			
		d			
Corbridge		d			
Riding Mill		d			
Stocksfield		d			
Prudhoe		d			
Wylam		d			
Blaydon		d			
Metrocentre		a			
		d			
Dunston		d			
Newcastle 8	⛴	a			
Sunderland	26,44 ⛴	a			
Newcastle 8	26 ⛴	d	20 43	21 38	21 51
Manors		d			
Cramlington		d			
Morpeth	26	d	20 59		22 07
Pegswood		d			
Widdrington		d			
Acklington		d			
Alnmouth for Alnwick	26	d	21a13	22a04	22a22
Chathill		a			

For connections to London Kings Cross please refer to Table 26

Route Diagram for Table 49

DM-4/09(2)
Design BAJS

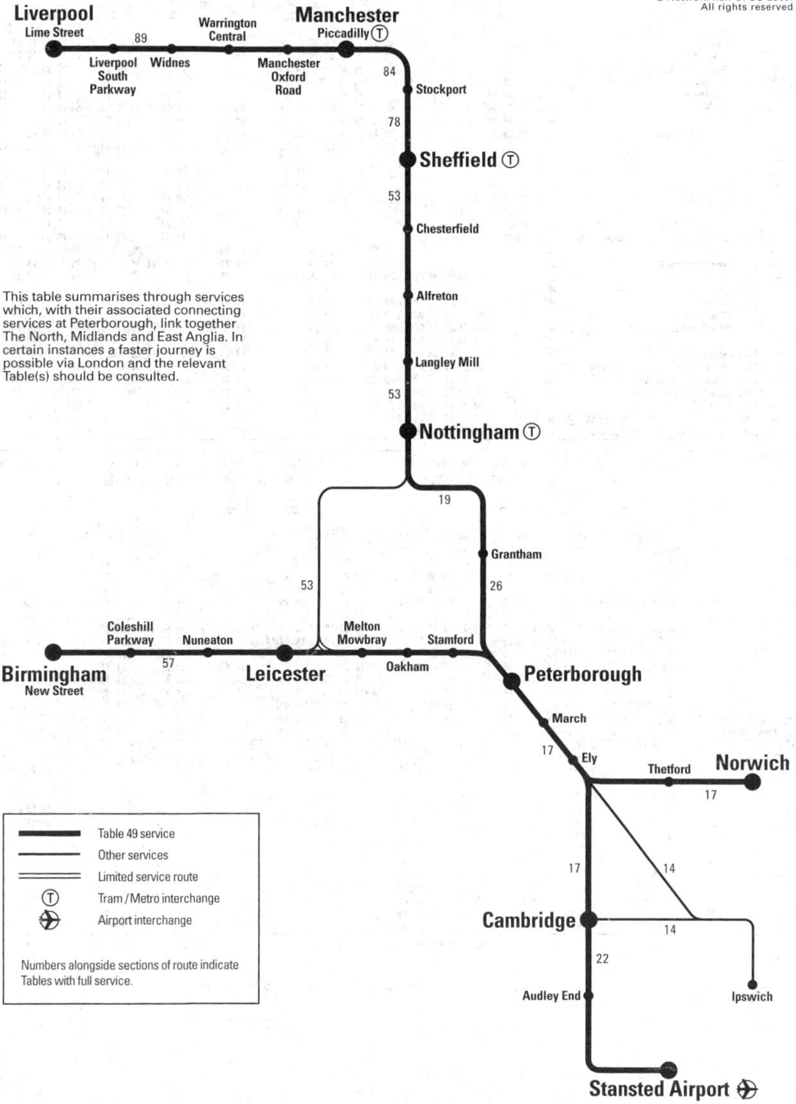

This table summarises through services which, with their associated connecting services at Peterborough, link together The North, Midlands and East Anglia. In certain instances a faster journey is possible via London and the relevant Table(s) should be consulted.

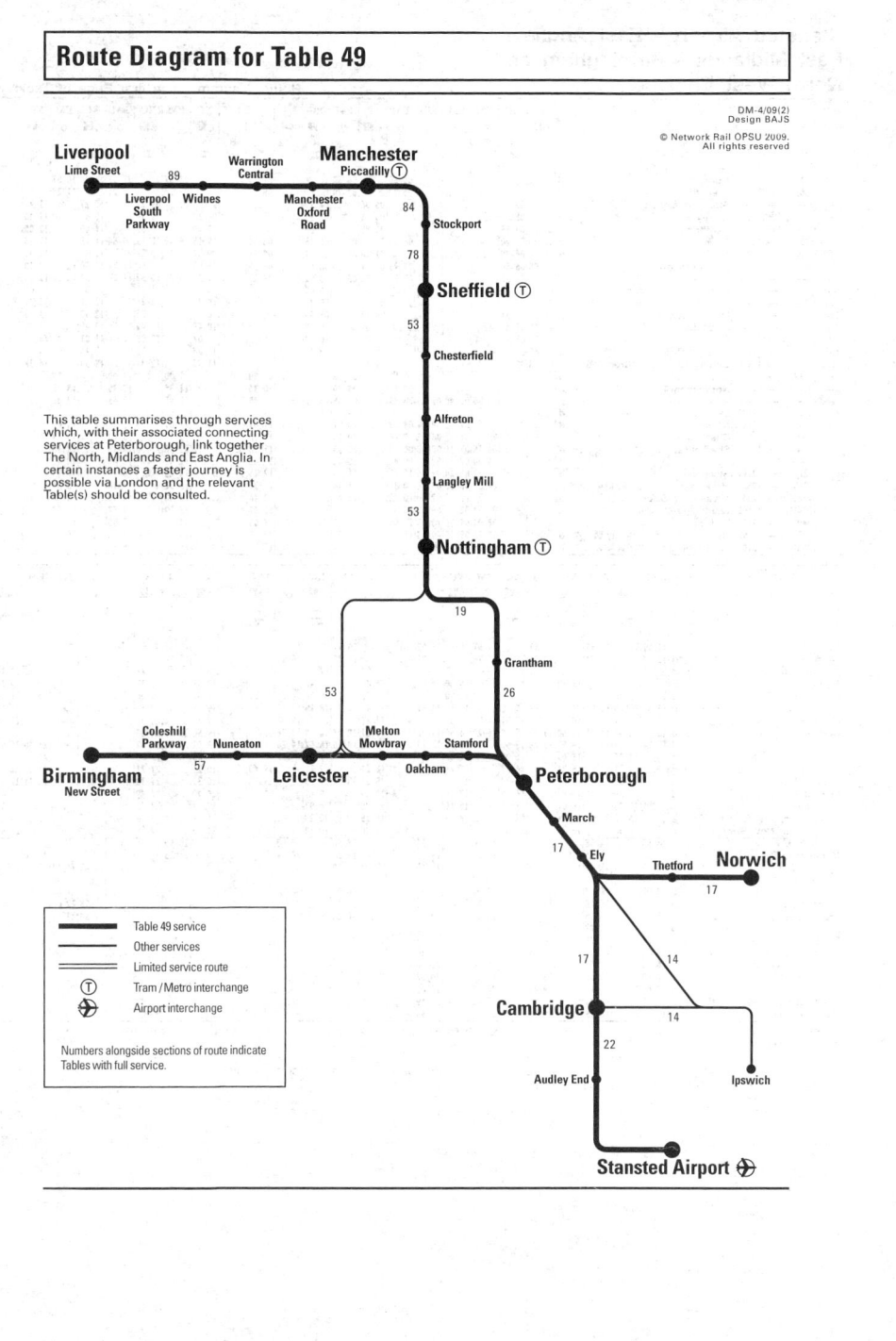

Stansted Airport - East Anglia - East Midlands - Birmingham and North West England

Route Diagram - see first Page of Table 49

Miles	Miles	Miles	Miles			XC	XC	EM	EM	EM	EM	XC	EM	XC		EM	EM	XC	EM	XC	EM	XC	EM	XC	
						◇1	◇1	◇	◇	◇	◇	◇1	◇	◇1		◇		◇1	◇	◇1	◇	◇1	◇	◇1	
							A					A		A			B	A		A		A		A	
0	0	—	0	**Norwich**	d						05 50		06 52			07 57			08 57		09 57		10 57		
30½	30½	—	30½	Thetford	d						06 23		07 20			08 24			09 24		10 24		11 24		
—	—	0	—	**Stansted Airport** ✈	d		05 16					06 06		07 21				08 21		09 21		10 27		11 27	
—	—	10¾	—	Audley End	d		05 37					06 23		07 37				08 37		09 39		10 40		11 40	
—	—	24¾	—	**Cambridge**	d	05 15	05 55					06 55		08 00				09 00		10 00		11 00		12 00	
53¾	53¾	39½	53¾	Ely 4	d	05 30	06 10				06 51	07 12	07 45	08 15		08 50		09 15	09 49	10 15	10 54	11 15	11 53	12 15	
69	69	—	69	March	d	05 46	06 28				07 07	07 28	08 01	08 31		09 07		09 31		10 31		11 31		12 31	
82¾	82¾	—	82¾	**Peterborough** 8	a	06 08	06 50				07 25	07 51	08 24	08 50		09 25		09 50	10 26	10 50	11 27	11 50	12 24	12 50	
—	—	—	—		d	06 10	06 52				07 27	07 52	08 26	08 52		09 27		09 52	10 28	10 52	11 28	11 52	12 26	12 52	
95¼	—	—	—	Stamford	d	06 23	07 05					08 05		09 05				10 05		11 05		12 05		13 05	
108¾	—	—	—	Oakham	d	06 39	07 21					08 21		09 21			09 49	10 21		11 21		12 21		13 21	
120¼	—	—	—	Melton Mowbray	d	06 50	07 33					08 33		09 33			10a00	10 33		11 33		12 33		13 33	
135¼	—	—	—	**Leicester**	d	07 10	07 49					08 49		09 49				10 49		11 49		12 49		13 49	
154	—	—	—	Nuneaton	a	07 29	08 15					09 08		10 08				11 07		12 08		13 07		14 08	
165½	—	—	—	Coleshill Parkway	a	07 45	08 32					09 25		10 25				11 24		12 25		13 24		14 25	
175	—	—	—	**Birmingham New Street** 12	a	07 58	08 45					09 38		10 38				11 38		12 39		13 38		14 38	
—	112	—	—	Grantham 7	d						07 58		08 55			09 58			11 00		12 00		12 59		
—	134¾	—	152½	**Nottingham** 8	a						08 40		09 36			10 36			11 35		12 36		13 36		
—	—	—	—		d			05 20	06 40	07 45	08 45		09 45			10 45			11 45		12 45		13 45		
—	146¾	—	164½	Langley Mill	d																				
—	153	—	170¾	Alfreton	d				07 02	08 07	09 07		10 07			11 07			12 07		13 07		14 07		
—	162¾	—	180¾	Chesterfield	d			05 49	07 13	08 18	09 18		10 18			11 18			12 18		13 18		14 19		
—	174¾	—	193	**Sheffield** 7	a			06 15	07 31	08 38	09 38		10 38			11 38			12 38		13 38		14 38		
—	—	—	—		d			06 20	07 35	08 42	09 42		10 42			11 42			12 42		13 42		14 42		
—	212	—	229¾	Stockport	a			07 22	08 24	09 25	10 25		11 25			12 25			13 25		14 25		15 25		
—	218	—	232¾	**Manchester Piccadilly** 10	a			07 34	08 36	09 36	10 36		11 36			12 36			13 36		14 36		15 36		
—	218½	—	236¼	Manchester Oxford Road	a			07 37	08 40	09 40	10 40		11 40			12 40			13 40		14 40		15 40		
—	234¼	—	252	Warrington Central	a			07 53	08 57	09 57	10 57		11 57			12 57			13 57		14 57		15 57		
—	240½	—	258¼	Widnes	a			08 01	09 05	10 05	11 05		12 05			13 05			14 05		15 05		16 05		
—	247¼	—	265	Liverpool South Parkway 7 ✈	a			08 18	09 15	10 15	11 15		12 15			13 15			14 15		15 15		16 15		
—	252¾	—	270½	**Liverpool Lime Street** 10	a			08 31	09 31	10 31	11 31		12 31			13 31			14 31		15 31		16 31		

		EM	XC	EM	XC	EM	XC	EM	XC	EM		XC	EM	XC	EM	EM		XC	EM	XC		NT	NT	EM	XC
		◇	◇1	◇	◇1	◇	◇1	◇	◇1	◇		◇1	◇	◇1	◇	◇1		◇1	◇	◇1					◇1
			A		A		A							A		C								E	
Norwich	d	11 57		12 57		13 57		14 57		15 52			16 57		17 54				18 57						
Thetford	d	12 24		13 24		14 24		15 24		16 27			17 27		18 27				19 24						
Stansted Airport ✈	d		12 27		13 27		14 27		15 27			16 27		17 27				18 21		19 21					20 21
Audley End	d		12 40		13 40		14 40		15 40			16 40		17 40				18 38		19 38					20 39
Cambridge	d		13 00		14 00		15 00		16 00			17 00		18 00				19 00		20 00					21 00
Ely 4	d	12 52	13 15	13 52	14 15	14f53	15 15	15 52	16 15	16 51		17 15	17 52	18 15	18 52			19 15	19 52	20 15					21 15
March	d		13 31		14 31		15 31		16 31			17 31		18 33	19 08			19 31		20 31					21 31
Peterborough 8	a	13 25	13 50	14 25	14 50	15 27	15 50	16 27	16 50	17 26		17 51	18 25	18 50	19 26			19 50	20 26	20 50					21 51
	d	13 27	13 52	14 26	14 52	15 28	15 52	16 28	16 52	17 27		17 52	18 26	18 52	19 26			19 52	20 28	20 52				21 30	21 52
Stamford	d		14 05		15 05		16 05		17 05			18 06		19 05				20 05		21 05				21 43	22 05
Oakham	d		14 21		15 21		16 21		17 21			18 21		19 21		19 40		20 21		21 21				21 58	22 21
Melton Mowbray	d		14 33		15 33		16 33		17 33			18 33		19 33		19a52		20 33		21 33				22 11	22 33
Leicester	d		14 49		15 49		16 49		17 49			18 49		19 49				20 49		21 49					22 49
Nuneaton	a		15 08		16 07		17 08		18 15			19 08		20 07				21 07		22 08					23 08
Coleshill Parkway	a		15 25		16 24		17 25		18 31			19 25		20 24				21 24		22 25					23 25
Birmingham New Street 12	a		15 38		16 38		17 38		18 45			19 38		20 38				21 37		22 38					23 41
Grantham 7	d	13 58		14 58		16 01		17 00		17 58			18 56		19 59				20 59						
Nottingham 8	a	14 36		15 36		16 36		17 36		18 36			19 36		20 31				21 35					22 50	
	d	14 45		15 45		16 45		17 45		18 45			19 40									20 45	21 11		
Langley Mill	d							18 02															21 38		
Alfreton	d	15 07		16 07		17 07		18 09		19 07			20 01										21 46		
Chesterfield	d	15 22		16 18		17 18		18 21		19 18			20 12									21 28	22 00		
Sheffield 7	a	15 38		16 38		17 36		18 39		19 39			20 28									21 54	22 19		
	d	15 42		16 42		17 40		18 43		19 42			20 32												
Stockport	a	16 25		17 25		18 25		19 25		20 25			21 20												
Manchester Piccadilly 10	a	16 36		17 37		18 36		19 36		20 36			21 32												
Manchester Oxford Road	a	16 40		17 40		18 40		19 40		20 40															
Warrington Central	a	16 57		18 03		18 57		19 57		20 57															
Widnes	a	17 05		18 11		19 05		20 05		21 05															
Liverpool South Parkway 7 ✈	a	17 15		18 21		19 18		20 16		21 19															
Liverpool Lime Street 10	a	17 31		18 35		19 35		20 35		21 35															

A from Peterborough
B From Corby. to Derby
C From St Pancras International
E From Spalding

For connections from Ipswich please refer to Table 14

Stansted Airport - East Anglia - East Midlands - Birmingham and North West England

Route Diagram - see first Page of Table 49

		XC	EM	XC	EM	EM	EM	XC	EM	XC		EM	XC	EM	XC	EM	XC	EM	XC	EM		XC	EM	XC	EM
		◇1	◇	◇1	◇	◇	◇	◇1	◇	◇1		◇	◇1	◇	◇1	◇	◇1	◇	◇1	◇		◇1	◇	◇1	◇
				A				A		A			A		A		A		A			A		A	
Norwich	d						05 52		06 53			07 57		08 57		09 57		10 57		11 57			12 57		13 57
Thetford	d						06 25		07 22			08 24		09 24		10 24		11 24		12 24			13 24		14 24
Stansted Airport ✈	d			05 25				06 27		07 27			08 27		09 27		10 27		11 27			12 27		13 27	
Audley End	d			05 37				06 40		07 40			08 40		09 40		10 40		11 40			12 40		13 40	
Cambridge	d	05 15		05 55				06 57		08 00			09 00		10 00		11 00		12 00			13 00		14 00	
Ely [4]	d	05 30		06 10			06 51	07 12	07 53	08 15		08 54	09 15	09 51	10 15	10 53	11 15	11 53	12 15	12 54		13 15	13 53	14 15	14 53
March	d	05 46		06 28			07 07	07 29	08 08	08 31		09 11	09 31		10 31		11 31		12 31			13 31		14 31	
Peterborough [8]	a	06 08		06 50			07 25	07 50	08 31	08 50		09 28	09 50	10 25	10 50	11 24	11 50	12 24	12 50	13 26		13 50	14 25	14 50	15 25
	d	06 10		06 52			07 27	07 52	08 33	08 52		09 30	09 52	10 26	10 52	11 25	11 52	12 25	12 52	13 28		13 52	14 26	14 52	15 25
Stamford	d	06 23		07 05				08 05		09 05			10 05		11 05		12 05		13 05			14 05		15 05	
Oakham	d	06 39		07 21				08 21		09 21			10 21		11 21		12 21		13 21			14 21		15 21	
Melton Mowbray	d	06 50		07 33				08 33		09 33			10 33		11 33		12 33		13 33			14 33		15 33	
Leicester	d	07 16		07 49				08 49		09 49			10 49		11 49		12 49		13 49			14 49		15 49	
Nuneaton	a	07 34		08 07				09 07		10 07			11 07		12 07		13 07		14 07			15 07		16 07	
Coleshill Parkway	a	07 50		08 23				09 24		10 24			11 24		12 24		13 24		14 24			15 24		16 24	
Birmingham New Street [12]	a	08 04		08 38				09 38		10 38			11 38		12 38		13 38		14 38			15 38		16 38	
Grantham [7]	d						07 58		09 09			09 58		10 58		11 58		12 58		13 58			14 58		15 58
Nottingham [8]	a						08 39		09 40			10 40		11 35		12 36		13 36		14 36			15 36		16 36
	d		05 20		06 40	07 45	08 45		09 45			10 45		11 45		12 45		13 45		14 45			15 45		16 45
Langley Mill	d																								
Alfreton	d				07 02	08 07	09 07		10 07			11 07		12 07		13 07		14 07		15 07			16 07		17 07
Chesterfield	d		05 49		07 13	08 18	09 18		10 18			11 18		12 18		13 18		14 18		15 18			16 18		17 18
Sheffield [7]	a		06 15		07 31	08 38	09 38		10 38			11 38		12 38		13 38		14 38		15 38			16 38		17 34
	d		06 20		07 35	08 42	09 42		10 42			11 42		12 42		13 42		14 42		15 42			16 42		17 40
Stockport	a		07 22		08 24	09 25	10 25		11 25			12 25		13 25		14 25		15 25		16 25			17 25		18 25
Manchester Piccadilly [10]	a		07 34		08 36	09 36	10 36		11 36			12 36		13 36		14 36		15 36		16 36			17 37		18 36
Manchester Oxford Road	a		07 37		08 40	09 40	10 40		11 40			12 40		13 40		14 40		15 40		16 40			17 40		18 40
Warrington Central	a		07 53		08 57	09 57	10 57		11 57			12 57		13 57		14 57		15 57		16 57			18 03		18 57
Widnes	a		08 01		09 05	10 05	11 05		12 05			13 05		14 05		15 05		16 05		17 05			18 11		19 05
Liverpool South Parkway [7] ✈	a		08 18		09 15	10 15	11 15		12 15			13 15		14 15		15 15		16 15		17 15			18 21		19 18
Liverpool Lime Street [10]	a		08 31		09 31	10 31	11 31		12 31			13 31		14 31		15 31		16 31		17 31			18 35		19 35

		XC	EM	XC	EM	XC		EM	XC	EM	XC	EM	XC	NT	NT	EM
		◇1	◇	◇1	◇	◇1		◇	◇1	◇	◇1	◇	◇1			
		A							A							B
Norwich	d		14 57		15 52			16 57		17 54		18 57				
Thetford	d		15 24		16 23			17 27		18 27		19 24				
Stansted Airport ✈	d	14 27		15 27		16 27			17 27		18 27		19 27			
Audley End	d	14 40		15 40		16 40			17 40		18 40		19 40			
Cambridge	d	15 00		16 00		17 00			18 00		19 00		20 00			
Ely [4]	d	15 15	15 52	16 15	16 52	17 15		17 52	18 15	18 53	19 15	19 51	20 15			
March	d	15 31		16 31		17 31			18 33	19 09	19 31		20 31			
Peterborough [8]	a	15 50	16 25	16 50	17 26	17 50		18 25	18 50	19 29	19 50	20 25	20 50			
	d	15 52	16 27	16 52	17 27	17 52		18 26	18 52	19 30	19 52	20 27	20 52			21 27
Stamford	d	16 05		17 05		18 05			19 05		20 05		21 05			
Oakham	d	16 21		17 21		18 21			19 21		20 21		21 21			
Melton Mowbray	d	16 33		17 33		18 33			19 33		20 33		21 33			
Leicester	d	16 49		17 49		18 49			19 49		20 49		21 49			
Nuneaton	a	17 07		18 07		19 07			20 07		21 07		22 07			
Coleshill Parkway	a	17 24		18 24		19 24			20 24		21 24		22 24			
Birmingham New Street [12]	a	17 38		18 38		19 38			20 38		21 38		22 38			
Grantham [7]	d		16 56		18 03			18 58		20 03		20 58				22 02
Nottingham [8]	a		17 36		18 36			19 36		20 37		21 32				22 32
	d		17 45		18 45			19 40						20 40	21 15	
Langley Mill	d		18 03											21 02	21 31	
Alfreton	d		18 10		19 07			20 01						21 10	21 39	
Chesterfield	d		18 22		19 18			20 11						21 22	21 50	
Sheffield [7]	a		18 39		19 39			20 27						21 40	22 13	
	d		18 42		19 42			20 31								
Stockport	a		19 25		20 25			21 20								
Manchester Piccadilly [10]	a		19 36		20 36			21 32								
Manchester Oxford Road	a		19 40		20 40											
Warrington Central	a		19 57		20 57											
Widnes	a		20 05		21 05											
Liverpool South Parkway [7] ✈	a		20 15		21 19											
Liverpool Lime Street [10]	a		20 30		21 35											

A from Peterborough

B From Spalding

For connections from Ipswich please refer to Table 14

Table 49

Sundays

until 1 January

Stansted Airport - East Anglia - East Midlands - Birmingham and North West England

Route Diagram - see first Page of Table 49

		EM	XC	EM	EM	EM	EM	XC	XC	XC	EM	EM	EM	XC	EM	XC	EM	XC	EM	XC	EM	XC	EM
		◇	◇1	◇	◇	◇	◇	◇1	◇1	◇1	◇	◇	◇	◇1	◇	◇1	◇	◇1	◇	◇1	◇	◇1	◇
			A					A	A	A				A									
Norwich	d						10 47						13 49		14 49		15 53		16 54		17 54		18 56
Thetford	d						11 14						14 16		15 16		16 20		17 21		18 21		19 23
Stansted Airport ✈	d		10 25					11 25	12 25	13 25				14 25		15 25		16 25		17 25		18 25	
Audley End	d		10 39					11 39	12 39	13 39				14 39		15 39		16 39		17 39		18 39	
Cambridge	d		11 00					12 00	13 00	14 00				15 00		16 00		17 00		18 00		19 00	
Ely 4	d		11 15				11 39	12 15	13 15	14 15			14 45	15 15	15 48	16 15		17 15	17 48	18 15	18 48	19 15	19 48
March	d		11 31					12 31	13 31	14 31				15 31		16 31		17 31		18 31		19 31	
Peterborough 8	a		11 50				12 16	12 50	13 50	14 50			15 24	15 50	16 22	16 50	17 10	17 50	18 23	18 50	19 24	19 50	20 29
	d		11 52				12 18	12 52	13 52	14 52			15 26	15 52	16 24	16 52	17 11	17 52	18 26	18 52	19 26	19 52	20 31
Stamford	d		12 05					13 05	14 05	15 05				16 05		17 05		18 05		19 05		20 05	
Oakham	d		12 19					13 19	14 19	15 19				16 19		17 19		18 19		19 19		20 19	
Melton Mowbray	d		12 30					13 30	14 30	15 30				16 30		17 30		18 30		19 31		20 30	
Leicester	d		12 49					13 49	14 49	15 49				16 49		17 49		18 49		19 49		20 49	
Nuneaton	a		13 07					14 07	15 07	16 05				17 07		18 07		19 07		20 07		21 07	
Coleshill Parkway	a		13 23					14 23	15 23	16 22				17 23		18 23		19 23		20 23		21 23	
Birmingham New Street 12	a		13 36					14 36	15 36	16 36				17 36		18 36		19 36		20 36		21 36	
Grantham 7	d						12 54						15 59		16 56		17 55		18 58		19 57		21 03
Nottingham 8	a						13 33						16 28		17 25		18 29		19 33		20 31		21 35
	d	09 31		10 41	11 46	12 39	13 38				14 37	15 44	16 40		17 35		18 37		19 38				
Langley Mill	d					12 56	13 55				14 54		17 00		17 54		18 54						
Alfreton	d	09 53		11 03	12 08	13 04	14 03				15 02	16 06	17 08		18 02		19 02		20 00				
Chesterfield	d	10 08		11 16	12 18	13 17	14 17				15 13	16 23	17 22		18 17		19 13		20 12				
Sheffield 7	a	10 33		11 35	12 36	13 33	14 35				15 31	16 39	17 40		18 34		19 31		20 31				
	d	10 41		11 38	12 41	13 38	14 39				15 38	16 44	17 44		18 37		19 35		20 35				
Stockport	a	11 25		12 25	13 25	14 25	15 25				16 25	17 28	18 25		19 25		20 25		21 24				
Manchester Piccadilly 10	a	11 37		12 35	13 37	14 37	15 37				16 37	17 37	18 37		19 37		20 38		21 36				
Manchester Oxford Road	a	11 41		12 41	13 41	14 41	15 41				16 41	17 41	18 41		19 41								
Warrington Central	a	11 58		12 58	13 58	14 58	15 58				16 58	17 58	18 58		19 58								
Widnes	a	12 06		13 06	14 06	15 06	16 06				17 06	18 06	19 06		20 06								
Liverpool South Parkway 7 ✈	a	12 16		13 16	14 16	15 16	16 16				17 16	18 16	19 16		20 16								
Liverpool Lime Street 10	a	12 30		13 30	14 30	15 30	16 30				17 30	18 30	19 30		20 30								

		XC	NT	EM
		◇1		◇
Norwich	d			20 52
Thetford	d			21 19
Stansted Airport ✈	d	19 25		
Audley End	d	19 39		
Cambridge	d	20 00		
Ely 4	d	20 15		21 44
March	d	20 31		
Peterborough 8	a	20 50		22 20
	d	20 52		22 22
Stamford	d	21 05		
Oakham	d	21 19		
Melton Mowbray	d	21 30		
Leicester	d	21 49		
Nuneaton	a	22 07		
Coleshill Parkway	a	22 23		
Birmingham New Street 12	a	22 36		
Grantham 7	d			22 54
Nottingham 8	a			23 28
	d		20 13	
Langley Mill	d		20 29	
Alfreton	d		20 37	
Chesterfield	d		20 48	
Sheffield 7	a		21 14	
	d			
Stockport	a			
Manchester Piccadilly 10	a			
Manchester Oxford Road	a			
Warrington Central	a			
Widnes	a			
Liverpool South Parkway 7 ✈	a			
Liverpool Lime Street 10	a			

A from Peterborough

For connections from Ipswich please refer to Table 14

Table 49

Sundays

8 January to 12 February

Stansted Airport - East Anglia - East Midlands - Birmingham and North West England

Route Diagram - see first Page of Table 49

		EM	XC	EM	EM	XC	XC	EM	EM			XC	XC	XC	XC	XC	XC	EM	EM			XC	XC	XC	EM
		◇	◇[1]	◇	◇			◇	◇								◇[1]	◇	◇					◇[1]	◇
			A														A							A	
						🚌	🚌					🚌	🚌	🚌	🚌	🚌						🚌	🚌		
			🛒														🛒							🛒	
Norwich	d								10 47																13 49
Thetford	d								11 14																14 16
Stansted Airport ✈	d		10 25														12 25							13 25	
Audley End	d		10 39														12 39							13 39	
Cambridge	d		11 00														13 00							14 00	
Ely [4]	d		11 15						11 39								13 15							14 15	14 45
March	d		11 31														13 31							14 31	
Peterborough [8]	a		11 50						12 16								13 50							14 50	15 24
	d		11 53				12 00		12 18			13 00		13 00		14 00	14 02						15 00	15 01	15 26
Stamford	d					12 05	12 25						13 05	13 25	14 05	14 25						15 05	15 25		
Oakham	d					12 30	12 50						13 30	13 50	14 30	14 50						15 30	15 50		
Melton Mowbray	d					12 50	13a10						13 50	14a10	14 50	15a10						15 50	16a10		
Leicester	d		13 19			13a30						14a25	14a30		15a30		15 49					16a30		16 49	
Nuneaton	a		13 42														16 07							17 07	
Coleshill Parkway	a		13 57														16 23							17 23	
Birmingham New Street [12]	a		14 16														16 36							17 36	
Grantham [7]	d								12 54																15 59
Nottingham [8] 🚊	a								13 33																16 28
	d	09 31		10 41	11 46			12 39	13 38									14 37	15 44						16 40
Langley Mill	d							12 56	13 55									14 54							17 00
Alfreton	d	09 53		11 03	12 08			13 04	14 03									15 02	16 06						17 08
Chesterfield	d	10 08		11 16	12 18			13 17	14 17									15 13	16 23						17 22
Sheffield [7] 🚊	a	10 33		11 35	12 36			13 33	14 35									15 31	16 39						17 40
	d	10 41		11 38	12 41			13 38	14 39									15 38	16 44						17 44
Stockport	a	11 25		12 25	13 25			14 25	15 25									16 25	17 28						18 25
Manchester Piccadilly [10] 🚊	a	11 37		12 35	13 37			14 37	15 37									16 37	17 37						18 37
Manchester Oxford Road	a	11 41		12 41	13 41			14 41	15 41									16 41	17 41						18 41
Warrington Central	a	11 58		12 58	13 58			14 58	15 58									16 58	17 58						18 58
Widnes	a	12 06		13 06	14 06			15 06	16 06									17 06	18 06						19 06
Liverpool South Parkway [7] ✈	a	12 16		13 16	14 16			15 16	16 16									17 16	18 16						19 16
Liverpool Lime Street [10]	a	12 30		13 30	14 30			15 30	16 30									17 30	18 30						19 30

			XC	XC	XC	EM		XC	XC	XC	EM		XC	XC	XC	EM			XC	XC	XC	XC	EM	NT	
						◇		◇[1]			◇			◇[1]		◇			◇[1]				◇		
								A						A											
			🚌	🚌	🚌				🚌	🚌			🚌		🚌					🚌	🚌	🚌			
								🛒						🛒											
Norwich	d					14 49					15 53					16 54							17 54		
Thetford	d					15 16					16 20					17 21							18 21		
Stansted Airport ✈	d							15 25						16 25					17 25						
Audley End	d							15 39						16 39					17 39						
Cambridge	d							16 00						17 00					18 00						
Ely [4]	d					15 48		16 15						17 15		17 48			18 15				18 48		
March	d							16 31						17 31					18 31						
Peterborough [8]	a					16 22		16 49			17 10			17 50		18 25			18 51				19 24		
	d		16 00		16 00	16 24		16 50		17 00	17 11			17 55	18 00	18 26			18 58	19 00		19 00	19 26		
Stamford	d			16 05	16 25				17 05	17 25			18 05		18 25						19 05	19 25			
Oakham	d			16 30	16 50				17 30	17 50			18 30		18 50						19 30	19 50			
Melton Mowbray	d			16 50	17a10				17 50	18a10			18 50		19a10						19 50	20a10			
Leicester	d		17a25	17a30				18 26	18a30				19a30	19 49					21 19	20a15	20a30				
Nuneaton	a							18 44						20 07					21 44						
Coleshill Parkway	a							18 59						20 22					22 00						
Birmingham New Street [12]	a							19 15						20 36					22 15						
Grantham [7]	d					16 56					17f55					18 58							19 57		
Nottingham [8] 🚊	a					17 25					18 29					19 33							20 31		
	d					17 35					18 37					19 38								20 13	
Langley Mill	d					17 54					18 54													20 29	
Alfreton	d					18 02					19 02					20 00								20 37	
Chesterfield	d					18 17					19 13					20 12								20 48	
Sheffield [7] 🚊	a					18 34					19 31					20 31								21 14	
	d					18 37					19 35					20 35									
Stockport	a					19 25					20 25					21 24									
Manchester Piccadilly [10] 🚊	a					19 37					20 38					21 36									
Manchester Oxford Road	a					19 41																			
Warrington Central	a					19 58																			
Widnes	a					20 06																			
Liverpool South Parkway [7] ✈	a					20 16																			
Liverpool Lime Street [10]	a					20 30																			

A 🛒 from Peterborough

For connections from Ipswich please refer to Table 14

Sundays
8 January to 12 February

Stansted Airport - East Anglia - East Midlands - Birmingham and North West England

Route Diagram - see first Page of Table 49

		XC	XC	XC	EM	XC	EM
					◇		◇
		bus	bus	bus		bus	
Norwich	d				18 56		20 52
Thetford	d				19 23		21 19
Stansted Airport (plane)	d						
Audley End	d						
Cambridge	d						
Ely 4	d				19 48		21 44
March	d						
Peterborough 8	a				20 29		22 20
	d	20 00		20 00	20 31	21 00	22 22
Stamford	d		20 05	20 25		21 25	
Oakham	d		20 30	20 50		21 50	
Melton Mowbray	d		20 50	21a10		22 10	
Leicester	d	21a25	21a30			22a50	
Nuneaton	a						
Coleshill Parkway	a						
Birmingham New Street 12	a						
Grantham 7	d				21 03		22 54
Nottingham 8 (tram)	a				21 35		23 28
	d						
Langley Mill	d						
Alfreton	d						
Chesterfield	d						
Sheffield 7 (tram)	a						
	d						
Stockport	a						
Manchester Piccadilly 10 (tram)	a						
Manchester Oxford Road	a						
Warrington Central	a						
Widnes	a						
Liverpool South Parkway 7 (plane)	a						
Liverpool Lime Street 10	a						

Sundays
from 19 February

		EM	XC	EM	EM	EM	EM	XC	XC	XC
		◇	◇ 1	◇	◇	◇	◇	◇ 1	◇ 1	◇ 1
			A (trolley)					A (trolley)	A (trolley)	A (trolley)
Norwich	d						10 47			
Thetford	d						11 14			
Stansted Airport (plane)	d		10 25					11 25	12 25	13 25
Audley End	d		10 39					11 39	12 39	13 39
Cambridge	d		11 00					12 00	13 00	14 00
Ely 4	d		11 15				11 39	12 15	13 15	14 15
March	d		11 31					12 31	13 31	14 31
Peterborough 8	a		11 50				12 16	12 50	13 50	14 50
	d		11 52				12 18	12 52	13 52	14 52
Stamford	d		12 05					13 05	14 05	15 05
Oakham	d		12 19					13 19	14 19	15 19
Melton Mowbray	d		12 30					13 30	14 30	15 30
Leicester	d		12 49					13 49	14 49	15 49
Nuneaton	a		13 07					14 07	15 07	16 05
Coleshill Parkway	a		13 23					14 23	15 23	16 22
Birmingham New Street 12	a		13 36					14 36	15 36	16 36
Grantham 7	d						12 54			
Nottingham 8 (tram)	a						13 33			
	d	09 31		10 41	11 46	12 39	13 38			
Langley Mill	d					12 56	13 55			
Alfreton	d	09 53		11 03	12 08	13 04	14 03			
Chesterfield	d	10 08		11 16	12 18	13 17	14 17			
Sheffield 7 (tram)	a	10 33		11 35	12 36	13 33	14 35			
	d	10 41		11 38	12 41	13 38	14 39			
Stockport	a	11 25		12 25	13 25	14 25	15 25			
Manchester Piccadilly 10 (tram)	a	11 37		12 35	13 37	14 37	15 37			
Manchester Oxford Road	a	11 41		12 41	13 41	14 41	15 41			
Warrington Central	a	11 58		12 58	13 58	14 58	15 58			
Widnes	a	12 06		13 06	14 06	15 06	16 06			
Liverpool South Parkway 7 (plane)	a	12 16		13 16	14 16	15 16	16 16			
Liverpool Lime Street 10	a	12 30		13 30	14 30	15 30	16 30			

		EM	EM	EM	XC	EM	XC	EM	XC	EM	XC	EM	XC	EM
		◇	◇	◇	◇ 1	◇	◇ 1	◇	◇ 1	◇	◇ 1	◇	◇ 1	◇
					A (trolley)									
Norwich	d			13 49		14 49		15 53		16 54		17 54		18 56
Thetford	d			14 16		15 16		16 20		17 21		18 21		19 23
Stansted Airport (plane)	d				14 25		15 25		16 25		17 25		18 25	
Audley End	d				14 39		15 39		16 39		17 39		18 39	
Cambridge	d				15 00		16 00		17 00		18 00		19 00	
Ely 4	d			14 45	15 15	15 48	16 15		17 15	17 48	18 15	18 48	19 15	19 48
March	d				15 31		16 31		17 31		18 31		19 31	
Peterborough 8	a			15 24	15 50	16 22	16 50	17 10	17 50	18 23	18 50	19 24	19 50	20 29
	d			15 26	15 52	16 24	16 52	17 11	17 52	18 26	18 52	19 26	19 52	20 31
Stamford	d				16 05		17 05		18 05		19 05		20 05	
Oakham	d				16 19		17 19		18 19		19 19		20 19	
Melton Mowbray	d				16 30		17 30		18 30		19 31		20 30	
Leicester	d				16 49		17 49		18 49		19 49		20 49	
Nuneaton	a				17 07		18 07		19 07		20 07		21 07	
Coleshill Parkway	a				17 23		18 23		19 23		20 23		21 23	
Birmingham New Street 12	a				17 36		18 36		19 36		20 36		21 36	
Grantham 7	d			15 59		16 56		17 55		18 58		19 57		21 03
Nottingham 8 (tram)	a			16 28		17 25		18 29		19 33		20 31		21 35
	d	14 37	15 44	16 40		17 35		18 37		19 38				
Langley Mill	d	14 54		17 00		17 54		18 54						
Alfreton	d	15 02	16 06	17 08		18 02		19 02		20 00				
Chesterfield	d	15 13	16 23	17 22		18 17		19 13		20 12				
Sheffield 7 (tram)	a	15 31	16 39	17 40		18 34		19 31		20 31				
	d	15 38	16 44	17 44		18 37		19 35		20 35				
Stockport	a	16 25	17 28	18 25		19 25		20 25		21 24				
Manchester Piccadilly 10 (tram)	a	16 37	17 37	18 37		19 37		20 38		21 36				
Manchester Oxford Road	a	16 41	17 41	18 41		19 41								
Warrington Central	a	16 58	17 58	18 58		19 58								
Widnes	a	17 06	18 06	19 06		20 06								
Liverpool South Parkway 7 (plane)	a	17 16	18 16	19 16		20 16								
Liverpool Lime Street 10	a	17 30	18 30	19 30		20 30								

A (trolley) from Peterborough

For connections from Ipswich please refer to Table 14

Table 49

Sundays

from 19 February

Stansted Airport - East Anglia - East Midlands - Birmingham and North West England

Route Diagram - see first Page of Table 49

		XC	NT	EM
		◇1		◇
Norwich	d			20 52
Thetford	d			21 19
Stansted Airport ✈	d	19 25		
Audley End	d	19 39		
Cambridge	d	20 00		
Ely 4	d	20 15		21 44
March	d	20 31		
Peterborough 8	a	20 50		22 20
	d	20 52		22 22
Stamford	d	21 05		
Oakham	d	21 19		
Melton Mowbray	d	21 30		
Leicester	d	21 49		
Nuneaton	a	22 07		
Coleshill Parkway	a	22 23		
Birmingham New Street 12	a	22 36		
Grantham 7	d			22 54
Nottingham 8 🚌	a			23 28
	d		20 13	
Langley Mill	d		20 29	
Alfreton	d		20 37	
Chesterfield	d		20 48	
Sheffield 7 🚌	a		21 14	
	d			
Stockport	a			
Manchester Piccadilly 10 🚌	a			
Manchester Oxford Road	a			
Warrington Central	a			
Widnes	a			
Liverpool South Parkway 7 ✈	a			
Liverpool Lime Street 10	a			

For connections from Ipswich please refer to Table 14

North West England and Birmingham - East Midlands - East Anglia - Stansted Airport

Route Diagram - see first Page of Table 49

Miles	Miles	Miles	Miles	Station		EM MO	EM MX	EM	EM	EM	XC	EM	NT	XC	NT	EM	XC	EM	XC	EM
						◇	◇	◇		◇1	◇1	◇		◇1		◇	◇1	◇	◇1	◇
									A	B ✉🚲				D 🚲		E	D 🚲		F 🚲	
—	0	—	0	**Liverpool Lime Street 10**	d	21p21	21p37													06 47
—	5½	—	5½	Liverpool South Parkway 7 ✈	d	21p31	21p47													06 57
—	12¼	—	12¼	Widnes	d	21p39	21p55													07 07
—	18½	—	18½	Warrington Central	d	21p47	22p03													07 15
—	34¼	—	34¼	Manchester Oxford Road	d	22p07	22p24													07 38
—	34¾	—	34¾	**Manchester Piccadilly 10**	d	22p11	22p28													07 42
—	40¾	—	40¾	Stockport	d	22b28	22p37													07 54
—	77½	—	77½	**Sheffield 7**	a	23p25	23p35													08 34
—	—	—	—		d	23p29	23p37						05 05		06 00					08 38
—	89¾	—	89¾	Chesterfield	d	23p43	00 02						05 20		06 16					08 53
—	99¾	—	99¾	Alfreton	d	23p54									06 30					09 03
—	106	—	106	Langley Mill	d	00 02									06 37					
—	118	—	118	**Nottingham 8**	a	00 25	00 40						06 12		07 06					09 30
—	—	—	—		d			05 03	05 10			05 56				07 52		08 34		09 34
—	140¾	—	—	Grantham 7	d				05 51							08 27		09 10		10 11
0	—	—	—	**Birmingham New Street 12**	d						05 22			06 22			07 22		08 22	
9½	—	—	—	Coleshill Parkway	d						05 35			06 35			07 35		08 35	
21	—	—	—	Nuneaton	d						05 52			06 52			07 51		08 52	
39¾	—	—	—	**Leicester**	d						06 15			07 18			08 18		09 18	
54¾	—	—	—	Melton Mowbray	d			05 36		06 01	06 31	06 52		07 34			08 33		09 34	
66¼	—	—	—	Oakham	d			05 48		06a12	06 42	07 05		07 45			08 45		09 45	
79¾	—	—	—	Stamford	d			06 03			06 57	07 18		08 01			09 01		10 01	
92¼	170	—	187¾	**Peterborough 8**	a			06 19	06 25		07 10	07 33		08 16		08 57	09 16	09 39	10 16	10 40
—	—	—	—		d			06 27			07 12	07 35		08 18		08 59	09 18	09 40	10 18	10 44
106¼	184	—	201¾	March	a			06 42			07 30	07 50		08 33			09 34		10 33	
121½	206¾	0	217	Ely 4	a			07 01			07 51	08 11		08 52		09 41	09 52	10 13	10 52	11 16
—	—	14¾	—	**Cambridge**	a						08 07			09 08			10 08		11 08	
—	—	28¾	—	Audley End	a						08 24			09 23			10 24		11 23	
—	—	39½	—	**Stansted Airport** ✈	a						08 39			09 39			10 40		11 40	
144½	222¼	—	240¼	Thetford	a			07 28				08 36				10 06		10 41		11 41
152	252¼	—	270½	**Norwich**	a			08 13				09 13				10 44		11 14		12 13

Station		XC	EM	XC	EM	XC	EM	XC	EM	XC	EM	XC	EM	XC	EM	EM	XC	EM	XC
		◇1	◇	◇1	◇	◇1	◇	◇1	◇	◇1	◇	◇1	◇	◇1	◇	◇1	◇1	◇	◇1
		D 🚲		D 🚲		D 🚲		D 🚲		D 🚲		D 🚲		D 🚲		G ☕	D 🚲		
Liverpool Lime Street 10	d		07 42		08 52		09 52		10 52		11 52		12 52		13 52			14 52	
Liverpool South Parkway 7 ✈	d		07 53		09 03		10 03		11 03		12 03		13 03		14 03			15 03	
Widnes	d		08 05		09 11		10 11		11 11		12 11		13 11		14 11			15 11	
Warrington Central	d		08 13		09 19		10 19		11 19		12 19		13 19		14 19			15 19	
Manchester Oxford Road	d		08 39		09 39		10 39		11 39		12 39		13 39		14 39			15 39	
Manchester Piccadilly 10	d		08 43		09 43		10 43		11 43		12 43		13 43		14 43			15 43	
Stockport	d		08 54		09 54		10 54		11 54		12 54		13 54		14 54			15 54	
Sheffield 7	a		09 35		10 35		11 34		12 35		13 35		14 35		15 35			16 34	
	d		09 38		10 38		11 38		12 38		13 38		14 38		15 38			16 38	
Chesterfield	d		09 53		10 52		11 53		12 53		13 52		14 53		15 53			16 56	
Alfreton	d		10 04		11 03		12 03		13 03		14 03		15 04		16 04			17 07	
Langley Mill	d																		
Nottingham 8	a		10 30		11 30		12 30		13 30		14 30		15 28		16 33			17 31	
	d		10 34		11 34		12 34		13 34		14 34		15 34		16 34			17 34	
Grantham 7	d		11 10		12 11		13 09		14 10		15 11		16 10		17 11			18 11	
Birmingham New Street 12	d	09 22		10 22		11 22		12 22		13 22		14 22		15 22			16 22		16 52
Coleshill Parkway	d	09 35		10 35		11 35		12 35		13 35		14 35		15 35			16 35		17 05
Nuneaton	d	09 52		10 52		11 52		12 52		13 52		14 52		15 52			16 52		17 22
Leicester	d	10 18		11 18		12 18		13 18		14 18		15 18		16 18			17 18		17 51
Melton Mowbray	d	10 34		11 34		12 34		13 34		14 34		15 34		16 33		17 12	17 34		18 07
Oakham	d	10 44		11 45		12 45		13 45		14 45		15 45		16 45		17a23	17 45		18 19
Stamford	d	11 00		12 01		13 01		14 01		15 01		16 01		17 01			18 01		18 40
Peterborough 8	a	11 17	11 39	12 16	12 40	13 16	13 39	14 16	14 39	15 16	15 38	16 16	16 39	17 16	17 40		18 16	18 38	18 57
	d	11 17	11 41	12 18	12 43	13 18	13 41	14 18	14 41	15 18	15 40	16 18	16 41	17 18	17 42		18 18	18 45	18 59
March	a	11 33		12 33		13 33		14 33		15 34		16 33		17 36			18 33	19 00	19 14
Ely 4	a	11 52	12 14	12 52	13 16	13 52	14 14	14 52	15 14	15 52	16 13	16 52	17 14	17 58	18 16		18 52	19 24	19 33
Cambridge	a	12 08		13 08		14 08		15 08		16 08		17 08		18 16			19 08		19 50
Audley End	a	12 23		13 23		14 23		15 23		16 23		17 23		18 31			19 23		
Stansted Airport ✈	a	12 40		13 40		14 40		15 40		16 40		17 40		18 54			19 39		
Thetford	a		12 39		13 40		14 38		15 38		16 37		17 38		18 40			19 50	
Norwich	a		13 13		14 13		15 13		16 14		17 13		18 18		19 15			20 22	

A To Spalding
B To St Pancras International
D 🚲 to Peterborough
E From Mansfield Woodhouse
F From Gloucester. 🚲 to Peterborough
G From Derby to St Pancras International
b Previous night, arr. 2220

For connections to Ipswich please refer to Table 14

North West England and Birmingham - East Midlands - East Anglia - Stansted Airport

Route Diagram - see first Page of Table 49

		XC ◇1	EM ◇	EM ◇	XC ◇1	XC ◇1	EM ◇	EM ◇	EM ◇	EM ◇	XC ◇1
Liverpool Lime Street 10	d		15 52	16 52			17 52	18 52	19 52	21 37	
Liverpool South Parkway 7 ✈	d		16 03	17 03			18 03	19 03	20 03	21 47	
Widnes	d		16 11	17 11			18 11	19 11	20 11	21 55	
Warrington Central	d		16 19	17 19			18 19	19 19	20 19	22 03	
Manchester Oxford Road	d		16 39	17 39			18 39	19 39	20 39	22 24	
Manchester Piccadilly 10	d		16 43	17 43			18 43	19 43	20 43	22 28	
Stockport	d		16 54	17 54			18 54	19 54	20 54	22 37	
Sheffield 7	a		17 40	18 41			19 33	20 36	21 35	23 35	
	d		17 44	18 45			19 38	20 41	21 39	23 37	
Chesterfield	d		18 02	19 01			19 53	20 58	21 55	00 02	
Alfreton	d		18 12	19 11			20 04	21 09	22 05		
Langley Mill	d								22 12		
Nottingham 8	a		18 34	19 38			20 31	21 38	22 38	00 40	
	d		18 37				20 34				
Grantham 7	d		19 08				21 10				
Birmingham New Street 12	d	17 22			18 22	19 22					20 22
Coleshill Parkway	d	17 35			18 35	19 35					20 35
Nuneaton	d	17 52			18 52	19 52					20 52
Leicester	d	18 18			19 18	20 18					21 18
Melton Mowbray	d	18 34			19 34	20 33					21 34
Oakham	d	18 45			19 45	20 44					21 45
Stamford	d	19 00			20 01	21 00					22 01
Peterborough 8	a	19 16	19 38		20 16	21 16	21 37				22 16
	d	19 18	19 40		20 18	21 18	21 38				22 18
March	a	19 34			20 34	21 34					22 35
Ely 4	a	19 53	20 13		20 53	21 52	22 11				22 53
Cambridge	a	20 08			21 08	22 08					23 10
Audley End	a	20 24			21 23	22 23					
Stansted Airport ✈	a	20 39			21 40	22 52					
Thetford	a		20 36				22 35				
Norwich	a		21 14				23 18				

Saturdays

		EM ◇	EM ◇	EM B	XC ◇1	EM ◇	LE 1 C	XC ◇1 D ⚲	EM	NT	EM ◇	XC ◇1 D ⚲	EM ◇	LE 1 C	XC ◇1 E ⚲	EM ◇	XC ◇1 D ⚲	EM ◇	XC ◇1 D ⚲	EM ◇	XC ◇1 D ⚲	EM ◇
Liverpool Lime Street 10	d	21p37														06 49		07 42		08 52		09 52
Liverpool South Parkway 7 ✈	d	21p47														06 59		07 52		09 03		10 03
Widnes	d	21p55														07 07		08 05		09 11		10 11
Warrington Central	d	22p03														07 15		08 13		09 19		10 19
Manchester Oxford Road	d	22p24														07 38		08 39		09 39		10 39
Manchester Piccadilly 10	d	22p28														07 42		08 43		09 43		10 43
Stockport	d	22p37														07 54		08 54		09 54		10 54
Sheffield 7	a	23p35														08 34		09 35		10 35		11 35
	d	23p37								05 54						08 38		09 38		10 38		11 38
Chesterfield	d	00 02								06 20						08 53		09 53		10 53		11 53
Alfreton	d									06 30						09 03		10 03		11 03		12 03
Langley Mill	d									06 38												
Nottingham 8	a	00 40								07 04						09 30		10 30		11 29		12 29
	d		05 04	05 10		05 54			06 55		07 45		08 32			09 34		10 34		11 34		12 34
Grantham 7	d			05 51							08 20		09 03			10 09		11 10		12 07		13 09
Birmingham New Street 12	d				05 22			06 22				07 22			08 22		09 22		10 22		11 22	
Coleshill Parkway	d				05 35			06 35				07 35			08 35		09 35		10 35		11 35	
Nuneaton	d				05 52			06 52				07 52			08 52		09 52		10 52		11 52	
Leicester	d				06 15			07 15				08 15			09 15		10 15		11 15		12 15	
Melton Mowbray	d		05 37		06 32	06 46		07 32				08 31			09 31		10 32		11 32		12 32	
Oakham	d		05 49		06 43	06 58		07 44				08 43			09 43		10 44		11 44		12 44	
Stamford	d		06 06		06 58	07 12		08 00				08 59			09 59		11 00		12 00		13 00	
Peterborough 8	a		06 19	06 25	07 12	07 29		08 16	09 27		08 58	09 16	09 41		10 14	10 38	11 16	11 39	12 14	12 38	13 16	13 38
	d		06 27		07 13	07 35	07 45	08 18			09 00	09 18	09 43	09 47	10 18	10 41	11 18	11 41	12 18	12 40	13 18	13 41
March	a		06 42		07 31	07 50	08 04	08 33				09 33		10 06	10 33		11 33		12 33		13 33	
Ely 4	a		07 01		07 52	08 11	08 22	08 52			09 35	09 52	10 14	10 29	10 52	11 17	11 52	12 14	12 52	13 13	13 52	14 14
Cambridge	a				08 08			09 07				10 07			11 07		12 07		13 07		14 07	
Audley End	a				08 23			09 23				10 23			11 23		12 23		13 23		14 23	
Stansted Airport ✈	a				08 39			09 40				10 40			11 40		12 40		13 40		14 40	
Thetford	a		07 30			08 36					10 04		10 40			11 44		12 38		13 39		14 38
Norwich	a		08 13			09 15					10 43		11 15			12 18		13 13		14 13		15 13

B To Spalding

D ⚲ to Peterborough

E From Gloucester. ⚲ to Peterborough

For connections to Ipswich please refer to Table 14

Table 49

Saturdays

North West England and Birmingham - East Midlands - East Anglia - Stansted Airport

Route Diagram - see first Page of Table 49

		XC ◇1 B	EM ◇	XC ◇1 B	EM ◇	XC ◇1 B	EM ◇	XC ◇1 B	EM ◇	XC ◇1 B	EM ◇	XC ◇1	EM ◇	EM ◇	XC ◇1	XC ◇1	EM ◇	EM ◇	EM ◇
Liverpool Lime Street 10	d		10 52		11 52		12 52		13 52		14 52		15 52	16 52			17 52	18 52	19 52
Liverpool South Parkway 7	d		11 03		12 03		13 03		14 03		15 03		16 03	17 03			18 03	19 03	20 03
Widnes	d		11 11		12 11		13 11		14 11		15 11		16 11	17 11			18 11	19 11	20 11
Warrington Central	d		11 19		12 19		13 19		14 19		15 19		16 19	17 19			18 19	19 19	20 19
Manchester Oxford Road	d		11 39		12 39		13 39		14 39		15 39		16 39	17 39			18 39	19 39	20 39
Manchester Piccadilly 10	d		11 43		12 43		13 43		14 43		15 43		16 43	17 43			18 43	19 43	20 43
Stockport	d		11 54		12 54		13 54		14 54		15 54		16 54	17 54			18 54	19 54	20 54
Sheffield 7	a		12 35		13 35		14 35		15 36		16 35		17 37	18 35			19 35	20 35	21 34
	d		12 38		13 38		14 38		15 38		16 38		17 44	18 38			19 38	20 41	21 38
Chesterfield	d		12 53		13 53		14 53		15 53		16 53		18 01	18 53			19 53	20 59	21 54
Alfreton	d		13 03		14 03		15 04		16 04		17 04		18 11	19 03			20 04	21 09	22 05
Langley Mill	d																		22 12
Nottingham 8	a		13 30		14 29		15 29		16 30		17 29		18 33	19 33			20 31	21 33	22 33
	d		13 34		14 34		15 34		16 34		17 34		18 34				20 34		
Grantham 7	d		14 07		15 10		16 07		17 06		18 15		19 08				21 07		
Birmingham New Street 12	d	12 22		13 22		14 22		15 22		16 22		17 22			18 22	19 22			
Coleshill Parkway	d	12 35		13 35		14 35		15 35		16 35		17 35			18 35	19 35			
Nuneaton	d	12 52		13 52		14 52		15 52		16 52		17 52			18 52	19 52			
Leicester	d	13 15		14 15		15 15		16 15		17 15		18 15			19 15	20 15			
Melton Mowbray	d	13 32		14 32		15 32		16 31		17 32		18 32			19 31	20 32			
Oakham	d	13 44		14 44		15 44		16 43		17 44		18 44			19 43	20 44			
Stamford	d	14 00		15 00		16 00		16 59		18 00		19 00			19 59	21 00			
Peterborough 8	a	14 16	14 41	15 16	15 39	16 16	16 40	17 16	17 37	18 15	18 42	19 17	19 39		20 14	21 16	21 36		
	d	14 18	14 43	15 18	15 41	16 18	16 41	17 19	17 39	18 18	18 44	19 18	19 41		20 18	21 18	21 38		
March	a	14 33		15 33		16 33		17 38		18 34	19 01	19 34			20 33	21 33			
Ely 6	a	14 52	15 14	15 52	16 14	16 52	17 13	17 59	18 12	18 52	19 19	19 51	20 14		20 51	21 51	22 12		
Cambridge	a	15 07		16 07		17 07		18 17		19 09		20 08			21 07	22 07			
Audley End	a	15 23		16 23		17 23		18 34		19 25		20 24			21 23	22 23			
Stansted Airport	a	15 40		16 40		17 40		18 53		19 40		20 40			21 40	22 40			
Thetford	a		15 40		16 38		17 39		18 36		19 43		20 36				22 36		
Norwich	a		16 15		17 13		18 18		19 19		20 18		21 14				23 20		

		EM ◇	EM ◇ D	EM ◇ E	XC ◇1
Liverpool Lime Street 10	d	20 52	21 37	21 37	
Liverpool South Parkway 7	d	21 03	21 47	21 47	
Widnes	d	21 11	21 55	21 55	
Warrington Central	d	21 19	22 03	22 03	
Manchester Oxford Road	d	21 39	22 27	22 27	
Manchester Piccadilly 10	d	21 43	22 31	22 31	
Stockport	d	21 52	22 42	22 42	
Sheffield 7	a	22 31	23 39	23 39	
	d	22 35	23 42	23 42	
Chesterfield	d	22 51	23 57	23 57	
Alfreton	d	23 02			
Langley Mill	d				
Nottingham 8	a	23 32	00 30	00 34	
	d				
Grantham 7	d				
Birmingham New Street 12	d				20 22
Coleshill Parkway	d				20 35
Nuneaton	d				20 52
Leicester	d				21 15
Melton Mowbray	d				21 31
Oakham	d				21 43
Stamford	d				21 59
Peterborough 8	a				22 16
	d				22 18
March	a				22 33
Ely 4	a				22 53
Cambridge	a				23 10
Audley End	a				
Stansted Airport	a				
Thetford	a				
Norwich	a				

B to Peterborough
D from 18 February until 24 March
E until 11 February and then from 31 March

For connections to Ipswich please refer to Table 14

Table 49

Sundays
until 1 January

North West England and Birmingham - East Midlands - East Anglia - Stansted Airport

Route Diagram - see first Page of Table 49

		EM	NT	XC	EM	XC	EM	XC	EM	XC	EM	XC	EM	XC	EM	XC	EM	EM
		◇		◇1	◇	◇1	◇	◇1	◇	◇1	◇	◇1	◇	◇1	◇	◇1	◇	◇
		A		C		C		C		C		C						
				⚲		⚲		⚲		⚲		⚲						
Liverpool Lime Street 10	d	21p37									12 52		13 52		14 52		15 52	16 52
Liverpool South Parkway 7 ✈	d	21p47									13 03		14 03		15 03		16 03	17 03
Widnes	d	21p55									13 11		14 11		15 11		16 11	17 11
Warrington Central	d	22p03									13 19		14 19		15 19		16 19	17 19
Manchester Oxford Road	d	22p27									13 39		14 39		15 39		16 39	17 39
Manchester Piccadilly 10	d	22p31							12 44		13 44		14 44		15 44		16 44	17 44
Stockport	d	22p42							12 55		13 54		14 54		15 54		16 54	17 54
Sheffield 7	a	23p39							13 37		14 39		15 37		16 36		17 36	18 37
	d	23p42	09 00				12 49		13 49		14 46		15 43		16 40		17 39	18 41
Chesterfield	d	23p57	09 17				13 03		14 03		15 00		15 57		16 56		17 55	18 56
Alfreton	d		09 28				13 14		14 14		15 11		16 08		17 07		18 05	19 06
Langley Mill	d		09 35								15 18		16 15		17 14		18 13	19 14
Nottingham 8	a	00 34	09 53				13 39		14 39		15 38		16 34		17 30		18 29	19 34
	d				12 37		13 49		14 45		15 49		16 45		17 36		18 47	
Grantham 7	d				13 12		14 22		15 20		16 22		17b21		18 17		19c27	
Birmingham New Street 12	d			11 22		12 22		13 22		14 22		15 22		16 22		17 22		
Coleshill Parkway	d			11 35		12 35		13 35		14 35		15 35		16 35		17 35		
Nuneaton	d			11 52		12 52		13 51		14 52		15 52		16 52		17 52		
Leicester	d			12 15		13 15		14 15		15 15		16 15		17 15		18 15		
Melton Mowbray	d			12 33		13 33		14 34		15 34		16 34		17 31		18 31		
Oakham	d			12 45		13 45		14 45		15 45		16 45		17 43		18 42		
Stamford	d			13 00		14 00		15 00		16 00		17 00		17 58		18 57		
Peterborough 8	a			13 16	13 41	14 16	14 51	15 16	15 58	16 16	16 55	17 16	17 50	18 16	18 46	19 14	19 56	
	d			13 18	13 43	14 18	14 53	15 18	16 03	16 18	16 59	17 18	17 56	18 18	18 48	19 18	19 58	
March	a			13 33		14 33		15 33		16 33		17 33	18 11	18 33		19 33		
Ely 4	a			13 52	14 16	14 52	15 29	15 52	16 38	16 52	17 32	17 52	18 32	18 52	19 21	19 52	20 31	
Cambridge	a			14 08		15 08		16 08		17 07		18 07		19 07		20 07		
Audley End	a			14 23		15 23		16 23		17 23		18 23		19 23		20 23		
Stansted Airport ✈	a			14 45		15 45		16 45		17 45		18 45		19 45		20 45		
Thetford	a				14 50		15 53		17 02		17 56		18 56		19 49		20 55	
Norwich	a				15 30		16 35		17 30		18 30		19 29		20 29		21 35	

		XC	XC	EM	EM	EM	XC	EM
		◇1	◇1	◇	◇	◇	◇1	◇
Liverpool Lime Street 10	d			17 52	18 52	19 52		21 21
Liverpool South Parkway 7 ✈	d			18 03	19 03	20 03		21 31
Widnes	d			18 11	19 11	20 11		21 39
Warrington Central	d			18 19	19 19	20 19		21 47
Manchester Oxford Road	d			18 39	19 39	20 39		22 07
Manchester Piccadilly 10	d			18 44	19 44	20 44		22 11
Stockport	d			18 54	19 54	20 54		22e28
Sheffield 7	a			19 34	20 34	21 36		23 25
	d			19 40	20 40	21 40		23 29
Chesterfield	d			19 55	20 55	21 56		23 43
Alfreton	d			20 06	21 06	22 07		23 54
Langley Mill	d			20 13	21 13	22 14		00 02
Nottingham 8	a			20 30	21 34	22 35		00 25
	d			20 44				
Grantham 7	d			21 19				
Birmingham New Street 12	d	18 22	19 22				20 22	
Coleshill Parkway	d	18 35	19 35				20 35	
Nuneaton	d	18 52	19 52				20 51	
Leicester	d	19 15	20 15				21 15	
Melton Mowbray	d	19 31	20 31				21 31	
Oakham	d	19 42	20 42				21 43	
Stamford	d	19 57	20 57				21 59	
Peterborough 8	a	20 14	21 13	21 52			22 14	
	d	20 18	21 18	21 53			22 18	
March	a	20 33	21 33				22 33	
Ely 4	a	20 52	21 52	22 28			22 52	
Cambridge	a	21 07	22 07				23 07	
Audley End	a	21 23	22 23					
Stansted Airport ✈	a	21 45	22 45					
Thetford	a			22 52				
Norwich	a			23 28				

A not 11 December

C ⚲ to Peterborough

For connections to Ipswich please refer to Table 14

Table 49

Sundays

8 January to 12 February

North West England and Birmingham - East Midlands - East Anglia - Stansted Airport

Route Diagram - see first Page of Table 49

		EM	NT		EM		XC	XC	XC			EM	XC	XC	XC		XC	EM	XC	XC			EM	XC	XC
		◇			◇							◇			◇[1]			◇					◇		
															C										
							🚌	🚌	🚌				🚌	🚌			🚌		🚌	🚌				🚌	🚌
															⚲										
Liverpool Lime Street [10]	d	21p37																					12 52		
Liverpool South Parkway [7] ✈	d	21p47																					13 03		
Widnes	d	21p55																					13 11		
Warrington Central	d	22p03																					13 19		
Manchester Oxford Road	d	22p27																					13 39		
Manchester Piccadilly [10] 🚋	d	22p31																12 44					13 44		
Stockport	d	22p42																12 55					13 54		
Sheffield [7] 🚋	a	23p39																13 37					14 39		
	d	23p42	09 00									12 49						13 49					14 46		
Chesterfield	d	23p57	09 17									13 03						14 03					15 00		
Alfreton	d		09 28									13 14						14 14					15 11		
Langley Mill	d		09 35																				15 18		
Nottingham [8] 🚋	a	00 34	09 53									13 39						14 39					15 38		
	d				12 37							13 49						14 45					15 49		
Grantham [7]	d				13 12							14 22						15 20					16 22		
Birmingham New Street [12]	d														12 44										
Coleshill Parkway	d														12 57										
Nuneaton	d														13 13										
Leicester	d						12 35		12 35					13 35	13 41		14 35			14 35					15 35
Melton Mowbray	d							12 50	13 10				13 50	14 10					14 50	15 10				15 50	16 10
Oakham	d							13 10	13 30				14 10	14 30					15 10	15 30				16 10	16 30
Stamford	d							13 35	13a55				14 35	14a55					15 35	15a55				16 35	16a55
Peterborough [8]	a				13 41		13 50	14 00				14 51	15 00		15 15		15 50	15 58	16 00				16 55	17 00	
	d				13 43							14 53			15 18			16 03					16 59		
March	a														15 33										
Ely [4]	a				14 16							15 29			15 52			16 38					17 32		
Cambridge	a														16 08										
Audley End	a														16 23										
Stansted Airport ✈	a														16 45										
Thetford	a				14 50							15 53						17 02					17 56		
Norwich	a				15 30							16 35						17 35					18 30		

		XC			EM	XC		XC	XC	EM	XC	XC	XC			EM		XC	XC	XC		EM	XC	XC	XC
		◇[1]			◇				◇[1]	◇						◇				◇[1]		◇			◇[1]
		C																							
						🚌		🚌			🚌	🚌	🚌					🚌	🚌				🚌	🚌	
		⚲																							
Liverpool Lime Street [10]	d				13 52					14 52						15 52						16 52			
Liverpool South Parkway [7] ✈	d				14 03					15 03						16 03						17 03			
Widnes	d				14 11					15 11						16 11						17 11			
Warrington Central	d				14 19					15 19						16 19						17 19			
Manchester Oxford Road	d				14 39					15 39						16 39						17 39			
Manchester Piccadilly [10] 🚋	d				14 44					15 44						16 44						17 44			
Stockport	d				14 54					15 54						16 54						17 54			
Sheffield [7] 🚋	a				15 37					16 36						17 36						18 37			
	d				15 43					16 40						17 39						18 41			
Chesterfield	d				15 57					16 56						17 55						18 56			
Alfreton	d				16 08					17 07						18 05						19 06			
Langley Mill	d				16 15					17 14						18 13						19 14			
Nottingham [8] 🚋	a				16 34					17 30						18 29						19 34			
	d				16 45					17 36						18 47									
Grantham [7]	d				17 21					18 17						19 27									
Birmingham New Street [12]	d	14 52							15 52											17 52					18 52
Coleshill Parkway	d	15 05							16 05											18 05					19 05
Nuneaton	d	15 22							16 22											18 22					19 22
Leicester	d	15 50						16 35	16 50		17 35		17 35						18 35	18 50				19 35	19 50
Melton Mowbray	d					16 50		17 10				17 50	18 10					18 50	19 10				19 50	20 10	
Oakham	d					17 10		17 30				18 10	18 30					19 10	19 30				20 10	20 30	
Stamford	d					17 35		17a55				18 35	18a55					19 35	19a55				20 35	20a55	
Peterborough [8]	a	17 16			17 50	18 00			18 38	18 46	18 50	19 00				19 56		20 00		20 23			21 00		21 24
	d	17 18			17 56				18 40	18 48						19 58				20 25					21 25
March	a	17 33			18 11				18 55											20 40					21 40
Ely [4]	a	17 52			18 32				19 15	19 21						20 31				21 04					22 01
Cambridge	a	18 07							19 31											21 22					22 16
Audley End	a	18 23							19 50											21 38					22 30
Stansted Airport ✈	a	18 45							20 08											21 59					22 45
Thetford	a				18 56					19 49						20 55									
Norwich	a				19 29					20 29						21 35									

C ⚲ to Peterborough

For connections to Ipswich please refer to Table 14

Table 49

Sundays
8 January to 12 February

North West England and Birmingham - East Midlands - East Anglia - Stansted Airport

Route Diagram - see first Page of Table 49

		EM	XC	XC	XC	EM	EM	EM	XC
		◇			◇1	◇	◇	◇	
			🚌	🚌					🚌
Liverpool Lime Street 10	d	17 52				18 52	19 52	21 21	
Liverpool South Parkway 7 ✈	d	18 03				19 03	20 03	21 31	
Widnes	d	18 11				19 11	20 11	21 39	
Warrington Central	d	18 19				19 19	20 19	21 47	
Manchester Oxford Road	d	18 39				19 39	20 39	22 07	
Manchester Piccadilly 10 ⛴	d	18 44				19 44	20 44	22 11	
Stockport	d	18 54				19 54	20 54	22b28	
Sheffield 7 ⛴	a	19 34				20 34	21 36	23 25	
	d	19 40				20 40	21 40	23 29	
Chesterfield	d	19 55				20 55	21 56	23 43	
Alfreton	d	20 06				21 06	22 07	23 54	
Langley Mill	d	20 13				21 13	22 14	00 02	
Nottingham 8 ⛴	a	20 30				21 34	22 35	00 25	
	d	20 44							
Grantham 7	d	21 19							
Birmingham New Street 12	d				19 52				
Coleshill Parkway	d				20 05				
Nuneaton	d				20 21				
Leicester	d			20 35	20 50				21 35
Melton Mowbray	d		20 50	21 10					22 10
Oakham	d		21 10	21 30					22 30
Stamford	d		21 35	21a55					22 55
Peterborough 8	a	21 52	22 00		22 16				23 20
	d	21 53			22 18				
March	a				22 33				
Ely 4	a	22 28			22 52				
Cambridge	a				23 07				
Audley End	a								
Stansted Airport ✈	a								
Thetford	a	22 52							
Norwich	a	23 28							

Sundays
from 19 February

		EM	EM	NT	XC	EM	XC	EM	XC	EM	XC	EM	XC	EM	EM	XC	EM	XC
		◇	◇		◇1	◇	◇1	◇	◇1	◇	◇1	◇	◇1	◇	◇	◇1	◇	◇1
		B	C		E		E		E		E		E	B	C			
					⚲		⚲		⚲		⚲		⚲					
Liverpool Lime Street 10	d	21p37	21p37									12 52		13 52	13 52		14 52	
Liverpool South Parkway 7 ✈	d	21p47	21p47									13 03		14 03	14 03		15 03	
Widnes	d	21p55	21p55									13 11		14 11	14 11		15 11	
Warrington Central	d	22p03	22p03									13 19		14 19	14 19		15 19	
Manchester Oxford Road	d	22p27	22p27									13 39		14 39	14 39		15 39	
Manchester Piccadilly 10 ⛴	d	22p31	22p31							12 44		13 44		14 44	14 44		15 44	
Stockport	d	22p42	22p42							12 55		13 54		14 54	14 54		15 54	
Sheffield 7 ⛴	a	23p39	23p39							13 37		14 39		15 37	15 37		16 36	
	d	23p42	23p42	09 00				12 49		13 49		14 46		15 43	15 43		16 40	
Chesterfield	d	23p57	23p57	09 17				13 03		14 03		15 00		15 57	15 57		16 56	
Alfreton	d			09 28				13 14		14 14		15 11		16 08	16 08		17 07	
Langley Mill	d			09 35								15 18		16 15	16 15		17 14	
Nottingham 8 ⛴	a	00 30	00 34	09 53				13 39		14 39		15 38		16 34	16 32		17 30	
	d					12 37		13 49		14 45		15 49		16 45	16 45		17 36	
Grantham 7	d					13 12		14 22		15 20		16 22		17 21	17 21		18 17	
Birmingham New Street 12	d				11 22		12 22		13 22		14 22		15 22			16 22		17 22
Coleshill Parkway	d				11 35		12 35		13 35		14 35		15 35			16 35		17 35
Nuneaton	d				11 52		12 52		13 51		14 52		15 52			16 52		17 52
Leicester	d				12 15		13 15		14 15		15 15		16 15			17 15		18 15
Melton Mowbray	d				12 33		13 33		14 34		15 34		16 34			17 31		18 31
Oakham	d				12 45		13 45		14 45		15 45		16 45			17 43		18 42
Stamford	d				13 00		14 00		15 00		16 00		17 00			17 58		18 57
Peterborough 8	a				13 16	13 41	14 16	14 51	15 16	15 58	16 16	16 55	17 16	17 50	17 50	18 16	18 46	19 14
	d				13 18	13 43	14 18	14 53	15 18	16 03	16 18	16 59	17 18	17 56	17 56	18 18	18 48	19 18
March	a				13 33		14 33		15 33		16 33		17 33	18 11	18 11	18 33		19 33
Ely 4	a				13 52	14 16	14 52	15 29	15 52	16 38	16 52	17 32	17 52	18 32	18 32	18 52	19 21	19 52
Cambridge	a				14 08		15 08		16 08		17 07		18 07			19 07		20 07
Audley End	a				14 23		15 23		16 23		17 23		18 23			19 23		20 23
Stansted Airport ✈	a				14 45		15 45		16 45		17 45		18 45			19 45		20 45
Thetford	a					14 50		15 53		17 02		17 56		18 56	18 56		19 49	
Norwich	a					15 30		16 35		17 35		18 30		19 29	19 29		20 29	

B from 19 February until 25 March
C from 1 April

E ⚲ to Peterborough

For connections to Ipswich please refer to Table 14

Table 49

Sundays
from 19 February

North West England and Birmingham - East Midlands - East Anglia - Stansted Airport

Route Diagram - see first Page of Table 49

		EM ◇	EM ◇	XC ◇1	XC ◇1	EM ◇		EM ◇	EM ◇	XC ◇1	EM ◇
Liverpool Lime Street 10	d	15 52	16 52			17 52		18 52	19 52		21 21
Liverpool South Parkway 7 ✈	d	16 03	17 03			18 03		19 03	20 03		21 31
Widnes	d	16 11	17 11			18 11		19 11	20 11		21 39
Warrington Central	d	16 19	17 19			18 19		19 19	20 19		21 47
Manchester Oxford Road	d	16 39	17 39			18 39		19 39	20 39		22 07
Manchester Piccadilly 10	d	16 44	17 44			18 44		19 44	20 44		22 11
Stockport	d	16 54	17 54			18 54		19 54	20 54		22 28
Sheffield 7	a	17 36	18 37			19 34		20 34	21 36		23 25
	d	17 39	18 41			19 40		20 40	21 40		23 29
Chesterfield	d	17 55	18 56			19 55		20 55	21 56		23 43
Alfreton	d	18 05	19 06			20 06		21 06	22 07		23 54
Langley Mill	d	18 13	19 14			20 13		21 13	22 14		00 02
Nottingham 8	a	18 29	19 34			20 30		21 34	22 35		00 25
	d	18 47				20 44					
Grantham 7	d	19 27				21 19					
Birmingham New Street 12	d			18 22	19 22					20 22	
Coleshill Parkway	d			18 35	19 35					20 35	
Nuneaton	d			18 52	19 52					20 52	
Leicester	d			19 15	20 15					21 15	
Melton Mowbray	d			19 31	20 31					21 31	
Oakham	d			19 42	20 42					21 43	
Stamford	d			19 57	20 57					21 59	
Peterborough 8	a	19 56		20 14	21 13	21 52				22 14	
	d	19 58		20 18	21 18	21 53				22 18	
March	a			20 33	21 33					22 33	
Ely 4	a	20 31		20 52	21 52	22 28				22 52	
Cambridge	a			21 07	22 07					23 07	
Audley End	a			21 23	22 23						
Stansted Airport ✈	a			21 45	22 45						
Thetford	a	20 55				22 52					
Norwich	a	21 35				23 28					

For connections to Ipswich please refer to Table 14

Network Diagram for Tables 50, 55, 56, 57

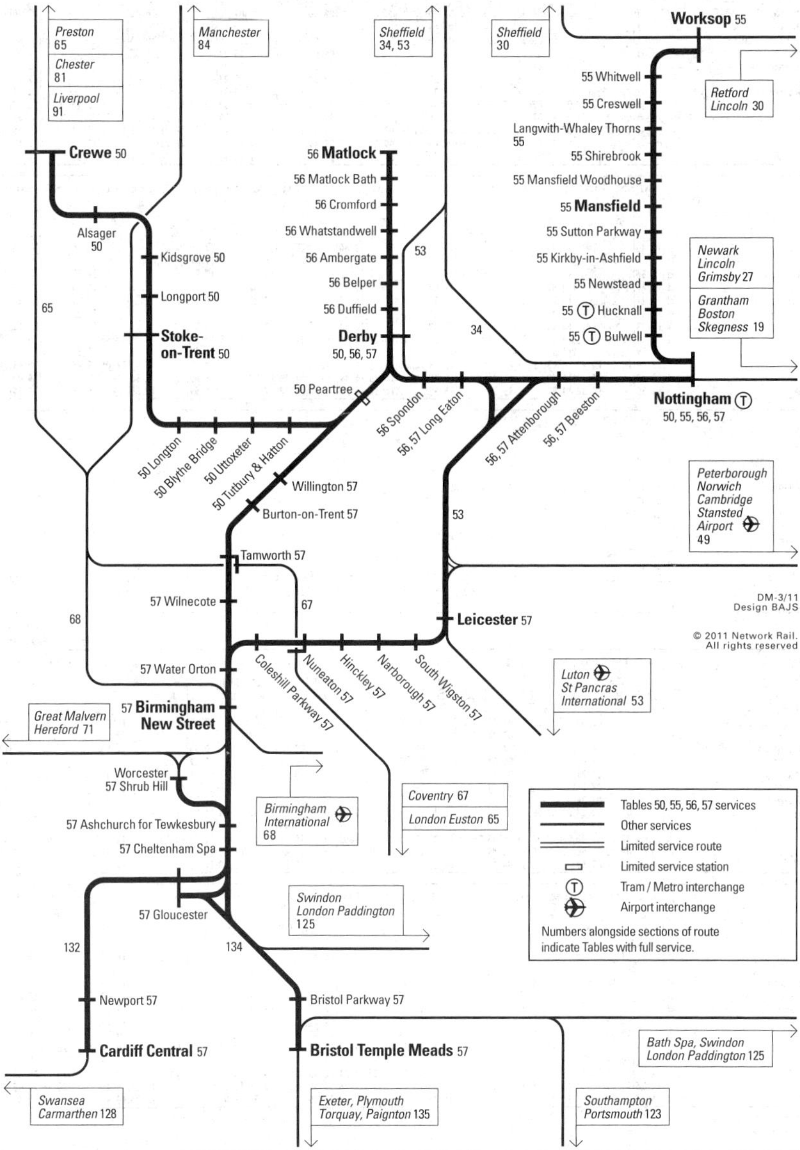

Derby - Stoke-on-Trent and Crewe

Network Diagram - see first Page of Table 50

Miles			NT	NT	LM	EM	NT	LM	EM	NT	LM		EM	NT	LM	EM	NT	LM	EM	NT	LM		EM	NT	LM
					◇1			◇1			◇1				◇1			◇1			◇1				◇1
			A	A	B		A	C		A	D			A	D		A	D		A	D			A	D
0	Derby 6	d				06 40			07 40				08 40			09 40			10 40				11 40		
1¼	Peartree	d							07 44																
11½	Tutbury & Hatton	d				06 54			07 56				08 56			09 56			10 56				11 56		
19¼	Uttoxeter	d				07 05			08 07				09 07			10 07			11 07				12 07		
30¼	Blythe Bridge	d				07 19			08 21				09 21			10 21			11 21				12 21		
33½	Longton	d				07 25			08 27				09 27			10 27			11 27				12 27		
36	Stoke-on-Trent	a				07 31			08 32				09 33			10 33			11 33				12 33		
—		d	06 30	07 17	07 26	07 33	07 57	08 13	08 34	08 58	09 13		09 34	09 58	10 13	10 34	10 58	11 13	11 34	11 58	12 13		12 34	12 58	13 13
39	Longport	d	06 34	07 21		07 38			08 39				09 39			10 39			11 39				12 39		
42¼	Kidsgrove	d	06a38	07a25	07 34	07 44	08a04	08 21	08 45	09a05	09 21		09 45	10a05	10 21	10 45	11a05	11 21	11 45	12a05	12 21		12 45	13a05	13 21
44½	Alsager	d			07 39	07 48		08 26	08 49		09 26		09 49		10 26	10 49		11 26	11 49		12 26		12 49		13 26
50¾	Crewe 10	a			07 49	07 59		08 38	08 59		09 38		09 59		10 38	10 59		11 38	11 59		12 38		12 59		13 38

		EM	NT	LM	EM	NT	LM		EM	NT	LM	EM	NT	LM	EM	NT	EM		LM	NT	EM	NT	EM	NT	LM
				◇1			◇1				◇1			◇1					◇1						◇1
			A	D		A	D			A	D		A	D		A			D	A		A		A	D
Derby 6	d	12 40			13 40				14 40			15 40			16 40		17 40				18 40		19 40		
Peartree	d														16 45		17 44								
Tutbury & Hatton	d	12 56			13 56				14 56			15 56			16 56		17 56				18 56		19 56		
Uttoxeter	d	13 07			14 07				15 07			16 07			17 07		18 07				19 07		20 07		
Blythe Bridge	d	13 21			14 21				15 21			16 21			17 21		18 21				19 21		20 21		
Longton	d	13 27			14 27				15 27			16 27			17 27		18 27				19 27		20 27		
Stoke-on-Trent	a	13 33			14 33				15 33			16 33			17 33		18 32				19 33		20 33		
	d	13 34	13 58	14 13	14 34	14 58	15 13		15 34	15 58	16 13	16 34	16 58	17 13	17 34	17 58	18 34		18 43	18 58	19 34	19 58	20 34	20 58	21 05
Longport	d	13 39			14 39				15 39			16 39			17 39		18 39				19 39		20 39		
Kidsgrove	d	13 45	14a05	14 21	14 45	15a05	15 21		15 45	16a05	16 21	16 45	17a05	17 21	17 46	18a05	18 45		18 51	19a05	19 45	20a05	20 45	21a05	21 14
Alsager	d	13 49		14 26	14 49		15 26		15 49		16 26	16 49		17 26	17 50		18 49		18 56		19 49		20 49		21 18
Crewe 10	a	13 59		14 38	14 59		15 38		15 59		16 38	16 59		17 38	17 59		18 59		19 05		19 59		20 59		21 27

		EM	NT
			A
Derby 6	d	20 40	
Peartree	d		
Tutbury & Hatton	d	20 56	
Uttoxeter	d	21 07	
Blythe Bridge	d	21 21	
Longton	d	21 27	
Stoke-on-Trent	a	21 33	
	d	21 34	22 18
Longport	d	21 39	
Kidsgrove	d	21 45	22a25
Alsager	d	21 49	
Crewe 10	a	21 59	

Saturdays

		NT	LM	EM	NT	LM	EM	NT	LM	EM		NT	LM	EM	NT	LM	EM	NT	LM	EM		NT	LM	EM	NT
			◇1			◇1			◇1				◇1			◇1			◇1				◇1		
		A	B		A	C		A	D			A	D		A	D		A	D			A	D		A
Derby 6	d			06 40			07 40			08 40				09 40			10 40			11 40				12 40	
Peartree	d						07 44																		
Tutbury & Hatton	d			06 56			07 56			08 56				09 56			10 56			11 56				12 56	
Uttoxeter	d			07 07			08 07			09 07				10 07			11 07			12 07				13 07	
Blythe Bridge	d			07 21			08 21			09 21				10 21			11 21			12 21				13 21	
Longton	d			07 28			08 27			09 27				10 27			11 27			12 27				13 27	
Stoke-on-Trent	a			07 34			08 32			09 33				10 33			11 33			12 33				13 33	
	d	06 57	07 13	07 34	07 57	08 13	08 34	08 58	09 13	09 34		09 58	10 13	10 34	10 58	11 13	11 34	11 58	12 13	12 34		12 58	13 13	13 34	13 58
Longport	d			07 39			08 39			09 39				10 39			11 39			12 39				13 39	
Kidsgrove	d	07a04	07 21	07 46	08a04	08 21	08 45	09a05	09 21	09 45		10a05	10 21	10 45	11a05	11 21	11 45	12a05	12 21	12 45		13a05	13 21	13 45	14a05
Alsager	d		07 26	07 50		08 26	08 49		09 26	09 49			10 26	10 49		11 26	11 49		12 26	12 49			13 26	13 49	
Crewe 10	a		07 36	07 59		08 37	08 59		09 38	09 59			10 38	10 59		11 38	11 59		12 38	12 59			13 38	13 59	

		LM	EM	NT	LM	EM		NT	LM	EM	NT	LM	EM	NT	EM	LM		NT	LM	EM	NT	LM	EM	NT	LM
		◇1			◇1				◇1			◇1				◇1			◇1			1			1
		D		A	D			A	D		A	D		A		D		A	D		A	D		A	D
Derby 6	d		13 40			14 40				15 40			16 40		17 40					18 40			19 40		
Peartree	d														17 45										
Tutbury & Hatton	d		13 56			14 56				15 56			16 56		17 57					18 56			19 56		
Uttoxeter	d		14 07			15 07				16 07			17 07		18 07					19 07			20 07		
Blythe Bridge	d		14 21			15 21				16 21			17 21		18 21					19 21			20 21		
Longton	d		14 27			15 27				16 27			17 27		18 27					19 27			20 27		
Stoke-on-Trent	a		14 33			15 33				16 33			17 32		18 32					19 33			20 33		
	d	14 13	14 34	14 58	15 13	15 34		15 58	16 13	16 34	16 58	17 13	17 34	17 58	18 34	18 41		18 58	19 13	19 34	19 58	20 13	20 34	20 58	21 15
Longport	d		14 39			15 39				16 39			17 39		18 39					19 39			20 39		
Kidsgrove	d	14 21	14 45	15a05	15 21	15 45		16a05	16 21	16 45	17a05	17 21	17 45	18a05	18 45	18 49		19a05	19 21	19 45	20a05	20 21	20 45	21a05	21 23
Alsager	d	14 26	14 49		15 26	15 49			16 26	16 49		17 26	17 49		18 49	18 54			19 26	19 49		20 26	20 49		21 28
Crewe 10	a	14 38	14 59		15 38	15 59			16 38	16 59		17 38	17 59		18 59	19 05			19 36	19 59		20 36	20 59		21 38

A To Manchester Piccadilly
B From Bletchley
C From Northampton
D From London Euston

Table 50

Saturdays

Derby - Stoke-on-Trent and Crewe

Network Diagram - see first Page of Table 50

		EM		NT A
Derby 6	d	20 40		
Peartree	d			
Tutbury & Hatton	d	20 56		
Uttoxeter	d	21 07		
Blythe Bridge	d	21 21		
Longton	d	21 27		
Stoke-on-Trent	a	21 33		
	d	21 34		22 18
Longport	d	21 39		
Kidsgrove	d	21 45		22a25
Alsager	d	21 49		
Crewe 10	a	21 59		

Sundays

		LM 1 B	LM ◇1 C	EM	LM ◇1 D	NT A	EM	EM	LM ◇1 D	EM		EM	LM ◇1 D	NT A	EM	EM	LM ◇1 D	NT A
Derby 6	d			14 38			15 38	16 38		17 40		18 41			19 38	20 40		
Peartree	d																	
Tutbury & Hatton	d			14 52			15 52	16 52		17 53		18 52			19 52	20 54		
Uttoxeter	d			15 03			16 03	17 03		18 03		19 03			20 03	21 05		
Blythe Bridge	d			15 17			16 17	17 17		18 17		19 17			20 17	21 19		
Longton	d			15 23			16 23	17 23		18 24		19 23			20 23	21 25		
Stoke-on-Trent	a			15 29			16 29	17 29		18 30		19 29			20 30	21 34		
	d	12 03	13 17	15 30	15 41	16 01	16 30	17 30	17 40	18 31		19 30	19 44	20 01	20 30	21 36	21 43	22 39
Longport	d			15 35			16 35	17 35		18 36		19 35			20 35	21 41		
Kidsgrove	d	12 11	13 25	15 41	15 50	16a08	16 41	17 41	17 48	18 41		19 41	19 52	20a08	20 41	21 47	21 52	22a46
Alsager	d	12 15	13 30	15 46	15 54		16 45	17 45	17 53	18 46		19 46	19 56		20 46	21 52	21 57	
Crewe 10	a	12 26	13 43	16 01	16 04		17 02	18 01	18 03	19 01		20 02	20 06		21 01	22 05	22 08	

A To Manchester Piccadilly
B From Stafford
C From Northampton
D From London Euston

Crewe and Stoke-on-Trent - Derby

Network Diagram - see first Page of Table 50

Miles			XC	NT	EM	LM	EM	LM	EM	NT	LM		EM	NT	LM	EM	NT	LM	EM	NT	LM		EM	NT	LM
			◇1			1		1			◇1				◇1			◇1			◇1				◇1
			A	B		C		C		D	C			D	C		D	C		D	C			D	C
0	**Crewe 10**	d	05 47		06 07	06 35	06 58	07 33	08 07		08 33		09 07		09 33	10 07		10 33	11 07		11 33		12 07		12 33
6¼	Alsager	d			06 16	06 44	07 07	07 41	08 16		08 41		09 16		09 41	10 16		10 41	11 16		11 41		12 16		12 41
8½	Kidsgrove	d		06 16	06 21	06 48	07 12	07 46	08 21	08 32	08 46		09 21	09 32	09 46	10 21	10 32	10 46	11 21	11 32	11 46		12 21	12 32	12 46
12	Longport	d			06 27		07 18		08 27				09 27			10 27			11 27				12 27		
15	**Stoke-on-Trent**	a	06 06	06 26	06 31	06 57	07 23	07 54	08 31	08 42	08 54		09 31	09 42	09 54	10 31	10 42	10 54	11 31	11 42	11 54		12 31	12 42	12 54
—		d			06 33		07 24		08 33				09 33			10 33			11 33				12 33		
17½	Longton	d			06 39		07 30		08 39				09 39			10 39			11 39				12 39		
20½	Blythe Bridge	d			06 45		07 37		08 45				09 45			10 45			11 45				12 45		
31½	Uttoxeter	d			06 58		07 49		08 58				09 58			10 58			11 58				12 58		
39½	Tutbury & Hatton	d			07 07		07 58		09 07				10 07			11 07			12 07				13 07		
49½	Peartree	d			07 20																				
50¾	**Derby 6**	a			07 24		08 16		09 24				10 24			11 24			12 24				13 24		

		EM	NT	LM	EM	NT	LM		EM	NT	LM	EM	NT	LM	EM	NT	LM		EM	NT	LM	EM	NT	NT	EM
				◇1			◇1				◇1			◇1			◇1				◇1				
			D	C		D	C			D	C		D	C		D	C			D	E		D	D	
Crewe 10	d	13 07		13 33	14 07		14 33		15 07		15 33	16 07		16 33	17 07		17 33		18 07		18 33	19 07			20 45
Alsager	d	13 16		13 41	14 16		14 41		15 16		15 41	16 16		16 41	17 16		17 41		18 16		18 41	19 16			20 58
Kidsgrove	d	13 21	13 32	13 46	14 21	14 32	14 46		15 21	15 32	15 46	16 21	16 32	16 46	17 21	17 32	17 46		18 21	18 32	18 46	19 21	19 32	20 32	21 07
Longport	d	13 27			14 27				15 27			16 27			17 27				18 27			19 27			21 12
Stoke-on-Trent	a	13 31	13 42	13 54	14 31	14 42	14 54		15 31	15 42	15 54	16 31	16 42	16 54	17 31	17 42	17 54		18 31	18 42	18 54	19 31	19 42	20 42	21 16
	d	13 33			14 33				15 33			16 33			17 33				18 33			19 33			21 18
Longton	d	13 39			14 39				15 39			16 39			17 39				18 39			19 39			21 24
Blythe Bridge	d	13 45			14 45				15 45			16 45			17 45				18 45			19 45			21 29
Uttoxeter	d	13 58			14 58				15 58			16 58			17 58				18 58			19 58			21 42
Tutbury & Hatton	d	14 07			15 07				16 07			17 07			18 07				19 07			20 07			21 51
Peartree	d								16 18																
Derby 6	a	14 24			15 24				16 24			17 24			18 24				19 24			20 24			22 09

		NT	NT
		D	D
Crewe 10	d		
Alsager	d		
Kidsgrove	d	21 32	22 32
Longport	d		
Stoke-on-Trent	a	21 42	22 42
	d		
Longton	d		
Blythe Bridge	d		
Uttoxeter	d		
Tutbury & Hatton	d		
Peartree	d		
Derby 6	a		

Saturdays

		XC	NT	EM	LM	EM	NT	LM	EM	NT		LM	EM	NT	LM	EM	NT	LM	EM	NT		LM	EM	NT	LM
		◇1			◇1			◇1				◇1			◇1			◇1				◇1			◇1
		A	B		C		D	C		D		C		D	C		D	C		D		C		D	C
Crewe 10	d	05 47		06 07	06 38	07 07		07 38	08 07			08 33	09 07		09 33	10 07		10 33	11 07			11 33	12 07		12 33
Alsager	d			06 16	06 47	07 16		07 47	08 16			08 41	09 16		09 41	10 16		10 41	11 16			11 41	12 16		12 41
Kidsgrove	d		06 16	06 21	06 51	07 21	07 28	07 51	08 21	08 32		08 46	09 21	09 32	09 46	10 21	10 32	10 46	11 21	11 32		11 46	12 21	12 32	12 46
Longport	d			06 27		07 27			08 27				09 27			10 27			11 27				12 27		
Stoke-on-Trent	a	06 07	06 26	06 31	06 59	07 31	07 40	07 59	08 31	08 42		08 54	09 31	09 42	09 54	10 31	10 42	10 54	11 31	11 42		11 54	12 31	12 42	12 54
	d			06 33		07 33			08 33				09 33			10 33			11 33				12 33		
Longton	d			06 39		07 39			08 39				09 39			10 39			11 39				12 39		
Blythe Bridge	d			06 45		07 45			08 45				09 45			10 45			11 45				12 45		
Uttoxeter	d			06 58		07 58			08 58				09 58			10 58			11 58				12 58		
Tutbury & Hatton	d			07 07		08 07			09 07				10 07			11 07			12 07				13 07		
Peartree	d			07 19																					
Derby 6	a			07 23		08 22			09 23				10 23			11 23			12 23				13 23		

		EM	NT	LM	EM	NT		LM	EM	NT	LM	EM	NT	LM	EM	NT		LM	EM	NT	LM	EM	NT	NT	EM
				◇1				◇1			◇1			◇1				◇1			◇1				
			D	C		D		C		D	C		D	C		D		E		D	E		D	D	
Crewe 10	d	13 07		13 33	14 07			14 33	15 07		15 33	16 07		16 33	17 07			17 33	18 07		18 33	19 07			20 45
Alsager	d	13 16		13 41	14 16			14 41	15 16		15 41	16 16		16 41	17 16			17 41	18 16		18 41	19 16			20 54
Kidsgrove	d	13 21	13 32	13 46	14 21	14 32		14 46	15 21	15 32	15 46	16 21	16 32	16 46	17 21	17 32		17 46	18 21	18 32	18 46	19 21	19 32	20 32	21 08
Longport	d	13 27			14 27				15 27			16 27			17 27				18 27			19 27			21 14
Stoke-on-Trent	a	13 31	13 42	13 54	14 31	14 42		14 54	15 31	15 42	15 54	16 31	16 42	16 54	17 31	17 42		17 54	18 31	18 42	18 54	19 31	19 42	20 42	21 18
	d	13 33			14 33				15 33			16 33			17 33				18 33			19 33			21 19
Longton	d	13 39			14 39				15 39			16 39			17 39				18 39			19 39			21 25
Blythe Bridge	d	13 45			14 45				15 45			16 45			17 45				18 45			19 45			21 31
Uttoxeter	d	13 58			14 58				15 58			16 58			17 58				18 58			19 58			21 44
Tutbury & Hatton	d	14 07			15 07				16 07			17 07			18 07				19 07			20 07			21 53
Peartree	d								16 19																
Derby 6	a	14 23			15 23				16 23			17 23			18 23				19 23			20 23			22 10

A From Manchester Piccadilly to Bournemouth
B From Macclesfield
C To London Euston
D From Manchester Piccadilly
E To Northampton

Table 50

Saturdays

Crewe and Stoke-on-Trent - Derby

Network Diagram - see first Page of Table 50

		NT		NT
		A		A
Crewe 10	d			
Alsager	d			
Kidsgrove	d	21 32		22 32
Longport	d			
Stoke-on-Trent	a	21 42		22 42
	d			
Longton	d			
Blythe Bridge	d			
Uttoxeter	d			
Tutbury & Hatton	d			
Peartree	d			
Derby 6	a			

Sundays

		LM	LM	LM	EM	EM	NT	LM	EM	EM		LM	EM	EM	NT	LM	EM	EM	NT
		1	◇1	◇1				◇1				◇1				◇1			
		B	C	C			A	C				C			A	C			A
Crewe 10	d	10 38	11 38	13 38	14 04	15 05		15 38	16 08	17 08		17 38	18 08	19 08		19 38	20 08	21 16	
Alsager	d	10 46	11 46	13 47	14 13	15 14		15 46	16 17	17 17		17 46	18 17	19 17		19 46	20 20	21 25	
Kidsgrove	d	10 50	11 50	13 51	14 18	15 21	15 25	15 50	16 22	17 22		17 50	18 22	19 22	19 28	19 50	20 25	21 30	22 26
Longport	d				14 24	15 26			16 29	17 29			18 29	19 29			20 33	21 36	
Stoke-on-Trent	a	10 58	11 58	13 59	14 29	15 30	15 37	15 58	16 35	17 33		17 58	18 34	19 33	19 40	19 58	20 37	21 40	22 36
	d				14 29	15 32			16 35	17 35			18 35	19 35			20 39	21 42	
Longton	d				14 35	15 38			16 41	17 41			18 41	19 41			20 46	21 53	
Blythe Bridge	d				14 41	15 44			16 47	17 47			18 47	19 47			20 52	21 59	
Uttoxeter	d				14 53	15 56			16 59	17 59			18 59	19 59			21 04	22 12	
Tutbury & Hatton	d				15 02	16 06			17 08	18 08			19 08	20 08			21 13	22 21	
Peartree	d																		
Derby 6	a				15 17	16 25			17 27	18 27			19 27	20 27			21 33	22 40	

A From Manchester Piccadilly

B To Stafford

C To London Euston

Route Diagram for Table 51

DM-5/10
Design BAJS

This Table summarises through services which, with their associated connecting services at Birmingham New Street, link centres in the North and South of the country. In certain instances a faster journey is possible via London and the relevant Table(s) should be consulted.

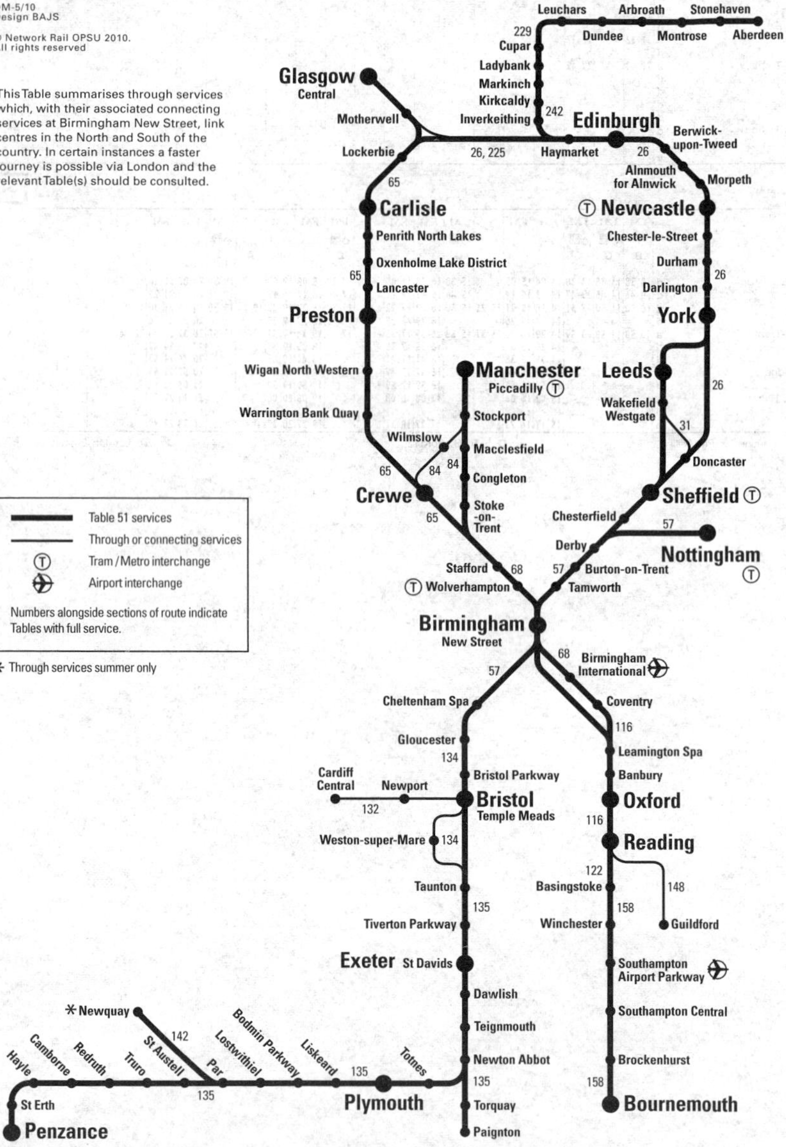

* Through services summer only

Scotland, The North East, North West England - The South West and South Coast

Route Diagram - see first Page of Table 51

		XC MX	XC	XC	XC	XC	XC	XC	XC	XC	XC	XC	VT	XC	XC	XC	XC	XC	XC	VT	XC	XC MO	XC MX
		◇1	◇1	◇1	◇1	◇1	◇1	◇1	◇1	◇1	◇1	◇1	◇1	◇1	◇1	◇1	◇1	◇1	1	◇1	◇1	◇1	◇1
		A							B	C				B		C							
		⌶			⌶		⌶	⌶	⌶	⌶		⌶	⊠	⌶	⌶	⌶	⌶	⌶		⊠	⌶	⌶	⌶
Aberdeen	d																						
Stonehaven	d																						
Montrose	d																						
Arbroath	d																						
Dundee	d																						
Leuchars 3	d																						
Cupar	d																						
Ladybank	d																						
Markinch	d																						
Kirkcaldy	d																						
Inverkeithing	d																						
Glasgow Central 15	d																						
Motherwell	d																						
Haymarket	d																						
Edinburgh 10	d	17p08																					
Haymarket	d																						
Lockerbie	d																						
Carlisle 8	d																						
Penrith North Lakes	d																						
Oxenholme Lake District	d																						
Lancaster 6	d																			06 58			
Preston 8	d												06 16							07 17			
Wigan North Western	d												06 27							07 28			
Warrington Bank Quay	d												06 38							07 39			
M'chester Piccadilly 10	d							05 11				06 00						07 07			07 26		
Stockport	d											06 08						07 16			07 35		
Wilmslow	d																						
Crewe 10	d							05 47				06 38	07 01							08 01			
Macclesfield	d																				07 49		
Congleton	d																						
Stoke-on-Trent	d							06 07										07 44			08 07		
Stafford	d							06 25				06 58						08 02			08 25		
Wolverhampton 7	d							06 41				07 15	07 32					08 16		08 32	08 41		
Dunbar	d	17p28																					
Berwick-upon-Tweed	d	17p51																					
Alnmouth for Alnwick	d																						
Morpeth	d																						
Newcastle 8	d	18p41																					
Chester-le-Street	d																						
Durham	d	18p53																					
Darlington 7	d	19p10																					
York 8	d	19p44																				06 32	06 32
Leeds 10	d	20p11													06 00		06 15					07 05	07 05
Wakefield Westgate 7	d	20p23													06 12		06 27					07 18	07 18
Doncaster 7	d																06 45						
Sheffield 7	d	20p54									06 01				06f50		07g18					07 53	07 53
Chesterfield	d	21p06									06 27				07 04		07 30					08 06	08 06
Nottingham 8	d									06 00				06 37		06 56			07 37				
Derby 6	d	21p29							06 10	06 36	06 48			07 06	07 27	07 36	07 50		08 06			08 28	08 28
Burton-on-Trent	d	21p40							06 20	06 48	06 58			07 18	07 38	07 50	08 00		08 18			08 38	08 38
Tamworth	d	21p50							06 31	07 01	07 09			07 30	07 50	08 03	08 11		08 30			08 49	08 50
Birmingham New Street 12	a	22p07						06 58	06 52	07 25	07 27	07 31	07 55	07 54	08 08	08 24	08 27	08 32	08 54	08 55	08 58	09 09	09 09
Birmingham New Street 12	d	22p12	05 00	05 42	06 04	06 33	06 42	07 04	07 12	07 30	07 33	07 42		08 04	08 12	08 30	08 33	08 42			09 04	09 12	09 12
Cheltenham Spa	a	23p30	06 01	06 43			07 21		07 51	08 14		08 23			08 51	09 11		09 23				09 51	09 51
Gloucester 7	a		06 16	06 53						08 27						09 22							
Bristol Parkway 7	a	00 01					07 57		08 25			08 54			09 24			09 54				10 25	10 25
Bristol Temple Meads 10	a	00 13					08 08		08 40			09 14			09 38			10 08				10 41	10 41
Newport (South Wales)	a		07 09	07 52						09 12						10 09							
Cardiff Central 7	a		07 26	08 08						09 30						10 25							
Weston-super-Mare	a																						
Taunton	a						08 41		09 15						10 16							11 16	11 16
Tiverton Parkway	a						08 54		09 28						10 29							11 29	11 29
Exeter St Davids 6	a						09 08		09 42						10 45							11 45	11 45
Dawlish	a																						
Teignmouth	a																						
Newton Abbot	a						09 29		10 02						11 06							12 06	12 06
Torquay	a						09 40																
Paignton	a						09 47																
Totnes	a								10 16						11 20							12 20	12 20
Plymouth	a								10 46						11 48							12 49	12 49
Liskeard 6	a																						
Bodmin Parkway	a																						
Lostwithiel	a																						
Par	a																						
Newquay (Summer Only)	a																						
St Austell	a																						
Truro	a																						
Redruth	a																						
Camborne	a																						
Hayle	a																						
St Erth	a																						
Penzance	a																						
Birmingham International	d				06 14			07 14						08 14							09 14		
Coventry	d				06 25			07 25						08 25							09 25		
Leamington Spa 8	d				06 38	07 00		07 38			08 04			08 38			09 00				09 38		
Banbury	a				06 56	07 21		07 54			08 20			08 54			09 18				09 54		
Oxford	a				07 14	07 41		08 14			08 41			09 14			09 41				10 14		
Reading 7	a				07 39	08 10		08 39			09 11			09 39			10 10				10 39		
Guildford	a																						
Basingstoke	a				08 08	08 40		09 08						10 08			10 39				11 08		
Winchester	a				08 24	08 56		09 24						10 24			10 54				11 24		
Southampton Airport Pkway	a				08 32	09 08		09 32						10 32			11 08				11 32		
Southampton Central	a				08 44	09 17		09 41						10 43			11 16				11 43		
Brockenhurst 3	a				08 59			09 56						10 58							11 58		
Bournemouth	a				09 14			10 12						11 12							12 12		

A from 27 March. ⌶ to Leeds

B ⌶ from Birmingham New Street

C ⌶ from Birmingham New Street to Newport (South Wales)

Scotland, The North East, North West England - The South West and South Coast

Route Diagram - see first Page of Table 51

		XC	XC	XC	XC	VT	XC	XC	XC	XC	XC	XC	XC	XC	XC	XC	XC	XC	VT	XC	XC	XC	XC
		◇1	◇1	◇1	1	◇1	◇1	◇1	◇1	◇1	◇1	1	◇1	◇1	◇1	◇1	◇1	1	◇1	◇1	◇1	◇1	◇1
		A							A						A						B	C	A
		🍴	🍴	🍴		⊠	🍴	🍴	🍴	🍴	🍴		🍴	🍴	🍴	🍴	🍴		⊠	🍴	🍴	🍴	🍴
Aberdeen	d																						
Stonehaven	d																						
Montrose	d																						
Arbroath	d																						
Dundee	d																						
Leuchars 3	d																						
Cupar	d																						
Ladybank	d																						
Markinch	d																						
Kirkcaldy	d																						
Inverkeithing	d																						
Glasgow Central 15	d					05 50													08 00		06 01	06 01	
Motherwell	d					06 04															06 16	06 16	
Haymarket	d																				06 57	06 57	
Edinburgh 10	d													06 06		07 00					07 07	07 07	
Haymarket	d																						
Lockerbie	d																						
Carlisle 8	d					07 04													09 10				
Penrith North Lakes	d					07 19																	
Oxenholme Lake District	d					07 42																	
Lancaster 6	d					07 57													09 57				
Preston 8	d					08 17													10 17				
Wigan North Western	d					08 28													10 28				
Warrington Bank Quay	d					08 39													10 39				
M'chester Piccadilly 10 ⛴	d			08 07			08 27				09 07		09 27				10 07			10 27			
Stockport	d			08 16			08 35				09 16		09 35				10 16			10 35			
Wilmslow	d																						
Crewe 10	d					09 01													11 01				
Macclesfield	d						08 49						09 49							10 49			
Congleton	d																						
Stoke-on-Trent	d			08 44			09 07				09 44		10 07				10 44			11 07			
Stafford	d			09 03			09 25				10 03		10 25				11 02			11 25			
Wolverhampton 7 ⛴	d			09 16		09 32	09 41				10 17		10 41				11 16		11 32	11 41			
Dunbar	d																				07 27	07 27	
Berwick-upon-Tweed	d													06 46		07 39							
Alnmouth for Alnwick	d													07 08		07 59							
Morpeth	d															08 13							
Newcastle 8	d		06 25					06 44		07 25				07 41		08 35					08 43	08 43	
Chester-le-Street	d																						
Durham	d		06 37					06 56		07 37				07 55		08 47					08 56	08 56	
Darlington 7	d		06 54					07 14		07 54				08 12		09 04					09 13	09 13	
York 8	d		07 23					07 44		08 24				08 44		09 35					09 45	09 45	
Leeds 10	d							08 11						09 11							10 11	10 11	
Wakefield Westgate 7	d							08 23						09 24							10 23	10 23	
Doncaster 7	d		07 55							08 50						09 58							
Sheffield 7 ⛴	d		08 20					08 54		09 23				09 54		10 23					10 54	10 54	
Chesterfield	d		08 32					09 06						10 06							11 06	11 06	
Nottingham 8 ⛴	d	08 08			08 37				09 11			09 37			10 11			10 37					11 08
Derby 6	d	08 36	08 53		09 10			09 28	09 36	09 53		10 10		10 28	10 37	10 53		11 10			11 28	11 28	11 36
Burton-on-Trent	d	08 49			09 21			09 38	09 49			10 21			10 49			11 21					11 49
Tamworth	d	09 02			09 33				10 02			10 33		10 48	11 02			11 33					12 02
Birmingham New Street 12	a	09 24	09 27	09 32	09 54	09 55	09 58	10 07	10 24	10 27	10 39	10 54	10 58	11 08	11 24	11 27	11 32	11 54	11 55	11 58	12 07	12 07	12 24
Birmingham New Street 12	d	09 30	09 33	09 42			10 04	10 12	10 30	10 33	10 42		11 04	11 12	11 30	11 33	11 42			12 04	12 12	12 12	12 30
Cheltenham Spa	a	10 10		10 23				10 50	11 10		11 23			11 51	12 10		12 23				12 50	12 50	13 10
Gloucester 7	a	10 22							11 22						12 22								13 22
Bristol Parkway 7	a			10 54				11 26			11 54			12 28			12 55				13 25	13 25	
Bristol Temple Meads 10	a			11 12				11 37			12 08			12 40			13 10				13 38	13 38	
Newport (South Wales)	a	11 11							12 10						13 11								14 09
Cardiff Central 7	a	11 27							12 28						13 29								14 29
Weston-super-Mare	a			11 32																			
Taunton	a			12 00				12 15						13 16							14 15	14 15	
Tiverton Parkway	a			12 13				12 28						13 29							14 28	14 28	
Exeter St Davids 6	a			12 30				12 42						13 45							14 42	14 42	
Dawlish	a			12 43																			
Teignmouth	a			12 48																			
Newton Abbot	a			12 55				13 02						14 06							15 02	15 02	
Torquay	a			13 06																			
Paignton	a			13 14																			
Totnes	a							13 15						14 20							15 15	15 15	
Plymouth	a							13 41						14 48							15 41	15 41	
Liskeard 6	a																						
Bodmin Parkway	a																						
Lostwithiel	a																						
Par	a																						
Newquay (Summer Only)	a																						
St Austell	a																						
Truro	a																						
Redruth	a																						
Camborne	a																						
Hayle	a																						
St Erth	a																						
Penzance	a																						
Birmingham International ✈	d						10 14						11 14							12 14			
Coventry	d						10 25						11 25							12 25			
Leamington Spa 8	d		10 00				10 38			11 00			11 38			12 00				12 38			
Banbury	a		10 17				10 54			11 17			11 54			12 17				12 54			
Oxford	a		10 41				11 14			11 40			12 14			12 40				13 14			
Reading 7	a		11 07				11 39			12 10			12 39			13 07				13 39			
Guildford	a																						
Basingstoke	a						12 08			12 39			13 08							14 08			
Winchester	a						12 24			12 54			13 24							14 24			
Southampton Airport Pkwy ✈	a						12 32			13 08			13 32							14 34			
Southampton Central ⛴	a						12 41			13 17			13 41							14 42			
Brockenhurst 3	a						12 56						13 56							14 56			
Bournemouth	a						13 10						14 10							15 11			

A 🍴 to Newport (South Wales)

B until 10 February. 🍴 from Edinburgh

C from 13 February

Scotland, The North East, North West England - The South West and South Coast

Route Diagram - see first Page of Table 51

		XC	XC	XC	VT	XC	XC	XC	XC	XC	XC	VT	XC	XC	XC	XC	XC	XC	VT	XC	XC	XC
		◇[1]	◇[1]	[1]	◇[1]	◇[1]	◇[1]	◇[1]	◇[1]	◇[1]	[1]	◇[1]	◇[1]	◇[1]	◇[1]	◇[1]	◇[1]	[1]	◇[1]	◇[1]	◇[1]	◇[1]
							A	B						A	B						C	D
		╤	╤	╤	⊠	╤	╤	╤	╤	╤	╤	⊏⊐	╤	╤	╤	╤	╤	╤	⊠	╤	╤	╤
Aberdeen	d																					
Stonehaven	d																					
Montrose	d																					
Arbroath	d																					
Dundee	d						06 32															
Leuchars [3]	d						06 46															
Cupar	d						06 54															
Ladybank	d						07 03															
Markinch	d						07 11															
Kirkcaldy	d						07 21															
Inverkeithing	d						07 43															
Glasgow Central [15]	d											10 00		07 50							09 00	
Motherwell	d													08 05							09 15	
Haymarket	d						08 01							08 50							09 58	
Edinburgh [10]	d				08 52		08 10							09 08					10 51		10 10	
Haymarket	d				08 57														10 57			
Lockerbie	d																					
Carlisle [8]	d				10 07							11 11							12 07			
Penrith North Lakes	d											11 26										
Oxenholme Lake District	d				10 42														12 43			
Lancaster [6]	d				10 57														12 57			
Preston [8]	d				11 17							12 17							13 17			
Wigan North Western	d				11 28							12 28							13 28			
Warrington Bank Quay	d				11 39							12 39							13 39			
M'chester Piccadilly [10] ⛴	d		11 07			11 27				12 07			12 27				13 07			13 27		
Stockport	d		11 16			11 35				12 16			12 35				13 16			13 35		
Wilmslow	d																					
Crewe [10]	d				12 01							13 01							14 01			
Macclesfield	d					11 49							12 49							13 49		
Congleton	d																					
Stoke-on-Trent	d		11 44			12 07				12 44			13 07				13 44			14 07		
Stafford	d		12 03			12 25				13 02			13 25				14 02			14 25		
Wolverhampton [7] ⛴	d		12 17		12 32	12 41				13 16		13 32	13 41				14 16		14 32	14 41		
Dunbar	d													09 28								
Berwick-upon-Tweed	d						08 50							09 51							10 49	
Alnmouth for Alnwick	d																					
Morpeth	d																				11 21	
Newcastle [8]	d	09 35					09 41		10 35					10 44		11 35					11 44	
Chester-le-Street	d																					
Durham	d	09 47					09 55		10 47					10 56		11 47					11 56	
Darlington [7]	d	10 05					10 12		11 04					11 13		12 05					12 13	
York [8]	d	10 34					10 44		11 34					11 45		12 34					12 44	
Leeds [10]	d						11 11							12 12							13 11	
Wakefield Westgate [7]	d						11 24							12 24							13 23	
Doncaster [7]	d	10 58							11 58							12 59						
Sheffield [7] ⛴	d	11 23					11 54		12 23					12 54		13 23					13 54	
Chesterfield	d						12 06							13 06							14 07	
Nottingham [8] ⛴	d			11 37				12 08			12 37				13 11			13 37				14 11
Derby [6]	d	11 53		12 10			12 28	12 36	12 53		13 06			13 28	13 36	13 53		14 10			14 28	14 36
Burton-on-Trent	d			12 21				12 49			13 21			13 38	13 49			14 21				14 49
Tamworth	d			12 33			12 48	13 02			13 33				14 02			14 33			14 47	15 02
Birmingham New Street [12]	a	12 27	12 39	12 54	12 55	12 58	13 07	13 24	13 27	13 39	13 54	13 55	13 58	14 06	14 24	14 27	14 32	14 54	14 55	14 58	15 07	15 24
Birmingham New Street [12]	d	12 33	12 42			13 04	13 12	13 30	13 33	13 42			14 04	14 12	14 30	14 33	14 42			15 04	15 12	15 30
Cheltenham Spa	a		13 23				13 53	14 10		14 23				14 50	15 10		15 23				15 50	16 10
Gloucester [7]	a							14 22							15 22							16 22
Bristol Parkway [7]	a		13 57				14 27			14 57				15 25			15 56				16 27	
Bristol Temple Meads [10]	a		14 09				14 41			15 10				15 39			16 08				16 40	
Newport (South Wales)	a							15 11							16 10							17 11
Cardiff Central [7]	a							15 29							16 29							17 28
Weston-super-Mare	a																					
Taunton	a						15 16			15 44				16 15							17 15	
Tiverton Parkway	a						15 29			15 57				16 28							17 28	
Exeter St Davids [6]	a						15 46			16 13				16 42							17 42	
Dawlish	a																					
Teignmouth	a																					
Newton Abbot	a						16 07							17 02							18 10	
Torquay	a																					
Paignton	a																					
Totnes	a						16 21							17 15							18 23	
Plymouth	a						16 49							17 42							18 50	
Liskeard [6]	a																				19 23	
Bodmin Parkway	a																				19 35	
Lostwithiel	a																					
Par	a																				19 46	
Newquay (Summer Only)	a																					
St Austell	a																				19 53	
Truro	a																				20 10	
Redruth	a																				20 25	
Camborne	a																				20 31	
Hayle	a																					
St Erth	a																				20 42	
Penzance	a																				20 52	
Birmingham International ✈	d					13 14							14 14							15 14		
Coventry	d					13 25							14 25							15 25		
Leamington Spa [8]	d	13 00				13 38			14 00				14 38			15 00				15 38		
Banbury	a	13 20				13 54			14 17				14 54			15 17				15 54		
Oxford	a	13 40				14 14			14 40				15 14			15 41				16 14		
Reading [7]	a	14 10				14 39			15 07				15 39			16 10				16 39		
Guildford	a																					
Basingstoke	a	14 39				15 08							16 08			16 39				17 08		
Winchester	a	14 54				15 24							16 24			16 59				17 24		
Southampton Airport Pkway ✈	a	15 08				15 32							16 32							17 32		
Southampton Central ⛴	a	15 17				15 41							16 41			17 17				17 41		
Brockenhurst [3]	a					15 56							16 56							17 56		
Bournemouth	a					16 10							17 10							18 15		

A ╤ from Edinburgh

B ╤ from Birmingham New Street to Newport (South Wales)

C ╤ from Edinburgh to Plymouth

D ╤ to Newport (South Wales)

Scotland, The North East, North West England - The South West and South Coast

Route Diagram - see first Page of Table 51

		XC	XC	XC	XC	XC	XC	XC	XC	XC	VT	XC	XC	XC	XC	XC	XC	VT	XC	XC	XC	XC	XC
		◇1	◇1	1	◇1	◇1	◇1	◇1	◇1	1	◇1	◇1	◇1	◇1	◇1	◇1	1	◇1	◇1	◇1	◇1	◇1	◇1
						A							B							C	D		
		🛒	🛒	🛒	🛒	🛒		🛒	🛒	🛒	☕	🛒	🛒		🛒	🛒	🛒	☕	🛒	🛒	🛒		🛒
																				FO			
Aberdeen	d					08 20																	
Stonehaven	d					08 38																	
Montrose	d					08 59																	
Arbroath	d					09 15																	
Dundee	d					09 32																	
Leuchars 3	d					09 47																	
Cupar	d					09 54																	
Ladybank	d					10 01																	
Markinch	d					10 09																	
Kirkcaldy	d					10 17																	
Inverkeithing	d					10 32																	
Glasgow Central 15	d												10 59					14 00					
Motherwell	d												11 14										
Haymarket	d					10 54							11 57										
Edinburgh 10	d					11 05					12 51		12 08							13 06	13 06		
Haymarket	d										12 57												
Lockerbie	d																						
Carlisle 8	d										14 07							15 09					
Penrith North Lakes	d										14 22												
Oxenholme Lake District	d																	15 44					
Lancaster 6	d										14 57												
Preston 8	d										15 17							16 17					
Wigan North Western	d										15 28							16 28					
Warrington Bank Quay	d										15 39							16 39					
M'chester Piccadilly 10 ⛴	d		14 07		14 27				15 07			15 27				16 07			16 27				
Stockport	d		14 16		14 35				15 16			15 35				16 16			16 35				
Wilmslow	d																						
Crewe 10	d										16 01							17 01					
Macclesfield	d				14 49							15 49							16 49				
Congleton	d																						
Stoke-on-Trent	d		14 44		15 07				15 44			16 07				16 44			17 07				
Stafford	d		15 03		15 25				16 03			16 25				17 03			17 25				
Wolverhampton 7 ⛴	d		15 17		15 41				16 17		16 32	16 41				17 16		17 32	17 41				
Dunbar	d					11 25														13 28	13 28		
Berwick-upon-Tweed	d					11 48							12 47										
Alnmouth for Alnwick	d					12 08														14 08	14 08		
Morpeth	d																						
Newcastle 8	d	12 35				12 41		13 35					13 42		14 35					14 42	14 42		15 03
Chester-le-Street	d																						
Durham	d	12 47				12 53		13 47					13 54		14 47					14 55	14 55		15 16
Darlington 7	d	13 04				13 11		14 05					14 11		15 04					15 12	15 12		15 33
York 8	d	13 34				13 44		14 34					14 44		15 34					15 44	15 44		16 04
Leeds 10	d					14 11							15 11							16 11	16 11		16 40
Wakefield Westgate 7	d					14 23							15 23							16 23	16 23		16 52
Doncaster 7	d	13 58						14 58							15 58								
Sheffield 7 ⛴	d	14 23				14 54		15 23					15 54		16 23					16 54	16 54		17 23
Chesterfield	d					15 06							16 06							17 06	17 06		
Nottingham 8 ⛴	d			14 37			15 11			15 37				16 08			16 37					17 08	
Derby 6	d	14 53		15 10		15 28	15 36	15 53		16 10			16 28	16 36	16 53		17 06			17 28	17 28	17 36	17 53
Burton-on-Trent	d			15 24		15 38	15 49			16 21				16 49			17 21			17 38	17 38	17 49	
Tamworth	d			15 35			16 02			16 33			16 47	17 02			17 33					18 02	
Birmingham New Street 12	a	15 27	15 39	15 54	15 58	16 04	16 24	16 27	16 39	16 54	16 55	16 58	17 09	17 24	17 27	17 32	17 52	17 55	17 58	18 08	18 07	18 24	18 27
Birmingham New Street 12	d	15 33	15 42		16 04	16 12	16 30	16 33	16 42			17 04	17 12	17 30	17 33	17 42			18 04	18 12	18 12	18 30	18 33
Cheltenham Spa	a		16 23			16 50	17 13		17 23				17 50	18 18		18 23				18 51	18 51	19 13	
Gloucester 7	a						17 26							18 29								19 27	
Bristol Parkway 7	a		16 56			17 25			17 58				18 28			18 55				19 27	19 27		
Bristol Temple Meads 10	a		17 10			17 39			18 10				18 41			19 06				19 38	19 38		
Newport (South Wales)	a						18 10							19 16								20 11	
Cardiff Central 7	a						18 27							19 33								20 27	
Weston-super-Mare	a																						
Taunton	a		17 44			18 15							19 15							20 16	20 16		
Tiverton Parkway	a		17 56			18 28							19 28							20 29	20 29		
Exeter St Davids 6	a		18 11			18 42							19 42							20 44	20 44		
Dawlish	a		18 23																				
Teignmouth	a		18 28																				
Newton Abbot	a		18 35			19 07							20 04							21 03	21 03		
Torquay	a		18 47																				
Paignton	a		18 55																				
Totnes	a					19 20							20 17							21 17	21 17		
Plymouth	a					19 46							20 44							21 48	21 48		
Liskeard 6	a					20 11							21 13										
Bodmin Parkway	a					20 23							21 25										
Lostwithiel	a												21 31										
Par	a					20 35							21 39										
Newquay (Summer Only)	a																						
St Austell	a					20 41							21 45										
Truro	a					21 00							22 03										
Redruth	a					21 15							22 14										
Camborne	a					21 22							22 21										
Hayle	a												22 29										
St Erth	a					21 33							22 34										
Penzance	a					21 42							22 43										
Birmingham International ✈	d				16 14							17 14							18 14				
Coventry	d				16 25							17 25							18 25				
Leamington Spa 8	d	16 00			16 38			17 00				17 38			18 00				18 38				19 00
Banbury	a	16 17			16 54			17 17				17 54			18 18				18 54				19 17
Oxford	a	16 40			17 14			17 39				18 14			18 40				19 14				19 39
Reading 7	a	17 07			17 39			18 09				18 39			19 07				19 39				20 10
Guildford	a																						
Basingstoke	a				18 08			18 47				19 08							20 09				
Winchester	a				18 24			19 08				19 24							20 24				
Southampton Airport Pkway ✈	a				18 32							19 32							20 32				
Southampton Central ⛴	a				18 44							19 41							20 41				
Brockenhurst 3	a				18 58							19 56							20 58				
Bournemouth	a				19 13							20 12							21 15				

A 🛒 from Edinburgh to Plymouth

B 🛒 to Plymouth

C from 17 February until 23 March

D until 16 February, FX from 20 February until 22 March and then from 26 March

Scotland, The North East, North West England - The South West and South Coast

Route Diagram - see first Page of Table 51

		XC	XC	VT	XC	XC	XC	XC	XC	XC	VT	XC	XC	XC	XC	XC	XC	LM	XC	VT	XC	XC
														FO	FX							
				R																R		
		◇1	1	1	◇1	◇1	◇1	◇1	◇1	1	◇1	◇1	◇1	◇1	◇1	◇1	◇1	◇1	1	1	◇1	◇1
		A			B	C			A			D	A			D	D				D	E
		🛒	🛒	🍽	🛒	🛒		🛒	🛒	🛒	🍽	🛒	🛒			🛒	🛒			🍽	🛒	🛒
Aberdeen	d																					
Stonehaven	d																					
Montrose	d																					
Arbroath	d																					
Dundee	d																					
Leuchars 3	d																					
Cupar	d																					
Ladybank	d																					
Markinch	d																					
Kirkcaldy	d																					
Inverkeithing	d																					
Glasgow Central 15	d					12 51					16 00											15 00
Motherwell	d					13 06																15 14
Haymarket	d																					15 56
Edinburgh 10	d			14 51		14 08							15 08							16 52		16 05
Haymarket	d			14 57																16 57		
Lockerbie	d																					
Carlisle 8	d			16 07							17 09									18 07		
Penrith North Lakes	d			16 21																		
Oxenholme Lake District	d										17 44									18 42		
Lancaster 6	d			16 57																18 57		
Preston 8	d			17 17							18 17									19 16		
Wigan North Western	d			17 28							18 28									19 29		
Warrington Bank Quay	d			17 39							18 39									19 39		
M'chester Piccadilly 10 🚌	d	17 05			17 27				18 05			18 27					19 07				19 27	
Stockport	d	17 13			17 35				18 13			18 35					19 16				19 35	
Wilmslow	d				17 44																	
Crewe 10	d			18 01	18 07						19 01							19 55		20 01		
Macclesfield	d	17 27							18 26												19 49	
Congleton	d											18 54										
Stoke-on-Trent	d	17 44							18 44			19 07					19 44				20 07	
Stafford	d	18 04			18 28				19 02			19 25					20 04	20 16			20 26	
Wolverhampton 7 🚌	d	18 16		18 32	18 41				19 16		19 33	19 41					20 17	20 29		20 34	20 43	
Dunbar	d												15 28									
Berwick-upon-Tweed	d					14 49																
Alnmouth for Alnwick	d																					17 01
Morpeth	d																					17 16
Newcastle 8	d					15 41		16 35					16 42			17 32						17 41
Chester-le-Street	d															17 41						
Durham	d					15 53		16 47					16 52			17 48						17 53
Darlington 7	d					16 10		17 04					17 10			18 05						18 10
York 8	d					16 44		17 34					17 44			18 34						18 45
Leeds 10	d					17 11							18 11									19 11
Wakefield Westgate 7	d					17 23							18 23									19 23
Doncaster 7	d							17 59								18 58						
Sheffield 7 🚌	d					17 54		18 23					18 54			19 23						19 54
Chesterfield	d					18 07							19 06									20 06
Nottingham 8 🚌	d		17 37				18 08			18 37				19 08	19 08				19 37			
Derby 6	d		18 10			18 28	18 37	18 53		19 10			19 28	19 36	19 36	19 54			20 10			20 28
Burton-on-Trent	d		18 22				18 49			19 21			19 38	19 49	19 49				20 21			
Tamworth	d		18 34			18 47	19 02			19 33				20 02	20 02				20 33			20 47
Birmingham New Street 12	a	18 38	18 54	18 55	18 58	19 08	19 24	19 27	19 32	19 54	19 55	19 58	20 09	20 24	20 24	20 27	20 33	20 47	20 54	20 55	21 00	21 07
Birmingham New Street 12	d	18 42			19 04	19 12	19 30	19 33	19 42			20 04	20 12	20 30	20 30	20 33	20 42				21 04	21 12
Cheltenham Spa	a	19 23				19 50	20 10		20 23				20 51	21 10	21 10		21 25					21 51
Gloucester 7	a						20 22							21 22	21 22							22 01
Bristol Parkway 7	a	19 56				20 27			20 55				21 25				22 01					22 32
Bristol Temple Meads 10	a	20 09				20 40			21 07				21 36				22 13					22 44
Newport (South Wales)	a	20 47					21 11							22 15	22 15							
Cardiff Central 7	a	21 02					21 27							22 31	22 35							
Weston-super-Mare	a																					
Taunton	a					21 16			21 43				22 15									
Tiverton Parkway	a					21 29			21 56				22 28									
Exeter St Davids 6	a					21 43			22 11				22 43									
Dawlish	a																					
Teignmouth	a																					
Newton Abbot	a					22 04			22 30				23 05									
Torquay	a																					
Paignton	a																					
Totnes	a					22 16			22 43				23 18									
Plymouth	a					22 43			23 14				23 45									
Liskeard 6	a																					
Bodmin Parkway	a																					
Lostwithiel	a																					
Par	a																					
Newquay (Summer Only)	a																					
St Austell	a																					
Truro	a																					
Redruth	a																					
Camborne	a																					
Hayle	a																					
St Erth	a																					
Penzance	a																					
Birmingham International ✈	d				19 14							20 14									21 14	
Coventry	d				19 25							20 25									21 25	
Leamington Spa 8	d				19 38			20 05				20 38				21 00					21 38	
Banbury	a				19 54			20 22				20 54				21 17					21 54	
Oxford	a				20 14			20 40				21 14				21 40					22 14	
Reading 7	a				20 39			21 07				21 40				22 17					22 41	
Guildford	a															22 59						
Basingstoke	a				21 09							22 09									23 06	
Winchester	a				21 24							22 24									23 24	
Southampton Airport Pkwy ✈	a				21 32							22 32									23 36	
Southampton Central ⛴	a				21 41							22 42									23 43	
Brockenhurst 3	a				21 56							22 56										
Bournemouth	a				22 16							23 21										

A 🛒 to Bristol Temple Meads
B 🛒 to Reading
C 🛒 from Edinburgh to Bristol Temple Meads
D 🛒 to Birmingham New Street
E 🛒 from Edinburgh to Birmingham New Street

Table 51

Mondays to Fridays

Scotland, The North East, North West England - The South West and South Coast

Route Diagram - see first Page of Table 51

		XC	XC	VT	XC	XC	XC	XC	XC	XC	VT	XC	XC	XC	XC	XC
		◇1	◇1	◇1	1	◇1	◇1	◇1	◇1	◇1	◇1	◇1	1	◇1	◇1	◇1
								A	B	C				D	E	F
		⚲		🛏				⚲	⚲	⚲	🛏			⚲		FX
Aberdeen	d															
Stonehaven	d															
Montrose	d															
Arbroath	d															
Dundee	d															
Leuchars 3	d															
Cupar	d															
Ladybank	d															
Markinch	d															
Kirkcaldy	d															
Inverkeithing	d															
Glasgow Central 15	d			17 40										16 52		
Motherwell	d													17 14		
Haymarket	d													17 54		
Edinburgh 10	d							17 08	17 08		18 52			18 04		
Haymarket	d										18 57					
Lockerbie	d			18 35												
Carlisle 8	d			18 54							20 08					
Penrith North Lakes	d			19 09												
Oxenholme Lake District	d			19 32							20 42					
Lancaster 6	d			19 47							20 57					
Preston 8	d			20 08							21 17					
Wigan North Western	d			20 19							21 28					
Warrington Bank Quay	d			20 31							21 39					
M'chester Piccadilly 10 ⛴	d		20 07			20 27						21 27			22 07	22 07
Stockport	d		20 16			20 35						21 35			22 16	22 16
Wilmslow	d															
Crewe 10	d			20 53							22 01					
Macclesfield	d					20 49						21 49			22 29	22 29
Congleton	d															
Stoke-on-Trent	d		20 44			21 07						22 08			22 47	22 47
Stafford	d		21 03	21 13		21 25						22 26			23 07	23 10
Wolverhampton 7 ⛴	d		21 16	21 32		21 41					22 32	22 41			23 21	23 23
Dunbar	d							17 28	17 28					18 25		
Berwick-upon-Tweed	d							17 51	17 51					18 48		
Alnmouth for Alnwick	d													19 08		
Morpeth	d															
Newcastle 8	d	18 35						18 41	18 41	19 33				19 40		
Chester-le-Street	d															
Durham	d	18 47						18 53	18 53	19 48				19 53		
Darlington 7	d	19 05						19 10	19 10	20 05				20 10		
York 8	d	19 34						19 44	19 44	20 34				20 44		
Leeds 10	d							20 11	20 11					21 11		
Wakefield Westgate 7	d							20 23	20 23					21 23		
Doncaster 7	d	19 58								21 02						
Sheffield 7 ⛴	d	20 23						20 54	20 54	21 28				22 00		
Chesterfield	d							21 06	21 06	21 41				22 24		
Nottingham 8 ⛴	d				20 37								21 37			
Derby 6	d	20 54			21 06			21 29	21 29	22 02			22 10	22 45		
Burton-on-Trent	d				21 21			21 40	21 40				22 21	22 56		
Tamworth	d				21 33			21 50	21 50				22 33	23 06		
Birmingham New Street 12	a	21 29	21 32	21 48	21 54	22 00		22 09	22 07	22 51	22 55	22 58	23 00	23 25	23 39	23 40
Birmingham New Street 12	d						22 04	22 12	22 12							
Cheltenham Spa	a							22 51	23 30							
Gloucester 7	a															
Bristol Parkway 7	a							23 21	00 01							
Bristol Temple Meads 10	a							23 40	00 13							
Newport (South Wales)	a															
Cardiff Central 7	a															
Weston-super-Mare	a															
Taunton	a															
Tiverton Parkway	a															
Exeter St Davids 6	a															
Dawlish	a															
Teignmouth	a															
Newton Abbot	a															
Torquay	a															
Paignton	a															
Totnes	a															
Plymouth	a															
Liskeard 6	a															
Bodmin Parkway	a															
Lostwithiel	a															
Par	a															
Newquay (Summer Only)	a															
St Austell	a															
Truro	a															
Redruth	a															
Camborne	a															
Hayle	a															
St Erth	a															
Penzance	a															
Birmingham International ✈	d						22 14									
Coventry	d						22 25									
Leamington Spa 8	d						22 38									
Banbury	a						22 54									
Oxford	a						23 14									
Reading 7	a						23 52									
Guildford	a															
Basingstoke	a															
Winchester	a															
Southampton Airport Pkwy ✈	a															
Southampton Central ⛴	a															
Brockenhurst 3	a															
Bournemouth	a															

A until 23 March. ⚲ to Leeds
B from 26 March. ⚲ to Leeds
C ⚲ to York
D ⚲ to Leeds
E until 23 March, FO from 30 March
F from 26 March

Table 51

Saturdays

until 11 February

Scotland, The North East, North West England - The South West and South Coast

Route Diagram - see first Page of Table 51

		XC	XC	XC	XC	XC	XC	XC	XC	XC	XC	VT	XC	XC	XC	XC	XC	XC	VT	XC	XC	XC	XC
		◇1	◇1	◇1	◇1	◇1	◇1	◇1	◇1	◇1	◇1	◇1	◇1	◇1	◇1	◇1	◇1	1	◇1	◇1	◇1	◇1	◇1
								A	B	A			C		B							D	
				🛒		🛒	🛒	🛒	🛒	🛒	🛒	🍽	🛒	🛒	🛒	🛒	🛒		🍽	🛒	🛒	🛒	🛒
Aberdeen	d																						
Stonehaven	d																						
Montrose	d																						
Arbroath	d																						
Dundee	d																						
Leuchars 8	d																						
Cupar	d																						
Ladybank	d																						
Markinch	d																						
Kirkcaldy	d																						
Inverkeithing	d																						
Glasgow Central 15	d																						
Motherwell	d																						
Haymarket	d																						
Edinburgh 10	d																						
Haymarket	d																						
Lockerbie	d																						
Carlisle 8	d																						
Penrith North Lakes	d																						
Oxenholme Lake District	d																						
Lancaster 6	d																		06 58				
Preston 8	d											06 17							07 17				
Wigan North Western	d											06 28							07 28				
Warrington Bank Quay	d											06 39							07 39				
M'chester Piccadilly 10	d						05 11				06 00						07 07			07 27			
Stockport	d										06 08						07 16			07 35			
Wilmslow	d																						
Crewe 10	d						05 47					07 01							08 01				
Macclesfield	d										06 21									07 49			
Congleton	d																						
Stoke-on-Trent	d						06 08				06 39						07 44			08 07			
Stafford	d						06 26				06 58						08 03			08 26			
Wolverhampton 7	d						06 41				07 15	07 32					08 18		08 32	08 41			
Dunbar	d																						
Berwick-upon-Tweed	d																						
Alnmouth for Alnwick	d																						
Morpeth	d																						
Newcastle 8	d																						06 22
Chester-le-Street	d																						
Durham	d																						06 37
Darlington 7	d																						06 54
York 8	d																				06 17		07 24
Leeds 10	d													06 00		06 15					07 10		
Wakefield Westgate 7	d													06 12		06 29					07 23		
Doncaster 7	d															06 47							07 52
Sheffield 7	d													06 50		07 18					07 56		08 20
Chesterfield	d													07 03		07 30					08 08		08 32
Nottingham 8	d								05 57				06 37		06 56			07 37				08 08	
Derby 6	d							06 10	06 36	06 48			07 06	07 26	07 36	07 50		08 06			08 28	08 36	08 53
Burton-on-Trent	d							06 20	06 48	06 59			07 18	07 37	07 50	08 00		08 18			08 39	08 49	
Tamworth	d							06 31	07 01	07 09			07 30	07 48	08 02	08 11		08 30			08 49	09 02	
Birmingham New Street 12	a						06 57	06 50	07 24	07 27	07 31	07 55	07 55	08 08	08 24	08 27	08 38	08 54	08 55	08 58	09 08	09 24	09 27
Birmingham New Street 12	d	05 00	05 42	06 04	06 33	06 42	07 04	07 12	07 30	07 33	07 42		08 04	08 12	08 30	08 33	08 42			09 04	09 12	09 30	09 33
Cheltenham Spa	a	06 02	06 41			07 23		07 50	08 10		08 23			08 51	09 10		09 23				09 50	10 10	
Gloucester 7	a	06 13	06 54						08 22						09 22							10 22	
Bristol Parkway 7	a					07 54		08 24			08 54			09 24			09 55				10 29		
Bristol Temple Meads 10	a					08 05		08 38			09 08			09 38			10 06				10 42		
Newport (South Wales)	a	07 06	07 52						09 07						10 07							11 08	
Cardiff Central 7	a	07 22	08 08						09 23						10 23							11 24	
Weston-super-Mare	a																						
Taunton	a					08 42		09 14						10 17							11 15		
Tiverton Parkway	a					08 54		09 28						10 30							11 28		
Exeter St Davids 6	a					09 09		09 41						10 46							11 42		
Dawlish	a																						
Teignmouth	a																						
Newton Abbot	a					09 28		10 02						11 09							12 03		
Torquay	a					09 40																	
Paignton	a					09 47																	
Totnes	a							10 15						11 23							12 16		
Plymouth	a							10 41						11 51							12 43		
Liskeard 6	a																						
Bodmin Parkway	a																						
Lostwithiel	a																						
Par	a																						
Newquay (Summer Only)	a																						
St Austell	a																						
Truro	a																						
Redruth	a																						
Camborne	a																						
Hayle	a																						
St Erth	a																						
Penzance	a																						
Birmingham International ✈	d			06 14			07 14						08 14							09 14			
Coventry	d			06 25			07 25						08 25							09 25			
Leamington Spa 8	d			06 38	07 00		07 38			08 00			08 38			09 00				09 38			10 00
Banbury	a			06 54	07 17		07 54			08 17			08 54			09 17				09 54			10 17
Oxford	a			07 14	07 40		08 14			08 40			09 14			09 40				10 14			10 40
Reading 7	a			07 39	08 06		08 39			09 11			09 39			10 07				10 39			11 09
Guildford	a																						
Basingstoke	a			08 08	08 40		09 08						10 08			10 39				11 08			
Winchester	a			08 24	08 55		09 24						10 24			10 54				11 24			
Southampton Airport Pkway ✈	a			08 32	09 08		09 32						10 32			11 08				11 32			
Southampton Central	a			08 41	09 17		09 40						10 43			11 17				11 41			
Brockenhurst 3	a			08 56			09 57						10 58							11 57			
Bournemouth	a			09 14			10 11						11 12							12 11			

A 🛒 from Birmingham New Street

B 🛒 from Birmingham New Street to Newport (South Wales)

C 🛒 from Derby

D 🛒 to Newport (South Wales)

Table 51

Saturdays
until 11 February

Scotland, The North East, North West England - The South West and South Coast

Route Diagram - see first Page of Table 51

		XC	XC	VT	XC	XC	XC	XC	XC	XC	VT	XC	XC	XC	XC	XC	XC	VT	XC	XC	XC	XC	XC
		◇1	1	◇1	◇1	◇1	◇1	◇1	◇1	1	◇1	◇1	◇1	◇1	◇1	◇1	1	◇1	◇1	◇1	◇1	◇1	◇1
							A							A						B	A		
		🛒		☕	🛒	🛒	🛒	🛒	🛒		☕	🛒	🛒	🛒	🛒	🛒		☕	🛒	🛒	🛒	🛒	🛒
Aberdeen	d																						
Stonehaven	d																						
Montrose	d																						
Arbroath	d																						
Dundee	d																						
Leuchars 3	d																						
Cupar	d																						
Ladybank	d																						
Markinch	d																						
Kirkcaldy	d																						
Inverkeithing	d																						
Glasgow Central 15	d			05 50														08 00		06 01			
Motherwell	d			06 04																06 16			
Haymarket	d																			06 57			
Edinburgh 10	d										06 52		06 06		07 00					07 07			
Haymarket	d										06 56												
Lockerbie	d																						
Carlisle 8	d			07 03							08 07							09 09					
Penrith North Lakes	d			07 18							08 22												
Oxenholme Lake District	d			07 42																			
Lancaster 6	d			07 57							08 57							09 57					
Preston 8	d			08 17							09 17							10 17					
Wigan North Western	d			08 28							09 28							10 28					
Warrington Bank Quay	d			08 39							09 39							10 39					
M'chester Piccadilly 10 ⛴	d	08 07			08 27				09 07			09 27				10 07			10 27				11 07
Stockport	d	08 16			08 35				09 16			09 35				10 16			10 35				11 16
Wilmslow	d																						
Crewe 10	d			09 01							10 01							11 01					
Macclesfield	d				08 49							09 49							10 49				
Congleton	d																						
Stoke-on-Trent	d	08 44			09 07				09 44			10 07				10 44			11 07				11 44
Stafford	d	09 03			09 26				10 03			10 26				11 03			11 26				12 03
Wolverhampton 7 ⛴	d	09 17		09 32	09 41				10 17		10 32	10 41				11 17		11 33	11 41				12 17
Dunbar	d																			07 27			
Berwick-upon-Tweed	d												06 48		07 40								
Alnmouth for Alnwick	d												07 08		08 00								
Morpeth	d														08 14								
Newcastle 8	d					06 45		07 35					07 40		08 36					08 43		09 35	
Chester-le-Street	d																						
Durham	d					06 57		07 47					07 52		08 48					08 56		09 47	
Darlington 7	d					07 14		08 04					08 10		09 05					09 13		10 05	
York 8	d					07 44		08 34					08 44		09 35					09 46		10 34	
Leeds 10	d					08 12							09 11							10 12			
Wakefield Westgate 7	d					08 24							09 24							10 24			
Doncaster 7	d							08 58							09 58							10 58	
Sheffield 7 ⛴	d					08 54		09 23					09 54		10 23					10 54		11 23	
Chesterfield	d					09 06							10 06							11 06			
Nottingham 8 ⛴	d		08 37				09 08			09 37				10 08			10 37				11 11		
Derby 6	d		09 10			09 27	09 36	09 53		10 10			10 28	10 37	10 53		11 10			11 27	11 36	11 54	
Burton-on-Trent	d		09 21			09 38	09 49			10 21				10 49			11 21			11 39	11 49		
Tamworth	d		09 33				10 02			10 33			10 48	11 02			11 33				12 02		
Birmingham New Street 12	a	09 39	09 54	09 55	09 58	10 04	10 24	10 27	10 39	10 54	10 55	10 58	11 04	11 24	11 27	11 39	11 54	11 55	11 58	12 07	12 24	12 27	12 39
Birmingham New Street 12	d	09 42			10 04	10 12	10 30	10 33	10 42			11 04	11 12	11 30	11 33	11 42			12 04	12 12	12 30	12 33	12 42
Cheltenham Spa	a	10 23				10 50	11 10		11 23				11 50	12 10		12 23				12 50	13 10		13 25
Gloucester 7	a						11 22							12 22							13 22		
Bristol Parkway 7	a	10 57				11 24			11 54				12 29			12 55				13 24			13 57
Bristol Temple Meads 10	a	11 09				11 37			12 08				12 42			13 07				13 38			14 08
Newport (South Wales)	a						12 07							13 11							14 08		
Cardiff Central 7	a						12 23							13 27							14 24		
Weston-super-Mare	a	11 29																					
Taunton	a	11 59				12 15							13 15							14 15			
Tiverton Parkway	a	12 12				12 28							13 28							14 28			
Exeter St Davids 6	a	12 26				12 42							13 42							14 42			
Dawlish	a	12 40																					
Teignmouth	a	12 45																					
Newton Abbot	a	12 52				13 03							14 02							15 02			
Torquay	a	13 03																					
Paignton	a	13 11																					
Totnes	a					13 16							14 15							15 15			
Plymouth	a					13 43							14 42							15 42			
Liskeard 6	a																						
Bodmin Parkway	a																						
Lostwithiel	a																						
Par	a																						
Newquay (Summer Only)	a																						
St Austell	a																						
Truro	a																						
Redruth	a																						
Camborne	a																						
Hayle	a																						
St Erth	a																						
Penzance	a																						
Birmingham International ✈	d				10 14							11 14							12 14				
Coventry	d				10 25							11 25							12 25				
Leamington Spa 8	d				10 38			11 00				11 38			12 00				12 38			13 02	
Banbury	a				10 54			11 17				11 54			12 17				12 54			13 19	
Oxford	a				11 14			11 40				12 14			12 40				13 14			13 40	
Reading 7	a				11 39			12 07				12 39			13 06				13 39			14 07	
Guildford	a																						
Basingstoke	a				12 08			12 40				13 08							14 08			14 40	
Winchester	a				12 24			12 55				13 24							14 24			14 55	
Southampton Airport Pkway ✈	a				12 32			13 08				13 32							14 32			15 08	
Southampton Central ⛴	a				12 41			13 17				13 41							14 41			15 17	
Brockenhurst 3	a				12 57							13 57							14 57				
Bournemouth	a				13 11							14 11							15 11				

A 🛒 to Newport (South Wales)

B 🛒 from Edinburgh

Table 51

Saturdays

until 11 February

Scotland, The North East, North West England - The South West and South Coast

Route Diagram - see first Page of Table 51

		XC	VT	XC	XC	XC	XC	XC	XC	VT	XC	XC	XC	XC	XC	XC	VT	XC	XC	XC	XC	XC
		1	◇1	◇1	◇1	◇1	◇1	◇1	1	◇1	◇1	◇1	◇1	◇1	◇1	1	◇1	◇1	◇1	◇1	◇1	◇1
						A							A						B	C		
		⌶	☕	⌶	⌶	⌶	⌶	⌶	⌶	☕	⌶	⌶	⌶	⌶	⌶	⌶	☕	⌶	⌶	⌶	⌶	⌶
Aberdeen	d																					
Stonehaven	d																					
Montrose	d																					
Arbroath	d																					
Dundee	d				06 32																	
Leuchars 3	d				06 46																	
Cupar	d				06 54																	
Ladybank	d				07 03																	
Markinch	d				07 11																	
Kirkcaldy	d				07 21																	
Inverkeithing	d				07 38																	
Glasgow Central 15	d									10 00		07 50							09 00			
Motherwell	d											08 05							09 15			
Haymarket	d				07 56							08 50							09 57			
Edinburgh 10	d		08 52		08 05							09 06					10 52		10 05			
Haymarket	d		08 57														10 57					
Lockerbie	d																					
Carlisle 8	d		10 07							11 09							12 07					
Penrith North Lakes	d									11 24												
Oxenholme Lake District	d		10 42														12 43					
Lancaster 6	d		10 57														12 57					
Preston 8	d		11 17							12 17							13 17					
Wigan North Western	d		11 28							12 28							13 28					
Warrington Bank Quay	d		11 39							12 39							13 39					
M'chester Piccadilly 10	d			11 27				12 07			12 27				13 07			13 27				14 07
Stockport	d			11 35				12 16			12 35				13 16			13 35				14 16
Wilmslow	d																					
Crewe 10	d		12 01							13 01							14 01					
Macclesfield	d			11 49							12 49							13 49				
Congleton	d																					
Stoke-on-Trent	d			12 07				12 44			13 07				13 44			14 07				14 44
Stafford	d			12 25				13 03			13 26				14 03			14 26				15 03
Wolverhampton 7	d		12 32	12 41				13 16		13 32	13 41				14 17		14 32	14 41				15 17
Dunbar	d											09 26										
Berwick-upon-Tweed	d				08 46							09 49							10 48			
Alnmouth for Alnwick	d				09 08																	
Morpeth	d																		11 19			
Newcastle 8	d				09 41		10 35					10 44		11 35					11 42		12 35	
Chester-le-Street	d																					
Durham	d				09 55		10 47					10 56		11 47					11 55		12 47	
Darlington 7	d				10 12		11 04					11 13		12 05					12 12		13 04	
York 8	d				10 45		11 34					11 45		12 34					12 45		13 34	
Leeds 10	d				11 11							12 11							13 11			
Wakefield Westgate 7	d				11 23							12 24							13 23			
Doncaster 7	d						11 58							12 58							13 58	
Sheffield 7	d				11 54		12 23					12 54		13 23					13 54		14 23	
Chesterfield	d				12 07							13 06							14 07			
Nottingham 8	d	11 37				12 08			12 37				13 08			13 37				14 08		
Derby 6	d	12 10			12 29	12 36	12 53		13 06			13 28	13 36	13 53		14 06			14 30	14 36	14 53	
Burton-on-Trent	d	12 21				12 49			13 21			13 38	13 49			14 18				14 49		
Tamworth	d	12 33			12 49	13 02			13 33				14 02			14 30			14 49	15 02		
Birmingham New Street 12	a	12 54	12 55	12 58	13 09	13 24	13 27	13 39	13 54	13 55	13 58	14 07	14 24	14 27	14 39	14 54	14 55	14 58	15 08	15 24	15 27	15 39
Birmingham New Street 12	d			13 04	13 12	13 30	13 33	13 42			14 04	14 12	14 30	14 33	14 42			15 04	15 12	15 30	15 33	15 42
Cheltenham Spa	a				13 51	14 10		14 23				14 50	15 10		15 23				15 50	16 10		16 23
Gloucester 7	a					14 22							15 22							16 22		
Bristol Parkway 7	a				14 26			14 57				15 23			15 55				16 29			16 54
Bristol Temple Meads 10	a				14 41			15 09				15 37			16 08				16 42			17 07
Newport (South Wales)	a					15 11							16 08							17 10		
Cardiff Central 7	a					15 27							16 25							17 26		
Weston-super-Mare	a																					
Taunton	a				15 16			15 43				16 15							17 17			17 41
Tiverton Parkway	a				15 29			15 55				16 28							17 30			17 53
Exeter St Davids 6	a				15 45			16 10				16 42							17 46			18 08
Dawlish	a																					18 21
Teignmouth	a																					18 26
Newton Abbot	a				16 06							17 02							18 10			18 33
Torquay	a																					18 45
Paignton	a																					18 53
Totnes	a				16 20							17 15							18 24			
Plymouth	a				16 48							17 42							18 52			
Liskeard 6	a																		19 18			
Bodmin Parkway	a																		19 32			
Lostwithiel	a																					
Par	a																		19 44			
Newquay (Summer Only)	a																					
St Austell	a																		19 52			
Truro	a																		20 10			
Redruth	a																		20 26			
Camborne	a																		20 33			
Hayle	a																					
St Erth	a																		20 45			
Penzance	a																		20 56			
Birmingham International ✈	d			13 14							14 14							15 14				
Coventry	d			13 25							14 25							15 25				
Leamington Spa 8	d			13 38			14 00				14 38			15 00				15 38			16 02	
Banbury	a			13 54			14 17				14 54			15 19				15 54			16 18	
Oxford	a			14 14			14 40				15 14			15 41				16 14			16 40	
Reading 7	a			14 39			15 07				15 39			16 08				16 39			17 07	
Guildford	a																					
Basingstoke	a			15 08							16 08			16 40				17 08				
Winchester	a			15 24							16 24			16 55				17 24				
Southampton Airport Pkway ✈	a			15 32							16 32			17 08				17 32				
Southampton Central	a			15 41							16 41			17 17				17 41				
Brockenhurst 3	a			15 57							16 57							17 57				
Bournemouth	a			16 11							17 11							18 11				

A ⌶ from Birmingham New Street to Newport (South Wales)

B ⌶ from Edinburgh to Plymouth

C ⌶ to Newport (South Wales)

Table 51

Saturdays
until 11 February

Scotland, The North East, North West England - The South West and South Coast

Route Diagram - see first Page of Table 51

		XC	VT	XC	XC	XC	XC	XC	XC	VT	XC	XC	XC	XC	XC	XC	VT	XC	XC	XC	XC	XC	XC
		1	◇1	◇1	◇1	◇1	◇1	◇1	1	◇1	◇1	◇1	◇1	◇1	◇1	1	◇1	◇1	◇1	◇1	◇1	◇1	1
					A							B											
		🛒	🛍	🛒	🛒	🛒	🛒	🛒	🛒	🛍	🛒	🛒		🛒	🛒	🛒	🛍	🛒	🛒		🛒	🛒	🛒
Aberdeen	d				08 20																		
Stonehaven	d				08 38																		
Montrose	d				08 59																		
Arbroath	d				09 15																		
Dundee	d				09 32																		
Leuchars 8	d				09 47																		
Cupar	d				09 54																		
Ladybank	d				10 01																		
Markinch	d				10 08																		
Kirkcaldy	d				10 17																		
Inverkeithing	d				10 32																		
Glasgow Central 15	d		12 00									10 59					14 00						
Motherwell	d											11 14											
Haymarket	d				10 52							11 56											
Edinburgh 10	d				11 05					12 52		12 09							13 08				
Haymarket	d									12 57													
Lockerbie	d																						
Carlisle 8	d		13 09							14 07							15 11						
Penrith North Lakes	d									14 22													
Oxenholme Lake District	d																15 46						
Lancaster 6	d		13 58							14 57													
Preston 8	d		14 17							15 17							16 17						
Wigan North Western	d		14 28							15 28							16 28						
Warrington Bank Quay	d		14 39							15 39							16 39						
M'chester Piccadilly 10 ⛴	d			14 27				15 07			15 27				16 07			16 27				17 06	
Stockport	d			14 35				15 16			15 35				16 16			16 35					
Wilmslow	d																						
Crewe 10	d		15 01							16 01							17 01						
Macclesfield	d			14 49							15 49							16 49				17 26	
Congleton	d																						
Stoke-on-Trent	d			15 07				15 44			16 07				16 44			17 07				17 44	
Stafford	d			15 26				16 03			16 25				17 03			17 26				18 04	
Wolverhampton 7 ⛴	d		15 32	15 41				16 17		16 32	16 41				17 17		17 32	17 41				18 17	
Dunbar	d				11 25														13 29				
Berwick-upon-Tweed	d				11 48							12 48											
Alnmouth for Alnwick	d				12 08														14 09				
Morpeth	d																						
Newcastle 8	d				12 44		13 35					13 44		14 35					14 44		15 07		
Chester-le-Street	d																						
Durham	d				12 56		13 47					13 56		14 47					14 56		15 19		
Darlington 7	d				13 13		14 05					14 13		15 04					15 13		15 36		
York 8	d				13 44		14 34					14 44		15 34					15 45		16 06		
Leeds 10	d				14 11							15 12							16 12		16 40		
Wakefield Westgate 7	d				14 24							15 24							16 24		16 52		
Doncaster 7	d						14 58							15 58									
Sheffield 7 ⛴	d				14 54		15 23					15 54		16 23					16 54		17 23		
Chesterfield	d				15 06							16 07							17 06				
Nottingham 8 ⛴	d	14 37				15 08			15 37				16 08			16 37				17 11			17 37
Derby 6	d	15 10			15 28	15 36	15 53		16 10			16 28	16 36	16 53		17 06			17 28	17 36	17 53		18 10
Burton-on-Trent	d	15 24			15 38	15 49			16 21				16 49			17 21			17 38	17 49			18 22
Tamworth	d	15 33				16 02			16 33			16 48	17 02			17 33				18 02			18 34
Birmingham New Street 12	a	15 54	15 55	15 58	16 04	16 24	16 27	16 39	16 54	16 55	16 58	17 07	17 24	17 27	17 39	17 54	17 55	17 58	18 07	18 24	18 27	18 38	18 54
Birmingham New Street 12	d			16 04	16 12	16 30	16 33	16 42			17 04	17 12	17 30	17 33	17 42			18 04	18 12	18 30	18 33	18 42	
Cheltenham Spa	a				16 50	17 10		17 23				17 50	18 17		18 23				18 50	19 10		19 23	
Gloucester 7	a					17 22							18 29							19 22			
Bristol Parkway 7	a				17 24			17 54				18 29			18 54				19 25			19 55	
Bristol Temple Meads 10	a				17 38			18 07				18 42			19 05				19 39			20 06	
Newport (South Wales)	a					18 05							19 12							20 05		20 55	
Cardiff Central 7	a					18 21							19 29							20 21		21 11	
Weston-super-Mare	a																						
Taunton	a				18 15							19 15							20 15				
Tiverton Parkway	a				18 28							19 28							20 28				
Exeter St Davids 6	a				18 42							19 43							20 42				
Dawlish	a																						
Teignmouth	a																						
Newton Abbot	a				19 04							20 03							21 03				
Torquay	a																						
Paignton	a																						
Totnes	a				19 17							20 16							21 16				
Plymouth	a				19 43							20 43							21 43				
Liskeard 6	a				20 10							21 24											
Bodmin Parkway	a				20 22							21 36											
Lostwithiel	a				20 28																		
Par	a				20 35							21 48											
Newquay (Summer Only)	a																						
St Austell	a				20 42							21 54											
Truro	a				21 00							22 12											
Redruth	a				21 12							22 27											
Camborne	a				21 18							22 34											
Hayle	a				21 26																		
St Erth	a				21 31							22 45											
Penzance	a				21 43							22 54											
Birmingham International ✈	d			16 14							17 14							18 14					
Coventry	d			16 25							17 25							18 25					
Leamington Spa 8	d			16 38			17 00				17 38			18 02				18 38			19 00		
Banbury	a			16 54			17 17				17 54			18 18				18 54			19 17		
Oxford	a			17 14			17 41				18 14			18 40				19 14			19 40		
Reading 7	a			17 39			18 07				18 39			19 07				19 39			20 10		
Guildford	a																						
Basingstoke	a			18 08			18 40				19 08							20 08					
Winchester	a			18 24			18 55				19 24							20 24					
Southampton Airport Pkway ✈	a			18 32			19 08				19 32							20 32					
Southampton Central ⛴	a			18 40			19 17				19 41							20 41					
Brockenhurst 3	a			18 57							19 57							20 57					
Bournemouth	a			19 11							20 11							21 11					

A 🛒 from Edinburgh to Plymouth

B 🛒 to Plymouth

Table 51

Saturdays
until 11 February

Scotland, The North East, North West England - The South West and South Coast

Route Diagram - see first Page of Table 51

		VT	XC	XC	XC	XC	XC	XC	VT	XC	XC	XC	XC	XC	LM	XC	VT	XC	XC	XC	XC	VT
		◇1	◇1	◇1	◇1	◇1	◇1	1	◇1	◇1	◇1	◇1	◇1	◇1	◇1	1	◇1	◇1	◇1	◇1	◇1	◇1
			A	B			C			A	C							D	D			
		🍴	⊥	⊥		⊥	⊥	⊥	🍴	⊥	⊥		⊥	⊥			🍴	⊥	⊥	⊥		🍴
Aberdeen	d																					
Stonehaven	d																					
Montrose	d																					
Arbroath	d																					
Dundee	d																					
Leuchars [3]	d																					
Cupar	d																					
Ladybank	d																					
Markinch	d																					
Kirkcaldy	d																					
Inverkeithing	d																					
Glasgow Central [15]	d			12 51					16 00										15 00			18 00
Motherwell	d			13 06															15 14			
Haymarket	d																		15 56			
Edinburgh [10]	d	14 52		14 08							15 08						16 52		16 05			
Haymarket	d	14 57															16 57					
Lockerbie	d																					
Carlisle [8]	d	16 07							17 09								18 08					19 09
Penrith North Lakes	d	16 22																				
Oxenholme Lake District	d								17 44								18 42					
Lancaster [6]	d	16 57															18 57					19 56
Preston [8]	d	17 17							18 17								19 17					20 17
Wigan North Western	d	17 28							18 28								19 28					20 28
Warrington Bank Quay	d	17 39							18 39								19 39					20 39
M'chester Piccadilly [10] ⛴	d		17 27				18 05			18 27				19 07				19 27			20 07	
Stockport	d		17 36				18 13			18 35				19 16				19 35			20 16	
Wilmslow	d																					
Crewe [10]	d	18 01							19 01						19 51		20 01					21 01
Macclesfield	d						18 26											19 49				
Congleton	d		17 54							18 54												
Stoke-on-Trent	d		18 08				18 44			19 07				19 44				20 07			20 44	
Stafford	d		18 27				19 03			19 25				20 03	20 12			20 26			21 03	
Wolverhampton [7] ⛴	d	18 32	18 41				19 17		19 32	19 41				20 17	20 28		20 33	20 41			21 16	21 33
Dunbar	d										15 28											
Berwick-upon-Tweed	d			14 49																		
Alnmouth for Alnwick	d																		17 03			
Morpeth	d																		17 17			
Newcastle [8]	d			15 41		16 35					16 41		17 32						17 44	18 35		
Chester-le-Street	d												17 41									
Durham	d			15 53		16 47					16 52		17 48						17 56	18 48		
Darlington [7]	d			16 11		17 04					17 10		18 05						18 13	19 05		
York [8]	d			16 44		17 34					17 44		18 34						18 44	19 34		
Leeds [10]	d			17 11							18 11								19 11			
Wakefield Westgate [7]	d			17 23							18 23								19 24			
Doncaster [7]	d					17 58							18 58							19 58		
Sheffield [7] ⛴	d			17 54		18 23					18 54		19 24						19 54	20 23		
Chesterfield	d			18 07							19 06								20 06			
Nottingham [8] ⛴	d				18 08			18 37				19 08				19 37						
Derby [6]	d			18 28	18 36	18 53		19 10			19 27	19 36	19 54			20 10			20 28	20 53		
Burton-on-Trent	d				18 49			19 21			19 37	19 49				20 21						
Tamworth	d			18 46	19 02			19 33				20 02				20 33			20 46			
Birmingham New Street [12]	a	18 55	18 58	19 06	19 24	19 27	19 33	19 54	19 55	19 58	20 06	20 24	20 27	20 33	20 47	20 54	20 55	20 58	21 03	21 25	21 32	21 54
Birmingham New Street [12]	d		19 04	19 12	19 30	19 33	19 42			20 04	20 12	20 30		20 42				21 04	21 10			
Cheltenham Spa	a			19 50	20 10		20 23				20 49	21 10		21 23					21 49			
Gloucester [7]	a				20 22							21 22							21 59			
Bristol Parkway [7]	a			20 29			20 54				21 22			21 58					22 30			
Bristol Temple Meads [10]	a			20 42			21 05				21 35			22 12					22 41			
Newport (South Wales)	a				21 11							22 21										
Cardiff Central [7]	a				21 29							22 43										
Weston-super-Mare	a																					
Taunton	a			21 15			21 42				22 15											
Tiverton Parkway	a			21 28			21 55				22 28											
Exeter St Davids [6]	a			21 42			22 09				22 43											
Dawlish	a																					
Teignmouth	a																					
Newton Abbot	a			22 04			22 29				23 10											
Torquay	a																					
Paignton	a																					
Totnes	a			22 20			22 42				23 24											
Plymouth	a			22 47			23 08				23 53											
Liskeard [6]	a																					
Bodmin Parkway	a																					
Lostwithiel	a																					
Par	a																					
Newquay (Summer Only)	a																					
St Austell	a																					
Truro	a																					
Redruth	a																					
Camborne	a																					
Hayle	a																					
St Erth	a																					
Penzance	a																					
Birmingham International ✈	d		19 14							20 14								21 14				
Coventry	d		19 25							20 25								21 25				
Leamington Spa [8]	d		19 38			20 03				20 38								21 38				
Banbury	a		19 54			20 19				20 54								21 54				
Oxford	a		20 14			20 40				21 14								22 16				
Reading [7]	a		20 39			21 10				21 40								22 41				
Guildford	a																					
Basingstoke	a		21 08							22 09								23 06				
Winchester	a		21 24							22 24								23 24				
Southampton Airport Pkway ✈	a		21 32							22 33								23 32				
Southampton Central ⛴	a		21 41							22 41								23 41				
Brockenhurst [3]	a		21 57							22 56												
Bournemouth	a		22 15							23 21												

A ⊥ to Reading
B ⊥ from Edinburgh to Bristol Temple Meads
C ⊥ to Bristol Temple Meads
D ⊥ to Birmingham New Street

Table 51

Saturdays
until 11 February

Scotland, The North East, North West England - The South West and South Coast

Route Diagram - see first Page of Table 51

		XC	XC	XC	XC	XC	VT	VT	VT	XC	XC	XC
		1	◇1	◇1	◇1	◇1	◇1	◇1	◇1	◇1	1	◇1
				A		B		C	D			E
				⚲		⚲	⊡	⊡	⊡			⚲
Aberdeen	d											
Stonehaven	d											
Montrose	d											
Arbroath	d											
Dundee	d											
Leuchars 3	d											
Cupar	d											
Ladybank	d											
Markinch	d											
Kirkcaldy	d											
Inverkeithing	d											
Glasgow Central 15	d						18 40					16 52
Motherwell	d											17 14
Haymarket	d											17 56
Edinburgh 10	d			17 08				18 42	18 52			18 05
Haymarket	d							18 46	18 57			
Lockerbie	d											
Carlisle 8	d						19 48	19 59	20 08			
Penrith North Lakes	d						20 02	20 14	20 23			
Oxenholme Lake District	d						20 25	20 37	20 46			
Lancaster 6	d						20 40	20 52	21 01			
Preston 8	d						21 00	21 21	21 21			
Wigan North Western	d						21 11	21 32	21 32			
Warrington Bank Quay	d						21 22	21 43	21 43			
M'chester Piccadilly 10	d		20 27		21 07					21 27		
Stockport	d		20 35							21 36		
Wilmslow	d											
Crewe 10	d						21 43	22 05	22 05			
Macclesfield	d		20 49							21 50		
Congleton	d											
Stoke-on-Trent	d		21 07		21 45					22 08		
Stafford	d		21 27		22 03		22 08	22 25	22 25	22 33		
Wolverhampton 7	d		21 41		22 16		22 23	22 40	22 40	22 46		
Dunbar	d			17 28								18 25
Berwick-upon-Tweed	d			17 51								18 48
Alnmouth for Alnwick	d											19 08
Morpeth	d											
Newcastle 8	d			18 44		19 35						19 44
Chester-le-Street	d											
Durham	d			18 56		19 49						19 56
Darlington 7	d			19 13		20 06						20 13
York 8	d			19 44		20 34						20 45
Leeds 10	d			20 11								21 11
Wakefield Westgate 7	d			20 23								21 23
Doncaster 7	d					21 00						
Sheffield 7	d			20 54		21 23						21 54
Chesterfield	d			21 06		21 35						22 06
Nottingham 8	d	20 37									21 37	
Derby 6	d	21 06		21 28		21 53					22 10	22 26
Burton-on-Trent	d	21 21		21 38							22 21	22 37
Tamworth	d	21 33		21 49							22 33	22 47
Birmingham New Street 12	a	21 54	21 58	22 05	22 32	22 43	22 46	22 59	22 59	23 02	23 02	23 05
Birmingham New Street 12	d											
Cheltenham Spa	a											
Gloucester 7	a											
Bristol Parkway 7	a											
Bristol Temple Meads 10	a											
Newport (South Wales)	a											
Cardiff Central 7	a											
Weston-super-Mare	a											
Taunton	a											
Tiverton Parkway	a											
Exeter St Davids 6	a											
Dawlish	a											
Teignmouth	a											
Newton Abbot	a											
Torquay	a											
Paignton	a											
Totnes	a											
Plymouth	a											
Liskeard 6	a											
Bodmin Parkway	a											
Lostwithiel	a											
Par	a											
Newquay (Summer Only)	a											
St Austell	a											
Truro	a											
Redruth	a											
Camborne	a											
Hayle	a											
St Erth	a											
Penzance	a											
Birmingham International	d											
Coventry	d											
Leamington Spa 8	d											
Banbury	a											
Oxford	a											
Reading 7	a											
Guildford	a											
Basingstoke	a											
Winchester	a											
Southampton Airport Pkway	a											
Southampton Central	a											
Brockenhurst 3	a											
Bournemouth	a											

A ⚲ to Leeds
B ⚲ to York
C from 7 January until 11 February
D until 31 December
E ⚲ from Edinburgh to Leeds

Table 51

Saturdays

18 February to 24 March

Scotland, The North East, North West England - The South West and South Coast

Route Diagram - see first Page of Table 51

		XC	XC	XC	XC	XC	XC	XC	XC	XC	XC	VT	XC	XC	XC	XC	XC	XC	VT	XC	XC	XC	XC
		◇1	◇1	◇1	◇1	◇1	◇1	◇1	◇1	◇1	◇1	◇1	◇1	◇1	◇1	◇1	◇1	1	◇1	◇1	◇1	◇1	◇1
								A	B	A			C		B							D	
				trolley		trolley	trolley	trolley	trolley	trolley	trolley	restaurant	trolley	trolley	trolley	trolley	trolley		restaurant	trolley	trolley	trolley	trolley
Aberdeen	d																						
Stonehaven	d																						
Montrose	d																						
Arbroath	d																						
Dundee	d																						
Leuchars [8]	d																						
Cupar	d																						
Ladybank	d																						
Markinch	d																						
Kirkcaldy	d																						
Inverkeithing	d																						
Glasgow Central [15]	d																						
Motherwell	d																						
Haymarket	d																						
Edinburgh [10]	d																						
Haymarket	d																						
Lockerbie	d																						
Carlisle [8]	d																						
Penrith North Lakes	d																						
Oxenholme Lake District	d																						
Lancaster [6]	d																		06 58				
Preston [8]	d											06 17							07 17				
Wigan North Western	d											06 28							07 28				
Warrington Bank Quay	d											06 39							07 39				
M'chester Piccadilly [10]	d						05 11				06 00						07 07			07 27			
Stockport	d										06 08						07 16			07 35			
Wilmslow	d																						
Crewe [10]	d						05 47					07 01							08 01				
Macclesfield	d										06 21									07 49			
Congleton	d																						
Stoke-on-Trent	d						06 08				06 39						07 44			08 07			
Stafford	d						06 26				06 58						08 03			08 26			
Wolverhampton [7]	d						06 41				07 15	07 32					08 18		08 32	08 41			
Dunbar	d																						
Berwick-upon-Tweed	d																						
Alnmouth for Alnwick	d																						
Morpeth	d																						
Newcastle [8]	d																						06 22
Chester-le-Street	d																						
Durham	d																						06 37
Darlington [7]	d																						06 54
York [8]	d																				06 17		07 24
Leeds [10]	d													06 00		06 15					07 10		
Wakefield Westgate [7]	d													06 12		06 29					07 23		
Doncaster [7]	d															06 47							07 52
Sheffield [7]	d													06 50		07 18					07 56		08 20
Chesterfield	d													07 03		07 30					08 08		08 32
Nottingham [8]	d								05 57				06 37		06 56			07 37				08 08	
Derby [6]	d							06 10	06 36	06 48			07 06	07 26	07 36	07 50		08 06			08 28	08 36	08 53
Burton-on-Trent	d							06 20	06 48	06 59			07 18	07 37	07 50	08 00		08 18			08 39	08 49	
Tamworth	d							06 31	07 01	07 09			07 30	07 48	08 02	08 11		08 30			08 49	09 02	
Birmingham New Street [12]	a						06 57	06 50	07 24	07 27	07 31	07 55	07 55	08 08	08 24	08 27	08 38	08 54	08 55	08 58	09 08	09 24	09 27
Birmingham New Street [12]	d	05 00	05 42	06 04	06 33	06 42	07 04	07 12	07 30	07 33	07 42		08 04	08 12	08 30	08 33	08 42			09 04	09 12	09 30	09 33
Cheltenham Spa	a	06 02	06 41			07 23		07 50	08 10		08 23			08 51	09 10		09 23				09 50	10 10	
Gloucester [7]	a	06 13	06 54						08 22						09 22							10 22	
Bristol Parkway [7]	a					07 54		08 24			08 54			09 24			09 55				10 29		
Bristol Temple Meads [10]	a					08 05		08 38			09 08			09 38			10 06				10 42		
Newport (South Wales)	a	07 06	07 52						09 07						10 07							11 08	
Cardiff Central [7]	a	07 22	08 08						09 23						10 23							11 24	
Weston-super-Mare	a																						
Taunton	a					08 42		09 14						10 17							11 15		
Tiverton Parkway	a					08 54		09 28						10 30							11 28		
Exeter St Davids [6]	a					09 09		09 41						10 46							11 42		
Dawlish	a																						
Teignmouth	a																						
Newton Abbot	a					09 28		10 02						11 09							12 03		
Torquay	a					09 40																	
Paignton	a					09 47																	
Totnes	a							10 15						11 23							12 16		
Plymouth	a							10 41						11 51							12 43		
Liskeard [6]	a																						
Bodmin Parkway	a																						
Lostwithiel	a																						
Par	a																						
Newquay (Summer Only)	a																						
St Austell	a																						
Truro	a																						
Redruth	a																						
Camborne	a																						
Hayle	a																						
St Erth	a																						
Penzance	a																						
Birmingham International	d			06 14			07 14						08 14							09 14			
Coventry	d			06 25			07 25						08 25							09 25			
Leamington Spa [8]	d			06 38	07 00		07 38			08 00			08 38			09 00				09 38			10 00
Banbury	a			06 54	07 17		07 54			08 17			08 54			09 17				09 54			10 17
Oxford	a			07 14	07 40		08 14			08 40			09 14			09 40				10 14			10 40
Reading [7]	a			07 39	08 06		08 39			09 11			09 39			10 07				10 39			11 09
Guildford	a																						
Basingstoke	a			08 08	08 40		09 08						10 08			10 39				11 08			
Winchester	a			08 24	08 55		09 24						10 24			10 54				11 24			
Southampton Airport Pkwy	a			08 32	09 08		09 32						10 32			11 08				11 32			
Southampton Central	a			08 41	09 17		09 40						10 43			11 17				11 41			
Brockenhurst [3]	a			08 56			09 57						10 58							11 57			
Bournemouth	a			09 14			10 11						11 12							12 11			

A trolley from Birmingham New Street

B trolley from Birmingham New Street to Newport (South Wales)

C trolley from Derby

D trolley to Newport (South Wales)

Table 51

Saturdays

18 February to 24 March

Scotland, The North East, North West England - The South West and South Coast

Route Diagram - see first Page of Table 51

		XC	XC	VT	XC	XC	XC	XC	XC	XC	VT	XC	XC	XC	XC	XC	XC	VT	XC	XC	XC	XC	XC
		◇1	1	◇1	◇1	◇1	◇1	◇1	◇1	1	◇1	◇1	◇1	◇1	◇1	◇1	1	◇1	◇1	◇1	◇1	◇1	◇1
							A							A						B	A		
		🛒		🍴	🛒	🛒	🛒	🛒	🛒		🍴	🛒	🛒	🛒	🛒	🛒		🍴	🛒	🛒	🛒	🛒	🛒
Aberdeen	d																						
Stonehaven	d																						
Montrose	d																						
Arbroath	d																						
Dundee	d																						
Leuchars 3	d																						
Cupar	d																						
Ladybank	d																						
Markinch	d																						
Kirkcaldy	d																						
Inverkeithing	d																						
Glasgow Central 15	d			05 50														08 00		06 01			
Motherwell	d			06 04																06 16			
Haymarket	d																			06 57			
Edinburgh 10	d										06 52		06 06		07 00					07 07			
Haymarket	d										06 56												
Lockerbie	d																						
Carlisle 8	d			07 03							08 07							09 09					
Penrith North Lakes	d			07 18							08 22												
Oxenholme Lake District	d			07 42																			
Lancaster 6	d			07 57							08 57							09 57					
Preston 8	d			08 17							09 17							10 17					
Wigan North Western	d			08 28							09 28							10 28					
Warrington Bank Quay	d			08 39							09 39							10 39					
M'chester Piccadilly 10 🚌	d	08 07			08 27				09 07			09 27				10 07			10 27				11 07
Stockport	d	08 16			08 35				09 16			09 35				10 16			10 35				11 16
Wilmslow	d																						
Crewe 10	d			09 01							10 01							11 01					
Macclesfield	d				08 49							09 49							10 49				
Congleton	d																						
Stoke-on-Trent	d	08 44			09 07				09 44			10 07				10 44			11 07				11 44
Stafford	d	09 03			09 26				10 03			10 26				11 03			11 26				12 03
Wolverhampton 7 🚌	d	09 17		09 32	09 41				10 17		10 32	10 41				11 17		11 33	11 41				12 17
Dunbar	d																			07 27			
Berwick-upon-Tweed	d												06 48		07 40								
Alnmouth for Alnwick	d												07 08		08 00								
Morpeth	d														08 14								
Newcastle 8	d					06 45		07 35					07 40		08 36					08 43		09 35	
Chester-le-Street	d																						
Durham	d					06 57		07 47					07 52		08 48					08 56		09 47	
Darlington 7	d					07 14		08 04					08 10		09 05					09 13		10 05	
York 8	d					07 44		08 34					08 44		09 35					09 46		10 34	
Leeds 10	d					08 12							09 11							10 12			
Wakefield Westgate 7	d					08 24							09 24							10 24			
Doncaster 7	d							08 58							09 58							10 58	
Sheffield 7 🚌	d					08 54		09 23					09 54		10 23					10 54		11 23	
Chesterfield	d					09 06							10 06							11 06			
Nottingham 8 🚌	d		08 37				09 08			09 37				10 08			10 37				11 11		
Derby 6	d		09 10			09 27	09 36	09 53		10 10			10 28	10 37	10 53		11 10			11 27	11 36	11 54	
Burton-on-Trent	d		09 21			09 38	09 49			10 21				10 49			11 21			11 39	11 49		
Tamworth	d		09 33				10 02			10 33			10 48	11 02			11 33				12 02		
Birmingham New Street 12	a	09 39	09 54	09 55	09 58	10 04	10 24	10 27	10 39	10 54	10 55	10 58	11 04	11 24	11 27	11 39	11 54	11 55	11 58	12 07	12 24	12 27	12 39
Birmingham New Street 12	d	09 42			10 04	10 12	10 30	10 33	10 42			11 04	11 12	11 30	11 33	11 42			12 04	12 12	12 30	12 33	12 42
Cheltenham Spa	a	10 23				10 50	11 10		11 23				11 50	12 10		12 23				12 50	13 10		13 25
Gloucester 7	a						11 22							12 22							13 22		
Bristol Parkway 7	a	10 57				11 24			11 54				12 29			12 55				13 24			13 57
Bristol Temple Meads 10	a	11 09				11 37			12 08				12 42			13 07				13 38			14 08
Newport (South Wales)	a						12 07							13 11							14 08		
Cardiff Central 7	a						12 23							13 27							14 24		
Weston-super-Mare	a	11 29																					
Taunton	a	11 59				12 15							13 15							14 15			
Tiverton Parkway	a	12 12				12 28							13 28							14 28			
Exeter St Davids 6	a	12 26				12 42							13 42							14 42			
Dawlish	a	12 40																					
Teignmouth	a	12 45																					
Newton Abbot	a	12 52				13 03							14 02							15 02			
Torquay	a	13 03																					
Paignton	a	13 11																					
Totnes	a					13 16							14 15							15 15			
Plymouth	a					13 43							14 42							15 42			
Liskeard 6	a																						
Bodmin Parkway	a																						
Lostwithiel	a																						
Par	a																						
Newquay (Summer Only)	a																						
St Austell	a																						
Truro	a																						
Redruth	a																						
Camborne	a																						
Hayle	a																						
St Erth	a																						
Penzance	a																						
Birmingham International ✈	d				10 14							11 14							12 14				
Coventry	d				10 25							11 25							12 25				
Leamington Spa 8	d				10 38			11 00				11 38			12 00				12 38			13 02	
Banbury	a				10 54			11 17				11 54			12 17				12 54			13 19	
Oxford	a				11 14			11 40				12 14			12 40				13 14			13 40	
Reading 7	a				11 39			12 07				12 39			13 06				13 39			14 07	
Guildford	a																						
Basingstoke	a				12 08			12 40				13 08							14 08			14 40	
Winchester	a				12 24			12 55				13 24							14 24			14 55	
Southampton Airport Pkway ✈	a				12 32			13 08				13 32							14 32			15 08	
Southampton Central ⛴	a				12 41			13 17				13 41							14 41			15 17	
Brockenhurst 3	a				12 57							13 57							14 57				
Bournemouth	a				13 11							14 11							15 11				

A 🛒 to Newport (South Wales)

B 🛒 from Edinburgh

Table 51

Saturdays

18 February to 24 March

Scotland, The North East, North West England - The South West and South Coast

Route Diagram - see first Page of Table 51

		XC	VT	XC	XC	XC	XC	XC	XC	VT	XC	XC	XC	XC	XC	XC	VT	XC	XC	XC	XC	XC
		1	◇1	◇1	◇1	◇1	◇1	◇1	1	◇1	◇1	◇1	◇1	◇1	◇1	1	◇1	◇1	◇1	◇1	◇1	◇1
						A							A						B	C		
Aberdeen	d																					
Stonehaven	d																					
Montrose	d																					
Arbroath	d																					
Dundee	d				06 32																	
Leuchars 3	d				06 46																	
Cupar	d				06 54																	
Ladybank	d				07 03																	
Markinch	d				07 11																	
Kirkcaldy	d				07 21																	
Inverkeithing	d				07 38																	
Glasgow Central 15	d									10 00		07 50							09 00			
Motherwell	d											08 05							09 15			
Haymarket	d				07 56							08 50							09 57			
Edinburgh 10	d		08 52		08 05							09 06					10 52		10 05			
Haymarket	d		08 57														10 57					
Lockerbie	d																					
Carlisle 8	d		10 07							11 09							12 07					
Penrith North Lakes	d									11 24												
Oxenholme Lake District	d		10 42														12 43					
Lancaster 6	d		10 57														12 57					
Preston 8	d		11 17							12 17							13 17					
Wigan North Western	d		11 28							12 28							13 28					
Warrington Bank Quay	d		11 39							12 39							13 39					
M'chester Piccadilly 10	d			11 27				12 07			12 27				13 07			13 27				14 07
Stockport	d			11 35				12 16			12 35				13 16			13 35				14 16
Wilmslow	d																					
Crewe 10	d		12 01							13 01							14 01					
Macclesfield	d			11 49							12 49							13 49				
Congleton	d																					
Stoke-on-Trent	d			12 07				12 44			13 07				13 44			14 07				14 44
Stafford	d			12 25				13 03			13 26				14 03			14 26				15 03
Wolverhampton 7	d		12 32	12 41				13 16		13 32	13 41				14 17		14 32	14 41				15 17
Dunbar	d											09 26										
Berwick-upon-Tweed	d				08 46							09 49							10 48			
Alnmouth for Alnwick	d				09 08																	
Morpeth	d																		11 19			
Newcastle 8	d				09 41		10 35					10 44		11 35					11 42		12 35	
Chester-le-Street	d																					
Durham	d				09 55		10 47					10 56		11 47					11 55		12 47	
Darlington 7	d				10 12		11 04					11 13		12 05					12 12		13 04	
York 8	d				10 45		11 34					11 45		12 34					12 45		13 34	
Leeds 10	d				11 11							12 11							13 11			
Wakefield Westgate 7	d				11 23							12 24							13 23			
Doncaster 7	d						11 58							12 58							13 58	
Sheffield 7	d				11 54		12 23					12 54		13 23					13 54		14 23	
Chesterfield	d				12 07							13 06							14 07			
Nottingham 8	d	11 37				12 08			12 37				13 08			13 37				14 08		
Derby 6	d	12 10			12 29	12 36	12 53		13 06			13 28	13 36	13 53		14 06			14 30	14 36	14 53	
Burton-on-Trent	d	12 21				12 49			13 21			13 38	13 49			14 18				14 49		
Tamworth	d	12 33			12 49	13 02			13 33				14 02			14 30			14 49	15 02		
Birmingham New Street 12	a	12 54	12 55	12 58	13 09	13 24	13 27	13 39	13 54	13 55	13 58	14 07	14 24	14 27	14 39	14 54	14 55	14 58	15 08	15 24	15 27	15 39
Birmingham New Street 12	d			13 04	13 12	13 30	13 33	13 42			14 04	14 12	14 30	14 33	14 42			15 04	15 12	15 30	15 33	15 42
Cheltenham Spa	a				13 51	14 10		14 23				14 50	15 10		15 23				15 50	16 10		16 23
Gloucester 7	a					14 22							15 22							16 22		
Bristol Parkway 7	a				14 26			14 57				15 23			15 55				16 29			16 54
Bristol Temple Meads 10	a				14 41			15 09				15 37			16 08				16 42			17 07
Newport (South Wales)	a					15 11							16 08							17 10		
Cardiff Central 7	a					15 27							16 25							17 26		
Weston-super-Mare	a																					
Taunton	a				15 16			15 43				16 15							17 17			17 41
Tiverton Parkway	a				15 29			15 55				16 28							17 30			17 53
Exeter St Davids 6	a				15 45			16 10				16 42							17 46			18 08
Dawlish	a																					18 21
Teignmouth	a																					18 26
Newton Abbot	a				16 06							17 02							18 10			18 33
Torquay	a																					18 45
Paignton	a																					18 53
Totnes	a				16 20							17 15							18 24			
Plymouth	a				16 48							17 42							18 52			
Liskeard 6	a																		19 18			
Bodmin Parkway	a																		19 32			
Lostwithiel	a																					
Par	a																		19 44			
Newquay (Summer Only)	a																					
St Austell	a																		19 52			
Truro	a																		20 10			
Redruth	a																		20 26			
Camborne	a																		20 33			
Hayle	a																					
St Erth	a																		20 45			
Penzance	a																		20 56			
Birmingham International	d			13 14							14 14							15 14				
Coventry	d			13 25							14 25							15 25				
Leamington Spa 8	d			13 38			14 00				14 38			15 00				15 38			16 02	
Banbury	a			13 54			14 17				14 54			15 19				15 54			16 18	
Oxford	a			14 14			14 40				15 14			15 41				16 14			16 40	
Reading 7	a			14 39			15 07				15 39			16 08				16 39			17 07	
Guildford	a																					
Basingstoke	a			15 08							16 08			16 40				17 08				
Winchester	a			15 24							16 24			16 55				17 24				
Southampton Airport Pkwy	a			15 32							16 32			17 08				17 32				
Southampton Central	a			15 41							16 41			17 17				17 41				
Brockenhurst 3	a			15 57							16 57							17 57				
Bournemouth	a			16 11							17 11							18 11				

A from Birmingham New Street to Newport (South Wales)

B from Edinburgh to Plymouth

C to Newport (South Wales)

Table 51

Saturdays

18 February to 24 March

Scotland, The North East, North West England - The South West and South Coast

Route Diagram - see first Page of Table 51

		XC	VT	XC	XC	XC	XC	XC	XC	VT	XC	XC	XC	XC	XC	XC	VT	XC	XC	XC	XC	XC	XC
		[1]	◇[1]	◇[1]	◇[1]	◇[1]	◇[1]	◇[1]	[1]	◇[1]	◇[1]	◇[1]	◇[1]	◇[1]	◇[1]	[1]	◇[1]	◇[1]	◇[1]	◇[1]	◇[1]	◇[1]	[1]
					A																		
		🛒	☕	🛒	🛒	🛒	🛒	🛒	🛒	☕	🛒	🛒		🛒	🛒	🛒	☕	🛒	🛒		🛒	🛒	🛒
Aberdeen	d				08 20																		
Stonehaven	d				08 38																		
Montrose	d				08 59																		
Arbroath	d				09 15																		
Dundee	d				09 32																		
Leuchars [3]	d				09 47																		
Cupar	d				09 54																		
Ladybank	d				10 01																		
Markinch	d				10 08																		
Kirkcaldy	d				10 17																		
Inverkeithing	d				10 32																		
Glasgow Central [15]	d		12 00									10 59					14 00						
Motherwell	d											11 14											
Haymarket	d				10 52							11 56											
Edinburgh [10]	d				11 05					12 52		12 09							13 08				
Haymarket	d									12 57													
Lockerbie	d																						
Carlisle [8]	d		13 09							14 07							15 11						
Penrith North Lakes	d									14 22													
Oxenholme Lake District	d																15 46						
Lancaster [6]	d		13 58							14 57													
Preston [8]	d		14 17							15 17							16 17						
Wigan North Western	d		14 28							15 28							16 28						
Warrington Bank Quay	d		14 39							15 39							16 39						
M'chester Piccadilly [10] ⛴	d			14 27				15 07			15 27			16 07				16 27				17 06	
Stockport	d			14 35				15 16			15 35			16 16				16 35					
Wilmslow	d																						
Crewe [10]	d		15 01							16 01							17 01						
Macclesfield	d			14 49							15 49							16 49				17 26	
Congleton	d																						
Stoke-on-Trent	d			15 07				15 44			16 07			16 44				17 07				17 44	
Stafford	d			15 26				16 03			16 25			17 03				17 26				18 04	
Wolverhampton [7] ⛴	d		15 32	15 41				16 17		16 32	16 41			17 17			17 32	17 41				18 17	
Dunbar	d				11 25														13 29				
Berwick-upon-Tweed	d				11 48							12 48											
Alnmouth for Alnwick	d				12 08														14 09				
Morpeth	d																						
Newcastle [8]	d				12 44		13 35					13 44	14 35						14 44		15 07		
Chester-le-Street	d																						
Durham	d				12 56		13 47					13 56	14 47						14 56		15 19		
Darlington [7]	d				13 13		14 05					14 13	15 04						15 13		15 36		
York [8]	d				13 44		14 34					14 44	15 34						15 45		16 06		
Leeds [10]	d				14 11							15 12							16 12		16 40		
Wakefield Westgate [7]	d				14 24							15 24							16 24		16 52		
Doncaster [7]	d						14 58						15 58										
Sheffield [7] ⛴	d				14 54		15 23					15 54	16 23						16 54		17 23		
Chesterfield	d				15 06							16 07							17 06				
Nottingham [8] ⛴	d	14 37				15 08			15 37				16 08			16 37				17 11			17 37
Derby [6]	d	15 10			15 28	15 36	15 53		16 10			16 28	16 36	16 53		17 06			17 28	17 36	17 53		18 10
Burton-on-Trent	d	15 24			15 38	15 49			16 21				16 49			17 21			17 38	17 49			18 22
Tamworth	d	15 33				16 02			16 33			16 48	17 02			17 33				18 02			18 34
Birmingham New Street [12]	a	15 54	15 55	15 58	16 04	16 24	16 27	16 39	16 54	16 55	16 58	17 07	17 24	17 27	17 39	17 54	17 55	17 58	18 07	18 24	18 27	18 38	18 54
Birmingham New Street [12]	d			16 04	16 12	16 30	16 33	16 42			17 04	17 12	17 30	17 33	17 42			18 04	18 12	18 30	18 33	18 42	
Cheltenham Spa	a				16 50	17 10		17 23				17 50	18 17		18 23				18 50	19 10		19 23	
Gloucester [7]	a					17 22							18 29							19 22			
Bristol Parkway [7]	a				17 24			17 54				18 29			18 54				19 25			19 55	
Bristol Temple Meads [10]	a				17 38			18 07				18 42			19 05				19 39			20 06	
Newport (South Wales)	a					18 05							19 12							20 05		20 55	
Cardiff Central [7]	a					18 21							19 29							20 21		21 11	
Weston-super-Mare	a																						
Taunton	a				18 15							19 15							20 15				
Tiverton Parkway	a				18 28							19 28							20 28				
Exeter St Davids [6]	a				18 42							19 43							20 42				
Dawlish	a																						
Teignmouth	a																						
Newton Abbot	a				19 04							20 03							21 03				
Torquay	a																						
Paignton	a																						
Totnes	a				19 17							20 16							21 16				
Plymouth	a				19 43							20 43							21 43				
Liskeard [6]	a				20 10							21 24											
Bodmin Parkway	a				20 22							21 36											
Lostwithiel	a				20 28																		
Par	a				20 35							21 48											
Newquay (Summer Only)	a																						
St Austell	a				20 42							21 54											
Truro	a				21 00							22 12											
Redruth	a				21 12							22 27											
Camborne	a				21 18							22 34											
Hayle	a				21 26																		
St Erth	a				21 31							22 45											
Penzance	a				21 43							22 54											
Birmingham International ✈	d			16 14							17 14							18 14					
Coventry	d			16 25							17 25							18 25					
Leamington Spa [8]	d			16 38			17 00				17 38			18 02				18 38			19 00		
Banbury	a			16 54			17 17				17 54			18 18				18 54			19 17		
Oxford	a			17 14			17 41				18 14			18 40				19 14			19 40		
Reading [7]	a			17 39			18 07				18 39			19 07				19 39			20 10		
Guildford	a																						
Basingstoke	a			18 08			18 40				19 08							20 08					
Winchester	a			18 24			18 55				19 24							20 24					
Southampton Airport Pkway ✈	a			18 32			19 08				19 32							20 32					
Southampton Central ⛴	a			18 40			19 17				19 41							20 41					
Brockenhurst [3]	a			18 57							19 57							20 57					
Bournemouth	a			19 11							20 11							21 11					

A 🛒 from Edinburgh to Plymouth

Table 51

Saturdays

18 February to 24 March

Scotland, The North East, North West England - The South West and South Coast

Route Diagram - see first Page of Table 51

		VT	XC	XC	XC	XC	XC	XC	VT	XC	XC	XC	XC	XC	LM	XC	VT	XC	XC	XC	XC	VT
		◇1	◇1	◇1	◇1	◇1	◇1	1	◇1	◇1	◇1	◇1	◇1	◇1	◇1	1	◇1	◇1	◇1	◇1	◇1	◇1
			A	B						A	C							D	D			
		🍽	🛒	🛒		🛒	🛒	🛒	🍽	🛒	🛒		🛒	🛒			🍽	🛒	🛒	🛒		🍽
Aberdeen	d																					
Stonehaven	d																					
Montrose	d																					
Arbroath	d																					
Dundee	d																					
Leuchars 3	d																					
Cupar	d																					
Ladybank	d																					
Markinch	d																					
Kirkcaldy	d																					
Inverkeithing	d																					
Glasgow Central 15	d			12 51					16 00										15 00			18 00
Motherwell	d			13 06															15 14			
Haymarket	d																		15 56			
Edinburgh 10	d	14 52		14 08							15 08						16 52		16 05			
Haymarket	d	14 57															16 57					
Lockerbie	d																					
Carlisle 8	d	16 07							17 09								18 08					19 09
Penrith North Lakes	d	16 22																				
Oxenholme Lake District	d								17 44								18 42					
Lancaster 6	d	16 57															18 57					19 56
Preston 8	d	17 17							18 17								19 17					20 17
Wigan North Western	d	17 28							18 28								19 28					20 28
Warrington Bank Quay	d	17 39							18 39								19 39					20 39
M'chester Piccadilly 10 ⛴	d		17 27				18 05			18 27				19 07				19 27			20 07	
Stockport	d		17 36				18 13			18 35				19 16				19 35			20 16	
Wilmslow	d																					
Crewe 10	d	18 01							19 01						19 51		20 01					21 01
Macclesfield	d						18 26											19 49				
Congleton	d		17 54							18 54												
Stoke-on-Trent	d		18 08				18 44			19 07				19 44				20 07			20 44	
Stafford	d		18 27				19 03			19 25				20 03	20 12			20 26			21 03	
Wolverhampton 7 ⛴	d	18 32	18 41				19 17		19 32	19 41				20 17	20 28		20 33	20 41			21 16	21 33
Dunbar	d										15 28											
Berwick-upon-Tweed	d			14 49																		
Alnmouth for Alnwick	d																		17 03			
Morpeth	d																		17 17			
Newcastle 8	d			15 41		16 35					16 41		17 32						17 44	18 35		
Chester-le-Street	d												17 41									
Durham	d			15 53		16 47					16 52		17 48						17 56	18 48		
Darlington 7	d			16 11		17 04					17 10		18 05						18 13	19 05		
York 8	d			16 44		17 34					17 44		18 34						18 44	19 34		
Leeds 10	d			17 11							18 11								19 11			
Wakefield Westgate 7	d			17 23							18 23								19 24			
Doncaster 7	d					17 58							18 58							19 58		
Sheffield 7 ⛴	d			17 54		18 23					18 54		19 24						19 54	20 23		
Chesterfield	d			18 07							19 06								20 06			
Nottingham 8 ⛴	d				18 08			18 37				19 08				19 37						
Derby 6	d			18 28	18 36	18 53		19 10			19 27	19 36	19 54			20 10			20 28	20 53		
Burton-on-Trent	d				18 49			19 21			19 37	19 49				20 21						
Tamworth	d			18 46	19 02			19 33				20 02				20 33			20 46			
Birmingham New Street 12	a	18 55	18 58	19 06	19 24	19 27	19 33	19 54	19 55	19 58	20 06	20 24	20 27	20 33	20 47	20 54	20 55	20 58	21 03	21 25	21 32	21 54
Birmingham New Street 12	d		19 04	19 12	19 30	19 33	19 42			20 04	20 12	20 30		20 42				21 04	21 10			
Cheltenham Spa	a			19 50	20 10		20 23				20 49	21 10		21 23					21 49			
Gloucester 7	a				20 22							21 22							21 59			
Bristol Parkway 7	a			20 29			20 54				21 22			21 58					22 30			
Bristol Temple Meads 10	a			20 42			21 06				21 35			22 12					22 41			
Newport (South Wales)	a				21 11							22 21										
Cardiff Central 7	a				21 29							22 43										
Weston-super-Mare	a																					
Taunton	a			21 15							22 15											
Tiverton Parkway	a			21 28							22 28											
Exeter St Davids 6	a			21 42							22 43											
Dawlish	a																					
Teignmouth	a																					
Newton Abbot	a			22 04																		
Torquay	a																					
Paignton	a																					
Totnes	a			22 20																		
Plymouth	a			22 47																		
Liskeard 6	a																					
Bodmin Parkway	a																					
Lostwithiel	a																					
Par	a																					
Newquay (Summer Only)	a																					
St Austell	a																					
Truro	a																					
Redruth	a																					
Camborne	a																					
Hayle	a																					
St Erth	a																					
Penzance	a																					
Birmingham International ✈	d		19 14							20 14								21 14				
Coventry	d		19 25							20 25								21 25				
Leamington Spa 8	d		19 38			20 03				20 38								21 38				
Banbury	a		19 54			20 19				20 54								21 54				
Oxford	a		20 14			20 40				21 14								22 16				
Reading 7	a		20 39			21 10				21 40								22 41				
Guildford	a																					
Basingstoke	a		21 08							22 09								23 06				
Winchester	a		21 24							22 24								23 24				
Southampton Airport Pkwy ✈	a		21 32							22 33								23 32				
Southampton Central ⛴	a		21 41							22 41								23 41				
Brockenhurst 3	a		21 57							22 56												
Bournemouth	a		22 15							23 21												

A 🛒 to Reading
B 🛒 from Edinburgh to Bristol Temple Meads
C 🛒 to Bristol Temple Meads
D 🛒 to Birmingham New Street

Table 51

Saturdays

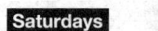

18 February to 24 March

Scotland, The North East, North West England - The South West and South Coast

Route Diagram - see first Page of Table 51

		XC	XC	XC	XC	XC	VT	VT	XC	XC		XC
		1	◇1	◇1	◇1	◇1	◇1	◇1	◇1	1		◇1
				A		B						C
				⚲		⚲	⊡	⊡				⚲
Aberdeen	d											
Stonehaven	d											
Montrose	d											
Arbroath	d											
Dundee	d											
Leuchars 3	d											
Cupar	d											
Ladybank	d											
Markinch	d											
Kirkcaldy	d											
Inverkeithing	d											
Glasgow Central 15	d						18 40					16 52
Motherwell	d											17 14
Haymarket	d											17 56
Edinburgh 10	d			17 08				18 42				18 05
Haymarket	d							18 46				
Lockerbie	d											
Carlisle 8	d						19 48	19 59				
Penrith North Lakes	d						20 02	20 14				
Oxenholme Lake District	d						20 25	20 37				
Lancaster 6	d						20 40	20 52				
Preston 8	d						21 00	21 21				
Wigan North Western	d						21 11	21 32				
Warrington Bank Quay	d						21 22	21 43				
M'chester Piccadilly 10 ⛴	d		20 27		21 07				21 27			
Stockport	d		20 35						21 36			
Wilmslow	d											
Crewe 10	d						21 43	22 05				
Macclesfield	d		20 49						21 50			
Congleton	d											
Stoke-on-Trent	d		21 07		21 45				22 08			
Stafford	d		21 27		22 03		22 08	22 25	22 33			
Wolverhampton 7 ⛴	d		21 41		22 16		22 23	22 40	22 46			
Dunbar	d			17 28								18 25
Berwick-upon-Tweed	d			17 51								18 48
Alnmouth for Alnwick	d											19 08
Morpeth	d											
Newcastle 8	d			18 44		19 35						19 44
Chester-le-Street	d											
Durham	d			18 56		19 49						19 56
Darlington 7	d			19 13		20 06						20 13
York 8	d			19 44		20 34						20 45
Leeds 10	d			20 11								21 11
Wakefield Westgate 7	d			20 23								21 23
Doncaster 7	d					21 00						
Sheffield 7 ⛴	d			20 54		21 23						21 54
Chesterfield	d			21 06		21 35						22 06
Nottingham 8 ⛴	d	20 37								21 37		
Derby 6	d	21 06		21 28		21 53				22 10		22 26
Burton-on-Trent	d	21 21		21 38						22 21		22 37
Tamworth	d	21 33		21 49						22 33		22 47
Birmingham New Street 12	a	21 54	21 58	22 05	22 32	22 43	22 46	22 59	23 02	23 02		23 05
Birmingham New Street 12	d											
Cheltenham Spa	a											
Gloucester 7	a											
Bristol Parkway 7	a											
Bristol Temple Meads 10	a											
Newport (South Wales)	a											
Cardiff Central 7	a											
Weston-super-Mare	a											
Taunton	a											
Tiverton Parkway	a											
Exeter St Davids 6	a											
Dawlish	a											
Teignmouth	a											
Newton Abbot	a											
Torquay	a											
Paignton	a											
Totnes	a											
Plymouth	a											
Liskeard 6	a											
Bodmin Parkway	a											
Lostwithiel	a											
Par	a											
Newquay (Summer Only)	a											
St Austell	a											
Truro	a											
Redruth	a											
Camborne	a											
Hayle	a											
St Erth	a											
Penzance	a											
Birmingham International ✈	d											
Coventry	d											
Leamington Spa 8	d											
Banbury	a											
Oxford	a											
Reading 7	a											
Guildford	a											
Basingstoke	a											
Winchester	a											
Southampton Airport Pkwy ✈	a											
Southampton Central ⛴	a											
Brockenhurst 3	a											
Bournemouth	a											

A ⚲ to Leeds

B ⚲ to York

C ⚲ from Edinburgh to Leeds

Scotland, The North East, North West England - The South West and South Coast

Route Diagram - see first Page of Table 51

		XC	XC	XC	XC	XC	XC	XC	XC	XC	XC	XC	VT	XC	XC	XC	XC	XC	XC	VT	XC	XC	XC
		◇1	◇1	◇1	◇1	◇1	◇1	◇1	◇1	◇1	◇1	◇1	◇1	◇1	◇1	◇1	◇1	◇1	1	◇1	◇1	◇1	◇1
		A							B	C	B			D		C							E
Aberdeen	d																						
Stonehaven	d																						
Montrose	d																						
Arbroath	d																						
Dundee	d																						
Leuchars 3	d																						
Cupar	d																						
Ladybank	d																						
Markinch	d																						
Kirkcaldy	d																						
Inverkeithing	d																						
Glasgow Central 15	d																						
Motherwell	d																						
Haymarket	d																						
Edinburgh 10	d	17p08																					
Haymarket	d																						
Lockerbie	d																						
Carlisle 8	d																						
Penrith North Lakes	d																						
Oxenholme Lake District	d																						
Lancaster 6	d																			06 58			
Preston 8	d												06 17							07 17			
Wigan North Western	d												06 28							07 28			
Warrington Bank Quay	d												06 39							07 39			
M'chester Piccadilly 10	d							05 11				06 00						07 07			07 27		
Stockport	d											06 08						07 16			07 35		
Wilmslow	d																						
Crewe 10	d							05 47					07 01							08 01			
Macclesfield	d											06 21									07 49		
Congleton	d																						
Stoke-on-Trent	d							06 08				06 39						07 44			08 07		
Stafford	d							06 26				06 58						08 03			08 26		
Wolverhampton 7	d							06 41				07 15	07 32					08 18		08 32	08 41		
Dunbar	d	17p28																					
Berwick-upon-Tweed	d	17p51																					
Alnmouth for Alnwick	d																						
Morpeth	d																						
Newcastle 8	d	18p41																					
Chester-le-Street	d																						
Durham	d	18p53																					
Darlington 7	d	19p10																					
York 8	d	19p44																				06 17	
Leeds 10	d	20p11													06 00		06 15					07 10	
Wakefield Westgate 7	d	20p23													06 12		06 29					07 23	
Doncaster 7	d																06 47						
Sheffield 7	d	20p54													06 50		07 18					07 56	
Chesterfield	d	21p06													07 03		07 30					08 08	
Nottingham 8	d									05 57				06 37		06 56			07 37				08 08
Derby 6	d	21p29							06 10	06 36	06 48			07 06	07 26	07 36	07 50		08 06			08 28	08 36
Burton-on-Trent	d	21p40							06 20	06 48	06 59			07 18	07 37	07 50	08 00		08 18			08 39	08 49
Tamworth	d	21p50							06 31	07 01	07 09			07 30	07 48	08 02	08 11		08 30			08 49	09 02
Birmingham New Street 12	a	22p07						06 57	06 50	07 24	07 27	07 31	07 55	07 55	08 08	08 24	08 27	08 38	08 54	08 55	08 58	09 08	09 24
Birmingham New Street 12	d	22p12	05 00	05 42	06 04	06 33	06 42	07 04	07 12	07 30	07 33	07 42		08 04	08 12	08 30	08 33	08 42			09 04	09 12	09 30
Cheltenham Spa	a	23p30	06 02	06 41			07 23		07 50	08 10		08 23			08 51	09 10		09 23				09 50	10 10
Gloucester 7	a		06 13	06 54						08 22						09 22							10 22
Bristol Parkway 7	a	00 01					07 54		08 24			08 54			09 24			09 55				10 29	
Bristol Temple Meads 10	a	00 13					08 05		08 38			09 08			09 38			10 06				10 42	
Newport (South Wales)	a		07 06	07 52						09 07						10 07							11 08
Cardiff Central 7	a		07 22	08 08						09 23						10 23							11 24
Weston-super-Mare	a																						
Taunton	a						08 42		09 14						10 17							11 15	
Tiverton Parkway	a						08 54		09 28						10 30							11 28	
Exeter St Davids 6	a						09 09		09 41						10 46							11 42	
Dawlish	a																						
Teignmouth	a																						
Newton Abbot	a						09 28		10 02						11 09							12 03	
Torquay	a						09 40																
Paignton	a						09 47																
Totnes	a								10 15						11 23							12 16	
Plymouth	a								10 41						11 51							12 43	
Liskeard 8	a																						
Bodmin Parkway	a																						
Lostwithiel	a																						
Par	a																						
Newquay (Summer Only)	a																						
St Austell	a																						
Truro	a																						
Redruth	a																						
Camborne	a																						
Hayle	a																						
St Erth	a																						
Penzance	a																						
Birmingham International	d				06 14			07 14						08 14							09 14		
Coventry	d				06 25			07 25						08 25							09 25		
Leamington Spa 8	d				06 38	07 00		07 38			08 00			08 38			09 00				09 38		
Banbury	a				06 54	07 17		07 54			08 17			08 54			09 17				09 54		
Oxford	a				07 14	07 40		08 14			08 40			09 14			09 40				10 14		
Reading 7	a				07 39	08 06		08 39			09 11			09 39			10 07				10 39		
Guildford	a																						
Basingstoke	a				08 08	08 40		09 08						10 08			10 39				11 08		
Winchester	a				08 24	08 55		09 24						10 24			10 54				11 24		
Southampton Airport Pkway	a				08 32	09 08		09 32						10 32			11 08				11 32		
Southampton Central	a				08 41	09 17		09 40						10 43			11 17				11 41		
Brockenhurst 3	a				08 56			09 57						10 58							11 57		
Bournemouth	a				09 14			10 11						11 12							12 11		

A to Leeds
B from Birmingham New Street
C from Birmingham New Street to Newport (South Wales)
D from Derby
E to Newport (South Wales)

Table 51

Saturdays
from 31 March

Scotland, The North East, North West England - The South West and South Coast

Route Diagram - see first Page of Table 51

		XC	XC	XC	VT	XC	XC	XC	XC	XC	XC	VT	XC	XC	XC	XC	XC	XC	VT	XC	XC	XC	XC
		◇1	◇1	1	◇1	◇1	◇1	◇1	◇1	◇1	1	◇1	◇1	◇1	◇1	◇1	◇1	1	◇1	◇1	◇1	◇1	◇1
								A							A						B	A	
		🛒	🛒		☕	🛒	🛒	🛒	🛒	🛒		☕	🛒	🛒	🛒	🛒	🛒		☕	🛒	🛒	🛒	🛒
Aberdeen	d																						
Stonehaven	d																						
Montrose	d																						
Arbroath	d																						
Dundee	d																						
Leuchars 3	d																						
Cupar	d																						
Ladybank	d																						
Markinch	d																						
Kirkcaldy	d																						
Inverkeithing	d																						
Glasgow Central 15	d				05 50														08 00		06 01		
Motherwell	d				06 04																06 16		
Haymarket	d																				06 57		
Edinburgh 10	d											06 52		06 06		07 00					07 07		
Haymarket	d											06 56											
Lockerbie	d																						
Carlisle 8	d				07 03							08 07							09 09				
Penrith North Lakes	d				07 18							08 22											
Oxenholme Lake District	d				07 42																		
Lancaster 6	d				07 57							08 57							09 57				
Preston 8	d				08 17							09 17							10 17				
Wigan North Western	d				08 28							09 28							10 28				
Warrington Bank Quay	d				08 39							09 39							10 39				
M'chester Piccadilly 10 ⛴	d		08 07			08 27				09 07			09 27				10 07			10 27			
Stockport	d		08 16			08 35				09 16			09 35				10 16			10 35			
Wilmslow	d																						
Crewe 10	d				09 01							10 01							11 01				
Macclesfield	d					08 49							09 49							10 49			
Congleton	d																						
Stoke-on-Trent	d		08 44			09 07				09 44			10 07				10 44			11 07			
Stafford	d		09 03			09 26				10 03			10 26				11 03			11 26			
Wolverhampton 7 ⛴	d		09 17		09 32	09 41				10 17		10 32	10 41				11 17		11 33	11 41			
Dunbar	d																				07 27		
Berwick-upon-Tweed	d													06 48		07 40							
Alnmouth for Alnwick	d													07 08		08 00							
Morpeth	d															08 14							
Newcastle 8	d	06 22					06 45		07 35					07 40		08 36					08 43		09 35
Chester-le-Street	d																						
Durham	d	06 37					06 57		07 47					07 52		08 48					08 56		09 47
Darlington 7	d	06 54					07 14		08 04					08 10		09 05					09 13		10 05
York 8	d	07 24					07 44		08 34					08 44		09 35					09 46		10 34
Leeds 10	d						08 12							09 11							10 12		
Wakefield Westgate 7	d						08 24							09 24							10 24		
Doncaster 7	d	07 52							08 58							09 58							10 58
Sheffield 7 ⛴	d	08 20					08 54		09 23					09 54		10 23					10 54		11 23
Chesterfield	d	08 32					09 06							10 06							11 06		
Nottingham 8 ⛴	d			08 37				09 08			09 37				10 08			10 37				11 11	
Derby 6	d	08 53		09 10			09 27	09 36	09 53		10 10			10 28	10 37	10 53		11 10			11 27	11 36	11 54
Burton-on-Trent	d			09 21			09 38	09 49			10 21				10 49			11 21			11 39	11 49	
Tamworth	d			09 33				10 02			10 33			10 48	11 02			11 33				12 02	
Birmingham New Street 12	a	09 27	09 39	09 54	09 55	09 58	10 04	10 24	10 27	10 39	10 54	10 55	10 58	11 04	11 24	11 27	11 39	11 54	11 55	11 58	12 07	12 24	12 27
Birmingham New Street 12	d	09 33	09 42			10 04	10 12	10 30	10 33	10 42			11 04	11 12	11 30	11 33	11 42			12 04	12 12	12 30	12 33
Cheltenham Spa	a		10 23				10 50	11 10		11 23				11 50	12 10		12 23				12 50	13 10	
Gloucester 7	a							11 22							12 22							13 22	
Bristol Parkway 7	a		10 57				11 24			11 54				12 29			12 55				13 24		
Bristol Temple Meads 10	a		11 09				11 37			12 08				12 42			13 07				13 38		
Newport (South Wales)	a							12 07							13 11							14 08	
Cardiff Central 7	a							12 23							13 27							14 24	
Weston-super-Mare	a		11 29																				
Taunton	a		11 59				12 15							13 15							14 15		
Tiverton Parkway	a		12 12				12 28							13 28							14 28		
Exeter St Davids 6	a		12 26				12 42							13 42							14 42		
Dawlish	a		12 40																				
Teignmouth	a		12 45																				
Newton Abbot	a		12 52				13 03							14 02							15 02		
Torquay	a		13 03																				
Paignton	a		13 11																				
Totnes	a						13 16							14 15							15 15		
Plymouth	a						13 43							14 42							15 42		
Liskeard 6	a																						
Bodmin Parkway	a																						
Lostwithiel	a																						
Par	a																						
Newquay (Summer Only)	a																						
St Austell	a																						
Truro	a																						
Redruth	a																						
Camborne	a																						
Hayle	a																						
St Erth	a																						
Penzance	a																						
Birmingham International ✈	d					10 14							11 14							12 14			
Coventry	d					10 25							11 25							12 25			
Leamington Spa 8	d	10 00				10 38			11 00				11 38			12 00				12 38			13 02
Banbury	a	10 17				10 54			11 17				11 54			12 17				12 54			13 19
Oxford	a	10 40				11 14			11 40				12 14			12 40				13 14			13 40
Reading 7	a	11 09				11 39			12 07				12 39			13 06				13 39			14 07
Guildford	a																						
Basingstoke	a					12 08			12 40				13 08							14 08			14 40
Winchester	a					12 24			12 55				13 24							14 24			14 55
Southampton Airport Pkway ✈	a					12 32			13 08				13 32							14 32			15 08
Southampton Central ⛴	a					12 41			13 17				13 41							14 41			15 17
Brockenhurst 3	a					12 57							13 57							14 57			
Bournemouth	a					13 11							14 11							15 11			

A 🛒 to Newport (South Wales)

B 🛒 from Edinburgh

Table 51

Saturdays
from 31 March

Scotland, The North East, North West England - The South West and South Coast

Route Diagram - see first Page of Table 51

		XC	XC	VT	XC	XC	XC	XC	XC	XC	VT	XC	XC	XC	XC	XC	XC	VT	XC	XC	XC	XC
		◇1	1	◇1	◇1	◇1	◇1	◇1	◇1	1	◇1	◇1	◇1	◇1	◇1	◇1	1	◇1	◇1	◇1	◇1	◇1
							A							A						B	C	
Aberdeen	d																					
Stonehaven	d																					
Montrose	d																					
Arbroath	d																					
Dundee	d					06 32																
Leuchars 3	d					06 46																
Cupar	d					06 54																
Ladybank	d					07 03																
Markinch	d					07 11																
Kirkcaldy	d					07 21																
Inverkeithing	d					07 38																
Glasgow Central 15	d										10 00		07 50							09 00		
Motherwell	d												08 05							09 15		
Haymarket	d					07 56							08 50							09 57		
Edinburgh 10	d			08 52		08 05							09 06					10 52		10 05		
Haymarket	d			08 57														10 57				
Lockerbie	d																					
Carlisle 8	d			10 07							11 09							12 07				
Penrith North Lakes	d										11 24											
Oxenholme Lake District	d			10 42														12 43				
Lancaster 6	d			10 57														12 57				
Preston 8	d			11 17							12 17							13 17				
Wigan North Western	d			11 28							12 28							13 28				
Warrington Bank Quay	d			11 39							12 39							13 39				
M'chester Piccadilly 10	d	11 07			11 27				12 07			12 27				13 07			13 27			
Stockport	d	11 16			11 35				12 16			12 35				13 16			13 35			
Wilmslow	d																					
Crewe 10	d			12 01							13 01							14 01				
Macclesfield	d				11 49							12 49							13 49			
Congleton	d																					
Stoke-on-Trent	d	11 44			12 07				12 44			13 07				13 44			14 07			
Stafford	d	12 03			12 25				13 03			13 26				14 03			14 26			
Wolverhampton 7	d	12 17		12 32	12 41				13 16		13 32	13 41				14 17		14 32	14 41			
Dunbar	d												09 26									
Berwick-upon-Tweed	d					08 46							09 49							10 48		
Alnmouth for Alnwick	d					09 08																
Morpeth	d																			11 19		
Newcastle 8	d					09 41		10 35					10 44		11 35					11 42		12 35
Chester-le-Street	d																					
Durham	d					09 55		10 47					10 56		11 47					11 55		12 47
Darlington 7	d					10 12		11 04					11 13		12 05					12 12		13 04
York 8	d					10 45		11 34					11 45		12 34					12 45		13 34
Leeds 10	d					11 11							12 11							13 11		
Wakefield Westgate 7	d					11 23							12 24							13 23		
Doncaster 7	d							11 58							12 58							13 58
Sheffield 7	d					11 54		12 23					12 54		13 23					13 54		14 23
Chesterfield	d					12 07							13 06							14 07		
Nottingham 8	d		11 37				12 08			12 37				13 08			13 37				14 08	
Derby 6	d		12 10			12 29	12 36	12 53		13 06			13 28	13 36	13 53		14 06			14 30	14 36	14 53
Burton-on-Trent	d		12 21				12 49			13 21			13 38	13 49			14 18				14 49	
Tamworth	d		12 33			12 49	13 02			13 33				14 02			14 30			14 49	15 02	
Birmingham New Street 12	a	12 39	12 54	12 55	12 58	13 09	13 24	13 27	13 39	13 54	13 55	13 58	14 07	14 24	14 27	14 39	14 54	14 55	14 58	15 08	15 24	15 27
Birmingham New Street 12	d	12 42			13 04	13 12	13 30	13 33	13 42			14 04	14 12	14 30	14 33	14 42			15 04	15 12	15 30	15 33
Cheltenham Spa	a	13 25				13 51	14 10		14 23				14 50	15 10		15 23				15 50	16 10	
Gloucester 7	a						14 22							15 22							16 22	
Bristol Parkway 7	a	13 57				14 26			14 57				15 23			15 55				16 29		
Bristol Temple Meads 10	a	14 08				14 41			15 09				15 37			16 08				16 42		
Newport (South Wales)	a						15 11							16 08							17 10	
Cardiff Central 7	a						15 27							16 25							17 26	
Weston-super-Mare	a																					
Taunton	a					15 16			15 43				16 15							17 17		
Tiverton Parkway	a					15 29			15 55				16 28							17 30		
Exeter St Davids 6	a					15 45			16 10				16 42							17 46		
Dawlish	a																					
Teignmouth	a																					
Newton Abbot	a					16 06							17 02							18 10		
Torquay	a																					
Paignton	a																					
Totnes	a					16 20							17 15							18 24		
Plymouth	a					16 48							17 42							18 52		
Liskeard 6	a																			19 18		
Bodmin Parkway	a																			19 32		
Lostwithiel	a																					
Par	a																			19 44		
Newquay (Summer Only)	a																					
St Austell	a																			19 52		
Truro	a																			20 10		
Redruth	a																			20 26		
Camborne	a																			20 33		
Hayle	a																					
St Erth	a																			20 45		
Penzance	a																			20 56		
Birmingham International	d				13 14							14 14							15 14			
Coventry	d				13 25							14 25							15 25			
Leamington Spa 8	d				13 38			14 00				14 38			15 00				15 38			16 02
Banbury	a				13 54			14 17				14 54			15 19				15 54			16 18
Oxford	a				14 14			14 40				15 14			15 41				16 14			16 40
Reading 7	a				14 39			15 07				15 39			16 08				16 39			17 07
Guildford	a																					
Basingstoke	a				15 08							16 08			16 40				17 08			
Winchester	a				15 24							16 24			16 55				17 24			
Southampton Airport Pkway	a				15 32							16 32			17 08				17 32			
Southampton Central	a				15 41							16 41			17 17				17 41			
Brockenhurst 3	a				15 57							16 57							17 57			
Bournemouth	a				16 11							17 11							18 11			

A from Birmingham New Street to Newport (South Wales)

B from Edinburgh to Plymouth

C to Newport (South Wales)

Table 51

Saturdays
from 31 March

Scotland, The North East, North West England - The South West and South Coast

Route Diagram - see first Page of Table 51

		XC	XC	VT	XC	XC	XC	XC	XC	XC	VT	XC	XC	XC	XC	XC	XC	VT	XC	XC	XC	XC	XC
		◇1	1	◇1	◇1	◇1	◇1	◇1	◇1	1	◇1	◇1	◇1	◇1	◇1	◇1	1	◇1	◇1	◇1	◇1	◇1	◇1
						A																	
		╤	╤	⊐	╤	╤	╤	╤	╤	╤	⊐	╤	╤		╤	╤	╤	⊐	╤	╤		╤	╤
Aberdeen	d					08 20																	
Stonehaven	d					08 38																	
Montrose	d					08 59																	
Arbroath	d					09 15																	
Dundee	d					09 32																	
Leuchars 3	d					09 47																	
Cupar	d					09 54																	
Ladybank	d					10 01																	
Markinch	d					10 08																	
Kirkcaldy	d					10 17																	
Inverkeithing	d					10 32																	
Glasgow Central 15	d			12 00									10 59					14 00					
Motherwell	d												11 14										
Haymarket	d					10 52							11 56										
Edinburgh 10	d					11 05					12 52		12 09							13 08			
Haymarket	d										12 57												
Lockerbie	d																						
Carlisle 8	d			13 09							14 07							15 11					
Penrith North Lakes	d										14 22												
Oxenholme Lake District	d																	15 46					
Lancaster 6	d			13 58							14 57												
Preston 8	d			14 17							15 17							16 17					
Wigan North Western	d			14 28							15 28							16 28					
Warrington Bank Quay	d			14 39							15 39							16 39					
M'chester Piccadilly 10 ⛴	d	14 07			14 27				15 07			15 27				16 07			16 27				17 06
Stockport	d	14 16			14 35				15 16			15 35				16 16			16 35				
Wilmslow	d																						
Crewe 10	d			15 01							16 01							17 01					
Macclesfield	d				14 49							15 49							16 49				17 26
Congleton	d																						
Stoke-on-Trent	d	14 44			15 07				15 44			16 07				16 44			17 07				17 44
Stafford	d	15 03			15 26				16 03			16 25				17 03			17 26				18 04
Wolverhampton 7 ⛴	d	15 17		15 32	15 41				16 17		16 32	16 41				17 17		17 32	17 41				18 17
Dunbar	d					11 25														13 29			
Berwick-upon-Tweed	d					11 48							12 48										
Alnmouth for Alnwick	d					12 08														14 09			
Morpeth	d																						
Newcastle 8	d					12 44		13 35					13 44		14 35					14 44		15 07	
Chester-le-Street	d																						
Durham	d					12 56		13 47					13 56		14 47					14 56		15 19	
Darlington 7	d					13 13		14 05					14 13		15 04					15 13		15 36	
York 8	d					13 44		14 34					14 44		15 34					15 45		16 06	
Leeds 10	d					14 11							15 12							16 12		16 40	
Wakefield Westgate 7	d					14 24							15 24							16 24		16 52	
Doncaster 7	d							14 58							15 58								
Sheffield 7 ⛴	d					14 54		15 23					15 54		16 23					16 54		17 23	
Chesterfield	d					15 06							16 07							17 06			
Nottingham 8 ⛴	d		14 37				15 08			15 37				16 08			16 37				17 11		
Derby 6	d		15 10			15 28	15 36	15 53		16 10			16 28	16 36	16 53		17 06			17 28	17 36	17 53	
Burton-on-Trent	d		15 24			15 38	15 49			16 21				16 49			17 21			17 38	17 49		
Tamworth	d		15 33				16 02			16 33			16 48	17 02			17 33				18 02		
Birmingham New Street 12	a	15 39	15 54	15 55	15 58	16 04	16 24	16 27	16 39	16 54	16 55	16 58	17 07	17 24	17 27	17 39	17 54	17 55	17 58	18 07	18 24	18 27	18 38
Birmingham New Street 12	d	15 42			16 04	16 12	16 30	16 33	16 42			17 04	17 12	17 30	17 33	17 42			18 04	18 12	18 30	18 33	18 42
Cheltenham Spa	a	16 23				16 50	17 10		17 23				17 50	18 17		18 23				18 50	19 10		19 23
Gloucester 7	a						17 22							18 29							19 22		
Bristol Parkway 7	a	16 54				17 24			17 54				18 29			18 54				19 25			19 55
Bristol Temple Meads 10	a	17 07				17 38			18 07				18 42			19 05				19 39			20 06
Newport (South Wales)	a						18 05							19 12							20 05		20 55
Cardiff Central 7	a						18 21							19 29							20 21		21 11
Weston-super-Mare	a																						
Taunton	a	17 41				18 15							19 15							20 15			
Tiverton Parkway	a	17 53				18 28							19 28							20 28			
Exeter St Davids 6	a	18 08				18 42							19 43							20 42			
Dawlish	a	18 21																					
Teignmouth	a	18 26																					
Newton Abbot	a	18 33				19 04							20 03							21 03			
Torquay	a	18 45																					
Paignton	a	18 53																					
Totnes	a					19 17							20 16							21 16			
Plymouth	a					19 43							20 43							21 43			
Liskeard 6	a					20 10							21 24										
Bodmin Parkway	a					20 22							21 36										
Lostwithiel	a					20 28																	
Par	a					20 35							21 48										
Newquay (Summer Only)	a																						
St Austell	a					20 42							21 54										
Truro	a					21 00							22 12										
Redruth	a					21 12							22 27										
Camborne	a					21 18							22 34										
Hayle	a					21 26																	
St Erth	a					21 31							22 45										
Penzance	a					21 43							22 54										
Birmingham International ✈	d				16 14							17 14							18 14				
Coventry	d				16 25							17 25							18 25				
Leamington Spa 8	d				16 38			17 00				17 38			18 02				18 38			19 00	
Banbury	a				16 54			17 17				17 54			18 18				18 54			19 17	
Oxford	a				17 14			17 41				18 14			18 40				19 14			19 40	
Reading 7	a				17 39			18 07				18 39			19 07				19 39			20 10	
Guildford	a																						
Basingstoke	a				18 08			18 40				19 08							20 08				
Winchester	a				18 24			18 55				19 24							20 24				
Southampton Airport Pkway ✈	a				18 32			19 08				19 32							20 32				
Southampton Central ⛴	a				18 40			19 17				19 41							20 41				
Brockenhurst 3	a				18 57							19 57							20 57				
Bournemouth	a				19 11							20 11							21 11				

A ╤ from Edinburgh to Plymouth

Table 51

Saturdays from 31 March

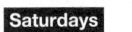

Scotland, The North East, North West England - The South West and South Coast

Route Diagram - see first Page of Table 51

		XC	VT	XC	XC	XC	XC	XC	XC	VT	XC	XC	XC	XC	XC	LM	XC	VT	XC	XC	XC	XC
		■1	◇■1	◇■1	◇■1	◇■1	◇■1	◇■1	■1	◇■1	◇■1	◇■1	◇■1	◇■1	◇■1	◇■1	■1	◇■1	◇■1	◇■1	◇■1	◇■1
				A	B			C			A	C							D	D		
		⚲	☕	⚲	⚲		⚲	⚲	⚲	☕	⚲	⚲		⚲	⚲			☕	⚲	⚲	⚲	
Aberdeen	d																					
Stonehaven	d																					
Montrose	d																					
Arbroath	d																					
Dundee	d																					
Leuchars ■3	d																					
Cupar	d																					
Ladybank	d																					
Markinch	d																					
Kirkcaldy	d																					
Inverkeithing	d																					
Glasgow Central ■15	d				12 51					16 00										15 00		
Motherwell	d				13 06															15 14		
Haymarket	d																			15 56		
Edinburgh ■10	d		14 52		14 08							15 08						16 52		16 05		
Haymarket	d		14 57															16 57				
Lockerbie	d																					
Carlisle ■8	d		16 07							17 09								18 08				
Penrith North Lakes	d		16 22																			
Oxenholme Lake District	d									17 44								18 42				
Lancaster ■6	d		16 57															18 57				
Preston ■8	d		17 17							18 17								19 17				
Wigan North Western	d		17 28							18 28								19 28				
Warrington Bank Quay	d		17 39							18 39								19 39				
M'chester Piccadilly ■10 🚊	d			17 27				18 05			18 27				19 07				19 27			20 07
Stockport	d			17 36				18 13			18 35				19 16				19 35			20 16
Wilmslow	d																					
Crewe ■10	d		18 01							19 01						19 51		20 01				
Macclesfield	d							18 26											19 49			
Congleton	d			17 54							18 54											
Stoke-on-Trent	d			18 08				18 44			19 07				19 44				20 07			20 44
Stafford	d			18 27				19 03			19 25				20 03	20 12			20 26			21 03
Wolverhampton ■7 🚊	d		18 32	18 41				19 17		19 32	19 41				20 17	20 28		20 33	20 41			21 16
Dunbar	d											15 28										
Berwick-upon-Tweed	d				14 49																	
Alnmouth for Alnwick	d																			17 03		
Morpeth	d																			17 17		
Newcastle ■8	d				15 41		16 35					16 41		17 32						17 44	18 35	
Chester-le-Street	d													17 41								
Durham	d				15 53		16 47					16 52		17 48						17 56	18 48	
Darlington ■7	d				16 11		17 04					17 10		18 05						18 13	19 05	
York ■8	d				16 44		17 34					17 44		18 34						18 44	19 34	
Leeds ■10	d				17 11							18 11								19 11		
Wakefield Westgate ■7	d				17 23							18 23								19 24		
Doncaster ■7	d						17 58							18 58							19 58	
Sheffield ■7 🚊	d				17 54		18 23					18 54		19 24						19 54	20 23	
Chesterfield	d				18 07							19 06								20 06		
Nottingham ■8 🚊	d	17 37				18 08			18 37				19 08				19 37					
Derby ■6	d	18 10			18 28	18 36	18 53		19 10			19 27	19 36	19 54			20 10			20 28	20 53	
Burton-on-Trent	d	18 22				18 49			19 21			19 37	19 49				20 21					
Tamworth	d	18 34			18 46	19 02			19 33				20 02				20 33			20 46		
Birmingham New Street ■12	a	18 54	18 55	18 58	19 06	19 24	19 27	19 33	19 54	19 55	19 58	20 06	20 24	20 27	20 33	20 47	20 54	20 55	20 58	21 03	21 25	21 32
Birmingham New Street ■12	d			19 04	19 12	19 30	19 33	19 42			20 04	20 12	20 30		20 42				21 04	21 10		
Cheltenham Spa	a				19 50	20 10		20 23				20 49	21 10		21 23					21 49		
Gloucester ■7	a					20 22							21 22							21 59		
Bristol Parkway ■7	a				20 29			20 54				21 22			21 58					22 30		
Bristol Temple Meads ■10	a				20 42			21 05				21 35			22 12					22 41		
Newport (South Wales)	a					21 11							22 21									
Cardiff Central ■7	a					21 29							22 43									
Weston-super-Mare	a																					
Taunton	a				21 15			21 42				22 15										
Tiverton Parkway	a				21 28			21 55				22 28										
Exeter St Davids ■6	a				21 42			22 09				22 43										
Dawlish	a																					
Teignmouth	a																					
Newton Abbot	a				22 04			22 29				23 10										
Torquay	a																					
Paignton	a																					
Totnes	a				22 20			22 42				23 24										
Plymouth	a				22 47			23 08				23 53										
Liskeard ■6	a																					
Bodmin Parkway	a																					
Lostwithiel	a																					
Par	a																					
Newquay (Summer Only)	a																					
St Austell	a																					
Truro	a																					
Redruth	a																					
Camborne	a																					
Hayle	a																					
St Erth	a																					
Penzance	a																					
Birmingham International ✈	d			19 14							20 14								21 14			
Coventry	d			19 25							20 25								21 25			
Leamington Spa ■8	d			19 38			20 03				20 38								21 38			
Banbury	a			19 54			20 19				20 54								21 54			
Oxford	a			20 14			20 40				21 14								22 16			
Reading ■7	a			20 39			21 10				21 40								22 41			
Guildford	a																					
Basingstoke	a			21 08							22 09								23 06			
Winchester	a			21 24							22 24								23 24			
Southampton Airport Pkway ✈	a			21 32							22 33								23 32			
Southampton Central ⛴	a			21 41							22 41								23 41			
Brockenhurst ■3	a			21 57							22 56											
Bournemouth	a			22 15							23 21											

A ⚲ to Reading
B ⚲ from Edinburgh to Bristol Temple Meads
C ⚲ to Bristol Temple Meads
D ⚲ to Birmingham New Street

Table 51

Saturdays
from 31 March

Scotland, The North East, North West England - The South West and South Coast

Route Diagram - see first Page of Table 51

		VT	XC	XC	XC	XC	XC	VT	XC	XC		XC
		◇1	1	◇1	◇1	◇1	◇1	◇1	◇1	1		◇1
					A		B					C
		⊡			⚲		⚲	⊡				⚲
Aberdeen	d											
Stonehaven	d											
Montrose	d											
Arbroath	d											
Dundee	d											
Leuchars 3	d											
Cupar	d											
Ladybank	d											
Markinch	d											
Kirkcaldy	d											
Inverkeithing	d											
Glasgow Central 15	d	18 00						18 30				16 52
Motherwell	d											17 14
Haymarket	d											17 56
Edinburgh 10	d				17 08							18 05
Haymarket	d											
Lockerbie	d											
Carlisle 8	d	19 09						19 40				
Penrith North Lakes	d							19 54				
Oxenholme Lake District	d							20 17				
Lancaster 6	d	19 56						20 32				
Preston 8	d	20 17						21 00				
Wigan North Western	d	20 28						21 11				
Warrington Bank Quay	d	20 39						21 22				
M'chester Piccadilly 10 ⛴	d			20 27		21 07			21 27			
Stockport	d			20 35					21 36			
Wilmslow	d											
Crewe 10	d	21 01						21 43				
Macclesfield	d			20 49					21 50			
Congleton	d											
Stoke-on-Trent	d			21 07		21 45			22 08			
Stafford	d			21 27		22 03		22 08	22 33			
Wolverhampton 7 ⛴	d	21 33		21 41		22 16		22 23	22 46			
Dunbar	d				17 28							18 25
Berwick-upon-Tweed	d				17 51							18 48
Alnmouth for Alnwick	d											19 08
Morpeth	d											
Newcastle 8	d				18 44		19 35					19 44
Chester-le-Street	d											
Durham	d				18 56		19 49					19 56
Darlington 7	d				19 13		20 06					20 13
York 8	d				19 44		20 34					20 45
Leeds 10	d				20 11							21 11
Wakefield Westgate 7	d				20 23							21 23
Doncaster 7	d						21 00					
Sheffield 7 ⛴	d				20 54		21 23					21 54
Chesterfield	d				21 06		21 35					22 06
Nottingham 8 ⛴	d		20 37							21 37		
Derby 6	d		21 06		21 28		21 53			22 10		22 26
Burton-on-Trent	d		21 21		21 38					22 21		22 37
Tamworth	d		21 33		21 49					22 33		22 47
Birmingham New Street 12	a	21 54	21 54	21 58	22 05	22 32	22 43	22 46	23 02	23 02		23 05
Birmingham New Street 12	d											
Cheltenham Spa	a											
Gloucester 7	a											
Bristol Parkway 7	a											
Bristol Temple Meads 10	a											
Newport (South Wales)	a											
Cardiff Central 7	a											
Weston-super-Mare	a											
Taunton	a											
Tiverton Parkway	a											
Exeter St Davids 6	a											
Dawlish	a											
Teignmouth	a											
Newton Abbot	a											
Torquay	a											
Paignton	a											
Totnes	a											
Plymouth	a											
Liskeard 6	a											
Bodmin Parkway	a											
Lostwithiel	a											
Par	a											
Newquay (Summer Only)	a											
St Austell	a											
Truro	a											
Redruth	a											
Camborne	a											
Hayle	a											
St Erth	a											
Penzance	a											
Birmingham International ✈	d											
Coventry	d											
Leamington Spa 8	d											
Banbury	a											
Oxford	a											
Reading 7	a											
Guildford	a											
Basingstoke	a											
Winchester	a											
Southampton Airport Pkway ✈	a											
Southampton Central ⛴	a											
Brockenhurst 3	a											
Bournemouth	a											

A ⚲ to Leeds

B ⚲ to York

C ⚲ from Edinburgh to Leeds

Table 51

Sundays
until 1 January

Scotland, The North East, North West England - The South West and South Coast

Route Diagram - see first Page of Table 51

		XC	XC	XC	XC	XC	XC	XC	XC	VT	XC	XC	XC	XC	VT	XC	XC	XC	XC	XC	VT	XC	XC
		◇1	◇1	◇1	◇1	◇1	◇1	◇1	◇1	◇1	◇1	◇1	◇1	◇1	◇1	◇1	◇1	◇1	◇1	◇1	◇1	◇1	◇1
			A	B			B				B		C			B		C				B	
		⊼	⊼	⊏⊼	⊼	⊼	⊏⊼	⊼	⊼	⊏	⊏⊼	⊼	⊼	⊼	⊏	⊏⊼	⊼	⊼	⊼	⊼	⊏	⊏⊼	⊼
Aberdeen	d																						
Stonehaven	d																						
Montrose	d																						
Arbroath	d																						
Dundee	d																						
Leuchars 3	d																						
Cupar	d																						
Ladybank	d																						
Markinch	d																						
Kirkcaldy	d																						
Inverkeithing	d																						
Glasgow Central 15	d																						
Motherwell	d																						
Haymarket	d																						
Edinburgh 10	d																						08 50
Haymarket	d																						
Lockerbie	d																						
Carlisle 8	d																						
Penrith North Lakes	d																						
Oxenholme Lake District	d																						
Lancaster 6	d																				12 00		
Preston 8	d									10 17					11 17						12 17		
Wigan North Western	d									10 28					11 28						12 28		
Warrington Bank Quay	d									10 39					11 39						12 39		
M'chester Piccadilly 10	d			08 27			09 27				10 27					11 27						12 26	
Stockport	d			08 36			09 36				10 36					11 36						12 35	
Wilmslow	d			08 43																			
Crewe 10	d			09 05						11 01					12 01						13 01		
Macclesfield	d						09 49				10 49					11 49						12 49	
Congleton	d																						
Stoke-on-Trent	d						10 07				11 07					12 07						13 07	
Stafford	d			09 26			10 27				11 28					12 25						13 25	
Wolverhampton 7	d			09 41			10 43			11 32	11 42				12 32	12 41					13 32	13 41	
Dunbar	d																						
Berwick-upon-Tweed	d																						09 33
Alnmouth for Alnwick	d																						
Morpeth	d																						
Newcastle 8	d																09 20						10 24
Chester-le-Street	d																						
Durham	d																09 33						10 37
Darlington 7	d																09 50						10 54
York 8	d											09 28					10 28						11 28
Leeds 10	d					08 10			09 00			10 00					11 00						12 00
Wakefield Westgate 7	d					08 23			09 11			10 12					11 12						12 12
Doncaster 7	d								09 32			10 30					11 30						12 30
Sheffield 7	d					08 54			09 57			10 57					11 57						12 57
Chesterfield	d					09 07			10 09			11 09					12 09						13 09
Nottingham 8	d												11 11					12 10					
Derby 6	d					09 28			10 34			11 30	11 36				12 30	12f36					13 32
Burton-on-Trent	d											11 41	11 48					12 48					13 43
Tamworth	d								10 53				12 00				12 48	13 00					
Birmingham New Street 12	a			09 58		10 19	10 59		11 20	11 55	12 00	12 04	12 24		12 55	12 58	13 05	13 24			13 55	13 58	14 08
Birmingham New Street 12	d	09 04	09 12	10 04	10 12	10 30	11 04	11 12	11 30		12 04	12 12	12 30	12 33		13 04	13 12	13 30	13 33	13 42		14 04	14 12
Cheltenham Spa	a		09 49		10 52	11 09		11 52	12 08			12 50	13 10				13 50	14 12		14 23			14 51
Gloucester 7	a				11 03			12 03					13 21					14 22					
Bristol Parkway 7	a		10 21			11 39			12 39			13 21					14 21			14 54			15 24
Bristol Temple Meads 10	a		10 32			11 52			12 51			13 32					14 32			15 07			15 36
Newport (South Wales)	a				11 48			12 52					14 06					15 08					
Cardiff Central 7	a				12 08			13 12					14 26					15 31					
Weston-super-Mare	a																						
Taunton	a		11 15			12 26			13 26			14 15					15 15						16 14
Tiverton Parkway	a		11 28			12 38			13 38			14 28					15 28						16 26
Exeter St Davids 6	a		11 42			12 56			13 55			14 44					15 43						16 44
Dawlish	a																						
Teignmouth	a																						
Newton Abbot	a		12 02			13 17			14 16			15 04					16 02						17 04
Torquay	a																						
Paignton	a																						
Totnes	a		12 15			13 31			14 30			15 17					16 15						17 18
Plymouth	a		12 42			13 59			14 57			15 43					16 42						17 46
Liskeard 6	a		13 17																				
Bodmin Parkway	a		13 29																				
Lostwithiel	a																						
Par	a		13 40																				
Newquay (Summer Only)	a																						
St Austell	a		13 47																				
Truro	a		14 04																				
Redruth	a		14 18																				
Camborne	a		14 24																				
Hayle	a																						
St Erth	a		14 35																				
Penzance	a		14 49																				
Birmingham International	d	09 14		10 14			11 14				12 14					13 14						14 14	
Coventry	d	09 25		10 25			11 25				12 25					13 25						14 25	
Leamington Spa 3	d	09 38		10 38			11 38				12 38			13 00		13 38			14 00			14 38	
Banbury	a	09 54		10 54			11 54				12 54			13 17		13 54			14 17			14 54	
Oxford	a	10 14		11 14			12 14				13 14			13 41		14 14			14 38			15 14	
Reading 7	a	10 38		11 43			12 40				13 42			14 09		14 43			15 07			15 45	
Guildford	a																						
Basingstoke	a	11 09		12 09			13 09				14 09					15 09						16 09	
Winchester	a	11 24		12 24			13 24				14 24					15 24						16 24	
Southampton Airport Pkway	a	11 33		12 33			13 33				14 33					15 33						16 33	
Southampton Central	a	11 42		12 42			13 42				14 42					15 42						16 42	
Brockenhurst 3	a	12 02		13 02			14 01				15 02					16 02						17 02	
Bournemouth	a	12 26		13 26			14 26				15 26					16 26						17 26	

A ⊼ to Plymouth

B ⊏ from Birmingham New Street ⊼ to Birmingham New Street

C ⊼ to Newport (South Wales)

Table 51

Sundays until 1 January

Scotland, The North East, North West England - The South West and South Coast

Route Diagram - see first Page of Table 51

		XC	XC	XC	VT	XC	XC	XC	XC	XC	VT	XC	XC	XC	XC	XC	VT	XC	XC	XC	XC	XC	VT
		◇1	◇1	◇1	◇1	◇1	◇1	◇1	◇1	◇1	◇1	◇1	◇1	◇1	◇1	◇1	◇1	◇1	◇1	◇1	◇1	◇1	◇1
		A				B	C	A				B						B	C	A			
		🛒	🛒	🛒	🍽	🍽🛒	🛒	🛒	🛒	🛒	🍽	🍽🛒	🛒	🛒	🛒	🛒	🍽	🍽🛒	🛒	🛒	🛒	🛒	🍽
Aberdeen	d																						
Stonehaven	d																						
Montrose	d																						
Arbroath	d																						
Dundee	d																						
Leuchars 3	d																						
Cupar	d																						
Ladybank	d																						
Markinch	d																						
Kirkcaldy	d																						
Inverkeithing	d																						
Glasgow Central 15	d										11 58								10 55				13 55
Motherwell	d																		11 10				
Haymarket	d																		11 51				
Edinburgh 10	d				10 52		09 50						11 05				12 52		12 08				
Haymarket	d				10 57												12 56						
Lockerbie	d																						
Carlisle 8	d				12 07						13 10						14 07						15 11
Penrith North Lakes	d																14 22						
Oxenholme Lake District	d				12 43																		15 46
Lancaster 6	d				12 57						13 58						14 57						
Preston 8	d				13 17						14 17						15 17						16 17
Wigan North Western	d				13 28						14 28						15 28						16 28
Warrington Bank Quay	d				13 39						14 39						15 39						16 39
M'chester Piccadilly 10	d			13 07		13 27				14 07		14 27				15 07		15 27				16 07	
Stockport	d					13 36						14 36						15 36					
Wilmslow	d																						
Crewe 10	d				14 01						15 01						16 01						17 00
Macclesfield	d					13 49						14 49						15 49					
Congleton	d																						
Stoke-on-Trent	d			13 43		14 07				14 43		15 07				15 43		16 07				16 43	
Stafford	d					14 25						15 25						16 25					
Wolverhampton 7	d			14 15	14 33	14 41				15 15	15 32	15 41				16 15	16 32	16 41				17 15	17 32
Dunbar	d												11 25										
Berwick-upon-Tweed	d												11 50						12 49				
Alnmouth for Alnwick	d						10 49						12 10										
Morpeth	d						11 04																
Newcastle 8	d						11 25						12 40		13 35				13 40		14 35		
Chester-le-Street	d																						
Durham	d						11 37						12 52		13 47				13 52		14 47		
Darlington 7	d						11 55						13 09		14 05				14 10		15 04		
York 8	d						12 28						13 40		14 34				14 40		15 34		
Leeds 10	d						13 00						14 10						15 10				
Wakefield Westgate 7	d						13 12						14 23						15 23				
Doncaster 7	d						13 30								14 59						15 59		
Sheffield 7	d						13 57		14 22				14 54		15 23				15 54		16 24		
Chesterfield	d						14 09		14 32				15 06						16 07				
Nottingham 8	d	13 06						14 10						15 10						16 10			
Derby 6	d	13 36	13 54				14 31	14 35	14 53				15 26	15 35	15 54				16 28	16 35	16 55		
Burton-on-Trent	d	13 48						14 48					15 38	15 48						16 48			
Tamworth	d	14 00					14 50	15 00						16 00					16 48	17 00			
Birmingham New Street 12	a	14 24	14 27	14 31	14 55	14 58	15 06	15 21	15 27	15 31	15 55	15 58	16 01	16 24	16 27	16 31	16 55	16 58	17 04	17 19	17 27	17 31	17 56
Birmingham New Street 12	d	14 30	14 33	14 42		15 04	15 12	15 30	15 33	15 42		16 04	16 12	16 30	16 33	16 42		17 04	17 12	17 30	17 33	17 42	
Cheltenham Spa	a	15 10		15 24			15 50	16 10		16 24			16 49	17 10		17 24			17 50	18 10		18 24	
Gloucester 7	a	15 21						16 21						17 21						18 22			
Bristol Parkway 7	a			15 59			16 21			16 55			17 20			18 02			18 22			18 56	
Bristol Temple Meads 10	a			16 11			16 35			17 08			17 35			18 13			18 40			19 08	
Newport (South Wales)	a	16 06						17 06						18 07						19 07			
Cardiff Central 7	a	16 26						17 27						18 29						19 27			
Weston-super-Mare	a																						
Taunton	a			16 45			17 15						18 18						19 15				
Tiverton Parkway	a			16 57			17 28						18 31						19 28				
Exeter St Davids 6	a			17 12			17 43						18 46						19 47				
Dawlish	a			17 25																			
Teignmouth	a			17 30																			
Newton Abbot	a			17 37			18 02						19 05						20 07				
Torquay	a			17 48																			
Paignton	a			17 56																			
Totnes	a						18 15						19 18						20 20				
Plymouth	a						18 42						19 45						20 46				
Liskeard 6	a						19 17												21 12				
Bodmin Parkway	a						19 29												21 24				
Lostwithiel	a																						
Par	a						19 40												21 35				
Newquay (Summer Only)	a																						
St Austell	a						19 47												21 42				
Truro	a						20 08												21 59				
Redruth	a						20 19												22 11				
Camborne	a						20 26												22 17				
Hayle	a																						
St Erth	a						20 38												22 29				
Penzance	a						20 47												22 38				
Birmingham International ✈	d					15 14						16 14						17 14					
Coventry	d					15 25						16 25						17 25					
Leamington Spa 8	d		15 00			15 38			16 00			16 38			17 00			17 38			18 01		
Banbury	a		15 18			15 54			16 17			16 54			17 17			17 54			18 19		
Oxford	a		15 41			16 14			16 41			17 14			17 38			18 14			18 41		
Reading 7	a		16 07			16 40			17 11			17 38			18 13			18 40			19 07		
Guildford	a																						
Basingstoke	a					17 09						18 09						19 09					
Winchester	a					17 24						18 24						19 24					
Southampton Airport Pkwy ✈	a					17 33						18 33						19 33					
Southampton Central ⛴	a					17 40						18 42						19 40					
Brockenhurst 3	a					18 02						19 01						20 02					
Bournemouth	a					18 26						19 26						20 26					

A 🛒 to Newport (South Wales)

B 🍽 from Birmingham New Street 🛒 to Birmingham New Street

C 🛒 to Plymouth

Table 51

Sundays
until 1 January

Scotland, The North East, North West England - The South West and South Coast

Route Diagram - see first Page of Table 51

		XC	XC	XC	XC	XC	VT	XC	XC	XC	XC	XC	VT	XC	XC	XC	XC	XC	VT	XC	XC	XC
		◇1	◇1	◇1	◇1	◇1	◇1	◇1	◇1	◇1	◇1	◇1	◇1	◇1	◇1	◇1	◇1	◇1	◇1	◇1	◇1	◇1
		A	B	C				D	E	F				D	E		G	F		F	H	
		[R][T]	[T]	[T]	[T]	[T]	[R]	[R][T]	[T]	[T]	[T]	[T]	[R]	[R][T]	[T]	[T]	[T]	[T]	[R]	[T]	[T]	
Aberdeen	d								11 12													
Stonehaven	d								11 29													
Montrose	d								11 50													
Arbroath	d								12 06													
Dundee	d								12 25													
Leuchars 3	d								12 38													
Cupar	d								12 45													
Ladybank	d																					
Markinch	d																					
Kirkcaldy	d								13 03													
Inverkeithing	d								13 18													
Glasgow Central 15	d		11 51										15 57		13 49						14 55	
Motherwell	d		12 07												14 04						15 11	
Haymarket	d		12 49						13 37						14 42						15 51	
Edinburgh 10	d		13 06		13 50		14 52		14 08						15 07				16 52		16 05	
Haymarket	d						14 57												16 56			
Lockerbie	d																					
Carlisle 8	d						16 07						17 09						18 07			
Penrith North Lakes	d						16 22															
Oxenholme Lake District	d												17 44						18 42			
Lancaster 6	d						16 57												18 57			
Preston 8	d						17 17						18 17						19 17			
Wigan North Western	d						17 28						18 28						19 28			
Warrington Bank Quay	d						17 39						18 39						19 39			
M'chester Piccadilly 10	d	16 27				17 07		17 27				18 07		18 27				19 07		19 27		
Stockport	d	16 36						17 36						18 36						19 36		
Wilmslow	d																					
Crewe 10	d						18 01						19 01						20 01			
Macclesfield	d	16 49						17 49						18 49						19 49		
Congleton	d																					
Stoke-on-Trent	d	17 08				17 43		18 08				18 43		19 07				19 43		20 07		
Stafford	d	17 26						18 26						19 25						20 27		
Wolverhampton 7	d	17 41				18 15	18 33	18 41				19 15	19 32	19 41				20 15	20 33	20 41		
Dunbar	d		13 25												15 27							
Berwick-upon-Tweed	d				14 33				14 49													
Alnmouth for Alnwick	d		14 08																		17 07	
Morpeth	d																				17 22	
Newcastle 8	d		14 40		15 23				15 40		16 35				16 40		17 35				17 40	
Chester-le-Street	d																					
Durham	d		14 52		15 36				15 52		16 47				16 52		17 47				17 52	
Darlington 7	d		15 09		15 53				16 09		17 04				17 09		18 05				18 09	
York 8	d		15 40		16 23				16 40		17 34				17 40		18 34				18 40	
Leeds 10	d		16 10						17 10						18 10						19 10	
Wakefield Westgate 7	d		16 22						17 22						18 22						19 22	
Doncaster 7	d				16 51						17 59						18 59					
Sheffield 7	d		16 54		17 24				17 54		18 24				18 54		19 24				19 54	
Chesterfield	d		17 06						18 06						19 06						20 06	
Nottingham 8	d			17 10						18 10						19 10						20 10
Derby 6	d		17 27	17 36	17 54				18 26	18 35	18 55				19 27	19 36	19 56				20 27	20 36
Burton-on-Trent	d		17 38	17 48						18 48					19 38	19 48						20 48
Tamworth	d			18 00					18 45	19 00						20 00					20 45	21 00
Birmingham New Street 12	a	17 58	18 01	18 19	18 24	18 31	18 55	18 58	19 04	19 20	19 27	19 31	19 55	19 58	20 05	20 24	20 27	20 31	20 50	20 58	21 03	21 19
Birmingham New Street 12	d	18 04	18 12	18 30	18 33	18 42		19 04	19 12	19 30	19 33	19 42		20 04	20 12		20 33	20 42		21 04	21 12	
Cheltenham Spa	a		18 50	19 11		19 24			19 50	20 10		20 24			20 50			21 24			21 50	
Gloucester 7	a			19 26						20 21											22 02	
Bristol Parkway 7	a		19 21			20 03			20 21			20 57			21 21			21 59			22 34	
Bristol Temple Meads 10	a		19 35			20 14			20 35			21 08			21 32			22 10			22 45	
Newport (South Wales)	a			20 11						21 06												
Cardiff Central 7	a			20 31						21 26												
Weston-super-Mare	a					20 36																
Taunton	a		20 18			20 58			21 15						22 15							
Tiverton Parkway	a		20 31			21 11			21 28						22 28							
Exeter St Davids 6	a		20 46			21 27			21 43						22 46							
Dawlish	a					21 41																
Teignmouth	a					21 46																
Newton Abbot	a		21 05			21 54			22 02						23 05							
Torquay	a																					
Paignton	a																					
Totnes	a		21 18						22 19						23 20							
Plymouth	a		21 45			22 37			22 45						23 47							
Liskeard 6	a																					
Bodmin Parkway	a																					
Lostwithiel	a																					
Par	a																					
Newquay (Summer Only)	a																					
St Austell	a																					
Truro	a																					
Redruth	a																					
Camborne	a																					
Hayle	a																					
St Erth	a																					
Penzance	a																					
Birmingham International	d	18 14						19 14						20 14						21 14		
Coventry	d	18 25						19 25						20 25						21 24		
Leamington Spa 8	d	18 38			19 00			19 38			20 00			20 38			21 00			21 35		
Banbury	a	18 54			19 17			19 54			20 18			20 54			21 17					
Oxford	a	19 14			19 38			20 14			20 40			21 14			21 38			22 08		
Reading 7	a	19 40			20 13			20 42			21 11			21 43			22 07			22 33		
Guildford	a																22 42					
Basingstoke	a	20 09						21 09						22 09								
Winchester	a	20 24						21 24						22 24								
Southampton Airport Pkway	a	20 33						21 33						22 33								
Southampton Central	a	20 42						21 43						22 42								
Brockenhurst 3	a	21 02						22 02														
Bournemouth	a	21 26						22 26														

A [R] from Birmingham New Street; [T] to Birmingham New Street
B [T] from Edinburgh
C [T] to Newport (South Wales)
D [R] from Birmingham New Street to Reading; [T] to Birmingham New Street
E [T] from Edinburgh to Bristol Temple Meads
F [T] to Birmingham New Street
G [T] to Reading
H [T] from Edinburgh to Birmingham New Street

Sundays
until 1 January

Scotland, The North East, North West England - The South West and South Coast

Route Diagram - see first Page of Table 51

		XC	XC	XC	XC	XC	VT	XC		VT	XC	XC
		◇1	◇1	◇1	◇1	◇1	◇1	◇1		◇1	◇1	◇1
				A							A	
		[trolley]		[trolley]		[trolley]	[buffet]			[buffet]	[trolley]	
Aberdeen	d											
Stonehaven	d											
Montrose	d											
Arbroath	d											
Dundee	d											
Leuchars 3	d											
Cupar	d											
Ladybank	d											
Markinch	d											
Kirkcaldy	d											
Inverkeithing	d											
Glasgow Central 15	d						18 30				16 55	
Motherwell	d										17 11	
Haymarket	d										17 51	
Edinburgh 10	d			17 07						18 52	18 07	
Haymarket	d									18 57		
Lockerbie	d											
Carlisle 8	d						19 44			20 07		
Penrith North Lakes	d									20 22		
Oxenholme Lake District	d						20 19					
Lancaster 6	d						20 34			20 57		
Preston 8	d						20 55			21 17		
Wigan North Western	d						21 07			21 28		
Warrington Bank Quay	d						21 18			21 39		
M'chester Piccadilly 10 ⛴	d		20 07					21 07				22 07
Stockport	d		20 16					21 16				22 16
Wilmslow	d											
Crewe 10	d						21 40			22 01		
Macclesfield	d		20 29					21 29				22 29
Congleton	d											
Stoke-on-Trent	d		20 47					21 47				22 47
Stafford	d		21 09				22 02	22 06				23 05
Wolverhampton 7 ⛴	d		21 22				22 18	22 22		22 32		23 19
Dunbar	d			17 27							18 26	
Berwick-upon-Tweed	d			17 52							18 52	
Alnmouth for Alnwick	d											
Morpeth	d											
Newcastle 8	d	18 20		18 39		19 25					19 40	
Chester-le-Street	d											
Durham	d	18 32		18 51		19 37					19 52	
Darlington 7	d	18 51		19 08		19 54					20 09	
York 8	d	19 24		19 40		20 24					20 40	
Leeds 10	d			20 10							21 10	
Wakefield Westgate 7	d			20 22							21 22	
Doncaster 7	d	19 50				20 50						
Sheffield 7 ⛴	d	20 20		20 54		21 20					21 54	
Chesterfield	d			21 06		21 32					22 06	
Nottingham 8 ⛴	d				21 08							
Derby 6	d	20 54		21 27	21 36	21 53					22 26	
Burton-on-Trent	d			21 37	21 48	22 03					22 37	
Tamworth	d			21 47	22 00	22 14					22 47	
Birmingham New Street 12	a	21 28	21 39	22 04	22 23	22 30	22 38	22 39		22 55	23 04	23 36
Birmingham New Street 12	d		21 43	22 12								
Cheltenham Spa	a		22 23	22 50								
Gloucester 7	a											
Bristol Parkway 7	a		22 53	23 22								
Bristol Temple Meads 10	a		23 07	23 33								
Newport (South Wales)	a											
Cardiff Central 7	a											
Weston-super-Mare	a											
Taunton	a											
Tiverton Parkway	a											
Exeter St Davids 6	a											
Dawlish	a											
Teignmouth	a											
Newton Abbot	a											
Torquay	a											
Paignton	a											
Totnes	a											
Plymouth	a											
Liskeard 6	a											
Bodmin Parkway	a											
Lostwithiel	a											
Par	a											
Newquay (Summer Only)	a											
St Austell	a											
Truro	a											
Redruth	a											
Camborne	a											
Hayle	a											
St Erth	a											
Penzance	a											
Birmingham International ✈	d											
Coventry	d											
Leamington Spa 8	d											
Banbury	a											
Oxford	a											
Reading 7	a											
Guildford	a											
Basingstoke	a											
Winchester	a											
Southampton Airport Pkway ✈	a											
Southampton Central ⛴	a											
Brockenhurst 3	a											
Bournemouth	a											

A [trolley] to Leeds

Table 51

Sundays

8 January to 12 February

Scotland, The North East, North West England - The South West and South Coast

Route Diagram - see first Page of Table 51

		XC	XC	XC	XC	XC	XC	XC	XC	VT	XC	XC	XC	VT	XC	XC	XC	XC	XC	VT	XC	XC	XC
		◇1	◇1	◇1	◇1	◇1	◇1	◇1	◇1	◇1	◇1	◇1	◇1	◇1	◇1	◇1	◇1	◇1	◇1	◇1	◇1	◇1	◇1
			A	B			B				B		C		B		C				B		
Aberdeen	d																						
Stonehaven	d																						
Montrose	d																						
Arbroath	d																						
Dundee	d																						
Leuchars 3	d																						
Cupar	d																						
Ladybank	d																						
Markinch	d																						
Kirkcaldy	d																						
Inverkeithing	d																						
Glasgow Central 15	d																						
Motherwell	d																						
Haymarket	d																						
Edinburgh 10	d																					08 50	
Haymarket	d																						
Lockerbie	d																						
Carlisle 8	d																						
Penrith North Lakes	d																						
Oxenholme Lake District	d																						
Lancaster 6	d																						
Preston 8	d									10 17				11 17						12 17			
Wigan North Western	d									10 28				11 28						12 28			
Warrington Bank Quay	d									10 39				11 39						12 39			
M'chester Piccadilly 10	d			08 27			09 27				10 27				11 27						12 26		
Stockport	d			08 36			09 36				10 36				11 36						12 35		
Wilmslow	d			08 43			09 43																
Crewe 10	d			09 05			10 05			11 01				12 01						13 01			
Macclesfield	d										10 49				11 49						12 49		
Congleton	d																						
Stoke-on-Trent	d										11 07				12 07						13 07		
Stafford	d			09 26			10 27				11 28				12 25						13 25		
Wolverhampton 7	d			09 41			10 43			11 32	11 42			12 32	12 41					13 32	13 41		
Dunbar	d																						
Berwick-upon-Tweed	d																					09 33	
Alnmouth for Alnwick	d																						
Morpeth	d																						
Newcastle 8	d															09 20						10 24	
Chester-le-Street	d																						
Durham	d															09 33						10 37	
Darlington 7	d															09 50						10 54	
York 8	d											09 28				10 28						11 28	
Leeds 10	d					08 10			09 00			10 00				11 00						12 00	
Wakefield Westgate 7	d					08 23			09 11			10 12				11 12						12 12	
Doncaster 7	d								09 32			10 30				11 30						12 30	
Sheffield 7	d					08 54			09 57			10 57				11 57						12 57	
Chesterfield	d					09 07			10 09			11 09				12 09						13 09	
Nottingham 8	d												11 11				12 10						12 53
Derby 6	d					09 28			10 34			11 30	11 36			12 30	12 36					13 32	
Burton-on-Trent	d											11 41	11 48				12 48					13 43	
Tamworth	d								10 53				12 00			12 48	13 00						
Birmingham New Street 12	a			09 58		10 19	10 59		11 20	11 55	12 00	12 04	12 24	12 55	12 58	13 05	13 24			13 55	13 58	14 08	14 16
Birmingham New Street 12	d	09 04	09 12	10 04	10 12	10 30	11 04	11 12	11 30		12 04	12 12	12 30		13 04	13 12	13 30	13 33	13 42		14 04	14 12	
Cheltenham Spa	a		09 49		10 52	11 09		11 52	12 08			12 50	13 10			13 50	14 12		14 23			14 51	
Gloucester 7	a				11 03			12 03					13 21				14 22						
Bristol Parkway 7	a		10 21			11 39			12 39			13 21				14 21			14 54			15 24	
Bristol Temple Meads 10	a		10 32			11 52			12 51			13 32				14 32			15 07			15 36	
Newport (South Wales)	a				11 48			12 52					14 06				15 08						
Cardiff Central 7	a				12 08			13 12					14 26				15 31						
Weston-super-Mare	a																						
Taunton	a		11 15			12 26			13 26			14 15				15 15						16 14	
Tiverton Parkway	a		11 28			12 38			13 38			14 28				15 28						16 26	
Exeter St Davids 6	a		11 42			12 56			13 55			14 44				15 43						16 44	
Dawlish	a																						
Teignmouth	a																						
Newton Abbot	a		12 02			13 17			14 16			15 04				16 02						17 04	
Torquay	a																						
Paignton	a																						
Totnes	a		12 15			13 31			14 30			15 17				16 15						17 18	
Plymouth	a		12 42			13 59			14 57			15 43				16 42						17 46	
Liskeard 6	a		13 17																				
Bodmin Parkway	a		13 29																				
Lostwithiel	a																						
Par	a		13 40																				
Newquay (Summer Only)	a																						
St Austell	a		13 47																				
Truro	a		14 04																				
Redruth	a		14 18																				
Camborne	a		14 24																				
Hayle	a																						
St Erth	a		14 35																				
Penzance	a		14 49																				
Birmingham International	d	09 14		10 14			11 14				12 14				13 14						14 14		
Coventry	d	09 25		10 25			11 25				12 25				13 25						14 25		
Leamington Spa 8	d	09a36		10a36			11a36				12a36				13a36			14 00			14 38		
Banbury	a																	14 17			14 54		
Oxford	a																	14 38			15 14		
Reading 7	a																	15 07			15 42		
Guildford	a																						
Basingstoke	a																				16 09		
Winchester	a																				16 24		
Southampton Airport Pkway	a																				16 33		
Southampton Central	a																				16 42		
Brockenhurst 3	a																				17 02		
Bournemouth	a																				17 26		

A to Plymouth

B from Birmingham New Street to Birmingham New Street

C to Newport (South Wales)

Table 51

Sundays

8 January to 12 February

Scotland, The North East, North West England - The South West and South Coast

Route Diagram - see first Page of Table 51

		XC	XC	XC	VT	XC	XC	XC	XC	XC	VT	XC	XC	XC	XC	XC	XC	VT	XC	XC	XC	XC	XC
		◇1	◇1	◇1	◇1	◇1	◇1	◇1	◇1	◇1	◇1	◇1	◇1	◇1	◇1	◇1	◇1	◇1	◇1	◇1	◇1	◇1	◇1
		A				B	C	A				B							B	C	A		
Aberdeen	d																						
Stonehaven	d																						
Montrose	d																						
Arbroath	d																						
Dundee	d																						
Leuchars 3	d																						
Cupar	d																						
Ladybank	d																						
Markinch	d																						
Kirkcaldy	d																						
Inverkeithing	d																						
Glasgow Central 15	d										11 58									10 55			
Motherwell	d																			11 10			
Haymarket	d																			11 51			
Edinburgh 10	d				10 52		09 50						11 05					12 52		12 08			
Haymarket	d				10 57													12 56					
Lockerbie	d																						
Carlisle 8	d				12 07						13 10							14 07					
Penrith North Lakes	d																	14 22					
Oxenholme Lake District	d				12 43																		
Lancaster 6	d				12 57						13 58							14 57					
Preston 8	d				13 17						14 17							15 17					
Wigan North Western	d				13 28						14 28							15 28					
Warrington Bank Quay	d				13 39						14 39							15 39					
M'chester Piccadilly 10	d			13 07		13 27				14 07		14 27					15 07		15 27				
Stockport	d					13 36						14 36							15 36				
Wilmslow	d																						
Crewe 10	d				14 01						15 01							16 01					
Macclesfield	d					13 49						14 49							15 49				
Congleton	d																						
Stoke-on-Trent	d			13 43		14 07				14 43		15 07					15 43		16 07				
Stafford	d					14 25						15 25							16 25				
Wolverhampton 7	d			14 15	14 33	14 41				15 15	15 32	15 41					16 15	16 32	16 41				
Dunbar	d												11 25										
Berwick-upon-Tweed	d												11 50							12 49			
Alnmouth for Alnwick	d						10 49						12 10										
Morpeth	d						11 04																
Newcastle 8	d						11 25						12 40		13 35					13 40		14 35	
Chester-le-Street	d																						
Durham	d						11 37						12 52		13 47					13 52		14 47	
Darlington 7	d						11 55						13 09		14 05					14 10		15 04	
York 8	d						12 28						13 40		14 34					14 40		15 34	
Leeds 10	d						13 00						14 10							15 10			
Wakefield Westgate 7	d						13 12						14 23							15 23			
Doncaster 7	d						13 30								14 59							15 59	
Sheffield 7	d						13 57		14 22				14 54		15 23					15 54		16 24	
Chesterfield	d						14 09		14 32				15 06							16 07			
Nottingham 8	d	13 06						14 10						15 10		15 04					16 10		16 04
Derby 6	d	13 36	13 54				14 31	14 35	14 53				15 26	15 35	15 54					16 28	16 35	16 55	
Burton-on-Trent	d	13 48						14 48					15 38	15 48							16 48		
Tamworth	d	14 00					14 50	15 00						16 00						16 48	17 00		
Birmingham New Street 12	a	14 24	14 27	14 31	14 55	14 58	15 06	15 21	15 27	15 31	15 55	15 58	16 01	16 24	16 27	16 36	16 31	16 55	16 58	17 04	17 19	17 27	17 36
Birmingham New Street 12	d	14 30	14 33	14 42		15 04	15 12	15 30	15 33	15 42		16 04	16 12	16 30	16 33		16 42		17 04	17 12	17 30	17 33	
Cheltenham Spa	a	15 10		15 24			15 50	16 10		16 24			16 49	17 10			17 24			17 50	18 10		
Gloucester 7	a	15 21						16 21						17 21							18 22		
Bristol Parkway 7	a			15 59			16 21			16 55			17 20				18 02			18 22			
Bristol Temple Meads 10	a			16 11			16 35			17 08			17 35				18 13			18 40			
Newport (South Wales)	a	16 06						17 06						18 07							19 07		
Cardiff Central 7	a	16 26						17 27						18 29							19 27		
Weston-super-Mare	a																						
Taunton	a			16 45			17 15						18 18							19 15			
Tiverton Parkway	a			16 57			17 28						18 31							19 28			
Exeter St Davids 6	a			17 12			17 43						18 46							19 47			
Dawlish	a			17 25																			
Teignmouth	a			17 30																			
Newton Abbot	a			17 37			18 02						19 05							20 07			
Torquay	a			17 48																			
Paignton	a			17 56																			
Totnes	a						18 15						19 18							20 20			
Plymouth	a						18 42						19 45							20 46			
Liskeard 6	a						19 17													21 12			
Bodmin Parkway	a						19 29													21 24			
Lostwithiel	a																						
Par	a						19 40													21 35			
Newquay (Summer Only)	a																						
St Austell	a						19 47													21 42			
Truro	a						20 08													21 59			
Redruth	a						20 19													22 11			
Camborne	a						20 26													22 17			
Hayle	a																						
St Erth	a						20 38													22 29			
Penzance	a						20 47													22 38			
Birmingham International	d					15 14						16 14							17 14				
Coventry	d					15 25						16 25							17 25				
Leamington Spa 8	d		15 00			15 38			16 00			16 38			17 00				17 38			18 01	
Banbury	a		15 18			15 54			16 17			16 54			17 17				17 54			18 19	
Oxford	a		15 41			16 14			16 41			17 14			17 38				18 14			18 41	
Reading 7	a		16 13			16 43			17 13			17 43			18 13				18 43			19 13	
Guildford	a																						
Basingstoke	a					17 09						18 09							19 09				
Winchester	a					17 24						18 24							19 24				
Southampton Airport Pkwy	a					17 33						18 33							19 33				
Southampton Central	a					17 40						18 42							19 40				
Brockenhurst 3	a					18 02						19 01							20 02				
Bournemouth	a					18 26						19 26							20 26				

A to Newport (South Wales)

B from Birmingham New Street to Birmingham New Street

C to Plymouth

Table 51

Sundays

8 January to 12 February

Scotland, The North East, North West England - The South West and South Coast

Route Diagram - see first Page of Table 51

		XC	VT	XC	XC	XC	XC	XC	VT	XC	XC	XC	XC	XC	XC	VT	XC	XC	XC	XC	XC	XC
		◇1	◇1	◇1	◇1	◇1	◇1	◇1	◇1	◇1	◇1	◇1	◇1	◇1	◇1	◇1	◇1	◇1	◇1	◇1	◇1	◇1
				A	B	C				D	E		F				D	E		G		F
		🚲	⊡	⊡🚲	🚲	🚲	🚲	🚲	⊡	⊡🚲	🚲	🚲	🚲	🚲	🚲	⊡	⊡🚲	🚲	🚲	🚲	🚲	🚲
Aberdeen	d										11 12											
Stonehaven	d										11 29											
Montrose	d										11 50											
Arbroath	d										12 06											
Dundee	d										12 25											
Leuchars 3	d										12 38											
Cupar	d										12 45											
Ladybank	d																					
Markinch	d																					
Kirkcaldy	d										13 03											
Inverkeithing	d										13 18											
Glasgow Central 15	d		13 55		11 51											15 57		13 49				
Motherwell	d				12 07													14 04				
Haymarket	d				12 49						13 37							14 42				
Edinburgh 10	d				13 06		13 50		14 52		14 08							15 07				
Haymarket	d								14 57													
Lockerbie	d																					
Carlisle 8	d		15 11						16 07							17 09						
Penrith North Lakes	d								16 22													
Oxenholme Lake District	d		15 46													17 44						
Lancaster 6	d								16 57													
Preston 8	d		16 17						17 17							18 17						
Wigan North Western	d		16 28						17 28							18 28						
Warrington Bank Quay	d		16 39						17 39							18 39						
M'chester Piccadilly 10 ⛴	d	16 07		16 27				17 07		17 27					18 07		18 27					19 07
Stockport	d			16 36						17 36							18 36					
Wilmslow	d																					
Crewe 10	d		17 00						18 01							19 01						
Macclesfield	d			16 49						17 49							18 49					
Congleton	d																					
Stoke-on-Trent	d	16 43		17 08				17 43		18 08					18 43		19 07					19 43
Stafford	d			17 26						18 26							19 25					
Wolverhampton 7 ⛴	d	17 15	17 32	17 41				18 15	18 33	18 41					19 15	19 32	19 41					20 15
Dunbar	d				13 25													15 27				
Berwick-upon-Tweed	d						14 33				14 49											
Alnmouth for Alnwick	d				14 08																	
Morpeth	d																					
Newcastle 8	d				14 40		15 23				15 40			16 35				16 40		17 35		
Chester-le-Street	d																					
Durham	d				14 52		15 36				15 52			16 47				16 52		17 47		
Darlington 7	d				15 09		15 53				16 09			17 04				17 09		18 05		
York 8	d				15 40		16 23				16 40			17 34				17 40		18 34		
Leeds 10	d				16 10						17 10							18 10				
Wakefield Westgate 7	d				16 22						17 22							18 22				
Doncaster 7	d						16 51							17 59						18 59		
Sheffield 7 ⛴	d				16 54		17 24				17 54			18 24				18 54		19 24		
Chesterfield	d				17 06						18 06							19 06				
Nottingham 8 ⛴	d					17 10						17 58	18 10						19 10		19 02	
Derby 6	d				17 27	17 36	17 54				18 26		18 35	18 55				19 27	19 36	19 56		
Burton-on-Trent	d				17 38	17 48							18 48					19 38	19 48			
Tamworth	d					18 00					18 45		19 00						20 00			
Birmingham New Street 12	a	17 31	17 56	17 58	18 01	18 19	18 24	18 31	18 55	18 58	19 04	19 15	19 20	19 27	19 31	19 55	19 58	20 05	20 24	20 27	20 36	20 31
Birmingham New Street 12	d	17 42		18 04	18 12	18 30	18 33	18 42		19 04	19 12		19 30	19 33	19 42		20 04	20 12		20 33		20 42
Cheltenham Spa	a	18 24			18 50	19 11		19 24			19 50		20 10		20 24			20 50				21 24
Gloucester 7	a					19 26							20 21									
Bristol Parkway 7	a	18 56			19 21			20 03			20 21				20 57			21 21				21 59
Bristol Temple Meads 10	a	19 08			19 35			20 14			20 35				21 08			21 32				22 10
Newport (South Wales)	a					20 11							21 06									
Cardiff Central 7	a					20 31							21 26									
Weston-super-Mare	a							20 36														
Taunton	a				20 18			20 58			21 15							22 15				
Tiverton Parkway	a				20 31			21 11			21 28							22 28				
Exeter St Davids 6	a				20 46			21 27			21 43							22 46				
Dawlish	a							21 41														
Teignmouth	a							21 46														
Newton Abbot	a				21 05			21 54			22 02							23 05				
Torquay	a																					
Paignton	a																					
Totnes	a				21 18						22 19							23 20				
Plymouth	a				21 45			22 37			22 45							23 47				
Liskeard 6	a																					
Bodmin Parkway	a																					
Lostwithiel	a																					
Par	a																					
Newquay (Summer Only)	a																					
St Austell	a																					
Truro	a																					
Redruth	a																					
Camborne	a																					
Hayle	a																					
St Erth	a																					
Penzance	a																					
Birmingham International ✈	d			18 14						19 14							20 14					
Coventry	d			18 25						19 25							20 25					
Leamington Spa 8	d			18 38			19 00			19 38				20 00			20 38			21 00		
Banbury	a			18 54			19 17			19 54				20 18			20 54			21 17		
Oxford	a			19 14			19 38			20 14				20 40			21 14			21 38		
Reading 7	a			19 43			20 13			20 42				21 11			21 43			22 11		
Guildford	a																			22 42		
Basingstoke	a			20 09						21 09							22 09					
Winchester	a			20 24						21 24							22 24					
Southampton Airport Pkway ✈	a			20 33						21 33							22 33					
Southampton Central ⛴	a			20 42						21 43							22 42					
Brockenhurst 3	a			21 02						22 02												
Bournemouth	a			21 26						22 26												

A ⊡ from Birmingham New Street 🚲 to Birmingham New Street

B 🚲 from Edinburgh

C 🚲 to Newport (South Wales)

D ⊡ from Birmingham New Street to Reading 🚲 to Birmingham New Street

E 🚲 from Edinburgh to Bristol Temple Meads

F 🚲 to Birmingham New Street

G 🚲 to Reading

Table 51

Sundays

8 January to 12 February

Scotland, The North East, North West England - The South West and South Coast

Route Diagram - see first Page of Table 51

		VT	XC	XC	XC	XC	XC	XC	XC	XC	XC	VT	XC	VT	XC	XC
		◇1	◇1	◇1	◇1	◇1	◇1	◇1	◇1	◇1	◇1	◇1	◇1	◇1	◇1	◇1
			A	B				C							C	
		🍽	🛒	🛒		🛒		🛒			🛒	🍽		🍽	🛒	
Aberdeen	d															
Stonehaven	d															
Montrose	d															
Arbroath	d															
Dundee	d															
Leuchars 3	d															
Cupar	d															
Ladybank	d															
Markinch	d															
Kirkcaldy	d															
Inverkeithing	d															
Glasgow Central 15	d			14 55								18 30			16 55	
Motherwell	d			15 11											17 11	
Haymarket	d			15 51											17 51	
Edinburgh 10	d	16 52		16 05				17 07						18 52	18 07	
Haymarket	d	16 56												18 57		
Lockerbie	d															
Carlisle 8	d	18 07										19 44		20 07		
Penrith North Lakes	d													20 22		
Oxenholme Lake District	d	18 42										20 19				
Lancaster 6	d	18 57										20 34		20 57		
Preston 8	d	19 17										20 55		21 17		
Wigan North Western	d	19 28										21 07		21 28		
Warrington Bank Quay	d	19 39										21 18		21 39		
M'chester Piccadilly 10	d		19 27				20 07						21 07			22 07
Stockport	d		19 36				20 16						21 16			22 16
Wilmslow	d															
Crewe 10	d	20 01										21 40		22 01		
Macclesfield	d		19 49				20 29						21 29			22 29
Congleton	d															
Stoke-on-Trent	d		20 07				20 47						21 47			22 47
Stafford	d		20 27				21 09					22 02	22 06			23 05
Wolverhampton 7	d	20 33	20 41				21 22					22 18	22 22	22 32		23 19
Dunbar	d							17 27							18 26	
Berwick-upon-Tweed	d							17 52							18 52	
Alnmouth for Alnwick	d			17 07												
Morpeth	d			17 22												
Newcastle 8	d			17 40		18 20		18 39			19 25				19 40	
Chester-le-Street	d															
Durham	d			17 52		18 32		18 51			19 37				19 52	
Darlington 7	d			18 09		18 51		19 08			19 54				20 09	
York 8	d			18 40		19 24		19 40			20 24				20 40	
Leeds 10	d			19 10				20 10							21 10	
Wakefield Westgate 7	d			19 22				20 22							21 22	
Doncaster 7	d					19 50					20 50					
Sheffield 7	d			19 54		20 20		20 54			21 20				21 54	
Chesterfield	d			20 06				21 06			21 32				22 06	
Nottingham 8	d				20 10				20 35	21 08						
Derby 6	d			20 27	20 36	20 54		21 27		21 36	21 53				22 26	
Burton-on-Trent	d				20 48			21 37		21 48	22 03				22 37	
Tamworth	d			20 45	21 00			21 47		22 00	22 14				22 47	
Birmingham New Street 12	a	20 50	20 58	21 03	21 19	21 28	21 39	22 04	22 15	22 23	22 30	22 38	22 39	22 55	23 04	23 36
Birmingham New Street 12	d		21 04	21 12			21 43	22 12								
Cheltenham Spa	a			21 50			22 23	22 50								
Gloucester 7	a			22 02												
Bristol Parkway 7	a			22 34			22 53	23 22								
Bristol Temple Meads 10	a			22 45			23 07	23 33								
Newport (South Wales)	a															
Cardiff Central 7	a															
Weston-super-Mare	a															
Taunton	a															
Tiverton Parkway	a															
Exeter St Davids 6	a															
Dawlish	a															
Teignmouth	a															
Newton Abbot	a															
Torquay	a															
Paignton	a															
Totnes	a															
Plymouth	a															
Liskeard 6	a															
Bodmin Parkway	a															
Lostwithiel	a															
Par	a															
Newquay (Summer Only)	a															
St Austell	a															
Truro	a															
Redruth	a															
Camborne	a															
Hayle	a															
St Erth	a															
Penzance	a															
Birmingham International ✈	d		21 14													
Coventry	d		21 24													
Leamington Spa 8	d		21 35													
Banbury	a															
Oxford	a		22 08													
Reading 7	a		22 45													
Guildford	a															
Basingstoke	a															
Winchester	a															
Southampton Airport Pkway ✈	a															
Southampton Central	a															
Brockenhurst 3	a															
Bournemouth	a															

A 🛒 to Birmingham New Street **B** 🛒 from Edinburgh to Birmingham New Street **C** 🛒 to Leeds

Table 51

Sundays

19 February to 25 March

Scotland, The North East, North West England - The South West and South Coast

Route Diagram - see first Page of Table 51

		XC	XC	XC	XC	XC	XC	XC	XC	VT	XC	XC	XC	VT	XC	XC	XC	XC	VT	XC	XC	XC	XC
		◇[1]	◇[1]	◇[1]	◇[1]	◇[1]	◇[1]	◇[1]	◇[1]	◇[1]	◇[1]	◇[1]	◇[1]	◇[1]	◇[1]	◇[1]	◇[1]	◇[1]	◇[1]	◇[1]	◇[1]	◇[1]	◇[1]
				A			A				A		B		A		B			A		B	
		⊼	⊼	ℛ⊼	⊼	⊼	ℛ⊼	⊼	⊼	ℛ	ℛ⊼	⊼	⊼	ℛ	ℛ⊼	⊼	⊼	⊼	ℛ	ℛ⊼	⊼	⊼	⊼
Aberdeen	d																						
Stonehaven	d																						
Montrose	d																						
Arbroath	d																						
Dundee	d																						
Leuchars [8]	d																						
Cupar	d																						
Ladybank	d																						
Markinch	d																						
Kirkcaldy	d																						
Inverkeithing	d																						
Glasgow Central [15]	d																						
Motherwell	d																						
Haymarket	d																						
Edinburgh [10]	d																				08 50		
Haymarket	d																						
Lockerbie	d																						
Carlisle [8]	d																						
Penrith North Lakes	d																						
Oxenholme Lake District	d																						
Lancaster [6]	d																						
Preston [8]	d									10 17				11 17					12 17				
Wigan North Western	d									10 28				11 28					12 28				
Warrington Bank Quay	d									10 39				11 39					12 39				
M'chester Piccadilly [10] ⛴	d			08 27			09 27				10 27				11 27					12 26			
Stockport	d			08 36			09 36				10 36				11 36					12 35			
Wilmslow	d			08 43			09 43																
Crewe [10]	d			09 05			10 05			11 01				12 01					13 01				
Macclesfield	d										10 49				11 49					12 49			
Congleton	d																						
Stoke-on-Trent	d										11 07				12 07					13 07			
Stafford	d			09 26			10 27				11 28				12 25					13 25			
Wolverhampton [7] ⛴	d			09 41			10 43			11 32	11 42			12 32	12 41				13 32	13 41			
Dunbar	d																						
Berwick-upon-Tweed	d																				09 33		
Alnmouth for Alnwick	d																						
Morpeth	d																						
Newcastle [8]	d															09 20					10 24		
Chester-le-Street	d																						
Durham	d															09 33					10 37		
Darlington [7]	d															09 50					10 54		
York [8]	d											09 28				10c28					11 28		
Leeds [10]	d					08 10			09 00			10b00				11e00					12g00		
Wakefield Westgate [7]	d					08 23			09 11			10 12				11 12					12 12		
Doncaster [7]	d								09 32			10 30				11 30					12 30		
Sheffield [7] ⛴	d					08 54			09 57			10 57				11 57					12 57		
Chesterfield	d					09 07			10 09			11 09				12 09					13 09		
Nottingham [8] ⛴	d												11 11				12 10					13 06	
Derby [6]	d					09 28			10 33			11 30	11 36			12 30	12f36				13 32	13h36	13 54
Burton-on-Trent	d											11 41	11 48				12 48				13 43	13 48	
Tamworth	d								10 53				12 00			12 48	13 00					14 00	
Birmingham New Street [12]	a			09 58		10 18	10 59		11 20	11 55	12 00	12 04	12 24	12 55	12 58	13 05	13 24		13 55	13 58	14 08	14 24	14 27
Birmingham New Street [12]	d	09 04	09 12	10 04	10 12	10 28	11 04	11 12	11 30		12 04	12 12	12 30		13 04	13 12	13 30	13 42		14 04	14 12	14 30	14 33
Cheltenham Spa	a		09 49		10 52	11 09		11 52	12 08			12 50	13 10			13 50	14 12	14 23			14 51	15 10	
Gloucester [7]	a				11 03			12 03					13 21				14 22					15 21	
Bristol Parkway [7]	a		10 21			11 39			12 39			13 21				14 21		14 54			15 24		
Bristol Temple Meads [10]	a		10 32			11 52			12 51			13 35				14 32		15 07			15 36		
Newport (South Wales)	a				11 48			12 52					14 06				15 08					16 06	
Cardiff Central [7]	a				12 08			13 12					14 26				15 31					16 26	
Weston-super-Mare	a																						
Taunton	a		11 15			12 26			13 26			14 15				15 15					16 14		
Tiverton Parkway	a		11 28			12 38			13 38			14 28				15 28					16 26		
Exeter St Davids [6]	a		11 42			12 56			13 55			14 44				15 43					16 44		
Dawlish	a																						
Teignmouth	a																						
Newton Abbot	a		12 03			13 17			14 16			15 05				16 05					17 06		
Torquay	a																						
Paignton	a																						
Totnes	a																						
Plymouth	a																						
Liskeard [6]	a																						
Bodmin Parkway	a																						
Lostwithiel	a																						
Par	a																						
Newquay (Summer Only)	a																						
St Austell	a																						
Truro	a																						
Redruth	a																						
Camborne	a																						
Hayle	a																						
St Erth	a																						
Penzance	a																						
Birmingham International ✈	d	09 14		10 14			11 14				12 14				13 14					14 14			
Coventry	d	09 25		10 25			11 25				12 25				13 25					14 25			
Leamington Spa [8]	d	09a36		10a36			11a36				12a36				13a36					14 38			15 00
Banbury	a																			14 54			15 18
Oxford	a																			15 14			15 41
Reading [7]	a																			15 42			16 13
Guildford	a																						
Basingstoke	a																			16 09			
Winchester	a																			16 24			
Southampton Airport Pkway ✈	a																			16 33			
Southampton Central ⛴	a																			16 42			
Brockenhurst [3]	a																			17 02			
Bournemouth	a																			17 26			

A ℛ from Birmingham New Street ⊼ to Birmingham New Street

B ⊼ to Newport (South Wales)

Table 51

Sundays

19 February to 25 March

Scotland, The North East, North West England - The South West and South Coast

Route Diagram - see first Page of Table 51

		XC	VT	XC	XC	XC	XC	XC	VT	XC	XC	XC	XC	XC	VT	XC	XC	XC	XC	XC	VT	XC	XC
		◇1	◇1	◇1	◇1	◇1	◇1	◇1	◇1	◇1	◇1	◇1	◇1	◇1	◇1	◇1	◇1	◇1	◇1	◇1	◇1	◇1	◇1
				A		B				A						A		B				A	C
		🛒	🍴	🍴🛒	🛒	🛒	🛒	🛒	🍴	🍴🛒	🛒	🛒	🛒	🛒	🍴	🍴🛒	🛒	🛒	🛒	🛒	🍴	🍴🛒	🛒
Aberdeen	d																						
Stonehaven	d																						
Montrose	d																						
Arbroath	d																						
Dundee	d																						
Leuchars 3	d																						
Cupar	d																						
Ladybank	d																						
Markinch	d																						
Kirkcaldy	d																						
Inverkeithing	d																						
Glasgow Central 15	d								11 58								10 55				13 55		11 51
Motherwell	d																11 10						12 07
Haymarket	d																11 51						12 49
Edinburgh 10	d		10 52		09 50						11 05				12 52		12 08						13 06
Haymarket	d		10 57												12 56								
Lockerbie	d																						
Carlisle 8	d		12 07						13 10						14 07						15 11		
Penrith North Lakes	d														14 22								
Oxenholme Lake District	d		12 43																		15 46		
Lancaster 6	d		12 57						13 58						14 57								
Preston 8	d		13 17						14 17						15 17						16 17		
Wigan North Western	d		13 28						14 28						15 28						16 28		
Warrington Bank Quay	d		13 39						14 39						15 39						16 39		
M'chester Piccadilly 10 🚊	d	13 07		13 27				14 07		14 27				15 07		15 27				16 07		16 27	
Stockport	d			13 36						14 36						15 36						16 36	
Wilmslow	d																						
Crewe 10	d		14 01						15 01						16 01						17 00		
Macclesfield	d			13 49						14 49						15 49						16 49	
Congleton	d																						
Stoke-on-Trent	d	13 43		14 07				14 43		15 07				15 43		16 07				16 43		17 08	
Stafford	d			14 25						15 25						16 25						17 26	
Wolverhampton 7 🚊	d	14 15	14 33	14 41				15 15	15 32	15 41				16 15	16 32	16 41				17 15	17 32	17 41	
Dunbar	d										11 25												13 25
Berwick-upon-Tweed	d										11 50						12 49						
Alnmouth for Alnwick	d				10 49						12 10												14 08
Morpeth	d				11 04																		
Newcastle 8	d				11 25						12 40		13 35				13 40		14 35				14 40
Chester-le-Street	d																						
Durham	d				11 37						12 52		13 47				13 52		14 47				14 52
Darlington 7	d				11 55						13 09		14 05				14 10		15 04				15 09
York 8	d				12 28						13 40		14 34				14 40		15 34				15 40
Leeds 10	d				13 00						14 10						15 10						16 10
Wakefield Westgate 7	d				13 12						14 23						15 23						16 22
Doncaster 7	d				13 30								14 59						15 59				
Sheffield 7 🚊	d				13 57		14 22				14 54		15 23				15 54		16 24				16 54
Chesterfield	d				14 09		14 32				15 06						16 07						17 06
Nottingham 8 🚊	d					14 10						15 10						16 10					
Derby 6	d				14 31	14f35	14 53				15 26	15 35	15 54				16 28	16 35	16 55				17 27
Burton-on-Trent	d					14 48					15 39	15 48						16 48					17 38
Tamworth	d				14 50	15 00						16 00					16 48	17 00					
Birmingham New Street 12	a	14 31	14 55	14 58	15 06	15 21	15 27	15 31	15 55	15 58	16 02	16 24	16 27	16 31	16 55	16 58	17 04	17 19	17 27	17 31	17 56	17 58	18 01
Birmingham New Street 12	d	14 42		15 04	15 12	15 30	15 33	15 42		16 04	16 12	16 30	16 33	16 42		17 04	17 12	17 30	17 33	17 42		18 04	18 12
Cheltenham Spa	a	15 24			15 50	16 10		16 24			16 49	17 10		17 24			17 50	18 10		18 24			18 50
Gloucester 7	a					16 21						17 21						18 22					
Bristol Parkway 7	a	15 59			16 21			16 55			17 20			18 02			18 26			18 56			19 21
Bristol Temple Meads 10	a	16 13			16 35			17 08			17 35			18 13			18 40			19 08			19 35
Newport (South Wales)	a					17 06						18 07						19 07					
Cardiff Central 7	a					17 27						18 29						19 29					
Weston-super-Mare	a																						
Taunton	a				17 15						18 18						19 15						20 18
Tiverton Parkway	a				17 28						18 31						19 28						20 31
Exeter St Davids 6	a				17 43						18 46						19 47						20 45
Dawlish	a																						
Teignmouth	a																						
Newton Abbot	a				18 13						19 06												
Torquay	a																						
Paignton	a																						
Totnes	a																						
Plymouth	a																						
Liskeard 6	a																						
Bodmin Parkway	a																						
Lostwithiel	a																						
Par	a																						
Newquay (Summer Only)	a																						
St Austell	a																						
Truro	a																						
Redruth	a																						
Camborne	a																						
Hayle	a																						
St Erth	a																						
Penzance	a																						
Birmingham International ✈	d			15 14						16 14						17 14						18 14	
Coventry	d			15 25						16 25						17 25						18 25	
Leamington Spa 8	d			15 38			16 00			16 38			17 00			17 38			18 01			18 38	
Banbury	a			15 54			16 17			16 54			17 17			17 54			18 19			18 54	
Oxford	a			16 14			16 41			17 14			17 38			18 14			18 41			19 14	
Reading 7	a			16 43			17 13			17 43			18 13			18 43			19 13			19 43	
Guildford	a																						
Basingstoke	a			17 09						18 09						19 09						20 09	
Winchester	a			17 24						18 24						19 24						20 24	
Southampton Airport Pkway ✈	a			17 33						18 33						19 33						20 33	
Southampton Central ⛴	a			17 40						18 42						19 40						20 42	
Brockenhurst 3	a			18 02						19 01						20 02						21 02	
Bournemouth	a			18 26						19 26						20 26						21 26	

A 🍴 from Birmingham New Street; 🛒 to Birmingham New Street

B 🛒 to Newport (South Wales)

C 🛒 from Edinburgh

Table 51

Sundays

19 February to 25 March

Scotland, The North East, North West England - The South West and South Coast

Route Diagram - see first Page of Table 51

		XC		XC	XC	VT	XC	XC	XC	XC	XC	VT		XC	XC	XC	XC	XC	VT	XC	XC	XC		XC	XC
		◇1		◇1	◇1	◇1	◇1	◇1	◇1	◇1	◇1	◇1		◇1	◇1	◇1	◇1	◇1	◇1	◇1	◇1	◇1		◇1	◇1
		A					B	C	D					B	C		E	D		D	F				
		🛒		🛒	🛒	☕	☕🛒	🛒	🛒	🛒	🛒	☕		☕🛒	🛒	🛒	🛒	🛒	☕	🛒	🛒			🛒	
Aberdeen	d							11 12																	
Stonehaven	d							11 29																	
Montrose	d							11 50																	
Arbroath	d							12 06																	
Dundee	d							12 25																	
Leuchars 3	d							12 38																	
Cupar	d							12 45																	
Ladybank	d																								
Markinch	d																								
Kirkcaldy	d							13 03																	
Inverkeithing	d							13 18																	
Glasgow Central 15	d											15 57			13 49						14 55				
Motherwell	d														14 04						15 11				
Haymarket	d							13 37							14 42						15 51				
Edinburgh 10	d			13 50		14 52		14 08							15 07				16 52		16 05				
Haymarket	d					14 57													16 56						
Lockerbie	d																								
Carlisle 8	d					16 07						17 09							18 07						
Penrith North Lakes	d					16 22																			
Oxenholme Lake District	d											17 44							18 42						
Lancaster 6	d					16 57													18 57						
Preston 8	d					17 17						18 17							19 17						
Wigan North Western	d					17 28						18 28							19 28						
Warrington Bank Quay	d					17 39						18 39							19 39						
M'chester Piccadilly 10 ⛴	d				17 07		17 27				18 07			18 27				19 07		19 27					20 07
Stockport	d						17 36							18 36						19 36					20 16
Wilmslow	d																								
Crewe 10	d					18 01						19 01							20 01						
Macclesfield	d						17 49							18 49						19 49					20 29
Congleton	d																								
Stoke-on-Trent	d				17 43		18 08				18 43			19 07				19 43		20 07					20 47
Stafford	d						18 26							19 25						20 27					21 09
Wolverhampton 7 ⛴	d				18 15	18 33	18 41				19 15	19 32		19 41				20 15	20 33	20 41					21 22
Dunbar	d														15 27										
Berwick-upon-Tweed	d			14 33				14 49																	
Alnmouth for Alnwick	d																				17 07				
Morpeth	d																				17 22				
Newcastle 8	d			15 23				15 40		16 35					16 40		17 35				17 40			18 20	
Chester-le-Street	d																								
Durham	d			15 36				15 52		16 47					16 52		17 47				17 52			18 32	
Darlington 7	d			15 53				16 09		17 04					17 09		18 05				18 09			18 51	
York 8	d			16 23				16 40		17 34					17 40		18 34				18 40			19 24	
Leeds 10	d							17 10							18 10						19k10				
Wakefield Westgate 7	d							17 22							18 22						19 22				
Doncaster 7	d			16 51						17 59							18 59							19 50	
Sheffield 7 ⛴	d			17 24				17 54		18 24					18 54		19 24				19 54			20 20	
Chesterfield	d							18 06							19 06						20 06				
Nottingham 8 ⛴	d	17 10							18 10							19 10						20 10			
Derby 6	d	17 36		17 54				18 26	18 35	18 55					19 27	19 36	19 56				20 27	20 36		20 54	
Burton-on-Trent	d	17 48							18 48						19 38	19 48						20 48			
Tamworth	d	18 00						18 45	19 00							20 00					20 45	21 00			
Birmingham New Street 12	a	18 19		18 24	18 31	18 55	18 58	19 04	19 24	19 27	19 31	19 55		19 58	20 05	20 24	20 27	20 31	20 50	20 58	21 03	21 19		21 28	21 39
Birmingham New Street 12	d	18 30		18 33	18 42		19 04	19 12	19 30	19 33	19 42			20 04	20 12		20 33	20 42		21 04	21 12				
Cheltenham Spa	a	19 11			19 24			19 50	20 10		20 24				20 50			21 24			21 50				
Gloucester 7	a	19 26							20 23												22 02				
Bristol Parkway 7	a				20 03			20 21			20 57				21 21			21 59			22 34				
Bristol Temple Meads 10	a				20 14			20 35			21 08				21 32			22 10			22 45				
Newport (South Wales)	a	20 11							21 12																
Cardiff Central 7	a	20 31							21 32																
Weston-super-Mare	a																								
Taunton	a							21 15							22 15										
Tiverton Parkway	a							21 28							22 28										
Exeter St Davids 6	a							21 42							22 45										
Dawlish	a																								
Teignmouth	a																								
Newton Abbot	a																								
Torquay	a																								
Paignton	a																								
Totnes	a																								
Plymouth	a																								
Liskeard 6	a																								
Bodmin Parkway	a																								
Lostwithiel	a																								
Par	a																								
Newquay (Summer Only)	a																								
St Austell	a																								
Truro	a																								
Redruth	a																								
Camborne	a																								
Hayle	a																								
St Erth	a																								
Penzance	a																								
Birmingham International ✈	d						19 14							20 14						21 14					
Coventry	d						19 25							20 25						21 24					
Leamington Spa 8	d			19 00			19 38			20 00				20 38			21 00			21 35					
Banbury	a			19 17			19 54			20 18				20 54			21 17								
Oxford	a			19 38			20 14			20 40				21 14			21 38			22 08					
Reading 7	a			20 13			20 42			21 11				21 43			22 11			22 45					
Guildford	a																22 42								
Basingstoke	a						21 09							22 09											
Winchester	a						21 24							22 24											
Southampton Airport Pkwy ✈	a						21 33							22 33											
Southampton Central ⛴	a						21 43							22 42											
Brockenhurst 3	a						22 02																		
Bournemouth	a						22 26																		

A 🛒 to Newport (South Wales)

B ☕ from Birmingham New Street to Reading; 🛒 to Birmingham New Street

C 🛒 from Edinburgh to Bristol Temple Meads

D 🛒 to Birmingham New Street

E 🛒 to Reading

F 🛒 from Edinburgh to Birmingham New Street

Table 51

Sundays

19 February to 25 March

Scotland, The North East, North West England - The South West and South Coast

Route Diagram - see first Page of Table 51

		XC	XC	XC	VT	XC	VT	XC		XC
		◇1	◇1	◇1	◇1	◇1	◇1	◇1		◇1
		A						A		
		🛒		🛒	☕		☕	🛒		
Aberdeen	d									
Stonehaven	d									
Montrose	d									
Arbroath	d									
Dundee	d									
Leuchars 3	d									
Cupar	d									
Ladybank	d									
Markinch	d									
Kirkcaldy	d									
Inverkeithing	d									
Glasgow Central 15	d				18 30			16 55		
Motherwell	d							17 11		
Haymarket	d							17 51		
Edinburgh 10	d	17 07					18 52	18 07		
Haymarket	d						18 57			
Lockerbie	d									
Carlisle 8	d				19 44		20 07			
Penrith North Lakes	d						20 22			
Oxenholme Lake District	d				20 19					
Lancaster 6	d				20 34		20 57			
Preston 8	d				20 55		21 17			
Wigan North Western	d				21 07		21 28			
Warrington Bank Quay	d				21 18		21 39			
M'chester Piccadilly 10	d					21 07				22 07
Stockport	d					21 16				22 16
Wilmslow	d									
Crewe 10	d				21 40		22 01			
Macclesfield	d					21 29				22 29
Congleton	d									
Stoke-on-Trent	d					21 47				22 47
Stafford	d				22 02	22 06				23 05
Wolverhampton 7	d				22 18	22 22	22 32			23 19
Dunbar	d	17 27						18 26		
Berwick-upon-Tweed	d	17 52						18 52		
Alnmouth for Alnwick	d									
Morpeth	d									
Newcastle 8	d	18 39		19 25				19 40		
Chester-le-Street	d									
Durham	d	18 51		19 37				19 52		
Darlington 7	d	19 08		19 54				20 09		
York 8	d	19 40		20 24				20 40		
Leeds 10	d	20 10						21 10		
Wakefield Westgate 7	d	20 22						21 22		
Doncaster 7	d			20 50						
Sheffield 7	d	20 54		21 20				21 54		
Chesterfield	d	21 06		21 32				22 06		
Nottingham 8	d		21 08							
Derby 6	d	21 27	21 36	21 53				22 26		
Burton-on-Trent	d	21 37	21 48	22 03				22 37		
Tamworth	d	21 47	22 00	22 14				22 47		
Birmingham New Street 12	a	22 04	22 23	22 30	22 38	22 39	22 55	23 04		23 36
Birmingham New Street 12	d	22 12								
Cheltenham Spa	a	22 50								
Gloucester 7	a									
Bristol Parkway 7	a	23 22								
Bristol Temple Meads 10	a	23 33								
Newport (South Wales)	a									
Cardiff Central 7	a									
Weston-super-Mare	a									
Taunton	a									
Tiverton Parkway	a									
Exeter St Davids 6	a									
Dawlish	a									
Teignmouth	a									
Newton Abbot	a									
Torquay	a									
Paignton	a									
Totnes	a									
Plymouth	a									
Liskeard 6	a									
Bodmin Parkway	a									
Lostwithiel	a									
Par	a									
Newquay (Summer Only)	a									
St Austell	a									
Truro	a									
Redruth	a									
Camborne	a									
Hayle	a									
St Erth	a									
Penzance	a									
Birmingham International	d									
Coventry	d									
Leamington Spa 8	d									
Banbury	a									
Oxford	a									
Reading 7	a									
Guildford	a									
Basingstoke	a									
Winchester	a									
Southampton Airport Pkwy	a									
Southampton Central	a									
Brockenhurst 3	a									
Bournemouth	a									

A 🛒 to Leeds

Table 51

Sundays
from 1 April

Scotland, The North East, North West England - The South West and South Coast

Route Diagram - see first Page of Table 51

		XC	XC	XC	XC	XC	XC	XC	XC	VT	XC	XC	XC	XC	VT	XC	XC	XC	XC	XC	VT	XC	XC
		◇1	◇1	◇1	◇1	◇1	◇1	◇1	◇1	◇1	◇1	◇1	◇1	◇1	◇1	◇1	◇1	◇1	◇1	◇1	◇1	◇1	◇1
			A	B			B				B		C			B		C				B	
		🛒	🛒	🍴🛒	🛒	🛒	🍴🛒	🛒	🛒	🍴	🍴🛒	🛒	🛒	🛒	🍴	🍴🛒	🛒	🛒	🛒	🛒	🍴	🍴🛒	🛒
Aberdeen	d																						
Stonehaven	d																						
Montrose	d																						
Arbroath	d																						
Dundee	d																						
Leuchars 3	d																						
Cupar	d																						
Ladybank	d																						
Markinch	d																						
Kirkcaldy	d																						
Inverkeithing	d																						
Glasgow Central 15	d																						
Motherwell	d																						
Haymarket	d																						
Edinburgh 10	d																						08 50
Haymarket	d																						
Lockerbie	d																						
Carlisle 8	d																						
Penrith North Lakes	d																						
Oxenholme Lake District	d																						
Lancaster 6	d																						
Preston 8	d									10 17					11 17						12 17		
Wigan North Western	d									10 28					11 28						12 28		
Warrington Bank Quay	d									10 39					11 39						12 39		
M'chester Piccadilly 10 ⛴	d			08 27			09 27				10 27					11 27						12 26	
Stockport	d			08 36			09 36				10 36					11 36						12 35	
Wilmslow	d			08 43																			
Crewe 10	d			09 05						11 01					12 01						13 01		
Macclesfield	d						09 49				10 49					11 49						12 49	
Congleton	d																						
Stoke-on-Trent	d						10 07				11 07					12 07						13 07	
Stafford	d			09 26			10 27				11 28					12 25						13 25	
Wolverhampton 7 ⛴	d			09 41			10 43			11 32	11 42				12 32	12 41					13 32	13 41	
Dunbar	d																						
Berwick-upon-Tweed	d																						09 33
Alnmouth for Alnwick	d																						
Morpeth	d																						
Newcastle 8	d																09 20						10 24
Chester-le-Street	d																						
Durham	d																09 33						10 37
Darlington 7	d																09 50						10 54
York 8	d											09 28					10 28						11 28
Leeds 10	d					08 10			09 00			10 00					11 00						12 00
Wakefield Westgate 7	d					08 23			09 11			10 12					11 12						12 12
Doncaster 7	d								09 32			10 30					11 30						12 30
Sheffield 7 ⛴	d					08 54			09 57			10 57					11 57						12 57
Chesterfield	d					09 07			10 09			11 09					12 09						13 09
Nottingham 8 ⛴	d												11 11					12 10					
Derby 6	d					09 28			10 34			11 30	11 36				12 30	12 36					13 32
Burton-on-Trent	d											11 41	11 48					12 48					13 43
Tamworth	d								10 53				12 00				12 48	13 00					
Birmingham New Street 12	a			09 58		10 19	10 59		11 20	11 55	12 00	12 04	12 24		12 55	12 58	13 05	13 24			13 55	13 58	14 08
Birmingham New Street 12	d	09 04	09 12	10 04	10 12	10 30	11 04	11 12	11 30		12 04	12 12	12 30	12 33		13 04	13 12	13 30	13 33	13 42		14 04	14 12
Cheltenham Spa	a		09 49		10 52	11 09		11 52	12 08			12 50	13 10				13 50	14 12		14 23			14 51
Gloucester 7	a				11 03			12 03					13 21					14 22					
Bristol Parkway 7	a		10 21			11 39			12 39			13 21					14 21			14 54			15 24
Bristol Temple Meads 10	a		10 32			11 52			12 51			13 32					14 32			15 07			15 36
Newport (South Wales)	a				11 48			12 52					14 06					15 08					
Cardiff Central 7	a				12 08			13 12					14 26					15 31					
Weston-super-Mare	a																						
Taunton	a		11 15			12 26			13 26			14 15					15 15						16 14
Tiverton Parkway	a		11 28			12 38			13 38			14 28					15 28						16 26
Exeter St Davids 6	a		11 42			12 56			13 55			14 44					15 43						16 44
Dawlish	a																						
Teignmouth	a																						
Newton Abbot	a		12 02			13 17			14 16			15 04					16 02						17 04
Torquay	a																						
Paignton	a																						
Totnes	a		12 15			13 31			14 30			15 17					16 15						17 18
Plymouth	a		12 42			13 59			14 57			15 43					16 42						17 46
Liskeard 6	a		13 17																				
Bodmin Parkway	a		13 29																				
Lostwithiel	a																						
Par	a		13 40																				
Newquay (Summer Only)	a																						
St Austell	a		13 47																				
Truro	a		14 04																				
Redruth	a		14 18																				
Camborne	a		14 24																				
Hayle	a																						
St Erth	a		14 35																				
Penzance	a		14 49																				
Birmingham International ✈	d	09 14		10 14			11 14				12 14					13 14						14 14	
Coventry	d	09 25		10 25			11 25				12 25					13 25						14 25	
Leamington Spa 8	d	09 38		10 38			11 38				12 38			13 00		13 38			14 00			14 38	
Banbury	a	09 54		10 54			11 54				12 54			13 17		13 54			14 17			14 54	
Oxford	a	10 14		11 14			12 14				13 14			13 41		14 14			14 38			15 14	
Reading 7	a	10 38		11 42			12 43				13 42			14 13		14 46			15 13			15 42	
Guildford	a																						
Basingstoke	a	11 09		12 09			13 09				14 09					15 09						16 09	
Winchester	a	11 24		12 24			13 24				14 24					15 24						16 24	
Southampton Airport Pkwy ✈	a	11 33		12 33			13 33				14 33					15 33						16 33	
Southampton Central ⛴	a	11 42		12 42			13 42				14 42					15 42						16 42	
Brockenhurst 3	a	12 02		13 02			14 01				15 02					16 02						17 02	
Bournemouth	a	12 26		13 26			14 26				15 26					16 26						17 26	

A 🛒 to Plymouth

B 🍴 from Birmingham New Street 🛒 to Birmingham New Street

C 🛒 to Newport (South Wales)

Table 51

Sundays

from 1 April

Scotland, The North East, North West England - The South West and South Coast

Route Diagram - see first Page of Table 51

		XC	XC	XC	VT	XC	XC	XC	XC	XC	VT	XC	XC	XC	XC	XC	VT	XC	XC	XC	XC	XC	VT
		◇1	◇1	◇1	◇1	◇1	◇1	◇1	◇1	◇1	◇1	◇1	◇1	◇1	◇1	◇1	◇1	◇1	◇1	◇1	◇1	◇1	◇1
		A				B	C	A				B						B	C	A			
Aberdeen	d																						
Stonehaven	d																						
Montrose	d																						
Arbroath	d																						
Dundee	d																						
Leuchars (3)	d																						
Cupar	d																						
Ladybank	d																						
Markinch	d																						
Kirkcaldy	d																						
Inverkeithing	d																						
Glasgow Central (15)	d										11 58								10 55				13 55
Motherwell	d																		11 10				
Haymarket	d																		11 51				
Edinburgh (10)	d				10 52		09 50						11 05				12 52		12 08				
Haymarket	d				10 57												12 56						
Lockerbie	d																						
Carlisle (8)	d				12 07						13 10						14 07						15 11
Penrith North Lakes	d																14 22						
Oxenholme Lake District	d				12 43																		15 46
Lancaster (6)	d				12 57						13 58						14 57						
Preston (8)	d				13 17						14 17						15 17						16 17
Wigan North Western	d				13 28						14 28						15 28						16 28
Warrington Bank Quay	d				13 39						14 39						15 39						16 39
M'chester Piccadilly (10) ⛴	d			13 07		13 27				14 07		14 27				15 07		15 27				16 07	
Stockport	d					13 36						14 36						15 36					
Wilmslow	d																						
Crewe (10)	d				14 01						15 01						16 01						17 00
Macclesfield	d					13 49						14 49						15 49					
Congleton	d																						
Stoke-on-Trent	d			13 43		14 07				14 43		15 07				15 43		16 07				16 43	
Stafford	d					14 25						15 25						16 25					
Wolverhampton (7) ⛴	d			14 15	14 33	14 41				15 15	15 32	15 41				16 15	16 32	16 41				17 15	17 32
Dunbar	d												11 25										
Berwick-upon-Tweed	d												11 50						12 49				
Alnmouth for Alnwick	d						10 49						12 10										
Morpeth	d						11 04																
Newcastle (8)	d						11 25						12 40		13 35				13 40		14 35		
Chester-le-Street	d																						
Durham	d						11 37						12 52		13 47				13 52		14 47		
Darlington (7)	d						11 55						13 09		14 05				14 10		15 04		
York (8)	d						12 28						13 40		14 34				14 40		15 34		
Leeds (10)	d						13 00						14 10						15 10				
Wakefield Westgate (7)	d						13 12						14 23						15 23				
Doncaster (7)	d						13 30								14 59						15 59		
Sheffield (7) ⛴	d						13 57		14 22				14 54		15 23				15 54		16 24		
Chesterfield	d						14 09		14 32				15 06						16 07				
Nottingham (8) ⛴	d	13 06						14 10						15 10						16 10			
Derby (6)	d	13 36	13 54				14 31	14 35	14 53				15 26	15 35	15 54				16 29	16 35	16 55		
Burton-on-Trent	d	13 48						14 48					15 38	15 48						16 48			
Tamworth	d	14 00					14 50	15 00						16 00					16 48	17 00			
Birmingham New Street (12)	a	14 24	14 27	14 31	14 55	14 58	15 06	15 21	15 27	15 31	15 55	15 58	16 01	16 24	16 27	16 31	16 55	16 58	17 04	17 19	17 27	17 31	17 56
Birmingham New Street (12)	d	14 30	14 33	14 42		15 04	15 12	15 30	15 33	15 42		16 04	16 12	16 30	16 33	16 42		17 04	17 12	17 30	17 33	17 42	
Cheltenham Spa	a	15 10		15 24			15 50	16 10		16 24			16 49	17 10		17 24			17 50	18 10		18 24	
Gloucester (7)	a	15 21						16 21						17 21						18 22			
Bristol Parkway (7)	a			15 59			16 21			16 55			17 20			18 02			18 22			18 56	
Bristol Temple Meads (10)	a			16 11			16 35			17 08			17 35			18 13			18 40			19 08	
Newport (South Wales)	a	16 06						17 06						18 07						19 07			
Cardiff Central (7)	a	16 26						17 27						18 29						19 27			
Weston-super-Mare	a																						
Taunton	a			16 45			17 15						18 18						19 15				
Tiverton Parkway	a			16 57			17 28						18 31						19 28				
Exeter St Davids (6)	a			17 12			17 43						18 46						19 47				
Dawlish	a			17 25																			
Teignmouth	a			17 30																			
Newton Abbot	a			17 37			18 02						19 05						20 07				
Torquay	a			17 48																			
Paignton	a			17 56																			
Totnes	a						18 15						19 18						20 20				
Plymouth	a						18 42						19 45						20 46				
Liskeard (6)	a						19 17												21 12				
Bodmin Parkway	a						19 29												21 24				
Lostwithiel	a																						
Par	a						19 40												21 35				
Newquay (Summer Only)	a																						
St Austell	a						19 47												21 42				
Truro	a						20 08												21 59				
Redruth	a						20 19												22 11				
Camborne	a						20 26												22 17				
Hayle	a																						
St Erth	a						20 38												22 29				
Penzance	a						20 47												22 38				
Birmingham International ✈	d					15 14						16 14						17 14					
Coventry	d					15 25						16 25						17 25					
Leamington Spa (8)	d		15 00			15 38			16 00			16 38			17 00			17 38			18 01		
Banbury	a		15 18			15 54			16 17			16 54			17 17			17 54			18 19		
Oxford	a		15 41			16 14			16 41			17 14			17 38			18 14			18 41		
Reading (7)	a		16 13			16 43			17 10			17 43			18 13			18 43			19 13		
Guildford	a																						
Basingstoke	a					17 09						18 09						19 09					
Winchester	a					17 24						18 24						19 24					
Southampton Airport Pkwy ✈	a					17 33						18 33						19 33					
Southampton Central ⛴	a					17 40						18 42						19 40					
Brockenhurst (3)	a					18 02						19 01						20 02					
Bournemouth	a					18 26						19 26						20 26					

A: Trolley service to Newport (South Wales)

B: Restaurant from Birmingham New Street; trolley service to Birmingham New Street

C: Trolley service to Plymouth

Table 51

Sundays
from 1 April

Scotland, The North East, North West England - The South West and South Coast

Route Diagram - see first Page of Table 51

		XC	XC	XC	XC	XC	VT	XC	XC	XC	XC	XC	VT	XC	XC	XC	XC	XC	VT	XC	XC	XC
		◇1	◇1	◇1	◇1	◇1	◇1	◇1	◇1	◇1	◇1	◇1	◇1	◇1	◇1	◇1	◇1	◇1	◇1	◇1	◇1	◇1
		A	B	C				D	E	F				D	E		G	F		F	H	
		🍴🛒	🛒	🛒	🛒	🛒	🍴	🍴🛒	🛒	🛒	🛒	🛒	🍴	🍴🛒	🛒	🛒	🛒	🛒	🍴	🛒	🛒	
Aberdeen	d								11 12													
Stonehaven	d								11 29													
Montrose	d								11 50													
Arbroath	d								12 06													
Dundee	d								12 25													
Leuchars [3]	d								12 38													
Cupar	d								12 45													
Ladybank	d																					
Markinch	d																					
Kirkcaldy	d								13 03													
Inverkeithing	d								13 18													
Glasgow Central [15]	d		11 51										15 57		13 49						14 55	
Motherwell	d		12 07												14 04						15 11	
Haymarket	d		12 49						13 37						14 42						15 51	
Edinburgh [10]	d		13 06		13 50		14 52		14 08						15 07				16 52		16 05	
Haymarket	d						14 57												16 56			
Lockerbie	d																					
Carlisle [8]	d						16 07						17 09						18 07			
Penrith North Lakes	d						16 22															
Oxenholme Lake District	d												17 44						18 42			
Lancaster [6]	d						16 57												18 57			
Preston [8]	d						17 17						18 17						19 17			
Wigan North Western	d						17 28						18 28						19 28			
Warrington Bank Quay	d						17 39						18 39						19 39			
M'chester Piccadilly [10] 🚌	d	16 27				17 07		17 27				18 07		18 27				19 07		19 27		
Stockport	d	16 36						17 36						18 36						19 36		
Wilmslow	d																					
Crewe [10]	d						18 01						19 01						20 01			
Macclesfield	d	16 49						17 49						18 49						19 49		
Congleton	d																					
Stoke-on-Trent	d	17 08				17 43		18 08				18 43		19 07				19 43		20 07		
Stafford	d	17 26						18 26						19 25						20 27		
Wolverhampton [7] 🚌	d	17 41				18 15	18 33	18 41				19 15	19 32	19 41				20 15	20 33	20 41		
Dunbar	d		13 25												15 27							
Berwick-upon-Tweed	d				14 33				14 49													
Alnmouth for Alnwick	d		14 08																		17 07	
Morpeth	d																				17 22	
Newcastle [8]	d		14 40		15 23				15g40		16 35				16i40		17 35				17 40	
Chester-le-Street	d																					
Durham	d		14 52		15 36				15 52		16 47				16 52		17 47				17 52	
Darlington [7]	d		15 09		15 53				16 09		17 04				17 09		18 05				18 09	
York [8]	d		15 40		16 23				16 40		17 34				17 40		18 34				18 40	
Leeds [10]	d		16 10						17 10						18 10						19ml	
Wakefield Westgate [7]	d		16 22						17 22						18 22						19 22	
Doncaster [7]	d				16 51						17 59						18 59					
Sheffield [7] 🚌	d		16 54		17 24				17 54		18 24				18 54		19 24				19 54	
Chesterfield	d		17 06						18 06						19 06						20 06	
Nottingham [8] 🚌	d			17 10						18 10						19 10						20 10
Derby [6]	d		17 27	17 36	17 54				18 26	18 35	18 55				19 27	19 36	19 55				20 27	20 36
Burton-on-Trent	d		17 38	17 48						18 48					19 38	19 48						20 48
Tamworth	d			18 00					18 45	19 00						20 00					20 45	21 00
Birmingham New Street [12]	a	17 58	18 01	18 19	18 24	18 31	18 55	18 58	19 04	19 20	19 27	19 31	19 55	19 58	20 05	20 24	20 27	20 31	20 50	20 58	21 03	21 19
Birmingham New Street [12]	d	18 04	18 12	18 30	18 33	18 42		19 04	19 12	19 30	19 33	19 42		20 04	20 12		20 33	20 42		21 04	21 12	
Cheltenham Spa	a		18 50	19 11		19 24			19 50	20 10		20 24			20 50			21 24			21 50	
Gloucester [7]	a			19 26						20 21											22 02	
Bristol Parkway [7]	a		19 21			20 03			20 21			20 57			21 21			21 59			22 34	
Bristol Temple Meads [10]	a		19 35			20 14			20 35			21 08			21 32			22 10			22 45	
Newport (South Wales)	a			20 11						21 06												
Cardiff Central [7]	a			20 31						21 26												
Weston-super-Mare	a					20 36																
Taunton	a		20 18			20 58			21 15						22 15							
Tiverton Parkway	a		20 31			21 11			21 28						22 28							
Exeter St Davids [6]	a		20 46			21 25			21 43						22 46							
Dawlish	a					21 39																
Teignmouth	a					21 44																
Newton Abbot	a		21 05			21 51			22 07						23 05							
Torquay	a																					
Paignton	a																					
Totnes	a		21 18						22 24						23 20							
Plymouth	a		21 45			22 32			22 50						23 47							
Liskeard [6]	a																					
Bodmin Parkway	a																					
Lostwithiel	a																					
Par	a																					
Newquay (Summer Only)	a																					
St Austell	a																					
Truro	a																					
Redruth	a																					
Camborne	a																					
Hayle	a																					
St Erth	a																					
Penzance	a																					
Birmingham International ✈	d	18 14						19 14						20 14						21 14		
Coventry	d	18 25						19 25						20 25						21 24		
Leamington Spa [8]	d	18 38			19 00			19 38			20 00			20 38			21 00			21 35		
Banbury	a	18 54			19 17			19 54			20 18			20 54			21 17					
Oxford	a	19 14			19 38			20 14			20 40			21 14			21 38			22 08		
Reading [7]	a	19 43			20 13			20 42			21 11			21 43			22 07			22 33		
Guildford	a																22 42					
Basingstoke	a	20 09						21 11						22 09								
Winchester	a	20 24						21 26						22 24								
Southampton Airport Pkway ✈	a	20 33						21 35						22 33								
Southampton Central ⛴	a	20 42						21 45						22 42								
Brockenhurst [3]	a	21 02						22 04														
Bournemouth	a	21 26						22 28														

A 🍴 from Birmingham New Street
🛒 to Birmingham New Street
B 🛒 from Edinburgh
C 🛒 to Newport (South Wales)
D 🍴 from Birmingham New Street to Reading 🛒 to Birmingham New Street
E 🛒 from Edinburgh to Bristol Temple Meads
F 🛒 to Birmingham New Street
G 🛒 to Reading
H 🛒 from Edinburgh to Birmingham New Street

Table 51

Sundays
from 1 April

Scotland, The North East, North West England - The South West and South Coast

Route Diagram - see first Page of Table 51

		XC	XC	XC	XC	XC	VT	XC	VT	XC	XC
		◇1	◇1	◇1	◇1	◇1	◇1	◇1	◇1	◇1	◇1
				A						A	
Aberdeen	d										
Stonehaven	d										
Montrose	d										
Arbroath	d										
Dundee	d										
Leuchars 3	d										
Cupar	d										
Ladybank	d										
Markinch	d										
Kirkcaldy	d										
Inverkeithing	d										
Glasgow Central 15	d						18 30			16 55	
Motherwell	d									17 11	
Haymarket	d									17 51	
Edinburgh 10	d			17 07					18 52	18 07	
Haymarket	d								18 57		
Lockerbie	d										
Carlisle 8	d						19 44		20 07		
Penrith North Lakes	d								20 22		
Oxenholme Lake District	d						20 19				
Lancaster 6	d						20 34		20 57		
Preston 8	d						20 55		21 17		
Wigan North Western	d						21 07		21 28		
Warrington Bank Quay	d						21 18		21 39		
M'chester Piccadilly 10	d		20 07					21 07			22 07
Stockport	d		20 16					21 16			22 16
Wilmslow	d										
Crewe 10	d						21 40		22 01		
Macclesfield	d		20 29					21 29			22 29
Congleton	d										
Stoke-on-Trent	d		20 47					21 47			22 47
Stafford	d		21 09				22 02	22 06			23 05
Wolverhampton 7	d		21 22				22 18	22 22	22 32		23 19
Dunbar	d			17 27						18 26	
Berwick-upon-Tweed	d			17 52						18 52	
Alnmouth for Alnwick	d										
Morpeth	d										
Newcastle 8	d	18 20		18 39		19 25				19 40	
Chester-le-Street	d										
Durham	d	18 32		18 51		19 37				19 52	
Darlington 7	d	18 51		19 08		19 54				20 09	
York 8	d	19 24		19 40		20 24				20 40	
Leeds 10	d			20 10						21 10	
Wakefield Westgate 7	d			20 22						21 22	
Doncaster 7	d	19 50				20 50					
Sheffield 7	d	20 20		20 54		21 20				21 54	
Chesterfield	d			21 06		21 32				22 06	
Nottingham 8	d				21 08						
Derby 6	d	20 54		21 27	21 36	21 53				22 26	
Burton-on-Trent	d			21 37	21 48	22 03				22 37	
Tamworth	d			21 47	22 00	22 14				22 47	
Birmingham New Street 12	a	21 28	21 39	22 04	22 23	22 30	22 38	22 39	22 55	23 04	23 36
Birmingham New Street 12	d		21 43	22 12							
Cheltenham Spa	a		22 23	22 50							
Gloucester 7	a										
Bristol Parkway 7	a		22 53	23 22							
Bristol Temple Meads 10	a		23 07	23 33							
Newport (South Wales)	a										
Cardiff Central 7	a										
Weston-super-Mare	a										
Taunton	a										
Tiverton Parkway	a										
Exeter St Davids 6	a										
Dawlish	a										
Teignmouth	a										
Newton Abbot	a										
Torquay	a										
Paignton	a										
Totnes	a										
Plymouth	a										
Liskeard 6	a										
Bodmin Parkway	a										
Lostwithiel	a										
Par	a										
Newquay (Summer Only)	a										
St Austell	a										
Truro	a										
Redruth	a										
Camborne	a										
Hayle	a										
St Erth	a										
Penzance	a										
Birmingham International	d										
Coventry	d										
Leamington Spa 8	d										
Banbury	a										
Oxford	a										
Reading 7	a										
Guildford	a										
Basingstoke	a										
Winchester	a										
Southampton Airport Pkway	a										
Southampton Central	a										
Brockenhurst 3	a										
Bournemouth	a										

A to Leeds

South Coast and the South West - North West England, The North East and Scotland

Route Diagram - see first Page of Table 51

		XC	XC	XC	XC	XC	XC	XC	XC	XC	VT	XC	XC	XC	XC	XC	XC	VT	XC	XC	XC	XC	XC
				MX	MX	MX	MX																
		◇1	◇1	◇1	◇1	◇1	◇1	◇1	◇1	1	◇1	◇1	◇1	1	◇1	◇1	1	◇1	◇1	◇1	◇1	1	◇1
		A	B	C	D				E												F		
		🛒	🛒						🛒	🛒	⊠	🛒	🛒		🛒	🛒	🛒	⊠	🛒	🛒	🛒		🛒
Bournemouth	d																						
Brockenhurst 3	d																						
Southampton Central	d																				05 15		
Southampton Airport Pkwy	d																				05 22		
Winchester	d																				05 31		
Basingstoke	d																				05 47		
Guildford	d																						
Reading 7	d																				06 11		
Oxford	d																				06 36		
Banbury	d																				06 54		
Leamington Spa 8	d																				07 12		
Coventry	d																				07 27		
Birmingham International	d																				07 38		
Penzance	d																						
St Erth	d																						
Hayle	d																						
Camborne	d																						
Redruth	d																						
Truro	d																						
St Austell	d																						
Newquay (Summer Only)	d																						
Par	d																						
Lostwithiel	d																						
Bodmin Parkway	d																						
Liskeard 6	d																						
Plymouth	d	18p23																					
Totnes	d	18p49																					
Paignton	d																						
Torquay	d																						
Newton Abbot	d	19p03	19p03																				
Teignmouth	d																						
Dawlish	d																						
Exeter St Davids 6	d	19p25	19p25																				
Tiverton Parkway	d	19p38	19p38																				
Taunton	d	19p54	19p54																				
Weston-super-Mare	d																						
Cardiff Central 7	d						21p50																
Newport (South Wales)	d						22p05																
Bristol Temple Meads 10	d	20p30	20p30																				06 27
Bristol Parkway 7	d	20p40	20p40																				06 40
Gloucester 7	d						22p47																
Cheltenham Spa	d	21p12	21p12				22p58																07 12
London Paddington	d																						
Birmingham New Street 12	a	21p51	21p51				00 01														07 48		07 56
Birmingham New Street 12	d	22p03	22p03	22p30	22p30	23p09		05 57	06 00	06 19	06 19	06 22	06 30	06 49	06 57	07 03	07 19	07 20	07 30	07 31	07 57	07 49	08 03
Tamworth	d	22p18	22p18			23p28				06 39				07 07		07 19	07 38					08 07	08 19
Burton-on-Trent	d					23p40				06 51				07 19		07 29	07 50					08 19	08 29
Derby 6	a	22p40	22p40			23p55			06 32	07 05			07 11	07 34		07 42	08 05		08 11			08 34	08 42
Nottingham 8	a					00 18				07 41				08 08			08 33					09 05	
Chesterfield	a	23p04	23p04						06 53				07 31			08 02			08 32				09 02
Sheffield 7	a	23p20	23p20						07 07				07 48			08 17			08 45				09 17
Doncaster 7	a												08 24						09 18				
Wakefield Westgate 7	a								07 36							08 46							09 46
Leeds 10	a	00 16	00 16						07 52							09 03							10 02
York 8	a								08 22				08 45			09 26			09 44				10 26
Darlington 7	a								08 55				09 16			09 57			10 13				11 00
Durham	a								09 12				09 33			10 16			10 30				11 19
Chester-le-Street	a																						
Newcastle 8	a								09 29				09 47			10 30			10 44				11 34
Morpeth	a																						
Alnmouth for Alnwick	a								09 58														
Berwick-upon-Tweed	a								10 19														12 21
Dunbar	a															11 36							
Wolverhampton 7	d			22p48	22p48			06 16			06 36	06 40			07 15			07 37		07 49	08 15		
Stafford	a			23p00	23p00			06 29				06 53			07 29					08 00	08 29		
Stoke-on-Trent	a			23p20	23p21			06 50				07 13								08 19	08 54		
Congleton	a							07 02															
Macclesfield	a							07 11				07 30								08 36	09 11		
Crewe 10	a										07 07				07 50			08 08					
Wilmslow	a														08 08								
Stockport	a							07 27				07 45			08 20					08 50	09 27		
M'chester Piccadilly 10	a			00 12	00 12			07 37				07 59			08 34					08 59	09 39		
Warrington Bank Quay	a										07 26							08 27					
Wigan North Western	a										07 37							08 38					
Preston 8	a										07 51							08 51					
Lancaster 6	a										08 08							09 08					
Oxenholme Lake District	a										08 21												
Penrith North Lakes	a																	09 44					
Carlisle 8	a										09 01							09 59					
Lockerbie	a																						
Haymarket	a										10 16												
Edinburgh 10	a								11 05		10 21					12 03							13 06
Haymarket	a								11 14														13 15
Motherwell	a								11 52														13 52
Glasgow Central 15	a								12 14									11 16					14 12
Inverkeithing	a																						
Kirkcaldy	a																						
Markinch	a																						
Ladybank	a																						
Cupar	a																						
Leuchars 3	a																						
Dundee	a																						
Arbroath	a																						
Montrose	a																						
Stonehaven	a																						
Aberdeen	a																						

A MO until 13 February and then from 2 April. 🛒 to Birmingham New Street

B MO from 20 February until 26 March. 🛒 to Birmingham New Street

C until 23 March

D from 27 March

E 🛒 to Edinburgh

F 🛒 from Reading

South Coast and the South West - North West England, The North East and Scotland

Route Diagram - see first Page of Table 51

		XC	XC	XC	VT	XC	XC	XC	XC	XC	VT	XC	XC	XC	XC	XC	XC	VT	XC	XC	XC	XC	XC
		◇1	1	◇1	◇1	◇1	◇1	◇1	1	◇1	◇1	◇1	◇1	◇1	◇1	1	◇1	◇1	◇1	◇1	◇1	◇1	1
				A								B	C		D					C			
			⊤	⊤	☒	⊤	⊤	⊤	⊤	⊤	☒	⊤	⊤	⊤	⊤		⊤	☒	⊤	⊤	⊤	⊤	
Bournemouth	d													06 30							07 30		
Brockenhurst 3	d													06 49							07 49		
Southampton Central ⛴	d						06 15							07 15							08 15		
Southampton Airport Pkwy ✈	d						06 22							07 22							08 22		
Winchester	d						06 31							07 31			08 01				08 31		
Basingstoke	d						06 47							07 47			08 18				08 47		
Guildford	d			06 02																			
Reading 7	d			06 41			07 09			07 40				08 11			08 41				09 11		
Oxford	d			07 07			07 36			08 07				08 36			09 07				09 36		
Banbury	d			07 26			07 54			08 27				08 54			09 26				09 54		
Leamington Spa 8	d			07 43			08 12			08 44				09 12			09 43				10 12		
Coventry	d						08 27							09 27							10 27		
Birmingham International ✈	d						08 38							09 38							10 38		
Penzance	d																						
St Erth	d																						
Hayle	d																						
Camborne	d																						
Redruth	d																						
Truro	d																						
St Austell	d																						
Newquay (Summer Only)	d																						
Par	d																						
Lostwithiel	d																						
Bodmin Parkway	d																						
Liskeard 6	d																						
Plymouth	d							05 20							06 25							07 25	
Totnes	d							05 45							06 50							07 50	
Paignton	d																		07 02				
Torquay	d																		07 08				
Newton Abbot	d							06 02							07 03				07 19			08 03	
Teignmouth	d																		07 26				
Dawlish	d																		07 31				
Exeter St Davids 6	d							06 22							07 23				07 45			08 23	
Tiverton Parkway	d							06 36							07 37				07 58			08 37	
Taunton	d							06 50							07 51				08 13			08 51	
Weston-super-Mare	d																		08 34				
Cardiff Central 7	d											07 00	07 45							08 45			
Newport (South Wales)	d											07 15	08 02							09 02			
Bristol Temple Meads 10	d					07 00		07 30				08 00			08 30				09 00			09 30	
Bristol Parkway 7	d					07 10		07 40				08 10			08 40				09 10			09 40	
Gloucester 7	d	07 10											08 46							09 46			
Cheltenham Spa	d	07 21				07 42		08 12				08 42	08 57		09 12				09 42	09 57		10 12	
London Paddington	d																						
Birmingham New Street 12	a	08 16		08 15		08 26	08 48	08 56		09 18		09 26	09 45	09 48	09 56		10 18		10 26	10 45	10 48	10 56	
Birmingham New Street 12	d		08 19	08 30	08 20	08 31	08 57	09 03	09 19	09 30	09 20	09 31	09 49	09 57	10 03	10 19	10 30	10 20	10 31	10 49	10 57	11 03	11 19
Tamworth	d		08 36						09 36				10 07		10 19	10 36				11 09			11 36
Burton-on-Trent	d		08 48					09 26	09 48				10 19			10 48				11 21		11 26	11 48
Derby 6	a		08 59	09 05				09 39	09 59	10 05			10 34		10 40	10 59	11 05			11 33		11 39	11 59
Nottingham 8 ⛴	a		09 33						10 32				11 05			11 32				12 05			12 32
Chesterfield	a							10 02							11 02							12 03	
Sheffield 7 ⛴	a			09 43				10 17		10 41					11 17		11 43					12 17	
Doncaster 7	a			10 18						11 18							12 18						
Wakefield Westgate 7	a							10 46							11 46							12 46	
Leeds 10	a							11 02							12 01							13 03	
York 8	a			10 45				11 26		11 46					12 26		12 46					13 26	
Darlington 7	a			11 13				11 57		12 13					12 58		13 13					13 59	
Durham	a			11 30				12 21		12 30					13 15		13 30					14 17	
Chester-le-Street	a																						
Newcastle 8	a			11 45				12 34		12 44					13 29		13 45					14 30	
Morpeth	a																					14 49	
Alnmouth for Alnwick	a														14 01								
Berwick-upon-Tweed	a														14 22								
Dunbar	a							13 39														15 40	
Wolverhampton 7 ⛴	d				08 37	08 49	09 15				09 37	09 49		10 15				10 37	10 49		11 15		
Stafford	a					09 00	09 29					10 00		10 29					11 00		11 28		
Stoke-on-Trent	a					09 19	09 54					10 19		10 54					11 19		11 54		
Congleton	a																						
Macclesfield	a						10 11							11 11							12 11		
Crewe 10	a				09 07						10 07							11 07					
Wilmslow	a																						
Stockport	a					09 49	10 27					10 49		11 27					11 49		12 27		
M'chester Piccadilly 10 ⛴	a					09 59	10 39					10 59		11 39					11 59		12 39		
Warrington Bank Quay	a				09 26						10 26							11 26					
Wigan North Western	a				09 37						10 37							11 37					
Preston 8	a				09 51						10 51							11 51					
Lancaster 6	a				10 08						11 08							12 08					
Oxenholme Lake District	a				10 22													12 22					
Penrith North Lakes	a										11 44												
Carlisle 8	a				11 02						12 00							13 01					
Lockerbie	a																						
Haymarket	a				12 14													14 15					
Edinburgh 10	a				12 21			14 10							15 06			14 21				16 05	
Haymarket	a														15 14								
Motherwell	a														15 52								
Glasgow Central 15	a										13 17				16 23								
Inverkeithing	a																						
Kirkcaldy	a																						
Markinch	a																						
Ladybank	a																						
Cupar	a																						
Leuchars 3	a																						
Dundee	a																						
Arbroath	a																						
Montrose	a																						
Stonehaven	a																						
Aberdeen	a																						

A ⊤ from Reading
B ⊤ from Bristol Temple Meads
C ⊤ from Newport (South Wales)
D ⊤ to Edinburgh

South Coast and the South West - North West England, The North East and Scotland

Route Diagram - see first Page of Table 51

		XC		XC	XC	XC	XC	XC	VT	XC	XC	XC		XC	XC	XC	VT	XC	XC	XC	XC	XC		VT	XC
		◇■1		◇■1	◇■1	◇■1	■1	◇■1	◇■1	◇■1	◇■1	◇■1		◇■1	■1	◇■1	◇■1	◇■1	◇■1	◇■1	■1	◇■1		◇■1	◇■1
						A					B			C						A					
		🛒		🛒	🛒	🛒	🛒	🛒	☕	🛒	🛒	🛒		🛒		🛒	☕	🛒	🛒	🛒		🛒		☕	🛒
Bournemouth	d				08 45							09 45							10 45						
Brockenhurst ■3	d				09 00							10 00							11 00						
Southampton Central ⛴	d				09 15			09 46				10 15							11 15			11 46			
Southampton Airport Pkwy ✈	d				09 22			09 53				10 22							11 22			11 53			
Winchester	d				09 31			10 03				10 31							11 31			12 02			
Basingstoke	d				09 47			10 19				10 47							11 47			12 18			
Guildford	d																								
Reading ■7	d	09 40			10 11			10 41				11 11				11 40			12 11			12 41			
Oxford	d	10 07			10 36			11 07				11 36				12 07			12 36			13 07			
Banbury	d	10 25			10 54			11 25				11 54				12 25			12 54			13 25			
Leamington Spa ■8	d	10 42			11 12			11 43				12 12				12 43			13 12			13 43			
Coventry	d				11 27							12 27							13 27						
Birmingham International ✈	d				11 38							12 38							13 38						
Penzance	d					06 28														08 28					
St Erth	d					06 36														08 36					
Hayle	d																								
Camborne	d					06 46														08 46					
Redruth	d					06 52														08 52					
Truro	d					07 04														09 04					
St Austell	d					07 20														09 20					
Newquay (Summer Only)	d																								
Par	d					07 28														09 28					
Lostwithiel	d																								
Bodmin Parkway	d					07 39														09 39					
Liskeard ■6	d					07 53														09 51					
Plymouth	d					08 25								09 25						10 25					
Totnes	d					08 50								09 50						10 50					
Paignton	d																	10 07							
Torquay	d																	10 13							
Newton Abbot	d					09 03								10 03				10 24		11 03					
Teignmouth	d																	10 31							
Dawlish	d																	10 36							
Exeter St Davids ■6	d					09 23								10 23				10 50		11 23					
Tiverton Parkway	d					09 37								10 37				11 03		11 37					
Taunton	d					09 51								10 51				11 18		11 51					
Weston-super-Mare	d																								
Cardiff Central ■7	d										10 45														
Newport (South Wales)	d										11 00														
Bristol Temple Meads ■10	d			10 00		10 30				11 00				11 30				12 00		12 30					13 00
Bristol Parkway ■7	d			10 10		10 40				11 10				11 40				12 10		12 40					13 10
Gloucester ■7	d										11 46														
Cheltenham Spa	d			10 42		11 12				11 42	11 57			12 12				12 42		13 12					13 42
London Paddington	d																								
Birmingham New Street ■12	a	11 18		11 26	11 48	11 58		12 18		12 26	12 45	12 48		12 56		13 18		13 26	13 48	13 56		14 18			14 26
Birmingham New Street ■12	d	11 30		11 31	11 57	12 03	12 19	12 30	12 20	12 31	12 49	12 57		13 03	13 19	13 30	13 20	13 31	13 57	14 03	14 19	14 30		14 20	14 31
Tamworth	d					12 19	12 37				13 09				13 36					14 19	14 36				
Burton-on-Trent	d						12 50				13 20			13 28	13 48						14 48				
Derby ■6	a	12 05				12 41	13 05	13 08			13 34			13 40	13 59	14 05				14 40	15 00	15 06			
Nottingham ■8 🚌	a						13 33				14 05				14 32						15 32				
Chesterfield	a					13 02								14 02						15 02					
Sheffield ■7 🚌	a	12 41				13 17		13 41						14 17		14 41				15 17		15 41			
Doncaster ■7	a	13 18						14 18								15 18						16 18			
Wakefield Westgate ■7	a					13 46								14 46						15 46					
Leeds ■10	a					14 02								15 01						16 02					
York ■8	a	13 40				14 26		14 44						15 26		15 45				16 28		16 45			
Darlington ■7	a	14 12				14 58		15 13						15 58		16 13				16 58		17 13			
Durham	a	14 29				15 15		15 30						16 16		16 30				17 15		17 30			
Chester-le-Street	a																								
Newcastle ■8	a	14 42				15 30		15 45						16 30		16 45				17 31		17 45			
Morpeth	a																								
Alnmouth for Alnwick	a					16 00								17 00						18 01					
Berwick-upon-Tweed	a					16 21														18 22					
Dunbar	a													17 42											
Wolverhampton ■7 🚌	d			11 49	12 15				12 37	12 49		13 15					13 37	13 49	14 15					14 37	14 49
Stafford	a			12 00	12 29					13 00		13 29						14 00	14 29						15 00
Stoke-on-Trent	a			12 19	12 54					13 19		13 54						14 19	14 54						15 19
Congleton	a																								
Macclesfield	a				13 11							14 11							15 11						
Crewe ■10	a								13 07								14 07							15 07	
Wilmslow	a																								
Stockport	a			12 49	13 27					13 49		14 27						14 49	15 27						15 49
M'chester Piccadilly ■10 🚌	a			12 59	13 39					13 59		14 39						14 59	15 39						15 59
Warrington Bank Quay	a								13 26								14 26							15 26	
Wigan North Western	a								13 37								14 37							15 37	
Preston ■8	a								13 51								14 51							15 51	
Lancaster ■6	a								14 08								15 08							16 08	
Oxenholme Lake District	a																15 22								
Penrith North Lakes	a								14 44															16 44	
Carlisle ■8	a								15 00								16 01							17 00	
Lockerbie	a																								
Haymarket	a								16 17															18 12	
Edinburgh ■10	a					17 06			16 21					18 07						19 06				18 22	
Haymarket	a					17 14								18 14						19 14					
Motherwell	a					17 52														19 54					
Glasgow Central ■15	a					18 16											17 14			20 15					
Inverkeithing	a													18 28											
Kirkcaldy	a													18 46											
Markinch	a													18 56											
Ladybank	a													19 03											
Cupar	a													19 15											
Leuchars ■3	a													19 22											
Dundee	a													19 35											
Arbroath	a													19 51											
Montrose	a													20 05											
Stonehaven	a													20 26											
Aberdeen	a													20 45											

A 🛒 from Plymouth to Edinburgh **B** 🛒 from Newport (South Wales) **C** 🛒 to Edinburgh

South Coast and the South West - North West England, The North East and Scotland

Route Diagram - see first Page of Table 51

		XC	XC	XC	XC	VT	XC	XC		XC	XC	XC	XC	XC	XC	XC	XC	XC		VT	XC	XC	XC	XC	XC
																				R					
		◇1	◇1	1	◇1	◇1	◇1	◇1		◇1	◇1	1	◇1	◇1	◇1	◇1	1	◇1		1	◇1	1	◇1	◇1	1
			A				B	C			A		D			E								F	
		🛒	🛒		🛒	🍴	🛒	🛒		🛒	🛒		🛒	🛒	🛒	🛒		🛒		🍴	🛒		🛒	🛒	
Bournemouth	d	11 45								12 45					13 45								14 45		
Brockenhurst 3	d	12 00								13 00					14 00								15 00		
Southampton Central ⛴	d	12 15								13 15			13 46		14 15								15 15		
Southampton Airport Pkwy ✈	d	12 22								13 22			13 53		14 22								15 22		
Winchester	d	12 31								13 31			14 03		14 31								15 31		
Basingstoke	d	12 47								13 47			14 19		14 47								15 47		
Guildford	d																								
Reading 7	d	13 11			13 40					14 11			14 41		15 11			15 40					16 11		
Oxford	d	13 36			14 07					14 36			15 07		15 36			16 07					16 36		
Banbury	d	13 54			14 26					14 54			15 25		15 54			16 26					16 54		
Leamington Spa 8	d	14 12			14 42					15 12			15 43		16 12			16 44					17 12		
Coventry	d	14 27								15 27					16 27								17 27		
Birmingham International ✈	d	14 38								15 38					16 38								17 38		
Penzance	d						09 40																		
St Erth	d						09 48																		
Hayle	d						09 52																		
Camborne	d						10 01																		
Redruth	d						10 08																		
Truro	d						10 19																		
St Austell	d						10 35																		
Newquay (Summer Only)	d																								
Par	d						10 43																		
Lostwithiel	d						10 50																		
Bodmin Parkway	d						10 57																		
Liskeard 6	d						11 09																		
Plymouth	d		11 25				11 50				12 23					13 23								14 25	
Totnes	d		11 50				12 15				12 49					13 49								14 50	
Paignton	d																				14 01				
Torquay	d																				14 07				
Newton Abbot	d		12 03				12 28				13 03					14 03					14 18			15 03	
Teignmouth	d																				14 25				
Dawlish	d																				14 30				
Exeter St Davids 6	d		12 23				12 48				13 25					14 25					14 44			15 23	
Tiverton Parkway	d		12 37				13 02				13 39					14 39					14 57			15 37	
Taunton	d		12 51				13 16				13 54					14 54					15 12			15 51	
Weston-super-Mare	d																				15 38				
Cardiff Central 7	d							13 45																	
Newport (South Wales)	d							14 00																	
Bristol Temple Meads 10	d		13 30				14 00				14 30			15 00		15 30					16 00			16 30	
Bristol Parkway 7	d		13 40				14 10				14 40			15 10		15 40					16 10			16 40	
Gloucester 7	d							14 46																	
Cheltenham Spa	d		14 12				14 42	14 57			15 12			15 42		16 12					16 42			17 12	
London Paddington	d																								
Birmingham New Street 12	a	14 48	14 56		15 18		15 26	15 45		15 48	15 56		16 18	16 26	16 48	16 58		17 18			17 26		17 48	17 56	
Birmingham New Street 12	d	14 57	15 03	15 19	15 30	15 20	15 31	15 49		15 57	16 03	16 19	16 30	16 31	16 57	17 03	17 19	17 30		17 20	17 31	17 39	17 57	18 03	18 19
Tamworth	d			15 36				16 09			16 19	16 39					17 36					18 02		18 19	18 36
Burton-on-Trent	d		15 26	15 48				16 21				16 51				17 26	17 48					18 13			18 48
Derby 6	a		15 39	16 00	16 06			16 34			16 40	17 05	17 08			17 38	17 59	18 05				18 31		18 40	18 59
Nottingham 8 ⛴	a			16 32				17 05				17 33					18 32								19 32
Chesterfield	a		16 02								17 03					18 01								19 00	
Sheffield 7 ⛴	a		16 17		16 41						17 19		17 44			18 18		18 44						19 19	
Doncaster 7	a				17 18													19 14							
Wakefield Westgate 7	a		16 49								17 47		18 13			18 47								19 50	
Leeds 10	a		17 04								18 03		18 31			19 03								20 05	
York 8	a		17 28		17 40						18 29		19 01			19 29		19 38						20 30	
Darlington 7	a		17 58		18 13						19 01		19 29			20 02		20 10						20 58	
Durham	a		18 15		18 31						19 19		19 47			20 20		20 27						21 17	
Chester-le-Street	a																								
Newcastle 8	a		18 33		18 46						19 35		20 03			20 34		20 42						21 31	
Morpeth	a															20 54									
Alnmouth for Alnwick	a										20 04		20 34											21 59	
Berwick-upon-Tweed	a		19 21								20 26					21 25									
Dunbar	a		19 44													21 50									
Wolverhampton 7 ⛴	d	15 15				15 37	15 50			16 15				16 49	17 15					17 37	17 50		18 15		
Stafford	a	15 29					16 01			16 30				17 00	17 29						18 01		18 29		
Stoke-on-Trent	a	15 54					16 20			16 54				17 19	17 54						18 20		18 54		
Congleton	a																								
Macclesfield	a	16 11								17 11					18 11								19 11		
Crewe 10	a					16 07														18 07					
Wilmslow	a																								
Stockport	a	16 27					16 49			17 27				17 49	18 27						18 49		19 27		
M'chester Piccadilly 10 ⛴	a	16 39					16 59			17 39				17 59	18 39						18 59		19 39		
Warrington Bank Quay	a					16 26														18 26					
Wigan North Western	a					16 37														18 37					
Preston 8	a					16 51														18 51					
Lancaster 6	a					17 08														19 08					
Oxenholme Lake District	a					17 22														19 22					
Penrith North Lakes	a					17 48																			
Carlisle 8	a					18 05														20 01					
Lockerbie	a																								
Haymarket	a																								
Edinburgh 10	a		20 09								21 11		21 35			22 16								23 04	
Haymarket	a		20 16								21 17														
Motherwell	a										22 01														
Glasgow Central 15	a					19 19					22 27									21 17					
Inverkeithing	a		20 30																						
Kirkcaldy	a																								
Markinch	a		21 01																						
Ladybank	a		21 09																						
Cupar	a		21 17																						
Leuchars 3	a		21 25																						
Dundee	a		21 41																						
Arbroath	a																								
Montrose	a																								
Stonehaven	a																								
Aberdeen	a																								

A 🛒 to Edinburgh
B 🛒 from Plymouth
C 🛒 from Newport (South Wales)
D 🛒 from Reading
E 🛒 to Newcastle
F 🛒 to Leeds

South Coast and the South West - North West England, The North East and Scotland

Route Diagram - see first Page of Table 51

		XC	VT	XC	XC	XC	XC	XC	XC	VT	XC	XC	XC	XC	XC	XC	XC	VT	VT	XC	XC	XC
		◇1	◇1	◇1	◇1	◇1	◇1	1	◇1	◇1	◇1	◇1	◇1	◇1	◇1	◇1	◇1	◇1	◇1	◇1	◇1	◇1
		A							B			C	C	C	C	C	C	D	E			F
		⚲	☕	⚲		⚲	⚲		⚲	☕	⚲	⚲	⚲	⚲	⚲	⚲	⚲	☕	☕			⚲
Bournemouth	d					15 45						16 45				17 45						18 45
Brockenhurst 3	d					16 00						17 00				18 00						19 00
Southampton Central	d	15 47				16 15						17 15		17 46		18 15						19 15
Southampton Airport Pkwy	d					16 22						17 22		17 53		18 22						19 22
Winchester	d					16 31						17 31		18 02		18 31						19 31
Basingstoke	d	16 18				16 47						17 47		18 18		18 47						19 47
Guildford	d																					
Reading 7	d	16 40				17 11			17 41			18 11		18 41		19 11				19 40		20 11
Oxford	d	17 07				17 36			18 07			18 36		19 12		19 36				20 07		20 36
Banbury	d	17 28				17 54			18 26			18 54		19 31		19 54				20 28		20 54
Leamington Spa 8	d	17 48				18 12			18 46			19 12		19 50		20 12				20 46		21 12
Coventry	d					18 27						19 27				20 27						21 27
Birmingham International	d					18 38						19 38				20 38						21 38
Penzance	d																					
St Erth	d																					
Hayle	d																					
Camborne	d																					
Redruth	d																					
Truro	d																					
St Austell	d																					
Newquay (Summer Only)	d																					
Par	d																					
Lostwithiel	d																					
Bodmin Parkway	d																					
Liskeard 6	d																					
Plymouth	d						15 23						16 25				17 23					
Totnes	d						15 49						16 50				17 49					
Paignton	d																					
Torquay	d																					
Newton Abbot	d						16 03						17 03				18 03					
Teignmouth	d																					
Dawlish	d																					
Exeter St Davids 6	d						16 25				16 54		17 23				18 25					
Tiverton Parkway	d						16 39				17 08		17 37				18 39					
Taunton	d						16 54				17 22		17 51				18 54					
Weston-super-Mare	d																					
Cardiff Central 7	d				16 45																	
Newport (South Wales)	d				17 00																	
Bristol Temple Meads 10	d			17 00			17 30				18 00		18 30		19 00		19 30				20 00	
Bristol Parkway 7	d			17 10			17 40				18 10		18 40		19 10		19 40				20 10	
Gloucester 7	d				17 46																20 46	
Cheltenham Spa	d			17 42	17 58		18 12				18 42		19 12		19 42		20 12				20 56	
London Paddington	d																					
Birmingham New Street 12	a	18 18		18 26	18 45	18 48	18 55		19 18		19 26	19 48	19 56	20 18	20 28	20 48	20 52			21 22	21 46	21 48
Birmingham New Street 12	d	18 30	18 20	18 31	18 49	18 57	19 03	19 19	19 30	19 20	19 31	19 57	20 03	20 30	20 31	20 57	21 03	21 20	21 20			21 57
Tamworth	d				19 09			19 36					20 19				21 19					
Burton-on-Trent	d				19 22		19 26	19 48									21 30					
Derby 6	a	19 05			19 34		19 39	19 59	20 05				20 42	21 11			21 43					
Nottingham 8	a				20 03			20 32														
Chesterfield	a	19 29					20 01						21 02	21 33			22 06					
Sheffield 7	a	19 47					20 18		20 48				21 18	21 51			22 24					
Doncaster 7	a	20 15							21 19					22 29								
Wakefield Westgate 7	a						20 46						21 46				22 59					
Leeds 10	a						21 05						22 02				23 15					
York 8	a	20 46							21 45					22 53								
Darlington 7	a	21 14							22 15													
Durham	a	21 31							22 33													
Chester-le-Street	a																					
Newcastle 8	a	21 44							22 50													
Morpeth	a																					
Alnmouth for Alnwick	a																					
Berwick-upon-Tweed	a																					
Dunbar	a																					
Wolverhampton 7	d		18 37	18 49		19 15				19 37	19 49	20 16			20 49	21 16		21 41	21 41			22 16
Stafford	a			19 00		19 27					20 00	20 29				21 31		21 53	21 53			22 29
Stoke-on-Trent	a			19 19		19 54					20 19	20 54			21 17	21 54						22 53
Congleton	a																					
Macclesfield	a					20 11						21 11				22 11						23 11
Crewe 10	a		19 07							20 07								22 17	22 17			
Wilmslow	a																					
Stockport	a			19 48		20 27					20 48	21 27			21 46	22 25						23 25
M'chester Piccadilly 10	a			19 59		20 39					20 58	21 39			21 59	22 35						23 37
Warrington Bank Quay	a		19 26							20 26								22 36	22 36			
Wigan North Western	a		19 37							20 37								22 46	22 46			
Preston 8	a		19 51							20 51								23 01	23 03			
Lancaster 6	a		20 08							21 08												
Oxenholme Lake District	a									21 22												
Penrith North Lakes	a		20 44																			
Carlisle 8	a		21 00							22 01												
Lockerbie	a																					
Haymarket	a		22 14																			
Edinburgh 10	a		22 22																			
Haymarket	a																					
Motherwell	a																					
Glasgow Central 15	a									23 18												
Inverkeithing	a																					
Kirkcaldy	a																					
Markinch	a																					
Ladybank	a																					
Cupar	a																					
Leuchars 3	a																					
Dundee	a																					
Arbroath	a																					
Montrose	a																					
Stonehaven	a																					
Aberdeen	a																					

A ⚲ to Doncaster
B ⚲ to Sheffield
C ⚲ to Birmingham New Street
D until 30 December and then from 26 March
E from 2 January until 23 March
F ⚲ to Reading

South Coast and the South West - North West England, The North East and Scotland

Route Diagram - see first Page of Table 51

		XC	XC	XC	XC	XC	XC	XC	XC	XC	XC	XC	XC
		◇1	◇1	◇1	◇1	◇1	◇1	◇1	◇1	◇1	◇1	◇1	◇1
			A		B	C	D						
			⊼			FX	FO						
Bournemouth	d							19 45					
Brockenhurst 3	d							20 00					
Southampton Central	d							20 15					
Southampton Airport Pkway	d							20 22					
Winchester	d							20 31					
Basingstoke	d							20 47					
Guildford	d												
Reading 7	d			20 40				21 11				21 46	
Oxford	d			21 08				21 36				22 30	
Banbury	d			21 33				21 54				22 54	
Leamington Spa 8	d			21 52				22 12				23 13	
Coventry	d							22 24				23 27	
Birmingham International	d							22 34				23 37	
Penzance	d												
St Erth	d												
Hayle	d												
Camborne	d												
Redruth	d												
Truro	d												
St Austell	d												
Newquay (Summer Only)	d												
Par	d												
Lostwithiel	d												
Bodmin Parkway	d												
Liskeard 6	d												
Plymouth	d		18 25										
Totnes	d		18 50										
Paignton	d										20 14		
Torquay	d										20 20		
Newton Abbot	d		19 03								20 31		
Teignmouth	d												
Dawlish	d												
Exeter St Davids 6	d		19 23								20 52		
Tiverton Parkway	d		19 37								21 04		
Taunton	d		19 51								21 19		
Weston-super-Mare	d												
Cardiff Central 7	d									21 05			21 50
Newport (South Wales)	d									21 21			22 05
Bristol Temple Meads 10	d		20 30								22 00		
Bristol Parkway 7	d		20 40								22 10		
Gloucester 7	d									22 04			22 47
Cheltenham Spa	d		21 17							22 15	22 42		22 58
London Paddington	d												
Birmingham New Street 12	a		22 06	22 17				22 45		23 36	23 44	23 57	00 01
Birmingham New Street 12	d	22 03			22 30	22 30	22 30		23 09				
Tamworth	d	22 28							23 28				
Burton-on-Trent	d	22 40							23 40				
Derby 6	a	22 54							23 55				
Nottingham 8	a	23 27							00 18				
Chesterfield	a												
Sheffield 7	a												
Doncaster 7	a												
Wakefield Westgate 7	a												
Leeds 10	a												
York 8	a												
Darlington 7	a												
Durham	a												
Chester-le-Street	a												
Newcastle 8	a												
Morpeth	a												
Alnmouth for Alnwick	a												
Berwick-upon-Tweed	a												
Dunbar	a												
Wolverhampton 7	d				22 48	22 48	22 48						
Stafford	a				23 00	23 00	23 00						
Stoke-on-Trent	a				23 20	23 21	23 21						
Congleton	a												
Macclesfield	a												
Crewe 10	a												
Wilmslow	a												
Stockport	a												
M'chester Piccadilly 10	a				00 12	00 12	00 13						
Warrington Bank Quay	a												
Wigan North Western	a												
Preston 8	a												
Lancaster 6	a												
Oxenholme Lake District	a												
Penrith North Lakes	a												
Carlisle 8	a												
Lockerbie	a												
Haymarket	a												
Edinburgh 10	a												
Haymarket	a												
Motherwell	a												
Glasgow Central 15	a												
Inverkeithing	a												
Kirkcaldy	a												
Markinch	a												
Ladybank	a												
Cupar	a												
Leuchars 8	a												
Dundee	a												
Arbroath	a												
Montrose	a												
Stonehaven	a												
Aberdeen	a												

A ⊼ to Bristol Temple Meads
B until 23 March
C from 26 March
D from 30 March

Table 51

Saturdays
until 11 February

South Coast and the South West - North West England, The North East and Scotland

Route Diagram - see first Page of Table 51

		XC	XC	XC	XC	XC	XC	VT	XC	XC	XC	XC	XC	XC	VT	XC	XC	XC	XC	XC	XC	XC	XC
		◇1	◇1	◇1	◇1	◇1	1	◇1	◇1	◇1	1	◇1	◇1	1	◇1	◇1	◇1	◇1	1	◇1	◇1	1	◇1
						A												B					B
						🛒	🛒	☕	🛒	🛒		🛒	🛒	🛒	☕	🛒	🛒	🛒		🛒		🛒	🛒
Bournemouth	d																						
Brockenhurst 3	d																						
Southampton Central	d																	05 09					
Southampton Airport Pkway ✈	d																	05 16					
Winchester	d																	05 25					
Basingstoke	d																	05 41					
Guildford	d																						06 09
Reading 7	d																	06 11					06 46
Oxford	d																	06 38					07 12
Banbury	d																	06 56					07 33
Leamington Spa 8	d																	07 14					07 51
Coventry	d																	07 27					
Birmingham International ✈	d																	07 38					
Penzance	d																						
St Erth	d																						
Hayle	d																						
Camborne	d																						
Redruth	d																						
Truro	d																						
St Austell	d																						
Newquay (Summer Only)	d																						
Par	d																						
Lostwithiel	d																						
Bodmin Parkway	d																						
Liskeard 6	d																						
Plymouth	d																						
Totnes	d																						
Paignton	d																						
Torquay	d																						
Newton Abbot	d																						
Teignmouth	d																						
Dawlish	d																						
Exeter St Davids 6	d																						
Tiverton Parkway	d																						
Taunton	d																						
Weston-super-Mare	d																						
Cardiff Central 7	d			21p50																			
Newport (South Wales)	d			22p05																			
Bristol Temple Meads 10	d																			06 15			
Bristol Parkway 7	d																			06 25			
Gloucester 7	d			22p47																07 01	07 07		
Cheltenham Spa	d			22p58																07 12	07 18		
London Paddington	d																						
Birmingham New Street 12	a			00 01														07 48		07 56	08 08		08 17
Birmingham New Street 12	d	22p30	23p09		05 57	05 57	06 19	06 20	06 30	06 31	06 49	06 57	07 03	07 19	07 20	07 30	07 31	07 57	07 49	08 03		08 19	08 30
Tamworth	d		23p28			06 13	06 39		06 46		07 07		07 19	07 38		07 45			08 07	08 19		08 36	
Burton-on-Trent	d		23p40			06 24	06 51		06 56		07 19		07 29	07 50		07 54			08 17	08 29		08 48	
Derby 6	a		23p55			06 35	07 05		07 09		07 34		07 42	08 05		08 09			08 34	08 42		08 59	09 06
Nottingham 8	a		00 18				07 38				08 08			08 34					09 05			09 33	
Chesterfield	a					06 55			07 29				08 02			08 29				09 02			
Sheffield 7	a					07 09			07 48				08 17			08 45				09 17			09 44
Doncaster 7	a								08 23							09 18							10 17
Wakefield Westgate 7	a					07 36							08 45							09 46			
Leeds 10	a					07 52							09 03							10 02			
York 8	a					08 23			08 48				09 27			09 44				10 26			10 40
Darlington 7	a					08 56			09 16				09 58			10 15				10 58			11 13
Durham	a					09 13			09 34				10 15			10 32				11 15			11 30
Chester-le-Street	a																						
Newcastle 8	a					09 26			09 47				10 31			10 45				11 29			11 46
Morpeth	a																						
Alnmouth for Alnwick	a					09 58																	
Berwick-upon-Tweed	a					10 19														12 19			
Dunbar	a												11 37										
Wolverhampton 7	d	22p48			06 16			06 37		06 49		07 15			07 37		07 49	08 15					
Stafford	a	23p00			06 29					07 00		07 29					08 00	08 29					
Stoke-on-Trent	a	23p20			06 50					07 18							08 19	08 54					
Congleton	a				07 02																		
Macclesfield	a				07 11					07 36							08 36	09 11					
Crewe 10	a							07 07				07 50			08 07								
Wilmslow	a											08 09											
Stockport	a				07 27					07 49		08 20					08 49	09 27					
M'chester Piccadilly 10	a	00 12			07 38					07 59		08 35					08 59	09 39					
Warrington Bank Quay	a							07 26							08 27								
Wigan North Western	a							07 37							08 38								
Preston 8	a							07 51							08 51								
Lancaster 6	a							08 08							09 08								
Oxenholme Lake District	a							08 21															
Penrith North Lakes	a														09 44								
Carlisle 8	a							09 00							10 02								
Lockerbie	a																						
Haymarket	a							10 16															
Edinburgh 10	a					11 05		10 22					12 07							13 04			
Haymarket	a					11 15														13 15			
Motherwell	a					11 52														13 52			
Glasgow Central 15	a					12 13									11 17					14 13			
Inverkeithing	a																						
Kirkcaldy	a																						
Markinch	a																						
Ladybank	a																						
Cupar	a																						
Leuchars 3	a																						
Dundee	a																						
Arbroath	a																						
Montrose	a																						
Stonehaven	a																						
Aberdeen	a																						

A 🛒 to Edinburgh

B 🛒 from Reading

Table 51

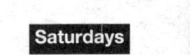

Saturdays
until 11 February

South Coast and the South West - North West England, The North East and Scotland

Route Diagram - see first Page of Table 51

		VT	XC	XC	XC	XC	XC	VT	XC	XC	XC	XC	XC	XC	VT	XC	XC	XC	XC	XC	XC	VT	XC
		◇1	◇1	◇1	◇1	1	◇1	◇1	◇1	◇1	◇1	◇1	1	◇1	◇1	◇1	◇1	◇1	◇1	1	◇1	◇1	◇1
			A						A	B		C				A	B						A
Bournemouth	d						06 25				06 37							07 45					
Brockenhurst 3	d						06 39				06 55							08 00					
Southampton Central	d			06 15			06 53				07 15			07 47				08 15					
Southampton Airport Pkwy	d			06 22			07 01				07 22			07 54				08 22					
Winchester	d			06 31			07 09				07 31			08 03				08 31					
Basingstoke	d			06 47			07 25				07 47			08 19				08 47					
Guildford	d																						
Reading 7	d			07 11			07 47				08 11			08 40				09 11			09 40		
Oxford	d			07 36			08 15				08 36			09 07				09 36			10 07		
Banbury	d			07 54			08 33				08 54			09 24				09 54			10 24		
Leamington Spa 8	d			08 12			08 50				09 12			09 42				10 13			10 42		
Coventry	d			08 27							09 27							10 27					
Birmingham International	d			08 38							09 38							10 38					
Penzance	d																						
St Erth	d																						
Hayle	d																						
Camborne	d																						
Redruth	d																						
Truro	d																						
St Austell	d																						
Newquay (Summer Only)	d																						
Par	d																						
Lostwithiel	d																						
Bodmin Parkway	d																						
Liskeard 6	d																						
Plymouth	d				05 25							06 25							07 25				
Totnes	d				05 50							06 50							07 50				
Paignton	d															07 02							
Torquay	d															07 08							
Newton Abbot	d				06 03							07 03				07 19			08 03				
Teignmouth	d															07 26							
Dawlish	d															07 31							
Exeter St Davids 6	d				06 23							07 23				07 45			08 23				
Tiverton Parkway	d				06 37							07 37				07 58			08 37				
Taunton	d				06 51							07 51				08 13			08 51				
Weston-super-Mare	d																						
Cardiff Central 7	d								07 00	07 45							08 45						
Newport (South Wales)	d								07 15	08 00							09 00						
Bristol Temple Meads 10	d		07 00		07 30				08 00			08h30				09 00			09 30				10 00
Bristol Parkway 7	d		07 10		07 40				08 10			08 40				09 10			09 40				10 10
Gloucester 7	d									08 47							09 46						
Cheltenham Spa	d		07 42		08 12				08 42	08 58		09 12				09 42	09 57		10 12				10 42
London Paddington	d																						
Birmingham New Street 12	a		08 26	08 48	08 56		09 19		09 26	09 45	09 48	09 56		10 18		10 26	10 45	10 48	10 56		11 18		11 26
Birmingham New Street 12	d	08 20	08 31	08 57	09 03	09 19	09 30	09 20	09 31	09 49	09 57	10 03	10 19	10 30	10 20	10 31	10 49	10 57	11 03	11 19	11 30	11 20	11 31
Tamworth	d					09 36				10 07		10 19	10 36				11 09			11 36			
Burton-on-Trent	d				09 28	09 48				10 19			10 48				11 21		11 28	11 48			
Derby 6	a				09 41	09 59	10 05			10 34		10 41	10 59	11 05			11 34		11 41	11 59	12 05		
Nottingham 8	a					10 33				11 05			11 33				12 05			12 33			
Chesterfield	a				10 02							11 02							12 02				
Sheffield 7	a				10 17		10 42					11 17		11 41					12 16		12 41		
Doncaster 7	a						11 15							12 15							13 17		
Wakefield Westgate 7	a				10 46							11 46							12 46				
Leeds 10	a				11 02							12 02							13 02				
York 8	a				11 26		11 40					12 26		12 39					13 26		13 40		
Darlington 7	a				11 57		12 13					12 58		13 13					13 57		14 12		
Durham	a				12 15		12 30					13 15		13 30					14 14		14 29		
Chester-le-Street	a																						
Newcastle 8	a				12 31		12 45					13 29		13 44					14 28		14 42		
Morpeth	a																		14 47				
Alnmouth for Alnwick	a											13 59											
Berwick-upon-Tweed	a											14 19											
Dunbar	a				13 37														15 39				
Wolverhampton 7	d	08 37	08 49	09 15				09 37	09 49		10 15				10 37	10 49		11 15				11 37	11 49
Stafford	a		09 00	09 29					10 00		10 29					11 00		11 29					12 00
Stoke-on-Trent	a		09 19	09 54					10 19		10 54					11 19		11 54					12 19
Congleton	a																						
Macclesfield	a			10 11							11 11							12 11					
Crewe 10	a	09 07						10 07							11 07							12 07	
Wilmslow	a																						
Stockport	a		09 49	10 27					10 49		11 27					11 49		12 27					12 49
M'chester Piccadilly 10	a		09 59	10 39					10 59		11 39					11 59		12 39					12 59
Warrington Bank Quay	a	09 26						10 26							11 26							12 26	
Wigan North Western	a	09 37						10 37							11 37							12 37	
Preston 8	a	09 51						10 51							11 51							12 51	
Lancaster 6	a	10 08						11 08							12 08							13 08	
Oxenholme Lake District	a	10 22													12 22							13 22	
Penrith North Lakes	a							11 44															
Carlisle 8	a	11 01						12 00							13 01							14 01	
Lockerbie	a																						
Haymarket	a	12 16													14 15								
Edinburgh 10	a	12 22			14 07							15 07			14 22				16 04				
Haymarket	a											15 15											
Motherwell	a											15 52											
Glasgow Central 15	a							13 17				16 23										15 17	
Inverkeithing	a																						
Kirkcaldy	a																						
Markinch	a																						
Ladybank	a																						
Cupar	a																						
Leuchars 3	a																						
Dundee	a																						
Arbroath	a																						
Montrose	a																						
Stonehaven	a																						
Aberdeen	a																						

A from Birmingham New Street; to Birmingham New Street

B from Newport (South Wales)

C to Edinburgh

Table 51

Saturdays
until 11 February

South Coast and the South West - North West England, The North East and Scotland

Route Diagram - see first Page of Table 51

		XC	XC	XC	XC	VT	XC	XC	XC	XC	XC	XC	VT	XC	XC	XC	XC	XC	VT	XC	XC	XC
		◇[1]	◇[1]	[1]	◇[1]	◇[1]	◇[1]	◇[1]	◇[1]	◇[1]	[1]	◇[1]	◇[1]	◇[1]	◇[1]	◇[1]	[1]	◇[1]	◇[1]	◇[1]	◇[1]	◇[1]
			A				B	C		D				B		A				B		D
		[trolley]	[trolley]	[trolley]	[trolley]	[restaurant]	[restaurant][trolley]	[trolley]	[trolley]	[trolley]		[trolley]	[restaurant]	[restaurant][trolley]	[trolley]	[trolley]		[trolley]	[restaurant]	[restaurant][trolley]	[trolley]	[trolley]
Bournemouth	d	08 45							09 45						10 45						11 45	
Brockenhurst [3]	d	09 00							10 00						11 00						12 00	
Southampton Central	d	09 15			09 47				10 15						11 15			11 47			12 15	
Southampton Airport Pkwy	d	09 22			09 54				10 22						11 22			11 54			12 22	
Winchester	d	09 31			10 03				10 31						11 31			12 03			12 31	
Basingstoke	d	09 47			10 19				10 47						11 47			12 19			12 47	
Guildford	d																					
Reading [7]	d	10 11			10 40				11 11			11 40			12 11			12 40			13 11	
Oxford	d	10 36			11 07				11 36			12 07			12 36			13 07			13 36	
Banbury	d	10 54			11 24				11 54			12 24			12 54			13 24			13 54	
Leamington Spa [8]	d	11 12			11 42				12 12			12 42			13 12			13 42			14 12	
Coventry	d	11 27							12 27						13 27						14 27	
Birmingham International	d	11 38							12 38						13 38						14 38	
Penzance	d		06 30													08 28						
St Erth	d		06 38													08 36						
Hayle	d		06 41																			
Camborne	d		06 51													08 46						
Redruth	d		06 57													08 52						
Truro	d		07 09													09 04						
St Austell	d		07 25													09 20						
Newquay (Summer Only)	d																					
Par	d		07 32													09 28						
Lostwithiel	d		07 39																			
Bodmin Parkway	d		07 46													09 39						
Liskeard [6]	d		07 58													09 51						
Plymouth	d		08 25							09 25						10 25						11 25
Totnes	d		08 50							09 50						10 50						11 50
Paignton	d													10 07								
Torquay	d													10 13								
Newton Abbot	d		09 03							10 03				10 24		11 03						12 03
Teignmouth	d													10 31								
Dawlish	d													10 36								
Exeter St Davids [6]	d		09 23							10 23				10 50		11 23						12 23
Tiverton Parkway	d		09 37							10 37				11 03		11 37						12 37
Taunton	d		09 51							10 51				11 18		11 51						12 51
Weston-super-Mare	d																					
Cardiff Central [7]	d							10 45														
Newport (South Wales)	d							11 00														
Bristol Temple Meads [10]	d		10 30				11 00			11 30				12 00		12 30				13 00		13 30
Bristol Parkway [7]	d		10 40				11 10			11 40				12 10		12 40				13 10		13 40
Gloucester [7]	d							11 46														
Cheltenham Spa	d		11 12				11 42	11 57		12 12				12 42		13 12				13 42		14 12
London Paddington	d																					
Birmingham New Street [12]	a	11 48	11 56		12 18		12 26	12 45	12 48	12 56		13 18		13 26	13 48	13 56		14 18		14 26	14 48	14 56
Birmingham New Street [12]	d	11 57	12 03	12 19	12 30	12 20	12 31	12 49	12 57	13 03	13 19	13 30	13 20	13 31	13 57	14 03	14 19	14 30	14 20	14 31	14 57	15 03
Tamworth	d		12 19	12 36				13 09			13 36					14 19	14 36					
Burton-on-Trent	d			12 48				13 21		13 27	13 50						14 47					15 27
Derby [6]	a		12 41	13 05	13 08			13 34		13 41	14 05	14 08				14 41	14 59	15 05				15 41
Nottingham [8]	a			13 33				14 05			14 33						15 33					
Chesterfield	a		13 02							14 02						15 02						16 02
Sheffield [7]	a		13 17		13 41					14 17		14 41				15 17		15 41				16 18
Doncaster [7]	a				14 18							15 17						16 18				
Wakefield Westgate [7]	a		13 46							14 46						15 46						16 46
Leeds [10]	a		14 02							15 02						16 02						17 02
York [8]	a		14 26		14 40					15 28		15 40				16 26		16 41				17 26
Darlington [7]	a		14 58		15 13					15 58		16 13				16 58		17 13				17 56
Durham	a		15 15		15 30					16 15		16 30				17 15		17 30				18 13
Chester-le-Street	a																					
Newcastle [8]	a		15 29		15 45					16 29		16 45				17 29		17 45				18 29
Morpeth	a																					
Alnmouth for Alnwick	a		15 58							16 58						18 00						
Berwick-upon-Tweed	a		16 18													18 20						19 17
Dunbar	a									17 38												19 40
Wolverhampton [7]	d	12 15				12 37	12 49		13 15				13 37	13 49	14 15				14 37	14 49	15 15	
Stafford	a	12 29					13 00		13 29					14 00	14 29					15 00	15 29	
Stoke-on-Trent	a	12 54					13 18		13 54					14 19	14 54					15 19	15 54	
Congleton	a																					
Macclesfield	a	13 11							14 11						15 11						16 11	
Crewe [10]	a					13 07							14 07						15 07			
Wilmslow	a																					
Stockport	a	13 27					13 49		14 27					14 49	15 27					15 49	16 27	
M'chester Piccadilly [10]	a	13 39					13 59		14 39					14 59	15 39					15 59	16 39	
Warrington Bank Quay	a					13 26							14 26						15 26			
Wigan North Western	a					13 37							14 37						15 37			
Preston [8]	a					13 51							14 51						15 51			
Lancaster [6]	a					14 08							15 08						16 08			
Oxenholme Lake District	a												15 22									
Penrith North Lakes	a					14 44													16 45			
Carlisle [8]	a					15 00							16 01						17 00			
Lockerbie	a																					
Haymarket	a					16 16													18 14			
Edinburgh [10]	a		17 07			16 22				18 05						19 08			18 22			20 06
Haymarket	a		17 15							18 14						19 15						20 17
Motherwell	a		17 52													19 52						
Glasgow Central [15]	a		18 11										17 17			20 11						
Inverkeithing	a									18 28												20 33
Kirkcaldy	a									18 46												20 50
Markinch	a									18 56												21 00
Ladybank	a									19 03												21 08
Cupar	a									19 10												21 17
Leuchars [3]	a									19 17												21 25
Dundee	a									19 32												21 43
Arbroath	a									19 49												
Montrose	a									20 03												
Stonehaven	a									20 23												
Aberdeen	a									20 43												

A [trolley] from Plymouth to Edinburgh

B [restaurant] from Birmingham New Street [trolley] to Birmingham New Street

C [trolley] from Newport (South Wales)

D [trolley] to Edinburgh

Table 51

Saturdays
until 11 February

South Coast and the South West - North West England, The North East and Scotland

Route Diagram - see first Page of Table 51

		XC	XC	VT	XC	XC	XC	XC		XC	XC	VT	XC	XC	XC	XC	XC	VT		XC	XC	XC	XC	XC	VT
		1	◇1	◇1	◇1	◇1	◇1	◇1		1	◇1	◇1	◇1	◇1	◇1	1	◇1	◇1		◇1	◇1	◇1	1	◇1	◇1
					A	B		C					A												
Bournemouth	d						12 45							13 45							14 45				
Brockenhurst [3]	d						13 00							14 00							15 00				
Southampton Central	d						13 15				13 47			14 15							15 15			15 47	
Southampton Airport Pkway	d						13 22				13 54			14 22							15 22			15 54	
Winchester	d						13 31				14 03			14 31							15 31			16 03	
Basingstoke	d						13 47				14 19			14 47							15 47			16 19	
Guildford	d																								
Reading [7]	d		13 40				14 11				14 40			15 11			15 40				16 11			16 40	
Oxford	d		14 07				14 36				15 07			15 36			16 07				16 36			17 07	
Banbury	d		14 24				14 54				15 24			15 54			16 24				16 54			17 24	
Leamington Spa [8]	d		14 42				15 12				15 42			16 12			16 42				17 12			17 42	
Coventry	d						15 27							16 27							17 27				
Birmingham International	d						15 38							16 38							17 38				
Penzance	d				09 43																				
St Erth	d				09 51																				
Hayle	d																								
Camborne	d				10 01																				
Redruth	d				10 07																				
Truro	d				10 19																				
St Austell	d				10 35																				
Newquay (Summer Only)	d																								
Par	d				10 42																				
Lostwithiel	d				10 49																				
Bodmin Parkway	d				10 56																				
Liskeard [6]	d				11 09																				
Plymouth	d				11 48			12 23							13 25							14 25			
Totnes	d				12 13			12 49							13 50							14 50			
Paignton	d																			13 53					
Torquay	d																			13 59					
Newton Abbot	d				12 25			13 03							14 03					14 10		15 03			
Teignmouth	d																			14 17					
Dawlish	d																			14 22					
Exeter St Davids [6]	d				12 48			13 25							14 23					14 36		15 23			
Tiverton Parkway	d				13 02			13 39							14 37					14 49		15 37			
Taunton	d				13 16			13 54							14 52					15 04		15 51			
Weston-super-Mare	d																			15 30					
Cardiff Central [7]	d					13 45																			
Newport (South Wales)	d					14 00																			
Bristol Temple Meads [10]	d				14 00			14 30					15 00		15 30					16 00		16 30			
Bristol Parkway [7]	d				14 10			14 40					15 10		15 40					16 10		16 40			
Gloucester [7]	d					14 46																			
Cheltenham Spa	d				14 42	14 57		15 12					15 42		16 12					16 42		17 12			
London Paddington	d																								
Birmingham New Street [12]	a		15 18		15 26	15 45	15 48	15 55			16 18		16 26	16 48	16 56		17 18			17 26	17 48	17 56		18 18	
Birmingham New Street [12]	d	15 19	15 30	15 20	15 31	15 49	15 57	16 03		16 19	16 30	16 20	16 31	16 57	17 03	17 19	17 30	17 20		17 31	17 57	18 03	18 19	18 30	18 20
Tamworth	d	15 36				16 09		16 17		16 38						17 36						18 19	18 36		
Burton-on-Trent	d	15 48				16 21				16 50					17 26	17 48							18 47		
Derby [6]	a	15 59	16 05			16 34		16 40		17 05	17 08				17 41	17 59	18 05					18 41	18 59	19 05	
Nottingham [8]	a	16 33				17 05				17 33						18 32							19 33		
Chesterfield	a							17 01							18 02							19 02		19 29	
Sheffield [7]	a		16 41					17 19			17 44				18 18		18 42					19 18		19 51	
Doncaster [7]	a		17 16														19 16							20 17	
Wakefield Westgate [7]	a							17 47			18 12				18 46							19 49			
Leeds [10]	a							18 02			18 31				19 01							20 05			
York [8]	a		17 37					18 28			18 58				19 26		19 39					20 29		20 40	
Darlington [7]	a		18 12					18 59			19 35				19 57		20 11					20 58		21 13	
Durham	a		18 29					19 17			19 52				20 14		20 28					21 15		21 30	
Chester-le-Street	a																								
Newcastle [8]	a		18 44					19 31			20 08				20 28		20 42					21 29		21 44	
Morpeth	a														20 50										
Alnmouth for Alnwick	a							20 03														22 01			
Berwick-upon-Tweed	a							20 24							21 23										
Dunbar	a														21 47										
Wolverhampton [7]	d			15 37	15 49		16 15					16 37	16 49	17 15				17 37		17 49	18 15				18 37
Stafford	a				16 00		16 29						17 00	17 29						18 00	18 29				
Stoke-on-Trent	a				16 19		16 54						17 19	17 54						18 19	18 54				
Congleton	a																								
Macclesfield	a						17 11							18 11							19 11				
Crewe [10]	a			16 08								17 07						18 07							19 07
Wilmslow	a																								
Stockport	a				16 49		17 27						17 49	18 27						18 49	19 27				
M'chester Piccadilly [10]	a				16 59		17 39						17 59	18 39						18 59	19 39				
Warrington Bank Quay	a			16 26								17 26						18 26							19 26
Wigan North Western	a			16 37								17 37						18 37							19 37
Preston [8]	a			16 51								17 51						18 51							19 54
Lancaster [6]	a			17 09								18 08						19 08							
Oxenholme Lake District	a			17 24								18 22						19 22							
Penrith North Lakes	a											18 48													
Carlisle [8]	a			18 03								19 04						20 01							
Lockerbie	a																								
Haymarket	a											20 16													
Edinburgh [10]	a							21 09				20 22			22 14							23 10			
Haymarket	a							21 16																	
Motherwell	a							22 00																	
Glasgow Central [15]	a			19 17				22 22										21 17							
Inverkeithing	a																								
Kirkcaldy	a																								
Markinch	a																								
Ladybank	a																								
Cupar	a																								
Leuchars [3]	a																								
Dundee	a																								
Arbroath	a																								
Montrose	a																								
Stonehaven	a																								
Aberdeen	a																								

A from Birmingham New Street; to Birmingham New Street

B from Newport (South Wales)

C to Edinburgh

Table 51

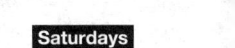

Saturdays
until 11 February

South Coast and the South West - North West England, The North East and Scotland

Route Diagram - see first Page of Table 51

		XC	XC	XC	XC	XC	XC	VT	XC	XC	XC	XC	VT	XC	XC	XC	XC	XC	XC	XC	XC	XC
		◇1	◇1	◇1	◇1	1	◇1	◇1	◇1	◇1	◇1	◇1	◇1	◇1	◇1	◇1	◇1	◇1	◇1	◇1	◇1	◇1
		A					B		A	C	C	C		A	C	C				D		
		🍽🛒		🛒	🛒		🛒	🍽	🍽🛒	🛒	🛒	🛒	🍽	🍽🛒	🛒	🛒			🛒	🛒		
Bournemouth	d			15 45						16 45					17 45					18 45		
Brockenhurst 3	d			16 00						17 00					18 00					19 00		
Southampton Central ⛴	d			16 15						17 15		17 47			18 15					19 15		
Southampton Airport Pkwy ✈	d			16 22						17 22		17 54			18 22					19 22		
Winchester	d			16 31						17 31		18 03			18 31					19 31		
Basingstoke	d			16 47						17 47		18 19			18 47					19 47		
Guildford	d																					
Reading 7	d			17 11			17 40			18 11		18 40			19 11		19 40			20 11	20 40	
Oxford	d			17 36			18 07			18 36		19 07			19 36		20 07			20 36	21 07	
Banbury	d			17 54			18 24			18 54		19 24			19 54		20 29			20 54	21 25	
Leamington Spa 8	d			18 12			18 42			19 12		19 42			20 12		20 46			21 12	21 45	
Coventry	d			18 27						19 27					20 27					21 27	21 56	
Birmingham International ✈	d			18 38						19 38					20 38					21 38	22 11	
Penzance	d																					
St Erth	d																					
Hayle	d																					
Camborne	d																					
Redruth	d																					
Truro	d																					
St Austell	d																					
Newquay (Summer Only)	d																					
Par	d																					
Lostwithiel	d																					
Bodmin Parkway	d																					
Liskeard 6	d																					
Plymouth	d				15 25						16 25					17 23			18 25			
Totnes	d				15 50						16 50					17 49			18 50			
Paignton	d																					
Torquay	d																					
Newton Abbot	d				16 03						17 03					18 03			19 03			
Teignmouth	d																					
Dawlish	d																					
Exeter St Davids 6	d				16 23				16 53		17 23					18 25			19 23			
Tiverton Parkway	d				16 37				17 07		17 37					18 39			19 37			
Taunton	d				16 51				17 21		17 51					18 54			19 51			
Weston-super-Mare	d																					
Cardiff Central 7	d		16 45																			
Newport (South Wales)	d		17 00																			
Bristol Temple Meads 10	d	17 00			17 30				18 00		18 30			19 00		19 30		20 00	20 30			
Bristol Parkway 7	d	17 10			17 40				18 10		18 40			19 10		19 40		20 10	20 40			
Gloucester 7	d		17 46																			
Cheltenham Spa	d	17 42	17 58		18 12				18 42		19 12			19 42		20 12		20 42	21 12			
London Paddington	d																					
Birmingham New Street 12	a	18 26	18 45	18 48	18 56		19 18		19 26	19 48	19 58	20 18		20 26	20 48	20 53	21 18	21 38	21 53	21 48	22 21	
Birmingham New Street 12	d	18 31	18 49	18 57	19 03	19 19	19 30	19 20	19 31	19 57	20 03	20 30	20 20	20 31	20 57	21 03				21 57		22 31
Tamworth	d		19 09			19 36					20 19					21 19						
Burton-on-Trent	d		19 21		19 27	19 48										21 31						
Derby 6	a		19 35		19 39	19 59	20 05				20 42	21 24				21 44						
Nottingham 8 🚌	a		20 05			20 32																
Chesterfield	a				20 04		20 29				21 04	21 45				22 07						
Sheffield 7 🚌	a				20 19		20 49				21 19	22 05				22 23						
Doncaster 7	a						21 21					22 30				22 51						
Wakefield Westgate 7	a				20 48						21 48					23 10						
Leeds 10	a				21 03						22 02					23 27						
York 8	a				21 57		21 44					22 57										
Darlington 7	a						22 13															
Durham	a						22 30															
Chester-le-Street	a																					
Newcastle 8	a						22 47															
Morpeth	a																					
Alnmouth for Alnwick	a																					
Berwick-upon-Tweed	a																					
Dunbar	a																					
Wolverhampton 7 🚌	d	18 49		19 15				19 37	19 49	20 15			20 37	20 49	21 15					22 16		22 49
Stafford	a	19 00		19 29					20 00	20 29			20 49	21 00	21 29					22 29		23 01
Stoke-on-Trent	a	19 19		19 54					20 19	20 54				21 20	21 52					22 50		23 20
Congleton	a																					
Macclesfield	a			20 11					20 36	21 11				21 38	22 11					23 07		23 38
Crewe 10	a							20 07					21 10									
Wilmslow	a																					
Stockport	a	19 49		20 27					20 49	21 27				21 53	22 27					23 21		23 53
M'chester Piccadilly 10 🚌	a	19 59		20 39					20 59	21 39				22 04	22 39					23 32		00 10
Warrington Bank Quay	a							20 26														
Wigan North Western	a							20 37														
Preston 8	a							20 59														
Lancaster 6	a																					
Oxenholme Lake District	a																					
Penrith North Lakes	a																					
Carlisle 8	a																					
Lockerbie	a																					
Haymarket	a																					
Edinburgh 10	a																					
Haymarket	a																					
Motherwell	a																					
Glasgow Central 15	a																					
Inverkeithing	a																					
Kirkcaldy	a																					
Markinch	a																					
Ladybank	a																					
Cupar	a																					
Leuchars 3	a																					
Dundee	a																					
Arbroath	a																					
Montrose	a																					
Stonehaven	a																					
Aberdeen	a																					

A 🍽 from Birmingham New Street; 🛒 to Birmingham New Street
B 🛒 to Sheffield
C 🛒 to Birmingham New Street
D 🛒 to Reading

Table 51

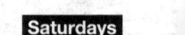

Saturdays
until 11 February

South Coast and the South West - North West England, The North East and Scotland

Route Diagram - see first Page of Table 51

		XC ◇[1]	XC ◇[1]	XC [1]
Bournemouth	d		19 45	
Brockenhurst [3]	d		20 00	
Southampton Central	d		20 15	
Southampton Airport Pkway	d		20 22	
Winchester	d		20 31	
Basingstoke	d		20 47	
Guildford	d			
Reading [7]	d		21 11	
Oxford	d		21 36	
Banbury	d		21 54	
Leamington Spa [8]	d		22 12	
Coventry	d		22 27	
Birmingham International	d		22 38	
Penzance	d			
St Erth	d			
Hayle	d			
Camborne	d			
Redruth	d			
Truro	d			
St Austell	d			
Newquay (Summer Only)	d			
Par	d			
Lostwithiel	d			
Bodmin Parkway	d			
Liskeard [6]	d			
Plymouth	d			
Totnes	d			
Paignton	d			
Torquay	d			
Newton Abbot	d			
Teignmouth	d			
Dawlish	d			
Exeter St Davids [6]	d			
Tiverton Parkway	d			
Taunton	d			
Weston-super-Mare	d			
Cardiff Central [7]	d	20 50		
Newport (South Wales)	d	21 05		
Bristol Temple Meads [10]	d			
Bristol Parkway [7]	d			
Gloucester [7]	d	21 49		
Cheltenham Spa	d	22 00		
London Paddington	d			
Birmingham New Street [12]	a	22 42	22 48	
Birmingham New Street [12]	d			22 49
Tamworth	d			23 08
Burton-on-Trent	d			23 20
Derby [6]	a			23 33
Nottingham [8]	a			
Chesterfield	a			
Sheffield [7]	a			
Doncaster [7]	a			
Wakefield Westgate [7]	a			
Leeds [10]	a			
York [8]	a			
Darlington [7]	a			
Durham	a			
Chester-le-Street	a			
Newcastle [8]	a			
Morpeth	a			
Alnmouth for Alnwick	a			
Berwick-upon-Tweed	a			
Dunbar	a			
Wolverhampton [7]	d			
Stafford	a			
Stoke-on-Trent	a			
Congleton	a			
Macclesfield	a			
Crewe [10]	a			
Wilmslow	a			
Stockport	a			
M'chester Piccadilly [10]	a			
Warrington Bank Quay	a			
Wigan North Western	a			
Preston [8]	a			
Lancaster [6]	a			
Oxenholme Lake District	a			
Penrith North Lakes	a			
Carlisle [8]	a			
Lockerbie	a			
Haymarket	a			
Edinburgh [10]	a			
Haymarket	a			
Motherwell	a			
Glasgow Central [15]	a			
Inverkeithing	a			
Kirkcaldy	a			
Markinch	a			
Ladybank	a			
Cupar	a			
Leuchars [3]	a			
Dundee	a			
Arbroath	a			
Montrose	a			
Stonehaven	a			
Aberdeen	a			

Table 51

Saturdays

18 February to 24 March

South Coast and the South West - North West England, The North East and Scotland

Route Diagram - see first Page of Table 51

		XC	XC	XC	XC	XC	XC	VT	XC	XC	XC	XC	XC	XC	VT	XC	XC	XC	XC	XC	XC	XC	XC
		◇1	◇1	◇1	◇1	◇1	1	◇1	◇1	◇1	1	◇1	◇1	1	◇1	◇1	◇1	◇1	1	◇1	◇1	1	◇1
						A												B					B
						⚒	⚒	⊡	⚒	⚒		⚒	⚒	⚒	⊡	⚒	⚒	⚒		⚒		⚒	⚒
Bournemouth	d																						
Brockenhurst 3	d																						
Southampton Central	d																	05 09					
Southampton Airport Pkwy	d																	05 16					
Winchester	d																	05 25					
Basingstoke	d																	05 41					
Guildford	d																						06 09
Reading 7	d																	06 11					06 46
Oxford	d																	06 38					07 12
Banbury	d																	06 56					07 33
Leamington Spa 8	d																	07 14					07 51
Coventry	d																	07 27					
Birmingham International	d																	07 38					
Penzance	d																						
St Erth	d																						
Hayle	d																						
Camborne	d																						
Redruth	d																						
Truro	d																						
St Austell	d																						
Newquay (Summer Only)	d																						
Par	d																						
Lostwithiel	d																						
Bodmin Parkway	d																						
Liskeard 6	d																						
Plymouth	d																						
Totnes	d																						
Paignton	d																						
Torquay	d																						
Newton Abbot	d																						
Teignmouth	d																						
Dawlish	d																						
Exeter St Davids 6	d																						
Tiverton Parkway	d																						
Taunton	d																						
Weston-super-Mare	d																						
Cardiff Central 7	d			21p50																			
Newport (South Wales)	d			22p05																			
Bristol Temple Meads 10	d																			06 15			
Bristol Parkway 7	d																			06 25			
Gloucester 7	d			22p47																07 01	07 07		
Cheltenham Spa	d			22p58																07 12	07 18		
London Paddington	d																						
Birmingham New Street 12	a			00 01														07 48		07 56	08 08		08 17
Birmingham New Street 12	d	22p30	23p09		05 57	05 57	06 19	06 20	06 30	06 31	06 49	06 57	07 03	07 19	07 20	07 30	07 31	07 57	07 49	08 03		08 19	08 30
Tamworth	d		23p28			06 13	06 39		06 46		07 07		07 19	07 38		07 45			08 07	08 19		08 36	
Burton-on-Trent	d		23p40			06 24	06 51		06 56		07 19		07 29	07 50		07 54			08 17	08 29		08 48	
Derby 6	a		23p55			06 35	07 05		07 09		07 34		07 42	08 05		08 09			08 34	08 42		08 59	09 06
Nottingham 8	a		00 18				07 38				08 08			08 34					09 05			09 33	
Chesterfield	a					06 55			07 29				08 02			08 29				09 02			
Sheffield 7	a					07 09			07 48				08 17			08 45				09 17			09 44
Doncaster 7	a								08 23							09 18							10 17
Wakefield Westgate 7	a					07 36							08 45							09 46			
Leeds 10	a					07 52							09 03							10 02			
York 8	a					08 23			08 48				09 27			09 44				10 26			10 40
Darlington 7	a					08 56			09 16				09 58			10 15				10 58			11 13
Durham	a					09 13			09 34				10 15			10 32				11 15			11 30
Chester-le-Street	a																						
Newcastle 8	a					09 26			09 47				10 31			10 45				11 29			11 46
Morpeth	a																						
Alnmouth for Alnwick	a					09 58																	
Berwick-upon-Tweed	a					10 19														12 19			
Dunbar	a												11 37										
Wolverhampton 7	d	22p48			06 16			06 37		06 49		07 15			07 37		07 49	08 15					
Stafford	a	23p00			06 29					07 00		07 29					08 00	08 29					
Stoke-on-Trent	a	23p20			06 50					07 18							08 19	08 54					
Congleton	a				07 02																		
Macclesfield	a				07 11					07 36							08 36	09 11					
Crewe 10	a							07 07				07 50			08 07								
Wilmslow	a											08 09											
Stockport	a				07 27					07 49		08 20					08 49	09 27					
M'chester Piccadilly 10	a	00 12			07 38					07 59		08 35					08 59	09 39					
Warrington Bank Quay	a							07 26							08 27								
Wigan North Western	a							07 37							08 38								
Preston 8	a							07 51							08 51								
Lancaster 6	a							08 08							09 08								
Oxenholme Lake District	a							08 21															
Penrith North Lakes	a														09 44								
Carlisle 8	a							09 00							10 02								
Lockerbie	a																						
Haymarket	a							10 16															
Edinburgh 10	a					11 05		10 22					12 07							13 04			
Haymarket	a					11 15														13 15			
Motherwell	a					11 52														13 52			
Glasgow Central 15	a					12 13									11 17					14 13			
Inverkeithing	a																						
Kirkcaldy	a																						
Markinch	a																						
Ladybank	a																						
Cupar	a																						
Leuchars 3	a																						
Dundee	a																						
Arbroath	a																						
Montrose	a																						
Stonehaven	a																						
Aberdeen	a																						

A ⚒ to Edinburgh

B ⚒ from Reading

Table 51

Saturdays

18 February to 24 March

South Coast and the South West - North West England, The North East and Scotland

Route Diagram - see first Page of Table 51

		VT	XC	XC	XC	XC	XC	VT	XC	XC	XC	XC	XC	XC	VT	XC	XC	XC	XC	XC	XC	VT	XC
		◇1	◇1	◇1	◇1	1	◇1	◇1	◇1	◇1	◇1	◇1	1	◇1	◇1	◇1	◇1	◇1	◇1	1	◇1	◇1	◇1
			A						A	B		C				A	B						A
		🍴	🍴🛒	🛒	🛒	🛒	🛒	🍴	🍴🛒	🛒	🛒	🛒		🛒	🍴	🍴🛒	🛒	🛒	🛒		🛒	🍴	🍴🛒
Bournemouth	d						06 25				06 37							07 45					
Brockenhurst 3	d						06 39				06 55							08 00					
Southampton Central ⛴	d			06 15			06 53				07f15			07 47				08 15					
Southampton Airport Pkwy ✈	d			06 22			07 01				07 22			07 54				08 22					
Winchester	d			06 31			07 09				07 31			08 03				08 31					
Basingstoke	d			06 47			07 25				07 47			08 19				08 47					
Guildford	d																						
Reading 7	d			07b11			07 47				08g11			08 40				09j11			09 40		
Oxford	d			07 36			08 15				08 36			09 07				09 36			10 07		
Banbury	d			07 54			08 33				08 54			09 24				09 54			10 24		
Leamington Spa 8	d			08 12			08 50				09 12			09 42				10 13			10 42		
Coventry	d			08 27							09 27							10k27					
Birmingham International ✈	d			08 38							09 38							10 38					
Penzance	d																						
St Erth	d																						
Hayle	d																						
Camborne	d																						
Redruth	d																						
Truro	d																						
St Austell	d																						
Newquay (Summer Only)	d																						
Par	d																						
Lostwithiel	d																						
Bodmin Parkway	d																						
Liskeard 6	d																						
Plymouth	d				05 25							06 25							07 25				
Totnes	d				05 50							06 50							07 50				
Paignton	d															07 02							
Torquay	d															07 08							
Newton Abbot	d				06 03							07 03				07 19			08 03				
Teignmouth	d															07 26							
Dawlish	d															07 31							
Exeter St Davids 6	d				06 23							07 23				07 45			08 23				
Tiverton Parkway	d				06 37							07 37				07 58			08 37				
Taunton	d				06 51							07 51				08 13			08 51				
Weston-super-Mare	d																						
Cardiff Central 7	d								07 00	07 45							08 45						
Newport (South Wales)	d								07 15	08 00							09 00						
Bristol Temple Meads 10	d		07 00		07c30				08e00			08h30				09i00			09 30				10 00
Bristol Parkway 7	d		07 10		07 40				08 10			08 40				09 10			09 40				10 10
Gloucester 7	d									08 47							09 46						
Cheltenham Spa	d		07 42		08 12				08 42	08 58		09 12				09 42	09 57		10 12				10 42
London Paddington	d																						
Birmingham New Street 12	a		08 26	08 48	08 56		09 19		09 26	09 45	09 48	09 56		10 18		10 26	10 45	10 48	10 56		11 18		11 26
Birmingham New Street 12	d	08 20	08 31	08 57	09 03	09 19	09 30	09 20	09 31	09 49	09 57	10 03	10 19	10 30	10 20	10 31	10 49	10 57	11 03	11 19	11 30	11 20	11 31
Tamworth	d					09 36				10 07		10 19	10 36				11 09			11 36			
Burton-on-Trent	d				09 28	09 48				10 19			10 48				11 21		11 28	11 48			
Derby 6	a				09 41	09 59	10 05			10 34		10 41	10 59	11 05			11 34		11 41	11 59	12 05		
Nottingham 8 ⛴	a					10 33				11 05			11 33				12 05			12 33			
Chesterfield	a				10 02							11 02							12 02				
Sheffield 7 ⛴	a				10 17		10 42					11 17		11 41					12 16		12 41		
Doncaster 7	a						11 15							12 15							13 17		
Wakefield Westgate 7	a				10 46							11 46							12 46				
Leeds 10	a				11 02							12 02							13 02				
York 8	a				11 26		11 40					12 26		12 39					13 26		13 40		
Darlington 7	a				11 57		12 13					12 58		13 13					13 57		14 12		
Durham	a				12 15		12 30					13 15		13 30					14 14		14 29		
Chester-le-Street	a																						
Newcastle 8	a				12 31		12 45					13 29		13 44					14 28		14 42		
Morpeth	a																		14 47				
Alnmouth for Alnwick	a											13 59											
Berwick-upon-Tweed	a											14 19											
Dunbar	a				13 37														15 39				
Wolverhampton 7 ⛴	d	08 37	08 49	09 15				09 37	09 49		10 15				10 37	10 49		11 15				11 37	11 49
Stafford	a		09 00	09 29					10 00		10 29					11 00		11 29					12 00
Stoke-on-Trent	a		09 19	09 54					10 19		10 54					11 19		11 54					12 19
Congleton	a																						
Macclesfield	a			10 11							11 11							12 11					
Crewe 10	a	09 07						10 07							11 07							12 07	
Wilmslow	a																						
Stockport	a		09 49	10 27					10 49		11 27					11 49		12 27					12 49
M'chester Piccadilly 10 ⛴	a		09 59	10 39					10 59		11 39					11 59		12 39					12 59
Warrington Bank Quay	a	09 26						10 26							11 26							12 26	
Wigan North Western	a	09 37						10 37							11 37							12 37	
Preston 8	a	09 51						10 51							11 51							12 51	
Lancaster 6	a	10 08						11 08							12 08							13 08	
Oxenholme Lake District	a	10 22													12 22							13 22	
Penrith North Lakes	a							11 44															
Carlisle 8	a	11 01						12 00							13 01							14 01	
Lockerbie	a																						
Haymarket	a	12 16													14 15								
Edinburgh 10	a	12 22			14 07							15 07			14 22				16 04				
Haymarket	a											15 15											
Motherwell	a											15 52											
Glasgow Central 15	a							13 17				16 23										15 17	
Inverkeithing	a																						
Kirkcaldy	a																						
Markinch	a																						
Ladybank	a																						
Cupar	a																						
Leuchars 3	a																						
Dundee	a																						
Arbroath	a																						
Montrose	a																						
Stonehaven	a																						
Aberdeen	a																						

A 🍴 from Birmingham New Street
🛒 to Birmingham New Street

B 🛒 from Newport (South Wales)

C 🛒 to Edinburgh

Table 51

Saturdays

18 February to 24 March

South Coast and the South West - North West England, The North East and Scotland

Route Diagram - see first Page of Table 51

		XC	XC	XC	XC	VT	XC	XC	XC	XC	XC	XC	VT	XC	XC	XC	XC	XC	VT	XC	XC	XC
		◇1	◇1	1	◇1	◇1	◇1	◇1	◇1	◇1	1	◇1	◇1	◇1	◇1	◇1	1	◇1	◇1	◇1	◇1	◇1
			A				B	C		D				B		A				B		D
		trolley	trolley	trolley	trolley	restaurant	restaurant trolley	trolley	trolley	trolley		trolley	restaurant	restaurant trolley	trolley	trolley		trolley	restaurant	restaurant trolley	trolley	trolley
Bournemouth	d	08 45							09 45						10 45						11 45	
Brockenhurst 3	d	09 00							10 00						11 00						12 00	
Southampton Central	d	09 15			09 47				10 15						11 15			11 47			12 15	
Southampton Airport Pkway	d	09 22			09 54				10 22						11 22			11 54			12 22	
Winchester	d	09 31			10 03				10 31						11 31			12 03			12 31	
Basingstoke	d	09 47			10 19				10 47						11 47			12 19			12 47	
Guildford	d																					
Reading 7	d	10 11			10 40				11 11			11 40			12 11			12 40			13 11	
Oxford	d	10 36			11 07				11 36			12 07			12 36			13 07			13 36	
Banbury	d	10 54			11 24				11 54			12 24			12 54			13 24			13 54	
Leamington Spa 8	d	11 12			11 42				12 12			12 42			13 12			13 42			14 12	
Coventry	d	11 27							12 27						13 27						14 27	
Birmingham International	d	11 38							12 38						13 38						14 38	
Penzance	d		06 30													08 28						
St Erth	d		06 38													08 36						
Hayle	d		06 41																			
Camborne	d		06 51													08 46						
Redruth	d		06 57													08 52						
Truro	d		07 09													09 04						
St Austell	d		07 25													09 20						
Newquay (Summer Only)	d																					
Par	d		07 32													09 28						
Lostwithiel	d		07 39																			
Bodmin Parkway	d		07 46													09 39						
Liskeard 6	d		07 58													09 51						
Plymouth	d		08 25							09 25						10 25						11 25
Totnes	d		08 50							09 50						10 50						11 50
Paignton	d													10 07								
Torquay	d													10 13								
Newton Abbot	d		09 03							10 03				10 24		11 03						12 03
Teignmouth	d													10 31								
Dawlish	d													10 36								
Exeter St Davids 6	d		09 23							10 23				10 50		11 23						12 23
Tiverton Parkway	d		09 37							10 37				11 03		11 37						12 37
Taunton	d		09 51							10 51				11 18		11 51						12 51
Weston-super-Mare	d																					
Cardiff Central 7	d							10 45														
Newport (South Wales)	d							11 00														
Bristol Temple Meads 10	d		10 30				11 00			11 30				12 00		12 30				13 00		13 30
Bristol Parkway 7	d		10 40				11 10			11 40				12 10		12 40				13 10		13 40
Gloucester 7	d							11 46														
Cheltenham Spa	d		11 12				11 42	11 57		12 12				12 42		13 12				13 42		14 12
London Paddington	d																					
Birmingham New Street 12	a	11 48	11 56		12 18		12 26	12 45	12 48	12 56		13 18		13 26	13 48	13 56		14 18		14 26	14 48	14 56
Birmingham New Street 12	d	11 57	12 03	12 19	12 30	12 20	12 31	12 49	12 57	13 03	13 19	13 30	13 20	13 31	13 57	14 03	14 19	14 30	14 20	14 31	14 57	15 03
Tamworth	d		12 19	12 36				13 09			13 36					14 19	14 36					
Burton-on-Trent	d			12 48				13 21		13 27	13 50						14 47					15 27
Derby 6	a		12 41	13 05	13 08			13 34		13 41	14 05	14 08				14 41	14 59	15 05				15 41
Nottingham 8	a			13 33				14 05			14 33						15 33					
Chesterfield	a		13 02							14 02						15 02						16 02
Sheffield 7	a		13 17		13 41					14 17		14 41				15 17		15 41				16 18
Doncaster 7	a				14 18							15 17						16 18				
Wakefield Westgate 7	a		13 46							14 46						15 46						16 46
Leeds 10	a		14 02							15 02						16 02						17 02
York 8	a		14 26		14 40					15 28		15 40				16 26		16 41				17 26
Darlington 7	a		14 58		15 13					15 58		16 13				16 58		17 13				17 56
Durham	a		15 15		15 30					16 15		16 30				17 15		17 30				18 13
Chester-le-Street	a																					
Newcastle 8	a		15 29		15 45					16 29		16 45				17 29		17 45				18 29
Morpeth	a																					
Alnmouth for Alnwick	a		15 58							16 58						18 00						
Berwick-upon-Tweed	a		16 18													18 20						19 17
Dunbar	a									17 38												19 40
Wolverhampton 7	d	12 15				12 37	12 49		13 15				13 37	13 49	14 15				14 37	14 49	15 15	
Stafford	a	12 29					13 00		13 29					14 00	14 29					15 00	15 29	
Stoke-on-Trent	a	12 54					13 18		13 54					14 19	14 54					15 19	15 54	
Congleton	a																					
Macclesfield	a	13 11							14 11						15 11						16 11	
Crewe 10	a					13 07							14 07						15 07			
Wilmslow	a																					
Stockport	a	13 27					13 49		14 27					14 49	15 27					15 49	16 27	
M'chester Piccadilly 10	a	13 39					13 59		14 39					14 59	15 39					15 59	16 39	
Warrington Bank Quay	a					13 26							14 26						15 26			
Wigan North Western	a					13 37							14 37						15 37			
Preston 8	a					13 51							14 51						15 51			
Lancaster 6	a					14 08							15 08						16 08			
Oxenholme Lake District	a												15 22									
Penrith North Lakes	a					14 44													16 45			
Carlisle 8	a					15 00							16 01						17 00			
Lockerbie	a																					
Haymarket	a					16 16													18 14			
Edinburgh 10	a		17 07			16 22				18 05						19 08			18 22			20 06
Haymarket	a		17 15							18 14						19 15						20 17
Motherwell	a		17 52													19 52						
Glasgow Central 15	a		18 11										17 17			20 11						
Inverkeithing	a									18 28												20 33
Kirkcaldy	a									18 46												20 50
Markinch	a									18 56												21 00
Ladybank	a									19 03												21 08
Cupar	a									19 10												21 17
Leuchars 3	a									19 17												21 25
Dundee	a									19 32												21 43
Arbroath	a									19 49												
Montrose	a									20 03												
Stonehaven	a									20 23												
Aberdeen	a									20 43												

A trolley from Plymouth to Edinburgh

B restaurant from Birmingham New Street trolley to Birmingham New Street

C trolley from Newport (South Wales)

D trolley to Edinburgh

Table 51

Saturdays

18 February to 24 March

South Coast and the South West - North West England, The North East and Scotland

Route Diagram - see first Page of Table 51

		XC	XC	VT	XC	XC	XC	XC	XC	XC	VT	XC	XC	XC	XC	XC	VT	XC	XC	XC	XC	XC	VT
		1	◇1	◇1	◇1	◇1	◇1	◇1	1	◇1	◇1	◇1	◇1	◇1	1	◇1	◇1	◇1	◇1	◇1	1	◇1	◇1
					A	B		C				A											
			⊼	ꝑ	ꝑ⊼	⊼	⊼	⊼		⊼	ꝑ	ꝑ⊼	⊼	⊼		⊼	ꝑ	⊼	⊼	⊼		⊼	ꝑ
Bournemouth	d						12 45						13 45						14 45				
Brockenhurst 3	d						13 00						14 00						15 00				
Southampton Central	d						13 15			13 47			14 15						15 15			15 47	
Southampton Airport Pkwy	d						13 22			13 54			14 22						15 22			15 54	
Winchester	d						13 31			14 03			14 31						15 31			16 03	
Basingstoke	d						13 47			14 19			14 47						15 47			16 19	
Guildford	d																						
Reading 7	d		13 40				14 11			14 40			15 11			15 40			16 11			16 40	
Oxford	d		14 07				14 36			15 07			15 36			16 07			16 36			17 07	
Banbury	d		14 24				14 54			15 24			15 54			16 24			16 54			17 24	
Leamington Spa 8	d		14 42				15 12			15 42			16 12			16 42			17 12			17 42	
Coventry	d						15 27						16 27						17 27				
Birmingham International	d						15 38						16 38						17 38				
Penzance	d				09 43																		
St Erth	d				09 51																		
Hayle	d																						
Camborne	d				10 01																		
Redruth	d				10 07																		
Truro	d				10 19																		
St Austell	d				10 35																		
Newquay (Summer Only)	d																						
Par	d				10 42																		
Lostwithiel	d				10 49																		
Bodmin Parkway	d				10 56																		
Liskeard 6	d				11 09																		
Plymouth	d				11 48			12 23						13 25						14 25			
Totnes	d				12 13			12 49						13 50						14 50			
Paignton	d																	13 53					
Torquay	d																	13 59					
Newton Abbot	d				12 25			13 03						14 03				14 10		15 03			
Teignmouth	d																	14 17					
Dawlish	d																	14 22					
Exeter St Davids 6	d				12 48			13 25						14 23				14 36		15 23			
Tiverton Parkway	d				13 02			13 39						14 37				14 49		15 37			
Taunton	d				13 16			13 54						14 52				15 04		15 51			
Weston-super-Mare	d																	15 30					
Cardiff Central 7	d					13 45																	
Newport (South Wales)	d					14 00																	
Bristol Temple Meads 10	d				14 00			14 30				15 00		15 30				16 00		16 30			
Bristol Parkway 7	d				14 10			14 40				15 10		15 40				16 10		16 40			
Gloucester 7	d					14 46																	
Cheltenham Spa	d				14 42	14 57		15 12				15 42		16 12				16 42		17 12			
London Paddington	d																						
Birmingham New Street 12	a		15 18		15 26	15 45	15 48	15 55		16 18		16 26	16 48	16 56		17 18		17 26	17 48	17 56		18 18	
Birmingham New Street 12	d	15 19	15 30	15 20	15 31	15 49	15 57	16 03	16 19	16 30	16 20	16 31	16 57	17 03	17 19	17 30	17 20	17 31	17 57	18 03	18 19	18 30	18 20
Tamworth	d	15 36				16 09		16 17	16 38						17 36					18 19	18 36		
Burton-on-Trent	d	15 48				16 21			16 50					17 26	17 48						18 47		
Derby 6	a	15 59	16 05			16 34		16 40	17 05	17 08				17 41	17 59	18 05				18 41	18 59	19 05	
Nottingham 8	a	16 33				17 05			17 33						18 32						19 33		
Chesterfield	a							17 01						18 02						19 02		19 29	
Sheffield 7	a		16 41					17 19		17 44				18 18		18 42				19 18		19 51	
Doncaster 7	a		17 16													19 16						20 17	
Wakefield Westgate 7	a							17 47		18 12				18 46						19 49			
Leeds 10	a							18 02		18 31				19 01						20 05			
York 8	a		17 37					18 28		18 58				19 26		19 39				20 29		20 40	
Darlington 7	a		18 12					18 59		19 35				19 57		20 11				20 58		21 13	
Durham	a		18 29					19 17		19 52				20 14		20 28				21 15		21 30	
Chester-le-Street	a																						
Newcastle 8	a		18 44					19 31		20 08				20 28		20 42				21 29		21 44	
Morpeth	a													20 50									
Alnmouth for Alnwick	a							20 03												22 01			
Berwick-upon-Tweed	a							20 24						21 23									
Dunbar	a													21 47									
Wolverhampton 7	d			15 37	15 49		16 15				16 37	16 49	17 15				17 37	17 49	18 15				18 37
Stafford	a				16 00		16 29					17 00	17 29					18 00	18 29				
Stoke-on-Trent	a				16 19		16 54					17 19	17 54					18 19	18 54				
Congleton	a																						
Macclesfield	a						17 11						18 11						19 11				
Crewe 10	a			16 08							17 07						18 07						19 07
Wilmslow	a																						
Stockport	a				16 49		17 27					17 49	18 27					18 49	19 27				
M'chester Piccadilly 10	a				16 59		17 39					17 59	18 39					18 59	19 39				
Warrington Bank Quay	a			16 26							17 26						18 26						19 26
Wigan North Western	a			16 37							17 37						18 37						19 37
Preston 8	a			16 51							17 51						18 51						19 54
Lancaster 6	a			17 09							18 08						19 08						
Oxenholme Lake District	a			17 24							18 22						19 22						
Penrith North Lakes	a										18 48												
Carlisle 8	a			18 03							19 04						20 01						
Lockerbie	a																						
Haymarket	a										20 16												
Edinburgh 10	a							21 09			20 22			22 14						23 10			
Haymarket	a							21 16															
Motherwell	a							22 00															
Glasgow Central 15	a			19 17				22 22									21 17						
Inverkeithing	a																						
Kirkcaldy	a																						
Markinch	a																						
Ladybank	a																						
Cupar	a																						
Leuchars 3	a																						
Dundee	a																						
Arbroath	a																						
Montrose	a																						
Stonehaven	a																						
Aberdeen	a																						

A ꝑ from Birmingham New Street; ⊼ to Birmingham New Street

B ⊼ from Newport (South Wales)

C ⊼ to Edinburgh

Table 51

Saturdays

18 February to 24 March

South Coast and the South West - North West England, The North East and Scotland

Route Diagram - see first Page of Table 51

		XC	XC	XC	XC	XC	XC	VT	XC	XC	XC	XC	VT	XC	XC	XC	XC	XC	XC	XC	XC	XC
		◇1	◇1	◇1	◇1	1	◇1	◇1	◇1	◇1	◇1	◇1	◇1	◇1	◇1	◇1	◇1	◇1	◇1	◇1	◇1	◇1
		A					B		A	C	C	C		A	C	C				D		
		🍴🛒		🛒	🛒		🛒	🍴	🍴🛒	🛒	🛒	🛒	🍴	🍴🛒	🛒	🛒			🛒	🛒		
Bournemouth	d			15 45						16 45					17 45					18 45		
Brockenhurst 3	d			16 00						17 00					18 00					19 00		
Southampton Central	d			16 15						17 15		17 47			18 15					19 15		
Southampton Airport Pkway	d			16 22						17 22		17 54			18 22					19 22		
Winchester	d			16 31						17 31		18 03			18 31					19 31		
Basingstoke	d			16 47						17 47		18 19			18 47					19 47		
Guildford	d																					
Reading 7	d			17b11			17 40			18f11		18 40			19h11		19 40			20j11	20 40	
Oxford	d			17 36			18 07			18 36		19 07			19 36		20 07			20 36	21 07	
Banbury	d			17 54			18 24			18 54		19 24			19 54		20 29			20 54	21 25	
Leamington Spa 8	d			18 12			18 42			19 12		19 42			20 12		20 46			21 12	21 45	
Coventry	d			18 27						19 27					20 27					21 27	21 56	
Birmingham International	d			18 38						19 38					20 38					21 38	22 11	
Penzance	d																					
St Erth	d																					
Hayle	d																					
Camborne	d																					
Redruth	d																					
Truro	d																					
St Austell	d																					
Newquay (Summer Only)	d																					
Par	d																					
Lostwithiel	d																					
Bodmin Parkway	d																					
Liskeard 6	d																					
Plymouth	d				15 25						16 25					17 23			18 25			
Totnes	d				15 50						16 50					17 49			18 50			
Paignton	d																					
Torquay	d																					
Newton Abbot	d				16 03						17 03					18 03			19 03			
Teignmouth	d																					
Dawlish	d																					
Exeter St Davids 6	d				16 23				16 53		17 23					18 25			19 23			
Tiverton Parkway	d				16 37				17 07		17 37					18 39			19 37			
Taunton	d				16 51				17 21		17 51					18 54			19 51			
Weston-super-Mare	d																					
Cardiff Central 7	d		16 45																			
Newport (South Wales)	d		17 00																			
Bristol Temple Meads 10	d	17 00			17c30				18e00		18g30			19 00		19 30		20 00	20i30			
Bristol Parkway 7	d	17 10			17 40				18 10		18 40			19 10		19 40		20 10	20 40			
Gloucester 7	d		17 46																			
Cheltenham Spa	d	17 42	17 58		18 12				18 42		19 12			19 42		20 12		20 42	21 12			
London Paddington	d																					
Birmingham New Street 12	a	18 26	18 45	18 48	18 56		19 18		19 26	19 48	19 58	20 18		20 26	20 48	20 53	21 18	21 38	21 53	21 48	22 21	
Birmingham New Street 12	d	18 31	18 49	18 57	19 03	19 19	19 30	19 20	19 31	19 57	20 03	20 30	20 20	20 31	20 57	21 03				21 57		22 31
Tamworth	d		19 09			19 36					20 19					21 19						
Burton-on-Trent	d		19 21		19 27	19 48										21 31						
Derby 6	a		19 35		19 39	19 59	20 05				20 42	21 24				21 44						
Nottingham 8	a		20 05			20 32																
Chesterfield	a				20 04		20 29				21 04	21 45				22 07						
Sheffield 7	a				20 19		20 49				21 19	22 05				22 23						
Doncaster 7	a						21 21					22 30				22 51						
Wakefield Westgate 7	a				20 48						21 48					23 10						
Leeds 10	a				21 03						22 02					23 27						
York 8	a				21 57		21 44					22 57										
Darlington 7	a						22 13															
Durham	a						22 30															
Chester-le-Street	a																					
Newcastle 8	a						22 47															
Morpeth	a																					
Alnmouth for Alnwick	a																					
Berwick-upon-Tweed	a																					
Dunbar	a																					
Wolverhampton 7	d	18 49		19 15				19 37	19 49	20 15			20 37	20 49	21 15					22 16		22 49
Stafford	a	19 00		19 29					20 00	20 29			20 49	21 00	21 29					22 29		23 01
Stoke-on-Trent	a	19 19		19 54					20 19	20 54				21 20	21 52					22 50		23 20
Congleton	a																					
Macclesfield	a			20 11					20 36	21 11				21 38	22 11					23 07		23 38
Crewe 10	a							20 07					21 10									
Wilmslow	a																					
Stockport	a	19 49		20 27					20 49	21 27				21 53	22 27					23 21		23 53
M'chester Piccadilly 10	a	19 59		20 39					20 59	21 39				22 04	22 39					23 32		00 10
Warrington Bank Quay	a							20 26														
Wigan North Western	a							20 37														
Preston 8	a							20 59														
Lancaster 6	a																					
Oxenholme Lake District	a																					
Penrith North Lakes	a																					
Carlisle 8	a																					
Lockerbie	a																					
Haymarket	a																					
Edinburgh 10	a																					
Haymarket	a																					
Motherwell	a																					
Glasgow Central 15	a																					
Inverkeithing	a																					
Kirkcaldy	a																					
Markinch	a																					
Ladybank	a																					
Cupar	a																					
Leuchars 3	a																					
Dundee	a																					
Arbroath	a																					
Montrose	a																					
Stonehaven	a																					
Aberdeen	a																					

A 🍴 from Birmingham New Street
🛒 to Birmingham New Street

B 🛒 to Sheffield

C 🛒 to Birmingham New Street

D 🛒 to Reading

Table 51

Saturdays

18 February to 24 March

South Coast and the South West - North West England, The North East and Scotland

Route Diagram - see first Page of Table 51

Station		XC ◇1	XC ◇1	XC 1
Bournemouth	d		19 45	
Brockenhurst 3	d		20 00	
Southampton Central	d		20 15	
Southampton Airport Pkway	d		20 22	
Winchester	d		20 31	
Basingstoke	d		20 47	
Guildford	d			
Reading 7	d		21 11	
Oxford	d		21 36	
Banbury	d		21 54	
Leamington Spa 8	d		22 12	
Coventry	d		22 27	
Birmingham International	d		22 38	
Penzance	d			
St Erth	d			
Hayle	d			
Camborne	d			
Redruth	d			
Truro	d			
St Austell	d			
Newquay (Summer Only)	d			
Par	d			
Lostwithiel	d			
Bodmin Parkway	d			
Liskeard 6	d			
Plymouth	d			
Totnes	d			
Paignton	d			
Torquay	d			
Newton Abbot	d			
Teignmouth	d			
Dawlish	d			
Exeter St Davids 6	d			
Tiverton Parkway	d			
Taunton	d			
Weston-super-Mare	d			
Cardiff Central 7	d	20 50		
Newport (South Wales)	d	21 05		
Bristol Temple Meads 10	d			
Bristol Parkway 7	d			
Gloucester 7	d	21 49		
Cheltenham Spa	d	22 00		
London Paddington	d			
Birmingham New Street 12	a	22 42	22 48	
Birmingham New Street 12	d			22 49
Tamworth	d			23 08
Burton-on-Trent	d			23 20
Derby 6	a			23 33
Nottingham 8	a			
Chesterfield	a			
Sheffield 7	a			
Doncaster 7	a			
Wakefield Westgate 7	a			
Leeds 10	a			
York 8	a			
Darlington 7	a			
Durham	a			
Chester-le-Street	a			
Newcastle 8	a			
Morpeth	a			
Alnmouth for Alnwick	a			
Berwick-upon-Tweed	a			
Dunbar	a			
Wolverhampton 7	d			
Stafford	a			
Stoke-on-Trent	a			
Congleton	a			
Macclesfield	a			
Crewe 10	a			
Wilmslow	a			
Stockport	a			
M'chester Piccadilly 10	a			
Warrington Bank Quay	a			
Wigan North Western	a			
Preston 8	a			
Lancaster 6	a			
Oxenholme Lake District	a			
Penrith North Lakes	a			
Carlisle 8	a			
Lockerbie	a			
Haymarket	a			
Edinburgh 10	a			
Haymarket	a			
Motherwell	a			
Glasgow Central 15	a			
Inverkeithing	a			
Kirkcaldy	a			
Markinch	a			
Ladybank	a			
Cupar	a			
Leuchars 3	a			
Dundee	a			
Arbroath	a			
Montrose	a			
Stonehaven	a			
Aberdeen	a			

Table 51

Saturdays
from 31 March

South Coast and the South West - North West England, The North East and Scotland

Route Diagram - see first Page of Table 51

		XC	XC	XC	XC	XC	XC	VT	XC	XC	XC	XC	XC	XC	VT	XC	XC	XC	XC	XC	XC	XC	XC
		◇1	◇1	◇1	◇1	◇1	1	◇1	◇1	◇1	1	◇1	◇1	1	◇1	◇1	◇1	◇1	1	◇1	◇1	1	◇1
						A												B					B
						🍴	🍴	🛒	🍴	🍴		🍴	🍴	🍴	🛒	🍴	🍴	🍴		🍴		🍴	🍴
Bournemouth	d																						
Brockenhurst 3	d																						
Southampton Central	d																	05 09					
Southampton Airport Pkway	d																	05 16					
Winchester	d																	05 25					
Basingstoke	d																	05 41					
Guildford	d																						06 09
Reading 7	d																	06b11					06 46
Oxford	d																	06 38					07 12
Banbury	d																	06 56					07 33
Leamington Spa 8	d																	07 14					07 51
Coventry	d																	07 27					
Birmingham International	d																	07 38					
Penzance	d																						
St Erth	d																						
Hayle	d																						
Camborne	d																						
Redruth	d																						
Truro	d																						
St Austell	d																						
Newquay (Summer Only)	d																						
Par	d																						
Lostwithiel	d																						
Bodmin Parkway	d																						
Liskeard 6	d																						
Plymouth	d																						
Totnes	d																						
Paignton	d																						
Torquay	d																						
Newton Abbot	d																						
Teignmouth	d																						
Dawlish	d																						
Exeter St Davids 6	d																						
Tiverton Parkway	d																						
Taunton	d																						
Weston-super-Mare	d																						
Cardiff Central 7	d			21p50																			
Newport (South Wales)	d			22p05																			
Bristol Temple Meads 10	d																			06 15			
Bristol Parkway 7	d																			06 25			
Gloucester 7	d			22p47																07c01	07 07		
Cheltenham Spa	d			22p58																07 12	07 18		
London Paddington	d																						
Birmingham New Street 12	a			00 01														07 48		07 56	08 08		08 17
Birmingham New Street 12	d	22p30	23p09		05 57	05 57	06 19	06 20	06 30	06 31	06 49	06 57	07 03	07 19	07 20	07 30	07 31	07 57	07 49	08 03		08 19	08 30
Tamworth	d		23p28			06 13	06 39		06 46		07 07		07 19	07 38		07 45			08 07	08 19		08 36	
Burton-on-Trent	d		23p40			06 24	06 51		06 56		07 19		07 29	07 50		07 54			08 17	08 29		08 48	
Derby 6	a		23p55			06 35	07 05		07 09		07 34		07 42	08 05		08 09			08 34	08 42		08 59	09 06
Nottingham 8	a		00 18				07 38				08 08			08 34					09 05			09 33	
Chesterfield	a					06 55			07 29				08 02			08 29				09 02			
Sheffield 7	a					07 09			07 48				08 17			08 45				09 17			09 44
Doncaster 7	a								08 23							09 18							10 17
Wakefield Westgate 7	a					07 36							08 45							09 46			
Leeds 10	a					07 52							09 03							10 02			
York 8	a					08 23			08 48				09 27			09 44				10 26			10 40
Darlington 7	a					08 56			09 16				09 58			10 15				10 58			11 13
Durham	a					09 13			09 34				10 15			10 32				11 15			11 30
Chester-le-Street	a																						
Newcastle 8	a					09 26			09 47				10 31			10 45				11 29			11 46
Morpeth	a																						
Alnmouth for Alnwick	a					09 58																	
Berwick-upon-Tweed	a					10 19														12 19			
Dunbar	a												11 37										
Wolverhampton 7	d	22p48			06 16			06 37		06 49		07 15			07 37		07 49	08 15					
Stafford	a	23p00			06 29					07 00		07 29					08 00	08 29					
Stoke-on-Trent	a	23p21			06 50					07 18							08 19	08 54					
Congleton	a				07 02																		
Macclesfield	a				07 11					07 36							08 36	09 11					
Crewe 10	a							07 07				07 50			08 07								
Wilmslow	a											08 09											
Stockport	a				07 27					07 49		08 20					08 49	09 27					
M'chester Piccadilly 10	a	00 13			07 38					07 59		08 35					08 59	09 39					
Warrington Bank Quay	a							07 26							08 27								
Wigan North Western	a							07 37							08 38								
Preston 8	a							07 51							08 51								
Lancaster 6	a							08 08							09 08								
Oxenholme Lake District	a							08 21															
Penrith North Lakes	a														09 44								
Carlisle 8	a							09 00							10 02								
Lockerbie	a																						
Haymarket	a							10 16															
Edinburgh 10	a					11 05		10 22					12 07							13 04			
Haymarket	a					11 15														13 15			
Motherwell	a					11 52														13 52			
Glasgow Central 15	a					12 13									11 17					14 13			
Inverkeithing	a																						
Kirkcaldy	a																						
Markinch	a																						
Ladybank	a																						
Cupar	a																						
Leuchars 3	a																						
Dundee	a																						
Arbroath	a																						
Montrose	a																						
Stonehaven	a																						
Aberdeen	a																						

A 🍴 to Edinburgh

B 🍴 from Reading

Table 51

Saturdays
from 31 March

South Coast and the South West - North West England, The North East and Scotland

Route Diagram - see first Page of Table 51

		VT	XC	XC	XC	XC	XC	VT	XC	XC	XC	XC	XC	XC	VT	XC	XC	XC	XC	XC	XC	VT	XC
		◇1	◇1	◇1	◇1	1	◇1	◇1	◇1	◇1	◇1	◇1	1	◇1	◇1	◇1	◇1	◇1	◇1	1	◇1	◇1	◇1
			A						A	B		C				A	B						A
		🍽	🍽🛒	🛒	🛒	🛒	🛒	🍽	🍽🛒	🛒	🛒	🛒		🛒	🍽	🍽🛒	🛒	🛒	🛒		🛒	🍽	🍽🛒
Bournemouth	d						06 25				06 37							07 45					
Brockenhurst 3	d						06 39				06 55							08 00					
Southampton Central	d			06 15			06 53				07 15			07 47				08 15					
Southampton Airport Pkway	d			06 22			07 01				07 22			07 54				08 22					
Winchester	d			06 31			07 09				07 31			08 03				08 31					
Basingstoke	d			06 47			07 25				07 47			08 19				08 47					
Guildford	d																						
Reading 7	d			07 11			07 47				08 11			08 40				09 11			09 40		
Oxford	d			07 36			08 15				08 36			09 07				09 36			10 07		
Banbury	d			07 54			08 33				08 54			09 24				09 54			10 24		
Leamington Spa 8	d			08 12			08 50				09 12			09 42				10 13			10 42		
Coventry	d			08 27							09 27							10 27					
Birmingham International	d			08 38							09 38							10 38					
Penzance	d																						
St Erth	d																						
Hayle	d																						
Camborne	d																						
Redruth	d																						
Truro	d																						
St Austell	d																						
Newquay (Summer Only)	d																						
Par	d																						
Lostwithiel	d																						
Bodmin Parkway	d																						
Liskeard 6	d																						
Plymouth	d				05 25							06 25							07 25				
Totnes	d				05 50							06 50							07 50				
Paignton	d															07 02							
Torquay	d															07 08							
Newton Abbot	d				06 03							07 03				07 19			08 03				
Teignmouth	d															07 26							
Dawlish	d															07 31							
Exeter St Davids 6	d				06 23							07 23				07 45			08 23				
Tiverton Parkway	d				06 37							07 37				07 58			08 37				
Taunton	d				06 51							07 51				08 13			08 51				
Weston-super-Mare	d																						
Cardiff Central 7	d								07 00	07 45							08 45						
Newport (South Wales)	d								07 15	08 00							09 00						
Bristol Temple Meads 10	d		07 00		07 30				08 00			08 30				09 00			09 30				10 00
Bristol Parkway 7	d		07 10		07 40				08 10			08 40				09 10			09 40				10 10
Gloucester 7	d									08 47							09 46						
Cheltenham Spa	d		07 42		08 12				08 42	08 58		09 12				09 42	09 57		10 12				10 42
London Paddington	d																						
Birmingham New Street 12	a		08 26	08 48	08 56		09 19		09 26	09 45	09 48	09 56		10 18		10 26	10 45	10 48	10 56		11 18		11 26
Birmingham New Street 12	d	08 20	08 31	08 57	09 03	09 19	09 30	09 20	09 31	09 49	09 57	10 03	10 19	10 30	10 20	10 31	10 49	10 57	11 03	11 19	11 30	11 20	11 31
Tamworth	d					09 36				10 07		10 19	10 36				11 09			11 36			
Burton-on-Trent	d				09 28	09 48				10 19			10 48				11 21		11 28	11 48			
Derby 6	a				09 41	09 59	10 05			10 34		10 41	10 59	11 05			11 34		11 41	11 59	12 05		
Nottingham 8	a					10 33				11 05			11 33				12 05			12 33			
Chesterfield	a				10 02							11 02							12 02				
Sheffield 7	a				10 17		10 42					11 17		11 41					12 16		12 41		
Doncaster 7	a						11 15							12 15							13 17		
Wakefield Westgate 7	a				10 46							11 46							12 46				
Leeds 10	a				11 02							12 02							13 02				
York 8	a				11 26		11 40					12 26		12 39					13 26		13 40		
Darlington 7	a				11 57		12 13					12 58		13 13					13 57		14 12		
Durham	a				12 15		12 30					13 15		13 30					14 14		14 29		
Chester-le-Street	a																						
Newcastle 8	a				12 31		12 45					13 29		13 44					14 28		14 42		
Morpeth	a																		14 47				
Alnmouth for Alnwick	a											13 59											
Berwick-upon-Tweed	a											14 19											
Dunbar	a				13 37														15 39				
Wolverhampton 7	d	08 37	08 49	09 15				09 37	09 49		10 15				10 37	10 49		11 15				11 37	11 49
Stafford	a		09 00	09 29					10 00		10 29					11 00		11 29					12 00
Stoke-on-Trent	a		09 19	09 54					10 19		10 54					11 19		11 54					12 19
Congleton	a																						
Macclesfield	a			10 11							11 11							12 11					
Crewe 10	a	09 07						10 07							11 07							12 07	
Wilmslow	a																						
Stockport	a		09 49	10 27					10 49		11 27					11 49		12 27					12 49
M'chester Piccadilly 10	a		09 59	10 39					10 59		11 39					11 59		12 39					12 59
Warrington Bank Quay	a	09 26						10 26							11 26							12 26	
Wigan North Western	a	09 37						10 37							11 37							12 37	
Preston 8	a	09 51						10 51							11 51							12 51	
Lancaster 6	a	10 08						11 08							12 08							13 08	
Oxenholme Lake District	a	10 22													12 22							13 22	
Penrith North Lakes	a							11 44															
Carlisle 8	a	11 01						12 00							13 01							14 01	
Lockerbie	a																						
Haymarket	a	12 16													14 15								
Edinburgh 10	a	12 22			14 07							15 07			14 22				16 04				
Haymarket	a											15 15											
Motherwell	a											15 52											
Glasgow Central 15	a							13 17				16 23										15 17	
Inverkeithing	a																						
Kirkcaldy	a																						
Markinch	a																						
Ladybank	a																						
Cupar	a																						
Leuchars 3	a																						
Dundee	a																						
Arbroath	a																						
Montrose	a																						
Stonehaven	a																						
Aberdeen	a																						

A 🍽 from Birmingham New Street
🛒 to Birmingham New Street

B 🛒 from Newport (South Wales)

C 🛒 to Edinburgh

Table 51

Saturdays
from 31 March

South Coast and the South West - North West England, The North East and Scotland

Route Diagram - see first Page of Table 51

		XC	XC	XC	XC	VT	XC	XC	XC	XC	XC	XC	VT	XC	XC	XC	XC	XC	VT	XC	XC	XC
		◇1	◇1	1	◇1	◇1	◇1	◇1	◇1	◇1	1	◇1	◇1	◇1	◇1	◇1	1	◇1	◇1	◇1	◇1	◇1
			A				B	C		D				B		A				B		D
		🛒	🛒	🛒	🛒	☕	☕🛒	🛒	🛒	🛒		🛒	☕	☕🛒	🛒	🛒		🛒	☕	☕🛒	🛒	🛒
Bournemouth	d	08 45							09 45						10 45						11 45	
Brockenhurst 3	d	09 00							10 00						11 00						12 00	
Southampton Central	d	09 15			09 47				10 15						11 15			11 47			12 15	
Southampton Airport Pkway ✈	d	09 22			09 54				10 22						11 22			11 54			12 22	
Winchester	d	09 31			10 03				10 31						11 31			12 03			12 31	
Basingstoke	d	09 47			10 19				10 47						11 47			12 19			12 47	
Guildford	d																					
Reading 7	d	10 11			10 40				11 11			11 40			12 11			12 40			13 11	
Oxford	d	10 36			11 07				11 36			12 07			12 36			13 07			13 36	
Banbury	d	10 54			11 24				11 54			12 24			12 54			13 24			13 54	
Leamington Spa 8	d	11 12			11 42				12 12			12 42			13 12			13 42			14 12	
Coventry	d	11 27							12 27						13 27						14 27	
Birmingham International ✈	d	11 38							12 38						13 38						14 38	
Penzance	d		06 30													08 28						
St Erth	d		06 38													08 36						
Hayle	d		06 41																			
Camborne	d		06 51													08 46						
Redruth	d		06 57													08 52						
Truro	d		07 09													09 04						
St Austell	d		07 25													09 20						
Newquay (Summer Only)	d																					
Par	d		07 32													09 28						
Lostwithiel	d		07 39																			
Bodmin Parkway	d		07 46													09 39						
Liskeard 6	d		07 58													09 51						
Plymouth	d		08 25							09 25						10 25						11 25
Totnes	d		08 50							09 50						10 50						11 50
Paignton	d													10 07								
Torquay	d													10 13								
Newton Abbot	d		09 03							10 03				10 24		11 03						12 03
Teignmouth	d													10 31								
Dawlish	d													10 36								
Exeter St Davids 6	d		09 23							10 23				10 50		11 23						12 23
Tiverton Parkway	d		09 37							10 37				11 03		11 37						12 37
Taunton	d		09 51							10 51				11 18		11 51						12 51
Weston-super-Mare	d																					
Cardiff Central 7	d							10 45														
Newport (South Wales)	d							11 00														
Bristol Temple Meads 10	d		10 30				11 00			11 30				12 00		12 30				13 00		13k30
Bristol Parkway 7	d		10 40				11 10			11 40				12 10		12 40				13 10		13 40
Gloucester 7	d							11 46														
Cheltenham Spa	d		11 12				11 42	11 57		12 12				12 42		13 12				13 42		14 12
London Paddington	d																					
Birmingham New Street 12	a	11 48	11 56		12 18		12 26	12 45	12 48	12 56		13 18		13 26	13 48	13 56		14 18		14 26	14 48	14 56
Birmingham New Street 12	d	11 57	12 03	12 19	12 30	12 20	12 31	12 49	12 57	13 03	13 19	13 30	13 20	13 31	13 57	14 03	14 19	14 30	14 20	14 31	14 57	15 03
Tamworth	d		12 19	12 36				13 09			13 36					14 19	14 36					
Burton-on-Trent	d			12 48				13 21		13 27	13 50						14 47					15 27
Derby 6	a		12 41	13 05	13 08			13 34		13 41	14 05	14 08				14 41	14 59	15 05				15 41
Nottingham 8 🚌	a			13 33				14 05			14 33						15 33					
Chesterfield	a		13 02							14 02						15 02						16 02
Sheffield 7 🚌	a		13 17		13 41					14 17		14 41				15 17		15 41				16 18
Doncaster 7	a				14 18							15 17						16 18				
Wakefield Westgate 7	a		13 46							14 46						15 46						16 46
Leeds 10	a		14 02							15 02						16 02						17 02
York 8	a		14 26		14 40					15 28		15 40				16 26		16 41				17 26
Darlington 7	a		14 58		15 13					15 58		16 13				16 58		17 13				17 56
Durham	a		15 15		15 30					16 15		16 30				17 15		17 30				18 13
Chester-le-Street	a																					
Newcastle 8	a		15 29		15 45					16 29		16 45				17 29		17 45				18 29
Morpeth	a																					
Alnmouth for Alnwick	a		15 58							16 58						18 00						
Berwick-upon-Tweed	a		16 18													18 20						19 17
Dunbar	a									17 38												19 40
Wolverhampton 7 🚌	d	12 15				12 37	12 49		13 15				13 37	13 49	14 15				14 37	14 49	15 15	
Stafford	a	12 29					13 00		13 29					14 00	14 29					15 00	15 29	
Stoke-on-Trent	a	12 54					13 18		13 54					14 19	14 54					15 19	15 54	
Congleton	a																					
Macclesfield	a	13 11							14 11						15 11						16 11	
Crewe 10	a					13 07							14 07						15 07			
Wilmslow	a																					
Stockport	a	13 27					13 49		14 27					14 49	15 27					15 49	16 27	
M'chester Piccadilly 10 🚌	a	13 39					13 59		14 39					14 59	15 39					15 59	16 39	
Warrington Bank Quay	a					13 26							14 26						15 26			
Wigan North Western	a					13 37							14 37						15 37			
Preston 8	a					13 51							14 51						15 51			
Lancaster 6	a					14 08							15 08						16 08			
Oxenholme Lake District	a												15 22									
Penrith North Lakes	a					14 44													16 45			
Carlisle 8	a					15 00							16 01						17 00			
Lockerbie	a																					
Haymarket	a					16 16													18 14			
Edinburgh 10	a		17 07			16 22				18 05						19 08			18 22			20 06
Haymarket	a		17 15							18 14						19 15						20 17
Motherwell	a		17 52													19 52						
Glasgow Central 15	a		18 11										17 17			20 11						
Inverkeithing	a									18 28												20 33
Kirkcaldy	a									18 46												20 50
Markinch	a									18 56												21 00
Ladybank	a									19 03												21 08
Cupar	a									19 10												21 17
Leuchars 3	a									19 17												21 25
Dundee	a									19 32												21 43
Arbroath	a									19 49												
Montrose	a									20 03												
Stonehaven	a									20 23												
Aberdeen	a									20 43												

A 🛒 from Plymouth to Edinburgh

B ☕ from Birmingham New Street 🛒 to Birmingham New Street

C 🛒 from Newport (South Wales)

D 🛒 to Edinburgh

Table 51

Saturdays
from 31 March

South Coast and the South West - North West England, The North East and Scotland

Route Diagram - see first Page of Table 51

		XC	XC	VT	XC	XC	XC	XC	XC	XC	VT	XC	XC	XC	XC	XC	VT	XC	XC	XC	XC	XC	VT
		1	◇1	◇1	◇1	◇1	◇1	◇1	1	◇1	◇1	◇1	◇1	◇1	1	◇1	◇1	◇1	◇1	◇1	1	◇1	◇1
					A	B		C				A											
			[trolley]	[restaurant]	[restaurant] [trolley]	[trolley]	[trolley]	[trolley]		[trolley]	[restaurant]	[restaurant] [trolley]	[trolley]	[trolley]		[trolley]	[restaurant]	[trolley]	[trolley]	[trolley]		[trolley]	[restaurant]
Bournemouth	d						12 45						13 45						14 45				
Brockenhurst 3	d						13 00						14 00						15 00				
Southampton Central	d						13 15			13 47			14 15						15 15			15 47	
Southampton Airport Pkway	d						13 22			13 54			14 22						15 22			15 54	
Winchester	d						13 31			14 03			14 31						15 31			16 03	
Basingstoke	d						13 47			14 19			14 47						15 47			16 19	
Guildford	d																						
Reading 7	d		13 40				14 11			14 40			15 11			15 40			16 11			16 40	
Oxford	d		14 07				14 36			15 07			15 36			16 07			16 36			17 07	
Banbury	d		14 24				14 54			15 24			15 54			16 24			16 54			17 24	
Leamington Spa 8	d		14 42				15 12			15 42			16 12			16 42			17 12			17 42	
Coventry	d						15 27						16 27						17 27				
Birmingham International	d						15 38						16 38						17 38				
Penzance	d				09 43																		
St Erth	d				09 51																		
Hayle	d																						
Camborne	d				10 01																		
Redruth	d				10 07																		
Truro	d				10 19																		
St Austell	d				10 35																		
Newquay (Summer Only)	d																						
Par	d				10 42																		
Lostwithiel	d				10 49																		
Bodmin Parkway	d				10 56																		
Liskeard 6	d				11 09																		
Plymouth	d				11 48			12 23						13 25						14 25			
Totnes	d				12 13			12 49						13 50						14 50			
Paignton	d																	13 53					
Torquay	d																	13 59					
Newton Abbot	d				12 25			13 03						14 03				14 10		15 03			
Teignmouth	d																	14 17					
Dawlish	d																	14 22					
Exeter St Davids 6	d				12 48			13 25						14 23				14 36		15 23			
Tiverton Parkway	d				13 02			13 39						14 37				14 49		15 37			
Taunton	d				13 16			13 54						14 52				15 04		15 51			
Weston-super-Mare	d																	15 30					
Cardiff Central 7	d					13 45																	
Newport (South Wales)	d					14 00																	
Bristol Temple Meads 10	d				14 00			14 30				15 00		15 30				16 00		16 30			
Bristol Parkway 7	d				14 10			14 40				15 10		15 40				16 10		16 40			
Gloucester 7	d					14 46																	
Cheltenham Spa	d				14 42	14 57		15 12				15 42		16 12				16 42		17 12			
London Paddington	d																						
Birmingham New Street 12	a		15 18		15 26	15 45	15 48	15 55		16 18		16 26	16 48	16 56		17 18		17 26	17 48	17 56		18 18	
Birmingham New Street 12	d	15 19	15 30	15 20	15 31	15 49	15 57	16 03	16 19	16 30	16 20	16 31	16 57	17 03	17 19	17 30	17 20	17 31	17 57	18 03	18 19	18 30	18 20
Tamworth	d	15 36				16 09		16 17	16 38						17 36					18 19	18 36		
Burton-on-Trent	d	15 48				16 21			16 50					17 26	17 48						18 47		
Derby 6	a	15 59	16 05			16 34		16 40	17 05	17 08				17 41	17 59	18 05				18 41	18 59	19 05	
Nottingham 8	a	16 33				17 05			17 33						18 32						19 33		
Chesterfield	a							17 01						18 02						19 02		19 29	
Sheffield 7	a		16 41					17 19		17 44				18 18		18 42				19 18		19 51	
Doncaster 7	a		17 16													19 16						20 17	
Wakefield Westgate 7	a							17 47		18 12				18 46						19 49			
Leeds 10	a							18 02		18 31				19 01						20 05			
York 8	a		17 37					18 28		18 58				19 26		19 39				20 29		20 40	
Darlington 7	a		18 12					18 59		19 35				19 57		20 11				20 58		21 13	
Durham	a		18 29					19 17		19 52				20 14		20 28				21 15		21 30	
Chester-le-Street	a																						
Newcastle 8	a		18 44					19 31		20 08				20 28		20 42				21 29		21 44	
Morpeth	a													20 50									
Alnmouth for Alnwick	a							20 03												22 01			
Berwick-upon-Tweed	a							20 24						21 23									
Dunbar	a													21 47									
Wolverhampton 7	d			15 37	15 49		16 15				16 37	16 49	17 15				17 37	17 49	18 15				18 37
Stafford	a				16 00		16 29					17 00	17 29					18 00	18 29				
Stoke-on-Trent	a				16 19		16 54					17 19	17 54					18 19	18 54				
Congleton	a																						
Macclesfield	a						17 11						18 11						19 11				
Crewe 10	a			16 08							17 07						18 07						19 07
Wilmslow	a																						
Stockport	a				16 49		17 27					17 49	18 27					18 49	19 27				
M'chester Piccadilly 10	a				16 59		17 39					17 59	18 39					18 59	19 39				
Warrington Bank Quay	a			16 26							17 26						18 26						19 26
Wigan North Western	a			16 37							17 37						18 37						19 37
Preston 8	a			16 51							17 51						18 51						19 54
Lancaster 6	a			17 09							18 08						19 08						
Oxenholme Lake District	a			17 24							18 22						19 22						
Penrith North Lakes	a										18 48												
Carlisle 8	a			18 03							19 04						20 01						
Lockerbie	a																						
Haymarket	a										20 16												
Edinburgh 10	a							21 09			20 22			22 14						23 10			
Haymarket	a							21 16															
Motherwell	a							22 00															
Glasgow Central 15	a			19 17				22 22									21 17						
Inverkeithing	a																						
Kirkcaldy	a																						
Markinch	a																						
Ladybank	a																						
Cupar	a																						
Leuchars 3	a																						
Dundee	a																						
Arbroath	a																						
Montrose	a																						
Stonehaven	a																						
Aberdeen	a																						

A [restaurant] from Birmingham New Street; [trolley] to Birmingham New Street
B [trolley] from Newport (South Wales)
C [trolley] to Edinburgh

Table 51

Saturdays
from 31 March

South Coast and the South West - North West England, The North East and Scotland

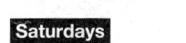

Route Diagram - see first Page of Table 51

		XC	XC	XC	XC	XC	XC	VT	XC	XC	XC	XC	VT	XC	XC	XC	XC	XC	XC	XC	XC	XC
		◇1	◇1	◇1	◇1	1	◇1	◇1	◇1	◇1	◇1	◇1	◇1	◇1	◇1	◇1	◇1	◇1	◇1	◇1	◇1	◇1
		A					B		A	C	C	C		A	C	C				D		
		⊡⊼		⊼	⊼		⊼	⊡	⊡⊼	⊼	⊼	⊼	⊡	⊡⊼	⊼	⊼			⊼	⊼		
Bournemouth	d			15 45						16 45					17 45					18 45		
Brockenhurst 3	d			16 00						17 00					18 00					19 00		
Southampton Central	d			16 15						17 15		17 47			18 15					19 15		
Southampton Airport Pkwy ✈	d			16 22						17 22		17 54			18 22					19 22		
Winchester	d			16 31						17 31		18 03			18 31					19 31		
Basingstoke	d			16 47						17 47		18 19			18 47					19 47		
Guildford	d																					
Reading 7	d			17 11			17 40			18 11		18 40			19 11		19 40			20 11	20 40	
Oxford	d			17 36			18 07			18 36		19 07			19 36		20 07			20 36	21 07	
Banbury	d			17 54			18 24			18 54		19 24			19 54		20 29			20 54	21 25	
Leamington Spa 8	d			18 12			18 42			19 12		19 42			20 12		20 46			21 12	21 45	
Coventry	d			18 27						19 27					20 27					21 27	21 56	
Birmingham International ✈	d			18 38						19 38					20 38					21 38	22 11	
Penzance	d																					
St Erth	d																					
Hayle	d																					
Camborne	d																					
Redruth	d																					
Truro	d																					
St Austell	d																					
Newquay (Summer Only)	d																					
Par	d																					
Lostwithiel	d																					
Bodmin Parkway	d																					
Liskeard 6	d																					
Plymouth	d				15 25						16 25					17 23			18 25			
Totnes	d				15 50						16 50					17 49			18 50			
Paignton	d																					
Torquay	d																					
Newton Abbot	d				16 03						17 03					18 03			19 03			
Teignmouth	d																					
Dawlish	d																					
Exeter St Davids 6	d				16 23				16 53		17 23					18 25			19 23			
Tiverton Parkway	d				16 37				17 07		17 37					18 39			19 37			
Taunton	d				16 51				17 21		17 51					18 54			19 51			
Weston-super-Mare	d																					
Cardiff Central 7	d		16 45																			
Newport (South Wales)	d		17 00																			
Bristol Temple Meads 10	d	17 00			17 30				18 00		18 30			19 00		19 30		20 00	20 30			
Bristol Parkway 7	d	17 10			17 40				18 10		18 40			19 10		19 40		20 10	20 40			
Gloucester 7	d		17 46																			
Cheltenham Spa	d	17 42	17 58		18 12				18 42		19 12			19 42		20 12		20 42	21 12			
London Paddington	d																					
Birmingham New Street 12	a	18 26	18 45	18 48	18 56		19 18		19 26	19 48	19 58	20 18		20 26	20 48	20 53	21 18	21 38	21 53	21 48	22 21	
Birmingham New Street 12	d	18 31	18 49	18 57	19 03	19 19	19 30	19 20	19 31	19 57	20 03	20 30	20 20	20 31	20 57	21 03				21 57		22 31
Tamworth	d		19 09			19 36					20 19					21 19						
Burton-on-Trent	d		19 21		19 27	19 48										21 31						
Derby 6	a		19 35		19 39	19 59	20 05				20 42	21 24				21 44						
Nottingham 8	a		20 05			20 32																
Chesterfield	a				20 04		20 29				21 04	21 45				22 07						
Sheffield 7	a				20 19		20 49				21 19	22 05				22 23						
Doncaster 7	a						21 21					22 30				22 51						
Wakefield Westgate 7	a				20 48						21 48					23 10						
Leeds 10	a				21 03						22 02					23 27						
York 8	a				21 57		21 44					22 57										
Darlington 7	a						22 13															
Durham	a						22 30															
Chester-le-Street	a																					
Newcastle 8	a						22 47															
Morpeth	a																					
Alnmouth for Alnwick	a																					
Berwick-upon-Tweed	a																					
Dunbar	a																					
Wolverhampton 7	d	18 49		19 15				19 37	19 49	20 15			20 37	20 49	21 15					22 16		22 49
Stafford	a	19 00		19 29					20 00	20 29			20 49	21 00	21 29					22 29		23 01
Stoke-on-Trent	a	19 19		19 54					20 19	20 54				21 20	21 52					22 50		23 20
Congleton	a																					
Macclesfield	a			20 11					20 36	21 11				21 38	22 11					23 07		23 38
Crewe 10	a							20 07					21 10									
Wilmslow	a																					
Stockport	a	19 49		20 27					20 49	21 27				21 53	22 27					23 21		23 53
M'chester Piccadilly 10	a	19 59		20 39					20 59	21 39				22 04	22 39					23 32		00 10
Warrington Bank Quay	a							20 26														
Wigan North Western	a							20 37														
Preston 8	a							20 59														
Lancaster 6	a																					
Oxenholme Lake District	a																					
Penrith North Lakes	a																					
Carlisle 8	a																					
Lockerbie	a																					
Haymarket	a																					
Edinburgh 10	a																					
Haymarket	a																					
Motherwell	a																					
Glasgow Central 15	a																					
Inverkeithing	a																					
Kirkcaldy	a																					
Markinch	a																					
Ladybank	a																					
Cupar	a																					
Leuchars 3	a																					
Dundee	a																					
Arbroath	a																					
Montrose	a																					
Stonehaven	a																					
Aberdeen	a																					

A ⊡ from Birmingham New Street
⊼ to Birmingham New Street

B ⊼ to Sheffield

C ⊼ to Birmingham New Street

D ⊼ to Reading

Table 51

Saturdays
from 31 March

South Coast and the South West - North West England, The North East and Scotland

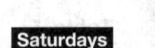

Route Diagram - see first Page of Table 51

		XC ◇1	XC ◇1	XC 1
Bournemouth	d		19 45	
Brockenhurst 3	d		20 00	
Southampton Central	d		20 15	
Southampton Airport Pkway	d		20 22	
Winchester	d		20 31	
Basingstoke	d		20 47	
Guildford	d			
Reading 7	d		21 11	
Oxford	d		21 36	
Banbury	d		21 54	
Leamington Spa 8	d		22 12	
Coventry	d		22 27	
Birmingham International	d		22 38	
Penzance	d			
St Erth	d			
Hayle	d			
Camborne	d			
Redruth	d			
Truro	d			
St Austell	d			
Newquay (Summer Only)	d			
Par	d			
Lostwithiel	d			
Bodmin Parkway	d			
Liskeard 6	d			
Plymouth	d			
Totnes	d			
Paignton	d			
Torquay	d			
Newton Abbot	d			
Teignmouth	d			
Dawlish	d			
Exeter St Davids 6	d			
Tiverton Parkway	d			
Taunton	d			
Weston-super-Mare	d			
Cardiff Central 7	d	20 50		
Newport (South Wales)	d	21 05		
Bristol Temple Meads 10	d			
Bristol Parkway 7	d			
Gloucester 7	d	21 49		
Cheltenham Spa	d	22 00		
London Paddington	d			
Birmingham New Street 12	a	22 42	22 48	
Birmingham New Street 12	d			22 49
Tamworth	d			23 08
Burton-on-Trent	d			23 20
Derby 6	a			23 33
Nottingham 8	a			
Chesterfield	a			
Sheffield 7	a			
Doncaster 7	a			
Wakefield Westgate 7	a			
Leeds 10	a			
York 8	a			
Darlington 7	a			
Durham	a			
Chester-le-Street	a			
Newcastle 8	a			
Morpeth	a			
Alnmouth for Alnwick	a			
Berwick-upon-Tweed	a			
Dunbar	a			
Wolverhampton 7	d			
Stafford	a			
Stoke-on-Trent	a			
Congleton	a			
Macclesfield	a			
Crewe 10	a			
Wilmslow	a			
Stockport	a			
M'chester Piccadilly 10	a			
Warrington Bank Quay	a			
Wigan North Western	a			
Preston 8	a			
Lancaster 6	a			
Oxenholme Lake District	a			
Penrith North Lakes	a			
Carlisle 8	a			
Lockerbie	a			
Haymarket	a			
Edinburgh 10	a			
Haymarket	a			
Motherwell	a			
Glasgow Central 15	a			
Inverkeithing	a			
Kirkcaldy	a			
Markinch	a			
Ladybank	a			
Cupar	a			
Leuchars 3	a			
Dundee	a			
Arbroath	a			
Montrose	a			
Stonehaven	a			
Aberdeen	a			

Table 51

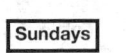

Sundays until 1 January

South Coast and the South West - North West England, The North East and Scotland

Route Diagram - see first Page of Table 51

		XC	VT	XC	XC	VT	XC	XC	VT	XC	XC	VT	XC	XC	XC	VT	XC	XC	XC	XC	VT	XC	XC
		◇1	◇1	◇1	◇1	◇1	◇1	◇1	◇1	◇1	◇1	◇1	◇1	◇1	◇1	◇1	◇1	◇1	◇1	◇1	◇1	◇1	◇1
		A						B							B			C	B				
Bournemouth	d																			09 40			
Brockenhurst [3]	d																			09 57			
Southampton Central	d													09 15						10 15			
Southampton Airport Pkway	d													09 22						10 22			
Winchester	d													09 31						10 31			
Basingstoke	d													09 47						10 47			
Guildford	d																						
Reading [7]	d									09 11				10 11						11 11			
Oxford	d									09 37				10 37						11 37			
Banbury	d									09 54				10 54						11 54			
Leamington Spa [8]	d									10 12				11 12						12 12			
Coventry	d									10 28				11 29						12 28			
Birmingham International	d									10 40				11 40						12 40			
Penzance	d																						
St Erth	d																						
Hayle	d																						
Camborne	d																						
Redruth	d																						
Truro	d																						
St Austell	d																						
Newquay (Summer Only)	d																						
Par	d																						
Lostwithiel	d																						
Bodmin Parkway	d																						
Liskeard [6]	d																						
Plymouth	d																		09 25				
Totnes	d																		09 50				
Paignton	d																						
Torquay	d																						
Newton Abbot	d																		10 03				
Teignmouth	d																						
Dawlish	d																						
Exeter St Davids [6]	d																		10 23				
Tiverton Parkway	d																		10 37				
Taunton	d																		10 51				
Weston-super-Mare	d																						
Cardiff Central [7]	d																	10 45					
Newport (South Wales)	d																	10 59					
Bristol Temple Meads [10]	d										09 15				10 30				11 30				
Bristol Parkway [7]	d										09 25				10 40				11 40				
Gloucester [7]	d										10 01							11 51					
Cheltenham Spa	d										10 12				11 12			12 03	12 12				
London Paddington	d																						
Birmingham New Street [12]	a									10 50	10 50			11 50	11 50			12 45	12 50	12 50			
Birmingham New Street [12]	d	22p31	08 45	09 01	09 03	09 20	10 01	10 03	10 20	11 01	11 03	11 20	11 49	12 01	12 03	12 20	12 30	12 49	13 03	13 01	13 20	13 30	13 31
Tamworth	d				09 19			10 18					12 07		12 19			13 07					
Burton-on-Trent	d				09 28			10 29			11 26		12 19					13 19	13 26				
Derby [6]	a				09 42			10 39			11 40		12 34		12 43		13 01	13 33	13 42			14 01	
Nottingham [8]	a												13 00					14 00					
Chesterfield	a				10 02			11 02			12 02				13 02		13 29		14 02			14 29	
Sheffield [7]	a				10 16			11 17			12 18				13 18		13 43		14 17			14 45	
Doncaster [7]	a																14 13					15 13	
Wakefield Westgate [7]	a				10 44			11 44			12 44				13 45				14 44				
Leeds [10]	a				11 02			12 01			13 02				14 02				15 02				
York [8]	a				11 29			12 29			13 29				14 29		14 40		15 29			15 43	
Darlington [7]	a				11 57			12 57			13 57				14 57		15 13		15 57			16 13	
Durham	a				12 14			13 14			14 14				15 14		15 30		16 14			16 30	
Chester-le-Street	a																						
Newcastle [8]	a				12 29			13 32			14 28				15 28		15 44		16 28			16 44	
Morpeth	a										14 48												
Alnmouth for Alnwick	a							13 59							16 01				16 58				
Berwick-upon-Tweed	a							14 20							16 21								
Dunbar	a				13 39						15 40								17 39				
Wolverhampton [7]	d	22p49	09 04	09 19		09 37	10 19		10 37	11 19		11 37		12 19		12 37				13 19	13 37		13 49
Stafford	a	23p01	09 16	09 32			10 32			11 31				12 32						13 33			
Stoke-on-Trent	a	23p20					10 51			11 51				12 52						13 56			14 19
Congleton	a																						
Macclesfield	a	23p38					11 08			12 09				13 10						14 14			
Crewe [10]	a		09 35	09 54		10 07			11 07			12 07				13 07					14 07		
Wilmslow	a			10 12																			
Stockport	a	23p53		10 21			11 22			12 22				13 28						14 28			
M'chester Piccadilly [10]	a	00 10		10 37			11 31			12 40				13 40						14 40			14 57
Warrington Bank Quay	a		09 54			10 26			11 26			12 26				13 26					14 26		
Wigan North Western	a		10 05			10 37			11 37			12 37				13 37					14 37		
Preston [8]	a		10 22			10 51			11 51			12 51				13 51					14 50		
Lancaster [6]	a					11 07			12 08			13 08				14 08					15 08		
Oxenholme Lake District	a					11 22			12 22			13 22									15 22		
Penrith North Lakes	a															14 44							
Carlisle [8]	a					12 01			13 01			14 01				15 00					16 01		
Lockerbie	a																						
Haymarket	a								14 13							16 14							
Edinburgh [10]	a				14 07			15 05	14 22		16 06				17 06	16 22			18 07				
Haymarket	a							15 14							17 14				18 16				
Motherwell	a							15 51							17 52								
Glasgow Central [15]	a					13 17		16 13				15 16			18 12						17 17		
Inverkeithing	a																		18 28				
Kirkcaldy	a																		18 44				
Markinch	a																		18 53				
Ladybank	a																		19 01				
Cupar	a																		19 07				
Leuchars [3]	a																		19 14				
Dundee	a																		19 29				
Arbroath	a																		19 46				
Montrose	a																		20 00				
Stonehaven	a																		20 23				
Aberdeen	a																		20 43				

A not 11 December **B** to Edinburgh **C** from Newport (South Wales)

Table 51

Sundays
until 1 January

South Coast and the South West - North West England, The North East and Scotland

Route Diagram - see first Page of Table 51

		XC	XC	XC	XC	VT	XC	XC	XC	XC	XC	VT	XC	XC	XC	XC	XC	VT	XC	XC	XC	XC	XC
		◇1	◇1	◇1	◇1	◇1	◇1	◇1	◇1	◇1	◇1	◇1	◇1	◇1	◇1	◇1	◇1	◇1	◇1	◇1	◇1	◇1	◇1
		A		B				A		C				A		B				A		D	
Bournemouth	d		10 40						11 40						12 40						13 40		
Brockenhurst 3	d		10 57						11 57						12 57						13 57		
Southampton Central	d		11 15						12 15						13 15						14 15		
Southampton Airport Pkway	d		11 22						12 22						13 22						14 22		
Winchester	d		11 31						12 31						13 31						14 31		
Basingstoke	d		11 47						12 47						13 47						14 47		
Guildford	d				12 14																		
Reading 7	d		12 11		12 54				13 11		13 40				14 11		14 40				15 11		15 40
Oxford	d		12 37		13 17				13 37		14 05				14 37		15 06				15 37		16 06
Banbury	d		12 54		13 35				13 54		14 24				14 54		15 25				15 54		16 25
Leamington Spa 8	d		13 12		13 52				14 12		14 42				15 12		15 43				16 12		16 43
Coventry	d		13 26						14 26						15 26						16 26		
Birmingham International	d		13 38						14 38						15 38						16 38		
Penzance	d									09 30													
St Erth	d									09 38													
Hayle	d																						
Camborne	d									09 48													
Redruth	d									09 54													
Truro	d									10 06													
St Austell	d									10 22													
Newquay (Summer Only)	d																						
Par	d									10 30													
Lostwithiel	d																						
Bodmin Parkway	d									10 41													
Liskeard 6	d									10 53													
Plymouth	d			10 25						11 25			12 00			12 25			12 52			13 23	
Totnes	d			10 50						11 50						12 50						13 49	
Paignton	d						10 50																
Torquay	d						10 56																
Newton Abbot	d			11 03			11 08			12 03			12 36			13 03			13 27			14 03	
Teignmouth	d						11 15																
Dawlish	d						11 20																
Exeter St Davids 6	d			11 23			11 32			12 23			12 57			13 23			13 48			14 25	
Tiverton Parkway	d			11 37			11 46			12 37			13 10			13 37						14 39	
Taunton	d			11 53			12 00			12 51			13 25			13 51						14 54	
Weston-super-Mare	d						12 21																
Cardiff Central 7	d	11 45						12 45						13 45						14 45			
Newport (South Wales)	d	11 59						12 59						13 59						14 59			
Bristol Temple Meads 10	d			12 30			13 00			13 30			14 00			14 30			15 00			15 30	
Bristol Parkway 7	d			12 40			13 10			13 40			14 10			14 40			15 10			15 40	
Gloucester 7	d	12 47						13 51						14 47						15 47			
Cheltenham Spa	d	12 58		13 12			13 42	14 02		14 12			14 42	14 58		15 12			15 42	15 58		16 12	
London Paddington	d																						
Birmingham New Street 12	a	13 41	13 48	13 50	14 19		14 26	14 45	14 48	14 50	15 09		15 27	15 41	15 48	15 50	16 12		16 26	16 41	16 48	16 50	17 12
Birmingham New Street 12	d	13 49	14 01	14 03	14 30	14 20	14 31	14 49	15 01	15 03	15 30	15 20	15 31	15 49	16 01	16 03	16 30	16 20	16 31	16 49	17 01	17 03	17 30
Tamworth	d	14 07		14 19				15 09						16 07		16 19				17 07			
Burton-on-Trent	d	14 19						15 21		15 28				16 19						17 19		17 28	
Derby 6	a	14 34		14 42	15 04			15 34		15 42	16 02			16 34		16 42	17 04			17 34		17 39	18 04
Nottingham 8	a	15 02						16 00						17 00						18 00			
Chesterfield	a			15 02						16 02						17 02						18 03	
Sheffield 7	a			15 17	15 47					16 18	16 48					17 17	17 48					18 19	18 46
Doncaster 7	a				16 15						17 13						18 13						19 15
Wakefield Westgate 7	a			15 44						16 44						17 47	18 33					18 47	
Leeds 10	a			16 02						17 02						18 02	18 51					19 04	
York 8	a			16 29	16 40					17 29	17 42					18 29	19 18					19 29	19 43
Darlington 7	a			16 57	17 15					17 57	18 11					18 57	19 46					19 59	20 11
Durham	a			17 14	17 33					18 14	18 29					19 14	20 03					20 17	20 28
Chester-le-Street	a																						
Newcastle 8	a			17 30	17 47					18 28	18 43					19 30	20 19					20 31	20 42
Morpeth	a																					20 52	
Alnmouth for Alnwick	a			18 01												20 04							
Berwick-upon-Tweed	a			18 22						19 17						20 24						21 25	
Dunbar	a									19 40												21 48	
Wolverhampton 7	d		14 19			14 37	14 49		15 19			15 37	15 49		16 19			16 37	16 49		17 19		
Stafford	a		14 33						15 33						16 34						17 35		
Stoke-on-Trent	a		14 56				15 19		15 56				16 19		16 56				17 19		17 56		
Congleton	a																						
Macclesfield	a		15 14						16 14						17 14						18 14		
Crewe 10	a					15 07						16 07						17 07					
Wilmslow	a																						
Stockport	a		15 28						16 28						17 28						18 28		
M'chester Piccadilly 10	a		15 40				15 59		16 40				16 59		17 40				17 56		18 40		
Warrington Bank Quay	a					15 26						16 26						17 26					
Wigan North Western	a					15 37						16 37						17 37					
Preston 8	a					15 51						16 51						17 51					
Lancaster 6	a					16 08						17 08						18 08					
Oxenholme Lake District	a											17 22						18 22					
Penrith North Lakes	a					16 44												18 48					
Carlisle 8	a					17 00						18 01						19 04					
Lockerbie	a																						
Haymarket	a					18 13																	
Edinburgh 10	a			19 06		18 22				20 05						21 08		20 22				22 16	22 23
Haymarket	a			19 22												21 15							
Motherwell	a			20 00												21 53							
Glasgow Central 15	a			20 20								19 17				22 14							
Inverkeithing	a																						
Kirkcaldy	a																						
Markinch	a																						
Ladybank	a																						
Cupar	a																						
Leuchars 3	a																						
Dundee	a																						
Arbroath	a																						
Montrose	a																						
Stonehaven	a																						
Aberdeen	a																						

A from Newport (South Wales)
B to Edinburgh
C from Plymouth
D from Birmingham New Street

Table 51

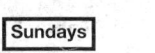

Sundays
until 1 January

South Coast and the South West - North West England, The North East and Scotland

Route Diagram - see first Page of Table 51

		VT	XC	XC	XC	XC	XC	VT	XC	XC	XC	XC	XC	VT	XC	XC	XC	XC	XC	VT	XC	XC
		◇1	◇1	◇1	◇1	◇1	◇1	◇1	◇1	◇1	◇1	◇1	◇1	R 1	◇1	◇1	◇1	◇1	◇1	◇1	◇1	◇1
						A			B				C				D	D				
Bournemouth	d				14 40						15 40						16 40					
Brockenhurst 3	d				14 57						15 57						16 57					
Southampton Central	d				15 15						16 15						17 15					
Southampton Airport Pkwy	d				15 22						16 22						17 22					
Winchester	d				15 31						16 31						17 31					
Basingstoke	d				15 47						16 47						17 47					
Guildford	d																					
Reading 7	d				16 11		16 41				17 11		17 40				18 11		18 41			
Oxford	d				16 37		17 06				17 37		18 06				18 37		19 06			
Banbury	d				16 54		17 25				17 54		18 25				18 54		19 25			
Leamington Spa 8	d				17 12		17 43				18 12		18 43				19 12		19 43			
Coventry	d				17 26						18 26						19 26		19 54			
Birmingham International	d				17 38						18 38						19 38		20 04			
Penzance	d								12 30													
St Erth	d								12 40													
Hayle	d								12 44													
Camborne	d								12 56													
Redruth	d								13 02													
Truro	d								13 14													
St Austell	d								13 30													
Newquay (Summer Only)	d																					
Par	d								13 38													
Lostwithiel	d								13 45													
Bodmin Parkway	d								13 52													
Liskeard 6	d								14 04													
Plymouth	d					14 23			14 35			15 23						16 25				
Totnes	d					14 49			15 00			15 49						16 50				
Paignton	d																					
Torquay	d																					
Newton Abbot	d					15 03			15 12			16 03						17 03				
Teignmouth	d																					
Dawlish	d																					
Exeter St Davids 6	d					15 25			15 33			16 24						17 23				
Tiverton Parkway	d					15 38			15 46			16 37						17 37				
Taunton	d					15 54			16 01			16 53						17 51				
Weston-super-Mare	d								16 30													
Cardiff Central 7	d			15 45						16 45						17 45						18 45
Newport (South Wales)	d			15 59						16 59						17 59						18 59
Bristol Temple Meads 10	d		16 00			16 30			17 00			17 30			18 00			18 30			19 00	
Bristol Parkway 7	d		16 10			16 40			17 10			17 40			18 10			18 40			19 10	
Gloucester 7	d			16 47						17 47						18 47						19 52
Cheltenham Spa	d		16 42	16 58		17 12			17 42	17 58		18 12			18 42	18 58		19 12			19 42	20 02
London Paddington	d																					
Birmingham New Street 12	a		17 26	17 41	17 48	17 49	18 09		18 27	18 41	18 48	18 51	19 11		19 26	19 41	19 48	19 50	20 15		20 26	20 44
Birmingham New Street 12	d	17 20	17 31	17 49	18 01	18 03	18 30	18 20	18 31	18 49	19 01	19 03	19 30	19 20	19 31	19 49	20 01	20 03		20 20	20 31	20 49
Tamworth	d			18 07		18 19				19 09						20 07		20 19				21 06
Burton-on-Trent	d			18 19						19 21		19 26				20 19						21 19
Derby 6	a			18 33		18 39	19 03			19 33		19 39	20 01			20 34		20 39				21 33
Nottingham 8	a			19 00						20 00						21 00						22 00
Chesterfield	a					19 04						20 01						21 02				
Sheffield 7	a					19 20	19 39					20 17	20 39					21 16				
Doncaster 7	a						20 16						21 19									
Wakefield Westgate 7	a					19 48						20 46						21 47				
Leeds 10	a					20 05						21 03						22 04				
York 8	a					20 29	20 45					21 31	21 44									
Darlington 7	a					20 59	21 12						22 22									
Durham	a					21 17	21 31						22 40									
Chester-le-Street	a																					
Newcastle 8	a					21 31	21 44						23 10									
Morpeth	a																					
Alnmouth for Alnwick	a					22 04																
Berwick-upon-Tweed	a																					
Dunbar	a																					
Wolverhampton 7	d	17 37	17 49		18 19			18 37	18 49		19 19			19 37	19 49		20 19			20 38	20 52	
Stafford	a				18 35						19 37						20 36			20 51		
Stoke-on-Trent	a		18 19		18 56				19 19		19 56				20 19		20 56				21 19	
Congleton	a																					
Macclesfield	a				19 15						20 14						21 15					
Crewe 10	a	18 07						19 07						20 07						21 10		
Wilmslow	a																					
Stockport	a				19 28						20 28						21 28					
M'chester Piccadilly 10	a		18 56		19 40				19 58		20 40				21 00		21 40				21 56	
Warrington Bank Quay	a	18 26						19 26						20 26								
Wigan North Western	a	18 37						19 37						20 37								
Preston 8	a	18 51						19 51						20 51								
Lancaster 6	a	19 08						20 08						21 08								
Oxenholme Lake District	a	19 22												21 22								
Penrith North Lakes	a							20 44														
Carlisle 8	a	20 01						21 00						22 01								
Lockerbie	a													22 22								
Haymarket	a							22 15														
Edinburgh 10	a					23 08		22 21														
Haymarket	a																					
Motherwell	a													23 07								
Glasgow Central 15	a	21 17												23 22								
Inverkeithing	a																					
Kirkcaldy	a																					
Markinch	a																					
Ladybank	a																					
Cupar	a																					
Leuchars 3	a																					
Dundee	a																					
Arbroath	a																					
Montrose	a																					
Stonehaven	a																					
Aberdeen	a																					

A to Leeds
B from Plymouth to Birmingham New Street
C to Sheffield
D to Birmingham New Street

Table 51

Sundays
until 1 January

South Coast and the South West - North West England, The North East and Scotland

Route Diagram - see first Page of Table 51

		XC	XC	XC	XC	VT	XC	XC	XC	XC	XC	XC	XC	XC
		◇1	◇1	◇1	◇1	◇1	◇1	◇1	◇1	◇1	◇1	◇1	◇1	◇1
		A	B					C	A					
		☕	☕	☕	☕	🍴		☕	☕					
Bournemouth	d	17 40						18 40			19 40			
Brockenhurst 3	d	17 57						18 57			19 57			
Southampton Central	d	18 15						19 15			20 15			
Southampton Airport Pkway	d	18 22						19 22			20 22			
Winchester	d	18 31						19 31			20 31			
Basingstoke	d	18 47						19 47			20 47			
Guildford	d													
Reading 7	d	19b11		19 40				20e10		20 41	21f11		21 40	
Oxford	d	19 37		20 06				20 37		21 06	21 37		22 06	
Banbury	d	19 54		20 25				20 54		21 24	21 54		22 24	
Leamington Spa 8	d	20 12		20 43				21 12		21 42	22 12		22 42	
Coventry	d	20 26		20 54				21 26		21 53	22 23		22 53	
Birmingham International	d	20 38		21 04				21 38		22 03	22 33		23 03	
Penzance	d		15 30											
St Erth	d		15 38											
Hayle	d													
Camborne	d		15 51											
Redruth	d		15 57											
Truro	d		16 09											
St Austell	d		16 25											
Newquay (Summer Only)	d													
Par	d		16 33											
Lostwithiel	d													
Bodmin Parkway	d		16 44											
Liskeard 6	d		16 56											
Plymouth	d		17c26						18 23					
Totnes	d		17 52						18 49					
Paignton	d				18 20									
Torquay	d				18 26									
Newton Abbot	d		18 04		18 37				19 03					
Teignmouth	d													
Dawlish	d													
Exeter St Davids 6	d		18 23		18 58				19 25					
Tiverton Parkway	d		18 38		19 11				19 38					
Taunton	d		18 52		19 25				19 54					
Weston-super-Mare	d													
Cardiff Central 7	d						19 45					20 45		
Newport (South Wales)	d						20 00					20 59		
Bristol Temple Meads 10	d		19 30		20 00				20 30					22 10
Bristol Parkway 7	d		19 40		20 10				20 40					22 20
Gloucester 7	d						20 50					21 48		
Cheltenham Spa	d		20 12		20 42		21 01		21 12			21 59		22 52
London Paddington	d													
Birmingham New Street 12	a	20 48	20 50	21 15	21 20		21 44	21 48	21 51	22 14	22 42	22 42	23 13	23 39
Birmingham New Street 12	d	21 01	21 03			21 20		22 01	22 03					
Tamworth	d		21 19						22 18					
Burton-on-Trent	d		21 30											
Derby 6	a		21 42						22 40					
Nottingham 8	a													
Chesterfield	a		22 02						23 04					
Sheffield 7	a		22 18						23 20					
Doncaster 7	a													
Wakefield Westgate 7	a		22 43											
Leeds 10	a		23 01						00 16					
York 8	a													
Darlington 7	a													
Durham	a													
Chester-le-Street	a													
Newcastle 8	a													
Morpeth	a													
Alnmouth for Alnwick	a													
Berwick-upon-Tweed	a													
Dunbar	a													
Wolverhampton 7	d	21 19				21 38		22 19						
Stafford	a	21 36				21 56		22 36						
Stoke-on-Trent	a	21 56						22 55						
Congleton	a													
Macclesfield	a	22 14						23 12						
Crewe 10	a					22 17								
Wilmslow	a													
Stockport	a	22 28						23 27						
M'chester Piccadilly 10	a	22 40						23 41						
Warrington Bank Quay	a					22 36								
Wigan North Western	a					22 47								
Preston 8	a					23 07								
Lancaster 6	a													
Oxenholme Lake District	a													
Penrith North Lakes	a													
Carlisle 8	a													
Lockerbie	a													
Haymarket	a													
Edinburgh 10	a													
Haymarket	a													
Motherwell	a													
Glasgow Central 15	a													
Inverkeithing	a													
Kirkcaldy	a													
Markinch	a													
Ladybank	a													
Cupar	a													
Leuchars 8	a													
Dundee	a													
Arbroath	a													
Montrose	a													
Stonehaven	a													
Aberdeen	a													

A ☕ to Birmingham New Street
B ☕ from Plymouth to Birmingham New Street
C ☕ to Reading

Table 51

Sundays

8 January to 12 February

South Coast and the South West - North West England, The North East and Scotland

Route Diagram - see first Page of Table 51

		XC	VT	XC	XC	VT	XC	XC	VT	XC	XC	VT	XC	XC	XC	VT	XC	XC	XC	XC	XC	VT	XC
		◇1	◇1	◇1	◇1	◇1	◇1	◇1	◇1	◇1	◇1	◇1	◇1	◇1	◇1	◇1	◇1	◇1	◇1	◇1	◇1	◇1	◇1
								A						A					B	A			
			☕	🛒	🛒	☕	🛒	🛒	☕	🛒	🛒	☕	🛒	🛒	🛒	☕	🛒	🛒	🛒	🛒	🛒	☕	🛒
Bournemouth	d																						
Brockenhurst 3	d																						
Southampton Central ⛴	d																						
Southampton Airport Pkwy ✈	d																						
Winchester	d																						
Basingstoke	d																						
Guildford	d																						
Reading 7	d																						
Oxford	d																						
Banbury	d																						
Leamington Spa 8	d										10 12				11 12						12 12		
Coventry	d										10 28				11 29						12 28		
Birmingham International ✈	d										10 40				11 40						12 40		
Penzance	d																						
St Erth	d																						
Hayle	d																						
Camborne	d																						
Redruth	d																						
Truro	d																						
St Austell	d																						
Newquay (Summer Only)	d																						
Par	d																						
Lostwithiel	d																						
Bodmin Parkway	d																						
Liskeard 6	d																						
Plymouth	d																			09 25			
Totnes	d																			09 50			
Paignton	d																						
Torquay	d																						
Newton Abbot	d																			10 03			
Teignmouth	d																						
Dawlish	d																						
Exeter St Davids 6	d																			10 23			
Tiverton Parkway	d																			10 37			
Taunton	d																			10 51			
Weston-super-Mare	d																						
Cardiff Central 7	d																		10 45				
Newport (South Wales)	d																		10 59				
Bristol Temple Meads 10	d									09 15				10 30						11 30			
Bristol Parkway 7	d									09 25				10 40						11 40			
Gloucester 7	d									10 01									11 51				
Cheltenham Spa	d									10 12				11 12					12 03	12 12			
London Paddington	d																						
Birmingham New Street 12	a									10 50	10 50			11 50	11 50				12 45	12 50	12 50		
Birmingham New Street 12	d	22p31	08 45	09 01	09 03	09 20	10 01	10 03	10 20	11 03	11 01	11 20	11 49	12 03	12 01	12 20	12 30	12 44	12 49	13 03	13 01	13 20	13 30
Tamworth	d				09 19			10 18					12 07	12 19					13 07				
Burton-on-Trent	d				09 28			10 29		11 26			12 19						13 19	13 26			
Derby 6	a				09 42			10 39		11 40			12 34	12 43			13 01		13 33	13 42			14 01
Nottingham 8 🚊	a												13 00					14 04	14 00				
Chesterfield	a				10 02			11 02		12 02				13 02			13 29			14 02			14 29
Sheffield 7 🚊	a				10 16			11 17		12 18				13 18			13 43			14 17			14 45
Doncaster 7	a																14 13						15 13
Wakefield Westgate 7	a				10 44			11 44		12 44				13 45						14 44			
Leeds 10	a				11 02			12 01		13 02				14 02						15 02			
York 8	a				11 29			12 29		13 29				14 29			14 40			15 29			15 43
Darlington 7	a				11 57			12 57		13 57				14 57			15 13			15 57			16 13
Durham	a				12 14			13 14		14 14				15 14			15 30			16 14			16 30
Chester-le-Street	a																						
Newcastle 8	a				12 29			13 32		14 28				15 28			15 44			16 28			16 44
Morpeth	a									14 48													
Alnmouth for Alnwick	a							13 59						16 01						16 58			
Berwick-upon-Tweed	a							14 20						16 21									
Dunbar	a				13 39					15 40										17 39			
Wolverhampton 7 🚊	d	22p49	09 04	09 19		09 37	10 19		10 37		11 19	11 37			12 19	12 37					13 19	13 37	
Stafford	a	23p01	09 16	09 32			10 32				11 31				12 32						13 33		
Stoke-on-Trent	a	23p20					10 51				11 51				12 52						13 56		
Congleton	a																						
Macclesfield	a	23p38					11 08				12 09				13 10						14 14		
Crewe 10	a		09 35	09 54		10 07			11 07			12 07				13 07						14 07	
Wilmslow	a			10 12																			
Stockport	a	23p53		10 21			11 22				12 22				13 28						14 28		
M'chester Piccadilly 10 🚊	a	00 10		10 37			11 31				12 40				13 40						14 40		
Warrington Bank Quay	a		09 54			10 26			11 26			12 26				13 26						14 26	
Wigan North Western	a		10 05			10 37			11 37			12 37				13 37						14 37	
Preston 8	a		10 22			10 51			11 51			12 51				13 51						14 50	
Lancaster 6	a					11 18			12 08			13 08				14 08						15 08	
Oxenholme Lake District	a					11 32			12 22			13 22										15 22	
Penrith North Lakes	a															14 44							
Carlisle 8	a					12 11			13 01			14 01				15 00						16 01	
Lockerbie	a																						
Haymarket	a								14 13							16 14							
Edinburgh 10	a				14 07			15 05	14 22	16 06				17 06		16 22				18 07			
Haymarket	a							15 14						17 14						18 16			
Motherwell	a							15 51						17 52									
Glasgow Central 15	a					13 22		16 13				15 16		18 12								17 17	
Inverkeithing	a																			18 28			
Kirkcaldy	a																			18 44			
Markinch	a																			18 53			
Ladybank	a																			19 01			
Cupar	a																			19 07			
Leuchars 3	a																			19 14			
Dundee	a																			19 29			
Arbroath	a																			19 46			
Montrose	a																			20 00			
Stonehaven	a																			20 23			
Aberdeen	a																			20 43			

A 🛒 to Edinburgh

B 🛒 from Newport (South Wales)

Table 51

Sundays

8 January to 12 February

South Coast and the South West - North West England, The North East and Scotland

Route Diagram - see first Page of Table 51

		XC	XC	XC	XC	VT	XC	XC	XC	XC	XC	XC	VT	XC	XC	XC	XC	XC	XC	XC	VT	XC	XC
		◇1	◇1	◇1	◇1	◇1	◇1	◇1	◇1	◇1	◇1	◇1	◇1	◇1	◇1	◇1	◇1	◇1	◇1	◇1	◇1	◇1	◇1
			A		B				A		C					A		B					A
		⊼	⊼	⊼	⊼	⊡	⊼	⊼	⊼	⊼	⊼	⊼	⊡	⊼	⊼	⊼	⊼	⊼		⊼	⊡	⊼	⊼
Bournemouth	d																12 40						
Brockenhurst 3	d																12 57						
Southampton Central ⛴	d																13 15						
Southampton Airport Pkway ✈	d																13 22						
Winchester	d																13 31						
Basingstoke	d																13 47						
Guildford	d																						
Reading 7	d																14 11			14 40			
Oxford	d																14 37			15 06			
Banbury	d																14 54			15 25			
Leamington Spa 8	d			13 12						14 12							15 12			15 43			
Coventry	d			13 26						14 26							15 26						
Birmingham International ✈	d			13 38						14 38							15 38						
Penzance	d										09 30												
St Erth	d										09 38												
Hayle	d																						
Camborne	d										09 48												
Redruth	d										09 54												
Truro	d										10 06												
St Austell	d										10 22												
Newquay (Summer Only)	d																						
Par	d										10 30												
Lostwithiel	d																						
Bodmin Parkway	d										10 41												
Liskeard 6	d										10 53												
Plymouth	d				10 25						11 25			12 00				12 25				12 52	
Totnes	d				10 50						11 50							12 50					
Paignton	d						10 50																
Torquay	d						10 56																
Newton Abbot	d				11 03		11 08				12 03			12 36				13 03				13 27	
Teignmouth	d						11 15																
Dawlish	d						11 20																
Exeter St Davids 6	d				11 23		11 32				12 23			12 57				13 23				13 48	
Tiverton Parkway	d				11 37		11 46				12 37			13 10				13 37					
Taunton	d				11 53		12 00				12 51			13 25				13 51					
Weston-super-Mare	d						12 21																
Cardiff Central 7	d		11 45						12 45							13 45							14 45
Newport (South Wales)	d		11 59						12 59							13 59							14 59
Bristol Temple Meads 10	d				12 30		13 00				13 30			14 00				14 30				15 00	
Bristol Parkway 7	d				12 40		13 10				13 40			14 10				14 40				15 10	
Gloucester 7	d		12 47						13 51							14 47							15 47
Cheltenham Spa	d		12 58		13 12		13 42		14 02		14 12			14 42		14 58		15 12				15 42	15 58
London Paddington	d																						
Birmingham New Street 12	a		13 41	13 48	13 50		14 26		14 45	14 48	14 50			15 27		15 41	15 48	15 50		16 12		16 26	16 41
Birmingham New Street 12	d	13 31	13 49	14 01	14 03	14 20	14 31	14 30	14 49	15 01	15 03	14 52	15 20	15 31	15 30	15 49	16 01	16 03	15 52	16 30	16 20	16 31	16 49
Tamworth	d		14 07		14 19				15 09							16 07		16 19					17 07
Burton-on-Trent	d		14 19						15 21		15 28					16 19							17 19
Derby 6	a		14 34		14 42			15 04	15 34		15 42				16 02	16 34		16 42		17 04			17 34
Nottingham 8	a		15 02						16 00			16 13				17 00			17 17				18 00
Chesterfield	a				15 02						16 02							17 02					
Sheffield 7	a				15 17			15 47			16 18				16 48			17 17		17 48			
Doncaster 7	a							16 15							17 13					18 13			
Wakefield Westgate 7	a				15 44						16 44							17 47		18 33			
Leeds 10	a				16 02						17 02							18 02		18 51			
York 8	a				16 29			16 40			17 29				17 42			18 29		19 18			
Darlington 7	a				16 57			17 15			17 57				18 11			18 57		19 46			
Durham	a				17 14			17 33			18 14				18 29			19 14		20 03			
Chester-le-Street	a																						
Newcastle 8	a				17 30			17 47			18 28				18 43			19 30		20 19			
Morpeth	a																						
Alnmouth for Alnwick	a				18 01													20 04					
Berwick-upon-Tweed	a				18 22						19 17							20 24					
Dunbar	a										19 40												
Wolverhampton 7	d	13 49		14 19		14 37	14 49			15 19			15 37	15 49			16 19				16 37	16 49	
Stafford	a			14 33						15 33							16 34						
Stoke-on-Trent	a	14 19		14 56			15 19			15 56				16 19			16 56					17 19	
Congleton	a																						
Macclesfield	a			15 14						16 14							17 14						
Crewe 10	a					15 07							16 07								17 07		
Wilmslow	a																						
Stockport	a			15 28						16 28							17 28						
M'chester Piccadilly 10	a	14 57		15 40			15 59			16 40				16 59			17 40					17 56	
Warrington Bank Quay	a					15 26							16 26								17 26		
Wigan North Western	a					15 37							16 37								17 37		
Preston 8	a					15 51							16 51								17 51		
Lancaster 6	a					16 08							17 08								18 08		
Oxenholme Lake District	a												17 22								18 22		
Penrith North Lakes	a					16 44															18 48		
Carlisle 8	a					17 00							18 01								19 04		
Lockerbie	a																						
Haymarket	a					18 13																	
Edinburgh 10	a				19 06	18 22					20 05							21 08			20 22		
Haymarket	a				19 22													21 15					
Motherwell	a				20 00													21 53					
Glasgow Central 15	a				20 20								19 17					22 14					
Inverkeithing	a																						
Kirkcaldy	a																						
Markinch	a																						
Ladybank	a																						
Cupar	a																						
Leuchars 3	a																						
Dundee	a																						
Arbroath	a																						
Montrose	a																						
Stonehaven	a																						
Aberdeen	a																						

A ⊼ from Newport (South Wales)

B ⊼ to Edinburgh

C ⊼ from Plymouth

Table 51

Sundays

8 January to 12 February

South Coast and the South West - North West England, The North East and Scotland

Route Diagram - see first Page of Table 51

		XC	XC	XC	VT	XC	XC	XC	XC	XC	XC	VT	XC	XC	XC	XC	XC	XC	VT	XC	XC	XC
		◇1	◇1	◇1	◇1	◇1	◇1	◇1	◇1	◇1	◇1	◇1	◇1	◇1	◇1	◇1	◇1	◇1	■ 1	◇1	◇1	◇1
			A						B				C					D				E
		⊼	⊼	⊼	⊐	⊼		⊼	⊼		⊼	⊐	⊼		⊼	⊼		⊼	⊐	⊼		⊼
Bournemouth	d	13 40						14 40							15 40							16 40
Brockenhurst 3	d	13 57						14 57							15 57							16 57
Southampton Central	d	14 15						15 15							16 15							17 15
Southampton Airport Pkway	d	14 22						15 22							16 22							17 22
Winchester	d	14 31						15 31							16 31							17 31
Basingstoke	d	14 47						15 47							16 47							17 47
Guildford	d																					
Reading 7	d	15 11		15 40				16 09			16 41				17 09			17 40				18 09
Oxford	d	15 37		16 06				16 37			17 06				17 37			18 06				18 37
Banbury	d	15 54		16 25				16 54			17 25				17 54			18 25				18 54
Leamington Spa 8	d	16 12		16 43				17 12			17 43				18 12			18 43				19 12
Coventry	d	16 26						17 26							18 26							19 26
Birmingham International	d	16 38						17 38							18 38							19 38
Penzance	d												12 30									
St Erth	d												12 40									
Hayle	d												12 44									
Camborne	d												12 56									
Redruth	d												13 02									
Truro	d												13 14									
St Austell	d												13 30									
Newquay (Summer Only)	d																					
Par	d												13 38									
Lostwithiel	d												13 45									
Bodmin Parkway	d												13 52									
Liskeard 6	d												14 04									
Plymouth	d		13 23						14 23				14 35			15 23						
Totnes	d		13 49						14 49				15 00			15 49						
Paignton	d																					
Torquay	d																					
Newton Abbot	d		14 03						15 03				15 12			16 03						
Teignmouth	d																					
Dawlish	d																					
Exeter St Davids 6	d		14 25						15 25				15 33			16 24						
Tiverton Parkway	d		14 39						15 38				15 46			16 37						
Taunton	d		14 54						15 54				16 01			16 53						
Weston-super-Mare	d												16 30									
Cardiff Central 7	d						15 45							16 45							17 45	
Newport (South Wales)	d						15 59							16 59							17 59	
Bristol Temple Meads 10	d		15 30			16 00			16 30				17 00			17 30				18 00		
Bristol Parkway 7	d		15 40			16 10			16 40				17 10			17 40				18 10		
Gloucester 7	d						16 47							17 47							18 47	
Cheltenham Spa	d		16 12			16 42	16 58		17 12				17 42	17 58		18 12				18 42	18 58	
London Paddington	d																					
Birmingham New Street 12	a	16 48	16 50	17 12		17 26	17 41	17 48	17 49		18 09		18 27	18 41	18 48	18 51		19 11		19 26	19 41	19 48
Birmingham New Street 12	d	17 01	17 03	17 30	17 20	17 31	17 49	18 01	18 03	17 52	18 30	18 20	18 31	18 49	19 01	19 03	18 52	19 30	19 20	19 31	19 49	20 01
Tamworth	d						18 07		18 19					19 09							20 07	
Burton-on-Trent	d		17 28				18 19							19 21		19 26					20 19	
Derby 6	a		17 39	18 04			18 33		18 39		19 03			19 33		19 39		20 01			20 34	
Nottingham 8	a						19 00			19 18				20 00			20 16				21 00	
Chesterfield	a		18 03						19 04							20 01						
Sheffield 7	a		18 19	18 46					19 20		19 39					20 17		20 38				
Doncaster 7	a			19 15							20 16							21 19				
Wakefield Westgate 7	a		18 47						19 48							20 46						
Leeds 10	a		19 04						20 05							21 03						
York 8	a		19 29	19 43					20 29		20 45					21 31		21 44				
Darlington 7	a		19 59	20 11					20 59		21 12							22 22				
Durham	a		20 17	20 28					21 17		21 31							22 40				
Chester-le-Street	a																					
Newcastle 8	a		20 31	20 42					21 31		21 44							23 10				
Morpeth	a		20 52																			
Alnmouth for Alnwick	a								22 04													
Berwick-upon-Tweed	a		21 25																			
Dunbar	a		21 48																			
Wolverhampton 7	d	17 19			17 37	17 49		18 19				18 37	18 49		19 19				19 37	19 49		20 19
Stafford	a	17 35						18 35							19 37							20 36
Stoke-on-Trent	a	17 56				18 19		18 56					19 19		19 56					20 19		20 56
Congleton	a																					
Macclesfield	a	18 14						19 15							20 14							21 15
Crewe 10	a				18 07							19 07							20 07			
Wilmslow	a																					
Stockport	a	18 28						19 28							20 28							21 28
M'chester Piccadilly 10	a	18 40				18 56		19 40					19 58		20 40					21 00		21 40
Warrington Bank Quay	a				18 26							19 26							20 26			
Wigan North Western	a				18 37							19 37							20 37			
Preston 8	a				18 51							19 51							20 51			
Lancaster 6	a				19 08							20 08							21 08			
Oxenholme Lake District	a				19 22														21 22			
Penrith North Lakes	a											20 44										
Carlisle 8	a				20 01							21 00							22 01			
Lockerbie	a																		22 22			
Haymarket	a											22 15										
Edinburgh 10	a		22 16	22 23					23 08			22 21										
Haymarket	a																					
Motherwell	a																		23 07			
Glasgow Central 15	a				21 17														23 22			
Inverkeithing	a																					
Kirkcaldy	a																					
Markinch	a																					
Ladybank	a																					
Cupar	a																					
Leuchars 3	a																					
Dundee	a																					
Arbroath	a																					
Montrose	a																					
Stonehaven	a																					
Aberdeen	a																					

A ⊼ from Birmingham New Street
B ⊼ to Leeds
C ⊼ from Plymouth to Birmingham New Street
D ⊼ to Sheffield
E ⊼ to Birmingham New Street

Table 51

Sundays

8 January to 12 February

South Coast and the South West - North West England, The North East and Scotland

Route Diagram - see first Page of Table 51

		XC	XC	XC	VT	XC	XC	XC		XC	XC	XC	VT	XC	XC	XC	XC	XC		XC	XC	XC			
		◇1	◇1	◇1	◇1	◇1	◇1	◇1		◇1	◇1	◇1	◇1	◇1	◇1	◇1	◇1	◇1		◇1	◇1	◇1			
		A						A		B					C	A									
		⊼		⊼	☕	⊼		⊼		⊼	⊼	⊼	☕		⊼	⊼									
Bournemouth	d							17 40							18 40			19 40							
Brockenhurst 3	d							17 57							18 57			19 57							
Southampton Central	d							18 15							19 15			20 15							
Southampton Airport Pkway	d							18 22							19 22			20 22							
Winchester	d							18 31							19 31			20 31							
Basingstoke	d							18 47							19 47			20 47							
Guildford	d																								
Reading 7	d			18 41				19 09			19 40				20 09		20 41	21 09			21 40				
Oxford	d			19 06				19 37			20 06				20 37		21 06	21 37			22 06				
Banbury	d			19 25				19 54			20 25				20 54		21 24	21 54			22 24				
Leamington Spa 8	d			19 43				20 12			20 43				21 12		21 42	22 12			22 42				
Coventry	d			19 54				20 26			20 54				21 26		21 53	22 23			22 53				
Birmingham International	d			20 04				20 38			21 04				21 38		22 03	22 33			23 03				
Penzance	d									15 30															
St Erth	d									15 38															
Hayle	d																								
Camborne	d									15 51															
Redruth	d									15 57															
Truro	d									16 09															
St Austell	d									16 25															
Newquay (Summer Only)	d																								
Par	d									16 33															
Lostwithiel	d																								
Bodmin Parkway	d									16 44															
Liskeard 6	d									16 56															
Plymouth	d	16 25								17 26						18 23									
Totnes	d	16 50								17 52						18 49									
Paignton	d											18 20													
Torquay	d											18 26													
Newton Abbot	d	17 03								18 04		18 37				19 03									
Teignmouth	d																								
Dawlish	d																								
Exeter St Davids 6	d	17 23								18 23		18 58				19 25									
Tiverton Parkway	d	17 37								18 38		19 11				19 38									
Taunton	d	17 51								18 52		19 25				19 54									
Weston-super-Mare	d																								
Cardiff Central 7	d						18 45							19 45						20 45					
Newport (South Wales)	d						18 59							20 00						20 59					
Bristol Temple Meads 10	d	18 30				19 00				19 30		20 00				20 30						22 10			
Bristol Parkway 7	d	18 40				19 10				19 40		20 10				20 40						22 20			
Gloucester 7	d						19 52							20 50						21 48					
Cheltenham Spa	d	19 12				19 42	20 02			20 12		20 42		21 01		21 12				21 59		22 52			
London Paddington	d																								
Birmingham New Street 12	a	19 50		20 15		20 26	20 44	20 48		20 50	21 15	21 20		21 44	21 48	21 51	22 14	22 42		22 42	23 13	23 39			
Birmingham New Street 12	d	20 03	19 52		20 20	20 31	20 49	21 01		21 03			21 20		22 01	22 03									
Tamworth	d	20 19					21 06			21 19						22 18									
Burton-on-Trent	d						21 19			21 30															
Derby 6	a	20 39					21 33			21 42						22 40									
Nottingham 8	a		21 13				22 00																		
Chesterfield	a	21 02								22 02						23 04									
Sheffield 7	a	21 16								22 18						23 20									
Doncaster 7	a																								
Wakefield Westgate 7	a	21 47								22 43															
Leeds 10	a	22 04								23 01						00 16									
York 8	a																								
Darlington 7	a																								
Durham	a																								
Chester-le-Street	a																								
Newcastle 8	a																								
Morpeth	a																								
Alnmouth for Alnwick	a																								
Berwick-upon-Tweed	a																								
Dunbar	a																								
Wolverhampton 7	d				20 38	20 52		21 19					21 38		22 19										
Stafford	a				20 51			21 36					21 56		22 36										
Stoke-on-Trent	a					21 19		21 56							22 55										
Congleton	a																								
Macclesfield	a							22 14							23 12										
Crewe 10	a				21 10								22 17												
Wilmslow	a																								
Stockport	a							22 28							23 27										
M'chester Piccadilly 10	a					21 56		22 40							23 41										
Warrington Bank Quay	a												22 36												
Wigan North Western	a												22 47												
Preston 8	a												23 07												
Lancaster 6	a																								
Oxenholme Lake District	a																								
Penrith North Lakes	a																								
Carlisle 8	a																								
Lockerbie	a																								
Haymarket	a																								
Edinburgh 10	a																								
Haymarket	a																								
Motherwell	a																								
Glasgow Central 15	a																								
Inverkeithing	a																								
Kirkcaldy	a																								
Markinch	a																								
Ladybank	a																								
Cupar	a																								
Leuchars 3	a																								
Dundee	a																								
Arbroath	a																								
Montrose	a																								
Stonehaven	a																								
Aberdeen	a																								

A ⊼ to Birmingham New Street **B** ⊼ from Plymouth to Birmingham New Street **C** ⊼ to Reading

Table 51

Sundays

19 February to 25 March

South Coast and the South West - North West England, The North East and Scotland

Route Diagram - see first Page of Table 51

		XC	VT	XC	XC	VT	XC	XC	VT	XC	XC	VT	XC	XC	XC	VT	XC	XC	XC	XC	VT	XC	XC
		◇1	◇1	◇1	◇1	◇1	◇1	◇1	◇1	◇1	◇1	◇1	◇1	◇1	◇1	◇1	◇1	◇1	◇1	◇1	◇1	◇1	◇1
								A						A				B	A				
			Shop	Trolley	Trolley	Shop	Trolley	Trolley	Shop	Trolley	Trolley	Shop	Trolley	Trolley	Trolley	Shop	Trolley	Trolley	Trolley	Trolley	Shop	Trolley	Trolley
Bournemouth	d																						
Brockenhurst 3	d																						
Southampton Central	d																						
Southampton Airport Pkway	d																						
Winchester	d																						
Basingstoke	d																						
Guildford	d																						
Reading 7	d																						
Oxford	d																						
Banbury	d																						
Leamington Spa 8	d										10 12				11 12					12 12			
Coventry	d										10 28				11 29					12 28			
Birmingham International	d										10 40				11 40					12 40			
Penzance	d																						
St Erth	d																						
Hayle	d																						
Camborne	d																						
Redruth	d																						
Truro	d																						
St Austell	d																						
Newquay (Summer Only)	d																						
Par	d																						
Lostwithiel	d																						
Bodmin Parkway	d																						
Liskeard 6	d																						
Plymouth	d																						
Totnes	d																						
Paignton	d																						
Torquay	d																						
Newton Abbot	d																						
Teignmouth	d																						
Dawlish	d																						
Exeter St Davids 6	d																						
Tiverton Parkway	d																						
Taunton	d																						
Weston-super-Mare	d																						
Cardiff Central 7	d																	10 45					
Newport (South Wales)	d																	10 59					
Bristol Temple Meads 10	d									09 15				10 30					11 30				
Bristol Parkway 7	d									09 25				10 40					11 40				
Gloucester 7	d									10 01								11 51					
Cheltenham Spa	d									10 12				11 12				12 03	12 12				
London Paddington	d																						
Birmingham New Street 12	a									10 50	10 50			11 50	11 50			12 45	12 50	12 50			
Birmingham New Street 12	d	22p31	08 45	09 01	09 03	09 20	10 01	10 03	10 20	11 03	11 01	11 20	11 49	12 03	12 01	12 20	12 30	12 49	13 03	13 01	13 20	13 30	13 31
Tamworth	d				09 19			10 18					12 07	12 19				13 07					
Burton-on-Trent	d				09 28			10 29		11 26			12 19					13 19	13 26				
Derby 6	a				09 42			10 39		11 40			12 34	12 43			13 01	13 33	13 44			14 01	
Nottingham 8	a												13 00					14 00					
Chesterfield	a				10 02			11 02		12 02				13 02			13 29		14 02			14 29	
Sheffield 7	a				10 16			11 17		12 18				13 18			13 43		14 17			14 45	
Doncaster 7	a																14 13					15 13	
Wakefield Westgate 7	a				10 44			11 44		12 44				13 45					14 44				
Leeds 10	a				11 02			12 01		13 02				14 02					15 02				
York 8	a				11 29			12 29		13 29				14 29			14 40		15 29			15 43	
Darlington 7	a				11 57			12 57		13 57				14 57			15 13		15 57			16 13	
Durham	a				12 14			13 14		14 14				15 14			15 30		16 14			16 30	
Chester-le-Street	a																						
Newcastle 8	a				12 29			13 32		14 28				15 28			15 44		16 28			16 44	
Morpeth	a									14 48													
Alnmouth for Alnwick	a							13 59						16 01					16 58				
Berwick-upon-Tweed	a							14 20						16 21									
Dunbar	a				13 39					15 40									17 39				
Wolverhampton 7	d	22p49	09 04	09 19		09 37	10 19		10 37		11 19	11 37			12 19	12 37				13 19	13 37		13 49
Stafford	a	23p01	09 16	09 32			10 32				11 31				12 32					13 33			
Stoke-on-Trent	a	23p20					10 51				11 51				12 52					13 56			14 19
Congleton	a																						
Macclesfield	a	23p38					11 08				12 09				13 10					14 14			
Crewe 10	a		09 35	09 54		10 07			11 07			12 07				13 07					14 07		
Wilmslow	a			10 12																			
Stockport	a	23p53		10 21			11 22				12 22				13 28					14 28			
M'chester Piccadilly 10	a	00 10		10 37			11 31				12 40				13 40					14 40			14 57
Warrington Bank Quay	a		09 54			10 26			11 26			12 26				13 26					14 26		
Wigan North Western	a		10 05			10 37			11 37			12 37				13 37					14 37		
Preston 8	a		10 22			10 51			11 51			12 51				13 51					14 50		
Lancaster 6	a					11 18			12 08			13 08				14 08					15 08		
Oxenholme Lake District	a					11 32			12 22			13 22									15 22		
Penrith North Lakes	a															14 44							
Carlisle 8	a					12 11			13 01			14 01				15 00					16 01		
Lockerbie	a																						
Haymarket	a								14 13							16 14							
Edinburgh 10	a				14 07			15 05	14 22	16 06				17 06		16 22			18 07				
Haymarket	a							15 14						17 14					18 16				
Motherwell	a							15 51						17 52									
Glasgow Central 15	a					13 22		16 13				15 16		18 12							17 17		
Inverkeithing	a																		18 28				
Kirkcaldy	a																		18 44				
Markinch	a																		18 53				
Ladybank	a																		19 01				
Cupar	a																		19 07				
Leuchars 3	a																		19 14				
Dundee	a																		19 29				
Arbroath	a																		19 46				
Montrose	a																		20 00				
Stonehaven	a																		20 23				
Aberdeen	a																		20 43				

A Trolley to Edinburgh

B Trolley from Newport (South Wales)

Table 51

Sundays

19 February to 25 March

South Coast and the South West - North West England, The North East and Scotland

Route Diagram - see first Page of Table 51

		XC	XC	XC	VT	XC	XC	XC	XC	XC	VT	XC	XC	XC	XC	XC	XC	VT	XC	XC	XC	XC	XC
		◇1	◇1	◇1	◇1	◇1	◇1	◇1	◇1	◇1	◇1	◇1	◇1	◇1	◇1	◇1	◇1	◇1	◇1	◇1	◇1	◇1	◇1
		A		B				A						A		B				A			
Bournemouth	d														12 40						13 40		
Brockenhurst 3	d														12 57						13 57		
Southampton Central	d														13 15						14 15		
Southampton Airport Pkway	d														13 22						14 22		
Winchester	d														13 31						14 31		
Basingstoke	d														13 47						14 47		
Guildford	d																						
Reading 7	d														14 11		14 40				15 11		15 40
Oxford	d														14 37		15 06				15 37		16 06
Banbury	d														14 54		15 25				15 54		16 25
Leamington Spa 8	d		13 12						14 12						15 12		15 43				16 12		16 43
Coventry	d		13 26						14 26						15 26						16 26		
Birmingham International	d		13 38						14 38						15 38						16 38		
Penzance	d																						
St Erth	d																						
Hayle	d																						
Camborne	d																						
Redruth	d																						
Truro	d																						
St Austell	d																						
Newquay (Summer Only)	d																						
Par	d																						
Lostwithiel	d																						
Bodmin Parkway	d																						
Liskeard 6	d																						
Plymouth	d																						
Totnes	d																						
Paignton	d					10 50																	
Torquay	d					10 56																	
Newton Abbot	d					11 08				12 00						13 03						14 03	
Teignmouth	d					11 15																	
Dawlish	d					11 20																	
Exeter St Davids 6	d					11 32				12 23						13 23						14 25	
Tiverton Parkway	d					11 46				12 37						13 37						14 39	
Taunton	d					12 00				12 51						13 51						14 54	
Weston-super-Mare	d					12 21																	
Cardiff Central 7	d	11 45						12 45						13 45						14 45			
Newport (South Wales)	d	11 59						12 59						13 59						14 59			
Bristol Temple Meads 10	d			12 30		13 00				13 30		14 00				14 30			15 00			15 30	
Bristol Parkway 7	d			12 40		13 10				13 40		14 10				14 40			15 10			15 40	
Gloucester 7	d	12 47						13 51						14 47						15 47			
Cheltenham Spa	d	12 58		13 12		13 42		14 02		14 12		14 42		14 58		15 12			15 42	15 58		16 12	
London Paddington	d																						
Birmingham New Street 12	a	13 41	13 48	13 50		14 26		14 45	14 48	14 50		15 27		15 41	15 48	15 50	16 12		16 26	16 41	16 48	16 50	17 12
Birmingham New Street 12	d	13 49	14 01	14 03	14 20	14 31	14 30	14 49	15 01	15 03	15 20	15 31	15 30	15 49	16 01	16 03	16 30	16 20	16 31	16 49	17 01	17 03	17 30
Tamworth	d	14 07		14 19				15 09						16 07		16 19				17 07			
Burton-on-Trent	d	14 19						15 21		15 28				16 19						17 19		17 28	
Derby 6	a	14 34		14 42			15 04	15 34		15 42			16 02	16 34		16 42	17 04			17 34		17 39	18 04
Nottingham 8	a	15 02						16 00						17 00						18 00			
Chesterfield	a			15 02						16 02						17 02						18 03	
Sheffield 7	a			15 17			15 47			16 18			16 48			17 17	17 48					18 19	18 46
Doncaster 7	a						16 15						17 13				18 13						19 15
Wakefield Westgate 7	a			15 44						16 44						17 48	18 33					18 47	
Leeds 10	a			16 02						17 02						18 02	18 51					19 04	
York 8	a			16 29			16 40			17 29			17 42			18 29	19 18					19 29	19 43
Darlington 7	a			16 57			17 15			17 57			18 11			18 57	19 46					19 59	20 11
Durham	a			17 14			17 33			18 14			18 29			19 14	20 03					20 17	20 28
Chester-le-Street	a																						
Newcastle 8	a			17 30			17 47			18 28			18 43			19 30	20 19					20 31	20 42
Morpeth	a																					20 52	
Alnmouth for Alnwick	a			18 01												20 04							
Berwick-upon-Tweed	a			18 22						19 17						20 24						21 25	
Dunbar	a									19 40												21 48	
Wolverhampton 7	d		14 19		14 37	14 49			15 19		15 37	15 49			16 19			16 37	16 49		17 19		
Stafford	a		14 33						15 33						16 34						17 35		
Stoke-on-Trent	a		14 56			15 19			15 56			16 19			16 56				17 19		17 56		
Congleton	a																						
Macclesfield	a		15 14						16 14						17 14						18 14		
Crewe 10	a				15 07						16 07							17 07					
Wilmslow	a																						
Stockport	a		15 28						16 28						17 28						18 28		
M'chester Piccadilly 10	a		15 40			16 00			16 40			16 59			17 40				17 56		18 40		
Warrington Bank Quay	a				15 26						16 26							17 26					
Wigan North Western	a				15 37						16 37							17 37					
Preston 8	a				15 51						16 51							17 51					
Lancaster 6	a				16 08						17 08							18 08					
Oxenholme Lake District	a										17 22							18 22					
Penrith North Lakes	a				16 44													18 48					
Carlisle 8	a				17 00						18 01							19 04					
Lockerbie	a																						
Haymarket	a				18 13																		
Edinburgh 10	a			19 06	18 22					20 05						21 08		20 22				22 16	22 23
Haymarket	a			19 22												21 15							
Motherwell	a			20 00												21 53							
Glasgow Central 15	a			20 20							19 17					22 14							
Inverkeithing	a																						
Kirkcaldy	a																						
Markinch	a																						
Ladybank	a																						
Cupar	a																						
Leuchars 3	a																						
Dundee	a																						
Arbroath	a																						
Montrose	a																						
Stonehaven	a																						
Aberdeen	a																						

A from Newport (South Wales)

B to Edinburgh

Sundays

19 February to 25 March

South Coast and the South West - North West England, The North East and Scotland

Route Diagram - see first Page of Table 51

		VT		XC	XC	XC	XC	XC	VT	XC	XC	XC		XC	XC	VT	XC	XC	XC	XC	XC	VT		XC	XC
																■									
		◇1		◇1	◇1	◇1	◇1	◇1	◇1	◇1	◇1	◇1		◇1	◇1	1	◇1	◇1	◇1	◇1	◇1	◇1		◇1	◇1
							A			B					C				B	B					
		⊒		⊼		⊼	⊼	⊼	⊒	⊼		⊼		⊼	⊼	⊒	⊼		⊼	⊼	⊼	⊒		⊼	
Bournemouth	d					14 40						15 40							16 40						
Brockenhurst 3	d					14 57						15 57							16 57						
Southampton Central	d					15 15						16 15							17 15						
Southampton Airport Pkwy	d					15 22						16 22							17 22						
Winchester	d					15 31						16 31							17 31						
Basingstoke	d					15 47						16 47							17 47						
Guildford	d																								
Reading 7	d					16 09		16 41				17 09			17 40				18 09		18 41				
Oxford	d					16 37		17 06				17 37			18 06				18 37		19 06				
Banbury	d					16 54		17 25				17 54			18 25				18 54		19 25				
Leamington Spa 8	d					17 12		17 43				18 12			18 43				19 12		19 43				
Coventry	d					17 26						18 26							19 26		19 54				
Birmingham International	d					17 38						18 38							19 38		20 04				
Penzance	d																								
St Erth	d																								
Hayle	d																								
Camborne	d																								
Redruth	d																								
Truro	d																								
St Austell	d																								
Newquay (Summer Only)	d																								
Par	d																								
Lostwithiel	d																								
Bodmin Parkway	d																								
Liskeard 6	d																								
Plymouth	d																								
Totnes	d																								
Paignton	d																								
Torquay	d																								
Newton Abbot	d						15 01							16 01						17 03					
Teignmouth	d																								
Dawlish	d																								
Exeter St Davids 6	d						15 25							16 25						17 23					
Tiverton Parkway	d						15 38							16 38						17 37					
Taunton	d						15 54							16 54						17 51					
Weston-super-Mare	d																								
Cardiff Central 7	d				15 45						16 45							17 45							18 45
Newport (South Wales)	d				15 59						16 59							17 59							18 59
Bristol Temple Meads 10	d			16 00			16 30			17 00				17 30			18 00			18 30				19 00	
Bristol Parkway 7	d			16 10			16 40			17 10				17 40			18 10			18 40				19 10	
Gloucester 7	d				16 47						17 47							18 47							19 52
Cheltenham Spa	d			16 42	16 58		17 12			17 42	17 58			18 12			18 42	18 58		19 12				19 42	20 02
London Paddington	d																								
Birmingham New Street 12	a			17 26	17 41	17 48	17 49	18 09		18 27	18 41	18 48		18 51	19 11		19 26	19 41	19 48	19 50	20 15			20 26	20 44
Birmingham New Street 12	d	17 20		17 31	17 49	18 01	18 03	18 30	18 20	18 31	18 49	19 01		19 03	19 30	19 20	19 31	19 49	20 01	20 03		20 20		20 31	20 49
Tamworth	d				18 07		18 19				19 09							20 07		20 19					21 06
Burton-on-Trent	d				18 19						19 21			19 26				20 19							21 19
Derby 6	a				18 33		18 39	19 03			19 33			19 39	20 01			20 34		20 39					21 33
Nottingham 8	a				19 00						20 00							21 00							22 00
Chesterfield	a						19 04							20 01						21 02					
Sheffield 7	a						19 20	19 39						20 17	20 38					21 16					
Doncaster 7	a							20 16							21 19										
Wakefield Westgate 7	a						19 48							20 46						21 47					
Leeds 10	a						20 05							21 03						22 04					
York 8	a						20 29	20 45						21 31	21 44										
Darlington 7	a						20 59	21 12							22 22										
Durham	a						21 17	21 31							22 40										
Chester-le-Street	a																								
Newcastle 8	a						21 31	21 44							23 10										
Morpeth	a																								
Alnmouth for Alnwick	a						22 04																		
Berwick-upon-Tweed	a																								
Dunbar	a																								
Wolverhampton 7	d	17 37		17 49		18 19			18 37	18 49		19 19				19 37	19 49		20 19			20 38		20 52	
Stafford	a					18 35						19 37							20 36			20 51			
Stoke-on-Trent	a			18 19		18 56				19 19		19 56					20 19		20 56					21 19	
Congleton	a																								
Macclesfield	a					19 15						20 14							21 15						
Crewe 10	a	18 07							19 07							20 07						21 10			
Wilmslow	a																								
Stockport	a					19 28						20 28							21 28						
M'chester Piccadilly 10	a			18 56		19 40				19 58		20 40					21 00		21 40					21 56	
Warrington Bank Quay	a	18 26							19 26							20 26									
Wigan North Western	a	18 37							19 37							20 37									
Preston 8	a	18 51							19 51							20 51									
Lancaster 6	a	19 08							20 08							21 08									
Oxenholme Lake District	a	19 22														21 22									
Penrith North Lakes	a								20 44																
Carlisle 8	a	20 01							21 00							22 01									
Lockerbie	a															22 22									
Haymarket	a								22 15																
Edinburgh 10	a						23 08		22 21																
Haymarket	a																								
Motherwell	a															23 07									
Glasgow Central 15	a	21 17														23 22									
Inverkeithing	a																								
Kirkcaldy	a																								
Markinch	a																								
Ladybank	a																								
Cupar	a																								
Leuchars 3	a																								
Dundee	a																								
Arbroath	a																								
Montrose	a																								
Stonehaven	a																								
Aberdeen	a																								

A ⊼ to Leeds

B ⊼ to Birmingham New Street

C ⊼ to Sheffield

Table 51

Sundays

19 February to 25 March

South Coast and the South West - North West England, The North East and Scotland

Route Diagram - see first Page of Table 51

		XC	XC	XC	XC	VT	XC	XC		XC	XC	XC	XC	XC	XC	XC
		◇1	◇1	◇1	◇1	◇1	◇1	◇1		◇1	◇1	◇1	◇1	◇1	◇1	◇1
		A	A					B		A						
		🛒	🛒	🛒	🛒	☕		🛒		🛒						
Bournemouth	d	17 40						18 40				19 40				
Brockenhurst [3]	d	17 57						18 57				19 57				
Southampton Central ⛴	d	18 15						19 15				20 15				
Southampton Airport Pkwy ✈	d	18 22						19 22				20 22				
Winchester	d	18 31						19 31				20 31				
Basingstoke	d	18 47						19 47				20 47				
Guildford	d															
Reading [7]	d	19 09		19 40				20 09			20 41	21 09			21 40	
Oxford	d	19 37		20 06				20 37			21 06	21 37			22 06	
Banbury	d	19 54		20 25				20 54			21 24	21 54			22 24	
Leamington Spa [8]	d	20 12		20 43				21 12			21 42	22 12			22 42	
Coventry	d	20 26		20 54				21 26			21 53	22 23			22 53	
Birmingham International ✈	d	20 38		21 04				21 38			22 03	22 33			23 03	
Penzance	d															
St Erth	d															
Hayle	d															
Camborne	d															
Redruth	d															
Truro	d															
St Austell	d															
Newquay (Summer Only)	d															
Par	d															
Lostwithiel	d															
Bodmin Parkway	d															
Liskeard [6]	d															
Plymouth	d															
Totnes	d															
Paignton	d															
Torquay	d															
Newton Abbot	d		18 04							19 03				19 50		
Teignmouth	d															
Dawlish	d															
Exeter St Davids [6]	d		18 23							19 25				20 10		20 45
Tiverton Parkway	d		18 38							19 38				20 24		20 58
Taunton	d		18 52							19 54				20 40		21 13
Weston-super-Mare	d															
Cardiff Central [7]	d						19 45						20 45			
Newport (South Wales)	d						20 00						20 59			
Bristol Temple Meads [10]	d		19 30		20 00					20 30				21 20		22 10
Bristol Parkway [7]	d		19 40		20 10					20 40				21 30		22 20
Gloucester [7]	d						20 50						21 48			
Cheltenham Spa	d		20 12		20 42		21 01			21 12			21 59	22 05		22 52
London Paddington	d															
Birmingham New Street [12]	a	20 48	20 50	21 15	21 20		21 44	21 48		21 51	22 14	22 42	22 42	22 46	23 13	23 39
Birmingham New Street [12]	d	21 01	21 03			21 20		22 01		22 03						
Tamworth	d		21 19							22 18						
Burton-on-Trent	d		21 30													
Derby [6]	a		21 42							22 40						
Nottingham [8] ⛴	a															
Chesterfield	a		22 02							23 04						
Sheffield [7] ⛴	a		22 18							23 20						
Doncaster [7]	a															
Wakefield Westgate [7]	a		22 43													
Leeds [10]	a		23 01							00 16						
York [8]	a															
Darlington [7]	a															
Durham	a															
Chester-le-Street	a															
Newcastle [8]	a															
Morpeth	a															
Alnmouth for Alnwick	a															
Berwick-upon-Tweed	a															
Dunbar	a															
Wolverhampton [7] ⛴	d	21 19				21 38		22 19								
Stafford	a	21 36				21 56		22 36								
Stoke-on-Trent	a	21 56						22 55								
Congleton	a															
Macclesfield	a	22 14						23 12								
Crewe [10]	a					22 17										
Wilmslow	a															
Stockport	a	22 28						23 27								
M'chester Piccadilly [10] ⛴	a	22 40						23 41								
Warrington Bank Quay	a					22 36										
Wigan North Western	a					22 47										
Preston [8]	a					23 07										
Lancaster [6]	a															
Oxenholme Lake District	a															
Penrith North Lakes	a															
Carlisle [8]	a															
Lockerbie	a															
Haymarket	a															
Edinburgh [10]	a															
Haymarket	a															
Motherwell	a															
Glasgow Central [15]	a															
Inverkeithing	a															
Kirkcaldy	a															
Markinch	a															
Ladybank	a															
Cupar	a															
Leuchars [3]	a															
Dundee	a															
Arbroath	a															
Montrose	a															
Stonehaven	a															
Aberdeen	a															

A 🛒 to Birmingham New Street

B 🛒 to Reading

Table 51

Sundays
from 1 April

South Coast and the South West - North West England, The North East and Scotland

Route Diagram - see first Page of Table 51

		XC	VT	XC	XC	VT	XC	XC	VT	XC	XC	VT	XC	XC	XC	VT	XC	XC	XC	XC	VT	XC	XC
		◇1	◇1	◇1	◇1	◇1	◇1	◇1	◇1	◇1	◇1	◇1	◇1	◇1	◇1	◇1	◇1	◇1	◇1	◇1	◇1	◇1	◇1
								A							A			B	A				
Bournemouth	d																			09 40			
Brockenhurst 3	d																			09 57			
Southampton Central	d													09 15						10 15			
Southampton Airport Pkwy	d													09 22						10 22			
Winchester	d													09 31						10 31			
Basingstoke	d													09 47						10 47			
Guildford	d																						
Reading 7	d									09 11				10 10						11 11			
Oxford	d									09 37				10 37						11 37			
Banbury	d									09 54				10 54						11 54			
Leamington Spa 8	d									10 12				11 12						12 12			
Coventry	d									10 28				11 29						12 28			
Birmingham International	d									10 40				11 40						12 40			
Penzance	d																						
St Erth	d																						
Hayle	d																						
Camborne	d																						
Redruth	d																						
Truro	d																						
St Austell	d																						
Newquay (Summer Only)	d																						
Par	d																						
Lostwithiel	d																						
Bodmin Parkway	d																						
Liskeard 6	d																						
Plymouth	d																		09 25				
Totnes	d																		09 50				
Paignton	d																						
Torquay	d																						
Newton Abbot	d																		10 03				
Teignmouth	d																						
Dawlish	d																						
Exeter St Davids 6	d																		10 23				
Tiverton Parkway	d																		10 37				
Taunton	d																		10 51				
Weston-super-Mare	d																						
Cardiff Central 7	d																	10 45					
Newport (South Wales)	d																	10 59					
Bristol Temple Meads 10	d										09 15				10 30				11 30				
Bristol Parkway 7	d										09 25				10 40				11 40				
Gloucester 7	d										10 01							11 51					
Cheltenham Spa	d										10 12				11 12			12 03	12 12				
London Paddington	d																						
Birmingham New Street 12	a									10 50	10 50			11 50	11 50			12 45	12 50	12 50			
Birmingham New Street 12	d	22p31	08 45	09 01	09 03	09 20	10 01	10 03	10 20	11 01	11 03	11 20	11 49	12 01	12 03	12 20	12 30	12 49	13 03	13 01	13 20	13 30	13 31
Tamworth	d				09 19			10 18					12 07		12 19			13 07					
Burton-on-Trent	d				09 28			10 29			11 26		12 19					13 19	13 26				
Derby 6	a				09 42			10 39			11 40		12 34		12 43		13 01	13 33	13 42			14 01	
Nottingham 8	a												13 00					14 00					
Chesterfield	a				10 02			11 02			12 02				13 02		13 29		14 02			14 29	
Sheffield 7	a				10 16			11 17			12 18				13 18		13 43		14 17			14 45	
Doncaster 7	a																14 13					15 13	
Wakefield Westgate 7	a				10 44			11 44			12 44				13 45				14 44				
Leeds 10	a				11 02			12 01			13 02				14 02				15 02				
York 8	a				11 29			12 29			13 29				14 29		14 40		15 29			15 43	
Darlington 7	a				11 57			12 57			13 57				14 57		15 13		15 57			16 13	
Durham	a				12 14			13 14			14 14				15 14		15 30		16 14			16 30	
Chester-le-Street	a																						
Newcastle 8	a				12 29			13 32			14 28				15 28		15 44		16 28			16 44	
Morpeth	a										14 48												
Alnmouth for Alnwick	a							13 59							16 01				16 58				
Berwick-upon-Tweed	a							14 20							16 21								
Dunbar	a				13 39						15 40								17 39				
Wolverhampton 7	d	22p49	09 04	09 19		09 37	10 19		10 37	11 19		11 37		12 19		12 37				13 19	13 37		13 49
Stafford	a	23p01	09 16	09 32			10 32			11 31				12 32						13 33			
Stoke-on-Trent	a	23p20					10 51			11 51				12 52						13 56			14 19
Congleton	a																						
Macclesfield	a	23p38					11 08			12 09				13 10						14 14			
Crewe 10	a		09 35	09 54		10 07			11 07			12 07				13 07					14 07		
Wilmslow	a			10 12																			
Stockport	a	23p53		10 21			11 22			12 22				13 28						14 28			
M'chester Piccadilly 10	a	00 10		10 37			11 31			12 40				13 40						14 40			14 57
Warrington Bank Quay	a		09 54			10 26			11 26			12 26				13 26					14 26		
Wigan North Western	a		10 05			10 37			11 37			12 37				13 37					14 37		
Preston 8	a		10 22			10 51			11 51			12 51				13 51					14 50		
Lancaster 6	a					11 18			12 08			13 08				14 08					15 08		
Oxenholme Lake District	a					11 32			12 22			13 22									15 22		
Penrith North Lakes	a															14 44							
Carlisle 8	a					12 11			13 01			14 01				15 00					16 01		
Lockerbie	a																						
Haymarket	a								14 13							16 14							
Edinburgh 10	a				14 07			15 05	14 22		16 06				17 06	16 22			18 07				
Haymarket	a							15 14							17 14				18 16				
Motherwell	a							15 51							17 52								
Glasgow Central 15	a					13 21		16 13				15 16			18 12						17 17		
Inverkeithing	a																		18 28				
Kirkcaldy	a																		18 44				
Markinch	a																		18 53				
Ladybank	a																		19 01				
Cupar	a																		19 07				
Leuchars 3	a																		19 14				
Dundee	a																		19 29				
Arbroath	a																		19 46				
Montrose	a																		20 00				
Stonehaven	a																		20 23				
Aberdeen	a																		20 43				

A to Edinburgh

B from Newport (South Wales)

Table 51

Sundays
from 1 April

South Coast and the South West - North West England, The North East and Scotland

Route Diagram - see first Page of Table 51

		XC	XC	XC	XC	VT	XC	XC	XC	XC	XC	VT	XC	XC	XC	XC	XC	VT	XC	XC	XC	XC	XC
		◇1	◇1	◇1	◇1	◇1	◇1	◇1	◇1	◇1	◇1	◇1	◇1	◇1	◇1	◇1	◇1	◇1	◇1	◇1	◇1	◇1	◇1
		A		B				A		C				A		B				A		D	
Bournemouth	d		10 40						11 40						12 40						13 40		
Brockenhurst 3	d		10 57						11 57						12 57						13 57		
Southampton Central	d		11 15						12 15						13 15						14 15		
Southampton Airport Pkwy	d		11 22						12 22						13 22						14 22		
Winchester	d		11 31						12 31						13 31						14 31		
Basingstoke	d		11 47						12 47						13 47						14 47		
Guildford	d				12 14																		
Reading 7	d		12 11		12 54				13 11		13 40				14 09		14 40				15 09		15 40
Oxford	d		12 36		13 17				13 37		14 05				14 37		15 06				15 37		16 06
Banbury	d		12 53		13 35				13 54		14 24				14 54		15 25				15 54		16 25
Leamington Spa 8	d		13 12		13 52				14 12		14 42				15 12		15 43				16 12		16 43
Coventry	d		13 25						14 26						15 26						16 26		
Birmingham International	d		13 37						14 38						15 38						16 38		
Penzance	d									09 30													
St Erth	d									09 38													
Hayle	d																						
Camborne	d									09 48													
Redruth	d									09 54													
Truro	d									10 06													
St Austell	d									10 22													
Newquay (Summer Only)	d																						
Par	d									10 30													
Lostwithiel	d																						
Bodmin Parkway	d									10 41													
Liskeard 6	d									10 53													
Plymouth	d			10 25						11 25			12 00			12 25			12 52			13 23	
Totnes	d			10 50						11 50						12 50						13 49	
Paignton	d						10 50																
Torquay	d						10 56																
Newton Abbot	d			11 03			11 08			12 03			12 36			13 03			13 27			14 03	
Teignmouth	d						11 15																
Dawlish	d						11 20																
Exeter St Davids 6	d			11 23			11 32			12 23			12 57			13 23			13 48			14 25	
Tiverton Parkway	d			11 37			11 46			12 37			13 10			13 37						14 39	
Taunton	d			11 53			12 00			12 51			13 25			13 51						14 54	
Weston-super-Mare	d						12 21																
Cardiff Central 7	d	11 45						12 45						13 45						14 45			
Newport (South Wales)	d	11 59						12 59						13 59						14 59			
Bristol Temple Meads 10	d			12 30			13 00			13 30			14 00			14 30			15 00			15 30	
Bristol Parkway 7	d			12 40			13 10			13 40			14 10			14 40			15 10			15 40	
Gloucester 7	d	12 47						13 51						14 47						15 47			
Cheltenham Spa	d	12 58		13 12			13 42	14 02		14 12			14 42	14 58		15 12			15 42	15 58		16 12	
London Paddington	d																						
Birmingham New Street 12	a	13 41	13 47	13 50	14 19		14 26	14 45	14 48	14 50	15 09		15 27	15 41	15 48	15 50	16 12		16 26	16 41	16 48	16 50	17 12
Birmingham New Street 12	d	13 49	14 00	14 03	14 30	14 20	14 31	14 49	15 01	15 03	15 30	15 20	15 31	15 49	16 01	16 03	16 30	16 20	16 31	16 49	17 01	17 03	17 30
Tamworth	d	14 07		14 19				15 09						16 07		16 19				17 07			
Burton-on-Trent	d	14 19						15 21		15 28				16 19						17 19		17 28	
Derby 6	a	14 34		14 42	15 04			15 34		15 42	16 02			16 34		16 42	17 04			17 34		17 39	18 04
Nottingham 8	a	15 02						16 00						17 00						18 00			
Chesterfield	a			15 02						16 02						17 02						18 03	
Sheffield 7	a			15 17	15 47					16 18	16 48					17 17	17 48					18 19	18 46
Doncaster 7	a				16 15						17 13						18 13						19 15
Wakefield Westgate 7	a			15 44						16 44						17 47	18 33					18 47	
Leeds 10	a			16 02						17 02						18 02	18 51					19 04	
York 8	a			16 29	16 40					17 29	17 42					18 29	19 18					19 29	19 43
Darlington 7	a			16 57	17 15					17 57	18 11					18 57	19 46					19 59	20 11
Durham	a			17 14	17 33					18 14	18 29					19 14	20 03					20 17	20 28
Chester-le-Street	a																						
Newcastle 8	a			17 30	17 47					18 28	18 43					19 30	20 19					20 31	20 42
Morpeth	a																					20 52	
Alnmouth for Alnwick	a			18 01												20 04							
Berwick-upon-Tweed	a			18 22						19 17						20 24						21 25	
Dunbar	a									19 40												21 48	
Wolverhampton 7	d		14 18			14 37	14 49		15 19			15 37	15 49		16 19			16 37	16 49		17 19		
Stafford	a		14 32						15 33						16 34						17 35		
Stoke-on-Trent	a		14 55				15 19		15 56				16 19		16 56				17 19		17 56		
Congleton	a																						
Macclesfield	a		15 13						16 14						17 14						18 14		
Crewe 10	a					15 07						16 07						17 07					
Wilmslow	a																						
Stockport	a		15 27						16 28						17 28						18 28		
M'chester Piccadilly 10	a		15 39				15 59		16 40				16 59		17 40				17 56		18 40		
Warrington Bank Quay	a					15 26						16 26						17 26					
Wigan North Western	a					15 37						16 37						17 37					
Preston 8	a					15 51						16 51						17 51					
Lancaster 6	a					16 08						17 08						18 08					
Oxenholme Lake District	a											17 22						18 22					
Penrith North Lakes	a					16 44												18 48					
Carlisle 8	a					17 00						18 01						19 04					
Lockerbie	a																						
Haymarket	a					18 13																	
Edinburgh 10	a			19 06		18 22				20 05						21 08		20 22				22 16	22 23
Haymarket	a			19 22												21 15							
Motherwell	a			20 00												21 53							
Glasgow Central 15	a			20 20								19 17				22 14							
Inverkeithing	a																						
Kirkcaldy	a																						
Markinch	a																						
Ladybank	a																						
Cupar	a																						
Leuchars 3	a																						
Dundee	a																						
Arbroath	a																						
Montrose	a																						
Stonehaven	a																						
Aberdeen	a																						

A from Newport (South Wales)
B to Edinburgh
C from Plymouth
D from Birmingham New Street

Table 51

Sundays
from 1 April

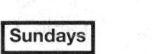

South Coast and the South West - North West England, The North East and Scotland

Route Diagram - see first Page of Table 51

		VT	XC	XC	XC	XC	XC	VT	XC	XC	XC	XC	XC	VT	XC	XC	XC	XC	XC	VT	XC	XC
														R								
		◇1	◇1	◇1	◇1	◇1	◇1	◇1	◇1	◇1	◇1	◇1	◇1	1	◇1	◇1	◇1	◇1	◇1	◇1	◇1	◇1
						A			B				C				D	D				
		⊡	⊼		⊼	⊼	⊼	⊡	⊼		⊼	⊼	⊼	⊡	⊼		⊼	⊼	⊼	⊡	⊼	
Bournemouth	d				14 40						15 40						16 40					
Brockenhurst 3	d				14 57						15 57						16 57					
Southampton Central	d				15 15						16 15						17 15					
Southampton Airport Pkway	d				15 22						16 22						17 22					
Winchester	d				15 31						16 31						17 31					
Basingstoke	d				15 47						16 47						17 47					
Guildford	d																					
Reading 7	d				16 09		16 41				17 09		17 40				18 09		18 41			
Oxford	d				16 37		17 06				17 37		18 06				18 37		19 06			
Banbury	d				16 54		17 25				17 54		18 25				18 54		19 25			
Leamington Spa 8	d				17 12		17 43				18 12		18 43				19 12		19 43			
Coventry	d				17 26						18 26						19 26		19 54			
Birmingham International	d				17 38						18 38						19 38		20 04			
Penzance	d								12 25													
St Erth	d								12 33													
Hayle	d								12 37													
Camborne	d								12 46													
Redruth	d								12 53													
Truro	d								13 04													
St Austell	d								13 21													
Newquay (Summer Only)	d																					
Par	d								13 28													
Lostwithiel	d								13 35													
Bodmin Parkway	d								13 42													
Liskeard 6	d								13 55													
Plymouth	d					14 23			14 35			15 23						16 25				
Totnes	d					14 49			15 00			15 49						16 50				
Paignton	d																					
Torquay	d																					
Newton Abbot	d					15 03			15 12			16 03						17 03				
Teignmouth	d																					
Dawlish	d																					
Exeter St Davids 6	d					15 25			15 33			16 24						17 23				
Tiverton Parkway	d					15 38			15 46			16 37						17 37				
Taunton	d					15 54			16 01			16 53						17 51				
Weston-super-Mare	d								16 30													
Cardiff Central 7	d			15 45						16 45						17 45						18 45
Newport (South Wales)	d			15 59						16 59						17 59						18 59
Bristol Temple Meads 10	d		16 00			16 30			17 00			17 30			18 00			18 30			19 00	
Bristol Parkway 7	d		16 10			16 40			17 10			17 40			18 10			18 40			19 10	
Gloucester 7	d			16 47						17 47						18 47						19 52
Cheltenham Spa	d		16 42	16 58		17 12			17 42	17 58		18 12			18 42	18 58		19 12			19 42	20 02
London Paddington	d																					
Birmingham New Street 12	a		17 26	17 41	17 48	17 49	18 09		18 27	18 41	18 48	18 51	19 11		19 26	19 41	19 48	19 50	20 15		20 26	20 44
Birmingham New Street 12	d	17 20	17 31	17 49	18 01	18 03	18 30	18 20	18 31	18 49	19 01	19 03	19 30	19 20	19 31	19 49	20 01	20 03		20 20	20 31	20 49
Tamworth	d			18 07		18 19				19 09						20 07		20 19				21 06
Burton-on-Trent	d			18 19						19 21		19 26				20 19						21 19
Derby 6	a			18 33		18 39	19 03			19 33		19 39	20 01			20 35		20 39				21 33
Nottingham 8	a			19 00						20 00						21 00						22 00
Chesterfield	a					19 04						20 01						21 02				
Sheffield 7	a					19 20	19 39					20 17	20 38					21 16				
Doncaster 7	a						20 16						21 19									
Wakefield Westgate 7	a					19 48						20 46						21 47				
Leeds 10	a					20 05						21 03						22 04				
York 8	a					20 29	20 45					21 31	21 44									
Darlington 7	a					20 59	21 12						22 22									
Durham	a					21 17	21 31						22 40									
Chester-le-Street	a																					
Newcastle 8	a					21 31	21 44						23 10									
Morpeth	a																					
Alnmouth for Alnwick	a					22 04																
Berwick-upon-Tweed	a																					
Dunbar	a																					
Wolverhampton 7	d	17 37	17 49		18 19			18 37	18 49		19 19			19 37	19 49		20 19			20 38	20 52	
Stafford	a				18 35						19 37						20 36			20 51		
Stoke-on-Trent	a		18 19		18 56				19 19		19 56				20 19		20 56				21 19	
Congleton	a																					
Macclesfield	a				19 15						20 14						21 15					
Crewe 10	a	18 07						19 07						20 07						21 10		
Wilmslow	a																					
Stockport	a				19 28						20 28						21 28					
M'chester Piccadilly 10	a		18 56		19 40				19 58		20 40				21 00		21 40				21 56	
Warrington Bank Quay	a	18 26						19 26						20 26								
Wigan North Western	a	18 37						19 37						20 37								
Preston 8	a	18 51						19 51						20 51								
Lancaster 6	a	19 08						20 08						21 08								
Oxenholme Lake District	a	19 22												21 22								
Penrith North Lakes	a							20 44														
Carlisle 8	a	20 01						21 00						22 01								
Lockerbie	a													22 22								
Haymarket	a							22 15														
Edinburgh 10	a					23 08		22 21														
Haymarket	a																					
Motherwell	a													23 07								
Glasgow Central 15	a	21 17												23 22								
Inverkeithing	a																					
Kirkcaldy	a																					
Markinch	a																					
Ladybank	a																					
Cupar	a																					
Leuchars 3	a																					
Dundee	a																					
Arbroath	a																					
Montrose	a																					
Stonehaven	a																					
Aberdeen	a																					

A ⊼ to Leeds
B ⊼ from Plymouth to Birmingham New Street
C ⊼ to Sheffield
D ⊼ to Birmingham New Street

Table 51

Sundays
from 1 April

South Coast and the South West - North West England, The North East and Scotland

Route Diagram - see first Page of Table 51

		XC	XC	XC	XC	VT	XC	XC	XC	XC	XC	XC	XC	XC
		◇1	◇1	◇1	◇1	◇1	◇1	◇1	◇1	◇1	◇1	◇1	◇1	◇1
		A	B					C	A					
		⚲	⚲	⚲	⚲	⊡		⚲	⚲					
Bournemouth	d	17 40						18 40			19 40			
Brockenhurst 3	d	17 57						18 57			19 57			
Southampton Central ⛴	d	18 15						19 15			20 15			
Southampton Airport Pkway ✈	d	18 22						19 22			20 22			
Winchester	d	18 31						19 31			20 31			
Basingstoke	d	18 47						19 47			20 47			
Guildford	d													
Reading 7	d	19 09		19 40				20 10		20 41	21 09		21 40	
Oxford	d	19 37		20 06				20 37		21 05	21 37		22 06	
Banbury	d	19 54		20 25				20 54		21 24	21 54		22 24	
Leamington Spa 8	d	20 12		20 43				21 12		21 42	22 12		22 42	
Coventry	d	20 26		20 54				21 26		21 53	22 23		22 53	
Birmingham International ✈	d	20 38		21 04				21 38		22 03	22 33		23 03	
Penzance	d		15 30											
St Erth	d		15 38											
Hayle	d													
Camborne	d		15 51											
Redruth	d		15 57											
Truro	d		16 09											
St Austell	d		16 25											
Newquay (Summer Only)	d													
Par	d		16 33											
Lostwithiel	d													
Bodmin Parkway	d		16 44											
Liskeard 6	d		16 56											
Plymouth	d		17 26						18 23					
Totnes	d		17 52						18 49					
Paignton	d				18 20									
Torquay	d				18 26									
Newton Abbot	d		18 04		18 37				19 03					
Teignmouth	d													
Dawlish	d													
Exeter St Davids 6	d		18 23		18 58				19 25					
Tiverton Parkway	d		18 38		19 11				19 38					
Taunton	d		18 52		19 25				19 54					
Weston-super-Mare	d													
Cardiff Central 7	d						19 45					20 45		
Newport (South Wales)	d						20 00					20 59		
Bristol Temple Meads 10	d		19 30		20 00				20 30					22 10
Bristol Parkway 7	d		19 40		20 10				20 40					22 20
Gloucester 7	d						20 50					21 48		
Cheltenham Spa	d		20 12		20 42		21 01		21 12			21 59		22 52
London Paddington	d													
Birmingham New Street 12	a	20 48	20 50	21 15	21 20		21 44	21 48	21 51	22 14	22 42	22 42	23 13	23 39
Birmingham New Street 12	d	21 01	21 03			21 20		22 01	22 03					
Tamworth	d		21 19						22 18					
Burton-on-Trent	d		21 30											
Derby 6	a		21 42						22 40					
Nottingham 8 🚌	a													
Chesterfield	a		22 02						23 04					
Sheffield 7 🚌	a		22 18						23 20					
Doncaster 7	a													
Wakefield Westgate 7	a		22 43											
Leeds 10	a		23 01						00 16					
York 8	a													
Darlington 7	a													
Durham	a													
Chester-le-Street	a													
Newcastle 8	a													
Morpeth	a													
Alnmouth for Alnwick	a													
Berwick-upon-Tweed	a													
Dunbar	a													
Wolverhampton 7 🚌	d	21 19				21 38		22 19						
Stafford	a	21 36				21 56		22 36						
Stoke-on-Trent	a	21 56						22 55						
Congleton	a													
Macclesfield	a	22 14						23 12						
Crewe 10	a					22 17								
Wilmslow	a													
Stockport	a	22 28						23 27						
M'chester Piccadilly 10 🚌	a	22 40						23 41						
Warrington Bank Quay	a					22 36								
Wigan North Western	a					22 47								
Preston 8	a					23 07								
Lancaster 6	a													
Oxenholme Lake District	a													
Penrith North Lakes	a													
Carlisle 8	a													
Lockerbie	a													
Haymarket	a													
Edinburgh 10	a													
Haymarket	a													
Motherwell	a													
Glasgow Central 15	a													
Inverkeithing	a													
Kirkcaldy	a													
Markinch	a													
Ladybank	a													
Cupar	a													
Leuchars 3	a													
Dundee	a													
Arbroath	a													
Montrose	a													
Stonehaven	a													
Aberdeen	a													

A ⚲ to Birmingham New Street   B ⚲ from Plymouth to Birmingham New Street   C ⚲ to Reading

Network Diagram for Table 52

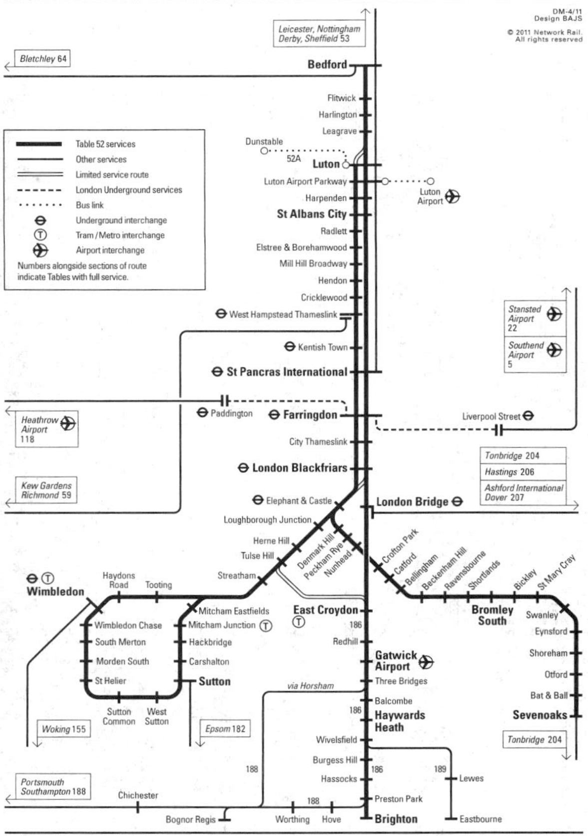

Bedford, Luton, St Albans and City of London - South London, Gatwick Airport and Brighton

Network Diagram - see first Page of Table 52

Miles	Miles	Miles	Miles			FC MX	FC MX	FC MX	SE MX	FC MX	FC	FC MO	FC MX	FC MO		FC	FC MO	FC MX	FC MO	FC MO	FC	FC MX	FC MO	FC
								1				1	1				1	1						
												A		B			A		B	C		D	C	
							bus				bus					bus					bus			bus
0	0	—	—	**Bedford** 7	d			22p52				23p10	23p12	23p12			23p30	23p32	23p32	00 02		00 02	01 02	
9½	—	—	—	Flitwick	d			23p02				23p20	23p22	23p22			23p40	23p42	23p42	00 12		00 12	01 12	
12½	—	—	—	Harlington	d			23p06				23p24	23p26	23p26			23p44	23p46	23p46	00 16		00 16	01 16	
17	—	—	—	Leagrave	d			23p12				23p32	23p32	23p32			23p52	23p52	23p52	00 22		00 22	01 22	
19½	19½	—	—	**Luton** 10	d			23p16				23p36	23p36	23p36			23p56	23p56	23p56	00 26		00 26	01 26	
20½	—	—	—	Luton Airport Parkway 7 ✈	d			23p19				23p39	23p39	23p39			23p59	23p59	23p59	00 29		00 29	01 29	
25	—	—	—	Harpenden	d			23p25				23p45	23p45	23p45			00 05	00 05	00 05	00 35		00 35	01 35	
29¾	—	—	—	**St Albans City**	d			23p31				23p51	23p51	23p51			00 11	00 11	00 11	00 41		00 41	01 41	
34¼	—	—	—	Radlett	d			23p36				23p56	23p56	23p56			00 16	00 16	00 16	00 46		00 46	01 46	
37¼	—	—	—	Elstree & Borehamwood	d			23p41				00 01	00 01	00 01			00 21	00 21	00 21	00 51		00 51	01 51	
40½	—	—	—	Mill Hill Broadway	d			23p45				00 05	00 05	00 05			00 25	00 25	00 25	00 55		00 55	01 55	
42¾	—	—	—	Hendon	d			23p48				00 09	00 08	00 08			00 28	00 28	00 28	00 58		00 58	01 58	
44¾	—	—	—	Cricklewood	d			23p52				00 12	00 12	00 12			00 32	00 32	00 32	01 02		01 02	02 02	
45¾	—	—	—	West Hampstead Thameslink ⊖	d			23p54				00 14	00 14	00 14			00 34	00 34	00 34	01 04		01 04	02 04	
48¼	—	—	—	Kentish Town ⊖	d			00 02				00 20	00 20	00 20			00 40	00 40	00 40	01 10		01 10	02 10	
49¾	—	—	—	**St Pancras International** 15 ⊖	a									00 26					00 46	01 16			02 16	
50	0	—	—	**St Pancras International** 15 ⊖	a			00 05				00 25	00 25				00 45	00 45				01 15		
—	—	—	—		d		23p42				00 12					00 30					01 00			01 30
51	0	—	—	Farringdon 3 ⊖	d		23p47				00 17					00 35								
51¾	0	—	—	City Thameslink 3	d																			
52¼	0	0	0	**London Blackfriars** 3 ⊖	d		23p52				00 22					00 40					01 10			01 40
1	1	—	—	Elephant & Castle ⊖	d																			
3	3	—	—	Loughborough Jn.	d																			
4	4	—	—	Herne Hill 4	d																			
53	—	—	—	**London Bridge** 4	a		00 07				00 35					00 55					01 25			01 55
—	—	—	—		d	23p29				23p59														
—	5	5	5	Tulse Hill 3	d	23p41				00 09														
—	62	62	0	Streatham 4	d	23p45				00 13														
—	—	—	1	Mitcham Eastfields	d																			
—	—	2	—	Mitcham Junction	d																			
—	—	4	—	Hackbridge	d																			
—	—	4¾	—	Carshalton	d																			
—	8	—	—	Tooting	d	23p50				00 18														
—	9¼	—	—	Haydons Road	d	23p53				00 21														
—	10½	—	—	**Wimbledon** 6 ⊖	d	23p57				00 25														
—	11½	—	—	Wimbledon Chase	d	00 01				00 28														
—	12	—	—	South Merton	d	00 03				00 30														
—	12½	—	—	Morden South	d	00 05				00 32														
—	13	—	—	St Helier	d	00 07				00 34														
—	14	—	—	Sutton Common	d	00 09				00 36														
—	15	—	—	West Sutton	d	00 12				00 39														
—	16	12½	6	**Sutton (Surrey)** 4	a	00 15				00 43														
63¼	—	—	10	**East Croydon**	d																			
—	—	—	—	Denmark Hill 4	d				23p52															
—	—	—	—	Peckham Rye 4	d				23p55															
—	—	—	—	Nunhead 4	d				23p57															
—	—	—	—	Crofton Park	d				23p59															
—	—	—	—	Catford	d				00 03															
—	—	—	—	Bellingham	d				00 05															
—	—	—	—	Beckenham Hill	d				00 07															
—	—	—	—	Ravensbourne	d				00 09															
—	—	—	—	Shortlands	d				00 11															
—	—	—	—	Bromley South 4	d				00 14															
—	—	—	—	Bickley 4	d				00a17															
—	—	—	—	St Mary Cray	d																			
—	—	—	—	Swanley 4	d																			
—	—	—	—	Eynsford	d																			
—	—	—	—	Shoreham (Kent)	d																			
—	—	—	—	Otford 4	d																			
—	—	—	—	Bat & Ball	d																			
—	—	—	—	Sevenoaks 4	a																			
73¾	—	—	—	Redhill	d																			
79½	—	—	—	**Gatwick Airport** 10 ✈	d																			
82¼	—	—	—	Three Bridges 4	d																			
86¾	—	—	—	Balcombe	d																			
90¾	—	—	—	**Haywards Heath** 3	d																			
93¾	—	—	—	Wivelsfield 4	d																			
94½	—	—	—	Burgess Hill 4	d																			
96½	—	—	—	Hassocks 4	d																			
102¼	—	—	—	Preston Park	d																			
103¾	—	—	—	**Brighton** 10	a																			

A From 2 April
B until 26 March
C until 19 March
D until 16 March and from 20 March

Table 52

Mondays to Fridays

Bedford, Luton, St Albans and City of London - South London, Gatwick Airport and Brighton

Network Diagram - see first Page of Table 52

		FC	FC	FC	FC	FC	FC	FC	FC	FC	FC	FC	FC	SE	FC	FC	FC	FC	FC	FC	FC
			1			1	1			1		1	1		1	1				1	
		A	B			A	B			A		C	D		C	D					
				🚌	🚌			🚌	🚌		🚌										
		MX	MO			MX	MO			MX											
Bedford 7	d	01 02	02 02			02 02	03 02			03 02		04 08	04 08		04 20	04 20				05 00	
Flitwick	d	01 12	02 12			02 12	03 12			03 12		04 18	04 18		04 30	04 30				05 10	
Harlington	d	01 16	02 16			02 16	03 16			03 16		04 22	04 22		04 34	04 34				05 14	
Leagrave	d	01 22	02 22			02 22	03 22			03 22		04 28	04 28		04 40	04 40				05 20	
Luton 10	d	01 26	02 26			02 26	03 26			03 26		04 32	04 33		04 44	04 45		05 08		05 24	
Luton Airport Parkway 7 ✈	d	01 29	02 29			02 29	03 29			03 29		04 35	04 35		04 47	04 47		05 10		05 27	
Harpenden	d	01 35	02 35			02 35	03 35			03 35		04 41	04 41		04 53	04 53		05 16		05 33	
St Albans City	d	01 41	02 41			02 41	03 41			03 41		04 47	04 47		04 59	04 59		05 22		05 39	
Radlett	d	01 46	02 46			02 46	03 46			03 46					05 04	05 04		05 28			
Elstree & Borehamwood	d	01 51	02 51			02 51	03 51			03 51					05 09	05 09		05 32			
Mill Hill Broadway	d	01 55	02 55			02 55	03 55			03 55					05 13	05 13		05 36			
Hendon	d	01 58	02 58			02 58	03 58			03 58					05 16	05 16		05 40			
Cricklewood	d	02 02	03 02			03 02	04 02			04 02					05 20	05 20		05 43			
West Hampstead Thameslink ⊖	d	02 04	03 04			03 04	04 04			04 04		05 04	05 04		05 22	05 22		05 46		05 54	06 04
Kentish Town ⊖	d	02 10	03 10			03 10	04 10			04 10					05 28	05 28		05 50	05 54		06 08
St Pancras International 15 ⊖	a		03 16				04 16														
St Pancras International 15 ⊖	a	02 15				03 15				04 15		05 12	05 12		05 32	05 32		05 54	05 58	06 02	06 12
	d			02 30	03 00			03 30	04 00		04 30	05 12	05 12		05 32	05 32	05 36	05 54	05 58	06 02	06 12
Farringdon 3 ⊖	d											05 18	05 18		05 38	05 38	05 42	06 00	06 04	06 08	06 18
City Thameslink 3	d											05 21	05 21	05 26	05 41	05 41	05 44	06 03	06 07	06 11	06 21
London Blackfriars 3 ⊖	d			02 40	03 10			03 40	04 10		04a40	05 24	05 24	05 28	05 44	05 44	05 47	06 06	06 10	06 14	06 24
Elephant & Castle ⊖	d													05 32			05 50	06 09	06 16		06 27
Loughborough Jn.	d																	06 13			06 31
Herne Hill 4	d																05 57	06 17			06 35
London Bridge 4	a			02 55	03 25			03 55	04 25			05 30	05 30		05 50	05 50				06 20	
	d											05 30	05 30		05 50	05 50				06 20	
Tulse Hill 3	d																06 02	06 22			06 42
Streatham 4	d																06 05	06 25			06 45
Mitcham Eastfields	d																	06 29			06 49
Mitcham Junction	d																	06 32			06 52
Hackbridge	d																	06 35			06 55
Carshalton	d																	06 38			06 58
Tooting	d																06 10				
Haydons Road	d																06 13				
Wimbledon 6 ⊖ 🚋	d																06 16				
Wimbledon Chase	d																06 19				
South Merton	d																06 21				
Morden South	d																06 23				
St Helier	d																06 25				
Sutton Common	d																06 27				
West Sutton	d																06 30				
Sutton (Surrey) 4	a																06 33	06 43			07 03
East Croydon 🚋	d											05 47	05 47		06 05	06 05				06 35	
Denmark Hill 4	d													05 39					06 22		
Peckham Rye 4	d													05 41					06 25		
Nunhead 4	d													05 44					06 27		
Crofton Park	d													05 47					06 30		
Catford	d													05 49					06 33		
Bellingham	d													05 52					06 35		
Beckenham Hill	d													05 54					06 37		
Ravensbourne	d													05 56					06 39		
Shortlands	d													05 58					06 41		
Bromley South 4	d													06 01					06 44		
Bickley 4	d													06 03					06 47		
St Mary Cray	d													06 08					06 51		
Swanley 4	d													06 12					06 56		
Eynsford	d													06 17					07 00		
Shoreham (Kent)	d													06 20					07 04		
Otford 4	d													06 23					07 07		
Bat & Ball	d													06 26					07 10		
Sevenoaks 4	a													06 29					07 14		
Redhill	d																				
Gatwick Airport 10 ✈	d											06 04	06 04		06 22	06 22				06 52	
Three Bridges 4	d											06 08	06 08		06 26	06 26				06 56	
Balcombe	d											06 14	06 14		06 33	06 33					
Haywards Heath 3	d											06 19	06 19		06 39	06 39				07 06	
Wivelsfield 4	d											06 23	06 23		06 43	06 43				07 10	
Burgess Hill 4	d											06 25	06 25		06 45	06 45				07 12	
Hassocks 4	d											06 29	06 29		06 49	06 49				07 16	
Preston Park	d											06 35	06 35		06 55	06 55				07 22	
Brighton 10	a											06 40	06 40		06 59	06 59				07 27	

A until 16 March and from 20 March
B until 19 March
C until 23 March
D from 26 March

Table 52

Mondays to Fridays

Bedford, Luton, St Albans and City of London - South London, Gatwick Airport and Brighton

Network Diagram - see first Page of Table 52

		FC	SE	FC	EM	FC	FC	FC	FC	FC	EM	FC	FC	FC	FC	FC	FC	EM	FC	FC	FC
		1			◇1	1		1		1	◇1		1		1		1	◇1		1	
					🛒						⊠							⊠			
Bedford 7	d	05 20			05 36	05 40		05 54		05 58			06 14		06 18		06 22	06 31		06 34	
Flitwick	d	05 30				05 50		06 04		06 08			06 24				06 32		06 36	06 44	
Harlington	d	05 34				05 54				06 12							06 36		06 40		
Leagrave	d	05 39				05 59				06 17					06 34		06 41		06 45		
Luton 10	d	05 44		05 48		06 04	06 06	06 14		06 22	06 24		06 34		06 39	06 43	06 46		06 50	06 54	
Luton Airport Parkway 7 ✈	d	05 46		05 50	05 53	06 06	06 08			06 24					06 41	06 45	06 48		06 52		
Harpenden	d	05 52		05 56		06 12	06 14	06 20		06 30			06 40		06 47	06 51	06 54		06 58	07 00	
St Albans City	d	05 58		06 02		06 18	06 20	06 26		06 36		06 40	06 46		06 53	06 57	07 00		07 04	07 06	
Radlett	d			06 07			06 25					06 45				07 02			07 09		
Elstree & Borehamwood	d			06 12			06 30					06 50				07 06			07 13		
Mill Hill Broadway	d			06 16			06 34					06 54				07 10			07 17		
Hendon	d			06 19			06 37					06 57				07 13					
Cricklewood	d			06 23			06 41					07 01				07 17					
West Hampstead Thameslink ⊖	d	06 12		06 26		06 30	06 44			06 50		07 04			07 08	07 20			07 24		
Kentish Town ⊖	d			06 30			06 48					07 08				07 24					
St Pancras International 15 ⊖	a				06 16				←		06 48			←				07 08			←
St Pancras International 15 ⊖	a	06 20		06 34		06 38	06 52	06 44	06 52	06 57		07 12	07 04	07 12	07 16	07 28	07 20		07 31	07 24	07 28
	d	06 22		06 34		06 38	06 52	06 44	06 52	06 58		07 12	07 04	07 12	07 16	07 28	07 20		07 32	07 24	07 28
Farringdon 3 ⊖	d	06 28		06 40		06 44	→	06 50	06 58	07 04		→	07 10	07 18	07 22	→	07 26		→	07 30	07 34
City Thameslink 3	d	06 31	06 39	06 43		06 47		06 53	07 01	07 07			07 13	07 21	07 25		07 29			07 33	07 37
London Blackfriars 3 ⊖	d	06 34	06 42	06 46		06 50		06 58	07 04	07 09			07 16	07 24	07 28		07 32			07 36	07 40
Elephant & Castle ⊖	d		06 46	06 49				07 02	07 07				07 19	07 28	07 33					07a39	07 44
Loughborough Jn.	d			06 53					07 11				07 23		07 37						
Herne Hill 4	d			06 57					07 15				07 27		07 41						
London Bridge 4	a	06 41				06 56				07 15							07 41				
	d	06 42				07 00				07 16							07 42				
Tulse Hill 3	d			07 02					07 20				07 31		07 45						
Streatham 4	d			07 05					07 23				07 34		07 48						
Mitcham Eastfields	d								07 27						07 52						
Mitcham Junction	d								07 30						07 55						
Hackbridge	d								07 33						07 58						
Carshalton	d								07 36						08 01						
Tooting	d			07 10									07 38								
Haydons Road	d			07 13									07 41								
Wimbledon 6 ⊖ 🚋	d			07 16									07 47								
Wimbledon Chase	d			07 19									07 50								
South Merton	d			07 21									07 52								
Morden South	d			07 23									07 54								
St Helier	d			07 25									07 56								
Sutton Common	d			07 27									07 58								
West Sutton	d			07 30									08 01								
Sutton (Surrey) 4	a			07 35					07 39				08 07		08 04						
East Croydon 🚋	d	06 55				07 15				07 31							07 55				
Denmark Hill 4	d		06 52					07 09						07 34							07 50
Peckham Rye 4	d		06 55					07 12						07 36							07 53
Nunhead 4	d		06 57					07 14						07 39							07 56
Crofton Park	d		07 00					07 17						07 42							
Catford	d		07 03					07 20						07 44							08 00
Bellingham	d		07 05					07 22						07 47							08 02
Beckenham Hill	d		07 07					07 24						07 49							
Ravensbourne	d		07 09					07 26						07 51							
Shortlands	d		07 11					07 28						07 54							
Bromley South 4	d		07 14					07 31						07 57							08a10
Bickley 4	d		07 17					07 34						08 00							
St Mary Cray	d		07 21					07 38						08 04							
Swanley 4	d		07 26					07 44						08 10							
Eynsford	d		07 30					07 48						08 15							
Shoreham (Kent)	d		07 34					07 52						08 18							
Otford 4	d		07 37					07 55						08 21							
Bat & Ball	d		07 40					07 58						08 24							
Sevenoaks 4	a		07 43					08 01						08 27							
Redhill	d																				
Gatwick Airport 10 ✈	d	07 11				07 31				07 47							08 12				
Three Bridges 4	d	07 15				07 35				07 51							08 16				
Balcombe	d	07 21								07 57							08 22				
Haywards Heath 3	d	07 26				07 46				08 02							08 27				
Wivelsfield 4	d					07 50				08 06							08 31				
Burgess Hill 4	d	07 31				07 52				08 08							08 33				
Hassocks 4	d	07 35				07 55				08 12							08 37				
Preston Park	d					08 02				08 18							08 43				
Brighton 10	a	07 44				08 06				08 23							08 48				

Bedford, Luton, St Albans and City of London - South London, Gatwick Airport and Brighton

Network Diagram - see first Page of Table 52

		FC	FC	EM ◇■	FC	FC	FC ■	FC	FC	FC	FC ■	EM ◇■	FC ■	FC	FC	EM ◇■	FC	FC ■	FC	FC ■	FC ■
Bedford 7	d				06 40		06 54				06 58	07 08	07 12					07 16	07 22	07 30	
Flitwick	d				06 50		07 04				07 08							07 26	07 32	07 40	
Harlington	d				06 54						07 12							07 30	07 36		
Leagrave	d				06 59						07 18		07 28					07 35	07 41		
Luton 10	d		07 00		07 04	07 10	07 14				07 22	07 24	07 32		07 30			07 40	07 46	07 50	
Luton Airport Parkway 7 ✈	d		07 02	07 04	07 06	07 12					07 25				07 32	07 41		07 42	07 48		
Harpenden	d		07 08		07 12	07 18	07 20				07 31		07 38		07 38			07 48	07 54	07 56	
St Albans City	d		07 16		07 18	07 24	07 26			07 34	07 38		07 44		07 44		07 52	07 55	08 00	08 02	
Radlett	d		07 21			07 29				07 39					07 49		07 57		08 05		
Elstree & Borehamwood	d		07 25			07 33				07 43					07 53		08 01		08 09		
Mill Hill Broadway	d		07 30			07 37				07 48					07 57		08 06		08 13		
Hendon	d		07 33							07 51							08 09				
Cricklewood	d		07 37							07 55							08 13				
West Hampstead Thameslink ⊖	d		07 40			07 44				08 00					08 04		08 16		08 20		
Kentish Town ⊖	d		07 44							08 04							08 20				
St Pancras International 15 ⊖	a	←		07 29				←	←			07 47		←		08 07					←
St Pancras International 15 ⊖	a	07 31	07 48		07 37	07 51	07 43	07 48	07 51	08 08	07 54		08 04	08 08	08 11		08 24	08 15	08 27	08 19	08 24
	d	07 32	07 48		07 38	07 52	07 44	07 48	07 52	08 08	07 56		08 04	08 08	08 12		08 24	08 16	08 28	08 20	08 24
Farringdon 3 ⊖	d	07 38	→		07 44	→	07 50	07 54	07 58	→	08 02		08 10	08 14	08 18		→	08 22	→	08 26	08 30
City Thameslink 3	d	07 41			07 47		07 53	07 57	08 01		08 05		08 13	08 17	08 21			08 25		08 29	08 33
London Blackfriars 3 ⊖	d	07 44			07 50		07 56	08 00	08 04		08 08		08a16	08 20	08 24			08 28		08 32	08 36
Elephant & Castle ⊖	d	07 47			07 54			08 04	08 07						08 27			08 32			
Loughborough Jn.	d	07 51							08 11						08 31						
Herne Hill 4	d	07 57							08 17						08 36						08 46
London Bridge 4	a										08 16										
	d										08 18										
Tulse Hill 3	d	08 05					08 10		08 21						08 40						08 50
Streatham 4	d	08 08							08 24						08 44						08 54
Mitcham Eastfields	d								08 28												08 58
Mitcham Junction	d								08 31												09 01
Hackbridge	d								08 34												09 04
Carshalton	d								08 37												09 07
Tooting	d	08 12													08 48						
Haydons Road	d	08 15													08 51						
Wimbledon 6 ⊖	d	08 19													08 55						
Wimbledon Chase	d	08 22													08 58						
South Merton	d	08 24													09 00						
Morden South	d	08 26													09 02						
St Helier	d	08 28													09 04						
Sutton Common	d	08 30													09 06						
West Sutton	d	08 33													09 09						
Sutton (Surrey) 4	a	08 37							08 40						09 12						09 10
East Croydon	d						08 26				08 37									08 58	
Denmark Hill 4	d				08 00			08 10										08 38			
Peckham Rye 4	d				08 03			08 13										08 41			
Nunhead 4	d				08 06			08 15										08 43			
Crofton Park	d				08 09			08 18										08 46			
Catford	d				08 12			08 21										08 49			
Bellingham	d				08 15			08 23										08 51			
Beckenham Hill	d				08 17			08 25										08 53			
Ravensbourne	d				08 19			08 27										08 55			
Shortlands	d				08 22			08 30										08 57			
Bromley South 4	d				08 25			08 33						08a37				09 00			
Bickley 4	d				08a28			08 35										09 03			
St Mary Cray	d							08 40										09 07			
Swanley 4	d							08 44										09 12			
Eynsford	d							08 49										09 16			
Shoreham (Kent)	d							08 52										09 20			
Otford 4	d							08 55										09 23			
Bat & Ball	d							08 58										09 26			
Sevenoaks 4	a							09 01										09 29			
Redhill	d																				
Gatwick Airport 10 ✈	d						08 42				08 53									09 13	
Three Bridges 4	d						08 46				08 58									09 17	
Balcombe	d						08 52														
Haywards Heath 3	d						08 58				09 08									09 27	
Wivelsfield 4	d						09 02														
Burgess Hill 4	d						09 04				09 13									09 32	
Hassocks 4	d						09 07													09 35	
Preston Park	d						09 14													09 42	
Brighton 10	a						09 18				09 25									09 46	

Bedford, Luton, St Albans and City of London - South London, Gatwick Airport and Brighton

Network Diagram - see first Page of Table 52

		FC	EM ◇■	FC	FC ■	FC ■	FC	FC	FC	FC ■	EM ◇■	EM ◇■	FC ■	FC	FC	FC	FC ■	FC	FC	FC ■	FC	EM ◇■	FC
Bedford 7	d				07 33	07 44				07 48	07 55		07 58				08 04			08 24		08 29	
Flitwick	d				07 43					07 58			08 08				08 14			08 34			
Harlington	d				07 47					08 02							08 18			08 38			
Leagrave	d				07 52	08 00				08 08							08 23			08 43			
Luton 10	d		07 56		07 57	08 04		08 02		08 12		08 15	08 20		08 20		08 28			08 48			08 54
Luton Airport Parkway 7 ✈	d				07 59			08 04		08 15	08 12				08 22		08 30			08 50			08 56
Harpenden	d				08 05	08 10		08 10		08 21			08 26		08 28		08 36			08 56			09 02
St Albans City	d			08 07	08 11	08 16		08 16	08 23	08 27			08 33		08 34	08 43	08 44		08 58	09 02			09 08
Radlett	d			08 12				08 21	08 28						08 39	08 48			09 03				09 13
Elstree & Borehamwood	d			08 16				08 25	08 32						08 43	08 52			09 07				09 17
Mill Hill Broadway	d			08 21				08 29	08 37							08 57			09 12				
Hendon	d			08 24					08 40							09 00			09 15				
Cricklewood	d			08 28					08 44							09 04			09 19				
West Hampstead Thameslink ⊖	d			08 32				08 36	08 48						08 52	09 08			09 22				09 26
Kentish Town ⊖	d			08 36					08 52							09 12			09 26				
St Pancras International 15 ⊖	a	←	08 24				←				08 39	08 43		←				←			←	09 06	
St Pancras International 15 ⊖	a	08 27		08 40	08 32	08 35	08 40	08 43	08 56	08 47			08 51	08 56	08 59	09 16	09 03	09 16	09 30	09 21	09 30		09 33
	d	08 28		08 40	08 32	08 36	08 40	08 44	08 56	08 48			08 52	08 56	09 00	09 16	09 04	09 16	09 30	09 22	09 30		09 34
Farringdon 3 ⊖	d	08 34		→	08 38	08 42	08 46	08 50	→	08 54			08 58	09 02	09 06	→	09 10	09 22	→	09 28	09 36		09 40
City Thameslink 3	d	08 37			08 41	08 45	08 49	08 53		08 57			09 01	09 05	09 09		09 13	09 25		09 31	09 39		09 43
London Blackfriars 3 ⊖	d	08 40			08 44	08 48	08 52	08 56		09 00			09 04	09 08	09 12		09 16	09 28		09 34	09 42		09 46
Elephant & Castle ⊖	d	08 44			08 47	08a52	08 56	09 00					09a09	09 12	09 16			09 31			09 46		09 49
Loughborough Jn.	d				08 51			09 04						09 16				09 35					09 53
Herne Hill 4	d				08 57			09 11						09 25				09 41					09 57
London Bridge 4	a									09 11							09 26			09 41			
	d									09 12							09 27			09 42			
Tulse Hill 3	d				09 01			09 16						09 31				09 46					10 01
Streatham 4	d				09 05			09 20						09 35				09 50					10 05
Mitcham Eastfields	d							09 24										09 54					
Mitcham Junction	d							09 27										09 57					
Hackbridge	d							09 30										10 00					
Carshalton	d							09 33										10 03					
Tooting	d				09 10									09 40									10 10
Haydons Road	d				09 13									09 43									10 13
Wimbledon 6 ⊖	d				09 17									09 47									10 17
Wimbledon Chase	d				09 20									09 50									10 20
South Merton	d				09 22									09 52									10 22
Morden South	d				09 24									09 54									10 24
St Helier	d				09 26									09 56									10 26
Sutton Common	d				09 28									09 58									10 28
West Sutton	d				09 31									10 01									10 31
Sutton (Surrey) 4	a				09 37			09 36						10 05				10 06					10 35
East Croydon	d									09 25							09 41			09 55			
Denmark Hill 4	d	08 52					09 02								09 22						09 52		
Peckham Rye 4	d	08 55													09 25						09 55		
Nunhead 4	d	08 57													09 27						09 57		
Crofton Park	d	09 00													09 30						10 00		
Catford	d	09 03					09 09								09 33						10 03		
Bellingham	d	09 05													09 35						10 05		
Beckenham Hill	d	09 07													09 37						10 07		
Ravensbourne	d	09 09													09 39						10 09		
Shortlands	d	09 11													09 41						10 11		
Bromley South 4	d	09 14					09 18								09 44						10 14		
Bickley 4	d	09 17					09 20								09 47						10 17		
St Mary Cray	d	09 21					09 25								09 51						10 21		
Swanley 4	d	09 26					09 36								09 56						10 26		
Eynsford	d	09 30					09 40								10 00						10 30		
Shoreham (Kent)	d	09 34					09 44								10 04						10 34		
Otford 4	d	09 37					09 47								10 07						10 37		
Bat & Ball	d	09 40					09 50								10 10						10 40		
Sevenoaks 4	a	09 45					09 53								10 13						10 43		
Redhill	d																						
Gatwick Airport 10 ✈	d									09 41							09 57			10 11			
Three Bridges 4	d									09 45							10 02			10 15			
Balcombe	d									09 51										10 21			
Haywards Heath 3	d									09 56							10 11			10 27			
Wivelsfield 4	d									10 00										10 31			
Burgess Hill 4	d									10 02										10 33			
Hassocks 4	d									10 06										10 36			
Preston Park	d									10 12										10 43			
Brighton 10	a									10 17							10 25			10 47			

Bedford, Luton, St Albans and City of London - South London, Gatwick Airport and Brighton

Network Diagram - see first Page of Table 52

Station		FC	FC 1	FC		FC	FC	FC 1	FC	FC	EM ◇1	FC	FC 1	EM ◇1		FC 1	FC	FC	FC	FC 1	FC	FC	FC	FC 1
Bedford 7	d		08 40					08 54			09 02		09 10	09 18		09 18				09 24				09 40
Flitwick	d		08 50					09 04					09 20			09 28				09 34				09 50
Harlington	d		08 54					09 08					09 24							09 38				09 54
Leagrave	d		08 59					09 13					09 29							09 43				09 59
Luton 10	d		09 04				09 14	09 18			09 18		09 34			09 39			09 44	09 48				10 04
Luton Airport Parkway 7 ✈	d		09 06				09 16	09 20					09 36	09 34		09 42			09 46	09 50				10 06
Harpenden	d		09 12				09 22	09 26					09 42			09 48			09 52	09 56				10 12
St Albans City	d	09 14	09 18				09 29	09 32				09 44	09 48			09 54			09 59	10 02			10 14	10 18
Radlett	d	09 19					09 34					09 49							10 04				10 19	
Elstree & Borehamwood	d	09 23					09 38					09 53							10 08				10 23	
Mill Hill Broadway	d	09 28					09 43					09 58							10 13				10 28	
Hendon	d	09 31					09 46					10 01							10 16				10 31	
Cricklewood	d	09 35					09 50					10 05							10 20				10 35	
West Hampstead Thameslink ⊖	d	09 39					09 54					10 09							10 24				10 39	
Kentish Town ⊖	d	09 44				09 54	10 00					10 14						10 26	10 30				10 44	
St Pancras International 15 ⊖	a			←					←	←	09 44			10 00			←				←	←		
St Pancras International 15 ⊖	a	09 47	09 39	09 47		09 58	10 03	09 51	09 58	10 03		10 18	10 09			10 13	10 18	10 29	10 33	10 23	10 29	10 33	10 48	10 38
	d	09 48	09 40	09 48		10 00	10 04	09 54	10 00	10 04		10 18	10 09			10 14	10 18	10 30	10 34	10 24	10 30	10 34	10 48	10 39
Farringdon 3 ⊖	d	→	09 45	09 53		→	→	09 59	10 05	10 09		→	10 14			10 20	10 24	→	→	10 29	10 35	10 39	→	10 44
City Thameslink 3	d		09 48	09 57				10 03	10 09	10 13			10 18			10 23	10 27			10 33	10 39	10 43		10 48
London Blackfriars 3 ⊖	d		09 50	10 00				10 05	10 12	10 16			10 20			10 26	10 30			10 35	10 42	10 46		10 50
Elephant & Castle ⊖	d			10 03					10 16	10 19						10a30	10 33				10 46	10 49		
Loughborough Jn	d			10 07						10 23							10 37					10 53		
Herne Hill 4	d			10 11						10 27							10 41					10 57		
London Bridge 4	a		09 56					10 11					10 26							10 41				10 56
	d		09 57					10 12					10 27							10 42				10 57
Tulse Hill 3	d			10 16						10 31							10 46					11 01		
Streatham 4	d			10 20						10 35							10 50					11 05		
Mitcham Eastfields	d			10 24													10 54							
Mitcham Junction	d			10 27													10 57							
Hackbridge	d			10 30													11 00							
Carshalton	d			10 33													11 03							
Tooting	d									10 40												11 10		
Haydons Road	d									10 43												11 13		
Wimbledon 6 ⊖ ⇌	d									10 47												11 17		
Wimbledon Chase	d									10 50												11 20		
South Merton	d									10 52												11 22		
Morden South	d									10 54												11 24		
St Helier	d									10 56												11 26		
Sutton Common	d									10 58												11 28		
West Sutton	d									11 01												11 31		
Sutton (Surrey) 4	a			10 36						11 05							11 06					11 35		
East Croydon ⇌	d		10 11					10 25					10 41							10 55				11 11
Denmark Hill 4	d								10 22												10 52			
Peckham Rye 4	d								10 25												10 55			
Nunhead 4	d								10 27												10 57			
Crofton Park	d								10 30												11 00			
Catford	d								10 33												11 03			
Bellingham	d								10 35												11 05			
Beckenham Hill	d								10 37												11 07			
Ravensbourne	d								10 39												11 09			
Shortlands	d								10 41												11 11			
Bromley South 4	d								10 44												11 14			
Bickley 4	d								10 47												11 17			
St Mary Cray	d								10 51												11 21			
Swanley 4	d								10 56												11 26			
Eynsford	d								11 00												11 30			
Shoreham (Kent)	d								11 04												11 34			
Otford 4	d								11 07												11 37			
Bat & Ball	d								11 10												11 40			
Sevenoaks 4	a								11 13												11 43			
Redhill	d																							
Gatwick Airport 10 ✈	d		10 27					10 41					10 57							11 11				11 27
Three Bridges 4	d		10 32					10 45					11 02							11 15				11 32
Balcombe	d																			11 21				
Haywards Heath 3	d		10 41					10 55					11 11							11 27				11 41
Wivelsfield 4	d							10 59												11 31				
Burgess Hill 4	d							11 01												11 33				
Hassocks 4	d							11 04												11 36				
Preston Park	d							11 11												11 43				
Brighton 10	a		10 55					11 15					11 25							11 47				11 55

Bedford, Luton, St Albans and City of London - South London, Gatwick Airport and Brighton

Network Diagram - see first Page of Table 52

Station		FC	FC	EM ◇1	FC	FC	FC 1	FC	FC	FC		FC 1	EM ◇1	FC	FC	FC	FC	FC 1	FC	FC		FC	FC 1	FC	EM ◇1
Bedford 7	d	09 48		09 49			09 54					10 10	10 18	10 18				10 25					10 40		10 49
Flitwick	d	09 58					10 04					10 20		10 28				10 35					10 50		
Harlington	d						10 08					10 24						10 39					10 54		
Leagrave	d						10 13					10 29						10 44					10 59		
Luton 10	d	10 09		10 04		10 14	10 18					10 34		10 39			10 44	10 49					11 04		11 05
Luton Airport Parkway 7 ✈	d	10 12				10 16	10 20					10 36	10 34	10 42			10 46	10 51					11 06		
Harpenden	d	10 18				10 22	10 26					10 42		10 48			10 52	10 57					11 12		
St Albans City	d	10 24				10 29	10 32			10 44		10 48		10 54			10 59	11 03				11 14	11 18		
Radlett	d					10 34				10 49							11 04					11 19			
Elstree & Borehamwood	d					10 38				10 53							11 08					11 23			
Mill Hill Broadway	d					10 43				10 58							11 13					11 28			
Hendon	d					10 46				11 01							11 16					11 31			
Cricklewood	d					10 50				11 05							11 20					11 35			
West Hampstead Thameslink ⊖	d					10 54				11 09							11 24					11 39			
Kentish Town ⊖	d				10 56	11 00				11 14						11 26	11 30					11 44			
St Pancras International 15 ⊖	a		←	10 29				←	←				11 01		←				←	←				←	11 29
St Pancras International 15 ⊖	a	10 43	10 48		10 59	11 03	10 51	10 59	11 03	11 18		11 09		11 13	11 18	11 29	11 33	11 21	11 29	11 33		11 47	11 38	11 47	
	d	10 44	10 48		11 00	11 04	10 54	11 00	11 04	11 18		11 09		11 14	11 18	11 30	11 34	11 24	11 30	11 34		11 48	11 39	11 48	
Farringdon 3 ⊖	d	10 50	10 54		→	→	10 59	11 05	11 09	→		11 14		11 20	11 24	→	→	11 29	11 35	11 39		→	11 44	11 53	
City Thameslink 3	d	10 53	10 57				11 03	11 09	11 13			11 18		11 23	11 27			11 33	11 39	11 43			11 48	11 57	
London Blackfriars 3 ⊖	d	10 56	11 00				11 05	11 12	11 16			11 20		11 26	11 30			11 35	11 42	11 46			11 50	12 00	
Elephant & Castle ⊖	d	11a00	11 03					11 16	11 19					11a30	11 33				11 46	11 49				12 03	
Loughborough Jn	d		11 07						11 23						11 37					11 53				12 07	
Herne Hill 4	d		11 11						11 27						11 41					11 57				12 11	
London Bridge 4	a						11 11					11 26						11 41					11 56		
	d						11 12					11 27						11 42					11 57		
Tulse Hill 3	d		11 16						11 31						11 46					12 01				12 16	
Streatham 4	d		11 20						11 35						11 50					12 05				12 20	
Mitcham Eastfields	d		11 24												11 54									12 24	
Mitcham Junction	d		11 27												11 57									12 27	
Hackbridge	d		11 30												12 00									12 30	
Carshalton	d		11 33												12 03									12 33	
Tooting	d								11 40											12 10					
Haydons Road	d								11 43											12 13					
Wimbledon 6 ⊖ ⇌	d								11 47											12 17					
Wimbledon Chase	d								11 50											12 20					
South Merton	d								11 52											12 22					
Morden South	d								11 54											12 24					
St Helier	d								11 56											12 26					
Sutton Common	d								11 58											12 28					
West Sutton	d								12 01											12 31					
Sutton (Surrey) 4	a		11 36						12 05						12 06					12 35				12 36	
East Croydon ⇌	d						11 25					11 41						11 55					12 11		
Denmark Hill 4	d							11 22											11 52						
Peckham Rye 4	d							11 25											11 55						
Nunhead 4	d							11 27											11 57						
Crofton Park	d							11 30											12 00						
Catford	d							11 33											12 03						
Bellingham	d							11 35											12 05						
Beckenham Hill	d							11 37											12 07						
Ravensbourne	d							11 39											12 09						
Shortlands	d							11 41											12 11						
Bromley South 4	d							11 44											12 14						
Bickley 4	d							11 47											12 17						
St Mary Cray	d							11 51											12 21						
Swanley 4	d							11 56											12 26						
Eynsford	d							12 00											12 30						
Shoreham (Kent)	d							12 04											12 34						
Otford 4	d							12 07											12 37						
Bat & Ball	d							12 10											12 40						
Sevenoaks 4	a							12 13											12 43						
Redhill	d																								
Gatwick Airport 10 ✈	d						11 41					11 57						12 11					12 27		
Three Bridges 4	d						11 45					12 02						12 15					12 32		
Balcombe	d																	12 21							
Haywards Heath 3	d						11 55					12 11						12 27					12 41		
Wivelsfield 4	d						11 59											12 31							
Burgess Hill 4	d						12 01											12 33							
Hassocks 4	d						12 04											12 36							
Preston Park	d						12 11											12 43							
Brighton 10	a						12 15					12 25						12 47					12 55		

Bedford, Luton, St Albans and City of London - South London, Gatwick Airport and Brighton

Network Diagram - see first Page of Table 52

		FC	FC	FC 1	FC	FC	FC	FC 1	FC	EM ◇1	FC	FC	FC 1	FC	FC	FC	FC 1	FC	EM ◇1	FC	FC	FC 1	FC
Bedford 7	d			10 54				11 10		11 18			11 24				11 40		11 49			11 54	
Flitwick	d			11 04				11 20					11 34				11 50					12 04	
Harlington	d			11 08				11 24					11 38				11 54					12 08	
Leagrave	d			11 13				11 29					11 43				11 59					12 13	
Luton 10	d		11 14	11 18				11 34				11 44	11 48				12 04		12 05		12 14	12 18	
Luton Airport Parkway 7 ✈	d		11 16	11 20				11 36		11 34		11 46	11 50				12 06				12 16	12 20	
Harpenden	d		11 22	11 26				11 42				11 52	11 56				12 12				12 22	12 26	
St Albans City	d		11 29	11 32			11 44	11 48				11 59	12 02			12 14	12 18				12 29	12 32	
Radlett	d		11 34				11 49					12 04				12 19					12 34		
Elstree & Borehamwood	d		11 38				11 53					12 08				12 23					12 38		
Mill Hill Broadway	d		11 43				11 58					12 13				12 28					12 43		
Hendon	d		11 46				12 01					12 16				12 31					12 46		
Cricklewood	d		11 50				12 05					12 20				12 35					12 50		
West Hampstead Thameslink ⊖	d		11 54				12 09					12 24				12 39					12 54		
Kentish Town ⊖	d	11 56	12 00				12 14				12 26	12 30				12 44				12 56	13 00		
St Pancras International 15 ⊖	a				←	←			←	12 00				←	←			←	12 29				←
St Pancras International 15 ⊖	a	11 59	12 03	11 51	11 59	12 03	12 17	12 09	12 17		12 29	12 33	12 21	12 29	12 33	12 47	12 39	12 47		12 59	13 03	12 51	12 59
	d	12 00	12 04	11 54	12 00	12 04	12 18	12 09	12 18		12 30	12 34	12 24	12 30	12 34	12 48	12 39	12 48		13 00	13 04	12 54	13 00
Farringdon 3 ⊖	d	→	→	11 59	12 05	12 09	→	12 14	12 23		→	→	12 29	12 35	12 39	→	12 44	12 53		→	→	12 59	13 05
City Thameslink 3	d			12 03	12 09	12 13		12 18	12 27				12 33	12 39	12 43		12 48	12 57				13 03	13 09
London Blackfriars 3 ⊖	d			12 05	12 12	12 16		12 20	12 30				12 35	12 42	12 46		12 50	13 00				13 05	13 12
Elephant & Castle ⊖	d				12 16	12 19			12 33					12 46	12 49			13 03					13 16
Loughborough Jn	d					12 23			12 37						12 53			13 07					
Herne Hill 4	d					12 27			12 41						12 57			13 11					
London Bridge 4	a			12 11				12 26					12 41				12 56					13 11	
	d			12 12				12 27					12 42				12 57					13 12	
Tulse Hill 3	d					12 31			12 46						13 01			13 16					
Streatham 4	d					12 35			12 50						13 05			13 20					
Mitcham Eastfields	d								12 54									13 24					
Mitcham Junction	d								12 57									13 27					
Hackbridge	d								13 00									13 30					
Carshalton	d								13 03									13 33					
Tooting	d					12 40									13 10								
Haydons Road	d					12 43									13 13								
Wimbledon 6 ⊖ 🚋	d					12 47									13 17								
Wimbledon Chase	d					12 50									13 20								
South Merton	d					12 52									13 22								
Morden South	d					12 54									13 24								
St Helier	d					12 56									13 26								
Sutton Common	d					12 58									13 28								
West Sutton	d					13 01									13 31								
Sutton (Surrey) 4	a					13 05			13 06						13 35			13 36					
East Croydon 🚋	d			12 25				12 41					12 55				13 11					13 25	
Denmark Hill 4	d				12 22									12 52									13 22
Peckham Rye 4	d				12 25									12 55									13 25
Nunhead 4	d				12 27									12 57									13 27
Crofton Park	d				12 30									13 00									13 30
Catford	d				12 33									13 03									13 33
Bellingham	d				12 35									13 05									13 35
Beckenham Hill	d				12 37									13 07									13 37
Ravensbourne	d				12 39									13 09									13 39
Shortlands	d				12 41									13 11									13 41
Bromley South 4	d				12 44									13 14									13 44
Bickley 4	d				12 47									13 17									13 47
St Mary Cray	d				12 51									13 21									13 51
Swanley 4	d				12 56									13 26									13 56
Eynsford	d				13 00									13 30									14 00
Shoreham (Kent)	d				13 04									13 34									14 04
Otford 4	d				13 07									13 37									14 07
Bat & Ball	d				13 10									13 40									14 10
Sevenoaks 4	a				13 13									13 43									14 13
Redhill	d																						
Gatwick Airport 10 ✈	d			12 41				12 57					13 11				13 27					13 41	
Three Bridges 4	d			12 45				13 02					13 15				13 32					13 45	
Balcombe	d												13 21										
Haywards Heath 3	d			12 55				13 11					13 27				13 41					13 55	
Wivelsfield 4	d			12 59									13 31									13 59	
Burgess Hill 4	d			13 01									13 33									14 01	
Hassocks 4	d			13 04									13 36									14 04	
Preston Park	d			13 11									13 43									14 11	
Brighton 10	a			13 15				13 25					13 47				13 55					14 15	

Bedford, Luton, St Albans and City of London - South London, Gatwick Airport and Brighton

Network Diagram - see first Page of Table 52

		FC	FC	FC 1	FC	EM ◇1	FC	FC	FC 1	FC	FC	FC	FC 1	FC	EM ◇1	FC	FC	FC 1	FC	FC	FC	FC 1
Bedford 7	d			12 10		12 18			12 24				12 40		12 49			12 54				13 10
Flitwick	d			12 20					12 34				12 50					13 04				13 20
Harlington	d			12 24					12 38				12 54					13 08				13 24
Leagrave	d			12 29					12 43				12 59					13 13				13 29
Luton 10	d			12 34				12 44	12 48				13 04		13 05		13 14	13 18				13 34
Luton Airport Parkway 7 ✈	d			12 36		12 34		12 46	12 50				13 06				13 16	13 20				13 36
Harpenden	d			12 42				12 52	12 56				13 12				13 22	13 26				13 42
St Albans City	d		12 44	12 48				12 59	13 02			13 14	13 18				13 29	13 32			13 44	13 48
Radlett	d		12 49					13 04				13 19					13 34				13 49	
Elstree & Borehamwood	d		12 53					13 08				13 23					13 38				13 53	
Mill Hill Broadway	d		12 58					13 13				13 28					13 43				13 58	
Hendon	d		13 01					13 16				13 31					13 46				14 01	
Cricklewood	d		13 05					13 20				13 35					13 50				14 05	
West Hampstead Thameslink ⊖	d		13 09					13 24				13 39					13 54				14 09	
Kentish Town ⊖	d		13 14				13 26	13 30				13 44				13 56	14 00				14 14	
St Pancras International 15 ⊖	a	←			←	13 00				←	←			←	13 29				←	←		
St Pancras International 15 ⊖	a	13 03	13 17	13 08	13 17		13 29	13 33	13 21	13 29	13 33	13 47	13 38	13 47		13 59	14 03	13 51	13 59	14 03	14 17	14 09
	d	13 04	13 18	13 09	13 18		13 30	13 34	13 24	13 30	13 34	13 48	13 39	13 48		14 00	14 04	13 54	14 00	14 04	14 18	14 09
Farringdon 3 ⊖	d	13 09	→	13 14	13 23		→	→	13 29	13 35	13 39	→	13 44	13 53		→	→	13 59	14 05	14 09	→	14 14
City Thameslink 3	d	13 13		13 18	13 27				13 33	13 39	13 43		13 48	13 57				14 03	14 09	14 13		14 18
London Blackfriars 3 ⊖	d	13 16		13 20	13 30				13 35	13 42	13 46		13 50	14 00				14 05	14 12	14 16		14 20
Elephant & Castle ⊖	d	13 19			13 33					13 46	13 49			14 03					14 16	14 19		
Loughborough Jn	d	13 23			13 37						13 53			14 07						14 23		
Herne Hill 4	d	13 27			13 41						13 57			14 11						14 27		
London Bridge 4	a			13 26					13 41				13 56					14 11				14 26
	d			13 27					13 42				13 57					14 12				14 27
Tulse Hill 3	d	13 31			13 46						14 01			14 16						14 31		
Streatham 4	d	13 35			13 50						14 05			14 20						14 35		
Mitcham Eastfields	d				13 54									14 24								
Mitcham Junction	d				13 57									14 27								
Hackbridge	d				14 00									14 30								
Carshalton	d				14 03									14 33								
Tooting	d	13 40									14 10									14 40		
Haydons Road	d	13 43									14 13									14 43		
Wimbledon 6 ⊖ 🚋	d	13 47									14 17									14 47		
Wimbledon Chase	d	13 50									14 20									14 50		
South Merton	d	13 52									14 22									14 52		
Morden South	d	13 54									14 24									14 54		
St Helier	d	13 56									14 26									14 56		
Sutton Common	d	13 58									14 28									14 58		
West Sutton	d	14 01									14 31									15 01		
Sutton (Surrey) 4	a	14 05			14 06						14 35			14 36						15 05		
East Croydon 🚋	d			13 41					13 55				14 11					14 25				14 41
Denmark Hill 4	d									13 52									14 22			
Peckham Rye 4	d									13 55									14 25			
Nunhead 4	d									13 57									14 27			
Crofton Park	d									14 00									14 30			
Catford	d									14 03									14 33			
Bellingham	d									14 05									14 35			
Beckenham Hill	d									14 07									14 37			
Ravensbourne	d									14 09									14 39			
Shortlands	d									14 11									14 41			
Bromley South 4	d									14 14									14 44			
Bickley 4	d									14 17									14 47			
St Mary Cray	d									14 21									14 51			
Swanley 4	d									14 26									14 56			
Eynsford	d									14 30									15 00			
Shoreham (Kent)	d									14 34									15 04			
Otford 4	d									14 37									15 07			
Bat & Ball	d									14 40									15 10			
Sevenoaks 4	a									14 43									15 13			
Redhill	d																					
Gatwick Airport 10 ✈	d			13 57					14 11				14 27					14 41				14 57
Three Bridges 4	d			14 02					14 15				14 32					14 45				15 02
Balcombe	d								14 21													
Haywards Heath 3	d			14 11					14 27				14 41					14 55				15 11
Wivelsfield 4	d								14 31									14 59				
Burgess Hill 4	d								14 33									15 01				
Hassocks 4	d								14 36									15 04				
Preston Park	d								14 43									15 11				
Brighton 10	a			14 25					14 47				14 55					15 15				15 25

Bedford, Luton, St Albans and City of London - South London, Gatwick Airport and Brighton

Network Diagram - see first Page of Table 52

		FC	EM ◇1	FC	FC	FC 1	FC	FC	FC	FC 1	FC	EM ◇1	FC	FC	FC 1	FC	FC	FC	FC 1	FC	EM ◇1	FC	FC
Bedford 7	d		13 18			13 24				13 40		13 49			13 54				14 10		14 18		
Flitwick	d					13 34				13 50					14 04				14 20				
Harlington	d					13 38				13 54					14 08				14 24				
Leagrave	d					13 43				13 59					14 13				14 29				
Luton 10	d				13 44	13 48				14 04		14 05		14 14	14 18				14 34				14 44
Luton Airport Parkway 7	d		13 34		13 46	13 50				14 06				14 16	14 20				14 36		14 34		14 46
Harpenden	d				13 52	13 56				14 12				14 22	14 26				14 42				14 52
St Albans City	d				13 59	14 02			14 14	14 18				14 29	14 32			14 44	14 48				14 59
Radlett	d				14 04				14 19					14 34				14 49					15 04
Elstree & Borehamwood	d				14 08				14 23					14 38				14 53					15 08
Mill Hill Broadway	d				14 13				14 28					14 43				14 58					15 13
Hendon	d				14 16				14 31					14 46				15 01					15 16
Cricklewood	d				14 20				14 35					14 50				15 05					15 20
West Hampstead Thameslink ⊖	d				14 24				14 39					14 54				15 09					15 24
Kentish Town ⊖	d			14 26	14 30				14 44				14 56	15 00				15 14				15 26	15 30
St Pancras International 15 ⊖	a	←	14 01				←	←			←	14 29				←	←			←	14 59		
St Pancras International 15 ⊖	a	14 17		14 29	14 33	14 21	14 29	14 33	14 47	14 38	14 47		14 59	15 03	14 51	14 59	15 03	15 17	15 08	15 17		15 29	15 33
	d	14 18		14 30	14 34	14 24	14 30	14 34	14 48	14 39	14 48		15 00	15 04	14 54	15 00	15 04	15 18	15 09	15 18		15 30	15 34
Farringdon 3 ⊖	d	14 23		→	→	14 29	14 35	14 39	→	14 44	14 53		→	→	14 59	15 05	15 09	→	15 14	15 23		→	→
City Thameslink 3	d	14 27				14 33	14 39	14 43		14 48	14 57				15 03	15 09	15 13		15 18	15 27			
London Blackfriars 3 ⊖	d	14 30				14 35	14 42	14 46		14 50	15 00				15 05	15 12	15 16		15 20	15 30			
Elephant & Castle ⊖	d	14 33					14 46	14 49			15 03					15 16	15 19			15 33			
Loughborough Jn.	d	14 37						14 53			15 07						15 23			15 37			
Herne Hill 4	d	14 41						14 57			15 11						15 27			15 41			
London Bridge 4	a					14 41				14 56					15 11				15 26				
	d					14 42				14 57					15 12				15 27				
Tulse Hill 3	d	14 46						15 01			15 16						15 31			15 46			
Streatham 4	d	14 50						15 05			15 20						15 35			15 50			
Mitcham Eastfields	d	14 54									15 24									15 54			
Mitcham Junction	d	14 57									15 27									15 57			
Hackbridge	d	15 00									15 30									16 00			
Carshalton	d	15 03									15 33									16 03			
Tooting	d							15 10									15 40						
Haydons Road	d							15 13									15 43						
Wimbledon 6 ⊖	d							15 17									15 47						
Wimbledon Chase	d							15 20									15 50						
South Merton	d							15 22									15 52						
Morden South	d							15 24									15 54						
St Helier	d							15 26									15 56						
Sutton Common	d							15 28									15 58						
West Sutton	d							15 31									16 01						
Sutton (Surrey) 4	a	15 06						15 35			15 36						16 05			16 06			
East Croydon	d					14 55				15 11					15 25				15 41				
Denmark Hill 4	d						14 52									15 22							
Peckham Rye 4	d						14 55									15 25							
Nunhead 4	d						14 57									15 27							
Crofton Park	d						15 00									15 30							
Catford	d						15 03									15 33							
Bellingham	d						15 05									15 35							
Beckenham Hill	d						15 07									15 37							
Ravensbourne	d						15 09									15 39							
Shortlands	d						15 11									15 41							
Bromley South 4	d						15 14									15 44							
Bickley 4	d						15 17									15 47							
St Mary Cray	d						15 21									15 51							
Swanley 4	d						15 26									15 56							
Eynsford	d						15 30									16 00							
Shoreham (Kent)	d						15 34									16 04							
Otford 4	d						15 37									16 07							
Bat & Ball	d						15 40									16 10							
Sevenoaks 4	a						15 43									16 13							
Redhill	d																						
Gatwick Airport 10 ✈	d					15 11				15 27					15 41				15 57				
Three Bridges 4	d					15 15				15 32					15 45				16 02				
Balcombe	d					15 21																	
Haywards Heath 3	d					15 27				15 41					15 55				16 11				
Wivelsfield 4	d					15 31									15 59								
Burgess Hill 4	d					15 33									16 01								
Hassocks 4	d					15 36									16 04								
Preston Park	d					15 43									16 11								
Brighton 10	a					15 47				15 55					16 15				16 25				

Bedford, Luton, St Albans and City of London - South London, Gatwick Airport and Brighton

Network Diagram - see first Page of Table 52

		FC 1	FC	FC	FC	FC 1	FC	EM ◇1	FC	FC	FC 1	FC	FC	FC	FC	FC 1	FC	FC	EM ◇1	FC	FC	FC 1
Bedford 7	d	14 24				14 40		14 49			14 54					15 10			15 18			15 24
Flitwick	d	14 34				14 50					15 04					15 20						15 34
Harlington	d	14 38				14 54					15 08					15 24						15 38
Leagrave	d	14 43				14 59					15 13					15 29						15 43
Luton 10	d	14 48				15 04		15 05		15 14	15 18					15 34					15 44	15 48
Luton Airport Parkway 7 ✈	d	14 50				15 06				15 16	15 20					15 36			15 34		15 46	15 50
Harpenden	d	14 56				15 12				15 22	15 26					15 42					15 52	15 56
St Albans City	d	15 02			15 14	15 18				15 29	15 32				15 44	15 48					15 59	16 02
Radlett	d				15 19					15 34					15 49						16 04	
Elstree & Borehamwood	d				15 23					15 38					15 53						16 08	
Mill Hill Broadway	d				15 28					15 43					15 58						16 13	
Hendon	d				15 31					15 46					16 01						16 16	
Cricklewood	d				15 35					15 50					16 05						16 20	
West Hampstead Thameslink ⊖	d				15 39					15 54					16 09						16 24	
Kentish Town ⊖	d				15 44				15 56	16 00				16 10	16 14					16 24	16 30	
St Pancras International 15 ⊖	a		←	←			←	15 29				←	←				←	←	15 59			
St Pancras International 15 ⊖	a	15 21	15 29	15 33	15 47	15 38	15 47		15 59	16 03	15 51	15 59	16 03	16 13	16 17	16 08	16 13	16 17		16 27	16 33	16 20
	d	15 24	15 30	15 34	15 48	15 39	15 48		16 00	16 04	15 54	16 00	16 04	16 14	16 18	16 09	16 14	16 18		16 28	16 34	16 22
Farringdon 3 ⊖	d	15 29	15 35	15 39	→	15 44	15 53		→	→	15 59	16 05	16 09	→	→	16 14	16 19	16 23		→	→	16 27
City Thameslink 3	d	15 33	15 39	15 43		15 48	15 57				16 03	16 09	16 13			16 18	16 23	16 27				16 31
London Blackfriars 3 ⊖	d	15 35	15 42	15 46		15 50	16 00				16 05	16 12	16 16			16 20	16 26	16 30				16 36
Elephant & Castle ⊖	d		15 46	15 49			16 03					16 16	16 19				16 30	16 33				
Loughborough Jn.	d			15 53			16 07						16 23					16 37				
Herne Hill 4	d			15 57			16 11						16 27					16 41				
London Bridge 4	a	15 41				15 56					16 11					16 26						16 42
	d	15 42				15 57					16 12					16 27						16 43
Tulse Hill 3	d			16 01			16 16						16 32					16 46				
Streatham 4	d			16 05			16 20						16 36					16 50				
Mitcham Eastfields	d						16 24											16 55				
Mitcham Junction	d						16 27											16 58				
Hackbridge	d						16 30											17 01				
Carshalton	d						16 33											17 04				
Tooting	d			16 10									16 40									
Haydons Road	d			16 13									16 43									
Wimbledon 6 ⊖	d			16 17									16 47									
Wimbledon Chase	d			16 20									16 50									
South Merton	d			16 22									16 52									
Morden South	d			16 24									16 54									
St Helier	d			16 26									16 56									
Sutton Common	d			16 28									16 58									
West Sutton	d			16 31									17 01									
Sutton (Surrey) 4	a			16 35			16 36						17 05					17 08				
East Croydon	d	15 55				16 11					16 25					16 41						17 00
Denmark Hill 4	d		15 52									16 22					16 39					
Peckham Rye 4	d		15 55									16 25					16 42					
Nunhead 4	d		15 57									16 27					16 44					
Crofton Park	d		16 00									16 30					16 47					
Catford	d		16 03									16 33					16 50					
Bellingham	d		16 05									16 35					16 52					
Beckenham Hill	d		16 07									16 37					16 54					
Ravensbourne	d		16 09									16 39					16 56					
Shortlands	d		16 11									16 41					16 58					
Bromley South 4	d		16 14									16 44					17 01					
Bickley 4	d		16 17									16 47					17a04					
St Mary Cray	d		16 21									16 51										
Swanley 4	d		16 26									16 56										
Eynsford	d		16 30									17 00										
Shoreham (Kent)	d		16 34									17 04										
Otford 4	d		16 37									17 07										
Bat & Ball	d		16 40									17 10										
Sevenoaks 4	a		16 43									17 14										
Redhill	d																					
Gatwick Airport 10 ✈	d	16 11				16 27					16 41					16 57						17 16
Three Bridges 4	d	16 15				16 32					16 45					17 02						17 21
Balcombe	d	16 21																				17 27
Haywards Heath 3	d	16 27				16 41					16 55					17 11						17 32
Wivelsfield 4	d	16 31									16 59											17 37
Burgess Hill 4	d	16 33									17 01					17 17						17 39
Hassocks 4	d	16 36									17 04					17 21						17 43
Preston Park	d	16 43									17 11											17 50
Brighton 10	a	16 47				16 55					17 15					17 30						17 54

Bedford, Luton, St Albans and City of London - South London, Gatwick Airport and Brighton

Network Diagram - see first Page of Table 52

		FC	FC	FC	FC 1	EM ◇1	FC 1	FC		FC		FC	FC	FC	FC 1	EM ◇1	FC 1	FC	FC			FC	FC 1	FC	FC 1
Bedford 7	d				15 40	15 49	15 52					15 56			16 10	16 18	16 22						16 26		16 36
Flitwick	d				15 50		16 02					16 06			16 20		16 32						16 36		16 46
Harlington	d				15 54							16 10			16 24								16 40		16 50
Leagrave	d				15 59							16 15			16 29								16 45		16 55
Luton 10	d				16 04	16 05	16 14			16 16		16 20			16 34		16 42					16 46	16 50		17 00
Luton Airport Parkway 7 ✈	d				16 06		16 17			16 18		16 22			16 36	16 34	16 44					16 48	16 52		17 02
Harpenden	d				16 12					16 24		16 28			16 42							16 54	16 58		17 08
St Albans City	d			16 14	16 18		16 25			16 30		16 34		16 44	16 48		16 54					17 00	17 04		17 14
Radlett	d			16 19						16 35				16 49								17 05			
Elstree & Borehamwood	d			16 23						16 39				16 53								17 09			
Mill Hill Broadway	d			16 28						16 44				16 58								17 14			
Hendon	d			16 31						16 47				17 01								17 17			
Cricklewood	d			16 35						16 51				17 05								17 21			
West Hampstead Thameslink ⊖	d			16 42						16 54		16 48		17 10								17 24	17 18		17 28
Kentish Town ⊖	d			16 46						16 58				17 14					17 18			17 28			
St Pancras International 15 ⊖	a	←	←			16 29		←					←			17 00		←						←	
St Pancras International 15 ⊖	a	16 27	16 33	16 50	16 39		16 44	16 50		17 02		16 55	17 02	17 18	17 09		17 13	17 18	17 21			17 32	17 25	17 32	17 35
	d	16 28	16 34	16 52	16 40		16 46	16 52		17 02		16 58	17 02	17 18	17 10		17 14	17 18	17 22			17 32	17 28	17 32	17 36
Farringdon 3 ⊖	d	16 33	16 39	→	16 45		16 51	16 57		→		17 03	17 07	→	17 15		17 19	17 23	17 27			→	17 33	17 37	17 41
City Thameslink 3	d	16 37	16 43		16 49		16 55	17 01				17 07	17 11		17 19		17 23	17 27	17 31				17 37	17 41	17 45
London Blackfriars 3 ⊖	d	16 42	16 46		16 52		16 58	17 04				17 10	17 14		17 22		17 25	17 30	17 36				17 40	17 44	17 48
Elephant & Castle ⊖	d	16 46	16 49		16 56		17 02	17 08				17 14	17 18				17 29	17 34	17 40					17 48	17 52
Loughborough Jn.	d		16 53		17 00			17 12					17 22					17 38						17 52	
Herne Hill 4	d		16 57		17a04			17 16					17 26				17 36	17 43						17 57	
London Bridge 4	a																								
	d																								
Tulse Hill 3	d		17 02					17 20					17 31					17 48						18 02	
Streatham 4	d		17 06					17 24					17 36					17 52						18 06	
Mitcham Eastfields	d							17 28										17 55							
Mitcham Junction	d							17 31										17 58							
Hackbridge	d							17 34										18 02							
Carshalton	d							17 37										18 04							
Tooting	d		17 10										17 40											18 10	
Haydons Road	d		17 13										17 43											18 13	
Wimbledon 6 ⊖ ⇌	d		17 19										17 49											18 19	
Wimbledon Chase	d		17 22										17 52											18 22	
South Merton	d		17 24										17 54											18 24	
Morden South	d		17 26										17 56											18 26	
St Helier	d		17 28										17 58											18 28	
Sutton Common	d		17 30										18 00											18 30	
West Sutton	d		17 33										18 03											18 33	
Sutton (Surrey) 4	a		17 37					17 40					18 07					18 08						18 37	
East Croydon ⇌	d						17 26								17 47								18 09		
Denmark Hill 4	d	16 52										17 20							17 47						
Peckham Rye 4	d	16 55										17 23							17 50						
Nunhead 4	d	16 57										17 26							17 52						
Crofton Park	d	17 00										17 29							17 55						
Catford	d	17 03										17 32							17 58						
Bellingham	d	17 05										17 35							18 01						
Beckenham Hill	d	17 07										17 37							18 03						
Ravensbourne	d	17 09										17 39							18 05						
Shortlands	d	17 11										17 43							18 07						
Bromley South 4	d	17 14										17 46					17 48		18 10						18 11
Bickley 4	d	17 17															17 50		18 12						
St Mary Cray	d	17 21															17 55		18 22						18 18
Swanley 4	d	17 30										17 55					17a59		18 26						18 22
Eynsford	d	17 34										18 00							18 31						
Shoreham (Kent)	d	17 38										18 03							18 34						
Otford 4	d	17 41										18 06							18 38						18a30
Bat & Ball	d	17 44										18 14							18 41						
Sevenoaks 4	a	17 49										18 23							18 50						
Redhill	d														18 03										
Gatwick Airport 10 ✈	d						17 42								18 14								18 25		
Three Bridges 4	d						17 46								18 19								18 30		
Balcombe	d						17 52								18 25										
Haywards Heath 3	d						17 58								18 31								18 39		
Wivelsfield 4	d																						18 44		
Burgess Hill 4	d						18 03								18 36								18 46		
Hassocks 4	d						18 07								18 40								18 50		
Preston Park	d						18 14								18 47								18 57		
Brighton 10	a						18 18								18 53								19 02		

Bedford, Luton, St Albans and City of London - South London, Gatwick Airport and Brighton

Network Diagram - see first Page of Table 52

		EM ◇1	FC 1	FC	FC	FC		FC	FC 1		FC	FC	FC 1	FC	EM ◇1	FC		FC 1	FC	EM ◇1	FC	FC 1	FC 1	FC 1	FC
Bedford 7	d	16 49							16 54				17 06		17 18			17 22				17 36	17 41		
Flitwick	d								17 04				17 16					17 32				17 46			
Harlington	d								17 08				17 20					17 36				17 50			
Leagrave	d								17 13				17 26					17 41				17 55			
Luton 10	d	17 05			17 10				17 18		17 22		17 30			17 38		17 46		17 51		18 00			
Luton Airport Parkway 7 ✈	d				17 12				17 20		17 24		17 33		17 30	17 40		17 48				18 02	17 59		
Harpenden	d				17 18				17 26		17 30		17 39			17 46		17 54				18 08			
St Albans City	d			17 20	17 24				17 32		17 36	17 40	17 45			17 52		18 00			18 06	18 14	18 09		
Radlett	d			17 25							17 41	17 45				17 57					18 11				
Elstree & Borehamwood	d			17 29							17 45	17 49				18 01					18 15				
Mill Hill Broadway	d			17 34							17 49	17 53				18 06					18 20				
Hendon	d			17 37								17 57				18 09					18 23				
Cricklewood	d			17 41								18 00				18 13					18 27				
West Hampstead Thameslink ⊖	d			17 44		17 40			17 48		17 56	18 04				18 16					18 30				
Kentish Town ⊖	d			17 48								18 08				18 20					18 34				
St Pancras International 15 ⊖	a	17 29						←						←	18 01				←	18 17				←	←
St Pancras International 15 ⊖	a			17 52	17 43	17 47		17 52	17 55		18 03	18 12	18 07	18 12		18 24		18 19	18 24		18 38	18 34	18 27	18 34	18 38
	d		17 40	17 52	17 44	17 48		17 52	17 56		18 04	18 12	18 08	18 12		18 24		18 20	18 24		18 38	18 34	18 30	18 34	18 38
Farringdon 3 ⊖	d		17 45	→	17 49	17 53		17 57	18 01		18 09	→	18 13	18 17		→		18 25	18 29		→	→	18 35	18 40	18 43
City Thameslink 3	d		17 49		17 53	17 57		18 01	18 05		18 13		18 17	18 21				18 29	18 33				18 39	18 43	18 47
London Blackfriars 3 ⊖	d		17 51		17 56	18 00		18 04	18 10		18 16		18 20	18 24				18 32	18 36				18 42	18 46	18 50
Elephant & Castle ⊖	d		17 55		18 00	18 05		18 08	18 14		18 20			18 28				18 36	18 40				18 46		18 54
Loughborough Jn.	d							18 12			18 24								18 44						18 58
Herne Hill 4	d				18a06			18 17	18 21		18 28								18 48						19 02
London Bridge 4	a												18 27											18 54	
	d												18 27											18 57	
Tulse Hill 3	d							18 22			18 32								18 52						19 09
Streatham 4	d							18 26			18 36								18 56						19 13
Mitcham Eastfields	d							18 29											18 59						
Mitcham Junction	d							18 32											19 02						
Hackbridge	d							18 36											19 06						
Carshalton	d							18 38											19 08						
Tooting	d										18 40														19 18
Haydons Road	d										18 43														19 21
Wimbledon 6 ⊖ ⇌	d										18 49														19 24
Wimbledon Chase	d										18 52														19 27
South Merton	d										18 54														19 29
Morden South	d										18 56														19 31
St Helier	d										18 58														19 33
Sutton Common	d										19 00														19 35
West Sutton	d										19 03														19 38
Sutton (Surrey) 4	a							18 42			19 07								19 12						19 41
East Croydon ⇌	d		18 25										18 41					19 01						19 11	
Denmark Hill 4	d					18 15								18 34									18 52		
Peckham Rye 4	d					18 18								18 38									18 55		
Nunhead 4	d					18 20								18 40									18 57		
Crofton Park	d					18 23								18 43									19 00		
Catford	d					18 26								18 46									19 03		
Bellingham	d					18 29								18 49									19 05		
Beckenham Hill	d					18 31								18 51									19 07		
Ravensbourne	d					18 33								18 53									19 09		
Shortlands	d					18 35								18 57									19 13		
Bromley South 4	d					18 38			18 31					19 00									19 16		
Bickley 4	d					18 40								19 03									19 19		
St Mary Cray	d					18 45			18 38					19 10									19 23		
Swanley 4	d					18 53			18a42					19 15									19 29		
Eynsford	d					18 57								19 19									19 33		
Shoreham (Kent)	d					19 01								19 23									19 37		
Otford 4	d					19 04								19 26									19 40		
Bat & Ball	d					19 07								19 29									19 43		
Sevenoaks 4	a					19 12								19 37									19 50		
Redhill	d		18 38																						
Gatwick Airport 10 ✈	d		18 50										18 57					19 18						19 26	
Three Bridges 4	d		18a56										19 02											19 31	
Balcombe	d												19 08											19 37	
Haywards Heath 3	d												19 14					19 30						19 42	
Wivelsfield 4	d																								
Burgess Hill 4	d												19 19					19 35						19 48	
Hassocks 4	d												19 23					19 39						19 51	
Preston Park	d																	19 46							
Brighton 10	a												19 33					19 52						20 01	

Bedford, Luton, St Albans and City of London - South London, Gatwick Airport and Brighton

Network Diagram - see first Page of Table 52

		EM ◇■	FC	EM ◇■	FC	FC ■	FC	FC	FC ■	EM ◇■	FC	SE	FC ■	SE	FC	FC ■	EM ◇■	FC	FC	FC ■	FC	FC
Bedford [7]	d	17 49				17 54		18 02	18 10	18 17			18 24		18 36	18 40	18 49			18 54		
Flitwick	d					18 04			18 20				18 34			18 50				19 04		
Harlington	d					18 08			18 24				18 38			18 54				19 08		
Leagrave	d					18 13			18 29				18 43			18 59				19 13		
Luton [10]	d	18 05	18 06	18 15		18 18		18 22	18 34			18 44	18 48		18 54	19 04	19 05		19 14	19 18		19 24
Luton Airport Parkway [7] ✈	d		18 08			18 20		18 24	18 36	18 33		18 46	18 50		18 57	19 06			19 16	19 20		19 27
Harpenden	d		18 14			18 26		18 30	18 42			18 52	18 56		19 02	19 12			19 22	19 26		19 32
St Albans City	d		18 20		18 26	18 32		18 36	18 48		18 52	18 58	19 02		19 08	19 18		19 22	19 28	19 32		19 38
Radlett	d		18 25		18 31			18 41			18 57	19 03			19 13			19 27	19 33			19 43
Elstree & Borehamwood	d		18 29		18 35			18 45			19 01	19 07			19 17			19 31	19 37			19 47
Mill Hill Broadway	d		18 33		18 40			18 49				19 12							19 42			
Hendon	d				18 43							19 15							19 45			
Cricklewood	d				18 47							19 19							19 49			
West Hampstead Thameslink ⊖	d		18 40		18 50	18 46		18 56	19 02		19 10	19 22			19 26	19 32		19 40	19 52			19 56
Kentish Town ⊖	d				18 54							19 26							19 56			
St Pancras International [15] ⊖	a	18 34		18 39			←			19 00				←			19 32				←	
St Pancras International [15] ⊖	a		18 47		18 58	18 53	18 58	19 04	19 08		19 17	19 30	19 22	19 30	19 33	19 38		19 47	20 00	19 51	20 00	20 03
	d		18 48		19 00	18 54	19 00	19 04	19 09		19 18	19 30	19 24	19 30	19 34	19 39		19 48	20 00	19 54	20 00	20 04
Farringdon [3] ⊖	d		18 53		→	18 59	19 05	19 09	19 14		19 23	→	19 29	19 36	19 39	19 44		19 53	→	19 59	20 05	20 09
City Thameslink [3]	d		18 57			19 03	19 09	19 13	19 18		19 27		19 33	19 39	19 43	19 48		19 57		20 03	20 09	20 13
London Blackfriars [3] ⊖	d		19 00			19 05	19 12	19 16	19 20		19 30		19 35	19 42	19 46	19 50		20 00		20 05	20 12	20 16
Elephant & Castle ⊖	d		19 04				19 16	19 19			19 33			19 46	19 49			20 03			20 16	20 19
Loughborough Jn.	d		19 08					19 23			19 37				19 53			20 07				20 23
Herne Hill [4]	d		19 12					19 27			19 41				19 57			20 11				20 27
London Bridge [4]	a					19 11			19 26				19 41			19 56				20 11		
	d					19 12			19 27				19 42			19 57				20 12		
Tulse Hill [3]	d		19 16					19 31			19 46				20 01			20 16				20 31
Streatham [4]	d		19 20					19 35			19 50				20 05			20 20				20 35
Mitcham Eastfields	d		19 24								19 54							20 24				
Mitcham Junction	d		19 27								19 57							20 27				
Hackbridge	d		19 30								20 00							20 30				
Carshalton	d		19 33								20 03							20 33				
Tooting	d							19 40							20 10							20 40
Haydons Road	d							19 43							20 13							20 43
Wimbledon [6] ⊖ ⛴	d							19 49							20 19							20 49
Wimbledon Chase	d							19 52							20 22							20 52
South Merton	d							19 54							20 24							20 54
Morden South	d							19 56							20 26							20 56
St Helier	d							19 58							20 28							20 58
Sutton Common	d							20 00							20 30							21 00
West Sutton	d							20 03							20 33							21 03
Sutton (Surrey) [4]	a		19 36					20 07			20 06				20 39			20 36				21 09
East Croydon ⛴	d					19 25			19 41				19 55			20 11				20 25		
Denmark Hill [4]	d						19 22							19 52							20 22	
Peckham Rye [4]	d						19 25							19 55							20 25	
Nunhead [4]	d						19 27							19 57							20 27	
Crofton Park	d						19 30							20 00							20 30	
Catford	d						19 33							20 03							20 33	
Bellingham	d						19 35							20 05							20 35	
Beckenham Hill	d						19 37							20 07							20 37	
Ravensbourne	d						19 39							20 09							20 39	
Shortlands	d						19 41							20 11							20 41	
Bromley South [4]	d						19 44							20 14							20 44	
Bickley [4]	d						19 47							20 17							20 47	
St Mary Cray	d						19 51							20 21							20 51	
Swanley [4]	d						19 56							20 26							20 56	
Eynsford	d						20 00							20 30							21 00	
Shoreham (Kent)	d						20 04							20 34							21 04	
Otford [4]	d						20 07							20 37							21 07	
Bat & Ball	d						20 10							20 40							21 10	
Sevenoaks [4]	a						20 13							20 43							21 13	
Redhill	d																					
Gatwick Airport [10] ✈	d					19 41			19 57				20 11			20 27				20 41		
Three Bridges [4]	d					19 45			20 02				20 15			20 32				20 45		
Balcombe	d					19 51														20 51		
Haywards Heath [3]	d					19 57			20 11				20 25			20 41				20 57		
Wivelsfield [4]	d					20 01							20 29							21 01		
Burgess Hill [4]	d					20 03			20 16				20 31			20 46				21 03		
Hassocks [4]	d					20 06			20 20				20 34							21 06		
Preston Park	d					20 13							20 41							21 13		
Brighton [10]	a					20 17			20 29				20 45			20 57				21 17		

Bedford, Luton, St Albans and City of London - South London, Gatwick Airport and Brighton

Network Diagram - see first Page of Table 52

		EM ◇■	FC	FC	FC	FC ■	FC	FC	EM ◇■	FC ■	FC	FC	EM ◇■	FC ■	FC	FC ■	EM ◇■	FC	EM ◇■	FC ■ A FX	FC ■ B FO	FC B FO	SE
Bedford [7]	d	19 18				19 26			19 49	19 52			20 18	20 22		20 52	20 54		21 22	21 22	21 22		
Flitwick	d					19 36				20 02				20 32		21 02				21 32	21 32		
Harlington	d					19 40				20 06				20 36		21 06				21 36	21 36		
Leagrave	d					19 45				20 11				20 41		21 11				21 41	21 41		
Luton [10]	d				19 46	19 50			20 05	20 16		20 20		20 46	20 50	21 16	21 08	21 20		21 46	21 46	21 50	
Luton Airport Parkway [7] ✈	d	19 34			19 48	19 52				20 18		20 22	20 34	20 48	20 52	21 18		21 22	21 39	21 48	21 48	21 53	
Harpenden	d				19 54	19 58				20 24		20 28		20 54	20 58	21 24		21 28		21 54	21 54	21 58	
St Albans City	d		19 52		20 00	20 04				20 30		20 34		21 00	21 04	21 30		21 34		22 00	22 00	22 05	
Radlett	d		19 57		20 05							20 39			21 09			21 39				22 10	
Elstree & Borehamwood	d		20 01		20 09							20 43			21 13			21 43				22 15	
Mill Hill Broadway	d				20 14							20 47			21 17			21 47				22 19	
Hendon	d				20 17							20 50			21 20			21 50				22 22	
Cricklewood	d				20 21							20 54			21 24			21 54				22 26	
West Hampstead Thameslink ⊖	d		20 10		20 24	20 17				20 44		20 56		21 14	21 26	21 44		21 56		22 14	22 14	22 28	
Kentish Town ⊖	d			20 26	20 30						20 56	21 01			21 31			22 01				22 34	
St Pancras International [15] ⊖	a	20 01					←	←	20 29				20 59				21 33		22 04		22 23	22 40	
St Pancras International [15] ⊖	a		20 17	20 29	20 33	20 24	20 29	20 33		20 51	20 59	21 05		21 21	21 35	21 51		22 05		22 23			
	d		20 18	20 30	20 34	20 24	20 30	20 34		20 54	21 00	21 06		21 24	21 36	21 54		22 06					
Farringdon [3] ⊖	d		20 23	→	→	20 29	20 35	20 39		20 59	21 05	21 10		21 29	21 40	21 59		22 10					
City Thameslink [3]	d		20 27			20 33	20 39	20 43		21 03	21 09	21 13		21 33	21 43	22 03		22 13					
London Blackfriars [3] ⊖	d		20 30			20 35	20 42	20 46		21 05	21 12	21 16		21 35	21 46	22 05		22 16					
Elephant & Castle ⊖	d		20 33				20 46	20 49			21 16	21 19			21 49			22 19					
Loughborough Jn.	d		20 37					20 53				21 23			21 53			22 23					
Herne Hill [4]	d		20 41					20 57				21 27			21 57			22 27					
London Bridge [4]	a					20 41				21 11				21 41		22 11							
	d					20 42				21 12				21 42		22 12							
Tulse Hill [3]	d		20 50					21 01				21 31			22 01			22 31					
Streatham [4]	d		20 53					21 05				21 35			22 05			22 35					
Mitcham Eastfields	d		20 57																				
Mitcham Junction	d		21 00																				
Hackbridge	d		21 03																				
Carshalton	d		21 06																				
Tooting	d							21 10				21 40			22 10			22 40					
Haydons Road	d							21 13				21 43			22 13			22 43					
Wimbledon [6] ⊖ ⛴	d							21 19				21 49			22 19			22 49					
Wimbledon Chase	d							21 22				21 52			22 22			22 52					
South Merton	d							21 24				21 54			22 24			22 54					
Morden South	d							21 26				21 56			22 26			22 56					
St Helier	d							21 28				21 58			22 28			22 58					
Sutton Common	d							21 30				22 00			22 30			23 00					
West Sutton	d							21 33				22 03			22 33			23 03					
Sutton (Surrey) [4]	a		21 10					21 39				22 09			22 39			23 09					
East Croydon ⛴	d					20 55				21 25				21 55		22 25							
Denmark Hill [4]	d						20 52				21 22												21 52
Peckham Rye [4]	d						20 55				21 25												21 55
Nunhead [4]	d						20 57				21 27												21 57
Crofton Park	d						21 00				21 30												22 00
Catford	d						21 03				21 33												22 03
Bellingham	d						21 05				21 35												22 05
Beckenham Hill	d						21 07				21 37												22 07
Ravensbourne	d						21 09				21 39												22 09
Shortlands	d						21 11				21 41												22 11
Bromley South [4]	d						21 14				21 44												22 14
Bickley [4]	d						21 17				21 47												22 17
St Mary Cray	d						21 21				21 51												22 21
Swanley [4]	d						21 26				21 56												22 26
Eynsford	d						21 30				22 00												22 30
Shoreham (Kent)	d						21 34				22 04												22 34
Otford [4]	d						21 37				22 07												22 37
Bat & Ball	d						21 40				22 10												22 40
Sevenoaks [4]	a						21 43				22 13												22 43
Redhill	d																						
Gatwick Airport [10] ✈	d					21 11				21 41				22 11		22 41							
Three Bridges [4]	d					21 15				21 45				22 15		22 45							
Balcombe	d									21 53						22 53							
Haywards Heath [3]	d					21 25				21 59				22 25		22 59							
Wivelsfield [4]	d					21 29				22 03				22 29		23 03							
Burgess Hill [4]	d					21 31				22 05				22 31		23 05							
Hassocks [4]	d					21 34				22 08				22 34		23 08							
Preston Park	d					21 41				22 15				22 41		23 15							
Brighton [10]	a					21 45				22 19				22 45		23 19							

A until 22 March and from 26 March **B** until 23 March

Bedford, Luton, St Albans and City of London - South London, Gatwick Airport and Brighton

Network Diagram - see first Page of Table 52

		SE	FC	FC	EM	FC	FC	FC	FC	SE	FC	FC	FC	FC	FC	FC	EM	FC	SE	FC	FC	FC
					◇1	1		1					1			1	◇1					
				A		B		A	B			A	B			A		B				A
			🚌				🚌				🚌				🚌						🚌	
					☕	FO							FO				☕	FO				
Bedford 7	d				21 44	21 52		21 52					22 16			22 16	22 19					
Flitwick	d					22 02		22 02					22 26			22 26						
Harlington	d					22 06		22 06					22 30			22 30						
Leagrave	d					22 11		22 11					22 35			22 35						
Luton 10	d			21 50	22 01	22 16		22 16	22 20			22 20	22 40			22 40	22 34	22 46				22 46
Luton Airport Parkway 7 ✈	d			21 53		22 18		22 18	22 23			22 23	22 42			22 42	22 38	22 49				22 49
Harpenden	d			21 58		22 24		22 24	22 29			22 29	22 48			22 48		22 55				22 55
St Albans City	d			22 05		22 30		22 30	22 35			22 35	22 54			22 54		23 01				23 01
Radlett	d			22 10					22 40			22 40						23 06				23 06
Elstree & Borehamwood	d			22 15					22 45			22 45						23 11				23 11
Mill Hill Broadway	d			22 19					22 49			22 49						23 15				23 15
Hendon	d			22 22					22 52			22 52						23 18				23 18
Cricklewood	d			22 26					22 56			22 56						23 22				23 22
West Hampstead Thameslink ⊖	d			22 28		22 44		22 44	22 58			22 58	23 10			23 10		23 24				23 24
Kentish Town ⊖	d			22 34					23 04			23 04						23 30				23 30
St Pancras International 15 ⊖	a				22 29	22 54			23 10				23 24				23 01	23 37				
St Pancras International 15 ⊖	a			22 39				22 53				23 09				23 21						23 35
	d		22 30				22 45				23 00				23 15						23 30	
Farringdon 3 ⊖	d		22 35				22 50				23 05				23 20						23 35	
City Thameslink 3	d		22 37				22 52				23 07											
London Blackfriars 3 ⊖	d		22 42				22 57				23 12				23 25						23 40	
Elephant & Castle ⊖	d																					
Loughborough Jn	d																					
Herne Hill 4	d																					
London Bridge 4	a		22 57				23 12				23 27				23 40						23 54	
	d													23 01						23 29		
Tulse Hill 3	d													23 11						23 41		
Streatham 4	d													23 15						23 45		
Mitcham Eastfields	d																					
Mitcham Junction	d																					
Hackbridge	d																					
Carshalton	d																					
Tooting	d													23 20						23 50		
Haydons Road	d													23 23						23 53		
Wimbledon 6 ⊖	d													23 27						23 57		
Wimbledon Chase	d													23 30						00 01		
South Merton	d													23 32						00 03		
Morden South	d													23 34						00 05		
St Helier	d													23 36						00 07		
Sutton Common	d													23 38						00 09		
West Sutton	d													23 41						00 12		
Sutton (Surrey) 4	a													23 45						00 15		
East Croydon	d																					
Denmark Hill 4	d	22 22								22 52									23 22			
Peckham Rye 4	d	22 25								22 55									23 25			
Nunhead 4	d	22 27								22 57									23 27			
Crofton Park	d	22 30								23 00									23 30			
Catford	d	22 33								23 03									23 33			
Bellingham	d	22 35								23 05									23 35			
Beckenham Hill	d	22 37								23 07									23 37			
Ravensbourne	d	22 39								23 09									23 39			
Shortlands	d	22 41								23 11									23 41			
Bromley South 4	d	22 44								23 14									23 44			
Bickley 4	d	22 47								23a17									23a47			
St Mary Cray	d	22 51																				
Swanley 4	d	22 56																				
Eynsford	d	23 00																				
Shoreham (Kent)	d	23 04																				
Otford 4	d	23 07																				
Bat & Ball	d	23 10																				
Sevenoaks 4	a	23 13																				
Redhill	d																					
Gatwick Airport 10 ✈	d																					
Three Bridges 4	d																					
Balcombe	d																					
Haywards Heath 3	d																					
Wivelsfield 4	d																					
Burgess Hill 4	d																					
Hassocks 4	d																					
Preston Park	d																					
Brighton 10	a																					

A until 22 March and from 26 March

B until 23 March

Bedford, Luton, St Albans and City of London - South London, Gatwick Airport and Brighton

Network Diagram - see first Page of Table 52

		EM	FC	FC	FC	FC	FC	FC	FC	SE	FC
		◇1	1		1	1	1	1	1		
			A		B	B	A	B	A		
				🚌							
		☕									
			FO		FX	FX	FO	FX	FO		
Bedford 7	d	22 45	22 52		22 52	23 12	23 12	23 32	23 32		
Flitwick	d		23 02		23 02	23 22	23 22	23 42	23 42		
Harlington	d		23 06		23 06	23 26	23 26	23 46	23 46		
Leagrave	d		23 12		23 12	23 32	23 32	23 52	23 52		
Luton 10	d	23 02	23 16		23 16	23 36	23 36	23 56	23 56		
Luton Airport Parkway 7 ✈	d		23 19		23 19	23 39	23 39	23 59	23 59		
Harpenden	d		23 25		23 25	23 45	23 45	00 05	00 05		
St Albans City	d		23 31		23 31	23 51	23 51	00 11	00 11		
Radlett	d		23 36		23 36	23 56	23 56	00 16	00 16		
Elstree & Borehamwood	d		23 41		23 41	00 01	00 01	00 21	00 21		
Mill Hill Broadway	d		23 45		23 45	00 05	00 05	00 25	00 25		
Hendon	d		23 48		23 48	00 08	00 08	00 28	00 28		
Cricklewood	d		23 52		23 52	00 12	00 12	00 32	00 32		
West Hampstead Thameslink ⊖	d		23 54		23 54	00 14	00 14	00 34	00 34		
Kentish Town ⊖	d		00 02		00 02	00 20	00 20	00 40	00 40		
St Pancras International 15 ⊖	a	23 34	00 08				00 26		00 46		
St Pancras International 15 ⊖	a				00 05	00 25		00 45			
	d			23 42							
Farringdon 3 ⊖	d			23 47							
City Thameslink 3	d										
London Blackfriars 3 ⊖	d			23 52							
Elephant & Castle ⊖	d										
Loughborough Jn	d										
Herne Hill 4	d										
London Bridge 4	a			00 07							
	d										23 59
Tulse Hill 3	d										00 09
Streatham 4	d										00 13
Mitcham Eastfields	d										
Mitcham Junction	d										
Hackbridge	d										
Carshalton	d										
Tooting	d										00 18
Haydons Road	d										00 21
Wimbledon 6 ⊖	d										00 25
Wimbledon Chase	d										00 28
South Merton	d										00 30
Morden South	d										00 32
St Helier	d										00 34
Sutton Common	d										00 36
West Sutton	d										00 39
Sutton (Surrey) 4	a										00 43
East Croydon	d										
Denmark Hill 4	d									23 52	
Peckham Rye 4	d									23 55	
Nunhead 4	d									23 57	
Crofton Park	d									23 59	
Catford	d									00 03	
Bellingham	d									00 05	
Beckenham Hill	d									00 07	
Ravensbourne	d									00 09	
Shortlands	d									00 11	
Bromley South 4	d									00 14	
Bickley 4	d									00a17	
St Mary Cray	d										
Swanley 4	d										
Eynsford	d										
Shoreham (Kent)	d										
Otford 4	d										
Bat & Ball	d										
Sevenoaks 4	a										
Redhill	d										
Gatwick Airport 10 ✈	d										
Three Bridges 4	d										
Balcombe	d										
Haywards Heath 3	d										
Wivelsfield 4	d										
Burgess Hill 4	d										
Hassocks 4	d										
Preston Park	d										
Brighton 10	a										

A until 23 March

B until 22 March and from 26 March

Brighton, Gatwick Airport and South London - City of London, St Albans, Luton and Bedford

Network Diagram - see first Page of Table 52

Miles	Miles	Miles	Miles	Miles	Station		FC MX	FC MX 1	FC MO 1 A	FC MO B	EM MX ◇1	FC MX	FC MX 1	FC MO 1 A	FC MO B		FC MX 1	FC MO 1	FC MX	FC MX 1	FC MO 1 C	FC MO 1 D	EM MX ◇1	FC MX E	FC MX F
0	—	—	—	—	**Brighton** [10]	d											23p37	23p45							
1½	—	—	—	—	Preston Park	d											23p41								
7¼	—	—	—	—	Hassocks [4]	d											23p47	23p53							
9¾	—	—	—	—	Burgess Hill [4]	d											23p51	23p57							
10	—	—	—	—	Wivelsfield [4]	d											23p53								
13	—	—	—	—	**Haywards Heath** [3]	d											23p59	00 02							
17	—	—	—	—	Balcombe	d											00 04								
21½	—	—	—	—	Three Bridges [4]	d											00 10	00 11							
24¾	—	—	—	—	**Gatwick Airport** [10] ✈	d											00 15	00 16							
30	—	—	—	—	Redhill	d											00 23	00 23							
40½	—	—	0	—	**East Croydon**	d											00a35	00a35							
—	—	—	—	—	Sevenoaks [4]	d																			
—	—	—	—	—	Bat & Ball	d																			
—	—	—	—	—	Otford [4]	d																			
—	—	—	—	—	Shoreham (Kent)	d																			
—	—	—	—	—	Eynsford	d																			
—	—	—	—	—	Swanley [4]	d																			
—	—	—	—	—	St Mary Cray [4]	d																			
—	—	—	—	—	Bickley	d																			
—	—	—	—	—	Bromley South	d																			
—	—	—	—	—	Shortlands [4]	d																			
—	—	—	—	—	Ravensbourne	d																			
—	—	—	—	—	Beckenham Hill	d																			
—	—	—	—	—	Bellingham	d																			
—	—	—	—	—	Catford	d																			
—	—	—	—	—	Crofton Park	d																			
—	—	—	—	—	Nunhead [4]	d																			
—	—	—	—	—	Peckham Rye [4]	d																			
—	—	—	—	—	Denmark Hill [4]	d																			
—	0	0	—	0	**Sutton (Surrey)** [4]	d																			
—	1	—	—	—	West Sutton	d																			
—	2	—	—	—	Sutton Common	d																			
—	3	—	—	—	St Helier	d																			
—	3½	—	—	—	Morden South	d																			
—	4	—	—	—	South Merton	d																			
—	4½	—	—	—	Wimbledon Chase	d																			
—	5½	—	—	—	**Wimbledon** [6] ⊖	d																			
—	6¼	—	—	—	Haydons Road	d																			
—	8	—	—	—	Tooting	d																			
—	—	—	—	1¼	Carshalton	d																			
—	—	—	—	2	Hackbridge	d																			
—	—	—	—	4	Mitcham Junction	d																			
—	—	—	—	5	Mitcham Eastfields	d																			
—	9½	6	—	6	Streatham [4]	d																			
—	11	7½	5	—	Tulse Hill [3]	d																			
50¼	—	—	—	—	**London Bridge** [4] ⊖	a																			
—	—	—	—	—		d																			
—	—	—	—	—	West Croydon	d																			
—	12	8½	—	—	Herne Hill [4]	d																			
—	13	9½	—	—	Loughborough Jn	d																			
—	15	11½	—	—	Elephant & Castle	d																			
51½	16	12½	10	—	**London Blackfriars** [3] ⊖	d																			
52	—	—	—	—	City Thameslink [3]	d																			
52¾	3	—	—	—	Farringdon [3] ⊖	d																			
53¾	0	—	—	—	**St Pancras International** [15] ⊖	d				23p04	23p15				23p34							00 06	00 15		
—	—	—	—	—	**St Pancras International** [15] ⊖	a				⌇					⌇							⌇			
—	—	—	—	—		d	22p48	23p02	23p04	⌇		23p18	23p32	23p34	⌇				23p48	00 02	00 02	⌇		00 18	00 18
55½	—	—	—	—	Kentish Town ⊖	d	22p51		23p07	23p09		23p21		23p37	23p39				23p51		00 05	00 11		00 21	00 21
58	—	—	—	—	West Hampstead Thameslink ⊖	d	22p55	23p10	23p11	23p13		23p25	23p40	23p41	23p43				23p55	00 10	00 10	00 15		00 25	00 25
59	—	—	—	—	Cricklewood	d	22p58		23p14	23p16		23p28		23p44	23p46				23p58		00 13	00 18		00 28	00 28
61	—	—	—	—	Hendon	d	23p01		23p17	23p19		23p31		23p47	23p49				00 01		00 16	00 21		00 31	00 31
63¼	—	—	—	—	Mill Hill Broadway	d	23p05		23p21	23p23		23p35		23p51	23p53				00 05		00 20	00 25		00 35	00 35
66½	—	—	—	—	Elstree & Borehamwood	d	23p09		23p25	23p27		23p39		23p55	23p57				00 09		00 24	00 29		00 39	00 39
69½	—	—	—	—	Radlett	d	23p14		23p30	23p32		23p44		00 02	00 02				00 14		00 29	00 34		00 44	00 44
74	—	—	—	—	**St Albans City**	d	23p20	23p27	23p36	23p38		23p50	23p57	00 08	00 08				00 20	00 27	00 36	00 40		00 50	00 51
78¾	—	—	—	—	Harpenden	d	23p26	23p33	23p42	23p44		23p56	00 03	00 14	00 14				00 26	00 33	00 42	00 46		00 56	00 57
83¼	—	—	—	—	Luton Airport Parkway [7] ✈	d	23p32	23p39	23p48	23p50		00 02	00 09	00 20	00 20				00 32	00 39	00 48	00 52	00 44	01 02	01 03
84¼	30¼	—	—	—	**Luton** [10]	d	23p35	23p42	23p51	23p53	23p46	00 05	00 12	00 23	00 23				00 35	00 42	00 51	00 55	00 47	01 05	01 06
86¾	—	—	—	—	Leagrave	d	23p39	23p46	23p54	23p56		00 09	00 16	00 26	00 26				00 39	00 46	00 54	00 58		01 09	01 09
91¾	—	—	—	—	Harlington	d	23p44	23p51	00 01	00 01		00 14	00 21	00 33	00 31				00 44	00 51	01 01	01 03		01 14	01 16
94¼	—	—	—	—	Flitwick	d	23p48	23p55	00 05	00 05		00 18	00 25	00 37	00 35				00 48	00 55	01 05	01 07		01 18	01 20
103¾	49¾	—	—	—	**Bedford** [7]	a	00 02	00 08	00 18	00 18	00 11	00 32	00 38	00 50	00 48				01 02	01 08	01 18	01 20	01 12	01 32	01 32

A from 2 April
B until 26 March
C from 26 March
D until 19 March
E until 23 March
F from 27 March

Brighton, Gatwick Airport and South London - City of London, St Albans, Luton and Bedford

Network Diagram - see first Page of Table 52

Station		FC MX 🚌	FC MX 1 A	FC 1 B	FC MO 1 C	FC 🚌	FC MX A	FC B	FC MO C	FC 🚌		FC MX A	FC B	FC MO C	FC 🚌	FC 1 B	FC MX 1 A	FC MO 1 C	FC 🚌	FC 🚌		FC 1 B	FC MX 1 A	FC MO 1 C
Brighton [10]	d																							
Preston Park	d																							
Hassocks [4]	d																							
Burgess Hill [4]	d																							
Wivelsfield [4]	d																							
Haywards Heath [3]	d																							
Balcombe	d																							
Three Bridges [4]	d																							
Gatwick Airport [10] ✈	d																							
Redhill	d																							
East Croydon	d																							
Sevenoaks [4]	d																							
Bat & Ball	d																							
Otford [4]	d																							
Shoreham (Kent)	d																							
Eynsford	d																							
Swanley [4]	d																							
St Mary Cray [4]	d																							
Bickley	d																							
Bromley South	d																							
Shortlands [4]	d																							
Ravensbourne	d																							
Beckenham Hill	d																							
Bellingham	d																							
Catford	d																							
Crofton Park	d																							
Nunhead [4]	d																							
Peckham Rye [4]	d																							
Denmark Hill [4]	d																							
Sutton (Surrey) [4]	d																							
West Sutton	d																							
Sutton Common	d																							
St Helier	d																							
Morden South	d																							
South Merton	d																							
Wimbledon Chase	d																							
Wimbledon [6] ⊖	d																							
Haydons Road	d																							
Tooting	d																							
Carshalton	d																							
Hackbridge	d																							
Mitcham Junction	d																							
Mitcham Eastfields	d																							
Streatham [4]	d																							
Tulse Hill [3]	d																							
London Bridge [4] ⊖	a																							
	d																							
West Croydon	d																							
Herne Hill [4]	d																							
Loughborough Jn	d																							
Elephant & Castle	d																							
London Blackfriars [3] ⊖	d	00 10				00 40				01 12					02 12				02 37	03 32				
City Thameslink [3]	d																							
Farringdon [3] ⊖	d	00 20				00 50																		
St Pancras International [15] ⊖	d				00 36				01 06					01 34				02 32						03 52
St Pancras International [15] ⊖	a	00 25			⌇	00 55			⌇	01 27				⌇	02 27			⌇	02 52	03 47				⌇
	d		00 32	00 32	⌇		01 02	01 02	⌇			01 34	01 34	⌇		02 32	02 32	⌇				03 52	03 52	⌇
Kentish Town ⊖	d		00 35	00 35	00 41		01 05	01 05	01 11			01 37	01 37	01 39		02 35	02 35	02 36				03 55	03 55	03 56
West Hampstead Thameslink ⊖	d		00 40	00 40	00 45		01 10	01 10	01 15			01 42	01 42	01 43		02 40	02 40	02 40				04 00	04 00	04 00
Cricklewood	d		00 43	00 43	00 48		01 13	01 13	01 18			01 45	01 45	01 46		02 43	02 43	02 43				04 03	04 03	04 03
Hendon	d		00 46	00 46	00 51		01 16	01 16	01 21			01 48	01 48	01 49		02 46	02 46	02 46				04 06	04 06	04 06
Mill Hill Broadway	d		00 50	00 50	00 55		01 20	01 20	01 25			01 52	01 52	01 53		02 50	02 50	02 50				04 10	04 10	04 10
Elstree & Borehamwood	d		00 54	00 54	00 59		01 24	01 24	01 29			01 56	01 56	01 57		02 54	02 54	02 54				04 14	04 14	04 14
Radlett	d		00 59	00 59	01 04		01 29	01 29	01 34			02 01	02 01	02 02		02 59	02 59	02 59				04 19	04 19	04 19
St Albans City	d		01 06	01 06	01 10		01 36	01 36	01 40			02 08	02 08	02 08		03 06	03 06	03 06				04 26	04 26	04 26
Harpenden	d		01 12	01 12	01 16		01 42	01 42	01 46			02 14	02 14	02 14		03 12	03 12	03 12				04 32	04 32	04 32
Luton Airport Parkway [7] ✈	d		01 18	01 18	01 22		01 48	01 48	01 52			02 20	02 20	02 20		03 18	03 18	03 18				04 38	04 38	04 38
Luton [10]	d		01 21	01 21	01 25		01 51	01 51	01 55			02 23	02 23	02 23		03 21	03 21	03 21				04 41	04 41	04 41
Leagrave	d		01 24	01 24	01 28		01 54	01 54	01 58			02 26	02 26	02 26		03 24	03 25	03 25				04 44	04 45	04 45
Harlington	d		01 29	01 31	01 33		01 59	02 01	02 03			02 31	02 33	02 31		03 31	03 30	03 30				04 51	04 50	04 50
Flitwick	d		01 33	01 35	01 37		02 03	02 05	02 07			02 35	02 37	02 35		03 35	03 34	03 34				04 55	04 54	04 54
Bedford [7]	a		01 47	01 48	01 50		02 17	02 18	02 20			02 49	02 50	02 49		03 48	03 47	03 47				05 08	05 07	05 07

A until 23 March
B from 26 March
C until 19 March

Brighton, Gatwick Airport and South London - City of London, St Albans, Luton and Bedford

Network Diagram - see first Page of Table 52

		FC	FC A	FC MX B	FC MO C	EM ◇1	FC	SE	SE	FC 1	EM ◇1	FC	FC 1	SE	FC 1	EM ◇1	EM ◇1	FC	SE	FC 1	FC	EM ◇1
Brighton 10	d														05 10					05 40		
Preston Park	d														05 14					05 44		
Hassocks 4	d														05 20					05 50		
Burgess Hill 4	d														05 24					05 54		
Wivelsfield 4	d														05 26					05 56		
Haywards Heath 3	d														05 31					06 01		
Balcombe	d														05 36					06 06		
Three Bridges 4	d						04 25			04 55					05 42					06 12		
Gatwick Airport 10	d						04 30			05 00			05 27		05 47					06 17		
Redhill	d												05 35									
East Croydon	d						04 47			05 17			05 47		06 02					06 32		
Sevenoaks 4	d																		05 40			
Bat & Ball	d																		05 43			
Otford 4	d																		05 46			
Shoreham (Kent)	d																		05 49			
Eynsford	d																		05 53			
Swanley 4	d																		05 58			
St Mary Cray 4	d																		06 02			
Bickley	d							04 41	05 02					05 41					06 06			
Bromley South	d							04 44	05 05					05 44					06 10			
Shortlands 4	d							04 47	05 08					05 47					06 13			
Ravensbourne	d							04 49						05 49					06 15			
Beckenham Hill	d							04 51						05 51					06 17			
Bellingham	d							04 53						05 53					06 19			
Catford	d							04 56						05 56					06 22			
Crofton Park	d							04 58						05 58					06 25			
Nunhead 4	d							05 01						06 01					06 27			
Peckham Rye 4	d							05 04						06 04					06 30			
Denmark Hill 4	d							05 07						06 07					06 33			
Sutton (Surrey) 4	d																				06 05	
West Sutton	d																				06 08	
Sutton Common	d																				06 10	
St Helier	d																				06 13	
Morden South	d																				06 15	
South Merton	d																				06 17	
Wimbledon Chase	d																				06 19	
Wimbledon 6	d																				06 28	
Haydons Road	d																				06 30	
Tooting	d																				06 33	
Carshalton	d																					
Hackbridge	d																					
Mitcham Junction	d																					
Mitcham Eastfields	d																					
Streatham 4	d											05 46						06 06			06 38	
Tulse Hill 3	d											05 50						06 10			06 42	
London Bridge 4	a									05 34			06 02		06 15					06 46		
	d									05 34			06 02		06 16					06 46		
West Croydon	d																					
Herne Hill 4	d								05 23			05 54						06 16			06 46	
Loughborough Jn	d																	06 19			06 49	
Elephant & Castle	d							05 13	05 29			06 00		06 13				06 24	06 40		06 54	
London Blackfriars 3	d	04 32					05 14	05 17	05 33	05 42		06 04	06 12	06 17	06 24			06 30	06 48	06 52	06 58	
City Thameslink 3	d						05 16	05a19	05 35	05 44		06 06	06 14	06a19	06 26			06 32	06 50	06 54	07 00	
Farringdon 3	d						05 20		05 38	05 48		06 10	06 18		06 30			06 36	06 54	06 58	07 04	
St Pancras International 15	d				04 52	05 45					06 37					06 55	07 00					07 30
St Pancras International 15	a	04 47					05 24		05 42	05 52		06 14	06 22		06 34			06 40	06 58	07 02	07 08	
	d		04 52	04 52			05 24		05 43	05 52		06 14	06 22		06 34			06 40	06 58	07 02	07 08	
Kentish Town	d		04 55	04 55	04 56		05 28		05a47	05 56		06 18						06 44	07 02			
West Hampstead Thameslink	d		05 00	05 00	05 00		05 32			06 00		06 22			06 42			06 48	07 06	07 10	07 16	
Cricklewood	d		05 03	05 03	05 03		05 35			06 03		06 25						06 51	07 09			
Hendon	d		05 06	05 06	05 06		05 38			06 06		06 28						06 54	07 12			
Mill Hill Broadway	d		05 10	05 10	05 10		05 42			06 10		06 32						06 58	07 16		07 23	
Elstree & Borehamwood	d		05 14	05 14	05 14		05 46			06 14		06 36						07 02	07 20		07 28	
Radlett	d		05 19	05 19	05 19		05 51			06 18		06 42						07 06	07 24		07 32	
St Albans City	d		05 26	05 26	05 26		05 58			06 24		06 48	06 44		06 58			07 12	07a31	07 23	07 38	
Harpenden	d		05 32	05 32	05 32		06 03			06 30		06 54	06 50		07 04			07 18		07 29	07 43	
Luton Airport Parkway 7	d		05 38	05 38	05 38		06 09			06 36		07 00	06 56		07 10	07a15		07 24		07 34	07 49	07 51
Luton 10	d		05 41	05 41	05 41	06 11	06 12			06 39	06a58	07a03	06 59		07 13		07 23	07 27		07 37	07a53	
Leagrave	d		05 44	05 45	05 45		06 16			06 43			07 03		07 17			07 31		07 41		
Harlington	d		05 51	05 50	05 50		06 21			06 48			07 08		07 22			07 36		07 46		
Flitwick	d		05 55	05 54	05 54		06 25			06 52			07 12		07 26			07 40		07 50		
Bedford 7	a		06 08	06 07	06 07	06 26	06 39			07 04			07 24		07 40		07 38	07 52		08 03		08 06

A from 26 March B until 23 March C until 19 March

Table 52 Mondays to Fridays

Brighton, Gatwick Airport and South London - City of London, St Albans, Luton and Bedford

Network Diagram - see first Page of Table 52

		FC 1	FC	SE	SE 1	FC 1	EM ◇1	FC	SE	SE	FC 1	FC	SE	SE	SE 1	FC
Brighton 10	d	05 50				06 08					06 24					
Preston Park	d	05 54				06 12					06 28					
Hassocks 4	d	06 00				06 19					06 35					
Burgess Hill 4	d	06 04				06 23					06 39					
Wivelsfield 4	d	06 06				06 25										
Haywards Heath 3	d	06 11				06 30					06 45					
Balcombe	d					06 36					06 51					
Three Bridges 4	d	06 20				06 42					06 57					
Gatwick Airport 10	d	06 25				06 47					07 02					
Redhill	d	06 33				06 56					07 11					
East Croydon	d	06 44				07 09					07 23					
Sevenoaks 4	d			06 13						06 42				07 11		
Bat & Ball	d			06 16						06 48				07 14		
Otford 4	d			06 19	06 38					06 51				07 18	07 23	
Shoreham (Kent)	d			06 22						06 54				07 21		
Eynsford	d			06 26						06 58				07 24		
Swanley 4	d			06 31	06 48					07 03				07 30	07 32	
St Mary Cray 4	d			06 35						07 07				07 34		
Bickley	d			06 39					07 05	07 11			07 35	07 39		
Bromley South	d			06 42	06 57				07 08	07 14			07 38	07 42	07 40	
Shortlands 4	d			06 45					07 11	07 17			07 41	07 44		
Ravensbourne	d			06 47						07 19				07 47		
Beckenham Hill	d			06 49						07 21				07 49		
Bellingham	d			06 51						07 23				07 51		
Catford	d			06 54						07 26				07 53		
Crofton Park	d			06 57						07 29				07 56		
Nunhead 4	d			06 59						07 31				07 58		
Peckham Rye 4	d			07 02						07 34				08 01		
Denmark Hill 4	d			07 05						07 37				08 04		
Sutton (Surrey) 4	d		06 34					06 45				07 05				07 37
West Sutton	d							06 48				07 08				
Sutton Common	d							06 50				07 10				
St Helier	d							06 53				07 13				
Morden South	d							06 55				07 15				
South Merton	d							06 57				07 17				
Wimbledon Chase	d							06 59				07 19				
Wimbledon 6	d							07 06				07 26				
Haydons Road	d							07 08				07 28				
Tooting	d							07 11				07 31				
Carshalton	d		06 37													07 40
Hackbridge	d		06 39													07 42
Mitcham Junction	d		06 42													07 45
Mitcham Eastfields	d		06 45													07 48
Streatham 4	d		06 49					07 16				07 38				07 52
Tulse Hill 3	d		06 53					07 20				07 43				07 57
London Bridge 4	a	06 58				07 23										
	d	06 58				07 24										
West Croydon	d															
Herne Hill 4	d		06 57					07 24	07 31		07 41	07 47	07 57			08 01
Loughborough Jn	d		07 00					07 27	07 34			07 50	08 00			08 04
Elephant & Castle	d		07 06	07 12	07 16			07 32	07 38	07 44	07 48	07 54	08 05	08 13	08 00	08 09
London Blackfriars 3	d	07 06	07 12	07 18	07 24	07 30		07 36	07 42	07 48	07 54	07 58	08 09	08 17	08 04	08 13
City Thameslink 3	d	07 08	07 14	07 20	07 26	07 33		07 38	07 44	07 50	07 56	08 01	08 11	08 19	08 06	08 15
Farringdon 3	d	07 12	07 18	07 24	07 30	07 36		07 42	07 48	07 54	08 00	08 04	08 15	08 23	08 10	08 19
St Pancras International 15	d						08 00									
St Pancras International 15	a	07 16	07 22	07 28	07 34	07 40		07 46	07 52	07 58	08 04	08 08	08 19	08 27	08 14	08 23
	d	07 18	07 22	07 28	07 34	07 40		07 46	07 52	07 58	08 04	08 10	08 20	08 28	08 16	08 24
Kentish Town	d			07 32						08 02		08 14		08 32		08 29
West Hampstead Thameslink	d	07 26	07 30	07 36				07 54	08 00	08 06		08 18	08 28	08a38	08 24	08 34
Cricklewood	d			07 39						08 09		08 21				08 37
Hendon	d			07 42						08 12		08 24				08 40
Mill Hill Broadway	d			07 46					08 07	08 16		08 28	08 35			08 44
Elstree & Borehamwood	d		07 40	07 50					08 11	08 20		08 32	08 39			08 48
Radlett	d		07 44	07 54					08 15	08 24		08 36	08 43			08 52
St Albans City	d	07 42	07a51	08a01	07 53			08 09	08a22	08 30	08 25	08a43	08 50		08 37	08a59
Harpenden	d	07 47			07 59			08 15		08 35	08 31		08 55		08 43	
Luton Airport Parkway 7	d	07 53			08 05	08 06		08 21		08 41	08 37		09 01		08 48	
Luton 10	d	07 57			08 08	08a10	08 23	08 24		08a45	08 40		09a04		08 52	
Leagrave	d	08 01			08 12			08 27			08 44				08 56	
Harlington	d	08 06			08 18			08 32			08 49				09 01	
Flitwick	d	08 10			08 22			08 36			08 53				09 05	
Bedford 7	a	08 23			08 35		08 37	08 49			09 05				09 17	

Brighton, Gatwick Airport and South London - City of London, St Albans, Luton and Bedford

Network Diagram - see first Page of Table 52

		EM ◇■	FC ■	SE ■	EM ◇■	SE	FC	SE	SE ■	FC	SE ■	FC ■	SE	FC	SE ■	EM ◇■	FC ■	FC	SE
Brighton 10	d		07 02									07 24					07 50		
Preston Park	d		07 06									07 28					07 54		
Hassocks 4	d		07 13									07 35					08 01		
Burgess Hill 4	d		07 17									07 39							
Wivelsfield 4	d		07 20																
Haywards Heath 3	d		07 25									07 47					08 09		
Balcombe	d																08 15		
Three Bridges 4	d		07 34									07 56							
Gatwick Airport 10 ✈	d		07 39									08 01					08 24		
Redhill	d											08 09							
East Croydon	d		07 54									08 23					08 39		
Sevenoaks 4	d							07 36					07 53						
Bat & Ball	d							07 39					07 56						
Otford 4	d							07 43					08 00						
Shoreham (Kent)	d							07 46					08 03						
Eynsford	d							07 49					08 06						
Swanley 4	d							07 54	07 55				08 11						
St Mary Cray 4	d							07 59	08 00				08 16						
Bickley	d					07 55		08 03					08 20						
Bromley South	d					07 58		08 08	08 06		08 18		08 26						08 44
Shortlands 4	d					08 00		08 10			08 20		08 29						08 46
Ravensbourne	d							08 13			08 23								08 49
Beckenham Hill	d							08 15			08 25								08 51
Bellingham	d					08 05		08 17			08 27		08 33						08 53
Catford	d					08 08		08 20			08 30		08 36						08 56
Crofton Park	d					08 10							08 39						08 58
Nunhead 4	d					08 14							08 41						09 01
Peckham Rye 4	d					08 16					08 36		08 44						09 04
Denmark Hill 4	d					08 19		08 26			08 39		08 47						09 07
Sutton (Surrey) 4	d						07 40			08 08				08 08				08 39	
West Sutton	d						07 43							08 11					
Sutton Common	d						07 45							08 13					
St Helier	d						07 48							08 16					
Morden South	d						07 50							08 18					
South Merton	d						07 52							08 20					
Wimbledon Chase	d						07 54							08 22					
Wimbledon 6 ⊖	d						07 58							08 28					
Haydons Road	d						08 00							08 30					
Tooting	d						08 03							08 33					
Carshalton	d									08 11								08 42	
Hackbridge	d									08 13								08 44	
Mitcham Junction	d									08 16								08 47	
Mitcham Eastfields	d									08 19								08 50	
Streatham 4	d						08 09			08 23				08 39				08 54	
Tulse Hill 3	d						08 13			08 28		08 37		08 43				08 58	
London Bridge 4 ⊖	a																		
	d																		
West Croydon	d																		
Herne Hill 4	d			08 13			08 20			08 32		08 41		08 47	08 52		08 57	09 02	
Loughborough Jn	d			08 16			08 23			08 36				08 50	08 55			09 05	
Elephant & Castle	d			08 21		08 25	08 28	08 35	08 31	08 40	08 45	08 50	08 54	08 58	09 02		09 06	09 10	09 14
London Blackfriars 3 ⊖	d		08 21	08 25		08 29	08 33	08 42	08 37	08 46	08 50	08 54	08 58	09 02	09 06		09 10	09 14	09 18
City Thameslink 3	d		08 23	08 27		08 31	08 35	08 44	08 39	08 48	08 52	08 56	09 00	09 04	09 08		09 12	09 16	09 20
Farringdon 3 ⊖	d		08 27	08 31		08 35	08 39	08 48	08 43	08 52	08 56	09 00	09 04	09 08	09 12		09 16	09 20	09 24
St Pancras International 15 ⊖	d	08 30			09 00											09 30			
St Pancras International 15 ⊖	a		08 31	08 35		08 39	08 43	08 52	08 47	08 56	09 00	09 04	09 08	09 12	09 16		09 20	09 24	09 28
	d		08 32	08 36		08 40	08 44	08 52	08 48	08 56	09 00	09 04	09 08	09 12	09 16		09 20	09 24	09 28
Kentish Town ⊖	d						08 48	08a57		09 00			09a13	09 16					09 34
West Hampstead Thameslink ⊖	d					08 50	08 54			09 04				09 20				09 32	09 40
Cricklewood	d						08 57			09 07				09 23					09 43
Hendon	d						09 00			09 10				09 26					09 46
Mill Hill Broadway	d					08 57	09 04			09 14				09 30					09 50
Elstree & Borehamwood	d					09 01	09 08			09 18				09 34				09 42	09 54
Radlett	d					09 06	09 12			09 22				09 38				09 46	09 58
St Albans City	d		08 52	08 57		09 13	09 18		09 09	09a29	09 20	09 25		09 46			09 40	09a53	10 04
Harpenden	d			09 04		09 19	09 24		09 15			09 32		09 53			09 46		10 09
Luton Airport Parkway 7 ✈	d	08 51	09 00	09 10		09 25	09 30		09 21		09 29	09 38		09 59	09 44	09 51	09 52		10 15
Luton 10	d		09 04	09 13	09 23	09a29	09a34		09 24		09 32	09 41		10a03	09 47		09 55		10a19
Leagrave	d			09 17					09 27			09 45			09 50		09 59		
Harlington	d			09 22					09 32			09 50					10 04		
Flitwick	d		09 14	09 26					09 36		09 43	09 56			10 00		10 08		
Bedford 7	a	09 07	09 26	09 38	09 37				09 49		09 56	10 08			10 12	10 07	10 20		

Brighton, Gatwick Airport and South London - City of London, St Albans, Luton and Bedford

Network Diagram - see first Page of Table 52

		FC ■	SE ■	SE	EM ◇■	FC	FC ■	SE	FC	FC ■	EM ◇■	FC	FC ■	FC	SE	FC ■	EM ◇■	FC	FC ■	FC	SE	FC ■
Brighton 10	d	08 02					08 16			08 34			09 00			09 07			09 34			09 37
Preston Park	d	08 06					08 20			08 38						09 11						09 41
Hassocks 4	d	08 13					08 27			08 44			09 09			09 17						09 47
Burgess Hill 4	d	08 17					08 31			08 48			09 12			09 21						09 51
Wivelsfield 4	d	08 20					08 34			08 50						09 23						09 53
Haywards Heath 3	d	08 25					08 39			09 00			09 18			09 32			09 48			10 02
Balcombe	d									09 06						09 37						
Three Bridges 4	d	08 34					08 48			09 12			09 27			09 43			09 57			10 12
Gatwick Airport 10 ✈	d	08 39					08 53			09 17			09 32			09 47			10 02			10 17
Redhill	d																					
East Croydon	d	08 54					09 09			09 32			09 47			10 02			10 17			10 32
Sevenoaks 4	d		08 24					08 43							09 13						09 42	
Bat & Ball	d		08 27					08 46							09 16						09 46	
Otford 4	d		08 31					08 49							09 21						09 50	
Shoreham (Kent)	d		08 34					08 52							09 24						09 53	
Eynsford	d		08 37					08 56							09 28						09 56	
Swanley 4	d		08 42					09 01							09 33						10 01	
St Mary Cray 4	d		08 46					09 05							09 37						10 05	
Bickley	d		08 51	08 55				09 09							09 42						10 10	
Bromley South	d		08 54	08 58				09 12							09 45						10 15	
Shortlands 4	d		08 56	09 00				09 15							09 48						10 18	
Ravensbourne	d			09 03				09 17							09 50						10 20	
Beckenham Hill	d			09 05				09 19							09 52						10 22	
Bellingham	d		09 01	09 07				09 21							09 54						10 24	
Catford	d		09 04	09 09				09 24							09 57						10 27	
Crofton Park	d			09 12				09 26							09 59						10 29	
Nunhead 4	d			09 14				09 29							10 02						10 32	
Peckham Rye 4	d		09 09	09 17				09 31							10 04						10 34	
Denmark Hill 4	d		09 12	09 19				09 34							10 07						10 37	
Sutton (Surrey) 4	d					08 41			09 13			09 11		09 38				09 37		10 08		
West Sutton	d					08 44						09 14						09 40				
Sutton Common	d					08 46						09 16						09 42				
St Helier	d					08 49						09 19						09 45				
Morden South	d					08 51						09 21						09 47				
South Merton	d					08 53						09 23						09 49				
Wimbledon Chase	d					08 55						09 25						09 51				
Wimbledon 6 ⊖	d					08 58						09 28						09 58				
Haydons Road	d					09 00						09 30						10 00				
Tooting	d					09 03						09 33						10 03				
Carshalton	d								09 16					09 41						10 11		
Hackbridge	d								09 18					09 43						10 13		
Mitcham Junction	d								09 21					09 46						10 16		
Mitcham Eastfields	d								09 24					09 49						10 19		
Streatham 4	d					09 08			09 28			09 38		09 53				10 08		10 23		
Tulse Hill 3	d					09 16			09 32			09 42		09 57				10 12		10 27		
London Bridge 4 ⊖	a	09 08								09 46			10 00			10 15			10 30			10 45
	d	09 09								09 46			10 00			10 16			10 30			10 45
West Croydon	d																					
Herne Hill 4	d					09 20			09 36			09 46		10 01				10 16		10 31		
Loughborough Jn	d					09 23			09 40			09 50		10 04				10 19		10 34		
Elephant & Castle	d		09 20	09 26		09 30	09 34	09 42	09 45			09 55		10 09	10 14			10 24		10 39	10 44	
London Blackfriars 3 ⊖	d	09 22	09 26	09 30		09 34	09 38	09 46	09 50	09 54		10 00	10 08	10 14	10 18	10 24		10 30	10 38	10 44	10 48	10 54
City Thameslink 3	d	09 24	09 28	09 32		09 36	09 40	09 48	09 52	09 56		10 02	10 10	10 16	10 20	10 26		10 32	10 40	10 46	10 50	10 56
Farringdon 3 ⊖	d	09 28	09 32	09 36		09 40	09 44	09 52	09 56	10 00		10 06	10 14	10 19	10 24	10 30		10 36	10 44	10 49	10 54	11 00
St Pancras International 15 ⊖	d				10 00						10 30						11 00					
St Pancras International 15 ⊖	a	09 32	09 36	09 40		09 44	09 48	09 56	10 00	10 04		10 10	10 18	10 23	10 28	10 34		10 40	10 48	10 53	10 58	11 04
	d	09 32	09 36	09 40		09 44	09 48	09 56	10 00	10 04		10 10	10 18	10 24	10 28	10 34		10 40	10 48	10 54	10 58	11 04
Kentish Town ⊖	d			09a45		09 48		10 00	10a05			10 14		10 27	10a33			10 44		10 57	11a03	
West Hampstead Thameslink ⊖	d					09 52		10 04				10 19		10 31				10 49		11 01		
Cricklewood	d					09 55		10 07				10 22		10 34				10 52		11 04		
Hendon	d					09 58		10 10				10 25		10 37				10 55		11 07		
Mill Hill Broadway	d					10 02		10 14				10 29		10 41				10 59		11 11		
Elstree & Borehamwood	d					10 06		10 18				10 33		10 45				11 03		11 15		
Radlett	d					10 10		10 22				10 37		10 49				11 09		11 19		
St Albans City	d	09 52	09 56			10 18	10 10	10a29		10 25		10 46	10 39	10a57		10 55		11 16	11 10	11a27		11 25
Harpenden	d		10 03			10 23	10 16			10 31		10 53	10 45			11 01		11 21	11 16			11 31
Luton Airport Parkway 7 ✈	d	10 01	10 09			10 29	10 22			10 37	10 51	10 59	10 51			11 07		11 27	11 22			11 37
Luton 10	d	10 04	10 12		10 23	10a33	10 25			10 40		11a03	10 54			11 10	11 23	11a31	11 25			11 40
Leagrave	d		10 16				10 29			10 44			10 57			11 14			11 28			11 44
Harlington	d		10 21				10 34			10 49			11 02			11 19			11 33			11 49
Flitwick	d	10 12	10 25				10 38			10 53			11 06			11 23			11 37			11 53
Bedford 7	a	10 24	10 38		10 37		10 50			11 05	11 06		11 19			11 35	11 37		11 50			12 05

Brighton, Gatwick Airport and South London - City of London, St Albans, Luton and Bedford

Network Diagram - see first Page of Table 52

		EM ◇1	FC	SE	FC 1	FC	FC 1	EM ◇1	FC	SE	FC 1	FC	FC 1	EM ◇1	FC	SE	FC 1	FC	FC 1	EM ◇1	FC	SE
Brighton 10	d				10 04		10 07				10 34		10 37				11 04		11 07			
Preston Park	d						10 11						10 41						11 11			
Hassocks 4	d						10 17						10 47						11 17			
Burgess Hill 4	d						10 21						10 51						11 21			
Wivelsfield 4	d						10 23						10 53						11 23			
Haywards Heath 3	d				10 18		10 32				10 48		11 02				11 18		11 32			
Balcombe	d						10 37												11 37			
Three Bridges 4	d				10 27		10 43				10 57		11 12				11 27		11 43			
Gatwick Airport 10 ✈	d				10 32		10 47				11 02		11 17				11 32		11 47			
Redhill	d																					
East Croydon	d				10 47		11 02				11 17		11 32				11 47		12 02			
Sevenoaks 4	d			10 02						10 32						11 02						11 32
Bat & Ball	d			10 05						10 35						11 05						11 35
Otford 4	d			10 08						10 38						11 08						11 38
Shoreham (Kent)	d			10 11						10 41						11 11						11 41
Eynsford	d			10 15						10 45						11 15						11 45
Swanley 4	d			10 20						10 50						11 20						11 50
St Mary Cray 4	d			10 24						10 54						11 24						11 54
Bickley	d			10 28						10 58						11 28						11 58
Bromley South	d			10 31						11 01						11 31						12 01
Shortlands 4	d			10 34						11 04						11 34						12 04
Ravensbourne	d			10 36						11 06						11 36						12 06
Beckenham Hill	d			10 38						11 08						11 38						12 08
Bellingham	d			10 40						11 10						11 40						12 10
Catford	d			10 43						11 13						11 43						12 13
Crofton Park	d			10 45						11 15						11 45						12 15
Nunhead 4	d			10 48						11 18						11 48						12 18
Peckham Rye 4	d			10 50						11 20						11 50						12 20
Denmark Hill 4	d			10 54						11 24						11 54						12 24
Sutton (Surrey) 4	d		10 07			10 38			10 37			11 08			11 07			11 38			11 37	
West Sutton	d		10 10						10 40						11 10						11 40	
Sutton Common	d		10 12						10 42						11 12						11 42	
St Helier	d		10 15						10 45						11 15						11 45	
Morden South	d		10 17						10 47						11 17						11 47	
South Merton	d		10 19						10 49						11 19						11 49	
Wimbledon Chase	d		10 21						10 51						11 21						11 51	
Wimbledon 6 ⊖	d		10 28						10 58						11 28						11 58	
Haydons Road	d		10 30						11 00						11 30						12 00	
Tooting	d		10 33						11 03						11 33						12 03	
Carshalton	d					10 41						11 11						11 41				
Hackbridge	d					10 43						11 13						11 43				
Mitcham Junction	d					10 46						11 16						11 46				
Mitcham Eastfields	d					10 49						11 19						11 49				
Streatham 4	d		10 38			10 53			11 08			11 23			11 38			11 53			12 08	
Tulse Hill 3	d		10 42			10 57			11 12			11 27			11 42			11 57			12 12	
London Bridge 4 ⊖	a				11 00		11 15				11 30		11 45				12 00		12 15			
	d				11 00		11 15				11 30		11 45				12 00		12 15			
West Croydon	d																					
Herne Hill 4	d		10 46			11 01			11 16			11 31			11 46			12 01			12 16	
Loughborough Jn.	d		10 49			11 04			11 19			11 34			11 49			12 04			12 19	
Elephant & Castle	d		10 54	11 00		11 09			11 24	11 30		11 39			11 54	12 00		12 09			12 24	12 30
London Blackfriars 3 ⊖	d		11 00	11 04	11 08	11 14	11 24		11 30	11 34	11 38	11 44	11 54		12 00	12 04	12 08	12 14	12 24		12 30	12 34
City Thameslink 3	d		11 02	11 06	11 10	11 16	11 26		11 32	11 36	11 40	11 46	11 56		12 02	12 06	12 10	12 16	12 26		12 32	12 36
Farringdon 3 ⊖	d		11 06	11 10	11 14	11 19	11 30		11 36	11 40	11 44	11 49	12 00		12 06	12 10	12 14	12 19	12 30		12 36	12 40
St Pancras International 15 ⊖	d	11 30						12 00						12 30						13 00		
St Pancras International 15 ⊖	a		11 10	11 14	11 18	11 23	11 34		11 40	11 44	11 48	11 53	12 04		12 10	12 14	12 18	12 23	12 34		12 40	12 44
	d		11 10	11 14	11 18	11 24	11 34		11 40	11 44	11 48	11 54	12 04		12 10	12 14	12 18	12 24	12 34		12 40	12 44
Kentish Town ⊖	d		11 14	11a19		11 27			11 44	11a49		11 57			12 14	12a19		12 27			12 44	12a49
West Hampstead Thameslink ⊖	d		11 19			11 31			11 49			12 01			12 19			12 31			12 49	
Cricklewood	d		11 22			11 34			11 52			12 04			12 22			12 34			12 52	
Hendon	d		11 25			11 37			11 55			12 07			12 25			12 37			12 55	
Mill Hill Broadway	d		11 29			11 41			11 59			12 11			12 29			12 41			12 59	
Elstree & Borehamwood	d		11 33			11 45			12 03			12 15			12 33			12 45			13 03	
Radlett	d		11 37			11 49			12 07			12 19			12 37			12 49			13 07	
St Albans City	d		11 44		11 39	11a57	11 55		12 14		12 09	12a27	12 25		12 44		12 39	12a57	12 55		13 14	
Harpenden	d		11 49		11 45		12 01		12 19		12 15		12 31		12 49		12 45		13 01		13 19	
Luton Airport Parkway 7 ✈	d	11 51	11 55		11 51		12 07		12 25		12 21		12 37	12 51	12 55		12 51		13 07		13 25	
Luton 10	d		11a59		11 54		12 10	12 23	12a29		12 24		12 40		12 58		12 54		13 10	13 22	13a29	
Leagrave	d				11 57		12 14				12 27		12 44				12 57		13 14			
Harlington	d				12 02		12 19				12 32		12 49				13 02		13 19			
Flitwick	d				12 06		12 23				12 36		12 53				13 06		13 23			
Bedford 7	a	12 06			12 19		12 35	12 37			12 49		13 05	13 06	13 24		13 19		13 35	13 37		

Brighton, Gatwick Airport and South London - City of London, St Albans, Luton and Bedford

Network Diagram - see first Page of Table 52

		FC 1	FC	FC 1	EM ◇1	FC	SE	FC 1	FC	FC 1	EM ◇1	FC	SE	FC 1	FC	FC 1	EM ◇1	FC	SE	FC 1	FC	FC 1	EM ◇1
Brighton 10	d	11 34		11 37				12 04		12 07				12 34		12 37				13 04		13 07	
Preston Park	d			11 41						12 11						12 41						13 11	
Hassocks 4	d			11 47						12 17						12 47						13 17	
Burgess Hill 4	d			11 51						12 21						12 51						13 21	
Wivelsfield 4	d			11 53						12 23						12 53						13 23	
Haywards Heath 3	d	11 48		12 02				12 18		12 32				12 48		13 02				13 18		13 32	
Balcombe	d									12 37												13 37	
Three Bridges 4	d	11 57		12 12				12 27		12 43				12 57		13 12				13 27		13 43	
Gatwick Airport 10 ✈	d	12 02		12 17				12 32		12 47				13 02		13 17				13 32		13 47	
Redhill	d																						
East Croydon	d	12 17		12 32				12 47		13 02				13 17		13 32				13 47		14 02	
Sevenoaks 4	d						12 02						12 32						13 02				
Bat & Ball	d						12 05						12 35						13 05				
Otford 4	d						12 08						12 38						13 08				
Shoreham (Kent)	d						12 11						12 41						13 11				
Eynsford	d						12 15						12 45						13 15				
Swanley 4	d						12 20						12 50						13 20				
St Mary Cray 4	d						12 24						12 54						13 24				
Bickley	d						12 28						12 58						13 28				
Bromley South	d						12 31						13 01						13 31				
Shortlands 4	d						12 34						13 04						13 34				
Ravensbourne	d						12 36						13 06						13 36				
Beckenham Hill	d						12 38						13 08						13 38				
Bellingham	d						12 40						13 10						13 40				
Catford	d						12 43						13 13						13 43				
Crofton Park	d						12 45						13 15						13 45				
Nunhead 4	d						12 48						13 18						13 48				
Peckham Rye 4	d						12 50						13 20						13 50				
Denmark Hill 4	d						12 54						13 24						13 54				
Sutton (Surrey) 4	d		12 08			12 07			12 38			12 37			13 08			13 07			13 38		
West Sutton	d					12 10						12 40						13 10					
Sutton Common	d					12 12						12 42						13 12					
St Helier	d					12 15						12 45						13 15					
Morden South	d					12 17						12 47						13 17					
South Merton	d					12 19						12 49						13 19					
Wimbledon Chase	d					12 21						12 51						13 21					
Wimbledon 6 ⊖	d					12 28						12 58						13 28					
Haydons Road	d					12 30						13 00						13 30					
Tooting	d					12 33						13 03						13 33					
Carshalton	d		12 11						12 41						13 11						13 41		
Hackbridge	d		12 13						12 43						13 13						13 43		
Mitcham Junction	d		12 16						12 46						13 16						13 46		
Mitcham Eastfields	d		12 19						12 49						13 19						13 49		
Streatham 4	d		12 23			12 38			12 53			13 08			13 23			13 38			13 53		
Tulse Hill 3	d		12 27			12 42			12 57			13 12			13 27			13 42			13 57		
London Bridge 4 ⊖	a	12 30		12 45				13 00		13 15				13 30		13 45				14 00		14 15	
	d	12 30		12 45				13 00		13 15				13 30		13 45				14 00		14 15	
West Croydon	d																						
Herne Hill 4	d		12 31			12 46			13 01			13 16			13 31			13 46			14 01		
Loughborough Jn.	d		12 34			12 49			13 04			13 19			13 34			13 49			14 04		
Elephant & Castle	d		12 39			12 54	13 00		13 09			13 24	13 30		13 39			13 54	14 00		14 09		
London Blackfriars 3 ⊖	d	12 38	12 44	12 54		13 00	13 04	13 08	13 14	13 24		13 30	13 34	13 38	13 44	13 54		14 00	14 04	14 08	14 14	14 24	
City Thameslink 3	d	12 40	12 46	12 56		13 02	13 06	13 10	13 16	13 26		13 32	13 36	13 40	13 46	13 56		14 02	14 06	14 10	14 16	14 26	
Farringdon 3 ⊖	d	12 44	12 49	13 00		13 06	13 10	13 14	13 19	13 30		13 36	13 40	13 44	13 49	14 00		14 06	14 10	14 14	14 19	14 30	
St Pancras International 15 ⊖	d				13 30						14 00						14 30						15 00
St Pancras International 15 ⊖	a	12 48	12 53	13 04		13 10	13 14	13 18	13 23	13 34		13 40	13 44	13 48	13 53	14 04		14 10	14 14	14 18	14 23	14 34	
	d	12 48	12 54	13 04		13 10	13 14	13 18	13 24	13 34		13 40	13 44	13 48	13 54	14 04		14 10	14 14	14 18	14 24	14 34	
Kentish Town ⊖	d		12 57			13 14	13a19		13 27			13 44	13a49		13 57			14 14	14a19		14 27		
West Hampstead Thameslink ⊖	d		13 01			13 19			13 31			13 49			14 01			14 19			14 31		
Cricklewood	d		13 04			13 22			13 34			13 52			14 04			14 22			14 34		
Hendon	d		13 07			13 25			13 37			13 55			14 07			14 25			14 37		
Mill Hill Broadway	d		13 11			13 29			13 41			13 59			14 11			14 29			14 41		
Elstree & Borehamwood	d		13 15			13 33			13 45			14 03			14 15			14 33			14 45		
Radlett	d		13 19			13 37			13 49			14 07			14 19			14 37			14 49		
St Albans City	d	13 09	13a27	13 25		13 44		13 39	13a57	13 55		14 14		14 09	14a27	14 25		14 44		14 39	14a57	14 55	
Harpenden	d	13 15		13 31		13 49		13 45		14 01		14 19		14 15		14 31		14 49		14 45		15 01	
Luton Airport Parkway 7 ✈	d	13 21		13 37	13 51	13 55		13 51		14 07		14 25		14 21		14 37	14 51	14 55		14 51		15 07	
Luton 10	d	13 24		13 40		13a59		13 54		14 10	14 23	14a29		14 24		14 40		14a59		14 54		15 10	15 23
Leagrave	d	13 27		13 44				13 57		14 14				14 27		14 44				14 57		15 14	
Harlington	d	13 32		13 49				14 02		14 19				14 32		14 49				15 02		15 19	
Flitwick	d	13 36		13 53				14 06		14 23				14 36		14 53				15 06		15 23	
Bedford 7	a	13 49		14 05	14 06			14 19		14 35	14 37			14 49		15 05	15 06			15 19		15 35	15 37

Brighton, Gatwick Airport and South London - City of London, St Albans, Luton and Bedford

Network Diagram - see first Page of Table 52

		FC	SE	FC ■	FC	FC ■	EM ◇■ ⊏⊐	FC	SE	FC ■	FC	FC ■	EM ◇■ ⊏⊐	FC	SE	FC ■	FC	FC ■	EM ◇■ ⊏⊐	FC	SE	FC ■
Brighton 10	d			13 34		13 37				14 04		14 07				14 34		14 37				15 04
Preston Park	d					13 41						14 11						14 41				
Hassocks 4	d					13 47						14 17						14 47				
Burgess Hill 4	d					13 51						14 21						14 51				
Wivelsfield 4	d					13 53						14 23						14 53				
Haywards Heath 3	d			13 48		14 02				14 18		14 32				14 48		15 02				15 18
Balcombe	d											14 37										
Three Bridges 4	d			13 57		14 12				14 27		14 43				14 57		15 12				15 27
Gatwick Airport 10 ✈	d			14 02		14 17				14 32		14 47				15 02		15 17				15 32
Redhill	d																					
East Croydon	d			14 17		14 32				14 47		15 02				15 17		15 32				15 47
Sevenoaks 4	d		13 32						14 02						14 32						15 02	
Bat & Ball	d		13 35						14 05						14 35						15 05	
Otford 4	d		13 38						14 08						14 38						15 08	
Shoreham (Kent)	d		13 41						14 11						14 41						15 11	
Eynsford	d		13 45						14 15						14 45						15 15	
Swanley 4	d		13 50						14 20						14 50						15 20	
St Mary Cray 4	d		13 54						14 24						14 54						15 24	
Bickley	d		13 58						14 28						14 58						15 28	
Bromley South	d		14 01						14 31						15 01						15 31	
Shortlands 4	d		14 04						14 34						15 04						15 34	
Ravensbourne	d		14 06						14 36						15 06						15 36	
Beckenham Hill	d		14 08						14 38						15 08						15 38	
Bellingham	d		14 10						14 40						15 10						15 40	
Catford	d		14 13						14 43						15 13						15 43	
Crofton Park	d		14 15						14 45						15 15						15 45	
Nunhead 4	d		14 18						14 48						15 18						15 48	
Peckham Rye 4	d		14 20						14 50						15 20						15 50	
Denmark Hill 4	d		14 24						14 54						15 24						15 54	
Sutton (Surrey) 4	d	13 37			14 08			14 07			14 38			14 37			15 08			15 07		
West Sutton	d	13 40						14 10						14 40						15 10		
Sutton Common	d	13 42						14 12						14 42						15 12		
St Helier	d	13 45						14 15						14 45						15 15		
Morden South	d	13 47						14 17						14 47						15 17		
South Merton	d	13 49						14 19						14 49						15 19		
Wimbledon Chase	d	13 51						14 21						14 51						15 21		
Wimbledon 6 ⊖	d	13 58						14 28						14 58						15 28		
Haydons Road	d	14 00						14 30						15 00						15 30		
Tooting	d	14 03						14 33						15 03						15 33		
Carshalton	d				14 11						14 41						15 11					
Hackbridge	d				14 13						14 43						15 13					
Mitcham Junction	d				14 16						14 46						15 16					
Mitcham Eastfields	d				14 19						14 49						15 19					
Streatham 4	d	14 08			14 23			14 38			14 53			15 08			15 23			15 38		
Tulse Hill 3	d	14 12			14 27			14 42			14 57			15 12			15 27			15 42		
London Bridge 4 ⊖	a			14 30		14 45				15 00		15 15				15 30		15 45				16 00
	d			14 30		14 45				15 00		15 15				15 30		15 45				16 00
West Croydon	d																					
Herne Hill 4	d	14 16			14 31			14 46			15 01			15 16			15 31			15 46		
Loughborough Jn	d	14 19			14 34			14 49			15 04			15 19			15 34			15 49		
Elephant & Castle	d	14 24	14 30		14 39			14 54	15 00		15 09			15 24	15 30		15 39			15 54	16 00	
London Blackfriars 3 ⊖	d	14 30	14 34	14 38	14 44	14 54		15 00	15 04	15 08	15 14	15 24		15 30	15 34	15 38	15 44	15 54		16 00	16 04	16 08
City Thameslink 3	d	14 32	14 36	14 40	14 46	14 56		15 02	15 06	15 10	15 16	15 26		15 32	15 36	15 40	15 46	15 56		16 02	16 06	16 10
Farringdon 3 ⊖	d	14 36	14 40	14 44	14 49	15 00		15 06	15 10	15 14	15 19	15 30		15 36	15 40	15 44	15 49	16 00		16 06	16 10	16 13
St Pancras International 15 ⊖	d						15 30						16 00						16 30			
St Pancras International 15 ⊖	a	14 40	14 44	14 48	14 53	15 04		15 10	15 14	15 18	15 23	15 34		15 40	15 44	15 48	15 53	16 04		16 10	16 14	16 17
	d	14 40	14 44	14 48	14 54	15 04		15 10	15 14	15 18	15 24	15 34		15 40	15 44	15 48	15 54	16 04		16 10	16 14	16 18
Kentish Town ⊖	d	14 44	14a49		14 57			15 14	15a19		15 27			15 44	15a49		15 57			16 14	16a19	
West Hampstead Thameslink ⊖	d	14 49			15 01			15 19			15 31			15 49			16 01			16 19		
Cricklewood	d	14 52			15 04			15 22			15 34			15 52			16 04			16 22		
Hendon	d	14 55			15 07			15 25			15 37			15 55			16 07			16 25		
Mill Hill Broadway	d	14 59			15 11			15 29			15 41			15 59			16 11			16 29		
Elstree & Borehamwood	d	15 03			15 15			15 33			15 45			16 03			16 15			16 33		
Radlett	d	15 07			15 19			15 37			15 49			16 07			16 19			16 38		
St Albans City	d	15 14		15 09	15a27	15 25		15 44		15 39	15a57	15 53		16 14		16 09	16a27	16 25		16 46		16 39
Harpenden	d	15 19		15 15		15 31		15 49		15 45		15 59		16 19		16 15		16 31		16 51		16 45
Luton Airport Parkway 7 ✈	d	15 25		15 21		15 37	15 51	15 55		15 51		16 04		16 25		16 21		16 37	16 51	16 57		16 51
Luton 10	d	15a29		15 24		15 40		15a59		15 54		16 07	16 22	16a29		16 24		16 40	16 55	17a01		16 54
Leagrave	d			15 27		15 44				15 57		16 12				16 27		16 44				16 57
Harlington	d			15 32		15 49				16 02		16 17				16 32		16 49				17 02
Flitwick	d			15 36		15 53				16 06		16 21				16 36		16 53				17 06
Bedford 7	a			15 49		16 05	16 06			16 19		16 33	16 37			16 49		17 05	17 09			17 19

Brighton, Gatwick Airport and South London - City of London, St Albans, Luton and Bedford

Network Diagram - see first Page of Table 52

		FC	FC ■	EM ◇■ ⊏⊐	FC ■	FC	SE ■	FC	FC ■	EM ◇■ ⊏⊐	EM ◇■ ⊏⊐	FC ■	FC	FC	SE ■	FC ■ A	SE	FC ■	FC ■	EM ◇■ ⊏⊐	EM ◇■ ⊏⊐	FC	FC ■
Brighton 10	d				15 07				15 34			15 37						16 04	16 07				16 24
Preston Park	d				15 11							15 41							16 11				
Hassocks 4	d				15 17							15 47							16 17				
Burgess Hill 4	d				15 21							15 51							16 21				
Wivelsfield 4	d				15 23							15 53											
Haywards Heath 3	d				15 32				15 48			15 58						16 18	16 26				16 38
Balcombe	d				15 37														16 32				
Three Bridges 4	d				15 43				15 57			16 07						16 27	16 37				16 47
Gatwick Airport 10 ✈	d				15 47				16 02			16 12						16 32	16 42				16 53
Redhill	d																						
East Croydon	d				16 02				16 17			16 28						16 47	16 58				17 09
Sevenoaks 4	d						15 32								16 02		16 22						
Bat & Ball	d						15 35								16 05		16 25						
Otford 4	d						15 38								16 08		16 28						
Shoreham (Kent)	d						15 41								16 11								
Eynsford	d						15 45								16 15								
Swanley 4	d						15 50								16 20		16 37						
St Mary Cray 4	d						15 54								16 24		16 41						
Bickley	d						15 58								16 28								
Bromley South	d						16 01								16 31		16 47						
Shortlands 4	d						16 04								16 34								
Ravensbourne	d						16 06								16 36								
Beckenham Hill	d						16 08								16 38								
Bellingham	d						16 10								16 40		16 52						
Catford	d						16 13								16 43		16 55						
Crofton Park	d						16 15								16 45								
Nunhead 4	d						16 18								16 48		16 59						
Peckham Rye 4	d						16 20								16 50		17 02						
Denmark Hill 4	d						16 24								16 54		17 05						
Sutton (Surrey) 4	d	15 38				15 37		16 08						16 07		16 38						16 37	
West Sutton	d					15 40								16 10								16 40	
Sutton Common	d					15 42								16 12								16 42	
St Helier	d					15 45								16 15								16 45	
Morden South	d					15 47								16 17								16 47	
South Merton	d					15 49								16 19								16 49	
Wimbledon Chase	d					15 51								16 21								16 51	
Wimbledon 6 ⊖	d					15 58								16 30								17 00	
Haydons Road	d					16 00								16 32								17 02	
Tooting	d					16 03								16 35								17 05	
Carshalton	d	15 41						16 11								16 41							
Hackbridge	d	15 43						16 13								16 43							
Mitcham Junction	d	15 46						16 16								16 46							
Mitcham Eastfields	d	15 49						16 19								16 49							
Streatham 4	d	15 53				16 08		16 23						16 40		16 53						17 10	
Tulse Hill 3	d	15 57				16 12		16 27	16 32					16 46		16 57			17 12			17 16	
London Bridge 4 ⊖	a				16 15																		17 27
	d				16 16																		17 27
West Croydon	d																						
Herne Hill 4	d	16 01				16 16		16 31						16 50		17 01						17 21	
Loughborough Jn	d	16 04				16 19		16 34						16 53								17 24	
Elephant & Castle	d	16 09	16 18			16 24	16 30	16 39	16 44				16 56	17 00	17 04	17 08	17 12		17 22			17 28	
London Blackfriars 3 ⊖	d	16 14	16 22		16 26	16 30	16 38	16 44	16 52			16 56	17 00	17 04	17 08	17 12	17 16	17 22	17 26			17 32	17 36
City Thameslink 3	d	16 16	16 24		16 28	16 32	16 40	16 46	16 54			16 58	17 02	17 06	17 10	17 14	17 18	17 24	17 28			17 34	17 38
Farringdon 3 ⊖	d	16 19	16 27		16 31	16 35	16 43	16 49	16 57			17 01	17 05	17 09	17 13	17 17	17 23	17 27	17 31			17 37	17 41
St Pancras International 15 ⊖	d			17 00						17 15	17 30									17 45	18 00		
St Pancras International 15 ⊖	a	16 23	16 31		16 35	16 39	16 47	16 53	17 01			17 05	17 09	17 13	17 17	17 21	17 27	17 31	17 35			17 41	17 45
	d	16 24	16 32		16 36	16 40	16 48	16 54	17 02			17 06	17 10	17 14	17 18	17 22	17 28	17 32	17 36			17 42	17 46
Kentish Town ⊖	d	16 28				16 44		16 58						17 18			17 32					17 46	
West Hampstead Thameslink ⊖	d	16 32				16 48		17 02					17 18	17 22			17 36					17 50	
Cricklewood	d	16 35				16 51		17 05						17 25			17 39					17 53	
Hendon	d	16 38				16 54		17 08						17 28			17 42					17 56	
Mill Hill Broadway	d	16 43				16 59		17 13					17 26	17 33			17 47					18 01	
Elstree & Borehamwood	d	16 47				17 03		17 17					17 30	17 37			17 51					18 05	
Radlett	d	16 51				17 07		17 21					17 34	17 43			17 54					18 09	
St Albans City	d	16a59	16 52		16 56	17 14	17 08	17a29	17 20			17 26	17 40	17a51	17 38	17 44	18a03	17 50	17 56			18 16	18 06
Harpenden	d		16 58		17 02	17 19	17 14		17 26			17 32	17 47			17 51		17 56	18 02			18 21	18 14
Luton Airport Parkway 7 ✈	d				17 08	17 25	17 20					17 38	17 52		17 48	17 57			18 08	18a08		18 27	18 20
Luton 10	d		17 04		17 11	17a29	17 23		17 32	17a38		17 41	17a56		17 51	18 00		18 02	18 11		18 23	18a31	18 23
Leagrave	d				17 15		17 27					17 45				18 04			18 15				18 27
Harlington	d				17 20		17 32					17 50				18 09			18 20				18 32
Flitwick	d		17 13		17 24		17 36		17 41			17 54			18 00	18 13		18 11	18 24				18 36
Bedford 7	a		17 25	17 33	17 36		17 49		17 53		18 03	18 06			18 12	18 26		18 23	18 36		18 38		18 48

Brighton, Gatwick Airport and South London - City of London, St Albans, Luton and Bedford

Network Diagram - see first Page of Table 52

		SE	FC	FC 1	SE 1	EM ◇1	FC	SE 1	EM ◇1	SE 1	FC	FC	FC 1	FC 1	EM ◇1	FC	SE 1	FC	FC	FC 1	FC 1	EM ◇1	FC
Brighton 10	d			16 30									17 02	17 07						17 24	17 37		
Preston Park	d			16 34										17 11						17 28	17 41		
Hassocks 4	d			16 40										17 17						17 34	17 47		
Burgess Hill 4	d			16 44									17 13	17 21						17 38	17 51		
Wivelsfield 4	d			16 46																17 40	17 53		
Haywards Heath 3	d			16 51									17 18	17 26						17 46	18 02		
Balcombe	d			16 56																	18 07		
Three Bridges 4	d			17 02									17 27							17 55	18 13		
Gatwick Airport 10 ✈	d			17 08									17 32	17 39						18 00	18 17		
Redhill	d																						
East Croydon	d			17 23									17 47	17 58						18 16	18 32		
Sevenoaks 4	d	16 32						17 02									17 32						
Bat & Ball	d	16 35						17 05									17 35						
Otford 4	d	16 38						17 08									17 38						
Shoreham (Kent)	d	16 41						17 11									17 41						
Eynsford	d	16 45						17 15									17 45						
Swanley 4	d	16 50						17 20									17 50						
St Mary Cray 4	d	16 54						17 24									17 54						
Bickley	d	16 58						17 28		17 42							17 58						
Bromley South	d	17 01						17 31		17 45							18 01						
Shortlands 4	d	17 04						17 34									18 04						
Ravensbourne	d	17 06						17 36									18 06						
Beckenham Hill	d	17 08						17 38									18 08						
Bellingham	d	17 10						17 40									18 10						
Catford	d	17 13						17 43									18 13						
Crofton Park	d	17 15						17 45									18 15						
Nunhead 4	d	17 18						17 48									18 18						
Peckham Rye 4	d	17 20						17 50									18 20						
Denmark Hill 4	d	17 24						17 54									18 23						
Sutton (Surrey) 4	d		17 08				17 11					17 42				17 41		18 08					18 09
West Sutton	d						17 14									17 44							18 12
Sutton Common	d						17 16									17 46							18 14
St Helier	d						17 19									17 49							18 17
Morden South	d						17 21									17 51							18 19
South Merton	d						17 23									17 53							18 21
Wimbledon Chase	d						17 25									17 55							18 23
Wimbledon 6 ⊖	d						17 30									18 00							18 28
Haydons Road	d						17 32									18 02							18 30
Tooting	d						17 35									18 05							18 33
Carshalton	d		17 11									17 45						18 11					
Hackbridge	d		17 13									17 47						18 13					
Mitcham Junction	d		17 16									17 50						18 16					
Mitcham Eastfields	d		17 19									17 53						18 19					
Streatham 4	d		17 23				17 40					17 57				18 10		18 23					18 40
Tulse Hill 3	d		17 27				17 44					18 01		18 12		18 16		18 28		18 32			18 44
London Bridge 4 ⊖	a												18 13								18 46		
	d												18 13								18 46		
West Croydon	d																						
Herne Hill 4	d		17 31		17 44		17 48					18 06				18 20		18 32		18 41			18 48
Loughborough Jn	d		17 34		17 47		17 51					18 09				18 23		18 35					18 51
Elephant & Castle	d	17 34	17 39		17 52		17 56	18 00		18 05	18 09	18 14		18 22		18 28	18 32	18 40	18 44	18 48			18 56
London Blackfriars 3 ⊖	d	17 40	17 46	17 52	17 56		18 00	18 06		18 10	18 14	18 18	18 22	18 26		18 32	18 36	18 44	18 48	18 52	18 56		19 00
City Thameslink 3	d	17 42	17 48	17 54	17 58		18 02	18 08		18 12	18 16	18 20	18 24	18 28		18 34	18 38	18 46	18 50	18 54	18 58		19 02
Farringdon 3 ⊖	d	17 45	17 51	17 57	18 01		18 05	18 11		18 15	18 19	18 23	18 27	18 31		18 37	18 41	18 49	18 53	18 57	19 01		19 05
St Pancras International 15 ⊖	d					18 25			18 30						19 00							19 30	
St Pancras International 15 ⊖	a	17 49	17 55	18 01	18 05		18 09	18 15		18 19	18 23	18 27	18 31	18 35		18 41	18 45	18 53	18 57	19 01	19 05		19 09
	d	17 50	17 56	18 02	18 06		18 10	18 16		18 20	18 24	18 28	18 32	18 36		18 42	18 46	18 54	18 58	19 02	19 06		19 10
Kentish Town ⊖	d		18 00				18 14					18 32				18 46			19 02				19 14
West Hampstead Thameslink ⊖	d	17 58	18 04				18 18				18 32	18 36		18 44		18 52		19 02	19 06				19 18
Cricklewood	d		18 07				18 21					18 39				18 55			19 09				19 21
Hendon	d		18 10				18 24					18 42				18 58			19 12				19 24
Mill Hill Broadway	d	18 06	18 15				18 29				18 40	18 47				19 03			19 17				19 28
Elstree & Borehamwood	d	18 10	18 19				18 33				18 44	18 51				19 07		19 12	19 21				19 32
Radlett	d	18 14	18 23				18 39				18 48	18 55				19 11		19 16	19 26				19 36
St Albans City	d	18 20	18a31	18 20	18 26		18 46	18 36		18 42	18 54	19a03	18 50	18 58		19 18	19 06	19 22	19a33	19 20	19 26		19 42
Harpenden	d	18 26		18 26	18 32		18 52			18 48	19 00		18 56	19 04		19 24	19 12	19 28		19 26	19 32		19 48
Luton Airport Parkway 7 ✈	d	18 32			18 38		18 58	18 47	18 53	18 54	19 06			19 10		19 30	19 18	19 34			19 38	19 51	19 54
Luton 10	d	18 36		18 32	18 41	18a49	19a01	18 50		18 57	19 09		19 02	19 13	19 23	19a33	19 23	19 37		19 32	19 41		19a57
Leagrave	d	18 40			18 45					19 01	19 13			19 17			19 27	19 41			19 45		
Harlington	d	18 45			18 50					19 06	19 18			19 22			19 32	19 46			19 50		
Flitwick	d	18 49		18 43	18 54			19 00		19 10	19 22		19 11	19 26			19 36	19 50		19 43	19 54		
Bedford 7	a	19 02		18 55	19 06			19 12	19 08	19 26	19 34		19 23	19 38	19 39		19 48	20 02		19 55	20 06	20 07	

Brighton, Gatwick Airport and South London - City of London, St Albans, Luton and Bedford

Network Diagram - see first Page of Table 52

		SE 1 A	FC 1	FC	FC 1	EM ◇1	FC	SE	FC 1	FC	FC 1	EM ◇1	FC	SE	FC 1	FC	FC 1	EM ◇1	FC	SE	FC 1
Brighton 10	d		18 02		18 07				18 34		18 37						19 07				19 34
Preston Park	d				18 11						18 41						19 11				
Hassocks 4	d				18 17						18 47						19 17				
Burgess Hill 4	d		18 13		18 21						18 51						19 21				
Wivelsfield 4	d				18 23						18 53						19 23				
Haywards Heath 3	d		18 18		18 32				18 48		19 02						19 32				19 48
Balcombe	d				18 37												19 37				
Three Bridges 4	d		18 27		18 43				18 57		19 12				19 27		19 43				19 57
Gatwick Airport 10 ✈	d		18 32		18 47				19 02		19 17				19 32		19 47				20 02
Redhill	d																				
East Croydon	d		18 47		19 02				19 17		19 32				19 47		20 02				20 17
Sevenoaks 4	d	18 02						18 32						19 02						19 32	
Bat & Ball	d	18 05						18 35						19 05						19 35	
Otford 4	d	18 08						18 38						19 08						19 38	
Shoreham (Kent)	d	18 11						18 41						19 11						19 41	
Eynsford	d	18 15						18 45						19 15						19 45	
Swanley 4	d	18 20						18 50						19 20						19 50	
St Mary Cray 4	d	18 24						18 54						19 24						19 54	
Bickley	d	18 28						18 58						19 28						19 58	
Bromley South	d	18 31						19 01						19 31						20 01	
Shortlands 4	d	18 34						19 04						19 34						20 04	
Ravensbourne	d	18 36						19 06						19 36						20 06	
Beckenham Hill	d	18 38						19 08						19 38						20 08	
Bellingham	d	18 40						19 10						19 40						20 10	
Catford	d	18 43						19 13						19 43						20 13	
Crofton Park	d	18 45						19 15						19 45						20 15	
Nunhead 4	d	18 48						19 18						19 48						20 18	
Peckham Rye 4	d	18 50						19 20						19 50						20 20	
Denmark Hill 4	d	18 54						19 24						19 54						20 24	
Sutton (Surrey) 4	d			18 38			18 43			19 08			19 13			19 42			19 37		
West Sutton	d						18 46						19 16						19 40		
Sutton Common	d						18 48						19 18						19 42		
St Helier	d						18 51						19 21						19 45		
Morden South	d						18 53						19 23						19 47		
South Merton	d						18 55						19 25						19 49		
Wimbledon Chase	d						18 57						19 27						19 51		
Wimbledon 6 ⊖	d						19 00						19 30						19 56		
Haydons Road	d						19 02						19 32						19 58		
Tooting	d						19 05						19 35						20 01		
Carshalton	d			18 41						19 11						19 45					
Hackbridge	d			18 43						19 13						19 47					
Mitcham Junction	d			18 46						19 16						19 50					
Mitcham Eastfields	d			18 49						19 19						19 53					
Streatham 4	d			18 53			19 10			19 23			19 40			19 57			20 06		
Tulse Hill 3	d			18 57			19 14			19 27			19 44			20 01			20 12		
London Bridge 4 ⊖	a		19 00		19 15				19 30		19 45				20 00		20 15				20 30
	d		19 01		19 17				19 30		19 45				20 00		20 15				20 30
West Croydon	d																				
Herne Hill 4	d			19 02			19 17			19 31			19 47			20 05			20 16		
Loughborough Jn	d			19 05			19 20			19 34			19 50			20 08			20 19		
Elephant & Castle	d	19 00		19 10			19 25	19 30		19 39			19 55	20 00		20 13			20 24	20 30	
London Blackfriars 3 ⊖	d	19 06	19 10	19 18	19 24		19 30	19 34	19 38	19 46	19 54		20 00	20 04	20 08	20 18	20 24		20 30	20 34	20 38
City Thameslink 3	d	19 08	19 12	19 20	19 26		19 32	19 36	19 40	19 48	19 56		20 02	20 06	20 10	20 20	20 26		20 32	20 36	20 40
Farringdon 3 ⊖	d	19 11	19 15	19 23	19 30		19 36	19 40	19 44	19 51	20 00		20 06	20 10	20 14	20 23	20 30		20 36	20 40	20 44
St Pancras International 15 ⊖	d					20 00						20 30						21 00			
St Pancras International 15 ⊖	a	19 15	19 19	19 27	19 34		19 40	19 44	19 48	19 55	20 04		20 10	20 14	20 18	20 27	20 34		20 40	20 44	20 48
	d	19 16	19 20	19 28	19 34		19 40	19 44	19 48	19 56	20 04		20 10	20 14	20 18	20 28	20 34		20 40	20 44	20 48
Kentish Town ⊖	d			19 32			19 44	19a49		19 59			20 14	20a19		20 31			20 44	20a49	
West Hampstead Thameslink ⊖	d		19 28	19 36	19 41		19 49			20 03	20 11		20 19			20 35	20 41		20 49		
Cricklewood	d			19 39			19 52			20 06			20 22			20 38			20 52		
Hendon	d			19 42			19 55			20 09			20 25			20 41			20 55		
Mill Hill Broadway	d			19 46			19 59			20 13			20 29			20 45			20 59		
Elstree & Borehamwood	d		19 38	19 50			20 03			20 17			20 33			20 49			21 03		
Radlett	d			19 54			20 07			20 21			20 37			20 53			21 07		
St Albans City	d	19 36	19 46	20a01	19 55		20 14		20 09	20a29	20 25		20 44		20 39	21a01	20 55		21 14		21 09
Harpenden	d	19 44	19 52		20 01		20 19		20 15		20 31		20 49		20 45		21 01		21 19		21 15
Luton Airport Parkway 7 ✈	d		19 58		20 07		20 25		20 21		20 37	20 51	20 55		20 51		21 07		21 25		21 21
Luton 10	d	19 50	20 01		20 10	20 23	20a29		20 24		20 40		20a59		20 54		21 10	21 23	21a29		21 24
Leagrave	d	19 54	20 04		20 14				20 27		20 44				20 57		21 14				21 27
Harlington	d		20 09		20 19				20 32		20 49				21 02		21 19				21 32
Flitwick	d		20 13		20 23				20 36		20 53				21 06		21 23				21 36
Bedford 7	a	20 12	20 26		20 35	20 37			20 49		21 05	21 06			21 19		21 35	21 37			21 49

Brighton, Gatwick Airport and South London - City of London, St Albans, Luton and Bedford

Network Diagram - see first Page of Table 52

		FC	FC 1	FC	SE	FC 1	SE	FC	SE	EM ◇1	FC 1	SE	EM ◇1	FC	FC 7	FC	FC 1	FC 1	FC 1	SE	FC 1	EM ◇1
Brighton 10	d		19 37			20 02					20 07				20 34		20 37	21 11	21 37		22 07	
Preston Park	d		19 41								20 11						20 41		21 41		22 11	
Hassocks 4	d		19 47								20 17						20 47	21 20	21 47		22 17	
Burgess Hill 4	d		19 51			20 13					20 21						20 51	21 23	21 51		22 21	
Wivelsfield 4	d		19 53								20 23						20 53		21 53		22 23	
Haywards Heath 3	d		20 02			20 19					20 32				20 48		21 02	21 32	22 02		22 32	
Balcombe	d										20 37							21 37			22 37	
Three Bridges 4	d		20 12			20 27					20 43				20 57		21 12	21 43	22 12		22 43	
Gatwick Airport 10 ✈	d		20 17			20 32					20 47				21 02		21 17	21 47	22 17		22 47	
Redhill	d																					
East Croydon	d		20 32			20 47					21 02				21 17		21 32	22a02	22a32		23a02	
Sevenoaks 4	d				20 02		20 32		21 02			21 32								22 02		
Bat & Ball	d				20 05		20 35		21 05			21 35								22 05		
Otford 4	d				20 08		20 38		21 08			21 38								22 08		
Shoreham (Kent)	d				20 11		20 41		21 11			21 41								22 11		
Eynsford	d				20 15		20 45		21 15			21 45								22 15		
Swanley 4	d				20 20		20 50		21 20			21 50								22 20		
St Mary Cray 4	d				20 24		20 54		21 24			21 54								22 24		
Bickley	d				20 28		20 58		21 28			21 58								22 28		
Bromley South	d				20 31		21 01		21 31			22 01								22 31		
Shortlands 4	d				20 34		21 04		21 34			22 04								22 34		
Ravensbourne	d				20 36		21 06		21 36			22 06								22 36		
Beckenham Hill	d				20 38		21 08		21 38			22 08								22 38		
Bellingham	d				20 40		21 10		21 40			22 10								22 40		
Catford	d				20 43		21 13		21 43			22 13								22 43		
Crofton Park	d				20 45		21 15		21 45			22 15								22 45		
Nunhead 4	d				20 48		21 18		21 48			22 18								22 48		
Peckham Rye 4	d				20 50		21 20		21 50			22 20								22 50		
Denmark Hill 4	d				20 54		21a23		21a53			22a23								22a53		
Sutton (Surrey) 4	d	20 12		20 07				20 42						20 37		21 12						
West Sutton	d			20 10										20 40								
Sutton Common	d			20 12										20 42								
St Helier	d			20 15										20 45								
Morden South	d			20 17										20 47								
South Merton	d			20 19										20 49								
Wimbledon Chase	d			20 21										20 51								
Wimbledon 5 ⊖	d			20 26										20 56								
Haydons Road	d			20 28										20 58								
Tooting	d			20 31										21 01								
Carshalton	d	20 15						20 45								21 15						
Hackbridge	d	20 17						20 47								21 17						
Mitcham Junction	d	20 20						20 50								21 20						
Mitcham Eastfields	d	20 23						20 53								21 23						
Streatham 4	d	20 27		20 36				20 57						21 06		21 27						
Tulse Hill 3	d	20 31		20 42				21 01						21 12		21 31						
London Bridge 4 ⊖	a		20 45			21 00					21 15				21 30		21 45					
	d		20 45			21 00					21 15				21 30		21 45					
West Croydon	d																					
Herne Hill 4	d	20 35		20 46				21 05						21 16		21 35						
Loughborough Jn.	d	20 38		20 49				21 08						21 19		21 38						
Elephant & Castle	d	20 43		20 54	21 00			21 13						21 24		21 43						
London Blackfriars 3 ⊖	d	20 48	20 54	21 00	21 04	21 08		21 18			21 24			21 30	21 38	21 48	21 54					
City Thameslink 3	d	20 50	20 56	21 02	21 06	21 10		21 20			21 26			21 32	21 40	21 50	21 56					
Farringdon 3 ⊖	d	20 53	21 00	21 06	21 10	21 14		21 23			21 30			21 36	21 44	21 53	22 00					
St Pancras International 15 ⊖	d									21 30			22 00									22 25
St Pancras International 15 ⊖	a	20 57	21 04	21 10	21 14	21 18		21 27			21 34			21 40	21 48	21 57	22 04					
	d	20 58	21 04	21 10	21 14	21 18		21 28			21 34			21 40	21 48	21 58	22 04					
Kentish Town ⊖	d	21 01		21 14	21a19			21 31						21 44		22 01						
West Hampstead Thameslink ⊖	d	21 05	21 11	21 19				21 35			21 41			21 49		22 05	22 11					
Cricklewood	d	21 08		21 22				21 38						21 52		22 08						
Hendon	d	21 11		21 25				21 41						21 55		22 11						
Mill Hill Broadway	d	21 15		21 29				21 45						21 59		22 15						
Elstree & Borehamwood	d	21 19		21 33				21 49						22 03		22 19						
Radlett	d	21 23		21 37				21 53						22 07		22 23						
St Albans City	d	21a31	21 25	21 44		21 39		22a01			21 55			22 14	22 09	22 30	22 25					
Harpenden	d		21 31	21 49		21 45					22 01			22 19	22 15	22 36	22 31					
Luton Airport Parkway 7 ✈	d		21 37	21 55		21 51				21 53	22 07			22 25	22 21	22 42	22 37					22 48
Luton 10	d		21 40	21a59		21 54					22 10		22 24	22a29	22 24	22 45	22 40					
Leagrave	d		21 44			21 57					22 14				22 27	22 49	22 44					
Harlington	d		21 49			22 02					22 19				22 32	22 54	22 49					
Flitwick	d		21 53			22 06					22 23				22 36	22 58	22 53					
Bedford 7	a		22 05			22 19				22 08	22 35		22 39		22 49	23 10	23 05					23 03

Brighton, Gatwick Airport and South London - City of London, St Albans, Luton and Bedford

Network Diagram - see first Page of Table 52

		FC	FC	SE	FC 1 A FX	FC 1 B FO	FC 1	FC A FX	FC bus	FC B FO	FC 1 A FX	FC bus	FC 1 B FO	FC 1	EM ◇1	FC A FX	FC bus	FC B FO	FC 1 A FX	FC bus	FC 1 B FO	FC 1
Brighton 10	d						22 33							23 11								23 37
Preston Park	d						22 37															23 41
Hassocks 4	d						22 43							23 20								23 47
Burgess Hill 4	d						22 47							23 23								23 51
Wivelsfield 4	d						22 49															23 53
Haywards Heath 3	d						22 54							23 29								23 59
Balcombe	d						22 59															00 04
Three Bridges 4	d						23 12							23 38								00 10
Gatwick Airport 10 ✈	d						23 17							23 43								00 15
Redhill	d																					00 23
East Croydon	d						23a32							00a01								00a35
Sevenoaks 4	d			22 32																		
Bat & Ball	d			22 35																		
Otford 4	d			22 38																		
Shoreham (Kent)	d			22 41																		
Eynsford	d			22 45																		
Swanley 4	d			22 50																		
St Mary Cray 4	d			22 54																		
Bickley	d			22 58																		
Bromley South	d			23 01																		
Shortlands 4	d			23 04																		
Ravensbourne	d			23 06																		
Beckenham Hill	d			23 08																		
Bellingham	d			23 10																		
Catford	d			23 13																		
Crofton Park	d			23 15																		
Nunhead 4	d			23 18																		
Peckham Rye 4	d			23 20																		
Denmark Hill 4	d			23a23																		
Sutton (Surrey) 4	d	21 17	22 12																			
West Sutton	d	21 20	22 15																			
Sutton Common	d	21 22	22 17																			
St Helier	d	21 25	22 20																			
Morden South	d	21 27	22 22																			
South Merton	d	21 29	22 24																			
Wimbledon Chase	d	21 31	22 26																			
Wimbledon 5 ⊖	d	21 38	22 30																			
Haydons Road	d	21 40	22 32																			
Tooting	d	21 43	22 35																			
Carshalton	d																					
Hackbridge	d																					
Mitcham Junction	d																					
Mitcham Eastfields	d																					
Streatham 4	d	21 49	22 40																			
Tulse Hill 3	d	21 53	22a44																			
London Bridge 4 ⊖	a																					
	d																					
West Croydon	d																					
Herne Hill 4	d	21 57																				
Loughborough Jn.	d	22 00																				
Elephant & Castle	d	22 04																				
London Blackfriars 3 ⊖	d	22 08							22 40			22 55					23 10			23 20		
City Thameslink 3	d	22 10							22 45			23 00					23 15			23 25		
Farringdon 3 ⊖	d	22 13							22 50			23 05					23 20			23 30		
St Pancras International 15 ⊖	d					22 32				22 48			23 02		23 15			23 18			23 32	
St Pancras International 15 ⊖	a	22 17							22 55			23 10					23 25			23 35		
	d	22 18			22 32			22 48			23 02					23 18			23 32			
Kentish Town ⊖	d	22 21						22 51		22 53						23 21		23 23				
West Hampstead Thameslink ⊖	d	22 25			22 40	22 40		22 55		22 57	23 10		23 10			23 25		23 27	23 40		23 40	
Cricklewood	d	22 28						22 58		23 00						23 28		23 30				
Hendon	d	22 31						23 01		23 03						23 31		23 33				
Mill Hill Broadway	d	22 35						23 05		23 07						23 35		23 37				
Elstree & Borehamwood	d	22 39						23 09		23 11						23 39		23 41				
Radlett	d	22 43						23 14		23 16						23 44		23 46				
St Albans City	d	22 50			22 57	22 57		23 20		23 22	23 27		23 27			23 50		23 52	23 57		23 57	
Harpenden	d	22 56			23 03	23 03		23 26		23 28	23 33		23 33			23 56		23 58	00 03		00 03	
Luton Airport Parkway 7 ✈	d	23 02			23 09	23 09		23 32		23 34	23 39		23 39			00 02		00 04	00 09		00 09	
Luton 10	d	23 05			23 12	23 12		23 35		23 37	23 42		23 42		23 46	00 05		00 07	00 12		00 12	
Leagrave	d	23 09			23 16	23 16		23 39		23 41	23 46		23 46			00 09		00 11	00 16		00 16	
Harlington	d	23 14			23 21	23 21		23 44		23 46	23 51		23 51			00 14		00 16	00 21		00 21	
Flitwick	d	23 18			23 25	23 25		23 48		23 50	23 55		23 55			00 18		00 20	00 25		00 25	
Bedford 7	a	23 30			23 38	23 38		00 02		00 02	00 08		00 08		00 11	00 32		00 32	00 38		00 38	

A until 22 March and from 26 March

B until 23 March

Brighton, Gatwick Airport and South London - City of London, St Albans, Luton and Bedford

Network Diagram - see first Page of Table 52

	FC A FX	FC (bus)	FC B FO
Brighton [10] d			
Preston Park d			
Hassocks [4] d			
Burgess Hill [4] d			
Wivelsfield [4] d			
Haywards Heath [3] d			
Balcombe d			
Three Bridges [4] d			
Gatwick Airport [10] ✈ d			
Redhill d			
East Croydon d			
Sevenoaks [4] d			
Bat & Ball d			
Otford [4] d			
Shoreham (Kent) d			
Eynsford d			
Swanley [4] d			
St Mary Cray [4] d			
Bickley d			
Bromley South d			
Shortlands [4] d			
Ravensbourne d			
Beckenham Hill d			
Bellingham d			
Catford d			
Crofton Park d			
Nunhead [4] d			
Peckham Rye [4] d			
Denmark Hill [4] d			
Sutton (Surrey) [4] d			
West Sutton d			
Sutton Common d			
St Helier d			
Morden South d			
South Merton d			
Wimbledon Chase d			
Wimbledon [5] ⊖ d			
Haydons Road d			
Tooting d			
Carshalton d			
Hackbridge d			
Mitcham Junction d			
Mitcham Eastfields d			
Streatham [4] d			
Tulse Hill [3] d			
London Bridge [4] ⊖ a			
d			
West Croydon d			
Herne Hill [4] d			
Loughborough Jn. d			
Elephant & Castle d			
London Blackfriars [3] ⊖ d		23 40	
City Thameslink [3] d			
Farringdon [3] ⊖ d		23 50	
St Pancras International [15] ⊖ d			23 48
St Pancras International [15] ⊖ a		23 55	
d	23 48		
Kentish Town ⊖ d	23 51		23 53
West Hampstead Thameslink ⊖ d	23 55		23 57
Cricklewood d	23 58		00 01
Hendon d	00 01		00 04
Mill Hill Broadway d	00 05		00 08
Elstree & Borehamwood d	00 09		00 12
Radlett d	00 14		00 16
St Albans City d	00 20		00 22
Harpenden d	00 26		00 28
Luton Airport Parkway [7] ✈ d	00 32		00 34
Luton [10] d	00 35		00 37
Leagrave d	00 39		00 41
Harlington d	00 44		00 46
Flitwick d	00 48		00 50
Bedford [7] a	01 02		01 02

A until 22 March and from 26 March

B until 23 March

Bedford, Luton, St Albans - London

Network Diagram - see first Page of Table 52

	FC [1]	FC [1]	FC [1]	FC (bus)	FC	FC (bus)	FC (bus)	FC (bus)	FC		FC (bus)	FC [1]	FC (bus)	FC (bus)	FC [1]	FC (bus)	FC [1]	FC (bus)	FC [1]		FC (bus)	FC [1]	FC (bus)	FC
Bedford [7] d	22p52	23p12	23p32		00 02				01 02			02 02			03 02		03 42		04 12			04 42		05 12
Flitwick d	23p02	23p22	23p42		00 12				01 12			02 12			03 12		03 52		04 22			04 52		05 22
Harlington d	23p06	23p26	23p46		00 16				01 16			02 16			03 16		03 56		04 26			04 56		05 26
Leagrave d	23p12	23p32	23p52		00 22				01 22			02 22			03 22		04 02		04 32			05 02		05 32
Luton [10] d	23p16	23p36	23p56		00 26				01 26			02 26			03 26		04 06		04 36			05 06		05 36
Luton Airport Parkway [7] ✈ d	23p19	23p39	23p59		00 29				01 29			02 29			03 29		04 09		04 39			05 09		05 39
Harpenden d	23p25	23p45	00 05		00 35				01 35			02 35			03 35		04 15		04 45			05 15		05 45
St Albans City d	23p31	23p51	00 11		00 41				01 41			02 41			03 41		04 21		04 51			05 21		05 51
Radlett d	23p36	23p56	00 16		00 46				01 46			02 46			03 46		04 26		04 56			05 26		05 56
Elstree & Borehamwood d	23p41	00 01	00 21		00 51				01 51			02 51			03 51		04 31		05 01			05 31		06 01
Mill Hill Broadway d	23p45	00 05	00 25		00 55				01 55			02 55			03 55		04 35		05 05			05 35		06 05
Hendon d	23p48	00 08	00 28		00 58				01 58			02 58			03 58		04 38		05 08			05 38		06 08
Cricklewood d	23p52	00 12	00 32		01 02				02 02			03 02			04 02		04 42		05 12			05 42		06 12
West Hampstead Thameslink ⊖ d	23p54	00 14	00 34		01 04				02 04			03 04			04 04		04 44		05 14			05 44		06 14
Kentish Town ⊖ a	00 02	00 20	00 40		01 10				02 10			03 10			04 10		04 50		05 20			05 50		06 20
St Pancras International [15] ⊖ a	00 08	00 26	00 46		01 16				02 16			03 16			04 16		04 56		05 26			05 56		06 26
d																								
St Pancras International [15] ⊖ a																								
d				23p42		00 12	00 30	01 00			01 30		02 30	03 00		03 30		04 00			04 30		05 00	
Farringdon [3] ⊖ d				23p47		00 17	00 35																05 05	
City Thameslink [3] d																								
London Blackfriars [3] ⊖ a				23p52		00 22	00 40	01 10			01 40		02 40	03 10		03 40		04 10			04 40		05 10	
London Bridge [4] a				00 07		00 37	00 55	01 25			01 55		02 55	03 25		03 55		04 25			04 55		05 25	

	FC (bus)	EM ◇[1] ☕	FC [1]	FC [1]	FC [1]		FC	FC [1]	FC	FC [1]	EM ◇[1] ☕	FC	FC [1]	FC	FC [1]		EM ◇[1] ☕	FC	FC [1]	FC	FC [1]	EM ◇[1] ☕	FC	FC [1]
Bedford [7] d		05 32	05 38	05 42	06 08			06 24		06 38	06 49		06 54		07 08		07 19		07 24		07 38	07 49		07 54
Flitwick d			05 48	05 52	06 18			06 34		06 48			07 04		07 18				07 34		07 48			08 04
Harlington d			05 52	05 56	06 22			06 38		06 52			07 08		07 22				07 38		07 52			08 08
Leagrave d			05 57	06 02	06 27			06 43		06 57			07 13		07 27				07 43		07 57			08 13
Luton [10] d			06 02	06 06	06 32		06 40	06 48		07 02	07 04	07 10	07 18		07 32			07 40	07 48		08 02	08 05	08 10	08 18
Luton Airport Parkway [7] ✈ d		05 55	06 04	06 09	06 34		06 42	06 50		07 04		07 12	07 20		07 34		07 35	07 42	07 50		08 04		08 12	08 20
Harpenden d			06 10	06 15	06 40		06 48	06 56		07 10		07 18	07 26		07 40			07 48	07 56		08 10		08 18	08 26
St Albans City d			06 16	06 21	06 46		06 55	07 02		07 16		07 25	07 32		07 46			07 55	08 02		08 16		08 25	08 32
Radlett d				06 26			07 00					07 30						08 00					08 30	
Elstree & Borehamwood d			06 25	06 31	06 55		07 04			07 23		07 34			07 53			08 04			08 23		08 34	
Mill Hill Broadway d				06 35			07 08					07 38						08 08					08 38	
Hendon d				06 38			07 12					07 42						08 12					08 42	
Cricklewood d				06 42			07 15		←			07 45		←				08 15		←			08 45	
West Hampstead Thameslink ⊖ d			06 33	06 44	07 03		07 18	07 15	07 18	07 32		07 48	07 45	07 48	08 02			08 18	08 15	08 18	08 32		08 48	08 45
Kentish Town ⊖ a				06 50			→		07 24			→		07 54				→		08 24			→	
St Pancras International [15] ⊖ a		06 21	06 42	06 56	07 12			07 24		07 42	07 31		07 54		08 12		08 00		08 24		08 42	08 31		08 54
d																								
St Pancras International [15] ⊖ a																								
d	05 30																							
Farringdon [3] ⊖ d	05 35																							
City Thameslink [3] d																								
London Blackfriars [3] ⊖ a	05 40																							
London Bridge [4] a	05 55																							

	FC		FC [1]	EM ◇[1] ☕	FC	FC [1]	FC	FC [1]	EM ◇[1] ☕	FC	FC [1]		FC	FC [1]	EM ◇[1] ☕	FC	FC [1]	FC	FC [1]	EM ◇[1] ☕	FC		FC [1]	FC
Bedford [7] d			08 08	08 19		08 24		08 38	08 49		08 54			09 08	09 19		09 24		09 38	09 49			09 54	
Flitwick d			08 18			08 34		08 48			09 04			09 18			09 34		09 48				10 04	
Harlington d			08 22			08 38		08 52			09 08			09 22			09 38		09 52				10 08	
Leagrave d			08 27			08 43		08 57			09 13			09 27			09 43		09 57				10 13	
Luton [10] d			08 32		08 40	08 48		09 02	09 05	09 10	09 18			09 32		09 40	09 48		10 02	10 05	10 10		10 18	
Luton Airport Parkway [7] ✈ d			08 34	08 35	08 42	08 50		09 04		09 12	09 20			09 34	09 35	09 42	09 50		10 04		10 12		10 20	
Harpenden d			08 40		08 48	08 56		09 10		09 18	09 26			09 40		09 48	09 56		10 10		10 18		10 26	
St Albans City d			08 46		08 55	09 02		09 16		09 25	09 32			09 46		09 55	10 02		10 16		10 25		10 32	
Radlett d					09 00					09 30						10 00					10 30			
Elstree & Borehamwood d			08 53		09 04			09 23		09 34				09 53		10 04			10 23		10 34			
Mill Hill Broadway d					09 08					09 38						10 08					10 38			
Hendon d					09 12					09 42						10 12					10 42			
Cricklewood d	←				09 15		←			09 45			←			10 15		←			10 45			←
West Hampstead Thameslink ⊖ d	08 48		09 02		09 18	09 15	09 18	09 32		09 48	09 45		09 48	10 02		10 18	10 15	10 18	10 32		10 48		10 45	10 48
Kentish Town ⊖ a	08 54				→		09 24			→			09 54			→		10 24			→			10 54
St Pancras International [15] ⊖ a			09 12	09 01		09 24		09 42	09 29		09 54			10 12	09 59		10 24		10 42	10 29			10 54	
d																								
St Pancras International [15] ⊖ a																								
d																								
Farringdon [3] ⊖ d																								
City Thameslink [3] d																								
London Blackfriars [3] ⊖ a																								
London Bridge [4] a																								

Please refer to separate pages within this table for services operating between South London and Brighton

At weekends please use local bus and tube services to travel to/from St Pancras International and London Bridge when no trains are operating. See local publicity for details of alternative routes and services that are available across central London

Bedford, Luton, St Albans - London

Saturdays until 24 March

Network Diagram - see first Page of Table 52

		FC	EM	FC	FC	FC	FC	EM		FC	FC	FC	FC	FC	FC	EM	FC	FC		FC	FC	EM	FC	FC	FC
Bedford	d	10 08	10 19		10 24		10 38	10 49				10 54			11 08	11 19		11 24			11 38	11 49		11 54	
Flitwick	d	10 18			10 34		10 48					11 04			11 18			11 34			11 48			12 04	
Harlington	d	10 22			10 38		10 52					11 08			11 22			11 38			11 52			12 08	
Leagrave	d	10 27			10 43		10 57					11 13			11 27			11 43			11 57			12 13	
Luton	d	10 32		10 40	10 48		11 02	11 05		11 10	11 14	11 18			11 32		11 40	11 48			12 02	12 05	12 10	12 18	
Luton Airport Parkway	d	10 34	10 35	10 42	10 50		11 04			11 12	11 16	11 20			11 34	11 35	11 42	11 50			12 04		12 12	12 20	
Harpenden	d	10 40		10 48	10 56		11 10			11 18	11 22	11 26			11 40		11 48	11 56			12 10		12 18	12 26	
St Albans City	d	10 46		10 55	11 02		11 16			11 25	11 29	11 32			11 46		11 55	12 02			12 16		12 25	12 32	
Radlett	d			11 00						11 30	11 34						12 00						12 30		
Elstree & Borehamwood	d	10 53		11 04			11 23			11 34	11 38				11 53		12 04				12 23		12 34		
Mill Hill Broadway	d			11 08						11 38	11 42						12 08						12 38		
Hendon	d			11 12						11 42	11 46						12 12						12 42		
Cricklewood	d			11 15		←				11 45	11 49		←	←			12 15			←			12 45		←
West Hampstead Thameslink	d	11 02		11 18	11 15	11 18	11 32			11 48	11 52	11 45	11 48	11 52	12 02		12 18	12 15		12 18	12 32		12 48	12 45	12 48
Kentish Town	a			→		11 24				→	→		11 54	11 57			→			12 24			→		12 54
St Pancras International	a	11 12	11 01		11 24		11 42	11 29				11 54			12 12	12 01		12 24			12 42	12 29		12 54	
	d																								
St Pancras International	a													12 02											
	d																								
Farringdon	d																								
City Thameslink	d																								
London Blackfriars	a																								
London Bridge	a																								

		FC	EM	FC		FC	FC	FC	EM	FC	FC	FC	FC	EM		FC	FC	FC	FC	EM	FC	FC	FC	FC	
Bedford	d	12 08	12 19			12 24		12 38	12 49		12 54		13 08	13 19			13 24		13 38	13 49		13 54		14 08	
Flitwick	d	12 18				12 34		12 48			13 04		13 18				13 34		13 48			14 04		14 18	
Harlington	d	12 22				12 38		12 52			13 08		13 22				13 38		13 52			14 08		14 22	
Leagrave	d	12 27				12 43		12 57			13 13		13 27				13 43		13 57			14 13		14 27	
Luton	d	12 32		12 40		12 48		13 02	13 05	13 10	13 18		13 32			13 40	13 48		14 02	14 05	14 10	14 18		14 32	
Luton Airport Parkway	d	12 34	12 35	12 42		12 50		13 04		13 12	13 20		13 34	13 35		13 42	13 50		14 04		14 12	14 20		14 34	
Harpenden	d	12 40		12 48		12 56		13 10		13 18	13 26		13 40			13 48	13 56		14 10		14 18	14 26		14 40	
St Albans City	d	12 46		12 55		13 02		13 16		13 25	13 32		13 46			13 55	14 02		14 16		14 25	14 32		14 46	
Radlett	d			13 00						13 30						14 00					14 30				
Elstree & Borehamwood	d	12 53		13 04				13 23		13 34			13 53			14 04			14 23		14 34			14 53	
Mill Hill Broadway	d			13 08						13 38						14 08					14 38				
Hendon	d			13 12						13 42						14 12					14 42				
Cricklewood	d			13 15			←			13 45		←				14 15		←			14 45		←		
West Hampstead Thameslink	d	13 02		13 18		13 15	13 18	13 32		13 48	13 45	13 48	14 02			14 18	14 15	14 18	14 32		14 48	14 45	14 48	15 02	
Kentish Town	a			→			13 24			→		13 54				→		14 24			→		14 54		
St Pancras International	a	13 12	13 01			13 24		13 42	13 29		13 54		14 12	14 01			14 24		14 42	14 29		14 54		15 12	
	d																								
St Pancras International	a																								
	d																								
Farringdon	d																								
City Thameslink	d																								
London Blackfriars	a																								
London Bridge	a																								

		EM	FC	FC	FC	FC	EM	FC	FC	FC		FC	EM	FC	FC	FC	FC	EM	FC	FC		FC	FC	EM	FC
Bedford	d	14 19		14 24		14 38	14 49		14 54			15 08	15 19		15 24		15 38	15 49		15 54			16 08	16 19	
Flitwick	d			14 34		14 48			15 04			15 18			15 34		15 48			16 04			16 18		
Harlington	d			14 38		14 52			15 08			15 22			15 38		15 52			16 08			16 22		
Leagrave	d			14 43		14 57			15 13			15 27			15 43		15 57			16 13			16 27		
Luton	d		14 40	14 48		15 02	15 05	15 10	15 18			15 32		15 40	15 48		16 02	16 05	16 10	16 18			16 32		16 40
Luton Airport Parkway	d	14 35	14 42	14 50		15 04		15 12	15 20			15 34	15 35	15 42	15 50		16 04		16 12	16 20			16 34	16 35	16 42
Harpenden	d		14 48	14 56		15 10		15 18	15 26			15 40		15 48	15 56		16 10		16 18	16 26			16 40		16 48
St Albans City	d		14 55	15 02		15 16		15 25	15 32			15 46		15 55	16 02		16 16		16 25	16 32			16 46		16 55
Radlett	d		15 00					15 30						16 00					16 30						17 00
Elstree & Borehamwood	d		15 04			15 23		15 34				15 53		16 04			16 23		16 34				16 53		17 04
Mill Hill Broadway	d		15 08					15 38						16 08					16 38						17 08
Hendon	d		15 12					15 42						16 12					16 42						17 12
Cricklewood	d		15 15		←			15 45		←				16 15		←			16 45			←			17 15
West Hampstead Thameslink	d		15 18	15 15	15 18	15 32		15 48	15 45	15 48		16 02		16 18	16 15	16 18	16 32		16 48	16 45		16 48	17 02		17 18
Kentish Town	a		→		15 24			→		15 54				→		16 24			→			16 54			→
St Pancras International	a	15 01		15 24		15 42	15 29		15 54			16 12	16 01		16 24		16 42	16 29		16 54			17 12	17 01	
	d																								
St Pancras International	a																								
	d																								
Farringdon	d																								
City Thameslink	d																								
London Blackfriars	a																								
London Bridge	a																								

Please refer to separate pages within this table for services operating between South London and Brighton

At weekends please use local bus and tube services to travel to/from St Pancras International and London Bridge when no trains are operating. See local publicity for details of alternative routes and services that are available across central London

Table 52

Bedford, Luton, St Albans - London

Saturdays until 24 March

Network Diagram - see first Page of Table 52

		FC	FC	FC	EM	FC		FC	FC	FC	EM	FC	FC	FC	FC	EM		FC	FC	FC	FC	EM	FC	EM	FC
Bedford	d	16 24		16 38	16 49			16 54		17 08	17 19		17 24		17 38	17 49			17 54		18 08	18 19	18 22	18 49	
Flitwick	d	16 34		16 48				17 04		17 18			17 34		17 48				18 04		18 18		18 32		
Harlington	d	16 38		16 52				17 08		17 22			17 38		17 52				18 08		18 22		18 36		
Leagrave	d	16 43		16 57				17 13		17 27			17 43		17 57				18 13		18 27		18 41		
Luton	d	16 48		17 02	17 05	17 10		17 18		17 32		17 40	17 48		18 02	18 05		18 10	18 18		18 32		18 46	19 05	18 50
Luton Airport Parkway	d	16 50		17 04		17 12		17 20		17 34	17 35	17 42	17 50		18 04			18 12	18 20		18 34	18 35	18 48		18 52
Harpenden	d	16 56		17 10		17 18		17 26		17 40		17 48	17 56		18 10			18 18	18 26		18 40		18 54		18 58
St Albans City	d	17 02		17 16		17 25		17 32		17 46		17 55	18 02		18 16			18 25	18 32		18 46		19 00		19 05
Radlett	d					17 30						18 00						18 30							19 10
Elstree & Borehamwood	d			17 23		17 34				17 53		18 04			18 23			18 34			18 53				19 14
Mill Hill Broadway	d					17 38						18 08						18 38							19 18
Hendon	d					17 42						18 12						18 42							19 22
Cricklewood	d		←			17 45			←			18 15		←				18 45		←					19 25
West Hampstead Thameslink	d	17 15	17 18	17 32		17 48		17 45	17 48	18 02		18 18	18 15	18 18	18 32			18 48	18 45	18 48	19 02		19 14		19 28
Kentish Town	a		17 24			→			17 54			→		18 24				→		18 54					19 33
St Pancras International	a	17 24		17 42	17 29			17 54		18 12	18 01		18 24		18 42	18 29			18 54		19 12	18 59	19 24	19 29	19 40
	d																								
St Pancras International	a																								
	d																								
Farringdon	d																								
City Thameslink	d																								
London Blackfriars	a																								
London Bridge	a																								

		FC		EM	FC	FC	EM	FC	FC	EM	FC	FC		EM	FC	FC	EM	FC	FC	EM	FC	FC		EM	FC
Bedford	d	18 52		19 18		19 22	19 49		19 52	20 18		20 22		20 49		20 52	21 22		21 22	21 47		21 50		22 01	
Flitwick	d	19 02				19 32			20 02			20 32				21 02			21 32			22 00			
Harlington	d	19 06				19 36			20 06			20 36				21 06			21 36			22 04			
Leagrave	d	19 11				19 41			20 11			20 41				21 11			21 41			22 09			
Luton	d	19 16			19 20	19 46	20 05	19 50	20 16		20 20	20 46		21 03	20 50	21 16		21 20	21 46	22 03	21 50	22 14		22 16	22 20
Luton Airport Parkway	d	19 18		19 30	19 22	19 48		19 52	20 18	20 30	20 22	20 48			20 52	21 18	21 38	21 22	21 48		21 52	22 17		22 19	22 22
Harpenden	d	19 24			19 28	19 54		19 58	20 24		20 28	20 54			20 58	21 24		21 28	21 54		21 58	22 22			22 28
St Albans City	d	19 30			19 35	20 00		20 05	20 30		20 35	21 00			21 05	21 30		21 35	22 00		22 05	22 28			22 35
Radlett	d				19 40			20 10			20 40				21 10			21 40			22 10				22 40
Elstree & Borehamwood	d				19 44			20 14			20 44				21 14			21 44			22 14				22 44
Mill Hill Broadway	d				19 48			20 18			20 48				21 18			21 48			22 18				22 48
Hendon	d				19 52			20 22			20 52				21 22			21 52			22 22				22 52
Cricklewood	d				19 55			20 25			20 55				21 25			21 55			22 25				22 55
West Hampstead Thameslink	d	19 44			19 58	20 14		20 28	20 44		20 58	21 14			21 28	21 44		21 58	22 14		22 29	22 44			22 58
Kentish Town	a				20 03			20 33			21 03				21 33			22 03			22 34				23 03
St Pancras International	a	19 54		20 01	20 10	20 24	20 29	20 40	20 54	21 01	21 10	21 24		21 29	21 40	21 54	22 05	22 10	22 24	22 29	22 40	22 54		22 46	23 10
	d																								
St Pancras International	a																								
	d																								
Farringdon	d																								
City Thameslink	d																								
London Blackfriars	a																								
London Bridge	a																								

		FC	EM	FC	FC	FC
Bedford	d	22 10	22 37	22 40	23 10	23 40
Flitwick	d	22 20		22 50	23 20	23 50
Harlington	d	22 24		22 54	23 24	23 54
Leagrave	d	22 30		23 00	23 30	00 01
Luton	d	22 34	22 59	23 04	23 34	00 06
Luton Airport Parkway	d	22 37		23 07	23 37	00 08
Harpenden	d	22 43		23 13	23 43	00 14
St Albans City	d	22 49		23 19	23 49	00 20
Radlett	d	22 54		23 24	23 54	00 26
Elstree & Borehamwood	d	22 59		23 29	23 59	00 30
Mill Hill Broadway	d	23 03		23 33	00 03	00 34
Hendon	d	23 06		23 36	00 06	00 38
Cricklewood	d	23 10		23 40	00 10	00 41
West Hampstead Thameslink	d	23 12		23 42	00 12	00 44
Kentish Town	a	23 18		23 48	00 18	00 49
St Pancras International	a	23 25	23 35	23 55	00 25	00 55
	d					
St Pancras International	a					
	d					
Farringdon	d					
City Thameslink	d					
London Blackfriars	a					
London Bridge	a					

Please refer to separate pages within this table for services operating between South London and Brighton

At weekends please use local bus and tube services to travel to/from St Pancras International and London Bridge when no trains are operating. See local publicity for details of alternative routes and services that are available across central London

Bedford, Luton, St Albans - London

Network Diagram - see first Page of Table 52

		FC	FC	FC	FC	FC	FC	FC	FC	FC	FC	FC	FC	FC	FC	FC	FC	FC	FC	FC	FC	FC	FC
		🚌	■1	🚌	■1	🚌	■1	🚌		🚌		🚌	🚌	■1	🚌	🚌	■1	🚌	■1	🚌	■1	🚌	■1
Bedford ■7	d		22p52		23p12		23p32		00 02		01 02			02 02			03 02		03 42		04 12		04 42
Flitwick	d		23p02		23p22		23p42		00 12		01 12			02 12			03 12		03 52		04 22		04 52
Harlington	d		23p06		23p26		23p46		00 16		01 16			02 16			03 16		03 56		04 26		04 56
Leagrave	d		23p12		23p32		23p52		00 22		01 22			02 22			03 22		04 02		04 32		05 02
Luton ■10	d		23p16		23p36		23p56		00 26		01 26			02 26			03 26		04 06		04 36		05 06
Luton Airport Parkway ■7 ✈	d		23p19		23p39		23p59		00 29		01 29			02 29			03 29		04 09		04 39		05 09
Harpenden	d		23p25		23p45		00 05		00 35		01 35			02 35			03 35		04 15		04 45		05 15
St Albans City	d		23p31		23p51		00 11		00 41		01 41			02 41			03 41		04 21		04 51		05 21
Radlett	d		23p36		23p56		00 16		00 46		01 46			02 46			03 46		04 26		04 56		05 26
Elstree & Borehamwood	d		23p41		00 01		00 21		00 51		01 51			02 51			03 51		04 31		05 01		05 31
Mill Hill Broadway	d		23p45		00 05		00 25		00 55		01 55			02 55			03 55		04 35		05 05		05 35
Hendon	d		23p48		00 08		00 28		00 58		01 58			02 58			03 58		04 38		05 08		05 38
Cricklewood	d		23p52		00 12		00 32		01 02		02 02			03 02			04 02		04 42		05 12		05 42
West Hampstead Thameslink ⊖	d		23p54		00 14		00 34		01 04		02 04			03 04			04 04		04 44		05 14		05 44
Kentish Town ⊖	a		00 02		00 20		00 40		01 10		02 10			03 10			04 10		04 50		05 20		05 50
St Pancras International ■15 ⊖	a																						
	d																						
St Pancras International ■15 ⊖	a		00 05		00 25		00 45		01 15		02 15			03 15			04 15		04 55		05 25		05 55
	d	23p42		00 12		00 30		01 00		01 30		02 30	03 00		03 30	04 00		04 30		05 00		05 30	
Farringdon ■3 ⊖	d	23p47		00 17		00 35														05 05		05 35	
City Thameslink ■3	d																						
London Blackfriars ■3 ⊖	a	23p52		00 22		00 40		01 10		01 40		02 40	03 10		03 40	04 10		04 40		05 10		05 40	
London Bridge ■4	a	00 07		00 37		00 55		01 25		01 55		02 55	03 25		03 55	04 25		04 55		05 25		05 55	

		FC	EM	FC	FC	FC	FC	FC	FC	FC	EM	FC	FC	FC	FC	EM	FC	FC	FC	FC	EM	FC	FC
			◇■1 ☕	■1	■1	■1		■1		■1	◇■1 ☕		■1		■1	◇■1 ☕		■1		■1	◇■1 ☕		■1
Bedford ■7	d	05 12	05 32	05 38	05 42	06 08		06 24		06 38	06 49		06 54		07 08	07 19		07 24		07 38	07 49		07 54
Flitwick	d	05 22		05 48	05 52	06 18		06 34		06 48			07 04		07 18			07 34		07 48			08 04
Harlington	d	05 26		05 52	05 56	06 22		06 38		06 52			07 08		07 22			07 38		07 52			08 08
Leagrave	d	05 32		05 57	06 02	06 27		06 43		06 57			07 13		07 27			07 43		07 57			08 13
Luton ■10	d	05 36		06 02	06 06	06 32	06 44	06 48		07 02	07 04	07 14	07 18		07 32		07 44	07 48		08 02	08 05	08 14	08 18
Luton Airport Parkway ■7 ✈	d	05 39	05 55	06 04	06 09	06 34	06 46	06 50		07 04		07 16	07 20		07 34	07 35	07 46	07 50		08 04		08 16	08 20
Harpenden	d	05 45		06 10	06 15	06 40	06 52	06 56		07 10		07 22	07 26		07 40		07 52	07 56		08 10		08 22	08 26
St Albans City	d	05 51		06 16	06 21	06 46	06 59	07 02		07 16		07 29	07 32		07 46		07 59	08 02		08 16		08 29	08 32
Radlett	d	05 56			06 26		07 04					07 34					08 04					08 34	
Elstree & Borehamwood	d	06 01		06 23	06 31	06 53	07 08			07 23		07 38			07 53		08 08			08 23		08 38	
Mill Hill Broadway	d	06 05			06 35		07 12					07 42					08 12					08 42	
Hendon	d	06 08			06 38		07 16					07 46					08 16					08 46	
Cricklewood	d	06 12			06 42		07 19		←			07 49		←			08 19		←			08 49	
West Hampstead Thameslink ⊖	d	06 14		06 32	06 44	07 02	07 22	07 15	07 22	07 32		07 52	07 45	07 52	08 02		08 22	08 15	08 22	08 32		08 52	08 45
Kentish Town ⊖	a	06 20			06 50		→		07 27			→		07 57			→		08 27			→	
St Pancras International ■15 ⊖	a		06 21								07 31					08 00					08 31		
	d																						
St Pancras International ■15 ⊖	a	06 25		06 41	06 55	07 11		07 24	07 32	07 41			07 54	08 02	08 11			08 24	08 32	08 41			08 54
	d																						
Farringdon ■3 ⊖	d																						
City Thameslink ■3	d																						
London Blackfriars ■3 ⊖	a																						
London Bridge ■4	a																						

		FC	FC	EM	FC	FC	FC	FC	EM	FC	FC	FC	FC	EM	FC	FC	FC	FC	EM	FC	FC	FC
			■1	◇■1 ☕		■1		■1	◇■1 ☕		■1		■1	◇■1 ☕		■1		■1	◇■1 ☕		■1	
Bedford ■7	d		08 08	08 19		08 24		08 38	08 49		08 54		09 08	09 19		09 24		09 38	09 49		09 54	
Flitwick	d		08 18			08 34		08 48			09 04		09 18			09 34		09 48			10 04	
Harlington	d		08 22			08 38		08 52			09 08		09 22			09 38		09 52			10 08	
Leagrave	d		08 27			08 43		08 57			09 13		09 27			09 43		09 57			10 13	
Luton ■10	d		08 32		08 44	08 48		09 02	09 05	09 14	09 18		09 32		09 44	09 48		10 02	10 05	10 14	10 18	
Luton Airport Parkway ■7 ✈	d		08 34	08 35	08 46	08 50		09 04		09 16	09 20		09 34	09 35	09 46	09 50		10 04		10 16	10 20	
Harpenden	d		08 40		08 52	08 56		09 10		09 22	09 26		09 40		09 52	09 56		10 10		10 22	10 26	
St Albans City	d		08 46		08 59	09 02		09 16		09 29	09 32		09 46		09 59	10 02		10 16		10 29	10 32	
Radlett	d				09 04					09 34					10 04					10 34		
Elstree & Borehamwood	d		08 53		09 08			09 23		09 38			09 53		10 08			10 23		10 38		
Mill Hill Broadway	d				09 12					09 42					10 12					10 42		
Hendon	d				09 16					09 46					10 16					10 46		
Cricklewood	d	←			09 19		←			09 49		←			10 19		←			10 49		←
West Hampstead Thameslink ⊖	d	08 52	09 02		09 22	09 15	09 22	09 32		09 52	09 45	09 52	10 02		10 22	10 15	10 22	10 32		10 52	10 45	10 52
Kentish Town ⊖	a	08 57			→		09 27			→		09 57			→		10 27			→		10 57
St Pancras International ■15 ⊖	a			09 01					09 29					09 59					10 29			
	d																					
St Pancras International ■15 ⊖	a	09 02	09 11			09 24	09 32	09 41			09 54	10 02	10 11			10 24	10 32	10 41			10 54	11 02
	d																					
Farringdon ■3 ⊖	d																					
City Thameslink ■3	d																					
London Blackfriars ■3 ⊖	a																					
London Bridge ■4	a																					

Please refer to separate pages within this table for services operating between South London and Brighton

At weekends please use local bus and tube services to travel to/from St Pancras International and London Bridge when no trains are operating. See local publicity for details of alternative routes and services that are available across central London

Bedford, Luton, St Albans - London

Network Diagram - see first Page of Table 52

		FC	EM	FC	FC	FC	FC	EM	FC	FC	FC	FC	EM	FC	FC	FC	FC	EM	FC	FC	FC	FC	EM
		■1	◇■1 ☕		■1		■1	◇■1 ☕		■1		■1	◇■1 ☕		■1		■1	◇■1 ☕		■1		■1	◇■1 ☕
Bedford ■7	d	10 08	10 19		10 24		10 38	10 49		10 54		11 08	11 19		11 24		11 38	11 49		11 54		12 08	12 19
Flitwick	d	10 18			10 34		10 48			11 04		11 18			11 34		11 48			12 04		12 18	
Harlington	d	10 22			10 38		10 52			11 08		11 22			11 38		11 52			12 08		12 22	
Leagrave	d	10 27			10 43		10 57			11 13		11 27			11 43		11 57			12 13		12 27	
Luton ■10	d	10 32		10 44	10 48		11 02	11 05	11 14	11 18		11 32		11 44	11 48		12 02	12 05	12 14	12 18		12 32	
Luton Airport Parkway ■7 ✈	d	10 34	10 35	10 46	10 50		11 04		11 16	11 20		11 34	11 35	11 46	11 50		12 04		12 16	12 20		12 34	12 35
Harpenden	d	10 40		10 52	10 56		11 10		11 22	11 26		11 40		11 52	11 56		12 10		12 22	12 26		12 40	
St Albans City	d	10 46		10 59	11 02		11 16		11 29	11 32		11 46		11 59	12 02		12 16		12 29	12 32		12 46	
Radlett	d			11 04					11 34					12 04					12 34				
Elstree & Borehamwood	d	10 53		11 08			11 23		11 38			11 53		12 08			12 23		12 38			12 53	
Mill Hill Broadway	d			11 12					11 42					12 12					12 42				
Hendon	d			11 16					11 46					12 16					12 46				
Cricklewood	d			11 19		←			11 49		←			12 19		←			12 49		←		
West Hampstead Thameslink ⊖	d	11 02		11 22	11 15	11 22	11 32		11 52	11 45	11 52	12 02		12 22	12 15	12 22	12 32		12 52	12 45	12 52	13 02	
Kentish Town ⊖	a			→		11 27			→		11 57			→		12 27			→		12 57		
St Pancras International ■15 ⊖	a		11 01					11 29					12 01					12 29					13 01
	d																						
St Pancras International ■15 ⊖	a	11 11			11 24	11 32	11 41			11 54	12 02	12 11			12 24	12 32	12 41			12 54	13 02	13 11	
	d																						
Farringdon ■3 ⊖	d																						
City Thameslink ■3	d																						
London Blackfriars ■3 ⊖	a																						
London Bridge ■4	a																						

		FC	FC	FC	FC	EM	FC	FC	FC	FC	EM	FC	FC	FC	FC	EM	FC	FC	FC	FC	EM	FC
			■1		■1	◇■1 ☕		■1		■1	◇■1 ☕		■1		■1	◇■1 ☕		■1		■1	◇■1 ☕	
Bedford ■7	d		12 24		12 38	12 49		12 54		13 08	13 19		13 24		13 38	13 49		13 54		14 08	14 19	
Flitwick	d		12 34		12 48			13 04		13 18			13 34		13 48			14 04		14 18		
Harlington	d		12 38		12 52			13 08		13 22			13 38		13 52			14 08		14 22		
Leagrave	d		12 43		12 57			13 13		13 27			13 43		13 57			14 13		14 27		
Luton ■10	d	12 44	12 48		13 02	13 05	13 14	13 18		13 32		13 44	13 48		14 02	14 05	14 14	14 18		14 32		14 44
Luton Airport Parkway ■7 ✈	d	12 46	12 50		13 04		13 16	13 20		13 34	13 35	13 46	13 50		14 04		14 16	14 20		14 34	14 35	14 46
Harpenden	d	12 52	12 56		13 10		13 22	13 26		13 40		13 52	13 56		14 10		14 22	14 26		14 40		14 52
St Albans City	d	12 59	13 02		13 16		13 29	13 32		13 46		13 59	14 02		14 16		14 29	14 32		14 46		14 59
Radlett	d	13 04					13 34					14 04					14 34					15 04
Elstree & Borehamwood	d	13 08			13 23		13 38			13 53		14 08			14 23		14 38			14 53		15 08
Mill Hill Broadway	d	13 12					13 42					14 12					14 42					15 12
Hendon	d	13 16					13 46					14 16					14 46					15 16
Cricklewood	d	13 19		←			13 49		←			14 19		←			14 49		←			15 19
West Hampstead Thameslink ⊖	d	13 22	13 15	13 22	13 32		13 52	13 45	13 52	14 02		14 22	14 15	14 22	14 32		14 52	14 45	14 52	15 02		15 22
Kentish Town ⊖	a	→		13 27			→		13 57			→		14 27			→		14 57			→
St Pancras International ■15 ⊖	a					13 29					14 01					14 29					15 01	
	d																					
St Pancras International ■15 ⊖	a		13 24	13 32	13 41			13 54	14 02	14 11			14 24	14 32	14 41			14 54	15 02	15 11		
	d																					
Farringdon ■3 ⊖	d																					
City Thameslink ■3	d																					
London Blackfriars ■3 ⊖	a																					
London Bridge ■4	a																					

		FC	FC	FC	EM	FC	FC	FC	FC	EM	FC	FC	FC	FC	EM	FC	FC	FC	FC	EM	FC	FC	FC
		■1		■1	◇■1 ☕		■1		■1	◇■1 ☕		■1		■1	◇■1 ☕		■1		■1	◇■1 ☕		■1	
Bedford ■7	d	14 24		14 38	14 49		14 54		15 08	15 19		15 24		15 38	15 49		15 54		16 08	16 19		16 24	
Flitwick	d	14 34		14 48			15 04		15 18			15 34		15 48			16 04		16 18			16 34	
Harlington	d	14 38		14 52			15 08		15 22			15 38		15 52			16 08		16 22			16 38	
Leagrave	d	14 43		14 57			15 13		15 27			15 43		15 57			16 13		16 27			16 43	
Luton ■10	d	14 48		15 02	15 05	15 14	15 18		15 32		15 44	15 48		16 02	16 05	16 14	16 18		16 32		16 44	16 48	
Luton Airport Parkway ■7 ✈	d	14 50		15 04		15 16	15 20		15 34	15 35	15 46	15 50		16 04		16 16	16 20		16 34	16 35	16 46	16 50	
Harpenden	d	14 56		15 10		15 22	15 26		15 40		15 52	15 56		16 10		16 22	16 26		16 40		16 52	16 56	
St Albans City	d	15 02		15 16		15 29	15 32		15 46		15 59	16 02		16 16		16 29	16 32		16 46		16 59	17 02	
Radlett	d					15 34					16 04					16 34					17 04		
Elstree & Borehamwood	d			15 23		15 38			15 53		16 08			16 23		16 38			16 53		17 08		
Mill Hill Broadway	d					15 42					16 12					16 42					17 12		
Hendon	d					15 46					16 16					16 46					17 16		
Cricklewood	d		←			15 49		←			16 19		←			16 49		←			17 19		←
West Hampstead Thameslink ⊖	d	15 15	15 22	15 32		15 52	15 45	15 52	16 02		16 22	16 15	16 22	16 32		16 52	16 45	16 52	17 02		17 22	17 15	17 22
Kentish Town ⊖	a		15 27			→		15 57			→		16 27			→		16 57			→		17 27
St Pancras International ■15 ⊖	a				15 29					16 01					16 29					17 01			
	d																						
St Pancras International ■15 ⊖	a	15 24	15 32	15 41			15 54	16 02	16 11			16 24	16 32	16 41			16 54	17 02	17 11			17 24	17 32
	d																						
Farringdon ■3 ⊖	d																						
City Thameslink ■3	d																						
London Blackfriars ■3 ⊖	a																						
London Bridge ■4	a																						

Please refer to separate pages within this table for services operating between South London and Brighton

At weekends please use local bus and tube services to travel to/from St Pancras International and London Bridge when no trains are operating. See local publicity for details of alternative routes and services that are available across central London

Table 52

Saturdays from 31 March

Bedford, Luton, St Albans - London

Network Diagram - see first Page of Table 52

		FC	EM	FC	FC	FC		FC	EM	FC	FC	FC	FC	EM	FC	FC		FC	FC	EM	FC	FC	EM	FC	FC
		1	◇1		1			1	◇1		1		1	◇1		1			1	◇1	1		◇1	1	
Bedford 7	d	16 38	16 49		16 54			17 08	17 19		17 24		17 38	17 49		17 54			18 08	18 19	18 22		18 49	18 52	
Flitwick	d	16 48			17 04			17 18			17 34		17 48			18 04			18 18		18 32			19 02	
Harlington	d	16 52			17 08			17 22			17 38		17 52			18 08			18 22		18 36			19 06	
Leagrave	d	16 57			17 13			17 27			17 43		17 57			18 13			18 27		18 41			19 11	
Luton 10	d	17 02	17 05	17 14	17 18			17 32		17 44	17 48		18 02	18 05	18 14	18 18			18 32		18 46	18 50	19 05	19 16	19 20
Luton Airport Parkway 7 ✈	d	17 04		17 16	17 20			17 34	17 35	17 46	17 50		18 04		18 16	18 20			18 34	18 35	18 48	18 52		19 18	19 22
Harpenden	d	17 10		17 22	17 26			17 40		17 52	17 56		18 10		18 22	18 26			18 40		18 54	18 58		19 24	19 28
St Albans City	d	17 16		17 29	17 32			17 46		17 59	18 02		18 16		18 29	18 32			18 46		19 00	19 05		19 30	19 35
Radlett	d			17 34						18 04					18 34							19 10			19 40
Elstree & Borehamwood	d	17 23		17 38				17 53		18 08			18 23		18 38				18 53			19 14			19 44
Mill Hill Broadway	d			17 42						18 12					18 42							19 18			19 48
Hendon	d			17 46						18 16					18 46							19 22			19 52
Cricklewood	d			17 49		←				18 19		←			18 49			←				19 25			19 55
West Hampstead Thameslink ⊖	d	17 32		17 52	17 45	17 52		18 02		18 22	18 15	18 22	18 32		18 52	18 45		18 52	19 02		19 14	19 28		19 44	19 58
Kentish Town ⊖	a			→		17 57				→		18 27			→			18 57				19 33			20 03
St Pancras International 15 ⊖	a		17 29						18 01					18 29						18 59			19 29		
	d																								
St Pancras International 15 ⊖	a	17 41			17 54	18 02		18 11			18 24	18 32	18 41			18 54		19 02	19 11		19 23	19 38		19 53	20 08
	d																								
Farringdon 3 ⊖	d																								
City Thameslink 3	d																								
London Blackfriars 3 ⊖	a																								
London Bridge 4	a																								

		EM		FC	FC	EM	FC	FC	EM	FC	FC	EM		FC	FC	EM	FC	FC	EM	FC	FC	EM		FC	EM
		◇1		1		◇1	1		◇1	1		◇1		1		◇1	1		◇1	1		◇1			◇1
Bedford 7	d	19 18		19 22		19 49	19 52		20 18	20 22		20 49		20 52		21 22	21 22		21 47	21 50		22 01		22 10	22 37
Flitwick	d			19 32			20 02			20 32				21 02			21 32			22 00				22 20	
Harlington	d			19 36			20 06			20 36				21 06			21 36			22 04				22 24	
Leagrave	d			19 41			20 11			20 41				21 11			21 41			22 11				22 32	
Luton 10	d			19 46	19 50	20 05	20 16	20 20		20 46	20 50	21 03		21 16	21 20		21 46	21 50	22 06	22 16	22 20	22 24		22 36	22 59
Luton Airport Parkway 7 ✈	d	19 30		19 48	19 52		20 18	20 22	20 30	20 48	20 52			21 18	21 22	21 38	21 48	21 52		22 18	22 22	22 28		22 39	
Harpenden	d			19 54	19 58		20 24	20 28		20 54	20 58			21 24	21 28		21 54	21 58		22 24	22 28			22 45	
St Albans City	d			20 00	20 05		20 30	20 35		21 00	21 05			21 30	21 34		22 00	22 05		22 30	22 35			22 51	
Radlett	d				20 10			20 40			21 10				21 39			22 10			22 40			22 56	
Elstree & Borehamwood	d				20 14			20 44			21 14				21 43			22 14			22 44			23 01	
Mill Hill Broadway	d				20 18			20 48			21 18				21 47			22 18			22 48			23 05	
Hendon	d				20 22			20 52			21 22				21 51			22 22			22 52			23 08	
Cricklewood	d				20 25			20 55			21 25				21 54			22 25			22 55			23 12	
West Hampstead Thameslink ⊖	d			20 14	20 28		20 44	20 58		21 14	21 28			21 44	21 57		22 14	22 28		22 46	22 58			23 14	
Kentish Town ⊖	a				20 33			21 03			21 33				22 02			22 33			23 03			23 20	
St Pancras International 15 ⊖	a	20 01				20 29			21 01			21 29				22 05			22 34			22 55			23 35
	d																								
St Pancras International 15 ⊖	a			20 23	20 38		20 53	21 08		21 23	21 38			21 53	22 07		22 23	22 38		22 53	23 08			23 25	
	d																								
Farringdon 3 ⊖	d																								
City Thameslink 3	d																								
London Blackfriars 3 ⊖	a																								
London Bridge 4	a																								

		FC	FC	FC
Bedford 7	d	22 40	23 10	23 40
Flitwick	d	22 50	23 20	23 50
Harlington	d	22 54	23 24	23 54
Leagrave	d	23 02	23 32	00 02
Luton 10	d	23 06	23 36	00 06
Luton Airport Parkway 7 ✈	d	23 09	23 39	00 09
Harpenden	d	23 15	23 45	00 15
St Albans City	d	23 21	23 51	00 21
Radlett	d	23 26	23 56	00 26
Elstree & Borehamwood	d	23 31	00 01	00 31
Mill Hill Broadway	d	23 35	00 05	00 35
Hendon	d	23 38	00 08	00 38
Cricklewood	d	23 42	00 12	00 42
West Hampstead Thameslink ⊖	d	23 44	00 14	00 44
Kentish Town ⊖	a	23 48	00 20	00 50
St Pancras International 15 ⊖	a			
	d			
St Pancras International 15 ⊖	a	23 53	00 25	00 55
	d			
Farringdon 3 ⊖	d			
City Thameslink 3	d			
London Blackfriars 3 ⊖	a			
London Bridge 4	a			

Please refer to separate pages within this table for services operating between South London and Brighton

At weekends please use local bus and tube services to travel to/from St Pancras International and London Bridge when no trains are operating. See local publicity for details of alternative routes and services that are available across central London

Table 52

Sundays until 25 March

Bedford, Luton, St Albans - London

Network Diagram - see first Page of Table 52

		FC	FC	FC	FC	FC	FC	FC	FC	FC		FC	FC	EM	FC	FC	EM	FC	FC	FC		EM	FC	FC	FC
		A	A	bus	bus				bus			1		◇1	1		◇1	1		1		◇1	1		1
Bedford 7	d	23p10	23p40			05 42	06 12	06 42		07 12		07 50		08 15	08 20		08 45	08 50		09 06		09 14	09 20		09 36
Flitwick	d	23p20	23p50			05 52	06 22	06 52		07 22		08 00			08 30			09 00		09 16			09 30		09 46
Harlington	d	23p24	23p54			05 56	06 26	06 56		07 26		08 04			08 34			09 04		09 20			09 34		09 50
Leagrave	d	23p30	00 01			06 02	06 32	07 02		07 32		08 09			08 39			09 09		09 25			09 39		09 55
Luton 10	d	23p34	00 06			06 06	06 36	07 06		07 36		08 14	08 18	08 34	08 44	08 48		09 14	09 18	09 30		09 39	09 44	09 48	10 00
Luton Airport Parkway 7 ✈	d	23p37	00 08			06 09	06 39	07 09		07 39		08 17	08 20		08 47	08 51	09 11	09 17	09 21	09 33			09 47	09 51	10 03
Harpenden	d	23p43	00 14			06 15	06 45	07 15		07 45		08 22	08 26		08 52	08 56		09 22	09 26	09 38			09 52	09 56	10 08
St Albans City	d	23p49	00 20			06 21	06 51	07 21		07 51		08 28	08 32		08 58	09 02		09 28	09 32	09 44			09 58	10 02	10 14
Radlett	d	23p54	00 26			06 26	06 56	07 26		07 56			08 38			09 08			09 38					10 08	
Elstree & Borehamwood	d	23p59	00 30			06 31	07 01	07 31		08 01			08 42			09 12			09 42					10 12	
Mill Hill Broadway	d	00 03	00 34			06 35	07 05	07 35		08 05			08 46			09 16			09 46					10 16	
Hendon	d	00 06	00 38			06 38	07 08	07 38		08 08			08 49			09 19			09 49					10 19	
Cricklewood	d	00 10	00 41			06 42	07 12	07 42		08 12			08 53			09 23			09 53					10 23	
West Hampstead Thameslink ⊖	d	00 12	00 44			06 44	07 14	07 44		08 14		08 44	08 55		09 14	09 25		09 44	09 55	09 58			10 14	10 25	10 28
Kentish Town ⊖	a	00 18	00 49			06 50	07 20	07 50		08 20			09 00			09 30			10 02					10 32	
St Pancras International 15 ⊖	a	00 25	00 55			06 56	07 26	07 56		08 26		08 53	09 07	09 13	09 24	09 37	09 50	09 54		10 09		10 20	10 24		10 39
	d																								
St Pancras International 15 ⊖	a																								
	d			00 30	01 00				07 00																
Farringdon 3 ⊖	d			00 35	01 05				07 05																
City Thameslink 3	d																								
London Blackfriars 3 ⊖	a			00 40	01 10				07 10																
London Bridge 4	a			00 55					07 25																

		EM	FC	FC	FC	EM		FC	FC	FC	EM	FC	FC	FC	EM	FC		FC	FC	EM	FC	FC	FC	EM	FC
		◇1	1		1	◇1		1		1	◇1	1		1	◇1	1			1	◇1	1		1	◇1	1
Bedford 7	d	09 45	09 50		10 06	10 16		10 20		10 36	10 45	10 50		11 06	11 16	11 20			11 36	11 45	11 50		12 06	12 15	12 20
Flitwick	d		10 00		10 16			10 30		10 46		11 00		11 16		11 30			11 46		12 00		12 16		12 30
Harlington	d		10 04		10 20			10 34		10 50		11 04		11 20		11 34			11 50		12 04		12 20		12 34
Leagrave	d		10 09		10 25			10 39		10 55		11 09		11 25		11 39			11 55		12 09		12 25		12 39
Luton 10	d		10 14	10 18	10 30	10 39		10 44	10 48	11 00		11 14	11 18	11 30	11 39	11 44		11 48	12 00		12 14	12 18	12 30	12 40	12 44
Luton Airport Parkway 7 ✈	d	10 10	10 17	10 21	10 33			10 47	10 51	11 03	11 10	11 17	11 21	11 33		11 47		11 51	12 03	12 09	12 17	12 21	12 33		12 47
Harpenden	d		10 22	10 26	10 38			10 52	10 56	11 08		11 22	11 26	11 38		11 52		11 56	12 08		12 22	12 26	12 38		12 52
St Albans City	d		10 28	10 32	10 44			10 58	11 02	11 14		11 28	11 32	11 44		11 58		12 02	12 14		12 28	12 32	12 44		12 58
Radlett	d			10 38					11 08				11 38					12 08				12 38			
Elstree & Borehamwood	d			10 42					11 12				11 42					12 12				12 42			
Mill Hill Broadway	d			10 46					11 16				11 46					12 16				12 46			
Hendon	d			10 49					11 19				11 49					12 19				12 49			
Cricklewood	d			10 53					11 23				11 53					12 23				12 53			
West Hampstead Thameslink ⊖	d		10 44	10 55	10 58			11 14	11 25	11 28		11 44	11 55	11 58		12 14		12 25	12 28		12 44	12 55	12 58		13 14
Kentish Town ⊖	a			11 02					11 32				12 02					12 32				13 02			
St Pancras International 15 ⊖	a	10 49	10 54		11 09	11 20		11 24		11 39	11 49	11 54		12 09	12 20	12 24			12 39	12 45	12 54		13 09	13 14	13 24
	d																								
St Pancras International 15 ⊖	a																								
	d																								
Farringdon 3 ⊖	d																								
City Thameslink 3	d																								
London Blackfriars 3 ⊖	a																								
London Bridge 4	a																								

		FC		FC	EM	FC	FC	FC	EM	FC	FC	FC		FC	EM	FC	FC	FC	EM	FC	FC	FC		EM	FC
				1	◇1	1		1	◇1	1		1		1	◇1		1	1	◇1		1	1		◇1	
Bedford 7	d			12 36	12 45	12 50		13 06	13 16	13 20		13 36		13 50	13 58		14 06	14 20	14 22		14 36	14 50		15 01	
Flitwick	d			12 46		13 00		13 16		13 30		13 46		14 00			14 16	14 30			14 46	15 00			
Harlington	d			12 50		13 04		13 20		13 34		13 50		14 04			14 20	14 34			14 50	15 04			
Leagrave	d			12 55		13 09		13 25		13 39		13 55		14 09			14 25	14 39			14 55	15 09			
Luton 10	d	12 48		13 00		13 14	13 18	13 30	13 39	13 44	13 48	14 00		14 14		14 18	14 30	14 44	14 39	14 48	15 00	15 14			15 18
Luton Airport Parkway 7 ✈	d	12 51		13 03	13 10	13 17	13 21	13 33		13 47	13 51	14 03		14 17	14 18	14 21	14 33	14 47		14 51	15 03	15 17		15 17	15 21
Harpenden	d	12 56		13 08		13 22	13 26	13 38		13 52	13 56	14 08		14 22		14 26	14 38	14 52		14 56	15 08	15 22			15 26
St Albans City	d	13 02		13 14		13 28	13 32	13 44		13 58	14 02	14 14		14 28		14 32	14 44	14 58		15 02	15 14	15 28			15 32
Radlett	d	13 08					13 38				14 08					14 38				15 08					15 38
Elstree & Borehamwood	d	13 12					13 42				14 12					14 42				15 12					15 42
Mill Hill Broadway	d	13 16					13 46				14 16					14 46				15 16					15 46
Hendon	d	13 19					13 49				14 19					14 49				15 19					15 49
Cricklewood	d	13 23					13 53				14 23					14 53				15 23					15 53
West Hampstead Thameslink ⊖	d	13 25		13 28		13 44	13 55	13 58		14 14	14 25	14 28		14 44		14 55	14 58	15 14		15 25	15 28	15 44			15 55
Kentish Town ⊖	a	13 32					14 02				14 32					15 02				15 32					16 02
St Pancras International 15 ⊖	a			13 39	13 48	13 54		14 09	14 14	14 24		14 39		14 54	14 44		15 09	15 24	15 04		15 39	15 54		15 43	
	d																								
St Pancras International 15 ⊖	a																								
	d																								
Farringdon 3 ⊖	d																								
City Thameslink 3	d																								
London Blackfriars 3 ⊖	a																								
London Bridge 4	a																								

A not 11 December

Please refer to separate pages within this table for services operating between South London and Brighton

At weekends please use local bus and tube services to travel to/from St Pancras International and London Bridge when no trains are operating. See local publicity for details of alternative routes and services that are available across central London

Bedford, Luton, St Albans - London

Sundays until 25 March

Network Diagram - see first Page of Table 52

		FC 1	FC 1	EM ◇1	FC	FC 1	FC 1	EM ◇1		EM ◇1	FC	FC 1	FC 1	FC	FC 1	EM ◇1	FC 1	FC		FC 1	FC 1	EM ◇1	FC	FC 1	FC 1
Bedford 7	d	15 06	15 20	15 24		15 36	15 50	15 52				16 06	16 20		16 36	16 43	16 50			17 06	17 20	17 23		17 36	17 50
Flitwick	d	15 16	15 30			15 46	16 00					16 16	16 30		16 46		17 00			17 16	17 30			17 46	18 00
Harlington	d	15 20	15 34			15 50	16 04					16 20	16 34		16 50		17 04			17 20	17 34			17 50	18 04
Leagrave	d	15 25	15 39			15 55	16 09					16 25	16 39		16 55		17 09			17 25	17 39			17 55	18 09
Luton 10	d	15 30	15 44	15 41	15 48	16 00	16 14			16 15	16 18	16 30	16 44	16 48	17 00		17 14	17 18		17 30	17 44	17 40	17 48	18 00	18 14
Luton Airport Parkway 7 ✈	d	15 33	15 47		15 51	16 03	16 17	16 08			16 21	16 33	16 47	16 51	17 03	17 00	17 17	17 21		17 33	17 47		17 51	18 03	18 17
Harpenden	d	15 38	15 52		15 56	16 08	16 22				16 26	16 38	16 52	16 56	17 08		17 22	17 26		17 38	17 52		17 56	18 08	18 22
St Albans City	d	15 44	15 58		16 02	16 14	16 28				16 32	16 44	16 58	17 02	17 14		17 28	17 32		17 44	17 58		18 02	18 14	18 28
Radlett	d				16 08						16 38			17 08				17 38					18 08		
Elstree & Borehamwood	d				16 12						16 42			17 12				17 42					18 12		
Mill Hill Broadway	d				16 16						16 46			17 16				17 46					18 16		
Hendon	d				16 19						16 49			17 19				17 49					18 19		
Cricklewood	d				16 23						16 53			17 23				17 53					18 23		
West Hampstead Thameslink ⊖	d	15 58	16 14		16 25	16 28	16 44				16 55	16 58	17 12	17 25	17 28		17 44	17 55		17 58	18 14		18 25	18 28	18 44
Kentish Town ⊖	a				16 32						17 02			17 32				18 02					18 32		
St Pancras International 15 ⊖	a	16 09	16 24	16 04		16 39	16 54	16 32		16 42		17 09	17 24		17 39	17 25	17 54			18 09	18 24	18 06		18 39	18 54
	d																								
St Pancras International 15 ⊖	a																								
	d																								
Farringdon 3 ⊖	d																								
City Thameslink 3	d																								
London Blackfriars 3 ⊖	a																								
London Bridge 4	a																								

		EM ◇1	FC	FC 1		EM ◇1	FC 1	EM ◇1	FC	FC 1	EM ◇1	FC	FC 1	FC		FC 1	EM ◇1	FC	FC	EM ◇1	FC	EM ◇1	FC	EM ◇1	
Bedford 7	d	17 53		18 06		18 11	18 20	18 46		18 50	19 09		19 20			19 50	19 54		20 10	20 19	20 40	20 46	21 10	21 18	
Flitwick	d			18 16			18 30			19 00			19 30			20 00			20 20		20 50		21 20		
Harlington	d			18 20			18 34			19 04			19 34			20 04			20 24		20 54		21 24		
Leagrave	d			18 25			18 39			19 09			19 39			20 09			20 30		21 00		21 30		
Luton 10	d		18 18	18 30		18 27	18 44		18 48	19 14	19 26	19 18	19 44	19 48		20 14		20 18	20 34	20 35	21 04		21 34	21 34	
Luton Airport Parkway 7 ✈	d	18 09	18 21	18 33			18 47	19 06	18 51	19 17		19 21	19 47	19 51		20 17	20 11	20 21	20 37		21 07	21 02	21 37		
Harpenden	d		18 26	18 38			18 52		18 56	19 22		19 26	19 52	19 56		20 22		20 26	20 43		21 13		21 43		
St Albans City	d		18 32	18 44			18 58		19 02	19 28		19 32	19 58	20 02		20 28		20 32	20 49		21 19		21 49		
Radlett	d		18 38						19 08			19 38		20 08				20 38	20 54		21 24		21 54		
Elstree & Borehamwood	d		18 42						19 12			19 42		20 12				20 42	20 59		21 29		21 59		
Mill Hill Broadway	d		18 46						19 16			19 46		20 16				20 46	21 03		21 33		22 03		
Hendon	d		18 49						19 19			19 49		20 19				20 49	21 06		21 36		22 06		
Cricklewood	d		18 53						19 23			19 53		20 23				20 53	21 10		21 40		22 10		
West Hampstead Thameslink ⊖	d		18 55	18 58			19 14		19 25	19 44		19 55	20 14	20 25		20 44		20 55	21 12		21 42		22 12		
Kentish Town ⊖	a		19 02						19 30			20 00		20 30				21 00	21 18		21 48		22 18		
St Pancras International 15 ⊖	a	18 32		19 09		18 50	19 24	19 29	19 38	19 54	19 49	20 08	20 24	20 38		20 54	20 34	21 08	21 26	20 58	21 56	21 27	22 24	21 57	
	d																								
St Pancras International 15 ⊖	a																								
	d																								
Farringdon 3 ⊖	d																								
City Thameslink 3	d																								
London Blackfriars 3 ⊖	a																								
London Bridge 4	a																								

		EM ◇1	FC	FC	EM ◇1	EM ◇1	FC	FC	FC
Bedford 7	d	21 41	21 42	22 10	22 31	22 41	22 42	23 12	23 32
Flitwick	d		21 52	22 20			22 52	23 22	23 42
Harlington	d		21 56	22 24			22 56	23 26	23 46
Leagrave	d		22 02	22 30			23 02	23 32	23 52
Luton 10	d	21 57	22 06	22 34	22 47	22 57	23 06	23 36	23 56
Luton Airport Parkway 7 ✈	d		22 09	22 37			23 09	23 39	23 59
Harpenden	d		22 15	22 43			23 15	23 45	00 05
St Albans City	d		22 21	22 49			23 21	23 51	00 11
Radlett	d		22 26	22 54			23 26	23 56	00 16
Elstree & Borehamwood	d		22 31	22 59			23 31	00 01	00 21
Mill Hill Broadway	d		22 35	23 03			23 35	00 05	00 25
Hendon	d		22 38	23 06			23 38	00 08	00 28
Cricklewood	d		22 42	23 10			23 42	00 12	00 32
West Hampstead Thameslink ⊖	d		22 44	23 12			23 44	00 14	00 34
Kentish Town ⊖	a		22 50	23 18			23 50	00 20	00 40
St Pancras International 15 ⊖	a	22 27	22 56	23 24	23 13	23 28	23 56	00 26	00 46
	d								
St Pancras International 15 ⊖	a								
	d								
Farringdon 3 ⊖	d								
City Thameslink 3	d								
London Blackfriars 3 ⊖	a								
London Bridge 4	a								

Please refer to separate pages within this table for services operating between South London and Brighton

At weekends please use local bus and tube services to travel to/from St Pancras International and London Bridge when no trains are operating. See local publicity for details of alternative routes and services that are available across central London

Bedford, Luton, St Albans - London

Sundays from 1 April

Network Diagram - see first Page of Table 52

		FC	FC bus	FC	FC bus	FC 1	FC bus	FC 1	FC 1	FC 1		FC 1	FC	EM ◇1	FC 1	FC	EM ◇1	FC 1	FC	FC		EM ◇1	FC 1	FC	FC
Bedford 7	d	23p10		23p40		05 40		06 10	06 40	07 10		07 49		08 15	08 19		08 45	08 49		09 04		09 14	09 19		09 34
Flitwick	d	23p20		23p50		05 50		06 20	06 50	07 20		07 58			08 28			08 58		09 14			09 28		09 44
Harlington	d	23p24		23p54		05 54		06 24	06 54	07 24		08 02			08 32			09 02		09 18			09 32		09 48
Leagrave	d	23p32		00 02		06 02		06 32	07 02	07 32		08 10			08 40			09 10		09 25			09 40		09 55
Luton 10	d	23p36		00 06		06 06		06 36	07 06	07 36		08 14	08 18	08 34	08 44	08 48		09 14	09 18	09 30		09 39	09 44	09 48	10 00
Luton Airport Parkway 7 ✈	d	23p39		00 09		06 09		06 39	07 09	07 39		08 17	08 21		08 47	08 51	09 11	09 17	09 21	09 32			09 47	09 51	10 02
Harpenden	d	23p45		00 15		06 15		06 45	07 15	07 45		08 22	08 26		08 52	08 56		09 22	09 26	09 38			09 52	09 56	10 08
St Albans City	d	23p51		00 21		06 21		06 51	07 21	07 51		08 28	08 33		08 58	09 03		09 28	09 33	09 44			09 58	10 03	10 14
Radlett	d	23p56		00 26		06 26		06 56	07 26	07 56			08 38			09 08			09 38					10 08	
Elstree & Borehamwood	d	00 01		00 31		06 31		07 01	07 31	08 01			08 42			09 12			09 42					10 12	
Mill Hill Broadway	d	00 05		00 35		06 35		07 05	07 35	08 05			08 46			09 16			09 46					10 16	
Hendon	d	00 08		00 38		06 38		07 08	07 38	08 08			08 49			09 19			09 49					10 19	
Cricklewood	d	00 12		00 42		06 42		07 12	07 42	08 12			08 53			09 23			09 53					10 23	
West Hampstead Thameslink ⊖	d	00 14		00 44		06 44		07 14	07 44	08 14		08 44	08 55		09 14	09 25		09 44	09 55	09 58			10 14	10 25	10 28
Kentish Town ⊖	a	00 20		00 50		06 50		07 20	07 50	08 20			09 00			09 30			10 00					10 30	
St Pancras International 15 ⊖	a													09 13			09 50					10 20			
	d																								
St Pancras International 15 ⊖	a	00 25		00 55		06 55		07 25	07 55	08 25		08 53	09 05		09 23	09 35		09 53	10 05	10 09			10 23	10 35	10 39
	d		00 30		01 00		07 00																		
Farringdon 3 ⊖	d		00 35		01 05		07 05																		
City Thameslink 3	d																								
London Blackfriars 3 ⊖	a		00 40		01 10		07 10																		
London Bridge 4	a		00 55				07 25																		

		EM ◇1	FC 1	FC	FC	EM ◇1		FC 1	FC	FC	EM ◇1	FC 1	FC	FC	EM ◇1	FC 1		FC	FC	FC	EM ◇1	FC 1	FC	FC	EM ◇1
Bedford 7	d	09 45	09 49		10 04	10 15		10 19		10 34	10 45	10 49		11 04	11 13	11 19				11 34	11 44	11 49		12 04	12 14
Flitwick	d		09 58		10 14			10 28		10 44		10 58		11 14		11 28				11 44		11 58		12 14	
Harlington	d		10 02		10 18			10 32		10 48		11 02		11 18		11 32				11 48		12 02		12 18	
Leagrave	d		10 10		10 25			10 40		10 55		11 10		11 25		11 40				11 55		12 10		12 25	
Luton 10	d		10 14	10 18	10 30	10 37		10 44	10 48	11 00		11 14	11 18	11 30	11 36	11 44		11 48	11 48	12 00		12 14	12 18	12 30	
Luton Airport Parkway 7 ✈	d	10 10	10 17	10 21	10 32			10 47	10 51	11 02	11 10	11 17	11 21	11 32		11 47		11 51	11 51	12 02	12 07	12 17	12 21	12 32	
Harpenden	d		10 22	10 26	10 38			10 52	10 56	11 08		11 22	11 26	11 38		11 52		11 56	11 56	12 08		12 22	12 26	12 38	
St Albans City	d		10 28	10 33	10 44			10 58	11 03	11 14		11 28	11 33	11 44		11 58		12 02	12 03	12 14		12 28	12 33	12 44	
Radlett	d			10 38					11 08				11 38					12 07	12 08				12 38		
Elstree & Borehamwood	d			10 42					11 12				11 42					12 11	12 12				12 42		
Mill Hill Broadway	d			10 46					11 16				11 46					12 15	12 16				12 46		
Hendon	d			10 49					11 19				11 49					12 19	12 19				12 49		
Cricklewood	d			10 53					11 23				11 53					12 22	12 23				12 53		
West Hampstead Thameslink ⊖	d		10 44	10 55	10 58			11 14	11 25	11 28		11 44	11 55	11 58		12 14		12 25	12 25	12 28		12 44	12 55	12 58	
Kentish Town ⊖	a			11 00					11 30				12 00					12 29	12 30				13 00		
St Pancras International 15 ⊖	a	10 49				11 18					11 49				12 11						12 45				13 14
	d																								
St Pancras International 15 ⊖	a		10 53	11 05	11 09			11 23	11 35	11 39		11 53	12 05	12 09		12 23		12 35	12 35	12 39		12 53	13 05	13 09	
	d																								
Farringdon 3 ⊖	d																								
City Thameslink 3	d																								
London Blackfriars 3 ⊖	a																								
London Bridge 4	a																								

		FC 1		FC	FC	EM ◇1	FC 1	FC	FC	EM ◇1	FC 1	FC		FC	FC 1	FC	EM ◇1	FC	FC 1	EM ◇1	FC	FC		EM ◇1	FC 1
Bedford 7	d	12 19			12 34	12 40	12 49		13 04	13 14	13 19			13 34	13 49		13 53	14 04	14 19	14 23		14 34		14 44	14 49
Flitwick	d	12 28			12 44		12 58		13 14		13 28			13 44	13 58			14 14	14 28			14 44			14 58
Harlington	d	12 32			12 48		13 02		13 18		13 32			13 48	14 02			14 18	14 32			14 48			15 02
Leagrave	d	12 40			12 55		13 10		13 25		13 40			13 55	14 10			14 25	14 40			14 55			15 10
Luton 10	d	12 44		12 48	13 00		13 14	13 18	13 30	13 37	13 44	13 48		14 00	14 14	14 18		14 30	14 44	14 50		15 00			15 14
Luton Airport Parkway 7 ✈	d	12 47		12 51	13 02	13 08	13 17	13 21	13 32		13 47	13 51		14 02	14 17	14 21	14 25	14 32	14 47			15 02		15 07	15 17
Harpenden	d	12 52		12 56	13 08		13 22	13 26	13 38		13 52	13 56		14 08	14 22	14 26		14 38	14 52			15 08			15 22
St Albans City	d	12 58		13 03	13 14		13 28	13 33	13 44		13 58	14 03		14 14	14 28	14 33		14 44	14 58		15 03	15 14			15 28
Radlett	d			13 08				13 38				14 08				14 38					15 08				
Elstree & Borehamwood	d			13 12				13 42				14 12				14 42					15 12				
Mill Hill Broadway	d			13 16				13 46				14 16				14 46					15 16				
Hendon	d			13 19				13 49				14 19				14 49					15 19				
Cricklewood	d			13 23				13 53				14 23				14 53					15 23				
West Hampstead Thameslink ⊖	d	13 14		13 25	13 28		13 44	13 55	13 58		14 14	14 25		14 28	14 44	14 55		14 58	15 14		15 25	15 28			15 44
Kentish Town ⊖	a			13 30				14 00				14 30				15 00					15 30				
St Pancras International 15 ⊖	a					13 46				14 14							14 54			15 17				15 35	
	d																								
St Pancras International 15 ⊖	a	13 23		13 35	13 39		13 53	14 05	14 09		14 23	14 35		14 39	14 53	15 05		15 09	15 23		15 35	15 39			15 53
	d																								
Farringdon 3 ⊖	d																								
City Thameslink 3	d																								
London Blackfriars 3 ⊖	a																								
London Bridge 4	a																								

Please refer to separate pages within this table for services operating between South London and Brighton

At weekends please use local bus and tube services to travel to/from St Pancras International and London Bridge when no trains are operating. See local publicity for details of alternative routes and services that are available across central London

Bedford, Luton, St Albans - London

Sundays from 1 April

Network Diagram - see first Page of Table 52

Station		FC	FC	FC 1	EM ◇1 ☕	FC	FC	EM ◇1 ☕	FC 1	EM ◇1 ☕	FC	FC	FC 1	EM ◇1 ☕	FC	FC	FC 1	FC	FC	EM ◇1 ☕	FC 1	FC	FC
Bedford 7	d		15 04	15 19	15 22		15 34	15 44	15 49			16 04	16 19	16 26		16 34	16 49		17 04	17 12	17 19		17 34
Flitwick	d		15 14	15 28			15 44		15 58			16 14	16 28			16 44	16 58		17 14		17 28		17 44
Harlington	d		15 18	15 32			15 48		16 02			16 18	16 32			16 48	17 02		17 18		17 32		17 48
Leagrave	d		15 25	15 40			15 55		16 10			16 25	16 40			16 55	17 10		17 25		17 40		17 55
Luton 10	d		15 30	15 44	15 50		16 00		16 14	16 20		16 30	16 44			17 00	17 14		17 30	17 35	17 44		18 00
Luton Airport Parkway 7 ✈	d		15 32	15 47			16 02	16 07	16 17			16 32	16 47	16 51		17 02	17 17		17 32		17 47		18 02
Harpenden	d		15 38	15 52			16 08		16 22			16 38	16 52			17 08	17 22		17 38		17 52		18 08
St Albans City	d	15 33	15 44	15 58		16 03	16 14		16 28		16 33	16 44	16 58		17 03	17 14	17 28	17 33	17 44		17 58	18 03	18 14
Radlett	d	15 38				16 08					16 38				17 08			17 38				18 08	
Elstree & Borehamwood	d	15 42				16 12					16 42				17 12			17 42				18 12	
Mill Hill Broadway	d	15 46				16 16					16 46				17 16			17 46				18 16	
Hendon	d	15 49				16 19					16 49				17 19			17 49				18 19	
Cricklewood	d	15 53				16 23					16 53				17 23			17 53				18 23	
West Hampstead Thameslink ⊖	d	15 55	15 58	16 14		16 25	16 28		16 44		16 55	16 58	17 14		17 25	17 28	17 44	17 55	17 58		18 14	18 25	18 28
Kentish Town ⊖	a	16 00				16 30					17 00				17 30			18 00				18 30	
St Pancras International 15 ⊖	a				16 17			16 33		16 47				17 16						18 06			
	d																						
St Pancras International 15 ⊖	a	16 05	16 09	16 23		16 35	16 39		16 53		17 05	17 09	17 23		17 35	17 39	17 53	18 05	18 09		18 23	18 35	18 39
	d																						
Farringdon 3 ⊖	d																						
City Thameslink 3	d																						
London Blackfriars 3 ⊖	a																						
London Bridge 4	a																						

Station		EM ◇1 ☕	FC 1	EM ◇1 ☕	FC	FC 1	EM ◇1 ☕	FC	FC 1	EM ◇1 ☕	FC	FC 1	FC	EM ◇1 ☕	FC 1	FC	EM ◇1 ☕	FC 1	EM ◇1 ☕	FC 1	EM ◇1 ☕	FC 1
Bedford 7	d	17 41	17 49	18 12		18 19	18 41		18 49	19 09		19 19		19 41	19 49		20 05	20 10	20 28	20 40	21 06	21 10
Flitwick	d		17 58			18 28			18 58			19 28			19 58			20 20		20 50		21 20
Harlington	d		18 02			18 32			19 02			19 32			20 02			20 24		20 54		21 24
Leagrave	d		18 10			18 40			19 10			19 40			20 10			20 32		21 02		21 32
Luton 10	d		18 14	18 31		18 44			19 14	19 31		19 44	19 49		20 14	20 18	20 27	20 36		21 06	21 28	21 36
Luton Airport Parkway 7 ✈	d	18 08	18 17			18 47	19 03		19 17			19 47	19 51	20 04	20 17	20 21		20 39	20 51	21 09		21 39
Harpenden	d		18 22			18 52			19 22			19 52	19 57		20 22	20 26		20 45		21 15		21 45
St Albans City	d		18 28		18 33	18 58		19 03	19 28		19 33	19 58	20 03		20 28	20 33		20 51		21 21		21 51
Radlett	d				18 38			19 08			19 38		20 08			20 38		20 56		21 26		21 56
Elstree & Borehamwood	d				18 42			19 12			19 42		20 12			20 42		21 01		21 31		22 01
Mill Hill Broadway	d				18 46			19 16			19 46		20 16			20 46		21 05		21 35		22 05
Hendon	d				18 49			19 19			19 49		20 19			20 49		21 08		21 38		22 08
Cricklewood	d				18 53			19 23			19 53		20 23			20 53		21 12		21 42		22 12
West Hampstead Thameslink ⊖	d		18 44		18 55	19 14		19 25	19 44		19 55	20 14	20 25		20 44	20 55		21 14		21 44		22 14
Kentish Town ⊖	a				19 00			19 30			20 00		20 30			21 00		21 20		21 50		22 20
St Pancras International 15 ⊖	a	18 35		18 57			19 29			19 57				20 30			20 53		21 17		21 54	
	d																					
St Pancras International 15 ⊖	a		18 53		19 05	19 23		19 35	19 53		20 05	20 23	20 35		20 53	21 05		21 25		21 55		22 25
	d																					
Farringdon 3 ⊖	d																					
City Thameslink 3	d																					
London Blackfriars 3 ⊖	a																					
London Bridge 4	a																					

Station		EM ◇1 ☕	FC 1	FC 1	EM ◇1 ☕	EM ◇1 ☕	FC 1	FC 1	FC 1
Bedford 7	d	21 36	21 40	22 10	22 25	22 30	22 40	23 10	23 30
Flitwick	d		21 50	22 20			22 50	23 20	23 40
Harlington	d		21 54	22 24			22 54	23 24	23 44
Leagrave	d		22 02	22 32			23 02	23 32	23 52
Luton 10	d	21 57	22 06	22 36	22 47	22 52	23 06	23 36	23 56
Luton Airport Parkway 7 ✈	d		22 09	22 39			23 09	23 39	23 59
Harpenden	d		22 15	22 45			23 15	23 45	00 05
St Albans City	d		22 21	22 51			23 21	23 51	00 11
Radlett	d		22 26	22 56			23 26	23 56	00 16
Elstree & Borehamwood	d		22 31	23 01			23 31	00 01	00 21
Mill Hill Broadway	d		22 35	23 05			23 35	00 05	00 25
Hendon	d		22 38	23 08			23 38	00 09	00 28
Cricklewood	d		22 42	23 12			23 42	00 12	00 32
West Hampstead Thameslink ⊖	d		22 44	23 14			23 44	00 14	00 34
Kentish Town ⊖	a		22 50	23 20			23 50	00 20	00 40
St Pancras International 15 ⊖	a	22 26			23 24	23 29			
	d								
St Pancras International 15 ⊖	a		22 55	23 25			23 55	00 25	00 45
	d								
Farringdon 3 ⊖	d								
City Thameslink 3	d								
London Blackfriars 3 ⊖	a								
London Bridge 4	a								

Please refer to separate pages within this table for services operating between South London and Brighton

At weekends please use local bus and tube services to travel to/from St Pancras International and London Bridge when no trains are operating. See local publicity for details of alternative routes and services that are available across central London

London, St Albans, Luton - Bedford

Saturdays until 24 March

Network Diagram - see first Page of Table 52

Station		FC	FC 1	EM ◇1 ☕	FC	FC 1	FC	FC 1	EM ◇1 ☕	FC	FC 🚌	FC 1	FC 🚌	FC	FC 🚌	FC	FC 🚌	FC 1	FC 🚌	FC 🚌	FC 1	FC	FC 🚌
London Bridge 4 ⊖	d										23p55		00 25		00 57		01 57		02 22	03 17			04 17
Elephant & Castle	d																						
London Blackfriars 3 ⊖	a										00 10		00 40		01 12		02 12		02 37	03 32			04 32
	d										00 10		00 40		01 12		02 12		02 37	03 32			04 32
City Thameslink 3	d																						
Farringdon 3 ⊖	d										00 20		00 50										
St Pancras International 15 ⊖	a										00 25		00 55		01 27		02 27		02 52	03 47			04 47
	d	22p48	23p02	23p15	23p18	23p32	23p48	00 02	00 15	00 18		00 36		01 06		01 34		02 32			03 52	04 32	
Kentish Town	d	22p53			23p23		23p53			00 23		00 41		01 11		01 39		02 36			03 56	04 36	
West Hampstead Thameslink	d	22p57	23p10		23p27	23p40	23p57	00 10		00 27		00 45		01 15		01 43		02 40			04 00	04 40	
Cricklewood	d	23p00			23p30		00 01			00 30		00 48		01 18		01 46		02 43			04 03	04 43	
Hendon	d	23p03			23p33		00 04			00 33		00 51		01 21		01 49		02 46			04 06	04 46	
Mill Hill Broadway	d	23p07			23p37		00 08			00 37		00 55		01 25		01 53		02 50			04 10	04 50	
Elstree & Borehamwood	d	23p11			23p41		00 12			00 41		00 59		01 29		01 57		02 54			04 14	04 54	
Radlett	d	23p16			23p46		00 16			00 45		01 04		01 34		02 02		02 59			04 19	04 59	
St Albans City	d	23p22	23p27		23p52	23p57	00 22	00 27		00 51		01 10		01 40		02 08		03 06			04 26	05 06	
Harpenden	d	23p28	23p33		23p58	00 03	00 28	00 33		00 57		01 16		01 46		02 14		03 12			04 32	05 12	
Luton Airport Parkway 7 ✈	d	23p34	23p39		00 04	00 09	00 34	00 39	00 44	01 03		01 22		01 52		02 20		03 18			04 38	05 18	
Luton 10	d	23p37	23p42	23p46	00 07	00 12	00 37	00 42	00 47	01 06		01 25		01 55		02 23		03 21			04 41	05 21	
Leagrave	d	23p41	23p46		00 11	00 16	00 41	00 46		01 09		01 28		01 58		02 26		03 25			04 45	05 25	
Harlington	d	23p46	23p51		00 16	00 21	00 46	00 51		01 14		01 33		02 03		02 31		03 30			04 50	05 30	
Flitwick	d	23p50	23p55		00 20	00 25	00 50	00 55		01 18		01 37		02 07		02 35		03 34			04 54	05 34	
Bedford 7	a	00 02	00 08	00 11	00 32	00 38	01 02	01 08	01 12	01 32		01 50		02 20		02 49		03 47			05 07	05 47	

Station		FC	FC	FC 🚌	FC	EM ◇1 ☕	FC	FC 1	FC	EM ◇1 ☕	FC 1	EM ◇1 ☕	EM ◇1 ☕	FC 1	FC	FC 1	EM ◇1 ☕	FC 1	FC	FC 1	EM ◇1 ☕	FC 1	FC 1
London Bridge 4 ⊖	d			05 20																			
Elephant & Castle	d																						
London Blackfriars 3 ⊖	a			05 35																			
	d			05 35																			
City Thameslink 3	d																						
Farringdon 3 ⊖	d			05 45																			
St Pancras International 15 ⊖	a			05 50																			
	d	05 02	05 32		06 02	06 10		06 20	06 32	06 37	06 50	06 55	07 00		07 04	07 20	07 30	07 34		07 50	08 00		08 04
Kentish Town	d	05 06	05 36		06 06				06 36						07 09				07 42				
West Hampstead Thameslink	d	05 10	05 40		06 10			06 29	06 40		06 59				07 13	07 29		07 41	07 46	07 59			08 11
Cricklewood	d	05 13	05 43		06 13				06 43						07 16				07 49				
Hendon	d	05 16	05 46		06 16				06 46						07 19				07 52				
Mill Hill Broadway	d	05 20	05 50		06 20				06 50						07 23				07 56				
Elstree & Borehamwood	d	05 24	05 54		06 24			06 39	06 54		07 09				07 27	07 39			08 00	08 09			
Radlett	d	05 29	05 59		06 29				06 59						07 32				08 04				
St Albans City	d	05 36	06 06		06 36			06 47	07 06		07 17				07 38	07 47		07 55	08 10	08 17			08 25
Harpenden	d	05 42	06 12		06 42			06 52	07 12		07 22				07 44	07 52		08 02	08 16	08 22			08 32
Luton Airport Parkway 7 ✈	d	05 48	06 18		06 48		←	06 58	07 18		07 28	07a15		←	07 50	07 58	07 51	08 08	08 22	08 28		←	08 38
Luton 10	d	05 51	06 21		06 51	06 33	06 51	07 01	07a22	06a58	07 31		07 23	07 31	07a54	08 01		08 11	08a26	08 31	08 23	08 31	08 41
Leagrave	d	05 55	06 25		→		06 55	07 05			→			07 35		08 05		08 15		→		08 35	08 45
Harlington	d	06 00	06 30				07 00	07 10						07 40		08 10		08 20				08 40	08 50
Flitwick	d	06 04	06 34				07 04	07 14						07 44		08 14		08 24				08 44	08 54
Bedford 7	a	06 17	06 47			06 47	07 17	07 26					07 38	07 56		08 26	08 06	08 36			08 37	08 56	09 06

Station		FC	FC 1	EM ◇1 ☕	FC 1	FC	FC 1	EM ◇1 ☕	FC 1	FC 1	FC	FC 1	EM ◇1 ☕	FC 1	FC	FC 1	EM ◇1 ☕	FC 1	FC 1	FC	FC 1	EM ◇1 ☕
London Bridge 4 ⊖	d																					
Elephant & Castle	d																					
London Blackfriars 3 ⊖	a																					
	d																					
City Thameslink 3	d																					
Farringdon 3 ⊖	d																					
St Pancras International 15 ⊖	a																					
	d		08 20	08 30	08 34		08 50	09 00		09 04		09 20	09 30	09 34		09 50	10 00		10 04		10 20	10 30
Kentish Town	d	08 12				08 42					09 12				09 42					10 12		
West Hampstead Thameslink	d	08 16	08 29		08 41	08 46	08 59			09 11	09 16	09 29		09 41	09 46	09 59			10 11	10 16	10 29	
Cricklewood	d	08 19				08 49					09 19				09 49					10 19		
Hendon	d	08 22				08 52					09 22				09 52					10 22		
Mill Hill Broadway	d	08 26				08 56					09 26				09 56					10 26		
Elstree & Borehamwood	d	08 30	08 39			09 00	09 09				09 30	09 39			10 00	10 09				10 30	10 39	
Radlett	d	08 34				09 04					09 34				10 04					10 34		
St Albans City	d	08 40	08 47		08 55	09 10	09 17			09 25	09 40	09 47		09 55	10 10	10 17			10 25	10 40	10 47	
Harpenden	d	08 46	08 52		09 02	09 16	09 22			09 32	09 46	09 52		10 02	10 16	10 22			10 32	10 46	10 52	
Luton Airport Parkway 7 ✈	d	08 52	08 58	08 51	09 08	09 22	09 28		←	09 38	09 52	09 58	09 51	10 08	10 22	10 28		←	10 38	10 52	10 58	10 51
Luton 10	d	08a56	09 01		09 11	09a26	09 31	09 23	09 31	09 41	09a56	10 01		10 11	10a26	10 31	10 23	10 31	10 41	10a56	11 01	
Leagrave	d		09 05		09 15		→		09 35	09 45		10 05		10 15		→		10 35	10 45		11 05	
Harlington	d		09 10		09 20				09 40	09 50		10 10		10 20				10 40	10 50		11 10	
Flitwick	d		09 14		09 24				09 44	09 54		10 14		10 24				10 44	10 54		11 14	
Bedford 7	a		09 26	09 06	09 36			09 37	09 56	10 06		10 26	10 06	10 36			10 37	10 56	11 06		11 26	11 06

Please refer to separate pages within this table for services operating between Brighton and South London

At weekends please use local bus and tube services to travel to/from St Pancras International and London Bridge when no trains are operating. See local publicity for details of alternative routes and services that are available across central London

Table 52

Saturdays
until 24 March

London, St Albans, Luton - Bedford

Network Diagram - see first Page of Table 52

	FC [1]	FC	FC [1]	EM ◇[1]	FC [1]	FC [1]	FC	FC [1]	EM ◇[1]	FC [1]	FC	FC [1]	EM ◇[1]	FC [1]	FC [1]	FC	FC [1]	EM ◇[1]	FC [1]	FC	FC [1]	EM ◇[1]
London Bridge [4] ⊖ d																						
Elephant & Castle d																						
London Blackfriars [3] ⊖ a																						
d																						
City Thameslink [3] d																						
Farringdon [3] ⊖ d																						
St Pancras International [15] ⊖ a																						
d	10 34		10 50	11 00		11 04		11 20	11 30	11 34		11 50	12 00		12 04		12 20	12 30	12 34		12 50	13 00
Kentish Town d		10 42					11 12				11 42					12 12				12 42		
West Hampstead Thameslink d	10 41	10 46	10 59			11 11	11 16	11 29		11 41	11 46	11 59			12 11	12 16	12 29		12 41	12 46	12 59	
Cricklewood d		10 49					11 19				11 49					12 19				12 49		
Hendon d		10 52					11 22				11 52					12 22				12 52		
Mill Hill Broadway d		10 56					11 26				11 56					12 26				12 56		
Elstree & Borehamwood d		11 00	11 09				11 30	11 39			12 00	12 09				12 30	12 39			13 00	13 09	
Radlett d		11 04					11 34				12 04					12 34				13 04		
St Albans City d	10 55	11 10	11 17			11 25	11 40	11 47		11 55	12 10	12 17			12 25	12 40	12 47		12 55	13 10	13 17	
Harpenden d	11 02	11 16	11 22			11 32	11 46	11 52		12 02	12 16	12 22			12 32	12 46	12 52		13 02	13 16	13 22	
Luton Airport Parkway [7] ✈ d	11 08	11 22	11 28		←	11 38	11 52	11 58	11 51	12 08	12 22	12 28		←	12 38	12 52	12 58	12 51	13 08	13 22	13 28	
Luton [10] d	11 11	11a26	11 31	11 23	11 31	11 41	11a56	12 01		12 11	12a26	12 31	12 23	12 31	12 41	12a56	13 01		13 11	13a26	13 31	13 23
Leagrave d	11 15		→		11 35	11 45		12 05		12 15		→		12 35	12 45		13 05		13 15		→	
Harlington d	11 20				11 40	11 50		12 10		12 20				12 40	12 50		13 10		13 20			
Flitwick d	11 24				11 44	11 54		12 14		12 24				12 44	12 54		13 14		13 24			
Bedford [7] a	11 36			11 37	11 56	12 06		12 26	12 06	12 36			12 37	12 56	13 06		13 26	13 06	13 36			13 37

	FC [1]	FC [1]	FC	FC [1]	EM ◇[1]	FC [1]	FC	FC [1]	EM ◇[1]	FC [1]	FC [1]	FC	FC [1]	EM ◇[1]	FC [1]	FC	FC [1]	EM ◇[1]	FC [1]	FC [1]	FC
London Bridge [4] ⊖ d																					
Elephant & Castle d																					
London Blackfriars [3] ⊖ a																					
d																					
City Thameslink [3] d																					
Farringdon [3] ⊖ d																					
St Pancras International [15] ⊖ a																					
d		13 04		13 20	13 30	13 34		13 50	14 00		14 04		14 20	14 30	14 34		14 50	15 00		15 04	
Kentish Town d			13 12				13 42					14 12				14 42					15 12
West Hampstead Thameslink d		13 11	13 16	13 29		13 41	13 46	13 59			14 11	14 16	14 29		14 41	14 46	14 59			15 11	15 16
Cricklewood d			13 19				13 49					14 19				14 49					15 19
Hendon d			13 22				13 52					14 22				14 52					15 22
Mill Hill Broadway d			13 26				13 56					14 26				14 56					15 26
Elstree & Borehamwood d			13 30	13 39			14 00	14 09				14 30	14 39			15 00	15 09				15 30
Radlett d			13 34				14 04					14 34				15 04					15 34
St Albans City d		13 25	13 40	13 47		13 55	14 10	14 17			14 25	14 40	14 47		14 55	15 10	15 17			15 25	15 40
Harpenden d		13 32	13 46	13 52		14 02	14 16	14 22			14 32	14 46	14 52		15 02	15 16	15 22			15 32	15 46
Luton Airport Parkway [7] ✈ d	←	13 38	13 52	13 58	13 51	14 08	14 22	14 28		←	14 38	14 52	14 58	14 51	15 08	15 22	15 28		←	15 38	15 52
Luton [10] d	13 31	13 41	13a56	14 01		14 11	14a26	14 31	14 23	14 31	14 41	14a56	15 01		15 11	15a26	15 31	15 23	15 31	15 41	15a56
Leagrave d	13 35	13 45		14 05		14 15		→		14 35	14 45		15 05		15 15		→		15 35	15 45	
Harlington d	13 40	13 50		14 10		14 20				14 40	14 50		15 10		15 20				15 40	15 50	
Flitwick d	13 44	13 54		14 14		14 24				14 44	14 54		15 14		15 24				15 44	15 54	
Bedford [7] a	13 56	14 06		14 26	14 06	14 36			14 37	14 56	15 06		15 26	15 06	15 36			15 37	15 56	16 06	

	FC [1]	EM ◇[1]	FC [1]	FC	FC [1]	EM ◇[1]	FC [1]	FC [1]	FC	FC [1]	EM ◇[1]	FC [1]	FC	FC [1]	EM ◇[1]	FC [1]	FC [1]	FC	FC [1]	EM ◇[1]	FC [1]	FC
London Bridge [4] ⊖ d																						
Elephant & Castle d																						
London Blackfriars [3] ⊖ a																						
d																						
City Thameslink [3] d																						
Farringdon [3] ⊖ d																						
St Pancras International [15] ⊖ a																						
d	15 20	15 30	15 34		15 50	16 00		16 04		16 20	16 30	16 34		16 50	17 00		17 04		17 20	17 30	17 34	
Kentish Town d				15 42					16 12				16 42					17 12				17 42
West Hampstead Thameslink d	15 29		15 41	15 46	15 59			16 11	16 16	16 29		16 41	16 46	16 59			17 11	17 16	17 29		17 41	17 46
Cricklewood d				15 49					16 19				16 49					17 19				17 49
Hendon d				15 52					16 22				16 52					17 22				17 52
Mill Hill Broadway d				15 56					16 26				16 56					17 26				17 56
Elstree & Borehamwood d	15 39			16 00	16 09				16 30	16 39			17 00	17 09				17 30	17 39			18 00
Radlett d				16 04					16 34				17 04					17 34				18 04
St Albans City d	15 47		15 55	16 10	16 17			16 25	16 40	16 47		16 55	17 10	17 17			17 25	17 40	17 47		17 55	18 10
Harpenden d	15 52		16 02	16 16	16 22			16 32	16 46	16 52		17 02	17 16	17 22			17 32	17 46	17 52		18 02	18 16
Luton Airport Parkway [7] ✈ d	15 58	15 51	16 08	16 22	16 28		←	16 38	16 52	16 58	16 51	17 08	17 22	17 28		←	17 38	17 52	17 58	17 51	18 08	18 22
Luton [10] d	16 01		16 11	16a26	16 31	16 23	16 31	16 41	16a56	17 01		17 11	17a26	17 31	17 23	17 31	17 41	17a56	18 01		18 11	18a26
Leagrave d	16 05		16 15		→		16 35	16 45		17 05		17 15		→		17 35	17 45		18 05		18 15	
Harlington d	16 10		16 20				16 40	16 50		17 10		17 20				17 40	17 50		18 10		18 20	
Flitwick d	16 14		16 24				16 44	16 54		17 14		17 24				17 44	17 54		18 14		18 24	
Bedford [7] a	16 26	16 06	16 36			16 37	16 56	17 06		17 26	17 06	17 36			17 37	17 56	18 06		18 26	18 06	18 36	

Please refer to separate pages within this table for services operating between Brighton and South London

At weekends please use local bus and tube services to travel to/from St Pancras International and London Bridge when no trains are operating. See local publicity for details of alternative routes and services that are available across central London

Table 52

Saturdays
until 24 March

London, St Albans, Luton - Bedford

Network Diagram - see first Page of Table 52

	FC [1]	EM ◇[1]	FC [1]	FC [1]	FC	FC [1]	EM ◇[1]	FC [1]	FC	FC [1]	EM ◇[1]	FC [1]	FC [1]	FC	FC [1]	EM ◇[1]	FC [1]	FC	EM ◇[1]	FC	FC [1]	FC
London Bridge [4] ⊖ d																						
Elephant & Castle d																						
London Blackfriars [3] ⊖ a																						
d																						
City Thameslink [3] d																						
Farringdon [3] ⊖ d																						
St Pancras International [15] ⊖ a																						
d	17 50	18 00		18 04		18 20	18 30	18 34		18 50	19 00		19 04		19 20	19 30	19 34	19 48	20 00		20 04	20 18
Kentish Town d					18 12				18 42					19 12				19 52				20 23
West Hampstead Thameslink d	17 59			18 11	18 16	18 29		18 41	18 46	18 59			19 11	19 16	19 29		19 41	19 58			20 11	20 28
Cricklewood d					18 19				18 49					19 19				20 01				20 31
Hendon d					18 22				18 52					19 22				20 04				20 34
Mill Hill Broadway d					18 26				18 56					19 26				20 08				20 38
Elstree & Borehamwood d	18 09				18 30	18 39			19 00	19 09				19 30	19 39			20 12				20 42
Radlett d					18 34				19 04					19 34				20 16				20 46
St Albans City d	18 17			18 25	18 40	18 47		18 55	19 10	19 17			19 25	19 40	19 47		19 55	20 22			20 25	20 52
Harpenden d	18 22			18 32	18 46	18 52		19 02	19 16	19 22			19 32	19 46	19 52		20 02	20 28			20 32	20 58
Luton Airport Parkway [7] ✈ d	18 28		←	18 38	18 52	18 58	18 51	19 08	19 22	19 28		←	19 38	19 52	19 58	19 51	20 08	20 34		←	20 38	21 04
Luton [10] d	18 31	18 23	18 31	18 41	18a56	19 01		19 11	19a26	19 31	19 23	19 31	19 41	19a56	20 01		20 11	20 37	20 23	20 37	20 41	21 07
Leagrave d	→		18 35	18 45		19 05		19 15		→		19 35	19 45		20 05		20 15	→		20 41	20 45	21 11
Harlington d			18 40	18 50		19 10		19 20				19 40	19 50		20 10		20 20			20 46	20 50	21 16
Flitwick d			18 44	18 54		19 14		19 24				19 44	19 54		20 14		20 24			20 50	20 54	21 20
Bedford [7] a		18 37	18 56	19 06		19 26	19 06	19 36			19 37	19 56	20 06		20 26	20 06	20 36		20 37	21 02	21 06	21 32

	EM ◇[1]	FC [1]	FC	EM ◇[1]	FC	FC [1]	FC	EM ◇[1]	FC [1]	FC	EM ◇[1]	FC	FC [1]	FC	EM ◇[1]	FC [1]	FC	FC [1]	FC	FC [1]	FC
London Bridge [4] ⊖ d																					
Elephant & Castle d																					
London Blackfriars [3] ⊖ a																					
d																					
City Thameslink [3] d																					
Farringdon [3] ⊖ d																					
St Pancras International [15] ⊖ a																					
d	20 30	20 34	20 48	21 00		21 04	21 18	21 30	21 34	21 48	22 00		22 04	22 18	22 25	22 34	22 48	23 04	23 18	23 34	23 48
Kentish Town d			20 52				21 23			21 53				22 23			22 53		23 23		23 53
West Hampstead Thameslink d		20 41	20 58			21 11	21 27		21 41	21 57			22 12	22 27		22 42	22 57	23 12	23 27	23 42	23 57
Cricklewood d			21 01				21 30			22 00				22 30			23 00		23 30		00 01
Hendon d			21 04				21 33			22 03				22 33			23 03		23 33		00 04
Mill Hill Broadway d			21 08				21 37			22 07				22 37			23 07		23 37		00 08
Elstree & Borehamwood d			21 12				21 41			22 11				22 41			23 11		23 41		00 12
Radlett d			21 16				21 45			22 15				22 45			23 15		23 45		00 16
St Albans City d		20 55	21 22			21 25	21 51		21 56	22 21			22 28	22 51		22 58	23 21	23 28	23 51	23 58	00 22
Harpenden d		21 02	21 28			21 32	21 57		22 02	22 27			22 34	22 57		23 04	23 27	23 34	23 57	00 04	00 28
Luton Airport Parkway [7] ✈ d	20 51	21 08	21 34		←	21 38	22 03	21 51	22 08	22 33		←	22 40	23 03	22 46	23 10	23 33	23 40	00 03	00 10	00 34
Luton [10] d		21 11	21 37	21 23	21 37	21 41	22 06		22 11	22 36	22 24	22 36	22 43	23 06		23 13	23 36	23 43	00 06	00 13	00 37
Leagrave d		21 15	→		21 41	21 45	22 09		22 14	→		22 39	22 47	23 09		23 16	23 39	23 46	00 09	00 16	00 40
Harlington d		21 20			21 46	21 50	22 14		22 19			22 44	22 52	23 14		23 21	23 44	23 51	00 14	00 21	00 45
Flitwick d		21 24			21 50	21 54	22 18		22 23			22 48	22 56	23 18		23 25	23 48	23 55	00 18	00 25	00 49
Bedford [7] a	21 06	21 36		21 38	22 02	22 06	22 32	22 06	22 36		22 41	23 02	23 08	23 32	23 01	23 38	00 02	00 08	00 32	00 38	01 02

Saturdays
from 31 March

	FC	FC [1]	EM ◇[1]	FC	FC [1]	FC	FC [1]	EM ◇[1]	FC	FC (bus)	FC [1]	FC (bus)	FC	FC (bus)	FC	FC (bus)	FC [1]	FC (bus)	FC (bus)	FC [1]	FC	FC (bus)
London Bridge [4] ⊖ d										23p55		00 25		00 57		01 57		02 22	03 17			04 17
Elephant & Castle d																						
London Blackfriars [3] ⊖ a										00 10		00 40		01 12		02 12		02 37	03 32			04 32
d										00 10		00 40		01 12		02 12		02 37	03 32			04 32
City Thameslink [3] d																						
Farringdon [3] ⊖ d										00 20		00 50										
St Pancras International [15] ⊖ a										00 25		00 55		01 27		02 27		02 52	03 47			04 47
d	22p48	23p02	23p15	23p18	23p32	23p48	00 02	00 15	00 18		00 32		01 02		01 34		02 32			03 52	04 32	
Kentish Town d	22p51			23p21		23p51			00 21		00 35		01 05		01 37		02 35			03 55	04 35	
West Hampstead Thameslink d	22p55	23p10		23p25	23p40	23p55	00 10		00 25		00 40		01 10		01 42		02 40			04 00	04 40	
Cricklewood d	22p58			23p28		23p58			00 28		00 43		01 13		01 45		02 43			04 03	04 43	
Hendon d	23p01			23p31		00 01			00 31		00 46		01 16		01 48		02 46			04 06	04 46	
Mill Hill Broadway d	23p05			23p35		00 05			00 35		00 50		01 20		01 52		02 50			04 10	04 50	
Elstree & Borehamwood d	23p09			23p39		00 09			00 39		00 54		01 24		01 56		02 54			04 14	04 54	
Radlett d	23p14			23p44		00 14			00 44		00 59		01 29		02 01		02 59			04 19	04 59	
St Albans City d	23p20	23p27		23p50	23p57	00 20	00 27		00 50		01 06		01 36		02 08		03 06			04 26	05 06	
Harpenden d	23p26	23p33		23p56	00 03	00 26	00 33		00 56		01 12		01 42		02 14		03 12			04 32	05 12	
Luton Airport Parkway [7] ✈ d	23p32	23p39		00 02	00 09	00 32	00 39	00 44	01 02		01 18		01 48		02 20		03 18			04 38	05 18	
Luton [10] d	23p35	23p42	23p46	00 05	00 12	00 35	00 42	00 47	01 05		01 21		01 51		02 23		03 21			04 41	05 21	
Leagrave d	23p39	23p46		00 09	00 16	00 39	00 46		01 09		01 25		01 55		02 27		03 25			04 45	05 25	
Harlington d	23p44	23p51		00 14	00 21	00 44	00 51		01 14		01 30		02 00		02 32		03 30			04 50	05 30	
Flitwick d	23p48	23p55		00 18	00 25	00 48	00 55		01 18		01 34		02 04		02 36		03 34			04 54	05 34	
Bedford [7] a	00 02	00 08	00 11	00 32	00 38	01 02	01 08	01 12	01 32		01 47		02 17		02 49		03 47			05 07	05 47	

Please refer to separate pages within this table for services operating between Brighton and South London

At weekends please use local bus and tube services to travel to/from St Pancras International and London Bridge when no trains are operating. See local publicity for details of alternative routes and services that are available across central London

Saturdays from 31 March

London, St Albans, Luton - Bedford

Network Diagram - see first Page of Table 52

		FC	FC	FC	FC	EM ◇■		FC	FC ■	FC	EM ◇■	FC ■	EM ◇■	EM ◇■	FC ■	FC		FC ■	EM ◇■	FC ■	FC	FC ■	EM ◇■	FC ■	FC ■
London Bridge ■ ⊖	d			05 20																					
Elephant & Castle	d																								
London Blackfriars ■ ⊖	a			05 35																					
	d			05 35																					
City Thameslink ■	d																								
Farringdon ■ ⊖	d			05 45																					
St Pancras International ■ ⊖	a			05 50																					
	d	05 02	05 32		06 02	06 10			06 20	06 32	06 37	06 50	06 55	07 00		07 08		07 20	07 30	07 34	07 38	07 50	08 00		08 04
Kentish Town	d	05 05	05 35		06 05					06 35						07 11					07 41				
West Hampstead Thameslink	d	05 10	05 40		06 10				06 27	06 40		06 57				07 16		07 27		07 41	07 46	07 57			08 11
Cricklewood	d	05 13	05 43		06 13					06 43						07 19					07 49				
Hendon	d	05 16	05 46		06 16					06 46						07 22					07 52				
Mill Hill Broadway	d	05 20	05 50		06 20					06 50						07 26					07 56				
Elstree & Borehamwood	d	05 24	05 54		06 24				06 37	06 54		07 07				07 30		07 37			08 00	08 07			
Radlett	d	05 29	05 59		06 29					06 58						07 34					08 04				
St Albans City	d	05 36	06 06		06 36				06 45	07 04		07 15				07 40		07 45		07 55	08 10	08 15			08 25
Harpenden	d	05 42	06 12		06 42				06 51	07 10		07 21				07 46		07 51		08 01	08 16	08 21			08 31
Luton Airport Parkway ■ ✈	d	05 48	06 18		06 48			←	06 57	07 16		07 27	07a15		←	07 52		07 57	07 51	08 07	08 22	08 27		←	08 37
Luton ■	d	05 51	06 21		06 51	06 33		06 51	07 00	07a20	06a58	07 30		07 23	07 30	07a56		08 00		08 10	08a26	08 30	08 23	08 30	08 40
Leagrave	d	05 55	06 25		→			06 55	07 04			→			07 34			08 04		08 14		→		08 34	08 44
Harlington	d	06 00	06 30					07 00	07 09						07 39			08 09		08 19				08 39	08 49
Flitwick	d	06 04	06 34					07 04	07 13						07 43			08 13		08 23				08 43	08 53
Bedford ■	a	06 17	06 47			06 47		07 17	07 25					07 38	07 55			08 25	08 06	08 35			08 37	08 55	09 05

		FC		FC ■	EM ◇■	FC ■	FC	FC ■	EM ◇■	FC ■	FC ■	FC		FC ■	EM ◇■	FC ■	FC	FC ■	EM ◇■	FC ■	FC ■	FC		FC ■	EM ◇■
London Bridge ■ ⊖	d																								
Elephant & Castle	d																								
London Blackfriars ■ ⊖	a																								
	d																								
City Thameslink ■	d																								
Farringdon ■ ⊖	d																								
St Pancras International ■ ⊖	a																								
	d	08 08		08 20	08 30	08 34	08 38	08 50	09 00		09 04	09 08		09 20	09 30	09 34	09 38	09 50	10 00		10 04	10 08		10 20	10 30
Kentish Town	d	08 11					08 41					09 11					09 41					10 11			
West Hampstead Thameslink	d	08 16		08 27		08 41	08 46	08 57			09 11	09 16		09 27		09 41	09 46	09 57			10 11	10 16		10 27	
Cricklewood	d	08 19					08 49					09 19					09 49					10 19			
Hendon	d	08 22					08 52					09 22					09 52					10 22			
Mill Hill Broadway	d	08 26					08 56					09 26					09 56					10 26			
Elstree & Borehamwood	d	08 30		08 37			09 00	09 07				09 30		09 37			10 00	10 07				10 30		10 37	
Radlett	d	08 34					09 04					09 34					10 04					10 34			
St Albans City	d	08 40		08 45		08 55	09 10	09 15			09 25	09 40		09 45		09 55	10 10	10 15			10 25	10 40		10 45	
Harpenden	d	08 46		08 51		09 01	09 16	09 21			09 31	09 46		09 51		10 01	10 16	10 21			10 31	10 46		10 51	
Luton Airport Parkway ■ ✈	d	08 52		08 57	08 51	09 07	09 22	09 27		←	09 37	09 52		09 57	09 51	10 07	10 22	10 27		←	10 37	10 52		10 57	10 51
Luton ■	d	08a56		09 00		09 10	09a26	09 30	09 23	09 30	09 40	09a56		10 00		10 10	10a26	10 30	10 23	10 30	10 40	10a56		11 00	
Leagrave	d			09 04		09 14		→		09 34	09 44			10 04		10 14		→		10 34	10 44			11 04	
Harlington	d			09 09		09 19				09 39	09 49			10 09		10 19				10 39	10 49			11 09	
Flitwick	d			09 13		09 23				09 43	09 53			10 13		10 23				10 43	10 53			11 13	
Bedford ■	a			09 25	09 06	09 35			09 37	09 55	10 05			10 25	10 06	10 35			10 37	10 55	11 05			11 25	11 06

		FC ■	FC	FC ■	EM ◇■	FC ■	FC ■	FC		FC ■	EM ◇■	FC ■	FC	FC ■	EM ◇■	FC ■	FC ■	FC		FC ■	EM ◇■	FC ■	FC	FC ■	EM ◇■
London Bridge ■ ⊖	d																								
Elephant & Castle	d																								
London Blackfriars ■ ⊖	a																								
	d																								
City Thameslink ■	d																								
Farringdon ■ ⊖	d																								
St Pancras International ■ ⊖	a																								
	d	10 34	10 38	10 50	11 00		11 04	11 08		11 20	11 30	11 34	11 38	11 50	12 00		12 04	12 08		12 20	12 30	12 34	12 38	12 50	13 00
Kentish Town	d		10 41					11 11					11 41					12 11					12 41		
West Hampstead Thameslink	d	10 41	10 46	10 57			11 11	11 16		11 27		11 41	11 46	11 57			12 11	12 16		12 27		12 41	12 46	12 57	
Cricklewood	d		10 49					11 19					11 49					12 19					12 49		
Hendon	d		10 52					11 22					11 52					12 22					12 52		
Mill Hill Broadway	d		10 56					11 26					11 56					12 26					12 56		
Elstree & Borehamwood	d		11 00	11 07				11 30		11 37			12 00	12 07				12 30		12 37			13 00	13 07	
Radlett	d		11 04					11 34					12 04					12 34					13 04		
St Albans City	d	10 55	11 10	11 15			11 25	11 40		11 45		11 55	12 10	12 15			12 25	12 40		12 45		12 55	13 10	13 15	
Harpenden	d	11 01	11 16	11 21			11 31	11 46		11 51		12 01	12 16	12 21			12 31	12 46		12 51		13 01	13 16	13 21	
Luton Airport Parkway ■ ✈	d	11 07	11 22	11 27		←	11 37	11 52		11 57	11 51	12 07	12 22	12 27		←	12 37	12 52		12 57	12 51	13 07	13 22	13 27	
Luton ■	d	11 10	11a26	11 30	11 23	11 30	11 40	11a56		12 00		12 10	12a26	12 30	12 23	12 30	12 40	12a56		13 00		13 10	13a26	13 30	13 23
Leagrave	d	11 14		→		11 34	11 44			12 04		12 14		→		12 34	12 44			13 04		13 14		→	
Harlington	d	11 19				11 39	11 49			12 09		12 19				12 39	12 49			13 09		13 19			
Flitwick	d	11 23				11 43	11 53			12 13		12 23				12 43	12 53			13 13		13 23			
Bedford ■	a	11 35			11 37	11 55	12 05			12 25	12 06	12 35			12 37	12 55	13 05			13 25	13 06	13 35			13 37

Please refer to separate pages within this table for services operating between Brighton and South London

At weekends please use local bus and tube services to travel to/from St Pancras International and London Bridge when no trains are operating. See local publicity for details of alternative routes and services that are available across central London

Saturdays from 31 March

London, St Albans, Luton - Bedford

Network Diagram - see first Page of Table 52

		FC ■	FC ■	FC		FC ■	EM ◇■	FC ■	FC	FC ■	EM ◇■	FC ■	FC ■	FC		FC ■	EM ◇■	FC ■	FC	FC ■	EM ◇■	FC ■	FC ■	FC	
London Bridge ■ ⊖	d																								
Elephant & Castle	d																								
London Blackfriars ■ ⊖	a																								
	d																								
City Thameslink ■	d																								
Farringdon ■ ⊖	d																								
St Pancras International ■ ⊖	a																								
	d		13 04	13 08		13 20	13 30	13 34	13 38	13 50	14 00		14 04	14 08		14 20	14 30	14 34	14 38	14 50	15 00		15 04	15 08	
Kentish Town	d			13 11					13 41					14 11					14 41					15 11	
West Hampstead Thameslink	d		13 11	13 16		13 27		13 41	13 46	13 57			14 11	14 16		14 27		14 41	14 46	14 57			15 11	15 16	
Cricklewood	d			13 19					13 49					14 19					14 49					15 19	
Hendon	d			13 22					13 52					14 22					14 52					15 22	
Mill Hill Broadway	d			13 26					13 56					14 26					14 56					15 26	
Elstree & Borehamwood	d			13 30		13 37			14 00	14 07				14 30		14 37			15 00	15 07				15 30	
Radlett	d			13 34					14 04					14 34					15 04					15 34	
St Albans City	d		13 25	13 40		13 45		13 55	14 10	14 15			14 25	14 40		14 45		14 55	15 10	15 15			15 25	15 40	
Harpenden	d		13 31	13 46		13 51		14 01	14 16	14 21			14 31	14 46		14 51		15 01	15 16	15 21			15 31	15 46	
Luton Airport Parkway ■ ✈	d	←	13 37	13 52		13 57	13 51	14 07	14 22	14 27		←	14 37	14 52		14 57	14 51	15 07	15 22	15 27		←	15 37	15 52	
Luton ■	d	13 30	13 40	13a56		14 00		14 10	14a26	14 30	14 23	14 30	14 40	14a56		15 00		15 10	15a26	15 30	15 23	15 30	15 40	15a56	
Leagrave	d	13 34	13 44			14 04		14 14		→		14 34	14 44			15 04		15 14		→		15 34	15 44		
Harlington	d	13 39	13 49			14 09		14 19				14 39	14 49			15 09		15 19				15 39	15 49		
Flitwick	d	13 43	13 53			14 13		14 23				14 43	14 53			15 13		15 23				15 43	15 53		
Bedford ■	a	13 55	14 05			14 25	14 06	14 35			14 37	14 55	15 05			15 25	15 06	15 35			15 37	15 55	16 05		

		FC ■	EM ◇■	FC ■	FC	FC ■	EM ◇■	FC ■	FC ■	FC		FC ■	EM ◇■	FC ■	FC	FC ■	EM ◇■	FC ■	FC ■	FC		FC ■	EM ◇■	FC ■	FC
London Bridge ■ ⊖	d																								
Elephant & Castle	d																								
London Blackfriars ■ ⊖	a																								
	d																								
City Thameslink ■	d																								
Farringdon ■ ⊖	d																								
St Pancras International ■ ⊖	a																								
	d	15 20	15 30	15 34	15 38	15 50	16 00		16 04	16 08		16 20	16 30	16 34	16 38	16 50	17 00		17 04	17 08		17 20	17 30	17 34	17 38
Kentish Town	d				15 41					16 11					16 41					17 11					17 41
West Hampstead Thameslink	d	15 27		15 41	15 46	15 57			16 11	16 16		16 27		16 41	16 46	16 57			17 11	17 16		17 27		17 41	17 46
Cricklewood	d				15 49					16 19					16 49					17 19					17 49
Hendon	d				15 52					16 22					16 52					17 22					17 52
Mill Hill Broadway	d				15 56					16 26					16 56					17 26					17 56
Elstree & Borehamwood	d	15 37			16 00	16 07				16 30		16 37			17 00	17 07				17 30		17 37			18 00
Radlett	d				16 04					16 34					17 04					17 34					18 04
St Albans City	d	15 45		15 55	16 10	16 15			16 25	16 40		16 45		16 55	17 10	17 15			17 25	17 40		17 45		17 55	18 10
Harpenden	d	15 51		16 01	16 16	16 21			16 31	16 46		16 51		17 01	17 16	17 21			17 31	17 46		17 51		18 01	18 16
Luton Airport Parkway ■ ✈	d	15 57	15 51	16 07	16 22	16 27		←	16 37	16 52		16 57	16 51	17 07	17 22	17 27		←	17 37	17 52		17 57	17 51	18 07	18 22
Luton ■	d	16 00		16 10	16a26	16 30	16 23	16 30	16 40	16a56		17 00		17 10	17a26	17 30	17 23	17 30	17 40	17a56		18 00		18 10	18a26
Leagrave	d	16 04		16 14		→		16 34	16 44			17 04		17 14		→		17 34	17 44			18 04		18 14	
Harlington	d	16 09		16 19				16 39	16 49			17 09		17 19				17 39	17 49			18 09		18 19	
Flitwick	d	16 13		16 23				16 43	16 53			17 13		17 23				17 43	17 53			18 13		18 23	
Bedford ■	a	16 25	16 06	16 35			16 37	16 55	17 05			17 25	17 06	17 35			17 37	17 55	18 05			18 25	18 06	18 35	

		FC ■	EM ◇■	FC ■	FC ■	FC		FC ■	EM ◇■	FC ■	FC	FC ■	EM ◇■	FC ■	FC ■	FC		FC ■	EM ◇■	FC ■	FC	EM ◇■	FC	FC ■	FC
London Bridge ■ ⊖	d																								
Elephant & Castle	d																								
London Blackfriars ■ ⊖	a																								
	d																								
City Thameslink ■	d																								
Farringdon ■ ⊖	d																								
St Pancras International ■ ⊖	a																								
	d	17 50	18 00		18 04	18 08		18 20	18 30	18 34	18 38	18 50	19 00		19 04	19 08		19 20	19 30	19 34	19 48	20 00		20 04	20 18
Kentish Town	d					18 11					18 41					19 11					19 51				20 21
West Hampstead Thameslink	d	17 57			18 11	18 16		18 27		18 41	18 46	18 57			19 11	19 16		19 27		19 41	19 56			20 11	20 26
Cricklewood	d					18 19					18 49					19 19					19 59				20 29
Hendon	d					18 22					18 52					19 22					20 02				20 32
Mill Hill Broadway	d					18 26					18 56					19 26					20 06				20 36
Elstree & Borehamwood	d	18 07				18 30		18 37			19 00	19 07				19 30		19 37			20 10				20 40
Radlett	d					18 34					19 04					19 34					20 14				20 44
St Albans City	d	18 15			18 25	18 40		18 45		18 55	19 10	19 15			19 25	19 40		19 45		19 55	20 20			20 25	20 50
Harpenden	d	18 21			18 31	18 46		18 51		19 01	19 16	19 21			19 31	19 46		19 51		20 01	20 26			20 31	20 56
Luton Airport Parkway ■ ✈	d	18 27		←	18 37	18 52		18 57	18 51	19 07	19 22	19 27		←	19 37	19 52		19 57	19 51	20 07	20 32		←	20 37	21 02
Luton ■	d	18 30	18 23	18 30	18 40	18a56		19 00		19 10	19a26	19 30	19 23	19 30	19 40	19a56		20 00		20 10	20 35	20 23	20 35	20 40	21 05
Leagrave	d	→		18 34	18 44			19 04		19 14		→		19 34	19 44			20 04		20 14	→		20 39	20 44	21 09
Harlington	d			18 39	18 49			19 09		19 19				19 39	19 49			20 09		20 19			20 44	20 49	21 14
Flitwick	d			18 43	18 53			19 13		19 23				19 43	19 53			20 13		20 23			20 48	20 53	21 18
Bedford ■	a		18 37	18 55	19 05			19 25	19 06	19 35			19 37	19 55	20 05			20 25	20 06	20 35		20 37	21 00	21 05	21 30

Please refer to separate pages within this table for services operating between Brighton and South London

At weekends please use local bus and tube services to travel to/from St Pancras International and London Bridge when no trains are operating. See local publicity for details of alternative routes and services that are available across central London

Saturdays from 31 March

London, St Albans, Luton - Bedford

Network Diagram - see first Page of Table 52

		EM ◇1		FC 1	FC	EM ◇1	FC	FC 1	FC	EM ◇1	FC 1	FC		EM ◇1	FC	FC 1	FC	EM ◇1	FC 1	FC	FC 1	FC		FC 1	FC
London Bridge 4 ⊖	d																								
Elephant & Castle	d																								
London Blackfriars 3 ⊖	a																								
	d																								
City Thameslink 3	d																								
Farringdon 3 ⊖	d																								
St Pancras International 15 ⊖	a																								
	d	20 30		20 34	20 48	21 00		21 04	21 18	21 30	21 34	21 48		22 00		22 04	22 18	22 25	22 34	22 48	23 04	23 18		23 34	23 48
Kentish Town	d				20 51				21 21			21 51					22 21			22 51		23 21			23 51
West Hampstead Thameslink	d			20 41	20 56			21 11	21 25		21 41	21 55				22 11	22 25		22 42	22 55	23 12	23 25		23 42	23 55
Cricklewood	d				20 59				21 28			21 58					22 28			22 58		23 28			23 58
Hendon	d				21 02				21 31			22 01					22 31			23 01		23 31			00 01
Mill Hill Broadway	d				21 06				21 35			22 05					22 35			23 05		23 35			00 05
Elstree & Borehamwood	d				21 10				21 39			22 09					22 39			23 09		23 39			00 09
Radlett	d				21 14				21 44			22 14					22 44			23 14		23 44			00 14
St Albans City	d			20 55	21 20			21 25	21 51		21 56	22 21				22 26	22 51		22 58	23 21	23 28	23 51		23 58	00 21
Harpenden	d			21 01	21 26			21 31	21 57		22 02	22 27				22 32	22 57		23 04	23 27	23 34	23 57		00 04	00 27
Luton Airport Parkway 7 ✈	d	20 51		21 07	21 32		←	21 37	22 03	21 51	22 08	22 33			←	22 38	23 03	22 49	23 10	23 33	23 40	00 03		00 10	00 33
Luton 10	d			21 10	21 35	21 23	21 35	21 40	22 06		22 11	22 36		22 26	22 36	22 41	23 06		23 13	23 36	23 43	00 06		00 13	00 36
Leagrave	d			21 14	→		21 39	21 44	22 09		22 14	→			22 39	22 44	23 09		23 16	23 39	23 46	00 09		00 16	00 39
Harlington	d			21 19			21 44	21 49	22 16		22 21				22 46	22 51	23 16		23 23	23 46	23 53	00 16		00 23	00 46
Flitwick	d			21 23			21 48	21 53	22 20		22 25				22 50	22 55	23 20		23 27	23 50	23 57	00 20		00 27	00 50
Bedford 7	a	21 06		21 35		21 38	22 00	22 05	22 32	22 06	22 37			22 47	23 02	23 08	23 32	23 10	23 40	00 02	00 10	00 32		00 40	01 02

Sundays until 25 March

		FC A	FC 1 A	FC A	FC 1 A	FC A	FC 1	FC	FC 1	FC		FC 🚌	FC	FC	FC 🚌	FC	FC	FC 🚌	FC	FC		EM ◇1	FC	EM ◇1	FC
London Bridge 4 ⊖	d											00 57			06 05			07 09							
Elephant & Castle	d																								
London Blackfriars 3 ⊖	a											01 12			06 20			07 24							
	d											01 12			06 20			07 24							
City Thameslink 3	d																								
Farringdon 3 ⊖	d																	07 34							
St Pancras International 15 ⊖	a											01 27			06 35			07 39							
	d	22p48	23p04	23p18	23p34	23p48	00 04	00 18	00 36	01 06			01 34	06 04		07 04	07 34		08 04	08 34		09 00	09 04	09 30	09 34
Kentish Town	d	22p53	≀	23p23	≀	23p53		00 23	00 41	01 11			01 39	06 09		07 09	07 39		08 09	08 39			09 09		09 39
West Hampstead Thameslink	d	22p57	23p12	23p27	23p42	23p57	00 12	00 27	00 45	01 15			01 43	06 13		07 13	07 43		08 13	08 43			09 13		09 43
Cricklewood	d	23p00	≀	23p30	≀	00 01		00 30	00 48	01 18			01 46	06 16		07 16	07 46		08 16	08 46			09 16		09 46
Hendon	d	23p03	≀	23p33	≀	00 04		00 33	00 51	01 21			01 49	06 19		07 19	07 49		08 19	08 49			09 19		09 49
Mill Hill Broadway	d	23p07	≀	23p37	≀	00 08		00 37	00 55	01 25			01 53	06 23		07 23	07 53		08 23	08 53			09 23		09 53
Elstree & Borehamwood	d	23p11	≀	23p41	≀	00 12		00 41	00 59	01 29			01 57	06 27		07 27	07 57		08 27	08 57			09 27		09 57
Radlett	d	23p15	≀	23p45	≀	00 16		00 45	01 04	01 34			02 02	06 32		07 32	08 02		08 32	09 02			09 32		10 02
St Albans City	d	23p21	23p28	23p51	23p58	00 22	00 28	00 51	01 10	01 40			02 08	06 38		07 38	08 08		08 38	09 08			09 38		10 08
Harpenden	d	23p27	23p34	23p57	00 04	00 28	00 34	00 57	01 16	01 46			02 14	06 44		07 44	08 14		08 44	09 14			09 44		10 14
Luton Airport Parkway 7 ✈	d	23p33	23p40	00 03	00 10	00 34	00 40	01 03	01 22	01 52			02 20	06 50		07 50	08 20		08 50	09 20		09 28	09 50		10 20
Luton 10	d	23p36	23p43	00 06	00 13	00 37	00 43	01 06	01 25	01 55			02 23	06 53		07 53	08 23		08 53	09 23			09 53	10 01	10 23
Leagrave	d	23p39	23p46	00 09	00 16	00 40	00 46	01 09	01 28	01 58			02 26	06 56		07 56	08 26		08 56	09 26			09 56		10 26
Harlington	d	23p44	23p51	00 14	00 21	00 45	00 51	01 14	01 33	02 03			02 31	07 01		08 01	08 31		09 01	09 31			10 01		10 31
Flitwick	d	23p48	23p55	00 18	00 25	00 49	00 55	01 18	01 37	02 07			02 35	07 05		08 05	08 35		09 05	09 35			10 05		10 35
Bedford 7	a	00 02	00 08	00 32	00 38	01 02	01 08	01 32	01 50	02 20			02 49	07 18		08 18	08 48		09 18	09 48		09 51	10 18	10 21	10 48

		FC	FC 1	EM ◇1	FC 1	FC		FC 1	EM ◇1	FC 1	FC	FC 1	EM ◇1	FC 1	FC	FC 1		EM ◇1	FC 1	FC	FC 1	EM ◇1	FC 1	FC	FC 1
London Bridge 4 ⊖	d																								
Elephant & Castle	d																								
London Blackfriars 3 ⊖	a																								
	d																								
City Thameslink 3	d																								
Farringdon 3 ⊖	d																								
St Pancras International 15 ⊖	a																								
	d	09 36	09 48	10 00	10 03			10 18	10 30	10 33		10 48	11 00	11 03		11 18		11 30	11 33		11 48	12 00	12 03		12 18
Kentish Town	d	09 40				10 09					10 39				11 09					11 39				12 09	
West Hampstead Thameslink	d	09 44	09 56		10 10	10 13		10 26		10 40	10 43	10 56		11 10	11 13	11 26			11 40	11 43	11 56		12 10	12 13	12 26
Cricklewood	d	09 47				10 16					10 46				11 16					11 46				12 16	
Hendon	d	09 50				10 19					10 49				11 19					11 49				12 19	
Mill Hill Broadway	d	09 54				10 23					10 53				11 23					11 53				12 23	
Elstree & Borehamwood	d	09 58				10 27					10 57				11 27					11 57				12 27	
Radlett	d	10 02				10 32					11 02				11 32					12 02				12 32	
St Albans City	d	10 08	10 12		10 26	10 38		10 42		10 56	11 08	11 12		11 26	11 38	11 42			11 56	12 08	12 12		12 26	12 38	12 42
Harpenden	d	10 14	10 18		10 32	10 44		10 48		11 02	11 14	11 18		11 32	11 44	11 48			12 02	12 14	12 18		12 32	12 44	12 48
Luton Airport Parkway 7 ✈	d	10 20	10 24	10 29	10 38	10 50		10 54		11 08	11 20	11 24	11 29	11 38	11 50	11 54		11 58	12 08	12 20	12 24	12 29	12 38	12 50	12 54
Luton 10	d	10a23	10 27		10 41	10a53		10 57	11 02	11 11	11a23	11 27	11 32	11 41	11a53	11 57		12 02	12 11	12a23	12 27	12 33	12 41	12a53	12 57
Leagrave	d		10 30		10 44			11 00		11 14		11 30		11 44		12 00			12 14		12 30		12 44		13 00
Harlington	d		10 35		10 49			11 05		11 19		11 35		11 49		12 05			12 19		12 35		12 49		13 05
Flitwick	d		10 39		10 53			11 09		11 23		11 39		11 53		12 09			12 23		12 39		12 53		13 09
Bedford 7	a		10 52	10 53	11 06			11 22	11 26	11 36		11 52	11 55	12 06		12 22		12 25	12 36		12 52	12 56	13 06		13 22

A not 11 December

Please refer to separate pages within this table for services operating between Brighton and South London

At weekends please use local bus and tube services to travel to/from St Pancras International and London Bridge when no trains are operating. See local publicity for details of alternative routes and services that are available across central London

Sundays until 25 March

London, St Albans, Luton - Bedford

Network Diagram - see first Page of Table 52

		EM ◇1		FC 1	FC	FC 1	EM ◇1	FC 1	FC	FC 1	EM ◇1	FC 1		FC	FC 1	EM ◇1	FC 1	FC	FC 1	EM ◇1	FC 1	FC 1		FC	FC 1
London Bridge 4 ⊖	d																								
Elephant & Castle	d																								
London Blackfriars 3 ⊖	a																								
	d																								
City Thameslink 3	d																								
Farringdon 3 ⊖	d																								
St Pancras International 15 ⊖	a																								
	d	12 30		12 33		12 48	13 00	13 03		13 18	13 30	13 33			13 48	14 00	14 03		14 18	14 30		14 33			14 48
Kentish Town	d				12 39				13 09					13 39				14 09						14 39	
West Hampstead Thameslink	d			12 40	12 43	12 56		13 10	13 13	13 26		13 40		13 43	13 56		14 10	14 13	14 26			14 40		14 43	14 56
Cricklewood	d				12 46				13 16					13 46				14 16						14 46	
Hendon	d				12 49				13 19					13 49				14 19						14 49	
Mill Hill Broadway	d				12 53				13 23					13 53				14 23						14 53	
Elstree & Borehamwood	d				12 57				13 27					13 57				14 27						14 57	
Radlett	d				13 02				13 32					14 02				14 32						15 02	
St Albans City	d			12 56	13 08	13 12		13 26	13 38	13 42		13 56		14 08	14 12		14 26	14 38	14 42			14 56		15 08	15 12
Harpenden	d			13 02	13 14	13 18		13 32	13 44	13 48		14 02		14 14	14 18		14 32	14 44	14 48			15 02		15 14	15 18
Luton Airport Parkway 7 ✈	d	12 59		13 08	13 20	13 24	13 29	13 38	13 50	13 54	14 00	14 08		14 20	14 24	14 22	14 38	14 50	14 54		←	15 08		15 20	15 24
Luton 10	d	13 03		13 11	13a23	13 27	13 33	13 41	13a53	13 57	14 05	14 11		14a23	14 27		14 41	14a53	14 57	14 54	14 57	15 11		15a23	15 27
Leagrave	d			13 14		13 30		13 44		14 00		14 14			14 30		14 44		→		15 00	15 14			15 30
Harlington	d			13 19		13 35		13 49		14 05		14 19			14 35		14 49				15 05	15 19			15 35
Flitwick	d			13 23		13 39		13 53		14 09		14 23			14 39		14 53				15 09	15 23			15 39
Bedford 7	a	13 26		13 36		13 52	13 56	14 06		14 22	14 19	14 36			14 52	14 38	15 06			15 10	15 22	15 36			15 52

		EM ◇1	FC 1	FC	FC 1	EM ◇1	FC 1	FC 1		FC	FC 1	EM ◇1	FC 1	FC	FC 1	EM ◇1	FC 1	FC 1		FC	FC 1	EM ◇1	FC 1	FC	FC 1
London Bridge 4 ⊖	d																								
Elephant & Castle	d																								
London Blackfriars 3 ⊖	a																								
	d																								
City Thameslink 3	d																								
Farringdon 3 ⊖	d																								
St Pancras International 15 ⊖	a																								
	d	15 00	15 03		15 18	15 30		15 33			15 48	16 00	16 03		16 18	16 30		16 33			16 48	17 00	17 03		17 18
Kentish Town	d			15 09						15 39				16 09						16 39				17 09	
West Hampstead Thameslink	d		15 10	15 13	15 26			15 40		15 43	15 56		16 10	16 13	16 26			16 40		16 43	16 56		17 10	17 13	17 26
Cricklewood	d			15 16						15 46				16 16						16 46				17 16	
Hendon	d			15 19						15 49				16 19						16 49				17 19	
Mill Hill Broadway	d			15 23						15 53				16 23						16 53				17 23	
Elstree & Borehamwood	d			15 27						15 57				16 27						16 57				17 27	
Radlett	d			15 32						16 02				16 32						17 02				17 32	
St Albans City	d		15 26	15 38	15 42			15 56		16 08	16 12		16 26	16 38	16 42			16 56		17 08	17 12		17 26	17 38	17 42
Harpenden	d		15 32	15 44	15 48			16 02		16 14	16 18		16 32	16 44	16 48			17 02		17 14	17 18		17 32	17 44	17 48
Luton Airport Parkway 7 ✈	d	15 23	15 38	15 50	15 54		←	16 08		16 20	16 24	16 21	16 38	16 50	16 54		←	17 08		17 20	17 24	17 21	17 38	17 50	17 54
Luton 10	d		15 41	15a53	15 57	15 54	15 57	16 11		16a23	16 27		16 41	16a53	16 57	16 53	16 57	17 11		17a23	17 27		17 41	17a53	17 57
Leagrave	d		15 44		→		16 00	16 14			16 30		16 44		→		17 00	17 14			17 30		17 44		→
Harlington	d		15 49				16 05	16 19			16 35		16 49				17 05	17 19			17 35		17 49		
Flitwick	d		15 53				16 09	16 23			16 39		16 53				17 09	17 23			17 39		17 53		
Bedford 7	a	15 39	16 06			16 10	16 22	16 36			16 52	16 37	17 06			17 08	17 22	17 36			17 52	17 38	18 06		

		EM ◇1	FC 1	FC 1		FC	FC 1	EM ◇1	FC 1	FC	FC 1	EM ◇1	FC 1	FC 1		FC	FC 1	EM ◇1	FC 1	FC	FC	EM ◇1	FC	FC 1	
London Bridge 4 ⊖	d																								
Elephant & Castle	d																								
London Blackfriars 3 ⊖	a																								
	d																								
City Thameslink 3	d																								
Farringdon 3 ⊖	d																								
St Pancras International 15 ⊖	a																								
	d	17 30		17 33			17 48	18 00	18 03		18 18	18 30		18 33			18 48	19 00	19 03		19 18	19 30		19 33	
Kentish Town	d					17 39				18 09						18 39				19 09	19 23				
West Hampstead Thameslink	d			17 40		17 43	17 56		18 10	18 13	18 26			18 40		18 43	18 56		19 10	19 13	19 27			19 40	
Cricklewood	d					17 46				18 16						18 46				19 16	19 30				
Hendon	d					17 49				18 19						18 49				19 19	19 33				
Mill Hill Broadway	d					17 53				18 23						18 53				19 23	19 37				
Elstree & Borehamwood	d					17 57				18 27						18 57				19 27	19 41				
Radlett	d					18 02				18 32						19 02				19 32	19 45				
St Albans City	d			17 56		18 08	18 12		18 26	18 38	18 42			18 56		19 08	19 12		19 26	19 38	19 51			19 56	
Harpenden	d			18 02		18 14	18 18		18 32	18 44	18 48			19 02		19 14	19 18		19 32	19 44	19 57			20 02	
Luton Airport Parkway 7 ✈	d		←	18 08		18 20	18 24	18 21	18 38	18 50	18 54		←	19 08		19 20	19 24	19 21	19 38	19 50	20 03		←	20 08	
Luton 10	d	17 52	17 57	18 11		18a23	18 27		18 41	18a53	18 57	18 53	18 57	19 11		19a23	19 27		19 41	19a53	20 06	19 53	20 06	20 11	
Leagrave	d		18 00	18 14			18 30		18 44		→		19 00	19 14			19 30		19 44		→		20 09	20 14	
Harlington	d		18 05	18 19			18 35		18 49				19 05	19 19			19 35		19 49				20 14	20 19	
Flitwick	d		18 09	18 23			18 39		18 53				19 09	19 23			19 39		19 53				20 18	20 23	
Bedford 7	a	18 08	18 22	18 36			18 52	18 38	19 06			19 08	19 22	19 36			19 52	19 38	20 06			20 08	20 32	20 36	

Please refer to separate pages within this table for services operating between Brighton and South London

At weekends please use local bus and tube services to travel to/from St Pancras International and London Bridge when no trains are operating. See local publicity for details of alternative routes and services that are available across central London

Table 52

Sundays
until 25 March

London, St Albans, Luton - Bedford

Network Diagram - see first Page of Table 52

		FC	EM	FC	FC	EM	FC	FC	FC	EM		FC	FC	EM	FC	FC	FC	FC	EM	FC		EM	FC	FC	
			◇1 ⊡	1		◇1 ⊡		1		◇1 ⊡		1		◇1 ⊡		1			◇1 ⊡			◇1 ⊡			
London Bridge 4 ⊖	d																								
Elephant & Castle	d																								
London Blackfriars 3 ⊖	a																								
	d																								
City Thameslink 3	d																								
Farringdon 3 ⊖	d																								
St Pancras International 15 ⊖	a																								
	d	19 48	20 00	20 03	20 18	20 30		20 33	20 48	21 00		21 03	21 18	21 30		21 33	21 48	22 04	22 30	22 34		23 00	23 04	23 34	
Kentish Town	d	19 53			20 23				20 53				21 23				21 53	22 09		22 39			23 09	23 39	
West Hampstead Thameslink	d	19 57		20 10	20 27			20 40	20 57			21 10	21 27			21 40	21 57	22 13		22 43			23 13	23 43	
Cricklewood	d	20 00			20 30				21 00				21 30				22 00	22 16		22 46			23 16	23 46	
Hendon	d	20 03			20 33				21 03				21 33				22 03	22 19		22 49			23 19	23 49	
Mill Hill Broadway	d	20 07			20 37				21 07				21 37				22 07	22 23		22 53			23 23	23 53	
Elstree & Borehamwood	d	20 11			20 41				21 11				21 41				22 11	22 27		22 57			23 27	23 57	
Radlett	d	20 15			20 45				21 15				21 45				22 15	22 32		23 02			23 32	00 02	
St Albans City	d	20 21		20 26	20 51			20 56	21 21			21 26	21 51			21 56	22 21	22 38		23 08			23 38	00 08	
Harpenden	d	20 27		20 32	20 57			21 02	21 27			21 32	21 57			22 02	22 27	22 44		23 14			23 44	00 14	
Luton Airport Parkway 7 ✈	d	20 33	20 22	20 38	21 03		←	21 08	21 33	21 21		21 38	22 03		←	22 08	22 33	22 50	22 53	23 20		23 27	23 50	00 20	
Luton 10	d	20 36		20 41	21 06	20 54	21 06	21 11	21 36			21 41	22 06	21 54	22 06	22 11	22 36	22 53		23 23			23 53	00 23	
Leagrave	d	20 39		20 44	→		21 09	21 14	21 39			21 44	→		22 09	22 14	22 39	22 56		23 26			23 56	00 26	
Harlington	d	20 44		20 49			21 14	21 19	21 44			21 49			22 14	22 19	22 44	23 01		23 31			00 01	00 31	
Flitwick	d	20 48		20 53			21 18	21 23	21 48			21 53			22 18	22 23	22 48	23 05		23 35			00 05	00 35	
Bedford 7	a	21 02	20 40	21 06		21 10	21 32	21 36	22 02	21 40		22 06		22 10	22 32	22 36	23 02	23 18	23 17	23 48		23 50	00 18	00 48	

Sundays
from 1 April

		FC	FC	FC	FC	FC	FC	FC	FC	FC		FC	FC	FC	FC	FC	FC	FC	FC	FC		EM	FC	EM	FC
			1		1		1		1	1		bus	1	1	bus	1		bus				◇1 ⊡		◇1 ⊡	1
London Bridge 4 ⊖	d											00 57			06 05			07 09							
Elephant & Castle	d																								
London Blackfriars 3 ⊖	a											01 12			06 20			07 24							
	d											01 12			06 20			07 24							
City Thameslink 3	d																								
Farringdon 3 ⊖	d																	07 34							
St Pancras International 15 ⊖	a											01 27			06 35			07 39							
	d	22p48	23p04	23p18	23p34	23p48	00 04	00 18	00 32	01 02			01 34	06 04		07 04	07 34		08 04	08 34		09 00	09 06	09 30	09 32
Kentish Town	d	22p51		23p21		23p51		00 21	00 35	01 05			01 37	06 07		07 07	07 37		08 07	08 37			09 09		
West Hampstead Thameslink	d	22p55	23p12	23p25	23p42	23p55	00 12	00 25	00 40	01 10			01 42	06 11		07 11	07 41		08 11	08 41			09 13		09 40
Cricklewood	d	22p58		23p28		23p58		00 28	00 43	01 13			01 45	06 14		07 14	07 44		08 14	08 44			09 16		
Hendon	d	23p01		23p31		00 01		00 31	00 46	01 16			01 48	06 17		07 17	07 47		08 17	08 47			09 19		
Mill Hill Broadway	d	23p05		23p35		00 05		00 35	00 50	01 20			01 52	06 21		07 21	07 51		08 21	08 51			09 23		
Elstree & Borehamwood	d	23p09		23p39		00 09		00 39	00 54	01 24			01 56	06 25		07 25	07 55		08 25	08 55			09 27		
Radlett	d	23p14		23p44		00 14		00 44	00 59	01 29			02 01	06 30		07 30	08 00		08 30	09 00			09 32		
St Albans City	d	23p21	23p28	23p51	23p58	00 21	00 28	00 51	01 06	01 36			02 08	06 36		07 36	08 06		08 36	09 06			09 38		09 56
Harpenden	d	23p27	23p34	23p57	00 04	00 27	00 34	00 57	01 12	01 42			02 14	06 42		07 42	08 12		08 42	09 12			09 44		10 02
Luton Airport Parkway 7 ✈	d	23p33	23p40	00 03	00 10	00 33	00 40	01 03	01 18	01 48			02 20	06 48		07 48	08 18		08 48	09 18		09 28	09 50		10 08
Luton 10	d	23p36	23p43	00 06	00 13	00 36	00 43	01 06	01 21	01 51			02 23	06 51		07 51	08 21		08 51	09 21			09 53	10 01	10 11
Leagrave	d	23p39	23p46	00 09	00 16	00 39	00 46	01 09	01 24	01 54			02 26	06 54		07 54	08 24		08 54	09 24			09 56		10 14
Harlington	d	23p46	23p53	00 16	00 23	00 46	00 53	01 16	01 31	02 01			02 33	07 01		08 01	08 31		09 01	09 31			10 03		10 21
Flitwick	d	23p50	23p57	00 20	00 27	00 50	00 57	01 20	01 35	02 05			02 37	07 05		08 05	08 35		09 05	09 35			10 07		10 25
Bedford 7	a	00 02	00 10	00 32	00 40	01 02	01 10	01 32	01 48	02 18			02 50	07 18		08 18	08 48		09 18	09 48		09 51	10 18	10 21	10 36

		FC	EM	FC	FC	FC		EM	FC	FC	FC	EM	FC	FC	FC	EM		FC	FC	FC	EM	FC	FC	FC	EM
			◇1 ⊡	1				◇1 ⊡	1			◇1 ⊡	1			◇1 ⊡		1			◇1 ⊡	1			◇1 ⊡
London Bridge 4 ⊖	d																								
Elephant & Castle	d																								
London Blackfriars 3 ⊖	a																								
	d																								
City Thameslink 3	d																								
Farringdon 3 ⊖	d																								
St Pancras International 15 ⊖	a																								
	d	09 36	10 00	10 02	10 06	10 19		10 30	10 32	10 36	10 49	11 00	11 02	11 06	11 19	11 30		11 32	11 36	11 49	12 00	12 02	12 06	12 19	12 30
Kentish Town	d	09 39			10 09					10 39				11 09					11 39				12 09		
West Hampstead Thameslink	d	09 43		10 10	10 13	10 26			10 40	10 43	10 56		11 10	11 13	11 26			11 40	11 43	11 56		12 10	12 13	12 26	
Cricklewood	d	09 46			10 16					10 46				11 16					11 46				12 16		
Hendon	d	09 49			10 19					10 49				11 19					11 49				12 19		
Mill Hill Broadway	d	09 53			10 23					10 53				11 23					11 53				12 23		
Elstree & Borehamwood	d	09 57			10 27					10 57				11 27					11 57				12 27		
Radlett	d	10 02			10 32					11 02				11 32					12 02				12 32		
St Albans City	d	10 08		10 26	10 38	10 42			10 56	11 08	11 12		11 26	11 38	11 42			11 56	12 08	12 12		12 26	12 38	12 42	
Harpenden	d	10 14		10 32	10 44	10 48			11 02	11 14	11 18		11 32	11 44	11 48			12 02	12 14	12 18		12 32	12 44	12 48	
Luton Airport Parkway 7 ✈	d	10 20	10 29	10 38	10 50	10 54			11 08	11 20	11 24	11 29	11 38	11 50	11 54	11 58		12 08	12 20	12 24	12 29	12 38	12 50	12 54	12 59
Luton 10	d	10a23		10 41	10a53	10 57		11 02	11 11	11a23	11 27	11 32	11 41	11a53	11 57	12 02		12 11	12a23	12 27	12 33	12 41	12a53	12 57	13 03
Leagrave	d			10 44		11 00			11 14		11 30		11 44		12 00			12 14		12 30		12 44		13 00	
Harlington	d			10 51		11 07			11 21		11 37		11 51		12 07			12 21		12 37		12 51		13 07	
Flitwick	d			10 55		11 11			11 25		11 41		11 55		12 11			12 25		12 41		12 55		13 11	
Bedford 7	a		10 53	11 06		11 22		11 26	11 36		11 52	11 55	12 06		12 22	12 25		12 36		12 52	12 56	13 06		13 22	13 26

Please refer to separate pages within this table for services operating between Brighton and South London

At weekends please use local bus and tube services to travel to/from St Pancras International and London Bridge when no trains are operating. See local publicity for details of alternative routes and services that are available across central London

Table 52

Sundays
from 1 April

London, St Albans, Luton - Bedford

Network Diagram - see first Page of Table 52

		FC		FC	FC	EM	FC	FC	FC	EM	FC	FC		FC	FC	FC	EM	FC	FC	FC	EM	FC		FC	FC
		1				◇1 ⊡	1			◇1 ⊡	1					1	◇1 ⊡			1	◇1 ⊡	1			
London Bridge 4 ⊖	d																								
Elephant & Castle	d																								
London Blackfriars 3 ⊖	a																								
	d																								
City Thameslink 3	d																								
Farringdon 3 ⊖	d																								
St Pancras International 15 ⊖	a																								
	d	12 32		12 36	12 49	13 00	13 02	13 06	13 19	13 30	13 32	13 36		13 36	13 49	14 02	14 05	14 06	14 19	14 32	14 35			14 36	14 49
Kentish Town	d			12 39				13 09				13 39		13 40				14 09						14 39	
West Hampstead Thameslink	d	12 40		12 43	12 56		13 10	13 13	13 26		13 40	13 43		13 44	13 56	14 10		14 13	14 26	14 40				14 43	14 56
Cricklewood	d			12 46				13 16				13 46		13 47				14 16						14 46	
Hendon	d			12 49				13 19				13 49		13 50				14 19						14 49	
Mill Hill Broadway	d			12 53				13 23				13 53		13 54				14 23						14 53	
Elstree & Borehamwood	d			12 57				13 27				13 57		13 58				14 27						14 57	
Radlett	d			13 02				13 32				14 02		14 02				14 32						15 02	
St Albans City	d	12 56		13 08	13 12		13 26	13 38	13 42		13 56	14 08		14 08	14 12	14 26		14a39	14 44	14 56				15a09	15 14
Harpenden	d	13 02		13 14	13 18		13 32	13 44	13 48		14 02	14 14		14 14	14 18	14 32			14 50	15 02					15 20
Luton Airport Parkway 7 ✈	d	13 08		13 20	13 24	13 29	13 38	13 50	13 54	13 57	14 08	14 20		14 20	14 24	14 38	14 30		14 56	15 08		←			15 26
Luton 10	d	13 11		13a23	13 27	13 33	13 41	13a53	13 57	14 03	14 11	14 23		14a23	14 27	14 41			14 59	15 11	15 04	15 11			15 29
Leagrave	d	13 14			13 30		13 44		14 00		14 14				14 30	14 44			15 02	→		15 14			15 32
Harlington	d	13 21			13 37		13 51		14 07		14 21				14 37	14 51			15 09			15 21			15 39
Flitwick	d	13 25			13 41		13 55		14 11		14 25				14 41	14 55			15 13			15 25			15 43
Bedford 7	a	13 36			13 52	13 55	14 06		14 22	14 24	14 36	14 44			14 52	15 06	14 54		15 24		15 28	15 36			15 54

		FC	EM	FC	FC	FC	EM	FC		FC	FC	FC	EM	FC	FC	FC	EM	FC		FC	FC	FC	EM	FC	FC
		1	◇1 ⊡			1	◇1 ⊡	1				1	◇1 ⊡			1	◇1 ⊡	1				1	◇1 ⊡		
London Bridge 4 ⊖	d																								
Elephant & Castle	d																								
London Blackfriars 3 ⊖	a																								
	d																								
City Thameslink 3	d																								
Farringdon 3 ⊖	d																								
St Pancras International 15 ⊖	a																								
	d	15 02	15 05	15 06	15 19	15 32	15 35			15 36	15 49	16 02	16 05	16 06	16 19	16 32	16 35			16 36	16 49	17 02	17 05	17 06	17 19
Kentish Town	d			15 09						15 39				16 09						16 39				17 09	
West Hampstead Thameslink	d	15 10		15 13	15 26	15 40				15 43	15 56	16 10		16 13	16 26	16 40				16 43	16 56	17 10		17 13	17 26
Cricklewood	d			15 16						15 46				16 16						16 46				17 16	
Hendon	d			15 19						15 49				16 19						16 49				17 19	
Mill Hill Broadway	d			15 23						15 53				16 23						16 53				17 23	
Elstree & Borehamwood	d			15 27						15 57				16 27						16 57				17 27	
Radlett	d			15 32						16 02				16 32						17 02				17 32	
St Albans City	d	15 26		15a39	15 44	15 56				16a09	16 14	16 26		16a39	16 44	16 56				17a09	17 14	17 26		17a39	17 44
Harpenden	d	15 32			15 50	16 02					16 20	16 32			16 50	17 02					17 20	17 32			17 50
Luton Airport Parkway 7 ✈	d	15 38	15 31		15 56	16 08		←			16 26	16 38	16 32		16 56	17 08		←			17 26	17 38	17 32		17 56
Luton 10	d	15 41			15 59	16 11	16 04	16 11			16 29	16 41			16 59	17 11	17 03	17 11			17 29	17 41			17 59
Leagrave	d	15 44			16 02	→		16 14			16 32	16 44			17 02	→		17 14			17 32	17 44			18 02
Harlington	d	15 51			16 09			16 21			16 39	16 51			17 09			17 21			17 39	17 51			18 09
Flitwick	d	15 55			16 13			16 25			16 43	16 55			17 13			17 25			17 43	17 55			18 13
Bedford 7	a	16 06	15 58		16 24		16 27	16 36			16 54	17 06	16 56		17 24		17 26	17 36			17 54	18 06	17 56		18 24

		FC	EM	FC		FC	FC	FC	EM	FC	FC	FC	EM	FC		FC	FC	FC	EM	FC	FC	EM	FC	FC	
		1	◇1 ⊡	1				1	◇1 ⊡			1	◇1 ⊡	1				1	◇1 ⊡			◇1 ⊡	1		
London Bridge 4 ⊖	d																								
Elephant & Castle	d																								
London Blackfriars 3 ⊖	a																								
	d																								
City Thameslink 3	d																								
Farringdon 3 ⊖	d																								
St Pancras International 15 ⊖	a																								
	d	17 32	17 35			17 36	17 49	18 02	18 05	18 06	18 19	18 32	18 35			18 36	18 49	19 02	19 05	19 12	19 19	19 30	19 32	19 48	
Kentish Town	d					17 39				18 09						18 39				19 15				19 51	
West Hampstead Thameslink	d	17 40				17 43	17 56	18 10		18 13	18 26	18 40				18 43	18 56	19 10		19 19	19 26		19 40	19 55	
Cricklewood	d					17 46				18 16						18 46				19 22				19 58	
Hendon	d					17 49				18 19						18 49				19 25				20 01	
Mill Hill Broadway	d					17 53				18 23						18 53				19 29				20 05	
Elstree & Borehamwood	d					17 57				18 27						18 57				19 33				20 09	
Radlett	d					18 02				18 32						19 02				19 40				20 14	
St Albans City	d	17 56				18a09	18 14	18 26		18a39	18 44	18 56				19a09	19 14	19 26		19a47	19 42		19 56	20 21	
Harpenden	d	18 02					18 20	18 32			18 50	19 02					19 20	19 32			19 50		20 02	20 27	
Luton Airport Parkway 7 ✈	d	18 08		←			18 26	18 38	18 32		18 56	19 08		←			19 26	19 38	19 32		19 56		20 08	20 33	
Luton 10	d	18 11	18 04	18 11			18 29	18 41			18 59	19 11	19 04	19 11			19 29	19 41			19 59	20 03	20 11	20 36	
Leagrave	d	→		18 14			18 32	18 44			19 02	→		19 14			19 32	19 44			20 02		20 14	20 39	
Harlington	d			18 21			18 39	18 51			19 09			19 21			19 39	19 51			20 09		20 21	20 46	
Flitwick	d			18 25			18 43	18 55			19 13			19 25			19 43	19 55			20 13		20 25	20 50	
Bedford 7	a		18 28	18 36			18 54	19 06	18 56		19 24		19 28	19 36			19 54	20 06	19 56		20 24	20 29	20 36	21 02	

Please refer to separate pages within this table for services operating between Brighton and South London

At weekends please use local bus and tube services to travel to/from St Pancras International and London Bridge when no trains are operating. See local publicity for details of alternative routes and services that are available across central London

London, St Albans, Luton - Bedford

Network Diagram - see first Page of Table 52

		EM ◇1	FC 1	FC	EM ◇1	FC	FC 1	FC	EM ◇1	FC 1		FC	EM ◇1	FC	FC 1	FC	FC 1	EM ◇1	FC 1	EM ◇1		FC 1	FC 1
London Bridge 4 ⊖	d																						
Elephant & Castle	d																						
London Blackfriars 3 ⊖	a																						
	d																						
City Thameslink 3	d																						
Farringdon 3 ⊖	d																						
St Pancras International 15 ⊖	a																						
	d	20 00	20 02	20 18	20 30		20 32	20 48	21 00	21 02		21 18	21 30		21 32	21 48	22 04	22 30	22 34	23 00		23 04	23 34
Kentish Town	d			20 21				20 51				21 21				21 51	22 07		22 37			23 07	23 37
West Hampstead Thameslink	d		20 10	20 25			20 40	20 55		21 10		21 25			21 40	21 55	22 11		22 41			23 11	23 41
Cricklewood	d			20 28				20 58				21 28				21 58	22 14		22 44			23 14	23 44
Hendon	d			20 31				21 01				21 31				22 01	22 17		22 47			23 17	23 47
Mill Hill Broadway	d			20 35				21 05				21 35				22 05	22 21		22 51			23 21	23 51
Elstree & Borehamwood	d			20 39				21 09				21 39				22 09	22 25		22 55			23 25	23 55
Radlett	d			20 44				21 14				21 44				22 14	22 30		23 00			23 30	00 02
St Albans City	d		20 26	20 51			20 56	21 21		21 26		21 51			21 56	22 21	22 36		23 06			23 36	00 08
Harpenden	d		20 32	20 57			21 02	21 27		21 32		21 57			22 02	22 27	22 42		23 12			23 42	00 14
Luton Airport Parkway 7 ✈	d	20 24	20 38	21 03		←	21 08	21 33	21 24	21 38		22 03		←	22 08	22 33	22 48	22 55	23 18	23 27		23 48	00 20
Luton 10	d		20 41	21 06	20 56	21 06	21 11	21 36		21 41		22 06	21 56	22 06	22 11	22 36	22 51		23 21			23 51	00 23
Leagrave	d		20 44	→		21 09	21 14	21 39		21 44		→		22 09	22 14	22 39	22 54		23 24			23 54	00 26
Harlington	d		20 51			21 16	21 21	21 46		21 51				22 16	22 21	22 46	23 01		23 31			00 01	00 33
Flitwick	d		20 55			21 20	21 25	21 50		21 55				22 20	22 25	22 50	23 05		23 35			00 05	00 37
Bedford 7	a	20 45	21 06		21 18	21 32	21 36	22 02	21 47	22 06			22 17	22 32	22 36	23 02	23 18	23 18	23 48	23 50		00 18	00 50

Please refer to separate pages within this table for services operating between Brighton and South London

At weekends please use local bus and tube services to travel to/from St Pancras International and London Bridge when no trains are operating. See local publicity for details of alternative routes and services that are available across central London

South London, Gatwick Airport - Brighton

Network Diagram - see first Page of Table 52

		FC 1	FC	FC 1	SE A	FC		FC (bus)	FC			FC (bus)		FC	FC (bus)	FC (bus)	FC (bus)	FC (bus)	FC (bus)	FC (bus)		FC (bus)	FC (bus)	FC (bus)	FC 1
St Pancras International 15 ⊖	d							23p42				00 12			00 30	01 00	01 30	02 30	03 00	03 30		04 00	04 30	05 00	
Farringdon 3 ⊖	d							23p47				00 17			00 35									05 05	
City Thameslink 3	d																								
London Blackfriars 3 ⊖	a							23p52				00 22			00 40	01 10	01 40	02 40	03 10	03 40		04 10	04 40	05 10	
	d							23p52				00 22			00 40	01 10	01 40	02 40	03 10	03 40		04 10	04 40	05 10	
Elephant & Castle ⊖	d																								
Loughborough Jn.	d																								
Herne Hill 4	d																								
Denmark Hill 4	d				23p52																				
Peckham Rye 4	d				23p55																				
Nunhead 4	d				23p57																				
Crofton Park	d				23p59																				
Catford	d				00 03																				
Bellingham	d				00 05																				
Beckenham Hill	d				00 07																				
Ravensbourne	d				00 09																				
Shortlands	d				00 11																				
Bromley South 4	d				00 14																				
Bickley 4	d				00a17																				
St Mary Cray	d																								
Swanley 4	d																								
Eynsford	d																								
Shoreham (Kent)	d																								
Otford 4	d																								
Bat & Ball	d																								
Sevenoaks 4	a																								
London Bridge 4	a							00 07				00 37			00 55	01 25	01 55	02 55	03 25	03 55		04 25	04 55	05 25	
	d	23p12	23p29	23p42		23p59			00 12					00 42											05 52
Tulse Hill 3	d		23p41			00 09																			
Streatham 4	d		23p45			00 13																			
Mitcham Eastfields	d																								
Mitcham Junction	d																								
Hackbridge	d																								
Carshalton	d																								
Tooting	d		23p50			00 18																			
Haydons Road	d		23p53			00 21																			
Wimbledon 3 ⊖	d		23p57			00 25																			
Wimbledon Chase	d		00 01			00 28																			
South Merton	d		00 03			00 30																			
Morden South	d		00 05			00 32																			
St Helier	d		00 07			00 34																			
Sutton Common	d		00 09			00 36																			
West Sutton	d		00 12			00 39																			
Sutton (Surrey) 4	a		00 15			00 43																			
East Croydon	d	23p25		23p57					00 27					00 57											06 05
Redhill	d																								
Gatwick Airport 10 ✈	d	23p41		00 19					00 49					01 22											06 20
Three Bridges 4	d	23p47		00a24					00a54					01a28											06 25
Balcombe	d	23p53																							06 31
Haywards Heath 3	d	23p59																							06 37
Wivelsfield 4	d	00 03																							06 41
Burgess Hill 4	d	00 05																							06 43
Hassocks 4	d	00 08																							06 46
Preston Park	d	00 15																							06 53
Brighton 10	a	00 19																							06 57

A From London Victoria to Orpington   B To Caterham   C From London Victoria

Please refer to separate pages within this table for services operating between Bedford and London

At weekends please use local bus and tube services to travel to/from St Pancras International and London Bridge when no trains are operating. See local publicity for details of alternative routes and services that are available across central London

South London, Gatwick Airport - Brighton

Network Diagram - see first Page of Table 52

		FC	FC	SE	FC	FC	FC	SE	FC	FC	FC	FC	SE	FC	FC	FC
					1		1			1		1			1	
				A				A					A			
St Pancras International 15 ⊖	d	05 30														
Farringdon 3 ⊖	d	05 35														
City Thameslink 3	d															
London Blackfriars 3 ⊖	a	05 40														
	d	05 40														
Elephant & Castle ⊖	d															
Loughborough Jn.	d															
Herne Hill 4	d					06 42					07 12					07 42
Denmark Hill 4	d			06 22				06 52					07 22			
Peckham Rye 4	d			06 25				06 55					07 25			
Nunhead 4	d			06 27				06 57					07 27			
Crofton Park	d			06 30				07 00					07 30			
Catford	d			06 33				07 03					07 33			
Bellingham	d			06 35				07 05					07 35			
Beckenham Hill	d			06 37				07 07					07 37			
Ravensbourne	d			06 39				07 09					07 39			
Shortlands	d			06 41				07 11					07 41			
Bromley South 4	d			06 44				07 14					07 44			
Bickley 4	d			06 47				07 17					07 47			
St Mary Cray	d			06 51				07 21					07 51			
Swanley 4	d			06 56				07 26					07 56			
Eynsford	d			07 00				07 30					08 00			
Shoreham (Kent)	d			07 04				07 34					08 04			
Otford 4	d			07 07				07 37					08 07			
Bat & Ball	d			07 10				07 40					08 10			
Sevenoaks 4	a			07 13				07 43					08 13			
London Bridge 4	a	05 55														
	d		06 21		06 27		06 42		06 45	06 57		07 12		07 15	07 27	
Tulse Hill 3	d		06 31			06 46			07 01		07 16			07 31		07 46
Streatham 4	d		06 35			06 50			07 05		07 20			07 35		07 50
Mitcham Eastfields	d					06 54					07 24					07 54
Mitcham Junction	d					06 57					07 27					07 57
Hackbridge	d					07 00					07 30					08 00
Carshalton	d					07 03					07 33					08 03
Tooting	d		06 40						07 10					07 40		
Haydons Road	d		06 43						07 13					07 43		
Wimbledon 6 ⊖	d		06 47						07 17					07 47		
Wimbledon Chase	d		06 50						07 20					07 50		
South Merton	d		06 52						07 22					07 52		
Morden South	d		06 54						07 24					07 54		
St Helier	d		06 56						07 26					07 56		
Sutton Common	d		06 58						07 28					07 58		
West Sutton	d		07 01						07 31					08 01		
Sutton (Surrey) 4	a		07 05			07 06			07 35		07 36			08 05		08 06
East Croydon	d				06 41		06 55			07 11		07 25			07 41	
Redhill	d															
Gatwick Airport 10 ✈	d				06 57		07 11			07 27		07 41			07 57	
Three Bridges 4	d				07 02		07 15			07 32		07 45			08 02	
Balcombe	d						07 21									
Haywards Heath 3	d				07 11		07 27			07 41		07 55			08 11	
Wivelsfield 4	d						07 31					07 59				
Burgess Hill 4	d						07 33					08 01				
Hassocks 4	d						07 36					08 04				
Preston Park	d						07 43					08 11				
Brighton 10	a				07 25		07 47			07 55		08 15			08 25	

A From London Victoria
B To Caterham
C From London Victoria to Dorking
D To Tattenham Corner
E From London Victoria to Epsom

Please refer to separate pages within this table for services operating between Bedford and London

At weekends please use local bus and tube services to travel to/from St Pancras International and London Bridge when no trains are operating. See local publicity for details of alternative routes and services that are available across central London

South London, Gatwick Airport - Brighton

Network Diagram - see first Page of Table 52

		FC	SE	FC	FC	FC	FC	SE	FC	FC	FC	FC	SE	FC
		1			1		1			1		1		
			A					A					A	
St Pancras International 15 ⊖	d													
Farringdon 3 ⊖	d													
City Thameslink 3	d													
London Blackfriars 3 ⊖	a													
	d													
Elephant & Castle ⊖	d													
Loughborough Jn.	d													
Herne Hill 4	d					08 12					08 42			
Denmark Hill 4	d		07 52					08 22					08 52	
Peckham Rye 4	d		07 55					08 25					08 55	
Nunhead 4	d		07 57					08 27					08 57	
Crofton Park	d		08 00					08 30					09 00	
Catford	d		08 03					08 33					09 03	
Bellingham	d		08 05					08 35					09 05	
Beckenham Hill	d		08 07					08 37					09 07	
Ravensbourne	d		08 09					08 39					09 09	
Shortlands	d		08 11					08 41					09 11	
Bromley South 4	d		08 14					08 44					09 14	
Bickley 4	d		08 17					08 47					09 17	
St Mary Cray	d		08 21					08 51					09 21	
Swanley 4	d		08 26					08 56					09 26	
Eynsford	d		08 30					09 00					09 30	
Shoreham (Kent)	d		08 34					09 04					09 34	
Otford 4	d		08 37					09 07					09 37	
Bat & Ball	d		08 40					09 10					09 40	
Sevenoaks 4	a		08 43					09 13					09 43	
London Bridge 4	a													
	d	07 42		07 45	07 57		08 12		08 15	08 27		08 42		08 45
Tulse Hill 3	d			08 01		08 16			08 31		08 46			09 01
Streatham 4	d			08 05		08 20			08 35		08 50			09 05
Mitcham Eastfields	d					08 24					08 54			
Mitcham Junction	d					08 27					08 57			
Hackbridge	d					08 30					09 00			
Carshalton	d					08 33					09 03			
Tooting	d			08 10					08 40					09 10
Haydons Road	d			08 13					08 43					09 13
Wimbledon 6 ⊖	d			08 17					08 47					09 17
Wimbledon Chase	d			08 20					08 50					09 20
South Merton	d			08 22					08 52					09 22
Morden South	d			08 24					08 54					09 24
St Helier	d			08 26					08 56					09 26
Sutton Common	d			08 28					08 58					09 28
West Sutton	d			08 31					09 01					09 31
Sutton (Surrey) 4	a			08 35		08 36			09 05		09 06			09 35
East Croydon	d	07 55			08 11		08 25			08 40		08 55		
Redhill	d													
Gatwick Airport 10 ✈	d	08 11			08 27		08 41			08 57		09 11		
Three Bridges 4	d	08 15			08 32		08 45			09 02		09 15		
Balcombe	d	08 21										09 21		
Haywards Heath 3	d	08 27			08 41		08 55			09 11		09 27		
Wivelsfield 4	d	08 31					08 59					09 31		
Burgess Hill 4	d	08 33					09 01					09 33		
Hassocks 4	d	08 36					09 04					09 36		
Preston Park	d	08 43					09 11					09 43		
Brighton 10	a	08 47			08 55		09 15			09 25		09 47		

A From London Victoria
B From London Victoria to Epsom
C To Tattenham Corner
D To Caterham

Please refer to separate pages within this table for services operating between Bedford and London

At weekends please use local bus and tube services to travel to/from St Pancras International and London Bridge when no trains are operating. See local publicity for details of alternative routes and services that are available across central London

South London, Gatwick Airport - Brighton

Network Diagram - see first Page of Table 52

		FC 1	FC	FC 1	SE B	FC	FC 1	FC	FC 1	SE B	FC	FC 1	FC	FC 1	SE B
St Pancras International 15 ⊖	d														
Farringdon 3 ⊖	d														
City Thameslink 3	d														
London Blackfriars 3 ⊖	a														
	d														
Elephant & Castle ⊖	d														
Loughborough Jn.	d														
Herne Hill 4	d		09 12					09 42					10 12		
Denmark Hill 4	d				09 22					09 52					10 22
Peckham Rye 4	d				09 25					09 55					10 25
Nunhead 4	d				09 27					09 57					10 27
Crofton Park	d				09 30					10 00					10 30
Catford	d				09 33					10 03					10 33
Bellingham	d				09 35					10 05					10 35
Beckenham Hill	d				09 37					10 07					10 37
Ravensbourne	d				09 39					10 09					10 39
Shortlands	d				09 41					10 11					10 41
Bromley South 4	d				09 44					10 14					10 44
Bickley 4	d				09 47					10 17					10 47
St Mary Cray	d				09 51					10 21					10 51
Swanley 4	d				09 56					10 26					10 56
Eynsford	d				10 00					10 30					11 00
Shoreham (Kent)	d				10 04					10 34					11 04
Otford 4	d				10 07					10 37					11 07
Bat & Ball	d				10 10					10 40					11 10
Sevenoaks 4	a				10 13					10 43					11 13
London Bridge 4	a														
	d	08 57		09 12		09 15	09 27		09 42		09 45	09 57		10 12	
Tulse Hill 4	d		09 16			09 31		09 46			10 01		10 16		
Streatham 4	d		09 20			09 35		09 50			10 05		10 20		
Mitcham Eastfields	d		09 24					09 54					10 24		
Mitcham Junction	d		09 27					09 57					10 27		
Hackbridge	d		09 30					10 00					10 30		
Carshalton	d		09 33					10 03					10 33		
Tooting	d					09 40					10 10				
Haydons Road	d					09 43					10 13				
Wimbledon 6 ⊖ ⇌	d					09 47					10 17				
Wimbledon Chase	d					09 50					10 20				
South Merton	d					09 52					10 22				
Morden South	d					09 54					10 24				
St Helier	d					09 56					10 26				
Sutton Common	d					09 58					10 28				
West Sutton	d					10 01					10 31				
Sutton (Surrey) 4	a		09 36			10 05		10 06			10 35		10 36		
East Croydon ⇌	d	09 11		09 25			09 41		09 55			10 11		10 25	
Redhill	d														
Gatwick Airport 10 ✈	d	09 27		09 41			09 57		10 11			10 27		10 41	
Three Bridges 4	d	09 32		09 45			10 02		10 15			10 32		10 45	
Balcombe	d								10 21						
Haywards Heath 3	d	09 41		09 55			10 11		10 27			10 41		10 55	
Wivelsfield 4	d			09 59					10 31					10 59	
Burgess Hill 4	d			10 01					10 33					11 01	
Hassocks 4	d			10 04					10 36					11 04	
Preston Park	d			10 11					10 43					11 11	
Brighton 10	a	09 55		10 15			10 25		10 47			10 55		11 15	

A To Caterham
B From London Victoria
C From London Victoria to Epsom
D To Tattenham Corner

Please refer to separate pages within this table for services operating between Bedford and London

At weekends please use local bus and tube services to travel to/from St Pancras International and London Bridge when no trains are operating. See local publicity for details of alternative routes and services that are available across central London

South London, Gatwick Airport - Brighton

Network Diagram - see first Page of Table 52

		FC	FC 1	FC	FC 1	SE C	FC	FC 1	FC	FC 1	SE C	FC	FC 1	FC
St Pancras International 15 ⊖	d													
Farringdon 3 ⊖	d													
City Thameslink 3	d													
London Blackfriars 3 ⊖	a													
	d													
Elephant & Castle ⊖	d													
Loughborough Jn.	d													
Herne Hill 4	d			10 42					11 12					11 42
Denmark Hill 4	d					10 52					11 22			
Peckham Rye 4	d					10 55					11 25			
Nunhead 4	d					10 57					11 27			
Crofton Park	d					11 00					11 30			
Catford	d					11 03					11 33			
Bellingham	d					11 05					11 35			
Beckenham Hill	d					11 07					11 37			
Ravensbourne	d					11 09					11 39			
Shortlands	d					11 11					11 41			
Bromley South 4	d					11 14					11 44			
Bickley 4	d					11 17					11 47			
St Mary Cray	d					11 21					11 51			
Swanley 4	d					11 26					11 56			
Eynsford	d					11 30					12 00			
Shoreham (Kent)	d					11 34					12 04			
Otford 4	d					11 37					12 07			
Bat & Ball	d					11 40					12 10			
Sevenoaks 4	a					11 43					12 13			
London Bridge 4	a													
	d	10 15	10 27		10 42		10 45	10 57		11 12		11 15	11 27	
Tulse Hill 4	d	10 31		10 46			11 01		11 16			11 31		11 46
Streatham 4	d	10 35		10 50			11 05		11 20			11 35		11 50
Mitcham Eastfields	d			10 54					11 24					11 54
Mitcham Junction	d			10 57					11 27					11 57
Hackbridge	d			11 00					11 30					12 00
Carshalton	d			11 03					11 33					12 03
Tooting	d	10 40					11 10					11 40		
Haydons Road	d	10 43					11 13					11 43		
Wimbledon 6 ⊖ ⇌	d	10 47					11 17					11 47		
Wimbledon Chase	d	10 50					11 20					11 50		
South Merton	d	10 52					11 22					11 52		
Morden South	d	10 54					11 24					11 54		
St Helier	d	10 56					11 26					11 56		
Sutton Common	d	10 58					11 28					11 58		
West Sutton	d	11 01					11 31					12 01		
Sutton (Surrey) 4	a	11 05		11 06			11 35		11 36			12 05		12 06
East Croydon ⇌	d		10 41		10 55			11 11		11 25			11 41	
Redhill	d													
Gatwick Airport 10 ✈	d		10 57		11 11			11 27		11 41			11 57	
Three Bridges 4	d		11 02		11 15			11 32		11 45			12 02	
Balcombe	d				11 21									
Haywards Heath 3	d		11 11		11 27			11 41		11 55			12 11	
Wivelsfield 4	d				11 31					11 59				
Burgess Hill 4	d				11 33					12 01				
Hassocks 4	d				11 36					12 04				
Preston Park	d				11 43					12 11				
Brighton 10	a		11 25		11 47			11 55		12 15			12 25	

A To Tattenham Corner
B To Caterham
C From London Victoria
D From London Victoria to Epsom

Please refer to separate pages within this table for services operating between Bedford and London

At weekends please use local bus and tube services to travel to/from St Pancras International and London Bridge when no trains are operating. See local publicity for details of alternative routes and services that are available across central London

Table 52

Saturdays

South London, Gatwick Airport - Brighton

Network Diagram - see first Page of Table 52

Station		FC 1	SE A	FC	FC 1	FC	FC 1	SE A	FC	FC 1	FC	FC 1	SE A	FC	FC 1
St Pancras International ⊖	d														
Farringdon ⊖	d														
City Thameslink	d														
London Blackfriars ⊖	a														
	d														
Elephant & Castle ⊖	d														
Loughborough Jn.	d														
Herne Hill	d					12 12					12 42				
Denmark Hill	d		11 52					12 22					12 52		
Peckham Rye	d		11 55					12 25					12 55		
Nunhead	d		11 57					12 27					12 57		
Crofton Park	d		12 00					12 30					13 00		
Catford	d		12 03					12 33					13 03		
Bellingham	d		12 05					12 35					13 05		
Beckenham Hill	d		12 07					12 37					13 07		
Ravensbourne	d		12 09					12 39					13 09		
Shortlands	d		12 11					12 41					13 11		
Bromley South	d		12 14					12 44					13 14		
Bickley	d		12 17					12 47					13 17		
St Mary Cray	d		12 21					12 51					13 21		
Swanley	d		12 26					12 56					13 26		
Eynsford	d		12 30					13 00					13 30		
Shoreham (Kent)	d		12 34					13 04					13 34		
Otford	d		12 37					13 07					13 37		
Bat & Ball	d		12 40					13 10					13 40		
Sevenoaks	a		12 43					13 13					13 43		
London Bridge	a														
	d	11 42		11 45	11 57		12 12		12 15	12 27		12 42		12 45	12 57
Tulse Hill	d			12 01		12 16			12 31		12 46			13 01	
Streatham	d			12 05		12 20			12 35		12 50			13 05	
Mitcham Eastfields	d					12 24					12 54				
Mitcham Junction	d					12 27					12 57				
Hackbridge	d					12 30					13 00				
Carshalton	d					12 33					13 03				
Tooting	d			12 10					12 40					13 10	
Haydons Road	d			12 13					12 43					13 13	
Wimbledon ⊖	d			12 17					12 47					13 17	
Wimbledon Chase	d			12 20					12 50					13 20	
South Merton	d			12 22					12 52					13 22	
Morden South	d			12 24					12 54					13 24	
St Helier	d			12 26					12 56					13 26	
Sutton Common	d			12 28					12 58					13 28	
West Sutton	d			12 31					13 01					13 31	
Sutton (Surrey)	a			12 35		12 36			13 05		13 06			13 35	
East Croydon	d	11 55			12 11		12 25			12 41		12 55			13 11
Redhill	d														
Gatwick Airport	d	12 11			12 27		12 41			12 57		13 11			13 27
Three Bridges	d	12 15			12 32		12 45			13 02		13 15			13 32
Balcombe	d	12 21										13 21			
Haywards Heath	d	12 27			12 41		12 55			13 11		13 27			13 41
Wivelsfield	d	12 31					12 59					13 31			
Burgess Hill	d	12 33					13 01					13 33			
Hassocks	d	12 36					13 04					13 36			
Preston Park	d	12 43					13 11					13 43			
Brighton	a	12 47			12 55		13 15			13 25		13 47			13 55

A From London Victoria
B From London Victoria to Epsom
C To Tattenham Corner
D To Caterham

Please refer to separate pages within this table for services operating between Bedford and London

At weekends please use local bus and tube services to travel to/from St Pancras International and London Bridge when no trains are operating. See local publicity for details of alternative routes and services that are available across central London

Table 52

Saturdays

South London, Gatwick Airport - Brighton

Network Diagram - see first Page of Table 52

Station		FC	FC 1	SE B	FC	FC 1	FC	FC 1	SE B	FC	FC 1	FC	FC 1	SE B	FC
St Pancras International ⊖	d														
Farringdon ⊖	d														
City Thameslink	d														
London Blackfriars ⊖	a														
	d														
Elephant & Castle ⊖	d														
Loughborough Jn.	d														
Herne Hill	d	13 12					13 42					14 12			
Denmark Hill	d			13 22					13 52					14 22	
Peckham Rye	d			13 25					13 55					14 25	
Nunhead	d			13 27					13 57					14 27	
Crofton Park	d			13 30					14 00					14 30	
Catford	d			13 33					14 03					14 33	
Bellingham	d			13 35					14 05					14 35	
Beckenham Hill	d			13 37					14 07					14 37	
Ravensbourne	d			13 39					14 09					14 39	
Shortlands	d			13 41					14 11					14 41	
Bromley South	d			13 44					14 14					14 44	
Bickley	d			13 47					14 17					14 47	
St Mary Cray	d			13 51					14 21					14 51	
Swanley	d			13 56					14 26					14 56	
Eynsford	d			14 00					14 30					15 00	
Shoreham (Kent)	d			14 04					14 34					15 04	
Otford	d			14 07					14 37					15 07	
Bat & Ball	d			14 10					14 40					15 10	
Sevenoaks	a			14 13					14 43					15 13	
London Bridge	a														
	d		13 12		13 15	13 27		13 42		13 45	13 57		14 12		14 15
Tulse Hill	d	13 16			13 31		13 46			14 01		14 16			14 31
Streatham	d	13 20			13 35		13 50			14 05		14 20			14 35
Mitcham Eastfields	d	13 24					13 54					14 24			
Mitcham Junction	d	13 27					13 57					14 27			
Hackbridge	d	13 30					14 00					14 30			
Carshalton	d	13 33					14 03					14 33			
Tooting	d				13 40					14 10					14 40
Haydons Road	d				13 43					14 13					14 43
Wimbledon ⊖	d				13 47					14 17					14 47
Wimbledon Chase	d				13 50					14 20					14 50
South Merton	d				13 52					14 22					14 52
Morden South	d				13 54					14 24					14 54
St Helier	d				13 56					14 26					14 56
Sutton Common	d				13 58					14 28					14 58
West Sutton	d				14 01					14 31					15 01
Sutton (Surrey)	a	13 36			14 05		14 06			14 35		14 36			15 05
East Croydon	d		13 25			13 41		13 55			14 11		14 25		
Redhill	d														
Gatwick Airport	d		13 41			13 57		14 11			14 27		14 41		
Three Bridges	d		13 45			14 02		14 15			14 32		14 45		
Balcombe	d							14 21							
Haywards Heath	d		13 55			14 11		14 27			14 41		14 55		
Wivelsfield	d		13 59					14 31					14 59		
Burgess Hill	d		14 01					14 33					15 01		
Hassocks	d		14 04					14 36					15 04		
Preston Park	d		14 11					14 43					15 11		
Brighton	a		14 15			14 25		14 47			14 55		15 15		

A To Caterham
B From London Victoria
C From London Victoria to Epsom
D To Tattenham Corner

Please refer to separate pages within this table for services operating between Bedford and London

At weekends please use local bus and tube services to travel to/from St Pancras International and London Bridge when no trains are operating. See local publicity for details of alternative routes and services that are available across central London

South London, Gatwick Airport - Brighton

Network Diagram - see first Page of Table 52

		FC	FC	FC	SE	FC	FC	FC	FC	SE	FC	FC	FC	FC
					C					C				
St Pancras International	d													
Farringdon	d													
City Thameslink	d													
London Blackfriars	a													
	d													
Elephant & Castle	d													
Loughborough Jn.	d													
Herne Hill	d		14 42					15 12					15 42	
Denmark Hill	d				14 52					15 22				
Peckham Rye	d				14 55					15 25				
Nunhead	d				14 57					15 27				
Crofton Park	d				15 00					15 30				
Catford	d				15 03					15 33				
Bellingham	d				15 05					15 35				
Beckenham Hill	d				15 07					15 37				
Ravensbourne	d				15 09					15 39				
Shortlands	d				15 11					15 41				
Bromley South	d				15 14					15 44				
Bickley	d				15 17					15 47				
St Mary Cray	d				15 21					15 51				
Swanley	d				15 26					15 56				
Eynsford	d				15 30					16 00				
Shoreham (Kent)	d				15 34					16 04				
Otford	d				15 37					16 07				
Bat & Ball	d				15 40					16 10				
Sevenoaks	a				15 43					16 13				
London Bridge	a													
	d	14 27		14 42		14 45	14 57		15 12		15 15	15 27		15 42
Tulse Hill	d		14 46			15 01		15 16			15 31		15 46	
Streatham	d		14 50			15 05		15 20			15 35		15 50	
Mitcham Eastfields	d		14 54					15 24					15 54	
Mitcham Junction	d		14 57					15 27					15 57	
Hackbridge	d		15 00					15 30					16 00	
Carshalton	d		15 03					15 33					16 03	
Tooting	d					15 10					15 40			
Haydons Road	d					15 13					15 43			
Wimbledon	d					15 17					15 47			
Wimbledon Chase	d					15 20					15 50			
South Merton	d					15 22					15 52			
Morden South	d					15 24					15 54			
St Helier	d					15 26					15 56			
Sutton Common	d					15 28					15 58			
West Sutton	d					15 31					16 01			
Sutton (Surrey)	a		15 06			15 35		15 36			16 05		16 06	
East Croydon	d	14 41		14 55			15 11		15 25			15 41		15 55
Redhill	d													
Gatwick Airport	d	14 57		15 11			15 27		15 41			15 57		16 11
Three Bridges	d	15 02		15 15			15 32		15 45			16 02		16 15
Balcombe	d			15 21										16 21
Haywards Heath	d	15 11		15 27			15 41		15 55			16 11		16 27
Wivelsfield	d			15 31					15 59					16 31
Burgess Hill	d			15 33					16 01					16 33
Hassocks	d			15 36					16 04					16 36
Preston Park	d			15 43					16 11					16 43
Brighton	a	15 25		15 47			15 55		16 15			16 25		16 47

A To Tattenham Corner
B To Caterham
C From London Victoria
D From London Victoria to Epsom

Please refer to separate pages within this table for services operating between Bedford and London

At weekends please use local bus and tube services to travel to/from St Pancras International and London Bridge when no trains are operating. See local publicity for details of alternative routes and services that are available across central London

South London, Gatwick Airport - Brighton

Network Diagram - see first Page of Table 52

		SE	FC	FC	FC	FC	SE	FC	FC	FC	FC	SE	FC	FC
		A					A					A		
St Pancras International	d													
Farringdon	d													
City Thameslink	d													
London Blackfriars	a													
	d													
Elephant & Castle	d													
Loughborough Jn.	d													
Herne Hill	d				16 12					16 42				
Denmark Hill	d	15 52					16 22					16 52		
Peckham Rye	d	15 55					16 25					16 55		
Nunhead	d	15 57					16 27					16 57		
Crofton Park	d	16 00					16 30					17 00		
Catford	d	16 03					16 33					17 03		
Bellingham	d	16 05					16 35					17 05		
Beckenham Hill	d	16 07					16 37					17 07		
Ravensbourne	d	16 09					16 39					17 09		
Shortlands	d	16 11					16 41					17 11		
Bromley South	d	16 14					16 44					17 14		
Bickley	d	16 17					16 47					17 17		
St Mary Cray	d	16 21					16 51					17 21		
Swanley	d	16 26					16 56					17 26		
Eynsford	d	16 30					17 00					17 30		
Shoreham (Kent)	d	16 34					17 04					17 34		
Otford	d	16 37					17 07					17 37		
Bat & Ball	d	16 40					17 10					17 40		
Sevenoaks	a	16 43					17 13					17 43		
London Bridge	a													
	d		15 45	15 57		16 12		16 15	16 27		16 42		16 45	16 57
Tulse Hill	d		16 01		16 16			16 31		16 46			17 01	
Streatham	d		16 05		16 20			16 35		16 50			17 05	
Mitcham Eastfields	d				16 24					16 54				
Mitcham Junction	d				16 27					16 57				
Hackbridge	d				16 30					17 00				
Carshalton	d				16 33					17 03				
Tooting	d		16 10					16 40					17 10	
Haydons Road	d		16 13					16 43					17 13	
Wimbledon	d		16 17					16 47					17 17	
Wimbledon Chase	d		16 20					16 50					17 20	
South Merton	d		16 22					16 52					17 22	
Morden South	d		16 24					16 54					17 24	
St Helier	d		16 26					16 56					17 26	
Sutton Common	d		16 28					16 58					17 28	
West Sutton	d		16 31					17 01					17 31	
Sutton (Surrey)	a		16 35		16 36			17 05		17 06			17 35	
East Croydon	d			16 11		16 25			16 41		16 55			17 11
Redhill	d													
Gatwick Airport	d			16 27		16 41			16 57		17 11			17 27
Three Bridges	d			16 32		16 45			17 02		17 15			17 32
Balcombe	d										17 21			
Haywards Heath	d			16 41		16 55			17 11		17 27			17 41
Wivelsfield	d					16 59					17 31			
Burgess Hill	d					17 01					17 33			
Hassocks	d					17 04					17 36			
Preston Park	d					17 11					17 43			
Brighton	a			16 55		17 15			17 25		17 47			17 55

A From London Victoria
B From London Victoria to Epsom
C To Tattenham Corner
D To Caterham

Please refer to separate pages within this table for services operating between Bedford and London

At weekends please use local bus and tube services to travel to/from St Pancras International and London Bridge when no trains are operating. See local publicity for details of alternative routes and services that are available across central London

Table 52

Saturdays

South London, Gatwick Airport - Brighton

Network Diagram - see first Page of Table 52

Station		FC	FC ■	SE A	FC	FC ■	FC	FC ■	SE A	FC	FC ■	FC	FC ■	SE A	FC
St Pancras International	d														
Farringdon	d														
City Thameslink	d														
London Blackfriars	a														
	d														
Elephant & Castle	d														
Loughborough Jn.	d														
Herne Hill	d	17 12					17 42					18 12			
Denmark Hill	d			17 22					17 52					18 22	
Peckham Rye	d			17 25					17 55					18 25	
Nunhead	d			17 27					17 57					18 27	
Crofton Park	d			17 30					18 00					18 30	
Catford	d			17 33					18 03					18 33	
Bellingham	d			17 35					18 05					18 35	
Beckenham Hill	d			17 37					18 07					18 37	
Ravensbourne	d			17 39					18 09					18 39	
Shortlands	d			17 41					18 11					18 41	
Bromley South	d			17 44					18 14					18 44	
Bickley	d			17 47					18 17					18 47	
St Mary Cray	d			17 51					18 21					18 51	
Swanley	d			17 56					18 26					18 56	
Eynsford	d			18 00					18 30					19 00	
Shoreham (Kent)	d			18 04					18 34					19 04	
Otford	d			18 07					18 37					19 07	
Bat & Ball	d			18 10					18 40					19 10	
Sevenoaks	a			18 13					18 43					19 13	
London Bridge	a														
	d		17 12		17 15	17 27		17 42		17 45	17 57		18 12		18 15
Tulse Hill	d	17 16			17 31		17 46			18 01		18 16			18 31
Streatham	d	17 20			17 35		17 50			18 05		18 20			18 35
Mitcham Eastfields	d	17 24					17 54					18 24			
Mitcham Junction	d	17 27					17 57					18 27			
Hackbridge	d	17 30					18 00					18 30			
Carshalton	d	17 33					18 03					18 33			
Tooting	d				17 40					18 10					18 40
Haydons Road	d				17 43					18 13					18 43
Wimbledon	d				17 47					18 17					18 47
Wimbledon Chase	d				17 50					18 20					18 50
South Merton	d				17 52					18 22					18 52
Morden South	d				17 54					18 24					18 54
St Helier	d				17 56					18 26					18 56
Sutton Common	d				17 58					18 28					18 58
West Sutton	d				18 01					18 31					19 01
Sutton (Surrey)	a	17 36			18 05		18 06			18 35		18 36			19 05
East Croydon	d		17 25			17 41		17 55			18 11		18 25		
Redhill	d														
Gatwick Airport	d		17 41			17 57		18 11			18 27		18 41		
Three Bridges	d		17 45			18 02		18 15			18 32		18 45		
Balcombe	d							18 21							
Haywards Heath	d		17 55			18 11		18 27			18 41		18 55		
Wivelsfield	d		17 59					18 31					18 59		
Burgess Hill	d		18 01					18 33					19 01		
Hassocks	d		18 04					18 36					19 04		
Preston Park	d		18 11					18 43					19 11		
Brighton	a		18 15			18 25		18 47			18 55		19 15		

A From London Victoria
B From London Victoria to Epsom
C To Tattenham Corner
D To Caterham

Please refer to separate pages within this table for services operating between Bedford and London

At weekends please use local bus and tube services to travel to/from St Pancras International and London Bridge when no trains are operating. See local publicity for details of alternative routes and services that are available across central London

Table 52

Saturdays

South London, Gatwick Airport - Brighton

Network Diagram - see first Page of Table 52

Station		FC ■	FC	FC ■	SE C	FC	FC ■	FC	FC ■	SE C	FC	FC ■	FC	FC ■	SE C
St Pancras International	d														
Farringdon	d														
City Thameslink	d														
London Blackfriars	a														
	d														
Elephant & Castle	d														
Loughborough Jn.	d														
Herne Hill	d		18 42					19 12					19 42		
Denmark Hill	d				18 52					19 22					19 52
Peckham Rye	d				18 55					19 25					19 55
Nunhead	d				18 57					19 27					19 57
Crofton Park	d				19 00					19 30					20 00
Catford	d				19 03					19 33					20 03
Bellingham	d				19 05					19 35					20 05
Beckenham Hill	d				19 07					19 37					20 07
Ravensbourne	d				19 09					19 39					20 09
Shortlands	d				19 11					19 41					20 11
Bromley South	d				19 14					19 44					20 14
Bickley	d				19 17					19 47					20 17
St Mary Cray	d				19 21					19 51					20 21
Swanley	d				19 26					19 56					20 26
Eynsford	d				19 30					20 00					20 30
Shoreham (Kent)	d				19 34					20 04					20 34
Otford	d				19 37					20 07					20 37
Bat & Ball	d				19 40					20 10					20 40
Sevenoaks	a				19 43					20 13					20 43
London Bridge	a														
	d	18 27		18 42		18 45	18 57		19 12		19 15	19 27		19 42	
Tulse Hill	d		18 46			19 01		19 16			19 31		19 46		
Streatham	d		18 50			19 05		19 20			19 35		19 51		
Mitcham Eastfields	d		18 54					19 24					19 55		
Mitcham Junction	d		18 57					19 27					19 58		
Hackbridge	d		19 00					19 30					20 01		
Carshalton	d		19 03					19 33					20 04		
Tooting	d					19 10					19 40				
Haydons Road	d					19 13					19 43				
Wimbledon	d					19 17					19 47				
Wimbledon Chase	d					19 20					19 50				
South Merton	d					19 22					19 52				
Morden South	d					19 24					19 54				
St Helier	d					19 26					19 56				
Sutton Common	d					19 28					19 58				
West Sutton	d					19 31					20 01				
Sutton (Surrey)	a		19 06			19 39		19 36			20 05		20 07		
East Croydon	d	18 41		18 55			19 11		19 25			19 41		19 55	
Redhill	d														
Gatwick Airport	d	18 57		19 11			19 27		19 41			19 57		20 11	
Three Bridges	d	19 02		19 15			19 32		19 45			20 02		20 15	
Balcombe	d			19 21										20 21	
Haywards Heath	d	19 11		19 27			19 41		19 55			20 11		20 27	
Wivelsfield	d			19 31					19 59					20 31	
Burgess Hill	d			19 33					20 01					20 33	
Hassocks	d			19 36					20 04					20 36	
Preston Park	d			19 43					20 11					20 43	
Brighton	a	19 25		19 47			19 55		20 15			20 25		20 47	

A To Tattenham Corner
B To Caterham
C From London Victoria
D From London Victoria to Epsom

Please refer to separate pages within this table for services operating between Bedford and London

At weekends please use local bus and tube services to travel to/from St Pancras International and London Bridge when no trains are operating. See local publicity for details of alternative routes and services that are available across central London

South London, Gatwick Airport - Brighton

Network Diagram - see first Page of Table 52

Station		FC	FC 1	FC 1	SE D	FC	FC 1	SE D	FC	FC 1	SE D	FC
St Pancras International 15 ⊖	d											
Farringdon 3 ⊖	d											
City Thameslink 3	d											
London Blackfriars 3 ⊖	a											
	d											
Elephant & Castle ⊖	d											
Loughborough Jn.	d											
Herne Hill 4	d											
Denmark Hill 4	d				20 22			20 52			21 22	
Peckham Rye 4	d				20 25			20 55			21 25	
Nunhead 4	d				20 27			20 57			21 27	
Crofton Park	d				20 30			21 00			21 30	
Catford	d				20 33			21 03			21 33	
Bellingham	d				20 35			21 05			21 35	
Beckenham Hill	d				20 37			21 07			21 37	
Ravensbourne	d				20 39			21 09			21 39	
Shortlands	d				20 41			21 11			21 41	
Bromley South 4	d				20 44			21 14			21 44	
Bickley 4	d				20 47			21 17			21 47	
St Mary Cray	d				20 51			21 21			21 51	
Swanley 4	d				20 56			21 26			21 56	
Eynsford	d				21 00			21 30			22 00	
Shoreham (Kent)	d				21 04			21 34			22 04	
Otford 4	d				21 07			21 37			22 07	
Bat & Ball	d				21 10			21 40			22 10	
Sevenoaks 4	a				21 13			21 43			22 13	
London Bridge 4	a											
	d	19 45	19 57	20 12		20 15	20 42		20 45	21 12		21 15
Tulse Hill 4	d	20 01				20 31			21 01			21 31
Streatham 4	d	20 05				20 35			21 05			21 35
Mitcham Eastfields	d											
Mitcham Junction	d											
Hackbridge	d											
Carshalton	d											
Tooting	d	20 10				20 40			21 10			21 40
Haydons Road	d	20 13				20 43			21 13			21 43
Wimbledon 3 ⊖	d	20 17				20 47			21 17			21 47
Wimbledon Chase	d	20 20				20 50			21 20			21 50
South Merton	d	20 22				20 52			21 22			21 52
Morden South	d	20 24				20 54			21 24			21 54
St Helier	d	20 26				20 56			21 26			21 56
Sutton Common	d	20 28				20 58			21 28			21 58
West Sutton	d	20 31				21 01			21 31			22 01
Sutton (Surrey) 4	a	20 37				21 05			21 37			22 05
East Croydon	d		20 11	20 25			20 54			21 25		
Redhill	d											
Gatwick Airport 10 ✈	d		20 27	20 41			21 11			21 41		
Three Bridges 4	d		20 32	20 45			21 15			21 45		
Balcombe	d			20 51						21 53		
Haywards Heath 3	d		20 41	20 57			21 25			21 59		
Wivelsfield 4	d			21 01			21 29			22 03		
Burgess Hill 4	d			21 03			21 31			22 05		
Hassocks 4	d			21 06			21 34			22 08		
Preston Park	d			21 13			21 41			22 15		
Brighton 10	a		20 55	21 17			21 45			22 19		

A From London Victoria to Epsom
B To Tattenham Corner
C To Caterham
D From London Victoria

Please refer to separate pages within this table for services operating between Bedford and London

At weekends please use local bus and tube services to travel to/from St Pancras International and London Bridge when no trains are operating. See local publicity for details of alternative routes and services that are available across central London

South London, Gatwick Airport - Brighton

Network Diagram - see first Page of Table 52

Station		FC 1	SE B	FC	FC 1	SE B	FC	FC 1	SE E	FC	FC 1	SE E
St Pancras International 15 ⊖	d											
Farringdon 3 ⊖	d											
City Thameslink 3	d											
London Blackfriars 3 ⊖	a											
	d											
Elephant & Castle ⊖	d											
Loughborough Jn.	d											
Herne Hill 4	d											
Denmark Hill 4	d		21 52			22 22			22 52			23 22
Peckham Rye 4	d		21 55			22 25			22 55			23 25
Nunhead 4	d		21 57			22 27			22 57			23 27
Crofton Park	d		22 00			22 30			23 00			23 30
Catford	d		22 03			22 33			23 03			23 33
Bellingham	d		22 05			22 35			23 05			23 35
Beckenham Hill	d		22 07			22 37			23 07			23 37
Ravensbourne	d		22 09			22 39			23 09			23 39
Shortlands	d		22 11			22 41			23 11			23 41
Bromley South 4	d		22 14			22 44			23 14			23 44
Bickley 4	d		22 17			22 47			23a17			23a47
St Mary Cray	d		22 21			22 51						
Swanley 4	d		22 26			22 56						
Eynsford	d		22 30			23 00						
Shoreham (Kent)	d		22 34			23 04						
Otford 4	d		22 37			23 07						
Bat & Ball	d		22 40			23 10						
Sevenoaks 4	a		22 43			23 13						
London Bridge 4	a											
	d	21 42		21 45	22 12		22 15	22 42		22 45	23 12	
Tulse Hill 4	d			22 01			22 31			23 01		
Streatham 4	d			22 05			22 35			23 05		
Mitcham Eastfields	d											
Mitcham Junction	d											
Hackbridge	d											
Carshalton	d											
Tooting	d			22 10			22 40			23 10		
Haydons Road	d			22 13			22 43			23 13		
Wimbledon 3 ⊖	d			22 17			22 47			23 17		
Wimbledon Chase	d			22 20			22 50			23 20		
South Merton	d			22 22			22 52			23 22		
Morden South	d			22 24			22 54			23 24		
St Helier	d			22 26			22 56			23 26		
Sutton Common	d			22 28			22 58			23 28		
West Sutton	d			22 31			23 01			23 31		
Sutton (Surrey) 4	a			22 39			23 05			23 35		
East Croydon	d	21 55			22 25			22 55			23 25	
Redhill	d											
Gatwick Airport 10 ✈	d	22 11			22 41			23 11			23 41	
Three Bridges 4	d	22 15			22 45			23 15			23 47	
Balcombe	d				22 53						23 53	
Haywards Heath 3	d	22 25			22 59			23 25			23 59	
Wivelsfield 4	d	22 29			23 03			23 29			00 03	
Burgess Hill 4	d	22 31			23 05			23 31			00 05	
Hassocks 4	d	22 34			23 08			23 34			00 08	
Preston Park	d	22 41			23 15			23 41			00 15	
Brighton 10	a	22 45			23 19			23 45			00 19	

A To Caterham
B From London Victoria
C From London Victoria to Epsom
D To Tattenham Corner
E From London Victoria to Orpington

Please refer to separate pages within this table for services operating between Bedford and London

At weekends please use local bus and tube services to travel to/from St Pancras International and London Bridge when no trains are operating. See local publicity for details of alternative routes and services that are available across central London

Table 52

Saturdays

South London, Gatwick Airport - Brighton

Network Diagram - see first Page of Table 52

		FC	FC 1	FC	SE C
St Pancras International 15 ⊖	d				
Farringdon 3 ⊖	d				
City Thameslink 3	d				
London Blackfriars 3 ⊖	a				
	d				
Elephant & Castle ⊖	d				
Loughborough Jn.	d				
Herne Hill 4	d				
Denmark Hill 4	d				23 52
Peckham Rye 4	d				23 55
Nunhead 4	d				23 57
Crofton Park	d				23 58
Catford	d				00 03
Bellingham	d				00 05
Beckenham Hill	d				00 07
Ravensbourne	d				00 09
Shortlands	d				00 11
Bromley South 4	d				00 14
Bickley 4	d				00a17
St Mary Cray	d				
Swanley 4	d				
Eynsford	d				
Shoreham (Kent)	d				
Otford 4	d				
Bat & Ball	d				
Sevenoaks 4	a				
London Bridge 4	a				
	d	23 15	23 42	23 45	
Tulse Hill 3	d	23 31		00 01	
Streatham 4	d	23 35		00 05	
Mitcham Eastfields	d				
Mitcham Junction	d				
Hackbridge	d				
Carshalton	d				
Tooting	d	23 40		00 10	
Haydons Road	d	23 43		00 13	
Wimbledon 6 ⊖ ⇌	d	23 47		00 17	
Wimbledon Chase	d	23 50		00 20	
South Merton	d	23 52		00 22	
Morden South	d	23 54		00 24	
St Helier	d	23 56		00 26	
Sutton Common	d	23 58		00 28	
West Sutton	d	00 01		00 31	
Sutton (Surrey) 4	a	00 05		00 35	
East Croydon ⇌	d		23 57		
Redhill	d				
Gatwick Airport 10 ✈	d		00 19		
Three Bridges 4	d		00a24		
Balcombe	d				
Haywards Heath 3	d				
Wivelsfield 4	d				
Burgess Hill 4	d				
Hassocks 4	d				
Preston Park	d				
Brighton 10	a				

A From London Victoria to Dorking
B To Caterham
C From London Victoria to Orpington

Please refer to separate pages within this table for services operating between Bedford and London

At weekends please use local bus and tube services to travel to/from St Pancras International and London Bridge when no trains are operating. See local publicity for details of alternative routes and services that are available across central London

Table 52

Sundays

South London, Gatwick Airport - Brighton

Network Diagram - see first Page of Table 52

		FC 1 A	FC A	FC 1 A	FC A	SE B	FC 1	FC 1	FC 🚌	FC 🚌	FC 1	FC 🚌	FC 1	SE F	FC 1
St Pancras International 15 ⊖	d								00 30	01 00		07 00			
Farringdon 3 ⊖	d								00 35	01 05		07 05			
City Thameslink 3	d														
London Blackfriars 3 ⊖	a								00 40	01 10		07 10			
	d								00 40			07 10			
Elephant & Castle ⊖	d														
Loughborough Jn.	d														
Herne Hill 4	d														
Denmark Hill 4	d					23p52								07 48	
Peckham Rye 4	d					23p55								07 51	
Nunhead 4	d					23p57								07 53	
Crofton Park	d					23p58								07 56	
Catford	d					00 03								07 59	
Bellingham	d					00 05								08 01	
Beckenham Hill	d					00 07								08 03	
Ravensbourne	d					00 09								08 05	
Shortlands	d					00 11								08 07	
Bromley South 4	d					00 14								08 10	
Bickley 4	d					00a17								08 13	
St Mary Cray	d													08 17	
Swanley 4	d													08 22	
Eynsford	d													08 26	
Shoreham (Kent)	d													08 30	
Otford 4	d													08 33	
Bat & Ball	d													08 36	
Sevenoaks 4	a													08 39	
London Bridge 4	a								00 55			07 25			
	d	23p12	23p15	23p42	23p45		00 12	00 42			07 12		07 42		08 12
Tulse Hill 3	d		23p31		00 01										
Streatham 4	d		23p35		00 05										
Mitcham Eastfields	d														
Mitcham Junction	d														
Hackbridge	d														
Carshalton	d														
Tooting	d		23p40		00 10										
Haydons Road	d		23p43		00 13										
Wimbledon 6 ⊖ ⇌	d		23p47		00 17										
Wimbledon Chase	d		23p50		00 20										
South Merton	d		23p52		00 22										
Morden South	d		23p54		00 24										
St Helier	d		23p56		00 26										
Sutton Common	d		23p58		00 28										
West Sutton	d		00 01		00 31										
Sutton (Surrey) 4	a		00 05		00 35										
East Croydon ⇌	d	23p25		23p57			00 27	00 57			07 27		07 57		08 27
Redhill	d														
Gatwick Airport 10 ✈	d	23p41		00 19			00 49	01 20			07 50		08 20		08 50
Three Bridges 4	d	23p47		00a24			00a54	01a24			07 54		08 24		08 54
Balcombe	d	23p53													
Haywards Heath 3	d	23p59									08 03		08 33		09 03
Wivelsfield 4	d	00 03													
Burgess Hill 4	d	00 05									08 08		08 38		09 08
Hassocks 4	d	00 08									08 12		08 42		09 12
Preston Park	d	00 15													
Brighton 10	a	00 19									08 22		08 52		09 22

A not 11 December
B not 11 December. From London Victoria to Orpington
C To Caterham
D To Tattenham Corner
E From London Victoria to Epsom
F From London Victoria

Please refer to separate pages within this table for services operating between Bedford and London

At weekends please use local bus and tube services to travel to/from St Pancras International and London Bridge when no trains are operating. See local publicity for details of alternative routes and services that are available across central London

South London, Gatwick Airport - Brighton

Network Diagram - see first Page of Table 52

		SE	FC	SE	FC	SE	FC	FC	SE	FC	FC
			1		1			1			1
		A		A		A			A		
St Pancras International 15 ⊖	d										
Farringdon 3 ⊖	d										
City Thameslink 3	d										
London Blackfriars 3 ⊖	a										
	d										
Elephant & Castle ⊖	d										
Loughborough Jn.	d										
Herne Hill 4	d										
Denmark Hill 4	d	08 18		08 48		09 18			09 48		
Peckham Rye 4	d	08 21		08 51		09 21			09 51		
Nunhead 4	d	08 23		08 53		09 23			09 53		
Crofton Park	d	08 26		08 56		09 26			09 56		
Catford	d	08 29		08 59		09 29			09 59		
Bellingham	d	08 31		09 01		09 31			10 01		
Beckenham Hill	d	08 33		09 03		09 33			10 03		
Ravensbourne	d	08 35		09 05		09 35			10 05		
Shortlands	d	08 37		09 07		09 37			10 07		
Bromley South 4	d	08 40		09 10		09 40			10 10		
Bickley 4	d	08 43		09 13		09 43			10 13		
St Mary Cray	d	08 47		09 17		09 47			10 17		
Swanley 4	d	08 52		09 22		09 52			10 22		
Eynsford	d	08 56		09 26		09 56			10 26		
Shoreham (Kent)	d	09 00		09 30		10 00			10 30		
Otford 4	d	09 03		09 33		10 03			10 33		
Bat & Ball	d	09 06		09 36		10 06			10 36		
Sevenoaks 4	a	09 09		09 39		10 09			10 39		
London Bridge 4	a										
	d		08 42		09 12		09 32	09 42		10 02	10 12
Tulse Hill 3	d						09 43			10 13	
Streatham 4	d						09 46			10 16	
Mitcham Eastfields	d										
Mitcham Junction	d										
Hackbridge	d										
Carshalton	d										
Tooting	d						09 50			10 20	
Haydons Road	d						09 53			10 23	
Wimbledon 6 ⊖	d						09 58			10 28	
Wimbledon Chase	d						10 01			10 31	
South Merton	d						10 03			10 33	
Morden South	d						10 05			10 35	
St Helier	d						10 07			10 37	
Sutton Common	d						10 09			10 39	
West Sutton	d						10 12			10 42	
Sutton (Surrey) 4	a						10 16			10 46	
East Croydon	d		08 57		09 27			09 57			10 27
Redhill	d										
Gatwick Airport 10 ✈	d		09 20		09 50			10 20			10 50
Three Bridges 4	d		09 24		09 54			10 24			10 54
Balcombe	d										
Haywards Heath 3	d		09 33		10 03			10 33			11 03
Wivelsfield 4	d										
Burgess Hill 4	d		09 38		10 08			10 38			11 08
Hassocks 4	d		09 42		10 12			10 42			11 12
Preston Park	d										
Brighton 10	a		09 52		10 22			10 52			11 22

A From London Victoria **B** To Tattenham Corner **C** From London Victoria to Epsom

Please refer to separate pages within this table for services operating between Bedford and London

At weekends please use local bus and tube services to travel to/from St Pancras International and London Bridge when no trains are operating. See local publicity for details of alternative routes and services that are available across central London

South London, Gatwick Airport - Brighton

Network Diagram - see first Page of Table 52

		SE	FC	FC	SE	FC	FC	SE	FC	FC	SE
				1			1			1	
		A			A			A			A
St Pancras International 15 ⊖	d										
Farringdon 3 ⊖	d										
City Thameslink 3	d										
London Blackfriars 3 ⊖	a										
	d										
Elephant & Castle ⊖	d										
Loughborough Jn.	d										
Herne Hill 4	d										
Denmark Hill 4	d	10 18			10 48			11 18			11 48
Peckham Rye 4	d	10 21			10 51			11 21			11 51
Nunhead 4	d	10 23			10 53			11 23			11 53
Crofton Park	d	10 26			10 56			11 26			11 56
Catford	d	10 29			10 59			11 29			11 59
Bellingham	d	10 31			11 01			11 31			12 01
Beckenham Hill	d	10 33			11 03			11 33			12 03
Ravensbourne	d	10 35			11 05			11 35			12 05
Shortlands	d	10 37			11 07			11 37			12 07
Bromley South 4	d	10 40			11 10			11 40			12 10
Bickley 4	d	10 43			11 13			11 43			12 13
St Mary Cray	d	10 47			11 17			11 47			12 17
Swanley 4	d	10 52			11 22			11 52			12 22
Eynsford	d	10 56			11 26			11 56			12 26
Shoreham (Kent)	d	11 00			11 30			12 00			12 30
Otford 4	d	11 03			11 33			12 03			12 33
Bat & Ball	d	11 06			11 36			12 06			12 36
Sevenoaks 4	a	11 09			11 39			12 09			12 39
London Bridge 4	a										
	d		10 32	10 42		11 02	11 12		11 32	11 42	
Tulse Hill 3	d		10 43			11 13			11 43		
Streatham 4	d		10 46			11 16			11 46		
Mitcham Eastfields	d										
Mitcham Junction	d										
Hackbridge	d										
Carshalton	d										
Tooting	d		10 50			11 20			11 50		
Haydons Road	d		10 53			11 23			11 53		
Wimbledon 6 ⊖	d		10 58			11 28			11 58		
Wimbledon Chase	d		11 01			11 31			12 01		
South Merton	d		11 03			11 33			12 03		
Morden South	d		11 05			11 35			12 05		
St Helier	d		11 07			11 37			12 07		
Sutton Common	d		11 09			11 39			12 09		
West Sutton	d		11 12			11 42			12 12		
Sutton (Surrey) 4	a		11 16			11 46			12 16		
East Croydon	d			10 57			11 27			11 57	
Redhill	d										
Gatwick Airport 10 ✈	d			11 20			11 50			12 20	
Three Bridges 4	d			11 24			11 54			12 24	
Balcombe	d										
Haywards Heath 3	d			11 33			12 03			12 33	
Wivelsfield 4	d										
Burgess Hill 4	d			11 38			12 08			12 38	
Hassocks 4	d			11 42			12 12			12 42	
Preston Park	d										
Brighton 10	a			11 52			12 22			12 52	

A From London Victoria **B** From London Victoria to Epsom **C** To Tattenham Corner

Please refer to separate pages within this table for services operating between Bedford and London

At weekends please use local bus and tube services to travel to/from St Pancras International and London Bridge when no trains are operating. See local publicity for details of alternative routes and services that are available across central London

Table 52

Sundays

South London, Gatwick Airport - Brighton

Network Diagram - see first Page of Table 52

		FC	FC ■	SE B	FC	FC ■	SE B	FC	FC ■	SE B	FC	FC ■	SE B
St Pancras International ⊖	d												
Farringdon ⊖	d												
City Thameslink	d												
London Blackfriars ⊖	a												
	d												
Elephant & Castle ⊖	d												
Loughborough Jn.	d												
Herne Hill	d												
Denmark Hill	d			12 18			12 48			13 18			13 48
Peckham Rye	d			12 21			12 51			13 21			13 51
Nunhead	d			12 23			12 53			13 23			13 53
Crofton Park	d			12 26			12 56			13 26			13 56
Catford	d			12 29			12 59			13 29			13 59
Bellingham	d			12 31			13 01			13 31			14 01
Beckenham Hill	d			12 33			13 03			13 33			14 03
Ravensbourne	d			12 35			13 05			13 35			14 05
Shortlands	d			12 37			13 07			13 37			14 07
Bromley South	d			12 40			13 10			13 40			14 10
Bickley	d			12 43			13 13			13 43			14 13
St Mary Cray	d			12 47			13 17			13 47			14 17
Swanley	d			12 52			13 22			13 52			14 22
Eynsford	d			12 56			13 26			13 56			14 26
Shoreham (Kent)	d			13 00			13 30			14 00			14 30
Otford	d			13 03			13 33			14 03			14 33
Bat & Ball	d			13 06			13 36			14 06			14 36
Sevenoaks	a			13 09			13 39			14 09			14 39
London Bridge	a												
	d	12 02	12 12		12 32	12 42		13 02	13 12		13 32	13 42	
Tulse Hill	d	12 13			12 43			13 13			13 43		
Streatham	d	12 16			12 46			13 16			13 46		
Mitcham Eastfields	d												
Mitcham Junction	d												
Hackbridge	d												
Carshalton	d												
Tooting	d	12 20			12 50			13 20			13 50		
Haydons Road	d	12 23			12 53			13 23			13 53		
Wimbledon ⊖	d	12 28			12 58			13 28			13 58		
Wimbledon Chase	d	12 31			13 01			13 31			14 01		
South Merton	d	12 33			13 03			13 33			14 03		
Morden South	d	12 35			13 05			13 35			14 05		
St Helier	d	12 37			13 07			13 37			14 07		
Sutton Common	d	12 39			13 09			13 39			14 09		
West Sutton	d	12 42			13 12			13 42			14 12		
Sutton (Surrey)	a	12 46			13 16			13 46			14 16		
East Croydon	d		12 27			12 57			13 27			13 57	
Redhill	d												
Gatwick Airport ✈	d		12 50			13 20			13 50			14 20	
Three Bridges	d		12 54			13 24			13 54			14 24	
Balcombe	d												
Haywards Heath	d		13 03			13 33			14 03			14 33	
Wivelsfield	d												
Burgess Hill	d		13 08			13 38			14 08			14 38	
Hassocks	d		13 12			13 42			14 12			14 42	
Preston Park	d												
Brighton	a		13 22			13 52			14 22			14 52	

A To Tattenham Corner B From London Victoria C From London Victoria to Epsom

Please refer to separate pages within this table for services operating between Bedford and London

At weekends please use local bus and tube services to travel to/from St Pancras International and London Bridge when no trains are operating. See local publicity for details of alternative routes and services that are available across central London

Table 52

Sundays

South London, Gatwick Airport - Brighton

Network Diagram - see first Page of Table 52

		FC	FC ■	SE C	FC	FC ■	SE C	FC	FC ■	SE C	FC
St Pancras International ⊖	d										
Farringdon ⊖	d										
City Thameslink	d										
London Blackfriars ⊖	a										
	d										
Elephant & Castle ⊖	d										
Loughborough Jn.	d										
Herne Hill	d										
Denmark Hill	d			14 18			14 48			15 18	
Peckham Rye	d			14 21			14 51			15 21	
Nunhead	d			14 23			14 53			15 23	
Crofton Park	d			14 26			14 56			15 26	
Catford	d			14 29			14 59			15 29	
Bellingham	d			14 31			15 01			15 31	
Beckenham Hill	d			14 33			15 03			15 33	
Ravensbourne	d			14 35			15 05			15 35	
Shortlands	d			14 37			15 07			15 37	
Bromley South	d			14 40			15 10			15 40	
Bickley	d			14 43			15 13			15 43	
St Mary Cray	d			14 47			15 17			15 47	
Swanley	d			14 52			15 22			15 52	
Eynsford	d			14 56			15 26			15 56	
Shoreham (Kent)	d			15 00			15 30			16 00	
Otford	d			15 03			15 33			16 03	
Bat & Ball	d			15 06			15 36			16 06	
Sevenoaks	a			15 09			15 39			16 09	
London Bridge	a										
	d	14 02	14 12		14 32	14 42		15 02	15 12		15 32
Tulse Hill	d	14 13			14 43			15 13			15 43
Streatham	d	14 16			14 46			15 16			15 46
Mitcham Eastfields	d										
Mitcham Junction	d										
Hackbridge	d										
Carshalton	d										
Tooting	d	14 20			14 50			15 20			15 50
Haydons Road	d	14 23			14 53			15 23			15 53
Wimbledon ⊖	d	14 28			14 58			15 28			15 58
Wimbledon Chase	d	14 31			15 01			15 31			16 01
South Merton	d	14 33			15 03			15 33			16 03
Morden South	d	14 35			15 05			15 35			16 05
St Helier	d	14 37			15 07			15 37			16 07
Sutton Common	d	14 39			15 09			15 39			16 09
West Sutton	d	14 42			15 12			15 42			16 12
Sutton (Surrey)	a	14 46			15 16			15 46			16 16
East Croydon	d		14 27			14 57			15 27		
Redhill	d										
Gatwick Airport ✈	d		14 50			15 20			15 50		
Three Bridges	d		14 54			15 24			15 54		
Balcombe	d										
Haywards Heath	d		15 03			15 33			16 03		
Wivelsfield	d										
Burgess Hill	d		15 08			15 38			16 08		
Hassocks	d		15 12			15 42			16 12		
Preston Park	d										
Brighton	a		15 22			15 52			16 22		

A From London Victoria to Epsom B To Tattenham Corner C From London Victoria

Please refer to separate pages within this table for services operating between Bedford and London

At weekends please use local bus and tube services to travel to/from St Pancras International and London Bridge when no trains are operating. See local publicity for details of alternative routes and services that are available across central London

South London, Gatwick Airport - Brighton

Network Diagram - see first Page of Table 52

		FC 1	SE B	FC	FC 1	SE B	FC	FC 1	SE B	FC	FC 1	SE B
St Pancras International 15 ⊖	d											
Farringdon 3 ⊖	d											
City Thameslink 3	d											
London Blackfriars 3 ⊖	a											
	d											
Elephant & Castle ⊖	d											
Loughborough Jn	d											
Herne Hill 4	d											
Denmark Hill 4	d		15 48			16 18			16 48			17 18
Peckham Rye 4	d		15 51			16 21			16 51			17 21
Nunhead 4	d		15 53			16 23			16 53			17 23
Crofton Park	d		15 56			16 26			16 56			17 26
Catford	d		15 59			16 29			16 59			17 29
Bellingham	d		16 01			16 31			17 01			17 31
Beckenham Hill	d		16 03			16 33			17 03			17 33
Ravensbourne	d		16 05			16 35			17 05			17 35
Shortlands	d		16 07			16 37			17 07			17 37
Bromley South 4	d		16 10			16 40			17 10			17 40
Bickley 4	d		16 13			16 43			17 13			17 43
St Mary Cray	d		16 17			16 47			17 17			17 47
Swanley 4	d		16 22			16 52			17 22			17 52
Eynsford	d		16 26			16 56			17 26			17 56
Shoreham (Kent)	d		16 30			17 00			17 30			18 00
Otford 4	d		16 33			17 03			17 33			18 03
Bat & Ball	d		16 36			17 06			17 36			18 06
Sevenoaks 4	a		16 39			17 09			17 39			18 09
London Bridge 4	a											
	d	15 42		16 02	16 12		16 32	16 42		17 02	17 12	
Tulse Hill 3	d			16 13			16 43			17 13		
Streatham 4	d			16 16			16 46			17 16		
Mitcham Eastfields	d											
Mitcham Junction	d											
Hackbridge	d											
Carshalton	d											
Tooting	d			16 20			16 50			17 20		
Haydons Road	d			16 23			16 53			17 23		
Wimbledon 6 ⊖ ⇌	d			16 28			16 58			17 28		
Wimbledon Chase	d			16 31			17 01			17 31		
South Merton	d			16 33			17 03			17 33		
Morden South	d			16 35			17 05			17 35		
St Helier	d			16 37			17 07			17 37		
Sutton Common	d			16 39			17 09			17 39		
West Sutton	d			16 42			17 12			17 42		
Sutton (Surrey) 4	a			16 46			17 16			17 46		
East Croydon ⇌	d	15 57			16 27			16 57			17 27	
Redhill	d											
Gatwick Airport 10 ✈	d	16 20			16 50			17 20			17 50	
Three Bridges 4	d	16 24			16 54			17 24			17 54	
Balcombe	d											
Haywards Heath 3	d	16 33			17 03			17 33			18 03	
Wivelsfield 4	d											
Burgess Hill 4	d	16 38			17 08			17 38			18 08	
Hassocks 4	d	16 42			17 12			17 42			18 12	
Preston Park	d											
Brighton 10	a	16 52			17 22			17 52			18 22	

A To Tattenham Corner **B** From London Victoria **C** From London Victoria to Epsom

Please refer to separate pages within this table for services operating between Bedford and London

At weekends please use local bus and tube services to travel to/from St Pancras International and London Bridge when no trains are operating. See local publicity for details of alternative routes and services that are available across central London

South London, Gatwick Airport - Brighton

Network Diagram - see first Page of Table 52

		FC	FC 1	SE C	FC	FC 1	SE C	FC	FC 1	SE C	FC	FC 1	SE C
St Pancras International 15 ⊖	d												
Farringdon 3 ⊖	d												
City Thameslink 3	d												
London Blackfriars 3 ⊖	a												
	d												
Elephant & Castle ⊖	d												
Loughborough Jn	d												
Herne Hill 4	d												
Denmark Hill 4	d			17 48			18 18			18 48			19 18
Peckham Rye 4	d			17 51			18 21			18 51			19 21
Nunhead 4	d			17 53			18 23			18 53			19 23
Crofton Park	d			17 56			18 26			18 56			19 26
Catford	d			17 59			18 29			18 59			19 29
Bellingham	d			18 01			18 31			19 01			19 31
Beckenham Hill	d			18 03			18 33			19 03			19 33
Ravensbourne	d			18 05			18 35			19 05			19 35
Shortlands	d			18 07			18 37			19 07			19 37
Bromley South 4	d			18 10			18 40			19 10			19 40
Bickley 4	d			18 13			18 43			19 13			19 43
St Mary Cray	d			18 17			18 47			19 17			19 47
Swanley 4	d			18 22			18 52			19 22			19 52
Eynsford	d			18 26			18 56			19 26			19 56
Shoreham (Kent)	d			18 30			19 00			19 30			20 00
Otford 4	d			18 33			19 03			19 33			20 03
Bat & Ball	d			18 36			19 06			19 36			20 06
Sevenoaks 4	a			18 39			19 09			19 39			20 09
London Bridge 4	a												
	d	17 32	17 42		18 02	18 12		18 32	18 42		19 02	19 12	
Tulse Hill 3	d	17 43			18 13			18 43			19 13		
Streatham 4	d	17 46			18 16			18 46			19 16		
Mitcham Eastfields	d												
Mitcham Junction	d												
Hackbridge	d												
Carshalton	d												
Tooting	d	17 50			18 20			18 50			19 20		
Haydons Road	d	17 53			18 23			18 53			19 23		
Wimbledon 6 ⊖ ⇌	d	17 58			18 28			18 58			19 28		
Wimbledon Chase	d	18 01			18 31			19 01			19 31		
South Merton	d	18 03			18 33			19 03			19 33		
Morden South	d	18 05			18 35			19 05			19 35		
St Helier	d	18 07			18 37			19 07			19 37		
Sutton Common	d	18 09			18 39			19 09			19 39		
West Sutton	d	18 12			18 42			19 12			19 42		
Sutton (Surrey) 4	a	18 16			18 46			19 16			19 46		
East Croydon ⇌	d		17 57			18 27			18 57			19 27	
Redhill	d												
Gatwick Airport 10 ✈	d		18 20			18 50			19 20			19 50	
Three Bridges 4	d		18 24			18 54			19 24			19 54	
Balcombe	d												
Haywards Heath 3	d		18 33			19 03			19 33			20 03	
Wivelsfield 4	d												
Burgess Hill 4	d		18 38			19 08			19 38			20 08	
Hassocks 4	d		18 42			19 12			19 42			20 12	
Preston Park	d												
Brighton 10	a		18 52			19 22			19 52			20 22	

A From London Victoria to Epsom **B** To Tattenham Corner **C** From London Victoria

Please refer to separate pages within this table for services operating between Bedford and London

At weekends please use local bus and tube services to travel to/from St Pancras International and London Bridge when no trains are operating. See local publicity for details of alternative routes and services that are available across central London

Table 52

Sundays

South London, Gatwick Airport - Brighton

Network Diagram - see first Page of Table 52

		FC	FC 1	SE B	FC	FC 1	SE B	FC	FC 1	SE B	FC	FC 1	SE B
St Pancras International 15 ⊖	d												
Farringdon 3 ⊖	d												
City Thameslink 3	d												
London Blackfriars 3 ⊖	a												
	d												
Elephant & Castle ⊖	d												
Loughborough Jn.	d												
Herne Hill 4	d												
Denmark Hill 4	d			19 48			20 18			20 48			21 18
Peckham Rye 4	d			19 51			20 21			20 51			21 21
Nunhead 4	d			19 53			20 23			20 53			21 23
Crofton Park	d			19 56			20 26			20 56			21 26
Catford	d			19 59			20 29			20 59			21 29
Bellingham	d			20 01			20 31			21 01			21 31
Beckenham Hill	d			20 03			20 33			21 03			21 33
Ravensbourne	d			20 05			20 35			21 05			21 35
Shortlands	d			20 07			20 37			21 07			21 37
Bromley South 4	d			20 10			20 40			21 10			21 40
Bickley 4	d			20 13			20 43			21 13			21 43
St Mary Cray	d			20 17			20 47			21 17			21 47
Swanley 4	d			20 22			20 52			21 22			21 52
Eynsford	d			20 26			20 56			21 26			21 56
Shoreham (Kent)	d			20 30			21 00			21 30			22 00
Otford 4	d			20 33			21 03			21 33			22 03
Bat & Ball	d			20 36			21 06			21 36			22 06
Sevenoaks 4	a			20 39			21 09			21 39			22 09
London Bridge 4	a												
	d	19 32	19 42		20 02	20 12		20 32	20 42		21 02	21 12	
Tulse Hill 3	d	19 43			20 13			20 43			21 13		
Streatham 4	d	19 46			20 16			20 46			21 16		
Mitcham Eastfields	d												
Mitcham Junction	d												
Hackbridge	d												
Carshalton	d												
Tooting	d	19 50			20 20			20 50			21 20		
Haydons Road	d	19 53			20 23			20 53			21 23		
Wimbledon 6 ⊖ ⇌	d	19 58			20 28			20 58			21 28		
Wimbledon Chase	d	20 01			20 31			21 01			21 31		
South Merton	d	20 03			20 33			21 03			21 33		
Morden South	d	20 05			20 35			21 05			21 35		
St Helier	d	20 07			20 37			21 07			21 37		
Sutton Common	d	20 09			20 39			21 09			21 39		
West Sutton	d	20 12			20 42			21 12			21 42		
Sutton (Surrey) 4	a	20 16			20 46			21 16			21 46		
East Croydon ⇌	d		19 57			20 27			20 57			21 27	
Redhill	d												
Gatwick Airport 10 ✈	d		20 20			20 50			21 20			21 50	
Three Bridges 4	d		20 24			20 54			21 24			21 54	
Balcombe	d												
Haywards Heath 3	d		20 33			21 03			21 33			22 03	
Wivelsfield 4	d												
Burgess Hill 4	d		20 38			21 08			21 38			22 08	
Hassocks 4	d		20 42			21 12			21 42			22 12	
Preston Park	d												
Brighton 10	a		20 52			21 22			21 52			22 22	

A To Tattenham Corner

B From London Victoria

Please refer to separate pages within this table for services operating between Bedford and London

At weekends please use local bus and tube services to travel to/from St Pancras International and London Bridge when no trains are operating. See local publicity for details of alternative routes and services that are available across central London

Table 52

Sundays

South London, Gatwick Airport - Brighton

Network Diagram - see first Page of Table 52

		FC 1	SE A	FC 1	SE A	FC 1	SE C	FC 1	SE C	FC 1
St Pancras International 15 ⊖	d									
Farringdon 3 ⊖	d									
City Thameslink 3	d									
London Blackfriars 3 ⊖	a									
	d									
Elephant & Castle ⊖	d									
Loughborough Jn.	d									
Herne Hill 4	d									
Denmark Hill 4	d		21 48		22 18		22 48		23 18	
Peckham Rye 4	d		21 51		22 21		22 51		23 21	
Nunhead 4	d		21 53		22 23		22 53		23 23	
Crofton Park	d		21 56		22 26		22 56		23 26	
Catford	d		21 59		22 29		22 59		23 29	
Bellingham	d		22 01		22 31		23 01		23 31	
Beckenham Hill	d		22 03		22 33		23 03		23 33	
Ravensbourne	d		22 05		22 35		23 05		23 35	
Shortlands	d		22 07		22 37		23 07		23 37	
Bromley South 4	d		22 10		22 40		23 10		23 40	
Bickley 4	d		22 13		22 43		23a13		23a43	
St Mary Cray	d		22 17		22 47					
Swanley 4	d		22 22		22 52					
Eynsford	d		22 26		22 56					
Shoreham (Kent)	d		22 30		23 00					
Otford 4	d		22 33		23 03					
Bat & Ball	d		22 36		23 06					
Sevenoaks 4	a		22 39		23 09					
London Bridge 4	a									
	d	21 42		22 12		22 42		23 12		23 42
Tulse Hill 3	d									
Streatham 4	d									
Mitcham Eastfields	d									
Mitcham Junction	d									
Hackbridge	d									
Carshalton	d									
Tooting	d									
Haydons Road	d									
Wimbledon 6 ⊖ ⇌	d									
Wimbledon Chase	d									
South Merton	d									
Morden South	d									
St Helier	d									
Sutton Common	d									
West Sutton	d									
Sutton (Surrey) 4	a									
East Croydon ⇌	d	21 57		22 27		22 57		23 27		23 57
Redhill	d									
Gatwick Airport 10 ✈	d	22 20		22 50		23 20		23 50		00 19
Three Bridges 4	d	22 24		22 54		23 24		23 54		00a24
Balcombe	d									
Haywards Heath 3	d	22 33		23 03		23 33		00 03		
Wivelsfield 4	d									
Burgess Hill 4	d	22 38		23 08		23 38		00 08		
Hassocks 4	d	22 42		23 12		23 42		00 12		
Preston Park	d									
Brighton 10	a	22 52		23 22		23 52		00 22		

A From London Victoria

B To Tattenham Corner

C From London Victoria to Orpington

D To Caterham

Please refer to separate pages within this table for services operating between Bedford and London

At weekends please use local bus and tube services to travel to/from St Pancras International and London Bridge when no trains are operating. See local publicity for details of alternative routes and services that are available across central London

Brighton, Gatwick Airport - South London

Network Diagram - see first Page of Table 52

		FC	FC	FC	FC	FC	FC	FC	FC	FC	FC	FC	SE	SE	FC	SE	FC	FC	SE
			1		1							1			1		1	1	
													B	C		C			C
		bus		bus		bus	bus	bus	bus	bus	bus								
Brighton 10	d		23p11		23p37							05 25			06 02		06 25	06 37	
Preston Park	d				23p41							05 29					06 29	06 41	
Hassocks 4	d		23p20		23p47							05 35					06 35	06 47	
Burgess Hill 4	d		23p23		23p51							05 39			06 12		06 39	06 51	
Wivelsfield 4	d				23p53							05 41					06 41	06 53	
Haywards Heath 3	d		23p29		23p59							05 46			06 17		06 46	07 02	
Balcombe	d				00 04							05 51					06 51		
Three Bridges 4	d		23p38		00 10							05 57			06 27		06 57	07 12	
Gatwick Airport 10 ✈	d		23p43		00 15							06 02			06 32		07 02	07 16	
Redhill	d				00 23														
East Croydon	d		00 04		00 36							06 17			06 47		07 17	07 32	
Sutton (Surrey) 4	d																		
West Sutton	d																		
Sutton Common	d																		
St Helier	d																		
Morden South	d																		
South Merton	d																		
Wimbledon Chase	d																		
Wimbledon 8	d																		
Haydons Road	d																		
Tooting	d																		
Carshalton	d																		
Hackbridge	d																		
Mitcham Junction	d																		
Mitcham Eastfields	d																		
Streatham 4	d																		
Tulse Hill 3	d																		
London Bridge 4 ⊖	a		00 19		00 52							06 32			07 02		07 32	07 47	
	d	23p55		00 25		00 57	01 57	02 22	03 17	04 17	05 20								
Sevenoaks 4	d													05 55		06 25			06 55
Bat & Ball	d													05 58		06 28			06 58
Otford 4	d													06 01		06 31			07 01
Shoreham (Kent)	d													06 04		06 34			07 04
Eynsford	d													06 08		06 38			07 08
Swanley 4	d													06 13		06 43			07 13
St Mary Cray 4	d													06 17		06 47			07 17
Bickley	d												05 51	06 21		06 51			07 21
Bromley South	d												05 54	06 24		06 54			07 24
Shortlands 4	d												05 57	06 27		06 57			07 27
Ravensbourne	d												05 59	06 29		06 59			07 29
Beckenham Hill	d												06 01	06 31		07 01			07 31
Bellingham	d												06 03	06 33		07 03			07 33
Catford	d												06 06	06 36		07 06			07 36
Crofton Park	d												06 08	06 38		07 08			07 38
Nunhead 4	d												06 11	06 41		07 11			07 41
Peckham Rye 4	d												06 13	06 43		07 13			07 43
Denmark Hill 4	d												06a16	06a46		07a16			07a46
Herne Hill 4	d																		
Loughborough Jn.	d																		
Elephant & Castle	d																		
London Blackfriars 3 ⊖	a	00 10		00 40		01 12	02 12	02 37	03 32	04 32	05 35								
	d	00 10		00 40		01 12	02 12	02 37	03 32	04 32	05 35								
City Thameslink 3	d																		
Farringdon 3 ⊖	d	00 20		00 50							05 45								
St Pancras International 15 ⊖	a	00 25		00 55		01 27	02 27	02 52	03 47	04 47	05 50								

A To London Victoria

B From Orpington to London Victoria

C To London Victoria

Please refer to separate pages within this table for services operating between London and Bedford

At weekends please use local bus and tube services to travel to/from St Pancras International and London Bridge when no trains are operating. See local publicity for details of alternative routes and services that are available across central London

Table 52 Saturdays

Brighton, Gatwick Airport - South London

Network Diagram - see first Page of Table 52

		FC	FC	FC	FC	SE	FC	FC	FC	FC	SE	FC	FC	FC	FC	SE	FC	FC	FC
			1	1				1	1				1	1				1	1
						B					B					B			
Brighton 10	d		07 04	07 07				07 34	07 37				08 04	08 07				08 34	08 37
Preston Park	d			07 11					07 41					08 11					08 41
Hassocks 4	d			07 17					07 47					08 17					08 47
Burgess Hill 4	d			07 21					07 51					08 21					08 51
Wivelsfield 4	d			07 23					07 53					08 23					08 53
Haywards Heath 3	d		07 18	07 32				07 48	08 02				08 18	08 32				08 48	09 02
Balcombe	d			07 37										08 37					
Three Bridges 4	d		07 27	07 42				07 57	08 12				08 27	08 42				08 57	09 12
Gatwick Airport 10 ✈	d		07 32	07 46				08 02	08 16				08 32	08 46				09 02	09 16
Redhill	d																		
East Croydon	d		07 47	08 01				08 17	08 32				08 47	09 01				09 17	09 32
Sutton (Surrey) 4	d	07 07			07 08		07 37			07 38		08 07			08 08		08 37		
West Sutton	d	07 10					07 40					08 10					08 40		
Sutton Common	d	07 12					07 42					08 12					08 42		
St Helier	d	07 15					07 45					08 15					08 45		
Morden South	d	07 17					07 47					08 17					08 47		
South Merton	d	07 19					07 49					08 19					08 49		
Wimbledon Chase	d	07 21					07 51					08 21					08 51		
Wimbledon 8	d	07 30					08 00					08 30					09 00		
Haydons Road	d	07 32					08 02					08 32					09 02		
Tooting	d	07 35					08 05					08 35					09 05		
Carshalton	d				07 11					07 41					08 11				
Hackbridge	d				07 13					07 43					08 13				
Mitcham Junction	d				07 16					07 46					08 16				
Mitcham Eastfields	d				07 19					07 49					08 19				
Streatham 4	d	07 40			07 23		08 10			07 53		08 40			08 23		09 10		
Tulse Hill 3	d	07 47			07 27		08 17			07 57		08 47			08 27		09 17		
London Bridge 4 ⊖	a	08 00	08 02	08 17			08 30	08 32	08 47			09 00	09 02	09 17			09 30	09 32	09 47
	d																		
Sevenoaks 4	d					07 25					07 55					08 25			
Bat & Ball	d					07 28					07 58					08 28			
Otford 4	d					07 31					08 01					08 31			
Shoreham (Kent)	d					07 34					08 04					08 34			
Eynsford	d					07 38					08 08					08 38			
Swanley 4	d					07 43					08 13					08 43			
St Mary Cray 4	d					07 47					08 17					08 47			
Bickley	d					07 51					08 21					08 51			
Bromley South	d					07 54					08 24					08 54			
Shortlands 4	d					07 57					08 27					08 57			
Ravensbourne	d					07 59					08 29					08 59			
Beckenham Hill	d					08 01					08 31					09 01			
Bellingham	d					08 03					08 33					09 03			
Catford	d					08 06					08 36					09 06			
Crofton Park	d					08 08					08 38					09 08			
Nunhead 4	d					08 11					08 41					09 11			
Peckham Rye 4	d					08 13					08 43					09 13			
Denmark Hill 4	d					08a16					08a46					09a16			
Herne Hill 4	d				07a31					08a01					08a31				
Loughborough Jn.	d																		
Elephant & Castle	d																		
London Blackfriars 3 ⊖	a																		
	d																		
City Thameslink 3	d																		
Farringdon 3 ⊖	d																		
St Pancras International 15 ⊖	a																		

A From Epsom to London Victoria

B To London Victoria

Please refer to separate pages within this table for services operating between London and Bedford

At weekends please use local bus and tube services to travel to/from St Pancras International and London Bridge when no trains are operating. See local publicity for details of alternative routes and services that are available across central London

Table 52

Saturdays

Brighton, Gatwick Airport - South London

Network Diagram - see first Page of Table 52

		FC	SE	FC	FC	FC	FC	SE	FC	FC	FC	FC	SE	FC	FC	FC	FC	SE
					1	1				1	1				1	1		
			A					A					A					A
Brighton 10	d				09 04	09 07				09 34	09 37				10 04	10 07		
Preston Park	d					09 11					09 41					10 11		
Hassocks 4	d					09 17					09 47					10 17		
Burgess Hill 4	d					09 21					09 51					10 21		
Wivelsfield 4	d					09 23					09 53					10 23		
Haywards Heath 3	d				09 18	09 32				09 48	10 02				10 18	10 32		
Balcombe	d					09 37										10 37		
Three Bridges 4	d				09 27	09 42				09 57	10 12				10 27	10 42		
Gatwick Airport 10 ✈	d				09 32	09 46				10 02	10 16				10 32	10 46		
Redhill	d																	
East Croydon	d				09 47	10 01				10 17	10 32				10 47	11 01		
Sutton (Surrey) 4	d	08 38		09 07			09 08		09 37			09 38		10 07			10 08	
West Sutton	d			09 10					09 40					10 10				
Sutton Common	d			09 12					09 42					10 12				
St Helier	d			09 15					09 45					10 15				
Morden South	d			09 17					09 47					10 17				
South Merton	d			09 19					09 49					10 19				
Wimbledon Chase	d			09 21					09 51					10 21				
Wimbledon 6	d			09 30					10 00					10 30				
Haydons Road	d			09 32					10 02					10 32				
Tooting	d			09 35					10 05					10 35				
Carshalton	d	08 41					09 11					09 41					10 11	
Hackbridge	d	08 43					09 13					09 43					10 13	
Mitcham Junction	d	08 46					09 16					09 46					10 16	
Mitcham Eastfields	d	08 49					09 19					09 49					10 19	
Streatham 4	d	08 53		09 40			09 23		10 10			09 53		10 40			10 23	
Tulse Hill 3	d	08 57		09 47			09 27		10 17			09 57		10 47			10 27	
London Bridge 4 ⊖	a			10 00	10 02	10 17			10 30	10 32	10 47			11 00	11 02	11 17		
	d																	
Sevenoaks 4	d		08 55					09 25					09 55					10 25
Bat & Ball	d		08 58					09 28					09 58					10 28
Otford 4	d		09 01					09 31					10 01					10 31
Shoreham (Kent)	d		09 04					09 34					10 04					10 34
Eynsford	d		09 08					09 38					10 08					10 38
Swanley 4	d		09 13					09 43					10 13					10 43
St Mary Cray 4	d		09 17					09 47					10 17					10 47
Bickley	d		09 21					09 51					10 21					10 51
Bromley South	d		09 24					09 54					10 24					10 54
Shortlands 4	d		09 27					09 57					10 27					10 57
Ravensbourne	d		09 29					09 59					10 29					10 59
Beckenham Hill	d		09 31					10 01					10 31					11 01
Bellingham	d		09 33					10 03					10 33					11 03
Catford	d		09 36					10 06					10 36					11 06
Crofton Park	d		09 38					10 08					10 38					11 08
Nunhead 4	d		09 41					10 11					10 41					11 11
Peckham Rye 4	d		09 43					10 13					10 43					11 13
Denmark Hill 4	d		09a46					10a16					10a46					11a16
Herne Hill 4	d	09a01					09a31					10a01					10a31	
Loughborough Jn	d																	
Elephant & Castle	d																	
London Blackfriars 3 ⊖	a																	
	d																	
City Thameslink 3	d																	
Farringdon 3 ⊖	d																	
St Pancras International 15 ⊖	a																	

A To London Victoria

B From Epsom to London Victoria

Please refer to separate pages within this table for services operating between London and Bedford

At weekends please use local bus and tube services to travel to/from St Pancras International and London Bridge when no trains are operating. See local publicity for details of alternative routes and services that are available across central London

Table 52

Saturdays

Brighton, Gatwick Airport - South London

Network Diagram - see first Page of Table 52

		FC	FC	FC	FC	SE	FC	FC	FC	FC	SE	FC	FC	FC	FC	SE	FC	FC	FC	FC
			1	1				1	1				1	1				1	1	
						A					A					A				
Brighton 10	d		10 34	10 37				11 04	11 07				11 34	11 37				12 04	12 07	
Preston Park	d			10 41					11 11					11 41					12 11	
Hassocks 4	d			10 47					11 17					11 47					12 17	
Burgess Hill 4	d			10 51					11 21					11 51					12 21	
Wivelsfield 4	d			10 53					11 23					11 53					12 23	
Haywards Heath 3	d		10 48	11 02				11 18	11 32				11 48	12 02				12 18	12 32	
Balcombe	d								11 37										12 37	
Three Bridges 4	d		10 57	11 12				11 27	11 42				11 57	12 12				12 27	12 42	
Gatwick Airport 10 ✈	d		11 02	11 16				11 32	11 46				12 02	12 16				12 32	12 46	
Redhill	d																			
East Croydon	d		11 17	11 32				11 47	12 01				12 17	12 32				12 47	13 01	
Sutton (Surrey) 4	d	10 37			10 38		11 07			11 08		11 37			11 38		12 07			12 08
West Sutton	d	10 40					11 10					11 40					12 10			
Sutton Common	d	10 42					11 12					11 42					12 12			
St Helier	d	10 45					11 15					11 45					12 15			
Morden South	d	10 47					11 17					11 47					12 17			
South Merton	d	10 49					11 19					11 49					12 19			
Wimbledon Chase	d	10 51					11 21					11 51					12 21			
Wimbledon 6	d	11 00					11 30					12 00					12 30			
Haydons Road	d	11 02					11 32					12 02					12 32			
Tooting	d	11 05					11 35					12 05					12 35			
Carshalton	d				10 41					11 11					11 41					12 11
Hackbridge	d				10 43					11 13					11 43					12 13
Mitcham Junction	d				10 46					11 16					11 46					12 16
Mitcham Eastfields	d				10 49					11 19					11 49					12 19
Streatham 4	d	11 10			10 53		11 40			11 23		12 10			11 53		12 40			12 23
Tulse Hill 3	d	11 17			10 57		11 47			11 27		12 17			11 57		12 47			12 27
London Bridge 4 ⊖	a	11 30	11 32	11 47			12 00	12 02	12 17			12 30	12 32	12 47			13 00	13 02	13 17	
	d																			
Sevenoaks 4	d					10 55					11 25					11 55				
Bat & Ball	d					10 58					11 28					11 58				
Otford 4	d					11 01					11 31					12 01				
Shoreham (Kent)	d					11 04					11 34					12 04				
Eynsford	d					11 08					11 38					12 08				
Swanley 4	d					11 13					11 43					12 13				
St Mary Cray 4	d					11 17					11 47					12 17				
Bickley	d					11 21					11 51					12 21				
Bromley South	d					11 24					11 54					12 24				
Shortlands 4	d					11 27					11 57					12 27				
Ravensbourne	d					11 29					11 59					12 29				
Beckenham Hill	d					11 31					12 01					12 31				
Bellingham	d					11 33					12 03					12 33				
Catford	d					11 36					12 06					12 36				
Crofton Park	d					11 38					12 08					12 38				
Nunhead 4	d					11 41					12 11					12 41				
Peckham Rye 4	d					11 43					12 13					12 43				
Denmark Hill 4	d					11a46					12a16					12a46				
Herne Hill 4	d				11a01					11a31					12a01					12a31
Loughborough Jn	d																			
Elephant & Castle	d																			
London Blackfriars 3 ⊖	a																			
	d																			
City Thameslink 3	d																			
Farringdon 3 ⊖	d																			
St Pancras International 15 ⊖	a																			

A To London Victoria

B From Epsom to London Victoria

Please refer to separate pages within this table for services operating between London and Bedford

At weekends please use local bus and tube services to travel to/from St Pancras International and London Bridge when no trains are operating. See local publicity for details of alternative routes and services that are available across central London

Brighton, Gatwick Airport - South London

Network Diagram - see first Page of Table 52

		SE	FC	FC	FC	FC	SE	FC	FC	FC	FC	SE	FC	FC	FC	FC	SE	FC
		A		1	1		A		1	1		A		1	1		A	
Brighton 10	d			12 34	12 37				13 04	13 07				13 34	13 37			
Preston Park	d				12 41					13 11					13 41			
Hassocks 4	d				12 47					13 17					13 47			
Burgess Hill 4	d				12 51					13 21					13 51			
Wivelsfield 4	d				12 53					13 23					13 53			
Haywards Heath 3	d			12 48	13 02				13 18	13 32				13 48	14 02			
Balcombe	d									13 37								
Three Bridges 4	d			12 57	13 12				13 27	13 42				13 57	14 12			
Gatwick Airport 10 ✈	d			13 02	13 16				13 32	13 46				14 02	14 16			
Redhill	d																	
East Croydon	d			13 17	13 32				13 47	14 01				14 17	14 32			
Sutton (Surrey) 4	d		12 37			12 38		13 07			13 08		13 37			13 38		14 07
West Sutton	d		12 40					13 10					13 40					14 10
Sutton Common	d		12 42					13 12					13 42					14 12
St Helier	d		12 45					13 15					13 45					14 15
Morden South	d		12 47					13 17					13 47					14 17
South Merton	d		12 49					13 19					13 49					14 19
Wimbledon Chase	d		12 51					13 21					13 51					14 21
Wimbledon 6	d		13 00					13 30					14 00					14 30
Haydons Road	d		13 02					13 32					14 02					14 32
Tooting	d		13 05					13 35					14 05					14 35
Carshalton	d					12 41					13 11					13 41		
Hackbridge	d					12 43					13 13					13 43		
Mitcham Junction	d					12 46					13 16					13 46		
Mitcham Eastfields	d					12 49					13 19					13 49		
Streatham 4	d		13 10			12 53		13 40			13 23		14 10			13 53		14 40
Tulse Hill 3	d		13 17			12 57		13 47			13 27		14 17			13 57		14 47
London Bridge 4 ⊖	a		13 30	13 32	13 47			14 00	14 02	14 17			14 30	14 32	14 47			15 00
	d																	
Sevenoaks 4	d	12 25					12 55					13 25					13 55	
Bat & Ball	d	12 28					12 58					13 28					13 58	
Otford 4	d	12 31					13 01					13 31					14 01	
Shoreham (Kent)	d	12 34					13 04					13 34					14 04	
Eynsford	d	12 38					13 08					13 38					14 08	
Swanley 4	d	12 43					13 13					13 43					14 13	
St Mary Cray 4	d	12 47					13 17					13 47					14 17	
Bickley	d	12 51					13 21					13 51					14 21	
Bromley South	d	12 54					13 24					13 54					14 24	
Shortlands 4	d	12 57					13 27					13 57					14 27	
Ravensbourne	d	12 59					13 29					13 59					14 29	
Beckenham Hill	d	13 01					13 31					14 01					14 31	
Bellingham	d	13 03					13 33					14 03					14 33	
Catford	d	13 06					13 36					14 06					14 36	
Crofton Park	d	13 08					13 38					14 08					14 38	
Nunhead 4	d	13 11					13 41					14 11					14 41	
Peckham Rye 4	d	13 13					13 43					14 13					14 43	
Denmark Hill 4	d	13a16					13a46					14a16					14a46	
Herne Hill 4	d					13a01					13a31					14a01		
Loughborough Jn.	d																	
Elephant & Castle	d																	
London Blackfriars 3 ⊖	a																	
	d																	
City Thameslink 3	d																	
Farringdon 3 ⊖	d																	
St Pancras International 15 ⊖	a																	

A To London Victoria

B From Epsom to London Victoria

Please refer to separate pages within this table for services operating between London and Bedford

At weekends please use local bus and tube services to travel to/from St Pancras International and London Bridge when no trains are operating. See local publicity for details of alternative routes and services that are available across central London

Brighton, Gatwick Airport - South London

Network Diagram - see first Page of Table 52

		FC	FC	FC	SE	FC	FC	FC	FC	SE	FC	FC	FC	FC	SE	FC	FC	FC	FC	SE
		1	1		A		1	1		A		1	1		A		1	1		A
Brighton 10	d	14 04	14 07				14 34	14 37				15 04	15 07				15 34	15 37		
Preston Park	d		14 11					14 41					15 11					15 41		
Hassocks 4	d		14 17					14 47					15 17					15 47		
Burgess Hill 4	d		14 21					14 51					15 21					15 51		
Wivelsfield 4	d		14 23					14 53					15 23					15 53		
Haywards Heath 3	d	14 18	14 32				14 48	15 02				15 18	15 32				15 48	16 02		
Balcombe	d		14 37										15 37							
Three Bridges 4	d	14 27	14 42				14 57	15 12				15 27	15 42				15 57	16 12		
Gatwick Airport 10 ✈	d	14 32	14 46				15 02	15 16				15 32	15 46				16 02	16 16		
Redhill	d																			
East Croydon	d	14 47	15 01				15 17	15 32				15 47	16 01				16 17	16 32		
Sutton (Surrey) 4	d			14 08		14 37			14 38		15 07			15 08		15 37			15 38	
West Sutton	d					14 40					15 10					15 40				
Sutton Common	d					14 42					15 12					15 42				
St Helier	d					14 45					15 15					15 45				
Morden South	d					14 47					15 17					15 47				
South Merton	d					14 49					15 19					15 49				
Wimbledon Chase	d					14 51					15 21					15 51				
Wimbledon 6	d					15 00					15 30					16 00				
Haydons Road	d					15 02					15 32					16 02				
Tooting	d					15 05					15 35					16 05				
Carshalton	d			14 11					14 41					15 11					15 41	
Hackbridge	d			14 13					14 43					15 13					15 43	
Mitcham Junction	d			14 16					14 46					15 16					15 46	
Mitcham Eastfields	d			14 19					14 49					15 19					15 49	
Streatham 4	d			14 23		15 10			14 53		15 40			15 23		16 10			15 53	
Tulse Hill 3	d			14 27		15 17			14 57		15 47			15 27		16 17			15 57	
London Bridge 4 ⊖	a	15 02	15 17			15 30	15 32	15 47			16 00	16 02	16 17			16 30	16 32	16 47		
	d																			
Sevenoaks 4	d				14 25					14 55					15 25					15 55
Bat & Ball	d				14 28					14 58					15 28					15 58
Otford 4	d				14 31					15 01					15 31					16 01
Shoreham (Kent)	d				14 34					15 04					15 34					16 04
Eynsford	d				14 38					15 08					15 38					16 08
Swanley 4	d				14 43					15 13					15 43					16 13
St Mary Cray 4	d				14 47					15 17					15 47					16 17
Bickley	d				14 51					15 21					15 51					16 21
Bromley South	d				14 54					15 24					15 54					16 24
Shortlands 4	d				14 57					15 27					15 57					16 27
Ravensbourne	d				14 59					15 29					15 59					16 29
Beckenham Hill	d				15 01					15 31					16 01					16 31
Bellingham	d				15 03					15 33					16 03					16 33
Catford	d				15 06					15 36					16 06					16 36
Crofton Park	d				15 08					15 38					16 08					16 38
Nunhead 4	d				15 11					15 41					16 11					16 41
Peckham Rye 4	d				15 13					15 43					16 13					16 43
Denmark Hill 4	d				15a16					15a46					16a16					16a46
Herne Hill 4	d			14a31					15a01					15a31					16a01	
Loughborough Jn.	d																			
Elephant & Castle	d																			
London Blackfriars 3 ⊖	a																			
	d																			
City Thameslink 3	d																			
Farringdon 3 ⊖	d																			
St Pancras International 15 ⊖	a																			

A To London Victoria

B From Epsom to London Victoria

Please refer to separate pages within this table for services operating between London and Bedford

At weekends please use local bus and tube services to travel to/from St Pancras International and London Bridge when no trains are operating. See local publicity for details of alternative routes and services that are available across central London

Table 52

Saturdays

Brighton, Gatwick Airport - South London

Network Diagram - see first Page of Table 52

		FC	FC 1	FC 1	FC	SE	FC	FC 1	FC 1	FC	SE	FC	FC 1	FC 1	FC	SE	FC	FC 1	FC 1
						B					B					B			
Brighton 10	d		16 04	16 07				16 34	16 37				17 04	17 07				17 34	17 37
Preston Park	d			16 11					16 41					17 11					17 41
Hassocks 4	d			16 17					16 47					17 17					17 47
Burgess Hill 4	d			16 21					16 51					17 21					17 51
Wivelsfield 4	d			16 23					16 53					17 23					17 53
Haywards Heath 3	d		16 18	16 32				16 48	17 02				17 18	17 32				17 48	18 02
Balcombe	d			16 37										17 37					
Three Bridges 4	d		16 27	16 42				16 57	17 12				17 27	17 42				17 57	18 12
Gatwick Airport 10 ✈	d		16 32	16 46				17 02	17 16				17 32	17 46				18 02	18 16
Redhill	d																		
East Croydon 🚋	d		16 47	17 01				17 17	17 32				17 47	18 01				18 17	18 32
Sutton (Surrey) 4	d	16 07			16 08		16 37			16 38		17 07			17 08		17 37		
West Sutton	d	16 10					16 40					17 10					17 40		
Sutton Common	d	16 12					16 42					17 12					17 42		
St Helier	d	16 15					16 45					17 15					17 45		
Morden South	d	16 17					16 47					17 17					17 47		
South Merton	d	16 19					16 49					17 19					17 49		
Wimbledon Chase	d	16 21					16 51					17 21					17 51		
Wimbledon 6 🚋	d	16 30					17 00					17 30					18 00		
Haydons Road	d	16 32					17 02					17 32					18 02		
Tooting	d	16 35					17 05					17 35					18 05		
Carshalton	d				16 11					16 41					17 11				
Hackbridge	d				16 13					16 43					17 13				
Mitcham Junction	d				16 16					16 46					17 16				
Mitcham Eastfields	d				16 19					16 49					17 19				
Streatham 4	d	16 40			16 23		17 10			16 53		17 40			17 23		18 10		
Tulse Hill 3	d	16 47			16 27		17 17			16 57		17 47			17 27		18 17		
London Bridge 4 ⊖	a	17 00	17 02	17 17			17 30	17 32	17 47			18 00	18 02	18 17			18 30	18 32	18 47
	d																		
Sevenoaks 4	d					16 25					16 55					17 25			
Bat & Ball	d					16 28					16 58					17 28			
Otford 4	d					16 31					17 01					17 31			
Shoreham (Kent)	d					16 34					17 04					17 34			
Eynsford	d					16 38					17 08					17 38			
Swanley 4	d					16 43					17 13					17 43			
St Mary Cray 4	d					16 47					17 17					17 47			
Bickley	d					16 51					17 21					17 51			
Bromley South	d					16 54					17 24					17 54			
Shortlands 4	d					16 57					17 27					17 57			
Ravensbourne	d					16 59					17 29					17 59			
Beckenham Hill	d					17 01					17 31					18 01			
Bellingham	d					17 03					17 33					18 03			
Catford	d					17 06					17 36					18 06			
Crofton Park	d					17 08					17 38					18 08			
Nunhead 4	d					17 11					17 41					18 11			
Peckham Rye 4	d					17 13					17 43					18 13			
Denmark Hill 4	d					17a16					17a46					18a16			
Herne Hill 4	d				16a31					17a01					17a31				
Loughborough Jn.	d																		
Elephant & Castle	d																		
London Blackfriars 3 ⊖	a																		
	d																		
City Thameslink 3	d																		
Farringdon 3 ⊖	d																		
St Pancras International 15 ⊖	a																		

A From Epsom to London Victoria

B To London Victoria

Please refer to separate pages within this table for services operating between London and Bedford

At weekends please use local bus and tube services to travel to/from St Pancras International and London Bridge when no trains are operating. See local publicity for details of alternative routes and services that are available across central London

Table 52

Saturdays

Brighton, Gatwick Airport - South London

Network Diagram - see first Page of Table 52

		FC	SE	FC	FC 1	FC 1	FC	SE	FC	FC 1	FC 1	FC	SE	FC	FC 1	FC 1	FC	SE
			A					A					A					A
Brighton 10	d				18 04	18 07				18 34	18 37				19 04	19 07		
Preston Park	d					18 11					18 41					19 11		
Hassocks 4	d					18 17					18 47					19 17		
Burgess Hill 4	d					18 21					18 51					19 21		
Wivelsfield 4	d					18 23					18 53					19 23		
Haywards Heath 3	d				18 18	18 32				18 48	19 02				19 18	19 32		
Balcombe	d					18 37										19 37		
Three Bridges 4	d				18 27	18 42				18 57	19 12				19 27	19 42		
Gatwick Airport 10 ✈	d				18 32	18 46				19 02	19 16				19 32	19 46		
Redhill	d																	
East Croydon 🚋	d				18 47	19 01				19 17	19 32				19 47	20 01		
Sutton (Surrey) 4	d	17 38		18 07			18 08		18 37			18 38		19 07			19 08	
West Sutton	d			18 10					18 40					19 10				
Sutton Common	d			18 12					18 42					19 12				
St Helier	d			18 15					18 45					19 15				
Morden South	d			18 17					18 47					19 17				
South Merton	d			18 19					18 49					19 19				
Wimbledon Chase	d			18 21					18 51					19 21				
Wimbledon 6 🚋	d			18 30					19 00					19 30				
Haydons Road	d			18 32					19 02					19 32				
Tooting	d			18 35					19 05					19 35				
Carshalton	d	17 41					18 11					18 41					19 11	
Hackbridge	d	17 43					18 13					18 43					19 13	
Mitcham Junction	d	17 46					18 16					18 46					19 16	
Mitcham Eastfields	d	17 49					18 19					18 49					19 19	
Streatham 4	d	17 53		18 40			18 23		19 10			18 53		19 40			19 23	
Tulse Hill 3	d	17 57		18 47			18 27		19 17			18 57		19 47			19 27	
London Bridge 4 ⊖	a			19 00	19 02	19 17			19 30	19 32	19 47			20 00	20 02	20 17		
	d																	
Sevenoaks 4	d		17 55					18 25					18 55					19 25
Bat & Ball	d		17 58					18 28					18 58					19 28
Otford 4	d		18 01					18 31					19 01					19 31
Shoreham (Kent)	d		18 04					18 34					19 04					19 34
Eynsford	d		18 08					18 38					19 08					19 38
Swanley 4	d		18 13					18 43					19 13					19 43
St Mary Cray 4	d		18 17					18 47					19 17					19 47
Bickley	d		18 21					18 51					19 21					19 51
Bromley South	d		18 24					18 54					19 24					19 54
Shortlands 4	d		18 27					18 57					19 27					19 57
Ravensbourne	d		18 29					18 59					19 29					19 59
Beckenham Hill	d		18 31					19 01					19 31					20 01
Bellingham	d		18 33					19 03					19 33					20 03
Catford	d		18 36					19 06					19 36					20 06
Crofton Park	d		18 38					19 08					19 38					20 08
Nunhead 4	d		18 41					19 11					19 41					20 11
Peckham Rye 4	d		18 43					19 13					19 43					20 13
Denmark Hill 4	d		18a46					19a16					19a46					20a16
Herne Hill 4	d	18a01					18a31					19a01					19a31	
Loughborough Jn.	d																	
Elephant & Castle	d																	
London Blackfriars 3 ⊖	a																	
	d																	
City Thameslink 3	d																	
Farringdon 3 ⊖	d																	
St Pancras International 15 ⊖	a																	

A To London Victoria

B From Epsom to London Victoria

Please refer to separate pages within this table for services operating between London and Bedford

At weekends please use local bus and tube services to travel to/from St Pancras International and London Bridge when no trains are operating. See local publicity for details of alternative routes and services that are available across central London

Brighton, Gatwick Airport - South London

Network Diagram - see first Page of Table 52

		FC	FC 1	FC 1	SE B	FC	FC 1	FC 1	SE B	FC	FC 1	FC 1	SE B	FC	FC 1	SE B	FC
Brighton 10	d		19 34	19 37			20 04	20 07			20 34	20 37			21 07		
Preston Park	d			19 41				20 11				20 41			21 11		
Hassocks 4	d			19 47				20 17				20 47			21 17		
Burgess Hill 4	d			19 51				20 21				20 51			21 21		
Wivelsfield 4	d			19 53				20 23				20 53			21 23		
Haywards Heath 3	d		19 48	20 02			20 18	20 32			20 48	21 02			21 32		
Balcombe	d							20 37							21 37		
Three Bridges 4	d		19 57	20 12			20 26	20 42			20 57	21 12			21 42		
Gatwick Airport 10 ✈	d		20 02	20 16			20 31	20 46			21 02	21 16			21 46		
Redhill	d																
East Croydon ⇌	d		20 17	20 32			20 47	21 01			21 17	21 32			22 01		
Sutton (Surrey) 4	d	19 37				20 08				20 37				21 07			21 37
West Sutton	d	19 40				20 11				20 40				21 10			21 40
Sutton Common	d	19 42				20 13				20 42				21 12			21 42
St Helier	d	19 45				20 16				20 45				21 15			21 45
Morden South	d	19 47				20 18				20 47				21 17			21 47
South Merton	d	19 49				20 20				20 49				21 19			21 49
Wimbledon Chase	d	19 51				20 22				20 51				21 21			21 51
Wimbledon 6 ⇌	d	20 00				20 30				21 00				21 30			22 00
Haydons Road	d	20 02				20 32				21 02				21 32			22 02
Tooting	d	20 05				20 35				21 05				21 35			22 05
Carshalton	d																
Hackbridge	d																
Mitcham Junction	d																
Mitcham Eastfields	d																
Streatham 4	d	20 10				20 40				21 10				21 40			22 10
Tulse Hill 3	d	20 17				20 47				21 17				21 47			22 17
London Bridge 4 ⊖	a	20 30	20 32	20 47		21 00	21 02	21 17		21 30	21 32	21 47		22 00	22 17		22 30
	d																
Sevenoaks 4	d				19 55				20 25				20 55			21 25	
Bat & Ball	d				19 58				20 28				20 58			21 28	
Otford 4	d				20 01				20 31				21 01			21 31	
Shoreham (Kent)	d				20 04				20 34				21 04			21 34	
Eynsford	d				20 08				20 38				21 08			21 38	
Swanley 4	d				20 13				20 43				21 13			21 43	
St Mary Cray 4	d				20 17				20 47				21 17			21 47	
Bickley	d				20 21				20 51				21 21			21 51	
Bromley South	d				20 24				20 54				21 24			21 54	
Shortlands 4	d				20 27				20 57				21 27			21 57	
Ravensbourne	d				20 29				20 59				21 29			21 59	
Beckenham Hill	d				20 31				21 01				21 31			22 01	
Bellingham	d				20 33				21 03				21 33			22 03	
Catford	d				20 36				21 06				21 36			22 06	
Crofton Park	d				20 38				21 08				21 38			22 08	
Nunhead 4	d				20 41				21 11				21 41			22 11	
Peckham Rye 4	d				20 43				21 13				21 43			22 13	
Denmark Hill 4	d				20a46				21a16				21a46			22a16	
Herne Hill 4	d																
Loughborough Jn.	d																
Elephant & Castle	d																
London Blackfriars 3 ⊖	a																
	d																
City Thameslink 3	d																
Farringdon 3 ⊖	d																
St Pancras International 15 ⊖	a																

A To London Victoria
B To London Victoria
C From Epsom to London Victoria

Please refer to separate pages within this table for services operating between London and Bedford

At weekends please use local bus and tube services to travel to/from St Pancras International and London Bridge when no trains are operating. See local publicity for details of alternative routes and services that are available across central London

Brighton, Gatwick Airport - South London

Network Diagram - see first Page of Table 52

		FC 1	SE A	FC	FC 1	SE A	FC 1	FC 1	FC 1
Brighton 10	d	21 37			22 07		22 33	23 11	23 37
Preston Park	d	21 41			22 11		22 37		23 41
Hassocks 4	d	21 47			22 17		22 43	23 20	23 47
Burgess Hill 4	d	21 51			22 21		22 47	23 23	23 51
Wivelsfield 4	d	21 53			22 23		22 49		23 53
Haywards Heath 3	d	22 02			22 32		22 54	23 29	23 59
Balcombe	d				22 37		22 59		00 04
Three Bridges 4	d	22 12			22 42		23b12	23 38	00 10
Gatwick Airport 10 ✈	d	22 16			22 46		23 16	23 43	00 15
Redhill	d								00 23
East Croydon ⇌	d	22 32			23 01		23 32	00 04	00 36
Sutton (Surrey) 4	d			22 07					
West Sutton	d			22 10					
Sutton Common	d			22 12					
St Helier	d			22 15					
Morden South	d			22 17					
South Merton	d			22 19					
Wimbledon Chase	d			22 21					
Wimbledon 6 ⇌	d			22 30					
Haydons Road	d			22 32					
Tooting	d			22 35					
Carshalton	d								
Hackbridge	d								
Mitcham Junction	d								
Mitcham Eastfields	d								
Streatham 4	d			22 40					
Tulse Hill 3	d			22 47					
London Bridge 4 ⊖	a	22 47		23 00	23 17		23 47	00 19	00 52
	d								
Sevenoaks 4	d		21 55			22 25			
Bat & Ball	d		21 58			22 28			
Otford 4	d		22 01			22 31			
Shoreham (Kent)	d		22 04			22 34			
Eynsford	d		22 08			22 38			
Swanley 4	d		22 13			22 43			
St Mary Cray 4	d		22 17			22 47			
Bickley	d		22 21			22 51			
Bromley South	d		22 24			22 54			
Shortlands 4	d		22 27			22 57			
Ravensbourne	d		22 29			22 59			
Beckenham Hill	d		22 31			23 01			
Bellingham	d		22 33			23 03			
Catford	d		22 36			23 06			
Crofton Park	d		22 38			23 08			
Nunhead 4	d		22 41			23 11			
Peckham Rye 4	d		22 43			23 13			
Denmark Hill 4	d		22a46			23a16			
Herne Hill 4	d								
Loughborough Jn.	d								
Elephant & Castle	d								
London Blackfriars 3 ⊖	a								
	d								
City Thameslink 3	d								
Farringdon 3 ⊖	d								
St Pancras International 15 ⊖	a								

A To London Victoria
B From Epsom to London Victoria
C To London Victoria

Please refer to separate pages within this table for services operating between London and Bedford

At weekends please use local bus and tube services to travel to/from St Pancras International and London Bridge when no trains are operating. See local publicity for details of alternative routes and services that are available across central London

Table 52

Sundays

Brighton, Gatwick Airport - South London

Network Diagram - see first Page of Table 52

		FC 1 A	FC 1 A	FC (bus)	FC (bus)	FC 1	SE B	FC (bus)	FC 1	FC 1	FC 1	SE B	FC 1	SE B	SE F	FC 1
Brighton 10	d	23p11	23p37			05 44			06 11	06 44	07 14		07 44			08 14
Preston Park	d		23p41													
Hassocks 4	d	23p20	23p47			05 52			06 20	06 53	07 23		07 53			08 23
Burgess Hill 4	d	23p23	23p51			05 56			06 25	06 56	07 26		07 56			08 26
Wivelsfield 4	d		23p53													
Haywards Heath 3	d	23p29	23p59			06 01			06 31	07 02	07 32		08 02			08 32
Balcombe	d		00 04													
Three Bridges 4	d	23p38	00 10			06 11			06 40	07 10	07 40		08 10			08 40
Gatwick Airport 10	d	23p43	00 15			06 16			06 45	07 15	07 45		08 15			08 45
Redhill	d		00 23													
East Croydon	d	00 04	00 36			06 32			07 02	07 32	08 02		08 32			09 02
Sutton (Surrey) 4	d															
West Sutton	d															
Sutton Common	d															
St Helier	d															
Morden South	d															
South Merton	d															
Wimbledon Chase	d															
Wimbledon 6	d															
Haydons Road	d															
Tooting	d															
Carshalton	d															
Hackbridge	d															
Mitcham Junction	d															
Mitcham Eastfields	d															
Streatham 4	d															
Tulse Hill 3	d															
London Bridge 4	a	00 19	00 52			06 59			07 15	07 45	08 15		08 45			09 15
	d			00 57	06 05			07 09								
Sevenoaks 4	d														07 54	
Bat & Ball	d														07 57	
Otford 4	d														08 00	
Shoreham (Kent)	d														08 03	
Eynsford	d														08 07	
Swanley 4	d														08 12	
St Mary Cray 4	d														08 16	
Bickley	d						06 50					07 20		07 50	08 20	
Bromley South	d						06 53					07 23		07 53	08 23	
Shortlands 4	d						06 56					07 26		07 56	08 26	
Ravensbourne	d						06 58					07 28		07 58	08 28	
Beckenham Hill	d						07 00					07 30		08 00	08 30	
Bellingham	d						07 02					07 32		08 02	08 32	
Catford	d						07 05					07 35		08 05	08 35	
Crofton Park	d						07 07					07 37		08 07	08 37	
Nunhead 4	d						07 10					07 40		08 10	08 40	
Peckham Rye 4	d						07 12					07 42		08 12	08 42	
Denmark Hill 4	d						07a15					07a45		08a15	08a45	
Herne Hill 4	d															
Loughborough Jn.	d															
Elephant & Castle	d															
London Blackfriars 3	a			01 12	06 20			07 24								
	d			01 12	06 20			07 24								
City Thameslink 3	d															
Farringdon 3	d							07 34								
St Pancras International 15	a			01 27	06 35			07 39								

A not 11 December
B From Orpington to London Victoria
C To London Victoria
D From Epsom to London Victoria
E From Dorking to London Victoria
F To London Victoria

Please refer to separate pages within this table for services operating between London and Bedford

At weekends please use local bus and tube services to travel to/from St Pancras International and London Bridge when no trains are operating. See local publicity for details of alternative routes and services that are available across central London

Table 52

Sundays

Brighton, Gatwick Airport - South London

Network Diagram - see first Page of Table 52

		SE A	FC 1	SE A	FC 1	SE A	FC 1	SE A	SE A	FC	FC 1
Brighton 10	d		08 44		09 14		09 44				10 14
Preston Park	d										
Hassocks 4	d		08 53		09 23		09 53				10 23
Burgess Hill 4	d		08 56		09 26		09 56				10 26
Wivelsfield 4	d										
Haywards Heath 3	d		09 02		09 32		10 02				10 32
Balcombe	d										
Three Bridges 4	d		09 10		09 40		10 10				10 40
Gatwick Airport 10	d		09 15		09 45		10 15				10 45
Redhill	d										
East Croydon	d		09 32		10 02		10 32				11 02
Sutton (Surrey) 4	d									10 28	
West Sutton	d									10 31	
Sutton Common	d									10 33	
St Helier	d									10 36	
Morden South	d									10 38	
South Merton	d									10 40	
Wimbledon Chase	d									10 42	
Wimbledon 6	d									10 45	
Haydons Road	d									10 48	
Tooting	d									10 51	
Carshalton	d										
Hackbridge	d										
Mitcham Junction	d										
Mitcham Eastfields	d										
Streatham 4	d									10 55	
Tulse Hill 3	d									10 59	
London Bridge 4	a		09 45		10 15		10 45			11 10	11 15
	d										
Sevenoaks 4	d	08 24		08 54		09 24		09 54	10 24		
Bat & Ball	d	08 27		08 57		09 27		09 57	10 27		
Otford 4	d	08 30		09 00		09 30		10 00	10 30		
Shoreham (Kent)	d	08 33		09 03		09 33		10 03	10 33		
Eynsford	d	08 37		09 07		09 37		10 07	10 37		
Swanley 4	d	08 42		09 12		09 42		10 12	10 42		
St Mary Cray 4	d	08 46		09 16		09 46		10 16	10 46		
Bickley	d	08 50		09 20		09 50		10 20	10 50		
Bromley South	d	08 53		09 23		09 53		10 23	10 53		
Shortlands 4	d	08 56		09 26		09 56		10 26	10 56		
Ravensbourne	d	08 58		09 28		09 58		10 28	10 58		
Beckenham Hill	d	09 00		09 30		10 00		10 30	11 00		
Bellingham	d	09 02		09 32		10 02		10 32	11 02		
Catford	d	09 05		09 35		10 05		10 35	11 05		
Crofton Park	d	09 07		09 37		10 07		10 37	11 07		
Nunhead 4	d	09 10		09 40		10 10		10 40	11 10		
Peckham Rye 4	d	09 12		09 42		10 12		10 42	11 12		
Denmark Hill 4	d	09a15		09a45		10a15		10a45	11a15		
Herne Hill 4	d										
Loughborough Jn.	d										
Elephant & Castle	d										
London Blackfriars 3	a										
	d										
City Thameslink 3	d										
Farringdon 3	d										
St Pancras International 15	a										

A To London Victoria
B From Epsom to London Victoria
C From Dorking to London Victoria
D To London Victoria

Please refer to separate pages within this table for services operating between London and Bedford

At weekends please use local bus and tube services to travel to/from St Pancras International and London Bridge when no trains are operating. See local publicity for details of alternative routes and services that are available across central London

Table 52

Sundays

Brighton, Gatwick Airport - South London

Network Diagram - see first Page of Table 52

		SE	FC	FC	SE	FC	FC	SE	FC	FC	SE	FC	FC
		A			A			A			A		
Brighton	d			10 44			11 14			11 44			12 14
Preston Park	d												
Hassocks	d			10 53			11 23			11 53			12 23
Burgess Hill	d			10 56			11 26			11 56			12 26
Wivelsfield	d												
Haywards Heath	d			11 02			11 32			12 02			12 32
Balcombe	d												
Three Bridges	d			11 10			11 40			12 10			12 40
Gatwick Airport ✈	d			11 15			11 45			12 15			12 45
Redhill	d												
East Croydon	d			11 32			12 02			12 32			13 02
Sutton (Surrey)	d		10 58			11 28			11 58			12 28	
West Sutton	d		11 01			11 31			12 01			12 31	
Sutton Common	d		11 03			11 33			12 03			12 33	
St Helier	d		11 06			11 36			12 06			12 36	
Morden South	d		11 08			11 38			12 08			12 38	
South Merton	d		11 10			11 40			12 10			12 40	
Wimbledon Chase	d		11 12			11 42			12 12			12 42	
Wimbledon	d		11 15			11 45			12 15			12 45	
Haydons Road	d		11 18			11 48			12 18			12 48	
Tooting	d		11 21			11 51			12 21			12 51	
Carshalton	d												
Hackbridge	d												
Mitcham Junction	d												
Mitcham Eastfields	d												
Streatham	d		11 25			11 55			12 25			12 55	
Tulse Hill	d		11 29			11 59			12 29			12 59	
London Bridge ⊖	a		11 40	11 45		12 10	12 15		12 40	12 45		13 10	13 15
	d												
Sevenoaks	d	10 54			11 24			11 54			12 24		
Bat & Ball	d	10 57			11 27			11 57			12 27		
Otford	d	11 00			11 30			12 00			12 30		
Shoreham (Kent)	d	11 03			11 33			12 03			12 33		
Eynsford	d	11 07			11 37			12 07			12 37		
Swanley	d	11 12			11 42			12 12			12 42		
St Mary Cray	d	11 16			11 46			12 16			12 46		
Bickley	d	11 20			11 50			12 20			12 50		
Bromley South	d	11 23			11 53			12 23			12 53		
Shortlands	d	11 26			11 56			12 26			12 56		
Ravensbourne	d	11 28			11 58			12 28			12 58		
Beckenham Hill	d	11 30			12 00			12 30			13 00		
Bellingham	d	11 32			12 02			12 32			13 02		
Catford	d	11 35			12 05			12 35			13 05		
Crofton Park	d	11 37			12 07			12 37			13 07		
Nunhead	d	11 40			12 10			12 40			13 10		
Peckham Rye	d	11 42			12 12			12 42			13 12		
Denmark Hill	d	11a45			12a15			12a45			13a15		
Herne Hill	d												
Loughborough Jn.	d												
Elephant & Castle	d												
London Blackfriars ⊖	a												
	d												
City Thameslink	d												
Farringdon ⊖	d												
St Pancras International ⊖	a												

A To London Victoria
B From Epsom to London Victoria
C To London Victoria
D From Dorking to London Victoria

Please refer to separate pages within this table for services operating between London and Bedford

At weekends please use local bus and tube services to travel to/from St Pancras International and London Bridge when no trains are operating. See local publicity for details of alternative routes and services that are available across central London

Table 52

Sundays

Brighton, Gatwick Airport - South London

Network Diagram - see first Page of Table 52

		SE	FC	FC	SE	FC	FC	SE	FC	FC	SE	FC	FC
		B			B			B			B		
Brighton	d			12 44			13 14			13 44			14 14
Preston Park	d												
Hassocks	d			12 53			13 23			13 53			14 23
Burgess Hill	d			12 56			13 26			13 56			14 26
Wivelsfield	d												
Haywards Heath	d			13 02			13 32			14 02			14 32
Balcombe	d												
Three Bridges	d			13 10			13 40			14 10			14 40
Gatwick Airport ✈	d			13 15			13 45			14 15			14 45
Redhill	d												
East Croydon	d			13 32			14 02			14 32			15 02
Sutton (Surrey)	d		12 58			13 28			13 58			14 28	
West Sutton	d		13 01			13 31			14 01			14 31	
Sutton Common	d		13 03			13 33			14 03			14 33	
St Helier	d		13 06			13 36			14 06			14 36	
Morden South	d		13 08			13 38			14 08			14 38	
South Merton	d		13 10			13 40			14 10			14 40	
Wimbledon Chase	d		13 12			13 42			14 12			14 42	
Wimbledon	d		13 15			13 45			14 15			14 45	
Haydons Road	d		13 18			13 48			14 18			14 48	
Tooting	d		13 21			13 51			14 21			14 51	
Carshalton	d												
Hackbridge	d												
Mitcham Junction	d												
Mitcham Eastfields	d												
Streatham	d		13 25			13 55			14 25			14 55	
Tulse Hill	d		13 29			13 59			14 29			14 59	
London Bridge ⊖	a		13 40	13 45		14 10	14 15		14 40	14 45		15 10	15 15
	d												
Sevenoaks	d	12 54			13 24			13 54			14 24		
Bat & Ball	d	12 57			13 27			13 57			14 27		
Otford	d	13 00			13 30			14 00			14 30		
Shoreham (Kent)	d	13 03			13 33			14 03			14 33		
Eynsford	d	13 07			13 37			14 07			14 37		
Swanley	d	13 12			13 42			14 12			14 42		
St Mary Cray	d	13 16			13 46			14 16			14 46		
Bickley	d	13 20			13 50			14 20			14 50		
Bromley South	d	13 23			13 53			14 23			14 53		
Shortlands	d	13 26			13 56			14 26			14 56		
Ravensbourne	d	13 28			13 58			14 28			14 58		
Beckenham Hill	d	13 30			14 00			14 30			15 00		
Bellingham	d	13 32			14 02			14 32			15 02		
Catford	d	13 35			14 05			14 35			15 05		
Crofton Park	d	13 37			14 07			14 37			15 07		
Nunhead	d	13 40			14 10			14 40			15 10		
Peckham Rye	d	13 42			14 12			14 42			15 12		
Denmark Hill	d	13a45			14a15			14a45			15a15		
Herne Hill	d												
Loughborough Jn.	d												
Elephant & Castle	d												
London Blackfriars ⊖	a												
	d												
City Thameslink	d												
Farringdon ⊖	d												
St Pancras International ⊖	a												

A From Dorking to London Victoria
B To London Victoria
C From Epsom to London Victoria
D To London Victoria

Please refer to separate pages within this table for services operating between London and Bedford

At weekends please use local bus and tube services to travel to/from St Pancras International and London Bridge when no trains are operating. See local publicity for details of alternative routes and services that are available across central London

Table 52

Sundays

Brighton, Gatwick Airport - South London

Network Diagram - see first Page of Table 52

		SE	FC	FC	SE	FC	FC	SE	FC	FC	SE	FC
		B		1	B		1	B		1	B	
Brighton 10	d			14 44			15 14			15 44		
Preston Park	d											
Hassocks 4	d			14 53			15 23			15 53		
Burgess Hill 4	d			14 56			15 26			15 56		
Wivelsfield 4	d											
Haywards Heath 3	d			15 02			15 32			16 02		
Balcombe	d											
Three Bridges 4	d			15 10			15 40			16 10		
Gatwick Airport 10 ✈	d			15 15			15 45			16 15		
Redhill	d											
East Croydon ⇌	d			15 32			16 02			16 32		
Sutton (Surrey) 4	d		14 58			15 28			15 58			16 28
West Sutton	d		15 01			15 31			16 01			16 31
Sutton Common	d		15 03			15 33			16 03			16 33
St Helier	d		15 06			15 36			16 06			16 36
Morden South	d		15 08			15 38			16 08			16 38
South Merton	d		15 10			15 40			16 10			16 40
Wimbledon Chase	d		15 12			15 42			16 12			16 42
Wimbledon 6 ⇌	d		15 15			15 45			16 15			16 45
Haydons Road	d		15 18			15 48			16 18			16 48
Tooting	d		15 21			15 51			16 21			16 51
Carshalton	d											
Hackbridge	d											
Mitcham Junction	d											
Mitcham Eastfields	d											
Streatham 4	d		15 25			15 55			16 25			16 55
Tulse Hill 3	d		15 29			15 59			16 29			16 59
London Bridge 4 ⊖	a		15 40	15 45		16 10	16 15		16 40	16 45		17 10
	d											
Sevenoaks 4	d	14 54			15 24			15 54			16 24	
Bat & Ball	d	14 57			15 27			15 57			16 27	
Otford 4	d	15 00			15 30			16 00			16 30	
Shoreham (Kent)	d	15 03			15 33			16 03			16 33	
Eynsford	d	15 07			15 37			16 07			16 37	
Swanley 4	d	15 12			15 42			16 12			16 42	
St Mary Cray 4	d	15 16			15 46			16 16			16 46	
Bickley	d	15 20			15 50			16 20			16 50	
Bromley South	d	15 23			15 53			16 23			16 53	
Shortlands 4	d	15 26			15 56			16 26			16 56	
Ravensbourne	d	15 28			15 58			16 28			16 58	
Beckenham Hill	d	15 30			16 00			16 30			17 00	
Bellingham	d	15 32			16 02			16 32			17 02	
Catford	d	15 35			16 05			16 35			17 05	
Crofton Park	d	15 37			16 07			16 37			17 07	
Nunhead 4	d	15 40			16 10			16 40			17 10	
Peckham Rye 4	d	15 42			16 12			16 42			17 12	
Denmark Hill 4	d	15a45			16a15			16a45			17a15	
Herne Hill 4	d											
Loughborough Jn.	d											
Elephant & Castle	d											
London Blackfriars 3 ⊖	a											
	d											
City Thameslink 3	d											
Farringdon 3 ⊖	d											
St Pancras International 15 ⊖	a											

A From Dorking to London Victoria
B To London Victoria
C From Epsom to London Victoria
D To London Victoria

Please refer to separate pages within this table for services operating between London and Bedford

At weekends please use local bus and tube services to travel to/from St Pancras International and London Bridge when no trains are operating. See local publicity for details of alternative routes and services that are available across central London

Table 52

Sundays

Brighton, Gatwick Airport - South London

Network Diagram - see first Page of Table 52

		FC	SE	FC	FC	SE	FC	FC	SE	FC	FC	SE	FC
		1	B		1	B		1	B		1	B	
Brighton 10	d	16 14			16 44			17 14			17 44		
Preston Park	d												
Hassocks 4	d	16 23			16 53			17 23			17 53		
Burgess Hill 4	d	16 26			16 56			17 26			17 56		
Wivelsfield 4	d												
Haywards Heath 3	d	16 32			17 02			17 32			18 02		
Balcombe	d												
Three Bridges 4	d	16 40			17 10			17 40			18 10		
Gatwick Airport 10 ✈	d	16 45			17 15			17 45			18 15		
Redhill	d												
East Croydon ⇌	d	17 02			17 32			18 02			18 32		
Sutton (Surrey) 4	d			16 58			17 28			17 58			18 28
West Sutton	d			17 01			17 31			18 01			18 31
Sutton Common	d			17 03			17 33			18 03			18 33
St Helier	d			17 06			17 36			18 06			18 36
Morden South	d			17 08			17 38			18 08			18 38
South Merton	d			17 10			17 40			18 10			18 40
Wimbledon Chase	d			17 12			17 42			18 12			18 42
Wimbledon 6 ⇌	d			17 15			17 45			18 15			18 45
Haydons Road	d			17 18			17 48			18 18			18 48
Tooting	d			17 21			17 51			18 21			18 51
Carshalton	d												
Hackbridge	d												
Mitcham Junction	d												
Mitcham Eastfields	d												
Streatham 4	d			17 25			17 55			18 25			18 55
Tulse Hill 3	d			17 29			17 59			18 29			18 59
London Bridge 4 ⊖	a	17 15		17 40	17 45		18 10	18 15		18 40	18 45		19 10
	d												
Sevenoaks 4	d		16 54			17 24			17 54			18 24	
Bat & Ball	d		16 57			17 27			17 57			18 27	
Otford 4	d		17 00			17 30			18 00			18 30	
Shoreham (Kent)	d		17 03			17 33			18 03			18 33	
Eynsford	d		17 07			17 37			18 07			18 37	
Swanley 4	d		17 12			17 42			18 12			18 42	
St Mary Cray 4	d		17 16			17 46			18 16			18 46	
Bickley	d		17 20			17 50			18 20			18 50	
Bromley South	d		17 23			17 53			18 23			18 53	
Shortlands 4	d		17 26			17 56			18 26			18 56	
Ravensbourne	d		17 28			17 58			18 28			18 58	
Beckenham Hill	d		17 30			18 00			18 30			19 00	
Bellingham	d		17 32			18 02			18 32			19 02	
Catford	d		17 35			18 05			18 35			19 05	
Crofton Park	d		17 37			18 07			18 37			19 07	
Nunhead 4	d		17 40			18 10			18 40			19 10	
Peckham Rye 4	d		17 42			18 12			18 42			19 12	
Denmark Hill 4	d		17a45			18a15			18a45			19a15	
Herne Hill 4	d												
Loughborough Jn.	d												
Elephant & Castle	d												
London Blackfriars 3 ⊖	a												
	d												
City Thameslink 3	d												
Farringdon 3 ⊖	d												
St Pancras International 15 ⊖	a												

A From Dorking to London Victoria
B To London Victoria
C From Epsom to London Victoria
D To London Victoria

Please refer to separate pages within this table for services operating between London and Bedford

At weekends please use local bus and tube services to travel to/from St Pancras International and London Bridge when no trains are operating. See local publicity for details of alternative routes and services that are available across central London

Table 52

Sundays

Brighton, Gatwick Airport - South London

Network Diagram - see first Page of Table 52

		FC 1	SE B	FC	FC 1	SE B	FC	FC 1	SE B	FC	FC 1	SE B	FC	FC 1	SE B
Brighton 10	d	18 14			18 44			19 14			19 44			20 14	
Preston Park	d														
Hassocks 4	d	18 23			18 53			19 23			19 53			20 23	
Burgess Hill 4	d	18 26			18 56			19 26			19 56			20 26	
Wivelsfield 4	d														
Haywards Heath 3	d	18 32			19 02			19 32			20 02			20 32	
Balcombe	d														
Three Bridges 4	d	18 40			19 10			19 40			20 10			20 40	
Gatwick Airport 10 ✈	d	18 45			19 15			19 45			20 15			20 45	
Redhill	d														
East Croydon	d	19 02			19 32			20 02			20 32			21 02	
Sutton (Surrey) 4	d			18 58			19 28			19 58			20 28		
West Sutton	d			19 01			19 31			20 01			20 31		
Sutton Common	d			19 03			19 33			20 03			20 33		
St Helier	d			19 06			19 36			20 06			20 36		
Morden South	d			19 08			19 38			20 08			20 38		
South Merton	d			19 10			19 40			20 10			20 40		
Wimbledon Chase	d			19 12			19 42			20 12			20 42		
Wimbledon 3	d			19 15			19 45			20 15			20 45		
Haydons Road	d			19 18			19 48			20 18			20 48		
Tooting	d			19 21			19 51			20 21			20 51		
Carshalton	d														
Hackbridge	d														
Mitcham Junction	d														
Mitcham Eastfields	d														
Streatham 4	d			19 25			19 55			20 25			20 55		
Tulse Hill 3	d			19 29			19 59			20 29			20 59		
London Bridge 4 ⊖	a	19 15		19 40	19 45		20 10	20 15		20 40	20 45		21 10	21 15	
	d														
Sevenoaks 4	d		18 54			19 24			19 54			20 24			20 54
Bat & Ball	d		18 57			19 27			19 57			20 27			20 57
Otford 4	d		19 00			19 30			20 00			20 30			21 00
Shoreham (Kent)	d		19 03			19 33			20 03			20 33			21 03
Eynsford	d		19 07			19 37			20 07			20 37			21 07
Swanley 4	d		19 12			19 42			20 12			20 42			21 12
St Mary Cray 4	d		19 16			19 46			20 16			20 46			21 16
Bickley	d		19 20			19 50			20 20			20 50			21 20
Bromley South	d		19 23			19 53			20 23			20 53			21 23
Shortlands 4	d		19 26			19 56			20 26			20 56			21 26
Ravensbourne	d		19 28			19 58			20 28			20 58			21 28
Beckenham Hill	d		19 30			20 00			20 30			21 00			21 30
Bellingham	d		19 32			20 02			20 32			21 02			21 32
Catford	d		19 35			20 05			20 35			21 05			21 35
Crofton Park	d		19 37			20 07			20 37			21 07			21 37
Nunhead 4	d		19 40			20 10			20 40			21 10			21 40
Peckham Rye 4	d		19 42			20 12			20 42			21 12			21 42
Denmark Hill 4	d		19a45			20a15			20a45			21a15			21a45
Herne Hill 4	d														
Loughborough Jn.	d														
Elephant & Castle	d														
London Blackfriars 3 ⊖	a														
	d														
City Thameslink 3	d														
Farringdon 3 ⊖	d														
St Pancras International 15 ⊖	a														

A From Dorking to London Victoria
B To London Victoria
C From Epsom to London Victoria
D To London Victoria

Please refer to separate pages within this table for services operating between London and Bedford

At weekends please use local bus and tube services to travel to/from St Pancras International and London Bridge when no trains are operating. See local publicity for details of alternative routes and services that are available across central London

Table 52

Sundays

Brighton, Gatwick Airport - South London

Network Diagram - see first Page of Table 52

		FC	FC 1	SE C	FC	FC 1	FC 1	SE C	FC 1	SE C	FC 1	SE C	FC 1	FC 1
Brighton 10	d		20 44			21 14	21 44		22 14		22 44		23 14	23 45
Preston Park	d													
Hassocks 4	d		20 53			21 23	21 53		22 23		22 53		23 23	23 53
Burgess Hill 4	d		20 56			21 26	21 56		22 26		22 56		23 26	23 57
Wivelsfield 4	d													
Haywards Heath 3	d		21 02			21 32	22 02		22 32		23 02		23 32	00 02
Balcombe	d													
Three Bridges 4	d		21 10			21 40	22 10		22 40		23 10		23 40	00 11
Gatwick Airport 10 ✈	d		21 15			21 45	22 15		22 45		23 15		23 45	00 16
Redhill	d													00 23
East Croydon	d		21 32			22 02	22 32		23 02		23 32		00 04	00 36
Sutton (Surrey) 4	d	20 58			21 28									
West Sutton	d	21 01			21 31									
Sutton Common	d	21 03			21 33									
St Helier	d	21 06			21 36									
Morden South	d	21 08			21 38									
South Merton	d	21 10			21 40									
Wimbledon Chase	d	21 12			21 42									
Wimbledon 3	d	21 15			21 45									
Haydons Road	d	21 18			21 48									
Tooting	d	21 21			21 51									
Carshalton	d													
Hackbridge	d													
Mitcham Junction	d													
Mitcham Eastfields	d													
Streatham 4	d	21 25			21 55									
Tulse Hill 3	d	21 29			21 59									
London Bridge 4 ⊖	a	21 40	21 45		22 10	22 15	22 45		23 15		23 45		00 19	00 52
	d													
Sevenoaks 4	d			21 24				21 54		22 24		22 54		
Bat & Ball	d			21 27				21 57		22 27		22 57		
Otford 4	d			21 30				22 00		22 30		23 00		
Shoreham (Kent)	d			21 33				22 03		22 33		23 03		
Eynsford	d			21 37				22 07		22 37		23 07		
Swanley 4	d			21 42				22 12		22 42		23 12		
St Mary Cray 4	d			21 46				22 16		22 46		23 16		
Bickley	d			21 50				22 20		22 50		23 20		
Bromley South	d			21 53				22 23		22 53		23 23		
Shortlands 4	d			21 56				22 26		22 56		23 26		
Ravensbourne	d			21 58				22 28		22 58		23 28		
Beckenham Hill	d			22 00				22 30		23 00		23 30		
Bellingham	d			22 02				22 32		23 02		23 32		
Catford	d			22 05				22 35		23 05		23 35		
Crofton Park	d			22 07				22 37		23 07		23 37		
Nunhead 4	d			22 10				22 40		23 10		23 40		
Peckham Rye 4	d			22 12				22 42		23 12		23 42		
Denmark Hill 4	d			22a15				22a45		23a15		23a45		
Herne Hill 4	d													
Loughborough Jn.	d													
Elephant & Castle	d													
London Blackfriars 3 ⊖	a													
	d													
City Thameslink 3	d													
Farringdon 3 ⊖	d													
St Pancras International 15 ⊖	a													

A To London Victoria
B From Dorking to London Victoria
C To London Victoria

Please refer to separate pages within this table for services operating between London and Bedford

At weekends please use local bus and tube services to travel to/from St Pancras International and London Bridge when no trains are operating. See local publicity for details of alternative routes and services that are available across central London

Route Diagram for Table 53

DM-7/09(2)
Design BAJS

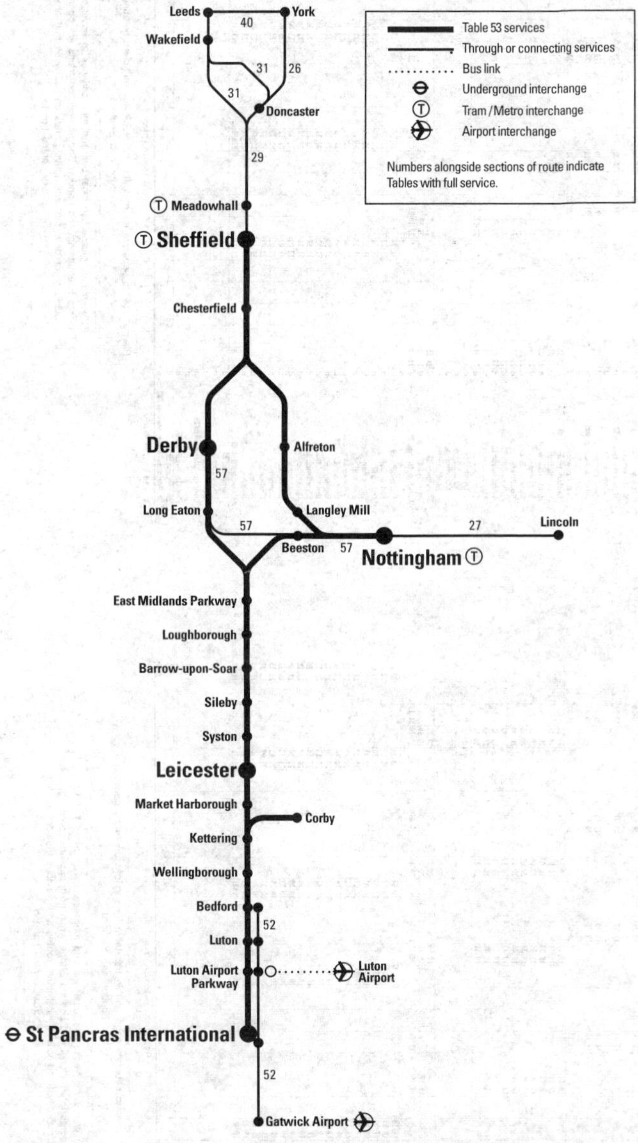

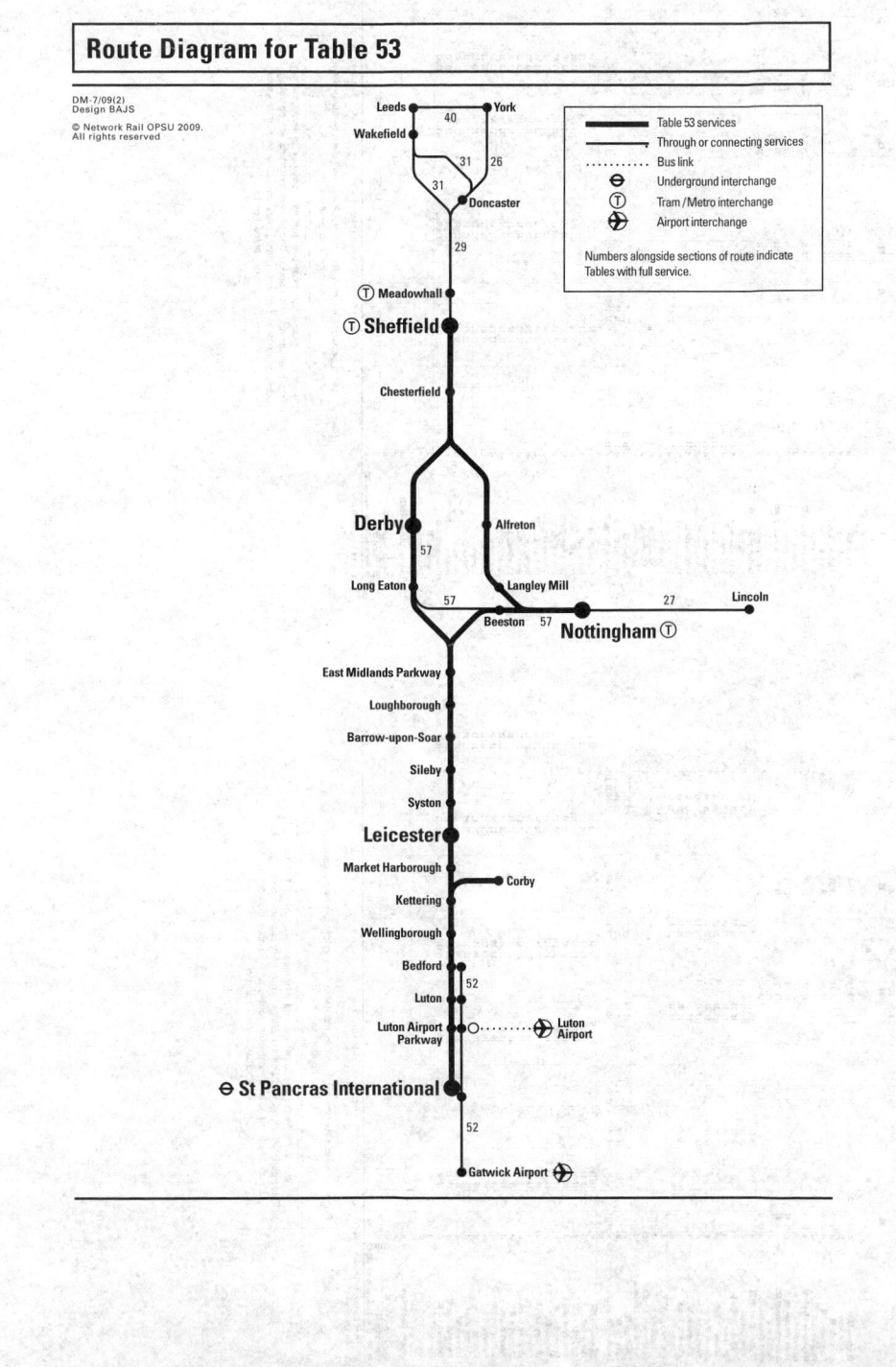

London - East Midlands - Sheffield

Route Diagram - see first Page of Table 53

Miles	Miles	Miles			NT MO	EM MO ◇1 A ☕	XC MO ◇1 B	EM ◇1 C ☕	EM MO ◇1 A ☕	EM ◇1 C ☕	EM MX ◇1 ☕	EM MX ◇1 ☕	EM MO ◇1 A ☕	EM ◇1 C ☕	EM MO ◇1 ☕	EM MX ◇1 ☕	EM MX ◇1 ☕	EM ◇ D	XC ◇1 E 🍴	NT	EM ◇1 ☕	XC ◇1 F 🍴	NT
0	0	—	**St Pancras International** ⊖	d		20p30		20p30	21p30	21p30	22p00	22p25	22p30	22p30	23p00	23p15	00 15						
29¼	29¼	—	Luton Airport Parkway 7 ✈	d		⌇		⌇	⌇	⌇		22p48	22p53	22p55	23p27		00 44						
30¼	30¼	—	Luton 10	d		20p54		20p56	21p54	21p56	22p24		⌇	⌇		23p46	00 47						
49¾	49¾	—	Bedford 7	d		21p11		21p19	22p10	22p17	22p40	23p04	23p17	23p18	23p50	00 12	01 12						
65¼	65¼	—	Wellingborough	d		21p24		21p32	22p23	22p31	22p53	23p17	23p31	23p32	00 04	00 25	01 33						
72	72	0	Kettering 4	a		21p31		21p39	22p30	22p37	23p00	23p25	23p37	23p38	00 10	00 41	01 43						
—	—	—		d		21p32		21p40	22p31	22p38	23p01	23p26	23p38	23p39	00 11	00 42	01 43						
—	—	7½	Corby	d		⌇		⌇	⌇	⌇			⌇	⌇									
—	—	21¾	Oakham	d		⌇		⌇	⌇	⌇			⌇	⌇									
—	—	33¼	Melton Mowbray	d		⌇		⌇	⌇	⌇			⌇	⌇									
83	83	—	**Market Harborough**	d		21p43		21p51	22p41	22p48	23p12	23p37	23p48	23p49	00 21	00 52	01 55						
99¼	99¼	48½	**Leicester**	a		22p04		22p12	23p00	23p08	23p29	23p53	00 07	00 08	00 42	01 05	02 10						
—	—	—		d		22p06		22p13	23p02	23p09	23p30	23p55	00 09	00 10	00 44	01 07							
103	103	—	Syston	d		⌇		⌇	⌇	⌇			⌇	⌇									
105¾	105¾	—	Sileby	d		⌇		⌇	⌇	⌇			⌇	⌇									
107¾	107¾	—	Barrow Upon Soar	d		⌇		⌇	⌇	⌇			⌇	⌇									
111¾	111¾	—	Loughborough	d		⌇		⌇	23p12	23p20	23p41	00 06	00 19	00 20	00 54	01 17							
117½	117½	—	East Midlands Parkway ✈	d		22p22		22p29	23p25	23p32	23p50	00 14	00 27	00 28	01 02	01 25							
123¼	—	—	Beeston	a		⌇		⌇	⌇	⌇	00 04		00 40	00 41		01 38							
126½	—	—	**Nottingham 8** 🚌	a		⌇		⌇	⌇	⌇	00 12		00 48	00 48		01 45							
—	—	—		d	21p30	⌇		⌇	⌇	⌇						01 52		05 20					06 23
—	—	—	Lincoln	a		⌇		⌇	⌇	⌇													
138½	—	—	Langley Mill	d	21p52	⌇		⌇	⌇	⌇													06 38
144¾	—	—	Alfreton	d	22p00	⌇		⌇	⌇	⌇													06 46
—	120½	—	Long Eaton	a		⌇		⌇	23p31	23p39													
—	128½	—	**Derby 6**	a		22p34		22p42	23p42	23p50		00 34			01 21	02 10							
—	—	—		d		22p36	22p44	22p51	23p44	23p51		00 35							05 56		06 20	06 34	
155	152¾	—	Chesterfield	d	22p13	22p58	23p05	23p13	00 03	00 11		00 58						05 49	06 15	06 26	06 42	06 54	06 58
167¼	165	—	**Sheffield 7** 🚌	a	22p36	23p13	23p20	23p28	00 17	00 24		01 13						06 15	06 28	06 46	07 13	07 07	07 18
—	—	—	Doncaster 7	a		⌇		⌇											06 57				
—	—	—	Wakefield Kirkgate 4	a	23p26	⌇		⌇												07 27			07 57
—	—	—	Wakefield Westgate 7	a		23p40		00 01														07 36	
—	—	—	Leeds 10	a	00 05	00 01	00 16	00 18												07 51		07 52	08 21
—	—	—	York 8	a															07 26			08 22	

		EM ◇ D	XC ◇1 G 🍴	EM ◇1 ☕	NT	EM	XC ◇1 H 🍴	EM ◇1 ☕	EM ◇ D	EM	XC ◇1 G 🍴	EM ◇1 ☕	EM ◇1 ☕	NT	EM ◇1 ☕	XC ◇1 I 🍴	EM ◇ J	XC ◇1 K 🍴	EM L	EM ◇1 ☕	EM M	EM ◇1 ☕	EM ◇1 ☕
St Pancras International ⊖	d							05 45				06 37			06 55					07 00		07 25	07 30
Luton Airport Parkway 7 ✈	d														07 16								07 51
Luton 10	d							06 11				06 59								07 23			
Bedford 7	d							06 27												07 38			08 07
Wellingborough	d							06 39				07 23								07 51			08 20
Kettering 4	a							06 46				07 30								08 00			08 26
	d							06 47				07 31	07 38							08 01			08 27
Corby	d												07a48										
Oakham	d																						
Melton Mowbray	d																						
Market Harborough	d							06 57				07 41								08 12		08 21	08 37
Leicester	a							07 11				07 56			08 04					08 29		08 36	08 52
	d					06 33		07 12		07 25		07 57			08 06				08 25	08 30		08 38	08 54
Syston	d					06 41				07 32									08 32				
Sileby	d					06 46				07 36									08 36				
Barrow Upon Soar	d					06 51				07 40									08 40				
Loughborough	d					06 56		07 24		07 45		08 08			08 16				08 45	08 41	←	08 48	09 04
East Midlands Parkway ✈	d					07 06		07 32		07 54					08 24				08 54	08 50	08 54	08 56	
Beeston	a					07 16				08 06					08 31				↪		09 02		09 16
Nottingham 8 🚌	a					07 23				08 15					08 39					09 02	09 13		09 26
	d	06 40			07 13				07 45					08 11			08 45				09 21		
Lincoln	a																				10 17		
Langley Mill	d				07 29									08 31									
Alfreton	d	07 02			07 37				08 07					08 39			09 07						
Long Eaton	a							07 35														08 59	
Derby 6	a							07 47				08 24										09 15	
	d		07 13	07 20			07 44	07 49			08 13	08 28				08 44		09 13				09 18	
Chesterfield	d	07 13	07 32	07 42	07 50		08 03	08 09	08 18		08 32	08 47		08 51		09 03	09 18					09 37	
Sheffield 7 🚌	a	07 31	07 48	08 00	08 08		08 17	08 25	08 38		08 45	09 04		09 16		09 17	09 38	09 43				09 52	
Doncaster 7	a		08 24								09 18							10 18					
Wakefield Kirkgate 4	a				08 57									09 57									
Wakefield Westgate 7	a						08 46									09 46							
Leeds 10	a				09 20		09 03							10 18		10 02							
York 8	a		08 45				09 26				09 44					10 26		10 45					

A until 26 March
B From Plymouth
C MO from 2 April
D To Liverpool Lime Street
E To Newcastle. 🍴 from Sheffield
F From Birmingham New Street to Glasgow Central
G From Birmingham New Street to Newcastle
H From Birmingham New Street to Edinburgh
I From Bath Spa to Glasgow Central
J From Norwich to Liverpool Lime Street
K From Guildford to Newcastle
L To Lincoln
M From Leicester

For connections from Gatwick Airport see Table 52

London - East Midlands - Sheffield

Route Diagram - see first Page of Table 53

		EM	EM	EM	NT		XC	EM	XC	EM	EM	EM	EM	EM	EM		EM	EM	NT	XC	EM	XC	EM	EM	EM
		◇1	◇1	◇1			◇1	◇	◇1		◇1	◇1		◇1	◇1		◇1	1		◇1	◇	◇1		◇1	◇1
							A	B	C	D			E							F	B	G	D		
		⊏P	⊏P	⊏P			⊼		⊼		⊏P	⊏P		⊏P	⊏P		⊏P			⊼		⊼		⊏P	⊏P
St Pancras International ⊖	d	07 55		08 00							08 15	08 25		08 30	08 55		09 00							09 15	09 25
Luton Airport Parkway [7] ✈	d													08 51											
Luton [10]	d			08 23													09 23								
Bedford [7]	d			08 38										09 07			09 38								
Wellingborough	d			08 51										09 20			09 51								
Kettering [4]	a			09 00										09 27			10 00								
	d		08 32	09 01										09 27											
Corby	d		08a42	09a10														09 30							
Oakham	d																	09 49							
Melton Mowbray	d																	10 01							
Market Harborough	d										09 12			09 37										10 12	
Leicester	a	09 02									09 29	09 34		09 53	10 02									10 29	10 34
	d	09 04								09 25	09 30	09 35		09 53	10 04								10 25	10 30	10 35
Syston	d									09 32													10 32		
Sileby	d									09 36													10 36		
Barrow Upon Soar	d									09 40													10 40		
Loughborough	d									09 45		09 45	←	10 04									10 45		10 46
East Midlands Parkway ✈	d									09 54	09 46	09 52	09 54					10 26					10 54	10 46	10 53
Beeston	a									→			10 02	10 16									→		
Nottingham [8] ⛴	a										09 59		10 13	10 25										10 59	
	d				09 15			09 45					10 29						10 15		10 45				
Lincoln	a												11 31												
Langley Mill	d				09 32														10 32						
Alfreton	d				09 40			10 07											10 40		11 07				
Long Eaton	a											09 56													10 56
Derby [6]	a	09 26										10 09			10 26			10 40							11 09
	d	09 28					09 44		10 11			10 18			10 28					10 44		11 11			11 18
Chesterfield	d	09 47			09 52		10 03	10 18				10 37			10 47				10 52	11 03	11 18				11 37
Sheffield [7] ⛴	a	10 00			10 16		10 17	10 38	10 41			10 52			11 02				11 17	11 17	11 38	11 43			11 52
Doncaster [7]	a								11 18													12 18			
Wakefield Kirkgate [4]	a				10 57														11 57						
Wakefield Westgate [7]	a						10 46													11 46					
Leeds [10]	a				11 18		11 02												12 18	12 01					
York [8]	a						11 26		11 46											12 26		12 46			

			EM	EM	EM	EM	NT	XC	EM	XC	EM		EM	EM	EM	EM	EM	EM	NT	XC	EM		XC	EM	EM
				◇1	◇1	◇1		◇1	◇	◇1			◇1	◇1		◇1	◇1	◇1		◇1	◇		◇1		◇1
			E					A	B	C	D				E					H	B		I	D	
				⊏P	⊏P	⊏P		⊼		⊼			⊏P	⊏P		⊏P	⊏P	⊏P		⊼			⊼		⊏P
St Pancras International ⊖	d			09 30	09 55	10 00							10 15	10 25		10 30	10 55	11 00							11 15
Luton Airport Parkway [7] ✈	d			09 51												10 51									
Luton [10]	d					10 23												11 23							
Bedford [7]	d			10 07		10 38										11 07		11 38							
Wellingborough	d			10 20		10 51										11 20		11 51							
Kettering [4]	a			10 26		11 00										11 26		12 00							
	d			10 27		11 01										11 27		12 01							
Corby	d					11a10												12a10							
Oakham	d																								
Melton Mowbray	d																								
Market Harborough	d			10 37									11 12			11 37									12 12
Leicester	a			10 54	11 02								11 29	11 33		11 52	12 02								12 29
	d			10 54	11 04						11 25		11 30	11 35		11 54	12 04							12 25	12 30
Syston	d										11 32													12 32	
Sileby	d										11 36													12 36	
Barrow Upon Soar	d										11 40													12 40	
Loughborough	d		←	11 04							11 45			11 45	←	12 04								12 46	
East Midlands Parkway ✈	d		10 54								11 54		11 46	11 53	11 54									12 58	12 46
Beeston	a		11 02	11 16							→				12 02	12 16								→	
Nottingham [8] ⛴	a		11 14	11 25									11 59		12 13	12 26									12 59
	d		11 17				11 15		11 45						12 27				12 15		12 45				
Lincoln	a		12 21												13 20										
Langley Mill	d						11 31												12 32						
Alfreton	d						11 39		12 07										12 40		13 07				
Long Eaton	a													11 56											
Derby [6]	a				11 26									12 09			12 26								
	d				11 28			11 44		12 11				12 18			12 28			12 44			13 11		
Chesterfield	d				11 47		11 52	12 04	12 18					12 37			12 47		12 52	13 03	13 18				
Sheffield [7] ⛴	a				12 04		12 16	12 17	12 38	12 41				12 52			13 04		13 16	13 17	13 38		13 41		
Doncaster [7]	a									13 18													14 18		
Wakefield Kirkgate [4]	a						12 57												13 57						
Wakefield Westgate [7]	a							12 46												13 46					
Leeds [10]	a						13 18	13 03											14 18	14 02					
York [8]	a							13 26		13 40										14 26			14 44		

A From Plymouth to Edinburgh
B From Norwich to Liverpool Lime Street
C From Reading to Newcastle
D To Lincoln
E From Leicester
F From Plymouth to Glasgow Central
G From Winchester to Newcastle
H From Penzance to Glasgow Central
I From Southampton Central to Newcastle

For connections from Gatwick Airport see Table 52

London - East Midlands - Sheffield

Route Diagram - see first Page of Table 53

		EM	EM	EM	EM	EM	NT		XC	EM	XC	EM	EM	EM	EM	EM	EM		EM	NT	XC	EM	XC	EM	EM
		◇[1]		◇[1]	◇[1]	◇[1]			◇[1]	◇	◇[1]		◇[1]	◇[1]		◇[1]	◇[1]		◇[1]		◇[1]	◇	◇[1]		◇[1]
			A						B	C	D	E			A						F	C	G	E	
		🍴		🍴	🍴	🍴			🛒		🛒		🍴	🍴		🍴	🍴		🍴		🛒		🛒		🍴
St Pancras International ⊖	d	11 25		11 30	11 55	12 00							12 15	12 25		12 30	12 55		13 00						13 15
Luton Airport Parkway [7] ✈	d			11 51												12 51									
Luton [10]	d					12 23													13 22						
Bedford [7]	d			12 07		12 38										13 07			13 38						
Wellingborough	d			12 20		12 51										13 20			13 50						
Kettering [4]	a			12 26		13 00										13 26			13 59						
	d			12 27		13 01										13 27			14 01						
Corby	d					13a10													14a10						
Oakham	d																								
Melton Mowbray	d																								
Market Harborough	d			12 37									13 12			13 37									14 12
Leicester	a	12 33		12 53	13 02								13 30	13 33		13 54	14 02								14 29
	d	12 35		12 54	13 04							13 25	13 30	13 35		13 54	14 04							14 25	14 30
Syston	d											13 32												14 32	
Sileby	d											13 36												14 36	
Barrow Upon Soar	d											13 40												14 40	
Loughborough	d	12 45	←	13 04								13 45		13 45	←	14 04								14 45	
East Midlands Parkway ✈	d	12 53	12 58									13 54	13 45	13 53	13 54									14 54	14 46
Beeston	a		13 07	13 16								↪			14 02	14 16								↪	
Nottingham [8]	a		13 14	13 25									13 59		14 13	14 26									14 59
	d		13 17				13 15			13 45					14 29					14 15		14 45			
Lincoln	a		14 23												15 22										
Langley Mill	d						13 32													14 30					
Alfreton	d						13 40			14 07										14 38		15 07			
Long Eaton	a	12 56												13 56											
Derby [6]	a	13 09			13 26									14 09			14 26								
	d	13 18			13 28				13 44		14 11			14 18			14 28				14 44		15 11		
Chesterfield	d	13 37			13 47		13 52		14 03	14 19				14 37			14 47			14 52	15 03	15 22			
Sheffield [7]	a	13 52			14 00		14 16		14 17	14 38	14 41			14 52			15 03			15 16	15 17	15 38	15 41		
Doncaster [7]	a										15 18												16 18		
Wakefield Kirkgate [4]	a						14 57													15 57					
Wakefield Westgate [7]	a								14 46												15 46				
Leeds [10]	a						15 18		15 01											16 18	16 02				
York [8]	a								15 26		15 45										16 28		16 45		

		EM	EM		EM	EM	EM	NT	XC	EM	XC	EM	EM		EM	EM	EM	EM	EM	NT	XC	EM	XC		EM
		◇[1]			◇[1]	◇[1]	◇[1]		◇[1]	◇	◇[1]		◇[1]		◇[1]		◇[1]	◇[1]	◇[1]		◇[1]	◇	◇[1]		
			A						H	C	D	I				J					K	C	L		E
		🍴			🍴	🍴	🍴		🛒		🛒		🍴		🍴		🍴	🍴	🍴		🛒		🛒		
St Pancras International ⊖	d	13 25			13 30	13 55	14 00						14 15		14 25		14 30	14 55	15 00						
Luton Airport Parkway [7] ✈	d				13 51												14 51								
Luton [10]	d						14 23												15 23						
Bedford [7]	d				14 07		14 38										15 07		15 38						
Wellingborough	d				14 20		14 51										15 20		15 51						
Kettering [4]	a				14 26		15 00										15 26		16 00						
	d				14 27		15 01										15 27		16 01						
Corby	d						15a10												16a10						
Oakham	d																								
Melton Mowbray	d																								
Market Harborough	d				14 37								15 12				15 37								
Leicester	a	14 33			14 54	15 02							15 29		15 33		15 54	16 02							
	d	14 35			14 54	15 04						15 25	15 30		15 35		15 54	16 04							16 25
Syston	d											15 32													16 32
Sileby	d											15 36													16 36
Barrow Upon Soar	d											15 40													16 40
Loughborough	d	14 45	←		15 04							15 45			15 45	←	16 04								16 45
East Midlands Parkway ✈	d	14 53	14 54									15 54	15 46		15 53	15 54									16 54
Beeston	a		15 02		15 16							↪				16 02	16 16								↪
Nottingham [8]	a		15 13		15 26								15 59			16 13	16 25								
	d		15 27					15 15		15 45						16 14				16 15		16 45			
Lincoln	a		16 25													17 18									
Langley Mill	d							15 32												16 32					
Alfreton	d							15 40		16 07										16 40		17 07			
Long Eaton	a	14 56													15 56										
Derby [6]	a	15 13				15 26									16 09			16 26							
	d	15 15				15 28			15 44		16 11				16 17			16 28			16 42		17 11		
Chesterfield	d	15 34				15 47		15 53	16 03	16 18					16 36			16 47		16 55	17 04	17 18			
Sheffield [7]	a	15 52				16 00		16 16	16 17	16 38	16 41				16 52			17 04		17 17	17 19	17 36	17 44		
Doncaster [7]	a										17 18														
Wakefield Kirkgate [4]	a							16 57												17 57					
Wakefield Westgate [7]	a								16 49												17 47		18 13		
Leeds [10]	a							17 18	17 04											18 18	18 03		18 31		
York [8]	a								17 28		17 40										18 29		19 01		

A From Leicester
B From Plymouth to Aberdeen
C From Norwich to Liverpool Lime Street
D From Reading to Newcastle
E To Lincoln
F From Penzance to Glasgow Central
G From Southampton Central to Newcastle
H From Plymouth to Dundee
I To Sleaford
J From Leicester to Sleaford
K From Plymouth to Glasgow Central
L From Southampton Central to Edinburgh

For connections from Gatwick Airport see Table 52

London - East Midlands - Sheffield

Route Diagram - see first Page of Table 53

		EM	EM	EM	EM	EM	EM	NT	XC		EM	XC	EM	EM	EM	EM	EM	EM	NT		XC	EM	XC	EM	EM
		◇1	◇1		◇1	◇1	◇1		◇1		◇	◇1		◇1	◇1		◇1	◇1			◇1	◇	◇1		◇1
				A					B		C	D	E			A					F	C	G	E	
		⊡	⊡		⊡	⊡	⊡		⊼			⊼		⊡	⊡		⊡	⊡			⊼		⊼		⊡
St Pancras International ⊖	d	15 15	15 25		15 30	15 55	16 00							16 15	16 25		16 30	16 55							
Luton Airport Parkway [7] ✈	d				15 51												16 51								
Luton [10]	d						16 22										16 55								
Bedford [7]	d				16 07		16 38										17 10								
Wellingborough	d				16 20		16 50										17 23								
Kettering [4]	a				16 26		16 59										17 29								
	d				16 27		17 00										17 30								18 04
Corby	d						17a09																		
Oakham	d																								
Melton Mowbray	d																								
Market Harborough	d	16 12			16 37									17 12			17 40								
Leicester	a	16 29	16 33		16 54	17 02								17 29	17 35		17 55	18 02							18 30
	d	16 30	16 35		16 54	17 04							17 25	17 30	17 35		17 55	18 04						18 25	18 32
Syston	d												17 32											18 32	
Sileby	d												17 36											18 36	
Barrow Upon Soar	d												17 40											18 40	
Loughborough	d		16 45	←	17 04								17 45		17 45	←	18 05							18 45	18 43
East Midlands Parkway ✈	d	16 46	16 53	16 54									17 54	17 46	17 52	17 54								18 54	18 50
Beeston	a			17 02	17 16								↪			18 02	18 17							↪	
Nottingham [8] 🚊	a	16 59		17 13	17 26									17 59		18 13	18 27								
	d			17 17				17 15			17 45					18 15			18 15			18 45			
Lincoln	a			18 26												19 23									
Langley Mill	d							17 32			18 02								18 32						
Alfreton	d							17 40			18 09								18 40			19 07			
Long Eaton	a		16 56												18 00										18 55
Derby [6]	a		17 09			17 26									18 14			18 26							19 09
	d		17 18			17 28			17 41			18 11			18 18			18 28			18 42		19 11		19 18
Chesterfield	d		17 37			17 47		17 52	18 02		18 21				18 42			18 47	18 52		19 01	19 18	19 30		19 37
Sheffield [7] 🚊	a		17 52			18 02		18 14	18 18		18 39	18 44			18 58			19 01	19 17		19 19	19 39	19 47		19 51
Doncaster [7]	a											19 14											20 15		
Wakefield Kirkgate [4]	a							18 59											19 58						
Wakefield Westgate [7]	a								18 47												19 50				
Leeds [10]	a							19 23	19 03										20 19		20 05				
York [8]	a								19 29			19 38									20 30		20 46		

		EM	EM	EM	EM		EM	NT	XC	EM	EM	XC	EM	EM	EM		EM	EM	EM	XC	EM	EM	NT	XC	EM
		◇1	◇1		◇1		◇1		◇1	◇	◇1	◇1		◇1			◇1	◇1	◇1	◇1	◇1	◇1		◇1	
				A					H	I		J	K		A					H				L	K
		⊡	⊡		⊡		⊡		⊼		⊡	⊼		⊡			⊡	⊡	⊡		⊡	⊡			
St Pancras International ⊖	d	17 00	17 15		17 30		17 55				17 45			18 15			18 00	18 25	18 30		18 55	19 00			
Luton Airport Parkway [7] ✈	d										18 09								18 53						
Luton [10]	d		17 40														18 23	18 50				19 23			
Bedford [7]	d	17 35			18 05												18 38		19 10			19 40			
Wellingborough	d	17 48			18 18						18 33			19 00			18 51		19 23			19 53			
Kettering [4]	a	17 56			18 24						18 44			19 07			19 05		19 29			20 04			
	d	18 08			18 25						18 46			19 08			19 10		19 31			20 05			
Corby	d	18a18															19 20					20a14			
Oakham	d																19 40								
Melton Mowbray	d																19a52								
Market Harborough	d		18 18		18 35						18 59							19 27			19 52				
Leicester	a		18 36		18 54		19 04				19 21			19 32				19 44	19 56		20 11				
	d		18 37		18 56		19 04				19 25		19 25	19 34				19 45	19 57		20 13				20 25
Syston	d												19 32												20 32
Sileby	d												19 36												20 36
Barrow Upon Soar	d												19 40												20 40
Loughborough	d			←	19 06						19 36		19 45	19 45	←			19 56			20 23				20 45
East Midlands Parkway ✈	d		18 53	18 54	19 13						19 44		19 54	19 53	19 54				20 12		20 31				20 54
Beeston	a		19 02	19 07	19 18								↪		20 07				20 17						↪
Nottingham [8] 🚊	a		19 10	19 14	19 27						19 58			20 08	20 15				20 28						
	d			19 20				19 15		19 40	20 07			20 15					20 29				20 45		
Lincoln	a			20 17															21 22						
Langley Mill	d							19 32						20 33											
Alfreton	d							19 40		20 01				20 41											
Long Eaton	a										20 22							20 06							
Derby [6]	a						19 28				20 35							20 19			20 46		21 05		
	d						19 28		19 41			20 11						20 21		20 44	20 48		21 06	21 13	
Chesterfield	d						19 47	19 52	20 02	20 12				20 53				20 41		21 03	21 09		21 28	21 34	
Sheffield [7] 🚊	a						20 03	20 15	20 18	20 28		20 48		21 14				20 56		21 18	21 25		21 54	21 51	
Doncaster [7]	a											21 19												22 29	
Wakefield Kirkgate [4]	a							20 57																	
Wakefield Westgate [7]	a								20 46					21 59						21 46					
Leeds [10]	a							21 20	21 05					22 19						22 02					
York [8]	a											21 45												22 53	

A From Leicester
B From Plymouth to Edinburgh
C From Norwich to Liverpool Lime Street
D From Reading to Newcastle
E To Lincoln
F From Plymouth to Edinburgh. ⊼ to Leeds
G From Southampton Central to Newcastle. ⊼ to Doncaster
H From Plymouth
I From Norwich to Manchester Piccadilly
J From Reading to Newcastle. ⊼ to Sheffield
K To Nottingham
L From Southampton Central to Crofton Depot

For connections from Gatwick Airport see Table 52

London - East Midlands - Sheffield

Route Diagram - see first Page of Table 53

		EM	EM	EM	EM	EM	EM	NT	EM	XC	EM	EM	EM	EM	EM	EM	EM	EM	EM	EM	EM	EM
		◇1		◇1	◇1	◇1	◇1		◇1	◇1		◇1		◇1	◇1	◇1	◇1	◇1	◇1	◇1	◇1	◇1
			A							B	C		A									
St Pancras International	d	19 15		19 25	19 30	19 55	20 00		20 15			20 25		20 30	20 55	21 00	21 25		21 30	22 00		22 25
Luton Airport Parkway 7	d				19 51									20 51					21 53			22 48
Luton 10	d						20 23									21 23				22 24		
Bedford 7	d				20 07		20 38							21 07		21 38			22 09	22 40		23 04
Wellingborough	d				20 20		20 51							21 20		21 51			22 22	22 53		23 17
Kettering 4	a			20 15			21 00							21 26		21 57			22 30	23 00		23 25
	d			20 17			21 01							21 27		21 58		22 05	22 31	23 01	23 05	23 26
Corby	d						21a10											22a15			23a15	
Oakham	d																					
Melton Mowbray	d																					
Market Harborough	d	20 11		20 27	20 37				21 11					21 37		22 08	22 23		22 42	23 12		23 37
Leicester	a	20 28		20 42	20 54	21 04			21 25			21 33		21 53	22 02	22 26	22 40		23 01	23 29		23 53
	d	20 28		20 43	20 54	21 04			21 26		21 25	21 35		21 54	22 04	22 28	22 41		23 02	23 30		23 55
Syston	d										21 32											
Sileby	d										21 36											
Barrow Upon Soar	d										21 40											
Loughborough	d		←	20 54	21 04						21 45	21 45	←	22 04		22 38	22 52		23 13	23 41		00 06
East Midlands Parkway	d	20 43	20 54	21 01					21 43		21 54	21 53	21 54			22 46	23 01		23 24	23 50		00 14
Beeston	a		21 03		21 18						↪		22 07	22 16						00 04		
Nottingham 8	a	21 04	21 15		21 29				21 58				22 15	22 26			23 11			00 12		
	d				21 43			21 11														
Lincoln	a																					
Langley Mill	d				22 01			21 38														
Alfreton	d				22 09			21 46														
Long Eaton	a			21 05								21 58							23 37			
Derby 6	a			21 16		21 32						22 10			22 26	22 59			23 50			00 34
	d					21 34				21 44					22 28							00 35
Chesterfield	d				22 21	21 55		22 00		22 07					22 47							00 58
Sheffield 7	a				22 37	22 16		22 19		22 24					23 03							01 13
Doncaster 7	a																					
Wakefield Kirkgate 4	a																					
Wakefield Westgate 7	a				23 21	22 46				22 59												
Leeds 10	a				23 41	23 04				23 15												
York 8	a																					

		EM
		◇1
St Pancras International	d	23 15
Luton Airport Parkway 7	d	
Luton 10	d	23 46
Bedford 7	d	00 12
Wellingborough	d	00 25
Kettering 4	a	00 41
	d	00 42
Corby	d	
Oakham	d	
Melton Mowbray	d	
Market Harborough	d	00 52
Leicester	a	01 05
	d	01 07
Syston	d	
Sileby	d	
Barrow Upon Soar	d	
Loughborough	d	01 17
East Midlands Parkway	d	01 25
Beeston	a	01 38
Nottingham 8	a	01 45
	d	01 52
Lincoln	a	
Langley Mill	d	
Alfreton	d	
Long Eaton	a	
Derby 6	a	02 10
	d	
Chesterfield	d	
Sheffield 7	a	
Doncaster 7	a	
Wakefield Kirkgate 4	a	
Wakefield Westgate 7	a	
Leeds 10	a	
York 8	a	

A From Leicester **B** From Plymouth **C** To Nottingham

For connections from Gatwick Airport see Table 52

Table 53

Saturdays
until 24 March

London - East Midlands - Sheffield

Route Diagram - see first Page of Table 53

		EM	EM	EM	EM	EM	XC	EM	XC	EM		XC	EM	NT	EM	XC	EM	EM	XC	EM		EM	EM	NT	EM
		◇1	◇1	◇1	◇1	◇	◇1	◇1	◇1	◇		◇1	◇1			◇1	◇		◇1	◇1		◇1	◇1		◇1
						A	B		C	A		D				E	A		D						
		🍴	🍴	🍴	🍴		🛒	🍴	🛒			🛒	🍴			🛒			🛒	🍴		🍴	🍴		🍴
St Pancras International ⊖	d	22p00	22p25	23p15	00 15															06 10		06 37			06 55
Luton Airport Parkway 7 ✈	d		22p48		00 44																				07 16
Luton 10	d	22p24		23p46	00 47															06 33		06 59			
Bedford 7	d	22p40	23p04	00 12	01 12															06 48					
Wellingborough	d	22p53	23p17	00 25	01 33															07 01					
Kettering 4	a	23p00	23p25	00 41	01 43															07 07		07 27			
	d	23p01	23p26	00 42	01 43															07 08		07 28	07 38		
Corby	d																						07a48		
Oakham	d																								
Melton Mowbray	d																								
Market Harborough	d	23p12	23p37	00 52	01 55															07 18		07 38			
Leicester	a	23p29	23p53	01 05	02 10															07 35		07 53			08 04
	d	23p30	23p55	01 07											06 36			07 25		07 36		07 55			08 06
Syston	d														06 43			07 32							
Sileby	d														06 47			07 36							
Barrow Upon Soar	d														06 51			07 40							
Loughborough	d	23p41	00 06	01 17											06 56			07 46		07 47		08 05			08 18
East Midlands Parkway ✈	d	23p50	00 14	01 25											07 06			07 57				08 13			
Beeston	a	00 04		01 38											07 15			08 04							08 31
Nottingham 8 🚌	a	00 12		01 45											07 24			08 13							08 42
	d			01 52		05 20				06 40				07 11			07 45							08 11	
Lincoln	a																								
Langley Mill	d													07 27										08 31	
Alfreton	d									07 02				07 35			08 07							08 39	
Long Eaton	a																			07 55					
Derby 6	a		00 34	02 10																08 09		08 26			
	d		00 35				05 55	06 26	06 37			07 11	07 20			07 44			08 11	08 18		08 28			
Chesterfield	d		00 58			05 49	06 31	06 45	06 56	07 13		07 30	07 42	07 50		08 03	08 18		08 30	08 37		08 47		08 51	
Sheffield 7 🚌	a		01 13			06 15	06 44	07 09	07 09	07 31		07 48	07 59	08 08		08 17	08 38		08 45	08 52		09 07		09 16	
Doncaster 7	a						07 16					08 23							09 18			09 53			
Wakefield Kirkgate 4	a													08 57										09 57	
Wakefield Westgate 7	a								07 36							08 45									
Leeds 10	a								07 52					09 20		09 03								10 18	
York 8	a						07 43		08 23			08 48				09 27			09 44			10 16			

		XC	EM	XC	EM	EM		EM	EM	EM	EM	EM	NT	XC	EM	XC		EM	EM	EM	EM	EM	EM	EM	NT
		◇1	◇	◇1		◇1		◇1		◇1	◇1	◇1		◇1	◇	◇1			◇1	◇1		◇1	◇1	◇1	
		F	G	H	I				J					K	G	L		I			J				
		🛒		🛒		🍴		🍴		🍴	🍴	🍴		🛒		🛒			🍴	🍴		🍴	🍴	🍴	
St Pancras International ⊖	d					07 00				07 30	07 55	08 00							08 15	08 25		08 30	08 55	09 00	
Luton Airport Parkway 7 ✈	d									07 51												08 51			
Luton 10	d					07 23						08 23												09 23	
Bedford 7	d					07 38				08 07		08 38										09 07		09 38	
Wellingborough	d					07 51				08 20		08 51										09 20		09 51	
Kettering 4	a					08 00				08 27		09 00										09 26		10 00	
	d					08 01				08 27		09 01										09 27		10 01	
Corby	d											09a10												10a10	
Oakham	d																								
Melton Mowbray	d																								
Market Harborough	d					08 12				08 37									09 12			09 37			
Leicester	a					08 29				08 53	09 02								09 29	09 33		09 52	10 02		
	d				08 25	08 30		08 38		08 54	09 04							09 25	09 30	09 35		09 54	10 04		
Syston	d				08 32													09 32							
Sileby	d				08 36													09 36							
Barrow Upon Soar	d				08 40													09 40							
Loughborough	d				08 45	08 41		08 49	←	09 04								09 45		09 45	←	10 04			
East Midlands Parkway ✈	d				08 57	08 50		08 56	08 57									09 54	09 46	09 53	09 54				
Beeston	a				↪				09 05	09 16								↪			10 02	10 16			
Nottingham 8 🚌	a					09 03			09 14	09 26									09 59		10 13	10 26			
	d		08 45						09 23				09 15		09 45						10 29				10 15
Lincoln	a								10 17												11 30				
Langley Mill	d												09 32												10 32
Alfreton	d		09 07										09 40		10 07										10 40
Long Eaton	a							09 00												09 56					
Derby 6	a							09 14			09 26									10 09			10 26		
	d	08 44		09 11				09 18			09 28			09 44		10 11				10 18			10 28		
Chesterfield	d	09 03	09 18					09 37			09 47		09 52	10 03	10 18					10 37			10 47		10 52
Sheffield 7 🚌	a	09 17	09 38	09 44				09 52			10 00		10 15	10 17	10 38	10 42				10 52			11 00		11 15
Doncaster 7	a			10 17												11 15									
Wakefield Kirkgate 4	a												10 57												11 57
Wakefield Westgate 7	a	09 46												10 46											
Leeds 10	a	10 02											11 18	11 02											12 18
York 8	a	10 26		10 40										11 26		11 40									

A To Liverpool Lime Street
B To Newcastle. 🛒 from Sheffield
C From Birmingham New Street to Glasgow Central
D From Birmingham New Street to Newcastle
E From Birmingham New Street to Edinburgh
F From Bristol Temple Meads to Glasgow Central
G From Norwich to Liverpool Lime Street
H From Guildford to Newcastle
I To Lincoln
J From Leicester
K From Plymouth to Edinburgh
L From Bournemouth to Newcastle

For connections from Gatwick Airport see Table 52

Table 53

Saturdays

until 24 March

London - East Midlands - Sheffield

Route Diagram - see first Page of Table 53

		XC		EM	XC	EM	EM	EM	EM	EM	EM	EM		NT	XC	EM	XC	EM	EM	EM	EM	EM		EM	EM
		◇1		◇	◇1		◇1	◇1		◇1	◇1	◇1			◇1	◇	◇1		◇1	◇1		◇1		◇1	◇1
		A		B	C	D			E						F	B	G	D			E				
		⊥o			⊥o		⊡	⊡		⊡	⊡	⊡			⊥o		⊥o		⊡	⊡		⊡		⊡	⊡
St Pancras International ⊖	d						09 15	09 25		09 30	09 55	10 00							10 15	10 25		10 30		10 55	11 00
Luton Airport Parkway 7 ✈	d									09 51												10 51			
Luton 10	d											10 23													11 23
Bedford 7	d									10 07		10 38										11 07			11 38
Wellingborough	d									10 20		10 51										11 20			11 51
Kettering 4	a									10 26		11 00										11 26			12 00
	d									10 27		11 01										11 27			12 01
Corby	d											11a10													12a10
Oakham	d																								
Melton Mowbray	d																								
Market Harborough	d						10 12			10 37									11 12			11 37			
Leicester	a						10 29	10 33		10 54	11 02								11 29	11 33		11 54		12 02	
	d					10 25	10 30	10 35		10 54	11 04							11 25	11 30	11 35		11 54		12 04	
Syston	d					10 32												11 32							
Sileby	d					10 36												11 36							
Barrow Upon Soar	d					10 40												11 40							
Loughborough	d					10 45		10 45	←	11 04								11 45		11 45	←	12 04			
East Midlands Parkway ✈	d					10 54	10 46	10 53	10 54									11 54	11 46	11 53	11 54				
Beeston	a					↪			11 02	11 16								↪			12 02	12 16			
Nottingham 8 ⛴	a						10 59		11 13	11 26									11 59		12 13	12 26			
	d			10 45					11 17					11 15		11 45					12 27				
Lincoln	a								12 27												13 18				
Langley Mill	d													11 31											
Alfreton	d			11 07										11 39		12 07									
Long Eaton	a							10 56												11 56					
Derby 6	a							11 09			11 26									12 09				12 26	
	d	10 44			11 11			11 18			11 28				11 44		12 11			12 18				12 28	
Chesterfield	d	11 03		11 18				11 37			11 47			11 52	12 03	12 18				12 37				12 47	
Sheffield 7 ⛴	a	11 17		11 38	11 41			11 52			12 00			12 16	12 16	12 38	12 41			12 52				13 04	
Doncaster 7	a				12 15												13 17								
Wakefield Kirkgate 4	a													12 57											
Wakefield Westgate 7	a	11 46													12 46										
Leeds 10	a	12 02												13 18	13 02										
York 8	a	12 26			12 39										13 26		13 40								

		NT	XC	EM	XC	EM	EM	EM		EM	EM	EM	EM	NT	XC	EM	XC	EM		EM	EM	EM	EM	EM	EM
			◇1	◇	◇1		◇1	◇1			◇1	◇1	◇1		◇1	◇	◇1			◇1	◇1		◇1	◇1	◇1
			H	B	C	D				E					I	B	G	D				E			
			⊥o		⊥o		⊡	⊡			⊡	⊡	⊡		⊥o		⊥o			⊡	⊡		⊡	⊡	⊡
St Pancras International ⊖	d						11 15	11 25			11 30	11 55	12 00							12 15	12 25		12 30	12 55	13 00
Luton Airport Parkway 7 ✈	d										11 51												12 51		
Luton 10	d												12 23												13 23
Bedford 7	d										12 07		12 38										13 07		13 38
Wellingborough	d										12 20		12 51										13 20		13 51
Kettering 4	a										12 26		13 00										13 26		14 00
	d										12 27		13 01										13 27		14 01
Corby	d												13a10												14a10
Oakham	d																								
Melton Mowbray	d																								
Market Harborough	d						12 12				12 37									13 12			13 37		
Leicester	a						12 29	12 33			12 54	13 02								13 29	13 33		13 52	14 02	
	d					12 25	12 30	12 35			12 54	13 04						13 25		13 30	13 35		13 54	14 04	
Syston	d					12 32												13 32							
Sileby	d					12 36												13 36							
Barrow Upon Soar	d					12 40												13 40							
Loughborough	d					12 45		12 45		←	13 04							13 45			13 45	←	14 04		
East Midlands Parkway ✈	d					12 54	12 46	12 53		12 54								13 54		13 46	13 53	13 54			
Beeston	a					↪				13 02	13 16							↪				14 02	14 16		
Nottingham 8 ⛴	a						12 59			13 13	13 27									13 59		14 13	14 26		
	d	12 15		12 45						13 17				13 15		13 45						14 29			
Lincoln	a									14 23												15 22			
Langley Mill	d	12 32												13 32											
Alfreton	d	12 40		13 07										13 40		14 07									
Long Eaton	a							12 56													13 56				
Derby 6	a							13 09				13 26									14 09			14 26	
	d		12 44		13 11			13 18				13 28			13 44		14 11				14 18			14 28	
Chesterfield	d	12 52	13 03	13 18				13 37				13 47		13 52	14 03	14 18					14 37			14 47	
Sheffield 7 ⛴	a	13 15	13 17	13 38	13 41			13 52				14 00		14 15	14 17	14 38	14 41				14 52			15 00	
Doncaster 7	a				14 18												15 17								
Wakefield Kirkgate 4	a	13 57												14 57											
Wakefield Westgate 7	a		13 46												14 46										
Leeds 10	a	14 18	14 02											15 18	15 02										
York 8	a		14 26		14 40										15 28		15 40								

A From Plymouth to Glasgow Central
B From Norwich to Liverpool Lime Street
C From Southampton Central to Newcastle
D To Lincoln
E From Leicester
F From Plymouth to Edinburgh
G From Reading to Newcastle
H From Penzance to Glasgow Central
I From Plymouth to Aberdeen

For connections from Gatwick Airport see Table 52

Table 53

Saturdays
until 24 March

London - East Midlands - Sheffield

Route Diagram - see first Page of Table 53

		NT	XC	EM		XC	EM	EM	EM	EM	EM	EM	EM	NT		XC	EM	XC	EM	EM	EM	EM	EM	EM	
			◇1	◇		◇1		◇1	◇1		◇1	◇1	◇1			◇1	◇	◇1		◇1	◇1		◇1	◇1	
			A	B		C	D			E						F	B	G	D			E			
			🛒			🛒		🍴	🍴		🍴	🍴	🍴			🛒		🛒		🍴	🍴		🍴	🍴	
St Pancras International ⊖	d							13 15	13 25		13 30	13 55	14 00							14 15	14 25		14 30	14 55	
Luton Airport Parkway [7] ✈	d										13 51												14 51		
Luton [10]	d												14 23												
Bedford [7]	d										14 07		14 38										15 07		
Wellingborough	d										14 20		14 51										15 20		
Kettering [4]	a										14 26		15 00										15 26		
	d										14 27		15 01										15 27		
Corby	d												15a10												
Oakham	d																								
Melton Mowbray	d																								
Market Harborough	d							14 12			14 37									15 12			15 37		
Leicester	a							14 29	14 33		14 54	15 02								15 29	15 33		15 53	16 02	
	d						14 25	14 30	14 35		14 54	15 04							15 25	15 30	15 35		15 54	16 04	
Syston	d						14 32												15 32						
Sileby	d						14 36												15 36						
Barrow Upon Soar	d						14 40												15 40						
Loughborough	d						14 45		14 45	←	15 04								15 45		15 45	←	16 04		
East Midlands Parkway ✈	d						14 54	14 46	14 53	14 54									15 54	15 46	15 53	15 54			
Beeston	a						↪			15 02	15 16								↪			16 02	16 16		
Nottingham [8] ⛴	a							14 59		15 13	15 26									16 01		16 13	16 26		
	d	14 15		14 45						15 23				15 15			15 45					16 14			
Lincoln	a									16 21												17 16			
Langley Mill	d	14 30												15 32											
Alfreton	d	14 38		15 07										15 40			16 07								
Long Eaton	a								14 56												15 56				
Derby [6]	a								15 09			15 26									16 09			16 26	
	d		14 44			15 11			15 18			15 28				15 44		16 11			16 18			16 28	
Chesterfield	d	14 52	15 03	15 18					15 37			15 47		15 53		16 03	16 18				16 37			16 47	
Sheffield [7] ⛴	a	15 15	15 17	15 38		15 41			15 52			16 00		16 14		16 18	16 38	16 41			16 52			17 00	
Doncaster [7]	a					16 18												17 16							
Wakefield Kirkgate [4]	a	15 57												16 57											
Wakefield Westgate [7]	a		15 46													16 46									
Leeds [10]	a	16 18	16 02											17 18		17 02									
York [8]	a		16 26			16 41										17 26		17 37							

		EM	NT	XC	EM	XC	EM	EM	EM	EM		EM	EM	EM	NT	XC	EM	XC	EM	EM		EM	EM	EM	EM
		◇1		◇1	◇	◇1		◇1	◇1			◇1	◇1	◇1		◇1	◇	◇1		◇1		◇1		◇1	◇1
				H	B	C	D			E						I	B	G	D				E		
		🍴		🛒		🛒		🍴	🍴			🍴	🍴	🍴		🛒		🛒		🍴		🍴		🍴	🍴
St Pancras International ⊖	d	15 00						15 15	15 25			15 30	15 55	16 00						16 15		16 25		16 30	16 55
Luton Airport Parkway [7] ✈	d											15 51												16 51	
Luton [10]	d	15 23												16 23											
Bedford [7]	d	15 38										16 07		16 38										17 07	
Wellingborough	d	15 51										16 20		16 51										17 20	
Kettering [4]	a	16 00										16 26		17 00										17 26	
	d	16 01										16 27		17 01										17 27	
Corby	d	16a10												17a10											
Oakham	d																								
Melton Mowbray	d																								
Market Harborough	d							16 12				16 37								17 12				17 37	
Leicester	a							16 29	16 33			16 54	17 02							17 29		17 33		17 52	18 02
	d						16 25	16 30	16 35			16 54	17 04						17 25	17 30		17 35		17 54	18 04
Syston	d						16 32												17 32						
Sileby	d						16 36												17 36						
Barrow Upon Soar	d						16 40												17 40						
Loughborough	d						16 45		16 45	←		17 04							17 45			17 45	←	18 04	
East Midlands Parkway ✈	d						16 54	16 45	16 52	16 54									17 54	17 46		17 53	17 54		
Beeston	a						↪			17 02		17 16							↪				18 02	18 16	
Nottingham [8] ⛴	a							16 59		17 13		17 26								17 59			18 12	18 26	
	d		16 15		16 45					17 13					17 15		17 45						18 15		
Lincoln	a									18 22													19 25		
Langley Mill	d		16 32												17 32		18 03								
Alfreton	d		16 40		17 07										17 40		18 10								
Long Eaton	a								16 56													17 56			
Derby [6]	a								17 09				17 26									18 09			18 26
	d			16 41		17 11			17 18				17 28			17 44		18 11				18 18			18 28
Chesterfield	d		16 55	17 02	17 18				17 37				17 47		17 52	18 03	18 22					18 39			18 47
Sheffield [7] ⛴	a		17 17	17 19	17 34	17 44			17 52				18 04		18 14	18 18	18 39	18 42				18 59			19 04
Doncaster [7]	a																	19 16							
Wakefield Kirkgate [4]	a		17 57												18 59										
Wakefield Westgate [7]	a			17 47		18 12										18 46									
Leeds [10]	a		18 18	18 02		18 31									19 23	19 01									
York [8]	a			18 28		18 58										19 26		19 39							

A From Penzance to Glasgow Central
B From Norwich to Liverpool Lime Street
C From Southampton Central to Newcastle
D To Lincoln
E From Leicester
F From Plymouth to Dundee
G From Reading to Newcastle
H From Plymouth to Glasgow Central
I From Plymouth to Edinburgh

For connections from Gatwick Airport see Table 52

Table 53

Saturdays

until 24 March

London - East Midlands - Sheffield

Route Diagram - see first Page of Table 53

		EM	NT	XC	EM	XC		EM	EM	EM	EM	EM	EM	EM	NT	XC		EM	XC	EM	EM	EM	EM	EM	EM
		◇1		◇1	◇	◇1			◇1	◇1		◇1	◇1	◇1		◇1		◇	◇1		◇1	◇1		◇1	◇1
				A	B	C		D			E					F		G	H	I			E		
		☕		🛒		🛒			☕	☕		☕	☕	☕		🛒			🛒		☕	☕		☕	☕
St Pancras International ⊖	d	17 00							17 15	17 25		17 30	17 55	18 00							18 15	18 25		18 30	18 55
Luton Airport Parkway 7 ✈	d											17 51												18 51	
Luton 10	d	17 23												18 23											
Bedford 7	d	17 38										18 07		18 38										19 07	
Wellingborough	d	17 51										18 20		18 51										19 20	
Kettering 4	a	18 00										18 26		19 00										19 26	
	d	18 01										18 27		19 01										19 27	
Corby	d	18a10												19a10											
Oakham	d																								
Melton Mowbray	d																								
Market Harborough	d								18 12			18 37									19 12			19 37	
Leicester	a								18 29	18 33		18 52	19 02								19 29	19 33		19 52	20 02
	d							18 25	18 30	18 35		18 54	19 04							19 25	19 30	19 35		19 54	20 04
Syston	d							18 32												19 32					
Sileby	d							18 36												19 36					
Barrow Upon Soar	d							18 40												19 40					
Loughborough	d							18 45		18 45	←	19 04								19 45		19 45	←	20 04	
East Midlands Parkway ✈	d							18 54	18 46	18 53	18 54									19 54	19 46	19 53	19 54		
Beeston	a							↪			19 02	19 16								↪			20 05	20 16	
Nottingham 8 ⛴	a								18 59		19 14	19 26									19 59		20 15	20 26	
	d		18 15		18 45							19 29			19 15			19 40			20 15		20 29		
Lincoln	a											20 26											21 23		
Langley Mill	d		18 32												19 32						20 33				
Alfreton	d		18 40		19 07										19 40			20 01			20 41				
Long Eaton	a									18 56												19 56			
Derby 6	a									19 09			19 26									20 09			20 26
	d			18 44		19 11				19 18			19 28			19 44			20 11			20 18			20 28
Chesterfield	d		18 55	19 03	19 18	19 30				19 37			19 47		19 52	20 05		20 11	20 30		20 53	20 37			20 47
Sheffield 7 ⛴	a		19 15	19 18	19 39	19 51				19 52			20 00		20 15	20 19		20 27	20 49		21 14	20 54			21 00
Doncaster 7	a					20 17													21 21						
Wakefield Kirkgate 4	a		19 58												20 57										
Wakefield Westgate 7	a			19 49												20 48					21 59				
Leeds 10	a		20 20	20 05											21 20	21 03					22 19				
York 8	a			20 29		20 40										21 57			21 44						

		EM		XC	NT	XC	EM	EM	EM	EM	NT	EM		EM	EM	XC	EM	EM	EM	EM	EM	EM		EM	EM
		◇1		◇1		◇1		◇1	◇1			◇1		◇1	◇1	◇1		◇1	◇1		◇1	◇1		◇1	◇1
				F		J	I			E						F	D			E					
		☕						☕	☕			☕		☕	☕			☕	☕		☕	☕		☕	☕
St Pancras International ⊖	d	19 00						19 15	19 25			19 30		19 55	20 00			20 15	20 25		20 30	20 55		21 00	21 25
Luton Airport Parkway 7 ✈	d											19 51									20 51				
Luton 10	d	19 23													20 23									21 23	
Bedford 7	d	19 38										20 07			20 38						21 07			21 38	
Wellingborough	d	19 51										20 20			20 51						21 20			21 51	
Kettering 4	a	20 00										20 26			21 00						21 26			22 00	
	d	20 01										20 27			21 01						21 27			22 01	
Corby	d	20a10													21a10										
Oakham	d																								
Melton Mowbray	d																								
Market Harborough	d							20 12				20 37						21 12			21 37			22 12	22 20
Leicester	a							20 29	20 33			20 52		21 04				21 29	21 33		21 52	22 02		22 29	22 36
	d						20 25	20 30	20 35			20 54		21 06			21 25	21 30	21 35		21 54	22 04		22 30	22 37
Syston	d						20 32										21 32								
Sileby	d						20 36										21 36								
Barrow Upon Soar	d						20 40										21 40								
Loughborough	d						20 45		20 45	←		21 04					21 45		21 45	←	22 04			22 41	22 48
East Midlands Parkway ✈	d						20 54	20 46	20 53	20 54							21 54	21 46	21 53	21 54	22 12				22 55
Beeston	a						↪			21 05		21 16					↪			22 06	22 17				
Nottingham 8 ⛴	a							20 59		21 15		21 26						22 01		22 14	22 27				23 05
	d				20 40					21 25	21 15														
Lincoln	a									22 40															
Langley Mill	d				21 02						21 31														
Alfreton	d				21 10						21 39														
Long Eaton	a								20 56										21 57						
Derby 6	a								21 10					21 32					22 10			22 26		23 02	
	d			20 44		21 26								21 34		21 48						22 28			
Chesterfield	d			21 05	21 22	21 46					21 50			21 56		22 08						22 47			
Sheffield 7 ⛴	a			21 19	21 40	22 05					22 13			22 16		22 23						23 00			
Doncaster 7	a					22 30										22 51									
Wakefield Kirkgate 4	a																								
Wakefield Westgate 7	a			21 48										22 44		23 10									
Leeds 10	a			22 02										23 04		23 27									
York 8	a					22 57																			

A From Plymouth to Edinburgh
B From Norwich to Liverpool Lime Street
C From Southampton Central to Newcastle
D To Nottingham
E From Leicester
F From Plymouth
G From Norwich to Manchester Piccadilly
H From Reading to Newcastle. 🛒 to Sheffield
I To Lincoln
J From Southampton Central

For connections from Gatwick Airport see Table 52

Table 53

Saturdays
until 24 March

London - East Midlands - Sheffield

Route Diagram - see first Page of Table 53

		EM	EM	EM	EM	EM
		◇1	◇1	◇1	◇1	◇1
St Pancras International	d		21 30		22 00	22 25
Luton Airport Parkway 7	d		21 51			22 46
Luton 10	d				22 24	
Bedford 7	d		22 07		22 42	23 02
Wellingborough	d		22 20		22 55	23 14
Kettering 4	a		22 26		23 02	23 21
	d	22 05	22 27	23 00	23 03	23 22
Corby	d	22a15		23a10		
Oakham	d					
Melton Mowbray	d					
Market Harborough	d		22 37		23 14	23 32
Leicester	a		22 51		23 31	23 46
	d		22 52		23 32	23 46
Syston	d					
Sileby	d					
Barrow Upon Soar	d					
Loughborough	d		23 04		23 44	23 59
East Midlands Parkway	d		23 12		23 52	00 07
Beeston	a				23 59	
Nottingham 8	a				00 08	
	d					
Lincoln	a					
Langley Mill	d					
Alfreton	d					
Long Eaton	a		23 15			00 10
Derby 6	a		23 26			00 21
	d					
Chesterfield	d					
Sheffield 7	a					
Doncaster 7	a					
Wakefield Kirkgate 4	a					
Wakefield Westgate 7	a					
Leeds 10	a					
York 8	a					

Saturdays
from 31 March

		EM	EM	EM	EM	EM	XC	EM	XC	EM		XC	EM	NT	EM	XC	EM	EM	XC	EM		EM	EM	NT	EM
		◇1	◇1	◇1	◇1	◇	◇1	◇1	◇1	◇		◇1	◇1			◇1	◇		◇1	◇1		◇1	◇1		◇1
						A	B		C	A		D				E	A		D						
St Pancras International	d	22p00	22p25	23p15	00 15															06 10		06 37			06 55
Luton Airport Parkway 7	d		22p48		00 44																				07 16
Luton 10	d	22p24		23p46	00 47															06 33		06 59			
Bedford 7	d	22p40	23p04	00 12	01 12															06 48					
Wellingborough	d	22p53	23p17	00 25	01 33															07 01					
Kettering 4	a	23p00	23p25	00 41	01 43															07 07		07 27			
	d	23p01	23p26	00 42	01 43															07 08		07 28	07 38		
Corby	d																						07a48		
Oakham	d																								
Melton Mowbray	d																								
Market Harborough	d	23p12	23p37	00 52	01 55															07 18		07 38			
Leicester	a	23p29	23p53	01 05	02 10															07 35		07 53			08 04
	d	23p30	23p55	01 07											06 36			07 25		07 36		07 55			08 06
Syston	d														06 43			07 32							
Sileby	d														06 47			07 36							
Barrow Upon Soar	d														06 51			07 40							
Loughborough	d	23p41	00 06	01 17											06 56			07 46		07 47		08 05			08 18
East Midlands Parkway	d	23p50	00 14	01 25											07 06			07 57				08 13			
Beeston	a	00 04		01 38											07 15			08 04							08 31
Nottingham 8	a	00 12		01 45											07 24			08 13							08 42
	d			01 52		05 20				06 40				07 11			07 45							08 11	
Lincoln	a																								
Langley Mill	d													07 27										08 31	
Alfreton	d									07 02				07 35			08 07							08 39	
Long Eaton	a																			07 55					
Derby 6	a		00 34	02 10																08 09		08 26			
	d		00 35				05 55	06 26	06 37			07 11	07 20			07 44			08 11	08 18		08 28			
Chesterfield	d		00 58			05 49	06 31	06 45	06 56	07 13		07 30	07 42	07 50		08 03	08 18		08 30	08 37		08 47		08 51	
Sheffield 7	a		01 13			06 15	06 44	07 09	07 09	07 31		07 48	07 59	08 08		08 17	08 38		08 45	08 52		09 07		09 16	
Doncaster 7	a						07 16					08 23							09 18			09 53			
Wakefield Kirkgate 4	a													08 57										09 57	
Wakefield Westgate 7	a								07 36							08 45									
Leeds 10	a								07 52					09 20		09 03								10 18	
York 8	a						07 43		08 23			08 48				09 27			09 44			10 16			

A To Liverpool Lime Street
B To Newcastle. from Sheffield
C From Birmingham New Street to Glasgow Central
D From Birmingham New Street to Newcastle
E From Birmingham New Street to Edinburgh

For connections from Gatwick Airport see Table 52

Saturdays
from 31 March

London - East Midlands - Sheffield

Route Diagram - see first Page of Table 53

		XC ◇1 A	EM ◇ B	XC ◇1 C	EM D	EM ◇1		EM ◇1	EM E	EM ◇1	EM ◇1	EM ◇1	NT	XC ◇1 F	EM ◇ B	XC ◇1 G		EM D	EM ◇1	EM ◇1	EM E	EM ◇1	EM ◇1	EM ◇1	NT
St Pancras International ⊖	d					07 00				07 30	07 55	08 00							08 15	08 25		08 30	08 55	09 00	
Luton Airport Parkway 7 ✈	d									07 51												08 51			
Luton 10	d					07 23						08 23												09 23	
Bedford 7	d					07 38				08 07		08 38										09 07		09 38	
Wellingborough	d					07 51				08 20		08 51										09 20		09 51	
Kettering 4	a					08 00				08 27		09 00										09 26		10 00	
	d					08 01				08 27		09 01										09 27		10 01	
Corby	d											09a10												10a10	
Oakham	d																								
Melton Mowbray	d																								
Market Harborough	d					08 12				08 37									09 12			09 37			
Leicester	a					08 29				08 53	09 02								09 29	09 33		09 52	10 02		
	d				08 25	08 30		08 38		08 54	09 04							09 25	09 30	09 35		09 54	10 04		
Syston	d				08 32													09 32							
Sileby	d				08 36													09 36							
Barrow Upon Soar	d				08 40													09 40							
Loughborough	d				08 45	08 41		08 49	←	09 04								09 45		09 45	←	10 04			
East Midlands Parkway ✈	d				08 57	08 50		08 56	08 57									09 54	09 46	09 53	09 54				
Beeston	a				↪				09 05	09 16								↪			10 02	10 16			
Nottingham 8	a					09 03			09 14	09 26									09 59		10 13	10 26			
	d		08 45						09 23				09 15		09 45						10 29				10 15
Lincoln	a								10 17												11 30				
Langley Mill	d												09 32												10 32
Alfreton	d		09 07										09 40		10 07										10 40
Long Eaton	a							09 00												09 56					
Derby 6	a							09 14			09 26									10 09			10 26		
	d	08 44		09 11				09 18			09 28			09 44		10 11				10 18			10 28		
Chesterfield	d	09 03	09 18					09 37			09 47		09 52	10 03	10 18					10 37			10 47		10 52
Sheffield 7	a	09 17	09 38	09 44				09 52			10 00		10 15	10 17	10 38	10 42				10 52			11 00		11 15
Doncaster 7	a			10 17												11 15									
Wakefield Kirkgate 4	a												10 57												11 57
Wakefield Westgate 7	a	09 46												10 46											
Leeds 10	a	10 02											11 18	11 02											12 18
York 8	a	10 26		10 40										11 26		11 40									

		XC ◇1 H		EM ◇ B	XC ◇1 I	EM D	EM ◇1	EM ◇1	EM E	EM ◇1	EM ◇1	EM ◇1		NT	XC ◇1 F	EM ◇ B	XC ◇1 J	EM D	EM ◇1	EM ◇1	EM E	EM ◇1		EM ◇1	EM ◇1
St Pancras International ⊖	d						09 15	09 25		09 30	09 55	10 00							10 15	10 25		10 30		10 55	11 00
Luton Airport Parkway 7 ✈	d									09 51												10 51			
Luton 10	d											10 23													11 23
Bedford 7	d									10 07		10 38										11 07			11 38
Wellingborough	d									10 20		10 51										11 20			11 51
Kettering 4	a									10 26		11 00										11 26			12 00
	d									10 27		11 01										11 27			12 01
Corby	d											11a10													12a10
Oakham	d																								
Melton Mowbray	d																								
Market Harborough	d						10 12			10 37									11 12			11 37			
Leicester	a						10 29	10 33		10 54	11 02								11 29	11 33		11 54		12 02	
	d					10 25	10 30	10 35		10 54	11 04							11 25	11 30	11 35		11 54		12 04	
Syston	d					10 32												11 32							
Sileby	d					10 36												11 36							
Barrow Upon Soar	d					10 40												11 40							
Loughborough	d					10 45		10 45	←	11 04								11 45		11 45	←	12 04			
East Midlands Parkway ✈	d					10 54	10 46	10 53	10 54									11 54	11 46	11 53	11 54				
Beeston	a					↪			11 02	11 16								↪			12 02	12 16			
Nottingham 8	a						10 59		11 13	11 26									11 59		12 13	12 26			
	d			10 45					11 17					11 15		11 45					12 27				
Lincoln	a								12 27												13 18				
Langley Mill	d													11 31											
Alfreton	d			11 07										11 39		12 07									
Long Eaton	a							10 56												11 56					
Derby 6	a							11 09			11 26									12 09				12 26	
	d	10 44			11 11			11 18			11 28				11 44		12 11			12 18				12 28	
Chesterfield	d	11 03		11 18				11 37			11 47			11 52	12 03	12 18				12 37				12 47	
Sheffield 7	a	11 17		11 38	11 41			11 52			12 00			12 16	12 16	12 38	12 41			12 52				13 04	
Doncaster 7	a				12 15												13 17								
Wakefield Kirkgate 4	a													12 57											
Wakefield Westgate 7	a	11 46													12 46										
Leeds 10	a	12 02												13 18	13 02										
York 8	a	12 26			12 39										13 26		13 40								

A From Bristol Temple Meads to Glasgow Central
B From Norwich to Liverpool Lime Street
C From Guildford to Newcastle
D To Lincoln
E From Leicester
F From Plymouth to Edinburgh
G From Bournemouth to Newcastle
H From Plymouth to Glasgow Central
I From Southampton Central to Newcastle
J From Reading to Newcastle

For connections from Gatwick Airport see Table 52

Table 53

Saturdays

from 31 March

London - East Midlands - Sheffield

Route Diagram - see first Page of Table 53

		NT	XC	EM	XC	EM	EM	EM	EM	EM	EM	EM	NT	XC	EM	XC	EM	EM	EM	EM	EM	EM	EM
			◇1	◇	◇1		◇1	◇1		◇1	◇1	◇1		◇1	◇	◇1		◇1	◇1		◇1	◇1	◇1
			A	B	C	D			E					F	B	G	D			E			
St Pancras International ⊖	d						11 15	11 25		11 30	11 55	12 00						12 15	12 25		12 30	12 55	13 00
Luton Airport Parkway 7	d									11 51											12 51		
Luton 10	d											12 23											13 23
Bedford 7	d									12 07		12 38									13 07		13 38
Wellingborough	d									12 20		12 51									13 20		13 51
Kettering 4	a									12 26		13 00									13 26		14 00
	d									12 27		13 01									13 27		14 01
Corby	d											13a10											14a10
Oakham	d																						
Melton Mowbray	d																						
Market Harborough	d						12 12			12 37								13 12			13 37		
Leicester	a						12 29	12 33		12 54	13 02							13 29	13 33		13 52	14 02	
	d					12 25	12 30	12 35		12 54	13 04						13 25	13 30	13 35		13 54	14 04	
Syston	d					12 32											13 32						
Sileby	d					12 36											13 36						
Barrow Upon Soar	d					12 40											13 40						
Loughborough	d					12 45		12 45	←	13 04							13 45		13 45	←	14 04		
East Midlands Parkway ✈	d					12 54	12 46	12 53	12 54								13 54	13 46	13 53	13 54			
Beeston	a					↪			13 02	13 16							↪			14 02	14 16		
Nottingham 8	a						12 59		13 13	13 27								13 59		14 13	14 26		
	d	12 15		12 45					13 17				13 15		13 45					14 29			
Lincoln	a								14 23											15 22			
Langley Mill	d	12 32											13 32										
Alfreton	d	12 40		13 07									13 40		14 07								
Long Eaton	a							12 56											13 56				
Derby 6	a							13 09				13 26							14 09				14 26
	d		12 44		13 11			13 18				13 28		13 44		14 11			14 18				14 28
Chesterfield	d	12 52	13 03	13 18				13 37				13 47	13 52	14 03	14 18				14 37				14 47
Sheffield 7	a	13 15	13 17	13 38	13 41			13 52				14 00	14 15	14 17	14 38	14 41			14 52				15 00
Doncaster 7	a				14 18											15 17							
Wakefield Kirkgate 4	a	13 57											14 57										
Wakefield Westgate 7	a		13 46											14 46									
Leeds 10	a	14 18	14 02										15 18	15 02									
York 8	a		14 26		14 40									15 28		15 40							

		NT	XC	EM	XC	EM	EM	EM	EM	EM	EM	EM	NT	XC	EM	XC	EM	EM	EM	EM	EM	EM
			◇1	◇	◇1		◇1	◇1		◇1	◇1	◇1		◇1	◇	◇1		◇1	◇1		◇1	◇1
			A	B	C	D			E					H	B	G	D			E		
St Pancras International ⊖	d						13 15	13 25		13 30	13 55	14 00						14 15	14 25		14 30	14 55
Luton Airport Parkway 7	d									13 51											14 51	
Luton 10	d											14 23										
Bedford 7	d									14 07		14 38									15 07	
Wellingborough	d									14 20		14 51									15 20	
Kettering 4	a									14 26		15 00									15 26	
	d									14 27		15 01									15 27	
Corby	d											15a10										
Oakham	d																					
Melton Mowbray	d																					
Market Harborough	d						14 12			14 37								15 12			15 37	
Leicester	a						14 29	14 33		14 54	15 02							15 29	15 33		15 53	16 02
	d					14 25	14 30	14 35		14 54	15 04						15 25	15 30	15 35		15 54	16 04
Syston	d					14 32											15 32					
Sileby	d					14 36											15 36					
Barrow Upon Soar	d					14 40											15 40					
Loughborough	d					14 45		14 45	←	15 04							15 45		15 45	←	16 04	
East Midlands Parkway ✈	d					14 54	14 46	14 53	14 54								15 54	15 46	15 53	15 54		
Beeston	a					↪			15 02	15 16							↪			16 02	16 16	
Nottingham 8	a						14 59		15 13	15 26								16 01		16 13	16 26	
	d	14 15		14 45					15 23				15 15		15 45					16 14		
Lincoln	a								16 21											17 16		
Langley Mill	d	14 30											15 32									
Alfreton	d	14 38		15 07									15 40		16 07							
Long Eaton	a							14 56											15 56			
Derby 6	a							15 09				15 26							16 09			16 26
	d		14 44		15 11			15 18				15 28		15 44		16 11			16 18			16 28
Chesterfield	d	14 52	15 03	15 18				15 37				15 47	15 53	16 03	16 18				16 37			16 47
Sheffield 7	a	15 15	15 17	15 38	15 41			15 52				16 00	16 14	16 18	16 38	16 41			16 52			17 00
Doncaster 7	a				16 18											17 16						
Wakefield Kirkgate 4	a	15 57											16 57									
Wakefield Westgate 7	a		15 46											16 46								
Leeds 10	a	16 18	16 02										17 18	17 02								
York 8	a		16 26		16 41									17 26		17 37						

A From Penzance to Glasgow Central
B From Norwich to Liverpool Lime Street
C From Southampton Central to Newcastle
D To Lincoln
E From Leicester
F From Plymouth to Aberdeen
G From Reading to Newcastle
H From Plymouth to Dundee

For connections from Gatwick Airport see Table 52

London - East Midlands - Sheffield

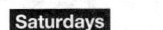

Route Diagram - see first Page of Table 53

		EM	NT	XC	EM	XC	EM	EM	EM	EM	EM	EM	EM	NT	XC	EM	XC	EM	EM	EM	EM	EM	EM
		◇1		◇1	◇	◇1		◇1	◇1		◇1	◇1	◇1		◇1	◇	◇1		◇1	◇1		◇1	◇1
				A	B	C	D			E					F	B	G	D			E		
		☕		🚲		🚲		☕	☕		☕	☕	☕		🚲		🚲		☕	☕		☕	☕
St Pancras International ⊖	d	15 00						15 15	15 25		15 30	15 55	16 00						16 15	16 25		16 30	16 55
Luton Airport Parkway 7 ✈	d										15 51											16 51	
Luton 10	d	15 23											16 23										
Bedford 7	d	15 38									16 07		16 38									17 07	
Wellingborough	d	15 51									16 20		16 51									17 20	
Kettering 4	a	16 00									16 26		17 00									17 26	
	d	16 01									16 27		17 01									17 27	
Corby	d	16a10											17a10										
Oakham	d																						
Melton Mowbray	d																						
Market Harborough	d							16 12			16 37								17 12			17 37	
Leicester	a							16 29	16 33		16 54	17 02							17 29	17 33		17 52	18 02
	d						16 25	16 30	16 35		16 54	17 04						17 25	17 30	17 35		17 54	18 04
Syston	d						16 32											17 32					
Sileby	d						16 36											17 36					
Barrow Upon Soar	d						16 40											17 40					
Loughborough	d						16 45		16 45	←	17 04							17 45		17 45	←	18 04	
East Midlands Parkway ✈	d						16 54	16 45	16 52	16 54								17 54	17 46	17 53	17 54		
Beeston	a						↪			17 02	17 16							↪			18 02	18 16	
Nottingham 8 🚊	a							16 59		17 13	17 26								17 59		18 12	18 26	
	d		16 15		16 45					17 13				17 15		17 45					18 15		
Lincoln	a									18 22											19 25		
Langley Mill	d		16 32											17 32		18 03							
Alfreton	d		16 40		17 07									17 40		18 10							
Long Eaton	a								16 56											17 56			
Derby 6	a								17 09			17 26								18 09			18 26
	d			16 41		17 11			17 18			17 28			17 44		18 11			18 18			18 28
Chesterfield	d		16 55	17 02	17 18				17 37			17 47		17 52	18 03	18 22				18 39			18 47
Sheffield 7 🚊	a		17 17	17 19	17 34	17 44			17 52			18 04		18 14	18 18	18 39	18 42			18 59			19 04
Doncaster 7	a																19 16						
Wakefield Kirkgate 4	a		17 57											18 59									
Wakefield Westgate 7	a			17 47		18 12									18 46								
Leeds 10	a		18 18	18 02		18 31								19 23	19 01								
York 8	a			18 28		18 58									19 26		19 39						

		EM	NT	XC	EM	XC	EM	EM	EM	EM	EM	EM	EM	NT	XC	EM	XC	EM	EM	EM	EM	EM	EM
		◇1		◇1	◇	◇1		◇1	◇1		◇1	◇1	◇1		◇1	◇	◇1		◇1	◇1		◇1	◇1
				F	B	C	H			E					I	J	K	D			E		
		☕		🚲		🚲		☕	☕		☕	☕	☕		🚲		🚲		☕	☕		☕	☕
St Pancras International ⊖	d	17 00						17 15	17 25		17 30	17 55	18 00						18 15	18 25		18 30	18 55
Luton Airport Parkway 7 ✈	d										17 51											18 51	
Luton 10	d	17 23											18 23										
Bedford 7	d	17 38									18 07		18 38									19 07	
Wellingborough	d	17 51									18 20		18 51									19 20	
Kettering 4	a	18 00									18 26		19 00									19 26	
	d	18 01									18 27		19 01									19 27	
Corby	d	18a10											19a10										
Oakham	d																						
Melton Mowbray	d																						
Market Harborough	d							18 12			18 37								19 12			19 37	
Leicester	a							18 29	18 33		18 52	19 02							19 29	19 33		19 52	20 02
	d						18 25	18 30	18 35		18 54	19 04						19 25	19 30	19 35		19 54	20 04
Syston	d						18 32											19 32					
Sileby	d						18 36											19 36					
Barrow Upon Soar	d						18 40											19 40					
Loughborough	d						18 45		18 45	←	19 04							19 45		19 45	←	20 04	
East Midlands Parkway ✈	d						18 54	18 46	18 53	18 54								19 54	19 46	19 53	19 54		
Beeston	a						↪			19 02	19 16							↪			20 05	20 16	
Nottingham 8 🚊	a							18 59		19 14	19 26								19 59		20 15	20 26	
	d		18 15		18 45						19 29			19 15		19 40			20 15		20 29		
Lincoln	a										20 26										21 23		
Langley Mill	d		18 32											19 32					20 33				
Alfreton	d		18 40		19 07									19 40		20 01			20 41				
Long Eaton	a								18 56											19 56			
Derby 6	a								19 09			19 26								20 09			20 26
	d			18 44		19 11			19 18			19 28			19 44		20 11			20 18			20 28
Chesterfield	d		18 55	19 03	19 18	19 30			19 37			19 47		19 52	20 05	20 11	20 30		20 53	20 37			20 47
Sheffield 7 🚊	a		19 15	19 18	19 39	19 51			19 52			20 00		20 15	20 19	20 27	20 49		21 14	20 54			21 00
Doncaster 7	a					20 17											21 21						
Wakefield Kirkgate 4	a		19 58											20 57									
Wakefield Westgate 7	a			19 49											20 48				21 59				
Leeds 10	a		20 20	20 05										21 20	21 03				22 19				
York 8	a			20 29		20 40									21 57		21 44						

A From Plymouth to Glasgow Central
B From Norwich to Liverpool Lime Street
C From Southampton Central to Newcastle
D To Lincoln
E From Leicester
F From Plymouth to Edinburgh
G From Reading to Newcastle
H To Nottingham
I From Plymouth
J From Norwich to Manchester Piccadilly
K From Reading to Newcastle.
🚲 to Sheffield

For connections from Gatwick Airport see Table 52

Table 53

Saturdays

from 31 March

London - East Midlands - Sheffield

Route Diagram - see first Page of Table 53

		EM	XC	NT	XC	EM	EM	EM	EM	NT	EM
		◇1	◇1		◇1		◇1	◇1			◇1
			A		B	C			D		
St Pancras International ⊖	d	19 00					19 15	19 25			19 30
Luton Airport Parkway 7 ✈	d										19 51
Luton 10	d	19 23									
Bedford 7	d	19 38									20 07
Wellingborough	d	19 51									20 20
Kettering 4	a	20 00									20 26
	d	20 01									20 27
Corby	d	20a10									
Oakham	d										
Melton Mowbray	d										
Market Harborough	d						20 12				20 37
Leicester	a						20 29	20 33			20 52
	d					20 25	20 30	20 35			20 54
Syston	d					20 32					
Sileby	d					20 36					
Barrow Upon Soar	d					20 40					
Loughborough	d					20 45		20 45	←		21 04
East Midlands Parkway ✈	d					20 54	20 46	20 53	20 54		
Beeston	a					→			21 05		21 16
Nottingham 8	a						20 59		21 15		21 26
	d			20 40					21 25	21 15	
Lincoln	a								22 40		
Langley Mill	d			21 02						21 31	
Alfreton	d			21 10						21 39	
Long Eaton	a							20 56			
Derby 6	a							21 10			
	d		20 44		21 26						
Chesterfield	d		21 05	21 22	21 46					21 50	
Sheffield 7	a		21 19	21 40	22 05					22 13	
Doncaster 7	a				22 30						
Wakefield Kirkgate 4	a										
Wakefield Westgate 7	a		21 48								
Leeds 10	a		22 02								
York 8	a				22 57						

		EM	EM	XC	EM	EM	EM	EM	EM	EM	EM	EM
		◇1	◇1	◇1		◇1	◇1		◇1	◇1	◇1	◇1
				A	E			D				
St Pancras International ⊖	d	19 55	20 00			20 15	20 25		20 30	20 55	21 00	21 25
Luton Airport Parkway 7 ✈	d								20 51			
Luton 10	d		20 23								21 23	
Bedford 7	d		20 38						21 07		21 38	
Wellingborough	d		20 51						21 20		21 51	
Kettering 4	a		21 00						21 26		22 00	
	d		21 01						21 27		22 01	
Corby	d		21a10									
Oakham	d											
Melton Mowbray	d											
Market Harborough	d					21 12			21 37		22 12	22 20
Leicester	a	21 04				21 29	21 33		21 52	22 02	22 29	22 36
	d	21 06			21 25	21 30	21 35		21 54	22 04	22 30	22 37
Syston	d				21 32							
Sileby	d				21 36							
Barrow Upon Soar	d				21 40							
Loughborough	d				21 45		21 45	←	22 04		22 41	22 48
East Midlands Parkway ✈	d				21 54	21 46	21 53	21 54	22 12			22 55
Beeston	a				→			22 06	22 17			
Nottingham 8	a					22 01		22 14	22 27			23 05
	d											
Lincoln	a											
Langley Mill	d											
Alfreton	d											
Long Eaton	a						21 57					
Derby 6	a	21 32					22 10			22 26	23 02	
	d	21 34		21 48						22 28		
Chesterfield	d	21 56		22 08						22 47		
Sheffield 7	a	22 16		22 23						23 00		
Doncaster 7	a			22 51								
Wakefield Kirkgate 4	a											
Wakefield Westgate 7	a	22 44		23 10								
Leeds 10	a	23 04		23 27								
York 8	a											

		EM	EM	EM	EM	EM
		◇1	◇1	◇1	◇1	◇1
St Pancras International ⊖	d		21 30		22 00	22 25
Luton Airport Parkway 7 ✈	d		21 51			22 49
Luton 10	d				22 26	
Bedford 7	d		22 07		22 48	23 11
Wellingborough	d		22 20		23 01	23 23
Kettering 4	a		22 26		23 09	23 29
	d	22 05	22 27	23 00	23 10	23 30
Corby	d	22a15		23a10		
Oakham	d					
Melton Mowbray	d					
Market Harborough	d		22 37		23 21	23 40
Leicester	a		22 51		23 37	23 54
	d		22 52		23 39	23 55
Syston	d					
Sileby	d					
Barrow Upon Soar	d					
Loughborough	d		23 04		23 50	00 11
East Midlands Parkway ✈	d		23 12		23 59	00 18
Beeston	a				00 06	
Nottingham 8	a				00 15	
	d					
Lincoln	a					
Langley Mill	d					
Alfreton	d					
Long Eaton	a		23 15			00 22
Derby 6	a		23 26			00 33
	d					
Chesterfield	d					
Sheffield 7	a					
Doncaster 7	a					
Wakefield Kirkgate 4	a					
Wakefield Westgate 7	a					
Leeds 10	a					
York 8	a					

A From Plymouth
B From Southampton Central
C To Lincoln
D From Leicester
E To Nottingham

For connections from Gatwick Airport see Table 52

Table 53

Sundays
until 25 March

London - East Midlands - Sheffield

Route Diagram - see first Page of Table 53

		EM	EM	XC	EM	EM	NT	XC	EM	EM		NT	EM	XC	EM	EM	EM	NT	EM	XC		EM	EM	EM	XC
		◇1	◇1	◇1	◇	◇1		◇1	◇1	◇			◇1	◇1	◇1	◇1	◇		◇1	◇1		◇1	◇1	◇	◇1
		A	A	B	C			D		C				E			C			F				C	G
		🍴	🍴	☕		🍴		☕	🍴				🍴	☕	🍴	🍴			🍴	☕		🍴	🍴		☕
St Pancras International ⊖	d	22p00	22p25										09 00		09 30				10 00			10 30			
Luton Airport Parkway 7 ✈	d		22p46										09 28						10 29						
Luton 10	d	22p24													10 01							11 02			
Bedford 7	d	22p42	23p02										09 51		10 21				10 53			11 27			
Wellingborough	d	22p55	23p14										10 05		10 35				11 07			11 39			
Kettering 4	a	23p02	23p21										10 13		10 40				11 14			11 46			
	d	23p03	23p22			09 55							10 14		10 41	10 55			11 15			11 46	11 55		
Corby	d					10a05										11a05							12a05		
Oakham	d																								
Melton Mowbray	d																								
Market Harborough	d	23p14	23p32										10 25		10 52				11 26			11 56			
Leicester	a	23p31	23p46										10 45		11 13				11 47			12 16			
	d	23p32	23p46						10 10				10 47		11 16				11 48			12 19			
Syston	d																								
Sileby	d																								
Barrow Upon Soar	d																								
Loughborough	d	23p44	23p59						10 21				10 58		11 27				11 59			12 29			
East Midlands Parkway ✈	d	23p52	00s07						10 29				11 06		11 35				12 08			12 37			
Beeston	a	23p59											11 12												
Nottingham 8 🚌	a	00s08											11 23						12 22						
	d				09 31		10 06			10 41		11 15					11 46	12 19						12 39	
Lincoln	a																								
Langley Mill	d						10 27					11 31						12 35						12 56	
Alfreton	d				09 53		10 35			11 03		11 39					12 08	12 43						13 04	
Long Eaton	a		00s10						10 32						11 38							12 40			
Derby 6	a		00s21						10 46						11 49							12 51			
	d			09 44				10 44	10 48					11 44	11 51					12 44		12 53			13 11
Chesterfield	d			10 03	10 08		10 54	11 03	11 09	11 16		11 51		12 03	12 10		12 18	12 54		13 03		13 12		13 17	13 30
Sheffield 7 🚌	a			10 16	10 33		11 15	11 17	11 28	11 35		12 15		12 18	12 30		12 36	13 16		13 18		13 28		13 33	13 43
Doncaster 7	a								11 52																14 13
Wakefield Kirkgate 4	a						11 52					12 52						13 52							
Wakefield Westgate 7	a			10 44				11 44						12 44						13 45					
Leeds 10	a			11 02			12 18	12 01				13 18		13 02				14 18		14 02					
York 8	a			11 29				12 29	12 15					13 29						14 29					14 40

		NT	EM	XC	EM	EM		EM	XC	XC	NT	EM	XC	EM	EM	EM		XC	NT	EM	XC	EM	EM	EM	EM
			◇1	◇1	◇1	◇1		◇	◇1	◇1		◇1	◇1	◇	◇1	◇1		◇1		◇1	◇1	◇1	◇1	◇	◇1
				H				I	J	G			K	C				L			M			C	
			🍴	☕	🍴	🍴			☕	☕		🍴	☕		🍴	🍴		☕		🍴	☕	🍴	🍴		🍴
St Pancras International ⊖	d		11 00		11 30							12 00			12 30					13 00		13 30			14 00
Luton Airport Parkway 7 ✈	d		11 29		11 58							12 29			12 59					13 29		14 00			14 22
Luton 10	d		11 32		12 02							12 33			13 03					13 33		14 05			
Bedford 7	d		11 55		12 26							12 56			13 26					13 56		14 19			14 38
Wellingborough	d		12 09		12 40							13 10			13 40					14 10		14 33			14 52
Kettering 4	a		12 15		12 47							13 16			13 48					14 16		14 40			14 58
	d		12 16		12 48	12 55						13 17			13 49	13 55				14 17		14 42	14 55		14 59
Corby	d					13a05										14a05							15a05		
Oakham	d																								
Melton Mowbray	d																								
Market Harborough	d		12 26		12 58							13 27			14 00					14 27		14 54			15 09
Leicester	a		12 45		13 17							13 46			14 20					14 46		15 16			15 32
	d		12 47		13 19				13s41			13 48			14 22					14 48		15 18			15 35
Syston	d																								
Sileby	d																								
Barrow Upon Soar	d																								
Loughborough	d		12 57		13 30							13 58			14 33					14 58		15 29			15 46
East Midlands Parkway ✈	d		13 05		13 37							14 06			14 41					15 06		15 37			15 53
Beeston	a		13 10									14 12								15 12					15 59
Nottingham 8 🚌	a		13 20						14s04			14 20								15 20					16 06
	d	13 09						13 38			14 19			14 37					15 12					15 44	
Lincoln	a																								
Langley Mill	d	13 27						13 55			14 35			14 54					15 34						
Alfreton	d	13 35						14 03			14 43			15 02					15 44					16 06	
Long Eaton	a				13 41										14 45							15 41			
Derby 6	a				13 52										14 57							15 53			
	d			13 44	13 54					14 11			14 44		15 01			15 11			15 44	15 55			
Chesterfield	d	13 46		14 03	14 13			14 17		14 30	14 54		15 03	15 13	15 22				15 53		16 03	16 16		16 23	
Sheffield 7 🚌	a	14 07		14 17	14 28			14 35		14 45	15 15		15 17	15 31	15 42			15 47	16 15		16 18	16 32		16 39	
Doncaster 7	a									15 13								16 15							
Wakefield Kirkgate 4	a	14 52									15 52								16 52						
Wakefield Westgate 7	a			14 44									15 44								16 44				
Leeds 10	a	15 18		15 02							16 18		16 02						17 18		17 02				
York 8	a			15 29						15 43			16 29					16 40			17 29				

A not 11 December
B From Birmingham New Street to Edinburgh
C To Liverpool Lime Street
D From Birmingham New Street to Glasgow Central
E From Bristol Temple Meads to Edinburgh
F From Bristol Temple Meads to Glasgow Central
G From Birmingham New Street to Newcastle
H From Plymouth to Aberdeen
I From Norwich to Liverpool Lime Street
J from 8 January until 12 February. From Birmingham New Street to Stansted Airport
K From Plymouth to Glasgow Central
L From Guildford to Newcastle
M From Penzance to Edinburgh

For connections from Gatwick Airport see Table 52

Table 53

Sundays
until 25 March

London - East Midlands - Sheffield

Route Diagram - see first Page of Table 53

		XC		XC	NT	XC	XC	EM	EM	EM	EM	XC		NT	XC	XC	EM	EM	EM	EM	XC	EM		EM	EM
		◇1		◇1		◇1	◇1	◇1	◇1	◇	◇1	◇1			◇1	◇1	◇1	◇1	◇	◇1	◇1	◇1		◇1	◇1
		A		B		C	D			E		B			A	F			E		G				
		🛒		🛒		🛒	🛒	☕	☕		☕	🛒				🛒	☕	☕		☕	🛒	☕		☕	☕
St Pancras International ⊖	d							14 30			15 00						15 30			16 00		16 25		16 30	
Luton Airport Parkway 7 ✈	d										15 23									16 21					
Luton 10	d							14 54									15 54							16 53	
Bedford 7	d							15 10			15 39						16 10			16 37				17 08	
Wellingborough	d							15 24			15 53						16 24			16 51				17 22	
Kettering 4	a							15 31			16 01						16 31			16 57				17 28	
	d							15 32	15 45		16 02						16 32	16 45		16 58				17 29	17 50
Corby	d								15a55									16a55							18a00
Oakham	d																								
Melton Mowbray	d																								
Market Harborough	d							15 46			16 13						16 43			17 08				17 39	
Leicester	a							16 07			16 34						17 04			17 31		17 40		18 00	
	d	15 50						16 08			16 35				16 50		17 05			17 35		17 42		18 02	
Syston	d																								
Sileby	d																								
Barrow Upon Soar	d																								
Loughborough	d							16 19			16 46						17 16			17 45				18 12	
East Midlands Parkway ✈	d							16 28			16 55						17 25			17 53		17 58		18 20	
Beeston	a																			17 59					
Nottingham 8	a	16 13									17 06				17 17					18 06					
	d				16 14					16 40				17 14					17 35						
Lincoln	a																								
Langley Mill	d				16 30					17 00				17 30					17 54						
Alfreton	d				16 38					17 08				17 38					18 02						
Long Eaton	a							16 31									17 28							18 23	
Derby 6	a							16 44									17 41					18 10		18 34	
	d			16 11		16 44	16 44	16 48				17 11				17 43	17 48				18 11	18 12			
Chesterfield	d				16 50	17 03	17 03	17 10		17 22				17 51		18 04			18 17			18 34			
Sheffield 7	a			16 48	17 15	17 17	17 17	17 30		17 40		17 48		18 14		18 19	18 29		18 34		18 46	18 51			
Doncaster 7	a			17 13								18 13									19 15				
Wakefield Kirkgate 4	a				17 52									18 52											
Wakefield Westgate 7	a					17 47	17 48	18 06				18 33				18 47									
Leeds 10	a				18 18	18 02	18 02	18 24				18 51		19 18		19 04									
York 8	a			17 42		18 29	18 29					19 18				19 29					19 43				

		NT	EM	XC	EM	EM	XC	EM		XC	EM	EM	NT	EM	XC	EM	EM	XC		XC	EM	NT	XC	EM	EM
			◇1	◇1	◇	◇1	◇1	◇1		◇1	◇1	◇1		◇1	◇1	◇	◇1	◇1		◇1	◇1		◇1	◇1	◇1
				H	I		B			A					J	I		K		L			A		
			☕	🛒		☕	🛒	☕			☕	☕		☕	🛒		☕	🛒		🛒	☕			☕	☕
St Pancras International ⊖	d		16 55			17 00		17 25			17 30			17 55			18 00				18 25			18 30	18 55
Luton Airport Parkway 7 ✈	d					17 21											18 21								
Luton 10	d										17 52													18 53	
Bedford 7	d					17 38					18 08						18 38							19 08	
Wellingborough	d					17 51					18 21						18 51							19 22	
Kettering 4	a					17 58					18 28						18 58							19 28	
	d					17 59					18 29	18 50					18 59							19 29	
Corby	d											19a00													
Oakham	d																								
Melton Mowbray	d																								
Market Harborough	d					18 09					18 39						19 09							19 39	
Leicester	a		18 07			18 29		18 37			19 01			19 08			19 31				19 40			20 01	20 07
	d		18 11			18 30		18 39		18 50	19 03			19 09			19 35				19 42		19 50	20 02	20 09
Syston	d																								
Sileby	d																								
Barrow Upon Soar	d																								
Loughborough	d					18 40					19 13						19 45							20 12	
East Midlands Parkway ✈	d		18 26			18 48		18 53			19 21			19 26			19 53				19 58			20 20	20 24
Beeston	a					19 00											19 59								
Nottingham 8	a		18 37			19 06				19 18				19 36			20 06						20 16		20 34
	d	18 14			18 37								19 19			19 38						20 13			
Lincoln	a																								
Langley Mill	d	18 30			18 54								19 35									20 29			
Alfreton	d	18 38			19 02								19 43			20 00						20 37			
Long Eaton	a										19 24													20 26	
Derby 6	a							19 04			19 35										20 10			20 37	
	d			18 43			19 05	19 06							19 41			20 03		20 03	20 12				
Chesterfield	d	18 52		19 05	19 13			19 27					19 54		20 02	20 12					20 33	20 48			
Sheffield 7	a	19 16		19 20	19 31		19 39	19 44					20 15		20 17	20 31		20 38		20 39	20 49	21 14			
Doncaster 7	a						20 16											21 19		21 19					
Wakefield Kirkgate 4	a	19 52											20 52												
Wakefield Westgate 7	a			19 48											20 46						21 27				
Leeds 10	a	20 18		20 05									21 16		21 03						21 44				
York 8	a			20 29			20 45								21 31			21 44		21 44					

A from 8 January until 12 February. From Birmingham New Street to Stansted Airport
B From Reading to Newcastle
C until 12 February. From Plymouth to Glasgow Central
D from 19 February until 25 March. From Newton Abbot to Glasgow Central
E From Norwich to Liverpool Lime Street
F From Plymouth to Edinburgh
G From Reading to Edinburgh
H From Plymouth to Edinburgh. 🛒 to Leeds
I From Norwich to Manchester Piccadilly
J From Plymouth
K from 8 January until 25 March. From Reading to Newcastle. 🛒 to Sheffield
L until 1 January. From Reading to Newcastle. 🛒 to Sheffield

For connections from Gatwick Airport see Table 52

Table 53

Sundays
until 25 March

London - East Midlands - Sheffield

Route Diagram - see first Page of Table 53

		EM	EM	XC		EM	XC	EM	EM	XC	NT	EM	EM	EM		EM	EM	EM	XC	EM	EM	EM			
		◇[1]	◇[1]	◇[1]		◇[1]	◇[1]	◇[1]	◇[1]	◇[1]		◇[1]	◇[1]	◇[1]		◇[1]	◇[1]	◇[1]	◇[1]	◇[1]	◇[1]	◇[1]			
				A			B			C									A						
		☕	☕			☕		☕	☕			☕	☕	☕		☕	☕	☕		☕	☕	☕			
St Pancras International ⊖	d		19 00			19 25		19 30				19 55	20 00	20 25		20 30		21 00		21 30	22 30	23 00			
Luton Airport Parkway [7] ✈	d		19 21										20 22					21 21			22 53	23 27			
Luton [10]	d							19 53								20 54				21 54					
Bedford [7]	d		19 38					20 08					20 41			21 11		21 40		22 10	23 17	23 50			
Wellingborough	d		19 51					20 22					20 53			21 24		21 53		22 23	23 31	00 04			
Kettering [4]	a		19 58					20 28					21 00			21 31		22 00		22 30	23 37	00 10			
	d	19 45	19 59					20 29	20 46				21 01			21 32	21 55	22 01		22 31	23 38	00 11			
Corby	d	19a55							20a56								22a05								
Oakham	d																								
Melton Mowbray	d																								
Market Harborough	d		20 09					20 39					21 11			21 43		22 11		22 41	23 48	00 21			
Leicester	a		20 31			20 40		21 01				21 09	21 31	21 37		22 04		22 30		23 00	00 07	00 42			
	d		20 35			20 42	20 50	21 02				21 11	21 34	21 39		22 06		22 32		23 02	00 09	00 44			
Syston	d																								
Sileby	d																								
Barrow Upon Soar	d																								
Loughborough	d		20 45					21 12				21 22	21 44	21 49				22 42		23 12	00 19	00 54			
East Midlands Parkway ✈	d		20 53			20 58		21 20				21 30	21 52	21 57		22 22		22 55		23 25	00 27	01 02			
Beeston	a		20 59										21 59					23 03			00 40				
Nottingham [8] 🚊	a		21 06				21 13					21 41	22 06					23 11			00 48				
	d										21 30														
Lincoln	a																								
Langley Mill	d										21 52														
Alfreton	d										22 00														
Long Eaton	a							21 23												23 31					
Derby [6]	a					21 10		21 35						22 08		22 34				23 42		01 21			
	d			20 43		21 12				21 44						22 36			22 44	23 44					
Chesterfield	d			21 03		21 33				22 03	22 13					22 58			23 05	00 03					
Sheffield [7] 🚊	a			21 16		21 47				22 18	22 36					23 13			23 20	00 17					
Doncaster [7]	a																								
Wakefield Kirkgate [4]	a										23 26														
Wakefield Westgate [7]	a			21 47						22 43						23 40									
Leeds [10]	a			22 04						23 01	00 05					00 01			00 16						
York [8]	a																								

Sundays
from 1 April

		EM	EM	XC	EM	EM	NT	XC	EM	EM		NT	EM	XC	EM	EM	EM	NT	EM	XC		EM	EM	EM	XC
		◇[1]	◇[1]	◇[1]	◇	◇[1]		◇[1]	◇[1]	◇			◇[1]	◇[1]	◇	◇[1]	◇[1]		◇[1]	◇[1]		◇	◇[1]	◇[1]	◇[1]
				D	E			F		E				G	E					H		E			I
		☕	☕	🛒		☕		🛒	☕				☕	🛒		☕	☕		☕	🛒			☕	☕	🛒
St Pancras International ⊖	d	22p00	22p25										09 00			09 30			10 00				10 30		
Luton Airport Parkway [7] ✈	d		22p49										09 28						10 29						
Luton [10]	d	22p26														10 01							11 02		
Bedford [7]	d	22p48	23p11										09 51			10 21			10 53				11 27		
Wellingborough	d	23p01	23p23										10 05			10 35			11 07				11 39		
Kettering [4]	a	23p09	23p29										10 13			10 40			11 14				11 46		
	d	23p10	23p30			09 55							10 14			10 42	10 55		11 15				11 46	11 55	
Corby	d					10a05											11a05							12a05	
Oakham	d																								
Melton Mowbray	d																								
Market Harborough	d	23p21	23p40										10 25			10 52			11 26				11 56		
Leicester	a	23p37	23p54										10 45			11 13			11 47				12 16		
	d	23p39	23p55						10 05				10 47			11 22			11 52				12 21		
Syston	d																								
Sileby	d																								
Barrow Upon Soar	d																								
Loughborough	d	23p50	00 11						10 19				11 05			11 40			12 10				12 39		
East Midlands Parkway ✈	d	23p59	00 18						10 27				11 13			11 47			12 19				12 47		
Beeston	a	00 06											11 19												
Nottingham [8] 🚊	a	00 15											11 27						12 30						
	d				09 31		10 06			10 41		11 15			11 46			12 19				12 39			
Lincoln	a																								
Langley Mill	d						10 27					11 31						12 35				12 56			
Alfreton	d				09 53		10 35			11 03		11 39			12 08			12 43				13 04			
Long Eaton	a		00 22						10 30							11 51							12 50		
Derby [6]	a		00 33						10 41							12 02							13 01		
	d			09 44				10 44	10 48					11 44		12 06				12 44			13 03		13 11
Chesterfield	d			10 03	10 08		10 54	11 03	11 09	11 16		11 51		12 03	12 18	12 26		12 54		13 03		13 17	13 23		13 30
Sheffield [7] 🚊	a			10 16	10 33		11 15	11 17	11 28	11 35		12 15		12 18	12 36	12 40		13 16		13 18		13 33	13 42		13 43
Doncaster [7]	a								11 52																14 13
Wakefield Kirkgate [4]	a						11 52					12 52						13 52							
Wakefield Westgate [7]	a			10 44				11 44						12 44						13 45					
Leeds [10]	a			11 02			12 18	12 01				13 18		13 02				14 18		14 02					
York [8]	a			11 29				12 29	12 15					13 29						14 29					14 40

A From Plymouth
B from 8 January until 12 February. From Birmingham New Street to Cambridge
C From Penzance
D From Birmingham New Street to Edinburgh
E To Liverpool Lime Street
F From Birmingham New Street to Glasgow Central
G From Bristol Temple Meads to Edinburgh
H From Bristol Temple Meads to Glasgow Central
I From Birmingham New Street to Newcastle

For connections from Gatwick Airport see Table 52

Table 53

Sundays

from 1 April

London - East Midlands - Sheffield

Route Diagram - see first Page of Table 53

		NT	EM	XC	EM	EM		EM	XC	NT	EM	XC	EM	XC	EM	EM		NT	EM	XC	EM	XC	EM	EM	NT
			◇1	◇1	◇	◇1		◇1	◇1		◇1	◇1	◇	◇1	◇1	◇1			◇1	◇1	◇	◇1	◇1	◇1	
				A	B				C			D	E	F						G	E	H			
			🍽	🛒		🍽		🍽	🛒		🍽	🛒		🛒	🍽	🍽			🍽	🛒		🛒	🍽	🍽	
St Pancras International ⊖	d		11 00			11 30					12 00				12 30				13 00				13 30		
Luton Airport Parkway 7 ✈	d		11 29			11 58					12 29				12 59				13 29				13 57		
Luton 10	d		11 32			12 02					12 33				13 03				13 33				14 03		
Bedford 7	d		11 55			12 26					12 56				13 26				13 55				14 24		
Wellingborough	d		12 09			12 40					13 10				13 40				14 09				14 38		
Kettering 4	a		12 15			12 47					13 16				13 48				14 15				14 45		
	d		12 16			12 48		12 55			13 17				13 49	13 55			14 16				14 46	14 55	
Corby	d							13a05								14a05								15a05	
Oakham	d																								
Melton Mowbray	d																								
Market Harborough	d		12 26			12 58					13 27				14 00				14 26				14 58		
Leicester	a		12 45			13 17					13 46				14 20				14 45				15 18		
	d		12 52			13 18					13 52				14 22				14 47				15 20		
Syston	d																								
Sileby	d																								
Barrow Upon Soar	d																								
Loughborough	d		13 10			13 36					14 10				14 40				15 05				15 38		
East Midlands Parkway ✈	d		13 17			13 43					14 17				14 48				15 12				15 46		
Beeston	a		13 23								14 26								15 18						
Nottingham 8 🚌	a		13 30								14 33								15 25						
	d	13 09			13 38					14 19			14 37					15 12			15 44				16 14
Lincoln	a																								
Langley Mill	d	13 27			13 55					14 35			14 54					15 34							16 30
Alfreton	d	13 35			14 03					14 43			15 02					15 44			16 06				16 38
Long Eaton	a					13 47									14 52								15 50		
Derby 6	a					13 58									15 04								16 02		
	d			13 44		14 04			14 11			14 44		15 11	15 15					15 44		16 11	16 15		
Chesterfield	d	13 46		14 03	14 17	14 24			14 30	14 54		15 03	15 13		15 36			15 53		16 03	16 23		16 36		16 50
Sheffield 7 🚌	a	14 07		14 17	14 35	14 42			14 45	15 15		15 17	15 31	15 47	15 51			16 15		16 18	16 39	16 48	16 52		17 15
Doncaster 7	a								15 13					16 15								17 13			
Wakefield Kirkgate 4	a	14 52								15 52								16 52							17 52
Wakefield Westgate 7	a			14 44								15 44								16 44					
Leeds 10	a	15 18		15 02						16 18		16 02						17 18		17 02					18 18
York 8	a			15 29					15 43			16 29		16 40						17 29		17 42			

		EM		EM	XC	EM	EM	XC	NT	EM	EM	XC		EM	EM	EM	XC	EM	EM	EM	NT	XC		EM	EM
		◇1		◇1	◇1	◇	◇1	◇1		◇1	◇1	◇1		◇	◇1	◇1	◇1	◇1	◇1	◇1		◇1		◇	◇1
					D	B		H				I		B			J					K		L	
		🍽		🍽	🛒		🍽	🛒		🍽	🍽	🛒			🍽	🍽	🛒	🍽	🍽	🍽		🛒			🍽
St Pancras International ⊖	d	14 05					14 35			15 05					15 35	16 05		16 25	16 35						16 55
Luton Airport Parkway 7 ✈	d	14 30								15 31						16 32									
Luton 10	d						15 04								16 04				17 03						
Bedford 7	d	14 54					15 28			15 58					16 27	16 56			17 26						
Wellingborough	d	15 06					15 42			16 12					16 41	17 09			17 40						
Kettering 4	a	15 13					15 49			16 19					16 48	17 16			17 46						
	d	15 14		15 45			15 50			16 20	16 45				16 49	17 17			17 47	17 50					
Corby	d			15a55							16a55									18a00					
Oakham	d																								
Melton Mowbray	d																								
Market Harborough	d	15 24					16 01			16 31					17 00	17 27			17 57						
Leicester	a	15 43					16 22			16 52					17 21	17 46		17 54	18 16						18 24
	d	15 46					16 23			16 54					17 22	17 47		17 56	18 20						18 26
Syston	d																								
Sileby	d																								
Barrow Upon Soar	d																								
Loughborough	d	16 04					16 34			17 05					17 34	17 58			18 30						
East Midlands Parkway ✈	d	16 11					16 43			17 13					17 42	18 05		18 12	18 38						18 43
Beeston	a	16 18														18 11									
Nottingham 8 🚌	a	16 24								17 30						18 18									18 53
	d					16 40			17 14					17 35							18 14			18 37	
Lincoln	a																								
Langley Mill	d					17 00			17 30					17 54							18 30			18 54	
Alfreton	d					17 08			17 38					18 02							18 38			19 02	
Long Eaton	a						16 46								17 46				18 41						
Derby 6	a						16 58								17 58			18 24	18 52						
	d				16 44		17 06	17 11				17 43			18 04		18 11	18 26				18 43			
Chesterfield	d				17 03	17 22	17 27		17 51			18 04		18 17				18 47			18 52	19 05		19 13	
Sheffield 7 🚌	a				17 17	17 40	17 42	17 48	18 14			18 19		18 34	18 41		18 46	19 01			19 16	19 20		19 31	
Doncaster 7	a							18 13									19 15								
Wakefield Kirkgate 4	a								18 52												19 52				
Wakefield Westgate 7	a				17 47		18 17	18 33				18 47										19 48			
Leeds 10	a				18 02		18 30	18 51	19 18			19 04									20 18	20 05			
York 8	a				18 29			19 18				19 29					19 43					20 29			

A From Plymouth to Aberdeen
B From Norwich to Liverpool Lime Street
C From Birmingham New Street to Newcastle
D From Plymouth to Glasgow Central
E To Liverpool Lime Street
F From Guildford to Newcastle
G From Penzance to Edinburgh
H From Reading to Newcastle
I From Plymouth to Edinburgh
J From Reading to Edinburgh
K From Plymouth to Edinburgh. 🛒 to Leeds
L From Norwich to Manchester Piccadilly

For connections from Gatwick Airport see Table 52

Table 53

Sundays

from 1 April

London - East Midlands - Sheffield

Route Diagram - see first Page of Table 53

		EM	XC	EM	EM	EM	NT	XC		EM	EM	EM	EM	XC	EM	EM	NT	EM		EM	XC	EM	EM	EM	XC
		◇1	◇1	◇1	◇1	◇1		◇1		◇	◇1	◇1	◇1	◇1	◇1	◇1		◇1		◇1	◇1	◇1	◇1	◇1	◇1
			A					B		C				D							B				E
St Pancras International ⊖	d	17 05		17 25	17 35						17 55	18 05			18 25	18 35		18 55		19 05		19 25		19 30	
Luton Airport Parkway 7 ✈	d	17 32										18 32								19 32					
Luton 10	d				18 04											19 04								20 03	
Bedford 7	d	17 56			18 28							18 56				19 28				19 56				20 29	
Wellingborough	d	18 09			18 42							19 09				19 41				20 09				20 42	
Kettering 4	a	18 16			18 48							19 16				19 48				20 16				20 49	
	d	18 17			18 49	18 50						19 17	19 45			19 49				20 17			20 46	20 50	
Corby	d					19a00							19a55										20a56		
Oakham	d																								
Melton Mowbray	d																								
Market Harborough	d	18 27			18 59							19 27				19 59				20 27				21 00	
Leicester	a	18 46		18 53	19 18						19 23	19 46			19 54	20 18		20 24		20 46		20 54		21 19	
	d	18 48		18 55	19 20						19 25	19 47			19 55	20 20		20 26		20 47		20 56		21 21	
Syston	d																								
Sileby	d																								
Barrow Upon Soar	d																								
Loughborough	d	18 58			19 30							19 58				20 30				20 57				21 31	
East Midlands Parkway ✈	d	19 06		19 12	19 38						19 42	20 05			20 11	20 38		20 42		21 05		21 12		21 39	
Beeston	a	19 12										20 11								21 10					
Nottingham 8	a	19 18									19 52	20 20						20 52		21 17					
	d						19 19			19 38							20 13								
Lincoln	a																								
Langley Mill	d						19 35										20 29								
Alfreton	d						19 43			20 00							20 37								
Long Eaton	a				19 41											20 41								21 42	
Derby 6	a			19 24	19 52										20 24	20 52						21 26		21 53	
	d		19 05	19 25				19 41						20 03	20 31						20 43	21 27			21 44
Chesterfield	d			19 45			19 54	20 02		20 12					20 52		20 48				21 03	21 48			22 03
Sheffield 7	a		19 39	19 59			20 15	20 17		20 31				20 38	21 11		21 14				21 16	22 03			22 18
Doncaster 7	a		20 16											21 19											
Wakefield Kirkgate 4	a						20 52																		
Wakefield Westgate 7	a							20 46							21 39						21 47				22 43
Leeds 10	a						21 16	21 03							21 57						22 04				23 01
York 8	a		20 45					21 31						21 44											

		NT	EM	EM		EM	XC	EM	EM	EM	EM	EM	EM
			◇1	◇1		◇1	◇1	◇1	◇1	◇1	◇1	◇1	◇1
							B						
St Pancras International ⊖	d		19 55	20 00		20 25		20 30		21 00	21 30	22 30	23 00
Luton Airport Parkway 7 ✈	d			20 24						21 24		22 55	23 27
Luton 10	d							20 56			21 56		
Bedford 7	d			20 46				21 19		21 47	22 17	23 18	23 50
Wellingborough	d			20 59				21 32		22 00	22 31	23 32	00 04
Kettering 4	a			21 05				21 39		22 07	22 37	23 38	00 10
	d			21 06				21 40	21 55	22 08	22 38	23 39	00 11
Corby	d								22a05				
Oakham	d												
Melton Mowbray	d												
Market Harborough	d			21 16				21 51		22 18	22 48	23 49	00 21
Leicester	a		21 23	21 35		21 45		22 12		22 37	23 08	00 08	00 42
	d		21 25	21 37		21 47		22 13		22 38	23 09	00 10	00 44
Syston	d												
Sileby	d												
Barrow Upon Soar	d												
Loughborough	d		21 37	21 47		21 57				22 48	23 20	00 20	00 54
East Midlands Parkway ✈	d		21 45	21 55		22 05		22 29		23 01	23 32	00 28	01 02
Beeston	a			22 00						23 09		00 41	
Nottingham 8	a		21 56	22 08						23 16		00 48	
	d	21 30											
Lincoln	a												
Langley Mill	d	21 52											
Alfreton	d	22 00											
Long Eaton	a										23 39		
Derby 6	a					22 16		22 42			23 50		01 21
	d						22 44	22 51			23 51		
Chesterfield	d	22 13					23 05	23 13			00 11		
Sheffield 7	a	22 36					23 20	23 28			00 24		
Doncaster 7	a												
Wakefield Kirkgate 4	a	23 26											
Wakefield Westgate 7	a							00 01					
Leeds 10	a	00 05					00 16	00 18					
York 8	a												

A From Reading to Newcastle
B From Plymouth
C From Norwich to Manchester Piccadilly
D From Reading to Newcastle. Trolley service to Sheffield
E From Penzance

For connections from Gatwick Airport see Table 52

Sheffield - East Midlands - London

Route Diagram - see first Page of Table 53

Miles	Miles	Miles			EM	EM	EM	EM	EM	EM	EM	EM	NT		EM	EM	EM	EM	EM	EM	NT	XC	EM		EM
					MX	MO	MX																		
					◇1	◇	◇	◇1	◇1	◇1	◇1				◇1	◇1	◇1	◇1	◇1	◇1		◇1			◇1
						A	A															B			
					🛒			🛒	⊠🍴	⊠🍴	⊠🍴				⊠🍴	⊠	🛒	⊠🍴	⊠🍴	⊠🍴					⊠
—	—	—	York 8	d																					
—	—	—	Leeds 10	d																					05 25
—	—	—	Wakefield Westgate 7	d																					05 37
—	—	—	Wakefield Kirkgate 4	d																					
—	—	—	Doncaster 7	d																					05 57
0	0	—	**Sheffield 7**	d	23p21	23p29	23p37						05 05			05 29			05 57		06 00	06 01			06 27
12¼	12¼	—	Chesterfield	d	23p45	23p43	00 02						05 20			05 41			06 10		06 16	06 27			06 39
—	36½	—	**Derby 6**	a	00 11											06 02			06 31			06 46			07 03
—	—	—		d					04 55	05 17						06 04			06 32						07 05
—	44	—	Long Eaton	d						05 27									06 43						
22½	—	—	Alfreton	d		23p54															06 30				
34½	—	—	Langley Mill	d		00 02															06 37				
—	—	—	Lincoln	d																					
40¾	—	—	**Nottingham 8**	a		00 25	00 40						06 12								07 06				
—	—	—		d							05 31	05 43						06 28		06 49					
44	—	—	Beeston	d														06 34		06 55					
—	—	—	East Midlands Parkway	d					05 06		05 42					06 17		06 40		07 02					
55½	53¼	—	Loughborough	d					05 14		05 50	06 05				06 25			06 52				06 53		07 22
59½	57¼	—	Barrow Upon Soar	d								06 09											06 57		
61½	59¼	—	Sileby	d								06 14											07 03		
64¼	62	—	Syston	d								06 20											07 08		
68	65¾	0	**Leicester**	a					05 24	05 42	06 02	06 28				06 37		06 54	07 04	07 16			07 19		07 34
—	—	—		d				04 44	05 26	05 43	06 04					06 39		06 57	07 06	07 17					07 35
84¼	82	—	Market Harborough	d					05 41	05 58	06 19					06 54		07 12		07 32					
—	—	15¼	Melton Mowbray	d											06 01										
—	—	26¾	Oakham	d											06 13										
—	—	41	Corby	d											06 34		07 08								
95¼	93	48½	Kettering 4	a				05 04	05 50	06 07	06 29				06 43	07 04	07 17	07 21	07 28	07 41					07 57
—	—	—		d				05 05	05 51	06 08	06 30				06 44	07 06		07 22	07 29	07 42					07 59
102¼	100	—	Wellingborough	d				05 23	05 59	06 16	06 38				06 53	07 14		07 30	07 38	07 50					08 07
117½	115¼	—	Bedford 7	d				05 36		06 31					07 08				07 55						
137	134¾	—	Luton 10	d					06 24						07 24			07 56		08 15					
138	135¾	—	Luton Airport Parkway 7	d				05 53			07 04					07 41			08 12						
167¼	165	—	**St Pancras International** ⊖	a				06 16	06 48	07 08	07 29				07 47	08 07		08 24	08 39	08 43					08 55

		EM	EM	EM	XC	EM	EM	EM	NT		XC	EM	EM	EM	EM	EM	XC	EM	NT		XC	EM	EM	EM	EM
		◇1	◇1	◇1	◇1	◇1		◇1			◇1	◇1	◇1	◇1	◇1	◇1	◇1				◇1	◇1	◇1	◇1	◇
					C						D			E		F	C	G			H				I
		⊠🍴	🛒	⊠🍴	🍴	🛒		🍴			🍴	⊠	🛒	🛒	⊠	🛒	🍴				🍴	🛒	🛒	🛒	
York 8	d																06 32				07 23				
Leeds 10	d				06 00				06 05		06 15			06 34			07 05		07 05						
Wakefield Westgate 7	d				06 12						06 27			06 46			07 18								
Wakefield Kirkgate 4	d								06 21										07 25						
Doncaster 7	d										06 45										07 55				
Sheffield 7	d			06 47	06 50				07 03		07 18	07 27		07 32	07 41		07 53		08 05		08 20		08 27		08 38
Chesterfield	d			06 59	07 04				07 20		07 30	07 39		07 45	07 55		08 06		08 24		08 32		08 39		08 53
Derby 6	a			07 19	07 25						07 49	07 59			08 14		08 26				08 51		08 59		
	d			07 20		07 26						08 01			08 16								09 01		
Long Eaton	d					07 36									08 26										
Alfreton	d								07 33					07 58					08 35						09 03
Langley Mill	d								07 40					08 06					08 42						
Lincoln	d												07 04					07 26							
Nottingham 8	a								08 02				07 57	08 21				08 30	09 02						09 30
	d	07 10					07 31	07 50					08 02	08 28				08 32						09 02	
Beeston	d	07 17					07 37						08 08			←		08 38						09 08	
East Midlands Parkway	d	07 25		07 33			07 46	08 01						08 39	08 32	08 39		08 46							
Loughborough	d			07 41		07 47	07 55						08 22	→	08 40			08 55						09 20	
Barrow Upon Soar	d						07 59											08 59							
Sileby	d						08 04											09 03							
Syston	d						08 09											09 08							
Leicester	a	07 41		07 52		07 59	08 21	08 17				08 23	08 32		08 52	08 57		09 22					09 23	09 31	
	d	07 42		07 54		08 00		08 18				08 25	08 33		08 52	08 57							09 25	09 33	
Market Harborough	d	07 58				08 16							08 47			09 12								09 47	
Melton Mowbray	d																								
Oakham	d																								
Corby	d		08 02																			09 17			
Kettering 4	a	08 08	08 11	08 14		08 26							08 56									09 26		09 56	
	d	08 09		08 16		08 27							08 56									09 27		09 56	
Wellingborough	d			08 24		08 38							09 04									09 35		10 04	
Bedford 7	d	08 29				09 02							09 18									09 49		10 18	
Luton 10	d					09 18																10 04			
Luton Airport Parkway 7	d												09 34											10 34	
St Pancras International ⊖	a	09 06		09 09		09 44		09 29				09 34	10 00		10 05	10 16						10 29	10 34	11 01	

A From Liverpool Lime Street
B To Reading
C To Plymouth
D To Southampton Central
E To St Pancras International
F From Leeds
G From Sleaford
H From Newcastle to Reading
I From Liverpool Lime Street to Norwich

For connections to Gatwick Airport see Table 52

Sheffield - East Midlands - London

Route Diagram - see first Page of Table 53

		EM	XC	EM	EM	NT	XC	EM	EM	EM	EM	EM	EM	EM	XC	NT	XC	EM	EM	EM	EM	EM	XC
		◇1	◇1	◇1			◇1	◇1	◇1	◇1	◇1	◇1		◇	◇1		◇1	◇1	◇1	◇1	◇	◇1	◇1
			A				B							C	D		E				C		F
		🍴	🚲	🍴			🚲	🍴	🍴	🍴	🍴	🍴			🚲		🚲	🍴	🍴	🍴		🍴	🚲
York 8	d		07 44				08 24								08 44		09 35						09 45
Leeds 10	d		08 11			08 02									09 11	09 05							10 11
Wakefield Westgate 7	d		08 23												09 24								10 23
Wakefield Kirkgate 4	d					08 23										09 23							
Doncaster 7	d						08 50										09 58						
Sheffield 7	d	08 47	08 54			09 05	09 23		09 27		09 35			09 38	09 54	10 05	10 23		10 27		10 38	10 47	10 54
Chesterfield	d	08 59	09 06			09 22			09 39		09 47			09 53	10 06	10 22			10 39		10 52	10 59	11 06
Derby 6	a	09 19	09 25				09 51		09 59		10 16				10 26		10 51		10 59			11 19	11 25
	d	09 20							10 01		10 20								11 01			11 20	
Long Eaton	d	09 30									10 30											11 30	
Alfreton	d					09 32								10 04		10 33					11 03		
Langley Mill	d					09 40										10 40							
Lincoln	d				08 35								09 32										
Nottingham 8	a				09 30	10 00							10 30	10 30		11 00					11 30		
	d			09 28	09 32					10 02		10 28	10 32							11 02			
Beeston	d				09 38					10 08			10 38							11 08			
East Midlands Parkway	d	09 35		09 39	09 46						10 35	10 39	10 46									11 35	
Loughborough	d	09 42			09 55					10 20	10 42		10 55							11 20		11 42	
Barrow Upon Soar	d				09 59								10 59										
Sileby	d				10 03								11 03										
Syston	d				10 08								11 08										
Leicester	a	09 54		09 57	10 21				10 23	10 33	10 54	10 57	11 21						11 23	11 31		11 54	
	d	09 55		09 57					10 25	10 33	10 55	10 57							11 25	11 33		11 55	
Market Harborough	d			10 12						10 47		11 12								11 47			
Melton Mowbray	d																						
Oakham	d																						
Corby	d																	11 17					
Kettering 4	a									10 55								11 26		11 56			
	d							10 27		10 56								11 27		11 56			
Wellingborough	d							10 35		11 04								11 35		12 04			
Bedford 7	d							10 49		11 18								11 49		12 18			
Luton 10	d							11 05										12 05					
Luton Airport Parkway 7	d									11 34										12 34			
St Pancras International	a	11 04		11 16				11 29	11 34	12 00	12 04	12 13						12 29	12 33	13 00		13 04	

		EM	EM	NT	XC	EM	EM	EM	EM	EM	XC	EM	EM	NT	XC	EM	EM	EM	EM	EM	EM	EM
		◇1			◇1	◇1	◇1	◇1	◇	◇1	◇1	◇1			◇1	◇1	◇1	◇1	◇1	◇1		◇
					G				C		H				I							C
		🍴			🚲	🍴	🍴	🍴		🍴	🚲	🍴			🚲	🍴	🍴	🍴	🍴	🍴		
York 8	d				10 34						10 44				11 34							
Leeds 10	d			10 05							11 11			11 05								
Wakefield Westgate 7	d										11 24											
Wakefield Kirkgate 4	d			10 23										11 23								
Doncaster 7	d				10 58										11 58							
Sheffield 7	d			11 05	11 23		11 27		11 38	11 47	11 54			12 05	12 23		12 27		12 35			12 38
Chesterfield	d			11 22			11 39		11 53	11 59	12 06			12 22			12 39		12 48			12 53
Derby 6	a				11 51		11 59			12 19	12 26				12 51		12 59		13 15			
	d						12 01			12 20							13 01		13 20			
Long Eaton	d									12 30									13 30			
Alfreton	d			11 33					12 03					12 33								13 03
Langley Mill	d			11 40										12 40								
Lincoln	d		10 36										11 42								12 30	
Nottingham 8	a		11 30	12 00					12 30				12 30	13 01							13 30	13 30
	d	11 28	11 32					12 02				12 28	12 32					13 02		13 28	13 32	
Beeston	d		11 38					12 08					12 38					13 08			13 38	
East Midlands Parkway	d	11 39	11 46							12 35		12 39	12 46						13 35	13 39	13 46	
Loughborough	d		11 55					12 20		12 42			12 55					13 20	13 42		13 55	
Barrow Upon Soar	d		11 59										12 59								13 59	
Sileby	d		12 03										13 03								14 03	
Syston	d		12 08										13 08								14 08	
Leicester	a	11 57	12 21				12 23	12 31		12 53		12 57	13 21				13 23	13 32	13 54	13 57	14 21	
	d	11 57					12 25	12 33		12 55		12 57					13 25	13 33	13 55	13 57		
Market Harborough	d	12 12						12 47				13 12						13 47		14 12		
Melton Mowbray	d																					
Oakham	d																					
Corby	d					12 17										13 17						
Kettering 4	a					12 26		12 56								13 26		13 56				
	d					12 27		12 56								13 27		13 56				
Wellingborough	d					12 35		13 04								13 35		14 04				
Bedford 7	d					12 49		13 18								13 49		14 18				
Luton 10	d					13 05										14 05						
Luton Airport Parkway 7	d							13 34										14 34				
St Pancras International	a	13 13				13 29	13 34	14 01		14 04		14 13				14 29	14 34	14 59	15 03	15 13		

A From Newcastle to Plymouth
B From Newcastle to Southampton Central
C From Liverpool Lime Street to Norwich
D From Edinburgh to Plymouth
E From Edinburgh to Reading
F From Glasgow Central to Plymouth
G From Newcastle to Southampton Central
H From Dundee to Plymouth
I From Newcastle to Reading

For connections to Gatwick Airport see Table 52

Sheffield - East Midlands - London

Route Diagram - see first Page of Table 53

		XC	NT	XC	EM	EM	EM		EM	EM	XC	EM	EM	NT	XC	EM	EM		EM	EM	EM	XC	EM	EM	NT
		◇1		◇1	◇1	◇1	◇1		◇	◇1	◇1	◇1			◇1	◇1	◇1		◇1	◇1	◇	◇1	◇1		
		A		B					C		D				E						C	F			
		🛒		🛒	☕	☕	☕			☕	🛒	☕			🛒	☕	☕		☕	☕		🛒	☕		
York 8	d	11 45		12 34							12 44				13 34							13 44			
Leeds 10	d	12 12	12 05								13 11			13 05								14 11			14 05
Wakefield Westgate 7	d	12 24									13 23											14 23			
Wakefield Kirkgate 4	d		12 23											13 23											14 23
Doncaster 7	d			12 59											13 58										
Sheffield 7	d	12 54	13 05	13 23		13 27			13 38	13 47	13 54			14 05	14 23		14 27			14 35	14 38	14 54			15 05
Chesterfield	d	13 06	13 22			13 39			13 52	13 59	14 07			14 22			14 39			14 47	14 53	15 06			15 22
Derby 6	a	13 25		13 51		13 59				14 19	14 26				14 51		14 59			15 16		15 25			
	d					14 01				14 20							15 01			15 20					
Long Eaton	d									14 30										15 30					
Alfreton	d		13 33						14 03					14 33							15 04				15 33
Langley Mill	d		13 40											14 40											15 40
Lincoln	d												13 40											14 33	
Nottingham 8	a		14 00						14 30				14 30	15 00							15 28			15 29	16 00
	d						14 02					14 28	14 32						15 02				15 28	15 32	
Beeston	d						14 08						14 38						15 08					15 38	
East Midlands Parkway	d									14 35		14 39	14 46							15 35			15 39	15 46	
Loughborough	d						14 20			14 42			14 55						15 20	15 42				15 55	
Barrow Upon Soar	d												14 59											15 59	
Sileby	d												15 03											16 03	
Syston	d												15 08											16 08	
Leicester	a					14 23	14 31			14 53		14 57	15 21				15 23		15 31	15 53			15 57	16 21	
	d					14 25	14 33			14 55		14 57					15 25		15 33	15 54			15 57		
Market Harborough	d						14 47					15 12							15 47				16 12		
Melton Mowbray	d																								
Oakham	d																								
Corby	d				14 17											15 17									
Kettering 4	a				14 26		14 56									15 26			15 56						
	d				14 27		14 56									15 27			15 56						
Wellingborough	d				14 35		15 04									15 35			16 04						
Bedford 7	d				14 49		15 18									15 49			16 18						
Luton 10	d				15 05											16 05									
Luton Airport Parkway 7	d						15 34												16 34						
St Pancras International ⊖	a				15 29	15 34	15 59			16 04		16 13				16 29	16 33		17 00	17 05			17 18		

		XC	EM		EM	EM	EM	EM	XC	EM	EM	EM	EM		NT	XC	EM	EM	EM	EM	EM	EM	EM		XC
		◇1	◇1		◇1	◇1	◇	◇1	◇1	◇1	◇1	◇1				◇1	◇1	◇1	◇1	◇1	◇1		◇		◇1
		G					C		D			H				E					I		C		J
		🛒	☕		☕	☕		☕	🛒	☕	☕	☕				🛒	☕	☕	☕	☕	☕				🛒
York 8	d	14 34							14 44							15 34									15 44
Leeds 10	d								15 11						15 05										16 11
Wakefield Westgate 7	d								15 23																16 23
Wakefield Kirkgate 4	d														15 23										
Doncaster 7	d	14 58														15 58									
Sheffield 7	d	15 23			15 27		15 38	15 47	15 54						16 04	16 23	16 27		16 35				16 38		16 54
Chesterfield	d				15 39		15 53		16 06						16 21		16 39		16 50				16 56		17 06
Derby 6	a	15 51			15 59			16 16	16 25							16 51	16 59		17 16						17 26
	d				16 01			16 18				16 34					17 01		17 18						
Long Eaton	d							16 28											17 28						
Alfreton	d						16 04								16 32								17 07		
Langley Mill	d														16 40										
Lincoln	d												15 30									16 34			
Nottingham 8	a						16 33						16 30		17 00							17 30	17 31		
	d					16 02				16 28			16 32					17 02		17 28		17 32			
Beeston	d					16 08							16 38					17 08				17 38			
East Midlands Parkway	d							16 32		16 39		16 47	16 48						17 32	17 39		17 48			
Loughborough	d					16 20		16 40					16 57					17 20	17 40			17 57			
Barrow Upon Soar	d												17 01									18 01			
Sileby	d												17 05									18 05			
Syston	d												17 09									18 09			
Leicester	a				16 23	16 31		16 51		16 55			17 22				17 23	17 31	17 52	17 57		18 22			
	d				16 25	16 33		16 53		16 57							17 25	17 33	17 54	17 57					
Market Harborough	d					16 47				17 12								17 47		18 12					
Melton Mowbray	d											17 12													
Oakham	d											17 24													
Corby	d		16 17								17 17	17 52													
Kettering 4	a		16 26			16 56		17 14			17 26	18 01						17 56	18 14						
	d		16 27			16 56		17 15			17 27	18 27						17 56	18 15						
Wellingborough	d		16 35			17 04					17 35	18 35						18 04							
Bedford 7	d		16 49			17 18					17 49	18 49						18 17			←				
Luton 10	d		17 05							17 51	18 05	19 05					18 15				19 05				
Luton Airport Parkway 7	d					17 30						→						18 33							
St Pancras International ⊖	a		17 29		17 33	18 01		18 08		18 17	18 34						18 39	19 00	19 06	19 19	19 32				

A From Glasgow Central to Plymouth
B From Newcastle to Southampton Central
C From Liverpool Lime Street to Norwich
D From Glasgow Central to Penzance
E From Newcastle to Reading
F From Aberdeen to Penzance
G From Newcastle to Eastleigh
H To St Pancras International
I From Derby
J From Edinburgh to Plymouth

For connections to Gatwick Airport see Table 52

Sheffield - East Midlands - London

Route Diagram - see first Page of Table 53

		NT	XC	EM	EM	EM	EM	EM	EM		XC	NT	XC	EM	EM	EM	EM	EM	EM		EM	XC	NT	XC	EM
			◇1	◇1	◇1	◇1	◇1		◇		◇1		◇1	◇1	◇1	◇1	◇1	◇1			◇	◇1		◇1	◇1
			A						B		C		A								D	E		F	
			🛒	☕	☕	☕	☕				🛒		🛒	☕	☕	☕	☕	☕				🛒		🛒	☕
York 8	d		16 04								16 44		17 34									17 44		18 34	
Leeds 10	d	16 05	16 40								17 11	17 05										18 11	18 05		
Wakefield Westgate 7	d		16 52								17 23											18 23			
Wakefield Kirkgate 4	d	16 23										17 23											18 23		
Doncaster 7	d												17 59											18 58	
Sheffield 7	d	17 05	17 23	17 27		17 35			17 44		17 54	18 05	18 23		18 27		18 35				18 45	18 54	19 05	19 23	
Chesterfield	d	17 22		17 39		17 50			18 02		18 07	18 22			18 39		18 47				19 01	19 06	19 22		
Derby 6	a		17 51	17 59		18 16					18 26		18 51		18 59		19 14					19 26		19 52	
	d			18 01		18 18									19 01		19 18								
Long Eaton	d					18 28											19 28								
Alfreton	d	17 33							18 12			18 33									19 11		19 33		
Langley Mill	d	17 40										18 40											19 40		
Lincoln	d							17 28											18 35						
Nottingham 8	a	18 00						18 32	18 34			19 00							19 29		19 38		20 00		
	d				18 02		18 28	18 33								19 02		19 28	19 32						
Beeston	d				18 08			18 39								19 08			19 38						
East Midlands Parkway	d					18 32	18 39	18 48									19 32	19 39	19 46						
Loughborough	d				18 20	18 40		18 56								19 20	19 40		19 55						
Barrow Upon Soar	d							19 01											19 59						
Sileby	d							19 05											20 03						
Syston	d							19 10											20 08						
Leicester	a			18 23	18 31	18 51	18 55	19 22							19 23	19 31	19 51	19 55	20 20						
	d			18 25	18 33	18 53	18 57								19 25	19 33	19 53	19 57							
Market Harborough	d				18 47		19 12									19 47		20 12							
Melton Mowbray	d																								
Oakham	d																								
Corby	d													18 57											19 43
Kettering 4	a				18 56									19 06		19 56									19 52
	d				18 56									19 27		19 56									20 27
Wellingborough	d				19 04									19 35		20 04									20 35
Bedford 7	d				19 18									19 49		20 18									20 54
Luton 10	d													20 05											21 08
Luton Airport Parkway 7	d				19 34											20 34									
St Pancras International	a			19 35	20 01	20 04	20 11							20 29	20 34	20 59	21 02	21 11							21 33

		EM	EM	EM	XC		EM	NT	XC	EM	EM	EM	EM	EM	EM		EM	XC	XC	EM	EM	XC	EM	EM	EM
		◇1	◇1	◇	◇1				◇1	◇1	◇1	◇1	◇1	◇1			◇	◇1	◇1	◇	◇1	◇1	◇1		◇1
				B	G				H								D	I	H	D		J			
		☕	☕		🛒				🛒	☕	☕	☕	☕	☕				🛒			☕	🛒	☕		☕
York 8	d				18 45				19 34									19 44	20 34			20 44			
Leeds 10	d				19 11			19 05										20 11				21 11			
Wakefield Westgate 7	d				19 23													20 23				21 23			
Wakefield Kirkgate 4	d							19 24																	
Doncaster 7	d								19 58										21 02						
Sheffield 7	d	19 27		19 38	19 54			20 05	20 23				20 39				20 41	20 54	21 28	21 39	21 42	22 00			23 21
Chesterfield	d	19 39		19 53	20 06			20 22					20 53				20 58	21 06	21 41	21 55	22 00	22 24			23 45
Derby 6	a	19 59			20 26				20 52				21 18					21 26	22 00		22 21	22 44			00 11
	d	20 01											21 20												
Long Eaton	d																								
Alfreton	d			20 04				20 33									21 09			22 05					
Langley Mill	d							20 40												22 12					
Lincoln	d																								
Nottingham 8	a			20 31				21 00									21 38			22 38					
	d		20 02				20 32					21 02		21 28	21 32									23 10	
Beeston	d		20 08				20 38					21 08			21 38									23 16	
East Midlands Parkway	d		20 16				20 46					21 15	21 33		21 46									23 25	
Loughborough	d		20 24				20 55					21 22	21 41	21 46	21 55									23 33	
Barrow Upon Soar	d						20 59								21 59										
Sileby	d						21 03								22 03										
Syston	d						21 08								22 08										
Leicester	a	20 23	20 34				21 22					21 32	21 52	21 58	22 21									23 58	
	d	20 25	20 36									21 33	21 55	21 59											
Market Harborough	d		20 50									21 47		22 13											
Melton Mowbray	d																								
Oakham	d																								
Corby	d									20 43	21 43												22 43		
Kettering 4	a		20 59							20 52	21 52	21 56		22 22									22 52		
	d		20 59							21 17		21 57		22 23											
Wellingborough	d		21 07							21 26		22 05		22 31											
Bedford 7	d		21 22							21 44		22 19		22 45											
Luton 10	d									22 01		22 34		23 02											
Luton Airport Parkway 7	d		21 39									22 38													
St Pancras International	a	21 36	22 04							22 29		23 01	23 04	23 34											

A From Newcastle to Reading
B From Liverpool Lime Street to Norwich
C From Glasgow Central to Plymouth
D From Liverpool Lime Street
E From Edinburgh to Plymouth
F From Newcastle to Guildford
G From Glasgow Central to Bristol Temple Meads
H From Newcastle to Birmingham New Street
I From Edinburgh to Bristol Temple Meads. 🛒 to Leeds
J From Glasgow Central to Birmingham New Street. 🛒 to Leeds

For connections to Gatwick Airport see Table 52

Sheffield - East Midlands - London

Route Diagram - see first Page of Table 53

		EM
		◇
		A
York [8]	d	
Leeds [10]	d	
Wakefield Westgate [7]	d	
Wakefield Kirkgate [4]	d	
Doncaster [7]	d	
Sheffield [7]	d	23 37
Chesterfield	d	00 02
Derby [6]	a	
	d	
Long Eaton	d	
Alfreton	d	
Langley Mill	d	
Lincoln	d	
Nottingham [8]	a	00 40
	d	
Beeston	d	
East Midlands Parkway ✈	d	
Loughborough	d	
Barrow Upon Soar	d	
Sileby	d	
Syston	d	
Leicester	a	
	d	
Market Harborough	d	
Melton Mowbray	d	
Oakham	d	
Corby	d	
Kettering [4]	a	
	d	
Wellingborough	d	
Bedford [7]	d	
Luton [10]	d	
Luton Airport Parkway [7] ✈	d	
St Pancras International ⊖	a	

Saturdays

until 24 March

		EM	EM	EM	EM	EM	EM	EM	EM	NT		EM	EM	EM	EM	EM	XC	EM	EM	NT		XC	EM	EM	EM
		◇[1]	◇	◇[1]	◇[1]	◇[1]	◇[1]	◇[1]	◇[1]				◇[1]	◇[1]	◇[1]	◇[1]	◇[1]	◇[1]				◇[1]	◇[1]	◇[1]	◇[1]
			A														B			C		D			
		☕		☕	☕	☕	☕	☕	☕				☕	☕	☕	☕	🛒	☕				🛒	☕	☕	☕
York [8]	d																								
Leeds [10]	d																06 00					06 15			
Wakefield Westgate [7]	d																06 12					06 29			
Wakefield Kirkgate [4]	d																								
Doncaster [7]	d																					06 47			
Sheffield [7]	d	23p21	23p37			05 27				05 54			06 25				06 50			07 03		07 18		07 27	
Chesterfield	d	23p45	00 02			05 39				06 20			06 37				07 03			07 20		07 30		07 39	
Derby [6]	a	00 11				05 59							06 59				07 24					07 49		07 59	
	d				05 25	06 01		06 18					07 01			07 18								08 01	
Long Eaton	d				05 35			06 28								07 28									
Alfreton	d									06 30										07 33					
Langley Mill	d									06 38										07 40					
Lincoln	d																								07 04
Nottingham [8]	a		00 40							07 04										08 02					07 58
	d						06 02		06 28						07 02			07 28	07 31						08 02
Beeston	d						06 08								07 08				07 37						08 08
East Midlands Parkway ✈	d				05 39			06 32	06 39							07 32		07 39	07 46						
Loughborough	d				05 47		06 20	06 40				06 50			07 20	07 40			07 55						08 20
Barrow Upon Soar	d											06 57							07 59						
Sileby	d											07 05							08 03						
Syston	d											07 10							08 08						
Leicester	a				05 57	06 23	06 31	06 51	06 55			07 21	07 23		07 31	07 51		07 55	08 21					08 23	08 31
	d			04 40	05 59	06 25	06 33	06 53	06 57				07 25		07 33	07 53		07 57						08 25	08 33
Market Harborough	d				06 14		06 47		07 12						07 47			08 12							08 47
Melton Mowbray	d																								
Oakham	d																								
Corby	d													07 08									08 15		
Kettering [4]	a			05 00	06 23		06 56	07 15						07 20	07 56								08 24		08 56
	d			05 01	06 26		06 56	07 26							07 56								08 26		08 56
Wellingborough	d			05 09	06 34		07 04	07 34							08 04								08 34		09 04
Bedford [7]	d			05 32	06 49		07 19	07 49							08 19								08 49		09 19
Luton [10]	d				07 04			08 05															09 05		
Luton Airport Parkway [7] ✈	d			05 55			07 35								08 35										09 35
St Pancras International ⊖	a			06 21	07 31	07 34	08 00	08 31	08 19				08 34		09 01	09 06		09 19					09 29	09 34	09 59

A From Liverpool Lime Street
B To Plymouth
C From Barnsley
D To Southampton Central

For connections to Gatwick Airport see Table 52

Table 53

Saturdays

until 24 March

Sheffield - East Midlands - London

Route Diagram - see first Page of Table 53

		EM	EM	XC	EM	NT		XC	EM	EM	EM	EM	EM	EM	EM	XC		EM	NT	XC	EM	EM	EM	EM	EM
		◇1	◇1	◇1				◇1	◇1	◇1	◇1	◇1	◇	◇1	◇1	◇1				◇1	◇1	◇1	◇1	◇	◇1
				A	B			C				D	E		F	G				H				E	
		☒	☕	🛒				🛒	☕	☕	☕	☕		☕	☕	🛒				🛒	☕	☕	☕		☕
York 8	d			06 17				07 24								07 44				08 34					
Leeds 10	d		06 34	07 10		07 05						07 34				08 12			08 05						
Wakefield Westgate 7	d		06 46	07 23								07 46				08 24									
Wakefield Kirkgate 4	d					07 25													08 23						
Doncaster 7	d							07 52												08 58					
Sheffield 7	d		07 32	07 56		08 05		08 20		08 27		08 32	08 38	08 47		08 54			09 05	09 23		09 27		09 38	09 47
Chesterfield	d		07 45	08 08		08 24		08 32		08 39		08 45	08 53	08 59		09 06			09 23			09 39		09 53	09 59
Derby 6	a			08 27				08 51		08 59				09 19		09 25				09 51		09 59			10 19
	d	08 18								09 01				09 20								10 01			10 20
Long Eaton	d	08 28												09 30											10 30
Alfreton	d		07 56			08 35						08 56	09 03						09 32					10 03	
Langley Mill	d		08 04			08 42													09 41						
Lincoln	d				07 26													08 35							
Nottingham 8	a		08 23		08 30	09 02						09 21	09 30					09 30	10 00					10 30	
	d		08 28		08 32						09 02	09 28						09 32					10 02		
Beeston	d				08 38						09 08				←			09 38					10 08		
East Midlands Parkway ✈	d	08 32	08 39		08 46							09 39		09 35	09 39			09 46							10 35
Loughborough	d	08 40			08 55						09 20	→		09 42				09 55					10 20		10 42
Barrow Upon Soar	d				08 59													09 59							
Sileby	d				09 03													10 03							
Syston	d				09 08													10 08							
Leicester	a	08 51	08 55		09 18					09 23	09 31			09 54	09 57			10 21				10 23	10 31		10 54
	d	08 53	08 57							09 25	09 33			09 55	09 57							10 25	10 33		10 55
Market Harborough	d		09 12								09 47				10 14								10 47		
Melton Mowbray	d																								
Oakham	d																								
Corby	d								09 17												10 17				
Kettering 4	a								09 26		09 56										10 26		10 56		
	d								09 27		09 57										10 27		10 56		
Wellingborough	d								09 35		10 04										10 35		11 04		
Bedford 7	d								09 49		10 19										10 49		11 19		
Luton 10	d								10 05												11 05				
Luton Airport Parkway 7 ✈	d										10 35												11 35		
St Pancras International ⊖	a	10 06	10 19						10 29	10 34	11 01			11 05	11 19						11 29	11 37	12 01		12 05

		XC		EM	EM	NT	XC	EM	EM	EM	EM	EM		XC	EM	EM	NT	XC	EM	EM	EM	EM		EM	XC
		◇1		◇1			◇1	◇1	◇1	◇1	◇	◇1		◇1	◇1			◇1	◇1	◇1	◇1	◇		◇1	◇1
		I					J				E			K				L				E			M
		🛒		☕			🛒	☕	☕	☕		☕		🛒	☕			🛒	☕	☕	☕			☕	🛒
York 8	d	08 44					09 35							09 46				10 34							10 45
Leeds 10	d	09 11				09 05								10 12			10 05								11 11
Wakefield Westgate 7	d	09 24												10 24											11 23
Wakefield Kirkgate 4	d					09 23											10 23								
Doncaster 7	d						09 58											10 58							
Sheffield 7	d	09 54				10 04	10 23		10 27		10 38	10 47		10 54			11 05	11 23		11 27		11 38		11 47	11 54
Chesterfield	d	10 06				10 21			10 39		10 53	10 59		11 06			11 22			11 39		11 53		11 59	12 07
Derby 6	a	10 25					10 51		10 59			11 19		11 25				11 51		11 59				12 19	12 26
	d								11 01			11 20								12 01				12 20	
Long Eaton	d											11 30												12 30	
Alfreton	d					10 32					11 03						11 35					12 03			
Langley Mill	d					10 40											11 40								
Lincoln	d				09 19											10 36									
Nottingham 8	a				10 25	11 00					11 29					11 29	12 00					12 29			
	d			10 28	10 32					11 02					11 28	11 32					12 02				
Beeston	d				10 38					11 08						11 38					12 08				
East Midlands Parkway ✈	d			10 39	10 46							11 35			11 39	11 46								12 35	
Loughborough	d				10 55					11 20		11 42				11 55					12 20			12 42	
Barrow Upon Soar	d				10 59											11 59									
Sileby	d				11 03											12 03									
Syston	d				11 08											12 08									
Leicester	a			10 57	11 20				11 23	11 31		11 54			11 57	12 19				12 23	12 31			12 54	
	d			10 57					11 25	11 33		11 55			11 57					12 25	12 33			12 55	
Market Harborough	d			11 12						11 47					12 12						12 47				
Melton Mowbray	d																								
Oakham	d																								
Corby	d							11 17											12 17						
Kettering 4	a							11 26		11 56									12 26		12 56				
	d							11 27		11 56									12 27		12 56				
Wellingborough	d							11 35		12 04									12 35		13 04				
Bedford 7	d							11 49		12 19									12 49		13 19				
Luton 10	d							12 05											13 05						
Luton Airport Parkway 7 ✈	d									12 35											13 35				
St Pancras International ⊖	a			12 19				12 29	12 34	13 01		13 05			13 19				13 29	13 34	14 01			14 05	

- **A** To Plymouth
- **B** From Sleaford
- **C** From Newcastle to Reading
- **D** To St Pancras International
- **E** From Liverpool Lime Street to Norwich
- **F** From Leeds
- **G** From Newcastle to Plymouth
- **H** From Newcastle to Southampton Central
- **I** From Edinburgh to Plymouth
- **J** From Edinburgh to Reading
- **K** From Glasgow Central to Plymouth
- **L** From Newcastle to Southampton Central
- **M** From Dundee to Plymouth

For connections to Gatwick Airport see Table 52

Table 53

Saturdays

until 24 March

Sheffield - East Midlands - London

Route Diagram - see first Page of Table 53

		EM	EM	NT	XC	EM	EM	EM		EM	EM	XC	EM	EM	NT	XC	EM	EM		EM	EM	EM	XC	EM	EM
		◇1			◇1	◇1	◇1	◇1		◇	◇1	◇1	◇1			◇1	◇1	◇1		◇1	◇	◇1	◇1	◇1	
					A					B		C				D					B		E		
		☕			🛒	☕	☕	☕			☕	🛒	☕			🛒	☕	☕		☕		☕	🛒	☕	
York [8]	d				11 34							11 45				12 34							12 45		
Leeds [10]	d			11 05								12 11			12 05								13 11		
Wakefield Westgate [7]	d											12 24											13 23		
Wakefield Kirkgate [4]	d			11 23											12 23										
Doncaster [7]	d				11 58											12 58									
Sheffield [7] 🚊	d			12 05	12 23		12 27			12 38	12 47	12 54			13 05	13 23		13 27			13 38	13 47	13 54		
Chesterfield	d			12 22			12 39			12 53	12 59	13 06			13 22			13 39			13 53	13 59	14 07		
Derby [6]	a				12 51		12 59				13 19	13 25				13 51		13 59				14 19	14 27		
	d						13 01				13 20							14 01				14 20			
Long Eaton	d										13 30											14 30			
Alfreton	d			12 33						13 03					13 33						14 03				
Langley Mill	d			12 40											13 40										
Lincoln	d		11 42											12 30											13 40
Nottingham [8] 🚊	a		12 30	13 01						13 30				13 30	14 00						14 29				14 30
	d	12 28	12 32					13 02					13 28	13 32						14 02				14 28	14 32
Beeston	d		12 38					13 08						13 38						14 08					14 38
East Midlands Parkway ✈	d	12 39	12 46								13 35		13 39	13 46								14 35		14 39	14 46
Loughborough	d		12 55					13 20			13 42			13 55						14 20		14 42			14 55
Barrow Upon Soar	d		12 59											13 59											14 59
Sileby	d		13 03											14 03											15 03
Syston	d		13 08											14 08											15 08
Leicester	a	12 57	13 19				13 23	13 31			13 54		13 57	14 19				14 23		14 31		14 54		14 57	15 21
	d	12 57					13 25	13 33			13 55		13 57					14 25		14 33		14 55		14 57	
Market Harborough	d	13 14						13 47					14 12							14 47				15 12	
Melton Mowbray	d																								
Oakham	d																								
Corby	d					13 17											14 17								
Kettering [4]	a					13 26		13 56									14 26			14 56					
	d					13 27		13 56									14 27			14 56					
Wellingborough	d					13 35		14 04									14 35			15 04					
Bedford [7]	d					13 49		14 19									14 49			15 19					
Luton [10]	d					14 05											15 05								
Luton Airport Parkway [7] ✈	d							14 35												15 35					
St Pancras International ⊖	a	14 19				14 29	14 34	15 01			15 05		15 19				15 29	15 34		16 01		16 05		16 19	

		NT	XC	EM		EM	EM	EM	EM	XC	EM	EM	NT	XC		EM	EM	EM	EM	EM	XC	EM	EM	NT	
			◇1	◇1		◇1	◇1	◇	◇1	◇1	◇1			◇1		◇1	◇1	◇1	◇	◇1	◇1	◇1			
			A					B		F				D					B		E				
			🛒	☕		☕	☕		☕	🛒	☕			🛒		☕	☕	☕		☕	🛒	☕			
York [8]	d		13 34							13 44				14 34							14 44				
Leeds [10]	d	13 05								14 11			14 05								15 12			15 05	
Wakefield Westgate [7]	d									14 24											15 24				
Wakefield Kirkgate [4]	d	13 23											14 23											15 23	
Doncaster [7]	d		13 58											14 58											
Sheffield [7] 🚊	d	14 05	14 23			14 27		14 38	14 47	14 54			15 05	15 23			15 27		15 38	15 47	15 54			16 04	
Chesterfield	d	14 22				14 39		14 53	14 59	15 06			15 22				15 39		15 53	15 59	16 07			16 21	
Derby [6]	a		14 51			14 59			15 19	15 26				15 51			15 59			16 19	16 26				
	d					15 01			15 20								16 01			16 20					
Long Eaton	d								15 30											16 30					
Alfreton	d	14 33						15 04					15 33						16 04					16 32	
Langley Mill	d	14 40											15 40											16 40	
Lincoln	d											14 35											15 27		
Nottingham [8] 🚊	a	15 00						15 29				15 30	16 00						16 30				16 30	17 00	
	d						15 02				15 28	15 32						16 02				16 28	16 32		
Beeston	d						15 08					15 38						16 08					16 38		
East Midlands Parkway ✈	d								15 35		15 39	15 46								16 35		16 39	16 48		
Loughborough	d						15 20		15 42			15 55						16 19		16 42			16 57		
Barrow Upon Soar	d											15 59											17 01		
Sileby	d											16 03											17 05		
Syston	d											16 08											17 10		
Leicester	a					15 23	15 31		15 54		15 57	16 21					16 23	16 31		16 54		16 57	17 22		
	d					15 25	15 33		15 55		15 57						16 25	16 33		16 55		16 57			
Market Harborough	d						15 47				16 12							16 47				17 12			
Melton Mowbray	d																								
Oakham	d																								
Corby	d			15 17												16 17									
Kettering [4]	a			15 26			15 56									16 26		16 56							
	d			15 27			15 56									16 27		16 56							
Wellingborough	d			15 35			16 04									16 35		17 04							
Bedford [7]	d			15 49			16 19									16 49		17 19							
Luton [10]	d			16 05												17 05									
Luton Airport Parkway [7] ✈	d						16 35											17 35							
St Pancras International ⊖	a			16 29		16 34	17 01		17 05		17 19					17 29	17 34	18 01		18 05		18 19			

A From Newcastle to Reading
B From Liverpool Lime Street to Norwich
C From Glasgow Central to Plymouth
D From Newcastle to Southampton Central
E From Glasgow Central to Penzance
F From Aberdeen to Penzance

For connections to Gatwick Airport see Table 52

Table 53

Saturdays until 24 March

Sheffield - East Midlands - London

Route Diagram - see first Page of Table 53

		XC	EM	EM	EM	EM	EM	EM	XC	EM		NT	XC	EM	EM	EM	EM	EM	EM	EM		XC	NT	XC	EM
		◇1	◇1	◇1	◇1	◇1	◇1	◇	◇1				◇1	◇1	◇1	◇1	◇1	◇1		◇		◇1		◇1	◇1
		A						B	C				A							B		D		A	
		🛒	☕	☕	☕	☕	☕		🛒				🛒	☕	☕	☕	☕	☕				🛒		🛒	☕
York 8	d	15 34							15 45				16 06									16 44		17 34	
Leeds 10	d								16 12			16 05	16 40									17 11	17 05		
Wakefield Westgate 7	d								16 24				16 52									17 23			
Wakefield Kirkgate 4	d											16 23											17 23		
Doncaster 7	d	15 58																						17 58	
Sheffield 7 🚌	d	16 23		16 27		16 35		16 38	16 54			17 05	17 23		17 27		17 35			17 44		17 54	18 06	18 23	
Chesterfield	d			16 39		16 47		16 53	17 06			17 22			17 39		17 51			18 01		18 07	18 22		
Derby 6	a	16 51		16 59		17 16			17 26				17 51		17 59		18 16					18 26		18 51	
	d			17 01		17 18									18 01		18 18								
Long Eaton	d					17 28											18 28								
Alfreton	d							17 04				17 33								18 11			18 33		
Langley Mill	d											17 40											18 40		
Lincoln	d									16 34									17 26						
Nottingham 8 🚌	a							17 29		17 30		18 00							18 31	18 33			19 00		
	d				17 02		17 28			17 32						18 02		18 28	18 32						
Beeston	d				17 08					17 38						18 08			18 38						
East Midlands Parkway ✈	d					17 32	17 39			17 48							18 32	18 39	18 47						
Loughborough	d				17 20	17 40				17 57						18 20	18 40		18 55						
Barrow Upon Soar	d									18 01									19 00						
Sileby	d									18 05									19 04						
Syston	d									18 10									19 09						
Leicester	a			17 23	17 31	17 51	17 55			18 22					18 23	18 31	18 51	18 55	19 21						
	d			17 25	17 33	17 53	17 57								18 25	18 33	18 53	18 57							
Market Harborough	d				17 47		18 12									18 47		19 12							
Melton Mowbray	d																								
Oakham	d																								
Corby	d		17 17											18 17											19 17
Kettering 4	a		17 26		17 56									18 26		18 56									19 26
	d		17 27		17 56									18 27		18 56									19 27
Wellingborough	d		17 35		18 04									18 35		19 04									19 35
Bedford 7	d		17 49		18 19									18 49		19 18									19 49
Luton 10	d		18 05											19 05											20 05
Luton Airport Parkway 7 ✈	d				18 35											19 30									
St Pancras International ⊖	a		18 29	18 34	18 59	19 06	19 19							19 29	19 34	20 01	20 05	20 19							20 29

		EM	EM	EM	EM	XC		EM	EM	NT	XC	EM	EM	EM	EM	XC		EM	EM	EM	NT	XC	EM	EM	EM
		◇1	◇1	◇	◇1	◇1		◇1			◇1	◇1	◇1	◇1	◇	◇1			◇1	◇1		◇1	◇1	◇1	◇1
				E		F					G				B	H						G			
		☕	☕		☕	🛒		☕			🛒	☕	☕	☕		🛒			☕	☕		🛒	☕	☕	☕
York 8	d				17 50	17 44					18 34					18 44						19 34			
Leeds 10	d					18 11				18 05						19 11					19 05				
Wakefield Westgate 7	d					18 23										19 24									
Wakefield Kirkgate 4	d									18 23											19 24				
Doncaster 7	d				18 18						18 58											19 58			
Sheffield 7 🚌	d	18 27		18 38	18 47	18 54				19 05	19 24		19 27		19 38	19 54					20 05	20 23	20 27		
Chesterfield	d	18 39		18 53		19 06				19 22			19 39		19 53	20 06					20 22		20 39		
Derby 6	a	18 59			19 19	19 25					19 52		19 59			20 26						20 51	21 00		
	d	19 01			19 21								20 01										21 01		
Long Eaton	d				19 31																				
Alfreton	d			19 03						19 33					20 04						20 33				
Langley Mill	d									19 40											20 40				
Lincoln	d								18 34																
Nottingham 8 🚌	a			19 33					19 29	20 00					20 31						21 00				
	d		19 02					19 28	19 32					20 02				20 32		20 43					21 18
Beeston	d		19 08						19 38					20 08				20 38		20 49					
East Midlands Parkway ✈	d				19 35			19 41	19 46					20 16				20 46		20 55			21 14		
Loughborough	d		19 20		19 41				19 55					20 24				20 55		21 03			21 23		21 32
Barrow Upon Soar	d								19 59									20 59							
Sileby	d								20 03									21 03							
Syston	d								20 08									21 08							
Leicester	a	19 23	19 31		19 54			19 58	20 20				20 23	20 34				21 19		21 13			21 36		21 42
	d	19 25	19 33		19 54			20 00					20 25	20 36						21 15					21 44
Market Harborough	d		19 47					20 15						20 50						21 29					21 58
Melton Mowbray	d																								
Oakham	d																								
Corby	d											19 43							20 43					21 43	
Kettering 4	a		19 56		20 16							19 52		20 59					20 52	21 38				21 52	22 07
	d		19 56		20 17							20 26		20 59					21 24	21 38					22 08
Wellingborough	d		20 04									20 35		21 07					21 32	21 47					22 15
Bedford 7	d		20 18									20 49		21 22					21 47	22 01					22 37
Luton 10	d											21 03							22 03	22 16					22 59
Luton Airport Parkway 7 ✈	d		20 30											21 38						22 19					
St Pancras International ⊖	a	20 34	21 01		21 06			21 15				21 29	21 34	22 05					22 29	22 46					23 35

A From Newcastle to Reading
B From Liverpool Lime Street to Norwich
C From Edinburgh to Plymouth
D From Glasgow Central to Plymouth
E From Liverpool Lime Street
F From Edinburgh to Exeter St Davids
G From Newcastle to Birmingham New Street
H From Glasgow Central to Bristol Temple Meads

For connections to Gatwick Airport see Table 52

Table 53

Saturdays
until 24 March

Sheffield - East Midlands - London

Route Diagram - see first Page of Table 53

		EM		EM	XC	XC	EM	XC	EM	EM	EM	EM		EM	EM
				◇	◇1	◇1	◇	◇1	◇1		◇	◇1		◇	◇
				A	B	C	A	D			A			E	F
					🍴			🍴	☕			☕			
York 8	d				19 44	20 34		20 45							
Leeds 10	d				20 11			21 11							
Wakefield Westgate 7	d				20 23			21 23							
Wakefield Kirkgate 4	d														
Doncaster 7	d					21 00									
Sheffield 7	d			20 41	20 54	21 23	21 38	21 54			22 35	23 20		23 42	23 42
Chesterfield	d			20 59	21 06	21 35	21 54	22 06			22 51	23 33		23 57	23 57
Derby 6	a				21 26	21 52		22 25				00 13			
	d														
Long Eaton	d														
Alfreton	d			21 09			22 05				23 02				
Langley Mill	d						22 12								
Lincoln	d														
Nottingham 8	a			21 33			22 33				23 32			00 30	00 34
	d	21 32								23 10					
Beeston	d	21 38								23 16					
East Midlands Parkway	d	21 46								23 25					
Loughborough	d	21 55								23 33					
Barrow Upon Soar	d	21 59													
Sileby	d	22 03													
Syston	d	22 13													
Leicester	a	22 21								23 52					
	d														
Market Harborough	d														
Melton Mowbray	d														
Oakham	d														
Corby	d								22 43						
Kettering 4	a								22 52						
	d														
Wellingborough	d														
Bedford 7	d														
Luton 10	d														
Luton Airport Parkway 7	d														
St Pancras International ⊖	a														

Saturdays
from 31 March

		EM	EM	EM	EM	EM	EM	EM	EM	NT		EM	EM	EM	EM	EM	XC	EM	EM	NT		XC	EM	EM	EM
		◇1	◇	◇1	◇1	◇1	◇1	◇1	◇1				◇1	◇1	◇1	◇1	◇1	◇1				◇1	◇1	◇1	◇1
			A														G			H		I			
		☕		☕	☕	☕	☕	☕	☕				☕	☕	☕	☕	🍴	☕				🍴	☕	☕	☕
York 8	d																								
Leeds 10	d																06 00					06 15			
Wakefield Westgate 7	d																06 12					06 29			
Wakefield Kirkgate 4	d																								
Doncaster 7	d																					06 47			
Sheffield 7	d	23p21	23p37			05 27				05 54			06 25				06 50			07 03		07 18		07 27	
Chesterfield	d	23p45	00 02			05 39				06 20			06 37				07 03			07 20		07 30		07 39	
Derby 6	a	00 11				05 59							06 59				07 24					07 49		07 59	
	d				05 25	06 01		06 18					07 01			07 18								08 01	
Long Eaton	d				05 35			06 28								07 28									
Alfreton	d									06 30										07 33					
Langley Mill	d									06 38										07 40					
Lincoln	d																								07 04
Nottingham 8	a		00 40							07 04										08 02					07 58
	d						06 02		06 28						07 02			07 28	07 31						08 02
Beeston	d						06 08								07 08				07 37						08 08
East Midlands Parkway	d				05 39			06 32	06 39							07 32		07 39	07 46						
Loughborough	d				05 47		06 20	06 40				06 50			07 20	07 40			07 55						08 20
Barrow Upon Soar	d											06 57							07 59						
Sileby	d											07 05							08 03						
Syston	d											07 10							08 08						
Leicester	a				05 57	06 23	06 31	06 51	06 55			07 21	07 23		07 31	07 51		07 55	08 21					08 23	08 31
	d			04 40	05 59	06 25	06 33	06 53	06 57				07 25		07 33	07 53		07 57						08 25	08 33
Market Harborough	d				06 14		06 47		07 12						07 47			08 12							08 47
Melton Mowbray	d																								
Oakham	d																								
Corby	d													07 08									08 15		
Kettering 4	a			05 00	06 23		06 56	07 15						07 20	07 56								08 24		08 56
	d			05 01	06 26		06 56	07 26							07 56								08 26		08 56
Wellingborough	d			05 09	06 34		07 04	07 34							08 04								08 34		09 04
Bedford 7	d			05 32	06 49		07 19	07 49							08 19								08 49		09 19
Luton 10	d				07 04			08 05															09 05		
Luton Airport Parkway 7	d			05 55			07 35								08 35										09 35
St Pancras International ⊖	a			06 21	07 31	07 34	08 00	08 31	08 12				08 34		09 01	09 06		09 12					09 29	09 34	09 59

A From Liverpool Lime Street
B From Edinburgh to Birmingham New Street. 🍴 to Leeds
C From Newcastle to Birmingham New Street
D From Glasgow Central to Birmingham New Street. 🍴 to Leeds
E from 18 February until 24 March. From Liverpool Lime Street
F until 11 February. From Liverpool Lime Street
G To Plymouth
H From Barnsley
I To Southampton Central

For connections to Gatwick Airport see Table 52

Table 53

Saturdays

from 31 March

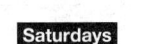

Sheffield - East Midlands - London

Route Diagram - see first Page of Table 53

		EM	EM	XC	EM	NT		XC	EM	EM	EM	EM	EM	EM	EM	XC		EM	NT	XC	EM	EM	EM	EM	EM
		◇1	◇1	◇1				◇1	◇1	◇1	◇1	◇1	◇	◇1	◇1	◇1				◇1	◇1	◇1	◇1	◇	◇1
				A	B			C				D	E		F	G				H				E	
		☒	☕	🛒				🛒	☕	☕	☕	☕		☕	☕	🛒				🛒	☕	☕	☕		☕
York 8	d			06 17				07 24								07 44				08 34					
Leeds 10	d		06 34	07 10		07 05						07 34				08 12			08 05						
Wakefield Westgate 7	d		06 46	07 23								07 46				08 24									
Wakefield Kirkgate 4	d					07 25													08 23						
Doncaster 7	d							07 52												08 58					
Sheffield 7	d		07 32	07 56		08 05		08 20		08 27		08 32	08 38	08 47		08 54			09 05	09 23		09 27		09 38	09 47
Chesterfield	d		07 45	08 08		08 24		08 32		08 39		08 45	08 53	08 59		09 06			09 23			09 39		09 53	09 59
Derby 6	a			08 27				08 51		08 59				09 19		09 25				09 51		09 59			10 19
	d	08 18								09 01				09 20								10 01			10 20
Long Eaton	d	08 28												09 30											10 30
Alfreton	d		07 56			08 35						08 56	09 03						09 32					10 03	
Langley Mill	d		08 04			08 42													09 41						
Lincoln	d				07 26													08 35							
Nottingham 8	a		08 23		08 30	09 02						09 21	09 30					09 30	10 00					10 30	
	d		08 28		08 32						09 02	09 28						09 32					10 02		
Beeston	d				08 38						09 08				←			09 38					10 08		
East Midlands Parkway	d	08 32	08 39		08 46							09 39		09 35	09 39			09 46							10 35
Loughborough	d	08 40			08 55						09 20	→		09 42				09 55					10 20		10 42
Barrow Upon Soar	d				08 59													09 59							
Sileby	d				09 03													10 03							
Syston	d				09 08													10 08							
Leicester	a	08 51	08 55		09 18					09 23	09 31			09 54	09 57			10 21				10 23	10 31		10 54
	d	08 53	08 57							09 25	09 33			09 55	09 57							10 25	10 33		10 55
Market Harborough	d		09 12								09 47				10 14								10 47		
Melton Mowbray	d																								
Oakham	d																								
Corby	d								09 17												10 17				
Kettering 4	a								09 26		09 56										10 26		10 56		
	d								09 27		09 57										10 27		10 56		
Wellingborough	d								09 35		10 04										10 35		11 04		
Bedford 7	d								09 49		10 19										10 49		11 19		
Luton 10	d								10 05												11 05				
Luton Airport Parkway 7	d										10 35												11 35		
St Pancras International	a	10 06	10 12						10 29	10 34	11 01			11 05	11 13						11 29	11 37	12 01		12 05

		XC		EM	EM	NT	XC	EM	EM	EM	EM	EM		XC	EM	EM	NT	XC	EM	EM	EM	EM		EM	XC
		◇1		◇1			◇1	◇1	◇1	◇1	◇	◇1		◇1	◇1			◇1	◇1	◇1	◇1	◇		◇1	◇1
		I					J				E			K				L				E			M
		🛒		☕			🛒	☕	☕	☕		☕		🛒	☕			🛒	☕	☕	☕			☕	🛒
York 8	d	08 44					09 35							09 46				10 34							10 45
Leeds 10	d	09 11				09 05								10 12			10 05								11 11
Wakefield Westgate 7	d	09 24												10 24											11 23
Wakefield Kirkgate 4	d					09 23											10 23								
Doncaster 7	d						09 58											10 58							
Sheffield 7	d	09 54				10 04	10 23		10 27		10 38	10 47		10 54			11 05	11 23		11 27		11 38		11 47	11 54
Chesterfield	d	10 06				10 21			10 39		10 53	10 59		11 06			11 22			11 39		11 53		11 59	12 07
Derby 6	a	10 25					10 51		10 59			11 19		11 25				11 51		11 59				12 19	12 26
	d								11 01			11 20								12 01				12 20	
Long Eaton	d											11 30												12 30	
Alfreton	d					10 32					11 03						11 35					12 03			
Langley Mill	d					10 40											11 40								
Lincoln	d				09 19											10 36									
Nottingham 8	a				10 25	11 00					11 29					11 29	12 00					12 29			
	d			10 28	10 32					11 02					11 28	11 32					12 02				
Beeston	d				10 38					11 08						11 38					12 08				
East Midlands Parkway	d			10 39	10 46							11 35			11 39	11 46								12 35	
Loughborough	d				10 55					11 20		11 42				11 55					12 20			12 42	
Barrow Upon Soar	d				10 59											11 59									
Sileby	d				11 03											12 03									
Syston	d				11 08											12 08									
Leicester	a			10 57	11 20				11 23	11 31		11 54			11 57	12 19				12 23	12 31			12 54	
	d			10 57					11 25	11 33		11 55			11 57					12 25	12 33			12 55	
Market Harborough	d			11 12						11 47					12 12						12 47				
Melton Mowbray	d																								
Oakham	d																								
Corby	d							11 17											12 17						
Kettering 4	a							11 26		11 56									12 26		12 56				
	d							11 27		11 56									12 27		12 56				
Wellingborough	d							11 35		12 04									12 35		13 04				
Bedford 7	d							11 49		12 19									12 49		13 19				
Luton 10	d							12 05											13 05						
Luton Airport Parkway 7	d									12 35											13 35				
St Pancras International	a			12 13				12 29	12 34	13 01		13 05			13 13				13 29	13 34	14 01			14 05	

- **A** To Plymouth
- **B** From Sleaford
- **C** From Newcastle to Reading
- **D** To St Pancras International
- **E** From Liverpool Lime Street to Norwich
- **F** From Leeds
- **G** From Newcastle to Plymouth
- **H** From Newcastle to Southampton Central
- **I** From Edinburgh to Plymouth
- **J** From Edinburgh to Reading
- **K** From Glasgow Central to Plymouth
- **L** From Newcastle to Southampton Central
- **M** From Dundee to Plymouth

For connections to Gatwick Airport see Table 52

Table 53

Saturdays

from 31 March

Sheffield - East Midlands - London

Route Diagram - see first Page of Table 53

		EM	EM	NT	XC	EM	EM	EM		EM	EM	XC	EM	EM	NT	XC	EM	EM		EM	EM	EM	XC	EM	EM
		◇1 🍴			◇1 A 🛒	◇1 🍴	◇1 🍴	◇1 🍴		◇ B	◇1 🍴	◇1 C 🛒	◇1 🍴			◇1 D 🛒	◇1 🍴	◇1 🍴		◇1 🍴	◇ B	◇1 🍴	◇1 E 🛒	◇1 🍴	
York 8	d				11 34							11 45				12 34							12 45		
Leeds 10	d			11 05								12 11			12 05								13 11		
Wakefield Westgate 7	d											12 24											13 23		
Wakefield Kirkgate 4	d			11 23											12 23										
Doncaster 7	d				11 58											12 58									
Sheffield 7	d			12 05	12 23		12 27			12 38	12 47	12 54			13 05	13 23		13 27			13 38	13 47	13 54		
Chesterfield	d			12 22			12 39			12 53	12 59	13 06			13 22			13 39			13 53	13 59	14 07		
Derby 6	a				12 51		12 59				13 19	13 25				13 51		13 59				14 19	14 27		
	d						13 01				13 20							14 01				14 20			
Long Eaton	d										13 30											14 30			
Alfreton	d			12 33						13 03					13 33						14 03				
Langley Mill	d			12 40											13 40										
Lincoln	d		11 42											12 30											13 40
Nottingham 8	a		12 30	13 01						13 30				13 30	14 00						14 29				14 30
	d	12 28	12 32					13 02					13 28	13 32						14 02				14 28	14 32
Beeston	d		12 38					13 08						13 38						14 08					14 38
East Midlands Parkway ✈	d	12 39	12 46								13 35		13 39	13 46								14 35		14 39	14 46
Loughborough	d		12 55					13 20			13 42			13 55						14 20		14 42			14 55
Barrow Upon Soar	d		12 59											13 59											14 59
Sileby	d		13 03											14 03											15 03
Syston	d		13 08											14 08											15 08
Leicester	a	12 57	13 19				13 23	13 31			13 54		13 57	14 19				14 23		14 31		14 54		14 57	15 21
	d	12 57					13 25	13 33			13 55		13 57					14 25		14 33		14 55		14 57	
Market Harborough	d	13 14						13 47					14 12							14 47				15 12	
Melton Mowbray	d																								
Oakham	d																								
Corby	d					13 17											14 17								
Kettering 4	a					13 26		13 56									14 26			14 56					
	d					13 27		13 56									14 27			14 56					
Wellingborough	d					13 35		14 04									14 35			15 04					
Bedford 7	d					13 49		14 19									14 49			15 19					
Luton 10	d					14 05											15 05								
Luton Airport Parkway 7 ✈	d							14 35												15 35					
St Pancras International ⊖	a	14 13				14 29	14 34	15 01			15 05		15 13				15 29	15 34		16 01		16 05		16 13	

		NT	XC	EM		EM	EM	EM	EM	XC	EM	EM	NT	XC		EM	EM	EM	EM	EM	XC	EM	EM	NT	
			◇1 A 🛒	◇1 🍴		◇1 🍴	◇1 🍴	◇ B	◇1 🍴	◇1 F 🛒	◇1 🍴			◇1 D 🛒		◇1 🍴	◇1 🍴	◇1 🍴	◇ B	◇1 🍴	◇1 E 🛒	◇1 🍴			
York 8	d		13 34							13 44				14 34							14 44				
Leeds 10	d	13 05								14 11			14 05								15 12			15 05	
Wakefield Westgate 7	d									14 24											15 24				
Wakefield Kirkgate 4	d	13 23											14 23											15 23	
Doncaster 7	d		13 58											14 58											
Sheffield 7	d	14 05	14 23			14 27		14 38	14 47	14 54			15 05	15 23			15 27		15 38	15 47	15 54			16 04	
Chesterfield	d	14 22				14 39		14 53	14 59	15 06			15 22				15 39		15 53	15 59	16 07			16 21	
Derby 6	a		14 51			14 59			15 19	15 26				15 51			15 59			16 19	16 26				
	d					15 01			15 20								16 01			16 20					
Long Eaton	d								15 30											16 30					
Alfreton	d	14 33						15 04					15 33						16 04					16 32	
Langley Mill	d	14 40											15 40											16 40	
Lincoln	d											14 35											15 27		
Nottingham 8	a	15 00						15 29				15 30	16 00						16 30				16 30	17 00	
	d						15 02				15 28	15 32						16 02				16 28	16 32		
Beeston	d						15 08					15 38						16 08					16 38		
East Midlands Parkway ✈	d								15 35		15 39	15 46								16 35		16 39	16 48		
Loughborough	d						15 20		15 42			15 55						16 19		16 42			16 57		
Barrow Upon Soar	d											15 59											17 01		
Sileby	d											16 03											17 05		
Syston	d											16 08											17 10		
Leicester	a					15 23	15 31		15 54		15 57	16 21					16 23	16 31		16 54		16 57	17 22		
	d					15 25	15 33		15 55		15 57						16 25	16 33		16 55		16 57			
Market Harborough	d						15 47				16 12							16 47				17 12			
Melton Mowbray	d																								
Oakham	d																								
Corby	d			15 17												16 17									
Kettering 4	a			15 26			15 56									16 26		16 56							
	d			15 27			15 56									16 27		16 56							
Wellingborough	d			15 35			16 04									16 35		17 04							
Bedford 7	d			15 49			16 19									16 49		17 19							
Luton 10	d			16 05												17 05									
Luton Airport Parkway 7 ✈	d						16 35											17 35							
St Pancras International ⊖	a			16 29		16 34	17 01		17 05		17 13					17 29	17 34	18 01		18 05		18 13			

A From Newcastle to Reading
B From Liverpool Lime Street to Norwich
C From Glasgow Central to Plymouth
D From Newcastle to Southampton Central
E From Glasgow Central to Penzance
F From Aberdeen to Penzance

For connections to Gatwick Airport see Table 52

Table 53

Saturdays
from 31 March

Sheffield - East Midlands - London

Route Diagram - see first Page of Table 53

		XC	EM	EM	EM	EM	EM	EM	XC	EM		NT	XC	EM	EM	EM	EM	EM	EM	EM		XC	NT	XC	EM
		◇1	◇1	◇1	◇1	◇1	◇1	◇	◇1				◇1	◇1	◇1	◇1	◇1	◇1		◇		◇1		◇1	◇1
		A						B	C				A							B		D		A	
		🛒	☕	☕	☕	☕	☕		🛒				🛒	☕	☕	☕	☕	☕				🛒		🛒	☕
York 8	d	15 34							15 45				16 06									16 44		17 34	
Leeds 10	d								16 12			16 05	16 40									17 11	17 05		
Wakefield Westgate 7	d								16 24				16 52									17 23			
Wakefield Kirkgate 4	d											16 23											17 23		
Doncaster 7	d	15 58																						17 58	
Sheffield 7	d	16 23		16 27		16 35		16 38	16 54			17 05	17 23		17 27		17 35			17 44		17 54	18 06	18 23	
Chesterfield	d			16 39		16 47		16 53	17 06			17 22			17 39		17 51			18 01		18 07	18 22		
Derby 6	a	16 51		16 59		17 16			17 26				17 51		17 59		18 16					18 26		18 51	
	d			17 01		17 18									18 01		18 18								
Long Eaton	d					17 28											18 28								
Alfreton	d							17 04				17 33								18 11			18 33		
Langley Mill	d											17 40											18 40		
Lincoln	d									16 34									17 26						
Nottingham 8	a							17 29		17 30		18 00							18 31	18 33			19 00		
	d				17 02		17 28			17 32						18 02		18 28	18 32						
Beeston	d				17 08					17 38						18 08			18 38						
East Midlands Parkway	d					17 32	17 39			17 48							18 32	18 39	18 47						
Loughborough	d				17 20	17 40				17 57						18 20	18 40		18 55						
Barrow Upon Soar	d									18 01									19 00						
Sileby	d									18 05									19 04						
Syston	d									18 10									19 09						
Leicester	a			17 23	17 31	17 51	17 55			18 22					18 23	18 31	18 51	18 55	19 21						
	d			17 25	17 33	17 53	17 57								18 25	18 33	18 53	18 57							
Market Harborough	d				17 47		18 12									18 47		19 12							
Melton Mowbray	d																								
Oakham	d																								
Corby	d		17 17											18 17											19 17
Kettering 4	a		17 26		17 56									18 26		18 56									19 26
	d		17 27		17 56									18 27		18 56									19 27
Wellingborough	d		17 35		18 04									18 35		19 04									19 35
Bedford 7	d		17 49		18 19									18 49		19 18									19 49
Luton 10	d		18 05											19 05											20 05
Luton Airport Parkway 7	d				18 35											19 30									
St Pancras International ⊖	a		18 29	18 34	18 59	19 06	19 12							19 29	19 34	20 01	20 05	20 12							20 29

		EM	EM	EM	EM	XC		EM	EM	NT	XC	EM	EM	EM	EM	XC		EM	EM	EM	NT	XC	EM	EM	EM
		◇1	◇1	◇	◇1	◇1		◇1			◇1	◇1	◇1	◇1	◇	◇1			◇1	◇1		◇1	◇1	◇1	◇1
				E		C					F				B	G						F			
		☕	☕		☕	🛒		☕			🛒	☕	☕	☕		🛒			☕	☕		🛒	☕	☕	☕
York 8	d				17 50	17 44					18 34					18 44						19 34			
Leeds 10	d					18 11				18 05						19 11					19 05				
Wakefield Westgate 7	d					18 23										19 24									
Wakefield Kirkgate 4	d									18 23											19 24				
Doncaster 7	d				18 18						18 58											19 58			
Sheffield 7	d	18 27		18 38	18 47	18 54				19 05	19 24		19 27		19 38	19 54					20 05	20 23	20 27		
Chesterfield	d	18 39		18 53		19 06				19 22			19 39		19 53	20 06					20 22		20 39		
Derby 6	a	18 59			19 19	19 25					19 52		19 59			20 26						20 51	21 00		
	d	19 01			19 21								20 01										21 01		
Long Eaton	d				19 31																				
Alfreton	d			19 03						19 33					20 04						20 33				
Langley Mill	d									19 40											20 40				
Lincoln	d								18 34																
Nottingham 8	a			19 33					19 29	20 00					20 31						21 00				
	d		19 02					19 28	19 32					20 02				20 32		20 43					21 18
Beeston	d		19 08						19 38					20 08				20 38		20 49					
East Midlands Parkway	d				19 35			19 41	19 46					20 16				20 46		20 55			21 14		
Loughborough	d		19 20		19 41				19 55					20 24				20 55		21 03			21 23		21 32
Barrow Upon Soar	d								19 59									20 59							
Sileby	d								20 03									21 03							
Syston	d								20 08									21 08							
Leicester	a	19 23	19 31		19 54			19 58	20 20				20 23	20 34				21 19		21 13			21 36		21 42
	d	19 25	19 33		19 54			20 00					20 25	20 36						21 15					21 44
Market Harborough	d		19 47					20 15						20 50						21 29					21 58
Melton Mowbray	d																								
Oakham	d																								
Corby	d											19 43							20 43					21 43	
Kettering 4	a		19 56		20 16							19 52		20 59					20 52	21 38				21 52	22 07
	d		19 56		20 17							20 26		20 59					21 24	21 38					22 08
Wellingborough	d		20 04									20 35		21 07					21 32	21 47					22 15
Bedford 7	d		20 18									20 49		21 22					21 47	22 01					22 37
Luton 10	d											21 03							22 06	22 24					22 59
Luton Airport Parkway 7	d		20 30											21 38						22 28					
St Pancras International ⊖	a	20 34	21 01		21 06			21 15				21 29	21 34	22 05					22 34	22 55					23 35

A From Newcastle to Reading
B From Liverpool Lime Street to Norwich
C From Edinburgh to Plymouth
D From Glasgow Central to Plymouth
E From Liverpool Lime Street
F From Newcastle to Birmingham New Street
G From Glasgow Central to Bristol Temple Meads

For connections to Gatwick Airport see Table 52

Table 53

Saturdays
from 31 March

Sheffield - East Midlands - London

Route Diagram - see first Page of Table 53

		EM		EM	XC	XC	EM	XC	EM	EM	EM	EM		EM
				◇	◇1	◇1	◇	◇1	◇1		◇	◇1		◇
				A	B	C	A	D			A			A
					🛒			🛒	☕			☕		
York 8	d				19 44	20 34		20 45						
Leeds 10	d				20 11			21 11						
Wakefield Westgate 7	d				20 23			21 23						
Wakefield Kirkgate 4	d													
Doncaster 7	d					21 00								
Sheffield 7	d			20 41	20 54	21 23	21 38	21 54			22 35	23 20		23 42
Chesterfield	d			20 59	21 06	21 35	21 54	22 06			22 51	23 33		23 57
Derby 6	a				21 26	21 52		22 25				00 13		
	d													
Long Eaton	d													
Alfreton	d			21 09			22 05				23 02			
Langley Mill	d						22 12							
Lincoln	d													
Nottingham 8	a			21 33			22 33				23 32			00 34
	d	21 32								23 10				
Beeston	d	21 38								23 16				
East Midlands Parkway ✈	d	21 46								23 25				
Loughborough	d	21 55								23 33				
Barrow Upon Soar	d	21 59												
Sileby	d	22 03												
Syston	d	22 13												
Leicester	a	22 21								23 52				
	d													
Market Harborough	d													
Melton Mowbray	d													
Oakham	d													
Corby	d								22 43					
Kettering 4	a								22 52					
	d													
Wellingborough	d													
Bedford 7	d													
Luton 10	d													
Luton Airport Parkway 7 ✈	d													
St Pancras International ⊖	a													

Sundays
until 25 March

		EM	EM	EM	EM	EM	EM	EM	EM	EM		EM	EM
		◇1	◇	◇	◇1	◇1	◇1	◇1	◇1	◇1		◇1	◇1
		E	F	G		H	I		H	I			
		☕			☕	☕	☕	☕	☕	☕		☕	☕
York 8	d												
Leeds 10	d												
Wakefield Westgate 7	d												
Wakefield Kirkgate 4	d												
Doncaster 7	d												
Sheffield 7	d	23p20	23p42	23p42									08 14
Chesterfield	d	23p33	23p57	23p57									08 27
Derby 6	a	00 13											08 46
	d				06 50			07 52					08 48
Long Eaton	d												08 58
Alfreton	d												
Langley Mill	d												
Lincoln	d												
Nottingham 8	a		00 30	00 34									
	d					07 28			08 19				
Beeston	d								08 25				
East Midlands Parkway ✈	d				07 03	07 38	07 38	08 03	08 32	08 32			09 02
Loughborough	d							08 11	08 39	08 39			09 10
Barrow Upon Soar	d												
Sileby	d												
Syston	d												
Leicester	a				07 19	07 52	07 52	08 22	08 50	08 50			09 21
	d				07 20	07 54	07 54	08 23	08 52	08 52			09 22
Market Harborough	d				07 38	08 11	08 11	08 40	09 09	09 09			09 39
Melton Mowbray	d												
Oakham	d												
Corby	d											09 30	
Kettering 4	a				07 48	08 20	08 20	08 49	09 18	09 18		09 39	09 48
	d				07 49	08 21	08 21	08 50	09 19	09 19			09 51
Wellingborough	d				08 01	08 32	08 32	09 02	09 30	09 30			10 03
Bedford 7	d				08 15	08 45	08 45	09 14	09 45	09 45			10 16
Luton 10	d				08 34			09 39					10 39
Luton Airport Parkway 7 ✈	d					09 11	09 11		10 10	10 10			
St Pancras International ⊖	a				09 13	09 50	09 50	10 20	10 49	10 49			11 20

		XC	EM	NT	EM	EM	EM	XC		EM	NT	EM	EM
		◇1	◇1		◇1	◇1	◇1	◇1		◇1		◇1	◇1
		J	H		I			J					
		🛒	☕		☕	☕	☕	🛒		☕		☕	☕
York 8	d												
Leeds 10	d	08 10						09 00			09 05		
Wakefield Westgate 7	d	08 23						09 11					
Wakefield Kirkgate 4	d										09 21		
Doncaster 7	d							09 32					
Sheffield 7	d	08 54		09 00			09 17	09 57			10 07		10 17
Chesterfield	d	09 07		09 17			09 29	10 09			10 23		10 29
Derby 6	a	09 28					09 49	10 32					10 50
	d						09 51						10 52
Long Eaton	d						10 01						11 02
Alfreton	d			09 28							10 33		
Langley Mill	d			09 35							10 41		
Lincoln	d												
Nottingham 8	a			09 53							10 57		
	d		09 15							10 15			
Beeston	d									10 22			
East Midlands Parkway ✈	d		09 26		09 26		10 05			10 30			11 06
Loughborough	d		09 34		09 34		10 13			10 38			11 14
Barrow Upon Soar	d												
Sileby	d												
Syston	d												
Leicester	a		09 47		09 47		10 23			10 51			11 24
	d		09 49		09 49		10 25			10 53			11 26
Market Harborough	d		10 07		10 07		10 39			11 08			11 40
Melton Mowbray	d												
Oakham	d												
Corby	d					10 25						11 25	
Kettering 4	a		10 17		10 17	10 34	10 48			11 18		11 34	11 49
	d		10 18		10 18		10 51			11 19			11 50
Wellingborough	d		10 26		10 26		10 58			11 27			11 58
Bedford 7	d		10 45		10 45		11 16			11 45			12 15
Luton 10	d						11 39						12 40
Luton Airport Parkway 7 ✈	d		11 10		11 10					12 09			
St Pancras International ⊖	a		11 49		11 49		12 20			12 45			13 14

A From Liverpool Lime Street
B From Edinburgh to Birmingham New Street. 🛒 to Leeds
C From Newcastle to Birmingham New Street
D From Glasgow Central to Birmingham New Street. 🛒 to Leeds
E not 11 December
F from 19 February until 25 March. From Liverpool Lime Street
G from 18 December until 12 February. From Liverpool Lime Street
H until 12 February
I from 19 February until 25 March
J To Newton Abbot

For connections to Gatwick Airport see Table 52

Sheffield - East Midlands - London

Route Diagram - see first Page of Table 53

		EM	XC	NT	EM	EM		XC	EM	NT	XC	EM	EM	NT	EM	EM		XC	EM	EM	NT	EM	EM	XC	EM
		◇1	◇1		◇1	◇1		◇1	◇1		◇1	◇1	◇1		◇1	◇		◇1	◇1	◇1		◇1	◇	◇1	◇1
			A					B			C					D		E					F	E	
York 8	d		09 28					10 28										11 28						12 28	
Leeds 10	d	09 44	10 00	10 02		10 15		11 00		10 57				11 29				12 00			12 29			13 00	
Wakefield Westgate 7	d	09 58	10 12			10 27		11 12										12 12						13 12	
Wakefield Kirkgate 4	d			10 18						11 13				11 46							12 46				
Doncaster 7	d		10 30					11 30										12 30						13 30	
Sheffield 7	d	10 26	10 57	11 03		11 06		11 57		12 00			12 24	12 31		12 49		12 57		13 24	13 31		13 49	13 57	14 16
Chesterfield	d	10 41	11 09	11 20		11 25		12 09		12 18			12 37	12 49		13 03		13 09		13 39	13 48		14 03	14 09	14 29
Derby 6	a		11 28			11 47		12 28					12 56					13 31		13 59				14 28	14 48
	d					11 48							12 58							14 02					14 50
Long Eaton	d												13 08							14 12					15 00
Alfreton	d			11 30						12 28				12 59		13 14					13 59		14 14		
Langley Mill	d			11 38						12 36				13 07							14 06				
Lincoln	d																								
Nottingham 8	a	11 11		11 53						12 52				13 24		13 39					14 22		14 39		
	d	11 18							12 28		12 53				13 31							14 32			
Beeston	d								12 35						13 38							14 38			
East Midlands Parkway	d	11 30				12 01			12 42				13 12		13 45					14 16		14 44			15 04
Loughborough	d	11 38				12 09			12 51				13 20		13 54					14 24		14 52			15 12
Barrow Upon Soar	d																								
Sileby	d																								
Syston	d																								
Leicester	a	11 51				12 21			13 04		13 16		13 30		14 06					14 34		15 02			15 22
	d	11 53				12 23			13 06				13 32		14 07					14 36		15 04			15 24
Market Harborough	d	12 08				12 38			13 21				13 46		14 22					14 50		15 18			
Melton Mowbray	d																								
Oakham	d																								
Corby	d				12 30							13 30							14 25						
Kettering 4	a	12 18			12 39	12 49			13 31			13 39	13 55		14 32				14 34	14 59		15 27			
	d	12 19				12 50			13 32				13 56		14 33					15 00		15 28			
Wellingborough	d	12 27				12 58			13 40				14 03		14 41					15 07		15 35			
Bedford 7	d	12 45				13 16			13 58				14 22		15 01					15 24		15 52			
Luton 10	d					13 39							14 39							15 41					16 15
Luton Airport Parkway 7	d	13 10							14 18						15 17							16 08			
St Pancras International	a	13 48				14 14			14 44				15 04		15 43					16 04		16 32			16 42

		XC		XC	EM	EM	EM	XC	XC	EM	EM	EM		NT	XC	XC	EM	EM	XC	EM	EM	NT		EM	EM
		◇1		◇1	◇1	◇1	◇	◇1	◇1	◇1	◇1	◇1			◇1	◇1	◇	◇1	◇1	◇1	◇1			◇1	◇1
		G		C			H	I	J						K	C	H		L						
York 8	d							13 40	13 40						14 34				14 40						
Leeds 10	d							14 10	14 10			13 59		14 05					15 10			15 05			
Wakefield Westgate 7	d							14 23	14 23			14 12							15 23						
Wakefield Kirkgate 4	d													14 21								15 22			
Doncaster 7	d														14 59										
Sheffield 7	d	14 22					14 46	14 54	14 54			15 00		15 07	15 23		15 43	15 50	15 54			16 07			
Chesterfield	d	14 32					15 00	15 06	15 06			15 16		15 24			15 57	16 02	16 07			16 23			
Derby 6	a	14 51						15 25	15 26			15 36			15 52			16 22	16 27						
	d											15 47						16 24							16 48
Long Eaton	d																								16 58
Alfreton	d						15 11							15 34			16 08					16 33			
Langley Mill	d						15 18							15 42			16 15					16 41			
Lincoln	d																								
Nottingham 8	a						15 38							15 59			16 34					16 56			
	d			15 04		15 21				15 48						16 04				16 31	16 45				
Beeston	d					15 27														16 37					
East Midlands Parkway	d					15 34				15 58		16 03						16 35		16 44	16 56				17 02
Loughborough	d					15 41						16 12								16 51					17 10
Barrow Upon Soar	d																								
Sileby	d																								
Syston	d																								
Leicester	a			15 27		15 53				16 12		16 24				16 28		16 50		17 03	17 11				17 20
	d					15 54				16 14		16 26						16 53		17 04	17 13				17 22
Market Harborough	d					16 08						16 41								17 18					17 36
Melton Mowbray	d																								
Oakham	d																								
Corby	d				15 25						16 25													17 20	
Kettering 4	a				15 34	16 17					16 34	16 51								17 27				17 29	17 45
	d					16 18						16 52								17 28					17 46
Wellingborough	d					16 26						17 00								17 36					17 53
Bedford 7	d					16 43						17 23								17 53					18 11
Luton 10	d											17 40													18 27
Luton Airport Parkway 7	d					17 00														18 09					
St Pancras International	a					17 25				17 29		18 06						18 12		18 32	18 35				18 50

A To Newton Abbot
B From Newcastle to Newton Abbot
C from 8 January until 12 February. From Stansted Airport to Birmingham New Street
D To Norwich
E From Edinburgh to Newton Abbot
F From Manchester Piccadilly to Norwich
G To Reading
H From Liverpool Lime Street to Norwich
I until 12 February. From Edinburgh to Plymouth
J from 19 February until 25 March. From Edinburgh to Newton Abbot
K From Newcastle to Reading
L From Glasgow Central to Exeter St Davids

For connections to Gatwick Airport see Table 52

Sundays

until 25 March

Sheffield - East Midlands - London

Route Diagram - see first Page of Table 53

		XC	EM	EM	EM	XC	EM	NT		EM	EM	XC	XC	EM	EM	XC	EM	EM		EM	NT	XC	XC	EM	EM
		◇1	◇1	◇1	◇	◇1	◇1			◇1	◇1	◇1	◇1	◇1	◇	◇1	◇1	◇1		◇1		◇1	◇1	◇	◇1
		A			B	C						D	E		B	F						A	E	G	
		🛒	☕	☕		🛒	☕			☕	☕	🛒	🛒	☕		🛒	☕	☕		☕		🛒	🛒		☕
York 8	d	15 34				15 40						16 23				16 40						17 34			17 40
Leeds 10	d					16 10		16 04								17 10					17 05				
Wakefield Westgate 7	d					16 22										17 22									
Wakefield Kirkgate 4	d							16 22													17 21				
Doncaster 7	d	15 59										16 51										17 59			18 08
Sheffield 7	d	16 24	16 36		16 40	16 54		17 07				17 24		17 29	17 39	17 54					18 07	18 24		18 41	18 46
Chesterfield	d		16 50		16 56	17 06		17 23						17 43	17 55	18 06					18 25			18 56	19 01
Derby 6	a	16 53	17 10			17 26						17 53		18 02		18 25						18 53			19 21
	d		17 11								17 47			18 04											19 22
Long Eaton	d										17 57														19 32
Alfreton	d				17 07			17 33							18 05						18 36			19 06	
Langley Mill	d				17 14			17 41							18 13						18 43			19 14	
Lincoln	d																								
Nottingham 8	a				17 30			17 58							18 29						19 00			19 34	
	d			17 26			17 39						17 58				18 34			18 57			19 02		
Beeston	d			17 32													18 40								
East Midlands Parkway	d		17 29	17 38			17 50				18 01			18 16			18 46			19 07					19 37
Loughborough	d			17 46							18 09						18 54			19 16					19 44
Barrow Upon Soar	d																								
Sileby	d																								
Syston	d																								
Leicester	a		17 51	17 56			18 07				18 19		18 24	18 34			19 04			19 28			19 34		19 55
	d		17 53	17 58			18 08				18 21			18 34			19 06			19 30					19 56
Market Harborough	d			18 12							18 35						19 20			19 44					20 10
Melton Mowbray	d																								
Oakham	d																								
Corby	d									18 20								19 25							
Kettering 4	a			18 21						18 29	18 44						19 29	19 34		19 53					20 19
	d			18 22							18 45						19 30			19 54					20 20
Wellingborough	d			18 29							18 52						19 37			20 01					20 28
Bedford 7	d			18 46							19 09						19 54			20 19					20 46
Luton 10	d										19 26									20 35					
Luton Airport Parkway 7	d			19 06													20 11								21 02
St Pancras International	a		19 08	19 29			19 34				19 49			19 59			20 34			20 58					21 27

		XC	EM	EM		NT	XC	EM	EM	XC	XC	NT	XC	EM		EM	EM	EM	XC	XC	EM	XC	EM	EM	
		◇1	◇1	◇1			◇1	◇1	◇	◇1	◇1		◇1	◇1		◇1	◇1	◇	◇1	◇1	◇	◇1	◇1	◇	
		C					H		B	I	E		J					G	K	J	G	L		G	
		🛒	☕	☕			🛒	☕		🛒			🛒	☕		☕	☕		🛒	🛒		🛒	☕		
York 8	d	17 40					18 34			18 40			19 24						19 40	20 24		20 40			
Leeds 10	d	18 10				18 05				19 10		19 04							20 10			21 10			
Wakefield Westgate 7	d	18 22								19 22									20 22			21 22			
Wakefield Kirkgate 4	d					18 22						19 21													
Doncaster 7	d						18 59						19 50							20 50					
Sheffield 7	d	18 54				19 07	19 24	19 31	19 40	19 54		20 06	20 20			20 31		20 40	20 54	21 20	21 40	21 54	22 35	23 29	
Chesterfield	d	19 06				19 25		19 44	19 55	20 06		20 23				20 45		20 55	21 06	21 32	21 56	22 06	22 49	23 43	
Derby 6	a	19 25					19 53	20 04		20 25			20 49			21 04			21 25	21 51		22 25	23 26		
	d							20 06								21 06									
Long Eaton	d							20 16																	
Alfreton	d					19 36			20 06			20 34						21 06			22 07			23 54	
Langley Mill	d					19 43			20 13			20 41						21 13			22 14			00 02	
Lincoln	d																								
Nottingham 8	a					19 59			20 30			20 57						21 34			22 35			00 25	
	d			19 57							20 35						21 20								
Beeston	d			20 03																					
East Midlands Parkway	d			20 09				20 21								21 18	21 30								
Loughborough	d			20 17				20 30									21 38								
Barrow Upon Soar	d																								
Sileby	d																								
Syston	d																								
Leicester	a			20 27				20 42			20 59					21 35	21 50								
	d			20 29				20 44								21 37	21 53								
Market Harborough	d			20 43				20 59								21 52	22 07								
Melton Mowbray	d																								
Oakham	d																								
Corby	d		20 25											21 25											
Kettering 4	a		20 34	20 52				21 09						21 34		22 02	22 16								
	d			20 53				21 10								22 03	22 17								
Wellingborough	d			21 00				21 18								22 11	22 24								
Bedford 7	d			21 18				21 41								22 31	22 41								
Luton 10	d			21 34				21 57								22 47	22 57								
Luton Airport Parkway 7	d																								
St Pancras International	a			21 57				22 27								23 13	23 28								

- **A** From Newcastle to Reading
- **B** From Liverpool Lime Street to Norwich
- **C** From Glasgow Central to Exeter St Davids
- **D** From Edinburgh to Reading
- **E** from 8 January until 12 February. From Stansted Airport to Birmingham New Street
- **F** From Aberdeen to Exeter St Davids
- **G** From Liverpool Lime Street
- **H** From Newcastle to Guildford
- **I** From Glasgow Central to Bristol Temple Meads
- **J** From Newcastle to Birmingham New Street
- **K** From Edinburgh to Bristol Temple Meads. 🛒 to Leeds
- **L** From Glasgow Central to Birmingham New Street. 🛒 to Leeds

For connections to Gatwick Airport see Table 52

Table 53

Sundays
from 1 April

Sheffield - East Midlands - London

Route Diagram - see first Page of Table 53

		EM	EM	EM	EM	EM	EM	EM	EM	XC	EM	NT	EM	EM	XC	EM	EM	EM	NT	EM	XC	NT	EM
		◇1	◇	◇1	◇1	◇1	◇1	◇1	◇1	◇1	◇1		◇1	◇1	◇1	◇1	◇1	◇1		◇1	◇1		◇1
			A							B					B						B		
		☕		☕	☕	☕	☕	☕	☕	🛒	☕		☕	☕	🛒	☕	☕	☕		☕	🛒		☕
York 8	d																				09 28		
Leeds 10	d									08 10					09 00				09 05	09 32	10 00	10 02	
Wakefield Westgate 7	d									08 23					09 11					09 46	10 12		
Wakefield Kirkgate 4	d																		09 21			10 18	
Doncaster 7	d														09 32						10 30		
Sheffield 7	d	23p20	23p42						08 08	08 54		09 00		09 08	09 57			10 03	10 07	10 14	10 57	11 03	
Chesterfield	d	23p33	23p57						08 20	09 07		09 17		09 22	10 09			10 17	10 23	10 29	11 09	11 20	
Derby 6	a	00 13							08 40	09 28				09 42	10 32			10 37			11 28		
	d			06 44		07 45			08 41					09 44				10 42					
Long Eaton	d								08 51					09 54				10 52					
Alfreton	d											09 28							10 33			11 30	
Langley Mill	d											09 35							10 41			11 38	
Lincoln	d																						
Nottingham 8	a		00 34									09 53							10 57	11 00		11 53	
	d				07 21		08 13				09 10					10 09				11 07			
Beeston	d						08 19									10 16							
East Midlands Parkway	d			06 57	07 31	07 57	08 25		08 56		09 21			09 58		10 24		10 56		11 18			
Loughborough	d					08 04	08 33		09 03		09 29			10 06		10 32		11 04		11 26			
Barrow Upon Soar	d																						
Sileby	d																						
Syston	d																						
Leicester	a			07 19	07 52	08 22	08 50		09 21		09 48			10 22		10 49		11 21		11 45			
	d			07 20	07 54	08 23	08 52		09 22		09 49			10 24		10 51		11 26		11 47			
Market Harborough	d			07 38	08 11	08 40	09 09		09 39		10 07			10 38		11 06		11 40		12 02			
Melton Mowbray	d																						
Oakham	d																						
Corby	d							09 30					10 25				11 25						12 30
Kettering 4	a			07 48	08 20	08 49	09 18	09 39	09 48		10 17		10 34	10 47		11 16	11 34	11 49		12 12			12 39
	d			07 49	08 21	08 50	09 19		09 50		10 18			10 49		11 17		11 50		12 13			
Wellingborough	d			08 01	08 32	09 02	09 30		10 02		10 26			10 56		11 25		11 58		12 21			
Bedford 7	d			08 15	08 45	09 14	09 45		10 15		10 45			11 13		11 44		12 14		12 40			
Luton 10	d			08 34		09 39			10 37					11 36									
Luton Airport Parkway 7	d				09 11		10 10				11 10					12 07				13 08			
St Pancras International	a			09 13	09 50	10 20	10 49		11 18		11 49			12 11		12 45		13 14		13 46			

		EM	XC	EM	NT	EM	EM	EM	NT	EM	XC	EM	EM	NT	EM	EM	XC	EM	XC	EM	EM	EM	EM
		◇1	◇1	◇1		◇1	◇1	◇1		◇	◇1	◇1	◇1		◇1	◇	◇1	◇1	◇1	◇1	◇1	◇1	◇
			C							D	E					F	G		H				I
		☕	🛒	☕		☕	☕	☕			🛒	☕	☕		☕		🛒	☕	🛒	☕	☕	☕	
York 8	d		10 28								11 28						12 28						
Leeds 10	d	10 15	11 00		10 57				11 29		12 00			12 29			13 00						
Wakefield Westgate 7	d	10 27	11 12								12 12						13 12						
Wakefield Kirkgate 4	d				11 13				11 46					12 46									
Doncaster 7	d		11 30								12 30						13 30						
Sheffield 7	d	11 06	11 57		12 00		12 24		12 31	12 49	12 57		13 21	13 31		13 49	13 57	14 04	14 22				14 46
Chesterfield	d	11 25	12 09		12 18		12 37		12 49	13 03	13 09		13 33	13 48		14 03	14 09	14 16	14 32				15 00
Derby 6	a	11 47	12 28				12 57				13 31		13 52				14 28	14 36	14 51				
	d	11 48					13 02						13 54					14 37					
Long Eaton	d						13 12						14 04					14 47					
Alfreton	d				12 28				12 59	13 14				13 59		14 14							15 11
Langley Mill	d				12 36				13 07					14 06									15 18
Lincoln	d																						
Nottingham 8	a				12 52				13 24	13 39				14 22		14 39							15 38
	d			12 15				13 15							14 24						15 05	15 36	
Beeston	d			12 22				13 22							14 30						15 11		
East Midlands Parkway	d	12 01		12 30			13 16	13 30					14 09		14 36			14 53			15 17	15 46	
Loughborough	d	12 09		12 38			13 24	13 38					14 19		14 44			15 00			15 25		
Barrow Upon Soar	d																						
Sileby	d																						
Syston	d																						
Leicester	a	12 21		12 52			13 34	13 51					14 29		14 55			15 11			15 36	16 02	
	d	12 23		12 53			13 36	13 53					14 31		14 57			15 13			15 38	16 03	
Market Harborough	d	12 38		13 08			13 50	14 08					14 45		15 11						15 52		
Melton Mowbray	d																						
Oakham	d																						
Corby	d					13 30						14 25								15 25			
Kettering 4	a	12 48		13 18		13 39	13 59	14 18				14 34	14 54		15 20					15 34	16 01		
	d	12 49		13 19			14 00	14 19					14 57		15 21						16 02		
Wellingborough	d	12 57		13 27			14 07	14 27					15 04		15 28						16 10		
Bedford 7	d	13 14		13 53			14 23	14 44					15 22		15 44						16 26		
Luton 10	d	13 37					14 50						15 50					16 20					
Luton Airport Parkway 7	d			14 25				15 07							16 07						16 51		
St Pancras International	a	14 14		14 54			15 17	15 35					16 17		16 33			16 47			17 16	17 40	

A From Liverpool Lime Street
B To Plymouth
C From Newcastle to Plymouth
D To Norwich
E From Edinburgh to Plymouth
F From Manchester Piccadilly to Norwich
G From Edinburgh to Penzance
H To Reading
I From Liverpool Lime Street to Norwich

For connections to Gatwick Airport see Table 52

Table 53

Sheffield - East Midlands - London

Route Diagram - see first Page of Table 53

		XC		EM	EM	NT	XC	EM	EM	EM	XC	EM		NT	EM	EM	XC	EM	EM	EM	XC	EM		NT	EM
		◇1		◇1	◇1		◇1	◇1	◇1	◇	◇1	◇1			◇1	◇1	◇1	◇1	◇1	◇	◇1	◇1			◇1
		A					B			C	D						B			C	E				
York 8	d	13 40					14 34				14 40						15 34				15 40				
Leeds 10	d	14 10			13 59	14 05					15 10			15 05							16 10			16 04	
Wakefield Westgate 7	d	14 23			14 12						15 23										16 22				
Wakefield Kirkgate 4	d					14 21								15 22										16 22	
Doncaster 7	d						14 59										15 59								
Sheffield 7	d	14 54			15 00	15 07	15 23	15 32		15 43	15 54			16 07			16 24	16 29		16 40	16 54			17 07	
Chesterfield	d	15 06			15 13	15 24		15 44		15 57	16 07			16 23				16 43		16 56	17 06			17 23	
Derby 6	a	15 25			15 36		15 52	16 09			16 27						16 53	17 04			17 26				
	d				15 42			16 14								16 47		17 05							
Long Eaton	d															16 57									
Alfreton	d					15 34				16 08				16 33						17 07				17 33	
Langley Mill	d					15 42				16 15				16 41						17 14				17 41	
Lincoln	d																								
Nottingham 8	a					15 59				16 32				16 56						17 30				17 58	
	d								16 18			16 45							17 19			17 39			
Beeston	d								16 24										17 25						
East Midlands Parkway	d				15 56			16 25	16 31			16 55				17 01		17 18	17 31			17 50			
Loughborough	d				16 05				16 39							17 09			17 39						
Barrow Upon Soar	d																								
Sileby	d																								
Syston	d																								
Leicester	a				16 17			16 40	16 52			17 12				17 20		17 35	17 50			18 07			
	d				16 19			16 41	16 54			17 13				17 23		17 36	17 53			18 09			
Market Harborough	d				16 34				17 08							17 37			18 07						
Melton Mowbray	d																								
Oakham	d																								
Corby	d			16 25											17 20										18 20
Kettering 4	a			16 34	16 44				17 17						17 29	17 46			18 16						18 29
	d				16 45				17 18							17 47			18 17						
Wellingborough	d				16 53				17 25							17 55			18 25						
Bedford 7	d				17 12				17 41							18 12			18 41						
Luton 10	d				17 35											18 31									
Luton Airport Parkway 7	d								18 08										19 03						
St Pancras International	a				18 06			18 16	18 35			18 46				18 57		19 03	19 29			19 35			

		EM	XC	EM	EM	EM	XC	EM		EM	NT	XC	EM	EM	XC	EM	EM	NT		XC	EM	EM	XC	NT	XC
		◇1	◇1	◇1	◇1	◇	◇1	◇1		◇1		◇1	◇1	◇	◇1	◇1	◇1			◇1	◇1	◇	◇1		◇1
			F			C	G					B		H	E					I		C	J		K
York 8	d		16 23				16 40					17 34	17 40		17 40					18 34			18 40		19 24
Leeds 10	d						17 10				17 05				18 10			18 05					19 10	19 04	
Wakefield Westgate 7	d						17 22								18 22								19 22		
Wakefield Kirkgate 4	d										17 21							18 22						19 21	
Doncaster 7	d		16 51									17 59	18 06							18 59					19 50
Sheffield 7	d		17 24	17 29		17 39	17 54				18 07	18 24	18 32	18 41	18 54			19 07		19 24	19 31	19 40	19 54	20 06	20 20
Chesterfield	d			17 43		17 55	18 06				18 25		18 44	18 56	19 06			19 25			19 44	19 55	20 06	20 23	
Derby 6	a		17 53	18 03			18 25					18 53	19 04		19 25					19 53	20 04		20 25		20 49
	d	17 47		18 04									19 05								20 05				
Long Eaton	d	17 57											19 15								20 16				
Alfreton	d					18 05					18 36			19 06				19 36				20 06		20 34	
Langley Mill	d					18 13					18 43			19 14				19 43				20 13		20 41	
Lincoln	d																								
Nottingham 8	a					18 29					19 00			19 34				19 59				20 30		20 57	
	d				18 20					18 43							19 43								
Beeston	d				18 26												19 49								
East Midlands Parkway	d	18 01		18 17	18 32					18 53			19 20				19 55				20 21				
Loughborough	d	18 09			18 40					19 01			19 27				20 03				20 29				
Barrow Upon Soar	d																								
Sileby	d																								
Syston	d																								
Leicester	a	18 19		18 33	18 51					19 12			19 38				20 13				20 41				
	d	18 21		18 34	18 53					19 14			19 39				20 15				20 43				
Market Harborough	d	18 35			19 07					19 30			19 53				20 29				20 58				
Melton Mowbray	d																								
Oakham	d																								
Corby	d							19 25								20 25									
Kettering 4	a	18 44			19 16			19 34		19 39			20 02			20 34	20 38				21 08				
	d	18 45			19 17					19 40			20 03				20 39				21 09				
Wellingborough	d	18 53			19 25					19 47			20 11				20 46				21 17				
Bedford 7	d	19 09			19 41					20 05			20 28				21 06				21 36				
Luton 10	d	19 31								20 27							21 28				21 57				
Luton Airport Parkway 7	d				20 04								20 51												
St Pancras International	a	19 57		20 04	20 30					20 53			21 17				21 54				22 26				

- **A** From Edinburgh to Plymouth
- **B** From Newcastle to Reading
- **C** From Liverpool Lime Street to Norwich
- **D** From Glasgow Central to Penzance
- **E** From Glasgow Central to Plymouth
- **F** From Edinburgh to Reading
- **G** From Aberdeen to Plymouth
- **H** From Liverpool Lime Street
- **I** From Newcastle to Guildford
- **J** From Glasgow Central to Bristol Temple Meads
- **K** From Newcastle to Birmingham New Street

For connections to Gatwick Airport see Table 52

Table 53

Sundays

from 1 April

Sheffield - East Midlands - London

Route Diagram - see first Page of Table 53

		EM	EM	EM	EM	XC	XC	EM	XC	EM	EM
		◇1	◇1	◇1	◇	◇1	◇1	◇	◇1	◇1	◇
					A	B	C	A	D		A
		🍴	🍴	🍴		⚲	⚲		⚲	🍴	
York 8	d					19 40	20 24		20 40		
Leeds 10	d					20 10			21 10		
Wakefield Westgate 7	d					20 22			21 22		
Wakefield Kirkgate 4	d										
Doncaster 7	d						20 50				
Sheffield 7 🚌	d		20 24		20 40	20 54	21 20	21 40	21 54	22 35	23 29
Chesterfield	d		20 38		20 55	21 06	21 32	21 56	22 06	22 49	23 43
Derby 6	a		20 57			21 25	21 51		22 25	23 26	
	d		21 01								
Long Eaton	d										
Alfreton	d				21 06			22 07			23 54
Langley Mill	d				21 13			22 14			00 02
Lincoln	d										
Nottingham 8 🚌	a				21 34			22 35			00 25
	d			21 13							
Beeston	d										
East Midlands Parkway ✈	d		21 13	21 23							
Loughborough	d			21 30							
Barrow Upon Soar	d										
Sileby	d										
Syston	d										
Leicester	a		21 31	21 41							
	d		21 32	21 42							
Market Harborough	d		21 47	21 56							
Melton Mowbray	d										
Oakham	d										
Corby	d	21 25									
Kettering 4	a	21 34	21 57	22 05							
	d		21 58	22 06							
Wellingborough	d		22 06	22 14							
Bedford 7	d		22 25	22 30							
Luton 10	d		22 47	22 52							
Luton Airport Parkway 7 ✈	d										
St Pancras International ⊖	a		23 24	23 29							

A From Liverpool Lime Street

B From Edinburgh to Bristol Temple Meads. ⚲ to Leeds

C From Newcastle to Birmingham New Street

D From Glasgow Central to Birmingham New Street. ⚲ to Leeds

For connections to Gatwick Airport see Table 52

Table 55

Mondays to Fridays

Nottingham - Mansfield - Worksop

Network Diagram - see first Page of Table 50

Miles			EM	EM	EM	EM	EM	EM	EM	EM	EM		EM	EM	EM	EM	EM	EM	EM	EM	EM		EM	EM	EM
0	**Nottingham** 8	d	05 40	06 05	07 00	08 25	08 53	09 25	09 55	10 25	10 55		11 25	11 55	12 25	12 55	13 25	13 55	14 25	14 55	15 25		15 55	16 25	16 55
5½	Bulwell	d	05 49	06 14	07 10	08 36	09 02		10 06		11 06			12 06		13 06		14 06		15 06			16 06		17 06
8¼	Hucknall	d	05 54	06 19	07 15	08 41	09 07	09 39	10 11	10 39	11 11		11 39	12 11	12 39	13 11	13 39	14 11	14 39	15 11	15 39		16 11	16 39	17 12
10¾	Newstead	d	05 59	06 24	07 21	08 46	09 12	09 44		10 44			11 44		12 44		13 44		14 44		15 44			16 44	17 17
13¾	Kirkby In Ashfield	d	06 05	06 30	07 31	08 52	09 18	09 49	10 19	10 49	11 19		11 49	12 19	12 49	13 19	13 49	14 19	14 49	15 19	15 49		16 19	16 49	17 23
14½	Sutton Parkway	d	06 08	06 33	07 34	08 55	09 21	09 52	10 22	10 52	11 22		11 52	12 22	12 52	13 22	13 52	14 22	14 52	15 22	15 52		16 22	16 52	17 27
17¼	**Mansfield**	d	06 13	06 38	07 40	09 00	09 26	09 57	10 27	10 57	11 27		11 57	12 27	12 57	13 27	13 57	14 27	14 57	15 27	15 57		16 27	16 57	17 32
18¾	Mansfield Woodhouse	d	06 18	06 47	07 45	09 04	09a33	10 02	10a34	11 02	11a34		12 02	12a34	13 02	13a34	14 02	14a34	15 02	15a34	16 02		16a34	17 02	17a39
21½	Shirebrook	d	06 24	06 54	07 51	09 11		10 08		11 08			12 08		13 08		14 08		15 08		16 08			17 08	
22¼	Langwith - Whaley Thorns	d	06 28	06 58	07 55	09 15		10 12		11 12			12 12		13 12		14 12		15 12		16 12			17 12	
25½	Creswell (Derbys)	d	06 32	07 02	07 59	09 19		10 16		11 16			12 16		13 16		14 16		15 16		16 16			17 16	
26¾	Whitwell	d	06 36	07 05	08 03	09 22		10 20		11 20			12 20		13 20		14 20		15 20		16 20			17 20	
31½	**Worksop**	a	06 48	07 20	08 18	09 33		10 33		11 33			12 33		13 33		14 33		15 33		16 33			17 33	

		EM	EM	EM	EM	EM	EM
Nottingham 8	d	17 25	17 55	18 55	19 55	20 55	22 05
Bulwell	d	17 39	18 11	19 05	20 05	21 05	22 19
Hucknall	d	17 44	18 16	19 10	20 16	21 16	22 24
Newstead	d	17 49	18 21	19 15	20 21	21 21	22 29
Kirkby In Ashfield	d	17 55	18 27	19 21	20 27	21 27	22 34
Sutton Parkway	d	17 58	18 30	19 24	20 30	21 30	22 37
Mansfield	d	18 03	18 35	19 29	20 35	21 35	22 42
Mansfield Woodhouse	d	18 08	18 39	19 33	20 39	21 40	22 47
Shirebrook	d	18 14	18 46	19 40	20 46	21 46	22 53
Langwith - Whaley Thorns	d	18 18	18 50	19 44	20 50	21 50	22 57
Creswell (Derbys)	d	18 22	18 54	19 48	20 54	21 54	23 01
Whitwell	d	18 26	18 57	19 51	20 57	21 58	23 05
Worksop	a	18 37	19 07	20 03	21 09	22 06	23 13

Saturdays

		EM	EM	EM	EM	EM	EM	EM	EM	EM		EM	EM	EM	EM	EM	EM	EM	EM	EM		EM	EM	EM	EM
Nottingham 8	d	05 40	06 05	06 59	08 25	08 53	09 25	09 55	10 25	10 55		11 25	11 55	12 25	12 55	13 25	13 55	14 25	14 55	15 25		15 55	16 25	16 55	17 25
Bulwell	d	05 49	06 14	07 09	08 36	09 02		10 06		11 06			12 06		13 06		14 06		15 06			16 06		17 06	17 39
Hucknall	d	05 54	06 19	07 14	08 41	09 07	09 39	10 11	10 39	11 11		11 39	12 11	12 39	13 11	13 39	14 11	14 39	15 11	15 39		16 11	16 39	17 12	17 44
Newstead	d	05 59	06 24	07 20	08 46	09 12	09 44		10 44			11 44		12 44		13 44		14 44		15 44			16 44	17 17	17 49
Kirkby In Ashfield	d	06 05	06 30	07 31	08 52	09 18	09 49	10 19	10 49	11 19		11 49	12 19	12 49	13 19	13 49	14 19	14 49	15 19	15 49		16 19	16 49	17 23	17 55
Sutton Parkway	d	06 08	06 33	07 34	08 55	09 21	09 52	10 22	10 52	11 22		11 52	12 22	12 52	13 22	13 52	14 22	14 52	15 22	15 52		16 22	16 52	17 27	17 58
Mansfield	d	06 13	06 38	07 40	09 00	09 26	09 57	10 27	10 57	11 27		11 57	12 27	12 57	13 27	13 57	14 27	14 57	15 27	15 57		16 27	16 57	17 32	18 03
Mansfield Woodhouse	d	06 18	06 47	07 45	09 04	09a33	10 02	10a34	11 02	11a34		12 02	12a34	13 02	13a34	14 02	14a34	15 02	15a34	16 02		16a34	17 02	17a39	18 08
Shirebrook	d	06 24	06 54	07 51	09 11		10 08		11 08			12 08		13 08		14 08		15 08		16 08			17 08		18 14
Langwith - Whaley Thorns	d	06 28	06 58	07 55	09 15		10 12		11 12			12 12		13 12		14 12		15 12		16 12			17 12		18 18
Creswell (Derbys)	d	06 32	07 02	07 59	09 19		10 16		11 16			12 16		13 16		14 16		15 16		16 16			17 16		18 22
Whitwell	d	06 36	07 05	08 03	09 22		10 20		11 20			12 20		13 20		14 20		15 20		16 20			17 20		18 26
Worksop	a	06 48	07 20	08 12	09 33		10 33		11 33			12 33		13 33		14 33		15 33		16 33			17 33		18 37

		EM	EM	EM	EM	EM		EM
Nottingham 8	d	17 55	18 55	19 55	20 55	22 05		23 05
Bulwell	d	18 11	19 05	20 05	21 05	22 19		23 18
Hucknall	d	18 16	19 10	20 16	21 16	22 24		23 23
Newstead	d	18 21	19 15	20 21	21 21	22 29		23 28
Kirkby In Ashfield	d	18 27	19 21	20 27	21 27	22 34		23 33
Sutton Parkway	d	18 30	19 24	20 30	21 30	22 37		23 36
Mansfield	d	18 35	19 29	20 35	21 35	22 42		23 41
Mansfield Woodhouse	d	18 39	19 33	20 39	21 40	22 47		23a46
Shirebrook	d	18 46	19 40	20 46	21 46	22 53		
Langwith - Whaley Thorns	d	18 50	19 44	20 50	21 50	22 57		
Creswell (Derbys)	d	18 54	19 48	20 54	21 54	23 01		
Whitwell	d	18 57	19 51	20 57	21 58	23 05		
Worksop	a	19 07	20 03	21 09	22 06	23 13		

Sundays

until 12 February

		EM	EM	EM	EM	EM	EM	EM	EM
Nottingham 8	d	08 07	09 36	11 26	13 26	15 25	16 53	18 29	20 26
Bulwell	d	08 16	09 46	11 36	13 36	15 35	17 03	18 40	20 37
Hucknall	d	08 21	09 51	11 41	13 41	15 40	17 08	18 45	20 42
Newstead	d	08 26	09 56	11 46	13 46	15 45	17 13	18 50	20 47
Kirkby In Ashfield	d	08 32	10 01	11 51	13 51	15 50	17 18	18 55	20 52
Sutton Parkway	d	08 35	10 04	11 54	13 54	15 53	17 21	18 58	20 55
Mansfield	d	08 40	10 09	11 59	13 59	15 58	17 26	19 03	21 00
Mansfield Woodhouse	d	08a47	10a16	12a06	14a06	16a05	17a33	19a10	21a07
Shirebrook	d								
Langwith - Whaley Thorns	d								
Creswell (Derbys)	d								
Whitwell	d								
Worksop	a								

Table 55

Sundays

19 February to 25 March

Nottingham - Mansfield - Worksop

Network Diagram - see first Page of Table 50

		EM	EM	EM	EM	EM	EM	EM	EM
		🚌							
Nottingham 8	d	07 20	09 36	11 26	13 26	15 25	16 53	18 29	20 26
Bulwell	d	07 40	09 46	11 36	13 36	15 35	17 03	18 40	20 37
Hucknall	d	07 45	09 51	11 41	13 41	15 40	17 08	18 45	20 42
Newstead	d	07 55	09 56	11 46	13 46	15 45	17 13	18 50	20 47
Kirkby In Ashfield	d	08 08	10 01	11 51	13 51	15 50	17 18	18 55	20 52
Sutton Parkway	d	08 15	10 04	11 54	13 54	15 53	17 21	18 58	20 55
Mansfield	d	08 30	10 09	11 59	13 59	15 58	17 26	19 03	21 00
Mansfield Woodhouse	d	08a40	10a16	12a06	14a06	16a05	17a33	19a10	21a07
Shirebrook	d								
Langwith - Whaley Thorns	d								
Creswell (Derbys)	d								
Whitwell	d								
Worksop	a								

Sundays

from 1 April

		EM	EM	EM	EM	EM	EM	EM	EM
Nottingham 8	d	08 07	09 36	11 26	13 26	15 25	16 53	18 29	20 27
Bulwell	d	08 16	09 46	11 36	13 36	15 35	17 03	18 40	20 37
Hucknall	d	08 21	09 51	11 41	13 41	15 40	17 08	18 45	20 42
Newstead	d	08 26	09 56	11 46	13 46	15 45	17 13	18 50	20 47
Kirkby In Ashfield	d	08 32	10 01	11 51	13 51	15 50	17 18	18 55	20 52
Sutton Parkway	d	08 35	10 04	11 54	13 54	15 53	17 21	18 58	20 55
Mansfield	d	08 40	10 09	11 59	13 59	15 58	17 26	19 03	21 00
Mansfield Woodhouse	d	08a47	10a16	12a06	14a06	16a05	17a33	19a10	21a07
Shirebrook	d								
Langwith - Whaley Thorns	d								
Creswell (Derbys)	d								
Whitwell	d								
Worksop	a								

Table 55

Mondays to Fridays

Worksop - Mansfield - Nottingham

Network Diagram - see first Page of Table 50

Miles			EM	EM	EM	EM	EM	EM	EM	EM	EM
0	**Worksop**	d	05 50		06 56		07 38	08 38		09 38	
4¾	Whitwell	d	05 59		07 05		07 47	08 47		09 47	
6	Creswell (Derbys)	d	06 02		07 08		07 50	08 50		09 50	
9¼	Langwith - Whaley Thorns	d	06 06		07 13		07 54	08 54		09 55	
10	Shirebrook	d	06 10		07 16		07 58	08 58		09 58	
12¾	Mansfield Woodhouse	d	06 17	07 07	07 25	07 39	08 06	09 06	09 37	10 07	10 37
14¼	**Mansfield**	d	06 22	07 11	07 29	07 43	08 10	09 10	09 40	10 10	10 40
17	Sutton Parkway	d	06 27	07 16	07 35	07 48	08 15	09 15	09 46	10 16	10 46
17¾	Kirkby In Ashfield	d	06 30	07 19	07 38	07 52	08 18	09 18	09 49	10 19	10 49
20¾	Newstead	d	06 35	07 26	07 43	07 57	08 23	09 23	09 54		10 54
23¼	Hucknall	d	06 39	07 31	07 48	08 02	08 28	09 27	09 58	10 26	10 58
26	Bulwell	d	06 43	07 35	07 53	08 06	08 32	09 31		10 30	
31½	**Nottingham** 8	a	06 58	07 48	08 04	08 18	08 44	09 44	10 14	10 44	11 14

Miles			EM	EM	EM	EM	EM	EM	EM	EM	EM	EM	EM	EM
0	**Worksop**	d	10 38		11 38		12 38		13 38		14 38		15 38	
4¾	Whitwell	d	10 47		11 47		12 47		13 47		14 47		15 47	
6	Creswell (Derbys)	d	10 50		11 50		12 50		13 50		14 50		15 50	
9¼	Langwith - Whaley Thorns	d	10 55		11 55		12 55		13 55		14 55		15 55	
10	Shirebrook	d	10 58		11 58		12 58		13 58		14 58		15 58	
12¾	Mansfield Woodhouse	d	11 07	11 37	12 07	12 37	13 07	13 37	14 07	14 37	15 07	15 37	16 07	16 37
14¼	**Mansfield**	d	11 10	11 40	12 10	12 40	13 10	13 40	14 10	14 40	15 10	15 40	16 10	16 40
17	Sutton Parkway	d	11 16	11 46	12 16	12 46	13 16	13 46	14 16	14 46	15 16	15 46	16 16	16 46
17¾	Kirkby In Ashfield	d	11 19	11 49	12 19	12 49	13 19	13 49	14 19	14 49	15 19	15 49	16 19	16 49
20¾	Newstead	d		11 54		12 54		13 54		14 54		15 54		16 54
23¼	Hucknall	d	11 26	11 58	12 26	12 58	13 26	13 58	14 26	14 58	15 26	15 58	16 26	16 58
26	Bulwell	d	11 30		12 30		13 30		14 30		15 30		16 30	
31½	**Nottingham** 8	a	11 44	12 14	12 44	13 19	13 44	14 14	14 44	15 14	15 44	16 14	16 44	17 14

		EM	EM	EM	EM	EM	EM	EM	EM
Worksop	d	16 42		17 46	18 41	19 22	20 15	21 20	22 21
Whitwell	d	16 51		17 55	18 50	19 31	20 24	21 29	22 30
Creswell (Derbys)	d	16 54		17 58	18 53	19 34	20 27	21 32	22 33
Langwith - Whaley Thorns	d	16 59		18 02	18 58	19 38	20 31	21 37	22 38
Shirebrook	d	17 02		18 07	19 01	19 42	20 35	21 40	22 41
Mansfield Woodhouse	d	17 10	17 43	18 14	19 09	19 49	20 43	21 48	22 49
Mansfield	d	17 14	17 46	18 18	19 13	19 53	20 50	21 53	22 53
Sutton Parkway	d	17 19	17 52	18 24	19 18	19 58	20 55	21 58	22 58
Kirkby In Ashfield	d	17 22	17 55	18 27	19 21	20 01	20 58	22 01	23 01
Newstead	d		17 59	18 31	19 26	20 06	21 03	22 06	23 06
Hucknall	d	17 30	18 04	18 36	19 30	20 10	21 07	22 10	23 10
Bulwell	d	17 34		18 40	19 34	20 14	21 14	22 14	23 14
Nottingham 8	a	17 48	18 20	18 51	19 47	20 36	21 26	22 26	23 26

Saturdays

		EM	EM	EM	EM	EM	EM	EM	EM	EM
Worksop	d	05 50	06 56	07 38	08 38		09 38		10 38	
Whitwell	d	05 59	07 05	07 47	08 47		09 47		10 47	
Creswell (Derbys)	d	06 02	07 08	07 50	08 50		09 50		10 50	
Langwith - Whaley Thorns	d	06 06	07 13	07 54	08 54		09 55		10 55	
Shirebrook	d	06 10	07 16	07 58	08 58		09 58		10 58	
Mansfield Woodhouse	d	06 17	07 25	08 06	09 06	09 37	10 07	10 37	11 07	11 37
Mansfield	d	06 22	07 29	08 10	09 10	09 40	10 10	10 40	11 10	11 40
Sutton Parkway	d	06 27	07 35	08 15	09 15	09 46	10 16	10 46	11 16	11 46
Kirkby In Ashfield	d	06 30	07 38	08 18	09 18	09 49	10 19	10 49	11 19	11 49
Newstead	d	06 35	07 43	08 23	09 23	09 54		10 54		11 54
Hucknall	d	06 39	07 48	08 28	09 27	09 58	10 26	10 58	11 26	11 58
Bulwell	d	06 43	07 53	08 32	09 31		10 30		11 30	
Nottingham 8	a	06 58	08 05	08 44	09 44	10 15	10 44	11 14	11 44	12 14

		EM	EM	EM	EM	EM	EM	EM	EM	EM	EM	EM	EM	EM
Worksop	d	11 38		12 38		13 38		14 38		15 38		16 42		17 46
Whitwell	d	11 47		12 47		13 47		14 47		15 47		16 51		17 55
Creswell (Derbys)	d	11 50		12 50		13 50		14 50		15 50		16 54		17 58
Langwith - Whaley Thorns	d	11 55		12 55		13 55		14 55		15 55		16 59		18 02
Shirebrook	d	11 58		12 58		13 58		14 58		15 58		17 02		18 07
Mansfield Woodhouse	d	12 07	12 37	13 07	13 37	14 07	14 37	15 07	15 37	16 07	16 37	17 10	17 43	18 14
Mansfield	d	12 10	12 40	13 10	13 40	14 10	14 40	15 10	15 40	16 10	16 40	17 14	17 46	18 18
Sutton Parkway	d	12 16	12 46	13 16	13 46	14 16	14 46	15 16	15 46	16 16	16 46	17 19	17 52	18 24
Kirkby In Ashfield	d	12 19	12 49	13 19	13 49	14 19	14 49	15 19	15 49	16 19	16 49	17 22	17 55	18 27
Newstead	d		12 54		13 54		14 54		15 54		16 54		17 59	18 31
Hucknall	d	12 26	12 58	13 26	13 58	14 26	14 58	15 26	15 58	16 26	16 58	17 30	18 04	18 36
Bulwell	d	12 30		13 30		14 30		15 30		16 30		17 34		18 40
Nottingham 8	a	12 44	13 15	13 44	14 14	14 44	15 14	15 44	16 15	16 44	17 14	17 48	18 20	18 51

		EM	EM	EM	EM	EM
Worksop	d	18 41	19 22	20 15	21 19	22 21
Whitwell	d	18 50	19 31	20 24	21 28	22 30
Creswell (Derbys)	d	18 53	19 34	20 27	21 31	22 33
Langwith - Whaley Thorns	d	18 58	19 38	20 31	21 36	22 38
Shirebrook	d	19 01	19 42	20 35	21 39	22 41
Mansfield Woodhouse	d	19 09	19 49	20 43	21 47	22 49
Mansfield	d	19 13	19 53	20 50	21 52	22 53
Sutton Parkway	d	19 18	19 58	20 55	21 57	22 58
Kirkby In Ashfield	d	19 21	20 01	20 58	22 00	23 01
Newstead	d	19 26	20 06	21 03	22 05	23 06
Hucknall	d	19 30	20 10	21 07	22 09	23 10
Bulwell	d	19 34	20 14	21 14	22 13	23 14
Nottingham 8	a	19 47	20 32	21 27	22 25	23 26

Sundays

until 12 February

		EM	EM	EM	EM	EM	EM	EM	EM
Worksop	d								
Whitwell	d								
Creswell (Derbys)	d								
Langwith - Whaley Thorns	d								
Shirebrook	d								
Mansfield Woodhouse	d	08 52	10 30	12 12	14 10	16 09	17 36	19 17	21 10
Mansfield	d	08 55	10 33	12 15	14 13	16 12	17 39	19 20	21 13
Sutton Parkway	d	09 01	10 39	12 21	14 19	16 18	17 45	19 26	21 19
Kirkby In Ashfield	d	09 04	10 42	12 24	14 22	16 21	17 48	19 29	21 22
Newstead	d	09 08	10 46	12 28	14 26	16 25	17 52	19 33	21 26
Hucknall	d	09 13	10 51	12 33	14 31	16 30	17 57	19 38	21 31
Bulwell	d	09 17	10 55	12 37	14 35	16 34	18 01	19 42	21 35
Nottingham 8	a	09 29	11 07	12 49	14 47	16 46	18 13	19 54	21 47

Sundays

19 February to 25 March

Worksop - Mansfield - Nottingham

Network Diagram - see first Page of Table 50

		EM 🚌	EM	EM	EM	EM	EM	EM	EM
Worksop	d								
Whitwell	d								
Creswell (Derbys)	d								
Langwith - Whaley Thorns	d								
Shirebrook	d								
Mansfield Woodhouse	d	08 45	10 30	12 12	14 10	16 09	17 36	19 17	21 10
Mansfield	d	08 57	10 33	12 15	14 13	16 12	17 39	19 20	21 13
Sutton Parkway	d	09 12	10 39	12 21	14 19	16 18	17 45	19 26	21 19
Kirkby In Ashfield	d	09 19	10 42	12 24	14 22	16 21	17 48	19 29	21 22
Newstead	d	09 32	10 46	12 28	14 26	16 25	17 52	19 33	21 26
Hucknall 🚊	d	09 42	10 51	12 33	14 31	16 30	17 57	19 38	21 31
Bulwell 🚊	d	09 47	10 55	12 37	14 35	16 34	18 01	19 42	21 35
Nottingham 8 🚊	a	10 07	11 07	12 49	14 47	16 46	18 13	19 54	21 47

Sundays

from 1 April

		EM	EM	EM	EM	EM	EM	EM	EM
Worksop	d								
Whitwell	d								
Creswell (Derbys)	d								
Langwith - Whaley Thorns	d								
Shirebrook	d								
Mansfield Woodhouse	d	08 52	10 30	12 12	14 10	16 09	17 36	19 17	21 10
Mansfield	d	08 55	10 33	12 15	14 13	16 12	17 39	19 20	21 13
Sutton Parkway	d	09 01	10 39	12 21	14 19	16 18	17 45	19 26	21 19
Kirkby In Ashfield	d	09 04	10 42	12 24	14 22	16 21	17 48	19 29	21 22
Newstead	d	09 08	10 46	12 28	14 26	16 25	17 52	19 33	21 26
Hucknall 🚊	d	09 13	10 51	12 33	14 31	16 30	17 57	19 38	21 31
Bulwell 🚊	d	09 17	10 55	12 37	14 35	16 34	18 01	19 42	21 35
Nottingham 8 🚊	a	09 29	11 07	12 49	14 47	16 46	18 13	19 57	21 47

Nottingham - Derby - Matlock

Network Diagram - see first Page of Table 50

Miles			EM MX	EM	XC	EM	EM	XC	EM	EM	XC		EM	EM	EM	EM	XC	EM	XC	EM	EM		XC	EM	EM
			◇1		◇1		◇1	◇1	◇1	◇1	◇1		◇1	◇1			1	◇1	◇1				1	◇1	◇1
			☕				🍴🛒		🍴🛒	☕			🍴🛒	☕				☕	🛒					☕	☕
0	**Nottingham 8**	d	01 52		06 00	06 18	06 28	06 37	06 49		06 56		07 10		07 19	07 31	07 37	08 02	08 08	08 15	08 32		08 37		09 02
3¼	Beeston	d			06 06	06 24	06a33	06 43	06a54		07 07		07a16		07 25	07a37	07 43	08a07		08 24	08a38		08 43		09a07
4¾	Attenborough	d			06 10	06 27					07 11				07 29					08 27					
7¾	Long Eaton	d			06 17	06 35					07 18			07 36	07 40		07 51			08 35			08 51	09 00	
13½	Spondon	d			06 24	06 42									07 47					08 42			08 57		
16	**Derby 6**	a	02 10		06 30	06 49		07 00			07 31			07 47	07 53		08 02		08 32	08 48			09 02	09 15	
—		d		05 40		06 50				07 20					07 54					08 50					
21¼	Duffield	d		05 47		06 57									08 02					08 57					
23¾	Belper	d		05 52		07 02				07a27					08 07					09 02					
26½	Ambergate	d		05 58		07 08									08 13					09 08					
28½	Whatstandwell	d		06 02		07 12									08 17					09 12					
31½	Cromford	d		06 07		07 17									08 22					09 17					
32¼	Matlock Bath	d		06 11		07 20									08 24					09 19					
33¼	**Matlock**	a		06 14		07 24									08 27					09 24					

		XC	EM	EM	XC	EM	EM		XC	EM	EM	XC	EM	EM	XC	EM	EM		XC	EM	EM	XC	EM	EM	XC
		◇1			1	◇1	◇1		◇1			1	◇1	◇1	◇1				1	◇1	◇1	◇1			1
		🛒				☕	☕		🛒				☕	☕	🛒				🛒	☕	☕				🛒
Nottingham 8	d	09 11	09 18	09 32	09 37		10 02		10 11	10 18	10 32	10 37		11 02	11 08	11 18	11 32		11 37		12 02	12 08	12 18	12 32	12 37
Beeston	d		09 24	09a38	09 43		10a07			10 24	10a38	10 43		11a07		11 24	11a38		11 43		12a07		12 24	12a38	12 43
Attenborough	d		09 27							10 27						11 27							12 27		
Long Eaton	d		09 35		09 51	09 56				10 35		10 51	10 56			11 35			11 51	11 57			12 35		12 51
Spondon	d																								
Derby 6	a	09 31	09 48		10 02	10 09			10 33	10 49		11 02	11 09		11 31	11 48			12 02	12 09		12 33	12 48		13 02
	d		09 50							10 50						11 54							12 50		
Duffield	d		09 57							10 57						12 01							12 57		
Belper	d		10 02							11 02						12 06							13 02		
Ambergate	d		10 08							11 08						12 12							13 08		
Whatstandwell	d		10 12							11 12						12 16							13 12		
Cromford	d		10 17							11 17						12 21							13 17		
Matlock Bath	d		10 20							11 20						12 24							13 20		
Matlock	a		10 24							11 24						12 28							13 24		

		EM	EM		XC	EM	EM	XC	EM	EM	XC	EM	EM		XC	EM	EM	XC	EM	EM	XC	EM	EM		XC
		◇1	◇1		◇1			1	◇1	◇1	◇1				1	◇1	◇1	◇1			1	◇1	◇1		◇1
		☕	☕					🛒	☕	☕	🛒				🛒	☕	☕				🛒	☕	☕		
Nottingham 8	d		13 02		13 11	13 18	13 32	13 37		14 02	14 11	14 18	14 32		14 37		15 02	15 11	15 18	15 32	15 37		16 02		16 08
Beeston	d		13a07			13 24	13a38	13 43		14a07		14 24	14a38		14 43		15a07		15 24	15a38	15 43		16a07		
Attenborough	d					13 27						14 27							15 27						
Long Eaton	d	12 57				13 35		13 51	13 57			14 35			14 51	14 57			15 35		15 51	15 57			
Spondon	d					13 43																			
Derby 6	a	13 09			13 31	13 48		14 02	14 09		14 31	14 47			15 03	15 13		15 31	15 48		16 03	16 09			16 31
	d					13 50						14 54							15 50						
Duffield	d					13 57						15 01							15 57						
Belper	d					14 02						15 06							16 02						
Ambergate	d					14 08						15 12							16 08						
Whatstandwell	d					14 12						15 16							16 12						
Cromford	d					14 17						15 21							16 17						
Matlock Bath	d					14 20						15 24							16 20						
Matlock	a					14 24						15 28							16 24						

		EM	EM	XC	EM	EM	EM	XC	EM		EM	XC	EM	EM	XC	EM	EM	XC	EM		EM	XC	EM	EM	XC
				1	◇1		◇1	◇1				1	◇1	◇1	◇1			1	◇1		◇1	◇1			1
				🛒	☕		☕					🛒	☕	☕				🛒	☕		☕				
Nottingham 8	d	16 18	16 32	16 37		16 50	17 02	17 08	17 18		17 32	17 37		18 02	18 08	18 18	18 33	18 37			19 02	19 08	19 18	19 32	19 37
Beeston	d	16 24	16 38	16 43		16 55	17a07		17 24		17 38	17 43		18a07		18 24	18a39	18 43			19a07		19 24	19a38	19 43
Attenborough	d	16 27	16a41			16 58			17 27		17a41					18 27							19 27		19 46
Long Eaton	d	16 35		16 51	16 57	17 07			17 35			17 51	18 01			18 37		18 51	18 56				19 35		19 53
Spondon	d								17 42			17 57													
Derby 6	a	16 48		17 02	17 09	17 23		17 31	17 49			18 02	18 14		18 33	18 48		19 02	19 09			19 32	19 48		20 02
	d	16 50							17 50							18 50							19 50		
Duffield	d	16 57							17 57							18 57							19 57		
Belper	d	17 02							18 02							19 02							20 02		
Ambergate	d	17 08							18 08							19 08							20 08		
Whatstandwell	d	17 12							18 12							19 12							20 12		
Cromford	d	17 17							18 17							19 17							20 17		
Matlock Bath	d	17 20							18 20							19 20							20 20		
Matlock	a	17 24							18 24							19 24							20 24		

		EM	EM	EM	EM		EM	XC	NT	EM	EM	EM	EM	XC	EM		EM	EM	EM	EM	EM				
		◇1	◇1	◇1				1		◇1	◇1			1	◇1						◇1				
		☕	☕	☕						☕	☕				☕						☕				
Nottingham 8	d	20 02		20 07	20 11		20 32	20 37	20 45	21 02		21 16	21 32	21 37				22 16	23 10	23 15					
Beeston	d	20a07			20 17		20a38	20 43		21a07		21 22	21a38	21 43				22 22	23a16	23 21					
Attenborough	d				20 20							21 25		21 46				22 25		23 24					
Long Eaton	d		20 07	20 23	20 28			20 51			21 06	21 33		21 53	21 59			22 33		23 33	23 38				
Spondon	d													21 59											
Derby 6	a		20 19	20 35	20 44			21 02	21 05		21 16	21 49		22 04	22 10			22 49		23 48	23 50				
	d				20 56												22 16								
Duffield	d				21 03												22 23								
Belper	d				21 08												22 28								
Ambergate	d				21 14												22 34								
Whatstandwell	d				21 18												22 38								
Cromford	d				21 23												22 43								
Matlock Bath	d				21 26												22 46								
Matlock	a				21 29												22 49								

For connections from St Pancras International please refer to Table 53

Table 56

Saturdays

Nottingham - Derby - Matlock

Network Diagram - see first Page of Table 50

		EM	EM	XC	EM	EM	XC	EM	XC	EM		EM	EM	XC	EM	EM	XC	EM	EM	XC		EM	EM	XC	EM
		◇1		◇1	◇1		◇1	◇1	◇1	◇1				1	◇1	◇1	◇1			1		◇1	◇1	◇1	
		☕			☕			☕		☕					☕	☕	🛒					☕	☕	🛒	
Nottingham 8	d	01 52		05 57	06 02	06 18	06 37		06 56	07 02		07 18	07 31	07 37		08 02	08 08	08 18	08 32	08 37			09 02	09 08	09 18
Beeston	d			06 03	06a07	06 24	06 43		07 02	07a07		07 24	07a37	07 43		08a07		08 24	08a38	08 43			09a07		09 24
Attenborough	d			06 06		06 27			07 06			07 27						08 27							09 27
Long Eaton	d			06 17		06 34			07 14			07 35		07 51	07 56			08 35		08 51		09 01			09 35
Spondon	d			06 24		06 43												08 42		08 58					
Derby 6	a	02 10		06 32		06 48	07 02		07 30			07 49		08 02	08 09		08 31	08 48		09 03		09 14		09 31	09 48
	d		05 40			06 50		07 20				07 50						08 50							09 50
Duffield	d		05 47			06 57						07 57						08 57							09 57
Belper	d		05 52			07 02		07a27				08 02						09 02							10 02
Ambergate	d		05 58			07 08						08 08						09 08							10 08
Whatstandwell	d		06 02			07 12						08 12						09 12							10 12
Cromford	d		06 07			07 17						08 17						09 17							10 17
Matlock Bath	d		06 11			07 20						08 20						09 21							10 20
Matlock	a		06 14			07 24						08 24						09 24							10 24

		EM	XC	EM	EM	XC		EM	EM	XC	EM	EM	XC	EM	EM	XC		EM	EM	XC	EM	EM	XC	EM	EM
			1	◇1	◇1	◇1				1	◇1	◇1	◇1			1		◇1	◇1	◇1			1	◇1	◇1
				☕	☕	🛒					☕	☕	🛒			🛒		☕	☕				🛒	☕	☕
Nottingham 8	d	09 32	09 37		10 02	10 08		10 18	10 32	10 37		11 02	11 11	11 18	11 32	11 37			12 02	12 08	12 18	12 32	12 37		13 02
Beeston	d	09a38	09 43		10a07			10 24	10a38	10 43		11a07		11 24	11a38	11 43			12a07		12 24	12a38	12 43		13a07
Attenborough	d							10 27						11 27							12 27				
Long Eaton	d		09 51	09 57				10 35		10 51	10 57			11 36		11 51		11 57			12 36		12 51	12 57	
Spondon	d																								
Derby 6	a		10 02	10 09		10 31		10 49		11 02	11 09		11 31	11 48		12 02		12 09		12 31	12 48		13 02	13 09	
	d							10 50						11 50							12 50				
Duffield	d							10 57						11 57							12 57				
Belper	d							11 02						12 02							13 02				
Ambergate	d							11 08						12 08							13 08				
Whatstandwell	d							11 12						12 12							13 12				
Cromford	d							11 17						12 17							13 17				
Matlock Bath	d							11 20						12 20							13 20				
Matlock	a							11 24						12 24							13 24				

		XC		EM	EM	XC	EM	EM	XC	EM	EM	XC		EM	EM	XC	EM	EM	XC	EM	EM	XC		EM	EM
		◇1				1	◇1	◇1	◇1			1		◇1	◇1	◇1			1	◇1	◇1	◇1			
						🛒	☕	☕	🛒			🛒		☕	☕	🛒			🛒	☕	☕				
Nottingham 8	d	13 08		13 18	13 32	13 37		14 02	14 08	14 18	14 32	14 37			15 02	15 08	15 18	15 32	15 37		16 02	16 08		16 18	16 32
Beeston	d			13 24	13a38	13 43		14a07		14 24	14a38	14 43			15a07		15 24	15a38	15 43		16a07			16 24	16 38
Attenborough	d			13 27						14 27							15 27							16 27	16a41
Long Eaton	d			13 35		13 51	13 57			14 36		14 51		14 57			15 36		15 51	15 57				16 36	
Spondon	d			13 43																					
Derby 6	a	13 31		13 48		14 02	14 09		14 32	14 48		15 02		15 09		15 31	15 48		16 02	16 09		16 31		16 48	
	d			13 50						14 50							15 50							16 50	
Duffield	d			13 57						14 57							15 57							16 57	
Belper	d			14 02						15 02							16 02							17 02	
Ambergate	d			14 08						15 08							16 08							17 08	
Whatstandwell	d			14 12						15 12							16 12							17 12	
Cromford	d			14 17						15 17							16 17							17 17	
Matlock Bath	d			14 20						15 20							16 20							17 20	
Matlock	a			14 24						15 24							16 24							17 24	

		XC	EM	EM	XC	EM	EM	XC		EM	EM	XC	EM	EM	XC	EM	EM	XC		EM	EM	XC	EM	EM	EM
		1	◇1	◇1	◇1			1		◇1	◇1	◇1			1	◇1	◇1	◇1				1	◇1	◇1	
		🛒	☕	☕				🛒		☕	☕				🛒	☕	☕						☕	☕	
Nottingham 8	d	16 37		17 02	17 11	17 18	17 32	17 37			18 02	18 08	18 19	18 32	18 37		19 02	19 08		19 18	19 32	19 37		20 02	20 09
Beeston	d	16 43		17a07		17 24	17 38	17 43			18a07		18 24	18a38	18 43		19a07			19 24	19a38	19 43		20a07	20 15
Attenborough	d					17 27	17a41						18 26							19 27		19 46			20 18
Long Eaton	d	16 51	16 56			17 35		17 51		17 57			18 37		18 51	18 57				19 35		19 53	19 57		20 27
Spondon	d					17 42												19 27							
Derby 6	a	17 02	17 09		17 31	17 48		18 02		18 09		18 31	18 48		19 02	19 09		19 32		19 48		20 02	20 09		20 42
	d					17 50							18 50							19 50					20 50
Duffield	d					17 57							18 57							19 57					20 57
Belper	d					18 02							19 02							20 02					21 02
Ambergate	d					18 08							19 08							20 08					21 08
Whatstandwell	d					18 12							19 12							20 12					21 12
Cromford	d					18 17							19 17							20 17					21 17
Matlock Bath	d					18 20							19 20							20 20					21 20
Matlock	a					18 24							19 24							20 24					21 24

		EM	XC	EM		EM	EM	EM	XC	EM	EM	EM	EM	EM		EM
			1	◇1		◇1			1	◇1				◇1		
				☕		☕				☕				☕		
Nottingham 8	d	20 32	20 37	20 43			21 08	21 32	21 37			22 15	23 10			23 15
Beeston	d	20a37	20 43	20a48			21 14	21a38	21 43			22 21	23a16			23 21
Attenborough	d						21 17		21 46			22 24				23 24
Long Eaton	d		20 51			20 57	21 26		21 53	21 57		22 33		23 16		23 32
Spondon	d								21 59							
Derby 6	a		21 02			21 10	21 41		22 04	22 10		22 48		23 26		23 47
	d										22 16					
Duffield	d										22 23					
Belper	d										22 28					
Ambergate	d										22 35					
Whatstandwell	d										22 39					
Cromford	d										22 44					
Matlock Bath	d										22 47					
Matlock	a										22 50					

For connections from St Pancras International please refer to Table 53

Table 56

Nottingham - Derby - Matlock

Sundays
until 25 March

Network Diagram - see first Page of Table 50

		EM ◇1 A ⊒	EM ◇1 B ⊒	EM	EM ◇1 ⊒	EM ◇1 ⊒	XC ◇1 🛒	EM ◇1 ⊒	EM	XC ◇1 🛒		EM ◇1 ⊒	EM ◇1 ⊒	XC ◇1 🛒	EM ◇1 ⊒	EM	EM ◇1 ⊒	XC ◇1 🛒	EM	EM ◇1 ⊒		EM ◇1 ⊒	XC ◇1 🛒	EM ◇1 ⊒	EM ◇1 ⊒
Nottingham 8	d		08 19	09 22	10 15		11 11		11 30	12 10		12 28		13 06		13 22	13 31	14 10	14 24	14 32			15 10	15 21	
Beeston	d		08a24	09 27	10a21				11 35			12a34				13 28	13a37		14 30	14a37				15a26	
Attenborough	d			09 31					11 39							13 34			14 33						
Long Eaton	d	00 11		09 39		10 32		11 39	11 47				12 41		13 42	13 46			14 41			14 46			15 42
Spondon	d																								
Derby 6	a	00 21		09 50		10 46	11 31	11 49	11 55	12 30			12 51	13 26	13 52	13 57		14 29	14 52			14 57	15 30		15 53
	d			09 52					12 00							13 59									
Duffield	d			09 59					12 07							14 06									
Belper	d			10 04					12 12							14 11									
Ambergate	d			10 10					12 18							14 17									
Whatstandwell	d			10 14					12 22							14 21									
Cromford	d			10 20					12 28							14 27									
Matlock Bath	d			10 22					12 30							14 29									
Matlock	a			10 25					12 33							14 32									

		EM	XC ◇1 🛒	EM ◇1 ⊒	EM	EM ◇1 ⊒		XC ◇1 🛒	EM ◇1 ⊒	EM ◇1 ⊒	EM	XC ◇1 🛒	EM ◇1 ⊒	EM	EM ◇1 ⊒	XC ◇1 🛒		EM ◇1 ⊒	EM	EM ◇1 ⊒	XC ◇1	EM ◇1 ⊒	EM	XC ◇1	EM ◇1 ⊒
Nottingham 8	d	15 29	16 10		16 22	16 31		17 10	17 26		17 29	18 10		18 23	18 34	19 10			19 22	19 57	20 10		20 21	21 08	
Beeston	d	15 34			16 27	16a36			17a31		17 35			18 29	18a39				19 27	20a02			20 27		
Attenborough	d	15 38			16 31						17 38			18 32					19 31				20 31		
Long Eaton	d	15 46		16 32	16 38					17 29	17 46		18 24	18 40				19 25	19 38			20 27	20 38		21 24
Spondon	d																								
Derby 6	a	15 57	16 30	16 44	16 50			17 29		17 41	17 58	18 30	18 34	18 51		19 30		19 35	19 50		20 29	20 37	20 51	21 31	21 35
	d	15 59									17 59								19 52						
Duffield	d	16 05									18 07								19 59						
Belper	d	16 10									18 11								20 04						
Ambergate	d	16 16									18 17								20 10						
Whatstandwell	d	16 20									18 21								20 14						
Cromford	d	16 26									18 27								20 20						
Matlock Bath	d	16 28									18 29								20 22						
Matlock	a	16 32									18 32								20 25						

		EM		EM ◇1 ⊒
Nottingham 8	d	21 24		
Beeston	d	21 29		
Attenborough	d	21 33		
Long Eaton	d	21 40		23 32
Spondon	d			
Derby 6	a	21 52		23 42
	d	21 54		
Duffield	d	22 01		
Belper	d	22 06		
Ambergate	d	22 12		
Whatstandwell	d	22 16		
Cromford	d	22 22		
Matlock Bath	d	22 24		
Matlock	a	22 27		

Sundays
from 1 April

		EM ◇1 ⊒	EM ◇1 ⊒	EM	EM ◇1 ⊒	EM ◇1 ⊒	XC ◇1 🛒	EM	EM ◇1 ⊒	XC ◇1 🛒		EM ◇1 ⊒	EM ◇1 ⊒	XC ◇1 🛒	EM ◇1 ⊒	EM	EM ◇1 ⊒	XC ◇1 🛒	EM ◇1 ⊒	EM		EM ◇1 ⊒	EM ◇1 ⊒	XC ◇1 🛒	EM
Nottingham 8	d		08 13	09 22	10 09		11 11	11 22		12 10		12 15		13 06	13 15	13 22		14 10	14 24	14 26			15 05	15 10	15 22
Beeston	d		08a18	09 27	10a15			11 27				12a21			13a21	13 27			14a29	14 31			15a10		15 27
Attenborough	d			09 31				11 31								13 31				14 35					15 31
Long Eaton	d	00 23		09 39		10 30		11 39	11 52				12 51			13 39	13 48			14 42		14 53			15 39
Spondon	d																								
Derby 6	a	00 33		09 50		10 41	11 31	11 47	12 02	12 30			13 01	13 26		13 50	13 58	14 29		14 56		15 04		15 30	15 50
	d			09 52				11 52								13 52									15 52
Duffield	d			09 59				11 59								13 59									15 58
Belper	d			10 04				12 04								14 04									16 03
Ambergate	d			10 10				12 10								14 10									16 09
Whatstandwell	d			10 14				12 14								14 14									16 13
Cromford	d			10 20				12 20								14 20									16 19
Matlock Bath	d			10 22				12 22								14 22									16 21
Matlock	a			10 25				12 25								14 25									16 25

A not 11 December

B until 12 February

For connections from St Pancras International please refer to Table 53

Table 56

Sundays

from 1 April

Nottingham - Derby - Matlock

Network Diagram - see first Page of Table 50

		EM	XC	EM	EM	EM		XC	EM	EM	EM	XC	EM	EM	EM	XC		EM	EM	EM	XC	EM	EM	XC	EM
		◇1	◇1	◇1		◇1		◇1	◇1		◇1	◇1	◇1	◇1		◇1			◇1	◇1	◇1		◇1	◇1	
		☕	🛒	☕		☕		🛒	☕		☕	🛒	☕	☕		🛒			☕	☕			☕		
Nottingham 8 🚌	d		16 10	16 18	16 22			17 10	17 19	17 23		18 10	18 20		18 26	19 10		19 14		19 43	20 10	20 19		21 08	21 20
Beeston	d			16a23	16 27				17a24	17 28			18a25		18 32			19 19		19a48		20 25			21 25
Attenborough	d				16 31					17 32					18 35			19 23				20 29			21 29
Long Eaton	d	15 51			16 38	16 47				17 40	17 47			18 42	18 46			19 30	19 42			20 36	20 42		21 36
Spondon	d																								
Derby 6	a	16 02	16 30		16 50	16 58		17 29		17 51	17 58	18 30		18 52	18 57	19 30		19 44	19 52		20 29	20 49	20 52	21 31	21 48
	d									17 53								19 52							21 52
Duffield	d									18 00								19 59							21 59
Belper	d									18 05								20 04							22 04
Ambergate	d									18 11								20 10							22 10
Whatstandwell	d									18 15								20 14							22 14
Cromford	d									18 21								20 20							22 20
Matlock Bath	d									18 23								20 22							22 22
Matlock	a									18 26								20 25							22 25

		EM		EM
		◇1		◇1
		☕		☕
Nottingham 8 🚌	d			
Beeston	d			
Attenborough	d			
Long Eaton	d	21 43		23 40
Spondon	d			
Derby 6	a	21 53		23 50
	d			
Duffield	d			
Belper	d			
Ambergate	d			
Whatstandwell	d			
Cromford	d			
Matlock Bath	d			
Matlock	a			

For connections from St Pancras International please refer to Table 53

Table 56

Matlock - Derby - Nottingham

Network Diagram - see first Page of Table 50

Miles			EM	EM	XC	EM	EM	EM	EM	XC	EM		EM	EM	EM	EM	XC	EM	EM	EM	XC		EM	EM	XC
			MX	MX	MX	MO	MO	MX																	
				◇1	◇1	◇1	◇1	◇1	◇1				◇1			◇1	1		◇1		1				1
						A	B																		
				☕		☕	☕	☕	⊠🛒				⊠🛒			⊠🛒	🛒		☕						🛒
0	**Matlock**	d	22p55											06 22											
1	Matlock Bath	d	22p57											06 24											
1¾	Cromford	d	23p00											06 27											
4¾	Whatstandwell	d	23p05											06 32											
6¾	Ambergate	d	23p10											06 37				06 56							
9½	Belper	d	23p17											06 44				07 01							
12	Duffield	d	23p21											06 48				07 05							
17¼	**Derby** 6	a	23p29											06 56				07 13							
—		d	23p31		23p59				05 17	06 00	06 24		06 32			07 01	07 10		07 26	07 33	07 40			07 53	08 10
19¾	Spondon	d									06 29						07 18				07 45				
25½	Long Eaton	d	23p41						05a26		06 36		06a42				07 25		07a35	07 44	07 49			08 03	08 19
28½	Attenborough	d	23p48								06 44				07 13		07 31			07 52				08 13	
30	Beeston	d	23p51	00 05		00∫41	00∫42	01 39		06 15	06 47				07 16		07 35			07 55	07 58		08 06	08 16	08 27
33¼	**Nottingham** 8 🚊	a	00 02	00 12	00 18	00∫48	00∫48	01 45		06 21	06 57				07 23	07 29	07 41			08 05	08 08		08 15	08 26	08 33

		EM	EM	EM	XC	EM	EM		XC	EM	EM	XC	EM	EM	XC	EM	EM		XC	EM	EM	XC	EM	EM	XC
		◇1	◇1		1		◇1		1	◇1		◇1		◇1	1	◇1			◇1		◇1	1	◇1		◇1
		⊠	☕				☕		🛒	☕				☕	🛒	☕			🛒		☕		☕		🛒
Matlock	d			07 36							08 36						09 36							10 36	
Matlock Bath	d			07 38							08 38						09 38							10 38	
Cromford	d			07 41							08 41						09 41							10 41	
Whatstandwell	d			07 46							08 46						09 46							10 46	
Ambergate	d			07 51							08 51						09 51							10 51	
Belper	d			07 58							08 58						09 58							10 58	
Duffield	d			08 02							09 02						10 02							11 02	
Derby 6	a			08 10							09 10						10 10							11 10	
	d	08 16		08 20	08 40				09 05	09 20	09 24	09 39			10 05	10 20	10 24		10 41			11 05	11 20	11 24	11 39
Spondon	d			08 25																					
Long Eaton	d	08a25		08 32					09 14	09a29	09 33				10 14	10a29	10 33					11 14	11a29	11 33	
Attenborough	d			08 39					09 21		09 40						10 40							11 40	
Beeston	d		08 32	08 42		09 02	09 17		09 24		09 43		10 02	10 17	10 22		10 43			11 02	11 17	11 22		11 43	
Nottingham 8 🚊	a		08 39	08 50	09 05	09 13	09 26		09 33		09 53	10 05	10 13	10 25	10 32		10 53		11 05	11 14	11 25	11 32		11 53	12 05

		EM	EM		XC	EM	EM	XC	EM	EM	XC	EM	EM		XC	EM	EM	XC	EM	EM	XC	EM	EM		XC
			◇1		1	◇1		◇1		◇1	1	◇1			◇1		◇1	1	◇1		◇1		◇1		1
			☕			☕		🛒		☕	🛒	☕			🛒		☕		☕		🛒		☕		
Matlock	d						11 36						12 36							13 36					
Matlock Bath	d						11 38						12 38							13 38					
Cromford	d						11 41						12 41							13 41					
Whatstandwell	d						11 46						12 46							13 46					
Ambergate	d						11 51						12 51							13 51					
Belper	d						11 58						12 58							13 58					
Duffield	d						12 02						13 02							14 02					
Derby 6	a						12 10						13 10							14 10					
	d				12 05	12 20	12 24	12 39			13 10	13 20	13 24		13 39			14 05	14 20	14 24	14 39				15 05
Spondon	d												13 29												
Long Eaton	d				12 14	12a29	12 33				13 19	13a29	13 34					14 14	14a29	14 33					15 14
Attenborough	d						12 40						13 41							14 40					
Beeston	d	12 02	12 17		12 22		12 43		13 07	13 17	13 27		13 44			14 02	14 16	14 24		14 43		15 02	15 17		15 22
Nottingham 8 🚊	a	12 13	12 26		12 32		12 53	13 05	13 14	13 25	13 33		13 53		14 05	14 13	14 26	14 32		14 53	15 05	15 13	15 26		15 32

		EM	EM	XC	EM	EM	XC	EM	EM		XC	EM	EM	XC	EM	EM	XC	EM	EM		EM	XC	EM	EM	XC
		◇1		◇1		◇1	1	◇1			◇1		◇1	1	◇1		◇1				◇1	1	◇1		◇1
		☕		🛒		☕		☕			🛒		☕		☕		🛒				☕		☕		
Matlock	d		14 36						15 36							16 36								17 36	
Matlock Bath	d		14 38						15 38							16 38								17 38	
Cromford	d		14 41						15 41							16 41								17 41	
Whatstandwell	d		14 46						15 46							16 46								17 46	
Ambergate	d		14 51						15 51							16 51								17 51	
Belper	d		14 58						15 58							16 58								17 58	
Duffield	d		15 02						16 02							17 02								18 02	
Derby 6	a		15 10						16 10							17 10								18 10	
	d	15 20	15 24	15 39			16 05	16 18	16 24		16 39			17 10	17 18	17 24	17 39		17 47			18 05	18 18	18 24	18 39
Spondon	d															17 29			17 53						
Long Eaton	d	15a29	15 33				16 14	16a27	16 33					17 19	17a28	17 36			18 01			18 14	18a27	18 33	
Attenborough	d		15 40						16 40							17 43			18 09					18 40	
Beeston	d		15 43		16 02	16 17	16 22		16 43			17 02	17 17	17 27		17 46		18 02	18 12		18 18	18 26		18 43	
Nottingham 8 🚊	a		15 53	16 05	16 13	16 25	16 32		16 54		17 05	17 13	17 26	17 33		17 54	18 05	18 13	18 22		18 27	18 32		18 54	19 05

A until 26 March

B from 2 April

For connections to St Pancras International please refer to Table 53

Matlock - Derby - Nottingham

Network Diagram - see first Page of Table 50

	EM	EM	EM	XC		EM	EM	XC	EM	EM	XC	EM	XC	EM		EM	EM	XC	EM	EM	EM	XC	EM	XC
	◇1 ☕		◇1 ☕	1		◇1 ☕		◇1		◇1 ☕	1		◇1			◇1 ☕		◇1			◇1 ☕	◇1		◇1
Matlock d							18 36					19 36					20 36		21 39				22 55	
Matlock Bath d							18 38					19 38					20 38		21 41				22 57	
Cromford d							18 41					19 41					20 41		21 44				23 00	
Whatstandwell d							18 46					19 46					20 46		21 49				23 05	
Ambergate d							18 51					19 51					20 51		21 54				23 10	
Belper d							18 58					19 58					20 58		22 01				23 17	
Duffield d							19 02					20 02					21 02		22 05				23 21	
Derby 6 a							19 10					20 10					21 10		22 13				23 29	
d				19 05		19 18	19 24	19 39			20 05	20 24	20 40				21 24	21 40				22 59	23 31	23 59
Spondon d																		21 45				23 04		
Long Eaton d				19 14		19a27	19 33				20 14	20 33	20 49				21 33	21 52				23 11	23 41	
Attenborough d							19 40					20 40					21 40	21 58				23 17	23 48	
Beeston d	19 03	19 07	19 19	19 23			19 43		20 07	20 18	20 23	20 43	20 58	21 03		21 19	21 43	22 02		22 07	22 17	23 20	23 51	
Nottingham 8 🚊 a	19 10	19 14	19 27	19 32			19 53	20 03	20 15	20 28	20 32	20 53	21 06	21 15		21 29	21 54	22 08		22 15	22 26	23 27	00 02	00 18

Saturdays

	EM	EM	XC	EM	EM	EM	EM	EM	EM		XC	EM	EM	XC	EM	XC	EM	EM	EM		XC	EM	EM	XC
		◇1 ☕	◇1	◇1 ☕	◇1 ☕	◇1 ☕					1 🛒	◇1 ☕		1		1 🛒	◇1 ⊠	◇1 ☕			1		◇1 ☕	1 🛒
Matlock d	22p55							06 22											07 36					
Matlock Bath d	22p57							06 24											07 38					
Cromford d	23p00							06 27											07 41					
Whatstandwell d	23p05							06 32											07 46					
Ambergate d	23p10							06 38											07 51					
Belper d	23p17							06 44											07 58					
Duffield d	23p21							06 48											08 02					
Derby 6 a	23p29							06 56											08 10					
d	23p31		23p59		05 25	06 18	06 24				07 10	07 18	07 33	07 39		08 10	08 18		08 24		08 39			09 05
Spondon d							06 29				07 15			07 44					08 29					
Long Eaton d	23p41				05a34	06a27	06 35				07 22	07a27	07 42	07 52		08 19	08a27		08 36					09 14
Attenborough d	23p48						06 44		07 12		07 28		07 51						08 43					09 21
Beeston d	23p51	00 05		01 39			06 47		07 15		07 32		07 54	07 59	08 04	08 27		08 31	08 46			09 05	09 17	09 24
Nottingham 8 🚊 a	00 02	00 12	00 18	01 45			06 57		07 24		07 38		08 05	08 08	08 13	08 34		08 42	08 53		09 05	09 14	09 26	09 33

	EM	EM	XC	EM	EM		XC	EM	EM	XC	EM	EM	XC	EM	EM		XC	EM	EM	XC	EM	EM	XC	EM
	◇1 ☕		◇1		◇1 ☕		1 🛒	◇1 ☕		◇1 🛒		◇1 ☕	1	◇1 ☕			◇1 🛒		◇1 ☕	1	◇1 ☕		◇1 🛒	
Matlock d		08 36							09 36						10 36							11 36		
Matlock Bath d		08 38							09 38						10 38							11 38		
Cromford d		08 41							09 41						10 41							11 41		
Whatstandwell d		08 46							09 46						10 46							11 46		
Ambergate d		08 51							09 51						10 51							11 51		
Belper d		08 58							09 58						10 58							11 58		
Duffield d		09 02							10 02						11 02							12 02		
Derby 6 a		09 10							10 10						11 10							12 10		
d	09 20	09 24	09 39				10 05	10 20	10 24	10 39			11 05	11 20	11 24		11 39			12 05	12 20	12 24	12 39	
Spondon d																								
Long Eaton d	09a29	09 33					10 14	10a29	10 33				11 14	11a29	11 33					12 15	12a29	12 33		
Attenborough d		09 40							10 40						11 40							12 40		
Beeston d		09 43		10 02	10 17		10 22		10 43		11 02	11 17	11 22		11 43			12 02	12 16	12 23		12 43		13 02
Nottingham 8 🚊 a		09 53	10 05	10 13	10 26		10 33		10 53	11 05	11 13	11 26	11 33		11 53		12 05	12 13	12 26	12 33		12 53	13 05	13 13

	EM		XC	EM	EM	XC	EM	EM	XC	EM	EM		XC	EM	EM	XC	EM	EM	XC	EM	EM		XC	EM
	◇1 ☕		1 🛒	◇1 ☕		◇1 🛒		◇1 ☕	1	◇1 ☕			◇1 🛒		◇1 ☕	1	◇1 ☕		◇1 🛒		◇1 ☕		1	◇1 ☕
Matlock d					12 36						13 36							14 36						
Matlock Bath d					12 38						13 38							14 38						
Cromford d					12 41						13 41							14 41						
Whatstandwell d					12 46						13 46							14 46						
Ambergate d					12 51						13 51							14 51						
Belper d					12 58						13 58							14 58						
Duffield d					13 02						14 02							15 02						
Derby 6 a					13 10						14 10							15 10						
d			13 10	13 20	13 24	13 39			14 10	14 20	14 24		14 39			15 05	15 20	15 24	15 39				16 05	16 20
Spondon d					13 29																			
Long Eaton d			13 19	13a29	13 35				14 19	14a30	14 33					15 14	15a29	15 33					16 14	16a29
Attenborough d					13 42						14 40							15 40						
Beeston d	13 16		13 27		13 45		14 02	14 17	14 27		14 43			15 02	15 17	15 24		15 43		16 02	16 17		16 24	
Nottingham 8 🚊 a	13 27		13 33		13 53	14 05	14 13	14 26	14 33		14 53		15 05	15 13	15 26	15 33		15 53	16 05	16 13	16 26		16 33	

	EM	XC	EM	EM	XC	EM	EM		XC	EM	EM	XC	EM	EM	XC	EM	EM		XC	EM	EM	XC	EM	EM
		◇1 🛒		◇1 ☕	1	◇1 ☕			◇1 🛒		◇1 ☕	1	◇1 ☕		◇1		◇1 ☕		1	◇1 ☕		◇1		◇1 ☕
Matlock d	15 36						16 36							17 36							18 36			
Matlock Bath d	15 38						16 38							17 38							18 38			
Cromford d	15 41						16 41							17 41							18 41			
Whatstandwell d	15 46						16 46							17 46							18 46			
Ambergate d	15 51						16 51							17 51							18 51			
Belper d	15 58						16 58							17 58							18 58			
Duffield d	16 02						17 02							18 02							19 02			
Derby 6 a	16 10						17 10							18 10							19 10			
d	16 24	16 39			17 10	17 18	17 24		17 39			18 05	18 18	18 24	18 39				19 05	19 21	19 25	19 39		
Spondon d							17 29																	
Long Eaton d	16 33				17 19	17a27	17 36					18 14	18a27	18 33					19 14	19a30	19 34			
Attenborough d	16 40						17 43							18 40							19 41			
Beeston d	16 43		17 02	17 17	17 27		17 46			18 02	18 16	18 22		18 43		19 02	19 17		19 24		19 44		20 05	20 16
Nottingham 8 🚊 a	16 53	17 05	17 13	17 26	17 33		17 53		18 05	18 12	18 26	18 32		18 53	19 05	19 14	19 26		19 33		19 51	20 05	20 15	20 26

For connections to St Pancras International please refer to Table 53

Table 56

Saturdays

Matlock - Derby - Nottingham

Network Diagram - see first Page of Table 50

		XC	EM	XC		EM	EM	EM	XC	EM	EM	EM	XC	EM
		1		◇1			◇1		◇1			◇1	◇1	
							☕					☕		
Matlock	d		19 36					20 36		21 36				22 55
Matlock Bath	d		19 38					20 38		21 38				22 57
Cromford	d		19 41					20 41		21 41				23 00
Whatstandwell	d		19 46					20 46		21 46				23 05
Ambergate	d		19 51					20 52		21 51				23 11
Belper	d		19 58					20 59		21 58				23 17
Duffield	d		20 02					21 03		22 02				23 21
Derby 6	a		20 10					21 11		22 10				23 29
	d	20 05	20 24	20 39				21 24	21 40				23 00	23 31
Spondon	d								21 45				23 05	
Long Eaton	d	20 14	20 33	20 49				21 33	21 52				23 12	23 41
Attenborough	d		20 40					21 40	21 58				23 18	23 48
Beeston	d	20 24	20 43	20 57		21 05	21 17	21 43	22 02		22 06	22 18	23 22	23 52
Nottingham 8	a	20 32	20 53	21 04		21 15	21 26	21 53	22 08		22 14	22 27	23 28	23 59

Sundays

until 25 March

		EM	EM	EM	EM	EM	EM	EM	XC	EM		EM	EM	XC	EM	EM	XC	EM	EM	EM		XC	EM	EM	XC
		◇1	◇1		◇1	◇1	◇1		◇1	◇1		◇1		◇1	◇1	◇1	◇1	◇1	◇1			◇1	◇1		◇1
		A																							
		☕	☕		☕	☕	☕		🛒	☕		☕		🛒	☕	☕	🛒	☕	☕			🛒	☕		🛒
Matlock	d							10 43					12 39							14 39					
Matlock Bath	d							10 45					12 41							14 41					
Cromford	d							10 48					12 44							14 44					
Whatstandwell	d							10 53					12 49							14 49					
Ambergate	d							10 59					12 54							14 54					
Belper	d							11 05					13 01							15 01					
Duffield	d							11 09					13 05							15 05					
Derby 6	a							11 15					13 13							15 13					
	d		08 48	09 18	09 51	10 52		11 18	12 40	12 58			13 18	13 40	14 02		14 40	14 50		15 18		15 40		16 18	16 40
Spondon	d																								
Long Eaton	d		08a57	09 28	10a00	11a01		11 28		13a07			13 28		14a11			14a59		15 28				16 27	
Attenborough	d			09 34				11 35					13 35							15 35				16 35	
Beeston	d	00(01		09 37			11 13	11 38				13 11	13 38			14 13			15 13	15 38			16 00	16 41	
Nottingham 8	a	00(08		09 44			11 23	11 45	13 00			13 20	13 46	14 00		14 20	15 02		15 20	15 45		16 00	16 06	16 48	17 00

		EM	EM	XC	EM	EM		EM	XC	EM	EM	EM	XC	EM	EM	EM		XC	EM	EM	XC	EM	EM	EM	EM
		◇1		◇1	◇1	◇1			◇1	◇1		◇1	◇1	◇1	◇1			◇1	◇1		◇1	◇1			◇1
		☕		🛒	☕	☕				☕		☕		☕	☕				☕			☕			☕
Matlock	d		16 45								18 39									20 39				22 45	
Matlock Bath	d		16 47								18 41									20 41				22 47	
Cromford	d		16 50								18 44									20 44				22 50	
Whatstandwell	d		16 55								18 49									20 49				22 55	
Ambergate	d		17 00								18 54									20 55				23 00	
Belper	d		17 07								19 01									21 01				23 07	
Duffield	d		17 11								19 05									21 06				23 11	
Derby 6	a		17 19								19 13									21 13				23 18	
	d	16 48	17 20	17 40	17 47			18 18	18 40		19 18	19 22	19 40		20 06	20 18		20 40		21 24	21 40		22 18		
Spondon	d																								
Long Eaton	d	16a57	17 30		17a56			18 28			19 28	19a31			20a15	20 27				21 35			22 28		
Attenborough	d		17 38					18 35			19 38					20 35				21 43			22 35		
Beeston	d		17 41			17 59		18 38		19 01	19 41			20 00		20 38			21 00	21 46		22 00	22 38		23 04
Nottingham 8	a		17 47	18 00		18 06		18 46	19 00	19 06	19 48		20 00	20 06		20 45		21 00	21 06	21 52	22 00	22 06	22 45		23 11

Sundays

from 1 April

		EM	EM	EM	EM	EM	EM	EM	XC	EM		EM	EM	XC	EM	EM	EM	XC	EM	EM		XC	EM	EM	XC
		◇1	◇1		◇1	◇1	◇1		◇1	◇1		◇1		◇1	◇1	◇1	◇1	◇1	◇1			◇1	◇1		◇1
		☕	☕		☕	☕	☕		🛒	☕		☕		🛒	☕	☕	☕	🛒	☕			🛒	☕		🛒
Matlock	d							10 43					12 39							14 39					
Matlock Bath	d							10 45					12 41							14 41					
Cromford	d							10 48					12 44							14 44					
Whatstandwell	d							10 53					12 49							14 49					
Ambergate	d							10 59					12 54							14 54					
Belper	d							11 05					13 01							15 01					
Duffield	d							11 09					13 05							15 05					
Derby 6	a							11 15					13 13							15 13					
	d		08 41	09 18	09 44	10 42		11 18	12 40	13 02			13 18	13 40	13 54		14 37	14 40		15 18		15 40		16 18	16 40
Spondon	d																								
Long Eaton	d		08a50	09 28	09a53	10a51		11 28		13a11			13 28		14a03		14a46			15 28				16 27	
Attenborough	d			09 34				11 35					13 35							15 35				16 35	
Beeston	d	00 07		09 37			11 20	11 38				13 24	13 38			14 27			15 19	15 38			16 19	16 41	
Nottingham 8	a	00 15		09 44			11 27	11 45	13 00			13 30	13 46	14 00		14 33		15 02	15 25	15 45		16 00	16 24	16 48	17 00

A not 11 December

For connections to St Pancras International please refer to Table 53

Table 56

Sundays

from 1 April

Matlock - Derby - Nottingham

Network Diagram - see first Page of Table 50

		EM	EM	XC	EM	EM		EM	XC	EM	EM	EM	XC
		◇1 (cup)		◇1 (trolley)	◇1 (cup)	◇1 (cup)			◇1	◇1 (cup)	◇1 (cup)		◇1
Matlock	d		16 39									18 39	
Matlock Bath	d		16 41									18 41	
Cromford	d		16 44									18 44	
Whatstandwell	d		16 49									18 49	
Ambergate	d		16 54									18 54	
Belper	d		17 01									19 01	
Duffield	d		17 05									19 05	
Derby 6	a		17 13									19 13	
	d	16 47	17 18	17 40	17 47			18 18	18 40	19 05		19 18	19 40
Spondon	d												
Long Eaton	d	16a56	17 28		17a56			18 28		19a14		19 28	
Attenborough	d		17 35					18 35				19 38	
Beeston	d		17 38			18 11		18 38			19 13	19 41	
Nottingham 8 (tram)	a		17 45	18 00		18 18		18 46	19 00		19 18	19 48	20 00

		EM	EM	EM		XC	EM	EM	XC	EM	EM	EM	EM
		◇1 (cup)	◇1 (cup)			◇1	◇1 (cup)		◇1	◇1 (cup)			◇1 (cup)
Matlock	d							20 39				22 45	
Matlock Bath	d							20 41				22 47	
Cromford	d							20 44				22 50	
Whatstandwell	d							20 49				22 55	
Ambergate	d							20 55				23 00	
Belper	d							21 01				23 07	
Duffield	d							21 06				23 11	
Derby 6	a							21 13				23 18	
	d	20 05		20 18		20 40		21 19	21 40		22 18		
Spondon	d												
Long Eaton	d	20a15		20 27				21 29			22 28		
Attenborough	d			20 35				21 36			22 35		
Beeston	d		20 12	20 38			21 11	21 39		22 01	22 38		23 10
Nottingham 8 (tram)	a		20 20	20 45		21 00	21 17	21 46	22 00	22 08	22 45		23 16

For connections to St Pancras International please refer to Table 53

Nottingham, Derby and Leicester
Birmingham - Cardiff and Bristol

Network Diagram - see first Page of Table 50

Miles	Miles	Miles			AW	XC	XC	EM	EM	AW	GW	XC	EM		GW	GW	XC	GW	XC	GW	AW	XC	XC		XC
					MX	MX	MO																		
						◇1	1	◇1	◇1		◇1	◇1	◇1			◇1	◇1	◇	◇1	◇1		◇1	1		◇1
						A		B	B	C	D		E		F	D		G	H	D	C	I			J
								⊠🛒	⊠🛒		☕		⊠			☕			🛒	☕		🛒			🛒
0	—	—	**Nottingham 8**	d																					06 00
3¼	—	—	Beeston	d																					06 06
4¾	—	—	Attenborough	d																					06 10
7¾	—	—	Long Eaton	d																					06 17
16	—	—	**Derby 6**	a																					06 30
—	—	—		d		21p29		04 55	05 17				06 04									06 10			06 36
22¼	—	—	Willington	d																					
27	—	—	Burton-on-Trent	d		21p40																06 20			06 48
40	—	—	Tamworth	d		21p50																06 31			07 01
41¾	—	—	Wilnecote	d																					07 05
—	0	—	**Leicester**	d			23p19	05a24	05a42				06a37										06 16		
—	1¾	—	South Wigston	d			23p24																06 22		
—	4¾	—	Narborough	d			23p29																06 27		
—	13½	—	Hinckley	d			23p38																06 35		
—	18¾	—	Nuneaton	d			23p45																06 42		
—	29¼	—	Coleshill Parkway	d			00 02																06 59		
—	31	—	Water Orton	d																					
56¾	38¾	0	**Birmingham New Street 12**	a		22p07	00 15															06 52	07 14		07 25
—	—	—		d		22p12						05 00					05 42		06 42			07 12			07 30
83¾	—	—	Worcester Shrub Hill 7	d							05 21							06 49		07 09					
98½	—	39¼	Ashchurch for Tewkesbury	d													06 34	07 05							
105¾	—	46½	Cheltenham Spa	d	23p00	23p31				05 37	05 54	06 03			06 24	06 31	06 43	07 16	07 22	07 30	07 45	07 52			08 16
112¼	—	—	Gloucester 7	a	23p12					05 48	06 03	06 16			06 34	06 40	06 53	07 26		07 39	07 57				08 27
—	—	87	Bristol Parkway 7	a		00 01									07 23			08 19	07 57			08 25			
—	—	92¾	**Bristol Temple Meads 10**	a		00 13									07 39			08 36	08 08			08 40			
157	—	—	Newport (South Wales)	a	00 06					06 41		07 09					07 52				08 50				09 12
168¾	—	—	**Cardiff Central 7**	a	00 35					07 00		07 26					08 08				09 07				09 30

		EM	XC	EM	XC	XC	XC	XC	EM		EM	EM	GW	AW	XC	XC	XC	EM	XC		EM	XC	XC	EM	XC
		◇1	◇1		◇1	1	◇1	◇1	◇1		◇1	◇1	◇1		◇1	1	◇1	◇1	◇1			◇1	◇1	◇1	1
		E	K	L	M		N	O	P		E	B	D	C	Q		J	R	S		L	M	T	E	
		⊠🛒			🛒				⊠		⊠🛒	☕	☕		🛒		🛒	☕	🛒			🛒	🛒	⊠	
Nottingham 8	d			06 18			06 37										06 56				07 19				07 37
Beeston	d			06 24			06 43										07 07				07 25				07 43
Attenborough	d			06 27													07 11				07 29				
Long Eaton	d			06 35													07 18	07 36			07 40				07 51
Derby 6	a			06 49			07 00										07 31	07 47			07 53				08 02
	d	06 32	06 48				07 06		07 05		07 20	07 26			07 27		07 36		07 50					08 01	08 06
Willington	d																07 44								
Burton-on-Trent	d		06 58				07 18								07 38		07 50		08 00						08 18
Tamworth	d		07 09				07 30								07 50		08 03		08 11						08 30
Wilnecote	d																08 07								08 34
Leicester	d	07a04				06 43		07 10	07a34		07a52	07a59				07 24							07 49	08a23	
South Wigston	d					06 49																	07 55		
Narborough	d					06 54										07 33							08 00		
Hinckley	d					07 02										07 42							08 08		
Nuneaton	d					07 10		07 30								07 50							08 17		
Coleshill Parkway	d					07 26		07 46								08 05							08 32		
Water Orton	d					07 30										08 09									
Birmingham New Street 12	a		07 27			07 44	07 54	07 58							08 08	08 19	08 24		08 27				08 45		08 54
	d				07 42										08 12		08 30					08 42			
Worcester Shrub Hill 7	d																								
Ashchurch for Tewkesbury	d																								
Cheltenham Spa	d				08 25								08 31	08 45	08 52		09 12					09 25			
Gloucester 7	a												08 40	08 58			09 22								
Bristol Parkway 7	a				08 54										09 24							09 54			
Bristol Temple Meads 10	a				09 14										09 38							10 08			
Newport (South Wales)	a													09 51			10 09								
Cardiff Central 7	a													10 07			10 25								

- **A** From 27 March. From Edinburgh
- **B** To St Pancras International
- **C** To Maesteg
- **D** To London Paddington
- **E** From Sheffield to St Pancras International
- **F** To Westbury
- **G** To Weymouth
- **H** To Paignton
- **I** To Plymouth. 🛒 from Birmingham New Street
- **J** 🛒 from Birmingham New Street to Newport (South Wales)
- **K** From Sheffield to Reading
- **L** To Matlock
- **M** From Manchester Piccadilly
- **N** To Bournemouth
- **O** From Cambridge
- **P** From Leeds to St Pancras International
- **Q** From Leeds to Plymouth
- **R** From St Pancras International to Sheffield
- **S** From Leeds to Southampton Central
- **T** From Stansted Airport

Nottingham, Derby and Leicester
Birmingham - Cardiff and Bristol

Network Diagram - see first Page of Table 50

		EM	GW	GW	XC	XC	XC	XC	EM	XC	XC	EM	XC	XC	EM	EM	GW	AW	XC	XC	XC	EM	XC
					MO	MX																	
		◇1			◇1	◇1	1	◇1		◇1	◇1	◇1	◇1	1	◇1	◇1	◇1		◇1	1	◇1		◇1
		A	B	C	D	D		E	F	G	H	A	I		J	A	K	L	M		E	F	N
		☒			🛒	🛒		🛒		🛒	🛒	☕	🛒		☕	☕	☕		🛒		🛒		🛒
Nottingham 8 🚊	d							08 08	08 15					08 37							09 11	09 18	
Beeston	d								08 24					08 43								09 24	
Attenborough	d								08 27													09 27	
Long Eaton	d								08 35					08 51	09 00							09 35	
Derby 6	a							08 32	08 48					09 02	09 15						09 31	09 48	
	d	08 16			08 28	08 28		08 36		08 53		09 01		09 10		09 20			09 28		09 36		09 53
Willington	d																						
Burton-on-Trent	d				08 38	08 38		08 49						09 21					09 38		09 49		
Tamworth	d				08 49	08 50		09 02						09 33							10 02		
Wilnecote	d													09 37									
Leicester	d	08a52					08 16				08 49	09a23				09a54				09 16			
South Wigston	d																						
Narborough	d						08 25													09 25			
Hinckley	d						08 34													09 34			
Nuneaton	d						08 42				09 10									09 42			
Coleshill Parkway	d						08 57				09 25									09 57			
Water Orton	d																			10 01			
Birmingham New Street 12	a				09 09	09 09	09 14	09 24		09 27	09 38			09 54					10 07	10 14	10 24		10 27
	d				09 12	09 12		09 30					09 42						10 12		10 30		
Worcester Shrub Hill 7	d		09 06																				
Ashchurch for Tewkesbury	d		09 24																				
Cheltenham Spa	d		09 34	09 40	09 52	09 52		10 11					10 25				10 31	10 45	10 52		11 11		
Gloucester 7	a		09 42	09 51				10 22									10 40	10 57			11 22		
Bristol Parkway 7	a		10 22		10 25	10 25							10 54						11 26				
Bristol Temple Meads 10	a		10 37		10 41	10 41							11 12						11 37				
Newport (South Wales)	a							11 11										11 50			12 10		
Cardiff Central 7	a							11 27										12 12			12 28		

		XC	EM	XC	XC	EM	EM	GW	GW	AW	XC	XC	XC	EM	XC	XC	EM	XC	XC	EM	EM	GW
								R														
		◇1	◇1	◇1	1	◇1	◇1				◇1	1	◇1		◇1	◇1	◇1	◇1	1	◇1	◇1	◇1
		H	A	O		J	A	P	C	L	Q		E	F	R	H	A	O		J	A	K
		🛒	☕	🛒		☕	☕				🛒		🛒		🛒	🛒	☕	🛒		☕	☕	☕
Nottingham 8 🚊	d				09 37								10 11	10 18					10 37			
Beeston	d				09 43									10 24					10 43			
Attenborough	d													10 27								
Long Eaton	d				09 51	09 56								10 35					10 51	10 56		
Derby 6	a				10 02	10 09							10 33	10 49					11 02	11 09		
	d		10 01		10 10		10 20				10 28		10 37		10 53		11 01		11 10		11 20	
Willington	d																					
Burton-on-Trent	d				10 21								10 49						11 21			
Tamworth	d				10 33						10 48		11 02						11 33			
Wilnecote	d				10 37														11 37			
Leicester	d	09 49	10a23				10a54					10 16				10 49	11a23				11a54	
South Wigston	d											10 22										
Narborough	d											10 27										
Hinckley	d											10 35										
Nuneaton	d	10 10										10 42				11 09						
Coleshill Parkway	d	10 25										10 58				11 24						
Water Orton	d																					
Birmingham New Street 12	a	10 38			10 54						11 08	11 14	11 24		11 27	11 38			11 54			
	d			10 42							11 12		11 30					11 42				
Worcester Shrub Hill 7	d							11 06														
Ashchurch for Tewkesbury	d							11 24														
Cheltenham Spa	d			11 25				11 32	11 40	11 45	11 52		12 11					12 25				12 31
Gloucester 7	a							11 42	11 51	11 57			12 22									12 40
Bristol Parkway 7	a			11 54				12 22			12 28							12 55				
Bristol Temple Meads 10	a			12 08				12 34			12 40							13 10				
Newport (South Wales)	a									12 50			13 11									
Cardiff Central 7	a									13 07			13 29									

A From Sheffield to St Pancras International
B From Great Malvern to Westbury
C To Swindon
D From York to Plymouth
E 🛒 to Newport (South Wales)
F To Matlock
G From Newcastle to Reading
H From Stansted Airport
I From Manchester Piccadilly to Paignton
J From St Pancras International to Sheffield
K To London Paddington
L To Maesteg
M From Newcastle to Plymouth
N From Newcastle to Southampton Central
O From Manchester Piccadilly
P From Great Malvern to Brighton
Q From Edinburgh to Plymouth
R From Edinburgh to Reading

Table 57

Nottingham, Derby and Leicester Birmingham - Cardiff and Bristol

Network Diagram - see first Page of Table 50

		XC	XC	XC	EM	XC	XC		EM	XC	XC	EM	EM	GW	GW	AW	XC		XC	XC	EM	XC	XC	EM	XC
		◇1	1	◇1		◇1	◇1		◇1	◇1	1	◇1	◇1	◇			◇1		1	◇1		◇1	◇1	◇1	◇1
		A		B	C	D	E		F	G		H	F	I	J	K	L			M	C	N	E	F	O
		🛒		🛒		🛒	🛒		☕	🛒	🛒	☕	☕				🛒			🛒		🛒	🛒	☕	🛒
Nottingham 8 🚊	d			11 08	11 18						11 37									12 08	12 18				
Beeston	d				11 24						11 43										12 24				
Attenborough	d				11 27																12 27				
Long Eaton	d				11 35						11 51	11 57									12 35				
Derby 6	a			11 31	11 48						12 02	12 09								12 33	12 48				
	d	11 28		11 36		11 53			12 01		12 10		12 20				12 28			12 36		12 53		13 01	
Willington	d																								
Burton-on-Trent	d			11 49							12 21									12 49					
Tamworth	d			12 02							12 33						12 48			13 02					
Wilnecote	d										12 37														
Leicester	d		11 16				11 49		12a23				12a53						12 16				12 49	13a23	
South Wigston	d																		12 22						
Narborough	d		11 25																12 27						
Hinckley	d		11 34																12 35						
Nuneaton	d		11 42				12 10												12 41				13 09		
Coleshill Parkway	d		11 57				12 25												12 58				13 24		
Water Orton	d		12 01																						
Birmingham New Street 12	a	12 07	12 14	12 24		12 27	12 39				12 54						13 07		13 14	13 24		13 27	13 38		
	d	12 12		12 30						12 42							13 12			13 30					13 42
Worcester Shrub Hill 7	d													13 06											
Ashchurch for Tewkesbury	d													13 24											
Cheltenham Spa	d	12 52		13 11						13 25				13 34	13 40	13 45	13 54			14 11					14 25
Gloucester 7	a			13 22										13 42	13 51	13 57				14 22					
Bristol Parkway 7	a	13 25								13 57				14 22			14 27								14 57
Bristol Temple Meads 10	a	13 38								14 09				14 38			14 41								15 10
Newport (South Wales)	a			14 09												14 50				15 11					
Cardiff Central 7	a			14 29												15 07				15 29					

		XC	EM		EM	GW	AW	XC	XC	XC	EM	XC	XC		EM	XC	XC	EM	EM	GW	GW	XC	XC		XC
		1	◇1		◇1	◇1		◇1	1	◇1		◇1	◇1		◇1	◇1	1	◇1	◇1	◇		◇1	1		◇1
			H		F	P	K	A		M	C	D	E		F	G		H	F	I	J	Q			B
		🛒	☕		☕	☕	🛒	🛒		🛒		🛒	🛒		☕	🛒	🛒	☕	☕			🛒			🛒
Nottingham 8 🚊	d	12 37								13 11	13 18						13 37								14 11
Beeston	d	12 43									13 24						13 43								
Attenborough	d										13 27														
Long Eaton	d	12 51	12 57								13 35						13 51	13 57							
Derby 6	a	13 02	13 09							13 31	13 48						14 02	14 09							14 31
	d	13 06			13 20			13 28		13 36		13 53			14 01		14 10		14 20			14 28			14 36
Willington	d	13 14																							
Burton-on-Trent	d	13 21						13 38		13 49							14 21								14 49
Tamworth	d	13 33								14 02							14 33					14 47			15 02
Wilnecote	d																14 37								
Leicester	d				13a54				13 16				13 49		14a23				14a53				14 16		
South Wigston	d																						14 22		
Narborough	d								13 25														14 27		
Hinckley	d								13 34														14 35		
Nuneaton	d								13 42				14 10										14 41		
Coleshill Parkway	d								13 57				14 25										14 58		
Water Orton	d								14 01																
Birmingham New Street 12	a	13 54						14 06	14 14	14 24		14 27	14 38				14 54					15 07	15 13		15 24
	d							14 12		14 30						14 42						15 12			15 30
Worcester Shrub Hill 7	d																			15 06					
Ashchurch for Tewkesbury	d																			15 24					
Cheltenham Spa	d					14 31	14 45	14 52		15 11						15 25				15 34	15 40	15 52			16 11
Gloucester 7	a					14 40	14 56			15 22										15 42	15 51				16 22
Bristol Parkway 7	a							15 25								15 56				16 22		16 27			
Bristol Temple Meads 10	a							15 39								16 08				16 37		16 40			
Newport (South Wales)	a						15 50			16 10															17 11
Cardiff Central 7	a						16 10			16 29															17 28

- **A** From Glasgow Central to Plymouth
- **B** 🛒 to Newport (South Wales)
- **C** To Matlock
- **D** From Newcastle to Southampton Central
- **E** From Stansted Airport
- **F** From Sheffield to St Pancras International
- **G** From Manchester Piccadilly
- **H** From St Pancras International to Sheffield
- **I** From Great Malvern to Weymouth
- **J** To Swindon
- **K** To Maesteg
- **L** From Dundee to Plymouth
- **M** 🛒 from Birmingham New Street to Newport (South Wales)
- **N** From Newcastle to Reading
- **O** From Manchester Piccadilly to Exeter St Davids
- **P** To London Paddington. **The Cheltenham Spa Express**
- **Q** From Glasgow Central to Penzance

Nottingham, Derby and Leicester
Birmingham - Cardiff and Bristol

Network Diagram - see first Page of Table 50

		EM	XC	XC	EM	XC	XC	EM	EM		GW	AW	XC	XC	XC	EM	XC	XC	EM		XC	XC	EM	EM	GW
			◇1	◇1	◇1	◇1	1	◇1	◇1		◇1		◇1	1	◇1		◇1	◇1	◇1		◇1	1	◇1	◇1	
		A	B	C	D	E		F	D		G	H	I			A	J	C	D		K		F	D	L
			⚲	⚲	☕	⚲	⚲	☕	☕		☕		⚲				⚲	⚲	☕		⚲	⚲	☕	☕	
Nottingham [8] ⛴	d	14 18					14 37								15 11	15 18						15 37			
Beeston	d	14 24					14 43									15 24						15 43			
Attenborough	d	14 27														15 27									
Long Eaton	d	14 35					14 51	14 57								15 35						15 51	15 57		
Derby [6]	a	14 47					15 03	15 13							15 31	15 48						16 03	16 09		
	d		14 53		15 01		15 10		15 20				15 28		15 36		15 53		16 01			16 10		16 18	
Willington	d						15 18																		
Burton-on-Trent	d						15 24						15 38		15 49							16 21			
Tamworth	d						15 35								16 02							16 33			
Wilnecote	d																					16 37			
Leicester	d			14 49	15a23				15a53					15 16				15 49	16a23					16a51	
South Wigston	d																								
Narborough	d													15 25											
Hinckley	d													15 34											
Nuneaton	d			15 10										15 42				16 09							
Coleshill Parkway	d			15 25										15 57				16 25							
Water Orton	d													16 01											
Birmingham New Street [12]	a		15 27	15 38			15 54						16 04	16 14	16 24		16 27	16 38				16 54			
	d					15 42							16 12		16 30						16 42				
Worcester Shrub Hill [7]	d																								17 06
Ashchurch for Tewkesbury	d														17 05										17 24
Cheltenham Spa	d					16 25					16 31	16 45	16 52		17 15						17 25				17 33
Gloucester [7]	a										16 40	16 56			17 26										17 42
Bristol Parkway [7]	a					16 56							17 25								17 58				18 22
Bristol Temple Meads [10]	a					17 10							17 39								18 10				18 38
Newport (South Wales)	a											17 50			18 10										
Cardiff Central [7]	a											18 10			18 27										

		GW	AW	XC	XC		XC	EM	XC	XC	EM	XC	XC	EM	EM		GW	AW	XC	XC	XC	XC	EM	XC	XC
		◇		◇1	1		◇1		◇1	◇1	◇1	◇1	1	◇1	◇1		◇1		◇1	◇1	1	◇1		◇1	◇1
		M	H	N				A	B	C	D	K		F	D		G	H	O	P			A	B	Q
				⚲					⚲	⚲	☕	⚲	⚲	☕	☕		☕		⚲ FO	⚲				⚲	⚲
Nottingham [8] ⛴	d						16 08	16 18					16 37									17 08	17 18		
Beeston	d							16 24					16 43										17 24		
Attenborough	d							16 27															17 27		
Long Eaton	d							16 35					16 51	16 57									17 35		
Derby [6]	a						16 31	16 48					17 02	17 09								17 31	17 49		
	d			16 28			16 36		16 53		17 01		17 06		17 18				17 28	17 28		17 36		17 53	
Willington	d												17 14												
Burton-on-Trent	d						16 49						17 21						17 38	17 38		17 49			
Tamworth	d			16 47			17 02						17 33									18 02			
Wilnecote	d																								
Leicester	d				16 16					16 49	17a23				17a52						17 16				
South Wigston	d				16 22																17 22				
Narborough	d				16 27																17 27				
Hinckley	d				16 35																17 35				
Nuneaton	d				16 41					17 10											17 41				
Coleshill Parkway	d				16 58					17 25											17 58				
Water Orton	d																								
Birmingham New Street [12]	a			17 09	17 14		17 24		17 27	17 38			17 52						18 08	18 07	18 14	18 24		18 27	
	d			17 12			17 30					17 42							18 12	18 12		18 30			18 42
Worcester Shrub Hill [7]	d																								
Ashchurch for Tewkesbury	d						18 09																		
Cheltenham Spa	d	17 40	17 45	17 52			18 18					18 25					18 34	18 45	18 52	18 52		19 15			19 25
Gloucester [7]	a	17 49	17 57				18 29										18 44	18 56				19 27			
Bristol Parkway [7]	a			18 28								18 55							19 27	19 27					19 56
Bristol Temple Meads [10]	a			18 41								19 06							19 38	19 38					20 09
Newport (South Wales)	a		18 51				19 16											19 50				20 11			20 47
Cardiff Central [7]	a		19 09				19 33											20 09				20 27			21 02

A To Matlock
B From Newcastle to Reading
C From Stansted Airport
D From Sheffield to St Pancras International
E From Manchester Piccadilly to Paignton
F From St Pancras International to Sheffield
G To London Paddington
H To Maesteg
I From Aberdeen to Penzance
J From Newcastle to Eastleigh
K From Manchester Piccadilly
L From Great Malvern to Westbury
M To Southampton Central
N From Glasgow Central to Penzance
O From 17 February until 23 March. From Edinburgh to Plymouth
P until 16 February, FX from 20 February until 22 March, from 26 March. From Edinburgh to Plymouth
Q From Manchester Piccadilly. ⚲ to Bristol Temple Meads

Table 57

Mondays to Fridays

Nottingham, Derby and Leicester
Birmingham - Cardiff and Bristol

Network Diagram - see first Page of Table 50

		XC	EM	XC	EM	EM	GW	AW	XC	XC	GW	XC	EM	XC	XC	EM	XC	XC	EM	EM	GW	XC
		◇1	◇1	1	◇1	◇1			◇1	1		◇1		◇1	◇1	◇1	◇1	1	◇1	◇1	1	◇1
		A	B		C	B	D	E	F		G		H	I	A	B	J		K	B	G	L
			🍽	🛒	🍽	🍽			🛒					🛒		🍽	🛒	🛒	🍽	🍽		🛒
Nottingham 8	d			17 37								18 08	18 18					18 37				
Beeston	d			17 43									18 24					18 43				
Attenborough	d												18 27									
Long Eaton	d			17 51	18 01								18 37					18 51	18 56			
Derby 6	a			18 02	18 14							18 33	18 48					19 02	19 09			
	d		18 01	18 10		18 18			18 28			18 37		18 53		19 01		19 10		19 18		19 28
Willington	d			18 16																		
Burton-on-Trent	d			18 22								18 49						19 21				19 38
Tamworth	d			18 34					18 47			19 02						19 33				
Wilnecote	d			18 37														19 37				
Leicester	d	17 49	18a23			18a51				18 16					18 49	19a23				19a51		
South Wigston	d	17 55								18 22												
Narborough	d	18 01								18 27												
Hinckley	d	18 09								18 35												
Nuneaton	d	18 16								18 41					19 10							
Coleshill Parkway	d	18 32								18 58					19 25							
Water Orton	d																					
Birmingham New Street 12	a	18 45		18 54					19 08	19 14		19 24		19 27	19 38			19 54				20 09
	d								19 12			19 30					19 42					20 12
Worcester Shrub Hill 7	d						19 07															
Ashchurch for Tewkesbury	d						19 24															
Cheltenham Spa	d						19 34	19 45	19 52		20 01	20 11					20 25				20 48	20 52
Gloucester 7	a						19 42	19 56			20 10	20 22									20 58	
Bristol Parkway 7	a						20 22		20 27								20 55					21 25
Bristol Temple Meads 10	a						20 38		20 40								21 07					21 36
Newport (South Wales)	a							20 51				21 11										
Cardiff Central 7	a							21 10				21 27										

		XC	GW	XC	XC	EM	XC	XC	EM	XC	XC	EM	XC	EM	XC	XC	XC	XC	NT	EM	GW	GW	XC
				FO	FX																		
		1		◇1	◇1		◇1	◇1	◇1	◇1	1	◇1	◇1		1	◇1	◇1	1		◇1			◇1
						H	M	A	B	N		C	O	H		P	A		Q	B	G	D	R
							🛒	🛒	🍽			🍽	🛒			🛒				🍽			
Nottingham 8	d			19 08	19 08	19 18					19 37			20 11				20 37	20 45				
Beeston	d					19 24					19 43			20 17				20 43					
Attenborough	d					19 27					19 46			20 20									
Long Eaton	d					19 35					19 53	20 07		20 28				20 51					
Derby 6	a			19 32	19 32	19 48					20 02	20 19		20 44				21 02	21 05				
	d			19 36	19 36		19 54		20 01		20 10		20 28			20 54		21 06		21 20			21 29
Willington	d																	21 14					
Burton-on-Trent	d			19 49	19 49						20 21							21 21					21 40
Tamworth	d			20 02	20 02						20 33		20 47					21 33					21 50
Wilnecote	d										20 37							21 37					
Leicester	d	19 16						19 49	20a23						20 18		20 49			21a52			
South Wigston	d	19 22													20 22								
Narborough	d	19 27													20 26								
Hinckley	d	19 35													20 35								
Nuneaton	d	19 41						20 09							20 41		21 09						
Coleshill Parkway	d	19 58						20 24							20 58		21 24						
Water Orton	d																						
Birmingham New Street 12	a	20 14		20 24	20 24		20 27	20 38			20 54		21 07		21 15	21 29	21 37	21 54					22 09
	d			20 30	20 30					20 42			21 12										22 12
Worcester Shrub Hill 7	d																					21 32	
Ashchurch for Tewkesbury	d																					21 52	
Cheltenham Spa	d		21 00	21 11	21 11					21 27			21 52								22 01	22 07	22 52
Gloucester 7	a		21 11	21 22	21 22								22 01								22 11	22 21	
Bristol Parkway 7	a		21 52							22 01			22 32									23 04	23 21
Bristol Temple Meads 10	a		22 10							22 13			22 44									23 19	23 40
Newport (South Wales)	a			22 15	22 15																		
Cardiff Central 7	a			22 31	22 35																		

- **A** From Stansted Airport
- **B** From Sheffield to St Pancras International
- **C** From St Pancras International to Sheffield
- **D** From Great Malvern
- **E** To Maesteg
- **F** From Glasgow Central to Plymouth
- **G** To Swindon
- **H** To Matlock
- **I** From Newcastle to Reading
- **J** From Manchester Piccadilly to Plymouth
- **K** From Kettering to Sheffield
- **L** From Edinburgh to Plymouth
- **M** From Newcastle to Guildford
- **N** From Manchester Piccadilly
- **O** From Glasgow Central. 🛒 to Birmingham New Street
- **P** From Newcastle
- **Q** To Sheffield
- **R** until 23 March. From Edinburgh

Nottingham, Derby and Leicester Birmingham - Cardiff and Bristol

Network Diagram - see first Page of Table 50

		AW FO	AW FX		GW	XC ◇1 A	XC 1	XC ◇1 B	XC ◇1 C	XC 1	LM D FO	LM E FO	XC 1		XC ◇1 F	XC ◇1 B
Nottingham 8	d									21 37						
Beeston	d									21 43						
Attenborough	d									21 46						
Long Eaton	d									21 53						
Derby 6	a									22 04						
	d					21 29			22 02	22 10					22 45	
Willington	d															
Burton-on-Trent	d					21 40				22 21					22 56	
Tamworth	d					21 50				22 33					23 06	
Wilnecote	d									22 36						
Leicester	d						21 16	21 49					22 27			22 49
South Wigston	d						21 22						22 33			
Narborough	d						21 27						22 38			
Hinckley	d						21 35						22 46			
Nuneaton	d						21 42	22 10					22 54			23 10
Coleshill Parkway	d						21 59	22 25					23 10			23 25
Water Orton	d															
Birmingham New Street 12	a					22 07	22 14	22 38	22 51	23 00			23 25		23 25	23 41
	d					22 12					23 00	23 16				
Worcester Shrub Hill 7	d				22 28						23 46	00 10				
Ashchurch for Tewkesbury	d				22 51						00 01	00 25				
Cheltenham Spa	d	23 00	23 00		23 05	23 31					00 09	00 33				
Gloucester 7	a	23 12	23 12		23 17						00 20	00 43				
Bristol Parkway 7	a					00 01										
Bristol Temple Meads 10	a					00 13										
Newport (South Wales)	a	00 06	00 06													
Cardiff Central 7	a	00 33	00 35													

Saturdays

		AW	XC ◇1 G	LM H	LM I	GW J	XC ◇1	XC ◇1	GW K	GW ◇ L		XC ◇1 M 🛒	XC 1	EM ◇1 N ☕	EM ◇1 O ☕	GW ◇1 P ☕	AW Q	XC ◇1 R 🛒	EM ◇1 N ☕	XC ◇1 S 🛒		EM T	XC ◇1 U	XC ◇1 V 🛒	XC 1
Nottingham 8	d																			05 57		06 18			
Beeston	d																			06 03		06 24			
Attenborough	d																			06 06		06 27			
Long Eaton	d																			06 17		06 34			
Derby 6	a																			06 32		06 48			
	d		21p29											05 25	06 01			06 10	06 18	06 36			06 48		
Willington	d																								
Burton-on-Trent	d		21p40															06 20		06 48			06 59		
Tamworth	d		21p50															06 31		07 01			07 09		
Wilnecote	d																			07 05					
Leicester	d												05 49	05a57	06a23				06a51						06 49
South Wigston	d												05 55												06 55
Narborough	d												06 00												07 00
Hinckley	d												06 08												07 08
Nuneaton	d												06 14												07 14
Coleshill Parkway	d												06 30												07 30
Water Orton	d																								07 35
Birmingham New Street 12	a		22p07										06 43					06 50		07 24			07 27		07 47
	d		22p12	23p00	23p16		05 00	05 42				06 42						07 12		07 30				07 42	
Worcester Shrub Hill 7	d			23b46	00 10					06 47															
Ashchurch for Tewkesbury	d			00 01	00 25			06 33		07 03															
Cheltenham Spa	d	23p00	23p31	00 09	00 33	05 30	06 04	06 43	06 48	07 13		07 25				07 30	07 45	07 52		08 11				08 25	
Gloucester 7	a	23p12		00 20	00 43	05 40	06 13	06 54	06 58	07 24						07 40	07 57			08 22					
Bristol Parkway 7	a		00 01						07 39	08 19		07 54						08 24						08 54	
Bristol Temple Meads 10	a		00 13						07 54	08 34		08 05						08 38						09 08	
Newport (South Wales)	a	00 06					07 06	07 52									08 50			09 07					
Cardiff Central 7	a	00 33					07 22	08 08									09 10			09 23					

- **A** from 26 March. From Edinburgh
- **B** From Stansted Airport
- **C** From Newcastle
- **D** Until 23 March
- **E** From 30 March
- **F** From Glasgow Central
- **G** from 31 March. From Edinburgh
- **H** until 24 March
- **I** from 31 March
- **J** To Swindon
- **K** To Weston-super-Mare
- **L** To Weymouth
- **M** To Paignton
- **N** To St Pancras International
- **O** From Sheffield to St Pancras International
- **P** To London Paddington
- **Q** To Maesteg
- **R** To Plymouth. 🛒 from Birmingham New Street
- **S** 🛒 from Birmingham New Street to Newport (South Wales)
- **T** To Matlock
- **U** To Reading
- **V** From Manchester Piccadilly
- **c** Previous night, arr. 2337

Table 57

Saturdays

Nottingham, Derby and Leicester Birmingham - Cardiff and Bristol

Network Diagram - see first Page of Table 50

		EM	XC	XC	EM	AW		XC	GW	XC	EM	XC	XC	EM	XC	XC		EM	EM	GW	XC	XC	GW	XC	EM
		◇1	◇1	◇1	◇1			◇1	◇1	◇1		◇1	◇1	◇1	◇1	1		◇1	◇1		◇1	1		◇1	
		A	B	C	D	E		F	G	H	I	J	K	A	L			M	D	N	O		P	Q	I
		☕	🛒		☕			🛒	☕	🛒		🛒	🛒	☕	🛒			☕	⊠		🛒			🛒	
Nottingham 8 🚌	d		06 37							06 56	07 18					07 37								08 08	08 18
Beeston	d		06 43							07 02	07 24					07 43									08 24
Attenborough	d									07 06	07 27														08 27
Long Eaton	d									07 14	07 35					07 51		07 56							08 35
Derby 6	a		07 02							07 30	07 49					08 02		08 09						08 31	08 48
	d	07 01	07 06		07 18			07 26		07 36		07 50		08 01		08 06			08 18		08 28			08 36	
Willington	d									07 43															
Burton-on-Trent	d		07 18					07 37		07 50		08 00				08 18					08 39			08 49	
Tamworth	d		07 30					07 48		08 02		08 11				08 30					08 49			09 02	
Wilnecote	d									08 05						08 34									
Leicester	d	07a23		07 16	07a51								07 49	08a23					08a51			08 16			
South Wigston	d																					08 22			
Narborough	d																					08 27			
Hinckley	d																					08 35			
Nuneaton	d			07 35									08 09									08 43			
Coleshill Parkway	d			07 51									08 24									09 01			
Water Orton	d																								
Birmingham New Street 12	a		07 55	08 04				08 08		08 24		08 27	08 38			08 54					09 08	09 14		09 24	
	d							08 12		08 30					08 42						09 12			09 30	
Worcester Shrub Hill 7	d																			09 08					
Ashchurch for Tewkesbury	d																			09 25					
Cheltenham Spa	d					08 45		08 52	08 59	09 11					09 25					09 35	09 52		10 01	10 11	
Gloucester 7	a					08 57			09 09	09 22										09 44			10 11	10 22	
Bristol Parkway 7	a							09 24							09 55					10 24	10 29				
Bristol Temple Meads 10	a							09 38							10 06					10 39	10 42				
Newport (South Wales)	a					09 50				10 07														11 08	
Cardiff Central 7	a					10 07				10 23														11 24	

		XC		XC	EM	XC	XC	EM	EM	AW	XC	XC		GW	XC	EM	XC	XC	EM	XC	XC	EM		EM	GW
																									■
		◇1		◇1	◇1	◇1	1	◇1	◇1		◇1	1		◇1	◇1		◇1	◇1	◇1	◇1	1	◇1		◇1	
		R		K	A	S		T	A	E	U			G	Q	I	V	K	A	L		M		A	W
		🛒		🛒	☕	🛒		☕	☕		🛒			☕	🛒		🛒	🛒	☕	🛒		☕		☕	
Nottingham 8 🚌	d						08 37								09 08	09 18					09 37				
Beeston	d						08 43									09 24					09 43				
Attenborough	d															09 27									
Long Eaton	d						08 51	09 01								09 35					09 51	09 57			
Derby 6	a						09 03	09 14							09 31	09 48					10 02	10 09			
	d	08 53			09 01		09 10		09 20		09 27				09 36		09 53		10 01		10 10			10 20	
Willington	d																								
Burton-on-Trent	d						09 21				09 38				09 49						10 21				
Tamworth	d						09 33								10 02						10 33				
Wilnecote	d						09 37														10 37				
Leicester	d			08 49	09a23				09a54			09 16						09 49	10a23					10a54	
South Wigston	d																								
Narborough	d											09 25													
Hinckley	d											09 34													
Nuneaton	d			09 09								09 41						10 09							
Coleshill Parkway	d			09 24								09 56						10 24							
Water Orton	d											10 01													
Birmingham New Street 12	a	09 27		09 38			09 54				10 04	10 14			10 24		10 27	10 38			10 54				
	d					09 42					10 12				10 30					10 42					
Worcester Shrub Hill 7	d																								11 06
Ashchurch for Tewkesbury	d																								11 24
Cheltenham Spa	d					10 25				10 45	10 52			11 00	11 11					11 25					11 34
Gloucester 7	a									10 56				11 09	11 22										11 44
Bristol Parkway 7	a					10 57					11 24									11 54					12 24
Bristol Temple Meads 10	a					11 09					11 37									12 08					12 39
Newport (South Wales)	a									11 50					12 07										
Cardiff Central 7	a									12 07					12 23										

- **A** From Sheffield to St Pancras International
- **B** To Bournemouth. 🛒 from Derby
- **C** From Cambridge
- **D** To St Pancras International
- **E** To Maesteg
- **F** From Leeds to Plymouth
- **G** To London Paddington
- **H** 🛒 from Birmingham New Street to Newport (South Wales)
- **I** To Matlock
- **J** From Leeds to Southampton Central
- **K** From Stansted Airport
- **L** From Manchester Piccadilly
- **M** From St Pancras International to Sheffield
- **N** To Westbury
- **O** From York to Plymouth
- **P** To Swindon
- **Q** 🛒 to Newport (South Wales)
- **R** From Newcastle to Reading
- **S** From Manchester Piccadilly to Paignton
- **T** From Leicester to Sheffield
- **U** From Newcastle to Plymouth
- **V** From Newcastle to Southampton Central
- **W** From Great Malvern to Brighton

Table 57

Saturdays

Nottingham, Derby and Leicester Birmingham - Cardiff and Bristol

Network Diagram - see first Page of Table 50

		AW	XC	XC	GW	XC	EM	XC		XC	EM	XC	XC	EM	EM	XC	XC	GW		XC	EM	XC	XC	EM	GW
			◇1	1		◇1		◇1		◇1	◇1	◇1	1	◇1	◇1	◇1	1	◇1		◇1		◇1	◇1	◇1	◇
		A	B		C	D	E	F		G	H	I		J	H	K		L		D	E	M	G	H	N
			🛒			🛒		🛒		🛒	☕	🛒		☕	☕	🛒		☕		🛒		🛒	🛒	☕	
Nottingham 8 🚌	d					10 08	10 18						10 37							11 11	11 18				
Beeston	d						10 24						10 43								11 24				
Attenborough	d						10 27														11 27				
Long Eaton	d						10 35						10 51	10 57							11 36				
Derby 6	a					10 31	10 49						11 02	11 09						11 31	11 48				
	d		10 28			10 37		10 53			11 01		11 10		11 20	11 27				11 36		11 54		12 01	
Willington	d																								
Burton-on-Trent	d					10 49							11 21			11 39				11 49					
Tamworth	d		10 48			11 02							11 33							12 02					
Wilnecote	d												11 37												
Leicester	d			10 16						10 49	11a23				11a54		11 16						11 49	12a23	
South Wigston	d			10 22																					
Narborough	d			10 27													11 25								
Hinckley	d			10 35													11 34								
Nuneaton	d			10 42						11 09							11 41						12 09		
Coleshill Parkway	d			10 58						11 24							11 56						12 24		
Water Orton	d																12 02								
Birmingham New Street 12	a		11 04	11 14		11 24		11 27		11 38			11 54			12 07	12 14			12 24		12 27	12 38		
	d		11 12			11 30						11 42				12 12				12 30					
Worcester Shrub Hill 7	d																								12 54
Ashchurch for Tewkesbury	d																								13 10
Cheltenham Spa	d	11 45	11 52		12 01	12 11						12 25				12 52		13 00		13 11					13 20
Gloucester 7	a	11 57			12 11	12 22												13 10		13 22					13 32
Bristol Parkway 7	a		12 29									12 55				13 24									14 20
Bristol Temple Meads 10	a		12 42									13 07				13 38									14 36
Newport (South Wales)	a	12 50				13 11														14 08					
Cardiff Central 7	a	13 07				13 27														14 24					

		XC	XC	EM		EM	AW	XC	XC	GW	XC	EM	XC	XC		EM	XC	XC	EM	EM	AW	XC	XC	GW	
		◇1	1	◇1		◇1		◇1	1		◇1		◇1	◇1		◇1	◇1	1	◇1	◇1		◇1	1	◇1	
		I		J		H	A	O		C	P	E	Q	G		H	R		J	H	A	K		L	
		🛒	🛒	☕		☕		🛒			🛒		🛒	🛒		☕	🛒	🛒	☕	☕	🛒	🛒		☕	
Nottingham 8 🚌	d		11 37								12 08	12 18						12 37							
Beeston	d		11 43									12 24						12 43							
Attenborough	d											12 27													
Long Eaton	d		11 51	11 57								12 36						12 51	12 57						
Derby 6	a		12 02	12 09							12 31	12 48						13 02	13 09						
	d		12 10			12 20		12 29			12 36		12 53			13 01		13 06		13 20		13 28			
Willington	d																	13 14							
Burton-on-Trent	d		12 21								12 49							13 21				13 38			
Tamworth	d		12 33					12 49			13 02							13 33							
Wilnecote	d		12 37																						
Leicester	d					12a54			12 16					12 49		13a23				13a54			13 16		
South Wigston	d								12 22																
Narborough	d								12 27														13 25		
Hinckley	d								12 35														13 34		
Nuneaton	d								12 42					13 09									13 41		
Coleshill Parkway	d								12 58					13 24									13 56		
Water Orton	d																						14 00		
Birmingham New Street 12	a		12 54					13 09	13 14		13 24		13 27	13 38				13 54				14 07	14 14		
	d	12 42						13 12			13 30						13 42					14 12			
Worcester Shrub Hill 7	d																								
Ashchurch for Tewkesbury	d																								
Cheltenham Spa	d	13 26					13 45	13 52		14 01	14 11						14 25				14 45	14 52		15 00	
Gloucester 7	a						13 57			14 11	14 22										14 56			15 10	
Bristol Parkway 7	a	13 57						14 26									14 57					15 23			
Bristol Temple Meads 10	a	14 08						14 41									15 09					15 37			
Newport (South Wales)	a						14 50				15 11										15 50				
Cardiff Central 7	a						15 09				15 27										16 07				

- **A** To Maesteg
- **B** From Edinburgh to Plymouth
- **C** To Swindon
- **D** 🛒 to Newport (South Wales)
- **E** To Matlock
- **F** From Edinburgh to Reading
- **G** From Stansted Airport
- **H** From Sheffield to St Pancras International
- **I** From Manchester Piccadilly
- **J** From St Pancras International to Sheffield
- **K** From Glasgow Central to Plymouth
- **L** To London Paddington
- **M** From Newcastle to Southampton Central
- **N** From Worcester Foregate Street to Weymouth
- **O** From Dundee to Plymouth
- **P** 🛒 from Birmingham New Street to Newport (South Wales)
- **Q** From Newcastle to Reading
- **R** From Manchester Piccadilly to Exeter St Davids

Table 57

Saturdays

Nottingham, Derby and Leicester Birmingham - Cardiff and Bristol

Network Diagram - see first Page of Table 50

		XC ◇1 A 🛒	EM B	XC ◇1 C 🛒	XC ◇1 D 🛒	EM ◇1 E 🍽	XC ◇1 F 🛒	XC 1 🛒	EM ◇1 G 🍽	EM ◇1 E 🍽		GW ◇ H	XC ◇1 I 🛒	XC 1	GW J	XC ◇1 K 🛒	EM B	XC ◇1 L 🛒	XC ◇1 D 🛒	EM ◇1 E 🍽		XC ◇1 M 🛒	XC 1 🛒	EM ◇1 G 🍽	EM ◇1 E 🍽
Nottingham 8	d	13 08	13 18					13 37								14 08	14 18						14 37		
Beeston	d		13 24					13 43									14 24						14 43		
Attenborough	d		13 27														14 27								
Long Eaton	d		13 35					13 51	13 57								14 36						14 51	14 57	
Derby 6	a	13 31	13 48					14 02	14 09							14 32	14 48						15 02	15 09	
	d	13 36		13 53		14 01		14 06		14 20			14 30			14 36		14 53		15 01			15 10		15 20
Willington	d																						15 18		
Burton-on-Trent	d	13 49						14 18								14 49							15 24		
Tamworth	d	14 02						14 30					14 49			15 02							15 33		
Wilnecote	d							14 34																	
Leicester	d				13 49	14a23				14a54				14 16					14 49	15a23					15a54
South Wigston	d													14 22											
Narborough	d													14 27											
Hinckley	d													14 35											
Nuneaton	d				14 09									14 42					15 09						
Coleshill Parkway	d				14 24									14 58					15 24						
Water Orton	d																								
Birmingham New Street 12	a	14 24		14 27	14 38			14 54					15 08	15 14		15 24		15 27	15 38				15 54		
	d	14 30					14 42						15 12			15 30						15 42			
Worcester Shrub Hill 7	d											15 06													
Ashchurch for Tewkesbury	d											15 24													
Cheltenham Spa	d	15 11					15 25					15 34	15 52		16 01	16 11						16 25			
Gloucester 7	a	15 22										15 42			16 11	16 22									
Bristol Parkway 7	a						15 55					16 24	16 29									16 54			
Bristol Temple Meads 10	a						16 08					16 39	16 42									17 07			
Newport (South Wales)	a	16 08														17 10									
Cardiff Central 7	a	16 25														17 26									

		AW N	XC ◇1 O 🛒	XC 1	GW ◇1 P 🍽	XC ◇1 🛒		EM B	XC ◇1 C 🛒	XC ◇1 D 🛒	EM ◇1 E 🍽	XC ◇1 F 🛒	XC 1 🛒	EM ◇1 G 🍽	EM ◇1 E 🍽	GW Q		AW N	XC ◇1 I 🛒	XC 1	GW J	XC ◇1	EM B	XC ◇1 L 🛒	XC ◇1 D 🛒
Nottingham 8	d					15 08		15 18					15 37									16 08	16 18		
Beeston	d							15 24					15 43										16 24		
Attenborough	d							15 27															16 27		
Long Eaton	d							15 36					15 51	15 57									16 36		
Derby 6	a					15 31		15 48					16 02	16 09								16 31	16 48		
	d		15 28			15 36			15 53		16 01		16 10		16 20				16 28			16 36		16 53	
Willington	d																								
Burton-on-Trent	d		15 38			15 49							16 21									16 49			
Tamworth	d					16 02							16 33						16 48			17 02			
Wilnecote	d												16 37												
Leicester	d			15 16						15 49	16a23				16a54					16 16					16 49
South Wigston	d																			16 22					
Narborough	d			15 25																16 27					
Hinckley	d			15 34																16 35					
Nuneaton	d			15 41						16 09										16 42					17 09
Coleshill Parkway	d			15 57						16 24										16 58					17 24
Water Orton	d			16 00																					
Birmingham New Street 12	a		16 04	16 14		16 24			16 27	16 38			16 54						17 07	17 14		17 24		17 27	17 38
	d		16 12			16 30						16 42							17 12			17 30			
Worcester Shrub Hill 7	d															17 08									
Ashchurch for Tewkesbury	d															17 24						18 08			
Cheltenham Spa	d	16 45	16 52		17 00	17 11						17 25				17 34		17 45	17 52		18 01	18 18			
Gloucester 7	a	16 56			17 10	17 22										17 44		17 56			18 11	18 29			
Bristol Parkway 7	a		17 24									17 54				18 24			18 29						
Bristol Temple Meads 10	a		17 38									18 07				18 39			18 42						
Newport (South Wales)	a	17 50				18 05												18 50				19 12			
Cardiff Central 7	a	18 10				18 21												19 10				19 29			

A 🛒 from Birmingham New Street to Newport (South Wales)
B To Matlock
C From Newcastle to Southampton Central
D From Stansted Airport
E From Sheffield to St Pancras International
F From Manchester Piccadilly
G From St Pancras International to Sheffield
H From Great Malvern to Weymouth
I From Glasgow Central to Penzance
J To Swindon
K 🛒 to Newport (South Wales)
L From Newcastle to Reading
M From Manchester Piccadilly to Paignton
N To Maesteg
O From Aberdeen to Penzance
P To London Paddington
Q From Great Malvern to Westbury

Table 57

Saturdays

Nottingham, Derby and Leicester Birmingham - Cardiff and Bristol

Network Diagram - see first Page of Table 50

		EM		XC	XC	EM	EM	AW	XC	XC	GW	XC		EM	XC	XC	EM	XC	XC	EM	EM	GW		AW	XC
		◇1		◇1	1	◇1	◇1		◇1	1	◇1	◇1			◇1	◇1	◇1	◇1	1	◇1	◇1				◇1
		A		B		C	A	D	E		F			G	H	I	A	B		C	A	J		D	K
Nottingham 8	d				16 37							17 11		17 18					17 37						
Beeston	d				16 43									17 24					17 43						
Attenborough	d													17 27											
Long Eaton	d				16 51	16 56								17 35					17 51	17 57					
Derby 6	a				17 02	17 09						17 31		17 48					18 02	18 09					
	d	17 01			17 06		17 18		17 28			17 36			17 53		18 01		18 10		18 18				18 28
Willington	d				17 14														18 16						
Burton-on-Trent	d				17 21				17 38			17 49							18 22						
Tamworth	d				17 33							18 02							18 34						18 46
Wilnecote	d																		18 37						
Leicester	d	17a23					17a51			17 16						17 49	18a23				18a51				
South Wigston	d									17 22															
Narborough	d									17 27															
Hinckley	d									17 35															
Nuneaton	d									17 41						18 09									
Coleshill Parkway	d									17 58						18 24									
Water Orton	d																								
Birmingham New Street 12	a				17 54				18 07	18 14		18 24			18 27	18 38			18 54						19 06
	d			17 42					18 12			18 30						18 42							19 12
Worcester Shrub Hill 7	d																					19 07			
Ashchurch for Tewkesbury	d																					19 24			
Cheltenham Spa	d			18 25				18 45	18 52		19 00	19 11						19 25				19 34		19 45	19 52
Gloucester 7	a							18 56			19 10	19 22										19 42		19 56	
Bristol Parkway 7	a			18 54					19 25									19 55				20 24			20 29
Bristol Temple Meads 10	a			19 05					19 39									20 06				20 39			20 42
Newport (South Wales)	a							19 50				20 05						20 55						20 50	
Cardiff Central 7	a							20 11				20 21						21 11						21 09	

		XC	GW	XC	EM	XC	XC	EM		XC	XC	XC	EM	EM	XC	XC	GW	XC		EM	XC	XC	EM	GW	XC
		1		◇1		◇1	◇1	◇1		◇1	◇1	1	◇1	◇1	◇1	1		◇1			◇1	◇1	◇1		◇1
			L		G	H	I	A		M	N		C	O	P					G	Q	I	A	R	B
Nottingham 8	d			18 08	18 19							18 37						19 08		19 18					
Beeston	d				18 24							18 43								19 24					
Attenborough	d				18 26															19 27					
Long Eaton	d				18 37							18 51	18 57							19 35					
Derby 6	a			18 31	18 48							19 02	19 09					19 32		19 48					
	d			18 36		18 53		19 01				19 10		19 21	19 27			19 36			19 54		20 01		
Willington	d																								
Burton-on-Trent	d			18 49								19 21			19 37			19 49							
Tamworth	d			19 02								19 33						20 02							
Wilnecote	d											19 37													
Leicester	d	18 16					18 49	19a23						19a54		19 16						19 49	20a23		
South Wigston	d	18 22														19 22									
Narborough	d	18 27														19 27									
Hinckley	d	18 35														19 35									
Nuneaton	d	18 42					19 09									19 42						20 09			
Coleshill Parkway	d	18 58					19 24									19 58						20 24			
Water Orton	d																								
Birmingham New Street 12	a	19 14		19 24		19 27	19 38					19 54			20 06	20 15		20 24			20 27	20 38			
	d			19 30						19 42	19 42				20 12			20 30							20 42
Worcester Shrub Hill 7	d																								
Ashchurch for Tewkesbury	d																								
Cheltenham Spa	d		20 01	20 11						20 25	20 25				20 50		21 02	21 11						21 19	21 25
Gloucester 7	a		20 11	20 22													21 12	21 22						21 29	
Bristol Parkway 7	a									20 54	20 54				21 22		21 53								21 58
Bristol Temple Meads 10	a									21 05	21 06				21 35		22 05								22 12
Newport (South Wales)	a			21 11														22 21							
Cardiff Central 7	a			21 29														22 43							

A From Sheffield to St Pancras International
B From Manchester Piccadilly
C From St Pancras International to Sheffield
D To Maesteg
E From Edinburgh to Plymouth
F To London Paddington
G To Matlock
H From Newcastle to Reading
I From Stansted Airport
J From Great Malvern
K From Glasgow Central to Plymouth
L To Westbury
M until 11 February, from 31 March. From Manchester Piccadilly to Plymouth
N from 18 February until 24 March. From Manchester Piccadilly
O From York to St Pancras International
P From Edinburgh to Exeter St Davids
Q From Newcastle
R To Swindon

Table 57

Saturdays

Nottingham, Derby and Leicester Birmingham - Cardiff and Bristol

Network Diagram - see first Page of Table 50

		XC	EM	XC		EM	XC	XC	XC	EM	XC	XC	XC	GW		XC	XC	XC	XC	XC					
		1	◇1	◇1			1	◇1	◇1	◇1	1	◇1	1			◇1	◇1	1	◇1	1					
			A	B		C		D	E	F		G		H		E	D		I						
			☕	🛒				🛒		☕															
Nottingham 8 🚌	d	19 37				20 09					20 37							21 37							
Beeston	d	19 43				20 15					20 43							21 43							
Attenborough	d	19 46				20 18												21 46							
Long Eaton	d	19 53	19 57			20 27					20 51							21 53							
Derby 6	a	20 02	20 09			20 42					21 02							22 04							
	d	20 10		20 28				20 53		21 01	21 06	21 28					21 53	22 10	22 26						
Willington	d										21 14														
Burton-on-Trent	d	20 21									21 21	21 38						22 21	22 37						
Tamworth	d	20 33		20 46							21 33	21 49						22 33	22 47						
Wilnecote	d	20 37									21 36							22 36							
Leicester	d						20 16		20 49	21a36			21 18			21 49				22 16					
South Wigston	d						20 22						21 22							22 22					
Narborough	d						20 27						21 27							22 27					
Hinckley	d						20 35						21 35							22 35					
Nuneaton	d						20 42		21 09				21 42			22 09				22 42					
Coleshill Parkway	d						20 58		21 24				21 58			22 24				22 58					
Water Orton	d																								
Birmingham New Street 12	a	20 54		21 03			21 14	21 25	21 38		21 54	22 05	22 14			22 38	22 43	23 02	23 05	23 13					
	d			21 10																					
Worcester Shrub Hill 7	d													21 31											
Ashchurch for Tewkesbury	d													21 51											
Cheltenham Spa	d			21 50										22 01											
Gloucester 7	a			21 59										22 10											
Bristol Parkway 7	a			22 30																					
Bristol Temple Meads 10	a			22 41																					
Newport (South Wales)	a																								
Cardiff Central 7	a																								

Sundays

until 1 January

		EM	EM	EM	GW	XC	GW	GW	XC	XC		EM	EM	GW	XC	GW	XC	EM	EM	AW		XC	XC	GW	XC
		◇1	◇1	◇1		◇1			◇1	◇1			◇1		◇1		◇1	◇1	◇1			◇1	1		◇1
		J	J	K	L	M	N	L		O		C	K	L			O	P	K			Q		L	R
		☕	☕	☕		🛒			🛒	🛒			☕		🛒		🛒	☕	☕			🛒			🛒
Nottingham 8 🚌	d											09 22													11 11
Beeston	d											09 27													
Attenborough	d											09 31													
Long Eaton	d											09 39						10 32							
Derby 6	a											09 50						10 46							11 31
	d	06 50	07 52	08 48						09 28			09 51				10 34		10 52			11 30			11 36
Willington	d																								
Burton-on-Trent	d																					11 41			11 48
Tamworth	d																10 53								12 00
Wilnecote	d																								
Leicester	d	07a19	08a22	09a21									10a23						11a24				11 19		
South Wigston	d																								
Narborough	d																						11 28		
Hinckley	d																						11 36		
Nuneaton	d																						11 42		
Coleshill Parkway	d																						11 57		
Water Orton	d																								
Birmingham New Street 12	a									10 19							11 20					12 04	12 14		12 24
	d					09 12			10 12	10 30					11 12		11 30					12 12			12 30
Worcester Shrub Hill 7	d																								
Ashchurch for Tewkesbury	d																								
Cheltenham Spa	d				09 24	09 52	10 05	10 24	10 53	11 10				11 24	11 53	12 00	12 10			12 18		12 52		13 01	13 11
Gloucester 7	a				09 34		10 15	10 34	11 03					11 34	12 03	12 11				12 28				13 11	13 21
Bristol Parkway 7	a					10 21	10 52			11 39						12 54	12 39					13 21			
Bristol Temple Meads 10	a					10 32	11 07			11 52						13 10	12 51					13 32			
Newport (South Wales)	a								11 48						12 52					13 33					14 06
Cardiff Central 7	a								12 08						13 12					13 52					14 26

A From St Pancras International to Sheffield
B From Glasgow Central. 🛒 to Birmingham New Street
C To Matlock
D From Newcastle
E From Stansted Airport
F From Sheffield
G From Edinburgh
H From Great Malvern
I From Glasgow Central
J To St Pancras International
K From Sheffield to St Pancras International
L To Swindon
M To Penzance
N To Taunton
O From Leeds to Plymouth
P From Leicester to York
Q From York to Plymouth
R 🛒 to Newport (South Wales)

Table 57

Sundays
until 1 January

Nottingham, Derby and Leicester
Birmingham - Cardiff and Bristol

Network Diagram - see first Page of Table 50

		EM	EM	EM	XC	XC		XC	EM	XC	EM	AW	XC	GW	XC	XC		GW	XC	EM	XC	EM	XC	EM	XC
		◇1	◇1		◇1	1		◇1	◇1	◇1	◇1		◇1		◇1	1			◇1	◇1	◇1		◇1	◇1	◇1
		A	B	C	D			E	B	F	G			H	I			J	E	B	K	C	F	G	L
		☕	☕		🛒			🛒	☕	🛒	☕		🛒		🛒				🛒	☕	🛒		🛒	☕	🛒
Nottingham 8 🚌	d			11 30				12 10											13 06			13 22			
Beeston	d			11 35																		13 28			
Attenborough	d			11 39																		13 34			
Long Eaton	d		11 39	11 47					12 41											13 42		13 46			
Derby 6	a		11 49	11 55				12 30	12 51										13 26	13 52		13 57			
	d	11 48			12 30			12 36			12 58				13 32				13 36		13 54			14 02	
Willington	d																								
Burton-on-Trent	d							12 48							13 43				13 48						
Tamworth	d				12 48			13 00											14 00						
Wilnecote	d																								
Leicester	d	12a21				12 19				12 49	13a30					13 19							13 49	14a34	
South Wigston	d					12 24																			
Narborough	d					12 29										13 28									
Hinckley	d					12 38										13 36									
Nuneaton	d					12 45				13 08						13 43							14 08		
Coleshill Parkway	d					13 00				13 23						13 59							14 23		
Water Orton	d																								
Birmingham New Street 12	a				13 05	13 15		13 24		13 36					14 08	14 15			14 24		14 27		14 36		
	d				13 12			13 30					13 42		14 12				14 30						14 42
Worcester Shrub Hill 7	d																	14 36							
Ashchurch for Tewkesbury	d																	14 51							
Cheltenham Spa	d				13 52			14 12				14 18	14 24	14 46	14 52			15 01	15 11						15 25
Gloucester 7	a							14 22				14 29		14 56				15 10	15 21						
Bristol Parkway 7	a				14 21								14 54		15 24			15 49							15 59
Bristol Temple Meads 10	a				14 32								15 07		15 36			16 09							16 11
Newport (South Wales)	a							15 08				15 34							16 06						
Cardiff Central 7	a							15 31				15 53							16 26						

		GW		XC	XC	XC	EM	XC	EM	XC	AW	XC		GW	XC	XC	GW	XC	EM	EM	XC	EM		XC	EM
		◇1		◇1	1	◇1	◇1	◇1	◇1	◇1		◇1			◇1	1		◇1	◇1	◇1	◇1			◇1	◇1
		M		N		E	G	O	B	F		P		H	I				A	B	Q	C		F	G
		☕		🛒		🛒	☕	🛒	☕	🛒		🛒			🛒			🛒	☕	☕	🛒			🛒	☕
Nottingham 8 🚌	d					14 10												15 10				15 29			
Beeston	d																					15 34			
Attenborough	d																					15 38			
Long Eaton	d								14 46											15 42		15 46			
Derby 6	a					14 29			14 57									15 30		15 53		15 57			
	d			14 31		14 35	14 50	14 53							15 26			15 35	15 47		15 54				16 24
Willington	d																								
Burton-on-Trent	d					14 48									15 38			15 48							
Tamworth	d			14 50		15 00												16 00							
Wilnecote	d																	16 03							
Leicester	d				14 19		15a22			14 49						15 19			16a24					15 49	16a50
South Wigston	d				14 24																				
Narborough	d				14 29											15 28									
Hinckley	d				14 38											15 36									
Nuneaton	d				14 45					15 08						15 43								16 07	
Coleshill Parkway	d				15 00					15 23						15 58								16 22	
Water Orton	d																								
Birmingham New Street 12	a			15 06	15 15	15 21		15 27		15 36					16 01	16 15		16 24			16 27			16 36	
	d			15 12		15 30						15 42			16 12			16 30							
Worcester Shrub Hill 7	d																16 40								
Ashchurch for Tewkesbury	d																16 58								
Cheltenham Spa	d	15 46		15 52		16 11					16 18	16 25		16 33	16 51		17 08	17 11							
Gloucester 7	a	15 57				16 21					16 29			16 43			17 16	17 21							
Bristol Parkway 7	a			16 21								16 55			17 20		17 57								
Bristol Temple Meads 10	a			16 35								17 08			17 35		18 10								
Newport (South Wales)	a					17 06					17 37							18 07							
Cardiff Central 7	a					17 27					17 57							18 29							

A From Leeds to St Pancras International
B From St Pancras International to Sheffield
C To Matlock
D From Newcastle to Plymouth
E 🛒 to Newport (South Wales)
F From Stansted Airport
G From Sheffield to St Pancras International
H To Swindon
I From Edinburgh to Plymouth
J To Weston-super-Mare
K To Reading
L From Manchester Piccadilly to Paignton
M To London Paddington
N From Edinburgh to Penzance
O From Sheffield to Reading
P From Manchester Piccadilly
Q From Newcastle to Reading

Table 57

Sundays

until 1 January

Nottingham, Derby and Leicester
Birmingham - Cardiff and Bristol

Network Diagram - see first Page of Table 50

		XC	GW	XC	XC	XC	EM	EM		XC	XC	EM	XC	AW	XC	XC	GW	XC		EM	EM	XC	EM	XC	EM
		◇1	◇1	◇1	1	◇1	◇1	◇1		◇1	◇1	◇1	◇1		◇1	1		◇1		◇1	◇1	◇1		◇1	◇1
		A	B	C		D	E	F		G	H	I	A		J			D		K	F	L	M	H	I
		[trolley]	[catering]	[trolley]		[trolley]	[catering]	[catering]		[trolley]	[trolley]	[catering]	[trolley]		[trolley]			[trolley]		[catering]	[catering]	[trolley]			[catering]
Nottingham 8	d					16 10												17 10					17 29		
Beeston	d																						17 35		
Attenborough	d																						17 38		
Long Eaton	d						16 32													17 29			17 46		
Derby 6	a					16 30	16 44											17 29		17 41			17 58		
	d			16 28		16 35		16 48		16 55		17 11			17 27			17 36			17 47	17 54			18 04
Willington	d																								
Burton-on-Trent	d					16 48									17 38			17 48							
Tamworth	d			16 48		17 00												18 00							
Wilnecote	d																								
Leicester	d				16 19			17a20			16 49	17a51				17 18					18a19			17 49	18a34
South Wigston	d				16 24											17 24									
Narborough	d				16 29											17 29									
Hinckley	d				16 38											17 38									
Nuneaton	d				16 45						17 08					17 45								18 08	
Coleshill Parkway	d				17 00						17 23					18 00								18 23	
Water Orton	d																								
Birmingham New Street 12	a			17 04	17 15	17 19				17 27	17 36				18 01	18 15		18 19				18 24		18 36	
	d	16 42		17 12		17 30							17 42		18 12			18 30							
Worcester Shrub Hill 7	d																18 40								
Ashchurch for Tewkesbury	d																18 55								
Cheltenham Spa	d	17 25	17 46	17 52		18 11							18 25	18 35	18 52		19 06	19 13							
Gloucester 7	a		17 56			18 22								18 46			19 17	19 26							
Bristol Parkway 7	a	18 02		18 22									18 56		19 21		19 57								
Bristol Temple Meads 10	a	18 13		18 40									19 08		19 35		20 11								
Newport (South Wales)	a					19 07								19 54				20 11							
Cardiff Central 7	a					19 27								20 12				20 31							

		XC	XC	XC		GW	XC	XC	XC	EM	AW	XC	XC	XC		XC	EM	XC	XC	EM	GW	XC	GW	XC	
		◇1	◇1	1		◇1	◇1	◇1	◇1	◇1		◇1	◇1	1		◇1		◇1	◇1	◇1		◇1		◇1	
		N	O			B	P	G	H	Q		A	J				M	R	H	I		A	S	T	
		[trolley]	[trolley]			[catering]	[trolley]	[trolley]		[catering]		[trolley]	[trolley]			[trolley]		[trolley]		[catering]				[trolley]	
Nottingham 8	d						18 10									19 10	19 22								
Beeston	d																19 27								
Attenborough	d																19 31								
Long Eaton	d																19 38								
Derby 6	a						18 30									19 30	19 50								
	d		18 26				18 35	18 55		19 22			19 27			19 36		19 56		20 06				20 27	
Willington	d																								
Burton-on-Trent	d						18 48						19 38			19 48									
Tamworth	d		18 45				19 00									20 00								20 45	
Wilnecote	d															20 04									
Leicester	d			18 16					18 49	19a55				19 19					19 49	20a42					
South Wigston	d													19 24											
Narborough	d			18 25										19 29											
Hinckley	d			18 34										19 37											
Nuneaton	d			18 41					19 08					19 43					20 08						
Coleshill Parkway	d			18 56					19 23					19 59					20 23						
Water Orton	d																								
Birmingham New Street 12	a		19 04	19 15			19 20	19 27	19 36				20 05	20 15		20 24		20 27	20 36					21 03	
	d	18 42	19 12				19 30					19 42	20 12									20 42		21 12	
Worcester Shrub Hill 7	d																				20 37				
Ashchurch for Tewkesbury	d																				20 53				
Cheltenham Spa	d	19 25	19 52			20 05	20 11				20 18	20 25	20 52								21 03	21 25	21 46	21 52	
Gloucester 7	a					20 15	20 21				20 29										21 13		21 56	22 02	
Bristol Parkway 7	a	20 03	20 21									20 57	21 21								21 53	21 59		22 34	
Bristol Temple Meads 10	a	20 14	20 35									21 08	21 32								22 07	22 10		22 45	
Newport (South Wales)	a						21 06				21 31														
Cardiff Central 7	a						21 26				21 49														

- **A** From Manchester Piccadilly
- **B** To London Paddington
- **C** From Glasgow Central to Penzance
- **D** [trolley] to Newport (South Wales)
- **E** From St Pancras International to Leeds
- **F** To St Pancras International
- **G** From Newcastle to Reading
- **H** From Stansted Airport
- **I** From Sheffield to St Pancras International
- **J** From Glasgow Central to Plymouth
- **K** From St Pancras International to Sheffield
- **L** From Edinburgh to Reading
- **M** To Matlock
- **N** From Manchester Piccadilly to Plymouth
- **O** From Aberdeen to Plymouth
- **P** [trolley] to Birmingham New Street
- **Q** From York to St Pancras International
- **R** From Newcastle to Guildford
- **S** To Swindon
- **T** From Glasgow Central. [trolley] to Birmingham New Street

Table 57

Nottingham, Derby and Leicester Birmingham - Cardiff and Bristol

Sundays until 1 January

Network Diagram - see first Page of Table 50

		XC	XC	XC	XC	EM	GW	XC	XC	XC		XC	EM	XC	XC	XC	XC	EM							
		■1	◇■1	◇■1	◇■1	◇■1		◇■1	◇■1	■1		◇■1		◇■1	◇■1	◇■1	■1	◇■1							
				A	B	C		D	E				F	A	B	G		H							
				🛒		☕								🛒				☕							
Nottingham ■8	d		20 10									21 08	21 24												
Beeston	d												21 29												
Attenborough	d												21 33												
Long Eaton	d												21 40					23 32							
Derby ■6	a		20 29									21 31	21 52					23 42							
	d		20 36	20 54		21 06			21 27			21 36		21 53		22 26									
Willington	d																								
Burton-on-Trent	d		20 48						21 37			21 48		22 03		22 37									
Tamworth	d		21 00						21 47			22 00		22 14		22 47									
Wilnecote	d											22 04													
Leicester	d	20 19			20 49	21a35				21 19					21 49		23 19								
South Wigston	d	20 24								21 24							23 24								
Narborough	d	20 29								21 29							23 29								
Hinckley	d	20 38								21 38							23 38								
Nuneaton	d	20 44			21 08					21 45					22 08		23 45								
Coleshill Parkway	d	21 00			21 23					22 00					22 23		00 02								
Water Orton	d																								
Birmingham New Street ■12	a	21 15	21 19	21 28	21 36				22 04	22 15		22 23		22 30	22 36	23 04	00 15								
	d							21 43	22 12																
Worcester Shrub Hill ■7	d																								
Ashchurch for Tewkesbury	d																								
Cheltenham Spa	d						22 01	22 24	22 52																
Gloucester ■7	a						22 12																		
Bristol Parkway ■7	a							22 53	23 22																
Bristol Temple Meads ■10	a							23 07	23 33																
Newport (South Wales)	a																								
Cardiff Central ■7	a																								

Sundays 8 January to 12 February

		EM	EM	EM	GW	XC	GW	GW	XC	XC		EM	EM	GW	XC	GW	XC	EM	EM	AW		XC	XC	GW	XC
		◇■1	◇■1	◇■1		◇■1			◇■1	◇■1			◇■1		◇■1		◇■1	◇■1	◇■1			◇■1	■1		◇■1
		I	I	C	J	K	L	J		M		F	C	J			M	N	C			O		J	P
		☕	☕	☕		🛒			🛒	🛒			☕		🛒		🛒	☕	☕			🛒			🛒
Nottingham ■8	d											09 22													11 11
Beeston	d											09 27													
Attenborough	d											09 31													
Long Eaton	d											09 39						10 32							
Derby ■6	a											09 50						10 46							11 31
	d	06 50	07 52	08 48						09 28			09 51				10 34		10 52			11 30			11 36
Willington	d																								
Burton-on-Trent	d																					11 41			11 48
Tamworth	d																10 53								12 00
Wilnecote	d																								
Leicester	d	07a19	08a22	09a21									10a23						11a24				11 19		
South Wigston	d																								
Narborough	d																						11 28		
Hinckley	d																						11 36		
Nuneaton	d																						11 42		
Coleshill Parkway	d																						11 57		
Water Orton	d																								
Birmingham New Street ■12	a									10 19							11 20					12 04	12 14		12 24
	d					09 12			10 12	10 30					11 12		11 30					12 12			12 30
Worcester Shrub Hill ■7	d																								
Ashchurch for Tewkesbury	d																								
Cheltenham Spa	d				09 24	09 52	10 05	10 24	10 53	11 10				11 24	11 53	12 00	12 10			12 18		12 52		13 01	13 11
Gloucester ■7	a				09 34		10 15	10 34	11 03					11 34	12 03	12 11				12 28				13 11	13 21
Bristol Parkway ■7	a					10 21	10 52			11 39						12 54	12 39					13 21			
Bristol Temple Meads ■10	a					10 32	11 07			11 52						13 10	12 51					13 32			
Newport (South Wales)	a								11 48						12 52					13 33					14 06
Cardiff Central ■7	a								12 08						13 12					13 52					14 26

A From Newcastle
B From Stansted Airport
C From Sheffield to St Pancras International
D From Manchester Piccadilly
E From Edinburgh
F To Matlock
G From Glasgow Central
H From St Pancras International to Sheffield
I To St Pancras International
J To Swindon
K To Penzance
L To Taunton
M From Leeds to Plymouth
N From Leicester to York
O From York to Plymouth
P 🛒 to Newport (South Wales)

Table 57

Sundays

8 January to 12 February

Nottingham, Derby and Leicester Birmingham - Cardiff and Bristol

Network Diagram - see first Page of Table 50

		EM	EM	EM	XC	XC		XC	EM	XC	EM	AW	XC	GW	XC	XC		GW	XC	EM	XC	EM	XC	EM	XC
		◇1	◇1		◇1	1		◇1	◇1	◇1	◇1		◇1		◇1	◇1			◇1	◇1	◇1		◇1	◇1	◇1
		A	B	C	D			E	B		F			G	H	I		J	E	B	K	C		F	L
		ꝓ	ꝓ		🛒			🛒	ꝓ	🛒	ꝓ		🛒		🛒	🛒			🛒	ꝓ	🛒		🛒	ꝓ	🛒
Nottingham 8	d			11 30				12 10								12 53			13 06			13 22			
Beeston	d			11 35																		13 28			
Attenborough	d			11 39																		13 34			
Long Eaton	d		11 39	11 47					12 41											13 42		13 46			
Derby 6	a		11 49	11 55				12 30	12 51										13 26	13 52		13 57			
	d	11 48			12 30			12 36			12 58				13 32				13 36		13 54			14 02	
Willington	d																								
Burton-on-Trent	d							12 48							13 43				13 48						
Tamworth	d				12 48			13 00											14 00						
Wilnecote	d																								
Leicester	d	12a21				12 19				12 49	13a30					13 19							13 49	14a34	
South Wigston	d					12 24																			
Narborough	d					12 29										13 28									
Hinckley	d					12 38										13 36									
Nuneaton	d					12 45				13 08						13 43							14 08		
Coleshill Parkway	d					13 00				13 23						13 58							14 23		
Water Orton	d																								
Birmingham New Street 12	a				13 05	13 15		13 24		13 36					14 08	14 16			14 24		14 27		14 36		
	d				13 12			13 30					13 42		14 12				14 30						14 42
Worcester Shrub Hill 7	d																	14 36							
Ashchurch for Tewkesbury	d																	14 51							
Cheltenham Spa	d				13 52			14 12				14 18	14 24	14 46	14 52			15 01	15 11						15 25
Gloucester 7	a							14 22				14 29		14 56				15 10	15 21						
Bristol Parkway 7	a				14 21								14 54		15 24			15 49							15 59
Bristol Temple Meads 10	a				14 32								15 07		15 36			16 09							16 11
Newport (South Wales)	a							15 08				15 34							16 06						
Cardiff Central 7	a							15 31				15 53							16 26						

		GW		XC	XC	XC	EM	XC	EM	XC	AW	XC		GW	XC	XC	GW	XC	EM	EM	XC	XC		EM	EM
		◇1		◇1	1	◇1	◇1	◇1	◇1	◇1		◇1			◇1	1		◇1	◇1	◇1	◇1	◇1			◇1
		M		N		E	F	O	B			P		G	H				A	B	Q	I		C	F
		ꝓ		🛒		🛒	ꝓ	🛒	ꝓ	🛒		🛒			🛒			🛒	ꝓ	ꝓ	🛒	🛒			ꝓ
Nottingham 8	d					14 10												15 10				15 04		15 29	
Beeston	d																							15 34	
Attenborough	d																							15 38	
Long Eaton	d								14 46											15 42				15 46	
Derby 6	a					14 29			14 57									15 30		15 53				15 57	
	d			14 31		14 35	14 50	14 53							15 26			15 35	15 47		15 54				16 24
Willington	d																								
Burton-on-Trent	d					14 48									15 38			15 48							
Tamworth	d			14 50		15 00												16 00							
Wilnecote	d																	16 03							
Leicester	d				14 19		15a22			14 49						15 19			16a24			15 49			16a50
South Wigston	d				14 24																				
Narborough	d				14 29											15 28									
Hinckley	d				14 38											15 36									
Nuneaton	d				14 45					15 08						15 43						16 08			
Coleshill Parkway	d				15 00					15 23						15 58						16 23			
Water Orton	d																								
Birmingham New Street 12	a			15 06	15 15	15 21		15 27		15 36					16 01	16 15		16 24			16 27	16 36			
	d			15 12		15 30						15 42			16 12			16 30							
Worcester Shrub Hill 7	d																16 40								
Ashchurch for Tewkesbury	d																16 58								
Cheltenham Spa	d	15 46		15 52		16 11					16 18	16 25		16 33	16 51		17 08	17 11							
Gloucester 7	a	15 57				16 21					16 29			16 43			17 16	17 21							
Bristol Parkway 7	a			16 21								16 55			17 20		17 57								
Bristol Temple Meads 10	a			16 35								17 08			17 35		18 10								
Newport (South Wales)	a					17 06					17 37							18 07							
Cardiff Central 7	a					17 27					17 57							18 29							

A From Leeds to St Pancras International
B From St Pancras International to Sheffield
C To Matlock
D From Newcastle to Plymouth
E 🛒 to Newport (South Wales)
F From Sheffield to St Pancras International
G To Swindon
H From Edinburgh to Plymouth
I From Stansted Airport
J To Weston-super-Mare
K To Reading
L From Manchester Piccadilly to Paignton
M To London Paddington
N From Edinburgh to Penzance
O From Sheffield to Reading
P From Manchester Piccadilly
Q From Newcastle to Reading

Table 57

Sundays

8 January to 12 February

Nottingham, Derby and Leicester Birmingham - Cardiff and Bristol

Network Diagram - see first Page of Table 50

		XC	GW	XC	XC	XC	EM	EM		XC	XC	EM	XC	AW	XC	XC	GW	XC		EM	EM	XC	EM	XC	EM
		◇1	◇1	◇1	1	◇1	◇1	◇1		◇1	◇1	◇1	◇1		◇1	1		◇1		◇1	◇1	◇1		◇1	◇1
		A	B	C		D	E	F		G	H	I	A		J			D		K	F	L	M		I
		🛒	☕	🛒		🛒	☕	☕		🛒	🛒	☕	🛒		🛒			🛒		☕	☕	🛒			☕
Nottingham 8	d					16 10					16 04							17 10					17 29		
Beeston	d																						17 35		
Attenborough	d																						17 38		
Long Eaton	d						16 32													17 29			17 46		
Derby 6	a					16 30	16 44											17 29		17 41			17 58		
	d			16 28		16 35		16 48		16 55		17 11			17 27			17 36			17 47	17 54			18 04
Willington	d																								
Burton-on-Trent	d					16 48									17 38			17 48							
Tamworth	d			16 48		17 00												18 00							
Wilnecote	d																								
Leicester	d				16 19			17a20			16 49	17a51				17 18					18a19			17 49	18a34
South Wigston	d				16 24											17 24									
Narborough	d				16 29											17 29									
Hinckley	d				16 38											17 38									
Nuneaton	d				16 45						17 08					17 45								18 08	
Coleshill Parkway	d				17 00						17 23					18 00								18 23	
Water Orton	d																								
Birmingham New Street 12	a			17 04	17 15	17 19				17 27	17 36				18 01	18 15		18 19				18 24		18 36	
	d	16 42		17 12		17 30							17 42		18 12			18 30							
Worcester Shrub Hill 7	d																18 40								
Ashchurch for Tewkesbury	d																18 55								
Cheltenham Spa	d	17 25	17 46	17 52		18 11							18 25	18 35	18 52		19 06	19 13							
Gloucester 7	a		17 56			18 22								18 46			19 17	19 26							
Bristol Parkway 7	a	18 02		18 22									18 56		19 21		19 57								
Bristol Temple Meads 10	a	18 13		18 40									19 08		19 35		20 11								
Newport (South Wales)	a					19 07								19 54				20 11							
Cardiff Central 7	a					19 27								20 12				20 31							

		XC	XC	XC		GW	XC	XC	XC	EM	AW	XC	XC	XC		XC	XC	XC	EM	EM	GW	XC	GW	XC	
		◇1	◇1	◇1		◇1	◇1	◇1	◇1	◇1		◇1	◇1	1		◇1	◇1	◇1		◇1		◇1		◇1	
		N	O	H		B	P	G		Q		A	J				R	H	M	I		A	S	T	
		🛒	🛒	🛒		☕	🛒	🛒		☕		🛒	🛒			🛒	🛒	🛒		☕				🛒	
Nottingham 8	d			17 58			18 10									19 10		19 02	19 22						
Beeston	d																		19 27						
Attenborough	d																		19 31						
Long Eaton	d																		19 38						
Derby 6	a						18 30									19 30			19 50						
	d		18 26				18 35	18 55		19 22			19 27			19 36	19 56			20 06				20 27	
Willington	d																								
Burton-on-Trent	d						18 48						19 38			19 48									
Tamworth	d		18 45				19 00									20 00								20 45	
Wilnecote	d															20 04									
Leicester	d			18 26					18 40	19a55				19 19				19 49		20a42					
South Wigston	d								18 45					19 24											
Narborough	d								18 50					19 29											
Hinckley	d								18 59					19 37											
Nuneaton	d			18 45					19 08					19 43				20 08							
Coleshill Parkway	d			18 59					19 23					19 59				20 22							
Water Orton	d																								
Birmingham New Street 12	a		19 04	19 15			19 20	19 27	19 36				20 05	20 15		20 24	20 27	20 36						21 03	
	d	18 42	19 12				19 30					19 42	20 12									20 42		21 12	
Worcester Shrub Hill 7	d																				20 37				
Ashchurch for Tewkesbury	d																				20 53				
Cheltenham Spa	d	19 25	19 52			20 05	20 11				20 18	20 25	20 52								21 03	21 25	21 46	21 52	
Gloucester 7	a					20 15	20 21				20 29										21 13		21 56	22 02	
Bristol Parkway 7	a	20 03	20 21									20 57	21 21								21 53	21 59		22 34	
Bristol Temple Meads 10	a	20 14	20 35									21 08	21 32								22 07	22 10		22 45	
Newport (South Wales)	a						21 06				21 31														
Cardiff Central 7	a						21 26				21 49														

A From Manchester Piccadilly
B To London Paddington
C From Glasgow Central to Penzance
D 🛒 to Newport (South Wales)
E From St Pancras International to Leeds
F To St Pancras International
G From Newcastle to Reading
H From Stansted Airport
I From Sheffield to St Pancras International
J From Glasgow Central to Plymouth
K From St Pancras International to Sheffield
L From Edinburgh to Reading
M To Matlock
N From Manchester Piccadilly to Plymouth
O From Aberdeen to Plymouth
P 🛒 to Birmingham New Street
Q From York to St Pancras International
R From Newcastle to Guildford
S To Swindon
T From Glasgow Central. 🛒 to Birmingham New Street

Table 57

Sundays

8 January to 12 February

Nottingham, Derby and Leicester
Birmingham - Cardiff and Bristol

Network Diagram - see first Page of Table 50

		XC	XC	XC	XC	EM	GW	XC	XC	XC		XC	EM	XC	XC	XC	EM
		1	◇1	◇1	◇1	◇1		◇1	◇1	◇1		◇1		◇1	◇1	1	◇1
				A		B		C	D	E			F	A	G		H
				[trolley]		[catering]								[trolley]			[catering]
Nottingham 8	d		20 10							20 35		21 08	21 24				
Beeston	d												21 29				
Attenborough	d												21 33				
Long Eaton	d												21 40				23 32
Derby 6	a		20 29									21 31	21 52				23 42
	d		20 36	20 54		21 06			21 27			21 36		21 53	22 26		
Willington	d																
Burton-on-Trent	d		20 48						21 37			21 48		22 03	22 37		
Tamworth	d		21 00						21 47			22 00		22 14	22 47		
Wilnecote	d											22 04					
Leicester	d	20 19			20 49	21a35				21 19						23 19	
South Wigston	d	20 24								21 24						23 24	
Narborough	d	20 29								21 29						23 29	
Hinckley	d	20 38								21 38						23 38	
Nuneaton	d	20 44			21 08					21 45						23 45	
Coleshill Parkway	d	21 00			21 23					22 00						00 02	
Water Orton	d																
Birmingham New Street 12	a	21 15	21 19	21 28	21 36				22 04	22 15		22 23		22 30	23 04	00 15	
	d							21 43	22 12								
Worcester Shrub Hill 7	d																
Ashchurch for Tewkesbury	d																
Cheltenham Spa	d						22 01	22 24	22 52								
Gloucester 7	a						22 12										
Bristol Parkway 7	a							22 53	23 22								
Bristol Temple Meads 10	a							23 07	23 33								
Newport (South Wales)	a																
Cardiff Central 7	a																

Sundays

19 February to 25 March

		EM	EM	EM	GW	XC	GW	XC	XC	EM		EM	XC	GW	XC	EM	EM	AW	XC	XC		XC	EM	EM	EM
		◇1	◇1	◇1		◇1		◇1	◇1			◇1	◇1		◇1	◇1	◇1		◇1	1		◇1	◇1	◇1	
		I	I	B		J	K		L	F		B			L	M	B		N			O	P	H	F
					[bus]																				
		[catering]	[catering]	[catering]		[trolley]		[trolley]	[trolley]			[catering]	[trolley]		[trolley]	[catering]	[catering]		[trolley]			[trolley]	[catering]	[catering]	
Nottingham 8	d									09 22												11 11			11 30
Beeston	d									09 27															11 35
Attenborough	d									09 31															11 39
Long Eaton	d									09 39						10 32								11 39	11 47
Derby 6	a									09 50						10 46						11 31		11 49	11 55
	d	06 50	07 52	08 48					09 28			09 51			10 33		10 52		11 30			11 36	11 48		
Willington	d																								
Burton-on-Trent	d																		11 41			11 48			
Tamworth	d														10 53							12 00			
Wilnecote	d																								
Leicester	d	07a19	08a22	09a21								10a23					11a24			11 19			12a21		
South Wigston	d																								
Narborough	d																			11 28					
Hinckley	d																			11 36					
Nuneaton	d																			11 42					
Coleshill Parkway	d																			11 57					
Water Orton	d																								
Birmingham New Street 12	a								10 18						11 20				12 04	12 14		12 24			
	d					09 12		10 12	10 28				11 12		11 30				12 12			12 30			
Worcester Shrub Hill 7	d																								
Ashchurch for Tewkesbury	d																								
Cheltenham Spa	d				09 30	09 52	10 05	10 53	11 10				11 53	12 00	12 10			12 18	12 52			13 11			
Gloucester 7	a				09 50		10 15	11 03					12 03	12 11				12 32				13 21			
Bristol Parkway 7	a					10 21	10 52		11 39					12 54	12 39				13 21						
Bristol Temple Meads 10	a					10 32	11 07		11 52					13 10	12 51				13 35						
Newport (South Wales)	a							11 48					12 52					13 33				14 06			
Cardiff Central 7	a							12 08					13 12					13 52				14 26			

A From Newcastle
B From Sheffield to St Pancras International
C From Manchester Piccadilly
D From Edinburgh
E From Stansted Airport
F To Matlock
G From Glasgow Central
H From St Pancras International to Sheffield
I To St Pancras International
J To Newton Abbot
K To Taunton
L From Leeds to Newton Abbot
M From Leicester to York
N From York to Newton Abbot
O [trolley] to Newport (South Wales)
P From Leeds to St Pancras International

Table 57

Nottingham, Derby and Leicester
Birmingham - Cardiff and Bristol

Network Diagram - see first Page of Table 50

		XC	XC	XC	EM	XC		EM	AW	XC	XC	XC	GW	XC	EM	XC		EM	XC	EM	XC	XC	XC	XC	EM
		◇1	1	◇1	◇1	◇1		◇1		◇1	◇1	1		◇1	◇1	◇1			◇1	◇1	◇1	◇1	1	◇1	◇1
		A		B	C	D		E			F		G	B	C	H		I	D	E	J	F		B	E
		trolley		trolley	buffet	trolley		buffet		trolley	trolley			trolley	buffet	trolley			trolley	buffet	trolley	trolley		trolley	buffet
Nottingham 8	d			12 10										13 06				13 22						14 10	
Beeston	d																	13 28							
Attenborough	d																	13 34							
Long Eaton	d				12 41										13 42			13 46							
Derby 6	a			12 30	12 51									13 26	13 52			13 57						14 29	
	d	12 30		12 36				12 58			13 32			13 36		13 54				14 02		14 31		14 35	14 50
Willington	d																								
Burton-on-Trent	d			12 48							13 43			13 48										14 48	
Tamworth	d	12 48		13 00										14 00								14 50		15 00	
Wilnecote	d																								
Leicester	d		12 19			12 49		13a30				13 19							13 49	14a34			14 19		15a22
South Wigston	d		12 24																				14 24		
Narborough	d		12 29									13 28											14 29		
Hinckley	d		12 38									13 36											14 38		
Nuneaton	d		12 45			13 08						13 43							14 08				14 45		
Coleshill Parkway	d		13 00			13 23						13 59							14 23				15 00		
Water Orton	d																								
Birmingham New Street 12	a	13 05	13 15	13 24		13 36					14 08	14 15		14 24		14 27			14 36			15 06	15 15	15 21	
	d	13 12		13 30						13 42	14 12			14 30							14 42	15 12		15 30	
Worcester Shrub Hill 7	d												14 36												
Ashchurch for Tewkesbury	d												14 51												
Cheltenham Spa	d	13 52		14 12					14 18	14 24	14 52		15 01	15 11							15 25	15 52		16 11	
Gloucester 7	a			14 22					14 33				15 10	15 21										16 21	
Bristol Parkway 7	a	14 21								14 54	15 24		15 49								15 59	16 21			
Bristol Temple Meads 10	a	14 32								15 07	15 36		16 09								16 13	16 35			
Newport (South Wales)	a			15 08					15 33					16 06										17 06	
Cardiff Central 7	a			15 31					15 53					16 26										17 27	

		XC		EM	XC	AW	XC	XC	XC	GW	XC	EM		EM	XC	EM	XC	EM	XC	GW	XC	XC		XC	EM
		◇1		◇1	◇1		◇1	◇1	1		◇1	◇1		◇1	◇1		◇1	◇1	◇1	◇1	◇1	1		◇1	◇1
		K		C	D		J	F				L		C	M	I	D	E	J	N	O			B	P
		trolley		buffet	trolley		trolley	trolley			trolley	buffet		buffet	trolley		trolley	buffet	trolley	buffet	trolley			trolley	buffet
Nottingham 8	d										15 10					15 29								16 10	
Beeston	d															15 34									
Attenborough	d															15 38									
Long Eaton	d			14 46										15 42		15 46									16 32
Derby 6	a			14 57							15 30			15 53		15 57								16 30	16 44
	d	14 53						15 26			15 35	15 47			15 54			16 24			16 28			16 35	
Willington	d																								
Burton-on-Trent	d							15 39			15 48													16 48	
Tamworth	d										16 00										16 48			17 00	
Wilnecote	d										16 03														
Leicester	d				14 49				15 19			16a24					15 49	16a50				16 19			
South Wigston	d																					16 24			
Narborough	d								15 28													16 29			
Hinckley	d								15 36													16 38			
Nuneaton	d				15 08				15 43								16 07					16 45			
Coleshill Parkway	d				15 23				15 58								16 22					17 00			
Water Orton	d																								
Birmingham New Street 12	a	15 27			15 36			16 02	16 15		16 24				16 27		16 36				17 04	17 15		17 19	
	d						15 42	16 12			16 30								16 42		17 12			17 30	
Worcester Shrub Hill 7	d									16 40															
Ashchurch for Tewkesbury	d									16 58															
Cheltenham Spa	d					16 18	16 25	16 51		17 08	17 11								17 25	17 46	17 52			18 11	
Gloucester 7	a					16 29				17 16	17 21									17 56				18 22	
Bristol Parkway 7	a						16 55	17 20		17 57									18 02		18 26				
Bristol Temple Meads 10	a						17 08	17 35		18 10									18 13		18 40				
Newport (South Wales)	a					17 37					18 07													19 07	
Cardiff Central 7	a					17 57					18 29													19 29	

- **A** From Newcastle to Newton Abbot
- **B** trolley to Newport (South Wales)
- **C** From St Pancras International to Sheffield
- **D** From Stansted Airport
- **E** From Sheffield to St Pancras International
- **F** From Edinburgh to Newton Abbot
- **G** To Weston-super-Mare
- **H** To Reading
- **I** To Matlock
- **J** From Manchester Piccadilly
- **K** From Sheffield to Reading
- **L** From Leeds to St Pancras International
- **M** From Newcastle to Reading
- **N** To London Paddington
- **O** From Glasgow Central to Exeter St Davids
- **P** From St Pancras International to Leeds

Table 57

19 February to 25 March

Nottingham, Derby and Leicester
Birmingham - Cardiff and Bristol

Network Diagram - see first Page of Table 50

		EM	XC	XC	EM	XC	AW	XC		XC	GW	XC	EM	EM	XC	EM	XC	EM		XC	XC	XC	XC	XC	XC
		◇1	◇1	◇1	◇1	◇1		◇1		1		◇1	◇1	◇1	◇1		◇1	◇1		◇1	◇1	1	◇1	◇1	◇1
		A	B	C	D	E		F				G	H	A	I	J	C	D		E	K		L	B	C
		🍴	☕	☕	🍴	☕		☕				☕	🍴	🍴	☕			🍴		☕	☕		☕	☕	
Nottingham 8	d											17 10				17 29							18 10		
Beeston	d															17 35									
Attenborough	d															17 38									
Long Eaton	d												17 29			17 46									
Derby 6	a											17 29	17 41			17 58							18 30		
	d	16 48	16 55		17 11			17 27				17 36		17 47	17 54			18 04			18 26		18 35	18 55	
Willington	d																								
Burton-on-Trent	d							17 38				17 48											18 48		
Tamworth	d											18 00									18 45		19 00		
Wilnecote	d																								
Leicester	d	17a20		16 49	17a51					17 18				18a19			17 49	18a34				18 16			18 49
South Wigston	d									17 24															
Narborough	d									17 29												18 25			
Hinckley	d									17 38												18 34			
Nuneaton	d			17 08						17 45							18 08					18 41			19 08
Coleshill Parkway	d			17 23						18 00							18 23					18 56			19 23
Water Orton	d																								
Birmingham New Street 12	a		17 27	17 36				18 01		18 15		18 19			18 24		18 36				19 04	19 15	19 24	19 27	19 36
	d					17 42		18 12				18 30								18 42	19 12		19 30		
Worcester Shrub Hill 7	d										18 40														
Ashchurch for Tewkesbury	d										18 55														
Cheltenham Spa	d					18 25	18 35	18 52			19 06	19 13								19 25	19 52		20 11		
Gloucester 7	a						18 46				19 17	19 26											20 23		
Bristol Parkway 7	a					18 56		19 21			19 57									20 03	20 21				
Bristol Temple Meads 10	a					19 08		19 35			20 11									20 14	20 35				
Newport (South Wales)	a						19 54					20 11											21 12		
Cardiff Central 7	a						20 12					20 31											21 32		

		EM	AW	XC		XC	XC	XC	EM	XC	XC	EM	GW	XC		XC	XC	XC	XC	XC	EM	GW	XC	XC
		◇1		◇1		◇1	1	◇1		◇1	◇1	◇1		◇1		◇1	1	◇1	◇1	◇1	◇1		◇1	1
		M		E		F			J	N	C	D		E		O			P	C	D		Q	
		🍴		☕		☕		☕		☕		🍴				☕			☕		🍴			
Nottingham 8	d							19 10	19 22									20 10						
Beeston	d								19 27															
Attenborough	d								19 31															
Long Eaton	d								19 38															
Derby 6	a							19 30	19 50									20 29						
	d	19 22				19 27		19 36		19 56		20 06				20 27		20 36	20 54		21 06		21 27	
Willington	d																							
Burton-on-Trent	d					19 38		19 48										20 48					21 37	
Tamworth	d							20 00								20 45		21 00					21 47	
Wilnecote	d							20 04																
Leicester	d	19a55					19 19				19 49	20a42					20 19			20 49	21a35			21 19
South Wigston	d						19 24										20 24							21 24
Narborough	d						19 29										20 29							21 29
Hinckley	d						19 37										20 38							21 38
Nuneaton	d						19 43				20 08						20 44			21 08				21 45
Coleshill Parkway	d						19 59				20 23						21 00			21 23				22 00
Water Orton	d																							
Birmingham New Street 12	a					20 05	20 15	20 24		20 27	20 36					21 03	21 15	21 19	21 28	21 36			22 04	22 15
	d			19 42		20 12								20 42		21 12							22 12	
Worcester Shrub Hill 7	d												20 37											
Ashchurch for Tewkesbury	d												20 53											
Cheltenham Spa	d		20 18	20 25		20 52							21 03	21 25		21 52						22 01	22 52	
Gloucester 7	a		20 29										21 13			22 02						22 12		
Bristol Parkway 7	a			20 57		21 21							21 53	21 59		22 34							23 22	
Bristol Temple Meads 10	a			21 08		21 32							22 07	22 10		22 45							23 33	
Newport (South Wales)	a		21 31																					
Cardiff Central 7	a		21 49																					

A To St Pancras International
B From Newcastle to Reading
C From Stansted Airport
D From Sheffield to St Pancras International
E From Manchester Piccadilly
F From Glasgow Central to Exeter St Davids
G ☕ to Newport (South Wales)
H From St Pancras International to Sheffield
I From Edinburgh to Reading
J To Matlock
K From Aberdeen to Exeter St Davids
L ☕ to Birmingham New Street
M From York to St Pancras International
N From Newcastle to Guildford
O From Glasgow Central. ☕ to Birmingham New Street
P From Newcastle
Q From Edinburgh

Table 57

Sundays

19 February to 25 March

Nottingham, Derby and Leicester Birmingham - Cardiff and Bristol

Network Diagram - see first Page of Table 50

		XC	EM	XC	XC	XC	XC	EM
		◇1		◇1	◇1	◇1	1	◇1
			A	B	C	D		E
				[trolley]				[restaurant]
Nottingham 8 [tram]	d	21 08	21 24					
Beeston	d		21 29					
Attenborough	d		21 33					
Long Eaton	d		21 40					23 32
Derby 6	a	21 31	21 52					23 42
	d	21 36		21 53		22 26		
Willington	d							
Burton-on-Trent	d	21 48		22 03		22 37		
Tamworth	d	22 00		22 14		22 47		
Wilnecote	d	22 04						
Leicester	d				21 49		23 19	
South Wigston	d						23 24	
Narborough	d						23 29	
Hinckley	d						23 38	
Nuneaton	d				22 08		23 45	
Coleshill Parkway	d				22 23		00 02	
Water Orton	d							
Birmingham New Street 12	a	22 23		22 30	22 36	23 04	00 15	
	d							
Worcester Shrub Hill 7	d							
Ashchurch for Tewkesbury	d							
Cheltenham Spa	d							
Gloucester 7	a							
Bristol Parkway 7	a							
Bristol Temple Meads 10	a							
Newport (South Wales)	a							
Cardiff Central 7	a							

Sundays

from 1 April

		EM	EM	EM	GW	XC	GW	GW	XC	XC	EM	EM	GW	XC	GW	XC	EM	EM	AW	XC	XC	GW	XC
		◇1	◇1	◇1		◇1			◇1	◇1	◇1			◇1		◇1	◇1	◇1		◇1	1		◇1
		F	F	G	H	I	J	H		K	G	A	H			K	L	G		M		H	N
		[restaurant]	[restaurant]	[restaurant]		[trolley]			[trolley]	[trolley]	[restaurant]			[trolley]		[trolley]	[restaurant]	[restaurant]		[trolley]			[trolley]
Nottingham 8 [tram]	d											09 22											11 11
Beeston	d											09 27											
Attenborough	d											09 31											
Long Eaton	d											09 39					10 30						
Derby 6	a											09 50					10 41						11 31
	d	06 44	07 45	08 41						09 28	09 44					10 34		10 42		11 30			11 36
Willington	d																						
Burton-on-Trent	d																			11 41			11 48
Tamworth	d															10 53							12 00
Wilnecote	d																						
Leicester	d	07a19	08a22	09a21							10a22							11a21			11 19		
South Wigston	d																						
Narborough	d																				11 28		
Hinckley	d																				11 36		
Nuneaton	d																				11 42		
Coleshill Parkway	d																				11 57		
Water Orton	d																						
Birmingham New Street 12	a									10 19						11 20				12 04	12 14		12 24
	d					09 12			10 12	10 30				11 12		11 30				12 12			12 30
Worcester Shrub Hill 7	d																						
Ashchurch for Tewkesbury	d																						
Cheltenham Spa	d				09 24	09 52	10 05	10 24	10 53	11 10			11 24	11 53	12 00	12 10			12 18	12 52		13 01	13 11
Gloucester 7	a				09 34		10 15	10 34	11 03				11 34	12 03	12 11				12 28			13 11	13 21
Bristol Parkway 7	a					10 21	10 52			11 39					12 54	12 39				13 21			
Bristol Temple Meads 10	a					10 32	11 07			11 52					13 10	12 51				13 32			
Newport (South Wales)	a								11 48					12 52					13 33				14 06
Cardiff Central 7	a								12 08					13 12					13 52				14 26

A To Matlock
B From Newcastle
C From Stansted Airport
D From Glasgow Central
E From St Pancras International to Sheffield
F To St Pancras International
G From Sheffield to St Pancras International
H To Swindon
I To Penzance
J To Taunton
K From Leeds to Plymouth
L From Leicester to York
M From York to Plymouth
N [trolley] to Newport (South Wales)

Table 57

Sundays

from 1 April

Nottingham, Derby and Leicester
Birmingham - Cardiff and Bristol

Network Diagram - see first Page of Table 50

		EM	EM	EM	XC	XC		XC	XC	EM	EM	AW	XC	GW	XC	XC		GW	XC	EM	XC	XC	EM	EM	XC
			◇1	◇1	◇1	1		◇1	◇1	◇1	◇1		◇1		◇1	1			◇1		◇1	◇1	◇1	◇1	◇1
		A	B	C	D			E	F	C	G			H	I			J	E	A	K	F	G	C	L
Nottingham 8	d	11 22						12 10											13 06	13 22					
Beeston	d	11 27																		13 27					
Attenborough	d	11 31																		13 31					
Long Eaton	d	11 39		11 52						12 51										13 39				13 48	
Derby 6	a	11 47		12 02				12 30		13 01									13 26	13 50				13 58	
	d		11 48		12 30			12 36			13 02				13 32				13 36		13 54		13 54		
Willington	d																								
Burton-on-Trent	d							12 48							13 43				13 48						
Tamworth	d				12 48			13 00											14 00						
Wilnecote	d																								
Leicester	d		12a21			12 19			12 49		13a34					13 19						13 49	14a29		
South Wigston	d					12 24																			
Narborough	d					12 29										13 28									
Hinckley	d					12 38										13 36									
Nuneaton	d					12 45			13 08							13 43						14 08			
Coleshill Parkway	d					13 00			13 23							13 59						14 23			
Water Orton	d																								
Birmingham New Street 12	a				13 05	13 15		13 24	13 36						14 08	14 15			14 24		14 27	14 36			
	d				13 12			13 30					13 42		14 12				14 30						14 42
Worcester Shrub Hill 7	d																	14 36							
Ashchurch for Tewkesbury	d																	14 51							
Cheltenham Spa	d				13 52			14 12				14 18	14 24	14 46	14 52			15 01	15 11						15 25
Gloucester 7	a							14 22				14 29		14 56				15 10	15 21						
Bristol Parkway 7	a				14 21								14 54		15 24			15 49							15 59
Bristol Temple Meads 10	a				14 32								15 07		15 36			16 09							16 11
Newport (South Wales)	a							15 08				15 34							16 06						
Cardiff Central 7	a							15 31				15 53							16 26						

		GW		XC	XC	XC	EM	XC	XC	EM	AW	XC		GW	XC	XC	GW	XC	EM	EM	XC	XC		EM	EM
		◇1		◇1	1	◇1	◇1	◇1	◇1	◇1		◇1			◇1	1		◇1	◇1		◇1	◇1		◇1	◇1
		M		N		E	G	O	F	C		P		H	I				B	A	Q	F		C	G
Nottingham 8	d					14 10												15 10		15 22					
Beeston	d																			15 27					
Attenborough	d																			15 31					
Long Eaton	d									14 53										15 39				15 51	
Derby 6	a					14 29				15 04								15 30		15 50				16 02	
	d			14 31		14 35	14 37	14 53							15 26			15 35	15 42		15 54				16 14
Willington	d																								
Burton-on-Trent	d					14 48									15 38			15 48							
Tamworth	d			14 50		15 00												16 00							
Wilnecote	d																	16 03							
Leicester	d				14 19		15a11		14 49							15 19			16a17			15 49			16a40
South Wigston	d				14 24																				
Narborough	d				14 29											15 28									
Hinckley	d				14 38											15 36									
Nuneaton	d				14 45				15 08							15 43						16 07			
Coleshill Parkway	d				15 00				15 23							15 58						16 22			
Water Orton	d																								
Birmingham New Street 12	a			15 06	15 15	15 21		15 27	15 36						16 01	16 15		16 24			16 27	16 36			
	d			15 12		15 30						15 42			16 12			16 30							
Worcester Shrub Hill 7	d																16 40								
Ashchurch for Tewkesbury	d																16 58								
Cheltenham Spa	d	15 46		15 52		16 11					16 18	16 25		16 33	16 51		17 08	17 11							
Gloucester 7	a	15 57				16 21					16 29			16 43			17 16	17 21							
Bristol Parkway 7	a			16 21								16 55			17 20		17 57								
Bristol Temple Meads 10	a			16 35								17 08			17 35		18 10								
Newport (South Wales)	a					17 06					17 37							18 07							
Cardiff Central 7	a					17 27					17 57							18 29							

A To Matlock
B From Leeds to St Pancras International
C From St Pancras International to Sheffield
D From Newcastle to Plymouth
E to Newport (South Wales)
F From Stansted Airport
G From Sheffield to St Pancras International
H To Swindon
I From Edinburgh to Plymouth
J To Weston-super-Mare
K To Reading
L From Manchester Piccadilly to Paignton
M To London Paddington
N From Edinburgh to Penzance
O From Sheffield to Reading
P From Manchester Piccadilly
Q From Newcastle to Reading

Table 57

Sundays
from 1 April

Nottingham, Derby and Leicester
Birmingham - Cardiff and Bristol

Network Diagram - see first Page of Table 50

		XC ◇1 A ⊼	GW ◇1 B ⊐P	XC ◇1 C ⊼	XC 1	XC ◇1 D ⊼	EM ◇1 E ⊐P	XC ◇1 F ⊼		EM ◇1 G ⊐P	XC ◇1 H ⊼	EM ◇1 I ⊐P	XC ◇1 A ⊼	AW	XC ◇1 J ⊼	XC 1	GW	XC ◇1 D ⊼		EM ◇1 E ⊐P	EM K	XC ◇1 L ⊼	EM ◇1 M ⊐P	XC ◇1 H	EM ◇1 I ⊐P
Nottingham 8	d					16 10												17 10			17 23				
Beeston	d																				17 28				
Attenborough	d																				17 32				
Long Eaton	d									16 47											17 40		17 47		
Derby 6	a					16 30				16 58								17 29			17 51		17 58		
	d			16 29		16 35	16 47	16 55				17 05			17 27			17 36		17 47		17 54			18 04
Willington	d																								
Burton-on-Trent	d					16 48									17 38			17 48							
Tamworth	d			16 48		17 00												18 00							
Wilnecote	d																								
Leicester	d				16 19		17a20				16 49	17a35				17 17				18a19				17 49	18a33
South Wigston	d				16 24											17 24									
Narborough	d				16 29											17 29									
Hinckley	d				16 38											17 38									
Nuneaton	d				16 45						17 08					17 45								18 08	
Coleshill Parkway	d				17 00						17 23					18 00								18 23	
Water Orton	d																								
Birmingham New Street 12	a			17 04	17 15	17 19		17 27			17 36				18 01	18 15		18 19				18 24		18 36	
	d	16 42		17 12		17 30							17 42		18 12			18 30							
Worcester Shrub Hill 7	d																18 40								
Ashchurch for Tewkesbury	d																18 55								
Cheltenham Spa	d	17 25	17 46	17 52		18 11							18 25	18 35	18 52		19 06	19 13							
Gloucester 7	a		17 56			18 22								18 46			19 17	19 26							
Bristol Parkway 7	a	18 02		18 22									18 56		19 21		19 57								
Bristol Temple Meads 10	a	18 13		18 40									19 08		19 35		20 11								
Newport (South Wales)	a					19 07								19 54				20 11							
Cardiff Central 7	a					19 27								20 12				20 31							

		XC ◇1 N ⊼	XC ◇1 O ⊼	XC 1		GW ◇1 B ⊐P	XC ◇1 P ⊼	XC ◇1 F ⊼	XC ◇1 H	EM ◇1 Q ⊐P	AW	XC ◇1 A ⊼	XC ◇1 J ⊼	XC 1		XC ◇1 ⊼	EM K	XC ◇1 R ⊼	XC ◇1 H	EM ◇1 I ⊐P	GW	XC ◇1 A	GW S	XC ◇1 T ⊼	
Nottingham 8	d						18 10									19 10	19 14								
Beeston	d																19 19								
Attenborough	d																19 23								
Long Eaton	d																19 30								
Derby 6	a						18 30									19 30	19 44								
	d		18 26				18 35	18 55		19 05			19 27			19 36		19 55		20 05				20 27	
Willington	d																								
Burton-on-Trent	d						18 48						19 38			19 48									
Tamworth	d		18 45				19 00									20 00								20 45	
Wilnecote	d															20 04									
Leicester	d			18 16					18 49	19a38				19 19					19 49	20a41					
South Wigston	d													19 24											
Narborough	d			18 25										19 29											
Hinckley	d			18 34										19 37											
Nuneaton	d			18 41					19 08					19 43					20 08						
Coleshill Parkway	d			18 56					19 23					19 59					20 23						
Water Orton	d																								
Birmingham New Street 12	a		19 04	19 15			19 20	19 27	19 36				20 05	20 15		20 24		20 27	20 36					21 03	
	d	18 42	19 12				19 30					19 42	20 12									20 42		21 12	
Worcester Shrub Hill 7	d																				20 37				
Ashchurch for Tewkesbury	d																				20 53				
Cheltenham Spa	d	19 25	19 52			20 05	20 11				20 18	20 25	20 52								21 03	21 25	21 46	21 52	
Gloucester 7	a					20 15	20 21				20 29										21 13		21 56	22 02	
Bristol Parkway 7	a	20 03	20 21									20 57	21 21								21 53	21 59		22 34	
Bristol Temple Meads 10	a	20 14	20 35									21 08	21 32								22 07	22 10		22 45	
Newport (South Wales)	a						21 06				21 31														
Cardiff Central 7	a						21 26				21 49														

A From Manchester Piccadilly
B To London Paddington
C From Glasgow Central to Penzance
D ⊼ to Newport (South Wales)
E To St Pancras International
F From Newcastle to Reading
G From St Pancras International to Leeds
H From Stansted Airport
I From Sheffield to St Pancras International
J From Glasgow Central to Plymouth
K To Matlock
L From Edinburgh to Reading
M From St Pancras International to Sheffield
N From Manchester Piccadilly to Plymouth
O From Aberdeen to Plymouth
P ⊼ to Birmingham New Street
Q From York to St Pancras International
R From Newcastle to Guildford
S To Swindon
T From Glasgow Central. ⊼ to Birmingham New Street

Table 57

Sundays
from 1 April

Nottingham, Derby and Leicester
Birmingham - Cardiff and Bristol

Network Diagram - see first Page of Table 50

		XC	XC	XC	XC	EM	GW	XC	XC	XC		XC	EM	XC	XC	XC	XC	EM
		1	◇1	◇1	◇1	◇1		◇1	◇1	1		◇1		◇1	◇1	◇1	1	◇1
				A	B	C		D	E				F	A	B	G		H
				✠		☕								✠				☕
Nottingham 8	d		20 10									21 08	21 20					
Beeston	d												21 25					
Attenborough	d												21 29					
Long Eaton	d												21 36					23 40
Derby 6	a		20 29									21 31	21 48					23 50
	d		20 36	20 54		21 01			21 27			21 36		21 53		22 26		
Willington	d																	
Burton-on-Trent	d		20 48						21 37			21 48		22 03		22 37		
Tamworth	d		21 00						21 47			22 00		22 14		22 47		
Wilnecote	d											22 04						
Leicester	d	20 19			20 49	21a31				21 19					21 49		23 19	
South Wigston	d	20 24								21 24							23 24	
Narborough	d	20 29								21 29							23 29	
Hinckley	d	20 38								21 38							23 38	
Nuneaton	d	20 44			21 08					21 45					22 08		23 45	
Coleshill Parkway	d	21 00			21 23					22 00					22 23		00 02	
Water Orton	d																	
Birmingham New Street 12	a	21 15	21 19	21 28	21 36				22 04	22 15		22 23		22 30	22 36	23 04	00 15	
	d							21 43	22 12									
Worcester Shrub Hill 7	d																	
Ashchurch for Tewkesbury	d																	
Cheltenham Spa	d						22 01	22 24	22 52									
Gloucester 7	a						22 12											
Bristol Parkway 7	a							22 53	23 22									
Bristol Temple Meads 10	a							23 07	23 33									
Newport (South Wales)	a																	
Cardiff Central 7	a																	

A From Newcastle
B From Stansted Airport
C From Sheffield to St Pancras International
D From Manchester Piccadilly
E From Edinburgh
F To Matlock
G From Glasgow Central
H From St Pancras International to Sheffield

Table 57

Bristol and Cardiff - Birmingham Leicester, Derby and Nottingham

Network Diagram - see first Page of Table 50

Miles	Miles	Miles			XC MX ◇1	XC MX ◇1	XC ◇1 A	XC 1	XC ◇1 B 🛒	GW	XC 1 🛒	XC ◇1 A 🛒	XC ◇1 C 🛒		XC 1	XC 1	XC ◇1 D 🛒	XC 1 🛒	XC ◇1 A 🛒	XC ◇1 C 🛒	XC 1	XC 1	XC ◇1 E 🛒		XC ◇1 F 🛒
0	—	—	**Cardiff Central 7**	d		21p50																			
11¾	—	—	Newport (South Wales)	d		22p05																			
—	—	0	**Bristol Temple Meads 10**	d																			06 27		
—	—	5¾	Bristol Parkway 7	d																			06 40		
56½	—	—	Gloucester 7	d		22p47				06 00															07 10
63	—	46¼	Cheltenham Spa	d		22p58				06 11													07 12		07 21
70¼	—	53½	Ashchurch for Tewkesbury	d						06 20															07 29
85	—	—	Worcester Shrub Hill 7	a						06 40															
112	0	92¾	**Birmingham New Street 12**	a		00 01																	07 56		08 16
—	—	—		d	23p09		05 22	05 52	06 00		06 19	06 22	06 30		06 49	06 52	07 03	07 19	07 22	07 30	07 49	07 52	08 03		08 22
119¾	7¾	—	Water Orton	d																					
—	9½	—	Coleshill Parkway	d			05 35	06 05				06 35				07 05			07 35			08 05			08 35
—	20	—	Nuneaton	d			05 52	06 21				06 52				07 22			07 51			08 22			08 52
—	25¼	—	Hinckley	d				06 29								07 29			07 58			08 29			
—	34	—	Narborough	d				06 37								07 37			08 06			08 37			
—	37	—	South Wigston	d				06 42								07 42			08 10			08 42			
—	38¾	—	**Leicester**	a			06 13	06 50				07 17				07 48			08 15			08 48			09 14
127	—	—	Wilnecote	d	23p24						06 35							07 34							
128¾	—	—	Tamworth	d	23p28						06 39				07 07		07 19	07 38			08 07		08 19		
141¾	—	—	Burton-on-Trent	d	23p40						06 51				07 19		07 29	07 50			08 19		08 29		
146½	—	—	Willington	d	23p45										07 25						08 25				
152¾	—	—	**Derby 6**	a	23p55				06 32		07 05		07 11		07 34		07 42	08 05		08 11	08 34		08 42		
—	—	—		d	23p59						07 10				07 40			08 10			08 40				
161	—	—	Long Eaton	d							07 25				07 49			08 19							
164	—	—	Attenborough	d							07 31														
165½	—	—	Beeston	d							07 35				07 58			08 27							
168¾	—	—	**Nottingham 8**	a	00 18						07 41				08 08			08 33			09 05				

		GW G	XC 1 🛒	XC ◇1 H 🛒	XC ◇1 I 🛒	XC ◇1	XC 1	XC ◇1 J 🛒	XC 1 🛒		XC ◇1 A 🛒	XC ◇1 K 🛒	XC ◇1 L 🛒	XC ◇1 M 🛒	XC 1	XC ◇1 N 🛒	XC 1	XC ◇1 A 🛒	XC ◇1 O 🛒		GW P	XC ◇1 Q 🛒	XC ◇1 M 🛒	XC 1	XC ◇1 J 🛒
Cardiff Central 7	d					06 40						07 00		07 45									08 45		
Newport (South Wales)	d					06 55						07 15		08 02									09 02		
Bristol Temple Meads 10	d			07 00				07 30				08 00				08 30			09 00		08 41				09 30
Bristol Parkway 7	d			07 10				07 40				08 10				08 40			09 10		08 52				09 40
Gloucester 7	d	07 14				07 46								08 46							09 37		09 46		
Cheltenham Spa	d	07 25		07 42		07 57		08 12				08 42		08 57		09 12			09 42		09 48		09 57		10 12
Ashchurch for Tewkesbury	d	07 34				08 05															09 56				
Worcester Shrub Hill 7	a	07 54																			10 14				
Birmingham New Street 12	a			08 26		08 45		08 56				09 26		09 45		09 56			10 26				10 45		10 56
	d		08 19		08 30	08 49	08 52	09 03	09 19		09 22		09 30	09 49	09 52	10 03	10 19	10 22				10 30	10 49	10 52	11 03
Water Orton	d						09 03																	11 03	
Coleshill Parkway	d						09 07				09 35				10 07			10 35						11 07	
Nuneaton	d						09 22				09 52				10 23			10 52						11 23	
Hinckley	d						09 30								10 30									11 30	
Narborough	d						09 39								10 39									11 39	
South Wigston	d														10 44										
Leicester	a						09 49				10 15				10 50			11 15						11 48	
Wilnecote	d					09 05																	11 05		
Tamworth	d		08 36			09 09			09 36					10 07		10 19	10 36						11 09		
Burton-on-Trent	d		08 48			09 21		09 26	09 48					10 19			10 48						11 21		11 26
Willington	d													10 25											
Derby 6	a		08 59		09 05	09 34		09 39	09 59				10 05	10 34		10 40	10 59					11 05	11 33		11 39
	d		09 05			09 39			10 05					10 41			11 05						11 39		
Long Eaton	d		09 14						10 14								11 14								
Attenborough	d		09 21																						
Beeston	d		09 24						10 22								11 22								
Nottingham 8	a		09 33			10 05			10 32					11 05			11 32						12 05		

A To Stansted Airport
B To Glasgow Central
C To Newcastle
D To Edinburgh
E From Bath Spa to Glasgow Central
F To Stansted Airport. 🛒 from Birmingham New Street
G To Great Malvern
H To Manchester Piccadilly
I From Guildford to Newcastle
J From Plymouth to Edinburgh
K To Manchester Piccadilly. 🛒 from Bristol Temple Meads
L From Reading to Newcastle
M 🛒 from Newport (South Wales)
N From Plymouth to Glasgow Central
O From Paignton to Manchester Piccadilly
P From Warminster to Great Malvern
Q From Winchester to Newcastle

Bristol and Cardiff - Birmingham
Leicester, Derby and Nottingham

Network Diagram - see first Page of Table 50

		XC	XC	XC	XC		XC	XC	XC	XC	XC	XC	GW	XC	XC		XC	XC	XC	XC	XC	XC	XC	XC	XC
		1	◇1	◇1	◇1		◇1	1	◇1	1	◇1	◇1	◇	◇1	◇1		1	◇1	1	◇1	◇1	◇1	◇1	1	◇1
			A	B	C		D		E		A	B	F	G	D			H		A	I	C	D		E
			🛒	🛒	🛒		🛒		🛒	🛒	🛒	🛒		🛒	🛒			🛒		🛒	🛒	🛒	🛒		🛒
Cardiff Central 7	d						09 45								10 45								11 45		
Newport (South Wales)	d						10 00								11 00								12 02		
Bristol Temple Meads 10	d			10 00					10 30			11 00	10 41					11 30			12 00				12 30
Bristol Parkway 7	d			10 10					10 40			11 10	10 52					11 40			12 10				12 40
Gloucester 7	d						10 46						11 35		11 46								12 46		
Cheltenham Spa	d			10 42			10 57		11 12			11 42	11 48		11 57			12 12			12 42		12 57		13 12
Ashchurch for Tewkesbury	d												11 56										13 05		
Worcester Shrub Hill 7	a												12 14												
Birmingham New Street 12	a			11 26			11 45		11 58			12 26			12 45			12 56			13 26		13 45		13 56
	d	11 19	11 22		11 30		11 49	11 52	12 03	12 19	12 22			12 30	12 49		12 52	13 03	13 19	13 22		13 30	13 49	13 52	14 03
Water Orton	d																13 03								
Coleshill Parkway	d		11 35					12 07			12 35						13 07			13 35				14 07	
Nuneaton	d		11 52					12 23			12 52						13 22			13 52				14 23	
Hinckley	d							12 30									13 29							14 30	
Narborough	d							12 38									13 38							14 39	
South Wigston	d							12 43																14 43	
Leicester	a		12 13					12 49			13 13						13 50			14 14				14 50	
Wilnecote	d														13 05								14 05		
Tamworth	d	11 36					12 07		12 19	12 37					13 09				13 36				14 09		14 19
Burton-on-Trent	d	11 48					12 19			12 50					13 20			13 28	13 48				14 21		
Willington	d						12 25																		
Derby 6	a	11 59			12 05		12 33		12 41	13 05				13 08	13 34			13 40	13 59			14 05	14 34		14 40
	d	12 05					12 39			13 10					13 39				14 05				14 39		
Long Eaton	d	12 14								13 19									14 14						
Attenborough	d																								
Beeston	d	12 22								13 27									14 24						
Nottingham 8 🚊	a	12 32					13 05			13 33					14 05				14 32				15 05		

			XC	XC	XC	GW	XC	XC	XC	XC	XC		XC	XC	XC	XC	XC	XC	XC	XC	XC		XC	GW	XC
			1	◇1	◇1	◇	◇1	◇1	1	◇1	1		◇1	◇1	◇1	◇1	1	◇1	1	1	◇1		◇1	◇	◇1
				A	B	J	G	D		K			A	L	C	D		M			A		B	F	N
				🛒	🛒		🛒	🛒		🛒			🛒	🛒	🛒	🛒		🛒			🛒		🛒		🛒
Cardiff Central 7	d							12 45								13 45									
Newport (South Wales)	d							13 01								14 00									
Bristol Temple Meads 10	d				13 00	12 41				13 30				14 00				14 30					15 00	14 41	
Bristol Parkway 7	d				13 10	12 52				13 40				14 10				14 40					15 10	14 52	
Gloucester 7	d					13 37		13 46								14 46								15 36	
Cheltenham Spa	d				13 42	13 48		13 57		14 12				14 42		14 57		15 12					15 42	15 48	
Ashchurch for Tewkesbury	d					13 56																		15 56	
Worcester Shrub Hill 7	a					14 14																		16 15	
Birmingham New Street 12	a				14 26			14 45		14 56				15 26		15 45		15 56					16 26		
	d		14 19	14 22			14 30	14 49	14 52	15 03	15 19		15 22		15 30	15 49	15 52	16 03	16 09	16 19	16 22				16 30
Water Orton	d								15 03										16 19						
Coleshill Parkway	d			14 35					15 07				15 35				16 07		16 23		16 35				
Nuneaton	d			14 52					15 22				15 52				16 23		16 39		16 52				
Hinckley	d								15 30								16 30		16 46						
Narborough	d								15 38								16 39		16 55						
South Wigston	d																16 43								
Leicester	a			15 14					15 50				16 14				16 50		17 06		17 14				
Wilnecote	d							15 05								16 05									
Tamworth	d		14 36					15 09			15 36					16 09		16 19		16 39					
Burton-on-Trent	d		14 48					15 21		15 26	15 48					16 21				16 51					
Willington	d																								
Derby 6	a		15 00				15 06	15 34		15 39	16 00				16 06	16 34		16 40		17 05					17 08
	d		15 05					15 39			16 05					16 39				17 10					
Long Eaton	d		15 14								16 14									17 19					
Attenborough	d																								
Beeston	d		15 22								16 22									17 27					
Nottingham 8 🚊	a		15 32					16 05			16 32					17 05				17 33					

A To Stansted Airport
B To Manchester Piccadilly
C From Reading to Newcastle
D 🛒 from Newport (South Wales)
E From Penzance to Glasgow Central
F From Southampton Central to Great Malvern
G From Southampton Central to Newcastle
H From Plymouth to Aberdeen
I From Paignton to Manchester Piccadilly
J From Brighton to Great Malvern
K From Plymouth to Dundee
L From Penzance to Manchester Piccadilly
M From Plymouth to Glasgow Central
N From Southampton Central to Edinburgh

Bristol and Cardiff - Birmingham Leicester, Derby and Nottingham

Network Diagram - see first Page of Table 50

		XC ◇1 A 🚲	XC ◇1 B	XC ◇1 C 🚲	XC 1	XC 1	XC ◇1 D		XC ◇1 E 🚲	XC ◇1 F 🚲	XC 1	XC ◇1	XC 1	XC ◇1 C 🚲	XC 1	XC ◇1 D	XC ◇1 G 🚲		GW H	XC ◇1 I 🚲	XC ◇1	XC 1	XC ◇1 J 🚲	XC 1	XC ◇1 D
Cardiff Central 7	d	14 45										15 45									16 45				
Newport (South Wales)	d	15 01										16 00									17 00				
Bristol Temple Meads 10	d			15 30					16 00					16 30			17 00		16 41				17 30		
Bristol Parkway 7	d			15 40					16 10					16 40			17 10		16 52				17 40		
Gloucester 7	d	15 46										16 46							17 37		17 46				
Cheltenham Spa	d	15 57		16 12					16 42			16 57		17 12			17 42		17 48		17 58		18 12		
Ashchurch for Tewkesbury	d																		17 56						
Worcester Shrub Hill 7	a																		18 18						
Birmingham New Street 12	a	16 45		16 58					17 26			17 45		17 56			18 26				18 45		18 55		
	d	16 49	16 52	17 03	17 09	17 19	17 22			17 30	17 39	17 49	17 52	18 03	18 19	18 22				18 30	18 49	18 52	19 03	19 19	19 22
Water Orton	d				17 23						17 50		18 03												
Coleshill Parkway	d		17 05		17 27		17 35						18 07			18 35						19 07			19 35
Nuneaton	d		17 22		17 44		17 52						18 23			18 52						19 23			19 52
Hinckley	d		17 29		17 51								18 30									19 30			
Narborough	d		17 39										18 39									19 39			
South Wigston	d				18 03								18 44									19 44			
Leicester	a		17 50		18 09		18 15						18 50			19 13						19 50			20 16
Wilnecote	d	17 05									17 58										19 05				
Tamworth	d	17 09				17 36					18 02	18 09		18 19	18 36						19 09			19 36	
Burton-on-Trent	d	17 21		17 26		17 48					18 13	18 21			18 48						19 22		19 26	19 48	
Willington	d										18 19														
Derby 6	a	17 34		17 38		17 59				18 05	18 31	18 34		18 40	18 59					19 05	19 34		19 39	19 59	
	d	17 39				18 05						18 39			19 05						19 39			20 05	
Long Eaton	d					18 14									19 14									20 14	
Attenborough	d																								
Beeston	d					18 26									19 23									20 23	
Nottingham 8	a	18 05				18 32						19 05			19 32						20 03			20 32	

		XC ◇1 K 🚲	XC ◇1 F 🚲		XC ◇1 L 🚲	XC 1	XC ◇1 M 🚲	XC ◇1 B	XC ◇1 G 🚲	GW H	XC ◇1 N	XC ◇1	XC ◇1 M 🚲		XC 1	XC ◇1	XC ◇1	XC ◇1	XC ◇1 O	GW	GW ◇1 P	XC 1	XC ◇1		XC ◇1
Cardiff Central 7	d				17 45							18 45					19 50								21 05
Newport (South Wales)	d				18 00							19 01					20 05								21 21
Bristol Temple Meads 10	d	18 00					18 30		19 00	18 41			19 30			20 00			20 30	20 41					
Bristol Parkway 7	d	18 10					18 40		19 10	18 52			19 40			20 10			20 40	20 52					
Gloucester 7	d				18 46					19 38		19 46				20 46	20 58			21 34	21 52				22 04
Cheltenham Spa	d	18 42			18 57		19 12		19 42	19 48		19 58	20 12			20 56	21 09		21 17	21 45	22 04				22 15
Ashchurch for Tewkesbury	d									19 56		20 05								21 54					22 23
Worcester Shrub Hill 7	a									20 15										22 14	22 24				
Birmingham New Street 12	a	19 26			19 45		19 56		20 28			20 45	20 52			21 46	21 51		22 06						23 36
	d		19 30		19 49	19 52	20 03	20 22			20 30	20 49	21 03		20 52			22 03				22 22	23 09		
Water Orton	d					20 03																			
Coleshill Parkway	d					20 07		20 35							21 05							22 35			
Nuneaton	d					20 23		20 52							21 22							22 52			
Hinckley	d					20 30									21 29							22 59			
Narborough	d					20 39									21 38							23 08			
South Wigston	d					20 44									21 42							23 12			
Leicester	a					20 50		21 14							21 50							23 18			
Wilnecote	d				20 05							21 05											23 24		
Tamworth	d				20 09		20 19					21 09	21 19					22 28					23 28		
Burton-on-Trent	d				20 21							21 21	21 30					22 40					23 40		
Willington	d																						23 45		
Derby 6	a		20 05		20 34		20 42				21 11	21 34	21 43					22 54					23 55		
	d				20 40							21 40						22 59					23 59		
Long Eaton	d				20 49							21 52						23 11							
Attenborough	d											21 58						23 17							
Beeston	d				20 58							22 02						23 20							
Nottingham 8	a				21 06							22 08						23 27					00 18		

A 🚲 from Newport (South Wales)
B To Cambridge
C From Plymouth to Edinburgh
D To Stansted Airport
E From Paignton to Manchester Piccadilly
F From Reading to Newcastle
G To Manchester Piccadilly
H From Warminster to Great Malvern
I From Southampton Central to Newcastle
J From Plymouth to Leeds
K From Exeter St Davids to Manchester Piccadilly
L 🚲 from Newport (South Wales) to Birmingham New Street
M From Plymouth to Leeds. 🚲 to Birmingham New Street
N From Southampton Central to Leeds
O From Plymouth
P From London Paddington

Bristol and Cardiff - Birmingham Leicester, Derby and Nottingham

Network Diagram - see first Page of Table 50

		XC ◇1 A	XC ◇1
Cardiff Central 7	d		21 50
Newport (South Wales)	d		22 05
Bristol Temple Meads 10	d	22 00	
Bristol Parkway 7	d	22 10	
Gloucester 7	d		22 47
Cheltenham Spa	d	22 42	22 58
Ashchurch for Tewkesbury	d		
Worcester Shrub Hill 7	a		
Birmingham New Street 12	a	23 44	00 01
	d		
Water Orton	d		
Coleshill Parkway	d		
Nuneaton	d		
Hinckley	d		
Narborough	d		
South Wigston	d		
Leicester	a		
Wilnecote	d		
Tamworth	d		
Burton-on-Trent	d		
Willington	d		
Derby 6	a		
	d		
Long Eaton	d		
Attenborough	d		
Beeston	d		
Nottingham 8 🚊	a		

Saturdays

		XC ◇1	XC ◇1	XC ◇1 B	GW	XC 1	XC ◇1 C 🛒	XC 1 🛒	XC ◇1 B 🛒	XC ◇1 D 🛒		XC 1	XC 1	XC ◇1 E 🛒	XC 1 🛒	XC ◇1 B 🛒	XC ◇1 D 🛒	XC 1	XC 1	XC ◇1 C 🛒		XC ◇1 F 🛒	GW	XC 1 🛒	XC ◇1 G 🛒
Cardiff Central 7	d		21p50																						
Newport (South Wales)	d		22p05																						
Bristol Temple Meads 10	d																			06 15					07 00
Bristol Parkway 7	d																			06 25					07 10
Gloucester 7	d		22p47		05 50															07 01		07 07	07 15		
Cheltenham Spa	d		22p58		06 00															07 12		07 18	07 25		07 42
Ashchurch for Tewkesbury	d				06 09																	07 25	07 34		
Worcester Shrub Hill 7	a				06 33																		07 52		
Birmingham New Street 12	a		00 01																	07 56		08 08			08 26
	d	23p09		05 22		05 52	05 57	06 19	06 22	06 30		06 49	06 52	07 03	07 19	07 22	07 30	07 49	07 52	08 03		08 22		08 19	
Water Orton	d												07 02												
Coleshill Parkway	d			05 35		06 05			06 35				07 06			07 35			08 05			08 35			
Nuneaton	d			05 52		06 21			06 52				07 22			07 52			08 22			08 52			
Hinckley	d					06 28							07 29						08 29						
Narborough	d					06 36							07 37						08 38						
South Wigston	d					06 41							07 42						08 42						
Leicester	a			06 13		06 47			07 13				07 48			08 13			08 48			09 13			
Wilnecote	d	23p24						06 35							07 34										
Tamworth	d	23p28					06 13	06 39		06 46		07 07		07 19	07 38		07 45	08 07		08 19				08 36	
Burton-on-Trent	d	23p40					06 24	06 51		06 56		07 19		07 29	07 50		07 54	08 17		08 29				08 48	
Willington	d	23p45										07 25						08 25							
Derby 6	a	23p55					06 35	07 05		07 09		07 34		07 42	08 05		08 09	08 34		08 42				08 59	
	d	23p59						07 10				07 39			08 10			08 39						09 05	
Long Eaton	d							07 22				07 52			08 19									09 14	
Attenborough	d							07 28																09 21	
Beeston	d							07 32				07 59			08 27									09 24	
Nottingham 8 🚊	a	00 18						07 38				08 08			08 34			09 05						09 33	

A From Paignton
B To Stansted Airport
C To Glasgow Central
D To Newcastle
E To Edinburgh
F To Stansted Airport..
🛒 from Birmingham New Street
G To Manchester Piccadilly

Table 57

Saturdays

Bristol and Cardiff - Birmingham Leicester, Derby and Nottingham

Network Diagram - see first Page of Table 50

		XC ◇1 A 🚲	XC ◇1	XC 1	XC ◇1 B 🚲	XC 1 🚲	XC ◇1 C 🚲	XC ◇1 D 🚲	XC ◇1 E 🚲	XC ◇1 F 🚲	XC 1	XC ◇1 G 🚲	XC 1	XC ◇1 C 🚲	XC ◇1 H 🚲	GW I	XC ◇1 J 🚲	XC ◇1 F 🚲	XC 1	XC ◇1 B 🚲	XC 1	XC ◇1 C 🚲	XC ◇1 D 🚲
Cardiff Central 7	d		06 40					07 00		07 45								08 45					
Newport (South Wales)	d		06 55					07 15		08 00								09 00					
Bristol Temple Meads 10	d				07 30			08 00				08 30			09 00	08 41				09 30			10 00
Bristol Parkway 7	d				07 40			08 10				08 40			09 10	08 52				09 40			10 10
Gloucester 7	d		07 46							08 47						09 38		09 46					
Cheltenham Spa	d		07 57		08 12			08 42		08 58		09 12			09 42	09 48		09 57		10 12			10 42
Ashchurch for Tewkesbury	d		08 04													09 57							
Worcester Shrub Hill 7	a															10 14							
Birmingham New Street 12	a		08 45		08 56			09 26		09 45		09 56			10 26			10 45		10 56			11 26
	d	08 30	08 49	08 52	09 03	09 19	09 22		09 30	09 49	09 52	10 03	10 19	10 22			10 30	10 49	10 52	11 03	11 19	11 22	
Water Orton	d			09 03															11 03				
Coleshill Parkway	d			09 07			09 35				10 07			10 35					11 07			11 35	
Nuneaton	d			09 23			09 52				10 24			10 52					11 23			11 52	
Hinckley	d			09 30							10 31								11 30				
Narborough	d			09 39							10 39								11 39				
South Wigston	d										10 44												
Leicester	a			09 48			10 14				10 50			11 14					11 48			12 14	
Wilnecote	d		09 05															11 05					
Tamworth	d		09 09			09 36				10 07		10 19	10 36					11 09			11 36		
Burton-on-Trent	d		09 21		09 28	09 48				10 19			10 48					11 21		11 28	11 48		
Willington	d									10 25													
Derby 6	a	09 06	09 34		09 41	09 59			10 05	10 34		10 41	10 59				11 05	11 34		11 41	11 59		
	d		09 39			10 05				10 39			11 05					11 39			12 05		
Long Eaton	d					10 14							11 14								12 15		
Attenborough	d																						
Beeston	d					10 22							11 22								12 23		
Nottingham 8	a		10 05			10 33				11 05			11 33					12 05			12 33		

		XC ◇1 K 🚲	XC ◇1 F 🚲	XC 1	XC ◇1 L 🚲	XC 1 🚲	XC ◇1 C 🚲	XC ◇1 D 🚲	GW ◇ M	XC ◇1 J 🚲	XC ◇1 F 🚲	XC 1	XC ◇1 N 🚲	XC 1	XC ◇1 C 🚲	XC ◇1 H 🚲	XC ◇1 K 🚲	XC ◇1 F 🚲	XC 1	XC ◇1 L 🚲	XC 1	XC ◇1 C 🚲
Cardiff Central 7	d		09 45								10 45							11 45				
Newport (South Wales)	d		10 00								11 00							12 00				
Bristol Temple Meads 10	d				10 30			11 00	10 41				11 30			12 00				12 30		
Bristol Parkway 7	d				10 40			11 10	10 52				11 40			12 10				12 40		
Gloucester 7	d		10 46						11 38		11 46							12 46				
Cheltenham Spa	d		10 57		11 12			11 42	11 48		11 57		12 12			12 42		12 57		13 12		
Ashchurch for Tewkesbury	d								11 58									13 05				
Worcester Shrub Hill 7	a								12 15													
Birmingham New Street 12	a		11 45		11 56			12 26			12 45		12 56			13 26		13 45		13 56		
	d	11 30	11 49	11 52	12 03	12 19	12 22			12 30	12 49	12 52	13 03	13 19	13 22		13 30	13 49	13 52	14 03	14 19	14 22
Water Orton	d											13 03										
Coleshill Parkway	d			12 08			12 35					13 07			13 35				14 08			14 35
Nuneaton	d			12 24			12 52					13 23			13 52				14 24			14 52
Hinckley	d			12 31								13 30							14 31			
Narborough	d			12 39								13 39							14 39			
South Wigston	d			12 43															14 44			
Leicester	a			12 49			13 14					13 48			14 14				14 50			15 14
Wilnecote	d										13 05							14 05				
Tamworth	d		12 07		12 19	12 36					13 09			13 36				14 09		14 19	14 36	
Burton-on-Trent	d		12 19			12 48					13 21		13 27	13 50				14 21			14 47	
Willington	d		12 25																			
Derby 6	a	12 05	12 34		12 41	13 05				13 08	13 34		13 41	14 05			14 08	14 35		14 41	14 59	
	d		12 39			13 10					13 39			14 10				14 39			15 05	
Long Eaton	d					13 19								14 19							15 14	
Attenborough	d																					
Beeston	d					13 27								14 27							15 24	
Nottingham 8	a		13 05			13 33					14 05			14 33				15 05			15 33	

A From Guildford to Newcastle
B From Plymouth to Edinburgh
C To Stansted Airport
D To Manchester Piccadilly
E From Bournemouth to Newcastle
F 🚲 from Newport (South Wales)
G From Plymouth to Glasgow Central
H From Paignton to Manchester Piccadilly
I From Warminster to Great Malvern
J From Southampton Central to Newcastle
K From Reading to Newcastle
L From Penzance to Glasgow Central
M From Southampton Central to Worcester Foregate Street
N From Plymouth to Aberdeen

Bristol and Cardiff - Birmingham
Leicester, Derby and Nottingham

Network Diagram - see first Page of Table 50

		XC ◇1 A ⚲	GW ◇ B	XC ◇1 C ⚲	XC ◇1 D ⚲	XC 1	XC ◇1 E ⚲	XC 1		XC ◇1 F ⚲	XC ◇1 G ⚲	XC ◇1 H ⚲	XC ◇1 D ⚲	XC 1	XC ◇1 I ⚲	XC 1	XC ◇1 F ⚲	XC ◇1 A ⚲		GW ◇ J	XC ◇1 C ⚲	XC ◇1 D ⚲	XC 1	XC ◇1 K ⚲	XC 1
Cardiff Central 7	d				12 45								13 45									14 45			
Newport (South Wales)	d				13 00								14 00									15 00			
Bristol Temple Meads 10	d	13 00	12 41				13 30				14 00				14 30			15 00		14 41				15 30	
Bristol Parkway 7	d	13 10	12 52				13 40				14 10				14 40			15 10		14 52				15 40	
Gloucester 7	d		13 38		13 46								14 46							15 38		15 46			
Cheltenham Spa	d	13 42	13 48		13 57		14 12				14 42		14 57		15 12			15 42		15 48		15 57		16 12	
Ashchurch for Tewkesbury	d		13 57																	15 57					
Worcester Shrub Hill 7	a		14 15																	16 14					
Birmingham New Street 12	a	14 26			14 45		14 56				15 26		15 45		15 55			16 26				16 45		16 56	
	d			14 30	14 49	14 52	15 03	15 19		15 22		15 30	15 49	15 52	16 03	16 19	16 22				16 30	16 49	16 52	17 03	17 19
Water Orton	d					15 03																	17 03		
Coleshill Parkway	d					15 07				15 35				16 08			16 35						17 07		
Nuneaton	d					15 23				15 52				16 24			16 52						17 23		
Hinckley	d					15 30								16 31									17 30		
Narborough	d					15 39								16 39									17 39		
South Wigston	d													16 44											
Leicester	a					15 48				16 14				16 50			17 14						17 48		
Wilnecote	d				15 05								16 05									17 05			
Tamworth	d				15 09			15 36					16 09		16 17	16 38						17 09			17 36
Burton-on-Trent	d				15 21		15 27	15 48					16 21			16 50						17 21		17 26	17 48
Willington	d																								
Derby 6	a			15 05	15 34		15 41	15 59				16 05	16 34		16 40	17 05					17 08	17 34		17 41	17 59
	d				15 39			16 05					16 39			17 10						17 39			18 05
Long Eaton	d							16 14								17 19									18 14
Attenborough	d																								
Beeston	d							16 24								17 27									18 22
Nottingham 8	a				16 05			16 33					17 05			17 33						18 05			18 32

		XC ◇1 F	XC ◇1 L ⚲	XC ◇1 H ⚲		XC ◇1	XC 1	XC ◇1 K ⚲	XC 1	XC ◇1 F	XC ◇1 A ⚲	GW M	XC ◇1 C ⚲	XC ◇1		XC 1	XC ◇1 N ⚲	XC 1	XC ◇1 F	XC ◇1 O ⚲	XC ◇1 H ⚲	XC ◇1 P ⚲	XC 1	XC ◇1 Q ⚲	
Cardiff Central 7	d					15 45								16 45								17 45			
Newport (South Wales)	d					16 00								17 00								18 00			
Bristol Temple Meads 10	d		16 00					16 30			17 00	16 41					17 30			18 00				18 30	
Bristol Parkway 7	d		16 10					16 40			17 10	16 52					17 40			18 10				18 40	
Gloucester 7	d					16 46						17 38		17 46								18 46			
Cheltenham Spa	d		16 42			16 57		17 12			17 42	17 48		17 58			18 12			18 42		18 57		19 12	
Ashchurch for Tewkesbury	d											17 57													
Worcester Shrub Hill 7	a											18 15													
Birmingham New Street 12	a		17 26			17 45		17 56			18 26			18 45			18 56			19 26		19 45		19 58	
	d	17 22		17 30		17 49	17 52	18 03	18 19	18 22			18 30	18 49		18 52	19 03	19 19	19 22		19 30	19 49	19 52	20 03	
Water Orton	d																						20 03		
Coleshill Parkway	d	17 35					18 05			18 35						19 05			19 35				20 07		
Nuneaton	d	17 52					18 22			18 52						19 22			19 52				20 23		
Hinckley	d						18 29									19 29							20 30		
Narborough	d						18 38									19 38							20 39		
South Wigston	d						18 42									19 42							20 43		
Leicester	a	18 14					18 48			19 13						19 48			20 14				20 49		
Wilnecote	d					18 05								19 05								20 05			
Tamworth	d					18 09		18 19	18 36					19 09				19 36				20 09		20 19	
Burton-on-Trent	d					18 21			18 47					19 21			19 27	19 48				20 21			
Willington	d					18 28																			
Derby 6	a			18 05		18 34		18 41	18 59				19 05	19 35			19 39	19 59			20 05	20 34		20 42	
	d					18 39			19 05					19 39				20 05				20 39			
Long Eaton	d								19 14									20 14				20 49			
Attenborough	d																								
Beeston	d								19 24									20 24				20 57			
Nottingham 8	a					19 05			19 33					20 05				20 32				21 04			

A To Manchester Piccadilly
B From Brighton to Great Malvern
C From Southampton Central to Newcastle
D ⚲ from Newport (South Wales)
E From Plymouth to Dundee
F To Stansted Airport
G From Penzance to Manchester Piccadilly
H From Reading to Newcastle
I From Plymouth to Glasgow Central
J From Southampton Central to Great Malvern
K From Plymouth to Edinburgh
L From Paignton to Manchester Piccadilly
M From Warminster to Great Malvern
N From Plymouth to York
O From Exeter St Davids to Manchester Piccadilly
P ⚲ from Newport (South Wales) to Birmingham New Street
Q From Plymouth to Leeds. ⚲ to Birmingham New Street

Table 57

Saturdays

Bristol and Cardiff - Birmingham
Leicester, Derby and Nottingham

Network Diagram - see first Page of Table 50

		XC	XC	GW	XC	XC	XC	XC	XC	XC	XC	GW	XC	XC	XC
		◇1	◇1		◇1	◇1	1	◇1	◇1	◇1	◇1		1	◇1	1
		A	B	C	D			E		F					
			🚲					🚲		🚲					
Cardiff Central 7	d					18 45					20 00			20 50	
Newport (South Wales)	d					19 00					20 15			21 05	
Bristol Temple Meads 10	d		19 00	18 41				19 30	20 00	20 30		20 43			
Bristol Parkway 7	d		19 10	18 52				19 40	20 10	20 40		20 52			
Gloucester 7	d			19 38		19 46					21 07	21 38		21 49	
Cheltenham Spa	d		19 42	19 48		19 57		20 12	20 42	21 12	21 18	21 48		22 00	
Ashchurch for Tewkesbury	d			19 57							21 25	21 58			
Worcester Shrub Hill 7	a			20 15								22 18			
Birmingham New Street 12	a		20 26			20 40		20 53	21 38	21 53	22 07			22 42	
	d	20 22			20 30	20 49	20 52	21 03			22 10		22 22		22 49
Water Orton	d														
Coleshill Parkway	d	20 35					21 05						22 35		
Nuneaton	d	20 52					21 21						22 52		
Hinckley	d						21 29						22 59		
Narborough	d						21 37						23 08		
South Wigston	d						21 42						23 12		
Leicester	a	21 13					21 48						23 18		
Wilnecote	d					21 04									23 04
Tamworth	d					21 09		21 19			22 27				23 08
Burton-on-Trent	d					21 21		21 31			22 39				23 20
Willington	d										22 45				
Derby 6	a				21 24	21 34		21 44			22 55				23 33
	d					21 40					23 00				
Long Eaton	d					21 52					23 12				
Attenborough	d					21 58					23 18				
Beeston	d					22 02					23 22				
Nottingham 8 🚌	a					22 08					23 28				

Sundays
until 1 January

		XC	XC	XC	XC	XC	XC	XC	XC	XC	XC	XC	XC	XC	XC	XC	XC	XC	XC	XC	XC	XC	GW
		◇1	1	◇1	◇1	1	◇1	◇1	◇1	1	◇1	◇1	◇1	◇1	1	◇1	◇1	◇1	◇1	1	◇1	◇1	
		G		H	G		I		H		I	J	K	L		I	J	K	M		I	N	
		🚲		🚲	🚲		🚲	🚲	🚲		🚲	🚲	🚲	🚲		🚲	🚲	🚲	🚲		🚲	🚲	
Cardiff Central 7	d												10 45					11 45					
Newport (South Wales)	d												10 59					11 59					
Bristol Temple Meads 10	d				09 15				10 30					11 30					12 30			13 00	12 41
Bristol Parkway 7	d				09 25				10 40					11 40					12 40			13 10	12 52
Gloucester 7	d				10b01								11 51					12 47					13 37
Cheltenham Spa	d				10 12				11 12				12 03	12 12				12 58	13 12			13 42	13 49
Ashchurch for Tewkesbury	d																						13 57
Worcester Shrub Hill 7	a																						14 17
Birmingham New Street 12	a				10 50				11 50				12 45	12 50				13 41	13 50			14 26	
	d	09 03	09 52	10 03	11 03	10 52	11 22	11 49	12 03	11 52	12 22	12 30	12 49	13 03	12 52	13 22	13 30	13 49	14 03	13 52	14 22		
Water Orton	d																						
Coleshill Parkway	d		10 05			11 05	11 35			12 05	12 35				13 05	13 35				14 04	14 35		
Nuneaton	d		10 22			11 22	11 52			12 22	12 52				13 22	13 51				14 20	14 52		
Hinckley	d		10 29			11 29				12 29					13 29					14 27			
Narborough	d		10 37			11 37				12 38					13 37					14 37			
South Wigston	d		10 42							12 42										14 41			
Leicester	a		10 50			11 50	12 13			12 48	13 12				13 50	14 12				14 50	15 12		
Wilnecote	d																						
Tamworth	d	09 19		10 18				12 07	12 19				13 07					14 07	14 19				
Burton-on-Trent	d	09 28		10 29	11 26			12 19					13 19	13 26				14 19					
Willington	d																						
Derby 6	a	09 42		10 39	11 40			12 34	12 43			13 01	13 33	13 42			14 01	14 34	14 42				
	d							12 40					13 40					14 40					
Long Eaton	d																						
Attenborough	d																						
Beeston	d																						
Nottingham 8 🚌	a							13 00					14 00					15 02					

A To Cambridge
B To Manchester Piccadilly
C From Warminster to Great Malvern
D From Southampton Central to York
E From Plymouth to Leeds. 🚲 to Birmingham New Street
F From Plymouth
G To Edinburgh
H To Glasgow Central
I To Stansted Airport
J To Newcastle
K 🚲 from Newport (South Wales)
L From Plymouth to Aberdeen
M From Plymouth to Glasgow Central
N From Paignton to Manchester Piccadilly

Sundays

until 1 January

Bristol and Cardiff - Birmingham Leicester, Derby and Nottingham

Network Diagram - see first Page of Table 50

		XC	XC	XC	XC	XC		XC	XC	XC	XC	XC	XC	XC	XC	XC		GW	XC	XC	XC	XC	XC	XC	XC
		◇1	◇1	◇1	1	◇1		◇1	◇1	◇1	◇1	1	◇1	◇1	◇1	◇1			◇1	1	◇1	◇1	◇1	◇1	◇1
		A	B	C		D		E	F	B	G		D	E	F	B			H		D	I	J		K
		🛒	🛒	🛒		🛒		🛒	🛒	🛒	🛒			🛒	🛒	🛒			🛒			🛒	🛒		🛒
Cardiff Central 7	d		12 45							13 45						14 45								15 45	
Newport (South Wales)	d		12 59							13 59						14 59								15 59	
Bristol Temple Meads 10	d			13 30				14 00			14 30			15 00				14 41	15 30			16 00			16 30
Bristol Parkway 7	d			13 40				14 10			14 40			15 10				14 53	15 40			16 10			16 40
Gloucester 7	d		13 51							14 47						15 47		15 52						16 47	
Cheltenham Spa	d		14 02	14 12				14 42		14 58	15 12			15 42		15 58		16 03	16 12			16 42		16 58	17 12
Ashchurch for Tewkesbury	d																	16 11							
Worcester Shrub Hill 7	a																	16 34							
Birmingham New Street 12	a		14 45	14 50				15 27		15 41	15 50			16 26		16 41			16 50			17 26		17 41	17 49
	d	14 30	14 49	15 03	14 52	15 22			15 30	15 49	16 03	15 52	16 22		16 30	16 49			17 03	16 52	17 22		17 30	17 49	18 03
Water Orton	d																								
Coleshill Parkway	d				15 05	15 35						16 05	16 35							17 05	17 35				
Nuneaton	d				15 22	15 52						16 22	16 52							17 22	17 52				
Hinckley	d				15 29							16 29								17 29					
Narborough	d				15 37							16 37								17 37					
South Wigston	d											16 42								17 42					
Leicester	a				15 48	16 13						16 48	17 12							17 47	18 12				
Wilnecote	d		15 04																						
Tamworth	d		15 09							16 07	16 19					17 07								18 07	18 19
Burton-on-Trent	d		15 21	15 28						16 19						17 19			17 28					18 19	
Willington	d																								
Derby 6	a	15 04	15 34	15 42					16 02	16 34	16 42				17 04	17 34			17 39				18 04	18 33	18 39
	d		15 40							16 40						17 40								18 40	
Long Eaton	d																								
Attenborough	d																								
Beeston	d																								
Nottingham 8 ⛴	a		16 00							17 00						18 00								19 00	

		XC		XC	XC	GW	XC	XC	XC	XC	XC	XC		XC	XC	XC	XC	XC	XC	GW	XC	XC		XC	XC
		1		◇1	◇1		◇1	◇1	◇1	1	◇1	◇1		◇1	◇1	◇1	1	◇1	◇1		◇1	◇1		1	◇1
				D	L		F		M		D	I		F		N		O	I			P			Q
					🛒		🛒		🛒			🛒		🛒		🛒			🛒			🛒			🛒
Cardiff Central 7	d							16 45							17 45						18 45				
Newport (South Wales)	d							16 59							17 59						18 59				
Bristol Temple Meads 10	d				17 00	16 41			17 30			18 00				18 30			19 00	18 41		19 30			20 00
Bristol Parkway 7	d				17 10	16 52			17 40			18 10				18 40			19 10	18 52		19 40			20 10
Gloucester 7	d					17 35		17 47							18 47					19 38	19 52				
Cheltenham Spa	d				17 42	17 46		17 58	18 12			18 42			18 58	19 12			19 42	19 48	20 02	20 12			20 42
Ashchurch for Tewkesbury	d					17 54														19 57					
Worcester Shrub Hill 7	a					18 14														20 18					
Birmingham New Street 12	a				18 27			18 41	18 51			19 26			19 41	19 50			20 26		20 44	20 50			21 20
	d	17 52		18 22			18 30	18 49	19 03	18 52	19 22			19 30	19 49	20 03	19 52	20 22			20 49	21 03		20 52	
Water Orton	d																								
Coleshill Parkway	d	18 05		18 35						19 05	19 35						20 05	20 35						21 05	
Nuneaton	d	18 22		18 52						19 22	19 52						20 22	20 52						21 22	
Hinckley	d	18 29								19 29							20 29							21 29	
Narborough	d	18 37								19 37							20 38							21 38	
South Wigston	d	18 42								19 41							20 42							21 42	
Leicester	a	18 49		19 12						19 48	20 12						20 48	21 12						21 48	
Wilnecote	d							19 04																	
Tamworth	d							19 09							20 07	20 19					21 06	21 19			
Burton-on-Trent	d							19 21	19 26						20 19						21 19	21 30			
Willington	d																								
Derby 6	a						19 03	19 33	19 39					20 01	20 34	20 39					21 33	21 42			
	d							19 40							20 40						21 40				
Long Eaton	d																								
Attenborough	d																								
Beeston	d																								
Nottingham 8 ⛴	a							20 00							21 00						22 00				

- **A** From Guildford to Newcastle
- **B** 🛒 from Newport (South Wales)
- **C** From Penzance to Edinburgh
- **D** To Stansted Airport
- **E** From Plymouth to Manchester Piccadilly
- **F** From Reading to Newcastle
- **G** From Plymouth to Glasgow Central
- **H** From Plymouth to Edinburgh. 🛒 from Birmingham New Street
- **I** To Manchester Piccadilly
- **J** From Reading to Edinburgh
- **K** From Plymouth to Edinburgh
- **L** From Penzance to Manchester Piccadilly
- **M** From Plymouth to York
- **N** From Plymouth to Leeds. 🛒 to Birmingham New Street
- **O** To Cambridge
- **P** From Penzance to Leeds. 🛒 to Birmingham New Street
- **Q** From Paignton

Table 57

Sundays
until 1 January

Bristol and Cardiff - Birmingham Leicester, Derby and Nottingham

Network Diagram - see first Page of Table 50

		XC ◇1	XC ◇1 A 🛒	XC 1	XC ◇1	XC ◇1
Cardiff Central 7	d	19 45			20 45	
Newport (South Wales)	d	20 00			20 59	
Bristol Temple Meads 10	d		20 30			22 10
Bristol Parkway 7	d		20 40			22 20
Gloucester 7	d	20 50			21 48	
Cheltenham Spa	d	21 01	21 12		21 59	22 52
Ashchurch for Tewkesbury	d					
Worcester Shrub Hill 7	a					
Birmingham New Street 12	a	21 44	21 51		22 42	23 39
	d		22 03	21 52		
Water Orton	d					
Coleshill Parkway	d			22 05		
Nuneaton	d			22 22		
Hinckley	d			22 29		
Narborough	d			22 37		
South Wigston	d			22 42		
Leicester	a			22 48		
Wilnecote	d					
Tamworth	d		22 18			
Burton-on-Trent	d					
Willington	d					
Derby 6	a		22 40			
	d					
Long Eaton	d					
Attenborough	d					
Beeston	d					
Nottingham 8	a					

Sundays
8 January to 12 February

		XC ◇1 B 🛒	XC 1	XC ◇1 C 🛒	XC ◇1 B 🛒	XC 1	XC ◇1 🛒	XC ◇1 🛒	XC ◇1 C 🛒	XC 1	XC ◇1 🛒	XC ◇1 D 🛒	XC ◇1 E 🛒	XC ◇1 F 🛒	XC ◇1 G 🛒	XC ◇1 🛒	XC ◇1 D 🛒	XC ◇1 F 🛒	XC ◇1 H 🛒	XC 1	XC ◇1 🛒	XC ◇1 I 🛒	GW
Cardiff Central 7	d													10 45				11 45					
Newport (South Wales)	d													10 59				11 59					
Bristol Temple Meads 10	d				09 15				10 30						11 30				12 30			13 00	12 41
Bristol Parkway 7	d				09 25				10 40						11 40				12 40			13 10	12 52
Gloucester 7	d				10 01									11 51				12 47					13 37
Cheltenham Spa	d				10 12				11 12					12 03	12 12			12 58	13 12			13 42	13 49
Ashchurch for Tewkesbury	d																						13 57
Worcester Shrub Hill 7	a																						14 17
Birmingham New Street 12	a				10 50				11 50					12 45	12 50			13 41	13 50			14 26	
	d	09 03	09 52	10 03	11 03	10 52	11 22	11 49	12 03	11 52	12 22	12 30	12 44	12 49	13 03	13 22	13 30	13 49	14 03	13 52	14 22		
Water Orton	d																						
Coleshill Parkway	d		10 05			11 05	11 35			12 05	12 35		12 57			13 35				14 04	14 35		
Nuneaton	d		10 22			11 22	11 52			12 22	12 52		13 13			13 51				14 20	14 52		
Hinckley	d		10 29			11 29				12 29			13 20							14 27			
Narborough	d		10 37			11 37				12 38			13 29							14 37			
South Wigston	d		10 42							12 42										14 41			
Leicester	a		10 50			11 50	12 13			12 48	13 12		13 39			14 12				14 50	15 12		
Wilnecote	d																						
Tamworth	d	09 19		10 18				12 07	12 19					13 07				14 07	14 19				
Burton-on-Trent	d	09 28		10 29	11 26			12 19						13 19	13 26			14 19					
Willington	d																						
Derby 6	a	09 42		10 39	11 40			12 34	12 43			13 01		13 33	13 42		14 01	14 34	14 42				
	d							12 40						13 40				14 40					
Long Eaton	d																						
Attenborough	d																						
Beeston	d																						
Nottingham 8	a							13 00					14 04	14 00				15 02					

A From Plymouth to Leeds. 🛒 to Birmingham New Street
B To Edinburgh
C To Glasgow Central
D To Newcastle
E To Stansted Airport
F 🛒 from Newport (South Wales)
G From Plymouth to Aberdeen
H From Plymouth to Glasgow Central
I From Paignton to Manchester Piccadilly

Table 57

Sundays

8 January to 12 February

Bristol and Cardiff - Birmingham
Leicester, Derby and Nottingham

Network Diagram - see first Page of Table 50

		XC	XC	XC	XC	XC		XC	XC	XC	XC	XC	XC	XC	XC	XC		GW	XC	XC	XC	XC	XC	XC	XC
		◇1	◇1	◇1	◇1	◇1		◇1	◇1	◇1	◇1	◇1	◇1	◇1	◇1	◇1			◇1	1	◇1	◇1	◇1	◇1	◇1
		A	B	C	D			E	A	B	F	D		E	G	B			H			I	J		K
		🚲	🚲	🚲	🚲	🚲		🚲	🚲	🚲	🚲			🚲	🚲	🚲			🚲			🚲	🚲		🚲
Cardiff Central 7	d		12 45							13 45						14 45								15 45	
Newport (South Wales)	d		12 59							13 59						14 59								15 59	
Bristol Temple Meads 10	d			13 30				14 00			14 30			15 00				14 41	15 30			16 00			16 30
Bristol Parkway 7	d			13 40				14 10			14 40			15 10				14 53	15 40			16 10			16 40
Gloucester 7	d		13 51							14 47						15 47		15 52						16 47	
Cheltenham Spa	d		14 02	14 12				14 42		14 58	15 12			15 42		15 58		16 03	16 12			16 42		16 58	17 12
Ashchurch for Tewkesbury	d																	16 11							
Worcester Shrub Hill 7	a																	16 34							
Birmingham New Street 12	a		14 45	14 50				15 27		15 41	15 50			16 26		16 41			16 50			17 26		17 41	17 49
	d	14 30	14 49	15 03	14 52	15 22			15 30	15 49	16 03	15 52	16 22		16 30	16 49			17 03	16 52	17 22		17 30	17 49	18 03
Water Orton	d																								
Coleshill Parkway	d				15 05	15 35						16 05	16 35							17 05	17 35				
Nuneaton	d				15 22	15 52						16 22	16 52							17 22	17 52				
Hinckley	d				15 29							16 29								17 29					
Narborough	d				15 37							16 37								17 37					
South Wigston	d											16 42								17 42					
Leicester	a				15 48	16 12						16 48	17 10							17 47	18 12				
Wilnecote	d		15 04																						
Tamworth	d		15 09							16 07	16 19					17 07								18 07	18 19
Burton-on-Trent	d		15 21	15 28						16 19						17 19			17 28					18 19	
Willington	d																								
Derby 6	a	15 04	15 34	15 42					16 02	16 34	16 42				17 04	17 34			17 39				18 04	18 33	18 39
	d		15 40							16 40						17 40								18 40	
Long Eaton	d																								
Attenborough	d																								
Beeston	d																								
Nottingham 8	a		16 00		16 13					17 00		17 17				18 00								19 00	

		XC		XC	XC	GW	XC	XC	XC	XC	XC	XC		XC	XC	XC	XC	XC	XC	GW	XC	XC		XC	XC
		◇1		◇1	◇1		◇1	◇1	◇1	◇1	◇1	◇1		◇1	◇1	◇1	◇1	◇1	◇1		◇1	◇1		1	◇1
		D			L		G		M	D		I		G		N	O		I			P			Q
					🚲		🚲		🚲			🚲		🚲		🚲			🚲			🚲			🚲
Cardiff Central 7	d							16 45							17 45						18 45				
Newport (South Wales)	d							16 59							17 59						18 59				
Bristol Temple Meads 10	d				17 00	16 41			17 30			18 00				18 30			19 00	18 41		19 30			20 00
Bristol Parkway 7	d				17 10	16 52			17 40			18 10				18 40			19 10	18 52		19 40			20 10
Gloucester 7	d					17 35		17 47							18 47					19 38	19 52				
Cheltenham Spa	d				17 42	17 46		17 58	18 12			18 42			18 58	19 12			19 42	19 48	20 02	20 12			20 42
Ashchurch for Tewkesbury	d					17 54														19 57					
Worcester Shrub Hill 7	a					18 14														20 18					
Birmingham New Street 12	a				18 27			18 41	18 51			19 26			19 41	19 50			20 26		20 44	20 50			21 20
	d	17 52		18 22			18 30	18 49	19 03	18 52	19 22			19 30	19 49	20 03	19 52	20 22			20 49	21 03		20 52	
Water Orton	d																								
Coleshill Parkway	d	18 05		18 35						19 05	19 35						20 05	20 35						21 05	
Nuneaton	d	18 22		18 52						19 22	19 52						20 21	20 52						21 22	
Hinckley	d	18 29								19 29							20 29							21 29	
Narborough	d	18 37								19 37							20 38							21 38	
South Wigston	d	18 42								19 42							20 42							21 42	
Leicester	a	18 48		19 11						19 48	20 12						20 48	21 12						21 48	
Wilnecote	d							19 04																	
Tamworth	d							19 09							20 07	20 19					21 06	21 19			
Burton-on-Trent	d							19 21	19 26						20 19						21 19	21 30			
Willington	d																								
Derby 6	a						19 03	19 33	19 39					20 01	20 34	20 39					21 33	21 42			
	d							19 40							20 40						21 40				
Long Eaton	d																								
Attenborough	d																								
Beeston	d																								
Nottingham 8	a	19 18						20 00		20 16					21 00		21 13				22 00				

A To Newcastle
B 🚲 from Newport (South Wales)
C From Penzance to Edinburgh
D To Stansted Airport
E From Plymouth to Manchester Piccadilly
F From Plymouth to Glasgow Central
G From Reading to Newcastle
H From Plymouth to Edinburgh. 🚲 from Birmingham New Street
I To Manchester Piccadilly
J From Reading to Edinburgh
K From Plymouth to Edinburgh
L From Penzance to Manchester Piccadilly
M From Plymouth to York
N From Plymouth to Leeds. 🚲 to Birmingham New Street
O To Cambridge
P From Penzance to Leeds. 🚲 to Birmingham New Street
Q From Paignton

Table 57

Sundays

8 January to 12 February

Bristol and Cardiff - Birmingham Leicester, Derby and Nottingham

Network Diagram - see first Page of Table 50

		XC ◇[1]	XC ◇[1] A 🚲	XC [1]	XC ◇[1]	XC ◇[1]
Cardiff Central [7]	d	19 45			20 45	
Newport (South Wales)	d	20 00			20 59	
Bristol Temple Meads [10]	d		20 30			22 10
Bristol Parkway [7]	d		20 40			22 20
Gloucester [7]	d	20 50			21 48	
Cheltenham Spa	d	21 01	21 12		21 59	22 52
Ashchurch for Tewkesbury	d					
Worcester Shrub Hill [7]	a					
Birmingham New Street [12]	a	21 44	21 51		22 42	23 39
	d		22 03	21 52		
Water Orton	d					
Coleshill Parkway	d			22 05		
Nuneaton	d			22 22		
Hinckley	d			22 29		
Narborough	d			22 37		
South Wigston	d			22 42		
Leicester	a			22 48		
Wilnecote	d					
Tamworth	d		22 18			
Burton-on-Trent	d					
Willington	d					
Derby [6]	a		22 40			
	d					
Long Eaton	d					
Attenborough	d					
Beeston	d					
Nottingham [8]	a					

Sundays

19 February to 25 March

		XC ◇[1] B 🚲	XC [1]	XC ◇[1] C 🚲	XC ◇[1] B 🚲	XC [1]	XC ◇[1] D 🚲	XC ◇[1] 🚲	XC ◇[1] C 🚲	XC [1]		XC ◇[1] D 🚲	XC ◇[1] E 🚲	XC ◇[1] F 🚲	XC ◇[1] G 🚲	XC [1]	XC ◇[1] D 🚲	XC ◇[1] E 🚲	XC ◇[1] F 🚲	XC ◇[1] C 🚲		XC [1]	XC ◇[1] D 🚲	XC ◇[1] H 🚲	GW
Cardiff Central [7]	d													10 45					11 45						
Newport (South Wales)	d													10 59					11 59						
Bristol Temple Meads [10]	d				09 15				10 30						11 30					12 30				13 00	12 41
Bristol Parkway [7]	d				09 25				10 40						11 40					12 40				13 10	12 52
Gloucester [7]	d				10b01									11 51					12 47						13 37
Cheltenham Spa	d				10 12				11 12					12 03	12 12				12 58	13 12				13 42	13 49
Ashchurch for Tewkesbury	d																								13 57
Worcester Shrub Hill [7]	a																								14 17
Birmingham New Street [12]	a				10 50				11 50					12 45	12 50				13 41	13 50				14 26	
	d	09 03	09 52	10 03	11 03	10 52	11 22	11 49	12 03	11 52		12 22	12 30	12 49	13 03	12 52	13 22	13 30	13 49	14 03		13 52	14 22		
Water Orton	d																								
Coleshill Parkway	d		10 05			11 05	11 35			12 05		12 35				13 05	13 35					14 04	14 35		
Nuneaton	d		10 22			11 22	11 52			12 22		12 52				13 22	13 51					14 20	14 52		
Hinckley	d		10 29			11 29				12 29						13 29						14 27			
Narborough	d		10 37			11 37				12 38						13 37						14 37			
South Wigston	d		10 42							12 42												14 41			
Leicester	a		10 50			11 50	12 13			12 48		13 12				13 50	14 12					14 50	15 12		
Wilnecote	d																								
Tamworth	d	09 19		10 18				12 07	12 19					13 07					14 07	14 19					
Burton-on-Trent	d	09 28		10 29	11 26			12 19						13 19	13 26				14 19						
Willington	d																								
Derby [6]	a	09 42		10 39	11 40			12 34	12 43				13 01	13 33	13 44			14 01	14 34	14 42					
	d							12 40						13 40					14 40						
Long Eaton	d																								
Attenborough	d																								
Beeston	d																								
Nottingham [8]	a							13 00						14 00					15 02						

A From Plymouth to Leeds. 🚲 to Birmingham New Street
B To Edinburgh
C To Glasgow Central
D To Stansted Airport
E To Newcastle
F 🚲 from Newport (South Wales)
G To Aberdeen
H From Paignton to Manchester Piccadilly

Table 57

Sundays

19 February to 25 March

Bristol and Cardiff - Birmingham
Leicester, Derby and Nottingham

Network Diagram - see first Page of Table 50

		XC	XC	XC	XC	XC		XC	XC	XC	XC	XC	XC	XC	XC	XC		GW	XC	XC	XC	XC	XC	XC	XC
		◇1	◇1	◇1	1	◇1		◇1	◇1	◇1	◇1	1	◇1	◇1	◇1	◇1			◇1	1	◇1	◇1	◇1	◇1	◇1
		A	B	C		D		E	A	B	F		D	E	G	B			C		D	E	H		C
		🚲	🚲	🚲		🚲		🚲	🚲	🚲	🚲			🚲	🚲	🚲			🚲			🚲	🚲		🚲
Cardiff Central 7	d		12 45							13 45						14 45								15 45	
Newport (South Wales)	d		12 59							13 59						14 59								15 59	
Bristol Temple Meads 10	d			13 30				14 00			14 30			15 00				14 41	15 30			16 00			16 30
Bristol Parkway 7	d			13 40				14 10			14 40			15 10				14 53	15 40			16 10			16 40
Gloucester 7	d		13 51							14 47						15 47		15 52						16 47	
Cheltenham Spa	d		14 02	14 12				14 42		14 58	15 12			15 42		15 58		16 03	16 12			16 42		16 58	17 12
Ashchurch for Tewkesbury	d																	16 11							
Worcester Shrub Hill 7	a																	16 34							
Birmingham New Street 12	a		14 45	14 50				15 27		15 41	15 50			16 26		16 41			16 50			17 26		17 41	17 49
	d	14 30	14 49	15 03	14 52	15 22			15 30	15 49	16 03	15 52	16 22		16 30	16 49			17 03	16 52	17 22		17 30	17 49	18 03
Water Orton	d																								
Coleshill Parkway	d				15 05	15 35						16 05	16 35							17 05	17 35				
Nuneaton	d				15 22	15 52						16 22	16 52							17 22	17 52				
Hinckley	d				15 29							16 29								17 29					
Narborough	d				15 37							16 37								17 37					
South Wigston	d											16 42								17 42					
Leicester	a				15 48	16 13						16 48	17 12							17 47	18 12				
Wilnecote	d		15 04																						
Tamworth	d		15 09							16 07	16 19					17 07								18 07	18 19
Burton-on-Trent	d		15 21	15 28						16 19						17 19			17 28					18 19	
Willington	d																								
Derby 6	a	15 04	15 34	15 42					16 02	16 34	16 42				17 04	17 34			17 39				18 04	18 33	18 39
	d		15 40							16 40						17 40								18 40	
Long Eaton	d																								
Attenborough	d																								
Beeston	d																								
Nottingham 8	a		16 00							17 00						18 00								19 00	

		XC		XC	XC	GW	XC	XC	XC	XC	XC	XC		XC	XC	XC	XC	XC	XC	GW	XC	XC		XC	XC
		1		◇1	◇1		◇1	◇1	◇1	1	◇1	◇1		◇1	◇1	◇1	1	◇1	◇1		◇1	◇1		1	◇1
				D	E		G		I		D	E		G		J		K	E			J			
					🚲		🚲		🚲			🚲		🚲		🚲			🚲			🚲			🚲
Cardiff Central 7	d							16 45							17 45						18 45				
Newport (South Wales)	d							16 59							17 59						18 59				
Bristol Temple Meads 10	d				17 00	16 41			17 30			18 00				18 30			19 00	18 41		19 30			20 00
Bristol Parkway 7	d				17 10	16 52			17 40			18 10				18 40			19 10	18 52		19 40			20 10
Gloucester 7	d					17 35		17 47							18 47					19 38	19 52				
Cheltenham Spa	d				17 42	17 46		17 58	18 12			18 42			18 58	19 12			19 42	19 48	20 02	20 12			20 42
Ashchurch for Tewkesbury	d					17 54														19 57					
Worcester Shrub Hill 7	a					18 14														20 18					
Birmingham New Street 12	a				18 27			18 41	18 51			19 26			19 41	19 50			20 26		20 44	20 50			21 20
	d	17 52		18 22			18 30	18 49	19 03	18 52	19 22			19 30	19 49	20 03	19 52	20 22			20 49	21 03		20 52	
Water Orton	d																								
Coleshill Parkway	d	18 05		18 35						19 05	19 35						20 05	20 35						21 05	
Nuneaton	d	18 22		18 52						19 22	19 52						20 22	20 52						21 22	
Hinckley	d	18 29								19 29							20 29							21 29	
Narborough	d	18 37								19 37							20 38							21 38	
South Wigston	d	18 42								19 41							20 42							21 42	
Leicester	a	18 49		19 12						19 48	20 12						20 48	21 12						21 48	
Wilnecote	d							19 04																	
Tamworth	d							19 09							20 07	20 19					21 06	21 19			
Burton-on-Trent	d							19 21	19 26						20 19						21 19	21 30			
Willington	d																								
Derby 6	a						19 03	19 33	19 39					20 01	20 34	20 39					21 33	21 42			
	d							19 40							20 40						21 40				
Long Eaton	d																								
Attenborough	d																								
Beeston	d																								
Nottingham 8	a							20 00							21 00						22 00				

A To Newcastle
B 🚲 from Newport (South Wales)
C From Newton Abbot to Edinburgh
D To Stansted Airport
E To Manchester Piccadilly
F From Newton Abbot to Glasgow Central
G From Reading to Newcastle
H From Reading to Edinburgh
I From Newton Abbot to York
J From Newton Abbot to Leeds. 🚲 to Birmingham New Street
K To Cambridge

Table 57

Sundays

19 February to 25 March

Bristol and Cardiff - Birmingham Leicester, Derby and Nottingham

Network Diagram - see first Page of Table 50

		XC	XC	XC	XC	XC	XC
		◇1	◇1	1	◇1	◇1	◇1
			A			B	C
			🚲				
Cardiff Central 7	d	19 45			20 45		
Newport (South Wales)	d	20 00			20 59		
Bristol Temple Meads 10	d		20 30			21 20	22 10
Bristol Parkway 7	d		20 40			21 30	22 20
Gloucester 7	d	20 50			21 48		
Cheltenham Spa	d	21 01	21 12		21 59	22 05	22 52
Ashchurch for Tewkesbury	d						
Worcester Shrub Hill 7	a						
Birmingham New Street 12	a	21 44	21 51		22 42	22 46	23 39
	d		22 03	21 52			
Water Orton	d						
Coleshill Parkway	d			22 05			
Nuneaton	d			22 22			
Hinckley	d			22 29			
Narborough	d			22 37			
South Wigston	d			22 42			
Leicester	a			22 48			
Wilnecote	d						
Tamworth	d		22 18				
Burton-on-Trent	d						
Willington	d						
Derby 6	a		22 40				
	d						
Long Eaton	d						
Attenborough	d						
Beeston	d						
Nottingham 8 ⛴	a						

Sundays

from 1 April

		XC	XC	XC	XC	XC	XC	XC	XC	XC		XC	XC	XC	XC	XC	XC	XC	XC	XC		XC	XC	XC	GW
		◇1	1	◇1	◇1	1	◇1	◇1	◇1	1		◇1	◇1	◇1	◇1	1	◇1	◇1	◇1	◇1		1	◇1	◇1	
		D		E	D		F		E			F	G	H	I		F	G	H	J			F	K	
		🚲		🚲	🚲		🚲	🚲	🚲			🚲	🚲	🚲	🚲		🚲	🚲	🚲	🚲			🚲	🚲	
Cardiff Central 7	d													10 45					11 45						
Newport (South Wales)	d													10 59					11 59						
Bristol Temple Meads 10	d				09 15				10 30						11 30					12 30				13 00	12 41
Bristol Parkway 7	d				09 25				10 40						11 40					12 40				13 10	12 52
Gloucester 7	d				10 01									11 51					12 47						13 37
Cheltenham Spa	d				10 12				11 12					12 03	12 12				12 58	13 12				13 42	13 49
Ashchurch for Tewkesbury	d																								13 57
Worcester Shrub Hill 7	a																								14 17
Birmingham New Street 12	a				10 50				11 50					12 45	12 50				13 41	13 50				14 26	
	d	09 03	09 52	10 03	11 03	10 52	11 22	11 49	12 03	11 52		12 22	12 30	12 49	13 03	12 52	13 22	13 30	13 49	14 03		13 52	14 22		
Water Orton	d																								
Coleshill Parkway	d		10 05			11 05	11 35			12 05		12 35				13 05	13 35					14 04	14 35		
Nuneaton	d		10 22			11 22	11 52			12 22		12 52				13 22	13 51					14 20	14 52		
Hinckley	d		10 29			11 29				12 29						13 29						14 27			
Narborough	d		10 37			11 37				12 38						13 37						14 37			
South Wigston	d		10 42							12 42												14 41			
Leicester	a		10 50			11 50	12 13			12 48		13 12				13 50	14 12					14 50	15 12		
Wilnecote	d																								
Tamworth	d	09 19		10 18				12 07	12 19					13 07					14 07	14 19					
Burton-on-Trent	d	09 28		10 29	11 26			12 19						13 19	13 26				14 19						
Willington	d																								
Derby 6	a	09 42		10 39	11 40			12 34	12 43				13 01	13 33	13 42			14 01	14 34	14 42					
	d							12 40						13 40					14 40						
Long Eaton	d																								
Attenborough	d																								
Beeston	d																								
Nottingham 8 ⛴	a							13 00						14 00					15 02						

A From Newton Abbot to Leeds. 🚲 to Birmingham New Street
B From Newton Abbot
C From Exeter St Davids
D To Edinburgh
E To Glasgow Central
F To Stansted Airport
G To Newcastle
H 🚲 from Newport (South Wales)
I From Plymouth to Aberdeen
J From Plymouth to Glasgow Central
K From Paignton to Manchester Piccadilly

Table 57

Sundays
from 1 April

Bristol and Cardiff - Birmingham
Leicester, Derby and Nottingham

Network Diagram - see first Page of Table 50

		XC ◇[1] A 🍴	XC ◇[1] B 🍴	XC ◇[1] C 🍴	XC [1]	XC ◇[1] D 🍴		XC ◇[1] E 🍴	XC ◇[1] F 🍴	XC ◇[1] B 🍴	XC ◇[1] G 🍴	XC [1]	XC ◇[1] D	XC ◇[1] E 🍴	XC ◇[1] F 🍴	XC ◇[1] B 🍴		GW	XC ◇[1] H 🍴	XC [1]	XC ◇[1] D	XC ◇[1] I 🍴	XC ◇[1] J 🍴	XC ◇[1]	XC ◇[1] K 🍴
Cardiff Central [7]	d		12 45							13 45						14 45								15 45	
Newport (South Wales)	d		12 59							13 59						14 59								15 59	
Bristol Temple Meads [10]	d			13 30				14 00			14 30			15 00				14 41	15 30			16 00			16 30
Bristol Parkway [7]	d			13 40				14 10			14 40			15 10				14 53	15 40			16 10			16 40
Gloucester [7]	d		13 51							14 47						15 47		15 52						16 47	
Cheltenham Spa	d		14 02	14 12				14 42		14 58	15 12			15 42		15 58		16 03	16 12			16 42		16 58	17 12
Ashchurch for Tewkesbury	d																	16 11							
Worcester Shrub Hill [7]	a																	16 34							
Birmingham New Street [12]	a		14 45	14 50				15 27		15 41	15 50			16 26		16 41			16 50			17 26		17 41	17 49
	d	14 30	14 49	15 03	14 52	15 22			15 30	15 49	16 03	15 52	16 22		16 30	16 49			17 03	16 52	17 22		17 30	17 49	18 03
Water Orton	d																								
Coleshill Parkway	d				15 05	15 35						16 05	16 35							17 05	17 35				
Nuneaton	d				15 22	15 52						16 22	16 52							17 22	17 52				
Hinckley	d				15 29							16 29								17 29					
Narborough	d				15 37							16 37								17 37					
South Wigston	d											16 42								17 42					
Leicester	a				15 48	16 13						16 48	17 12							17 48	18 12				
Wilnecote	d		15 04																						
Tamworth	d		15 09							16 07	16 19					17 07								18 07	18 19
Burton-on-Trent	d		15 21	15 28						16 19						17 19			17 28					18 19	
Willington	d																								
Derby [6]	a	15 04	15 34	15 42					16 02	16 34	16 42				17 04	17 34			17 39				18 04	18 33	18 39
	d		15 40							16 40						17 40								18 40	
Long Eaton	d																								
Attenborough	d																								
Beeston	d																								
Nottingham [8]	a		16 00							17 00						18 00								19 00	

		XC [1]		XC ◇[1] D	XC ◇[1] L 🍴	GW	XC ◇[1] F 🍴	XC ◇[1]	XC ◇[1] M 🍴	XC [1]	XC ◇[1] D	XC ◇[1] I 🍴		XC ◇[1] F 🍴	XC ◇[1]	XC ◇[1] N 🍴	XC [1]	XC ◇[1] O	XC ◇[1] I 🍴	GW	XC ◇[1]	XC ◇[1] P 🍴		XC [1]	XC ◇[1] Q 🍴
Cardiff Central [7]	d							16 45							17 45						18 45				
Newport (South Wales)	d							16 59							17 59						18 59				
Bristol Temple Meads [10]	d				17 00	16 41			17 30			18 00				18 30			19 00	18 41		19 30			20 00
Bristol Parkway [7]	d				17 10	16 52			17 40			18 10				18 40			19 10	18 52		19 40			20 10
Gloucester [7]	d					17 35		17 47							18 47					19 38	19 52				
Cheltenham Spa	d				17 42	17 46		17 58	18 12			18 42			18 58	19 12			19 42	19 48	20 02	20 12			20 42
Ashchurch for Tewkesbury	d					17 54														19 57					
Worcester Shrub Hill [7]	a					18 14														20 18					
Birmingham New Street [12]	a				18 27			18 41	18 51			19 26			19 41	19 50			20 26		20 44	20 50			21 20
	d	17 52		18 22			18 30	18 49	19 03	18 52	19 22			19 30	19 49	20 03	19 52	20 22			20 49	21 03		20 52	
Water Orton	d																								
Coleshill Parkway	d	18 05		18 35						19 05	19 35						20 05	20 35						21 05	
Nuneaton	d	18 22		18 52						19 22	19 52						20 22	20 52						21 22	
Hinckley	d	18 29								19 29							20 29							21 29	
Narborough	d	18 37								19 37							20 38							21 38	
South Wigston	d	18 42								19 41							20 42							21 42	
Leicester	a	18 49		19 12						19 48	20 12						20 48	21 12						21 48	
Wilnecote	d							19 04																	
Tamworth	d							19 09							20 07	20 19					21 06	21 19			
Burton-on-Trent	d							19 21	19 26						20 19						21 19	21 30			
Willington	d																								
Derby [6]	a						19 03	19 33	19 39					20 01	20 35	20 39					21 33	21 42			
	d							19 40							20 40						21 40				
Long Eaton	d																								
Attenborough	d																								
Beeston	d																								
Nottingham [8]	a							20 00							21 00						22 00				

A From Guildford to Newcastle
B 🍴 from Newport (South Wales)
C From Penzance to Edinburgh
D To Stansted Airport
E From Plymouth to Manchester Piccadilly
F From Reading to Newcastle
G From Plymouth to Glasgow Central
H From Plymouth to Edinburgh. 🍴 from Birmingham New Street
I To Manchester Piccadilly
J From Reading to Edinburgh
K From Plymouth to Edinburgh
L From Penzance to Manchester Piccadilly
M From Plymouth to York
N From Plymouth to Leeds. 🍴 to Birmingham New Street
O To Cambridge
P From Penzance to Leeds. 🍴 to Birmingham New Street
Q From Paignton

Table 57

Sundays
from 1 April

Bristol and Cardiff - Birmingham Leicester, Derby and Nottingham

Network Diagram - see first Page of Table 50

		XC	XC	XC	XC	XC
		◇1	◇1	1	◇1	◇1
			A			
			⚲			
Cardiff Central 7	d	19 45			20 45	
Newport (South Wales)	d	20 00			20 59	
Bristol Temple Meads 10	d		20 30			22 10
Bristol Parkway 7	d		20 40			22 20
Gloucester 7	d	20 50			21 48	
Cheltenham Spa	d	21 01	21 12		21 59	22 52
Ashchurch for Tewkesbury	d					
Worcester Shrub Hill 7	a					
Birmingham New Street 12	a	21 44	21 51		22 42	23 39
	d		22 03	21 52		
Water Orton	d					
Coleshill Parkway	d			22 05		
Nuneaton	d			22 22		
Hinckley	d			22 29		
Narborough	d			22 37		
South Wigston	d			22 42		
Leicester	a			22 48		
Wilnecote	d					
Tamworth	d		22 18			
Burton-on-Trent	d					
Willington	d					
Derby 6	a		22 40			
	d					
Long Eaton	d					
Attenborough	d					
Beeston	d					
Nottingham 6 ⇌	a					

A From Plymouth to Leeds.
⚲ to Birmingham New Street

Network Diagram for Tables 59, 60, 61, 62, 64, 66

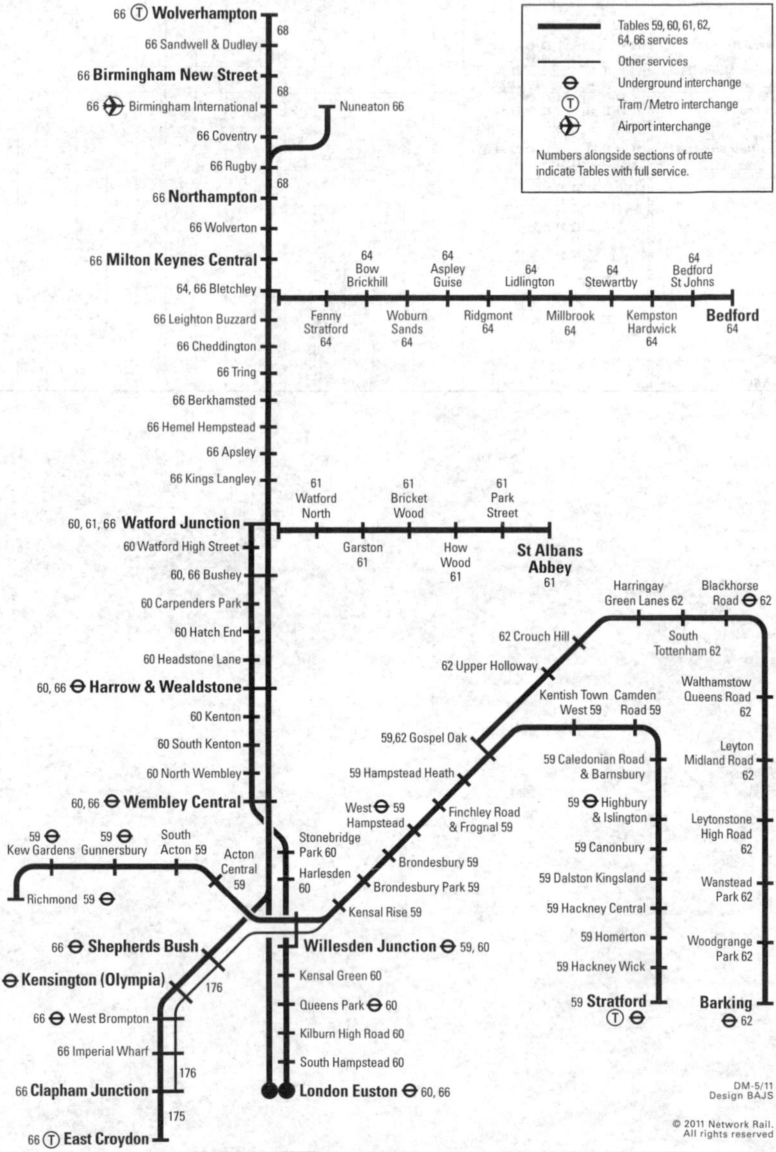

Stratford - Highbury and Islington, West Hampstead, Willesden Junction and Richmond

Network Diagram - see first Page of Table 59

Miles			LO MX	LO	LO	LO	LO	LO	LO	LO	LO		LO	LO	LO	LO	LO	LO	LO	LO	LO		LO	LO	LO
0	**Stratford 7** ⊖	d	23p45		05 47		06 05	06 12	06 20	06 27	06 35		06 42	06 50	06 55	07 00	07 12	07 20	07 27	07 35	07 42		07 50	07 57	08 05
1	Hackney Wick	d	23p48		05 50		06 08	06 15	06 23	06 30	06 38		06 45	06 54	06 58	07 03	07 15	07 23	07 30	07 38	07 45		07 53	08 00	08 08
1¾	Homerton	d	23p51		05 53		06 11	06 18	06 26	06 33	06 41		06 48	06 56	07 01	07 06	07 18	07 26	07 33	07 42	07 48		07 56	08 03	08 11
2½	Hackney Central	d	23p53		05 55		06 13	06 20	06 28	06 35	06 43		06 50	06 58	07 03	07 08	07 20	07 28	07 35	07 43	07 50		07 58	08 05	08 13
3¼	Dalston Kingsland	d	23p55		05 57		06 15	06 22	06 30	06 37	06 45		06 52	07 00	07 05	07 10	07 22	07 30	07 37	07 45	07 52		08 00	08 07	08 15
4¼	Canonbury	d	23p57		05 59		06 17	06 24	06 32	06 39	06 47		06 54	07 02	07 07	07 12	07 24	07 32	07 39	07 47	07 54		08 02	08 09	08 17
4¾	**Highbury & Islington** ⊖	d	23p59		06 02		06 19	06 27	06 35	06 41	06 50		06 57	07 05	07 10	07 15	07 27	07 35	07 42	07 50	07 57		08 05	08 12	08 20
5¼	Caledonian Rd & Barnsbury	d	00 02		06 04		06 21	06 29	06 37	06 43	06 52		06 59	07 07	07 12	07 17	07 29	07 37	07 44	07 52	07 59		08 07	08 14	08 22
6¼	Camden Road	d	00 05		06 07		06 24	06 32	06 40	06 46	06 55		07 02	07 10	07 15	07 20	07 32	07 40	07 47	07 55	08 02		08 10	08 17	08 25
6½	Kentish Town West	d	00 07		06 09		06 27	06 34	06 42	06 49	06 57		07 04	07 13	07 17	07 22	07 34	07 42	07 49	07 57	08 04		08 12	08 19	08 27
7½	**Gospel Oak**	d	00 10		06 12		06 30	06 37	06 45	06 51	07 00		07 07	07 15	07 20	07 25	07 37	07 45	07 52	08 00	08 07		08 15	08 22	08 30
8	Hampstead Heath	d	00 12		06 14		06 32	06 39	06 47	06 53	07 02		07 09	07 17	07 22	07 27	07 39	07 47	07 54	08 02	08 09		08 17	08 24	08 32
9	Finchley Road & Frognal	d	00 14		06 16		06 34	06 41	06 49	06 55	07 04		07 11	07 19	07 24	07 29	07 41	07 49	07 56	08 04	08 11		08 19	08 26	08 34
9½	West Hampstead ⊖	d	00 16		06 18		06 36	06 43	06 51	06 57	07 06		07 13	07 21	07 26	07 31	07 43	07 51	07 58	08 06	08 13		08 21	08 28	08 36
10	Brondesbury	d	00 18		06 20		06 38	06 45	06 53	06 58	07 08		07 15	07 22	07 28	07 33	07 45	07 53	08 00	08 08	08 15		08 23	08 30	08 38
10¼	Brondesbury Park	d	00 19		06 21		06 39	06 46	06 54	07 00	07 09		07 16	07 24	07 29	07 34	07 46	07 54	08 01	08 09	08 16		08 24	08 31	08 39
11	Kensal Rise	d	00a21		06 23		06 41	06 48	06 56	07 02	07 11		07 18	07 26	07 31	07 36	07 48	07 56	08 03	08 11	08 18		08 26	08 33	08 41
12	**Willesden Jn. High Level** ⊖	a			06 27		06 45	06 52	07 00	07 06	07 15		07 22	07 30	07 35	07 40	07 52	08 00	08 07	08 15	08 22		08 30	08 37	08 45
—		d		06 09	06 28	06 41		06 53		07 07			07 23		07 36		07 53		08 08		08 23			08 38	
13½	Acton Central	d		06 14	06 33	06 46		06 58		07 13			07 28		07 41		07 58		08 13		08 28			08 43	
14½	South Acton	d		06 16	06 36	06 49		07 01		07 16			07 31		07 44		08 01		08 16		08 31			08 46	
15¼	Gunnersbury ⊖	d		06 20	06 39	06 53		07 04		07 19			07 34		07 48		08 04		08 19		08 34			08 51	
16¼	Kew Gardens ⊖	d		06 23	06 42	06 56		07 07		07 22			07 37		07 51		08 07		08 22		08 37			08 54	
17½	**Richmond** ⊖	a		06 31	06 49	07 04		07 14		07 30			07 42		07 55		08 12		08 29		08 42			09 00	

		LO	LO	LO	LO	LO	LO		LO	LO	LO	LO	LO	LO	LO	LO	LO		LO	LO	LO	LO	LO	LO	LO
Stratford 7 ⊖	d	08 12	08 20	08 27	08 35	08 42	08 50		08 57	09 03	09 15	09 25	09 35	09 45	09 55	10 05	10 15		10 25	10 35	10 45	10 55	11 05	11 15	11 25
Hackney Wick	d	08 15	08 23	08 30	08 38	08 45	08 53		09 00	09 06	09 18	09 28	09 38	09 48	09 58	10 08	10 18		10 28	10 38	10 48	10 58	11 08	11 18	11 28
Homerton	d	08 18	08 26	08 33	08 41	08 48	08 56		09 03	09 09	09 21	09 31	09 41	09 51	10 01	10 11	10 21		10 31	10 41	10 51	11 01	11 11	11 21	11 31
Hackney Central	d	08 20	08 28	08 35	08 43	08 50	08 58		09 05	09 11	09 23	09 33	09 43	09 53	10 03	10 13	10 23		10 33	10 43	10 53	11 03	11 13	11 23	11 33
Dalston Kingsland	d	08 22	08 30	08 37	08 45	08 52	09 00		09 07	09 13	09 25	09 35	09 45	09 55	10 05	10 15	10 25		10 35	10 45	10 55	11 05	11 15	11 25	11 35
Canonbury	d	08 24	08 32	08 39	08 47	08 54	09 02		09 09	09 15	09 27	09 37	09 47	09 57	10 07	10 17	10 27		10 37	10 47	10 57	11 07	11 17	11 27	11 37
Highbury & Islington ⊖	d	08 27	08 35	08 42	08 50	08 57	09 05		09 12	09 18	09 30	09 40	09 50	10 00	10 10	10 20	10 30		10 40	10 50	11 00	11 10	11 20	11 30	11 40
Caledonian Rd & Barnsbury	d	08 29	08 37	08 44	08 52	08 59	09 07		09 14	09 20	09 32	09 42	09 52	10 02	10 12	10 22	10 32		10 42	10 52	11 02	11 12	11 22	11 32	11 42
Camden Road	d	08 32	08 40	08 47	08 55	09 02	09 10		09 17	09 23	09 35	09 45	09 55	10 05	10 15	10 25	10 35		10 45	10 55	11 05	11 15	11 25	11 35	11 45
Kentish Town West	d	08 34	08 42	08 49	08 59	09 04	09 12		09 19	09 25	09 37	09 47	09 57	10 07	10 17	10 27	10 37		10 47	10 57	11 07	11 17	11 27	11 37	11 47
Gospel Oak	d	08 37	08 45	08 52	09 02	09 08	09 15		09 22	09 27	09 40	09 50	10 00	10 10	10 20	10 30	10 40		10 50	11 00	11 10	11 20	11 30	11 40	11 51
Hampstead Heath	d	08 39	08 47	08 54	09 04	09 10	09 17		09 24	09 29	09 42	09 52	10 02	10 12	10 22	10 32	10 42		10 52	11 02	11 12	11 22	11 32	11 42	11 53
Finchley Road & Frognal	d	08 41	08 49	08 56	09 06	09 12	09 19		09 26	09 31	09 44	09 54	10 04	10 14	10 24	10 34	10 44		10 54	11 04	11 14	11 24	11 34	11 44	11 55
West Hampstead ⊖	d	08 43	08 51	08 58	09 08	09 14	09 21		09 28	09 33	09 46	09 56	10 06	10 16	10 26	10 36	10 46		10 56	11 06	11 16	11 26	11 36	11 46	11 57
Brondesbury	d	08 45	08 53	09 00	09 10	09 15	09 23		09 30	09 35	09 48	09 58	10 08	10 18	10 28	10 38	10 48		10 58	11 08	11 18	11 28	11 38	11 48	11 59
Brondesbury Park	d	08 46	08 54	09 01	09 11	09 17	09 24		09 31	09 36	09 49	09 59	10 09	10 19	10 29	10 39	10 49		10 59	11 09	11 19	11 29	11 39	11 49	12 00
Kensal Rise	d	08 48	08 56	09 03	09 13	09 19	09 26		09 33	09 38	09 51	10 01	10 11	10 21	10 31	10 41	10 51		11 01	11 11	11 21	11 31	11 41	11 51	12 02
Willesden Jn. High Level ⊖	a	08 52	09 00	09 07	09 16	09 23	09 30		09 37	09 42	09 55	10 05	10 15	10 25	10 35	10 45	10 55		11 05	11 15	11 25	11 35	11 44	11 55	12 06
	d	08 53		09 08		09 24			09 38		09 56	10 06		10 26	10 36		10 56		11 06		11 26	11 36		11 56	12 07
Acton Central	d	08 58		09 13		09 29			09 43		10 01	10 11		10 31	10 41		11 01		11 11		11 31	11 41		12 01	12 12
South Acton	d	09 01		09 16		09 31			09 46		10 04	10 14		10 34	10 44		11 04		11 14		11 34	11 44		12 04	12 15
Gunnersbury ⊖	d	09 04		09 19		09 37			09 49		10 08	10 19		10 38	10 48		11 08		11 18		11 38	11 48		12 08	12 19
Kew Gardens ⊖	d	09 07		09 22		09 40			09 52		10 11	10 22		10 41	10 51		11 11		11 21		11 41	11 51		12 11	12 22
Richmond ⊖	a	09 14		09 29		09 46			10 00		10 18	10 29		10 48	10 58		11 18		11 26		11 48	11 58		12 18	12 29

		LO	LO		LO	LO	LO	LO	LO	LO	LO	LO	LO		LO	LO	LO	LO	LO	LO	LO	LO	LO		LO
Stratford 7 ⊖	d	11 37	11 45		11 55	12 05	12 15	12 25	12 35	12 45	12 55	13 05	13 15		13 25	13 35	13 45	13 55	14 05	14 15	14 25	14 35	14 45		14 55
Hackney Wick	d	11 40	11 48		11 58	12 08	12 18	12 28	12 38	12 48	12 58	13 08	13 18		13 28	13 38	13 48	13 58	14 08	14 18	14 28	14 38	14 48		14 58
Homerton	d	11 43	11 51		12 01	12 11	12 21	12 31	12 41	12 51	13 01	13 11	13 21		13 31	13 41	13 51	14 01	14 11	14 21	14 31	14 41	14 51		15 01
Hackney Central	d	11 45	11 53		12 03	12 13	12 23	12 33	12 43	12 53	13 03	13 13	13 23		13 33	13 43	13 53	14 03	14 13	14 23	14 33	14 43	14 53		15 03
Dalston Kingsland	d	11 47	11 55		12 05	12 15	12 25	12 35	12 45	12 55	13 05	13 15	13 25		13 35	13 45	13 55	14 05	14 15	14 25	14 35	14 45	14 55		15 05
Canonbury	d	11 49	11 57		12 07	12 17	12 27	12 37	12 47	12 57	13 07	13 17	13 27		13 37	13 47	13 57	14 07	14 17	14 27	14 37	14 47	14 57		15 07
Highbury & Islington ⊖	d	11 52	12 00		12 10	12 20	12 30	12 40	12 50	13 00	13 10	13 20	13 30		13 40	13 50	14 00	14 10	14 20	14 30	14 40	14 50	15 00		15 10
Caledonian Rd & Barnsbury	d	11 54	12 02		12 12	12 22	12 32	12 42	12 52	13 02	13 12	13 22	13 32		13 42	13 52	14 02	14 12	14 22	14 32	14 42	14 52	15 02		15 12
Camden Road	d	11 57	12 05		12 15	12 25	12 35	12 45	12 55	13 05	13 15	13 25	13 35		13 45	13 55	14 05	14 15	14 25	14 35	14 45	14 55	15 05		15 15
Kentish Town West	d	11 59	12 07		12 17	12 27	12 37	12 47	12 57	13 07	13 17	13 27	13 37		13 47	13 57	14 07	14 17	14 27	14 37	14 47	14 57	15 07		15 17
Gospel Oak	d	12 02	12 10		12 20	12 30	12 40	12 50	13 00	13 10	13 20	13 30	13 41		13 50	14 00	14 10	14 20	14 30	14 40	14 50	15 00	15 10		15 20
Hampstead Heath	d	12 04	12 12		12 22	12 32	12 42	12 52	13 02	13 12	13 22	13 32	13 43		13 52	14 02	14 12	14 22	14 32	14 42	14 52	15 02	15 12		15 22
Finchley Road & Frognal	d	12 06	12 14		12 24	12 34	12 44	12 54	13 04	13 14	13 24	13 34	13 45		13 54	14 04	14 14	14 24	14 34	14 44	14 54	15 04	15 14		15 24
West Hampstead ⊖	d	12 08	12 16		12 26	12 36	12 46	12 56	13 06	13 16	13 26	13 36	13 47		13 56	14 06	14 16	14 26	14 36	14 46	14 56	15 06	15 16		15 26
Brondesbury	d	12 10	12 18		12 28	12 38	12 48	12 58	13 08	13 18	13 28	13 38	13 49		13 58	14 08	14 18	14 28	14 38	14 48	14 58	15 08	15 18		15 28
Brondesbury Park	d	12 11	12 19		12 29	12 39	12 49	12 59	13 09	13 19	13 29	13 39	13 50		13 59	14 09	14 19	14 29	14 39	14 49	14 59	15 09	15 19		15 29
Kensal Rise	d	12 13	12 21		12 31	12 41	12 51	13 01	13 11	13 21	13 31	13 41	13 52		14 01	14 11	14 21	14 31	14 41	14 51	15 01	15 11	15 21		15 31
Willesden Jn. High Level ⊖	a	12 16	12 25		12 35	12 45	12 55	13 05	13 15	13 25	13 35	13 45	13 56		14 05	14 15	14 25	14 35	14 45	14 55	15 05	15 15	15 25		15 35
	d		12 26		12 36		12 56	13 06		13 26	13 36		13 57		14 06		14 26	14 36		14 56	15 06		15 26		15 36
Acton Central	d		12 31		12 41		13 01	13 11		13 31	13 41		14 02		14 11		14 31	14 41		15 01	15 11		15 31		15 41
South Acton	d		12 34		12 44		13 04	13 14		13 34	13 44		14 05		14 14		14 34	14 44		15 04	15 14		15 34		15 44
Gunnersbury ⊖	d		12 38		12 48		13 08	13 18		13 38	13 48		14 09		14 18		14 38	14 48		15 08	15 18		15 38		15 48
Kew Gardens ⊖	d		12 41		12 51		13 11	13 21		13 41	13 51		14 12		14 21		14 41	14 51		15 11	15 21		15 41		15 51
Richmond ⊖	a		12 48		12 58		13 18	13 29		13 49	13 59		14 20		14 29		14 48	14 59		15 19	15 29		15 49		15 58

Stratford - Highbury and Islington, West Hampstead, Willesden Junction and Richmond

Network Diagram - see first Page of Table 59

		LO	LO	LO	LO	LO	LO	LO	LO	LO	LO	LO	LO	LO	LO	LO	LO	LO	LO	LO	LO	LO	LO
Stratford 7 ⊖	d	15 05	15 15	15 25	15 35	15 42	15 50	15 59	16 12	16 20	16 27	16 35	16 42	16 50	16 57	17 05	17 12	17 21	17 27	17 36	17 42	17 51	17 57
Hackney Wick	d	15 08	15 18	15 28	15 38	15 45	15 53	16 02	16 15	16 23	16 30	16 38	16 45	16 53	17 00	17 08	17 15	17 23	17 30	17 38	17 45	17 54	18 00
Homerton	d	15 11	15 21	15 31	15 41	15 48	15 56	16 05	16 18	16 26	16 33	16 40	16 48	16 56	17 03	17 11	17 18	17 26	17 33	17 41	17 48	17 57	18 03
Hackney Central	d	15 13	15 23	15 33	15 43	15 50	15 58	16 07	16 20	16 28	16 35	16 42	16 50	16 58	17 05	17 13	17 20	17 28	17 35	17 43	17 50	17 59	18 05
Dalston Kingsland	d	15 15	15 25	15 35	15 45	15 52	16 00	16 09	16 22	16 30	16 37	16 44	16 52	17 00	17 07	17 15	17 22	17 30	17 37	17 45	17 52	18 01	18 07
Canonbury	d	15 17	15 27	15 37	15 47	15 54	16 02	16 11	16 24	16 32	16 39	16 46	16 54	17 02	17 09	17 17	17 24	17 32	17 39	17 47	17 54	18 03	18 09
Highbury & Islington ⊖	d	15 20	15 30	15 40	15 50	15 57	16 05	16 14	16 27	16 35	16 42	16 49	16 57	17 05	17 12	17 20	17 27	17 35	17 42	17 50	17 57	18 06	18 12
Caledonian Rd & Barnsbury	d	15 22	15 32	15 42	15 52	15 59	16 07	16 16	16 29	16 37	16 44	16 51	16 59	17 07	17 14	17 22	17 29	17 37	17 44	17 52	17 59	18 08	18 14
Camden Road	d	15 25	15 35	15 45	15 55	16 03	16 10	16 19	16 32	16 40	16 47	16 54	17 02	17 10	17 17	17 25	17 32	17 40	17 47	17 55	18 02	18 12	18 17
Kentish Town West	d	15 27	15 37	15 48	15 57	16 06	16 12	16 21	16 34	16 42	16 49	16 58	17 04	17 13	17 19	17 27	17 34	17 42	17 49	17 58	18 05	18 15	18 19
Gospel Oak	d	15 30	15 40	15 50	16 02	16 08	16 15	16 24	16 37	16 45	16 52	17 03	17 08	17 17	17 23	17 30	17 37	17 45	17 52	18 02	18 08	18 18	18 22
Hampstead Heath	d	15 32	15 42	15 52	16 04	16 10	16 17	16 26	16 39	16 47	16 54	17 05	17 10	17 19	17 25	17 32	17 39	17 47	17 54	18 04	18 10	18 20	18 24
Finchley Road & Frognal	d	15 34	15 44	15 54	16 06	16 12	16 19	16 28	16 41	16 49	16 56	17 07	17 12	17 21	17 27	17 34	17 41	17 49	17 56	18 06	18 12	18 22	18 26
West Hampstead ⊖	d	15 36	15 46	15 56	16 08	16 14	16 21	16 30	16 43	16 51	16 58	17 09	17 14	17 23	17 29	17 36	17 43	17 51	17 58	18 08	18 14	18 24	18 28
Brondesbury	d	15 38	15 48	15 58	16 10	16 15	16 23	16 32	16 45	16 53	17 00	17 10	17 16	17 25	17 30	17 38	17 45	17 53	18 00	18 09	18 16	18 26	18 30
Brondesbury Park	d	15 39	15 49	15 59	16 11	16 17	16 24	16 33	16 46	16 54	17 01	17 12	17 17	17 26	17 32	17 39	17 46	17 54	18 01	18 11	18 17	18 27	18 31
Kensal Rise	d	15 41	15 51	16 01	16 13	16 19	16 26	16 35	16 48	16 56	17 03	17 14	17 19	17 28	17 34	17 41	17 48	17 56	18 03	18 13	18 19	18 29	18 33
Willesden Jn. High Level ⊖	a	15 45	15 55	16 05	16 16	16 23	16 30	16 39	16 52	17 00	17 07	17 18	17 23	17 31	17 38	17 45	17 52	18 00	18 07	18 17	18 23	18 32	18 37
	d		15 56	16 06		16 24		16 40	16 53		17 08		17 24		17 39		17 53		18 08		18 24		18 38
Acton Central	d		16 01	16 11		16 29		16 45	16 58		17 13		17 29		17 44		17 58		18 13		18 29		18 43
South Acton	d		16 04	16 14		16 31		16 48	17 01		17 16		17 34		17 46		18 00		18 16		18 32		18 46
Gunnersbury ⊖	d		16 08	16 18		16 34		16 51	17 04		17 19		17 39		17 49		18 03		18 19		18 38		18 49
Kew Gardens ⊖	d		16 11	16 21		16 37		16 54	17 07		17 22		17 42		17 52		18 06		18 22		18 41		18 52
Richmond ⊖	a		16 18	16 29		16 45		17 01	17 12		17 29		17 47		18 00		18 11		18 29		18 46		18 57

		LO	LO	LO	LO	LO	LO	LO	LO	LO	LO	LO	LO	LO	LO	LO	LO	LO	LO	LO	LO	LO	LO
Stratford 7 ⊖	d	18 05	18 12	18 20	18 27	18 35	18 42	18 48	18 57	19 05	19 15	19 25	19 37	19 45	19 55	20 05	20 15	20 25	20 35	20 45	20 55	21 05	21 15
Hackney Wick	d	18 08	18 15	18 23	18 30	18 38	18 45	18 51	19 00	19 08	19 18	19 28	19 40	19 48	19 58	20 08	20 18	20 28	20 38	20 48	20 58	21 08	21 18
Homerton	d	18 11	18 18	18 26	18 33	18 41	18 48	18 54	19 03	19 11	19 21	19 31	19 43	19 51	20 01	20 11	20 21	20 31	20 41	20 51	21 01	21 11	21 21
Hackney Central	d	18 13	18 20	18 28	18 35	18 43	18 50	18 56	19 05	19 13	19 23	19 33	19 45	19 53	20 03	20 13	20 23	20 33	20 43	20 53	21 03	21 13	21 23
Dalston Kingsland	d	18 15	18 22	18 31	18 37	18 45	18 52	18 58	19 07	19 15	19 25	19 35	19 47	19 55	20 05	20 15	20 25	20 35	20 45	20 55	21 05	21 15	21 25
Canonbury	d	18 17	18 24	18 32	18 39	18 47	18 54	19 00	19 09	19 17	19 27	19 37	19 49	19 57	20 07	20 17	20 27	20 37	20 47	20 57	21 07	21 17	21 27
Highbury & Islington ⊖	d	18 20	18 27	18 35	18 42	18 50	18 57	19 03	19 12	19 20	19 30	19 40	19 52	20 00	20 10	20 20	20 30	20 40	20 50	21 00	21 10	21 20	21 30
Caledonian Rd & Barnsbury	d	18 22	18 29	18 37	18 44	18 52	18 59	19 05	19 14	19 22	19 32	19 42	19 54	20 02	20 12	20 22	20 32	20 42	20 52	21 02	21 12	21 22	21 32
Camden Road	d	18 25	18 32	18 40	18 47	18 55	19 02	19 08	19 17	19 25	19 35	19 45	19 57	20 05	20 15	20 25	20 35	20 45	20 55	21 05	21 15	21 25	21 35
Kentish Town West	d	18 27	18 34	18 42	18 49	18 57	19 05	19 10	19 19	19 27	19 37	19 47	19 59	20 07	20 18	20 27	20 37	20 47	20 57	21 07	21 17	21 27	21 37
Gospel Oak	d	18 30	18 37	18 45	18 52	19 00	19 09	19 13	19 24	19 30	19 40	19 50	20 01	20 10	20 22	20 30	20 40	20 50	21 00	21 10	21 20	21 30	21 40
Hampstead Heath	d	18 32	18 39	18 47	18 54	19 02	19 11	19 15	19 26	19 32	19 42	19 52	20 03	20 12	20 24	20 32	20 42	20 52	21 02	21 12	21 22	21 32	21 42
Finchley Road & Frognal	d	18 34	18 41	18 49	18 56	19 04	19 13	19 17	19 28	19 34	19 44	19 54	20 05	20 14	20 26	20 34	20 44	20 54	21 04	21 14	21 24	21 34	21 44
West Hampstead ⊖	d	18 36	18 43	18 51	18 58	19 06	19 15	19 19	19 30	19 36	19 46	19 56	20 07	20 16	20 28	20 36	20 46	20 56	21 06	21 16	21 26	21 36	21 46
Brondesbury	d	18 38	18 45	18 53	19 00	19 08	19 16	19 21	19 32	19 38	19 48	19 58	20 09	20 18	20 29	20 38	20 48	20 57	21 08	21 18	21 28	21 38	21 48
Brondesbury Park	d	18 39	18 46	18 54	19 01	19 09	19 18	19 22	19 33	19 39	19 49	19 59	20 10	20 19	20 31	20 39	20 49	20 59	21 09	21 19	21 29	21 39	21 49
Kensal Rise	d	18 41	18 48	18 56	19 03	19 11	19 20	19 24	19 35	19 41	19 51	20 01	20 12	20 21	20 33	20 41	20 51	21 01	21 11	21 21	21 31	21 41	21 51
Willesden Jn. High Level ⊖	a	18 45	18 52	19 00	19 07	19 15	19 24	19 29	19 39	19 45	19 55	20 05	20 16	20 25	20 36	20 45	20 55	21 05	21 15	21 25	21 35	21 45	21 55
	d		18 53		19 08		19 25		19 40		19 56	20 06		20 26	20 37		20 57	21 06		21 26	21 36		21 56
Acton Central	d		18 58		19 13		19 30		19 45		20 01	20 11		20 31	20 42		21 02	21 11		21 31	21 41		22 01
South Acton	d		19 01		19 16		19 32		19 48		20 04	20 14		20 34	20 44		21 05	21 13		21 34	21 44		22 04
Gunnersbury ⊖	d		19 06		19 19		19 38		19 51		20 09	20 18		20 38	20 49		21 08	21 18		21 38	21 48		22 08
Kew Gardens ⊖	d		19 09		19 22		19 41		19 54		20 12	20 21		20 41	20 52		21 11	21 21		21 41	21 51		22 11
Richmond ⊖	a		19 16		19 28		19 46		20 01		20 19	20 28		20 48	20 58		21 19	21 27		21 48	21 58		22 18

		LO	LO	LO	LO	LO	LO	LO	LO	LO	LO
Stratford 7 ⊖	d	21 25	21 35	21 45	21 55	22 15	22 25	22 45	22 55	23 15	23 45
Hackney Wick	d	21 28	21 38	21 48	21 58	22 18	22 28	22 48	22 58	23 18	23 48
Homerton	d	21 31	21 41	21 51	22 01	22 21	22 31	22 51	23 01	23 21	23 51
Hackney Central	d	21 33	21 43	21 53	22 03	22 23	22 33	22 53	23 03	23 23	23 53
Dalston Kingsland	d	21 35	21 45	21 55	22 05	22 25	22 35	22 55	23 05	23 25	23 55
Canonbury	d	21 37	21 47	21 57	22 07	22 27	22 37	22 57	23 07	23 27	23 57
Highbury & Islington ⊖	d	21 40	21 50	22 00	22 10	22 30	22 40	23 00	23 10	23 30	23 59
Caledonian Rd & Barnsbury	d	21 42	21 52	22 02	22 12	22 32	22 42	23 02	23 12	23 32	00 02
Camden Road	d	21 45	21 55	22 05	22 15	22 35	22a46	23 05	23a16	23 35	00 05
Kentish Town West	d	21 47	21 57	22 07	22 17	22 37		23 07		23 37	00 07
Gospel Oak	d	21 50	22 00	22 10	22 20	22 40		23 10		23 40	00 10
Hampstead Heath	d	21 52	22 02	22 12	22 22	22 42		23 12		23 42	00 12
Finchley Road & Frognal	d	21 54	22 04	22 14	22 24	22 44		23 14		23 44	00 14
West Hampstead ⊖	d	21 56	22 06	22 16	22 26	22 46		23 16		23 46	00 16
Brondesbury	d	21 58	22 08	22 18	22 28	22 48		23 18		23 48	00 18
Brondesbury Park	d	21 59	22 09	22 19	22 29	22 49		23 19		23 49	00 19
Kensal Rise	d	22 01	22 11	22 21	22 31	22 51		23 21		23a51	00a21
Willesden Jn. High Level ⊖	a	22 05	22 15	22 25	22 35	22 55		23 25			
	d	22 06		22 26	22 36	22 56		23 26			
Acton Central	d	22 11		22 31	22 41	23 01		23 31			
South Acton	d	22 14		22 34	22 44	23 04		23 34			
Gunnersbury ⊖	d	22 18		22 38	22 48	23 08		23 38			
Kew Gardens ⊖	d	22 21		22 41	22 51	23 11		23 41			
Richmond ⊖	a	22 27		22 48	22 58	23 18		23 48			

Table 59

Saturdays

Stratford - Highbury and Islington, West Hampstead, Willesden Junction and Richmond

Network Diagram - see first Page of Table 59

		LO	LO	LO	LO	LO	LO	LO	LO	LO		LO	LO	LO	LO	LO	LO	LO	LO	LO		LO	LO	LO	LO
Stratford 7 ⊖	d	23p45		05 42	05 55	06 05	06 15	06 25	06 35	06 45		06 55	07 05	07 15	07 25	07 35	07 45	07 55	08 05	08 15		08 25	08 35	08 45	08 55
Hackney Wick	d	23p48		05 45	05 58	06 08	06 18	06 28	06 38	06 48		06 58	07 08	07 18	07 28	07 38	07 48	07 58	08 08	08 18		08 28	08 38	08 48	08 58
Homerton	d	23p51		05 48	06 01	06 11	06 21	06 31	06 41	06 51		07 01	07 11	07 21	07 31	07 41	07 51	08 01	08 11	08 21		08 31	08 41	08 51	09 01
Hackney Central	d	23p53		05 50	06 03	06 13	06 23	06 33	06 43	06 53		07 03	07 13	07 23	07 33	07 43	07 53	08 03	08 13	08 23		08 33	08 43	08 53	09 03
Dalston Kingsland	d	23p55		05 52	06 05	06 15	06 25	06 35	06 45	06 55		07 05	07 15	07 25	07 35	07 45	07 55	08 05	08 15	08 25		08 35	08 45	08 55	09 05
Canonbury	d	23p57		05 54	06 07	06 17	06 27	06 37	06 47	06 57		07 07	07 17	07 27	07 37	07 47	07 57	08 07	08 17	08 27		08 37	08 47	08 57	09 07
Highbury & Islington ⊖	d	23p59		05 57	06 10	06 20	06 30	06 40	06 50	07 00		07 10	07 20	07 30	07 40	07 50	08 00	08 10	08 20	08 30		08 40	08 50	09 00	09 10
Caledonian Rd & Barnsbury	d	00 02		05 59	06 12	06 22	06 32	06 42	06 52	07 02		07 12	07 22	07 32	07 42	07 52	08 02	08 12	08 22	08 32		08 42	08 52	09 02	09 12
Camden Road	d	00 05		06 02	06 15	06 25	06 35	06 45	06 55	07 05		07 15	07 25	07 35	07 45	07 55	08 05	08 15	08 25	08 35		08 45	08 55	09 05	09 15
Kentish Town West	d	00 07		06 07	06 17	06 27	06 37	06 47	06 57	07 07		07 17	07 27	07 37	07 47	07 57	08 07	08 17	08 27	08 37		08 47	08 57	09 07	09 17
Gospel Oak	d	00 10		06 11	06 20	06 30	06 40	06 50	07 00	07 10		07 20	07 30	07 40	07 50	08 00	08 10	08 20	08 30	08 40		08 50	09 00	09 10	09 20
Hampstead Heath	d	00 12		06 13	06 22	06 32	06 42	06 52	07 02	07 12		07 22	07 32	07 42	07 52	08 02	08 12	08 22	08 32	08 42		08 52	09 02	09 12	09 22
Finchley Road & Frognal	d	00 14		06 15	06 24	06 34	06 44	06 54	07 04	07 14		07 24	07 34	07 44	07 54	08 04	08 14	08 24	08 34	08 44		08 54	09 04	09 14	09 24
West Hampstead ⊖	d	00 16		06 17	06 26	06 36	06 46	06 56	07 06	07 16		07 26	07 36	07 46	07 56	08 06	08 16	08 26	08 36	08 46		08 56	09 06	09 16	09 26
Brondesbury	d	00 18		06 19	06 28	06 38	06 48	06 58	07 08	07 18		07 28	07 38	07 48	07 58	08 08	08 18	08 28	08 38	08 48		08 58	09 08	09 18	09 28
Brondesbury Park	d	00 19		06 20	06 29	06 39	06 49	06 59	07 09	07 19		07 29	07 39	07 49	07 59	08 09	08 19	08 29	08 39	08 49		08 59	09 09	09 19	09 29
Kensal Rise	d	00a21		06 22	06 31	06 41	06 51	07 01	07 11	07 21		07 31	07 41	07 51	08 01	08 11	08 21	08 31	08 41	08 51		09 01	09 11	09 21	09 31
Willesden Jn. High Level ⊖	a			06 25	06 35	06 45	06 55	07 05	07 15	07 25		07 35	07 45	07 55	08 05	08 15	08 25	08 35	08 45	08 55		09 05	09 15	09 25	09 35
	d		06 06	06 26	06 36		06 56	07 06		07 26		07 36		07 56	08 06		08 26	08 36		08 56		09 06		09 26	09 36
Acton Central	d		06 11	06 31	06 41		07 01	07 11		07 31		07 41		08 01	08 11		08 31	08 41		09 01		09 11		09 31	09 41
South Acton	d		06 14	06 34	06 44		07 04	07 14		07 34		07 44		08 04	08 14		08 34	08 44		09 04		09 14		09 34	09 44
Gunnersbury ⊖	d		06 19	06 37	06 47		07 07	07 17		07 37		07 48		08 08	08 18		08 38	08 48		09 08		09 18		09 38	09 48
Kew Gardens ⊖	d		06 22	06 40	06 50		07 10	07 20		07 40		07 51		08 11	08 21		08 41	08 51		09 11		09 21		09 41	09 51
Richmond ⊖	a		06 29	06 47	06 57		07 17	07 27		07 47		07 57		08 17	08 27		08 47	08 57		09 17		09 28		09 47	09 57

		LO	LO	LO	LO	LO		LO	LO	LO	LO	LO	LO	LO	LO	LO		LO	LO	LO	LO	LO	LO	LO	LO
Stratford 7 ⊖	d	09 05	09 15	09 25	09 35	09 45		09 55	10 05	10 15	10 25	10 35	10 45	10 55	11 05	11 15		11 25	11 35	11 45	11 55	12 05	12 15	12 25	12 35
Hackney Wick	d	09 08	09 18	09 28	09 38	09 48		09 58	10 08	10 18	10 28	10 38	10 48	10 58	11 08	11 18		11 28	11 38	11 48	11 58	12 08	12 18	12 28	12 38
Homerton	d	09 11	09 21	09 31	09 41	09 51		10 01	10 11	10 21	10 31	10 41	10 51	11 01	11 11	11 21		11 31	11 41	11 51	12 01	12 11	12 21	12 31	12 41
Hackney Central	d	09 13	09 23	09 33	09 43	09 53		10 03	10 13	10 23	10 33	10 43	10 53	11 03	11 13	11 23		11 33	11 43	11 53	12 03	12 13	12 23	12 33	12 43
Dalston Kingsland	d	09 15	09 25	09 35	09 45	09 55		10 05	10 15	10 25	10 35	10 45	10 55	11 05	11 15	11 25		11 35	11 45	11 55	12 05	12 15	12 25	12 35	12 45
Canonbury	d	09 17	09 27	09 37	09 47	09 57		10 07	10 17	10 27	10 37	10 47	10 57	11 07	11 17	11 27		11 37	11 47	11 57	12 07	12 17	12 27	12 37	12 47
Highbury & Islington ⊖	d	09 20	09 30	09 40	09 50	10 00		10 10	10 20	10 30	10 40	10 50	11 00	11 10	11 20	11 30		11 40	11 50	12 00	12 10	12 20	12 30	12 40	12 50
Caledonian Rd & Barnsbury	d	09 22	09 32	09 42	09 52	10 02		10 12	10 22	10 32	10 42	10 52	11 02	11 12	11 22	11 32		11 42	11 52	12 02	12 12	12 22	12 32	12 42	12 52
Camden Road	d	09 25	09 35	09 45	09 55	10 05		10 15	10 25	10 35	10 45	10 55	11 05	11 15	11 25	11 35		11 45	11 55	12 05	12 15	12 25	12 35	12 45	12 55
Kentish Town West	d	09 27	09 37	09 47	09 57	10 07		10 17	10 27	10 37	10 47	10 57	11 07	11 17	11 27	11 37		11 47	11 57	12 07	12 17	12 27	12 37	12 47	12 57
Gospel Oak	d	09 30	09 40	09 50	10 00	10 10		10 20	10 30	10 40	10 50	11 00	11 10	11 20	11 30	11 40		11 50	12 00	12 10	12 20	12 30	12 40	12 50	13 00
Hampstead Heath	d	09 32	09 42	09 52	10 02	10 12		10 22	10 32	10 42	10 52	11 02	11 12	11 22	11 32	11 42		11 52	12 02	12 12	12 22	12 32	12 42	12 52	13 02
Finchley Road & Frognal	d	09 34	09 44	09 54	10 04	10 14		10 24	10 34	10 44	10 54	11 04	11 14	11 24	11 34	11 44		11 54	12 04	12 14	12 24	12 34	12 44	12 54	13 04
West Hampstead ⊖	d	09 36	09 46	09 56	10 06	10 16		10 26	10 36	10 46	10 56	11 06	11 16	11 26	11 36	11 46		11 56	12 06	12 16	12 26	12 36	12 46	12 56	13 06
Brondesbury	d	09 38	09 48	09 58	10 08	10 18		10 28	10 38	10 48	10 58	11 08	11 18	11 28	11 38	11 48		11 58	12 08	12 18	12 28	12 38	12 48	12 58	13 08
Brondesbury Park	d	09 39	09 49	09 59	10 09	10 19		10 29	10 39	10 49	10 59	11 09	11 19	11 29	11 39	11 49		11 59	12 09	12 19	12 29	12 39	12 49	12 59	13 09
Kensal Rise	d	09 41	09 51	10 01	10 11	10 21		10 31	10 41	10 51	11 01	11 11	11 21	11 31	11 41	11 51		12 01	12 11	12 21	12 31	12 41	12 51	13 01	13 11
Willesden Jn. High Level ⊖	a	09 45	09 55	10 05	10 15	10 25		10 35	10 45	10 55	11 05	11 15	11 25	11 35	11 45	11 55		12 05	12 15	12 25	12 35	12 45	12 55	13 05	13 15
	d		09 56	10 06		10 26		10 36		10 56	11 06		11 26	11 36		11 56		12 06		12 26	12 36		12 56	13 06	
Acton Central	d		10 01	10 11		10 31		10 41		11 01	11 11		11 31	11 41		12 01		12 11		12 31	12 41		13 01	13 11	
South Acton	d		10 04	10 14		10 34		10 45		11 04	11 14		11 34	11 44		12 04		12 14		12 34	12 44		13 04	13 14	
Gunnersbury ⊖	d		10 08	10 18		10 38		10 48		11 08	11 18		11 38	11 48		12 08		12 18		12 38	12 48		13 08	13 18	
Kew Gardens ⊖	d		10 11	10 21		10 41		10 51		11 11	11 21		11 41	11 51		12 11		12 21		12 41	12 51		13 11	13 21	
Richmond ⊖	a		10 17	10 27		10 47		10 57		11 17	11 27		11 47	11 57		12 17		12 27		12 47	12 57		13 17	13 28	

		LO		LO	LO	LO	LO		LO	LO	LO		LO	LO	LO	LO	LO	LO	LO	LO	LO		LO	LO
Stratford 7 ⊖	d	12 45		12 55	13 05	13 15	13 25		17 25	17 35	17 45		17 55	18 05	18 15	18 25	18 35	18 45	18 55	19 05	19 15		19 25	19 35
Hackney Wick	d	12 48		12 58	13 08	13 18	13 28		17 28	17 38	17 48		17 58	18 08	18 18	18 28	18 38	18 48	18 58	19 08	19 18		19 28	19 38
Homerton	d	12 51		13 01	13 11	13 21	13 31		17 31	17 41	17 51		18 01	18 11	18 21	18 31	18 41	18 51	19 01	19 11	19 21		19 31	19 41
Hackney Central	d	12 53		13 03	13 13	13 23	13 33		17 33	17 43	17 53		18 03	18 13	18 23	18 33	18 43	18 53	19 03	19 13	19 23		19 33	19 43
Dalston Kingsland	d	12 55		13 05	13 15	13 25	13 35		17 35	17 45	17 55		18 05	18 15	18 25	18 35	18 45	18 55	19 05	19 15	19 25		19 35	19 45
Canonbury	d	12 57		13 07	13 17	13 27	13 37		17 37	17 47	17 57		18 07	18 17	18 27	18 37	18 47	18 57	19 07	19 17	19 27		19 37	19 47
Highbury & Islington ⊖	d	13 00		13 10	13 20	13 30	13 40		17 40	17 50	18 00		18 10	18 20	18 30	18 40	18 50	19 00	19 10	19 20	19 30		19 40	19 50
Caledonian Rd & Barnsbury	d	13 02		13 12	13 22	13 32	13 42		17 42	17 52	18 02		18 12	18 22	18 32	18 42	18 52	19 02	19 12	19 22	19 32		19 42	19 52
Camden Road	d	13 05		13 15	13 25	13 35	13 45	and at the same minutes past each hour until	17 45	17 55	18 05		18 15	18 25	18 35	18 45	18 55	19 05	19 15	19 25	19 35		19 45	19 55
Kentish Town West	d	13 07		13 17	13 27	13 37	13 47		17 47	17 57	18 07		18 17	18 27	18 37	18 47	18 57	19 07	19 17	19 27	19 37		19 47	19 57
Gospel Oak	d	13 10		13 20	13 30	13 40	13 50		17 50	18 00	18 10		18 20	18 30	18 40	18 50	19 00	19 10	19 20	19 30	19 40		19 50	20 00
Hampstead Heath	d	13 12		13 22	13 32	13 42	13 52		17 52	18 02	18 12		18 22	18 32	18 42	18 52	19 02	19 12	19 22	19 32	19 42		19 52	20 02
Finchley Road & Frognal	d	13 14		13 24	13 34	13 44	13 54		17 54	18 04	18 14		18 24	18 34	18 44	18 54	19 04	19 14	19 24	19 34	19 44		19 54	20 04
West Hampstead ⊖	d	13 16		13 26	13 36	13 46	13 56		17 56	18 06	18 16		18 26	18 36	18 46	18 56	19 06	19 16	19 26	19 36	19 46		19 56	20 06
Brondesbury	d	13 18		13 28	13 38	13 48	13 58		17 58	18 08	18 18		18 28	18 38	18 48	18 58	19 08	19 18	19 28	19 38	19 48		19 58	20 08
Brondesbury Park	d	13 19		13 29	13 39	13 49	13 59		17 59	18 09	18 19		18 29	18 39	18 49	18 59	19 09	19 19	19 29	19 39	19 49		19 59	20 09
Kensal Rise	d	13 21		13 31	13 41	13 51	14 01		18 01	18 11	18 21		18 31	18 41	18 51	19 01	19 11	19 21	19 31	19 41	19 51		20 01	20 11
Willesden Jn. High Level ⊖	a	13 25		13 35	13 45	13 55	14 05		18 05	18 15	18 25		18 35	18 45	18 55	19 05	19 15	19 25	19 35	19 45	19 55		20 05	20 15
	d	13 26		13 36		13 56	14 06		18 06		18 26		18 36		18 56	19 05		19 26	19 36		19 56		20 06	
Acton Central	d	13 31		13 41		14 01	14 11		18 11		18 31		18 41		19 01	19 10		19 31	19 41		20 01		20 11	
South Acton	d	13 34		13 44		14 04	14 14		18 14		18 34		18 44		19 04	19 13		19 34	19 44		20 04		20 14	
Gunnersbury ⊖	d	13 38		13 48		14 08	14 18		18 18		18 38		18 48		19 08	19 17		19 38	19 48		20 08		20 18	
Kew Gardens ⊖	d	13 41		13 51		14 11	14 21		18 21		18 41		18 51		19 11	19 20		19 41	19 51		20 11		20 21	
Richmond ⊖	a	13 47		13 57		14 17	14 27		18 27		18 47		18 57		19 17	19 28		19 47	19 57		20 17		20 27	

Table 59

Saturdays

Stratford - Highbury and Islington, West Hampstead, Willesden Junction and Richmond

Network Diagram - see first Page of Table 59

			LO	LO	LO	LO	LO	LO	LO	LO	LO	LO	LO	LO	LO	LO	LO	LO	LO	LO	LO	LO
Stratford 7	⊖	d	19 45	19 55	20 05	20 15	20 25	20 35	20 45	20 55	21 05	21 15	21 25	21 35	21 45	21 55	22 15	22 25	22 45	22 55	23 15	23 45
Hackney Wick		d	19 48	19 58	20 08	20 18	20 28	20 38	20 48	20 58	21 08	21 18	21 28	21 38	21 48	21 58	22 18	22 28	22 48	22 58	23 18	23 48
Homerton		d	19 51	20 01	20 11	20 21	20 31	20 41	20 51	21 01	21 11	21 21	21 31	21 41	21 51	22 01	22 21	22 31	22 51	23 01	23 21	23 51
Hackney Central		d	19 53	20 03	20 13	20 23	20 33	20 43	20 53	21 03	21 13	21 23	21 33	21 43	21 53	22 03	22 23	22 33	22 53	23 03	23 23	23 53
Dalston Kingsland		d	19 55	20 05	20 15	20 25	20 35	20 45	20 55	21 05	21 15	21 25	21 35	21 45	21 55	22 05	22 25	22 35	22 55	23 05	23 25	23 55
Canonbury		d	19 57	20 07	20 17	20 27	20 37	20 47	20 57	21 07	21 17	21 27	21 37	21 47	21 57	22 07	22 27	22 37	22 57	23 07	23 27	23 57
Highbury & Islington	⊖	d	20 00	20 10	20 20	20 30	20 40	20 50	21 00	21 10	21 20	21 30	21 40	21 50	22 00	22 10	22 30	22 40	23 00	23 10	23 30	23 59
Caledonian Rd & Barnsbury		d	20 02	20 12	20 22	20 32	20 42	20 52	21 02	21 12	21 22	21 32	21 42	21 52	22 02	22 12	22 32	22 42	23 02	23 12	23 32	00 02
Camden Road		d	20 05	20 15	20 25	20 35	20 45	20 55	21 05	21 15	21 25	21 35	21 45	21 55	22 05	22 15	22 35	22a45	23 05	23a15	23 35	00 05
Kentish Town West		d	20 07	20 17	20 27	20 37	20 47	20 57	21 07	21 17	21 27	21 37	21 47	21 57	22 07	22 17	22 37		23 07		23 37	00 07
Gospel Oak		d	20 10	20 20	20 30	20 40	20 50	21 00	21 10	21 20	21 30	21 40	21 50	22 00	22 10	22 20	22 40		23 10		23 40	00 10
Hampstead Heath		d	20 12	20 22	20 32	20 42	20 52	21 02	21 12	21 22	21 32	21 42	21 52	22 02	22 12	22 22	22 42		23 12		23 42	00 12
Finchley Road & Frognal		d	20 14	20 24	20 34	20 44	20 54	21 04	21 14	21 24	21 34	21 44	21 54	22 04	22 14	22 24	22 44		23 14		23 44	00 14
West Hampstead	⊖	d	20 16	20 26	20 36	20 46	20 56	21 06	21 16	21 26	21 36	21 46	21 56	22 06	22 16	22 26	22 46		23 16		23 46	00 16
Brondesbury		d	20 18	20 28	20 38	20 48	20 58	21 08	21 18	21 28	21 38	21 48	21 58	22 08	22 18	22 28	22 48		23 18		23 48	00 18
Brondesbury Park		d	20 19	20 29	20 39	20 49	20 59	21 09	21 19	21 29	21 39	21 49	21 59	22 09	22 19	22 29	22 49		23 19		23 49	00 19
Kensal Rise		d	20 21	20 31	20 41	20 51	21 01	21 11	21 21	21 31	21 41	21 51	22 01	22 11	22 21	22 31	22 51		23 21		23 51	00a21
Willesden Jn. High Level	⊖	a	20 25	20 35	20 45	20 55	21 05	21 15	21 25	21 35	21 45	21 55	22 05	22 15	22 25	22 35	22 55		23 25		23 54	
		d	20 26	20 36		20 56	21 06		21 26	21 36		21 56	22 06		22 26	22 36	22 56		23 26			
Acton Central		d	20 31	20 41		21 01	21 11		21 31	21 41		22 01	22 11		22 31	22 41	23 01		23 31			
South Acton		d	20 34	20 44		21 04	21 14		21 34	21 44		22 04	22 14		22 34	22 44	23 04		23 34			
Gunnersbury	⊖	d	20 38	20 48		21 08	21 18		21 38	21 48		22 08	22 18		22 38	22 48	23 08		23 38			
Kew Gardens	⊖	d	20 41	20 51		21 11	21 21		21 41	21 51		22 11	22 21		22 41	22 51	23 11		23 41			
Richmond	⊖	a	20 47	20 57		21 17	21 27		21 47	21 58		22 17	22 27		22 47	22 57	23 17		23 47			

Sundays

			LO A	LO	LO	LO	LO	LO	LO	LO	LO	LO	LO	LO	LO	LO	LO	LO	LO		LO	LO	LO
Stratford 7	⊖	d	23p45				09 15	09 30	09 45	10 00	10 20	10 35		10 45	10 55	11 05	11 15	11 25	11 35		14 35	14 45	14 55
Hackney Wick		d	23p48				09 18	09 33	09 48	10 03	10 23	10 38		10 48	10 58	11 08	11 18	11 28	11 38		14 38	14 48	14 58
Homerton		d	23p51				09 21	09 36	09 51	10 06	10 26	10 41		10 51	11 01	11 11	11 21	11 31	11 41		14 41	14 51	15 01
Hackney Central		d	23p53				09 23	09 38	09 53	10 08	10 28	10 43		10 53	11 03	11 13	11 23	11 33	11 43		14 43	14 53	15 03
Dalston Kingsland		d	23p55				09 25	09 40	09 55	10 10	10 30	10 45		10 55	11 05	11 15	11 25	11 35	11 45		14 45	14 55	15 05
Canonbury		d	23p57				09 27	09 42	09 57	10 12	10 32	10 47		10 57	11 07	11 17	11 27	11 37	11 47		14 47	14 57	15 07
Highbury & Islington	⊖	d	23p59				09 30	09 45	10 00	10 15	10 35	10 50		11 00	11 10	11 20	11 30	11 40	11 50		14 50	15 00	15 10
Caledonian Rd & Barnsbury		d	00 02				09 32	09 47	10 02	10 17	10 37	10 52		11 02	11 12	11 22	11 32	11 42	11 52	and at the same minutes past each hour until	14 52	15 02	15 12
Camden Road		d	00 05				09 35	09 50	10 05	10 20	10 40	10 55		11 05	11 15	11 25	11 35	11 45	11 55		14 55	15 05	15 15
Kentish Town West		d	00 07				09 37	09 52	10 07	10 22	10 42	10 57		11 07	11 17	11 27	11 37	11 47	11 57		14 57	15 07	15 17
Gospel Oak		d	00 10			09 24	09 40	09 55	10 10	10 25	10 45	11 00		11 10	11 20	11 30	11 40	11 50	12 00		15 00	15 10	15 20
Hampstead Heath		d	00 12			09 26	09 42	09 57	10 12	10 27	10 47	11 02		11 12	11 22	11 32	11 42	11 52	12 02		15 02	15 12	15 22
Finchley Road & Frognal		d	00 14			09 28	09 44	09 59	10 14	10 29	10 49	11 04		11 14	11 24	11 34	11 44	11 54	12 04		15 04	15 14	15 24
West Hampstead	⊖	d	00 16			09 30	09 46	10 01	10 16	10 31	10 51	11 06		11 16	11 26	11 36	11 46	11 56	12 06		15 06	15 16	15 26
Brondesbury		d	00 18			09 32	09 48	10 03	10 18	10 33	10 53	11 08		11 18	11 28	11 38	11 48	11 58	12 08		15 08	15 18	15 28
Brondesbury Park		d	00 19			09 33	09 49	10 04	10 19	10 34	10 54	11 09		11 19	11 29	11 39	11 49	11 59	12 09		15 09	15 19	15 29
Kensal Rise		d	00a21			09 35	09 51	10 06	10 21	10 36	10 56	11 11		11 21	11 31	11 41	11 51	12 01	12 11		15 11	15 21	15 31
Willesden Jn. High Level	⊖	a				09 39	09 55	10 10	10 25	10 40	11 00	11 15		11 25	11 35	11 45	11 55	12 05	12 15		15 15	15 25	15 35
		d		08 56	09 26	09 40	09 56	10 11	10 26	10 41	11 01		11 16	11 26	11 36		11 56	12 06				15 26	15 36
Acton Central		d		09 01	09 31	09 45	10 01	10 16	10 31	10 46	11 06		11 21	11 31	11 41		12 01	12 11				15 31	15 41
South Acton		d		09 03	09 34	09 47	10 04	10 19	10 34	10 49	11 09		11 24	11 34	11 44		12 04	12 14				15 34	15 44
Gunnersbury	⊖	d		09 08	09 38	09 50	10 08	10 22	10 38	10 52	11 12		11 28	11 38	11 48		12 08	12 18				15 38	15 48
Kew Gardens	⊖	d		09 11	09 41	09 53	10 11	10 25	10 41	10 55	11 15		11 31	11 41	11 51		12 11	12 21				15 41	15 51
Richmond	⊖	a		09 19	09 49	10 03	10 18	10 34	10 47	11 04	11 22		11 38	11 47	11 57		12 17	12 27				15 47	15 57

			LO	LO	LO	LO	LO	LO	LO	LO	LO	LO	LO	LO	LO	LO	LO	LO	LO	LO	LO	LO	LO	LO
Stratford 7	⊖	d	15 05	15 15	15 25	15 35	15 45	15 55	16 05	16 15	16 25	16 35	16 45	16 55	17 05	17 15	17 25	17 35	17 45	17 55	18 05	18 15	18 25	18 35
Hackney Wick		d	15 08	15 18	15 28	15 38	15 48	15 58	16 08	16 18	16 28	16 38	16 48	16 58	17 08	17 18	17 28	17 38	17 48	17 58	18 08	18 18	18 28	18 38
Homerton		d	15 11	15 21	15 31	15 41	15 51	16 01	16 11	16 21	16 31	16 41	16 51	17 01	17 11	17 21	17 31	17 41	17 51	18 01	18 11	18 21	18 31	18 41
Hackney Central		d	15 13	15 23	15 33	15 43	15 53	16 03	16 13	16 23	16 33	16 43	16 53	17 03	17 13	17 23	17 33	17 43	17 53	18 03	18 13	18 23	18 33	18 43
Dalston Kingsland		d	15 15	15 25	15 35	15 45	15 55	16 05	16 15	16 25	16 35	16 45	16 55	17 05	17 15	17 25	17 35	17 45	17 55	18 05	18 15	18 25	18 35	18 45
Canonbury		d	15 17	15 27	15 37	15 47	15 57	16 07	16 17	16 27	16 37	16 47	16 57	17 07	17 17	17 27	17 37	17 47	17 57	18 07	18 17	18 27	18 37	18 47
Highbury & Islington	⊖	d	15 20	15 30	15 40	15 50	16 00	16 10	16 20	16 30	16 40	16 50	17 00	17 10	17 20	17 30	17 40	17 50	18 00	18 10	18 20	18 30	18 40	18 50
Caledonian Rd & Barnsbury		d	15 22	15 32	15 42	15 52	16 02	16 12	16 22	16 32	16 42	16 52	17 02	17 12	17 22	17 32	17 42	17 52	18 02	18 12	18 22	18 32	18 42	18 52
Camden Road		d	15 25	15 35	15 45	15 55	16 05	16 15	16 25	16 35	16 45	16 55	17 05	17 15	17 25	17 35	17 45	17 55	18 05	18 15	18 25	18 35	18 45	18 55
Kentish Town West		d	15 27	15 37	15 47	15 57	16 07	16 17	16 27	16 37	16 47	16 57	17 07	17 17	17 27	17 37	17 47	17 57	18 07	18 17	18 27	18 37	18 47	18 57
Gospel Oak		d	15 30	15 40	15 50	16 00	16 10	16 20	16 30	16 40	16 50	17 01	17 10	17 20	17 31	17 40	17 50	18 02	18 10	18 20	18 30	18 40	18 50	19 00
Hampstead Heath		d	15 32	15 42	15 52	16 02	16 12	16 22	16 32	16 42	16 52	17 02	17 12	17 22	17 32	17 42	17 52	18 02	18 12	18 22	18 32	18 42	18 52	19 02
Finchley Road & Frognal		d	15 34	15 44	15 54	16 04	16 14	16 24	16 34	16 44	16 54	17 04	17 14	17 24	17 34	17 44	17 54	18 04	18 14	18 24	18 34	18 44	18 54	19 04
West Hampstead	⊖	d	15 36	15 46	15 56	16 06	16 16	16 26	16 36	16 46	16 56	17 06	17 16	17 26	17 36	17 46	17 56	18 06	18 16	18 26	18 36	18 46	18 56	19 06
Brondesbury		d	15 38	15 48	15 58	16 08	16 18	16 28	16 38	16 48	16 58	17 08	17 18	17 28	17 38	17 48	17 58	18 08	18 18	18 28	18 38	18 48	18 58	19 08
Brondesbury Park		d	15 39	15 49	15 59	16 09	16 19	16 29	16 39	16 49	16 59	17 09	17 19	17 29	17 39	17 49	17 59	18 09	18 19	18 29	18 39	18 49	18 59	19 09
Kensal Rise		d	15 41	15 51	16 01	16 11	16 21	16 31	16 41	16 51	17 01	17 11	17 21	17 31	17 41	17 51	18 01	18 11	18 21	18 31	18 41	18 51	19 01	19 11
Willesden Jn. High Level	⊖	a	15 45	15 55	16 05	16 15	16 25	16 35	16 45	16 55	17 05	17 15	17 25	17 35	17 45	17 55	18 05	18 15	18 25	18 35	18 45	18 55	19 05	19 15
		d		15 56	16 06		16 26	16 36		16 56	17 06		17 26	17 36		17 56	18 06		18 26	18 36		18 56	19 06	
Acton Central		d		16 01	16 11		16 31	16 41		17 01	17 11		17 31	17 41		18 01	18 11		18 31	18 41		19 01	19 11	
South Acton		d		16 04	16 14		16 34	16 44		17 04	17 14		17 34	17 44		18 04	18 14		18 34	18 44		19 04	19 14	
Gunnersbury	⊖	d		16 08	16 18		16 38	16 48		17 08	17 18		17 38	17 48		18 08	18 18		18 38	18 48		19 08	19 18	
Kew Gardens	⊖	d		16 11	16 21		16 41	16 51		17 11	17 21		17 41	17 51		18 11	18 21		18 41	18 51		19 11	19 21	
Richmond	⊖	a		16 18	16 27		16 47	16 57		17 17	17 27		17 47	17 57		18 17	18 27		18 47	18 57		19 17	19 27	

A not 11 December

Table 59

Sundays

Stratford - Highbury and Islington, West Hampstead, Willesden Junction and Richmond

Network Diagram - see first Page of Table 59

			LO	LO	LO		LO	LO	LO	LO	LO	LO	LO	LO	LO		LO	LO	LO	LO	LO	LO	LO	LO	LO	
Stratford 7	⊖	d	18 45	18 55	19 05		19 15	19 25	19 35	19 45	19 55	20 05	20 15	20 25	20 35		20 45	20 55	21 05	21 15	21 30	21 45	22 00			
Hackney Wick		d	18 48	18 58	19 08		19 18	19 28	19 38	19 48	19 58	20 08	20 18	20 28	20 38		20 48	20 58	21 08	21 18	21 33	21 48	22 03			
Homerton		d	18 51	19 01	19 11		19 21	19 31	19 41	19 51	20 01	20 11	20 21	20 31	20 41		20 51	21 01	21 11	21 21	21 36	21 51	22 06			
Hackney Central		d	18 53	19 03	19 13		19 23	19 33	19 43	19 53	20 03	20 13	20 23	20 33	20 43		20 53	21 03	21 13	21 23	21 38	21 53	22 08			
Dalston Kingsland		d	18 55	19 05	19 15		19 25	19 35	19 45	19 55	20 05	20 15	20 25	20 35	20 45		20 55	21 05	21 15	21 25	21 40	21 55	22 10			
Canonbury		d	18 57	19 07	19 17		19 27	19 37	19 47	19 57	20 07	20 17	20 27	20 37	20 47		20 57	21 07	21 17	21 27	21 42	21 57	22 12			
Highbury & Islington	⊖	d	19 00	19 10	19 20		19 30	19 40	19 50	20 00	20 10	20 20	20 30	20 40	20 50		21 00	21 10	21 20	21 30	21 45	22 00	22 15			
Caledonian Rd & Barnsbury		d	19 02	19 12	19 22		19 32	19 42	19 52	20 02	20 12	20 22	20 32	20 42	20 52		21 02	21 12	21 22	21 32	21 47	22 02	22 17			
Camden Road		d	19 05	19 15	19 25		19 35	19 45	19 55	20 05	20 15	20 25	20 35	20 45	20 55		21 05	21 15	21 25	21 35	21 50	22 05	22 20			
Kentish Town West		d	19 07	19 17	19 27		19 37	19 47	19 57	20 07	20 17	20 27	20 37	20 47	20 57		21 07	21 17	21 27	21 37	21 52	22 07	22 22			
Gospel Oak		d	19 10	19 20	19 30		19 40	19 50	20 00	20 10	20 20	20 30	20 40	20 50	21 00		21 10	21 20	21 30	21 40	21 55	22 10	22 25	22 55	23 30	
Hampstead Heath		d	19 12	19 22	19 32		19 42	19 52	20 02	20 12	20 22	20 32	20 42	20 52	21 02		21 12	21 22	21 32	21 42	21 57	22 12	22 27	22 57	23 32	
Finchley Road & Frognal		d	19 14	19 24	19 34		19 44	19 54	20 04	20 14	20 24	20 34	20 44	20 54	21 04		21 14	21 24	21 34	21 44	21 59	22 14	22 29	22 59	23 34	
West Hampstead	⊖	d	19 16	19 26	19 36		19 46	19 56	20 06	20 16	20 26	20 36	20 46	20 56	21 06		21 16	21 26	21 36	21 46	22 01	22 16	22 31	23 01	23 36	
Brondesbury		d	19 18	19 28	19 38		19 48	19 58	20 08	20 18	20 28	20 38	20 48	20 58	21 08		21 18	21 28	21 38	21 48	22 03	22 18	22 33	23 03	23 38	
Brondesbury Park		d	19 19	19 29	19 39		19 49	19 59	20 09	20 19	20 29	20 39	20 49	20 59	21 09		21 19	21 29	21 39	21 49	22 04	22 19	22 34	23 04	23 39	
Kensal Rise		d	19 21	19 31	19 41		19 51	20 01	20 11	20 21	20 31	20 41	20 51	21 01	21 11		21 21	21 31	21 41	21 51	22 06	22 21	22 36	23 06	23a41	
Willesden Jn. High Level	⊖	a	19 25	19 35	19 45		19 55	20 05	20 15	20 25	20 35	20 45	20 55	21 05	21 15		21 25	21 35	21 45	21 55	22 10	22 25	22 40	23 10		
		d	19 26	19 36			19 56	20 06		20 26	20 36		20 56	21 06			21 26	21 39		21 56	22 11	22 26	22 41	23 11		
Acton Central		d	19 31	19 41			20 01	20 11		20 31	20 41		21 01	21 11			21 31	21 44		22 01	22 16	22 31	22 46	23 16		
South Acton		d	19 34	19 44			20 04	20 14		20 34	20 44		21 04	21 14			21 34	21 47		22 04	22 19	22 34	22 49	23 19		
Gunnersbury	⊖	d	19 38	19 48			20 08	20 18		20 38	20 48		21 08	21 18			21 38	21 50		22 08	22 22	22 38	22 52	23 22		
Kew Gardens	⊖	d	19 41	19 51			20 11	20 21		20 41	20 51		21 11	21 21			21 41	21 53		22 11	22 25	22 41	22 55	23 25		
Richmond	⊖	a	19 47	19 57			20 17	20 27		20 47	20 57		21 17	21 27			21 47	21 57		22 18	22 33	22 48	23 02	23 32		

Richmond - Willesden Junction, West Hampstead, Highbury and Islington and Stratford

Network Diagram - see first Page of Table 59

Miles			LO MX	LO	LO	LO	LO	LO	LO	LO	LO		LO	LO	LO	LO	LO	LO	LO	LO	LO		LO	LO	LO
0	**Richmond**	⊖ d	23p00			05 54	06 09		06 24		06 37			06 53		07 06		07 24		07 36			07 53		08 08
1½	Kew Gardens	⊖ d	23p03			05 57	06 12		06 27		06 40			06 56		07 09		07 27		07 39			07 56		08 11
2½	Gunnersbury	⊖ d	23p06			06 00	06 15		06 30		06 43			06 59		07 12		07 30		07 42			07 59		08 14
3¼	South Acton	d	23p09			06 03	06 18		06 33		06 46			07 02		07 15		07 33		07 45			08 02		08 17
4	Acton Central	d	23p12			06 06	06 21		06 36		06 51			07 06		07 21		07 36		07 51			08 06		08 21
5¾	**Willesden Jn. High Level**	⊖ a	23p17			06 11	06 26		06 41		06 56			07 11		07 26		07 41		07 56			08 11		08 26
—		d	23p18			06 12	06 27	06 35	06 42	06 50	06 57		07 05	07 12	07 20	07 27	07 35	07 42	07 50	07 57	08 06		08 12	08 20	08 27
6¾	Kensal Rise	d	23p20		06 02	06 14	06 29	06 37	06 44	06 52	06 59		07 07	07 14	07 22	07 29	07 37	07 44	07 52	07 59	08 08		08 14	08 22	08 29
7½	Brondesbury Park	d	23p22		06 04	06 16	06 31	06 39	06 46	06 54	07 01		07 09	07 16	07 24	07 31	07 39	07 46	07 54	08 01	08 10		08 16	08 24	08 31
7¾	Brondesbury	d	23p24		06 06	06 18	06 33	06 41	06 48	06 56	07 03		07 11	07 18	07 26	07 33	07 41	07 48	07 56	08 03	08 12		08 18	08 26	08 33
8¼	West Hampstead	⊖ d	23p26		06 08	06 20	06 35	06 43	06 50	06 58	07 05		07 13	07 20	07 28	07 35	07 43	07 50	07 58	08 05	08 14		08 20	08 28	08 35
8¾	Finchley Road & Frognal	d	23p27		06 09	06 21	06 36	06 44	06 51	06 59	07 06		07 14	07 21	07 29	07 36	07 44	07 51	07 59	08 06	08 15		08 21	08 29	08 36
9¾	Hampstead Heath	d	23p30		06 12	06 24	06 39	06 47	06 54	07 02	07 09		07 17	07 24	07 32	07 39	07 47	07 54	08 02	08 09	08 18		08 24	08 32	08 39
10¼	**Gospel Oak**	d	23p32		06 14	06 26	06 41	06 49	06 56	07 04	07 11		07 19	07 26	07 34	07 41	07 49	07 56	08 04	08 11	08 20		08 26	08 34	08 41
11	Kentish Town West	d	23p34		06 16	06 28	06 43	06 51	06 58	07 06	07 13		07 21	07 28	07 36	07 43	07 51	07 58	08 06	08 13	08 22		08 28	08 36	08 43
11¼	Camden Road	d	23p38	06 11	06 20	06 32	06 47	06 55	07 02	07 10	07 17		07 25	07 32	07 40	07 47	07 55	08 02	08 10	08 17	08 26		08 32	08 40	08 47
12½	Caledonian Rd & Barnsbury	d	23p41	06 14	06 23	06 35	06 50	06 58	07 05	07 13	07 20		07 28	07 35	07 43	07 50	07 58	08 05	08 13	08 20	08 29		08 35	08 43	08 50
13	**Highbury & Islington**	⊖ d	23p44	06 16	06 26	06 38	06 53	07 01	07 08	07 16	07 23		07 31	07 38	07 46	07 53	08 01	08 08	08 16	08 23	08 32		08 38	08 46	08 53
13½	Canonbury	⊖ d	23p46	06 18	06 28	06 40	06 55	07 03	07 10	07 18	07 25		07 33	07 40	07 48	07 55	08 03	08 10	08 18	08 25	08 34		08 40	08 48	08 55
14½	Dalston Kingsland	d	23p48	06 20	06 30	06 42	06 57	07 05	07 12	07 20	07 27		07 35	07 42	07 50	07 57	08 05	08 12	08 20	08 27	08 36		08 42	08 50	08 57
15¼	Hackney Central	d	23p50	06 22	06 32	06 44	06 59	07 07	07 14	07 22	07 29		07 37	07 44	07 52	07 59	08 07	08 14	08 22	08 29	08 38		08 44	08 52	08 59
16	Homerton	d	23p52	06 24	06 34	06 46	07 01	07 09	07 16	07 24	07 31		07 39	07 46	07 54	08 01	08 09	08 16	08 24	08 31	08 40		08 46	08 54	09 01
16¾	Hackney Wick	d	23p54	06 26	06 36	06 48	07 03	07 11	07 18	07 26	07 33		07 41	07 48	07 56	08 03	08 11	08 18	08 26	08 33	08 42		08 48	08 56	09 03
17¾	**Stratford** 7	⊖ a	00 02	06 32	06 44	06 56	07 11	07 18	07 24	07 33	07 40		07 48	07 56	08 03	08 10	08 18	08 26	08 33	08 40	08 49		08 56	09 03	09 11

		LO	LO	LO	LO	LO	LO		LO	LO	LO	LO	LO	LO	LO	LO	LO		LO	LO	LO	LO	LO	LO	LO
Richmond	⊖ d		08 22		08 36		08 52			09 10		09 27	09 36		09 57	10 08			10 28	10 38		10 58	11 08		11 28
Kew Gardens	⊖ d		08 25		08 39		08 55			09 13		09 30	09 39		10 00	10 11			10 31	10 41		11 01	11 11		11 31
Gunnersbury	⊖ d		08 28		08 42		08 58			09 16		09 33	09 42		10 03	10 14			10 34	10 44		11 04	11 14		11 34
South Acton	d		08 31		08 45		09 01			09 19		09 36	09 45		10 06	10 17			10 37	10 47		11 07	11 17		11 37
Acton Central	d		08 36		08 51		09 06			09 22		09 40	09 50		10 10	10 20			10 40	10 50		11 10	11 20		11 40
Willesden Jn. High Level	⊖ a		08 41		08 56		09 11			09 27		09 45	09 55		10 15	10 25			10 45	10 55		11 15	11 25		11 45
	d	08 36	08 42	08 50	08 57	09 06	09 13		09 20	09 28	09 36	09 46	09 56	10 06	10 16	10 26	10 36		10 46	10 56	11 06	11 16	11 26	11 36	11 46
Kensal Rise	d	08 39	08 44	08 52	08 59	09 08	09 15		09 24	09 30	09 38	09 48	09 58	10 08	10 18	10 28	10 38		10 48	10 58	11 08	11 18	11 28	11 38	11 48
Brondesbury Park	d	08 41	08 46	08 54	09 01	09 10	09 17		09 26	09 32	09 40	09 50	10 00	10 10	10 20	10 30	10 40		10 50	11 00	11 10	11 20	11 30	11 40	11 50
Brondesbury	d	08 42	08 48	08 56	09 03	09 12	09 19		09 27	09 34	09 42	09 52	10 02	10 12	10 22	10 32	10 42		10 52	11 02	11 12	11 22	11 32	11 42	11 52
West Hampstead	⊖ d	08 44	08 50	08 58	09 05	09 14	09 21		09 30	09 36	09 44	09 54	10 04	10 14	10 24	10 34	10 44		10 54	11 04	11 14	11 24	11 34	11 44	11 54
Finchley Road & Frognal	d	08 46	08 51	08 59	09 06	09 15	09 22		09 31	09 37	09 45	09 55	10 05	10 15	10 25	10 35	10 45		10 55	11 05	11 15	11 25	11 35	11 45	11 55
Hampstead Heath	d	08 48	08 54	09 02	09 09	09 18	09 25		09 34	09 40	09 48	09 58	10 08	10 18	10 28	10 38	10 48		10 58	11 08	11 18	11 28	11 38	11 48	11 58
Gospel Oak	d	08 52	08 56	09 04	09 11	09 20	09 27		09 36	09 42	09 50	10 00	10 10	10 20	10 30	10 40	10 50		11 00	11 10	11 20	11 30	11 40	11 50	12 00
Kentish Town West	d	08 54	08 58	09 06	09 13	09 22	09 29		09 38	09 44	09 52	10 02	10 12	10 22	10 32	10 42	10 52		11 02	11 12	11 22	11 32	11 42	11 52	12 02
Camden Road	d	08 57	09 02	09 10	09 17	09 26	09 33		09 42	09 48	09 56	10 06	10 16	10 26	10 36	10 46	10 56		11 06	11 16	11 26	11 36	11 46	11 56	12 06
Caledonian Rd & Barnsbury	d	09 00	09 05	09 13	09 20	09 29	09 36		09 45	09 51	09 59	10 09	10 19	10 29	10 39	10 49	10 59		11 09	11 19	11 29	11 39	11 49	11 59	12 09
Highbury & Islington	⊖ d	09 03	09 08	09 16	09 23	09 32	09 39		09 48	09 54	10 02	10 12	10 22	10 32	10 42	10 52	11 02		11 12	11 22	11 32	11 42	11 52	12 02	12 12
Canonbury	⊖ d	09 05	09 10	09 18	09 25	09 34	09 41		09 50	09 56	10 04	10 14	10 24	10 34	10 44	10 54	11 04		11 14	11 24	11 34	11 45	11 54	12 04	12 14
Dalston Kingsland	d	09 07	09 12	09 20	09 27	09 36	09 43		09 52	09 58	10 06	10 16	10 26	10 36	10 46	10 56	11 06		11 16	11 26	11 36	11 47	11 56	12 06	12 16
Hackney Central	d	09 09	09 14	09 22	09 29	09 38	09 45		09 54	10 00	10 08	10 18	10 28	10 38	10 48	10 58	11 08		11 18	11 28	11 38	11 49	11 58	12 08	12 18
Homerton	d	09 11	09 16	09 24	09 31	09 40	09 47		09 56	10 02	10 10	10 20	10 30	10 40	10 50	11 00	11 10		11 20	11 30	11 40	11 51	12 00	12 10	12 20
Hackney Wick	d	09 14	09 18	09 26	09 33	09 42	09 49		09 58	10 04	10 12	10 22	10 32	10 42	10 52	11 02	11 12		11 22	11 32	11 42	11 53	12 02	12 12	12 22
Stratford 7	⊖ a	09 19	09 29	09 33	09 39	09 51	09 55		10 05	10 10	10 20	10 30	10 39	10 50	11 00	11 10	11 20		11 30	11 40	11 49	11 59	12 10	12 20	12 30

		LO	LO		LO	LO	LO	LO	LO	LO	LO	LO	LO		LO	LO	LO	LO	LO	LO	LO	LO	LO		LO
Richmond	⊖ d	11 38			11 58	12 08		12 28	12 38		12 58	13 08			13 28	13 38		13 58	14 10		14 28	14 38			14 58
Kew Gardens	⊖ d	11 41			12 01	12 11		12 31	12 41		13 01	13 11			13 31	13 41		14 01	14 13		14 31	14 41			15 01
Gunnersbury	⊖ d	11 44			12 04	12 14		12 34	12 44		13 04	13 14			13 34	13 44		14 04	14 16		14 34	14 44			15 04
South Acton	d	11 47			12 07	12 17		12 37	12 47		13 07	13 17			13 37	13 47		14 07	14 19		14 37	14 47			15 07
Acton Central	d	11 50			12 10	12 20		12 40	12 50		13 10	13 20			13 40	13 50		14 10	14 22		14 40	14 50			15 10
Willesden Jn. High Level	⊖ a	11 55			12 15	12 25		12 45	12 55		13 15	13 25			13 45	13 55		14 15	14 27		14 45	14 55			15 15
	d	11 56	12 06		12 16	12 26	12 36	12 46	12 56	13 06	13 16	13 26	13 36		13 46	13 56	14 06	14 16	14 28	14 36	14 46	14 56	15 11		15 16
Kensal Rise	d	11 58	12 08		12 18	12 28	12 38	12 48	12 58	13 08	13 18	13 28	13 38		13 48	13 58	14 08	14 18	14 30	14 38	14 48	14 58	15 14		15 18
Brondesbury Park	d	12 00	12 10		12 20	12 30	12 40	12 50	13 00	13 10	13 20	13 30	13 40		13 50	14 00	14 10	14 20	14 32	14 40	14 50	15 00	15 16		15 20
Brondesbury	d	12 02	12 12		12 22	12 32	12 42	12 52	13 02	13 12	13 22	13 32	13 42		13 52	14 02	14 12	14 22	14 34	14 42	14 52	15 02	15 17		15 22
West Hampstead	⊖ d	12 04	12 14		12 24	12 34	12 44	12 54	13 04	13 14	13 24	13 34	13 44		13 54	14 04	14 14	14 24	14 36	14 44	14 54	15 04	15 19		15 24
Finchley Road & Frognal	d	12 05	12 15		12 25	12 35	12 45	12 55	13 05	13 15	13 25	13 35	13 45		13 55	14 05	14 15	14 25	14 37	14 45	14 55	15 05	15 21		15 25
Hampstead Heath	d	12 08	12 18		12 28	12 38	12 48	12 58	13 08	13 18	13 28	13 38	13 48		13 58	14 08	14 18	14 28	14 40	14 48	14 58	15 08	15 23		15 28
Gospel Oak	d	12 10	12 20		12 30	12 40	12 50	13 00	13 10	13 20	13 30	13 40	13 50		14 00	14 10	14 20	14 30	14 42	14 50	15 00	15 10	15 26		15 30
Kentish Town West	d	12 12	12 22		12 32	12 42	12 52	13 02	13 12	13 22	13 32	13 42	13 52		14 02	14 12	14 22	14 32	14 44	14 52	15 02	15 12	15 28		15 32
Camden Road	d	12 16	12 26		12 36	12 46	12 56	13 06	13 16	13 26	13 36	13 46	13 56		14 06	14 16	14 26	14 36	14 48	14 56	15 06	15 16	15 32		15 36
Caledonian Rd & Barnsbury	d	12 19	12 29		12 39	12 49	12 59	13 09	13 19	13 29	13 39	13 49	13 59		14 09	14 19	14 29	14 39	14 51	14 59	15 09	15 19	15 35		15 39
Highbury & Islington	⊖ d	12 22	12 32		12 42	12 52	13 02	13 12	13 22	13 32	13 42	13 52	14 02		14 12	14 22	14 32	14 42	14 54	15 02	15 12	15 22	15 38		15 42
Canonbury	⊖ d	12 24	12 34		12 44	12 54	13 04	13 14	13 24	13 34	13 45	13 54	14 04		14 14	14 24	14 34	14 44	14 56	15 04	15 14	15 24	15 40		15 44
Dalston Kingsland	d	12 26	12 36		12 46	12 56	13 06	13 16	13 26	13 36	13 47	13 56	14 06		14 16	14 26	14 36	14 46	14 58	15 06	15 16	15 26	15 42		15 46
Hackney Central	d	12 28	12 38		12 48	12 58	13 08	13 18	13 28	13 38	13 49	13 58	14 08		14 18	14 28	14 38	14 48	15 00	15 08	15 18	15 28	15 44		15 48
Homerton	d	12 30	12 40		12 50	13 00	13 10	13 20	13 30	13 40	13 51	14 00	14 10		14 20	14 30	14 40	14 50	15 02	15 10	15 20	15 30	15 46		15 50
Hackney Wick	d	12 32	12 42		12 52	13 02	13 12	13 22	13 33	13 42	13 53	14 02	14 12		14 22	14 32	14 42	14 52	15 04	15 12	15 22	15 32	15 49		15 52
Stratford 7	⊖ a	12 40	12 50		13 00	13 10	13 20	13 30	13 41	13 50	14 01	14 10	14 20		14 30	14 40	14 50	15 00	15 12	15 20	15 30	15 40	15 56		16 00

Table 59

Mondays to Fridays

Richmond - Willesden Junction, West Hampstead, Highbury and Islington and Stratford

Network Diagram - see first Page of Table 59

Station		LO	LO	LO	LO	LO	LO	LO	LO	LO	LO	LO	LO	LO	LO	LO	LO	LO	LO	LO	LO	LO	LO
Richmond	⊖ d	15 08		15 26	15 38		15 53		16 09		16 23		16 36		16 53		17 06		17 23		17 36		17 53
Kew Gardens	⊖ d	15 11		15 29	15 41		15 56		16 12		16 26		16 39		16 56		17 09		17 26		17 39		17 56
Gunnersbury	⊖ d	15 14		15 32	15 44		15 59		16 15		16 29		16 42		16 59		17 12		17 29		17 42		17 59
South Acton	d	15 17		15 35	15 47		16 02		16 18		16 32		16 45		17 02		17 15		17 32		17 45		18 02
Acton Central	d	15 20		15 38	15 50		16 06		16 21		16 36		16 51		17 06		17 21		17 36		17 51		18 06
Willesden Jn. High Level	⊖ a	15 25		15 44	15 55		16 11		16 26		16 41		16 56		17 11		17 26		17 41		17 56		18 11
	d	15 26	15 36	15 45	15 56	16 06	16 12	16 20	16 27	16 35	16 42	16 50	16 57	17 05	17 12	17 20	17 27	17 35	17 42	17 50	17 57	18 05	18 12
Kensal Rise	d	15 28	15 38	15 47	15 58	16 08	16 14	16 22	16 29	16 37	16 44	16 52	16 59	17 07	17 14	17 22	17 29	17 37	17 44	17 52	17 59	18 07	18 14
Brondesbury Park	d	15 30	15 40	15 49	16 00	16 10	16 16	16 24	16 31	16 40	16 46	16 54	17 01	17 09	17 16	17 24	17 31	17 39	17 46	17 54	18 01	18 09	18 16
Brondesbury	d	15 32	15 42	15 51	16 02	16 12	16 18	16 26	16 33	16 41	16 48	16 56	17 03	17 11	17 18	17 26	17 33	17 41	17 48	17 56	18 03	18 11	18 18
West Hampstead	⊖ d	15 34	15 44	15 53	16 04	16 14	16 20	16 28	16 35	16 43	16 50	16 58	17 05	17 13	17 20	17 28	17 35	17 43	17 50	17 58	18 05	18 13	18 20
Finchley Road & Frognal	d	15 35	15 45	15 54	16 05	16 15	16 21	16 29	16 36	16 44	16 51	16 59	17 06	17 14	17 21	17 29	17 36	17 44	17 51	17 59	18 06	18 14	18 21
Hampstead Heath	d	15 38	15 48	15 57	16 08	16 18	16 24	16 32	16 39	16 47	16 54	17 02	17 09	17 17	17 24	17 32	17 39	17 47	17 54	18 02	18 09	18 17	18 24
Gospel Oak	d	15 40	15 50	16 00	16 10	16 20	16 26	16 34	16 41	16 49	16 56	17 04	17 11	17 19	17 26	17 34	17 41	17 49	17 56	18 04	18 11	18 19	18 26
Kentish Town West	d	15 42	15 52	16 02	16 12	16 22	16 28	16 36	16 43	16 51	16 58	17 06	17 13	17 21	17 28	17 36	17 43	17 51	17 58	18 06	18 13	18 21	18 28
Camden Road	d	15 46	15 56	16 05	16 16	16 26	16 32	16 40	16 47	16 55	17 02	17 10	17 17	17 25	17 32	17 40	17 47	17 55	18 02	18 10	18 17	18 25	18 32
Caledonian Rd & Barnsbury	d	15 49	15 59	16 08	16 19	16 29	16 35	16 43	16 50	16 58	17 05	17 13	17 20	17 28	17 35	17 43	17 50	17 58	18 05	18 13	18 20	18 28	18 35
Highbury & Islington	⊖ d	15 52	16 02	16 11	16 22	16 32	16 38	16 46	16 53	17 01	17 08	17 16	17 23	17 31	17 38	17 46	17 53	18 01	18 08	18 16	18 23	18 31	18 38
Canonbury	⊖ d	15 54	16 04	16 13	16 24	16 34	16 40	16 48	16 55	17 03	17 10	17 18	17 25	17 33	17 40	17 48	17 55	18 03	18 10	18 18	18 25	18 33	18 40
Dalston Kingsland	d	15 56	16 06	16 15	16 26	16 36	16 42	16 50	16 57	17 05	17 12	17 20	17 27	17 35	17 42	17 50	17 57	18 05	18 12	18 20	18 27	18 35	18 42
Hackney Central	d	15 58	16 08	16 17	16 28	16 38	16 44	16 52	16 59	17 07	17 14	17 22	17 29	17 37	17 44	17 52	17 59	18 07	18 14	18 22	18 29	18 37	18 44
Homerton	d	16 00	16 10	16 19	16 30	16 40	16 46	16 54	17 01	17 09	17 16	17 24	17 31	17 39	17 46	17 54	18 01	18 09	18 16	18 24	18 31	18 39	18 46
Hackney Wick	d	16 02	16 12	16 21	16 32	16 42	16 48	16 56	17 03	17 11	17 18	17 26	17 33	17 41	17 48	17 56	18 03	18 11	18 18	18 26	18 33	18 41	18 48
Stratford 7	⊖ a	16 11	16 20	16 30	16 42	16 49	16 54	17 05	17 11	17 20	17 26	17 35	17 40	17 50	17 56	18 05	18 10	18 20	18 26	18 35	18 39	18 50	18 56

Station		LO	LO	LO	LO	LO	LO	LO	LO	LO	LO	LO	LO	LO	LO	LO	LO	LO	LO	LO	LO	LO	LO
Richmond	⊖ d		18 06		18 22		18 36		18 54		19 09		19 26	19 41		19 56	20 11		20 26	20 40		20 58	21 10
Kew Gardens	⊖ d		18 09		18 26		18 39		18 57		19 12		19 29	19 44		19 59	20 14		20 29	20 43		21 01	21 13
Gunnersbury	⊖ d		18 12		18 29		18 42		19 00		19 15		19 32	19 47		20 02	20 17		20 32	20 46		21 04	21 16
South Acton	d		18 15		18 31		18 45		19 03		19 18		19 35	19 50		20 05	20 20		20 35	20 49		21 07	21 19
Acton Central	d		18 21		18 34		18 51		19 06		19 23		19 40	19 54		20 08	20 23		20 40	20 52		21 10	21 23
Willesden Jn. High Level	⊖ a		18 26		18 39		18 56		19 11		19 28		19 45	19 59		20 15	20 28		20 45	20 57		21 16	21 28
	d	18 20	18 27	18 35	18 40	18 50	18 57	19 05	19 12	19 20	19 29	19 36	19 46	20 00	20 06	20 16	20 29	20 36	20 46	20 59	21 06	21 17	21 29
Kensal Rise	d	18 22	18 29	18 37	18 43	18 52	18 59	19 07	19 14	19 22	19 31	19 38	19 48	20 02	20 08	20 18	20 31	20 38	20 48	21 01	21 08	21 19	21 31
Brondesbury Park	d	18 24	18 31	18 39	18 45	18 54	19 01	19 09	19 16	19 24	19 33	19 40	19 50	20 04	20 10	20 20	20 33	20 40	20 50	21 03	21 10	21 21	21 33
Brondesbury	d	18 26	18 33	18 41	18 46	18 56	19 03	19 11	19 18	19 26	19 35	19 42	19 52	20 06	20 12	20 22	20 35	20 42	20 52	21 05	21 12	21 23	21 35
West Hampstead	⊖ d	18 28	18 35	18 43	18 48	18 58	19 05	19 13	19 20	19 28	19 37	19 44	19 54	20 08	20 14	20 24	20 37	20 44	20 54	21 07	21 14	21 25	21 37
Finchley Road & Frognal	d	18 29	18 36	18 44	18 50	18 59	19 06	19 14	19 21	19 29	19 38	19 45	19 55	20 09	20 15	20 25	20 38	20 45	20 55	21 08	21 15	21 26	21 38
Hampstead Heath	d	18 32	18 39	18 47	18 52	19 02	19 09	19 17	19 24	19 32	19 41	19 48	19 58	20 12	20 18	20 28	20 41	20 48	20 58	21 11	21 18	21 29	21 41
Gospel Oak	d	18 34	18 41	18 49	18 55	19 04	19 11	19 19	19 26	19 34	19 43	19 50	20 00	20 14	20 20	20 30	20 43	20 50	21 00	21 13	21 20	21 30	21 43
Kentish Town West	d	18 36	18 43	18 51	18 57	19 06	19 13	19 21	19 28	19 36	19 45	19 52	20 02	20 16	20 22	20 32	20 45	20 52	21 02	21 15	21 22	21 32	21 45
Camden Road	d	18 40	18 47	18 55	19 00	19 10	19 17	19 25	19 32	19 40	19 49	19 56	20 06	20 20	20 26	20 36	20 49	20 56	21 06	21 19	21 26	21 36	21 49
Caledonian Rd & Barnsbury	d	18 44	18 50	18 58	19 03	19 13	19 20	19 28	19 35	19 43	19 52	19 59	20 09	20 23	20 29	20 39	20 52	20 59	21 09	21 22	21 29	21 39	21 52
Highbury & Islington	⊖ d	18 46	18 53	19 01	19 06	19 16	19 23	19 31	19 38	19 46	19 55	20 02	20 12	20 26	20 33	20 42	20 55	21 02	21 12	21 25	21 32	21 42	21 55
Canonbury	⊖ d	18 48	18 55	19 03	19 08	19 18	19 25	19 33	19 40	19 48	19 57	20 04	20 14	20 28	20 35	20 44	20 57	21 04	21 14	21 27	21 34	21 44	21 57
Dalston Kingsland	d	18 50	18 57	19 05	19 10	19 20	19 27	19 35	19 42	19 50	19 59	20 06	20 16	20 30	20 37	20 46	20 59	21 06	21 16	21 29	21 36	21 46	21 59
Hackney Central	d	18 52	18 59	19 07	19 12	19 22	19 29	19 37	19 44	19 52	20 01	20 08	20 18	20 32	20 39	20 48	21 01	21 08	21 18	21 31	21 38	21 48	22 01
Homerton	d	18 54	19 01	19 09	19 14	19 24	19 31	19 39	19 46	19 54	20 03	20 10	20 20	20 34	20 41	20 50	21 03	21 10	21 20	21 33	21 40	21 50	22 03
Hackney Wick	d	18 56	19 03	19 11	19 17	19 26	19 33	19 41	19 48	19 56	20 05	20 12	20 22	20 36	20 43	20 52	21 05	21 12	21 22	21 35	21 42	21 52	22 05
Stratford 7	⊖ a	19 05	19 09	19 21	19 25	19 35	19 40	19 50	19 57	20 04	20 12	20 20	20 30	20 43	20 51	21 00	21 13	21 20	21 30	21 43	21 50	22 00	22 13

Station			LO	LO	LO	LO	LO	LO	LO	LO
Richmond	⊖ d			21 28	21 38		21 56	22 28	23 00	23 28
Kew Gardens	⊖ d			21 31	21 41		21 59	22 31	23 03	23 31
Gunnersbury	⊖ d			21 34	21 44		22 02	22 34	23 06	23 34
South Acton	d			21 37	21 47		22 05	22 37	23 09	23 37
Acton Central	d			21 40	21 50		22 10	22 40	23 12	23 40
Willesden Jn. High Level	⊖ a			21 45	21 55		22 15	22 45	23 17	23 45
	d		21 36	21 46	21 56	22 06	22 16	22 46	23 18	
Kensal Rise	d		21 38	21 48	21 58	22 08	22 18	22 48	23 20	
Brondesbury Park	d		21 40	21 50	22 00	22 10	22 20	22 50	23 22	
Brondesbury	d		21 42	21 52	22 02	22 12	22 22	22 52	23 24	
West Hampstead	⊖ d		21 44	21 54	22 04	22 14	22 24	22 54	23 26	
Finchley Road & Frognal	d		21 45	21 55	22 05	22 15	22 25	22 55	23 27	
Hampstead Heath	d		21 48	21 58	22 08	22 18	22 28	22 58	23 30	
Gospel Oak	d		21 50	22 00	22 10	22 20	22 30	23 00	23 32	
Kentish Town West	d		21 52	22 02	22 12	22 22	22 32	23 02	23 34	
Camden Road	d		21 56	22 06	22 16	22 26	22 36	23 06	23 38	
Caledonian Rd & Barnsbury	d		21 59	22 09	22 19	22 29	22 39	23 09	23 41	
Highbury & Islington	⊖ d		22 02	22 12	22 22	22 32	22 42	23 12	23 44	
Canonbury	⊖ d		22 04	22 14	22 24	22 34	22 44	23 14	23 46	
Dalston Kingsland	d		22 06	22 16	22 26	22 36	22 46	23 16	23 48	
Hackney Central	d		22 08	22 18	22 28	22 38	22 48	23 18	23 50	
Homerton	d		22 10	22 20	22 30	22 40	22 50	23 20	23 52	
Hackney Wick	d		22 12	22 22	22 32	22 42	22 52	23 22	23 54	
Stratford 7	⊖ a		22 20	22 30	22 40	22 50	23 00	23 30	00 02	

Richmond - Willesden Junction, West Hampstead, Highbury and Islington and Stratford

Network Diagram - see first Page of Table 59

		LO	LO	LO	LO	LO	LO	LO	LO	LO	LO	LO	LO	LO	LO	LO	LO	LO	LO	LO	LO	LO
Richmond	⊖ d	23p00		05 58	06 10		06 28	06 40		06 58	07 10		07 28	07 40		07 58	08 08		08 28	08 38		08 58
Kew Gardens	⊖ d	23p03		06 01	06 13		06 31	06 43		07 01	07 13		07 31	07 43		08 01	08 11		08 31	08 41		09 01
Gunnersbury	⊖ d	23p06		06 04	06 16		06 34	06 46		07 04	07 16		07 34	07 46		08 04	08 14		08 34	08 44		09 04
South Acton	d	23p09		06 07	06 19		06 37	06 49		07 07	07 19		07 37	07 49		08 07	08 17		08 37	08 47		09 07
Acton Central	d	23p12		06 10	06 23		06 40	06 53		07 10	07 23		07 40	07 52		08 10	08 20		08 40	08 50		09 10
Willesden Jn. High Level	⊖ a	23p17		06 15	06 28		06 45	06 58		07 15	07 28		07 45	07 57		08 15	08 25		08 45	08 55		09 15
	d	23p18		06 16	06 29	06 36	06 46	06 59	07 06	07 16	07 29	07 36	07 46	07 58	08 06	08 16	08 26	08 36	08 46	08 56	09 06	09 16
Kensal Rise	d	23p20	06 01	06 18	06 31	06 38	06 48	07 01	07 08	07 18	07 31	07 38	07 48	08 00	08 08	08 18	08 28	08 38	08 48	08 58	09 08	09 18
Brondesbury Park	d	23p22	06 03	06 20	06 33	06 40	06 50	07 03	07 10	07 20	07 33	07 40	07 50	08 02	08 10	08 20	08 30	08 40	08 50	09 00	09 10	09 20
Brondesbury	d	23p24	06 05	06 22	06 35	06 42	06 52	07 05	07 12	07 22	07 35	07 42	07 52	08 04	08 12	08 22	08 32	08 42	08 52	09 02	09 12	09 22
West Hampstead	⊖ d	23p26	06 07	06 24	06 37	06 44	06 54	07 07	07 14	07 24	07 37	07 44	07 54	08 06	08 14	08 24	08 34	08 44	08 54	09 04	09 14	09 24
Finchley Road & Frognal	d	23p27	06 08	06 25	06 38	06 45	06 55	07 08	07 15	07 25	07 38	07 45	07 55	08 07	08 15	08 25	08 35	08 45	08 55	09 05	09 15	09 25
Hampstead Heath	d	23p30	06 11	06 28	06 41	06 48	06 58	07 11	07 18	07 28	07 41	07 48	07 58	08 10	08 18	08 28	08 38	08 48	08 58	09 08	09 18	09 28
Gospel Oak	d	23p32	06 13	06 30	06 43	06 50	07 00	07 13	07 20	07 30	07 43	07 50	08 00	08 12	08 20	08 30	08 41	08 50	09 00	09 10	09 20	09 30
Kentish Town West	d	23p34	06 15	06 32	06 45	06 52	07 02	07 15	07 22	07 32	07 45	07 52	08 02	08 14	08 22	08 32	08 43	08 52	09 02	09 12	09 22	09 32
Camden Road	d	23p38	06 19	06 36	06 49	06 56	07 06	07 19	07 26	07 36	07 49	07 56	08 06	08 18	08 26	08 36	08 46	08 56	09 06	09 16	09 26	09 36
Caledonian Rd & Barnsbury	d	23p41	06 22	06 39	06 52	06 59	07 09	07 22	07 29	07 39	07 52	07 59	08 09	08 21	08 29	08 39	08 49	08 59	09 09	09 19	09 29	09 39
Highbury & Islington	⊖ d	23p44	06 25	06 42	06 55	07 02	07 12	07 25	07 32	07 42	07 55	08 02	08 12	08 24	08 32	08 42	08 52	09 02	09 12	09 22	09 32	09 42
Canonbury	⊖ d	23p46	06 27	06 44	06 57	07 04	07 14	07 27	07 34	07 44	07 57	08 04	08 14	08 26	08 34	08 44	08 54	09 04	09 14	09 24	09 34	09 44
Dalston Kingsland	d	23p48	06 29	06 46	06 59	07 06	07 16	07 29	07 36	07 46	07 59	08 06	08 16	08 28	08 36	08 46	08 56	09 06	09 16	09 26	09 36	09 46
Hackney Central	d	23p50	06 31	06 48	07 01	07 08	07 18	07 31	07 38	07 48	08 01	08 08	08 18	08 30	08 38	08 48	08 58	09 08	09 18	09 28	09 38	09 48
Homerton	d	23p52	06 33	06 50	07 03	07 10	07 20	07 33	07 40	07 50	08 03	08 10	08 20	08 32	08 40	08 50	09 00	09 10	09 20	09 30	09 40	09 50
Hackney Wick	d	23p54	06 35	06 52	07 05	07 12	07 22	07 35	07 42	07 52	08 05	08 12	08 22	08 34	08 42	08 52	09 02	09 12	09 22	09 32	09 42	09 52
Stratford 7	⊖ a	00 02	06 43	07 01	07 13	07 20	07 30	07 43	07 50	08 01	08 13	08 20	08 30	08 43	08 50	09 01	09 11	09 20	09 30	09 41	09 50	10 01

		LO		LO	LO	LO	LO	LO	LO	LO	LO	LO	LO		LO		LO	LO	LO	LO	LO
Richmond	⊖ d	09 08		16 08		16 28	16 38		16 58	17 08		17 28	17 38		21 38		21 58	22 28	23 00	23 28
Kew Gardens	⊖ d	09 11		16 11		16 31	16 41		17 01	17 11		17 31	17 41		21 41		22 01	22 31	23 03	23 31
Gunnersbury	⊖ d	09 14		16 14		16 34	16 44		17 04	17 14		17 34	17 44		21 44		22 04	22 34	23 06	23 34
South Acton	d	09 17		16 17		16 37	16 47		17 07	17 17		17 37	17 47		21 47		22 07	22 37	23 09	23 37
Acton Central	d	09 20		16 20		16 40	16 50		17 10	17 20		17 40	17 50		21 50		22 10	22 40	23 12	23 40
Willesden Jn. High Level	⊖ a	09 25		16 25		16 45	16 55		17 15	17 25		17 45	17 55		21 55		22 15	22 45	23 17	23 45
	d	09 26		16 26	16 36	16 46	16 56	17 06	17 16	17 26	17 36	17 46	17 56		21 56	22 06	22 16	22 46	23 18	
Kensal Rise	d	09 28		16 28	16 38	16 48	16 58	17 08	17 18	17 28	17 38	17 48	17 58		21 58	22 08	22 18	22 48	23 20	
Brondesbury Park	d	09 30	and at	16 30	16 40	16 50	17 00	17 10	17 20	17 30	17 40	17 50	18 00	and at	22 00	22 10	22 20	22 50	23 22	
Brondesbury	d	09 32	the same	16 32	16 42	16 52	17 02	17 12	17 22	17 32	17 42	17 52	18 02	the same	22 02	22 12	22 22	22 52	23 24	
West Hampstead	⊖ d	09 34	minutes	16 34	16 44	16 54	17 04	17 14	17 24	17 34	17 44	17 54	18 04	minutes	22 04	22 14	22 24	22 54	23 26	
Finchley Road & Frognal	d	09 35	past	16 35	16 45	16 55	17 05	17 15	17 25	17 35	17 45	17 55	18 05	past	22 05	22 15	22 25	22 55	23 27	
Hampstead Heath	d	09 38	each	16 38	16 48	16 58	17 08	17 18	17 28	17 38	17 48	17 58	18 08	each	22 08	22 18	22 28	22 58	23 30	
Gospel Oak	d	09 40	hour until	16 40	16 50	17 00	17 11	17 20	17 30	17 40	17 50	18 00	18 10	hour until	22 10	22 20	22 30	23 00	23 32	
Kentish Town West	d	09 42		16 42	16 52	17 02	17 13	17 22	17 32	17 42	17 52	18 02	18 12		22 12	22 22	22 32	23 02	23 34	
Camden Road	d	09 46		16 46	16 56	17 06	17 16	17 26	17 36	17 46	17 56	18 06	18 16		22 16	22 26	22 36	23 06	23 38	
Caledonian Rd & Barnsbury	d	09 49		16 49	16 59	17 09	17 19	17 29	17 39	17 49	17 59	18 09	18 19		22 19	22 29	22 39	23 09	23 41	
Highbury & Islington	⊖ d	09 52		16 52	17 02	17 12	17 22	17 32	17 42	17 52	18 02	18 12	18 22		22 22	22 32	22 42	23 12	23 44	
Canonbury	⊖ d	09 54		16 54	17 04	17 14	17 24	17 34	17 44	17 54	18 04	18 14	18 24		22 24	22 34	22 44	23 14	23 46	
Dalston Kingsland	d	09 56		16 56	17 06	17 16	17 26	17 36	17 46	17 56	18 06	18 16	18 26		22 26	22 36	22 46	23 16	23 48	
Hackney Central	d	09 58		16 58	17 08	17 18	17 28	17 38	17 48	17 58	18 08	18 18	18 28		22 28	22 38	22 48	23 18	23 50	
Homerton	d	10 00		17 00	17 10	17 20	17 30	17 40	17 50	18 00	18 10	18 20	18 30		22 30	22 40	22 50	23 20	23 52	
Hackney Wick	d	10 02		17 02	17 12	17 22	17 32	17 42	17 52	18 02	18 12	18 22	18 32		22 32	22 42	22 52	23 22	23 54	
Stratford 7	⊖ a	10 11		17 11	17 20	17 30	17 41	17 50	18 01	18 11	18 20	18 30	18 41		22 41	22 50	23 01	23 30	00 02	

Sundays

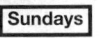

		LO A	LO	LO	LO	LO	LO	LO	LO	LO	LO	LO	LO	LO	LO	LO	LO	LO	LO	LO	LO
Richmond	⊖ d	23p00		08 59	09 17	09 29	09 47	09 59	10 10		10 29	10 40		10 59	11 10		11 29	11 40		11 59	12 10
Kew Gardens	⊖ d	23p03		09 02	09 20	09 32	09 50	10 02	10 13		10 32	10 43		11 02	11 13		11 32	11 43		12 02	12 13
Gunnersbury	⊖ d	23p06		09 05	09 23	09 35	09 53	10 05	10 16		10 35	10 46		11 05	11 16		11 35	11 46		12 05	12 16
South Acton	d	23p09		09 08	09 26	09 38	09 56	10 08	10 19		10 38	10 49		11 08	11 19		11 38	11 49		12 08	12 19
Acton Central	d	23p12		09 11	09 29	09 41	09 59	10 11	10 22		10 41	10 52		11 11	11 22		11 41	11 52		12 11	12 22
Willesden Jn. High Level	⊖ a	23p17		09 16	09 34	09 45	10 04	10 16	10 27		10 46	10 57		11 16	11 27		11 46	11 57		12 16	12 27
	d	23p18		09 17	09 35	09 47	10 05	10 17	10 28	10 41	10 47	10 58	11 06	11 17	11 28	11 41	11 47	11 58	12 06	12 17	12 28
Kensal Rise	d	23p20	09 04	09 19	09 37	09 49	10 07	10 19	10 30	10 43	10 49	11 00	11 08	11 19	11 30	11 43	11 49	12 00	12 08	12 19	12 30
Brondesbury Park	d	23p22	09 06	09 21	09 39	09 51	10 09	10 21	10 32	10 45	10 51	11 02	11 10	11 21	11 32	11 45	11 51	12 02	12 10	12 21	12 32
Brondesbury	d	23p24	09 08	09 23	09 41	09 53	10 11	10 23	10 34	10 47	10 53	11 04	11 12	11 23	11 34	11 47	11 53	12 04	12 12	12 23	12 34
West Hampstead	⊖ d	23p26	09 10	09 25	09 43	09 55	10 13	10 25	10 36	10 49	10 55	11 06	11 14	11 25	11 36	11 49	11 55	12 06	12 14	12 25	12 36
Finchley Road & Frognal	d	23p27	09 11	09 26	09 44	09 56	10 14	10 26	10 37	10 50	10 56	11 07	11 15	11 26	11 37	11 50	11 56	12 07	12 15	12 26	12 37
Hampstead Heath	d	23p30	09 14	09 30	09 47	09 59	10 17	10 29	10 40	10 53	10 59	11 10	11 18	11 29	11 40	11 53	11 59	12 10	12 18	12 29	12 40
Gospel Oak	d	23p32	09 16	09 32	09 49	10 01	10 19	10 31	10 42	10 55	11 01	11 12	11 20	11 31	11 42	11 55	12 01	12 12	12 20	12 31	12 42
Kentish Town West	d	23p34	09 18	09 34	09 51	10 03	10 21	10 33	10 44	10 57	11 03	11 14	11 22	11 33	11 44	11 57	12 03	12 14	12 22	12 33	12 44
Camden Road	d	23p38	09 22	09 37	09 55	10 07	10 25	10 37	10 48	11 01	11 07	11 18	11 26	11 37	11 48	12 01	12 07	12 18	12 26	12 37	12 48
Caledonian Rd & Barnsbury	d	23p41	09 25	09 40	09 58	10 10	10 28	10 40	10 51	11 04	11 10	11 21	11 29	11 40	11 51	12 04	12 10	12 21	12 29	12 40	12 51
Highbury & Islington	⊖ d	23p44	09 28	09 43	10 01	10 13	10 31	10 43	10 54	11 07	11 13	11 24	11 32	11 43	11 54	12 07	12 13	12 24	12 32	12 43	12 54
Canonbury	⊖ d	23p46	09 30	09 45	10 03	10 15	10 33	10 45	10 56	11 09	11 15	11 26	11 34	11 45	11 56	12 09	12 15	12 26	12 34	12 45	12 56
Dalston Kingsland	d	23p48	09 32	09 47	10 05	10 17	10 35	10 47	10 58	11 11	11 17	11 28	11 36	11 47	11 58	12 11	12 17	12 28	12 36	12 47	12 58
Hackney Central	d	23p50	09 34	09 49	10 07	10 19	10 37	10 49	11 00	11 13	11 19	11 30	11 38	11 49	12 00	12 13	12 19	12 30	12 38	12 49	13 00
Homerton	d	23p52	09 36	09 51	10 09	10 21	10 39	10 51	11 02	11 15	11 21	11 32	11 40	11 51	12 02	12 15	12 21	12 32	12 40	12 51	13 02
Hackney Wick	d	23p54	09 38	09 53	10 11	10 23	10 41	10 53	11 04	11 17	11 23	11 34	11 42	11 53	12 04	12 17	12 23	12 34	12 42	12 53	13 04
Stratford 7	⊖ a	00 02	09 46	10 01	10 19	10 30	10 48	11 01	11 12	11 25	11 30	11 42	11 50	12 00	12 12	12 25	12 30	12 42	12 50	13 00	13 12

A not 11 December

Table 59

Sundays

Richmond - Willesden Junction, West Hampstead, Highbury and Islington and Stratford

Network Diagram - see first Page of Table 59

		LO		LO	LO	LO	LO		LO	LO	LO	LO	LO	LO	LO	LO	LO		LO	LO
Richmond ⊖	d				19 29	19 40			19 59	20 10	20 29	20 40	20 59	21 17	21 29	21 47	21 59		22 28	22 58
Kew Gardens ⊖	d				19 32	19 43			20 02	20 13	20 32	20 43	21 02	21 20	21 32	21 50	22 02		22 31	23 02
Gunnersbury ⊖	d				19 35	19 46			20 05	20 16	20 35	20 46	21 05	21 23	21 35	21 53	22 05		22 34	23 05
South Acton	d				19 38	19 49			20 08	20 19	20 38	20 49	21 08	21 26	21 38	21 56	22 08		22 37	23 08
Acton Central	d				19 41	19 52			20 11	20 22	20 41	20 52	21 11	21 29	21 41	21 59	22 11		22 40	23 11
Willesden Jn. High Level ⊖	a				19 46	19 57			20 16	20 27	20 46	20 57	21 16	21 34	21 46	22 04	22 16		22 45	23 16
	d	12 36		19 36	19 47	19 58	20 06		20 17	20 28	20 47	20 58	21 17	21 35	21 47	22 05	22 17		22 46	23 17
Kensal Rise	d	12 38		19 38	19 49	20 00	20 08		20 19	20 30	20 49	21 00	21 19	21 37	21 49	22 07	22 19		22 48	23 19
Brondesbury Park	d	12 40	and at the same minutes past each hour until	19 40	19 51	20 02	20 10		20 21	20 32	20 51	21 02	21 21	21 39	21 51	22 09	22 21		22 50	23 21
Brondesbury	d	12 42		19 42	19 53	20 04	20 12		20 23	20 34	20 53	21 04	21 23	21 41	21 53	22 11	22 23		22 52	23 23
West Hampstead ⊖	d	12 44		19 44	19 55	20 06	20 14		20 25	20 36	20 55	21 06	21 25	21 43	21 55	22 13	22 25		22 54	23 25
Finchley Road & Frognal	d	12 45		19 45	19 56	20 07	20 15		20 26	20 37	20 56	21 07	21 26	21 44	21 56	22 14	22 26		22 55	23 26
Hampstead Heath	d	12 48		19 48	19 59	20 10	20 18		20 29	20 40	20 59	21 10	21 29	21 47	21 59	22 17	22 29		22 58	23 29
Gospel Oak	d	12 50		19 50	20 01	20 12	20 20		20 31	20 42	21 01	21 12	21 31	21 49	22 01	22a22	22a36		23a03	23a35
Kentish Town West	d	12 52		19 52	20 03	20 14	20 22		20 33	20 44	21 03	21 14	21 33	21 51	22 03					
Camden Road	d	12 56		19 56	20 07	20 18	20 26		20 37	20 48	21 07	21 18	21 37	21 55	22 07					
Caledonian Rd & Barnsbury	d	12 59		19 59	20 10	20 21	20 29		20 40	20 51	21 10	21 21	21 40	21 58	22 10					
Highbury & Islington ⊖	d	13 02		20 02	20 13	20 24	20 32		20 43	20 54	21 13	21 24	21 43	22 01	22 13					
Canonbury ⊖	d	13 04		20 04	20 15	20 26	20 34		20 45	20 56	21 15	21 26	21 45	22 03	22 15					
Dalston Kingsland	d	13 06		20 06	20 17	20 28	20 36		20 47	20 58	21 17	21 28	21 47	22 05	22 17					
Hackney Central	d	13 08		20 08	20 19	20 30	20 38		20 49	21 00	21 19	21 30	21 49	22 07	22 19					
Homerton	d	13 10		20 10	20 21	20 32	20 40		20 51	21 02	21 21	21 32	21 51	22 09	22 21					
Hackney Wick	d	13 12		20 12	20 23	20 34	20 42		20 53	21 04	21 23	21 34	21 53	22 11	22 23					
Stratford 7 ⊖	a	13 20		20 20	20 30	20 42	20 49		21 01	21 12	21 30	21 39	22 01	22 19	22 31					

London, Queen's Park and Harrow & Wealdstone - Watford Junction

Network Diagram - see first Page of Table 59

Miles				LO MO	LO MX	LO MO	LO MX	LO	LO	LO	LO	LO	LO	LO	LO	LO		LO	LO	LO	LO	LO	LO
0	**London Euston** 15	⊖	d	23p17	23p27	23p47	23p57	05 37	06 07	06 37	06 57	07 17	07 37	07 57	08 17	08 37		15 37	15 57	16 17	16 37	16 57	17 17
2½	South Hampstead		d	23p23	23p33	23p53	00 03	05 43	06 13	06 43	07 03	07 23	07 43	08 03	08 23	08 43		15 43	16 03	16 23	16 43	17 03	17 23
3	Kilburn High Road		d	23p24	23p34	23p54	00 04	05 44	06 14	06 44	07 04	07 24	07 44	08 04	08 24	08 44		15 44	16 04	16 24	16 44	17 04	17 24
3¾	**Queen's Park (London)**	⊖	d	23p26	23p36	23p56	00 06	05 46	06 16	06 46	07 06	07 26	07 46	08 06	08 26	08 46		15 46	16 06	16 27	16 47	17 07	17 27
4½	Kensal Green		d	23p28	23p38	23p58	00 08	05 48	06 18	06 48	07 08	07 28	07 48	08 08	08 28	08 48		15 48	16 08	16 29	16 49	17 09	17 29
5½	**Willesden Jn Low Level**		d	23p31	23p41	00 01	00 11	05 51	06 21	06 51	07 11	07 31	07 51	08 11	08 31	08 51	and at	15 51	16 11	16 32	16 52	17 12	17 32
6	Harlesden		d	23p33	23p43	00 03	00 13	05 53	06 23	06 53	07 13	07 33	07 53	08 13	08 33	08 53	the same	15 53	16 13	16 34	16 54	17 14	17 34
7	Stonebridge Park		d	23p35	23p45	00 05	00 15	05 55	06 25	06 55	07 15	07 35	07 55	08 15	08 35	08 55	minutes	15 55	16 15	16 36	16 56	17 16	17 36
8	Wembley Central		d	23p38	23p48	00 08	00 18	05 58	06 28	06 58	07 18	07 38	07 58	08 18	08 38	08 58	past	15 58	16 18	16 39	16 59	17 19	17 39
9	North Wembley		d	23p40	23p50	00 10	00 20	06 00	06 30	07 00	07 20	07 40	08 00	08 20	08 40	09 00	each	16 00	16 20	16 41	17 01	17 21	17 41
9½	South Kenton		d	23p42	23p52	00 12	00 22	06 02	06 32	07 02	07 22	07 42	08 02	08 22	08 42	09 02	hour until	16 02	16 22	16 43	17 03	17 23	17 43
10¼	Kenton		d	23p44	23p54	00 14	00 24	06 04	06 34	07 04	07 24	07 44	08 04	08 24	08 44	09 04		16 04	16 24	16 45	17 05	17 25	17 45
11¼	**Harrow & Wealdstone**		d	23p46	23p56	00 16	00 26	06 06	06 36	07 06	07 26	07 46	08 06	08 26	08 46	09 06		16 06	16 26	16 48	17 08	17 28	17 48
12½	Headstone Lane		d	23p49	23p59	00 19	00 29	06 09	06 39	07 09	07 29	07 49	08 09	08 29	08 49	09 09		16 09	16 29	16 51	17 11	17 31	17 51
13¼	Hatch End		d	23p51	00 01	00 21	00 31	06 11	06 41	07 11	07 31	07 51	08 11	08 31	08 51	09 11		16 11	16 31	16 53	17 13	17 33	17 53
14¾	Carpenders Park		d	23p54	00 04	00 24	00 34	06 14	06 44	07 14	07 34	07 54	08 14	08 34	08 54	09 14		16 14	16 34	16 56	17 16	17 36	17 56
16	Bushey		d	23p57	00 07	00 27	00 37	06 17	06 47	07 17	07 37	07 57	08 17	08 37	08 57	09 17		16 17	16 37	16 59	17 19	17 39	17 59
16¾	Watford High Street		d	23p59	00 10	00 30	00 40	06 20	06 50	07 20	07 40	08 00	08 20	08 40	09 00	09 20		16 20	16 40	17 01	17 21	17 41	18 01
17¾	**Watford Junction**		a	00 04	00 14	00 35	00 44	06 24	06 54	07 24	07 44	08 04	08 28	08 44	09 04	09 24		16 24	16 44	17 08	17 28	17 48	18 08

			LO	LO	LO	LO	LO	LO	LO	LO	LO	LO	LO	LO	LO	LO	LO	LO	LO	LO
London Euston 15	⊖	d	17 37	17 57	18 17	18 37	18 57	19 17	19 37	19 57	20 17	20 37	20 57	21 17	21 37	21 57	22 27	22 57	23 27	23 57
South Hampstead		d	17 43	18 03	18 23	18 43	19 03	19 23	19 43	20 03	20 23	20 43	21 03	21 23	21 43	22 03	22 33	23 03	23 33	00 03
Kilburn High Road		d	17 44	18 04	18 24	18 44	19 04	19 24	19 44	20 04	20 24	20 44	21 04	21 24	21 44	22 04	22 34	23 04	23 34	00 04
Queen's Park (London)	⊖	d	17 47	18 07	18 27	18 47	19 07	19 26	19 46	20 06	20 26	20 46	21 06	21 26	21 46	22 06	22 36	23 06	23 36	00 06
Kensal Green		d	17 49	18 09	18 29	18 49	19 09	19 28	19 48	20 08	20 28	20 48	21 08	21 28	21 48	22 08	22 38	23 08	23 38	00 08
Willesden Jn Low Level		d	17 52	18 12	18 32	18 52	19 12	19 31	19 51	20 11	20 31	20 51	21 11	21 31	21 51	22 11	22 41	23 11	23 41	00 11
Harlesden		d	17 54	18 14	18 34	18 54	19 14	19 33	19 53	20 13	20 33	20 53	21 13	21 33	21 53	22 13	22 43	23 13	23 43	00 13
Stonebridge Park		d	17 56	18 16	18 36	18 56	19 16	19 35	19 55	20 15	20 35	20 55	21 15	21 35	21 55	22 15	22 45	23 15	23 45	00 15
Wembley Central		d	17 59	18 19	18 39	18 59	19 19	19 38	19 58	20 18	20 38	20 58	21 18	21 38	21 58	22 18	22 48	23 18	23 48	00 18
North Wembley		d	18 01	18 21	18 41	19 01	19 21	19 40	20 00	20 20	20 40	21 00	21 20	21 40	22 00	22 20	22 50	23 20	23 50	00 20
South Kenton		d	18 03	18 23	18 43	19 03	19 23	19 42	20 02	20 22	20 42	21 02	21 22	21 42	22 02	22 22	22 52	23 22	23 52	00 22
Kenton		d	18 05	18 25	18 45	19 05	19 25	19 44	20 04	20 24	20 44	21 04	21 24	21 44	22 04	22 24	22 54	23 24	23 54	00 24
Harrow & Wealdstone		d	18 08	18 28	18 48	19 08	19 28	19 46	20 06	20 26	20 46	21 06	21 26	21 46	22 06	22 26	22 56	23 26	23 56	00 26
Headstone Lane		d	18 11	18 31	18 51	19 11	19 31	19 49	20 09	20 29	20 49	21 09	21 29	21 49	22 09	22 29	22 59	23 29	23 59	00 29
Hatch End		d	18 13	18 33	18 53	19 13	19 33	19 51	20 11	20 31	20 51	21 11	21 31	21 51	22 11	22 31	23 01	23 31	00 01	00 31
Carpenders Park		d	18 16	18 36	18 56	19 16	19 36	19 54	20 14	20 34	20 54	21 14	21 34	21 54	22 14	22 34	23 04	23 34	00 04	00 34
Bushey		d	18 19	18 39	18 59	19 19	19 39	19 57	20 17	20 37	20 57	21 17	21 37	21 57	22 17	22 37	23 07	23 37	00 07	00 37
Watford High Street		d	18 21	18 41	19 01	19 21	19 41	20 00	20 20	20 40	21 00	21 20	21 40	22 00	22 20	22 40	23 10	23 40	00 10	00 40
Watford Junction		a	18 28	18 48	19 08	19 28	19 48	20 04	20 28	20 44	21 08	21 28	21 44	22 04	22 25	22 44	23 14	23 44	00 14	00 44

Saturdays

			LO	LO	LO	LO	LO	LO	LO		LO	LO	LO	LO	LO	LO		LO	LO	LO	LO	LO
London Euston 15	⊖	d	23p27	23p57	05 37	06 07	06 37	06 57	07 17		14 17	14 37	14 57	15 17	15 37	15 57		19 57	20 17	20 37	20 57	21 17
South Hampstead		d	23p33	00 03	05 43	06 13	06 43	07 03	07 23		14 23	14 43	15 03	15 23	15 43	16 03		20 03	20 23	20 43	21 03	21 23
Kilburn High Road		d	23p34	00 04	05 44	06 14	06 44	07 04	07 24		14 24	14 44	15 04	15 24	15 44	16 04		20 04	20 24	20 44	21 04	21 24
Queen's Park (London)	⊖	d	23p36	00 06	05 46	06 16	06 46	07 06	07 26		14 26	14 46	15 06	15 26	15 46	16 06		20 06	20 26	20 46	21 06	21 26
Kensal Green		d	23p38	00 08	05 48	06 18	06 48	07 08	07 28		14 28	14 48	15 08	15 28	15 48	16 08		20 08	20 28	20 48	21 08	21 28
Willesden Jn Low Level		d	23p41	00 11	05 51	06 21	06 51	07 11	07 31	and at	14 31	14 51	15 11	15 31	15 51	16 11	and at	20 11	20 31	20 51	21 11	21 31
Harlesden		d	23p43	00 13	05 53	06 23	06 53	07 13	07 33	the same	14 33	14 53	15 13	15 33	15 53	16 13	the same	20 13	20 33	20 53	21 13	21 33
Stonebridge Park		d	23p45	00 15	05 55	06 25	06 55	07 15	07 35	minutes	14 35	14 55	15 15	15 35	15 55	16 15	minutes	20 15	20 35	20 55	21 15	21 35
Wembley Central		d	23p48	00 18	05 58	06 28	06 58	07 18	07 38	past	14 38	14 58	15 18	15 38	15 58	16 18	past	20 18	20 38	20 58	21 18	21 38
North Wembley		d	23p50	00 20	06 00	06 30	07 00	07 20	07 40	each	14 40	15 00	15 20	15 40	16 00	16 20	each	20 20	20 40	21 00	21 20	21 40
South Kenton		d	23p52	00 22	06 02	06 32	07 02	07 22	07 42	hour until	14 42	15 02	15 22	15 42	16 02	16 22	hour until	20 22	20 42	21 02	21 22	21 42
Kenton		d	23p54	00 24	06 04	06 34	07 04	07 24	07 44		14 44	15 04	15 24	15 44	16 04	16 24		20 24	20 44	21 04	21 24	21 44
Harrow & Wealdstone		d	23p56	00 26	06 06	06 36	07 06	07 26	07 46		14 46	15 06	15 26	15 46	16 06	16 26		20 26	20 46	21 06	21 26	21 46
Headstone Lane		d	23p59	00 29	06 09	06 39	07 09	07 29	07 49		14 49	15 09	15 29	15 49	16 09	16 29		20 29	20 49	21 09	21 29	21 49
Hatch End		d	00 01	00 31	06 11	06 41	07 11	07 31	07 51		14 51	15 11	15 31	15 51	16 11	16 31		20 31	20 51	21 11	21 31	21 51
Carpenders Park		d	00 04	00 34	06 14	06 44	07 14	07 34	07 54		14 54	15 14	15 34	15 54	16 14	16 34		20 34	20 54	21 14	21 34	21 54
Bushey		d	00 07	00 37	06 17	06 47	07 17	07 37	07 57		14 57	15 17	15 37	15 57	16 17	16 37		20 37	20 57	21 17	21 37	21 57
Watford High Street		d	00 10	00 40	06 20	06 50	07 20	07 40	08 00		15 00	15 20	15 40	16 00	16 20	16 40		20 40	21 00	21 20	21 40	22 00
Watford Junction		a	00 14	00 44	06 24	06 55	07 24	07 44	08 04		15 04	15 24	15 44	16 08	16 28	16 48		20 48	21 04	21 24	21 44	22 08

			LO	LO	LO	LO	LO	LO
London Euston 15	⊖	d	21 37	21 57	22 27	22 57	23 27	23 57
South Hampstead		d	21 43	22 03	22 33	23 03	23 33	00 03
Kilburn High Road		d	21 44	22 04	22 34	23 04	23 34	00 04
Queen's Park (London)	⊖	d	21 46	22 06	22 36	23 06	23 36	00 06
Kensal Green		d	21 48	22 08	22 38	23 08	23 38	00 08
Willesden Jn Low Level		d	21 51	22 11	22 41	23 11	23 41	00 11
Harlesden		d	21 53	22 13	22 43	23 13	23 43	00 13
Stonebridge Park		d	21 55	22 15	22 45	23 15	23 45	00 15
Wembley Central		d	21 58	22 18	22 48	23 18	23 48	00 18
North Wembley		d	22 00	22 20	22 50	23 20	23 50	00 20
South Kenton		d	22 02	22 22	22 52	23 22	23 52	00 22
Kenton		d	22 04	22 24	22 54	23 24	23 54	00 24
Harrow & Wealdstone		d	22 06	22 26	22 56	23 26	23 56	00 26
Headstone Lane		d	22 09	22 29	22 59	23 29	23 59	00 29
Hatch End		d	22 11	22 31	23 01	23 31	00 01	00 31
Carpenders Park		d	22 14	22 34	23 04	23 34	00 04	00 34
Bushey		d	22 17	22 37	23 07	23 37	00 07	00 37
Watford High Street		d	22 20	22 40	23 10	23 40	00 10	00 40
Watford Junction		a	22 24	22 44	23 14	23 44	00 14	00 44

Stations Queen's Park to Harrow & Wealdstone inclusive are also served by London Underground Bakerloo Line Services

Table 60

Sundays

London, Queen's Park and Harrow & Wealdstone - Watford Junction

Network Diagram - see first Page of Table 59

		LO A	LO A	LO		LO	LO	LO	LO	LO	LO	LO	LO		LO	LO	LO	LO	LO	LO	LO
London Euston [15] ⊖	d	23p27	23p57	06 47	and every 30 minutes until	08 17	08 47	09 17	09 37	09 57	10 17	10 37	10 57	and at the same minutes past each hour until	14 57	15 17	15 37	15 57	16 17	16 37	16 57
South Hampstead	d	23p33	00 03	06 53		08 23	08 53	09 23	09 43	10 03	10 23	10 43	11 03		15 03	15 23	15 43	16 03	16 23	16 43	17 03
Kilburn High Road	d	23p34	00 04	06 54		08 24	08 54	09 24	09 44	10 04	10 24	10 44	11 04		15 04	15 24	15 44	16 04	16 24	16 44	17 04
Queen's Park (London) ⊖	d	23p36	00 06	06 56		08 26	08 56	09 26	09 46	10 06	10 26	10 46	11 06		15 06	15 26	15 46	16 06	16 26	16 46	17 06
Kensal Green	d	23p38	00 08	06 58		08 28	08 58	09 28	09 48	10 08	10 28	10 48	11 08		15 08	15 28	15 48	16 08	16 28	16 48	17 08
Willesden Jn Low Level	d	23p41	00 11	07 01		08 31	09 01	09 31	09 51	10 11	10 31	10 51	11 11		15 11	15 31	15 51	16 11	16 31	16 51	17 11
Harlesden	d	23p43	00 13	07 03		08 33	09 03	09 33	09 53	10 13	10 33	10 53	11 13		15 13	15 33	15 53	16 13	16 33	16 53	17 13
Stonebridge Park	d	23p45	00 15	07 05		08 35	09 05	09 35	09 55	10 15	10 35	10 55	11 15		15 15	15 35	15 55	16 15	16 35	16 55	17 15
Wembley Central	d	23p48	00 18	07 08		08 38	09 08	09 38	09 58	10 18	10 38	10 58	11 18		15 18	15 38	15 58	16 18	16 38	16 58	17 18
North Wembley	d	23p50	00 20	07 10		08 40	09 10	09 40	10 00	10 20	10 40	11 00	11 20		15 20	15 40	16 00	16 20	16 40	17 00	17 20
South Kenton	d	23p52	00 22	07 12		08 42	09 12	09 42	10 02	10 22	10 42	11 02	11 22		15 22	15 42	16 02	16 22	16 42	17 02	17 22
Kenton	d	23p54	00 24	07 14		08 44	09 14	09 44	10 04	10 24	10 44	11 04	11 24		15 24	15 44	16 04	16 24	16 44	17 04	17 24
Harrow & Wealdstone	d	23p56	00 26	07 16		08 46	09 16	09 46	10 06	10 26	10 46	11 06	11 26		15 26	15 46	16 06	16 26	16 46	17 06	17 26
Headstone Lane	d	23p59	00 29	07 19		08 49	09 19	09 49	10 09	10 29	10 49	11 09	11 29		15 29	15 49	16 09	16 29	16 49	17 09	17 29
Hatch End	d	00 01	00 31	07 21		08 51	09 21	09 51	10 11	10 31	10 51	11 11	11 31		15 31	15 51	16 11	16 31	16 51	17 11	17 31
Carpenders Park	d	00 04	00 34	07 24		08 54	09 24	09 54	10 14	10 34	10 54	11 14	11 34		15 34	15 54	16 14	16 34	16 54	17 14	17 34
Bushey	d	00 07	00 37	07 27		08 57	09 27	09 57	10 17	10 37	10 57	11 17	11 37		15 37	15 57	16 17	16 37	16 57	17 17	17 37
Watford High Street	d	00 10	00 40	07 30		09 00	09 30	10 00	10 20	10 40	11 00	11 20	11 40		15 40	16 00	16 20	16 40	17 00	17 20	17 40
Watford Junction	a	00 14	00 44	07 34		09 04	09 35	10 04	10 24	10 45	11 04	11 24	11 44		15 44	16 08	16 28	16 48	17 08	17 24	17 44

		LO	LO	LO	LO	LO	LO	LO	LO	LO	LO	LO	LO	LO	LO	LO	LO	LO	LO	LO
London Euston [15] ⊖	d	17 17	17 37	17 57	18 17	18 37	18 57	19 17	19 37	19 57	20 17	20 37	20 57	21 17	21 37	21 57	22 17	22 47	23 17	23 47
South Hampstead	d	17 23	17 43	18 03	18 23	18 43	19 03	19 23	19 43	20 03	20 23	20 43	21 03	21 23	21 43	22 03	22 23	22 53	23 23	23 53
Kilburn High Road	d	17 24	17 44	18 04	18 24	18 44	19 04	19 24	19 44	20 04	20 24	20 44	21 04	21 24	21 44	22 04	22 24	22 54	23 24	23 54
Queen's Park (London) ⊖	d	17 26	17 46	18 06	18 26	18 46	19 06	19 26	19 46	20 06	20 26	20 46	21 06	21 26	21 46	22 06	22 26	22 56	23 26	23 56
Kensal Green	d	17 28	17 48	18 08	18 28	18 48	19 08	19 28	19 48	20 08	20 28	20 48	21 08	21 28	21 48	22 08	22 28	22 58	23 28	23 58
Willesden Jn Low Level	d	17 31	17 51	18 11	18 31	18 51	19 11	19 31	19 51	20 11	20 31	20 51	21 11	21 31	21 51	22 11	22 31	23 01	23 31	00 01
Harlesden	d	17 33	17 53	18 13	18 33	18 53	19 13	19 33	19 53	20 13	20 33	20 53	21 13	21 33	21 53	22 13	22 33	23 03	23 33	00 03
Stonebridge Park	d	17 35	17 55	18 15	18 35	18 55	19 15	19 35	19 55	20 15	20 35	20 55	21 15	21 35	21 55	22 15	22 35	23 05	23 35	00 05
Wembley Central	d	17 38	17 58	18 18	18 38	18 58	19 18	19 38	19 58	20 18	20 38	20 58	21 18	21 38	21 58	22 18	22 38	23 08	23 38	00 08
North Wembley	d	17 40	18 00	18 20	18 40	19 00	19 20	19 40	20 00	20 20	20 40	21 00	21 20	21 40	22 00	22 20	22 40	23 10	23 40	00 10
South Kenton	d	17 42	18 02	18 22	18 42	19 02	19 22	19 42	20 02	20 22	20 42	21 02	21 22	21 42	22 02	22 22	22 42	23 12	23 42	00 12
Kenton	d	17 44	18 04	18 24	18 44	19 04	19 24	19 44	20 04	20 24	20 44	21 04	21 24	21 44	22 04	22 24	22 44	23 14	23 44	00 14
Harrow & Wealdstone	d	17 46	18 06	18 26	18 46	19 06	19 26	19 46	20 06	20 26	20 46	21 06	21 26	21 46	22 06	22 26	22 46	23 16	23 46	00 16
Headstone Lane	d	17 49	18 09	18 29	18 49	19 09	19 29	19 49	20 09	20 29	20 49	21 09	21 29	21 49	22 09	22 29	22 49	23 19	23 49	00 19
Hatch End	d	17 51	18 11	18 31	18 51	19 11	19 31	19 51	20 11	20 31	20 51	21 11	21 31	21 51	22 11	22 31	22 51	23 21	23 51	00 21
Carpenders Park	d	17 54	18 14	18 34	18 54	19 14	19 34	19 54	20 14	20 34	20 54	21 14	21 34	21 54	22 14	22 34	22 54	23 24	23 54	00 24
Bushey	d	17 57	18 17	18 37	18 57	19 17	19 37	19 57	20 17	20 37	20 57	21 17	21 37	21 57	22 17	22 37	22 57	23 27	23 57	00 27
Watford High Street	d	18 00	18 20	18 40	19 00	19 20	19 40	20 00	20 20	20 40	21 00	21 20	21 40	22 00	22 20	22 40	23 00	23 30	23 59	00 30
Watford Junction	a	18 08	18 28	18 48	19 08	19 28	19 48	20 08	20 28	20 48	21 04	21 24	21 45	22 04	22 24	22 44	23 04	23 34	00 04	00 35

A not 11 December

Stations Queen's Park to Harrow & Wealdstone inclusive are also served by London Underground Bakerloo Line Services

Watford Junction - Harrow & Wealdstone, Queen's Park and London

Network Diagram - see first Page of Table 59

Miles			LO MX	LO MO	LO	LO	LO	LO	LO	LO	LO		LO	LO	LO	LO	LO	LO	LO	LO	LO		LO	
0	**Watford Junction**	d	23p21	23p21	05 11	05 41	06 11	06 40	07 00	07 20	07 40		08 00	08 20	08 40	09 00	09 21	09 41	10 01	10 21	10 41		11 01	
1	Watford High Street	d	23p24	23p24	05 14	05 44	06 14	06 43	07 03	07 23	07 43		08 03	08 23	08 43	09 03	09 24	09 44	10 04	10 24	10 44		11 04	
13	Bushey	d	23p26	23p26	05 16	05 46	06 16	06 45	07 05	07 25	07 45		08 05	08 25	08 45	09 05	09 26	09 46	10 06	10 26	10 46		11 06	
3	Carpenders Park	d	23p29	23p29	05 19	05 49	06 19	06 48	07 08	07 28	07 48		08 08	08 28	08 48	09 08	09 29	09 49	10 09	10 29	10 49		11 09	
4½	Hatch End	d	23p32	23p32	05 22	05 52	06 22	06 51	07 11	07 31	07 51		08 11	08 31	08 51	09 11	09 32	09 52	10 12	10 32	10 52		11 12	
5¼	Headstone Lane	d	23p34	23p34	05 24	05 54	06 24	06 53	07 13	07 33	07 53		08 13	08 33	08 53	09 13	09 34	09 54	10 14	10 34	10 54		11 14	and at the same minutes past each hour until
6½	**Harrow & Wealdstone**	d	23p37	23p37	05 27	05 57	06 27	06 56	07 16	07 36	07 56		08 16	08 36	08 56	09 16	09 37	09 57	10 17	10 37	10 57		11 17	
7½	Kenton	d	23p39	23p39	05 29	05 59	06 29	06 59	07 19	07 39	07 59		08 19	08 39	08 59	09 19	09 39	09 59	10 19	10 39	10 59		11 19	
8¼	South Kenton	d	23p41	23p41	05 31	06 01	06 31	07 01	07 21	07 41	08 01		08 21	08 41	09 01	09 21	09 41	10 01	10 21	10 41	11 01		11 21	
8¾	North Wembley	d	23p43	23p43	05 33	06 03	06 33	07 03	07 23	07 43	08 03		08 23	08 43	09 03	09 23	09 43	10 03	10 23	10 43	11 03		11 23	
9¾	Wembley Central	d	23p45	23p45	05 35	06 05	06 35	07 05	07 25	07 45	08 05		08 25	08 45	09 05	09 25	09 45	10 05	10 25	10 45	11 05		11 25	
10¾	Stonebridge Park	d	23p48	23p48	05 38	06 08	06 38	07 08	07 28	07 48	08 08		08 28	08 48	09 08	09 28	09 48	10 08	10 28	10 48	11 08		11 28	
11¾	Harlesden	d	23p50	23p50	05 40	06 10	06 40	07 10	07 30	07 50	08 10		08 30	08 50	09 10	09 30	09 50	10 10	10 30	10 50	11 10		11 30	
12¼	**Willesden Jn Low Level**	d	23p52	23p52	05 42	06 12	06 42	07 13	07 33	07 53	08 13		08 33	08 53	09 13	09 33	09 52	10 12	10 32	10 52	11 12		11 32	
13¼	Kensal Green	d	23p55	23p55	05 45	06 15	06 45	07 15	07 35	07 55	08 15		08 35	08 55	09 15	09 35	09 55	10 15	10 35	10 55	11 15		11 35	
14	**Queen's Park (London)** ⊖	d	23p57	23p57	05 47	06 17	06 47	07 18	07 38	07 58	08 18		08 38	08 58	09 18	09 38	09 57	10 17	10 37	10 57	11 17		11 37	
14¾	Kilburn High Road	d	23p59	23p59	05 49	06 19	06 49	07 20	07 40	08 00	08 20		08 40	09 00	09 20	09 40	09 59	10 19	10 39	10 59	11 19		11 39	
15¼	South Hampstead	d	00 01	00 01	05 51	06 21	06 51	07 22	07 42	08 02	08 22		08 42	09 02	09 22	09 42	10 01	10 21	10 41	11 01	11 21		11 41	
17¾	**London Euston** 15 ⊖	a	00 09	00 12	05 59	06 32	06 58	07 29	07 52	08 12	08 31		08 52	09 12	09 29	09 52	10 11	10 30	10 49	11 11	11 30		11 50	

		LO	LO	LO	LO	LO	LO		LO	LO	LO	LO	LO	LO	LO	LO	LO		LO	LO	LO	LO	LO	LO	LO
Watford Junction	d	15 01	15 21	15 41	16 01	16 21	16 41		17 01	17 21	17 41	18 01	18 21	18 41	19 01	19 21	19 41		20 01	20 21	20 41	21 01	21 21	21 41	22 01
Watford High Street	d	15 04	15 24	15 44	16 04	16 24	16 44		17 04	17 24	17 44	18 04	18 24	18 44	19 04	19 24	19 44		20 04	20 24	20 44	21 04	21 24	21 44	22 04
Bushey	d	15 06	15 26	15 46	16 06	16 26	16 46		17 06	17 26	17 46	18 06	18 26	18 46	19 06	19 26	19 46		20 06	20 26	20 46	21 06	21 26	21 46	22 06
Carpenders Park	d	15 09	15 29	15 49	16 09	16 29	16 49		17 09	17 29	17 49	18 09	18 29	18 49	19 09	19 29	19 49		20 09	20 29	20 49	21 09	21 29	21 49	22 09
Hatch End	d	15 12	15 32	15 52	16 12	16 32	16 52		17 12	17 32	17 52	18 12	18 32	18 52	19 12	19 32	19 52		20 12	20 32	20 52	21 12	21 32	21 52	22 12
Headstone Lane	d	15 14	15 34	15 54	16 14	16 34	16 54		17 14	17 34	17 54	18 14	18 34	18 54	19 14	19 34	19 54		20 14	20 34	20 54	21 14	21 34	21 54	22 14
Harrow & Wealdstone	d	15 17	15 37	15 57	16 17	16 37	16 57		17 17	17 37	17 57	18 17	18 37	18 57	19 17	19 37	19 57		20 17	20 37	20 57	21 17	21 37	21 57	22 17
Kenton	d	15 19	15 39	15 59	16 19	16 39	16 59		17 19	17 39	17 59	18 19	18 39	18 59	19 19	19 39	19 59		20 19	20 39	20 59	21 19	21 39	21 59	22 19
South Kenton	d	15 21	15 41	16 01	16 21	16 41	17 01		17 21	17 41	18 01	18 21	18 41	19 01	19 21	19 41	20 01		20 21	20 41	21 01	21 21	21 41	22 01	22 21
North Wembley	d	15 23	15 43	16 03	16 23	16 43	17 03		17 23	17 43	18 03	18 23	18 43	19 03	19 23	19 43	20 03		20 23	20 43	21 03	21 23	21 43	22 03	22 23
Wembley Central	d	15 25	15 45	16 05	16 25	16 45	17 05		17 25	17 45	18 05	18 25	18 45	19 05	19 25	19 45	20 05		20 25	20 45	21 05	21 25	21 45	22 05	22 25
Stonebridge Park	d	15 28	15 48	16 08	16 28	16 48	17 08		17 28	17 48	18 08	18 28	18 48	19 08	19 28	19 48	20 08		20 28	20 48	21 08	21 28	21 48	22 08	22 28
Harlesden	d	15 30	15 50	16 10	16 30	16 50	17 10		17 30	17 50	18 10	18 30	18 50	19 10	19 30	19 50	20 10		20 30	20 50	21 10	21 30	21 50	22 10	22 30
Willesden Jn Low Level	d	15 32	15 52	16 12	16 32	16 52	17 12		17 32	17 52	18 12	18 32	18 52	19 12	19 32	19 52	20 12		20 32	20 52	21 12	21 32	21 52	22 12	22 32
Kensal Green	d	15 35	15 55	16 15	16 35	16 55	17 15		17 35	17 55	18 15	18 35	18 55	19 15	19 35	19 55	20 15		20 35	20 55	21 15	21 35	21 55	22 15	22 35
Queen's Park (London) ⊖	d	15 37	15 57	16 17	16 37	16 57	17 17		17 37	17 57	18 17	18 37	18 57	19 17	19 37	19 57	20 17		20 37	20 57	21 17	21 37	21 57	22 17	22 37
Kilburn High Road	d	15 39	15 59	16 19	16 39	16 59	17 19		17 39	17 59	18 19	18 39	18 59	19 19	19 39	19 59	20 19		20 39	20 59	21 19	21 39	21 59	22 19	22 39
South Hampstead	d	15 41	16 01	16 21	16 41	17 01	17 21		17 41	18 01	18 21	18 41	19 01	19 21	19 41	20 01	20 21		20 41	21 01	21 21	21 41	22 01	22 21	22 41
London Euston 15 ⊖	a	15 50	16 11	16 30	16 49	17 11	17 30		17 53	18 13	18 30	18 50	19 11	19 30	19 52	20 10	20 30		20 48	21 11	21 30	21 51	22 11	22 30	22 50

		LO	LO		LO
Watford Junction	d	22 21	22 51		23 21
Watford High Street	d	22 24	22 54		23 24
Bushey	d	22 26	22 56		23 26
Carpenders Park	d	22 29	22 59		23 29
Hatch End	d	22 32	23 02		23 32
Headstone Lane	d	22 34	23 04		23 34
Harrow & Wealdstone	d	22 37	23 07		23 37
Kenton	d	22 39	23 09		23 39
South Kenton	d	22 41	23 11		23 41
North Wembley	d	22 43	23 13		23 43
Wembley Central	d	22 45	23 15		23 45
Stonebridge Park	d	22 48	23 18		23 48
Harlesden	d	22 50	23 20		23 50
Willesden Jn Low Level	d	22 52	23 22		23 52
Kensal Green	d	22 55	23 25		23 55
Queen's Park (London) ⊖	d	22 57	23 27		23 57
Kilburn High Road	d	22 59	23 29		23 59
South Hampstead	d	23 01	23 31		00 01
London Euston 15 ⊖	a	23 10	23 39		00 09

Saturdays

		LO	LO	LO	LO	LO	LO	LO	LO	LO		LO	LO	LO	LO	LO	LO	LO	LO	LO		LO		LO
Watford Junction	d	23p21	05 11	05 41	06 11	06 41	07 01	07 21	07 41	08 01		08 21	08 41	09 01	09 21	09 41	10 01	10 21	10 41	11 01		21 01		21 21
Watford High Street	d	23p24	05 14	05 44	06 14	06 44	07 04	07 24	07 44	08 04		08 24	08 44	09 04	09 24	09 44	10 04	10 24	10 44	11 04		21 04		21 24
Bushey	d	23p26	05 16	05 46	06 16	06 46	07 06	07 26	07 46	08 06		08 26	08 46	09 06	09 26	09 46	10 06	10 26	10 46	11 06		21 06		21 26
Carpenders Park	d	23p29	05 19	05 49	06 19	06 49	07 09	07 29	07 49	08 09		08 29	08 49	09 09	09 29	09 49	10 09	10 29	10 49	11 09		21 09		21 29
Hatch End	d	23p32	05 22	05 52	06 22	06 52	07 12	07 32	07 52	08 12		08 32	08 52	09 12	09 32	09 52	10 12	10 32	10 52	11 12		21 12		21 32
Headstone Lane	d	23p34	05 24	05 54	06 24	06 54	07 14	07 34	07 54	08 14		08 34	08 54	09 14	09 34	09 54	10 14	10 34	10 54	11 14	and at the same minutes past each hour until	21 14		21 34
Harrow & Wealdstone	d	23p37	05 27	05 57	06 27	06 57	07 17	07 37	07 57	08 17		08 37	08 57	09 17	09 37	09 57	10 17	10 37	10 57	11 17		21 17		21 37
Kenton	d	23p39	05 29	05 59	06 29	06 59	07 19	07 39	07 59	08 19		08 39	08 59	09 19	09 39	09 59	10 19	10 39	10 59	11 19		21 19		21 39
South Kenton	d	23p41	05 31	06 01	06 31	07 01	07 21	07 41	08 01	08 21		08 41	09 01	09 21	09 41	10 01	10 21	10 41	11 01	11 21		21 21		21 41
North Wembley	d	23p43	05 33	06 03	06 33	07 03	07 23	07 43	08 03	08 23		08 43	09 03	09 23	09 43	10 03	10 23	10 43	11 03	11 23		21 23		21 43
Wembley Central	d	23p45	05 35	06 05	06 35	07 05	07 25	07 45	08 05	08 25		08 45	09 05	09 25	09 45	10 05	10 25	10 45	11 05	11 25		21 25		21 45
Stonebridge Park	d	23p48	05 38	06 08	06 38	07 08	07 28	07 48	08 08	08 28		08 48	09 08	09 28	09 48	10 08	10 28	10 48	11 08	11 28		21 28		21 48
Harlesden	d	23p50	05 40	06 10	06 40	07 10	07 30	07 50	08 10	08 30		08 50	09 10	09 30	09 50	10 10	10 30	10 50	11 10	11 30		21 30		21 50
Willesden Jn Low Level	d	23p52	05 42	06 12	06 42	07 12	07 32	07 52	08 12	08 32		08 52	09 12	09 32	09 52	10 12	10 32	10 52	11 12	11 32		21 32		21 52
Kensal Green	d	23p55	05 45	06 15	06 45	07 15	07 35	07 55	08 15	08 35		08 55	09 15	09 35	09 55	10 15	10 35	10 55	11 15	11 35		21 35		21 55
Queen's Park (London) ⊖	d	23p57	05 47	06 17	06 47	07 17	07 37	07 57	08 17	08 37		08 57	09 17	09 37	09 57	10 17	10 37	10 57	11 17	11 37		21 37		21 57
Kilburn High Road	d	23p59	05 49	06 19	06 49	07 19	07 39	07 59	08 19	08 39		08 59	09 19	09 39	09 59	10 19	10 39	10 59	11 19	11 39		21 39		21 59
South Hampstead	d	00 01	05 51	06 21	06 51	07 21	07 41	08 01	08 21	08 41		09 01	09 21	09 41	10 01	10 21	10 41	11 01	11 21	11 41		21 41		22 01
London Euston 15 ⊖	a	00 09	06 00	06 31	06 59	07 30	07 49	08 13	08 30	08 50		09 12	09 30	09 50	10 13	10 30	10 49	11 13	11 30	11 50		21 50		22 10

Stations Harrow & Wealdstone to Queen's Park inclusive are also served by London Underground Bakerloo Line Services

Table 60

Saturdays

Watford Junction - Harrow & Wealdstone, Queen's Park and London

Network Diagram - see first Page of Table 59

			LO	LO	LO	LO	LO
Watford Junction		d	21 41	22 01	22 21	22 51	23 21
Watford High Street		d	21 44	22 04	22 24	22 54	23 24
Bushey		d	21 46	22 06	22 26	22 56	23 26
Carpenders Park		d	21 49	22 09	22 29	22 59	23 29
Hatch End		d	21 52	22 12	22 32	23 02	23 32
Headstone Lane		d	21 54	22 14	22 34	23 04	23 34
Harrow & Wealdstone		d	21 57	22 17	22 37	23 07	23 37
Kenton		d	21 59	22 19	22 39	23 09	23 39
South Kenton		d	22 01	22 21	22 41	23 11	23 41
North Wembley		d	22 03	22 23	22 43	23 13	23 43
Wembley Central		d	22 05	22 25	22 45	23 15	23 45
Stonebridge Park		d	22 08	22 28	22 48	23 17	23 48
Harlesden		d	22 10	22 30	22 50	23 19	23 50
Willesden Jn Low Level		d	22 12	22 32	22 52	23 21	23 52
Kensal Green		d	22 15	22 35	22 55	23 23	23 55
Queen's Park (London)	⊖	d	22 17	22 37	22 57	23 25	23 57
Kilburn High Road		d	22 19	22 39	22 59	23 27	23 59
South Hampstead		d	22 21	22 41	23 01	23 29	00 01
London Euston 15	⊖	a	22 30	22 53	23 11	23 38	00 08

Sundays

			LO A	LO	LO	LO	LO	LO	LO	LO	LO	LO	LO	LO	LO	LO	LO		LO	LO	LO	LO	LO
Watford Junction		d	23p21	06 51	07 21	07 51	08 51	09 21	09 41	10 01	10 21	10 41	11 01	11 21	11 41	12 01	12 21	and at the same minutes past each hour until	18 21	18 41	19 01	19 21	19 41
Watford High Street		d	23p24	06 54	07 24	07 54	08 54	09 24	09 44	10 04	10 24	10 44	11 04	11 24	11 44	12 04	12 24		18 24	18 44	19 04	19 24	19 44
Bushey		d	23p26	06 56	07 26	07 56	08 56	09 26	09 46	10 06	10 26	10 46	11 06	11 26	11 46	12 06	12 26		18 26	18 46	19 06	19 26	19 46
Carpenders Park		d	23p29	06 59	07 29	07 59	08 59	09 29	09 49	10 09	10 29	10 49	11 09	11 29	11 49	12 09	12 29		18 29	18 49	19 09	19 29	19 49
Hatch End		d	23p32	07 02	07 32	08 02	09 02	09 32	09 52	10 12	10 32	10 52	11 12	11 32	11 52	12 12	12 32		18 32	18 52	19 12	19 32	19 52
Headstone Lane		d	23p34	07 04	07 34	08 04	09 04	09 34	09 54	10 14	10 34	10 54	11 14	11 34	11 54	12 14	12 34		18 34	18 54	19 14	19 34	19 54
Harrow & Wealdstone		d	23p37	07 07	07 37	08 07	09 07	09 37	09 57	10 17	10 37	10 57	11 17	11 37	11 57	12 17	12 37		18 37	18 57	19 17	19 37	19 57
Kenton		d	23p39	07 09	07 39	08 09	09 09	09 39	09 59	10 19	10 39	10 59	11 19	11 39	11 59	12 19	12 39		18 39	18 59	19 19	19 39	19 59
South Kenton		d	23p41	07 11	07 41	08 11	09 11	09 41	10 01	10 21	10 41	11 01	11 21	11 41	12 01	12 21	12 41		18 41	19 01	19 21	19 41	20 01
North Wembley		d	23p43	07 13	07 43	08 13	09 13	09 43	10 03	10 23	10 43	11 03	11 23	11 43	12 03	12 23	12 43		18 43	19 03	19 23	19 43	20 03
Wembley Central		d	23p45	07 15	07 45	08 15	09 15	09 45	10 05	10 25	10 45	11 05	11 25	11 45	12 05	12 25	12 45		18 45	19 05	19 25	19 45	20 05
Stonebridge Park		d	23p48	07 18	07 48	08 18	09 18	09 48	10 08	10 28	10 48	11 08	11 28	11 48	12 08	12 28	12 48		18 48	19 08	19 28	19 48	20 08
Harlesden		d	23p50	07 20	07 50	08 20	09 20	09 50	10 10	10 30	10 50	11 10	11 30	11 50	12 10	12 30	12 50		18 50	19 10	19 30	19 50	20 10
Willesden Jn Low Level		d	23p52	07 22	07 52	08 22	09 22	09 52	10 12	10 32	10 52	11 12	11 32	11 52	12 12	12 32	12 52		18 52	19 12	19 32	19 52	20 12
Kensal Green		d	23p55	07 25	07 55	08 25	09 25	09 55	10 15	10 35	10 55	11 15	11 35	11 55	12 15	12 35	12 55		18 55	19 15	19 35	19 55	20 15
Queen's Park (London)	⊖	d	23p57	07 27	07 57	08 27	09 27	09 57	10 17	10 37	10 57	11 17	11 37	11 57	12 17	12 37	12 57		18 57	19 17	19 37	19 57	20 17
Kilburn High Road		d	23p59	07 29	07 59	08 29	09 29	09 59	10 19	10 39	10 59	11 19	11 39	11 59	12 19	12 39	12 59		18 59	19 19	19 39	19 59	20 19
South Hampstead		d	00 01	07 31	08 01	08 31	09 31	10 01	10 21	10 41	11 01	11 21	11 41	12 01	12 21	12 41	13 01		19 01	19 21	19 41	20 01	20 21
London Euston 15	⊖	a	00 08	07 40	08 10	08 40	09 40	10 10	10 30	10 50	11 13	11 30	11 50	12 11	12 31	12 50	13 10		19 10	19 31	19 49	20 10	20 31

			LO	LO	LO	LO	LO	LO	LO	LO	LO	LO
Watford Junction		d	20 01	20 21	20 41	21 01	21 21	21 41	22 01	22 21	22 51	23 21
Watford High Street		d	20 04	20 24	20 44	21 04	21 24	21 44	22 04	22 24	22 54	23 24
Bushey		d	20 06	20 26	20 46	21 06	21 26	21 46	22 06	22 26	22 56	23 26
Carpenders Park		d	20 09	20 29	20 49	21 09	21 29	21 49	22 09	22 29	22 59	23 29
Hatch End		d	20 12	20 32	20 52	21 12	21 32	21 52	22 12	22 32	23 02	23 32
Headstone Lane		d	20 14	20 34	20 54	21 14	21 34	21 54	22 14	22 34	23 04	23 34
Harrow & Wealdstone		d	20 17	20 37	20 57	21 17	21 37	21 57	22 17	22 37	23 07	23 37
Kenton		d	20 19	20 39	20 59	21 19	21 39	21 59	22 19	22 39	23 09	23 39
South Kenton		d	20 21	20 41	21 01	21 21	21 41	22 01	22 21	22 41	23 11	23 41
North Wembley		d	20 23	20 43	21 03	21 23	21 43	22 03	22 23	22 43	23 13	23 43
Wembley Central		d	20 25	20 45	21 05	21 25	21 45	22 05	22 25	22 45	23 15	23 45
Stonebridge Park		d	20 28	20 48	21 08	21 28	21 48	22 08	22 28	22 48	23 18	23 48
Harlesden		d	20 30	20 50	21 10	21 30	21 50	22 10	22 30	22 50	23 20	23 50
Willesden Jn Low Level		d	20 32	20 52	21 12	21 32	21 52	22 12	22 32	22 52	23 22	23 52
Kensal Green		d	20 35	20 55	21 15	21 35	21 55	22 15	22 35	22 55	23 25	23 55
Queen's Park (London)	⊖	d	20 37	20 57	21 17	21 37	21 57	22 17	22 37	22 57	23 27	23 57
Kilburn High Road		d	20 39	20 59	21 19	21 39	21 59	22 19	22 39	22 59	23 29	23 59
South Hampstead		d	20 41	21 01	21 21	21 41	22 01	22 21	22 41	23 01	23 31	00 01
London Euston 15	⊖	a	20 49	21 13	21 30	21 51	22 10	22 30	22 49	23 10	23 40	00 12

A not 11 December

Stations Harrow & Wealdstone to Queen's Park inclusive are also served by London Underground Bakerloo Line Services

Table 61

Mondays to Fridays

Watford Junction - St. Albans

Miles			LM 1	LM 1	LM 1	LM 1	LM 1	LM 1	LM 1	LM 1	LM 1	LM 1	LM 1	LM 1	LM 1	LM 1	LM 1	LM 1	LM 1	LM 1	LM 1	LM 1	LM 1
0	**Watford Junction**	d	05 57	06 39	07 21	08 04	09 01	09 46	10 31	11 16	12 01	12 46	13 31	14 16	15 01	15 46	16 31	17 21	18 10	18 55	19 38	20 31	21 31
0¾	Watford North	d	05 59	06 41	07 23	08 06	09 03	09 48	10 33	11 18	12 03	12 48	13 33	14 18	15 03	15 48	16 33	17 23	18 12	18 57	19 40	20 33	21 33
1¾	Garston (Hertfordshire)	d	06 02	06 44	07 26	08 09	09 06	09 51	10 36	11 21	12 06	12 51	13 36	14 21	15 06	15 51	16 36	17 26	18 15	19 00	19 43	20 36	21 36
3¼	Bricket Wood	d	06 05	06 47	07 29	08 12	09 09	09 54	10 39	11 24	12 09	12 54	13 39	14 24	15 09	15 54	16 39	17 29	18 18	19 03	19 46	20 39	21 39
4½	How Wood	d	06 07	06 49	07 31	08 14	09 11	09 56	10 41	11 26	12 11	12 56	13 41	14 26	15 11	15 56	16 41	17 31	18 20	19 05	19 48	20 41	21 41
5	Park Street	d	06 09	06 51	07 33	08 16	09 13	09 58	10 43	11 28	12 13	12 58	13 43	14 28	15 13	15 58	16 43	17 33	18 22	19 07	19 50	20 43	21 43
6½	**St Albans Abbey**	a	06 13	06 55	07 37	08 20	09 17	10 02	10 47	11 32	12 17	13 02	13 47	14 32	15 17	16 02	16 47	17 37	18 26	19 11	19 54	20 47	21 47

Saturdays

		LM 1	LM 1	LM 1	LM 1	LM 1	LM 1	LM 1	LM 1	LM 1	LM 1	LM 1	LM 1	LM 1	LM 1	LM 1	LM 1	LM 1	LM 1	LM 1	LM 1	LM 1
Watford Junction	d	06 01	06 45	07 31	08 15	09 01	09 46	10 31	11 16	12 01	12 46	13 31	14 16	15 01	15 46	16 31	17 16	18 01	18 46	19 31	20 31	21 31
Watford North	d	06 03	06 47	07 33	08 17	09 03	09 48	10 33	11 18	12 03	12 48	13 33	14 18	15 03	15 48	16 33	17 18	18 03	18 48	19 33	20 33	21 33
Garston (Hertfordshire)	d	06 06	06 50	07 36	08 20	09 06	09 51	10 36	11 21	12 06	12 51	13 36	14 21	15 06	15 51	16 36	17 21	18 06	18 51	19 36	20 36	21 36
Bricket Wood	d	06 09	06 53	07 39	08 23	09 09	09 54	10 39	11 24	12 09	12 54	13 39	14 24	15 09	15 54	16 39	17 24	18 09	18 54	19 39	20 39	21 39
How Wood	d	06 11	06 55	07 41	08 25	09 11	09 56	10 41	11 26	12 11	12 56	13 41	14 26	15 11	15 56	16 41	17 26	18 11	18 56	19 41	20 41	21 41
Park Street	d	06 13	06 57	07 43	08 27	09 13	09 58	10 43	11 28	12 13	12 58	13 43	14 28	15 13	15 58	16 43	17 28	18 13	18 58	19 43	20 43	21 43
St Albans Abbey	a	06 17	07 01	07 47	08 31	09 17	10 02	10 47	11 32	12 17	13 02	13 47	14 32	15 17	16 02	16 47	17 32	18 17	19 02	19 47	20 47	21 47

Sundays

		LM 1	LM 1	LM 1	LM 1	LM 1	LM 1	LM 1	LM 1	LM 1	LM 1	LM 1	LM 1	LM 1	LM 1	LM 1
Watford Junction	d	08 07	09 07	10 20	11 20	12 07	13 07	14 07	15 07	16 07	17 07	18 07	19 07	20 07	21 02	22 04
Watford North	d	08 09	09 09	10 22	11 22	12 09	13 09	14 09	15 09	16 09	17 09	18 09	19 09	20 09	21 04	22 06
Garston (Hertfordshire)	d	08 12	09 12	10 25	11 25	12 12	13 12	14 12	15 12	16 12	17 12	18 12	19 12	20 12	21 07	22 09
Bricket Wood	d	08 15	09 15	10 28	11 28	12 15	13 15	14 15	15 15	16 15	17 15	18 15	19 15	20 15	21 10	22 12
How Wood	d	08 17	09 17	10 30	11 30	12 17	13 17	14 17	15 17	16 17	17 17	18 17	19 17	20 17	21 12	22 14
Park Street	d	08 19	09 19	10 32	11 32	12 19	13 19	14 19	15 19	16 19	17 19	18 19	19 19	20 19	21 14	22 16
St Albans Abbey	a	08 23	09 23	10 36	11 36	12 23	13 23	14 23	15 23	16 23	17 23	18 23	19 23	20 23	21 18	22 20

For connections to London Euston please refer to Table 66

Table 61

Mondays to Fridays

St. Albans - Watford Junction

Miles			LM 1	LM 1	LM 1	LM 1	LM 1	LM 1	LM 1	LM 1	LM 1	LM 1	LM 1	LM 1	LM 1	LM 1	LM 1	LM 1	LM 1	LM 1	LM 1	LM 1	LM 1
0	**St Albans Abbey**	d	06 18	07 00	07 42	08 25	09 22	10 07	10 52	11 37	12 22	13 07	13 52	14 37	15 22	16 07	16 52	17 42	18 32	19 16	20 00	20 52	21 52
1½	Park Street	d	06 21	07 03	07 45	08 28	09 25	10 10	10 55	11 40	12 25	13 10	13 55	14 40	15 25	16 10	16 55	17 45	18 35	19 19	20 03	20 55	21 55
2¼	How Wood	d	06 23	07 05	07 47	08 30	09 27	10 12	10 57	11 42	12 27	13 12	13 57	14 42	15 27	16 12	16 57	17 47	18 37	19 21	20 05	20 57	21 57
3	Bricket Wood	d	06 26	07 08	07 50	08 33	09 30	10 15	11 00	11 45	12 30	13 15	14 00	14 45	15 30	16 15	17 00	17 50	18 40	19 24	20 08	21 00	22 00
4¾	Garston (Hertfordshire)	d	06 29	07 11	07 53	08 36	09 33	10 18	11 03	11 48	12 33	13 18	14 03	14 48	15 33	16 18	17 03	17 53	18 43	19 27	20 11	21 03	22 03
5½	Watford North	d	06 31	07 13	07 55	08 38	09 35	10 20	11 05	11 50	12 35	13 20	14 05	14 50	15 35	16 20	17 05	17 55	18 45	19 29	20 13	21 05	22 05
6½	**Watford Junction**	a	06 34	07 16	07 58	08 41	09 38	10 23	11 08	11 53	12 38	13 23	14 08	14 53	15 38	16 24	17 08	17 58	18 48	19 32	20 16	21 08	22 08

Saturdays

		LM 1	LM 1	LM 1	LM 1	LM 1	LM 1	LM 1	LM 1	LM 1	LM 1	LM 1	LM 1	LM 1	LM 1	LM 1	LM 1	LM 1	LM 1	LM 1	LM 1	LM 1
St Albans Abbey	d	06 22	07 06	07 52	08 36	09 22	10 07	10 52	11 37	12 22	13 07	13 52	14 37	15 22	16 07	16 52	17 37	18 22	19 07	19 52	20 52	21 52
Park Street	d	06 25	07 09	07 55	08 39	09 25	10 10	10 55	11 40	12 25	13 10	13 55	14 40	15 25	16 10	16 55	17 40	18 25	19 10	19 55	20 55	21 55
How Wood	d	06 27	07 11	07 57	08 41	09 27	10 12	10 57	11 42	12 27	13 12	13 57	14 42	15 27	16 12	16 57	17 42	18 27	19 12	19 57	20 57	21 57
Bricket Wood	d	06 30	07 14	08 00	08 44	09 30	10 15	11 00	11 45	12 30	13 15	14 00	14 45	15 30	16 15	17 00	17 45	18 30	19 15	20 00	21 00	22 00
Garston (Hertfordshire)	d	06 33	07 17	08 03	08 47	09 33	10 18	11 03	11 48	12 33	13 18	14 03	14 48	15 33	16 18	17 03	17 48	18 33	19 18	20 03	21 03	22 03
Watford North	d	06 35	07 19	08 05	08 49	09 35	10 20	11 05	11 50	12 35	13 20	14 05	14 50	15 35	16 20	17 05	17 50	18 35	19 20	20 05	21 05	22 05
Watford Junction	a	06 38	07 22	08 08	08 52	09 38	10 23	11 08	11 53	12 38	13 23	14 08	14 53	15 38	16 23	17 08	17 53	18 38	19 23	20 08	21 08	22 08

Sundays

		LM 1	LM 1	LM 1	LM 1	LM 1	LM 1	LM 1	LM 1	LM 1	LM 1	LM 1	LM 1	LM 1	LM 1	LM 1
St Albans Abbey	d	08 28	09 28	10 42	11 42	12 28	13 28	14 28	15 28	16 28	17 28	18 28	19 28	20 28	21 23	22 25
Park Street	d	08 31	09 31	10 45	11 45	12 31	13 31	14 31	15 31	16 31	17 31	18 31	19 31	20 31	21 26	22 28
How Wood	d	08 33	09 33	10 47	11 47	12 33	13 33	14 33	15 33	16 33	17 33	18 33	19 33	20 33	21 28	22 30
Bricket Wood	d	08 36	09 36	10 50	11 50	12 36	13 36	14 36	15 36	16 36	17 36	18 36	19 36	20 36	21 31	22 33
Garston (Hertfordshire)	d	08 39	09 39	10 53	11 53	12 39	13 39	14 39	15 39	16 39	17 39	18 39	19 39	20 39	21 34	22 36
Watford North	d	08 41	09 41	10 55	11 55	12 41	13 41	14 41	15 41	16 41	17 41	18 41	19 41	20 41	21 36	22 38
Watford Junction	a	08 44	09 44	10 58	11 58	12 44	13 44	14 44	15 44	16 44	17 44	18 44	19 44	20 44	21 39	22 41

For connections to London Euston please refer to Table 66

Table 62

Mondays to Fridays

Gospel Oak - Barking

Network Diagram - see first Page of Table 59

Miles			LO MX	LO	LO	LO	LO	LO	LO	LO	LO	LO	LO	LO	LO	LO	LO	LO	LO	LO	LO	
0	**Gospel Oak**	d	23p35	06 20	06 35	06 50	07 05	07 20	07 35	07 50	08 05	08 20	08 35	08 50	09 05	09 20	09 35	09 50	10 05	10 20	10 35	and at the same minutes past each hour until
1¼	Upper Holloway	d	23p39	06 24	06 39	06 54	07 09	07 24	07 39	07 54	08 09	08 24	08 39	08 54	09 09	09 24	09 39	09 54	10 09	10 24	10 39	
2	Crouch Hill	d	23p42	06 27	06 42	06 57	07 12	07 27	07 42	07 57	08 12	08 27	08 42	08 57	09 12	09 27	09 42	09 57	10 12	10 27	10 42	
3	Harringay Green Lanes	d	23p45	06 30	06 45	07 00	07 15	07 30	07 45	08 00	08 15	08 30	08 45	09 00	09 15	09 30	09 45	10 00	10 15	10 30	10 45	
4¼	South Tottenham	d	23p48	06 33	06 48	07 03	07 18	07 33	07 48	08 03	08 18	08 33	08 48	09 03	09 18	09 33	09 48	10 03	10 18	10 33	10 48	
5¾	Blackhorse Road ⊖	d	23p51	06 36	06 51	07 06	07 21	07 36	07 51	08 06	08 21	08 36	08 51	09 06	09 21	09 36	09 51	10 06	10 21	10 36	10 51	
6½	Walthamstow Queen's Road	d	23p54	06 39	06 54	07 09	07 24	07 39	07 54	08 09	08 24	08 39	08 54	09 09	09 24	09 39	09 54	10 09	10 24	10 39	10 54	
7½	Leyton Midland Road	d	23p57	06 42	06 57	07 12	07 27	07 42	07 57	08 12	08 27	08 42	08 57	09 12	09 27	09 42	09 57	10 12	10 27	10 42	10 57	
8¼	Leytonstone High Road	d	23p59	06 45	07 00	07 15	07 30	07 45	08 00	08 15	08 30	08 45	09 00	09 15	09 30	09 45	10 00	10 15	10 30	10 45	11 00	
9½	Wanstead Park	d	00 03	06 48	07 03	07 18	07 33	07 48	08 03	08 18	08 33	08 48	09 03	09 18	09 33	09 48	10 03	10 18	10 33	10 48	11 03	
10½	Woodgrange Park	d	00 05	06 50	07 05	07 20	07 35	07 50	08 05	08 20	08 35	08 50	09 05	09 20	09 35	09 50	10 05	10 20	10 35	10 50	11 05	
12¼	**Barking** ⊖	a	00 12	06 57	07 11	07 27	07 41	07 56	08 11	08 26	08 42	08 56	09 11	09 26	09 41	09 56	10 12	10 26	10 41	10 56	11 11	

		LO	LO	LO	LO	LO	LO	LO	LO	LO	LO	LO	LO	LO	LO	LO	LO	LO	LO
Gospel Oak	d	18 35	18 50	19 05	19 20	19 35	19 50	20 05	20 20	20 35	20 50	21 05	21 20	21 35	21 50	22 05	22 35	23 05	23 35
Upper Holloway	d	18 39	18 54	19 09	19 24	19 39	19 54	20 09	20 24	20 39	20 54	21 09	21 24	21 39	21 54	22 09	22 39	23 09	23 39
Crouch Hill	d	18 42	18 57	19 12	19 27	19 42	19 57	20 12	20 27	20 42	20 57	21 12	21 27	21 42	21 57	22 12	22 42	23 12	23 42
Harringay Green Lanes	d	18 45	19 00	19 15	19 30	19 45	20 00	20 15	20 30	20 45	21 00	21 15	21 30	21 45	22 00	22 15	22 45	23 15	23 45
South Tottenham	d	18 48	19 03	19 18	19 33	19 48	20 03	20 18	20 33	20 48	21 03	21 18	21 33	21 48	22 03	22 18	22 48	23 18	23 48
Blackhorse Road ⊖	d	18 51	19 06	19 21	19 36	19 51	20 06	20 21	20 36	20 51	21 06	21 21	21 36	21 51	22 06	22 21	22 51	23 21	23 51
Walthamstow Queen's Road	d	18 54	19 09	19 24	19 39	19 54	20 09	20 24	20 39	20 54	21 09	21 24	21 39	21 54	22 09	22 24	22 54	23 24	23 54
Leyton Midland Road	d	18 57	19 12	19 27	19 42	19 57	20 12	20 27	20 42	20 57	21 12	21 27	21 42	21 57	22 12	22 27	22 57	23 27	23 57
Leytonstone High Road	d	19 00	19 15	19 30	19 45	20 00	20 15	20 30	20 45	21 00	21 15	21 30	21 45	22 00	22 15	22 30	23 00	23 30	23 59
Wanstead Park	d	19 03	19 18	19 33	19 48	20 03	20 18	20 33	20 48	21 03	21 18	21 33	21 48	22 03	22 18	22 33	23 03	23 33	00 03
Woodgrange Park	d	19 05	19 20	19 35	19 50	20 05	20 20	20 35	20 50	21 05	21 20	21 35	21 50	22 05	22 20	22 35	23 05	23 35	00 05
Barking ⊖	a	19 11	19 26	19 41	19 57	20 11	20 26	20 42	20 56	21 11	21 26	21 41	21 56	22 11	22 26	22 41	23 11	23 41	00 12

Saturdays

		LO	LO	LO	LO	LO	LO		LO	LO	LO	LO	LO	LO	LO	LO	LO	LO	LO	LO	
Gospel Oak	d	23p35	06 20	06 35	06 50	07 05	07 20	and at the same minutes past each hour until	15 20	15 35	15 50	16 05	16 20	16 35	16 50	17 05	17 20	17 35	17 50	18 05	and at the same minutes past each hour until
Upper Holloway	d	23p39	06 24	06 39	06 54	07 09	07 24		15 24	15 39	15 54	16 09	16 24	16 39	16 54	17 09	17 24	17 39	17 54	18 09	
Crouch Hill	d	23p42	06 27	06 42	06 57	07 12	07 27		15 27	15 42	15 57	16 12	16 27	16 42	16 57	17 12	17 27	17 42	17 57	18 12	
Harringay Green Lanes	d	23p45	06 30	06 45	07 00	07 15	07 30		15 30	15 45	16 00	16 15	16 30	16 45	17 00	17 15	17 30	17 45	18 00	18 15	
South Tottenham	d	23p48	06 33	06 48	07 03	07 18	07 33		15 33	15 48	16 03	16 18	16 33	16 48	17 03	17 18	17 33	17 48	18 03	18 18	
Blackhorse Road ⊖	d	23p51	06 36	06 51	07 06	07 21	07 36		15 36	15 51	16 06	16 21	16 36	16 51	17 06	17 21	17 36	17 51	18 06	18 21	
Walthamstow Queen's Road	d	23p54	06 39	06 54	07 09	07 24	07 39		15 39	15 54	16 09	16 24	16 39	16 54	17 09	17 24	17 39	17 54	18 09	18 24	
Leyton Midland Road	d	23p57	06 42	06 57	07 12	07 27	07 42		15 42	15 57	16 12	16 27	16 42	16 57	17 12	17 27	17 42	17 57	18 12	18 27	
Leytonstone High Road	d	23p59	06 45	07 00	07 15	07 30	07 45		15 45	16 00	16 15	16 30	16 45	17 00	17 15	17 30	17 45	18 00	18 15	18 30	
Wanstead Park	d	00 03	06 48	07 03	07 18	07 33	07 48		15 48	16 03	16 18	16 33	16 48	17 03	17 18	17 33	17 48	18 03	18 18	18 33	
Woodgrange Park	d	00 05	06 50	07 05	07 20	07 35	07 50		15 50	16 05	16 20	16 35	16 50	17 05	17 20	17 35	17 50	18 05	18 20	18 35	
Barking ⊖	a	00 12	06 57	07 09	07 24	07 39	07 54		15 54	16 09	16 24	16 42	16 57	17 12	17 27	17 42	17 54	18 09	18 24	18 39	

		LO	LO	LO	LO
Gospel Oak	d	22 05	22 35	23 05	23 35
Upper Holloway	d	22 09	22 39	23 09	23 39
Crouch Hill	d	22 12	22 42	23 12	23 42
Harringay Green Lanes	d	22 15	22 45	23 15	23 45
South Tottenham	d	22 18	22 48	23 18	23 48
Blackhorse Road ⊖	d	22 21	22 51	23 21	23 51
Walthamstow Queen's Road	d	22 24	22 54	23 24	23 54
Leyton Midland Road	d	22 27	22 57	23 27	23 57
Leytonstone High Road	d	22 30	23 00	23 30	00 01
Wanstead Park	d	22 33	23 03	23 33	00 03
Woodgrange Park	d	22 35	23 05	23 35	00 05
Barking ⊖	a	22 39	23 09	23 39	00 12

Sundays

		LO A	LO	LO	LO	LO		LO	LO	LO	LO	LO	LO	LO	LO	LO
Gospel Oak	d	23p35	08 55	09 10	09 25	09 40	and at the same minutes past each hour until	20 40	20 55	21 10	21 25	21 40	21 55	22 10	22 40	23 10
Upper Holloway	d	23p39	08 59	09 14	09 29	09 44		20 44	20 59	21 14	21 29	21 44	21 59	22 14	22 44	23 14
Crouch Hill	d	23p42	09 02	09 17	09 32	09 47		20 47	21 02	21 17	21 32	21 47	22 02	22 17	22 47	23 17
Harringay Green Lanes	d	23p45	09 05	09 20	09 35	09 50		20 50	21 05	21 20	21 35	21 50	22 05	22 20	22 50	23 20
South Tottenham	d	23p48	09 08	09 23	09 38	09 53		20 53	21 08	21 23	21 38	21 53	22 08	22 23	22 53	23 23
Blackhorse Road ⊖	d	23p51	09 11	09 26	09 41	09 56		20 56	21 11	21 26	21 41	21 56	22 11	22 26	22 56	23 26
Walthamstow Queen's Road	d	23p54	09 14	09 29	09 44	09 59		20 59	21 14	21 29	21 44	21 59	22 14	22 29	22 59	23 29
Leyton Midland Road	d	23p57	09 17	09 32	09 47	10 02		21 02	21 17	21 32	21 47	22 02	22 17	22 32	23 02	23 32
Leytonstone High Road	d	00 01	09 20	09 35	09 50	10 05		21 05	21 20	21 35	21 50	22 05	22 20	22 35	23 05	23 35
Wanstead Park	d	00 03	09 23	09 38	09 53	10 08		21 08	21 23	21 38	21 53	22 08	22 23	22 38	23 08	23 38
Woodgrange Park	d	00 05	09 25	09 40	09 55	10 10		21 10	21 25	21 40	21 55	22 10	22 25	22 40	23 10	23 40
Barking ⊖	a	00 12	09 29	09 44	09 59	10 14		21 14	21 29	21 47	21 59	22 14	22 29	22 44	23 14	23 44

A not 11 December

Barking - Gospel Oak

Network Diagram - see first Page of Table 59

Miles			LO MO	LO MX	LO	LO	LO	LO	LO	LO	LO		LO	LO	LO	LO	LO	LO	LO	LO	LO		LO	LO	LO
0	**Barking** ⊖	d	23p38	23p47	06 17	06 32	06 47	07 02	07 17	07 32	07 47		08 02	08 17	08 32	08 47	09 02	09 17	09 32	09 47	10 02		10 17	10 32	10 47
1¾	Woodgrange Park	d	23p41	23p50	06 20	06 35	06 50	07 05	07 20	07 35	07 50		08 05	08 20	08 35	08 50	09 05	09 20	09 35	09 50	10 05		10 20	10 35	10 50
2¾	Wanstead Park	d	23p44	23p53	06 23	06 38	06 53	07 08	07 23	07 38	07 53		08 08	08 23	08 38	08 53	09 08	09 23	09 38	09 53	10 08		10 23	10 38	10 53
4	Leytonstone High Road	d	23p48	23p57	06 27	06 42	06 57	07 12	07 27	07 42	07 57		08 12	08 27	08 42	08 57	09 12	09 27	09 42	09 57	10 12		10 27	10 42	10 57
4¾	Leyton Midland Road	d	23p50	23p59	06 29	06 44	06 59	07 14	07 29	07 44	07 59		08 14	08 29	08 44	08 59	09 14	09 29	09 44	09 59	10 14		10 29	10 44	10 59
5¾	Walthamstow Queen's Road	d	23p53	00 02	06 32	06 47	07 02	07 17	07 32	07 47	08 02		08 17	08 32	08 47	09 02	09 17	09 32	09 47	10 02	10 17		10 32	10 47	11 02
6½	Blackhorse Road ⊖	d	23p56	00 05	06 35	06 50	07 05	07 20	07 35	07 50	08 05		08 20	08 35	08 50	09 05	09 20	09 35	09 50	10 05	10 20		10 35	10 50	11 05
8¼	South Tottenham	d	23p59	00 09	06 39	06 54	07 09	07 24	07 39	07 54	08 09		08 24	08 39	08 54	09 09	09 24	09 39	09 54	10 09	10 24		10 39	10 54	11 09
9¼	Harringay Green Lanes	d	00 03	00 12	06 42	06 57	07 12	07 27	07 42	07 57	08 12		08 27	08 42	08 57	09 12	09 27	09 42	09 57	10 12	10 27		10 42	10 57	11 12
10¼	Crouch Hill	d	00 06	00 15	06 45	07 00	07 15	07 30	07 45	08 00	08 15		08 30	08 45	09 00	09 15	09 30	09 45	10 00	10 19	10 30		10 45	11 00	11 15
11	Upper Holloway	d	00 08	00 17	06 47	07 02	07 17	07 32	07 47	08 02	08 17		08 32	08 47	09 02	09 17	09 32	09 47	10 02	10 22	10 32		10 47	11 02	11 17
12¼	**Gospel Oak**	a	00 13	00 24	06 55	07 09	07 23	07 39	07 53	08 08	08 23		08 38	08 53	09 08	09 23	09 38	09 53	10 08	10 29	10 38		10 54	11 11	11 23

		LO	LO	LO	LO	LO	LO		LO	LO	LO	LO	LO	LO	LO	LO	LO		LO	LO	LO	LO	LO	LO	LO
Barking ⊖	d	11 02	11 17	11 32	11 47	12 02	12 17		12 32	12 47	13 02	13 17	13 32	13 47	14 02	14 17	14 32		14 47	15 02	15 17	15 32	15 47	16 02	16 17
Woodgrange Park	d	11 05	11 20	11 35	11 50	12 05	12 20		12 35	12 50	13 05	13 20	13 35	13 50	14 05	14 20	14 35		14 50	15 05	15 20	15 35	15 50	16 05	16 20
Wanstead Park	d	11 08	11 23	11 38	11 53	12 08	12 23		12 38	12 53	13 08	13 23	13 38	13 53	14 08	14 23	14 38		14 53	15 08	15 23	15 38	15 53	16 08	16 23
Leytonstone High Road	d	11 12	11 27	11 42	11 57	12 12	12 27		12 42	12 57	13 12	13 27	13 42	13 57	14 12	14 27	14 42		14 57	15 12	15 27	15 42	15 57	16 12	16 27
Leyton Midland Road	d	11 14	11 29	11 44	11 59	12 14	12 29		12 44	12 59	13 14	13 29	13 44	13 59	14 14	14 29	14 44		14 59	15 14	15 29	15 44	15 59	16 14	16 29
Walthamstow Queen's Road	d	11 17	11 32	11 47	12 02	12 17	12 32		12 47	13 02	13 17	13 32	13 47	14 02	14 17	14 32	14 47		15 02	15 17	15 32	15 47	16 02	16 17	16 32
Blackhorse Road ⊖	d	11 20	11 35	11 50	12 05	12 20	12 35		12 50	13 05	13 20	13 35	13 50	14 05	14 20	14 35	14 50		15 05	15 20	15 35	15 50	16 05	16 20	16 35
South Tottenham	d	11 24	11 39	11 54	12 09	12 24	12 39		12 54	13 09	13 24	13 39	13 54	14 09	14 24	14 39	14 54		15 09	15 24	15 39	15 54	16 09	16 24	16 39
Harringay Green Lanes	d	11 27	11 42	11 57	12 12	12 27	12 42		12 57	13 12	13 27	13 42	13 57	14 12	14 27	14 42	14 57		15 12	15 27	15 42	15 57	16 12	16 27	16 42
Crouch Hill	d	11 30	11 45	12 00	12 15	12 30	12 45		13 00	13 15	13 30	13 45	14 00	14 15	14 30	14 45	15 00		15 15	15 30	15 45	16 00	16 15	16 30	16 45
Upper Holloway	d	11 32	11 47	12 02	12 17	12 32	12 47		13 02	13 17	13 32	13 47	14 02	14 17	14 32	14 47	15 02		15 17	15 32	15 47	16 02	16 17	16 32	16 47
Gospel Oak	a	11 38	11 55	12 11	12 23	12 41	12 54		13 11	13 23	13 41	13 53	14 08	14 23	14 38	14 53	15 08		15 24	15 38	15 53	16 08	16 23	16 40	16 53

		LO	LO		LO	LO	LO	LO	LO	LO	LO	LO	LO		LO	LO	LO	LO	LO	LO	LO	LO	LO		LO
Barking ⊖	d	16 32	16 47		17 02	17 17	17 32	17 47	18 02	18 17	18 32	18 47	19 02		19 17	19 32	19 47	20 02	20 17	20 32	20 47	21 02	21 17		21 32
Woodgrange Park	d	16 35	16 50		17 05	17 20	17 35	17 50	18 05	18 20	18 35	18 50	19 05		19 20	19 35	19 50	20 05	20 20	20 35	20 50	21 05	21 20		21 35
Wanstead Park	d	16 38	16 53		17 08	17 23	17 38	17 53	18 08	18 23	18 38	18 53	19 08		19 23	19 38	19 53	20 08	20 23	20 38	20 53	21 08	21 23		21 38
Leytonstone High Road	d	16 42	16 57		17 12	17 27	17 42	17 57	18 12	18 27	18 42	18 57	19 12		19 27	19 42	19 57	20 12	20 27	20 42	20 57	21 12	21 27		21 42
Leyton Midland Road	d	16 44	16 59		17 14	17 29	17 44	17 59	18 14	18 29	18 44	18 59	19 14		19 29	19 44	19 59	20 14	20 29	20 44	20 59	21 14	21 29		21 44
Walthamstow Queen's Road	d	16 47	17 02		17 17	17 32	17 47	18 02	18 17	18 32	18 47	19 02	19 17		19 32	19 47	20 02	20 17	20 32	20 47	21 02	21 17	21 32		21 47
Blackhorse Road ⊖	d	16 50	17 05		17 20	17 35	17 50	18 05	18 20	18 35	18 50	19 05	19 20		19 35	19 50	20 05	20 20	20 35	20 50	21 05	21 20	21 35		21 50
South Tottenham	d	16 54	17 09		17 24	17 39	17 54	18 09	18 24	18 39	18 54	19 09	19 24		19 39	19 54	20 09	20 24	20 39	20 54	21 09	21 24	21 39		21 54
Harringay Green Lanes	d	16 57	17 12		17 27	17 42	17 57	18 12	18 27	18 42	18 57	19 12	19 27		19 42	19 57	20 12	20 27	20 42	20 57	21 12	21 27	21 42		21 57
Crouch Hill	d	17 00	17 15		17 30	17 45	18 00	18 15	18 30	18 45	19 00	19 15	19 30		19 45	20 00	20 15	20 30	20 45	21 00	21 15	21 30	21 45		22 00
Upper Holloway	d	17 02	17 17		17 32	17 47	18 02	18 17	18 32	18 47	19 02	19 17	19 32		19 47	20 02	20 17	20 32	20 47	21 02	21 17	21 32	21 47		22 02
Gospel Oak	a	17 08	17 23		17 38	17 53	18 08	18 23	18 38	18 53	19 09	19 26	19 38		19 53	20 08	20 23	20 38	20 53	21 08	21 24	21 38	21 54		22 08

		LO	LO	LO	LO	LO	LO
Barking ⊖	d	21 47	22 02	22 17	22 47	23 17	23 47
Woodgrange Park	d	21 50	22 05	22 20	22 50	23 20	23 50
Wanstead Park	d	21 53	22 08	22 23	22 53	23 23	23 53
Leytonstone High Road	d	21 57	22 12	22 27	22 57	23 27	23 57
Leyton Midland Road	d	21 59	22 14	22 29	22 59	23 29	23 59
Walthamstow Queen's Road	d	22 02	22 17	22 32	23 02	23 32	00 02
Blackhorse Road ⊖	d	22 05	22 20	22 35	23 05	23 35	00 05
South Tottenham	d	22 09	22 24	22 39	23 09	23 39	00 09
Harringay Green Lanes	d	22 12	22 27	22 42	23 12	23 42	00 12
Crouch Hill	d	22 16	22 30	22 45	23 15	23 45	00 15
Upper Holloway	d	22 18	22 32	22 47	23 17	23 47	00 17
Gospel Oak	a	22 23	22 38	22 53	23 25	23 53	00 24

Saturdays

		LO	LO	LO	LO	LO	LO	LO	LO	LO		LO	LO	LO	LO	LO	LO	LO	LO	LO		LO	LO	LO	LO
Barking ⊖	d	23p47	06 17	06 32	06 47	07 02	07 17	07 32	07 47	08 02		08 17	08 32	08 47	09 02	09 17	09 32	09 47	10 02	10 17		10 32	10 47	11 02	11 17
Woodgrange Park	d	23p50	06 20	06 35	06 50	07 05	07 20	07 35	07 50	08 05		08 20	08 35	08 50	09 05	09 20	09 35	09 50	10 05	10 20		10 35	10 50	11 05	11 20
Wanstead Park	d	23p53	06 23	06 38	06 53	07 08	07 23	07 38	07 53	08 08		08 23	08 38	08 53	09 08	09 23	09 38	09 53	10 08	10 23		10 38	10 53	11 08	11 23
Leytonstone High Road	d	23p57	06 27	06 42	06 57	07 12	07 27	07 42	07 57	08 12		08 27	08 42	08 57	09 12	09 27	09 42	09 57	10 12	10 27		10 42	10 57	11 12	11 27
Leyton Midland Road	d	23p59	06 29	06 44	06 59	07 14	07 29	07 44	07 59	08 14		08 29	08 44	08 59	09 14	09 29	09 44	09 59	10 14	10 29		10 44	10 59	11 14	11 29
Walthamstow Queen's Road	d	00 02	06 32	06 47	07 02	07 17	07 32	07 47	08 02	08 17		08 32	08 47	09 02	09 17	09 32	09 47	10 02	10 17	10 32		10 47	11 02	11 17	11 32
Blackhorse Road ⊖	d	00 05	06 35	06 50	07 05	07 20	07 35	07 50	08 05	08 20		08 35	08 50	09 05	09 20	09 35	09 50	10 05	10 20	10 35		10 50	11 05	11 20	11 35
South Tottenham	d	00 09	06 39	06 54	07 09	07 24	07 39	07 54	08 09	08 24		08 39	08 54	09 09	09 24	09 39	09 54	10 09	10 24	10 39		10 54	11 09	11 24	11 39
Harringay Green Lanes	d	00 12	06 42	06 57	07 12	07 27	07 42	07 57	08 12	08 27		08 42	08 57	09 12	09 27	09 42	09 57	10 12	10 27	10 42		10 57	11 12	11 27	11 42
Crouch Hill	d	00 15	06 45	07 00	07 15	07 30	07 45	08 00	08 15	08 30		08 45	09 00	09 15	09 30	09 45	10 00	10 15	10 30	10 45		11 00	11 15	11 30	11 45
Upper Holloway	d	00 17	06 47	07 02	07 17	07 32	07 47	08 02	08 17	08 32		08 47	09 02	09 17	09 32	09 47	10 02	10 17	10 32	10 48		11 02	11 17	11 32	11 47
Gospel Oak	a	00 24	06 54	07 08	07 23	07 38	07 53	08 08	08 23	08 38		08 53	09 08	09 24	09 38	09 53	10 08	10 23	10 40	10 53		11 11	11 23	11 40	11 53

		LO	LO	LO	LO	LO		LO	LO		LO	LO	LO	LO	LO		LO	LO	LO	LO
Barking ⊖	d	11 32	11 47	12 02	12 17	12 32		12 47	13 02	and at the same minutes past each hour until	21 02	21 17	21 32	21 47	22 02		22 17	22 47	23 17	23 47
Woodgrange Park	d	11 35	11 50	12 05	12 20	12 35		12 50	13 05		21 05	21 20	21 35	21 50	22 05		22 20	22 50	23 20	23 50
Wanstead Park	d	11 38	11 53	12 08	12 23	12 38		12 53	13 08		21 08	21 23	21 38	21 53	22 08		22 23	22 53	23 23	23 53
Leytonstone High Road	d	11 42	11 57	12 12	12 27	12 42		12 57	13 12		21 12	21 27	21 42	21 57	22 12		22 27	22 57	23 27	23 57
Leyton Midland Road	d	11 44	11 59	12 14	12 29	12 44		12 59	13 14		21 14	21 29	21 44	21 59	22 14		22 29	22 59	23 29	23 59
Walthamstow Queen's Road	d	11 47	12 02	12 17	12 32	12 47		13 02	13 17		21 17	21 32	21 47	22 02	22 17		22 32	23 02	23 32	00 02
Blackhorse Road ⊖	d	11 50	12 05	12 20	12 35	12 50		13 05	13 20		21 20	21 35	21 50	22 05	22 20		22 35	23 05	23 35	00 05
South Tottenham	d	11 54	12 09	12 24	12 39	12 54		13 09	13 24		21 24	21 39	21 54	22 09	22 24		22 39	23 09	23 39	00 09
Harringay Green Lanes	d	11 57	12 12	12 27	12 42	12 57		13 12	13 27		21 27	21 42	21 57	22 12	22 27		22 42	23 12	23 42	00 12
Crouch Hill	d	12 00	12 15	12 30	12 45	13 00		13 15	13 30		21 30	21 45	22 00	22 15	22 30		22 45	23 15	23 45	00 15
Upper Holloway	d	12 02	12 17	12 32	12 47	13 02		13 17	13 32		21 32	21 47	22 02	22 17	22 32		22 47	23 17	23 47	00 17
Gospel Oak	a	12 10	12 23	12 40	12 53	13 08		13 23	13 38		21 38	21 53	22 08	22 22	22 38		22 52	23 22	23 52	00 24

Table 62

Sundays

Barking - Gospel Oak

Network Diagram - see first Page of Table 59

			LO A	LO	LO	LO	LO		LO	LO	LO	LO	LO	LO
Barking	⊖	d	23p47	08 53	09 08	09 23	09 38	and at the same minutes past each hour until	21 38	21 53	22 08	22 38	23 08	23 38
Woodgrange Park		d	23p50	08 56	09 11	09 26	09 41		21 41	21 56	22 11	22 41	23 11	23 41
Wanstead Park		d	23p53	08 59	09 14	09 29	09 44		21 44	21 59	22 14	22 44	23 14	23 44
Leytonstone High Road		d	23p57	09 03	09 18	09 33	09 48		21 48	22 03	22 18	22 48	23 18	23 48
Leyton Midland Road		d	23p59	09 05	09 20	09 35	09 50		21 50	22 05	22 20	22 50	23 20	23 50
Walthamstow Queen's Road		d	00 02	09 08	09 23	09 38	09 53		21 53	22 08	22 23	22 53	23 23	23 53
Blackhorse Road	⊖	d	00 05	09 11	09 26	09 41	09 56		21 56	22 11	22 26	22 56	23 26	23 56
South Tottenham		d	00 09	09 15	09 30	09 45	10 00		22 00	22 15	22 30	23 00	23 30	23 59
Harringay Green Lanes		d	00 12	09 18	09 33	09 48	10 03		22 03	22 18	22 33	23 03	23 33	00 03
Crouch Hill		d	00 15	09 21	09 36	09 51	10 06		22 06	22 21	22 36	23 06	23 36	00 06
Upper Holloway		d	00 17	09 23	09 38	09 53	10 08		22 08	22 23	22 38	23 08	23 38	00 08
Gospel Oak		a	00 24	09 28	09 43	09 58	10 13		22 13	22 28	22 43	23 13	23 43	00 13

A not 11 December

Table 64

Mondays to Fridays

Bletchley - Bedford

Network Diagram - see first Page of Table 59

Miles			LM	LM	LM	LM	LM	LM	LM	LM	LM	LM	LM	LM	LM	LM	LM	LM
0	**Bletchley**	d	05 41	06 41	07 32	08 39	10 01	11 01	12 01	13 01	14 01	15 01	15 47	16 47	17 31	18 31	20 01	21 01
1	Fenny Stratford	d	05 44	06 44	07 35	08 42	10 04	11 04	12 04	13 04	14 04	15 04	15 50	16 50	17 34	18 34	20 04	21 04
2	Bow Brickhill	d	05 48	06 48	07 39	08 46	10 08	11 08	12 08	13 08	14 08	15 08	15 54	16 54	17 38	18 38	20 08	21 08
4	Woburn Sands	d	05 52	06 52	07 43	08 50	10 12	11 12	12 12	13 12	14 12	15 12	15 58	16 58	17 42	18 42	20 12	21 12
5	Aspley Guise	d	05 55	06 55	07 46	08 53	10 15	11 15	12 15	13 15	14 15	15 15	16 01	17 01	17 45	18 45	20 15	21 15
6¾	Ridgmont	d	05 58	06 58	07 49	08 56	10 18	11 18	12 18	13 18	14 18	15 18	16 04	17 04	17 48	18 48	20 18	21 18
8½	Lidlington	d	06 02	07 02	07 53	09 00	10 22	11 22	12 22	13 22	14 22	15 22	16 08	17 08	17 52	18 52	20 22	21 22
10	Millbrook (Bedfordshire)	d	06 05	07 05	07 56	09 03	10 25	11 25	12 25	13 25	14 25	15 25	16 11	17 11	17 55	18 55	20 25	21 25
11¼	Stewartby	d	06 09	07 09	08 00	09 07	10 29	11 29	12 29	13 29	14 29	15 29	16 15	17 15	17 59	18 59	20 29	21 29
13	Kempston Hardwick	d	06 12	07 12	08 03	09 10	10 32	11 32	12 32	13 32	14 32	15 32	16 18	17 18	18 02	19 02	20 32	21 32
16	Bedford St Johns	d	06 19	07 20	08 10	09 17	10 39	11 39	12 39	13 39	14 39	15 39	16 25	17 25	18 09	19 09	20 39	21 39
16¾	**Bedford** 7	a	06 25	07 25	08 16	09 23	10 45	11 45	12 45	13 45	14 45	15 45	16 31	17 31	18 15	19 15	20 45	21 45

Saturdays

		LM	LM	LM	LM	LM	LM	LM	LM	LM	LM	LM	LM	LM	LM	LM	LM
Bletchley	d	05 41	06 37	07 32	08 39	10 01	11 01	12 01	13 01	14 01	15 01	15 47	16 47	17 31	18 31	20 01	21 01
Fenny Stratford	d	05 44	06 40	07 35	08 42	10 04	11 04	12 04	13 04	14 04	15 04	15 50	16 50	17 34	18 34	20 04	21 04
Bow Brickhill	d	05 48	06 44	07 39	08 46	10 08	11 08	12 08	13 08	14 08	15 08	15 54	16 54	17 38	18 38	20 08	21 08
Woburn Sands	d	05 52	06 48	07 43	08 50	10 12	11 12	12 12	13 12	14 12	15 12	15 58	16 58	17 42	18 42	20 12	21 12
Aspley Guise	d	05 55	06 51	07 46	08 53	10 15	11 15	12 15	13 15	14 15	15 15	16 01	17 01	17 45	18 45	20 15	21 15
Ridgmont	d	05 58	06 54	07 49	08 56	10 18	11 18	12 18	13 18	14 18	15 18	16 04	17 04	17 48	18 48	20 18	21 18
Lidlington	d	06 02	06 58	07 53	09 00	10 22	11 22	12 22	13 22	14 22	15 22	16 08	17 08	17 52	18 52	20 22	21 22
Millbrook (Bedfordshire)	d	06 05	07 01	07 56	09 03	10 25	11 25	12 25	13 25	14 25	15 25	16 11	17 11	17 55	18 55	20 25	21 25
Stewartby	d	06 09	07 05	08 00	09 07	10 29	11 29	12 29	13 29	14 29	15 29	16 15	17 15	17 59	18 59	20 29	21 29
Kempston Hardwick	d	06 12	07 08	08 03	09 10	10 32	11 32	12 32	13 32	14 32	15 32	16 18	17 18	18 02	19 02	20 32	21 32
Bedford St Johns	d	06 19	07 15	08 10	09 17	10 39	11 39	12 39	13 39	14 39	15 39	16 25	17 25	18 09	19 09	20 39	21 39
Bedford 7	a	06 25	07 21	08 16	09 23	10 45	11 45	12 45	13 45	14 45	15 45	16 31	17 31	18 15	19 15	20 45	21 45

No Sunday Service

For connections to Milton Keynes Central please refer to Table 66

Table 64

Mondays to Fridays

Bedford - Bletchley

Network Diagram - see first Page of Table 59

Miles			LM	LM	LM	LM	LM	LM	LM	LM	LM	LM	LM	LM	LM	LM	LM	LM
0	**Bedford** 7	d	06 31	07 31	08 31	09 33	10 55	11 55	12 55	13 55	14 55	15 55	16 37	17 37	18 25	19 35	20 55	21 56
0¾	Bedford St Johns	d	06 34	07 34	08 34	09 36	10 58	11 58	12 58	13 58	14 58	15 58	16 40	17 40	18 28	19 38	20 58	21 59
3¾	Kempston Hardwick	d	06 41	07 41	08 41	09 43	11 05	12 05	13 05	14 05	15 05	16 05	16 47	17 47	18 35	19 45	21 05	22 06
5½	Stewartby	d	06 44	07 44	08 44	09 46	11 08	12 08	13 08	14 08	15 08	16 08	16 50	17 50	18 38	19 48	21 08	22 09
6¾	Millbrook (Bedfordshire)	d	06 48	07 48	08 48	09 50	11 12	12 12	13 12	14 12	15 12	16 12	16 54	17 54	18 42	19 52	21 12	22 13
8¼	Lidlington	d	06 51	07 51	08 51	09 53	11 15	12 15	13 15	14 15	15 15	16 15	16 57	17 57	18 45	19 55	21 15	22 16
10	Ridgmont	d	06 56	07 56	08 56	09 58	11 20	12 20	13 20	14 20	15 20	16 20	17 02	18 02	18 50	20 00	21 20	22 21
11¾	Aspley Guise	d	06 59	07 59	08 59	10 01	11 23	12 23	13 23	14 23	15 23	16 23	17 05	18 05	18 53	20 03	21 23	22 24
12¾	Woburn Sands	d	07 02	08 02	09 02	10 04	11 26	12 26	13 26	14 26	15 26	16 26	17 08	18 08	18 56	20 06	21 26	22 27
14¾	Bow Brickhill	d	07 06	08 06	09 06	10 08	11 30	12 30	13 30	14 30	15 30	16 30	17 12	18 12	19 00	20 10	21 30	22 31
15¾	Fenny Stratford	d	07 09	08 09	09 09	10 11	11 33	12 33	13 33	14 33	15 33	16 33	17 15	18 15	19 03	20 13	21 33	22 34
16¾	**Bletchley**	a	07 14	08 14	09 14	10 16	11 38	12 38	13 38	14 38	15 38	16 38	17 20	18 20	19 08	20 18	21 38	22 39

Saturdays

		LM	LM	LM	LM	LM	LM	LM	LM	LM	LM	LM	LM	LM	LM	LM	LM
Bedford 7	d	06 31	07 31	08 31	09 33	10 55	11 55	12 55	13 55	14 55	15 55	16 37	17 37	18 25	19 35	20 55	21 56
Bedford St Johns	d	06 34	07 34	08 34	09 36	10 58	11 58	12 58	13 58	14 58	15 58	16 40	17 40	18 28	19 38	20 58	21 59
Kempston Hardwick	d	06 41	07 41	08 41	09 43	11 05	12 05	13 05	14 05	15 05	16 05	16 47	17 47	18 35	19 45	21 05	22 06
Stewartby	d	06 44	07 44	08 44	09 46	11 08	12 08	13 08	14 08	15 08	16 08	16 50	17 50	18 38	19 48	21 08	22 09
Millbrook (Bedfordshire)	d	06 48	07 48	08 48	09 50	11 12	12 12	13 12	14 12	15 12	16 12	16 54	17 54	18 42	19 52	21 12	22 13
Lidlington	d	06 51	07 51	08 51	09 53	11 15	12 15	13 15	14 15	15 15	16 15	16 57	17 57	18 45	19 55	21 15	22 16
Ridgmont	d	06 56	07 56	08 56	09 58	11 20	12 20	13 20	14 20	15 20	16 20	17 02	18 02	18 50	20 00	21 20	22 21
Aspley Guise	d	06 59	07 59	08 59	10 01	11 23	12 23	13 23	14 23	15 23	16 23	17 05	18 05	18 53	20 03	21 23	22 24
Woburn Sands	d	07 02	08 02	09 02	10 04	11 26	12 26	13 26	14 26	15 26	16 26	17 08	18 08	18 56	20 06	21 26	22 27
Bow Brickhill	d	07 06	08 06	09 06	10 08	11 30	12 30	13 30	14 30	15 30	16 30	17 12	18 12	19 00	20 10	21 30	22 31
Fenny Stratford	d	07 09	08 09	09 09	10 11	11 33	12 33	13 33	14 33	15 33	16 33	17 15	18 15	19 03	20 13	21 33	22 34
Bletchley	a	07 14	08 14	09 14	10 16	11 38	12 38	13 38	14 38	15 38	16 38	17 20	18 20	19 08	20 18	21 38	22 39

No Sunday Service

For connections to Milton Keynes Central please refer to Table 66

Route Diagram for Table 65

London-Scotland
See Tables 400-404 for Sleeper trains.

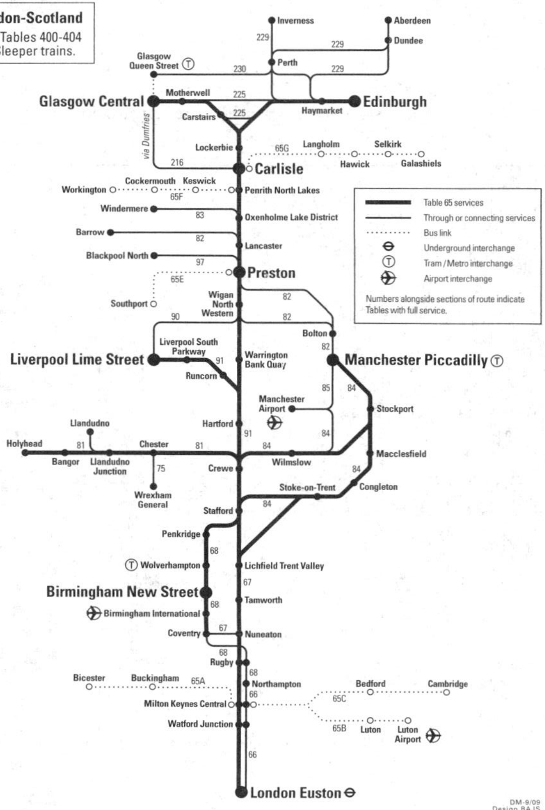

DM-9/09
Design BAJS

London and West Midlands - North West England and Scotland

Route Diagram - see first Page of Table 65

Miles	Miles	Miles	Miles	Miles			AW MO	XC MX	XC MX	VT MO	VT MX	VT MO	TP MX	TP MX	TP MX	TP MX	NT MO	TP MO	TP MX	SR MO	SR TWThO	VT MO
							◇	◇1	◇1	◇1	1	◇1	◇1	◇1	◇1	◇1		◇1	◇1			◇1
								A	B				C	D	C	D	E	F			G	
0	—	—	—	—	London Euston 15 ⊖	d				19p25	19p30									20p55	21p15	21p21
17½	—	—	—	—	Watford Junction	d														21b17	21b33	
49¾	—	—	—	—	Milton Keynes Central	d																
82½	0	—	—	—	Rugby	d																
97	—	—	—	—	Nuneaton	d																22p52
110	—	—	—	—	Tamworth Low Level	d																
116¾	—	0	—	—	Lichfield Trent Valley	d																
—	11½	—	—	—	Coventry	d																
—	22	—	—	—	Birmingham International ✈	d																
—	30½	—	—	—	Birmingham New Street 12	d		22p30	22p30													
—	43¼	—	—	—	Wolverhampton 7	d		22p48	22p48													
—	53¼	—	—	—	Penkridge	d																
133½	59½	—	—	—	Stafford	a		23p00	23p00													23p16
—	—	—	—	—		d		23p01	23p01													23p17
—	75¾	30¼	—	—	Stoke-on-Trent	a		23p20	23p21													
—	87½	42	—	—	Congleton	a																
—	95¼	50¼	—	—	Macclesfield	a																
158	—	—	0	—	Crewe 10	a																23p43
—	—	—	—	—		d	22p29													23b39	23b54	23p45
—	—	—	—	—	Chester	a	22p52															
—	—	—	—	—		d	23p00															
—	—	—	—	—	Wrexham General	a																
—	—	—	—	—	Llandudno	a																
—	—	—	—	—	Bangor (Gwynedd)	a	00 12															
—	—	—	—	—	Holyhead	a	00 49															
—	—	—	—	—	Wilmslow	a																
—	107¼	62¼	—	—	Stockport	a																
—	113	68	—	—	Manchester Piccadilly 10	a		00 12	00 12													
169¾	—	—	11¾	—	Hartford	a																
182	—	—	—	—	Warrington Bank Quay	a				21p16	21p15											
—	—	—	—	—		d				21p16	21p15											
—	—	—	22½	—	Runcorn	a																00 07
—	—	—	30	—	Liverpool South Parkway 7 ✈	a																
—	—	—	35½	—	Liverpool Lime Street 10	a																00 30
—	—	—	—	—		d																
—	—	—	—	—	Manchester Airport ✈	d							22p00	22p00	22p29	22p29		22p30				
—	—	—	—	—	Manchester Piccadilly 10	d							22p16	22p16	22p46	22p46		22p46				
—	—	79¼	—	—	Bolton	d						←	22p33	22p33	23p07	23p07		23p05				
193¾	—	—	—	—	Wigan North Western	a				21p27	21p26	21p27	22p48	22p48								
—	—	—	—	—		d				21p27	21p26	21p27	22p51	22p51			23p13					
209	—	99¼	—	—	Preston 8	a				→	21p39	21p40	23p09	23p12	23p33	23p34	23p35	23p42				
—	—	—	—	—	Preston 8	d					21p41	21p42	23p13	23p15	23p35	23p37	23p36	23p47	23p51	00u30	00u52	
—	—	—	—	—	Blackpool North	a									00 02	00 04	00 05	00 14	00 16			
230	—	—	—	—	Lancaster 6	a					21p55	21p56	23p28	23p31								
—	—	—	—	—		d					21p56	21p57	23p29	23p31								
—	—	—	—	—	Barrow-in-Furness	a							00 31	00 34								
249	—	—	—	—	Oxenholme Lake District	a					22p09	22p10										
—	—	—	—	—		d					22p09	22p11										
—	—	—	—	—	Windermere	a																
281¼	—	—	—	—	Penrith North Lakes	d					22p35	22p36										
299	—	—	—	—	Carlisle 8	a					22p50	22p51										
—	—	—	—	—		d					22p51	22p53										
324¼	—	—	0	—	Lockerbie	d																
372½	—	—	—	0	Carstairs	a																
388½	—	—	—	—	Motherwell	a																
401¼	—	—	—	—	Glasgow Central 15	a					00 06	00 02										
—	—	—	75	26¼	Haymarket	a																
—	—	—	76¼	27½	Edinburgh 10	a														03 58	03 58	
—	—	—	—	97¼	Perth	a														05s39	05s39	
—	—	—	135½	—	Dundee	a														06s08	06s08	
—	—	—	206¾	—	Aberdeen	a														07 35	07 36	
—	—	—	—	215¾	Inverness	a														08 38	08 38	

A until 23 March
B from 27 March
C until 30 December and then from 27 March
D from 3 January until 23 March
E from 20 February until 26 March
F from 9 January until 13 February
G to Edinburgh, from Edinburgh, to Edinburgh; from Edinburgh
b Previous night, stops to pick up only

OVERNIGHT SLEEPERS. For sleeper trains, operated by First ScotRail, please refer to Tables 400 - 404

London and West Midlands - North West England and Scotland

Route Diagram - see first Page of Table 65

		VT	AW	AW	VT	VT	LM	SR	SR	SR	TP	NT	AW	TP	NT	LM	TP
		MO	MX	MO	MO	MX	MX	MO	TWThO	FO		MX					
		◇1	◇	◇	◇1	◇1	◇1				◇1			◇1		◇1	◇1
			A						B				C				
London Euston 15 ⊖	d	21p25			21p51	22p00		23p27	23p50	23 50							
Watford Junction	d							23c47	00u10	00u10							
Milton Keynes Central	d	22p14			22p38	22p31											
Rugby	d				23p18	22p54											
Nuneaton	d				23p29	23p04											
Tamworth Low Level	d					23b15											
Lichfield Trent Valley	d					23b22											
Coventry	d																
Birmingham International ✈	d			22p40													
Birmingham New Street 12	d		22p55	22p55			23p09										
Wolverhampton 7 ⇌	d		23p13	23p15			23p36										
Penkridge	d						23p46										
Stafford	a		23p30	23p30	23b53	23b38	23p52										
	d		23p30	23p31			23p53										
Stoke-on-Trent	a	23p29															
Congleton	a																
Macclesfield	a	23p45															
Crewe 10	a		23p55	23p55	00s21	00s03	00 16										
	d		23p57	00 01								00 44	01 37			05 40	
Chester	a		00 18	00 22									01 59				
	d		00 40	00 38													
Wrexham General	a																
Llandudno	a																
Bangor (Gwynedd)	a		01 45	01 44													
Holyhead	a		02 15	02 20													
Wilmslow	a																
Stockport	a	23p59			00s50	00s26											
Manchester Piccadilly 10 ⇌	a	00 12			01 00	00 35											
Hartford	a																
Warrington Bank Quay	a																
	d																
Runcorn	a															05 58	
Liverpool South Parkway 7 ✈	a															06 10	
Liverpool Lime Street 10	a															06 22	
	d																
Manchester Airport ✈	d										00 01	01 20		04 00			
Manchester Piccadilly 10 ⇌	d										00 16	01a36		04 15			05 46
Bolton	d										00s31			04s29			
Wigan North Western	a													04 44			06 15
	d													04 44			06 15
Preston 8	a										01s05			05s04			06 35
Preston 8	d														05 22		06 37
Blackpool North	a										01 30			05 33			07 06
Lancaster 6	a														05 42		
	d														05 42		
Barrow-in-Furness	a														06 47		
Oxenholme Lake District	a																
	d																
Windermere	a																
Penrith North Lakes	d																
Carlisle 8	a							05s04	05s16	05s15					09 22		
	d																
Lockerbie	d																
Carstairs	a							06s20	06s20	06s20							
Motherwell	a							06s56	06s56	06s56							
Glasgow Central 15	a							07 20	07 20	07 20							
Haymarket	a																
Edinburgh 10	a							07 16	07 16								
Perth	a																
Dundee	a																
Aberdeen	a																
Inverness	a																

A until 23 March
B to Carstairs from Carstairs to Carstairs from Carstairs
C from 3 January until 6 January
b Previous night, stops to set down only
c Previous night, stops to pick up only

OVERNIGHT SLEEPERS. For sleeper trains, operated by First ScotRail, please refer to Tables 400 - 404

London and West Midlands - North West England and Scotland

Route Diagram - see first Page of Table 65

		VT	TP	LM	VT	VT	TP	XC	NT	TP	NT	LM	LM	VT	XC	TP
		◇1 ⊠	◇1 ✕	◇1	◇1	◇1 ⊠	◇1 ✕	◇1		◇1		◇1	1	◇1 ⊠	◇1 ✕	◇1 ✕
London Euston 15 ⊖	d															
Watford Junction	d															
Milton Keynes Central	d															
Rugby	d															
Nuneaton	d															
Tamworth Low Level	d															
Lichfield Trent Valley	d															
Coventry	d															
Birmingham International ✈	d															
Birmingham New Street 12	d					05 30		05 57					06 01	06 19	06 22	
Wolverhampton 7 ⇌	d					05 48		06 16					06 19	06 36	06 40	
Penkridge	d												06 29			
Stafford	a					06 01		06 29					06 35		06 53	
	d					06 02		06 30					06 36		06 55	
Stoke-on-Trent	a							06 50							07 13	
Congleton	a							07 02								
Macclesfield	a							07 11							07 30	
Crewe 10	a					06 21							06 56	07 07		
	d	05 57		06 02	06 11	06 23						06 32	06 57	07 09		
Chester	a					06 43										
	d					06 44										
Wrexham General	a															
Llandudno	a															
Bangor (Gwynedd)	a					07 49										
Holyhead	a					08 23										
Wilmslow	a				06 26											
Stockport	a				06 36			07 27							07 45	
Manchester Piccadilly 10 ⇌	a				06 49			07 37							07 59	
Hartford	a			06 14								06 46	07 10			
Warrington Bank Quay	a	06 13												07 26		
	d	06 14												07 27		
Runcorn	a			06 27								06 59	07 22			
Liverpool South Parkway 7 ✈	a			06 36								07 08	07 31			
Liverpool Lime Street 10	a			06 49								07 22	07 43			
	d										06 57					
Manchester Airport ✈	d		05 45				06 18									07 00
Manchester Piccadilly 10 ⇌	d		06 03				06 33									07 15
Bolton	d		06 19				06 50		07 01							07 31
Wigan North Western	a	06 24							07 19		07 30			07 37		
	d	06 25									07 31			07 38		
Preston 8	a	06 37	06 42				07 11				07 56			07 51		07 57
Preston 8	d	06 40	06 44				07 14			07 20				07 53		07 59
Blackpool North	a															08 29
Lancaster 6	a	06 54	06 59				07 30			07 36				08 08		
	d	06 54	07 00				07 30			07 36				08 08		
Barrow-in-Furness	a									08 39						
Oxenholme Lake District	a	07 08	07 15											08 21		
	d	07 10	07 15											08 22		
Windermere	a															
Penrith North Lakes	d	07 35					08 07									
Carlisle 8	a	07 50	07 55				08 24							09 01		
	d	07 51	07 56				08 25							09 01		
Lockerbie	d	08 10	08 16													
Carstairs	a															
Motherwell	a															
Glasgow Central 15	a	09 14					09 45									
Haymarket	a		09s17											10 16		
Edinburgh 10	a		09 22											10 21		
Perth	a															
Dundee	a															
Aberdeen	a															
Inverness	a															

OVERNIGHT SLEEPERS. For sleeper trains, operated by First ScotRail, please refer to Tables 400 - 404

London and West Midlands - North West England and Scotland

Route Diagram - see first Page of Table 65

		VT	VT	VT	TP	NT	NT	LM	XC	LM	VT	VT	XC	VT	TP
		◇1	◇1	◇1	◇1			◇1	◇1	◇1	◇1	◇1	◇1	◇1	◇1
		⊠	⊠	⊠	⊤				⊤		⊠	⊠	⊤	⊠	⊤
London Euston 15 ⊖	d	05 27	05 39	06 17								06 36		06 55	
Watford Junction	d	05u45	06u02									06u51			
Milton Keynes Central	d	06 10	06 22	06 47										07 27	
Rugby	d		06 45												
Nuneaton	d	06 39													
Tamworth Low Level	d														
Lichfield Trent Valley	d														
Coventry	d														
Birmingham International ✈	d														
Birmingham New Street 12	d							06 36	06 57	07 01	07 20		07 31		
Wolverhampton 7	d							06 53	07 15	07 19	07 37		07 49		
Penkridge	d									07 29					
Stafford	a	07 03						07 08	07 29	07 36			08 00		
	d	07 03						07 08	07 30	07 36			08 01		
Stoke-on-Trent	a			07 45									08 19	08 24	
Congleton	a														
Macclesfield	a			08 01									08 36	08 41	
Crewe 10	a	07 22	07 30					07 33	07 50	07 56	08 08	08 10			
	d	07 24	07 32					07 34	07 52	07 57	08 09	08 11			
Chester	a														
	d														
Wrexham General	a														
Llandudno	a														
Bangor (Gwynedd)	a														
Holyhead	a														
Wilmslow	a								08 08			08 27			
Stockport	a			08 16					08 20			08 37	08 50	08 55	
Manchester Piccadilly 10	a			08 28					08 34			08 49	08 59	09 07	
Hartford	a							07 47		08 09					
Warrington Bank Quay	a		07 49								08 27				
	d		07 49								08 27				
Runcorn	a	07 41						08 00		08 22					
Liverpool South Parkway 7 ✈	a							08 09		08 31					
Liverpool Lime Street 10	a	08 01						08 21		08 44					
	d						07 57								
Manchester Airport ✈	d				07 25										07 56
Manchester Piccadilly 10	d				07 45										08 15
Bolton	d				07 59										08 32
Wigan North Western	a		08 00				08 30				08 38				
	d		08 00				08 31				08 38				
Preston 8	a		08 13		08 22		08 56				08 51				08 58
Preston 8	d		08 15		08 24	08 38					08 53				08 59
Blackpool North	a														09 25
Lancaster 6	a		08 29		08 39	08 58					09 08				
	d		08 30		08 40	08 58					09 08				
Barrow-in-Furness	a					10 04									
Oxenholme Lake District	a		08 43		08 54										
	d		08 43		08 54										
Windermere	a														
Penrith North Lakes	d				09 20						09 45				
Carlisle 8	a		09 21		09 34	12 39					09 59				
	d		09 22		09 36						10 01				
Lockerbie	d				09 55										
Carstairs	a														
Motherwell	a														
Glasgow Central 15	a		10 36								11 16				
Haymarket	a				10s56										
Edinburgh 10	a				11 04										
Perth	a														
Dundee	a														
Aberdeen	a														
Inverness	a														

OVERNIGHT SLEEPERS. For sleeper trains, operated by First ScotRail, please refer to Tables 400 - 404

Table 65 — Mondays to Fridays

London and West Midlands - North West England and Scotland

Route Diagram - see first Page of Table 65

		LM	VT	VT	VT	XC	TP	VT	NT	LM	VT	VT	XC	VT
		◇1	◇1	◇1	◇1	◇1	◇1	◇1		1	◇1	◇1	◇1	◇1
			⊠	⊠	⊠	⊤	⊤	⊠			⊠	⊠	⊤	⊠
London Euston 15 ⊖	d		07 07	07 10	07 20			07 30				07 35		08 00
Watford Junction	d													
Milton Keynes Central	d			07 41	07 50							08 06		
Rugby	d													
Nuneaton	d													
Tamworth Low Level	d													
Lichfield Trent Valley	d													
Coventry	d					07 27								
Birmingham International ✈	d	07 17				07 38								
Birmingham New Street 12	d	07 36				07 57				08 01	08 20		08 31	
Wolverhampton 7	d	07 53				08 15				08 19	08 37		08 49	
Penkridge	d	08 03								08 29				
Stafford	a	08 09	08 22			08 29				08 35			09 00	
	d	08 09	08 23			08 30				08 36			09 01	
Stoke-on-Trent	a				08 48	08 54							09 19	09 24
Congleton	a													
Macclesfield	a					09 11								09 41
Crewe 10	a	08 30		08 47						08 56	09 07	09 10		
	d	08 31		08 49						08 57	09 09	09 11		
Chester	a			09 12										
	d													
Wrexham General	a													
Llandudno	a													
Bangor (Gwynedd)	a													
Holyhead	a													
Wilmslow	a											09 27		
Stockport	a				09 16	09 27						09 36	09 49	09 55
Manchester Piccadilly 10	a				09 28	09 39						09 49	09 59	10 07
Hartford	a									09 11				
Warrington Bank Quay	a							09 14			09 26			
	d							09 14			09 27			
Runcorn	a	08 50	08 55							09 22				
Liverpool South Parkway 7 ✈	a	08 59								09 31				
Liverpool Lime Street 10	a	09 10	09 15							09 43				
	d								08 57					
Manchester Airport ✈	d						08 25							
Manchester Piccadilly 10	d						08 46							
Bolton	d						09 07							
Wigan North Western	a							09 25	09 30		09 37			
	d							09 25	09 31		09 38			
Preston 8	a						09 33	09 38	09 54		09 51			
Preston 8	d						09 38	09 41	09 55		09 53			
Blackpool North	a						10 05		10 21					
Lancaster 6	a							09 54			10 08			
	d							09 55			10 08			
Barrow-in-Furness	a													
Oxenholme Lake District	a										10 22			
	d										10 23			
Windermere	a													
Penrith North Lakes	d							10 31						
Carlisle 8	a							10 46			11 02			
	d							10 47			11 04			
Lockerbie	d													
Carstairs	a													
Motherwell	a													
Glasgow Central 15	a							12 01						
Haymarket	a										12 14			
Edinburgh 10	a										12 21			
Perth	a													
Dundee	a													
Aberdeen	a													
Inverness	a													

OVERNIGHT SLEEPERS. For sleeper trains, operated by First ScotRail, please refer to Tables 400 - 404

London and West Midlands - North West England and Scotland

Route Diagram - see first Page of Table 65

		TP	TP	LM	VT	VT	VT	XC	NT	VT	TP	TP	NT	LM
		◇1		◇1	◇1	◇1	◇1	◇1		◇1	◇1			◇1
		⌶			⊠	⊠	⊠	⌶		⊠	⌶			
London Euston 15 ⊖	d				08 07	08 10	08 20			08 30				
Watford Junction	d													
Milton Keynes Central	d					08 41	08 50							
Rugby	d													
Nuneaton	d													
Tamworth Low Level	d													
Lichfield Trent Valley	d													
Coventry	d							08 27						
Birmingham International ✈	d							08 38						
Birmingham New Street 12	d			08 36				08 57						09 01
Wolverhampton 7 ⇌	d			08 53				09 15						09 19
Penkridge	d			09 03										
Stafford	a			09 09	09 22			09 29						09 34
	d			09 09	09 23			09 30						09 35
Stoke-on-Trent	a						09 48	09 54						
Congleton	a													
Macclesfield	a							10 11						
Crewe 10	a			09 30		09 47								09 56
	d			09 31		09 49								09 57
Chester	a					10 09								
	d					10 16								
Wrexham General	a													
Llandudno	a													
Bangor (Gwynedd)	a					11 27								
Holyhead	a													
Wilmslow	a													
Stockport	a						10 16	10 27						
Manchester Piccadilly 10 ⇌	a						10 28	10 39						
Hartford	a													10 10
Warrington Bank Quay	a									10 14				
	d									10 14				
Runcorn	a			09 50	09 55									10 22
Liverpool South Parkway 7 ✈	a			09 59										10 31
Liverpool Lime Street 10	a			10 10	10 15									10 43
	d												09 57	
Manchester Airport ✈	d	09 00									09 29			
Manchester Piccadilly 10 ⇌	d	09 16									09 46			
Bolton	d	09 33									10 07			
Wigan North Western	a									10 25			10 30	
	d									10 25			10 31	
Preston 8	a	09 55								10 38	10 33		10 54	
Preston 8	d	09 58	10 07						10 34	10 41	10 38	10 45	10 55	
Blackpool North	a								11 01		11 05		11 21	
Lancaster 6	a	10 13	10 22							10 54		11 00		
	d	10 14	10 23							10 55		11 01		
Barrow-in-Furness	a		11 17											
Oxenholme Lake District	a									11 08		11 17		
	d									11 08		11 18		
Windermere	a											11 39		
Penrith North Lakes	d													
Carlisle 8	a	11 07								11 46				
	d	11 10								11 47				
Lockerbie	d	11 29												
Carstairs	a													
Motherwell	a													
Glasgow Central 15	a	12 28								13 01				
Haymarket	a													
Edinburgh 10	a													
Perth	a													
Dundee	a													
Aberdeen	a													
Inverness	a													

OVERNIGHT SLEEPERS. For sleeper trains, operated by First ScotRail, please refer to Tables 400 - 404

London and West Midlands - North West England and Scotland

Route Diagram - see first Page of Table 65

		VT	VT	XC	VT	TP	LM	VT	VT	VT	XC	TP	VT
		◇1	◇1	◇1	◇1	◇1	◇1	◇1	◇1	◇1	◇1	◇1	◇1
		⊠	⊠	⌶	⊠	⌶		⊠	⊠	⊠	⌶	⌶	⊠
London Euston 15 ⊖	d		08 40		09 00			09 07	09 10	09 20			09 30
Watford Junction	d												
Milton Keynes Central	d								09 41	09 50			
Rugby	d												
Nuneaton	d												
Tamworth Low Level	d												
Lichfield Trent Valley	d												
Coventry	d										09 27		
Birmingham International ✈	d										09 38		
Birmingham New Street 12	d	09 20		09 31			09 36				09 57		
Wolverhampton 7 ⇌	d	09 37		09 49			09 53				10 15		
Penkridge	d						10 03						
Stafford	a			10 00			10 09	10 22			10 29		
	d			10 01			10 09	10 23			10 30		
Stoke-on-Trent	a			10 19	10 24					10 48	10 54		
Congleton	a												
Macclesfield	a				10 41						11 11		
Crewe 10	a	10 07	10 10				10 30		10 47				
	d	10 09	10 11				10 31		10 49				
Chester	a								11 09				
	d								11 16				
Wrexham General	a												
Llandudno	a												
Bangor (Gwynedd)	a								12 16				
Holyhead	a								12 50				
Wilmslow	a		10 27										
Stockport	a		10 36	10 49	10 55					11 16	11 27		
Manchester Piccadilly 10 ⇌	a		10 49	10 59	11 07					11 28	11 39		
Hartford	a												
Warrington Bank Quay	a	10 26											11 14
	d	10 27											11 14
Runcorn	a						10 50	10 55					
Liverpool South Parkway 7 ✈	a						10 59						
Liverpool Lime Street 10	a						11 10	11 15					
	d												
Manchester Airport ✈	d					10 00						10 29	
Manchester Piccadilly 10 ⇌	d					10 16						10 46	
Bolton	d					10 33						11 07	
Wigan North Western	a	10 37											11 25
	d	10 38											11 25
Preston 8	a	10 51				10 55						11 33	11 38
Preston 8	d	10 53				10 58						11 38	11 41
Blackpool North	a											12 05	
Lancaster 6	a	11 08				11 13							11 54
	d	11 08				11 14							11 55
Barrow-in-Furness	a												
Oxenholme Lake District	a					11 28							
	d					11 28							
Windermere	a												
Penrith North Lakes	d	11 45				11 53							12 30
Carlisle 8	a	12 00				12 10							12 45
	d	12 01				12 11							12 47
Lockerbie	d					12 30							
Carstairs	a												
Motherwell	a												
Glasgow Central 15	a	13 17											14 01
Haymarket	a					13s33							
Edinburgh 10	a					13 39							
Perth	a												
Dundee	a												
Aberdeen	a												
Inverness	a												

OVERNIGHT SLEEPERS. For sleeper trains, operated by First ScotRail, please refer to Tables 400 - 404

London and West Midlands - North West England and Scotland

Route Diagram - see first Page of Table 65

		NT	LM	VT	VT	XC	TP		LM		XC	LM	NT	TP	VT	VT	VT	VT	VT		VT		VT
			◇1	◇1	◇1	◇1	◇1		◇1		◇1	◇1		◇1	◇1	◇1	◇1	◇1	◇1		◇1		◇1
							A																
				⊠	⊠	⊥	⊥				⊥			⊥	⊏	⊠	⊠	⊠	⊠		⊠		⊠
London Euston 15 ⊖	d				09 40										09 43	10 00	10 07	10 10	10 20		10 30		10 40
Watford Junction	d																						
Milton Keynes Central	d														10 13			10 41	10 50				
Rugby	d																						
Nuneaton	d																						
Tamworth Low Level	d																						
Lichfield Trent Valley	d																						
Coventry	d										10 27				10 42								
Birmingham International ✈	d										10 38				10 53								
Birmingham New Street 12	d		10 01	10 20		10 31			10 36		10 57	11 01			11 20								
Wolverhampton 7 ⛴	d		10 19	10 37		10 49			10 53		11 15	11 19			11 37								
Penkridge	d								11 03														
Stafford	a		10 34			11 00			11 09		11 28	11 34					11 22						
	d		10 35			11 01			11 09		11 30	11 35					11 23						
Stoke-on-Trent	a					11 19					11 54					11 24			11 48				
Congleton	a																						
Macclesfield	a										12 11					11 41							
Crewe 10	a		10 56	11 07	11 10				11 30			11 56			12 07			11 47					12 10
	d		10 57	11 09	11 11				11 31			11 57			12 09			11 49					12 11
Chester	a																	12 12					
	d																						
Wrexham General	a																						
Llandudno	a																						
Bangor (Gwynedd)	a																						
Holyhead	a																						
Wilmslow	a				11 27																		12 27
Stockport	a				11 36	11 49					12 27					11 55			12 16				12 36
Manchester Piccadilly 10 ⛴	a				11 49	11 59					12 39					12 07			12 28				12 49
Hartford	a		11 11									12 10											
Warrington Bank Quay	a			11 26											12 26						12 14		
	d			11 27											12 27						12 14		
Runcorn	a		11 21						11 50			12 22					11 55						
Liverpool South Parkway 7 ✈	a		11 30						11 59			12 31											
Liverpool Lime Street 10	a		11 43						12 10			12 43					12 15						
	d	10 57																					
Manchester Airport ✈	d						11 00							11 29									
Manchester Piccadilly 10 ⛴	d						11 16							11 46									
Bolton	d						11 33							12 07									
Wigan North Western	a	11 30		11 37											12 37						12 25		
	d	11 31		11 38											12 38						12 25		
Preston 8	a	11 54		11 51			11 57							12 33	→						12 38		
Preston 8	d	11 55		11 53			11 58						12 34	12 38							12 41		
Blackpool North	a	12 21											13 00	13 05									
Lancaster 6	a			12 08			12 13														13 00		
	d			12 08			12 14																
Barrow-in-Furness	a						13 11																
Oxenholme Lake District	a			12 22																			
	d			12 24																			
Windermere	a																						
Penrith North Lakes	d																						
Carlisle 8	a			13 01																			
	d			13 03																			
Lockerbie	d																						
Carstairs	a																						
Motherwell	a																						
Glasgow Central 15	a																						
Haymarket	a			14 15																			
Edinburgh 10	a			14 21																			
Perth	a																						
Dundee	a																						
Aberdeen	a																						
Inverness	a																						

A ⊥ to Preston

OVERNIGHT SLEEPERS. For sleeper trains, operated by First ScotRail, please refer to Tables 400 - 404

London and West Midlands - North West England and Scotland

Route Diagram - see first Page of Table 65

		XC	VT	NT	VT	TP	LM	VT	VT	VT	XC
		◇1	◇1		◇1	◇1	◇1	◇1	◇1	◇1	◇1
		⊥	⊏		⊏	⊥		⊏	⊏	⊏	⊥
London Euston 15 ⊖	d		11 00					11 07	11 10	11 20	
Watford Junction	d										
Milton Keynes Central	d								11 41	11 50	
Rugby	d										
Nuneaton	d										
Tamworth Low Level	d										
Lichfield Trent Valley	d										
Coventry	d										11 27
Birmingham International ✈	d										11 38
Birmingham New Street 12	d	11 31					11 36				11 57
Wolverhampton 7 ⛴	d	11 49					11 53				12 15
Penkridge	d						12 03				
Stafford	a	12 00					12 09	12 22			12 29
	d	12 01					12 09	12 23			12 30
Stoke-on-Trent	a	12 19	12 24							12 48	12 54
Congleton	a										
Macclesfield	a		12 41								13 11
Crewe 10	a						12 30		12 47		
	d						12 31		12 49		
Chester	a								13 12		
	d										
Wrexham General	a										
Llandudno	a										
Bangor (Gwynedd)	a										
Holyhead	a										
Wilmslow	a										
Stockport	a	12 49	12 55							13 16	13 27
Manchester Piccadilly 10 ⛴	a	12 59	13 07							13 28	13 39
Hartford	a										
Warrington Bank Quay	a										
	d										
Runcorn	a						12 50	12 55			
Liverpool South Parkway 7 ✈	a						12 59				
Liverpool Lime Street 10	a						13 10	13 15			
	d			11 57							
Manchester Airport ✈	d					12 00					
Manchester Piccadilly 10 ⛴	d					12 16					
Bolton	d				←	12 33					
Wigan North Western	a			12 30	12 37						
	d			12 31	12 38						
Preston 8	a			12 54	12 51	12 55					
Preston 8	d			12 55	12 53	12 58					
Blackpool North	a			13 21							
Lancaster 6	a				13 08	13 13					
	d				13 08	13 14					
Barrow-in-Furness	a										
Oxenholme Lake District	a				13 22	13 28					
	d				13 23	13 28					
Windermere	a										
Penrith North Lakes	d					13 53					
Carlisle 8	a				14 00	14 10					
	d				14 02	14 11					
Lockerbie	d					14 30					
Carstairs	a										
Motherwell	a										
Glasgow Central 15	a				15 25						
Haymarket	a					15s34					
Edinburgh 10	a					15 39					
Perth	a										
Dundee	a										
Aberdeen	a										
Inverness	a										

OVERNIGHT SLEEPERS. For sleeper trains, operated by First ScotRail, please refer to Tables 400 - 404

London and West Midlands - North West England and Scotland

Route Diagram - see first Page of Table 65

		TP	TP	VT	NT	LM	VT	VT	XC	VT	TP		LM	VT	VT	VT	XC
		◇1	◇1	1 ⊠		◇1	◇1	◇1	◇1	◇1	◇1		◇1	◇1	◇1	◇1	◇1
London Euston 15 ⊖	d			11 30				11 40		12 00				12 07	12 10	12 20	
Watford Junction	d																
Milton Keynes Central	d														12 41	12 50	
Rugby	d																
Nuneaton	d																
Tamworth Low Level	d																
Lichfield Trent Valley	d																
Coventry	d																12 27
Birmingham International ✈	d																12 38
Birmingham New Street 12	d					12 01	12 20		12 31				12 36				12 57
Wolverhampton 7	d					12 19	12 37		12 49				12 53				13 15
Penkridge	d												13 03				
Stafford	a					12 34			13 00				13 09	13 22			13 29
	d					12 35			13 01				13 09	13 23			13 30
Stoke-on-Trent	a								13 19	13 24						13 48	13 54
Congleton	a																
Macclesfield	a									13 41							14 11
Crewe 10	a					12 56	13 07	13 10					13 30		13 47		
	d					12 57	13 09	13 11					13 31		13 49		
Chester	a														14 12		
	d																
Wrexham General	a																
Llandudno	a																
Bangor (Gwynedd)	a																
Holyhead	a																
Wilmslow	a							13 27									
Stockport	a							13 36	13 49	13 55						14 16	14 27
Manchester Piccadilly 10	a							13 49	13 59	14 07						14 28	14 39
Hartford	a					13 11											
Warrington Bank Quay	a			13 14			13 26										
	d			13 14			13 27										
Runcorn	a					13 21							13 50	13 55			
Liverpool South Parkway 7 ✈	a					13 30							13 59				
Liverpool Lime Street 10	a					13 43							14 10	14 15			
	d				12 57												
Manchester Airport ✈	d		12 29								13 00						
Manchester Piccadilly 10	d		12 46								13 16						
Bolton	d		13 07								13 33						
Wigan North Western	a			13 25	13 30		13 37										
	d			13 25	13 31		13 38										
Preston 8	a		13 33	13 38	13 54		13 51				13 55						
Preston 8	d	13 04	13 38	13 41	13 55		13 53				13 58	14 04					
Blackpool North	a		14 05		14 21												
Lancaster 6	a	13 19		13 54			14 08				14 13	14 19					
	d	13 20		13 55			14 08				14 14	14 20					
Barrow-in-Furness	a											15 15					
Oxenholme Lake District	a	13 36		14 08													
	d	13 37		14 08													
Windermere	a	13 56															
Penrith North Lakes	d						14 45										
Carlisle 8	a			14 46			15 00				15 06						
	d			14 47			15 02				15 07						
Lockerbie	d										15 27						
Carstairs	a																
Motherwell	a																
Glasgow Central 15	a			16 06							16 30						
Haymarket	a						16 17										
Edinburgh 10	a						16 21										
Perth	a																
Dundee	a																
Aberdeen	a																
Inverness	a																

OVERNIGHT SLEEPERS. For sleeper trains, operated by First ScotRail, please refer to Tables 400 - 404

London and West Midlands - North West England and Scotland

Route Diagram - see first Page of Table 65

		TP	VT	NT	LM	VT	VT	XC	VT	TP	LM	VT	VT	VT	XC
		◇1	◇1		◇1	◇1	◇1	◇1	◇1	◇1	◇1	◇1	◇1	◇1	◇1
London Euston 15 ⊖	d		12 30				12 40		13 00			13 07	13 10	13 20	
Watford Junction	d														
Milton Keynes Central	d												13 41	13 50	
Rugby	d														
Nuneaton	d														
Tamworth Low Level	d														
Lichfield Trent Valley	d														
Coventry	d														13 27
Birmingham International ✈	d														13 38
Birmingham New Street 12	d				13 01	13 20		13 31			13 36				13 57
Wolverhampton 7	d				13 19	13 37		13 49			13 53				14 15
Penkridge	d										14 03				
Stafford	a				13 34			14 00			14 09	14 22			14 29
	d				13 35			14 01			14 09	14 23			14 30
Stoke-on-Trent	a							14 19	14 24					14 48	14 54
Congleton	a														
Macclesfield	a								14 41						15 11
Crewe 10	a				13 56	14 07	14 10				14 30		14 47		
	d				13 57	14 09	14 11				14 31		14 49		
Chester	a												15 12		
	d														
Wrexham General	a														
Llandudno	a														
Bangor (Gwynedd)	a														
Holyhead	a														
Wilmslow	a						14 27								
Stockport	a						14 36	14 49	14 55					15 16	15 27
Manchester Piccadilly 10	a						14 49	14 59	15 07					15 28	15 39
Hartford	a				14 11										
Warrington Bank Quay	a		14 14			14 26									
	d		14 14			14 27									
Runcorn	a				14 21						14 50	14 55			
Liverpool South Parkway 7 ✈	a				14 30						14 59				
Liverpool Lime Street 10	a				14 43						15 10	15 15			
	d			13 57											
Manchester Airport ✈	d	13 29								14 00					
Manchester Piccadilly 10	d	13 46								14 16					
Bolton	d	14 07								14 33					
Wigan North Western	a		14 25	14 30		14 37									
	d		14 25	14 31		14 38									
Preston 8	a	14 33	14 38	14 54		14 51				14 55					
Preston 8	d	14 38	14 41	14 55		14 53				14 58					
Blackpool North	a	15 05		15 21											
Lancaster 6	a		15 00			15 08				15 13					
	d					15 09				15 14					
Barrow-in-Furness	a														
Oxenholme Lake District	a					15 22				15 28					
	d					15 24				15 28					
Windermere	a														
Penrith North Lakes	d									15 53					
Carlisle 8	a					16 01				16 10					
	d					16 03				16 11					
Lockerbie	d									16 30					
Carstairs	a														
Motherwell	a														
Glasgow Central 15	a					17 14									
Haymarket	a									17s31					
Edinburgh 10	a									17 39					
Perth	a														
Dundee	a														
Aberdeen	a														
Inverness	a														

OVERNIGHT SLEEPERS. For sleeper trains, operated by First ScotRail, please refer to Tables 400 - 404

London and West Midlands - North West England and Scotland

Route Diagram - see first Page of Table 65

		TP	VT	NT	LM	VT	TP	VT FO	VT	XC	VT	LM	VT	VT	VT
		◇1	◇1		◇1	◇1	◇1 A	◇	◇1	◇1	◇1	◇1	◇1	◇1	◇1
		🛒	⊠			🍴	🛒	🍴	🍴	🛒	🍴		🍴	🍴	🍴
London Euston 15 ⊖	d		13 30					13 33	13 40		14 00		14 07	14 10	14 20
Watford Junction	d														
Milton Keynes Central	d													14 41	14 50
Rugby	d														
Nuneaton	d														
Tamworth Low Level	d														
Lichfield Trent Valley	d														
Coventry	d														
Birmingham International ✈	d														
Birmingham New Street 12	d				14 01	14 20				14 31		14 36			
Wolverhampton 7 ⛴	d				14 19	14 37				14 49		14 53			
Penkridge	d											15 03			
Stafford	a				14 34					15 00		15 09	15 22		
	d				14 35					15 01		15 09	15 23		
Stoke-on-Trent	a									15 19	15 24				15 48
Congleton	a														
Macclesfield	a										15 41				
Crewe 10	a				14 56	15 07		15 16	15 10			15 30		15 47	
	d				14 57	15 09		15 19	15 11			15 31		15 49	
Chester	a													16 12	
	d														
Wrexham General	a														
Llandudno	a														
Bangor (Gwynedd)	a														
Holyhead	a														
Wilmslow	a								15 27						
Stockport	a								15 36	15 49	15 55				16 16
Manchester Piccadilly 10 ⛴	a								15 49	15 59	16 07				16 28
Hartford	a				15 11										
Warrington Bank Quay	a		15 14			15 26		15 38							
	d		15 14			15 27		15 39							
Runcorn	a				15 21							15 50	15 55		
Liverpool South Parkway 7 ✈	a				15 30							15 59			
Liverpool Lime Street 10	a				15 43							16 10	16 15		
	d			14 57											
Manchester Airport ✈	d	14 29					15 00								
Manchester Piccadilly 10 ⛴	d	14 46					15 16								
Bolton	d	15 07					15 33								
Wigan North Western	a		15 25	15 30		15 37		15 49							
	d		15 25	15 31		15 38		15 50							
Preston 8	a	15 33	15 38	15 54		15 51	15 57	16 03							
Preston 8	d	15 38	15 41	15 55		15 53	15 58	16 06							
Blackpool North	a	16 05		16 21											
Lancaster 6	a					16 08	16 14	16 26							
	d					16 08	16 15								
Barrow-in-Furness	a						17 18								
Oxenholme Lake District	a		16 04												
	d		16 06												
Windermere	a														
Penrith North Lakes	d		16 31			16 45									
Carlisle 8	a		16 46			17 00									
	d		16 47			17 02									
Lockerbie	d														
Carstairs	a														
Motherwell	a														
Glasgow Central 15	a		18 01												
Haymarket	a					18 12									
Edinburgh 10	a					18 22									
Perth	a														
Dundee	a														
Aberdeen	a														
Inverness	a														

A 🛒 to Preston

OVERNIGHT SLEEPERS. For sleeper trains, operated by First ScotRail, please refer to Tables 400 - 404

London and West Midlands - North West England and Scotland

Route Diagram - see first Page of Table 65

		XC	TP	VT FX	VT FO	NT	LM	VT	VT	XC	TP		LM	XC
					■									
		◇1	◇1	◇1	1		◇1	◇1	◇1	◇1	◇1		◇1	◇1
		🛒	🛒	🍴	🍴			🍴	🍴	🛒	🛒			🛒
London Euston 15 ⊖	d			14 30	14 30				14 40					
Watford Junction	d													
Milton Keynes Central	d													
Rugby	d													
Nuneaton	d													
Tamworth Low Level	d													
Lichfield Trent Valley	d													
Coventry	d	14 27												15 27
Birmingham International ✈	d	14 38												15 38
Birmingham New Street 12	d	14 57					15 01	15 20		15 31			15 36	15 57
Wolverhampton 7 ⛴	d	15 15					15 19	15 37		15 50			15 53	16 15
Penkridge	d												16 03	
Stafford	a	15 29					15 34			16 01			16 09	16 30
	d	15 30					15 35			16 02			16 09	16 31
Stoke-on-Trent	a	15 54								16 20				16 54
Congleton	a													
Macclesfield	a	16 11												17 11
Crewe 10	a						15 56	16 07	16 11				16 30	
	d						15 57	16 09	16 12				16 31	
Chester	a													
	d													
Wrexham General	a													
Llandudno	a													
Bangor (Gwynedd)	a													
Holyhead	a													
Wilmslow	a								16 27					
Stockport	a	16 27							16 36	16 49				17 27
Manchester Piccadilly 10 ⛴	a	16 39							16 49	16 59				17 39
Hartford	a						16 10							
Warrington Bank Quay	a			16 17	16 16			16 26						
	d			16 17	16 17			16 27						
Runcorn	a						16 22						16 50	
Liverpool South Parkway 7 ✈	a						16 31						16 59	
Liverpool Lime Street 10	a						16 44						17 10	
	d					15 57								
Manchester Airport ✈	d		15 29								16 00			
Manchester Piccadilly 10 ⛴	d		15 46								16 16			
Bolton	d		16 07								16 33			
Wigan North Western	a			16 29	16 28	16 30		16 37						
	d			16 29	16 29	16 30		16 38						
Preston 8	a		16 35	16 42	16 42	16 54		16 51			16 55			
Preston 8	d		16 38	16 43	16 43	16 56		16 53			17 00	17 04		
Blackpool North	a		17 07			17 21								
Lancaster 6	a			17 00	17 00			17 08			17 15	17 23		
	d				17 00			17 08			17 16	17 25		
Barrow-in-Furness	a													
Oxenholme Lake District	a				17 15			17 22			17 30	17 43		
	d				17 16			17 23			17 30	17 49		
Windermere	a											18 08		
Penrith North Lakes	d				17 42			17 49						
Carlisle 8	a				18 00			18 05			18 10			
	d				18 00			18 06			18 11			
Lockerbie	d										18 30			
Carstairs	a													
Motherwell	a													
Glasgow Central 15	a				19 14			19 19						
Haymarket	a										19s31			
Edinburgh 10	a										19 39			
Perth	a													
Dundee	a													
Aberdeen	a													
Inverness	a													

OVERNIGHT SLEEPERS. For sleeper trains, operated by First ScotRail, please refer to Tables 400 - 404

London and West Midlands - North West England and Scotland

Route Diagram - see first Page of Table 65

		LM	TP	TP	VT	VT	VT	VT	VT	VT	VT	XC	VT	NT	VT
		◇1	◇1	◇1	1	◇1	◇1	◇1	◇1	◇1	◇1	◇1	◇1		1
London Euston 15 ⊖	d				14 43	15 00	15 07	15 10	15 20	15 30	15 40		16 00		
Watford Junction	d														
Milton Keynes Central	d				15 13			15 41	15 50						
Rugby	d														
Nuneaton	d														
Tamworth Low Level	d														
Lichfield Trent Valley	d														
Coventry	d				15 42										
Birmingham International ✈	d				15 53										
Birmingham New Street 12	d	16 01			16 20							16 31			
Wolverhampton 7	d	16 19			16 37							16 49			
Penkridge	d														
Stafford	a	16 34					16 22					17 00			
	d	16 35					16 23					17 01			
Stoke-on-Trent	a					16 24			16 48			17 19	17 24		
Congleton	a														
Macclesfield	a					16 41							17 41		
Crewe 10	a	16 56			17 07			16 47			17 10				
	d	16 57			17 09			16 49			17 11				
Chester	a							17 12							
	d														
Wrexham General	a														
Llandudno	a														
Bangor (Gwynedd)	a														
Holyhead	a														
Wilmslow	a										17 27				
Stockport	a					16 54			17 16		17 36	17 49	17 55		
Manchester Piccadilly 10	a					17 07			17 28		17 49	17 59	18 07		
Hartford	a	17 11													
Warrington Bank Quay	a				17 26					17 14					
	d				17 27					17 14					
Runcorn	a	17 21					16 55								
Liverpool South Parkway 7 ✈	a	17 30													
Liverpool Lime Street 10	a	17 43					17 15								
	d													16 57	
Manchester Airport ✈	d			16 29											
Manchester Piccadilly 10	d			16 46											
Bolton	d			17 06											←
Wigan North Western	a				17 37					17 25				17 30	17 37
	d				17 38					17 25				17 31	17 38
Preston 8	a			17 30	→					17 38				17 54	17 51
Preston 8	d		17 04	17 32						17 41				17 55	17 53
Blackpool North	a			18 02										18 24	
Lancaster 6	a		17 23							17 54					18 08
	d		17 25							17 55					18 08
Barrow-in-Furness	a														
Oxenholme Lake District	a		17 43							18 08					18 22
	d		17 49							18 08					18 23
Windermere	a		18 08												
Penrith North Lakes	d														18 49
Carlisle 8	a									18 47					19 04
	d									18 47					19 04
Lockerbie	d														
Carstairs	a														
Motherwell	a														
Glasgow Central 15	a									19 57					
Haymarket	a														20 16
Edinburgh 10	a														20 22
Perth	a														
Dundee	a														
Aberdeen	a														
Inverness	a														

OVERNIGHT SLEEPERS. For sleeper trains, operated by First ScotRail, please refer to Tables 400 - 404

London and West Midlands - North West England and Scotland

Route Diagram - see first Page of Table 65

		TP		NT	LM	VT	VT	VT	VT	XC	LM	TP
		◇1			◇1	◇1	◇1	◇1	◇1	◇1	◇1	◇1
London Euston 15 ⊖	d					16 07	16 10	16 20	16 30			
Watford Junction	d											
Milton Keynes Central	d						16u40	16u50				
Rugby	d											
Nuneaton	d											
Tamworth Low Level	d											
Lichfield Trent Valley	d											
Coventry	d									16 27		
Birmingham International ✈	d									16 38		
Birmingham New Street 12	d				16 36					16 57	17 01	
Wolverhampton 7	d				16 53					17 15	17 19	
Penkridge	d				17 03						17 29	
Stafford	a				17 09	17 22				17 29	17 35	
	d				17 09	17 23				17 30	17 36	
Stoke-on-Trent	a							17 48		17 54		
Congleton	a											
Macclesfield	a									18 11		
Crewe 10	a				17 30		17 47				17 56	
	d				17 31		17 49				17 57	
Chester	a						18 08					
	d						18 10					
Wrexham General	a											
Llandudno	a											
Bangor (Gwynedd)	a						19 21					
Holyhead	a											
Wilmslow	a											
Stockport	a							18 16		18 27		
Manchester Piccadilly 10	a							18 28		18 39		
Hartford	a										18 11	
Warrington Bank Quay	a											
	d											
Runcorn	a				17 50	17 55					18 21	
Liverpool South Parkway 7 ✈	a				17 59						18 30	
Liverpool Lime Street 10	a				18 10	18 15					18 43	
	d			17 19								
Manchester Airport ✈	d	17 00										17 29
Manchester Piccadilly 10	d	17 15										17 46
Bolton	d	17 32										18 07
Wigan North Western	a			18 04								
	d											
Preston 8	a	17 55							18 30			18 38
Preston 8	d	17 58	18 08						18 30			18 40
Blackpool North	a											19 10
Lancaster 6	a	18 13	18 23									
	d	18 14	18 24									
Barrow-in-Furness	a		19 29									
Oxenholme Lake District	a	18 28										
	d	18 28										
Windermere	a											
Penrith North Lakes	d	18 53										
Carlisle 8	a	19 09										
	d	19 11										
Lockerbie	d											
Carstairs	a											
Motherwell	a	20s16										
Glasgow Central 15	a	20 33							20 38			
Haymarket	a											
Edinburgh 10	a											
Perth	a											
Dundee	a											
Aberdeen	a											
Inverness	a											

OVERNIGHT SLEEPERS. For sleeper trains, operated by First ScotRail, please refer to Tables 400 - 404

London and West Midlands - North West England and Scotland

Route Diagram - see first Page of Table 65

		VT	VT	VT	XC	TP		LM	VT	VT	VT	VT	VT	VT	XC	LM
		1 ☕	◇1 ☕	◇1 ☕	◇1 ⊼	◇1 ⊼		1	◇1 ⊠	◇1 ⊠	◇1 ⊠	◇1 ⊠	◇1 ⊠	◇1 ⊠	◇1 ⊼	◇1
London Euston 15 ⊖	d		16 33	16 40					16 57	17 00	17 07	17 10	17 10	17 20		
Watford Junction	d															
Milton Keynes Central	d											17u40	17u40	17u50		
Rugby	d		17 22													
Nuneaton	d											18 12	18 12			
Tamworth Low Level	d								18 00							
Lichfield Trent Valley	d								18 07							
Coventry	d														17 27	
Birmingham International ✈	d														17 38	
Birmingham New Street 12	d	17 20			17 31			17 36							17 57	18 01
Wolverhampton 7 🚊	d	17 37			17 50			17 53							18 15	18 19
Penkridge	d							18 02								18 29
Stafford	a		17 52		18 01			18 09			18 23				18 29	18 35
	d		17 56		18 02			18 09			18 24				18 30	18 35
Stoke-on-Trent	a				18 20					18 24				18 49	18 54	
Congleton	a															
Macclesfield	a									18 41					19 11	
Crewe 10	a	18 07	18 16	18 10				18 30			18 42	18 53	18 53			19 00
	d	18 09	18 18	18 11				18 31			18 44	18 56	18 56			19 02
Chester	a											19 15	19 15			
	d												19 21			
Wrexham General	a															
Llandudno	a															
Bangor (Gwynedd)	a												20 27			
Holyhead	a												20 59			
Wilmslow	a			18 27												
Stockport	a			18 37	18 49					18 55				19 16	19 27	
Manchester Piccadilly 10 🚊	a			18 49	18 59					19 07				19 28	19 39	
Hartford	a							18 44								
Warrington Bank Quay	a	18 26	18 35						18 49							
	d	18 27	18 36						18 50							
Runcorn	a							18 56			19 02					19 22
Liverpool South Parkway 7 ✈	a							19 05								19 31
Liverpool Lime Street 10	a							19 16			19 22					19 44
	d															
Manchester Airport ✈	d					18 00										
Manchester Piccadilly 10 🚊	d					18 16										
Bolton	d					18 33										
Wigan North Western	a	18 37	18 46						19 00							
	d	18 38	18 47						19 01							
Preston 8	a	18 51	19 01			18 55			19 14							
Preston 8	d	18 53				19 00	19 04		19 15							
Blackpool North	a															
Lancaster 6	a	19 08				19 15	19 20		19 30							
	d	19 08				19 16	19 20		19 30							
Barrow-in-Furness	a						20 24									
Oxenholme Lake District	a	19 22				19 30			19 43							
	d	19 24				19 32			19 45							
Windermere	a															
Penrith North Lakes	d					19 57			20 10							
Carlisle 8	a	20 01				20 13			20 25							
	d	20 03				20 13			20 25							
Lockerbie	d								20 44							
Carstairs	a															
Motherwell	a								21 26							
Glasgow Central 15	a	21 17							21 47							
Haymarket	a					21s31										
Edinburgh 10	a					21 39										
Perth	a															
Dundee	a															
Aberdeen	a															
Inverness	a															

OVERNIGHT SLEEPERS. For sleeper trains, operated by First ScotRail, please refer to Tables 400 - 404

London and West Midlands - North West England and Scotland

Route Diagram - see first Page of Table 65

		TP	VT	VT	TP	NT	VT	VT	VT	XC	VT	LM	VT	VT	VT	XC	LM
		◇1 ⊼	◇1 ⊠	◇1 ☕	◇1		◇1 ⊠	◇1 ⊠	◇1 ⊠	◇1 ⊼	◇1 ⊠	◇1	◇1 ⊠	◇1 ⊠	◇1 ⊠	◇1 ⊼	◇1
London Euston 15 ⊖	d		17 30				17 33	17 40	17 57		18 00		18 07	18 10	18 20		
Watford Junction	d																
Milton Keynes Central	d													18u40	18u50		
Rugby	d						18 23										
Nuneaton	d													19 13			
Tamworth Low Level	d								19 00								
Lichfield Trent Valley	d								19 08								
Coventry	d															18 27	
Birmingham International ✈	d															18 38	
Birmingham New Street 12	d			18 20						18 31		18 36				18 57	19 01
Wolverhampton 7 🚊	d			18 37						18 49		18 53				19 15	19 19
Penkridge	d											19 03					19 29
Stafford	a						18 52			19 00		19 09	19 23			19 27	19 36
	d						18 55			19 01		19 09	19 24			19 29	19 36
Stoke-on-Trent	a									19 19	19 24				19 48	19 54	
Congleton	a																
Macclesfield	a										19 41					20 11	
Crewe 10	a			19 07			19 14	19 10				19 30	19 42	19 53			20 01
	d			19 09			19 16	19 11				19 31	19 44	19 56			
Chester	a													20 15			
	d													20 26			
Wrexham General	a																
Llandudno	a																
Bangor (Gwynedd)	a													21 25			
Holyhead	a													21 59			
Wilmslow	a							19 27									
Stockport	a							19 36		19 48	19 55				20 16	20 27	
Manchester Piccadilly 10 🚊	a							19 49		19 59	20 07				20 28	20 39	
Hartford	a											19 47					
Warrington Bank Quay	a		19 14	19 26					19 49								
	d		19 14	19 27					19 50								
Runcorn	a						19 33					19 57	20 01				
Liverpool South Parkway 7 ✈	a											20 06					
Liverpool Lime Street 10	a						19 51					20 18	20 19				
	d					19 23											
Manchester Airport ✈	d	18 29			19 00												
Manchester Piccadilly 10 🚊	d	18 46			19 16												
Bolton	d	19 07			19 33												
Wigan North Western	a		19 25	19 37		19 54			20 00								
	d		19 25	19 38		19 55			20 01								
Preston 8	a	19 33	19 38	19 51	19 55	20 18			20 14								
Preston 8	d	19 38	19 41	19 53	19 58	20 19			20 15								
Blackpool North	a	20 06				20 44											
Lancaster 6	a		19 54	20 08	20 13				20 30								
	d		19 55	20 08	20 14				20 30								
Barrow-in-Furness	a				21 17												
Oxenholme Lake District	a		20 08														
	d		20 08														
Windermere	a																
Penrith North Lakes	d			20 45													
Carlisle 8	a		20 46	21 00					21 17								
	d		20 47	21 02					21 18								
Lockerbie	d								21 37								
Carstairs	a																
Motherwell	a								22 21								
Glasgow Central 15	a		22 01						22 39								
Haymarket	a			22 14													
Edinburgh 10	a			22 22													
Perth	a																
Dundee	a																
Aberdeen	a																
Inverness	a																

OVERNIGHT SLEEPERS. For sleeper trains, operated by First ScotRail, please refer to Tables 400 - 404

Table 65

Mondays to Fridays

London and West Midlands - North West England and Scotland

Route Diagram - see first Page of Table 65

		TP	VT	VT	TP	NT	VT	VT		XC		LM	XC	VT	TP	VT	VT	VT		VT	VT	VT
																FO	FO					
		◇1	◇1	◇1	◇1		◇1	◇1		◇1		◇1	◇1	◇1	◇1	◇	◇	■1		■1	■1	■1
			⊠	☕			⊠	⊠		⊤			A ⊤	⊠		☕	☕	☕		☕	B ☕	☕
London Euston 15 ⊖	d		18 30				18 33	18 40						18 43		18 46	18 57	19 00		19 07	19 10	19 10
Watford Junction	d																					
Milton Keynes Central	d													19 13							19u40	19u40
Rugby	d						19 23									19 39						
Nuneaton	d																			20 03		
Tamworth Low Level	d															19s59						
Lichfield Trent Valley	d															20s07						
Coventry	d												19 27	19 42								
Birmingham International ✈	d												19 38	19 53								
Birmingham New Street 12	d			19 20						19 31		19 36	19 57	20 20								
Wolverhampton 7	d			19 37						19 49		19 53	20 16	20 36								
Penkridge	d											20 03										
Stafford	a						19 53			20 00		20 09	20 29	20 49		20s35				20 26		
	d						19 56			20 01		20 09	20 30	20 52						20 27		
Stoke-on-Trent	a									20 19			20 54					20 24				
Congleton	a																					
Macclesfield	a												21 11					20 41				
Crewe 10	a			20 07			20 15	20 11				20 30		21 15		21s01	20s33				20 48	20 48
	d			20 09			20 17	20 12				20 31									20 50	20 50
Chester	a																				21 13	21 10
	d																					21 17
Wrexham General	a																					
Llandudno	a																					
Bangor (Gwynedd)	a																					22 22
Holyhead	a																					22 56
Wilmslow	a							20 27														
Stockport	a							20 36		20 48			21 27					20 55				
Manchester Piccadilly 10	a							20 49		20 58			21 39				21 09	21 07				
Hartford	a											20 45										
Warrington Bank Quay	a		20 14	20 26												21s20						
	d		20 14	20 27																		
Runcorn	a						20 34					20 56								21 01		
Liverpool South Parkway 7 ✈	a											21 05										
Liverpool Lime Street 10	a						20 53					21 16								21 21		
	d					20 25																
Manchester Airport ✈	d	19 29			20 00										20 29							
Manchester Piccadilly 10	d	19 46			20 16										20 46							
Bolton	d	20 07			20 33										21 07							
Wigan North Western	a		20 25	20 37		20 57										21s31						
	d		20 25	20 38		20 57																
Preston 8	a	20 33	20 38	20 51	20 57	21 22									21 33	→						
Preston 8	d	20 38	20 41	20 53	20 59	21 24									21 38							
Blackpool North	a	21 06				21 53									22 06							
Lancaster 6	a		20 54	21 08	21 14																	
	d		20 55	21 08	21 15																	
Barrow-in-Furness	a				22 18																	
Oxenholme Lake District	a		21 08	21 22																		
	d		21 09	21 24																		
Windermere	a																					
Penrith North Lakes	d		21 34																			
Carlisle 8	a		21 49	22 01																		
	d		21 51	22 03																		
Lockerbie	d																					
Carstairs	a																					
Motherwell	a																					
Glasgow Central 15	a		23 04	23 18																		
Haymarket	a																					
Edinburgh 10	a																					
Perth	a																					
Dundee	a																					
Aberdeen	a																					
Inverness	a																					

A ⊤ to Birmingham New Street

B not 26 December

OVERNIGHT SLEEPERS. For sleeper trains, operated by First ScotRail, please refer to Tables 400 - 404

Table 65

Mondays to Fridays

London and West Midlands - North West England and Scotland

Route Diagram - see first Page of Table 65

		VT	VT	VT		VT		VT	XC	VT	LM	VT		XC		NT			VT
				FO															
		■1	■1	◇		◇1		◇1	◇1	◇1	◇1	◇1		◇1					◇1
		☕	☕	☕				☕		☕		☕		A ⊤					☕
London Euston 15 ⊖	d	19 20	19 30					19 40		20 00		20 07							20 10
Watford Junction	d																		
Milton Keynes Central	d	19u50																	20 40
Rugby	d																		
Nuneaton	d											21 03							
Tamworth Low Level	d							20 43											
Lichfield Trent Valley	d							20 50											
Coventry	d													20 27					
Birmingham International ✈	d													20 38					
Birmingham New Street 12	d								20 31		20 36			20 57					
Wolverhampton 7	d								20 49		20 53			21 16					
Penkridge	d										21 03								
Stafford	a							21 02			21 09	21 27		21 31					
	d							21 04			21 09	21 27		21 32					
Stoke-on-Trent	a	20 48							21 17	21 23				21 54					
Congleton	a																		
Macclesfield	a									21 40				22 11					
Crewe 10	a							21 21			21 30								21 48
	d							21 23			21 31								21 50
Chester	a																		22 15
	d					20 22													
Wrexham General	a					20 38													
Llandudno	a																		
Bangor (Gwynedd)	a																		
Holyhead	a																		
Wilmslow	a							21 38											
Stockport	a	21 16							21 46	21 55				22 25					
Manchester Piccadilly 10	a	21 28						21 57	21 59	22 07				22 35					
Hartford	a										21 43								
Warrington Bank Quay	a		21 15																
	d		21 15																
Runcorn	a										21 54	21 59							
Liverpool South Parkway 7 ✈	a										22 05								
Liverpool Lime Street 10	a										22 15	22 20							
	d																		
Manchester Airport ✈	d																		
Manchester Piccadilly 10	d																		
Bolton	d			←															
Wigan North Western	a		21 26	21s31															
	d		21 26																
Preston 8	a		21 39	21 46															
Preston 8	d		21 41													21 51			
Blackpool North	a																		
Lancaster 6	a		21 55													22 11			
	d		21 56													22 11			
Barrow-in-Furness	a															23 16			
Oxenholme Lake District	a		22 09																
	d		22 09																
Windermere	a																		
Penrith North Lakes	d		22 35																
Carlisle 8	a		22 50																
	d		22 51																
Lockerbie	d																		
Carstairs	a																		
Motherwell	a																		
Glasgow Central 15	a		00 06																
Haymarket	a																		
Edinburgh 10	a																		
Perth	a																		
Dundee	a																		
Aberdeen	a																		
Inverness	a																		

A ⊤ to Birmingham New Street

OVERNIGHT SLEEPERS. For sleeper trains, operated by First ScotRail, please refer to Tables 400 - 404

London and West Midlands - North West England and Scotland

Route Diagram - see first Page of Table 65

		TP	VT	VT	VT	VT	AW	VT	VT	TP	TP	LM	VT	XC	TP	TP	VT
							FX										
		◇1	◇1	◇1	◇1	◇1		◇1	◇1	◇1	◇1	◇1	◇1	◇1	◇1	◇1	◇1
			A	B				A	B	A	B				A	B	
London Euston 15 ⊖	d		20 30	20 30	20 40	21 00							21 07				21 10
Watford Junction	d																21u25
Milton Keynes Central	d					21 31							21 38				
Rugby	d																22 04
Nuneaton	d												22 08				
Tamworth Low Level	d		21 34	21 34													
Lichfield Trent Valley	d		21 42	21 42													
Coventry	d													21 27			
Birmingham International ✈	d													21 38			
Birmingham New Street 12	d							21 20	21 20			21 36		21 57			
Wolverhampton 7	d							21 41	21 41			21 53		22 16			
Penkridge	d											22 03					
Stafford	a							21 53	21 53			22 09		22 29			22 34
	d							21 55	21 55			22 09		22 30			22 34
Stoke-on-Trent	a					22 28								22 53			
Congleton	a																
Macclesfield	a					22 44								23 11			
Crewe 10	a				22 12			22 17	22 17			22 30	22 46				22 53
	d				22 13			22 18	22 18			22 31	22 48				22 54
Chester	a																
	d																
Wrexham General	a																
Llandudno	a																
Bangor (Gwynedd)	a																
Holyhead	a																
Wilmslow	a				22 29												
Stockport	a				22 38	22 58								23 25			
Manchester Piccadilly 10	a				22 48	23 11								23 37			
Hartford	a											22 43					
Warrington Bank Quay	a		22 22	22 22				22 36	22 36								23 12
	d		22 23	22 23			22 28	22 36	22 36								23 12
Runcorn	a											22 56	23 05				
Liverpool South Parkway 7 ✈	a											23 07					
Liverpool Lime Street 10	a											23 23	23 29				
	d																
Manchester Airport ✈	d	21 29								22 00	22 00				22 29	22 29	
Manchester Piccadilly 10	d	21 46					23a38			22 16	22 16				22 46	22 46	
Bolton	d	22 07								22 33	22 33				23 07	23 07	
Wigan North Western	a		22 33	22 33				22 46	22 46	22 48	22 48						23 23
	d		22 34	22 34				22 46	22 46	22 51	22 51						23 23
Preston 8	a	22 36	22 53	22 58				23 01	23 03	23 09	23 12				23 33	23 34	23 39
Preston 8	d	22 38								23 13	23 15				23 35	23 37	
Blackpool North	a	23 04													00 02	00 04	
Lancaster 6	a									23 28	23 31						
	d									23 29	23 31						
Barrow-in-Furness	a									00 31	00 34						
Oxenholme Lake District	a																
	d																
Windermere	a																
Penrith North Lakes	d																
Carlisle 8	a																
	d																
Lockerbie	d																
Carstairs	a																
Motherwell	a																
Glasgow Central 15	a																
Haymarket	a																
Edinburgh 10	a																
Perth	a																
Dundee	a																
Aberdeen	a																
Inverness	a																

A until 30 December and then from 26 March

B from 2 January until 23 March

OVERNIGHT SLEEPERS. For sleeper trains, operated by First ScotRail, please refer to Tables 400 - 404

Table 65
Mondays to Fridays

London and West Midlands - North West England and Scotland

Route Diagram - see first Page of Table 65

		TP	SR	SR	VT	XC	XC	XC	LM	AW	VT	LM	AW	SR	SR
			MT WO				FX	FO					FX	MTWO	FO
		◇1			◇1	◇1	◇1	◇1	◇1	◇	◇1	◇1			
			A			B	C	D		B				E	
London Euston 15 ⊖	d		21 15	21 15	21 40						22 00			23 50	23 50
Watford Junction	d		21u33	21u33										00u10	00u10
Milton Keynes Central	d										22 31				
Rugby	d										22 54				
Nuneaton	d										23 04				
Tamworth Low Level	d										23s15				
Lichfield Trent Valley	d										23s22				
Coventry	d														
Birmingham International ✈	d														
Birmingham New Street 12	d					22 30	22 30	22 30	22 36	22 55		23 09			
Wolverhampton 7	d					22 48	22 48	22 48	22 57	23 13		23 36			
Penkridge	d								23 07			23 46			
Stafford	a					23 00	23 00	23 00	23 13	23 30	23s38	23 52			
	d					23 01	23 01	23 01	23 13	23 30		23 53			
Stoke-on-Trent	a				23 06	23 20	23 21	23 21							
Congleton	a														
Macclesfield	a				23 23										
Crewe 10	a								23 43	23 55	00s03	00 16			
	d		23u54	23u54						23 57					
Chester	a									00 18					
	d									00 40					
Wrexham General	a														
Llandudno	a														
Bangor (Gwynedd)	a									01 45					
Holyhead	a									02 15					
Wilmslow	a														
Stockport	a				23 37						00s26				
Manchester Piccadilly 10	a				23 46	00 12	00 12	00 13			00 35				
Hartford	a														
Warrington Bank Quay	a														
	d												23 59		
Runcorn	a														
Liverpool South Parkway 7 ✈	a														
Liverpool Lime Street 10	a														
	d														
Manchester Airport ✈	d														
Manchester Piccadilly 10	d												01a09		
Bolton	d														
Wigan North Western	a														
	d														
Preston 8	a														
Preston 8	d	23 51	00u52	00u52											
Blackpool North	a	00 16													
Lancaster 6	a														
	d														
Barrow-in-Furness	a														
Oxenholme Lake District	a														
	d														
Windermere	a														
Penrith North Lakes	d														
Carlisle 8	a													05s16	05s15
	d														
Lockerbie	d														
Carstairs	a													06s20	06s20
Motherwell	a													06s56	06s56
Glasgow Central 15	a													07 20	07 20
Haymarket	a														
Edinburgh 10	a		03 58	03 58										07 16	
Perth	a			05s39											
Dundee	a		06s08												
Aberdeen	a		07 36												
Inverness	a			08 38											

A to Edinburgh from Edinburgh; to Edinburgh from Edinburgh

B until 23 March

C from 26 March

D from 30 March

E to Carstairs from Carstairs; to Carstairs from Carstairs

OVERNIGHT SLEEPERS. For sleeper trains, operated by First ScotRail, please refer to Tables 400 - 404

Table 65

Saturdays

London and West Midlands - North West England and Scotland

Route Diagram - see first Page of Table 65

		VT	TP	TP	TP	TP	XC	XC	TP	SR	AW	VT	LM	SR	TP	NT	TP	TP	LM
		1	◇1	◇1	◇1	◇1	◇1	◇1	◇1		◇	◇1	◇1		◇1		◇1	◇1	1
			A	B	A	B	C	D			C								
London Euston 15 ⊖	d	19p30								21p15		22p00		23p50					
Watford Junction	d									21b33				00u10					
Milton Keynes Central	d											22p31							
Rugby	d											22p54							
Nuneaton	d											23p04							
Tamworth Low Level	d											23c15							
Lichfield Trent Valley	d											23c22							
Coventry	d																		
Birmingham International ✈	d																		
Birmingham New Street 12	d						22p30	22p30			22p55		23p09						
Wolverhampton 7	d						22p48	22p48			23p13		23p36						
Penkridge	d												23p46						
Stafford	a						23p00	23p00			23p30	23c38	23p52						
	d						23p01	23p01			23p30		23p53						
Stoke-on-Trent	a						23p20	23p21											
Congleton	a																		
Macclesfield	a																		
Crewe 10	a										23p55	00s03	00 16						
	d									23b54	23p57					00 44			05 48
Chester	a										00 18								
	d										00 40								
Wrexham General	a																		
Llandudno	a																		
Bangor (Gwynedd)	a										01 45								
Holyhead	a										02 15								
Wilmslow	a																		
Stockport	a											00s26							
Manchester Piccadilly 10	a						00 12	00 13				00 35							
Hartford	a																		
Warrington Bank Quay	a	21p15												03 15					
	d	21p15												03 17					
Runcorn	a																		06 07
Liverpool South Parkway 7 ✈	a																		06 15
Liverpool Lime Street 10	a																		06 26
	d																		
Manchester Airport ✈	d		22p00	22p00	22p29	22p29									00 01	01 20	04 00		
Manchester Piccadilly 10	d		22p16	22p16	22p46	22p46									00 16	01a36	04 15	05 43	
Bolton	d		22p33	22p33	23p07	23p07									00s31		04s29	05 59	
Wigan North Western	a	21p26	22p48	22p48															
	d	21p26	22p51	22p51															
Preston 8	a	21p39	23p09	23p12	23p33	23p34									01s05		05s04	06 26	
Preston 8	d	21p41	23p13	23p15	23p35	23p37			23p51	00u52								06 37	
Blackpool North	a				00 02	00 04			00 16						01 30		05 33	07 06	
Lancaster 6	a	21p55	23p28	23p31															
	d	21p56	23p29	23p31															
Barrow-in-Furness	a		00 31	00 34															
Oxenholme Lake District	a	22p09																	
	d	22p09																	
Windermere	a																		
Penrith North Lakes	d	22p35																	
Carlisle 8	a	22p50												05s15					
	d	22p51																	
Lockerbie	d																		
Carstairs	a													06s20					
Motherwell	a													06s56					
Glasgow Central 15	a	00 06												07 20					
Haymarket	a																		
Edinburgh 10	a									03 58									
Perth	a									05s39									
Dundee	a																		
Aberdeen	a																		
Inverness	a									08 38									

A until 31 December and then from 31 March
B from 7 January until 24 March
C until 24 March
D from 31 March
b Previous night, stops to pick up only
c Previous night, stops to set down only

OVERNIGHT SLEEPERS. For sleeper trains, operated by First ScotRail, please refer to Tables 400 - 404

Table 65

Saturdays

London and West Midlands - North West England and Scotland

Route Diagram - see first Page of Table 65

		VT	TP	TP	NT	NT	LM	VT	XC	TP	NT	LM	LM	NT	VT	XC
		◇1	◇1	◇1			1	◇1	◇1	◇1		◇1	◇1		◇1	◇1
						A					B			A		
London Euston 15 ⊖	d															
Watford Junction	d															
Milton Keynes Central	d															
Rugby	d															
Nuneaton	d															
Tamworth Low Level	d															
Lichfield Trent Valley	d															
Coventry	d															
Birmingham International ✈	d															
Birmingham New Street 12	d							05 30	05 57				06 01		06 20	06 31
Wolverhampton 7	d							05 48	06 16				06 18		06 37	06 49
Penkridge	d												06 29			
Stafford	a							06 00	06 29				06 35			07 00
	d							06 01	06 30				06 36			07 01
Stoke-on-Trent	a								06 50							07 18
Congleton	a								07 02							
Macclesfield	a								07 11							07 36
Crewe 10	a							06 20					06 56		07 07	
	d	05 57					06 12	06 23				06 32	06 57		07 09	
Chester	a							06 43								
	d							06 44								
Wrexham General	a															
Llandudno	a															
Bangor (Gwynedd)	a							07 49								
Holyhead	a							08 23								
Wilmslow	a															
Stockport	a								07 27							07 49
Manchester Piccadilly 10	a								07 38							07 59
Hartford	a											06 46	07 10			
Warrington Bank Quay	a	06 13													07 26	
	d	06 14													07 27	
Runcorn	a						06 31					06 59	07 20			
Liverpool South Parkway 7 ✈	a						06 39					07 08	07 30			
Liverpool Lime Street 10	a						06 53					07 22	07 42			
	d					06 20					06 57					
Manchester Airport ✈	d		05 45	06 18												
Manchester Piccadilly 10	d		06 03	06 33												
Bolton	d		06 19	06 50	07 01											
Wigan North Western	a	06 24			07 19	07 20					07 30				07 37	
	d	06 25									07 31			07 30	07 38	
Preston 8	a	06 37	06 42	07 11							07 54			07 54	07 51	
Preston 8	d	06 40	06 44	07 14						07 20	07 55			07 55	07 53	
Blackpool North	a										08 21			08 21		
Lancaster 6	a	06 54	06 59	07 30						07 36					08 08	
	d	06 54	07 00	07 30						07 36					08 08	
Barrow-in-Furness	a									08 39						
Oxenholme Lake District	a	07 08	07 15												08 21	
	d	07 10	07 15												08 22	
Windermere	a															
Penrith North Lakes	d	07 37		08 07												
Carlisle 8	a	07 50	07 55	08 24											09 00	
	d	07 51	07 56	08 25											09 02	
Lockerbie	d	08 10	08 16													
Carstairs	a															
Motherwell	a															
Glasgow Central 15	a	09 13		09 45												
Haymarket	a		09s17												10 16	
Edinburgh 10	a		09 22												10 22	
Perth	a															
Dundee	a															
Aberdeen	a															
Inverness	a															

A from 18 February until 24 March
B until 11 February

OVERNIGHT SLEEPERS. For sleeper trains, operated by First ScotRail, please refer to Tables 400 - 404

London and West Midlands - North West England and Scotland

Route Diagram - see first Page of Table 65

		TP	NT	TP	LM	XC	VT	LM	NT	NT	VT	VT	XC	VT	TP	NT
		◇1		◇1	◇1	◇1	◇1	◇1			◇1	◇1	◇1	◇1	◇1	
			A							B						A
		⊼		⊼		⊼	☕				☕	☕	⊼	☕	⊼	
London Euston 15 ⊖	d						06 05					06 36		06 55		
Watford Junction	d						06u20					06u51				
Milton Keynes Central	d						06 41							07 27		
Rugby	d						07 03									
Nuneaton	d															
Tamworth Low Level	d															
Lichfield Trent Valley	d															
Coventry	d															
Birmingham International ✈	d															
Birmingham New Street 12	d				06 36	06 57		07 01			07 20		07 31			
Wolverhampton 7	d				06 54	07 15		07 18			07 37		07 49			
Penkridge	d							07 30								
Stafford	a				07 08	07 29	07 33	07 36					08 00			
	d				07 08	07 30	07 34	07 38					08 01			
Stoke-on-Trent	a												08 19	08 24		
Congleton	a															
Macclesfield	a												08 36	08 41		
Crewe 10	a				07 33	07 50	07 53	07 58			08 07	08 10				
	d				07 35	07 53	07 55	08 00			08 09	08 11				
Chester	a															
	d															
Wrexham General	a															
Llandudno	a															
Bangor (Gwynedd)	a															
Holyhead	a															
Wilmslow	a					08 09						08 27				
Stockport	a					08 20						08 36	08 49	08 55		
Manchester Piccadilly 10	a					08 35						08 49	08 59	09 07		
Hartford	a				07 48			08 11								
Warrington Bank Quay	a						08 11				08 27					
	d						08 12				08 27					
Runcorn	a				08 02			08 24								
Liverpool South Parkway 7 ✈	a				08 11			08 33								
Liverpool Lime Street 10	a				08 24			08 46								
	d		07 20													08 20
Manchester Airport ✈	d	07 00		07 25											07 56	
Manchester Piccadilly 10	d	07 15		07 45											08 15	
Bolton	d	07 31		07 59											08 32	
Wigan North Western	a		08 20				08 22				08 38					09 20
	d						08 23			08 30	08 38					
Preston 8	a	07 57		08 22			08 36			08 54	08 51				08 58	
Preston 8	d	07 59		08 24			08 37		08 42	08 55	08 53				08 59	
Blackpool North	a	08 29								09 21					09 25	
Lancaster 6	a			08 39			08 52		09 02		09 08					
	d			08 40			08 52		09 03		09 08					
Barrow-in-Furness	a								10 07							
Oxenholme Lake District	a						09 05									
	d						09 06									
Windermere	a															
Penrith North Lakes	d						09 32				09 45					
Carlisle 8	a			09 30			09 47		12 39		10 02					
	d			09 30			09 48				10 04					
Lockerbie	d			09 50												
Carstairs	a															
Motherwell	a															
Glasgow Central 15	a						11 03				11 17					
Haymarket	a			10s48												
Edinburgh 10	a			10 56												
Perth	a															
Dundee	a															
Aberdeen	a															
Inverness	a															

A from 18 February until 24 March
B until 11 February

OVERNIGHT SLEEPERS. For sleeper trains, operated by First ScotRail, please refer to Tables 400 - 404

London and West Midlands - North West England and Scotland

Route Diagram - see first Page of Table 65

		LM	VT	VT	XC	TP	VT	TP	NT	LM	NT	VT	VT	XC
		◇1	◇1	◇1	◇1	◇1	◇1	◇1		◇1		◇1	◇1	◇1
						A			B		C			
			☕	☕	⊼	⊼	☕					☕	☕	☕
London Euston 15 ⊖	d		07 07	07 20			07 30						07 35	
Watford Junction	d													
Milton Keynes Central	d			07 50									08 06	
Rugby	d													
Nuneaton	d													
Tamworth Low Level	d													
Lichfield Trent Valley	d													
Coventry	d				07 27									
Birmingham International ✈	d				07 38									
Birmingham New Street 12	d	07 36			07 57					08 01		08 20		08 31
Wolverhampton 7	d	07 53			08 15					08 19		08 37		08 49
Penkridge	d	08 03								08 29				
Stafford	a	08 09	08 22		08 29					08 35				09 00
	d	08 09	08 23		08 30					08 36				09 01
Stoke-on-Trent	a			08 48	08 54									09 19
Congleton	a													
Macclesfield	a				09 11									
Crewe 10	a	08 30	08 41							08 56		09 07	09 10	
	d	08 31	08 43							08 57		09 09	09 11	
Chester	a													
	d													
Wrexham General	a													
Llandudno	a													
Bangor (Gwynedd)	a													
Holyhead	a													
Wilmslow	a												09 27	
Stockport	a			09 16	09 27								09 36	09 49
Manchester Piccadilly 10	a			09 28	09 39								09 49	09 59
Hartford	a									09 11				
Warrington Bank Quay	a						09 14					09 26		
	d						09 14					09 27		
Runcorn	a	08 50	09 00							09 21				
Liverpool South Parkway 7 ✈	a	08 59								09 30				
Liverpool Lime Street 10	a	09 12	09 21							09 43				
	d								08 57					
Manchester Airport ✈	d					08 25								
Manchester Piccadilly 10	d					08 46								
Bolton	d					09 07								
Wigan North Western	a						09 25		09 30			09 37		
	d						09 25		09 31		09 30	09 38		
Preston 8	a					09 30	09 38		09 54		09 54	09 51		
Preston 8	d					09 32	09 41	09 45	09 55		09 55	09 53		
Blackpool North	a								10 21		10 21			
Lancaster 6	a					09 47	09 54	10 00				10 08		
	d					09 48	09 55	10 01				10 08		
Barrow-in-Furness	a							11 04						
Oxenholme Lake District	a					10 04						10 22		
	d					10 05						10 24		
Windermere	a					10 26								
Penrith North Lakes	d						10 30							
Carlisle 8	a						10 46					11 01		
	d						10 47					11 03		
Lockerbie	d													
Carstairs	a													
Motherwell	a													
Glasgow Central 15	a						12 01							
Haymarket	a											12 16		
Edinburgh 10	a											12 22		
Perth	a													
Dundee	a													
Aberdeen	a													
Inverness	a													

A ⊼ to Preston
B until 11 February
C from 18 February until 24 March

OVERNIGHT SLEEPERS. For sleeper trains, operated by First ScotRail, please refer to Tables 400 - 404

Table 65

Saturdays

London and West Midlands - North West England and Scotland

Route Diagram - see first Page of Table 65

		VT	TP	TP	NT	LM	VT	VT	VT	XC	TP	VT	TP
		◇1	◇1			◇1	◇1	◇1	◇1	◇1	◇1	◇1	◇1
			A		B								
		⊡	⫟				⊡	⊡	⊡	⫟	⫟	⊡	
London Euston 15 ⊖	d	08 00					08 07	08 10	08 20			08 30	
Watford Junction	d												
Milton Keynes Central	d							08 41	08 50				
Rugby	d												
Nuneaton	d												
Tamworth Low Level	d												
Lichfield Trent Valley	d												
Coventry	d									08 27			
Birmingham International ✈	d									08 38			
Birmingham New Street 12	d					08 36				08 57			
Wolverhampton 7 ⇌	d					08 53				09 15			
Penkridge	d					09 03							
Stafford	a					09 09	09 22			09 29			
	d					09 09	09 23			09 30			
Stoke-on-Trent	a	09 24							09 48	09 54			
Congleton	a												
Macclesfield	a	09 41								10 11			
Crewe 10	a					09 30		09 47					
	d					09 31		09 49					
Chester	a							10 12					
	d												
Wrexham General	a												
Llandudno	a												
Bangor (Gwynedd)	a												
Holyhead	a												
Wilmslow	a												
Stockport	a	09 55							10 16	10 27			
Manchester Piccadilly 10 ⇌	a	10 07							10 28	10 39			
Hartford	a												
Warrington Bank Quay	a											10 14	
	d											10 14	
Runcorn	a					09 50	09 55						
Liverpool South Parkway 7 ✈	a					09 59							
Liverpool Lime Street 10	a					10 10	10 15						
	d				09 20								
Manchester Airport ✈	d		09 00								09 29		
Manchester Piccadilly 10 ⇌	d		09 16								09 46		
Bolton	d		09 33								10 07		
Wigan North Western	a				10 20							10 25	
	d											10 25	
Preston 8	a		09 55								10 33	10 38	
Preston 8	d		10 08	09 58							10 38	10 41	10 45
Blackpool North	a		10 35								11 05		
Lancaster 6	a			10 13								10 54	11 00
	d			10 14								10 55	11 01
Barrow-in-Furness	a												
Oxenholme Lake District	a											11 08	11 17
	d											11 08	11 18
Windermere	a												11 39
Penrith North Lakes	d			10 53									
Carlisle 8	a			11 10								11 46	
	d			11 11								11 47	
Lockerbie	d			11 30									
Carstairs	a												
Motherwell	a												
Glasgow Central 15	a			12 32								13 01	
Haymarket	a												
Edinburgh 10	a												
Perth	a												
Dundee	a												
Aberdeen	a												
Inverness	a												

A ⫟ to Preston

B from 18 February until 24 March

OVERNIGHT SLEEPERS. For sleeper trains, operated by First ScotRail, please refer to Tables 400 - 404

Table 65

Saturdays

London and West Midlands - North West England and Scotland

Route Diagram - see first Page of Table 65

		NT	LM	NT	VT	VT	XC	TP	NT	LM	VT	VT	VT	VT	XC
			◇1		◇1	◇1	◇1	◇1		◇1	◇1	◇1	◇1	◇1	◇1
		A		B					B						
					⊡	⊡	⊡	⫟			⊡	⊡	⊡	⊡	⫟
London Euston 15 ⊖	d					08 40					08 50	09 00	09 07	09 20	
Watford Junction	d										09 05				
Milton Keynes Central	d										09 25			09 50	
Rugby	d														
Nuneaton	d														
Tamworth Low Level	d														
Lichfield Trent Valley	d														
Coventry	d														09 27
Birmingham International ✈	d														09 38
Birmingham New Street 12	d		09 01		09 20		09 31			09 36					09b57
Wolverhampton 7 ⇌	d		09 19		09 37		09 49			09 53					10 15
Penkridge	d									10 03					
Stafford	a		09 34				10 00			10 09			10 22		10 29
	d		09 35				10 01			10 09			10 23		10 30
Stoke-on-Trent	a						10 19					10 24		10 48	10 54
Congleton	a														
Macclesfield	a											10 41			11 11
Crewe 10	a		09 56		10 07	10 10				10 30	10 32				
	d		09 57		10 09	10 11				10 31	10 43				
Chester	a										11 10				
	d										11 12				
Wrexham General	a														
Llandudno	a														
Bangor (Gwynedd)	a										12 19				
Holyhead	a										12 55				
Wilmslow	a					10 27									
Stockport	a					10 36	10 49					10 55		11 16	11 27
Manchester Piccadilly 10 ⇌	a					10 49	10 59					11 07		11 28	11 39
Hartford	a		10 10												
Warrington Bank Quay	a				10 26										
	d				10 27										
Runcorn	a		10 22							10 50			10 55		
Liverpool South Parkway 7 ✈	a		10 31							10 59					
Liverpool Lime Street 10	a		10 44							11 10			11 15		
	d	09 57							10 20						
Manchester Airport ✈	d							10 00							
Manchester Piccadilly 10 ⇌	d							10 16							
Bolton	d							10 33							
Wigan North Western	a	10 30			10 37				11 20						
	d	10 31		10 30	10 38										
Preston 8	a	10 54		10 54	10 51			10 55							
Preston 8	d	10 55		10 55	10 53			10 58							
Blackpool North	a	11 21		11 21											
Lancaster 6	a				11 08			11 13							
	d				11 08			11 14							
Barrow-in-Furness	a														
Oxenholme Lake District	a							11 28							
	d							11 28							
Windermere	a														
Penrith North Lakes	d				11 45			11 53							
Carlisle 8	a				12 00			12 10							
	d				12 03			12 11							
Lockerbie	d							12 30							
Carstairs	a														
Motherwell	a														
Glasgow Central 15	a				13 17										
Haymarket	a							13s33							
Edinburgh 10	a							13 39							
Perth	a														
Dundee	a														
Aberdeen	a														
Inverness	a														

A until 11 February

B from 18 February until 24 March

OVERNIGHT SLEEPERS. For sleeper trains, operated by First ScotRail, please refer to Tables 400 - 404

London and West Midlands - North West England and Scotland

Route Diagram - see first Page of Table 65

Station		TP ◇1	VT ◇1	NT A	LM ◇1	NT B	VT ◇1	VT ◇1	XC ◇1	VT ◇1	TP ◇1 C	NT B	LM ◇1	VT ◇1	VT ◇1	VT ◇1	XC ◇1
London Euston 15 ⊖	d		09 30					09 40		10 00				10 07	10 10	10 20	
Watford Junction	d																
Milton Keynes Central	d														10 41	10 50	
Rugby	d																
Nuneaton	d																
Tamworth Low Level	d																
Lichfield Trent Valley	d																
Coventry	d																10 27
Birmingham International ✈	d																10 38
Birmingham New Street 12	d				10 01		10 20		10 31				10 36				10 57
Wolverhampton 7	d				10 19		10 37		10 49				10 53				11 15
Penkridge	d												11 03				
Stafford	a				10 35				11 00				11 09	11 22			11 29
	d				10 35				11 01				11 09	11 23			11 30
Stoke-on-Trent	a								11 19	11 24						11 48	11 54
Congleton	a																
Macclesfield	a									11 41							12 11
Crewe 10	a				10 56		11 07	11 10					11 30		11 47		
	d				10 57		11 09	11 11					11 31		11 49		
Chester	a														12 12		
	d																
Wrexham General	a																
Llandudno	a																
Bangor (Gwynedd)	a																
Holyhead	a																
Wilmslow	a							11 27									
Stockport	a							11 36	11 49	11 55						12 16	12 27
Manchester Piccadilly 10	a							11 49	11 59	12 07						12 28	12 39
Hartford	a				11 11												
Warrington Bank Quay	a		11 14				11 26										
	d		11 14				11 27										
Runcorn	a				11 21								11 50	11 55			
Liverpool South Parkway 7 ✈	a				11 30								11 59				
Liverpool Lime Street 10	a				11 43								12 10	12 15			
	d			10 57								11 20					
Manchester Airport ✈	d	10 29									11 00						
Manchester Piccadilly 10	d	10 46									11 16						
Bolton	d	11 07									11 33						
Wigan North Western	a		11 25	11 30			11 37					12 20					
	d		11 25	11 31		11 30	11 38										
Preston 8	a	11 33	11 38	11 54		11 54	11 51				11 55						
Preston 8	d	11 38	11 41	11 55		11 55	11 53				11 58						
Blackpool North	a	12 05		12 21		12 21											
Lancaster 6	a		11 54				12 08				12 13						
	d		11 55				12 08				12 14						
Barrow-in-Furness	a										13 11						
Oxenholme Lake District	a						12 22										
	d						12 24										
Windermere	a																
Penrith North Lakes	d		12 30														
Carlisle 8	a		12 46				13 01										
	d		12 47				13 03										
Lockerbie	d																
Carstairs	a																
Motherwell	a																
Glasgow Central 15	a		14 01														
Haymarket	a						14 15										
Edinburgh 10	a						14 22										
Perth	a																
Dundee	a																
Aberdeen	a																
Inverness	a																

A until 11 February
B from 18 February until 24 March
C to Preston

OVERNIGHT SLEEPERS. For sleeper trains, operated by First ScotRail, please refer to Tables 400 - 404

London and West Midlands - North West England and Scotland

Route Diagram - see first Page of Table 65

Station		TP ◇1	VT ◇1	NT A	LM ◇1	NT B	VT ◇1	VT ◇1	XC ◇1	VT ◇1	TP ◇1	NT B	LM ◇1	VT ◇1	VT ◇1	VT ◇1	NT
London Euston 15 ⊖	d		10 30					10 40		11 00				11 07	11 10	11 20	
Watford Junction	d																
Milton Keynes Central	d														11 41	11 50	
Rugby	d																
Nuneaton	d																
Tamworth Low Level	d																
Lichfield Trent Valley	d																
Coventry	d																
Birmingham International ✈	d																
Birmingham New Street 12	d				11 01		11 20		11 31				11 36				
Wolverhampton 7	d				11 19		11 37		11 49				11 53				
Penkridge	d												12 03				
Stafford	a				11 35				12 00				12 09	12 22			
	d				11 35				12 01				12 09	12 23			
Stoke-on-Trent	a								12 19	12 24						12 48	
Congleton	a																
Macclesfield	a									12 41							
Crewe 10	a				11 56		12 07	12 10					12 30		12 47		
	d				11 57		12 09	12 11					12 31		12 49		
Chester	a														13 12		
	d																12 07
Wrexham General	a																
Llandudno	a																
Bangor (Gwynedd)	a																
Holyhead	a																
Wilmslow	a							12 27									
Stockport	a							12 36	12 49	12 55						13 16	13 21
Manchester Piccadilly 10	a							12 49	12 59	13 07						13 28	13 36
Hartford	a				12 10												
Warrington Bank Quay	a		12 14				12 26										
	d		12 14				12 27										
Runcorn	a				12 22								12 50	12 55			
Liverpool South Parkway 7 ✈	a				12 31								12 59				
Liverpool Lime Street 10	a				12 44								13 10	13 15			
	d			11 57								12 20					
Manchester Airport ✈	d	11 29									12 00						
Manchester Piccadilly 10	d	11 46									12 16						
Bolton	d	12 07									12 33						
Wigan North Western	a		12 25	12 30			12 37					13 20					
	d		12 25	12 31		12 30	12 38										
Preston 8	a	12 33	12 38	12 54		12 54	12 51				12 55						
Preston 8	d	12 38	12 41	12 55		12 55	12 53				12 58						
Blackpool North	a	13 05		13 21		13 21											
Lancaster 6	a		12 54				13 08				13 13						
	d		12 55				13 08				13 14						
Barrow-in-Furness	a																
Oxenholme Lake District	a		13 08				13 22				13 28						
	d		13 08				13 24				13 28						
Windermere	a																
Penrith North Lakes	d										13 53						
Carlisle 8	a		13 46				14 01				14 10						
	d		13 47				14 03				14 11						
Lockerbie	d										14 30						
Carstairs	a																
Motherwell	a																
Glasgow Central 15	a		15 01				15 17										
Haymarket	a										15s30						
Edinburgh 10	a										15 39						
Perth	a																
Dundee	a																
Aberdeen	a																
Inverness	a																

A until 11 February
B from 18 February until 24 March

OVERNIGHT SLEEPERS. For sleeper trains, operated by First ScotRail, please refer to Tables 400 - 404

London and West Midlands - North West England and Scotland

Route Diagram - see first Page of Table 65

		XC	TP	TP	VT	NT	LM	NT	VT	VT	XC	VT	TP	NT	LM
		◇1	◇1	◇1	◇1		◇1		◇1	◇1	◇1	◇1	◇1		◇1
						A		B						B	
		🛒		🛒	⊡				⊡	⊡	⊡	⊡	🛒	🚌	
London Euston 15 ⊖	d				11 30					11 40		12 00			
Watford Junction	d														
Milton Keynes Central	d														
Rugby	d														
Nuneaton	d														
Tamworth Low Level	d														
Lichfield Trent Valley	d														
Coventry	d	11 27													
Birmingham International ✈	d	11 38													
Birmingham New Street 12	d	11 57					12 01		12 20		12 31				12 36
Wolverhampton 7 ⇌	d	12 15					12 19		12 37		12 49				12 53
Penkridge	d														13 03
Stafford	a	12 29					12 35				13 00				13 09
	d	12 30					12 35				13 01				13 09
Stoke-on-Trent	a	12 54									13 18	13 24			
Congleton	a														
Macclesfield	a	13 11										13 41			
Crewe 10	a						12 56		13 07	13 10					13 30
	d						12 57		13 09	13 11					13 31
Chester	a														
	d														
Wrexham General	a														
Llandudno	a														
Bangor (Gwynedd)	a														
Holyhead	a														
Wilmslow	a									13 27					
Stockport	a	13 27								13 36	13 49	13 55			
Manchester Piccadilly 10 ⇌	a	13 39								13 49	13 59	14 07			
Hartford	a						13 11								
Warrington Bank Quay	a				13 14				13 26						
	d				13 14				13 27						
Runcorn	a						13 21								13 50
Liverpool South Parkway 7 ✈	a						13 30								13 59
Liverpool Lime Street 10	a						13 43								14 10
	d					12{57								13{20	
Manchester Airport ✈	d			12 29									13 00		
Manchester Piccadilly 10 ⇌	d			12 46									13 16		
Bolton	d			13 07									13 33		
Wigan North Western	a				13 25	13{30			13 37					14{20	
	d				13 25	13{31		13{30	13 38						
Preston 8	a			13 33	13 38	13{54		13{54	13 51				13 55		
Preston 8	d		13 04	13 38	13 41	13{55		13{55	13 53				13 58		
Blackpool North	a			14 05		14{21		14{21							
Lancaster 6	a		13 19		13 54				14 08				14 13		
	d		13 20		13 55				14 08				14 14		
Barrow-in-Furness	a														
Oxenholme Lake District	a		13 36		14 08								14 28		
	d		13 37		14 08								14 28		
Windermere	a		13 56												
Penrith North Lakes	d								14 45						
Carlisle 8	a				14 46				15 00				15 06		
	d				14 47				15 02				15 07		
Lockerbie	d												15 27		
Carstairs	a														
Motherwell	a														
Glasgow Central 15	a				16 01								16 30		
Haymarket	a								16 16						
Edinburgh 10	a								16 22						
Perth	a														
Dundee	a														
Aberdeen	a														
Inverness	a														

A until 11 February

B from 18 February until 24 March

OVERNIGHT SLEEPERS. For sleeper trains, operated by First ScotRail, please refer to Tables 400 - 404

London and West Midlands - North West England and Scotland

Route Diagram - see first Page of Table 65

		VT	VT	VT	XC	TP	VT	NT	LM	NT	VT	VT	XC	VT
		◇1	◇1	◇1	◇1	◇1	◇1		◇1		◇1	◇1	◇1	◇1
								A		B				
		⊡	⊡	⊡	🛒	🛒	⊡				⊡	⊡	⊡	⊡
London Euston 15 ⊖	d	12 07	12 10	12 20			12 30					12 40		13 00
Watford Junction	d													
Milton Keynes Central	d		12 41	12 50										
Rugby	d													
Nuneaton	d													
Tamworth Low Level	d													
Lichfield Trent Valley	d													
Coventry	d				12 27									
Birmingham International ✈	d				12 38									
Birmingham New Street 12	d				12 57				13 01		13 20		13 31	
Wolverhampton 7 ⇌	d				13 15				13 19		13 37		13 49	
Penkridge	d													
Stafford	a	13 22			13 29				13 35				14 00	
	d	13 23			13 30				13 35				14 01	
Stoke-on-Trent	a			13 48	13 54								14 19	14 24
Congleton	a													
Macclesfield	a				14 11									14 41
Crewe 10	a		13 47						13 56		14 07	14 10		
	d		13 49						13 57		14 09	14 11		
Chester	a		14 12											
	d													
Wrexham General	a													
Llandudno	a													
Bangor (Gwynedd)	a													
Holyhead	a													
Wilmslow	a											14 27		
Stockport	a			14 16	14 27							14 36	14 49	14 55
Manchester Piccadilly 10 ⇌	a			14 28	14 39							14 49	14 59	15 07
Hartford	a								14 11					
Warrington Bank Quay	a						14 14				14 26			
	d						14 14				14 27			
Runcorn	a	13 55							14 21					
Liverpool South Parkway 7 ✈	a								14 30					
Liverpool Lime Street 10	a	14 15							14 43					
	d							13{57						
Manchester Airport ✈	d					13 29								
Manchester Piccadilly 10 ⇌	d					13 46								
Bolton	d					14 07								
Wigan North Western	a						14 25	14{30			14 37			
	d						14 25	14{31		14{30	14 38			
Preston 8	a					14 33	14 38	14{54		14{54	14 51			
Preston 8	d					14 38	14 41	14{55		14{55	14 53			
Blackpool North	a					15 05		15{21		15{21				
Lancaster 6	a						14 54				15 08			
	d						14 55				15 09			
Barrow-in-Furness	a													
Oxenholme Lake District	a										15 22			
	d										15 24			
Windermere	a													
Penrith North Lakes	d						15 30							
Carlisle 8	a						15 46				16 01			
	d						15 47				16 03			
Lockerbie	d													
Carstairs	a													
Motherwell	a													
Glasgow Central 15	a						17 01				17 17			
Haymarket	a													
Edinburgh 10	a													
Perth	a													
Dundee	a													
Aberdeen	a													
Inverness	a													

A until 11 February

B from 18 February until 24 March

OVERNIGHT SLEEPERS. For sleeper trains, operated by First ScotRail, please refer to Tables 400 - 404

London and West Midlands - North West England and Scotland

Route Diagram - see first Page of Table 65

		TP		NT	LM	VT	VT	VT	XC	TP	VT	NT	LM	NT
		◇1			◇1	◇1	◇1	◇1	◇1	◇1	◇1		◇1	
				A								B		A
		✠		🚌		🍴	🍴	🍴	✠	✠	🍴			
London Euston 15 ⊖	d					13 07	13 10	13 20			13 30			
Watford Junction	d													
Milton Keynes Central	d						13 41	13 50						
Rugby	d													
Nuneaton	d													
Tamworth Low Level	d													
Lichfield Trent Valley	d													
Coventry	d								13 27					
Birmingham International ✈	d								13 38					
Birmingham New Street 12	d				13 36				13 57				14 01	
Wolverhampton 7 🚌	d				13 53				14 15				14 19	
Penkridge	d				14 03									
Stafford	a				14 09	14 22			14 29				14 35	
	d				14 09	14 23			14 30				14 35	
Stoke-on-Trent	a							14 48	14 54					
Congleton	a													
Macclesfield	a								15 11					
Crewe 10	a				14 30		14 47						14 56	
	d				14 31		14 49						14 57	
Chester	a						15 12							
	d													
Wrexham General	a													
Llandudno	a													
Bangor (Gwynedd)	a													
Holyhead	a													
Wilmslow	a													
Stockport	a							15 16	15 27					
Manchester Piccadilly 10 🚌	a							15 28	15 39					
Hartford	a												15 11	
Warrington Bank Quay	a										15 14			
	d										15 14			
Runcorn	a				14 50	14 55							15 21	
Liverpool South Parkway 7 ✈	a				14 59								15 30	
Liverpool Lime Street 10	a				15 10	15 15							15 43	
	d			14 20								14 57		
Manchester Airport ✈	d	14 00								14 29				
Manchester Piccadilly 10 🚌	d	14 16								14 46				
Bolton	d	14 33								15 07				
Wigan North Western	a			15 20							15 25	15 30		
	d										15 25	15 31		15 30
Preston 8	a	14 55								15 33	15 38	15 54		15 54
Preston 8	d	14 58	15 04							15 38	15 41	15 55		15 55
Blackpool North	a									16 05		16 21		16 21
Lancaster 6	a	15 13	15 20								15 54			
	d	15 14	15 20								15 55			
Barrow-in-Furness	a		16 15											
Oxenholme Lake District	a	15 28									16 08			
	d	15 28									16 08			
Windermere	a													
Penrith North Lakes	d	15 53												
Carlisle 8	a	16 10									16 46			
	d	16 11									16 47			
Lockerbie	d	16 30												
Carstairs	a													
Motherwell	a													
Glasgow Central 15	a										18 01			
Haymarket	a	17s31												
Edinburgh 10	a	17 39												
Perth	a													
Dundee	a													
Aberdeen	a													
Inverness	a													

A from 18 February until 24 March

B until 11 February

OVERNIGHT SLEEPERS. For sleeper trains, operated by First ScotRail, please refer to Tables 400 - 404

London and West Midlands - North West England and Scotland

Route Diagram - see first Page of Table 65

		VT	VT	XC	VT	TP	NT	LM	VT	VT	VT	XC	TP	VT
		◇1	◇1	◇1	◇1	◇1		◇1	◇1	◇1	◇1	◇1	◇1	◇1
						A	B							
		🍴	🍴	🍴	🍴	✠	🚌		🍴	🍴	🍴	✠	✠	🍴
London Euston 15 ⊖	d		13 40		14 00				14 07	14 10	14 20			14 30
Watford Junction	d													
Milton Keynes Central	d									14 41	14 50			
Rugby	d													
Nuneaton	d													
Tamworth Low Level	d													
Lichfield Trent Valley	d													
Coventry	d											14 27		
Birmingham International ✈	d											14 38		
Birmingham New Street 12	d	14 20		14 31				14 36				14 57		
Wolverhampton 7 🚌	d	14 37		14 49				14 53				15 15		
Penkridge	d							15 03						
Stafford	a			15 00				15 09	15 22			15 29		
	d			15 01				15 09	15 23			15 30		
Stoke-on-Trent	a			15 19	15 24						15 48	15 54		
Congleton	a													
Macclesfield	a				15 41							16 11		
Crewe 10	a	15 07	15 10					15 30		15 47				
	d	15 09	15 11					15 31		15 49				
Chester	a									16 10				
	d									16 12				
Wrexham General	a													
Llandudno	a													
Bangor (Gwynedd)	a									17 17				
Holyhead	a									17 51				
Wilmslow	a		15 27											
Stockport	a		15 36	15 49	15 55						16 16	16 27		
Manchester Piccadilly 10 🚌	a		15 49	15 59	16 07						16 28	16 39		
Hartford	a													
Warrington Bank Quay	a	15 26												16 14
	d	15 27												16 14
Runcorn	a							15 50	15 55					
Liverpool South Parkway 7 ✈	a							15 59						
Liverpool Lime Street 10	a							16 10	16 15					
	d						15 20							
Manchester Airport ✈	d					15 00							15 29	
Manchester Piccadilly 10 🚌	d					15 16							15 46	
Bolton	d					15 33							16 07	
Wigan North Western	a	15 37					16 20							16 25
	d	15 38												16 25
Preston 8	a	15 51				15 57							16 33	16 38
Preston 8	d	15 53				15 58							16 38	16 41
Blackpool North	a												17 07	
Lancaster 6	a	16 08				16 14								16 54
	d	16 08				16 15								16 55
Barrow-in-Furness	a					17 18								
Oxenholme Lake District	a													
	d													
Windermere	a													
Penrith North Lakes	d	16 45												17 30
Carlisle 8	a	17 00												17 46
	d	17 03												17 47
Lockerbie	d													
Carstairs	a													
Motherwell	a													
Glasgow Central 15	a													19 01
Haymarket	a	18 14												
Edinburgh 10	a	18 22												
Perth	a													
Dundee	a													
Aberdeen	a													
Inverness	a													

A ✠ to Preston

B from 18 February until 24 March

OVERNIGHT SLEEPERS. For sleeper trains, operated by First ScotRail, please refer to Tables 400 - 404

London and West Midlands - North West England and Scotland

Route Diagram - see first Page of Table 65

		NT	LM	NT	VT	VT	XC	VT	TP		NT	LM	VT	VT	VT	XC	TP
			◇1		◇1	◇1	◇1	◇1	◇1			◇1	◇1	◇1	◇1	◇1	◇1
		A		B							B						
London Euston 15 ⊖	d					14 40		15 00					15 07	15 10	15 20		
Watford Junction	d																
Milton Keynes Central	d													15 41	15 50		
Rugby	d																
Nuneaton	d																
Tamworth Low Level	d																
Lichfield Trent Valley	d																
Coventry	d															15 27	
Birmingham International ✈	d															15 38	
Birmingham New Street 12	d		15 01		15 20		15 31					15 36				15 57	
Wolverhampton 7	d		15 19		15 37		15 49					15 53				16 15	
Penkridge	d											16 03					
Stafford	a		15 35				16 00					16 09	16 22			16 29	
	d		15 35				16 01					16 09	16 23			16 30	
Stoke-on-Trent	a						16 19	16 24							16 48	16 54	
Congleton	a																
Macclesfield	a							16 41								17 11	
Crewe 10	a		15 56		16 08	16 10						16 30		16 47			
	d		15 57		16 09	16 11						16 31		16 49			
Chester	a													17 12			
	d																
Wrexham General	a																
Llandudno	a																
Bangor (Gwynedd)	a																
Holyhead	a																
Wilmslow	a					16 27											
Stockport	a					16 36	16 49	16 54							17 16	17 27	
Manchester Piccadilly 10	a					16 49	16 59	17 07							17 28	17 39	
Hartford	a		16 10														
Warrington Bank Quay	a				16 26												
	d				16 27												
Runcorn	a		16 22									16 50	16 55				
Liverpool South Parkway 7 ✈	a		16 31									16 59					
Liverpool Lime Street 10	a		16 44									17 10	17 15				
	d	15 57									16 20						
Manchester Airport ✈	d								16 00								16 29
Manchester Piccadilly 10	d								16 16								16 46
Bolton	d								16 33								17 06
Wigan North Western	a	16 30			16 37						17 20						
	d	16 31		16 30	16 38												
Preston 8	a	16 54		16 54	16 51				16 55								17 30
Preston 8	d	16 55		16 55	16 53				17 00	17 04							17 32
Blackpool North	a	17 21		17 21													18 02
Lancaster 6	a				17 09				17 16	17 20							
	d				17 10				17 16	17 21							
Barrow-in-Furness	a																
Oxenholme Lake District	a				17 24				17 30	17 37							
	d				17 25				17 30	17 38							
Windermere	a									18 00							
Penrith North Lakes	d																
Carlisle 8	a				18 03				18 10								
	d				18 04				18 11								
Lockerbie	d								18 30								
Carstairs	a																
Motherwell	a																
Glasgow Central 15	a				19 17												
Haymarket	a								19s31								
Edinburgh 10	a								19 39								
Perth	a																
Dundee	a																
Aberdeen	a																
Inverness	a																

A until 11 February

B from 18 February until 24 March

OVERNIGHT SLEEPERS. For sleeper trains, operated by First ScotRail, please refer to Tables 400 - 404

London and West Midlands - North West England and Scotland

Route Diagram - see first Page of Table 65

		VT	NT	LM	NT	VT	VT	XC	VT	TP	NT	NT	LM	VT	VT	VT	XC
		◇1		◇1		◇1	◇1	◇1	◇1	◇1			◇1	◇1	◇1	◇1	◇1
			A		B						A	B					
London Euston 15 ⊖	d	15 30					15 40		16 00					16 07	16 10	16 20	
Watford Junction	d																
Milton Keynes Central	d														16 41	16 50	
Rugby	d																
Nuneaton	d																
Tamworth Low Level	d																
Lichfield Trent Valley	d																
Coventry	d																16 27
Birmingham International ✈	d																16 38
Birmingham New Street 12	d			16 01		16 20		16 31					16 36				16 57
Wolverhampton 7	d			16 19		16 37		16 49					16 53				17 15
Penkridge	d												17 03				
Stafford	a			16 35				17 00					17 09	17 22			17 29
	d			16 35				17 01					17 09	17 23			17 30
Stoke-on-Trent	a							17 19	17 24							17 48	17 54
Congleton	a																
Macclesfield	a								17 41								18 11
Crewe 10	a			16 56		17 07	17 10						17 30		17 47		
	d			16 57		17 09	17 11						17 31		17 49		
Chester	a														18 09		
	d														18 16		
Wrexham General	a																
Llandudno	a																
Bangor (Gwynedd)	a														19 21		
Holyhead	a														19 55		
Wilmslow	a						17 27										
Stockport	a						17 36	17 49	17 55							18 16	18 27
Manchester Piccadilly 10	a						17 49	17 59	18 07							18 28	18 39
Hartford	a			17 11													
Warrington Bank Quay	a	17 14				17 26											
	d	17 14				17 27											
Runcorn	a			17 21									17 50	17 55			
Liverpool South Parkway 7 ✈	a			17 30									17 59				
Liverpool Lime Street 10	a			17 43									18 10	18 15			
	d		16 57								17 19	17 20					
Manchester Airport ✈	d									17 00							
Manchester Piccadilly 10	d									17 15							
Bolton	d									17 32							
Wigan North Western	a	17 25	17 30			17 37					18 04	18 20					
	d	17 25	17 31		17 30	17 38											
Preston 8	a	17 38	17 54		17 54	17 51				17 55							
Preston 8	d	17 41	17 55		17 55	17 53				17 58							
Blackpool North	a		18 24		18 24												
Lancaster 6	a	17 54				18 08				18 13							
	d	17 55				18 08				18 14							
Barrow-in-Furness	a																
Oxenholme Lake District	a	18 08				18 22				18 28							
	d	18 08				18 23				18 28							
Windermere	a																
Penrith North Lakes	d					18 49				18 53							
Carlisle 8	a	18 46				19 04				19 09							
	d	18 47				19 04				19 11							
Lockerbie	d									19 30							
Carstairs	a																
Motherwell	a									20s16							
Glasgow Central 15	a	20 01								20 33							
Haymarket	a					20 16											
Edinburgh 10	a					20 22											
Perth	a																
Dundee	a																
Aberdeen	a																
Inverness	a																

A until 11 February

B from 18 February until 24 March

OVERNIGHT SLEEPERS. For sleeper trains, operated by First ScotRail, please refer to Tables 400 - 404

London and West Midlands - North West England and Scotland

Route Diagram - see first Page of Table 65

		TP	TP	VT	TP	NT	LM	VT	NT	VT	VT	XC	VT	TP
		◇1	◇1	◇1	◇1		◇1	◇1		◇1	◇1	◇1	◇1	◇1
		A	B			A			C					D
London Euston 15 ⊖	d			16 30				16 33			16 40		17 00	
Watford Junction	d													
Milton Keynes Central	d													
Rugby	d													
Nuneaton	d													
Tamworth Low Level	d							17 38						
Lichfield Trent Valley	d							17 45						
Coventry	d													
Birmingham International ✈	d													
Birmingham New Street 12	d						17 01			17 20		17 31		
Wolverhampton 7	d						17 19			17 37		17 49		
Penkridge	d						17 29							
Stafford	a						17 35	17 58				18 00		
	d						17 36	17 59				18 01		
Stoke-on-Trent	a											18 19	18 24	
Congleton	a													
Macclesfield	a												18 41	
Crewe 10	a						17 56			18 07	18 10			
	d						17 57			18 09	18 11			
Chester	a													
	d													
Wrexham General	a													
Llandudno	a													
Bangor (Gwynedd)	a													
Holyhead	a													
Wilmslow	a										18 27			
Stockport	a										18 36	18 49	18 55	
Manchester Piccadilly 10	a										18 49	18 59	19 07	
Hartford	a						18 11							
Warrington Bank Quay	a			18 14						18 26				
	d			18 14						18 27				
Runcorn	a						18 21	18 31						
Liverpool South Parkway 7 ✈	a						18 30							
Liverpool Lime Street 10	a						18 43	18 52						
	d					17 31								
Manchester Airport ✈	d				17 29									18 00
Manchester Piccadilly 10	d				17 46									18 16
Bolton	d				18 07									18 33
Wigan North Western	a			18 25		18 17				18 37				
	d			18 25		18 30			18 30	18 38				
Preston 8	a			18 38	18 38	18 54			18 54	18 51				18 55
Preston 8	d	18 02	18 02	18 41	18 40	18 55			18 55	18 53				18 58
Blackpool North	a				19 10	19 21			19 21					
Lancaster 6	a	18 18	18 18	18 54						19 08				19 13
	d	18 18	18 18	18 55						19 08				19 15
Barrow-in-Furness	a	19 22	19 26											20 19
Oxenholme Lake District	a			19 08						19 22				
	d			19 08						19 24				
Windermere	a													
Penrith North Lakes	d			19 34										
Carlisle 8	a			19 49						20 01				
	d			19 51						20 03				
Lockerbie	d													
Carstairs	a													
Motherwell	a													
Glasgow Central 15	a			21 01						21 17				
Haymarket	a													
Edinburgh 10	a													
Perth	a													
Dundee	a													
Aberdeen	a													
Inverness	a													

A from 31 March
B until 24 March
C from 18 February until 24 March
D to Preston

OVERNIGHT SLEEPERS. For sleeper trains, operated by First ScotRail, please refer to Tables 400 - 404

London and West Midlands - North West England and Scotland

Route Diagram - see first Page of Table 65

		LM	VT	VT	VT	XC	LM	TP	VT	VT	VT	XC	VT	LM	NT	TP
		◇1	◇1	◇1	◇1	◇1	◇1	◇1	◇1	◇1	◇1	◇1	◇1	◇1		◇1
															A	
London Euston 15 ⊖	d		17 07	17 10	17 20				17 30		17 40		18 00			
Watford Junction	d															
Milton Keynes Central	d			17 41	17 50											
Rugby	d															
Nuneaton	d		18 03													
Tamworth Low Level	d															
Lichfield Trent Valley	d															
Coventry	d					17 27										
Birmingham International ✈	d					17 38										
Birmingham New Street 12	d	17 36				17 57	18 01			18 20		18 31		18 36		
Wolverhampton 7	d	17 53				18 15	18 19			18 37		18 49		18 53		
Penkridge	d	18 03					18 29							19 03		
Stafford	a	18 09	18 26			18 29	18 35					19 00		19 09		
	d	18 09	18 27			18 30	18 35					19 01		19 09		
Stoke-on-Trent	a				18 48	18 54						19 19	19 24			
Congleton	a															
Macclesfield	a					19 11							19 41			
Crewe 10	a	18 30		18 48			18 56			19 07	19 10			19 30		
	d	18 33		18 50			18 59			19 09	19 11					
Chester	a			19 10												
	d			19 17												
Wrexham General	a															
Llandudno	a															
Bangor (Gwynedd)	a			20 22												
Holyhead	a			20 56												
Wilmslow	a										19 27					
Stockport	a				19 16	19 27					19 36	19 49	19 55			
Manchester Piccadilly 10	a				19 28	19 39					19 49	19 59	20 07			
Hartford	a	18 43					19 12									
Warrington Bank Quay	a								19 14	19 26						
	d								19 14	19 27						
Runcorn	a	18 52	18 59				19 22									
Liverpool South Parkway 7 ✈	a	19 02					19 31									
Liverpool Lime Street 10	a	19 14	19 17				19 44									
	d														18 40	
Manchester Airport ✈	d							18 29								19 00
Manchester Piccadilly 10	d							18 46								19 16
Bolton	d							19 07								19 33
Wigan North Western	a								19 25	19 37					19 40	
	d								19 25	19 38						
Preston 8	a							19 33	19 38	19 54						19 58
Preston 8	d							19 38	19 41							20 01
Blackpool North	a							20 06								
Lancaster 6	a								19 54							20 17
	d								19 55							20 17
Barrow-in-Furness	a															21 20
Oxenholme Lake District	a								20 08							
	d								20 08							
Windermere	a															
Penrith North Lakes	d								20 34							
Carlisle 8	a								20 49							
	d								20 51							
Lockerbie	d															
Carstairs	a															
Motherwell	a															
Glasgow Central 15	a								22 01							
Haymarket	a															
Edinburgh 10	a															
Perth	a															
Dundee	a															
Aberdeen	a															
Inverness	a															

A from 18 February until 24 March

OVERNIGHT SLEEPERS. For sleeper trains, operated by First ScotRail, please refer to Tables 400 - 404

London and West Midlands - North West England and Scotland

Route Diagram - see first Page of Table 65

		NT	VT	VT	VT	XC	LM	NT	VT	TP	VT	TP	VT	NT	TP	NT	NT
			◇[1]	◇[1]	◇[1]	◇[1]	◇[1]		◇[1]	◇[1]	◇[1]	◇[1]	◇[1]		◇[1]		
		A						B	C		D	E		B 🚌	F	E 🚌	G
			🍴	🍴	🍴	🛒			🍴		🍴		🍴				
London Euston [15] ⊖	d		18 07	18 10	18 20				18⌇30		18⌇30						
Watford Junction	d																
Milton Keynes Central	d			18 41	18 50												
Rugby	d																
Nuneaton	d																
Tamworth Low Level	d																
Lichfield Trent Valley	d																
Coventry	d					18 27											
Birmingham International ✈	d					18 38											
Birmingham New Street [12]	d					18 57	19 01						19 20				
Wolverhampton [7] ⇌	d					19 15	19 19						19 37				
Penkridge	d						19 29										
Stafford	a		19 22			19 29	19 35										
	d		19 23			19 30	19 36										
Stoke-on-Trent	a				19 48	19 54											
Congleton	a																
Macclesfield	a					20 11											
Crewe [10]	a			19 47			19 58						20 07				
	d			19 49			19 58						20 09				
Chester	a			20 12													
	d																
Wrexham General	a																
Llandudno	a																
Bangor (Gwynedd)	a																
Holyhead	a																
Wilmslow	a																
Stockport	a				20 16	20 27											
Manchester Piccadilly [10] ⇌	a				20 28	20 39											
Hartford	a						20 11										
Warrington Bank Quay	a								20⌇14		20⌇14		20 26				
	d								20⌇14		20⌇14		20 27				
Runcorn	a		19 55				20 24										
Liverpool South Parkway [7] ✈	a						20 33										
Liverpool Lime Street [10]	a		20 15				20 46										
	d	19⌇23												19⌇40			
Manchester Airport ✈	d									19 29		20⌇00			20⌇00		
Manchester Piccadilly [10] ⇌	d									19 46		20⌇16			20⌇16		
Bolton	d									20 07		20⌇33			20⌇33		
Wigan North Western	a	19⌇54							20⌇25		20⌇25		20 37	20⌇40			
	d	19⌇55						19⌇54	20⌇25		20⌇25		20 38				20⌇56
Preston [8]	a	20⌇18						20⌇18	20⌇38	20 33	20⌇38	20⌇57	20 59		20⌇57		21⌇22
Preston [8]	d	20⌇19						20⌇19		20 38	20⌇41				21⌇02	21⌇15	21⌇24
Blackpool North	a	20⌇44						20⌇44		21 06							21⌇53
Lancaster [6]	a										20⌇54				21⌇17	22⌇05	
	d										20⌇55				21⌇18		
Barrow-in-Furness	a														22⌇21		
Oxenholme Lake District	a										21⌇08						
	d										21⌇09						
Windermere	a																
Penrith North Lakes	d										21⌇34						
Carlisle [8]	a										21⌇49						
	d										21⌇51						
Lockerbie	d																
Carstairs	a																
Motherwell	a										22⌇44						
Glasgow Central [15]	a										23⌇04						
Haymarket	a																
Edinburgh [10]	a																
Perth	a																
Dundee	a																
Aberdeen	a																
Inverness	a																

A until 11 February
B from 18 February until 24 March
C from 31 March
D until 24 March
E from 7 January
F Until 31 December
G from 18 February

OVERNIGHT SLEEPERS. For sleeper trains, operated by First ScotRail, please refer to Tables 400 - 404

London and West Midlands - North West England and Scotland

Route Diagram - see first Page of Table 65

		NT	VT	VT	XC	VT	VT	VT	XC	TP	VT	NT	LM	VT	VT
			◇[1]	◇[1]	◇[1]	◇[1]	◇[1]	◇[1]	◇[1]	◇[1]	◇[1]		◇[1]	◇[1]	◇[1]
		A							B			C 🚌			
			🍴	🍴	🍴	🍴	🍴	🍴	🛒		🍴			🍴	🍴
London Euston [15] ⊖	d		18 33	18 40		19 00	19 07	19 20			19 30			19 40	
Watford Junction	d														
Milton Keynes Central	d							19 50							
Rugby	d														
Nuneaton	d						20 03								
Tamworth Low Level	d		19 38												
Lichfield Trent Valley	d		19 45												
Coventry	d								19 27						
Birmingham International ✈	d								19 38						
Birmingham New Street [12]	d				19 31				19 57				20 01		20 20
Wolverhampton [7] ⇌	d				19 49				20 15				20 22		20 37
Penkridge	d												20 31		
Stafford	a		19 58		20 00		20 26		20 29				20 37		20 49
	d		19 59		20 01		20 27		20 30				20 38		20 50
Stoke-on-Trent	a				20 19	20 24		20 48	20 54						
Congleton	a														
Macclesfield	a				20 36	20 41			21 11						
Crewe [10]	a			20 10			20 45				21 04		20 58	21 18	21 10
	d			20 11			20 47				21 05		21 06	21 19	
Chester	a														
	d														
Wrexham General	a														
Llandudno	a														
Bangor (Gwynedd)	a														
Holyhead	a														
Wilmslow	a			20 27										21 34	
Stockport	a			20 36	20 49	20 55		21 16	21 27					21 44	
Manchester Piccadilly [10] ⇌	a			20 49	20 59	21 07		21 28	21 39					21 53	
Hartford	a												21 19		
Warrington Bank Quay	a										21 22				
	d										21 22				
Runcorn	a		20 31				21 05						21 29		
Liverpool South Parkway [7] ✈	a												21 38		
Liverpool Lime Street [10]	a		20 52				21 25						21 50		
	d	20⌇25										21⌇15			
Manchester Airport ✈	d									20 29					
Manchester Piccadilly [10] ⇌	d									20 46					
Bolton	d									21 07					
Wigan North Western	a	20⌇57									21 33	22⌇15			
	d	20⌇57									21 33				
Preston [8]	a	21⌇22								21 33	21 49				
Preston [8]	d	21⌇24								21 38					
Blackpool North	a	21⌇53								22 06					
Lancaster [6]	a														
	d														
Barrow-in-Furness	a														
Oxenholme Lake District	a														
	d														
Windermere	a														
Penrith North Lakes	d														
Carlisle [8]	a														
	d														
Lockerbie	d														
Carstairs	a														
Motherwell	a														
Glasgow Central [15]	a														
Haymarket	a														
Edinburgh [10]	a														
Perth	a														
Dundee	a														
Aberdeen	a														
Inverness	a														

A until 11 February
B 🛒 to Birmingham New Street
C from 18 February until 24 March

OVERNIGHT SLEEPERS. For sleeper trains, operated by First ScotRail, please refer to Tables 400 - 404

London and West Midlands - North West England and Scotland

Route Diagram - see first Page of Table 65

		XC	LM	XC	VT	VT	LM	XC	NT	TP	TP	TP	NT	VT	VT
		◇1	◇1	◇1	◇1	◇1	◇1	◇1		◇1	◇1	◇1		◇1	◇1
				A					B		B	C	D		
		🍴		🍴	🍴	🍴								🍴	🍴
London Euston 15 ⊖	d				20 11	20 20								20 31	21 00
Watford Junction	d													20u46	
Milton Keynes Central	d					21 05									21 45
Rugby	d				21 15									21 36	
Nuneaton	d					21 33									
Tamworth Low Level	d													21 53	
Lichfield Trent Valley	d													22 00	
Coventry	d			20 27				21 27							
Birmingham International ✈	d			20 38				21 38							
Birmingham New Street 12	d	20 31	20 36	20 57			21 36	21 57							
Wolverhampton 7	d	20 49	20 53	21 15			21 59	22 16							
Penkridge	d		21 03				22 09								
Stafford	a	21 00	21 09	21 29	21 46		22 15	22 29							22 32
	d	21 01	21 09	21 30	21 46		22 16	22 30							22 34
Stoke-on-Trent	a	21 20		21 52		22 05		22 50							
Congleton	a														
Macclesfield	a	21 38		22 11		22 21		23 07							
Crewe 10	a		21 30		22 05		22 40							22 35	22 58
	d				22 06									22 37	22 59
Chester	a														
	d														
Wrexham General	a														
Llandudno	a														
Bangor (Gwynedd)	a														
Holyhead	a														
Wilmslow	a														23 14
Stockport	a	21 53		22 27		22 35		23 21							23 25
Manchester Piccadilly 10	a	22 04		22 39		22 51		23 32							23 38
Hartford	a														
Warrington Bank Quay	a													22 53	
	d													22 54	
Runcorn	a				22 24										
Liverpool South Parkway 7 ✈	a														
Liverpool Lime Street 10	a				22 46										
	d														
Manchester Airport ✈	d									21 29	22§00	22§00			
Manchester Piccadilly 10	d									21 46	22§16	22§16			
Bolton	d									22 07	22§33	22§33			
Wigan North Western	a													23 04	
	d												22§27	23 05	
Preston 8	a									22 36	22§54	22§54	22§55	23 19	
Preston 8	d								21§59	22 38	22§55		22§57		
Blackpool North	a									23 04			23§22		
Lancaster 6	a								22§19		23§11				
	d								22§19		23§11				
Barrow-in-Furness	a								23§24		00§15				
Oxenholme Lake District	a														
	d														
Windermere	a														
Penrith North Lakes	d														
Carlisle 8	a														
	d														
Lockerbie	d														
Carstairs	a														
Motherwell	a														
Glasgow Central 15	a														
Haymarket	a														
Edinburgh 10	a														
Perth	a														
Dundee	a														
Aberdeen	a														
Inverness	a														

A 🍴 to Birmingham New Street
B until 31 December
C from 7 January
D from 18 February until 24 March

OVERNIGHT SLEEPERS. For sleeper trains, operated by First ScotRail, please refer to Tables 400 - 404

London and West Midlands - North West England and Scotland

Route Diagram - see first Page of Table 65

		TP	XC	NT	LM	NT
		◇1	◇1		◇1	
				A		A
				🚌		
London Euston 15 ⊖	d					
Watford Junction	d					
Milton Keynes Central	d					
Rugby	d					
Nuneaton	d					
Tamworth Low Level	d					
Lichfield Trent Valley	d					
Coventry	d					
Birmingham International ✈	d					
Birmingham New Street 12	d		22 31		22 36	
Wolverhampton 7	d		22 49		22 56	
Penkridge	d				23 06	
Stafford	a		23 01		23 13	
	d		23 02		23 13	
Stoke-on-Trent	a		23 20			
Congleton	a					
Macclesfield	a		23 38			
Crewe 10	a				23 37	
	d					
Chester	a					
	d					
Wrexham General	a					
Llandudno	a					
Bangor (Gwynedd)	a					
Holyhead	a					
Wilmslow	a					
Stockport	a		23 53			
Manchester Piccadilly 10	a		00 10			
Hartford	a					
Warrington Bank Quay	a					
	d					
Runcorn	a					
Liverpool South Parkway 7 ✈	a					
Liverpool Lime Street 10	a					
	d			22§35		
Manchester Airport ✈	d	22 29				
Manchester Piccadilly 10	d	22 46				
Bolton	d	23 07				
Wigan North Western	a			23§35		
	d					23§47
Preston 8	a	23 33				00§13
Preston 8	d	23 35				
Blackpool North	a	00 02				
Lancaster 6	a					
	d					
Barrow-in-Furness	a					
Oxenholme Lake District	a					
	d					
Windermere	a					
Penrith North Lakes	d					
Carlisle 8	a					
	d					
Lockerbie	d					
Carstairs	a					
Motherwell	a					
Glasgow Central 15	a					
Haymarket	a					
Edinburgh 10	a					
Perth	a					
Dundee	a					
Aberdeen	a					
Inverness	a					

A from 18 February until 24 March

OVERNIGHT SLEEPERS. For sleeper trains, operated by First ScotRail, please refer to Tables 400 - 404

London and West Midlands - North West England and Scotland

Route Diagram - see first Page of Table 65

		TP	TP	XC	TP	TP	TP	TP	TP	VT	XC
		◇1	◇1	◇1			◇1	◇1	◇1	◇1	◇1
		A	A	A							
London Euston 15	d										
Watford Junction	d										
Milton Keynes Central	d										
Rugby	d										
Nuneaton	d										
Tamworth Low Level	d										
Lichfield Trent Valley	d										
Coventry	d										
Birmingham International	d										
Birmingham New Street 12	d			22p31						08 45	09 01
Wolverhampton 7	d			22p49						09 04	09 19
Penkridge	d										
Stafford	a			23p01						09 16	09 32
	d			23p02						09 17	09 33
Stoke-on-Trent	a			23p20							
Congleton	a										
Macclesfield	a			23p38							
Crewe 10	a									09 35	09 54
	d									09 37	09 56
Chester	a										
	d										
Wrexham General	a										
Llandudno	a										
Bangor (Gwynedd)	a										
Holyhead	a										
Wilmslow	a										10 12
Stockport	a			23p53							10 21
Manchester Piccadilly 10	a			00 10							10 37
Hartford	a										
Warrington Bank Quay	a									09 54	
	d									09 54	
Runcorn	a										
Liverpool South Parkway 7	a										
Liverpool Lime Street 10	a										
	d										
Manchester Airport	d	22p00	22p29		00 05	05 30		08 47	09 00		
Manchester Piccadilly 10	d	22p16	22p46		00 30	05 55	07 46	09 03	09 16		
Bolton	d	22p33	23p07		00s55	06s20	08 05	09 23	09 33		
Wigan North Western	a									10 05	
	d									10 05	
Preston 8	a	22p54	23p33		01s30	06s55	08 32	09 50	09 57	10 22	
Preston 8	d	22p55	23p35				08 33	09 52	10 00		
Blackpool North	a		00 02		02 10	07 35	08 57	10 18			
Lancaster 6	a	23p11							10 15		
	d	23p11							10 16		
Barrow-in-Furness	a	00 15									
Oxenholme Lake District	a								10 30		
	d								10 30		
Windermere	a										
Penrith North Lakes	d								10 55		
Carlisle 8	a								11 12		
	d								11 13		
Lockerbie	d								11 32		
Carstairs	a										
Motherwell	a										
Glasgow Central 15	a										
Haymarket	a								12s32		
Edinburgh 10	a								12 39		
Perth	a										
Dundee	a										
Aberdeen	a										
Inverness	a										

A not 11 December

OVERNIGHT SLEEPERS. For sleeper trains, operated by First ScotRail, please refer to Tables 400 - 404

London and West Midlands - North West England and Scotland

Route Diagram - see first Page of Table 65

		TP		VT	VT	TP	VT	VT	VT	LM	XC	VT	TP	VT	VT
		◇1		◇1	◇1	◇1	◇1	◇1	◇1	◇1	◇1	◇1	◇1	◇1	◇1
London Euston 15	d				08 10			08 15	08 20					08 45	
Watford Junction	d														
Milton Keynes Central	d				08 56				09 06					09 32	
Rugby	d													10 09	
Nuneaton	d							09 44							
Tamworth Low Level	d														
Lichfield Trent Valley	d														
Coventry	d														
Birmingham International	d														
Birmingham New Street 12	d			09 20						09 42	10 01				10 20
Wolverhampton 7	d			09 37						10 00	10 19				10 37
Penkridge	d									10 10					
Stafford	a							10 08		10 16	10 32				
	d							10 08		10 17	10 33				
Stoke-on-Trent	a								10 19		10 51				
Congleton	a														
Macclesfield	a								10 36		11 08				
Crewe 10	a			10 07	10 17			10 28		10 37				10 55	11 07
	d			10 08	10 19		10 21	10 30		10 38		10 42		10 57	11 09
Chester	a											11 02			
	d											11 07			
Wrexham General	a														
Llandudno	a														
Bangor (Gwynedd)	a											12 09			
Holyhead	a											12 43			
Wilmslow	a				10 33										
Stockport	a				10 43				10 50		11 22				
Manchester Piccadilly 10	a				10 55				11 03		11 31				
Hartford	a									10 50					
Warrington Bank Quay	a			10 26			10 37							11 14	11 26
	d			10 27			10 37							11 14	11 27
Runcorn	a							10 47		11 00					
Liverpool South Parkway 7	a									11 09					
Liverpool Lime Street 10	a							11 09		11 21					
	d														
Manchester Airport	d	09 29				10 00							10 30		
Manchester Piccadilly 10	d	09 46				10 16							10 46		
Bolton	d	10 05				10 33							11 05		
Wigan North Western	a			10 37			10 48							11 25	11 37
	d			10 38			10 48							11 25	11 38
Preston 8	a	10 33		10 51		10 57	11 02						11 33	11 38	11 51
Preston 8	d	10 35	10 41	10 52		10 58	11 04						11 35	11 40	11 53
Blackpool North	a	11 01											12 01		
Lancaster 6	a		10 56	11 07		11 13	11 20							11 54	12 08
	d		10 57	11 08		11 14								11 55	12 08
Barrow-in-Furness	a		12 00												
Oxenholme Lake District	a			11 22		11 28								12 08	12 22
	d			11 23		11 28								12 08	12 24
Windermere	a														
Penrith North Lakes	d					11 53								12 34	
Carlisle 8	a			12 01		12 10								12 49	13 01
	d			12 02		12 11								12 50	13 03
Lockerbie	d					12 30									
Carstairs	a														
Motherwell	a														
Glasgow Central 15	a			13 17		13 35								14 01	
Haymarket	a														14 13
Edinburgh 10	a														14 22
Perth	a														
Dundee	a														
Aberdeen	a														
Inverness	a														

OVERNIGHT SLEEPERS. For sleeper trains, operated by First ScotRail, please refer to Tables 400 - 404

London and West Midlands - North West England and Scotland

Route Diagram - see first Page of Table 65

Station		VT	VT	LM	XC	TP	VT	TP	VT	TP	VT	VT	LM	XC
		◇1	◇1	◇1	◇1	◇1	◇1	◇1	◇1	◇1	◇1	◇1	◇1	◇1
		⊡	⊡		⚒		⊡		⊡	⚒	⊡	⊡		⚒
London Euston 15 ⊖	d	09 15	09 20				09 45				10 15	10 20		
Watford Junction	d													
Milton Keynes Central	d		10 07				10 33					11 07		
Rugby	d						11 09							
Nuneaton	d	10 45									11 47			
Tamworth Low Level	d													
Lichfield Trent Valley	d													
Coventry	d				10 28									11 29
Birmingham International ✈	d				10 40									11 40
Birmingham New Street 12	d			10 42	11 01				11 20				11 42	12 01
Wolverhampton 7	d			11 00	11 19				11 37				12 00	12 19
Penkridge	d			11 10									12 10	
Stafford	a	11 09		11 16	11 31						12 13		12 16	12 32
	d	11 09		11 17	11 32						12 13		12 17	12 33
Stoke-on-Trent	a		11 20		11 51							12 24		12 52
Congleton	a													
Macclesfield	a		11 37		12 09							12 40		13 10
Crewe 10	a	11 30		11 37			11 55		12 07		12 32		12 37	
	d	11 32		11 38			11 57		12 09		12 34		12 38	
Chester	a													
	d													
Wrexham General	a													
Llandudno	a													
Bangor (Gwynedd)	a													
Holyhead	a													
Wilmslow	a													
Stockport	a		11 51		12 22							12 55		13 28
Manchester Piccadilly 10	a		12 04		12 40							13 08		13 40
Hartford	a			11 50									12 50	
Warrington Bank Quay	a						12 14		12 26					
	d						12 14		12 27					
Runcorn	a	11 49		12 01							12 51		13 01	
Liverpool South Parkway 7 ✈	a			12 10									13 10	
Liverpool Lime Street 10	a	12 10		12 21							13 12		13 21	
	d													
Manchester Airport ✈	d					11 30				12 00				
Manchester Piccadilly 10	d					11 46				12 16				
Bolton	d					12 05				12 33				
Wigan North Western	a						12 25		12 37					
	d						12 25		12 38					
Preston 8	a					12 33	12 38		12 51	12 57				
Preston 8	d					12 35	12 40	12 48	12 53	12 58				
Blackpool North	a					13 01								
Lancaster 6	a						12 54	13 03	13 08	13 13				
	d						12 55	13 04	13 08	13 14				
Barrow-in-Furness	a							14 07						
Oxenholme Lake District	a						13 08		13 22	13 28				
	d						13 08		13 24	13 28				
Windermere	a													
Penrith North Lakes	d						13 34			13 53				
Carlisle 8	a						13 49		14 01	14 10				
	d						13 50		14 03	14 11				
Lockerbie	d									14 30				
Carstairs	a													
Motherwell	a													
Glasgow Central 15	a						15 02		15 16					
Haymarket	a									15s29				
Edinburgh 10	a									15 39				
Perth	a													
Dundee	a													
Aberdeen	a													
Inverness	a													

OVERNIGHT SLEEPERS. For sleeper trains, operated by First ScotRail, please refer to Tables 400 - 404

until 1 January

London and West Midlands - North West England and Scotland

Route Diagram - see first Page of Table 65

Station		TP	VT	VT	VT	VT	TP	LM	VT	VT	XC	TP	VT	VT	VT
		◇1	◇1	◇1	◇1	◇1	◇1	◇1	◇1	◇1	◇1	◇1	◇1	◇1	◇1
			⊡	⊡	⊡	⊡	⚒		⊡	⊡	⚒		⊡	⊡	⊡
London Euston 15 ⊖	d		10 45		11 15	11 20			12 02	12 15			12 25		12 35
Watford Junction	d														
Milton Keynes Central	d		11 33		12 03	12 08				12 48					
Rugby	d		12 09												
Nuneaton	d														
Tamworth Low Level	d														
Lichfield Trent Valley	d														
Coventry	d										12 28				
Birmingham International ✈	d										12 40				
Birmingham New Street 12	d			12 20				12 35			13 01			13 20	
Wolverhampton 7	d			12 37				12 53			13 19			13 37	
Penkridge	d							13 03							
Stafford	a				12 53			13 09	13 24		13 33				
	d				12 53			13 09	13 25		13 34				
Stoke-on-Trent	a					13 09				13 50	13 56				
Congleton	a														
Macclesfield	a					13 26					14 14				
Crewe 10	a		12 56	13 07	13 13			13 30	13 43					14 07	14 12
	d		12 58	13 09	13 15			13 31	13 45					14 09	14 13
Chester	a														
	d														
Wrexham General	a														
Llandudno	a														
Bangor (Gwynedd)	a														
Holyhead	a														
Wilmslow	a														14 29
Stockport	a					13 41				14 18	14 28				14 38
Manchester Piccadilly 10	a					13 53				14 29	14 40				14 50
Hartford	a							13 43							
Warrington Bank Quay	a		13 15	13 26									14 16	14 26	
	d		13 15	13 27									14 16	14 27	
Runcorn	a				13 32			13 54	14 02						
Liverpool South Parkway 7 ✈	a							14 03							
Liverpool Lime Street 10	a				13 54			14 14	14 24						
	d														
Manchester Airport ✈	d	12 30					12 59					13 30			
Manchester Piccadilly 10	d	12 46					13 16					13 46			
Bolton	d	13 05					13 33					14 05			
Wigan North Western	a		13 26	13 37									14 27	14 37	
	d		13 26	13 38									14 27	14 38	
Preston 8	a	13 33	13 40	13 51			13 57					14 33	14 40	14 50	
Preston 8	d	13 35	13 42	13 53			14 00					14 35	14 42	14 53	
Blackpool North	a	14 01										15 01			
Lancaster 6	a		13 56	14 08			14 15						14 56	15 08	
	d		13 57	14 08			14 16						14 58	15 09	
Barrow-in-Furness	a														
Oxenholme Lake District	a		14 10				14 30							15 22	
	d		14 10				14 30							15 24	
Windermere	a														
Penrith North Lakes	d		14 36	14 45			14 55						15 32		
Carlisle 8	a		14 51	15 00			15 12						15 47	16 01	
	d		14 52	15 03			15 17						15 48	16 03	
Lockerbie	d														
Carstairs	a														
Motherwell	a														
Glasgow Central 15	a		16 05				16 35						17 00	17 17	
Haymarket	a			16 14											
Edinburgh 10	a			16 22											
Perth	a														
Dundee	a														
Aberdeen	a														
Inverness	a														

OVERNIGHT SLEEPERS. For sleeper trains, operated by First ScotRail, please refer to Tables 400 - 404

London and West Midlands - North West England and Scotland

Route Diagram - see first Page of Table 65

		XC ◇1	VT ◇1	TP ◇1	LM ◇1	VT ◇1	VT ◇1	XC ◇1	TP ◇1	VT ◇1	VT ◇1	VT ◇1	XC ◇1	VT ◇1	TP ◇1
London Euston 15 ⊖	d		12 55			13 02	13 15			13 25		13 35		13 55	
Watford Junction	d														
Milton Keynes Central	d						13 48								
Rugby	d														
Nuneaton	d														
Tamworth Low Level	d														
Lichfield Trent Valley	d														
Coventry	d							13 26							
Birmingham International ✈	d							13 38							
Birmingham New Street 12	d	13 31			13 35			14 01			14 20		14 31		
Wolverhampton 7	d	13 49			13 53			14 19			14 37		14 49		
Penkridge	d				14 03										
Stafford	a				14 09	14 21		14 33							
	d				14 09	14 22		14 34							
Stoke-on-Trent	a	14 19	14 26				14 50	14 56					15 19	15 25	
Congleton	a														
Macclesfield	a		14 42					15 14						15 42	
Crewe 10	a				14 29	14 43					15 07	15 12			
	d				14 31	14 45					15 09	15 13			
Chester	a														
	d														
Wrexham General	a														
Llandudno	a														
Bangor (Gwynedd)	a														
Holyhead	a														
Wilmslow	a											15 29			
Stockport	a		14 56				15 18	15 28				15 38		15 56	
Manchester Piccadilly 10	a	14 57	15 09				15 29	15 40				15 50	15 59	16 09	
Hartford	a				14 42										
Warrington Bank Quay	a									15 16	15 26				
	d									15 16	15 27				
Runcorn	a				14 53	15 02									
Liverpool South Parkway 7 ✈	a				15 02										
Liverpool Lime Street 10	a				15 14	15 24									
	d														
Manchester Airport ✈	d			14 00					14 30						15 00
Manchester Piccadilly 10	d			14 16					14 46						15 16
Bolton	d			14 33					15 05						15 33
Wigan North Western	a									15 27	15 37				
	d									15 27	15 38				
Preston 8	a			14 57					15 33	15 40	15 51				15 57
Preston 8	d			15 00					15 35	15 42	15 53				16 00
Blackpool North	a								16 01						
Lancaster 6	a			15 15						15 56	16 08				16 15
	d			15 16						15 58	16 08				16 16
Barrow-in-Furness	a														17 19
Oxenholme Lake District	a			15 30						16 10					
	d			15 30						16 11					
Windermere	a														
Penrith North Lakes	d			15 55							16 45				
Carlisle 8	a			16 12						16 48	17 00				
	d			16 13						16 49	17 02				
Lockerbie	d			16 32											
Carstairs	a														
Motherwell	a														
Glasgow Central 15	a									18 01					
Haymarket	a			17s30							18 13				
Edinburgh 10	a			17 39							18 22				
Perth	a														
Dundee	a														
Aberdeen	a														
Inverness	a														

OVERNIGHT SLEEPERS. For sleeper trains, operated by First ScotRail, please refer to Tables 400 - 404

London and West Midlands - North West England and Scotland

Route Diagram - see first Page of Table 65

		LM ◇1	VT ◇1	VT ◇1	XC ◇1	TP ◇1	VT ◇1	VT ◇1	VT ◇1	XC ◇1	VT ◇1	TP ◇1	LM ◇1	VT ◇1	VT ◇1	VT ◇1	XC ◇1
London Euston 15 ⊖	d		14 02	14 15			14 25		14 35		14 55			15 02	15 05	15 15	
Watford Junction	d																
Milton Keynes Central	d			14 48											15 39	15 48	
Rugby	d																
Nuneaton	d																
Tamworth Low Level	d																
Lichfield Trent Valley	d																
Coventry	d				14 26												15 26
Birmingham International ✈	d				14 38												15 38
Birmingham New Street 12	d	14 35			15 01			15 20		15 31			15 35				16 01
Wolverhampton 7	d	14 53			15 19			15 37		15 49			15 53				16 19
Penkridge	d	15 03											16 03				
Stafford	a	15 09	15 24		15 33								16 09	16 20			16 34
	d	15 09	15 25		15 34								16 09	16 21			16 34
Stoke-on-Trent	a			15 50	15 56					16 19	16 24					16 50	16 56
Congleton	a																
Macclesfield	a				16 14						16 42						17 14
Crewe 10	a	15 29	15 43					16 07	16 12				16 29		16 50		
	d	15 31	15 45					16 09	16 13				16 31		16 52		
Chester	a														17 14		
	d																
Wrexham General	a																
Llandudno	a																
Bangor (Gwynedd)	a																
Holyhead	a																
Wilmslow	a								16 29								
Stockport	a			16 18	16 28				16 38		16 56					17 18	17 28
Manchester Piccadilly 10	a			16 29	16 40				16 50	16 59	17 09					17 29	17 40
Hartford	a	15 42											16 43				
Warrington Bank Quay	a						16 16	16 26									
	d						16 16	16 27									
Runcorn	a	15 53	16 02										16 54	16 57			
Liverpool South Parkway 7 ✈	a	16 02											17 03				
Liverpool Lime Street 10	a	16 14	16 24										17 14	17 16			
	d																
Manchester Airport ✈	d					15 30						16 00					
Manchester Piccadilly 10	d					15 46						16 16					
Bolton	d					16 05						16 33					
Wigan North Western	a						16 27	16 37									
	d						16 27	16 38									
Preston 8	a					16 33	16 40	16 51				16 57					
Preston 8	d					16 35	16 42	16 53				17 00					
Blackpool North	a					17 01											
Lancaster 6	a						16 56	17 08				17 15					
	d						16 57	17 08				17 16					
Barrow-in-Furness	a																
Oxenholme Lake District	a							17 22				17 30					
	d							17 23				17 30					
Windermere	a																
Penrith North Lakes	d						17 32					17 55					
Carlisle 8	a						17 47	18 01				18 12					
	d						17 48	18 03				18 13					
Lockerbie	d																
Carstairs	a																
Motherwell	a																
Glasgow Central 15	a						19 00	19 17									
Haymarket	a											19s28					
Edinburgh 10	a											19 35					
Perth	a																
Dundee	a																
Aberdeen	a																
Inverness	a																

OVERNIGHT SLEEPERS. For sleeper trains, operated by First ScotRail, please refer to Tables 400 - 404

London and West Midlands - North West England and Scotland

Route Diagram - see first Page of Table 65

		TP	VT	VT	VT	XC	VT	TP	LM	VT	VT	VT	XC	TP	VT	VT	VT
		◇1	◇1	◇1	◇1	◇1	◇1	◇1	◇1	◇1	◇1	◇1	◇1	◇1	◇1	◇1	◇1
London Euston 15 ⊖	d		15 25		15 35		15 55			16 02	16 05	16 15			16 25		16 35
Watford Junction	d																
Milton Keynes Central	d										16 39	16 48					
Rugby	d																
Nuneaton	d																
Tamworth Low Level	d																
Lichfield Trent Valley	d																
Coventry	d												16 26				
Birmingham International ✈	d												16 38				
Birmingham New Street 12	d			16 20		16 31			16 35				17 01			17 20	
Wolverhampton 7	d			16 37		16 49			16 53				17 19			17 37	
Penkridge	d								17 03								
Stafford	a								17 09	17 24			17 35				
	d								17 09	17 25			17 36				
Stoke-on-Trent	a					17 19	17 25					17 50	17 56				
Congleton	a																
Macclesfield	a						17 42						18 14				
Crewe 10	a			17 07	17 12				17 30		17 50					18 07	18 12
	d			17 09	17 13				17 31		17 52					18 09	18 13
Chester	a										18 14						
	d																
Wrexham General	a																
Llandudno	a																
Bangor (Gwynedd)	a																
Holyhead	a																
Wilmslow	a				17 29												18 29
Stockport	a				17 38		17 56					18 18	18 28				18 38
Manchester Piccadilly 10	a				17 50	17 56	18 09					18 29	18 40				18 50
Hartford	a								17 43								
Warrington Bank Quay	a		17 16	17 26											18 16	18 26	
	d		17 16	17 27											18 17	18 27	
Runcorn	a								17 54	17 57							
Liverpool South Parkway 7 ✈	a								18 03								
Liverpool Lime Street 10	a								18 14	18 16							
	d																
Manchester Airport ✈	d	16 30						17 00						17 30			
Manchester Piccadilly 10	d	16 46						17 16						17 46			
Bolton	d	17 05						17 33						18 05			
Wigan North Western	a		17 27	17 37											18 27	18 37	
	d		17 27	17 38											18 28	18 38	
Preston 8	a	17 33	17 40	17 51				17 57						18 33	18 40	18 51	
Preston 8	d	17 35	17 42	17 53				18 00						18 35	18 42	18 53	
Blackpool North	a	18 01												19 01			
Lancaster 6	a		17 56	18 08				18 15							18 56	19 08	
	d		17 57	18 08				18 16							18 58	19 08	
Barrow-in-Furness	a																
Oxenholme Lake District	a		18 10	18 22				18 30							19 10	19 22	
	d		18 10	18 23				18 30							19 11	19 24	
Windermere	a																
Penrith North Lakes	d			18 49				18 55							19 36		
Carlisle 8	a		18 48	19 04				19 12							19 51	20 01	
	d		18 49	19 04				19 13							19 53	20 03	
Lockerbie	d							19 32									
Carstairs	a																
Motherwell	a							20s18									
Glasgow Central 15	a		20 01					20 35							21 09	21 17	
Haymarket	a																
Edinburgh 10	a			20 22													
Perth	a																
Dundee	a																
Aberdeen	a																
Inverness	a																

OVERNIGHT SLEEPERS. For sleeper trains, operated by First ScotRail, please refer to Tables 400 - 404

London and West Midlands - North West England and Scotland

Route Diagram - see first Page of Table 65

		XC	VT	TP		LM	VT	VT	VT	XC	TP	VT	VT	VT	XC	VT	TP
		◇1	◇1	◇1		◇1	◇1	◇1	◇1	◇1	◇1	◇1	◇1	◇1	◇1	◇1	◇1
London Euston 15 ⊖	d		16 55				17 02	17 05	17 15			17 25		17 35		17 55	
Watford Junction	d																
Milton Keynes Central	d							17 39	17 48								
Rugby	d																
Nuneaton	d							18 10									
Tamworth Low Level	d																
Lichfield Trent Valley	d																
Coventry	d									17 26							
Birmingham International ✈	d									17 38							
Birmingham New Street 12	d	17 31				17 35				18 01			18 20		18 31		
Wolverhampton 7	d	17 49				17 53				18 19			18 37		18 49		
Penkridge	d					18 03											
Stafford	a					18 09	18 24			18 35							
	d					18 09	18 25			18 36							
Stoke-on-Trent	a	18 19	18 25						18 50	18 56					19 19	19 25	
Congleton	a																
Macclesfield	a		18 42							19 15						19 42	
Crewe 10	a					18 30		18 53					19 07	19 12			
	d					18 31		18 56					19 09	19 13			
Chester	a							19 14									
	d							19 22									
Wrexham General	a																
Llandudno	a																
Bangor (Gwynedd)	a							20 27									
Holyhead	a							20 59									
Wilmslow	a													19 29			
Stockport	a		18 56						19 18	19 28				19 38		19 56	
Manchester Piccadilly 10	a	18 56	19 09						19 29	19 40				19 50	19 58	20 09	
Hartford	a					18 43											
Warrington Bank Quay	a											19 16	19 26				
	d											19 16	19 27				
Runcorn	a					18 54	18 57										
Liverpool South Parkway 7 ✈	a					19 03											
Liverpool Lime Street 10	a					19 14	19 19										
	d																
Manchester Airport ✈	d			18 00							18 30						19 00
Manchester Piccadilly 10	d			18 16							18 46						19 16
Bolton	d			18 33							19 05						19 33
Wigan North Western	a											19 27	19 37				
	d											19 27	19 38				
Preston 8	a			18 57							19 33	19 40	19 51				19 57
Preston 8	d			19 00	19 06						19 35	19 42	19 53				20 06
Blackpool North	a										20 01						
Lancaster 6	a			19 15	19 22							19 56	20 08				20 21
	d			19 16	19 22							19 57	20 08				20 22
Barrow-in-Furness	a				20 26												21 17
Oxenholme Lake District	a			19 30								20 10					
	d			19 30								20 10					
Windermere	a																
Penrith North Lakes	d			19 55								20 36	20 45				
Carlisle 8	a			20 12								20 51	21 00				
	d			20 13								20 52	21 02				
Lockerbie	d			20 32													
Carstairs	a																
Motherwell	a																
Glasgow Central 15	a											22 07					
Haymarket	a			21s30									22 15				
Edinburgh 10	a			21 39									22 21				
Perth	a																
Dundee	a																
Aberdeen	a																
Inverness	a																

OVERNIGHT SLEEPERS. For sleeper trains, operated by First ScotRail, please refer to Tables 400 - 404

Table 65

Sundays until 1 January

London and West Midlands - North West England and Scotland

Route Diagram - see first Page of Table 65

		LM	VT	VT	VT	XC	TP	VT	VT	VT	XC	VT	LM	VT	VT
		◇1	◇1	◇1	◇1	◇1	◇1	◇1	1	◇1	◇1	◇1	◇1	◇1	◇1
London Euston 15 ⊖	d		18 02	18 05	18 15			18 25		18 35		18 55		19 02	19 05
Watford Junction	d														
Milton Keynes Central	d			18 39	18 48										19 39
Rugby	d														
Nuneaton	d													20 01	
Tamworth Low Level	d														
Lichfield Trent Valley	d														
Coventry	d					18 26									
Birmingham International ✈	d					18 38									
Birmingham New Street 12	d	18 35				19 01			19 20		19 31		19 35		
Wolverhampton 7	d	18 53				19 19			19 37		19 49		19 53		
Penkridge	d	19 03											20 03		
Stafford	a	19 09	19 24			19 37							20 09	20 25	
	d	19 09	19 25			19 38							20 09	20 30	
Stoke-on-Trent	a				19 50	19 56					20 19	20 25			
Congleton	a														
Macclesfield	a					20 14						20 42			
Crewe 10	a	19 29		19 50					20 07	20 12			20 30	20 48	20 53
	d	19 31		19 52					20 09	20 13			20 31	20 50	20 55
Chester	a			20 11											21 14
	d			20 18											21 17
Wrexham General	a														
Llandudno	a														
Bangor (Gwynedd)	a			21 23											22 22
Holyhead	a			21 57											22 56
Wilmslow	a									20 29					
Stockport	a				20 18	20 28				20 38		20 56			
Manchester Piccadilly 10	a				20 29	20 40				20 50	21 00	21 09			
Hartford	a	19 42											20 43		
Warrington Bank Quay	a							20 16	20 26						
	d							20 16	20 27						
Runcorn	a	19 53	19 58										20 54	21 07	
Liverpool South Parkway 7 ✈	a	20 02											21 03		
Liverpool Lime Street 10	a	20 14	20 16										21 14	21 28	
	d														
Manchester Airport ✈	d						19 30								
Manchester Piccadilly 10	d						19 46								
Bolton	d						20 05								
Wigan North Western	a							20 27	20 37						
	d							20 27	20 38						
Preston 8	a						20 33	20 40	20 51						
Preston 8	d						20 35	20 42	20 53						
Blackpool North	a						21 01								
Lancaster 6	a							20 56	21 08						
	d							20 57	21 08						
Barrow-in-Furness	a														
Oxenholme Lake District	a							21 10	21 22						
	d							21 11	21 24						
Windermere	a														
Penrith North Lakes	d							21 36							
Carlisle 8	a							21 51	22 01						
	d							21 52	22 03						
Lockerbie	d								22 23						
Carstairs	a														
Motherwell	a							22 48	23 07						
Glasgow Central 15	a							23 09	23 22						
Haymarket	a														
Edinburgh 10	a														
Perth	a														
Dundee	a														
Aberdeen	a														
Inverness	a														

OVERNIGHT SLEEPERS. For sleeper trains, operated by First ScotRail, please refer to Tables 400 - 404

Table 65

Sundays until 1 January

London and West Midlands - North West England and Scotland

Route Diagram - see first Page of Table 65

		VT	XC	VT	TP	VT	VT	XC	VT	VT	VT	VT	XC
		◇1	◇1	◇1	◇1	◇1	◇1	◇1	◇1	◇1	◇1	◇1	◇1
			A										A
London Euston 15 ⊖	d	19 15				19 25	19 35		19 55	20 02	20 05	20 15	
Watford Junction	d												
Milton Keynes Central	d	19 48									20 38	20 48	
Rugby	d												
Nuneaton	d									21 01			
Tamworth Low Level	d												
Lichfield Trent Valley	d												
Coventry	d		19 26										20 26
Birmingham International ✈	d		19 38										20 38
Birmingham New Street 12	d		20 01	20 20				20 31					21 01
Wolverhampton 7	d		20 19	20 38				20 52					21 19
Penkridge	d												
Stafford	a		20 36	20 51							21 31		21 36
	d		20 37	20 52							21 33		21 37
Stoke-on-Trent	a	20 50	20 56					21 19	21 25			21 50	21 56
Congleton	a												
Macclesfield	a		21 15						21 42				22 14
Crewe 10	a			21 10			21 13			21 44	21 53		
	d						21 14			21 46	21 55		
Chester	a												
	d												
Wrexham General	a												
Llandudno	a												
Bangor (Gwynedd)	a												
Holyhead	a												
Wilmslow	a						21 30						
Stockport	a	21 18	21 28				21 39		21 56			22 18	22 28
Manchester Piccadilly 10	a	21 29	21 40				21 50	21 56	22 09			22 29	22 40
Hartford	a												
Warrington Bank Quay	a					21 16							
	d					21 16							
Runcorn	a									22 03	22 12		
Liverpool South Parkway 7 ✈	a												
Liverpool Lime Street 10	a									22 23	22 33		
	d												
Manchester Airport ✈	d				20 30								
Manchester Piccadilly 10	d				20 46								
Bolton	d				21 05								
Wigan North Western	a					21 27							
	d					21 27							
Preston 8	a				21 33	21 40							
Preston 8	d				21 35	21 42							
Blackpool North	a				22 01								
Lancaster 6	a					21 56							
	d					21 57							
Barrow-in-Furness	a												
Oxenholme Lake District	a					22 10							
	d					22 11							
Windermere	a												
Penrith North Lakes	d					22 36							
Carlisle 8	a					22 51							
	d					22 53							
Lockerbie	d												
Carstairs	a												
Motherwell	a												
Glasgow Central 15	a					00 02							
Haymarket	a												
Edinburgh 10	a												
Perth	a												
Dundee	a												
Aberdeen	a												
Inverness	a												

A to Birmingham New Street

OVERNIGHT SLEEPERS. For sleeper trains, operated by First ScotRail, please refer to Tables 400 - 404

Sundays
until 1 January

London and West Midlands - North West England and Scotland

Route Diagram - see first Page of Table 65

		TP	VT	VT	VT	LM	XC	VT	SR	VT	VT	AW	VT	SR
		◇1	◇1	◇1	◇1	◇1	◇1	◇1		◇1	◇1	◇	◇1	
London Euston 15 ⊖	d		20 25		20 35			20 50	20 55	21 21	21 25		21 51	23 27
Watford Junction	d								21u17					23u47
Milton Keynes Central	d							21 37			22 14		22 38	
Rugby	d							22 01					23 18	
Nuneaton	d									22 52			23 29	
Tamworth Low Level	d		21 32											
Lichfield Trent Valley	d		21 39											
Coventry	d						21 26							
Birmingham International ✈	d						21 38					22 40		
Birmingham New Street 12	d			21 20		21 35	22b01					22 55		
Wolverhampton 7	d			21 38		21 57	22 19					23 15		
Penkridge	d					22 07								
Stafford	a			21 56	21 59	22 13	22 36			23 16		23 30	23s53	
	d			21 57	22 00	22 16	22 37			23 17		23 31		
Stoke-on-Trent	a						22 55				23 29			
Congleton	a													
Macclesfield	a						23 12				23 45			
Crewe 10	a		22 10	22 17	22 20	22 38		22 49		23 43		23 55	00s21	
	d		22 13	22 18	22 21			22 51	23u39	23 45		00 01		
Chester	a											00 22		
	d											00 38		
Wrexham General	a													
Llandudno	a													
Bangor (Gwynedd)	a											01 44		
Holyhead	a											02 20		
Wilmslow	a				22 36									
Stockport	a				22 45		23 27				23 59		00s50	
Manchester Piccadilly 10	a				22 57		23 41				00 12		01 00	
Hartford	a													
Warrington Bank Quay	a		22 29	22 36				23 08						
	d		22 30	22 36				23 08						
Runcorn	a									00 07				
Liverpool South Parkway 7 ✈	a													
Liverpool Lime Street 10	a									00 30				
	d													
Manchester Airport ✈	d	21 30												
Manchester Piccadilly 10	d	21 46												
Bolton	d	22 05												
Wigan North Western	a		22 40	22 47				23 19						
	d		22 41	22 47				23 19						
Preston 8	a	22 28	22 58	23 07				23 41						
Preston 8	d	22 29							00u30					
Blackpool North	a	22 55												
Lancaster 6	a													
	d													
Barrow-in-Furness	a													
Oxenholme Lake District	a													
	d													
Windermere	a													
Penrith North Lakes	d													
Carlisle 8	a													05s04
	d													
Lockerbie	d													
Carstairs	a													06s20
Motherwell	a													06s56
Glasgow Central 15	a													07 20
Haymarket	a													
Edinburgh 10	a								03s58					07 16
Perth	a								05s39					
Dundee	a								06s08					
Aberdeen	a								07 35					
Inverness	a								08 38					

OVERNIGHT SLEEPERS. For sleeper trains, operated by First ScotRail, please refer to Tables 400 - 404

Sundays
8 January to 12 February

London and West Midlands - North West England and Scotland

Route Diagram - see first Page of Table 65

		TP	XC	TP	TP	TP	TP	TP	VT	XC
		◇1	◇1			◇1	◇1		◇1	◇1
London Euston 15 ⊖	d									
Watford Junction	d									
Milton Keynes Central	d									
Rugby	d									
Nuneaton	d									
Tamworth Low Level	d									
Lichfield Trent Valley	d									
Coventry	d									
Birmingham International ✈	d									
Birmingham New Street 12	d		22p31						08 45	09 01
Wolverhampton 7	d		22p49						09 04	09 19
Penkridge	d									
Stafford	a		23p01						09 16	09 32
	d		23p02						09 17	09 33
Stoke-on-Trent	a		23p20							
Congleton	a									
Macclesfield	a		23p38							
Crewe 10	a								09 35	09 54
	d								09 37	09 56
Chester	a									
	d									
Wrexham General	a									
Llandudno	a									
Bangor (Gwynedd)	a									
Holyhead	a									
Wilmslow	a									10 12
Stockport	a		23p53							10 21
Manchester Piccadilly 10	a		00 10							10 37
Hartford	a									
Warrington Bank Quay	a								09 54	
	d								09 54	
Runcorn	a									
Liverpool South Parkway 7 ✈	a									
Liverpool Lime Street 10	a									
	d									
Manchester Airport ✈	d	22p29		00 05	05 30		08 47			
Manchester Piccadilly 10	d	22p46		00 30	05 55	07 50	09 03			
Bolton	d	23p07		00s55	06s20	08 09	09 23	09 30		
Wigan North Western	a						09 35		10 05	
	d						09 39		10 05	
Preston 8	a	23p33		01s30	06s55	08 52	09 55	10 11	10 22	
Preston 8	d	23p35				08 53	09 56			
Blackpool North	a	00 02		02 10	07 35	09 20	10 22			
Lancaster 6	a									
	d									
Barrow-in-Furness	a									
Oxenholme Lake District	a									
	d									
Windermere	a									
Penrith North Lakes	d									
Carlisle 8	a									
	d									
Lockerbie	d									
Carstairs	a									
Motherwell	a									
Glasgow Central 15	a									
Haymarket	a									
Edinburgh 10	a									
Perth	a									
Dundee	a									
Aberdeen	a									
Inverness	a									

OVERNIGHT SLEEPERS. For sleeper trains, operated by First ScotRail, please refer to Tables 400 - 404

Table 65

Sundays
8 January to 12 February

London and West Midlands - North West England and Scotland

Route Diagram - see first Page of Table 65

		TP	VT	VT	VT	VT	VT	LM	TP	XC	VT	TP	TP	TP	VT	VT	TP
		◇1	◇1	◇1	◇1	◇1	◇1	◇1	◇1	◇1	◇1	◇1	bus	◇1	◇1	◇1	◇1
London Euston 15 ⊖	d			08 10		08 15	08 20								08 45		
Watford Junction	d																
Milton Keynes Central	d			08 56			09 06								09 32		
Rugby	d														10 09		
Nuneaton	d					09 44											
Tamworth Low Level	d																
Lichfield Trent Valley	d																
Coventry	d																
Birmingham International ✈	d																
Birmingham New Street 12	d		09 20					09 42		10 01						10 20	
Wolverhampton 7	d		09 37					10 00		10 19						10 37	
Penkridge	d							10 10									
Stafford	a					10 08		10 16		10 32							
	d					10 08		10 17		10 33							
Stoke-on-Trent	a						10 19			10 51							
Congleton	a																
Macclesfield	a						10 36			11 08							
Crewe 10	a		10 07	10 17		10 28		10 37							10 55	11 07	
	d		10 08	10 19	10 21	10 30		10 38			10 42				10 57	11 09	
Chester	a										11 02						
	d										11 07						
Wrexham General	a																
Llandudno	a																
Bangor (Gwynedd)	a										12 09						
Holyhead	a										12 43						
Wilmslow	a			10 33													
Stockport	a			10 43			10 50			11 22							
Manchester Piccadilly 10	a			10 55			11 03			11 31							
Hartford	a							10 50									
Warrington Bank Quay	a		10 26		10 37										11 14	11 26	
	d		10 27		10 37										11 14	11 27	
Runcorn	a					10 47		11 00									
Liverpool South Parkway 7 ✈	a							11 09									
Liverpool Lime Street 10	a					11 09		11 21									
	d																
Manchester Airport ✈	d	09 29							10 00					10 30			11 00
Manchester Piccadilly 10	d	09 46							10 16					10 46			11 16
Bolton	d	10 05							10 33				10 40	11 05			11 33
Wigan North Western	a		10 37		10 48				10 45						11 25	11 37	
	d		10 38		10 48				10 51						11 25	11 38	
Preston 8	a	10 33	10 51		11 02				11 08				11 21	11 33	11 38	11 51	12 01
Preston 8	d	10 35	11 04						11 10			11 14		11 35	11 40	11 53	12 02
Blackpool North	a	11 01												12 01			
Lancaster 6	a		11 18						11 25			11 29			11 54	12 08	12 17
	d		11 19						11 26			11 30			11 55	12 08	12 18
Barrow-in-Furness	a											12 25					
Oxenholme Lake District	a		11 32						11 40						12 08	12 22	12 32
	d		11 33						11 40						12 08	12 24	12 32
Windermere	a																
Penrith North Lakes	d								12 05						12 34		12 57
Carlisle 8	a		12 11						12 22						12 49	13 01	13 14
	d		12 12						12 23						12 50	13 03	13 15
Lockerbie	d								12 42								13 36
Carstairs	a																
Motherwell	a																
Glasgow Central 15	a		13 22												14 01		14 35
Haymarket	a								13s41							14 13	
Edinburgh 10	a								13 48							14 22	
Perth	a																
Dundee	a																
Aberdeen	a																
Inverness	a																

OVERNIGHT SLEEPERS. For sleeper trains, operated by First ScotRail, please refer to Tables 400 - 404

Table 65

Sundays
8 January to 12 February

London and West Midlands - North West England and Scotland

Route Diagram - see first Page of Table 65

		VT	VT	LM	XC	LM	TP	TP	VT	TP	VT	TP	VT	VT	LM
		◇1	◇1	◇1	◇1	1	bus	◇1	◇1	◇1	◇1	◇1	◇1	◇1	◇1
London Euston 15 ⊖	d	09 15	09 20						09 45				10 15	10 20	
Watford Junction	d														
Milton Keynes Central	d		10 07						10 33					11 07	
Rugby	d								11 09						
Nuneaton	d	10 45											11 47		
Tamworth Low Level	d														
Lichfield Trent Valley	d														
Coventry	d				10 28										
Birmingham International ✈	d				10 40										
Birmingham New Street 12	d			10 42	11 01						11 20				11 42
Wolverhampton 7	d			11 00	11 19						11 37				12 00
Penkridge	d			11 10											12 10
Stafford	a	11 09		11 16	11 31								12 13		12 16
	d	11 09		11 17	11 32	11 45							12 13		12 17
Stoke-on-Trent	a		11 20		11 51	12 02								12 24	
Congleton	a														
Macclesfield	a		11 37		12 09									12 40	
Crewe 10	a	11 30		11 37		12 26			11 55		12 07		12 32		12 37
	d	11 32		11 38					11 57		12 09		12 34		12 38
Chester	a														
	d														
Wrexham General	a														
Llandudno	a														
Bangor (Gwynedd)	a														
Holyhead	a														
Wilmslow	a														
Stockport	a		11 51		12 22									12 55	
Manchester Piccadilly 10	a		12 04		12 40									13 08	
Hartford	a			11 50											12 50
Warrington Bank Quay	a								12 14		12 26				
	d								12 14		12 27				
Runcorn	a	11 49		12 01									12 51		13 01
Liverpool South Parkway 7 ✈	a			12 10											13 10
Liverpool Lime Street 10	a	12 10		12 21									13 12		13 21
	d														
Manchester Airport ✈	d							11 30				12 00			
Manchester Piccadilly 10	d							11 46				12 16			
Bolton	d						11 40	12 05				12 33			
Wigan North Western	a								12 25		12 37				
	d								12 25		12 38				
Preston 8	a						12 21	12 33	12 38		12 51	13 04			
Preston 8	d							12 35	12 40	12 48	12 53	13 04			
Blackpool North	a							13 01							
Lancaster 6	a								12 54	13 03	13 08	13 19			
	d								12 55	13 04	13 08	13 20			
Barrow-in-Furness	a									14 07					
Oxenholme Lake District	a								13 08		13 22	13 34			
	d								13 08		13 24	13 34			
Windermere	a														
Penrith North Lakes	d								13 34			13 59			
Carlisle 8	a								13 49		14 01	14 15			
	d								13 50		14 03	14 16			
Lockerbie	d														
Carstairs	a														
Motherwell	a														
Glasgow Central 15	a								15 02		15 16				
Haymarket	a											15s29			
Edinburgh 10	a											15 39			
Perth	a														
Dundee	a														
Aberdeen	a														
Inverness	a														

OVERNIGHT SLEEPERS. For sleeper trains, operated by First ScotRail, please refer to Tables 400 - 404

London and West Midlands - North West England and Scotland

Route Diagram - see first Page of Table 65

		XC	TP	TP	VT	VT	VT	VT	TP	LM	VT	VT	XC	TP
		◇1		◇1	◇1	◇1	◇1	◇1	◇1	◇1	◇1	◇1	◇1	
London Euston 15 ⊖	d				10 45		11 15	11 20			12 02	12 15		
Watford Junction	d													
Milton Keynes Central	d				11 33		12 03	12 08				12 48		
Rugby	d				12 09									
Nuneaton	d													
Tamworth Low Level	d													
Lichfield Trent Valley	d													
Coventry	d	11 29											12 28	
Birmingham International ✈	d	11 40											12 40	
Birmingham New Street 12	d	12 01				12 20				12 35			13 01	
Wolverhampton 7	d	12 19				12 37				12 53			13 19	
Penkridge	d									13 03				
Stafford	a	12 32					12 53			13 09	13 24		13 33	
	d	12 33					12 53			13 09	13 25		13 34	
Stoke-on-Trent	a	12 52						13 09				13 50	13 56	
Congleton	a													
Macclesfield	a	13 10						13 26					14 14	
Crewe 10	a				12 56	13 07	13 13			13 30	13 43			
	d				12 58	13 09	13 15			13 31	13 45			
Chester	a													
	d													
Wrexham General	a													
Llandudno	a													
Bangor (Gwynedd)	a													
Holyhead	a													
Wilmslow	a													
Stockport	a	13 28						13 41				14 18	14 28	
Manchester Piccadilly 10	a	13 40						13 53				14 29	14 40	
Hartford	a									13 43				
Warrington Bank Quay	a				13 15	13 26								
	d				13 15	13 27								
Runcorn	a						13 32			13 54	14 02			
Liverpool South Parkway 7 ✈	a									14 03				
Liverpool Lime Street 10	a						13 54			14 14	14 24			
	d													
Manchester Airport ✈	d			12 30					13 00					
Manchester Piccadilly 10	d			12 46					13 16					
Bolton	d		12 40	13 05					13 33					13 40
Wigan North Western	a				13 26	13 37								
	d				13 26	13 38								
Preston 8	a		13 21	13 33	13 40	13 51			14 02					14 21
Preston 8	d			13 35	13 42	13 53			14 02					
Blackpool North	a			14 01										
Lancaster 6	a				13 56	14 08			14 18					
	d				13 57	14 08			14 18					
Barrow-in-Furness	a													
Oxenholme Lake District	a				14 10				14 32					
	d				14 10				14 32					
Windermere	a													
Penrith North Lakes	d				14 36	14 45			14 57					
Carlisle 8	a				14 51	15 00			15 15					
	d				14 52	15 03			15 17					
Lockerbie	d													
Carstairs	a													
Motherwell	a													
Glasgow Central 15	a				16 05				16 35					
Haymarket	a					16 14								
Edinburgh 10	a					16 22								
Perth	a													
Dundee	a													
Aberdeen	a													
Inverness	a													

OVERNIGHT SLEEPERS. For sleeper trains, operated by First ScotRail, please refer to Tables 400 - 404

London and West Midlands - North West England and Scotland

Route Diagram - see first Page of Table 65

		TP	VT	VT	VT	XC	VT	TP	LM	VT	VT	XC	TP	TP	VT	VT	VT
		◇1	◇1	◇1	◇1	◇1	◇1	◇1	◇1	◇1	◇1	◇1		◇1	◇1	◇1	◇1
London Euston 15 ⊖	d		12 25		12 35		12 55			13 02	13 15				13 25		13 35
Watford Junction	d																
Milton Keynes Central	d										13 48						
Rugby	d																
Nuneaton	d																
Tamworth Low Level	d																
Lichfield Trent Valley	d																
Coventry	d											13 26					
Birmingham International ✈	d											13 38					
Birmingham New Street 12	d			13 20		13 31			13 35			14 01				14 20	
Wolverhampton 7	d			13 37		13 49			13 53			14 19				14 37	
Penkridge	d								14 03								
Stafford	a								14 09	14 21		14 33					
	d								14 09	14 22		14 34					
Stoke-on-Trent	a					14 19	14 26				14 50	14 56					
Congleton	a																
Macclesfield	a						14 42					15 14					
Crewe 10	a			14 07	14 12				14 29	14 43						15 07	15 12
	d			14 09	14 13				14 31	14 45						15 09	15 13
Chester	a																
	d																
Wrexham General	a																
Llandudno	a																
Bangor (Gwynedd)	a																
Holyhead	a																
Wilmslow	a				14 29												15 29
Stockport	a				14 38		14 56				15 18	15 28					15 38
Manchester Piccadilly 10	a				14 50	14 57	15 09				15 29	15 40					15 50
Hartford	a								14 42								
Warrington Bank Quay	a		14 16	14 26											15 16	15 26	
	d		14 16	14 27											15 16	15 27	
Runcorn	a								14 53	15 02							
Liverpool South Parkway 7 ✈	a								15 02								
Liverpool Lime Street 10	a								15 14	15 24							
	d																
Manchester Airport ✈	d	13 30						14 00						14 30			
Manchester Piccadilly 10	d	13 46						14 16						14 46			
Bolton	d	14 05						14 33					14 40	15 05			
Wigan North Western	a		14 27	14 37											15 27	15 37	
	d		14 27	14 38											15 27	15 38	
Preston 8	a	14 33	14 40	14 50				15 02					15 21	15 33	15 40	15 51	
Preston 8	d	14 35	14 42	14 53				15 03						15 35	15 42	15 53	
Blackpool North	a	15 01												16 01			
Lancaster 6	a		14 56	15 08											15 56	16 08	
	d		14 58	15 09											15 58	16 08	
Barrow-in-Furness	a																
Oxenholme Lake District	a			15 22				15 30							16 10		
	d			15 24				15 30							16 11		
Windermere	a																
Penrith North Lakes	d		15 32					15 55								16 45	
Carlisle 8	a		15 47	16 01				16 12							16 48	17 00	
	d		15 48	16 03				16 13							16 49	17 02	
Lockerbie	d							16 32									
Carstairs	a																
Motherwell	a																
Glasgow Central 15	a		17 00	17 17											18 01		
Haymarket	a							17s30								18 13	
Edinburgh 10	a							17 39								18 22	
Perth	a																
Dundee	a																
Aberdeen	a																
Inverness	a																

OVERNIGHT SLEEPERS. For sleeper trains, operated by First ScotRail, please refer to Tables 400 - 404

Table 65

Sundays
8 January to 12 February

London and West Midlands - North West England and Scotland

Route Diagram - see first Page of Table 65

		XC	VT	LM	VT	VT	XC	TP	TP	VT	VT	VT	XC	VT	TP	LM
		◇1	◇1	◇1	◇1	◇1	◇1		◇1	◇1	◇1	◇1	◇1	◇1	◇1	◇1
London Euston 15 ⊖	d		13 55		14 02	14 15				14 25		14 35		14 55		
Watford Junction	d															
Milton Keynes Central	d					14 48										
Rugby	d															
Nuneaton	d															
Tamworth Low Level	d															
Lichfield Trent Valley	d															
Coventry	d						14 26									
Birmingham International ✈	d						14 38									
Birmingham New Street 12	d	14 31		14 35			15 01				15 20		15 31			15 35
Wolverhampton 7	d	14 49		14 53			15 19				15 37		15 49			15 53
Penkridge	d			15 03												16 03
Stafford	a			15 09	15 24		15 33									16 09
	d			15 09	15 25		15 34									16 09
Stoke-on-Trent	a	15 19	15 25			15 50	15 56						16 19	16 24		
Congleton	a															
Macclesfield	a		15 42				16 14							16 42		
Crewe 10	a			15 29	15 43						16 07	16 12				16 29
	d			15 31	15 45						16 09	16 13				16 31
Chester	a															
	d															
Wrexham General	a															
Llandudno	a															
Bangor (Gwynedd)	a															
Holyhead	a															
Wilmslow	a											16 29				
Stockport	a		15 56			16 18	16 28					16 38		16 56		
Manchester Piccadilly 10	a	15 59	16 09			16 29	16 40					16 50	16 59	17 09		
Hartford	a			15 42												16 43
Warrington Bank Quay	a									16 16	16 26					
	d									16 16	16 27					
Runcorn	a			15 53	16 02											16 54
Liverpool South Parkway 7 ✈	a			16 02												17 03
Liverpool Lime Street 10	a			16 14	16 24											17 14
	d															
Manchester Airport ✈	d								15 30						16 00	
Manchester Piccadilly 10	d								15 46						16 16	
Bolton	d							15 40	16 05						16 33	
Wigan North Western	a									16 27	16 37					
	d									16 27	16 38					
Preston 8	a							16 21	16 33	16 40	16 51				17 02	
Preston 8	d								16 35	16 42	16 53				17 04	
Blackpool North	a								17 02							
Lancaster 6	a									16 56	17 08				17 19	
	d									16 57	17 08				17 20	
Barrow-in-Furness	a															
Oxenholme Lake District	a										17 22					
	d										17 23					
Windermere	a															
Penrith North Lakes	d									17 32					17 57	
Carlisle 8	a									17 47	18 01				18 13	
	d									17 48	18 03				18 15	
Lockerbie	d															
Carstairs	a															
Motherwell	a															
Glasgow Central 15	a									19 00	19 17					
Haymarket	a														19s28	
Edinburgh 10	a														19 35	
Perth	a															
Dundee	a															
Aberdeen	a															
Inverness	a															

OVERNIGHT SLEEPERS. For sleeper trains, operated by First ScotRail, please refer to Tables 400 - 404

Table 65

Sundays
8 January to 12 February

London and West Midlands - North West England and Scotland

Route Diagram - see first Page of Table 65

		VT	VT	VT	XC	TP	TP	VT	VT	VT	XC	VT	TP	LM	VT	VT	VT
		◇1	◇1	◇1	◇1		◇1	◇1	◇1	◇1	◇1	◇1	◇1	◇1	◇1	◇1	◇1
London Euston 15 ⊖	d	15 02	15 05	15 15				15 25		15 35		15 55			16 02	16 05	16 15
Watford Junction	d																
Milton Keynes Central	d		15 39	15 48												16 39	16 48
Rugby	d																
Nuneaton	d																
Tamworth Low Level	d																
Lichfield Trent Valley	d																
Coventry	d				15 26												
Birmingham International ✈	d				15 38												
Birmingham New Street 12	d				16 01				16 20		16 31			16 35			
Wolverhampton 7	d				16 19				16 37		16 49			16 53			
Penkridge	d													17 03			
Stafford	a	16 20			16 34									17 09	17 24		
	d	16 21			16 34									17 09	17 25		
Stoke-on-Trent	a			16 50	16 56						17 19	17 25					17 50
Congleton	a																
Macclesfield	a				17 14							17 42					
Crewe 10	a		16 50						17 07	17 12				17 30		17 50	
	d		16 52						17 09	17 13				17 31		17 52	
Chester	a		17 14													18 14	
	d																
Wrexham General	a																
Llandudno	a																
Bangor (Gwynedd)	a																
Holyhead	a																
Wilmslow	a									17 29							
Stockport	a			17 18	17 28					17 38		17 56					18 18
Manchester Piccadilly 10	a			17 29	17 40					17 50	17 56	18 09					18 29
Hartford	a													17 43			
Warrington Bank Quay	a							17 16	17 26								
	d							17 16	17 27								
Runcorn	a	16 57												17 54	17 57		
Liverpool South Parkway 7 ✈	a													18 03			
Liverpool Lime Street 10	a	17 16												18 14	18 16		
	d																
Manchester Airport ✈	d						16 30						17 00				
Manchester Piccadilly 10	d						16 46						17 16				
Bolton	d					16 40	17 05						17 33				
Wigan North Western	a							17 27	17 37								
	d							17 27	17 38								
Preston 8	a					17 21	17 33	17 40	17 51				18 02				
Preston 8	d						17 35	17 42	17 53				18 02				
Blackpool North	a						18 01										
Lancaster 6	a							17 56	18 08				18 18				
	d							17 57	18 08				18 18				
Barrow-in-Furness	a																
Oxenholme Lake District	a							18 10	18 22				18 32				
	d							18 10	18 23				18 32				
Windermere	a																
Penrith North Lakes	d								18 49				18 57				
Carlisle 8	a							18 48	19 04				19 15				
	d							18 49	19 04				19 15				
Lockerbie	d												19 35				
Carstairs	a																
Motherwell	a												20s22				
Glasgow Central 15	a							20 01					20 42				
Haymarket	a																
Edinburgh 10	a								20 22								
Perth	a																
Dundee	a																
Aberdeen	a																
Inverness	a																

OVERNIGHT SLEEPERS. For sleeper trains, operated by First ScotRail, please refer to Tables 400 - 404

Table 65

Sundays

8 January to 12 February

London and West Midlands - North West England and Scotland

Route Diagram - see first Page of Table 65

		XC	TP	TP	VT	VT	VT	XC	VT	TP	TP	LM	VT	VT	VT	XC
		◇1		◇1	◇1	◇1	◇1	◇1	◇1	◇1		◇1	◇1	◇1	◇1	◇1
London Euston 15 ⊖	d				16 25		16 35		16 55				17 02	17 05	17 15	
Watford Junction	d															
Milton Keynes Central	d													17 39	17 48	
Rugby	d															
Nuneaton	d													18 10		
Tamworth Low Level	d															
Lichfield Trent Valley	d															
Coventry	d	16 26														17 26
Birmingham International ✈	d	16 38														17 38
Birmingham New Street 12	d	17 01				17 20		17 31				17 35				18 01
Wolverhampton 7	d	17 19				17 37		17 49				17 53				18 19
Penkridge	d											18 03				
Stafford	a	17 35										18 09	18 24			18 35
	d	17 36										18 09	18 25			18 36
Stoke-on-Trent	a	17 56						18 19	18 25						18 50	18 56
Congleton	a															
Macclesfield	a	18 14							18 42							19 15
Crewe 10	a					18 07	18 12					18 30		18 53		
	d					18 09	18 13					18 31		18 56		
Chester	a													19 14		
	d													19 22		
Wrexham General	a															
Llandudno	a															
Bangor (Gwynedd)	a													20 27		
Holyhead	a													20 59		
Wilmslow	a						18 29									
Stockport	a	18 28					18 38		18 56						19 18	19 28
Manchester Piccadilly 10	a	18 40					18 50	18 56	19 09						19 29	19 40
Hartford	a											18 43				
Warrington Bank Quay	a				18 16	18 26										
	d				18 17	18 27										
Runcorn	a											18 54	18 57			
Liverpool South Parkway 7 ✈	a											19 03				
Liverpool Lime Street 10	a											19 14	19 19			
	d															
Manchester Airport ✈	d			17 30						18 00						
Manchester Piccadilly 10	d			17 46						18 16						
Bolton	d		17 40	18 05						18 33						
Wigan North Western	a				18 27	18 37										
	d				18 28	18 38										
Preston 8	a		18 21	18 33	18 40	18 51				19 02						
Preston 8	d			18 35	18 42	18 53				19 07	19 12					
Blackpool North	a			19 01												
Lancaster 6	a				18 56	19 08				19 22	19 28					
	d				18 58	19 08				19 23	19 28					
Barrow-in-Furness	a										20 32					
Oxenholme Lake District	a				19 10	19 22				19 37						
	d				19 11	19 24				19 37						
Windermere	a															
Penrith North Lakes	d				19 36					20 02						
Carlisle 8	a				19 51	20 01				20 19						
	d				19 53	20 03				20 20						
Lockerbie	d									20 39						
Carstairs	a															
Motherwell	a															
Glasgow Central 15	a				21 09	21 17										
Haymarket	a									21s44						
Edinburgh 10	a									21 51						
Perth	a															
Dundee	a															
Aberdeen	a															
Inverness	a															

OVERNIGHT SLEEPERS. For sleeper trains, operated by First ScotRail, please refer to Tables 400 - 404

Table 65

Sundays

8 January to 12 February

London and West Midlands - North West England and Scotland

Route Diagram - see first Page of Table 65

		TP	TP	VT	VT	VT	XC	VT	TP	LM	VT	VT	VT	XC	TP	TP	VT	VT
			◇1	◇1	◇1	◇1	◇1	◇1	◇1	◇1	◇1	◇1	◇1	◇1		◇1	◇1	1
London Euston 15 ⊖	d			17 25		17 35		17 55			18 02	18 05	18 15				18 25	
Watford Junction	d																	
Milton Keynes Central	d											18 39	18 48					
Rugby	d																	
Nuneaton	d																	
Tamworth Low Level	d																	
Lichfield Trent Valley	d																	
Coventry	d													18 26				
Birmingham International ✈	d													18 38				
Birmingham New Street 12	d				18 20		18 31			18 35				19 01				19 20
Wolverhampton 7	d				18 37		18 49			18 53				19 19				19 37
Penkridge	d									19 03								
Stafford	a									19 09	19 24			19 37				
	d									19 09	19 25			19 38				
Stoke-on-Trent	a						19 19	19 25					19 50	19 56				
Congleton	a																	
Macclesfield	a							19 42						20 14				
Crewe 10	a				19 07	19 12				19 29		19 50						20 07
	d				19 09	19 13				19 31		19 52						20 09
Chester	a											20 11						
	d											20 18						
Wrexham General	a																	
Llandudno	a																	
Bangor (Gwynedd)	a											21 23						
Holyhead	a											21 57						
Wilmslow	a					19 29												
Stockport	a					19 38		19 56					20 18	20 28				
Manchester Piccadilly 10	a					19 50	19 58	20 09					20 29	20 40				
Hartford	a									19 42								
Warrington Bank Quay	a			19 16	19 26												20 16	20 26
	d			19 16	19 27												20 16	20 27
Runcorn	a									19 53	19 58							
Liverpool South Parkway 7 ✈	a									20 02								
Liverpool Lime Street 10	a									20 14	20 16							
	d																	
Manchester Airport ✈	d		18 30						19 00							19 30		
Manchester Piccadilly 10	d		18 46						19 16							19 46		
Bolton	d	18 40	19 05						19 33						19 40	20 05		
Wigan North Western	a			19 27	19 37												20 27	20 37
	d			19 27	19 38												20 27	20 38
Preston 8	a	19 21	19 33	19 40	19 51				20 05						20 21	20 33	20 40	20 51
Preston 8	d		19 35	19 42	19 53				20 13							20 35	20 42	20 53
Blackpool North	a		20 01													21 01		
Lancaster 6	a			19 56	20 08				20 29								20 56	21 08
	d			19 57	20 08				20 29								20 57	21 08
Barrow-in-Furness	a								21 25									
Oxenholme Lake District	a			20 10													21 10	21 22
	d			20 10													21 11	21 24
Windermere	a																	
Penrith North Lakes	d			20 36	20 45												21 36	
Carlisle 8	a			20 51	21 00												21 51	22 01
	d			20 52	21 02												21 52	22 03
Lockerbie	d																	22 23
Carstairs	a																	
Motherwell	a																22 48	23 07
Glasgow Central 15	a			22 07													23 09	23 22
Haymarket	a				22 15													
Edinburgh 10	a				22 21													
Perth	a																	
Dundee	a																	
Aberdeen	a																	
Inverness	a																	

OVERNIGHT SLEEPERS. For sleeper trains, operated by First ScotRail, please refer to Tables 400 - 404

Table 65

Sundays

8 January to 12 February

London and West Midlands - North West England and Scotland

Route Diagram - see first Page of Table 65

		VT	XC	VT	LM	VT	VT	VT	XC	VT	TP	VT	VT	XC	VT	VT
		◇1	◇1	◇1	◇1	◇1	◇1	◇1	◇1	◇1	◇1	◇1	◇1	◇1	◇1	◇1
									A							
		🍴	⊼	🍴		🍴	🍴	🍴	⊼	🍴		🍴	🍴	⊼	🍴	🍴
London Euston 15 ⊖	d	18 35		18 55		19 02	19 05	19 15				19 25	19 35		19 55	20 02
Watford Junction	d															
Milton Keynes Central	d						19 39	19 48								
Rugby	d															
Nuneaton	d					20 01										21 01
Tamworth Low Level	d															
Lichfield Trent Valley	d															
Coventry	d								19 26							
Birmingham International ✈	d								19 38							
Birmingham New Street 12	d		19 31		19 35				20 01	20 20				20 31		
Wolverhampton 7	d		19 49		19 53				20 19	20 38				20 52		
Penkridge	d				20 03											
Stafford	a				20 09	20 25			20 36	20 51						
	d				20 09	20 30			20 37	20 52						
Stoke-on-Trent	a		20 19	20 25				20 50	20 56					21 19	21 25	
Congleton	a															
Macclesfield	a			20 42					21 15						21 42	
Crewe 10	a	20 12			20 30	20 48	20 53			21 10			21 13			21 44
	d	20 13			20 31	20 50	20 55						21 14			21 46
Chester	a						21 14									
	d						21 17									
Wrexham General	a															
Llandudno	a															
Bangor (Gwynedd)	a						22 22									
Holyhead	a						22 56									
Wilmslow	a	20 29											21 30			
Stockport	a	20 38		20 56				21 18	21 28				21 39		21 56	
Manchester Piccadilly 10	a	20 50	21 00	21 09				21 29	21 40				21 50	21 56	22 09	
Hartford	a				20 43											
Warrington Bank Quay	a											21 16				
	d											21 16				
Runcorn	a				20 54	21 07										22 03
Liverpool South Parkway 7 ✈	a				21 03											
Liverpool Lime Street 10	a				21 14	21 28										22 23
	d															
Manchester Airport ✈	d										20 30					
Manchester Piccadilly 10	d										20 46					
Bolton	d										21 05					
Wigan North Western	a											21 27				
	d											21 27				
Preston 8	a										21 33	21 40				
Preston 8	d										21 35	21 42				
Blackpool North	a										22 01					
Lancaster 6	a											21 56				
	d											21 57				
Barrow-in-Furness	a															
Oxenholme Lake District	a											22 10				
	d											22 11				
Windermere	a															
Penrith North Lakes	d											22 36				
Carlisle 8	a											22 51				
	d											22 53				
Lockerbie	d															
Carstairs	a															
Motherwell	a															
Glasgow Central 15	a											00 02				
Haymarket	a															
Edinburgh 10	a															
Perth	a															
Dundee	a															
Aberdeen	a															
Inverness	a															

A ⊼ to Birmingham New Street

OVERNIGHT SLEEPERS. For sleeper trains, operated by First ScotRail, please refer to Tables 400 - 404

Table 65

Sundays

8 January to 12 February

London and West Midlands - North West England and Scotland

Route Diagram - see first Page of Table 65

		VT	VT	XC	TP	VT	VT	VT	LM	XC	VT	TP
		◇1	◇1	◇1	◇1	◇1	◇1	◇1	◇1	◇1	◇1	◇1
				A								
		🍴	🍴	⊼		🍴	🍴	🍴			🍴	
London Euston 15 ⊖	d	20 05	20 15			20 25		20 35			20 50	
Watford Junction	d											
Milton Keynes Central	d	20 38	20 48								21 37	
Rugby	d										22 01	
Nuneaton	d											
Tamworth Low Level	d					21 32						
Lichfield Trent Valley	d					21 39						
Coventry	d			20 26						21 26		
Birmingham International ✈	d			20 38						21 38		
Birmingham New Street 12	d			21 01			21 20		21 35	22 01		
Wolverhampton 7	d			21 19			21 38		21 57	22 19		
Penkridge	d								22 07			
Stafford	a	21 31		21 36			21 56	21 59	22 13	22 36		
	d	21 33		21 37			21 57	22 00	22 16	22 37		
Stoke-on-Trent	a		21 50	21 56						22 55		
Congleton	a											
Macclesfield	a			22 14						23 12		
Crewe 10	a	21 53				22 10	22 17	22 20	22 38		22 49	
	d	21 55				22 13	22 18	22 21			22 51	
Chester	a											
	d											
Wrexham General	a											
Llandudno	a											
Bangor (Gwynedd)	a											
Holyhead	a											
Wilmslow	a							22 36				
Stockport	a		22 18	22 28				22 45		23 27		
Manchester Piccadilly 10	a		22 29	22 40				22 57		23 41		
Hartford	a											
Warrington Bank Quay	a					22 29	22 36				23 08	
	d					22 30	22 36				23 08	
Runcorn	a	22 12										
Liverpool South Parkway 7 ✈	a											
Liverpool Lime Street 10	a	22 33										
	d											
Manchester Airport ✈	d				21 30							22 30
Manchester Piccadilly 10	d				21 46							22 46
Bolton	d				22 05							23 05
Wigan North Western	a					22 40	22 47				23 19	
	d					22 41	22 47				23 19	
Preston 8	a				22 33	22 58	23 07				23 41	23 42
Preston 8	d				22 34							23 47
Blackpool North	a				23 00							00 14
Lancaster 6	a											
	d											
Barrow-in-Furness	a											
Oxenholme Lake District	a											
	d											
Windermere	a											
Penrith North Lakes	d											
Carlisle 8	a											
	d											
Lockerbie	d											
Carstairs	a											
Motherwell	a											
Glasgow Central 15	a											
Haymarket	a											
Edinburgh 10	a											
Perth	a											
Dundee	a											
Aberdeen	a											
Inverness	a											

A ⊼ to Birmingham New Street

OVERNIGHT SLEEPERS. For sleeper trains, operated by First ScotRail, please refer to Tables 400 - 404

Sundays

8 January to 12 February

London and West Midlands - North West England and Scotland

Route Diagram - see first Page of Table 65

		SR	VT	VT	AW	VT	SR
		🛏	◇1	◇1	◇	◇1	🛏
London Euston 15 ⊖	d	20 55	21 21	21 25		21 51	23 27
Watford Junction	d	21u17					23u47
Milton Keynes Central	d			22 14		22 38	
Rugby	d					23 18	
Nuneaton	d		22 52			23 29	
Tamworth Low Level	d						
Lichfield Trent Valley	d						
Coventry	d						
Birmingham International ✈	d				22 40		
Birmingham New Street 12	d				22 55		
Wolverhampton 7	d				23 15		
Penkridge	d						
Stafford	a		23 16		23 30	23s53	
	d		23 17		23 31		
Stoke-on-Trent	a			23 29			
Congleton	a						
Macclesfield	a			23 45			
Crewe 10	a		23 43		23 55	00s21	
	d	23u39	23 45		00 01		
Chester	a				00 22		
	d				00 38		
Wrexham General	a						
Llandudno	a						
Bangor (Gwynedd)	a				01 44		
Holyhead	a				02 20		
Wilmslow	a						
Stockport	a			23 59		00s50	
Manchester Piccadilly 10	a			00 12		01 00	
Hartford	a						
Warrington Bank Quay	a						
	d						
Runcorn	a		00 07				
Liverpool South Parkway 7 ✈	a						
Liverpool Lime Street 10	a		00 30				
	d						
Manchester Airport ✈	d						
Manchester Piccadilly 10	d						
Bolton	d						
Wigan North Western	a						
	d						
Preston 8	a						
Preston 8	d	00u30					
Blackpool North	a						
Lancaster 6	a						
	d						
Barrow-in-Furness	a						
Oxenholme Lake District	a						
	d						
Windermere	a						
Penrith North Lakes	d						
Carlisle 8	a						05s04
	d						
Lockerbie	d						
Carstairs	a						06s20
Motherwell	a						06s56
Glasgow Central 15	a						07 20
Haymarket	a						
Edinburgh 10	a	03s58					07 16
Perth	a	05s39					
Dundee	a	06s08					
Aberdeen	a	07 35					
Inverness	a	08 38					

OVERNIGHT SLEEPERS. For sleeper trains, operated by First ScotRail, please refer to Tables 400 - 404

Table 65

Sundays

19 February to 25 March

London and West Midlands - North West England and Scotland

Route Diagram - see first Page of Table 65

		TP	XC	NT	NT	TP	TP	TP	NT	TP	VT	XC
		◇1	◇1			🚌	🚌	◇1		◇1	◇1	◇1
London Euston 15 ⊖	d											
Watford Junction	d											
Milton Keynes Central	d											
Rugby	d											
Nuneaton	d											
Tamworth Low Level	d											
Lichfield Trent Valley	d											
Coventry	d											
Birmingham International ✈	d											
Birmingham New Street 12	d		22p31								08 45	09 01
Wolverhampton 7	d		22p49								09 04	09 19
Penkridge	d											
Stafford	a		23p01								09 16	09 32
	d		23p02								09 17	09 33
Stoke-on-Trent	a		23p20									
Congleton	a											
Macclesfield	a		23p38									
Crewe 10	a										09 35	09 54
	d										09 37	09 56
Chester	a											
	d			22p49								
Wrexham General	a											
Llandudno	a											
Bangor (Gwynedd)	a											
Holyhead	a											
Wilmslow	a											10 12
Stockport	a		23p53	00 02								10 21
Manchester Piccadilly 10	a		00 10	00 15								10 37
Hartford	a											
Warrington Bank Quay	a										09 54	
	d										09 54	
Runcorn	a											
Liverpool South Parkway 7 ✈	a											
Liverpool Lime Street 10	a											
	d											
Manchester Airport ✈	d	22p29				00 05	05 30	07 30		08 47		
Manchester Piccadilly 10	d	22p46				00 30	05 55	07 46		09 03		
Bolton	d	23p07				00s55	06s20	08 05		09 23		
Wigan North Western	a										10 05	
	d				23p47				09 13		10 05	
Preston 8	a	23p33			00 13	01s30	06s55	08 32	09 37	09 50	10 22	
Preston 8	d	23p35						08 33	09 39	09 52		
Blackpool North	a	00 02				02 10	07 35	08 57	10 07	10 18		
Lancaster 6	a											
	d											
Barrow-in-Furness	a											
Oxenholme Lake District	a											
	d											
Windermere	a											
Penrith North Lakes	d											
Carlisle 8	a											
	d											
Lockerbie	d											
Carstairs	a											
Motherwell	a											
Glasgow Central 15	a											
Haymarket	a											
Edinburgh 10	a											
Perth	a											
Dundee	a											
Aberdeen	a											
Inverness	a											

OVERNIGHT SLEEPERS. For sleeper trains, operated by First ScotRail, please refer to Tables 400 - 404

Table 65

Sundays
19 February to 25 March

London and West Midlands - North West England and Scotland

Route Diagram - see first Page of Table 65

		TP	NT	VT	VT	TP	VT	VT	VT	LM	XC	VT	TP	TP	NT	VT
		◇1		◇1	◇1	◇1	◇1	◇1	◇1	◇1	◇1	◇1	◇1	◇1		◇1
London Euston 15 ⊖	d				08 10			08 15	08 20							08 45
Watford Junction	d															
Milton Keynes Central	d				08 56				09 06							09 32
Rugby	d															10 09
Nuneaton	d							09 44								
Tamworth Low Level	d															
Lichfield Trent Valley	d															
Coventry	d															
Birmingham International ✈	d															
Birmingham New Street 12	d			09 20						09 42	10 01					
Wolverhampton 7	d			09 37						10 00	10 19					
Penkridge	d									10 10						
Stafford	a							10 08		10 16	10 32					
	d							10 08		10 17	10 33					
Stoke-on-Trent	a								10 19		10 51					
Congleton	a															
Macclesfield	a								10 36		11 08					
Crewe 10	a			10 07	10 17			10 28		10 37						10 55
	d			10 08	10 19		10 21	10 30		10 38		10 42				10 57
Chester	a											11 02				
	d											11 07				
Wrexham General	a															
Llandudno	a															
Bangor (Gwynedd)	a											12 09				
Holyhead	a											12 43				
Wilmslow	a				10 33											
Stockport	a				10 43				10 50		11 22					
Manchester Piccadilly 10	a				10 55				11 03		11 31					
Hartford	a									10 50						
Warrington Bank Quay	a			10 26			10 37									11 14
	d			10 27			10 37									11 14
Runcorn	a							10 47		11 00						
Liverpool South Parkway 7 ✈	a									11 09						
Liverpool Lime Street 10	a							11 09		11 21						
	d															
Manchester Airport ✈	d	09 29				10 00								10 30		
Manchester Piccadilly 10	d	09 46				10 16								10 46		
Bolton	d	10 05				10 33								11 05		
Wigan North Western	a			10 37			10 48									11 25
	d		10 15	10 38			10 48								11 13	11 25
Preston 8	a	10 34	10 39	10 51		10 57	11 02							11 33	11 37	11 38
Preston 8	d	10 35	10 40	11 04		11 10							11 14	11 35	11 39	11 40
Blackpool North	a	11 01	11 07											12 01	12 07	
Lancaster 6	a			11 18		11 25							11 29			11 54
	d			11 19		11 26							11 30			11 55
Barrow-in-Furness	a												12 25			
Oxenholme Lake District	a			11 32		11 40										12 08
	d			11 33		11 40										12 08
Windermere	a															
Penrith North Lakes	d					12 05										12 34
Carlisle 8	a			12 11		12 22										12 49
	d			12 12		12 23										12 50
Lockerbie	d					12 42										
Carstairs	a															
Motherwell	a															
Glasgow Central 15	a			13 22												14 01
Haymarket	a					13s41										
Edinburgh 10	a					13 48										
Perth	a															
Dundee	a															
Aberdeen	a															
Inverness	a															

OVERNIGHT SLEEPERS. For sleeper trains, operated by First ScotRail, please refer to Tables 400 - 404

Table 65

Sundays
19 February to 25 March

London and West Midlands - North West England and Scotland

Route Diagram - see first Page of Table 65

		VT	TP	VT	VT	LM	XC	LM	TP	NT	VT	TP
		◇1	◇1	◇1	◇1	◇1	◇1	1	◇1		◇1	◇1
London Euston 15 ⊖	d			09 15	09 20						09 45	
Watford Junction	d											
Milton Keynes Central	d				10 07						10 33	
Rugby	d										11 09	
Nuneaton	d			10 45								
Tamworth Low Level	d											
Lichfield Trent Valley	d											
Coventry	d						10 28					
Birmingham International ✈	d						10 40					
Birmingham New Street 12	d	10 20				10 42	11 01					
Wolverhampton 7	d	10 37				11 00	11 19					
Penkridge	d					11 10						
Stafford	a			11 09		11 16	11 31					
	d			11 09		11 17	11 32	11 45				
Stoke-on-Trent	a				11 20		11 51	12 02				
Congleton	a											
Macclesfield	a				11 37		12 09					
Crewe 10	a	11 07		11 30		11 37		12 26			11 55	
	d	11 09		11 32		11 38					11 57	
Chester	a											
	d											
Wrexham General	a											
Llandudno	a											
Bangor (Gwynedd)	a											
Holyhead	a											
Wilmslow	a											
Stockport	a				11 51		12 22					
Manchester Piccadilly 10	a				12 04		12 40					
Hartford	a					11 50						
Warrington Bank Quay	a	11 26									12 14	
	d	11 27									12 14	
Runcorn	a			11 49		12 01						
Liverpool South Parkway 7 ✈	a					12 10						
Liverpool Lime Street 10	a			12 10		12 21						
	d											
Manchester Airport ✈	d		11 00						11 30			
Manchester Piccadilly 10	d		11 16						11 46			
Bolton	d		11 33						12 05			
Wigan North Western	a	11 37									12 25	
	d	11 38								12 13	12 25	
Preston 8	a	11 51	11 56						12 33	12 37	12 38	
Preston 8	d	11 53	11 58						12 35	12 39	12 40	12 48
Blackpool North	a								13 01	13 07		
Lancaster 6	a	12 08	12 13								12 54	13 03
	d	12 08	12 14								12 55	13 04
Barrow-in-Furness	a											14 07
Oxenholme Lake District	a	12 22	12 28								13 08	
	d	12 24	12 28								13 08	
Windermere	a											
Penrith North Lakes	d		12 53								13 34	
Carlisle 8	a	13 01	13 10								13 49	
	d	13 03	13 15								13 50	
Lockerbie	d		13 36									
Carstairs	a											
Motherwell	a											
Glasgow Central 15	a		14 35								15 02	
Haymarket	a	14 13										
Edinburgh 10	a	14 22										
Perth	a											
Dundee	a											
Aberdeen	a											
Inverness	a											

OVERNIGHT SLEEPERS. For sleeper trains, operated by First ScotRail, please refer to Tables 400 - 404

London and West Midlands - North West England and Scotland

Route Diagram - see first Page of Table 65

		VT	TP	VT	VT	LM	XC	TP	NT	VT	VT	VT	VT	TP	LM
		◇1	◇1	◇1	◇1	◇1	◇1	◇1		◇1	◇1	◇1	◇1	◇1	◇1
London Euston 15 ⊖	d			10 15	10 20					10 45		11 15	11 20		
Watford Junction	d														
Milton Keynes Central	d				11 07					11 33		12 03	12 08		
Rugby	d									12 09					
Nuneaton	d			11 47											
Tamworth Low Level	d														
Lichfield Trent Valley	d														
Coventry	d						11 29								
Birmingham International ✈	d						11 40								
Birmingham New Street 12	d	11 20				11 42	12 01				12 20				12 35
Wolverhampton 7	d	11 37				12 00	12 19				12 37				12 53
Penkridge	d					12 10									13 03
Stafford	a			12 13		12 16	12 32					12 53			13 09
	d			12 13		12 17	12 33					12 53			13 09
Stoke-on-Trent	a				12 24		12 52						13 09		
Congleton	a														
Macclesfield	a				12 40		13 10						13 26		
Crewe 10	a	12 07		12 32		12 37				12 56	13 07	13 13			13 30
	d	12 09		12 34		12 38				12 58	13 09	13 15			13 31
Chester	a														
	d														
Wrexham General	a														
Llandudno	a														
Bangor (Gwynedd)	a														
Holyhead	a														
Wilmslow	a														
Stockport	a				12 55		13 28						13 41		
Manchester Piccadilly 10	a				13 08		13 40						13 53		
Hartford	a					12 50									13 43
Warrington Bank Quay	a	12 26								13 15	13 26				
	d	12 27								13 15	13 27				
Runcorn	a			12 51		13 01						13 32			13 54
Liverpool South Parkway 7 ✈	a					13 10									14 03
Liverpool Lime Street 10	a			13 12		13 21						13 54			14 14
	d														
Manchester Airport ✈	d		12 00					12 30						12 59	
Manchester Piccadilly 10	d		12 16					12 46						13 16	
Bolton	d		12 33					13 05						13 33	
Wigan North Western	a	12 37								13 26	13 37				
	d	12 38							13 13	13 26	13 38				
Preston 8	a	12 51	12 57					13 33	13 37	13 40	13 51			13 57	
Preston 8	d	12 53	12 58					13 35	13 39	13 42	13 53			14 00	
Blackpool North	a							14 01	14 09						
Lancaster 6	a	13 08	13 13							13 56	14 08			14 15	
	d	13 08	13 14							13 57	14 08			14 16	
Barrow-in-Furness	a														
Oxenholme Lake District	a	13 22	13 28							14 10				14 30	
	d	13 24	13 28							14 10				14 30	
Windermere	a														
Penrith North Lakes	d		13 53							14 36	14 45			14 55	
Carlisle 8	a	14 01	14 10							14 51	15 00			15 12	
	d	14 03	14 11							14 52	15 03			15 17	
Lockerbie	d		14 30												
Carstairs	a														
Motherwell	a														
Glasgow Central 15	a	15 16								16 05				16 35	
Haymarket	a		15s29								16 14				
Edinburgh 10	a		15 39								16 22				
Perth	a														
Dundee	a														
Aberdeen	a														
Inverness	a														

OVERNIGHT SLEEPERS. For sleeper trains, operated by First ScotRail, please refer to Tables 400 - 404

London and West Midlands - North West England and Scotland

Route Diagram - see first Page of Table 65

		VT	VT	XC	TP	NT	VT	VT	VT	XC	VT	TP	LM	VT	VT	XC
		◇1	◇1	◇1	◇1		◇1	◇1	◇1	◇1	◇1	◇1	◇1	◇1	◇1	◇1
London Euston 15 ⊖	d	12 02	12 15				12 25		12 35		12 55			13 02	13 15	
Watford Junction	d															
Milton Keynes Central	d		12 48												13 48	
Rugby	d															
Nuneaton	d															
Tamworth Low Level	d															
Lichfield Trent Valley	d															
Coventry	d			12 28												13 26
Birmingham International ✈	d			12 40												13 38
Birmingham New Street 12	d			13 01				13 20		13 31			13 35			14 01
Wolverhampton 7	d			13 19				13 37		13 49			13 53			14 19
Penkridge	d												14 03			
Stafford	a	13 24		13 33									14 09	14 21		14 33
	d	13 25		13 34									14 09	14 22		14 34
Stoke-on-Trent	a		13 50	13 56						14 19	14 26				14 50	14 56
Congleton	a															
Macclesfield	a			14 14							14 42					15 14
Crewe 10	a	13 43						14 07	14 12				14 29	14 43		
	d	13 45						14 09	14 13				14 31	14 45		
Chester	a															
	d															
Wrexham General	a															
Llandudno	a															
Bangor (Gwynedd)	a															
Holyhead	a															
Wilmslow	a								14 29							
Stockport	a		14 18	14 28					14 38		14 56				15 18	15 28
Manchester Piccadilly 10	a		14 29	14 40					14 50	14 57	15 09				15 29	15 40
Hartford	a												14 42			
Warrington Bank Quay	a						14 16	14 26								
	d						14 16	14 27								
Runcorn	a	14 02											14 53	15 02		
Liverpool South Parkway 7 ✈	a												15 02			
Liverpool Lime Street 10	a	14 24											15 14	15 24		
	d															
Manchester Airport ✈	d				13 30							14 00				
Manchester Piccadilly 10	d				13 46							14 16				
Bolton	d				14 05							14 33				
Wigan North Western	a						14 27	14 37								
	d					14 13	14 27	14 38								
Preston 8	a				14 33	14 37	14 40	14 50				14 57				
Preston 8	d				14 35	14 39	14 42	14 53				15 00				
Blackpool North	a				15 01	15 07										
Lancaster 6	a						14 56	15 08				15 15				
	d						14 58	15 09				15 16				
Barrow-in-Furness	a															
Oxenholme Lake District	a							15 22				15 30				
	d							15 24				15 30				
Windermere	a															
Penrith North Lakes	d						15 32					15 55				
Carlisle 8	a						15 47	16 01				16 12				
	d						15 48	16 03				16 13				
Lockerbie	d											16 32				
Carstairs	a															
Motherwell	a															
Glasgow Central 15	a						17 00	17 17								
Haymarket	a											17s30				
Edinburgh 10	a											17 39				
Perth	a															
Dundee	a															
Aberdeen	a															
Inverness	a															

OVERNIGHT SLEEPERS. For sleeper trains, operated by First ScotRail, please refer to Tables 400 - 404

Table 65

Sundays

19 February to 25 March

London and West Midlands - North West England and Scotland

Route Diagram - see first Page of Table 65

		TP	NT	VT	VT	VT	XC	VT	TP	LM	VT	VT	XC
		◇1		◇1	◇1	◇1	◇1	◇1	◇1	◇1	◇1	◇1	◇1
London Euston 15 ⊖	d			13 25		13 35		13 55			14 02	14 15	
Watford Junction	d												
Milton Keynes Central	d											14 48	
Rugby	d												
Nuneaton	d												
Tamworth Low Level	d												
Lichfield Trent Valley	d												
Coventry	d												14 26
Birmingham International ✈	d												14 38
Birmingham New Street 12	d				14 20		14 31			14 35			15 01
Wolverhampton 7	d				14 37		14 49			14 53			15 19
Penkridge	d									15 03			
Stafford	a									15 09	15 24		15 33
	d									15 09	15 25		15 34
Stoke-on-Trent	a						15 19	15 25				15 50	15 56
Congleton	a												
Macclesfield	a							15 42					16 14
Crewe 10	a				15 07	15 12				15 29	15 43		
	d				15 09	15 13				15 31	15 45		
Chester	a												
	d												
Wrexham General	a												
Llandudno	a												
Bangor (Gwynedd)	a												
Holyhead	a												
Wilmslow	a					15 29							
Stockport	a					15 38		15 56				16 18	16 28
Manchester Piccadilly 10	a					15 50	16 00	16 09				16 29	16 40
Hartford	a									15 42			
Warrington Bank Quay	a			15 16	15 26								
	d			15 16	15 27								
Runcorn	a									15 53	16 02		
Liverpool South Parkway 7 ✈	a									16 02			
Liverpool Lime Street 10	a									16 14	16 24		
	d												
Manchester Airport ✈	d	14 30							15 00				
Manchester Piccadilly 10	d	14 46							15 16				
Bolton	d	15 05							15 33				
Wigan North Western	a			15 27	15 37								
	d		15 13	15 27	15 38								
Preston 8	a	15 33	15 37	15 40	15 51				15 57				
Preston 8	d	15 35	15 39	15 42	15 53				16 00				
Blackpool North	a	16 01	16 07										
Lancaster 6	a			15 56	16 08				16 15				
	d			15 58	16 08				16 16				
Barrow-in-Furness	a								17 19				
Oxenholme Lake District	a			16 10									
	d			16 11									
Windermere	a												
Penrith North Lakes	d				16 45								
Carlisle 8	a			16 48	17 00								
	d			16 49	17 02								
Lockerbie	d												
Carstairs	a												
Motherwell	a												
Glasgow Central 15	a			18 01									
Haymarket	a				18 13								
Edinburgh 10	a				18 22								
Perth	a												
Dundee	a												
Aberdeen	a												
Inverness	a												

OVERNIGHT SLEEPERS. For sleeper trains, operated by First ScotRail, please refer to Tables 400 - 404

Table 65

Sundays

19 February to 25 March

London and West Midlands - North West England and Scotland

Route Diagram - see first Page of Table 65

		TP	NT	VT	VT	VT	XC	VT	TP	LM	VT	VT	VT	XC	TP	VT	VT	VT
		◇1		◇1	◇1	◇1	◇1	◇1	◇1	◇1	◇1	◇1	◇1	◇1	◇1	◇1	◇1	◇1
London Euston 15 ⊖	d			14 25		14 35		14 55			15 02	15 05	15 15			15 25		15 35
Watford Junction	d																	
Milton Keynes Central	d											15 39	15 48					
Rugby	d																	
Nuneaton	d																	
Tamworth Low Level	d																	
Lichfield Trent Valley	d																	
Coventry	d													15 26				
Birmingham International ✈	d													15 38				
Birmingham New Street 12	d				15 20		15 31			15 35				16 01			16 20	
Wolverhampton 7	d				15 37		15 49			15 53				16 19			16 37	
Penkridge	d									16 03								
Stafford	a									16 09	16 20			16 34				
	d									16 09	16 21			16 34				
Stoke-on-Trent	a						16 19	16 24					16 50	16 56				
Congleton	a																	
Macclesfield	a							16 42						17 14				
Crewe 10	a				16 07	16 12				16 29		16 50					17 07	17 12
	d				16 09	16 13				16 31		16 52					17 09	17 13
Chester	a											17 14						
	d																	
Wrexham General	a																	
Llandudno	a																	
Bangor (Gwynedd)	a																	
Holyhead	a																	
Wilmslow	a					16 29												17 29
Stockport	a					16 38		16 56					17 18	17 28				17 38
Manchester Piccadilly 10	a					16 50	16 59	17 09					17 29	17 40				17 50
Hartford	a									16 43								
Warrington Bank Quay	a			16 16	16 26											17 16	17 26	
	d			16 16	16 27											17 16	17 27	
Runcorn	a									16 54	16 57							
Liverpool South Parkway 7 ✈	a									17 03								
Liverpool Lime Street 10	a									17 14	17 16							
	d																	
Manchester Airport ✈	d	15 30							16 00						16 30			
Manchester Piccadilly 10	d	15 46							16 16						16 46			
Bolton	d	16 05							16 33						17 05			
Wigan North Western	a			16 27	16 37											17 27	17 37	
	d		16 13	16 27	16 38											17 27	17 38	
Preston 8	a	16 33	16 37	16 40	16 51				16 57						17 33	17 40	17 51	
Preston 8	d	16 35	16 39	16 42	16 53				17 00						17 35	17 42	17 53	
Blackpool North	a	17 01	17 07												18 01			
Lancaster 6	a			16 56	17 08				17 15							17 56	18 08	
	d			16 57	17 08				17 16							17 57	18 08	
Barrow-in-Furness	a																	
Oxenholme Lake District	a				17 22				17 30							18 10	18 22	
	d				17 23				17 30							18 10	18 23	
Windermere	a																	
Penrith North Lakes	d			17 32					17 55								18 49	
Carlisle 8	a			17 47	18 01				18 12							18 48	19 04	
	d			17 48	18 03				18 13							18 49	19 04	
Lockerbie	d																	
Carstairs	a																	
Motherwell	a																	
Glasgow Central 15	a			19 00	19 17											20 01		
Haymarket	a								19s28									
Edinburgh 10	a								19 35								20 22	
Perth	a																	
Dundee	a																	
Aberdeen	a																	
Inverness	a																	

OVERNIGHT SLEEPERS. For sleeper trains, operated by First ScotRail, please refer to Tables 400 - 404

London and West Midlands - North West England and Scotland

Route Diagram - see first Page of Table 65

		XC	VT	TP	LM	VT	VT	VT	XC	TP	NT	VT	VT	VT	XC	VT
		◇1	◇1	◇1	◇1	◇1	◇1	◇1	◇1	◇1		◇1	◇1	◇1	◇1	◇1
		🍴	☕	🍴		☕	☕	☕	🍴			☕	☕	☕	🍴	☕
London Euston [15] ⊖	d		15 55			16 02	16 05	16 15				16 25		16 35		16 55
Watford Junction	d															
Milton Keynes Central	d						16 39	16 48								
Rugby	d															
Nuneaton	d															
Tamworth Low Level	d															
Lichfield Trent Valley	d															
Coventry	d								16 26							
Birmingham International ✈	d								16 38							
Birmingham New Street [12]	d	16 31			16 35				17 01				17 20		17 31	
Wolverhampton [7] ⛴	d	16 49			16 53				17 19				17 37		17 49	
Penkridge	d				17 03											
Stafford	a				17 09	17 24			17 35							
	d				17 09	17 25			17 36							
Stoke-on-Trent	a	17 19	17 25					17 50	17 56						18 19	18 25
Congleton	a															
Macclesfield	a		17 42						18 14							18 42
Crewe [10]	a				17 30		17 50						18 07	18 12		
	d				17 31		17 52						18 09	18 13		
Chester	a						18 14									
	d															
Wrexham General	a															
Llandudno	a															
Bangor (Gwynedd)	a															
Holyhead	a															
Wilmslow	a													18 29		
Stockport	a		17 56					18 18	18 28					18 38		18 56
Manchester Piccadilly [10] ⛴	a	17 56	18 09					18 29	18 40					18 50	18 56	19 09
Hartford	a				17 43											
Warrington Bank Quay	a											18 16	18 26			
	d											18 17	18 27			
Runcorn	a				17 54	17 57										
Liverpool South Parkway [7] ✈	a				18 03											
Liverpool Lime Street [10]	a				18 14	18 16										
	d															
Manchester Airport ✈	d			17 00						17 30						
Manchester Piccadilly [10] ⛴	d			17 16						17 46						
Bolton	d			17 33						18 05						
Wigan North Western	a											18 27	18 37			
	d										18 13	18 28	18 38			
Preston [8]	a			17 57						18 33	18 37	18 40	18 51			
Preston [8]	d			18 00						18 35	18 39	18 42	18 53			
Blackpool North	a									19 01	19 07					
Lancaster [6]	a			18 15								18 56	19 08			
	d			18 16								18 58	19 08			
Barrow-in-Furness	a															
Oxenholme Lake District	a			18 30								19 10	19 22			
	d			18 30								19 11	19 24			
Windermere	a															
Penrith North Lakes	d			18 55								19 36				
Carlisle [8]	a			19 12								19 51	20 01			
	d			19 13								19 53	20 03			
Lockerbie	d			19 32												
Carstairs	a															
Motherwell	a			20s18												
Glasgow Central [15]	a			20 35								21 09	21 17			
Haymarket	a															
Edinburgh [10]	a															
Perth	a															
Dundee	a															
Aberdeen	a															
Inverness	a															

OVERNIGHT SLEEPERS. For sleeper trains, operated by First ScotRail, please refer to Tables 400 - 404

London and West Midlands - North West England and Scotland

Route Diagram - see first Page of Table 65

		TP		LM	VT	VT	VT	XC	TP	NT	VT	VT	VT	XC	VT	TP
		◇1		◇1	◇1	◇1	◇1	◇1	◇1		◇1	◇1	◇1	◇1	◇1	◇1
		🍴			☕	☕	☕	🍴			☕	☕	☕		☕	
London Euston [15] ⊖	d				17 02	17 05	17 15				17 25		17 35		17 55	
Watford Junction	d															
Milton Keynes Central	d					17 39	17 48									
Rugby	d															
Nuneaton	d					18 10										
Tamworth Low Level	d															
Lichfield Trent Valley	d															
Coventry	d							17 26								
Birmingham International ✈	d							17 38								
Birmingham New Street [12]	d			17 35				18 01				18 20		18 31		
Wolverhampton [7] ⛴	d			17 53				18 19				18 37		18 49		
Penkridge	d			18 03												
Stafford	a			18 09	18 24			18 35								
	d			18 09	18 25			18 36								
Stoke-on-Trent	a						18 50	18 56						19 19	19 25	
Congleton	a															
Macclesfield	a							19 15							19 42	
Crewe [10]	a			18 30		18 53						19 07	19 12			
	d			18 31		18 56						19 09	19 13			
Chester	a					19 14										
	d					19 22										
Wrexham General	a															
Llandudno	a															
Bangor (Gwynedd)	a					20 27										
Holyhead	a					20 59										
Wilmslow	a												19 29			
Stockport	a						19 18	19 28					19 38		19 56	
Manchester Piccadilly [10] ⛴	a						19 29	19 40					19 50	19 58	20 09	
Hartford	a			18 43												
Warrington Bank Quay	a										19 16	19 26				
	d										19 16	19 27				
Runcorn	a			18 54	18 57											
Liverpool South Parkway [7] ✈	a			19 03												
Liverpool Lime Street [10]	a			19 14	19 19											
	d															
Manchester Airport ✈	d	18 00							18 30							19 00
Manchester Piccadilly [10] ⛴	d	18 16							18 46							19 16
Bolton	d	18 33							19 05							19 33
Wigan North Western	a										19 27	19 37				
	d									19 13	19 27	19 38				
Preston [8]	a	18 57							19 33	19 37	19 40	19 51				19 57
Preston [8]	d	19 00	19 06						19 35	19 39	19 42	19 53				20 06
Blackpool North	a								20 01	20 07						
Lancaster [6]	a	19 15	19 22								19 56	20 08				20 21
	d	19 16	19 22								19 57	20 08				20 22
Barrow-in-Furness	a		20 26													21 17
Oxenholme Lake District	a	19 30									20 10					
	d	19 30									20 10					
Windermere	a															
Penrith North Lakes	d	19 55									20 36	20 45				
Carlisle [8]	a	20 12									20 51	21 00				
	d	20 13									20 52	21 02				
Lockerbie	d	20 32														
Carstairs	a															
Motherwell	a															
Glasgow Central [15]	a										22 07					
Haymarket	a	21s30										22 15				
Edinburgh [10]	a	21 39										22 21				
Perth	a															
Dundee	a															
Aberdeen	a															
Inverness	a															

OVERNIGHT SLEEPERS. For sleeper trains, operated by First ScotRail, please refer to Tables 400 - 404

Table 65

Sundays

19 February to 25 March

London and West Midlands - North West England and Scotland

Route Diagram - see first Page of Table 65

		LM	VT	VT	VT	XC	TP	NT	VT	VT	VT	XC	VT	LM	VT
		◇■1	◇■1	◇■1	◇■1	◇■1	◇■1		◇■1	■ ■1	◇■1	◇■1	◇■1	◇■1	◇■1
			☕	☕	☕	🛒			☕	☕	☕	🛒	☕		☕
London Euston ■15 ⊖	d		18 02	18 05	18 15				18 25		18 35		18 55		19 02
Watford Junction	d														
Milton Keynes Central	d			18 39	18 48										
Rugby	d														
Nuneaton	d														20 01
Tamworth Low Level	d														
Lichfield Trent Valley	d														
Coventry	d					18 26									
Birmingham International ✈	d					18 38									
Birmingham New Street ■12	d	18 35				19 01				19 20		19 31		19 35	
Wolverhampton ■7 ⇌	d	18 53				19 19				19 37		19 49		19 53	
Penkridge	d	19 03												20 03	
Stafford	a	19 09	19 24			19 37								20 09	20 25
	d	19 09	19 25			19 38								20 09	20 30
Stoke-on-Trent	a				19 50	19 56						20 19	20 25		
Congleton	a														
Macclesfield	a					20 14							20 42		
Crewe ■10	a	19 29		19 50						20 07	20 12			20 30	20 48
	d	19 31		19 52						20 09	20 13			20 31	20 50
Chester	a			20 11											
	d			20 18											
Wrexham General	a														
Llandudno	a														
Bangor (Gwynedd)	a			21 23											
Holyhead	a			21 57											
Wilmslow	a										20 29				
Stockport	a				20 18	20 28					20 38		20 56		
Manchester Piccadilly ■10 ⇌	a				20 29	20 40					20 50	21 00	21 09		
Hartford	a	19 42												20 43	
Warrington Bank Quay	a								20 16	20 26					
	d								20 16	20 27					
Runcorn	a	19 53	19 58											20 54	21 07
Liverpool South Parkway ■7 ✈	a	20 02												21 03	
Liverpool Lime Street ■10	a	20 14	20 16											21 14	21 28
	d														
Manchester Airport ✈	d						19 30								
Manchester Piccadilly ■10 ⇌	d						19 46								
Bolton	d						20 05								
Wigan North Western	a								20 27	20 37					
	d							20 13	20 27	20 38					
Preston ■8	a						20 33	20 37	20 40	20 51					
Preston ■8	d						20 35	20 39	20 42	20 53					
Blackpool North	a						21 01	21 07							
Lancaster ■6	a								20 56	21 08					
	d								20 57	21 08					
Barrow-in-Furness	a														
Oxenholme Lake District	a								21 10	21 22					
	d								21 11	21 24					
Windermere	a														
Penrith North Lakes	d								21 36						
Carlisle ■8	a								21 51	22 01					
	d								21 52	22 03					
Lockerbie	d									22 23					
Carstairs	a														
Motherwell	a								22 48	23 07					
Glasgow Central ■15	a								23 09	23 22					
Haymarket	a														
Edinburgh ■10	a														
Perth	a														
Dundee	a														
Aberdeen	a														
Inverness	a														

OVERNIGHT SLEEPERS. For sleeper trains, operated by First ScotRail, please refer to Tables 400 - 404

Table 65

Sundays

19 February to 25 March

London and West Midlands - North West England and Scotland

Route Diagram - see first Page of Table 65

		VT	VT	XC	VT	TP	NT	VT	VT	XC	VT	VT	VT	VT	XC
		◇■1	◇■1	◇■1	◇■1	◇■1		◇■1	◇■1	◇■1	◇■1	◇■1	◇■1	◇■1	◇■1
				A											A
		☕	☕	🛒	☕			☕	☕	🛒	☕	☕	☕	☕	🛒
London Euston ■15 ⊖	d	19 05	19 15					19 25	19 35		19 55	20 02	20 05	20 15	
Watford Junction	d														
Milton Keynes Central	d	19 39	19 48										20 38	20 48	
Rugby	d														
Nuneaton	d											21 01			
Tamworth Low Level	d														
Lichfield Trent Valley	d														
Coventry	d			19 26											20 26
Birmingham International ✈	d			19 38											20 38
Birmingham New Street ■12	d			20 01	20 20					20 31					21 01
Wolverhampton ■7 ⇌	d			20 19	20 38					20 52					21 19
Penkridge	d														
Stafford	a			20 36	20 51								21 31		21 36
	d			20 37	20 52								21 33		21 37
Stoke-on-Trent	a		20 50	20 56						21 19	21 25			21 50	21 56
Congleton	a														
Macclesfield	a			21 15							21 42				22 14
Crewe ■10	a	20 53			21 10				21 13			21 44	21 53		
	d	20 55							21 14			21 46	21 55		
Chester	a	21 14													
	d	21 17													
Wrexham General	a														
Llandudno	a														
Bangor (Gwynedd)	a	22 22													
Holyhead	a	22 56													
Wilmslow	a								21 30						
Stockport	a		21 18	21 28					21 39		21 56			22 18	22 28
Manchester Piccadilly ■10 ⇌	a		21 29	21 40					21 50	21 56	22 09			22 29	22 40
Hartford	a														
Warrington Bank Quay	a							21 16							
	d							21 16							
Runcorn	a											22 03	22 12		
Liverpool South Parkway ■7 ✈	a														
Liverpool Lime Street ■10	a											22 23	22 33		
	d														
Manchester Airport ✈	d					20 30									
Manchester Piccadilly ■10 ⇌	d					20 46									
Bolton	d					21 05									
Wigan North Western	a							21 27							
	d						21 13	21 27							
Preston ■8	a					21 33	21 37	21 40							
Preston ■8	d					21 35	21 39	21 42							
Blackpool North	a					22 01	22 07								
Lancaster ■6	a							21 56							
	d							21 57							
Barrow-in-Furness	a														
Oxenholme Lake District	a							22 10							
	d							22 11							
Windermere	a														
Penrith North Lakes	d							22 36							
Carlisle ■8	a							22 51							
	d							22 53							
Lockerbie	d														
Carstairs	a														
Motherwell	a														
Glasgow Central ■15	a							00 02							
Haymarket	a														
Edinburgh ■10	a														
Perth	a														
Dundee	a														
Aberdeen	a														
Inverness	a														

A 🛒 to Birmingham New Street

OVERNIGHT SLEEPERS. For sleeper trains, operated by First ScotRail, please refer to Tables 400 - 404

London and West Midlands - North West England and Scotland

Route Diagram - see first Page of Table 65

		TP	NT	VT	VT	VT	LM	XC	NT	VT	SR	VT	VT	AW	VT	SR
		◇1		◇1	◇1	◇1	◇1	◇1		◇1		◇1	◇1	◇	◇1	
London Euston 15 ⊖	d			20 25		20 35				20 50	20 55	21 21	21 25		21 51	23 27
Watford Junction	d										21u17					23u47
Milton Keynes Central	d									21 37			22 14		22 38	
Rugby	d									22 01					23 18	
Nuneaton	d											22 52			23 29	
Tamworth Low Level	d			21 32												
Lichfield Trent Valley	d			21 39												
Coventry	d							21 26								
Birmingham International ✈	d							21 38						22 40		
Birmingham New Street 12	d				21 20		21 35	22 01						22 55		
Wolverhampton 7	d				21 38		21 57	22 19						23 15		
Penkridge	d						22 07									
Stafford	a				21 56	21 59	22 13	22 36				23 16		23 30	23s53	
	d				21 57	22 00	22 16	22 37				23 17		23 31		
Stoke-on-Trent	a							22 55					23 29			
Congleton	a															
Macclesfield	a							23 12					23 45			
Crewe 10	a			22 10	22 17	22 20	22 38			22 49		23 43		23 55	00s21	
	d			22 13	22 18	22 21				22 51	23u39	23 45		00 01		
Chester	a													00 22		
	d													00 38		
Wrexham General	a															
Llandudno	a															
Bangor (Gwynedd)	a													01 44		
Holyhead	a													02 20		
Wilmslow	a					22 36										
Stockport	a					22 45		23 27					23 59		00s50	
Manchester Piccadilly 10	a					22 57		23 41					00 12		01 00	
Hartford	a															
Warrington Bank Quay	a			22 29	22 36					23 08						
	d			22 30	22 36					23 08						
Runcorn	a											00 07				
Liverpool South Parkway 7 ✈	a															
Liverpool Lime Street 10	a											00 30				
	d															
Manchester Airport ✈	d	21 30														
Manchester Piccadilly 10	d	21 46														
Bolton	d	22 05														
Wigan North Western	a			22 40	22 47					23 19						
	d		22 13	22 41	22 47				23 13	23 19						
Preston 8	a	22 28	22 37	22 58	23 07				23 35	23 41						
Preston 8	d	22 29	22 39						23 36		00u30					
Blackpool North	a	22 55	23 07						00 05							
Lancaster 6	a															
	d															
Barrow-in-Furness	a															
Oxenholme Lake District	a															
	d															
Windermere	a															
Penrith North Lakes	d															
Carlisle 8	a															05s04
	d															
Lockerbie	d															
Carstairs	a															06s20
Motherwell	a															06s56
Glasgow Central 15	a															07 20
Haymarket	a															
Edinburgh 10	a										03s58					07 16
Perth	a										05s39					
Dundee	a										06s08					
Aberdeen	a										07 35					
Inverness	a										08 38					

OVERNIGHT SLEEPERS. For sleeper trains, operated by First ScotRail, please refer to Tables 400 - 404

London and West Midlands - North West England and Scotland

Route Diagram - see first Page of Table 65

		TP	XC	NT	TP	TP	TP	NT	TP	VT	XC
		◇1	◇1				◇1		◇1	◇1	◇1
London Euston 15 ⊖	d										
Watford Junction	d										
Milton Keynes Central	d										
Rugby	d										
Nuneaton	d										
Tamworth Low Level	d										
Lichfield Trent Valley	d										
Coventry	d										
Birmingham International ✈	d										
Birmingham New Street 12	d		22p31							08 45	09 01
Wolverhampton 7	d		22p49							09 04	09 19
Penkridge	d										
Stafford	a		23p01							09 16	09 32
	d		23p02							09 17	09 33
Stoke-on-Trent	a		23p20								
Congleton	a										
Macclesfield	a		23p38								
Crewe 10	a									09 35	09 54
	d									09 37	09 56
Chester	a										
	d			22p49							
Wrexham General	a										
Llandudno	a										
Bangor (Gwynedd)	a										
Holyhead	a										
Wilmslow	a										10 12
Stockport	a		23p53	00 02							10 21
Manchester Piccadilly 10	a		00 10	00 15							10 37
Hartford	a										
Warrington Bank Quay	a									09 54	
	d									09 54	
Runcorn	a										
Liverpool South Parkway 7 ✈	a										
Liverpool Lime Street 10	a										
	d										
Manchester Airport ✈	d	22p29			00 05	05 30	07 55		08 47		
Manchester Piccadilly 10	d	22p46			00 30	05 55	08 11		09 03		
Bolton	d	23p07			00s55	06s20	08 30		09 23		
Wigan North Western	a									10 05	
	d									10 05	
Preston 8	a	23p33			01s30	06s55	08 57		09 50	10 22	
Preston 8	d	23p35					08 58	09 05	09 52		
Blackpool North	a	00 02			02 10	07 35	09 23		10 18		
Lancaster 6	a										
	d										
Barrow-in-Furness	a										
Oxenholme Lake District	a										
	d										
Windermere	a										
Penrith North Lakes	d										
Carlisle 8	a							12 17			
	d										
Lockerbie	d										
Carstairs	a										
Motherwell	a										
Glasgow Central 15	a										
Haymarket	a										
Edinburgh 10	a										
Perth	a										
Dundee	a										
Aberdeen	a										
Inverness	a										

OVERNIGHT SLEEPERS. For sleeper trains, operated by First ScotRail, please refer to Tables 400 - 404

Table 65

Sundays from 1 April

London and West Midlands - North West England and Scotland

Route Diagram - see first Page of Table 65

		TP	VT	VT	TP	VT	VT	VT	LM	XC	VT	TP	TP	VT	VT	TP
		◇1	◇1	◇1	◇1	◇1	◇1	◇1	◇1	◇1	◇1	◇1	◇1	◇1	◇1	◇1
London Euston 15 ⊖	d			08 10			08 15	08 20						08 45		
Watford Junction	d															
Milton Keynes Central	d			08 56				09 06						09 32		
Rugby	d													10 09		
Nuneaton	d						09 44									
Tamworth Low Level	d															
Lichfield Trent Valley	d															
Coventry	d															
Birmingham International ✈	d															
Birmingham New Street 12	d		09 20						09 42	10 01					10 20	
Wolverhampton 7	d		09 37						10 00	10 19					10 37	
Penkridge	d								10 10							
Stafford	a						10 08		10 16	10 32						
	d						10 08		10 17	10 33						
Stoke-on-Trent	a							10 19		10 51						
Congleton	a															
Macclesfield	a							10 36		11 08						
Crewe 10	a		10 07	10 17			10 28		10 37					10 55	11 07	
	d		10 08	10 19		10 21	10 30		10 38		10 42			10 57	11 09	
Chester	a										11 02					
	d										11 07					
Wrexham General	a															
Llandudno	a															
Bangor (Gwynedd)	a										12 09					
Holyhead	a										12 43					
Wilmslow	a			10 33												
Stockport	a			10 43				10 50		11 22						
Manchester Piccadilly 10	a			10 55				11 03		11 31						
Hartford	a								10 50							
Warrington Bank Quay	a		10 26			10 37								11 14	11 26	
	d		10 27			10 37								11 14	11 27	
Runcorn	a						10 47		11 00							
Liverpool South Parkway 7 ✈	a								11 09							
Liverpool Lime Street 10	a						11 09		11 21							
	d															
Manchester Airport ✈	d	09 30			10 00								10 30			11 00
Manchester Piccadilly 10	d	09 46			10 16								10 46			11 16
Bolton	d	10 05			10 33								11 05			11 33
Wigan North Western	a		10 37			10 48								11 25	11 37	
	d		10 38			10 48								11 25	11 38	
Preston 8	a	10 33	10 51		10 57	11 02							11 33	11 38	11 51	11 56
Preston 8	d	10 35	11 04		11 10							11 14	11 35	11 40	11 53	11 58
Blackpool North	a	11 01											12 01			
Lancaster 6	a		11 18		11 25							11 29		11 54	12 08	12 13
	d		11 19		11 26							11 30		11 55	12 08	12 14
Barrow-in-Furness	a											12 25				
Oxenholme Lake District	a		11 32		11 40									12 08	12 22	12 28
	d		11 33		11 40									12 08	12 24	12 28
Windermere	a															
Penrith North Lakes	d				12 05									12 34		12 53
Carlisle 8	a		12 11		12 22									12 49	13 01	13 10
	d		12 12		12 23									12 50	13 03	13 15
Lockerbie	d				12 42											13 36
Carstairs	a															
Motherwell	a															
Glasgow Central 15	a		13 21											14 01		14 35
Haymarket	a				13s41										14 13	
Edinburgh 10	a				13 48										14 22	
Perth	a															
Dundee	a															
Aberdeen	a															
Inverness	a															

OVERNIGHT SLEEPERS. For sleeper trains, operated by First ScotRail, please refer to Tables 400 - 404

Table 65

Sundays from 1 April

London and West Midlands - North West England and Scotland

Route Diagram - see first Page of Table 65

		VT	VT	LM	XC	LM	TP	VT	TP	VT	TP	VT	VT	LM	XC
		◇1	◇1	◇1	◇1	1	◇1	◇1	◇1	◇1	◇1	◇1	◇1	◇1	◇1
London Euston 15 ⊖	d	09 15	09 20					09 45				10 15	10 20		
Watford Junction	d														
Milton Keynes Central	d		10 07					10 33					11 07		
Rugby	d							11 09							
Nuneaton	d	10 45										11 47			
Tamworth Low Level	d														
Lichfield Trent Valley	d														
Coventry	d				10 28										11 29
Birmingham International ✈	d				10 40										11 40
Birmingham New Street 12	d			10 42	11 01					11 20				11 42	12 01
Wolverhampton 7	d			11 00	11 19					11 37				12 00	12 19
Penkridge	d			11 10										12 10	
Stafford	a	11 09		11 16	11 31							12 13		12 16	12 32
	d	11 09		11 17	11 32	11 45						12 13		12 17	12 33
Stoke-on-Trent	a		11 20		11 51	12 02							12 24		12 52
Congleton	a														
Macclesfield	a		11 37		12 09								12 40		13 10
Crewe 10	a	11 30		11 37		12 26		11 55		12 07		12 32		12 37	
	d	11 32		11 38				11 57		12 09		12 34		12 38	
Chester	a														
	d														
Wrexham General	a														
Llandudno	a														
Bangor (Gwynedd)	a														
Holyhead	a														
Wilmslow	a														
Stockport	a		11 51		12 22								12 55		13 28
Manchester Piccadilly 10	a		12 04		12 40								13 08		13 40
Hartford	a			11 50										12 50	
Warrington Bank Quay	a							12 14		12 26					
	d							12 14		12 27					
Runcorn	a	11 49		12 01								12 51		13 01	
Liverpool South Parkway 7 ✈	a			12 10										13 10	
Liverpool Lime Street 10	a	12 10		12 21								13 12		13 21	
	d														
Manchester Airport ✈	d						11 30				12 00				
Manchester Piccadilly 10	d						11 46				12 16				
Bolton	d						12 05				12 33				
Wigan North Western	a							12 25		12 37					
	d							12 25		12 38					
Preston 8	a						12 33	12 38		12 51	12 57				
Preston 8	d						12 35	12 40	12 48	12 53	12 58				
Blackpool North	a						13 01								
Lancaster 6	a							12 54	13 03	13 08	13 13				
	d							12 55	13 04	13 08	13 14				
Barrow-in-Furness	a								14 07						
Oxenholme Lake District	a							13 08		13 22	13 28				
	d							13 08		13 24	13 28				
Windermere	a														
Penrith North Lakes	d							13 34			13 53				
Carlisle 8	a							13 49		14 01	14 10				
	d							13 50		14 03	14 11				
Lockerbie	d										14 30				
Carstairs	a														
Motherwell	a														
Glasgow Central 15	a							15 02		15 16					
Haymarket	a										15s29				
Edinburgh 10	a										15 39				
Perth	a														
Dundee	a														
Aberdeen	a														
Inverness	a														

OVERNIGHT SLEEPERS. For sleeper trains, operated by First ScotRail, please refer to Tables 400 - 404

London and West Midlands - North West England and Scotland

Route Diagram - see first Page of Table 65

		TP ◇1	VT ◇1	VT ◇1	VT ◇1	VT ◇1	TP ◇1	LM ◇1	VT ◇1	VT ◇1	XC ◇1	TP ◇1	VT ◇1	VT ◇1	VT ◇1
London Euston 15 ⊖	d		10 45		11 15	11 20			12 02	12 15			12 25		12 35
Watford Junction	d														
Milton Keynes Central	d		11 33		12 03	12 08				12 48					
Rugby	d		12 09												
Nuneaton	d														
Tamworth Low Level	d														
Lichfield Trent Valley	d														
Coventry	d										12 28				
Birmingham International ✈	d										12 40				
Birmingham New Street 12	d			12 20				12 35			13 01			13 20	
Wolverhampton 7	d			12 37				12 53			13 19			13 37	
Penkridge	d							13 03							
Stafford	a				12 53			13 09	13 24		13 33				
	d				12 53			13 09	13 25		13 34				
Stoke-on-Trent	a					13 09				13 50	13 56				
Congleton	a														
Macclesfield	a					13 26					14 14				
Crewe 10	a		12 56	13 07	13 13			13 30	13 43					14 07	14 12
	d		12 58	13 09	13 15			13 31	13 45					14 09	14 13
Chester	a														
	d														
Wrexham General	a														
Llandudno	a														
Bangor (Gwynedd)	a														
Holyhead	a														
Wilmslow	a														14 29
Stockport	a					13 41				14 18	14 28				14 38
Manchester Piccadilly 10	a					13 53				14 29	14 40				14 50
Hartford	a							13 43							
Warrington Bank Quay	a		13 15	13 26									14 16	14 26	
	d		13 15	13 27									14 16	14 27	
Runcorn	a				13 32			13 54	14 02						
Liverpool South Parkway 7 ✈	a							14 03							
Liverpool Lime Street 10	a				13 54			14 14	14 24						
	d														
Manchester Airport ✈	d	12 30					12 58					13 30			
Manchester Piccadilly 10	d	12 46					13 16					13 46			
Bolton	d	13 05					13 33					14 05			
Wigan North Western	a		13 26	13 37									14 27	14 37	
	d		13 26	13 38									14 27	14 38	
Preston 8	a	13 33	13 40	13 51			13 57					14 33	14 40	14 50	
Preston 8	d	13 35	13 42	13 53			14 00					14 35	14 42	14 53	
Blackpool North	a	14 01										15 01			
Lancaster 6	a		13 56	14 08			14 15						14 56	15 08	
	d		13 57	14 08			14 16						14 58	15 09	
Barrow-in-Furness	a														
Oxenholme Lake District	a		14 10				14 30							15 22	
	d		14 10				14 30							15 24	
Windermere	a														
Penrith North Lakes	d		14 36	14 45			14 55						15 32		
Carlisle 8	a		14 51	15 00			15 12						15 47	16 01	
	d		14 52	15 03			15 17						15 48	16 03	
Lockerbie	d														
Carstairs	a														
Motherwell	a														
Glasgow Central 15	a		16 05				16 35						17 00	17 17	
Haymarket	a			16 14											
Edinburgh 10	a			16 22											
Perth	a														
Dundee	a														
Aberdeen	a														
Inverness	a														

OVERNIGHT SLEEPERS. For sleeper trains, operated by First ScotRail, please refer to Tables 400 - 404

London and West Midlands - North West England and Scotland

Route Diagram - see first Page of Table 65

		XC ◇1	VT ◇1	TP ◇1	LM ◇1	VT ◇1	VT ◇1	XC ◇1	TP ◇1	VT ◇1	VT ◇1	VT ◇1	XC ◇1	VT ◇1	TP ◇1
London Euston 15 ⊖	d		12 55			13 02	13 15			13 25		13 35		13 55	
Watford Junction	d														
Milton Keynes Central	d						13 48								
Rugby	d														
Nuneaton	d														
Tamworth Low Level	d														
Lichfield Trent Valley	d														
Coventry	d							13 25							
Birmingham International ✈	d							13 37							
Birmingham New Street 12	d	13 31			13 35			14 00			14 20		14 31		
Wolverhampton 7	d	13 49			13 53			14 18			14 37		14 49		
Penkridge	d				14 03										
Stafford	a				14 09	14 21		14 32							
	d				14 09	14 22		14 33							
Stoke-on-Trent	a	14 19	14 26				14 50	14 55					15 19	15 25	
Congleton	a														
Macclesfield	a		14 42					15 13						15 42	
Crewe 10	a				14 29	14 43					15 07	15 12			
	d				14 31	14 45					15 09	15 13			
Chester	a														
	d														
Wrexham General	a														
Llandudno	a														
Bangor (Gwynedd)	a														
Holyhead	a														
Wilmslow	a											15 29			
Stockport	a		14 56				15 18	15 27				15 38		15 56	
Manchester Piccadilly 10	a	14 57	15 09				15 29	15 39				15 50	15 59	16 09	
Hartford	a				14 42										
Warrington Bank Quay	a									15 16	15 26				
	d									15 16	15 27				
Runcorn	a				14 53	15 02									
Liverpool South Parkway 7 ✈	a				15 02										
Liverpool Lime Street 10	a				15 14	15 24									
	d														
Manchester Airport ✈	d			13 58					14 30						14 58
Manchester Piccadilly 10	d			14 16					14 46						15 16
Bolton	d			14 33					15 05						15 33
Wigan North Western	a									15 27	15 37				
	d									15 27	15 38				
Preston 8	a			14 57					15 33	15 40	15 51				15 57
Preston 8	d			15 00					15 35	15 42	15 53				16 00
Blackpool North	a								16 01						
Lancaster 6	a			15 15						15 56	16 08				16 15
	d			15 16						15 58	16 08				16 16
Barrow-in-Furness	a														17 19
Oxenholme Lake District	a			15 30						16 10					
	d			15 30						16 11					
Windermere	a														
Penrith North Lakes	d			15 55							16 45				
Carlisle 8	a			16 12						16 48	17 00				
	d			16 13						16 49	17 02				
Lockerbie	d			16 32											
Carstairs	a														
Motherwell	a														
Glasgow Central 15	a									18 01					
Haymarket	a			17s30							18 13				
Edinburgh 10	a			17 39							18 22				
Perth	a														
Dundee	a														
Aberdeen	a														
Inverness	a														

OVERNIGHT SLEEPERS. For sleeper trains, operated by First ScotRail, please refer to Tables 400 - 404

Table 65

Sundays
from 1 April

London and West Midlands - North West England and Scotland

Route Diagram - see first Page of Table 65

Station		LM ◇1	VT ◇1	VT ◇1	XC ◇1	TP ◇1	VT ◇1	VT ◇1	VT ◇1	XC ◇1	VT ◇1	TP ◇1	LM ◇1	VT ◇1	VT ◇1	VT ◇1	XC ◇1
London Euston 15 ⊖	d		14 02	14 15			14 25		14 35		14 55			15 02	15 05	15 15	
Watford Junction	d																
Milton Keynes Central	d			14 48											15 39	15 48	
Rugby	d																
Nuneaton	d																
Tamworth Low Level	d																
Lichfield Trent Valley	d																
Coventry	d				14 26												15 26
Birmingham International ✈	d				14 38												15 38
Birmingham New Street 12	d	14 35			15 01			15 20		15 31			15 35				16 01
Wolverhampton 7	d	14 53			15 19			15 37		15 49			15 53				16 19
Penkridge	d	15 03											16 03				
Stafford	a	15 09	15 24		15 33								16 09	16 20			16 34
	d	15 09	15 25		15 34								16 09	16 21			16 34
Stoke-on-Trent	a			15 50	15 56					16 19	16 24					16 50	16 56
Congleton	a																
Macclesfield	a				16 14						16 42						17 14
Crewe 10	a	15 29	15 43					16 07	16 12				16 29		16 50		
	d	15 31	15 45					16 09	16 13				16 31		16 52		
Chester	a														17 14		
	d																
Wrexham General	a																
Llandudno	a																
Bangor (Gwynedd)	a																
Holyhead	a																
Wilmslow	a								16 29								
Stockport	a			16 18	16 28				16 38		16 56					17 18	17 28
Manchester Piccadilly 10	a			16 29	16 40				16 50	16 59	17 09					17 29	17 40
Hartford	a	15 42											16 43				
Warrington Bank Quay	a						16 16	16 26									
	d						16 16	16 27									
Runcorn	a	15 53	16 02										16 54	16 57			
Liverpool South Parkway 7 ✈	a	16 02											17 03				
Liverpool Lime Street 10	a	16 14	16 24										17 14	17 16			
	d																
Manchester Airport ✈	d					15 30						15 58					
Manchester Piccadilly 10	d					15 46						16 16					
Bolton	d					16 05						16 33					
Wigan North Western	a						16 27	16 37									
	d						16 27	16 38									
Preston 8	a					16 33	16 40	16 51				16 57					
Preston 8	d					16 35	16 42	16 53				17 00					
Blackpool North	a					17 01											
Lancaster 6	a						16 56	17 08				17 15					
	d						16 57	17 08				17 16					
Barrow-in-Furness	a																
Oxenholme Lake District	a							17 22				17 30					
	d							17 23				17 30					
Windermere	a																
Penrith North Lakes	d						17 32					17 55					
Carlisle 8	a						17 47	18 01				18 12					
	d						17 48	18 03				18 13					
Lockerbie	d																
Carstairs	a																
Motherwell	a																
Glasgow Central 15	a						19 00	19 17									
Haymarket	a											19s28					
Edinburgh 10	a											19 35					
Perth	a																
Dundee	a																
Aberdeen	a																
Inverness	a																

OVERNIGHT SLEEPERS. For sleeper trains, operated by First ScotRail, please refer to Tables 400 - 404

Table 65

Sundays
from 1 April

London and West Midlands - North West England and Scotland

Route Diagram - see first Page of Table 65

Station		TP ◇1	VT ◇1	VT ◇1	VT ◇1	XC ◇1	VT ◇1	TP ◇1	LM ◇1	VT ◇1	VT ◇1	VT ◇1	XC ◇1	TP ◇1	VT ◇1	VT ◇1	VT ◇1
London Euston 15 ⊖	d		15 25		15 35		15 55			16 02	16 05	16 15			16 25		16 35
Watford Junction	d																
Milton Keynes Central	d										16 39	16 48					
Rugby	d																
Nuneaton	d																
Tamworth Low Level	d																
Lichfield Trent Valley	d																
Coventry	d												16 26				
Birmingham International ✈	d												16 38				
Birmingham New Street 12	d			16 20		16 31			16 35				17 01			17 20	
Wolverhampton 7	d			16 37		16 49			16 53				17 19			17 37	
Penkridge	d								17 03								
Stafford	a								17 09	17 24			17 35				
	d								17 09	17 25			17 36				
Stoke-on-Trent	a					17 19	17 25					17 50	17 56				
Congleton	a																
Macclesfield	a						17 42						18 14				
Crewe 10	a			17 07	17 12				17 30		17 50					18 07	18 12
	d			17 09	17 13				17 31		17 52					18 09	18 13
Chester	a										18 14						
	d																
Wrexham General	a																
Llandudno	a																
Bangor (Gwynedd)	a																
Holyhead	a																
Wilmslow	a				17 29												18 29
Stockport	a				17 38		17 56					18 18	18 28				18 38
Manchester Piccadilly 10	a				17 50	17 56	18 09					18 29	18 40				18 50
Hartford	a								17 43								
Warrington Bank Quay	a		17 16	17 26											18 16	18 26	
	d		17 16	17 27											18 17	18 27	
Runcorn	a								17 54	17 57							
Liverpool South Parkway 7 ✈	a								18 03								
Liverpool Lime Street 10	a								18 14	18 16							
	d																
Manchester Airport ✈	d	16 30						16 58						17 30			
Manchester Piccadilly 10	d	16 46						17 16						17 46			
Bolton	d	17 05						17 33						18 05			
Wigan North Western	a		17 27	17 37											18 27	18 37	
	d		17 27	17 38											18 28	18 38	
Preston 8	a	17 33	17 40	17 51				17 57						18 33	18 40	18 51	
Preston 8	d	17 35	17 42	17 53				18 00						18 35	18 42	18 53	
Blackpool North	a	18 01												19 01			
Lancaster 6	a		17 56	18 08				18 15							18 56	19 08	
	d		17 57	18 08				18 16							18 58	19 08	
Barrow-in-Furness	a																
Oxenholme Lake District	a		18 10	18 22				18 30							19 10	19 22	
	d		18 10	18 23				18 30							19 11	19 24	
Windermere	a																
Penrith North Lakes	d			18 49				18 55							19 36		
Carlisle 8	a		18 48	19 04				19 12							19 51	20 01	
	d		18 49	19 04				19 13							19 53	20 03	
Lockerbie	d							19 32									
Carstairs	a																
Motherwell	a							20s18									
Glasgow Central 15	a		20 01					20 35							21 09	21 17	
Haymarket	a																
Edinburgh 10	a			20 22													
Perth	a																
Dundee	a																
Aberdeen	a																
Inverness	a																

OVERNIGHT SLEEPERS. For sleeper trains, operated by First ScotRail, please refer to Tables 400 - 404

London and West Midlands - North West England and Scotland

Route Diagram - see first Page of Table 65

		XC	VT	TP		LM	VT	VT	VT	XC	TP	VT	VT	VT	XC	VT	TP
		◇1	◇1	◇1		◇1	◇1	◇1	◇1	◇1	◇1	◇1	◇1	◇1	◇1	◇1	◇1
London Euston 15 ⊖	d		16 55				17 02	17 05	17 15			17 25		17 35		17 55	
Watford Junction	d																
Milton Keynes Central	d							17 39	17 48								
Rugby	d																
Nuneaton	d							18 10									
Tamworth Low Level	d																
Lichfield Trent Valley	d																
Coventry	d									17 26							
Birmingham International ✈	d									17 38							
Birmingham New Street 12	d	17 31				17 35				18 01			18 20		18 31		
Wolverhampton 7	d	17 49				17 53				18 19			18 37		18 49		
Penkridge	d					18 03											
Stafford	a					18 09	18 24			18 35							
	d					18 09	18 25			18 36							
Stoke-on-Trent	a	18 19	18 25						18 50	18 56					19 19	19 25	
Congleton	a																
Macclesfield	a		18 42							19 15						19 42	
Crewe 10	a					18 30		18 53					19 07	19 12			
	d					18 31		18 56					19 09	19 13			
Chester	a							19 14									
	d							19 22									
Wrexham General	a																
Llandudno	a																
Bangor (Gwynedd)	a							20 27									
Holyhead	a							20 59									
Wilmslow	a													19 29			
Stockport	a		18 56						19 18	19 28				19 38		19 56	
Manchester Piccadilly 10	a	18 56	19 09						19 29	19 40				19 50	19 58	20 09	
Hartford	a					18 43											
Warrington Bank Quay	a											19 16	19 26				
	d											19 16	19 27				
Runcorn	a					18 54	18 57										
Liverpool South Parkway 7 ✈	a					19 03											
Liverpool Lime Street 10	a					19 14	19 19										
	d																
Manchester Airport ✈	d			17 58							18 30						18 58
Manchester Piccadilly 10	d			18 16							18 46						19 16
Bolton	d			18 33							19 05						19 33
Wigan North Western	a											19 27	19 37				
	d											19 27	19 38				
Preston 8	a			18 57							19 33	19 40	19 51				19 57
Preston 8	d			19 00	19 06						19 35	19 42	19 53				20 06
Blackpool North	a										20 01						
Lancaster 6	a			19 15	19 22							19 56	20 08				20 21
	d			19 16	19 22							19 57	20 08				20 22
Barrow-in-Furness	a				20 26												21 17
Oxenholme Lake District	a			19 30								20 10					
	d			19 30								20 10					
Windermere	a																
Penrith North Lakes	d			19 55								20 36	20 45				
Carlisle 8	a			20 12								20 51	21 00				
	d			20 13								20 52	21 02				
Lockerbie	d			20 32													
Carstairs	a																
Motherwell	a																
Glasgow Central 15	a											22 07					
Haymarket	a			21s30									22 15				
Edinburgh 10	a			21 39									22 21				
Perth	a																
Dundee	a																
Aberdeen	a																
Inverness	a																

OVERNIGHT SLEEPERS. For sleeper trains, operated by First ScotRail, please refer to Tables 400 - 404

Table 65 **Sundays** from 1 April

London and West Midlands - North West England and Scotland

Route Diagram - see first Page of Table 65

		LM	VT	VT	VT	XC	TP	VT	VT	VT	XC	VT	LM	VT	VT
		◇1	◇1	◇1	◇1	◇1	◇1	◇1	1	◇1	◇1	◇1	◇1	◇1	◇1
London Euston 15 ⊖	d		18 02	18 05	18 15			18 25		18 35		18 55		19 02	19 05
Watford Junction	d														
Milton Keynes Central	d			18 39	18 48										19 39
Rugby	d														
Nuneaton	d													20 01	
Tamworth Low Level	d														
Lichfield Trent Valley	d														
Coventry	d					18 26									
Birmingham International ✈	d					18 38									
Birmingham New Street 12	d	18 35				19 01			19 20		19 31		19 35		
Wolverhampton 7	d	18 53				19 19			19 37		19 49		19 53		
Penkridge	d	19 03											20 03		
Stafford	a	19 09	19 24			19 37							20 09	20 25	
	d	19 09	19 25			19 38							20 09	20 30	
Stoke-on-Trent	a				19 50	19 56					20 19	20 25			
Congleton	a														
Macclesfield	a					20 14						20 42			
Crewe 10	a	19 29		19 50					20 07	20 12			20 30	20 48	20 53
	d	19 31		19 52					20 09	20 13			20 31	20 50	20 55
Chester	a			20 11											21 14
	d			20 18											21 17
Wrexham General	a														
Llandudno	a														
Bangor (Gwynedd)	a			21 23											22 22
Holyhead	a			21 57											22 56
Wilmslow	a									20 29					
Stockport	a				20 18	20 28				20 38		20 56			
Manchester Piccadilly 10	a				20 29	20 40				20 50	21 00	21 09			
Hartford	a	19 42											20 43		
Warrington Bank Quay	a							20 16	20 26						
	d							20 16	20 27						
Runcorn	a	19 53	19 58										20 54	21 07	
Liverpool South Parkway 7 ✈	a	20 02											21 03		
Liverpool Lime Street 10	a	20 14	20 16										21 14	21 28	
	d														
Manchester Airport ✈	d						19 30								
Manchester Piccadilly 10	d						19 46								
Bolton	d						20 05								
Wigan North Western	a							20 27	20 37						
	d							20 27	20 38						
Preston 8	a						20 33	20 40	20 51						
Preston 8	d						20 35	20 42	20 53						
Blackpool North	a						21 01								
Lancaster 6	a							20 56	21 08						
	d							20 57	21 08						
Barrow-in-Furness	a														
Oxenholme Lake District	a							21 10	21 22						
	d							21 11	21 24						
Windermere	a														
Penrith North Lakes	d							21 36							
Carlisle 8	a							21 51	22 01						
	d							21 52	22 03						
Lockerbie	d								22 23						
Carstairs	a														
Motherwell	a							22 48	23 07						
Glasgow Central 15	a							23 09	23 22						
Haymarket	a														
Edinburgh 10	a														
Perth	a														
Dundee	a														
Aberdeen	a														
Inverness	a														

OVERNIGHT SLEEPERS. For sleeper trains, operated by First ScotRail, please refer to Tables 400 - 404

Table 65

Sundays from 1 April

London and West Midlands - North West England and Scotland

Route Diagram - see first Page of Table 65

		VT	XC	VT	TP	VT	VT	XC	VT	VT	VT	VT	XC
		◇1	◇1	◇1	◇1	◇1	◇1	◇1	◇1	◇1	◇1	◇1	◇1
			A										A
London Euston 15 ⊖	d	19 15				19 25	19 35		19 55	20 02	20 05	20 15	
Watford Junction	d												
Milton Keynes Central	d	19 48									20 38	20 48	
Rugby	d												
Nuneaton	d									21 01			
Tamworth Low Level	d												
Lichfield Trent Valley	d												
Coventry	d		19 26										20 26
Birmingham International ✈	d		19 38										20 38
Birmingham New Street 12	d		20 01	20 20				20 31					21 01
Wolverhampton 7	d		20 19	20 38				20 52					21 19
Penkridge	d												
Stafford	a		20 36	20 51							21 31		21 36
	d		20 37	20 52							21 33		21 37
Stoke-on-Trent	a	20 50	20 56					21 19	21 25			21 50	21 56
Congleton	a												
Macclesfield	a		21 15						21 42				22 14
Crewe 10	a			21 10			21 13			21 44	21 53		
	d						21 14			21 46	21 55		
Chester	a												
	d												
Wrexham General	a												
Llandudno	a												
Bangor (Gwynedd)	a												
Holyhead	a												
Wilmslow	a						21 30						
Stockport	a	21 18	21 28				21 39		21 56			22 18	22 28
Manchester Piccadilly 10	a	21 29	21 40				21 50	21 56	22 09			22 29	22 40
Hartford	a												
Warrington Bank Quay	a					21 16							
	d					21 16							
Runcorn	a									22 03	22 12		
Liverpool South Parkway 7 ✈	a												
Liverpool Lime Street 10	a									22 23	22 33		
	d												
Manchester Airport ✈	d				20 30								
Manchester Piccadilly 10	d				20 46								
Bolton	d				21 05								
Wigan North Western	a					21 27							
	d					21 27							
Preston 8	a				21 33	21 40							
Preston 8	d				21 35	21 42							
Blackpool North	a				22 01								
Lancaster 6	a					21 56							
	d					21 57							
Barrow-in-Furness	a												
Oxenholme Lake District	a					22 10							
	d					22 11							
Windermere	a												
Penrith North Lakes	d					22 36							
Carlisle 8	a					22 51							
	d					22 53							
Lockerbie	d												
Carstairs	a												
Motherwell	a												
Glasgow Central 15	a					00 02							
Haymarket	a												
Edinburgh 10	a												
Perth	a												
Dundee	a												
Aberdeen	a												
Inverness	a												

A to Birmingham New Street

OVERNIGHT SLEEPERS. For sleeper trains, operated by First ScotRail, please refer to Tables 400 - 404

Table 65

Sundays from 1 April

London and West Midlands - North West England and Scotland

Route Diagram - see first Page of Table 65

		TP	VT	VT	VT	LM	XC	VT	SR	VT	VT	AW	VT	SR
		◇1	◇1	◇1	◇1	◇1	◇1	◇1		◇1	◇1	◇	◇1	
London Euston 15 ⊖	d		20 25		20 35			20 50	20 55	21 21	21 25		21 51	23 27
Watford Junction	d								21u17					23u47
Milton Keynes Central	d							21 37			22 14		22 38	
Rugby	d							22 01					23 18	
Nuneaton	d									22 52			23 29	
Tamworth Low Level	d		21 32											
Lichfield Trent Valley	d		21 39											
Coventry	d						21 26							
Birmingham International ✈	d						21 38					22 40		
Birmingham New Street 12	d			21 20		21 35	22 01					22 55		
Wolverhampton 7	d			21 38		21 57	22 19					23 15		
Penkridge	d					22 07								
Stafford	a			21 56	21 59	22 13	22 36			23 16		23 30	23s53	
	d			21 57	22 00	22 16	22 37			23 17		23 31		
Stoke-on-Trent	a						22 55				23 29			
Congleton	a													
Macclesfield	a						23 12				23 45			
Crewe 10	a		22 10	22 17	22 20	22 38		22 49		23 43		23 55	00s21	
	d		22 13	22 18	22 21			22 51	23u39	23 45		00 01		
Chester	a											00 22		
	d											00 38		
Wrexham General	a													
Llandudno	a													
Bangor (Gwynedd)	a											01 44		
Holyhead	a											02 20		
Wilmslow	a				22 36									
Stockport	a				22 45		23 27				23 59		00s50	
Manchester Piccadilly 10	a				22 57		23 41				00 12		01 00	
Hartford	a													
Warrington Bank Quay	a		22 29	22 36				23 08						
	d		22 30	22 36				23 08						
Runcorn	a									00 07				
Liverpool South Parkway 7 ✈	a													
Liverpool Lime Street 10	a									00 30				
	d													
Manchester Airport ✈	d	21 30												
Manchester Piccadilly 10	d	21 46												
Bolton	d	22 05												
Wigan North Western	a		22 40	22 47				23 19						
	d		22 41	22 47				23 19						
Preston 8	a	22 28	22 58	23 07				23 41						
Preston 8	d	22 29							00u30					
Blackpool North	a	22 55												
Lancaster 6	a													
	d													
Barrow-in-Furness	a													
Oxenholme Lake District	a													
	d													
Windermere	a													
Penrith North Lakes	d													
Carlisle 8	a													05s04
	d													
Lockerbie	d													
Carstairs	a													06s20
Motherwell	a													06s56
Glasgow Central 15	a													07 20
Haymarket	a													
Edinburgh 10	a								03s58					07 16
Perth	a								05s39					
Dundee	a								06s08					
Aberdeen	a								07 35					
Inverness	a								08 38					

OVERNIGHT SLEEPERS. For sleeper trains, operated by First ScotRail, please refer to Tables 400 - 404

Scotland and North West England - West Midlands and London

Route Diagram - see first Page of Table 65

Miles	Miles	Miles	Miles	Miles			TP	TP	TP	SR	LM	SR	SR	AW	TP	AW	TP	TP	LM	VT	SR	SR
							MX	MO	MO	MO	MX	MX	MX			MO					MO	
										B		B	B								B	B
							◇1	◇1	◇1		◇1				◇1		◇1	◇1	1	◇1		
								A	B			C	D	E		F						C
										sleeper		sleeper	sleeper							⊠	sleeper	sleeper
—	0	—	—	—	Inverness	d															20p25	20p47
—	—	0	—	—	Aberdeen	d																
—	—	71¼	—	—	Dundee	d																
—	118	—	—	—	Perth	d															23b00	23b21
—	130¼	187¼	—	—	**Edinburgh** 10	d															01 06	01 24
—	131½	188½	—	—	Haymarket	d																
0	—	—	—	—	**Glasgow Central** 15	d				23p15		23p40	23p40									
12¾	—	—	—	—	Motherwell	d				23b31		23b56	23b56									
28¾	158	—	—	—	Carstairs	d				23b47		00u16	00u16									
77	—	263½	—	—	Lockerbie	d																
102¾	—	—	—	—	**Carlisle** 8	a															02 51	02 53
—	—	—	—	—		d				01u12		01u41	01u41								02 53	02 54
120	—	—	—	—	Penrith North Lakes	d																
—	—	—	—	—	Windermere	d																
152¾	—	—	—	—	Oxenholme Lake District	a																
—	—	—	—	—		d																
—	—	—	—	—	Barrow-in-Furness	d											04 35					
171¼	—	—	—	—	Lancaster 6	a											05 28					
—	—	—	—	—		d																
—	—	—	—	—	Blackpool North	d	22p44	23p03	23p03						03 33							
192¾	—	—	—	—	**Preston** 8	a	23p08	23p28	23p28	03 02		03 07	03 07								04s41	04s32
—	—	—	0	—	**Preston** 8	d	23p10	23p28	23p28	03 07		03 13	03 13		03u58			05 16				
207½	—	—	—	—	Wigan North Western	a																
—	—	—	—	—		d																
—	—	—	—	—	Blackrod	d			23p50													
—	—	—	—	—	Lostock	d			23p57													
—	—	—	20	—	Bolton	a	23p34	00 01	00 02						04c31			05 42				
—	—	—	31¼	—	**Manchester Piccadilly** 10	a	23p53	00 16	00 18						04 48			06 01				
—	—	—	—	—	Manchester Airport ✈	a	00 24	00 30	00 32						05 07			06 18				
—	0	—	—	—	**Liverpool Lime Street** 10	a																
—	—	—	—	—		d					23p34											
—	5½	—	—	—	Liverpool South Parkway ✈	d					23p45											
—	13	—	—	—	Runcorn	d					23p53											
219¼	—	—	—	—	Warrington Bank Quay	a				03 34		03 40	03 44									
—	—	—	—	—		d				03 36		03 41	03 45									
231½	23¾	—	—	—	Hartford	d					00 07											
—	—	—	—	0	**Manchester Piccadilly** 10	d								00 50						05 05		
—	—	—	37	5¾	Stockport	d														05 13		
—	—	—	—	—	Wilmslow	d																
—	—	—	—	—	Holyhead	d																
—	—	—	—	—	Bangor (Gwynedd)	d																
—	—	—	—	—	Llandudno Junction	d																
—	—	—	—	—	Wrexham General	d																
—	—	—	—	—	Chester	d										04 22						
243½	35½	—	—	—	**Crewe** 10	a					00 22			01 31		04 44				05 34	05s37	05s34
—	—	—	—	—		d										04 59			05 18	05 36		
—	—	—	49	17¾	Macclesfield	d																
—	—	—	57	25¾	Congleton	d																
—	—	—	68¾	37¼	**Stoke-on-Trent**	d																
267¾	—	—	—	53½	**Stafford**	a										05 24				05 53		
—	—	—	—	—		d										05 25				05 55		
—	—	—	—	59¾	Penkridge	a																
—	—	—	—	69¾	Wolverhampton 7	a										05 39						
—	—	—	—	82½	**Birmingham New Street** 12	a										06 01						
—	—	—	—	91	Birmingham International ✈	a																
—	—	—	—	101½	Coventry	a																
285	—	—	99¼	—	Lichfield Trent Valley	a													06 06			
291¼	—	—	—	—	Tamworth Low Level	a													06 13			
304¼	—	—	—	—	Nuneaton	a													06 29	06 17		
318¾	—	—	—	113	Rugby	a													06 47	06 30		
351½	—	—	—	—	Milton Keynes Central	a														06 51		
383½	—	—	—	—	Watford Junction	a				06s23		06s19	06s22									
401¼	—	—	—	—	**London Euston** 15 ⊖	a				06 46		06 43	06 43							07 28	07 47	07 47

A from 9 January until 13 February
B until 2 January and then from 20 February
C until 30 December and then from 27 March
D from 3 January until 23 March
E from 3 January until 6 January
F until 26 March, from 2 April
b Previous night, stops to pick up only
c Stops to pick up only

OVERNIGHT SLEEPERS. For sleeper trains, operated by First ScotRail, please refer to Tables 400 - 404

Scotland and North West England - West Midlands and London

Route Diagram - see first Page of Table 65

		SR	XC	VT	XC	VT	VT	TP	LM	VT	VT	XC	VT	TP	LM	VT	VT	TP
		MX																
		B	◇1	◇1	◇1	◇1	◇1	◇1	◇1	◇1	◇1	◇1	◇1	◇1	◇1	◇1	◇1	◇1
		A																B
		sleeper	T	⊠	T	⊠	⊠	T		⊠	⊠	T	⊠	T		⊠	⊠	T
Inverness	d	20p47																
Aberdeen	d																	
Dundee	d																	
Perth	d	23b21																
Edinburgh 10	d	01c24																
Haymarket	d																	
Glasgow Central 15	d																	
Motherwell	d																	
Carstairs	d																	
Lockerbie	d																	
Carlisle 8	a	02 53																
	d	02 54																
Penrith North Lakes	d																	
Windermere	d																	
Oxenholme Lake District	a																	
	d																	
Barrow-in-Furness	d																	05 31
Lancaster 6	a																	06 23
	d						05 35											06 23
Blackpool North	d							05 39										
Preston 8	a	04s32					05 52	06 03										06 42
Preston 8	d					05 33	06 00	06 05									06 16	06 44
Wigan North Western	a					05 44	06 11										06 27	
	d					05 45	06 11										06 27	
Blackrod	d							06 22										
Lostock	d							06 30										
Bolton	a							06 34										07 08
Manchester Piccadilly 10	a							06 56										07 27
Manchester Airport ✈	a							07 17										07 47
Liverpool Lime Street 10	a																	
	d			05 27							06 05			06 15				
Liverpool South Parkway ✈	d													06 25				
Runcorn	d			05 43							06 21							
Warrington Bank Quay	a					05 55	06 22										06 38	
	d					05 56	06 22										06 38	
Hartford	d																	
Manchester Piccadilly 10	d		05 11							05 55		06 00	06 10	07a09				
Stockport	d									06 03		06 08	06 18					
Wilmslow	d									06 11								
Holyhead	d															04 48		
Bangor (Gwynedd)	d															05 14		
Llandudno Junction	d															05 32		
Wrexham General	d																	
Chester	d															06 26		
Crewe 10	a	05s38	05 44	06 00			06 42			06 27		06 32				06 47	06 58	
	d		05 47	06 02					06 20	06 29		06 38			06 47	06 53	07 01	
Macclesfield	d												06 31					
Congleton	d																	
Stoke-on-Trent	d		06 07		←								06 48					
Stafford	a		06 24	06 20	06 24				06 40		06 52	06 57			07 10			
	d		06 25	06 21	06 25				06 41		06 53	06 58			07 12			
Penkridge	a		→						06 46						07 17			
Wolverhampton 7	a				06 39				06 57			07 12			07 28		07 31	
Birmingham New Street 12	a				06 58				07 18			07 31			07 48		07 55	
Birmingham International ✈	a				07 13													
Coventry	a				07 24													
Lichfield Trent Valley	a					06 40					07 07							
Tamworth Low Level	a					06 46					07 14							
Nuneaton	a									07 06						07 32		
Rugby	a			06 52		07 06							07 28					
Milton Keynes Central	a			07 12														
Watford Junction	a																	
London Euston 15 ⊖	a	07 47		07 50		07 57				08 07	08 22		08 22			08 33		

A from 3 January until 23 March
B T from Preston
b Previous night, stops to pick up only

OVERNIGHT SLEEPERS. For sleeper trains, operated by First ScotRail, please refer to Tables 400 - 404

Scotland and North West England - West Midlands and London

Route Diagram - see first Page of Table 65

		VT	VT	LM	VT	LM	VT	VT	TP	XC	LM	VT	VT	VT	TP	TP	XC	VT	EM
		◇**1**	◇**1**	◇**1**	◇**1**	◇**1**	◇**1**	◇**1**	◇**1**	◇**1**	◇**1**	◇**1**	◇**1**	◇**1**	◇**1**	◇**1**	◇**1**	◇**1**	◇
															A				
		⊠	⊠		⊠		⊠	⊠	⌶	⌶		⊠	⊠	⊠	⌶	⌶	⌶	⊠	
Inverness	d																		
Aberdeen	d																		
Dundee	d																		
Perth	d																		
Edinburgh **10**	d																		
Haymarket	d																		
Glasgow Central **15**	d							04 28											
Motherwell	d																		
Carstairs	d																		
Lockerbie	d																		
Carlisle **8**	a							05 42											
	d							05 43											
Penrith North Lakes	d							05 57											
Windermere	d																		
Oxenholme Lake District	a							06 20											
	d							06 20											
Barrow-in-Furness	d														06 20				
Lancaster **6**	a							06 35							07 21				
	d							06 35						06 58	07 22				
Blackpool North	d								06 40							07 10			
Preston **8**	a							06 53	07 07					07 15	07 41	07 37			
Preston **8**	d							06 56	07 09					07 17	07 47				
Wigan North Western	a							07 06						07 28					
	d							07 08						07 28					
Blackrod	d																		
Lostock	d								07 30										
Bolton	a								07 34						08 08				
Manchester Piccadilly **10**	a								07 56						08 27				
Manchester Airport ✈	a								08 17						08 47				
Liverpool Lime Street **10**	a																		
	d			06 30			07 00				07 04								06 47
Liverpool South Parkway ✈	d			06 40							07 14								06 57
Runcorn	d			06 48			07u15				07 22								
Warrington Bank Quay	a							07 17						07 39					
	d							07 18						07 39					
Hartford	d			07 02							07 36								
Manchester Piccadilly **10**	d	06 27	06 35		06 43					07 07		07 15					07 26	07 35	07 42
Stockport	d	06 35	06 43		06 51					07 16		07 23					07 35	07 43	07a53
Wilmslow	d				06 59														
Holyhead	d												05 51						
Bangor (Gwynedd)	d												06 18						
Llandudno Junction	d												06 36						
Wrexham General	d																		
Chester	d												07 35						
Crewe **10**	a			07 14	07 15						07 48		07 54	07 58					
	d			07 16	07 17						07 49		07 57	08 01					
Macclesfield	d	06 48	06 56														07 49	07 56	
Congleton	d																		
Stoke-on-Trent	d	07 06	07 12			←				07 44		07 50					08 07	08 12	
Stafford	a	07 27		07 40	07 34	07 40				08 01	08 10						08 24		
	d	07 28		07 41	07 35	07 41				08 02	08 10						08 25		
Penkridge	a			→		07 46					08 16								
Wolverhampton **7**	a	07 43				07 57				08 15	08 26			08 31			08 39		
Birmingham New Street **12**	a	08 06				08 17				08 32	08 47			08 55			08 58		
Birmingham International ✈	a	08 19															09 13		
Coventry	a	08 30															09 24		
Lichfield Trent Valley	a																		
Tamworth Low Level	a																		
Nuneaton	a																	08 44	
Rugby	a		07 52										08 45						
Milton Keynes Central	a											08s46							
Watford Junction	a	09s15																09s31	
London Euston **15** ⊖	a	09 34	08 45		08 52		09 01	09 04				09 23	09 38					09 52	

A ⌶ from Preston

OVERNIGHT SLEEPERS. For sleeper trains, operated by First ScotRail, please refer to Tables 400 - 404

Scotland and North West England - West Midlands and London

Route Diagram - see first Page of Table 65

		TP	LM	VT	LM	VT	VT	TP	TP	XC	LM	VT	VT	VT	NT	TP	XC	VT	EM
		◇**1**	◇**1**	◇**1**	◇**1**	◇**1**	◇**1**	◇**1**	◇**1**	◇**1**	◇**1**	◇**1**	◇**1**	◇**1**		◇**1**	◇**1**	◇**1**	◇
																A			
		⌶		⊠		⊠	⊠	⌶	⌶	⌶		⊠	⊠	⊠		⌶	⌶	⊠	
Inverness	d																		
Aberdeen	d																		
Dundee	d																		
Perth	d																		
Edinburgh **10**	d							05 36											
Haymarket	d							05u40											
Glasgow Central **15**	d						05 40							05 50					
Motherwell	d													06 04					
Carstairs	d																		
Lockerbie	d																		
Carlisle **8**	a						06 46	06 58						07 02					
	d						06 49	06 59						07 04					
Penrith North Lakes	d													07 19					
Windermere	d																		
Oxenholme Lake District	a						07 22							07 42					
	d						07 24							07 42					
Barrow-in-Furness	d														07 00	07 29			
Lancaster **6**	a						07 37	07 47						07 56	08 04	08 26			
	d						07 38	07 47						07 57	08 05	08 27			
Blackpool North	d								07 36										
Preston **8**	a						07 56	08 07	08 03					08 15	08 30	08 45			
Preston **8**	d						07 58	08 12						08 17		08 47			
Wigan North Western	a						08 09							08 28					
	d						08 09							08 28					
Blackrod	d																		
Lostock	d																		
Bolton	a							08 34								09 08			
Manchester Piccadilly **10**	a							08 56								09 27			
Manchester Airport ✈	a							09 19								09 47			
Liverpool Lime Street **10**	a																		
	d	07 15	07 34	07 48							08 04								07 42
Liverpool South Parkway ✈	d	07 25	07 44								08 15								07 53
Runcorn	d		07 52	08 04							08 24								
Warrington Bank Quay	a						08 20							08 39					
	d						08 20							08 39					
Hartford	d		08 04																
Manchester Piccadilly **10**	d	08a08				07 55				08 07		08 15					08 27	08 35	08 43
Stockport	d					08 04				08 16		08 23					08 35	08 43	08a53
Wilmslow	d					08 11													
Holyhead	d												06 55						
Bangor (Gwynedd)	d												07 22						
Llandudno Junction	d												07 40						
Wrexham General	d																		
Chester	d												08 35						
Crewe **10**	a		08 19			08 27					08 47		08 54	08 58					
	d		08 22			08 29					08 49		08 56	09 01					
Macclesfield	d																08 49	08 56	
Congleton	d																		
Stoke-on-Trent	d				←					08 44		08 50					09 07	09 12	
Stafford	a		08 42	08 35	08 42					09 02	09 09						09 24		
	d		08 43	08 36	08 43					09 03	09 10						09 25		
Penkridge	a		→		08 48						09 15								
Wolverhampton **7**	a				08 58					09 15	09 27			09 31			09 39		
Birmingham New Street **12**	a				09 18					09 32	09 47			09 55			09 58		
Birmingham International ✈	a																10 13		
Coventry	a																10 24		
Lichfield Trent Valley	a																		
Tamworth Low Level	a																		
Nuneaton	a																		
Rugby	a																		
Milton Keynes Central	a											09 46	10 01						
Watford Junction	a																		
London Euston **15** ⊖	a			09 56		10 04	10 12					10 23	10 38					10 42	

A ⌶ from Preston

OVERNIGHT SLEEPERS. For sleeper trains, operated by First ScotRail, please refer to Tables 400 - 404

Scotland and North West England - West Midlands and London

Route Diagram - see first Page of Table 65

					TP		LM	VT	LM		VT	VT	SR	XC	LM	VT	XC	VT	VT		EM				TP
					◇1 🛒		◇1	◇1 ⊠	◇1		◇1 ⊠	◇1 ⊠		◇1 🛒	◇1	◇1 ⊠	◇1 🛒	◇1 ⊠	◇1 ⊠		◇				◇1 🛒
Inverness	d																								
Aberdeen	d																								
Dundee	d																								
Perth	d																								
Edinburgh 10	d																								
Haymarket	d																								
Glasgow Central 15	d											06 30	07 07												
Motherwell	d											06 44													
Carstairs	d																								
Lockerbie	d											07 25													
Carlisle 8	a											07 43	09 37												
	d											07 46													
Penrith North Lakes	d											08 00													
Windermere	d																								
Oxenholme Lake District	a											08 22													
	d											08 23													
Barrow-in-Furness	d																								
Lancaster 6	a											08 37													
	d											08 38													
Blackpool North	d																								
Preston 8	a											08 56													
Preston 8	d											08 58													
Wigan North Western	a											09 09													
	d											09 09													
Blackrod	d																								
Lostock	d																								
Bolton	a																								
Manchester Piccadilly 10 🚊	a																								
Manchester Airport ✈	a																								
Liverpool Lime Street 10	a																								
	d				08 22		08 34	08 48							09 04						08 52				09 22
Liverpool South Parkway ✈	d				08 32		08 44								09 15						09 03				09 32
Runcorn	d						08 52	09 04							09 25										
Warrington Bank Quay	a											09 20													
	d											09 20													
Hartford	d						09 06																		
Manchester Piccadilly 10 🚊	d				09a09						08 55			09 07		09 15	09 27		09 35		09 43				10a09
Stockport	d										09 04			09 16		09 23	09 35		09 43		09a53				
Wilmslow	d										09 11														
Holyhead	d																								
Bangor (Gwynedd)	d																								
Llandudno Junction	d																								
Wrexham General	d																								
Chester	d																	09 35							
Crewe 10	a						09 20				09 27				09 44			09 54							
	d						09 22				09 29				09 49			09 56							
Macclesfield	d																09 49		09 56						
Congleton	d																								
Stoke-on-Trent	d								←					09 44		09 50	10 07		10 12						
Stafford	a						09 42	09 35	09 42					10 02	10 09		10 24								
	d						09 43	09 36	09 43					10 03	10 10		10 25								
Penkridge	a						→								10 15										
Wolverhampton 7 🚊	a								09 56					10 15	10 27		10 39								
Birmingham New Street 12	a								10 17					10 39	10 47		10 58								
Birmingham International ✈	a																11 13								
Coventry	a																11 24								
Lichfield Trent Valley	a																								
Tamworth Low Level	a																								
Nuneaton	a																								
Rugby	a																								
Milton Keynes Central	a															10 46		11 01							
Watford Junction	a																								
London Euston 15 ⊖	a							10 56			11 04	11 12				11 23		11 38	11 42						

OVERNIGHT SLEEPERS. For sleeper trains, operated by First ScotRail, please refer to Tables 400 - 404

Scotland and North West England - West Midlands and London

Route Diagram - see first Page of Table 65

			NT	TP	VT		TP		LM	VT	LM	VT	VT	XC	LM		NT	TP	TP	VT	VT	VT	XC	VT	EM
				◇1 🛒	◇1 ⊠		◇1 🛒		◇1	◇1 ⊠	◇1	◇1 ⊠	◇1 ⊠	◇1 🛒	◇1			◇1 🛒	◇1 🛒	◇1 ⊠	◇1 ⊠	◇1 ⊠	◇1 🛒	◇1 ⊠	◇
Inverness	d																								
Aberdeen	d																								
Dundee	d																								
Perth	d																								
Edinburgh 10	d				06 52													07 42							
Haymarket	d				06 56													07u46							
Glasgow Central 15	d						07 10						07 37									08 00			
Motherwell	d												07 52												
Carstairs	d																								
Lockerbie	d						08 06																		
Carlisle 8	a				08 05		08 29						08 46					08 59				09 08			
	d				08 07		08 29						08 49					08 59				09 10			
Penrith North Lakes	d				08 22		08 45																		
Windermere	d																								
Oxenholme Lake District	a						09 09						09 22												
	d						09 11						09 23												
Barrow-in-Furness	d																								
Lancaster 6	a				08 56		09 25						09 37									09 56			
	d				08 57		09 26						09 38									09 57			
Blackpool North	d			08 44													09 37		09 43						
Preston 8	a			09 08	09 15		09 45						09 56				10 02	10 05	10 07			10 15			
Preston 8	d		09 04	09 10	09 17		09 47						09 58				10 04	10 12				10 17			
Wigan North Western	a		09 24		09 28								10 09				10 24					10 28			
	d		09 24		09 28								10 09				10 24					10 28			
Blackrod	d																								
Lostock	d																								
Bolton	a			09 34			10 08											10 34							
Manchester Piccadilly 10 🚊	a			09 56			10 27											10 56							
Manchester Airport ✈	a			10 17			10 47											11 17							
Liverpool Lime Street 10	a		10 02														11 02								
	d		10 16						09 34	09 48					10 04		11 16								09 52
Liverpool South Parkway ✈	d		10a27						09 44						10 15		11a27								10 03
Runcorn	d								09 52	10 04					10 25										
Warrington Bank Quay	a				09 39								10 20									10 39			
	d				09 39								10 20									10 39			
Hartford	d								10 04																
Manchester Piccadilly 10 🚊	d											09 55		10 07						10 15			10 27	10 35	10 43
Stockport	d											10 04		10 16						10 23			10 35	10 43	10a53
Wilmslow	d											10 11													
Holyhead	d																				08 55				
Bangor (Gwynedd)	d																				09 22				
Llandudno Junction	d																				09 40				
Wrexham General	d																								
Chester	d																				10 35				
Crewe 10	a				09 58				10 19			10 27			10 45						10 54	10 58			
	d				10 01				10 22			10 29			10 49						10 56	11 01			
Macclesfield	d																						10 49	10 56	
Congleton	d																								
Stoke-on-Trent	d										←			10 44						10 50			11 07	11 12	
Stafford	a								10 42	10 35	10 42			11 01	11 09								11 24		
	d								10 43	10 36	10 43			11 02	11 10								11 25		
Penkridge	a								→						11 15										
Wolverhampton 7 🚊	a				10 33						10 56			11 15	11 27							11 31	11 39		
Birmingham New Street 12	a				11 10						11 18			11 32	11 47							11 55	11 58		
Birmingham International ✈	a				11 19																		12 13		
Coventry	a				11 30																		12 24		
Lichfield Trent Valley	a																								
Tamworth Low Level	a																								
Nuneaton	a																								
Rugby	a																								
Milton Keynes Central	a																			11 46	12 01				
Watford Junction	a				12s15																				
London Euston 15 ⊖	a				12 32					11 56		12 04	12 12							12 23	12 38			12 42	

OVERNIGHT SLEEPERS. For sleeper trains, operated by First ScotRail, please refer to Tables 400 - 404

Table 65

Mondays to Fridays

Scotland and North West England - West Midlands and London

Route Diagram - see first Page of Table 65

		VT	TP	NT	TP	LM	VT	LM	VT	VT	XC	LM	NT	TP	VT	VT	VT
		FO															
		◇	◇[1]		◇[1]	◇[1]	◇[1]	◇[1]	◇[1]	◇[1]	◇[1]	◇[1]		◇[1]	◇[1]	◇[1]	◇[1]
			A														
		⊡	⊥		⊥		⊠		⊠	⊠	⊥			⊥	⊡	⊡	⊠
Inverness	d																
Aberdeen	d																
Dundee	d																
Perth	d																
Edinburgh [10]	d																08 52
Haymarket	d																08 57
Glasgow Central [15]	d									08 40							
Motherwell	d																
Carstairs	d																
Lockerbie	d																
Carlisle [8]	a									09 47							10 05
	d									09 49							10 07
Penrith North Lakes	d									10 03							
Windermere	d																
Oxenholme Lake District	a																10 41
	d																10 42
Barrow-in-Furness	d		09 23	10 16													
Lancaster [6]	a		10 25	11 20						10 37							10 56
	d		10 26							10 38							10 57
Blackpool North	d												10 37	10 44			
Preston [8]	a		10 45							10 56			11 02	11 08			11 15
Preston [8]	d	10 36	10 47							10 58			11 04	11 10			11 17
Wigan North Western	a	10 47								11 09			11 24				11 28
	d	10 47								11 09			11 24				11 28
Blackrod	d																
Lostock	d																
Bolton	a		11 08											11 34			
Manchester Piccadilly [10]	a		11 27											11 56			
Manchester Airport	a		11 50											12 17			
Liverpool Lime Street [10]	a												12 02				
	d				10 22	10 34	10 48					11 04	12 16				
Liverpool South Parkway	d				10 32	10 44						11 15	12a27				
Runcorn	d					10 52	11 04					11 25					
Warrington Bank Quay	a	10 58								11 20							11 39
	d	10 58								11 20							11 39
Hartford	d					11 04											
Manchester Piccadilly [10]	d				11a09				10 55		11 07				11 15		
Stockport	d								11 04		11 16				11 23		
Wilmslow	d								11 11								
Holyhead	d																
Bangor (Gwynedd)	d																
Llandudno Junction	d																
Wrexham General	d																
Chester	d															11 35	
Crewe [10]	a					11 19			11 27			11 45				11 54	11 58
	d					11 22			11 29			11 49				11 56	12 01
Macclesfield	d																
Congleton	d																
Stoke-on-Trent	d							←			11 44				11 50		
Stafford	a					11 43	11 33	11 43			12 02	12 09					
	d					11 43	11 34	11 43			12 03	12 10					
Penkridge	a					↪						12 15					
Wolverhampton [7]	a							11 57			12 15	12 27					12 31
Birmingham New Street [12]	a							12 17			12 39	12 47					12 55
Birmingham International	a																
Coventry	a																
Lichfield Trent Valley	a																
Tamworth Low Level	a																
Nuneaton	a																
Rugby	a																
Milton Keynes Central	a														12 46	13 01	
Watford Junction	a																
London Euston [15]	a	12 52					12 56		13 03	13 12					13 23	13 38	

A ⊥ from Preston

OVERNIGHT SLEEPERS. For sleeper trains, operated by First ScotRail, please refer to Tables 400 - 404

Table 65

Mondays to Fridays

Scotland and North West England - West Midlands and London

Route Diagram - see first Page of Table 65

		TP	XC	VT	EM	TP	LM	VT	LM	VT	VT	TP	XC	LM	NT	TP	TP	VT
																FO	FX	
		◇[1]	◇[1]	◇[1]	◇	◇[1]	◇[1]	◇[1]	◇[1]	◇[1]	◇[1]	◇[1]	◇[1]	◇[1]		◇[1]	◇[1]	◇[1]
		A																
		⊥	⊥	⊡		⊥		⊡		⊡	⊠		⊥			⊥	⊥	⊡
Inverness	d																	
Aberdeen	d																	
Dundee	d																	
Perth	d																	
Edinburgh [10]	d																	
Haymarket	d																	
Glasgow Central [15]	d										09 40							
Motherwell	d																	
Carstairs	d																	
Lockerbie	d																	
Carlisle [8]	a										10 47							
	d										10 49							
Penrith North Lakes	d																	
Windermere	d	10 49																
Oxenholme Lake District	a	11 08									11 22							
	d	11 09									11 23							
Barrow-in-Furness	d											11 25						
Lancaster [6]	a	11 26									11 37	12 18						
	d	11 26									11 38	12 18						
Blackpool North	d														11 37	11 44	11 44	
Preston [8]	a	11 45									11 56	12 37			12 02	12 08	12 08	
Preston [8]	d	11 47									11 58				12 04	12 10	12 10	
Wigan North Western	a										12 09				12 24			
	d										12 09				12 24			
Blackrod	d																	
Lostock	d																	
Bolton	a	12 08														12 34	12 34	
Manchester Piccadilly [10]	a	12 27														12 56	12 56	
Manchester Airport	a	12 47														13 16	13 17	
Liverpool Lime Street [10]	a														13 02			
	d				10 52	11 22	11 34	11 48						12 04	13 16			
Liverpool South Parkway	d				11 03	11 32	11 44							12 15	13a27			
Runcorn	d						11 52	12 04						12 25				
Warrington Bank Quay	a										12 20							
	d										12 20							
Hartford	d						12 04											
Manchester Piccadilly [10]	d		11 27	11 35	11 43	12a09				11 55			12 07					12 15
Stockport	d		11 35	11 43	11a53					12 04			12 16					12 23
Wilmslow	d									12 11								
Holyhead	d																	
Bangor (Gwynedd)	d																	
Llandudno Junction	d																	
Wrexham General	d																	
Chester	d																	
Crewe [10]	a						12 19			12 27				12 45				
	d						12 22			12 29				12 49				
Macclesfield	d		11 49	11 56														
Congleton	d																	
Stoke-on-Trent	d		12 07	12 12					←				12 44					12 50
Stafford	a		12 24				12 42	12 35	12 42				13 01	13 09				
	d		12 25				12 43	12 36	12 43				13 02	13 10				
Penkridge	a						↪							13 15				
Wolverhampton [7]	a		12 39						12 56				13 15	13 27				
Birmingham New Street [12]	a		12 58						13 17				13 39	13 47				
Birmingham International	a		13 13															
Coventry	a		13 24															
Lichfield Trent Valley	a																	
Tamworth Low Level	a																	
Nuneaton	a																	
Rugby	a																	
Milton Keynes Central	a																	13 46
Watford Junction	a																	
London Euston [15]	a			13 42				13 56		14 04	14 12							14 23

A ⊥ from Preston

OVERNIGHT SLEEPERS. For sleeper trains, operated by First ScotRail, please refer to Tables 400 - 404

Scotland and North West England - West Midlands and London

Route Diagram - see first Page of Table 65

		VT	VT		TP FX	TP	XC	VT	EM				TP			TP FO	LM	VT	LM	VT	VT	XC	LM		NT
		◇1	◇1		◇1	◇1	◇1	◇1	◇				◇1			◇1	◇1	◇1	◇1	◇1	◇1	◇1	◇1		
		☕	☕		⊼	⊼	⊼	☕					⊼					☕		☕	⊠	⊼			
Inverness	d																								
Aberdeen	d																								
Dundee	d																								
Perth	d																								
Edinburgh 10	d				09 51																				
Haymarket	d				09u56																				
Glasgow Central 15	d		10 00			10 10															10 40				
Motherwell	d																								
Carstairs	d																								
Lockerbie	d				11 01																				
Carlisle 8	a		11 10		11 22	11 26															11 47				
	d		11 11		11 29																11 49				
Penrith North Lakes	d		11 26		11 45																				
Windermere	d																								
Oxenholme Lake District	a				12 09																12 22				
	d				12 10																12 23				
Barrow-in-Furness	d															13 25									
Lancaster 6	a				12 26											14 18					12 37				
	d				12 26																12 38				
Blackpool North	d																								12 37
Preston 8	a		12 15		12 45																12 56				13 02
Preston 8	d		12 17		12 47																12 58				13 04
Wigan North Western	a		12 28																		13 09				13 24
	d		12 28																		13 09				13 24
Blackrod	d																								
Lostock	d																								
Bolton	a				13 08																				
Manchester Piccadilly 10	a				13 27																				
Manchester Airport ✈	a				13 47																				
Liverpool Lime Street 10	a																								14 02
	d								11 52				12 22				12 34	12 48					13 04		14 16
Liverpool South Parkway ✈	d								12 03				12 32				12 44						13 15		14a27
Runcorn	d																12 52	13 04					13 25		
Warrington Bank Quay	a		12 39																		13 20				
	d		12 39																		13 20				
Hartford	d																13 06								
Manchester Piccadilly 10	d						12 27	12 35	12 43				13a09							12 55		13 07			
Stockport	d						12 35	12 43	12a53											13 04		13 16			
Wilmslow	d																			13 11					
Holyhead	d																								
Bangor (Gwynedd)	d																								
Llandudno Junction	d																								
Wrexham General	d																								
Chester	d	12 35																							
Crewe 10	a	12 54	12 58														13 20			13 27			13 45		
	d	12 56	13 01														13 22			13 29			13 49		
Macclesfield	d						12 49	12 56																	
Congleton	d																								
Stoke-on-Trent	d						13 07	13 12											←			13 44			
Stafford	a						13 24										13 42	13 35	13 42			14 01	14 09		
	d						13 25										13 43	13 36	13 43			14 02	14 10		
Penkridge	a																→						14 15		
Wolverhampton 7	a		13 31				13 39												13 56			14 15	14 27		
Birmingham New Street 12	a		13 55				13 58												14 17			14 32	14 47		
Birmingham International ✈	a						14 13																		
Coventry	a						14 24																		
Lichfield Trent Valley	a																								
Tamworth Low Level	a																								
Nuneaton	a																								
Rugby	a																								
Milton Keynes Central	a	14 01																							
Watford Junction	a																								
London Euston 15 ⊖	a	14 38						14 42										14 56		15 04	15 12				

OVERNIGHT SLEEPERS. For sleeper trains, operated by First ScotRail, please refer to Tables 400 - 404

Scotland and North West England - West Midlands and London

Route Diagram - see first Page of Table 65

		TP	VT	VT	VT	TP	XC	VT	EM					TP		LM	VT	LM	VT			VT	VT	XC	LM
		◇1	◇1	◇1	◇1	◇1	◇1	◇1	◇					◇1		◇1	◇1	◇1	◇1			◇1	◇1	◇1	1
						A																			
		⊼	☕	☕	⊠	⊼	⊼	☕						⊼			☕		⊠			☕	☕	⊼	
Inverness	d																								
Aberdeen	d																								
Dundee	d																								
Perth	d																								
Edinburgh 10	d				10 51																				
Haymarket	d				10 57																				
Glasgow Central 15	d																		11 40						
Motherwell	d																								
Carstairs	d																								
Lockerbie	d																								
Carlisle 8	a				12 05														12 46						
	d				12 07														12 49						
Penrith North Lakes	d																		13 03						
Windermere	d					12 51																			
Oxenholme Lake District	a				12 41	13 07																			
	d				12 43	13 09																			
Barrow-in-Furness	d																								
Lancaster 6	a				12 56	13 26																			
	d				12 57	13 26																	13 39		
Blackpool North	d	12 44																							
Preston 8	a	13 08			13 15	13 45													13 50				13 56		
Preston 8	d	13 10			13 17	13 47													13 53				13 59		
Wigan North Western	a				13 28																		14 09		
	d				13 28																		14 10		
Blackrod	d																								
Lostock	d																								
Bolton	a	13 34				14 08																			
Manchester Piccadilly 10	a	13 56				14 27																			
Manchester Airport ✈	a	14 17				14 47																			
Liverpool Lime Street 10	a																								
	d								12 52					13 22		13 34	13 48								14 04
Liverpool South Parkway ✈	d								13 03					13 32		13 44									14 15
Runcorn	d															13 52	14 04								14 25
Warrington Bank Quay	a				13 39																		14 20		
	d				13 39																		14 21		
Hartford	d															14 04									
Manchester Piccadilly 10	d		13 15				13 27	13 35	13 43					14a09								13 55		14 07	
Stockport	d		13 23				13 35	13 43	13a53													14 04		14 16	
Wilmslow	d																					14 11			
Holyhead	d																								
Bangor (Gwynedd)	d			12 24																					
Llandudno Junction	d			12 42																					
Wrexham General	d																								
Chester	d			13 35																					
Crewe 10	a			13 54	13 58											14 19						14 27			14 45
	d			13 56	14 01											14 22						14 29			14 49
Macclesfield	d						13 49	13 56																	
Congleton	d																								
Stoke-on-Trent	d		13 50				14 07	14 12										←						14 44	
Stafford	a						14 24									14 46	14 35	14 46						15 02	15 09
	d						14 25									14 46	14 36	14 46						15 03	15 10
Penkridge	a															→									15 15
Wolverhampton 7	a				14 31		14 39											14 59						15 15	15 27
Birmingham New Street 12	a				14 55		14 58											15 20						15 39	15 47
Birmingham International ✈	a						15 13																		
Coventry	a						15 24																		
Lichfield Trent Valley	a																								
Tamworth Low Level	a																								
Nuneaton	a																								
Rugby	a																								
Milton Keynes Central	a		14 46	15 01																					
Watford Junction	a																								
London Euston 15 ⊖	a		15 23	15 38				15 42									15 56		16 03			16 04	16 11		

A ⊼ from Preston

OVERNIGHT SLEEPERS. For sleeper trains, operated by First ScotRail, please refer to Tables 400 - 404

Table 65

Mondays to Fridays

Scotland and North West England - West Midlands and London

Route Diagram - see first Page of Table 65

		VT	XC	VT	VT	EM	TP	NT	TP	VT	SR	TP FX	TP	NT	LM	VT	LM	VT
		◇1 ☕	◇1 🛒	◇1 ☕	◇1 ☕	◇	◇1 🛒		◇1 🛒	◇1 ☕		◇1	◇1 🛒		◇1	◇1 ☕	◇1	◇1 ☕
Inverness	d																	
Aberdeen	d																	
Dundee	d																	
Perth	d																	
Edinburgh 10	d												12 12					
Haymarket	d												12u16					
Glasgow Central 15	d									12 00	12 12							
Motherwell	d																	
Carstairs	d																	
Lockerbie	d												13 11					
Carlisle 8	a									13 08	14 32		13 33					
	d									13 09			13 34					
Penrith North Lakes	d																	
Windermere	d																	
Oxenholme Lake District	a												14 09					
	d												14 10					
Barrow-in-Furness	d											13 25		14 16				
Lancaster 6	a									13 56		14 18	14 26	15 20				
	d									13 58		14 18	14 26					
Blackpool North	d							13 37	13 44									
Preston 8	a							14 02	14 08	14 15		14 37	14 45					
Preston 8	d							14 04	14 10	14 17			14 47					
Wigan North Western	a							14 24		14 28								
	d							14 24		14 28								
Blackrod	d																	
Lostock	d																	
Bolton	a								14 34				15 08					
Manchester Piccadilly 10	a								14 56				15 27					
Manchester Airport ✈	a								15 17				15 47					
Liverpool Lime Street 10	a							15 02										
	d					13 52	14 22	15 16							14 34	14 48		
Liverpool South Parkway ✈	d					14 03	14 32	15a27							14 44			
Runcorn	d														14 52	15 04		
Warrington Bank Quay	a									14 39								
	d									14 39								
Hartford	d														15 04			
Manchester Piccadilly 10	d	14 15	14 27		14 35	14 43	15a09											14 55
Stockport	d	14 23	14 35		14 43	14a53												15 04
Wilmslow	d																	15 11
Holyhead	d																	
Bangor (Gwynedd)	d																	
Llandudno Junction	d																	
Wrexham General	d																	
Chester	d			14 35														
Crewe 10	a			14 54						14 58					15 19			15 27
	d			14 56						15 01					15 22			15 29
Macclesfield	d		14 49		14 56													
Congleton	d																	
Stoke-on-Trent	d	14 50	15 07		15 12												←	
Stafford	a		15 24												15 42	15 35	15 42	
	d		15 25												15 43	15 36	15 43	
Penkridge	a														→			
Wolverhampton 7	a		15 39							15 33							15 56	
Birmingham New Street 12	a		15 58							16 10							16 17	
Birmingham International ✈	a		16 13							16 19								
Coventry	a		16 24							16 30								
Lichfield Trent Valley	a																	
Tamworth Low Level	a																	
Nuneaton	a																	
Rugby	a																	
Milton Keynes Central	a	15 46		16 01														
Watford Junction	a									17 15								
London Euston 15 ⊖	a	16 23		16 38	16 42					17 34						16 59		17 04

OVERNIGHT SLEEPERS. For sleeper trains, operated by First ScotRail, please refer to Tables 400 - 404

Table 65

Mondays to Fridays

Scotland and North West England - West Midlands and London

Route Diagram - see first Page of Table 65

		VT	XC	LM	NT	TP	VT	VT	VT	TP	XC	VT	EM	TP	LM	VT	LM	VT
		◇1 ⊠	◇1 🛒	◇1		◇1 🛒	◇1 ☕	◇1 ☕	◇1 ☕	◇1 🛒	◇1 🛒	◇1 ☕	◇	◇1 🛒	◇1	◇1 ☕	◇1	◇1 ⊠
Inverness	d																	
Aberdeen	d																	
Dundee	d																	
Perth	d																	
Edinburgh 10	d								12 51									
Haymarket	d								12 57									
Glasgow Central 15	d	12 40								13 09								13 40
Motherwell	d																	
Carstairs	d																	
Lockerbie	d									14 06								
Carlisle 8	a	13 47							14 05	14 29								14 46
	d	13 49							14 07	14 29								14 49
Penrith North Lakes	d								14 22	14 45								
Windermere	d																	
Oxenholme Lake District	a	14 22																15 22
	d	14 24																15 24
Barrow-in-Furness	d																	
Lancaster 6	a	14 37							14 56	15 22								
	d	14 38							14 57	15 22								
Blackpool North	d				14 37	14 44												
Preston 8	a	14 56			15 02	15 08			15 15	15 41								15 50
Preston 8	d	14 58			15 04	15 10			15 17	15 47								15 53
Wigan North Western	a	15 09			15 24				15 28									
	d	15 09			15 24				15 28									
Blackrod	d																	
Lostock	d																	
Bolton	a					15 34				16 08								
Manchester Piccadilly 10	a					15 56				16 27								
Manchester Airport ✈	a					16 17				16 47								
Liverpool Lime Street 10	a				16 02													
	d			15 04	16 16								14 52	15 22	15 34	15 48		
Liverpool South Parkway ✈	d			15 15	16a27								15 03	15 32	15 44			
Runcorn	d			15 25											15 52	16 04		
Warrington Bank Quay	a	15 20							15 39									
	d	15 20							15 39									
Hartford	d														16 04			
Manchester Piccadilly 10	d		15 07				15 15				15 27	15 35	15 43	16a09				
Stockport	d		15 16				15 23				15 35	15 43	15a53					
Wilmslow	d																	
Holyhead	d							13 58										
Bangor (Gwynedd)	d							14 25										
Llandudno Junction	d							14 43										
Wrexham General	d																	
Chester	d							15 35										
Crewe 10	a			15 45				15 54	15 58						16 19			
	d			15 49				15 57	16 01						16 22			
Macclesfield	d										15 49	15 56						
Congleton	d																	
Stoke-on-Trent	d		15 44				15 50				16 07	16 12					←	
Stafford	a		16 02	16 09							16 24				16 46	16 35	16 46	
	d		16 03	16 10							16 25				16 46	16 36	16 46	
Penkridge	a			16 15											→			
Wolverhampton 7	a		16 15	16 26					16 31		16 39						16 59	
Birmingham New Street 12	a		16 39	16 47					16 55		16 58						17 20	
Birmingham International ✈	a										17 13							
Coventry	a										17 24							
Lichfield Trent Valley	a																	
Tamworth Low Level	a																	
Nuneaton	a																	
Rugby	a																	
Milton Keynes Central	a						16 46	17 01										
Watford Junction	a																	
London Euston 15 ⊖	a	17 12					17 23	17 38				17 42				17 56		18 01

OVERNIGHT SLEEPERS. For sleeper trains, operated by First ScotRail, please refer to Tables 400 - 404

Scotland and North West England - West Midlands and London

Route Diagram - see first Page of Table 65

		VT	VT	TP FO	XC	LM	NT	TP	VT	VT	VT	TP FX	TP	NT	XC	VT	EM	TP	TP
		◇1	◇1	◇1	◇1	◇1		◇1	◇1	◇1	◇1	◇1 A	◇1		◇1	◇1	◇	◇1	◇1
		🍴	🍴		🛒			🛒	🍴	🍴	🍴	🛒	🛒		🛒	🍴		🛒	
Inverness	d																		
Aberdeen	d																		
Dundee	d																		
Perth	d																		
Edinburgh [10]	d												14 07						
Haymarket	d												14u11						
Glasgow Central [15]	d										14 00								
Motherwell	d																		
Carstairs	d																		
Lockerbie	d												15 06						
Carlisle [8]	a										15 08		15 27						
	d										15 09		15 27						
Penrith North Lakes	d												15 43						
Windermere	d																		
Oxenholme Lake District	a										15 44		16 06						
	d										15 44		16 07						
Barrow-in-Furness	d			15 24								15 24		16 20					17 21
Lancaster [6]	a			16 18								16 18	16 21	17 26					18 20
	d		15 39	16 18								16 18	16 22						
Blackpool North	d						15 37	15 44											
Preston [8]	a		15 56	16 37			16 02	16 08			16 15	16 37	16 42						
Preston [8]	d		15 59				16 04	16 10			16 17		16 47						
Wigan North Western	a		16 09				16 24				16 28								
	d		16 10				16 24				16 28								
Blackrod	d																		
Lostock	d																		
Bolton	a							16 34					17 08						
Manchester Piccadilly [10]	a							16 56					17 29						
Manchester Airport ✈	a							17 17					17 48						
Liverpool Lime Street [10]	a						17 05												
	d					16 04											15 52	16 22	
Liverpool South Parkway ✈	d					16 15											16 03	16 32	
Runcorn	d					16 25													
Warrington Bank Quay	a		16 20								16 39								
	d		16 21								16 39								
Hartford	d																		
Manchester Piccadilly [10]	d	15 55			16 07				16 15						16 27	16 35	16 43	17a09	
Stockport	d	16 04			16 16				16 23						16 35	16 43	16a53		
Wilmslow	d	16 11																	
Holyhead	d																		
Bangor (Gwynedd)	d																		
Llandudno Junction	d																		
Wrexham General	d																		
Chester	d									16 35									
Crewe [10]	a	16 27				16 45				16 54	16 58								
	d	16 29				16 49				16 56	17 01								
Macclesfield	d														16 49	16 56			
Congleton	d																		
Stoke-on-Trent	d				16 44				16 50						17 07	17 12			
Stafford	a				17 02	17 10									17 24				
	d				17 03	17 10									17 25				
Penkridge	a					17 15													
Wolverhampton [7]	a				17 15	17 27					17 31				17 39				
Birmingham New Street [12]	a				17 32	17 47					17 55				17 58				
Birmingham International ✈	a														18 13				
Coventry	a														18 24				
Lichfield Trent Valley	a																		
Tamworth Low Level	a																		
Nuneaton	a																		
Rugby	a																		
Milton Keynes Central	a								17 46	18 01									
Watford Junction	a																		
London Euston [15] ⊖	a	18 03	18 09						18 23	18 38						18 42			

A 🛒 from Preston

OVERNIGHT SLEEPERS. For sleeper trains, operated by First ScotRail, please refer to Tables 400 - 404

Scotland and North West England - West Midlands and London

Route Diagram - see first Page of Table 65

		LM	VT	LM	VT	VT	XC	LM	NT	TP	VT	VT	VT	TP	XC	VT	EM	TP	LM
		◇1	◇1	◇1	◇1	◇1	◇1	◇1		◇1	◇1	◇1	1	◇1	◇1	◇1	◇	◇1	◇1
			🍴		🍴	⊠	🛒			🛒	⊠	⊠	🍴	🛒	🛒	⊠		🛒	
Inverness	d																		
Aberdeen	d																		
Dundee	d																		
Perth	d																		
Edinburgh [10]	d												14 51						
Haymarket	d												14 57						
Glasgow Central [15]	d					14 40													
Motherwell	d																		
Carstairs	d																		
Lockerbie	d																		
Carlisle [8]	a					15 47							16 05						
	d					15 49							16 07						
Penrith North Lakes	d												16 21						
Windermere	d																		
Oxenholme Lake District	a					16 22													
	d					16 24													
Barrow-in-Furness	d																		
Lancaster [6]	a					16 37							16 56						
	d					16 38							16 57						
Blackpool North	d								16 35	16 40				17 20					
Preston [8]	a					16 56			17 02	17 08			17 15	17 45					
Preston [8]	d					16 58			17 04	17 10			17 17	17 47					
Wigan North Western	a					17 09			17 24				17 28						
	d					17 09			17 24				17 28						
Blackrod	d																		
Lostock	d																		
Bolton	a									17 34				18 08					
Manchester Piccadilly [10]	a									17 56				18 27					
Manchester Airport ✈	a									18 17				18 47					
Liverpool Lime Street [10]	a								18 02										
	d	16 34	16 48					17 04									16 52	17 22	17 34
Liverpool South Parkway ✈	d	16 44						17 15									17 03	17 32	17 44
Runcorn	d	16 52	17 04					17 25											17 52
Warrington Bank Quay	a					17 20							17 39						
	d					17 20							17 39						
Hartford	d	17 06																	18 06
Manchester Piccadilly [10]	d				16 55		17 05				17 15				17 27	17 35	17 43	18a09	
Stockport	d				17 04		17 13				17 23				17 35	17 43	17a53		
Wilmslow	d				17 11										17 44				
Holyhead	d																		
Bangor (Gwynedd)	d																		
Llandudno Junction	d																		
Wrexham General	d																		
Chester	d											17 35							
Crewe [10]	a	17 19			17 27			17 47				17 54	17 59		18 04				18 20
	d	17 22			17 29			17 49				17 56	18 01		18 07				18 22
Macclesfield	d						17 27									17 56			
Congleton	d																		
Stoke-on-Trent	d			←			17 44				17 50					18 12			
Stafford	a	17 42	17 35	17 42			18 03	18 09							18 27				18 42
	d	17 43	17 36	17 43			18 04	18 10							18 28				18 43
Penkridge	a	→						18 15											→
Wolverhampton [7]	a			17 56			18 15	18 27					18 31		18 39				
Birmingham New Street [12]	a			18 17			18 38	18 48					18 55		18 58				
Birmingham International ✈	a														19 13				
Coventry	a														19 24				
Lichfield Trent Valley	a																		
Tamworth Low Level	a																		
Nuneaton	a																		
Rugby	a																		
Milton Keynes Central	a		18 23								18 47	19 02							
Watford Junction	a				18s48														
London Euston [15] ⊖	a		18 59		19 08	19 13					19 23	19 38				19 42			

OVERNIGHT SLEEPERS. For sleeper trains, operated by First ScotRail, please refer to Tables 400 - 404

Scotland and North West England - West Midlands and London

Route Diagram - see first Page of Table 65

		VT	LM	VT	VT	XC	LM	NT	TP	VT	TP	SR	VT	XC	VT	EM	TP	LM	VT
		◇1	◇1	◇1	◇1	◇1	◇1		◇1	◇1	◇1		◇1	◇1	◇1	◇	◇1	◇1	◇1
									A					B					
		⊠		⊠	⊠	✕			✕	▭	✕		⊠	✕	⊠				⊠
Inverness	d																		
Aberdeen	d																		
Dundee	d																		
Perth	d																		
Edinburgh 10	d										16 12								
Haymarket	d										16u16								
Glasgow Central 15	d									16 00		16 12							
Motherwell	d																		
Carstairs	d																		
Lockerbie	d										17 11								
Carlisle 8	a									17 08	17 33	18 35							
	d									17 09	17 34								
Penrith North Lakes	d										17 49								
Windermere	d								17 06										
Oxenholme Lake District	a								17 25	17 44									
	d								17 30	17 44									
Barrow-in-Furness	d																		
Lancaster 6	a								17 47		18 26								
	d				17 36				17 48		18 26								
Blackpool North	d							17 37											
Preston 8	a				17 54			18 02	18 06	18 15	18 45								
Preston 8	d				17 56			18 04	18 08	18 17	18 47								
Wigan North Western	a				18 07			18 24		18 28									
	d				18 08			18 24		18 28									
Blackrod	d																		
Lostock	d								18 30										
Bolton	a								18 34		19 08								
Manchester Piccadilly 10	a								18 56		19 27								
Manchester Airport ✈	a								19 17		19 47								
Liverpool Lime Street 10	a							19 03											
	d	17 48					18 04									17 52	18 22	18 34	18 48
Liverpool South Parkway ✈	d						18 15									18 03	18 32	18 44	
Runcorn	d	18 04					18 24											18 52	19 04
Warrington Bank Quay	a				18 19					18 39									
	d				18 19					18 39									
Hartford	d																	19 04	
Manchester Piccadilly 10	d			17 55		18 05							18 15	18 27	18 35	18 43	19a09		
Stockport	d			18 04		18 13							18 23	18 35	18 43	18a53			
Wilmslow	d			18 11															
Holyhead	d																		
Bangor (Gwynedd)	d																		
Llandudno Junction	d																		
Wrexham General	d																		
Chester	d																		
Crewe 10	a			18 27			18 47			18 59								19 16	19 21
	d			18 29			18 49			19 01								19 18	19 23
Macclesfield	d					18 26									18 56				
Congleton	d													18 54					
Stoke-on-Trent	d		←			18 44							18 50	19 07	19 12				
Stafford	a	18 35	18 42			19 01	19 09							19 24				19 41	19 41
	d	18 36	18 43			19 02	19 10							19 25				19 42	19 42
Penkridge	a						19 15											19 47	
Wolverhampton 7	a		18 56			19 15	19 27			19 32				19 39				19 57	
Birmingham New Street 12	a		19 17			19 32	19 47			19 55				19 58				20 18	
Birmingham International ✈	a													20 13					
Coventry	a													20 24					
Lichfield Trent Valley	a																		
Tamworth Low Level	a																		
Nuneaton	a																		
Rugby	a																		
Milton Keynes Central	a			19 31									19 46						
Watford Junction	a	19s42																	20s46
London Euston 15 ⊖	a	20 02		20 06	20 11								20 23		20 42				21 05

A ✕ from Preston
B ✕ to Birmingham New Street

OVERNIGHT SLEEPERS. For sleeper trains, operated by First ScotRail, please refer to Tables 400 - 404

Scotland and North West England - West Midlands and London

Route Diagram - see first Page of Table 65

		VT	XC	LM	NT	VT	TP	TP	VT	VT	VT	TP	XC	EM	TP	LM	VT	VT	VT	XC	LM	NT
		◇1	◇1	◇1		◇1	◇1	◇1	◇1	◇1	1	◇1	◇1	◇	◇1	◇1	◇1	◇1	◇1	◇1	◇1	
													A									
		⊠	✕			⊠	✕		▭	▭	▭	✕	✕				▭	▭	▭			
Inverness	d																					
Aberdeen	d																					
Dundee	d																					
Perth	d																					
Edinburgh 10	d										16 52											
Haymarket	d										16 57											
Glasgow Central 15	d					16 40						17 06										
Motherwell	d					16 54																
Carstairs	d																					
Lockerbie	d											18 06										
Carlisle 8	a					17 49					18 05	18 28										
	d					17 51					18 07	18 29										
Penrith North Lakes	d					18 05						18 45										
Windermere	d							18 15														
Oxenholme Lake District	a					18 27		18 34			18 41	19 09										
	d					18 29		18 36			18 42	19 10										
Barrow-in-Furness	d																					
Lancaster 6	a					18 43		18 52			18 56	19 26										
	d					18 44		18 52			18 57	19 26										
Blackpool North	d				18 37		18 44															19 37
Preston 8	a				19 02	19 02	19 08	19 11			19 15	19 45										20 02
Preston 8	d				19 04	19 05	19 10	19 16			19 16	19 47							19 58			20 04
Wigan North Western	a				19 24	19 16					19 28								20 09			20 24
	d				19 24	19 16					19 29								20 09			20 24
Blackrod	d																					
Lostock	d																					
Bolton	a						19 33	19 42				20 08										
Manchester Piccadilly 10	a						19 56	20 01				20 27										
Manchester Airport ✈	a						20 17	20 24				20 47										
Liverpool Lime Street 10	a				20 02																	21 02
	d			19 11										18 52	19 22	19 34	19 48				20 04	
Liverpool South Parkway ✈	d			19 21										19 03	19 32	19 44					20 15	
Runcorn	d			19 29												19 52	20 04				20 24	
Warrington Bank Quay	a					19 27					19 39								20 20			
	d					19 27					19 39								20 20			
Hartford	d															20 04						
Manchester Piccadilly 10	d	18 55	19 07						19 15				19 27	19 43	20a09			19 55		20 07		
Stockport	d	19 04	19 16						19 23				19 35	19a53				20 04		20 16		
Wilmslow	d	19 11																20 11				
Holyhead	d																					
Bangor (Gwynedd)	d																					
Llandudno Junction	d																					
Wrexham General	d																					
Chester	d									19 35												
Crewe 10	a	19 27		19 53						19 54	19 59					20 16	20 21	20 27	20 39		20 45	
	d	19 29		19 55						19 56	20 01					20 18	20 23	20 29	20 41		20 47	
Macclesfield	d								19 36				19 49									
Congleton	d																					
Stoke-on-Trent	d		19 44						19 52				20 07							20 44		
Stafford	a		20 03	20 15									20 25			20 38		20 47		21 02	21 08	
	d		20 04	20 16									20 26			20 42		20 48		21 03	21 10	
Penkridge	a															20 47					21 15	
Wolverhampton 7	a		20 16	20 29							20 33		20 40			20 57				21 15	21 26	
Birmingham New Street 12	a		20 33	20 47							20 55		21 00			21 18				21 32	21 47	
Birmingham International ✈	a												21 13									
Coventry	a												21 24									
Lichfield Trent Valley	a																					
Tamworth Low Level	a																					
Nuneaton	a																21 02					
Rugby	a																		21 27			
Milton Keynes Central	a	20 32				20 45			20 48	21 03								21 35	21 47			
Watford Junction	a																21s48					
London Euston 15 ⊖	a	21 06				21 24			21 26	21 42							22 09	22 12	22 22			

A ✕ to Birmingham New Street

OVERNIGHT SLEEPERS. For sleeper trains, operated by First ScotRail, please refer to Tables 400 - 404

Scotland and North West England - West Midlands and London

Route Diagram - see first Page of Table 65

		VT	TP	TP ThX	TP ThO	VT	VT	XC	EM	TP	LM	TP	VT	VT	VT	VT	TP	XC	LM
		◇1	◇1	◇1	◇1	◇1	◇1	◇1	◇	◇1	◇1	◇1	◇1	◇1	◇1	◇1	◇1	◇1	◇1
Inverness	d																		
Aberdeen	d																		
Dundee	d																		
Perth	d																		
Edinburgh 10	d			18 12	18 12											18 52			
Haymarket	d			18u16	18u16											18 57			
Glasgow Central 15	d	17 40					18 40												
Motherwell	d																		
Carstairs	d																		
Lockerbie	d	18 35		19 11	19 11														
Carlisle 8	a	18 52		19 34	19 34		19 47									20 06			
	d	18 54		19 34	19 34		19 49									20 08			
Penrith North Lakes	d	19 09		19 49	19 49														
Windermere	d																		
Oxenholme Lake District	a	19 32		20 12	20 12		20 22									20 42			
	d	19 32		20 13	20 13		20 24									20 42			
Barrow-in-Furness	d																20 08		
Lancaster 6	a	19 47		20 26	20 26		20 37									20 57	21 10		
	d	19 47		20 26	20 26		20 38									20 57	21 10		
Blackpool North	d		19 44									20 44							
Preston 8	a	20 05	20 08	20 45	20 45		20 56					21 08				21 15	21 29		
Preston 8	d	20 08	20 10	20 47	20 47		20 58					21 10				21 17	21 31		
Wigan North Western	a	20 19					21 09									21 28	21 47		
	d	20 19					21 09									21 28	21 48		
Blackrod	d																		
Lostock	d																		
Bolton	a		20 34	21 08	21 08							21 34							
Manchester Piccadilly 10	a		20 56	21 27	21 27							21 56					22 30		
Manchester Airport ✈	a		21 17	21 46	21 47							22 17					22 47		
Liverpool Lime Street 10	a																		
	d								19 52	20 22	20 34			20 48					21 34
Liverpool South Parkway ✈	d								20 03	20 32	20 44								21 44
Runcorn	d										20 52			21 04					21 52
Warrington Bank Quay	a	20 30					21 20									21 39			
	d	20 31					21 20									21 39			
Hartford	d										21 04								22 04
Manchester Piccadilly 10	d					20 15		20 27	20 43	21a09			21 15					21 27	
Stockport	d					20 23		20 35	20a53				21 23					21 35	
Wilmslow	d																		
Holyhead	d																		
Bangor (Gwynedd)	d														20 20				
Llandudno Junction	d														20 38				
Wrexham General	d																		
Chester	d														21 35				
Crewe 10	a	20 50									21 16			21 21	21 54	21 59			22 18
	d	20 53									21 18			21 24	21 56	22 01			22 20
Macclesfield	d					20 36		20 49					21 36					21 49	
Congleton	d																		
Stoke-on-Trent	d					20 53		21 07					21 53					22 08	
Stafford	a	21 11						21 24			21 38			21 42				22 25	22 40
	d	21 13						21 25			21 41			21 44				22 26	22 41
Penkridge	a										21 46								22 46
Wolverhampton 7	a	21 29						21 39			21 57				22 27	22 32		22 39	22 57
Birmingham New Street 12	a	21 48						22 00			22 17				22 50	22 55		22 58	23 18
Birmingham International ✈	a																		
Coventry	a																		
Lichfield Trent Valley	a													21 57					
Tamworth Low Level	a													22 03					
Nuneaton	a													22 16					
Rugby	a													22 30					
Milton Keynes Central	a					21 50	22 39						22 52	22 58					
Watford Junction	a					22s11	23s14						23s25	23s30					
London Euston 15 ⊖	a					22 33	23 38						23 48	23 56					

OVERNIGHT SLEEPERS. For sleeper trains, operated by First ScotRail, please refer to Tables 400 - 404

Table 65

Mondays to Fridays

Scotland and North West England - West Midlands and London

Route Diagram - see first Page of Table 65

		TP	VT FO	VT FX	VT FX	TP FO	NT	XC FO	XC FX	EM	TP	LM	TP	TP	LM	SR FX	SR FX	SR FO	SR FO	SR FX
		◇1	◇1	◇1	◇1	◇1		◇1	◇1	◇	◇1	◇1	◇1	◇1	◇1	B	B	B	B	B
				A	B			C	D							B	A	E	F	B
Inverness	d																			20 47
Aberdeen	d																			
Dundee	d																			
Perth	d																			23u21
Edinburgh 10	d					20 12														01 24
Haymarket	d					20u16														
Glasgow Central 15	d		20 10	20 10	20 10											23 40	23 40	23 40	23 40	
Motherwell	d															23u56	23u56	23u56	23u56	
Carstairs	d			20 36	20 36											00u16	00u16	00u16	00u16	
Lockerbie	d		21 05	21 05	21 05	21 11														
Carlisle 8	a		21 25	21 25	21 25	21 34														02 53
	d		21 26	21 26	21 26	21 34										01u41	01u41	01u41	01u41	02 54
Penrith North Lakes	d		21 40	21 41	21 41															
Windermere	d													22 45						
Oxenholme Lake District	a		22 04	22 04	22 04	22 09								23 04						
	d		22 04	22 05	22 05	22 10								23 06						
Barrow-in-Furness	d						21 43													
Lancaster 6	a		22 19	22 19	22 19	22 26	22 45							23 23						
	d		22 19	22 20	22 20	22 26	22 46							23 24						
Blackpool North	d	21 44											22 44							
Preston 8	a	22 08	22 36	22 37	22 37	22 45	23 11						23 08	23 45						04s32
Preston 8	d	22 10	22 40	22 40	22 40	22 47							23 10							
Wigan North Western	a		22 51	22 51	22 51															
	d		22 52	22 52	22 52															
Blackrod	d																			
Lostock	d																			
Bolton	a	22 34				23 06							23 34							
Manchester Piccadilly 10	a	22 56				23 31							23 53							
Manchester Airport ✈	a	23 17											00 24							
Liverpool Lime Street 10	a																			
	d									21 37	22 30	22 34			23 34					
Liverpool South Parkway ✈	d									21 47	22 40	22 45			23 45					
Runcorn	d											22 54			23 53					
Warrington Bank Quay	a		23 02	23 01	23 02											03 40	03 44	03 40	03 46	
	d		23 03	23 02	23 03											03 41	03 45	03 42	03 48	
Hartford	d											23 08			00 07					
Manchester Piccadilly 10	d							22 07	22 07	22 28	23a19									
Stockport	d							22 16	22 16	22a37										
Wilmslow	d																			
Holyhead	d																			
Bangor (Gwynedd)	d																			
Llandudno Junction	d																			
Wrexham General	d																			
Chester	d																			
Crewe 10	a		23 24	23 24	23 24							23 21			00 22					05s34
	d																			
Macclesfield	d							22 29	22 29											
Congleton	d																			
Stoke-on-Trent	d							22 47	22 47											
Stafford	a							23 06	23 09											
	d							23 07	23 10											
Penkridge	a																			
Wolverhampton 7	a							23 19	23 22											
Birmingham New Street 12	a							23 39	23 40											
Birmingham International ✈	a																			
Coventry	a																			
Lichfield Trent Valley	a																			
Tamworth Low Level	a																			
Nuneaton	a																			
Rugby	a																			
Milton Keynes Central	a																			
Watford Junction	a															06s19	06s22	06s27	06s33	
London Euston 15 ⊖	a															06 43	06 43	06 50	06 56	07 47

A from 2 January until 22 March
B until 29 December and then from 26 March
C until 23 March and then from 30 March
D from 26 March
E Until 30 December and then from 30 March
F from 6 January until 23 March

OVERNIGHT SLEEPERS. For sleeper trains, operated by First ScotRail, please refer to Tables 400 - 404

Table 65

Mondays to Fridays

Scotland and North West England - West Midlands and London

Route Diagram - see first Page of Table 65

		SR FX	SR FO	SR FO
		A	B	C
Inverness	d	20 47	20 47	20 47
Aberdeen	d			
Dundee	d			
Perth	d	23u21	23u21	23u21
Edinburgh 10	d	01 24	01 24	01 24
Haymarket	d			
Glasgow Central 15	d			
Motherwell	d			
Carstairs	d			
Lockerbie	d			
Carlisle 8	a	02 53	03 03	03 03
	d	02 54	03 11	03 11
Penrith North Lakes	d			
Windermere	d			
Oxenholme Lake District	a			
	d			
Barrow-in-Furness	d			
Lancaster 6	a			
	d			
Blackpool North	d			
Preston 8	a	04s32	04s32	04s32
Preston 8	d			
Wigan North Western	a			
	d			
Blackrod	d			
Lostock	d			
Bolton	a			
Manchester Piccadilly 10	a			
Manchester Airport	a			
Liverpool Lime Street 10	a			
	d			
Liverpool South Parkway	d			
Runcorn	d			
Warrington Bank Quay	a			
	d			
Hartford	d			
Manchester Piccadilly 10	d			
Stockport	d			
Wilmslow	d			
Holyhead	d			
Bangor (Gwynedd)	d			
Llandudno Junction	d			
Wrexham General	d			
Chester	d			
Crewe 10	a	05s38	05s34	05s38
	d			
Macclesfield	d			
Congleton	d			
Stoke-on-Trent	d			
Stafford	a			
	d			
Penkridge	a			
Wolverhampton 7	a			
Birmingham New Street 12	a			
Birmingham International	a			
Coventry	a			
Lichfield Trent Valley	a			
Tamworth Low Level	a			
Nuneaton	a			
Rugby	a			
Milton Keynes Central	a			
Watford Junction	a			
London Euston 15	a	07 47	07 47	07 47

A from 2 January until 22 March
B Until 30 December and then from 30 March
C from 6 January until 23 March

OVERNIGHT SLEEPERS. For sleeper trains, operated by First ScotRail, please refer to Tables 400 - 404

Table 65

Saturdays

Scotland and North West England - West Midlands and London

Route Diagram - see first Page of Table 65

		TP	LM	SR	SR	SR	SR	TP	AW	TP	TP	XC	VT	XC	VT	TP	LM
		◇1	◇1					◇1		◇1	◇1	◇1	◇1	◇1	◇1	◇1	◇1
				A	B	A	B										
Inverness	d					20p47	20p47										
Aberdeen	d																
Dundee	d																
Perth	d					23b21	23b21										
Edinburgh 10	d					01 24	01 24										
Haymarket	d																
Glasgow Central 15	d			23p40	23p40												
Motherwell	d			23b56	23b56												
Carstairs	d			00u16	00u16												
Lockerbie	d																
Carlisle 8	a					03 03	03 03										
	d			01u41	01u41	03 11	03 11										
Penrith North Lakes	d																
Windermere	d																
Oxenholme Lake District	a																
	d																
Barrow-in-Furness	d									04 35							
Lancaster 6	a									05 28							
	d																
Blackpool North	d	22p44						03 33									
Preston 8	a	23p08		03 07	03 07	04s32	04s32										
Preston 8	d	23p10		03 14	03 14			03u58			05 16						
Wigan North Western	a																
	d																
Blackrod	d																
Lostock	d																
Bolton	a	23p34						04e31			05 42						
Manchester Piccadilly 10	a	23p53						04 48			06 01						
Manchester Airport	a	00 24						05 07			06 18						
Liverpool Lime Street 10	a																
	d		23p34												05 47	06 15	
Liverpool South Parkway	d		23p45													06 25	
Runcorn	d		23p53												06 03		
Warrington Bank Quay	a			03 40	03 46												
	d			03 42	03 48												
Hartford	d		00 07														
Manchester Piccadilly 10	d											05 11	05 25			07a09	
Stockport	d												05 34				
Wilmslow	d												05 41				
Holyhead	d																
Bangor (Gwynedd)	d																
Llandudno Junction	d																
Wrexham General	d																
Chester	d								04 22								
Crewe 10	a		00 22			05s34	05s38		04 44			05 41	05 57				
	d								04 59			05 47	06 00				06 20
Macclesfield	d																
Congleton	d																
Stoke-on-Trent	d											06 08		←			
Stafford	a								05 24			06 25	06 17	06 25	06 34		06 41
	d								05 25			06 26	06 19	06 26	06 35		06 41
Penkridge	a											→					06 47
Wolverhampton 7	a								05 39					06 39			06 57
Birmingham New Street 12	a								05 58					06 57			07 17
Birmingham International	a													07 13			
Coventry	a													07 24			
Lichfield Trent Valley	a																
Tamworth Low Level	a																
Nuneaton	a														06 57		
Rugby	a												06 49				
Milton Keynes Central	a												07 11				
Watford Junction	a			06s27	06s33								07s32		07s44		
London Euston 15	a			06 50	06 56	07 47	07 47						07 52		08 05		

A Until 31 December and then from 31 March
B from 7 January until 24 March
b Previous night, stops to pick up only
e Stops to pick up only

OVERNIGHT SLEEPERS. For sleeper trains, operated by First ScotRail, please refer to Tables 400 - 404

Table 65

Saturdays

Scotland and North West England - West Midlands and London

Route Diagram - see first Page of Table 65

		VT	VT	TP	XC	VT	VT	LM	VT	TP	LM	VT	LM	VT	VT	TP	XC	VT	VT	LM
		◇1	◇1	◇1	◇1	◇1	◇1	◇1	◇1	◇1	◇1	◇1	◇1	◇1	◇1	◇1	◇1	◇1	◇1	◇1
		□	□		✕	□	□		□			□		□	□	✕	✕	□	□	
Inverness	d																			
Aberdeen	d																			
Dundee	d																			
Perth	d																			
Edinburgh 10	d																			
Haymarket	d																			
Glasgow Central 15	d														04 26					
Motherwell	d																			
Carstairs	d																			
Lockerbie	d																			
Carlisle 8	a														05 43					
	d														05 44					
Penrith North Lakes	d														05 59					
Windermere	d																			
Oxenholme Lake District	a														06 21					
	d														06 22					
Barrow-in-Furness	d									05 31										
Lancaster 6	a									06 23					06 36					
	d		05 40							06 23					06 37					
Blackpool North	d			05 39												06 40				
Preston 8	a		05 55	06 03						06 42					06 55	07 07				
Preston 8	d		05 58	06 05					06 17	06 44					06 58	07 09				
Wigan North Western	a		06 09						06 28						07 09					
	d		06 09						06 28						07 10					
Blackrod	d			06 22																
Lostock	d			06 30												07 30				
Bolton	a			06 34						07 08						07 34				
Manchester Piccadilly 10	a			06 56						07 27						07 56				
Manchester Airport ✈	a			07 17						07 47						08 17				
Liverpool Lime Street 10	a																			
	d										06 32	06 45								07 04
Liverpool South Parkway ✈	d										06 42									07 14
Runcorn	d										06 50	07 01								07 22
Warrington Bank Quay	a		06 20						06 39						07 20					
	d		06 20						06 39						07 20					
Hartford	d										07 02									07 36
Manchester Piccadilly 10	d	05 55			06 00	06 10	06 35							06 55			07 07	07 15		
Stockport	d	06 03			06 08	06 18	06 43							07 04			07 16	07 23		
Wilmslow	d	06 11												07 11						
Holyhead	d																			
Bangor (Gwynedd)	d																			
Llandudno Junction	d																			
Wrexham General	d																			
Chester	d																		07 17	
Crewe 10	a	06 27							06 58		07 14	07 18		07 27					07 36	07 47
	d	06 29						06 47	07 01		07 16	07 20		07 29					07 39	07 49
Macclesfield	d				06 21	06 31	06 56													
Congleton	d																			
Stoke-on-Trent	d				06 39	06 48	07 12						←				07 44	07 50		
Stafford	a				06 57			07 10			07 40	07 38	07 40				08 02			08 10
	d				06 58			07 12			07 41	07 39	07 41				08 03			08 10
Penkridge	a							07 17			→		07 46							08 16
Wolverhampton 7	a				07 12			07 28	07 32				07 57				08 16			08 28
Birmingham New Street 12	a				07 31			07 47	07 55				08 17				08 38			08 47
Birmingham International ✈	a																			
Coventry	a																			
Lichfield Trent Valley	a					07 11														
Tamworth Low Level	a					07 17														
Nuneaton	a																			
Rugby	a						07 52													
Milton Keynes Central	a	07 31	07 37															08 46		
Watford Junction	a																			
London Euston 15 ⊖	a	08 09	08 14			08 27	08 46					08 59		09 04	09 12			09 23	09 30	

A until 11 February and then from 31 March

OVERNIGHT SLEEPERS. For sleeper trains, operated by First ScotRail, please refer to Tables 400 - 404

Table 65

Saturdays

Scotland and North West England - West Midlands and London

Route Diagram - see first Page of Table 65

		VT	VT	TP	XC	VT	EM	TP	LM	VT	LM	VT	XC	LM	NT	VT	TP	VT
		◇1	◇1	◇1	◇1	◇1	◇	◇1	◇1	◇1	◇1	◇1	◇1	◇1		◇1	◇1	◇1
				A											C			
		□	□	✕	✕	□		✕		□		□	✕			□	✕	□
Inverness	d																	
Aberdeen	d																	
Dundee	d																	
Perth	d																	
Edinburgh 10	d																	
Haymarket	d																	
Glasgow Central 15	d															05 40		
Motherwell	d																	
Carstairs	d																	
Lockerbie	d																	
Carlisle 8	a															06 46		
	d															06 49		
Penrith North Lakes	d																	
Windermere	d																	
Oxenholme Lake District	a															07 22		
	d															07 24		
Barrow-in-Furness	d			06 20														
Lancaster 6	a			07 21												07 37		
	d		06 58	07 22												07 38		
Blackpool North	d																07 44	
Preston 8	a		07 15	07 41												07 56	08 11	
Preston 8	d		07 17	07 47												07 58	08 12	
Wigan North Western	a		07 28													08 09		
	d		07 28												08⌇05	08 09		
Blackrod	d														⌇			
Lostock	d														⌇			
Bolton	a			08 08											⌇		08 34	
Manchester Piccadilly 10	a			08 27											⌇		08 56	
Manchester Airport ✈	a			08 47											⌇		09 19	
Liverpool Lime Street 10	a														09⌇05			
	d	07 19					06 49	07 15	07 34	07 48				08 04				
Liverpool South Parkway ✈	d						06 59	07 25	07 44					08 15				
Runcorn	d	07 36							07 52	08 04				08 24				
Warrington Bank Quay	a		07 39													08 20		
	d		07 39													08 20		
Hartford	d								08 04									
Manchester Piccadilly 10	d				07 27	07 35	07 42	08a08				07 55	08 07					08 15
Stockport	d				07 35	07 43	07a53					08 04	08 16					08 23
Wilmslow	d											08 11						
Holyhead	d																	
Bangor (Gwynedd)	d																	
Llandudno Junction	d																	
Wrexham General	d																	
Chester	d																	
Crewe 10	a	07 52	07 58						08 19			08 27		08 47				
	d	07 55	08 01						08 22			08 29		08 49				
Macclesfield	d				07 49	07 56												
Congleton	d																	
Stoke-on-Trent	d				08 07	08 12					←		08 44					08 50
Stafford	a	08 14			08 25				08 42	08 35	08 42		09 02	09 09				
	d	08 16			08 26				08 43	08 36	08 43		09 03	09 10				
Penkridge	a								→		08 48			09 15				
Wolverhampton 7	a		08 31		08 39						08 58		09 15	09 27				
Birmingham New Street 12	a		08 55		08 58						09 18		09 39	09 47				
Birmingham International ✈	a				09 13													
Coventry	a				09 24													
Lichfield Trent Valley	a	08 30																
Tamworth Low Level	a	08 36																
Nuneaton	a									08 58								
Rugby	a																	
Milton Keynes Central	a																	09 46
Watford Junction	a																	
London Euston 15 ⊖	a	09 46				09 42				10 00		10 04				10 12		10 23

A ✕ from Preston

C from 18 February until 24 March

OVERNIGHT SLEEPERS. For sleeper trains, operated by First ScotRail, please refer to Tables 400 - 404

Table 65

Saturdays

Scotland and North West England - West Midlands and London

Route Diagram - see first Page of Table 65

		VT	VT	TP	XC	VT	EM	TP	LM	VT	LM	VT	VT	SR	XC	LM	NT	NT
		◇1	◇1	◇1	◇1	◇1	◇	◇1	◇1	◇1	◇1	◇1	◇1		◇1	◇1		
				A													C	D
		☕	☕	⌶	⌶	☕		⌶		☕		☕	☕		⌶			
Inverness	d																	
Aberdeen	d																	
Dundee	d																	
Perth	d																	
Edinburgh 10	d																	
Haymarket	d																	
Glasgow Central 15	d		05 50										06 30	07 07				
Motherwell	d		06 04										06 44					
Carstairs	d																	
Lockerbie	d												07 25					
Carlisle 8	a		07 02										07 43	09 37				
	d		07 03										07 46					
Penrith North Lakes	d		07 18										08 00					
Windermere	d																	
Oxenholme Lake District	a		07 41										08 22					
	d		07 42										08 23					
Barrow-in-Furness	d			07 29														
Lancaster 6	a		07 56	08 26									08 37					
	d		07 57	08 27									08 38					
Blackpool North	d																08 38	08 38
Preston 8	a		08 15	08 45									08 56				09 02	09 02
Preston 8	d		08 17	08 47									08 58				09 04	09 04
Wigan North Western	a		08 28										09 09				09 24	09 27
	d		08 28										09 09				09 24	
Blackrod	d																	
Lostock	d																	
Bolton	a			09 08														
Manchester Piccadilly 10	a			09 27														
Manchester Airport ✈	a			09 47														
Liverpool Lime Street 10	a																10 02	
	d						07 42	08 22	08 34	08 48						09 04	10 16	
Liverpool South Parkway ✈	d						07 52	08 32	08 44							09 15	10a27	
Runcorn	d								08 52	09 04						09 24		
Warrington Bank Quay	a		08 39										09 20					
	d		08 39										09 20					
Hartford	d								09 06									
Manchester Piccadilly 10	d				08 27	08 35	08 43	09a09				08 55			09 07			
Stockport	d				08 35	08 43	08a53					09 04			09 16			
Wilmslow	d											09 11						
Holyhead	d	06 52																
Bangor (Gwynedd)	d	07 20																
Llandudno Junction	d	07 38																
Wrexham General	d																	
Chester	d	08 35																
Crewe 10	a	08 54	08 58						09 20			09 27				09 44		
	d	08 56	09 01						09 22			09 29				09 49		
Macclesfield	d				08 49	08 56												
Congleton	d																	
Stoke-on-Trent	d				09 07	09 12					←				09 44			
Stafford	a				09 25				09 42	09 35	09 42				10 02	10 10		
	d				09 26				09 43	09 36	09 43				10 03	10 10		
Penkridge	a								→							10 16		
Wolverhampton 7	a		09 31		09 39						09 56				10 15	10 27		
Birmingham New Street 12	a		09 55		09 58						10 17				10 39	10 47		
Birmingham International ✈	a				10 13													
Coventry	a				10 24													
Lichfield Trent Valley	a																	
Tamworth Low Level	a																	
Nuneaton	a									09 58								
Rugby	a																	
Milton Keynes Central	a	10 01																
Watford Junction	a																	
London Euston 15 ⊖	a	10 37				10 42				11 01		11 04	11 12					

A ⌶ from Preston
C until 11 February
D from 18 February until 24 March

OVERNIGHT SLEEPERS. For sleeper trains, operated by First ScotRail, please refer to Tables 400 - 404

Table 65

Saturdays

Scotland and North West England - West Midlands and London

Route Diagram - see first Page of Table 65

		TP	VT	VT	VT	TP	XC	VT	EM	TP	LM	VT	LM	VT	XC	LM	NT
		◇1	◇1	◇1	◇1	◇1	◇1	◇1	◇	◇1	◇1	◇1	◇1	◇1	◇1	◇1	
																	B
		⌶	☕	☕	☕	⌶	⌶	☕		⌶		☕		☕	⌶		🚌
Inverness	d																
Aberdeen	d																
Dundee	d																
Perth	d																
Edinburgh 10	d				06 52												
Haymarket	d				06 56												
Glasgow Central 15	d					07 10											
Motherwell	d																
Carstairs	d																
Lockerbie	d					08 06											
Carlisle 8	a				08 05	08 29											
	d				08 07	08 29											
Penrith North Lakes	d				08 22	08 45											
Windermere	d																
Oxenholme Lake District	a					09 09											
	d					09 11											
Barrow-in-Furness	d																
Lancaster 6	a				08 56	09 26											
	d				08 57	09 26											
Blackpool North	d	08 44															
Preston 8	a	09 08			09 15	09 45											
Preston 8	d	09 10			09 17	09 47											
Wigan North Western	a				09 28												
	d				09 28												09 35
Blackrod	d																
Lostock	d																
Bolton	a	09 34				10 08											
Manchester Piccadilly 10	a	09 56				10 27											
Manchester Airport ✈	a	10 17				10 47											
Liverpool Lime Street 10	a																10 35
	d								08 52	09 22	09 34	09 48				10 04	
Liverpool South Parkway ✈	d								09 03	09 32	09 44					10 15	
Runcorn	d										09 52	10 04				10 25	
Warrington Bank Quay	a				09 39												
	d				09 39												
Hartford	d										10 04						
Manchester Piccadilly 10	d		09 15				09 27	09 35	09 43	10a09				09 55	10 07		
Stockport	d		09 23				09 35	09 43	09a53					10 04	10 16		
Wilmslow	d													10 11			
Holyhead	d			07 55													
Bangor (Gwynedd)	d			08 22													
Llandudno Junction	d			08 40													
Wrexham General	d																
Chester	d			09 35													
Crewe 10	a			09 54	09 58						10 19			10 27		10 45	
	d			09 56	10 01						10 22			10 29		10 49	
Macclesfield	d						09 49	09 56									
Congleton	d																
Stoke-on-Trent	d		09 50				10 07	10 12					←		10 44		
Stafford	a						10 25				10 42	10 35	10 42		11 02	11 09	
	d						10 26				10 43	10 36	10 43		11 03	11 10	
Penkridge	a										→					11 15	
Wolverhampton 7	a				10 31		10 39						10 56		11 16	11 27	
Birmingham New Street 12	a				10 55		10 58						11 17		11 39	11 47	
Birmingham International ✈	a						11 13										
Coventry	a						11 24										
Lichfield Trent Valley	a																
Tamworth Low Level	a																
Nuneaton	a																
Rugby	a																
Milton Keynes Central	a		10 46	11 01													
Watford Junction	a																
London Euston 15 ⊖	a		11 23	11 38				11 42				11 56		12 04			

B from 18 February until 24 March

OVERNIGHT SLEEPERS. For sleeper trains, operated by First ScotRail, please refer to Tables 400 - 404

Scotland and North West England - West Midlands and London

Route Diagram - see first Page of Table 65

		VT	NT	NT	TP	TP	VT	VT	VT	TP		TP	NT	XC	NT	VT	EM					TP		LM	VT
		◇1			◇1	◇1	◇1	◇1	◇1	◇1		◇1		◇1		◇1	◇					◇1		◇1	◇1
			A	B								C													
		🍴			🛒	🛒	🍴	🍴	🍴			🛒		🛒		🍴						🛒			🍴
Inverness	d																								
Aberdeen	d																								
Dundee	d																								
Perth	d																								
Edinburgh 10	d				07 42																				
Haymarket	d				07u46																				
Glasgow Central 15	d	07 35							08 00																
Motherwell	d	07 52																							
Carstairs	d																								
Lockerbie	d																								
Carlisle 8	a	08 46			08 59				09 08																
	d	08 49			08 59				09 09																
Penrith North Lakes	d																								
Windermere	d									09 38															
Oxenholme Lake District	a	09 22								09 57															
	d	09 23								09 58															
Barrow-in-Furness	d											09 23	10 16												
Lancaster 6	a	09 37							09 56	10 16		10 25	11 21												
	d	09 38							09 57	10 16		10 26													
Blackpool North	d		09 37	09 37		09 43									10 29										
Preston 8	a	09 56	10 02	10 02	10 04	10 07			10 15	10 35		10 45			10 52										
Preston 8	d	09 58	10 04	10 04	10 12				10 17			10 47			16a32										
Wigan North Western	a	10 09	10 24	10 27					10 28																
	d	10 09	10 24						10 28																
Blackrod	d																								
Lostock	d																								
Bolton	a				10 34							11 08													
Manchester Piccadilly 10	a				10 56							11 27													
Manchester Airport	a				11 17							11 47													
Liverpool Lime Street 10	a		11 02																						
	d		11 16														09 52					10 22		10 34	10 48
Liverpool South Parkway	d		11a27														10 03					10 32		10 44	
Runcorn	d																							10 52	11 04
Warrington Bank Quay	a	10 20							10 39																
	d	10 20							10 39																
Hartford	d																							11 04	
Manchester Piccadilly 10	d						10 15							10 27		10 35	10 43					11a09			
Stockport	d						10 23							10 35		10 43	10a53								
Wilmslow	d																								
Holyhead	d							08 55																	
Bangor (Gwynedd)	d							09 22																	
Llandudno Junction	d							09 40																	
Wrexham General	d																								
Chester	d							10 35																	
Crewe 10	a							10 54	10 58															11 19	
	d							10 56	11 01															11 22	
Macclesfield	d													10 49		10 56									
Congleton	d																								
Stoke-on-Trent	d						10 50							11 07		11 12									
Stafford	a													11 25										11 42	11 35
	d													11 26										11 43	11 36
Penkridge	a																							→	
Wolverhampton 7	a								11 32					11 39											
Birmingham New Street 12	a								11 55					11 58											
Birmingham International	a													12 13											
Coventry	a													12 24											
Lichfield Trent Valley	a																								
Tamworth Low Level	a																								
Nuneaton	a																								
Rugby	a																								
Milton Keynes Central	a						11 46	12 01																	
Watford Junction	a																								
London Euston 15	a	12 12					12 23	12 38								12 42									12 56

A until 11 February
B from 18 February until 24 March
C 🛒 from Preston

OVERNIGHT SLEEPERS. For sleeper trains, operated by First ScotRail, please refer to Tables 400 - 404

Scotland and North West England - West Midlands and London

Route Diagram - see first Page of Table 65

		LM	VT	XC	LM	NT		VT	NT	NT	TP	VT	VT	VT	TP	XC			VT	EM				TP	
		◇1	◇1	◇1	◇1			◇1			◇1	◇1	◇1	◇1	◇1	◇1			◇1	◇				◇1	
						A			B	A					C										
			🍴	🛒		🚌		🍴			🛒	🍴	🍴	🍴	🛒	🛒			🍴					🛒	
Inverness	d																								
Aberdeen	d																								
Dundee	d																								
Perth	d																								
Edinburgh 10	d													08 52											
Haymarket	d													08 57											
Glasgow Central 15	d							08 40																	
Motherwell	d																								
Carstairs	d																								
Lockerbie	d																								
Carlisle 8	a							09 46						10 05											
	d							09 49						10 07											
Penrith North Lakes	d							10 03																	
Windermere	d														10 49										
Oxenholme Lake District	a													10 41	11 08										
	d													10 42	11 09										
Barrow-in-Furness	d																								
Lancaster 6	a							10 37						10 56	11 26										
	d							10 38						10 57	11 26										
Blackpool North	d								10 37	10 37	10 44														
Preston 8	a							10 56	11 02	11 02	11 08			11 15	11 45										
Preston 8	d							10 58	11 04	11 04	11 10			11 17	11 47										
Wigan North Western	a							11 09	11 24	11 27				11 28											
	d					10 35		11 09	11 24					11 28											
Blackrod	d																								
Lostock	d																								
Bolton	a										11 34				12 08										
Manchester Piccadilly 10	a										11 56				12 27										
Manchester Airport	a										12 17				12 47										
Liverpool Lime Street 10	a					11 35			12 02																
	d				11 04				12 16											10 52				11 22	
Liverpool South Parkway	d				11 15				12a27											11 03				11 32	
Runcorn	d				11 25																				
Warrington Bank Quay	a							11 20						11 39											
	d							11 20						11 39											
Hartford	d																								
Manchester Piccadilly 10	d		10 55	11 07								11 15				11 27			11 35	11 43				12a09	
Stockport	d		11 04	11 16								11 23				11 35			11 43	11a53					
Wilmslow	d		11 11																						
Holyhead	d																								
Bangor (Gwynedd)	d																								
Llandudno Junction	d																								
Wrexham General	d																								
Chester	d												11 35												
Crewe 10	a		11 27		11 45								11 54	11 58											
	d		11 29		11 49								11 56	12 01											
Macclesfield	d															11 49			11 56						
Congleton	d																								
Stoke-on-Trent	d	←		11 44								11 50				12 07			12 12						
Stafford	a	11 42		12 02	12 09											12 24									
	d	11 43		12 03	12 10											12 25									
Penkridge	a				12 15																				
Wolverhampton 7	a	11 56		12 16	12 27									12 31		12 39									
Birmingham New Street 12	a	12 17		12 39	12 47									12 55		12 58									
Birmingham International	a															13 13									
Coventry	a															13 24									
Lichfield Trent Valley	a																								
Tamworth Low Level	a																								
Nuneaton	a																								
Rugby	a																								
Milton Keynes Central	a											12 46	13 01												
Watford Junction	a																								
London Euston 15	a		13 04					13 12				13 23	13 38						13 42						

A from 18 February until 24 March
B until 11 February
C 🛒 from Preston

OVERNIGHT SLEEPERS. For sleeper trains, operated by First ScotRail, please refer to Tables 400 - 404

Scotland and North West England - West Midlands and London

Route Diagram - see first Page of Table 65

		LM		VT	LM	VT	XC	LM	NT	VT	TP	NT		NT	TP	VT	VT	VT	TP	TP	XC			VT	EM
		◇1		◇1	◇1	◇1	◇1	◇1		◇1	◇1				◇1	◇1	◇1	◇1	◇1	◇1	◇1			◇1	◇
									A 🚌			B		A											
				🍴		🍴	🛒			🍴					🛒	🍴	🍴	🍴	🛒	🛒	🛒			🍴	
Inverness	d																								
Aberdeen	d																								
Dundee	d																								
Perth	d																								
Edinburgh 10	d																		09 51						
Haymarket	d																		09u56						
Glasgow Central 15	d									09 40								10 00		10 10					
Motherwell	d																								
Carstairs	d																								
Lockerbie	d																		11 01						
Carlisle 8	a									10 47								11 08	11 22	11 26					
	d									10 49								11 09	11 29						
Penrith North Lakes	d																	11 24	11 45						
Windermere	d																								
Oxenholme Lake District	a									11 22									12 09						
	d									11 23									12 10						
Barrow-in-Furness	d										11 25														
Lancaster 6	a									11 37	12 18								12 26						
	d									11 38	12 18								12 26						
Blackpool North	d											11 37		11 37	11 44										
Preston 8	a									11 56	12 37	12 02		12 02	12 08			12 15	12 45						
Preston 8	d									11 58		12 04		12 04	12 10			12 17	12 47						
Wigan North Western	a									12 09		12 24		12 27				12 28							
	d								11 35	12 09		12 24						12 28							
Blackrod	d																								
Lostock	d																								
Bolton	a														12 34				13 08						
Manchester Piccadilly 10 🚊	a														12 56				13 27						
Manchester Airport ✈	a														13 17				13 47						
Liverpool Lime Street 10	a								12 35			13 02													
	d	11 34		11 48				12 04				13 16													11 52
Liverpool South Parkway ✈	d	11 44						12 15				13a27													12 03
Runcorn	d	11 52		12 04				12 25																	
Warrington Bank Quay	a									12 20								12 39							
	d									12 20								12 39							
Hartford	d	12 04																							
Manchester Piccadilly 10 🚊	d					11 55	12 07									12 15					12 27			12 35	12 43
Stockport	d					12 04	12 16									12 23					12 35			12 43	12a53
Wilmslow	d					12 11																			
Holyhead	d																								
Bangor (Gwynedd)	d																								
Llandudno Junction	d																								
Wrexham General	d																								
Chester	d																12 35								
Crewe 10	a	12 19				12 27		12 45									12 54	12 58							
	d	12 22				12 29		12 49									12 57	13 01							
Macclesfield	d																				12 49			12 56	
Congleton	d																								
Stoke-on-Trent	d				←		12 44									12 50					13 07			13 12	
Stafford	a	12 42		12 35	12 42		13 02	13 09													13 25				
	d	12 43		12 36	12 43		13 03	13 10													13 26				
Penkridge	a	→						13 15																	
Wolverhampton 7 🚊	a				12 56		13 15	13 27										13 31			13 39				
Birmingham New Street 12	a				13 17		13 39	13 47										13 55			13 58				
Birmingham International ✈	a																				14 13				
Coventry	a																				14 24				
Lichfield Trent Valley	a																								
Tamworth Low Level	a																								
Nuneaton	a																								
Rugby	a																								
Milton Keynes Central	a															13 46	14 01								
Watford Junction	a																								
London Euston 15 ⊖	a			13 56		14 04				14 12						14 23	14 38							14 42	

A from 18 February until 24 March

B until 11 February

OVERNIGHT SLEEPERS. For sleeper trains, operated by First ScotRail, please refer to Tables 400 - 404

Scotland and North West England - West Midlands and London

Route Diagram - see first Page of Table 65

					TP		LM	VT		LM	VT	XC	LM	NT	VT	NT	NT	TP		VT	VT	VT	TP	XC	
					◇1		◇1	◇1		◇1	◇1	◇1	◇1		◇1			◇1		◇1	◇1	◇1	◇1	◇1	
														B 🚌		C	B						D		
					🛒			🍴			🍴	🛒			🍴			🛒		🍴	🍴	🍴	🛒	🛒	
Inverness	d																								
Aberdeen	d																								
Dundee	d																								
Perth	d																								
Edinburgh 10	d																					10 52			
Haymarket	d																					10 57			
Glasgow Central 15	d														10 40										
Motherwell	d																								
Carstairs	d																								
Lockerbie	d																								
Carlisle 8	a														11 47							12 05			
	d														11 49							12 07			
Penrith North Lakes	d																								
Windermere	d																						12 51		
Oxenholme Lake District	a														12 22							12 41	13 07		
	d														12 23							12 43	13 09		
Barrow-in-Furness	d																								
Lancaster 6	a														12 37							12 56	13 26		
	d														12 38							12 57	13 26		
Blackpool North	d															12 37	12 37	12 44							
Preston 8	a														12 56	13 02	13 02	13 08				13 15	13 45		
Preston 8	d														12 58	13 04	13 04	13 10				13 17	13 47		
Wigan North Western	a														13 09	13 24	13 27					13 28			
	d													12 35	13 09	13 24						13 28			
Blackrod	d																								
Lostock	d																								
Bolton	a																	13 34					14 08		
Manchester Piccadilly 10 🚊	a																	13 56					14 27		
Manchester Airport ✈	a																	14 17					14 47		
Liverpool Lime Street 10	a													13 35		14 02									
	d				12 22		12 34	12 48					13 04			14 16									
Liverpool South Parkway ✈	d				12 32		12 44						13 15			14a27									
Runcorn	d						12 52	13 04					13 25												
Warrington Bank Quay	a														13 20							13 39			
	d														13 20							13 39			
Hartford	d						13 06																		
Manchester Piccadilly 10 🚊	d				13a09						12 55	13 07								13 15				13 27	
Stockport	d										13 04	13 16								13 23				13 35	
Wilmslow	d										13 11														
Holyhead	d																								
Bangor (Gwynedd)	d																								
Llandudno Junction	d																								
Wrexham General	d																								
Chester	d																				13 35				
Crewe 10	a						13 20				13 27		13 45								13 54	13 58			
	d						13 22				13 29		13 49								13 56	14 01			
Macclesfield	d																							13 49	
Congleton	d																								
Stoke-on-Trent	d									←		13 44								13 50				14 07	
Stafford	a						13 42	13 35		13 42		14 02	14 09											14 25	
	d						13 43	13 36		13 43		14 03	14 10											14 26	
Penkridge	a						→						14 15												
Wolverhampton 7 🚊	a									13 56		14 16	14 27									14 31		14 39	
Birmingham New Street 12	a									14 17		14 39	14 47									14 55		14 58	
Birmingham International ✈	a																							15 13	
Coventry	a																							15 24	
Lichfield Trent Valley	a																								
Tamworth Low Level	a																								
Nuneaton	a																								
Rugby	a																								
Milton Keynes Central	a																			14 46	15 01				
Watford Junction	a																								
London Euston 15 ⊖	a							14 56			15 04				15 12					15 23	15 38				

B from 18 February until 24 March

C until 11 February

D 🛒 from Preston

OVERNIGHT SLEEPERS. For sleeper trains, operated by First ScotRail, please refer to Tables 400 - 404

Scotland and North West England - West Midlands and London

Route Diagram - see first Page of Table 65

		VT	EM	TP	LM	VT	LM	VT	XC	LM	NT	VT	NT	NT	TP	VT	VT	VT
		◇1	◇	◇1	◇1	◇1	◇1	◇1	◇1	◇1		◇1			◇1	◇1	◇1	◇1
											B 🚌		C	B				
		☕		🍴		☕		☕	🍴			☕			🍴	☕	☕	☕
Inverness	d																	
Aberdeen	d																	
Dundee	d																	
Perth	d																	
Edinburgh 10	d																	
Haymarket	d																	
Glasgow Central 15	d											11 40						12 00
Motherwell	d																	
Carstairs	d																	
Lockerbie	d																	
Carlisle 8	a											12 46						13 08
	d											12 49						13 09
Penrith North Lakes	d											13 03						
Windermere	d																	
Oxenholme Lake District	a																	
	d																	
Barrow-in-Furness	d																	
Lancaster 6	a											13 37						13 56
	d											13 38						13 58
Blackpool North	d												13 37	13 37	13 44			
Preston 8	a											13 56	14 02	14 02	14 08			14 15
Preston 8	d											13 58	14 04	14 04	14 10			14 17
Wigan North Western	a											14 09	14 24	14 27				14 28
	d										13 35	14 09	14 24					14 28
Blackrod	d																	
Lostock	d																	
Bolton	a														14 34			
Manchester Piccadilly 10	a														14 56			
Manchester Airport ✈	a														15 17			
Liverpool Lime Street 10	a										14 35		15 02					
	d		12 52	13 22	13 34	13 48				14 04			15 16					
Liverpool South Parkway ✈	d		13 03	13 32	13 44					14 15			15a27					
Runcorn	d				13 52	14 04				14 25								
Warrington Bank Quay	a											14 20						14 39
	d											14 20						14 39
Hartford	d				14 04													
Manchester Piccadilly 10	d	13 35	13 43	14a09				13 55	14 07							14 15		
Stockport	d	13 43	13a53					14 04	14 16							14 23		
Wilmslow	d							14 11										
Holyhead	d																	
Bangor (Gwynedd)	d																	
Llandudno Junction	d																	
Wrexham General	d																	
Chester	d																14 35	
Crewe 10	a				14 19			14 27		14 45							14 54	14 58
	d				14 22			14 29		14 49							14 56	15 01
Macclesfield	d	13 56																
Congleton	d																	
Stoke-on-Trent	d	14 12					←		14 44							14 50		
Stafford	a				14 46	14 35	14 46		15 02	15 09								
	d				14 46	14 36	14 46		15 03	15 10								
Penkridge	a				→					15 15								
Wolverhampton 7	a						14 59		15 16	15 27								15 31
Birmingham New Street 12	a						15 18		15 39	15 47								15 55
Birmingham International ✈	a																	
Coventry	a																	
Lichfield Trent Valley	a																	
Tamworth Low Level	a																	
Nuneaton	a																	
Rugby	a																	
Milton Keynes Central	a															15 46	16 01	
Watford Junction	a																	
London Euston 15 ⊖	a	15 42				15 56		16 04				16 12				16 23	16 38	

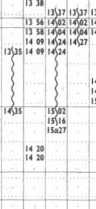

A until 11 February and then from 31 March **B** from 18 February until 24 March **C** until 11 February

OVERNIGHT SLEEPERS. For sleeper trains, operated by First ScotRail, please refer to Tables 400 - 404

Scotland and North West England - West Midlands and London

Route Diagram - see first Page of Table 65

		SR	TP	TP	NT	XC	VT	EM	TP	LM	VT	LM	VT	XC	LM	NT	VT	NT
			◇1	◇1		◇1	◇1	◇	◇1	◇1	◇1	◇1	◇1	◇1	◇1		◇1	
			A													C 🚌		D
			🍴	🍴		🍴	☕		🍴		☕		☕	🍴			☕	
Inverness	d																	
Aberdeen	d																	
Dundee	d																	
Perth	d																	
Edinburgh 10	d			12 08														
Haymarket	d			12u12														
Glasgow Central 15	d	12 12															12 40	
Motherwell	d																	
Carstairs	d																	
Lockerbie	d			13 07														
Carlisle 8	a	14 32		13 29													13 47	
	d			13 29													13 49	
Penrith North Lakes	d																	
Windermere	d																	
Oxenholme Lake District	a			14 06													14 22	
	d			14 07													14 24	
Barrow-in-Furness	d		13 25		14 16													
Lancaster 6	a		14 18	14 21	15 20												14 37	
	d		14 18	14 22													14 38	
Blackpool North	d																	14 37
Preston 8	a		14 37	14 41													14 56	15 02
Preston 8	d		14 47														14 58	15 04
Wigan North Western	a																15 09	15 24
	d															14 35	15 09	15 24
Blackrod	d																	
Lostock	d																	
Bolton	a		15 08															
Manchester Piccadilly 10	a		15 27															
Manchester Airport ✈	a		15 47															
Liverpool Lime Street 10	a															15 35		16 02
	d							13 52	14 22	14 34	14 48				15 04			16 16
Liverpool South Parkway ✈	d							14 03	14 32	14 44					15 15			16a27
Runcorn	d									14 52	15 04				15 25			
Warrington Bank Quay	a																15 20	
	d																15 20	
Hartford	d									15 04								
Manchester Piccadilly 10	d					14 27	14 35	14 43	15a09				14 55	15 07				
Stockport	d					14 35	14 43	14a53					15 04	15 16				
Wilmslow	d												15 11					
Holyhead	d																	
Bangor (Gwynedd)	d																	
Llandudno Junction	d																	
Wrexham General	d																	
Chester	d																	
Crewe 10	a									15 19			15 27		15 45			
	d									15 22			15 29		15 49			
Macclesfield	d					14 49	14 56											
Congleton	d																	
Stoke-on-Trent	d					15 07	15 12					←		15 44				
Stafford	a					15 25				15 42	15 35	15 42		16 02	16 09			
	d					15 26				15 43	15 36	15 43		16 03	16 10			
Penkridge	a									→					16 15			
Wolverhampton 7	a					15 39						15 56		16 16	16 27			
Birmingham New Street 12	a					15 58						16 17		16 39	16 47			
Birmingham International ✈	a					16 13												
Coventry	a					16 24												
Lichfield Trent Valley	a																	
Tamworth Low Level	a																	
Nuneaton	a																	
Rugby	a																	
Milton Keynes Central	a																	
Watford Junction	a																	
London Euston 15 ⊖	a						16 42				16 56		17 04				17 12	

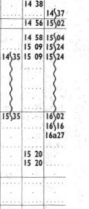

A 🍴 from Preston **C** from 18 February until 24 March **D** until 11 February

OVERNIGHT SLEEPERS. For sleeper trains, operated by First ScotRail, please refer to Tables 400 - 404

Scotland and North West England - West Midlands and London

Route Diagram - see first Page of Table 65

		NT	TP	VT	VT	VT	TP	XC	NT	VT	EM	TP	LM	VT	LM	VT	XC	LM	NT
			◇1	◇1	◇1	◇1	◇1	◇1		◇1	◇	◇1	◇1	◇1	◇1	◇1	◇1	◇1	
		A																	A 🚌
			⊥	⊏	⊏	⊏	⊥	⊥		⊏				⊏		⊏	⊥		
Inverness	d																		
Aberdeen	d																		
Dundee	d																		
Perth	d																		
Edinburgh 10	d					12 52													
Haymarket	d					12 57													
Glasgow Central 15	d						13 09												
Motherwell	d																		
Carstairs	d																		
Lockerbie	d						14 06												
Carlisle 8	a					14 05	14 29												
	d					14 07	14 29												
Penrith North Lakes	d					14 22	14 45												
Windermere	d																		
Oxenholme Lake District	a						15 09												
	d						15 10												
Barrow-in-Furness	d																		
Lancaster 6	a					14 56	15 26												
	d					14 57	15 26												
Blackpool North	d	14 37	14 44						15 29										
Preston 8	a	15 02	15 08			15 15	15 45		15 52										
Preston 8	d	15 04	15 10			15 17	15 47		22a31										
Wigan North Western	a	15 27				15 28													
	d					15 28													15 35
Blackrod	d																		
Lostock	d																		
Bolton	a		15 34				16 08												
Manchester Piccadilly 10 ⇌	a		15 56				16 27												
Manchester Airport ✈	a		16 17				16 47												
Liverpool Lime Street 10	a																		16 35
	d										14 52	15 22	15 34	15 48				16 04	
Liverpool South Parkway ✈	d										15 03	15 32	15 44					16 15	
Runcorn	d												15 52	16 04				16 25	
Warrington Bank Quay	a					15 39													
	d					15 39													
Hartford	d												16 04						
Manchester Piccadilly 10 ⇌	d			15 15				15 27		15 35	15 43	16a09				15 55	16 07		
Stockport	d			15 23				15 35		15 43	15a53					16 04	16 16		
Wilmslow	d															16 11			
Holyhead	d																		
Bangor (Gwynedd)	d																		
Llandudno Junction	d																		
Wrexham General	d																		
Chester	d				15 35														
Crewe 10	a				15 54	15 58							16 19			16 27		16 45	
	d				15 56	16 01							16 22			16 29		16 49	
Macclesfield	d							15 49		15 56									
Congleton	d																		
Stoke-on-Trent	d			15 50				16 07		16 12					←		16 44		
Stafford	a							16 24					16 46	16 35	16 46		17 02	17 09	
	d							16 25					16 46	16 36	16 46		17 03	17 10	
Penkridge	a												→					17 15	
Wolverhampton 7 ⇌	a					16 31		16 39							16 59		17 16	17 27	
Birmingham New Street 12	a					16 55		16 58							17 18		17 39	17 47	
Birmingham International ✈	a							17 13											
Coventry	a							17 24											
Lichfield Trent Valley	a																		
Tamworth Low Level	a																		
Nuneaton	a																		
Rugby	a																		
Milton Keynes Central	a			16 46	17 01														
Watford Junction	a																		
London Euston 15 ⊖	a			17 23	17 38					17 42				17 56		18 04			

A from 18 February until 24 March

OVERNIGHT SLEEPERS. For sleeper trains, operated by First ScotRail, please refer to Tables 400 - 404

Scotland and North West England - West Midlands and London

Route Diagram - see first Page of Table 65

		VT	NT	NT	TP	VT	VT	VT	TP	XC	VT	EM	TP	LM	VT	LM	VT	XC	LM
		◇1			◇1	◇1	◇1	◇1	◇1	◇1	◇1	◇	◇1	◇1	◇1	◇1	◇1	◇1	◇1
			A	B															
		⊏			⊥	⊏	⊏	⊏	⊥	⊥	⊏				⊏		⊏	⊥	
Inverness	d																		
Aberdeen	d																		
Dundee	d																		
Perth	d																		
Edinburgh 10	d								14 07										
Haymarket	d								14u11										
Glasgow Central 15	d	13 40						14 00											
Motherwell	d																		
Carstairs	d																		
Lockerbie	d								15 06										
Carlisle 8	a	14 46						15 09	15 27										
	d	14 49						15 11	15 27										
Penrith North Lakes	d								15 43										
Windermere	d																		
Oxenholme Lake District	a	15 22						15 45	16 06										
	d	15 23						15 46	16 07										
Barrow-in-Furness	d																		
Lancaster 6	a	15 37							16 26										
	d	15 38							16 26										
Blackpool North	d		15 37	15 37	15 44														
Preston 8	a	15 56	16 02	16 02	16 08			16 15	16 45										
Preston 8	d	15 58	16 04	16 04	16 10			16 17	16 47										
Wigan North Western	a	16 09	16 24	16 27				16 28											
	d	16 09	16 24					16 28											
Blackrod	d																		
Lostock	d																		
Bolton	a				16 34				17 08										
Manchester Piccadilly 10 ⇌	a				16 56				17 27										
Manchester Airport ✈	a				17 17				17 48										
Liverpool Lime Street 10	a		17 05																
	d											15 52	16 22	16 34	16 48				17 04
Liverpool South Parkway ✈	d											16 03	16 32	16 44					17 15
Runcorn	d													16 52	17 04				17 25
Warrington Bank Quay	a	16 20						16 39											
	d	16 20						16 39											
Hartford	d													17 06					
Manchester Piccadilly 10 ⇌	d					16 15				16 27	16 35	16 43	17a09				16 55	17 06	
Stockport	d					16 23				16 35	16 43	16a53					17 04		
Wilmslow	d																17 11		
Holyhead	d						14 38												
Bangor (Gwynedd)	d						15 07												
Llandudno Junction	d						15 27												
Wrexham General	d																		
Chester	d						16 24												
Crewe 10	a						16 47	16 58						17 20			17 27		17 47
	d						16 56	17 01						17 22			17 29		17 49
Macclesfield	d									16 49	16 56							17 26	
Congleton	d																		
Stoke-on-Trent	d					16 50				17 07	17 12					←		17 44	
Stafford	a									17 25				17 42	17 35	17 42		18 03	18 09
	d									17 26				17 43	17 36	17 43		18 04	18 10
Penkridge	a													→					18 15
Wolverhampton 7 ⇌	a							17 31		17 39						17 56		18 16	18 27
Birmingham New Street 12	a							17 55		17 58						18 17		18 38	18 47
Birmingham International ✈	a									18 13									
Coventry	a									18 24									
Lichfield Trent Valley	a																		
Tamworth Low Level	a																		
Nuneaton	a																		
Rugby	a																		
Milton Keynes Central	a					17 46	18 01												
Watford Junction	a																		
London Euston 15 ⊖	a	18 12				18 23	18 38				18 42				18 56		19 04		

A until 11 February

B from 18 February until 24 March

OVERNIGHT SLEEPERS. For sleeper trains, operated by First ScotRail, please refer to Tables 400 - 404

Scotland and North West England - West Midlands and London

Route Diagram - see first Page of Table 65

		NT	VT	NT	NT	TP	VT	TP		VT	TP	XC	VT	EM			TP			LM	VT	LM	VT	XC	LM
			◇1			◇1	◇1	◇1		◇1	◇1	◇1	◇1	◇			◇1			◇1	◇1	◇1	◇1	◇1	◇1
		A		B	A																				
		🚌	ᑭ			⌶	ᑭ			ᑭ	⌶	⌶	ᑭ								ᑭ		ᑭ	⌶	
Inverness	d																								
Aberdeen	d																								
Dundee	d																								
Perth	d																								
Edinburgh 10	d						14 52																		
Haymarket	d						14 57																		
Glasgow Central 15	d		14 40																						
Motherwell	d																								
Carstairs	d																								
Lockerbie	d																								
Carlisle 8	a		15 46				16 05																		
	d		15 49				16 07																		
Penrith North Lakes	d						16 22																		
Windermere	d																								
Oxenholme Lake District	a		16 22																						
	d		16 24																						
Barrow-in-Furness	d							16 22																	
Lancaster 6	a		16 37				16 56	17 19																	
	d		16 38				16 57	17 20																	
Blackpool North	d			16 35	16 35	16 40					17 20														
Preston 8	a		16 56	17 02	17 02	17 08	17 15	17 39			17 45														
Preston 8	d		16 58	17 04	17 04	17 10	17 17				17 47														
Wigan North Western	a		17 09	17 24	17 27		17 28																		
	d	16 35	17 09	17 24			17 28																		
Blackrod	d																								
Lostock	d																								
Bolton	a					17 34					18 08														
Manchester Piccadilly 10	a					17 56					18 27														
Manchester Airport ✈	a					18 17					18 47														
Liverpool Lime Street 10	a	17 35		18 02																					
	d													16 52			17 22			17 34	17 48				18 04
Liverpool South Parkway ✈	d													17 03			17 32			17 44					18 15
Runcorn	d																			17 52	18 04				18 24
Warrington Bank Quay	a		17 20				17 39																		
	d		17 20				17 39																		
Hartford	d																			18 06					
Manchester Piccadilly 10	d									17 15		17 27	17 35	17 43			18a09						17 55	18 05	
Stockport	d									17 23		17 36	17 43	17a53									18 04	18 13	
Wilmslow	d																						18 11		
Holyhead	d																								
Bangor (Gwynedd)	d																								
Llandudno Junction	d																								
Wrexham General	d																								
Chester	d																								
Crewe 10	a						17 59													18 20			18 27		18 46
	d						18 01													18 22			18 29		18 49
Macclesfield	d												17 56											18 26	
Congleton	d											17 54													
Stoke-on-Trent	d									17 50		18 08	18 12									←		18 44	
Stafford	a											18 26								18 42	18 35	18 42		19 02	19 09
	d											18 27								18 43	18 36	18 43		19 03	19 10
Penkridge	a																			↦					19 15
Wolverhampton 7	a						18 31					18 40										18 56		19 16	19 27
Birmingham New Street 12	a						18 55					18 58										19 17		19 33	19 47
Birmingham International ✈	a											19 13													
Coventry	a											19 24													
Lichfield Trent Valley	a																								
Tamworth Low Level	a																								
Nuneaton	a																								
Rugby	a																								
Milton Keynes Central	a									18 46															
Watford Junction	a																								
London Euston 15 ⊖	a		19 12							19 23			19 42								19 56		20 04		

A from 18 February until 24 March

B until 11 February

OVERNIGHT SLEEPERS. For sleeper trains, operated by First ScotRail, please refer to Tables 400 - 404

Scotland and North West England - West Midlands and London

Route Diagram - see first Page of Table 65

		NT	VT	NT		NT	TP	VT	SR	TP	TP	VT	XC	VT		EM				TP		LM	VT	LM	
			◇1				◇1	◇1		◇1	◇1	◇1	◇1	◇1		◇				◇1		◇1	◇1	◇1	
		A		B		A	C																		
		🚌	ᑭ				⌶	ᑭ			⌶	ᑭ	⌶	ᑭ									ᑭ		
Inverness	d																								
Aberdeen	d																								
Dundee	d																								
Perth	d																								
Edinburgh 10	d										16 12														
Haymarket	d										16u16														
Glasgow Central 15	d		15 40					16 00	16 12																
Motherwell	d																								
Carstairs	d																								
Lockerbie	d										17 11														
Carlisle 8	a		16 46					17 08	18 35		17 33														
	d		16 49					17 09			17 34														
Penrith North Lakes	d		17 03								17 49														
Windermere	d						17 06																		
Oxenholme Lake District	a						17 25	17 44																	
	d						17 30	17 44																	
Barrow-in-Furness	d									17 21															
Lancaster 6	a		17 37				17 47			18 16	18 26														
	d		17 38				17 48			18 17	18 26														
Blackpool North	d			17 37		17 37																			
Preston 8	a		17 56	18 02		18 02	18 06	18 15		18 36	18 45														
Preston 8	d		17 58	18 04		18 04	18 08	18 17			18 47														
Wigan North Western	a		18 09	18 24		18 27		18 28																	
	d	17 35	18 09	18 24				18 28																	
Blackrod	d																								
Lostock	d						18 30																		
Bolton	a						18 34				19 08														
Manchester Piccadilly 10	a						18 56				19 27														
Manchester Airport ✈	a						19 17				19 50														
Liverpool Lime Street 10	a	18 35		19 02																					
	d															17 52				18 22		18 34	18 48		
Liverpool South Parkway ✈	d															18 03				18 32		18 44			
Runcorn	d																					18 52	19 04		
Warrington Bank Quay	a		18 20					18 39																	
	d		18 20					18 39																	
Hartford	d																					19 04			
Manchester Piccadilly 10	d											18 15	18 27	18 35		18 43				19a09					
Stockport	d											18 23	18 35	18 43		18a53									
Wilmslow	d																								
Holyhead	d																								
Bangor (Gwynedd)	d																								
Llandudno Junction	d																								
Wrexham General	d																								
Chester	d																								
Crewe 10	a							18 59														19 19			
	d							19 01														19 22			
Macclesfield	d													18 56											
Congleton	d												18 54												
Stoke-on-Trent	d											18 49	19 07	19 12										←	
Stafford	a												19 25									19 42	19 35	19 42	
	d												19 25									19 43	19 36	19 43	
Penkridge	a																					↦		19 48	
Wolverhampton 7	a							19 31					19 39											19 59	
Birmingham New Street 12	a							19 55					19 58											20 17	
Birmingham International ✈	a												20 13												
Coventry	a												20 24												
Lichfield Trent Valley	a																								
Tamworth Low Level	a																								
Nuneaton	a																								
Rugby	a																								
Milton Keynes Central	a											19 45													
Watford Junction	a																								
London Euston 15 ⊖	a		20 15									20 24		20 59									21 15		

A from 18 February until 24 March

B until 11 February

C ⌶ from Preston

OVERNIGHT SLEEPERS. For sleeper trains, operated by First ScotRail, please refer to Tables 400 - 404

Scotland and North West England - West Midlands and London

Route Diagram - see first Page of Table 65

		VT	XC	LM	NT	VT	NT	NT	TP	VT	TP	XC	VT	EM	TP	LM	VT	LM	NT	VT	NT	NT
		◇1	◇1	◇1		◇1			◇1	◇1	◇1	◇1	◇1	◇	◇1	◇1	◇1	◇1		◇1		
					A		B	A				C							A		B	A
Inverness	d																					
Aberdeen	d																					
Dundee	d																					
Perth	d																					
Edinburgh 10	d									16 52												
Haymarket	d									16 57												
Glasgow Central 15	d					16 40					17 06									17 40		
Motherwell	d					16 54																
Carstairs	d																					
Lockerbie	d										18 06									18 32		
Carlisle 8	a					17 49				18 06	18 28									18 50		
	d					17 52				18 08	18 29									18 52		
Penrith North Lakes	d										18 45									19 06		
Windermere	d																					
Oxenholme Lake District	a					18 25				18 41	19 09									19 28		
	d					18 26				18 42	19 10									19 29		
Barrow-in-Furness	d																					
Lancaster 6	a					18 40				18 56	19 26									19 43		
	d					18 41				18 57	19 26									19 44		
Blackpool North	d						18 37	18 37	18 44												19 37	19 37
Preston 8	a					18 59	19 00	19 00	19 08	19 15	19 45									20 02	20 02	20 02
Preston 8	d					19 01	19 04	19 04	19 10	19 17	19 47									20 04	20 04	20 04
Wigan North Western	a					19 12	19 24	19 27		19 28										20 15	20 24	20 27
	d				18 35	19 12	19 24			19 28									19 35	20 15	20 24	
Blackrod	d																					
Lostock	d																					
Bolton	a								19 34		20 08											
Manchester Piccadilly 10	a								19 56		20 27											
Manchester Airport ✈	a								20 17		20 47											
Liverpool Lime Street 10	a				19 35		20 02												20 35		21 02	
	d			19 04										18 52	19 22	19 34	19 48					
Liverpool South Parkway ✈	d			19 14										19 03	19 32	19 44						
Runcorn	d			19 23												19 52	20 04					
Warrington Bank Quay	a					19 23				19 39										20 26		
	d					19 23				19 39										20 26		
Hartford	d															20 04						
Manchester Piccadilly 10	d	18 55	19 07									19 27	19 35	19 43	20a09							
Stockport	d	19 04	19 16									19 35	19 43	19a53								
Wilmslow	d	19 11																				
Holyhead	d																					
Bangor (Gwynedd)	d																					
Llandudno Junction	d																					
Wrexham General	d																					
Chester	d																					
Crewe 10	a	19 27		19 49						19 59						20 16				20 45		
	d	19 29		19 51						20 01						20 22				20 47		
Macclesfield	d											19 49	19 56									
Congleton	d																					
Stoke-on-Trent	d		19 44									20 07	20 12					←				
Stafford	a		20 02	20 11								20 25				20 44	20 35	20 44				
	d		20 03	20 12								20 26				20 45	20 36	20 45				
Penkridge	a															→		20 50				
Wolverhampton 7	a		20 16	20 28						20 32		20 39						21 01				
Birmingham New Street 12	a		20 33	20 47						20 55		20 58						21 19				
Birmingham International ✈	a											21 13										
Coventry	a											21 24										
Lichfield Trent Valley	a																					
Tamworth Low Level	a																					
Nuneaton	a																					
Rugby	a																					
Milton Keynes Central	a					20 41							21 10							21 50		
Watford Junction	a					21s15																
London Euston 15 ⊖	a	21 18				21 38							22 00				22 14			22 44		

A from 18 February until 24 March
B until 11 February
C to Birmingham New Street

OVERNIGHT SLEEPERS. For sleeper trains, operated by First ScotRail, please refer to Tables 400 - 404

Scotland and North West England - West Midlands and London

Route Diagram - see first Page of Table 65

		TP	XC	VT	XC	VT	EM	TP	LM	NT	XC	TP	TP	TP	TP	TP	VT	VT	NT	TP	VT
		◇1	◇1	◇1	◇1	◇1	◇	◇1	◇1		◇1	◇1	◇1	◇1	◇1	◇1	◇1	◇1		◇1	◇1
										B		C	D	D	C	C	C	D	B		E
Inverness	d																				
Aberdeen	d																				
Dundee	d																				
Perth	d																				
Edinburgh 10	d													18 12	18 12						18 42
Haymarket	d													18u16	18u16						18 46
Glasgow Central 15	d			18 00													18 30	18 40			
Motherwell	d																				
Carstairs	d																				
Lockerbie	d													19 11	19 11						
Carlisle 8	a			19 08										19 34	19 34		19 38	19 46			19 58
	d			19 09										19 34	19 34		19 40	19 48			19 59
Penrith North Lakes	d													19 49			19 54	20 02			20 14
Windermere	d																				
Oxenholme Lake District	a													20 12	20 12		20 16	20 24			20 37
	d													20 13	20 12		20 17	20 25			20 37
Barrow-in-Furness	d											19 25	19 33								
Lancaster 6	a			19 55								20 21	20 34	20 26	20 26		20 31	20 39			20 52
	d			19 56								20 22	20 35	20 26	20 27		20 32	20 40			20 52
Blackpool North	d	19 44																	20 37	20 42	
Preston 8	a	20 08		20 15								20 41	20 53	20 45	20 45		20 50	20 58	21 01	21 06	21 10
Preston 8	d	20 10		20 17								21 10		20 47	20 47		21 00	21 00	21 04	21 10	21 21
Wigan North Western	a			20 28													21 11	21 11	21 27		21 32
	d			20 28						20 35							21 11	21 11			21 32
Blackrod	d																				
Lostock	d															←					
Bolton	a	20 34										21 34		21 08	21 08	21 34				21 34	
Manchester Piccadilly 10	a	20 56										→		21 27	21 27	21 56				21 56	
Manchester Airport ✈	a	21 17												21 46	21 47	22 17				22 17	
Liverpool Lime Street 10	a									21 35											
	d						19 52	20 22	20 34												
Liverpool South Parkway ✈	d						20 03	20 32	20 44												
Runcorn	d								20 52												
Warrington Bank Quay	a			20 39													21 22	21 22			21 43
	d			20 39													21 22	21 22			21 43
Hartford	d								21 03												
Manchester Piccadilly 10	d		20 07		20 27	20 35	20 43	21a09			21 07										
Stockport	d		20 16		20 35	20 43	20a53														
Wilmslow	d																				
Holyhead	d																				
Bangor (Gwynedd)	d																				
Llandudno Junction	d																				
Wrexham General	d																				
Chester	d																				
Crewe 10	a			20 59					21 16								21 41	21 41			22 03
	d			21 01					21 17								21 43	21 43			22 05
Macclesfield	d				20 49	20 56															
Congleton	d																				
Stoke-on-Trent	d		20 44		21 07	21 12					21 45										
Stafford	a		21 02		21 26				21 42		22 02						22 07	22 07			22 24
	d		21 03		21 27				21 42		22 03						22 08	22 08			22 25
Penkridge	a								21 48												
Wolverhampton 7	a		21 15	21 31	21 39				21 58		22 14						22 22	22 22			22 39
Birmingham New Street 12	a		21 32	21 54	21 58				22 20		22 32						22 46	22 46			22 59
Birmingham International ✈	a																				
Coventry	a																				
Lichfield Trent Valley	a																				
Tamworth Low Level	a																				
Nuneaton	a																				
Rugby	a																				
Milton Keynes Central	a					22 10															
Watford Junction	a					22s40															
London Euston 15 ⊖	a					23 02															

B from 18 February until 24 March
C from 31 March
D until 24 March
E from 7 January until 24 March

OVERNIGHT SLEEPERS. For sleeper trains, operated by First ScotRail, please refer to Tables 400 - 404

Scotland and North West England - West Midlands and London

Route Diagram - see first Page of Table 65

		VT	XC	EM	LM	EM	TP	NT	TP	LM	TP	NT	VT	NT	TP	NT	NT
		◇1	◇1	◇	◇1	◇	◇1		◇1	1	◇1		◇1		◇1		
		A					A	A				B	C	B		D	E
		⊏										🚌	⊏			🚌	🚌
Inverness	d																
Aberdeen	d																
Dundee	d																
Perth	d																
Edinburgh 10	d	18 52											18 52				
Haymarket	d	18 57											18 57				
Glasgow Central 15	d																
Motherwell	d																
Carstairs	d																
Lockerbie	d																
Carlisle 8	a	20 06											20 06				
	d	20 08											20 09				
Penrith North Lakes	d	20 23															
Windermere	d						21 40										
Oxenholme Lake District	a	20 46					21 59										
	d	20 46					22 01										
Barrow-in-Furness	d							21 43									
Lancaster 6	a	21 00					22 17	22 45									
	d	21 01					22 17	22 46								23 07	
Blackpool North	d								21 44					22 14	22 44		
Preston 8	a	21 19					22 38	23 11	22 08				22 22	22 41	23 08	23 47	
Preston 8	d	21 21							22 10				22 26	22 43	23 10		
Wigan North Western	a	21 32											22 37	23 06			
	d	21 32										21 35	22 37				23 15
Blackrod	d																
Lostock	d																
Bolton	a								22 34						23 34		
Manchester Piccadilly 10	a								22 56						23 53		
Manchester Airport ✈	a								23 17						00 23		
Liverpool Lime Street 10	a											22 35					00 15
	d			20 52	21 34	21 37				22 04	22 30						
Liverpool South Parkway ✈	d			21 03	21 44	21 47				22 14	22 40						
Runcorn	d				21 52					22 23							
Warrington Bank Quay	a	21 43											22 48				
	d	21 43											22 48				
Hartford	d				22 04					22 34							
Manchester Piccadilly 10	d		21 27	21 43		22 31					23a19						
Stockport	d		21 36	21a52		22a41											
Wilmslow	d																
Holyhead	d																
Bangor (Gwynedd)	d																
Llandudno Junction	d																
Wrexham General	d																
Chester	d																
Crewe 10	a	22 03			22 21					22 48			23 08				
	d	22 05			22 23												
Macclesfield	d		21 50														
Congleton	d																
Stoke-on-Trent	d		22 08														
Stafford	a	22 24	22 32		22 47												
	d	22 25	22 33		22 47												
Penkridge	a				22 53												
Wolverhampton 7	a	22 39	22 45		23 03												
Birmingham New Street 12	a	22 59	23 02		23 21												
Birmingham International ✈	a																
Coventry	a																
Lichfield Trent Valley	a																
Tamworth Low Level	a																
Nuneaton	a																
Rugby	a																
Milton Keynes Central	a																
Watford Junction	a																
London Euston 15 ⊖	a																

A Until 31 December
B from 18 February until 24 March
C from 31 March
D from 7 January
E from 18 February

OVERNIGHT SLEEPERS. For sleeper trains, operated by First ScotRail, please refer to Tables 400 - 404

Scotland and North West England - West Midlands and London

Route Diagram - see first Page of Table 65

		TP	TP	TP	VT	TP	VT	VT	TP	XC	VT	VT	TP	VT	TP	XC	VT	LM
		◇1			◇1	◇1	◇1	◇1	◇1	◇1	◇1	◇1	◇1	◇1	◇1	◇1	◇1	◇1
		A								B						B		
			🚌	🚌	⊏		⊏	⊏		⊏	⊏	⊏		⊏		⊏	⊏	
Inverness	d																	
Aberdeen	d																	
Dundee	d																	
Perth	d																	
Edinburgh 10	d																	
Haymarket	d																	
Glasgow Central 15	d																	
Motherwell	d																	
Carstairs	d																	
Lockerbie	d																	
Carlisle 8	a																	
	d																	
Penrith North Lakes	d																	
Windermere	d																	
Oxenholme Lake District	a																	
	d																	
Barrow-in-Furness	d																	
Lancaster 6	a																	
	d																	
Blackpool North	d	22p44	03 20	05 20		08 14							08 44					
Preston 8	a	23p08				08 38							09 08					
Preston 8	d	23p10	04u00	06u00		08 42						09 00	09 10					
Wigan North Western	a											09 10						
	d											09 11						
Blackrod	d																	
Lostock	d																	
Bolton	a	23p34	04b35	06b35		09 05							09 34					
Manchester Piccadilly 10	a	23p53	05b00	07b00		09 28							09 56					
Manchester Airport ✈	a	00 23	05 25	07 25		09 48							10 17					
Liverpool Lime Street 10	a																	
	d							08 15	08 22		08 38				09 22		09 38	
Liverpool South Parkway ✈	d								08 32						09 32			
Runcorn	d							08 35			08 54						09 54	
Warrington Bank Quay	a											09 21						
	d											09 22						
Hartford	d																	
Manchester Piccadilly 10	d				08 05		08 20		09a11	08 27				09 20	10a09	09 27		
Stockport	d				08 14		08 28			08 36				09 27		09 36		
Wilmslow	d				08 22					08 43								
Holyhead	d																	
Bangor (Gwynedd)	d																	
Llandudno Junction	d																	
Wrexham General	d																	
Chester	d																	
Crewe 10	a				08 39			08 52		09 01	09 11	09 41					10 12	
	d				08 43			08 53		09 05	09 13	09 43					10 14	10 20
Macclesfield	d						08 42							09 40		09 49		
Congleton	d																	
Stoke-on-Trent	d						08 59							09 57		10 07		
Stafford	a				09 01					09 25	09 31					10 26	10 32	10 41
	d				09 02					09 26	09 32					10 27	10 33	10 41
Penkridge	a																	10 48
Wolverhampton 7	a									09 40						10 42		11 00
Birmingham New Street 12	a									09 58						10 59		11 17
Birmingham International ✈	a									10 13						11 13		
Coventry	a									10 24						11 24		
Lichfield Trent Valley	a																	
Tamworth Low Level	a																	
Nuneaton	a										09 54						10 55	
Rugby	a											10 31						
Milton Keynes Central	a							10 17				11 06		11 16			11 46	
Watford Junction	a				10s35		10s41				11s16	11s43						
London Euston 15 ⊖	a				10 57		11 02	11 06			11 37	12 05		12 08			12 32	

A not 11 December
B ⊏ from Birmingham New Street ⊤ to Birmingham New Street
b Stops to pick up only

OVERNIGHT SLEEPERS. For sleeper trains, operated by First ScotRail, please refer to Tables 400 - 404

Table 65

Sundays
until 1 January

Scotland and North West England - West Midlands and London

Route Diagram - see first Page of Table 65

		TP	LM	VT	TP	VT	VT	TP	XC	VT	VT	VT	TP	VT	TP	VT	VT	TP	XC	VT
		◇1	1	◇1	◇1	◇1	◇1	◇1	◇1	◇1	◇1	◇1	◇1	◇1	◇1	◇1	◇1	◇1	◇1	◇1
									A										A	
				⊡		⊡	⊡		⊡⊼	⊡	⊡	⊡		⊡		⊡	⊡		⊡⊼	⊡
Inverness	d																			
Aberdeen	d																			
Dundee	d																			
Perth	d																			
Edinburgh 10	d																			
Haymarket	d																			
Glasgow Central 15	d																			
Motherwell	d																			
Carstairs	d																			
Lockerbie	d																			
Carlisle 8	a																			
	d																			
Penrith North Lakes	d																			
Windermere	d																			
Oxenholme Lake District	a																			
	d																			
Barrow-in-Furness	d							09 17										10 30		
Lancaster 6	a							10 17										11 22		
	d							10 21										11 22		
Blackpool North	d				09 44								10 44							
Preston 8	a				10 07			10 40					11 08					11 42		
Preston 8	d			10 00	10 10		10 17	10 47				10 58	11 10				11 17	11 47		
Wigan North Western	a			10 10			10 28					11 09					11 28			
	d			10 11			10 28					11 09					11 28			
Blackrod	d																			
Lostock	d																			
Bolton	a				10 34			11 08					11 34					12 08		
Manchester Piccadilly 10	a				10 56			11 27					11 58					12 27		
Manchester Airport	a				11 17			11 47					12 17					12 48		
Liverpool Lime Street 10	a																			
	d	10 22									10 38				11 22					
Liverpool South Parkway	d	10 32													11 32					
Runcorn	d										10 54									
Warrington Bank Quay	a			10 21			10 39					11 20					11 39			
	d			10 22			10 39					11 20					11 39			
Hartford	d																			
Manchester Piccadilly 10	d	11a09				10 20			10 27	10 35				11 15	12a09				11 27	11 35
Stockport	d					10 29			10 36	10 42				11 23					11 36	11 43
Wilmslow	d					10 36														
Holyhead	d																			
Bangor (Gwynedd)	d																			
Llandudno Junction	d																			
Wrexham General	d																			
Chester	d															11 28				
Crewe 10	a			10 41		10 53	10 59				11 12					11 47	11 59			
	d		10 38	10 43		10 55	11 01				11 14					11 49	12 01			
Macclesfield	d								10 49	10 55									11 49	11 56
Congleton	d																			
Stoke-on-Trent	d		10 59						11 07	11 12				11 51					12 07	12 13
Stafford	a		11 17						11 27		11 34								12 24	
	d								11 28		11 36								12 25	
Penkridge	a																			
Wolverhampton 7	a						11 31		11 41								12 32		12 40	
Birmingham New Street 12	a						11 55		12 00								12 55		12 58	
Birmingham International	a								12 13										13 13	
Coventry	a								12 24										13 24	
Lichfield Trent Valley	a																			
Tamworth Low Level	a																			
Nuneaton	a										11 58					12 31				
Rugby	a			11 31																
Milton Keynes Central	a			12 06						12 20				12 50		13 03				
Watford Junction	a					12s35					12s50									
London Euston 15	a			12 45		12 56				12 59	13 11	13 21		13 28		13 44				13 47

A ⊡ from Birmingham New Street
⊼ to Birmingham New Street

OVERNIGHT SLEEPERS. For sleeper trains, operated by First ScotRail, please refer to Tables 400 - 404

Table 65

Sundays
until 1 January

Scotland and North West England - West Midlands and London

Route Diagram - see first Page of Table 65

		LM	VT	LM	VT	VT	TP	VT	VT	VT	TP	TP	XC	VT	LM	VT	LM	VT	VT	TP
		◇1	◇1	◇1	◇1	◇1	◇1	◇1	◇1	◇1	◇1	◇1	◇1	◇1	◇1	◇1	◇1	◇1	◇1	◇1
													A							
			⊡		⊡	⊡	⊼	⊡	⊡	⊡	⊼		⊡⊼	⊡		⊡		⊡	⊡	
Inverness	d																			
Aberdeen	d																			
Dundee	d																			
Perth	d																			
Edinburgh 10	d										10 10									
Haymarket	d										10u14									
Glasgow Central 15	d					09 37													10 34	
Motherwell	d																		10 49	
Carstairs	d																			
Lockerbie	d										11 08									
Carlisle 8	a					10 44					11 29								11 44	
	d					10 46					11 29								11 46	
Penrith North Lakes	d					11 00					11 45								12 00	
Windermere	d																			
Oxenholme Lake District	a					11 22					12 09								12 22	
	d					11 23					12 10								12 24	
Barrow-in-Furness	d																			
Lancaster 6	a					11 37					12 26								12 37	
	d					11 38				12 00	12 26								12 38	
Blackpool North	d						11 44													12 44
Preston 8	a					11 56	12 08			12 15	12 45								12 56	13 08
Preston 8	d					11 58	12 10			12 17	12 47								12 58	13 10
Wigan North Western	a					12 09				12 28									13 09	
	d					12 09				12 28									13 09	
Blackrod	d																			
Lostock	d																			
Bolton	a						12 34				13 08									13 34
Manchester Piccadilly 10	a						12 59				13 27									13 56
Manchester Airport	a						13 17				13 47									14 17
Liverpool Lime Street 10	a																			
	d	11 34	11 48									12 22			12 34	12 48				
Liverpool South Parkway	d	11 44										12 32			12 44					
Runcorn	d	11 52	12 04												12 52	13 04				
Warrington Bank Quay	a					12 20				12 39									13 20	
	d					12 20				12 39									13 20	
Hartford	d	12 03													13 03					
Manchester Piccadilly 10	d				11 55			12 15				13a09	12 26	12 35				12 55		
Stockport	d				12 05			12 23					12 35	12 44				13 05		
Wilmslow	d				12 12													13 12		
Holyhead	d								10 55											
Bangor (Gwynedd)	d								11 22											
Llandudno Junction	d								11 40											
Wrexham General	d																			
Chester	d								12 33											
Crewe 10	a	12 20			12 28				12 52	12 59					13 19			13 28		
	d	12 22			12 30				12 56	13 01					13 22			13 30		
Macclesfield	d												12 49	12 57						
Congleton	d																			
Stoke-on-Trent	d			←				12 51					13 07	13 14			←			
Stafford	a	12 41	12 35	12 41									13 24		13 42	13 35	13 42			
	d	12 42	12 36	12 42									13 25		13 43	13 36	13 43			
Penkridge	a	→		12 48											→		13 48			
Wolverhampton 7	a			12 59						13 31			13 40				13 59			
Birmingham New Street 12	a			13 16						13 55			13 58				14 15			
Birmingham International	a												14 13							
Coventry	a												14 24							
Lichfield Trent Valley	a																			
Tamworth Low Level	a																			
Nuneaton	a																			
Rugby	a																			
Milton Keynes Central	a							13 49	14 02											
Watford Junction	a																			
London Euston 15	a		14 01		14 09	14 16		14 27	14 43					14 47		15 01		15 09	15 15	

A ⊡ from Birmingham New Street
⊼ to Birmingham New Street

OVERNIGHT SLEEPERS. For sleeper trains, operated by First ScotRail, please refer to Tables 400 - 404

Scotland and North West England - West Midlands and London

Route Diagram - see first Page of Table 65

		XC	VT	VT	VT	TP	NT	XC	VT	EM	TP	LM	VT	LM	VT	VT	TP	XC	VT	VT	VT
		◇1	◇1	◇1	◇1	◇1		◇1	◇1	◇	◇1	◇1	◇1	◇1	◇1	◇1	◇1	◇1	◇1	◇1	◇1
								A													
		⊼	⊐	⊐	⊐			⊐⊼	⊐				⊐		⊐	⊐		⊼	⊐	⊐	⊐
Inverness	d																				
Aberdeen	d																				
Dundee	d																				
Perth	d																				
Edinburgh 10	d				10 52																
Haymarket	d				10 57																
Glasgow Central 15	d															11 36					11 58
Motherwell	d																				
Carstairs	d																				
Lockerbie	d																				
Carlisle 8	a				12 05											12 47					13 09
	d				12 07											12 49					13 10
Penrith North Lakes	d																				
Windermere	d																				
Oxenholme Lake District	a				12 41											13 22					
	d				12 43											13 23					
Barrow-in-Furness	d					12 25	13 10														
Lancaster 6	a				12 56	13 26	14 15									13 37					13 56
	d				12 57	13 26										13 38					13 58
Blackpool North	d																13 44				
Preston 8	a				13 15	13 45										13 56	14 08				14 15
Preston 8	d				13 17	13 47										13 58	14 10				14 17
Wigan North Western	a				13 28											14 09					14 28
	d				13 28											14 09					14 28
Blackrod	d																				
Lostock	d																				
Bolton	a					14 08											14 34				
Manchester Piccadilly 10	a					14 27											14 56				
Manchester Airport	a					14 47											15 17				
Liverpool Lime Street 10	a																				
	d									12 52	13 22	13 34	13 48								
Liverpool South Parkway	d									13 03	13 32	13 44									
Runcorn	d											13 52	14 04								
Warrington Bank Quay	a				13 39											14 20					14 39
	d				13 39											14 20					14 39
Hartford	d											14 03									
Manchester Piccadilly 10	d	13 07	13 15					13 27	13 35	13 44	14a09				13 55			14 07	14 15		
Stockport	d		13 22					13 36	13 42	13a53					14 04				14 22		
Wilmslow	d														14 11						
Holyhead	d			11 50																12 50	
Bangor (Gwynedd)	d			12 17																13 18	
Llandudno Junction	d			12 35																13 36	
Wrexham General	d																				
Chester	d			13 30																14 33	
Crewe 10	a			13 50	13 59							14 18			14 27					14 52	14 59
	d			13 51	14 01							14 22			14 29					14 54	15 01
Macclesfield	d							13 49	13 55												
Congleton	d																				
Stoke-on-Trent	d	13 43	13 50					14 07	14 12					←				14 43	14 50		
Stafford	a							14 24				14 42	14 35	14 42							
	d							14 25				14 43	14 36	14 43							
Penkridge	a											→		14 48							
Wolverhampton 7	a	14 13			14 32			14 40						14 59				15 13			15 31
Birmingham New Street 12	a	14 31			14 55			14 58						15 15				15 31			15 55
Birmingham International	a							15 13													
Coventry	a							15 24													
Lichfield Trent Valley	a																				
Tamworth Low Level	a																				
Nuneaton	a			14 31																	
Rugby	a																				
Milton Keynes Central	a		14 49	15 04															15 49	16 04	
Watford Junction	a																				
London Euston 15	a		15 27	15 45					15 47				16 01		16 09	16 15			16 27	16 44	

A ⊐ from Birmingham New Street
⊼ to Birmingham New Street

OVERNIGHT SLEEPERS. For sleeper trains, operated by First ScotRail, please refer to Tables 400 - 404

Scotland and North West England - West Midlands and London

Route Diagram - see first Page of Table 65

		TP	XC	VT	EM	TP	LM	VT	LM	VT	VT	TP	XC	VT	VT	VT	TP	XC	VT	EM
		◇1	◇1	◇1	◇	◇1	◇1	◇1	◇1	◇1	◇1	◇1	◇1	◇1	◇1	◇1	◇1	◇1	◇1	◇
			A															A		
		⊼	⊐⊼	⊐				⊐		⊐	⊐		⊼	⊐	⊐	⊐		⊐⊼	⊐	
Inverness	d																			
Aberdeen	d																			
Dundee	d																			
Perth	d																			
Edinburgh 10	d	12 10														12 52				
Haymarket	d	12u14														12 56				
Glasgow Central 15	d										12 42									
Motherwell	d																			
Carstairs	d																			
Lockerbie	d	13 08																		
Carlisle 8	a	13 29									13 51					14 05				
	d	13 29									13 54					14 07				
Penrith North Lakes	d	13 45														14 22				
Windermere	d																			
Oxenholme Lake District	a	14 09									14 27									
	d	14 10									14 28									
Barrow-in-Furness	d																14 25			
Lancaster 6	a	14 26									14 42					14 56	15 26			
	d	14 26									14 43					14 57	15 26			
Blackpool North	d											14 44								
Preston 8	a	14 45									15 01	15 08				15 15	15 45			
Preston 8	d	14 47									15 03	15 10				15 17	15 47			
Wigan North Western	a										15 14					15 28				
	d										15 14					15 28				
Blackrod	d																			
Lostock	d																			
Bolton	a	15 08										15 34					16 08			
Manchester Piccadilly 10	a	15 27										15 56					16 27			
Manchester Airport	a	15 47										16 17					16 46			
Liverpool Lime Street 10	a																			
	d				13 52	14 22	14 34	14 48												14 52
Liverpool South Parkway	d				14 03	14 32	14 44													15 03
Runcorn	d						14 52	15 04												
Warrington Bank Quay	a										15 25					15 39				
	d										15 25					15 39				
Hartford	d						15 03													
Manchester Piccadilly 10	d		14 27	14 35	14 44	15a09				14 55			15 07	15 15				15 27	15 35	15 44
Stockport	d		14 36	14 42	14a53					15 04				15 22				15 36	15 42	15a53
Wilmslow	d									15 11										
Holyhead	d														13 55					
Bangor (Gwynedd)	d														14 22					
Llandudno Junction	d														14 40					
Wrexham General	d																			
Chester	d														15 33					
Crewe 10	a						15 20			15 27					15 52	15 59				
	d						15 22			15 29					15 54	16 01				
Macclesfield	d		14 49	14 55														15 49	15 55	
Congleton	d																			
Stoke-on-Trent	d		15 07	15 12					←				15 43	15 50				16 07	16 12	
Stafford	a		15 24				15 42	15 35	15 42									16 24		
	d		15 25				15 43	15 36	15 43									16 25		
Penkridge	a						→		15 48											
Wolverhampton 7	a		15 40						15 59				16 13			16 32		16 40		
Birmingham New Street 12	a		15 58						16 15				16 31			16 55		16 58		
Birmingham International	a		16 13															17 13		
Coventry	a		16 24															17 24		
Lichfield Trent Valley	a																			
Tamworth Low Level	a																			
Nuneaton	a																			
Rugby	a																			
Milton Keynes Central	a													16 49	17 03					
Watford Junction	a																			
London Euston 15	a			16 47				17 01		17 09	17 20			17 27	17 44				17 47	

A ⊐ from Birmingham New Street
⊼ to Birmingham New Street

OVERNIGHT SLEEPERS. For sleeper trains, operated by First ScotRail, please refer to Tables 400 - 404

Table 65

Sundays
until 1 January

Scotland and North West England - West Midlands and London

Route Diagram - see first Page of Table 65

		TP	LM	VT	LM	VT	VT	TP	XC	VT	VT	VT	TP	XC	VT	EM	TP	LM	VT
		◇1	◇1	◇1	◇1	◇1	◇1	◇1	◇1	◇1	◇1	◇1	◇1	◇1	◇1	◇	◇1	◇1	◇1
														A					
				⊡		⊡	⊡		⊼	⊡	⊡	⊡	⊼	⊡⊼	⊡				⊡
Inverness	d																		
Aberdeen	d																		
Dundee	d																		
Perth	d																		
Edinburgh 10	d												14 10						
Haymarket	d												14u14						
Glasgow Central 15	d						13 36					13 55							
Motherwell	d																		
Carstairs	d																		
Lockerbie	d												15 08						
Carlisle 8	a						14 46					15 09	15 29						
	d						14 49					15 11	15 29						
Penrith North Lakes	d												15 45						
Windermere	d																		
Oxenholme Lake District	a						15 22					15 46	16 09						
	d						15 23					15 46	16 10						
Barrow-in-Furness	d																		
Lancaster 6	a						15 37						16 26						
	d						15 38						16 26						
Blackpool North	d							15 44											
Preston 8	a						15 56	16 08				16 15	16 46						
Preston 8	d						15 58	16 10				16 17	16 47						
Wigan North Western	a						16 09					16 28							
	d						16 09					16 28							
Blackrod	d																		
Lostock	d																		
Bolton	a							16 34					17 08						
Manchester Piccadilly 10 ⇌	a							16 56					17 27						
Manchester Airport ✈	a							17 17					17 47						
Liverpool Lime Street 10	a																		
	d	15 22	15 34	15 48							16 18					15 52	16 22	16 34	16 48
Liverpool South Parkway ✈	d	15 32	15 44													16 03	16 32	16 44	
Runcorn	d		15 52	16 04							16 34							16 52	17 04
Warrington Bank Quay	a						16 20					16 39							
	d						16 20					16 39							
Hartford	d		16 03															17 03	
Manchester Piccadilly 10 ⇌	d	16a09				15 55			16 07	16 15				16 27	16 35	16 44	17a09		
Stockport	d					16 04				16 23				16 36	16 42	16a53			
Wilmslow	d					16 11													
Holyhead	d																		
Bangor (Gwynedd)	d																		
Llandudno Junction	d																		
Wrexham General	d																		
Chester	d																		
Crewe 10	a		16 18			16 27					16 51	16 58						17 18	
	d		16 22			16 29					16 54	17 00						17 22	
Macclesfield	d													16 49	16 55				
Congleton	d																		
Stoke-on-Trent	d				←				16 43	16 50				17 08	17 12				
Stafford	a		16 42	16 36	16 42									17 25				17 42	17 35
	d		16 43	16 37	16 43									17 26				17 43	17 36
Penkridge	a		→		16 48													→	
Wolverhampton 7 ⇌	a				16 59				17 13			17 31		17 40					
Birmingham New Street 12	a				17 15				17 31			17 56		17 58					
Birmingham International ✈	a													18 13					
Coventry	a													18 24					
Lichfield Trent Valley	a										17 26								
Tamworth Low Level	a																		
Nuneaton	a																		
Rugby	a																		
Milton Keynes Central	a									17 49	18 04								
Watford Junction	a																		
London Euston 15 ⊖	a			18 01		18 09	18 15			18 27	18 44				18 47				19 01

A ⊡ from Birmingham New Street
⊼ to Birmingham New Street

OVERNIGHT SLEEPERS. For sleeper trains, operated by First ScotRail, please refer to Tables 400 - 404

Table 65

Sundays
until 1 January

Scotland and North West England - West Midlands and London

Route Diagram - see first Page of Table 65

		LM	VT	VT	TP	XC	VT	VT	VT	TP	XC	VT	EM	TP	LM	VT	LM	VT	VT	TP	XC
		◇1	◇1	◇1	◇1	◇1	◇1	◇1	◇1	◇1	◇1	◇1	◇	◇1	◇1	◇1	◇1	◇1	◇1	◇1	◇1
											A										
			⊡	⊡		⊼	⊡	⊡	⊡	⊼	⊡⊼	⊡				⊡		⊡	⊡		⊼
Inverness	d																				
Aberdeen	d																				
Dundee	d																				
Perth	d																				
Edinburgh 10	d								14 52												
Haymarket	d								14 57												
Glasgow Central 15	d			14 36						15 06									15 36		
Motherwell	d																				
Carstairs	d																				
Lockerbie	d									16 06											
Carlisle 8	a			15 46					16 05	16 26									16 46		
	d			15 49					16 07	16 26									16 49		
Penrith North Lakes	d								16 22	16 42									17 03		
Windermere	d																				
Oxenholme Lake District	a			16 22						17 07											
	d			16 23						17 07											
Barrow-in-Furness	d																				
Lancaster 6	a			16 37					16 56	17 22									17 37		
	d			16 38					16 57	17 22									17 38		
Blackpool North	d				16 44															17 44	
Preston 8	a			16 56	17 08				17 15	17 41									17 56	18 08	
Preston 8	d			16 58	17 10				17 17	17 47									17 58	18 10	
Wigan North Western	a			17 09					17 28										18 09		
	d			17 09					17 28										18 09		
Blackrod	d																				
Lostock	d																				
Bolton	a				17 34					18 08										18 34	
Manchester Piccadilly 10 ⇌	a				17 56					18 27										18 56	
Manchester Airport ✈	a				18 17					18 45										19 17	
Liverpool Lime Street 10	a																				
	d												16 52	17 22	17 34	17 48					
Liverpool South Parkway ✈	d												17 03	17 32	17 44						
Runcorn	d														17 52	18 04					
Warrington Bank Quay	a			17 20					17 39										18 20		
	d			17 20					17 39										18 20		
Hartford	d														18 03						
Manchester Piccadilly 10 ⇌	d		16 55			17 07	17 15				17 27	17 35	17 44	18a09				17 55			18 07
Stockport	d		17 04				17 22				17 36	17 42	17a53					18 04			
Wilmslow	d		17 11															18 11			
Holyhead	d																				
Bangor (Gwynedd)	d																				
Llandudno Junction	d																				
Wrexham General	d																				
Chester	d							17 35													
Crewe 10	a		17 27					17 53	17 59						18 20			18 27			
	d		17 29					17 55	18 01						18 22			18 29			
Macclesfield	d										17 49	17 55									
Congleton	d																				
Stoke-on-Trent	d	←				17 43	17 50				18 08	18 12					←				18 43
Stafford	a	17 42									18 25				18 42	18 35	18 42				
	d	17 43									18 26				18 43	18 36	18 43				
Penkridge	a	17 48													→		18 48				
Wolverhampton 7 ⇌	a	17 59				18 13			18 32		18 40						18 59				19 13
Birmingham New Street 12	a	18 15				18 31			18 55		18 58						19 15				19 31
Birmingham International ✈	a										19 13										
Coventry	a										19 24										
Lichfield Trent Valley	a																				
Tamworth Low Level	a																				
Nuneaton	a																				
Rugby	a																				
Milton Keynes Central	a						18 49	19 02													
Watford Junction	a																				
London Euston 15 ⊖	a		19 09	19 15			19 27	19 43				19 47				20 01		20 09	20 15		

A ⊡ from Birmingham New Street
⊼ to Birmingham New Street

OVERNIGHT SLEEPERS. For sleeper trains, operated by First ScotRail, please refer to Tables 400 - 404

Scotland and North West England - West Midlands and London

Route Diagram - see first Page of Table 65

		VT	VT	VT	TP	XC	VT	EM	TP	LM	VT	LM	VT	VT	TP	XC	VT	TP	TP	VT
		◇1	◇1	◇1	◇1	◇1	◇1	◇	◇1	◇1	◇1	◇1	◇1	◇1	◇1	◇1	◇1	◇1	◇1	◇1
						A														
Inverness	d																			
Aberdeen	d																			
Dundee	d																			
Perth	d																			
Edinburgh 10	d				16 10												16 52			
Haymarket	d				16u14												16 56			
Glasgow Central 15	d			15 57										16 40					17 06	
Motherwell	d													16 54						
Carstairs	d																			
Lockerbie	d				17 08															
Carlisle 8	a			17 08	17 29									17 49			18 05		18 25	
	d			17 09	17 29									17 51			18 07		18 26	
Penrith North Lakes	d				17 45									18 05					18 42	
Windermere	d																			
Oxenholme Lake District	a			17 44	18 09									18 27			18 41		19 07	
	d			17 44	18 10									18 28			18 42		19 07	
Barrow-in-Furness	d																	18 17		
Lancaster 6	a				18 26									18 42			18 56	19 17	19 22	
	d				18 26									18 43			18 57	19 17	19 22	
Blackpool North	d														18 44					
Preston 8	a			18 13	18 45									19 01	19 08		19 15	19 37	19 41	
Preston 8	d			18 17	18 47									19 03	19 10		19 17		19 47	
Wigan North Western	a			18 28										19 14			19 28			
	d			18 28										19 14			19 28			
Blackrod	d																			
Lostock	d																			
Bolton	a				19 08										19 34				20 08	
Manchester Piccadilly 10	a				19 27										19 56				20 27	
Manchester Airport	a				19 47										20 17				20 45	
Liverpool Lime Street 10	a																			
	d							17 52	18 22	18 34	18 48									
Liverpool South Parkway	d							18 03	18 32	18 44										
Runcorn	d									18 52	19 04									
Warrington Bank Quay	a			18 39										19 25			19 39			
	d			18 39										19 25			19 39			
Hartford	d									19 03										
Manchester Piccadilly 10	d	18 15				18 27	18 35	18 44	19a09				18 55			19 07				19 15
Stockport	d	18 22				18 36	18 42	18a53					19 04							19 22
Wilmslow	d												19 11							
Holyhead	d																			
Bangor (Gwynedd)	d																			
Llandudno Junction	d																			
Wrexham General	d																			
Chester	d		18 35																	
Crewe 10	a		18 53	18 59						19 20			19 27				19 59			
	d		18 55	19 01						19 22			19 29				20 01			
Macclesfield	d					18 49	18 55													
Congleton	d																			
Stoke-on-Trent	d	18 50				19 07	19 12					←				19 43				19 50
Stafford	a					19 24				19 42	19 35	19 42								
	d					19 25				19 43	19 36	19 43								
Penkridge	a									→		19 48								
Wolverhampton 7	a			19 31		19 40						19 59				20 13	20 32			
Birmingham New Street 12	a			19 55		19 58						20 15				20 31	20 50			
Birmingham International	a					20 13														
Coventry	a					20 24														
Lichfield Trent Valley	a																			
Tamworth Low Level	a																			
Nuneaton	a																			
Rugby	a																			
Milton Keynes Central	a	19 49	20 03																	20 46
Watford Junction	a																			
London Euston 15	a	20 27	20 44				20 47				21 01		21 09	21 21						21 31

A from Birmingham New Street
to Birmingham New Street

OVERNIGHT SLEEPERS. For sleeper trains, operated by First ScotRail, please refer to Tables 400 - 404

Table 65

Sundays
until 1 January

Scotland and North West England - West Midlands and London

Route Diagram - see first Page of Table 65

		XC	VT	EM	TP	LM	VT	VT	TP	TP	NT	XC	AW	VT	EM	TP	LM	VT	VT
		◇1	◇1	◇	◇1	◇1	◇1	◇1	◇1	◇1		◇1	◇	◇1	◇	◇1	◇1	◇1	◇1
		A																	
Inverness	d																		
Aberdeen	d																		
Dundee	d																		
Perth	d																		
Edinburgh 10	d									18 10									
Haymarket	d									18u14									
Glasgow Central 15	d							17 36											
Motherwell	d																		
Carstairs	d																		
Lockerbie	d							18 32		19 08									
Carlisle 8	a							18 50		19 29									
	d							18 52		19 29									
Penrith North Lakes	d							19 06		19 45									
Windermere	d																		
Oxenholme Lake District	a							19 28		20 09									
	d							19 29		20 10									
Barrow-in-Furness	d										20 02								
Lancaster 6	a							19 43		20 26	21 07								
	d							19 44		20 26									
Blackpool North	d								19 44										
Preston 8	a							20 02	20 08	20 45									
Preston 8	d							20 04	20 10	20 47									
Wigan North Western	a							20 15											
	d							20 15											
Blackrod	d																		
Lostock	d																		
Bolton	a								20 34	21 08									
Manchester Piccadilly 10	a								20 56	21 27									
Manchester Airport	a								21 16	21 46									
Liverpool Lime Street 10	a																		
	d			18 52	19 22	19 34	19 48								19 52	20 22	20 34		20 48
Liverpool South Parkway	d			19 03	19 32	19 44									20 03	20 32	20 44		
Runcorn	d					19 52	20 04										20 52		21 04
Warrington Bank Quay	a							20 26											
	d							20 26											
Hartford	d					20 03											21 03		
Manchester Piccadilly 10	d	19 27	19 35	19 44	20a09							20 07		20 20	20 44	21a09		20 55	
Stockport	d	19 36	19 41	19a53								20 16		20 27	20a53			21 03	
Wilmslow	d																		
Holyhead	d												18 25						
Bangor (Gwynedd)	d												19 04						
Llandudno Junction	d												19 24						
Wrexham General	d																		
Chester	d												20 27						
Crewe 10	a					20 16	20 22	20 45					20 48				21 16		21 21
	d					20 18	20 24	20 47					20 52				21 18		21 23
Macclesfield	d	19 49	19 54									20 29		20 40				21 15	
Congleton	d																		
Stoke-on-Trent	d	20 07	20 11									20 47		20 57				21 33	
Stafford	a	20 26				20 38	20 41					21 08	21 16				21 38		21 42
	d	20 27				20 39	20 43					21 09	21 16				21 39		21 43
Penkridge	a					20 44											21 44		
Wolverhampton 7	a	20 39				20 55						21 21	21 34				21 55		
Birmingham New Street 12	a	20 58				21 15						21 39	21 52				22 15		
Birmingham International	a	21 13											22 09						
Coventry	a	21 23																	
Lichfield Trent Valley	a																		21 59
Tamworth Low Level	a																		22 05
Nuneaton	a																		22 17
Rugby	a																		22 31
Milton Keynes Central	a						21 36	21 55						22 03				22 46	23 04
Watford Junction	a							22s31										23s25	23s34
London Euston 15	a		21 58				22 27	22 53						22 56				23 49	23 54

A to Birmingham New Street

OVERNIGHT SLEEPERS. For sleeper trains, operated by First ScotRail, please refer to Tables 400 - 404

Table 65

Sundays
until 1 January

Scotland and North West England - West Midlands and London

Route Diagram - see first Page of Table 65

		VT	TP	TP	XC	VT	LM	TP	TP	VT	XC	EM	TP	TP	SR	SR
		◇1	◇1	◇1	◇1	◇1	◇1	◇1	◇1	◇1	◇1	◇	◇1	◇1	B	B
									A							
Inverness	d															20 25
Aberdeen	d															
Dundee	d															
Perth	d															23u00
Edinburgh 10	d					18 52		19 57								01 06
Haymarket	d					18 57		20u01								
Glasgow Central 15	d	18 30								20 08					23 15	
Motherwell	d														23u31	
Carstairs	d														23u47	
Lockerbie	d									21 02						
Carlisle 8	a	19 43				20 05		21 13		21 21						02 51
	d	19 44				20 07		21 14		21 24					01u12	02 53
Penrith North Lakes	d					20 22				21 39						
Windermere	d		20 40													
Oxenholme Lake District	a	20 19	20 59							22 02						
	d	20 19	21 01							22 03						
Barrow-in-Furness	d															
Lancaster 6	a	20 34	21 18			20 56		22 03		22 17						
	d	20 34				20 57		22 03		22 18						
Blackpool North	d			20 44					21 56					23 03		
Preston 8	a	20 52		21 08		21 15		22 23	22 20	22 35				23 28		04s41
Preston 8	d	20 55		21 10		21 17			22 29	22 38				23 28		
Wigan North Western	a	21 06				21 28				22 49						
	d	21 07				21 28				22 50						
Blackrod	d													23 50		
Lostock	d													23 57		
Bolton	a			21 34					22 50					00 02		
Manchester Piccadilly 10	a			21 56					23 14					00 18		
Manchester Airport ✈	a			22 17					23 30					00 32		
Liverpool Lime Street 10	a															
	d						21 34					21 21	21 52			
Liverpool South Parkway ✈	d						21 44					21 31	22 02			
Runcorn	d						21 52									
Warrington Bank Quay	a	21 18				21 39				23 00					03 34	
	d	21 18				21 39				23 01					03 36	
Hartford	d						22 03									
Manchester Piccadilly 10	d				21 07						22 07	22 11	22a39			
Stockport	d				21 16						22 16	22a20				
Wilmslow	d															
Holyhead	d															
Bangor (Gwynedd)	d															
Llandudno Junction	d															
Wrexham General	d															
Chester	d															
Crewe 10	a	21 38				21 59	22 18			23 20						05s37
	d	21 40				22 01	22 22									
Macclesfield	d				21 29						22 29					
Congleton	d															
Stoke-on-Trent	d				21 47						22 47					
Stafford	a	22 01			22 06		22 42				23 04					
	d	22 02			22 06		22 45				23 05					
Penkridge	a						22 50									
Wolverhampton 7	a	22 17			22 20	22 31	23 01				23 18					
Birmingham New Street 12	a	22 38			22 39	22 55	23 17				23 36					
Birmingham International ✈	a															
Coventry	a															
Lichfield Trent Valley	a															
Tamworth Low Level	a															
Nuneaton	a															
Rugby	a															
Milton Keynes Central	a															
Watford Junction	a														06s23	
London Euston 15 ⊖	a														06 46	07 47

A from Preston

OVERNIGHT SLEEPERS. For sleeper trains, operated by First ScotRail, please refer to Tables 400 - 404

Table 65

Sundays
8 January to 12 February

Scotland and North West England - West Midlands and London

Route Diagram - see first Page of Table 65

		TP	TP	TP	VT	NT	TP	VT	VT	TP	XC	VT	VT	TP	NT	VT	TP	XC
		◇1			◇1		◇1	◇1	◇1	◇1	◇1	◇1	◇1	◇1		◇1	◇1	◇1
											A							A
Inverness	d																	
Aberdeen	d																	
Dundee	d																	
Perth	d																	
Edinburgh 10	d																	
Haymarket	d																	
Glasgow Central 15	d																	
Motherwell	d																	
Carstairs	d																	
Lockerbie	d																	
Carlisle 8	a																	
	d																	
Penrith North Lakes	d																	
Windermere	d																	
Oxenholme Lake District	a																	
	d																	
Barrow-in-Furness	d																	
Lancaster 6	a																	
	d																	
Blackpool North	d	22p44	03 20	05 20			08 14							08 44				
Preston 8	a	23p08					08 38							09 08				
Preston 8	d	23p10	04u00	06u00		08 14	08 42						09 00	09 10	09 14			
Wigan North Western	a												09 10					
	d												09 11					
Blackrod	d					09 00									10 00			
Lostock	d					09 10									10 10			
Bolton	a	23p34	04b35	06b35		09 25	09 09							09 37	10 25			
Manchester Piccadilly 10	a	23p53	05b00	07b00			09 32							09 59				
Manchester Airport ✈	a	00 23	05 25	07 25			09 49							10 17				
Liverpool Lime Street 10	a																	
	d								08 15	08 22		08 38					09 22	
Liverpool South Parkway ✈	d									08 32							09 32	
Runcorn	d								08 35			08 54						
Warrington Bank Quay	a												09 21					
	d												09 22					
Hartford	d																	
Manchester Piccadilly 10	d				08 05			08 20		09a11	08 27					09 20	10a09	09 27
Stockport	d				08 14			08 28			08 36					09 27		09 36
Wilmslow	d				08 22						08 43							09 43
Holyhead	d																	
Bangor (Gwynedd)	d																	
Llandudno Junction	d																	
Wrexham General	d																	
Chester	d																	
Crewe 10	a				08 39				08 52		09 01	09 11	09 41					10 01
	d				08 43				08 53		09 05	09 13	09 43					10 05
Macclesfield	d							08 42								09 40		
Congleton	d																	
Stoke-on-Trent	d							08 59								09 57		
Stafford	a				09 01						09 25	09 31						10 26
	d				09 02						09 26	09 32						10 27
Penkridge	a																	
Wolverhampton 7	a										09 40							10 42
Birmingham New Street 12	a										09 58							10 59
Birmingham International ✈	a										10 13							11 13
Coventry	a										10 24							11 24
Lichfield Trent Valley	a																	
Tamworth Low Level	a																	
Nuneaton	a											09 54						
Rugby	a												10 31					
Milton Keynes Central	a								10 17				11 06			11 16		
Watford Junction	a				10s35			10s41				11s16	11s43					
London Euston 15 ⊖	a				10 57			11 02	11 06			11 37	12 05			12 08		

A from Birmingham New Street; to Birmingham New Street

b Stops to pick up only

OVERNIGHT SLEEPERS. For sleeper trains, operated by First ScotRail, please refer to Tables 400 - 404

Scotland and North West England - West Midlands and London

Route Diagram - see first Page of Table 65

		VT		LM	TP			LM	VT	TP	NT	VT	VT	TP	XC	VT		VT	TP	VT	TP		NT	VT	TP
		◇1		◇1	◇1			1	◇1	◇1		◇1	◇1		◇1	◇1		◇1	◇1	◇1	◇1			◇1	◇1
															A										
		⊡							⊡		▭	⊡	⊡	▭	⊡⊼	⊡		⊡		⊡			▭	⊡	
Inverness	d																								
Aberdeen	d																								
Dundee	d																								
Perth	d																								
Edinburgh 10	d																								
Haymarket	d																								
Glasgow Central 15	d																								
Motherwell	d																								
Carstairs	d																								
Lockerbie	d																								
Carlisle 8	a																								
	d																								
Penrith North Lakes	d																								
Windermere	d																								
Oxenholme Lake District	a																								
	d																								
Barrow-in-Furness	d																								
Lancaster 6	a																								
	d																								
Blackpool North	d									09 44											10 44				
Preston 8	a									10 07											11 08				
Preston 8	d								10 00	10 10	10 14		10 17	10 19					10 44	10 58	11 10		11 14		
Wigan North Western	a								10 10				10 28							11 09					
	d								10 11				10 28							11 09					
Blackrod	d										11 00												12 00		
Lostock	d										11 10												12 10		
Bolton	a									10 37	11 25			11 00					11 11		11 37		12 25		
Manchester Piccadilly 10	a									10 59									11 30		11 59				
Manchester Airport	a									11 17									11 47		12 17				
Liverpool Lime Street 10	a																								
	d	09 38			10 22													10 38							11 22
Liverpool South Parkway	d				10 32																				11 32
Runcorn	d	09 54																10 54							
Warrington Bank Quay	a								10 21				10 39							11 20					
	d								10 22				10 39							11 20					
Hartford	d																								
Manchester Piccadilly 10	d				11a09							10 20			10 27	10 35								11 15	12a09
Stockport	d											10 29			10 36	10 42								11 23	
Wilmslow	d											10 36													
Holyhead	d																								
Bangor (Gwynedd)	d																								
Llandudno Junction	d																								
Wrexham General	d																								
Chester	d																								
Crewe 10	a	10 12							10 41			10 53	10 59					11 12							
	d	10 14		10 20				10 38	10 43			10 55	11 01					11 14							
Macclesfield	d														10 49	10 55									
Congleton	d																								
Stoke-on-Trent	d							10 59							11 07	11 12								11 51	
Stafford	a	10 32		10 41				11 17							11 27			11 34							
	d	10 33		10 41											11 28			11 36							
Penkridge	a			10 48																					
Wolverhampton 7	a			11 00									11 31		11 41										
Birmingham New Street 12	a			11 17									11 55		12 00										
Birmingham International	a														12 13										
Coventry	a														12 24										
Lichfield Trent Valley	a																								
Tamworth Low Level	a																								
Nuneaton	a	10 55																11 58							
Rugby	a								11 31																
Milton Keynes Central	a	11 46							12 06							12 20								12 50	
Watford Junction	a											12s35						12s50							
London Euston 15	a	12 32							12 45			12 56				12 59		13 11		13 21				13 28	

A ⊡ from Birmingham New Street
⊼ to Birmingham New Street

OVERNIGHT SLEEPERS. For sleeper trains, operated by First ScotRail, please refer to Tables 400 - 404

Scotland and North West England - West Midlands and London

Route Diagram - see first Page of Table 65

				VT	VT	TP	TP	XC	VT	LM	VT	LM		VT	VT	TP	NT	NT	VT	VT	VT	TP		TP	TP
				◇1	◇1		◇1	◇1	◇1	◇1	◇1	◇1		◇1	◇1	◇1			◇1	◇1	◇1			◇1	◇1
								A																	
				⊡	⊡	▭		⊡⊼	⊡		⊡			⊡	⊡	⊼		▭	⊡	⊡	⊡	▭		⊼	
Inverness	d																								
Aberdeen	d																								
Dundee	d																								
Perth	d																								
Edinburgh 10	d																							10 03	
Haymarket	d																							10u07	
Glasgow Central 15	d														09 37										
Motherwell	d																								
Carstairs	d																								
Lockerbie	d																							11 03	
Carlisle 8	a														10 44									11 24	
	d														10 46									11 24	
Penrith North Lakes	d														11 00									11 39	
Windermere	d																								
Oxenholme Lake District	a														11 22									12 03	
	d														11 23									12 04	
Barrow-in-Furness	d						10 22																		
Lancaster 6	a						11 22								11 37									12 19	
	d						11 22								11 38									12 19	
Blackpool North	d															11 44									
Preston 8	a						11 42								11 56	12 08								12 38	
Preston 8	d				11 17	11 19	11 44								11 58	12 09		12 14			12 17	12 19		12 40	
Wigan North Western	a				11 28										12 09						12 28				
	d				11 28										12 09						12 28				
Blackrod	d																	13 00							
Lostock	d																	13 10							
Bolton	a					12 00	12 11									12 37		13 25				13 00		13 08	
Manchester Piccadilly 10	a						12 30									12 58								13 27	
Manchester Airport	a						12 47									13 17								13 47	
Liverpool Lime Street 10	a																								
	d									11 34	11 48						12 01								12 22
Liverpool South Parkway	d									11 44															12 32
Runcorn	d									11 52	12 04														
Warrington Bank Quay	a				11 39										12 20						12 39				
	d				11 39										12 20						12 39				
Hartford	d									12 03															
Manchester Piccadilly 10	d							11 27	11 35					11 55			13a03		12 15						13a09
Stockport	d							11 36	11 43					12 05					12 23						
Wilmslow	d													12 12											
Holyhead	d																			10 55					
Bangor (Gwynedd)	d																			11 22					
Llandudno Junction	d																			11 40					
Wrexham General	d																								
Chester	d			11 28																12 33					
Crewe 10	a			11 47	11 59					12 20				12 28						12 52	12 59				
	d			11 49	12 01					12 22				12 30						12 56	13 01				
Macclesfield	d							11 49	11 56																
Congleton	d																								
Stoke-on-Trent	d							12 07	12 13			←							12 51						
Stafford	a							12 24		12 41	12 35	12 41													
	d							12 25		12 42	12 36	12 42													
Penkridge	a									→		12 48													
Wolverhampton 7	a				12 32			12 40				12 59									13 31				
Birmingham New Street 12	a				12 55			12 58				13 16									13 55				
Birmingham International	a							13 13																	
Coventry	a							13 24																	
Lichfield Trent Valley	a																								
Tamworth Low Level	a																								
Nuneaton	a			12 31																					
Rugby	a																								
Milton Keynes Central	a			13 03															13 49	14 02					
Watford Junction	a																								
London Euston 15	a			13 44					13 47		14 01			14 09	14 16				14 27	14 43					

A ⊡ from Birmingham New Street
⊼ to Birmingham New Street

OVERNIGHT SLEEPERS. For sleeper trains, operated by First ScotRail, please refer to Tables 400 - 404

Table 65

Sundays
8 January to 12 February

Scotland and North West England - West Midlands and London

Route Diagram - see first Page of Table 65

		XC	VT	LM	VT	LM	VT	VT	TP	XC	NT	VT	VT	VT	TP	TP	NT	XC	VT	EM	TP
		◇1	◇1	◇1	◇1	◇1	◇1	◇1	◇1	◇1		◇1	◇1	◇1		◇1		◇1	◇1	◇	◇1
		A																A			
Inverness	d																				
Aberdeen	d																				
Dundee	d																				
Perth	d																				
Edinburgh 10	d													10 52							
Haymarket	d													10 57							
Glasgow Central 15	d							10 34													
Motherwell	d							10 49													
Carstairs	d																				
Lockerbie	d																				
Carlisle 8	a							11 44						12 05							
	d							11 46						12 07							
Penrith North Lakes	d							12 00													
Windermere	d																				
Oxenholme Lake District	a							12 22						12 41							
	d							12 24						12 43							
Barrow-in-Furness	d															12 30	13 10				
Lancaster 6	a							12 37						12 56		13 20	14 15				
	d							12 38						12 57		13 20					
Blackpool North	d								12 44												
Preston 8	a							12 56	13 08					13 15		13 40					
Preston 8	d							12 58	13 10		13 14			13 17	13 19	13 40					
Wigan North Western	a							13 09						13 28							
	d							13 09						13 28							
Blackrod	d										14 00										
Lostock	d										14 10										
Bolton	a								13 37		14 25				14 00	14 08					
Manchester Piccadilly 10	a								13 59							14 27					
Manchester Airport	a								14 17							14 47					
Liverpool Lime Street 10	a																				
	d			12 34	12 48															12 52	13 22
Liverpool South Parkway	d			12 44																13 03	13 32
Runcorn	d			12 52	13 04																
Warrington Bank Quay	a							13 20						13 39							
	d							13 20						13 39							
Hartford	d			13 03																	
Manchester Piccadilly 10	d	12 26	12 35				12 55			13 07		13 15						13 27	13 35	13 44	14a09
Stockport	d	12 35	12 44				13 05					13 22						13 36	13 42	13a53	
Wilmslow	d						13 12														
Holyhead	d												11 50								
Bangor (Gwynedd)	d												12 17								
Llandudno Junction	d												12 35								
Wrexham General	d																				
Chester	d												13 30								
Crewe 10	a			13 19			13 28						13 50	13 59							
	d			13 22			13 30						13 51	14 01							
Macclesfield	d	12 49	12 57															13 49	13 55		
Congleton	d																				
Stoke-on-Trent	d	13 07	13 14			←				13 43		13 50						14 07	14 12		
Stafford	a	13 24		13 42	13 35	13 42												14 24			
	d	13 25		13 43	13 36	13 43												14 25			
Penkridge	a			→		13 48															
Wolverhampton 7	a	13 40				13 59				14 13				14 32				14 40			
Birmingham New Street 12	a	13 58				14 15				14 31				14 55				14 58			
Birmingham International	a	14 13																15 13			
Coventry	a	14 24																15 24			
Lichfield Trent Valley	a																				
Tamworth Low Level	a																				
Nuneaton	a												14 31								
Rugby	a																				
Milton Keynes Central	a											14 49	15 04								
Watford Junction	a																				
London Euston 15	a		14 47		15 01		15 09	15 15				15 27	15 45						15 47		

A from Birmingham New Street
to Birmingham New Street

OVERNIGHT SLEEPERS. For sleeper trains, operated by First ScotRail, please refer to Tables 400 - 404

Table 65

Sundays
8 January to 12 February

Scotland and North West England - West Midlands and London

Route Diagram - see first Page of Table 65

		LM	VT	LM	VT	VT	TP	XC	NT	VT	VT	VT	TP	TP	XC	VT	EM	TP	LM
		◇1	◇1	◇1	◇1	◇1	◇1	◇1		◇1	◇1	◇1		◇1	◇1	◇1	◇	◇1	◇1
															A				
Inverness	d																		
Aberdeen	d																		
Dundee	d																		
Perth	d																		
Edinburgh 10	d													12 03					
Haymarket	d													12u08					
Glasgow Central 15	d					11 36						11 58							
Motherwell	d																		
Carstairs	d																		
Lockerbie	d													13 03					
Carlisle 8	a					12 47						13 09		13 24					
	d					12 49						13 10		13 24					
Penrith North Lakes	d													13 39					
Windermere	d																		
Oxenholme Lake District	a					13 22								14 04					
	d					13 23								14 04					
Barrow-in-Furness	d																		
Lancaster 6	a					13 37						13 56		14 20					
	d					13 38						13 58		14 20					
Blackpool North	d						13 44												
Preston 8	a					13 56	14 08					14 15		14 39					
Preston 8	d					13 58	14 10		14 14			14 17	14 19	14 40					
Wigan North Western	a					14 09						14 28							
	d					14 09						14 28							
Blackrod	d								15 00										
Lostock	d								15 10										
Bolton	a						14 37		15 25				15 00	15 08					
Manchester Piccadilly 10	a						14 59							15 27					
Manchester Airport	a						15 17							15 47					
Liverpool Lime Street 10	a																		
	d	13 34	13 48														13 52	14 22	14 34
Liverpool South Parkway	d	13 44															14 03	14 32	14 44
Runcorn	d	13 52	14 04																14 52
Warrington Bank Quay	a					14 20						14 39							
	d					14 20						14 39							
Hartford	d	14 03																	15 03
Manchester Piccadilly 10	d				13 55			14 07		14 15					14 27	14 35	14 44	15a09	
Stockport	d				14 04					14 22					14 36	14 42	14a53		
Wilmslow	d				14 11														
Holyhead	d										12 50								
Bangor (Gwynedd)	d										13 18								
Llandudno Junction	d										13 36								
Wrexham General	d																		
Chester	d										14 33								
Crewe 10	a	14 18			14 27						14 52	14 59							15 20
	d	14 22			14 29						14 54	15 01							15 22
Macclesfield	d														14 49	14 55			
Congleton	d																		
Stoke-on-Trent	d			←				14 43		14 50					15 07	15 12			
Stafford	a	14 42	14 35	14 42											15 24				15 42
	d	14 43	14 36	14 43											15 25				15 43
Penkridge	a	→		14 48															→
Wolverhampton 7	a			14 59				15 13				15 31			15 40				
Birmingham New Street 12	a			15 15				15 31				15 55			15 58				
Birmingham International	a														16 13				
Coventry	a														16 24				
Lichfield Trent Valley	a																		
Tamworth Low Level	a																		
Nuneaton	a																		
Rugby	a																		
Milton Keynes Central	a									15 49	16 04								
Watford Junction	a																		
London Euston 15	a		16 01		16 09	16 15				16 27	16 44					16 47			

A from Birmingham New Street
to Birmingham New Street

OVERNIGHT SLEEPERS. For sleeper trains, operated by First ScotRail, please refer to Tables 400 - 404

Scotland and North West England - West Midlands and London

Route Diagram - see first Page of Table 65

		VT	LM	VT	VT	TP	XC	NT	VT	VT		VT	TP	TP	XC	VT	EM		TP			LM	VT	LM	VT
		◇1	◇1	◇1	◇1	◇1	◇1		◇1	◇1		◇1		◇1	◇1	◇1	◇		◇1			◇1	◇1	◇1	◇1
															A										
		🛒		🛒	🛒		🍴	🚌	🛒	🛒		🛒	🚌		🛒🍴	🛒							🛒		🛒
Inverness	d																								
Aberdeen	d																								
Dundee	d																								
Perth	d																								
Edinburgh 10	d											12 52													
Haymarket	d											12 56													
Glasgow Central 15	d				12 42																				
Motherwell	d																								
Carstairs	d																								
Lockerbie	d																								
Carlisle 8	a				13 51							14 05													
	d				13 54							14 07													
Penrith North Lakes	d											14 22													
Windermere	d																								
Oxenholme Lake District	a				14 27																				
	d				14 28																				
Barrow-in-Furness	d													14 18											
Lancaster 6	a				14 42							14 56		15 18											
	d				14 43							14 57		15 20											
Blackpool North	d					14 44																			
Preston 8	a				15 01	15 08						15 15		15 38											
Preston 8	d				15 03	15 10		15 14				15 17	15 19	15 40											
Wigan North Western	a				15 14							15 28													
	d				15 14							15 28													
Blackrod	d							16 00																	
Lostock	d							16 10																	
Bolton	a					15 37		16 25					16 00	16 08											
Manchester Piccadilly 10	a					15 59								16 27											
Manchester Airport ✈	a					16 17								16 47											
Liverpool Lime Street 10	a																								
	d	14 48															14 52		15 22			15 34	15 48		
Liverpool South Parkway ✈	d																15 03		15 32			15 44			
Runcorn	d	15 04																				15 52	16 04		
Warrington Bank Quay	a				15 25							15 39													
	d				15 25							15 39													
Hartford	d																					16 03			
Manchester Piccadilly 10	d			14 55			15 07		15 15						15 27	15 35	15 44		16a09						15 55
Stockport	d			15 04					15 22						15 36	15 42	15a53								16 04
Wilmslow	d			15 11																					16 11
Holyhead	d									13 55															
Bangor (Gwynedd)	d									14 22															
Llandudno Junction	d									14 40															
Wrexham General	d																								
Chester	d									15 33															
Crewe 10	a			15 27						15 52		15 59										16 18			16 27
	d			15 29						15 54		16 01										16 22			16 29
Macclesfield	d														15 49	15 55									
Congleton	d																								
Stoke-on-Trent	d		←				15 43		15 50						16 07	16 12								←	
Stafford	a	15 35	15 42												16 24							16 42	16 36	16 42	
	d	15 36	15 43												16 25							16 43	16 37	16 43	
Penkridge	a		15 48																			→		16 48	
Wolverhampton 7	a		15 59				16 13					16 32			16 40									16 59	
Birmingham New Street 12	a		16 15				16 31					16 55			16 58									17 15	
Birmingham International ✈	a														17 13										
Coventry	a														17 24										
Lichfield Trent Valley	a																								
Tamworth Low Level	a																								
Nuneaton	a																								
Rugby	a																								
Milton Keynes Central	a								16 49	17 03															
Watford Junction	a																								
London Euston 15 ⊖	a	17 01		17 09	17 20				17 27	17 44						17 47							18 01		18 09

A 🛒 from Birmingham New Street
🍴 to Birmingham New Street

OVERNIGHT SLEEPERS. For sleeper trains, operated by First ScotRail, please refer to Tables 400 - 404

Scotland and North West England - West Midlands and London

Route Diagram - see first Page of Table 65

		VT	TP	XC	NT	VT		VT	VT	TP	TP	XC	VT	EM		TP			LM	VT	LM	VT	VT	TP	XC
		◇1	◇1	◇1		◇1		◇1	◇1		◇1	◇1	◇1	◇		◇1			◇1	◇1	◇1	◇1	◇1	◇1	◇1
												A													
		🛒		🍴	🚌	🛒		🛒	🛒	🚌	🍴	🛒🍴	🛒							🛒		🛒	🛒		🍴
Inverness	d																								
Aberdeen	d																								
Dundee	d																								
Perth	d																								
Edinburgh 10	d										14 03														
Haymarket	d										14u08														
Glasgow Central 15	d	13 36							13 55														14 36		
Motherwell	d																								
Carstairs	d																								
Lockerbie	d										15 03														
Carlisle 8	a	14 46							15 09		15 24												15 46		
	d	14 49							15 11		15 24												15 49		
Penrith North Lakes	d										15 39														
Windermere	d																								
Oxenholme Lake District	a	15 22							15 46		16 04												16 22		
	d	15 23							15 46		16 04												16 23		
Barrow-in-Furness	d																								
Lancaster 6	a	15 37									16 20												16 37		
	d	15 38									16 20												16 38		
Blackpool North	d		15 44																					16 44	
Preston 8	a	15 56	16 08						16 15		16 39												16 56	17 08	
Preston 8	d	15 58	16 10		16 14				16 17	16 19	16 40												16 58	17 10	
Wigan North Western	a	16 09							16 28														17 09		
	d	16 09							16 28														17 09		
Blackrod	d				17 00																				
Lostock	d				17 10																				
Bolton	a		16 37		17 25					17 00	17 08													17 37	
Manchester Piccadilly 10	a		16 59								17 27													17 59	
Manchester Airport ✈	a		17 17								17 47													18 17	
Liverpool Lime Street 10	a																								
	d							16 18						15 52		16 22			16 34	16 48					
Liverpool South Parkway ✈	d													16 03		16 32			16 44						
Runcorn	d							16 34											16 52	17 04					
Warrington Bank Quay	a	16 20							16 39														17 20		
	d	16 20							16 39														17 20		
Hartford	d																		17 03						
Manchester Piccadilly 10	d			16 07		16 15						16 27	16 35	16 44		17a09						16 55			17 07
Stockport	d					16 23						16 36	16 42	16a53								17 04			
Wilmslow	d																					17 11			
Holyhead	d																								
Bangor (Gwynedd)	d																								
Llandudno Junction	d																								
Wrexham General	d																								
Chester	d																								
Crewe 10	a							16 51	16 58										17 18			17 27			
	d							16 54	17 00										17 22			17 29			
Macclesfield	d											16 49	16 55												
Congleton	d																								
Stoke-on-Trent	d			16 43		16 50						17 08	17 12								←				17 43
Stafford	a											17 25							17 42	17 35	17 42				
	d											17 26							17 43	17 36	17 43				
Penkridge	a																		→		17 48				
Wolverhampton 7	a			17 13					17 31			17 40									17 59				18 13
Birmingham New Street 12	a			17 31					17 56			17 58									18 15				18 31
Birmingham International ✈	a											18 13													
Coventry	a											18 24													
Lichfield Trent Valley	a							17 26																	
Tamworth Low Level	a																								
Nuneaton	a																								
Rugby	a																								
Milton Keynes Central	a					17 49		18 04																	
Watford Junction	a																								
London Euston 15 ⊖	a	18 15				18 27		18 44					18 47							19 01		19 09	19 15		

A 🛒 from Birmingham New Street
🍴 to Birmingham New Street

OVERNIGHT SLEEPERS. For sleeper trains, operated by First ScotRail, please refer to Tables 400 - 404

Table 65

Sundays
8 January to 12 February

Scotland and North West England - West Midlands and London

Route Diagram - see first Page of Table 65

		NT		VT	VT	VT	TP	TP	XC	VT	EM			TP		LM	VT	LM	VT	VT	TP	XC		NT	VT
				◇1	◇1	◇1		◇1	◇1	◇1	◇			◇1		◇1	◇1	◇1	◇1	◇1	◇1	◇1			◇1
									A																
Inverness	d																								
Aberdeen	d																								
Dundee	d																								
Perth	d																								
Edinburgh 10	d					14 52																			
Haymarket	d					14 57																			
Glasgow Central 15	d							15 06												15 36					
Motherwell	d																								
Carstairs	d																								
Lockerbie	d																								
Carlisle 8	a					16 05		16 24												16 46					
	d					16 07		16 24												16 49					
Penrith North Lakes	d					16 22		16 39												17 03					
Windermere	d																								
Oxenholme Lake District	a							17 04																	
	d							17 04																	
Barrow-in-Furness	d																								
Lancaster 6	a					16 56		17 20												17 37					
	d					16 57		17 20												17 38					
Blackpool North	d																				17 44				
Preston 8	a					17 15		17 39												17 56	18 08				
Preston 8	d	17 14				17 17	17 19	17 40												17 58	18 10			18 14	
Wigan North Western	a					17 28														18 09					
	d					17 28														18 09					
Blackrod	d	18 00																						19 00	
Lostock	d	18 10																						19 10	
Bolton	a	18 25					18 00	18 08													18 37			19 25	
Manchester Piccadilly 10	a							18 27													18 59				
Manchester Airport	a							18 47													19 17				
Liverpool Lime Street 10	a																								
	d										16 52			17 22		17 34	17 48								
Liverpool South Parkway	d										17 03			17 32		17 44									
Runcorn	d															17 52	18 04								
Warrington Bank Quay	a					17 39														18 20					
	d					17 39														18 20					
Hartford	d															18 03									
Manchester Piccadilly 10	d			17 15					17 27	17 35	17 44			18a09					17 55			18 07			18 15
Stockport	d			17 22					17 36	17 42	17a53								18 04						18 22
Wilmslow	d																		18 11						
Holyhead	d																								
Bangor (Gwynedd)	d																								
Llandudno Junction	d																								
Wrexham General	d																								
Chester	d				17 35																				
Crewe 10	a				17 53	17 59										18 20			18 27						
	d				17 55	18 01										18 22			18 29						
Macclesfield	d								17 49	17 55															
Congleton	d																								
Stoke-on-Trent	d			17 50					18 08	18 12								←				18 43			18 50
Stafford	a								18 25							18 42	18 35	18 42							
	d								18 26							18 43	18 36	18 43							
Penkridge	a															→		18 48							
Wolverhampton 7	a					18 32			18 40									18 59				19 13			
Birmingham New Street 12	a					18 55			18 58									19 15				19 31			
Birmingham International	a								19 13																
Coventry	a								19 24																
Lichfield Trent Valley	a																								
Tamworth Low Level	a																								
Nuneaton	a																								
Rugby	a																								
Milton Keynes Central	a			18 49	19 02																				19 49
Watford Junction	a																								
London Euston 15	a			19 27	19 43					19 47							20 01		20 09	20 15					20 27

A from Birmingham New Street
to Birmingham New Street

OVERNIGHT SLEEPERS. For sleeper trains, operated by First ScotRail, please refer to Tables 400 - 404

Table 65

Sundays
8 January to 12 February

Scotland and North West England - West Midlands and London

Route Diagram - see first Page of Table 65

		VT	VT	TP	TP	XC	VT	EM			TP		LM	VT	LM	VT	VT	TP		XC	NT	VT	TP	VT	TP
		◇1	◇1		◇1	◇1	◇1	◇			◇1		◇1	◇1	◇1	◇1	◇1	◇1		◇1		◇1	◇1	◇1	
						A																			
Inverness	d																								
Aberdeen	d																								
Dundee	d																								
Perth	d																								
Edinburgh 10	d				16 03																	16 52			
Haymarket	d				16u08																	16 56			
Glasgow Central 15	d		15 57														16 40								
Motherwell	d																16 54								
Carstairs	d																								
Lockerbie	d				17 03																				
Carlisle 8	a		17 08		17 24												17 49					18 05			
	d		17 09		17 24												17 51					18 07			
Penrith North Lakes	d				17 39												18 05								
Windermere	d																								
Oxenholme Lake District	a		17 44		18 04												18 27					18 41			
	d		17 44		18 04												18 28					18 42			
Barrow-in-Furness	d																						18 14		
Lancaster 6	a				18 20												18 42					18 56	19 14		
	d				18 20												18 43					18 57	19 15		
Blackpool North	d																	18 44							
Preston 8	a		18 13		18 39												19 01	19 08				19 15	19 34		
Preston 8	d		18 17	18 19	18 40												19 03	19 10			19 14	19 17			19 19
Wigan North Western	a		18 28														19 14					19 28			
	d		18 28														19 14					19 28			
Blackrod	d																				20 00				
Lostock	d																				20 10				
Bolton	a			19 00	19 08													19 37			20 25				20 00
Manchester Piccadilly 10	a				19 27													19 59							
Manchester Airport	a				19 47													20 17							
Liverpool Lime Street 10	a																								
	d							17 52			18 22		18 34	18 48											
Liverpool South Parkway	d							18 03			18 32		18 44												
Runcorn	d												18 52	19 04											
Warrington Bank Quay	a		18 39														19 25					19 39			
	d		18 39														19 25					19 39			
Hartford	d												19 03												
Manchester Piccadilly 10	d					18 27	18 35	18 44			19a09					18 55				19 07				19 15	
Stockport	d					18 36	18 42	18a53								19 04								19 22	
Wilmslow	d															19 11									
Holyhead	d																								
Bangor (Gwynedd)	d																								
Llandudno Junction	d																								
Wrexham General	d																								
Chester	d	18 35																							
Crewe 10	a	18 53	18 59										19 20			19 27						19 59			
	d	18 55	19 01										19 22			19 29						20 01			
Macclesfield	d					18 49	18 55																		
Congleton	d																								
Stoke-on-Trent	d					19 07	19 12								←					19 43				19 50	
Stafford	a					19 24							19 42	19 35	19 42										
	d					19 25							19 43	19 36	19 43										
Penkridge	a												→		19 48										
Wolverhampton 7	a		19 31			19 40									19 59					20 13		20 32			
Birmingham New Street 12	a		19 55			19 58									20 15					20 31		20 50			
Birmingham International	a					20 13																			
Coventry	a					20 24																			
Lichfield Trent Valley	a																								
Tamworth Low Level	a																								
Nuneaton	a																								
Rugby	a																								
Milton Keynes Central	a	20 03																						20 46	
Watford Junction	a																								
London Euston 15	a	20 44					20 47							21 01		21 09	21 21							21 31	

A from Birmingham New Street
to Birmingham New Street

OVERNIGHT SLEEPERS. For sleeper trains, operated by First ScotRail, please refer to Tables 400 - 404

Scotland and North West England - West Midlands and London

Route Diagram - see first Page of Table 65

		TP	XC	VT	EM	TP	LM	VT	VT	TP	NT	XC	AW	NT	TP	TP	VT	EM	TP
		◇1	◇1	◇1	◇	◇1	◇1	◇1	◇1	◇1		◇1	◇			◇1	◇1	◇	◇1
			A																
Inverness	d																		
Aberdeen	d																		
Dundee	d																		
Perth	d																		
Edinburgh 10	d															18 03			
Haymarket	d															18u08			
Glasgow Central 15	d	17 06							17 36										
Motherwell	d																		
Carstairs	d																		
Lockerbie	d								18 32							19 03			
Carlisle 8	a	18 24							18 50							19 24			
	d	18 24							18 52							19 24			
Penrith North Lakes	d	18 39							19 06							19 39			
Windermere	d																		
Oxenholme Lake District	a								19 28							20 03			
	d								19 29							20 04			
Barrow-in-Furness	d										20 02								
Lancaster 6	a	19 20							19 43		21 07					20 20			
	d	19 20							19 44							20 20			
Blackpool North	d									19 44									
Preston 8	a	19 39							20 02	20 08						20 39			
Preston 8	d	19 40							20 04	20 10				20 14	20 19	20 40			
Wigan North Western	a								20 15										
	d								20 15										
Blackrod	d													21 00					
Lostock	d													21 10					
Bolton	a	20 08								20 37				21 25	21 00	21 08			
Manchester Piccadilly 10	a	20 27								20 59						21 27			
Manchester Airport	a	20 47								21 17						21 47			
Liverpool Lime Street 10	a																		
	d				18 52	19 22	19 34	19 48										19 52	20 22
Liverpool South Parkway	d				19 03	19 32	19 44											20 03	20 32
Runcorn	d						19 52	20 04											
Warrington Bank Quay	a								20 26										
	d								20 26										
Hartford	d						20 03												
Manchester Piccadilly 10	d		19 27	19 35	19 44	20a09						20 07					20 20	20 44	21a09
Stockport	d		19 36	19 41	19a53							20 16					20 27	20a53	
Wilmslow	d																		
Holyhead	d												18 25						
Bangor (Gwynedd)	d												19 04						
Llandudno Junction	d												19 24						
Wrexham General	d																		
Chester	d												20 27						
Crewe 10	a						20 16	20 22	20 45				20 48						
	d						20 18	20 24	20 47				20 52						
Macclesfield	d		19 49	19 54								20 29					20 40		
Congleton	d																		
Stoke-on-Trent	d		20 07	20 11								20 47					20 57		
Stafford	a		20 26				20 38	20 41				21 08	21 16						
	d		20 27				20 39	20 43				21 09	21 16						
Penkridge	a						20 44												
Wolverhampton 7	a		20 39				20 55					21 21	21 34						
Birmingham New Street 12	a		20 58				21 15					21 39	21 52						
Birmingham International	a		21 13										22 09						
Coventry	a		21 23																
Lichfield Trent Valley	a																		
Tamworth Low Level	a																		
Nuneaton	a																		
Rugby	a																		
Milton Keynes Central	a							21 36	21 55								22 03		
Watford Junction	a								22s31										
London Euston 15	a			21 58				22 27	22 53								22 56		

A to Birmingham New Street

OVERNIGHT SLEEPERS. For sleeper trains, operated by First ScotRail, please refer to Tables 400 - 404

Scotland and North West England - West Midlands and London

Route Diagram - see first Page of Table 65

		LM	VT	VT	VT	TP	TP	XC	NT	VT	LM	TP	TP	VT	XC	EM	TP
		◇1	◇1	◇1	◇1	◇1	◇1	◇1		◇1	◇1	◇1	◇1	◇1	◇1	◇	◇1
													A				
Inverness	d																
Aberdeen	d																
Dundee	d																
Perth	d																
Edinburgh 10	d									18 52		19 57					
Haymarket	d									18 57		20u01					
Glasgow Central 15	d				18 30									20 08			
Motherwell	d																
Carstairs	d																
Lockerbie	d													21 02			
Carlisle 8	a				19 43					20 05		21 13		21 21			
	d				19 44					20 07		21 14		21 24			
Penrith North Lakes	d									20 22				21 39			
Windermere	d					20 40											
Oxenholme Lake District	a				20 19	20 59								22 02			
	d				20 19	21 01								22 03			
Barrow-in-Furness	d																
Lancaster 6	a				20 34	21 18				20 56		22 03		22 17			
	d				20 34					20 57		22 03		22 18			
Blackpool North	d						20 44						21 56				
Preston 8	a				20 52		21 08			21 15		22 23	22 20	22 35			
Preston 8	d				20 55		21 10		21 14	21 17		22 28		22 38			
Wigan North Western	a				21 06					21 28				22 49			
	d				21 07					21 28				22 50			
Blackrod	d								22 00								
Lostock	d								22 10								
Bolton	a						21 37		22 25			22 58					
Manchester Piccadilly 10	a						21 59					23 24					
Manchester Airport	a						22 17					23 42					
Liverpool Lime Street 10	a																
	d	20 34		20 48							21 34					21 21	21 52
Liverpool South Parkway	d	20 44									21 44					21 31	22 02
Runcorn	d	20 52		21 04							21 52						
Warrington Bank Quay	a				21 18					21 39				23 00			
	d				21 18					21 39				23 01			
Hartford	d	21 03									22 03						
Manchester Piccadilly 10	d		20 55					21 07							22 07	22 11	22a39
Stockport	d		21 03					21 16							22 16	22a20	
Wilmslow	d																
Holyhead	d																
Bangor (Gwynedd)	d																
Llandudno Junction	d																
Wrexham General	d																
Chester	d																
Crewe 10	a	21 16		21 21	21 38					21 59	22 18			23 20			
	d	21 18		21 23	21 40					22 01	22 22						
Macclesfield	d		21 15					21 29							22 29		
Congleton	d																
Stoke-on-Trent	d		21 33					21 47							22 47		
Stafford	a	21 38		21 42	22 01			22 06			22 42				23 04		
	d	21 39		21 43	22 02			22 06			22 45				23 05		
Penkridge	a	21 44									22 50						
Wolverhampton 7	a	21 55			22 17			22 20		22 31	23 01				23 18		
Birmingham New Street 12	a	22 15			22 38			22 39		22 55	23 17				23 36		
Birmingham International	a																
Coventry	a																
Lichfield Trent Valley	a			21 59													
Tamworth Low Level	a			22 05													
Nuneaton	a			22 17													
Rugby	a			22 31													
Milton Keynes Central	a		22 46	23 04													
Watford Junction	a		23s25	23s34													
London Euston 15	a		23 49	23 54													

A from Preston

OVERNIGHT SLEEPERS. For sleeper trains, operated by First ScotRail, please refer to Tables 400 - 404

Table 65

Sundays

8 January to 12 February

Scotland and North West England - West Midlands and London

Route Diagram - see first Page of Table 65

		TP	SR	SR
			8	8
		◇1		
Inverness	d			20 25
Aberdeen	d			
Dundee	d			
Perth	d			23u00
Edinburgh 10	d			01 06
Haymarket	d			
Glasgow Central 15	d		23 15	
Motherwell	d		23u31	
Carstairs	d		23u47	
Lockerbie	d			
Carlisle 8	a			02 51
	d		01u12	02 53
Penrith North Lakes	d			
Windermere	d			
Oxenholme Lake District	a			
	d			
Barrow-in-Furness	d			
Lancaster 6	a			
	d			
Blackpool North	d	23 03		
Preston 8	a	23 28		04s41
Preston 8	d	23 28		
Wigan North Western	a			
	d			
Blackrod	d			
Lostock	d			
Bolton	a	00 01		
Manchester Piccadilly 10	a	00 16		
Manchester Airport	a	00 30		
Liverpool Lime Street 10	a			
	d			
Liverpool South Parkway	d			
Runcorn	d			
Warrington Bank Quay	a		03 34	
	d		03 36	
Hartford	d			
Manchester Piccadilly 10	d			
Stockport	d			
Wilmslow	d			
Holyhead	d			
Bangor (Gwynedd)	d			
Llandudno Junction	d			
Wrexham General	d			
Chester	d			
Crewe 10	a			05s37
	d			
Macclesfield	d			
Congleton	d			
Stoke-on-Trent	d			
Stafford	a			
	d			
Penkridge	a			
Wolverhampton 7	a			
Birmingham New Street 12	a			
Birmingham International	a			
Coventry	a			
Lichfield Trent Valley	a			
Tamworth Low Level	a			
Nuneaton	a			
Rugby	a			
Milton Keynes Central	a			
Watford Junction	a		06s23	
London Euston 15	a		06 46	07 47

OVERNIGHT SLEEPERS. For sleeper trains, operated by First ScotRail, please refer to Tables 400 - 404

Table 65

Sundays

19 February to 25 March

Scotland and North West England - West Midlands and London

Route Diagram - see first Page of Table 65

		TP	NT	TP	TP	VT	TP	VT	VT	TP	XC	VT	VT	TP	NT	VT	TP	XC	VT
		◇1				◇1	◇1	◇1	◇1	◇1	◇1	◇1	◇1	◇1		◇1	◇1	◇1	◇1
											A							A	
Inverness	d																		
Aberdeen	d																		
Dundee	d																		
Perth	d																		
Edinburgh 10	d																		
Haymarket	d																		
Glasgow Central 15	d																		
Motherwell	d																		
Carstairs	d																		
Lockerbie	d																		
Carlisle 8	a																		
	d																		
Penrith North Lakes	d																		
Windermere	d																		
Oxenholme Lake District	a																		
	d																		
Barrow-in-Furness	d																		
Lancaster 6	a																		
	d																		
Blackpool North	d	22p44		03 20	05 20		08 14							08 44	08 50				
Preston 8	a	23p08					08 38							09 08	09 14				
Preston 8	d	23p10		04u00	06u00		08 42						09 00	09 10	09 15				
Wigan North Western	a												09 10		09 37				
	d		23p15										09 11						
Blackrod	d																		
Lostock	d																		
Bolton	a	23p34		04b35	06b35		09 05							09 34					
Manchester Piccadilly 10	a	23p53		05b00	07b00		09 28							09 56					
Manchester Airport	a	00 23		05 25	07 25		09 48							10 17					
Liverpool Lime Street 10	a		00 15																
	d								08 15	08 22		08 38					09 22		09 38
Liverpool South Parkway	d									08 32							09 32		
Runcorn	d								08 35			08 54							09 54
Warrington Bank Quay	a												09 21						
	d												09 22						
Hartford	d																		
Manchester Piccadilly 10	d					08 05		08 20		09a11	08 27					09 20	10a09	09 27	
Stockport	d					08 14		08 28			08 36					09 27		09 36	
Wilmslow	d					08 22					08 43							09 43	
Holyhead	d																		
Bangor (Gwynedd)	d																		
Llandudno Junction	d																		
Wrexham General	d																		
Chester	d																		
Crewe 10	a					08 39			08 52		09 01	09 11	09 41					10 01	10 12
	d					08 43			08 53		09 05	09 13	09 43					10 05	10 14
Macclesfield	d							08 42								09 40			
Congleton	d																		
Stoke-on-Trent	d							08 59								09 57			
Stafford	a					09 01					09 25	09 31						10 26	10 32
	d					09 02					09 26	09 32						10 27	10 33
Penkridge	a																		
Wolverhampton 7	a										09 40							10 42	
Birmingham New Street 12	a										09 58							10 59	
Birmingham International	a										10 13							11 13	
Coventry	a										10 24							11 24	
Lichfield Trent Valley	a																		
Tamworth Low Level	a																		
Nuneaton	a											09 54							10 55
Rugby	a												10 31						
Milton Keynes Central	a								10 17				11 06			11 16			11 46
Watford Junction	a					10s35		10s41				11s16	11s43						
London Euston 15	a					10 57		11 02	11 06			11 37	12 05			12 08			12 32

A from Birmingham New Street; to Birmingham New Street

b Stops to pick up only

OVERNIGHT SLEEPERS. For sleeper trains, operated by First ScotRail, please refer to Tables 400 - 404

Scotland and North West England - West Midlands and London

Route Diagram - see first Page of Table 65

		LM ◇1	TP ◇1	LM 1	VT ◇1	TP ◇1	NT	VT ◇1	VT ◇1	XC ◇1	VT ◇1	VT ◇1	TP ◇1	VT ◇1	TP ◇1	NT	VT ◇1	TP ◇1	VT ◇1	VT ◇1
					⊏⊐			⊏⊐	⊏⊐	A ⊏⊐⌶	⊏⊐	⊏⊐		⊏⊐			⊏⊐		⊏⊐	⊏⊐
Inverness	d																			
Aberdeen	d																			
Dundee	d																			
Perth	d																			
Edinburgh 10	d																			
Haymarket	d																			
Glasgow Central 15	d																			
Motherwell	d																			
Carstairs	d																			
Lockerbie	d																			
Carlisle 8	a																			
	d																			
Penrith North Lakes	d																			
Windermere	d																			
Oxenholme Lake District	a																			
	d																			
Barrow-in-Furness	d																			
Lancaster 6	a																			
	d																			
Blackpool North	d					09 44	09 50								10 44	10 50				
Preston 8	a					10 07	10 14								11 08	11 14				
Preston 8	d				10 00	10 10	10 15		10 17				10 47	10 58	11 10	11 15				11 17
Wigan North Western	a				10 10		10 38		10 28					11 09		11 38				11 28
	d				10 11				10 28					11 09						11 28
Blackrod	d																			
Lostock	d																			
Bolton	a					10 34							11 08		11 34					
Manchester Piccadilly 10	a					10 56							11 27		11 58					
Manchester Airport ✈	a					11 17							11 47		12 17					
Liverpool Lime Street 10	a																			
	d		10 22									10 38						11 22		
Liverpool South Parkway ✈	d		10 32															11 32		
Runcorn	d											10 54								
Warrington Bank Quay	a				10 21				10 39					11 20						11 39
	d				10 22				10 39					11 20						11 39
Hartford	d																			
Manchester Piccadilly 10	d		11a09					10 20		10 27	10 35						11 15	12a09		
Stockport	d							10 29		10 36	10 42						11 23			
Wilmslow	d							10 36												
Holyhead	d																			
Bangor (Gwynedd)	d																			
Llandudno Junction	d																			
Wrexham General	d																			
Chester	d																		11 28	
Crewe 10	a				10 41			10 53	10 59			11 12							11 47	11 59
	d	10 20		10 38	10 43			10 55	11 01			11 14							11 49	12 01
Macclesfield	d									10 49	10 55									
Congleton	d																			
Stoke-on-Trent	d			10 59						11 07	11 12						11 51			
Stafford	a	10 41		11 17						11 27		11 34								
	d	10 41								11 28		11 36								
Penkridge	a	10 48																		
Wolverhampton 7	a	11 00							11 31	11 41										12 32
Birmingham New Street 12	a	11 17							11 55	12 00										12 55
Birmingham International ✈	a									12 13										
Coventry	a									12 24										
Lichfield Trent Valley	a																			
Tamworth Low Level	a																			
Nuneaton	a											11 58							12 31	
Rugby	a				11 31															
Milton Keynes Central	a				12 06						12 20						12 50		13 03	
Watford Junction	a							12s35				12s50								
London Euston 15 ⊖	a				12 45			12 56			12 59	13 11		13 21			13 28		13 44	

A ⊏⊐ from Birmingham New Street
⌶ to Birmingham New Street

OVERNIGHT SLEEPERS. For sleeper trains, operated by First ScotRail, please refer to Tables 400 - 404

Scotland and North West England - West Midlands and London

Route Diagram - see first Page of Table 65

		TP ◇1	XC ◇1	VT ◇1	LM ◇1	VT ◇1	LM ◇1	VT ◇1	VT ◇1	TP ◇1	NT	VT ◇1	VT ◇1	VT ◇1	TP ◇1	TP ◇1	XC ◇1	VT ◇1	LM ◇1	VT ◇1
			A ⊏⊐⌶	⊏⊐		⊏⊐		⊏⊐	⊏⊐	⌶		⊏⊐	⊏⊐	⊏⊐	⌶		A ⊏⊐⌶	⊏⊐		⊏⊐
Inverness	d																			
Aberdeen	d																			
Dundee	d																			
Perth	d																			
Edinburgh 10	d														10 10					
Haymarket	d														10u14					
Glasgow Central 15	d								09 37											
Motherwell	d																			
Carstairs	d																			
Lockerbie	d														11 08					
Carlisle 8	a								10 44						11 29					
	d								10 46						11 29					
Penrith North Lakes	d								11 00						11 45					
Windermere	d																			
Oxenholme Lake District	a								11 22						12 09					
	d								11 23						12 10					
Barrow-in-Furness	d	10 22																		
Lancaster 6	a	11 22							11 37						12 26					
	d	11 22							11 38						12 26					
Blackpool North	d									11 44	11 50									
Preston 8	a	11 42							11 56	12 08	12 14				12 45					
Preston 8	d	11 47							11 58	12 10	12 15			12 17	12 47					
Wigan North Western	a								12 09		12 38			12 28						
	d								12 09					12 28						
Blackrod	d																			
Lostock	d																			
Bolton	a	12 08								12 34					13 08					
Manchester Piccadilly 10	a	12 27								12 59					13 27					
Manchester Airport ✈	a	12 48								13 17					13 47					
Liverpool Lime Street 10	a																			
	d				11 34	11 48										12 22			12 34	12 48
Liverpool South Parkway ✈	d				11 44											12 32			12 44	
Runcorn	d				11 52	12 04													12 52	13 04
Warrington Bank Quay	a								12 20					12 39						
	d								12 20					12 39						
Hartford	d				12 03														13 03	
Manchester Piccadilly 10	d		11 27	11 35				11 55				12 15				13a09	12 26	12 35		
Stockport	d		11 36	11 43				12 05				12 23					12 35	12 44		
Wilmslow	d							12 12												
Holyhead	d												10 55							
Bangor (Gwynedd)	d												11 22							
Llandudno Junction	d												11 40							
Wrexham General	d																			
Chester	d												12 33							
Crewe 10	a				12 20			12 28					12 52	12 59					13 19	
	d				12 22			12 30					12 56	13 01					13 22	
Macclesfield	d		11 49	11 56													12 49	12 57		
Congleton	d																			
Stoke-on-Trent	d		12 07	12 13			←					12 51					13 07	13 14		
Stafford	a		12 24		12 41	12 35	12 41										13 24		13 42	13 35
	d		12 25		12 42	12 36	12 42										13 25		13 43	13 36
Penkridge	a				→		12 48												→	
Wolverhampton 7	a		12 40				12 59							13 31			13 40			
Birmingham New Street 12	a		12 58				13 16							13 55			13 58			
Birmingham International ✈	a		13 13														14 13			
Coventry	a		13 24														14 24			
Lichfield Trent Valley	a																			
Tamworth Low Level	a																			
Nuneaton	a																			
Rugby	a																			
Milton Keynes Central	a											13 49	14 02							
Watford Junction	a																			
London Euston 15 ⊖	a			13 47		14 01		14 09	14 16			14 27	14 43					14 47		15 01

A ⊏⊐ from Birmingham New Street
⌶ to Birmingham New Street

OVERNIGHT SLEEPERS. For sleeper trains, operated by First ScotRail, please refer to Tables 400 - 404

Table 65

Sundays

19 February to 25 March

Scotland and North West England - West Midlands and London

Route Diagram - see first Page of Table 65

		LM	VT	VT	TP	NT	XC	VT		VT	VT	TP	NT	XC	VT	EM		TP			LM	VT	LM	VT	VT
		◇■	◇■	◇■	◇■		◇■	◇■		◇■	◇■	◇■		◇■	◇■	◇		◇■			◇■	◇■	◇■	◇■	◇■
														A											
			⊡	⊡			✕	⊡		⊡	⊡			⊡✕	⊡							⊡		⊡	⊡
Inverness	d																								
Aberdeen	d																								
Dundee	d																								
Perth	d																								
Edinburgh 10	d										10 52														
Haymarket	d										10 57														
Glasgow Central 15	d			10 34																					11 36
Motherwell	d			10 49																					
Carstairs	d																								
Lockerbie	d																								
Carlisle 8	a			11 44							12 05														12 47
	d			11 46							12 07														12 49
Penrith North Lakes	d			12 00																					
Windermere	d																								
Oxenholme Lake District	a			12 22							12 41														13 22
	d			12 24							12 43														13 23
Barrow-in-Furness	d											12 34	13 10												
Lancaster 6	a			12 37							12 56	13 26	14 15												13 37
	d			12 38							12 57	13 26													13 38
Blackpool North	d				12 44	12 50																			
Preston 8	a			12 56	13 08	13 14					13 15	13 45													13 56
Preston 8	d			12 58	13 10	13 15					13 17	13 47													13 58
Wigan North Western	a			13 09		13 39					13 28														14 09
	d			13 09							13 28														14 09
Blackrod	d																								
Lostock	d																								
Bolton	a				13 34							14 08													
Manchester Piccadilly 10	a				13 56							14 27													
Manchester Airport	a				14 17							14 47													
Liverpool Lime Street 10	a																								
	d															12 52		13 22			13 34	13 48			
Liverpool South Parkway	d															13 03		13 32			13 44				
Runcorn	d																				13 52	14 04			
Warrington Bank Quay	a			13 20							13 39														14 20
	d			13 20							13 39														14 20
Hartford	d																				14 03				
Manchester Piccadilly 10	d		12 55				13 07	13 15						13 27	13 35	13 44		14a09						13 55	
Stockport	d		13 05					13 22						13 36	13 42	13a53								14 04	
Wilmslow	d		13 12																					14 11	
Holyhead	d									11 50															
Bangor (Gwynedd)	d									12 17															
Llandudno Junction	d									12 35															
Wrexham General	d																								
Chester	d									13 30															
Crewe 10	a		13 28							13 50	13 59										14 18			14 27	
	d		13 30							13 51	14 01										14 22			14 29	
Macclesfield	d													13 49	13 55										
Congleton	d																								
Stoke-on-Trent	d	←					13 43	13 50						14 07	14 12								←		
Stafford	a	13 42												14 24							14 42	14 35	14 42		
	d	13 43												14 25							14 43	14 36	14 43		
Penkridge	a	13 48																			→		14 48		
Wolverhampton 7	a	13 59					14 13				14 32			14 40									14 59		
Birmingham New Street 12	a	14 15					14 31				14 55			14 58									15 15		
Birmingham International	a													15 13											
Coventry	a													15 24											
Lichfield Trent Valley	a																								
Tamworth Low Level	a																								
Nuneaton	a									14 31															
Rugby	a																								
Milton Keynes Central	a							14 49		15 04															
Watford Junction	a																								
London Euston 15	a		15 09	15 15				15 27		15 45					15 47							16 01		16 09	16 15

A ⊡ from Birmingham New Street
✕ to Birmingham New Street

OVERNIGHT SLEEPERS. For sleeper trains, operated by First ScotRail, please refer to Tables 400 - 404

Table 65

Sundays

19 February to 25 March

Scotland and North West England - West Midlands and London

Route Diagram - see first Page of Table 65

		TP	NT	XC		VT	VT	VT	TP	XC	VT	EM		TP			LM	VT	LM	VT	VT	TP	NT	XC
		◇■		◇■		◇■	◇■	◇■	◇■	◇■	◇■	◇		◇■			◇■	◇■	◇■	◇■	◇■	◇■		◇■
										A														
				✕		⊡	⊡	⊡	✕	⊡✕	⊡							⊡		⊡	⊡			✕
Inverness	d																							
Aberdeen	d																							
Dundee	d																							
Perth	d																							
Edinburgh 10	d								12 10															
Haymarket	d								12u14															
Glasgow Central 15	d							11 58													12 42			
Motherwell	d																							
Carstairs	d																							
Lockerbie	d								13 08															
Carlisle 8	a							13 09	13 29												13 51			
	d							13 10	13 29												13 54			
Penrith North Lakes	d								13 45															
Windermere	d																							
Oxenholme Lake District	a								14 09												14 27			
	d								14 10												14 28			
Barrow-in-Furness	d																							
Lancaster 6	a							13 56	14 26												14 42			
	d							13 58	14 26												14 43			
Blackpool North	d	13 44	13 50																			14 44	14 50	
Preston 8	a	14 08	14 14					14 15	14 45												15 01	15 08	15 14	
Preston 8	d	14 10	14 15					14 17	14 47												15 03	15 10	15 15	
Wigan North Western	a		14 38					14 28													15 14		15 38	
	d							14 28													15 14			
Blackrod	d																							
Lostock	d																							
Bolton	a	14 34							15 08													15 34		
Manchester Piccadilly 10	a	14 56							15 27													15 56		
Manchester Airport	a	15 17							15 47													16 17		
Liverpool Lime Street 10	a																							
	d											13 52		14 22			14 34	14 48						
Liverpool South Parkway	d											14 03		14 32			14 44							
Runcorn	d																14 52	15 04						
Warrington Bank Quay	a							14 39													15 25			
	d							14 39													15 25			
Hartford	d																15 03							
Manchester Piccadilly 10	d			14 07		14 15				14 27	14 35	14 44		15a09						14 55				15 07
Stockport	d					14 22				14 36	14 42	14a53								15 04				
Wilmslow	d																			15 11				
Holyhead	d						12 50																	
Bangor (Gwynedd)	d						13 18																	
Llandudno Junction	d						13 36																	
Wrexham General	d																							
Chester	d						14 33																	
Crewe 10	a						14 52	14 59									15 20			15 27				
	d						14 54	15 01									15 22			15 29				
Macclesfield	d									14 49	14 55													
Congleton	d																							
Stoke-on-Trent	d			14 43		14 50				15 07	15 12								←					15 43
Stafford	a									15 24							15 42	15 35	15 42					
	d									15 25							15 43	15 36	15 43					
Penkridge	a																→		15 48					
Wolverhampton 7	a			15 13				15 31		15 40									15 59					16 13
Birmingham New Street 12	a			15 31				15 55		15 58									16 15					16 31
Birmingham International	a									16 13														
Coventry	a									16 24														
Lichfield Trent Valley	a																							
Tamworth Low Level	a																							
Nuneaton	a																							
Rugby	a																							
Milton Keynes Central	a					15 49	16 04																	
Watford Junction	a																							
London Euston 15	a					16 27	16 44				16 47							17 01		17 09	17 20			

A ⊡ from Birmingham New Street
✕ to Birmingham New Street

OVERNIGHT SLEEPERS. For sleeper trains, operated by First ScotRail, please refer to Tables 400 - 404

Table 65

Sundays

19 February to 25 March

Scotland and North West England - West Midlands and London

Route Diagram - see first Page of Table 65

		VT	VT	VT	TP	XC	VT	EM	TP	LM	VT	LM	VT	VT	TP	NT	XC	VT	VT	VT	TP
		◇1	◇1	◇1	◇1	◇1	◇1	◇	◇1	◇1	◇1	◇1	◇1	◇1	◇1		◇1	◇1	◇1	◇1	◇1
						A															
Inverness	d																				
Aberdeen	d																				
Dundee	d																				
Perth	d																				
Edinburgh 10	d			12 52																	14 10
Haymarket	d			12 56																	14u14
Glasgow Central 15	d													13 36						13 55	
Motherwell	d																				
Carstairs	d																				
Lockerbie	d																				15 08
Carlisle 8	a			14 05										14 46						15 09	15 29
	d			14 07										14 49						15 11	15 29
Penrith North Lakes	d			14 22																	15 45
Windermere	d																				
Oxenholme Lake District	a													15 22						15 46	16 09
	d													15 23						15 46	16 10
Barrow-in-Furness	d				14 25																
Lancaster 6	a			14 56	15 26									15 37							16 26
	d			14 57	15 26									15 38							16 26
Blackpool North	d														15 44	15 50					
Preston 8	a			15 15	15 45									15 56	16 08	16 14				16 15	16 46
Preston 8	d			15 17	15 47									15 58	16 10	16 15				16 17	16 47
Wigan North Western	a			15 28										16 09		16 38				16 28	
	d			15 28										16 09						16 28	
Blackrod	d																				
Lostock	d																				
Bolton	a				16 08										16 34						17 08
Manchester Piccadilly 10	a				16 27										16 56						17 27
Manchester Airport	a				16 46										17 17						17 47
Liverpool Lime Street 10	a																				
	d							14 52	15 22	15 34	15 48								16 18		
Liverpool South Parkway	d							15 03	15 32	15 44											
Runcorn	d									15 52	16 04								16 34		
Warrington Bank Quay	a			15 39										16 20						16 39	
	d			15 39										16 20						16 39	
Hartford	d									16 03											
Manchester Piccadilly 10	d	15 15				15 27	15 35	15 44	16a09				15 55				16 07	16 15			
Stockport	d	15 22				15 36	15 42	15a53					16 04					16 23			
Wilmslow	d												16 11								
Holyhead	d		13 55																		
Bangor (Gwynedd)	d		14 22																		
Llandudno Junction	d		14 40																		
Wrexham General	d																				
Chester	d		15 33																		
Crewe 10	a		15 52	15 59						16 18			16 27						16 51	16 58	
	d		15 54	16 01						16 22			16 29						16 54	17 00	
Macclesfield	d					15 49	15 55														
Congleton	d																				
Stoke-on-Trent	d	15 50				16 07	16 12					←					16 43	16 50			
Stafford	a					16 24				16 42	16 36	16 42									
	d					16 25				16 43	16 37	16 43									
Penkridge	a									→		16 48									
Wolverhampton 7	a			16 32		16 40						16 59					17 13			17 31	
Birmingham New Street 12	a			16 55		16 58						17 15					17 31			17 56	
Birmingham International	a					17 13															
Coventry	a					17 24															
Lichfield Trent Valley	a																		17 26		
Tamworth Low Level	a																				
Nuneaton	a																				
Rugby	a																				
Milton Keynes Central	a	16 49	17 03															17 49	18 04		
Watford Junction	a																				
London Euston 15	a	17 27	17 44				17 47				18 01		18 09	18 15				18 27	18 44		

A from Birmingham New Street
to Birmingham New Street

OVERNIGHT SLEEPERS. For sleeper trains, operated by First ScotRail, please refer to Tables 400 - 404

Table 65

Sundays

19 February to 25 March

Scotland and North West England - West Midlands and London

Route Diagram - see first Page of Table 65

		XC	VT	EM	TP	LM	VT	LM	VT	VT	TP	NT	XC	VT	VT	VT	TP	XC	VT	EM
		◇1	◇1	◇	◇1	◇1	◇1	◇1	◇1	◇1	◇1		◇1	◇1	◇1	◇1	◇1	◇1	◇1	◇
		A																A		
Inverness	d																			
Aberdeen	d																			
Dundee	d																			
Perth	d																			
Edinburgh 10	d															14 52				
Haymarket	d															14 57				
Glasgow Central 15	d									14 36							15 06			
Motherwell	d																			
Carstairs	d																			
Lockerbie	d																16 06			
Carlisle 8	a									15 46						16 05	16 26			
	d									15 49						16 07	16 26			
Penrith North Lakes	d															16 22	16 42			
Windermere	d																			
Oxenholme Lake District	a									16 22							17 07			
	d									16 23							17 07			
Barrow-in-Furness	d																			
Lancaster 6	a									16 37						16 56	17 22			
	d									16 38						16 57	17 22			
Blackpool North	d										16 44	16 50								
Preston 8	a									16 56	17 08	17 14				17 15	17 41			
Preston 8	d									16 58	17 10	17 15				17 17	17 47			
Wigan North Western	a									17 09		17 38				17 28				
	d									17 09						17 28				
Blackrod	d																			
Lostock	d																			
Bolton	a										17 34						18 08			
Manchester Piccadilly 10	a										17 56						18 27			
Manchester Airport	a										18 17						18 45			
Liverpool Lime Street 10	a																			
	d			15 52	16 22	16 34	16 48													16 52
Liverpool South Parkway	d			16 03	16 32	16 44														17 03
Runcorn	d					16 52	17 04													
Warrington Bank Quay	a									17 20						17 39				
	d									17 20						17 39				
Hartford	d					17 03														
Manchester Piccadilly 10	d	16 27	16 35	16 44	17a09				16 55				17 07	17 15				17 27	17 35	17 44
Stockport	d	16 36	16 42	16a53					17 04					17 22				17 36	17 42	17a53
Wilmslow	d								17 11											
Holyhead	d																			
Bangor (Gwynedd)	d																			
Llandudno Junction	d																			
Wrexham General	d																			
Chester	d														17 35					
Crewe 10	a					17 18			17 27						17 53	17 59				
	d					17 22			17 29						17 55	18 01				
Macclesfield	d	16 49	16 55															17 49	17 55	
Congleton	d																			
Stoke-on-Trent	d	17 08	17 12					←					17 43	17 50				18 08	18 12	
Stafford	a	17 25				17 42	17 35	17 42										18 25		
	d	17 26				17 43	17 36	17 43										18 26		
Penkridge	a					→		17 48												
Wolverhampton 7	a	17 40						17 59					18 13			18 32		18 40		
Birmingham New Street 12	a	17 58						18 15					18 31			18 55		18 58		
Birmingham International	a	18 13																19 13		
Coventry	a	18 24																19 24		
Lichfield Trent Valley	a																			
Tamworth Low Level	a																			
Nuneaton	a																			
Rugby	a																			
Milton Keynes Central	a													18 49	19 02					
Watford Junction	a																			
London Euston 15	a		18 47				19 01		19 09	19 15				19 27	19 43				19 47	

A from Birmingham New Street
to Birmingham New Street

OVERNIGHT SLEEPERS. For sleeper trains, operated by First ScotRail, please refer to Tables 400 - 404

Table 65

Sundays
19 February to 25 March

Scotland and North West England - West Midlands and London

Route Diagram - see first Page of Table 65

		TP ◇1			LM ◇1	VT ◇1 ⊏	LM ◇1	VT ◇1 ⊏	VT ◇1 ⊏	TP ◇1	NT	XC ◇1 ⊤		VT ◇1 ⊏	VT ◇1 ⊏	VT ◇1 ⊏	TP ◇1 ⊤	XC ◇1 A ⊏⊤	VT ◇1 ⊏	EM ◇		TP ◇1			LM ◇1
Inverness	d																								
Aberdeen	d																								
Dundee	d																								
Perth	d																								
Edinburgh 10	d																16 10								
Haymarket	d																16u14								
Glasgow Central 15	d								15 36							15 57									
Motherwell	d																								
Carstairs	d																								
Lockerbie	d																17 08								
Carlisle 8	a								16 46							17 08	17 29								
	d								16 49							17 09	17 29								
Penrith North Lakes	d								17 03								17 45								
Windermere	d																								
Oxenholme Lake District	a															17 44	18 09								
	d															17 44	18 10								
Barrow-in-Furness	d																								
Lancaster 6	a								17 37								18 26								
	d								17 38								18 26								
Blackpool North	d									17 44	17 50														
Preston 8	a								17 56	18 08	18 14					18 13	18 45								
Preston 8	d								17 58	18 10	18 15					18 17	18 47								
Wigan North Western	a								18 09		18 38					18 28									
	d								18 09							18 28									
Blackrod	d																								
Lostock	d																								
Bolton	a									18 34							19 08								
Manchester Piccadilly 10	a									18 56							19 27								
Manchester Airport	a									19 17							19 47								
Liverpool Lime Street 10	a																								
	d	17 22			17 34	17 48														17 52		18 22			18 34
Liverpool South Parkway	d	17 32			17 44															18 03		18 32			18 44
Runcorn	d				17 52	18 04																			18 52
Warrington Bank Quay	a								18 20							18 39									
	d								18 20							18 39									
Hartford	d				18 03																				19 03
Manchester Piccadilly 10	d	18a09						17 55				18 07		18 15				18 27	18 35	18 44		19a09			
Stockport	d							18 04						18 22				18 36	18 42	18a53					
Wilmslow	d							18 11																	
Holyhead	d																								
Bangor (Gwynedd)	d																								
Llandudno Junction	d																								
Wrexham General	d																								
Chester	d														18 35										
Crewe 10	a				18 20			18 27							18 53	18 59									19 20
	d				18 22			18 29							18 55	19 01									19 22
Macclesfield	d																	18 49	18 55						
Congleton	d																								
Stoke-on-Trent	d						←					18 43		18 50				19 07	19 12						
Stafford	a				18 42	18 35	18 42											19 24							19 42
	d				18 43	18 36	18 43											19 25							19 43
Penkridge	a				→		18 48																		↪
Wolverhampton 7	a						18 59					19 13				19 31		19 40							
Birmingham New Street 12	a						19 15					19 31				19 55		19 58							
Birmingham International	a																	20 13							
Coventry	a																	20 24							
Lichfield Trent Valley	a																								
Tamworth Low Level	a																								
Nuneaton	a																								
Rugby	a																								
Milton Keynes Central	a													19 49	20 03										
Watford Junction	a																								
London Euston 15	a					20 01		20 09	20 15					20 27	20 44				20 47						

A ⊏ from Birmingham New Street
⊤ to Birmingham New Street

OVERNIGHT SLEEPERS. For sleeper trains, operated by First ScotRail, please refer to Tables 400 - 404

Table 65

Sundays
19 February to 25 March

Scotland and North West England - West Midlands and London

Route Diagram - see first Page of Table 65

		VT ◇1 ⊏	LM ◇1	VT ◇1 ⊏	VT ◇1 ⊏	TP ◇1	NT	XC ◇1 ⊤		VT ◇1 ⊏	TP ◇1	TP ◇1 ⊤	VT ◇1 ⊏	XC ◇1 A ⊤	VT ◇1 ⊏	EM ◇		TP ◇1			LM ◇1	VT ◇1 ⊏	VT ◇1 ⊏	TP ◇1	NT
Inverness	d																								
Aberdeen	d																								
Dundee	d																								
Perth	d																								
Edinburgh 10	d									16 52															
Haymarket	d									16 56															
Glasgow Central 15	d				16 40							17 06											17 36		
Motherwell	d				16 54																				
Carstairs	d																								
Lockerbie	d																						18 32		
Carlisle 8	a				17 49					18 05		18 25											18 50		
	d				17 51					18 07		18 26											18 52		
Penrith North Lakes	d				18 05							18 42											19 06		
Windermere	d																								
Oxenholme Lake District	a				18 27					18 41		19 07											19 28		
	d				18 28					18 42		19 07											19 29		
Barrow-in-Furness	d										18 17														
Lancaster 6	a				18 42					18 56	19 17	19 22											19 43		
	d				18 43					18 57	19 17	19 22											19 44		
Blackpool North	d					18 44	18 50																	19 44	19 50
Preston 8	a				19 01	19 08	19 14			19 15	19 37	19 41											20 02	20 08	20 14
Preston 8	d				19 03	19 10	19 15			19 17		19 47											20 04	20 10	20 15
Wigan North Western	a				19 14		19 38			19 28													20 15		20 38
	d				19 14					19 28													20 15		
Blackrod	d																								
Lostock	d																								
Bolton	a					19 34						20 08												20 34	
Manchester Piccadilly 10	a					19 56						20 27												20 56	
Manchester Airport	a					20 17						20 45												21 16	
Liverpool Lime Street 10	a																								
	d	18 48														18 52		19 22			19 34	19 48			
Liverpool South Parkway	d															19 03		19 32			19 44				
Runcorn	d	19 04																			19 52	20 04			
Warrington Bank Quay	a				19 25					19 39													20 26		
	d				19 25					19 39													20 26		
Hartford	d																				20 03				
Manchester Piccadilly 10	d			18 55				19 07					19 15	19 27	19 35	19 44		20a09							
Stockport	d			19 04									19 22	19 36	19 41	19a53									
Wilmslow	d			19 11																					
Holyhead	d																								
Bangor (Gwynedd)	d																								
Llandudno Junction	d																								
Wrexham General	d																								
Chester	d																								
Crewe 10	a			19 27						19 59											20 16	20 22	20 45		
	d			19 29						20 01											20 18	20 24	20 47		
Macclesfield	d													19 49	19 54										
Congleton	d																								
Stoke-on-Trent	d		←					19 43					19 50	20 07	20 11										
Stafford	a	19 35	19 42											20 26							20 38	20 41			
	d	19 36	19 43											20 27							20 39	20 43			
Penkridge	a		19 48																		20 44				
Wolverhampton 7	a		19 59					20 13		20 32				20 39							20 55				
Birmingham New Street 12	a		20 15					20 31		20 50				20 58							21 15				
Birmingham International	a													21 13											
Coventry	a													21 23											
Lichfield Trent Valley	a																								
Tamworth Low Level	a																								
Nuneaton	a																								
Rugby	a																								
Milton Keynes Central	a												20 46									21 36	21 55		
Watford Junction	a																						22s31		
London Euston 15	a	21 01		21 09	21 21								21 31		21 58							22 27	22 53		

A ⊤ to Birmingham New Street

OVERNIGHT SLEEPERS. For sleeper trains, operated by First ScotRail, please refer to Tables 400 - 404

Table 65

Sundays

19 February to 25 March

Scotland and North West England - West Midlands and London

Route Diagram - see first Page of Table 65

		TP	NT	XC	AW	VT	EM	TP	LM	VT	VT	VT	TP	TP	NT	XC	VT	LM	NT
		◇1		◇1	◇	◇1	◇	◇1	◇1	◇1	◇1	◇1	◇1	◇1		◇1	◇1	◇1	
		⊤			⊤	☕				☕	☕	☕					☕		
Inverness	d																		
Aberdeen	d																		
Dundee	d																		
Perth	d																		
Edinburgh 10	d	18 10															18 52		
Haymarket	d	18u14															18 57		
Glasgow Central 15	d											18 30							
Motherwell	d																		
Carstairs	d																		
Lockerbie	d	19 08																	
Carlisle 8	a	19 29										19 43					20 05		
	d	19 29										19 44					20 07		
Penrith North Lakes	d	19 45															20 22		
Windermere	d												20 40						
Oxenholme Lake District	a	20 09										20 19	20 59						
	d	20 10										20 19	21 01						
Barrow-in-Furness	d		20 02																
Lancaster 6	a	20 26	21 07									20 34	21 18				20 56		
	d	20 26										20 34					20 57		
Blackpool North	d													20 44	20 50				21 50
Preston 8	a	20 45										20 52		21 08	21 14		21 15		22 14
Preston 8	d	20 47										20 55		21 10	21 15		21 17		22 15
Wigan North Western	a											21 06			21 38		21 28		22 38
	d											21 07					21 28		
Blackrod	d																		
Lostock	d																		
Bolton	a	21 08												21 34					
Manchester Piccadilly 10	a	21 27												21 56					
Manchester Airport ✈	a	21 46												22 17					
Liverpool Lime Street 10	a																		
	d						19 52	20 22	20 34		20 48							21 34	
Liverpool South Parkway ✈	d						20 03	20 32	20 44									21 44	
Runcorn	d								20 52		21 04							21 52	
Warrington Bank Quay	a											21 18					21 39		
	d											21 18					21 39		
Hartford	d								21 03									22 03	
Manchester Piccadilly 10	d			20 07		20 20	20 44	21a09		20 55						21 07			
Stockport	d			20 16		20 27	20a53			21 03						21 16			
Wilmslow	d																		
Holyhead	d				18 25														
Bangor (Gwynedd)	d				19 04														
Llandudno Junction	d				19 24														
Wrexham General	d																		
Chester	d				20 27														
Crewe 10	a				20 48				21 16		21 21	21 38					21 59	22 18	
	d				20 52				21 18		21 23	21 40					22 01	22 22	
Macclesfield	d			20 29		20 40				21 15						21 29			
Congleton	d																		
Stoke-on-Trent	d			20 47		20 57				21 33						21 47			
Stafford	a			21 08	21 16				21 38		21 42	22 01				22 06		22 42	
	d			21 09	21 16				21 39		21 43	22 02				22 06		22 45	
Penkridge	a								21 44									22 50	
Wolverhampton 7	a			21 21	21 34				21 55			22 17				22 20	22 31	23 01	
Birmingham New Street 12	a			21 39	21 52				22 15			22 38				22 39	22 55	23 17	
Birmingham International ✈	a				22 09														
Coventry	a																		
Lichfield Trent Valley	a										21 59								
Tamworth Low Level	a										22 05								
Nuneaton	a										22 17								
Rugby	a										22 31								
Milton Keynes Central	a					22 03				22 46	23 04								
Watford Junction	a									23s25	23s34								
London Euston 15 ⊖	a					22 56				23 49	23 54								

OVERNIGHT SLEEPERS. For sleeper trains, operated by First ScotRail, please refer to Tables 400 - 404

Table 65

Sundays

19 February to 25 March

Scotland and North West England - West Midlands and London

Route Diagram - see first Page of Table 65

		TP	TP	VT	XC	EM	TP	NT	TP	SR	SR
										B	B
		◇1	◇1 A	◇1	◇1	◇	◇1		◇1		
		⊤	⊤	☕						🛏 ☕	🛏 ☕
Inverness	d										20 25
Aberdeen	d										
Dundee	d										
Perth	d										23u00
Edinburgh 10	d	19 57									01 06
Haymarket	d	20u01									
Glasgow Central 15	d			20 08						23 15	
Motherwell	d									23u31	
Carstairs	d									23u47	
Lockerbie	d			21 02							
Carlisle 8	a	21 13		21 21							02 51
	d	21 14		21 24						01u12	02 53
Penrith North Lakes	d			21 39							
Windermere	d										
Oxenholme Lake District	a			22 02							
	d			22 03							
Barrow-in-Furness	d										
Lancaster 6	a	22 03		22 17							
	d	22 03		22 18							
Blackpool North	d		21 56					22 44	23 03		
Preston 8	a	22 23	22 20	22 35				23 08	23 28		04s41
Preston 8	d		22 29	22 38				23 09	23 28		
Wigan North Western	a			22 49				23 32			
	d			22 50							
Blackrod	d								23 50		
Lostock	d								23 57		
Bolton	a		22 50						00 02		
Manchester Piccadilly 10	a		23 14						00 18		
Manchester Airport ✈	a		23 30						00 32		
Liverpool Lime Street 10	a										
	d					21 21	21 52				
Liverpool South Parkway ✈	d					21 31	22 02				
Runcorn	d										
Warrington Bank Quay	a			23 00						03 34	
	d			23 01						03 36	
Hartford	d										
Manchester Piccadilly 10	d				22 07	22 11	22a39				
Stockport	d				22 16	22a20					
Wilmslow	d										
Holyhead	d										
Bangor (Gwynedd)	d										
Llandudno Junction	d										
Wrexham General	d										
Chester	d										
Crewe 10	a			23 20							05s37
	d										
Macclesfield	d				22 29						
Congleton	d										
Stoke-on-Trent	d				22 47						
Stafford	a				23 04						
	d				23 05						
Penkridge	a										
Wolverhampton 7	a				23 18						
Birmingham New Street 12	a				23 36						
Birmingham International ✈	a										
Coventry	a										
Lichfield Trent Valley	a										
Tamworth Low Level	a										
Nuneaton	a										
Rugby	a										
Milton Keynes Central	a										
Watford Junction	a									06s23	
London Euston 15 ⊖	a									06 46	07 47

A ⊤ from Preston

OVERNIGHT SLEEPERS. For sleeper trains, operated by First ScotRail, please refer to Tables 400 - 404

Sundays
from 1 April

Scotland and North West England - West Midlands and London

Route Diagram - see first Page of Table 65

	TP	NT	TP	TP	TP	VT	VT	VT	XC	VT	VT	TP	VT	XC	VT	TP	LM
	◇1				◇1	◇1	◇1	◇1	◇1	◇1	◇1	◇1	◇1	◇1	◇1	◇1	◇1
									A					A			
Inverness d																	
Aberdeen d																	
Dundee d																	
Perth d																	
Edinburgh d																	
Haymarket d																	
Glasgow Central d																	
Motherwell d																	
Carstairs d																	
Lockerbie d																	
Carlisle a																	
d																	
Penrith North Lakes d																	
Windermere d																	
Oxenholme Lake District a																	
d																	
Barrow-in-Furness d																	
Lancaster a																	
d																	
Blackpool North d	22p44		03 20	05 20	07 48							08 44					
Preston a	23p08				08 12							09 08					
Preston d	23p10		04u00	06u00	08 14						09 00	09 10					
Wigan North Western a											09 10						
d		23p15									09 11						
Blackrod d																	
Lostock d																	
Bolton a	23p34		04b35	06b35	08 37							09 34					
Manchester Piccadilly a	23p53		05b00	07b00	08 59							09 56					
Manchester Airport a	00 23		05 25	07 25	09 17							10 17					
Liverpool Lime Street a		00 15														09 56	
d								08 15		08 38					09 38		
Liverpool South Parkway d																	
Runcorn d								08 35		08 54					09 54		
Warrington Bank Quay a											09 21						
d											09 22						
Hartford d																	
Manchester Piccadilly d						08 05	08 20		08 27				09 20	09 27			
Stockport d						08 14	08 28		08 36				09 27	09 36			
Wilmslow d						08 22			08 43								
Holyhead d																	
Bangor (Gwynedd) d																	
Llandudno Junction d																	
Wrexham General d																	
Chester d																	
Crewe a						08 39		08 52	09 01	09 11	09 41				10 12		
d						08 43		08 53	09 05	09 13	09 43				10 14		10 20
Macclesfield d							08 42						09 40	09 49			
Congleton d																	
Stoke-on-Trent d							08 59						09 57	10 07			
Stafford a						09 01			09 25	09 31				10 26	10 32		10 41
d						09 02			09 26	09 32				10 27	10 33		10 41
Penkridge a																	10 48
Wolverhampton a									09 40					10 42			11 00
Birmingham New Street a									09 58					10 59			11 17
Birmingham International a									10 13					11 13			
Coventry a									10 24					11 24			
Lichfield Trent Valley a																	
Tamworth Low Level a																	
Nuneaton a										09 54					10 55		
Rugby a											10 31						
Milton Keynes Central a								10 17			11 06		11 16		11 46		
Watford Junction a						10s35	10s41			11s16	11s43						
London Euston a						10 57	11 02	11 06		11 37	12 05		12 08		12 32		

A from Birmingham New Street; to Birmingham New Street

b Stops to pick up only

OVERNIGHT SLEEPERS. For sleeper trains, operated by First ScotRail, please refer to Tables 400 - 404

Sundays
from 1 April

Scotland and North West England - West Midlands and London

Route Diagram - see first Page of Table 65

	LM	VT	TP	VT	VT	XC	VT	VT	TP	TP	VT	TP	VT	VT	VT	XC	VT	TP	LM
	1	◇1	◇1	◇1	◇1	◇1	◇1	◇1		◇1	◇1	◇1	◇1	◇1	◇1	◇1	◇1	◇1	◇1
						A										A			
Inverness d																			
Aberdeen d																			
Dundee d																			
Perth d																			
Edinburgh d																			
Haymarket d																			
Glasgow Central d																			
Motherwell d																			
Carstairs d																			
Lockerbie d																			
Carlisle a																			
d																			
Penrith North Lakes d																			
Windermere d																			
Oxenholme Lake District a																			
d																			
Barrow-in-Furness d																			
Lancaster a																			
d									10 45										
Blackpool North d			09 44									10 44							
Preston a			10 08						11 35			11 08							
Preston d		10 00	10 10		10 17					10 47	10 58	11 10			11 17			11 47	
Wigan North Western a		10 10			10 28						11 09				11 28				
d		10 11			10 28						11 09				11 28				
Blackrod d																			
Lostock d																			
Bolton a			10 34							11 08		11 34						12 08	
Manchester Piccadilly a			10 56							11 27		11 56						12 27	
Manchester Airport a			11 17							11 47		12 17						12 47	
Liverpool Lime Street a																			
d								10 38											11 34
Liverpool South Parkway d																			11 44
Runcorn d								10 54											11 52
Warrington Bank Quay a		10 21			10 39						11 20				11 39				
d		10 22			10 39						11 20				11 39				
Hartford d																			12 03
Manchester Piccadilly d				10 20		10 27	10 35						11 15			11 27	11 35		
Stockport d				10 29		10 36	10 42						11 23			11 36	11 43		
Wilmslow d				10 36															
Holyhead d																			
Bangor (Gwynedd) d																			
Llandudno Junction d																			
Wrexham General d																			
Chester d														11 28					
Crewe a		10 41		10 53	10 59			11 12						11 47	11 59				12 20
d	10 38	10 43		10 55	11 01			11 14						11 49	12 01				12 22
Macclesfield d						10 49	10 55									11 49	11 56		
Congleton d																			
Stoke-on-Trent d	10 59					11 07	11 12						11 51			12 07	12 13		
Stafford a	11 17					11 27		11 34								12 24			12 41
d						11 28		11 36								12 25			12 42
Penkridge a																			→
Wolverhampton a					11 31	11 41									12 32	12 40			
Birmingham New Street a					11 55	12 00									12 55	12 58			
Birmingham International a						12 13										13 13			
Coventry a						12 24										13 24			
Lichfield Trent Valley a																			
Tamworth Low Level a																			
Nuneaton a								11 58						12 31					
Rugby a		11 31																	
Milton Keynes Central a		12 06					12 20						12 50	13 03					
Watford Junction a				12s35				12s50											
London Euston a		12 45		12 56			12 59	13 11			13 21		13 28	13 44			13 47		

A from Birmingham New Street; to Birmingham New Street

OVERNIGHT SLEEPERS. For sleeper trains, operated by First ScotRail, please refer to Tables 400 - 404

Table 65

Sundays
from 1 April

Scotland and North West England - West Midlands and London

Route Diagram - see first Page of Table 65

		VT		LM	VT	VT	TP		VT	VT	VT	TP			XC	VT	LM	VT	LM	VT	VT	TP		XC	VT
		◇1		◇1	◇1	◇1	◇1		◇1	◇1	◇1	◇1			◇1	◇1	◇1	◇1	◇1	◇1	◇1	◇1		◇1	◇1
															A										
		⊏⊐			⊏⊐	⊏⊐	⌶		⊏⊐	⊏⊐	⊏⊐				⊏⊐⌶	⊏⊐		⊏⊐		⊏⊐	⊏⊐			⌶	⊏⊐
Inverness	d																								
Aberdeen	d																								
Dundee	d																								
Perth	d																								
Edinburgh 10	d																								
Haymarket	d																								
Glasgow Central 15	d																				10 34				
Motherwell	d																				10 49				
Carstairs	d																								
Lockerbie	d																								
Carlisle 8	a																				11 44				
	d																				11 46				
Penrith North Lakes	d																				12 00				
Windermere	d																								
Oxenholme Lake District	a																				12 22				
	d																				12 24				
Barrow-in-Furness	d											11 22													
Lancaster 6	a											12 22									12 37				
	d											12 22									12 38				
Blackpool North	d						11 44															12 44			
Preston 8	a						12 08					12 41									12 56	13 08			
Preston 8	d					11 58	12 10				12 17	12 47									12 58	13 10			
Wigan North Western	a					12 09					12 28										13 09				
	d					12 09					12 28										13 09				
Blackrod	d																								
Lostock	d																								
Bolton	a						12 34					13 08										13 34			
Manchester Piccadilly 10 ⇌	a						12 59					13 27										13 56			
Manchester Airport ✈	a						13 17					13 47										14 17			
Liverpool Lime Street 10	a																								
	d	11 48															12 34	12 48							
Liverpool South Parkway ✈	d																12 44								
Runcorn	d	12 04															12 52	13 04							
Warrington Bank Quay	a					12 20					12 39										13 20				
	d					12 20					12 39										13 20				
Hartford	d																13 03								
Manchester Piccadilly 10 ⇌	d				11 55				12 15						12 26	12 35				12 55				13 07	13 15
Stockport	d				12 05				12 23						12 35	12 44				13 05					13 22
Wilmslow	d				12 12															13 12					
Holyhead	d									10 55															
Bangor (Gwynedd)	d									11 22															
Llandudno Junction	d									11 40															
Wrexham General	d																								
Chester	d									12 33															
Crewe 10	a				12 28					12 52	12 59						13 19			13 28					
	d				12 30					12 56	13 01						13 22			13 30					
Macclesfield	d														12 49	12 57									
Congleton	d																								
Stoke-on-Trent	d			←					12 51						13 07	13 14			←					13 43	13 50
Stafford	a	12 35		12 41											13 24		13 42	13 35	13 42						
	d	12 36		12 42											13 25		13 43	13 36	13 43						
Penkridge	a			12 48													→		13 48						
Wolverhampton 7 ⇌	a			12 59							13 31				13 40				13 59					14 13	
Birmingham New Street 12	a			13 16							13 55				13 58				14 15					14 31	
Birmingham International ✈	a														14 13										
Coventry	a														14 24										
Lichfield Trent Valley	a																								
Tamworth Low Level	a																								
Nuneaton	a																								
Rugby	a																								
Milton Keynes Central	a								13 49	14 02															14 49
Watford Junction	a																								
London Euston 15 ⊖	a	14 01			14 09	14 16			14 27	14 43						14 47		15 01		15 09	15 15				15 27

A ⊏⊐ from Birmingham New Street
⌶ to Birmingham New Street

OVERNIGHT SLEEPERS. For sleeper trains, operated by First ScotRail, please refer to Tables 400 - 404

Table 65

Sundays
from 1 April

Scotland and North West England - West Midlands and London

Route Diagram - see first Page of Table 65

		VT	VT	TP	NT	XC	VT	EM				LM	VT	LM	VT	VT	TP	XC		VT	VT	VT	TP	XC	VT
		◇1	◇1	◇1		◇1	◇1	◇				◇1	◇1	◇1	◇1	◇1	◇1	◇1		◇1	◇1	◇1	◇1	◇1	◇1
						A																		A	
		⊏⊐	⊏⊐			⊏⊐⌶	⊏⊐						⊏⊐		⊏⊐	⊏⊐		⌶		⊏⊐	⊏⊐	⊏⊐	⌶	⊏⊐⌶	⊏⊐
Inverness	d																								
Aberdeen	d																								
Dundee	d																								
Perth	d																								
Edinburgh 10	d		10 52																				12 10		
Haymarket	d		10 57																				12u14		
Glasgow Central 15	d															11 36						11 58			
Motherwell	d																								
Carstairs	d																								
Lockerbie	d																						13 08		
Carlisle 8	a		12 05													12 47						13 09	13 29		
	d		12 07													12 49						13 10	13 29		
Penrith North Lakes	d																						13 45		
Windermere	d																								
Oxenholme Lake District	a		12 41													13 22							14 09		
	d		12 43													13 23							14 10		
Barrow-in-Furness	d			12 34	13 10																				
Lancaster 6	a		12 56	13 26	14 15											13 37						13 56	14 26		
	d		12 57	13 26												13 38						13 58	14 26		
Blackpool North	d																13 44								
Preston 8	a		13 15	13 45												13 56	14 08					14 15	14 45		
Preston 8	d		13 17	13 47												13 58	14 10					14 17	14 47		
Wigan North Western	a		13 28													14 09						14 28			
	d		13 28													14 09						14 28			
Blackrod	d																								
Lostock	d																								
Bolton	a			14 08													14 34						15 08		
Manchester Piccadilly 10 ⇌	a			14 27													14 56						15 27		
Manchester Airport ✈	a			14 47													15 17						15 47		
Liverpool Lime Street 10	a																								
	d							12 52				13 34	13 48												
Liverpool South Parkway ✈	d							13 03				13 44													
Runcorn	d											13 52	14 04												
Warrington Bank Quay	a		13 39													14 20						14 39			
	d		13 39													14 20						14 39			
Hartford	d											14 03													
Manchester Piccadilly 10 ⇌	d					13 27	13 35	13 44							13 55			14 07		14 15				14 27	14 35
Stockport	d					13 36	13 42	13a53							14 04					14 22				14 36	14 42
Wilmslow	d														14 11										
Holyhead	d	11 50																			12 50				
Bangor (Gwynedd)	d	12 17																			13 18				
Llandudno Junction	d	12 35																			13 36				
Wrexham General	d																								
Chester	d	13 30																			14 33				
Crewe 10	a	13 50	13 59									14 18			14 27						14 52	14 59			
	d	13 51	14 01									14 22			14 29						14 54	15 01			
Macclesfield	d					13 49	13 55																	14 49	14 55
Congleton	d																								
Stoke-on-Trent	d					14 07	14 12							←				14 43		14 50				15 07	15 12
Stafford	a					14 24						14 42	14 35	14 42										15 24	
	d					14 25						14 43	14 36	14 43										15 25	
Penkridge	a											→		14 48											
Wolverhampton 7 ⇌	a		14 32			14 40								14 59				15 13				15 31		15 40	
Birmingham New Street 12	a		14 55			14 58								15 15				15 31				15 55		15 58	
Birmingham International ✈	a					15 13																		16 13	
Coventry	a					15 24																		16 24	
Lichfield Trent Valley	a																								
Tamworth Low Level	a																								
Nuneaton	a	14 31																							
Rugby	a																								
Milton Keynes Central	a	15 04																		15 49	16 04				
Watford Junction	a																								
London Euston 15 ⊖	a	15 45					15 47						16 01		16 09	16 15				16 27	16 44				16 47

A ⊏⊐ from Birmingham New Street
⌶ to Birmingham New Street

OVERNIGHT SLEEPERS. For sleeper trains, operated by First ScotRail, please refer to Tables 400 - 404

Table 65

Sundays
from 1 April

Scotland and North West England - West Midlands and London

Route Diagram - see first Page of Table 65

		EM	LM	VT	LM	VT	VT	TP	XC	VT	VT	VT	TP	XC	VT	EM	LM	VT
		◇	◇■	◇■	◇■	◇■	◇■	◇■	◇■	◇■	◇■	◇■	◇■	◇■	◇■	◇	◇■	◇■
														A				
				🍽		🍽	🍽		🛒	🍽	🍽	🍽		🍽🛒	🍽			🍽
Inverness	d																	
Aberdeen	d																	
Dundee	d																	
Perth	d																	
Edinburgh [10]	d											12 52						
Haymarket	d											12 56						
Glasgow Central [15]	d						12 42											
Motherwell	d																	
Carstairs	d																	
Lockerbie	d																	
Carlisle [8]	a						13 51					14 05						
	d						13 54					14 07						
Penrith North Lakes	d											14 22						
Windermere	d																	
Oxenholme Lake District	a						14 27											
	d						14 28											
Barrow-in-Furness	d												14 25					
Lancaster [6]	a						14 42					14 56	15 26					
	d						14 43					14 57	15 26					
Blackpool North	d							14 44										
Preston [8]	a						15 01	15 08				15 15	15 45					
Preston [8]	d						15 03	15 10				15 17	15 47					
Wigan North Western	a						15 14					15 28						
	d						15 14					15 28						
Blackrod	d																	
Lostock	d																	
Bolton	a							15 34					16 08					
Manchester Piccadilly [10]	a							15 56					16 27					
Manchester Airport ✈	a							16 17					16 46					
Liverpool Lime Street [10]	a																	
	d	13 52	14 34	14 48												14 52	15 34	15 48
Liverpool South Parkway ✈	d	14 03	14 44													15 03	15 44	
Runcorn	d		14 52	15 04													15 52	16 04
Warrington Bank Quay	a						15 25					15 39						
	d						15 25					15 39						
Hartford	d		15 03														16 03	
Manchester Piccadilly [10]	d	14 44				14 55			15 07	15 15				15 27	15 35	15 44		
Stockport	d	14a53				15 04				15 22				15 36	15 42	15a53		
Wilmslow	d					15 11												
Holyhead	d										13 55							
Bangor (Gwynedd)	d										14 22							
Llandudno Junction	d										14 40							
Wrexham General	d																	
Chester	d										15 33							
Crewe [10]	a		15 20			15 27					15 52	15 59					16 18	
	d		15 22			15 29					15 54	16 01					16 22	
Macclesfield	d													15 49	15 55			
Congleton	d																	
Stoke-on-Trent	d				←				15 43	15 50				16 07	16 12			
Stafford	a		15 42	15 35	15 42									16 24			16 42	16 36
	d		15 43	15 36	15 43									16 25			16 43	16 37
Penkridge	a		→		15 48												→	
Wolverhampton [7]	a				15 59				16 13			16 32		16 40				
Birmingham New Street [12]	a				16 15				16 31			16 55		16 58				
Birmingham International ✈	a													17 13				
Coventry	a													17 24				
Lichfield Trent Valley	a																	
Tamworth Low Level	a																	
Nuneaton	a																	
Rugby	a																	
Milton Keynes Central	a									16 49	17 03							
Watford Junction	a																	
London Euston [15] ⊖	a			17 01		17 09	17 20			17 27	17 44				17 47			18 01

A 🍽 from Birmingham New Street
🛒 to Birmingham New Street

OVERNIGHT SLEEPERS. For sleeper trains, operated by First ScotRail, please refer to Tables 400 - 404

Table 65

Sundays
from 1 April

Scotland and North West England - West Midlands and London

Route Diagram - see first Page of Table 65

		LM	VT	VT	TP	XC	VT	VT	VT	TP	XC	VT	EM	LM	VT	LM	VT	VT	TP	XC	VT
		◇■	◇■	◇■	◇■	◇■	◇■	◇■	◇■	◇■	◇■	◇■	◇	◇■	◇■	◇■	◇■	◇■	◇■	◇■	◇■
											A										
			🍽	🍽		🛒	🍽	🍽	🍽	🛒	🍽🛒	🍽			🍽		🍽	🍽		🛒	🍽
Inverness	d																				
Aberdeen	d																				
Dundee	d																				
Perth	d																				
Edinburgh [10]	d									14 10											
Haymarket	d									14u14											
Glasgow Central [15]	d			13 36					13 55									14 36			
Motherwell	d																				
Carstairs	d																				
Lockerbie	d									15 08											
Carlisle [8]	a			14 46					15 09	15 29								15 46			
	d			14 49					15 11	15 29								15 49			
Penrith North Lakes	d									15 45											
Windermere	d																				
Oxenholme Lake District	a			15 22					15 46	16 09								16 22			
	d			15 23					15 46	16 10								16 23			
Barrow-in-Furness	d																				
Lancaster [6]	a			15 37						16 26								16 37			
	d			15 38						16 26								16 38			
Blackpool North	d				15 44														16 44		
Preston [8]	a			15 56	16 08				16 15	16 46								16 56	17 08		
Preston [8]	d			15 58	16 10				16 17	16 47								16 58	17 10		
Wigan North Western	a			16 09					16 28									17 09			
	d			16 09					16 28									17 09			
Blackrod	d																				
Lostock	d																				
Bolton	a				16 34					17 08									17 34		
Manchester Piccadilly [10]	a				16 56					17 27									17 56		
Manchester Airport ✈	a				17 17					17 47									18 17		
Liverpool Lime Street [10]	a																				
	d							16 18					15 52	16 34	16 48						
Liverpool South Parkway ✈	d												16 03	16 44							
Runcorn	d							16 34						16 52	17 04						
Warrington Bank Quay	a			16 20					16 39									17 20			
	d			16 20					16 39									17 20			
Hartford	d													17 03							
Manchester Piccadilly [10]	d		15 55			16 07	16 15				16 27	16 35	16 44				16 55			17 07	17 15
Stockport	d		16 04				16 23				16 36	16 42	16a53				17 04				17 22
Wilmslow	d		16 11														17 11				
Holyhead	d																				
Bangor (Gwynedd)	d																				
Llandudno Junction	d																				
Wrexham General	d																				
Chester	d																				
Crewe [10]	a		16 27					16 51	16 58					17 18			17 27				
	d		16 29					16 54	17 00					17 22			17 29				
Macclesfield	d										16 49	16 55									
Congleton	d																				
Stoke-on-Trent	d	←				16 43	16 50				17 08	17 12				←				17 43	17 50
Stafford	a	16 42									17 25			17 42	17 35	17 42					
	d	16 43									17 26			17 43	17 36	17 43					
Penkridge	a	16 48												→		17 48					
Wolverhampton [7]	a	16 59				17 13			17 31		17 40					17 59				18 13	
Birmingham New Street [12]	a	17 15				17 31			17 56		17 58					18 15				18 31	
Birmingham International ✈	a										18 13										
Coventry	a										18 24										
Lichfield Trent Valley	a							17 26													
Tamworth Low Level	a																				
Nuneaton	a																				
Rugby	a																				
Milton Keynes Central	a						17 49	18 04													18 49
Watford Junction	a																				
London Euston [15] ⊖	a		18 09	18 15			18 27	18 44				18 47			19 01		19 09	19 15			19 27

A 🍽 from Birmingham New Street
🛒 to Birmingham New Street

OVERNIGHT SLEEPERS. For sleeper trains, operated by First ScotRail, please refer to Tables 400 - 404

Table 65

Sundays
from 1 April

Scotland and North West England - West Midlands and London

Route Diagram - see first Page of Table 65

		VT	VT	TP	XC	VT	EM	LM	VT	LM	VT	VT	TP	XC	VT	VT	VT	TP	NT	XC	VT
		◇1	◇1	◇1	◇1	◇1	◇	◇1	◇1	◇1	◇1	◇1	◇1	◇1	◇1	◇1	◇1	◇1		◇1	◇1
					A															A	
		⊡	⊡	⌶	⊡⌶	⊡			⊡		⊡	⊡		⌶	⊡	⊡	⊡	⌶	⌶	⊡⌶	⊡
Inverness	d																				
Aberdeen	d																				
Dundee	d																				
Perth	d																				
Edinburgh [10]	d		14 52															16 10			
Haymarket	d		14 57															16u14			
Glasgow Central [15]	d			15 06								15 36					15 57				
Motherwell	d																				
Carstairs	d																				
Lockerbie	d			16 06														17 08			
Carlisle [8]	a		16 05	16 26								16 46					17 08	17 29			
	d		16 07	16 26								16 49					17 09	17 29	17 41		
Penrith North Lakes	d		16 22	16 42								17 03						17 45			
Windermere	d																				
Oxenholme Lake District	a			17 07													17 44	18 09			
	d			17 07													17 44	18 10			
Barrow-in-Furness	d																				
Lancaster [6]	a		16 56	17 22								17 37						18 26			
	d		16 57	17 22								17 38						18 26			
Blackpool North	d												17 44								
Preston [8]	a		17 15	17 41								17 56	18 08				18 13	18 45	20 47		
Preston [8]	d		17 17	17 47								17 58	18 10				18 17	18 47			
Wigan North Western	a		17 28									18 09					18 28				
	d		17 28									18 09					18 28				
Blackrod	d																				
Lostock	d																				
Bolton	a			18 08									18 34					19 08			
Manchester Piccadilly [10]	a			18 27									18 56					19 27			
Manchester Airport	a			18 45									19 17					19 47			
Liverpool Lime Street [10]	a																				
	d						16 52	17 34	17 48												
Liverpool South Parkway	d						17 03	17 44													
Runcorn	d							17 52	18 04												
Warrington Bank Quay	a		17 39									18 20					18 39				
	d		17 39									18 20					18 39				
Hartford	d							18 03													
Manchester Piccadilly [10]	d				17 27	17 35	17 44				17 55			18 07	18 15					18 27	18 35
Stockport	d				17 36	17 42	17a53				18 04				18 22					18 36	18 42
Wilmslow	d										18 11										
Holyhead	d																				
Bangor (Gwynedd)	d																				
Llandudno Junction	d																				
Wrexham General	d																				
Chester	d	17 35														18 35					
Crewe [10]	a	17 53	17 59					18 20			18 27					18 53	18 59				
	d	17 55	18 01					18 22			18 29					18 55	19 01				
Macclesfield	d				17 49	17 55														18 49	18 55
Congleton	d																				
Stoke-on-Trent	d				18 08	18 12				←				18 43	18 50					19 07	19 12
Stafford	a				18 25			18 42	18 35	18 42										19 24	
	d				18 26			18 43	18 36	18 43										19 25	
Penkridge	a							→		18 48											
Wolverhampton [7]	a		18 32		18 40					18 59				19 13			19 31			19 40	
Birmingham New Street [12]	a		18 55		18 58					19 15				19 31			19 55			19 58	
Birmingham International	a				19 13															20 13	
Coventry	a				19 24															20 24	
Lichfield Trent Valley	a																				
Tamworth Low Level	a																				
Nuneaton	a																				
Rugby	a																				
Milton Keynes Central	a	19 02													19 49	20 03					
Watford Junction	a																				
London Euston [15] ⊖	a	19 43				19 47			20 01		20 09	20 15			20 27	20 44					20 47

A ⊡ from Birmingham New Street
⌶ to Birmingham New Street

OVERNIGHT SLEEPERS. For sleeper trains, operated by First ScotRail, please refer to Tables 400 - 404

Table 65

Sundays
from 1 April

Scotland and North West England - West Midlands and London

Route Diagram - see first Page of Table 65

		EM	LM	VT	LM	VT	VT	TP	XC	VT	TP	TP	VT	XC	VT	EM	LM	VT
		◇	◇1	◇1	◇1	◇1	◇1	◇1	◇1	◇1	◇1	◇1	◇1	◇1	◇1	◇	◇1	◇1
														A				
				⊡		⊡	⊡		⌶	⊡		⌶	⊡	⌶	⊡			⊡
Inverness	d																	
Aberdeen	d																	
Dundee	d																	
Perth	d																	
Edinburgh [10]	d									16 52								
Haymarket	d									16 56								
Glasgow Central [15]	d						16 40					17 06						
Motherwell	d						16 54											
Carstairs	d																	
Lockerbie	d																	
Carlisle [8]	a						17 49			18 05		18 25						
	d						17 51			18 07		18 26						
Penrith North Lakes	d						18 05					18 42						
Windermere	d																	
Oxenholme Lake District	a						18 27			18 41		19 07						
	d						18 28			18 42		19 07						
Barrow-in-Furness	d										18 17							
Lancaster [6]	a						18 42			18 56	19 17	19 22						
	d						18 43			18 57	19 17	19 22						
Blackpool North	d							18 44										
Preston [8]	a						19 01	19 08		19 15	19 37	19 41						
Preston [8]	d						19 03	19 10		19 17		19 47						
Wigan North Western	a						19 14			19 28								
	d						19 14			19 28								
Blackrod	d																	
Lostock	d																	
Bolton	a							19 34				20 08						
Manchester Piccadilly [10]	a							19 56				20 27						
Manchester Airport	a							20 17				20 45						
Liverpool Lime Street [10]	a																	
	d	17 52	18 34	18 48												18 52	19 34	19 48
Liverpool South Parkway	d	18 03	18 44													19 03	19 44	
Runcorn	d		18 52	19 04													19 52	20 04
Warrington Bank Quay	a						19 25			19 39								
	d						19 25			19 39								
Hartford	d		19 03														20 03	
Manchester Piccadilly [10]	d	18 44				18 55			19 07				19 15	19 27	19 35	19 44		
Stockport	d	18a53				19 04							19 22	19 36	19 41	19a53		
Wilmslow	d					19 11												
Holyhead	d																	
Bangor (Gwynedd)	d																	
Llandudno Junction	d																	
Wrexham General	d																	
Chester	d																	
Crewe [10]	a		19 20			19 27				19 59							20 16	20 22
	d		19 22			19 29				20 01							20 18	20 24
Macclesfield	d													19 49	19 54			
Congleton	d																	
Stoke-on-Trent	d				←				19 43				19 50	20 07	20 11			
Stafford	a		19 42	19 35	19 42									20 26			20 38	20 41
	d		19 43	19 36	19 43									20 27			20 39	20 43
Penkridge	a		→		19 48												20 44	
Wolverhampton [7]	a				19 59				20 13	20 32				20 39			20 55	
Birmingham New Street [12]	a				20 15				20 31	20 50				20 58			21 15	
Birmingham International	a													21 13				
Coventry	a													21 23				
Lichfield Trent Valley	a																	
Tamworth Low Level	a																	
Nuneaton	a																	
Rugby	a																	
Milton Keynes Central	a												20 46					21 36
Watford Junction	a																	
London Euston [15] ⊖	a			21 01		21 09	21 21						21 31		21 58			22 27

A ⌶ to Birmingham New Street

OVERNIGHT SLEEPERS. For sleeper trains, operated by First ScotRail, please refer to Tables 400 - 404

Sundays
from 1 April

Scotland and North West England - West Midlands and London

Route Diagram - see first Page of Table 65

		VT	TP	TP	NT	XC	AW	VT	EM	LM	VT	VT	VT	TP	TP	XC	VT	TP	VT	LM
		◇1	◇1	◇1		◇1	◇	◇1	◇	◇1	◇1	◇1	◇1	◇1	◇1	◇1	◇1	◇1	◇1	◇1
Inverness	d																			
Aberdeen	d																			
Dundee	d																			
Perth	d																			
Edinburgh 10	d			18 10													18 52	19 57		
Haymarket	d			18u14													18 57	20u01		
Glasgow Central 15	d	17 36											18 30						20 08	
Motherwell	d																			
Carstairs	d																			
Lockerbie	d	18 32		19 08															21 02	
Carlisle 8	a	18 50		19 29									19 43				20 05	21 13	21 21	
	d	18 52		19 29									19 44				20 07	21 14	21 24	
Penrith North Lakes	d	19 06		19 45													20 22		21 39	
Windermere	d													20 40						
Oxenholme Lake District	a	19 28		20 09									20 19	20 59					22 02	
	d	19 29		20 10									20 19	21 01					22 03	
Barrow-in-Furness	d				20 02															
Lancaster 6	a	19 43		20 26	21 07								20 34	21 18			20 56	22 03	22 17	
	d	19 44		20 26									20 34				20 57	22 03	22 18	
Blackpool North	d		19 44												20 44					
Preston 8	a	20 02	20 08	20 45									20 52		21 08		21 15	22 23	22 35	
Preston 8	d	20 04	20 10	20 47									20 55		21 10		21 17	22 29	22 38	
Wigan North Western	a	20 15											21 06				21 28		22 49	
	d	20 15											21 07				21 28		22 50	
Blackrod	d																			
Lostock	d																			
Bolton	a		20 34	21 08											21 34			22 50		
Manchester Piccadilly 10	a		20 56	21 27											21 56			23 14		
Manchester Airport	a		21 16	21 46											22 17			23 30		
Liverpool Lime Street 10	a																			
	d								19 52	20 34		20 48								21 34
Liverpool South Parkway	d								20 03	20 44										21 44
Runcorn	d									20 52		21 04								21 52
Warrington Bank Quay	a	20 26											21 18				21 39		23 00	
	d	20 26											21 18				21 39		23 01	
Hartford	d									21 03										22 03
Manchester Piccadilly 10	d					20 07		20 20	20 44		20 55					21 07				
Stockport	d					20 16		20 27	20a53		21 03					21 16				
Wilmslow	d																			
Holyhead	d						18 25													
Bangor (Gwynedd)	d						19 04													
Llandudno Junction	d						19 24													
Wrexham General	d																			
Chester	d						20 27													
Crewe 10	a	20 45					20 48			21 16		21 21	21 38				21 59		23 20	22 18
	d	20 47					20 52			21 18		21 23	21 40				22 01			22 22
Macclesfield	d					20 29		20 40			21 15					21 29				
Congleton	d																			
Stoke-on-Trent	d					20 47		20 57			21 33					21 47				
Stafford	a					21 08	21 16			21 38		21 42	22 01			22 06				22 42
	d					21 09	21 16			21 39		21 43	22 02			22 06				22 45
Penkridge	a									21 44										22 50
Wolverhampton 7	a					21 21	21 34			21 55			22 17			22 20	22 31			23 01
Birmingham New Street 12	a					21 39	21 52			22 15			22 38			22 39	22 55			23 17
Birmingham International	a						22 09													
Coventry	a																			
Lichfield Trent Valley	a											21 59								
Tamworth Low Level	a											22 05								
Nuneaton	a											22 17								
Rugby	a											22 31								
Milton Keynes Central	a	21 55						22 03			22 46	23 04								
Watford Junction	a	22s31									23s25	23s34								
London Euston 15	a	22 53						22 56			23 49	23 54								

OVERNIGHT SLEEPERS. For sleeper trains, operated by First ScotRail, please refer to Tables 400 - 404

Table 65

Sundays
from 1 April

Scotland and North West England - West Midlands and London

Route Diagram - see first Page of Table 65

		XC	EM	TP	SR	SR
					B	B
		◇1	◇	◇1		
Inverness	d					20 25
Aberdeen	d					
Dundee	d					
Perth	d					23u00
Edinburgh 10	d					01 06
Haymarket	d					
Glasgow Central 15	d				23 15	
Motherwell	d				23u31	
Carstairs	d				23u47	
Lockerbie	d					
Carlisle 8	a					02 51
	d				01u12	02 53
Penrith North Lakes	d					
Windermere	d					
Oxenholme Lake District	a					
	d					
Barrow-in-Furness	d					
Lancaster 6	a					
	d					
Blackpool North	d			23 03		
Preston 8	a			23 28		04s41
Preston 8	d			23 28		
Wigan North Western	a					
	d					
Blackrod	d			23 50		
Lostock	d			23 57		
Bolton	a			00 02		
Manchester Piccadilly 10	a			00 18		
Manchester Airport	a			00 32		
Liverpool Lime Street 10	a					
	d		21 21			
Liverpool South Parkway	d		21 31			
Runcorn	d					
Warrington Bank Quay	a				03 34	
	d				03 36	
Hartford	d					
Manchester Piccadilly 10	d	22 07	22 11			
Stockport	d	22 16	22a20			
Wilmslow	d					
Holyhead	d					
Bangor (Gwynedd)	d					
Llandudno Junction	d					
Wrexham General	d					
Chester	d					
Crewe 10	a					05s37
	d					
Macclesfield	d	22 29				
Congleton	d					
Stoke-on-Trent	d	22 47				
Stafford	a	23 04				
	d	23 05				
Penkridge	a					
Wolverhampton 7	a	23 18				
Birmingham New Street 12	a	23 36				
Birmingham International	a					
Coventry	a					
Lichfield Trent Valley	a					
Tamworth Low Level	a					
Nuneaton	a					
Rugby	a					
Milton Keynes Central	a					
Watford Junction	a				06s23	
London Euston 15	a				06 46	07 47

OVERNIGHT SLEEPERS. For sleeper trains, operated by First ScotRail, please refer to Tables 400 - 404

London - Watford Junction, Milton Keynes Central, Northampton and West Midlands

Network Diagram - see first Page of Table 59

Miles	Miles	Miles			LM	LM	VT	LM	VT	VT	LM	LM	LM	VT	VT	LM	LM	LM	LM	LM	LM	LM	SN
					MO	MX	MO	MO	MO	MX	MX	MO	MX	MO	MX	MO	MX		MO	MX	MO	MX	
					◇1	1	◇1	1	◇1	◇1	1	◇1	1	◇1	◇1	◇1	1	1	1	1	1	1	1
							(restaurant)		(restaurant)	(restaurant)				(restaurant)	(restaurant)								
0	0	—	**London Euston** 15 ⊖	d	21p28	21p46	21p55	22p00	22p25	22p30	22p54	22p58	23p24	23p25	23p30	23p34	23p34	00 04	00 34	00 34	01 34	01 34	
—	—	0	East Croydon	d																			
—	—	—	Clapham Junction	d																			05 03
—	—	8¾	Imperial Wharf	d																			05 07
—	—	9¼	West Brompton ⊖	d																			05 10
—	—	11¼	Kensington (Olympia) ⊖	d																			05 14
—	—	12½	Shepherd's Bush	d																			05 17
8	—	16¾	Wembley Central ⊖	d															00 43	00 45	01 45	01 45	
11½	11½	—	Harrow & Wealdstone ⊖	d	21p40			22p12				23p10				23p46	23p46	00 16	00 48	00 50	01 50	01 50	05 33
16	—	—	Bushey	d													23p51			00 55			
17½	17½	—	**Watford Junction**	a	21p46			22p18			23p09	23p16	23p39			23p52	23p54	00 22	00 54	00 57	01 56	01 56	05 40
—	—	—		d	21p46		22b09	22p19	22b39	22b45	23p10	23p17	23p40	23b39		23p53	23p54	00 23	00 58	00 58	01 57	01 57	
21	—	—	Kings Langley	d	21p51						23p14	23p21				23p57	23p59		01 02	01 02			
23	—	—	Apsley	d	21p55						23p18	23p25				00 01	00 02		01 06	01 06			
24½	—	—	Hemel Hempstead	d	21p57			22p26			23p21	23p28	23p47			00 04	00 05	00 30	01 09	01 09	02 04	02 04	
28	—	—	Berkhamsted	d	22p02			22p31			23p26	23p33	23p52			00 09	00 09	00 35	01 14	01 14	02 09	02 09	
31¾	—	—	Tring	d				22p35			23p33	23p37				00 13	00 15	00 41	01 18	01 19	02 13	02 14	
36	—	—	Cheddington	d				22p41				23p43				00 19	00 20		01 24	01 25			
40¼	—	—	Leighton Buzzard	d	22p15	22p18		22p47			23p40	23p49	00 05			00 25	00 26	00 50	01 30	01 31	02 22	02 23	
46¾	—	—	Bletchley	d	22p22			22p54			23p47	23p56	00 13			00 32	00 33	00 57	01 37	01 38	02 29	02 30	
49¾	49¾	—	**Milton Keynes Central** 10	a	22p30	22p32	22p42	23p02	23p11	23p28	23p55	00 04	00 21	00 11	00 27	00 40	00 41	01 05	01 45	01 46	02 37	02 38	
—	—	—		d	22p31	22p32	22p44	23p03	23p12	23p29	23p55	00 05	00 21	00 12	00 28	00 41		01 05	01 46	01 47			
52½	52½	—	Wolverton	d	22p34	22p36		23p06			23p59	00 08	00 25			00 44		01 09	01 49	01 50			
65¾	—	—	**Northampton**	a	22p48	22p49		23p20			00 13	00 22	00 38			00 58		01 22	02 03	02 04			
84½	82½	—	**Rugby**	a	23p13	23p17	23p20	23p54	23p46	23p58				00s46	01 00								
—	—	—	Nuneaton	a																			
96	—	—	Coventry	a	23p25	23p29	23p31	00 05	23p57	00 10				00s58	01 13								
106¾	—	—	Birmingham International ✈	a	23p52	23p47	23p42		00 08	00 21				01s09	01 24								
115¼	—	—	**Birmingham New Street** 12	a	00 04	00 04	23p54		00 21	00 32				01s22	01 36								
120½	—	—	Sandwell & Dudley	a																			
128	—	—	Wolverhampton 7	a			00 15		00 43	01 03				01 53	02 07								

		LM	VT	LM	VT	SN	VT	LM	SN	VT	VT	LM	LM	VT	VT	LM	VT	SN	VT	LM	VT	LM	VT
		◇1	◇1	1	◇1	1	◇1	1	1	◇1	◇1	◇1	1	◇1	◇1	1	◇1	1	◇1	1	◇1	1	◇1
			(☒)		(☒)		(☒)			(☒)	(☒)			(☒)	(☒)		(☒)		(☒)		(☒)		(☒)
London Euston 15 ⊖	d		05 27	05 30	05 39		06 03	06 04		06 17	06 23	06 24	06 34	06 36	06 43	06 53	06 55		07 03	07 04	07 10	07 13	07 20
East Croydon	d																						
Clapham Junction	d					05 30			05 55									06 38					
Imperial Wharf	d					05 39			06 00									06 42					
West Brompton ⊖	d					05 41			06 03									06 45					
Kensington (Olympia) ⊖	d					05 44			06 07									06 49					
Shepherd's Bush	d					05 47			06 10									06 52					
Wembley Central ⊖	d					06s00			06 24									07s07					
Harrow & Wealdstone ⊖	d			05 43		06 07		06 16	06 29				06 47					07 12		07 17			
Bushey	d																						
Watford Junction	a			05 50		06 14		06 22	06 36			06 39	06 53			07 08		07 19		07 24			
	d		05u45	05 50	06u02	06 14		06 23			06u37	06 41	06 54			07 10		07 19		07 24			
Kings Langley	d			05 55				06 27					06 58							07 29			
Apsley	d			05 59				06 31					07 02							07 32			
Hemel Hempstead	d			06 01		06 22		06 34				06 48	07 05			07 17		07 27		07 35			
Berkhamsted	d			06 06		06 26		06 39				06 53	07 10			07 22		07 32		07 40			
Tring	d			06 13		06 33		06a46				06 59	07 16					07 39		07a47			
Cheddington	d			06 18								07 05	07 21										
Leighton Buzzard	d			06 23		06 42						07 10	07 26			07 35		07 51				07 42	
Bletchley	d	05 17		06 30		06 49						07 17	07 33			07 43		07 58				07 50	
Milton Keynes Central 10	a	05 21	06 09	06 35	06 22	06 55				06 47		07 22	07 38		07 13	07 48	07 25	08 03			07 40	07 54	07 50
	d	05 21	06 10	06 36	06 22							07 22			07 13	07 48						07 54	
Wolverton	d	05 25		06 39								07 26				07 52						07 58	
Northampton	a	05 37		06 52								07 38				08 05						08 11	
Rugby	a	06 02		07 17	06 44		06 51					08 04							07 51			08 38	
Nuneaton	a	06 16	06 38									08 17											
Coventry	a			07 29			07 02				07 22				07 42				08 02			08 49	
Birmingham International ✈	a			07 45			07 13				07 33				07 53				08 12			09 04	
Birmingham New Street 12	a			08 03			07 27				07 45				08 08				08 27			09 16	
Sandwell & Dudley	a										07 57												
Wolverhampton 7	a										08 11												

b Previous night, stops to pick up only

Table 66

Mondays to Fridays

until 30 March

London - Watford Junction, Milton Keynes Central, Northampton and West Midlands

Network Diagram - see first Page of Table 59

		VT ◇1 ⊠	LM 1	LM 1	VT ◇1 ⊠		VT ◇1 ⊠	LM ◇1	LM 1	SN 1	VT ◇1 ⊠	LM 1	VT ◇1 ⊠	LM 1	VT ◇1 ⊠		VT ◇1 ⊠	LM 1	LM 1	VT ◇1 ⊠	LM ◇1		LM 1	SN 1	VT ◇1 ⊠
London Euston 15 ⊖	d	07 23	07 24	07 34	07 35		07 43	07 47	07 54		08 03	08 05	08 10	08 13	08 20		08 23	08 24	08 34	08 43	08 46		08 54		09 03
East Croydon	d																							08 07	
Clapham Junction	d									07 39														08 39	
Imperial Wharf	d									07 44														08 44	
West Brompton ⊖	d									07 47														08 47	
Kensington (Olympia) ⊖	d									07 50														08 50	
Shepherd's Bush	d									07 53														08 53	
Wembley Central ⊖	d									08s08														09s08	
Harrow & Wealdstone ⊖	d			07 46						08 13		08 21						08 36	08 46					09 13	
Bushey	d											08 26							08 51						
Watford Junction	a		07 40	07 52				08 01	08 11	08 20		08 29						08 43	08 54		09 00		09 09	09 20	
	d	07u37	07 42	07 53				08 02	08 12	08 20		08 29					08u37	08 44	08 55		09 01		09 11	09 20	
Kings Langley	d			07 58								08 34							08 59						
Apsley	d			08 01								08 38							09 03						
Hemel Hempstead	d		07 49	08 04					08 19	08 28		08 40						08 51	09 06				09 18	09 28	
Berkhamsted	d		07 54	08 09					08 24	08 32		08 45						08 56	09 11				09 23	09 32	
Tring	d		08 01	08a16						08 39		08a52						09 02	09a17					09 39	
Cheddington	d		08 06															09 07							
Leighton Buzzard	d		08 11						08 37	08 48				08 42				09 12					09 36	09 48	
Bletchley	d		08 18						08 44	08 55				08 50				09 20					09 43	09 55	
Milton Keynes Central 10	a		08 23		08 05		08 13	08 25	08 49	09 01			08 40	08 54	08 50			09 26		09 13	09 24		09 48	10 01	
	d						08 13	08 31	08 50					08 54						09 13	09 25		09 49		
Wolverton	d								08 53					08 58									09 52		
Northampton	a							08 44	09 07					09 11							09 40		10 05		
Rugby	a							09 04			08 51			09 38							10 04	10 17			09 51
Nuneaton	a							09 16													10 16				
Coventry	a	08 22					08 42				09 02			09 49			09 22			09 42		10 29			10 02
Birmingham International ✈	a	08 33					08 53				09 13			10 04			09 33			09 53		10 45			10 13
Birmingham New Street 12	a	08 45					09 08				09 27			10 16			09 45			10 08		11 01			10 27
Sandwell & Dudley	a	08 57															09 57								
Wolverhampton 7	a	09 11															10 11								

			LM 1	VT ◇1 ⊠	LM 1	VT ◇1 ⊠	VT ◇1 ⊠	LM 1	LM 1	VT ◇1 ☕	LM ◇1		LM 1	SN 1	VT ◇1 ⊠	LM 1	VT ◇1 ⊠	LM 1	VT ◇1 ⊠	VT ◇1 ⊠	LM 1		LM 1	VT ◇1 ⊠	LM ◇1
London Euston 15 ⊖	d		09 05	09 10	09 13	09 20	09 23	09 24	09 34	09 43	09 46		09 54		10 03	10 05	10 10	10 13	10 20	10 23	10 24		10 34	10 43	10 46
East Croydon	d													09 08											
Clapham Junction	d													09 39											
Imperial Wharf	d													09 44											
West Brompton ⊖	d													09 47											
Kensington (Olympia) ⊖	d													09 50											
Shepherd's Bush	d													09 53											
Wembley Central ⊖	d													10s08											
Harrow & Wealdstone ⊖	d		09 17						09 48					10 13		10 17							10 46		
Bushey	d		09 22						09 53							10 22							10 51		
Watford Junction	a		09 25					09 39	09 56		10 00		10 09	10 20		10 25					10 39		10 54		11 00
	d		09 26				09u37	09 41	09 57		10 01		10 11	10 20		10 26				10u37	10 41		10 55		11 01
Kings Langley	d		09 30						10 01							10 30							10 59		
Apsley	d		09 34						10 05							10 34							11 03		
Hemel Hempstead	d		09 37					09 48	10 08				10 18	10 28		10 37					10 48		11 06		
Berkhamsted	d		09 42					09 53	10 13				10 23	10 32		10 42					10 53		11 11		
Tring	d		09a48					09 59	10a19					10 39		10a48					10 59		11a17		
Cheddington	d							10 04													11 04				
Leighton Buzzard	d				09 42			10 09					10 36	10 48				10 42			11 09				
Bletchley	d				09 50			10 16					10 43	10 57				10 50			11 16				
Milton Keynes Central 10	a			09 40	09 54	09 50		10 21		10 13	10 24		10 48	11 02			10 40	10 54	10 50		11 21			11 13	11 24
	d				09 54					10 13	10 25		10 49					10 54						11 13	11 25
Wolverton	d				09 58								10 52					10 58							
Northampton	a				10 11						10 40		11 08					11 11							11 40
Rugby	a				10 38						11 04				10 51			11 38							12 04
Nuneaton	a										11 16														12 16
Coventry	a				10 49		10 22			10 42					11 02			11 49		11 22				11 42	
Birmingham International ✈	a				11 04		10 33			10 53					11 13			12 04		11 33				11 53	
Birmingham New Street 12	a				11 16		10 45			11 08					11 27			12 16		11 45				12 08	
Sandwell & Dudley	a						10 57													11 57					
Wolverhampton 7	a						11 11			11 37										12 11					

Table 66

Mondays to Fridays

until 30 March

London - Watford Junction, Milton Keynes Central, Northampton and West Midlands

Network Diagram - see first Page of Table 59

		LM 1	SN 1	VT ◇1 ⊡	LM 1	VT ◇1 ⊡	LM 1	VT ◇1 ⊡	VT ◇1 ⊡	LM 1	LM 1	VT ◇1 ⊡	LM ◇1		LM 1	SN 1	VT ◇1 ⊡	LM 1	VT ◇1 ⊡	LM 1	VT ◇1 ⊡	VT ◇1 ⊡	LM 1
London Euston [15] ⊖	d	10 54		11 03	11 04	11 10	11 13	11 20	11 23	11 24	11 34	11 43	11 46		11 54		12 03	12 04	12 10	12 13	12 20	12 23	12 24
East Croydon	d		10 10													11 11							
Clapham Junction	d		10 39													11 39							
Imperial Wharf	d		10 44													11 44							
West Brompton ⊖	d		10 47													11 47							
Kensington (Olympia) ⊖	d		10 50													11 50							
Shepherd's Bush	d		10 53													11 53							
Wembley Central ⊖	d		11s08													12s08							
Harrow & Wealdstone ⊖	d		11 13		11 17						11 46					12 13		12 17					
Bushey	d				11 22						11 51							12 22					
Watford Junction	a	11 10	11 20		11 25					11 39	11 54		12 00		12 09	12 20		12 25					12 40
	d	11 11	11 20		11 26				11u37	11 41	11 55		12 01		12 11	12 20		12 26				12u37	12 41
Kings Langley	d				11 30						11 59							12 30					
Apsley	d				11 34						12 03							12 34					
Hemel Hempstead	d	11 18	11 28		11 37					11 48	12 06				12 18	12 28		12 37					12 48
Berkhamsted	d	11 23	11 32		11 42					11 53	12 11				12 23	12 32		12 42					12 53
Tring	d		11 39		11a48					11 59	12a17					12 39		12a48					12 59
Cheddington	d									12 04													13 04
Leighton Buzzard	d	11 36	11 48				11 42			12 09					12 36	12 48				12 42			13 09
Bletchley	d	11 43	11 55				11 50			12 16					12 43	12 55				12 50			13 16
Milton Keynes Central [10]	a	11 48	12 01			11 40	11 54	11 50		12 21		12 13	12 24		12 48	13 01			12 40	12 54	12 50		13 21
	d	11 49					11 54					12 13	12 25		12 49					12 54			
Wolverton	d	11 52					11 58								12 52					12 58			
Northampton	a	12 06					12 11						12 40		13 05					13 11			
Rugby	a			11 51			12 38						13 04	13 17			12 51			13 38			
Nuneaton	a												13 16										
Coventry	a			12 02			12 49		12 22			12 42		13 29			13 02			13 49		13 22	
Birmingham International ✈	a			12 13			13 04		12 33			12 53		13 45			13 13			14 04		13 33	
Birmingham New Street [12]	a			12 27			13 16		12 45			13 08		14 01			13 27			14 16		13 45	
Sandwell & Dudley	a								12 57													13 57	
Wolverhampton [7]	a								13 11													14 11	

		LM 1	VT ◇1 ⊡	LM ◇1		LM 1	SN 1	VT ◇1 ⊡	LM 1	VT ◇1 ⊡	LM 1	VT ◇1 ⊡	VT ◇1 ⊡	LM 1	LM 1	VT ◇1 ⊡	LM ◇1	LM 1	SN 1	VT ◇1 ⊡	LM 1	VT ◇1 ⊡
London Euston [15] ⊖	d	12 34	12 43	12 46		12 54		13 03	13 04	13 10	13 13	13 20	13 23	13 24	13 34	13 43	13 46	13 54		14 03	14 04	14 10
East Croydon	d						12 10												13 10			
Clapham Junction	d						12 39												13 39			
Imperial Wharf	d						12 44												13 44			
West Brompton ⊖	d						12 47												13 47			
Kensington (Olympia) ⊖	d						12 50												13 50			
Shepherd's Bush	d						12 53												13 53			
Wembley Central ⊖	d						13s08												14s08			
Harrow & Wealdstone ⊖	d	12 46					13 13		13 17						13 47				14 13		14 17	
Bushey	d	12 51							13 22						13 52						14 22	
Watford Junction	a	12 54		13 00		13 09	13 20		13 25					13 40	13 54		14 00	14 10	14 20		14 25	
	d	12 55		13 01		13 11	13 20		13 26				13u37	13 41	13 55		14 01	14 11	14 20		14 26	
Kings Langley	d	12 59							13 30						13 59						14 30	
Apsley	d	13 03							13 34						14 03						14 34	
Hemel Hempstead	d	13 06				13 18	13 28		13 37					13 48	14 06			14 18	14 28		14 37	
Berkhamsted	d	13 11				13 23	13 32		13 42					13 53	14 11			14 23	14 32		14 42	
Tring	d	13a17					13 39		13a48					13 59	14a17				14 39		14a48	
Cheddington	d													14 04								
Leighton Buzzard	d					13 36	13 48				13 42			14 09				14 36	14 48			
Bletchley	d					13 43	13 55				13 50			14 16				14 43	14 55			
Milton Keynes Central [10]	a		13 13	13 24		13 48	14 01			13 40	13 54	13 50		14 23		14 13	14 24	14 48	15 01			14 40
	d		13 13	13 25		13 49					13 54					14 13	14 25	14 49				
Wolverton	d					13 52					13 58							14 52				
Northampton	a			13 40		14 05					14 11						14 40	15 05				
Rugby	a			14 04	14 17			13 51			14 38						15 04			14 51		
Nuneaton	a			14 16													15 16					
Coventry	a		13 42		14 29			14 02			14 49		14 22			14 42				15 02		
Birmingham International ✈	a		13 53		14 45			14 13			15 04		14 33			14 53				15 13		
Birmingham New Street [12]	a		14 08		15 01			14 27			15 16		14 45			15 08				15 27		
Sandwell & Dudley	a												14 57									
Wolverhampton [7]	a												15 11									

London - Watford Junction, Milton Keynes Central, Northampton and West Midlands

Network Diagram - see first Page of Table 59

		LM	VT	VT	LM	LM	VT	LM			LM	SN	VT	LM	VT	LM	VT	VT	LM		LM	VT	LM		LM
		1	◇1 ☕	◇1 ☕	1	1	R 1 ☕	◇1			1	1	◇1 ☕	1	◇1 ☕	1	◇1 ☕	◇1 ☕	1		1	◇1 ☕	◇1		1
London Euston 15 ⊖	d	14 13	14 20	14 23	14 24	14 34	14 43	14 46			14 54		15 03	15 04	15 10	15 13	15 20	15 23	15 24		15 34	15 43	15 46		15 54
East Croydon	d											14 10													
Clapham Junction	d											14 39													
Imperial Wharf	d											14 44													
West Brompton ⊖	d											14 47													
Kensington (Olympia) ⊖	d											14 50													
Shepherd's Bush	d											14 53													
Wembley Central ⊖	d											15s08													
Harrow & Wealdstone ⊖	d					14 46						15 13		15 17							15 47				
Bushey	d					14 51								15 22							15 52				
Watford Junction	a				14 39	14 54		15 00			15 09	15 20		15 25					15 39		15 54		16 00		16 09
	d			14u37	14 41	14 55		15 01			15 11	15 20		15 26				15u37	15 41		15 55		16 01		16 11
Kings Langley	d					14 59								15 30							15 59				
Apsley	d					15 03								15 34							16 03				
Hemel Hempstead	d				14 48	15 06					15 18	15 28		15 37					15 48		16 06				16 18
Berkhamsted	d				14 53	15 11					15 23	15 32		15 42					15 53		16 11				16 23
Tring	d				14 59	15a17						15 39		15a48					15 59		16a17				
Cheddington	d				15 04														16 04						
Leighton Buzzard	d	14 42			15 09						15 36	15 48				15 42			16 09						16 36
Bletchley	d	14 50			15 16						15 43	15 55				15 50			16 16						16 43
Milton Keynes Central 10	a	14 54	14 50		15 21		15 13	15 24			15 48	16 01			15 40	15 54	15 50		16 21			16 13	16 24		16 48
	d	14 54					15 13	15 25			15 49					15 54						16 13	16 25		16 49
Wolverton	d	14 58									15 52					15 58									16 52
Northampton	a	15 11						15 40			16 05					16 11							16 40		17 05
Rugby	a	15 38						16 04	16 17				15 51			16 38							17 04	17 17	17 38
Nuneaton	a							16 16															17 16		
Coventry	a	15 49		15 22			15 42		16 29				16 02			16 49		16 22				16 42		17 29	17 49
Birmingham International ✈	a	16 04		15 33			15 53		16 45				16 13			17 04		16 33				16 53		17 45	18 04
Birmingham New Street 12	a	16 16		15 45			16 08		17 02				16 27			17 16		16 45				17 08		18 01	18 17
Sandwell & Dudley	a			15 57														16 57							
Wolverhampton 7	a			16 11			16 37											17 11							

		SN	VT	LM	VT		LM	VT	VT	LM	VT	LM	VT	LM	LM		SN	VT	LM	VT	LM	LM	VT	VT	LM
		1	◇1 ☕	1	◇1 ☕		1	◇1 ☕	◇1 ☕	1	◇1 ☕	1	◇1 ☕	◇1	1		1	◇1 ⊠	1	◇1 ⊠	1	1	◇1 ⊠	◇1 ⊠	1
London Euston 15 ⊖	d		16 03	16 04	16 10		16 13	16 20	16 23	16 24	16 33	16 34	16 43	16 48	16 54			17 03	17 05	17 10	17 13	17 14	17 20	17 23	17 24
East Croydon	d	15 10															16 10								
Clapham Junction	d	15 39															16 39								
Imperial Wharf	d	15 44															16 44								
West Brompton ⊖	d	15 47															16 47								
Kensington (Olympia) ⊖	d	15 50															16 50								
Shepherd's Bush	d	15 53															16 53								
Wembley Central ⊖	d	16s08															17s08								
Harrow & Wealdstone ⊖	d	16 13		16 17								16 46			17 06		17 13		17 19			17 26			
Bushey	d			16 22								16 51			17 11							17 31			
Watford Junction	a	16 20		16 25						16 39		16 54			17 14		17 20		17 26			17 34			17 43
	d	16 20		16 26					16u37	16 41		16 55			17 14		17 21		17 27			17 34		17u37	17 44
Kings Langley	d			16 30								16 59							17 31			17 39			
Apsley	d			16 34								17 03			17 20							17 42			
Hemel Hempstead	d	16 28		16 37						16 48		17 06			17 23		17 28		17 36						17 51
Berkhamsted	d	16 32		16 42						16 53		17 11			17 28		17 33		17 41						17 56
Tring	d	16 39		16a48						16 59		17a19			17a36		17 38		17 46			17a52			
Cheddington	d									17 04									17 51						
Leighton Buzzard	d	16 48					16 42			17 09				17 19			17 47				17 42				18 09
Bletchley	d	16 56					16 50			17 16							17 54		18 01						18 16
Milton Keynes Central 10	a	17 00					16 54			17 22				17 28			17 59		18 06		17 51				18 21
	d						16 54						17u13	17 29						17u40	17 52				18 21
Wolverton	d						16 58							17 33							17 56				18 25
Northampton	a						17 13							17 46							18 10				18 37
Rugby	a		16 51								17 21			18 17				17 51			18 38				19 03
Nuneaton	a																			18 11					
Coventry	a		17 02						17 22				17 42	18 29				18 02			18 49			18 22	
Birmingham International ✈	a		17 13						17 33				17 53	18 45				18 13			19 04			18 33	
Birmingham New Street 12	a		17 27						17 45				18 08	19 01				18 27			19 17			18 45	
Sandwell & Dudley	a								17 57															18 57	
Wolverhampton 7	a								18 11															19 11	

London - Watford Junction, Milton Keynes Central, Northampton and West Midlands

Network Diagram - see first Page of Table 59

		LM	VT	LM	LM	VT	LM	LM	SN	VT	LM	VT	LM	LM	VT	LM	VT	LM	VT	LM	LM	VT
		1	◇1	1	1	◇1	1	1	1	◇1	1	◇1	1	◇1	◇1	1	◇1	◇1	◇1	1	1	◇1
											A			B								
			⊠			⊠				⊠		⊠			⊠		⊠		⊠			⊠
London Euston 15 ⊖	d	17 30	17 33	17 34	17 41	17 43	17 46	17 51		18 03	18 05	18 10	18 12	18 13	18 20	18 21	18 23	18 29	18 33	18 34	18 40	18 43
East Croydon	d								17 10													
Clapham Junction	d								17 39													
Imperial Wharf	d								17 44													
West Brompton ⊖	d								17 47													
Kensington (Olympia) ⊖	d								17 50													
Shepherd's Bush	d								17 53													
Wembley Central ⊖	d								18s08													
Harrow & Wealdstone ⊖	d			17 46				18 03	18 13		18 18					18 34				18 46		
Bushey	d			17 52	17 56								18 27							18 52	18 57	
Watford Junction	a	17 48		17 55	18 00			18 09	18 20		18 25		18 30			18 40		18 46		18 55	19 00	
	d	17 49			18 01			18 11	18 20		18 25		18 31			18 41	18u37	18 47		18 56	19 01	
Kings Langley	d				18 05						18 30					18 46					19 05	
Apsley	d	17 55									18 33							18 53			19 09	
Hemel Hempstead	d	17 58			18 10			18 18	18 28				18 38			18 51				19 03	19 12	
Berkhamsted	d				18 15			18 23	18 32				18 43					18 59			19 16	
Tring	d	18 05			18a22				18 38		18 43		18a53			18 59				19 12	19a26	
Cheddington	d	18 10									18 48							19 08		19 17		
Leighton Buzzard	d						18 19		18 47		18 53			18 42		19 07				19 23		
Bletchley	d	18 22						18 41	18 54		19 01							19 18		19a31		
Milton Keynes Central 10	a	18 28					18 30	18 45	19 00		19 06			18 52		19 19		19 23				19 13
	d					18u13	18 32	18 46			19 07	18u40		18 54				19 23				19 13
Wolverton	d						18 36	18 49			19 10			18 57				19 27				
Northampton	a						18 50	19 03			19 25			19 10				19 39				
Rugby	a		18 21				19 17			18 51				19 38				20 04	19 22			
Nuneaton	a											19 12						20 16				
Coventry	a					18 42	19 29			19 02				19 49			19 22					19 42
Birmingham International ✈	a					18 53	19 45			19 13				20 04			19 33					19 53
Birmingham New Street 12	a					19 08	20 01			19 27				20 16			19 45					20 06
Sandwell & Dudley	a																19 58					
Wolverhampton 7	a																20 12					20 36

		VT	LM	LM	SN	VT	LM	VT	VT	LM	VT	VT	LM	LM	VT	LM	LM	SN	VT	LM	VT	VT	LM
		FO																					
						R		R	R		R	R											
		◇	1	1	1	1	1	1	1	1	1	1	1	1	◇1	1	1	1	◇1	1	◇1	◇1	◇1
		☕				☕		☕	☕		☕	☕			☕				☕		☕	☕	
London Euston 15 ⊖	d	18 46	18 49	18 54		19 03	19 04	19 07	19 10	19 13	19 20	19 23	19 24	19 34	19 43	19 46	19 54		20 03	20 04	20 07	20 10	20 13
East Croydon	d				18 10													19 10					
Clapham Junction	d				18 39													19 39					
Imperial Wharf	d				18 44													19 44					
West Brompton ⊖	d				18 47													19 47					
Kensington (Olympia) ⊖	d				18 50													19 50					
Shepherd's Bush	d				18 53													19 53					
Wembley Central ⊖	d				19s08													20s08					
Harrow & Wealdstone ⊖	d			19 06	19 13		19 17							19 46				20 13		20 17			
Bushey	d						19 22							19 51						20 22			
Watford Junction	a			19 12	19 20		19 25						19 40	19 54			20 09	20 20		20 25			
	d			19 13	19 21		19 26					19u37	19 42	19 55			20 11	20 20		20 26			
Kings Langley	d						19 30							19 59						20 30			
Apsley	d						19 34							20 03						20 34			
Hemel Hempstead	d			19 20	19 28		19 37						19 49	20 06			20 18	20 28		20 37			
Berkhamsted	d			19 25	19 33		19 42						19 54	20 11			20 23	20 32		20 42			
Tring	d			19 30	19 40		19a48						20 01	20a17				20 39		20a48			
Cheddington	d												20 06										
Leighton Buzzard	d		19 19	19 38	19 52					19 43			20 12			20 18	20 36	20 48					20 42
Bletchley	d		19 25	19 46	20 01								20 19				20 43	20 55					20 50
Milton Keynes Central 10	a		19 30	19 52	20 06					19 55			20 24		20 13	20 28	20 48	21 01				20 40	20 54
	d		19 31							19 56					20 13	20 30	20 49						20 55
Wolverton	d		19 35							19 59						20 33	20 52						20 59
Northampton	a		19 49							20 11						20 47	21 05						21 13
Rugby	a	19 38	20 17			19 51				20 38						21 17	21 38		20 51				
Nuneaton	a							20 02													21 02		
Coventry	a		20 29			20 02				20 49		20 22			20 42	21 29	21 49		21 02				
Birmingham International ✈	a		20 45			20 13				21 04		20 33			20 53	21 45	22 04		21 13				
Birmingham New Street 12	a		21 01			20 27				21 16		20 45			21 06	22 01	22 16		21 25				
Sandwell & Dudley	a											20 58			21 23								
Wolverhampton 7	a											21 12			21 38				21 56				

A not from 26 December until 2 January

B ◇ from Coventry

Table 66

Mondays to Fridays

until 30 March

London - Watford Junction, Milton Keynes Central, Northampton and West Midlands

Network Diagram - see first Page of Table 59

		VT	LM		LM	VT	LM	LM	VT	VT	SN	LM	VT		VT	LM		LM	LM	VT	LM	LM	SN		VT
		◇1	1		1	◇1	1	1	◇1	◇1	1	1	◇1		◇1	1		1	1	◇1	1	1	1		◇1
		☕				☕			☕	☕			☕		☕					☕					☕
London Euston 15 ⊖	d	20 23	20 24		20 34	20 43	20 46	20 54	21 00	21 03		21 04	21 07		21 10	21 13		21 24	21 34	21 43	21 46	21 54			22 00
East Croydon	d																								
Clapham Junction	d										20 39												21 39		
Imperial Wharf	d										20 44												21 44		
West Brompton ⊖	d										20 47												21 47		
Kensington (Olympia) ⊖	d										20 50												21 50		
Shepherd's Bush	d										20 53												21 53		
Wembley Central ⊖	d										21s08														
Harrow & Wealdstone ⊖	d				20 46						21 13	21 17							21 46				22 16		
Bushey	d				20 51							21 22							21 51						
Watford Junction	a		20 40		20 54			21 10			21 20	21 25						21 39	21 53			22 09	22 23		
	d	20u37	20 42		20 55			21 11			21 20	21 26			21u25			21 41	21 54	21u58		22 11			
Kings Langley	d				20 59							21 30							21 58						
Apsley	d				21 03							21 34							22 02						
Hemel Hempstead	d		20 49		21 06			21 18			21 28	21 36						21 48	22 05			22 18			
Berkhamsted	d		20 55		21 11			21 23			21 32	21 41						21 53	22 10			22 23			
Tring	d		21 00		21a17						21 39	21 48							22 16			22 27			
Cheddington	d		21 05									21 53							22 22						
Leighton Buzzard	d		21 10				21 18	21 36			21 50	21 57				21 44		22 07	22 26		22 18	22 37			
Bletchley	d		21 17					21 43			21 58	22a04				21 52		22 15	22 33			22 45			
Milton Keynes Central 10	a		21 23			21 13	21 27	21 48	21 30	21 33	22 05		21 37			21 56		22 21	22 38	22 17	22 32	22 53			22 30
	d					21 13	21 29	21 49		21 34			21 38			21 57				22 17	22 32	22 56			22 31
Wolverton	d						21 32	21 52								22 00					22 36	22 59			
Northampton	a						21 46	22 05								22 14					22 49	23 13			
Rugby	a						22 17			21 56					22 02	22 38					23 17				22 52
Nuneaton	a												22 07												23 03
Coventry	a	21 22				21 42	22 29			22 06						22 49				22 46	23 29				
Birmingham International ✈	a	21 33				21 53	22 45			22 18						23 06				23 00	23 47				
Birmingham New Street 12	a	21 46				22 06	23 02			22 29						23 19				23 16	00 04				
Sandwell & Dudley	a	21 58				22 23				22 40										23 33					
Wolverhampton 7	a	22 12				22 38				22 56										23 47					

		LM	LM	VT	LM	LM	SN	LM	VT FX		VT FO	LM
		1	1	◇1	1	1	1	1	◇1		◇1	1
				☕					☕		☕	
London Euston 15 ⊖	d	22 04	22 24	22 30	22 34	22 54		23 24	23 30		23 30	23 34
East Croydon	d											
Clapham Junction	d						22 39					
Imperial Wharf	d						22 44					
West Brompton ⊖	d						22 47					
Kensington (Olympia) ⊖	d						22 50					
Shepherd's Bush	d						22 53					
Wembley Central ⊖	d											
Harrow & Wealdstone ⊖	d	22 19			22 49		23 16					23 46
Bushey	d				22 54							23 51
Watford Junction	a	22 25	22 39		22 57	23 09	23 23	23 39				23 54
	d	22 26	22 40	22u45	22 58	23 10		23 40				23 54
Kings Langley	d	22 30			23 02	23 14						23 59
Apsley	d	22 33			23 06	23 18						00 02
Hemel Hempstead	d	22 36	22 47		23 09	23 21		23 47				00 05
Berkhamsted	d	22 40	22 52		23 14	23 26		23 52				00 09
Tring	d	22 45			23 18	23 33						00 15
Cheddington	d				23 24							00 20
Leighton Buzzard	d	22 56	23 06		23 30	23 40		00 05				00 26
Bletchley	d	23 05	23 13		23 37	23 47		00 13				00 33
Milton Keynes Central 10	a	23 11	23 21	23 28	23 45	23 55		00 21	00 27		00 27	00 41
	d		23 22	23 29		23 55		00 21	00 28		00 28	
Wolverton	d		23 25			23 59		00 25				
Northampton	a		23 39			00 13		00 38				
Rugby	a			23 58					01 00		01 05	
Nuneaton	a											
Coventry	a			00 10					01 13		01 18	
Birmingham International ✈	a			00 21					01 24		01 29	
Birmingham New Street 12	a			00 32					01 36		01 41	
Sandwell & Dudley	a											
Wolverhampton 7	a			01 03					02 07		02 10	

Table 66

Mondays to Fridays

from 2 April

London - Watford Junction, Milton Keynes Central, Northampton and West Midlands

Network Diagram - see first Page of Table 59

		LM MO ◇1	LM MX 1	VT MO ◇1 ☕	LM MO 1	VT MO ◇1 ☕	VT MX ◇1 ☕	LM MX 1	LM MO ◇1	LM MX 1	VT MO ◇1 ☕	VT MX ◇1 ☕	LM MO ◇1	LM MX 1	LM 1	LM MO 1	LM MX 1	LM MO 1	LM MX 1	SN 1	LM ◇1	VT ◇1 ⊠	LM 1
London Euston 15 ⊖	d	21p28	21p46	21p55	22p00	22p25	22p30	22p54	22p58	23p24	23p25	23p30	23p34	23p34	00 04	00 34	00 34	01 34	01 34			05 27	05 30
East Croydon	d																						
Clapham Junction	d																			05 03			
Imperial Wharf	d																			05 07			
West Brompton ⊖	d																			05 10			
Kensington (Olympia) ⊖	d																			05 14			
Shepherd's Bush	d																			05 17			
Wembley Central ⊖	d															00 43	00 45	01 45	01 45				
Harrow & Wealdstone ⊖	d	21p40			22p12				23p10				23p46	23p46	00 16	00 48	00 50	01 50	01 50	05 33			05 43
Bushey	d													23p51			00 55						
Watford Junction	a	21p46			22p18			23p09	23p16	23p39			23p52	23p54	00 22	00 54	00 57	01 56	01 56	05 40			05 50
	d	21p46		22b09	22p19	22b39	22b45	23p10	23p17	23p40	23b39		23p53	23p54	00 23	00 58	00 58	01 57	01 57			05u45	05 50
Kings Langley	d	21p51						23p14	23p21				23p57	23p59		01 02	01 02						05 55
Apsley	d	21p55						23p18	23p25				00 01	00 02		01 06	01 06						05 59
Hemel Hempstead	d	21p57			22p26			23p21	23p28	23p47			00 04	00 05	00 30	01 09	01 09	02 04	02 04				06 01
Berkhamsted	d	22p02			22p31			23p26	23p33	23p52			00 09	00 09	00 35	01 14	01 14	02 09	02 09				06 06
Tring	d				22p35			23p33	23p37				00 13	00 15	00 41	01 18	01 19	02 13	02 14				06 13
Cheddington	d				22p41				23p43				00 19	00 20		01 24	01 25						06 18
Leighton Buzzard	d	22p15	22p18		22p47			23p40	23p49	00 05			00 25	00 26	00 50	01 30	01 31	02 22	02 23				06 23
Bletchley	d	22p22			22p54			23p47	23p56	00 13			00 32	00 33	00 57	01 37	01 38	02 29	02 30		05 17		06 30
Milton Keynes Central 10	a	22p30	22p32	22p42	23p02	23p11	23p28	23p55	00 04	00 21	00 11	00 27	00 40	00 41	01 05	01 45	01 46	02 37	02 38		05 21	06 09	06 35
	d	22p31	22p32	22p44	23p03	23p12	23p29	23p55	00 05	00 21	00 12	00 28	00 41		01 05	01 46	01 47				05 21	06 10	06 36
Wolverton	d	22p34	22p36		23p06			23p59	00 08	00 25			00 44		01 09	01 49	01 50				05 25		06 39
Northampton	a	22p48	22p49		23p20			00 13	00 22	00 38			00 58		01 22	02 03	02 04				05 37		06 52
Rugby	a	23p13	23p17	23p20	23p54	23p46	23p58				00s46	01 00									06 02		07 17
Nuneaton	a																				06 16	06 38	
Coventry	a	23p25	23p29	23p31	00 05	23p57	00 10				00s58	01 13											07 29
Birmingham International ✈	a	23p52	23p47	23p42		00 08	00 21				01s09	01 24											07 45
Birmingham New Street 12	a	00 04	00 04	23p54		00 21	00 32				01s22	01 36											08 03
Sandwell & Dudley	a																						
Wolverhampton 7	a			00 15		00 43	01 03				01 53	02 07											

		VT ◇1 ⊠	SN 1	VT ◇1 ⊠	LM 1	SN 1	VT ◇1 ⊠	VT ◇1 ⊠	LM ◇1	LM 1	VT ◇1 ⊠	VT ◇1 ⊠	LM 1	VT ◇1 ⊠	SN 1	VT ◇1 ⊠	LM 1	VT ◇1 ⊠	LM 1	VT ◇1 ⊠	VT ◇1 ⊠	LM 1	LM 1
London Euston 15 ⊖	d	05 39		06 03	06 04		06 17	06 23	06 24	06 34	06 36	06 43	06 53	06 55		07 03	07 04	07 10	07 13	07 20	07 23	07 24	07 34
East Croydon	d																						
Clapham Junction	d		05 30			05 55									06 38								
Imperial Wharf	d		05 39			06 00									06 42								
West Brompton ⊖	d		05 41			06 03									06 45								
Kensington (Olympia) ⊖	d		05 44			06 07									06 49								
Shepherd's Bush	d		05 47			06 10									06 52								
Wembley Central ⊖	d		06 02			06 24									07 07								
Harrow & Wealdstone ⊖	d		06 07		06 16	06 29				06 47					07 12		07 17						07 46
Bushey	d																						
Watford Junction	a		06 14		06 22	06 36			06 39	06 53			07 08		07 19		07 24					07 40	07 52
	d	06u02	06 14		06 23			06u37	06 41	06 54			07 10		07 19		07 24				07u37	07 42	07 53
Kings Langley	d				06 27					06 58							07 29						07 58
Apsley	d				06 31					07 02							07 32						08 01
Hemel Hempstead	d		06 22		06 34				06 48	07 05			07 17		07 27		07 35					07 49	08 04
Berkhamsted	d		06 26		06 39				06 53	07 10			07 22		07 32		07 40					07 54	08 09
Tring	d		06 33		06a46				06 59	07 16					07 39		07a47					08 01	08a16
Cheddington	d								07 05	07 21												08 06	
Leighton Buzzard	d		06 42						07 10	07 26			07 35		07 51				07 42			08 11	
Bletchley	d		06 49						07 17	07 33			07 43		07 58				07 50			08 18	
Milton Keynes Central 10	a	06 22	06 55				06 47		07 22	07 38		07 13	07 48	07 25	08 03			07 40	07 54	07 50		08 23	
	d	06 22							07 22			07 13	07 48						07 54				
Wolverton	d								07 26				07 52						07 58				
Northampton	a								07 38				08 05						08 11				
Rugby	a	06 44		06 51					08 04							07 51			08 38				
Nuneaton	a								08 17														
Coventry	a			07 02				07 22				07 42				08 02			08 49		08 22		
Birmingham International ✈	a			07 13				07 33				07 53				08 12			09 04		08 33		
Birmingham New Street 12	a			07 27				07 45				08 08				08 27			09 16		08 45		
Sandwell & Dudley	a							07 57													08 57		
Wolverhampton 7	a							08 11													09 11		

b Previous night, stops to pick up only

Table 66

Mondays to Fridays

from 2 April

London - Watford Junction, Milton Keynes Central, Northampton and West Midlands

Network Diagram - see first Page of Table 59

		VT		VT	LM	LM	SN	VT	LM	VT	LM	VT		VT	LM	LM	VT	LM		LM	SN	VT		LM	VT
		◇1		◇1	◇1	1	1	◇1	1	◇1	1	◇1		◇1	1	1	◇1	◇1		1	1	◇1		1	◇1
		⊠		⊠				⊠		⊠		⊠		⊠			⊠					⊠			⊠
London Euston 15 ⊖	d	07 35		07 43	07 47	07 54		08 03	08 05	08 10	08 13	08 20		08 23	08 24	08 34	08 43	08 46		08 54		09 03		09 05	09 10
East Croydon	d																				08 07				
Clapham Junction	d						07 39														08 39				
Imperial Wharf	d						07 44														08 44				
West Brompton ⊖	d						07 47														08 47				
Kensington (Olympia) ⊖	d						07 50														08 50				
Shepherd's Bush	d						07 53														08 53				
Wembley Central ⊖	d						08 08														09 08				
Harrow & Wealdstone ⊖	d						08 13		08 21						08 36	08 46					09 13			09 17	
Bushey	d								08 26							08 51								09 22	
Watford Junction	a				08 01	08 11	08 20		08 29						08 43	08 54		09 00		09 09	09 20			09 25	
	d				08 02	08 12	08 20		08 29					08u37	08 44	08 55		09 01		09 11	09 20			09 26	
Kings Langley	d								08 34							08 59								09 30	
Apsley	d								08 38							09 03								09 34	
Hemel Hempstead	d					08 19	08 28		08 40						08 51	09 06				09 18	09 28			09 37	
Berkhamsted	d					08 24	08 32		08 45						08 56	09 11				09 23	09 32			09 42	
Tring	d						08 39		08a52						09 02	09a17					09 39			09a48	
Cheddington	d														09 07										
Leighton Buzzard	d					08 37	08 48				08 42				09 12					09 36	09 48				
Bletchley	d					08 44	08 55				08 50				09 20					09 43	09 55				
Milton Keynes Central 10	a	08 05		08 13	08 25	08 49	09 01			08 40	08 54	08 50			09 26		09 13	09 24		09 48	10 01				09 40
	d			08 13	08 31	08 50					08 54						09 13	09 25		09 49					
Wolverton	d					08 53					08 58									09 52					
Northampton	a				08 44	09 07					09 11							09 40		10 05					
Rugby	a				09 04			08 51			09 38							10 04	10 17			09 51			
Nuneaton	a				09 16													10 16							
Coventry	a			08 42				09 02			09 49			09 22			09 42		10 29			10 02			
Birmingham International ✈	a			08 53				09 13			10 04			09 33			09 53		10 45			10 13			
Birmingham New Street 12	a			09 08				09 27			10 16			09 45			10 08		11 01			10 27			
Sandwell & Dudley	a													09 57											
Wolverhampton 7	a													10 11											

		LM	VT	VT	LM	LM	VT	LM		LM	SN	VT	LM	VT	LM	VT	VT	LM		LM	VT	LM	LM	SN	VT
		1	◇1	◇1	1	1	◇1	◇1		1	1	◇1	1	◇1	1	◇1	◇1	1		1	◇1	◇1	1	1	◇1
			⊠	⊠			☕					⊠		⊠		⊠	⊠				⊠				☕
London Euston 15 ⊖	d	09 13	09 20	09 23	09 24	09 34	09 43	09 46		09 54		10 03	10 05	10 10	10 13	10 20	10 23	10 24		10 34	10 43	10 46	10 54		11 03
East Croydon	d										09 08													10 10	
Clapham Junction	d										09 39													10 39	
Imperial Wharf	d										09 44													10 44	
West Brompton ⊖	d										09 47													10 47	
Kensington (Olympia) ⊖	d										09 50													10 50	
Shepherd's Bush	d										09 53													10 53	
Wembley Central ⊖	d										10 08													11 08	
Harrow & Wealdstone ⊖	d					09 48					10 13		10 17							10 46				11 13	
Bushey	d					09 53							10 22							10 51					
Watford Junction	a				09 39	09 56		10 00		10 09	10 20		10 25					10 39		10 54		11 00	11 10	11 20	
	d			09u37	09 41	09 57		10 01		10 11	10 20		10 26				10u37	10 41		10 55		11 01	11 11	11 20	
Kings Langley	d					10 01							10 30							10 59					
Apsley	d					10 05							10 34							11 03					
Hemel Hempstead	d				09 48	10 08				10 18	10 28		10 37					10 48		11 06			11 18	11 28	
Berkhamsted	d				09 53	10 13				10 23	10 32		10 42					10 53		11 11			11 23	11 32	
Tring	d				09 59	10a19					10 39		10a48					10 59		11a17				11 39	
Cheddington	d				10 04													11 04							
Leighton Buzzard	d	09 42			10 09					10 36	10 48				10 42			11 09					11 36	11 48	
Bletchley	d	09 50			10 16					10 43	10 57				10 50			11 16					11 43	11 55	
Milton Keynes Central 10	a	09 54	09 50		10 21		10 13	10 24		10 48	11 02			10 40	10 54	10 50		11 21			11 13	11 24	11 48	12 01	
	d	09 54					10 13	10 25		10 49					10 54						11 13	11 25	11 49		
Wolverton	d	09 58								10 52					10 58								11 52		
Northampton	a	10 11						10 40		11 08					11 11							11 40	12 06		
Rugby	a	10 38						11 04				10 51			11 38							12 04			11 51
Nuneaton	a							11 16														12 16			
Coventry	a	10 49		10 22			10 42					11 02			11 49		11 22				11 42				12 02
Birmingham International ✈	a	11 04		10 33			10 53					11 13			12 04		11 33				11 53				12 13
Birmingham New Street 12	a	11 16		10 45			11 08					11 27			12 16		11 45				12 08				12 27
Sandwell & Dudley	a			10 57													11 57								
Wolverhampton 7	a			11 11			11 37										12 11								

Table 66

Mondays to Fridays

from 2 April

London - Watford Junction, Milton Keynes Central, Northampton and West Midlands

Network Diagram - see first Page of Table 59

		LM	VT	LM		VT	VT	LM	LM	VT	LM		LM	SN		VT	LM	VT	LM	VT	VT	LM	LM	VT	
		1	◇1	1		◇1	◇1	1	1	◇1	◇1		1	1		◇1	1	◇1	1	◇1	◇1	1	1	◇1	
			☕			☕	☕			☕						☕		☕		☕	☕			☕	
London Euston 15 ⊖	d	11 04	11 10	11 13		11 20	11 23	11 24	11 34	11 43	11 46		11 54			12 03	12 04	12 10	12 13	12 20	12 23	12 24	12 34	12 43	
East Croydon	d													11 11											
Clapham Junction	d													11 39											
Imperial Wharf	d													11 44											
West Brompton ⊖	d													11 47											
Kensington (Olympia) ⊖	d													11 50											
Shepherd's Bush	d													11 53											
Wembley Central ⊖	d													12 08											
Harrow & Wealdstone ⊖	d	11 17							11 46					12 13			12 17						12 46		
Bushey	d	11 22							11 51								12 22						12 51		
Watford Junction	a	11 25						11 39	11 54		12 00		12 09	12 20			12 25					12 40	12 54		
	d	11 26					11u37	11 41	11 55		12 01		12 11	12 20			12 26				12u37	12 41	12 55		
Kings Langley	d	11 30							11 59								12 30						12 59		
Apsley	d	11 34							12 03								12 34						13 03		
Hemel Hempstead	d	11 37						11 48	12 06				12 18	12 28			12 37					12 48	13 06		
Berkhamsted	d	11 42						11 53	12 11				12 23	12 32			12 42					12 53	13 11		
Tring	d	11a48						11 59	12a17					12 39			12a48					12 59	13a17		
Cheddington	d							12 04														13 04			
Leighton Buzzard	d			11 42				12 09					12 36	12 48					12 42			13 09			
Bletchley	d			11 50				12 16					12 43	12 55					12 50			13 16			
Milton Keynes Central 10	a		11 40	11 54		11 50		12 21		12 13	12 24		12 48	13 01				12 40	12 54	12 50		13 21		13 13	
	d			11 54						12 13	12 25		12 49						12 54					13 13	
Wolverton	d			11 58									12 52						12 58						
Northampton	a			12 11							12 40		13 05						13 11						
Rugby	a			12 38							13 04	13 17				12 51			13 38						
Nuneaton	a										13 16														
Coventry	a			12 49			12 22			12 42		13 29				13 02			13 49		13 22			13 42	
Birmingham International ✈	a			13 04			12 33			12 53		13 45				13 13			14 04		13 33			13 53	
Birmingham New Street 12	a			13 16			12 45			13 08		14 01				13 27			14 16		13 45			14 08	
Sandwell & Dudley	a						12 57														13 57				
Wolverhampton 7	a						13 11														14 11				

		LM		LM	SN	VT	LM	VT	LM	VT		VT	LM	LM	VT	LM	LM	SN	VT	LM		VT	LM	VT	VT
		◇1		1	1	◇1	1	◇1	1	◇1		◇1	1	1	◇1	◇1	1	1	◇1	1		◇1	1	◇1	◇1
						☕		☕		☕		☕			☕				☕			☕		☕	☕
London Euston 15 ⊖	d	12 46		12 54		13 03	13 04	13 10	13 13	13 20		13 23	13 24	13 34	13 43	13 46	13 54		14 03	14 04		14 10	14 13	14 20	14 23
East Croydon	d				12 10													13 10							
Clapham Junction	d				12 39													13 39							
Imperial Wharf	d				12 44													13 44							
West Brompton ⊖	d				12 47													13 47							
Kensington (Olympia) ⊖	d				12 50													13 50							
Shepherd's Bush	d				12 53													13 53							
Wembley Central ⊖	d				13 08													14 08							
Harrow & Wealdstone ⊖	d				13 13		13 17							13 47				14 13		14 17					
Bushey	d						13 22							13 52						14 22					
Watford Junction	a	13 00		13 09	13 20		13 25						13 40	13 54		14 00	14 10	14 20		14 25					
	d	13 01		13 11	13 20		13 26					13u37	13 41	13 55		14 01	14 11	14 20		14 26					14u37
Kings Langley	d						13 30							13 59						14 30					
Apsley	d						13 34							14 03						14 34					
Hemel Hempstead	d			13 18	13 28		13 37						13 48	14 06			14 18	14 28		14 37					
Berkhamsted	d			13 23	13 32		13 42						13 53	14 11			14 23	14 32		14 42					
Tring	d				13 39		13a48						13 59	14a17				14 39		14a48					
Cheddington	d												14 04												
Leighton Buzzard	d			13 36	13 48				13 42				14 09				14 36	14 48					14 42		
Bletchley	d			13 43	13 55				13 50				14 16				14 43	14 55					14 50		
Milton Keynes Central 10	a	13 24		13 48	14 01			13 40	13 54	13 50			14 23		14 13	14 24	14 48	15 01				14 40	14 54	14 50	
	d	13 25		13 49					13 54						14 13	14 25	14 49						14 54		
Wolverton	d			13 52					13 58								14 52						14 58		
Northampton	a	13 40		14 05					14 11							14 40	15 05						15 11		
Rugby	a	14 04	14 17			13 51			14 38							15 04			14 51				15 38		
Nuneaton	a	14 16														15 16									
Coventry	a		14 29			14 02			14 49			14 22			14 42				15 02				15 49		15 22
Birmingham International ✈	a		14 45			14 13			15 04			14 33			14 53				15 13				16 04		15 33
Birmingham New Street 12	a		15 01			14 27			15 16			14 45			15 08				15 27				16 16		15 45
Sandwell & Dudley	a											14 57													15 57
Wolverhampton 7	a											15 11													16 11

London - Watford Junction, Milton Keynes Central, Northampton and West Midlands

Network Diagram - see first Page of Table 59

		LM	LM	VT	LM		LM	SN	VT	LM	VT	LM	VT	VT	LM		LM	VT	LM	LM	SN	VT	LM
		1	1	R 1 ☕	◇1		1	1	◇1 ☕	1	◇1 ☕	1	◇1 ☕	◇1 ☕	1		1	◇1 ☕	◇1	1	1	◇1 ☕	1
London Euston 15 ⊖	d	14 24	14 34	14 43	14 46		14 54		15 03	15 04	15 10	15 13	15 20	15 23	15 24		15 34	15 43	15 46	15 54		16 03	16 04
East Croydon	d							14 10													15 10		
Clapham Junction	d							14 39													15 39		
Imperial Wharf	d							14 44													15 44		
West Brompton ⊖	d							14 47													15 47		
Kensington (Olympia) ⊖	d							14 50													15 50		
Shepherd's Bush	d							14 53													15 53		
Wembley Central ⊖	d							15 08													16 08		
Harrow & Wealdstone ⊖	d		14 46					15 13		15 17							15 47				16 13		16 17
Bushey	d		14 51							15 22							15 52						16 22
Watford Junction	a	14 39	14 54		15 00		15 09	15 20		15 25					15 39		15 54		16 00	16 09	16 20		16 25
	d	14 41	14 55		15 01		15 11	15 20		15 26				15u37	15 41		15 55		16 01	16 11	16 20		16 26
Kings Langley	d		14 59							15 30							15 59						16 30
Apsley	d		15 03							15 34							16 03						16 34
Hemel Hempstead	d	14 48	15 06				15 18	15 28		15 37					15 48		16 06			16 18	16 28		16 37
Berkhamsted	d	14 53	15 11				15 23	15 32		15 42					15 53		16 11			16 23	16 32		16 42
Tring	d	14 59	15a17					15 39		15a48					15 59		16a17				16 39		16a48
Cheddington	d	15 04													16 04								
Leighton Buzzard	d	15 09					15 36	15 48				15 42			16 09					16 36	16 48		
Bletchley	d	15 16					15 43	15 55				15 50			16 16					16 43	16 56		
Milton Keynes Central 10	a	15 21		15 13	15 24		15 48	16 01			15 40	15 54	15 50		16 21			16 13	16 24	16 48	17 00		
	d			15 13	15 25		15 49					15 54						16 13	16 25	16 49			
Wolverton	d						15 52					15 58								16 52			
Northampton	a				15 40		16 05					16 11							16 40	17 05			
Rugby	a				16 04 / 16 17				15 51			16 38							17 04 / 17 17	17 38		16 51	
Nuneaton	a				16 16														17 16				
Coventry	a			15 42	16 29				16 02			16 49		16 22				16 42	17 29	17 49		17 02	
Birmingham International ✈	a			15 53	16 45				16 13			17 04		16 33				16 53	17 45	18 04		17 13	
Birmingham New Street 12	a			16 08	17 02				16 27			17 16		16 45				17 08	18 01	18 17		17 27	
Sandwell & Dudley	a													16 57									
Wolverhampton 7	a			16 37										17 11									

		VT		LM	VT	VT	LM	VT	LM	VT	LM	LM		SN	VT	LM	VT	LM	LM	VT	VT	LM		LM	VT
		◇1 ☕		1	◇1 ☕	◇1 ☕	1	◇1 ☕	1	◇1 ☕	◇1	1		1	◇1 ⊠	1	◇1 ⊠	1	1	◇1 ⊠	◇1 ⊠	1		1	◇1 ⊠
London Euston 15 ⊖	d	16 10		16 13	16 20	16 23	16 24	16 33	16 34	16 43	16 48	16 54			17 03	17 05	17 10	17 13	17 14	17 20	17 23	17 24		17 30	17 33
East Croydon	d													16 10											
Clapham Junction	d													16 39											
Imperial Wharf	d													16 44											
West Brompton ⊖	d													16 47											
Kensington (Olympia) ⊖	d													16 50											
Shepherd's Bush	d													16 53											
Wembley Central ⊖	d													17 08											
Harrow & Wealdstone ⊖	d								16 46			17 06		17 13		17 19			17 26						
Bushey	d								16 51			17 11							17 31						
Watford Junction	a						16 39		16 54			17 14		17 20		17 26			17 34			17 43		17 48	
	d					16u37	16 41		16 55			17 14		17 21		17 27			17 34		17u37	17 44		17 49	
Kings Langley	d								16 59							17 31			17 39						
Apsley	d								17 03			17 20							17 42					17 55	
Hemel Hempstead	d						16 48		17 06			17 23		17 28		17 36						17 51		17 58	
Berkhamsted	d						16 53		17 11			17 28		17 33		17 41						17 56			
Tring	d						16 59		17a19			17a36		17 38		17 46			17a52					18 05	
Cheddington	d						17 04									17 51								18 10	
Leighton Buzzard	d			16 42			17 09				17 19			17 47				17 42				18 09			
Bletchley	d			16 50			17 16							17 54		18 01						18 16		18 22	
Milton Keynes Central 10	a			16 54			17 22				17 28			17 59		18 06		17 51				18 21		18 28	
	d			16 54						17u13	17 29						17u40	17 52				18 21			
Wolverton	d			16 58							17 33							17 56				18 25			
Northampton	a			17 13							17 46							18 10				18 37			
Rugby	a							17 21			18 17				17 51			18 38				19 03			18 21
Nuneaton	a																18 11								
Coventry	a					17 22				17 42	18 29				18 02			18 49			18 22				
Birmingham International ✈	a					17 33				17 53	18 45				18 13			19 04			18 33				
Birmingham New Street 12	a					17 45				18 08	19 01				18 27			19 17			18 45				
Sandwell & Dudley	a					17 57															18 57				
Wolverhampton 7	a					18 11															19 11				

London - Watford Junction, Milton Keynes Central, Northampton and West Midlands

Network Diagram - see first Page of Table 59

		LM	LM	VT	LM	LM	SN	VT		LM	VT	LM	LM	VT	LM	VT	LM	VT		LM	LM	VT	VT	LM	LM
																							FO		
		1	1	◇1	1	1	1	◇1		1	◇1	1	◇1	◇1	1	◇1	◇1	◇1		1	1	◇1	◇	1	1
													A												
				⊠				⊠			⊠			⊠		⊠		⊠				⊠	☕		
London Euston 15 ⊖	d	17 34	17 41	17 43	17 46	17 51		18 03		18 05	18 10	18 12	18 13	18 20	18 21	18 23	18 29	18 33		18 34	18 40	18 43	18 46	18 49	18 54
East Croydon	d						17 10																		
Clapham Junction	d						17 39																		
Imperial Wharf	d						17 44																		
West Brompton ⊖	d						17 47																		
Kensington (Olympia) ⊖	d						17 50																		
Shepherd's Bush	d						17 53																		
Wembley Central ⊖	d						18 08																		
Harrow & Wealdstone ⊖	d	17 46				18 03	18 13			18 18					18 34					18 46					19 06
Bushey	d	17 52	17 56									18 27								18 52	18 57				
Watford Junction	a	17 55	18 00			18 09	18 20			18 25		18 30			18 40		18 46			18 55	19 00				19 12
	d		18 01			18 11	18 20			18 25		18 31			18 41	18u37	18 47			18 56	19 01				19 13
Kings Langley	d		18 05							18 30					18 46						19 05				
Apsley	d									18 33							18 53				19 09				
Hemel Hempstead	d		18 10			18 18	18 28					18 38			18 51					19 03	19 12				19 20
Berkhamsted	d		18 15			18 23	18 32					18 43					18 59				19 16				19 25
Tring	d		18a22				18 38			18 43		18a53			18 59					19 12	19a26				19 30
Cheddington	d									18 48							19 08			19 17					
Leighton Buzzard	d				18 19		18 47			18 53			18 42		19 07					19 23				19 19	19 38
Bletchley	d					18 41	18 54			19 01							19 18			19a31				19 25	19 46
Milton Keynes Central 10	a				18 30	18 45	19 00			19 06			18 52		19 19		19 23					19 13		19 30	19 52
	d			18u13	18 32	18 46				19 07	18u40		18 54				19 23					19 13		19 31	
Wolverton	d				18 36	18 49				19 10			18 57				19 27							19 35	
Northampton	a				18 50	19 03				19 25			19 10				19 39							19 49	
Rugby	a				19 17			18 51					19 38				20 04	19 22					19 38	20 17	
Nuneaton	a										19 12						20 16								
Coventry	a			18 42	19 29			19 02					19 49			19 22						19 42		20 29	
Birmingham International ✈	a			18 53	19 45			19 13					20 04			19 33						19 53		20 45	
Birmingham New Street 12	a			19 08	20 01			19 27					20 16			19 45						20 06		21 01	
Sandwell & Dudley	a															19 58									
Wolverhampton 7	a															20 12						20 36			

		SN	VT	LM		VT	VT	LM	VT	VT	LM	LM	VT	LM		LM	SN	VT	LM	VT	VT	LM	VT	LM	
			R			R	R		R	R															
		1	1	1		1	1	1	1	1	1	1	◇1	1		1	1	◇1	1	◇1	◇1	◇1	◇1	1	
			☕			☕	☕		☕	☕			☕					☕		☕	☕		☕		
London Euston 15 ⊖	d		19 03	19 04		19 07	19 10	19 13	19 20	19 23	19 24	19 34	19 43	19 46		19 54		20 03	20 04	20 07	20 10	20 13	20 23	20 24	
East Croydon	d	18 10															19 10								
Clapham Junction	d	18 39															19 39								
Imperial Wharf	d	18 44															19 44								
West Brompton ⊖	d	18 47															19 47								
Kensington (Olympia) ⊖	d	18 50															19 50								
Shepherd's Bush	d	18 53															19 53								
Wembley Central ⊖	d	19 08															20 08								
Harrow & Wealdstone ⊖	d	19 13		19 17								19 46					20 13		20 17						
Bushey	d			19 22								19 51							20 22						
Watford Junction	a	19 20		19 25							19 40	19 54				20 09	20 20		20 25					20 40	
	d	19 21		19 26						19u37	19 42	19 55				20 11	20 20		20 26				20u37	20 42	
Kings Langley	d			19 30								19 59							20 30						
Apsley	d			19 34								20 03							20 34						
Hemel Hempstead	d	19 28		19 37							19 49	20 06				20 18	20 28		20 37					20 49	
Berkhamsted	d	19 33		19 42							19 54	20 11				20 23	20 32		20 42					20 55	
Tring	d	19 40		19a48							20 01	20a17					20 39		20a48					21 00	
Cheddington	d										20 06													21 05	
Leighton Buzzard	d	19 52						19 43			20 12			20 18		20 36	20 48					20 42		21 10	
Bletchley	d	20 01									20 19					20 43	20 55					20 50		21 17	
Milton Keynes Central 10	a	20 06						19 55			20 24		20 13	20 28		20 48	21 01				20 40	20 54		21 23	
	d							19 56					20 13	20 30		20 49						20 55			
Wolverton	d							19 59						20 33		20 52						20 59			
Northampton	a							20 11						20 47		21 05						21 13			
Rugby	a		19 51					20 38						21 17		21 38		20 51							
Nuneaton	a					20 02														21 02					
Coventry	a		20 02					20 49		20 22			20 42	21 29		21 49		21 02					21 22		
Birmingham International ✈	a		20 13					21 04		20 33			20 53	21 45		22 04		21 13					21 33		
Birmingham New Street 12	a		20 27					21 16		20 45			21 06	22 01		22 16		21 25					21 46		
Sandwell & Dudley	a									20 58			21 23										21 58		
Wolverhampton 7	a									21 12			21 38					21 56					22 12		

A ◇ from Coventry

Table 66

Mondays to Fridays

from 2 April

London - Watford Junction, Milton Keynes Central, Northampton and West Midlands

Network Diagram - see first Page of Table 59

Station		LM	VT	LM	LM	VT	VT	SN	LM	VT		VT	LM		LM	LM	VT	LM	LM	SN		VT	LM	LM	VT
		1	◇1	1	1	◇1	◇1	1	1	◇1		◇1	1		1	1	◇1	1	1	1		◇1	1	1	◇1
			☕			☕	☕			☕		☕					☕					☕			☕
London Euston 15 ⊖	d	20 34	20 43	20 46	20 54	21 00	21 03		21 04	21 07		21 10	21 13		21 24	21 34	21 43	21 46	21 54			22 00	22 04	22 24	22 30
East Croydon 🚢	d																								
Clapham Junction	d							20 39												21 39					
Imperial Wharf	d							20 44												21 44					
West Brompton ⊖	d							20 47												21 47					
Kensington (Olympia) ⊖	d							20 50												21 50					
Shepherd's Bush	d							20 53												21 53					
Wembley Central ⊖	d							21 08																	
Harrow & Wealdstone ⊖	d	20 46						21 13	21 17							21 46				22 16			22 19		
Bushey	d	20 51							21 22							21 51									
Watford Junction	a	20 54			21 10			21 20	21 25						21 39	21 53			22 09	22 23			22 25	22 39	
	d	20 55			21 11			21 20	21 26			21u25			21 41	21 54	21u58		22 11				22 26	22 40	22u45
Kings Langley	d	20 59							21 30							21 58							22 30		
Apsley	d	21 03							21 34							22 02							22 33		
Hemel Hempstead	d	21 06			21 18			21 28	21 36						21 48	22 05			22 18				22 36	22 47	
Berkhamsted	d	21 11			21 23			21 32	21 41						21 53	22 10			22 23				22 40	22 52	
Tring	d	21a17						21 39	21 48							22 16			22 27				22 45		
Cheddington	d								21 53							22 22									
Leighton Buzzard	d			21 18	21 36			21 50	21 57				21 44		22 07	22 26		22 18	22 37				22 56	23 06	
Bletchley	d				21 43			21 58	22a04				21 52		22 15	22 33			22 45				23 05	23 13	
Milton Keynes Central 10	a		21 13	21 27	21 48	21 30	21 33	22 05		21 37			21 56		22 21	22 38	22 17	22 32	22 53			22 30	23 11	23 21	23 28
	d		21 13	21 29	21 49		21 34			21 38			21 57				22 17	22 32	22 56			22 31		23 22	23 29
Wolverton	d			21 32	21 52								22 00					22 36	22 59					23 25	
Northampton	a			21 46	22 05								22 14					22 49	23 13					23 39	
Rugby	a			22 17			21 56					22 02	22 38					23 17				22 52			23 58
Nuneaton	a									22 07												23 03			
Coventry	a		21 42	22 29			22 06						22 49				22 46	23 29							00 10
Birmingham International ✈	a		21 53	22 45			22 18						23 06				23 00	23 47							00 21
Birmingham New Street 12	a		22 06	23 02			22 29						23 19				23 16	00 04							00 32
Sandwell & Dudley	a		22 23				22 40										23 33								
Wolverhampton 7 🚢	a		22 38				22 56										23 47								01 03

Station		LM	LM	SN	LM	VT FX		VT FO	LM
		1	1	1	1	◇1		◇1	1
						☕		☕	
London Euston 15 ⊖	d	22 34	22 54		23 24	23 30		23 30	23 34
East Croydon 🚢	d								
Clapham Junction	d			22 39					
Imperial Wharf	d			22 44					
West Brompton ⊖	d			22 47					
Kensington (Olympia) ⊖	d			22 50					
Shepherd's Bush	d			22 53					
Wembley Central ⊖	d								
Harrow & Wealdstone ⊖	d	22 49		23 16					23 46
Bushey	d	22 54							23 51
Watford Junction	a	22 57	23 09	23 23	23 39				23 54
	d	22 58	23 10		23 40				23 54
Kings Langley	d	23 02	23 14						23 59
Apsley	d	23 06	23 18						00 02
Hemel Hempstead	d	23 09	23 21		23 47				00 05
Berkhamsted	d	23 14	23 26		23 52				00 09
Tring	d	23 18	23 33						00 15
Cheddington	d	23 24							00 20
Leighton Buzzard	d	23 30	23 40		00 05				00 26
Bletchley	d	23 37	23 47		00 13				00 33
Milton Keynes Central 10	a	23 45	23 55		00 21	00 27		00 27	00 41
	d		23 55		00 21	00 28		00 28	
Wolverton	d		23 59		00 25				
Northampton	a		00 13		00 38				
Rugby	a					01 00		01 05	
Nuneaton	a								
Coventry	a					01 13		01 18	
Birmingham International ✈	a					01 24		01 29	
Birmingham New Street 12	a					01 36		01 41	
Sandwell & Dudley	a								
Wolverhampton 7 🚢	a					02 07		02 10	

Table 66

Saturdays
until 31 March

London - Watford Junction, Milton Keynes Central, Northampton and West Midlands

Network Diagram - see first Page of Table 59

		LM 1	VT ◇1 ☕	LM 1	LM 1	VT ◇1 ☕	LM 1	LM 1	LM 1	LM 1		SN 1	LM ◇1	LM ◇1	SN 1	VT ◇1 ☕	VT ◇1 ☕	LM ◇1	SN 1	VT ◇1 ☕		VT ◇1 ☕	SN 1	VT ◇1 ☕	LM 1
London Euston 15 ⊖	d	21p46	22p30	22p54	23p24	23p30	23p34	00 04	00 34	01 34				05 34		06 05	06 23	06 24		06 36		06 55		07 03	07 04
East Croydon	d																						06 10		
Clapham Junction	d											05 08			05 38				06 09				06 39		
Imperial Wharf	d											05 12			05 42				06 13				06 44		
West Brompton ⊖	d											05 15			05 45				06 16				06 47		
Kensington (Olympia) ⊖	d											05 19			05 49				06 20				06 50		
Shepherd's Bush	d											05 22			05 52				06 23				06 53		
Wembley Central ⊖	d								00 45	01 45					06s07				06 38				07s07		
Harrow & Wealdstone ⊖	d						23p46	00 16	00 50	01 50		05 40		05 46	06 12				06 43				07 12		07 16
Bushey	d						23p51		00 55																07 21
Watford Junction	a			23p09	23p39		23p54	00 22	00 57	01 56		05 47		05 52	06 19			06 39	06 50				07 19		07 24
	d		22b45	23p10	23p40		23p54	00 23	00 58	01 57				05 52	06 19	06u20	06u37	06 41					07 19		07 24
Kings Langley	d			23p14			23p59		01 02					05 57											07 29
Apsley	d			23p18			00 02		01 06					06 01											07 32
Hemel Hempstead	d			23p21	23p47		00 05	00 30	01 09	02 04				06 03	06 27			06 48					07 27		07 35
Berkhamsted	d			23p26	23p52		00 09	00 35	01 14	02 09				06 08	06 31			06 53					07 32		07 40
Tring	d			23p33			00 15	00 40	01 18	02 13				06 13	06 37			06 59					07 39		07 47
Cheddington	d						00 20		01 24					06 18				07 05							07 52
Leighton Buzzard	d	22p18		23p40	00 05		00 26	00 49	01 30	02 22				06 25	06 47			07 10					07 48		07 57
Bletchley	d			23p47	00 13		00 33	00 56	01 37	02 29			05 17	06 32	06 55			07 17					07 55		08 04
Milton Keynes Central 10	a	22p32	23p28	23p55	00 21	00 27	00 41	01 04	01 45	02 37			05 21	06 37	07 00	06 39		07 22				07 25	08 00		08 09
	d	22p32	23p29	23p55	00 21	00 28		01 04	01 46				05 21	06 37		06 41		07 23							08 10
Wolverton	d	22p36		23p59	00 25			01 08	01 49				05 25	06 41				07 26							08 13
Northampton	a	22p49		00 13	00 38			01 21	02 03				05 37	06 53				07 39							08 26
Rugby	a	23p17	23p58			01 05							06 01	07 17		07 02		08 04						07 51	08 59
Nuneaton	a												06 16					08 16							
Coventry	a	23p29	00 10			01 18								07 29			07 22							08 02	09 10
Birmingham International ✈	a	23p47	00 21			01 29								07 45			07 33							08 13	09 28
Birmingham New Street 12	a	00 04	00 32			01 41								08 01			07 45							08 27	09 42
Sandwell & Dudley	a																07 57								
Wolverhampton 7	a		01 03			02 10											08 11								

		VT ◇1 ☕	VT ◇1 ☕	LM 1	LM 1	VT ◇1 ☕		VT ◇1 ☕	LM ◇1	LM ◇1	SN 1	VT ◇1 ☕	LM 1	VT ◇1 ☕	VT ◇1 ☕	VT ◇1 ☕		LM 1	LM 1	VT ◇1 ☕	LM ◇1		VT ◇1 ☕	LM ◇1	SN 1
London Euston 15 ⊖	d	07 20	07 23	07 24	07 34	07 35		07 43	07 46	07 54		08 03	08 04	08 10	08 20	08 23		08 24	08 34	08 43	08 46		08 50	08 54	
East Croydon	d										07 10														08 10
Clapham Junction	d										07 39														08 39
Imperial Wharf	d										07 44														08 44
West Brompton ⊖	d										07 47														08 47
Kensington (Olympia) ⊖	d										07 50														08 50
Shepherd's Bush	d										07 53														08 53
Wembley Central ⊖	d										08s07														09s07
Harrow & Wealdstone ⊖	d				07 46						08 12		08 16						08 46						09 12
Bushey	d												08 21						08 51						
Watford Junction	a			07 39	07 52				08 00	08 09	08 19		08 24					08 39	08 54				09 04	09 09	09 19
	d		07u37	07 42	07 53				08 01	08 11	08 19		08 25			08u37		08 41	08 55				09 05	09 11	09 19
Kings Langley	d				07 58								08 29						08 59						
Apsley	d				08 01								08 33						09 03						
Hemel Hempstead	d			07 49	08 04					08 18	08 27		08 36					08 48	09 06					09 18	09 27
Berkhamsted	d			07 54	08 09					08 23	08 31		08 41					08 53	09 11					09 23	09 33
Tring	d			08 01	08a16						08 37		08a47					08 59	09a17						09 38
Cheddington	d			08 06														09 04							
Leighton Buzzard	d			08 11						08 36	08 47							09 09						09 36	09 47
Bletchley	d			08 18						08 43	08 55							09 16						09 43	09 55
Milton Keynes Central 10	a	07 50		08 23		08 05		08 13	08 24	08 48	09 00			08 40	08 50			09 21		09 13	09 21		09 24	09 48	10 00
	d							08 13	08 25	08 49										09 13	09 23			09 49	
Wolverton	d									08 52														09 52	
Northampton	a								08 41	09 05											09 39			10 05	
Rugby	a								09 04	09 38		08 51									10 04	10 17			
Nuneaton	a								09 16												10 16				
Coventry	a		08 22					08 42		09 49		09 02				09 22				09 42		10 29			
Birmingham International ✈	a		08 33					08 53		10 04		09 13				09 33				09 53		10 45			
Birmingham New Street 12	a		08 45					09 08		10 16		09 27				09 45				10 08		11 01			
Sandwell & Dudley	a		08 57													09 57									
Wolverhampton 7	a		09 11													10 11									

b Previous night, stops to pick up only

Table 66

Saturdays
until 31 March

London - Watford Junction, Milton Keynes Central, Northampton and West Midlands

Network Diagram - see first Page of Table 59

		VT ◇1 ☕		LM 1	LM ◇1	VT ◇1 ☕	VT ◇1 ☕	LM 1	LM 1	VT ◇1 ☕	LM ◇1			LM 1	SN 1	VT ◇1 ☕	LM 1	VT ◇1 ☕	LM ◇1	VT ◇1 ☕	VT ◇1 ☕	LM 1		LM 1	VT ◇1 ☕
London Euston [15] ⊖	d	09 03		09 04	09 13	09 20	09 23	09 24	09 34	09 43	09 46			09 54		10 03	10 04	10 10	10 13	10 20	10 23	10 24		10 34	10 43
East Croydon	d														09 10										
Clapham Junction	d														09 39										
Imperial Wharf	d														09 44										
West Brompton ⊖	d														09 47										
Kensington (Olympia) ⊖	d														09 50										
Shepherd's Bush	d														09 53										
Wembley Central ⊖	d														10s07										
Harrow & Wealdstone ⊖	d			09 16					09 46						10 12		10 16							10 46	
Bushey	d			09 21					09 51								10 21							10 51	
Watford Junction	a			09 24				09 39	09 54		10 00			10 09	10 19		10 24					10 39		10 54	
	d			09 25			09u37	09 41	09 55		10 01			10 11	10 19		10 25				10u37	10 41		10 55	
Kings Langley	d			09 29					09 59								10 29							10 59	
Apsley	d			09 33					10 03								10 33							11 03	
Hemel Hempstead	d			09 36				09 48	10 06					10 18	10 27		10 36					10 48		11 06	
Berkhamsted	d			09 41				09 53	10 11					10 23	10 31		10 41					10 53		11 11	
Tring	d			09a47				09 59	10a17						10 37		10a47					10 59		11a17	
Cheddington	d							10 04														11 04			
Leighton Buzzard	d				09 42			10 09						10 36	10 47				10 42			11 09			
Bletchley	d				09 50			10 16						10 43	10 55				10 50			11 16			
Milton Keynes Central [10]	a				09 54	09 50		10 21		10 13	10 24			10 48	11 00			10 40	10 54	10 50		11 21			11 13
	d				09 54					10 13	10 25			10 49					10 54						11 13
Wolverton	d				09 58									10 52					10 58						
Northampton	a				10 12						10 40			11 05					11 12						
Rugby	a	09 51			10 38						11 04	11 17				10 51			11 38						
Nuneaton	a										11 16														
Coventry	a	10 02			10 49		10 22			10 42		11 29				11 02			11 49		11 22				11 42
Birmingham International ✈	a	10 13			11 04		10 33			10 53		11 45				11 13			12 04		11 33				11 53
Birmingham New Street [12]	a	10 27			11 16		10 45			11 08		12 01				11 27			12 16		11 45				12 08
Sandwell & Dudley	a						10 57														11 57				
Wolverhampton [7]	a						11 11														12 11				

		LM ◇1		LM ◇1	SN 1	VT ◇1 ☕	LM 1	VT ◇1 ☕		LM ◇1	VT ◇1 ☕	VT ◇1 ☕	LM 1	LM 1	VT ◇1 ☕	LM ◇1		LM ◇1		SN 1	VT ◇1 ☕	LM 1	VT ◇1 ☕	LM ◇1	VT ◇1 ☕
London Euston [15] ⊖	d	10 46		10 54		11 03	11 04	11 10		11 13	11 20	11 23	11 24	11 34	11 43	11 46		11 54			12 03	12 04	12 10	12 13	12 20
East Croydon	d				10 10															11 10					
Clapham Junction	d				10 39															11 39					
Imperial Wharf	d				10 44															11 44					
West Brompton ⊖	d				10 47															11 47					
Kensington (Olympia) ⊖	d				10 50															11 50					
Shepherd's Bush	d				10 53															11 53					
Wembley Central ⊖	d				11s08															12s07					
Harrow & Wealdstone ⊖	d				11 13		11 17							11 46						12 13		12 16			
Bushey	d						11 22							11 51								12 21			
Watford Junction	a	11 00		11 10	11 20		11 25						11 39	11 54		12 00		12 09		12 20		12 24			
	d	11 01		11 11	11 20		11 25					11u37	11 41	11 55		12 01		12 11		12 20		12 25			
Kings Langley	d						11 30							11 59								12 29			
Apsley	d						11 33							12 03								12 33			
Hemel Hempstead	d			11 18	11 28		11 36						11 48	12 06				12 18		12 28		12 36			
Berkhamsted	d			11 23	11 33		11 41						11 53	12 11				12 23		12 32		12 41			
Tring	d				11 38		11a47						11 59	12a17						12 37		12a47			
Cheddington	d												12 04												
Leighton Buzzard	d			11 36	11 47					11 42			12 09					12 36		12 47				12 42	
Bletchley	d			11 43	11 55					11 50			12 16					12 43		12 55				12 50	
Milton Keynes Central [10]	a	11 24		11 48	12 00			11 40		11 54	11 50		12 21		12 13	12 24		12 48		13 00			12 40	12 54	12 50
	d	11 25		11 49						11 54					12 13	12 25		12 49						12 54	
Wolverton	d			11 52						11 58								12 52						12 58	
Northampton	a	11 41		12 05						12 12						12 41		13 05						13 12	
Rugby	a	12 04	12 17			11 51				12 38						13 04	13 17				12 51			13 38	
Nuneaton	a	12 16														13 16									
Coventry	a		12 29			12 02				12 49		12 22			12 42		13 29				13 02			13 49	
Birmingham International ✈	a		12 45			12 13				13 04		12 33			12 53		13 45				13 13			14 04	
Birmingham New Street [12]	a		13 01			12 27				13 16		12 45			13 08		14 01				13 27			14 16	
Sandwell & Dudley	a											12 57													
Wolverhampton [7]	a											13 11													

Table 66

Saturdays
until 31 March

London - Watford Junction, Milton Keynes Central, Northampton and West Midlands

Network Diagram - see first Page of Table 59

		VT ◇1 ☕	LM 1	LM 1		VT ◇1 ☕	LM ◇1		LM ◇1	SN 1	VT ◇1 ☕	LM 1	VT ◇1 ☕	LM ◇1		VT ◇1 ☕	VT ◇1 ☕	LM 1	LM 1	VT ◇1 ☕	LM ◇1		LM ◇1	SN 1	
London Euston 15 ⊖	d	12 23	12 24	12 34		12 43	12 46		12 54		13 03	13 04	13 10	13 13		13 20	13 23	13 24	13 34	13 43	13 46		13 54		
East Croydon	d									12 10														13 10	
Clapham Junction	d									12 39														13 39	
Imperial Wharf	d									12 44														13 44	
West Brompton ⊖	d									12 47														13 47	
Kensington (Olympia) ⊖	d									12 50														13 50	
Shepherd's Bush	d									12 53														13 53	
Wembley Central ⊖	d									13s07														14s08	
Harrow & Wealdstone ⊖	d			12 46						13 12		13 16							13 46					14 13	
Bushey	d			12 51								13 21							13 51						
Watford Junction	a		12 39	12 54			13 00		13 09	13 19		13 24						13 39	13 54		14 00		14 09	14 20	
	d	12u37	12 41	12 55			13 01		13 11	13 19		13 25					13u37	13 41	13 55		14 01		14 11	14 20	
Kings Langley	d			12 59								13 29							13 59						
Apsley	d			13 03								13 33							14 03						
Hemel Hempstead	d		12 48	13 06					13 18	13 27		13 36						13 48	14 06				14 18	14 28	
Berkhamsted	d		12 53	13 11					13 23	13 32		13 41						13 53	14 11				14 23	14 32	
Tring	d		12 59	13a17						13 37		13a47						13 59	14a17					14 37	
Cheddington	d		13 04															14 04							
Leighton Buzzard	d		13 09						13 36	13 47				13 42				14 09					14 36	14 47	
Bletchley	d		13 16						13 43	13 55				13 50				14 16					14 43	14 55	
Milton Keynes Central 10	a		13 21			13 13	13 24		13 48	14 00			13 40	13 54		13 50		14 21		14 13	14 24		14 48	15 00	
	d					13 13	13 25		13 49					13 54						14 13	14 25		14 49		
Wolverton	d								13 52					13 58									14 52		
Northampton	a						13 41		14 05					14 12							14 41		15 05		
Rugby	a						14 04	14 17			13 51			14 38							15 04	15 17			
Nuneaton	a						14 16														15 16				
Coventry	a	13 22				13 42		14 29			14 02			14 49			14 22			14 42		15 29			
Birmingham International ✈	a	13 33				13 53		14 45			14 13			15 04			14 33			14 53		15 45			
Birmingham New Street 12	a	13 45				14 08		15 01			14 27			15 16			14 45			15 08		16 01			
Sandwell & Dudley	a	13 57															14 57								
Wolverhampton 7	a	14 11															15 11								

		VT ◇1 ☕	LM 1	VT ◇1 ☕	LM ◇1	VT ◇1 ☕	VT ◇1 ☕	LM 1	LM 1	VT ◇1 ☕		LM ◇1		LM ◇1	SN 1	VT ◇1 ☕	LM 1	VT ◇1 ☕	LM ◇1	VT ◇1 ☕		VT ◇1 ☕	LM 1	LM 1	VT ◇1 ☕
London Euston 15 ⊖	d	14 03	14 04	14 10	14 13	14 20	14 23	14 24	14 34	14 43		14 46		14 54		15 03	15 04	15 10	15 13	15 20		15 23	15 24	15 34	15 43
East Croydon	d														14 10										
Clapham Junction	d														14 39										
Imperial Wharf	d														14 44										
West Brompton ⊖	d														14 47										
Kensington (Olympia) ⊖	d														14 50										
Shepherd's Bush	d														14 53										
Wembley Central ⊖	d														15s07										
Harrow & Wealdstone ⊖	d		14 17						14 46						15 12		15 16							15 46	
Bushey	d		14 22						14 51								15 21							15 51	
Watford Junction	a		14 25					14 39	14 54			15 00		15 09	15 19		15 24						15 39	15 54	
	d		14 26				14u37	14 41	14 55			15 01		15 11	15 19		15 25					15u37	15 41	15 55	
Kings Langley	d		14 30						14 59								15 29							15 59	
Apsley	d		14 34						15 03								15 33							16 03	
Hemel Hempstead	d		14 37					14 48	15 06					15 18	15 27		15 36						15 48	16 06	
Berkhamsted	d		14 42					14 53	15 11					15 23	15 32		15 41						15 53	16 11	
Tring	d		14a48					14 59	15a17						15 37		15a47						15 59	16a17	
Cheddington	d							15 04															16 04		
Leighton Buzzard	d				14 42			15 09						15 36	15 47				15 42				16 09		
Bletchley	d				14 50			15 16						15 43	15 55				15 50				16 16		
Milton Keynes Central 10	a			14 40	14 54	14 50		15 21		15 13		15 24		15 48	16 00			15 40	15 54	15 50			16 21		16 13
	d				14 54					15 13		15 25		15 49					15 54						16 13
Wolverton	d				14 58									15 52					15 58						
Northampton	a				15 12							15 41		16 05					16 12						
Rugby	a	14 51			15 38							16 04	16 17			15 51			16 38						
Nuneaton	a											16 16													
Coventry	a	15 02			15 49		15 22			15 42			16 29			16 02			16 49			16 22			16 42
Birmingham International ✈	a	15 13			16 04		15 33			15 53			16 45			16 13			17 04			16 33			16 53
Birmingham New Street 12	a	15 27			16 16		15 45			16 08			17 01			16 27			17 16			16 45			17 08
Sandwell & Dudley	a						15 57															16 57			
Wolverhampton 7	a						16 11															17 11			

Table 66

Saturdays
until 31 March

London - Watford Junction, Milton Keynes Central, Northampton and West Midlands

Network Diagram - see first Page of Table 59

		LM ◇1	LM ◇1	SN 1	VT ◇1 ☕		LM 1	VT ◇1 ☕	LM ◇1	VT ◇1 ☕	VT ◇1 ☕	LM 1	LM 1	VT ◇1 ☕	LM ◇1		LM ◇1	SN 1	VT ◇1 ☕	LM 1	VT ◇1 ☕	VT ◇1 ☕	LM ◇1
London Euston 15 ⊖	d	15 46	15 54		16 03		16 04	16 10	16 13	16 20	16 23	16 24	16 34	16 43	16 46		16 54		17 03	17 04	17 07	17 10	17 13
East Croydon	d			15 10														16 10					
Clapham Junction	d			15 39														16 39					
Imperial Wharf	d			15 44														16 44					
West Brompton ⊖	d			15 47														16 47					
Kensington (Olympia) ⊖	d			15 50														16 50					
Shepherd's Bush	d			15 53														16 53					
Wembley Central ⊖	d			16s07														17s07					
Harrow & Wealdstone ⊖	d			16 12			16 16						16 46					17 12		17 16			
Bushey	d						16 21						16 51							17 21			
Watford Junction	a	16 00	16 09	16 19			16 24					16 39	16 54		17 00		17 09	17 19		17 24			
	d	16 01	16 11	16 19			16 25				16u37	16 41	16 55		17 01		17 11	17 19		17 25			
Kings Langley	d						16 29						16 59							17 29			
Apsley	d						16 33						17 03							17 33			
Hemel Hempstead	d		16 18	16 27			16 36					16 48	17 06				17 18	17 27		17 36			
Berkhamsted	d		16 23	16 32			16 41					16 53	17 11				17 23	17 32		17 41			
Tring	d			16 37			16a47					16 59	17a17					17 37		17a47			
Cheddington	d											17 04											
Leighton Buzzard	d		16 36	16 47					16 42			17 09					17 36	17 47					17 42
Bletchley	d		16 43	16 55					16 50			17 16					17 43	17 55					17 50
Milton Keynes Central 10	a	16 24	16 48	17 00				16 40	16 54	16 50		17 21		17 13	17 24		17 48	18 00				17 40	17 54
	d	16 25	16 49						16 54					17 13	17 25		17 49						17 54
Wolverton	d		16 52						16 58								17 52						17 58
Northampton	a	16 41	17 05						17 12						17 41		18 05						18 12
Rugby	a	17 04 17 17			16 51				17 38						18 04 18 17				17 51				18 38
Nuneaton	a	17 16													18 16						18 02		
Coventry	a	17 29			17 02				17 49		17 22			17 42	18 29				18 02				18 49
Birmingham International ✈	a	17 45			17 13				18 04		17 33			17 53	18 45				18 13				19 04
Birmingham New Street 12	a	18 01			17 27				18 16		17 45			18 08	19 01				18 27				19 16
Sandwell & Dudley	a										17 57												
Wolverhampton 7	a										18 11												

		VT ◇1 ☕	VT ◇1 ☕		LM 1	LM 1	VT ◇1 ☕	LM 1	LM ◇1	SN 1	VT ◇1 ☕	LM 1		VT ◇1 ☕	LM ◇1	VT ◇1 ☕	VT ◇1 ☕	LM 1	LM 1	VT ◇1 ☕	LM 1		LM ◇1
London Euston 15 ⊖	d	17 20	17 23		17 24	17 34	17 43	17 46	17 54		18 03	18 04		18 10	18 13	18 20	18 23	18 24	18 34	18 43	18 46		18 54
East Croydon	d									17 10													
Clapham Junction	d									17 39													
Imperial Wharf	d									17 44													
West Brompton ⊖	d									17 47													
Kensington (Olympia) ⊖	d									17 50													
Shepherd's Bush	d									17 53													
Wembley Central ⊖	d									18s07													
Harrow & Wealdstone ⊖	d					17 46				18 12		18 16							18 46				
Bushey	d					17 51						18 21							18 51				
Watford Junction	a				17 39	17 54		18 00	18 09	18 19		18 24						18 39	18 54		19 00		19 09
	d		17u37		17 41	17 55		18 01	18 11	18 19		18 25					18u37	18 41	18 55		19 01		19 11
Kings Langley	d					17 59						18 29							18 59				
Apsley	d					18 03						18 33							19 03				
Hemel Hempstead	d				17 48	18 06			18 18	18 27		18 36						18 48	19 06				19 18
Berkhamsted	d				17 53	18 11			18 23	18 32		18 41						18 53	19 11				19 23
Tring	d				17 59	18a17				18 37		18a47						18 59	19a17				
Cheddington	d				18 04													19 04					
Leighton Buzzard	d				18 09				18 36	18 47					18 42			19 09					19 36
Bletchley	d				18 16				18 43	18 55					18 50			19 16					19 43
Milton Keynes Central 10	a	17 50			18 21		18 13	18 24	18 48	19 00				18 40	18 54	18 50		19 21		19 13	19 24		19 48
	d						18 13	18 25	18 49						18 54					19 13	19 25		19 49
Wolverton	d								18 52						18 58								19 52
Northampton	a							18 40	19 05						19 12						19 40		20 05
Rugby	a							19 04 19 17			18 51				19 38						20 04 20 17		
Nuneaton	a							19 16													20 16		
Coventry	a		18 22				18 42	19 29			19 02				19 49		19 22			19 42	20 29		
Birmingham International ✈	a		18 33				18 53	19 45			19 13				20 04		19 33			19 53	20 45		
Birmingham New Street 12	a		18 45				19 08	20 01			19 25				20 16		19 45			20 08	21 01		
Sandwell & Dudley	a		18 57								19 53						19 58						
Wolverhampton 7	a		19 11								20 08						20 12						

Table 66

Saturdays
until 31 March

London - Watford Junction, Milton Keynes Central, Northampton and West Midlands

Network Diagram - see first Page of Table 59

		SN	VT	LM	VT	LM	LM	VT	VT		LM	VT	LM	SN	LM	VT	VT	VT	VT		LM	LM	SN	VT	VT
		1	◇1	1	◇1	◇1	1	◇1	◇1		1	◇1	◇1	1	1	◇1	◇1	◇1	◇1		◇1	1	1	◇1	◇1
			☕		☕			☕	☕			☕				☕	☕	☕	☕					☕	☕
London Euston 15 ⊖	d		19 03	19 04	19 07	19 13	19 14	19 20	19 23		19 30	19 43	19 46		20 02	20 11	20 20	20 25	20 31		20 34	20 40		21 00	21 03
East Croydon	d	18 10												19 10											
Clapham Junction	d	18 39												19 38									20 25		
Imperial Wharf	d	18 44												19 42									20 29		
West Brompton ⊖	d	18 47												19 45									20 32		
Kensington (Olympia) ⊖	d	18 50												19 48									20 36		
Shepherd's Bush	d	18 53												19 50									20 39		
Wembley Central ⊖	d	19 08																							
Harrow & Wealdstone ⊖	d	19 13		19 17							19 42			20 08								20 52	21 02		
Bushey	d			19 22							19 47														
Watford Junction	a	19 21		19 25			19 30				19 50		20 01	20 15	20 18						20 49	20 58	21 09		
	d			19 26			19 32		19u37		19 51		20 02		20 19			20u40	20u46		20 50	21 00			21u18
Kings Langley	d			19 30							19 55		20 06									21 04			
Apsley	d			19 34							19 59		20 10									21 08			
Hemel Hempstead	d						19 39				20 02		20 13		20 26						20 57				
Berkhamsted	d			19 40			19 45				20 07		20 18		20 31						21 02				
Tring	d			19a46			19 50				20 11		20 23									21 18			
Cheddington	d						19 55						20 28								21 10				
Leighton Buzzard	d					19 42	20 00				20 20		20 35		20 42						21 15				
Bletchley	d					19 50	20 06				20a26		20 42		20 49						21 22	21 30			
Milton Keynes Central 10	a					19 54	20 12	19 50				20 20	20 49		20 54		21 03				21 30	21 38		21 43	21 50
	d					19 54						20 20	20 49				21 05				21 30				21 50
Wolverton	d					19 58							20 53								21 34				
Northampton	a					20 12							21 07								21 51				
Rugby	a		19 51			20 42							21 38			21 15			21 34		22 17				22 11
Nuneaton	a				20 02												21 32								
Coventry	a		20 02			20 54			20 22			20 49	21 49					21 36			22 29				22 22
Birmingham International ✈	a		20 13			21 12			20 33			21 00	22 04					21 50			22 45				22 33
Birmingham New Street 12	a		20 25			21 24			20 45			21 12	22 16					22 04			23 01				22 45
Sandwell & Dudley	a		20 53						20 58									22 24							22 56
Wolverhampton 7	a		21 08						21 12			21 38						22 38							23 10

		LM	LM	VT	LM		SN	LM	SN	LM	LM
		◇1	◇1	◇1	◇1		1	◇1	1	◇1	◇1
				☕							
London Euston 15 ⊖	d	21 08	21 28	21 43	21 54			22 34		23 04	23 44
East Croydon	d										
Clapham Junction	d						21 39		22 39		
Imperial Wharf	d						21 44		22 44		
West Brompton ⊖	d						21 47		22 47		
Kensington (Olympia) ⊖	d						21 50		22 50		
Shepherd's Bush	d						21 53		22 53		
Wembley Central ⊖	d										
Harrow & Wealdstone ⊖	d				22 06		22 13		23 12	23 16	23 56
Bushey	d										
Watford Junction	a	21 24	21 43		22 12		22 20	22 49	23 19	23 23	00 02
	d	21 25	21 44	21u58	22 13			22 50		23 24	00 02
Kings Langley	d				22 17					23 28	00 07
Apsley	d				22 21					23 32	00 11
Hemel Hempstead	d	21 32	21 51		22 24			22 57		23 35	00 13
Berkhamsted	d	21 37	21 56		22 29			23 02		23 40	00 18
Tring	d				22 33					23 44	00 24
Cheddington	d				22 39					23 49	00 29
Leighton Buzzard	d	21 50	22 07		22 45			23 13		23 56	00 34
Bletchley	d	21 57	22 14		22 52			23 20		00 03	00 41
Milton Keynes Central 10	a	22 05	22 22	22 29	23 00			23 28		00 11	00 48
	d	22 06	22 22	22 30	23 01			23 28		00 11	00 48
Wolverton	d	22 09	22 26		23 04			23 32		00 15	00 52
Northampton	a	22 27	22 43		23 18			23 49		00 28	01 10
Rugby	a		23 17	22 51							
Nuneaton	a										
Coventry	a		23 29	23 02							
Birmingham International ✈	a		23 47	23 13							
Birmingham New Street 12	a		00 04	23 25							
Sandwell & Dudley	a			23 36							
Wolverhampton 7	a			23 50							

Table 66

Saturdays
from 7 April

London - Watford Junction, Milton Keynes Central, Northampton and West Midlands

Network Diagram - see first Page of Table 59

		LM	VT	LM	LM	VT	LM	LM	LM	LM		SN	LM	LM	SN	VT	VT	LM	SN	VT		VT	SN	VT	LM
		1	◇1 ☕	1	1	◇1 ☕	1	1	1	1		1	◇1	◇1	1	◇1 ☕	◇1 ☕	◇1	1	◇1 ☕		◇1 ☕	1	◇1 ☕	1
London Euston 15 ⊖	d	21p46	22p30	22p54	23p24	23p30	23p34	00 04	00 34	01 34				05 34		06 05	06 23	06 24		06 36		06 55		07 03	07 04
East Croydon ⇌	d																						06 10		
Clapham Junction	d											05 08			05 38				06 09				06 39		
Imperial Wharf	d											05 12			05 42				06 13				06 44		
West Brompton ⊖	d											05 15			05 45				06 16				06 47		
Kensington (Olympia) ⊖	d											05 19			05 49				06 20				06 50		
Shepherd's Bush	d											05 22			05 52				06 23				06 53		
Wembley Central ⊖	d								00 45	01 45					06 07				06 38				07 07		
Harrow & Wealdstone ⊖	d						23p46	00 16	00 50	01 50		05 40		05 46	06 12				06 43				07 12		07 16
Bushey	d						23p51		00 55																07 21
Watford Junction	a			23p09	23p39		23p54	00 22	00 57	01 56		05 47		05 52	06 19			06 39	06 50				07 19		07 24
	d		22b45	23p10	23p40		23p54	00 23	00 58	01 57				05 52	06 19	06u20	06u37	06 41					07 19		07 24
Kings Langley	d			23p14			23p59		01 02					05 57											07 29
Apsley	d			23p18			00 02		01 06					06 01											07 32
Hemel Hempstead	d			23p21	23p47		00 05	00 30	01 09	02 04				06 03	06 27			06 48					07 27		07 35
Berkhamsted	d			23p26	23p52		00 09	00 35	01 14	02 09				06 08	06 31			06 53					07 32		07 40
Tring	d			23p33			00 15	00 40	01 18	02 13				06 13	06 37			06 59					07 39		07 47
Cheddington	d						00 20		01 24					06 18				07 05							07 52
Leighton Buzzard	d	22p18		23p40	00 05		00 26	00 49	01 30	02 22				06 25	06 47			07 10					07 48		07 57
Bletchley	d			23p47	00 13		00 33	00 56	01 37	02 29			05 17	06 32	06 55			07 17					07 55		08 04
Milton Keynes Central 10	a	22p32	23p28	23p55	00 21	00 27	00 41	01 04	01 45	02 37			05 21	06 37	07 00	06 39		07 22				07 25	08 00		08 09
	d	22p32	23p29	23p55	00 21	00 28		01 04	01 46				05 21	06 37		06 41		07 23							08 10
Wolverton	d	22p36		23p59	00 25			01 08	01 49				05 25	06 41				07 26							08 13
Northampton	a	22p49		00 13	00 38			01 21	02 03				05 37	06 53				07 39							08 26
Rugby	a	23p17	23p58			01 05							06 01	07 17		07 02		08 04						07 51	08 59
Nuneaton	a												06 16					08 16							
Coventry	a	23p29	00 10			01 18								07 29			07 22							08 02	09 10
Birmingham International ✈	a	23p47	00 21			01 29								07 45			07 33							08 13	09 28
Birmingham New Street 12	a	00 04	00 32			01 41								08 01			07 45							08 27	09 42
Sandwell & Dudley	a																07 57								
Wolverhampton 7 ⇌	a		01 03			02 10											08 11								

		VT	VT	LM	LM	VT		VT	LM	LM	SN	VT	LM	VT	VT	VT		LM	LM	VT	LM		VT	LM	SN
		◇1 ☕	◇1 ☕	1	1	◇1 ☕		◇1 ☕	◇1	◇1	1	◇1 ☕	1	◇1 ☕	◇1 ☕	◇1 ☕		1	1	◇1 ☕	◇1		◇1 ☕	◇1	1
London Euston 15 ⊖	d	07 20	07 23	07 24	07 34	07 35		07 43	07 46	07 54		08 03	08 04	08 10	08 20	08 23		08 24	08 34	08 43	08 46		08 50	08 54	
East Croydon ⇌	d										07 10														08 10
Clapham Junction	d										07 39														08 39
Imperial Wharf	d										07 44														08 44
West Brompton ⊖	d										07 47														08 47
Kensington (Olympia) ⊖	d										07 50														08 50
Shepherd's Bush	d										07 53														08 53
Wembley Central ⊖	d										08 07														09 07
Harrow & Wealdstone ⊖	d				07 46						08 12		08 16						08 46						09 12
Bushey	d												08 21						08 51						
Watford Junction	a			07 39	07 52				08 00	08 09	08 19		08 24					08 39	08 54				09 04	09 09	09 19
	d		07u37	07 42	07 53				08 01	08 11	08 19		08 25			08u37		08 41	08 55				09 05	09 11	09 19
Kings Langley	d				07 58								08 29						08 59						
Apsley	d				08 01								08 33						09 03						
Hemel Hempstead	d			07 49	08 04					08 18	08 27		08 36					08 48	09 06					09 18	09 27
Berkhamsted	d			07 54	08 09					08 23	08 31		08 41					08 53	09 11					09 23	09 33
Tring	d			08 01	08a16						08 37		08a47					08 59	09a17						09 38
Cheddington	d			08 06														09 04							
Leighton Buzzard	d			08 11						08 36	08 47							09 09						09 36	09 47
Bletchley	d			08 18						08 43	08 55							09 16						09 43	09 55
Milton Keynes Central 10	a	07 50		08 23		08 05		08 13	08 24	08 48	09 00			08 40	08 50			09 21		09 13	09 21		09 24	09 48	10 00
	d							08 13	08 25	08 49										09 13	09 23			09 49	
Wolverton	d									08 52														09 52	
Northampton	a								08 41	09 05											09 39			10 05	
Rugby	a								09 04	09 38		08 51									10 04	10 17			
Nuneaton	a								09 16												10 16				
Coventry	a		08 22					08 42		09 49		09 02				09 22				09 42		10 29			
Birmingham International ✈	a		08 33					08 53		10 04		09 13				09 33				09 53		10 45			
Birmingham New Street 12	a		08 45					09 08		10 16		09 27				09 45				10 08		11 01			
Sandwell & Dudley	a		08 57													09 57									
Wolverhampton 7 ⇌	a		09 11													10 11									

b Previous night, stops to pick up only

Table 66

Saturdays
from 7 April

London - Watford Junction, Milton Keynes Central, Northampton and West Midlands

Network Diagram - see first Page of Table 59

		VT		LM	LM	VT	VT	LM	LM	VT	LM			LM	SN	VT	LM	VT	LM	VT	VT	LM		LM	VT
		◇1		1	◇1	◇1	◇1	1	1	◇1	◇1			1	1	◇1	1	◇1	◇1	◇1	◇1	1		1	◇1
		☕				☕	☕			☕						☕		☕		☕	☕				☕
London Euston [15] ⊖	d	09 03		09 04	09 13	09 20	09 23	09 24	09 34	09 43	09 46			09 54		10 03	10 04	10 10	10 13	10 20	10 23	10 24		10 34	10 43
East Croydon	d														09 10										
Clapham Junction	d														09 39										
Imperial Wharf	d														09 44										
West Brompton ⊖	d														09 47										
Kensington (Olympia) ⊖	d														09 50										
Shepherd's Bush	d														09 53										
Wembley Central ⊖	d														10 07										
Harrow & Wealdstone ⊖	d			09 16					09 46						10 12		10 16							10 46	
Bushey	d			09 21					09 51								10 21							10 51	
Watford Junction	a			09 24				09 39	09 54		10 00			10 09	10 19		10 24					10 39		10 54	
	d			09 25			09u37	09 41	09 55		10 01			10 11	10 19		10 25				10u37	10 41		10 55	
Kings Langley	d			09 29					09 59								10 29							10 59	
Apsley	d			09 33					10 03								10 33							11 03	
Hemel Hempstead	d			09 36				09 48	10 06					10 18	10 27		10 36					10 48		11 06	
Berkhamsted	d			09 41				09 53	10 11					10 23	10 31		10 41					10 53		11 11	
Tring	d			09a47				09 59	10a17						10 37		10a47					10 59		11a17	
Cheddington	d							10 04														11 04			
Leighton Buzzard	d				09 42			10 09						10 36	10 47				10 42			11 09			
Bletchley	d				09 50			10 16						10 43	10 55				10 50			11 16			
Milton Keynes Central [10]	a				09 54	09 50		10 21		10 13	10 24			10 48	11 00			10 40	10 54	10 50		11 21			11 13
	d				09 54					10 13	10 25			10 49					10 54						11 13
Wolverton	d				09 58									10 52					10 58						
Northampton	a				10 12						10 40			11 05					11 12						
Rugby	a	09 51			10 38						11 04	11 17				10 51			11 38						
Nuneaton	a										11 16														
Coventry	a	10 02			10 49		10 22			10 42		11 29				11 02			11 49		11 22				11 42
Birmingham International ✈	a	10 13			11 04		10 33			10 53		11 45				11 13			12 04		11 33				11 53
Birmingham New Street [12]	a	10 27			11 16		10 45			11 08		12 01				11 27			12 16		11 45				12 08
Sandwell & Dudley	a						10 57														11 57				
Wolverhampton [7]	a						11 11														12 11				

		LM		LM	SN	VT	LM	VT		LM	VT	VT	LM	LM	VT	LM		LM		SN	VT	LM	VT	LM	VT
		◇1		◇1	1	◇1	1	◇1		◇1	◇1	◇1	1	1	◇1	◇1		◇1		1	◇1	1	◇1	◇1	◇1
						☕		☕			☕	☕			☕						☕		☕		☕
London Euston [15] ⊖	d	10 46		10 54		11 03	11 04	11 10		11 13	11 20	11 23	11 24	11 34	11 43	11 46		11 54			12 03	12 04	12 10	12 13	12 20
East Croydon	d				10 10															11 10					
Clapham Junction	d				10 39															11 39					
Imperial Wharf	d				10 44															11 44					
West Brompton ⊖	d				10 47															11 47					
Kensington (Olympia) ⊖	d				10 50															11 50					
Shepherd's Bush	d				10 53															11 53					
Wembley Central ⊖	d				11 08															12 07					
Harrow & Wealdstone ⊖	d				11 13		11 17							11 46						12 13		12 16			
Bushey	d						11 22							11 51								12 21			
Watford Junction	a	11 00		11 10	11 20		11 25						11 39	11 54		12 00		12 09		12 20		12 24			
	d	11 01		11 11	11 20		11 25					11u37	11 41	11 55		12 01		12 11		12 20		12 25			
Kings Langley	d						11 30							11 59								12 29			
Apsley	d						11 33							12 03								12 33			
Hemel Hempstead	d			11 18	11 28		11 36						11 48	12 06				12 18		12 28		12 36			
Berkhamsted	d			11 23	11 33		11 41						11 53	12 11				12 23		12 32		12 41			
Tring	d				11 38		11a47						11 59	12a17						12 37		12a47			
Cheddington	d												12 04												
Leighton Buzzard	d			11 36	11 47					11 42			12 09					12 36		12 47				12 42	
Bletchley	d			11 43	11 55					11 50			12 16					12 43		12 55				12 50	
Milton Keynes Central [10]	a	11 24		11 48	12 00			11 40		11 54	11 50		12 21		12 13	12 24		12 48		13 00			12 40	12 54	12 50
	d	11 25		11 49						11 54					12 13	12 25		12 49						12 54	
Wolverton	d			11 52						11 58								12 52						12 58	
Northampton	a	11 41		12 05						12 12						12 41		13 05						13 12	
Rugby	a	12 04	12 17			11 51				12 38						13 04	13 17				12 51			13 38	
Nuneaton	a	12 16														13 16									
Coventry	a		12 29			12 02				12 49		12 22			12 42		13 29				13 02			13 49	
Birmingham International ✈	a		12 45			12 13				13 04		12 33			12 53		13 45				13 13			14 04	
Birmingham New Street [12]	a		13 01			12 27				13 16		12 45			13 08		14 01				13 27			14 16	
Sandwell & Dudley	a											12 57													
Wolverhampton [7]	a											13 11													

Table 66

Saturdays

from 7 April

London - Watford Junction, Milton Keynes Central, Northampton and West Midlands

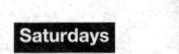

Network Diagram - see first Page of Table 59

		VT ◇1 ☕	LM 1	LM 1		VT ◇1 ☕	LM ◇1		LM ◇1	SN 1	VT ◇1 ☕	LM 1	VT ◇1 ☕	LM ◇1		VT ◇1 ☕	VT ◇1 ☕	LM 1	LM 1	VT ◇1 ☕	LM ◇1		LM ◇1	SN 1	
London Euston 15 ⊖	d	12 23	12 24	12 34		12 43	12 46		12 54		13 03	13 04	13 10	13 13		13 20	13 23	13 24	13 34	13 43	13 46		13 54		
East Croydon 🚊	d									12 10														13 10	
Clapham Junction	d									12 39														13 39	
Imperial Wharf	d									12 44														13 44	
West Brompton ⊖	d									12 47														13 47	
Kensington (Olympia) ⊖	d									12 50														13 50	
Shepherd's Bush	d									12 53														13 53	
Wembley Central ⊖	d									13 07														14 08	
Harrow & Wealdstone ⊖	d			12 46						13 12		13 16							13 46					14 13	
Bushey	d			12 51								13 21							13 51						
Watford Junction	a		12 39	12 54			13 00		13 09	13 19		13 24						13 39	13 54		14 00		14 09	14 20	
	d	12u37	12 41	12 55			13 01		13 11	13 19		13 25					13u37	13 41	13 55		14 01		14 11	14 20	
Kings Langley	d			12 59								13 29							13 59						
Apsley	d			13 03								13 33							14 03						
Hemel Hempstead	d		12 48	13 06					13 18	13 27		13 36						13 48	14 06				14 18	14 28	
Berkhamsted	d		12 53	13 11					13 23	13 32		13 41						13 53	14 11				14 23	14 32	
Tring	d		12 59	13a17						13 37		13a47						13 59	14a17					14 37	
Cheddington	d		13 04															14 04							
Leighton Buzzard	d		13 09						13 36	13 47				13 42				14 09					14 36	14 47	
Bletchley	d		13 16						13 43	13 55				13 50				14 16					14 43	14 55	
Milton Keynes Central 10	a		13 21			13 13	13 24		13 48	14 00			13 40	13 54		13 50		14 21		14 13	14 24		14 48	15 00	
	d					13 13	13 25		13 49					13 54						14 13	14 25		14 49		
Wolverton	d								13 52					13 58									14 52		
Northampton	a						13 41		14 05					14 12							14 41		15 05		
Rugby	a						14 04	14 17			13 51			14 38							15 04	15 17			
Nuneaton	a						14 16														15 16				
Coventry	a	13 22				13 42		14 29			14 02			14 49			14 22			14 42		15 29			
Birmingham International ✈	a	13 33				13 53		14 45			14 13			15 04			14 33			14 53		15 45			
Birmingham New Street 12	a	13 45				14 08		15 01			14 27			15 16			14 45			15 08		16 01			
Sandwell & Dudley	a	13 57															14 57								
Wolverhampton 7 🚊	a	14 11															15 11								

		VT ◇1 ☕	LM 1	VT ◇1 ☕	LM ◇1	VT ◇1 ☕	VT ◇1 ☕	LM 1	LM 1	VT ◇1 ☕		LM ◇1		LM ◇1	SN 1	VT ◇1 ☕	LM 1	VT ◇1 ☕	LM ◇1	VT ◇1 ☕		VT ◇1 ☕	LM 1	LM 1	VT ◇1 ☕
London Euston 15 ⊖	d	14 03	14 04	14 10	14 13	14 20	14 23	14 24	14 34	14 43		14 46		14 54		15 03	15 04	15 10	15 13	15 20		15 23	15 24	15 34	15 43
East Croydon 🚊	d														14 10										
Clapham Junction	d														14 39										
Imperial Wharf	d														14 44										
West Brompton ⊖	d														14 47										
Kensington (Olympia) ⊖	d														14 50										
Shepherd's Bush	d														14 53										
Wembley Central ⊖	d														15 07										
Harrow & Wealdstone ⊖	d		14 17						14 46						15 12		15 16							15 46	
Bushey	d		14 22						14 51								15 21							15 51	
Watford Junction	a		14 25					14 39	14 54			15 00		15 09	15 19		15 24						15 39	15 54	
	d		14 26				14u37	14 41	14 55			15 01		15 11	15 19		15 25					15u37	15 41	15 55	
Kings Langley	d		14 30						14 59								15 29							15 59	
Apsley	d		14 34						15 03								15 33							16 03	
Hemel Hempstead	d		14 37					14 48	15 06					15 18	15 27		15 36						15 48	16 06	
Berkhamsted	d		14 42					14 53	15 11					15 23	15 32		15 41						15 53	16 11	
Tring	d		14a48					14 59	15a17						15 37		15a47						15 59	16a17	
Cheddington	d							15 04															16 04		
Leighton Buzzard	d				14 42			15 09						15 36	15 47				15 42				16 09		
Bletchley	d				14 50			15 16						15 43	15 55				15 50				16 16		
Milton Keynes Central 10	a			14 40	14 54	14 50		15 21		15 13		15 24		15 48	16 00			15 40	15 54	15 50			16 21		16 13
	d				14 54					15 13		15 25		15 49					15 54						16 13
Wolverton	d				14 58									15 52					15 58						
Northampton	a				15 12							15 41		16 05					16 12						
Rugby	a	14 51			15 38							16 04	16 17			15 51			16 38						
Nuneaton	a											16 16													
Coventry	a	15 02			15 49		15 22			15 42			16 29			16 02			16 49			16 22			16 42
Birmingham International ✈	a	15 13			16 04		15 33			15 53			16 45			16 13			17 04			16 33			16 53
Birmingham New Street 12	a	15 27			16 16		15 45			16 08			17 01			16 27			17 16			16 45			17 08
Sandwell & Dudley	a						15 57															16 57			
Wolverhampton 7 🚊	a						16 11															17 11			

Table 66

Saturdays
from 7 April

London - Watford Junction, Milton Keynes Central, Northampton and West Midlands

Network Diagram - see first Page of Table 59

		LM		LM	SN	VT		LM	VT	LM	VT	VT	LM	LM	VT	LM			LM	SN	VT	LM	VT	VT	LM
		◇1		◇1	1	◇1		1	◇1	◇1	◇1	◇1	1	1	◇1	◇1			◇1	1	◇1	1	◇1	◇1	◇1
						☕			☕		☕	☕			☕						☕		☕	☕	
London Euston 15 ⊖	d	15 46		15 54		16 03		16 04	16 10	16 13	16 20	16 23	16 24	16 34	16 43	16 46			16 54		17 03	17 04	17 07	17 10	17 13
East Croydon	d				15 10															16 10					
Clapham Junction	d				15 39															16 39					
Imperial Wharf	d				15 44															16 44					
West Brompton ⊖	d				15 47															16 47					
Kensington (Olympia) ⊖	d				15 50															16 50					
Shepherd's Bush	d				15 53															16 53					
Wembley Central ⊖	d				16 07															17 07					
Harrow & Wealdstone ⊖	d				16 12			16 16						16 46						17 12		17 16			
Bushey	d							16 21						16 51								17 21			
Watford Junction	a	16 00		16 09	16 19			16 24					16 39	16 54		17 00			17 09	17 19		17 24			
	d	16 01		16 11	16 19			16 25				16u37	16 41	16 55		17 01			17 11	17 19		17 25			
Kings Langley	d							16 29						16 59								17 29			
Apsley	d							16 33						17 03								17 33			
Hemel Hempstead	d			16 18	16 27			16 36					16 48	17 06					17 18	17 27		17 36			
Berkhamsted	d			16 23	16 32			16 41					16 53	17 11					17 23	17 32		17 41			
Tring	d				16 37			16a47					16 59	17a17						17 37		17a47			
Cheddington	d												17 04												
Leighton Buzzard	d			16 36	16 47					16 42			17 09						17 36	17 47					17 42
Bletchley	d			16 43	16 55					16 50			17 16						17 43	17 55					17 50
Milton Keynes Central 10	a	16 24		16 48	17 00				16 40	16 54	16 50		17 21		17 13	17 24			17 48	18 00				17 40	17 54
	d	16 25		16 49						16 54					17 13	17 25			17 49						17 54
Wolverton	d			16 52						16 58									17 52						17 58
Northampton	a	16 41		17 05						17 12						17 41			18 05						18 12
Rugby	a	17 04	17 17			16 51				17 38						18 04	18 17				17 51				18 38
Nuneaton	a	17 16														18 16							18 02		
Coventry	a		17 29			17 02				17 49		17 22			17 42		18 29				18 02				18 49
Birmingham International ✈	a		17 45			17 13				18 04		17 33			17 53		18 45				18 13				19 04
Birmingham New Street 12	a		18 01			17 27				18 16		17 45			18 08		19 01				18 27				19 16
Sandwell & Dudley	a											17 57													
Wolverhampton 7	a											18 11													

		VT	VT		LM	LM	VT	LM		LM	SN	VT	LM		VT	LM	VT	VT	LM	LM	VT	LM			LM
		◇1	◇1		1	1	◇1	1		◇1	1	◇1	1		◇1	◇1	◇1	◇1	1	1	◇1	1			◇1
		☕	☕				☕					☕			☕		☕	☕			☕				
London Euston 15 ⊖	d	17 20	17 23		17 24	17 34	17 43	17 46		17 54		18 03	18 04		18 10	18 13	18 20	18 23	18 24	18 34	18 43	18 46			18 54
East Croydon	d										17 10														
Clapham Junction	d										17 39														
Imperial Wharf	d										17 44														
West Brompton ⊖	d										17 47														
Kensington (Olympia) ⊖	d										17 50														
Shepherd's Bush	d										17 53														
Wembley Central ⊖	d										18 07														
Harrow & Wealdstone ⊖	d					17 46					18 12		18 16							18 46					
Bushey	d					17 51							18 21							18 51					
Watford Junction	a				17 39	17 54		18 00		18 09	18 19		18 24						18 39	18 54		19 00			19 09
	d		17u37		17 41	17 55		18 01		18 11	18 19		18 25					18u37	18 41	18 55		19 01			19 11
Kings Langley	d					17 59							18 29							18 59					
Apsley	d					18 03							18 33							19 03					
Hemel Hempstead	d				17 48	18 06				18 18	18 27		18 36						18 48	19 06					19 18
Berkhamsted	d				17 53	18 11				18 23	18 32		18 41						18 53	19 11					19 23
Tring	d				17 59	18a17					18 37		18a47						18 59	19a17					
Cheddington	d				18 04														19 04						
Leighton Buzzard	d				18 09					18 36	18 47					18 42			19 09						19 36
Bletchley	d				18 16					18 43	18 55					18 50			19 16						19 43
Milton Keynes Central 10	a	17 50			18 21		18 13	18 24		18 48	19 00				18 40	18 54	18 50		19 21		19 13	19 24			19 48
	d						18 13	18 25		18 49						18 54					19 13	19 25			19 49
Wolverton	d									18 52						18 58									19 52
Northampton	a							18 40		19 05						19 12						19 40			20 05
Rugby	a							19 04	19 17			18 51				19 38						20 04	20 17		
Nuneaton	a							19 16														20 16			
Coventry	a		18 22				18 42		19 29			19 02				19 49		19 22			19 42		20 29		
Birmingham International ✈	a		18 33				18 53		19 45			19 13				20 04		19 33			19 53		20 45		
Birmingham New Street 12	a		18 45				19 08		20 01			19 25				20 16		19 45			20 08		21 01		
Sandwell & Dudley	a		18 57									19 53						19 58							
Wolverhampton 7	a		19 11									20 08						20 12							

Table 66

Saturdays
from 7 April

London - Watford Junction, Milton Keynes Central, Northampton and West Midlands

Network Diagram - see first Page of Table 59

		SN	VT	LM	VT	LM	LM	VT	VT		LM	VT	LM	SN	LM	VT	VT	VT	VT		LM	LM	SN	VT	VT
		1	◇1	1	◇1	◇1	1	◇1	◇1		1	◇1	◇1	1	1	◇1	◇1	◇1	◇1		◇1	1	1	◇1	◇1
			☕		☕			☕	☕			☕				☕	☕	☕	☕					☕	☕
London Euston 15 ⊖	d		19 03	19 04	19 07	19 13	19 14	19 20	19 23		19 30	19 43	19 46		20 02	20 11	20 20	20 25	20 31		20 34	20 40		21 00	21 03
East Croydon	d	18 10												19 10											
Clapham Junction	d	18 39												19 38									20 25		
Imperial Wharf	d	18 44												19 42									20 29		
West Brompton ⊖	d	18 47												19 45									20 32		
Kensington (Olympia) ⊖	d	18 50												19 48									20 36		
Shepherd's Bush	d	18 53												19 50									20 39		
Wembley Central ⊖	d	19 08																							
Harrow & Wealdstone ⊖	d	19 13		19 17							19 42			20 08								20 52	21 02		
Bushey	d			19 22							19 47														
Watford Junction	a	19 21		19 25			19 30				19 50		20 01	20 15	20 18						20 49	20 58	21 09		
	d			19 26			19 32		19u37		19 51		20 02		20 19			20u40	20u46		20 50	21 00			21u18
Kings Langley	d			19 30							19 55		20 06									21 04			
Apsley	d			19 34							19 59		20 10									21 08			
Hemel Hempstead	d						19 39				20 02		20 13		20 26						20 57				
Berkhamsted	d			19 40			19 45				20 07		20 18		20 31						21 02				
Tring	d			19a46			19 50				20 11		20 23									21 18			
Cheddington	d						19 55						20 28								21 10				
Leighton Buzzard	d					19 42	20 00				20 20		20 35		20 42						21 15				
Bletchley	d					19 50	20 06				20a26		20 42		20 49						21 22	21 30			
Milton Keynes Central 10	a					19 54	20 12	19 50				20 20	20 49		20 54		21 03				21 30	21 38		21 43	21 50
	d					19 54						20 20	20 49				21 05				21 30				21 50
Wolverton	d					19 58							20 53								21 34				
Northampton	a					20 12							21 07								21 51				
Rugby	a		19 51			20 42							21 38			21 15			21 34		22 17				22 11
Nuneaton	a				20 02												21 32								
Coventry	a		20 02			20 54			20 22			20 49	21 49					21 36			22 29				22 22
Birmingham International ✈	a		20 13			21 12			20 33			21 00	22 04					21 50			22 45				22 33
Birmingham New Street 12	a		20 25			21 24			20 45			21 12	22 16					22 04			23 01				22 45
Sandwell & Dudley	a		20 53						20 58									22 24							22 56
Wolverhampton 7	a		21 08						21 12			21 38						22 38							23 10

		LM	LM	VT	LM		SN	LM	SN	LM	LM
		◇1	◇1	◇1	◇1		1	◇1	1	◇1	◇1
				☕							
London Euston 15 ⊖	d	21 08	21 28	21 43	21 54			22 34		23 04	23 44
East Croydon	d										
Clapham Junction	d						21 39		22 39		
Imperial Wharf	d						21 44		22 44		
West Brompton ⊖	d						21 47		22 47		
Kensington (Olympia) ⊖	d						21 50		22 50		
Shepherd's Bush	d						21 53		22 53		
Wembley Central ⊖	d										
Harrow & Wealdstone ⊖	d				22 06		22 13		23 12	23 16	23 56
Bushey	d										
Watford Junction	a	21 24	21 43		22 12		22 20	22 49	23 19	23 23	00 02
	d	21 25	21 44	21u58	22 13			22 50		23 24	00 02
Kings Langley	d				22 17					23 28	00 07
Apsley	d				22 21					23 32	00 11
Hemel Hempstead	d	21 32	21 51		22 24			22 57		23 35	00 13
Berkhamsted	d	21 37	21 56		22 29			23 02		23 40	00 18
Tring	d				22 33					23 44	00 24
Cheddington	d				22 39					23 49	00 29
Leighton Buzzard	d	21 50	22 07		22 45			23 13		23 56	00 34
Bletchley	d	21 57	22 14		22 52			23 20		00 03	00 41
Milton Keynes Central 10	a	22 05	22 22	22 29	23 00			23 28		00 11	00 48
	d	22 06	22 22	22 30	23 01			23 28		00 11	00 48
Wolverton	d	22 09	22 26		23 04			23 32		00 15	00 52
Northampton	a	22 27	22 43		23 18			23 49		00 28	01 10
Rugby	a		23 17	22 51							
Nuneaton	a										
Coventry	a		23 29	23 02							
Birmingham International ✈	a		23 47	23 13							
Birmingham New Street 12	a		00 04	23 25							
Sandwell & Dudley	a			23 36							
Wolverhampton 7	a			23 50							

Table 66

Sundays

London - Watford Junction, Milton Keynes Central, Northampton and West Midlands

Network Diagram - see first Page of Table 59

		LM	LM	LM	LM	LM	LM	LM	LM	LM		VT	VT	VT	LM	SN	VT	VT	LM	VT		VT	LM	SN	VT
		◇1	◇1	◇1	◇1			◇1	◇1	◇1		◇1	◇1	◇1	◇1	1	◇1	◇1	◇1	◇1		◇1	◇1	1	◇1
		A	A	A																					
						bus	bus					☕	☕	☕			☕	☕		☕		☕			☕
London Euston 15 ⊖	d	21p28	23p04	23p44	00 15			06 53	07 23	07 50		08 10	08 15	08 20	08 23		08 45	08 50	08 53	09 15		09 20	09 23		09 45
East Croydon	d																								
Clapham Junction	d															08 15								09 15	
Imperial Wharf	d															08 19								09 19	
West Brompton ⊖	d															08 22								09 22	
Kensington (Olympia) ⊖	d															08 26								09 26	
Shepherd's Bush	d															08 29								09 29	
Wembley Central ⊖	d				00 24																				
Harrow & Wealdstone ⊖	d		23p16	23p56	00 29			07 05	07 35	08 02					08 35	08 48			09 05				09 35	09 48	
Bushey	d																								
Watford Junction	a	21p43	23p23	00 02	00 35			07 11	07 41	08 08					08 41	08 56			09 11				09 41	09 58	
	d	21p44	23p24	00 02	00 35	02 50	02 55	07 12	07 42	08 08					08 42			09u05	09 12				09 42		
Kings Langley	d		23p28	00 07	00 40		03 11		07 46						08 46								09 46		
Apsley	d		23p32	00 11	00 44		03 22		07 50						08 50								09 50		
Hemel Hempstead	d	21p51	23p35	00 13	00 46	03 16	03 28	07 19	07 53	08 15					08 53				09 19				09 53		
Berkhamsted	d	21p56	23p40	00 18	00 51		03 39	07 24	07 58	08 20					08 58				09 24				09 58		
Tring	d		23p44	00 24	00 56		03 55	07 28		08 25									09 28						
Cheddington	d		23p49	00 29	01 01		04 16	07 34		08 30									09 34						
Leighton Buzzard	d	22p07	23p56	00 34	01 06	03 53	04 37	07 40	08 11	08 37					09 11				09 40				10 11		
Bletchley	d	22p14	00 03	00 41	01 13	04 19	05 03	07 47	08 18	08 44					09 18				09 47				10 18		
Milton Keynes Central 10	a	22p22	00 11	00 48	01 19	04 34	05 18	07 55	08 26	08 50		08 55		09 05	09 26		09 31	09 37	09 55			10 06	10 26		10 32
	d	22p22	00 11	00 48	01 19			07 56	08 26	08 51					09 26		09 32	09 38	09 56				10 26		10 33
Wolverton	d	22p26	00 15	00 52	01 23			07 59	08 30	08 54					09 30				09 59				10 30		
Northampton	a	22p43	00 28	01 10	01 36			08 13	08 43	09 09					09 43				10 13				10 43		
Rugby	a	23p17								09 52					10 22		10 07	10 12					11 22		11 07
Nuneaton	a												09 43							10 44					
Coventry	a	23p29								10 03					10 33			10 23					11 33		
Birmingham International	a	23p47								10 13					10 51			10 34					11 51		
Birmingham New Street 12	a	00 04								10 30					11 03			10 47					12 03		
Sandwell & Dudley	a																	10 59							
Wolverhampton 7	a																	11 13							

		VT	LM	VT	VT	LM		SN	VT	VT	LM	VT	VT	LM	SN	VT		LM	LM	VT	VT	SN	LM	VT	LM
		◇1	◇1	◇1	◇1	◇1		1	◇1	◇1	◇1	◇1	◇1	◇1	1	◇1		◇1	1	◇1	◇1	1	◇1	◇1	◇1
		☕		☕	☕				☕	☕		☕	☕			☕				☕	☕			☕	
London Euston 15 ⊖	d	09 50	09 53	10 15	10 20	10 23			10 45	10 50	10 53	11 15	11 20	11 23		11 45		11 53	12 14	12 15	12 18		12 34	12 38	12 50
East Croydon	d																								
Clapham Junction	d							10 15							11 15							12 05			
Imperial Wharf	d							10 19							11 19							12 09			
West Brompton ⊖	d							10 22							11 22							12 12			
Kensington (Olympia) ⊖	d							10 26							11 26							12 16			
Shepherd's Bush	d							10 29							11 29							12 19			
Wembley Central ⊖	d																								
Harrow & Wealdstone ⊖	d		10 05			10 35		10 48			11 05			11 35	11 48			12 05	12 26			12 36			
Bushey	d																		12 31						
Watford Junction	a		10 11			10 41		10 56			11 11			11 41	11 56			12 11	12 34			12 44	12 49		13 06
	d	10u06	10 12			10 42				11u04	11 12			11 42		12u03		12 12	12 34		12u32		12 50		13 06
Kings Langley	d					10 46								11 46					12 39						
Apsley	d					10 50								11 50					12 43						
Hemel Hempstead	d		10 19			10 53					11 19			11 53				12 19	12 45				12 57		
Berkhamsted	d		10 24			10 58					11 24			11 58				12 24	12 50				13 02		
Tring	d		10 28								11 28							12 28	12a57						
Cheddington	d		10 34								11 34							12 34							
Leighton Buzzard	d		10 40			11 11					11 40			12 11				12 40					13 15		13 26
Bletchley	d		10 47			11 18					11 47			12 18				12 47					13 22		
Milton Keynes Central 10	a	10 38	10 55		11 06	11 26			11 32	11 37	11 55	12 02	12 08	12 23		12 26		12 55		12 48			13 27	13 11	13 36
	d	10 39	10 56			11 26			11 33	11 39	11 56			12 23		12 27		12 56					13 28	13 11	13 36
Wolverton	d		10 59			11 30					11 59			12 27				12 59					13 31		
Northampton	a		11 13			11 43					12 13			12 39				13 13					13 44		13 54
Rugby	a	11 13				12 22			12 07	12 13				13 13		12 46							14 13		14 18
Nuneaton	a			11 46																					14 30
Coventry	a	11 25				12 33				12 24				13 28		12 56					13 20		14 28	13 40	
Birmingham International	a	11 36				12 51				12 35				13 46		13 07					13 31		14 46	13 51	
Birmingham New Street 12	a	11 49				13 03				12 48				13 58		13 22					13 44		14 58	14 05	
Sandwell & Dudley	a	12 01								13 00											13 56				
Wolverhampton 7	a	12 15								13 14											14 10				

A not 11 December

Table 66

Sundays

London - Watford Junction, Milton Keynes Central, Northampton and West Midlands

Network Diagram - see first Page of Table 59

		LM		VT	LM	VT	VT	SN	LM	VT	LM	LM		VT	LM	VT	VT	SN	LM	VT	LM	LM		VT	VT
		1		◇1 ☕	1	◇1 ☕	◇1 ☕	1	◇1	◇1 ☕	◇1	1		◇1 ☕	1	◇1 ☕	◇1 ☕	1	◇1	◇1 ☕	◇1	1		◇1 ☕	◇1 ☕
London Euston 15 ⊖	d	12 54		12 58	13 14	13 15	13 18		13 34	13 38	13 50	13 54		13 58	14 14	14 15	14 18		14 34	14 38	14 50	14 54		14 58	15 05
East Croydon	d																								
Clapham Junction	d							13 05										14 05							
Imperial Wharf	d							13 09										14 09							
West Brompton ⊖	d							13 12										14 12							
Kensington (Olympia) ⊖	d							13 16										14 16							
Shepherd's Bush	d							13 19										14 19							
Wembley Central ⊖	d																								
Harrow & Wealdstone ⊖	d	13 06			13 26			13 36				14 06			14 26			14 36				15 06			
Bushey	d				13 31										14 31										
Watford Junction	a	13 12			13 34			13 44	13 49		14 06	14 12			14 34			14 44	14 49		15 06	15 12			
	d	13 13			13 34		13u32		13 50		14 06	14 13			14 34		14u32		14 50		15 06	15 13			
Kings Langley	d				13 39										14 39										
Apsley	d				13 43										14 43										
Hemel Hempstead	d	13 20			13 45				13 57			14 20			14 45				14 57			15 20			
Berkhamsted	d	13 25			13 50				14 02			14 25			14 50				15 02			15 25			
Tring	d	13 29			13a57							14 29			14a57							15 29			
Cheddington	d	13 35										14 35										15 35			
Leighton Buzzard	d	13 41							14 15		14 26	14 41							15 15		15 26	15 41			
Bletchley	d	13 48							14 22			14 48							15 22			15 48			
Milton Keynes Central 10	a	13 54				13 48			14 27	14 11	14 36	14 54				14 48			15 27	15 11	15 36	15 54			15 38
	d								14 28	14 11	14 36								15 28	15 11	15 36				
Wolverton	d								14 31										15 31						
Northampton	a								14 44		14 54								15 46		15 51				
Rugby	a			13 49					15 13		15 18			14 49					16 10		16 18			15 49	
Nuneaton	a																				16 30				
Coventry	a			14 00			14 20		15 28	14 40				15 00			15 20		16 28	15 40				16 00	
Birmingham International ✈	a			14 11			14 31		15 46	14 51				15 11			15 31		16 46	15 51				16 11	
Birmingham New Street 12	a			14 25			14 44		15 58	15 05				15 25			15 44		16 58	16 05				16 25	
Sandwell & Dudley	a						14 56										15 56								
Wolverhampton 7	a						15 10										16 10								

		LM	VT	VT	SN	LM	VT	LM		LM	VT	VT	LM	VT	VT	SN	LM	VT		LM	LM	VT	VT	LM	VT
		1	◇1 ☕	◇1 ☕	1	◇1	◇1 ☕	◇1		1	◇1 ☕	◇1 ☕	1	◇1 ☕	◇1 ☕	1	◇1	◇1 ☕		◇1	1	◇1 ☕	◇1 ☕	1	◇1 ☕
London Euston 15 ⊖	d	15 14	15 15	15 18		15 34	15 38	15 50		15 54	15 58	16 05	16 14	16 15	16 18		16 34	16 38		16 50	16 54	16 58	17 05	17 14	17 15
East Croydon	d																								
Clapham Junction	d				15 05											16 05									
Imperial Wharf	d				15 09											16 09									
West Brompton ⊖	d				15 12											16 12									
Kensington (Olympia) ⊖	d				15 16											16 16									
Shepherd's Bush	d				15 19											16 19									
Wembley Central ⊖	d																								
Harrow & Wealdstone ⊖	d	15 26			15 36					16 06			16 26			16 36					17 06			17 26	
Bushey	d	15 31											16 31											17 31	
Watford Junction	a	15 34			15 44	15 49		16 06		16 12			16 34			16 44	16 49			17 06	17 12			17 34	
	d	15 34		15u32		15 50		16 06		16 13			16 34		16u32		16 50			17 06	17 13			17 34	
Kings Langley	d	15 39											16 39											17 39	
Apsley	d	15 43											16 43											17 43	
Hemel Hempstead	d	15 45				15 57				16 20			16 45				16 57				17 20			17 45	
Berkhamsted	d	15 50				16 02				16 25			16 50				17 02				17 25			17 50	
Tring	d	15a57								16 29			16a57								17 29			17a57	
Cheddington	d									16 35											17 35				
Leighton Buzzard	d					16 15		16 26		16 41							17 15			17 26	17 41				
Bletchley	d					16 22				16 48							17 22				17 48				
Milton Keynes Central 10	a		15 48			16 27	16 11	16 36		16 54		16 38		16 48			17 27	17 11		17 36	17 54		17 38		17 48
	d					16 28	16 11	16 36									17 28	17 11		17 36			17 39		
Wolverton	d					16 31											17 31								
Northampton	a					16 44		16 54									17 44			17 54					
Rugby	a					17 13		17 18			16 49						18 13			18 18		17 49			
Nuneaton	a																			18 30			18 09		
Coventry	a			16 20		17 28	16 40				17 00				17 20		18 28	17 40				18 00			
Birmingham International ✈	a			16 31		17 46	16 51				17 11				17 31		18 46	17 51				18 11			
Birmingham New Street 12	a			16 44		17 58	17 05				17 25				17 44		18 58	18 05				18 25			
Sandwell & Dudley	a			16 56											17 56										
Wolverhampton 7	a			17 10											18 10										

Table 66

Sundays

London - Watford Junction, Milton Keynes Central, Northampton and West Midlands

Network Diagram - see first Page of Table 59

		VT	SN	LM		VT	LM	LM	VT	VT	LM	VT	VT	SN		LM	VT	LM	LM	VT	VT	VT	LM	VT	
		◇ 1	1	◇ 1		◇ 1	◇ 1	1	◇ 1	◇ 1	1	◇ 1	◇ 1	1		◇ 1	◇ 1	◇ 1	1	◇ 1	◇ 1	◇ 1	1	◇ 1	
		☕				☕			☕	☕		☕	☕				☕			☕	☕	☕		☕	
London Euston 15 ⊖	d	17 18		17 34		17 38	17 50	17 54	17 58	18 05	18 14	18 15	18 18			18 34	18 38	18 50	18 54	18 58	19 02	19 05	19 14	19 15	
East Croydon	d																								
Clapham Junction	d		17 05											18 05											
Imperial Wharf	d		17 09											18 09											
West Brompton ⊖	d		17 12											18 12											
Kensington (Olympia) ⊖	d		17 16											18 16											
Shepherd's Bush	d		17 19											18 19											
Wembley Central ⊖	d																								
Harrow & Wealdstone ⊖	d		17 36					18 06			18 26			18 36					19 06				19 26		
Bushey	d										18 31												19 31		
Watford Junction	a		17 44	17 49			18 06	18 12			18 34			18 44		18 49		19 06	19 12				19 34		
	d	17u32		17 50			18 06	18 13			18 34		18u32			18 50		19 06	19 13				19 34		
Kings Langley	d										18 39												19 39		
Apsley	d										18 43												19 43		
Hemel Hempstead	d			17 57				18 20			18 45					18 57			19 20				19 45		
Berkhamsted	d			18 02				18 25			18 50					19 02			19 25				19 50		
Tring	d							18 29			18a57								19 29				19a57		
Cheddington	d							18 35											19 35						
Leighton Buzzard	d			18 15			18 26	18 41								19 15		19 26	19 41						
Bletchley	d			18 22				18 48								19 22			19 48						
Milton Keynes Central 10	a			18 27		18 11	18 36	18 54		18 38		18 48				19 27	19 11	19 36	19 54			19 38		19 48	
	d			18 28		18 11	18 36									19 28	19 11	19 36							
Wolverton	d			18 31												19 31									
Northampton	a			18 44			18 54									19 44		19 54							
Rugby	a			19 13			19 21		18 49							20 13		20 18		19 49					
Nuneaton	a																	20 30			20 00				
Coventry	a	18 20		19 28		18 40			19 00				19 20			20 28	19 40			20 00					
Birmingham International ✈	a	18 31		19 46		18 51			19 11				19 31			20 46	19 51			20 11					
Birmingham New Street 12	a	18 44		19 58		19 05			19 24				19 44			20 58	20 05			20 23					
Sandwell & Dudley	a	18 56							19 48				19 56							20 35					
Wolverhampton 7	a	19 10							20 02				20 10							20 46					

		VT	SN	LM	VT	LM	LM	VT	VT	VT		LM	VT	VT	SN	LM	VT	VT	VT	SR		LM	VT	VT	LM
																				R					
		◇ 1	1	◇ 1	◇ 1	◇ 1	1	◇ 1	◇ 1	◇ 1		1	◇ 1	◇ 1	1	◇ 1	◇ 1	◇ 1	◇ 1	🛏		◇ 1	◇ 1	◇ 1	◇ 1
		☕			☕			☕	☕	☕			☕	☕			☕	☕	☕	☕			☕	☕	
London Euston 15 ⊖	d	19 18		19 34	19 38	19 50	19 54	19 58	20 02	20 05		20 14	20 15	20 18		20 34	20 38	20 50	20 54	20 55		21 02	21 21	21 25	21 28
East Croydon	d																								
Clapham Junction	d		19 05												20 05										
Imperial Wharf	d		19 09												20 09										
West Brompton ⊖	d		19 12												20 12										
Kensington (Olympia) ⊖	d		19 16												20 16										
Shepherd's Bush	d		19 19												20 19										
Wembley Central ⊖	d																								
Harrow & Wealdstone ⊖	d		19 36				20 06					20 26			20 36										21 40
Bushey	d											20 31													
Watford Junction	a		19 43	19 50		20 06	20 12					20 34			20 44	20 49						21 22			21 46
	d	19u32		19 51		20 06	20 13					20 34		20u32		20 50			21u10			21 23			21 46
Kings Langley	d											20 39													21 51
Apsley	d											20 43													21 55
Hemel Hempstead	d			19 58			20 20					20 45				20 57						21 30			21 57
Berkhamsted	d			20 03			20 25					20 50				21 03						21 35			22 02
Tring	d						20 29					20a57										21 39			
Cheddington	d						20 35															21 45			
Leighton Buzzard	d			20 15		20 26	20 41									21 16						21 49			22 15
Bletchley	d			20 22			20 48									21 23						21 56			22 22
Milton Keynes Central 10	a			20 27	20 11	20 36	20 54			20 38			20 48			21 28	21 16	21 35	21 41			22 04		22 13	22 30
	d			20 28	20 11	20 36										21 29	21 16	21 37	21 43			22 05			22 31
Wolverton	d			20 31												21 32						22 08			22 34
Northampton	a			20 44		20 56										21 45						22 22			22 48
Rugby	a			21 13		21 21		20 49								22 14		21 59	22 05						23 13
Nuneaton	a								21 00														22 51		
Coventry	a	20 20		21 27	20 40			21 00						21 20		22 27	21 46		22 16						23 25
Birmingham International ✈	a	20 31		21 46	20 51			21 11						21 31		22 46	21 57		22 27						23 52
Birmingham New Street 12	a	20 44		21 58	21 04			21 24						21 44		22 58	22 09		22 39						00 04
Sandwell & Dudley	a	20 56			21 15			21 36						21 56			22 24		22 52						
Wolverhampton 7	a	21 10			21 31			21 51						22 10			22 38		23 06						

London - Watford Junction, Milton Keynes Central, Northampton and West Midlands

Network Diagram - see first Page of Table 59

		SN	VT	VT	LM	VT		LM	SN	LM	VT		LM
		1	◇1	◇1	1	◇1		◇1	1	◇1	◇1		◇1
			☕	☕		☕					☕		
London Euston 15 ⊖	d		21 51	21 55	22 00	22 25		22 28		22 58	23 25		23 34
East Croydon ⛴	d												
Clapham Junction	d	21 15							22 15				
Imperial Wharf	d	21 19							22 19				
West Brompton ⊖	d	21 22							22 22				
Kensington (Olympia) ⊖	d	21 26							22 26				
Shepherd's Bush	d	21 29							22 29				
Wembley Central ⊖	d												
Harrow & Wealdstone ⊖	d	21 47			22 12			22 40	22 48	23 10			23 46
Bushey	d												
Watford Junction	a	21 54			22 18			22 46	22 56	23 16			23 52
	d			22u09	22 19	22u39		22 47		23 17	23u39		23 53
Kings Langley	d							22 51		23 21			23 57
Apsley	d							22 55		23 25			00 01
Hemel Hempstead	d				22 26			22 58		23 28			00 04
Berkhamsted	d				22 31			23 03		23 33			00 09
Tring	d				22 35					23 37			00 13
Cheddington	d				22 41					23 43			00 19
Leighton Buzzard	d				22 47			23 16		23 49			00 25
Bletchley	d				22 54			23 23		23 56			00 32
Milton Keynes Central 10	a		22 36	22 42	23 02	23 11		23 31		00 04	00 11		00 40
	d		22 38	22 44	23 03	23 12		23 31		00 05	00 12		00 41
Wolverton	d				23 06			23 35		00 08			00 44
Northampton	a				23 20			23 48		00 22			00 58
Rugby	a		23 16	23 20	23 54	23 46					00s46		
Nuneaton	a		23 28										
Coventry	a			23 31	00 05	23 57					00s58		
Birmingham International ✈	a			23 42		00 08					01s09		
Birmingham New Street 12	a			23 54		00 21					01s22		
Sandwell & Dudley	a												
Wolverhampton 7 ⛴	a			00 15		00 43					01 53		

Table 66

Mondays to Fridays

until 30 March

West Midlands, Northampton, Milton Keynes Central and Watford Junction - London

Network Diagram - see first Page of Table 59

Miles	Miles	Miles			SN	SN	SN	LM	VT	LM	VT	LM	LM	VT	VT	LM	LM	LM	SN	LM	LM
					MX	MO	MX	MX	MX	MO	MO	TO	WTh FO	MO	MX						
					1	1	1	1	◇1	◇1	◇1	1	1	◇1	◇1	1	1	1	1	1	1
									☕		☕			☕	☕						
0	—	—	Wolverhampton 7	d					21p45		22p05			22p37	22p45						
7½	—	—	Sandwell & Dudley	d					21p56		22p15			22p47	22p55						
12¾	—	—	**Birmingham New Street 12**	d				21p33	22p10		22g30			23p00	23p10						
21¼	—	—	Birmingham International ✈	d				21p45	22p20		22p40			23p10	23p20						
32	—	—	Coventry	d				22p01	22p31		22p51			23p21	23p31						
—	—	—	Nuneaton	d																	
43½	0	—	**Rugby**	d				22p12	22p43		23p04			23p34	23p44						
62¼	—	—	**Northampton**	d				22e55		23p00		23p30	23p46	23f53	00s05		04 15	04 48		05 05	
75¼	30	—	Wolverton	d				23p07		23p12		23p46	00 02				04 27	05 00		05 17	
78¼	32¾	—	**Milton Keynes Central 10**	a				23p12	23f05	23p15	23p36	23p50	00 05	00s12	00s23		04 30	05 03		05 20	
—	—	—		d	22p11			23p13		23p16	23p37	23p50	00 06			03 30	04 31	05 04		05 21	
81¼	—	—	Bletchley	d	22p15			23p18		23p21		23p55	00 11			03 35	04 36	05 09		05 26	05 38
87¾	—	—	Leighton Buzzard	d	22p22			23p24		23p27		00 02	00 17			03 41	04 42	05 15		05 33	05 45
92	—	—	Cheddington	d				23p29		23p32		00 08	00 24					05 20			05 50
96¼	—	—	Tring	d	22p34			23p38		23p41		00 14	00 30			03 53	04 54	05 29			05 56
100	—	—	Berkhamsted	d	22p39			23p43		23p45		00 18	00 34			03 58	04 59	05 34		05 47	06 01
103½	—	—	Hemel Hempstead	d	22p43			23p47		23p50		00 22	00 39			04 02	05 03	05 38		05 52	06 05
105	—	—	Apsley	d				23p50										05 41			06 08
107	—	—	Kings Langley	d				23p53										05 44			06 11
110½	65	—	**Watford Junction**	a	22p52			23p58	23f37	23p57	00s06	00 29	00 46	00s42	00s52	04 09	05 10	05 49		05 59	06 16
—	—	—		d	22p53	23p17	23p29	23p58		23p57		00 30	00 47			04 10	05 11	05 50	05 54	06 01	06 17
112	—	—	Bushey	d				00 01													
116½	71	—	Harrow & Wealdstone ⊖	d	23p00	23p23	23p35	00 06		00 03		00 36	00 53			04 16	05 17	05 56	06 00		06 23
119¾	—	0	Wembley Central ⊖	d								00 40	00 57			04 20	05 21		06 05		
—	—	4¼	Shepherd's Bush	a	23p21	23p45	23p53												06 19		
—	—	5½	Kensington (Olympia) ⊖	a	23p23	23p47	23p56												06 21		
—	—	7½	West Brompton ⊖	a	23p26	23p50	23p59												06 24		
—	—	8	Imperial Wharf	a	23p28	23p53	00 02												06 27		
—	—	—	Clapham Junction	d	23b40	00 05	00a07												06a32		
—	—	16¾	East Croydon	a	00 01	00 22															
128	82½	—	**London Euston 15** ⊖	a				00 21	00 04	00 17	00 27	00 53	01 09	01 04	01 15	04 35	05 35	06 10		06 19	06 40

		LM	LM	LM	VT	LM	SN	LM	VT	LM	LM	LM	LM	VT	VT	VT	VT	SN	LM	VT	LM	LM	LM
		1	1	1	◇1	1	1		◇1	1	1	1	1	◇1	◇1	◇1	◇1	1	1	◇1	1	1	1
					⊠				⊠					⊠	⊠	⊠	⊠			⊠			
Wolverhampton 7	d				05 00				05 24							05 45	06 04						
Sandwell & Dudley	d								05 34							05 56	06 15						
Birmingham New Street 12	d				05 29				05 50							06 10	06 30		05 53				
Birmingham International ✈	d				05 40				06 00							06 20	06 40		06 05				
Coventry	d				05 51				06 11							06 31	06 51		06 21				
Nuneaton	d														06 18								
Rugby	d		05 20		06 03								06 13	06 20	06 32				06 32	06 53			
Northampton	d		05 45					06 17					06 38	06 42					07 00				
Wolverton	d		05 57					06 29					06 50						07 12				
Milton Keynes Central 10	a		06 00		06 22			06 33	06 38				06 53		06 51	06 59			07 15	07 12			
	d	05 54	06 02	06 20	06 23			06 34	06 38			06 48	06 55		06 52	06 59		07 01	07 17	07 14			07 21
Bletchley	d	05 59	06 07	06 25				06 39		06 34		06 53	07 00					07 05			07 13		07 26
Leighton Buzzard	d	06 05	06 14	06 31				06 46		06 41		06 59	07 07					07 13	07 26				07 33
Cheddington	d			06 37								07 05											07 38
Tring	d			06 42		06 24				06 52	07 00	07 11						07 22			07 28		07 45
Berkhamsted	d	06 17		06 47		06 28				06 56	07 05	07 16						07 26			07 32		07 49
Hemel Hempstead	d	06 22		06 52		06 33				07 01	07 09	07 20						07 31			07 37		07 54
Apsley	d					06 36				07 04		07 24											07 57
Kings Langley	d					06 39				07 07		07 27											08 00
Watford Junction	a	06 29	06 31	06 59	06s43	06 44		07 04		07 12	07 17	07 31					07s36	07 38			07 44		08 05
	d	06 30	06 33	07 00		06 45	06 53	07 05		07 12	07 19	07 32						07 38			07 45	07 55	08 05
Bushey	d					06 48				07 15	07 22	07 34										07 59	
Harrow & Wealdstone ⊖	d			07 06		06 53	06 59			07 20		07 40						07 45				08 05	
Wembley Central ⊖	d						07 04											07u49					
Shepherd's Bush	a						07 19											08 04					
Kensington (Olympia) ⊖	a						07 21											08 06					
West Brompton ⊖	a						07 24											08 09					
Imperial Wharf	a						07 27											08 12					
Clapham Junction	d						07a32											08 36					
East Croydon	a																	09 04					
London Euston 15 ⊖	a	06 49	06 50	07 20	07 02	07 07		07 22	07 13	07 34	07 40	07 54	07 40	07 30	07 28	07 34	07 53		08 02	07 50	08 05	08 18	08 24

b Previous night, arr. 2333
e Previous night, arr. 2234
f Previous night, stops to set down only
g Previous night, arr. 2224

Table 66

Mondays to Fridays

until 30 March

West Midlands, Northampton, Milton Keynes Central and Watford Junction - London

Network Diagram - see first Page of Table 59

		LM	VT	LM	LM		LM	LM	VT	VT	VT	VT	VT	LM	VT		LM	LM	SN	LM	VT	VT	LM	LM	VT
		1	◇1 ⊠	1	1		1	1	◇1 ⊠	◇1 ⊠	◇1 ⊠	◇1 ⊠	◇1 ⊠	1	◇1 ⊠		1	1	1	1	◇1 ⊠	◇1 ⊠	1	1	◇1 ⊠
Wolverhampton 7	d		06 27									06 45			07 04										07 45
Sandwell & Dudley	d		06 37									06 56			07 15										07 56
Birmingham New Street 12	d		06 50									07 10			07 30					06 53					08 10
Birmingham International ✈	d		07 00									07 20								07 05		07 41			08 20
Coventry	d		07 11									07 31								07 21		07 52			08 31
Nuneaton	d									07 07			07 33												
Rugby	d							07 02	07 08		07 29									07 32	07 55				
Northampton	d	07 13						07 32						07 39						08 05			08 25		
Wolverton	d	07 25												07 51						08 17			08 37		
Milton Keynes Central 10	a	07 29	07s40					07 46						07 54						08 21			08 41		
	d	07 30						07 46						07 55			07 59		08 13	08 21			08 41		
Bletchley	d			07 39				07 51									08 04		08 17	08 27			08 46		
Leighton Buzzard	d	07 39		07 46				07 58						08 05			08 11		08 24	08 34			08 53		
Cheddington	d							08 04																	
Tring	d						08 04	08 10										08 25	08 34					08 48	
Berkhamsted	d			07 59				08 15										08 29	08 39					08 53	
Hemel Hempstead	d			08 03				08 19									08 28	08 34	08 43					08 57	
Apsley	d						08 13											08 37							
Kings Langley	d						08 16											08 40							
Watford Junction	a			08 10			08 20	08 26									08 35	08 45	08 51					09 04	09s15
	d			08 11	08 15		08 22	08 28									08 36	08 46	08 51					09 05	
Bushey	d				08 19													08 48						09 08	
Harrow & Wealdstone ⊖	d			08 17	08 24		08 29	08 34										08 54	08 58					09 13	
Wembley Central ⊖	d																		09u05						
Shepherd's Bush	a																		09 18						
Kensington (Olympia) ⊖	a																		09 20						
West Brompton ⊖	a																		09 23						
Imperial Wharf	a																		09 26						
Clapham Junction	d																		09 34						
East Croydon	a																		09 57						
London Euston 15 ⊖	a	08 11	08 14	08 33	08 38		08 42	08 49	07 57	08 07	08 22	08 30	08 33	08 39	08 42		08 55	09 08		09 10	08 45	08 49	09 27	09 27	09 34

			LM	LM	LM	VT	VT	VT	LM	SN	VT		LM	VT	LM	VT	VT	LM	LM	VT	LM	LM		VT	LM
			1	1	1	◇1 ⊠	◇1 ⊠	◇1 ⊠	1	1	◇1 ⊠		1	◇1 ⊠	1	◇1 ⊠	◇1 ⊠	1	1	◇1 ⊠	1	1		◇1 ⊠	1
Wolverhampton 7	d																08 45								
Sandwell & Dudley	d																08 56								
Birmingham New Street 12	d					07 50					08 30		07 53				09 10				08 33			08 50	
Birmingham International ✈	d					08 00					08 40		08 05				09 20				08 45			09 00	
Coventry	d					08 11					08 51		08 21				09 31				09 01			09 11	
Nuneaton	d				08 02			08 46														09 02			
Rugby	d				08 20	08 23							08 32	08 46							09 12	09 20		09 23	
Northampton	d				08 47								09 05		09 25						09 50				
Wolverton	d												09 17		09 37										
Milton Keynes Central 10	a				09 01						09 18		09 20		09 41						10 04				
	d			08 47	09 01					09 13	09 19		09 22		09 41	09 47			09 47	10 02	10 05				
Bletchley	d			08 52						09 17			09 27		09 46				09 52						
Leighton Buzzard	d			08 58						09 24			09 33		09 53				09 58						
Cheddington	d			09 04															10 04						
Tring	d		09 01	09 10					09 26	09 34								09 56	10 10						10 26
Berkhamsted	d		09 05	09 15					09 30	09 39			09 46					10 00	10 15						10 30
Hemel Hempstead	d		09 10	09 19					09 35	09 43			09 51					10 05	10 19						10 35
Apsley	d		09 13						09 38									10 08							10 38
Kings Langley	d		09 16						09 41									10 11							10 41
Watford Junction	a		09 20	09 26	09 27			09s31	09 46	09 51			09 58				10s15	10 16	10 26		10 30				10 46
	d		09 21	09 27	09 28				09 46	09 51			09 59					10 16	10 27		10 31				10 46
Bushey	d		09 23						09 49									10 19							10 49
Harrow & Wealdstone ⊖	d		09 28	09 33					09 54	09 58								10 24							10 54
Wembley Central ⊖	d									10u05															
Shepherd's Bush	a									10 21															
Kensington (Olympia) ⊖	a									10 23															
West Brompton ⊖	a									10 26															
Imperial Wharf	a									10 29															
Clapham Junction	d									10 34															
East Croydon	a									10 57															
London Euston 15 ⊖	a		09 42	09 47	09 44	09 13	09 23	09 52	10 08		09 54		10 18	09 38	10 27	10 23	10 28	10 38	10 46	10 38	10 49			10 14	11 08

Table 66

Mondays to Fridays

until 30 March

West Midlands, Northampton, Milton Keynes Central and Watford Junction - London

Network Diagram - see first Page of Table 59

		SN	VT	LM	LM	VT	VT	LM		LM	VT	LM	LM	VT	LM	SN	VT	LM		LM	VT	VT	LM	LM	VT
		1	◇1	1	1	◇1	◇1	1		1	◇1	◇1	◇1	◇1	1	1	◇1	1		1	◇1	◇1	1	1	◇1
												A													
			⊠			⊠	⊠				⊠			⊠			⊠				⊠	⊠			⊠
Wolverhampton 7	d						09 45															10 45			
Sandwell & Dudley	d						09 56															10 56			
Birmingham New Street 12	d		09 30	08 53	09 13		10 10					09 33		09 50			10 30	09 53		10 13		11 10			
Birmingham International	d		09 40	09 05	09 29		10 20					09 45		09 59			10 40	10 05		10 29		11 20			
Coventry	d		09 51	09 21	09 48		10 31					10 01		10 10			10 51	10 21		10 48		11 31			
Nuneaton	d												10 02												
Rugby	d			09 32	09 59							10 12	10 20	10 24				10 32		10 59					
Northampton	d			10 05	10 25							10 50						11 05		11 25					
Wolverton	d			10 17	10 37													11 17		11 37					
Milton Keynes Central 10	a		10 18	10 20	10 41							11 04					11 18	11 20		11 41					
	d	10 13	10 19	10 22	10 41	10 47				10 47	11 02	11 05				11 13	11 19	11 22		11 41	11 47			11 47	12 02
Bletchley	d	10 17		10 27	10 46					10 52						11 17		11 27		11 46				11 52	
Leighton Buzzard	d	10 24		10 33	10 53					10 58						11 24		11 33		11 53				11 58	
Cheddington	d									11 04														12 04	
Tring	d	10 34						10 56		11 10					11 26	11 34							11 56	12 10	
Berkhamsted	d	10 39		10 46				11 00		11 15					11 30	11 39		11 46					12 00	12 15	
Hemel Hempstead	d	10 43		10 51				11 05		11 19					11 35	11 43		11 51					12 05	12 19	
Apsley	d							11 08							11 38								12 08		
Kings Langley	d							11 11							11 41								12 11		
Watford Junction	a	10 51		10 58			11s15	11 16		11 26		11 30			11 46	11 51		11 58				12s15	12 16	12 26	
	d	10 51		10 59				11 16		11 27		11 31			11 46	11 51		11 59					12 16	12 27	
Bushey	d							11 19							11 49								12 19		
Harrow & Wealdstone ⊖	d	10 59						11 24							11 54	11 59							12 24		
Wembley Central ⊖	d	11u04														12u04									
Shepherd's Bush	a	11 19														12 19									
Kensington (Olympia) ⊖	a	11 21														12 21									
West Brompton ⊖	a	11 23														12 24									
Imperial Wharf	a	11 26														12 27									
Clapham Junction	d	11 34														12 34									
East Croydon	a	11 57														12 57									
London Euston 15 ⊖	a		10 54	11 17	11 27	11 23	11 32	11 38		11 46	11 38	11 49		11 14	12 08		11 54	12 17		12 27	12 23	12 32	12 38	12 45	12 38

		LM	LM	VT		LM	SN	VT	LM	LM	VT	VT	LM	LM		VT	LM	LM	VT	LM	SN	VT	LM	LM
		◇1	◇1	◇1		1	1	◇1	1	1	◇1	◇1	1	1		◇1	◇1	◇1	◇1	1	1	◇1	1	1
		A															A							
				⊠				☕			☕	☕				☕			☕			☕		
Wolverhampton 7	d											11 45												
Sandwell & Dudley	d											11 56												
Birmingham New Street 12	d	10 33		10 50				11 30	10 53	11 13		12 10					11 33		11 50			12 30	11 53	12 13
Birmingham International	d	10 45		11 00				11 40	11 05	11 29		12 20					11 45		12 00			12 40	12 05	12 29
Coventry	d	11 01		11 11				11 51	11 21	11 48		12 31					12 01		12 11			12 51	12 21	12 48
Nuneaton	d		11 02															12 02						
Rugby	d	11 12	11 20	11 24					11 32	11 59							12 12	12 20	12 24				12 32	13 00
Northampton	d	11 50							12 05	12 25							12 50						13 05	13 25
Wolverton	d								12 17	12 37													13 17	13 37
Milton Keynes Central 10	a	12 04						12 18	12 20	12 41							13 04					13 18	13 20	13 41
	d	12 05					12 13	12 19	12 22	12 41	12 46			12 47		13 02	13 05				13 13	13 19	13 22	13 41
Bletchley	d						12 17		12 27	12 46				12 52							13 17		13 27	13 46
Leighton Buzzard	d						12 24		12 33	12 53				12 58							13 24		13 33	13 53
Cheddington	d													13 04										
Tring	d					12 26	12 34						12 56	13 10						13 26	13 34			
Berkhamsted	d					12 30	12 39		12 46				13 00	13 15						13 30	13 39		13 46	
Hemel Hempstead	d					12 35	12 43		12 51				13 05	13 19						13 35	13 43		13 51	
Apsley	d					12 38							13 08							13 38				
Kings Langley	d					12 41							13 11							13 41				
Watford Junction	a	12 30				12 46	12 51		12 58			13s15	13 16	13 26			13 30			13 46	13 51		13 58	
	d	12 31				12 46	12 51		12 59				13 16	13 27			13 31			13 46	13 51		13 59	
Bushey	d					12 49							13 19							13 49				
Harrow & Wealdstone ⊖	d					12 54	12 59						13 24							13 54	13 59			
Wembley Central ⊖	d						13u04														14u04			
Shepherd's Bush	a						13 19														14 19			
Kensington (Olympia) ⊖	a						13 21														14 21			
West Brompton ⊖	a						13 24														14 24			
Imperial Wharf	a						13 27														14 27			
Clapham Junction	d						13 34														14 34			
East Croydon	a						13 57														14 57			
London Euston 15 ⊖	a	12 49		12 14		13 08		12 54	13 17	13 27	13 23	13 32	13 38	13 45		13 38	13 49		13 14	14 08		13 54	14 17	14 27

A ◇ from Northampton

Table 66

Mondays to Fridays

until 30 March

West Midlands, Northampton, Milton Keynes Central and Watford Junction - London

Network Diagram - see first Page of Table 59

		VT	VT	LM	LM	VT	VT	LM	LM	LM	SN	VT	LM	LM	VT	VT	LM	LM	VT	LM	LM	VT	LM
		◇1	◇1	1	1	◇1	◇1	◇1	◇1	1	1	◇1	1	1	◇1	◇1	1	1	◇1	◇1	◇1	◇1	1
								A												A			
		☕	☕			☕	☕					☕			☕	☕			☕			☕	
Wolverhampton 7	d		12 45													13 45							
Sandwell & Dudley	d		12 56													13 56							
Birmingham New Street 12	d		13 10				12 50	12 33				13 30	12 53	13 13		14 10				13 33		13 50	
Birmingham International	d		13 20				13 00	12 45				13 40	13 05	13 29		14 20				13 45		14 00	
Coventry	d		13 31				13 11	13 01				13 51	13 21	13 48		14 31				14 01		14 11	
Nuneaton	d								13 02												14 02		
Rugby	d						13 24	13 12	13 25				13 32	13 59						14 12	14 20	14 24	
Northampton	d							13 50					14 05	14 25						14 50			
Wolverton	d												14 17	14 37									
Milton Keynes Central 10	a							14 04				14 19	14 20	14 41						15 04			
	d	13 47			13 47	14 02		14 05			14 13	14 19	14 22	14 41	14 47			14 47	15 02	15 05			
Bletchley	d				13 52						14 17		14 27	14 46				14 52					
Leighton Buzzard	d				13 58						14 24		14 33	14 53				14 58					
Cheddington	d				14 04													15 04					
Tring	d			13 56	14 10					14 26	14 34						14 56	15 10					15 26
Berkhamsted	d			14 00	14 15					14 30	14 39		14 46				15 00	15 15					15 30
Hemel Hempstead	d			14 05	14 19					14 35	14 43		14 51				15 05	15 19					15 35
Apsley	d			14 08						14 38							15 08						15 38
Kings Langley	d			14 11						14 41							15 11						15 41
Watford Junction	a		14s14	14 16	14 26			14 30		14 46	14 51		14 58			15s15	15 16	15 26		15 30			15 46
	d			14 16	14 27			14 31		14 46	14 51		14 59				15 16	15 27		15 31			15 46
Bushey	d			14 19						14 49							15 19						15 49
Harrow & Wealdstone ⊖	d			14 24						14 54	14 59						15 24						15 54
Wembley Central ⊖	d										15u04												
Shepherd's Bush	a										15 22												
Kensington (Olympia) ⊖	a										15 24												
West Brompton ⊖	a										15 26												
Imperial Wharf	a										15 29												
Clapham Junction	d										15 34												
East Croydon	a										15 57												
London Euston 15 ⊖	a	14 23	14 32	14 38	14 45	14 38	14 14	14 49		15 08		14 54	15 17	15 27	15 23	15 32	15 38	15 45	15 38	15 49		15 14	16 08

		SN	VT	LM	LM	VT	VT	LM	LM	VT	LM	LM	VT	LM	SN	VT	LM	LM	VT	VT	LM	LM	VT
		1	◇1	1	1	◇1	◇1	1	1	◇1	◇1	◇1	◇1	1	1	◇1	1	1	◇1	◇1	1	1	◇1
											A												
			☕			☕	☕			☕			☕			☕			☕	☕			☕
Wolverhampton 7	d						14 45													15 45			
Sandwell & Dudley	d						14 56													15 56			
Birmingham New Street 12	d		14 30	13 53	14 13		15 10				14 33		14 50			15 30	14 53	15 13		16 10			
Birmingham International	d		14 40	14 05	14 29		15 20				14 45		15 00			15 40	15 05	15 29		16 20			
Coventry	d		14 51	14 21	14 48		15 31				15 01		15 11			15 51	15 21	15 48		16 32			
Nuneaton	d											15 02											
Rugby	d			14 32	14 59						15 12	15 20	15 24				15 32	15 59					
Northampton	d			15 05	15 25						15 50						16 05	16 25					
Wolverton	d			15 17	15 37												16 17	16 37					
Milton Keynes Central 10	a		15 18	15 20	15 41						16 04					16 18	16 20	16 41					
	d	15 13	15 19	15 22	15 41	15 47			15 47	16 02	16 05				16 13	16 19	16 22	16 41	16 47			16 47	17 02
Bletchley	d	15 17		15 27	15 46				15 52						16 17		16 27	16 46				16 52	
Leighton Buzzard	d	15 24		15 33	15 53				15 58						16 24		16 33	16 53				16 58	
Cheddington	d								16 04													17 04	
Tring	d	15 34						15 56	16 10					16 26	16 34						16 56	17 10	
Berkhamsted	d	15 39		15 46				16 00	16 15					16 30	16 39		16 46				17 00	17 15	
Hemel Hempstead	d	15 43		15 51				16 05	16 19					16 35	16 43		16 51				17 05	17 19	
Apsley	d							16 08						16 38							17 08		
Kings Langley	d							16 11						16 41							17 11		
Watford Junction	a	15 51		15 58			16s15	16 16	16 26		16 30			16 46	16 51		16 58			17 15	17 16	17 26	
	d	15 51		15 59				16 16	16 27		16 31			16 46	16 51		16 59			17 16	17 16	17 27	
Bushey	d							16 19						16 49							17 19		
Harrow & Wealdstone ⊖	d	15 59						16 24						16 54	16 59						17 24		
Wembley Central ⊖	d	16u05													17u05								
Shepherd's Bush	a	16 19													17 19								
Kensington (Olympia) ⊖	a	16 21													17 21								
West Brompton ⊖	a	16 24													17 24								
Imperial Wharf	a	16 27													17 27								
Clapham Junction	d	16 34													17 33								
East Croydon	a	16 58													17 59								
London Euston 15 ⊖	a		15 54	16 17	16 27	16 23	16 32	16 38	16 45	16 38	16 49		16 14	17 08		16 57	17 18	17 27	17 23	17 34	17 38	17 47	17 38

A ◇ from Northampton

Table 66

Mondays to Fridays

until 30 March

West Midlands, Northampton, Milton Keynes Central and Watford Junction - London

Network Diagram - see first Page of Table 59

		LM	LM		VT	LM	SN	VT	LM	LM	VT	VT	LM		LM	VT	LM	LM	VT	LM	SN	VT	LM		VT
		◇1	◇1		◇1	1	1	◇1	1	1	◇1	◇1	1		1	◇1	◇1	◇1	◇1	1	1	◇1	1		◇1
		A															A								
					☕			☕			☕	☕				☕			☕			⊠			☕
Wolverhampton 7	d											16 45													
Sandwell & Dudley	d											16 56													
Birmingham New Street 12	d	15 33			15 50			16 30	15 53			17 10					16 33		16 50			17 30	16 53		
Birmingham International	d	15 45			16 00			16 40	16 05			17 20					16 45		17 00			17 40	17 05		
Coventry	d	16 01			16 11			16 51	16 21			17 31					17 01		17 11			17 51	17 21		
Nuneaton	d		16 02															17 02							
Rugby	d	16 12	16 20		16 24				16 32								17 12	17 20	17 24				17 32		
Northampton	d	16 50							17 05	17 25							17 50						18 05		
Wolverton	d								17 17	17 37													18 17		
Milton Keynes Central 10	a	17 04						17 18	17 20	17 41							18 04					18 18	18 20		
	d	17 05					17 13	17 19	17 22	17 41	17 47				17 47	18 02	18 05				18 13	18 19	18 22		18 24
Bletchley	d						17 17		17 27	17 46					17 52						18 17		18 27		
Leighton Buzzard	d						17 24		17 33	17 53					17 58						18 24		18 33		
Cheddington	d														18 04										
Tring	d					17 26	17 34						17 59		18 10					18 27	18 34				
Berkhamsted	d					17 30	17 39		17 46				18 03		18 15					18 31	18 39		18 46		
Hemel Hempstead	d					17 35	17 43		17 51				18 08		18 19					18 36	18 43		18 51		
Apsley	d					17 38							18 11							18 39					
Kings Langley	d					17 41							18 14							18 42					
Watford Junction	a	17 30				17 46	17 51		17 59			18s15	18 19		18 26		18 31			18 46	18 51		18 58		
	d	17 31				17 46	17 51		17 59				18 19		18 27		18 31			18 47	18 51		18 59		
Bushey	d					17 49							18 22							18 49					
Harrow & Wealdstone ⊖	d					17 54	17 59						18 27							18 54	18 59				
Wembley Central ⊖	d						18u05														19u05				
Shepherd's Bush	a						18 19														19 18				
Kensington (Olympia) ⊖	a						18 21														19 20				
West Brompton ⊖	a						18 24														19 23				
Imperial Wharf	a						18 27														19 25				
Clapham Junction	d						18 34														19a30				
East Croydon	a						19 02																		
London Euston 15 ⊖	a	17 49			17 14	18 10		17 54	18 18	18 27	18 23	18 34	18 41		18 45	18 38	18 49		18 14	19 09		18 54	19 18		18 59

		VT	LM	VT	LM	LM	VT	VT	LM		VT	LM	SN	VT	VT	LM	VT	LM	VT		VT	LM	LM	LM	LM
		◇1	1	◇1	1	1	◇1	◇1	◇1		◇1	1	1	◇1	◇1	1	◇1	1	◇1		◇1	1	1	◇1	◇1
																								A	
		☕		⊠			⊠	⊠			⊠			⊠	⊠		⊠		⊠		⊠				
Wolverhampton 7	d			17 45																	18 45				
Sandwell & Dudley	d			17 56																	18 56				
Birmingham New Street 12	d		17 13	18 10							17 50			18 30		17 53					19 10			18 33	
Birmingham International	d		17 25	18 20							18 00			18 40		18 05					19 20			18 45	
Coventry	d		17 40	18 31							18 11			18 51		18 21					19 31			19 01	
Nuneaton	d								18 02																19 02
Rugby	d		17 51						18 20		18 24					18 32								19 12	19 20
Northampton	d		18 25						18 50							19 05		19 25						19 51	
Wolverton	d		18 37													19 17		19 37							
Milton Keynes Central 10	a		18 41						19 04					19 18		19 20		19 41						20 05	
	d		18 41			18 47	18 48	19 03	19 05				19 15	19 19		19 22	19 32	19 41	19 47				19 47	20 09	
Bletchley	d		18 46			18 52							19 19			19 27		19 46					19 52		
Leighton Buzzard	d		18 53			18 58							19 26			19 33		19 53					19 58		
Cheddington	d					19 06																	20 04		
Tring	d				19 00	19 12						19 29	19 36									19 56	20 10		
Berkhamsted	d				19 04	19 17						19 33	19 41			19 46						20 00	20 15		
Hemel Hempstead	d				19 09	19 21						19 38	19 45			19 51						20 05	20 19		
Apsley	d				19 12							19 41										20 08			
Kings Langley	d				19 15							19 44										20 11			
Watford Junction	a			19s16	19 20	19 28			19 30			19 49	19 54			19 59					20s15	20 16	20 26	20 31	
	d				19 20	19 29			19 31			19 49	19 54			19 59						20 16	20 27	20 32	
Bushey	d				19 23							19 52										20 19			
Harrow & Wealdstone ⊖	d				19 28							19 57	20 01									20 24			
Wembley Central ⊖	d												20u06												
Shepherd's Bush	a												20 21												
Kensington (Olympia) ⊖	a												20 23												
West Brompton ⊖	a												20 25												
Imperial Wharf	a												20 28												
Clapham Junction	d												20a33												
East Croydon	a																								
London Euston 15 ⊖	a	19 08	19 29	19 34	19 42	19 47	19 23	19 38	19 50		19 14	20 11		19 54	20 02	20 19	20 06	20 27	20 23		20 34	20 38	20 51	20 49	

A ◇ from Northampton

Table 66

Mondays to Fridays

until 30 March

West Midlands, Northampton, Milton Keynes Central and Watford Junction - London

Network Diagram - see first Page of Table 59

		VT	LM	SN	VT		VT	LM	VT	VT	LM	VT	LM	LM	VT		VT	VT	LM	VT	SN	LM	VT	VT	VT
		◇1	1	1	◇1		◇1	1	◇1	◇1	1	◇1	1	1	◇1		◇1	◇1	1	◇1	1	1	◇1	◇1	◇1
		☒			☕		☒		☒	☕		☒			☕		☕	☕		☕			☕	☕	☕
Wolverhampton 7 🚋	d																19 45								
Sandwell & Dudley	d																19 56								
Birmingham New Street 12	d	18 50			19 30			18 53		19 50							20 10					19 53	20 50		
Birmingham International ✈	d	19 00			19 40			19 05		20 00							20 20					20 05	21 00		
Coventry	d	19 11			19 51			19 21		20 11							20 31					20 21	21 11		
Nuneaton	d																			21 03					
Rugby	d	19 24						19 32		20 23												20 32	21 23		21 28
Northampton	d							20 05			20 25											21 05			
Wolverton	d							20 17			20 37											21 17			
Milton Keynes Central 10	a				20 18			20 20			20 41						20 58					21 20			21 47
	d			20 13	20 19			20 22	20 33		20 41	20 46		20 47	20 50		20 59	21 04			21 13	21 22		21 36	21 49
Bletchley	d			20 17				20 27			20 46			20 52							21 17	21 27			
Leighton Buzzard	d			20 24				20 33			20 53			20 58							21 24	21 33			
Cheddington	d													21 06											
Tring	d		20 26	20 34									20 56	21 11					21 26		21 34				
Berkhamsted	d		20 30	20 39				20 46					21 00	21 16					21 30		21 39	21 46			
Hemel Hempstead	d		20 35	20 43				20 51					21 05	21 20					21 35		21 43	21 51			
Apsley	d		20 38										21 08						21 38						
Kings Langley	d		20 41										21 11						21 41						
Watford Junction	a		20 46	20 51				20 58					21 16	21 27			21s19		21 46	21s48	21 51	21 58			
	d		20 46	20 51				20 59					21 16	21 27					21 46		21 51	21 59			
Bushey	d		20 49										21 19						21 49						
Harrow & Wealdstone ⊖	d		20 54	20 59									21 24						21 54		21 59				
Wembley Central ⊖	d			21u04																					
Shepherd's Bush	a			21 22																	22 23				
Kensington (Olympia) ⊖	a			21 24																	22 25				
West Brompton ⊖	a			21 27																	22 27				
Imperial Wharf	a			21 29																	22 30				
Clapham Junction	d			21a34																	22a34				
East Croydon 🚋	a																								
London Euston 15 ⊖	a	20 14	21 08		20 54		21 05	21 17	21 06	21 14	21 29	21 24	21 38	21 46	21 26		21 38	21 42	22 08	22 09		22 20	22 12	22 12	22 22

			VT	LM	VT	SN	LM	SN	LM	VT	VT		SN	LM	VT	VT	LM MO	LM MX	VT
			◇1	1	◇1	1	1	1	1	◇1	◇1		1	1	◇1	◇1	1	1	◇1
			☕		☕					☒	☕				☕	☕			☕
Wolverhampton 7 🚋	d				20 47											21 45			22 45
Sandwell & Dudley	d				20 57											21 56			22 55
Birmingham New Street 12	d				21 10				20 53					21 33		22 10			23 10
Birmingham International ✈	d				21 20				21 05					21 45		22 20			23 20
Coventry	d				21 31				21 21					22 01		22 31			23 31
Nuneaton	d														22 17				
Rugby	d								21 32					22 12	22 34	22 43			23 44
Northampton	d			21 37					22 05					22 55			23 30	23 46	00s05
Wolverton	d			21 49					22 17					23 07			23 46	00 02	
Milton Keynes Central 10	a			21 52	21 58				22 20					23 12	22 58	23s05	23 50	00 05	00s23
	d		21 52	21 53	21 59		22 05	22 11	22 22	22 41	22 53			23 13	22 59		23 50	00 06	
Bletchley	d			21 58			22 10	22 15	22 27					23 18			23 55	00 11	
Leighton Buzzard	d			22 04			22 17	22 22	22 33					23 24			00 02	00 17	
Cheddington	d			22 10			22 23							23 29			00 08	00 24	
Tring	d			22 16			22 28	22 34						23 38			00 14	00 30	
Berkhamsted	d			22 20			22 33	22 39	22 48					23 43			00 18	00 34	
Hemel Hempstead	d			22 25			22 37	22 43	22 53					23 47			00 22	00 39	
Apsley	d						22 41							23 50					
Kings Langley	d						22 44							23 53					
Watford Junction	a		22s11	22 32	22s20		22 48	22 52	23 00	23s14	23s25			23 58	23s30	23s37	00 29	00 46	00s52
	d			22 33		22 27	22 49	22 53	23 01				23 29	23 58			00 30	00 47	
Bushey	d						22 51							00 01					
Harrow & Wealdstone ⊖	d					22 33	22 57	23 00					23 35	00 06			00 36	00 53	
Wembley Central ⊖	d																00 40	00 57	
Shepherd's Bush	a					22 49		23 21					23 53						
Kensington (Olympia) ⊖	a					22 51		23 23					23 56						
West Brompton ⊖	a					22 54		23 26					23 59						
Imperial Wharf	a					22 56		23 28					00 02						
Clapham Junction	d					23a01		23e40					00a07						
East Croydon 🚋	a							00 01											
London Euston 15 ⊖	a		22 33	22 52	22 43		23 12		23 21	23 38	23 48			00 21	23 56	00 04	00 53	01 09	01 15

Table 66

Mondays to Fridays

from 2 April

West Midlands, Northampton, Milton Keynes Central and Watford Junction - London

Network Diagram - see first Page of Table 59

		SN MX	SN MO	SN MX	LM MX	VT MX	LM MO	VT MO	LM TO	LM WThFO		VT MO	VT MX	LM	LM	LM	SN	LM	LM				LM	LM	LM
		■1	■1	■1	■1	◇■1	◇■1	◇■1	■1	■1		◇■1	◇■1	■1	■1	■1	■1	■1	■1				■1	■1	■1
						☕		☕				☕	☕												
Wolverhampton [7] 🚊	d					21p45		22p05				22p37	22p45												
Sandwell & Dudley	d					21p56		22p15				22p47	22p55												
Birmingham New Street [12]	d				21p33	22p10		22g30				23p00	23p10												
Birmingham International ✈	d				21p45	22p20		22p40				23p10	23p20												
Coventry	d				22p01	22p31		22p51				23p21	23p31												
Nuneaton	d																								
Rugby	d				22p12	22p43		23p04				23p34	23p44											05 20	
Northampton	d				22e55		23p00		23p30	23p46		23f53	00s05		04 15	04 48		05 05						05 45	
Wolverton	d				23p07		23p12		23p46	00 02					04 27	05 00		05 17						05 57	
Milton Keynes Central [10]	a				23p12	23f05	23p15	23p36	23p50	00 05		00s12	00s23		04 30	05 03		05 20						06 00	
	d	22p11			23p13		23p16	23p37	23p50	00 06				03 30	04 31	05 04		05 21					05 54	06 02	06 20
Bletchley	d	22p15			23p18		23p21		23p55	00 11				03 35	04 36	05 09		05 26	05 38				05 59	06 07	06 25
Leighton Buzzard	d	22p22			23p24		23p27		00 02	00 17				03 41	04 42	05 15		05 33	05 45				06 05	06 14	06 31
Cheddington	d				23p29		23p32		00 08	00 24						05 20			05 50						06 37
Tring	d	22p34			23p38		23p41		00 14	00 30				03 53	04 54	05 29			05 56						06 42
Berkhamsted	d	22p39			23p43		23p45		00 18	00 34				03 58	04 59	05 34		05 47	06 01				06 17		06 47
Hemel Hempstead	d	22p43			23p47		23p50		00 22	00 39				04 02	05 03	05 38		05 52	06 05				06 22		06 52
Apsley	d				23p50											05 41			06 08						
Kings Langley	d				23p53											05 44			06 11						
Watford Junction	a	22p52			23p58	23f37	23p57	00s06	00 29	00 46		00s42	00s52	04 09	05 10	05 49		05 59	06 16				06 29	06 31	06 59
	d	22p53	23p17	23p29	23p58		23p57		00 30	00 47				04 10	05 11	05 50	05 54	06 01	06 17				06 30	06 33	07 00
Bushey	d				00 01																				
Harrow & Wealdstone ⊖	d	23p00	23p23	23p35	00 06		00 03		00 36	00 53				04 16	05 17	05 56	06 00		06 23						07 06
Wembley Central ⊖	d								00 40	00 57				04 20	05 21		06 05								
Shepherd's Bush	a	23p21	23p45	23p53													06 19								
Kensington (Olympia) ⊖	a	23p23	23p47	23p56													06 21								
West Brompton ⊖	a	23p26	23p50	23p59													06 24								
Imperial Wharf	a	23p28	23p53	00 02													06 27								
Clapham Junction	d	23b40	00c05	00a07													06a32								
East Croydon 🚊	a	00 01	00 22																						
London Euston [15] ⊖	a				00 21	00 04	00 17	00 27	00 53	01 09		01 04	01 15	04 35	05 35	06 10		06 19	06 40				06 49	06 50	07 20

		VT	LM	SN	LM	VT		LM	LM	LM	LM	VT	VT	VT	VT	SN		LM	VT	LM	LM	LM	LM	VT	LM
		◇■1	■1	■1		◇■1		■1	■1	■1	■1	◇■1	◇■1	◇■1	◇■1	■1		■1	◇■1	■1	■1	■1	■1	◇■1	■1
		⊠				⊠						⊠	⊠	⊠	⊠				⊠					⊠	
Wolverhampton [7] 🚊	d	05 00				05 24								05 45	06 04									06 27	
Sandwell & Dudley	d					05 34								05 56	06 15									06 37	
Birmingham New Street [12]	d	05 29				05 50								06 10	06 30			05 53						06 50	
Birmingham International ✈	d	05 40				06 00								06 20	06 40			06 05						07 00	
Coventry	d	05 51				06 11								06 31	06 51			06 21						07 11	
Nuneaton	d												06 18												
Rugby	d	06 03									06 13	06 20	06 32					06 32	06 53						
Northampton	d				06 17						06 38	06 42						07 00					07 13		
Wolverton	d				06 29						06 50							07 12					07 25		
Milton Keynes Central [10]	a	06 22			06 33	06 38					06 53		06 51	06 59				07 15	07 12				07 29	07s40	
	d	06 23			06 34	06 38				06 48	06 55		06 52	06 59		07 01		07 17	07 14			07 21	07 30		
Bletchley	d				06 39			06 34		06 53	07 00					07 05				07 13		07 26			07 39
Leighton Buzzard	d				06 46			06 41		06 59	07 07					07 13		07 26				07 33	07 39		07 46
Cheddington	d									07 05												07 38			
Tring	d		06 24					06 52	07 00	07 11						07 22				07 28		07 45			
Berkhamsted	d		06 28					06 56	07 05	07 16						07 26				07 32		07 49			07 59
Hemel Hempstead	d		06 33					07 01	07 09	07 20						07 31				07 37		07 54			08 03
Apsley	d		06 36					07 04		07 24												07 57			
Kings Langley	d		06 39					07 07		07 27												08 00			
Watford Junction	a	06s43	06 44		07 04			07 12	07 17	07 31					07s36	07 38				07 44		08 05			08 10
	d		06 45	06 53	07 05			07 12	07 19	07 32						07 38				07 45	07 55	08 05			08 11
Bushey	d		06 48					07 15	07 22	07 34											07 59				
Harrow & Wealdstone ⊖	d		06 53	06 59				07 20		07 40						07 45					08 05				08 17
Wembley Central ⊖	d			07 04												07 49									
Shepherd's Bush	a			07 19												08 04									
Kensington (Olympia) ⊖	a			07 21												08 06									
West Brompton ⊖	a			07 24												08 09									
Imperial Wharf	a			07 27												08 12									
Clapham Junction	d			07a32												08j36									
East Croydon 🚊	a															09 04									
London Euston [15] ⊖	a	07 02	07 07		07 22	07 13		07 34	07 40	07 54	07 40	07 30	07 28	07 34	07 53			08 02	07 50	08 05	08 18	08 24	08 11	08 14	08 33

b Previous night, arr. 2333

e Previous night, arr. 2234

f Previous night, stops to set down only

g Previous night, arr. 2224

from 2 April

West Midlands, Northampton, Milton Keynes Central and Watford Junction - London

Network Diagram - see first Page of Table 59

		LM 1		LM 1	LM 1	VT ◇1 ⊠	VT ◇1 ⊠	VT ◇1 ⊠	VT ◇1 ⊠	VT ◇1 ⊠	LM 1	VT ◇1 ⊠		LM 1	LM 1	SN 1	LM 1	VT ◇1 ⊠	VT ◇1 ⊠	LM 1	LM 1	VT ◇1 ⊠		LM 1	LM 1
Wolverhampton 7 ⛴	d								06 45			07 04										07 45			
Sandwell & Dudley	d								06 56			07 15										07 56			
Birmingham New Street 12	d								07 10			07 30					06 53					08 10			
Birmingham International ✈	d								07 20								07 05		07 41			08 20			
Coventry	d								07 31								07 21		07 52			08 31			
Nuneaton	d						07 07			07 33															
Rugby	d				07 02	07 08		07 29									07 32	07 55							
Northampton	d				07 32						07 39						08 05			08 25					
Wolverton	d										07 51						08 17			08 37					
Milton Keynes Central 10	a				07 46						07 54						08 21			08 41					
	d				07 46						07 55			07 59		08 13	08 21			08 41					08 47
Bletchley	d				07 51									08 04		08 17	08 27			08 46					08 52
Leighton Buzzard	d				07 58						08 05			08 11		08 24	08 34			08 53					08 58
Cheddington	d				08 04																				09 04
Tring	d			08 04	08 10										08 25	08 34					08 48			09 01	09 10
Berkhamsted	d				08 15										08 29	08 39					08 53			09 05	09 15
Hemel Hempstead	d				08 19									08 28	08 34	08 43					08 57			09 10	09 19
Apsley	d			08 13											08 37									09 13	
Kings Langley	d			08 16											08 40									09 16	
Watford Junction	a			08 20	08 26									08 35	08 45	08 51					09 04	09s15		09 20	09 26
	d	08 15		08 22	08 28									08 36	08 46	08 51					09 05			09 21	09 27
Bushey	d	08 19													08 48						09 08			09 23	
Harrow & Wealdstone ⊖	d	08 24		08 29	08 34										08 54	08 58					09 13			09 28	09 33
Wembley Central ⊖	d															09 05									
Shepherd's Bush	a															09 18									
Kensington (Olympia) ⊖	a															09 20									
West Brompton ⊖	a															09 23									
Imperial Wharf	a															09 26									
Clapham Junction	d															09 34									
East Croydon ⛴	a															09 57									
London Euston 15 ⊖	a	08 38		08 42	08 49	07 57	08 07	08 22	08 30	08 33	08 39	08 42		08 55	09 08		09 10	08 45	08 49	09 27	09 27	09 34		09 42	09 47

		LM 1	VT ◇1 ⊠	VT ◇1 ⊠	VT ◇1 ⊠	LM 1	SN 1	VT ◇1 ⊠		LM 1	VT ◇1 ⊠	LM 1	VT ◇1 ⊠	VT ◇1 ⊠	LM 1	LM 1	VT ◇1 ⊠	LM 1	LM 1		VT ◇1 ⊠	LM 1	SN 1	VT ◇1 ⊠	LM 1
Wolverhampton 7 ⛴	d													08 45											
Sandwell & Dudley	d													08 56											
Birmingham New Street 12	d		07 50					08 30		07 53				09 10				08 33			08 50			09 30	08 53
Birmingham International ✈	d		08 00					08 40		08 05				09 20				08 45			09 00			09 40	09 05
Coventry	d		08 11					08 51		08 21				09 31				09 01			09 11			09 51	09 21
Nuneaton	d	08 02			08 46														09 02						
Rugby	d	08 20	08 23							08 32	08 46							09 12	09 20		09 23				09 32
Northampton	d	08 47								09 05		09 25						09 50							10 05
Wolverton	d									09 17		09 37													10 17
Milton Keynes Central 10	a	09 01						09 18		09 20		09 41						10 04						10 18	10 20
	d	09 01					09 13	09 19		09 22		09 41	09 47			09 47	10 02	10 05					10 13	10 19	10 22
Bletchley	d						09 17			09 27		09 46				09 52							10 17		10 27
Leighton Buzzard	d						09 24			09 33		09 53				09 58							10 24		10 33
Cheddington	d															10 04									
Tring	d					09 26	09 34								09 56	10 10						10 26	10 34		
Berkhamsted	d					09 30	09 39			09 46					10 00	10 15						10 30	10 39		10 46
Hemel Hempstead	d					09 35	09 43			09 51					10 05	10 19						10 35	10 43		10 51
Apsley	d					09 38									10 08							10 38			
Kings Langley	d					09 41									10 11							10 41			
Watford Junction	a	09 27			09s31	09 46	09 51			09 58				10s15	10 16	10 26		10 30				10 46	10 51		10 58
	d	09 28				09 46	09 51			09 59					10 16	10 27		10 31				10 46	10 51		10 59
Bushey	d					09 49									10 19							10 49			
Harrow & Wealdstone ⊖	d					09 54	09 58								10 24							10 54	10 59		
Wembley Central ⊖	d						10 05																11 04		
Shepherd's Bush	a						10 21																11 19		
Kensington (Olympia) ⊖	a						10 23																11 21		
West Brompton ⊖	a						10 26																11 23		
Imperial Wharf	a						10 29																11 26		
Clapham Junction	d						10 34																11 34		
East Croydon ⛴	a						10 57																11 57		
London Euston 15 ⊖	a	09 44	09 13	09 23	09 52	10 08		09 54		10 18	09 38	10 27	10 23	10 28	10 38	10 46	10 38	10 49			10 14	11 08		10 54	11 17

Table 66

Mondays to Fridays

from 2 April

West Midlands, Northampton, Milton Keynes Central and Watford Junction - London

Network Diagram - see first Page of Table 59

Station		LM	VT	VT	LM		LM	VT	LM	LM	VT	LM	SN	VT	LM		LM	VT	VT	LM	LM	VT	LM	LM	VT
		[1]	◇[1]	◇[1]	[1]		[1]	◇[1]	◇[1]	◇[1]	◇[1]	[1]	[1]	◇[1]	[1]		[1]	◇[1]	◇[1]	[1]	[1]	◇[1]	◇[1]	◇[1]	◇[1]
									A														A		
			⊠	⊠				⊠			⊠			⊠				⊠	⊠			⊠			⊠
Wolverhampton [7]	d			09 45															10 45						
Sandwell & Dudley	d			09 56															10 56						
Birmingham New Street [12]	d	09 13		10 10					09 33		09 50			10 30	09 53		10 13		11 10				10 33		10 50
Birmingham International	d	09 29		10 20					09 45		09 59			10 40	10 05		10 29		11 20				10 45		11 00
Coventry	d	09 48		10 31					10 01		10 10			10 51	10 21		10 48		11 31				11 01		11 11
Nuneaton	d									10 02														11 02	
Rugby	d	09 59							10 12	10 20	10 24				10 32		10 59						11 12	11 20	11 24
Northampton	d	10 25							10 50						11 05		11 25						11 50		
Wolverton	d	10 37													11 17		11 37								
Milton Keynes Central [10]	a	10 41							11 04					11 18	11 20		11 41						12 04		
	d	10 41	10 47				10 47	11 02	11 05				11 13	11 19	11 22		11 41	11 47			11 47	12 02	12 05		
Bletchley	d	10 46					10 52						11 17		11 27		11 46				11 52				
Leighton Buzzard	d	10 53					10 58						11 24		11 33		11 53				11 58				
Cheddington	d						11 04														12 04				
Tring	d				10 56		11 10					11 26	11 34							11 56	12 10				
Berkhamsted	d				11 00		11 15					11 30	11 39		11 46					12 00	12 15				
Hemel Hempstead	d				11 05		11 19					11 35	11 43		11 51					12 05	12 19				
Apsley	d				11 08							11 38								12 08					
Kings Langley	d				11 11							11 41								12 11					
Watford Junction	a			11s15	11 16		11 26		11 30			11 46	11 51		11 58				12s15	12 16	12 26		12 30		
	d				11 16		11 27		11 31			11 46	11 51		11 59					12 16	12 27		12 31		
Bushey	d				11 19							11 49								12 19					
Harrow & Wealdstone ⊖	d				11 24							11 54	11 59							12 24					
Wembley Central ⊖	d												12 04												
Shepherd's Bush	a												12 19												
Kensington (Olympia) ⊖	a												12 21												
West Brompton ⊖	a												12 24												
Imperial Wharf	a												12 27												
Clapham Junction	d												12 34												
East Croydon	a												12 57												
London Euston [15] ⊖	a	11 27	11 23	11 32	11 38		11 46	11 38	11 49		11 14	12 08		11 54	12 17		12 27	12 23	12 32	12 38	12 45	12 38	12 49		12 14

Station			LM	SN	VT	LM	LM	VT	VT	LM	LM		VT	LM	LM	VT	LM	SN	VT	LM	LM		VT	VT	LM
			[1]	[1]	◇[1]	[1]	[1]	◇[1]	◇[1]	[1]	[1]		◇[1]	◇[1]	◇[1]	◇[1]	[1]	[1]	◇[1]	[1]	[1]		◇[1]	◇[1]	[1]
														A											
					☕			☕	☕				☕			☕			☕				☕	☕	
Wolverhampton [7]	d								11 45															12 45	
Sandwell & Dudley	d								11 56															12 56	
Birmingham New Street [12]	d				11 30	10 53	11 13		12 10					11 33		11 50			12 30	11 53	12 13			13 10	
Birmingham International	d				11 40	11 05	11 29		12 20					11 45		12 00			12 40	12 05	12 29			13 20	
Coventry	d				11 51	11 21	11 48		12 31					12 01		12 11			12 51	12 21	12 48			13 31	
Nuneaton	d														12 02										
Rugby	d					11 32	11 59							12 12	12 20	12 24				12 32	13 00				
Northampton	d					12 05	12 25							12 50						13 05	13 25				
Wolverton	d					12 17	12 37													13 17	13 37				
Milton Keynes Central [10]	a				12 18	12 20	12 41							13 04					13 18	13 20	13 41				
	d			12 13	12 19	12 22	12 41	12 46			12 47		13 02	13 05				13 13	13 19	13 22	13 41		13 47		
Bletchley	d			12 17		12 27	12 46				12 52							13 17		13 27	13 46				
Leighton Buzzard	d			12 24		12 33	12 53				12 58							13 24		13 33	13 53				
Cheddington	d										13 04														
Tring	d		12 26	12 34						12 56	13 10						13 26	13 34							13 56
Berkhamsted	d		12 30	12 39		12 46				13 00	13 15						13 30	13 39		13 46					14 00
Hemel Hempstead	d		12 35	12 43		12 51				13 05	13 19						13 35	13 43		13 51					14 05
Apsley	d		12 38							13 08							13 38								14 08
Kings Langley	d		12 41							13 11							13 41								14 11
Watford Junction	a		12 46	12 51		12 58			13s15	13 16	13 26			13 30			13 46	13 51		13 58				14s14	14 16
	d		12 46	12 51		12 59				13 16	13 27			13 31			13 46	13 51		13 59					14 16
Bushey	d		12 49							13 19							13 49								14 19
Harrow & Wealdstone ⊖	d		12 54	12 59						13 24							13 54	13 59							14 24
Wembley Central ⊖	d			13 04														14 04							
Shepherd's Bush	a			13 19														14 19							
Kensington (Olympia) ⊖	a			13 21														14 21							
West Brompton ⊖	a			13 24														14 24							
Imperial Wharf	a			13 27														14 27							
Clapham Junction	d			13 34														14 34							
East Croydon	a			13 57														14 57							
London Euston [15] ⊖	a		13 08		12 54	13 17	13 27	13 23	13 32	13 38	13 45		13 38	13 49		13 14	14 08		13 54	14 17	14 27		14 23	14 32	14 38

A ◇ from Northampton

from 2 April

West Midlands, Northampton, Milton Keynes Central and Watford Junction - London

Network Diagram - see first Page of Table 59

		LM	VT	VT	LM	LM	LM		SN	VT	LM	LM	VT	VT	LM	LM	VT		LM	LM	VT	LM	SN	VT	LM
		1	◇1	◇1	◇1	◇1	1		1	◇1	1	1	◇1	◇1	1	1	◇1		◇1	◇1	◇1	1	1	◇1	1
					A														A						
			☕	☕						☕			☕	☕			☕				☕			☕	
Wolverhampton 7	d													13 45											
Sandwell & Dudley	d													13 56											
Birmingham New Street 12	d			12 50	12 33					13 30	12 53	13 13		14 10					13 33		13 50			14 30	13 53
Birmingham International	d			13 00	12 45					13 40	13 05	13 29		14 20					13 45		14 00			14 40	14 05
Coventry	d			13 11	13 01					13 51	13 21	13 48		14 31					14 01		14 11			14 51	14 21
Nuneaton	d					13 02														14 02					
Rugby	d			13 24	13 12	13c25					13 32	13 59							14 12	14 20	14 24				14 32
Northampton	d				13 50						14 05	14 25							14 50						15 05
Wolverton	d										14 17	14 37													15 17
Milton Keynes Central 10	a				14 04					14 19	14 20	14 41							15 04					15 18	15 20
	d	13 47	14 02		14 05				14 13	14 19	14 22	14 41	14 47			14 47	15 02		15 05				15 13	15 19	15 22
Bletchley	d	13 52							14 17		14 27	14 46				14 52							15 17		15 27
Leighton Buzzard	d	13 58							14 24		14 33	14 53				14 58							15 24		15 33
Cheddington	d	14 04														15 04									
Tring	d	14 10					14 26		14 34						14 56	15 10						15 26	15 34		
Berkhamsted	d	14 15					14 30		14 39		14 46				15 00	15 15						15 30	15 39		15 46
Hemel Hempstead	d	14 19					14 35		14 43		14 51				15 05	15 19						15 35	15 43		15 51
Apsley	d						14 38								15 08							15 38			
Kings Langley	d						14 41								15 11							15 41			
Watford Junction	a	14 26			14 30		14 46		14 51		14 58			15s15	15 16	15 26			15 30			15 46	15 51		15 58
	d	14 27			14 31		14 46		14 51		14 59				15 16	15 27			15 31			15 46	15 51		15 59
Bushey	d						14 49								15 19							15 49			
Harrow & Wealdstone ⊖	d						14 54		14 59						15 24							15 54	15 59		
Wembley Central ⊖	d								15 04														16 05		
Shepherd's Bush	a								15 22														16 19		
Kensington (Olympia) ⊖	a								15 24														16 21		
West Brompton ⊖	a								15 26														16 24		
Imperial Wharf	a								15 29														16 27		
Clapham Junction	d								15 34														16 34		
East Croydon	a								15 57														16 58		
London Euston 15 ⊖	a	14 45	14 38	14 14	14 49		15 08			14 54	15 17	15 27	15 23	15 32	15 38	15 45	15 38		15 49		15 14	16 08		15 54	16 17

		LM	VT		VT	LM	LM	VT	LM	LM	VT	LM	SN		VT	LM	LM	VT	VT	LM	LM	VT	LM	LM	
		1	◇1		◇1	1	1	◇1	◇1	◇1	◇1	1	1		◇1	1	1	◇1	◇1	1	1	◇1	◇1	◇1	
									A														A		
			☕		☕			☕			☕				☕			☕	☕			☕			
Wolverhampton 7	d				14 45														15 45						
Sandwell & Dudley	d				14 56														15 56						
Birmingham New Street 12	d	14 13			15 10				14 33		14 50				15 30	14 53	15 13		16 10				15 33		
Birmingham International	d	14 29			15 20				14 45		15 00				15 40	15 05	15 29		16 20				15 45		
Coventry	d	14 48			15 31				15 01		15 11				15 51	15 21	15 48		16 32				16 01		
Nuneaton	d									15 02														16 02	
Rugby	d	14 59							15 12	15 20	15 24					15 32	15 59						16 12	16 20	
Northampton	d	15 25							15 50							16 05	16 25						16 50		
Wolverton	d	15 37														16 17	16 37								
Milton Keynes Central 10	a	15 41							16 04						16 18	16 20	16 41						17 04		
	d	15 41	15 47				15 47	16 02	16 05				16 13		16 19	16 22	16 41	16 47			16 47	17 02	17 05		
Bletchley	d	15 46					15 52						16 17			16 27	16 46				16 52				
Leighton Buzzard	d	15 53					15 58						16 24			16 33	16 53				16 58				
Cheddington	d						16 04														17 04				
Tring	d					15 56	16 10					16 26	16 34							16 56	17 10				
Berkhamsted	d					16 00	16 15					16 30	16 39			16 46				17 00	17 15				
Hemel Hempstead	d					16 05	16 19					16 35	16 43			16 51				17 05	17 19				
Apsley	d					16 08						16 38								17 08					
Kings Langley	d					16 11						16 41								17 11					
Watford Junction	a				16s15	16 16	16 26		16 30			16 46	16 51			16 58			17 15	17 16	17 26		17 30		
	d					16 16	16 27		16 31			16 46	16 51			16 59			17 16	17 16	17 27		17 31		
Bushey	d					16 19						16 49								17 19					
Harrow & Wealdstone ⊖	d					16 24						16 54	16 59							17 24					
Wembley Central ⊖	d												17 05												
Shepherd's Bush	a												17 19												
Kensington (Olympia) ⊖	a												17 21												
West Brompton ⊖	a												17 24												
Imperial Wharf	a												17 27												
Clapham Junction	d												17 33												
East Croydon	a												17 59												
London Euston 15 ⊖	a	16 27	16 23		16 32	16 38	16 45	16 38	16 49		16 14	17 08			16 57	17 18	17 27	17 23	17 34	17 38	17 47	17 38	17 49		

A ◇ from Northampton

West Midlands, Northampton, Milton Keynes Central and Watford Junction - London

Network Diagram - see first Page of Table 59

		VT	LM	SN	VT	LM	LM	VT	VT	LM		LM	VT	LM	LM	VT	LM	SN	VT	LM		VT	VT	LM	VT
		◇1	1	1	◇1	1	1	◇1	◇1	1		1	◇1	◇1	◇1	◇1	1	1	◇1	1		◇1	◇1	1	◇1
														A											
		☕			☕			☕	☕				☕			☕			☒			☕	☕		☒
Wolverhampton 7	d								16 45																17 45
Sandwell & Dudley	d								16 56																17 56
Birmingham New Street 12	d	15 50			16 30	15 53			17 10					16 33		16 50			17 30	16 53				17 13	18 10
Birmingham International	d	16 00			16 40	16 05			17 20					16 45		17 00			17 40	17 05				17 25	18 20
Coventry	d	16 11			16 51	16 21			17 31					17 01		17 11			17 51	17 21				17 40	18 31
Nuneaton	d														17 02										
Rugby	d	16 24				16 32								17 12	17 20	17 24				17 32				17 51	
Northampton	d					17 05	17 25							17 50						18 05				18 25	
Wolverton	d					17 17	17 37													18 17				18 37	
Milton Keynes Central 10	a				17 18	17 20	17 41							18 04					18 18	18 20				18 41	
	d			17 13	17 19	17 22	17 41	17 47				17 47	18 02	18 05				18 13	18 19	18 22		18 24		18 41	
Bletchley	d			17 17		17 27	17 46					17 52						18 17		18 27				18 46	
Leighton Buzzard	d			17 24		17 33	17 53					17 58						18 24		18 33				18 53	
Cheddington	d											18 04													
Tring	d		17 26	17 34						17 59		18 10					18 27	18 34							
Berkhamsted	d		17 30	17 39		17 46				18 03		18 15					18 31	18 39		18 46					
Hemel Hempstead	d		17 35	17 43		17 51				18 08		18 19					18 36	18 43		18 51					
Apsley	d		17 38							18 11							18 39								
Kings Langley	d		17 41							18 14							18 42								
Watford Junction	a		17 46	17 51		17 59			18s15	18 19		18 26		18 31			18 46	18 51		18 58					19s16
	d		17 46	17 51		17 59				18 19		18 27		18 31			18 47	18 51		18 59					
Bushey	d		17 49							18 22							18 49								
Harrow & Wealdstone ⊖	d		17 54	17 59						18 27							18 54	18 59							
Wembley Central ⊖	d			18 05														19 05							
Shepherd's Bush	a			18 19														19 18							
Kensington (Olympia) ⊖	a			18 21														19 20							
West Brompton ⊖	a			18 24														19 23							
Imperial Wharf	a			18 27														19 25							
Clapham Junction	d			18 34														19a30							
East Croydon	a			19 02																					
London Euston 15 ⊖	a	17 14	18 10		17 54	18 18	18 27	18 23	18 34	18 41		18 45	18 38	18 49		18 14	19 09		18 54	19 18		18 59	19 08	19 29	19 34

		LM	LM	VT	VT	LM		VT	LM	SN	VT	VT	LM	VT	LM	VT		VT	LM	LM	LM	LM	VT	LM	SN
		1	1	◇1	◇1	◇1		◇1	1	1	◇1	◇1	1	◇1	1	◇1		◇1	1	1	◇1	◇1	◇1	1	1
																					A				
				☒	☒			☒			☒	☒		☒		☒		☒					☒		
Wolverhampton 7	d																	18 45							
Sandwell & Dudley	d																	18 56							
Birmingham New Street 12	d							17 50			18 30		17 53					19 10			18 33		18 50		
Birmingham International	d							18 00			18 40		18 05					19 20			18 45		19 00		
Coventry	d							18 11			18 51		18 21					19 31			19 01		19 11		
Nuneaton	d					18 02																19 02			
Rugby	d					18 20		18 24					18 32								19 12	19 20	19 24		
Northampton	d					18 50							19 05		19 25						19 51				
Wolverton	d												19 17		19 37										
Milton Keynes Central 10	a					19 04					19 18		19 20		19 41						20 05				
	d		18 47	18 48	19 03	19 05				19 15	19 19		19 22	19 32	19 41	19 47				19 47	20 09				20 13
Bletchley	d		18 52							19 19			19 27		19 46					19 52					20 17
Leighton Buzzard	d		18 58							19 26			19 33		19 53					19 58					20 24
Cheddington	d		19 06																	20 04					
Tring	d	19 00	19 12						19 29	19 36									19 56	20 10				20 26	20 34
Berkhamsted	d	19 04	19 17						19 33	19 41			19 46						20 00	20 15				20 30	20 39
Hemel Hempstead	d	19 09	19 21						19 38	19 45			19 51						20 05	20 19				20 35	20 43
Apsley	d	19 12							19 41										20 08					20 38	
Kings Langley	d	19 15							19 44										20 11					20 41	
Watford Junction	a	19 20	19 28			19 30			19 49	19 54			19 59					20s15	20 16	20 26	20 31			20 46	20 51
	d	19 20	19 29			19 31			19 49	19 54			19 59						20 16	20 27	20 32			20 46	20 51
Bushey	d	19 23							19 52										20 19					20 49	
Harrow & Wealdstone ⊖	d	19 28							19 57	20 01									20 24					20 54	20 59
Wembley Central ⊖	d									20 06															21 04
Shepherd's Bush	a									20 21															21 22
Kensington (Olympia) ⊖	a									20 23															21 24
West Brompton ⊖	a									20 25															21 27
Imperial Wharf	a									20 28															21 29
Clapham Junction	d									20a33															21a34
East Croydon	a																								
London Euston 15 ⊖	a	19 42	19 47	19 23	19 38	19 50		19 14	20 11		19 54	20 02	20 19	20 06	20 27	20 23		20 34	20 38	20 51	20 49		20 14	21 08	

A ◇ from Northampton

Table 66

Mondays to Fridays

from 2 April

West Midlands, Northampton, Milton Keynes Central and Watford Junction - London

Network Diagram - see first Page of Table 59

		VT		VT	LM	VT	VT	LM	VT	LM	LM	VT		VT	VT	LM	VT	SN	LM	VT	VT	VT		VT	LM
		◇1 ☕		◇1 ⊠	1	◇1 ⊠	◇1 ☕	1	◇1 ⊠	1	1	◇1 ☕		◇1 ☕	◇1 ☕	1	◇1 ☕	1	1	◇1 ☕	◇1 ☕	◇1 ☕		◇1 ☕	1
Wolverhampton 7 🚌	d													19 45											
Sandwell & Dudley	d													19 56											
Birmingham New Street 12	d	19 30			18 53		19 50							20 10					19 53	20 50					
Birmingham International ✈	d	19 40			19 05		20 00							20 20					20 05	21 00					
Coventry	d	19 51			19 21		20 11							20 31					20 21	21 11					
Nuneaton	d																21 03								
Rugby	d				19 32		20 23												20 32	21 23		21 28			
Northampton	d				20 05			20 25											21 05						21 37
Wolverton	d				20 17			20 37											21 17						21 49
Milton Keynes Central 10	a	20 18			20 20			20 41						20 58					21 20			21 47			21 52
	d	20 19			20 22	20 33		20 41	20 46		20 47	20 50		20 59	21 04			21 13	21 22		21 36	21 49		21 52	21 53
Bletchley	d				20 27			20 46			20 52							21 17	21 27						21 58
Leighton Buzzard	d				20 33			20 53			20 58							21 24	21 33						22 04
Cheddington	d										21 06														22 10
Tring	d									20 56	21 11					21 26		21 34							22 16
Berkhamsted	d				20 46					21 00	21 16					21 30		21 39	21 46						22 20
Hemel Hempstead	d				20 51					21 05	21 20					21 35		21 43	21 51						22 25
Apsley	d									21 08						21 38									
Kings Langley	d									21 11						21 41									
Watford Junction	a				20 58					21 16	21 27			21s19		21 46	21s48	21 51	21 58					22s11	22 32
	d				20 59					21 16	21 27					21 46		21 51	21 59						22 33
Bushey	d									21 19						21 49									
Harrow & Wealdstone ⊖	d									21 24						21 54		21 59							
Wembley Central ⊖	d																								
Shepherd's Bush	a																	22 23							
Kensington (Olympia) ⊖	a																	22 25							
West Brompton ⊖	a																	22 27							
Imperial Wharf	a																	22 30							
Clapham Junction	d																	22a34							
East Croydon 🚌	a																								
London Euston 15 ⊖	a	20 54		21 05	21 17	21 06	21 14	21 29	21 24	21 38	21 46	21 26		21 38	21 42	22 08	22 09		22 20	22 12	22 12	22 22		22 33	22 52

		VT	SN	LM	SN	LM	VT	VT		SN	LM	VT	VT	LM MO	LM MX	VT
		◇1 ☕	1	1	1	1	◇1 ⊠	◇1 ☕		1	1	◇1 ☕	◇1 ☕	1	1	◇1 ☕
Wolverhampton 7 🚌	d	20 47											21 45			22 45
Sandwell & Dudley	d	20 57											21 56			22 55
Birmingham New Street 12	d	21 10				20 53					21 33		22 10			23 10
Birmingham International ✈	d	21 20				21 05					21 45		22 20			23 20
Coventry	d	21 31				21 21					22 01		22 31			23 31
Nuneaton	d											22 17				
Rugby	d					21 32					22 12	22 34	22 43			23 44
Northampton	d					22 05					22 55			23 30	23 46	00s05
Wolverton	d					22 17					23 07			23 46	00 02	
Milton Keynes Central 10	a	21 58				22 20					23 12	22 58	23s05	23 50	00 05	00s23
	d	21 59		22 05	22 11	22 22	22 41	22 53			23 13	22 59		23 50	00 06	
Bletchley	d			22 10	22 15	22 27					23 18			23 55	00 11	
Leighton Buzzard	d			22 17	22 22	22 33					23 24			00 02	00 17	
Cheddington	d			22 23							23 29			00 08	00 24	
Tring	d			22 28	22 34						23 38			00 14	00 30	
Berkhamsted	d			22 33	22 39	22 48					23 43			00 18	00 34	
Hemel Hempstead	d			22 37	22 43	22 53					23 47			00 22	00 39	
Apsley	d			22 41							23 50					
Kings Langley	d			22 44							23 53					
Watford Junction	a	22s20		22 48	22 52	23 00	23s14	23s25			23 58	23s30	23s37	00 29	00 46	00s52
	d		22 27	22 49	22 53	23 01				23 29	23 58			00 30	00 47	
Bushey	d			22 51							00 01					
Harrow & Wealdstone ⊖	d		22 33	22 57	23 00					23 35	00 06			00 36	00 53	
Wembley Central ⊖	d													00 40	00 57	
Shepherd's Bush	a		22 49		23 21					23 53						
Kensington (Olympia) ⊖	a		22 51		23 23					23 56						
West Brompton ⊖	a		22 54		23 26					23 59						
Imperial Wharf	a		22 56		23 28					00 02						
Clapham Junction	d		23a01		23 40					00a07						
East Croydon 🚌	a				00 01											
London Euston 15 ⊖	a	22 43		23 12		23 21	23 38	23 48			00 21	23 56	00 04	00 53	01 09	01 15

Table 66

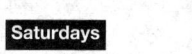

Saturdays
until 31 March

West Midlands, Northampton, Milton Keynes Central and Watford Junction - London

Network Diagram - see first Page of Table 59

		SN	SN	LM	VT	LM	VT	LM	LM	SN		LM			LM	VT	SN	LM	LM	LM		VT	VT	VT	VT
		1	**1**	**1**	◇**1**	**1**	◇**1**	**1**	**1**	**1**		◇**1**			**1**	◇**1**	**1**	◇**1**	**1**	**1**		◇**1**	◇**1**	◇**1**	◇**1**
					☕		☕									☕						☕	☕	☕	☕
Wolverhampton **7** 🚌	d				21p45		22p45															05 45		06 06	
Sandwell & Dudley	d				21p56		22p55															05 56		06 17	
Birmingham New Street 12	d			21p33	22p10		23p10									05 50						06 10		06 30	
Birmingham International ✈	d			21p45	22p20		23p20									06 00						06 20		06 40	
Coventry	d			22p01	22p31		23p31									06 10						06 31		06 51	
Nuneaton	d																								06 59
Rugby	d			22p12	22p43		23p44									06 24							06 51		
Northampton	d			22c55		23p46	00s05					05 16						06 05							
Wolverton	d			23p07		00 02						05 28						06 17							
Milton Keynes Central 10	a			23p12	23e05	00 05	00s23					05 31						06 20				06 58	07 11		
	d	22p11		23p13		00 06		03 40	04 35			05 32						06 22		06 47		06 59	07 12		
Bletchley	d	22p15		23p18		00 11		03 45	04 40			05 37			06 10			06 27	06 40	06 52					
Leighton Buzzard	d	22p22		23p24		00 17		03 51	04 46			05 43			06 17			06 33	06 47	06 58					
Cheddington	d			23p29		00 24						05 49								07 04					
Tring	d	22p34		23p38		00 30		04 03	04 58			05 55			06 26			06 43	06 56	07 10					
Berkhamsted	d	22p39		23p43		00 34		04 08	05 03			06 00			06 31			06 47	07 01	07 15					
Hemel Hempstead	d	22p43		23p47		00 39		04 12	05 07			06 04			06 35			06 52	07 05	07 19					
Apsley	d			23p50								06 07			06 38				07 08						
Kings Langley	d			23p53								06 10			06 41				07 11						
Watford Junction	a	22p52		23p58	23e37	00 46	00s52	04 19	05 14			06 15			06 46			06 59	07 16	07 26		07s19	07s32	07s36	07s44
	d	22p53	23p29	23p58		00 47		04 20	05 15	05 52		06 16			06 47		06 55	07 01	07 17	07 27					
Bushey	d			00 01								06 18			06 49				07 20						
Harrow & Wealdstone ⊖	d	23p00	23p35	00 06		00 53		04 26	05 21	05 58		06 24			06 55		07 01		07 25						
Wembley Central ⊖	d					00 57		04 34	05 25								07 06								
Shepherd's Bush	a	23p21	23p53							06 20							07 19								
Kensington (Olympia) ⊖	a	23p23	23p56							06 22							07 21								
West Brompton ⊖	a	23p26	23p59							06 25							07 24								
Imperial Wharf	a	23p28	00 02							06 28							07 27								
Clapham Junction	d	23b40	00a07							06 34							07 34								
East Croydon 🚌	a	00 01								06 57							07 57								
London Euston 15 ⊖	a			00 21	00 04	01 09	01 15	04 46	05 41			06 38			07 09	07 16		07 20	07 39	07 45		07 38	07 52	07 55	08 05

		LM	SN	LM	VT	VT		VT	VT	LM	LM	LM	LM	SN	VT	LM		VT	LM	VT	LM	VT	LM	LM	LM
		1	**1**	◇**1**	◇**1**	◇**1**		◇**1**	◇**1**	**1**	**1**	◇**1**	**1**	**1**	◇**1**	◇**1**		◇**1**	◇**1**	◇**1**	**1**	◇**1**	**1**	◇**1**	◇**1**
					☕	☕		☕	☕						☕			☕		☕		☕			
Wolverhampton **7** 🚌	d					06 27			06 45						07 04							07 45			
Sandwell & Dudley	d					06 37			06 56						07 15							07 56			
Birmingham New Street 12	d					06 50			07 10						07 30	06 53			07 13			08 10		07 33	
Birmingham International ✈	d					07 00			07 20						07 40	07 05			07 29			08 20		07 45	
Coventry	d					07 11			07 31						07 52	07 21			07 48			08 31		08 01	
Nuneaton	d																								08 02
Rugby	d					07 23										07 32		07 54	07 59					08 12	08 20
Northampton	d			07 05								07 33				08 05			08 25					08 50	
Wolverton	d			07 17								07 45				08 17			08 37						
Milton Keynes Central 10	a			07 20								07 49			08 18	08 20			08 41					09 04	
	d		07 13	07 22	07 32			07 38			07 44	07 49		08 13	08 19	08 22			08 41	08 47			08 47	09 05	
Bletchley	d	07 10	07 17	07 27							07 49	07 54		08 17		08 27			08 46				08 52		
Leighton Buzzard	d	07 17	07 24	07 33							07 55	08 01		08 24		08 33			08 53				08 58		
Cheddington	d										08 01												09 04		
Tring	d	07 26	07 34							07 56	08 07		08 26	08 34							08 56		09 10		
Berkhamsted	d	07 31	07 39	07 46						08 00	08 11		08 30	08 39		08 46					09 00		09 15		
Hemel Hempstead	d	07 35	07 43	07 51						08 05	08 16		08 35	08 43		08 51					09 05		09 19		
Apsley	d	07 38								08 08			08 38								09 08				
Kings Langley	d	07 41								08 11			08 41								09 11				
Watford Junction	a	07 46	07 51	07 58					08s15	08 16	08 23	08 20	08 46	08 51		08 58					09 16	09s17	09 26	09 33	
	d	07 47	07 52	07 59						08 16	08 24	08 20	08 46	08 52		08 59					09 16		09 27	09 34	
Bushey	d	07 49								08 19			08 49								09 19				
Harrow & Wealdstone ⊖	d	07 55	07 59							08 24			08 54	08 59							09 24				
Wembley Central ⊖	d		08u04											09u04											
Shepherd's Bush	a		08 19											09 19											
Kensington (Olympia) ⊖	a		08 21											09 21											
West Brompton ⊖	a		08 24											09 24											
Imperial Wharf	a		08 27											09 27											
Clapham Junction	d		08 34											09 34											
East Croydon 🚌	a		08 57											09 57											
London Euston 15 ⊖	a	08 09		08 17	08 09	08 14		08 14	08 34	08 38	08 42	08 38	09 08		08 54	09 17		08 46	09 27	09 23	09 38	09 35	09 45	09 50	

b Previous night, arr. 2333
c Previous night, arr. 2234
e Previous night, stops to set down only

Table 66

Saturdays

until 31 March

West Midlands, Northampton, Milton Keynes Central and Watford Junction - London

Network Diagram - see first Page of Table 59

		VT		LM	SN	VT	VT	LM	LM	VT	VT	LM		LM	VT	LM	LM	VT	LM	SN	VT	VT		LM	LM
		◇1		1	1	◇1	◇1	◇1	◇1	◇1	◇1	1		1	◇1	◇1	◇1	◇1	1	1	◇1	◇1		◇1	◇1
		☕				☕	☕			☕	☕				☕			☕			☕	☕			
Wolverhampton 7	d					08 06					08 45														
Sandwell & Dudley	d										08 56														
Birmingham New Street 12	d	07 50				08 30		07 53	08 13		09 10					08 33		08 50			09 30			08 53	09 13
Birmingham International	d	08 00				08 40		08 05	08 29		09 20					08 45		09 00			09 40			09 05	09 29
Coventry	d	08 11				08 51		08 21	08 48		09 31					09 01		09 11			09 51			09 21	09 48
Nuneaton	d						08 59										09 02					09 59			
Rugby	d	08 23						08 32	08 59							09 12	09 20	09 23						09 32	09 59
Northampton	d							09 05	09 25							09 50								10 05	10 25
Wolverton	d							09 17	09 37															10 17	10 37
Milton Keynes Central 10	a					09 18		09 20	09 41							10 04					10 18			10 20	10 41
	d				09 13	09 19		09 22	09 41	09 47				09 47	10 02	10 05				10 13	10 19			10 22	10 41
Bletchley	d				09 17			09 27	09 46					09 52						10 17				10 27	10 46
Leighton Buzzard	d				09 24			09 33	09 53					09 58						10 24				10 33	10 53
Cheddington	d													10 04											
Tring	d			09 26	09 34							09 56		10 10					10 26	10 34					
Berkhamsted	d			09 30	09 39			09 46				10 00		10 15					10 30	10 39				10 46	
Hemel Hempstead	d			09 35	09 43			09 51				10 05		10 19					10 35	10 43				10 51	
Apsley	d			09 38								10 08							10 38						
Kings Langley	d			09 41								10 11							10 41						
Watford Junction	a			09 46	09 51			09 58			10s15	10 16		10 26		10 30			10 46	10 51				10 58	
	d			09 46	09 52			09 59				10 16		10 27		10 31			10 46	10 52				10 59	
Bushey	d			09 49								10 19							10 49						
Harrow & Wealdstone ⊖	d			09 54	09 59							10 24							10 54	10 59					
Wembley Central ⊖	d				10u04															11u04					
Shepherd's Bush	a				10 19															11 19					
Kensington (Olympia) ⊖	a				10 21															11 21					
West Brompton ⊖	a				10 24															11 24					
Imperial Wharf	a				10 27															11 27					
Clapham Junction	d				10 34															11 34					
East Croydon	a				10 57															11 57					
London Euston 15 ⊖	a	09 14		10 08		09 55	10 00	10 17	10 27	10 23	10 34	10 38		10 45	10 37	10 49		10 14	11 08		10 54	11 01		11 17	11 27

		VT	VT	LM	LM	VT	LM	LM		VT	LM	SN	VT	LM	LM	VT	VT	LM		LM	VT	LM	LM	VT	LM
		◇1	◇1	1	1	◇1	◇1	◇1		◇1	1	1	◇1	◇1	◇1	◇1	◇1	1		1	◇1	◇1	◇1	◇1	1
		☕	☕			☕				☕			☕			☕	☕				☕			☕	
Wolverhampton 7	d		09 45														10 45								
Sandwell & Dudley	d		09 56														10 56								
Birmingham New Street 12	d		10 10				09 33			09 50			10 30	09 53	10 13		11 10					10 33		10 50	
Birmingham International	d		10 20				09 45			10 00			10 40	10 05	10 29		11 20					10 45		11 00	
Coventry	d		10 31				10 01			10 11			10 51	10 21	10 48		11 31					11 01		11 11	
Nuneaton	d							10 02															11 02		
Rugby	d						10 12	10 20		10 23				10 32	10 59							11 12	11 20	11 23	
Northampton	d						10 50							11 05	11 25							11 50			
Wolverton	d													11 17	11 37										
Milton Keynes Central 10	a						11 04						11 18	11 20	11 41							12 04			
	d	10 47			10 47	11 02	11 05					11 13	11 20	11 22	11 41	11 47				11 47	12 02	12 05			
Bletchley	d				10 52							11 17		11 27	11 46					11 52					
Leighton Buzzard	d				10 58							11 24		11 33	11 53					11 58					
Cheddington	d				11 04															12 04					
Tring	d			10 56	11 10						11 26	11 34						11 56		12 10					12 26
Berkhamsted	d			11 00	11 15						11 30	11 39		11 46				12 00		12 15					12 30
Hemel Hempstead	d			11 05	11 19						11 35	11 43		11 51				12 05		12 19					12 35
Apsley	d			11 08							11 38							12 08							12 38
Kings Langley	d			11 11							11 41							12 11							12 41
Watford Junction	a		11s15	11 16	11 26		11 30				11 46	11 51		11 58			12s15	12 16		12 26		12 30			12 46
	d			11 16	11 27		11 31				11 46	11 52		11 59				12 16		12 27		12 31			12 46
Bushey	d			11 19							11 49							12 19							12 49
Harrow & Wealdstone ⊖	d			11 24							11 54	11 59						12 24							12 54
Wembley Central ⊖	d											12u04													
Shepherd's Bush	a											12 19													
Kensington (Olympia) ⊖	a											12 21													
West Brompton ⊖	a											12 24													
Imperial Wharf	a											12 27													
Clapham Junction	d											12 34													
East Croydon	a											12 57													
London Euston 15 ⊖	a	11 23	11 34	11 38	11 45	11 38	11 49			11 14	12 08		11 55	12 17	12 27	12 23	12 34	12 38		12 45	12 38	12 49		12 14	13 08

Table 66

Saturdays
until 31 March

West Midlands, Northampton, Milton Keynes Central and Watford Junction - London

Network Diagram - see first Page of Table 59

		SN	VT	LM		LM	VT	VT	LM	LM	VT	LM	LM	VT		LM	SN	VT	LM	LM	VT	VT	LM	LM
		1	◇1	◇1		◇1	◇1	◇1	1	1	◇1	◇1	◇1	◇1		1	1	◇1	◇1	◇1	◇1	◇1	1	1
			☕				☕	☕			☕			☕				☕			☕	☕		
Wolverhampton 7 ⇌	d							11 45														12 45		
Sandwell & Dudley	d							11 56														12 56		
Birmingham New Street 12	d		11 30	10 53		11 13		12 10				11 33		11 50				12 30	11 53	12 13		13 10		
Birmingham International ✈	d		11 40	11 05		11 29		12 20				11 45		12 00				12 40	12 05	12 29		13 20		
Coventry	d		11 51	11 21		11 48		12 31				12 01		12 11				12 51	12 21	12 48		13 31		
Nuneaton	d												12 02											
Rugby	d			11 32		11 59						12 12	12 20	12 23					12 32	12 59				
Northampton	d			12 05		12 25						12 50							13 05	13 25				
Wolverton	d			12 17		12 37													13 17	13 37				
Milton Keynes Central 10	a		12 18	12 20		12 41						13 04						13 18	13 20	13 41				
	d	12 13	12 19	12 22		12 41	12 47			12 47	13 02	13 05					13 13	13 19	13 22	13 41	13 47			13 47
Bletchley	d	12 17		12 27		12 46				12 52							13 17		13 27	13 46				13 52
Leighton Buzzard	d	12 24		12 33		12 53				12 58							13 24		13 33	13 53				13 58
Cheddington	d									13 04														14 04
Tring	d	12 34							12 56	13 10						13 26	13 34						13 56	14 10
Berkhamsted	d	12 39		12 46					13 00	13 15						13 30	13 39		13 46				14 00	14 15
Hemel Hempstead	d	12 43		12 51					13 05	13 19						13 35	13 43		13 51				14 05	14 19
Apsley	d								13 08							13 38							14 08	
Kings Langley	d								13 11							13 41							14 11	
Watford Junction	a	12 51		12 58				13s15	13 16	13 26		13 30				13 46	13 51		13 58			14s15	14 16	14 26
	d	12 52		12 59					13 16	13 27		13 31				13 46	13 52		13 59				14 16	14 27
Bushey	d								13 19							13 49							14 19	
Harrow & Wealdstone ⊖	d	12 59							13 24							13 54	13 59						14 24	
Wembley Central ⊖	d	13u04															14u04							
Shepherd's Bush	a	13 19															14 19							
Kensington (Olympia) ⊖	a	13 21															14 21							
West Brompton ⊖	a	13 24															14 24							
Imperial Wharf	a	13 27															14 27							
Clapham Junction	d	13 34															14 34							
East Croydon ⇌	a	13 57															14 57							
London Euston 15 ⊖	a		12 54	13 17		13 27	13 23	13 34	13 38	13 47	13 38	13 49		13 14		14 08		13 54	14 17	14 27	14 23	14 34	14 38	14 45

		VT	LM	LM	VT	LM	SN	VT	LM	LM		VT	VT	LM	LM	VT	LM	LM	VT	LM		SN	VT	LM	LM
		◇1	◇1	◇1	◇1	1	1	◇1	◇1	◇1		◇1	◇1	1	1	◇1	◇1	◇1	◇1	1		1	◇1	◇1	◇1
		☕			☕			☕				☕	☕			☕			☕				☕		
Wolverhampton 7 ⇌	d												13 45												
Sandwell & Dudley	d												13 56												
Birmingham New Street 12	d		12 33		12 50			13 30	12 53	13 13			14 10				13 33		13 50				14 30	13 53	14 13
Birmingham International ✈	d		12 45		13 00			13 40	13 05	13 29			14 20				13 45		14 00				14 40	14 05	14 29
Coventry	d		13 01		13 11			13 51	13 21	13 48			14 31				14 01		14 11				14 51	14 21	14 48
Nuneaton	d			13 02														14 02							
Rugby	d		13 12	13 20	13 23				13 32	13 59							14 12	14 20	14 23					14 32	14 59
Northampton	d		13 50						14 05	14 25							14 50							15 05	15 25
Wolverton	d								14 17	14 37														15 17	15 37
Milton Keynes Central 10	a		14 04					14 18	14 20	14 41							15 04						15 18	15 20	15 41
	d	14 02	14 05				14 13	14 19	14 22	14 41		14 47			14 47	15 02	15 05					15 13	15 19	15 22	15 41
Bletchley	d						14 17		14 27	14 46					14 52							15 17		15 27	15 46
Leighton Buzzard	d						14 24		14 33	14 53					14 58							15 24		15 33	15 53
Cheddington	d														15 04										
Tring	d					14 26	14 34							14 56	15 10					15 26		15 34			
Berkhamsted	d					14 30	14 39		14 46					15 00	15 15					15 30		15 39		15 46	
Hemel Hempstead	d					14 35	14 43		14 51					15 05	15 19					15 35		15 43		15 51	
Apsley	d					14 38								15 08						15 38					
Kings Langley	d					14 41								15 11						15 41					
Watford Junction	a		14 30			14 46	14 51		14 58				15s15	15 16	15 26		15 30			15 46		15 51		15 58	
	d		14 31			14 46	14 52		14 59					15 16	15 27		15 31			15 46		15 52		15 59	
Bushey	d					14 49								15 19						15 49					
Harrow & Wealdstone ⊖	d					14 54	14 59							15 24						15 54		15 59			
Wembley Central ⊖	d						15u04															16u04			
Shepherd's Bush	a						15 19															16 19			
Kensington (Olympia) ⊖	a						15 21															16 21			
West Brompton ⊖	a						15 24															16 24			
Imperial Wharf	a						15 27															16 27			
Clapham Junction	d						15 34															16 34			
East Croydon ⇌	a						15 57															16 57			
London Euston 15 ⊖	a	14 38	14 49		14 14	15 08		14 54	15 18	15 27		15 23	15 34	15 38	15 45	15 38	15 49		15 14	16 08			15 54	16 18	16 27

Table 66

Saturdays
until 31 March

West Midlands, Northampton, Milton Keynes Central and Watford Junction - London

Network Diagram - see first Page of Table 59

	VT	VT	LM	LM	VT		LM	LM	VT	LM	SN	VT	LM	LM	VT		VT	LM	LM	VT	LM	LM	VT	LM
	◇1	◇1	1	1	◇1		◇1	◇1	◇1	1	1	◇1	◇1	◇1	◇1		◇1	1	1	◇1	◇1	◇1	◇1	1
	☕	☕			☕				☕			☕			☕		☕			☕			☕	
Wolverhampton 7 d		14 45															15 45							
Sandwell & Dudley d		14 56															15 56							
Birmingham New Street 12 d		15 10					14 33		14 50			15 30	14 53	15 13			16 10				15 33		15 50	
Birmingham International d		15 20					14 45		15 00			15 40	15 05	15 29			16 20				15 45		16 00	
Coventry d		15 31					15 01		15 11			15 51	15 21	15 48			16 31				16 01		16 11	
Nuneaton d								15 02														16 02		
Rugby d							15 12	15 20	15 23				15 32	15 59							16 12	16 20	16 23	
Northampton d							15 50						16 05	16 25							16 50			
Wolverton d													16 17	16 37										
Milton Keynes Central 10 a							16 04					16 18	16 20	16 41							17 04			
d	15 47			15 47	16 02		16 05				16 13	16 19	16 22	16 41	16 47				16 47	17 02	17 05			
Bletchley d				15 52							16 17		16 27	16 46					16 52					
Leighton Buzzard d				15 58							16 24		16 33	16 53					16 58					
Cheddington d				16 04															17 04					
Tring d			15 56	16 10						16 26	16 34							16 56	17 10					17 26
Berkhamsted d			16 00	16 15						16 30	16 39		16 46					17 00	17 15					17 30
Hemel Hempstead d			16 05	16 19						16 35	16 43		16 51					17 05	17 19					17 35
Apsley d			16 08							16 38								17 08						17 38
Kings Langley d			16 11							16 41								17 11						17 41
Watford Junction a		16s15	16 16	16 26			16 30			16 46	16 51		16 58				17s15	17 16	17 26		17 30			17 46
d			16 16	16 27			16 31			16 46	16 52		16 59					17 16	17 27		17 31			17 46
Bushey d			16 19							16 49								17 19						17 49
Harrow & Wealdstone ⊖ d			16 24							16 54	16 59							17 24						17 54
Wembley Central ⊖ d											17u04													
Shepherd's Bush a											17 19													
Kensington (Olympia) ⊖ a											17 21													
West Brompton ⊖ a											17 24													
Imperial Wharf a											17 27													
Clapham Junction d											17 34													
East Croydon a											17 57													
London Euston 15 ⊖ a	16 23	16 34	16 38	16 45	16 38		16 49		16 14	17 08		16 54	17 17	17 27	17 23		17 34	17 38	17 45	17 38	17 49		17 14	18 08

	SN		VT	LM	LM	VT	VT	LM	LM	VT	LM	LM		VT	LM	SN	VT	LM	VT	VT	LM	LM		
	1		◇1	◇1	◇1	◇1	◇1	1	1	◇1	◇1	◇1		◇1	1	1	◇1	◇1	◇1	◇1	1	◇1		
			☕			☕	☕			☕				☕			☕		☕	☕				
Wolverhampton 7 d							16 45													17 45				
Sandwell & Dudley d							16 56													17 56				
Birmingham New Street 12 d			16 30	15 53	16 13		17 10				16 33			16 50			17 30	16 53		18 10		17 13		
Birmingham International d			16 40	16 05	16 29		17 20				16 45			17 00			17 40	17 05		18 20		17 30		
Coventry d			16 51	16 21	16 48		17 31				17 01			17 11			17 51	17 21		18 31		17 48		
Nuneaton d												17 02												
Rugby d				16 32	16 59						17 12	17 20		17 23				17 32				17 59		
Northampton d				17 05	17 25						17 50							18 05				18 31		
Wolverton d				17 17	17 37													18 17				18 43		
Milton Keynes Central 10 a			17 18	17 20	17 41						18 05						18 18	18 20				18 46		
d	17 13		17 19	17 22	17 41	17 47			17 47	18 02	18 05					18 13	18 19	18 22	18 47			18 47		
Bletchley d	17 17			17 27	17 46				17 52							18 17		18 27				18 52		
Leighton Buzzard d	17 24			17 33	17 53				17 58							18 24		18 33				18 58		
Cheddington d									18 04													19 04		
Tring d	17 34							17 56	18 10						18 26	18 34					18 56	19 10		
Berkhamsted d	17 39			17 46				18 00	18 15						18 30	18 39		18 46			19 00	19 15		
Hemel Hempstead d	17 43			17 51				18 05	18 19						18 35	18 43		18 51			19 05	19 19		
Apsley d								18 08							18 38						19 08			
Kings Langley d								18 11							18 41						19 11			
Watford Junction a	17 51			17 58			18s15	18 16	18 26		18 31				18 46	18 51		18 58		19s15	19 16	19 26		
d	17 52			17 59				18 16	18 27		18 31				18 46	18 52		18 59			19 16	19 27		
Bushey d								18 19							18 49						19 19			
Harrow & Wealdstone ⊖ d	17 59							18 24							18 54	18 59					19 24			
Wembley Central ⊖ d	18u04															19u04								
Shepherd's Bush a	18 19															19 19								
Kensington (Olympia) ⊖ a	18 21															19 21								
West Brompton ⊖ a	18 24															19 24								
Imperial Wharf a	18 27															19 27								
Clapham Junction d	18 34															19 34								
East Croydon a	18 57															19 57								
London Euston 15 ⊖ a			17 52	18 17	18 27	18 23	18 34	18 38	18 45	18 38	18 49			18 14	19 08		18 54	19 17	19 23	19 34	19 38	19 45		

Table 66

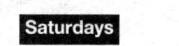

Saturdays
until 31 March

West Midlands, Northampton, Milton Keynes Central and Watford Junction - London

Network Diagram - see first Page of Table 59

		LM	LM	VT	SN	LM	SN	VT	LM	LM		LM	VT	VT	LM	VT	SN	VT	LM	LM		LM	VT	VT	SN
		◇1	◇1	◇1	1	1	1	◇1	◇1	1		◇1	◇1	◇1	◇1	◇1	1	◇1	◇1	1		◇1	◇1	◇1	1
				☕				☕					☕	☕		☕		☕					☕	☕	
Wolverhampton 7 ⛴	d															18 45							19 45		
Sandwell & Dudley	d															18 56							19 56		
Birmingham New Street 12	d	17 33		17 50				18 30	17 53			18 13	18 50		18 53	19 10			19 13			19 53	20 10		
Birmingham International ✈	d	17 45		18 00				18 40	18 05			18 29	19 00		19 05	19 20			19 29			20 05	20 20		
Coventry	d	18 01		18 11				18 51	18 21			18 48	19 11		19 21	19 31			19 48			20 21	20 31		
Nuneaton	d		18 02																						
Rugby	d	18 12	18 20	18 23					18 32			18 59	19 23		19 32	19 44			19 59			20 32	20 43		
Northampton	d	18 50							19 05			19 31			20 00				20 32			21 00			
Wolverton	d								19 17			19 43			20 12							21 12			
Milton Keynes Central 10	a	19 04						19 18	19 20			19 46			20 15	20 05			20 47			21 15	21 04		
	d	19 05					19 13	19 19	19 22			19 47		19 46	20 16	20 07		20 43	20 47	20 50		21 16	21 05	21 11	
Bletchley	d						19 17		19 27			19 52			20 21					20 55					
Leighton Buzzard	d						19 24		19 33			19 58			20 27				20 56						
Cheddington	d											20 04							21 03						
Tring	d					19 24	19 34			19 58		20 10							21 08	21 12					
Berkhamsted	d					19 28	19 39		19 46	20 02		20 15								21 17		21 38			
Hemel Hempstead	d					19 33	19 43		19 51	20 07		20 19							21 15	21 21		21 42			
Apsley	d					19 36				20 10									21 18						
Kings Langley	d					19 39				20 13									21 21						
Watford Junction	a	19 30				19 44	19 50		19 58	20 18		20 26			20 50	20s34		21s15	21 26	21 30		21 49	21s34		
	d	19 31			19 31	19 44	19 51		20 03	20 19		20 27			20 51		20 43		21 27	21 31		21 51			21 43
Bushey	d					19 47																			
Harrow & Wealdstone ⊖	d				19 38	19 52	19 58			20 25							20 50			21 37					21 50
Wembley Central ⊖	d				19 43																				
Shepherd's Bush	a				19 57		20 19										21 07								22 07
Kensington (Olympia) ⊖	a				19 59		20 21										21 09								22 09
West Brompton ⊖	a				20 02		20 24										21 12								22 12
Imperial Wharf	a				20 05		20 27										21 15								22 15
Clapham Junction	d				20a10		20 34										21a20								22a20
East Croydon ⛴	a						20 59																		
London Euston 15 ⊖	a	19 49		19 14		20 06		19 54	20 21	20 39		20 45	20 15	20 24	21 09	20 55		21 38	21 45	21 52		22 11	21 56	22 00	

		LM	VT	LM	VT	VT		SN	VT	SN	LM	LM
		◇1	◇1	◇1	◇1	◇1		1	◇1	1	◇1	◇1
			☕		☕	☕			☕			
Wolverhampton 7 ⛴	d				20 45				21 07			
Sandwell & Dudley	d				20 56				21 17			
Birmingham New Street 12	d			20 53	21 10				21 30		21 53	
Birmingham International ✈	d			21 05	21 20				21 40		22 05	
Coventry	d			21 21	21 31				21 51		22 21	
Nuneaton	d											
Rugby	d			21 32	21 43				22 03		22 32	
Northampton	d	21 20		22 05							22 55	23 30
Wolverton	d			22 17							23 07	23 42
Milton Keynes Central 10	a	21 34		22 20	22 04				22 28		23 10	23 45
	d	21 34	21 52	22 21	22 05	22 11			22 29		23 11	23 46
Bletchley	d	21 39		22 26							23 16	23 51
Leighton Buzzard	d	21 46		22 32							23 22	23 57
Cheddington	d	21 51		22 37							23 27	
Tring	d	21 58		22 44							23 36	
Berkhamsted	d	22 02		22 49							23 41	
Hemel Hempstead	d	22 07		22 53							23 45	
Apsley	d	22 10		22 56							23 49	
Kings Langley	d	22 13		23 00							23 52	
Watford Junction	a	22 18		23 06	22s34	22s40			23s11		23 56	00 19
	d	22 19		23 07				22 48		23 25	23 57	00 20
Bushey	d											
Harrow & Wealdstone ⊖	d			23 13				22 55		23 31	00 03	
Wembley Central ⊖	d											
Shepherd's Bush	a							23 14		23 48		
Kensington (Olympia) ⊖	a							23 16		23 51		
West Brompton ⊖	a							23 19		23 54		
Imperial Wharf	a							23 21		23 57		
Clapham Junction	d							23a26		00a02		
East Croydon ⛴	a											
London Euston 15 ⊖	a	22 37	22 44	23 27	22 55	23 02			23 30		00 17	00 40

Table 66

Saturdays

from 7 April

West Midlands, Northampton, Milton Keynes Central and Watford Junction - London

Network Diagram - see first Page of Table 59

		SN	SN	LM	VT	LM	VT	LM	LM	SN	LM	LM	VT	SN	LM	LM	LM	VT	VT	VT	VT	LM
		1	1	1	◇1	1	◇1	1	1	1	◇1	1	◇1	1	◇1	1	1	◇1	◇1	◇1	◇1	1
					☕		☕						☕					☕	☕	☕	☕	
Wolverhampton 7	d				21p45		22p45											05 45		06 06		
Sandwell & Dudley	d				21p56		22p55											05 56		06 17		
Birmingham New Street 12	d			21p33	22p10		23p10						05 50					06 10		06 30		
Birmingham International ✈	d			21p45	22p20		23p20						06 00					06 20		06 40		
Coventry	d			22p01	22p31		23p31						06 10					06 31		06 51		
Nuneaton	d																				06 59	
Rugby	d			22p12	22p43		23p44						06 24						06 51			
Northampton	d			22c55		23p46	00s05				05 16				06 05							
Wolverton	d			23p07		00 02					05 28				06 17							
Milton Keynes Central 10	a			23p12	23e05	00 05	00s23				05 31				06 20			06 58	07 11			
	d	22p11		23p13		00 06		03 40	04 35		05 32				06 22		06 47	06 59	07 12			
Bletchley	d	22p15		23p18		00 11		03 45	04 40		05 37	06 10			06 27	06 40	06 52					07 10
Leighton Buzzard	d	22p22		23p24		00 17		03 51	04 46		05 43	06 17			06 33	06 47	06 58					07 17
Cheddington	d			23p29		00 24					05 49						07 04					
Tring	d	22p34		23p38		00 30		04 03	04 58		05 55	06 26			06 43	06 56	07 10					07 26
Berkhamsted	d	22p39		23p43		00 34		04 08	05 03		06 00	06 31			06 47	07 01	07 15					07 31
Hemel Hempstead	d	22p43		23p47		00 39		04 12	05 07		06 04	06 35			06 52	07 05	07 19					07 35
Apsley	d			23p50							06 07	06 38				07 08						07 38
Kings Langley	d			23p53							06 10	06 41				07 11						07 41
Watford Junction	a	22p52		23p58	23e37	00 46	00s52	04 19	05 14		06 15	06 46			06 59	07 16	07 26	07s19	07s32	07s36	07s44	07 46
	d	22p53	23p29	23p58		00 47		04 20	05 15	05 52	06 16	06 47		06 55	07 01	07 17	07 27					07 47
Bushey	d			00 01							06 18	06 49				07 20						07 49
Harrow & Wealdstone ⊖	d	23p00	23p35	00 06		00 53		04 26	05 21	05 58	06 24	06 55		07 01		07 25						07 55
Wembley Central ⊖	d					00 57		04 34	05 25					07 06								
Shepherd's Bush	a	23p21	23p53							06 20				07 19								
Kensington (Olympia) ⊖	a	23p23	23p56							06 22				07 21								
West Brompton ⊖	a	23p26	23p59							06 25				07 24								
Imperial Wharf	a	23p28	00 02							06 28				07 27								
Clapham Junction	d	23b40	00a07							06 34				07 34								
East Croydon	a	00 01								06 57				07 57								
London Euston 15 ⊖	a			00 21	00 04	01 09	01 15	04 46	05 41		06 38	07 09	07 16		07 20	07 39	07 45	07 38	07 52	07 55	08 05	08 09

		SN	LM	VT	VT	VT	VT	LM	LM	LM	LM	SN	VT	LM	VT	LM	VT	LM	VT	LM	LM	LM	VT
		1	◇1	◇1	◇1	◇1	◇1	1	1	◇1	1	1	◇1	◇1	◇1	◇1	◇1	1	◇1	1	◇1	◇1	◇1
				☕	☕	☕	☕						☕		☕		☕		☕				☕
Wolverhampton 7	d				06 27		06 45						07 04						07 45				
Sandwell & Dudley	d				06 37		06 56						07 15						07 56				
Birmingham New Street 12	d				06 50		07 10						07 30	06 53		07 13			08 10		07 33		07 50
Birmingham International ✈	d				07 00		07 20						07 40	07 05		07 29			08 20		07 45		08 00
Coventry	d				07 11		07 31						07 52	07 21		07 48			08 31		08 01		08 11
Nuneaton	d																					08 02	
Rugby	d				07 23									07 32	07 54	07 59					08 12	08 20	08 23
Northampton	d		07 05							07 33				08 05		08 25					08 50		
Wolverton	d		07 17							07 45				08 17		08 37							
Milton Keynes Central 10	a		07 20							07 49			08 18	08 20		08 41					09 04		
	d	07 13	07 22	07 32		07 38			07 44	07 49		08 13	08 19	08 22		08 41	08 47			08 47	09 05		
Bletchley	d	07 17	07 27						07 49	07 54		08 17		08 27		08 46				08 52			
Leighton Buzzard	d	07 24	07 33						07 55	08 01		08 24		08 33		08 53				08 58			
Cheddington	d								08 01											09 04			
Tring	d	07 34						07 56	08 07		08 26	08 34						08 56		09 10			
Berkhamsted	d	07 39	07 46					08 00	08 11		08 30	08 39		08 46				09 00		09 15			
Hemel Hempstead	d	07 43	07 51					08 05	08 16		08 35	08 43		08 51				09 05		09 19			
Apsley	d							08 08			08 38							09 08					
Kings Langley	d							08 11			08 41							09 11					
Watford Junction	a	07 51	07 58				08s15	08 16	08 23	08 20	08 46	08 51		08 58				09 16	09s17	09 26	09 33		
	d	07 52	07 59					08 16	08 24	08 20	08 46	08 52		08 59				09 16		09 27	09 34		
Bushey	d							08 19			08 49							09 19					
Harrow & Wealdstone ⊖	d	07 59						08 24			08 54	08 59						09 24					
Wembley Central ⊖	d	08 04										09 04											
Shepherd's Bush	a	08 19										09 19											
Kensington (Olympia) ⊖	a	08 21										09 21											
West Brompton ⊖	a	08 24										09 24											
Imperial Wharf	a	08 27										09 27											
Clapham Junction	d	08 34										09 34											
East Croydon	a	08 57										09 57											
London Euston 15 ⊖	a		08 17	08 09	08 14	08 14	08 34	08 38	08 42	08 38	09 08		08 54	09 17	08 46	09 27	09 23	09 38	09 35	09 45	09 50		09 14

b Previous night, arr. 2333

c Previous night, arr. 2234

e Previous night, stops to set down only

Table 66

Saturdays
from 7 April

West Midlands, Northampton, Milton Keynes Central and Watford Junction - London

Network Diagram - see first Page of Table 59

		LM		SN	VT	VT	LM	LM	VT	VT	LM	LM		VT	LM	LM	VT	LM	SN	VT	VT	LM		LM	VT
		1		1	◇1	◇1	◇1	◇1	◇1	◇1	1	1		◇1	◇1	◇1	◇1	1	1	◇1	◇1	◇1		◇1	◇1
					☕	☕			☕	☕				☕			☕			☕	☕				☕
Wolverhampton 7	d				08 06					08 45															
Sandwell & Dudley	d									08 56															
Birmingham New Street 12	d				08 30		07 53	08 13		09 10					08 33		08 50			09 30		08 53		09 13	
Birmingham International	d				08 40		08 05	08 29		09 20					08 45		09 00			09 40		09 05		09 29	
Coventry	d				08 51		08 21	08 48		09 31					09 01		09 11			09 51		09 21		09 48	
Nuneaton	d					08 59										09 02					09 59				
Rugby	d						08 32	08 59							09 12	09 20	09 23					09 32		09 59	
Northampton	d						09 05	09 25							09 50							10 05		10 25	
Wolverton	d						09 17	09 37														10 17		10 37	
Milton Keynes Central 10	a				09 18		09 20	09 41							10 04					10 18		10 20		10 41	
	d			09 13	09 19		09 22	09 41	09 47			09 47		10 02	10 05				10 13	10 19		10 22		10 41	10 47
Bletchley	d			09 17			09 27	09 46				09 52							10 17			10 27		10 46	
Leighton Buzzard	d			09 24			09 33	09 53				09 58							10 24			10 33		10 53	
Cheddington	d											10 04													
Tring	d	09 26		09 34							09 56	10 10						10 26	10 34						
Berkhamsted	d	09 30		09 39			09 46				10 00	10 15						10 30	10 39			10 46			
Hemel Hempstead	d	09 35		09 43			09 51				10 05	10 19						10 35	10 43			10 51			
Apsley	d	09 38									10 08							10 38							
Kings Langley	d	09 41									10 11							10 41							
Watford Junction	a	09 46		09 51			09 58			10s15	10 16	10 26			10 30			10 46	10 51			10 58			
	d	09 46		09 52			09 59				10 16	10 27			10 31			10 46	10 52			10 59			
Bushey	d	09 49									10 19							10 49							
Harrow & Wealdstone ⊖	d	09 54		09 59							10 24							10 54	10 59						
Wembley Central ⊖	d			10 04															11 04						
Shepherd's Bush	a			10 19															11 19						
Kensington (Olympia) ⊖	a			10 21															11 21						
West Brompton ⊖	a			10 24															11 24						
Imperial Wharf	a			10 27															11 27						
Clapham Junction	d			10 34															11 34						
East Croydon	a			10 57															11 57						
London Euston 15 ⊖	a	10 08			09 55	10 00	10 17	10 27	10 23	10 34	10 38	10 45		10 37	10 49		10 14	11 08		10 54	11 01	11 17		11 27	11 23

		VT	LM	LM	VT	LM	LM	VT		LM	SN	VT	LM	LM	VT	VT	LM	LM		VT	LM	LM	VT	LM	SN
		◇1	1	1	◇1	◇1	◇1	◇1		1	1	◇1	◇1	◇1	◇1	◇1	1	1		◇1	◇1	◇1	◇1	1	1
		☕			☕			☕				☕			☕	☕				☕			☕		
Wolverhampton 7	d	09 45														10 45									
Sandwell & Dudley	d	09 56														10 56									
Birmingham New Street 12	d	10 10				09 33		09 50				10 30	09 53	10 13		11 10					10 33		10 50		
Birmingham International	d	10 20				09 45		10 00				10 40	10 05	10 29		11 20					10 45		11 00		
Coventry	d	10 31				10 01		10 11				10 51	10 21	10 48		11 31					11 01		11 11		
Nuneaton	d						10 02															11 02			
Rugby	d					10 12	10 20	10 23					10 32	10 59							11 12	11 20	11 23		
Northampton	d					10 50							11 05	11 25							11 50				
Wolverton	d												11 17	11 37											
Milton Keynes Central 10	a					11 04						11 18	11 20	11 41							12 04				
	d			10 47	11 02	11 05					11 13	11 20	11 22	11 41	11 47			11 47		12 02	12 05				12 13
Bletchley	d			10 52							11 17		11 27	11 46				11 52							12 17
Leighton Buzzard	d			10 58							11 24		11 33	11 53				11 58							12 24
Cheddington	d			11 04														12 04							
Tring	d		10 56	11 10						11 26	11 34						11 56	12 10						12 26	12 34
Berkhamsted	d		11 00	11 15						11 30	11 39		11 46				12 00	12 15						12 30	12 39
Hemel Hempstead	d		11 05	11 19						11 35	11 43		11 51				12 05	12 19						12 35	12 43
Apsley	d		11 08							11 38							12 08							12 38	
Kings Langley	d		11 11							11 41							12 11							12 41	
Watford Junction	a	11s15	11 16	11 26		11 30				11 46	11 51		11 58			12s15	12 16	12 26			12 30			12 46	12 51
	d		11 16	11 27		11 31				11 46	11 52		11 59				12 16	12 27			12 31			12 46	12 52
Bushey	d		11 19							11 49							12 19							12 49	
Harrow & Wealdstone ⊖	d		11 24							11 54	11 59						12 24							12 54	12 59
Wembley Central ⊖	d										12 04														13 04
Shepherd's Bush	a										12 19														13 19
Kensington (Olympia) ⊖	a										12 21														13 21
West Brompton ⊖	a										12 24														13 24
Imperial Wharf	a										12 27														13 27
Clapham Junction	d										12 34														13 34
East Croydon	a										12 57														13 57
London Euston 15 ⊖	a	11 34	11 38	11 45	11 38	11 49		11 14		12 08		11 55	12 17	12 27	12 23	12 34	12 38	12 45		12 38	12 49		12 14	13 08	

Table 66

Saturdays
from 7 April

West Midlands, Northampton, Milton Keynes Central and Watford Junction - London

Network Diagram - see first Page of Table 59

		VT	LM	LM		VT	VT	LM	LM	VT	LM	LM	VT	LM		SN	VT	LM	LM	VT	VT	LM	LM	VT	
		◇1	◇1	◇1		◇1	◇1	1	1	◇1	◇1	◇1	◇1	1		1	◇1	◇1	◇1	◇1	◇1	1	1	◇1	
		☕				☕	☕			☕			☕				☕			☕	☕			☕	
Wolverhampton 7	d						11 45														12 45				
Sandwell & Dudley	d						11 56														12 56				
Birmingham New Street 12	d	11 30	10 53	11 13			12 10				11 33		11 50				12 30	11 53	12 13		13 10				
Birmingham International	d	11 40	11 05	11 29			12 20				11 45		12 00				12 40	12 05	12 29		13 20				
Coventry	d	11 51	11 21	11 48			12 31				12 01		12 11				12 51	12 21	12 48		13 31				
Nuneaton	d											12 02													
Rugby	d		11 32	11 59							12 12	12 20	12 23					12 32	12 59						
Northampton	d		12 05	12 25							12 50							13 05	13 25						
Wolverton	d		12 17	12 37														13 17	13 37						
Milton Keynes Central 10	a	12 18	12 20	12 41							13 04						13 18	13 20	13 41						
	d	12 19	12 22	12 41		12 47			12 47	13 02	13 05					13 13	13 19	13 22	13 41	13 47			13 47	14 02	
Bletchley	d		12 27	12 46					12 52							13 17		13 27	13 46				13 52		
Leighton Buzzard	d		12 33	12 53					12 58							13 24		13 33	13 53				13 58		
Cheddington	d								13 04														14 04		
Tring	d							12 56	13 10					13 26		13 34						13 56	14 10		
Berkhamsted	d		12 46					13 00	13 15					13 30		13 39		13 46				14 00	14 15		
Hemel Hempstead	d		12 51					13 05	13 19					13 35		13 43		13 51				14 05	14 19		
Apsley	d							13 08						13 38								14 08			
Kings Langley	d							13 11						13 41								14 11			
Watford Junction	a		12 58				13s15	13 16	13 26		13 30			13 46		13 51		13 58			14s15	14 16	14 26		
	d		12 59					13 16	13 27		13 31			13 46		13 52		13 59				14 16	14 27		
Bushey	d							13 19						13 49								14 19			
Harrow & Wealdstone ⊖	d							13 24						13 54		13 59						14 24			
Wembley Central ⊖	d															14 04									
Shepherd's Bush	a															14 19									
Kensington (Olympia) ⊖	a															14 21									
West Brompton ⊖	a															14 24									
Imperial Wharf	a															14 27									
Clapham Junction	d															14 34									
East Croydon	a															14 57									
London Euston 15 ⊖	a	12 54	13 17	13 27		13 23	13 34	13 38	13 47	13 38	13 49		13 14	14 08			13 54	14 17	14 27	14 23	14 34	14 38	14 45	14 38	

		LM	LM	VT	LM	SN	VT	LM	LM	VT		VT	LM	LM	VT	LM	LM	VT	LM	SN		VT	LM	LM	VT
		◇1	◇1	◇1	1	1	◇1	◇1	◇1	◇1		◇1	1	1	◇1	◇1	◇1	◇1	1	1		◇1	◇1	◇1	◇1
				☕			☕			☕		☕			☕			☕				☕			☕
Wolverhampton 7	d											13 45													
Sandwell & Dudley	d											13 56													
Birmingham New Street 12	d	12 33		12 50			13 30	12 53	13 13			14 10				13 33		13 50				14 30	13 53	14 13	
Birmingham International	d	12 45		13 00			13 40	13 05	13 29			14 20				13 45		14 00				14 40	14 05	14 29	
Coventry	d	13 01		13 11			13 51	13 21	13 48			14 31				14 01		14 11				14 51	14 21	14 48	
Nuneaton	d		13 02														14 02								
Rugby	d	13 12	13 20	13 23				13 32	13 59							14 12	14 20	14 23					14 32	14 59	
Northampton	d	13 50						14 05	14 25							14 50							15 05	15 25	
Wolverton	d							14 17	14 37														15 17	15 37	
Milton Keynes Central 10	a	14 04					14 18	14 20	14 41							15 04						15 18	15 20	15 41	
	d	14 05				14 13	14 19	14 22	14 41	14 47				14 47	15 02	15 05				15 13		15 19	15 22	15 41	15 47
Bletchley	d					14 17		14 27	14 46					14 52						15 17			15 27	15 46	
Leighton Buzzard	d					14 24		14 33	14 53					14 58						15 24			15 33	15 53	
Cheddington	d													15 04											
Tring	d				14 26	14 34							14 56	15 10					15 26	15 34					
Berkhamsted	d				14 30	14 39		14 46					15 00	15 15					15 30	15 39			15 46		
Hemel Hempstead	d				14 35	14 43		14 51					15 05	15 19					15 35	15 43			15 51		
Apsley	d				14 38								15 08						15 38						
Kings Langley	d				14 41								15 11						15 41						
Watford Junction	a	14 30			14 46	14 51		14 58				15s15	15 16	15 26		15 30			15 46	15 51			15 58		
	d	14 31			14 46	14 52		14 59					15 16	15 27		15 31			15 46	15 52			15 59		
Bushey	d				14 49								15 19						15 49						
Harrow & Wealdstone ⊖	d				14 54	14 59							15 24						15 54	15 59					
Wembley Central ⊖	d					15 04														16 04					
Shepherd's Bush	a					15 19														16 19					
Kensington (Olympia) ⊖	a					15 21														16 21					
West Brompton ⊖	a					15 24														16 24					
Imperial Wharf	a					15 27														16 27					
Clapham Junction	d					15 34														16 34					
East Croydon	a					15 57														16 57					
London Euston 15 ⊖	a	14 49		14 14	15 08		14 54	15 18	15 27	15 23		15 34	15 38	15 45	15 38	15 49		15 14	16 08			15 54	16 18	16 27	16 23

Table 66

Saturdays
from 7 April

West Midlands, Northampton, Milton Keynes Central and Watford Junction - London

Network Diagram - see first Page of Table 59

		VT ◇1 ☕	LM 1	LM 1	VT ◇1 ☕	LM ◇1	LM ◇1		VT ◇1 ☕	LM 1	SN 1	VT ◇1 ☕	LM ◇1	LM ◇1	VT ◇1 ☕	VT ◇1 ☕	LM 1		LM 1	VT ◇1 ☕	LM ◇1	LM ◇1	VT ◇1 ☕	LM 1	SN 1
Wolverhampton 7	d	14 45														15 45									
Sandwell & Dudley	d	14 56														15 56									
Birmingham New Street 12	d	15 10				14 33			14 50			15 30	14 53	15 13		16 10					15 33		15 50		
Birmingham International	d	15 20				14 45			15 00			15 40	15 05	15 29		16 20					15 45		16 00		
Coventry	d	15 31				15 01			15 11			15 51	15 21	15 48		16 31					16 01		16 11		
Nuneaton	d						15 02															16 02			
Rugby	d					15 12	15 20		15 23				15 32	15 59							16 12	16 20	16 23		
Northampton	d					15 50							16 05	16 25							16 50				
Wolverton	d												16 17	16 37											
Milton Keynes Central 10	a					16 04						16 18	16 20	16 41							17 04				
	d			15 47	16 02	16 05					16 13	16 19	16 22	16 41	16 47				16 47	17 02	17 05				17 13
Bletchley	d			15 52							16 17		16 27	16 46					16 52						17 17
Leighton Buzzard	d			15 58							16 24		16 33	16 53					16 58						17 24
Cheddington	d			16 04															17 04						
Tring	d		15 56	16 10						16 26	16 34						16 56		17 10					17 26	17 34
Berkhamsted	d		16 00	16 15						16 30	16 39		16 46				17 00		17 15					17 30	17 39
Hemel Hempstead	d		16 05	16 19						16 35	16 43		16 51				17 05		17 19					17 35	17 43
Apsley	d		16 08							16 38							17 08							17 38	
Kings Langley	d		16 11							16 41							17 11							17 41	
Watford Junction	a	16s15	16 16	16 26		16 30				16 46	16 51		16 58			17s15	17 16		17 26		17 30			17 46	17 51
	d		16 16	16 27		16 31				16 46	16 52		16 59				17 16		17 27		17 31			17 46	17 52
Bushey	d		16 19							16 49							17 19							17 49	
Harrow & Wealdstone ⊖	d		16 24							16 54	16 59						17 24							17 54	17 59
Wembley Central ⊖	d										17 04														18 04
Shepherd's Bush	a										17 19														18 19
Kensington (Olympia) ⊖	a										17 21														18 21
West Brompton ⊖	a										17 24														18 24
Imperial Wharf	a										17 27														18 27
Clapham Junction	d										17 34														18 34
East Croydon	a										17 57														18 57
London Euston 15 ⊖	a	16 34	16 38	16 45	16 38	16 49			16 14	17 08		16 54	17 17	17 27	17 23	17 34	17 38		17 45	17 38	17 49		17 14	18 08	

		VT ◇1 ☕	LM ◇1		LM ◇1	VT ◇1 ☕	VT ◇1 ☕	LM 1	LM 1	VT ◇1 ☕	LM ◇1	LM ◇1	VT ◇1 ☕		LM 1	SN 1	VT ◇1 ☕	LM ◇1	VT ◇1 ☕	VT ◇1 ☕	LM 1	LM ◇1	LM ◇1	LM ◇1	
Wolverhampton 7	d						16 45													17 45					
Sandwell & Dudley	d						16 56													17 56					
Birmingham New Street 12	d	16 30	15 53		16 13		17 10				16 33		16 50				17 30	16 53		18 10		17 13	17 33		
Birmingham International	d	16 40	16 05		16 29		17 20				16 45		17 00				17 40	17 05		18 20		17 30	17 45		
Coventry	d	16 51	16 21		16 48		17 31				17 01		17 11				17 51	17 21		18 31		17 48	18 01		
Nuneaton	d											17 02												18 02	
Rugby	d		16 32		16 59						17 12	17 20	17 23					17 32				17 59	18 12	18 20	
Northampton	d		17 05		17 25						17 50							18 05				18 31	18 50		
Wolverton	d		17 17		17 37													18 17				18 43			
Milton Keynes Central 10	a	17 18	17 20		17 41						18 05						18 18	18 20				18 46	19 04		
	d	17 19	17 22		17 41	17 47			17 47	18 02	18 05					18 13	18 19	18 22	18 47			18 47	19 05		
Bletchley	d		17 27		17 46				17 52							18 17		18 27				18 52			
Leighton Buzzard	d		17 33		17 53				17 58							18 24		18 33				18 58			
Cheddington	d								18 04													19 04			
Tring	d							17 56	18 10						18 26	18 34					18 56	19 10			
Berkhamsted	d		17 46					18 00	18 15						18 30	18 39		18 46			19 00	19 15			
Hemel Hempstead	d		17 51					18 05	18 19						18 35	18 43		18 51			19 05	19 19			
Apsley	d							18 08							18 38						19 08				
Kings Langley	d							18 11							18 41						19 11				
Watford Junction	a		17 58				18s15	18 16	18 26		18 31				18 46	18 51		18 58		19s15	19 16	19 26	19 30		
	d		17 59					18 16	18 27		18 31				18 46	18 52		18 59			19 16	19 27	19 31		
Bushey	d							18 19							18 49						19 19				
Harrow & Wealdstone ⊖	d							18 24							18 54	18 59					19 24				
Wembley Central ⊖	d															19 04									
Shepherd's Bush	a															19 19									
Kensington (Olympia) ⊖	a															19 21									
West Brompton ⊖	a															19 24									
Imperial Wharf	a															19 27									
Clapham Junction	d															19 34									
East Croydon	a															19 57									
London Euston 15 ⊖	a	17 52	18 17		18 27	18 23	18 34	18 38	18 45	18 38	18 49		18 14		19 08		18 54	19 17	19 23	19 34	19 38	19 45	19 49		

Table 66

Saturdays

from 7 April

West Midlands, Northampton, Milton Keynes Central and Watford Junction - London

Network Diagram - see first Page of Table 59

		VT ◇1 ☕	SN 1	LM 1	SN 1	VT ◇1 ☕	LM ◇1	LM 1	LM ◇1	VT ◇1 ☕	VT ◇1 ☕	LM ◇1	VT ◇1 ☕	SN 1	VT ◇1 ☕	LM ◇1	LM 1	LM ◇1	VT ◇1 ☕	VT ◇1 ☕	SN 1	LM ◇1	VT ◇1 ☕
Wolverhampton 7 ⛴	d												18 45						19 45				
Sandwell & Dudley	d												18 56						19 56				
Birmingham New Street 12	d	17 50				18 30	17 53		18 13	18 50		18 53	19 10			19 13		19 53	20 10				
Birmingham International ✈	d	18 00				18 40	18 05		18 29	19 00		19 05	19 20			19 29		20 05	20 20				
Coventry	d	18 11				18 51	18 21		18 48	19 11		19 21	19 31			19 48		20 21	20 31				
Nuneaton	d																						
Rugby	d	18 23					18 32		18 59	19 23		19 32	19 44			19 59		20 32	20 43				
Northampton	d						19 05		19 31			20 00				20 32		21 00				21 20	
Wolverton	d						19 17		19 43			20 12						21 12					
Milton Keynes Central 10	a					19 18	19 20		19 46			20 15	20 05			20 47		21 15	21 04			21 34	
	d				19 13	19 19	19 22		19 47		19 46	20 16	20 07		20 43	20 47	20 50	21 16	21 05	21 11		21 34	21 52
Bletchley	d				19 17		19 27		19 52			20 21					20 55					21 39	
Leighton Buzzard	d				19 24		19 33		19 58			20 27				20 56						21 46	
Cheddington	d								20 04							21 03						21 51	
Tring	d			19 24	19 34			19 58	20 10							21 08	21 12					21 58	
Berkhamsted	d			19 28	19 39		19 46	20 02	20 15								21 17	21 38				22 02	
Hemel Hempstead	d			19 33	19 43		19 51	20 07	20 19							21 15	21 21	21 42				22 07	
Apsley	d			19 36				20 10								21 18						22 10	
Kings Langley	d			19 39				20 13								21 21						22 13	
Watford Junction	a			19 44	19 50		19 58	20 18	20 26			20 50	20s34		21s15	21 26	21 30	21 49	21s34			22 18	
	d		19 31	19 44	19 51		20 03	20 19	20 27			20 51		20 43		21 27	21 31	21 51			21 43	22 19	
Bushey	d			19 47																			
Harrow & Wealdstone ⊖	d		19 38	19 52	19 58			20 25						20 50			21 37				21 50		
Wembley Central ⊖	d		19 43																				
Shepherd's Bush	a		19 57		20 19									21 07							22 07		
Kensington (Olympia) ⊖	a		19 59		20 21									21 09							22 09		
West Brompton ⊖	a		20 02		20 24									21 12							22 12		
Imperial Wharf	a		20 05		20 27									21 15							22 15		
Clapham Junction	d		20a10		20 34									21a20							22a20		
East Croydon ⛴	a				20 59																		
London Euston 15 ⊖	a	19 14		20 06		19 54	20 21	20 39	20 45	20 15	20 24	21 09	20 55		21 38	21 45	21 52	22 11	21 56	22 00		22 37	22 44

		LM ◇1	VT ◇1 ☕	VT ◇1 ☕	SN 1	VT ◇1 ☕	SN 1	LM ◇1	LM ◇1
Wolverhampton 7 ⛴	d		20 45			21 07			
Sandwell & Dudley	d		20 56			21 17			
Birmingham New Street 12	d	20 53	21 10			21 30		21 53	
Birmingham International ✈	d	21 05	21 20			21 40		22 05	
Coventry	d	21 21	21 31			21 51		22 21	
Nuneaton	d								
Rugby	d	21 32	21 43			22 03		22 32	
Northampton	d	22 05						22 55	23 30
Wolverton	d	22 17						23 07	23 42
Milton Keynes Central 10	a	22 20	22 04			22 28		23 10	23 45
	d	22 21	22 05	22 11		22 29		23 11	23 46
Bletchley	d	22 26						23 16	23 51
Leighton Buzzard	d	22 32						23 22	23 57
Cheddington	d	22 37						23 27	
Tring	d	22 44						23 36	
Berkhamsted	d	22 49						23 41	
Hemel Hempstead	d	22 53						23 45	
Apsley	d	22 56						23 49	
Kings Langley	d	23 00						23 52	
Watford Junction	a	23 06	22s34	22s40		23s11		23 56	00 19
	d	23 07			22 48		23 25	23 57	00 20
Bushey	d								
Harrow & Wealdstone ⊖	d	23 13			22 55		23 31	00 03	
Wembley Central ⊖	d								
Shepherd's Bush	a				23 14		23 48		
Kensington (Olympia) ⊖	a				23 16		23 51		
West Brompton ⊖	a				23 19		23 54		
Imperial Wharf	a				23 21		23 57		
Clapham Junction	d				23a26		00a02		
East Croydon ⛴	a								
London Euston 15 ⊖	a	23 27	22 55	23 02		23 30		00 17	00 40

Table 66

Sundays

West Midlands, Northampton, Milton Keynes Central and Watford Junction - London

Network Diagram - see first Page of Table 59

		LM	LM	LM	LM	LM	LM	LM	LM	SN	LM	LM	VT	SN	LM	VT	VT	VT	LM	LM		VT	VT	SN	VT
		◇1	◇1		1		1	1	◇1	1	◇1	◇1	◇1	1	◇1	◇1	◇1	◇1	◇1	◇1		◇1	◇1	1	◇1
		A	A																						
						🚌							☕			☕	☕	☕				☕	☕		☕
Wolverhampton 7	d												08 05									09 05			
Sandwell & Dudley	d												08 15									09 15			
Birmingham New Street 12	d	21p53											08 30							09 14		09 30			
Birmingham International ✈	d	22p05											08 40							09 25		09 40			
Coventry	d	22p21											08 51							09 44		09 51			
Nuneaton	d																						09 55		
Rugby	d	22p32											09 04							09 55		10 04			10 33
Northampton	d	22p55	23p30			06 20			07 53		08 23	08 53			09 30				10 08	10 37					
Wolverton	d	23p07	23p42			06 52			08 05		08 37	09 05			09 42				10 20	10 51					
Milton Keynes Central 10	a	23p10	23p45			07 00			08 08		08 40	09 08	09 37		09 45				10 23	10 54		10 37			11 06
	d	23p11	23p46		06 42		07 11	07 41	08 09		08 41	09 09	09 39		09 46			10 19	10 24	10 55		10 39			11 08
Bletchley	d	23p16	23p51		06 47		07 16	07 46	08 14		08 46	09 14			09 51				10 29	11 00					
Leighton Buzzard	d	23p22	23p57		06 53		07 22	07 52	08 20		08 52	09 20			09 57				10 35	11 06					
Cheddington	d	23p27					07 27		08 25			09 25							10 44						
Tring	d	23p36					07 36		08 34			09 34							10 49						
Berkhamsted	d	23p41			07 08		07 41	08 07	08 39		09 07	09 38			10 12				10 54	11 21					
Hemel Hempstead	d	23p45			07 13		07 45	08 12	08 43		09 12	09 42			10 17				10 58	11 26					
Apsley	d	23p49			07 16			08 15			09 15				10 20					11 29					
Kings Langley	d	23p52			07 19			08 18			09 18				10 23					11 32					
Watford Junction	a	23p56	00 19		07 24		07 52	08 23	08 50		09 23	09 49	10s07		10 28				11 05	11 37		11s11	11s16		11s43
	d	23p57	00 20	00 40	07 24		07 53	08 23	08 53	09 17	09 25	09 53		10 17	10 30				11 05	11 37				11 22	
Bushey	d																								
Harrow & Wealdstone ⊖	d	00 03		00 52	07 30		07 59	08 29	08 59	09 23	09 31	09 59		10 23	10 36				11 11	11 43				11 28	
Wembley Central ⊖	d			00 58																					
Shepherd's Bush	a									09 45				10 45										11 45	
Kensington (Olympia) ⊖	a									09 47				10 47										11 47	
West Brompton ⊖	a									09 50				10 50										11 50	
Imperial Wharf	a									09 53				10 53										11 53	
Clapham Junction	d									09a58				10a58										11a58	
East Croydon	a																								
London Euston 15 ⊖	a	00 17	00 40	01 19	07 44		08 13	08 43	09 13		09 45	10 13	10 28		10 51	10 57	11 02	11 06	11 25	11 57		11 31	11 37		12 05

		VT	LM	LM	VT	VT		VT	SN	LM	VT	VT	LM	VT	LM	VT		VT	VT	VT	VT	SN	LM	LM	LM
		◇1	◇1	◇1	◇1	◇1		◇1	1	1	◇1	◇1	1	◇1	◇1	◇1		◇1	◇1	◇1	◇1	1	◇1	1	1
		☕			☕	☕		☕			☕	☕		☕		☕		☕	☕	☕	☕				
Wolverhampton 7	d				10 05											11 05				11 45					
Sandwell & Dudley	d				10 15											11 15				11 57					
Birmingham New Street 12	d			10 14	10 30										11 14	11 30		11 50		12 10					
Birmingham International ✈	d			10 25	10 40										11 25	11 40		12 00		12 20					
Coventry	d			10 44	10 51										11 44	11 51		12 11		12 31					
Nuneaton	d					10 56						11 59									12 32				
Rugby	d			10 55	11 04			11 33							11 55	12 05		12 25					12 25		
Northampton	d		11 08	11 25											12 25								12 50		
Wolverton	d		11 20	11 37											12 37										
Milton Keynes Central 10	a		11 23	11 42	11 37	11 46		12 06							12 40	12 24					13 03		13 04		
	d	11 17	11 24	11 42	11 39	11 47		12 07					12 12	12 22	12 41	12 26			12 52		13 04		13 05		13 12
Bletchley	d		11 29	11 47						11 56			12 17		12 46										13 17
Leighton Buzzard	d		11 35	11 54						12 02			12 23		12 52								13 18		13 23
Cheddington	d		11 40							12 08			12 29												13 29
Tring	d		11 49							12 14			12 35											13 15	13 35
Berkhamsted	d		11 53	12 06						12 19			12 39		13 05									13 19	13 39
Hemel Hempstead	d		11 58	12 10						12 23			12 44		13 10									13 24	13 44
Apsley	d									12 26														13 27	
Kings Langley	d									12 29														13 30	
Watford Junction	a		12 06	12 17	12s07					12 34		12s50	12 52		13 17					13s18			13 33	13 35	13 52
	d		12 06	12 18					12 22	12 34			12 52		13 17							13 22	13 33	13 35	13 52
Bushey	d									12 37														13 38	
Harrow & Wealdstone ⊖	d		12 12	12 24					12 29	12 42			12 58		13 23							13 28		13 43	13 58
Wembley Central ⊖	d																								
Shepherd's Bush	a								12 45													13 45			
Kensington (Olympia) ⊖	a								12 47													13 47			
West Brompton ⊖	a								12 50													13 50			
Imperial Wharf	a								12 53													13 53			
Clapham Junction	d								12a58													13a58			
East Croydon	a																								
London Euston 15 ⊖	a	12 08	12 25	12 37	12 27	12 32		12 45		12 56	12 56	13 11	13 11	12 59	13 37	13 04		13 19	13 28	13 37	13 44		13 53	13 57	14 11

A not 11 December

Table 66

Sundays

West Midlands, Northampton, Milton Keynes Central and Watford Junction - London

Network Diagram - see first Page of Table 59

		VT		VT	LM	VT	VT	SN	LM	VT	LM	LM		VT	VT	LM	VT	VT	VT	SN	LM	LM		LM	VT
		◇1		◇1	◇1	◇1	◇1	1	◇1	◇1	1	1		◇1	◇1	◇1	◇1	◇1	◇1	1	◇1	1		1	◇1
		☕		☕		☕	☕			☕				☕	☕		☕	☕	☕						☕
Wolverhampton 7	d			12 45											13 45										
Sandwell & Dudley	d			12 55											13 56										
Birmingham New Street 12	d	12 30		13 10	12 14					12 50				13 30	14 10	13 14	13 50								14 30
Birmingham International ✈	d	12 39		13 20	12 25					13 00				13 39	14 20	13 25	14 01								14 39
Coventry	d	12 51		13 31	12 44					13 11				13 51	14 31	13 44	14 11								14 51
Nuneaton	d								12 58										14 32						
Rugby	d				12 55				13 20	13 25						13 55	14 26				14 26				
Northampton	d				13 25				13 50							14 25					14 50				
Wolverton	d				13 37											14 37									
Milton Keynes Central 10	a	13 18			13 40				14 04					14 18		14 40			15 04		15 04				15 18
	d	13 19			13 41	13 51	14 03		14 06			14 12		14 19		14 41		14 51	15 05		15 05			15 12	15 19
Bletchley	d				13 46							14 17				14 46								15 17	
Leighton Buzzard	d				13 52				14 15			14 23				14 52					15 17			15 23	
Cheddington	d											14 29												15 29	
Tring	d										14 15	14 35										15 15		15 35	
Berkhamsted	d				14 05						14 19	14 39				15 05						15 19		15 39	
Hemel Hempstead	d				14 10						14 24	14 44				15 10						15 24		15 44	
Apsley	d										14 27											15 27			
Kings Langley	d										14 30											15 30			
Watford Junction	a			14s16	14 17				14 35		14 35	14 52			15s16	15 17					15 33	15 35		15 52	
	d				14 17			14 22	14 36		14 35	14 52				15 17				15 22	15 33	15 35		15 52	
Bushey	d										14 38											15 38			
Harrow & Wealdstone ⊖	d				14 23			14 28			14 43	14 58				15 23				15 28		15 43		15 58	
Wembley Central ⊖	d																								
Shepherd's Bush	a							14 45												15 45					
Kensington (Olympia) ⊖	a							14 47												15 47					
West Brompton ⊖	a							14 50												15 50					
Imperial Wharf	a							14 53												15 53					
Clapham Junction	d							14a58												15a58					
East Croydon	a																								
London Euston 15 ⊖	a	13 57		14 37	14 37	14 27	14 43		14 53	14 17	14 57	15 11		14 57	15 37	15 37	15 17	15 27	15 45		15 53	15 57		16 11	15 57

		VT	LM	VT	SN	LM	VT	VT		LM	LM	VT	VT	LM	VT	VT	VT	SN		LM	LM	LM	VT	VT	LM
		◇1	◇1	◇1	1	◇1	◇1	◇1		1	1	◇1	◇1	◇1	◇1	◇1	◇1	1		◇1	1	1	◇1	◇1	◇1
		☕		☕			☕	☕				☕	☕		☕	☕	☕						☕	☕	
Wolverhampton 7	d	14 45											15 45											16 45	
Sandwell & Dudley	d	14 56											15 56											16 56	
Birmingham New Street 12	d	15 10	14 14				14 50					15 30	16 10	15 14	15 50								16 30	17 10	16 14
Birmingham International ✈	d	15 20	14 25				15 01					15 39	16 20	15 25	16 01								16 39	17 20	16 25
Coventry	d	15 31	14 44				15 11					15 51	16 31	15 44	16 11								16 51	17 31	16 44
Nuneaton	d					14 58																			
Rugby	d		14 55			15 20	15 26							15 55	16 24					16 25					16 55
Northampton	d		15 25			15 50								16 25						16 50					17 25
Wolverton	d		15 37											16 37											17 37
Milton Keynes Central 10	a		15 40			16 04						16 18		16 40						17 04			17 18		17 40
	d		15 41	15 51		16 06		16 05			16 12	16 19		16 41		16 51	17 04			17 05		17 12	17 19		17 41
Bletchley	d		15 46								16 17			16 46								17 17			17 46
Leighton Buzzard	d		15 52			16 15					16 23			16 52						17 17		17 23			17 52
Cheddington	d										16 29											17 29			
Tring	d									16 15	16 35										17 15	17 35			
Berkhamsted	d		16 05							16 19	16 39			17 05							17 19	17 39			18 05
Hemel Hempstead	d		16 10							16 24	16 44			17 10							17 24	17 44			18 10
Apsley	d									16 27											17 27				
Kings Langley	d									16 30											17 30				
Watford Junction	a	16s16	16 17			16 35				16 35	16 52		17s16	17 17						17 33	17 35	17 52		18s16	18 17
	d		16 17		16 22	16 35				16 35	16 52			17 17				17 22		17 33	17 35	17 52			18 17
Bushey	d									16 38											17 38				
Harrow & Wealdstone ⊖	d		16 23		16 28					16 43	16 58			17 23				17 28			17 43	17 58			18 23
Wembley Central ⊖	d																								
Shepherd's Bush	a				16 45													17 45							
Kensington (Olympia) ⊖	a				16 47													17 47							
West Brompton ⊖	a				16 50													17 50							
Imperial Wharf	a				16 53													17 53							
Clapham Junction	d				16a58													17a58							
East Croydon	a																								
London Euston 15 ⊖	a	16 37	16 37	16 27		16 53	16 17	16 44		16 57	17 11	16 57	17 37	17 37	17 17	17 27	17 44			17 53	17 57	18 11	17 57	18 37	18 37

Table 66

Sundays

West Midlands, Northampton, Milton Keynes Central and Watford Junction - London

Network Diagram - see first Page of Table 59

		VT	SN	LM		VT	VT	LM	LM	VT	VT	LM	VT	VT		SN	LM	VT	LM	LM	VT	VT	LM	VT	
		◇1	1	◇1		◇1	◇1	1	1	◇1	◇1	◇1	◇1	◇1		1	◇1	◇1	1	1	◇1	◇1	◇1	◇1	
		☕				☕	☕			☕	☕		☕	☕				☕			☕	☕		☕	
Wolverhampton 7 🚌	d										17 45											18 45			
Sandwell & Dudley	d										17 56											18 56			
Birmingham New Street 12	d					16 50				17 30	18 10	17 14						17 50			18 30	19 10	18 14		
Birmingham International ✈	d					17 01				17 39	18 20	17 25						18 01			18 39	19 20	18 25		
Coventry	d					17 11				17 51	18 31	17 44						18 11			18 51	19 31	18 44		
Nuneaton	d			16 58																					
Rugby	d			17 20		17 26						17 55					18 24	18 26					18 55		
Northampton	d			17 50								18 25					18 50						19 25		
Wolverton	d											18 37											19 37		
Milton Keynes Central 10	a			18 04						18 18		18 40					19 04				19 18		19 40		
	d	17 51		18 06			18 05		18 12	18 19		18 41	18 51	19 03			19 05			19 12	19 19		19 41	19 51	
Bletchley	d								18 17			18 46								19 17			19 46		
Leighton Buzzard	d			18 15					18 23			18 52					19 17			19 23			19 52		
Cheddington	d								18 29											19 29					
Tring	d							18 15	18 35										19 15	19 35					
Berkhamsted	d							18 19	18 39			19 05							19 19	19 39			20 05		
Hemel Hempstead	d							18 24	18 44			19 10							19 24	19 44			20 10		
Apsley	d							18 27											19 27						
Kings Langley	d							18 30											19 30						
Watford Junction	a			18 35				18 35	18 52		19s16	19 17					19 33		19 35	19 52		20s16	20 17		
	d		18 22	18 35				18 35	18 52			19 17				19 22	19 33		19 35	19 52			20 17		
Bushey	d							18 38											19 38						
Harrow & Wealdstone ⊖	d		18 28					18 43	18 58			19 23				19 28			19 43	19 58			20 23		
Wembley Central ⊖	d																								
Shepherd's Bush	a		18 45													19 45									
Kensington (Olympia) ⊖	a		18 47													19 47									
West Brompton ⊖	a		18 50													19 50									
Imperial Wharf	a		18 53													19 53									
Clapham Junction	d		18a58													19a58									
East Croydon 🚌	a																								
London Euston 15 ⊖	a	18 27		18 53		18 17	18 44	18 57	19 11	18 57	19 37	19 37	19 27	19 43			19 53	19 17	19 57	20 11	19 57	20 37	20 37	20 27	

		VT	SN	LM	VT	LM	LM	VT	SN	LM		VT	VT	LM	LM	LM	VT	VT	SN	VT		VT	LM	LM	VT
		◇1	1	◇1	◇1	1	1	◇1	1	◇1		◇1	◇1	◇1	1	◇1	◇1	◇1	1	◇1		◇1	◇1	◇1	◇1
		☕			☕			☕				☕	☕				☕	☕		☕		☕			☕
Wolverhampton 7 🚌	d												19 45												21 05
Sandwell & Dudley	d												19 58												21 17
Birmingham New Street 12	d				18 50			19 30		19 14			20 10			20 14	20 30							21 14	21 30
Birmingham International ✈	d				19 01			19 39		19 25			20 20			20 25	20 40							21 25	21 40
Coventry	d				19 11			19 51		19 44			20 31			20 43	20 51							21 44	21 51
Nuneaton	d			18 58																			20 57		
Rugby	d			1920	19 26					19 55				20 20		20 55	21 05						21 19	21 55	22 04
Northampton	d			19 50						20 25				20 45		21 25							21 54	22 25	
Wolverton	d			20 02						20 37				21 02		21 38							22 06	22 37	
Milton Keynes Central 10	a			20 06				20 18		20 40				21 05		21 42	21 26						22 09	22 40	22 35
	d	20 04		20 06			20 12	20 19		20 41		20 48		21 05	21 17	21 42	21 28	21 38		21 57		22 04	22 10	22 41	22 37
Bletchley	d						20 17			20 46					21 22	21 47							22 15	22 46	
Leighton Buzzard	d			20 15			20 23			20 52				21 15	21 28	21 54							22 21	22 52	
Cheddington	d						20 28								21 33								22 26		
Tring	d					20 15	20 37								21 41								22 35		
Berkhamsted	d					20 19	20 42			21 07					21 45	22 09							22 40	23 05	
Hemel Hempstead	d					20 24	20 46			21 11					21 50	22 13							22 44	23 10	
Apsley	d					20 27				21 14						22 16								23 13	
Kings Langley	d					20 30				21 17						22 19								23 16	
Watford Junction	a			20 35		20 35	20 53			21 22			21s26	21 34	21 57	22 23	22s02			22s31			22 51	23 20	23s05
	d		20 22	20 35		20 35	20 54		21 17	21 22				21 34	21 58	22 24			22 17				22 52	23 21	
Bushey	d					20 38																			
Harrow & Wealdstone ⊖	d		20 28			20 43	21 00		21 23	21 28					22 04	22 30			22 23				22 58	23 27	
Wembley Central ⊖	d																								
Shepherd's Bush	a		20 45						21 45										22 45						
Kensington (Olympia) ⊖	a		20 47						21 47										22 47						
West Brompton ⊖	a		20 50						21 50										22 50						
Imperial Wharf	a		20 53						21 53										22 53						
Clapham Junction	d		20a58						21a58										22a58						
East Croydon 🚌	a																								
London Euston 15 ⊖	a	20 44		20 53	20 17	20 59	21 14	20 57		21 42		21 31	21 47	21 55	22 18	22 44	22 23	22 27		22 53		22 56	23 13	23 41	23 25

Table 66

Sundays

West Midlands, Northampton, Milton Keynes Central and Watford Junction - London

Network Diagram - see first Page of Table 59

		SN	VT	VT	LM	VT	VT
		1	◇1	◇1	◇1	◇1	◇1
			🍴	🍴		🍴	🍴
Wolverhampton 7	d					22 05	22 37
Sandwell & Dudley	d					22 15	22 47
Birmingham New Street 12	d					22 30	23 00
Birmingham International	d					22 40	23 10
Coventry	d					22 51	23 21
Nuneaton	d			22 18			
Rugby	d			22 32		23 04	23 34
Northampton	d				23 00		23s53
Wolverton	d				23 12		
Milton Keynes Central 10	a			23 04	23 15	23 36	00s12
	d		22 48	23 05	23 16	23 37	
Bletchley	d				23 21		
Leighton Buzzard	d				23 27		
Cheddington	d				23 32		
Tring	d				23 41		
Berkhamsted	d				23 45		
Hemel Hempstead	d				23 50		
Apsley	d						
Kings Langley	d						
Watford Junction	a		23s25	23s34	23 57	00s06	00s42
	d	23 17			23 57		
Bushey	d						
Harrow & Wealdstone ⊖	d	23 23			00 03		
Wembley Central ⊖	d						
Shepherd's Bush	a	23 45					
Kensington (Olympia) ⊖	a	23 47					
West Brompton ⊖	a	23 50					
Imperial Wharf	a	23 53					
Clapham Junction	d	00 05					
East Croydon	a	00 22					
London Euston 15 ⊖	a		23 49	23 54	00 17	00 27	01 04

Network Diagram for Tables 67, 68, 69, 70

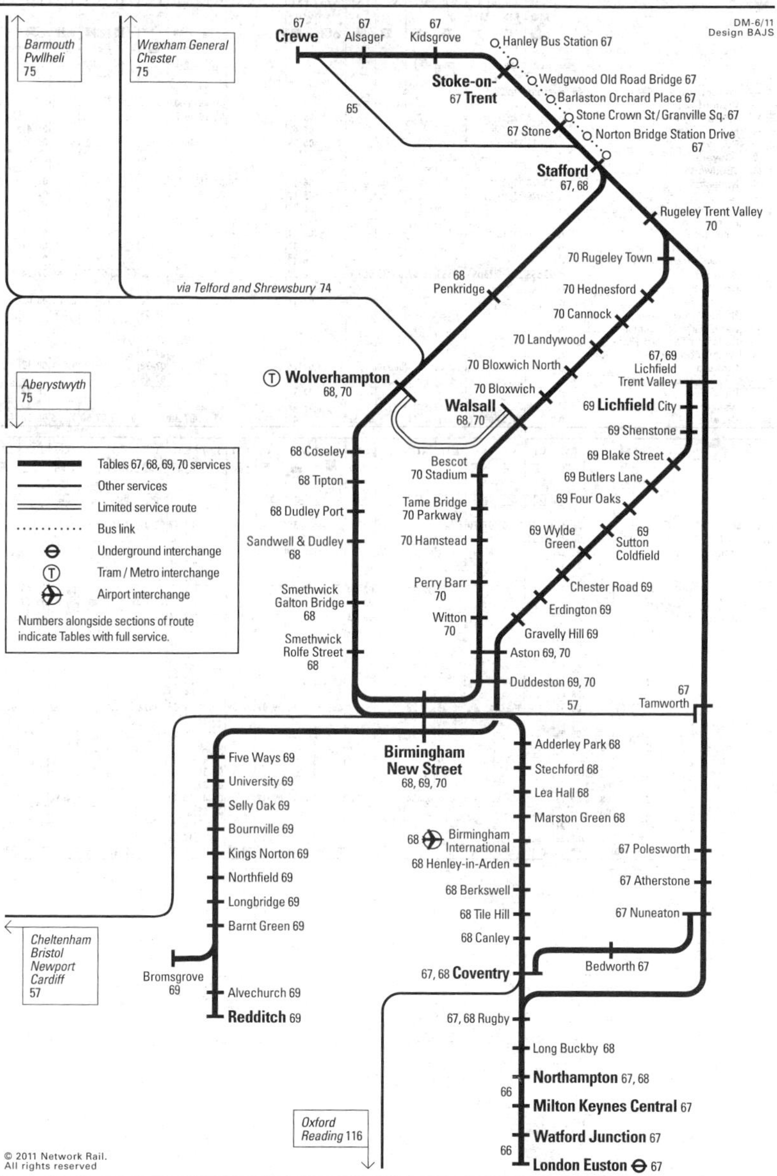

London - Stoke-on-Trent and Crewe
Coventry - Nuneaton

Network Diagram - see first Page of Table 67

Miles	Miles	Miles			VT	VT	LM	VT	VT	XC	LM	XC	LM		LM	VT	VT	LM	LM	XC	LM	LM	LM		XC
					MO	MX	MX	MO																	
					◇1	◇1	◇1	◇1	◇1	◇1	1	◇1	◇1			◇1	◇1		◇1	◇1	◇1	◇1			◇1
					🛏	🛏		🛏	⊠			⊥				⊠	⊠	bus		⊥					⊥
0	—	—	**London Euston** 15 ⊖	d	21p51	22p00										05 27	05 39								
17½	—	—	Watford Junction	d												05u45	06u02								
49¾	—	—	Milton Keynes Central	d	22p38	22p31							05 21			06 10	06 22								
65¾	—	—	Northampton	d									05 42									06 41			
84½	—	—	Rugby	d	23p18	22p54							06 05				06 45					07 01			
—	—	0	**Coventry**	d											06 12								07 06		
—	—	6¼	Bedworth	d											06 23								07 17		
99	—	10	Nuneaton	a	23p28	23p03							06 16		06 30	06 38						07 13	07 27		
—	—	—		d	23p29	23p04							06 17			06 39						07 15			
104	—	—	Atherstone	d									06 23									07 21			
108	—	—	Polesworth	d																		07 26			
111½	—	—	Tamworth	d		23b15							06 31									07 31			
117¾	—	—	Lichfield Trent Valley	d		23b22							06 37									07 37			
125¾	—	—	Rugeley Trent Valley	d				←					06 44									07 43			
135½	0	—	**Stafford**	d	23b53	23b38	23p53	23b53	06 02	06 30	06 36	06 55	06 58			07 03			07 08	07 30	07 36	07 54			08 01
—	—	—	Norton Bridge Station Drv	d	↪																				
144½	—	—	Stone	d									07 18									08 05			
—	—	—	Stone Crown Street	d														07 05							
—	—	—	Stone Granville Square	a																					
—	—	—	Barlaston Orchard Place	d														07 15							
—	—	—	Wedgwood Old Road Bridge	d														07 17							
151¾	—	—	**Stoke-on-Trent**	d						06a50		07a13	07 26					07 38				08 13			08a19
—	—	—	Hanley Bus Station	a														07 45							
159	—	—	Kidsgrove	d									07 34									08 21			
161¼	—	—	Alsager	d									07 39									08 26			
167¾	24½	—	**Crewe**	a		00s03	00 16	00s21	06 21		06 56		07 49			07 22	07 30		07 33	07 50	07 56	08 38			

		LM	LM	LM	VT	VT	VT	LM	XC		LM	LM	VT	XC	LM	LM	LM	VT	VT		XC	LM	LM	VT	XC
		◇1		◇1	◇1	◇1	◇1		◇1			1	◇1	◇1	◇1		◇1	◇1	◇1		◇1		◇1	◇1	◇1
			bus		⊠	⊠	⊠	bus	⊥				⊠	⊥		bus		⊠	⊠		⊥			⊠	⊥
London Euston 15 ⊖	d			06 24	06 36	07 07	07 10						07 35				07 47	08 07	08 10					08 40	
Watford Junction	d			06 41	06u51												08 02								
Milton Keynes Central	d			07 22			07 41						08 06				08f31		08 41						
Northampton	d			07 45													08 45								
Rugby	d			08 04													09 04								
Coventry	d								07 27		08 04										08 27	09 06			
Bedworth	d										08 15											09 17			
Nuneaton	a			08 17							08 23						09 16					09 25			
	d			08 17													09 17								
Atherstone	d			08 23													09 23								
Polesworth	d																								
Tamworth	d			08 31													09 31								
Lichfield Trent Valley	d			08 37													09 37								
Rugeley Trent Valley	d			08 43													09 43								
Stafford	d	08 09		08 54		08a22		08 25	08 30			08 36		09 01	09 09		09 54	09a22			09 30		09 35		10 01
Norton Bridge Station Drv	d							08 40																	
Stone	d			09 05													10 05								
Stone Crown Street	d		08 15													09 20									
Stone Granville Square	a							09 02																	
Barlaston Orchard Place	d		08 25													09 30									
Wedgwood Old Road Bridge	d		08 27													09 32									
Stoke-on-Trent	d		08 48	09 13					08a54					09a19		09 48	10 13				09a54				10a19
Hanley Bus Station	a		08 55													09 55									
Kidsgrove	d			09 21													10 21								
Alsager	d			09 26													10 26								
Crewe	a	08 30		09 38	08 10		08 47					08 56	09 10		09 30		10 38		09 47				09 56	10 10	

b Previous night, stops to set down only

London - Stoke-on-Trent and Crewe
Coventry - Nuneaton

Network Diagram - see first Page of Table 67

		LM	LM	LM	VT		VT		LM	XC	LM	VT	LM	XC	LM	VT	LM	LM	VT	VT	XC	LM	VT	LM	XC
		◇1		◇1	◇1		◇1			◇1	◇1	◇1		◇1	◇1	◇1		◇1	◇1	◇1	◇1	◇1	◇1		◇1
			🚌						🚌								🚌								
					⊠		⊠			🛒		⊠		🛒		☕			⊠	⊠	🛒		⊠		🛒
London Euston 15 ⊖	d			08 46	09 07		09 10					09 40				09 43		09 46	10 07	10 10			10 40		
Watford Junction	d			09 01														10 01							
Milton Keynes Central	d			09 25			09 41									10 13		10 25		10 41					
Northampton	d			09 45														10 45							
Rugby	d			10 04														11 04							
Coventry	d									09 27			10 42			10 42					10 27			11 42	
Bedworth	d												10 53											11 53	
Nuneaton	a			10 16									11 00					11 16						12 00	
	d			10 17														11 17							
Atherstone	d			10 23														11 23							
Polesworth	d																								
Tamworth	d			10 31														11 31							
Lichfield Trent Valley	d			10 37														11 37							
Rugeley Trent Valley	d			10 43														11 43							
Stafford	d	10 09		10 54	10a22				10 25	10 30	10 35			11 01	11 09			11 54	11a22		11 30	11 35			12 01
Norton Bridge Station Drv	d								10 40																
Stone	d			11 05														12 05							
Stone Crown Street	d		10 20														11 20								
Stone Granville Square	a								11 02																
Barlaston Orchard Place	d		10 30														11 30								
Wedgwood Old Road Bridge	d		10 32														11 32								
Stoke-on-Trent	d		10 48	11 13						10a54				11a19			11 48	12 13			11a54				12a19
Hanley Bus Station	a		10 55														11 55								
Kidsgrove	d			11 21														12 21							
Alsager	d			11 26														12 26							
Crewe	a	10 30		11 38			10 47				10 56	11 10			11 30	12 07		12 38		11 47		11 56	12 10		

			LM	LM	LM	VT	VT	XC	LM	VT	LM		LM	XC	LM	LM	LM	VT	VT	XC	LM		VT	LM	XC
			◇1		◇1	◇1	◇1	◇1	◇1	◇1				◇1	◇1		◇1	◇1	◇1	◇1	◇1		◇1		◇1
				🚌							🚌					🚌									
						☕	☕	🛒		☕				🛒				☕	☕	🛒			☕		🛒
London Euston 15 ⊖	d				10 46	11 07	11 10			11 40							11 46	12 07	12 10				12 40		
Watford Junction	d				11 01												12 01								
Milton Keynes Central	d				11 25		11 41										12 25		12 41						
Northampton	d				11 45												12 45								
Rugby	d				12 04												13 04								
Coventry	d							11 27					12 42							12 27				13 42	
Bedworth	d												12 53											13 53	
Nuneaton	a				12 16								13 00				13 16							14 00	
	d				12 17												13 17								
Atherstone	d				12 23												13 23								
Polesworth	d																								
Tamworth	d				12 31												13 31								
Lichfield Trent Valley	d				12 37												13 37								
Rugeley Trent Valley	d				12 43												13 43								
Stafford	d		12 09		12 54	12a22		12 30	12 35		12 35			13 01	13 09		13 54	13a22		13 30	13 35				14 01
Norton Bridge Station Drv	d										12 59														
Stone	d				13 05												14 05								
Stone Crown Street	d			12 20												13 20									
Stone Granville Square	a										13 39														
Barlaston Orchard Place	d			12 30												13 30									
Wedgwood Old Road Bridge	d			12 32												13 32									
Stoke-on-Trent	d			12 48	13 13			12a54						13a19		13 48	14 13			13a54					14a19
Hanley Bus Station	a			12 55												13 55									
Kidsgrove	d				13 21												14 21								
Alsager	d				13 26												14 26								
Crewe	a		12 30		13 38		12 47		12 56	13 10					13 30		14 38		13 47		13 56		14 10		

		LM	LM	LM	LM	VT	VT		XC	LM	VT FO	VT	LM	XC	LM	LM	LM		VT	VT	XC	LM	VT	LM	XC
		◇1			◇1	◇1	◇1		◇1	◇1	◇	◇1		◇1	◇1		◇1		◇1	◇1	◇1	◇1	◇1		◇1
			🚌	🚌												🚌									
						☕	☕		🛒		☕	☕		🛒					☕	☕	🛒		☕		🛒
London Euston 15 ⊖	d				12 46	13 07	13 10				13 33	13 40					13 46		14 07	14 10			14 40		
Watford Junction	d				13 01												14 01								
Milton Keynes Central	d				13 25		13 41										14 25			14 41					
Northampton	d				13 45												14 45								
Rugby	d				14 04												15 04								
Coventry	d								13 27				14 42								14 27			15 42	
Bedworth	d												14 53											15 53	
Nuneaton	a				14 16								15 00				15 16							16 00	
	d				14 17												15 17								
Atherstone	d				14 23												15 23								
Polesworth	d																								
Tamworth	d				14 31												15 31								
Lichfield Trent Valley	d				14 37												15 37								
Rugeley Trent Valley	d				14 43												15 43								
Stafford	d	14 09	14 18		14 54	14a22			14 30	14 35				15 01	15 09		15 54		15a22		15 30	15 35			16 02
Norton Bridge Station Drv	d		14 42																						
Stone	d				15 05												16 05								
Stone Crown Street	d			14 20												15 20									
Stone Granville Square	a		14 54																						
Barlaston Orchard Place	d			14 30												15 30									
Wedgwood Old Road Bridge	d			14 32												15 32									
Stoke-on-Trent	d			14 48	15 13				14a54					15a19		15 48	16 13				15a54				16a20
Hanley Bus Station	a			14 55												15 55									
Kidsgrove	d				15 21												16 21								
Alsager	d				15 26												16 26								
Crewe	a	14 30			15 38		14 47			14 56	15 16	15 10			15 30		16 38			15 47		15 56	16 11		

London - Stoke-on-Trent and Crewe
Coventry - Nuneaton

Network Diagram - see first Page of Table 67

		LM	LM	VT	LM	LM	VT	VT	XC	LM	VT	LM	XC		LM	LM	LM	VT	VT	XC	LM	LM	VT		VT
		◇[1]		[R]		◇[1]	◇[1]	◇[1]	◇[1]	◇[1]	◇[1]		◇[1]		◇[1]		◇[1]	◇[1]	◇[1]	◇[1]	◇[1]		◇[1]		◇[1]
			[bus]	[1]	[bus]											[bus]						[bus]			
				[at-seat]			[at-seat]	[at-seat]	[trolley]		[at-seat]		[trolley]					[at-seat]	[at-seat]	[trolley]			[at-seat]		[at-seat]
London Euston [15] ⊖	d			14 43		14 46	15 07	15 10			15 40						15 46	16 07	16 10				16 33		16 40
Watford Junction	d					15 01											16 01								
Milton Keynes Central	d			15 13		15 25		15 41									16 25		16u40						
Northampton	d					15 45											16 45								
Rugby	d					16 04											17 04						17 22		
Coventry	d			15 42					15 27			16 42								16 27					
Bedworth	d											16 53													
Nuneaton	a					16 16						17 00					17 16								
	d					16 17											17 17								
Atherstone	d					16 23											17 23								
Polesworth	d																								
Tamworth	d					16 31											17 31								
Lichfield Trent Valley	d					16 37											17 37								
Rugeley Trent Valley	d					16 43											17 43								
Stafford	d	16 09	16 18			16 54	16a22		16 31	16 35			17 01		17 09		18 20	17a22		17 30	17 36	17 40	17 56		
Norton Bridge Station Drv	d		16a42														↦					18a04			
Stone	d					17 05																			
Stone Crown Street	d				16 20											17 20									
Stone Granville Square	a																								
Barlaston Orchard Place	d				16 30											17 30									
Wedgwood Old Road Bridge	d				16 32											17 32									
Stoke-on-Trent	d				16 48	17 13			16a54				17a19			17 48				17a54					
Hanley Bus Station	a				16 55											17 55									
Kidsgrove	d					17 21																			
Alsager	d					17 26																			
Crewe	a	16 30		17 07		17 38		16 47		16 56	17 10				17 30				17 47		17 56		18 16		18 10

		XC	LM	LM	VT	LM	XC	LM	VT		LM	VT	VT	LM	XC	LM	VT	XC	LM		VT	LM	LM	LM	VT
		◇[1]	[1]	◇[1]	◇[1]		◇[1]		◇[1]		◇[1]	◇[1]	◇[1]		◇[1]	◇[1]	◇[1]	◇[1]			◇[1]	◇[1]		◇[1]	◇[1]
						[bus]								[bus]											
		[trolley]			[restaurant]		[trolley]		[restaurant]			[restaurant]	[restaurant]		[trolley]		[restaurant]	[trolley]			[restaurant]				[restaurant]
London Euston [15] ⊖	d				17 07				17 10			17 33	17 40				18 07				18 10			18 29	18 33
Watford Junction	d																							18 47	
Milton Keynes Central	d								17u40												18u40			19 23	
Northampton	d																							19 45	
Rugby	d											18 23												20 04	19 23
Coventry	d						17 27	17 42										18 27	18 42				19 43		
Bedworth	d							17 53											18 53				19 54		
Nuneaton	a							18 00	18 11										19 00		19 12		20 01	20 16	
	d								18 12												19 13			20 17	
Atherstone	d																							20 23	
Polesworth	d																								
Tamworth	d																							20 31	
Lichfield Trent Valley	d																							↦	
Rugeley Trent Valley	d			↤																					
Stafford	d	18 02	18 09	18 20	18 24		18 30				18 35	18 55			19 01	19 09	19 24	19 29				19 36			19 56
Norton Bridge Station Drv	d																								
Stone	d			18 31																					
Stone Crown Street	d					18 20								18 45											
Stone Granville Square	a																								
Barlaston Orchard Place	d					18 30								18 55											
Wedgwood Old Road Bridge	d					18 32								18 57											
Stoke-on-Trent	d	18a20		18 43		18 48	18a54							19 13	19a19			19a54							
Hanley Bus Station	a					19 00								19 20											
Kidsgrove	d			18 51																					
Alsager	d			18 56																					
Crewe	a		18 30	19 05	18 42				18 53		19 00	19 14	19 10			19 30	19 42				19 53	20 01			20 15

Table 67

London - Stoke-on-Trent and Crewe
Coventry - Nuneaton

Network Diagram - see first Page of Table 67

		VT	XC	LM	VT		VT FO	VT FO	VT	VT	XC	VT	LM	VT	LM		LM	VT	VT	XC	VT	VT	LM	XC	LM
		◇1 ⊠	◇1 🛒	◇1	◇1 ⊠		◇ 🍴	◇ 🍴	R 1 🍴	R 1 🍴	◇1	◇1 ⊠	◇1	◇1 🍴			◇1	◇1 🍴	◇1 🍴	◇1	◇1 🍴	◇1 🍴	◇1	◇1	
London Euston 15 ⊖	d	18 40			18 43		18 46	18 57	19 07	19 10				19 40				20 07	20 10		20 40				
Watford Junction	d																								
Milton Keynes Central	d				19 13					19u40									20 40						
Northampton	d																								
Rugby	d						19 39																		
Coventry	d				19 42						19 27				20 42					20 27				21 27	21 42
Bedworth	d														20 53										21 53
Nuneaton	a								20 02						21 00			21 02							22 02
	d								20 03									21 03							
Atherstone	d																								
Polesworth	d												←												
Tamworth	d						19s59						20 31	20 43											
Lichfield Trent Valley	d						20s07						20 37	20 50											
Rugeley Trent Valley	d											←	20 43												
Stafford	d		20 01	20 09	20 52		20s35		20a26		20 30	20 52		21 04			21 09	21a27		21 32		21 55	22 09	22 30	
Norton Bridge Station Drv	d				→																				
Stone	d																								
Stone Crown Street	d																								
Stone Granville Square	a																								
Barlaston Orchard Place	d																								
Wedgwood Old Road Bridge	d																								
Stoke-on-Trent	d		20a19								20a54		21 05							21a54				22a53	
Hanley Bus Station	a																								
Kidsgrove	d												21 14												
Alsager	d												21 18												
Crewe	a	20 11		20 30			21s01	20s33		20 48		21 15	21 27	21 21			21 30		21 48		22 12	22 17	22 30		

			VT	VT		XC	LM	AW	VT	LM
			◇1 🍴	◇1 🍴		◇1	◇1	◇	◇1 🍴	◇1
London Euston 15 ⊖	d		21 07	21 10					22 00	
Watford Junction	d			21u25						
Milton Keynes Central	d		21 38						22 31	
Northampton	d									
Rugby	d			22 04					22 54	
Coventry	d									
Bedworth	d									
Nuneaton	a		22 07						23 03	
	d		22 08						23 04	
Atherstone	d									
Polesworth	d									
Tamworth	d								23s15	
Lichfield Trent Valley	d								23s22	
Rugeley Trent Valley	d									
Stafford	d			22 34		23 01	23 13	23 30	23s38	23 53
Norton Bridge Station Drv	d									
Stone	d									
Stone Crown Street	d									
Stone Granville Square	a									
Barlaston Orchard Place	d									
Wedgwood Old Road Bridge	d									
Stoke-on-Trent	d					23a20				
Hanley Bus Station	a									
Kidsgrove	d									
Alsager	d									
Crewe	a		22 46	22 53			23 43	23 55	00s03	00 16

Table 67

Saturdays

London - Stoke-on-Trent and Crewe
Coventry - Nuneaton

Network Diagram - see first Page of Table 67

		VT	LM	VT	XC	LM	LM	LM	XC	LM		LM	XC	VT	LM	LM	LM	XC	LM	LM		VT	LM	VT	LM
		◇1	◇1	◇1	◇1	◇1	◇1		◇1	◇1			◇1	◇1	◇1	◇1		◇1		◇1		◇1	◇1	◇1	
		P		P					trolley			🚌	trolley	P				trolley	🚌			P		P	🚌
London Euston 15 ⊖	d	22p00												06 05						06 24		06 36		07 07	
Watford Junction	d													06u20						06 41		06u51			
Milton Keynes Central	d	22p31					05 21							06 41						07 23					
Northampton	d						05 42									06 38				07 45					
Rugby	d	22p54					06 05							07 03		06 58				08 04					
Coventry	d							06 16									07 16								
Bedworth	d							06 27									07 27								
Nuneaton	a	23p03					06 16	06 34								07 09	07 35			08 16					
	d	23p04					06 17									07 15				08 17					
Atherstone	d						06 23									07 21				08 23					
Polesworth	d															07 26									
Tamworth	d	23b15					06 31									07 31				08 31					
Lichfield Trent Valley	d	23b22					06 37									07 37				08 37					
Rugeley Trent Valley	d						06 44									07 43				08 43					
Stafford	d	23b38	23p53	06 01	06 30	06 36	06 54		07 01	07 08			07 30	07 34	07 38	07 54		08 01		08 54			08 09	08 23	08 25
Norton Bridge Station Drv	d																			→					08 40
Stone	d						07 05									08 05									
Stone Crown Street	d											07 20							08 20						
Stone Granville Square	a																								09 02
Barlaston Orchard Place	d											07 28							08 28						
Wedgwood Old Road Bridge	d											07 30							08 30						
Stoke-on-Trent	d				06a50		07 13		07a18			07 41				08 13		08a19	08 41						
Hanley Bus Station	a											07 47							08 47						
Kidsgrove	d						07 21									08 21									
Alsager	d						07 26									08 26									
Crewe	a	00s03	00 16	06 20		06 56	07 36			07 33			07 50	07 53	07 58	08 37						08 10	08 30	08 41	

		XC	LM	VT	LM	LM		XC	LM	LM	LM	VT	VT	XC	LM	VT		LM	XC	LM	LM	LM	VT	VT	LM
		◇1	◇1	◇1	◇1			◇1	◇1		◇1	◇1	◇1	◇1	◇1	◇1			◇1	◇1		◇1	◇1	◇1	
		trolley		P				P		🚌		P	P	trolley		P			P		🚌		P	P	🚌
London Euston 15 ⊖	d			07 35							07 46	08 07	08 10			08 40						08 46	08 50	09 07	
Watford Junction	d										08 01												09 05		
Milton Keynes Central	d			08 06							08 25		08 41									09 23	09 25		
Northampton	d										08 45											09 45			
Rugby	d										09 04											10 04			
Coventry	d	07 27				08 42								08 27				09 42							
Bedworth	d					08 53												09 53							
Nuneaton	a					09 00					09 16							10 00				10 16			
	d										09 17											10 17			
Atherstone	d										09 23											10 23			
Polesworth	d																								
Tamworth	d										09 31											10 31			
Lichfield Trent Valley	d										09 37											10 37			
Rugeley Trent Valley	d				←						09 43											10 43			
Stafford	d	08 30	08 36		08 54			09 01	09 09		09 54	09a22		09 30	09 35				10 01	10 09		10 54		10a22	10 25
Norton Bridge Station Drv	d																								10 40
Stone	d				09 05						10 05											11 05			
Stone Crown Street	d									09 20											10 20				
Stone Granville Square	a																								11 02
Barlaston Orchard Place	d									09 28											10 28				
Wedgwood Old Road Bridge	d									09 30											10 30				
Stoke-on-Trent	d	08a54			09 13			09a19		09 41	10 13			09a54					10a19		10 41	11 13			
Hanley Bus Station	a									09 47											10 47				
Kidsgrove	d				09 21						10 21											11 21			
Alsager	d				09 26						10 26											11 26			
Crewe	a		08 56	09 10	09 38				09 30		10 38		09 47		09 56	10 10				10 30		11 38	10 32		

		XC		LM	VT	LM	XC	LM	LM	LM	VT	VT		XC	LM	VT	LM	XC	LM	LM	LM	VT		VT	XC
		◇1		◇1	◇1		◇1	◇1		◇1	◇1	◇1		◇1	◇1	◇1		◇1	◇1		◇1	◇1		◇1	◇1
		trolley			P		P		🚌		P	P		trolley		P		P		🚌		P		P	trolley
London Euston 15 ⊖	d				09 40					09 46	10 07	10 10				10 40					10 46	11 07		11 10	
Watford Junction	d									10 01											11 01				
Milton Keynes Central	d									10 25		10 41									11 25			11 41	
Northampton	d									10 45											11 45				
Rugby	d									11 04											12 04				
Coventry	d	09 27				10 42								10 27			11 42								11 27
Bedworth	d					10 53											11 53								
Nuneaton	a					11 00				11 16							12 00				12 16				
	d									11 17											12 17				
Atherstone	d									11 23											12 23				
Polesworth	d																								
Tamworth	d									11 31											12 31				
Lichfield Trent Valley	d									11 37											12 37				
Rugeley Trent Valley	d									11 43											12 43				
Stafford	d	10 30		10 35			11 01	11 09		11 54	11a22			11 30	11 35			12 01	12 09		12 54	12a22			12 30
Norton Bridge Station Drv	d																								
Stone	d									12 05											13 05				
Stone Crown Street	d								11 20											12 20					
Stone Granville Square	a																								
Barlaston Orchard Place	d								11 28											12 28					
Wedgwood Old Road Bridge	d								11 30											12 30					
Stoke-on-Trent	d	10a54					11a19		11 41	12 13				11a54				12a19		12 41	13 13				12a54
Hanley Bus Station	a								11 47											12 47					
Kidsgrove	d									12 21											13 21				
Alsager	d									12 26											13 26				
Crewe	a			10 56	11 10			11 30		12 38		11 47			11 56	12 10			12 30		13 38			12 47	

b Previous night, stops to set down only

Table 67

Saturdays

London - Stoke-on-Trent and Crewe
Coventry - Nuneaton

Network Diagram - see first Page of Table 67

		LM	VT	LM	LM	XC	LM	LM		LM	VT	VT	XC	LM	VT	LM	XC	LM		LM	LM	LM	VT	VT	XC
		◇1	◇1 ☕	🚌		◇1 ☕	◇1	🚌		◇1	◇1 ☕	◇1 ☕	◇1 🛒	◇1	◇1 ☕		◇1 ☕	◇1		🚌	🚌	◇1	◇1 ☕	◇1 ☕	◇1 🛒
London Euston 15 ⊖	d		11 40							11 46	12 07	12 10			12 40							12 46	13 07	13 10	
Watford Junction	d									12 01												13 01			
Milton Keynes Central	d									12 25		12 41										13 25		13 41	
Northampton	d									12 45												13 45			
Rugby	d									13 04												14 04			
Coventry	d				12 42								12 27			13 42									13 27
Bedworth	d				12 53											13 53									
Nuneaton	a				13 00					13 16						14 00						14 16			
	d									13 17												14 17			
Atherstone	d									13 23												14 23			
Polesworth	d																								
Tamworth	d									13 31												14 31			
Lichfield Trent Valley	d									13 37												14 37			
Rugeley Trent Valley	d									13 43												14 43			
Stafford	d	12 35		12 35		13 01	13 09			13 54	13a22		13 30	13 35			14 01	14 09		14 18		14 54	14a22		14 30
Norton Bridge Station Drv	d			12 59																14 42					
Stone	d									14 05												15 05			
Stone Crown Street	d							13 20													14 20				
Stone Granville Square	a			13 39																14 54					
Barlaston Orchard Place	d							13 28													14 28				
Wedgwood Old Road Bridge	d							13 30													14 30				
Stoke-on-Trent	d					13a18		13 41		14 13			13a54				14a19				14 41	15 13			14a54
Hanley Bus Station	a							13 47													14 47				
Kidsgrove	d									14 21												15 21			
Alsager	d									14 26												15 26			
Crewe	a	12 56	13 10				13 30			14 38		13 47		13 56	14 10			14 30				15 38		14 47	

		LM	VT	LM		XC	LM	LM	LM	VT	VT	XC	LM	VT		LM	XC	LM	LM	LM	LM	VT	VT	XC	
		◇1	◇1 ☕			◇1 ☕	◇1	🚌	◇1	◇1 ☕	◇1 ☕	◇1 🛒	◇1	◇1 ☕			◇1 ☕	◇1	🚌	🚌	◇1	◇1 ☕	◇1 ☕	◇1 🛒	
London Euston 15 ⊖	d		13 40						13 46	14 07	14 10			14 40							14 46	15 07	15 10		
Watford Junction	d								14 01												15 01				
Milton Keynes Central	d								14 25		14 41										15 25		15 41		
Northampton	d								14 45												15 45				
Rugby	d								15 04												16 04				
Coventry	d			14 42								14 27				15 42								15 27	
Bedworth	d			14 53												15 53									
Nuneaton	a			15 00					15 16							16 00					16 16				
	d								15 17												16 17				
Atherstone	d								15 23												16 23				
Polesworth	d																								
Tamworth	d								15 31												16 31				
Lichfield Trent Valley	d								15 37												16 37				
Rugeley Trent Valley	d								15 43												16 43				
Stafford	d	14 35				15 01	15 09		15 54	15a22		15 30	15 35				16 01	16 09	16 18		16 54	16a22		16 30	
Norton Bridge Station Drv	d																		16a42						
Stone	d								16 05												17 05				
Stone Crown Street	d							15 20												16 20					
Stone Granville Square	a																								
Barlaston Orchard Place	d							15 28												16 28					
Wedgwood Old Road Bridge	d							15 30												16 30					
Stoke-on-Trent	d					15a19		15 41	16 13			15a54					16a19			16 41	17 13			16a54	
Hanley Bus Station	a							15 47												16 47					
Kidsgrove	d								16 21												17 21				
Alsager	d								16 26												17 26				
Crewe	a	14 56	15 10				15 30		16 38		15 47		15 56	16 10				16 30			17 38		16 47		

		LM	VT	LM	XC	LM	LM	LM	VT	VT		XC	LM	LM	VT	VT	LM	XC	LM	LM		VT	VT	XC	LM
		◇1	◇1 ☕		◇1 ☕	◇1	🚌	◇1	◇1 ☕	◇1 ☕		◇1 🛒	◇1	🚌	◇1 ☕	◇1 ☕		◇1 🛒	◇1	◇1		◇1 ☕	◇1 ☕	◇1 🛒	◇1
London Euston 15 ⊖	d		15 40					15 46	16 07	16 10					16 33	16 40				16 46		17 07	17 10		
Watford Junction	d							16 01												17 01					
Milton Keynes Central	d							16 25		16 41										17 25			17 41		
Northampton	d							16 45												17 45					
Rugby	d							17 04												18 04					
Coventry	d			16 42								16 27					17 42							17 27	
Bedworth	d			16 53													17 53								
Nuneaton	a			17 00				17 16									18 00			18 16		18 02			
	d							17 17												18 17		18 03			
Atherstone	d							17 23												18 23					
Polesworth	d																								
Tamworth	d							17 31							17 38					18 31					
Lichfield Trent Valley	d							17 37							17 45					18 37					
Rugeley Trent Valley	d							17 43												18 43					
Stafford	d	16 35			17 01	17 09		18 20	17a22			17 30	17 36	17 40	17a58			18 01	18 09	18 54		18a26		18 30	18 35
Norton Bridge Station Drv	d													18a06											
Stone	d							18 31												19 05					
Stone Crown Street	d						17 20																		
Stone Granville Square	a																								
Barlaston Orchard Place	d						17 28																		
Wedgwood Old Road Bridge	d						17 30																		
Stoke-on-Trent	d				17a19		17 41	18 41				17a54						18a19		19 13				18a54	
Hanley Bus Station	a						17 47																		
Kidsgrove	d							18 49												19 21					
Alsager	d							18 54												19 26					
Crewe	a	16 56	17 10			17 30		19 05		17 47			17 56			18 10			18 30	19 36			18 48		18 56

Table 67

Saturdays

London - Stoke-on-Trent and Crewe
Coventry - Nuneaton

Network Diagram - see first Page of Table 67

		VT	LM	LM	XC	LM		LM	VT	VT	XC	LM	VT	VT	XC	LM		VT	XC	LM	LM	VT	VT	VT	LM
		◇1			◇1	◇1		1	◇1	◇1	◇1	◇1	◇1	◇1	◇1	1		◇1	◇1		◇1	◇1	◇1	◇1	1
				🚌																					
		☕			☕				☕	☕	🛒		☕	☕	☕			☕				☕	☕	☕	
London Euston 15 ⊖	d	17 40						17 46	18 07	18 10			18 33	18 40		18 46		19 07				19 30		19 40	
Watford Junction	d							18 01								19 01									
Milton Keynes Central	d							18 25		18 41						19 25									
Northampton	d							18 45								19 45									
Rugby	d							19 04								20 04									
Coventry	d		18 42								18 27								19 27	20 15					
Bedworth	d		18 53																	20 26					
Nuneaton	a		19 00					19 16								20 16		20 02		20 34					
	d							19 17								20 17		20 03							
Atherstone	d							19 23								20 23									
Polesworth	d																								
Tamworth	d							19 31					19 38			20 31									
Lichfield Trent Valley	d							19 37					19 45			20 37									
Rugeley Trent Valley	d							19 43								20 43									←
Stafford	d				19 01	19 09		19 54	19a22		19 30	19 36	19a58		20 01	20 55		20 27	20 30		20 38		20 50		20 55
Norton Bridge Station Drv	d															↪									
Stone	d							20 05																	21 07
Stone Crown Street	d			18 45																					
Stone Granville Square	a																								
Barlaston Orchard Place	d			18 53																					
Wedgwood Old Road Bridge	d			18 55																					
Stoke-on-Trent	d			19 06	19a19			20 13			19a54				20a19				20a54						21 15
Hanley Bus Station	a			19 12																					
Kidsgrove	d							20 21																	21 23
Alsager	d							20 26																	21 28
Crewe	a	19 10				19 30		20 36		19 47		19 58		20 10				20 45			20 58	21 04	21 10	21 18	21 38

		XC		LM	XC	VT	VT	VT	LM	XC	VT	LM		XC	LM
		◇1		◇1	◇1	◇1	◇1	◇1	◇1	◇1	◇1			◇1	◇1
		☕				☕	☕	☕			☕				
London Euston 15 ⊖	d					20 11	20 20	20 31			21 00				
Watford Junction	d							20u46							
Milton Keynes Central	d						21 05				21 45				
Northampton	d														
Rugby	d					21 15		21 36							
Coventry	d				20 27					21 27		21 45			
Bedworth	d											21 56			
Nuneaton	a						21 32					22 03			
	d						21 33								
Atherstone	d														
Polesworth	d														
Tamworth	d							21 53							
Lichfield Trent Valley	d							22 00							
Rugeley Trent Valley	d														
Stafford	d	21 01		21 09	21 30	21 46			22 16	22 30	22 34			23 02	23 13
Norton Bridge Station Drv	d														
Stone	d														
Stone Crown Street	d														
Stone Granville Square	a														
Barlaston Orchard Place	d														
Wedgwood Old Road Bridge	d														
Stoke-on-Trent	d	21a20			21a52		22a05			22a50				23a20	
Hanley Bus Station	a														
Kidsgrove	d														
Alsager	d														
Crewe	a			21 30		22 05		22 35	22 40		22 58				23 37

Sundays

		VT	XC	VT	VT	LM	VT	XC	VT	LM		VT	XC	LM	VT	LM	VT	XC	VT	LM	LM	LM	VT	XC	VT
		◇1	◇1	◇1	◇1	◇1	◇1	◇1	◇1	◇1		◇1	◇1	1	◇1	◇1	◇1	◇1	◇1		◇1	◇1	◇1	◇1	◇1
		☕	🛒	☕	☕		☕	🛒	☕			☕	🛒		☕		☕	🛒	☕				☕	🛒	☕
London Euston 15 ⊖	d			08 10	08 15		08 45		09 15			09 45			10 15		10 45		11 15				12 02		12 35
Watford Junction	d																								
Milton Keynes Central	d			08 56			09 32					10 33					11 33		12 03						
Northampton	d																				11 36				
Rugby	d						10 09					11 09					12 09				12 03				
Coventry	d												10 28					11 29		11 55				12 28	
Bedworth	d																			12 06					
Nuneaton	a				09 43				10 44						11 46					12 13	12 16				
	d				09 44				10 45						11 47						12 17				
Atherstone	d																				12 23				
Polesworth	d																								
Tamworth	d																				12 31				
Lichfield Trent Valley	d																				12 37				
Rugeley Trent Valley	d																				12 44				
Stafford	d	09 17	09 33		10 08	10 17		10 33	11 09	11 17			11 32	11 45	12 13	12 17		12 33	12 53		12 59	13 09	13 25	13 34	
Norton Bridge Station Drv	d																								
Stone	d													11 55							13 09				
Stone Crown Street	d																								
Stone Granville Square	a																								
Barlaston Orchard Place	d																								
Wedgwood Old Road Bridge	d																								
Stoke-on-Trent	d							10a51					11a51	12 03				12a52			13 17			13a56	
Hanley Bus Station	a																								
Kidsgrove	d													12 11							13 25				
Alsager	d													12 15							13 30				
Crewe	a	09 35	09 54	10 17	10 28	10 37	10 55		11 30	11 37		11 55		12 26	12 32	12 37	12 56		13 13		13 43	13 30	13 43		14 12

Table 67

Sundays

London - Stoke-on-Trent and Crewe
Coventry - Nuneaton

Network Diagram - see first Page of Table 67

		LM	LM	LM	VT	XC		XC	VT	LM	LM	VT	XC	VT	LM	LM		LM	LM	VT	VT	XC	VT	LM	VT
			◇1	◇1	◇1	◇1		◇1	◇1	◇1	◇1	◇1	◇1	◇1				◇1	◇1	◇1	◇1	◇1	◇1	◇1	◇1
						A		B																	
					☕	🛒		🛒	☕			☕	🛒	☕						☕	☕	🛒	☕		☕
London Euston 15 ⊖	d			12 50	13 02				13 35			14 02		14 35					14 50	15 02	15 05		15 35		16 02
Watford Junction	d			13 06															15 06						
Milton Keynes Central	d			13 36															15 36		15 39				
Northampton	d			13 56															15 56						
Rugby	d			14 18															16 18						
Coventry	d	13 46				13 25		13 26					14 26		14 46	15 46						15 26			
Bedworth	d	13 57													14 57	15 57									
Nuneaton	a	14 04		14 30											15 04	16 04			16 30						
	d			14 31															16 31						
Atherstone	d			14 37															16 37						
Polesworth	d																								
Tamworth	d			14 45															16 45						
Lichfield Trent Valley	d			14 51															16 51						
Rugeley Trent Valley	d			14 58							←								16 58						
Stafford	d		14 09	15 18	14 22	14 33		14 34		15 09	15 18	15 25	15 34					16 09	17 18	16a20		16 34		17 09	17a24
Norton Bridge Station Drv	d			→																					
Stone	d										15 29								17 29						
Stone Crown Street	d																								
Stone Granville Square	a																								
Barlaston Orchard Place	d																								
Wedgwood Old Road Bridge	d																								
Stoke-on-Trent	d					14a55		14a56			15 41		15a56						17 40			16a56			
Hanley Bus Station	a																								
Kidsgrove	d										15 50								17 48						
Alsager	d										15 54								17 53						
Crewe	a		14 29		14 43				15 12	15 29	16 04	15 43		16 12				16 29	18 03		16 50		17 12	17 30	

		VT		XC	VT	LM	LM	LM	LM	VT	VT	XC		VT	LM	VT	VT	XC	VT	LM	LM	VT		VT	XC
		◇1		◇1	◇1			◇1	◇1	◇1	◇1	◇1		◇1	◇1	◇1	◇1	◇1	◇1	◇1	◇1	◇1		◇1	◇1
		☕		🛒	☕					☕	☕	🛒		☕		☕	☕	🛒	☕			☕		☕	
London Euston 15 ⊖	d	16 05			16 35				16 50	17 02	17 05			17 35		18 02	18 05		18 35		18 50	19 02		19 05	
Watford Junction	d								17 06												19 06				
Milton Keynes Central	d	16 39							17 36		17 39						18 39				19 36			19 39	
Northampton	d								17 56												19 56				
Rugby	d								18 18												20 18				
Coventry	d			16 26		16 46	17 46					17 26						18 26							19 26
Bedworth	d					16 57	17 57																		
Nuneaton	a					17 04	18 04		18 30		18 09										20 30	20 00			
	d								18 31		18 10										20 31	20 01			
Atherstone	d								18 37												20 37				
Polesworth	d																								
Tamworth	d								18 45												20 45				
Lichfield Trent Valley	d								18 51												20 51				
Rugeley Trent Valley	d								18 58												20 58				
Stafford	d			17 36				18 09	19 18	18a24		18 36			19 09	19a24		19 38		20 09	21 18	20 30			20 37
Norton Bridge Station Drv	d																				→				
Stone	d								19 29																
Stone Crown Street	d																								
Stone Granville Square	a																								
Barlaston Orchard Place	d																								
Wedgwood Old Road Bridge	d																								
Stoke-on-Trent	d			17a56					19 44			18a56						19a56							20a56
Hanley Bus Station	a																								
Kidsgrove	d								19 52																
Alsager	d								19 56																
Crewe	a	17 50			18 12			18 30	20 06		18 53			19 12	19 29		19 50		20 12	20 30		20 48		20 53	

A from 1 April

B until 25 March

Table 67

Sundays

London - Stoke-on-Trent and Crewe
Coventry - Nuneaton

Network Diagram - see first Page of Table 67

		LM	VT	VT	VT	LM	VT	VT		XC	VT	LM	VT		XC	LM	VT	AW		VT				
			◇1	◇1	◇1	◇1	◇1	◇1		◇1	◇1	◇1	◇1		◇1		◇1	◇		◇1				
			☕	☕	☕		☕	☕			☕		☕				☕			☕				
London Euston 15 ⊖	d			19 35	20 02		20 05	20 25			20 35		20 50				21 21			21 51				
Watford Junction	d																							
Milton Keynes Central	d						20 38						21 37							22 38				
Northampton	d																							
Rugby	d												22 01							23 18				
Coventry	d	19 46								20 26					21 26	21 35								
Bedworth	d	19 57														21 46								
Nuneaton	a	20 04			21 00											21 53	22 51			23 28				
	d				21 01												22 52			23 29				
Atherstone	d																							
Polesworth	d																							
Tamworth	d							21 32																
Lichfield Trent Valley	d							21 39																
Rugeley Trent Valley	d					←																		
Stafford	d		20 52			21 18	21 33			21 37	22 00	22 16			22 37		23 17	23 31		23s53				
Norton Bridge Station Drv	d																							
Stone	d					21 29																		
Stone Crown Street	d																							
Stone Granville Square	a																							
Barlaston Orchard Place	d																							
Wedgwood Old Road Bridge	d																							
Stoke-on-Trent	d					21 43				21a56					22a55									
Hanley Bus Station	a																							
Kidsgrove	d					21 52																		
Alsager	d					21 57																		
Crewe	a		21 10	21 13	21 44	22 08	21 53	22 10			22 20	22 38	22 49				23 43	23 55		00s21				

Crewe and Stoke-on-Trent - London
Nuneaton - Coventry

Network Diagram - see first Page of Table 67

Miles	Miles	Miles			AW	LM	VT	LM		XC	VT	XC	LM		VT	LM	VT	LM	XC	LM	VT	LM	VT		LM
						1	◇1			◇1	◇1	◇1	◇1		◇1		◇1	1	◇1	◇1	◇1		◇1		◇1
							⊠			🛒	⊠	🛒			⊠	🚌	⊠		🛒		⊠		⊠		
0	0	—	**Crewe**	d	04 59	05 18	05 36			05 47	06 02		06 20		06 29			06 35	06 38	06 47	06 53				07 16
6½	—	—	Alsager	d														06 44							
8¾	—	—	Kidsgrove	d														06 48							
—	—	—	Hanley Bus Station	d												06 45									
16	—	—	**Stoke-on-Trent**	d						06 07						06 51		06 58					07 06		
—	—	—	Wedgwood Old Road Bridge	d												07 06									
—	—	—	Barlaston Orchard Place	d												07 10									
—	—	—	Stone Granville Square	d												07a20									
23¼	—	—	Stone	d														07 06							
—	—	—	Norton Bridge Station Drv	d								←													
32¼	24½	—	**Stafford**	d	05a24		05 55			06 25	06 21	06 25	06a40				06 53	07 22	06a57	07a10			07 28		07a40
42	—	—	Rugeley Trent Valley	d		06 00				→								07 33							
50	—	—	Lichfield Trent Valley	d		06 07											07 08	07 40							
56¼	—	—	Tamworth	d		06 14											07 15	07 47							
59¾	—	—	Polesworth	d																					
63¾	—	—	Atherstone	d		06 23												07 56							
68¾	—	0	Nuneaton	a		06 29	06 17								07 06			08 02			07 32				
—	—	—		d		06 30	06 18	06 37							07 07			08 02			07 33	07 37			
—	—	3¾	Bedworth	d				06 44														07 44			
—	—	10	**Coventry**	a				06 56				07 24										07 57	08 30		
83¼	—	—	Rugby	a		06 47	06 30				06 52							08 17							
102	—	—	Northampton	a														08 41							
118	—	—	Milton Keynes Central	a			06 51				07 12							09 01							
150¼	—	—	Watford Junction	a														09 27					09s15		
167¾	—	—	**London Euston** 15 ⊖	a			07 28				07 50				08 07		08 22	09 44			08 33		09 34		

		VT	XC	LM	LM	LM	LM	LM	VT		XC	VT	VT	LM	VT	XC	LM	LM	LM		VT	LM	LM	XC	VT
		◇1	◇1		1	◇1			◇1		◇1	◇1	◇1	◇1	◇1	◇1		◇1	◇1		◇1	1		◇1	◇1
		⊠	🛒				🚌	🚌	⊠		🛒	⊠	⊠		⊠	🛒					⊠		🚌	🛒	⊠
Crewe	d	07 17			07 33	07 49			07 57					08 22	08 29			08 33	08 49		08 56				
Alsager	d				07 41													08 41							
Kidsgrove	d				07 46													08 46							
Hanley Bus Station	d						07 50																09 00		
Stoke-on-Trent	d		07 44		07 54		08 01				08 07	08 12				08 44		08 54					09 06	09 07	
Wedgwood Old Road Bridge	d						08 10																09 21		
Barlaston Orchard Place	d						08 11																09 25		
Stone Granville Square	d						08a25																09a35		
Stone	d				08 02													09 02							
Norton Bridge Station Drv	d							07 52																	
Stafford	d	07 35	08a01		08 21	08a10		08a22			08 25		08 36	08a42		09a02		09 21	09a09					09 25	09 36
Rugeley Trent Valley	d				08 33													09 33							
Lichfield Trent Valley	d				08 40													09 40							
Tamworth	d				08 47													09 47							
Polesworth	d																								
Atherstone	d				08 56													09 56							
Nuneaton	a				09 02							08 44						10 02							
	d			08 28	09 02							08 46					09 30	10 02							
Bedworth	d			08 35													09 37								
Coventry	a			08 47							09 24						09 56							10 24	
Rugby	a				09 17				08 45									10 17							
Northampton	a				09 39													10 39				←			
Milton Keynes Central	a				10 04													11 04			10 01	10 04			
Watford Junction	a				→							09s31						→				10 30			
London Euston 15 ⊖	a	08 52							09 38			09 52	09 56		10 04						10 38	10 49			10 56

		LM	VT	XC	LM		LM	LM	VT	LM	LM	XC	VT	LM	VT		XC	LM	LM	LM	VT	LM	LM	XC	VT
		◇1	◇1	◇1	◇1		◇1		◇1	◇1		◇1	◇1	◇1	◇1		◇1		◇1	◇1	◇1	◇1		◇1	◇1
			⊠	🛒				🚌	⊠		🚌	🛒	⊠		⊠		🛒				⊠		🚌	🛒	⊠
Crewe	d	09 22	09 29		09 33		09 49		09 56					10 22	10 29				10 33	10 49	10 56				
Alsager	d				09 41														10 41						
Kidsgrove	d				09 46														10 46						
Hanley Bus Station	d										10 00												11 00		
Stoke-on-Trent	d			09 44	09 54						10 06	10 07					10 44		10 54				11 06	11 07	
Wedgwood Old Road Bridge	d										10 21												11 21		
Barlaston Orchard Place	d										10 25												11 25		
Stone Granville Square	d										10a35												11a35		
Stone	d				10 02														11 02						
Norton Bridge Station Drv	d							09 52																	
Stafford	d	09a42		10a02	10 21		10a09	10a22				10 25	10 36	10a42			11a01		11 21	11a09				11 25	11 34
Rugeley Trent Valley	d				10 33														11 33						
Lichfield Trent Valley	d				10 40														11 40						
Tamworth	d				10 47														11 47						
Polesworth	d																								
Atherstone	d				10 56														11 56						
Nuneaton	a				11 02														12 02						
	d				11 02													11 15	12 02						
Bedworth	d																	11 22							
Coventry	a											11 24						11 34						12 24	
Rugby	a				11 17														12 17						
Northampton	a				11 39					←									12 43			←			
Milton Keynes Central	a				12 04				11 01	11 04									13 04		12 01	12 04			
Watford Junction	a				→					11 30									→			12 30			
London Euston 15 ⊖	a		11 04						11 38	11 49			11 56		12 04						12 38	12 49			12 56

Crewe and Stoke-on-Trent - London
Nuneaton - Coventry

Network Diagram - see first Page of Table 67

		LM	VT	XC	LM	LM	LM	VT	LM	LM		XC	LM	VT	LM	VT	XC	LM	LM	LM		VT	LM	LM
		◇1	◇1 ⊠	◇1 🛒		◇1	◇1	◇1 ☕	◇1	🚌		◇1 🛒	🚌	◇1 ☕	◇1	◇1 ☕	◇1 🛒		◇1	◇1		◇1 ☕	◇1	🚌
Crewe	d	11 22	11 29			11 33	11 49	11 56							12 22	12 29			12 33	12 49		12 56		
Alsager	d					11 41													12 41					
Kidsgrove	d					11 46													12 46					
Hanley Bus Station	d									12 00														13 00
Stoke-on-Trent	d			11 44		11 54				12 06		12 07					12 44		12 54					13 06
Wedgwood Old Road Bridge	d									12 21														13 21
Barlaston Orchard Place	d									12 25														13 25
Stone Granville Square	d									12a35			11 39											13a35
Stone	d					12 02													13 02					
Norton Bridge Station Drv	d												12 02											
Stafford	d	11a43		12a02		12 21	12a09					12 25	12a32	12 36	12a42		13a01		13 21	13a09				
Rugeley Trent Valley	d					12 33													13 33					
Lichfield Trent Valley	d					12 40													13 40					
Tamworth	d					12 47													13 47					
Polesworth	d																							
Atherstone	d					12 56													13 56					
Nuneaton	a					13 02													14 02					
	d				12 15	13 02												13 15	14 02					
Bedworth	d				12 22													13 22						
Coventry	a				12 34							13 24						13 36						
Rugby	a					13 17													14 17					
Northampton	a					13 46			←										14 42				←	
Milton Keynes Central	a					14 04		13 01	13 04										15 04			14 01	14 04	
Watford Junction	a					→			13 30										→				14 30	
London Euston 15 ⊖	a		13 03					13 38	13 49					13 56		14 04						14 38	14 49	

		XC	VT	LM	VT	XC	LM		LM	LM	LM	VT	LM	LM	XC	VT	LM		VT	XC	LM	LM	LM	VT	LM
		◇1 🛒	◇1 ☕	◇1	◇1 ☕	◇1 🛒			◇1	◇1	🚌	◇1 ☕	◇1	🚌	◇1 🛒	◇1 ☕	◇1		◇1 ☕	◇1 🛒		◇1	1	◇1 ☕	◇1
Crewe	d			13 22	13 29				13 33	13 49		13 56					14 22		14 29			14 33	14 49	14 56	
Alsager	d								13 41													14 41			
Kidsgrove	d								13 46													14 46			
Hanley Bus Station	d													14 00											
Stoke-on-Trent	d	13 07				13 44			13 54					14 06	14 07					14 44		14 54			
Wedgwood Old Road Bridge	d													14 21											
Barlaston Orchard Place	d													14 25											
Stone Granville Square	d										13 39			14a35											
Stone	d								14 02													15 02			
Norton Bridge Station Drv	d										13 54														
Stafford	d	13 25	13 36	13a42		14a01			14 21	14a09	14a15				14 25	14 36	14a46			15a02		15 21	15a09		
Rugeley Trent Valley	d								14 33													15 33			
Lichfield Trent Valley	d								14 40													15 40			
Tamworth	d								14 47													15 47			
Polesworth	d																								
Atherstone	d								14 56													15 56			
Nuneaton	a								15 02													16 02			
	d						14 15		15 02												15 15	16 02			
Bedworth	d						14 22														15 22				
Coventry	a	14 24					14 34								15 24						15 34				
Rugby	a								15 17													16 17			
Northampton	a								15 42				←									16 43			←
Milton Keynes Central	a								16 04			15 01	15 04									17 04		16 01	16 04
Watford Junction	a								→				15 30									→			16 30
London Euston 15 ⊖	a		14 56		15 04							15 38	15 49			15 56			16 04					16 38	16 49

		LM	XC		VT	LM	VT	XC	LM	LM	LM	LM	VT		VT	LM	LM	XC	VT	LM	VT	XC	LM		LM
		🚌	◇1 🛒		◇1 ☕	◇1	◇1 ☕	◇1 🛒		◇1	◇1	🚌	◇1 ☕		◇1 ☕	◇1	🚌	◇1 🛒	◇1 ☕	◇1	◇1 ☕	◇1 🛒			◇1
Crewe	d					15 22	15 29			15 33	15 49		15 56		15 57					16 22	16 29				16 33
Alsager	d									15 41															16 41
Kidsgrove	d									15 46															16 46
Hanley Bus Station	d	15 00															16 00								
Stoke-on-Trent	d	15 06	15 07					15 44		15 54							16 06	16 07				16 44			16 54
Wedgwood Old Road Bridge	d	15 21															16 21								
Barlaston Orchard Place	d	15 25															16 25								
Stone Granville Square	d	15a35										15 29					16a35								
Stone	d									16 02															17 02
Norton Bridge Station Drv	d											15 52													
Stafford	d		15 25		15 36	15a42		16a02		16 21	16a09	16a13						16 25	16 36	16a46		17a02			17h21
Rugeley Trent Valley	d									16 33															17 33
Lichfield Trent Valley	d									16 40															17 40
Tamworth	d									16 47															17 47
Polesworth	d																								
Atherstone	d									16 56															17 56
Nuneaton	a									17 02															18 02
	d								16 13	17 02													17 15		18 02
Bedworth	d								16 20														17 22		
Coventry	a		16 24						16 34									17 24					17 34		
Rugby	a									17 17															18 17
Northampton	a									17 39						←									18 39
Milton Keynes Central	a									18 04			17s01		17 01	17 04									19 04
Watford Junction	a									→						17 30									→
London Euston 15 ⊖	a				16 59		17 04						17 38		17 38	17 49			17 56		18 03				

Crewe and Stoke-on-Trent - London Nuneaton - Coventry

Network Diagram - see first Page of Table 67

		LM	VT	LM	LM	XC	VT	LM	VT		XC	LM	LM	LM	VT	LM	LM	XC	VT		LM	VT	LM	XC	LM
		◇1	◇1	◇1		◇1	◇1	◇1	◇1		◇1		◇1	◇1	◇1	◇1		◇1	◇1		◇1	◇1	◇1	◇1	
			☕		🚌	🛒	☕		☕		🛒				⊠		🚌	🛒	⊠			⊠		🛒	
Crewe	d	16 49	16 56					17 22	17 29				17 33	17 49	17 56			18 07			18 22	18 29			
Alsager	d												17 41												
Kidsgrove	d												17 46												
Hanley Bus Station	d				17 00												18 00								
Stoke-on-Trent	d				17 06	17 07					17 44		17 54				18 06							18 44	
Wedgwood Old Road Bridge	d				17 21												18 21								
Barlaston Orchard Place	d				17 25												18 25								
Stone Granville Square	d				17a35												18a33								
Stone	d												18 02												
Norton Bridge Station Drv	d																								
Stafford	d	17a10				17 25	17 36	17a42			18a03		18b21	18a09				18 28	18 36		18a42			19a01	
Rugeley Trent Valley	d												18 33												
Lichfield Trent Valley	d												18 40												
Tamworth	d												18 47												
Polesworth	d																								
Atherstone	d												18 56												
Nuneaton	a												19 02												
	d											18 10	19 02												19 15
Bedworth	d											18 17													19 22
Coventry	a					18 24						18 34						19 24							19 38
Rugby	a												19 18												
Northampton	a			←									19 45			←							←		
Milton Keynes Central	a		18 01	18 04			18 23						20 05		19 01	19 04						19 31	20 05		
Watford Junction	a			18 31					18s48				↪			19 30			19s42				20 31		
London Euston 15 ⊖	a		18 38	18 49			18 59		19 08						19 38	19 50			20 02			20 06	20 49		

		LM	LM	XC	LM		VT	VT	XC	LM	VT	LM	XC	LM	VT		VT	VT	XC	LM	VT	XC	LM	LM	VT
		◇1	◇1	◇1	◇1		◇1	◇1	◇1	◇1	◇1		◇1	◇1	◇1		◇1	◇1	◇1	◇1	◇1	◇1		◇1	◇1
				A									A												
				🛒			⊠	⊠	🛒		☕		🛒		☕		☕	☕			☕				☕
Crewe	d	18 33	18 49		19 18		19 23	19 29		19 55	19 56			20 18	20 23		20 29	20 41		20 47	20 53			21 18	21 24
Alsager	d	18 41																							
Kidsgrove	d	18 46																							
Hanley Bus Station	d																								
Stoke-on-Trent	d	18 54		19 07					19 44				20 07						20 44			21 07			
Wedgwood Old Road Bridge	d																								
Barlaston Orchard Place	d																								
Stone Granville Square	d																								
Stone	d	19 02																							
Norton Bridge Station Drv	d																								
Stafford	d	19c21	19a09	19 25	19a41		19 42		20a03	20a15			20 26	20a38			20 48		21a02	21a08	21a11	21a24		21a38	21 44
Rugeley Trent Valley	d	19 33																							
Lichfield Trent Valley	d	19 40																							21 58
Tamworth	d	19 47																							22 05
Polesworth	d																								
Atherstone	d	19 56																							
Nuneaton	a	20 02													21 02										22 16
	d	20 02										20 15			21 03								21 15		22 17
Bedworth	d											20 22											21 22		
Coventry	a			20 24								20 34	21 24										21 34		
Rugby	a	20 17																21 27							22 30
Northampton	a	20 43																							
Milton Keynes Central	a							20 32			21 03						21 35	21 47							22 58
Watford Junction	a						20s46								21s48										23s30
London Euston 15 ⊖	a						21 05	21 06			21 42				22 09		22 12	22 22							23 56

		XC	LM	LM	XC
		◇1	◇1		◇1
Crewe	d		22 20		
Alsager	d				
Kidsgrove	d				
Hanley Bus Station	d				
Stoke-on-Trent	d	22 08			22 47
Wedgwood Old Road Bridge	d				
Barlaston Orchard Place	d				
Stone Granville Square	d				
Stone	d				
Norton Bridge Station Drv	d				
Stafford	d	22a25	22a40		23a06
Rugeley Trent Valley	d				
Lichfield Trent Valley	d				
Tamworth	d				
Polesworth	d				
Atherstone	d				
Nuneaton	a				
	d			22 20	
Bedworth	d			22 27	
Coventry	a			22 39	
Rugby	a				
Northampton	a				
Milton Keynes Central	a				
Watford Junction	a				
London Euston 15 ⊖	a				

A 🛒 to Stafford

Table 67

Saturdays

Crewe and Stoke-on-Trent - London
Nuneaton - Coventry

Network Diagram - see first Page of Table 67

		AW	LM		XC	VT	XC	VT	LM	VT		XC	LM	LM	LM	VT	VT	XC	LM	LM		LM	VT	LM	VT
					◇1 🛒	◇1 ☕	◇1 🛒	◇1 ☕	◇1	◇1 ☕		◇1 🛒	◇1	◇1	◇1	◇1 ☕	◇1 ☕	◇1 🛒	🚌			◇1	◇1 ☕	◇1	◇1 ☕
Crewe	d	04 59			05 47	06 00			06 20	06 29			06 38	06 47	07 16	07 20	07 29					07 38	07 39	07 49	07 55
Alsager	d												06 47									07 47			
Kidsgrove	d												06 51									07 51			
Hanley Bus Station	d																		07 50						
Stoke-on-Trent	d				06 08							06 39	07 00					07 44	07 56			08 00			
Wedgwood Old Road Bridge	d																		08 05						
Barlaston Orchard Place	d																		08 06						
Stone Granville Square	d																		08a12						
Stone	d												07 08									08 08			
Norton Bridge Station Drv	d						←																		
Stafford	d	05a24			06 26	06 19	06 26	06 35	06a41			06a57	07 24	07a10	07a40	07 39		08a02				08 23		08a10	08 16
Rugeley Trent Valley	d				→								07 33									→			
Lichfield Trent Valley	d												07 40												08 31
Tamworth	d												07 47												08 37
Polesworth	d																								
Atherstone	d												07 56												
Nuneaton	a							06 57					08 02												
	d		06 47					06 59					08 02							08 14					
Bedworth	d		06 54																	08 21					
Coventry	a		07 06				07 24													08 33					
Rugby	a					06 49							08 17												
Northampton	a												08 40												
Milton Keynes Central	a					07 11				07 31			09 04												
Watford Junction	a					07s32		07s44					09 33												
London Euston 15 ⊖	a					07 52		08 05		08 09			09 50			08 59	09 04						09 30		09 46

		LM	LM	XC	VT	LM		VT	XC	LM	LM	LM	LM	VT	LM	XC		VT	LM	VT	XC	LM	LM	LM	LM
		◇1	🚌	◇1 🛒	◇1 ☕	◇1		◇1 ☕	◇1 🛒		◇1	◇1	🚌	◇1 ☕	◇1	◇1 🛒		◇1 ☕	◇1	◇1 ☕	◇1 🛒		◇1	◇1	🚌
Crewe	d					08 22		08 29			08 33	08 49		08 56					09 22	09 29			09 33	09 49	
Alsager	d										08 41												09 41		
Kidsgrove	d										08 46												09 46		
Hanley Bus Station	d												08 50												09 50
Stoke-on-Trent	d			08 07					08 44		08 54		08 56			09 07					09 44		09 54		09 56
Wedgwood Old Road Bridge	d												09 05												10 05
Barlaston Orchard Place	d												09 06												10 06
Stone Granville Square	d												09a12												10a12
Stone	d										09 02												10 02		
Norton Bridge Station Drv	d	←	07 52																						
Stafford	d	08 23	08a22	08 26	08 36	08a42			09a02		09 21	09a09				09 26		09 36	09a42		10a02		10 21	10a10	
Rugeley Trent Valley	d	08 33									09 33												10 33		
Lichfield Trent Valley	d	08 40									09 40												10 40		
Tamworth	d	08 47									09 47												10 47		
Polesworth	d																								
Atherstone	d	08 56									09 56												10 56		
Nuneaton	a	09 02			08 58						10 02							09 58					11 02		
	d	09 02			08 59					09 15	10 02							09 59				10 15	11 02		
Bedworth	d									09 22												10 22			
Coventry	a			09 24						09 34						10 24						10 34			
Rugby	a	09 17									10 17												11 17		
Northampton	a	09 39									10 39				←								11 39		
Milton Keynes Central	a	10 04									11 04			10 01	10 04								12 04		
Watford Junction	a	→									→				10 30								→		
London Euston 15 ⊖	a				10 00			10 04						10 37	10 49			11 01		11 04					

		LM		VT	LM	XC	VT	LM	VT	XC	LM	LM		LM	LM	VT	LM	XC	VT	LM	VT	XC		LM	LM
		🚌		◇1 ☕	◇1	◇1 🛒	◇1 ☕	◇1	◇1 ☕	◇1 🛒		◇1		◇1	🚌	◇1 ☕	◇1	◇1 🛒	◇1 ☕	◇1	◇1 ☕	◇1 🛒			◇1
Crewe	d			09 56				10 22	10 29			10 33		10 49		10 56				11 22	11 29				11 33
Alsager	d											10 41													11 41
Kidsgrove	d											10 46													11 46
Hanley Bus Station	d														10 50										
Stoke-on-Trent	d					10 07				10 44		10 54			10 56			11 07				11 44			11 54
Wedgwood Old Road Bridge	d														11 05										
Barlaston Orchard Place	d														11 06										
Stone Granville Square	d														11a12										
Stone	d											11 02													12 02
Norton Bridge Station Drv	d	09 52																							
Stafford	d	10a22				10 26	10 36	10a42		11a02		11 21		11a09				11 26	11 36	11a42		12a02			12 21
Rugeley Trent Valley	d											11 33													12 33
Lichfield Trent Valley	d											11 40													12 40
Tamworth	d											11 47													12 47
Polesworth	d																								
Atherstone	d											11 56													12 56
Nuneaton	a											12 02													13 02
	d										11 15	12 02												12 15	13 02
Bedworth	d										11 22													12 22	
Coventry	a					11 24					11 34							12 24						12 34	
Rugby	a											12 17													13 17
Northampton	a				←							12 39					←								13 39
Milton Keynes Central	a			11 01	11 04							13 04				12 01	12 04								14 04
Watford Junction	a				11 30							→					12 30								→
London Euston 15 ⊖	a			11 38	11 49		11 56		12 04							12 38	12 49		12 56		13 04				

Crewe and Stoke-on-Trent - London
Nuneaton - Coventry

Network Diagram - see first Page of Table 67

		LM	LM	VT	LM	XC	LM	VT		LM	VT	XC	LM	LM	LM	LM	VT	LM		XC	VT	LM	VT	XC	LM
		◇1		◇1	◇1	◇1		◇1		◇1	◇1	◇1		◇1	◇1		◇1	◇1		◇1	◇1	◇1	◇1	◇1	
			🚌				🚌									🚌									
				🍴		🛒		🍴			🍴	🛒					🍴			🛒	🍴		🍴	🛒	
Crewe	d	11 49		11 56						12 22	12 29			12 33	12 49		12 57					13 22	13 29		
Alsager	d													12 41											
Kidsgrove	d													12 46											
Hanley Bus Station	d		11 50													12 50									
Stoke-on-Trent	d		11 56			12 07						12 44		12 54		12 56				13 07				13 44	
Wedgwood Old Road Bridge	d		12 05													13 05									
Barlaston Orchard Place	d		12 06													13 06									
Stone Granville Square	d		12a12				11 39									13a12									
Stone	d													13 02											
Norton Bridge Station Drv	d						12 02																		
Stafford	d	12a09				12 25	12a32	12 36		12a42		13a02		13b21	13a09					13 26	13 36	13a42		14a02	
Rugeley Trent Valley	d													13 33											
Lichfield Trent Valley	d													13 40											
Tamworth	d													13 47											
Polesworth	d																								
Atherstone	d													13 56											
Nuneaton	a													14 02											
	d												13 15	14 02											14 15
Bedworth	d												13 22												14 22
Coventry	a					13 24							13 34							14 24					14 34
Rugby	a													14 17											
Northampton	a				←									14 39				←							
Milton Keynes Central	a			13 01	13 04									15 04			14 01	14 04							
Watford Junction	a				13 30									↪				14 30							
London Euston 15 ⊖	a			13 38	13 49			13 56			14 04						14 38	14 49			14 56		15 04		

		LM	LM	LM		LM	VT	LM	XC	VT	LM	VT	XC	LM		LM	LM	LM	VT	LM	XC	VT	LM	VT	
		◇1	◇1				◇1	◇1	◇1	◇1	◇1	◇1	◇1			◇1	◇1		◇1	◇1	◇1	◇1	◇1	◇1	
				🚌		🚌												🚌							
							🍴		🛒	🍴		🍴	🛒						🍴		🛒	🍴		🍴	
Crewe	d	13 33	13 49				13 56				14 22	14 29				14 33	14 49		14 56				15 22	15 29	
Alsager	d	13 41														14 41									
Kidsgrove	d	13 46														14 46									
Hanley Bus Station	d					13 50												14 50							
Stoke-on-Trent	d	13 54				13 56			14 07				14 44			14 54		14 56			15 07				
Wedgwood Old Road Bridge	d					14 05												15 05							
Barlaston Orchard Place	d					14 06												15 06							
Stone Granville Square	d			13 39		14a12												15a12							
Stone	d	14 02														15 02									
Norton Bridge Station Drv	d			13 54																					
Stafford	d	14 21	14a09	14a15					14 26	14 36	14a46		15a02			15 21	15a09				15 26	15 36	15a42		
Rugeley Trent Valley	d	14 33														15 33									
Lichfield Trent Valley	d	14 40														15 40									
Tamworth	d	14 47														15 47									
Polesworth	d																								
Atherstone	d	14 56														15 56									
Nuneaton	a	15 02														16 02									
	d	15 02												15 15		16 02									
Bedworth	d													15 22											
Coventry	a								15 24					15 34							16 24				
Rugby	a	15 17														16 17									
Northampton	a	15 39						←								16 39				←					
Milton Keynes Central	a	16 04					15 01	15 04								17 04			16 01	16 04					
Watford Junction	a	↪						15 30								↪				16 30					
London Euston 15 ⊖	a						15 38	15 49		15 56		16 04							16 38	16 49		16 56		17 04	

		XC	LM	LM	LM	LM	LM	VT	LM	XC		VT	LM	VT	XC	LM	LM	LM	LM	VT		LM	XC	VT	LM
		◇1		◇1	◇1			◇1	◇1	◇1		◇1	◇1	◇1	◇1		◇1	◇1		◇1		◇1	◇1	◇1	◇1
						🚌	🚌												🚌						
		🛒						🍴		🛒		🍴		🍴	🛒					🍴			🛒	🍴	
Crewe	d			15 33	15 49			15 56					16 22	16 29			16 33	16 49		16 56					17 22
Alsager	d			15 41													16 41								
Kidsgrove	d			15 46													16 46								
Hanley Bus Station	d						15 50												16 50						
Stoke-on-Trent	d	15 44		15 54			15 56			16 07					16 44		16 54		16 56				17 07		
Wedgwood Old Road Bridge	d						16 05												17 05						
Barlaston Orchard Place	d						16 06												17 06						
Stone Granville Square	d					15 29	16a12												17a12						
Stone	d			16 02													17 02								
Norton Bridge Station Drv	d					15 52																			
Stafford	d	16a02		16 21	16a09	16a13				16 25		16 36	16a46		17a02		17 21	17a09					17 26	17 36	17a42
Rugeley Trent Valley	d			16 33													17 33								
Lichfield Trent Valley	d			16 40													17 40								
Tamworth	d			16 47													17 47								
Polesworth	d																								
Atherstone	d			16 56													17 56								
Nuneaton	a			17 02													18 02								
	d		16 15	17 02												17 15	18 02								
Bedworth	d		16 22													17 22									
Coventry	a		16 34							17 24						17 34							18 24		
Rugby	a			17 17													18 17								
Northampton	a			17 39					←								18 39					←			
Milton Keynes Central	a			18 05				17 01	17 04								19 04			18 01		18 05			
Watford Junction	a			↪					17 30								↪					18 31			
London Euston 15 ⊖	a							17 38	17 49			17 56		18 04						18 38		18 49		18 56	

Crewe and Stoke-on-Trent - London Nuneaton - Coventry

Network Diagram - see first Page of Table 67

		VT	LM	XC	LM	LM		LM	LM	XC	VT	LM	VT	XC	LM	LM		LM	XC	VT	LM	VT	XC	LM	XC
		◇1	◇1	◇1		◇1		◇1		◇1	◇1	◇1	◇1	◇1		◇1		◇1	◇1	◇1	◇1	◇1	◇1	◇1	◇1
																									A
		⊡		🛒					🚌	🛒	⊡		⊡	🛒					🛒	⊡		⊡	🛒		🛒
Crewe	d	17 29				17 33		17 49				18 22	18 29			18 33		18 49			19 22	19 29		19 51	
Alsager	d					17 41										18 41									
Kidsgrove	d					17 46										18 46									
Hanley Bus Station	d								17 50																
Stoke-on-Trent	d			17 44		17 54			17 56	18 08				18 44		18 54			19 07				19 44		20 07
Wedgwood Old Road Bridge	d								18 05																
Barlaston Orchard Place	d								18 06																
Stone Granville Square	d								18a12																
Stone	d					18 02										19 02									
Norton Bridge Station Drv	d																								
Stafford	d			18a03		18 21		18a09		18 27	18 36	18a42		19a02		19 21		19a09	19 25	19 36	19a42		20a02	20a11	20 26
Rugeley Trent Valley	d					18 33										19 33									
Lichfield Trent Valley	d					18 40										19 40									
Tamworth	d					18 47										19 47									
Polesworth	d																								
Atherstone	d					18 56										19 56									
Nuneaton	a					19 02										20 02									
	d				18 15	19 02									19 46	20 02									
Bedworth	d				18 22										19 53										
Coventry	a				18 34					19 24					20 05				20 24						21 24
Rugby	a					19 17										20 17									
Northampton	a		←			19 41										20 40									
Milton Keynes Central	a		19 04																						
Watford Junction	a		19 30																						
London Euston 15 ⊖	a	19 04	19 49								19 56		20 04							21 15		21 18			

		VT		LM	XC	VT	XC	LM	LM	XC	VT	VT		XC	LM	LM
		◇1		◇1	◇1	◇1	◇1		◇1	◇1	◇1	◇1		◇1		◇1
												B				
		⊡				⊡					⊡	⊡				
Crewe	d			20 22		20 47			21 17		21 43	22 05				22 23
Alsager	d											≀				
Kidsgrove	d											≀				
Hanley Bus Station	d											≀				
Stoke-on-Trent	d				20 44		21 07			21 45		≀		22 08		
Wedgwood Old Road Bridge	d											≀				
Barlaston Orchard Place	d											≀				
Stone Granville Square	d											≀				
Stone	d											≀				
Norton Bridge Station Drv	d											≀				
Stafford	d	20 36		20a44	21a02		21a26		21a42	22a02	22a07	22a24		22a32		22a47
Rugeley Trent Valley	d															
Lichfield Trent Valley	d															
Tamworth	d															
Polesworth	d															
Atherstone	d															
Nuneaton	a															
	d							21 15							22 15	
Bedworth	d							21 22							22 22	
Coventry	a							21 34							22 34	
Rugby	a															
Northampton	a															
Milton Keynes Central	a					21 50										
Watford Junction	a															
London Euston 15 ⊖	a	22 14				22 44										

A 🛒 to Stafford

B until 24 March

Table 67

Sundays

Crewe and Stoke-on-Trent - London
Nuneaton - Coventry

Network Diagram - see first Page of Table 67

		LM	VT ◇1 ☕	VT ◇1 ☕	XC ◇1 A 🛒	VT ◇1 ☕	VT ◇1 ☕	XC ◇1 B 🛒	XC ◇1 C 🛒	VT ◇1 ☕	LM ◇1	LM 1	VT ◇1 ☕	VT ◇1 ☕	XC ◇1 A 🛒	VT ◇1 ☕	LM	LM ◇1	VT ◇1 ☕	XC ◇1 A 🛒		VT ◇1 ☕	LM ◇1	VT ◇1 ☕	VT ◇1 ☕
Crewe	d		08 43	08 53	09 05	09 13	09 43	10 05		10 14	10 20	10 38	10 43	10 55		11 14		11 38	11 49				12 22	12 30	12 56
Alsager	d											10 46						11 46							
Kidsgrove	d											10 50						11 50							
Hanley Bus Station	d																								
Stoke-on-Trent	d								10 07			10 59			11 07			11 59		12 07					
Wedgwood Old Road Bridge	d																								
Barlaston Orchard Place	d																								
Stone Granville Square	d																								
Stone	d											11 07						12 07							
Norton Bridge Station Drv	d																								
Stafford	d		09 02		09 26	09 32		10 27	10 27	10 33	10a41	11a17			11 28	11 36		12 19		12 25		12 36	12a41		
Rugeley Trent Valley	d																	12 28							
Lichfield Trent Valley	d																	12 35							
Tamworth	d																	12 42							
Polesworth	d																								
Atherstone	d																	12 51							
Nuneaton	a					09 54				10 55						11 58		12 57	12 31						
	d					09 55				10 56						11 59	12 30	12 58	12 32						
Bedworth	d																12 36								
Coventry	a				10 24			11 24	11 24						12 24		12 54			13 24					
Rugby	a						10 31						11 31					13 13							
Northampton	a																	13 41							
Milton Keynes Central	a			10 17			11 06			11 46			12 06					14 04	13 03						14 02
Watford Junction	a	00 39	10s35			11s16	11s43							12s35		12s50		↪							
London Euston 15 ⊖	a	01 14	10 57	11 06		11 37	12 05			12 32			12 45	12 56		13 11			13 44			14 01		14 09	14 43

		LM ◇1	XC ◇1 A 🛒	VT ◇1 ☕	LM ◇1	VT ◇1 ☕		LM	LM ◇1	VT ◇1 ☕	XC ◇1 A 🛒	VT ◇1 ☕	LM ◇1	VT ◇1 ☕	VT ◇1 ☕	LM ◇1		LM	XC ◇1 A 🛒	VT ◇1 ☕	LM ◇1	VT ◇1 ☕	LM	LM ◇1	VT ◇1 ☕
Crewe	d				13 22	13 30			13 38	13 51			14 22	14 29	14 54						15 22	15 29		15 38	15 54
Alsager	d								13 47															15 46	
Kidsgrove	d								13 51															15 50	
Hanley Bus Station	d																								
Stoke-on-Trent	d		13 07						13 59		14 07								15 07					15 59	
Wedgwood Old Road Bridge	d																								
Barlaston Orchard Place	d																								
Stone Granville Square	d																								
Stone	d								14 07															16 07	
Norton Bridge Station Drv	d																								
Stafford	d		13 25	13 36	13a42				14 19		14 25	14 36	14a42						15 25	15 36	15a42			16 19	
Rugeley Trent Valley	d								14 28															16 28	
Lichfield Trent Valley	d								14 35															16 35	
Tamworth	d								14 42															16 42	
Polesworth	d																								
Atherstone	d								14 51															16 51	
Nuneaton	a								14 57	14 31														16 57	
	d							14 11	14 58	14 32								15 11					16 11	16 58	
Bedworth	d							14 17										15 17					16 17		
Coventry	a		14 24					14 34			15 24							15 34	16 24				16 34		
Rugby	a								15 13															17 13	
Northampton	a	↤							15 41							↤								17 41	
Milton Keynes Central	a	14 04							16 04	15 04					16 04	16 04								18 04	17 03
Watford Junction	a	14 35							↪							16 35								↪	
London Euston 15 ⊖	a	14 53		15 01		15 09				15 45		16 01		16 09	16 44	16 53				17 01		17 09			17 44

		XC ◇1 A 🛒		VT ◇1 ☕	LM ◇1	VT ◇1 ☕	VT ◇1 ☕	LM ◇1	LM	XC ◇1 A 🛒	VT ◇1 ☕	LM ◇1		VT ◇1 ☕	LM	LM ◇1	VT ◇1 ☕	XC ◇1 A 🛒	VT ◇1 ☕	LM ◇1	VT ◇1 ☕	VT ◇1 ☕		LM ◇1	XC ◇1 A 🛒
Crewe	d				16 22	16 29	16 54					17 22		17 29		17 38	17 55			18 22	18 29	18 55			
Alsager	d															17 46									
Kidsgrove	d															17 50									
Hanley Bus Station	d																								
Stoke-on-Trent	d	16 07								17 08						17 59		18 08							19 07
Wedgwood Old Road Bridge	d																								
Barlaston Orchard Place	d																								
Stone Granville Square	d																								
Stone	d															18 07									
Norton Bridge Station Drv	d																								
Stafford	d	16 25		16 37	16a42					17 26	17 36	17a42				18 19		18 26	18 36	18a42					19 25
Rugeley Trent Valley	d															18 28									
Lichfield Trent Valley	d						17 27									18 35									
Tamworth	d															18 42									
Polesworth	d																								
Atherstone	d															18 51									
Nuneaton	a															18 57									
	d								17 11						18 11	18 58									
Bedworth	d								17 17						18 17										
Coventry	a	17 24							17 34	18 24					18 34			19 24							20 24
Rugby	a															19 13									
Northampton	a							↤								19 41								↤	
Milton Keynes Central	a						18 04	18 04								20 06	19 02					20 03		20 06	
Watford Junction	a							18 35								↪								20 35	
London Euston 15 ⊖	a			18 01		18 09	18 44	18 53			19 01			19 09			19 43		20 01		20 09	20 44		20 53	

A 🛒 to Stafford

B from 8 January until 25 March. 🛒 to Stafford

C until 1 January and then from 1 April. 🛒 to Stafford

Table 67

Sundays

Crewe and Stoke-on-Trent - London
Nuneaton - Coventry

Network Diagram - see first Page of Table 67

		VT	LM	VT	LM	LM	XC	LM		VT	VT	LM	XC	AW	LM	LM	VT	VT		XC	LM	XC			
		◇1	◇1	◇1		◇1	◇1	◇1		◇1	◇1	◇1	◇1	◇	◇1		◇1	◇1		◇1	◇1	◇1			
							A																		
		☕		☕			🛒			☕	☕			🛒			☕	☕							
Crewe	d		19 22	19 29		19 38		20 18		20 24	20 47			20 52	21 18		21 23	21 40			22 22				
Alsager	d					19 46																			
Kidsgrove	d					19 50																			
Hanley Bus Station	d																								
Stoke-on-Trent	d					19 59	20 07						20 47							21 47		22 47			
Wedgwood Old Road Bridge	d																								
Barlaston Orchard Place	d																								
Stone Granville Square	d																								
Stone	d					20 07																			
Norton Bridge Station Drv	d																								
Stafford	d	19 36	19a42			20 18	20 27	20a38		20 43			21a08	21a16	21a38		21 43	22a01		22a06	22a42	23a04			
Rugeley Trent Valley	d					20 27																			
Lichfield Trent Valley	d					20 34											22 00								
Tamworth	d					20 41											22 06								
Polesworth	d																								
Atherstone	d					20 50																			
Nuneaton	a					20 56											22 17								
	d				20 11	20 57										22 00	22 18								
Bedworth	d				20 17											22 06									
Coventry	a				20 34		21 23									22 21									
Rugby	a					21 12											22 31								
Northampton	a					21 40						←													
Milton Keynes Central	a					22 09				21 36	21 55	22 09					23 04								
Watford Junction	a					↪					22s31	22 51					23s34								
London Euston 15 ⊖	a	21 01		21 09						22 27	22 53	23 13					23 54								

A 🛒 to Stafford

Northampton - Coventry - Birmingham - Wolverhampton - Stafford

Network Diagram - see first Page of Table 67

Miles			AW	AW	LM	LM	VT	VT	LM	VT	VT		VT	VT	LM	XC	LM	LM	LM	VT	XC		LM	AW	LM
			TThO	WFO	MO	MX	MO	MO	MO	MX	MO		MX												
					◇1	1	◇1	◇1	1	◇1	◇1		◇1	◇1		◇1	1		1	◇1	◇1		◇1	◇	
							☕	☕		☕	☕		☕	⊠						⊠	🍴			🍴	
—	London Euston 15 ⊖	d			21p28	21p46	21p55	22p25	22p00	22p30	23p25		23p30												
0	**Northampton**	d			22p51	22b55			23c32										05 16				05 42		
9½	Long Buckby	d			23p02	23p06			23p43										05 27						
18¾	Rugby	d			23p13	23p17	23p21	23p48	23p54	00 01	00s46		01 00						05 38				06 05		
32¼	**Coventry**	a			23p25	23p29	23p31	23p57	00 05	00 10	00s58		01 13						05 49						
—		d			23p35	23p30	23p31	23p58		00 10			01 13						05 50						
34	Canley	d			23p38	23p33																			
36	Tile Hill	d			23p42	23p37													05 55						
38	Berkswell	d			23p45	23p40																			
41¼	Hampton-in-Arden	d			23p49	23p44													06 01						
43	**Birmingham International** ✈	a			23p52	23p47	23p42	00 08		00 21	01s09		01 24						06 04						
—		d			23p53	23p48	23p42	00 09		00 21			01 24						06 05						06 17
45	Marston Green	d			23p56	23p51													06 08						
46½	Lea Hall	d				23p54																			06 22
47¾	Stechford	d				23p57																			06 25
49½	Adderley Park	d																							06 28
51½	**Birmingham New Street** 12	a			00 04	00 04	23p54	00 21		00 32	01s22		01 36						06 16						06 33
—		d	23p32	23p32			23p57	00 24		00 35			01 37	05 30	05 51	05 57	06 01	06 06		06 19	06 22			06 24	
54¾	Smethwick Rolfe Street	d																06 12							
55½	Smethwick Galton Bridge 7	d															06 08	06 14						06 30	
56¾	Sandwell & Dudley	d													05 59			06 17							
57¾	Dudley Port	d																06 20							
58½	Tipton	d																06 22							
60	Coseley	d																06 25							
64¼	**Wolverhampton** 7 🚌	a	00 01	00 02			00 15	00 43		01 03	01 53		02 07	05 47	06 09	06 14	06 19	06 31		06 35	06 39			06 42	
—		d												05 48		06 16	06 19				06 40				
74¼	Penkridge	d															06 29								
79½	**Stafford**	a												06 01		06 29	06 35				06 53		06 58		

		LM	LM	LM	XC	LM	LM		LM	LM	VT	AW	VT	LM	LM	XC	LM		LM	VT	XC	LM	LM	LM	VT
		◇1		1	◇1	1	◇1			1	◇1	◇	◇1	◇1		◇1	◇1			◇1	◇1	1	1		◇1
					🍴						⊠	🍴	⊠			🍴				⊠	🍴				⊠
London Euston 15 ⊖	d												06 03							06 23			05 30		06 43
Northampton	d					05 55				06 16				06 41									06 55		
Long Buckby	d					06 06				06 27													07 06		
Rugby	d					06 17				06 38			06 51	07 01									07 17		
Coventry	a					06 29				06 49			07 02							07 22			07 29		07 42
	d			06 10		06 30				06 50			07 02						07 07	07 22	07 27		07 30		07 42
Canley	d			06 13		06 33													07 09				07 33		
Tile Hill	d			06 17		06 37				06 55									07 13				07 37		
Berkswell	d			06 20		06 40													07 16				07 40		
Hampton-in-Arden	d			06 24						07 01									07 20						
Birmingham International ✈	a			06 27		06 45				07 04			07 13						07 23	07 33	07 37		07 45		07 53
	d			06 28		06 46				07 05		07 09	07 13				07 17		07 24	07 33	07 38		07 46		07 53
Marston Green	d			06 31		06 49				07 08									07 27				07 49		
Lea Hall	d					06 52											07 22						07 52		
Stechford	d					06 55											07 25						07 55		
Adderley Park	d																07 28						07 58		
Birmingham New Street 12	a			06 39		07 01				07 16		07 19	07 27				07 32		07 36	07 45	07 48		08 03		08 08
	d	06 36	06 38		06 57		07 01		07 08		07 20	07 24			07 27	07 31	07 36		07 38	07 49	07 57	08 01		08 05	
Smethwick Rolfe Street	d		06 44						07 14										07 44						
Smethwick Galton Bridge 7	d		06 46				07 08		07 16			07 30							07 46			08 08			
Sandwell & Dudley	d		06 49						07 19										07 49	07 58				08 13	
Dudley Port	d		06 52						07 22										07 52						
Tipton	d		06 54						07 24										07 54						
Coseley	d		06 57						07 27								07 46		07 57						
Wolverhampton 7 🚌	a	06 52	07 03		07 14		07 19		07 33		07 37	07 41			07 45	07 48	07 53		08 03	08 11	08 14	08 19		08 24	
	d	06 53			07 15		07 19									07 49	07 53				08 15	08 19			
Penkridge	d						07 29										08 03					08 29			
Stafford	a	07 08			07 29		07 36							07 53		08 00	08 09				08 29	08 35			

b Previous night, arr. 2249

c Previous night, arr. 2320

Northampton - Coventry - Birmingham - Wolverhampton - Stafford

Network Diagram - see first Page of Table 67

		LM	LM 1		VT ◇1 ⊠	AW ◇ ⊥	VT ◇1 ⊠	LM ◇1	XC ◇1 ⊥	LM	LM ◇1	LM	LM 1		VT ◇1 ⊠	XC ◇1 ⊥	LM 1	LM ◇1	LM	VT ◇1 ⊠	LM	LM 1	VT ◇1 ⊠		AW ◇ ⊥
London Euston 15 ⊖	d						07 03	06 24							07 23					07 43		07 13			
Northampton	d		07 16					07 45									07 55					08 16			
Long Buckby	d		07 27														08 06					08 27			
Rugby	d		07 38				07 51	08 04									08 17					08 38			
Coventry	a		07 49				08 02								08 22		08 29			08 42		08 49			
	d		07 50				08 02						08 11		08 22	08 27	08 30			08 42		08 50			
Canley	d												08 14				08 33								
Tile Hill	d		07 55										08 18				08 37					08 55			
Berkswell	d												08 21				08 40								
Hampton-in-Arden	d		08 01										08 25									09 01			
Birmingham International ✈	a		08 04				08 12						08 28		08 33	08 37	08 45			08 53		09 04			
	d		08 05			08 09	08 13			08 17			08 29		08 33	08 38	08 46			08 53		09 05			09 09
Marston Green	d		08 08							08 20			08 32				08 49					09 08			
Lea Hall	d									08 23							08 52								
Stechford	d									08 26							08 55								
Adderley Park	d									08 29															
Birmingham New Street 12	a		08 16			08 19	08 27			08 33			08 42		08 45	08 48	09 01			09 08		09 16			09 20
	d	08 08			08 20	08 24			08 31		08 36	08 38			08 49	08 57		09 01	09 05		09 08		09 20		09 24
Smethwick Rolfe Street	d	08 14										08 44									09 14				
Smethwick Galton Bridge 7	d	08 16				08 30						08 46						09 08			09 16				09 30
Sandwell & Dudley	d	08 19										08 49			08 58				09 13		09 19				
Dudley Port	d	08 22										08 52									09 22				
Tipton	d	08 24										08 54									09 24				
Coseley	d	08 27									08 46	08 57									09 27				
Wolverhampton 7 ⛴	a	08 33			08 37	08 42			08 48		08 53	09 03			09 11	09 14		09 19	09 24		09 33		09 37		09 43
	d								08 49		08 53					09 15		09 19							
Penkridge	d										09 03														
Stafford	a							08 53	09 00		09 09					09 29		09 34							

		VT ◇1 ⊠	LM ◇1	XC ◇1 ⊥	LM	LM ◇1	LM	LM 1	VT ◇1 ⊠		XC ◇1 ⊥	LM 1	LM ◇1	LM	VT ◇1 ⊠	LM	LM 1	VT ◇1 ⊠	AW ◇ ⊥		LM 1	VT ◇1 ⊠	XC ◇1 ⊥	LM	LM ◇1
London Euston 15 ⊖	d	08 03	07 47						08 23						08 43		08 13					09 03			
Northampton	d		08 45									08 55					09 16				09 25				
Long Buckby	d											09 06					09 27				09 36				
Rugby	d	08 51	09 04									09 17					09 38				09 47	09 51			
Coventry	a	09 02							09 22			09 29			09 42		09 49				09 58	10 02			
	d	09 02						09 11	09 22		09 27	09 30			09 42		09 50				10 11	10 02			
Canley	d							09 14				09 33									10 14				
Tile Hill	d							09 18				09 37					09 55				10 18				
Berkswell	d							09 21				09 40									10 21				
Hampton-in-Arden	d							09 25									10 01				10 25				
Birmingham International ✈	a	09 12						09 28	09 33		09 37	09 45			09 53		10 04				10 28	10 13			
	d	09 13			09 17			09 29	09 33		09 38	09 46			09 53		10 05		10 09		10 29	10 13		10 17	
Marston Green	d							09 32				09 49					10 08				10 32				
Lea Hall	d				09 22							09 52												10 21	
Stechford	d				09 25							09 55												10 24	
Adderley Park	d				09 28																			10 27	
Birmingham New Street 12	a	09 27			09 33			09 42	09 45		09 48	10 01			10 08		10 16		10 19		10 42	10 27		10 33	
	d			09 31		09 36	09 38		09 49		09 57		10 01	10 05		10 08		10 20	10 24				10 31		10 36
Smethwick Rolfe Street	d						09 44									10 14									
Smethwick Galton Bridge 7	d						09 46						10 08			10 16			10 30						
Sandwell & Dudley	d						09 49		09 58					10 13		10 19									
Dudley Port	d						09 52									10 22									
Tipton	d						09 54									10 24									
Coseley	d					09 46	09 57									10 27									10 46
Wolverhampton 7 ⛴	a			09 48		09 53	10 03		10 11		10 14		10 19	10 24		10 33		10 37	10 42				10 48		10 53
	d			09 49		09 53					10 15		10 19										10 49		10 53
Penkridge	d					10 03																			11 03
Stafford	a		09 53	10 00		10 09					10 29		10 34										11 00		11 09

Table 68

Mondays to Fridays

Northampton - Coventry - Birmingham - Wolverhampton - Stafford

Network Diagram - see first Page of Table 67

		LM	VT	XC	LM			LM	LM	LM	VT	LM		AW	LM	VT		LM	XC	LM	LM	LM	VT	XC	LM
			◇1	◇1	◇1			◇1			◇1	1		◇	1	◇1		◇1	◇1		◇1		◇1	◇1	1
			⊠	🛒							🍽			🛒		⊠			🛒				⊠	🛒	
London Euston 15 ⊖	d		09 23		08 46						09 43	09 13				10 03		09 46					10 23		
Northampton	d				09 45	09 55						10 16			10 25			10 45							10 55
Long Buckby	d					10 06						10 27			10 36										11 06
Rugby	d				10 04	10 17						10 38			10 47	10 51		11 04							11 17
Coventry	a		10 22			10 29					10 42	10 49			10 58	11 02							11 22		11 29
	d		10 22	10 27		10 30					10 42	10 50			11 11	11 02							11 22	11 27	11 30
Canley	d					10 33									11 14										11 33
Tile Hill	d					10 37						10 55			11 18										11 37
Berkswell	d					10 40									11 21										11 40
Hampton-in-Arden	d											11 01			11 25										
Birmingham International ✈	a		10 33	10 37		10 45					10 53	11 04			11 28	11 13							11 33	11 37	11 45
	d		10 33	10 38		10 46					10 53	11 05		11 09	11 29	11 13				11 17			11 33	11 38	11 46
Marston Green	d					10 49						11 08			11 32										11 49
Lea Hall	d					10 52														11 21					11 52
Stechford	d					10 55														11 24					11 55
Adderley Park	d																			11 27					
Birmingham New Street 12	a		10 45	10 48		11 01					11 08	11 16		11 20	11 42	11 27				11 33			11 45	11 48	12 01
	d	10 38	10 49	10 57				11 01	11 05	11 08	11 20			11 24					11 31		11 36	11 38	11 49	11 57	
Smethwick Rolfe Street	d	10 44								11 14												11 44			
Smethwick Galton Bridge 7	d	10 46						11 08		11 16				11 30								11 46			
Sandwell & Dudley	d	10 49	10 58						11 13	11 19												11 49	11 58		
Dudley Port	d	10 52								11 22												11 52			
Tipton	d	10 54								11 24												11 54			
Coseley	d	10 57								11 27											11 46	11 57			
Wolverhampton 7 ⛴	a	11 03	11 11	11 14				11 19	11 24	11 33	11 37			11 42					11 48		11 53	12 03	12 11	12 14	
	d			11 15				11 19											11 49		11 53			12 15	
Penkridge	d																				12 03				
Stafford	a			11 28	10 53			11 34										11 53	12 00		12 09			12 29	

		LM		LM	VT	LM	LM	VT	AW	LM	VT	LM		XC	LM	LM	LM	VT	XC	LM	LM	LM		VT FX	LM
		◇1			◇1		1	◇1	◇	1	◇1	◇1		◇1		◇1		◇1	◇1	1	◇1			◇1	
					⊠			🍽	🛒		🍽			🛒				🍽	🛒					🍽	
London Euston 15 ⊖	d				10 43		10 13				11 03	10 46						11 23						11 43	
Northampton	d						11 16			11 25		11 45								11 55					
Long Buckby	d						11 27			11 36										12 06					
Rugby	d						11 38			11 47	11 51	12 04								12 17					
Coventry	a				11 42		11 49			11 58	12 02							12 22		12 29				12 43	
	d				11 42		11 50			12 11	12 02							12 22	12 27	12 30				12 43	
Canley	d									12 14										12 33					
Tile Hill	d						11 55			12 18										12 37					
Berkswell	d									12 21										12 40					
Hampton-in-Arden	d						12 01			12 25															
Birmingham International ✈	a				11 53		12 04			12 28	12 13							12 33	12 37	12 45				12 54	
	d				11 53		12 05		12 09	12 29	12 13				12 17			12 33	12 38	12 46				12 54	
Marston Green	d						12 08			12 32										12 49					
Lea Hall	d														12 21					12 52					
Stechford	d														12 24					12 55					
Adderley Park	d														12 27										
Birmingham New Street 12	a				12 08		12 16		12 20	12 42	12 27				12 33			12 45	12 48	13 01				13 08	
	d	12 01		12 05		12 08		12 20	12 24					12 31		12 36	12 38	12 49	12 57		13 01	13 05			13 08
Smethwick Rolfe Street	d					12 14											12 44								13 14
Smethwick Galton Bridge 7	d	12 08				12 16			12 30								12 46				13 08				13 16
Sandwell & Dudley	d			12 13		12 19											12 49	12 58				13 13			13 19
Dudley Port	d					12 22											12 52								13 22
Tipton	d					12 24											12 54								13 24
Coseley	d					12 27										12 46	12 57								13 27
Wolverhampton 7 ⛴	a	12 19		12 24		12 33		12 37	12 42					12 48		12 53	13 03	13 11	13 14		13 19	13 24			13 33
	d	12 19												12 49		12 53			13 15		13 19				
Penkridge	d															13 03									
Stafford	a	12 34										12 53		13 00		13 09			13 29		13 34				

Northampton - Coventry - Birmingham - Wolverhampton - Stafford

Network Diagram - see first Page of Table 67

		LM	VT	AW	LM	VT	XC	LM	LM	LM	VT	XC	LM		LM	LM	VT	LM	LM	VT	AW	LM	VT
		■1	◇■1	◇	■1	◇■1	◇■1		◇■1		◇■1	◇■1	◇■1		◇■1		◇■1		■1	◇■1	◇	■1	◇■1
			☕	🛒		☕	🛒				☕	🛒					☕			☕	🛒		☕
London Euston [15] ⊖	d	11 13				12 03					12 23		11 46				12 43		12 13				13 03
Northampton	d	12 16			12 25								12 45	12 55					13 16			13 25	
Long Buckby	d	12 27			12 36									13 06					13 27			13 36	
Rugby	d	12 38			12 47	12 51							13 04	13 17					13 38			13 47	13 51
Coventry	a	12 49			12 58	13 02					13 22			13 29			13 42		13 49			13 58	14 02
	d	12 50			13 11	13 02					13 22	13 27		13 30			13 42		13 50			14 11	14 02
Canley	d				13 14									13 33								14 14	
Tile Hill	d	12 55			13 18									13 37					13 55			14 18	
Berkswell	d				13 21									13 40								14 21	
Hampton-in-Arden	d	13 01			13 25														14 01			14 25	
Birmingham International ✈	a	13 04			13 28	13 13					13 33	13 37		13 45			13 53		14 04			14 28	14 13
	d	13 05		13 09	13 29	13 13		13 17			13 33	13 38		13 46			13 53		14 05		14 09	14 29	14 13
Marston Green	d	13 08			13 32									13 49					14 08			14 32	
Lea Hall	d							13 21						13 52									
Stechford	d							13 24						13 55									
Adderley Park	d							13 27															
Birmingham New Street [12]	a	13 16		13 22	13 42	13 27		13 33			13 45	13 48		14 01			14 08		14 16		14 19	14 42	14 27
	d		13 20	13 24			13 31		13 36	13 38	13 49	13 57			14 01	14 05		14 08		14 20	14 24		
Smethwick Rolfe Street	d									13 44								14 14					
Smethwick Galton Bridge [7]	d			13 30						13 46					14 08			14 16			14 30		
Sandwell & Dudley	d									13 49	13 58					14 13		14 19					
Dudley Port	d									13 52								14 22					
Tipton	d									13 54								14 24					
Coseley	d								13 46	13 57								14 27					
Wolverhampton [7] 🚢	a		13 37	13 42			13 48		13 53	14 03	14 11	14 14			14 19	14 24		14 33		14 37	14 42		
	d						13 49		13 53			14 15			14 19								
Penkridge	d								14 03														
Stafford	a						14 00		14 09			14 29	13 53		14 34								

		XC	LM	LM	LM	VT	XC	LM		LM	LM	VT	LM	LM	VT	AW	LM	VT	LM	XC	LM	LM
		◇■1		◇■1		◇■1	◇■1	◇■1		◇■1		◇■1		■1	◇■1	◇	■1	◇■1	◇■1	◇■1		◇■1
		🛒				☕	🛒					☕			☕	🛒		☕		🛒		
London Euston [15] ⊖	d					13 23		12 46				13 43		13 13				14 03	13 46			
Northampton	d							13 45	13 55					14 16			14 25		14 45			
Long Buckby	d								14 06					14 27			14 36					
Rugby	d							14 04	14 17					14 38			14 47	14 51	15 04			
Coventry	a					14 22			14 29			14 42		14 49			14 58	15 02				
	d					14 22	14 27		14 30			14 42		14 50			15 11	15 02				
Canley	d								14 33								15 14					
Tile Hill	d								14 37					14 55			15 18					
Berkswell	d								14 40								15 21					
Hampton-in-Arden	d													15 01			15 25					
Birmingham International ✈	a					14 33	14 37		14 45			14 53		15 04			15 28	15 13				
	d		14 17			14 33	14 38		14 46			14 53		15 05		15 09	15 29	15 13			15 17	
Marston Green	d								14 49					15 08			15 32					
Lea Hall	d		14 21						14 52												15 21	
Stechford	d		14 24						14 55												15 24	
Adderley Park	d		14 27																		15 27	
Birmingham New Street [12]	a		14 33			14 45	14 48		15 01			15 08		15 16		15 19	15 42	15 27			15 33	
	d	14 31		14 36	14 38	14 49	14 57			15 01	15 05		15 08		15 20	15 26				15 31		15 36
Smethwick Rolfe Street	d				14 44								15 14									
Smethwick Galton Bridge [7]	d				14 46					15 08			15 16			15 32						
Sandwell & Dudley	d				14 49	14 58					15 13		15 19									
Dudley Port	d				14 52								15 22									
Tipton	d				14 54								15 24									
Coseley	d			14 46	14 57								15 27									15 46
Wolverhampton [7] 🚢	a	14 48		14 53	15 03	15 11	15 14			15 19	15 24		15 33		15 37	15 44				15 49		15 53
	d	14 49		14 53			15 15			15 19										15 50		15 53
Penkridge	d			15 03																		16 03
Stafford	a	15 00		15 09			15 29	14 53		15 34									15 53	16 01		16 09

Northampton - Coventry - Birmingham - Wolverhampton - Stafford

Network Diagram - see first Page of Table 67

		LM	VT	XC	LM	LM	LM	VT	LM	LM		VT	AW	VT	XC	LM	LM	LM	LM	VT		XC	LM	LM	
			◇1 🍴	◇1 🛒	1	◇1		◇1 🍴		1		R 1 🍴	R 🛒	◇1 🍴	◇1 🛒		◇1		1	◇1 🍴		◇1 🛒	◇1	◇1	
London Euston 15 ⊖	d		14 23					14 43		14 13				15 03						15 23				14 46	
Northampton	d				14 55					15 16									15 35					15 45	15 55
Long Buckby	d				15 06					15 27									15 46						16 06
Rugby	d				15 17					15 38				15 51					15 59					16 04	16 17
Coventry	a		15 22		15 29			15 42		15 49				16 02					16 10	16 22					16 29
	d		15 22	15 27	15 30			15 42		15 50				16 02					16 11	16 22		16 27			16 30
Canley	d				15 33														16 14						16 33
Tile Hill	d				15 37					15 55									16 18						16 37
Berkswell	d				15 40														16 21						16 40
Hampton-in-Arden	d									16 01									16 25						
Birmingham International ✈	a		15 33	15 37	15 45			15 53		16 04				16 13					16 28	16 33		16 37			16 45
	d		15 33	15 38	15 46			15 53		16 05			16 09	16 13		16 17			16 29	16 33		16 38			16 46
Marston Green	d				15 49					16 08									16 32						16 49
Lea Hall	d				15 52											16 21									16 52
Stechford	d				15 55											16 24									16 55
Adderley Park	d															16 27									
Birmingham New Street 12	a		15 45	15 48	16 01			16 08		16 16			16 20	16 27		16 33			16 42	16 45		16 48			17 02
	d	15 38	15 49	15 57		16 01	16 05		16 08			16 20	16 24		16 31		16 36	16 38		16 49		16 57	17 01		
Smethwick Rolfe Street	d	15 44							16 14									16 44							
Smethwick Galton Bridge 7	d	15 46				16 08			16 16				16 30					16 46					17 08		
Sandwell & Dudley	d	15 49	15 58				16 13		16 19									16 49		16 58					
Dudley Port	d	15 52							16 22									16 53							
Tipton	d	15 54							16 24									16 55							
Coseley	d	15 57							16 27								16 46	16 58							
Wolverhampton 7 🚌	a	16 03	16 11	16 14		16 19	16 24		16 33			16 37	16 42		16 48		16 53	17 04		17 11		17 14	17 19		
	d			16 15		16 19									16 49		16 53					17 15	17 19		
Penkridge	d																17 03						17 29		
Stafford	a			16 30		16 34									17 00		17 09					17 29	17 35	16 54	

		LM	VT	LM	LM	VT		AW	VT	XC	LM	LM	LM	LM	LM	VT		XC	LM		LM	LM	VT	LM	LM
			◇1 🍴		1	R 1 🍴		◇ 🛒	◇1 🍴	◇1 🛒		1		1		◇1 🍴		◇1 🛒	◇1		◇1		◇1 🍴		1
London Euston 15 ⊖	d		15 43		15 13				16 03							16 23			15 46				16 43		15 54
Northampton	d				16 16														16 45	16 55					17 16
Long Buckby	d				16 27															17 06					17 27
Rugby	d				16 38				16 51										17 04	17 17					17 38
Coventry	a		16 42		16 49				17 02							17 22				17 29			17 42		17 49
	d		16 42		16 50				17 02					17 11		17 22		17 27		17 30			17 42		17 50
Canley	d													17 14						17 33					
Tile Hill	d				16 55									17 18						17 37					17 55
Berkswell	d													17 21						17 40					
Hampton-in-Arden	d				17 01									17 25											18 01
Birmingham International ✈	a		16 53		17 04				17 13					17 28		17 33		17 37		17 45			17 53		18 04
	d		16 53		17 05			17 09	17 13		17 17			17 29		17 33		17 38		17 46			17 53		18 05
Marston Green	d				17 08									17 32						17 49					18 08
Lea Hall	d										17 21									17 52					
Stechford	d										17 24									17 55					
Adderley Park	d										17 27														
Birmingham New Street 12	a		17 08		17 16			17 19	17 27		17 33			17 42		17 45		17 48		18 01			18 08		18 17
	d	17 05		17 08		17 20		17 26		17 31		17 36	17 38		17 46	17 49		17 57			18 01	18 05		18 08	
Smethwick Rolfe Street	d			17 14									17 44											18 14	
Smethwick Galton Bridge 7	d			17 16				17 32					17 46								18 08			18 16	
Sandwell & Dudley	d	17 13		17 19									17 49			17 58						18 13		18 19	
Dudley Port	d			17 22									17 52		17 56									18 22	
Tipton	d			17 24									17 54		17 58									18 24	
Coseley	d			17 27								17 46	17 57											18 27	
Wolverhampton 7 🚌	a	17 24		17 33		17 37		17 44		17 49		17 53	18 03		18 06	18 11		18 14			18 19	18 24		18 33	
	d									17 50		17 53						18 15			18 19				
Penkridge	d											18 02									18 29				
Stafford	a									18 01		18 09						18 29	18 01		18 35				

Northampton - Coventry - Birmingham - Wolverhampton - Stafford

Network Diagram - see first Page of Table 67

		VT		AW	VT	XC	LM	LM	LM	LM	VT	XC		LM	LM	LM	VT	LM	LM	VT	AW	VT		LM	XC
		◇1 ☕		◇ 🛒	◇1 ⊠	◇1 🛒		◇1		1	◇1 ⊠	◇1 🛒		◇1	◇1		◇1 ⊠		1	◇1 ☕	◇ 🛒	◇1 ⊠		1	◇1 🛒
London Euston 15 ⊖	d				17 03						17 23			16 48			17 43		17 13			18 03		17 24	
Northampton	d													17 55					18 16					18 40	
Long Buckby	d													18 06					18 27					18 51	
Rugby	d				17 51									18 17					18 38			18 51		19a03	
Coventry	a				18 02						18 22			18 29			18 42		18 49			19 02			
	d				18 02					18 11	18 22	18 27		18 30			18 42		18 50			19 02			
Canley	d									18 14				18 33											
Tile Hill	d									18 18				18 37					18 55						
Berkswell	d									18 21				18 40											
Hampton-in-Arden	d									18 25									19 01						
Birmingham International ✈	a				18 13					18 28	18 33	18 37		18 45			18 53		19 04			19 13			
	d			18 09	18 13		18 17			18 29	18 33	18 38		18 46			18 53		19 05		19 09	19 13			
Marston Green	d									18 32				18 49					19 08						
Lea Hall	d						18 21							18 52											
Stechford	d						18 24							18 55											
Adderley Park	d						18 27																		
Birmingham New Street 12	a			18 20	18 27		18 33			18 42	18 45	18 48		19 01			19 08		19 17		19 20	19 27			
	d	18 20		18 24		18 31		18 36	18 38		18 49	18 57			19 01	19 05		19 08		19 20	19 24				19 31
Smethwick Rolfe Street	d								18 44									19 14							
Smethwick Galton Bridge 7	d			18 30					18 46						19 08			19 16			19 30				
Sandwell & Dudley	d								18 49		18 58					19 13		19 19							
Dudley Port	d								18 52									19 22							
Tipton	d								18 54									19 24							
Coseley	d							18 46	18 57									19 27							
Wolverhampton 7 ⛴	a	18 37		18 42		18 48		18 53	19 03		19 11	19 14			19 19	19 24		19 33		19 37	19 42				19 48
	d					18 49		18 53				19 15			19 19										19 49
Penkridge	d							19 03							19 29										
Stafford	a					19 00		19 09				19 27			19 36										20 00

		LM	LM	LM	LM	VT	XC	LM		LM	LM	VT	LM	AW	VT	LM	XC	LM		LM	LM	LM	VT	XC	LM
			◇1		1	◇1 ⊠	◇1 A 🛒	1				◇1 ⊠	◇1	◇	Ⓡ 1 ☕	◇1	◇1			◇1		1	Ⓡ 1 ☕	◇1 A 🛒	1
London Euston 15 ⊖	d					18 23		17 46				18 43	18 13		19 03	18 29							19 23		18 49
Northampton	d							18 55					19 16			19 45									19 55
Long Buckby	d							19 06					19 27												20 06
Rugby	d							19 17					19 38		19 51	20a04									20 17
Coventry	a					19 22		19 29				19 42	19 49		20 02								20 22		20 29
	d				19 11	19 22	19 27	19 30				19 42	19 50		20 02							20 11	20 22	20 27	20 30
Canley	d				19 14			19 33														20 14			20 33
Tile Hill	d				19 18			19 37					19 55									20 18			20 37
Berkswell	d				19 21			19 40														20 21			20 40
Hampton-in-Arden	d				19 25								20 01									20 25			
Birmingham International ✈	a				19 28	19 33	19 37	19 45				19 53	20 04		20 13							20 28	20 33	20 37	20 45
	d	19 17			19 29	19 33	19 38	19 46				19 53	20 05	20 09	20 13			20 17				20 29	20 33	20 38	20 46
Marston Green	d				19 32			19 49					20 08									20 32			20 49
Lea Hall	d	19 21						19 52										20 21							20 52
Stechford	d	19 24						19 55										20 24							20 55
Adderley Park	d	19 27																20 27							
Birmingham New Street 12	a	19 33			19 42	19 45	19 48	20 01				20 06	20 16	20 20	20 27			20 33				20 42	20 45	20 48	21 01
	d		19 36	19 38		19 50	19 57			20 05	20 08	20 20		20 24			20 31			20 36	20 38		20 50	20 57	
Smethwick Rolfe Street	d			19 44							20 14										20 44				
Smethwick Galton Bridge 7	d			19 46							20 16			20 30							20 46				
Sandwell & Dudley	d			19 49		19 59				20 13	20 19										20 49		20 59		
Dudley Port	d			19 52							20 22										20 52				
Tipton	d			19 54							20 24										20 54				
Coseley	d		19 46	19 57							20 27									20 46	20 57				
Wolverhampton 7 ⛴	a		19 53	20 03		20 12	20 14			20 24	20 33	20 36		20 42			20 48			20 53	21 04		21 12	21 14	
	d		19 53				20 16					20 36								20 53				21 16	
Penkridge	d		20 03																	21 03					
Stafford	a		20 09				20 29					20 49								21 09				21 31	

A 🛒 to Birmingham New Street

Northampton - Coventry - Birmingham - Wolverhampton - Stafford

Network Diagram - see first Page of Table 67

Station		LM	LM	VT		LM	VT	AW	VT	LM	LM	LM	LM	VT		XC	LM	LM	VT	LM	LM	XC	VT	LM
				◇1 ☕		1	◇1 ☕		◇1 ☕		◇1		1	◇1 ☕		◇1	1		◇1 ☕	1		◇1	◇1 ☕	◇1
London Euston 15 ⊖	d			19 43		19 13			20 03					20 23			19 46		20 43	19 54			21 03	
Northampton	d					20 16											20 55			21 16				
Long Buckby	d					20 27											21 06			21 27				
Rugby	d					20 38			20 51								21 17			21 38			21 57	
Coventry	a			20 42		20 49			21 02					21 22			21 29		21 42	21 49			22 06	
	d			20 42		20 50			21 02				21 11	21 22		21 27	21 30		21 42	21 50			22 07	
Canley	d												21 14				21 33							
Tile Hill	d					20 55							21 18				21 37			21 55				
Berkswell	d												21 21				21 40							
Hampton-in-Arden	d					21 01							21 25							22 01				
Birmingham International ✈	a			20 53		21 04			21 13				21 28	21 33		21 37	21 45		21 53	22 04			22 18	
	d			20 53		21 05		21 09	21 13	21 17			21 29	21 33		21 38	21 46		21 53	22 05			22 18	
Marston Green	d					21 08							21 32				21 49			22 08				
Lea Hall	d									21 21							21 52							
Stechford	d									21 24							21 55							
Adderley Park	d									21 27														
Birmingham New Street 12	a			21 06		21 16		21 19	21 25	21 33			21 42	21 46		21 48	22 01		22 06	22 16			22 29	
	d	21 05	21 08	21 13			21 20	21 24	21 28		21 36	21 38		21 50		21 57		22 08	22 13		22 21	22 30	22 32	22 36
Smethwick Rolfe Street	d		21 14									21 44						22 14						
Smethwick Galton Bridge 7	d		21 16					21 30				21 46						22 16						22 43
Sandwell & Dudley	d	21 13	21 19	21 24								21 49		21 59				22 19	22 24		22 29		22 41	
Dudley Port	d		21 22									21 52						22 22						
Tipton	d		21 24									21 54						22 24						
Coseley	d		21 27								21 46	21 57						22 27						22 50
Wolverhampton 7	a	21 24	21 33	21 38			21 40	21 42	21 56		21 53	22 03		22 12		22 14		22 33	22 38		22 41	22 47	22 56	22 57
	d						21 41				21 53					22 16						22 48		22 57
Penkridge	d										22 03													23 07
Stafford	a						21 53				22 09					22 29						23 00		23 13

Station		LM	LM	LM	XC	AW	LM	LM	VT	LM		AW MW FO	AW TThO	XC	LM	VT	VT FX	VT FO
				1	◇1	◇	1	◇1	◇1 ☕	1		A	B	◇1	1	◇1 ☕	◇1 ☕	◇1 ☕
London Euston 15 ⊖	d						20 46		21 43	21 13					21 46	22 30	23 30	23 30
Northampton	d						21 55			22 16					22 55			
Long Buckby	d						22 06			22 27					23 06			
Rugby	d						22 17			22 38					23 17	00 01	01 00	01 05
Coventry	a						22 29		22 46	22 49					23 29	00 10	01 13	01 18
	d			22 11	22 24		22 30		22 46	22 50				23 27	23 30	00 10	01 13	01 18
Canley	d			22 14			22 33								23 33			
Tile Hill	d			22 18			22 37			22 55					23 37			
Berkswell	d			22 21			22 40								23 40			
Hampton-in-Arden	d			22 25						23 01					23 44			
Birmingham International ✈	a			22 28	22 33		22 45		23 00	23 06				23 36	23 47	00 21	01 24	01 29
	d	22 22		22 29	22 34		22 46		23 01	23 07				23 37	23 48	00 21	01 24	01 29
Marston Green	d			22 32			22 49			23 10					23 51			
Lea Hall	d	22 26					22 52								23 54			
Stechford	d	22 29					22 55								23 57			
Adderley Park	d	22 32																
Birmingham New Street 12	a	22 38		22 42	22 45		23 02		23 16	23 19				23 57	00 04	00 32	01 36	01 41
	d		22 38			22 55		23 09	23 20			23 32	23 32			00 35	01 37	01 42
Smethwick Rolfe Street	d		22 44					23 15										
Smethwick Galton Bridge 7	d		22 46					23 17										
Sandwell & Dudley	d		22 49					23 20	23 34									
Dudley Port	d		22 52					23 24										
Tipton	d		22 54					23 26										
Coseley	d		22 57					23 29										
Wolverhampton 7	a		23 03			23 11		23 35	23 47			00 01	00 02			01 03	02 07	02 10
	d					23 13		23 36										
Penkridge	d							23 46										
Stafford	a					23 30		23 52										

Northampton - Coventry - Birmingham - Wolverhampton - Stafford

Network Diagram - see first Page of Table 67

		AW	LM	VT	VT	VT	XC	LM	LM	LM		VT	AW	XC	LM	LM	LM	LM	XC	LM		LM	LM	LM	LM
			1	◇1 🍴	◇1 🍴	◇1 🍴	◇1	◇1	◇1			◇1 🍴	◇ 🛒	◇1 🛒		◇1		1	◇1 🛒	◇1		◇1			◇1
London Euston 15 ⊖	d		21p46	22p30	23p30																				
Northampton	d		22b55						05 42											05 55					06 16
Long Buckby	d		23p06																	06 06					06 27
Rugby	d		23p17	00 01	01 05				06 05											06 17					06 38
Coventry	a		23p29	00 10	01 18															06 29					06 49
	d		23p30	00 10	01 18													06 10		06 30					06 50
Canley	d		23p33															06 13		06 33					
Tile Hill	d		23p37															06 17		06 37					06 55
Berkswell	d		23p40															06 20		06 40					
Hampton-in-Arden	d		23p44															06 24							07 01
Birmingham International ✈	a		23p47	00 21	01 29													06 27		06 45					07 04
	d		23p48	00 21	01 29										06 17			06 28		06 46					07 05
Marston Green	d		23p51															06 31		06 49					07 08
Lea Hall	d		23p54												06 21					06 52					
Stechford	d		23p57												06 24					06 55					
Adderley Park	d														06 27										
Birmingham New Street 12	a		00 04	00 32	01 41										06 32			06 39		07 01					07 16
	d	23p32		00 35	01 42	05 30	05 57	06 01		06 08		06 20	06 24	06 31		06 36	06 38		06 57			07 01	07 05	07 08	
Smethwick Rolfe Street	d									06 14							06 44							07 14	
Smethwick Galton Bridge 7	d							06 07		06 16			06 30				06 46					07 07		07 16	
Sandwell & Dudley	d									06 19							06 49						07 13	07 19	
Dudley Port	d									06 22							06 52							07 22	
Tipton	d									06 24							06 54							07 24	
Coseley	d									06 27							06 57							07 27	
Wolverhampton 7 🚌	a	00 01		01 03	02 10	05 47	06 14	06 18		06 33		06 37	06 42	06 48		06 54	07 03		07 14			07 18	07 24	07 33	
	d					05 48	06 16	06 18						06 49		06 54			07 15			07 18			
Penkridge	d							06 29														07 30			
Stafford	a					06 00	06 29	06 35	06 54					07 00		07 08			07 29			07 36			

		LM	VT	AW	XC	LM		LM	LM	LM	VT	XC	LM	LM	LM	LM		LM	VT	AW	VT	XC	LM	LM	LM
		◇1	◇1 🍴	◇ 🛒	◇1 🛒			◇1		1	◇1 🍴	◇1 🛒	◇1	◇1				◇1	◇1 🍴	◇ 🛒	◇1 🍴	◇1 🍴		◇1	
London Euston 15 ⊖	d										06 23		05 34								07 03				
Northampton	d	06 38											06 55					07 16							
Long Buckby	d												07 06					07 27							
Rugby	d	06 58											07 17					07 38			07 51				
Coventry	a										07 22		07 29					07 49			08 02				
	d									07 10	07 22	07 27	07 30					07 50			08 02				
Canley	d									07 13			07 33												
Tile Hill	d									07 17			07 37					07 55							
Berkswell	d									07 20			07 40												
Hampton-in-Arden	d									07 24								08 01							
Birmingham International ✈	a									07 27	07 33	07 37	07 45					08 04			08 13				
	d			07 09		07 17				07 28	07 33	07 38	07 46					08 05		08 09	08 13		08 17		
Marston Green	d									07 31			07 49					08 08							
Lea Hall	d					07 21							07 52										08 21		
Stechford	d					07 24							07 55										08 24		
Adderley Park	d					07 27																	08 27		
Birmingham New Street 12	a			07 19		07 32				07 42	07 45	07 48	08 01					08 16		08 20	08 27		08 32		
	d		07 20	07 23	07 31			07 36	07 38		07 49	07 57		08 01	08 05	08 08			08 20	08 24		08 31		08 36	08 38
Smethwick Rolfe Street	d								07 44							08 14									08 44
Smethwick Galton Bridge 7	d			07 29					07 46					08 08		08 16				08 30					08 46
Sandwell & Dudley	d								07 49		07 58				08 13	08 19									08 49
Dudley Port	d								07 52							08 22									08 52
Tipton	d								07 54							08 24									08 54
Coseley	d							07 46	07 57							08 27								08 46	08 57
Wolverhampton 7 🚌	a		07 37	07 40	07 48			07 53	08 03		08 11	08 14		08 19	08 24	08 33			08 37	08 42		08 48		08 53	09 03
	d				07 49			07 53				08 15		08 19								08 49		08 53	
Penkridge	d							08 03						08 29										09 03	
Stafford	a	07 53			08 00			08 09				08 29		08 35								09 00		09 09	

Table 68

Saturdays

Northampton - Coventry - Birmingham - Wolverhampton - Stafford

Network Diagram - see first Page of Table 67

		LM		LM	VT	XC	LM	LM	LM	VT	LM	LM		VT	AW	VT	XC	LM	LM	LM	LM	LM		VT	XC
		1		◇1	◇1 ☕	◇1 🛒	◇1	◇1		◇1 ☕		◇1		◇1 ☕	◇ 🛒	◇1 ☕	◇1 ☕		◇1		1	◇1		◇1 ☕	◇1 🛒
London Euston 15 ⊖	d			06 24	07 23					07 43						08 03					07 04	07 46		08 23	
Northampton	d	07 37		07 45			07 55					08 16									08 37	08 45			
Long Buckby	d	07 48					08 06					08 27									08 48				
Rugby	d	07 59		08 04			08 17					08 38				08 51					08 59	09 04			
Coventry	a	08 10			08 22		08 29			08 42		08 49				09 02					09 10			09 22	
	d	08 11			08 22	08 27	08 30			08 42		08 50				09 02					09 11			09 22	09 27
Canley	d	08 14					08 33														09 14				
Tile Hill	d	08 18					08 37					08 55									09 18				
Berkswell	d	08 21					08 40														09 21				
Hampton-in-Arden	d	08 25										09 01									09 25				
Birmingham International ✈	a	08 28			08 33	08 37	08 45			08 53		09 04				09 13					09 28			09 33	09 37
	d	08 29			08 33	08 38	08 46			08 53		09 05			09 09	09 13		09 17			09 29			09 33	09 38
Marston Green	d	08 32					08 49					09 08									09 32				
Lea Hall	d						08 52											09 21							
Stechford	d						08 55											09 24							
Adderley Park	d																	09 27							
Birmingham New Street 12	a	08 42			08 45	08 48	09 01			09 08		09 16			09 20	09 27		09 32			09 42			09 45	09 48
	d				08 49	08 57		09 01	09 05		09 08			09 20	09 24		09 31		09 36	09 38				09 49	09 57
Smethwick Rolfe Street	d										09 14									09 44					
Smethwick Galton Bridge 7	d							09 08			09 16				09 30					09 46					
Sandwell & Dudley	d				08 58				09 13		09 19									09 49				09 58	
Dudley Port	d										09 22									09 52					
Tipton	d										09 24									09 54					
Coseley	d										09 27								09 46	09 57					
Wolverhampton 7 ⛴	a				09 11	09 14		09 19	09 24		09 33			09 37	09 43		09 48		09 53	10 03				10 11	10 14
	d					09 15		09 19									09 49		09 53						10 15
Penkridge	d																		10 03						
Stafford	a			08 53		09 29		09 34									10 00		10 09			09 53			10 29

		LM	LM	LM	VT	LM	LM	VT		AW	LM	VT	XC	LM	LM	LM	VT	XC		LM		LM	LM	VT	LM
		◇1	◇1		◇1 ☕		◇1	◇1 ☕		◇ 🛒	1	◇1 ☕	◇1 ☕		◇1		◇1 ☕	◇1 🛒		◇1		◇1		◇1 ☕	
London Euston 15 ⊖	d				08 43		07 54					09 03					09 23			08 46				09 43	
Northampton	d	08 55					09 16				09 25									09 45	09 55				
Long Buckby	d	09 06					09 27				09 36										10 06				
Rugby	d	09 17					09 38				09 47	09 51								10 04	10 17				
Coventry	a	09 29			09 42		09 49				09 58	10 02					10 22				10 29			10 42	
	d	09 30			09 42		09 50				10 11	10 02					10 22	10 27			10 30			10 42	
Canley	d	09 33									10 14										10 33				
Tile Hill	d	09 37					09 55				10 18										10 37				
Berkswell	d	09 40									10 21										10 40				
Hampton-in-Arden	d						10 01				10 25														
Birmingham International ✈	a	09 45			09 53		10 04				10 28	10 13					10 33	10 37			10 45			10 53	
	d	09 46			09 53		10 05			10 09	10 29	10 13		10 17			10 33	10 38			10 46			10 53	
Marston Green	d	09 49					10 08				10 32										10 49				
Lea Hall	d	09 52												10 21							10 52				
Stechford	d	09 55												10 24							10 55				
Adderley Park	d													10 27											
Birmingham New Street 12	a	10 01			10 08		10 16			10 19	10 42	10 27		10 32			10 45	10 48			11 01			11 08	
	d		10 01	10 05		10 08		10 20		10 24			10 31		10 36	10 38	10 49	10 57				11 01	11 05		11 08
Smethwick Rolfe Street	d					10 14										10 44									11 14
Smethwick Galton Bridge 7	d		10 08			10 16				10 30						10 46						11 08			11 16
Sandwell & Dudley	d			10 13		10 19										10 49	10 58						11 13		11 19
Dudley Port	d					10 22										10 52									11 22
Tipton	d					10 24										10 54									11 24
Coseley	d					10 27									10 46	10 57									11 27
Wolverhampton 7 ⛴	a		10 19	10 24		10 33		10 37		10 42			10 48		10 53	11 03	11 11	11 14				11 19	11 24		11 33
	d		10 19										10 49		10 53			11 15				11 19			
Penkridge	d														11 03										
Stafford	a		10 35										11 00		11 09			11 29		10 53		11 35			

Northampton - Coventry - Birmingham - Wolverhampton - Stafford

Network Diagram - see first Page of Table 67

		LM	VT	AW		LM	VT	XC	LM	LM	LM	VT	XC	LM			LM	LM	VT	LM	LM	VT	AW	LM	VT
		◇1	◇1	◇		1	◇1	◇1		◇1		◇1	◇1	◇1			◇1		◇1		◇1	◇1	◇	1	◇1
			☕	🛒			☕	☕				☕	🛒						☕			☕	🛒		☕
London Euston 15 ⊖	d	09 13					10 03					10 23		09 46					10 43		10 13				11 03
Northampton	d	10 16				10 25								10 45	10 55						11 16			11 25	
Long Buckby	d	10 27				10 36									11 06						11 27			11 36	
Rugby	d	10 38				10 48	10 51							11 04	11 17						11 38			11 47	11 51
Coventry	a	10 49				10 59	11 02					11 22			11 29				11 42		11 49			11 58	12 02
	d	10 50				11 11	11 02					11 22	11 27		11 30				11 42		11 50			12 11	12 02
Canley	d					11 14									11 33									12 14	
Tile Hill	d	10 55				11 18									11 37						11 55			12 18	
Berkswell	d					11 21									11 40									12 21	
Hampton-in-Arden	d	11 01				11 25															12 01			12 25	
Birmingham International ✈	a	11 04				11 28	11 13					11 33	11 37		11 45				11 53		12 04			12 28	12 13
	d	11 05		11 09		11 29	11 13		11 17			11 33	11 38		11 46				11 53		12 05		12 09	12 29	12 13
Marston Green	d	11 08				11 32									11 49						12 08			12 32	
Lea Hall	d								11 21						11 52										
Stechford	d								11 24						11 55										
Adderley Park	d								11 27																
Birmingham New Street 12	a	11 16		11 20		11 42	11 27		11 32			11 45	11 48		12 01				12 08		12 16		12 20	12 42	12 27
	d		11 20	11 24				11 31		11 36	11 38	11 49	11 57				12 01	12 05		12 08		12 20	12 24		
Smethwick Rolfe Street	d										11 44									12 14					
Smethwick Galton Bridge 7	d			11 30							11 46						12 08			12 16			12 30		
Sandwell & Dudley	d										11 49	11 58						12 13		12 19					
Dudley Port	d										11 52									12 22					
Tipton	d										11 54									12 24					
Coseley	d									11 46	11 57									12 27					
Wolverhampton 7 ⛴	a		11 37	11 42				11 48		11 53	12 03	12 11	12 14				12 19	12 24		12 33		12 37	12 42		
	d							11 49		11 53			12 15				12 19								
Penkridge	d									12 03															
Stafford	a							12 00		12 09			12 29	11 53			12 35								

			XC	LM	LM	LM	VT	XC	LM		LM		LM	VT	LM	LM	VT	AW	LM	VT	XC		LM	LM	LM
			◇1		◇1		◇1	◇1	◇1		◇1			◇1		◇1	◇1	◇	1	◇1	◇1			◇1	
			☕				☕	🛒						☕			☕	🛒		☕	☕				
London Euston 15 ⊖	d						11 23		10 46					11 43		11 13				12 03					
Northampton	d								11 45	11 55						12 16			12 25						
Long Buckby	d									12 06						12 27			12 36						
Rugby	d								12 04	12 17						12 38			12 47	12 51					
Coventry	a						12 22			12 29				12 42		12 49			12 58	13 02					
	d						12 22	12 27		12 30				12 42		12 50			13 11	13 02					
Canley	d									12 33									13 14						
Tile Hill	d									12 37						12 55			13 18						
Berkswell	d									12 40									13 21						
Hampton-in-Arden	d															13 01			13 25						
Birmingham International ✈	a						12 33	12 37		12 45				12 53		13 04			13 28	13 13					
	d			12 17			12 33	12 38		12 46				12 53		13 05		13 09	13 29	13 13			13 17		
Marston Green	d									12 49						13 08			13 32						
Lea Hall	d			12 21						12 52													13 21		
Stechford	d			12 24						12 55													13 24		
Adderley Park	d			12 27																			13 27		
Birmingham New Street 12	a			12 32			12 45	12 48		13 01				13 08		13 16		13 21	13 42	13 27			13 32		
	d		12 31		12 36	12 38	12 49	12 57			13 01		13 05		13 08		13 20	13 24			13 31			13 36	13 38
Smethwick Rolfe Street	d					12 44									13 14										13 44
Smethwick Galton Bridge 7	d					12 46					13 08				13 16			13 30							13 46
Sandwell & Dudley	d					12 49	12 58						13 13		13 19										13 49
Dudley Port	d					12 52									13 22										13 52
Tipton	d					12 54									13 24										13 54
Coseley	d				12 46	12 57									13 27									13 46	13 57
Wolverhampton 7 ⛴	a		12 48		12 53	13 03	13 11	13 14			13 19		13 24		13 33		13 37	13 42			13 48			13 53	14 03
	d		12 49		12 53			13 15			13 19										13 49			13 53	
Penkridge	d				13 03																			14 03	
Stafford	a		13 00		13 09			13 29	12 53		13 35										14 00			14 09	

Table 68

Saturdays

Northampton - Coventry - Birmingham - Wolverhampton - Stafford

Network Diagram - see first Page of Table 67

		VT	XC	LM	LM	LM	LM		VT	LM	LM	VT	AW	LM	VT	XC	LM		LM	LM	VT	XC	LM	LM	LM
		◇1	◇1	◇1		◇1			◇1		◇1	◇1	◇	1	◇1	◇1			◇1		◇1	◇1	◇1		◇1
		☕	🛒						☕			☕	🛒		☕	☕					☕	🛒			
London Euston 15 ⊖	d	12 23		11 46					12 43		12 13				13 03						13 23		12 46		
Northampton	d			12 45	12 55						13 16			13 25									13 45	13 55	
Long Buckby	d				13 06						13 27			13 36										14 06	
Rugby	d			13 04	13 17						13 38			13 47	13 51								14 04	14 17	
Coventry	a	13 22			13 29				13 42		13 49			13 58	14 02						14 22			14 29	
	d	13 22	13 27		13 30				13 42		13 50			14 11	14 02						14 22	14 27		14 30	
Canley	d				13 33									14 14										14 33	
Tile Hill	d				13 37						13 55			14 18										14 37	
Berkswell	d				13 40									14 21										14 40	
Hampton-in-Arden	d										14 01			14 25											
Birmingham International ✈	a	13 33	13 37		13 45				13 53		14 04			14 28	14 13						14 33	14 37		14 45	
	d	13 33	13 38		13 46				13 53		14 05		14 09	14 29	14 13		14 17				14 33	14 38		14 46	
Marston Green	d				13 49						14 08			14 32										14 49	
Lea Hall	d				13 52												14 21							14 52	
Stechford	d				13 55												14 24							14 55	
Adderley Park	d																14 27								
Birmingham New Street 12	a	13 45	13 48		14 01				14 08		14 16		14 19	14 42	14 27		14 32				14 45	14 48		15 01	
	d	13 49	13 57			14 01	14 05			14 08		14 20	14 24			14 31			14 36	14 38	14 49	14 57			15 01
Smethwick Rolfe Street	d									14 14										14 44					
Smethwick Galton Bridge 7	d					14 08				14 16			14 30							14 46					15 08
Sandwell & Dudley	d	13 58					14 13			14 19										14 49	14 58				
Dudley Port	d									14 22										14 52					
Tipton	d									14 24										14 54					
Coseley	d									14 27									14 46	14 57					
Wolverhampton 7 🚌	a	14 11	14 14			14 19	14 24			14 33		14 37	14 42			14 48			14 53	15 03	15 11	15 14			15 19
	d		14 15			14 19										14 49			14 53			15 15			15 19
Penkridge	d																		15 03						
Stafford	a		14 29	13 53		14 35										15 00			15 09			15 29	14 53		15 35

		LM	VT		LM	LM	VT	AW	LM	VT	XC	LM	LM		LM	VT	XC	LM	LM	LM	LM	VT	LM		LM
			◇1			◇1	◇1	◇	1	◇1	◇1		◇1			◇1	◇1	◇1		◇1		◇1			◇1
			☕				☕	🛒		☕	☕					☕	🛒					☕			
London Euston 15 ⊖	d		13 43			13 13				14 03						14 23		13 46				14 43			14 13
Northampton	d					14 16			14 25									14 45	14 55						15 16
Long Buckby	d					14 27			14 36										15 06						15 27
Rugby	d					14 38			14 47	14 51								15 04	15 17						15 38
Coventry	a		14 42			14 49			14 58	15 02						15 22			15 29			15 42			15 49
	d		14 42			14 50			15 11	15 02						15 22	15 27		15 30			15 42			15 50
Canley	d								15 14										15 33						
Tile Hill	d					14 55			15 18										15 37						15 55
Berkswell	d								15 21										15 40						
Hampton-in-Arden	d					15 01			15 25																16 01
Birmingham International ✈	a		14 53			15 04			15 28	15 13						15 33	15 37		15 45			15 53			16 04
	d		14 53			15 05		15 09	15 29	15 13		15 17				15 33	15 38		15 46			15 53			16 05
Marston Green	d					15 08			15 32										15 49						16 08
Lea Hall	d											15 21							15 52						
Stechford	d											15 24							15 55						
Adderley Park	d											15 27													
Birmingham New Street 12	a		15 08			15 16		15 20	15 42	15 27		15 32				15 45	15 48		16 01			16 08			16 16
	d	15 05			15 08		15 20	15 24			15 31		15 36		15 38	15 49	15 57			16 01	16 05		16 08		
Smethwick Rolfe Street	d				15 14										15 44								16 14		
Smethwick Galton Bridge 7	d				15 16			15 30							15 46					16 08			16 16		
Sandwell & Dudley	d	15 13			15 19										15 49	15 58					16 13		16 19		
Dudley Port	d				15 22										15 52								16 22		
Tipton	d				15 24										15 54								16 24		
Coseley	d				15 27								15 46		15 57								16 27		
Wolverhampton 7 🚌	a	15 24			15 33		15 37	15 42			15 48		15 53		16 03	16 11	16 14			16 19	16 24		16 33		
	d										15 49		15 53				16 15			16 19					
Penkridge	d												16 03												
Stafford	a										16 00		16 09				16 29	15 53		16 35					

Northampton - Coventry - Birmingham - Wolverhampton - Stafford

Network Diagram - see first Page of Table 67

		VT	AW	LM	VT	XC	LM	LM	LM		VT	XC	LM		LM	LM	VT	LM	LM		VT	AW	LM	VT	XC
			R																						
		◇1		1	◇1	◇1		◇1			◇1	◇1	◇1		◇1		◇1		◇1		◇1	◇	1	◇1	◇1
		⊐P	⚲		⊐P	⊐P					⊐P	⚲					⊐P				⊐P	⚲		⊐P	⚲
London Euston 15 ⊖	d				15 03						15 23		14 46				15 43		15 13					16 03	
Northampton	d			15 25									15 45	15 55					16 16				16 25		
Long Buckby	d			15 36										16 06					16 27				16 36		
Rugby	d			15 47	15 51								16 04	16 17					16 38				16 47	16 51	
Coventry	a			15 58	16 02						16 22			16 29			16 42		16 49				16 58	17 02	
	d			16 11	16 02						16 22	16 27		16 30			16 42		16 50				17 11	17 02	
Canley	d			16 14										16 33									17 14		
Tile Hill	d			16 18										16 37					16 55				17 18		
Berkswell	d			16 21										16 40									17 21		
Hampton-in-Arden	d			16 25															17 01				17 25		
Birmingham International ✈	a			16 28	16 13						16 33	16 37		16 45			16 53		17 04				17 28	17 13	
	d		16 09	16 29	16 13		16 17				16 33	16 38		16 46			16 53		17 05			17 09	17 29	17 13	
Marston Green	d			16 32										16 49					17 08				17 32		
Lea Hall	d						16 21							16 52											
Stechford	d						16 24							16 55											
Adderley Park	d						16 27																		
Birmingham New Street 12	a		16 20	16 42	16 27		16 32				16 45	16 48		17 01			17 08		17 16			17 20	17 42	17 27	
	d	16 20	16 24			16 31		16 36	16 38		16 49	16 57			17 01	17 05		17 08			17 20	17 24			17 31
Smethwick Rolfe Street	d								16 44									17 14							
Smethwick Galton Bridge 7	d		16 30						16 46						17 08			17 16				17 31			
Sandwell & Dudley	d								16 49		16 58					17 13		17 19							
Dudley Port	d								16 52									17 22							
Tipton	d								16 54									17 24							
Coseley	d							16 46	16 57									17 27							
Wolverhampton 7	a	16 37	16 42			16 48		16 53	17 04		17 11	17 14			17 19	17 24		17 33			17 37	17 42			17 48
	d					16 49		16 53				17 15			17 19										17 49
Penkridge	d							17 03							17 29										
Stafford	a					17 00		17 09				17 29	16 53		17 35										18 00

		LM	LM	LM	VT		XC	LM		LM	LM	VT	LM	LM	VT		AW	LM	VT	XC	LM	LM	LM	VT	XC
			◇1		◇1		◇1	◇1		◇1		◇1		◇1	◇1		◇	1	◇1	◇1		◇1		◇1	◇1
					⊐P		⚲					⊐P			⊐P		⚲		⊐P	⊐P				⊐P	⚲
London Euston 15 ⊖	d				16 23			15 46				16 43		16 13					17 03					17 23	
Northampton	d							16 45	16 55					17 16				17 25							
Long Buckby	d								17 06					17 27				17 36							
Rugby	d							17 04	17 17					17 38				17 47	17 51						
Coventry	a				17 22				17 29			17 42		17 49				17 58	18 02					18 22	
	d				17 22		17 27		17 30			17 42		17 50				18 11	18 02					18 22	18 27
Canley	d								17 33									18 14							
Tile Hill	d								17 37					17 55				18 18							
Berkswell	d								17 40									18 21							
Hampton-in-Arden	d													18 01				18 25							
Birmingham International ✈	a				17 33		17 37		17 45			17 53		18 04				18 28	18 13					18 33	18 37
	d	17 17			17 33		17 38		17 46			17 53		18 05			18 09	18 29	18 13		18 17			18 33	18 38
Marston Green	d								17 49					18 08				18 32							
Lea Hall	d	17 21							17 52												18 21				
Stechford	d	17 24							17 55												18 24				
Adderley Park	d	17 27																			18 27				
Birmingham New Street 12	a	17 32			17 45		17 48		18 01			18 08		18 16			18 20	18 42	18 27		18 32			18 45	18 48
	d		17 36	17 38	17 49		17 57			18 01	18 05		18 08		18 20		18 24			18 31		18 36	18 38	18 49	18 57
Smethwick Rolfe Street	d			17 44									18 14										18 44		
Smethwick Galton Bridge 7	d			17 46						18 08			18 16				18 30						18 46		
Sandwell & Dudley	d			17 49	17 58						18 13		18 19										18 49	18 58	
Dudley Port	d			17 52									18 22										18 52		
Tipton	d			17 54									18 24										18 54		
Coseley	d		17 46	17 57									18 27									18 46	18 57		
Wolverhampton 7	a		17 53	18 03	18 11		18 14			18 19	18 24		18 33		18 37		18 42			18 48		18 53	19 03	19 11	19 14
	d		17 53				18 15			18 19										18 49		18 53			19 15
Penkridge	d		18 03							18 29												19 03			
Stafford	a		18 09				18 29	18 04		18 35										19 00		19 09			19 29

Table 68

Saturdays

Northampton - Coventry - Birmingham - Wolverhampton - Stafford

Network Diagram - see first Page of Table 67

			LM		LM	LM	VT	LM	LM	VT	AW		XC	LM	VT	LM	LM	VT	XC	LM			LM	LM	VT
			◇1		◇1		◇1		◇1	◇1	◇		◇1	1	◇1			◇1	◇1	1			◇1		◇1
																			A						
							☕			☕	🛒		☕		☕			☕	🛒						☕
London Euston 15 ⊖	d		16 46				17 43		17 13						18 03			18 23		17 46					18 43
Northampton	d		17 45	17 55					18 16					18 25						18 45	18 55				
Long Buckby	d			18 06					18 27					18 36							19 06				
Rugby	d		18 04	18 17					18 38					18 47	18 51					19 04	19 17				
Coventry	a			18 29			18 42		18 49					18 58	19 02			19 22			19 29				19 42
	d			18 30			18 42		18 50					19 11	19 02			19 22	19 27		19 30				19 42
Canley	d			18 33										19 14							19 33				
Tile Hill	d			18 37					18 55					19 18							19 37				
Berkswell	d			18 40										19 21							19 40				
Hampton-in-Arden	d								19 01					19 25											
Birmingham International ✈	a			18 45			18 53		19 04					19 28	19 13			19 33	19 37		19 45				19 53
	d			18 46			18 53		19 05		19 09			19 29	19 13	19 17		19 33	19 38		19 46				19 53
Marston Green	d			18 49					19 08					19 32							19 49				
Lea Hall	d			18 52												19 21					19 52				
Stechford	d			18 55												19 24					19 55				
Adderley Park	d															19 27									
Birmingham New Street 12	a			19 01			19 08		19 16		19 20			19 42	19 25	19 32		19 45	19 48		20 01				20 08
	d				19 01	19 05		19 08		19 20	19 24		19 31		19 42		19 38	19 50	19 57				20 01	20 05	
Smethwick Rolfe Street	d							19 14									19 44								
Smethwick Galton Bridge 7	d				19 08			19 16			19 30						19 46						20 08		
Sandwell & Dudley	d					19 13		19 19							19 54		19 49	19 59						20 13	
Dudley Port	d							19 22									19 52								
Tipton	d							19 24									19 54								
Coseley	d							19 27									19 57								
Wolverhampton 7	a				19 19	19 24		19 33		19 37	19 42		19 48		20 08		20 03	20 12	20 14				20 20	20 24	
	d				19 19								19 49						20 15				20 22		
Penkridge	d				19 29																		20 31		
Stafford	a		18 53		19 35								20 00						20 29	19 53			20 37		

		LM	LM	VT	AW	XC	LM		VT	LM	LM	LM	VT	XC	LM		LM		LM	VT	AW	LM	LM	LM	LM
			◇1	◇1	◇	◇1	1		◇1		◇1		◇1	◇1	1					◇1	◇	◇1		◇1	
														A											
				☕		☕			☕				☕	🛒						☕					
London Euston 15 ⊖	d		18 13						19 03				19 23		18 46					19 43		19 13			
Northampton	d		19 16				19 37								19 45	19 55						20 20			
Long Buckby	d		19 27				19 48									20 06						20 31			
Rugby	d		19 38				19 59		19 51						20 04	20 17						20 43			
Coventry	a		19 49				20 10		20 02				20 22			20 29				20 49		20 54			
	d		19 50				20 11		20 02				20 22	20 27		20 30				20 49		20 55			
Canley	d						20 14									20 33						20 58			
Tile Hill	d		19 55				20 18									20 37						21 02			
Berkswell	d						20 21									20 40						21 05			
Hampton-in-Arden	d		20 01				20 25															21 09			
Birmingham International ✈	a		20 04				20 28		20 13				20 33	20 37		20 45				21 00		21 12			
	d		20 05		20 09		20 29		20 13	20 17			20 33	20 38		20 46				21 00	21 09	21 13	21 17		
Marston Green	d		20 08				20 32									20 49						21 16			
Lea Hall	d									20 21						20 52							21 21		
Stechford	d									20 24						20 55							21 24		
Adderley Park	d									20 27													21 27		
Birmingham New Street 12	a		20 16		20 20		20 42		20 25	20 32			20 45	20 48		21 01				21 12	21 19	21 24	21 32		
	d	20 08		20 20	20 24	20 31			20 42		20 36	20 38	20 50	20 57			21 05		21 08	21 16	21 24			21 36	21 38
Smethwick Rolfe Street	d	20 14										20 44							21 14						21 44
Smethwick Galton Bridge 7	d	20 16			20 30							20 46							21 16		21 30				21 46
Sandwell & Dudley	d	20 19							20 54			20 49	20 59				21 13		21 19						21 49
Dudley Port	d	20 22										20 52							21 22						21 52
Tipton	d	20 24										20 54							21 24						21 54
Coseley	d	20 27									20 46	20 57							21 27					21 46	21 57
Wolverhampton 7	a	20 33		20 37	20 42	20 48			21 08		20 53	21 03	21 12	21 14			21 24		21 33	21 38	21 42			21 53	22 03
	d			20 37		20 49					20 53			21 15										21 59	
Penkridge	d										21 03													22 09	
Stafford	a			20 49		21 00					21 09			21 29	20 54									22 15	

A 🛒 to Birmingham New Street

Table 68

Saturdays

Northampton - Coventry - Birmingham - Wolverhampton - Stafford

Network Diagram - see first Page of Table 67

		LM	XC		LM	LM	LM	VT	LM	XC	XC	LM	LM		LM	LM	VT	XC	AW	LM	LM	LM	VT		AW
		1	◇1		◇1			◇1 ⊡	◇1	◇1	◇1		◇1			1	◇1 ⊡	◇1		◇1		◇1	◇1 ⊡		
London Euston 15 ⊖	d							20 25	19 46								21 03			20 34			21 43		
Northampton	d				20 55				21 16											21 55		22 16			
Long Buckby	d				21 06				21 27											22 06		22 27			
Rugby	d				21 17				21 38								22 12			22 17		22 38	22 53		
Coventry	a				21 29			21 36	21 49								22 22			22 29		22 49	23 02		
	d	21 11	21 27		21 30			21 36	21 50	21 56						22 11	22 23	22 27		22 30		22 50	23 02		
Canley	d	21 14			21 33											22 14				22 33					
Tile Hill	d	21 18			21 37				21 55							22 18				22 37		22 55			
Berkswell	d	21 21			21 40											22 21				22 40					
Hampton-in-Arden	d	21 25							22 01							22 25						23 01			
Birmingham International ✈	a	21 28	21 37		21 45			21 50	22 04	22 10						22 28	22 33	22 36		22 45		23 04	23 13		
	d	21 29	21 38		21 46			21 50	22 05	22 11		22 21				22 29	22 34	22 38		22 46		23 05	23 13		
Marston Green	d	21 32			21 49				22 08							22 32				22 49		23 08			
Lea Hall	d				21 52							22 25								22 52					
Stechford	d				21 55							22 28								22 55					
Adderley Park	d											22 31													
Birmingham New Street 12	a	21 42	21 48		22 01			22 04	22 16	22 21		22 36				22 42	22 45	22 48		23 01		23 16	23 25		
	d		21 57			22 05	22 08	22 16			22 31		22 36		22 38		22 48		22 55		23 08		23 28		23 35
Smethwick Rolfe Street	d						22 14								22 44						23 14				
Smethwick Galton Bridge 7	d						22 16						22 42		22 46						23 16				
Sandwell & Dudley	d					22 13	22 19	22 25							22 49		22 57				23 19		23 37		
Dudley Port	d						22 22								22 52						23 22				
Tipton	d						22 24								22 54						23 24				
Coseley	d						22 27						22 48		22 57						23 27				
Wolverhampton 7	a		22 14			22 24	22 33	22 38			22 48		22 55		23 03		23 10		23 12		23 33		23 50		23 53
	d		22 16								22 49		22 56												
Penkridge	d												23 06												
Stafford	a		22 29								23 01		23 13												

		LM
		◇1
London Euston 15 ⊖	d	21 28
Northampton	d	22 55
Long Buckby	d	23 06
Rugby	d	23 17
Coventry	a	23 29
	d	23 30
Canley	d	23 33
Tile Hill	d	23 37
Berkswell	d	23 40
Hampton-in-Arden	d	23 44
Birmingham International ✈	a	23 47
	d	23 48
Marston Green	d	23 51
Lea Hall	d	23 54
Stechford	d	23 57
Adderley Park	d	
Birmingham New Street 12	a	00 04
	d	
Smethwick Rolfe Street	d	
Smethwick Galton Bridge 7	d	
Sandwell & Dudley	d	
Dudley Port	d	
Tipton	d	
Coseley	d	
Wolverhampton 7	a	
	d	
Penkridge	d	
Stafford	a	

Table 68

Sundays

Northampton - Coventry - Birmingham - Wolverhampton - Stafford

Network Diagram - see first Page of Table 67

		LM	VT	XC	LM	LM	LM	VT	LM	LM		XC	AW	VT	LM	LM	LM	LM	VT	XC		AW	LM	LM	VT
		◇1 A	◇1	◇1	1		1	◇1	1	◇1		◇1		◇1		◇1	1	◇1	◇1	◇1		◇	◇1		◇1
			🍴	🛒				🍴				🛒		🍴					🍴	🛒					🍴
London Euston 15 ⊖	d	21p28														07 50			08 50				08 23		
Northampton	d	22 55														09 30							10 00		
Long Buckby	d	23p06														09 41							10 11		
Rugby	d	23p17														09 52			10 14				10 22		
Coventry	a	23p29														10 05			10 23				10 33		
	d	23p30			08 37				09 07							10 05	10 08		10 24	10 28			10 34		
Canley	d	23p33			08 40				09 10								10 11						10 37		
Tile Hill	d	23p37			08 44				09 14								10 15						10 41		
Berkswell	d	23p40			08 47				09 17								10 18						10 44		
Hampton-in-Arden	d	23p44			08 51				09 21								10 22						10 48		
Birmingham International ✈	a	23p47			08 54				09 24							10 14	10 26		10 34	10 38			10 51		
	d	23p48			08 55		09 03		09 25				09 51			10 15	10 26		10 35	10 40		10 48	10 52		
Marston Green	d	23p51			08 58		09 06		09 28							10 18	10 29						10 55		
Lea Hall	d	23p54					09 09									10 21									
Stechford	d	23p57					09 12									10 24									
Adderley Park	d						09 15									10 27									
Birmingham New Street 12	a	00 04			09 06		09 20		09 36				10 02			10 32	10 38		10 47	10 50		10 58	11 03		
	d		08 45	09 01		09 09		09 20		09 42		10 01	10 05	10 20	10 23			10 42	10 51	11 01		11 05		11 09	11 20
Smethwick Rolfe Street	d					09 15									10 29									11 15	
Smethwick Galton Bridge 7	d					09 17									10 31									11 17	
Sandwell & Dudley	d					09 19									10 33				11 00					11 19	
Dudley Port	d					09 22									10 36									11 22	
Tipton	d					09 24									10 38									11 24	
Coseley	d					09 27									10 41									11 27	
Wolverhampton 7	a		09 02	09 18		09 32		09 37		09 59		10 18	10 21	10 37	10 46			10 59	11 13	11 18		11 26		11 32	11 37
	d		09 04	09 19						10 00		10 19						11 00		11 19					
Penkridge	d									10 10								11 10							
Stafford	a		09 16	09 32						10 16		10 32						11 16		11 31					

		LM	LM	VT	XC	LM		LM	VT	AW	LM	LM	VT	XC	LM	LM	VT	VT	XC	LM	LM	XC	XC	VT	LM
		1	◇1	◇1	◇1	◇1			◇1	◇	◇1	1	◇1	◇1	◇1		◇1	◇1	◇1	◇1	1	◇1 C	◇1 B	◇1	◇1
				🍴	🛒				🍴	🛒			🍴	🛒			🍴	🍴	🛒			🛒	🛒	🍴	
London Euston 15 ⊖	d			09 50		09 23							10 50		10 23			11 45						12 18	11 23
Northampton	d					11 00									12 00										12 51
Long Buckby	d					11 11									12 11										13 02
Rugby	d			11 15		11 22							12 14		12 22			12 48							13 15
Coventry	a			11 25		11 33							12 24		12 33			12 56						13 20	13 28
	d	11 08		11 25	11 28	11 34						12 08	12 25	12 28	12 34			12 57			13 10	13 25	13 26	13 21	13 29
Canley	d					11 37									12 37										13 32
Tile Hill	d					11 41									12 41						13 15				13 36
Berkswell	d					11 44									12 44										13 39
Hampton-in-Arden	d					11 48									12 48										13 43
Birmingham International ✈	a	11 18		11 36	11 38	11 51						12 17	12 35	12 38	12 51			13 07			13 22	13 36	13 37	13 31	13 46
	d	11 18		11 36	11 40	11 52				12 08		12 18	12 36	12 40	12 52			13 08			13 22	13 37	13 38	13 32	13 47
Marston Green	d	11 21				11 55						12 21			12 55						13 25				13 50
Lea Hall	d	11 24										12 24									13 29				
Stechford	d	11 27										12 27									13 31				
Adderley Park	d	11 30										12 30									13 35				
Birmingham New Street 12	a	11 36		11 49	11 50	12 03				12 18		12 36	12 48	12 50	13 03			13 22			13 40	13 47	13 48	13 44	13 58
	d		11 42	11 52	12 01			12 09	12 20	12 24	12 35		12 52	13 01		13 09	13 20		13 31	13 35		14 00	14 01	13 48	
Smethwick Rolfe Street	d							12 15								13 15									
Smethwick Galton Bridge 7	d							12 17								13 17									
Sandwell & Dudley	d			12 02				12 19					13 01			13 19								13 57	
Dudley Port	d							12 22								13 22									
Tipton	d							12 24								13 24									
Coseley	d							12 27								13 27									
Wolverhampton 7	a		11 59	12 15	12 19			12 32	12 37	12 42	12 52		13 14	13 18		13 32	13 37		13 48	13 52		14 17	14 18	14 10	
	d		12 00		12 19						12 53			13 19						13 53		14 18	14 19		
Penkridge	d		12 10								13 03									14 03					
Stafford	a		12 16		12 32						13 09			13 33						14 09		14 32	14 33		

A not 11 December
C until 25 March
C from 1 April
b Previous night, arr. 2243

Table 68

Sundays

Northampton - Coventry - Birmingham - Wolverhampton - Stafford

Network Diagram - see first Page of Table 67

		VT		LM	VT	AW	VT	XC	LM	LM	VT	XC		LM	LM	VT	LM	VT	AW	VT	XC	LM		LM	VT
		◇1			◇1	◇	◇1	◇1	◇1	1	◇1	◇1		◇1	◇1	◇1		◇1	◇	◇1	◇1	◇1		1	◇1
		☕			☕	🛒	☕	🛒			☕	🛒				☕		☕	🛒	☕	🛒				☕
London Euston 15 ⊖	d	12 38					12 58				13 18			12 34	12 50	13 38				13 58					14 18
Northampton	d													13 51	13 56										
Long Buckby	d													14 02	14 07										
Rugby	d						13 49							14 15	14 18					14 49					
Coventry	a	13 40					14 00				14 20			14 28		14 40				15 00					15 20
	d	13 40					14 00			14 10	14 20	14 26		14 29		14 40				15 00				15 10	15 20
Canley	d													14 32											
Tile Hill	d									14 15				14 36										15 15	
Berkswell	d													14 39											
Hampton-in-Arden	d													14 43											
Birmingham International ✈	a	13 51					14 11			14 22	14 31	14 35		14 46		14 51				15 11				15 22	15 31
	d	13 51				14 07	14 11			14 22	14 31	14 38		14 47		14 51			15 07	15 11				15 22	15 31
Marston Green	d									14 25				14 50										15 25	
Lea Hall	d									14 29														15 29	
Stechford	d									14 31														15 31	
Adderley Park	d									14 35														15 35	
Birmingham New Street 12	a	14 05				14 18	14 25			14 40	14 44	14 48		14 58		15 05			15 18	15 25				15 40	15 44
	d			14 09	14 20	14 24		14 31	14 35		14 48	15 01					15 09	15 20	15 24		15 31	15 35			15 48
Smethwick Rolfe Street	d			14 15													15 15								
Smethwick Galton Bridge 7	d			14 17													15 17								
Sandwell & Dudley	d			14 19							14 57						15 19								15 57
Dudley Port	d			14 22													15 22								
Tipton	d			14 24													15 24								
Coseley	d			14 27													15 27								
Wolverhampton 7 🚌	a			14 32	14 37	14 42		14 48	14 52		15 10	15 18					15 32	15 37	15 42		15 48	15 52			16 10
	d								14 53			15 19										15 53			
Penkridge	d								15 03													16 03			
Stafford	a								15 09			15 33			15 07							16 09			

		XC	LM	LM	VT	LM	VT	AW		VT	XC	LM	LM	VT	XC	LM	LM	VT		LM	VT	AW	VT	XC	LM
		◇1	◇1	◇1	◇1		◇1	◇		◇1	◇1	◇1	1	◇1	◇1	◇1	◇1	◇1			◇1	◇	◇1	◇1	◇1
		🛒			☕		☕	🛒		☕	🛒			☕	🛒			☕			☕	🛒	☕	🛒	
London Euston 15 ⊖	d		13 34	13 50	14 38					14 58				15 18		14 33	14 50	15 38					15 58		
Northampton	d		14 51	14 56												15 47	15 56								
Long Buckby	d		15 02	15 07												15 58	16 07								
Rugby	d		15 15	15a18						15 49						16 16	16 18						16 49		
Coventry	a		15 28		15 40					16 00				16 20		16 29		16 40					17 00		
	d	15 26	15 29		15 40					16 00			16 10	16 20	16 26	16 30		16 40					17 00		
Canley	d		15 32													16 33									
Tile Hill	d		15 36										16 15			16 37									
Berkswell	d		15 39													16 40									
Hampton-in-Arden	d		15 43													16 44									
Birmingham International ✈	a	15 35	15 46		15 51					16 11			16 22	16 31	16 35	16 47		16 51					17 11		
	d	15 38	15 47		15 51			16 07		16 11			16 22	16 31	16 38	16 48		16 51				17 07	17 11		
Marston Green	d		15 50										16 25			16 51									
Lea Hall	d												16 29												
Stechford	d												16 31												
Adderley Park	d												16 35												
Birmingham New Street 12	a	15 48	15 58		16 05			16 18		16 25			16 41	16 44	16 48	16 59		17 05				17 18	17 25		
	d	16 01				16 09	16 20	16 24			16 31	16 35		16 48	17 01					17 09	17 20	17 24		17 31	17 35
Smethwick Rolfe Street	d					16 15														17 15					
Smethwick Galton Bridge 7	d					16 17														17 17					
Sandwell & Dudley	d					16 19								16 57						17 19					
Dudley Port	d					16 22														17 22					
Tipton	d					16 24														17 24					
Coseley	d					16 27														17 27					
Wolverhampton 7 🚌	a	16 18				16 32	16 37	16 42			16 48	16 52		17 10	17 18					17 32	17 37	17 42		17 48	17 52
	d	16 19										16 53			17 19										17 53
Penkridge	d											17 03													18 03
Stafford	a	16 34										17 09			17 35		17 07								18 09

Northampton - Coventry - Birmingham - Wolverhampton - Stafford

Network Diagram - see first Page of Table 67

Station		LM	VT	XC	LM	LM	VT	LM	VT	AW	VT	XC	LM	LM	VT	XC	LM	LM	VT	LM	VT	AW
		1	◇1 ⊥P	◇1 trolley	◇1	◇1	◇1 ⊥P		◇1 ⊥P	◇ trolley	◇1 ⊥P	◇1	◇1	1	◇1 ⊥P	◇1 trolley	◇1	◇1	◇1 ⊥P		R 1 ⊥P	◇ trolley
London Euston 15 ⊖	d		16 18		15 34	15 50	16 38				16 58				17 18		16 34	16 50	17 38			
Northampton	d				16 51	16 56											17 51	17 56				
Long Buckby	d				17 02	17 07											18 02	18 07				
Rugby	d				17 15	17a18					17 49						18 15	18 18				
Coventry	a		17 20		17 28		17 40				18 00				18 20		18 28		18 40			
	d	17 10	17 20	17 26	17 29		17 40				18 00			18 10	18 20	18 26	18 29		18 40			
Canley	d				17 32												18 32					
Tile Hill	d	17 15			17 36									18 15			18 36					
Berkswell	d				17 39												18 39					
Hampton-in-Arden	d				17 43												18 43					
Birmingham International ✈	a	17 22	17 31	17 35	17 46		17 51				18 11			18 22	18 31	18 35	18 46		18 51			
	d	17 22	17 31	17 38	17 47		17 51			18 07	18 11			18 22	18 31	18 38	18 47		18 51			19 07
Marston Green	d	17 25			17 50									18 25			18 50					
Lea Hall	d	17 29												18 29								
Stechford	d	17 31												18 31								
Adderley Park	d	17 35												18 35								
Birmingham New Street 12	a	17 41	17 44	17 48	17 58		18 05			18 18	18 25			18 41	18 44	18 48	18 58		19 05			19 18
	d		17 48	18 01				18 09	18 20	18 24		18 31	18 35		18 48	19 01				19 09	19 20	19 24
Smethwick Rolfe Street	d							18 15												19 15		
Smethwick Galton Bridge 7	d							18 17												19 17		
Sandwell & Dudley	d		17 57					18 19							18 57					19 19		
Dudley Port	d							18 22												19 22		
Tipton	d							18 24												19 24		
Coseley	d							18 27												19 27		
Wolverhampton 7	a		18 10	18 18				18 32	18 37	18 42		18 48	18 52		19 10	19 18				19 32	19 37	19 42
	d			18 19									18 53			19 19						
Penkridge	d												19 03									
Stafford	a			18 35									19 09			19 37		19 07				

Station		XC	LM	VT	LM	VT	XC	LM	LM	VT	LM	XC	VT	AW	VT	XC	LM	VT	XC	LM	LM	VT	LM
		◇1 trolley	◇1	◇1 ⊥P	1	◇1 ⊥P	◇1 A trolley	◇1	◇1	◇1 ⊥P		◇1 trolley	◇1 ⊥P	◇	◇1 ⊥P	◇1 trolley	1	◇1 ⊥P	◇1 A trolley	◇1	◇1	◇1 ⊥P	
London Euston 15 ⊖	d			17 58		18 18		17 34	17 50	18 38					18 58			19 18		18 34	18 50	19 38	
Northampton	d							18 51	18 58											19 51	19 56		
Long Buckby	d							19 02	19 09											20 02	20 07		
Rugby	d			18 49				19 15	19a21						19 49					20 15	20 18		
Coventry	a			19 00		19 20		19 28		19 40					20 00			20 20		20 28		20 40	
	d			19 01	19 10	19 20	19 26	19 29		19 40		19 54			20 00		20 10	20 20	20 26	20 29		20 40	
Canley	d							19 32												20 32			
Tile Hill	d				19 15			19 36									20 15			20 36			
Berkswell	d							19 39												20 39			
Hampton-in-Arden	d							19 43												20 43			
Birmingham International ✈	a			19 11	19 22	19 31	19 35	19 46		19 51		20 03			20 11		20 22	20 31	20 35	20 46		20 51	
	d			19 12	19 22	19 31	19 38	19 47		19 51		20 04		20 07	20 11		20 22	20 31	20 38	20 47		20 51	
Marston Green	d				19 25			19 50									20 25			20 50			
Lea Hall	d				19 29												20 29						
Stechford	d				19 31												20 31						
Adderley Park	d				19 35												20 35						
Birmingham New Street 12	a			19 24	19 40	19 44	19 48	19 58		20 05		20 15		20 18	20 23		20 41	20 44	20 48	20 58		21 04	
	d	19 31	19 35	19 39		19 48	20 01				20 09		20 20	20 24	20 26	20 31		20 48	21 01			21 07	21 09
Smethwick Rolfe Street	d										20 15												21 15
Smethwick Galton Bridge 7	d										20 17												21 17
Sandwell & Dudley	d			19 49		19 57					20 19				20 36			20 57				21 16	21 19
Dudley Port	d										20 22												21 22
Tipton	d										20 24												21 24
Coseley	d										20 27												21 27
Wolverhampton 7	a	19 48	19 52	20 02		20 10	20 18				20 32		20 36	20 42	20 46	20 50		21 10	21 18			21 31	21 33
	d		19 53				20 19						20 38						21 19				
Penkridge	d		20 03																				
Stafford	a		20 09				20 36						20 51						21 36		21 14		

A trolley to Birmingham New Street

Table 68

Sundays

Northampton - Coventry - Birmingham - Wolverhampton - Stafford

Network Diagram - see first Page of Table 67

		XC	AW	VT	LM	LM		VT	XC	LM	LM	LM	VT	XC	AW	LM		VT	XC	AW	LM	LM	XC	AW	LM
		◇1	◇	◇1	◇1	1		◇1	◇1	◇1	◇1		◇1	◇1		1		◇1	◇1	◇	◇1		◇1		1
			A																						
		🛒		☕				☕					☕					☕	🛒						
London Euston 15 ⊖	d			19 58				20 18		19 34	19 50		20 38					20 54			20 34				
Northampton	d									20 51	20 58										21 52				
Long Buckby	d									21 02	21 09										22 03				
Rugby	d			20 49						21 15	21a21							22 07			22 15				
Coventry	a			21 00				21 20		21 27			21 46					22 16			22 27				
	d	20 54		21 00		21 10		21 20	21 26	21 29			21 46	21 53		22 08		22 16	22 23		22 29		22 53		23 08
Canley	d									21 32											22 32				
Tile Hill	d					21 15				21 36											22 36				
Berkswell	d									21 39											22 39				
Hampton-in-Arden	d									21 43											22 43				
Birmingham International ✈	a	21 03		21 11		21 22		21 31	21 35	21 46			21 57	22 02		22 17		22 27	22 32		22 46		23 02		23 17
	d	21 04	21 07	21 11		21 22		21 31	21 38	21 47			21 57	22 03	22 11	22 18		22 27	22 33	22 40	22 47		23 03	23 08	23 18
Marston Green	d					21 25				21 50						22 21					22 50				23 21
Lea Hall	d					21 29										22 24									23 24
Stechford	d					21 31										22 27									23 27
Adderley Park	d					21 35										22 30									23 30
Birmingham New Street 12	a	21 15	21 18	21 24		21 40		21 44	21 48	21 58			22 09	22 14	22 21	22 36		22 39	22 42	22 50	22 58		23 13	23 19	23 36
	d		21 24	21 28	21 35			21 48	22 01			22 09	22 16		22 24			22 44		22 55		23 09		23 24	
Smethwick Rolfe Street	d											22 15										23 15			
Smethwick Galton Bridge 7	d											22 17										23 17			
Sandwell & Dudley	d			21 37				21 57				22 19	22 25					22 53				23 19			
Dudley Port	d											22 22										23 22			
Tipton	d											22 24										23 24			
Coseley	d											22 27										23 27			
Wolverhampton 7 ⛴	a		21 42	21 51	21 56			22 10	22 18			22 32	22 38		22 41			23 06		23 13		23 32		23 40	
	d				21 57				22 19											23 15					
Penkridge	d				22 07																				
Stafford	a				22 13				22 36											23 30					

		LM		VT	VT	LM	VT
		◇1		◇1	◇1	1	◇1
				☕	☕		☕
London Euston 15 ⊖	d	21 28		21 55	22 25	22 00	23 25
Northampton	d	22 51				23 32	
Long Buckby	d	23 02				23 43	
Rugby	d	23 13		23 21	23 48	23 54	00s46
Coventry	a	23 25		23 31	23 57	00 05	00s58
	d	23 35		23 31	23 58		
Canley	d	23 38					
Tile Hill	d	23 42					
Berkswell	d	23 45					
Hampton-in-Arden	d	23 49					
Birmingham International ✈	a	23 52		23 42	00 08		01s09
	d	23 53		23 42	00 09		
Marston Green	d	23 56					
Lea Hall	d						
Stechford	d						
Adderley Park	d						
Birmingham New Street 12	a	00 04		23 54	00 21		01s22
	d			23 57	00 24		
Smethwick Rolfe Street	d						
Smethwick Galton Bridge 7	d						
Sandwell & Dudley	d						
Dudley Port	d						
Tipton	d						
Coseley	d						
Wolverhampton 7 ⛴	a			00 15	00 43		01 53
	d						
Penkridge	d						
Stafford	a						

A until 25 March

Table 68

Mondays to Fridays

Stafford - Wolverhampton - Birmingham - Coventry - Northampton

Network Diagram - see first Page of Table 67

Miles			LM MX 1	VT MX ◇1 ☕	VT MO ◇1 ☕	VT MO ◇1 ☕	VT MX ◇1 ☕	LM MX 1	LM 1	VT ◇1 ⊠	VT ◇1 ⊠		LM 1	VT ◇1 ⊠	LM 1	AW	XC ◇1 🛒	VT ◇1 ⊠	LM 1	AW	VT ◇1 ⊠		LM	LM 1	LM 1
—	**Stafford**	d														05 25									
0	Penkridge	d																							
9½	**Wolverhampton 7** ⛴	a														05 39									
—		d		21p45	22p05	22p37	22p45			05 00	05 24					05 40		05 45		05 59	06 04		06 15		
18¾	Coseley	d																							
32¼	Tipton	d																							
34	Dudley Port	d																							
36	Sandwell & Dudley	d		21p56	22p15	22p47	22p55				05 34							05 56			06 15				
38	Smethwick Galton Bridge 7	d																		06 10					
41¼	Smethwick Rolfe Street	d																							
43	**Birmingham New Street 12**	a		22p06	22p24	22p56	23p06			05 26	05 43					06 01		06 06		06 15	06 24		06 32		
—		d	21p33	22p10	22p30	23p00	23p10	23p53		05 29	05 50				05 53		06 04	06 10	06 13	06 36	06 30				06 33
45	Adderley Park	d																		↦					
46½	Stechford	d																	06 20						
47¾	Lea Hall	d																	06 23						
49½	Marston Green	d	21p41					00 01							06 01				06 26						06 41
51½	**Birmingham International** ✈	a	21p45	22p19	22p39	23p09	23p19	00 04		05 38	05 59				06 05		06 13	06 19	06 29		06 39				06 45
—		d	21p45	22p20	22p40	23p10	23p20	00 05		05 40	06 00				06 05		06 14	06 20	06 29		06 40				06 45
54¾	Hampton-in-Arden	d	21p48																06 32						06 48
55½	Berkswell	d													06 11				06 37						
56¾	Tile Hill	d	21p55												06 14				06 40						06 55
57¾	Canley	d													06 17				06 44						
58½	**Coventry**	a	22p00	22p30	22p50	23p20	23p30	00 15		05 50	06 10				06 20		06 24	06 30	06 47		06 49				07 00
—		d	22p01	22p31	22p51	23p21	23p31			05 51	06 11				06 21			06 31			06 51				07 01
60	Rugby	d	22p12	22p43	23p04	23p34	23p44		05 20	06 03			06 13	06 20	06 32									07 02	07 12
64¼	Long Buckby	d	22p22						05 30				06 23		06 42									07 12	07 21
74¼	**Northampton**	a	22p34			23b53	00s05		05 42				06 35	06 39	06 54									07 25	07 33
79½	London Euston 15 ⊖	a	00 21	00 04	00 27	01 04	01 15		06 50	07 02	07 13		07 40	07 30	08 02			07 34			07 53			08 49	

		AW	LM	LM 1	VT ◇1 ⊠	LM 1	XC ◇1 🛒		VT ◇1 ⊠	LM 1	LM	LM ◇1	VT ◇1 ⊠	VT ◇1 ⊠	AW	XC ◇1 🛒	LM		LM	LM ◇1	LM 1	LM 1	VT ◇1 ⊠	LM 1	VT ◇1 ⊠
Stafford	d						06 25					06 41				06 58				07 12		07 22			
Penkridge	d											06 47								07 18					
Wolverhampton 7 ⛴	a						06 39					06 57				07 12				07 28					
	d			06 19	06 27		06 41		06 45		06 49	06 59	07 04		07 10	07 15			07 19	07 28					07 32
Coseley	d			06 24							06 54	07 04							07 24						
Tipton	d			06 26							06 57								07 26						
Dudley Port	d			06 28							06 59								07 28						
Sandwell & Dudley	d			06 32	06 37				06 56		07 03		07 15						07 32						
Smethwick Galton Bridge 7	d			06 34							07 06				07 21				07 34	07 40					
Smethwick Rolfe Street	d	↤		06 36							07 09								07 36						
Birmingham New Street 12	a	06 15		06 43	06 46		06 58		07 06		07 15	07 18	07 24		07 26	07 31			07 44	07 48					07 55
	d	06 36	06 39		06 50	06 53	07 04		07 10	07 13			07 30		07 36		07 39				07 33		07 50	07 53	
Adderley Park	d		06 44														07 44								
Stechford	d		06 47							07 20							07 47								
Lea Hall	d		06 50							07 23							07 50								
Marston Green	d					07 01				07 26											07 41			08 01	
Birmingham International ✈	a	06 50	06 55		06 59	07 05	07 13		07 19	07 29					07 50		07 55				07 45		07 59	08 05	
	d				07 00	07 05	07 14		07 20	07 29				07 41							07 45		08 00	08 05	
Hampton-in-Arden	d					07 08															07 48				
Berkswell	d					07 13				07 35														08 11	
Tile Hill	d									07 38											07 55			08 14	
Canley	d					07 18															07 58			08 17	
Coventry	a				07 10	07 21	07 24		07 30	07 43				07 51							08 02		08 10	08 20	
	d				07 11	07 21			07 31					07 52							08 03		08 11	08 21	
Rugby	d					07 32															08 14	08 20	08 23	08 32	
Long Buckby	d					07 42															08 24			08 42	
Northampton	a					07 54															08 37	08 41		08 56	
London Euston 15 ⊖	a				08 14	09 10			08 30				08 42	08 49							09 44		09 13	10 18	

b Previous night, stops to set down only

Stafford - Wolverhampton - Birmingham - Coventry - Northampton

Network Diagram - see first Page of Table 67

		LM	LM		XC	VT	LM	LM	LM	LM	VT	AW	XC		LM	LM	LM	LM	LM	LM	VT	LM	VT		LM
					◇1	◇1	1		◇1		◇1	◇	◇1					◇1	1	1	◇1	1	◇1		
					🛒	⊠					⊠	🛒	🛒								⊠		⊠		
Stafford	d					07 28			07 41				08 02					08 10		08 21					
Penkridge	d								07 47									08 16							
Wolverhampton 7	a					07 43			07 57				08 15					08 26							
	d	07 35	07 39			07 45		07 49	07 57	08 04		08 09	08 16			08 19	08 19	08 28					08 32		08 37
Coseley	d		07 44					07 54	08 03							08 24	08 25								
Tipton	d		07 47					07 57								08 26	08 27								
Dudley Port	d		07 49					07 59								08 28	08 29								
Sandwell & Dudley	d	07 45				07 56		08 02								08 32	08 33								08 46
Smethwick Galton Bridge 7	d		07 53					08 05				08 21				08 34	08 35	08 40							
Smethwick Rolfe Street	d		07 55					08 07								08 36	08 37								
Birmingham New Street 12	a	07 54	08 03			08 06		08 14	08 17	08 20		08 26	08 32			08 44	08 44	08 47					08 55		08 55
	d				08 04	08 10	08 13				08 30	08 36			08 39				08 33		08 50	08 53			
Adderley Park	d														08 44										
Stechford	d						08 20								08 47										
Lea Hall	d						08 23								08 50										
Marston Green	d						08 26												08 41			09 01			
Birmingham International ✈	a				08 13	08 19	08 29				08 39	08 50			08 55				08 45		08 59	09 05			
	d				08 14	08 20	08 29				08 40								08 45		09 00	09 05			
Hampton-in-Arden	d						08 32												08 48						
Berkswell	d						08 37															09 11			
Tile Hill	d						08 40												08 55			09 14			
Canley	d						08 44															09 17			
Coventry	a				08 24	08 30	08 47				08 49								09 00		09 10	09 20			
	d					08 31					08 51								09 01		09 11	09 21			
Rugby	d																		09 12	09 20	09 23	09 32			
Long Buckby	d																		09 22			09 42			
Northampton	a																		09 34	09 39		09 54			
London Euston 15 ⊖	a					09 34					09 54								10 49		10 14	11 17			

		XC	VT	LM	LM	LM	VT	AW	XC		LM	LM	LM	LM	LM	VT	LM	VT	LM		XC	VT	LM	LM	LM
		◇1	◇1	1		◇1	◇1	◇	◇1				◇1	◇1	◇1	◇1	1	◇1			◇1	◇1	1		◇1
														A											
		🛒	⊠				⊠	🛒	🛒							⊠		⊠			🛒	⊠			
Stafford	d	08 25				08 43			09 03				09 10		09 21						09 25				09 43
Penkridge	d					08 48							09 16												
Wolverhampton 7	a	08 39				08 58			09 15				09 27								09 39				09 56
	d	08 41	08 45		08 49	08 58		09 09	09 16			09 19	09 28					09 32	09 37		09 41	09 45		09 49	09 57
Coseley	d				08 54	09 04						09 24												09 54	10 03
Tipton	d				08 56							09 26												09 56	
Dudley Port	d				08 58							09 28												09 58	
Sandwell & Dudley	d		08 56		09 02							09 32							09 46			09 56		10 02	
Smethwick Galton Bridge 7	d				09 04			09 20				09 34	09 40											10 04	
Smethwick Rolfe Street	d				09 06							09 36												10 06	
Birmingham New Street 12	a	08 58	09 06		09 14	09 18		09 25	09 32			09 44	09 47					09 55	09 55		09 58	10 06		10 14	10 17
	d	09 04	09 10	09 13			09 30	09 36			09 39			09 33		09 50	09 53				10 04	10 10	10 13		
Adderley Park	d										09 44														
Stechford	d			09 20							09 47												10 20		
Lea Hall	d			09 23							09 50												10 23		
Marston Green	d			09 26										09 41			10 01						10 26		
Birmingham International ✈	a	09 13	09 19	09 29			09 39	09 50			09 55			09 45		09 59	10 05				10 13	10 19	10 29		
	d	09 14	09 20	09 29			09 40							09 45		10 00	10 05				10 14	10 20	10 29		
Hampton-in-Arden	d			09 32										09 48									10 32		
Berkswell	d			09 37													10 11						10 37		
Tile Hill	d			09 40										09 55			10 14						10 40		
Canley	d			09 44													10 17						10 44		
Coventry	a	09 24	09 30	09 47			09 49							10 00		10 10	10 20				10 24	10 30	10 47		
	d		09 31	09 48			09 51							10 01		10 11	10 21					10 31	10 48		
Rugby	d			09 59										10 12	10 20	10 24	10 32						10 59		
Long Buckby	d			10 09										10 22			10 42						11 09		
Northampton	a			10 21										10 34	10 39		10 54						11 21		
London Euston 15 ⊖	a		10 34	11 27			10 54							11 49		11 14	12 17					11 34	12 27		

A ◇ from Northampton

Stafford - Wolverhampton - Birmingham - Coventry - Northampton

Network Diagram - see first Page of Table 67

		VT	AW	XC	LM		LM	LM	LM	LM	VT	LM	LM	XC	VT		LM	LM	LM	VT	AW	XC	LM	LM	LM
		◇1	◇	◇1				◇1	◇1	◇1	◇1	1		◇1	◇1		1		◇1	◇1	◇	◇1	1		
									A																
		⊠	🛒	🛒							⊠			🛒	⊠					☕	🛒	🛒			
Stafford	d			10 03				10 10		10 21				10 25					10 43			11 02			
Penkridge	d							10 16																	
Wolverhampton 7	a			10 15				10 27						10 39					10 56			11 15			
	d		10 08	10 17			10 19	10 28					10 37	10 41	10 45			10 49	10 57		11 09	11 16			11 19
Coseley	d						10 24											10 54	11 03						11 24
Tipton	d						10 26											10 56							11 26
Dudley Port	d						10 28											10 58							11 28
Sandwell & Dudley	d						10 32						10 46		10 56			11 02							11 32
Smethwick Galton Bridge 7	d		10 19				10 34	10 40										11 04			11 21				11 34
Smethwick Rolfe Street	d						10 36											11 06							11 36
Birmingham New Street 12	a		10 25	10 39			10 44	10 47					10 55	10 58	11 06			11 14	11 18		11 27	11 32			11 44
	d	10 30	10 36		10 39				10 33		10 50	10 53		11 04	11 10		11 13			11 30	11 36		11 33	11 39	
Adderley Park	d				10 44																			11 44	
Stechford	d				10 47												11 20							11 47	
Lea Hall	d				10 50												11 23							11 50	
Marston Green	d								10 41			11 01					11 26						11 41		
Birmingham International ✈	a	10 39	10 50		10 55				10 45		10 59	11 05		11 13	11 19		11 29			11 39	11 50		11 45	11 55	
	d	10 40							10 45		11 00	11 05		11 14	11 20		11 29			11 40			11 45		
Hampton-in-Arden	d								10 48								11 32						11 48		
Berkswell	d											11 11					11 37								
Tile Hill	d								10 55			11 14					11 40						11 55		
Canley	d											11 17					11 44								
Coventry	a	10 49							11 00		11 10	11 20		11 24	11 30		11 47			11 49			12 00		
	d	10 51							11 01		11 11	11 21			11 31		11 48			11 51			12 01		
Rugby	d								11 12	11 20	11 24	11 32					11 59						12 12		
Long Buckby	d								11 22			11 42					12 09						12 22		
Northampton	a								11 35	11 39		11 54					12 21						12 34		
London Euston 15 ⊖	a	11 54							12 49		12 14	13 17			12 34		13 27			12 54					

			LM	LM	VT	LM	VT	LM	XC	VT	LM		LM	LM	VT	AW	XC	LM	LM	LM	VT		LM	LM	LM
			◇1	◇1	◇1	1	◇1		◇1	◇1	1			◇1	◇1	◇	◇1			◇1	◇1		◇1	◇1	1
																							A		
					☕		⊠		🛒	☕					☕	🛒	🛒				☕				
Stafford	d		11 10	11 21					11 25					11 43			12 03			12 10				12 21	
Penkridge	d		11 16																	12 16					
Wolverhampton 7	a		11 27						11 39					11 57			12 15			12 27					
	d		11 28				11 32	11 37	11 41	11 45			11 49	11 57		12 09	12 17		12 19	12 28					
Coseley	d												11 54	12 03					12 24						
Tipton	d												11 56						12 26						
Dudley Port	d												11 58						12 28						
Sandwell & Dudley	d							11 46		11 56			12 02						12 32						
Smethwick Galton Bridge 7	d		11 40										12 04			12 20			12 34	12 40					
Smethwick Rolfe Street	d												12 06						12 36						
Birmingham New Street 12	a		11 47				11 55	11 55	11 58	12 06			12 14	12 17		12 26	12 39		12 44	12 47					
	d				11 50	11 53			12 04	12 10	12 13				12 30	12 36		12 39			12 50		12 33		12 53
Adderley Park	d																	12 44							
Stechford	d										12 20							12 47							
Lea Hall	d										12 23							12 50							
Marston Green	d					12 01					12 26												12 41		13 01
Birmingham International ✈	a				11 59	12 05			12 13	12 19	12 29				12 39	12 50		12 55			12 59		12 45		13 05
	d				12 00	12 05			12 14	12 20	12 29				12 40						13 00		12 45		13 05
Hampton-in-Arden	d										12 32												12 48		
Berkswell	d					12 11					12 37														13 11
Tile Hill	d					12 14					12 40												12 55		13 14
Canley	d					12 17					12 44														13 17
Coventry	a				12 10	12 20			12 24	12 30	12 47				12 49						13 10		13 00		13 20
	d				12 11	12 21				12 31	12 48				12 51						13 11		13 01		13 21
Rugby	d			12 20	12 24	12 32					13 00										13 24		13 12	13 25	13 32
Long Buckby	d					12 42					13 10												13 22		13 42
Northampton	a			12 43		12 58					13 22												13 34	13 46	13 54
London Euston 15 ⊖	a			13 49	13 14	14 17				13 34	14 27				13 54						14 14		14 49		15 17

A ◇ from Northampton

Stafford - Wolverhampton - Birmingham - Coventry - Northampton

Network Diagram - see first Page of Table 67

		VT	LM	XC	VT	LM	LM		LM	VT	AW	XC	LM	LM	LM	LM	LM		VT	LM	VT	LM	XC	VT	LM
		◇1		◇1	◇1	1			◇1	◇1	◇	◇1			◇1	◇1	◇1		◇1	1	◇1		◇1	◇1	1
																A									
		⊠		🛒	🍴					🍴	🛒	🛒							🍴		🍴		🛒	🍴	
Stafford	d			12 25					12 43			13 02			13 10		13 21						13 25		
Penkridge	d														13 16										
Wolverhampton 7	a			12 39					12 56			13 15			13 27								13 39		
	d	12 32	12 37	12 41	12 45		12 49		12 57		13 09	13 16		13 19	13 28						13 32	13 37	13 41	13 45	
Coseley	d						12 54		13 03					13 24											
Tipton	d						12 56							13 26											
Dudley Port	d						12 58							13 28											
Sandwell & Dudley	d		12 46		12 56		13 02							13 32								13 46		13 56	
Smethwick Galton Bridge 7	d						13 04				13 20			13 34	13 40										
Smethwick Rolfe Street	d						13 06							13 36											
Birmingham New Street 12	a	12 55	12 55	12 58	13 06		13 14		13 17		13 26	13 39		13 44	13 47						13 55	13 55	13 58	14 06	
	d			13 04	13 10	13 13				13 30	13 36		13 39			13 33			13 50	13 53			14 04	14 10	14 13
Adderley Park	d												13 44												
Stechford	d					13 20							13 47												14 20
Lea Hall	d					13 23							13 50												14 23
Marston Green	d					13 26										13 41				14 01					14 26
Birmingham International ✈	a			13 13	13 19	13 29				13 39	13 50		13 55			13 45			13 59	14 05			14 13	14 19	14 29
	d			13 14	13 20	13 29				13 40						13 45			14 00	14 05			14 14	14 20	14 29
Hampton-in-Arden	d					13 32										13 48									14 32
Berkswell	d					13 37														14 11					14 37
Tile Hill	d					13 40										13 55				14 14					14 40
Canley	d					13 44														14 17					14 44
Coventry	a			13 24	13 30	13 47				13 49						14 00			14 10	14 20			14 24	14 30	14 47
	d				13 31	13 48				13 51						14 01			14 11	14 21				14 31	14 48
Rugby	d					13 59										14 12	14 20		14 24	14 32					14 59
Long Buckby	d					14 09										14 22				14 42					15 09
Northampton	a					14 21										14 35	14 42			14 54					15 21
London Euston 15 ⊖	a				14 33	15 27				14 54						15 49			15 14	16 17				15 34	16 27

		LM	LM		VT	AW	XC	LM	LM	LM	LM	LM	VT		LM	VT	LM	XC	VT	LM	LM	LM	VT		AW
			◇1		◇1	◇	◇1			◇1	◇1	◇1	◇1		1	◇1		◇1	◇1	1		◇1	◇1		◇
											A														
					🍴	🛒	🛒						🍴			⊠		🛒	🍴				🍴		🛒
Stafford	d		13 43				14 02			14 10		14 21						14 25				14 46			
Penkridge	d									14 16															
Wolverhampton 7	a		13 56				14 15			14 27								14 39				14 59			
	d	13 49	13 57			14 09	14 16		14 19	14 28						14 32	14 37	14 41	14 45		14 49	14 59			15 09
Coseley	d	13 54	14 03						14 24												14 54	15 05			
Tipton	d	13 56							14 26												14 56				
Dudley Port	d	13 58							14 28												14 58				
Sandwell & Dudley	d	14 02							14 32								14 46		14 56		15 02				
Smethwick Galton Bridge 7	d	14 04				14 20			14 34	14 40											15 04				15 20
Smethwick Rolfe Street	d	14 06							14 36												15 06				
Birmingham New Street 12	a	14 14	14 17			14 26	14 32		14 44	14 47						14 55	14 55	14 58	15 06		15 14	15 20			15 26
	d				14 30	14 36		14 39			14 33		14 50		14 53			15 04	15 10	15 13			15 30		15 36
Adderley Park	d							14 44																	
Stechford	d							14 47												15 20					
Lea Hall	d							14 50												15 23					
Marston Green	d										14 41				15 01					15 26					
Birmingham International ✈	a				14 39	14 50		14 55			14 45		14 59		15 05			15 13	15 19	15 29			15 39		15 50
	d				14 40						14 45		15 00		15 05			15 14	15 20	15 29			15 40		
Hampton-in-Arden	d										14 48									15 32					
Berkswell	d														15 11					15 37					
Tile Hill	d										14 55				15 14					15 40					
Canley	d														15 17					15 44					
Coventry	a				14 49						15 00		15 10		15 20			15 24	15 30	15 47			15 49		
	d				14 51						15 01		15 11		15 21				15 31	15 48			15 51		
Rugby	d										15 12	15 20	15 24		15 32					15 59					
Long Buckby	d										15 22				15 42										
Northampton	a										15 34	15 42			15 54					16 18					
London Euston 15 ⊖	a				15 54						16 49		16 14		17 18				16 34	17 27			16 57		

A ◇ from Northampton

Stafford - Wolverhampton - Birmingham - Coventry - Northampton

Network Diagram - see first Page of Table 67

		LM	LM	LM	LM	LM	VT	LM	VT	LM	XC	VT	LM	LM	LM	VT	AW	XC	LM	LM	LM
				1	◇1	◇1	◇1	1	◇1		◇1	◇1	1		◇1	◇1	◇	◇1			◇1
					A																
							☕		☕		🛒	☕				☕	🛒	🛒			
Stafford	d			15 10		15 21					15 25				15 43			16 03			16 10
Penkridge	d			15 16																	16 16
Wolverhampton 7	a			15 27							15 39				15 56			16 15			16 26
	d		15 19	15 28					15 32	15 37	15 41	15 45		15 49	15 57		16 09	16 17		16 19	16 28
Coseley	d		15 24											15 54	16 03					16 24	
Tipton	d		15 26											15 56						16 26	
Dudley Port	d		15 28											15 58						16 28	
Sandwell & Dudley	d		15 32							15 46		15 56		16 02						16 32	
Smethwick Galton Bridge 7	d		15 34	15 40										16 04			16 20			16 34	16 40
Smethwick Rolfe Street	d		15 36											16 06						16 36	
Birmingham New Street 12	a		15 44	15 47					15 55	15 55	15 58	16 06		16 14	16 17		16 26	16 39		16 44	16 47
	d	15 39			15 33		15 50	15 53			16 04	16 10	16 13			16 30	16 36		16 39		
Adderley Park	d	15 44																	16 44		
Stechford	d	15 47											16 20						16 47		
Lea Hall	d	15 50											16 23						16 50		
Marston Green	d				15 41			16 01					16 26								
Birmingham International ✈	a	15 55			15 45		15 59	16 05			16 13	16 19	16 29			16 39	16 50		16 55		
	d				15 45		16 00	16 05			16 14	16 20	16 29			16 40					
Hampton-in-Arden	d				15 48								16 32								
Berkswell	d							16 11					16 37								
Tile Hill	d				15 55			16 14					16 40								
Canley	d							16 17					16 44								
Coventry	a				16 00		16 10	16 20			16 24	16 30	16 47			16 49					
	d				16 01		16 11	16 21				16 31				16 51					
Rugby	d				16 12	16 20	16 24	16 32													
Long Buckby	d				16 22			16 42													
Northampton	a				16 34	16 43		16 54													
London Euston 15 ⊖	a				17 49		17 14	18 18				17 34				17 54					

		LM	LM	VT	LM	VT	LM	XC	VT	LM	LM	LM	LM	VT	AW	XC	LM	LM	LM	LM	LM	VT	LM
		◇1	◇1	◇1	1	◇1		◇1	◇1	1		1	◇1	◇1	◇	◇1			◇1	◇1	◇1	◇1	1
		A																		A			
				☕		☕		🛒	☕					⊠	🛒	🛒						⊠	
Stafford	d		16 21					16 25					16 46			17 03			17 10		17 21		
Penkridge	d																		17 16				
Wolverhampton 7	a							16 39					16 59			17 15			17 27				
	d					16 32	16 37	16 41	16 45		16 49		16 59		17 10	17 16		17 19	17 28				
Coseley	d										16 54		17 05					17 24					
Tipton	d										16 56							17 26					
Dudley Port	d										16 58							17 28					
Sandwell & Dudley	d						16 46		16 56		17 02							17 32					
Smethwick Galton Bridge 7	d										17 04				17 21			17 34	17 40				
Smethwick Rolfe Street	d										17 06							17 36					
Birmingham New Street 12	a					16 55	16 55	16 58	17 06		17 14		17 20		17 27	17 32		17 44	17 47				
	d	16 33		16 50	16 53			17 04	17 10	17 13		17 16		17 30	17 36		17 39			17 33		17 50	17 53
Adderley Park	d											17 21					17 44						
Stechford	d									17 20							17 47						
Lea Hall	d											17 25					17 50						
Marston Green	d	16 41			17 01							17 28								17 41			18 01
Birmingham International ✈	a	16 45		16 59	17 05			17 13	17 19	17 25		17 32		17 39	17 50		17 55			17 45		17 59	18 05
	d	16 45		17 00	17 05			17 14	17 20	17 25		17 32		17 40						17 45		18 00	18 05
Hampton-in-Arden	d	16 48										17 35								17 48			
Berkswell	d				17 11							17 40											18 11
Tile Hill	d	16 55			17 14					17 32										17 55			18 14
Canley	d				17 17					17 36													18 17
Coventry	a	17 00		17 10	17 20			17 24	17 30	17 40		17 47		17 49						18 00		18 10	18 20
	d	17 01		17 11	17 21				17 31	17 40				17 51						18 01		18 11	18 21
Rugby	d	17 12	17 20	17 24	17 32					17 51										18 12	18 20	18 24	18 32
Long Buckby	d	17 22			17 42					18 01										18 22			18 42
Northampton	a	17 34	17 39		17 54					18 13										18 34	18 39		18 54
London Euston 15 ⊖	a	18 49		18 14	19 18				18 34	19 29				18 54						19 50		19 14	20 19

A ◇ from Northampton

Stafford - Wolverhampton - Birmingham - Coventry - Northampton

Network Diagram - see first Page of Table 67

		VT		LM	XC	VT	LM	LM	LM	VT	AW	XC		LM	LM	LM	LM	LM	VT	LM	VT	LM		XC	VT
		◇1			◇1	◇1	1		◇1	◇1	◇	◇1				◇1	◇1 A	◇1	◇1	1	R 1			◇1	◇1
		⊡			⊼	⊠				⊠	⊼	⊼							⊠		⊡			⊼	⊠
Stafford	d				17 25				17 43			18 04				18 10		18 21						18 28	
Penkridge	d															18 16									
Wolverhampton 7	a				17 39				17 56			18 15				18 27								18 39	
	d	17 32		17 37	17 41	17 45		17 49	17 57		18 09	18 16			18 19	18 28					18 32	18 37		18 41	18 45
Coseley	d							17 54	18 03						18 24										
Tipton	d							17 56							18 26										
Dudley Port	d							17 58							18 28										
Sandwell & Dudley	d			17 46		17 56		18 02							18 32							18 46			18 56
Smethwick Galton Bridge 7	d							18 04			18 20				18 34	18 40									
Smethwick Rolfe Street	d							18 06							18 36										
Birmingham New Street 12	a	17 55		17 55	17 58	18 06		18 14	18 17		18 26	18 38			18 44	18 48					18 55	18 55		18 58	19 06
	d				18 04	18 10	18 13			18 30	18 36			18 39			18 33		18 50	18 53				19 04	19 10
Adderley Park	d													18 44											
Stechford	d						18 20							18 47											
Lea Hall	d						18 23							18 50											
Marston Green	d						18 26										18 41			19 01					
Birmingham International	a				18 13	18 19	18 29			18 39	18 50			18 55			18 45		18 59	19 05				19 13	19 19
	d				18 14	18 20	18 29			18 40							18 45		19 00	19 05				19 14	19 20
Hampton-in-Arden	d						18 32										18 48								
Berkswell	d						18 37													19 11					
Tile Hill	d						18 40										18 55			19 14					
Canley	d						18 44													19 17					
Coventry	a				18 24	18 30	18 47			18 49							19 00		19 10	19 20				19 24	19 30
	d					18 31				18 51							19 01		19 11	19 21					19 31
Rugby	d																19 12	19 20	19 24	19 32					
Long Buckby	d																19 22			19 42					
Northampton	a																19 34	19 45		19 55					
London Euston 15 ⊖	a					19 34				19 54							20 49		20 14	21 17					20 34

		LM	LM	LM	VT	AW	XC	LM		LM	LM	LM	LM	VT	LM	VT	LM	XC		VT	LM	LM	LM	LM	AW
		1		◇1	◇1	◇	◇1	1				◇1	◇1	◇1	1	◇1		◇1 B		◇1	1		◇1	1	◇
					⊡	⊼	⊼							⊡		⊡		⊼		⊡					⊼
Stafford	d			18 43			19 02					19 10	19 21					19 25					19 42		
Penkridge	d											19 16											19 47		
Wolverhampton 7	a			18 56			19 15					19 27						19 39					19 57		
	d		18 49	18 57		19 09	19 16				19 19	19 28				19 32	19 37	19 41		19 45		19 49	19 57		20 10
Coseley	d		18 54	19 03							19 24											19 54	20 03		
Tipton	d		18 56								19 26											19 56			
Dudley Port	d		18 58								19 28											19 58			
Sandwell & Dudley	d		19 02								19 32						19 46			19 56		20 02			
Smethwick Galton Bridge 7	d		19 04			19 20					19 34	19 40										20 04			20 21
Smethwick Rolfe Street	d		19 06								19 36											20 06			
Birmingham New Street 12	a		19 14	19 17		19 26	19 32				19 44	19 47				19 55	19 55	19 58		20 06		20 14	20 18		20 26
	d	19 13			19 30	19 36		19 33		19 39				19 50	19 53			20 04		20 10	20 13			20 33	20 36
Adderley Park	d									19 44															
Stechford	d	19 20								19 47											20 20				
Lea Hall	d	19 23								19 50											20 23				
Marston Green	d	19 26						19 41							20 01						20 26			20 41	
Birmingham International	a	19 29			19 39	19 50		19 45		19 55				19 59	20 05			20 13		20 19	20 29			20 45	20 50
	d	19 29			19 40			19 45						20 00	20 05			20 14		20 20	20 29			20 45	
Hampton-in-Arden	d	19 32						19 48													20 32			20 48	
Berkswell	d	19 37													20 11						20 37				
Tile Hill	d	19 40						19 55							20 14						20 40			20 55	
Canley	d	19 44													20 17						20 44				
Coventry	a	19 47			19 49			20 00						20 10	20 20			20 24		20 30	20 47			21 00	
	d				19 51			20 01						20 11	20 21					20 31				21 01	
Rugby	d							20 12					20 20	20 23	20 32									21 12	
Long Buckby	d							20 22							20 42									21 22	
Northampton	a							20 37					20 43		20 54									21 34	
London Euston 15 ⊖	a				20 54									21 14	22 20					21 38					

A ◇ from Northampton

B ⊼ to Birmingham New Street

Stafford - Wolverhampton - Birmingham - Coventry - Northampton

Network Diagram - see first Page of Table 67

		XC	LM	LM	LM	VT	LM	VT	LM	XC	VT	LM	LM	LM	XC	LM	LM	LM	LM	VT	LM	LM
								R														
		◇1			◇1	◇1	1	1		◇1	◇1	1		◇1	◇1	1			◇1	◇1	1	
										A												
		🛒				☕		☕		🛒	☕									☕		
Stafford	d	20 04			20 16					20 26				20 42	21 03				21 10	21 13		
Penkridge	d													20 47					21 16			
Wolverhampton 7	a	20 16			20 29					20 40				20 57	21 15				21 26	21 29		
	d	20 17		20 19	20 29			20 34	20 38	20 43	20 47		20 49	20 57	21 16			21 19	21 28	21 32		21 37
Coseley	d			20 24									20 54	21 03				21 24				
Tipton	d			20 26									20 56					21 26				
Dudley Port	d			20 28									20 58					21 28				
Sandwell & Dudley	d			20 32					20 47		20 57		21 02					21 32				21 46
Smethwick Galton Bridge 7	d			20 34	20 41								21 04					21 34	21 40			
Smethwick Rolfe Street	d			20 36									21 06					21 36				
Birmingham New Street 12	a	20 33		20 44	20 47			20 55	20 56	21 00	21 06		21 14	21 18	21 32			21 44	21 47	21 48		21 55
	d		20 39			20 50	20 53			21 04	21 10	21 13				21 33	21 39				21 53	
Adderley Park	d		20 44														21 44					
Stechford	d		20 47									21 20					21 48					
Lea Hall	d		20 50									21 23					21 50					
Marston Green	d						21 01					21 26				21 41					22 01	
Birmingham International ✈	a		20 55			20 59	21 05			21 13	21 19	21 29				21 45	21 55				22 05	
	d					21 00	21 05			21 14	21 20	21 29				21 45					22 05	
Hampton-in-Arden	d											21 32				21 48						
Berkswell	d						21 11					21 37									22 11	
Tile Hill	d						21 14					21 40				21 55					22 14	
Canley	d						21 17					21 44									22 17	
Coventry	a					21 10	21 20			21 24	21 30	21 53				22 00					22 20	
	d					21 11	21 21				21 31					22 01					22 21	
Rugby	d					21 23	21 32									22 12					22 32	
Long Buckby	d						21 42									22 22					22 42	
Northampton	a						21 54									22 34					22 55	
London Euston 15 ⊖	a					22 12	23 21				22 43					00 21						

		XC	XC	VT	LM	LM	LM	AW	LM	LM	VT	LM	VT	LM	XC	VT	LM	LM	AW MW FO	AW TThO	LM	XC	LM
									R														
		◇1	◇1	◇1	1		◇1	◇	1		◇1	1	◇1		◇1	◇1	1		◇	◇	◇1	◇1	1
																			B	C			
				☕							☕		☕			☕							
Stafford	d	21 25					21 41								22 26						22 41	23 07	
Penkridge	d						21 47														22 47		
Wolverhampton 7	a	21 39					21 57								22 39						22 57	23 19	
	d	21 41		21 45		21 49	21 57	22 09		22 19	22 28		22 32	22 37	22 41	22 45		22 49	22 55	22 55	22 57	23 21	
Coseley	d					21 54	22 03			22 24								22 54			23 03		
Tipton	d					21 56				22 26								22 56					
Dudley Port	d					21 58				22 28								22 58					
Sandwell & Dudley	d			21 56		22 02				22 32				22 46		22 55		23 02					
Smethwick Galton Bridge 7	d					22 04		22 20		22 34								23 04					
Smethwick Rolfe Street	d					22 06				22 36								23 06					
Birmingham New Street 12	a	22 00		22 06		22 14	22 17	22 32		22 44	22 50		22 55	22 55	22 58	23 06		23 14	23 27	23 28	23 18	23 39	
	d		22 04	22 10	22 13				22 33			22 53				23 10	23 13						23 53
Adderley Park	d																23 18						
Stechford	d				22 20												23 21						
Lea Hall	d				22 23												23 24						
Marston Green	d				22 26				22 41			23 01					23 27						00 01
Birmingham International ✈	a		22 13	22 19	22 29				22 45			23 05				23 19	23 30						00 04
	d		22 14	22 20	22 29				22 45			23 05				23 20	23 30						00 05
Hampton-in-Arden	d				22 32				22 48								23 33						
Berkswell	d				22 37							23 11					23 38						
Tile Hill	d				22 40				22 55			23 14					23 41						
Canley	d				22 44							23 17					23 45						
Coventry	a		22 24	22 30	22 47				23 00			23 20				23 30	23 48						00 15
	d			22 31								23 21				23 31							
Rugby	d			22 43								23 32				23 44							
Long Buckby	d											23 42											
Northampton	a											23 54				00s05							
London Euston 15 ⊖	a			00 04												01 15							

A 🛒 to Birmingham New Street

Table 68

Saturdays

Stafford - Wolverhampton - Birmingham - Coventry - Northampton

Network Diagram - see first Page of Table 67

		LM	VT	VT	LM	VT	AW	XC	VT	LM		AW	VT	LM	AW	LM	LM	VT	LM	XC		VT	LM	LM	LM
		1	◇1 ☕	◇1 ☕	1	◇1 ☕		◇1 🛒	◇1 ☕	1			◇1 ☕	◇1				◇1 ☕	◇1	◇1 🛒		◇1 ☕	◇1		◇1
Stafford	d						05 25													06 26					06 41
Penkridge	d																								06 47
Wolverhampton 7	a						05 39													06 39					06 57
	d		21p45	22p45			05 40		05 45			06 03	06 06				06 19	06 27		06 41		06 45		06 49	06 57
Coseley	d																06 24							06 54	07 03
Tipton	d																06 26							06 56	
Dudley Port	d																06 28							06 58	
Sandwell & Dudley	d		21p56	22p55					05 56				06 17				06 32	06 37				06 56		07 02	
Smethwick Galton Bridge 7	d											06 14					06 34							07 04	
Smethwick Rolfe Street	d														←		06 36							07 06	
Birmingham New Street 12	a		22p06	23p06			05 58		06 06			06 20	06 26		06 20		06 44	06 47		06 57		07 06		07 14	07 17
	d	21p33	22p10	23p10	23p53	05 50		06 04	06 10	06 13		06 36	06 30	06 33	06 36	06 39		06 50	06 53	07 04		07 10	07 13		
Adderley Park	d											↪				06 44									
Stechford	d									06 20						06 47							07 20		
Lea Hall	d									06 23						06 50							07 23		
Marston Green	d	21p41			00 01					06 26				06 41					07 01				07 26		
Birmingham International ✈	a	21p45	22p19	23p19	00 04	05 59		06 13	06 19	06 29			06 39	06 45	06 50	06 54		06 59	07 05	07 13		07 19	07 29		
	d	21p45	22p20	23p20	00 05	06 00		06 14	06 20	06 29			06 40	06 45				07 00	07 05	07 14		07 20	07 29		
Hampton-in-Arden	d	21p48								06 32				06 48									07 32		
Berkswell	d									06 37									07 11				07 37		
Tile Hill	d	21p55								06 40				06 55					07 14				07 40		
Canley	d									06 44									07 17				07 44		
Coventry	a	22p00	22p30	23p30	00 15	06 10		06 24	06 30	06 47			06 50	07 00				07 10	07 20	07 24		07 30	07 47		
	d	22p01	22p31	23p31		06 10			06 31				06 51	07 01				07 11	07 21			07 31	07 48		
Rugby	d	22p12	22p43	23p44		06 24								07 12				07 23	07 32				07 59		
Long Buckby	d	22p22												07 22					07 42				08 09		
Northampton	a	22p34		00s05										07 34					07 54				08 21		
London Euston 15 ⊖	a	00 21	00 04	01 15		07 16			07 38				07 55					08 14	09 17			08 34	09 27		

		VT	AW	XC	LM	LM		LM	LM	LM	VT	LM	VT	LM	XC	VT		LM	LM	LM	VT	AW	XC	LM	LM
		◇1 ☕	🛒	◇1 🛒				◇1	◇1	◇1	◇1 ☕	◇1	◇1 ☕		◇1 🛒	◇1 ☕		◇1		◇1	◇1 ☕	◇ 🛒	◇1 🛒		
Stafford	d			06 58				07 12		07 24										07 41			08 03		
Penkridge	d							07 18												07 47					
Wolverhampton 7	a			07 12				07 28												07 57			08 16		
	d	07 04	07 10	07 15		07 19		07 28					07 32	07 37		07 45			07 49	07 57	08 06	08 09	08 18		08 19
Coseley	d					07 24													07 54	08 03					08 24
Tipton	d					07 26													07 56						08 26
Dudley Port	d					07 28													07 58						08 28
Sandwell & Dudley	d	07 15				07 32								07 46		07 56			08 02						08 32
Smethwick Galton Bridge 7	d		07 21			07 34		07 40											08 04			08 21			08 34
Smethwick Rolfe Street	d					07 36													08 06						08 36
Birmingham New Street 12	a	07 24	07 26	07 31		07 44		07 47					07 55	07 55		08 06			08 14	08 17	08 23	08 26	08 38		08 44
	d	07 30	07 36		07 39				07 33		07 50	07 53			08 04	08 10		08 13			08 30	08 36		08 39	
Adderley Park	d				07 44																			08 44	
Stechford	d				07 47													08 20						08 47	
Lea Hall	d				07 50													08 23						08 50	
Marston Green	d								07 41			08 01						08 26							
Birmingham International ✈	a	07 39	07 50		07 54				07 45		07 59	08 05			08 13	08 19		08 29			08 39	08 50		08 54	
	d	07 40							07 45		08 00	08 05			08 14	08 20		08 29			08 40				
Hampton-in-Arden	d								07 48									08 32							
Berkswell	d											08 11						08 37							
Tile Hill	d								07 55			08 14						08 40							
Canley	d											08 17						08 44							
Coventry	a	07 50							08 00		08 10	08 20			08 24	08 30		08 47			08 49				
	d	07 52							08 01		08 11	08 21				08 31		08 48			08 51				
Rugby	d								08 12	08 20	08 23	08 32						08 59							
Long Buckby	d								08 22			08 42						09 09							
Northampton	a								08 34	08 40		08 54						09 21							
London Euston 15 ⊖	a	08 54							09 50		09 14	10 17				09 35		10 27			09 55				

Table 68

Saturdays

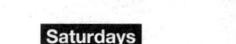

Stafford - Wolverhampton - Birmingham - Coventry - Northampton

Network Diagram - see first Page of Table 67

		LM ◇1		LM ◇1	LM ◇1	VT ◇1 🍴	LM ◇1	VT ◇1 🍴	LM	XC ◇1 🛒	VT ◇1 🍴	LM ◇1		LM	LM ◇1	VT ◇1 🍴	AW ◇ 🛒	XC ◇1 🛒	LM	LM	LM ◇1	LM ◇1	LM ◇1		VT ◇1 🍴
Stafford	d	08 10			08 23					08 26					08 43			09 03			09 10		09 21		
Penkridge	d	08 16													08 48						09 16				
Wolverhampton 7 🚢	a	08 28								08 39					08 58			09 15			09 27				
	d	08 28						08 32	08 37	08 41	08 45			08 49	08 59		09 10	09 17		09 19	09 28				
Coseley	d													08 54	09 04					09 24					
Tipton	d													08 56						09 26					
Dudley Port	d													08 58						09 28					
Sandwell & Dudley	d								08 46		08 56			09 02						09 32					
Smethwick Galton Bridge 7	d	08 40												09 04			09 22			09 34	09 40				
Smethwick Rolfe Street	d													09 06						09 36					
Birmingham New Street 12	a	08 47						08 55	08 55	08 58	09 05			09 14	09 18		09 26	09 39		09 44	09 47				
	d			08 33		08 50	08 53			09 04	09 10	09 13				09 30	09 36		09 39			09 33			09 50
Adderley Park	d																		09 44						
Stechford	d											09 20							09 47						
Lea Hall	d											09 23							09 50						
Marston Green	d			08 41			09 01					09 26										09 41			
Birmingham International ✈	a			08 45		08 59	09 05			09 13	09 19	09 29				09 39	09 50		09 54			09 45			09 59
	d			08 45		09 00	09 05			09 14	09 20	09 29				09 40						09 45			10 00
Hampton-in-Arden	d			08 48								09 32										09 48			
Berkswell	d						09 11					09 37													
Tile Hill	d			08 55			09 14					09 40										09 55			
Canley	d						09 17					09 44													
Coventry	a			09 00		09 10	09 20			09 24	09 30	09 47				09 49						10 00			10 10
	d			09 01		09 11	09 21				09 31	09 48				09 51						10 01			10 11
Rugby	d			09 12	09 20	09 23	09 32					09 59										10 12	10 20		10 23
Long Buckby	d			09 22			09 42					10 09										10 22			
Northampton	a			09 34	09 41		09 58					10 21										10 34	10 39		
London Euston 15 ⊖	a			10 49		10 14	11 17				10 34	11 27				10 54						11 49			11 14

		LM ◇1	VT ◇1 🍴	LM	XC ◇1 🛒	VT ◇1 🍴	LM ◇1	LM	LM ◇1		VT ◇1 🍴	AW ◇ 🛒	XC ◇1 🛒	LM	LM	LM ◇1	LM ◇1	LM ◇1	VT ◇1 🍴		LM ◇1	VT ◇1 🍴	LM	XC ◇1 🛒	VT ◇1 🍴
Stafford	d				09 26				09 43				10 03			10 10		10 21						10 26	
Penkridge	d															10 16									
Wolverhampton 7 🚢	a				09 39				09 56				10 15			10 27								10 39	
	d		09 32	09 37	09 41	09 45		09 49	09 57			10 09	10 17		10 19	10 28						10 32	10 37	10 41	10 45
Coseley	d							09 54	10 03						10 24										
Tipton	d							09 56							10 26										
Dudley Port	d							09 58							10 28										
Sandwell & Dudley	d			09 46		09 56		10 02							10 32								10 46		10 56
Smethwick Galton Bridge 7	d							10 04				10 20			10 34	10 40									
Smethwick Rolfe Street	d							10 06							10 36										
Birmingham New Street 12	a		09 55	09 55	09 58	10 06		10 14	10 17			10 26	10 39		10 44	10 47						10 55	10 55	10 58	11 06
	d	09 53			10 04	10 10	10 13				10 30	10 36		10 39			10 33		10 50		10 53			11 04	11 10
Adderley Park	d													10 44											
Stechford	d						10 20							10 47											
Lea Hall	d						10 23							10 50											
Marston Green	d	10 01					10 26										10 41				11 01				
Birmingham International ✈	a	10 05			10 13	10 19	10 29				10 39	10 50		10 54			10 45		10 59		11 05			11 13	11 19
	d	10 05			10 14	10 20	10 29				10 40						10 45		11 00		11 05			11 14	11 20
Hampton-in-Arden	d						10 32										10 48								
Berkswell	d	10 11					10 37														11 11				
Tile Hill	d	10 14					10 40										10 55				11 14				
Canley	d	10 17					10 44														11 17				
Coventry	a	10 20			10 24	10 30	10 47				10 49						11 00		11 10		11 20			11 24	11 30
	d	10 21				10 31	10 48				10 51						11 01		11 11		11 21				11 31
Rugby	d	10 32					10 59										11 12	11 20	11 23		11 32				
Long Buckby	d	10 42					11 09										11 22				11 42				
Northampton	a	10 54					11 21										11 34	11 39			11 54				
London Euston 15 ⊖	a	12 17				11 34	12 27				11 55						12 49		12 14		13 17				12 34

Table 68

Saturdays

Stafford - Wolverhampton - Birmingham - Coventry - Northampton

Network Diagram - see first Page of Table 67

Station		LM	LM	LM	VT		AW	XC	LM	LM	LM	LM	LM	VT	LM		VT	LM	XC	VT	LM	LM	LM	VT	AW
		◇1		◇1	◇1		◇	◇1			◇1	◇1	◇1	◇1	◇1		◇1		◇1	◇1	◇1		◇1	◇1	◇
					☕		🛒	🛒						☕			☕		🛒	☕				☕	🛒
Stafford	d			10 43				11 03			11 10		11 21						11 26				11 43		
Penkridge	d										11 16														
Wolverhampton 7 ⇌	a			10 56				11 16			11 27								11 39				11 56		
	d		10 49	10 57			11 09	11 17		11 19	11 28						11 33	11 37	11 41	11 45		11 49	11 57		12 09
Coseley	d		10 54	11 03						11 24												11 54	12 03		
Tipton	d		10 56							11 26												11 56			
Dudley Port	d		10 58							11 28												11 58			
Sandwell & Dudley	d		11 02							11 32								11 46		11 56		12 02			
Smethwick Galton Bridge 7	d		11 04				11 20			11 34	11 40											12 04			12 20
Smethwick Rolfe Street	d		11 06							11 36												12 06			
Birmingham New Street 12	a		11 14	11 17			11 26	11 39		11 44	11 47						11 55	11 55	11 58	12 06		12 14	12 17		12 26
	d	11 13			11 30		11 36		11 39			11 33		11 50	11 53				12 04	12 10	12 13			12 30	12 36
Adderley Park	d								11 44																
Stechford	d	11 20							11 47												12 20				
Lea Hall	d	11 23							11 50												12 23				
Marston Green	d	11 26										11 41			12 01						12 26				
Birmingham International ✈	a	11 29			11 39		11 50		11 54			11 45		11 59	12 05				12 13	12 19	12 29			12 39	12 50
	d	11 29			11 40							11 45		12 00	12 05				12 14	12 20	12 29			12 40	
Hampton-in-Arden	d	11 32										11 48									12 32				
Berkswell	d	11 37													12 11						12 37				
Tile Hill	d	11 40										11 55			12 14						12 40				
Canley	d	11 44													12 17						12 44				
Coventry	a	11 47			11 49							12 00		12 10	12 20				12 24	12 30	12 47			12 49	
	d	11 48			11 51							12 01		12 11	12 21					12 31	12 48			12 51	
Rugby	d	11 59										12 12	12 20	12 23	12 32						12 59				
Long Buckby	d	12 09										12 22			12 42						13 09				
Northampton	a	12 21										12 34	12 39		12 54						13 21				
London Euston 15 ⊖	a	13 27			12 54							13 49		13 14	14 17					13 34	14 27			13 54	

Station			XC	LM	LM	LM	LM	LM	VT	LM	VT		LM	XC	VT	LM	LM	LM	VT	AW	XC		LM	LM	LM
			◇1			◇1	◇1	◇1	◇1	◇1	◇1			◇1	◇1	◇1		◇1	◇1		◇1				◇1
			🛒						☕		☕			🛒	☕				☕		🛒				
Stafford	d		12 03			12 10		12 21						12 25				12 43			13 03				13 10
Penkridge	d					12 16																			13 16
Wolverhampton 7 ⇌	a		12 16			12 27								12 39				12 56			13 15				13 27
	d		12 17		12 19	12 28					12 32		12 37	12 41	12 45		12 49	12 57		13 09	13 16			13 19	13 28
Coseley	d				12 24												12 54	13 03						13 24	
Tipton	d				12 26												12 56							13 26	
Dudley Port	d				12 28												12 58							13 28	
Sandwell & Dudley	d				12 32								12 46		12 56		13 02							13 32	
Smethwick Galton Bridge 7	d				12 34	12 40											13 04			13 20				13 34	13 40
Smethwick Rolfe Street	d				12 36												13 06							13 36	
Birmingham New Street 12	a		12 39		12 44	12 47					12 55		12 55	12 58	13 06		13 14	13 17		13 26	13 39			13 44	13 47
	d			12 39			12 33		12 50	12 53				13 04	13 10	13 13			13 30	13 36			13 39		
Adderley Park	d			12 44																			13 44		
Stechford	d			12 47												13 20							13 47		
Lea Hall	d			12 50												13 23							13 50		
Marston Green	d						12 41			13 01						13 26									
Birmingham International ✈	a			12 54			12 45		12 59	13 05				13 13	13 19	13 29			13 39	13 50			13 54		
	d						12 45		13 00	13 05				13 14	13 20	13 29			13 40						
Hampton-in-Arden	d						12 48									13 32									
Berkswell	d									13 11						13 37									
Tile Hill	d						12 55			13 14						13 40									
Canley	d									13 17						13 44									
Coventry	a						13 00		13 10	13 20				13 24	13 30	13 47			13 49						
	d						13 01		13 11	13 21					13 31	13 48			13 51						
Rugby	d						13 12	13 20	13 23	13 32						13 59									
Long Buckby	d						13 22			13 42						14 09									
Northampton	a						13 34	13 39		13 54						14 21									
London Euston 15 ⊖	a						14 49		14 14	15 18					14 34	15 27			14 54						

Table 68

Saturdays

Stafford - Wolverhampton - Birmingham - Coventry - Northampton

Network Diagram - see first Page of Table 67

		LM	LM	VT	LM	VT	LM		XC	VT	LM	LM	LM	VT	AW	XC	LM		LM	LM	LM	LM	VT	LM	VT
		◇1	◇1	◇1	◇1	◇1			◇1	◇1	◇1		◇1	◇1	◇	◇1				◇1	◇1	◇1	◇1	◇1	◇1
				☕		☕			🛒	☕				☕	🛒	🛒							☕		☕
Stafford	d		13 21						13 26				13 43			14 03				14 10		14 21			
Penkridge	d																			14 16					
Wolverhampton 7	a								13 39				13 56			14 16				14 27					
	d					13 32	13 37		13 41	13 45		13 49	13 57		14 09	14 17			14 19	14 28					14 32
Coseley	d											13 54	14 03						14 24						
Tipton	d											13 56							14 26						
Dudley Port	d											13 58							14 28						
Sandwell & Dudley	d						13 46			13 56		14 02							14 32						
Smethwick Galton Bridge 7	d											14 04			14 20				14 34	14 40					
Smethwick Rolfe Street	d											14 06							14 36						
Birmingham New Street 12	a					13 55	13 55		13 58	14 06		14 14	14 17		14 26	14 39			14 44	14 47					14 55
	d	13 33		13 50	13 53				14 04	14 10	14 13			14 30	14 36		14 39				14 33		14 50	14 53	
Adderley Park	d																14 44								
Stechford	d										14 20						14 47								
Lea Hall	d										14 23						14 50								
Marston Green	d	13 41			14 01						14 26										14 41			15 01	
Birmingham International ✈	a	13 45		13 59	14 05				14 13	14 19	14 29			14 39	14 50		14 54				14 45		14 59	15 05	
	d	13 45		14 00	14 05				14 14	14 20	14 29			14 40							14 45		15 00	15 05	
Hampton-in-Arden	d	13 48									14 32										14 48				
Berkswell	d				14 11						14 37													15 11	
Tile Hill	d	13 55			14 14						14 40										14 55			15 14	
Canley	d				14 17						14 44													15 17	
Coventry	a	14 00		14 10	14 20				14 24	14 30	14 47			14 49							15 00		15 10	15 20	
	d	14 01		14 11	14 21					14 31	14 48			14 51							15 01		15 11	15 21	
Rugby	d	14 12	14 20	14 23	14 32						14 59										15 12	15 20	15 23	15 32	
Long Buckby	d	14 22			14 42						15 09										15 22			15 42	
Northampton	a	14 34	14 39		14 54						15 21										15 34	15 39		15 54	
London Euston 15 ⊖	a	15 49		15 14	16 18					15 34	16 27			15 54							16 49		16 14	17 17	

		LM	XC		VT	LM	LM	LM	VT	AW	XC	LM	LM		LM	LM	LM	VT	LM	VT	LM	XC	VT		LM
			◇1		◇1	◇1		◇1	◇1	◇	◇1				◇1	◇1	◇1	◇1	◇1	◇1		◇1	◇1		◇1
			🛒		☕				☕	🛒	🛒							☕		☕		🛒	☕		
Stafford	d		14 26					14 46			15 03				15 10		15 21					15 26			
Penkridge	d														15 16										
Wolverhampton 7	a		14 39					14 59			15 16				15 27							15 39			
	d	14 37	14 41		14 45		14 49	14 59		15 09	15 17		15 19		15 28					15 32	15 37	15 41	15 45		
Coseley	d						14 54	15 05					15 24												
Tipton	d						14 56						15 26												
Dudley Port	d						14 58						15 28												
Sandwell & Dudley	d	14 46			14 56		15 02						15 32								15 46		15 56		
Smethwick Galton Bridge 7	d						15 04			15 20			15 34		15 40										
Smethwick Rolfe Street	d						15 06						15 36												
Birmingham New Street 12	a	14 55	14 58		15 06		15 14	15 18		15 26	15 39		15 44		15 47					15 55	15 55	15 58	16 06		
	d		15 04		15 10	15 13			15 30	15 36		15 39				15 33		15 50	15 53			16 04	16 10		16 13
Adderley Park	d											15 44													
Stechford	d					15 20						15 47													16 20
Lea Hall	d					15 23						15 50													16 23
Marston Green	d					15 26										15 41			16 01						16 26
Birmingham International ✈	a		15 13		15 19	15 29			15 39	15 50		15 54				15 45		15 59	16 05			16 13	16 19		16 29
	d		15 14		15 20	15 29			15 40							15 45		16 00	16 05			16 14	16 20		16 29
Hampton-in-Arden	d					15 32										15 48									16 32
Berkswell	d					15 37													16 11						16 37
Tile Hill	d					15 40										15 55			16 14						16 40
Canley	d					15 44													16 17						16 44
Coventry	a		15 24		15 30	15 47			15 49							16 00		16 10	16 20			16 24	16 30		16 47
	d				15 31	15 48			15 51							16 01		16 11	16 21				16 31		16 48
Rugby	d					15 59										16 12	16 20	16 23	16 32						16 59
Long Buckby	d					16 09										16 22			16 42						17 09
Northampton	a					16 21										16 34	16 39		16 54						17 21
London Euston 15 ⊖	a				16 34	17 27			16 54							17 49		17 14	18 17				17 34		18 27

Table 68

Saturdays

Stafford - Wolverhampton - Birmingham - Coventry - Northampton

Network Diagram - see first Page of Table 67

		LM	LM	VT	AW	XC	LM	LM	LM		LM	LM	VT	LM	VT	LM	XC	VT	LM		LM	LM	VT	AW	XC
			◇1	◇1	◇	◇1			◇1		◇1	◇1	◇1	◇1	◇1		◇1	◇1	◇1			◇1	◇1	◇	◇1
				🍴	🛒	🛒							🍴		🍴		🛒	🍴					🍴	🛒	🛒
Stafford	d		15 43			16 03			16 10			16 21					16 25					16 46			17 03
Penkridge	d								16 16																
Wolverhampton 7	a		15 56			16 16			16 27								16 39					16 59			17 16
	d	15 49	15 57		16 09	16 17		16 19	16 28						16 32	16 37	16 41	16 45			16 49	16 59		17 10	17 17
Coseley	d	15 54	16 03					16 24													16 54	17 05			
Tipton	d	15 56						16 26													16 56				
Dudley Port	d	15 58						16 28													16 58				
Sandwell & Dudley	d	16 02						16 32								16 46		16 56			17 02				
Smethwick Galton Bridge 7	d	16 04			16 20			16 34	16 40												17 04			17 22	
Smethwick Rolfe Street	d	16 06						16 36													17 06				
Birmingham New Street 12	a	16 14	16 17		16 26	16 39		16 44	16 47						16 55	16 55	16 58	17 06			17 14	17 18		17 28	17 39
	d			16 30	16 36		16 39				16 33		16 50	16 53			17 04	17 10	17 13				17 30	17 37	
Adderley Park	d						16 44												17 17						
Stechford	d						16 47												17 21						
Lea Hall	d						16 50												17 23						
Marston Green	d										16 41			17 01					17 26						
Birmingham International ✈	a			16 39	16 50		16 54				16 45		16 59	17 05			17 13	17 19	17 29				17 39	17 50	
	d			16 40							16 45		17 00	17 05			17 14	17 20	17 30				17 40		
Hampton-in-Arden	d										16 48								17 33						
Berkswell	d													17 11					17 38						
Tile Hill	d										16 55			17 14					17 41						
Canley	d													17 17					17 44						
Coventry	a			16 49							17 00		17 10	17 20			17 24	17 30	17 47				17 49		
	d			16 51							17 01		17 11	17 21				17 31	17 48				17 51		
Rugby	d										17 12	17 20	17 23	17 32					17 59						
Long Buckby	d										17 22			17 42					18 09						
Northampton	a										17 34	17 39		17 54					18 21						
London Euston 15 ⊖	a			17 52							18 49		18 14	19 17				18 34	19 45				18 54		

		LM	LM	LM	LM	LM		VT	LM	VT	LM	XC	VT	LM	LM	LM		VT	LM	AW	XC	LM	LM	LM	LM
				◇1	◇1	◇1		◇1	◇1	◇1		◇1	◇1	◇1		◇1		◇1	◇1	◇	◇1			◇1	◇1
								🍴		🍴		🛒	🍴					🍴		🛒	🛒				
Stafford	d			17 10		17 21						17 26				17 43					18 04			18 10	18 21
Penkridge	d			17 16																				18 16	
Wolverhampton 7	a			17 27								17 39				17 56					18 16			18 27	
	d		17 19	17 28						17 32	17 37	17 41	17 45		17 49	17 57				18 09	18 17		18 19	18 28	
Coseley	d		17 24												17 54	18 03							18 24		
Tipton	d		17 26												17 56								18 26		
Dudley Port	d		17 28												17 58								18 28		
Sandwell & Dudley	d		17 32								17 46		17 56		18 02								18 32		
Smethwick Galton Bridge 7	d		17 34	17 40											18 04					18 20			18 34	18 40	
Smethwick Rolfe Street	d		17 36												18 06								18 36		
Birmingham New Street 12	a		17 44	17 47						17 55	17 55	17 58	18 06		18 14	18 17				18 26	18 38		18 44	18 47	
	d	17 39			17 33			17 50	17 53			18 04	18 10	18 13				18 30	18 33	18 36		18 39			
Adderley Park	d	17 44																				18 44			
Stechford	d	17 47												18 20								18 47			
Lea Hall	d	17 50												18 23								18 50			
Marston Green	d				17 41				18 01					18 26					18 41						
Birmingham International ✈	a	17 54			17 45			17 59	18 05			18 13	18 19	18 29				18 39	18 45	18 50		18 54			
	d				17 45			18 00	18 05			18 14	18 20	18 29				18 40	18 45						
Hampton-in-Arden	d				17 48									18 32					18 48						
Berkswell	d								18 11					18 37											
Tile Hill	d				17 55				18 14					18 40					18 55						
Canley	d								18 17					18 44											
Coventry	a				18 00			18 10	18 20			18 24	18 30	18 47				18 49	19 00						
	d				18 01			18 11	18 21				18 31	18 48				18 51	19 01						
Rugby	d				18 12	18 20		18 23	18 32					18 59					19 12						19 20
Long Buckby	d				18 22				18 42					19 09					19 22						
Northampton	a				18 34	18 39			18 54					19 21					19 34						19 41
London Euston 15 ⊖	a				19 49			19 14	20 21				19 34	20 45				19 54							

Table 68

Stafford - Wolverhampton - Birmingham - Coventry - Northampton

Network Diagram - see first Page of Table 67

		VT		LM	VT	LM	XC	VT	LM	LM	LM	LM		AW	XC	LM	LM	LM	LM	LM	VT	LM		XC	VT
		◇1		◇1	◇1		◇1	◇1	◇1		◇1	◇1		◇	◇1			◇1	◇1	◇1	◇1			◇1	◇1
		🍽			🍽		🛒	🍽						🛒	🛒						🍽			🛒	🍽
Stafford	d						18 27				18 43				19 03			19 10	19 21					19 25	
Penkridge	d																	19 16							
Wolverhampton 7	a						18 40				18 56				19 16			19 27						19 39	
	d				18 32	18 37	18 41	18 45		18 49	18 57			19 09	19 17		19 19	19 28			19 32	19 37		19 41	19 45
Coseley	d									18 54	19 03						19 24								
Tipton	d									18 56							19 26								
Dudley Port	d									18 58							19 28								
Sandwell & Dudley	d					18 46		18 56		19 02							19 32					19 46			19 56
Smethwick Galton Bridge 7	d									19 04				19 20			19 34	19 40							
Smethwick Rolfe Street	d									19 06							19 36								
Birmingham New Street 12	a				18 55	18 55	18 58	19 06		19 14	19 17			19 26	19 33		19 44	19 47			19 55	19 55		19 58	20 06
	d	18 50		18 53			19 04	19 10	19 13			19 33		19 36		19 39				19 53				20 04	20 10
Adderley Park	d															19 44									
Stechford	d								19 20							19 47									
Lea Hall	d								19 23							19 50									
Marston Green	d			19 01					19 26			19 41								20 01					
Birmingham International ✈	a	18 59		19 05			19 13	19 19	19 29			19 45		19 50		19 54				20 05				20 13	20 19
	d	19 00		19 05			19 14	19 20	19 29			19 45								20 05				20 14	20 20
Hampton-in-Arden	d								19 32			19 48													
Berkswell	d			19 11					19 37											20 11					
Tile Hill	d			19 14					19 40			19 55								20 14					
Canley	d			19 17					19 44											20 17					
Coventry	a	19 10		19 20			19 24	19 30	19 47			20 00								20 20				20 24	20 30
	d	19 11		19 21				19 31	19 48			20 01								20 21					20 31
Rugby	d	19 23		19 32				19 44	19 59			20 12							20 20	20 32					20 43
Long Buckby	d			19 42					20 09			20 22								20 42					
Northampton	a			19 54					20 21			20 34							20 40	20 54					
London Euston 15 ⊖	a	20 15		21 09				20 55	21 45											22 11					21 56

		LM	LM	LM	LM	AW	XC	LM		LM	LM	LM	VT	LM	XC	VT	LM	LM		LM	VT	XC	LM	LM	LM
		1		◇1	◇1	◇	◇1				◇1	◇1	◇1		◇1	◇1	1			◇1	◇1	◇1	◇1		
															A										
						🛒	🛒						🍽		🛒	🍽					🍽				
Stafford	d			19 43			20 03				20 12				20 26					20 45		21 03			
Penkridge	d			19 49																20 51					
Wolverhampton 7	a			19 59			20 16				20 28				20 39					21 01		21 15			
	d		19 49	19 59		20 09	20 17			20 19	20 28		20 33	20 37	20 41	20 45		20 49		21 01	21 07	21 16			21 19
Coseley	d		19 54	20 04						20 24								20 54		21 06					21 24
Tipton	d		19 56							20 26								20 56							21 26
Dudley Port	d		19 58							20 28								20 58							21 28
Sandwell & Dudley	d		20 02							20 32				20 46		20 56		21 02			21 17				21 32
Smethwick Galton Bridge 7	d		20 04			20 20				20 34	20 40							21 04							21 34
Smethwick Rolfe Street	d		20 06							20 36								21 06							21 36
Birmingham New Street 12	a		20 14	20 17		20 25	20 33			20 44	20 47		20 55	20 57	20 58	21 06		21 14		21 19	21 26	21 32			21 44
	d	20 13			20 33	20 36		20 39				20 53			21 04	21 10	21 13				21 30		21 33	21 39	
Adderley Park	d							20 44																21 44	
Stechford	d	20 20						20 47									21 20							21 47	
Lea Hall	d	20 23						20 50									21 23							21 50	
Marston Green	d	20 26			20 41							21 01					21 26						21 41		
Birmingham International ✈	a	20 29			20 45	20 49		20 54				21 05			21 13	21 19	21 29				21 39		21 45	21 54	
	d	20 29			20 45							21 05			21 14	21 20	21 29				21 40		21 45		
Hampton-in-Arden	d	20 32			20 48												21 32						21 48		
Berkswell	d	20 37										21 11					21 37								
Tile Hill	d	20 40			20 55							21 14					21 40						21 55		
Canley	d	20 44										21 17					21 44								
Coventry	a	20 47			21 00							21 20			21 24	21 30	21 47				21 50		22 00		
	d				21 01							21 21				21 31					21 51		22 01		
Rugby	d				21 12							21 32				21 43					22 03		22 12		
Long Buckby	d				21 22							21 42											22 22		
Northampton	a				21 34							21 54											22 34		
London Euston 15 ⊖	a											23 27				22 55					23 30				

A 🛒 to Birmingham New Street

Table 68

Saturdays

Stafford - Wolverhampton - Birmingham - Coventry - Northampton

Network Diagram - see first Page of Table 67

		LM	VT	LM		XC	LM	LM	LM	AW	XC	LM	LM	VT		LM	LM	VT	XC	LM	LM	LM	AW		
		◇1	◇1			◇1	1		◇1	◇	◇1	1		◇1		◇1		◇1	◇1	1		◇1	◇		
																		A							
			catering											catering				catering							
Stafford	d					21 27			21 42		22 03			22 08				22 25	22 33			22 47			
Penkridge	d								21 48													22 53			
Wolverhampton [7]	a					21 39			21 58		22 14			22 22				22 39	22 45			23 03			
	d		21 33	21 37		21 41		21 49	21 58	22 08	22 16		22 19	22 23			22 37	22 40	22 46		22 49	23 03	23 08		
Coseley	d							21 54	22 04				22 24								22 54	23 09			
Tipton	d							21 56					22 26								22 56				
Dudley Port	d							21 58					22 28								22 58				
Sandwell & Dudley	d			21 46				22 02					22 32				22 46				23 02				
Smethwick Galton Bridge [7]	d							22 04		22 19			22 34								23 04				
Smethwick Rolfe Street	d							22 06					22 36								23 06				
Birmingham New Street [12]	a		21 54	21 55		21 58		22 14	22 20	22 31	22 32		22 44	22 46			22 55	22 59	23 02		23 14	23 21	23 28		
	d	21 53					22 13					22 33				22 53				23 13					
Adderley Park	d																			23 18					
Stechford	d						22 20													23 21					
Lea Hall	d						22 23													23 24					
Marston Green	d	22 01					22 26					22 41				23 01				23 27					
Birmingham International	a	22 05					22 29					22 45				23 05				23 30					
	d	22 05					22 29					22 45				23 05				23 30					
Hampton-in-Arden	d						22 32					22 48								23 33					
Berkswell	d	22 11					22 37									23 11				23 38					
Tile Hill	d	22 14					22 40					22 55				23 14				23 41					
Canley	d	22 17					22 44									23 17				23 45					
Coventry	a	22 20					22 47					23 00				23 20				23 48					
	d	22 21														23 21									
Rugby	d	22 32														23 32									
Long Buckby	d	22 41														23 42									
Northampton	a	22 53														23 55									
London Euston [15] ⊖	a	00 17																							

Sundays

		LM	VT	LM	LM	LM	XC	LM	AW	VT		LM	LM	XC	LM	AW	VT	LM	LM	XC		LM	AW	LM	VT
		◇1	◇1	1	1		◇1	◇1		◇1		1		◇1	◇1		◇1	1		◇1		◇1	◇	◇1	◇1
		B												D						D					
			catering				trolley			catering				catering trolley			catering			catering trolley					catering
Stafford	d													09 26						10 27				10 41	
Penkridge	d																							10 49	
Wolverhampton [7]	a													09 40						10 42				11 00	
	d		08 05			08 22			09 00	09 05			09 22	09 41		09 59	10 05		10 22	10 43			10 57	11 01	11 05
Coseley	d					08 27							09 27						10 27						
Tipton	d					08 29							09 29						10 29						
Dudley Port	d					08 31							09 31						10 31						
Sandwell & Dudley	d		08 15			08 35				09 15			09 35				10 15		10 35						11 15
Smethwick Galton Bridge [7]	d					08 37							09 37						10 37						
Smethwick Rolfe Street	d					08 39							09 39						10 39						
Birmingham New Street [12]	a		08 24			08 46			09 15	09 24			09 46	09 58		10 14	10 24		10 46	10 59			11 13	11 17	11 26
	d	21p53	08 30	08 34	08 38		09 04	09 14	09 20	09 30		09 34		10 04	10 14	10 20	10 30	10 34		11 04		11 14	11 19		11 30
Adderley Park	d				08 42							09 38						10 38							
Stechford	d				08 46							09 42						10 42							
Lea Hall	d				08 48							09 44						10 44							
Marston Green	d	22p01		08 42	08 52			09 22				09 48			10 22			10 48				11 22			
Birmingham International	a	22p05	08 39	08 45	08 55		09 13	09 25	09 31	09 39		09 51		10 13	10 25	10 32	10 39	10 52		11 13		11 25	11 31		11 39
	d	22p05	08 40	08 45			09 14	09 25		09 40		09 51		10 14	10 25		10 40	10 52		11 14		11 25			11 40
Hampton-in-Arden	d							09 28							10 28							11 28			
Berkswell	d	22p11		08 51				09 33							10 33							11 33			
Tile Hill	d	22p14		08 54				09 36							10 36							11 36			
Canley	d	22p17		08 57				09 40							10 40							11 40			
Coventry	a	22p20	08 50	09 00			09 24	09 44		09 50		10 01		10 24	10 44		10 50	11 03		11 24		11 44			11 50
	d	22p21	08 51					09 44		09 51					10 44		10 51					11 44			11 51
Rugby	d	22p32	09 04					09 55		10 04					10 55		11 04					11 55			12 05
Long Buckby	d	22p41						10 05							11 05							12 05			
Northampton	a	22p53						10 17							11 17							12 17			
London Euston [15] ⊖	a	00 17	10 28					11 57		11 31					12 37		12 27					13 37			13 04

A until 24 March
B not 11 December

D catering from Birmingham New Street
trolley to Birmingham New Street

Table 68

Sundays

Stafford - Wolverhampton - Birmingham - Coventry - Northampton

Network Diagram - see first Page of Table 67

		LM	LM	VT	VT	XC		VT	LM	LM	VT	LM	LM	AW	LM	VT		VT	XC	VT	LM	LM	VT	LM	AW
		1		◇1	◇1	◇1		◇1	◇1	◇1	◇1	◇1	1	◇		◇1		◇1	◇1	◇1	◇1	◇1	◇1	1	◇
						A													A						
				☕	☕	☕🚲		☕			☕			🚲		☕		☕	☕🚲	☕			☕		🚲
Stafford	d					11 28						12 19							12 25			12 42			
Penkridge	d																					12 49			
Wolverhampton 7 🚊	a					11 41													12 40			12 59			
	d		11 22		11 32	11 42		11 45						12 17	12 22			12 32	12 41	12 45		13 00			13 08
Coseley	d		11 27												12 27										
Tipton	d		11 29												12 29										
Dudley Port	d		11 31												12 31										
Sandwell & Dudley	d		11 35					11 57							12 35					12 55					
Smethwick Galton Bridge 7	d		11 37												12 37										
Smethwick Rolfe Street	d		11 39												12 39										
Birmingham New Street 12	a		11 48		11 55	12 00		12 06						12 32	12 46			12 55	12 58	13 06		13 16			13 23
	d	11 34		11 50		12 04		12 10		12 14	12 30		12 34	12 37		12 50			13 04	13 10	13 14		13 30	13 34	13 36
Adderley Park	d	11 38											12 38											13 38	
Stechford	d	11 42											12 42											13 42	
Lea Hall	d	11 44											12 44											13 44	
Marston Green	d	11 48								12 22			12 48								13 22			13 48	
Birmingham International ✈	a	11 51		11 59		12 13		12 19		12 25	12 38		12 51	12 56		12 59			13 13	13 19	13 25		13 38	13 51	13 55
	d	11 51		12 00		12 14		12 20		12 25	12 39		12 51			13 00			13 14	13 20	13 25		13 39	13 51	
Hampton-in-Arden	d									12 28											13 28				
Berkswell	d									12 33											13 33				
Tile Hill	d									12 36			12 58								13 36			13 58	
Canley	d									12 40											13 40				
Coventry	a	12 01		12 10		12 24		12 30		12 44	12 49		13 04			13 10			13 24	13 30	13 44		13 49	14 04	
	d			12 11				12 31		12 44	12 51					13 11				13 31	13 44		13 51		
Rugby	d			12 25					12 25	12 55		13 20				13 25					13 55				
Long Buckby	d								12 36	13 05		13 29									14 05				
Northampton	a								12 48	13 17		13 41									14 17				
London Euston 15 ⊖	a			13 19				13 37	13 53	14 37	13 57	14 53				14 17				14 37	15 37		14 57		

		LM		VT	VT	XC	VT	LM	LM	LM	VT	AW		XC	LM	LM	LM	VT	VT	XC	VT	LM		LM	VT
				◇1	◇1	◇1	◇1	◇1	◇1	◇1	◇1	◇		◇1	◇1	1		◇1	◇1	◇1	◇1	◇1		◇1	◇1
						A														A					
				☕	☕	☕🚲	☕				☕	🚲		🚲				☕	☕	☕🚲	☕				☕
Stafford	d					13 25				13 43					14 19					14 25				14 43	
Penkridge	d									13 49														14 49	
Wolverhampton 7 🚊	a					13 40				13 59										14 40				14 59	
	d	13 22			13 32	13 41	13 45			13 59		14 08		14 15			14 22		14 33	14 41	14 45			14 59	
Coseley	d	13 27															14 27								
Tipton	d	13 29															14 29								
Dudley Port	d	13 31															14 31								
Sandwell & Dudley	d	13 35					13 56										14 35				14 56				
Smethwick Galton Bridge 7	d	13 37															14 37								
Smethwick Rolfe Street	d	13 39															14 39								
Birmingham New Street 12	a	13 46			13 55	13 58	14 06			14 15		14 23		14 31			14 46		14 55	14 58	15 06			15 15	
	d			13 50		14 04	14 10		14 14		14 30	14 36				14 34		14 50		15 04	15 10	15 14			15 30
Adderley Park	d															14 38									
Stechford	d															14 42									
Lea Hall	d															14 44									
Marston Green	d								14 22							14 48						15 22			
Birmingham International ✈	a			13 59		14 13	14 19		14 25		14 38	14 55				14 51		14 59		15 13	15 19	15 25			15 38
	d			14 01		14 14	14 20		14 25		14 39					14 51		15 01		15 14	15 20	15 25			15 39
Hampton-in-Arden	d								14 28													15 28			
Berkswell	d								14 33													15 33			
Tile Hill	d								14 36							14 58						15 36			
Canley	d								14 40													15 40			
Coventry	a			14 11		14 24	14 30		14 44		14 49					15 04		15 11		15 24	15 30	15 44			15 49
	d			14 11			14 31		14 44		14 51							15 11			15 31	15 44			15 51
Rugby	d			14 26				14 26	14 55						15 20			15 26				15 55			
Long Buckby	d							14 37	15 05						15 29							16 05			
Northampton	a							14 49	15 17						15 41							16 17			
London Euston 15 ⊖	a			15 17			15 37	15 53	16 37		15 57				16 53			16 17			16 37	17 37			16 57

A ☕ from Birmingham New Street 🚲 to Birmingham New Street

Table 68

Sundays

Stafford - Wolverhampton - Birmingham - Coventry - Northampton

Network Diagram - see first Page of Table 67

	AW	XC	LM	LM	VT	VT	XC	VT	LM	LM	LM	VT	AW	XC	LM	LM	LM		VT	VT	XC	VT	LM	LM
	◇	◇1	1		◇1	◇1	◇1	◇1	◇1	◇1	◇1	◇1	◇	◇1	◇1	1			◇1	◇1	◇1	◇1	◇1	◇1
							A														A			
		🛒			☕	☕	☕🛒	☕				☕	🛒	🛒					☕	☕	☕🛒	☕		
Stafford d							15 25				15 43				16 19						16 25			16 43
Penkridge d											15 49													16 49
Wolverhampton 7 a							15 40				15 59										16 40			16 59
d	15 09	15 15		15 22		15 32	15 41	15 45			15 59		16 09	16 15			16 22			16 32	16 41	16 45		16 59
Coseley d				15 27													16 27							
Tipton d				15 29													16 29							
Dudley Port d				15 31													16 31							
Sandwell & Dudley d				15 35				15 56									16 35					16 56		
Smethwick Galton Bridge 7 d				15 37													16 37							
Smethwick Rolfe Street d				15 39													16 39							
Birmingham New Street 12 a	15 24	15 31		15 46		15 55	15 58	16 06			16 15		16 24	16 31			16 46			16 55	16 58	17 06		17 15
d	15 36		15 34		15 50		16 04	16 10		16 14		16 30	16 35			16 34			16 50		17 04	17 10	17 14	
Adderley Park d			15 38													16 38								
Stechford d			15 42													16 42								
Lea Hall d			15 44													16 44								
Marston Green d			15 48							16 22						16 48							17 22	
Birmingham International ✈ a	15 55		15 51		15 59		16 13	16 19		16 25		16 38	16 55			16 51			16 59		17 13	17 19	17 25	
d			15 51		16 01		16 14	16 20		16 25		16 39				16 51			17 01		17 14	17 20	17 25	
Hampton-in-Arden d										16 28													17 28	
Berkswell d										16 33													17 33	
Tile Hill d			15 58							16 36						16 58							17 36	
Canley d										16 40													17 40	
Coventry a			16 04		16 11		16 24	16 30		16 44		16 49				17 05			17 11		17 24	17 30	17 44	
d					16 11			16 31		16 44		16 51							17 11			17 31	17 44	
Rugby d					16 24				16 25	16 55					17 20				17 26				17 55	
Long Buckby d									16 36	17 05					17 29								18 05	
Northampton a									16 48	17 17					17 41								18 17	
London Euston 15 ⊖ a					17 17			17 37	17 53	18 37		17 57			18 53				18 17			18 37	19 37	

	VT	XC	LM		AW	LM	VT	VT	XC	LM	LM	LM	VT		AW	XC	LM	LM	LM	VT	VT	XC	VT	
	◇1	◇1	1		◇		◇1	◇1	◇1	◇1	◇1	◇1	◇1		◇	◇1	◇1	1		◇1	◇1	◇1	◇1	
									A													A		
	☕	🛒			🛒		☕	☕	☕🛒				☕		🛒	🛒				☕	☕	☕🛒	☕	
Stafford d									17 26			17 43					18 19					18 26		
Penkridge d												17 49												
Wolverhampton 7 a									17 40			17 59										18 40		
d		17 15			17 19	17 22		17 32	17 41			17 59			18 09	18 15			18 22		18 33	18 41	18 45	
Coseley d						17 27													18 27					
Tipton d						17 29													18 29					
Dudley Port d						17 31													18 31					
Sandwell & Dudley d						17 35													18 35				18 56	
Smethwick Galton Bridge 7 d						17 37													18 37					
Smethwick Rolfe Street d						17 39													18 39					
Birmingham New Street 12 a		17 31			17 35	17 46		17 55	17 58			18 15			18 27	18 31			18 46		18 55	18 58	19 06	
d	17 30		17 34		17 38		17 50		18 04		18 14		18 30		18 36			18 34		18 50		19 04	19 10	
Adderley Park d			17 38															18 38						
Stechford d			17 42															18 42						
Lea Hall d			17 44															18 44						
Marston Green d			17 48								18 22							18 48						
Birmingham International ✈ a	17 38		17 51		17 56		17 59		18 13		18 25		18 38		18 55			18 51		18 59		19 13	19 19	
d	17 39		17 51				18 01		18 14		18 25		18 39					18 51		19 01		19 14	19 20	
Hampton-in-Arden d											18 28													
Berkswell d											18 33													
Tile Hill d			17 58								18 36							18 58						
Canley d											18 40													
Coventry a	17 49		18 05				18 11		18 24		18 44		18 49					19 05		19 11		19 24	19 30	
d	17 51						18 11				18 44		18 51							19 11			19 31	
Rugby d							18 26			18 24	18 55						19 20			19 26				
Long Buckby d										18 37	19 05						19 29							
Northampton a										18 49	19 17						19 41							
London Euston 15 ⊖ a	18 57						19 17			19 53	20 37		19 57				20 53			20 17			20 37	

A ☕ from Birmingham New Street 🛒 to Birmingham New Street

Table 68

Sundays

Stafford - Wolverhampton - Birmingham - Coventry - Northampton

Network Diagram - see first Page of Table 67

		LM	LM	VT	AW	XC	LM	LM	VT	XC		VT	LM	LM	LM	VT	AW	XC	LM	LM		LM	VT	XC	LM
		◇1	◇1	◇1	◇	◇1	1		◇1	◇1		◇1	◇1	◇1	◇1	◇1	◇	◇1	◇1	1			◇1	◇1	◇1
										A														B	
				[P]		[trolley]			[P]	[P][trolley]		[P]				[P]	[trolley]	[trolley]					[P]	[trolley]	
Stafford	d		18 43							19 25					19 43				20 18					20 27	
Penkridge	d		18 49												19 49										
Wolverhampton 7	a		18 59							19 40					19 59									20 39	
	d		18 59		19 08	19 15		19 22	19 32	19 41		19 45			19 59		20 08	20 15				20 22	20 33	20 41	
Coseley	d							19 27														20 27			
Tipton	d							19 29														20 29			
Dudley Port	d							19 31														20 31			
Sandwell & Dudley	d							19 35				19 58										20 35			
Smethwick Galton Bridge 7	d							19 37														20 37			
Smethwick Rolfe Street	d							19 39														20 39			
Birmingham New Street 12	a		19 15		19 26	19 31		19 46	19 55	19 58		20 07			20 15		20 23	20 31				20 46	20 50	20 58	
	d	19 14		19 30	19 36		19 34			20 04		20 10		20 14		20 30	20 36			20 34				21 04	21 14
Adderley Park	d						19 38													20 38					
Stechford	d						19 42													20 42					
Lea Hall	d						19 44													20 44					
Marston Green	d	19 22					19 48							20 22						20 48					21 22
Birmingham International ✈	a	19 25		19 38	19 55		19 51			20 13		20 19		20 25		20 39	20 55			20 51				21 13	21 25
	d	19 25		19 39			19 51			20 14		20 20		20 25		20 40				20 51				21 14	21 25
Hampton-in-Arden	d	19 28												20 28											21 28
Berkswell	d	19 33												20 33											21 33
Tile Hill	d	19 36					19 58							20 36						20 58					21 36
Canley	d	19 40												20 40											21 40
Coventry	a	19 44		19 49			20 05			20 24		20 30		20 43		20 50				21 04				21 23	21 44
	d	19 44		19 51								20 31		20 43		20 51									21 44
Rugby	d	19 55											20 20	20 55		21 05			21 19						21 55
Long Buckby	d	20 05											20 32	21 05					21 28						22 05
Northampton	a	20 17											20 44	21 17					21 40						22 17
London Euston 15 ⊖	a	21 42		20 57								21 47	21 55	22 42		22 23			23 13						23 42

		LM	VT	LM	AW	XC		LM	AW	LM	LM	VT	LM	AW	VT	XC		LM	VT	VT	LM	LM	XC		
		◇1	◇1	1		◇1			◇	◇1	◇1	◇1	1	◇	◇1	◇1			◇1	◇1	1	◇1	◇1		
			[P]						[trolley]			[P]			[P]				[P]	[P]					
Stafford	d	20 39				21 09			21 16		21 39				22 02	22 06						22 45	23 05		
Penkridge	d	20 45									21 45											22 51			
Wolverhampton 7	a	20 55				21 21			21 34		21 55				22 17	22 20						23 01	23 18		
	d	20 59	21 05		21 12	21 22		21 25	21 35		21 59	22 05		22 08	22 18	22 22		22 25	22 32	22 37		23 01	23 19		
Coseley	d							21 30										22 30							
Tipton	d							21 32										22 32							
Dudley Port	d							21 34										22 34							
Sandwell & Dudley	d		21 17					21 38				22 15						22 38		22 47					
Smethwick Galton Bridge 7	d							21 40										22 40							
Smethwick Rolfe Street	d							21 42										22 42							
Birmingham New Street 12	a	21 15	21 26		21 29	21 39		21 49	21 52		22 15	22 24		22 27	22 38	22 39		22 49	22 55	22 56		23 17	23 36		
	d		21 30	21 34	21 37				21 55	22 14		22 30	22 34	22 40						23 00	23 14				
Adderley Park	d			21 38									22 38								23 19				
Stechford	d			21 42									22 42								23 22				
Lea Hall	d			21 44									22 45								23 25				
Marston Green	d			21 48						22 22			22 48								23 28				
Birmingham International ✈	a		21 39	21 51	21 56				22 09	22 25		22 39	22 51	22 55						23 09	23 31				
	d		21 40	21 51						22 25		22 40	22 52							23 10	23 32				
Hampton-in-Arden	d									22 28											23 35				
Berkswell	d									22 33											23 40				
Tile Hill	d									22 36											23 43				
Canley	d									22 40											23 46				
Coventry	a		21 50	22 01						22 44		22 50	23 01							23 20	23 50				
	d		21 51							22 44		22 51								23 21					
Rugby	d		22 04							22 55		23 04								23 34					
Long Buckby	d									23 05															
Northampton	a									23 17										23s53					
London Euston 15 ⊖	a		23 25									00 27								01 04					

A [P] from Birmingham New Street [trolley] to Birmingham New Street

B [trolley] to Birmingham New Street

Lichfield - Birmingham - Longbridge and Redditch

Network Diagram - see first Page of Table 67

Miles	Miles			LM	LM	LM	LM	LM	LM	LM	LM	LM		LM	LM	LM	XC ◇1	LM	LM	LM	LM	LM		LM	LM
0	—	**Lichfield Trent Valley**	d							06 09		06 20						06 50		07 10		07 20			07 38
1¼	—	**Lichfield City**	d							06 12		06 24				06 45		06 54		07 13		07 24			07 42
4¼	—	Shenstone	d							06 17						06 50				07 18					07 47
6¾	—	Blake Street	d					06 03		06 21		06 32				06 54		07 02		07 22		07 32			07 51
8½	—	Butlers Lane	d					06 05		06 23		06 34				06 56		07 04		07 24		07 34			07 53
9½	—	Four Oaks	d					06 08	06 17	06 26		06 37		06 47		06 59		07 07	07 17	07 27		07 37		07 47	07 56
11	—	Sutton Coldfield	d					06 11	06 20	06 30		06 40		06 50		07 02		07 10	07 20	07 31		07 40		07 50	08 00
12	—	Wylde Green	d					06 14	06 23	06 32		06 43		06 53		07 05		07 13	07 23	07 33		07 43		07 53	08 03
12¾	—	Chester Road	d					06 16	06 25	06 35		06 45		06 55		07 07		07 15	07 25	07 36		07 45		07 55	08 05
13¾	—	Erdington	d					06 17	06 27	06 36		06 47		06 57		07 09		07 17	07 27	07 37		07 47		07 57	08 07
14½	—	Gravelly Hill	d					06 20	06 29	06 39		06 49		06 59		07 11		07 19	07 29	07 40		07 49		07 59	08 10
15¾	—	Aston	d					06 23	06 33	06 42		06 53		07 03		07 14		07 23	07 33	07 43		07 53		08 03	08 13
17	—	Duddeston	d					06 26	06 35	06 45				07 05					07 35	07 46				08 05	08 16
18½	0	**Birmingham New Street** 12	a					06 31	06 40	06 49		06 59		07 10		07 21		07 30	07 41	07 51		08 01		08 10	08 21
—	—		d	05 53	06 03	06 13	06 23	06 33	06 43	06 53	06 59	07 03		07 13	07 19	07 23	07 30	07 33	07 43	07 53	07 59	08 03		08 13	08 23
19½	—	Five Ways	d	05 56	06 06	06 16	06 26	06 36	06 46	06 56		07 06		07 16		07 26		07 36	07 46	07 56		08 06		08 16	08 26
20	1½	University	d	06 00	06 10	06 20	06 30	06 40	06 50	07 00	07 05	07 10		07 20	07 25	07 30	07a36	07 40	07 50	08 00	08 05	08 10		08 20	08 30
20¾	—	Selly Oak	d	06 03	06 13	06 23	06 33	06 43	06 53	07 03		07 13		07 23		07 33		07 43	07 53	08 03		08 13		08 23	08 33
21¾	—	Bournville	d	06 05	06 15	06 25	06 35	06 45	06 55	07 05		07 15		07 25		07 35		07 45	07 55	08 05		08 15		08 25	08 35
22¾	—	Kings Norton	d	06 07	06 17	06 27	06 37	06 47	06 57	07 07		07 17		07 27		07 37		07 47	07 57	08 07		08 17		08 27	08 37
24¼	—	Northfield	d	06 10	06 20	06 30	06 40	06 50	07 00	07 10		07 20		07 30		07 40		07 50	08 00	08 10		08 20		08 30	08 40
25¼	—	Longbridge	d	06a14	06a24	06 34	06a44	06a54	07 04	07a14		07a24		07 34		07a44		07a54	08 04	08a14		08a24		08 34	08a44
28	9½	Barnt Green	d			06 39			07 09					07 39	07 41				08 09		08 18			08 39	
29¾	—	Alvechurch	d			06 43			07 13					07 43					08 13					08 43	
33	—	**Redditch**	a			06 52			07 22					07 52					08 22					08 52	
—	13	Bromsgrove	a								07 21				07 46						08 22				

		XC ◇1	LM	LM	LM	LM	LM	LM		LM	LM	XC ◇1	LM	LM	LM	LM	LM	LM		LM	XC ◇1	LM	LM	LM	LM
Lichfield Trent Valley	d		07 50				08 11				08 41		08 50				09 20					09 50			
Lichfield City	d		07 54		08 10		08 15	08 26			08 44		08 54			09 13	09 24			09 43		09 54			10 13
Shenstone	d						08 20				08 49					09 18				09 48					10 18
Blake Street	d		08 01				08 23	08 33			08 53		09 02			09 22	09 32			09 52		10 02			10 22
Butlers Lane	d		08 03				08 25	08 35			08 55		09 04			09 24	09 34			09 54		10 04			10 24
Four Oaks	d		08 06	08 15	08 20		08 28	08 38		08 47	08 58		09 07	09 17		09 27	09 37	09 47		09 57		10 07	10 17		10 27
Sutton Coldfield	d		08 10	08 18	08 23		08 32	08 42		08 50	09 02		09 10	09 20		09 30	09 40	09 50		10 00		10 10	10 20		10 30
Wylde Green	d		08 13	08 21	08 26		08 34	08 44		08 53	09 04		09 13	09 23		09 33	09 43	09 53		10 03		10 13	10 23		10 33
Chester Road	d		08 15	08 23	08 28		08 37	08 47		08 55	09 07		09 15	09 25		09 35	09 45	09 55		10 05		10 15	10 25		10 35
Erdington	d		08 17	08 25	08 29		08 38	08 48		08 57	09 08		09 17	09 27		09 37	09 47	09 57		10 07		10 17	10 27		10 37
Gravelly Hill	d		08 20		08 32		08 41	08 51		08 59	09 11		09 19	09 29		09 39	09 49	09 59		10 09		10 19	10 29		10 39
Aston	d		08 23		08 35		08 44	08 54		09 03	09 14		09 23	09 33		09 43	09 53	10 03		10 13		10 23	10 33		10 43
Duddeston	d				08 37		08 47	08 57		09 05				09 35				10 05					10 35		
Birmingham New Street 12	a		08 31	08 36	08 42		08 51	09 01		09 11	09 20		09 30	09 41		09 50	10 00	10 10		10 21		10 30	10 41		10 50
	d	08 30	08 33		08 43	08 49	08 53	09 03		09 13	09 23	09 30	09 33	09 43	09 49	09 53	10 03	10 13		10 23	10 30	10 33	10 43	10 49	10 53
Five Ways	d		08 36		08 46		08 56	09 06		09 16	09 26		09 36	09 46		09 56	10 06	10 16		10 26		10 36	10 46		10 56
University	d	08a36	08 40		08 50	08 55	09 00	09 10		09 20	09 30	09a36	09 41	09 50	09 55	10 00	10 10	10 20		10 30	10a36	10 40	10 50	10 55	11 00
Selly Oak	d		08 43		08 53		09 03	09 13		09 23	09 33		09 43	09 53		10 03	10 13	10 23		10 33		10 43	10 53		11 03
Bournville	d		08 45		08 55		09 05	09 15		09 25	09 35		09 45	09 55		10 05	10 15	10 25		10 35		10 45	10 55		11 05
Kings Norton	d		08 47		08 57		09 07	09 17		09 27	09 37		09 47	09 57		10 07	10 17	10 27		10 37		10 47	10 57		11 07
Northfield	d		08 50		09 00		09 10	09 20		09 30	09 40		09 50	10 00		10 10	10 20	10 30		10 40		10 50	11 00		11 10
Longbridge	d		08a54		09 06		09a14	09a24		09 34	09a44		09a54	10 06		10a14	10a24	10 34		10a44		10a54	11 06		11a14
Barnt Green	d				09 10					09 39				10 10				10 39					11 10		
Alvechurch	d				09 15					09 43				10 15				10 43					11 15		
Redditch	a				09 22					09 52				10 22				10 52					11 22		
Bromsgrove	a					09 09									10 09									11 09	

		LM	LM	LM		XC ◇1	LM	LM	LM	LM	LM	LM	LM	XC ◇1		LM	LM	LM	LM	LM	LM	LM	XC ◇1	LM	
Lichfield Trent Valley	d	10 20					10 50				11 20					11 50				12 20				12 50	
Lichfield City	d	10 24		10 43			10 54			11 13	11 24		11 43			11 54			12 13	12 24		12 43		12 54	
Shenstone	d			10 48						11 18			11 48						12 18			12 48			
Blake Street	d	10 32		10 52			11 02			11 22	11 32		11 52			12 02			12 22	12 32		12 52		13 02	
Butlers Lane	d	10 34		10 54			11 04			11 24	11 34		11 54			12 04			12 24	12 34		12 54		13 04	
Four Oaks	d	10 37	10 47	10 57			11 07	11 17		11 27	11 37	11 47	11 57			12 07	12 17		12 27	12 37	12 47	12 57		13 07	
Sutton Coldfield	d	10 40	10 50	11 00			11 10	11 20		11 30	11 40	11 50	12 00			12 10	12 20		12 30	12 40	12 50	13 00		13 10	
Wylde Green	d	10 43	10 53	11 03			11 13	11 23		11 33	11 43	11 53	12 03			12 13	12 23		12 33	12 43	12 53	13 03		13 13	
Chester Road	d	10 45	10 55	11 05			11 15	11 25		11 35	11 45	11 55	12 05			12 15	12 25		12 35	12 45	12 55	13 05		13 15	
Erdington	d	10 47	10 57	11 07			11 17	11 27		11 37	11 47	11 57	12 07			12 17	12 27		12 37	12 47	12 57	13 07		13 17	
Gravelly Hill	d	10 49	10 59	11 09			11 19	11 29		11 39	11 49	11 59	12 09			12 19	12 29		12 39	12 49	12 59	13 09		13 19	
Aston	d	10 53	11 03	11 13			11 23	11 33		11 43	11 53	12 03	12 13			12 23	12 33		12 43	12 53	13 03	13 13		13 23	
Duddeston	d		11 05					11 35				12 05					12 35				13 05				
Birmingham New Street 12	a	11 00	11 10	11 21			11 30	11 41		11 50	12 00	12 10	12 21			12 30	12 41		12 50	13 00	13 10	13 21		13 31	
	d	11 03	11 13	11 23		11 30	11 33	11 43	11 49	11 53	12 03	12 13	12 23	12 30		12 33	12 43	12 49	12 53	13 03	13 13	13 23	13 30	13 33	
Five Ways	d	11 06	11 16	11 26			11 36	11 46		11 56	12 06	12 16	12 26			12 36	12 46		12 56	13 06	13 16	13 26		13 36	
University	d	11 10	11 20	11 30		11a36	11 40	11 50	11 55	12 00	12 10	12 20	12 30	12a36		12 40	12 50	12 55	13 00	13 10	13 20	13 30	13a36	13 40	
Selly Oak	d	11 13	11 23	11 33			11 43	11 53		12 03	12 13	12 23	12 33			12 43	12 53		13 03	13 13	13 23	13 33		13 43	
Bournville	d	11 15	11 25	11 35			11 45	11 55		12 05	12 15	12 25	12 35			12 45	12 55		13 05	13 15	13 25	13 35		13 45	
Kings Norton	d	11 17	11 27	11 37			11 47	11 57		12 07	12 17	12 27	12 37			12 47	12 57		13 07	13 17	13 27	13 37		13 47	
Northfield	d	11 20	11 30	11 40			11 50	12 00		12 10	12 20	12 30	12 40			12 50	13 00		13 10	13 20	13 30	13 40		13 50	
Longbridge	d	11a24	11 34	11a44			11a54	12 06		12a14	12a24	12 34	12a44			12a54	13 06		13a14	13a24	13 34	13a44		13a54	
Barnt Green	d		11 39					12 10				12 39					13 10				13 39				
Alvechurch	d		11 43					12 15				12 43					13 15				13 43				
Redditch	a		11 52					12 22				12 52					13 22				13 52				
Bromsgrove	a								12 09									13 09							

Table 69

Mondays to Fridays

Lichfield - Birmingham - Longbridge and Redditch

Network Diagram - see first Page of Table 67

		LM	LM	LM	LM	LM	LM	XC	LM	LM		LM	LM	LM	LM	LM	XC	LM	LM	LM		LM	LM	LM	LM
								◇1 ⌶									◇1 ⌶								
Lichfield Trent Valley	d				13 20				13 50					14 20				14 50					15 20		
Lichfield City	d			13 13	13 24		13 43		13 54				14 13	14 24		14 43		14 54				15 13	15 24		
Shenstone	d			13 18			13 48						14 18			14 48						15 18			
Blake Street	d			13 22	13 32		13 52		14 02				14 22	14 32		14 52		15 02				15 22	15 32		
Butlers Lane	d			13 24	13 34		13 54		14 04				14 24	14 34		14 54		15 04				15 24	15 34		
Four Oaks	d	13 17		13 27	13 37	13 47	13 57		14 07	14 17			14 27	14 37	14 47	14 57		15 07	15 17			15 27	15 37	15 47	
Sutton Coldfield	d	13 20		13 30	13 40	13 50	14 00		14 10	14 20			14 30	14 40	14 50	15 00		15 10	15 20			15 30	15 40	15 50	
Wylde Green	d	13 23		13 33	13 43	13 53	14 03		14 13	14 23			14 33	14 43	14 53	15 03		15 13	15 23			15 33	15 43	15 53	
Chester Road	d	13 25		13 35	13 45	13 55	14 05		14 15	14 25			14 35	14 45	14 55	15 05		15 15	15 25			15 35	15 45	15 55	
Erdington	d	13 27		13 37	13 47	13 57	14 07		14 17	14 27			14 37	14 47	14 57	15 07		15 17	15 27			15 37	15 47	15 57	
Gravelly Hill	d	13 29		13 39	13 49	13 59	14 09		14 19	14 29			14 39	14 49	14 59	15 09		15 19	15 29			15 39	15 49	15 59	
Aston	d	13 33		13 43	13 53	14 03	14 13		14 23	14 33			14 43	14 53	15 03	15 13		15 23	15 33			15 43	15 53	16 03	
Duddeston	d	13 35				14 05				14 35					15 05				15 35					16 05	
Birmingham New Street 12	a	13 41		13 50	14 00	14 10	14 21		14 30	14 41			14 50	15 00	15 10	15 21		15 30	15 42			15 50	16 01	16 10	
	d	13 43	13 49	13 53	14 03	14 13	14 23	14 30	14 33	14 43		14 49	14 53	15 03	15 13	15 23	15 30	15 33	15 43	15 49		15 53	16 03	16 13	16 19
Five Ways	d	13 46		13 56	14 06	14 16	14 26		14 36	14 46			14 56	15 06	15 16	15 26		15 36	15 46			15 56	16 06	16 16	
University	d	13 50	13 55	14 00	14 10	14 20	14 30	14a36	14 40	14 50		14 55	15 00	15 10	15 20	15 30	15a36	15 40	15 50	15 55		16 00	16 10	16 20	16 25
Selly Oak	d	13 53		14 03	14 13	14 23	14 33		14 43	14 53			15 03	15 13	15 23	15 33		15 43	15 53			16 03	16 13	16 23	
Bournville	d	13 55		14 05	14 15	14 25	14 35		14 45	14 55			15 05	15 15	15 25	15 35		15 45	15 55			16 05	16 15	16 25	
Kings Norton	d	13 57		14 07	14 17	14 27	14 37		14 47	14 57			15 07	15 17	15 27	15 37		15 47	15 57			16 07	16 17	16 27	
Northfield	d	14 00		14 10	14 20	14 30	14 40		14 50	15 00			15 10	15 20	15 30	15 40		15 50	16 00			16 10	16 20	16 30	
Longbridge	d	14 06		14a14	14a24	14 34	14a44		14a54	15 06			15a14	15a24	15 34	15a44		15a54	16 06			16a14	16a24	16 36	
Barnt Green	d	14 10				14 39				15 10					15 39				16 10					16 40	
Alvechurch	d	14 15				14 43				15 15					15 43				16 15					16 45	
Redditch	a	14 22				14 52				15 22					15 52				16 22					16 52	
Bromsgrove	a		14 09									15 09								16 09					16 40

		LM	XC	LM	LM	LM		LM	LM	LM	LM	LM	XC	LM	LM	LM		LM	LM	LM	LM	LM	LM	XC	LM
			◇1										◇1											◇1	
Lichfield Trent Valley	d			15 50					16 20					16 50						17 20			17 40		17 50
Lichfield City	d	15 43		15 54				16 13	16 24			16 43		16 54	17 05					17 24			17 44		17 54
Shenstone	d	15 48		15 59				16 18				16 48								17 29			17 49		
Blake Street	d	15 52		16 03				16 22	16 32			16 52		17 02	17 13					17 33			17 53		18 02
Butlers Lane	d	15 54		16 05				16 24	16 34			16 54		17 04	17 15					17 35			17 55		18 04
Four Oaks	d	15 57		16 08	16 17			16 27	16 37	16 47		16 57		17 07	17 18			17 28		17 38	17 47		17 58		18 07
Sutton Coldfield	d	16 00		16 11	16 20			16 30	16 40	16 50		17 00		17 10	17 21			17 31		17 41	17 50		18 01		18 10
Wylde Green	d	16 03		16 14	16 23			16 33	16 43	16 53		17 03		17 13	17 24			17 34		17 44	17 53		18 04		18 13
Chester Road	d	16 05		16 16	16 25			16 35	16 45	16 55		17 05		17 15	17 26			17 36		17 46	17 55		18 06		18 15
Erdington	d	16 07		16 18	16 27			16 37	16 47	16 57		17 07		17 17	17 28			17 38		17 48	17 57		18 08		18 17
Gravelly Hill	d	16 09		16 20	16 29			16 39	16 49	16 59		17 09		17 19	17 30			17 40		17 50	17 59		18 10		18 19
Aston	d	16 13		16 24	16 33			16 43	16 53	17 03		17 13		17 23	17 34			17 44		17 54	18 03		18 14		18 23
Duddeston	d				16 35					17 05					17 36						18 05				
Birmingham New Street 12	a	16 21		16 31	16 41			16 50	17 00	17 12		17 21		17 30	17 41			17 51		18 01	18 12		18 21		18 31
	d	16 23	16 30	16 33	16 43	16 49		16 53	17 03	17 13	17 19	17 23	17 30	17 33	17 43	17 49		17 53	17 59	18 03	18 13	18 19	18 23	18 30	18 33
Five Ways	d	16 26		16 36	16 46			16 56	17 06	17 16		17 26		17 36	17 46			17 56		18 06	18 16		18 26		18 36
University	d	16 30	16a36	16 40	16 50	16 55		17 01	17 10	17 20	17 25	17 31	17 36	17 40	17 50	17a55		18 00	18 05	18 10	18 20	18 25	18 30	18 36	18 40
Selly Oak	d	16 33		16 43	16 53			17 03	17 13	17 23		17 33		17 43	17 53			18 03		18 13	18 23		18 33		18 43
Bournville	d	16 35		16 45	16 55			17 06	17 15	17 25		17 35		17 45	17 55			18 05		18 15	18 25		18 35		18 45
Kings Norton	d	16 37		16 47	16 57			17 07	17 17	17 27		17 37		17 47	17 57			18 07		18 17	18 27		18 37		18 47
Northfield	d	16 40		16 50	17 00			17 10	17 20	17 30		17 40		17 50	18 00			18 10		18 20	18 30		18 40		18 50
Longbridge	d	16a44		16a54	17 06			17a14	17a24	17 36		17a44		17a54	18 06			18a14		18a24	18 34		18a44		18a54
Barnt Green	d				17 10					17 40					18 10						18 39				
Alvechurch	d				17 15					17 44					18 15						18 43				
Redditch	a				17 22					17 52					18 22						18 52				
Bromsgrove	a					17 09					17 40		17 51						18 21			18 44		18 49	

		LM		LM	LM	LM	LM	LM	XC	LM	LM	LM		LM	LM	LM	LM	XC	LM	LM	LM	LM		LM	LM
									◇1									◇1							
Lichfield Trent Valley	d			18 10	18 20					18 50					19 20				20 00			20 30			21 00
Lichfield City	d			18 14	18 24			18 43		18 54				19 13	19 24		19 43		20 04			20 34			21 04
Shenstone	d			18 19				18 48						19 18			19 48		20 09			20 39			21 09
Blake Street	d			18 23	18 32			18 52		19 02				19 22	19 32		19 52		20 13			20 43			21 13
Butlers Lane	d			18 25	18 34			18 54		19 04				19 24	19 34		19 54		20 15			20 45			21 15
Four Oaks	d	18 17		18 28	18 37	18 47		18 57		19 07	19 17			19 27	19 37	19 50	19 57		20 18			20 48			21 18
Sutton Coldfield	d	18 20		18 31	18 40	18 50		19 00		19 10	19 20			19 30	19 40	19 53	20 00		20 21			20 51			21 21
Wylde Green	d	18 23		18 34	18 43	18 53		19 03		19 13	19 23			19 33	19 43	19 56	20 03		20 24			20 54			21 24
Chester Road	d	18 25		18 36	18 45	18 55		19 05		19 15	19 25			19 35	19 45	19 58	20 05		20 26			20 56			21 26
Erdington	d	18 27		18 38	18 47	18 57		19 07		19 17	19 27			19 37	19 47	20 00	20 07		20 28			20 58			21 28
Gravelly Hill	d	18 29		18 40	18 49	18 59		19 09		19 19	19 29			19 39	19 49	20 02	20 09		20 30			21 00			21 30
Aston	d	18 33		18 44	18 53	19 03		19 13		19 23	19 33			19 43	19 53	20 06	20 13		20 33			21 03			21 33
Duddeston	d	18 35				19 05					19 35				19 55				20 36			21 06			21 36
Birmingham New Street 12	a	18 40		18 50	19 00	19 11		19 21		19 30	19 41			19 50	20 02	20 13	20 20		20 40			21 12			21 41
	d	18 43		18 53	19 03	19 13	19 19	19 23	19 30	19 33	19 43	19 49		19 53		20 13	20 23	20 30	20 43	20 53	20 59	21 13		21 23	21 43
Five Ways	d	18 46		18 56	19 06	19 16		19 26		19 36	19 46			19 56		20 16	20 26		20 46	20 56		21 16		21 26	21 46
University	d	18 50		19 00	19 10	19 20	19 25	19 30	19a36	19 40	19 50	19 55		20 00		20 20	20 30	20a36	20 50	21 00	21 05	21 20		21 30	21 50
Selly Oak	d	18 53		19 03	19 13	19 23		19 33		19 43	19 53			20 03		20 23	20 33		20 53	21 03		21 23		21 33	21 53
Bournville	d	18 55		19 05	19 15	19 25		19 35		19 45	19 55			20 05		20 25	20 35		20 55	21 05		21 25		21 35	21 55
Kings Norton	d	18 57		19 07	19 17	19 27		19 37		19 47	19 57			20 07		20 27	20 37		20 57	21 07		21 27		21 37	21 57
Northfield	d	19 00		19 10	19 20	19 30		19 40		19 50	20 00			20 10		20 30	20 40		21 00	21 10		21 30		21 40	22 00
Longbridge	d	19 04		19a14	19a24	19 34		19a44		19a54	20 06			20a14		20 34	20a44		21 04	21a14		21 34		21a44	22 04
Barnt Green	d	19 09				19 39					20 10					20 39			21 09			21 39			22 09
Alvechurch	d	19 13				19 44					20 15					20 43			21 13			21 43			22 13
Redditch	a	19 22				19 52					20 22					20 52			21 22			21 52			22 22
Bromsgrove	a						19 40					20 10									21 19				

Lichfield - Birmingham - Longbridge and Redditch

Network Diagram - see first Page of Table 67

		LM	LM A	LM B 🚌	LM	LM	LM	LM		LM A	LM B 🚌	LM	LM	LM
Lichfield Trent Valley	d				21 30		22 00					22 30	22 56	
Lichfield City	d				21 34		22 04					22 34	23 00	
Shenstone	d				21 39		22 09					22 39	23 05	
Blake Street	d				21 43		22 13					22 43	23 09	23 36
Butlers Lane	d				21 45		22 15					22 45	23 11	23 38
Four Oaks	d				21 48		22 18					22 48	23 14	23 41
Sutton Coldfield	d				21 51		22 21					22 51	23 17	23 44
Wylde Green	d				21 54		22 24					22 54	23 20	
Chester Road	d				21 56		22 26					22 56		
Erdington	d				21 58		22 28					22 58		
Gravelly Hill	d				22 00		22 30					23 00		
Aston	d				22 03		22 33					23 03		
Duddeston	d				22 06		22 36					23 06		
Birmingham New Street 12	a				22 11		22 41					23 11	23 31	23 59
	d	21 53	22 00		22 13	22 23	22 43	22 53		23 00		23 13	23 33	
Five Ways	d	21 56			22 16	22 26	22 46	22 56				23 16	23 36	
University	d	22 00	22 06		22 20	22 30	22 50	23 00		23 06		23 20	23 40	
Selly Oak	d	22 03			22 23	22 33	22 53	23 03				23 23	23 43	
Bournville	d	22 05			22 25	22 35	22 55	23 05				23 25	23 45	
Kings Norton	d	22 07			22 27	22 37	22 57	23 07				23 27	23 47	
Northfield	d	22 10			22 30	22 40	23 00	23 10				23 30	23 50	
Longbridge	d	22a14		22 20	22 34	22a44	23 04	23a14			23 20	23 34	23a54	
Barnt Green	d				22 39		23 09					23 39		
Alvechurch	d				22 43		23 13					23 43		
Redditch	a				22 52		23 22					23 52		
Bromsgrove	a		22 19	22 40						23 19	23 40			

Saturdays

		XC ◇1	LM	LM	LM	LM	LM	LM	LM	LM		LM	LM	LM	XC ◇1 🛒	LM	LM	LM	LM	LM		LM	LM	XC ◇1 🛒	LM
Lichfield Trent Valley	d											06 20				06 50				07 20					07 50
Lichfield City	d											06 24	06 38			06 54	07 07			07 24			07 43		07 54
Shenstone	d											06 29				06 59				07 29			07 48		
Blake Street	d						06 03					06 33				07 03				07 33			07 52		08 02
Butlers Lane	d						06 05					06 35				07 05				07 35			07 54		08 04
Four Oaks	d						06 08					06 38	06 48			07 08	07 17			07 38		07 47	07 57		08 07
Sutton Coldfield	d						06 11					06 41	06 51			07 11	07 20			07 41		07 50	08 00		08 10
Wylde Green	d						06 14					06 44	06 54			07 14	07 23			07 44		07 53	08 03		08 13
Chester Road	d						06 16					06 46	06 56			07 16	07 25			07 46		07 55	08 05		08 15
Erdington	d						06 17					06 48	06 58			07 18	07 27			07 47		07 57	08 07		08 17
Gravelly Hill	d						06 20					06 50	07 00			07 20	07 29			07 50		07 59	08 09		08 19
Aston	d						06 23					06 53	07 04			07 23	07 33			07 53		08 03	08 13		08 23
Duddeston	d						06 26					06 56	07 06			07 26	07 35					08 05			
Birmingham New Street 12	a						06 31					07 00	07 11			07 31	07 40			08 00		08 11	08 21		08 31
	d	05 42	05 53	06 03	06 13	06 23	06 33	06 43	06 49	06 53		07 03	07 13	07 23	07 30	07 33	07 43	07 49	07 53	08 03		08 13	08 23	08 30	08 33
Five Ways	d		05 56	06 06	06 16	06 26	06 36	06 46		06 56		07 06	07 16	07 26		07 36	07 46		07 56	08 06		08 16	08 26		08 36
University	d		06 00	06 10	06 20	06 30	06 40	06 50	06 55	07 00		07 10	07 20	07 30	07a36	07 40	07 50	07 55	08 00	08 10		08 20	08 30	08a36	08 40
Selly Oak	d		06 03	06 13	06 23	06 33	06 43	06 53		07 03		07 13	07 23	07 33		07 43	07 53		08 03	08 13		08 23	08 33		08 43
Bournville	d		06 05	06 15	06 25	06 35	06 45	06 55		07 05		07 15	07 25	07 35		07 45	07 55		08 05	08 15		08 25	08 35		08 45
Kings Norton	d		06 07	06 17	06 27	06 37	06 47	06 57		07 07		07 17	07 27	07 37		07 47	07 57		08 07	08 17		08 27	08 37		08 47
Northfield	d		06 10	06 20	06 30	06 40	06 50	07 00		07 10		07 20	07 30	07 40		07 50	08 00		08 10	08 20		08 30	08 40		08 50
Longbridge	d		06a14	06a24	06 34	06a44	06a54	07 06		07a14		07a24	07 34	07a44		07a54	08 06		08a14	08a24		08 34	08a44		08a54
Barnt Green	d				06 39			07 10					07 39				08 10					08 39			
Alvechurch	d				06 43			07 15					07 43				08 15					08 43			
Redditch	a				06 52			07 22					07 52				08 22					08 52			
Bromsgrove	a	06 03							07 09									08 09							

		LM	LM	LM	LM	LM		LM	XC ◇1 🛒	LM	LM	LM	LM	LM	LM	LM		XC ◇1 🛒	LM	LM	LM	LM	LM	LM	LM
Lichfield Trent Valley	d				08 20					08 50				09 20					09 50				10 20		
Lichfield City	d			08 13	08 24			08 43		08 54			09 13	09 24		09 43			09 54			10 13	10 24		10 43
Shenstone	d			08 18				08 48					09 18			09 48						10 18			10 48
Blake Street	d			08 22	08 32			08 52		09 02			09 22	09 32		09 52			10 02			10 22	10 32		10 52
Butlers Lane	d			08 24	08 34			08 54		09 04			09 24	09 34		09 54			10 04			10 24	10 34		10 54
Four Oaks	d	08 17		08 27	08 37	08 47		08 57		09 07	09 17		09 27	09 37	09 47	09 57			10 07	10 17		10 27	10 37	10 47	10 57
Sutton Coldfield	d	08 20		08 30	08 40	08 50		09 00		09 10	09 20		09 30	09 40	09 50	10 00			10 10	10 20		10 30	10 40	10 50	11 00
Wylde Green	d	08 23		08 33	08 43	08 53		09 03		09 13	09 23		09 33	09 43	09 53	10 03			10 13	10 23		10 33	10 43	10 53	11 03
Chester Road	d	08 25		08 35	08 45	08 55		09 05		09 15	09 25		09 35	09 45	09 55	10 05			10 15	10 25		10 35	10 45	10 55	11 05
Erdington	d	08 27		08 37	08 47	08 57		09 07		09 17	09 27		09 37	09 47	09 57	10 07			10 17	10 27		10 37	10 47	10 57	11 07
Gravelly Hill	d	08 29		08 39	08 49	08 59		09 09		09 19	09 29		09 39	09 49	09 59	10 09			10 19	10 29		10 39	10 49	10 59	11 09
Aston	d	08 33		08 43	08 53	09 03		09 13		09 23	09 33		09 43	09 53	10 03	10 13			10 23	10 33		10 43	10 53	11 03	11 13
Duddeston	d	08 35				09 05					09 35				10 05					10 35				11 05	
Birmingham New Street 12	a	08 41		08 50	09 00	09 10		09 21		09 31	09 41		09 50	10 00	10 10	10 21			10 31	10 41		10 50	11 00	11 10	11 21
	d	08 43	08 49	08 53	09 03	09 13		09 23	09 30	09 33	09 43	09 49	09 53	10 03	10 13	10 23		10 30	10 33	10 43	10 49	10 53	11 03	11 13	11 23
Five Ways	d	08 46		08 56	09 06	09 16		09 26		09 36	09 46		09 56	10 06	10 16	10 26			10 36	10 46		10 56	11 06	11 16	11 26
University	d	08 50	08 55	09 00	09 10	09 20		09 30	09a36	09 40	09 50	09 55	10 00	10 10	10 20	10 30		10a36	10 40	10 50	10 55	11 00	11 10	11 20	11 30
Selly Oak	d	08 53		09 03	09 13	09 23		09 33		09 43	09 53		10 03	10 13	10 23	10 33			10 43	10 53		11 03	11 13	11 23	11 33
Bournville	d	08 55		09 05	09 15	09 25		09 35		09 45	09 55		10 05	10 15	10 25	10 35			10 45	10 55		11 05	11 15	11 25	11 35
Kings Norton	d	08 57		09 07	09 17	09 27		09 37		09 47	09 57		10 07	10 17	10 27	10 37			10 47	10 57		11 07	11 17	11 27	11 37
Northfield	d	09 00		09 10	09 20	09 30		09 40		09 50	10 00		10 10	10 20	10 30	10 40			10 50	11 00		11 10	11 20	11 30	11 40
Longbridge	d	09 06		09a14	09a24	09 34		09a44		09a54	10 06		10a14	10a24	10 34	10a44			10a54	11 06		11a14	11a24	11 34	11a44
Barnt Green	d	09 10				09 39					10 10				10 39					11 10				11 39	
Alvechurch	d	09 15				09 43					10 15				10 43					11 15				11 43	
Redditch	a	09 22				09 52					10 22				10 52					11 22				11 52	
Bromsgrove	a		09 09									10 09									11 10				

A until 23 March

B from 26 March

Table 69

Saturdays

Lichfield - Birmingham - Longbridge and Redditch

Network Diagram - see first Page of Table 67

		XC ◇1	LM	LM	LM	LM	LM	LM	LM	XC ◇1	LM	LM	LM	LM	LM	LM	LM	XC ◇1	LM	LM	LM	LM
Lichfield Trent Valley	d		10 50				11 20				11 50				12 20				12 50			
Lichfield City	d		10 54			11 13	11 24		11 43		11 54			12 13	12 24		12 43		12 54			13 13
Shenstone	d					11 18			11 48					12 18			12 48					13 18
Blake Street	d		11 02			11 22	11 32		11 52		12 02			12 22	12 32		12 52		13 02			13 22
Butlers Lane	d		11 04			11 24	11 34		11 54		12 04			12 24	12 34		12 54		13 04			13 24
Four Oaks	d		11 07	11 17		11 27	11 37	11 47	11 57		12 07	12 17		12 27	12 37	12 47	12 57		13 07	13 17		13 27
Sutton Coldfield	d		11 10	11 20		11 30	11 40	11 50	12 00		12 10	12 20		12 30	12 40	12 50	13 00		13 10	13 20		13 30
Wylde Green	d		11 13	11 23		11 33	11 43	11 53	12 03		12 13	12 23		12 33	12 43	12 53	13 03		13 13	13 23		13 33
Chester Road	d		11 15	11 25		11 35	11 45	11 55	12 05		12 15	12 25		12 35	12 45	12 55	13 05		13 15	13 25		13 35
Erdington	d		11 17	11 27		11 37	11 47	11 57	12 07		12 17	12 27		12 37	12 47	12 57	13 07		13 17	13 27		13 37
Gravelly Hill	d		11 19	11 29		11 39	11 49	11 59	12 09		12 19	12 29		12 39	12 49	12 59	13 09		13 19	13 29		13 39
Aston	d		11 23	11 33		11 43	11 53	12 03	12 13		12 23	12 33		12 43	12 53	13 03	13 13		13 23	13 33		13 43
Duddeston	d			11 35				12 05				12 35				13 05				13 35		
Birmingham New Street 12	a		11 30	11 41		11 50	12 00	12 10	12 21		12 30	12 41		12 50	13 00	13 10	13 21		13 30	13 41		13 50
	d	11 30	11 33	11 43	11 49	11 53	12 03	12 13	12 23	12 30	12 33	12 43	12 49	12 53	13 03	13 13	13 23	13 30	13 33	13 43	13 49	13 53
Five Ways	d		11 36	11 46		11 56	12 06	12 16	12 26		12 36	12 46		12 56	13 06	13 16	13 26		13 36	13 46		13 56
University	d	11a36	11 40	11 50	11 55	12 00	12 10	12 20	12 30	12a36	12 40	12 50	12 55	13 00	13 10	13 20	13 30	13a36	13 40	13 50	13 55	14 00
Selly Oak	d		11 43	11 53		12 03	12 13	12 23	12 33		12 43	12 53		13 03	13 13	13 23	13 33		13 43	13 53		14 03
Bournville	d		11 45	11 55		12 05	12 15	12 25	12 35		12 45	12 55		13 05	13 15	13 25	13 35		13 45	13 55		14 05
Kings Norton	d		11 47	11 57		12 07	12 17	12 27	12 37		12 47	12 57		13 07	13 17	13 27	13 37		13 47	13 57		14 07
Northfield	d		11 50	12 00		12 10	12 20	12 30	12 40		12 50	13 00		13 10	13 20	13 30	13 40		13 50	14 00		14 10
Longbridge	d		11a54	12 06		12a14	12a24	12 34	12a44		12a54	13 06		13a14	13a24	13 34	13a44		13a54	14 06		14a14
Barnt Green	d			12 10				12 39				13 10				13 39				14 10		
Alvechurch	d			12 15				12 43				13 15				13 43				14 15		
Redditch	a			12 22				12 52				13 22				13 52				14 22		
Bromsgrove	a				12 09								13 09								14 10	

		LM	LM	LM	XC ◇1	LM	LM	LM	LM	LM	LM	LM	XC ◇1	LM	LM	LM	LM	LM	LM	LM	LM	XC ◇1	LM
Lichfield Trent Valley	d	13 20				13 50				14 20				14 50				15 20					15 50
Lichfield City	d	13 24		13 43		13 54			14 13	14 24		14 43		14 54			15 13	15 24			15 43		15 54
Shenstone	d			13 48					14 18			14 48					15 18				15 48		
Blake Street	d	13 32		13 52		14 02			14 22	14 32		14 52		15 02			15 22	15 32			15 52		16 02
Butlers Lane	d	13 34		13 54		14 04			14 24	14 34		14 54		15 04			15 24	15 34			15 54		16 04
Four Oaks	d	13 37	13 47	13 57		14 07	14 17		14 27	14 37	14 47	14 57		15 07	15 17		15 27	15 37	15 47		15 57		16 07
Sutton Coldfield	d	13 40	13 50	14 00		14 10	14 20		14 30	14 40	14 50	15 00		15 10	15 20		15 30	15 40	15 50		16 00		16 10
Wylde Green	d	13 43	13 53	14 03		14 13	14 23		14 33	14 43	14 53	15 03		15 13	15 23		15 33	15 43	15 53		16 03		16 13
Chester Road	d	13 45	13 55	14 05		14 15	14 25		14 35	14 45	14 55	15 05		15 15	15 25		15 35	15 45	15 55		16 05		16 15
Erdington	d	13 47	13 57	14 07		14 17	14 27		14 37	14 47	14 57	15 07		15 17	15 27		15 37	15 47	15 57		16 07		16 17
Gravelly Hill	d	13 49	13 59	14 09		14 19	14 29		14 39	14 49	14 59	15 09		15 19	15 29		15 39	15 49	15 59		16 09		16 19
Aston	d	13 53	14 03	14 13		14 23	14 33		14 43	14 53	15 03	15 13		15 23	15 33		15 43	15 53	16 03		16 13		16 23
Duddeston	d		14 05				14 35				15 05				15 35				16 05				
Birmingham New Street 12	a	14 00	14 10	14 21		14 30	14 41		14 50	15 00	15 10	15 20		15 30	15 41		15 50	16 00	16 10		16 21		16 30
	d	14 03	14 13	14 23	14 30	14 33	14 43	14 49	14 53	15 03	15 13	15 23	15 30	15 33	15 43	15 49	15 53	16 03	16 13	16 19	16 23	16 30	16 33
Five Ways	d	14 06	14 16	14 26		14 36	14 46		14 56	15 06	15 16	15 26		15 36	15 46		15 56	16 06	16 16		16 26		16 36
University	d	14 10	14 20	14 30	14a36	14 40	14 50	14 55	15 00	15 10	15 20	15 30	15a36	15 40	15 50	15 55	16 00	16 10	16 20		16 30	16a36	16 40
Selly Oak	d	14 13	14 23	14 33		14 43	14 53		15 03	15 13	15 23	15 33		15 43	15 53		16 03	16 13	16 23		16 33		16 43
Bournville	d	14 15	14 25	14 35		14 45	14 55		15 05	15 15	15 25	15 35		15 45	15 55		16 05	16 15	16 25		16 35		16 45
Kings Norton	d	14 17	14 27	14 37		14 47	14 57		15 07	15 17	15 27	15 37		15 47	15 57		16 07	16 17	16 27		16 37		16 47
Northfield	d	14 20	14 30	14 40		14 50	15 00		15 10	15 20	15 30	15 40		15 50	16 00		16 10	16 20	16 30		16 40		16 50
Longbridge	d	14a24	14 34	14a44		14a54	15 06		15a14	15a24	15 34	15a44		15a54	16 06		16a14	16a24	16 36		16a44		16a54
Barnt Green	d		14 39				15 10				15 39				16 10				16 40				
Alvechurch	d		14 43				15 15				15 43				16 15				16 45				
Redditch	a		14 52				15 22				15 52				16 22				16 52				
Bromsgrove	a							15 09								16 09				16 43			

		LM	LM	LM	LM	LM	LM	LM	XC ◇1	LM	LM	LM	LM	LM	LM	LM	XC ◇1	LM	LM	LM	LM	LM
Lichfield Trent Valley	d				16 20					16 50				17 20				17 50				18 20
Lichfield City	d			16 13	16 24			16 43		16 54			17 13	17 24		17 43		17 54			18 13	18 24
Shenstone	d			16 18				16 48					17 18			17 48					18 18	
Blake Street	d			16 22	16 32			16 52		17 02			17 22	17 32		17 52		18 02			18 22	18 32
Butlers Lane	d			16 24	16 34			16 54		17 04			17 24	17 34		17 54		18 04			18 24	18 34
Four Oaks	d	16 17		16 27	16 37	16 47		16 57		17 07	17 17		17 27	17 37	17 47	17 57		18 07	18 17		18 27	18 37
Sutton Coldfield	d	16 20		16 30	16 40	16 50		17 00		17 10	17 20		17 30	17 40	17 50	18 00		18 10	18 20		18 30	18 40
Wylde Green	d	16 23		16 33	16 43	16 53		17 03		17 13	17 23		17 33	17 43	17 53	18 03		18 13	18 23		18 33	18 43
Chester Road	d	16 25		16 35	16 45	16 55		17 05		17 15	17 25		17 35	17 45	17 55	18 05		18 15	18 25		18 35	18 45
Erdington	d	16 27		16 37	16 47	16 57		17 07		17 17	17 27		17 37	17 47	17 57	18 07		18 17	18 27		18 37	18 47
Gravelly Hill	d	16 29		16 39	16 49	16 59		17 09		17 19	17 29		17 39	17 49	17 59	18 09		18 19	18 29		18 39	18 49
Aston	d	16 33		16 43	16 53	17 03		17 13		17 23	17 33		17 43	17 53	18 03	18 13		18 23	18 33		18 43	18 53
Duddeston	d	16 35				17 05					17 35				18 05				18 35			
Birmingham New Street 12	a	16 41		16 50	17 00	17 10		17 21		17 30	17 41		17 50	18 00	18 10	18 21		18 30	18 41		18 50	19 00
	d	16 43	16 49	16 53	17 03	17 13	17 19	17 23	17 30	17 33	17 43	17 49	17 53	18 03	18 13	18 23	18 30	18 33	18 43	18 49	18 53	19 03
Five Ways	d	16 46		16 56	17 06	17 16		17 26		17 36	17 46		17 56	18 06	18 16	18 26		18 36	18 46		18 56	19 06
University	d	16 50	16 55	17 00	17 10	17 20		17 30	17 36	17 40	17 50	17 55	18 00	18 10	18 20	18 30	18a36	18 40	18 50	18 55	19 00	19 10
Selly Oak	d	16 53		17 03	17 13	17 23		17 33		17 43	17 53		18 03	18 13	18 23	18 33		18 43	18 53		19 03	19 13
Bournville	d	16 55		17 05	17 15	17 25		17 35		17 45	17 55		18 05	18 15	18 25	18 35		18 45	18 55		19 05	19 15
Kings Norton	d	16 57		17 07	17 17	17 27		17 37		17 47	17 57		18 07	18 17	18 27	18 37		18 47	18 57		19 07	19 17
Northfield	d	17 00		17 10	17 20	17 30		17 40		17 50	18 00		18 10	18 20	18 30	18 40		18 50	19 00		19 10	19 20
Longbridge	d	17 06		17a14	17a24	17 36		17a44		17a54	18 06		18a14	18a24	18 34	18a44		18a54	19 06		19a14	19a24
Barnt Green	d	17 10				17 40					18 10				18 39				19 10			
Alvechurch	d	17 15				17 45					18 15				18 43				19 15			
Redditch	a	17 22				17 52					18 22				18 52				19 22			
Bromsgrove	a		17 10				17 40		17 49			18 09								19 09		

Table 69

Saturdays

Lichfield - Birmingham - Longbridge and Redditch

Network Diagram - see first Page of Table 67

Station		LM	LM	LM	XC ◇1	LM	LM	LM	LM	LM	LM	XC ◇1	LM	LM	LM	LM	LM	LM	LM	LM	LM	LM	LM
Lichfield Trent Valley	d					18 50			19 20				20 00			20 30		21 00		21 30		22 00	
Lichfield City	d			18 43		18 54		19 13	19 24		19 43		20 04			20 34		21 04		21 34		22 04	
Shenstone	d			18 48				19 18			19 48		20 09			20 39		21 09		21 39		22 09	
Blake Street	d			18 52		19 02		19 22	19 32		19 52		20 13			20 43		21 13		21 43		22 13	
Butlers Lane	d			18 54		19 04		19 24	19 34		19 54		20 15			20 45		21 15		21 45		22 15	
Four Oaks	d	18 47		18 57		19 07	19 17	19 27	19 37	19 50	19 57		20 18			20 48		21 18		21 48		22 18	
Sutton Coldfield	d	18 50		19 00		19 10	19 20	19 30	19 40	19 53	20 00		20 21			20 51		21 21		21 51		22 21	
Wylde Green	d	18 53		19 03		19 13	19 23	19 33	19 43	19 56	20 03		20 24			20 54		21 24		21 54		22 24	
Chester Road	d	18 55		19 05		19 15	19 25	19 35	19 45	19 58	20 05		20 26			20 56		21 26		21 56		22 26	
Erdington	d	18 57		19 07		19 17	19 27	19 37	19 47	20 00	20 07		20 28			20 58		21 28		21 58		22 28	
Gravelly Hill	d	18 59		19 09		19 19	19 29	19 39	19 49	20 02	20 09		20 30			21 00		21 30		22 00		22 30	
Aston	d	19 03		19 13		19 23	19 33	19 43	19 53	20 06	20 13		20 33			21 03		21 33		22 03		22 33	
Duddeston	d	19 05					19 35		19 55				20 36			21 06		21 36		22 06		22 36	
Birmingham New Street 12	a	19 10		19 21		19 30	19 41	19 50	20 02	20 13	20 20		20 41			21 12		21 41		22 11		22 41	
	d	19 13	19 19	19 23	19 30	19 33	19 43	19 53		20 13	20 23	20 30	20 43	20 53	20 59	21 13	21 23	21 43	21 53	22 13	22 23	22 43	22 53
Five Ways	d	19 16		19 26		19 36	19 46	19 56		20 16	20 26		20 46	20 56		21 16	21 26	21 46	21 56	22 16	22 26	22 46	22 56
University	d	19 20	19 25	19 30	19a36	19 40	19 50	20 00		20 20	20 30	20a36	20 50	21 00	21 05	21 20	21 30	21 50	22 00	22 20	22 30	22 50	23 00
Selly Oak	d	19 23		19 33		19 43	19 53	20 03		20 23	20 33		20 53	21 03		21 23	21 33	21 53	22 03	22 23	22 33	22 53	23 03
Bournville	d	19 25		19 35		19 45	19 55	20 05		20 25	20 35		20 55	21 05		21 25	21 35	21 55	22 05	22 25	22 35	22 55	23 05
Kings Norton	d	19 27		19 37		19 47	19 57	20 07		20 27	20 37		20 57	21 07		21 27	21 37	21 57	22 07	22 27	22 37	22 57	23 07
Northfield	d	19 30		19 40		19 50	20 00	20 10		20 30	20 40		21 00	21 10		21 30	21 40	22 00	22 10	22 30	22 40	23 00	23 10
Longbridge	d	19 36		19a44		19a54	20 04	20a14		20 34	20a44		21 04	21a14		21 34	21a44	22 04	22a14	22 34	22a44	23 04	23a14
Barnt Green	d	19 40					20 09			20 39			21 09			21 39		22 09		22 39		23 09	
Alvechurch	d	19 45					20 13			20 43			21 13			21 43		22 13		22 43		23 13	
Redditch	a	19 52					20 22			20 52			21 22			21 52		22 22		22 52		23 22	
Bromsgrove	a		19 39												21 19								

Station		LM	LM	LM
Lichfield Trent Valley	d	22 30	22 56	
Lichfield City	d	22 34	23 00	
Shenstone	d	22 39	23 05	
Blake Street	d	22 43	23 09	23 36
Butlers Lane	d	22 45	23 11	23 38
Four Oaks	d	22 48	23 14	23 41
Sutton Coldfield	d	22 51	23 17	23 44
Wylde Green	d	22 54	23 20	
Chester Road	d	22 56		
Erdington	d	22 58		
Gravelly Hill	d	23 00		
Aston	d	23 03		
Duddeston	d	23 06		
Birmingham New Street 12	a	23 11	23 31	23 59
	d	23 13	23 33	
Five Ways	d	23 16	23 36	
University	d	23 20	23 40	
Selly Oak	d	23 23	23 43	
Bournville	d	23 25	23 45	
Kings Norton	d	23 27	23 47	
Northfield	d	23 30	23 50	
Longbridge	d	23 34	23a54	
Barnt Green	d	23 39		
Alvechurch	d	23 43		
Redditch	a	23 53		
Bromsgrove	a			

Sundays

Station		LM	LM	LM	XC ◇1 🛒	LM	LM	XC ◇1 🛒	LM	LM	LM	XC ◇1 🛒	LM	LM	LM	XC ◇1 🛒	LM	LM	XC ◇1 🛒	LM	LM	XC ◇1 🛒	LM
Lichfield Trent Valley	d					09 31	10 01		10 31	11 01	11 31		12 01	12 31			13 01	13 31		14 01	14 31		15 01
Lichfield City	d					09 35	10 05		10 35	11 05	11 35		12 05	12 35			13 05	13 35		14 05	14 35		15 05
Shenstone	d					09 40	10 10		10 40	11 10	11 40		12 10	12 40			13 10	13 40		14 10	14 40		15 10
Blake Street	d					09 44	10 14		10 44	11 14	11 44		12 14	12 44			13 14	13 44		14 14	14 44		15 14
Butlers Lane	d					09 46	10 16		10 46	11 16	11 46		12 16	12 46			13 16	13 46		14 16	14 46		15 16
Four Oaks	d			09 19		09 49	10 19		10 49	11 19	11 49		12 19	12 49			13 19	13 49		14 19	14 49		15 19
Sutton Coldfield	d			09 22		09 52	10 22		10 52	11 22	11 52		12 22	12 52			13 22	13 52		14 22	14 52		15 22
Wylde Green	d			09 25		09 55	10 25		10 55	11 25	11 55		12 25	12 55			13 25	13 55		14 25	14 55		15 25
Chester Road	d			09 27		09 57	10 27		10 57	11 27	11 57		12 27	12 57			13 27	13 57		14 27	14 57		15 27
Erdington	d			09 29		09 59	10 29		10 59	11 29	11 59		12 29	12 59			13 29	13 59		14 29	14 59		15 29
Gravelly Hill	d			09 31		10 01	10 31		11 01	11 31	12 01		12 31	13 01			13 31	14 01		14 31	15 01		15 31
Aston	d			09 35		10 05	10 35		11 05	11 35	12 05		12 35	13 05			13 35	14 05		14 35	15 05		15 35
Duddeston	d			09 37		10 07	10 37		11 07	11 37	12 07		12 38	13 07			13 37	14 07		14 37	15 07		15 37
Birmingham New Street 12	a			09 42		10 12	10 42		11 12	11 42	12 12		12 42	13 12			13 42	14 12		14 42	15 12		15 42
	d	08 55	09 15	09 45	10 12	10 15	10 45	11 12	11 15	11 45	12 15	12 30	12 45	13 15	13 24	13 30	13 45	14 15	14 30	14 45	15 15	15 30	15 45
Five Ways	d		09 19	09 49		10 19	10 49		11 19	11 49	12 19		12 49	13 19			13 49	14 19		14 49	15 19		15 49
University	d	09 01	09 23	09 53	10a18	10 23	10 53	11a18	11 23	11 53	12 23	12a36	12 53	13 23		13a36	13 53	14 23	14a36	14 53	15 23	15a36	15 53
Selly Oak	d		09 25	09 55		10 25	10 55		11 25	11 55	12 25		12 55	13 25			13 55	14 25		14 55	15 25		15 55
Bournville	d		09 27	09 57		10 27	10 57		11 27	11 57	12 27		12 57	13 27			13 57	14 27		14 57	15 27		15 57
Kings Norton	d		09 30	10 00		10 30	11 00		11 30	12 00	12 30		13 00	13 30			14 00	14 30		15 00	15 30		16 00
Northfield	d		09 33	10 03		10 33	11 03		11 33	12 03	12 33		13 03	13 33			14 03	14 33		15 03	15 33		16 03
Longbridge	d	09 09	09 36	10 06		10 36	11 06		11 36	12 06	12 36		13 06	13 36			14 06	14 36		15 06	15 36		16 06
Barnt Green	d		09 40	10 10		10 40	11 10		11 40	12 10	12 40		13 10	13 40			14 10	14 40		15 10	15 40		16 10
Alvechurch	d		09 45	10 15		10 45	11 15		11 45	12 15	12 45		13 15	13 45			14 15	14 45		15 15	15 45		16 15
Redditch	a	09 24	09 53	10 23		10 53	11 23		11 53	12 23	12 53		13 23	13 53			14 23	14 53		15 23	15 53		16 23
Bromsgrove	a														13 41								

Table 69

Sundays

Lichfield - Birmingham - Longbridge and Redditch

Network Diagram - see first Page of Table 67

		LM	LM	XC ◇1	LM	LM		XC ◇1	LM	LM	LM	XC ◇1	LM	LM	LM	XC ◇1		LM	LM	LM	LM	LM	LM	LM	LM
Lichfield Trent Valley	d		15 31		16 01	16 31			17 01		17 31		18 01		18 31			19 01	19 31	20 01		20 31	21 01	21 31	22 01
Lichfield City	d		15 35		16 05	16 35			17 05		17 35		18 05		18 35			19 05	19 35	20 05		20 35	21 05	21 35	22 05
Shenstone	d		15 40		16 10	16 40			17 10		17 40		18 10		18 40			19 10	19 40	20 10		20 40	21 10	21 40	22 10
Blake Street	d		15 44		16 14	16 44			17 14		17 44		18 14		18 44			19 14	19 44	20 14		20 44	21 14	21 44	22 14
Butlers Lane	d		15 46		16 16	16 46			17 16		17 46		18 16		18 46			19 16	19 46	20 16		20 46	21 16	21 46	22 16
Four Oaks	d		15 49		16 19	16 49			17 19		17 49		18 19		18 49			19 19	19 49	20 19		20 49	21 19	21 49	22 19
Sutton Coldfield	d		15 52		16 22	16 52			17 22		17 52		18 22		18 52			19 22	19 52	20 22		20 52	21 22	21 52	22 22
Wylde Green	d		15 55		16 25	16 55			17 25		17 55		18 25		18 55			19 25	19 55	20 25		20 55	21 25	21 55	22 25
Chester Road	d		15 57		16 27	16 57			17 27		17 57		18 27		18 57			19 27	19 57	20 27		20 57	21 27	21 57	22 27
Erdington	d		15 59		16 29	16 59			17 29		17 59		18 29		18 59			19 29	19 59	20 29		20 59	21 29	21 59	22 29
Gravelly Hill	d		16 01		16 31	17 01			17 31		18 01		18 31		19 01			19 31	20 01	20 31		21 01	21 31	22 01	22 31
Aston	d		16 05		16 35	17 05			17 35		18 05		18 35		19 05			19 35	20 05	20 35		21 05	21 35	22 05	22 35
Duddeston	d		16 07		16 37	17 07			17 37		18 07		18 37		19 07			19 37	20 07	20 37		21 07	21 37	22 07	22 37
Birmingham New Street 12	a		16 12		16 42	17 12			17 42		18 12		18 42		19 12			19 42	20 12	20 42		21 12	21 42	22 12	22 42
	d	16 00	16 15	16 30	16 45	17 15		17 30	17 45	18 00	18 15	18 30	18 45	19 00	19 15	19 30		19 45	20 15	20 45	21 00	21 15	21 45	22 15	22 45
Five Ways	d		16 19		16 49	17 19			17 49		18 19		18 49		19 19			19 49	20 19	20 49		21 19	21 49	22 19	22 49
University	d		16 23	16a36	16 53	17 23		17a36	17 53		18 23	18a36	18 53		19 23	19a36		19 53	20 23	20 53		21 23	21 53	22 23	22 53
Selly Oak	d		16 25		16 55	17 25			17 55		18 25		18 55		19 25			19 55	20 25	20 55		21 25	21 55	22 25	22 55
Bournville	d		16 27		16 57	17 27			17 57		18 27		18 57		19 27			19 57	20 27	20 57		21 27	21 57	22 27	22 57
Kings Norton	d		16 30		17 00	17 30			18 00		18 30		19 00		19 30			20 00	20 30	21 00		21 30	22 00	22 30	23 00
Northfield	d		16 33		17 03	17 33			18 03		18 33		19 03		19 33			20 03	20 33	21 03		21 33	22 03	22 33	23 03
Longbridge	d		16 36		17 06	17 36			18 06		18 36		19 06		19 36			20 06	20 36	21 06		21 36	22 06	22 36	23 06
Barnt Green	d		16 40		17 10	17 40			18 10		18 40		19 10		19 40			20 10	20 40	21 10		21 40	22 10	22 40	23 10
Alvechurch	d		16 45		17 15	17 45			18 15		18 45		19 15		19 45			20 15	20 45	21 15		21 45	22 15	22 45	23 15
Redditch	a		16 53		17 23	17 53			18 23		18 53		19 23		19 53			20 23	20 53	21 23		21 53	22 23	22 53	23 23
Bromsgrove	a	16 20								18 20				19 21							21 19				

		LM		LM
Lichfield Trent Valley	d	22 31		23 01
Lichfield City	d	22 35		23 05
Shenstone	d	22 40		23 10
Blake Street	d	22 44		23 14
Butlers Lane	d	22 46		23 16
Four Oaks	d	22 49		23 19
Sutton Coldfield	d	22 52		23 22
Wylde Green	d	22 55		23 25
Chester Road	d	22 57		
Erdington	d	22 59		
Gravelly Hill	d	23 01		
Aston	d	23 05		
Duddeston	d	23 07		
Birmingham New Street 12	a	23 12		23 39
	d	23 15		
Five Ways	d	23 19		
University	d	23 23		
Selly Oak	d	23 25		
Bournville	d	23 27		
Kings Norton	d	23 30		
Northfield	d	23 33		
Longbridge	d	23 36		
Barnt Green	d	23 40		
Alvechurch	d	23 45		
Redditch	a	23 53		
Bromsgrove	a			

Redditch and Longbridge - Birmingham - Lichfield

Network Diagram - see first Page of Table 67

Miles	Miles			LM	LM	LM	LM	LM	LM	LM	LM	LM		LM	LM	LM	LM	LM	LM	LM	LM	LM		XC ◇1	LM
—	0	Bromsgrove	d					06 22			06 44						07 24							07 49	
0	—	**Redditch**	d							06 27					06 57					07 27					
3¼	—	Alvechurch	d							06 32					07 02					07 32					
5	3½	Barnt Green	d							06 38					07 08					07 38					
7¼	—	Longbridge	d			06 12	06 22		06 32	06 42		06 52		07 02	07 12	07 22			07 32	07 42		07 52			08 02
8¾	—	Northfield	d			06 14	06 24		06 34	06 44		06 54		07 04	07 14	07 24			07 34	07 44		07 54			08 04
10¼	—	Kings Norton	d			06 17	06 27		06 37	06 47		06 57		07 07	07 17	07 27			07 37	07 47		07 57			08 07
11¼	—	Bournville	d			06 19	06 29		06 39	06 49		06 59		07 09	07 19	07 29			07 39	07 49		07 59			08 09
12¼	—	Selly Oak	d			06 22	06 32		06 42	06 52		07 02		07 12	07 22	07 32			07 42	07 52		08 02			08 12
13	11½	University	d			06 25	06 35	06 39	06 45	06 55	06 59	07 05		07 15	07 25	07 35	07 39		07 45	07 55	07 59	08 05		08 09	08 15
13½	—	Five Ways	d			06 29	06 39		06 49	06 59		07 09		07 19	07 29	07 39			07 49	07 59		08 09			08 19
14½	13	**Birmingham New Street** 12	a			06 33	06 42	06 45	06 52	07 02	07 07	07 13		07 22	07 33	07 42	07 46		07 52	08 03	08 09	08 12		08 16	08 22
—	—		d	06 03	06 25	06 35	06 45		06 55	07 05		07 15		07 25	07 35	07 45		07 47	07 55	08 05		08 15			08 25
16	—	Duddeston	d	06 07	06 29					07 09				07 29				07 52	07 59						08 29
17¼	—	Aston	d	06 10	06 32	06 41	06 51		07 00	07 12		07 21		07 32	07 41			07 54	08 02	08 11		08 21			08 32
18½	—	Gravelly Hill	d	06 13	06 35	06 44	06 54		07 03	07 15		07 24		07 35	07 44			07 57	08 05	08 14		08 24			08 35
19¼	—	Erdington	d	06 16	06 38	06 46	06 56		07 06	07 17		07 26		07 38	07 46			08 00	08 08	08 16		08 26			08 38
20¼	—	Chester Road	d	06 18	06 40	06 48	06 58		07 08	07 19		07 28		07 40	07 48			08 02	08 10	08 18		08 28			08 40
21	—	Wylde Green	d	06 20	06 42	06 50	07 00		07 10	07 21		07 30		07 42	07 50			08 04	08 12	08 20		08 30			08 42
22	—	Sutton Coldfield	d	06 23	06 45	06 54	07 04		07 13	07 24		07 34		07 45	07 53	07 59		08 07	08 15	08 24		08 34			08 45
23½	—	Four Oaks	d	06 26	06 48	06 58	07a11		07 16	07 28		07a41		07 48		08 03		08a12	08 18	08 28		08a41			08 48
24½	—	Butlers Lane	d	06 28	06 50	07 00			07 18	07 30				07 50		08 05			08 20	08 30					08 50
26¼	—	Blake Street	d	06 31	06 53	07 02			07 21	07 32				07 53		08 07			08 23	08 32					08 53
28¾	—	Shenstone	d	06 35	06 57				07 25					07 57		08 11			08 27	08 36					08 57
31¾	—	**Lichfield City**	d	06a41	07 02	07 11			07 30	07 40				08 02	08a08	08a17			08 32	08 41					09a02
33	—	**Lichfield Trent Valley**	a		07 06	07 16			07 34	07 46				08 06					08 36	08 46					

		LM	LM	LM	XC ◇1	LM	LM	LM		LM	LM	LM	LM	LM	XC ◇1	LM	LM	LM		LM	LM	LM	LM	XC ◇1	LM
Bromsgrove	d				08 24			08 42					09 11							09 54					
Redditch	d	07 57					08 27					08 57					09 27					09 57			
Alvechurch	d	08 02					08 32					09 02					09 32					10 02			
Barnt Green	d	08 08					08 38					09 08					09 38					10 08			
Longbridge	d	08 12		08 22		08 32	08 42			08 52	09 02	09 12		09 22		09 32	09 42	09 52			10 02	10 12	10 22		10 32
Northfield	d	08 14		08 24		08 34	08 44			08 54	09 04	09 14		09 24		09 34	09 44	09 54			10 04	10 14	10 24		10 34
Kings Norton	d	08 17		08 27		08 37	08 47			08 57	09 07	09 17		09 27		09 37	09 47	09 57			10 07	10 17	10 27		10 37
Bournville	d	08 19		08 29		08 39	08 49			08 59	09 09	09 19		09 29		09 39	09 49	09 59			10 09	10 19	10 29		10 39
Selly Oak	d	08 22		08 32		08 42	08 52			09 02	09 12	09 22		09 32		09 42	09 52	10 02			10 12	10 22	10 32		10 42
University	d	08 25	08 29	08 35	08 39	08 45	08 55	08 59		09 05	09 15	09 25	09 29	09 35	09 39	09 45	09 55	10 05		10 09	10 15	10 25	10 35	10 39	10 45
Five Ways	d	08 29		08 39		08 49	08 59			09 09	09 19	09 29		09 39		09 49	09 59	10 09			10 19	10 29	10 39		10 49
Birmingham New Street 12	a	08 33	08 37	08 42	08 45	08 52	09 03	09 07		09 13	09 22	09 33	09 42	09 42	09 45	09 52	10 03	10 12		10 24	10 22	10 33	10 42	10 45	10 53
	d	08 35		08 45		08 55	09 05			09 15	09 25	09 35		09 45		09 55	10 05	10 15			10 25	10 35	10 45		10 55
Duddeston	d					08 59					09 29					09 59					10 29				10 59
Aston	d	08 41		08 51		09 02	09 11			09 21	09 32	09 41		09 51		10 02	10 11	10 21			10 32	10 41	10 51		11 02
Gravelly Hill	d	08 44		08 54		09 05	09 14			09 24	09 35	09 44		09 54		10 05	10 14	10 24			10 35	10 44	10 54		11 05
Erdington	d	08 46		08 56		09 08	09 16			09 26	09 38	09 46		09 56		10 08	10 16	10 26			10 38	10 46	10 56		11 08
Chester Road	d	08 48		08 58		09 10	09 18			09 28	09 40	09 48		09 58		10 10	10 18	10 28			10 40	10 48	10 58		11 10
Wylde Green	d	08 50		09 00		09 12	09 20			09 30	09 42	09 50		10 00		10 12	10 20	10 30			10 42	10 50	11 00		11 12
Sutton Coldfield	d	08 54		09 04		09 15	09 24			09 34	09 45	09 54		10 04		10 15	10 24	10 34			10 45	10 54	11 04		11 15
Four Oaks	d	08 58		09a11		09 18	09 28			09a41	09 48	09 58		10a11		10 18	10 28	10a41			10 48	10 58	11a11		11 18
Butlers Lane	d	09 00				09 20	09 30				09 50	10 00				10 20	10 30				10 50	11 00			11 20
Blake Street	d	09 02				09 23	09 32				09 53	10 02				10 23	10 32				10 53	11 02			11 23
Shenstone	d					09 27					09 57					10 27					10 57				11 27
Lichfield City	d	09 11				09a34	09 41				10a02	10 11				10a32	10 41				11a02	11 11			11a32
Lichfield Trent Valley	a	09 15					09 45					10 15					10 45					11 15			

		LM	LM	LM		LM	LM	LM	XC ◇1	LM	LM	LM	LM	LM		LM	LM	XC ◇1	LM	LM	LM	LM	LM	LM	
Bromsgrove	d		10 42									11 42									12 42				
Redditch	d	10 27					10 57				11 27					11 57				12 27				12 57	
Alvechurch	d	10 32					11 02				11 32					12 02				12 32				13 02	
Barnt Green	d	10 38					11 08				11 38					12 08				12 38				13 08	
Longbridge	d	10 42		10 52		11 02	11 12	11 22		11 32	11 42		11 52	12 02		12 12	12 22		12 32	12 42		12 52	13 02	13 12	
Northfield	d	10 44		10 54		11 04	11 14	11 24		11 34	11 44		11 54	12 04		12 14	12 24		12 34	12 44		12 54	13 04	13 14	
Kings Norton	d	10 47		10 57		11 07	11 17	11 27		11 37	11 47		11 57	12 07		12 17	12 27		12 37	12 47		12 57	13 07	13 17	
Bournville	d	10 49		10 59		11 09	11 19	11 29		11 39	11 49		11 59	12 09		12 19	12 29		12 39	12 49		12 59	13 09	13 19	
Selly Oak	d	10 52		11 02		11 12	11 22	11 32		11 42	11 52		12 02	12 12		12 22	12 32		12 42	12 52		13 02	13 12	13 22	
University	d	10 55	10 59	11 05		11 15	11 25	11 35	11 39	11 45	11 55	11 59	12 05	12 15		12 25	12 35	12 39	12 45	12 55	12 59	13 05	13 15	13 25	
Five Ways	d	10 59		11 09		11 19	11 29	11 39		11 49	11 59		12 09	12 19		12 29	12 39		12 49	12 59		13 09	13 19	13 29	
Birmingham New Street 12	a	11 02	11 13	11 12		11 22	11 33	11 42	11 45	11 53	12 03	12 11	12 12	12 22		12 33	12 42	12 45	12 53	13 03	13 13	13 12	13 22	13 33	
	d	11 05		11 15		11 25	11 35	11 45		11 55	12 05		12 15	12 25		12 35	12 45		12 55	13 05		13 15	13 25	13 35	
Duddeston	d					11 29				11 59				12 29					12 59				13 29		
Aston	d	11 11		11 21		11 32	11 41	11 51		12 02	12 11		12 21	12 32		12 41	12 51		13 02	13 11		13 21	13 32	13 41	
Gravelly Hill	d	11 14		11 24		11 35	11 44	11 54		12 05	12 14		12 24	12 35		12 44	12 54		13 05	13 14		13 24	13 35	13 44	
Erdington	d	11 16		11 26		11 38	11 46	11 56		12 08	12 16		12 26	12 38		12 46	12 56		13 08	13 16		13 26	13 38	13 46	
Chester Road	d	11 18		11 28		11 40	11 48	11 58		12 10	12 18		12 28	12 40		12 48	12 58		13 10	13 18		13 28	13 40	13 48	
Wylde Green	d	11 20		11 30		11 42	11 50	12 00		12 12	12 20		12 30	12 42		12 50	13 00		13 12	13 20		13 30	13 42	13 50	
Sutton Coldfield	d	11 24		11 34		11 45	11 54	12 04		12 15	12 24		12 34	12 45		12 54	13 04		13 15	13 24		13 34	13 45	13 54	
Four Oaks	d	11 28		11a41		11 48	11 58	12a11		12 18	12 28		12a41	12 48		12 58	13a11		13 18	13 28		13a41	13 48	13 58	
Butlers Lane	d	11 30				11 50	12 00			12 20	12 30			12 50		13 00			13 20	13 30			13 50	14 00	
Blake Street	d	11 32				11 53	12 02			12 23	12 32			12 53		13 02			13 23	13 32			13 53	14 02	
Shenstone	d					11 57				12 27				12 57					13 27				13 57		
Lichfield City	d	11 41				12a02	12 11			12a32	12 41			13a02		13 11			13a32	13 41			14a02	14 11	
Lichfield Trent Valley	a	11 45					12 15				12 45					13 15				13 45				14 15	

Redditch and Longbridge - Birmingham - Lichfield

Network Diagram - see first Page of Table 67

		LM	XC	LM	LM	LM	LM	LM	LM	LM		XC	LM	LM	LM	LM	LM	LM	LM	XC		LM	LM	LM	LM
			◇1									◇1								◇1					
Bromsgrove	d					13 42									14 42									15 42	
Redditch	d				13 27				13 57					14 27				14 57					15 27		
Alvechurch	d				13 32				14 02					14 32				15 02					15 32		
Barnt Green	d				13 38				14 08					14 38				15 08					15 38		
Longbridge	d	13 22		13 32	13 42		13 52	14 02	14 12	14 22			14 32	14 42		14 52	15 02	15 12	15 22			15 32	15 42		15 52
Northfield	d	13 24		13 34	13 44		13 54	14 04	14 14	14 24			14 34	14 44		14 54	15 04	15 14	15 24			15 34	15 44		15 54
Kings Norton	d	13 27		13 37	13 47		13 57	14 07	14 17	14 27			14 37	14 47		14 57	15 07	15 17	15 27			15 37	15 47		15 57
Bournville	d	13 29		13 39	13 49		13 59	14 09	14 19	14 29			14 39	14 49		14 59	15 09	15 19	15 29			15 39	15 49		15 59
Selly Oak	d	13 32		13 42	13 52		14 02	14 12	14 22	14 32			14 42	14 52		15 02	15 12	15 22	15 32			15 42	15 52		16 02
University	d	13 35	13 39	13 45	13 55	13 59	14 05	14 15	14 25	14 35		14 39	14 45	14 55	14 59	15 05	15 15	15 25	15 35	15 39		15 45	15 55	15 59	16 05
Five Ways	d	13 39		13 49	13 59		14 09	14 19	14 29	14 39			14 49	14 59		15 09	15 19	15 29	15 39			15 49	15 59		16 09
Birmingham New Street 12	a	13 42	13 45	13 53	14 03	14 12	14 12	14 22	14 33	14 42		14 45	14 53	15 03	15 13	15 12	15 22	15 33	15 42	15 45		15 53	16 03	16 13	16 12
	d	13 45		13 55	14 05		14 15	14 25	14 35	14 45			14 55	15 05		15 15	15 25	15 35	15 45			15 55	16 05		16 15
Duddeston	d			13 59				14 29					14 59				15 29					15 59			
Aston	d	13 51		14 02	14 11		14 21	14 32	14 41	14 51			15 02	15 11		15 21	15 32	15 41	15 51			16 02	16 11		16 21
Gravelly Hill	d	13 54		14 05	14 14		14 24	14 35	14 44	14 54			15 05	15 14		15 24	15 35	15 44	15 54			16 05	16 14		16 24
Erdington	d	13 56		14 08	14 16		14 26	14 38	14 46	14 56			15 08	15 16		15 26	15 38	15 46	15 56			16 08	16 16		16 26
Chester Road	d	13 58		14 10	14 18		14 28	14 40	14 48	14 58			15 10	15 18		15 28	15 40	15 48	15 58			16 10	16 18		16 28
Wylde Green	d	14 00		14 12	14 20		14 30	14 42	14 50	15 00			15 12	15 20		15 30	15 42	15 50	16 00			16 12	16 20		16 30
Sutton Coldfield	d	14 04		14 15	14 24		14 34	14 45	14 54	15 04			15 15	15 24		15 34	15 45	15 54	16 04			16 15	16 24		16 34
Four Oaks	d	14a11		14 18	14 28		14a41	14 48	14 58	15a11			15 18	15 28		15a41	15 48	15 58	16a11			16 18	16 28		16a41
Butlers Lane	d			14 20	14 30			14 50	15 00				15 20	15 30			15 50	16 00				16 20	16 30		
Blake Street	d			14 23	14 32			14 53	15 02				15 23	15 32			15 53	16 02				16 23	16 32		
Shenstone	d			14 27				14 57					15 27				15 57					16 27			
Lichfield City	d			14a32	14 41			15a02	15 11				15a32	15 41			16a02	16 11				16a32	16 41		
Lichfield Trent Valley	a				14 45				15 15					15 45				16 15					16 45		

		LM	LM	LM	XC	LM		LM	LM	LM	LM	LM	LM	XC	LM	LM		LM	LM	LM	LM	LM	XC	LM	LM
					◇1									◇1									◇1		
Bromsgrove	d								16 42									17 42							
Redditch	d		15 57					16 27				16 57				17 27					17 57				18 27
Alvechurch	d		16 02					16 32				17 02				17 32					18 02				18 32
Barnt Green	d		16 08					16 38	16 49			17 08				17 38					18 08				18 38
Longbridge	d	16 02	16 12	16 22		16 32		16 42		16 52	17 02	17 12	17 22		17 32	17 42			17 52	18 02	18 12	18 22		18 32	18 42
Northfield	d	16 04	16 14	16 24		16 34		16 44		16 54	17 04	17 14	17 24		17 34	17 44			17 54	18 04	18 14	18 24		18 34	18 44
Kings Norton	d	16 07	16 17	16 27		16 37		16 47		16 57	17 07	17 17	17 27		17 37	17 47			17 57	18 07	18 17	18 27		18 37	18 47
Bournville	d	16 09	16 19	16 29		16 39		16 49		16 59	17 09	17 19	17 29		17 39	17 49			17 59	18 09	18 19	18 29		18 39	18 49
Selly Oak	d	16 12	16 22	16 32		16 42		16 52		17 02	17 12	17 22	17 32		17 42	17 52			18 02	18 12	18 22	18 32		18 42	18 52
University	d	16 15	16 25	16 35	16 39	16 45		16 55	16 59	17 05	17 15	17 25	17 35	17 39	17 45	17 55		17 59	18 05	18 15	18 25	18 35	18 39	18 45	18 55
Five Ways	d	16 19	16 29	16 39		16 49		16 59		17 09	17 19	17 29	17 39		17 49	17 59			18 09	18 19	18 29	18 39		18 49	18 59
Birmingham New Street 12	a	16 22	16 33	16 42	16 45	16 53		17 03	17 13	17 12	17 23	17 33	17 42	17 45	17 53	18 03		18 13	18 12	18 23	18 33	18 42	18 45	18 53	19 03
	d	16 25	16 35	16 45		16 55		17 05		17 15	17 25	17 35	17 45		17 55	18 05			18 15	18 25	18 35	18 45		18 55	19 05
Duddeston	d	16 29				16 59					17 29				17 59					18 29				18 59	
Aston	d	16 32	16 41	16 51		17 02		17 11		17 21	17 32	17 41	17 51		18 02	18 11			18 21	18 32	18 41	18 51		19 02	19 11
Gravelly Hill	d	16 35	16 44	16 54		17 05		17 14		17 24	17 35	17 44	17 54		18 05	18 14			18 24	18 35	18 44	18 54		19 05	19 14
Erdington	d	16 38	16 46	16 56		17 08		17 16		17 26	17 38	17 46	17 56		18 08	18 16			18 26	18 38	18 46	18 56		19 08	19 16
Chester Road	d	16 39	16 48	16 58		17 10		17 18		17 28	17 40	17 48	17 58		18 10	18 18			18 28	18 40	18 48	18 58		19 10	19 18
Wylde Green	d	16 41	16 50	17 00		17 12		17 20		17 30	17 42	17 50	18 00		18 12	18 20			18 30	18 42	18 50	19 00		19 12	19 20
Sutton Coldfield	d	16 44	16 54	17 04		17 15		17 24		17 34	17 45	17 54	18 04		18 15	18 24			18 34	18 45	18 54	19 04		19 15	19 24
Four Oaks	d	16 48	16 58	17a11		17 18		17 28		17a41	17 48	17 58	18a11		18 18	18 28			18a41	18 48	18 58	19a11		19 18	19 28
Butlers Lane	d	16 50	17 00			17 20		17 30			17 50	18 00			18 20	18 30				18 50	19 00			19 20	19 30
Blake Street	d	16 52	17 02			17 23		17 32			17 53	18 02			18 23	18 32				18 53	19 02			19 23	19 32
Shenstone	d	16 56				17 27		17 36			17 57	18 06			18 27					18 57				19 27	
Lichfield City	d	17a02	17 11			17 32		17 41			18 02	18 11			18a32	18 41				19a02	19 11			19a32	19 41
Lichfield Trent Valley	a		17 15			17 36		17 46			18 06	18 16				18 45					19 15				19 45

		LM		LM	LM	LM	LM	XC	LM	LM	LM	LM		LM	LM	XC	LM	LM	LM	LM	LM	LM		XC	LM
								◇1								◇1			A					◇1	
Bromsgrove	d	18 43										19 46								20 55					
Redditch	d					18 57				19 27					19 57			20 27			20 57				21 27
Alvechurch	d					19 02				19 32					20 02			20 32			21 02				21 32
Barnt Green	d	18 49				19 08				19 38					20 08			20 38			21 08				21 38
Longbridge	d			18 52	19 02	19 12	19 22		19 32	19 42	19 52			20 02	20 12		20 30	20 42	20 57		21 12	21 27			21 42
Northfield	d			18 54	19 04	19 14	19 24		19 34	19 44	19 54			20 04	20 14		20 32	20 44	20 59		21 14	21 29			21 44
Kings Norton	d			18 57	19 07	19 17	19 27		19 37	19 47	19 57			20 07	20 17		20 35	20 47	21 02		21 17	21 32			21 47
Bournville	d			18 59	19 09	19 19	19 29		19 39	19 49	19 59			20 09	20 19		20 37	20 49	21 04		21 19	21 34			21 49
Selly Oak	d			19 02	19 12	19 22	19 32		19 42	19 52	20 02			20 12	20 22		20 40	20 52	21 07		21 22	21 37			21 52
University	d	18 59		19 05	19 15	19 25	19 35	19 39	19 45	19 55	20 05	20 09		20 15	20 25	20 39	20 42	20 55	21 10	21 14	21 25	21 40		21 45	21 55
Five Ways	d			19 09	19 19	19 29	19 39		19 49	19 59	20 09			20 19	20 29		20 46	20 59	21 14		21 29	21 44			21 59
Birmingham New Street 12	a	19 12		19 12	19 22	19 33	19 42	19 45	19 52	20 03	20 12	20 20		20 22	20 33	20 45	20 50	21 02	21 17	21 20	21 33	21 47		21 51	22 02
	d			19 15		19 35				20 05					20 35			21 05			21 35				22 05
Duddeston	d					19 39				20 09					20 39			21 09			21 39				22 09
Aston	d			19 21		19 42				20 12					20 42			21 12			21 42				22 12
Gravelly Hill	d			19 24		19 45				20 15					20 45			21 15			21 45				22 15
Erdington	d			19 26		19 48				20 18					20 48			21 18			21 48				22 18
Chester Road	d			19 28		19 50				20 20					20 50			21 20			21 50				22 20
Wylde Green	d			19 30		19 52				20 22					20 52			21 22			21 52				22 22
Sutton Coldfield	d			19 34		19 55				20 25					20 55			21 25			21 55				22 25
Four Oaks	d			19a41		19 58				20 28					20 58			21 28			21 58				22 28
Butlers Lane	d					20 00				20 30					21 00			21 30			22 00				22 30
Blake Street	d					20 03				20 33					21 03			21 33			22 03				22 33
Shenstone	d					20 07				20 37					21 07			21 37			22 07				22 37
Lichfield City	d					20 12				20 42					21 12			21 42			22 12				22 42
Lichfield Trent Valley	a					20 16				20 46					21 16			21 46			22 16				22 46

A not from 26 December until 28 December

Table 69

Mondays to Fridays

Redditch and Longbridge - Birmingham - Lichfield

Network Diagram - see first Page of Table 67

		LM	LM	LM	LM A	LM	LM	LM B 🚌		LM	LM
Bromsgrove	d				22 28			22 46			
Redditch	d		21 57			22 27				22 57	
Alvechurch	d		22 02			22 32				23 02	
Barnt Green	d		22 08			22 38				23 08	
Longbridge	d	21 57	22 12	22 27		22 42	22 52	23a06		23 12	23 30
Northfield	d	21 59	22 14	22 29		22 44	22 54			23 14	23 32
Kings Norton	d	22 02	22 17	22 32		22 47	22 57			23 17	23 35
Bournville	d	22 04	22 19	22 34		22 49	22 59			23 19	23 37
Selly Oak	d	22 07	22 22	22 37		22 52	23 02			23 22	23 40
University	d	22 10	22 25	22 40	22 44	22 55	23 05			23 25	23 43
Five Ways	d	22 14	22 29	22 44		22 59	23 09			23 29	23 47
Birmingham New Street 12	a	22 17	22 33	22 47	22 50	23 03	23 12			23 34	23 50
	d		22 35	22 55			23 15				
Duddeston	d		22 39	22 59			23 19				
Aston	d		22 42	23 02			23 22				
Gravelly Hill	d		22 45	23 05			23 25				
Erdington	d		22 48	23 08			23 28				
Chester Road	d		22 50	23 10			23 30				
Wylde Green	d		22 52	23 12			23 32				
Sutton Coldfield	d		22 55	23 15			23 35				
Four Oaks	d		22 58	23 18			23 38				
Butlers Lane	d		23 00	23 20			23 40				
Blake Street	d		23 03	23a24			23 43				
Shenstone	d		23 07				23 47				
Lichfield City	d		23 12				23a52				
Lichfield Trent Valley	a		23 16								

Saturdays

		LM	LM	LM	LM	LM	LM	LM	LM	LM		LM	LM	LM	LM	XC ◇1	LM	LM	LM	LM		LM	XC ◇1	LM	LM
Bromsgrove	d								06 51							07 44		07 52							
Redditch	d						06 27					06 57			07 27					07 57					08 27
Alvechurch	d						06 32					07 02			07 32					08 02					08 32
Barnt Green	d						06 38					07 08			07 38					08 08					08 38
Longbridge	d			06 12	06 22	06 32	06 42	06 52		07 02		07 12	07 22	07 32	07 42		07 52		08 02	08 12		08 22		08 32	08 42
Northfield	d			06 14	06 24	06 34	06 44	06 54		07 04		07 14	07 24	07 34	07 44		07 54		08 04	08 14		08 24		08 34	08 44
Kings Norton	d			06 17	06 27	06 37	06 47	06 57		07 07		07 17	07 27	07 37	07 47		07 57		08 07	08 17		08 27		08 37	08 47
Bournville	d			06 19	06 29	06 39	06 49	06 59		07 09		07 19	07 29	07 39	07 49		07 59		08 09	08 19		08 29		08 39	08 49
Selly Oak	d			06 22	06 32	06 42	06 52	07 02		07 12		07 22	07 32	07 42	07 52		08 02		08 12	08 22		08 32		08 42	08 52
University	d			06 25	06 35	06 45	06 55	07 05	07 09	07 15		07 25	07 35	07 45	07 55	08 00	08 05	08 09	08 15	08 25		08 35	08 39	08 45	08 55
Five Ways	d			06 29	06 39	06 49	06 59	07 09		07 19		07 29	07 39	07 49	07 59		08 09		08 19	08 29		08 39		08 49	08 59
Birmingham New Street 12	a			06 33	06 43	06 53	07 02	07 13	07 16	07 23		07 33	07 43	07 53	08 03	08 08	08 13	08 16	08 23	08 33		08 43	08 45	08 52	09 03
	d	05 57	06 25	06 35		06 55	07 05	07 15		07 25		07 35	07 45	07 55	08 05		08 15		08 25	08 35		08 45		08 55	09 05
Duddeston	d	06 01	06 29			06 59				07 29				07 59					08 29					08 59	
Aston	d	06 04	06 32			07 02	07 11	07 21		07 32		07 41	07 51	08 02	08 11		08 21		08 32	08 41		08 51		09 02	09 11
Gravelly Hill	d	06 07	06 35			07 05	07 14	07 24		07 35		07 44	07 54	08 05	08 14		08 24		08 35	08 44		08 54		09 05	09 14
Erdington	d	06 10	06 38	06 44		07 08	07 16	07 26		07 38		07 46	07 56	08 08	08 16		08 26		08 38	08 46		08 56		09 08	09 16
Chester Road	d	06 12	06 40	06 46		07 10	07 18	07 28		07 40		07 48	07 58	08 10	08 18		08 28		08 40	08 48		08 58		09 10	09 18
Wylde Green	d	06 14	06 42	06 48		07 12	07 20	07 30		07 42		07 50	08 00	08 12	08 20		08 30		08 42	08 50		09 00		09 12	09 20
Sutton Coldfield	d	06 17	06 45	06 52		07 15	07 24	07 34		07 45		07 54	08 04	08 15	08 24		08 34		08 45	08 54		09 04		09 15	09 24
Four Oaks	d	06 20	06 48	06 55		07 18	07 28	07a41		07 48		07 58	08a11	08 18	08 28		08a41		08 48	08 58		09a11		09 18	09 28
Butlers Lane	d	06 22	06 50	06 57		07 20	07 30			07 50		08 00		08 20	08 30				08 50	09 00				09 20	09 30
Blake Street	d	06 24	06 53	07 00		07 23	07 32			07 53		08 02		08 23	08 32				08 53	09 02				09 23	09 32
Shenstone	d	06 28	06 57			07 27				07 57				08 27	08 36				08 57					09 27	
Lichfield City	d	06a34	07a02	07 08		07a32	07 41			08a02		08 11		08a32	08 41				09a02	09 11				09a32	09 41
Lichfield Trent Valley	a			07 12			07 45					08 15			08 45					09 15					09 45

		LM	LM	LM	LM	LM		XC ◇1	LM	LM	LM	LM	LM	LM	LM	LM		XC ◇1	LM	LM	LM	LM	LM	LM	LM
Bromsgrove	d	08 42									09 42				10 13						10 42				11 15
Redditch	d				08 57					09 27				09 57						10 27				10 57	
Alvechurch	d				09 02					09 32				10 02						10 32				11 02	
Barnt Green	d				09 08					09 38				10 08						10 38				11 08	
Longbridge	d		08 52	09 02	09 12	09 22			09 32	09 42		09 52	10 02	10 12		10 22			10 32	10 42		10 52	11 02	11 12	
Northfield	d		08 54	09 04	09 14	09 24			09 34	09 44		09 54	10 04	10 14		10 24			10 34	10 44		10 54	11 04	11 14	
Kings Norton	d		08 57	09 07	09 17	09 27			09 37	09 47		09 57	10 07	10 17		10 27			10 37	10 47		10 57	11 07	11 17	
Bournville	d		08 59	09 09	09 19	09 29			09 39	09 49		09 59	10 09	10 19		10 29			10 39	10 49		10 59	11 09	11 19	
Selly Oak	d		09 02	09 12	09 22	09 32			09 42	09 52		10 02	10 12	10 22		10 32			10 42	10 52		11 02	11 12	11 22	
University	d	08 59	09 05	09 15	09 25	09 35		09 39	09 45	09 55	09 59	10 05	10 15	10 25		10 35		10 39	10 45	10 55	10 59	11 05	11 15	11 25	
Five Ways	d		09 09	09 19	09 29	09 39			09 49	09 59		10 09	10 19	10 29		10 39			10 49	10 59		11 09	11 19	11 29	
Birmingham New Street 12	a	09 11	09 13	09 23	09 33	09 43		09 45	09 53	10 03	10 11	10 13	10 23	10 33	10 41	10 43		10 45	10 53	11 03	11 11	11 13	11 23	11 33	11 38
	d		09 15	09 25	09 35	09 45			09 55	10 05		10 15	10 25	10 35		10 45			10 55	11 05		11 15	11 25	11 35	
Duddeston	d			09 29					09 59				10 29						10 59				11 29		
Aston	d		09 21	09 32	09 41	09 51			10 02	10 11		10 21	10 32	10 41		10 51			11 02	11 11		11 21	11 32	11 41	
Gravelly Hill	d		09 24	09 35	09 44	09 54			10 05	10 14		10 24	10 35	10 44		10 54			11 05	11 14		11 24	11 35	11 44	
Erdington	d		09 26	09 38	09 46	09 56			10 08	10 16		10 26	10 38	10 46		10 56			11 08	11 16		11 26	11 38	11 46	
Chester Road	d		09 28	09 40	09 48	09 58			10 10	10 18		10 28	10 40	10 48		10 58			11 10	11 18		11 28	11 40	11 48	
Wylde Green	d		09 30	09 42	09 50	10 00			10 12	10 20		10 30	10 42	10 50		11 00			11 12	11 20		11 30	11 42	11 50	
Sutton Coldfield	d		09 34	09 45	09 54	10 04			10 15	10 24		10 34	10 45	10 54		11 04			11 15	11 24		11 34	11 45	11 54	
Four Oaks	d		09a41	09 48	09 58	10a11			10 18	10 28		10a41	10 48	10 58		11a11			11 18	11 28		11a41	11 48	11 58	
Butlers Lane	d			09 50	10 00				10 20	10 30			10 50	11 00					11 20	11 30			11 50	12 00	
Blake Street	d			09 53	10 02				10 23	10 32			10 53	11 02					11 23	11 32			11 53	12 02	
Shenstone	d			09 57					10 27				10 57						11 27				11 57		
Lichfield City	d			10a02	10 11				10a32	10 41			11a02	11 11					11a32	11 41			12a02	12 11	
Lichfield Trent Valley	a				10 15					10 45				11 15						11 45				12 15	

A until 23 March

B from 26 March

Table 69

Saturdays

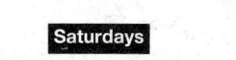

Redditch and Longbridge - Birmingham - Lichfield

Network Diagram - see first Page of Table 67

		LM		XC ◇1	LM	LM	LM	LM	LM	LM	LM	XC ◇1		LM	LM	LM	LM	LM	LM	LM	XC ◇1	LM		LM	LM
Bromsgrove	d						11 42									12 42									13 42
Redditch	d					11 27				11 57					12 27				12 57					13 27	
Alvechurch	d					11 32				12 02					12 32				13 02					13 32	
Barnt Green	d					11 38				12 08					12 38				13 08					13 38	
Longbridge	d	11 22			11 32	11 42		11 52	12 02	12 12	12 22			12 32	12 42		12 52	13 02	13 12	13 22		13 32		13 42	
Northfield	d	11 24			11 34	11 44		11 54	12 04	12 14	12 24			12 34	12 44		12 54	13 04	13 14	13 24		13 34		13 44	
Kings Norton	d	11 27			11 37	11 47		11 57	12 07	12 17	12 27			12 37	12 47		12 57	13 07	13 17	13 27		13 37		13 47	
Bournville	d	11 29			11 39	11 49		11 59	12 09	12 19	12 29			12 39	12 49		12 59	13 09	13 19	13 29		13 39		13 49	
Selly Oak	d	11 32			11 42	11 52		12 02	12 12	12 22	12 32			12 42	12 52		13 02	13 12	13 22	13 32		13 42		13 52	
University	d	11 35		11 39	11 45	11 55	11 59	12 05	12 15	12 25	12 35	12 39		12 45	12 55	12 59	13 05	13 15	13 25	13 35	13 39	13 45		13 55	13 59
Five Ways	d	11 39			11 49	11 59		12 09	12 19	12 29	12 39			12 49	12 59		13 09	13 19	13 29	13 39		13 49		13 59	
Birmingham New Street 12	a	11 43		11 45	11 53	12 03	12 11	12 13	12 23	12 33	12 43	12 45		12 53	13 03	13 11	13 13	13 23	13 33	13 43	13 45	13 53		14 03	14 11
	d	11 45			11 55	12 05		12 15	12 25	12 35	12 45			12 55	13 05		13 15	13 25	13 35	13 45		13 55		14 05	
Duddeston	d				11 59				12 29					12 59				13 29				13 59			
Aston	d	11 51			12 02	12 11		12 21	12 32	12 41	12 51			13 02	13 11		13 21	13 32	13 41	13 51		14 02		14 11	
Gravelly Hill	d	11 54			12 05	12 14		12 24	12 35	12 44	12 54			13 05	13 14		13 24	13 35	13 44	13 54		14 05		14 14	
Erdington	d	11 56			12 08	12 16		12 26	12 38	12 46	12 56			13 08	13 16		13 26	13 38	13 46	13 56		14 08		14 16	
Chester Road	d	11 58			12 10	12 18		12 28	12 40	12 48	12 58			13 10	13 18		13 28	13 40	13 48	13 58		14 10		14 18	
Wylde Green	d	12 00			12 12	12 20		12 30	12 42	12 50	13 00			13 12	13 20		13 30	13 42	13 50	14 00		14 12		14 20	
Sutton Coldfield	d	12 04			12 15	12 24		12 34	12 45	12 54	13 04			13 15	13 24		13 34	13 45	13 54	14 04		14 15		14 24	
Four Oaks	d	12a11			12 18	12 28		12a41	12 48	12 58	13a11			13 18	13 28		13a41	13 48	13 58	14a11		14 18		14 28	
Butlers Lane	d				12 20	12 30			12 50	13 00				13 20	13 30			13 50	14 00			14 20		14 30	
Blake Street	d				12 23	12 32			12 53	13 02				13 23	13 32			13 53	14 02			14 23		14 32	
Shenstone	d				12 27				12 57					13 27				13 57				14 27			
Lichfield City	d				12a32	12 41			13a02	13 11				13a32	13 41			14a02	14 11			14a32		14 41	
Lichfield Trent Valley	a					12 45				13 15					13 45				14 15					14 45	

		LM	LM	LM	LM	XC ◇1	LM	LM		LM	LM	LM	LM	LM	XC ◇1	LM	LM	LM		LM	LM	LM	LM	LM	XC ◇1
Bromsgrove	d									14 42								15 42					16 12		
Redditch	d			13 57				14 27					14 57				15 27					15 57			
Alvechurch	d			14 02				14 32					15 02				15 32					16 02			
Barnt Green	d			14 08				14 38					15 08				15 38					16 08			
Longbridge	d	13 52	14 02	14 12	14 22		14 32	14 42			14 52	15 02	15 12	15 22		15 32	15 42			15 52	16 02	16 12		16 22	
Northfield	d	13 54	14 04	14 14	14 24		14 34	14 44			14 54	15 04	15 14	15 24		15 34	15 44			15 54	16 04	16 14		16 24	
Kings Norton	d	13 57	14 07	14 17	14 27		14 37	14 47			14 57	15 07	15 17	15 27		15 37	15 47			15 57	16 07	16 17		16 27	
Bournville	d	13 59	14 09	14 19	14 29		14 39	14 49			14 59	15 09	15 19	15 29		15 39	15 49			15 59	16 09	16 19		16 29	
Selly Oak	d	14 02	14 12	14 22	14 32		14 42	14 52			15 02	15 12	15 22	15 32		15 42	15 52			16 02	16 12	16 22		16 32	
University	d	14 05	14 15	14 25	14 35	14 39	14 45	14 55		14 59	15 05	15 15	15 25	15 35	15 39	15 45	15 55	15 59		16 05	16 15	16 25		16 35	16 39
Five Ways	d	14 09	14 19	14 29	14 39		14 49	14 59			15 09	15 19	15 29	15 39		15 49	15 59			16 09	16 19	16 29		16 39	
Birmingham New Street 12	a	14 13	14 23	14 33	14 43	14 45	14 53	15 03		15 11	15 13	15 23	15 33	15 43	15 45	15 53	16 03	16 11		16 13	16 23	16 33	16 45	16 43	16 45
	d	14 15	14 25	14 35	14 45		14 55	15 05			15 15	15 25	15 35	15 45		15 55	16 05			16 15	16 25	16 35		16 45	
Duddeston	d		14 29				14 59					15 29				15 59					16 29				
Aston	d	14 21	14 32	14 41	14 51		15 02	15 11			15 21	15 32	15 41	15 51		16 02	16 11			16 21	16 32	16 41		16 51	
Gravelly Hill	d	14 24	14 35	14 44	14 54		15 05	15 14			15 24	15 35	15 44	15 54		16 05	16 14			16 24	16 35	16 44		16 54	
Erdington	d	14 26	14 38	14 46	14 56		15 08	15 16			15 26	15 38	15 46	15 56		16 08	16 16			16 26	16 38	16 46		16 56	
Chester Road	d	14 28	14 40	14 48	14 58		15 10	15 18			15 28	15 40	15 48	15 58		16 10	16 18			16 28	16 40	16 48		16 58	
Wylde Green	d	14 30	14 42	14 50	15 00		15 12	15 20			15 30	15 42	15 50	16 00		16 12	16 20			16 30	16 42	16 50		17 00	
Sutton Coldfield	d	14 34	14 45	14 54	15 04		15 15	15 24			15 34	15 45	15 54	16 04		16 15	16 24			16 34	16 45	16 54		17 04	
Four Oaks	d	14a41	14 48	14 58	15a11		15 18	15 28			15a41	15 48	15 58	16a11		16 18	16 28			16a41	16 48	16 58		17a11	
Butlers Lane	d		14 50	15 00			15 20	15 30				15 50	16 00			16 20	16 30				16 50	17 00			
Blake Street	d		14 53	15 02			15 23	15 32				15 53	16 02			16 23	16 32				16 53	17 02			
Shenstone	d		14 57				15 27					15 57				16 27					16 57				
Lichfield City	d		15a02	15 11			15a32	15 41				16a02	16 11			16a32	16 41				17a02	17 11			
Lichfield Trent Valley	a			15 15				15 45					16 15				16 45					17 15			

		LM	LM	LM		LM	LM	LM	LM	XC ◇1	LM	LM	LM	LM		LM	LM	LM	XC ◇1	LM	LM	LM	LM	LM	
Bromsgrove	d			16 42									17 44									18 42			
Redditch	d		16 27					16 57				17 27					17 57				18 27				
Alvechurch	d		16 32					17 02				17 32					18 02				18 32				
Barnt Green	d		16 38					17 08				17 38					18 08				18 38				
Longbridge	d	16 32	16 42			16 52	17 02	17 12	17 22		17 32	17 42		17 52		18 02	18 12	18 22		18 32	18 42		18 52	19 02	
Northfield	d	16 34	16 44			16 54	17 04	17 14	17 24		17 34	17 44		17 54		18 04	18 14	18 24		18 34	18 44		18 54	19 04	
Kings Norton	d	16 37	16 47			16 57	17 07	17 17	17 27		17 37	17 47		17 57		18 07	18 17	18 27		18 37	18 47		18 57	19 07	
Bournville	d	16 39	16 49			16 59	17 09	17 19	17 29		17 39	17 49		17 59		18 09	18 19	18 29		18 39	18 49		18 59	19 09	
Selly Oak	d	16 42	16 52			17 02	17 12	17 22	17 32		17 42	17 52		18 02		18 12	18 22	18 32		18 42	18 52		19 02	19 12	
University	d	16 45	16 55	16 59		17 05	17 15	17 25	17 35	17 39	17 45	17 55	17 59	18 05		18 15	18 25	18 35	18 39	18 45	18 55	18 59	19 05	19 15	
Five Ways	d	16 49	16 59			17 09	17 19	17 29	17 39		17 49	17 59		18 09		18 19	18 29	18 39		18 49	18 59		19 09	19 19	
Birmingham New Street 12	a	16 53	17 03	17 11		17 13	17 23	17 33	17 43	17 45	17 53	18 03	18 11	18 13		18 23	18 33	18 43	18 45	18 53	19 03	19 11	19 13	19 23	
	d	16 55	17 05			17 15	17 25	17 35	17 45		17 55	18 05		18 15		18 25	18 35	18 45		18 55	19 05		19 15		
Duddeston	d	16 59					17 29				17 59					18 29				18 59					
Aston	d	17 02	17 11			17 21	17 32	17 41	17 51		18 02	18 11		18 21		18 32	18 41	18 51		19 02	19 11		19 21		
Gravelly Hill	d	17 05	17 14			17 24	17 35	17 44	17 54		18 05	18 14		18 24		18 35	18 44	18 54		19 05	19 14		19 24		
Erdington	d	17 08	17 16			17 26	17 38	17 46	17 56		18 08	18 16		18 26		18 38	18 46	18 56		19 08	19 16		19 26		
Chester Road	d	17 10	17 18			17 28	17 40	17 48	17 58		18 10	18 18		18 28		18 40	18 48	18 58		19 10	19 18		19 28		
Wylde Green	d	17 12	17 20			17 30	17 42	17 50	18 00		18 12	18 20		18 30		18 42	18 50	19 00		19 12	19 20		19 30		
Sutton Coldfield	d	17 15	17 24			17 34	17 45	17 54	18 04		18 15	18 24		18 34		18 45	18 54	19 04		19 15	19 24		19 34		
Four Oaks	d	17 18	17 28			17a41	17 48	17 58	18a11		18 18	18 28		18a41		18 48	18 58	19a11		19 18	19 28		19a41		
Butlers Lane	d	17 20	17 30				17 50	18 00			18 20	18 30				18 50	19 00			19 20	19 30				
Blake Street	d	17 23	17 32				17 53	18 02			18 23	18 32				18 53	19 02			19 23	19 32				
Shenstone	d	17 27					17 57				18 27					18 57				19 27					
Lichfield City	d	17a32	17 41				18a02	18 11			18a32	18 41				19a02	19 11			19a32	19 41				
Lichfield Trent Valley	a		17 45					18 15				18 45					19 15				19 45				

Table 69

Saturdays

Redditch and Longbridge - Birmingham - Lichfield

Network Diagram - see first Page of Table 67

		LM	LM	XC	LM	LM	LM	LM	LM	XC	LM	LM	LM	LM	LM	LM	LM	XC	LM	LM	XC	LM	LM
				◇1 🛒						◇1								◇1			◇1		
Bromsgrove	d													20 59				21 44					
Redditch	d	18 57				19 27			19 57			20 27			20 57		21 27			21 57			22 27
Alvechurch	d	19 02				19 32			20 02			20 32			21 02		21 32			22 02			22 32
Barnt Green	d	19 08				19 38			20 08			20 38			21 08		21 38			22 08			22 38
Longbridge	d	19 12	19 22		19 32	19 42	19 52	20 02	20 12		20 30	20 42	20 57		21 12	21 27	21 42		21 57	22 12		22 27	22 42
Northfield	d	19 14	19 24		19 34	19 44	19 54	20 04	20 14		20 32	20 44	20 59		21 14	21 29	21 44		21 59	22 14		22 29	22 44
Kings Norton	d	19 17	19 27		19 37	19 47	19 57	20 07	20 17		20 35	20 47	21 02		21 17	21 32	21 47		22 02	22 17		22 32	22 47
Bournville	d	19 19	19 29		19 39	19 49	19 59	20 09	20 19		20 37	20 49	21 04		21 19	21 34	21 49		22 04	22 19		22 34	22 49
Selly Oak	d	19 22	19 32		19 42	19 52	20 02	20 12	20 22		20 40	20 52	21 07		21 22	21 37	21 52		22 07	22 22		22 37	22 52
University	d	19 25	19 35	19 39	19 45	19 55	20 05	20 15	20 25	20 34	20 42	20 55	21 10	21 14	21 25	21 40	21 55	22 01	22 10	22 25	22 36	22 40	22 55
Five Ways	d	19 29	19 39		19 49	19 59	20 09	20 19	20 29		20 46	20 59	21 14		21 29	21 44	21 59		22 14	22 29		22 44	22 59
Birmingham New Street 12	a	19 33	19 43	19 45	19 53	20 03	20 13	20 23	20 33	20 40	20 51	21 03	21 18	21 21	21 33	21 48	22 03	22 07	22 18	22 33	22 42	22 48	23 03
	d	19 35				20 05			20 35			21 05			21 35		22 05			22 35		22 55	
Duddeston	d	19 39				20 09			20 39			21 09			21 39		22 09			22 39		22 59	
Aston	d	19 42				20 12			20 42			21 12			21 42		22 12			22 42		23 02	
Gravelly Hill	d	19 45				20 15			20 45			21 15			21 45		22 15			22 45		23 05	
Erdington	d	19 48				20 18			20 48			21 18			21 48		22 18			22 48		23 08	
Chester Road	d	19 50				20 20			20 50			21 20			21 50		22 20			22 50		23 10	
Wylde Green	d	19 52				20 22			20 52			21 22			21 52		22 22			22 52		23 12	
Sutton Coldfield	d	19 55				20 25			20 55			21 25			21 55		22 25			22 55		23 15	
Four Oaks	d	19 58				20 28			20 58			21 28			21 58		22 28			22 58		23 18	
Butlers Lane	d	20 00				20 30			21 00			21 30			22 00		22 30			23 00		23 20	
Blake Street	d	20 03				20 33			21 03			21 33			22 03		22 33			23 03		23a24	
Shenstone	d	20 07				20 37			21 07			21 37			22 07		22 37			23 07			
Lichfield City	d	20 12				20 42			21 12			21 42			22 12		22 42			23 12			
Lichfield Trent Valley	a	20 16				20 46			21 16			21 46			22 16		22 46			23 16			

		LM	LM	LM
Bromsgrove	d			
Redditch	d		22 57	
Alvechurch	d		23 02	
Barnt Green	d		23 08	
Longbridge	d	22 52	23 12	23 30
Northfield	d	22 54	23 14	23 32
Kings Norton	d	22 57	23 17	23 35
Bournville	d	22 59	23 19	23 37
Selly Oak	d	23 02	23 22	23 40
University	d	23 05	23 25	23 43
Five Ways	d	23 09	23 29	23 47
Birmingham New Street 12	a	23 13	23 33	23 51
	d	23 15		
Duddeston	d	23 19		
Aston	d	23 22		
Gravelly Hill	d	23 25		
Erdington	d	23 28		
Chester Road	d	23 30		
Wylde Green	d	23 32		
Sutton Coldfield	d	23 35		
Four Oaks	d	23 38		
Butlers Lane	d	23 40		
Blake Street	d	23 43		
Shenstone	d	23 47		
Lichfield City	d	23a52		
Lichfield Trent Valley	a			

Sundays

		LM	LM	LM	LM	LM	LM	LM	LM	XC	LM	LM	XC	LM	LM	XC	LM	LM	LM	XC	LM	LM	XC
										◇1 🛒			◇1 🛒			◇1 🛒				◇1 🛒			◇1 🛒
Bromsgrove	d																		15 10				
Redditch	d			09 27	09 57	10 27	10 57	11 27	11 57		12 27	12 57		13 27	13 57		14 27	14 57			15 27	15 57	
Alvechurch	d			09 32	10 02	10 32	11 02	11 32	12 02		12 32	13 02		13 32	14 02		14 32	15 02			15 32	16 02	
Barnt Green	d			09 38	10 08	10 38	11 08	11 38	12 08		12 38	13 08		13 38	14 08		14 38	15 08			15 38	16 08	
Longbridge	d			09 43	10 13	10 43	11 13	11 43	12 13		12 43	13 13		13 43	14 13		14 43	15 13			15 43	16 13	
Northfield	d			09 45	10 15	10 45	11 15	11 45	12 15		12 45	13 15		13 45	14 15		14 45	15 15			15 45	16 15	
Kings Norton	d			09 48	10 18	10 48	11 18	11 48	12 18		12 48	13 18		13 48	14 18		14 48	15 18			15 48	16 18	
Bournville	d			09 51	10 21	10 51	11 21	11 51	12 21		12 51	13 21		13 51	14 21		14 51	15 21			15 51	16 21	
Selly Oak	d			09 53	10 23	10 53	11 23	11 53	12 23		12 53	13 23		13 53	14 23		14 53	15 23			15 53	16 23	
University	d			09 56	10 26	10 56	11 26	11 56	12 26	12 39	12 56	13 26	13 35	13 56	14 26	14 38	14 56	15 26		15 35	15 56	16 26	16 35
Five Ways	d			10 00	10 30	11 00	11 30	12 00	12 30		13 00	13 30		14 00	14 30		15 00	15 30			16 00	16 30	
Birmingham New Street 12	a			10 03	10 33	11 03	11 33	12 03	12 33	12 45	13 03	13 34	13 41	14 03	14 33	14 45	15 03	15 33	15 37	15 41	16 03	16 33	16 41
	d	09 06	09 36	10 06	10 36	11 06	11 36	12 06	12 36		13 06	13 36		14 06	14 36		15 06	15 36			16 06	16 36	
Duddeston	d	09 10	09 40	10 10	10 40	11 10	11 40	12 10	12 40		13 10	13 40		14 10	14 40		15 10	15 40			16 10	16 40	
Aston	d	09 13	09 43	10 13	10 43	11 13	11 43	12 13	12 43		13 13	13 43		14 13	14 43		15 13	15 43			16 13	16 43	
Gravelly Hill	d	09 16	09 46	10 16	10 46	11 16	11 46	12 16	12 46		13 16	13 46		14 16	14 46		15 16	15 46			16 16	16 46	
Erdington	d	09 19	09 49	10 19	10 49	11 19	11 49	12 19	12 49		13 19	13 49		14 19	14 49		15 19	15 49			16 19	16 49	
Chester Road	d	09 21	09 51	10 21	10 51	11 21	11 51	12 21	12 51		13 21	13 51		14 21	14 51		15 21	15 51			16 21	16 51	
Wylde Green	d	09 23	09 53	10 23	10 53	11 23	11 53	12 23	12 53		13 23	13 53		14 23	14 53		15 23	15 53			16 23	16 53	
Sutton Coldfield	d	09 26	09 56	10 26	10 56	11 26	11 56	12 26	12 56		13 26	13 56		14 26	14 56		15 26	15 56			16 26	16 56	
Four Oaks	d	09 29	09 59	10 29	10 59	11 29	11 59	12 29	12 59		13 29	13 59		14 29	14 59		15 29	15 59			16 29	16 59	
Butlers Lane	d	09 31	10 01	10 31	11 01	11 31	12 01	12 31	13 01		13 31	14 01		14 31	15 01		15 31	16 01			16 31	17 01	
Blake Street	d	09 34	10 04	10 34	11 04	11 34	12 04	12 34	13 04		13 34	14 04		14 34	15 04		15 34	16 04			16 34	17 04	
Shenstone	d	09 38	10 08	10 38	11 08	11 38	12 08	12 38	13 08		13 38	14 08		14 38	15 08		15 38	16 08			16 38	17 08	
Lichfield City	d	09 43	10 13	10 43	11 13	11 43	12 13	12 43	13 13		13 43	14 13		14 43	15 13		15 43	16 13			16 43	17 13	
Lichfield Trent Valley	a	09 47	10 17	10 47	11 17	11 47	12 17	12 47	13 17		13 47	14 17		14 47	15 17		15 47	16 17			16 47	17 17	

Table 69

Sundays

Redditch and Longbridge - Birmingham - Lichfield

Network Diagram - see first Page of Table 67

		LM	LM	LM	XC ◇🅱	LM		LM	LM	XC ◇🅱	LM	LM	XC ◇🅱	LM	LM	LM		XC ◇🅱	LM	LM	LM	XC ◇🅱	LM	LM	XC ◇🅱
Bromsgrove	d		16 51					17 53								20 10					21 09				
Redditch	d	16 27		16 57		17 27			17 57		18 27	18 57		19 27	19 57				20 27	20 57			21 27	21 57	
Alvechurch	d	16 32		17 02		17 32			18 02		18 32	19 02		19 32	20 02				20 32	21 02			21 32	22 02	
Barnt Green	d	16 38		17 08		17 38			18 08		18 38	19 08		19 38	20 08				20 38	21 08			21 38	22 08	
Longbridge	d	16 43		17 13		17 43			18 13		18 43	19 13		19 43	20 13				20 43	21 13			21 43	22 13	
Northfield	d	16 45		17 15		17 45			18 15		18 45	19 15		19 45	20 15				20 45	21 15			21 45	22 15	
Kings Norton	d	16 48		17 18		17 48			18 18		18 48	19 18		19 48	20 18				20 48	21 18			21 48	22 18	
Bournville	d	16 51		17 21		17 51			18 21		18 51	19 21		19 51	20 21				20 51	21 21			21 51	22 21	
Selly Oak	d	16 53		17 23		17 53			18 23		18 53	19 23		19 53	20 23				20 53	21 23			21 53	22 23	
University	d	16 56		17 26	17 35	17 56			18 26	18 35	18 56	19 26	19 35	19 56	20 26			20 38	20 56	21 26		21 38	21 56	22 26	22 36
Five Ways	d	17 00		17 30		18 00			18 30		19 00	19 30		20 00	20 30				21 00	21 30			22 00	22 30	
Birmingham New Street 🅱	a	17 03	17 17	17 33	17 41	18 03		18 15	18 33	18 41	19 03	19 33	19 41	20 03	20 33	20 36		20 44	21 03	21 33	21 42	21 44	22 03	22 33	22 42
	d	17 06		17 36		18 06			18 36		19 06	19 36		20 06	20 36				21 06	21 36			22 06	22 36	
Duddeston	d	17 10		17 40		18 10			18 40		19 10	19 40		20 10	20 40				21 10	21 40			22 10	22 40	
Aston	d	17 13		17 43		18 13			18 43		19 13	19 43		20 13	20 43				21 13	21 43			22 13	22 43	
Gravelly Hill	d	17 16		17 46		18 16			18 46		19 16	19 46		20 16	20 46				21 16	21 46			22 16	22 46	
Erdington	d	17 19		17 49		18 19			18 49		19 19	19 49		20 19	20 49				21 19	21 49			22 19	22 49	
Chester Road	d	17 21		17 51		18 21			18 51		19 21	19 51		20 21	20 51				21 21	21 51			22 21	22 51	
Wylde Green	d	17 23		17 53		18 23			18 53		19 23	19 53		20 23	20 53				21 23	21 53			22 23	22 53	
Sutton Coldfield	d	17 26		17 56		18 26			18 56		19 26	19 56		20 26	20 56				21 26	21 56			22 26	22 56	
Four Oaks	d	17 29		17 59		18 29			18 59		19 29	19 59		20 29	20 59				21 29	21 59			22 29	22 59	
Butlers Lane	d	17 31		18 01		18 31			19 01		19 31	20 01		20 31	21 01				21 31	22 01			22 31	23 01	
Blake Street	d	17 34		18 04		18 34			19 04		19 34	20 04		20 34	21 04				21 34	22 04			22 34	23 04	
Shenstone	d	17 38		18 08		18 38			19 08		19 38	20 08		20 38	21 08				21 38	22 08			22 38	23 08	
Lichfield City	d	17 43		18 13		18 43			19 13		19 43	20 13		20 43	21 13				21 43	22 13			22 43	23 13	
Lichfield Trent Valley	a	17 47		18 17		18 47			19 17		19 47	20 17		20 47	21 18				21 47	22 17			22 47	23 17	

		LM		LM
Bromsgrove	d			
Redditch	d	22 27		22 57
Alvechurch	d	22 32		23 02
Barnt Green	d	22 38		23 08
Longbridge	d	22 43		23 13
Northfield	d	22 45		23 15
Kings Norton	d	22 48		23 18
Bournville	d	22 51		23 21
Selly Oak	d	22 53		23 23
University	d	22 56		23 26
Five Ways	d	23 00		23 30
Birmingham New Street 🅱	a	23 03		23 33
	d	23 06		
Duddeston	d	23 10		
Aston	d	23 13		
Gravelly Hill	d	23 16		
Erdington	d	23 19		
Chester Road	d	23 21		
Wylde Green	d	23 23		
Sutton Coldfield	d	23 26		
Four Oaks	d	23 29		
Butlers Lane	d	23 31		
Blake Street	d	23 34		
Shenstone	d	23 38		
Lichfield City	d	23 43		
Lichfield Trent Valley	a	23 47		

Birmingham - Walsall and Rugeley

Network Diagram - see first Page of Table 67

Mondays to Fridays

Miles			LM MX	LM	LM	LM 1	LM	LM 1	LM 1	LM	LM		LM	LM	LM	LM	LM	LM	LM	LM	LM		LM	LM	LM
—	Wolverhampton 7	d						06 19						07 49		08 19		08 49		09 19			09 49		10 19
0	**Birmingham New Street 12**	d	23p18	05 33	05 56	06 21	06 39	06 46	07 21	07 39	07 59		08 07	08 17	08 39	08 47	09 07	09 17	09 39	09 47	10 07		10 17	10 39	10 47
1½	Duddeston	d	23p23		06 00	06 25		06 51	07 25		08 03			08 22		08 52		09 22		09 52			10 22		10 52
2¾	Aston	d	23p26		06 03	06 28		06 54	07 28		08 06			08 25		08 55		09 25		09 55			10 25		10 55
3½	Witton	d	23p28		06 05	06 30		06 56	07 30		08 08			08 27		08 57		09 27		09 57			10 27		10 57
4¼	Perry Barr	d	23p31		06 07	06 33		06 58	07 33		08 10			08 29		08 59		09 29		09 59			10 29		10 59
5¾	Hamstead	d	23p34	05 41	06 10	06 36		07 00	07 36		08 13			08 31		09 01		09 31		10 01			10 31		11 01
8½	Tame Bridge Parkway	d	23p39	05 45	06 15	06 41	06 51	07 04	07 41	07 50	08 18		08 20	08 35	08 50	09 05	09 20	09 35	09 50	10 05	10 20		10 35	10 50	11 05
9½	Bescot Stadium	d	23p41	05 48	06 18	06 43		07 07	07 43		08 21			08 38		09 08		09 38		10 08			10 38		11 08
10¾	**Walsall**	a	23p47	05 55	06 23	06 48	06 58	07 13	07 48	07 59	08 25		08 29	08 44	08 59	09 14	09 29	09 44	09 59	10 14	10 35		10 46	10 59	11 14
—		d	23p47		06 24		06 59			08 00			08 30		09 00		09 30		10 00					11 00	
14	Bloxwich	d	23p54		06 31		07 06			08 07					09 07				10 07					11 07	
14½	Bloxwich North	d	23p57		06 33		07 08			08 09					09 09				10 09					11 09	
16¾	Landywood	d	00 01		06 37		07 12			08 13					09 13				10 13					11 13	
18¾	Cannock	d	00 06		06 42		07 16			08 18			08 44		09 18		09 44		10 18					11 18	
20¾	Hednesford	d	00a12		06 47		07 21			08 23			08 49		09 23		09 49		10 23					11 23	
24¾	Rugeley Town	d			06 55		07 29			08 31			08 57		09 31		09 57		10 31					11 31	
26¼	**Rugeley Trent Valley**	a			07 00		07 35			08 36			09 04		09 36		10 04		10 36					11 36	

		LM	LM	LM	LM	LM	LM		LM	LM	LM	LM	LM	LM	LM	LM	LM		LM	LM	LM	LM	LM	LM	LM
Wolverhampton 7	d		10 49		11 19		11 49			12 19		12 49		13 19		13 49			14 19		14 49		15 19		15 49
Birmingham New Street 12	d	11 07	11 17	11 39	11 47	12 07	12 17		12 39	12 47	13 07	13 17	13 39	13 47	14 07	14 17	14 39		14 47	15 07	15 17	15 39	15 47	16 07	16 17
Duddeston	d		11 22		11 52		12 22			12 52		13 22		13 52		14 22			14 52		15 22		15 52		16 22
Aston	d		11 25		11 55		12 25			12 55		13 25		13 55		14 25			14 55		15 25		15 55		16 25
Witton	d		11 27		11 57		12 27			12 57		13 27		13 57		14 27			14 57		15 27		15 57		16 27
Perry Barr	d		11 29		11 59		12 29			12 59		13 29		13 59		14 29			14 59		15 29		15 59		16 29
Hamstead	d		11 31		12 01		12 31			13 01		13 31		14 01		14 31			15 01		15 31		16 01		16 31
Tame Bridge Parkway	d	11 20	11 35	11 50	12 05	12 20	12 35		12 50	13 05	13 20	13 35	13 50	14 05	14 20	14 35	14 50		15 05	15 20	15 35	15 50	16 05	16 20	16 35
Bescot Stadium	d		11 38		12 08		12 38			13 08		13 38		14 08		14 38			15 08		15 38		16 08		16 38
Walsall	a	11 35	11 44	11 59	12 14	12 34	12 44		12 59	13 14	13 35	13 44	13 59	14 14	14 35	14 44	14 59		15 14	15 35	15 44	15 59	16 14	16 29	16 44
	d			12 00					13 00				14 00				15 00					16 00		16 31	
Bloxwich	d			12 07					13 07				14 07				15 07					16 07		16 38	
Bloxwich North	d			12 09					13 09				14 09				15 09					16 09		16 40	
Landywood	d			12 13					13 13				14 13				15 13					16 13		16 45	
Cannock	d			12 18					13 18				14 18				15 18					16 18		16 49	
Hednesford	d			12 23					13 23				14 23				15 23					16 23		16 54	
Rugeley Town	d			12 31					13 31				14 31				15 31					16 31		17 02	
Rugeley Trent Valley	a			12 36					13 36				14 36				15 36					16 36		17 08	

		LM	LM		LM	LM	LM	LM	LM	LM	LM	LM	LM		LM	LM	LM	LM	LM	LM	LM	LM			
Wolverhampton 7	d		16 19			16 49		17 19		17 49		18 19			19 19										
Birmingham New Street 12	d	16 39	16 47		17 07	17 17	17 42	17 47	18 12	18 17	18 39	18 47	19 17		19 47	20 17	20 47	21 17	21 47	22 17	22 47	23 18			
Duddeston	d		16 52			17 22		17 52		18 22		18 52	19 22		19 52		20 52		21 52		22 52	23 23			
Aston	d		16 55			17 25		17 55		18 25		18 55	19 25		19 55		20 55		21 55		22 55	23 26			
Witton	d		16 57			17 27		17 57		18 27		18 57	19 27		19 57		20 57		21 57		22 57	23 28			
Perry Barr	d		16 59			17 29		17 59		18 29		18 59	19 29		19 59		20 59		21 59		22 59	23 31			
Hamstead	d		17 01			17 31		18 01		18 31		19 01	19 32		20 01		21 01		22 01		23 01	23 34			
Tame Bridge Parkway	d	16 50	17 05		17 20	17 35	17 54	18 05	18 23	18 35	18 50	19 05	19 37		20 05	20 30	21 05	21 30	22 05	22 30	23 05	23 39			
Bescot Stadium	d		17 08			17 38		18 08		18 38		19 08	19 40		20 08		21 08		22 08		23 10	23 41			
Walsall	a	16 59	17 14		17 29	17 44	18 01	18 14	18 30	18 44	18 59	19 15	19 45		20 14	20 38	21 14	21 38	22 14	22 38	23 14	23 47			
	d	17 00			17 30		18 02		18 31		19 00		19 46			20 39		21 39		22 39		23 47			
Bloxwich	d	17 07			17 37		18 09		18 38		19 07		19 53			20 46		21 46		22 46		23 54			
Bloxwich North	d	17 09			17 39		18 11		18 40		19 09		19 56			20 49		21 49		22 49		23 57			
Landywood	d	17 13			17 43		18 15		18 44		19 13		20 00			20 53		21 53		22 53		00 01			
Cannock	d	17 18			17 48		18 20		18 48		19 18		20 05			20 57		21 57		22 57		00 06			
Hednesford	d	17 23			17 53		18 25		18 53		19 23		20 10			21 02		22 02		23 02		00a12			
Rugeley Town	d	17 31			18 01		18 33		19 01		19 31		20 18			21 10		22 10		23 10					
Rugeley Trent Valley	a	17 36			18 06		18 38		19 07		19 36		20 22			21 15		22 15		23 15					

Saturdays

		LM	LM	LM	LM	LM	LM	LM	LM	LM		LM	LM	LM	LM	LM	LM	LM	LM	LM		LM	LM	LM	LM
Wolverhampton 7	d					06 49		07 19		07 49			08 19		08 49		09 19		09 49			10 19		10 49	
Birmingham New Street 12	d	23p18	06 02	06 27	07 00	07 17	07 39	07 47	08 07	08 17		08 39	08 47	09 07	09 17	09 39	09 47	10 07	10 17	10 39		10 47	11 07	11 17	11 39
Duddeston	d	23p23	06 06	06 32		07 22		07 52		08 22			08 52		09 22		09 52		10 22			10 52		11 22	
Aston	d	23p26	06 09	06 35	07 06	07 25		07 55		08 25			08 55		09 25		09 55		10 25			10 55		11 25	
Witton	d	23p28	06 11	06 37		07 27		07 57		08 27			08 57		09 27		09 57		10 27			10 57		11 27	
Perry Barr	d	23p31	06 13	06 40	07 09	07 29		07 59		08 29			08 59		09 29		09 59		10 29			10 59		11 29	
Hamstead	d	23p34	06 16	06 43	07 12	07 31		08 01		08 31			09 01		09 31		10 01		10 31			11 01		11 31	
Tame Bridge Parkway	d	23p39	06 21	06 48	07 17	07 35	07 50	08 05	08 20	08 35		08 50	09 05	09 20	09 35	09 50	10 05	10 20	10 35	10 50		11 05	11 20	11 35	11 50
Bescot Stadium	d	23p41	06 24	06 50		07 38		08 08		08 38			09 08		09 38		10 08		10 38			11 08		11 38	
Walsall	a	23p47	06 29	06 56	07 25	07 44	07 57	08 14	08 29	08 44		08 59	09 14	09 29	09 44	09 59	10 14	10 29	10 44	10 59		11 14	11 29	11 44	11 59
	d	23p47	06 30	06 57	07 26		07 57		08 30			09 00		09 30		10 00		10 30		11 00			11 30		12 00
Bloxwich	d	23p54	06 37	07 04	07 33		08 04					09 07				10 07				11 07					12 07
Bloxwich North	d	23p57	06 39	07 06	07 35		08 06					09 09				10 09				11 09					12 09
Landywood	d	00 01	06 43	07 10	07 39		08 10					09 13				10 13				11 13					12 13
Cannock	d	00 06	06 48	07 15	07 44		08 15		08 44			09 18		09 44		10 18		10 44		11 18			11 44		12 18
Hednesford	d	00a12	06a53	07 20	07 49		08 20		08 49			09 23		09 49		10 23		10 49		11 23			11 49		12 23
Rugeley Town	d			07 28	07 57		08 28		08 57			09 31		09 57		10 31		10 57		11 31			11 57		12 31
Rugeley Trent Valley	a			07 32	08 04		08 35		09 04			09 36		10 04		10 36		11 04		11 36			12 04		12 36

For connections to Stafford please refer to Table 67

Table 70

Saturdays

Birmingham - Walsall and Rugeley

Network Diagram - see first Page of Table 67

		LM	LM	LM	LM	LM		LM	LM	LM	LM	LM	LM	LM	LM	LM		LM	LM	LM	LM	LM	LM	LM	LM
Wolverhampton 7	d	11 19		11 49		12 19			12 49		13 19		13 49		14 19			14 49		15 19		15 49		16 19	
Birmingham New Street 12	d	11 47	12 07	12 17	12 39	12 47		13 07	13 17	13 39	13 47	14 07	14 17	14 39	14 47	15 07		15 17	15 39	15 47	16 07	16 17	16 39	16 47	17 07
Duddeston	d	11 52		12 22		12 52			13 22		13 52		14 22		14 52			15 22		15 52		16 22		16 52	
Aston	d	11 55		12 25		12 55			13 25		13 55		14 25		14 55			15 25		15 55		16 25		16 55	
Witton	d	11 57		12 27		12 57			13 27		13 57		14 27		14 57			15 27		15 57		16 27		16 57	
Perry Barr	d	11 59		12 29		12 59			13 29		13 59		14 29		14 59			15 29		15 59		16 29		16 59	
Hamstead	d	12 01		12 31		13 01			13 31		14 01		14 31		15 01			15 31		16 01		16 31		17 01	
Tame Bridge Parkway	d	12 05	12 20	12 35	12 50	13 05		13 20	13 35	13 50	14 05	14 20	14 35	14 50	15 05	15 20		15 35	15 50	16 05	16 20	16 35	16 50	17 05	17 20
Bescot Stadium	d	12 08		12 38		13 08			13 38		14 08		14 38		15 08			15 38		16 08		16 38		17 08	
Walsall	a	12 14	12 29	12 44	12 59	13 14		13 29	13 44	13 59	14 14	14 29	14 44	14 59	15 14	15 29		15 46	15 59	16 14	16 29	16 44	16 59	17 14	17 29
	d		12 30		13 00			13 30		14 00		14 30		15 00		15 30			16 00		16 30		17 00		17 30
Bloxwich	d				13 07					14 07				15 07					16 07				17 07		17 37
Bloxwich North	d				13 09					14 09				15 09					16 09				17 09		17 39
Landywood	d				13 13					14 13				15 13					16 13				17 13		17 43
Cannock	d		12 44		13 18			13 44		14 18		14 44		15 18		15 44			16 18		16 44		17 18		17 48
Hednesford	d		12 49		13 23			13 49		14 23		14 49		15 23		15 49			16 23		16 49		17 23		17 53
Rugeley Town	d		12 57		13 31			13 57		14 31		14 57		15 31		15 57			16 31		16 57		17 31		18 01
Rugeley Trent Valley	a		13 04		13 36			14 04		14 36		15 04		15 36		16 04			16 36		17 04		17 36		18 06

		LM		LM	LM	LM	LM	LM	LM	LM	LM	LM		LM	LM	LM	LM	LM	LM
Wolverhampton 7	d	16 49			17 19		17 49		18 19		19 19								
Birmingham New Street 12	d	17 17		17 39	17 47	18 07	18 17	18 39	18 47	19 17	19 47	20 17		20 47	21 17	21 47	22 17	22 47	23 18
Duddeston	d	17 22			17 52		18 22		18 52	19 22	19 52			20 52		21 52		22 52	23 23
Aston	d	17 25			17 55		18 25		18 55	19 25	19 55			20 55		21 55		22 55	23 26
Witton	d	17 27			17 57		18 27		18 57	19 27	19 57			20 57		21 57		22 57	23 28
Perry Barr	d	17 29			17 59		18 29		18 59	19 29	19 59			20 59		21 59		22 59	23 31
Hamstead	d	17 31			18 01		18 31		19 01	19 32	20 01			21 01		22 01		23 01	23 34
Tame Bridge Parkway	d	17 35		17 50	18 05	18 20	18 35	18 50	19 05	19 37	20 05	20 31		21 05	21 31	22 05	22 31	23 05	23 39
Bescot Stadium	d	17 38			18 08		18 38		19 08	19 40	20 08			21 08		22 08		23 08	23 41
Walsall	a	17 44		17 59	18 14	18 29	18 44	18 59	19 14	19 45	20 14	20 38		21 14	21 38	22 14	22 38	23 14	23 47
	d			18 00		18 30		19 00		19 46		20 39			21 39		22 39		23 47
Bloxwich	d			18 07		18 37		19 07		19 53		20 46			21 46		22 46		23 54
Bloxwich North	d			18 09		18 39		19 09		19 56		20 49			21 49		22 49		23 57
Landywood	d			18 13		18 43		19 13		20 00		20 53			21 53		22 53		00 01
Cannock	d			18 18		18 48		19 18		20 05		20 57			21 57		22 57		00 06
Hednesford	d			18 23		18 53		19 23		20 10		21 02			22 02		23 02		00a12
Rugeley Town	d			18 31		19 01		19 31		20 18		21 10			22 10		23 10		
Rugeley Trent Valley	a			18 36		19 06		19 36		20 22		21 15			22 15		23 15		

Sundays

		LM A	LM	LM	LM	LM	LM	LM	LM	LM		LM	LM	LM	LM	LM	LM	LM	LM	LM		LM	LM	LM	LM
Wolverhampton 7	d																								
Birmingham New Street 12	d	23p18	09 17	09 40	10 17	10 40	11 17	11 40	12 17	12 40		13 17	13 40	14 17	14 40	15 17	15 40	16 17	16 40	17 17		17 40	18 17	18 40	19 17
Duddeston	d	23p23	09 21		10 21		11 21		12 21			13 21		14 21		15 21		16 21		17 21			18 21		19 21
Aston	d	23p26	09 24		10 24		11 24		12 24			13 24		14 24		15 24		16 24		17 24			18 24		19 24
Witton	d	23p28	09 26		10 26		11 26		12 26			13 26		14 26		15 26		16 26		17 26			18 26		19 26
Perry Barr	d	23p31	09 29		10 29		11 29		12 29			13 29		14 29		15 29		16 29		17 29			18 29		19 29
Hamstead	d	23p34	09 32		10 32		11 32		12 32			13 32		14 32		15 32		16 32		17 32			18 32		19 32
Tame Bridge Parkway	d	23p39	09 37	09 52	10 37	10 52	11 37	11 52	12 37	12 52		13 37	13 52	14 37	14 52	15 37	15 52	16 37	16 52	17 37		17 52	18 37	18 52	19 37
Bescot Stadium	d	23p41	09 39		10 39		11 39		12 39			13 39		14 39		15 39		16 39		17 39			18 39		19 39
Walsall	a	23p47	09 44	10 00	10 44	11 00	11 44	12 00	12 44	13 00		13 44	14 00	14 44	15 00	15 44	16 00	16 44	17 00	17 44		18 00	18 44	19 00	19 44
	d	23p47		10 01		11 01		12 01		13 01			14 01		15 01		16 01		17 01			18 01		19 01	
Bloxwich	d	23p54		10 08		11 08		12 08		13 08			14 08		15 08		16 08		17 08			18 08		19 08	
Bloxwich North	d	23p57		10 10		11 10		12 10		13 10			14 10		15 10		16 10		17 10			18 10		19 10	
Landywood	d	00 01		10 15		11 15		12 15		13 15			14 15		15 15		16 15		17 15			18 15		19 15	
Cannock	d	00 06		10 19		11 19		12 19		13 19			14 19		15 19		16 19		17 19			18 19		19 19	
Hednesford	d	00a12		10 24		11 24		12 24		13 24			14 24		15 24		16 24		17 24			18 24		19 24	
Rugeley Town	d			10 32		11 32		12 32		13 32			14 32		15 32		16 32		17 32			18 32		19 32	
Rugeley Trent Valley	a			10 37		11 37		12 37		13 37			14 37		15 37		16 37		17 37			18 37		19 37	

		LM	LM	LM	LM	LM		LM	LM	LM
Wolverhampton 7	d									
Birmingham New Street 12	d	19 40	20 17	20 40	21 17	21 40		22 17	22 40	23 17
Duddeston	d		20 21		21 21			22 21		23 21
Aston	d		20 24		21 24			22 24		23 24
Witton	d		20 26		21 26			22 26		23 26
Perry Barr	d		20 29		21 29			22 29		23 29
Hamstead	d		20 32		21 32			22 32		23 32
Tame Bridge Parkway	d	19 52	20 37	20 52	21 37	21 52		22 37	22 52	23 37
Bescot Stadium	d		20 39		21 39			22 39		23 39
Walsall	a	20 00	20 44	21 00	21 44	22 00		22 44	23 00	23 44
	d	20 01		21 01		22 01			23 01	
Bloxwich	d	20 08		21 08		22 08			23 08	
Bloxwich North	d	20 10		21 10		22 10			23 10	
Landywood	d	20 15		21 15		22 15			23 15	
Cannock	d	20 19		21 19		22 19			23 19	
Hednesford	d	20 24		21 24		22 24			23 24	
Rugeley Town	d	20 32		21 32		22 32			23 32	
Rugeley Trent Valley	a	20 37		21 37		22 37			23 37	

A not 11 December

For connections to Stafford please refer to Table 67

Rugeley and Walsall - Birmingham

Network Diagram - see first Page of Table 67

Miles			LM MX	LM	LM	LM	LM	LM [1]	LM	LM	LM		LM	LM	LM	LM	LM	LM	LM	LM	LM		LM	LM	LM
0	**Rugeley Trent Valley**	d			05 55		06 39		07 04		07 40			08 06		08 42		09 06		09 42			10 06		
1½	Rugeley Town	d			05 59		06 43		07 08		07 44			08 10		08 46		09 10		09 46			10 10		
5½	Hednesford	d			06 07		06 51		07 16		07 52			08 18		08 54		09 18		09 54			10 18		
7½	Cannock	d			06 11		06 55		07 20		07 56			08 22		08 58		09 22		09 58			10 22		
9½	Landywood	d			06 14		06 58		07 23		07 59			08 25				09 25					10 25		
11¾	Bloxwich North	d			06 19		07 03		07 27		08 04			08 30				09 30					10 30		
12¼	Bloxwich	d			06 21		07 05		07 29		08 06			08 32				09 32					10 32		
15½	**Walsall**	a			06 28		07 12		07 37		08 13			08 39		09 12		09 39		10 12			10 39		
—		d	23p40	06 01	06 29	07 01	07 13	07 30	07 37	08 01	08 14		08 30	08 40	09 01	09 13	09 30	09 40	10 01	10 13	10 31		10 40	11 01	11 10
16¾	Bescot Stadium	d	23p44	06 04	06 34	07 04		07 34		08 04			08 34		09 04		09 34		10 04		10 34			11 04	
17¾	Tame Bridge Parkway	d	23p47	06 07	06 37	07 07	07 19	07 37	07 43	08 07	08 20		08 37	08 47	09 07	09 19	09 37	09 46	10 07	10 19	10 37		10 46	11 07	11 19
20½	Hamstead	d	23p51	06 11	06 41	07 11		07 41		08 11			08 41		09 11		09 41		10 11		10 41			11 11	
22	Perry Barr	d	23p55	06 14	06 44	07 14		07 44		08 14			08 44		09 14		09 44		10 14		10 44			11 14	
22¾	Witton	d	23p57	06 16	06 46	07 16		07 47		08 16			08 46		09 16		09 46		10 16		10 46			11 16	
23½	Aston	d	00 01	06 19	06 49	07 19		07 49		08 19			08 49		09 19		09 49		10 19		10 49			11 19	
24¾	Duddeston	d	00 04	06 21	06 52	07 21		07 52		08 21			08 52		09 21		09 51		10 21		10 51			11 21	
26¼	**Birmingham New Street** [12]	a	00 09	06 28	06 57	07 28	07 36	07 57	08 00	08 28	08 37		08 58	09 03	09 28	09 36	09 58	10 03	10 28	10 36	10 58		11 03	11 28	11 36
—	Wolverhampton [7]	a		07 03				08 19							10 03				11 03		11 33			12 03	

		LM	LM	LM	LM	LM	LM		LM	LM	LM	LM	LM	LM	LM	LM	LM		LM	LM	LM	LM	LM	LM	LM
Rugeley Trent Valley	d		11 06				12 06					13 06				14 06					15 06				16 06
Rugeley Town	d		11 10				12 10					13 10				14 10					15 10				16 10
Hednesford	d		11 18				12 18					13 18				14 18					15 18				16 18
Cannock	d		11 22				12 22					13 22				14 22					15 22				16 22
Landywood	d		11 25				12 25					13 25				14 25					15 25				16 25
Bloxwich North	d		11 30				12 30					13 30				14 30					15 30				16 30
Bloxwich	d		11 32				12 32					13 32				14 32					15 32				16 32
Walsall	a		11 39				12 39					13 39				14 39					15 39				16 39
	d	11 31	11 40	12 01	12 10	12 31	12 40		13 01	13 10	13 31	13 40	14 01	14 10	14 31	14 40	15 01		15 10	15 31	15 40	16 01	16 10	16 31	16 40
Bescot Stadium	d	11 34		12 04		12 34			13 04		13 34		14 04		14 34		15 04			15 34		16 04		16 34	
Tame Bridge Parkway	d	11 37	11 46	12 07	12 19	12 37	12 46		13 07	13 19	13 37	13 46	14 07	14 19	14 37	14 46	15 07		15 19	15 37	15 46	16 07	16 19	16 37	16 46
Hamstead	d	11 41		12 11		12 41			13 11		13 41		14 11		14 41		15 11			15 41		16 11		16 41	
Perry Barr	d	11 44		12 14		12 44			13 14		13 44		14 14		14 44		15 14			15 44		16 14		16 44	
Witton	d	11 46		12 16		12 46			13 16		13 46		14 16		14 46		15 16			15 46		16 16		16 46	
Aston	d	11 49		12 19		12 49			13 19		13 49		14 19		14 49		15 19			15 49		16 19		16 49	
Duddeston	d	11 51		12 21		12 51			13 21		13 51		14 21		14 51		15 21			15 51		16 21		16 51	
Birmingham New Street [12]	a	11 58	12 03	12 28	12 36	12 58	13 03		13 28	13 36	13 58	14 03	14 28	14 36	14 58	15 03	15 28		15 36	15 58	16 03	16 30	16 36	16 59	17 03
Wolverhampton [7]	a	12 33		13 03		13 33			14 03		14 33		15 03		15 33		16 03			16 33		17 04		17 33	

		LM	LM		LM	LM	LM	LM	LM	LM	LM	LM	LM		LM	LM	LM	LM	LM	LM	LM	LM	LM		
Rugeley Trent Valley	d		16 42			17 13		17 42		18 12		18 46			19 10	19 42		20 35		21 40		22 33			
Rugeley Town	d		16 46			17 17		17 46		18 16		18 50			19 14	19 46		20 39		21 44		22 37			
Hednesford	d		16 54			17 25		17 54		18 24		18 58			19 22	19 54		20 47		21 52		22 45			
Cannock	d		16 58			17 29		17 58		18 28		19 02			19 26	19 58		20 51		21 56		22 49			
Landywood	d					17 32				18 31					19 29	20 01		20 54		21 59		22 53			
Bloxwich North	d					17 37				18 36					19 34	20 06		20 59		22 04		22 58			
Bloxwich	d					17 39				18 38					19 36	20 08		21 01		22 06		23 00			
Walsall	a		17 12			17 46		18 12		18 45		19 16			19 43	20 15		21 08		22 16		23 07			
	d	17 01	17 13		17 31	17 47	18 01	18 13	18 31	18 46	19 01	19 18	19 36		19 44	20 16	20 40	21 10	21 40	22 17	22 40	23 10	23 40		
Bescot Stadium	d	17 04			17 34		18 04		18 34		19 04	19 23			19 48		20 44		21 44		22 44		23 44		
Tame Bridge Parkway	d	17 07	17 19		17 37	17 53	18 07	18 19	18 37	18 52	19 07	19 26			19 51	20 22	20 47	21 16	21 47	22 23	22 47	23 16	23 47		
Hamstead	d	17 11			17 41		18 11		18 41		19 11	19 30			19 55		20 51		21 51		22 51		23 51		
Perry Barr	d	17 14			17 44		18 14		18 44		19 14	19 33			19 59		20 55		21 55		22 55		23 55		
Witton	d	17 16			17 46		18 16		18 46		19 16	19 36			20 01		20 57		21 57		22 57		23 57		
Aston	d	17 19			17 49		18 19		18 49		19 19	19 39			20 04		21 00		22 00		23 00		00 01		
Duddeston	d	17 21			17 51		18 21		18 51		19 21	19 42			20 07		21 03		22 03		23 03		00 04		
Birmingham New Street [12]	a	17 28	17 36		17 58	18 10	18 28	18 36	18 58	19 09	19 28	19 46			20 11	20 39	21 09	21 35	22 09	22 40	23 09	23 33	00 09		
Wolverhampton [7]	a	18 03			18 33		19 03		19 33		20 03		19 50												

Saturdays

		LM	LM	LM	LM	LM	LM	LM	LM	LM		LM	LM	LM	LM	LM	LM	LM	LM	LM		LM	LM	LM	LM
Rugeley Trent Valley	d				06 26				07 39			08 06		08 42		09 06		09 42		10 06			10 42		11 06
Rugeley Town	d				06 30				07 43			08 10		08 46		09 10		09 46		10 10			10 46		11 10
Hednesford	d				06 38	06 58			07 51			08 18		08 54		09 18		09 54		10 18			10 54		11 18
Cannock	d				06 42	07 02			07 55			08 22		08 58		09 22		09 58		10 22			10 58		11 22
Landywood	d				06 45	07 05			07 58			08 25				09 25				10 25					11 25
Bloxwich North	d				06 50	07 10			08 03			08 30				09 30				10 30					11 30
Bloxwich	d				06 52	07 12			08 05			08 32				09 32				10 32					11 32
Walsall	a				06 59	07 19			08 12			08 39		09 12		09 39		10 12		10 39			11 12		11 39
	d	23p40	06 01	06 31	07 00	07 20	07 31	08 01	08 13	08 31		08 40	09 01	09 13	09 31	09 40	10 01	10 13	10 31	10 40		11 01	11 13	11 31	11 40
Bescot Stadium	d	23p44	06 04	06 34	07 04		07 34	08 04		08 34			09 04		09 34		10 04		10 34			11 04		11 34	
Tame Bridge Parkway	d	23p47	06 07	06 37	07 07	07 26	07 37	08 07	08 19	08 37		08 46	09 07	09 19	09 37	09 46	10 07	10 19	10 37	10 46		11 07	11 19	11 37	11 46
Hamstead	d	23p51	06 11	06 41	07 12		07 41	08 11		08 41			09 11		09 41		10 11		10 41			11 11		11 41	
Perry Barr	d	23p55	06 14	06 44	07 15		07 44	08 14		08 44			09 14		09 44		10 14		10 44			11 14		11 44	
Witton	d	23p57	06 16	06 46	07 17		07 46	08 16		08 46			09 16		09 46		10 16		10 46			11 16		11 46	
Aston	d	00 01	06 19	06 49	07 20		07 49	08 19		08 49			09 19		09 49		10 19		10 49			11 19		11 49	
Duddeston	d	00 04	06 21	06 51	07 23		07 51	08 21		08 51			09 21		09 51		10 21		10 51			11 21		11 51	
Birmingham New Street [12]	a	00 09	06 28	06 58	07 28	07 44	07 58	08 28	08 36	08 58		09 03	09 29	09 36	09 58	10 03	10 29	10 36	10 58	11 03		11 28	11 36	11 58	12 03
Wolverhampton [7]	a		07 03	07 33			08 33	09 03		09 33			10 03		10 33		11 03		11 33			12 03		12 33	

For connections from Stafford please refer to Table 67

Table 70

Saturdays

Rugeley and Walsall - Birmingham

Network Diagram - see first Page of Table 67

		LM	LM	LM	LM	LM		LM	LM	LM	LM	LM	LM	LM	LM	LM		LM	LM	LM	LM	LM	LM	LM	LM
Rugeley Trent Valley	d		11 42		12 06			12 42		13 06		13 42		14 06		14 42			15 06		15 42		16 06		16 42
Rugeley Town	d		11 46		12 10			12 46		13 10		13 46		14 10		14 46			15 10		15 46		16 10		16 46
Hednesford	d		11 54		12 18			12 54		13 18		13 54		14 18		14 54			15 18		15 54		16 18		16 54
Cannock	d		11 58		12 22			12 58		13 22		13 58		14 22		14 58			15 22		15 58		16 22		16 58
Landywood	d				12 25					13 25				14 25					15 25				16 25		
Bloxwich North	d				12 30					13 30				14 30					15 30				16 30		
Bloxwich	d				12 32					13 32				14 32					15 32				16 32		
Walsall	a		12 12		12 39			13 12		13 39		14 12		14 39		15 12			15 39		16 12		16 39		17 12
	d	12 01	12 13	12 31	12 40	13 01		13 13	13 31	13 40	14 01	14 13	14 31	14 40	15 01	15 13		15 31	15 40	16 01	16 13	16 31	16 40	17 01	17 13
Bescot Stadium	d	12 04		12 34		13 04			13 34		14 04		14 34		15 04			15 34		16 04		16 34		17 04	
Tame Bridge Parkway	d	12 07	12 19	12 37	12 46	13 07		13 19	13 37	13 46	14 07	14 19	14 37	14 46	15 07	15 19		15 37	15 46	16 07	16 19	16 37	16 46	17 07	17 19
Hamstead	d	12 11		12 41		13 11			13 41		14 11		14 41		15 11			15 41		16 11		16 41		17 11	
Perry Barr	d	12 14		12 44		13 14			13 44		14 14		14 44		15 14			15 44		16 14		16 44		17 14	
Witton	d	12 16		12 46		13 16			13 46		14 16		14 46		15 16			15 46		16 16		16 46		17 16	
Aston	d	12 19		12 49		13 19			13 49		14 19		14 49		15 19			15 49		16 19		16 49		17 19	
Duddeston	d	12 21		12 51		13 21			13 51		14 21		14 51		15 21			15 51		16 21		16 51		17 21	
Birmingham New Street 12	a	12 28	12 36	12 58	13 03	13 28		13 36	13 58	14 03	14 28	14 36	14 58	15 03	15 28	15 36		15 58	16 03	16 28	16 36	16 58	17 03	17 28	17 36
Wolverhampton 7	a	13 03		13 33		14 03			14 33		15 03		15 33		16 03			16 33		17 04		17 33		18 03	

		LM		LM	LM	LM	LM	LM	LM	LM	LM	LM		LM	LM	LM	LM	LM	LM	LM
Rugeley Trent Valley	d			17 06		17 42		18 12		18 45	19 10	19 42			20 39		21 35		22 35	
Rugeley Town	d			17 10		17 46		18 16		18 49	19 14	19 46			20 43		21 39		22 39	
Hednesford	d			17 18		17 54		18 24		18 57	19 21	19 54			20 51		21 47		22 47	
Cannock	d			17 22		17 58		18 28		19 01	19 25	19 58			20 55		21 51		22 51	
Landywood	d			17 25				18 31			19 29	20 01			20 58		21 54		22 54	
Bloxwich North	d			17 30				18 36			19 33	20 06			21 03		21 59		22 59	
Bloxwich	d			17 32				18 38			19 35	20 08			21 05		22 01		23 01	
Walsall	a			17 39		18 12		18 45		19 15	19 43	20 15			21 12		22 08		23 08	
	d	17 31		17 40	18 01	18 13	18 31	18 46	19 01	19 18	19 43	20 16		20 40	21 13	21 40	22 10	22 40	23 10	23 40
Bescot Stadium	d	17 34			18 04		18 34		19 04	19 23	19 48			20 44		21 44		22 44		23 44
Tame Bridge Parkway	d	17 37		17 46	18 07	18 19	18 37	18 52	19 07	19 26	19 51	20 22		20 47	21 19	21 47	22 16	22 47	23 16	23 47
Hamstead	d	17 41			18 11		18 41		19 11	19 30	19 55			20 51		21 51		22 51		23 51
Perry Barr	d	17 44			18 14		18 44		19 14	19 33	19 58			20 55		21 55		22 55		23 55
Witton	d	17 46			18 16		18 46		19 16	19 36	20 01			20 57		21 57		22 57		23 57
Aston	d	17 49			18 19		18 49		19 19	19 39	20 03			21 00		22 00		23 00		00 01
Duddeston	d	17 51			18 21		18 51		19 21	19 42	20 06			21 03		22 03		23 03		00 04
Birmingham New Street 12	a	17 58		18 03	18 28	18 36	18 58	19 09	19 28	19 46	20 12	20 39		21 09	21 36	22 09	22 33	23 09	23 34	00 09
Wolverhampton 7	a	18 33			19 03		19 33		20 03											

Sundays

		LM A	LM	LM	LM	LM	LM	LM	LM	LM		LM	LM	LM	LM	LM	LM	LM	LM	LM		LM	LM	LM	LM
Rugeley Trent Valley	d			09 48		10 48		11 48		12 48			13 48		14 48		15 48		16 48			17 48		18 48	
Rugeley Town	d			09 52		10 52		11 52		12 52			13 52		14 52		15 52		16 52			17 52		18 52	
Hednesford	d			10 00		11 00		12 00		13 00			14 00		15 00		16 00		17 00			18 00		19 00	
Cannock	d			10 04		11 04		12 04		13 04			14 04		15 04		16 04		17 04			18 04		19 04	
Landywood	d			10 07		11 07		12 07		13 07			14 07		15 07		16 07		17 07			18 07		19 07	
Bloxwich North	d			10 12		11 12		12 12		13 12			14 12		15 12		16 12		17 12			18 12		19 12	
Bloxwich	d			10 14		11 14		12 14		13 14			14 14		15 14		16 14		17 14			18 14		19 14	
Walsall	a			10 21		11 21		12 21		13 21			14 21		15 21		16 21		17 21			18 21		19 21	
	d	23p40	10 00	10 23	11 00	11 23	12 00	12 23	13 00	13 23		14 00	14 23	15 00	15 23	16 00	16 23	17 00	17 23	18 00		18 23	19 00	19 23	20 00
Bescot Stadium	d	23p44	10 04		11 04		12 04		13 04			14 04		15 04		16 04		17 04		18 04			19 04		20 04
Tame Bridge Parkway	d	23p47	10 07	10 29	11 07	11 29	12 07	12 29	13 07	13 29		14 07	14 29	15 07	15 29	16 07	16 29	17 07	17 29	18 07		18 29	19 07	19 29	20 07
Hamstead	d	23p51	10 11		11 11		12 11		13 11			14 11		15 11		16 11		17 11		18 11			19 11		20 11
Perry Barr	d	23p55	10 14		11 14		12 14		13 14			14 14		15 14		16 14		17 14		18 14			19 14		20 14
Witton	d	23p57	10 17		11 17		12 17		13 17			14 17		15 17		16 17		17 17		18 17			19 17		20 17
Aston	d	00 01	10 20		11 20		12 20		13 20			14 20		15 20		16 20		17 20		18 20			19 20		20 20
Duddeston	d	00 04	10 23		11 23		12 23		13 23			14 23		15 23		16 23		17 23		18 23			19 23		20 23
Birmingham New Street 12	a	00 09	10 27	10 46	11 27	11 46	12 27	12 46	13 27	13 46		14 27	14 46	15 30	15 46	16 30	16 46	17 30	17 46	18 28		18 46	19 27	19 47	20 27
Wolverhampton 7	a																								

		LM	LM	LM	LM	LM		LM	LM
Rugeley Trent Valley	d	19 48		20 48		21 48			22 48
Rugeley Town	d	19 52		20 52		21 52			22 52
Hednesford	d	20 00		21 00		22 00			23 00
Cannock	d	20 04		21 04		22 04			23 04
Landywood	d	20 07		21 07		22 07			23 07
Bloxwich North	d	20 12		21 12		22 12			23 12
Bloxwich	d	20 14		21 14		22 14			23 14
Walsall	a	20 21		21 21		22 21			23 21
	d	20 23	21 00	21 23	22 00	22 23		23 00	23 23
Bescot Stadium	d		21 04		22 04			23 04	
Tame Bridge Parkway	d	20 29	21 07	21 29	22 07	22 29		23 07	23 29
Hamstead	d		21 11		22 11			23 11	
Perry Barr	d		21 14		22 14			23 14	
Witton	d		21 17		22 17			23 17	
Aston	d		21 20		22 20			23 20	
Duddeston	d		21 23		22 23			23 23	
Birmingham New Street 12	a	20 46	21 27	21 46	22 27	22 48		23 27	23 46
Wolverhampton 7	a								

A not 11 December

For connections from Stafford please refer to Table 67

Network Diagram for Tables 71, 72

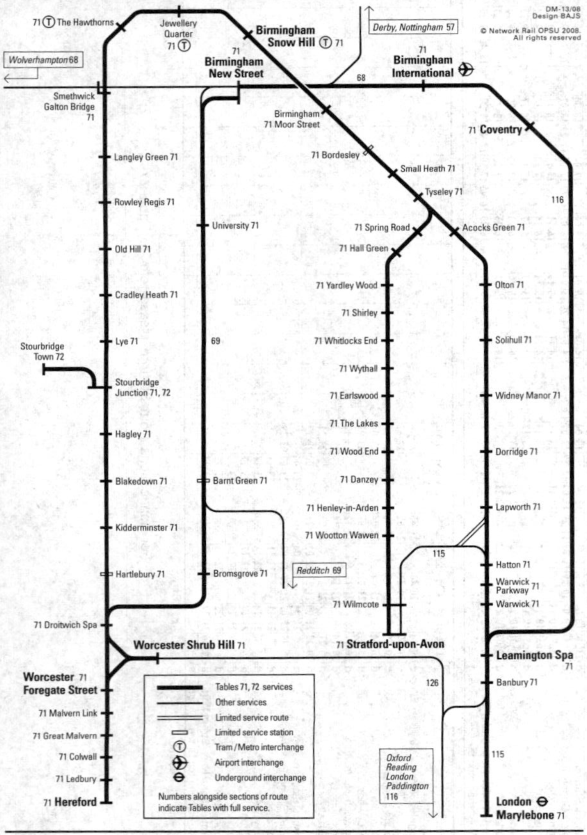

Table 71

Mondays to Fridays

Hereford, Worcester and Stourbridge - Birmingham - Leamington Spa, Marylebone and Stratford-upon-Avon

Network Diagram - see first Page of Table 71

Miles	Miles	Miles			CH MX	CH	CH	LM	XC	CH	CH	LM	GW		LM	CH	XC	LM	LM	CH	CH	CH	XC		LM
							◇		◇1				◇1				◇1				◇		◇1		
						🍴	🍴		🍴		🍴		🍽								🍴		🍴		
0	—	—	**Hereford** 7	d																					
13¾	—	—	Ledbury	a																					
—	—	—		d																					
18	—	—	Colwall	d																					
20¼	—	—	**Great Malvern**	a																					
—	—	—		d									05 18					05 52							
22	—	—	Malvern Link	d									05 21					05 55							
28¾	0	—	**Worcester Foregate Street** 7	a									05 31					06 02							
—	—	—		d									05 32					06 04							
29½	—	—	**Worcester Shrub Hill** 7	a									05 36												
—	—	—		d								05 30													
34¼	5½	—	Droitwich Spa	d								05 38						06 13							
40½	—	—	Bromsgrove	d														06 22							
44	—	—	Barnt Green	d																					
52	—	—	University	d														06 39							
—	11	—	Hartlebury	d																					
—	14¼	—	**Kidderminster**	d								05 48										06 10			
—	17¾	—	Blakedown	d																					
—	19½	—	Hagley	d																					
—	21½	—	**Stourbridge Junction** 4	d								05 57										06 18			06 24
—	22¾	—	Lye	d								06 01													06 28
—	24	—	Cradley Heath	d								06 04										06 23			06 31
—	25½	—	Old Hill	d								06 08													06 35
—	26¾	—	Rowley Regis	d								06 12										06 29			06 39
—	28½	0	Langley Green	d								06 15													06 42
54½	—	6¼	**Birmingham New Street** 12	a														06 45							
—	—	—		d					06 04								06 33						07 04		
—	—	—	**Birmingham International** ✈	d					06 14														07 14		
—	—	—	**Coventry**	d					06 25														07 25		
—	29½	—	Smethwick Galton Bridge 7	d								06 18										06 34			06 46
—	30¼	—	The Hawthorns 🚊	d								06 21										06 37			06 48
—	32¾	—	Jewellery Quarter 🚊	d								06 25													06 52
—	33½	—	**Birmingham Snow Hill** 🚊	a								06 28										06 45			06 55
—	—	—		d	23p30			05 55				06 29			06 35				06 40			06 46			07 02
—	34	—	**Birmingham Moor Street**	d	23p33		05 46	05 58			06 19	06 32			06 38				06 43		06 55	06 59			07 05
—	34¼	—	Bordesley	d																					
—	35¾	9¼	Small Heath	d				06 02							06 42				06 47						07 09
—	36¾	10¼	Tyseley	d	23p38			06 04				06 36			06 45				06 49						07 11
—	—	11¾	Acocks Green	d	23p41			06 07							06 48										07 14
—	—	12¾	Olton	d	23p44			06 10							06 50										07 17
—	—	14	Solihull	d	23p48		05 54	06 13			06 29				06 54						07 03	07 09			07 20
—	—	15½	Widney Manor	d	23p51			06 17							06 58										07 24
—	—	17½	Dorridge	d	23p55		05 59	06 21			06 35				07a03							07 14			07 28
—	—	20	Lapworth	d	23p59			06 25																	07 32
—	—	24¼	Hatton	d	00 05					06 31												07 22			07 38
—	—	27	Warwick Parkway	d	00 10	05 40	06 09				06 45									07 07	07 15	07 27			07 42
—	—	28¼	Warwick	d	00 13		06 12			06 39										07 11		07 30			07 45
—	—	30¼	**Leamington Spa** 8	a	00 16	05 45	06 17		06 36	06 45	06 50						06 58			07 15		07 34	07 37		07 51
—	—	—		d	00 17	05 45	06 17		06 38		06 52					06 52	07 00			07 22		07 34	07 38		
—	—	—	Banbury	d	00a38	06 03	06 36		06a56		07 11						07a21			07 40		07 52	07a54		
—	—	—	**London Marylebone** 10 ⊖	a		07 09	07 38				08 06									08 48	08 25	09 07			
—	37¾	—	Spring Road	d								06 39							06 52						
—	38¼	—	Hall Green	d								06 42							06 55						
—	39½	—	Yardley Wood	d								06 45							06 58						
—	40¾	—	Shirley	d								06 48							07 01						
—	41¾	—	Whitlocks End	d								06 51							07 04						
—	42¾	—	Wythall	d								06 53							07 06						
—	43¾	—	Earlswood (West Midlands)	d															07 09						
—	44½	—	The Lakes	d															07x11						
—	45¾	—	Wood End	d															07x13						
—	47½	—	Danzey	d															07x17						
—	50¼	—	Henley-in-Arden	d								07 04							07 22						
—	52¼	—	Wootton Wawen	d															07x24						
—	56	—	Wilmcote	d				06 42								07 20			07 30						
—	58¾	—	**Stratford-upon-Avon**	a				06 48				07 16				07 27			07 36						

Hereford, Worcester and Stourbridge - Birmingham - Leamington Spa, Marylebone and Stratford-upon-Avon

Network Diagram - see first Page of Table 71

		LM	LM	GW	LM	CH	XC	LM	CH	CH	LM	GW	LM	LM	XC	CH	LM	LM	GW	CH	XC	CH	LM
				◇1		◇	◇1			◇		1			◇1	◇			◇1		◇1	◇	
																			A				
				Ø						⌶					⌶	⌶			Ø		⌶		
Hereford 7	d			05 35															06 44				
Ledbury	a			05 51															07 00				
	d			05 52															07 01				
Colwall	d			05 59															07 08				
Great Malvern	a			06 04															07 13				
	d			06 04									06 47					07 04	07 14				
Malvern Link	d			06 08									06 50					07 07	07 18				
Worcester Foregate Street 7	a			06 19									06 58					07 15	07 28				
	d			06 19								06 53	06 59				07 14	07 17	07 29				
Worcester Shrub Hill 2	a			06 21								06 55	07 01					07 19	07 32				
	d		06 15		06 28						06 47		07 06					07 25					
Droitwich Spa	d		06 23		06 35						06 55		07 14				07 23	07 34					
Bromsgrove	d				06 44								07 24										
Barnt Green	d																						
University	d				06 59								07 39					07 59					
Hartlebury	d		06 30								07 02						07 30						
Kidderminster	d		06 36							06 59	07 09			07 18		07 30	07 36						
Blakedown	d		06 41								07 14			07 24			07 41						
Hagley	d		06 44								07 18			07 28			07 45						
Stourbridge Junction 2	d		06 49							07 07	07 22			07 32		07 40	07 49						07 55
Lye	d		06 53							07 11				07 36									07 59
Cradley Heath	d		06 56							07 14	07 28			07 39		07 45	07 55						08 02
Old Hill	d		07 00							07 18				07 43									08 06
Rowley Regis	d		07 04							07 22	07 34			07 47		07 53	08 00						08 10
Langley Green	d		07 07							07 25				07 50									08 13
Birmingham New Street 12	a				07 07								07 46					08 09					
	d						07 33								08 04						08 33		
Birmingham International ✈	d														08 14								
Coventry	d														08 25								
Smethwick Galton Bridge 7	d		07 11							07 29	07 39			07 54		07 59	08 06						08 16
The Hawthorns 🚋	d		07 13							07 32	07 42			07 56		08 02	08 08						08 19
Jewellery Quarter 🚋	d		07 17							07 36	07 46			08 00		08 06	08 12						08 23
Birmingham Snow Hill 🚋	a		07 21							07 40	07 49			08 03		08 11	08 15						08 26
	d	07 19	07 23					07 39		07 44	07 50			08 05		08 12	08 17					08 22	08 27
Birmingham Moor Street	d	07 22	07 26			07 33		07 42		07 47	07 53			08 08		08 15	08 20					08 25	08 30
Bordesley	d																						
Small Heath	d		07 30					07 46						08 12									
Tyseley	d		07 32					07 48			07 57			08 14									
Acocks Green	d	07 27									08 00						08 25						
Olton	d	07 30									08 03						08 28						
Solihull	d	07 34				07 41				07 55	08 07					08 24	08 32					08 37	
Widney Manor	d	07 37									08 10						08 35						
Dorridge	d	07a42								08 00	08a16					08 29	08a41					08 50	
Lapworth	d									08 04												08 54	
Hatton	d								08 00	08 10												09 00	
Warwick Parkway	d					07 52			08 06	08 16						08 39							
Warwick	d									08 19						08 43						09 06	
Leamington Spa 8	a					07 57	08 03		08 11	08 24					08 36	08 46					08 59	09 09	
	d					07 58	08 04		08 12	08 24					08 38	08 47				08 51	09 00	09 10	
Banbury	d					08 16	08a20		08 31	08 43					08a54	09 06					09a18	09 29	
London Marylebone 10 ⊖	a					09 07			09 40	09 58						09 59						10 28	
Spring Road	d		07 35					07 51						08 17									08 36
Hall Green	d		07 38					07 54						08 20									08 39
Yardley Wood	d		07 41					07 57						08 23									08 42
Shirley	d		07 44					08 00						08 26									08 45
Whitlocks End	d		07 47					08a02						08a28									08 48
Wythall	d		07 50																				08 50
Earlswood (West Midlands)	d		07 52																				08 53
The Lakes	d		07x55																				08x55
Wood End	d		07x57																				08x58
Danzey	d		08x01																				09x01
Henley-in-Arden	d		08 07																				09 07
Wootton Wawen	d		08x10																				09x10
Wilmcote	d		08 15																	09 19			09 15
Stratford-upon-Avon	a		08 21																	09 31			09 21

A The Cathedrals Express

Hereford, Worcester and Stourbridge - Birmingham - Leamington Spa, Marylebone and Stratford-upon-Avon

Network Diagram - see first Page of Table 71

		LM	LM	LM	CH	LM	LM	XC	LM	GW	CH	LM	LM	LM	LM	XC	LM	GW	CH	LM	LM	CH	CH
					◇			◇1		◇1	◇					◇1			◇			◇	◇
					⌶			⌶		⌶						⌶							⌶
Hereford 7	d		07 10						07 34														
Ledbury	a		07 25						07 49														
	d		07 26						07 50														
Colwall	d		07 32						07 56														
Great Malvern	a		07 37						08 00														
	d		07 39						08 05								08 38	08 50					
Malvern Link	d		07 42						08 08								08 41	08 53					
Worcester Foregate Street 7	a		07 50						08 16								08 49	09 03					
	d		07 51				08 04		08 24	08 26					08 38		08 52	09 03			09 06		
Worcester Shrub Hill 2	a		07 53							08 28					08 40			09 06					
	d	07 35	07 57												08 44								
Droitwich Spa	d	07 43	08 05				08 13		08 33						08 52		09 01				09 15		
Bromsgrove	d								08 42								09 11						
Barnt Green	d																						
University	d		08 29						08 59								09 29						
Hartlebury	d																						
Kidderminster	d	07 54			08 09		08 23							08 57	09 06						09 26		
Blakedown	d	07 59			08 14		08 28							09 02	09 11						09 31		
Hagley	d	08 03			08 19		08 32							09 05	09 15						09 35		
Stourbridge Junction 2	d	08 07		08 14	08 23		08 36					08 45	08 54	09 09	09 19					09 25	09 39		
Lye	d			08 18			08 40						08 58							09 29			
Cradley Heath	d	08 13		08 21	08 28		08 43					08 51	09 01	09 15	09 24					09 32	09 44		
Old Hill	d			08 25			08 47						09 05							09 36			
Rowley Regis	d	08 19		08 29	08 34		08 51					08 57	09 09	09 21	09 30					09 39	09 50		
Langley Green	d			08 32			08 54						09 12							09 42			
Birmingham New Street 12	a		08 37						09 07								09 42						
	d							09 04								09 33							
Birmingham International ✈	d							09 14															
Coventry	d							09 25															
Smethwick Galton Bridge 7	d	08 25		08 36	08 40		08 57					09 02	09 15	09 26	09 36					09 46	09 56		
The Hawthorns 🚋	d	08 28		08 38	08 42		08 59					09 05	09 17	09 29	09 38					09 48	09 58		
Jewellery Quarter 🚋	d	08 32		08 42	08 47		09 03					09 09	09 21	09 33	09 42					09 52	10 02		
Birmingham Snow Hill 🚋	a	08 35		08 45	08 51		09 06					09 12	09 25	09 36	09 45					09 55	10 05		
	d	08 37		08 47	08 52	08 57	09 07				09 12	09 17	09 27	09 37	09 47					09 57	10 07		
Birmingham Moor Street	d	08 40		08 50	08 55	09 00	09 10				09 15	09 20	09 30	09 40	09 50				09 55	10 00	10 10		
Bordesley	d																						
Small Heath	d	08 44					09 14							09 44							10 14		
Tyseley	d	08 47					09 16							09 46							10 16		
Acocks Green	d	08 50				09 05						09 25		09 49						10 05			
Olton	d	08 53				09 08						09 28		09 52						10 08			
Solihull	d	08 57			09 03	09 12					09 23	09 32		09 56					10 03	10 12			
Widney Manor	d	09 00				09 15						09 35		09 59						10 15			
Dorridge	d	09a05				09a22					09 28	09a41		10a04						10a22			
Lapworth	d										09 32												
Hatton	d																					10 16	
Warwick Parkway	d				09 15						09 40								10 14				
Warwick	d										09 44											10 23	
Leamington Spa 8	a							09 36			09 48					09 58			10 20			10 27	
	d							09 38			09 49					10 00			10 21			10 27	10 33
Banbury	d							09a54			10 07					10a17			10 38			10 48	
London Marylebone 10 ⊖	a				10 29						11 14								11 32			12 00	
Spring Road	d			08 56			09 19						09 36		09 56						10 19		
Hall Green	d			08 59			09 22						09 39		09 59						10 22		
Yardley Wood	d			09 02			09 25						09 42		10 02						10 25		
Shirley	d			09 05			09 28						09 45		10 05						10 28		
Whitlocks End	d			09a07			09a30						09 48		10a07						10a30		
Wythall	d												09 50										
Earlswood (West Midlands)	d												09 53										
The Lakes	d												09x55										
Wood End	d												09x58										
Danzey	d												10x01										
Henley-in-Arden	d												10 07										
Wootton Wawen	d												10x10										
Wilmcote	d												10 15										
Stratford-upon-Avon	a												10 21										11 09

Hereford, Worcester and Stourbridge - Birmingham - Leamington Spa, Marylebone and Stratford-upon-Avon

Network Diagram - see first Page of Table 71

		XC	LM	CH	LM	LM	LM	LM	GW	XC	CH	LM	LM	XC	CH	LM	LM	LM	CH	XC	CH	LM
		◇1 🚲		◇					◇1 🚲	◇1 🚲	◇			◇1 🚲	◇					◇1 🚲	🚲	
Hereford 7	d		08 49														09 40					
Ledbury	a		09 05														09 56					
	d		09 08														09 58					
Colwall	d		09 14														10 04					
Great Malvern	a		09 18														10 08					
	d		09 19						09 54								10 10					
Malvern Link	d		09 22						09 56								10 13					
Worcester Foregate Street 7	a		09 30						10 05								10 22					
	d		09 31						10 05							10 16	10 24					
Worcester Shrub Hill 7	a		09 33						10 08													
	d		09 37					09 47														
Droitwich Spa	d		09 45					09 55								10 25	10 33					
Bromsgrove	d		09 54														10 42					
Barnt Green	d																					
University	d		10 09														10 59					
Hartlebury	d																					
Kidderminster	d				09 36		09 58	10 06					10 26			10 36						10 56
Blakedown	d				09 41			10 11								10 41						
Hagley	d				09 45			10 15								10 45						
Stourbridge Junction 2	d				09 49	09 55	10 09	10 19				10 25	10 39			10 49		10 55				11 09
Lye	d					09 59						10 29						10 59				
Cradley Heath	d				09 54	10 02	10 14	10 24				10 32	10 44			10 54		11 02				11 14
Old Hill	d					10 06						10 36						11 06				
Rowley Regis	d				10 00	10 10	10 20	10 30				10 40	10 50			11 00		11 10				11 20
Langley Green	d					10 13						10 43						11 13				
Birmingham New Street 12	a		10 24														11 13					
	d	10 04								10 33				11 04						11 33		
Birmingham International ✈	d	10 14												11 14								
Coventry	d	10 25												11 25								
Smethwick Galton Bridge 7	d				10 06	10 16	10 26	10 36				10 46	10 56			11 06		11 16				11 26
The Hawthorns 🚋	d				10 08	10 18	10 28	10 38				10 48	10 58			11 08		11 18				11 28
Jewellery Quarter 🚋	d				10 12	10 22	10 32	10 42				10 52	11 02			11 12		11 22				11 32
Birmingham Snow Hill 🚋	a				10 15	10 25	10 35	10 45				10 55	11 05			11 15		11 25				11 35
	d			10 12	10 17	10 27	10 37	10 47				10 57	11 07		11 12	11 17		11 27				11 37
Birmingham Moor Street	d			10 15	10 20	10 30	10 40	10 50			10 55	11 00	11 10		11 15	11 20		11 30			11 33	11 40
Bordesley	d																					
Small Heath	d						10 44						11 14									11 44
Tyseley	d						10 46						11 16									11 46
Acocks Green	d				10 25		10 49					11 05				11 25						11 49
Olton	d				10 28		10 52					11 08				11 28						11 52
Solihull	d			10 23	10 32		10 56				11 03	11 12			11 23	11 32					11 42	11 56
Widney Manor	d				10 35		10 59					11 15				11 35						11 59
Dorridge	d			10 28	10a41		11a04					11a21			11 28	11a41					11 50	12a04
Lapworth	d																				11 54	
Hatton	d																		11 39		12 00	
Warwick Parkway	d			10 39							11 14				11 39						12 05	
Warwick	d			10 42											11 42				11 46		12 08	
Leamington Spa 8	a	10 36		10 46						10 58	11 20			11 36	11 46				11 50	11 59	12 15	
	d	10 38		10 46						11 00	11 21			11 38	11 46				11 50	12 00		
Banbury	d	10a54		11 04						11a17	11 38			11a54	12 04				12 10	12a17		
London Marylebone 10 ⊖	a			12 09							12 32				13 07				13 31			
Spring Road	d					10 36		10 56					11 19					11 36				
Hall Green	d					10 39		10 59					11 22					11 39				
Yardley Wood	d					10 42		11 02					11 25					11 42				
Shirley	d					10 45		11 05					11 28					11 45				
Whitlocks End	d					10 48		11a07					11a30					11 48				
Wythall	d					10 50												11 50				
Earlswood (West Midlands)	d					10 53												11 53				
The Lakes	d					10x55												11x55				
Wood End	d					10x58												11x58				
Danzey	d					11x01												12x01				
Henley-in-Arden	d					11 07												12 07				
Wootton Wawen	d					11x10												12x10				
Wilmcote	d					11 15												12 15				
Stratford-upon-Avon	a					11 21												12 21				

Hereford, Worcester and Stourbridge - Birmingham - Leamington Spa, Marylebone and Stratford-upon-Avon

Network Diagram - see first Page of Table 71

		LM	GW	CH	CH	LM	LM	XC	CH	LM	LM	LM	LM	LM	GW	XC	CH	LM	LM	XC	CH	CH	LM
			■	◇				◇1 🚲	◇						◇1 🚲	◇1 🚲	◇			◇1 🚲		◇	
Hereford 7	d										10 40												
Ledbury	a										10 56												
	d										10 58												
Colwall	d										11 04												
Great Malvern	a										11 08												
	d		10 50								11 10			11 34									
Malvern Link	d		10 53								11 13			11 36									
Worcester Foregate Street 7	a		11 03								11 22			11 45									
	d		11 03							11 16	11 24			11 46	12 06								12 16
Worcester Shrub Hill 7	a		11 06												12 08								
	d	10 47																					
Droitwich Spa	d	10 55								11 25	11 33			11 55									12 25
Bromsgrove	d										11 42												
Barnt Green	d																						
University	d										11 59												
Hartlebury	d																						
Kidderminster	d	11 06					11 26			11 36			11 56	12 06					12 26				12 36
Blakedown	d	11 11								11 41				12 11									12 41
Hagley	d	11 14								11 44				12 14									12 44
Stourbridge Junction 2	d	11 19				11 25	11 39			11 49		11 55	12 09	12 19				12 25	12 39				12 49
Lye	d					11 29						11 59						12 29					
Cradley Heath	d	11 24				11 32	11 44			11 54		12 02	12 14	12 24				12 32	12 44				12 54
Old Hill	d					11 36						12 06						12 36					
Rowley Regis	d	11 30				11 40	11 50			12 00		12 10	12 20	12 30				12 40	12 50				13 00
Langley Green	d					11 43						12 13						12 43					
Birmingham New Street 12	a										12 11												
	d							12 04								12 33				13 04			
Birmingham International ✈	d							12 14												13 14			
Coventry	d							12 25												13 25			
Smethwick Galton Bridge 7	d	11 36				11 46	11 56			12 06		12 16	12 26	12 36				12 46	12 56				13 06
The Hawthorns 🚋	d	11 38				11 48	11 58			12 08		12 18	12 28	12 38				12 48	12 58				13 08
Jewellery Quarter 🚋	d	11 42				11 52	12 02			12 12		12 22	12 32	12 42				12 52	13 02				13 12
Birmingham Snow Hill 🚋	a	11 45				11 55	12 05			12 15		12 25	12 35	12 45				12 55	13 05				13 15
	d	11 47				11 57	12 07		12 12	12 17		12 27	12 37	12 47				12 57	13 07			13 12	13 17
Birmingham Moor Street	d	11 50			11 55	12 00	12 10		12 15	12 20		12 30	12 40	12 50			12 55	13 00	13 10			13 15	13 20
Bordesley	d																						
Small Heath	d						12 14						12 44						13 14				
Tyseley	d						12 16						12 46						13 16				
Acocks Green	d					12 05				12 25			12 49					13 05					13 25
Olton	d					12 08				12 28			12 52					13 08					13 28
Solihull	d				12 03	12 12			12 23	12 32			12 56				13 03	13 12				13 23	13 32
Widney Manor	d					12 15				12 35			12 59					13 15					13 35
Dorridge	d					12a22			12 28	12a41			13a04					13a21				13 28	13a41
Lapworth	d																						
Hatton	d																				13 28		
Warwick Parkway	d				12 14				12 39								13 14					13 39	
Warwick	d								12 42												13 36	13 42	
Leamington Spa 8	a				12 19			12 36	12 46							12 58	13 19			13 36	13 41	13 46	
	d			12 18	12 20			12 38	12 46							13 00	13 20			13 38		13 46	
Banbury	d				12 38			12a54	13 04							13a20	13 38			13a54		14 04	
London Marylebone 10 ⊖	a				13 32				14 09								14 32					15 07	
Spring Road	d	11 56					12 19					12 36		12 56					13 19				
Hall Green	d	11 59					12 22					12 39		12 59					13 22				
Yardley Wood	d	12 02					12 25					12 42		13 02					13 25				
Shirley	d	12 05					12 28					12 45		13 05					13 28				
Whitlocks End	d	12a07					12a30					12 48		13a07					13a30				
Wythall	d											12 50											
Earlswood (West Midlands)	d											12 53											
The Lakes	d											12x55											
Wood End	d											12x58											
Danzey	d											13x01											
Henley-in-Arden	d											13 07											
Wootton Wawen	d											13x10											
Wilmcote	d											13 15											
Stratford-upon-Avon	a			12 52								13 21											

Hereford, Worcester and Stourbridge - Birmingham - Leamington Spa, Marylebone and Stratford-upon-Avon

Network Diagram - see first Page of Table 71

		LM	LM		XC	CH	LM	LM	GW	CH	LM	LM	CH		XC	CH	LM	LM	LM	LM	LM	GW	XC		CH
					◇1				◇	◇			◇		◇1	◇						◇1	◇1		◇
					🛒	🛒							🛒		🛒							🍽	🛒		
Hereford 7	d	11 40																12 40				13 14			
Ledbury	a	11 56																12 56				13 30			
	d	11 58																12 58				13 31			
Colwall	d	12 04																13 04				13 39			
Great Malvern	a	12 09																13 08				13 44			
	d	12 10							12 50									13 10				13 44			
Malvern Link	d	12 13							12 53									13 13				13 48			
Worcester Foregate Street 7	a	12 22							13 03									13 21				13 58			
	d	12 24						12 46	13 03									13 24				13 59			
Worcester Shrub Hill 7	a								13 06													14 03			
	d																13 17				13 47				
Droitwich Spa	d	12 33						12 55									13 25	13 33			13 55				
Bromsgrove	d	12 42																13 42							
Barnt Green	d																								
University	d	12 59																13 59							
Hartlebury	d																								
Kidderminster	d						12 56	13 06									13 36			13 56	14 06				
Blakedown	d							13 11									13 41				14 11				
Hagley	d							13 14									13 44				14 14				
Stourbridge Junction 2	d		12 55				13 09	13 19			13 25	13 39					13 49		13 55	14 09	14 19				
Lye	d		12 59								13 29								13 59						
Cradley Heath	d		13 02				13 14	13 24			13 32	13 44					13 54		14 02	14 14	14 24				
Old Hill	d		13 06								13 36								14 06						
Rowley Regis	d		13 10				13 20	13 30			13 40	13 50					14 00		14 10	14 20	14 30				
Langley Green	d		13 13								13 43								14 13						
Birmingham New Street 12	a	13 13																14 12							
	d				13 33										14 04								14 33		
Birmingham International ✈	d														14 14										
Coventry	d														14 25										
Smethwick Galton Bridge 7	d		13 16				13 26	13 36			13 46	13 56					14 06		14 16	14 26	14 36				
The Hawthorns 🚊	d		13 18				13 28	13 38			13 48	13 58					14 08		14 18	14 28	14 38				
Jewellery Quarter 🚊	d		13 22				13 32	13 42			13 52	14 02					14 12		14 22	14 32	14 42				
Birmingham Snow Hill 🚊	a		13 25				13 35	13 45			13 55	14 05					14 15		14 25	14 35	14 45				
	d		13 27				13 37	13 47			13 57	14 07				14 12	14 17		14 27	14 37	14 47				
Birmingham Moor Street	d		13 30			13 33	13 40	13 50		13 55	14 00	14 10				14 15	14 20		14 30	14 40	14 50				14 55
Bordesley	d																								
Small Heath	d						13 44					14 14								14 44					
Tyseley	d						13 46					14 16								14 46					
Acocks Green	d						13 49				14 05						14 25			14 49					
Olton	d						13 52				14 08						14 28			14 52					
Solihull	d					13 42	13 56			14 03	14 12					14 23	14 32			14 56					15 03
Widney Manor	d						13 59				14 15						14 35			14 59					
Dorridge	d					13 50	14a04				14a22					14 28	14a41			15a04					
Lapworth	d					13 54																			
Hatton	d					14 00																			
Warwick Parkway	d					14 05				14 14						14 39									15 14
Warwick	d					14 08										14 42									
Leamington Spa 8	a				13 59	14 16				14 20					14 36	14 46							14 58		15 19
	d				14 00					14 21			14 34		14 38	14 46							15 00		15 20
Banbury	d				14a17					14 38					14a54	15 04							15a17		15 38
London Marylebone 10 ⊖	a									15 32						16 11									16 32
Spring Road	d		13 36					13 56				14 19							14 36		14 56				
Hall Green	d		13 39					13 59				14 22							14 39		14 59				
Yardley Wood	d		13 42					14 02				14 25							14 42		15 02				
Shirley	d		13 45					14 05				14 28							14 45		15 05				
Whitlocks End	d		13 48					14a07				14a30							14 48		15a07				
Wythall	d		13 50																14 50						
Earlswood (West Midlands)	d		13 53																14 53						
The Lakes	d		13x55																14x55						
Wood End	d		13x58																14x58						
Danzey	d		14x01																15x01						
Henley-in-Arden	d		14 07																15 07						
Wootton Wawen	d		14x10																15x10						
Wilmcote	d		14 15										15 01						15 15						
Stratford-upon-Avon	a		14 21										15 09						15 21						

Hereford, Worcester and Stourbridge - Birmingham - Leamington Spa, Marylebone and Stratford-upon-Avon

Network Diagram - see first Page of Table 71

		LM	LM	XC	CH	LM	LM	GW	LM		XC	CH	CH	LM	LM	GW	CH	LM	LM		CH	XC	CH	LM	LM
				◇1	◇			◇1			◇1	◇				◇	◇					◇1			
				🛒				🛒			🛒		🛒									🛒			
Hereford 7	d						13 43																		14 40
Ledbury	a						14 00																		14 56
	d						14 00																		14 58
Colwall	d						14 06																		15 04
Great Malvern	a						14 11																		15 08
	d					14 00	14 11	14 26								14 50									15 10
Malvern Link	d					14 02	14 14	14 28								14 53									15 13
Worcester Foregate Street 7	a					14 10	14 23	14 38								15 03									15 22
	d					14 16	14 24	14 38								15 03								15 16	15 24
Worcester Shrub Hill 7	a							14 41								15 06									
	d														14 47										
Droitwich Spa	d					14 25	14 33								14 55									15 25	15 33
Bromsgrove	d						14 42																		15 42
Barnt Green	d																								
University	d						14 59																		15 59
Hartlebury	d																								
Kidderminster	d		14 26			14 36								14 56	15 06				15 26					15 36	
Blakedown	d					14 41									15 11				15 31					15 41	
Hagley	d					14 44									15 14				15 34					15 44	
Stourbridge Junction 2	d	14 25	14 39			14 49			14 55					15 09	15 19			15 25	15 39					15 49	
Lye	d	14 29							14 59									15 29							
Cradley Heath	d	14 32	14 44			14 54			15 02					15 14	15 24			15 32	15 44					15 54	
Old Hill	d	14 36							15 06									15 36							
Rowley Regis	d	14 40	14 50			15 00			15 10					15 20	15 30			15 40	15 50					16 00	
Langley Green	d	14 43							15 13									15 43							
Birmingham New Street 12	a						15 13																		16 13
	d			15 04							15 33											16 04			
Birmingham International ✈	d			15 14																		16 14			
Coventry	d			15 25																		16 25			
Smethwick Galton Bridge 7	d	14 46	14 56			15 06			15 16					15 26	15 36			15 46	15 56					16 06	
The Hawthorns 🚊	d	14 48	14 58			15 08			15 18					15 28	15 38			15 48	15 58					16 08	
Jewellery Quarter 🚊	d	14 52	15 02			15 12			15 22					15 32	15 42			15 52	16 02					16 12	
Birmingham Snow Hill 🚊	a	14 55	15 05			15 15			15 25					15 35	15 45			15 55	16 05					16 15	
	d	14 57	15 07		15 12	15 17			15 26					15 37	15 47			15 57	16 07				16 12	16 17	
Birmingham Moor Street	d	15 00	15 10		15 15	15 20			15 29				15 33	15 40	15 50		15 55	16 00	16 10				16 15	16 20	
Bordesley	d																								
Small Heath	d		15 14											15 44					16 14						
Tyseley	d		15 16											15 46					16 16						
Acocks Green	d	15 05				15 25								15 49				16 05						16 25	
Olton	d	15 08				15 28								15 52				16 08						16 28	
Solihull	d	15 12			15 23	15 32							15 42	15 56			16 03	16 12					16 23	16 32	
Widney Manor	d	15 15				15 35								15 59				16 15						16 35	
Dorridge	d	15a21			15 28	15a41							15 50	16a04				16a22					16 28	16a41	
Lapworth	d												15 54												
Hatton	d											15 57	16 00												
Warwick Parkway	d				15 39								16 05				16 15						16 39		
Warwick	d				15 42							16 04	16 08										16 42		
Leamington Spa 8	a			15 36	15 46						15 58	16 12	16 17				16 21					16 36	16 46		
	d			15 38	15 46						16 00						16 22				16 35	16 38	16 46		
Banbury	d			15a54	16 04						16a17						16 40					16a54	17 05		
London Marylebone 10 ⊖	a				17 11												17 46						18 19		
Spring Road	d		15 19						15 35						15 56				16 19						
Hall Green	d		15 22						15 38						15 59				16 22						
Yardley Wood	d		15 25						15 41						16 02				16 25						
Shirley	d		15 28						15 44						16 05				16 28						
Whitlocks End	d		15a30						15 47						16a07				16a30						
Wythall	d								15 49																
Earlswood (West Midlands)	d								15 52																
The Lakes	d								15x54																
Wood End	d								15x56																
Danzey	d								15x59																
Henley-in-Arden	d								16 04																
Wootton Wawen	d								16x07																
Wilmcote	d								16 12												17 02				
Stratford-upon-Avon	a								16 21												17 14				

Hereford, Worcester and Stourbridge - Birmingham - Leamington Spa, Marylebone and Stratford-upon-Avon

Network Diagram - see first Page of Table 71

		GW	LM	XC	CH		LM	LM	GW	CH	LM	LM	XC	CH	CH		LM	LM	LM	LM	XC	CH	LM	LM	LM
		1		◇1					◇1				◇1	◇	◇						◇1				
				H	H				▭				H								H				
Hereford 7	d								15 14										15 40						
Ledbury	a								15 30										15 56						
	d								15 31										15 58						
Colwall	d								15 38										16 04						
Great Malvern	a								15 43										16 09						
	d	15 22						15 30	15 44										16 10						
Malvern Link	d							15 32	15 48										16 13						
Worcester Foregate Street 7	a	15 30						15 40	15 58										16 21						
	d	15 34						15 41	15 59								16 07		16 24					16 34	16 47
Worcester Shrub Hill 7	a	15 37						15 43	16 02															16 36	
	d							15 47										16 17						16 40	
Droitwich Spa	d							15 55									16 16	16 25	16 33					16 48	16 56
Bromsgrove	d																		16 42						
Barnt Green	d																		16 49						
University	d																		16 59						
Hartlebury	d																16 23								
Kidderminster	d						15 56	16 06				16 23					16 30	16 37					16 53	16 59	17 06
Blakedown	d							16 11				16 28					16 35	16 43						17 04	17 11
Hagley	d							16 14				16 31					16 39	16 47						17 08	17 15
Stourbridge Junction 2	d		15 55				16 09	16 19			16 25	16 35					16 44	16 51		16 55			17 06	17 13	17 19
Lye	d		15 59								16 29									16 59					
Cradley Heath	d		16 02				16 14	16 24			16 32	16 41					16 50	16 57		17 02			17 12	17 19	17 24
Old Hill	d		16 06								16 36									17 06					
Rowley Regis	d		16 10				16 20	16 30			16 40	16 47					16 55	17 03		17 10			17 17	17 24	17 30
Langley Green	d		16 13								16 43									17 13					
Birmingham New Street 12	a																		17 13						
	d			16 33									17 04								17 33				
Birmingham International ✈	d												17 14												
Coventry	d												17 25												
Smethwick Galton Bridge 7	d		16 16				16 26	16 36			16 46	16 52					17 01	17 08		17 16			17 23	17 30	17 36
The Hawthorns 🚊	d		16 18				16 28	16 38			16 48	16 55					17 03	17 11		17 19			17 25	17 32	17 38
Jewellery Quarter 🚊	d		16 22				16 32	16 42			16 52	16 59					17 07	17 15		17 22			17 29	17 36	17 42
Birmingham Snow Hill 🚊	a		16 25				16 35	16 45			16 55	17 02					17 10	17 18		17 25			17 32	17 39	17 45
	d		16 27				16 37	16 47		16 52	16 57	17 03			17 10		17 14	17 22		17 27			17 35	17 42	17 47
Birmingham Moor Street	d		16 30		16 33		16 40	16 50		16 55	17 00	17 06		17 10	17 13		17 17	17 25		17 30			17 38	17 45	17 50
Bordesley	d																								
Small Heath	d						16 44	16 54									17 21						17 42	17 49	17 54
Tyseley	d		16 34				16 46	16 56			17 04						17 23			17 34			17 45	17 51	17 56
Acocks Green	d						16 49				17 07							17 30					17 48	17 54	
Olton	d						16 52				17 10							17 33					17 50	17 57	
Solihull	d				16 42		16 56			17 03	17 14			17 18	17 23			17 37					17 54	18 01	
Widney Manor	d						16 59				17 17				17 26			17 40					17 58	18 04	
Dorridge	d				16 50		17a04				17a22			17 26	17 30			17a46					18 02	18a09	
Lapworth	d				16 54										17 34								18 06		
Hatton	d				17 00										17 39							18 01	18 12		
Warwick Parkway	d				17 05					17 14				17 35	17 44								18 16		
Warwick	d				17 08					17 18				17 39	17 47							18 08	18 19		
Leamington Spa 8	a			16 58	17 18					17 22			17 36	17 42	17 51						17 59	18 11	18 24		
	d			17 00						17 23			17 38	17 43	17 51						18 00	18 12			
Banbury	d			17a17						17 41			17a54	18 00	18 12						18a18	18 30			
London Marylebone 10 ⊖	a									18 47				19 09	19 38							19 39			
Spring Road	d		16 37					16 59				17 12					17 26			17 37					17 59
Hall Green	d		16 40					17 02				17 15					17 29			17 40					18 02
Yardley Wood	d		16 43					17 05				17 18					17 32			17 43					18 05
Shirley	d		16 46					17 08				17 21					17 35			17 46					18 08
Whitlocks End	d		16 49					17a10				17 24					17a37			17 49					18 11
Wythall	d		16 51									17 26								17 51					18 13
Earlswood (West Midlands)	d		16 54																	17 54					18 16
The Lakes	d		16x56																	17x56					18x18
Wood End	d		16x59																	17x59					18x21
Danzey	d		17x02																	18x02					18x24
Henley-in-Arden	d		17 07									17 37								18 08					18 30
Wootton Wawen	d		17x10																	18x11					18x33
Wilmcote	d		17 16																	18 16					18 38
Stratford-upon-Avon	a		17 22									17 51								18 23					18 45

Hereford, Worcester and Stourbridge - Birmingham - Leamington Spa, Marylebone and Stratford-upon-Avon

Network Diagram - see first Page of Table 71

			GW	CH	XC	CH	LM	LM	CH	LM	LM		GW	LM	LM	XC	CH	LM	LM	XC	LM		CH	CH	LM
					◇1				◇				◇1			◇1				◇1			◇		
					H								H			H				H				H	
Hereford 7	d										16 40										17 40				
Ledbury	a										16 56										17 56				
	d										16 58										18 01				
Colwall	d										17 04										18 07				
Great Malvern	a										17 08										18 11				
	d		16 48								17 10			17 41							18 12				
Malvern Link	d		16 51								17 13			17 44							18 15				
Worcester Foregate Street 7	a		17 01								17 21			17 52							18 23				
	d		17 02							17 16	17 24		17 28	17 53					17 56		18 24				
Worcester Shrub Hill 7	a		17 04										17 30	17 55											
	d																								
Droitwich Spa	d									17 25	17 33								18 05		18 33				
Bromsgrove	d										17 42										18 43				
Barnt Green	d																				18 49				
University	d										17 59										18 59				
Hartlebury	d									17 32															
Kidderminster	d							17 27		17 38								18 00	18 16						18 38
Blakedown	d							17 32		17 43								18 05							18 43
Hagley	d							17 35		17 46								18 09							18 46
Stourbridge Junction 2	d						17 25	17 39		17 50					17 55			18 13	18 25						18 50
Lye	d						17 29								17 59				18 29						18 54
Cradley Heath	d						17 32	17 45		17 56					18 02			18 19	18 32						18 57
Old Hill	d						17 36								18 06				18 36						19 01
Rowley Regis	d						17 40	17 51		18 02					18 10			18 25	18 40						19 05
Langley Green	d						17 43								18 13				18 43						19 08
Birmingham New Street 12	a										18 13										19 12				
	d				18 04											18 33				19 04					
Birmingham International ✈	d				18 14															19 14					
Coventry	d				18 25															19 25					
Smethwick Galton Bridge 7	d						17 46	17 56		18 08					18 16			18 30	18 46						19 11
The Hawthorns 🚊	d						17 48	17 58		18 10					18 19			18 33	18 48						19 14
Jewellery Quarter 🚊	d						17 52	18 02		18 14					18 23			18 37	18 52						19 18
Birmingham Snow Hill 🚊	a						17 55	18 05		18 17					18 26			18 41	18 55						19 21
	d			17 52			17 57	18 07	18 12	18 22					18 27		18 40	18 45	18 57						19 22
Birmingham Moor Street	d			17 55			18 00	18 10	18 15	18 25					18 30		18 43	18 48	19 00					19 16	19 25
Bordesley	d																								
Small Heath	d						18 04	18 14							18 34			18 52	19 04						
Tyseley	d						18 06	18 16							18 36			18 54	19 06						
Acocks Green	d						18 09			18 30								18 57							19 30
Olton	d						18 12			18 33								19 00							19 33
Solihull	d			18 04			18 16		18 24	18 37							18 51	19 04						19 25	19 37
Widney Manor	d						18 19			18 40								19 07							19 40
Dorridge	d			18 11			18 23		18 29	18a45							18 56	19 11						19 30	19a47
Lapworth	d						18 27		18 33									19 15						19 34	
Hatton	d						18 33		18 39									19 21					19 37	19 41	
Warwick Parkway	d			18 21			18 38		18 44								19 06							19 46	
Warwick	d						18 41		18 47									19 27					19 44	19 49	
Leamington Spa 8	a			18 27	18 36		18 47		18 52							18 58	19 11	19 32		19 37			19 48	19 57	
	d			18 28	18 38	18 36			18 52							19 00	19 11			19 38			19 48		
Banbury	d			18 45	18a54				19 12							19a17	19 30			19a54			20 07		
London Marylebone 10 ⊖	a			19 56					20 27								20 43						21 28		
Spring Road	d							18 19							18 39				19 09						
Hall Green	d							18 22							18 42				19 12						
Yardley Wood	d							18 25							18 45				19 15						
Shirley	d							18 28							18 48				19 18						
Whitlocks End	d							18a30							18 51				19a20						
Wythall	d														18 53										
Earlswood (West Midlands)	d														18 56										
The Lakes	d														18x58										
Wood End	d														19x00										
Danzey	d														19x03										
Henley-in-Arden	d														19 08										
Wootton Wawen	d														19x10										
Wilmcote	d					19 00									19 16										
Stratford-upon-Avon	a					19 12									19 22										

Hereford, Worcester and Stourbridge - Birmingham - Leamington Spa, Marylebone and Stratford-upon-Avon

Network Diagram - see first Page of Table 71

		LM	LM	XC ◇1 🍴	CH ◇	LM	GW ◇1 🍴	GW	LM	XC ◇1	LM	XC ◇1	CH ◇	LM	GW ◇1	CH ◇	XC ◇1	LM	CH 🍴	LM	CH ◇	LM	GW ◇1
Hereford 7	d										18 48							19 50					
Ledbury	a										19 03							20 06					
	d										19 04							20 10					
Colwall	d										19 10							20 16					
Great Malvern	a										19 14							20 20					
	d							18 50			19 15				19 44			20 21					
Malvern Link	d							18 53			19 18				19 46			20 24					
Worcester Foregate Street 7	a							19 03			19 26				19 54			20 32					
	d					18 46	18 49	19 03			19 28			19 46	19 54			20 37					20 59
Worcester Shrub Hill 7	a						18 52	19 06							19 57								21 02
	d		18 37																			20 52	
Droitwich Spa	d		18 45			18 55					19 37			19 55				20 46				21 00	
Bromsgrove	d										19 46							20 55					
Barnt Green	d																						
University	d										20 09							21 14					
Hartlebury	d					19 02																	
Kidderminster	d		18 55			19 10								20 10								21 10	
Blakedown	d		19 00			19 15								20 15								21 15	
Hagley	d		19 04			19 19								20 19								21 19	
Stourbridge Junction 2	d		19 09			19 25			19 55					20 25						20 55		21 25	
Lye	d					19 29			19 59					20 29						20 59		21 29	
Cradley Heath	d		19 14			19 32			20 02					20 32						21 02		21 32	
Old Hill	d					19 36			20 06					20 36						21 06		21 36	
Rowley Regis	d		19 20			19 40			20 10					20 40						21 10		21 40	
Langley Green	d					19 43			20 13					20 43						21 13		21 43	
Birmingham New Street 12	a										20 20							21 20					
	d			19 33						20 04		20 33					21 04						
Birmingham International ✈	d									20 14							21 14						
Coventry	d									20 25							21 25						
Smethwick Galton Bridge 7	d		19 26			19 46			20 16					20 46						21 16		21 46	
The Hawthorns 🚊	d		19 28			19 48			20 18					20 48						21 18		21 48	
Jewellery Quarter 🚊	d		19 32			19 52			20 22					20 52						21 22		21 52	
Birmingham Snow Hill 🚊	a		19 35			19 55			20 25					20 55						21 25		21 55	
	d	19 27	19 37		19 48	19 57			20 27				20 42	20 57						21 27	21 42	21 57	
Birmingham Moor Street	d	19 30	19a39		19 51	20 00			20 30				20 45	21 00					21 17	21 30	21 45	22 00	
Bordesley	d																						
Small Heath	d	19 34				20 04			20 34					21 04						21 34		22 04	
Tyseley	d	19 36				20 06			20 36					21 06						21 36		22 06	
Acocks Green	d					20 09								21 09								22 09	
Olton	d					20 12								21 12								22 12	
Solihull	d				19 59	20 16							20 53	21 16					21 26		21 53	22 16	
Widney Manor	d					20 19								21 19								22 19	
Dorridge	d				20 04	20a24							20 58	21a24					21 31		21 58	22a24	
Lapworth	d																		21 35				
Hatton	d																		21 41				
Warwick Parkway	d				20 14								21 08						21 46		22 08		
Warwick	d				20 17								21 11						21 49		22 11		
Leamington Spa 8	a			20 04	20 21					20 36		20 58	21 16				21 36		21 59		22 16		
	d			20 05	20 21					20 38		21 00	21 16			21 17	21 38				22 16		
Banbury	d			20a22	20 41					20a54		21a17	21 34				21a54				22 34		
London Marylebone 10 ⊖	a				21 51								22 52								23 50		
Spring Road	d	19 39							20 39											21 39			
Hall Green	d	19 42							20 42											21 42			
Yardley Wood	d	19 45							20 45											21 45			
Shirley	d	19 48							20 48											21 48			
Whitlocks End	d	19 51							20 51											21a50			
Wythall	d	19 53							20 53														
Earlswood (West Midlands)	d	19 56							20 56														
The Lakes	d	19x58							20x58														
Wood End	d	20x00							21x00														
Danzey	d	20x03							21x03														
Henley-in-Arden	d	20 08							21 08														
Wootton Wawen	d	20x10							21x10														
Wilmcote	d	20 16							21 16							21 43							
Stratford-upon-Avon	a	20 23							21 23							21 54							

Hereford, Worcester and Stourbridge - Birmingham - Leamington Spa, Marylebone and Stratford-upon-Avon

Network Diagram - see first Page of Table 71

		GW	LM	CH	XC ◇1	CH	CH	LM	CH	LM	LM A	LM B	LM	GW ◇1	LM	CH
Hereford 7	d		20 54								21 29	21 29		21 51	23 00	
Ledbury	a		21 10								21 44	21 44		22 07	23 15	
	d		21 14								21 45	21 45		22 09	23 16	
Colwall	d		21 20								21 51	21 51		22 17	23 22	
Great Malvern	a		21 24								21 55	21 55		22 22	23 26	
	d	21 15	21 25								21 56	21 56		22 22	23 27	
Malvern Link	d	21 18	21 28								21 59	21 59			23 30	
Worcester Foregate Street 7	a	21 27	21 36								22 07	22 07		22 33	23 38	
	d	21 28	21 37								22 10	22 10	22 17	22 34	23 39	
Worcester Shrub Hill 7	a	21 31	21 39										22 19	22 38	23 44	
	d									21 52			22 27			
Droitwich Spa	d									22 00	22 19	22 19	22 35			
Bromsgrove	d										22 28					
Barnt Green	d															
University	d										22 44					
Hartlebury	d															
Kidderminster	d									22 10			22 45			
Blakedown	d									22 15						
Hagley	d									22 19						
Stourbridge Junction 2	d							21 55		22 25			22 55			
Lye	d							21 59		22 29			22 59			
Cradley Heath	d							22 02		22 32			23 02			
Old Hill	d							22 06		22 36			23 06			
Rowley Regis	d							22 10		22 40			23 10			
Langley Green	d							22 13		22 43			23 13			
Birmingham New Street 12	a										22 50	23 01				
	d				22 04											
Birmingham International ✈	d				22 14											
Coventry	d				22 25											
Smethwick Galton Bridge 7	d							22 16		22 46			23 16			
The Hawthorns 🚊	d							22 18		22 48			23 18			
Jewellery Quarter 🚊	d							22 22		22 52			23 22			
Birmingham Snow Hill 🚊	a							22 25		22 55			23 24			
	d						22 15	22 27		22 57			23 25			23 30
Birmingham Moor Street	d						22 18	22 30		23 00			23 28			23 33
Bordesley	d															
Small Heath	d							22 34		23 04			23 32			
Tyseley	d						22 23	22 36		23 06			23 34			23 38
Acocks Green	d						22 26			23 09						23 41
Olton	d						22 29			23 12						23 44
Solihull	d						22 33			23 16						23 48
Widney Manor	d						22 36			23 19						23 51
Dorridge	d						22 40			23 23						23 55
Lapworth	d						22 44			23 27						23 59
Hatton	d			22 17			22 49			23 33						00 05
Warwick Parkway	d						22 54			23 38						00 10
Warwick	d			22 24			22 57		23 34	23 41						00 13
Leamington Spa 8	a			22 28	22 37		23 01		23 37	23 46						00 16
	d				22 38	22 40	23 01		23 38							00 17
Banbury	d				22a54		23a23		23a56							00a38
London Marylebone 10 ⊖	a															
Spring Road	d							22 39					23 37			
Hall Green	d							22 42					23 40			
Yardley Wood	d							22 45					23 43			
Shirley	d							22 48					23 46			
Whitlocks End	d							22a50					23a48			
Wythall	d															
Earlswood (West Midlands)	d															
The Lakes	d															
Wood End	d															
Danzey	d															
Henley-in-Arden	d															
Wootton Wawen	d															
Wilmcote	d															
Stratford-upon-Avon	a					23 11										

A until 23 March

B from 26 March

Table 71

Saturdays

Hereford, Worcester and Stourbridge - Birmingham - Leamington Spa, Marylebone and Stratford-upon-Avon

Network Diagram - see first Page of Table 71

		CH	XC	CH	XC	CH	LM	LM	GW	XC	CH	LM	XC	CH	LM	LM	CH	LM	GW	CH	CH	XC	LM
			◇1 🍴	◇	◇1	◇			◇1 ☕	◇1 🍴	◇		◇1 🍴	🍴					◇1 ☕	◇		◇1 🍴	
Hereford 7	d																		06 17				
Ledbury	a																		06 33				
	d																		06 34				
Colwall	d																		06 41				
Great Malvern	a																		06 46				
	d								05 56							06 21			06 49				
Malvern Link	d								05 59							06 24			06 53				
Worcester Foregate Street 7	a								06 08							06 31			07 02				
	d								06 09							06 33			07 04				
Worcester Shrub Hill 7	a								06 11										07 07				
	d						05 44	06 07							06 25			07 01					07 35
Droitwich Spa	d						05 52	06 15							06 33	06 42		07 09					07 43
Bromsgrove	d															06 51							07 52
Barnt Green	d																						
University	d															07 09							08 09
Hartlebury	d														06 40			07 16					
Kidderminster	d						06 02				06 37				06 46		07 14	07 22					
Blakedown	d						06 07								06 51			07 27					
Hagley	d						06 11								06 54			07 30					
Stourbridge Junction 2	d						06 15				06 45				07 02		07 22	07 35					
Lye	d						06 19								07 06			07 39					
Cradley Heath	d						06 22				06 50				07 09		07 27	07 42					
Old Hill	d						06 26								07 13			07 46					
Rowley Regis	d						06 30				06 56				07 17		07 33	07 50					
Langley Green	d						06 33								07 20			07 53					
Birmingham New Street 12	a							06 48								07 16							08 16
	d		06 04		06 33					07 04			07 33									08 04	
Birmingham International ✈	d		06 14							07 14												08 14	
Coventry	d		06 25							07 25												08 25	
Smethwick Galton Bridge 7	d						06 36				07 02				07 23		07 39	07 56					
The Hawthorns 🚊	d						06 38				07 04				07 25		07 41	07 58					
Jewellery Quarter 🚊	d						06 42								07 29			08 02					
Birmingham Snow Hill 🚊	a						06 45				07 10				07 32		07 50	08 05					
	d	23p30					06 51				07 12	07 20			07 37		07 52	08 07					
Birmingham Moor Street	d	23p33		06 15		06 44	06 54				07 15	07 23		07 33	07 40		07 55	08 10					
Bordesley	d																						
Small Heath	d						06 58					07 27						08 14					
Tyseley	d	23p38					07 00					07 29						08 16					
Acocks Green	d	23p41					07 03								07 45								
Olton	d	23p44					07 06								07 48								
Solihull	d	23p48		06 24		06 52	07 10				07 24			07 42	07 52		08 04						
Widney Manor	d	23p51					07 13								07 55								
Dorridge	d	23p55		06 29		06 57	07a18				07 29			07 50	08a01								
Lapworth	d	23p59		06 33										07 54									
Hatton	d	00 05		06 39										08 00						08 17			
Warwick Parkway	d	00 10		06 44		07 07					07 39			08 05			08 18						
Warwick	d	00 13		06 47							07 43			08 08						08 24			
Leamington Spa 8	a	00 16	06 36	06 51	06 58	07 13				07 36	07 46		07 58	08 17			08 23			08 27		08 36	
	d	00 17	06 38	06 52	07 00	07 13				07 38	07 47		08 00				08 23			08 28	08 31	08 38	
Banbury	d	00a38	06a54	07 09	07a17	07 31				07a54	08 05		08a17				08 44			08 48		08a54	
London Marylebone 10 ⊖	a			08 21		08 31					09 11						09 37			10 09			
Spring Road	d											07 32						08 19					
Hall Green	d											07 35						08 22					
Yardley Wood	d											07 38						08 25					
Shirley	d											07 41						08 28					
Whitlocks End	d											07 44						08a30					
Wythall	d											07 46											
Earlswood (West Midlands)	d											07 49											
The Lakes	d											07x51											
Wood End	d											07x54											
Danzey	d											07x57											
Henley-in-Arden	d											08 03											
Wootton Wawen	d											08x06											
Wilmcote	d											08 11									09 00		
Stratford-upon-Avon	a											08 17									09 11		

Table 71

Saturdays

Hereford, Worcester and Stourbridge - Birmingham - Leamington Spa, Marylebone and Stratford-upon-Avon

Network Diagram - see first Page of Table 71

		CH	LM	LM	LM	LM	GW	XC	CH	LM	LM	XC	CH	LM	LM	GW	LM	XC	CH	CH	CH	LM	LM
		◇					◇1 Ø	◇1 🍴	◇			◇1 🍴	◇			◇1 ☕		◇1 🍴		◇	🍴		
Hereford 7	d						07 10								07 40								
Ledbury	a						07 28								07 56								
	d						07 30								07 58								
Colwall	d						07 37								08 04								
Great Malvern	a						07 42								08 08								
	d					07 32	07 43								08 10	08 43							
Malvern Link	d					07 35	07 46								08 13	08 47							
Worcester Foregate Street 7	a					07 43	07 58								08 21	08 56							
	d					07 46	07 59								08 24	08 58							
Worcester Shrub Hill 7	a						08 02									09 01							
	d													08 15									
Droitwich Spa	d					07 55								08 23	08 33								
Bromsgrove	d														08 42								
Barnt Green	d																						
University	d														08 59								
Hartlebury	d													08 30									
Kidderminster	d			07 46		08 06			08 13					08 36									
Blakedown	d			07 51		08 11								08 41									
Hagley	d			07 54		08 14								08 44									
Stourbridge Junction 2	d			07 59	08 05	08 19			08 26		08 35			08 49			08 55					09 09	
Lye	d				08 09						08 39						08 59						
Cradley Heath	d			08 04	08 12	08 24			08 32		08 42			08 54			09 02					09 14	
Old Hill	d				08 16						08 46						09 06						
Rowley Regis	d			08 10	08 20	08 30			08 37		08 50			09 00			09 10					09 20	
Langley Green	d				08 23						08 53						09 13						
Birmingham New Street 12	a														09 11								
	d							08 33				09 04						09 33					
Birmingham International ✈	d											09 14											
Coventry	d											09 25											
Smethwick Galton Bridge 7	d			08 16	08 26	08 36			08 43		08 56			09 06			09 16					09 26	
The Hawthorns 🚊	d			08 18	08 28	08 38			08 45		08 58			09 08			09 18					09 28	
Jewellery Quarter 🚊	d			08 22	08 32	08 42					09 02			09 12			09 22					09 32	
Birmingham Snow Hill 🚊	a			08 25	08 35	08 45			08 51		09 05			09 15			09 25					09 35	
	d	08 12	08 17	08 27	08 37	08 47			08 52	08 57	09 07		09 12	09 17			09 27					09 37	09 47
Birmingham Moor Street	d	08 15	08 20	08 30	08 40	08 50			08 55	09 00	09 10		09 15	09 20			09 30				09 33	09 40	09 50
Bordesley	d																						
Small Heath	d				08 44						09 14											09 44	
Tyseley	d				08 46						09 16											09 46	
Acocks Green	d		08 25		08 49					09 05				09 25								09 49	
Olton	d		08 28		08 52					09 08				09 28								09 52	
Solihull	d	08 25	08 32		08 56				09 05	09 12			09 23	09 32							09 42	09 56	
Widney Manor	d		08 35		08 59					09 15				09 35								09 59	
Dorridge	d	08 30	08a41		09a04					09a21			09 28	09a41							09 50	10a04	
Lapworth	d																				09 54		
Hatton	d																		09 58		10 00		
Warwick Parkway	d	08 39							09 19				09 38								10 05		
Warwick	d	08 43											09 41						10 04		10 08		
Leamington Spa 8	a	08 47						08 58	09 24			09 36	09 46					09 58	10 08		10 18		
	d	08 47						09 00	09 24			09 38	09 46					10 00	10 08	10 09			
Banbury	d	09 10						09a17	09 44			09a54	10 05					10a17	10 26				
London Marylebone 10 ⊖	a	10 14							10 41				11 11						11 41				
Spring Road	d			08 36		08 56					09 19						09 36						09 56
Hall Green	d			08 39		08 59					09 22						09 39						09 59
Yardley Wood	d			08 42		09 02					09 25						09 42						10 02
Shirley	d			08 45		09 05					09 28						09 45						10 05
Whitlocks End	d			08 48		09a08					09a30						09 48						10a08
Wythall	d			08 50													09 50						
Earlswood (West Midlands)	d			08 53													09 53						
The Lakes	d			08x55													09x55						
Wood End	d			08x58													09x58						
Danzey	d			09x01													10x01						
Henley-in-Arden	d			09 07													10 07						
Wootton Wawen	d			09x10													10x10						
Wilmcote	d			09 15													10 15						
Stratford-upon-Avon	a			09 21													10 21			10 40			

Hereford, Worcester and Stourbridge - Birmingham - Leamington Spa, Marylebone and Stratford-upon-Avon

Network Diagram - see first Page of Table 71

Station		CH	LM	LM	XC	CH	LM	LM	LM	LM	LM	XC	LM	GW	CH	LM	LM	XC	CH	LM	LM	LM
		◇			◇1 ⚲	◇						◇1 ⚲		◇1 ⚲	◇			◇1 ⚲	◇			
Hereford ■7	d							08 40													09 40	
Ledbury	a							08 56													09 56	
	d							08 58													09 58	
Colwall	d							09 04													10 04	
Great Malvern	a							09 09													10 08	
	d						09 00	09 10						09 51							10 10	
Malvern Link	d						09 03	09 13						09 54							10 13	
Worcester Foregate Street ■7	a						09 11	09 22						10 02							10 21	
	d		08 56				09 16	09 24						10 04						10 16	10 24	
Worcester Shrub Hill ■7	a													10 06								
	d										09 47		09 56									
Droitwich Spa	d		09 05				09 25	09 33			09 55		10 04							10 25	10 33	
Bromsgrove	d							09 42					10 13								10 42	
Barnt Green	d																					
University	d							09 59													10 59	
Hartlebury	d																					
Kidderminster	d	09 03	09 16	09 26			09 36			09 56	10 06						10 26			10 36		
Blakedown	d	09 08		09 31			09 41				10 11									10 41		
Hagley	d	09 12		09 34			09 44				10 14									10 44		
Stourbridge Junction ■2	d	09 16	09 25	09 39			09 49		09 55	10 09	10 19					10 25	10 39			10 49		10 55
Lye	d		09 29						09 59							10 29						10 59
Cradley Heath	d	09 21	09 32	09 44			09 54		10 02	10 14	10 24					10 32	10 44			10 54		11 02
Old Hill	d		09 36						10 06							10 36						11 06
Rowley Regis	d	09 27	09 40	09 50			10 00		10 10	10 20	10 30					10 40	10 50			11 00		11 10
Langley Green	d		09 43						10 13							10 43						11 13
Birmingham New Street ■12	a							10 11					10 41								11 11	
	d				10 04							10 33						11 04				
Birmingham International ✈	d				10 14													11 14				
Coventry	d				10 25													11 25				
Smethwick Galton Bridge ■7	d	09 33	09 46	09 56			10 06		10 16	10 26	10 36					10 46	10 56			11 06		11 16
The Hawthorns 🚊	d	09 35	09 48	09 58			10 08		10 18	10 28	10 38					10 48	10 58			11 08		11 18
Jewellery Quarter 🚊	d		09 52	10 02			10 12		10 22	10 32	10 42					10 52	11 02			11 12		11 22
Birmingham Snow Hill 🚊	a	09 42	09 55	10 05			10 15		10 25	10 35	10 45					10 55	11 05			11 15		11 25
	d	09 52	09 57	10 07		10 12	10 17		10 27	10 37	10 47					10 57	11 07		11 12	11 17		11 27
Birmingham Moor Street	d	09 55	10 00	10 10		10 15	10 20		10 30	10 40	10 50				10 55	11 00	11 10		11 15	11 20		11 30
Bordesley	d																					
Small Heath	d			10 14						10 44							11 14					
Tyseley	d			10 16						10 46							11 16					
Acocks Green	d		10 05				10 25			10 49						11 05				11 25		
Olton	d		10 08				10 28			10 52						11 08				11 28		
Solihull	d	10 05	10 12			10 24	10 32			10 56					11 03	11 12			11 23	11 32		
Widney Manor	d		10 15				10 35			10 59						11 15				11 35		
Dorridge	d		10a22			10 30	10a41			11a04						11a22			11 28	11a41		
Lapworth	d																					
Hatton	d																					
Warwick Parkway	d	10 19				10 39									11 14				11 38			
Warwick	d					10 43													11 41			
Leamington Spa ■8	a	10 24			10 36	10 48						10 58			11 19			11 36	11 46			
	d	10 25			10 38	10 48						11 00			11 20			11 38	11 46			
Banbury	d	10 46			10a54	11 09						11a17			11 39			11a54	12 04			
London Marylebone ■10 ⊖	a	11 45				12 14									12 44				13 14			
Spring Road	d			10 19					10 36		10 56						11 19					11 36
Hall Green	d			10 22					10 39		10 59						11 22					11 39
Yardley Wood	d			10 25					10 42		11 02						11 25					11 42
Shirley	d			10 28					10 45		11 05						11 28					11 45
Whitlocks End	d			10a30					10 48		11a08						11a30					11 48
Wythall	d								10 50													11 50
Earlswood (West Midlands)	d								10 53													11 53
The Lakes	d								10x55													11x55
Wood End	d								10x58													11x58
Danzey	d								11x01													12x01
Henley-in-Arden	d								11 07													12 07
Wootton Wawen	d								11x10													12x10
Wilmcote	d								11 15													12 15
Stratford-upon-Avon	a								11 21													12 21

Hereford, Worcester and Stourbridge - Birmingham - Leamington Spa, Marylebone and Stratford-upon-Avon

Network Diagram - see first Page of Table 71

Station		XC	CH	CH	LM	LM	GW	GW	CH	CH	LM	LM	XC	CH	LM	LM	LM	LM	LM	XC	CH	LM	LM
		◇1 ⚲		⚲			■	◇1 ⚲	◇				◇1 ⚲							◇1 ⚲			
Hereford ■7	d															10 40							
Ledbury	a															10 56							
	d															10 58							
Colwall	d															11 04							
Great Malvern	a															11 08							
	d						10 46	10 58								11 10			11 35				
Malvern Link	d						10 48	11 01								11 13			11 37				
Worcester Foregate Street ■7	a						10 56	11 09								11 21			11 45				
	d						10 57	11 11								11 24			11 46				
Worcester Shrub Hill ■7	a						11 00	11 13															
	d					10 47									11 17								
Droitwich Spa	d					10 55									11 25	11 33			11 55				
Bromsgrove	d															11 42							
Barnt Green	d																						
University	d															11 59							
Hartlebury	d																						
Kidderminster	d				10 56	11 06						11 26			11 36			11 56	12 06				12 26
Blakedown	d					11 11									11 41				12 11				
Hagley	d					11 14									11 44				12 14				
Stourbridge Junction ■2	d				11 09	11 19					11 25	11 39			11 49		11 55	12 09	12 19			12 25	12 39
Lye	d										11 29						11 59					12 29	
Cradley Heath	d				11 14	11 24					11 32	11 44			11 54		12 02	12 14	12 24			12 32	12 44
Old Hill	d										11 36						12 06					12 36	
Rowley Regis	d				11 20	11 30					11 40	11 50			12 00		12 10	12 20	12 30			12 40	12 50
Langley Green	d										11 43						12 13					12 43	
Birmingham New Street ■12	a															12 11							
	d	11 33											12 04							12 33			
Birmingham International ✈	d												12 14										
Coventry	d												12 25										
Smethwick Galton Bridge ■7	d				11 26	11 36					11 46	11 56			12 06		12 16	12 26	12 36			12 46	12 56
The Hawthorns 🚊	d				11 28	11 38					11 48	11 58			12 08		12 18	12 28	12 38			12 48	12 58
Jewellery Quarter 🚊	d				11 32	11 42					11 52	12 02			12 12		12 22	12 32	12 42			12 52	13 02
Birmingham Snow Hill 🚊	a				11 35	11 45					11 55	12 05			12 15		12 25	12 35	12 45			12 55	13 05
	d				11 37	11 47					11 57	12 07		12 12	12 17		12 27	12 37	12 47			12 57	13 07
Birmingham Moor Street	d			11 33	11 40	11 50				11 55	12 00	12 10		12 15	12 20		12 30	12 40	12 50		12 55	13 00	13 10
Bordesley	d																						
Small Heath	d				11 44							12 14						12 44					13 14
Tyseley	d				11 46							12 16						12 46					13 16
Acocks Green	d				11 49						12 05				12 25			12 49				13 05	
Olton	d				11 52						12 08				12 28			12 52				13 08	
Solihull	d			11 42	11 56					12 04	12 12			12 23	12 32			12 56			13 05	13 12	
Widney Manor	d				11 59						12 15				12 35			12 59				13 15	
Dorridge	d			11 50	12a04						12a22			12 28	12a41			13a04				13a21	
Lapworth	d			11 54																			
Hatton	d		11 56	12 00																			
Warwick Parkway	d			12 05						12 20				12 38							13 18		
Warwick	d		12 03	12 08										12 41									
Leamington Spa ■8	a	11 58	12 07	12 17						12 25			12 36	12 46						12 59	13 23		
	d	12 00	12 07						12 17	12 26			12 38	12 46						13 02	13 24		
Banbury	d	12a17	12 25							12 48			12a54	13 08						13a19	13 44		
London Marylebone ■10 ⊖	a		13 41							13 45				14 14							14 41		
Spring Road	d					11 56						12 19					12 36		12 56				13 19
Hall Green	d					11 59						12 22					12 39		12 59				13 22
Yardley Wood	d					12 02						12 25					12 42		13 02				13 25
Shirley	d					12 05						12 28					12 45		13 05				13 28
Whitlocks End	d					12a08						12a30					12 48		13a08				13a30
Wythall	d																12 50						
Earlswood (West Midlands)	d																12 53						
The Lakes	d																12x55						
Wood End	d																12x58						
Danzey	d																13x01						
Henley-in-Arden	d																13 07						
Wootton Wawen	d																13x10						
Wilmcote	d								12 42								13 15						
Stratford-upon-Avon	a								12 52								13 21						

Table 71

Saturdays

Hereford, Worcester and Stourbridge - Birmingham - Leamington Spa, Marylebone and Stratford-upon-Avon

Network Diagram - see first Page of Table 71

		XC	CH	LM	LM	GW	LM	CH	XC	CH	LM	LM	GW	CH	CH	LM	LM	XC	CH	LM	LM	LM
		◇1 ✕	◇			◇		◇	◇1 ✕	✕			◇1 A 🚌	◇	◇			◇1 ✕				
Hereford [7]	d				11 40								12 13								12 40	
Ledbury	a				11 56								12 30								12 56	
	d				11 58								12 31								12 58	
Colwall	d				12 04								12 38								13 04	
Great Malvern	a				12 08								12 43								13 08	
	d				12 10								12 44								13 10	
Malvern Link	d				12 13								12 48								13 13	
Worcester Foregate Street [7]	a				12 21								12 58								13 21	
	d			12 16	12 24	12 40						12 46	12 59								13 24	
Worcester Shrub Hill [7]	a					12 42							13 02									
	d																			13 17		
Droitwich Spa	d			12 25	12 33							12 55								13 25	13 33	
Bromsgrove	d				12 42																13 42	
Barnt Green	d																					
University	d				12 59																13 59	
Hartlebury	d																					
Kidderminster	d			12 36							12 56	13 06					13 26			13 36		
Blakedown	d			12 41								13 11								13 41		
Hagley	d			12 44								13 14								13 44		
Stourbridge Junction [2]	d			12 49			12 55				13 09	13 19				13 25	13 39			13 49		13 55
Lye	d						12 59									13 29						13 59
Cradley Heath	d			12 54			13 02				13 14	13 24				13 32	13 44			13 54		14 02
Old Hill	d						13 06									13 36						14 06
Rowley Regis	d			13 00			13 10				13 20	13 30				13 40	13 50			14 00		14 10
Langley Green	d						13 13									13 43						14 13
Birmingham New Street [12]	a				13 11																14 11	
	d	13 04							13 33									14 04				
Birmingham International ✈	d	13 14																14 14				
Coventry	d	13 25																14 25				
Smethwick Galton Bridge [7]	d			13 06			13 16				13 26	13 36				13 46	13 56			14 06		14 16
The Hawthorns 🚊	d			13 08			13 18				13 28	13 38				13 48	13 58			14 08		14 18
Jewellery Quarter 🚊	d			13 12			13 22				13 32	13 42				13 52	14 02			14 12		14 22
Birmingham Snow Hill 🚊	a			13 15			13 25				13 35	13 45				13 55	14 05			14 15		14 25
	d		13 12	13 17			13 27				13 37	13 47				13 57	14 07		14 12	14 17		14 27
Birmingham Moor Street	d		13 15	13 20			13 30			13 33	13 40	13 50			13 55	14 00	14 10		14 15	14 20		14 30
Bordesley	d																					
Small Heath	d										13 44						14 14					
Tyseley	d										13 46						14 16					
Acocks Green	d			13 25							13 49					14 05				14 25		
Olton	d			13 28							13 52					14 08				14 28		
Solihull	d		13 23	13 32						13 42	13 56				14 03	14 12			14 23	14 32		
Widney Manor	d			13 35							13 59					14 15				14 35		
Dorridge	d		13 28	13a41						13 50	14a04					14a22			14 28	14a41		
Lapworth	d									13 54												
Hatton	d							13 42		14 00												
Warwick Parkway	d		13 38							14 05					14 14				14 38			
Warwick	d		13 41					13 50		14 08									14 41			
Leamington Spa [8]	a	13 36	13 46					13 54	13 58	14 16					14 20			14 36	14 46			
	d	13 38	13 46					13 55	14 00					14 17	14 21			14 38	14 46			
Banbury	d	13a54	14 08					14 14	14a17						14 44			14a54	15 08			
London Marylebone [10] ⊖	a		15 15					15 36							15 41				16 14			
Spring Road	d						13 36					13 56					14 19					14 36
Hall Green	d						13 39					13 59					14 22					14 39
Yardley Wood	d						13 42					14 02					14 25					14 42
Shirley	d						13 45					14 05					14 28					14 45
Whitlocks End	d						13 48					14a08					14a30					14 48
Wythall	d						13 50															14 50
Earlswood (West Midlands)	d						13 53															14 53
The Lakes	d						13x55															14x55
Wood End	d						13x58															14x58
Danzey	d						14x01															15x01
Henley-in-Arden	d						14 07															15 07
Wootton Wawen	d						14x10															15x10
Wilmcote	d						14 15															15 15
Stratford-upon-Avon	a						14 21							14 49								15 21

A until 11 February and then from 31 March

Table 71

Saturdays

Hereford, Worcester and Stourbridge - Birmingham - Leamington Spa, Marylebone and Stratford-upon-Avon

Network Diagram - see first Page of Table 71

		LM	LM	XC	CH	LM	LM	XC	CH	LM	LM	LM	CH	XC	CH	CH	LM	LM	GW	GW	CH	LM	LM
				◇1 ✕	◇			◇1 ✕						◇1 ✕		✕			◇1 ✕	◇	◇		
Hereford [7]	d										13 40												
Ledbury	a										13 56												
	d										13 58												
Colwall	d										14 04												
Great Malvern	a										14 08												
	d		13 35								14 10								14 34	14 50			
Malvern Link	d		13 37								14 13								14 37	14 52			
Worcester Foregate Street [7]	a		13 45								14 21								14 55	15 02			
	d		13 46							14 16	14 24								14 57	15 02			
Worcester Shrub Hill [7]	a																		14 59	15 06			
	d																	14 43					
Droitwich Spa	d		13 55							14 25	14 33							14 55					
Bromsgrove	d										14 42												
Barnt Green	d																						
University	d										14 59												
Hartlebury	d																						
Kidderminster	d	13 56	14 06				14 26			14 36							14 56	15 06					15 26
Blakedown	d		14 11							14 41								15 11					15 31
Hagley	d		14 14							14 44								15 14					15 34
Stourbridge Junction [2]	d	14 09	14 19			14 25	14 39			14 49		14 55					15 09	15 19				15 25	15 39
Lye	d					14 29						14 59										15 29	
Cradley Heath	d	14 14	14 24			14 32	14 44			14 54		15 02					15 14	15 24				15 32	15 44
Old Hill	d					14 36						15 06										15 36	
Rowley Regis	d	14 20	14 30			14 40	14 50			15 00		15 10					15 20	15 30				15 40	15 50
Langley Green	d					14 43						15 13										15 43	
Birmingham New Street [12]	a										15 11												
	d			14 33				15 04						15 33									
Birmingham International ✈	d							15 14															
Coventry	d							15 25															
Smethwick Galton Bridge [7]	d	14 26	14 36			14 46	14 56			15 06		15 16					15 26	15 36				15 46	15 56
The Hawthorns 🚊	d	14 28	14 38			14 48	14 58			15 08		15 18					15 28	15 38				15 48	15 58
Jewellery Quarter 🚊	d	14 32	14 42			14 52	15 02			15 12		15 22					15 32	15 42				15 52	16 02
Birmingham Snow Hill 🚊	a	14 35	14 45			14 55	15 05			15 15		15 25					15 35	15 45				15 55	16 05
	d	14 37	14 47			14 57	15 07		15 12	15 17		15 27					15 37	15 47				15 57	16 07
Birmingham Moor Street	d	14 40	14 50		14 55	15 00	15 10		15 15	15 20		15 30				15 33	15 40	15 50			15 55	16 00	16 10
Bordesley	d																						
Small Heath	d	14 44					15 14										15 44						16 14
Tyseley	d	14 46					15 16										15 46						16 16
Acocks Green	d	14 49				15 05				15 25							15 49					16 05	
Olton	d	14 52				15 08				15 28							15 52					16 08	
Solihull	d	14 56			15 03	15 12			15 23	15 32						15 42	15 56				16 03	16 12	
Widney Manor	d	14 59				15 15				15 35							15 59					16 15	
Dorridge	d	15a04				15a21			15 28	15a41						15 50	16a04					16a21	
Lapworth	d															15 54							
Hatton	d												15 44			16 00							
Warwick Parkway	d				15 14				15 38							16 05					16 14		
Warwick	d								15 41				15 51			16 08							
Leamington Spa [8]	a			14 58	15 20			15 36	15 46				15 56	16 00		16 16					16 20		
	d			15 00	15 21			15 38	15 46				15 56	16 02	16 05						16 21		
Banbury	d			15a19	15 45			15a54	16 08				16 15	16a18							16 45		
London Marylebone [10] ⊖	a				16 44				17 14				17 40								17 44		
Spring Road	d		14 56				15 19					15 36						15 56					16 19
Hall Green	d		14 59				15 22					15 39						15 59					16 22
Yardley Wood	d		15 02				15 25					15 42						16 02					16 25
Shirley	d		15 05				15 28					15 45						16 05					16 28
Whitlocks End	d		15a08				15a30					15 48						16a08					16a30
Wythall	d											15 50											
Earlswood (West Midlands)	d											15 53											
The Lakes	d											15x55											
Wood End	d											15x58											
Danzey	d											16x01											
Henley-in-Arden	d											16 07											
Wootton Wawen	d											16x10											
Wilmcote	d											16 15			16 31								
Stratford-upon-Avon	a											16 21			16 42								

Hereford, Worcester and Stourbridge - Birmingham - Leamington Spa, Marylebone and Stratford-upon-Avon

Network Diagram - see first Page of Table 71

		XC	CH	LM	LM	LM	LM	LM	XC	LM	GW	CH	LM	LM	XC	CH	LM	LM	LM	XC	CH	CH	LM
		◇1							◇1		◇1	◇			◇1					◇1			
Hereford 7	d				14 40						15 13							15 40					
Ledbury	a				14 56						15 30							15 56					
	d				14 58						15 31							15 58					
Colwall	d				15 04						15 38							16 04					
Great Malvern	a				15 08						15 43							16 08					
	d				15 10			15 30			15 44							16 10					
Malvern Link	d				15 13			15 32			15 48							16 13					
Worcester Foregate Street 7	a				15 21			15 40			15 58							16 21					
	d			15 16	15 24			15 46			15 59						16 15	16 24					
Worcester Shrub Hill 7	a										16 02												
	d									15 54													
Droitwich Spa	d			15 25	15 33			15 55		16 02							16 24	16 33					
Bromsgrove	d				15 42					16 12								16 42					
Barnt Green	d																						
University	d				15 59													16 59					
Hartlebury	d																16 31						
Kidderminster	d			15 36			15 56	16 06						16 26			16 37						16 56
Blakedown	d			15 41				16 11						16 31			16 42						
Hagley	d			15 44				16 14						16 34			16 45						
Stourbridge Junction 2	d			15 49		15 55	16 09	16 19					16 25	16 39			16 49		16 55				17 09
Lye	d					15 59							16 29						16 59				
Cradley Heath	d			15 54		16 02	16 14	16 24					16 32	16 44			16 54		17 02				17 14
Old Hill	d					16 06							16 36						17 06				
Rowley Regis	d			16 00		16 10	16 20	16 30					16 40	16 50			17 00		17 10				17 20
Langley Green	d					16 13							16 43						17 13				
Birmingham New Street 12	a				16 11					16 45								17 11					
	d	16 04							16 33						17 04					17 33			
Birmingham International ✈	d	16 14													17 14								
Coventry	d	16 25													17 25								
Smethwick Galton Bridge 7	d			16 06		16 16	16 26	16 36					16 46	16 56			17 06		17 16				17 26
The Hawthorns	d			16 08		16 18	16 28	16 38					16 48	16 58			17 08		17 18				17 28
Jewellery Quarter	d			16 12		16 22	16 32	16 42					16 52	17 02			17 12		17 22				17 32
Birmingham Snow Hill	a			16 15		16 25	16 35	16 45					16 55	17 05			17 16		17 25				17 35
	d		16 12	16 17		16 27	16 37	16 47					16 57	17 07		17 12	17 17		17 27				17 37
Birmingham Moor Street	d		16 15	16 20		16 30	16 40	16 50				16 55	17 00	17 10		17 15	17 20		17 30			17 33	17 40
Bordesley	d																						
Small Heath	d						16 44	16 54						17 14									17 44
Tyseley	d					16 34	16 46	16 56					17 04	17 16					17 34				17 46
Acocks Green	d			16 25			16 49						17 07				17 25						17 49
Olton	d			16 28			16 52						17 10				17 28						17 52
Solihull	d		16 23	16 32			16 56					17 02	17 14			17 23	17 32					17 42	17 56
Widney Manor	d			16 35			16 59						17 17				17 35						17 59
Dorridge	d		16 28	16a41			17a04						17a22			17 28	17a41					17 50	18a04
Lapworth	d																					17 54	
Hatton	d																					18 00	
Warwick Parkway	d		16 38									17 14				17 38						18 05	
Warwick	d		16 41													17 41					18 01	18 08	
Leamington Spa 8	a	16 36	16 46						16 59			17 20			17 36	17 46				18 00	18 05	18 17	
	d	16 38	16 46						17 00			17 21			17 38	17 46				18 02	18 06		
Banbury	d	16a54	17 08						17a17			17 44			17a54	18 06				18a18	18 23		
London Marylebone 10 ⊖	a		18 14									18 44				19 11					19 17		
Spring Road	d					16 37		16 59						17 19					17 37				
Hall Green	d					16 40		17 02						17 22					17 40				
Yardley Wood	d					16 43		17 05						17 25					17 43				
Shirley	d					16 46		17 08						17 28					17 46				
Whitlocks End	d					16 49		17a11						17 31					17a49				
Wythall	d					16 51								17 33									
Earlswood (West Midlands)	d					16 54								17 36									
The Lakes	d					16x56								17x38									
Wood End	d					16x59								17x41									
Danzey	d					17x02								17x44									
Henley-in-Arden	d					17 07								17 49									
Wootton Wawen	d					17x10								17x52									
Wilmcote	d					17 16								17 58									
Stratford-upon-Avon	a					17 22								18 04									

Hereford, Worcester and Stourbridge - Birmingham - Leamington Spa, Marylebone and Stratford-upon-Avon

Network Diagram - see first Page of Table 71

		LM	GW	GW	CH	CH	LM	LM	LM	LM	XC	LM	XC	CH	LM	GW	LM	XC	CH	LM	LM	GW
			◇1 A								◇1		◇1	◇		◇1		◇1				◇1
Hereford 7	d											16 40									17 40	
Ledbury	a											16 56									17 56	
	d											16 58									17 58	
Colwall	d											17 04									18 04	
Great Malvern	a											17 08									18 08	
	d		16ʃ34	16 50								17 10				17 49				18 00	18 10	18 35
Malvern Link	d		16ʃ37	16 52								17 13				17 52				18 02	18 13	18 38
Worcester Foregate Street 7	a		16ʃ52	17 04								17 21				18 00				18 10	18 21	18 46
	d		16ʃ54	17 04								17 24			17 48	18 02				18 11	18 24	18 48
Worcester Shrub Hill 7	a		16ʃ56	17 07												18 04				18 13		18 50
	d	16 47							17 15											18 17		
Droitwich Spa	d	16 55							17 23			17 35			17 57					18 25	18 33	
Bromsgrove	d											17 44									18 42	
Barnt Green	d																					
University	d											17 59									18 59	
Hartlebury	d								17 30													
Kidderminster	d	17 06						17 26	17 36						18 07					18 36		
Blakedown	d	17 11						17 31	17 41						18 12					18 41		
Hagley	d	17 14						17 34	17 44						18 16					18 44		
Stourbridge Junction 2	d	17 19					17 25	17 39	17 49	17 55					18 20		18 27			18 49		
Lye	d						17 29			17 59							18 30					
Cradley Heath	d	17 24					17 32	17 44	17 54	18 02					18 25		18 33			18 54		
Old Hill	d						17 36			18 06							18 37					
Rowley Regis	d	17 30					17 40	17 50	18 00	18 10					18 31		18 41			19 00		
Langley Green	d						17 43			18 13							18 44					
Birmingham New Street 12	a											18 11									19 11	
	d										18 04		18 33					19 04				
Birmingham International ✈	d										18 14							19 14				
Coventry	d										18 25							19 25				
Smethwick Galton Bridge 7	d	17 36					17 46	17 56	18 06	18 16					18 37		18 47			19 06		
The Hawthorns	d	17 38					17 48	17 58	18 08	18 18					18 39		18 50			19 08		
Jewellery Quarter	d	17 42					17 52	18 02	18 12	18 22					18 43		18 53			19 12		
Birmingham Snow Hill	a	17 45					17 55	18 05	18 15	18 25					18 46		18 56			19 15		
	d	17 47					17 57	18 07	18 17	18 27				18 42	18 47		18 57			19 17		
Birmingham Moor Street	d	17 50				17 55	18 00	18 10	18 20	18 30				18 45	18 50		19 00		19 09	19 20		
Bordesley	d																					
Small Heath	d	17 54						18 14	18 24						18 54		19 04			19 24		
Tyseley	d	17 56						18 16	18 26						18 56		19 06			19 26		
Acocks Green	d						18 05		18 29						18 59					19 29		
Olton	d						18 08		18 32						19 02					19 32		
Solihull	d					18 03	18 12		18 36					18 53	19 06				19 19	19 36		
Widney Manor	d						18 15		18 39						19 09					19 39		
Dorridge	d						18a22		18a44					18 58	19a14				19 24	19a44		
Lapworth	d																		19 28			
Hatton	d																		19 33			
Warwick Parkway	d					18 14								19 08					19 38			
Warwick	d					18 18								19 11					19 41			
Leamington Spa 8	a					18 22					18 36		18 58	19 16				19 36	19 46			
	d				18 19	18 23					18 38		19 00	19 16				19 38				
Banbury	d					18 45					18a54		19a17	19 34				19a54				
London Marylebone 10 ⊖	a					19 45								20 40								
Spring Road	d	17 59						18 19		18 36							19 09					
Hall Green	d	18 02						18 22		18 39							19 12					
Yardley Wood	d	18 05						18 25		18 42							19 15					
Shirley	d	18 08						18 28		18 45							19 18					
Whitlocks End	d	18 11						18a30		18 48							19a21					
Wythall	d	18 13								18 50												
Earlswood (West Midlands)	d	18 16								18 53												
The Lakes	d	18x18								18x55												
Wood End	d	18x21								18x58												
Danzey	d	18x24								19x01												
Henley-in-Arden	d	18 30								19 07												
Wootton Wawen	d	18x33								19x10												
Wilmcote	d	18 38			18 45					19 15												
Stratford-upon-Avon	a	18 45			18 59					19 21												

A until 11 February and then from 31 March

Table 71

Saturdays

Hereford, Worcester and Stourbridge - Birmingham - Leamington Spa, Marylebone and Stratford-upon-Avon

Network Diagram - see first Page of Table 71

		LM	CH ◇	XC ◇1	CH ◇	LM	GW	CH	LM	XC ◇1	CH ◇	LM	GW ◇1	CH A	XC ◇1	LM	CH	CH ◇ B	CH ◇ C	CH ◇ D	LM	LM	GW ◇1
Hereford 7	d											19 11				20 00							20 20
Ledbury	a											19 27				20 15							20 36
	d											19 28				20 16							20 40
Colwall	d											19 34				20 22							20 47
Great Malvern	a											19 39				20 26							20 52
	d						18 50					19 39				20 28							20 53
Malvern Link	d						18 52					19 42				20 31							20 57
Worcester Foregate Street 7	a						19 03					19 51				20 39							21 09
	d					18 51	19 03					19 51	20 02			20 41							21 11
Worcester Shrub Hill 7	a						19 06						20 05										21 14
	d																					20 52	
Droitwich Spa	d					19 00						20 00				20 50						21 00	
Bromsgrove	d															20 59							
Barnt Green	d																						
University	d															21 14							
Hartlebury	d					19 07																	
Kidderminster	d					19 13			19 40			20 10										21 10	
Blakedown	d					19 18			19 45			20 15										21 15	
Hagley	d					19 21			19 49			20 19										21 19	
Stourbridge Junction 2	d	18 55				19 25			19 55			20 25									20 55	21 25	
Lye	d	18 59				19 29			19 59			20 29									20 59	21 29	
Cradley Heath	d	19 02				19 32			20 02			20 32									21 02	21 32	
Old Hill	d	19 06				19 36			20 06			20 36									21 06	21 36	
Rowley Regis	d	19 10				19 40			20 10			20 40									21 10	21 40	
Langley Green	d	19 13				19 43			20 13			20 43									21 13	21 43	
Birmingham New Street 12	a															21 21							
	d			19 33						20 04					21 04								
Birmingham International ✈	d									20 14					21 14								
Coventry	d									20 25					21 25								
Smethwick Galton Bridge 7	d	19 16				19 46			20 16			20 46									21 16	21 46	
The Hawthorns	d	19 18				19 48			20 18			20 48									21 18	21 48	
Jewellery Quarter	d	19 22				19 52			20 22			20 52									21 22	21 52	
Birmingham Snow Hill	a	19 25				19 55			20 25			20 55									21 25	21 55	
	d	19 27			19 42	19 57			20 27		20 42	20 57						21 20	21 20	21 20	21 27	21 57	
Birmingham Moor Street	d	19 30			19 45	20 00			20 30		20 45	21 00						21 23	21 23	21 23	21 30	22 00	
Bordesley	d																						
Small Heath	d	19 34				20 04			20 34			21 04									21 34	22 04	
Tyseley	d	19 36				20 06			20 36			21 06									21 36	22 06	
Acocks Green	d					20 09						21 09										22 09	
Olton	d					20 12						21 12										22 12	
Solihull	d				19 53	20 16					20 53	21 16						21 31	21 31	21 31		22 16	
Widney Manor	d					20 19						21 19						21 34	21 34	21 34		22 19	
Dorridge	d				19 58	20a24					20 58	21a24						21 38	21 38	21 38		22a24	
Lapworth	d										21 02							21 42	21 42	21 42			
Hatton	d		19 37								21 08							21 48	21 48	21 48			
Warwick Parkway	d				20 08						21 13							21 53	21 53	21 53			
Warwick	d		19 45		20 11						21 16						21 35	21 56	21 56	21 56			
Leamington Spa 8	a		19 50	20 01	20 16					20 36	21 21				21 36		21 45	22 01	22 02	22 01			
	d		19 51	20 03	20 16			20 29		20 38	21 21			21 30	21 38					22 02			
Banbury	d		20 10	20a19	20 34					20a54	21 39			22a10	21a54					22 19			
London Marylebone 10 ⊖	a		21 44		21 47						22 58									23 33			
Spring Road	d	19 39							20 39												21 39		
Hall Green	d	19 42							20 42												21 42		
Yardley Wood	d	19 45							20 45												21 45		
Shirley	d	19 48							20 48												21 48		
Whitlocks End	d	19 51							20 51												21a50		
Wythall	d	19 53							20 53														
Earlswood (West Midlands)	d	19 56							20 56														
The Lakes	d	19x58							20x58														
Wood End	d	20x00							21x00														
Danzey	d	20x03							21x03														
Henley-in-Arden	d	20 08							21 08														
Wootton Wawen	d	20x10							21x10														
Wilmcote	d	20 16						20 55	21 16														
Stratford-upon-Avon	a	20 23						21 05	21 23														

A from 7 January until 24 March
B from 7 January until 11 February
C from 18 February until 24 March
D until 31 December and then from 31 March

Table 71

Saturdays

Hereford, Worcester and Stourbridge - Birmingham - Leamington Spa, Marylebone and Stratford-upon-Avon

Network Diagram - see first Page of Table 71

		GW	CH A	CH A	CH B	CH C	CH D	LM	LM	LM	LM	CH A	LM	GW 1	LM
Hereford 7	d									21 35					22 50
Ledbury	a									21 50					23 05
	d									21 51					23 06
Colwall	d									21 57					23 12
Great Malvern	a									22 02					23 16
	d	21 15							21 30	22 05				22 41	23 17
Malvern Link	d	21 17							21 32	22 08				22 44	23 20
Worcester Foregate Street 7	a	21 27							21 41	22 17				22 51	23 27
	d	21 27							21 42	22 18				22 53	23 28
Worcester Shrub Hill 7	a	21 30							21 44	22 20				22 55	23 34
	d								21 52				22 47		
Droitwich Spa	d								22 00				22 55		
Bromsgrove	d														
Barnt Green	d														
University	d														
Hartlebury	d														
Kidderminster	d								22 10				23 05		
Blakedown	d								22 15				23 10		
Hagley	d								22 19				23 14		
Stourbridge Junction 2	d							21 55	22 25		22 55		23 18		
Lye	d							21 59	22 29		22 59				
Cradley Heath	d							22 02	22 32		23 02				
Old Hill	d							22 06	22 36		23 06				
Rowley Regis	d							22 10	22 40		23 10				
Langley Green	d							22 13	22 43		23 13				
Birmingham New Street 12	a														
	d														
Birmingham International ✈	d														
Coventry	d														
Smethwick Galton Bridge 7	d							22 16	22 46		23 16				
The Hawthorns	d							22 18	22 48		23 18				
Jewellery Quarter	d							22 22	22 52		23 22				
Birmingham Snow Hill	a							22 25	22 55		23 25		23 36		
	d				22 15	22 15	22 15	22 27	22 57		23 27		23 37		
Birmingham Moor Street	d				22 18	22 18	22 18	22 30	23 00		23 30		23 40		
Bordesley	d														
Small Heath	d							22 34	23 04		23 34		23 44		
Tyseley	d				22 23	22 23	22 23	22 36	23 06		23 36		23 46		
Acocks Green	d				22 26	22 26	22 26		23 09				23 49		
Olton	d				22 29	22 29	22 29		23 12				23 52		
Solihull	d				22 33	22 33	22 33		23 16				23 56		
Widney Manor	d				22 36	22 36	22 36		23 19				23 59		
Dorridge	d				22 40	22 40	22 40		23a24				00 03		
Lapworth	d				22 44	22 44	22 44						00 07		
Hatton	d				22 49	22 49	22 49						00 13		
Warwick Parkway	d				22 54	22 54	22 54						00 18		
Warwick	d				22 57	22 57	22 57						00 21		
Leamington Spa 8	a				23 02	23 03	23 04						00 26		
	d		22 10	22 10	23 02							23 15			
Banbury	d		22 40	22 40	23a23							23a45			
London Marylebone 10 ⊖	a		00 10	01 55											
Spring Road	d							22 39			23 39				
Hall Green	d							22 42			23 42				
Yardley Wood	d							22 45			23 45				
Shirley	d							22 48			23 48				
Whitlocks End	d							22a50			23a50				
Wythall	d														
Earlswood (West Midlands)	d														
The Lakes	d														
Wood End	d														
Danzey	d														
Henley-in-Arden	d														
Wootton Wawen	d														
Wilmcote	d														
Stratford-upon-Avon	a														

A from 7 January until 24 March
B until 31 December and then from 31 March
C from 7 January until 11 February
D from 18 February until 24 March

Hereford, Worcester and Stourbridge - Birmingham - Leamington Spa, Marylebone and Stratford-upon-Avon

Network Diagram - see first Page of Table 71

		LM	CH	XC	CH	LM	CH	XC	CH	LM		GW	CH	LM	CH	XC	CH	LM	CH	LM		XC	CH	LM	GW
		A	◇	◇1	◇			◇1	◇			◇1	◇			◇1	◇					◇1			◇1
Hereford 7	d																								
Ledbury	a																								
	d																								
Colwall	d																								
Great Malvern	a																								
	d									09 03		09 20						10 02						10 56	11 15
Malvern Link	d									09 06		09 23						10 04						10 58	11 18
Worcester Foregate Street 7	a									09 15		09 30						10 12						11 06	11 26
	d									09 15		09 31						10 16						11 20	11 27
Worcester Shrub Hill 7	a									09 18		09 33						10 18							11 29
	d	22p47								09 23								10 22							
Droitwich Spa	d	22p55								09 32								10 30						11 29	
Bromsgrove	d																								
Barnt Green	d																								
University	d																								
Hartlebury	d																								
Kidderminster	d	23p05								09 42				10 08				10 40						11 39	
Blakedown	d	23p10								09 47				10 13											
Hagley	d	23p14								09 51				10 17				10 47						11 46	
Stourbridge Junction 2	d	23p18								09 55				10 22				10 52		11 22				11 52	
Lye	d													10 25						11 25					
Cradley Heath	d									10 01				10 29				10 58		11 29				11 58	
Old Hill	d													10 33						11 33					
Rowley Regis	d									10 06				10 36				11 03		11 36				12 03	
Langley Green	d													10 39						11 39					
Birmingham New Street 12	a																								
	d			09 04				10 04								11 04						12 04			
Birmingham International ✈	d			09 14				10 14								11 14						12 14			
Coventry	d			09 25				10 25								11 25						12 25			
Smethwick Galton Bridge 7	d									10 12				10 43				11 09		11 43				12 08	
The Hawthorns	d									10 15				10 45				11 12		11 45				12 11	
Jewellery Quarter	d									10 18				10 49				11 15		11 49				12 14	
Birmingham Snow Hill	a	23p36								10 20				10 52				11 17		11 52				12 17	
	d	23p37				09 19	09 40			10 22			10 40	10 53				11 19	11 40	11 53				12 19	
Birmingham Moor Street	d	23p40	08 55		09 13	09 22	09 43		10 13	10 25			10 43	10 56			11 13	11 22	11 43	11 56			12 13	12 22	
Bordesley	d																								
Small Heath	d	23p44																							
Tyseley	d	23p46				09 26				10 29								11 26						12 26	
Acocks Green	d	23p49												11 02						12 02					
Olton	d	23p52												11 04						12 04					
Solihull	d	23p56	09 04		09 22		09 52		10 21				10 52	11 08			11 21		11 51	12 08			12 21		
Widney Manor	d	23p59												11 11						12 11					
Dorridge	d	00 03	09 09		09 27		09 57		10 26				10 57	11a17			11 26		11 56	12a17			12 26		
Lapworth	d	00 07											11 01												
Hatton	d	00 13											11 06												
Warwick Parkway	d	00 18	09 18		09 35		10 06		10 35				11 11				11 35		12 06				12 35		
Warwick	d	00 21	09 22		09 40				10 39								11 39						12 39		
Leamington Spa 8	a	00 26	09 26	09 36	09 44		10 13	10 36	10 44				11 16			11 36	11 43		12 12			12 36	12 43		
	d		09 27	09 38	09 45		10 14	10 38	10 44				11 18		11 20	11 38	11 43		12 13			12 38	12 43		
Banbury	d		09 44	09a54	10 02		10 31	10a54	11 06				11 35			11a54	12 01		12 30			12a54	13 01		
London Marylebone 10 ⊖	a		10 47		11 09		11 44		12 12				12 40				13 12		13 37				14 12		
Spring Road	d					09 29				10 32								11 29						12 29	
Hall Green	d					09 32				10 35								11 32						12 32	
Yardley Wood	d					09 35				10 38								11 35						12 35	
Shirley	d					09 38				10 41								11 38						12 38	
Whitlocks End	d					09 41				10 44								11 41						12 41	
Wythall	d					09 43				10 46								11 43						12 43	
Earlswood (West Midlands)	d																								
The Lakes	d					09x46				10x49								11x46						12x46	
Wood End	d																								
Danzey	d																								
Henley-in-Arden	d					09 54				10 57								11 54						12 54	
Wootton Wawen	d																								
Wilmcote	d					10 04				11 05					11 42			12 02						13 02	
Stratford-upon-Avon	a					10 09				11 12					11 54			12 09						13 09	

A not 11 December

Hereford, Worcester and Stourbridge - Birmingham - Leamington Spa, Marylebone and Stratford-upon-Avon

Network Diagram - see first Page of Table 71

		XC	CH	LM	CH	XC		CH	LM	XC	CH	LM	CH	XC	CH	LM		GW	XC	CH	LM	CH	XC	CH	LM
		◇1				◇1		◇		◇1			◇	◇1	◇			◇1	◇1			◇	◇1		
Hereford 7	d																								
Ledbury	a																								
	d																								
Colwall	d																								
Great Malvern	a																								
	d								12 04									13 15							
Malvern Link	d								12 06									13 18							
Worcester Foregate Street 7	a								12 15									13 25							
	d								12 16							13 20		13 26							14 20
Worcester Shrub Hill 7	a								12 18									13 29							
	d								12 24																
Droitwich Spa	d								12 32							13 29									14 29
Bromsgrove	d																								
Barnt Green	d																								
University	d																								
Hartlebury	d																								
Kidderminster	d								12 42							13 39									14 39
Blakedown	d								12 47																14 44
Hagley	d								12 51							13 46									14 48
Stourbridge Junction 2	d			12 22					12 55			13 22				13 52					14 22				14 52
Lye	d			12 25								13 25									14 25				
Cradley Heath	d			12 29					13 01			13 29				13 58					14 29				14 58
Old Hill	d			12 33								13 33									14 33				
Rowley Regis	d			12 36					13 06			13 36				14 03					14 36				15 03
Langley Green	d			12 39								13 39									14 39				
Birmingham New Street 12	a																								
	d	12 33				13 04				13 33				14 04					14 33				15 04		
Birmingham International ✈	d					13 14								14 14									15 14		
Coventry	d					13 25								14 25									15 25		
Smethwick Galton Bridge 7	d			12 43					13 11			13 43				14 08					14 43				15 08
The Hawthorns	d			12 45					13 14			13 45				14 11					14 45				15 11
Jewellery Quarter	d			12 49					13 17			13 49				14 14					14 49				15 14
Birmingham Snow Hill	a			12 52					13 20			13 52				14 17					14 52				15 17
	d		12 40	12 53					13 22		13 40	13 53				14 19				14 40	14 53				15 19
Birmingham Moor Street	d		12 43	12 56				13 11	13 25		13 43	13 56			14 13	14 22				14 43	14 56			15 13	15 22
Bordesley	d																								
Small Heath	d																								
Tyseley	d								13 29							14 26									15 26
Acocks Green	d			13 02								14 02									15 02				
Olton	d			13 04								14 04									15 04				
Solihull	d		12 50	13 08				13 20			13 51	14 08			14 21					14 51	15 08			15 21	
Widney Manor	d			13 11								14 11									15 11				
Dorridge	d		12 56	13a18				13 25			13 56	14a17			14 26					14 56	15a17			15 26	
Lapworth	d										14 00														
Hatton	d										14 06		14 15												
Warwick Parkway	d		13 06					13 34			14 11				14 37					15 05				15 37	
Warwick	d							13 39					14 22		14 39									15 40	
Leamington Spa 8	a	12 59	13 11			13 36		13 43		13 59	14 17		14 26	14 36	14 44				14 59	15 10			15 36	15 44	
	d	13 00	13 11		13 20	13 38		13 43		14 00	14 17		14 26	14 38	14 44				15 00	15 11		15 20	15 38	15 45	
Banbury	d	13a17	13 29			13a54		14 05		14a17	14 35		14 45	14a54	15 04				15a18	15 30			15a54	16 05	
London Marylebone 10 ⊖	a		14 38					15 12			15 46		16 08		16 12					16 45				17 13	
Spring Road	d								13 32							14 29									15 29
Hall Green	d								13 35							14 32									15 32
Yardley Wood	d								13 38							14 35									15 35
Shirley	d								13 41							14 38									15 38
Whitlocks End	d								13 44							14 40									15 41
Wythall	d								13 46							14 43									15 43
Earlswood (West Midlands)	d																								
The Lakes	d								13x49							14x46									15x46
Wood End	d																								
Danzey	d																								
Henley-in-Arden	d								13 57							14 54									15 54
Wootton Wawen	d																								
Wilmcote	d				13 42				14 05							15 02						15 42			16 02
Stratford-upon-Avon	a				13 54				14 12							15 07						15 54			16 09

Hereford, Worcester and Stourbridge - Birmingham - Leamington Spa, Marylebone and Stratford-upon-Avon

Network Diagram - see first Page of Table 71

		GW	XC	LM	CH	LM	CH	XC	CH	LM	GW	LM	XC	CH	LM	CH	XC	LM	CH	LM	GW	XC
		◇1	◇1				◇	◇1			◇1		◇1			◇	◇1				◇1	◇1
Hereford 7	d	13 32									14 32							15 30			16 35	
Ledbury	a	13 49									14 49							15 47			16 51	
	d	13 50									14 55							15 51			16 52	
Colwall	d	13 57									15 02							15 58			17 00	
Great Malvern	a	14 02									15 07							16 02			17 04	
	d	14 11		14 35							15 08							16 03			17 05	
Malvern Link	d	14 15		14 37							15 12							16 05			17 09	
Worcester Foregate Street 7	a	14 24		14 45							15 21							16 14			17 20	
	d	14 26		14 45						15 20	15 23							16 15		16 20	17 22	
Worcester Shrub Hill 7	a	14 29		14 48							15 26							16 18			17 27	
	d			14 53								15 46						16 33				
Droitwich Spa	d			15 01						15 29		15 54						16 41		16 29		
Bromsgrove	d			15 10														16 51				
Barnt Green	d																					
University	d																					
Hartlebury	d																					
Kidderminster	d									15 40		16 04								16 39		
Blakedown	d																					
Hagley	d									15 47		16 11								16 46		
Stourbridge Junction 2	d					15 22				15 52		16 16			16 22					16 52		
Lye	d					15 25									16 25							
Cradley Heath	d					15 29				15 58					16 29					16 58		
Old Hill	d					15 33									16 33							
Rowley Regis	d					15 36				16 03					16 36					17 03		
Langley Green	d					15 39									16 39							
Birmingham New Street 12	a			15 37														17 17				
	d		15 33					16 04					16 33				17 04					17 33
Birmingham International ✈	d							16 14									17 14					
Coventry	d							16 25									17 25					
Smethwick Galton Bridge 7	d					15 43				16 08		16 29			16 43					17 08		
The Hawthorns	d					15 45				16 11					16 45					17 11		
Jewellery Quarter	d					15 49				16 14					16 49					17 14		
Birmingham Snow Hill	a					15 52				16 17		16 35			16 52					17 17		
	d				15 40	15 53				16 19		16 45		16 40	16 53					17 19		
Birmingham Moor Street	d				15 43	15 56			16 13	16 22		16a47		16 43	16 56				17 13	17 22		
Bordesley	d																					
Small Heath	d																					
Tyseley	d									16 26										17 26		
Acocks Green	d					16 02									17 02							
Olton	d					16 04									17 04							
Solihull	d				15 51	16 08			16 21					16 51	17 08				17 21			
Widney Manor	d					16 11									17 11							
Dorridge	d				15 56	16a17			16 26					16 56	17a17				17 26			
Lapworth	d				16 00																	
Hatton	d				16 06		16 14															
Warwick Parkway	d				16 11				16 37					17 05					17 36			
Warwick	d						16 23		16 40										17 40			
Leamington Spa 8	a		15 59		16 17		16 26	16 36	16 44				16 59	17 12			17 36		17 44			18 00
	d		16 00		16 17		16 27	16 38	16 45				17 00	17 12		17 20	17 38		17 45			18 01
Banbury	d		16a17		16 35		16 46	16a54	17 05				17a17	17 30			17a54		18 05			18a19
London Marylebone 10 ⊖	a				17 46		18 08		18 12					18 45					19 13			
Spring Road	d									16 29										17 29		
Hall Green	d									16 32										17 32		
Yardley Wood	d									16 35										17 35		
Shirley	d									16 38										17 38		
Whitlocks End	d									16 41										17 41		
Wythall	d									16 43										17 43		
Earlswood (West Midlands)	d																					
The Lakes	d									16x46										17x46		
Wood End	d																					
Danzey	d																					
Henley-in-Arden	d									16 55										17 54		
Wootton Wawen	d																					
Wilmcote	d									17 03						17 42				18 02		
Stratford-upon-Avon	a									17 10						17 54				18 09		

Hereford, Worcester and Stourbridge - Birmingham - Leamington Spa, Marylebone and Stratford-upon-Avon

Network Diagram - see first Page of Table 71

		CH	LM	CH	XC	CH	LM	LM	XC	CH	CH	XC	CH	LM	GW	GW	XC	CH	XC	CH	LM	XC	LM
				◇	◇1	◇			◇1		◇	◇1			◇1	◇1	◇1	◇	◇1	◇		◇1	
Hereford 7	d															18 30							
Ledbury	a															18 47							
	d															18 48							
Colwall	d															18 55							
Great Malvern	a															19 00							
	d							17 17								19 11							
Malvern Link	d							17 20								19 14							
Worcester Foregate Street 7	a							17 28								19 23							
	d						17 20	17 28						18 20	18 25	19 25							
Worcester Shrub Hill 7	a							17 31							18 26	19 26							
	d							17 36													19 38		19 53
Droitwich Spa	d						17 29	17 44						18 29							19 46		20 01
Bromsgrove	d							17 53															20 10
Barnt Green	d																						
University	d																						
Hartlebury	d																						
Kidderminster	d						17 39							18 39							19 56		
Blakedown	d						17 44																
Hagley	d						17 48							18 46							20 03		
Stourbridge Junction 2	d		17 22				17 52							18 52							20 07		
Lye	d		17 25																				
Cradley Heath	d		17 29				17 58							18 58							20 13		
Old Hill	d		17 33																				
Rowley Regis	d		17 36				18 03							19 03							20 19		
Langley Green	d		17 39																				
Birmingham New Street 12	a							18 15															20 36
	d				18 04				18 33			19 04					19 33		20 04			20 33	
Birmingham International ✈	d				18 14							19 14							20 14				
Coventry	d				18 25							19 25							20 25				
Smethwick Galton Bridge 7	d		17 43				18 08							19 08							20 24		
The Hawthorns	d		17 45				18 11							19 11							20 26		
Jewellery Quarter	d		17 49				18 14							19 14							20 30		
Birmingham Snow Hill	a		17 53				18 17							19 19							20 33		
	d	17 40	17 53				18 19			18 40			19 15	19 21						20 15	20 33		
Birmingham Moor Street	d	17 43	17 56			18 13	18 22			18 43			19 18	19a23						20 18	20a36		
Bordesley	d																						
Small Heath	d																						
Tyseley	d						18 26																
Acocks Green	d		18 02																				
Olton	d		18 04																				
Solihull	d	17 51	18 08			18 21				18 51			19 26							20 28			
Widney Manor	d		18 11										19 29							20 31			
Dorridge	d	17 56	18a17			18 26				18 56			19 33							20 35			
Lapworth	d	18 00											19 37										
Hatton	d	18 06		18 14									19 43					20 15					
Warwick Parkway	d	18 11				18 36				19 05			19 47							20 45			
Warwick	d			18 22		18 40							19 51					20 21		20 48			
Leamington Spa 8	a	18 17		18 26	18 36	18 44			18 59	19 11		19 36	19 56				19 59	20 25	20 36	20 53		20 58	
	d	18 17		18 26	18 38	18 45			19 00	19 11	19 20	19 38	19 56				20 00	20 26	20 38	20 53		21 00	
Banbury	d	18 35		18 45	18a54	19 05			19a17	19 29		19a54	20 14				20a18	20 46	20a54	21 12		21a17	
London Marylebone 10 ⊖	a	19 45		20 08		20 12				20 45			21 46					21 53		22 50			
Spring Road	d						18 29																
Hall Green	d						18 32																
Yardley Wood	d						18 35																
Shirley	d						18 38																
Whitlocks End	d						18 41																
Wythall	d						18 43																
Earlswood (West Midlands)	d																						
The Lakes	d						18x46																
Wood End	d																						
Danzey	d																						
Henley-in-Arden	d						18 54																
Wootton Wawen	d																						
Wilmcote	d						19 02				19 42												
Stratford-upon-Avon	a						19 09				19 54												

Table 71

Sundays
until 1 January

Hereford, Worcester and Stourbridge - Birmingham - Leamington Spa, Marylebone and Stratford-upon-Avon

Network Diagram - see first Page of Table 71

Station		GW ◇1	XC ◇1	CH ◇	LM	LM	LM	LM
Hereford 7	d					20 05		
Ledbury	a					20 21		
	d					20 22		
Colwall	d					20 28		
Great Malvern	a					20 33		
	d	20 15				20 33		22 10
Malvern Link	d	20 18				20 36		22 13
Worcester Foregate Street 7	a	20 25				20 44		22 22
	d	20 26				20 45		22 23
Worcester Shrub Hill 7	a	20 29				20 47		22 25
	d				20 34	20 52	21 25	22 29
Droitwich Spa	d				20 42	21 00	21 33	22 37
Bromsgrove	d					21 09		
Barnt Green	d							
University	d							
Hartlebury	d							
Kidderminster	d				20 52		21 43	22 47
Blakedown	d							
Hagley	d				20 59		21 50	22 54
Stourbridge Junction 2	d				21 03		21 54	22 58
Lye	d							
Cradley Heath	d				21 08		21 59	23 04
Old Hill	d							
Rowley Regis	d				21 14		22 05	23 09
Langley Green	d							
Birmingham New Street 12	a					21 42		
	d		21 04					
Birmingham International ✈	d		21 14					
Coventry	d		21 24					
Smethwick Galton Bridge 7	d				21 19		22 10	23 14
The Hawthorns 🚊	d				21 21		22 12	23 17
Jewellery Quarter 🚊	d				21 25		22 16	23 20
Birmingham Snow Hill 🚊	a				21 28		22 19	23 24
	d			21 15	21 28		22 20	
Birmingham Moor Street	d			21 18	21a31		22a22	
Bordesley	d							
Small Heath	d							
Tyseley	d							
Acocks Green	d							
Olton	d							
Solihull	d			21 28				
Widney Manor	d			21 31				
Dorridge	d			21 35				
Lapworth	d							
Hatton	d							
Warwick Parkway	d			21 45				
Warwick	d			21 48				
Leamington Spa 8	a		21 34	21 53				
	d			21 53				
Banbury	d			22 15				
London Marylebone 10 ⊖	a			23 50				
Spring Road	d							
Hall Green	d							
Yardley Wood	d							
Shirley	d							
Whitlocks End	d							
Wythall	d							
Earlswood (West Midlands)	d							
The Lakes	d							
Wood End	d							
Danzey	d							
Henley-in-Arden	d							
Wootton Wawen	d							
Wilmcote	d							
Stratford-upon-Avon	a							

Table 71

Sundays
8 January to 12 February

Hereford, Worcester and Stourbridge - Birmingham - Leamington Spa, Marylebone and Stratford-upon-Avon

Network Diagram - see first Page of Table 71

Station		CH 🚌	CH 🚌	LM	CH 🚌	CH ◇	CH 🚌	XC ◇1	XC 🚌	CH ◇	LM	CH 🚌	CH ◇	CH 🚌	CH ◇	XC ◇1	XC 🚌	CH ◇	LM	GW ◇1	CH 🚌	CH	CH ◇
Hereford 7	d																						
Ledbury	a																						
	d																						
Colwall	d																						
Great Malvern	a																						
	d																		09 03	09 20			
Malvern Link	d																		09 06	09 23			
Worcester Foregate Street 7	a																		09 15	09 30			
	d																		09 15	09 31			
Worcester Shrub Hill 7	a																		09 18	09 33			
	d			22p47															09 23				
Droitwich Spa	d			22p55															09 32				
Bromsgrove	d																						
Barnt Green	d																						
University	d																						
Hartlebury	d																						
Kidderminster	d			23p05															09 42				
Blakedown	d			23p10															09 47				
Hagley	d			23p14															09 51				
Stourbridge Junction 2	d			23p18															09 55				
Lye	d																						
Cradley Heath	d																		10 01				
Old Hill	d																						
Rowley Regis	d																		10 06				
Langley Green	d																						
Birmingham New Street 12	a																						
	d							09 04								10 04							
Birmingham International ✈	d							09 14								10 14							
Coventry	d							09 25								10 25							
Smethwick Galton Bridge 7	d																		10 12				
The Hawthorns 🚊	d																		10 15				
Jewellery Quarter 🚊	d																		10 18				
Birmingham Snow Hill 🚊	a			23p36															10 20				
	d			23p37							09 19		09 40						10 22				10 40
Birmingham Moor Street	d			23p40		08 43				09 13	09 22		09 43					10 13	10 25				10 43
Bordesley	d																						
Small Heath	d			23p44																			
Tyseley	d			23p46							09 26								10 29				
Acocks Green	d			23p49																			
Olton	d			23p52																			
Solihull	d			23p56		08 51				09 21			09 51					10 21					10 51
Widney Manor	d			23p59																			
Dorridge	d			00 03		08 56				09 26			09 56					10 26					10 56
Lapworth	d			00 07																			11 00
Hatton	d			00 13											10 15								11 06
Warwick Parkway	d			00 18	08 10	09 06				09 36			10 06					10 36					11 11
Warwick	d			00 21	08 20	09 09				09 39					10 23			10 39					
Leamington Spa 8	a			00 26	08 30	09 15		09 36		09 46			10 14		10 29	10 36		10 46					11 23
	d	22p10	22p10		08 30		09 30		09 45			09 55		10 20			10 45				10 55	11 20	
Banbury	d	22p40	22p40		09a05		10a05		10a25			10a30		10a55			11a25				11a30		
London Marylebone 10 ⊖	a	00 10	01 55																				
Spring Road	d										09 29								10 32				
Hall Green	d										09 32								10 35				
Yardley Wood	d										09 35								10 38				
Shirley	d										09 38								10 41				
Whitlocks End	d										09 41								10 44				
Wythall	d										09 43								10 46				
Earlswood (West Midlands)	d																						
The Lakes	d										09x46								10x49				
Wood End	d																						
Danzey	d																						
Henley-in-Arden	d										09 54								10 57				
Wootton Wawen	d																						
Wilmcote	d										10 04								11 05			11 42	
Stratford-upon-Avon	a										10 09								11 12			11 54	

Table 71

Sundays

8 January to 12 February

Hereford, Worcester and Stourbridge - Birmingham - Leamington Spa, Marylebone and Stratford-upon-Avon

Network Diagram - see first Page of Table 71

		LM	CH	XC	XC	CH	LM	CH	CH	LM	CH	CH	XC	XC	CH	LM	GW	CH	CH	LM	CH	CH	XC
			▬	◇1 ⊐P	▬	◇		▬	◇		▬	◇	◇1 ⊐P	▬	◇		◇1	▬	◇			▬	◇1 ⊐P
Hereford 7	d																						
Ledbury	a																						
	d																						
Colwall	d																						
Great Malvern	a																						
	d						10 02									10 56	11 15						
Malvern Link	d						10 04									10 58	11 18						
Worcester Foregate Street 7	a						10 12									11 06	11 26						
	d						10 16									11 20	11 27						
Worcester Shrub Hill 7	a						10 18										11 29						
	d						10 22																
Droitwich Spa	d						10 30									11 29							
Bromsgrove	d																						
Barnt Green	d																						
University	d																						
Hartlebury	d																						
Kidderminster	d	10 08					10 40									11 39							
Blakedown	d	10 13																					
Hagley	d	10 17					10 47									11 46							
Stourbridge Junction 2	d	10 22					10 52			11 22						11 52				12 22			
Lye	d	10 25								11 25										12 25			
Cradley Heath	d	10 29					10 58			11 29						11 58				12 29			
Old Hill	d	10 33								11 33										12 33			
Rowley Regis	d	10 36					11 03			11 36						12 03				12 36			
Langley Green	d	10 39								11 39										12 39			
Birmingham New Street 12	a																						
	d			11 04									12 04										13 04
Birmingham International ✈	d			11 14									12 14										13 14
Coventry	d			11 25									12 25										13 25
Smethwick Galton Bridge 7	d	10 43					11 09			11 43						12 08				12 43			
The Hawthorns	d	10 45					11 12			11 45						12 11				12 45			
Jewellery Quarter	d	10 49					11 15			11 49						12 14				12 49			
Birmingham Snow Hill	a	10 52					11 17			11 52						12 17				12 52			
	d	10 53					11 19		11 40	11 53						12 19			12 40	12 53			
Birmingham Moor Street	d	10 56				11 13	11 22		11 43	11 56					12 13	12 22			12 43	12 56			
Bordesley	d																						
Small Heath	d																						
Tyseley	d						11 26									12 26							
Acocks Green	d	11 02								12 02										13 02			
Olton	d	11 04								12 04										13 04			
Solihull	d	11 08				11 21			11 51	12 08					12 21				12 51	13 08			
Widney Manor	d	11 11								12 11										13 11			
Dorridge	d	11a17				11 26			11 56	12a17					12 26				12 56	13a18			
Lapworth	d																						
Hatton	d											12 15											
Warwick Parkway	d					11 36			12 06						12 37				13 06				
Warwick	d					11 39						12 22			12 40								
Leamington Spa 8	a			11 36		11 46			12 15			12 28	12 36		12 46				13 14				13 36
	d		11 30		11 45			11 55			12 25			12 45				12 55			13 20	13 20	
Banbury	d		12a05		12a25			12a30			13a00			13a25				13a30				13a55	
London Marylebone 10 ⊖	a																						
Spring Road	d						11 29									12 29							
Hall Green	d						11 32									12 32							
Yardley Wood	d						11 35									12 35							
Shirley	d						11 38									12 38							
Whitlocks End	d						11 41									12 41							
Wythall	d						11 43									12 43							
Earlswood (West Midlands)	d																						
The Lakes	d						11x46									12x46							
Wood End	d																						
Danzey	d																						
Henley-in-Arden	d						11 54									12 54							
Wootton Wawen	d																						
Wilmcote	d						12 02									13 02					13 42		
Stratford-upon-Avon	a						12 09									13 09					13 54		

Table 71

Sundays

8 January to 12 February

Hereford, Worcester and Stourbridge - Birmingham - Leamington Spa, Marylebone and Stratford-upon-Avon

Network Diagram - see first Page of Table 71

		XC	CH	LM	XC	CH	LM	CH	XC	CH	LM	GW	XC	CH	LM	CH	XC	CH	LM	GW	XC	LM
		▬	◇		◇1 H			◇	◇1 ⊐P	◇		◇1	◇1 H			◇	◇1 ⊐P			◇1 ⊐P	◇1 H	
Hereford 7	d																			13 32		
Ledbury	a																			13 49		
	d																			13 50		
Colwall	d																			13 57		
Great Malvern	a																			14 02		
	d			12 04								13 15								14 11		14 35
Malvern Link	d			12 06								13 18								14 15		14 37
Worcester Foregate Street 7	a			12 15								13 25								14 24		14 45
	d			12 16							13 20	13 26							14 20	14 26		14 45
Worcester Shrub Hill 7	a			12 18								13 29								14 29		14 48
	d			12 24																		14 53
Droitwich Spa	d			12 32							13 29								14 29			15 01
Bromsgrove	d																					15 10
Barnt Green	d																					
University	d																					
Hartlebury	d																					
Kidderminster	d			12 42							13 39								14 39			
Blakedown	d			12 47															14 44			
Hagley	d			12 51							13 46								14 48			
Stourbridge Junction 2	d			12 55			13 22				13 52				14 22				14 52			
Lye	d						13 25								14 25							
Cradley Heath	d			13 01			13 29				13 58				14 29				14 58			
Old Hill	d						13 33								14 33							
Rowley Regis	d			13 06			13 36				14 03				14 36				15 03			
Langley Green	d						13 39								14 39							
Birmingham New Street 12	a																					15 37
	d				13 33				14 04				14 33				15 04				15 33	
Birmingham International ✈	d								14 14								15 14					
Coventry	d								14 25								15 25					
Smethwick Galton Bridge 7	d			13 11			13 43				14 08				14 43				15 08			
The Hawthorns	d			13 14			13 45				14 11				14 45				15 11			
Jewellery Quarter	d			13 17			13 49				14 14				14 49				15 14			
Birmingham Snow Hill	a			13 20			13 52				14 17				14 52				15 17			
	d			13 22		13 40	13 53				14 19			14 40	14 53				15 19			
Birmingham Moor Street	d		13 13	13 25		13 43	13 56			14 13	14 22			14 43	14 56			15 13	15 22			
Bordesley	d																					
Small Heath	d																					
Tyseley	d			13 29							14 26								15 26			
Acocks Green	d						14 02								15 02							
Olton	d						14 04								15 04							
Solihull	d		13 21			13 51	14 08			14 21				14 51	15 08			15 21				
Widney Manor	d						14 11								15 11							
Dorridge	d		13 26			13 56	14a17			14 26				14 56	15a17			15 26				
Lapworth	d					14 00																
Hatton	d					14 06		14 15														
Warwick Parkway	d		13 36			14 11				14 37				15 05				15 37				
Warwick	d		13 39					14 22		14 39								15 40				
Leamington Spa 8	a		13 46		13 59	14 17		14 26	14 36	14 44			14 59	15 10			15 36	15 44			15 59	
	d	13 45			14 00	14 17		14 26	14 38	14 44			15 00	15 11		15 20	15 38	15 45			16 00	
Banbury	d	14a25			14a17	14 35		14 45	14a54	15 04			15a18	15 30			15a54	16 05			16a17	
London Marylebone 10 ⊖	a					15 46		16 08		16 12				16 45				17 13				
Spring Road	d			13 32							14 29								15 29			
Hall Green	d			13 35							14 32								15 32			
Yardley Wood	d			13 38							14 35								15 35			
Shirley	d			13 41							14 38								15 38			
Whitlocks End	d			13 44							14 40								15 41			
Wythall	d			13 46							14 43								15 43			
Earlswood (West Midlands)	d																					
The Lakes	d			13x49							14x46								15x46			
Wood End	d																					
Danzey	d																					
Henley-in-Arden	d			13 57							14 54								15 54			
Wootton Wawen	d																					
Wilmcote	d			14 05							15 02					15 42			16 02			
Stratford-upon-Avon	a			14 12							15 07					15 54			16 09			

Hereford, Worcester and Stourbridge - Birmingham - Leamington Spa, Marylebone and Stratford-upon-Avon

Network Diagram - see first Page of Table 71

		CH	LM	CH	XC	CH	LM	GW	LM	XC	CH	LM	CH	XC	LM	CH	LM	GW	XC	CH	LM	CH	XC
				◇	◇1			◇1		◇1			◇	◇1				◇1	◇1			◇	◇1
					⊡			⊡		⊼				⊡				⊡	⊼				⊡
Hereford [7]	d							14 32							15 30			16 35					
Ledbury	a							14 49							15 47			16 51					
	d							14 55							15 51			16 52					
Colwall	d							15 02							15 58			17 00					
Great Malvern	a							15 07							16 02			17 04					
	d							15 08							16 03			17 05					
Malvern Link	d							15 12							16 05			17 09					
Worcester Foregate Street [7]	a							15 21							16 14			17 20					
	d						15 20	15 23							16 15		16 20	17 22					
Worcester Shrub Hill [7]	a							15 26							16 18			17 27					
	d								15 46						16 33								
Droitwich Spa	d						15 29		15 54						16 41		16 29						
Bromsgrove	d														16 51								
Barnt Green	d																						
University	d																						
Hartlebury	d																						
Kidderminster	d						15 40		16 04								16 39						
Blakedown	d																						
Hagley	d						15 47		16 11								16 46						
Stourbridge Junction [2]	d		15 22				15 52		16 16			16 22					16 52				17 22		
Lye	d		15 25									16 25									17 25		
Cradley Heath	d		15 29				15 58					16 29					16 58				17 29		
Old Hill	d		15 33									16 33									17 33		
Rowley Regis	d		15 36				16 03					16 36					17 03				17 36		
Langley Green	d		15 39									16 39									17 39		
Birmingham New Street [12]	a														17 17								
	d				16 04					16 33				17 04					17 33				18 04
Birmingham International ✈	d				16 14									17 14									18 14
Coventry	d				16 25									17 25									18 25
Smethwick Galton Bridge [7]	d		15 43				16 08		16 29			16 43					17 08				17 43		
The Hawthorns	d		15 45				16 11					16 45					17 11				17 45		
Jewellery Quarter	d		15 49				16 14					16 49					17 14				17 49		
Birmingham Snow Hill	a		15 52				16 17		16 35			16 52					17 17				17 53		
	d	15 40	15 53				16 19		16 45		16 40	16 53					17 19			17 40	17 53		
Birmingham Moor Street	d	15 43	15 56			16 13	16 22		16a47		16 43	16 56				17 13	17 22			17 43	17 56		
Bordesley	d																						
Small Heath	d																						
Tyseley	d						16 26										17 26						
Acocks Green	d		16 02									17 02									18 02		
Olton	d		16 04									17 04									18 04		
Solihull	d	15 51	16 08			16 21					16 51	17 08				17 21				17 51	18 08		
Widney Manor	d		16 11									17 11									18 11		
Dorridge	d	15 56	16a17			16 26					16 56	17a17				17 26				17 56	18a17		
Lapworth	d	16 00																		18 00			
Hatton	d	16 06		16 14																18 06		18 14	
Warwick Parkway	d	16 11				16 37					17 05					17 36				18 11			
Warwick	d			16 23		16 40										17 40						18 22	
Leamington Spa [8]	a	16 17		16 26	16 36	16 44				16 59	17 12			17 36		17 44			18 00	18 17		18 26	18 36
	d	16 17		16 27	16 38	16 45				17 00	17 12		17 20	17 38		17 45			18 01	18 17		18 26	18 38
Banbury	d	16 35		16 46	16a54	17 05				17a17	17 30			17a54		18 05			18a19	18 35		18 45	18a54
London Marylebone [10] ⊖	a	17 46		18 08		18 12					18 45					19 13				19 45		20 08	
Spring Road	d						16 29										17 29						
Hall Green	d						16 32										17 32						
Yardley Wood	d						16 35										17 35						
Shirley	d						16 38										17 38						
Whitlocks End	d						16 41										17 41						
Wythall	d						16 43										17 43						
Earlswood (West Midlands)	d																						
The Lakes	d						16x46										17x46						
Wood End	d																						
Danzey	d																						
Henley-in-Arden	d						16 55										17 54						
Wootton Wawen	d																						
Wilmcote	d						17 03						17 42				18 02						
Stratford-upon-Avon	a						17 10						17 54				18 09						

Hereford, Worcester and Stourbridge - Birmingham - Leamington Spa, Marylebone and Stratford-upon-Avon

Network Diagram - see first Page of Table 71

		CH	LM	LM	XC	CH	CH	XC	CH	LM	GW	GW	XC	CH	XC	CH	LM	XC	LM	GW	XC	CH
		◇			◇1		◇	◇1			◇1	◇1	◇1	◇	◇1	◇		◇1		◇1	◇1	◇
					⊼			⊡					⊼		⊡			⊼				
Hereford [7]	d											18 30										
Ledbury	a											18 47										
	d											18 48										
Colwall	d											18 55										
Great Malvern	a											19 00										
	d			17 17								19 11								20 15		
Malvern Link	d			17 20								19 14								20 18		
Worcester Foregate Street [7]	a			17 28								19 23								20 25		
	d		17 20	17 28						18 20	18 25	19 25								20 26		
Worcester Shrub Hill [7]	a			17 31							18 26	19 26								20 29		
	d			17 36													19 38		19 53			
Droitwich Spa	d		17 29	17 44						18 29							19 46		20 01			
Bromsgrove	d			17 53															20 10			
Barnt Green	d																					
University	d																					
Hartlebury	d																					
Kidderminster	d		17 39							18 39							19 56					
Blakedown	d		17 44																			
Hagley	d		17 48							18 46							20 03					
Stourbridge Junction [2]	d		17 52							18 52							20 07					
Lye	d																					
Cradley Heath	d		17 58							18 58							20 13					
Old Hill	d																					
Rowley Regis	d		18 03							19 03							20 19					
Langley Green	d																					
Birmingham New Street [12]	a			18 15															20 36			
	d				18 33			19 04					19 33		20 04			20 33			21 04	
Birmingham International ✈	d							19 14							20 14						21 14	
Coventry	d							19 25							20 25						21 24	
Smethwick Galton Bridge [7]	d		18 08							19 08							20 24					
The Hawthorns	d		18 11							19 11							20 26					
Jewellery Quarter	d		18 14							19 14							20 30					
Birmingham Snow Hill	a		18 17							19 19							20 33					
	d		18 19			18 40			19 15	19 21						20 15	20 33					21 15
Birmingham Moor Street	d	18 13	18 22			18 43			19 18	19a23						20 18	20a36					21 18
Bordesley	d																					
Small Heath	d																					
Tyseley	d		18 26																			
Acocks Green	d																					
Olton	d																					
Solihull	d	18 21				18 51			19 26							20 28						21 28
Widney Manor	d								19 29							20 31						21 31
Dorridge	d	18 26				18 56			19 33							20 35						21 35
Lapworth	d								19 37													
Hatton	d								19 43					20 15								
Warwick Parkway	d	18 36				19 05			19 47							20 45						21 45
Warwick	d	18 40							19 51					20 21		20 48						21 48
Leamington Spa [8]	a	18 44			18 59	19 11		19 36	19 56				19 59	20 25	20 36	20 53		20 58			21 34	21 53
	d	18 45			19 00	19 11	19 20	19 38	19 56				20 00	20 26	20 38	20 53		21 00				21 53
Banbury	d	19 05			19a17	19 29		19a54	20 14				20a18	20 46	20a54	21 12		21a17				22 15
London Marylebone [10] ⊖	a	20 12				20 45			21 46					21 53		22 50						23 50
Spring Road	d		18 29																			
Hall Green	d		18 32																			
Yardley Wood	d		18 35																			
Shirley	d		18 38																			
Whitlocks End	d		18 41																			
Wythall	d		18 43																			
Earlswood (West Midlands)	d																					
The Lakes	d		18x46																			
Wood End	d																					
Danzey	d																					
Henley-in-Arden	d		18 54																			
Wootton Wawen	d																					
Wilmcote	d		19 02				19 42															
Stratford-upon-Avon	a		19 09				19 54															

Sundays
8 January to 12 February

Hereford, Worcester and Stourbridge - Birmingham - Leamington Spa, Marylebone and Stratford-upon-Avon

Network Diagram - see first Page of Table 71

		LM	LM	LM	LM
Hereford [7]	d		20 05		
Ledbury	a		20 21		
	d		20 22		
Colwall	d		20 28		
Great Malvern	a		20 33		
	d		20 33		22 10
Malvern Link	d		20 36		22 13
Worcester Foregate Street [7]	a		20 44		22 22
	d		20 45		22 23
Worcester Shrub Hill [7]	a		20 47		22 25
	d	20 34	20 52	21 25	22 29
Droitwich Spa	d	20 42	21 00	21 33	22 37
Bromsgrove	d		21 09		
Barnt Green	d				
University	d				
Hartlebury	d				
Kidderminster	d	20 52		21 43	22 47
Blakedown	d				
Hagley	d	20 59		21 50	22 54
Stourbridge Junction [2]	d	21 03		21 54	22 58
Lye	d				
Cradley Heath	d	21 08		21 59	23 04
Old Hill	d				
Rowley Regis	d	21 14		22 05	23 09
Langley Green	d				
Birmingham New Street [12]	a		21 42		
	d				
Birmingham International ✈	d				
Coventry	d				
Smethwick Galton Bridge [7]	d	21 19		22 10	23 14
The Hawthorns (tram)	d	21 21		22 12	23 17
Jewellery Quarter (tram)	d	21 25		22 16	23 20
Birmingham Snow Hill (tram)	a	21 28		22 19	23 24
	d	21 28		22 20	
Birmingham Moor Street	d	21a31		22a22	
Bordesley	d				
Small Heath	d				
Tyseley	d				
Acocks Green	d				
Olton	d				
Solihull	d				
Widney Manor	d				
Dorridge	d				
Lapworth	d				
Hatton	d				
Warwick Parkway	d				
Warwick	d				
Leamington Spa [8]	a				
	d				
Banbury	d				
London Marylebone [10] ⊖	a				
Spring Road	d				
Hall Green	d				
Yardley Wood	d				
Shirley	d				
Whitlocks End	d				
Wythall	d				
Earlswood (West Midlands)	d				
The Lakes	d				
Wood End	d				
Danzey	d				
Henley-in-Arden	d				
Wootton Wawen	d				
Wilmcote	d				
Stratford-upon-Avon	a				

Sundays
19 February to 25 March

Hereford, Worcester and Stourbridge - Birmingham - Leamington Spa, Marylebone and Stratford-upon-Avon

Network Diagram - see first Page of Table 71

		CH	CH	LM	CH	CH	CH	XC	XC	CH		LM	CH	CH	CH	CH	XC	XC	CH	LM		GW	CH	CH	CH
						◇		◇[1]		◇				◇		◇	◇[1]		◇			◇[1]			◇
		🚌	🚌		🚌		🚌	✠	🚌				🚌		🚌		⊡	🚌					🚌		
Hereford [7]	d																								
Ledbury	a																								
	d																								
Colwall	d																								
Great Malvern	a																								
	d																			09 03		09 20			
Malvern Link	d																			09 06		09 23			
Worcester Foregate Street [7]	a																			09 15		09 30			
	d																			09 15		09 31			
Worcester Shrub Hill [7]	a																			09 18		09 33			
	d			22p47																09 23					
Droitwich Spa	d			22p55																09 32					
Bromsgrove	d																								
Barnt Green	d																								
University	d																								
Hartlebury	d																								
Kidderminster	d			23p05																09 42					
Blakedown	d			23p10																09 47					
Hagley	d			23p14																09 51					
Stourbridge Junction [2]	d			23p18																09 55					
Lye	d																								
Cradley Heath	d																			10 01					
Old Hill	d																								
Rowley Regis	d																			10 06					
Langley Green	d																								
Birmingham New Street [12]	a																								
	d							09 04									10 04								
Birmingham International ✈	d							09 14									10 14								
Coventry	d							09 25									10 25								
Smethwick Galton Bridge [7]	d																			10 12					
The Hawthorns (tram)	d																			10 15					
Jewellery Quarter (tram)	d																			10 18					
Birmingham Snow Hill (tram)	a			23p36																10 20					
	d			23p37								09 19		09 40						10 22					10 40
Birmingham Moor Street	d			23p40		08 43				09 13		09 22		09 43					10 13	10 25					10 43
Bordesley	d																								
Small Heath	d			23p44																					
Tyseley	d			23p46								09 26								10 29					
Acocks Green	d			23p49																					
Olton	d			23p52																					
Solihull	d			23p56		08 51				09 21				09 51					10 21						10 51
Widney Manor	d			23p59																					
Dorridge	d			00 03		08 56				09 26				09 56					10 26						10 56
Lapworth	d			00 07																					11 00
Hatton	d			00 13												10 15									11 06
Warwick Parkway	d			00 18	08 10	09 06				09 36				10 06					10 36						11 11
Warwick	d			00 21	08 20	09 09				09 39						10 23			10 39						
Leamington Spa [8]	a			00 26	08 30	09 15		09 36		09 46				10 14		10 29	10 36		10 46						11 23
	d	22p10	22p10		08 30		09 30		09 45				09 55		10 20			10 45					10 55	11 20	
Banbury	d	22p40	22p40		09a05		10a05		10a25				10a30		10a55			11a25					11a30		
London Marylebone [10] ⊖	a	00 10	01 55																						
Spring Road	d											09 29								10 32					
Hall Green	d											09 32								10 35					
Yardley Wood	d											09 35								10 38					
Shirley	d											09 38								10 41					
Whitlocks End	d											09 41								10 44					
Wythall	d											09 43								10 46					
Earlswood (West Midlands)	d																								
The Lakes	d											09x46								10x49					
Wood End	d																								
Danzey	d																								
Henley-in-Arden	d											09 54								10 57					
Wootton Wawen	d																								
Wilmcote	d											10 04								11 05				11 42	
Stratford-upon-Avon	a											10 09								11 12				11 54	

Sundays

19 February to 25 March

Hereford, Worcester and Stourbridge - Birmingham - Leamington Spa, Marylebone and Stratford-upon-Avon

Network Diagram - see first Page of Table 71

		LM	CH	XC	XC	CH	LM	CH	CH	LM	CH	CH	XC	XC	CH	LM	GW	CH	CH	LM	CH	CH	XC
				◇1		◇			◇			◇	◇1		◇		◇1		◇				◇1
			🚌	☕	🚌			🚌			🚌		☕	🚌				🚌				🚌	☕
Hereford 7	d																						
Ledbury	a																						
	d																						
Colwall	d																						
Great Malvern	a																						
	d						10 02									10 56	11 15						
Malvern Link	d						10 04									10 58	11 18						
Worcester Foregate Street 7	a						10 12									11 06	11 26						
	d						10 16									11 20	11 27						
Worcester Shrub Hill 7	a						10 18										11 29						
	d						10 22																
Droitwich Spa	d						10 30									11 29							
Bromsgrove	d																						
Barnt Green	d																						
University	d																						
Hartlebury	d																						
Kidderminster	d	10 08					10 40									11 39							
Blakedown	d	10 13																					
Hagley	d	10 17					10 47									11 46							
Stourbridge Junction 2	d	10 22					10 52			11 22						11 52				12 22			
Lye	d	10 25								11 25										12 25			
Cradley Heath	d	10 29					10 58			11 29						11 58				12 29			
Old Hill	d	10 33								11 33										12 33			
Rowley Regis	d	10 36					11 03			11 36						12 03				12 36			
Langley Green	d	10 39								11 39										12 39			
Birmingham New Street 12	a																						
	d			11 04									12 04										13 04
Birmingham International ✈	d			11 14									12 14										13 14
Coventry	d			11 25									12 25										13 25
Smethwick Galton Bridge 7	d	10 43					11 09			11 43						12 08				12 43			
The Hawthorns	d	10 45					11 12			11 45						12 11				12 45			
Jewellery Quarter	d	10 49					11 15			11 49						12 14				12 49			
Birmingham Snow Hill	a	10 52					11 17			11 52						12 17				12 52			
	d	10 53					11 19		11 40	11 53						12 19			12 40	12 53			
Birmingham Moor Street	d	10 56				11 13	11 22		11 43	11 56					12 13	12 22			12 43	12 56			
Bordesley	d																						
Small Heath	d																						
Tyseley	d						11 26									12 26							
Acocks Green	d	11 02								12 02										13 02			
Olton	d	11 04								12 04										13 04			
Solihull	d	11 08				11 21			11 51	12 08					12 21				12 51	13 08			
Widney Manor	d	11 11								12 11										13 11			
Dorridge	d	11a17				11 26			11 56	12a17					12 26				12 56	13a18			
Lapworth	d																						
Hatton	d											12 15											
Warwick Parkway	d					11 36			12 06						12 37				13 06				
Warwick	d					11 39						12 22			12 40								
Leamington Spa 8	a			11 36		11 46			12 15			12 28	12 36		12 46				13 14				13 36
	d		11 30		11 45			11 55			12 25			12 45				12 55			13 20	13 20	
Banbury	d		12a05		12a25			12a30			13a00			13a25				13a30				13a55	
London Marylebone 10 ⊖	a																						
Spring Road	d						11 29									12 29							
Hall Green	d						11 32									12 32							
Yardley Wood	d						11 35									12 35							
Shirley	d						11 38									12 38							
Whitlocks End	d						11 41									12 41							
Wythall	d						11 43									12 43							
Earlswood (West Midlands)	d																						
The Lakes	d						11x46									12x46							
Wood End	d																						
Danzey	d																						
Henley-in-Arden	d						11 54									12 54							
Wootton Wawen	d																						
Wilmcote	d						12 02									13 02					13 42		
Stratford-upon-Avon	a						12 09									13 09					13 54		

Table 71

Sundays

19 February to 25 March

Hereford, Worcester and Stourbridge - Birmingham - Leamington Spa, Marylebone and Stratford-upon-Avon

Network Diagram - see first Page of Table 71

		XC	CH	LM	CH	LM	CH	XC	CH	LM	GW	XC	CH	LM	CH	XC	CH	LM	GW	XC	LM	CH
			◇				◇	◇1	◇		◇1	◇1			◇	◇1			◇1	◇1		
		🚌						☕				🛒				☕			☕	🛒		
Hereford 7	d																		13 32			
Ledbury	a																		13 49			
	d																		13 50			
Colwall	d																		13 57			
Great Malvern	a																		14 02			
	d			12 04							13 15								14 11		14 35	
Malvern Link	d			12 06							13 18								14 15		14 37	
Worcester Foregate Street 7	a			12 15							13 25								14 24		14 45	
	d			12 16						13 20	13 26							14 20	14 26		14 45	
Worcester Shrub Hill 7	a			12 18							13 29								14 29		14 48	
	d			12 24																	14 53	
Droitwich Spa	d			12 32						13 29								14 29			15 01	
Bromsgrove	d																				15 10	
Barnt Green	d																					
University	d																					
Hartlebury	d																					
Kidderminster	d			12 42						13 39								14 39				
Blakedown	d			12 47														14 44				
Hagley	d			12 51						13 46								14 48				
Stourbridge Junction 2	d			12 55		13 22				13 52				14 22				14 52				
Lye	d					13 25								14 25								
Cradley Heath	d			13 01		13 29				13 58				14 29				14 58				
Old Hill	d					13 33								14 33								
Rowley Regis	d			13 06		13 36				14 03				14 36				15 03				
Langley Green	d					13 39								14 39								
Birmingham New Street 12	a																				15 37	
	d							14 04				14 33				15 04				15 33		
Birmingham International ✈	d							14 14								15 14						
Coventry	d							14 25								15 25						
Smethwick Galton Bridge 7	d			13 11		13 43				14 08				14 43				15 08				
The Hawthorns	d			13 14		13 45				14 11				14 45				15 11				
Jewellery Quarter	d			13 17		13 49				14 14				14 49				15 14				
Birmingham Snow Hill	a			13 20		13 52				14 17				14 52				15 17				
	d			13 22	13 40	13 53				14 19			14 40	14 53				15 19				15 40
Birmingham Moor Street	d		13 13	13 25	13 43	13 56			14 13	14 22			14 43	14 56			15 13	15 22				15 43
Bordesley	d																					
Small Heath	d																					
Tyseley	d			13 29						14 26								15 26				
Acocks Green	d					14 02								15 02								
Olton	d					14 04								15 04								
Solihull	d		13 21		13 51	14 08			14 21				14 51	15 08			15 21					15 51
Widney Manor	d					14 11								15 11								
Dorridge	d		13 26		13 56	14a17			14 26				14 56	15a17			15 26					15 56
Lapworth	d				14 00																	16 00
Hatton	d				14 06		14 15															16 06
Warwick Parkway	d		13 36		14 11				14 37				15 05				15 37					16 11
Warwick	d		13 39				14 22		14 39								15 40					
Leamington Spa 8	a		13 46		14 17		14 26	14 36	14 44			14 59	15 10			15 36	15 44			15 59		16 17
	d	13 45			14 17		14 26	14 38	14 44			15 00	15 11		15 20	15 38	15 45			16 00		16 17
Banbury	d	14a25			14 35		14 45	14a54	15 04			15a18	15 30			15a54	16 05			16a17		16 35
London Marylebone 10 ⊖	a				15 46		16 08		16 12				16 45				17 13					17 46
Spring Road	d			13 32						14 29								15 29				
Hall Green	d			13 35						14 32								15 32				
Yardley Wood	d			13 38						14 35								15 35				
Shirley	d			13 41						14 38								15 38				
Whitlocks End	d			13 44						14 40								15 41				
Wythall	d			13 46						14 43								15 43				
Earlswood (West Midlands)	d																					
The Lakes	d			13x49						14x46								15x46				
Wood End	d																					
Danzey	d																					
Henley-in-Arden	d			13 57						14 54								15 54				
Wootton Wawen	d																					
Wilmcote	d			14 05						15 02					15 42			16 02				
Stratford-upon-Avon	a			14 12						15 07					15 54			16 09				

Table 71

Sundays

19 February to 25 March

Hereford, Worcester and Stourbridge - Birmingham - Leamington Spa, Marylebone and Stratford-upon-Avon

Network Diagram - see first Page of Table 71

		LM	CH	XC	CH	LM	GW	LM		XC	CH	LM	CH	XC	LM	CH	LM	GW		XC	CH	LM	CH	XC	CH
			◇	◇1			◇1			◇1			◇	◇1				◇1		◇1			◇	◇1	◇
Hereford 7	d						14 32								15 30			16 35							
Ledbury	a						14 49								15 47			16 51							
	d						14 55								15 51			16 52							
Colwall	d						15 02								15 58			17 00							
Great Malvern	a						15 07								16 02			17 04							
	d						15 08								16 03			17 05							
Malvern Link	d						15 12								16 05			17 09							
Worcester Foregate Street 7	a						15 21								16 14			17 20							
	d					15 20	15 23								16 15		16 20	17 22							
Worcester Shrub Hill 7	a						15 26								16 18			17 27							
	d							15 46							16 33										
Droitwich Spa	d					15 29		15 54							16 41		16 29								
Bromsgrove	d														16 51										
Barnt Green	d																								
University	d																								
Hartlebury	d																								
Kidderminster	d					15 40		16 04									16 39								
Blakedown	d																								
Hagley	d					15 47		16 11									16 46								
Stourbridge Junction 2	d	15 22				15 52		16 16				16 22					16 52					17 22			
Lye	d	15 25										16 25										17 25			
Cradley Heath	d	15 29				15 58						16 29					16 58					17 29			
Old Hill	d	15 33										16 33										17 33			
Rowley Regis	d	15 36				16 03						16 36					17 03					17 36			
Langley Green	d	15 39										16 39										17 39			
Birmingham New Street 12	a														17 17										
	d			16 04						16 33				17 04						17 33				18 04	
Birmingham International ✈	d			16 14										17 14										18 14	
Coventry	d			16 25										17 25										18 25	
Smethwick Galton Bridge 7	d	15 43				16 08		16 29				16 43					17 08					17 43			
The Hawthorns	d	15 45				16 11						16 45					17 11					17 45			
Jewellery Quarter	d	15 49				16 14						16 49					17 14					17 49			
Birmingham Snow Hill	a	15 52				16 17		16 35				16 52					17 17					17 53			
	d	15 53				16 19		16 45			16 40	16 53					17 19				17 40	17 53			
Birmingham Moor Street	d	15 56			16 13	16 22		16a47			16 43	16 56				17 13	17 22				17 43	17 56			18 13
Bordesley	d																								
Small Heath	d																								
Tyseley	d					16 26											17 26								
Acocks Green	d	16 02										17 02										18 02			
Olton	d	16 04										17 04										18 04			
Solihull	d	16 08			16 21						16 51	17 08				17 21					17 51	18 08			18 21
Widney Manor	d	16 11										17 11										18 11			
Dorridge	d	16a17			16 26						16 56	17a17				17 26					17 56	18a17			18 26
Lapworth	d																				18 00				
Hatton	d		16 14																		18 06		18 14		
Warwick Parkway	d				16 37						17 05					17 36					18 11				18 36
Warwick	d		16 23		16 40											17 40							18 22		18 40
Leamington Spa 8	a		16 26	16 36	16 44					16 59	17 12			17 36		17 44				18 00	18 17		18 26	18 36	18 44
	d		16 27	16 38	16 45					17 00	17 12		17 20	17 38		17 45				18 01	18 17		18 26	18 38	18 45
Banbury	d		16 46	16a54	17 05					17a17	17 30			17a54		18 05				18a19	18 35		18 45	18a54	19 05
London Marylebone 10 ⊖	a		18 08		18 12						18 45					19 13					19 45		20 08		20 12
Spring Road	d					16 29											17 29								
Hall Green	d					16 32											17 32								
Yardley Wood	d					16 35											17 35								
Shirley	d					16 38											17 38								
Whitlocks End	d					16 41											17 41								
Wythall	d					16 43											17 43								
Earlswood (West Midlands)	d																								
The Lakes	d					16x46											17x46								
Wood End	d																								
Danzey	d																								
Henley-in-Arden	d					16 55											17 54								
Wootton Wawen	d																								
Wilmcote	d					17 03							17 42				18 02								
Stratford-upon-Avon	a					17 10							17 54				18 09								

Table 71

Sundays

19 February to 25 March

Hereford, Worcester and Stourbridge - Birmingham - Leamington Spa, Marylebone and Stratford-upon-Avon

Network Diagram - see first Page of Table 71

		LM	LM	XC		CH	CH	XC	CH	LM	GW	GW	XC	CH		XC	CH	LM	XC	LM	GW	XC	CH	LM	
				◇1			◇	◇1			◇1	◇1	◇1	◇		◇1	◇		◇1		◇1	◇1	◇		
Hereford 7	d											18 30													
Ledbury	a											18 47													
	d											18 48													
Colwall	d											18 55													
Great Malvern	a											19 00													
	d		17 17									19 11									20 15				
Malvern Link	d		17 20									19 14									20 18				
Worcester Foregate Street 7	a		17 28									19 23									20 25				
	d	17 20	17 28							18 20	18 25	19 25									20 26				
Worcester Shrub Hill 7	a		17 31								18 26	19 26									20 29				
	d		17 36															19 38		19 53				20 34	
Droitwich Spa	d	17 29	17 44							18 29								19 46		20 01				20 42	
Bromsgrove	d		17 53																	20 10					
Barnt Green	d																								
University	d																								
Hartlebury	d																								
Kidderminster	d	17 39								18 39								19 56						20 52	
Blakedown	d	17 44																							
Hagley	d	17 48								18 46								20 03						20 59	
Stourbridge Junction 2	d	17 52								18 52								20 07						21 03	
Lye	d																								
Cradley Heath	d	17 58								18 58								20 13						21 08	
Old Hill	d																								
Rowley Regis	d	18 03								19 03								20 19						21 14	
Langley Green	d																								
Birmingham New Street 12	a		18 15																	20 36					
	d			18 33				19 04					19 33			20 04			20 33			21 04			
Birmingham International ✈	d							19 14								20 14						21 14			
Coventry	d							19 25								20 25						21 24			
Smethwick Galton Bridge 7	d	18 08								19 08								20 24						21 19	
The Hawthorns	d	18 11								19 11								20 26						21 21	
Jewellery Quarter	d	18 14								19 14								20 30						21 25	
Birmingham Snow Hill	a	18 17								19 19								20 33						21 28	
	d	18 19				18 40			19 15	19 21							20 15	20 33					21 15	21 28	
Birmingham Moor Street	d	18 22				18 43			19 18	19a23							20 18	20a36					21 18	21a31	
Bordesley	d																								
Small Heath	d																								
Tyseley	d	18 26																							
Acocks Green	d																								
Olton	d																								
Solihull	d					18 51			19 26								20 28						21 28		
Widney Manor	d								19 29								20 31						21 31		
Dorridge	d					18 56			19 33								20 35						21 35		
Lapworth	d								19 37																
Hatton	d								19 43					20 15											
Warwick Parkway	d					19 05			19 47								20 45						21 45		
Warwick	d								19 51					20 21			20 48						21 48		
Leamington Spa 8	a			18 59		19 11		19 36	19 56				19 59	20 25		20 36	20 53		20 58			21 34	21 53		
	d			19 00		19 11	19 20	19 38	19 56				20 00	20 26		20 38	20 53		21 00				21 53		
Banbury	d			19a17		19 29		19a54	20 14				20a18	20 46		20a54	21 12		21a17				22 15		
London Marylebone 10 ⊖	a					20 45			21 46					21 53			22 50						23 50		
Spring Road	d	18 29																							
Hall Green	d	18 32																							
Yardley Wood	d	18 35																							
Shirley	d	18 38																							
Whitlocks End	d	18 41																							
Wythall	d	18 43																							
Earlswood (West Midlands)	d																								
The Lakes	d	18x46																							
Wood End	d																								
Danzey	d																								
Henley-in-Arden	d	18 54																							
Wootton Wawen	d																								
Wilmcote	d	19 02					19 42																		
Stratford-upon-Avon	a	19 09					19 54																		

Table 71

Sundays
19 February to 25 March

Hereford, Worcester and Stourbridge - Birmingham - Leamington Spa, Marylebone and Stratford-upon-Avon

Network Diagram - see first Page of Table 71

		LM	LM	LM
Hereford 7	d	20 05		
Ledbury	a	20 21		
	d	20 22		
Colwall	d	20 28		
Great Malvern	a	20 33		
	d	20 33		22 10
Malvern Link	d	20 36		22 13
Worcester Foregate Street 7	a	20 44		22 22
	d	20 45		22 23
Worcester Shrub Hill 7	a	20 47		22 25
	d	20 52	21 25	22 29
Droitwich Spa	d	21 00	21 33	22 37
Bromsgrove	d	21 09		
Barnt Green	d			
University	d			
Hartlebury	d			
Kidderminster	d		21 43	22 47
Blakedown	d			
Hagley	d		21 50	22 54
Stourbridge Junction 2	d		21 54	22 58
Lye	d			
Cradley Heath	d		21 59	23 04
Old Hill	d			
Rowley Regis	d		22 05	23 09
Langley Green	d			
Birmingham New Street 12	a	21 42		
	d			
Birmingham International ✈	d			
Coventry	d			
Smethwick Galton Bridge 7	d		22 10	23 14
The Hawthorns 🚊	d		22 12	23 17
Jewellery Quarter 🚊	d		22 16	23 20
Birmingham Snow Hill 🚊	a		22 19	23 24
	d		22 20	
Birmingham Moor Street	d		22a22	
Bordesley	d			
Small Heath	d			
Tyseley	d			
Acocks Green	d			
Olton	d			
Solihull	d			
Widney Manor	d			
Dorridge	d			
Lapworth	d			
Hatton	d			
Warwick Parkway	d			
Warwick	d			
Leamington Spa 8	a			
	d			
Banbury	d			
London Marylebone 10 ⊖	a			
Spring Road	d			
Hall Green	d			
Yardley Wood	d			
Shirley	d			
Whitlocks End	d			
Wythall	d			
Earlswood (West Midlands)	d			
The Lakes	d			
Wood End	d			
Danzey	d			
Henley-in-Arden	d			
Wootton Wawen	d			
Wilmcote	d			
Stratford-upon-Avon	a			

Table 71

Sundays
from 1 April

Hereford, Worcester and Stourbridge - Birmingham - Leamington Spa, Marylebone and Stratford-upon-Avon

Network Diagram - see first Page of Table 71

		LM	CH	XC	CH	LM	CH	XC	CH	LM		GW	CH	LM	CH	XC	CH	LM	CH	LM		XC	CH	LM	GW
			◇	◇1	◇			◇1	◇			◇1	◇			◇1	◇					◇1			◇1
Hereford 7	d																								
Ledbury	a																								
	d																								
Colwall	d																								
Great Malvern	a																								
	d									09 03		09 20						10 02						10 56	11 15
Malvern Link	d									09 06		09 23						10 04						10 58	11 18
Worcester Foregate Street 7	a									09 15		09 30						10 12						11 06	11 26
	d									09 15		09 31						10 16						11 20	11 27
Worcester Shrub Hill 7	a									09 18		09 33						10 18							11 29
	d	22p47								09 23								10 22							
Droitwich Spa	d	22p55								09 32								10 30						11 29	
Bromsgrove	d																								
Barnt Green	d																								
University	d																								
Hartlebury	d																								
Kidderminster	d	23p05								09 42				10 08				10 40						11 39	
Blakedown	d	23p10								09 47				10 13											
Hagley	d	23p14								09 51				10 17				10 47						11 46	
Stourbridge Junction 2	d	23p18								09 55				10 22				10 52		11 22				11 52	
Lye	d													10 25						11 25					
Cradley Heath	d									10 01				10 29				10 58		11 29				11 58	
Old Hill	d													10 33						11 33					
Rowley Regis	d									10 06				10 36				11 03		11 36				12 03	
Langley Green	d													10 39						11 39					
Birmingham New Street 12	a																								
	d			09 04				10 04								11 04						12 04			
Birmingham International ✈	d			09 14				10 14								11 14						12 14			
Coventry	d			09 25				10 25								11 25						12 25			
Smethwick Galton Bridge 7	d									10 12				10 43				11 09		11 43				12 08	
The Hawthorns 🚊	d									10 15				10 45				11 12		11 45				12 11	
Jewellery Quarter 🚊	d									10 18				10 49				11 15		11 49				12 14	
Birmingham Snow Hill 🚊	a	23p36								10 20				10 52				11 17		11 52				12 17	
	d	23p37				09 19	09 40			10 22			10 40	10 53				11 19	11 40	11 53				12 19	
Birmingham Moor Street	d	23p40	08 55		09 13	09 22	09 43		10 13	10 25			10 43	10 56			11 13	11 22	11 43	11 56			12 13	12 22	
Bordesley	d																								
Small Heath	d	23p44																							
Tyseley	d	23p46				09 26				10 29								11 26						12 26	
Acocks Green	d	23p49												11 02						12 02					
Olton	d	23p52												11 04						12 04					
Solihull	d	23p56	09 04		09 22		09 52		10 21				10 52	11 08			11 21		11 51	12 08			12 21		
Widney Manor	d	23p59												11 11						12 11					
Dorridge	d	00 03	09 09		09 27		09 57		10 26				10 57	11a17			11 26		11 56	12a17			12 26		
Lapworth	d	00 07											11 01												
Hatton	d	00 13											11 06												
Warwick Parkway	d	00 18	09 18		09 35		10 06		10 35				11 11				11 35		12 06				12 35		
Warwick	d	00 21	09 22		09 40				10 39								11 39						12 39		
Leamington Spa 8	a	00 26	09 26	09 36	09 44		10 13	10 36	10 44				11 16			11 36	11 43		12 12			12 37	12 43		
	d		09 27	09 38	09 45		10 14	10 38	10 44				11 18		11 20	11 38	11 43		12 13			12 38	12 43		
Banbury	d		09 44	09a54	10 02		10 31	10a54	11 06				11 35			11a54	12 01		12 30			12a54	13 01		
London Marylebone 10 ⊖	a		10 47		11 09		11 44		12 12				12 40				13 12		13 37				14 12		
Spring Road	d					09 29				10 32								11 29						12 29	
Hall Green	d					09 32				10 35								11 32						12 32	
Yardley Wood	d					09 35				10 38								11 35						12 35	
Shirley	d					09 38				10 41								11 38						12 38	
Whitlocks End	d					09 41				10 44								11 41						12 41	
Wythall	d					09 43				10 46								11 43						12 43	
Earlswood (West Midlands)	d																								
The Lakes	d					09x46				10x49								11x46						12x46	
Wood End	d																								
Danzey	d																								
Henley-in-Arden	d					09 54				10 57								11 54						12 54	
Wootton Wawen	d																								
Wilmcote	d					10 04				11 05					11 42			12 02						13 02	
Stratford-upon-Avon	a					10 09				11 12					11 54			12 09						13 09	

Table 71

Sundays
from 1 April

Hereford, Worcester and Stourbridge - Birmingham - Leamington Spa, Marylebone and Stratford-upon-Avon

Network Diagram - see first Page of Table 71

		XC	CH	LM	CH	XC	CH	LM	XC	CH	LM	CH	XC	CH	LM	GW	XC	CH	LM	CH	XC	CH	LM
		◇1				◇1	◇		◇1			◇	◇1	◇		◇1	◇1			◇	◇1		
		⊼				⊏			⊼				⊏				⊼				⊏		
Hereford 7	d																						
Ledbury	a																						
	d																						
Colwall	d																						
Great Malvern	a																						
	d							12 04								13 15							
Malvern Link	d							12 06								13 18							
Worcester Foregate Street 7	a							12 15								13 25							
	d							12 16							13 20	13 26							14 20
Worcester Shrub Hill 7	a							12 18								13 29							
	d							12 24															
Droitwich Spa	d							12 32							13 29								14 29
Bromsgrove	d																						
Barnt Green	d																						
University	d																						
Hartlebury	d																						
Kidderminster	d							12 42							13 39								14 39
Blakedown	d							12 47															14 44
Hagley	d							12 51							13 46								14 48
Stourbridge Junction 2	d			12 22				12 55			13 22				13 52				14 22				14 52
Lye	d			12 25							13 25								14 25				
Cradley Heath	d			12 29				13 01			13 29				13 58				14 29				14 58
Old Hill	d			12 33							13 33								14 33				
Rowley Regis	d			12 36				13 06			13 36				14 03				14 36				15 03
Langley Green	d			12 39							13 39								14 39				
Birmingham New Street 12	a																						
	d	12 33				13 04			13 33				14 04				14 33				15 04		
Birmingham International ✈	d					13 14							14 14								15 14		
Coventry	d					13 25							14 25								15 25		
Smethwick Galton Bridge 7	d			12 43				13 11			13 43				14 08				14 43				15 08
The Hawthorns 🚊	d			12 45				13 14			13 45				14 11				14 45				15 11
Jewellery Quarter 🚊	d			12 49				13 17			13 49				14 14				14 49				15 14
Birmingham Snow Hill 🚊	a			12 52				13 20			13 52				14 17				14 52				15 17
	d		12 40	12 53				13 22		13 40	13 53				14 19			14 40	14 53				15 19
Birmingham Moor Street	d		12 43	12 56			13 11	13 25		13 43	13 56			14 13	14 22			14 43	14 56			15 13	15 22
Bordesley	d																						
Small Heath	d																						
Tyseley	d							13 29							14 26								15 26
Acocks Green	d			13 02							14 02								15 02				
Olton	d			13 04							14 04								15 04				
Solihull	d		12 50	13 08			13 20			13 51	14 08			14 21				14 51	15 08			15 21	
Widney Manor	d			13 11							14 11								15 11				
Dorridge	d		12 56	13a18			13 25			13 56	14a17			14 26				14 56	15a17			15 26	
Lapworth	d									14 00													
Hatton	d									14 06		14 15											
Warwick Parkway	d		13 06				13 34			14 11				14 37				15 05				15 37	
Warwick	d						13 39					14 22		14 39								15 40	
Leamington Spa 8	a	12 59	13 11			13 36	13 43		13 59	14 17		14 26	14 36	14 44			14 59	15 10			15 36	15 44	
	d	13 00	13 11		13 20	13 38	13 43		14 00	14 17		14 26	14 38	14 44			15 00	15 11		15 20	15 38	15 45	
Banbury	d	13a17	13 29			13a54	14 05		14a17	14 35		14 45	14a54	15 04			15a18	15 30			15a54	16 05	
London Marylebone 10 ⊖	a		14 38				15 12			15 46		16 08		16 12				16 45				17 13	
Spring Road	d							13 32							14 29								15 29
Hall Green	d							13 35							14 32								15 32
Yardley Wood	d							13 38							14 35								15 35
Shirley	d							13 41							14 38								15 38
Whitlocks End	d							13 44							14 40								15 41
Wythall	d							13 46							14 43								15 43
Earlswood (West Midlands)	d																						
The Lakes	d							13x49							14x46								15x46
Wood End	d																						
Danzey	d																						
Henley-in-Arden	d							13 57							14 54								15 54
Wootton Wawen	d																						
Wilmcote	d				13 42			14 05							15 02					15 42			16 02
Stratford-upon-Avon	a				13 54			14 12							15 07					15 54			16 09

Table 71

Sundays
from 1 April

Hereford, Worcester and Stourbridge - Birmingham - Leamington Spa, Marylebone and Stratford-upon-Avon

Network Diagram - see first Page of Table 71

		GW	XC	LM	CH	LM	CH	XC	CH	LM	GW	LM	XC	CH	LM	CH	XC	LM	CH	LM	GW	XC
		◇1	◇1				◇	◇1			◇1		◇1			◇	◇1				◇1	◇1
		⊏	⊼					⊏			⊏		⊼				⊏				⊏	⊼
Hereford 7	d	13 32									14 32							15 30			16 35	
Ledbury	a	13 49									14 49							15 47			16 51	
	d	13 50									14 55							15 51			16 52	
Colwall	d	13 57									15 02							15 58			17 00	
Great Malvern	a	14 02									15 07							16 02			17 04	
	d	14 11		14 35							15 08							16 03			17 05	
Malvern Link	d	14 15		14 37							15 12							16 05			17 09	
Worcester Foregate Street 7	a	14 24		14 45							15 21							16 14			17 20	
	d	14 26		14 45						15 20	15 23							16 15		16 20	17 22	
Worcester Shrub Hill 7	a	14 29		14 48							15 26							16 18			17 27	
	d			14 53								15 46						16 33				
Droitwich Spa	d			15 01						15 29		15 54						16 41		16 29		
Bromsgrove	d			15 10														16 51				
Barnt Green	d																					
University	d																					
Hartlebury	d																					
Kidderminster	d									15 40		16 04								16 39		
Blakedown	d																					
Hagley	d									15 47		16 11								16 46		
Stourbridge Junction 2	d					15 22				15 52		16 16			16 22					16 52		
Lye	d					15 25									16 25							
Cradley Heath	d					15 29				15 58					16 29					16 58		
Old Hill	d					15 33									16 33							
Rowley Regis	d					15 36				16 03					16 36					17 03		
Langley Green	d					15 39									16 39							
Birmingham New Street 12	a			15 37														17 17				
	d		15 33					16 04					16 33				17 04					17 33
Birmingham International ✈	d							16 14									17 14					
Coventry	d							16 25									17 25					
Smethwick Galton Bridge 7	d					15 43				16 08		16 29			16 43					17 08		
The Hawthorns 🚊	d					15 45				16 11					16 45					17 11		
Jewellery Quarter 🚊	d					15 49				16 14					16 49					17 14		
Birmingham Snow Hill 🚊	a					15 52				16 17		16 35			16 52					17 17		
	d				15 40	15 53				16 19		16 45		16 40	16 53					17 19		
Birmingham Moor Street	d				15 43	15 56			16 13	16 22		16a47		16 43	16 56				17 13	17 22		
Bordesley	d																					
Small Heath	d																					
Tyseley	d									16 26										17 26		
Acocks Green	d					16 02									17 02							
Olton	d					16 04									17 04							
Solihull	d				15 51	16 08			16 21					16 51	17 08				17 21			
Widney Manor	d					16 11									17 11							
Dorridge	d				15 56	16a17			16 26					16 56	17a17				17 26			
Lapworth	d				16 00																	
Hatton	d				16 06		16 14															
Warwick Parkway	d				16 11				16 37					17 05					17 36			
Warwick	d						16 23		16 40										17 40			
Leamington Spa 8	a		15 59		16 17		16 26	16 36	16 44				16 59	17 12			17 36		17 44			18 00
	d		16 00		16 17		16 27	16 38	16 45				17 00	17 12		17 20	17 38		17 45			18 01
Banbury	d		16a17		16 35		16 46	16a54	17 05				17a17	17 30			17a54		18 05			18a19
London Marylebone 10 ⊖	a				17 46		18 08		18 12					18 45					19 13			
Spring Road	d									16 29										17 29		
Hall Green	d									16 32										17 32		
Yardley Wood	d									16 35										17 35		
Shirley	d									16 38										17 38		
Whitlocks End	d									16 41										17 41		
Wythall	d									16 43										17 43		
Earlswood (West Midlands)	d																					
The Lakes	d									16x46										17x46		
Wood End	d																					
Danzey	d																					
Henley-in-Arden	d									16 55										17 54		
Wootton Wawen	d																					
Wilmcote	d									17 03						17 42				18 02		
Stratford-upon-Avon	a									17 10						17 54				18 09		

Hereford, Worcester and Stourbridge - Birmingham - Leamington Spa, Marylebone and Stratford-upon-Avon

Network Diagram - see first Page of Table 71

		CH	LM	CH	XC	CH	LM	LM	XC	CH	CH	XC	CH	LM	GW	GW	XC	CH	XC	CH	LM	XC	LM
				◇	◇1	◇			◇1		◇	◇1			◇1	◇1	◇1	◇	◇1	◇		◇1	
Hereford 7	d															18 30							
Ledbury	a															18 47							
	d															18 48							
Colwall	d															18 55							
Great Malvern	a															19 00							
	d							17 17								19 11							
Malvern Link	d							17 20								19 14							
Worcester Foregate Street 7	a							17 28								19 23							
	d						17 20	17 28						18 20	18 25	19 25							
Worcester Shrub Hill 7	a							17 31							18 26	19 26							
	d							17 36													19 38		19 53
Droitwich Spa	d						17 29	17 44						18 29							19 46		20 01
Bromsgrove	d							17 53															20 10
Barnt Green	d																						
University	d																						
Hartlebury	d																						
Kidderminster	d						17 39							18 39							19 56		
Blakedown	d						17 44																
Hagley	d						17 48							18 46							20 03		
Stourbridge Junction 2	d		17 22				17 52							18 52							20 07		
Lye	d		17 25																				
Cradley Heath	d		17 29				17 58							18 58							20 13		
Old Hill	d		17 33																				
Rowley Regis	d		17 36				18 03							19 03							20 19		
Langley Green	d		17 39																				
Birmingham New Street 12	a							18 15															20 36
	d				18 04				18 33			19 04					19 33		20 04			20 33	
Birmingham International ✈	d				18 14							19 14							20 14				
Coventry	d				18 25							19 25							20 25				
Smethwick Galton Bridge 7	d		17 43				18 08							19 08							20 24		
The Hawthorns ⇌	d		17 45				18 11							19 11							20 26		
Jewellery Quarter ⇌	d		17 49				18 14							19 14							20 30		
Birmingham Snow Hill ⇌	a		17 53				18 17							19 19							20 33		
	d	17 40	17 53				18 19			18 40			19 15	19 21						20 15	20 33		
Birmingham Moor Street	d	17 43	17 56			18 13	18 22			18 43			19 18	19a23						20 18	20a36		
Bordesley	d																						
Small Heath	d																						
Tyseley	d						18 26																
Acocks Green	d		18 02																				
Olton	d		18 04																				
Solihull	d	17 51	18 08			18 21				18 51			19 26							20 28			
Widney Manor	d		18 11										19 29							20 31			
Dorridge	d	17 56	18a17			18 26				18 56			19 33							20 35			
Lapworth	d	18 00											19 37										
Hatton	d	18 06		18 14									19 43					20 15					
Warwick Parkway	d	18 11				18 36				19 05			19 47							20 45			
Warwick	d			18 22		18 40							19 51					20 21		20 48			
Leamington Spa 8	a	18 17		18 26	18 36	18 44			18 59	19 11		19 36	19 56				19 59	20 25	20 36	20 53		20 58	
	d	18 17		18 26	18 38	18 45			19 00	19 11	19 20	19 38	19 56				20 00	20 26	20 38	20 53		21 00	
Banbury	d	18 35		18 45	18a54	19 05			19a17	19 29		19a54	20 14				20a18	20 46	20a54	21 12		21a17	
London Marylebone 10 ⊖	a	19 45		20 08		20 12				20 45			21 46					21 53		22 50			
Spring Road	d						18 29																
Hall Green	d						18 32																
Yardley Wood	d						18 35																
Shirley	d						18 38																
Whitlocks End	d						18 41																
Wythall	d						18 43																
Earlswood (West Midlands)	d																						
The Lakes	d						18x46																
Wood End	d																						
Danzey	d																						
Henley-in-Arden	d						18 54																
Wootton Wawen	d																						
Wilmcote	d						19 02				19 42												
Stratford-upon-Avon	a						19 09				19 54												

Hereford, Worcester and Stourbridge - Birmingham - Leamington Spa, Marylebone and Stratford-upon-Avon

Network Diagram - see first Page of Table 71

		GW	XC	CH	LM	LM	LM	LM
		◇1	◇1	◇				
Hereford 7	d					20 05		
Ledbury	a					20 21		
	d					20 22		
Colwall	d					20 28		
Great Malvern	a					20 33		
	d	20 15				20 33		22 10
Malvern Link	d	20 18				20 36		22 13
Worcester Foregate Street 7	a	20 25				20 44		22 22
	d	20 26				20 45		22 23
Worcester Shrub Hill 7	a	20 29				20 47		22 25
	d				20 34	20 52	21 25	22 29
Droitwich Spa	d				20 42	21 00	21 33	22 37
Bromsgrove	d					21 09		
Barnt Green	d							
University	d							
Hartlebury	d							
Kidderminster	d				20 52		21 43	22 47
Blakedown	d							
Hagley	d				20 59		21 50	22 54
Stourbridge Junction 2	d				21 03		21 54	22 58
Lye	d							
Cradley Heath	d				21 08		21 59	23 04
Old Hill	d							
Rowley Regis	d				21 14		22 05	23 09
Langley Green	d							
Birmingham New Street 12	a					21 42		
	d		21 04					
Birmingham International ✈	d		21 14					
Coventry	d		21 24					
Smethwick Galton Bridge 7	d				21 19		22 10	23 14
The Hawthorns ⇌	d				21 21		22 12	23 17
Jewellery Quarter ⇌	d				21 25		22 16	23 20
Birmingham Snow Hill ⇌	a				21 28		22 19	23 24
	d			21 15	21 28		22 20	
Birmingham Moor Street	d			21 18	21a31		22a22	
Bordesley	d							
Small Heath	d							
Tyseley	d							
Acocks Green	d							
Olton	d							
Solihull	d			21 28				
Widney Manor	d			21 31				
Dorridge	d			21 35				
Lapworth	d							
Hatton	d							
Warwick Parkway	d			21 45				
Warwick	d			21 48				
Leamington Spa 8	a		21 34	21 53				
	d			21 53				
Banbury	d			22 15				
London Marylebone 10 ⊖	a			23 50				
Spring Road	d							
Hall Green	d							
Yardley Wood	d							
Shirley	d							
Whitlocks End	d							
Wythall	d							
Earlswood (West Midlands)	d							
The Lakes	d							
Wood End	d							
Danzey	d							
Henley-in-Arden	d							
Wootton Wawen	d							
Wilmcote	d							
Stratford-upon-Avon	a							

Stratford-upon-Avon, Marylebone and Leamington Spa - Birmingham - Stourbridge, Worcester and Hereford

Network Diagram - see first Page of Table 71

Miles	Miles	Miles			LM MX	CH MX ◇	CH MX ◇	LM MX A	LM	GW ■1	LM	LM	LM		LM	CH ◇	LM	GW	LM	GW ◇■1	LM	CH	LM		CH
—	0	—	**Stratford-upon-Avon**	d																		06 10	06 27		
—	2¾	—	Wilmcote	d																		06 16	06 32		
—	6½	—	Wootton Wawen	d																			06x37		
—	8¾	—	Henley-in-Arden	d																			06 41		
—	11¼	—	Danzey	d																			06x46		
—	13	—	Wood End	d																			06x50		
—	14¾	—	The Lakes	d																			06x53		
—	15	—	Earlswood (West Midlands)	d																			06 55		
—	16	—	Wythall	d																			06 58		
—	17	—	Whitlocks End	d											06 28		06 46						07 00		
—	18	—	Shirley	d											06 31		06 52						07 03		
—	19¼	—	Yardley Wood	d											06 34		06 55						07 06		
—	20½	—	Hall Green	d											06 37		06 58						07 09		
—	21	—	Spring Road	d											06 39		07 00						07 11		
—	—	—	**London Marylebone** ■10 ⊖	d		22p37	23p07																		
—	—	—	Banbury	d		23p39	00 04									06 07									
—	—	0	**Leamington Spa** ■8	a		23p56	00 21									06 24						06 45			
—	—	—		d		23p56	00 22					05 47				06 25					06 29				06 52
—	—	2	Warwick	d		00 01	00 26					05 51				06 29					06 33				06 56
—	—	3¾	Warwick Parkway	d		00 04	00 29					05 55				06 32					06 37				06 59
—	—	6	Hatton	d								06 00									06 42				07a04
—	—	10¼	Lapworth	d								06 06									06 48				
—	—	12¾	Dorridge	d	22p33	00 14					05 40	06 11				06 44					06 53				
—	—	14¾	Widney Manor	d	22p37						05 45	06 14									06 56				
—	—	16¼	Solihull	d	22p41	00 19	00 41				05 48	06 18				06 49					07 00				
—	—	18	Olton	d	22p44						05 52	06 21									07 03				
—	—	19	Acocks Green	d	22p47						05 54	06 24									07 06				
—	22	20	Tyseley	d	22p50						05 57	06 27			06 42		07 03				07 09		07 14		
—	23	21	Small Heath	d	22p52						06 00	06 29			06 44		07 05				07 11		07 17		
—	24	—	Bordesley	d																					
—	24¾	—	**Birmingham Moor Street**	d	22p56	00a32	00a55				06 04	06 33			06 48	07a03	07 09				07 16		07 22		
—	25¼	—	**Birmingham Snow Hill** 🚊	a	22p59						06 06	06 37			06 51		07 12				07 19		07 24		
—	—	—		d	23p00						06 08				06 53		07 13				07 23				
—	26	—	Jewellery Quarter 🚊	d	23p02						06 10				06 55		07 15				07 25				
—	28½	—	The Hawthorns 🚊	d	23p07						06 15				07 00		07 20				07 30				
—	29¼	29	Smethwick Galton Bridge ■7	d	23p10						06 17				07 03		07 23				07 33				
—	—	—	**Coventry**	a																					
—	—	—	**Birmingham International** ✈	a																					
0	—	24	**Birmingham New Street** ■12	a																					
—	—	—		d				23p16					06 59						07 19						
—	30½	30¼	Langley Green	d	23p13						06 20				07 06						07 36				
—	32¼	—	Rowley Regis	d	23p16						06 24				07 09		07 28				07 39				
—	33½	—	Old Hill	d	23p19						06 27				07 12						07 42				
—	34¾	—	Cradley Heath	d	23p23						06 30				07 16		07 33				07 46				
—	36¼	—	Lye	d	23p26						06 33				07 19						07 49				
—	37¼	—	**Stourbridge Junction** ■2	d	23p30						06 37				07 23		07a39				07 53				
—	39¼	—	Hagley	d	23p33						06 40				07 26						07 56				
—	41	—	Blakedown	d	23p36						06 43				07 29						07 59				
—	44¼	—	**Kidderminster**	d	23p41						06 48				07 34						08 04				
—	47¾	—	Hartlebury	d											07 39						08 09				
2½	—	—	University	d									07 05						07 25						
10½	—	—	Barnt Green	d															07 41						
13	—	—	Bromsgrove	d									07 22						07 46						
19¼	53½	—	Droitwich Spa	d	23p52			00 01			06 59		07 32		07 46				07 56		08 17				
25	—	—	**Worcester Shrub Hill** ■7	a	00 01			00 11											08 03		08 25				
—	—	—		d					06 00	06 33								07 55	08 07	08 14	08 29				
25¾	58¾	—	**Worcester Foregate Street** ■7	a					06 02	06 39	07 09		07 42		07 57			07 58	08 09	08 17	08 31				
—	—	—		d					06 03				07 43					07 58	08 11						
32½	—	—	Malvern Link	d					06 12				07 53					08 07	08 20						
33¾	—	—	**Great Malvern**	a					06 15				07 56					08 12	08 22						
—	—	—		d					06 15				07 59												
36½	—	—	Colwall	d					06 20				08 04												
40¾	—	—	Ledbury	a					06 27				08 11												
—	—	—		d					06 29				08 12												
54½	—	—	**Hereford** ■7	a					06 50				08 32												

A from 27 March

Stratford-upon-Avon, Marylebone and Leamington Spa - Birmingham - Stourbridge, Worcester and Hereford

Network Diagram - see first Page of Table 71

		LM	LM	LM	LM	XC ◇■1	CH	CH	LM		XC ◇■1	LM	LM	LM	GW ■1	LM	LM	LM	CH		XC ◇■1	LM	CH ◇	LM	XC ◇■1
Stratford-upon-Avon	d			06 52			06 47		07 23							07 42			07 35						
Wilmcote	d			06 57												07 47			07 41						
Wootton Wawen	d			07x02												07x52									
Henley-in-Arden	d			07 06					07 34							07 57									
Danzey	d			07x11												08x02									
Wood End	d			07x15												08x06									
The Lakes	d			07x18												08x08									
Earlswood (West Midlands)	d			07 20					07 42							08 11									
Wythall	d			07 23					07 44							08 14									
Whitlocks End	d			07 26					07 47				08 07			08 16						08 35			
Shirley	d			07 29					07 50				08 10			08 20						08 38			
Yardley Wood	d			07 32					07 53				08 13			08 23						08 41			
Hall Green	d			07 36					07 57				08 16			08 27						08 44			
Spring Road	d			07 38					07 59				08 18			08 29						08 46			
London Marylebone ■10 ⊖	d																						07 00		
Banbury	d					06 54		07 02			07 26										07 54		08 04		08 27
Leamington Spa ■8	a					07 10	07 15	07 21			07 42								08 11		08 11		08 25		08 43
	d				07 08	07 12		07 22			07 43			07 46				08 00			08 12		08 26		08 44
Warwick	d				07 12			07 26						07 50				08 04					08 30		
Warwick Parkway	d				07 16			07 29						07 54				08 08					08 33		
Hatton	d				07 21			07 34						07 59				08 13							
Lapworth	d				07 28									08 05				08 19							
Dorridge	d	07 09			07 34			07 42				07 56		08 10			08 20	08 25					08 43		
Widney Manor	d	07 14			07 37			07 46				08 01		08 14			08 24	08 28							
Solihull	d	07 17			07 41			07 50				08 04		08 17			08 28	08 32					08 49		
Olton	d	07 21			07 44			07 54				08 08		08 21			08 32	08 36							
Acocks Green	d	07 23			07 47							08 11		08 24			08 35	08 38							
Tyseley	d	07 26		07 41	07 50							08 14	08 21	08 27		08 32	08 38	08 42				08 49			
Small Heath	d	07 29		07 43	07 53								08 24	08 29		08 35		08 45				08 51			
Bordesley	d																								
Birmingham Moor Street	d	07 33		07 47	07 57			08 01	08 06			08 19	08 28	08 33		08 39	08 42	08 49				08 55	08 59		
Birmingham Snow Hill 🚊	a	07 35		07 52	07 59			08 10	08 10			08 21	08 30	08 37		08 41	08 47	08 51				08 58	09 07		
	d	07 37		07 53	08 03				08 13			08 23	08 33			08 43		08 53				09 03			
Jewellery Quarter 🚊	d	07 39		07 55	08 05				08 15			08 25	08 35			08 45		08 55				09 05			
The Hawthorns 🚊	d	07 44		08 00	08 10				08 20			08 30	08 40			08 50		09 00				09 10			
Smethwick Galton Bridge ■7	d	07 47		08 03	08 13				08 23			08 33	08 43			08 53		09 03				09 13			
Coventry	a					07 22															08 23				
Birmingham International ✈	a					07 37															08 37				
Birmingham New Street ■12	a					07 48					08 15										08 48				09 18
	d		07 59																					08 49	
Langley Green	d	07 50			08 16								08 46									09 16			
Rowley Regis	d	07 53		08 08	08 19				08 28			08 38	08 49			08 58		09 08				09 19			
Old Hill	d	07 56			08 22								08 52									09 22			
Cradley Heath	d	08 00		08 13	08 26				08 33			08 43	08 56			09 03		09 13				09 26			
Lye	d	08 03			08 29								08 59									09 29			
Stourbridge Junction ■2	d	08a07		08 19	08 33				08a39			08a49	09 03			09 09		09a19				09 33			
Hagley	d			08 23	08 36											09 12									
Blakedown	d			08 26	08 39											09 15									
Kidderminster	d			08 31	08a45								09a12			09 20						09a42			
Hartlebury	d			08 36																					
University	d		08 05																					08 55	
Barnt Green	d		08 18																						
Bromsgrove	d		08 23																					09 10	
Droitwich Spa	d		08 32	08 44												09 31								09 20	
Worcester Shrub Hill ■7	a															09 40									
	d														09 15										
Worcester Foregate Street ■7	a		08 41	08 59											09 18									09 28	
	d		08 42												09 18									09 32	
Malvern Link	d		08 52												09 27									09 42	
Great Malvern	a		08 54												09 32									09 44	
	d		08 55																					09 45	
Colwall	d		09 00																					09 50	
Ledbury	a		09 07																					09 57	
	d		09 08																					09 59	
Hereford ■7	a		09 28																					10 17	

r

Stratford-upon-Avon, Marylebone and Leamington Spa - Birmingham - Stourbridge, Worcester and Hereford

Network Diagram - see first Page of Table 71

		CH	LM	LM	LM	LM	CH	XC	GW	LM	LM	LM	CH	XC	LM	GW	LM	CH	LM	LM	CH	XC	LM
							◇	◇1					◇	◇1		◇1		◇			◇	◇1	
								H						H		⊏					H	H	
Stratford-upon-Avon	d			08 26															09 26				
Wilmcote	d			08 31															09 31				
Wootton Wawen	d			08x36															09x36				
Henley-in-Arden	d			08 41															09 41				
Danzey	d			08x46															09x46				
Wood End	d			08x50															09x50				
The Lakes	d			08x52															09x52				
Earlswood (West Midlands)	d			08 55															09 55				
Wythall	d			08 57															09 57				
Whitlocks End	d			09 00							09 19				09 39				10 00				
Shirley	d			09 03							09 22				09 42				10 03				
Yardley Wood	d			09 06							09 25				09 45				10 06				
Hall Green	d			09 09							09 28				09 48				10 09				
Spring Road	d			09 11							09 30				09 50				10 11				
London Marylebone 10 ⊖	d	07 08					07 33						08 03					08 37					
Banbury	d	08 32					08 38	08 54					09 05	09 26				09 30				09 54	
Leamington Spa 8	a	08 50					08 56	09 10					09 22	09 42				09 47				10 11	
	d	08 51					08 57	09 12					09 23	09 43				09 47			09 55	10 12	
Warwick	d	08 55					09 01						09 27								09 59		
Warwick Parkway	d						09 04						09 30					09 53			10 02		
Hatton	d	09a02					09 09														10 07		
Lapworth	d						09 14														10 13		
Dorridge	d		08 46			09 10	09 20					09 28	09 40				09 46			10 09	10 17		
Widney Manor	d		08 50			09 14						09 32					09 50			10 13			
Solihull	d		08 54			09 18	09 25					09 36	09 46				09 54	10 05		10 17	10 23		
Olton	d		08 57			09 21						09 39					09 57			10 20			
Acocks Green	d		09 00			09 24						09 42					10 00			10 23			
Tyseley	d		09 03								09 33						10 03						
Small Heath	d		09 05								09 35						10 05						
Bordesley	d																						
Birmingham Moor Street	d		09 09	09 18		09 31	09a38				09 39	09 48	09 55		09 59		10 09	10a17	10 18	10 29	10a37		
Birmingham Snow Hill	a		09 12	09 21		09 34					09 42	09 51	10 05		10 02		10 12		10 21	10 32			
	d		09 13	09 23	09 33						09 43	09 53			10 03		10 13		10 23	10 33			
Jewellery Quarter	d		09 15	09 25	09 35						09 45	09 55			10 05		10 15		10 25	10 35			
The Hawthorns	d		09 20	09 30	09 40						09 50	10 00			10 10		10 20		10 30	10 40			
Smethwick Galton Bridge 7	d		09 23	09 33	09 43						09 53	10 03			10 13		10 23		10 33	10 43			
Coventry	a							09 22														10 23	
Birmingham International ✈	a							09 37														10 37	
Birmingham New Street 12	a							09 48						10 18								10 48	
	d									09 49													10 49
Langley Green	d				09 46										10 16					10 46			
Rowley Regis	d		09 28	09 38	09 49						09 58	10 08			10 19		10 28		10 38	10 49			
Old Hill	d				09 52										10 22					10 52			
Cradley Heath	d		09 33	09 43	09 56						10 03	10 13			10 26		10 33		10 43	10 56			
Lye	d				09 59										10 29					10 59			
Stourbridge Junction 2	d		09 39	09a49	10 03						10 09	10a19			10 33		10 39		10a49	11 03			
Hagley	d		09 42								10 12						10 42						
Blakedown	d		09 45								10 15						10 45						
Kidderminster	d		09 50		10a13						10 20				10a43		10 50			11a13			
Hartlebury	d																						
University	d									09 55													10 55
Barnt Green	d																						
Bromsgrove	d									10 10													11 10
Droitwich Spa	d		10 01							10 20	10 31						11 01						11 20
Worcester Shrub Hill 7	a																						
	d								10 15							10 45							
Worcester Foregate Street 7	a		10 10						10 17	10 30	10 40					10 48	11 10						11 30
	d								10 18	10 32	10 42					10 49							11 32
Malvern Link	d								10 27	10 42	10 52					11 03							11 42
Great Malvern	a								10 32	10 44	10 55					11 06							11 44
	d									10 45						11 07							11 45
Colwall	d									10 50						11 14							11 50
Ledbury	a									10 57						11 22							11 57
	d									10 59						11 24							11 59
Hereford 7	a									11 19						11 42							12 19

Stratford-upon-Avon, Marylebone and Leamington Spa - Birmingham - Stourbridge, Worcester and Hereford

Network Diagram - see first Page of Table 71

		GW	LM	LM	CH	CH	CH	XC	LM	LM	LM	CH	XC	LM	GW	LM	LM	LM	CH	XC	CH	LM
		◇1			◇	◇	◇	◇1				◇	◇1		◇				◇	◇1		
		H			H		H	H				H	H						H	H		
Stratford-upon-Avon	d					09 55					10 26										11 20	
Wilmcote	d					10 00					10 31										11 25	
Wootton Wawen	d										10x36											
Henley-in-Arden	d										10 41											
Danzey	d										10x46											
Wood End	d										10x50											
The Lakes	d										10x52											
Earlswood (West Midlands)	d										10 55											
Wythall	d										10 57											
Whitlocks End	d		10 19						10 39		11 00						11 19					11 39
Shirley	d		10 22						10 42		11 03						11 22					11 42
Yardley Wood	d		10 25						10 45		11 06						11 25					11 45
Hall Green	d		10 28						10 48		11 09						11 28					11 48
Spring Road	d		10 30						10 50		11 11						11 30					11 50
London Marylebone 10 ⊖	d				09 07		09 10					09 37							10 07			
Banbury	d				10 05		10 16	10 25				10 30	10 54						11 05	11 25		
Leamington Spa 8	a				10 23	10 27	10 33	10 41				10 48	11 10						11 23	11 41	11 50	
	d				10 23		10 33	10 42				10 48	11 12						11 23	11 43		
Warwick	d				10 27		10a37												11 27			
Warwick Parkway	d				10 31							10 54							11 31			
Hatton	d																					
Lapworth	d																					
Dorridge	d			10 28	10 41					10 46				11 09				11 28	11 41			
Widney Manor	d			10 32						10 50				11 13				11 32				
Solihull	d			10 36	10 46					10 54		11 06		11 17				11 36	11 46			
Olton	d			10 39						10 57				11 20				11 39				
Acocks Green	d			10 42						11 00				11 23				11 42				
Tyseley	d		10 33							11 03							11 33					
Small Heath	d		10 35							11 05							11 35					
Bordesley	d																					
Birmingham Moor Street	d		10 39	10 48	10 55				10 59	11 09	11 19	11a19		11 29			11 39	11 48	11 55			11 59
Birmingham Snow Hill	a		10 42	10 51	11 04				11 02	11 12	11 22			11 32			11 42	11 51	12 04			12 02
	d		10 43	10 53					11 03	11 13	11 23			11 33			11 43	11 53				12 03
Jewellery Quarter	d		10 45	10 55					11 05	11 15	11 25			11 35			11 45	11 55				12 05
The Hawthorns	d		10 50	11 00					11 10	11 20	11 30			11 40			11 50	12 00				12 10
Smethwick Galton Bridge 7	d		10 53	11 03					11 13	11 23	11 33			11 43			11 53	12 03				12 13
Coventry	a												11 22									
Birmingham International ✈	a												11 37									
Birmingham New Street 12	a							11 18					11 48							12 18		
	d															11 49						
Langley Green	d								11 16					11 46								12 16
Rowley Regis	d		10 58	11 08					11 19	11 28	11 38			11 49			11 58	12 08				12 19
Old Hill	d								11 22					11 52								12 22
Cradley Heath	d		11 03	11 13					11 26	11 33	11 43			11 56			12 03	12 13				12 26
Lye	d								11 29					11 59								12 29
Stourbridge Junction 2	d		11 09	11a19					11 33	11 39	11a49			12 03			12 09	12a19				12 33
Hagley	d		11 12							11 42							12 12					
Blakedown	d		11 15							11 45							12 15					
Kidderminster	d		11 20						11a43	11 50				12a13			12 20					12a43
Hartlebury	d																					
University	d															11 55						
Barnt Green	d																					
Bromsgrove	d															12 10						
Droitwich Spa	d		11 31							12 01						12 20	12 31					
Worcester Shrub Hill 7	a		11 39																			
	d	11 35													12 15							
Worcester Foregate Street 7	a	11 40								12 10					12 17	12 30	12 40					
	d														12 18	12 32						
Malvern Link	d														12 27	12 42						
Great Malvern	a														12 34	12 44						
	d															12 45						
Colwall	d															12 50						
Ledbury	a															12 57						
	d															12 59						
Hereford 7	a															13 19						

Table 71

Mondays to Fridays

Stratford-upon-Avon, Marylebone and Leamington Spa - Birmingham - Stourbridge, Worcester and Hereford

Network Diagram - see first Page of Table 71

		GW	LM	LM	CH	LM	CH	XC	CH	LM	GW	LM	LM	CH	XC	LM	LM	LM	CH	XC	LM	GW	LM
		◇1			◇		◇	◇1	◇		◇1			◇	◇1					◇1		◇	
		🍴			🛒		🛒	🛒			🛒			🛒	🛒				🛒	🛒			
Stratford-upon-Avon	d			11 26														12 26					
Wilmcote	d			11 31														12 31					
Wootton Wawen	d			11x36														12x36					
Henley-in-Arden	d			11 41														12 41					
Danzey	d			11x46														12x46					
Wood End	d			11x50														12x50					
The Lakes	d			11x52														12x52					
Earlswood (West Midlands)	d			11 55														12 55					
Wythall	d			11 57														12 57					
Whitlocks End	d			12 00								12 19				12 39		13 00					
Shirley	d			12 03								12 22				12 42		13 03					
Yardley Wood	d			12 06								12 25				12 45		13 06					
Hall Green	d			12 09								12 28				12 48		13 09					
Spring Road	d			12 11								12 30				12 50		13 11					
London Marylebone 10 ⊖	d				10 37				10 40					11 07					11 37				
Banbury	d				11 33			11 54	11 59					12 06	12 25				12 29	12 54			
Leamington Spa 8	a				11 50			12 11	12 18					12 23	12 42				12 46	13 10			
	d				11 50		11 55	12 12	12 18					12 23	12 43				12 47	13 12			
Warwick	d						11 59		12 22					12 27									
Warwick Parkway	d				11 56		12 02							12 31					12 52				
Hatton	d						12 07		12a29														
Lapworth	d						12 12																
Dorridge	d		11 46			12 09	12 17						12 28	12 41			12 46				13 09		
Widney Manor	d		11 50			12 13							12 32				12 50				13 13		
Solihull	d		11 54		12 08	12 17	12 22						12 36	12 46			12 54		13 05		13 17		
Olton	d		11 57			12 20							12 39				12 57				13 20		
Acocks Green	d		12 00			12 23							12 42				13 00				13 23		
Tyseley	d		12 03									12 33					13 03						
Small Heath	d		12 05									12 35					13 05						
Bordesley	d																						
Birmingham Moor Street	d		12 09	12 18	12a25	12 29	12a39					12 39	12 48	12 55		12 59	13 09	13 18	13a19		13 29		
Birmingham Snow Hill 🚊	a		12 12	12 22		12 32						12 42	12 51	13 04		13 02	13 12	13 21			13 32		
	d		12 13	12 23		12 33						12 43	12 53			13 03	13 13	13 23			13 33		
Jewellery Quarter 🚊	d		12 15	12 25		12 35						12 45	12 55			13 05	13 15	13 25			13 35		
The Hawthorns 🚊	d		12 20	12 30		12 40						12 50	13 00			13 10	13 20	13 30			13 40		
Smethwick Galton Bridge 7	d		12 23	12 33		12 43						12 53	13 03			13 13	13 23	13 33			13 43		
Coventry	a							12 24												13 22			
Birmingham International ✈	a							12 37												13 37			
Birmingham New Street 12	a							12 48							13 18					13 48			
	d									12 49													13 49
Langley Green	d					12 46										13 16					13 46		
Rowley Regis	d		12 28	12 38		12 49						12 58	13 08			13 19	13 28	13 38			13 49		
Old Hill	d					12 52										13 22					13 52		
Cradley Heath	d		12 33	12 43		12 56						13 03	13 13			13 26	13 33	13 43			13 56		
Lye	d					12 59										13 29					13 59		
Stourbridge Junction 2	d		12 39	12a49		13 03						13 09	13a19			13a33	13 44	13a49			14 03		
Hagley	d		12 42									13 12					13 47						
Blakedown	d		12 45									13 15					13 50						
Kidderminster	d		12 50			13a13						13 20					13 55				14a13		
Hartlebury	d																						
University	d									12 55													13 55
Barnt Green	d																						
Bromsgrove	d									13 10													14 10
Droitwich Spa	d		13 01							13 20		13 31					14 06						14 20
Worcester Shrub Hill 7	a											13 39					14 14						
	d	12 45									13 32											14 15	
Worcester Foregate Street 7	a	12 48	13 10							13 30	13 35											14 18	14 30
	d	12 49	13 11							13 32	13 36											14 18	14 32
Malvern Link	d	12 58	13 20							13 42	13 51											14 27	14 42
Great Malvern	a	13 02	13 24							13 44	13 56											14 37	14 44
	d	13 09								13 45													14 45
Colwall	d	13 16								13 50													14 50
Ledbury	a	13 24								13 58													14 57
	d	13 31								14 00													14 59
Hereford 7	a	13 48								14 21													15 19

Table 71

Mondays to Fridays

Stratford-upon-Avon, Marylebone and Leamington Spa - Birmingham - Stourbridge, Worcester and Hereford

Network Diagram - see first Page of Table 71

		LM	LM	CH	CH	XC	LM	GW	LM	LM	CH	LM	CH	XC	LM	LM	LM	CH	CH	XC	LM	LM
				◇		◇1		◇1					◇	◇1				◇	◇	◇1		
				🛒		🛒		🛒					🛒	🛒					🛒	🛒		
Stratford-upon-Avon	d				13 06					13 26												
Wilmcote	d				13 11					13 31												
Wootton Wawen	d									13x36												
Henley-in-Arden	d									13 41												
Danzey	d									13x46												
Wood End	d									13x50												
The Lakes	d									13x52												
Earlswood (West Midlands)	d									13 55												
Wythall	d									13 57												
Whitlocks End	d	13 19					13 39			14 00						14 19					14 39	
Shirley	d	13 22					13 42			14 03						14 22					14 42	
Yardley Wood	d	13 25					13 45			14 06						14 25					14 45	
Hall Green	d	13 28					13 48			14 09						14 28					14 48	
Spring Road	d	13 30					13 50			14 11						14 30					14 50	
London Marylebone 10 ⊖	d			12 07							12 37							13 07				
Banbury	d			13 06		13 25					13 29			13 54				14 06		14 26		
Leamington Spa 8	a			13 23	13 41	13 42					13 46			14 10				14 23		14 41		
	d			13 23		13 43					13 47		13 52	14 12				14 23	14 34	14 42		
Warwick	d			13 27									13 57					14 27	14 38			
Warwick Parkway	d			13 31							13 52		14 00					14 31				
Hatton	d												14 05						14a45			
Lapworth	d												14 10									
Dorridge	d		13 28	13 41					13 46			14 09	14 17				14 28	14 41				14 46
Widney Manor	d		13 32						13 50			14 13					14 32					14 50
Solihull	d		13 36	13 46					13 54		14 05	14 17	14 22				14 36	14 46				14 54
Olton	d		13 39						13 57			14 20					14 39					14 57
Acocks Green	d		13 42						14 00			14 23					14 42					15 00
Tyseley	d	13 33							14 03							14 33						15 03
Small Heath	d	13 35							14 05							14 35						15 05
Bordesley	d																					
Birmingham Moor Street	d	13 39	13 48	13 55			13 58		14 09	14 18	14a18	14 29	14a38			14 39	14 48	14 55			14 59	15 09
Birmingham Snow Hill 🚊	a	13 42	13 51	14 04			14 02		14 12	14 21		14 32				14 42	14 51	15 04			15 02	15 12
	d	13 43	13 53				14 03		14 13	14 23		14 33				14 43	14 53				15 03	15 13
Jewellery Quarter 🚊	d	13 45	13 55				14 05		14 15	14 25		14 35				14 45	14 55				15 05	15 15
The Hawthorns 🚊	d	13 50	14 00				14 10		14 20	14 30		14 40				14 50	15 00				15 10	15 20
Smethwick Galton Bridge 7	d	13 53	14 03				14 13		14 23	14 33		14 43				14 53	15 03				15 13	15 23
Coventry	a													14 22								
Birmingham International ✈	a													14 37								
Birmingham New Street 12	a					14 18								14 48						15 18		
	d														14 49							
Langley Green	d						14 16					14 46									15 16	
Rowley Regis	d	13 58	14 08				14 19		14 28	14 38		14 49				14 58	15 08				15 19	15 28
Old Hill	d						14 22					14 52									15 22	
Cradley Heath	d	14 03	14 13				14 26		14 33	14 43		14 56				15 03	15 13				15 26	15 33
Lye	d						14 29					14 59									15 29	
Stourbridge Junction 2	d	14 09	14a19				14 33		14 39	14a49		15 03				15 09	15a19				15 33	15 39
Hagley	d	14 12							14 42							15 12					15 37	15 43
Blakedown	d	14 15							14 45							15 15						15 46
Kidderminster	d	14 20					14a43		14 50			15a13				15 20					15a44	15 51
Hartlebury	d																					
University	d														14 55							
Barnt Green	d																					
Bromsgrove	d														15 10							
Droitwich Spa	d	14 31							15 01						15 20	15 31						16 03
Worcester Shrub Hill 7	a	14 39																				16 11
	d	14 43						14 49														
Worcester Foregate Street 7	a	14 45						14 51	15 10						15 30	15 40						
	d	14 46						14 53							15 32							
Malvern Link	d	14 54						15 06							15 42							
Great Malvern	a	14 58						15 09							15 44							
	d														15 45							
Colwall	d														15 50							
Ledbury	a														15 57							
	d														15 59							
Hereford 7	a														16 19							

Stratford-upon-Avon, Marylebone and Leamington Spa - Birmingham - Stourbridge, Worcester and Hereford

Network Diagram - see first Page of Table 71

		LM	CH	LM	GW ◇	LM	LM	CH ◇	XC ◇1	LM	CH ◇	XC ◇1	LM	GW ◇1	LM	LM	CH	LM	CH ◇	XC ◇1	LM	LM	LM
Stratford-upon-Avon	d	14 26																15 26	15 37				
Wilmcote	d	14 31																15 31	15 42				
Wootton Wawen	d	14x36																15x36					
Henley-in-Arden	d	14 41																15 41					
Danzey	d	14x46																15x46					
Wood End	d	14x50																15x50					
The Lakes	d	14x52																15x52					
Earlswood (West Midlands)	d	14 55																15 55					
Wythall	d	14 57																15 57					
Whitlocks End	d	15 00					15 19						15 39					16 00					16 18
Shirley	d	15 03					15 22						15 42					16 03					16 21
Yardley Wood	d	15 06					15 25						15 45					16 06					16 24
Hall Green	d	15 09					15 28						15 48					16 09					16 27
Spring Road	d	15 11					15 30						15 50					16 11					16 29
London Marylebone 10 ⊖	d		13 37								14 07						14 37						
Banbury	d		14 30						14 54		15 06	15 25					15 29			15 54			
Leamington Spa 8	a		14 47						15 11		15 23	15 42					15 46		16 12	16 10			
	d		14 47					14 52	15 12		15 23	15 43					15 47			16 12			
Warwick	d							14 57			15 27												
Warwick Parkway	d		14 53					15 00			15 31						15 52						
Hatton	d							15 05															
Lapworth	d							15 10															
Dorridge	d			15 09				15 15		15 28	15 41					15 46					16 09		
Widney Manor	d			15 13						15 32						15 50					16 13		
Solihull	d		15 05	15 17				15 22		15 36	15 46					15 54	16 05				16 17		
Olton	d			15 20						15 39						15 57					16 20		
Acocks Green	d			15 23						15 42						16 00					16 23		
Tyseley	d						15 33									16 03							16 32
Small Heath	d						15 35									16 05							16 34
Bordesley	d																						
Birmingham Moor Street	d	15 18	15a19	15 29			15 39	15a41		15 48	15 55		15 59			16 09	16 13	16 18			16 29		16 38
Birmingham Snow Hill	a	15 21		15 32			15 42			15 51	16 04		16 02			16 12	16 21	16 21			16 32		16 41
	d	15 23		15 33			15 43			15 53			16 03			16 13		16 23			16 33		16 43
Jewellery Quarter	d	15 25		15 35			15 45			15 55			16 05			16 15		16 25			16 35		16 46
The Hawthorns	d	15 30		15 40			15 50			16 00			16 10			16 20		16 30			16 40		16 51
Smethwick Galton Bridge 7	d	15 33		15 43			15 53			16 03			16 13			16 23		16 33			16 43		16 54
Coventry	a								15 24											16 22			
Birmingham International ✈	a								15 37											16 37			
Birmingham New Street 12	a								15 48			16 18								16 48			
	d					15 49									16 19							16 49	
Langley Green	d			15 46									16 16								16 46		
Rowley Regis	d	15 38		15 49			15 58			16 08			16 19			16 28		16 38			16 49		16 59
Old Hill	d			15 52									16 22								16 52		
Cradley Heath	d	15 43		15 56			16 03			16 13			16 26			16 33		16 43			16 56		17 05
Lye	d			15 59									16 29								16 59		
Stourbridge Junction 2	d	15a49		16 03			16 09			16a19			16 33			16 39		16a49			17 03		17 11
Hagley	d			16 06			16 12									16 42					17 06		17 15
Blakedown	d						16 15									16 45					17 09		17 19
Kidderminster	d			16a14			16 20						16a43			16 50					17a15		17 24
Hartlebury	d																						17 29
University	d					15 55									16 25							16 55	
Barnt Green	d																						
Bromsgrove	d					16 10									16 41							17 10	
Droitwich Spa	d					16 20	16 31								16 51	17 01						17 20	17 37
Worcester Shrub Hill 7	a														16 58							17 27	
	d				16 15									16 40	17 06							17 32	
Worcester Foregate Street 7	a				16 18	16 30	16 40							16 43	17 08	17 10						17 34	17 47
	d				16 18	16 32									17 09							17 35	
Malvern Link	d				16 27	16 42									17 18							17 44	
Great Malvern	a				16 33	16 44									17 21							17 46	
	d					16 45																17 47	
Colwall	d					16 50																17 52	
Ledbury	a					16 57																17 59	
	d					16 59																18 00	
Hereford 7	a					17 19																18 22	

Stratford-upon-Avon, Marylebone and Leamington Spa - Birmingham - Stourbridge, Worcester and Hereford

Network Diagram - see first Page of Table 71

		LM	LM	CH ◇	CH	XC ◇1	LM	LM	CH	LM	XC ◇1	GW	LM	LM	LM	LM	LM	CH ◇	XC ◇1	LM	CH	LM	LM
Stratford-upon-Avon	d									16 23												17 26	
Wilmcote	d									16 28												17 31	
Wootton Wawen	d									16x33												17x36	
Henley-in-Arden	d									16 38												17 41	
Danzey	d									16x43												17x46	
Wood End	d									16x47												17x50	
The Lakes	d									16x49												17x52	
Earlswood (West Midlands)	d									16 52												17 55	
Wythall	d									16 55												17 57	
Whitlocks End	d		16 39							16 58					17 18					17 42		18 00	
Shirley	d		16 42							17 01					17 21					17 44		18 03	
Yardley Wood	d		16 45							17 04					17 24					17 47		18 06	
Hall Green	d		16 48							17 07					17 27					17 50		18 09	
Spring Road	d		16 50							17 09					17 29					17 52		18 11	
London Marylebone 10 ⊖	d			15 07	15 10				15 37									16 07			16 30		
Banbury	d			16 06	16 17	16 26			16 30		16 54							17 03	17 28				
Leamington Spa 8	a			16 23	16 34	16 43			16 47		17 11							17 20	17 47				
	d			16 24	16 35	16 44			16 47		17 12							17 21	17 48				
Warwick	d			16 28	16 39													17 25					
Warwick Parkway	d			16 31					16 53									17 29			17 39		
Hatton	d				16a46																		
Lapworth	d																						
Dorridge	d	16 27		16 41				16 46						17 09			17 27	17 39					18 03
Widney Manor	d	16 31						16 50						17 13			17 31						18 08
Solihull	d	16 35		16 47				16 54	17 05					17 17			17 35	17 44			17 51		18 11
Olton	d	16 38						16 57						17 20			17 38						18 15
Acocks Green	d	16 41						17 00						17 23			17 41						18 17
Tyseley	d	16 44	16 53					17 03							17 32		17 44						18 20
Small Heath	d							17 05							17 34		17 46						18 23
Bordesley	d																						
Birmingham Moor Street	d	16 49	16 59	17a01				17 09	17 13	17 16				17 29	17 38		17 50	17 56		17 59	18 04	18 18	18 27
Birmingham Snow Hill	a	16 51	17 02					17 12	17 21	17 19				17 32	17 41		17 53	18 03		18 02	18 12	18 21	18 29
	d	16 53	17 03					17 13		17 20				17 33	17 43		17 54			18 03		18 23	18 33
Jewellery Quarter	d	16 55	17 05					17 16		17 23				17 36	17 45		17 57			18 05		18 25	18 35
The Hawthorns	d	17 00	17 10					17 21		17 27				17 41	17 50		18 02			18 10		18 30	18 40
Smethwick Galton Bridge 7	d	17 03	17 13					17 24		17 30				17 44	17 53		18 05			18 13		18 33	18 43
Coventry	a										17 23												
Birmingham International ✈	a										17 37												
Birmingham New Street 12	a					17 18					17 48								18 18				
	d						17 19						17 49			17 59							
Langley Green	d		17 16							17 33					17 56					18 16			18 46
Rowley Regis	d	17 08	17 19					17 30		17 37				17 50	17 59		18 10			18 19		18 38	18 49
Old Hill	d		17 22							17 40					18 02					18 22			18 52
Cradley Heath	d	17 13	17 26					17 35		17 43				17 55	18 06		18 15			18 26		18 43	18 56
Lye	d		17 29							17 46					18 09					18 29			18 59
Stourbridge Junction 2	d	17a19	17 33					17 42		17a51				18 01	18 13		18 21			18 33		18 50	19a03
Hagley	d		17 37					17 46						18 05	18 17		18 25			18 37		18 54	
Blakedown	d		17 40					17 49						18 08	18 20		18 28			18 40		18 57	
Kidderminster	d		17a45					17 54						18 13	18a26		18 33			18a45		19a02	
Hartlebury	d													18 18			18 38						
University	d						17 25						17 55			18 05							
Barnt Green	d																						
Bromsgrove	d						17 40									18 21							
Droitwich Spa	d						17 52	18 05					18 17	18 26		18 34	18 49						
Worcester Shrub Hill 7	a						17 59	18 18					18 25			18 42	18 58						
	d						18 04					18 18	18 32			18 53							
Worcester Foregate Street 7	a						18 06					18 21	18 34	18 36		18 55							
	d						18 07					18 21	18 35			18 56							
Malvern Link	d						18 16					18 29	18 44			19 05							
Great Malvern	a						18 18					18 36	18 47			19 08							
	d						18 19						18 49										
Colwall	d						18 24						18 54										
Ledbury	a						18 31						19 02										
	d						18 31						19 04										
Hereford 7	a						18 51						19 24										

Stratford-upon-Avon, Marylebone and Leamington Spa - Birmingham - Stourbridge, Worcester and Hereford

Network Diagram - see first Page of Table 71

		CH	GW	LM	GW	LM	LM	LM	CH	CH	XC	CH	CH	XC	LM	LM	GW	LM	CH	LM	CH	XC
			1		◇1 🍴				◇ 🛒		◇1 🛒	◇ 🛒		◇1 🛒							◇	◇1 🛒
Stratford-upon-Avon	d					17 58				17 40					18 26					18 50		
Wilmcote	d									17 46					18 31					18 55		
Wootton Wawen	d														18x36					19x00		
Henley-in-Arden	d					18 08									18 40					19 04		
Danzey	d														18x45							
Wood End	d														18x49							
The Lakes	d														18x51							
Earlswood (West Midlands)	d														18 54							
Wythall	d														18 56							
Whitlocks End	d							18 36							18 59					19 15		
Shirley	d					18 21		18 39							19 02					19 18		
Yardley Wood	d					18 24		18 42							19 05					19 21		
Hall Green	d					18 27		18 45							19 08					19 24		
Spring Road	d					18 29		18 47							19 10					19 26		
London Marylebone [10] ⊖	d	16 46										17 07	17 10						17 37		18 07	
Banbury	d	17 43									17 54	18 04	18 19	18 26					18 35			18 54
Leamington Spa [8]	a	18 00								18 11	18 11	18 21	18 36	18 45					18 53			19 10
	d	18 01							18 08		18 12	18 21	18 36	18 46					18 54			19 12
Warwick	d								18 13				18 40						18 58			
Warwick Parkway	d	18 07							18 16			18 27							19 01		19 20	
Hatton	d								18 21				18a47									
Lapworth	d								18 26													
Dorridge	d	18 17					18 23		18 31			18 39						18 59	19 11			
Widney Manor	d						18 27											19 03				
Solihull	d	18 23					18 31		18 36			18 45						19 07	19 17		19 32	
Olton	d						18 34											19 10				
Acocks Green	d						18 37											19 13				
Tyseley	d					18 32	18 40	18 50										19 16				
Small Heath	d					18 34	18 42											19 18				
Bordesley	d																					
Birmingham Moor Street	d	18a35				18 38	18 46	18 55	18a55			19 02			19 17			19 22	19 28	19 33	19 41	
Birmingham Snow Hill ⇌	a					18 41	18 49	18 57				19 04			19 20			19 25	19 36	19 36	19 43	
	d					18 43		18 59				19 10						19 27		19 40	19 50	
Jewellery Quarter ⇌	d					18 45		19 01										19 29		19 42		
The Hawthorns ⇌	d					18 50		19 06				19 16						19 34		19 47		
Smethwick Galton Bridge [7]	d					18 53		19 09				19 19						19 37		19 50		
Coventry	a										18 22											19 22
Birmingham International ✈	a										18 37											19 37
Birmingham New Street [12]	a										18 48			19 18								19 48
	d			18 19												19 19						
Langley Green	d							19 12										19 40				
Rowley Regis	d					18 58		19 15				19 24						19 43		19 55	20 02	
Old Hill	d							19 18										19 46				
Cradley Heath	d					19 04		19 22				19 29						19 50		20 00		
Lye	d							19 25										19 53				
Stourbridge Junction [2]	d					19 10		19a29				19 36						19 57		20a06	20 16	
Hagley	d					19 13												20 00				
Blakedown	d					19 16												20 03				
Kidderminster	d					19 21						19a48						20 08			20a30	
Hartlebury	d																					
University	d			18 25												19 25						
Barnt Green	d																					
Bromsgrove	d			18 45												19 41						
Droitwich Spa	d			18 57		19 32										19 52		20 19				
Worcester Shrub Hill [7]	a			19 10												19 59		20 27				
	d		19 09		19 35											20 10	20 20					
Worcester Foregate Street [7]	a		19 11		19 38	19 41										20 12	20 22					
	d		19 12		19 39											20 13	20 25					
Malvern Link	d		19 21		19 48											20 22	20 34					
Great Malvern	a		19 24		19 52											20 24	20 40					
	d				19 52											20 25						
Colwall	d				19 58											20 30						
Ledbury	a				20 06											20 37						
	d				20 09											20 38						
Hereford [7]	a				20 27											21 02						

Stratford-upon-Avon, Marylebone and Leamington Spa - Birmingham - Stourbridge, Worcester and Hereford

Network Diagram - see first Page of Table 71

		LM	LM	GW	LM	CH	CH	LM	XC	CH	CH	XC	CH	LM	GW	LM	CH	LM	XC	CH	GW	LM	XC
				◇1 A 🍴		◇ B 🛒	◇		◇1 🛒		◇ 🛒	◇1 🛒			◇1 🍴		◇ 🛒		◇1		◇1	D	◇1
Stratford-upon-Avon	d						19 20	19 26										20 26					
Wilmcote	d						19 25	19 31										20 31					
Wootton Wawen	d							19x36										20x36					
Henley-in-Arden	d							19 40										20 40					
Danzey	d							19x44										20x44					
Wood End	d							19x48										20x48					
The Lakes	d							19x50										20x50					
Earlswood (West Midlands)	d							19 53										20 53					
Wythall	d							19 55										20 55					
Whitlocks End	d	19 25						19 58										20 58					
Shirley	d	19 27						20 01										21 01					
Yardley Wood	d	19 30						20 04										21 04					
Hall Green	d	19 33						20 07										21 07					
Spring Road	d	19 35						20 09										21 09					
London Marylebone [10] ⊖	d					18 10				18 40			18 44				19 15			19 37			
Banbury	d					19 05			19 31	19 37		19 54	20 00				20 13		20 28	20 40			20 54
Leamington Spa [8]	a					19 23	19 48		19 49	19 54		20 10	20 24				20 30		20 45	20 57			21 10
	d					19 23			19 50	19 55	20 05	20 12					20 31		20 46	20 57			21 12
Warwick	d					19 27				19 59	20 09									21 01			
Warwick Parkway	d					19 31				20 02	20 12						20 36			21 05			
Hatton	d										20 17												
Lapworth	d										20 22												
Dorridge	d				19 30	19 41				20 13	20 27					20 29	20 46			21 15			
Widney Manor	d				19 34											20 33							
Solihull	d				19 38	19 46				20 19	20 32					20 36	20 52			21 20			
Olton	d				19 41											20 40							
Acocks Green	d				19 44											20 42							
Tyseley	d	19 38			19 47											20 45							
Small Heath	d	19 40			19 49											20 48							
Bordesley	d																						
Birmingham Moor Street	d	19 44			19 53	19 58		20 16		20 28	20a46					20 52	21 00	21 16		21 29			
Birmingham Snow Hill ⇌	a	19 47			19 56	20 00		20 19		20 37						20 54	21 04	21 19		21 37			
	d				19 58	20 10		20 20								20 55	21 05	21 20					
Jewellery Quarter ⇌	d				20 00			20 22								20 58		21 22					
The Hawthorns ⇌	d				20 05	20 16		20 27								21 02	21 11	21 27					
Smethwick Galton Bridge [7]	d				20 08	20 19		20 30								21 05	21 14	21 30					
Coventry	a											20 22											21 22
Birmingham International ✈	a											20 37											21 37
Birmingham New Street [12]	a								20 18			20 48							21 22				21 48
	d		19 49											20 59								21 45	
Langley Green	d				20 11			20 33								21 08		21 33					
Rowley Regis	d				20 14	20 24		20 36								21 11	21 20	21 36					
Old Hill	d				20 17			20 39								21 14		21 39					
Cradley Heath	d				20 21	20 29		20 43								21 17	21 25	21 43					
Lye	d				20 24			20 46								21 20		21 46					
Stourbridge Junction [2]	d				20 28	20a40		20a51								21 24	21 33	21a50					
Hagley	d				20 31											21 28							
Blakedown	d				20 34											21 31							
Kidderminster	d				20 39											21 36	21a49						
Hartlebury	d																						
University	d		19 55											21 05									
Barnt Green	d																						
Bromsgrove	d		20 10											21 20									
Droitwich Spa	d		20 26		20 50									21 30		21 47						22 34	
Worcester Shrub Hill [7]	a		20 34		20 59											21 57						22 47	
	d			20 42											21 47	22 03					22 40		
Worcester Foregate Street [7]	a			20 45										21 38	21 50	22 05					22 43		
	d			20 46										21 41	21 51						22 44		
Malvern Link	d			20 55										21 51	22 02						22 52		
Great Malvern	a			20 58										21 53	22 06						22 58		
	d			20 59										21 54	22 19								
Colwall	d			21 05										21 59	22 26								
Ledbury	a			21 12										22 06	22 33								
	d			21 14										22 09	22 35								
Hereford [7]	a			21 33										22 29	22 54								

A The Cathedrals Express

B 🛒 to Birmingham Snow Hill

D from 26 March

Stratford-upon-Avon, Marylebone and Leamington Spa - Birmingham - Stourbridge, Worcester and Hereford

Network Diagram - see first Page of Table 71

		CH ◇	LM A	LM	CH	XC ◇1	LM	LM	CH ◇	XC ◇1	LM A	LM	CH ◇ 🚌	CH	CH ◇	CH	LM	CH ◇	LM FO C	LM FX D	XC ◇1	CH ◇
Stratford-upon-Avon	d						21 36							22 00								
Wilmcote	d													22 05								
Wootton Wawen	d																					
Henley-in-Arden	d																					
Danzey	d																					
Wood End	d																					
The Lakes	d																					
Earlswood (West Midlands)	d																					
Wythall	d																					
Whitlocks End	d							21 55									22 55					
Shirley	d							21 57									22 57					
Yardley Wood	d							22 00									23 00					
Hall Green	d							22 03									23 03					
Spring Road	d							22 05									23 05					
London Marylebone [10] ⊖	d	19 40			20 10				20 37						21 07			21 37				22 07
Banbury	d	20 57			21 06	21 33			21 45	21 54					22 14			22 43			22 54	23 04
Leamington Spa [8]	a	21 16			21 24	21 51			22 04	22 10				22 28	22 32			23 00			23 12	23 21
	d	21 17			21 24	21 52			22 04	22 12			22 18		22 32	22 40		23 00			23 13	23 22
Warwick	d	21 21							22 08				22 23		22 36	22a43		23 04				23 26
Warwick Parkway	d				21 30				22 12				22 26		22 40			23 08				23 30
Hatton	d	21a28											22 31									
Lapworth	d												22 36									
Dorridge	d			21 31	21 40				22 22			22 33	22 41		22 50			23 19				23 40
Widney Manor	d			21 35								22 37	22 44									
Solihull	d			21 38	21 45				22 27			22 41	22 48		22 55			23 24				23 45
Olton	d			21 42								22 44										
Acocks Green	d			21 44								22 47										
Tyseley	d			21 47				22 08				22 50					23 08					
Small Heath	d			21 50				22 11				22 52					23 10					
Bordesley	d																					
Birmingham Moor Street	d			21 54	21 58		22 08	22 14	22a42			22 56	23 00		23 07		23 14	23a37				23a59
Birmingham Snow Hill	a			21 56	22 00		22 10	22 17				22 59	23 07		23 11		23 17					
	d			21 57	22 10			22 20				23 00			23 22							
Jewellery Quarter	d			22 00				22 22				23 02			23 24							
The Hawthorns	d			22 04	22 16			22 27				23 07			23 29							
Smethwick Galton Bridge [7]	d			22 07	22 19			22 30				23 10			23 32							
Coventry	a									22 22											23 25	
Birmingham International ✈	a									22 33											23 36	
Birmingham New Street [12]	a					22 17				22 45											23 57	
	d		22 00								23 00								23 16	23 16		
Langley Green	d			22 10				22 33				23 13			23 35							
Rowley Regis	d			22 13	22 24			22 36				23 16			23 38							
Old Hill	d			22 16				22 39				23 19			23 41							
Cradley Heath	d			22 19	22 29			22 43				23 23			23 45							
Lye	d			22 22				22 46				23 26			23 48							
Stourbridge Junction [2]	d			22 26	22 36			22a50				23 30			23a52							
Hagley	d			22 30								23 33										
Blakedown	d			22 33								23 36										
Kidderminster	d			22 38	22a50							23 41										
Hartlebury	d																					
University	d		22 06								23 06											
Barnt Green	d																					
Bromsgrove	d		22 20								23 19											
Droitwich Spa	d		22 34	22 49							23 29	23 52							00 01	00 01		
Worcester Shrub Hill [7]	a		22 47	22 57							23 37	00 01							00 09	00 11		
	d			23 05																		
Worcester Foregate Street [7]	a			23 07																		
	d			23 08																		
Malvern Link	d			23 16																		
Great Malvern	a			23 19																		
	d																					
Colwall	d																					
Ledbury	a																					
	d																					
Hereford [7]	a																					

A until 23 March C from 30 March D FX from 26 March

Stratford-upon-Avon, Marylebone and Leamington Spa - Birmingham - Stourbridge, Worcester and Hereford

Network Diagram - see first Page of Table 71

		CH	CH ◇	CH ◇
Stratford-upon-Avon	d	23 15		
Wilmcote	d			
Wootton Wawen	d			
Henley-in-Arden	d			
Danzey	d			
Wood End	d			
The Lakes	d			
Earlswood (West Midlands)	d			
Wythall	d			
Whitlocks End	d			
Shirley	d			
Yardley Wood	d			
Hall Green	d			
Spring Road	d			
London Marylebone [10] ⊖	d		22 37	23 07
Banbury	d		23 39	00 04
Leamington Spa [8]	a	23 37	23 56	00 21
	d		23 56	00 22
Warwick	d		00 01	00 26
Warwick Parkway	d		00 04	00 29
Hatton	d			
Lapworth	d			
Dorridge	d		00 14	
Widney Manor	d			
Solihull	d		00 19	00 41
Olton	d			
Acocks Green	d			
Tyseley	d			
Small Heath	d			
Bordesley	d			
Birmingham Moor Street	d		00a32	00a55
Birmingham Snow Hill	a			
	d			
Jewellery Quarter	d			
The Hawthorns	d			
Smethwick Galton Bridge [7]	d			
Coventry	a			
Birmingham International ✈	a			
Birmingham New Street [12]	a			
	d			
Langley Green	d			
Rowley Regis	d			
Old Hill	d			
Cradley Heath	d			
Lye	d			
Stourbridge Junction [2]	d			
Hagley	d			
Blakedown	d			
Kidderminster	d			
Hartlebury	d			
University	d			
Barnt Green	d			
Bromsgrove	d			
Droitwich Spa	d			
Worcester Shrub Hill [7]	a			
	d			
Worcester Foregate Street [7]	a			
	d			
Malvern Link	d			
Great Malvern	a			
	d			
Colwall	d			
Ledbury	a			
	d			
Hereford [7]	a			

Stratford-upon-Avon, Marylebone and Leamington Spa - Birmingham - Stourbridge, Worcester and Hereford

Network Diagram - see first Page of Table 71

		LM	CH	CH	LM	CH	LM	LM	LM	GW	LM	LM	XC	LM	LM	GW	LM	LM	CH	XC	LM	LM	LM
			◇	◇	A	◇				◇1			◇1			◇1				◇1			
Stratford-upon-Avon	d																	07 00				07 44	
Wilmcote	d																	07 05				07 49	
Wootton Wawen	d																	07x10				07x54	
Henley-in-Arden	d																	07 14				07 59	
Danzey	d																	07x19				08x04	
Wood End	d																	07x23				08x08	
The Lakes	d																	07x26				08x10	
Earlswood (West Midlands)	d																	07 28				08 13	
Wythall	d																	07 31				08 15	
Whitlocks End	d													07 03				07 33				08 18	
Shirley	d													07 05				07 36				08 21	
Yardley Wood	d													07 08				07 39				08 24	
Hall Green	d													07 11				07 42				08 27	
Spring Road	d													07 13				07 44				08 29	
London Marylebone 10 ⊖	d		22p37	23p07		00 05																	
Banbury	d		23p39	00 04		01 19							06 56						07 07	07 33			
Leamington Spa 8	a		23p56	00 21		01 50							07 12						07 25	07 50			
	d		23p56	00 22								06 26	07 14						07 26	07 51			
Warwick	d		00 01	00 26								06 30							07 30				
Warwick Parkway	d		00 04	00 29								06 34							07 33				
Hatton	d											06 39											
Lapworth	d											06 45											
Dorridge	d	22p33	00 14									06 50					07 25		07 44		08 05		
Widney Manor	d	22p37										06 53					07 29				08 09		
Solihull	d	22p41	00 19	00 41								06 57					07 33		07 50		08 13		
Olton	d	22p44										07 00					07 36				08 16		
Acocks Green	d	22p47										07 03					07 39				08 19		
Tyseley	d	22p50										07 06		07 16			07 42	07 47			08 22	08 32	
Small Heath	d	22p52										07 08		07 19			07 44	07 50				08 34	
Bordesley	d																						
Birmingham Moor Street	d	22p56	00a32	00a55					06 31		07 01	07 12		07 23			07 48	07 55	08 00		08 27	08 38	
Birmingham Snow Hill ⇌	a	22p59							06 33		07 03	07 15		07 25			07 51	07 57	08 07		08 29	08 42	
	d	23p00							06 35		07 05			07 28			07 53	08 03			08 30	08 43	
Jewellery Quarter ⇌	d	23p02							06 37		07 07			07 30			07 55	08 05			08 33	08 45	
The Hawthorns ⇌	d	23p07							06 42		07 12			07 35			08 00	08 10			08 37	08 50	
Smethwick Galton Bridge 7	d	23p10							06 45		07 15			07 38			08 03	08 13			08 40	08 53	
Coventry	a												07 24										
Birmingham International ✈	a												07 37										
Birmingham New Street 12	a												07 48							08 17			
	d				23p16			06 49							07 49								08 49
Langley Green	d	23p13							06 48		07 18			07 41				08 16			08 43		
Rowley Regis	d	23p16							06 51		07 21			07 44			08 08	08 19			08 47	08 58	
Old Hill	d	23p19							06 54		07 24			07 47				08 22			08 50		
Cradley Heath	d	23p23							06 57		07 27			07 51			08 12	08 26			08 53	09 02	
Lye	d	23p26							07 00		07 30			07 54				08 29			08 56		
Stourbridge Junction 2	d	23p30							07 04		07 35			07a58			08 18	08a33			09a00	09a08	
Hagley	d	23p33							07 08		07 38						08 21						
Blakedown	d	23p36							07 11		07 41						08 24						
Kidderminster	d	23p41							07 16		07 46						08 29						
Hartlebury	d								07 21														
University	d							06 55							07 55								08 55
Barnt Green	d																						
Bromsgrove	d							07 10							08 10								09 10
Droitwich Spa	d	23p52			00 01			07 20	07 28		07 57				08 20		08 40						09 20
Worcester Shrub Hill 7	a	00 01			00 09				07 39		08 05												
	d						06 30			07 46	08 11					08 41							
Worcester Foregate Street 7	a						06 32	07 30		07 48	08 13				08 30	08 44	08 49						09 30
	d						06 33	07 32		07 50	08 14				08 32	08 45							09 32
Malvern Link	d						06 42	07 42		07 59	08 23				08 42	08 54							09 42
Great Malvern	a						06 44	07 44		08 03	08 26				08 44	09 00							09 44
	d						06 45	07 45							08 45								09 45
Colwall	d						06 50	07 50							08 50								09 50
Ledbury	a						06 57	07 57							08 57								09 57
	d						06 58	07 59							08 59								09 59
Hereford 7	a						07 14	08 19							09 19								10 19

A from 31 March

Stratford-upon-Avon, Marylebone and Leamington Spa - Birmingham - Stourbridge, Worcester and Hereford

Network Diagram - see first Page of Table 71

		GW	LM	XC	LM	CH	CH	CH	XC	LM	LM	CH	XC	LM	GW	LM	LM	LM	LM	CH	XC	GW	LM
		◇1		◇1		◇	◇		◇1			◇	◇1							◇	◇1	◇1	
Stratford-upon-Avon	d						08 00				08 26												
Wilmcote	d										08 31												
Wootton Wawen	d										08x36												
Henley-in-Arden	d										08 41												
Danzey	d										08x46												
Wood End	d										08x50												
The Lakes	d										08x52												
Earlswood (West Midlands)	d										08 55												
Wythall	d										08 57												
Whitlocks End	d				08 35						09 00						09 19		09 39				
Shirley	d				08 38						09 03						09 22		09 42				
Yardley Wood	d				08 41						09 06						09 25		09 45				
Hall Green	d				08 44						09 09						09 28		09 48				
Spring Road	d				08 46						09 11						09 30		09 50				
London Marylebone 10 ⊖	d					07 00														08 00			
Banbury	d			07 54		08 04			08 33			08 36	08 54							09 08	09 24		
Leamington Spa 8	a			08 10		08 21	08 27		08 49			08 54	09 10							09 26	09 41		
	d		07 56	08 12		08 22		08 31	08 50			08 54	09 12							09 26	09 42		
Warwick	d		08 00			08 26		08 35												09 30			
Warwick Parkway	d		08 04			08 29		08 38				09 00								09 34			
Hatton	d		08 09			08 34		08a44															
Lapworth	d		08 15			08 39																	
Dorridge	d		08 21			08 44				08 46				09 09				09 28		09 44			09 46
Widney Manor	d		08 24							08 50				09 13				09 32					09 50
Solihull	d		08 28			08 50				08 54		09 12		09 17				09 36		09 49			09 54
Olton	d		08 31							08 57				09 20				09 39					09 57
Acocks Green	d		08 34							09 00				09 23				09 42					10 00
Tyseley	d		08 37		08 49					09 03							09 33						10 03
Small Heath	d		08 39		08 51					09 05							09 35						10 05
Bordesley	d																						
Birmingham Moor Street	d		08 43		08 55	09 00				09 09	09 18	09a24		09 29			09 39	09 48	09 58	10 02			10 09
Birmingham Snow Hill ⇌	a		08 47		08 58	09 07				09 12	09 20			09 32			09 42	09 51	10 00	10 09			10 12
	d		08 53		09 03					09 13	09 23			09 33			09 43	09 53	10 03				10 13
Jewellery Quarter ⇌	d		08 55		09 05					09 15	09 25			09 35			09 45	09 55	10 05				10 15
The Hawthorns ⇌	d		09 00		09 10					09 20	09 30			09 40			09 50	10 00	10 10				10 20
Smethwick Galton Bridge 7	d		09 03		09 13					09 23	09 33			09 43			09 53	10 03	10 13				10 23
Coventry	a			08 22									09 22										
Birmingham International ✈	a			08 37									09 37										
Birmingham New Street 12	a			08 48					09 19				09 48								10 18		
	d															09 49							
Langley Green	d				09 16									09 46					10 16				
Rowley Regis	d		09 08		09 19					09 28	09 38			09 49			09 58	10 08	10 19				10 28
Old Hill	d				09 22									09 52					10 22				
Cradley Heath	d		09 13		09 26					09 33	09 43			09 56			10 03	10 13	10 26				10 33
Lye	d				09 29									09 59					10 29				
Stourbridge Junction 2	d		09 19		09 33					09 39	09a49			10 03			10 09	10a19	10 33				10 39
Hagley	d		09 22							09 42							10 12						10 42
Blakedown	d		09 25							09 45							10 15						10 45
Kidderminster	d		09 30		09a42					09 50				10a12			10 20		10a42				10 50
Hartlebury	d																						
University	d															09 55							
Barnt Green	d																						
Bromsgrove	d															10 10							
Droitwich Spa	d		09 41							10 01						10 20	10 31						11 01
Worcester Shrub Hill 7	a		09 49														10 39						
	d	09 41													10 15							10 46	
Worcester Foregate Street 7	a	09 44								10 10					10 17	10 30						10 48	11 10
	d	09 45													10 18	10 32						10 50	11 11
Malvern Link	d	09 54													10 27	10 42						10 58	11 19
Great Malvern	a	10 00													10 32	10 44						11 05	11 22
	d															10 45						11 06	
Colwall	d															10 50						11 12	
Ledbury	a															10 57						11 20	
	d															10 59						11 22	
Hereford 7	a															11 19						11 41	

Stratford-upon-Avon, Marylebone and Leamington Spa - Birmingham - Stourbridge, Worcester and Hereford

Network Diagram - see first Page of Table 71

		LM		LM	CH	CH	CH	XC	LM	LM	LM	CH		XC	LM	LM	CH	LM	LM	CH	XC	GW		LM	LM
					◇	◇		◇1				◇		◇1			◇			◇	◇1	◇			
Stratford-upon-Avon	d	09 26					09 37											10 26							
Wilmcote	d	09 31					09 43											10 31							
Wootton Wawen	d	09x36																10x36							
Henley-in-Arden	d	09 41																10 41							
Danzey	d	09x46																10x46							
Wood End	d	09x50																10x50							
The Lakes	d	09x52																10x52							
Earlswood (West Midlands)	d	09 55																10 55							
Wythall	d	09 57																10 57							
Whitlocks End	d	10 00								10 19					10 39			11 00							11 19
Shirley	d	10 03								10 22					10 42			11 03							11 22
Yardley Wood	d	10 06								10 25					10 45			11 06							11 25
Hall Green	d	10 09								10 28					10 48			11 09							11 28
Spring Road	d	10 11								10 30					10 50			11 11							11 30
London Marylebone 10 ⊖	d				08 20	08 54						09 00					09 30								
Banbury	d				09 36	09 51		09 54				10 05		10 24			10 28				10 54				
Leamington Spa 8	a				09 54	10 08	10 08	10 12				10 23		10 41			10 45				11 10				
	d				09 55	10 09		10 13				10 23		10 42			10 46			10 55	11 12				
Warwick	d				09 59	10a13						10 27								10 59					
Warwick Parkway	d				10 02							10 31					10 51			11 02					
Hatton	d				10 07															11 07					
Lapworth	d				10 12															11 12					
Dorridge	d			10 09	10 17						10 28	10 41				10 46			11 09	11 17					
Widney Manor	d			10 13							10 32					10 50			11 13						
Solihull	d			10 17	10 23						10 36	10 46				10 54	11 04		11 17	11 22					
Olton	d			10 20							10 39					10 57			11 20						
Acocks Green	d			10 23							10 42					11 00			11 23						
Tyseley	d									10 33						11 03									11 33
Small Heath	d									10 35						11 05									11 35
Bordesley	d																								
Birmingham Moor Street	d	10 18		10 29	10a35					10 39	10 48	10 55			10 57	11 09	11a17	11 18	11 29	11a37					11 39
Birmingham Snow Hill ⇌	a	10 21		10 32						10 42	10 51	11 02			11 01	11 12		11 21	11 32						11 42
	d	10 23		10 33						10 43	10 53				11 03	11 13		11 23	11 33						11 43
Jewellery Quarter ⇌	d	10 25		10 35						10 45	10 55				11 05	11 15		11 25	11 35						11 45
The Hawthorns ⇌	d	10 30		10 40						10 50	11 00				11 10	11 20		11 30	11 40						11 50
Smethwick Galton Bridge 7	d	10 33		10 43						10 53	11 03				11 13	11 23		11 33	11 43						11 53
Coventry	a							10 22													11 22				
Birmingham International ✈	a							10 37													11 37				
Birmingham New Street 12	a							10 48						11 18							11 48				
	d								10 49															11 49	
Langley Green	d			10 46											11 16				11 46						
Rowley Regis	d	10 38		10 49						10 58	11 08				11 19	11 28		11 38	11 49						11 58
Old Hill	d			10 52											11 22				11 52						
Cradley Heath	d	10 43		10 56						11 03	11 13				11 26	11 33		11 43	11 56						12 03
Lye	d			10 59											11 29				11 59						
Stourbridge Junction 2	d	10a49		11 03						11 09	11a19				11 33	11 39		11a49	12 03						12 09
Hagley	d									11 12						11 42									12 12
Blakedown	d									11 15						11 45									12 15
Kidderminster	d			11a12						11 20					11a42	11 50			12a12						12 20
Hartlebury	d																								
University	d								10 55															11 55	
Barnt Green	d																								
Bromsgrove	d								11 10															12 10	
Droitwich Spa	d								11 20	11 31						12 01								12 20	12 31
Worcester Shrub Hill 7	a									11 39															
	d																					12 16			
Worcester Foregate Street 7	a								11 30							12 10						12 18		12 30	12 40
	d								11 32															12 32	
Malvern Link	d								11 42															12 42	
Great Malvern	a								11 44															12 44	
	d								11 45															12 45	
Colwall	d								11 50															12 50	
Ledbury	a								11 57															12 57	
	d								11 59															12 59	
Hereford 7	a								12 19															13 19	

Table 71

Saturdays

Stratford-upon-Avon, Marylebone and Leamington Spa - Birmingham - Stourbridge, Worcester and Hereford

Network Diagram - see first Page of Table 71

		LM	CH	XC	LM	GW	LM	CH		LM	CH	XC	CH	LM	LM	LM	LM	CH		XC	LM	GW	LM	CH	LM
			◇	◇1		◇1		◇				◇1	◇							◇1		◇1		◇	
Stratford-upon-Avon	d									11 26	11 34														12 26
Wilmcote	d									11 31	11 40														12 31
Wootton Wawen	d									11x36															12x36
Henley-in-Arden	d									11 41															12 41
Danzey	d									11x46															12x46
Wood End	d									11x50															12x50
The Lakes	d									11x52															12x52
Earlswood (West Midlands)	d									11 55															12 55
Wythall	d									11 57															12 57
Whitlocks End	d				11 39					12 00						12 19					12 39				13 00
Shirley	d				11 42					12 03						12 22					12 42				13 03
Yardley Wood	d				11 45					12 06						12 25					12 45				13 06
Hall Green	d				11 48					12 09						12 28					12 48				13 09
Spring Road	d				11 50					12 11						12 30					12 50				13 11
London Marylebone 10 ⊖	d		10 00					10 30					10 33					11 00						11 30	
Banbury	d		11 05	11 24				11 29				11 54	11 58					12 04		12 24				12 28	
Leamington Spa 8	a		11 22	11 41				11 47			12 07	12 10	12 16					12 22		12 41				12 46	
	d		11 22	11 42				11 47				12 12	12 17					12 22		12 42				12 47	
Warwick	d		11 27										12 21					12 26							
Warwick Parkway	d		11 31					11 53										12 30						12 52	
Hatton	d												12a27												
Lapworth	d																								
Dorridge	d	11 28	11 41				11 46							12 09			12 28	12 40					12 46		
Widney Manor	d	11 32					11 50							12 13			12 32						12 50		
Solihull	d	11 36	11 46				11 54	12 05						12 17			12 36	12 45					12 54	13 04	
Olton	d	11 39					11 57							12 20			12 39						12 57		
Acocks Green	d	11 42					12 00							12 23			12 42						13 00		
Tyseley	d						12 03									12 33							13 03		
Small Heath	d						12 05									12 35							13 05		
Bordesley	d																								
Birmingham Moor Street	d	11 48	11 55		11 57		12 09	12a17		12 18				12 29		12 39	12 48	12 55			12 57		13 09	13a17	13 18
Birmingham Snow Hill ⇌	a	11 51	12 02		12 01		12 12			12 21				12 32		12 42	12 51	13 02			13 01		13 12		13 21
	d	11 53			12 03		12 13			12 23				12 33		12 43	12 53				13 03		13 13		13 23
Jewellery Quarter ⇌	d	11 55			12 05		12 15			12 25				12 35		12 45	12 55				13 05		13 15		13 25
The Hawthorns ⇌	d	12 00			12 10		12 20			12 30				12 40		12 50	13 00				13 10		13 20		13 30
Smethwick Galton Bridge 7	d	12 03			12 13		12 23			12 33				12 43		12 53	13 03				13 13		13 23		13 33
Coventry	a											12 22													
Birmingham International ✈	a											12 37													
Birmingham New Street 12	a			12 18								12 48								13 18					
	d														12 49										
Langley Green	d				12 16									12 46							13 16				
Rowley Regis	d	12 08			12 19		12 28			12 38				12 49		12 58	13 08				13 19		13 28		13 38
Old Hill	d				12 22									12 52							13 22				
Cradley Heath	d	12 13			12 26		12 33			12 43				12 56		13 03	13 13				13 26		13 33		13 43
Lye	d				12 29									12 59							13 29				
Stourbridge Junction 2	d	12a19			12 33		12 39			12a49				13 03		13 09	13a19				13 33		13 39		13a49
Hagley	d						12 42									13 12							13 42		
Blakedown	d						12 45									13 15							13 45		
Kidderminster	d				12a42		12 50							13a12		13 20					13a42		13 50		
Hartlebury	d																								
University	d														12 55										
Barnt Green	d																								
Bromsgrove	d														13 10										
Droitwich Spa	d						13 01								13 20	13 31							14 01		
Worcester Shrub Hill 7	a															13 39									
	d					12 45																13 41			
Worcester Foregate Street 7	a					12 47	13 10								13 30							13 44	14 10		
	d					12 49	13 11								13 32							13 45			
Malvern Link	d					12 57	13 19								13 42							13 54			
Great Malvern	a					13 02	13 22								13 44							14 00			
	d					13 06									13 45										
Colwall	d					13 13									13 50										
Ledbury	a					13 21									13 57										
	d					13 23									13 59										
Hereford 7	a					13 40									14 19										

Table 71

Saturdays

Stratford-upon-Avon, Marylebone and Leamington Spa - Birmingham - Stourbridge, Worcester and Hereford

Network Diagram - see first Page of Table 71

		LM	CH ◇ ✕	XC ◇1 ✕	GW ◇	LM	LM	LM	CH	XC ◇1 ✕	LM	LM	CH ◇	CH ◇	LM	XC ◇1 ✕	CH ◇	LM	LM	LM	LM	CH
Stratford-upon-Avon	d													13 18	13 26							
Wilmcote	d													13 23	13 31							
Wootton Wawen	d														13x36							
Henley-in-Arden	d														13 41							
Danzey	d														13x46							
Wood End	d														13x50							
The Lakes	d														13x52							
Earlswood (West Midlands)	d														13 55							
Wythall	d														13 57							
Whitlocks End	d						13 19				13 39				14 00					14 19		
Shirley	d						13 22				13 42				14 03					14 22		
Yardley Wood	d						13 25				13 45				14 06					14 25		
Hall Green	d						13 28				13 48				14 09					14 28		
Spring Road	d						13 30				13 50				14 11					14 30		
London Marylebone 10 ⊖	d								12 00				12 30				12 37					13 00
Banbury	d			12 54					13 05	13 24			13 29			13 54	13 58					14 05
Leamington Spa 8	a			13 10					13 22	13 41			13 47	13 54		14 10	14 17					14 23
	d		12 55	13 12					13 22	13 42			13 47			14 12	14 17					14 23
Warwick	d		12 59						13 26								14 21					14 27
Warwick Parkway	d		13 02						13 30				13 53									14 31
Hatton	d		13 07														14a28					
Lapworth	d		13 13																			
Dorridge	d	13 09	13 17					13 28	13 40			13 46						14 09			14 28	14 41
Widney Manor	d	13 13						13 32				13 50						14 13			14 32	
Solihull	d	13 17	13 23					13 36	13 45			13 54	14 05					14 17			14 36	14 46
Olton	d	13 20						13 39				13 57						14 20			14 39	
Acocks Green	d	13 23						13 42				14 00						14 23			14 42	
Tyseley	d						13 33					14 03								14 33		
Small Heath	d						13 35					14 05								14 35		
Bordesley	d						13 37															
Birmingham Moor Street	d	13 29	13a37				13 40	13 48	13 54		13 57	14 09	14a17		14 18			14 29		14 39	14 48	14 55
Birmingham Snow Hill ⇌	a	13 32					13 43	13 51	14 02		14 01	14 12			14 21			14 32		14 42	14 51	15 02
	d	13 33					13 43	13 53			14 03	14 13			14 23			14 33		14 43	14 53	
Jewellery Quarter ⇌	d	13 35					13 45	13 55			14 05	14 15			14 25			14 35		14 45	14 55	
The Hawthorns ⇌	d	13 40					13 50	14 00			14 10	14 20			14 30			14 40		14 50	15 00	
Smethwick Galton Bridge 7	d	13 43					13 53	14 03			14 13	14 23			14 33			14 43		14 53	15 03	
Coventry	a			13 22												14 22						
Birmingham International ✈	a			13 37												14 37						
Birmingham New Street 12	a			13 48						14 18						14 48						
	d					13 49													14 49			
Langley Green	d	13 46									14 16							14 46				
Rowley Regis	d	13 49					13 58	14 08			14 19	14 28			14 38			14 49		14 58	15 08	
Old Hill	d	13 52									14 22							14 52				
Cradley Heath	d	13 56					14 03	14 13			14 26	14 33			14 43			14 56		15 03	15 13	
Lye	d	13 59									14 29							14 59				
Stourbridge Junction 2	d	14 03					14 09	14a19			14 33	14 39			14a49			15 03		15 09	15a19	
Hagley	d						14 12					14 42								15 12		
Blakedown	d						14 15					14 45								15 15		
Kidderminster	d	14a12					14 20				14a42	14 50						15a12		15 20		
Hartlebury	d																					
University	d					13 55													14 55			
Barnt Green	d																					
Bromsgrove	d					14 10													15 10			
Droitwich Spa	d					14 20	14 31					15 01							15 20	15 31		
Worcester Shrub Hill 7	a						14 40													15 39		
	d				14 15		14 46															
Worcester Foregate Street 7	a				14 18	14 30	14 48					15 10							15 30			
	d				14 18	14 32	14 49												15 32			
Malvern Link	d				14 27	14 42	14 57												15 42			
Great Malvern	a				14 31	14 44	15 00												15 44			
	d					14 45													15 45			
Colwall	d					14 50													15 50			
Ledbury	a					14 57													15 57			
	d					14 59													15 59			
Hereford 7	a					15 19													16 17			

Table 71

Saturdays

Stratford-upon-Avon, Marylebone and Leamington Spa - Birmingham - Stourbridge, Worcester and Hereford

Network Diagram - see first Page of Table 71

		XC ◇1 ✕	LM	GW ◇1 ✕	LM	CH ◇	LM	LM	CH ◇ ✕	XC ◇1 ✕	GW ◇	LM	LM	LM	CH ◇	XC ◇1 ✕	LM	GW ◇1 ✕	LM	CH ◇	CH	CH	LM
Stratford-upon-Avon	d						14 26														15 19		15 26
Wilmcote	d						14 31														15 24		15 31
Wootton Wawen	d						14x36																15x36
Henley-in-Arden	d						14 41																15 41
Danzey	d						14x46																15x46
Wood End	d						14x50																15x50
The Lakes	d						14x52																15x52
Earlswood (West Midlands)	d						14 55																15 55
Wythall	d						14 57																15 57
Whitlocks End	d		14 39				15 00						15 19				15 39						16 00
Shirley	d		14 42				15 03						15 22				15 42						16 03
Yardley Wood	d		14 45				15 06						15 25				15 45						16 06
Hall Green	d		14 48				15 09						15 28				15 48						16 09
Spring Road	d		14 50				15 11						15 30				15 50						16 11
London Marylebone 10 ⊖	d					13 30									14 00					14 30		14 33	
Banbury	d	14 24				14 29				14 54					15 05	15 24				15 28		15 46	
Leamington Spa 8	a	14 41				14 47				15 10					15 23	15 41				15 46	15 56	16 04	
	d	14 42				14 47			14 55	15 12					15 23	15 42				15 47		16 05	
Warwick	d								14 59						15 27							16 09	
Warwick Parkway	d					14 53			15 02						15 31					15 52			
Hatton	d								15 07													16a16	
Lapworth	d								15 13														
Dorridge	d				14 46			15 09	15 17					15 28	15 41				15 46				
Widney Manor	d				14 50			15 13						15 32					15 50				
Solihull	d				14 54	15 05		15 17	15 23					15 36	15 46				15 54	16 04			
Olton	d				14 57			15 20						15 39					15 57				
Acocks Green	d				15 00			15 23						15 42					16 00				
Tyseley	d				15 03								15 33						16 03				
Small Heath	d				15 05								15 35						16 05				
Bordesley	d																						
Birmingham Moor Street	d		14 57		15 09	15a17	15 18	15 29	15a37				15 39	15 48	15 55		15 57		16 09	16a17			16 18
Birmingham Snow Hill ⇌	a		15 01		15 12		15 21	15 32					15 42	15 51	16 02		16 01		16 12				16 21
	d		15 03		15 13		15 23	15 33					15 43	15 53			16 03		16 13				16 23
Jewellery Quarter ⇌	d		15 05		15 15		15 25	15 35					15 45	15 55			16 05		16 15				16 25
The Hawthorns ⇌	d		15 10		15 20		15 30	15 40					15 50	16 00			16 10		16 20				16 30
Smethwick Galton Bridge 7	d		15 13		15 23		15 33	15 43					15 53	16 03			16 13		16 23				16 33
Coventry	a									15 22													
Birmingham International ✈	a									15 37													
Birmingham New Street 12	a	15 18								15 48						16 18							
	d											15 49											
Langley Green	d		15 16					15 46									16 16						
Rowley Regis	d		15 19		15 28		15 38	15 49					15 58	16 08			16 19		16 28				16 38
Old Hill	d		15 22					15 52									16 22						
Cradley Heath	d		15 26		15 33		15 43	15 56					16 03	16 13			16 26		16 33				16 43
Lye	d		15 29					15 59									16 29						
Stourbridge Junction 2	d		15 33		15 39		15a49	16 03					16 09	16a19			16 33		16 39				16a49
Hagley	d				15 42								16 12						16 42				
Blakedown	d				15 45								16 15						16 45				
Kidderminster	d		15a42		15 50			16a12					16 20				16a42		16 50				
Hartlebury	d																						
University	d											15 55											
Barnt Green	d																						
Bromsgrove	d											16 10											
Droitwich Spa	d				16 01							16 20	16 31						17 01				
Worcester Shrub Hill 7	a												16 39										
	d			15 41							16 15							16 41					
Worcester Foregate Street 7	a			15 44	16 10						16 17	16 30						16 44	17 10				
	d			15 45							16 18	16 32						16 45	17 11				
Malvern Link	d			15 54							16 26	16 42						16 54	17 20				
Great Malvern	a			16 00							16 32	16 44						17 00	17 23				
	d											16 45											
Colwall	d											16 50											
Ledbury	a											16 57											
	d											16 59											
Hereford 7	a											17 19											

Stratford-upon-Avon, Marylebone and Leamington Spa - Birmingham - Stourbridge, Worcester and Hereford

Network Diagram - see first Page of Table 71

		XC ◇1 H	LM	LM	LM	LM		CH	XC ◇1 H	LM	GW ◇1	LM	LM	CH	LM	LM		CH ◇ H	XC ◇1 H	GW	LM	LM	LM	CH	XC ◇1 H
Stratford-upon-Avon	d														16 26										
Wilmcote	d														16 31										
Wootton Wawen	d														16x36										
Henley-in-Arden	d														16 41										
Danzey	d														16x46										
Wood End	d														16x50										
The Lakes	d														16x52										
Earlswood (West Midlands)	d														16 55										
Wythall	d														16 57										
Whitlocks End	d				16 19					16 39					17 00							17 19			
Shirley	d				16 22					16 42					17 03							17 22			
Yardley Wood	d				16 25					16 45					17 06							17 25			
Hall Green	d				16 28					16 48					17 09							17 28			
Spring Road	d				16 30					16 50					17 11							17 30			
London Marylebone 10 ⊖	d							15 00						15 30										16 00	
Banbury	d	15 54						16 05	16 24					16 28					16 54					17 05	17 24
Leamington Spa 8	a	16 10						16 23	16 41					16 46					17 10					17 23	17 41
	d	16 12						16 23	16 42					16 47				16 55	17 12					17 23	17 42
Warwick	d							16 27										16 59						17 27	
Warwick Parkway	d							16 31						16 52				17 02						17 31	
Hatton	d																	17 07							
Lapworth	d																	17 13							
Dorridge	d		16 09			16 27		16 41					16 46			17 09		17 17					17 27	17 41	
Widney Manor	d		16 13			16 31							16 50			17 13							17 31		
Solihull	d		16 17			16 35		16 46					16 54	17 05		17 17		17 23					17 35	17 46	
Olton	d		16 20			16 38							16 57			17 20							17 38		
Acocks Green	d		16 23			16 41							17 00			17 23							17 41		
Tyseley	d				16 33	16 44				16 53			17 03									17 33	17 44		
Small Heath	d				16 35								17 05									17 35			
Bordesley	d																								
Birmingham Moor Street	d		16 29		16 39	16 49		16 55		16 58			17 09	17a17	17 18	17 29		17a37				17 39	17 49	17 55	
Birmingham Snow Hill ⇌	a		16 32		16 42	16 51		17 02		17 01			17 12		17 21	17 32						17 42	17 51	18 02	
	d		16 33		16 43	16 53				17 03			17 13		17 23	17 33						17 43	17 53		
Jewellery Quarter ⇌	d		16 35		16 45	16 55				17 05			17 15		17 25	17 35						17 45	17 55		
The Hawthorns ⇌	d		16 40		16 50	17 00				17 10			17 20		17 30	17 40						17 50	18 00		
Smethwick Galton Bridge 7	d		16 43		16 53	17 03				17 13			17 23		17 33	17 43						17 53	18 03		
Coventry	a	16 22																	17 22						
Birmingham International ✈	a	16 37																	17 37						
Birmingham New Street 12	a	16 48							17 18										17 48						18 18
	d			16 49								17 19									17 49				
Langley Green	d		16 46							17 16						17 46							18 06		
Rowley Regis	d		16 49		16 58	17 08				17 19			17 28		17 38	17 49						17 58	18 09		
Old Hill	d		16 52							17 22						17 52							18 12		
Cradley Heath	d		16 56		17 03	17 13				17 26			17 33		17 43	17 56						18 03	18 16		
Lye	d		16 59							17 29						17 59							18 19		
Stourbridge Junction 2	d		17 03		17 11	17a19				17 33			17 39		17a49	18 03						18 10	18a23		
Hagley	d		17 06		17 14								17 42			18 06						18 13			
Blakedown	d		17 09		17 17								17 45			18 09						18 16			
Kidderminster	d		17a15		17 22					17a42			17 50			18a15						18 21			
Hartlebury	d				17 27								17 55									18 26			
University	d			16 55																	17 55				
Barnt Green	d																								
Bromsgrove	d			17 10								17 40									18 10				
Droitwich Spa	d			17 20	17 35							17 50	18 03								18 20	18 34			
Worcester Shrub Hill 7	a											17 58	18 12								18 27				
	d										17 41									18 19	18 31				
Worcester Foregate Street 7	a			17 29	17 43						17 44									18 21	18 33	18 43			
	d			17 32							17 45									18 22	18 34				
Malvern Link	d			17 42							17 54									18 30	18 44				
Great Malvern	a			17 45							18 00									18 36	18 46				
	d			17 45																	18 47				
Colwall	d			17 50																	18 52				
Ledbury	a			17 57																	18 59				
	d			17 59																	19 00				
Hereford 7	a			18 16																	19 20				

Stratford-upon-Avon, Marylebone and Leamington Spa - Birmingham - Stourbridge, Worcester and Hereford

Network Diagram - see first Page of Table 71

		LM		CH	GW ◇1	LM	CH	XC ◇1 H	CH	LM	LM	LM		GW ◇1	LM	CH	LM	XC ◇1 H	CH ◇	LM	GW	LM		CH ◇ H	LM
Stratford-upon-Avon	d					17 26	17 40										18 08								18 49
Wilmcote	d					17 31											18 13								18 54
Wootton Wawen	d					17x36											18x18								18x59
Henley-in-Arden	d					17 41											18 23								19 03
Danzey	d					17x46											18x28								19x08
Wood End	d					17x50											18x32								19x12
The Lakes	d					17x52											18x34								19x14
Earlswood (West Midlands)	d					17 55											18 37								19 17
Wythall	d					17 57											18 39								19 19
Whitlocks End	d					18 00					18 19						18 42								19 22
Shirley	d					18 03					18 22						18 45								19 25
Yardley Wood	d					18 06					18 25						18 48								19 28
Hall Green	d					18 09					18 28						18 51								19 31
Spring Road	d					18 11					18 30						18 53								19 33
London Marylebone 10 ⊖	d			16 30					16 33							17 00			17 30						
Banbury	d			17 28				17 54	17 59							18 05		18 24	18 28						
Leamington Spa 8	a			17 46			18 05	18 10	18 19							18 23		18 41	18 45						
	d			17 47				18 12	18 19							18 23		18 42	18 46					18 55	
Warwick	d								18 23							18 27								18 59	
Warwick Parkway	d			17 52												18 31			18 51					19 02	
Hatton	d								18a30															19 07	
Lapworth	d																							19 13	
Dorridge	d	17 46								18 09					18 28	18 41						19 01		19 17	
Widney Manor	d	17 50								18 13					18 32							19 05			
Solihull	d	17 54		18 06						18 17					18 36	18 46			19 05			19 09		19 23	
Olton	d	17 57								18 20					18 39							19 12			
Acocks Green	d	18 00								18 23					18 42							19 15			
Tyseley	d	18 03									18 33				18 45		18 56					19 18			19 36
Small Heath	d	18 05									18 35				18 47		18 58					19 20			19 39
Bordesley	d																								
Birmingham Moor Street	d	18 09		18a17		18 18				18 29	18 39				18 51	18 56	19 02		19a17			19 24		19a38	19 43
Birmingham Snow Hill ⇌	a	18 12				18 21				18 32	18 42				18 54	19 03	19 06					19 27			19 46
	d	18 13				18 23				18 33					18 58							19 28			
Jewellery Quarter ⇌	d	18 15				18 25				18 35					19 00							19 30			
The Hawthorns ⇌	d	18 20				18 30				18 40					19 05							19 35			
Smethwick Galton Bridge 7	d	18 23				18 33				18 43					19 08							19 38			
Coventry	a							18 22																	
Birmingham International ✈	a							18 37																	
Birmingham New Street 12	a							18 48										19 18							
	d											18 49								19 19					
Langley Green	d	18 26								18 46					19 11							19 41			
Rowley Regis	d	18 29				18 38				18 49					19 14							19 44			
Old Hill	d	18 32								18 52					19 17							19 47			
Cradley Heath	d	18 36				18 43				18 56					19 21							19 51			
Lye	d	18 39								18 59					19 24							19 54			
Stourbridge Junction 2	d	18a43				18 49				19 03					19 28							19 58			
Hagley	d					18 52				19 06					19 31							20 01			
Blakedown	d					18 55				19 09					19 34							20 04			
Kidderminster	d					19 00				19a15					19 39							20 09			
Hartlebury	d					19 05																			
University	d											18 55								19 25					
Barnt Green	d																								
Bromsgrove	d											19 10								19 40					
Droitwich Spa	d					19 13						19 20			19 50					19 57		20 20			
Worcester Shrub Hill 7	a											19 27			19 58							20 30			
	d				18 53							19 35		19 42							20 20				
Worcester Foregate Street 7	a				18 55	19 22						19 37		19 44						20 05	20 22				
	d				18 57	19 23						19 38								20 06	20 25				
Malvern Link	d				19 05	19 32						19 48								20 16	20 34				
Great Malvern	a				19 09	19 35						19 50								20 18	20 40				
	d				19 09															20 25					
Colwall	d				19 15															20 30					
Ledbury	a				19 23															20 38					
	d				19 29															20 39					
Hereford 7	a				19 45															21 02					

Table 71

Saturdays

Stratford-upon-Avon, Marylebone and Leamington Spa - Birmingham - Stourbridge, Worcester and Hereford

Network Diagram - see first Page of Table 71

		XC	GW	LM	CH	XC	LM	CH		CH	CH	XC	LM	LM	CH	CH	LM	XC		CH	XC	GW	LM	CH	CH
		◇■	◇■			◇■		◇		◇	◇	◇■						◇■		◇	◇■	◇■ A		◇	
Stratford-upon-Avon	d						19 26			19 16							20 26								21 15
Wilmcote	d						19 31			19 22							20 31								
Wootton Wawen	d						19x36										20x36								
Henley-in-Arden	d						19 40										20 40								
Danzey	d						19x44										20x44								
Wood End	d						19x48										20x48								
The Lakes	d						19x50										20x50								
Earlswood (West Midlands)	d						19 53										20 53								
Wythall	d						19 55										20 55								
Whitlocks End	d						19 58										20 58								
Shirley	d						20 01										21 01								
Yardley Wood	d						20 04										21 04								
Hall Green	d						20 07										21 07								
Spring Road	d						20 09										21 09								
London Marylebone ⊖	d				18 00			18 30							19 00	18 33				19 30				20 00	
Banbury	d	18 54			19 05	19 24		19 28				19 54			20 05	20 08		20 29		20 33	20 54			21 04	
Leamington Spa	a	19 10			19 23	19 41		19 46		19 50		20 10			20 23	20 28		20 45		20 51	21 10			21 22	21 45
	d	19 12			19 23	19 42		19 47			19 55	20 12			20 23	20 29		20 46		20 52	21 12			21 23	
Warwick	d				19 27						19 59				20 27	20 33								21 27	
Warwick Parkway	d				19 31			19 52			20 02				20 31					20 57				21 30	
Hatton	d										20 07					20a39									
Lapworth	d										20 13														
Dorridge	d			19 28	19 42						20 17			20 28	20 41								21 28	21 40	
Widney Manor	d			19 32										20 32									21 32		
Solihull	d			19 36	19 47			20 04			20 23			20 36	20 46					21 09			21 36	21 46	
Olton	d			19 39										20 39									21 39		
Acocks Green	d			19 42										20 42									21 42		
Tyseley	d			19 45										20 45									21 45		
Small Heath	d			19 47										20 47									21 47		
Bordesley	d																								
Birmingham Moor Street	d			19 51	19 56		20 16	20a17			20a37			20 51	20 56		21 16			21a22			21 51	21 56	
Birmingham Snow Hill	a			19 54	20 03		20 19							20 54	21 03		21 19						21 54	22 03	
	d			19 55			20 20							20 55			21 20						21 55		
Jewellery Quarter	d			19 57			20 22							20 57			21 22						21 57		
The Hawthorns	d			20 02			20 27							21 02			21 27						22 02		
Smethwick Galton Bridge	d			20 05			20 30							21 05			21 30						22 05		
Coventry	a	19 22										20 22									21 22				
Birmingham International	a	19 37										20 37									21 37				
Birmingham New Street	a	19 48				20 18						20 48						21 18			21 48				
	d												20 59												
Langley Green	d			20 08			20 33							21 08			21 33						22 08		
Rowley Regis	d			20 11			20 36							21 11			21 36						22 11		
Old Hill	d			20 14			20 39							21 14			21 39						22 14		
Cradley Heath	d			20 18			20 43							21 18			21 43						22 18		
Lye	d			20 21			20 46							21 21			21 46						22 21		
Stourbridge Junction	d			20 25			20a50							21 25			21a50						22 25		
Hagley	d			20 28										21 28									22 28		
Blakedown	d			20 31										21 31									22 31		
Kidderminster	d			20 36										21 36									22 36		
Hartlebury	d																								
University	d												21 05												
Barnt Green	d																								
Bromsgrove	d												21 20												
Droitwich Spa	d			20 47									21 30	21 47									22 47		
Worcester Shrub Hill	a			20 55									21 37	21 55									22 55		
	d		20 46	20 59									21 47									22 04	23 00		
Worcester Foregate Street	a		20 48	21 01									21 49									22 06	23 02		
	d		20 50	21 02									21 50									22 08	23 03		
Malvern Link	d		20 58	21 11									21 59									22 17	23 11		
Great Malvern	a		21 02	21 14									22 01									22 22	23 14		
	d		21 02										22 02												
Colwall	d		21 08										22 07												
Ledbury	a		21 16										22 14												
	d		21 18										22 15												
Hereford	a		21 34										22 35												

A until 11 February and then from 31 March

Table 71

Saturdays

Stratford-upon-Avon, Marylebone and Leamington Spa - Birmingham - Stourbridge, Worcester and Hereford

Network Diagram - see first Page of Table 71

		XC	LM	CH		XC	LM	CH	CH	CH	LM	CH	CH
		◇■		◇		◇■		◇ A	◇ B	A		◇ B	◇ A
Stratford-upon-Avon	d												
Wilmcote	d												
Wootton Wawen	d												
Henley-in-Arden	d												
Danzey	d												
Wood End	d												
The Lakes	d												
Earlswood (West Midlands)	d												
Wythall	d												
Whitlocks End	d		21 55								22 57		
Shirley	d		21 58								23 00		
Yardley Wood	d		22 01								23 03		
Hall Green	d		22 04								23 06		
Spring Road	d		22 06								23 08		
London Marylebone ⊖	d								21 00			22 10	
Banbury	d	21 25				21 54			22 05	22 25		23 06	
Leamington Spa	a	21 44				22 10			22 23	23 05		23 24	
	d	21 45		21 55		22 12		22 21	22 23			23 25	23 25
Warwick	d			21 59				22 27	22 27			23 29	23 29
Warwick Parkway	d			22 02				22 31	22 31			23 32	23 32
Hatton	d			22 07									
Lapworth	d			22 13									
Dorridge	d			22 17			22 33	22 41	22 41			23 42	23 42
Widney Manor	d						22 37					23 46	23 46
Solihull	d			22 23			22 41	22 46	22 46			23 49	23 49
Olton	d						22 44						
Acocks Green	d						22 47						
Tyseley	d		22 09				22 50				23 11		
Small Heath	d		22 11				22 52				23 13		
Bordesley	d												
Birmingham Moor Street	d		22 15	22a34			22 56	23 01	23 01		23 17	00a01	00a01
Birmingham Snow Hill	a		22 18				22 59	23 09	23 09		23 20		
	d		22 20				23 00				23 23		
Jewellery Quarter	d		22 22				23 02				23 25		
The Hawthorns	d		22 27				23 07				23 30		
Smethwick Galton Bridge	d		22 30				23 10				23 33		
Coventry	a	21 55				22 22							
Birmingham International	a	22 10				22 36							
Birmingham New Street	a	22 21				22 48							
	d												
Langley Green	d		22 33				23 13				23 36		
Rowley Regis	d		22 36				23 16				23 39		
Old Hill	d		22 39				23 19				23 42		
Cradley Heath	d		22 43				23 23				23 46		
Lye	d		22 46				23 26				23 49		
Stourbridge Junction	d		22a50				23 30				23a52		
Hagley	d						23 33						
Blakedown	d						23 36						
Kidderminster	d						23 41						
Hartlebury	d												
University	d												
Barnt Green	d												
Bromsgrove	d												
Droitwich Spa	d						23 52						
Worcester Shrub Hill	a						00 01						
	d												
Worcester Foregate Street	a												
	d												
Malvern Link	d												
Great Malvern	a												
	d												
Colwall	d												
Ledbury	a												
	d												
Hereford	a												

A from 7 January until 24 March

B until 31 December and then from 31 March

Stratford-upon-Avon, Marylebone and Leamington Spa - Birmingham - Stourbridge, Worcester and Hereford

Network Diagram - see first Page of Table 71

		LM	LM	GW	LM	CH	XC	LM	GW	LM		CH	XC	CH	LM	CH	GW	LM	CH	XC		LM	CH	LM	CH
				◇1		◇	◇1		◇1			◇	◇1			◇	◇1		◇	◇1					◇
		A																							
Stratford-upon-Avon	d				09 30					10 30								11 30						12 30	
Wilmcote	d				09 35					10 35								11 35						12 35	
Wootton Wawen	d																								
Henley-in-Arden	d				09 42					10 42								11 42						12 42	
Danzey	d																								
Wood End	d																								
The Lakes	d				09x49					10x49								11x49						12x49	
Earlswood (West Midlands)	d																								
Wythall	d				09 53					10 53								11 53						12 53	
Whitlocks End	d				09 55					10 55								11 55						12 55	
Shirley	d				09 59					10 59								11 59						12 59	
Yardley Wood	d				10 02					11 02								12 02						13 02	
Hall Green	d				10 05					11 05								12 05						13 05	
Spring Road	d				10 07					11 07								12 07						13 07	
London Marylebone 10 ⊖	d					08 25						09 23				10 03			10 33				11 03		11 33
Banbury	d					09 33	09 54					10 33	10 54			11 10			11 30	11 54			12 07		12 30
Leamington Spa 8	a					09 50	10 11					10 51	11 11			11 27			11 48	12 11			12 24		12 47
	d					09 51	10 12					10 51	11 12	11 20		11 29			11 48	12 12			12 25		12 48
Warwick	d					09 55						10 55		11 24		11 33							12 29		
Warwick Parkway	d					09 58						10 59				11 36			11 54				12 33		12 53
Hatton	d					10 03								11a31									12 37		
Lapworth	d					10 08																	12 43		
Dorridge	d	22p33				10 13		10 25				11 09			11 25	11 46			12 04			12 25	12 48		13 02
Widney Manor	d	22p37						10 29							11 29							12 29			
Solihull	d	22p41				10 19		10 32				11 13			11 32	11 52			12 09			12 32	12 53		13 08
Olton	d	22p44						10 36							11 36							12 36			
Acocks Green	d	22p47						10 38							11 38							12 38			
Tyseley	d	22p50			10 10					11 10								12 10						13 10	
Small Heath	d	22p52																							
Bordesley	d																								
Birmingham Moor Street	d	22p56	09 26		10 17	10 25		10 45		11 17		11 21			11 45	12 00		12 17	12a19			12 45	13 03	13 15	13a16
Birmingham Snow Hill	a	22p59	09 28		10 19	10 39		10 47		11 19		11 31			11 47	12 09		12 19				12 47	13 05	13 18	
	d	23p00	09 30		10 20			10 48		11 20					11 48			12 20				12 48		13 20	
Jewellery Quarter	d	23p02	09 32		10 22			10 51		11 22					11 51			12 22				12 51		13 22	
The Hawthorns	d	23p07	09 37		10 27			10 55		11 27					11 55			12 27				12 55		13 27	
Smethwick Galton Bridge 7	d	23p10	09 39		10 29			10 58		11 29					11 58			12 29				12 58		13 29	
Coventry	a						10 22						11 22							12 22					
Birmingham International ✈	a						10 38						11 38							12 38					
Birmingham New Street 12	a						10 50						11 50							12 50					
	d																								
Langley Green	d	23p13						11 01							12 01							13 01			
Rowley Regis	d	23p16	09 44		10 34			11 04		11 34					12 04			12 34				13 04		13 34	
Old Hill	d	23p19						11 07							12 07							13 07			
Cradley Heath	d	23p23	09 49		10 39			11 10		11 39					12 10			12 39				13 10		13 39	
Lye	d	23p26						11 13							12 13							13 13			
Stourbridge Junction 2	d	23p30	09 54		10 45			11a17		11 45					12a17			12 45				13a17		13 45	
Hagley	d	23p33	09 58		10 48					11 49								12 48						13 49	
Blakedown	d	23p36								11 52								12 51							
Kidderminster	d	23p41	10 04		10 55					11 57								12 56						13 55	
Hartlebury	d																								
University	d																								
Barnt Green	d																								
Bromsgrove	d																								
Droitwich Spa	d	23p52	10 15		11 06					12 08								13 08						14 07	
Worcester Shrub Hill 7	a	00 01	10 23		11 14					12 16								13 15							
	d		10 26	10 32	11 32				12 06								13 10	13 31							
Worcester Foregate Street 7	a		10 29	10 35	11 34				12 09								13 12	13 33						14 15	
	d		10 29	10 36	11 35				12 10								13 13	13 34							
Malvern Link	d		10 38	10 47	11 43				12 19								13 23	13 42							
Great Malvern	a		10 41	10 50	11 46				12 22								13 26	13 45							
	d								12 23								13 27								
Colwall	d								12 29								13 33								
Ledbury	a								12 36								13 41								
	d								12 38								13 49								
Hereford 7	a								12 54								14 06								

A not 11 December

Stratford-upon-Avon, Marylebone and Leamington Spa - Birmingham - Stourbridge, Worcester and Hereford

Network Diagram - see first Page of Table 71

		LM	XC	CH	LM	CH		XC	GW	LM	CH	XC	LM	CH	CH	XC		LM	CH	XC	CH	LM	CH	LM	XC
			◇1			◇		◇1	◇1			◇1		◇		◇1				◇1	◇		◇		◇1
Stratford-upon-Avon	d									13 30					14 00			14 30							
Wilmcote	d									13 35					14 04			14 35							
Wootton Wawen	d																								
Henley-in-Arden	d									13 42								14 42							
Danzey	d																								
Wood End	d																								
The Lakes	d									13x49								14x49							
Earlswood (West Midlands)	d																								
Wythall	d									13 53								14 53							
Whitlocks End	d									13 55								14 55							
Shirley	d									13 59								14 59							
Yardley Wood	d									14 02								15 02							
Hall Green	d									14 05								15 05							
Spring Road	d									14 07								15 07							
London Marylebone 10 ⊖	d					12 03					12 33			13 03					13 33		13 36		14 00		
Banbury	d		12 54			13 09		13 35			13 38	13 54		14 08		14 24			14 35	14 54	15 00		15 10		15 25
Leamington Spa 8	a		13 11			13 27		13 50			13 56	14 11		14 25	14 26	14 40			14 52	15 11	15 19		15 27		15 41
	d		13 12	13 20		13 28		13 52			13 56	14 12		14 25		14 42			14 52	15 12	15 20		15 28		15 43
Warwick	d			13 24		13 32								14 29							15 24		15 31		
Warwick Parkway	d					13 35					14 02			14 33					14 59				15 35		
Hatton	d			13a31										14 37							15a31		15 39		
Lapworth	d													14 43									15 45		
Dorridge	d				13 25	13 44					14 12		14 25	14 48					15 08			15 25	15 49		
Widney Manor	d				13 29								14 29									15 29			
Solihull	d				13 32	13 50					14 16		14 32	14 53					15 14			15 32	15 55		
Olton	d				13 36								14 36									15 36			
Acocks Green	d				13 38								14 38									15 38			
Tyseley	d									14 10								15 10							
Small Heath	d																								
Bordesley	d																								
Birmingham Moor Street	d				13 45	13 58				14 17	14a23		14 45	15 02				15 15	15a28			15 45	16 04		
Birmingham Snow Hill	a				13 48	14 03				14 19			14 47	15 05				15 19				15 48	16 12		
	d				13 48					14 20			14 48					15 20				15 48			
Jewellery Quarter	d				13 51					14 22			14 51					15 22				15 51			
The Hawthorns	d				13 55					14 27			14 55					15 27				15 55			
Smethwick Galton Bridge 7	d				13 58					14 29			14 58					15 29				15 58			
Coventry	a		13 22									14 22								15 22					
Birmingham International ✈	a		13 37									14 35								15 35					
Birmingham New Street 12	a		13 48					14 19				14 48				15 09				15 48					16 12
	d	13 24																						16 00	
Langley Green	d				14 01								15 01									16 01			
Rowley Regis	d				14 04					14 34			15 04					15 34				16 04			
Old Hill	d				14 07								15 07									16 07			
Cradley Heath	d				14 10					14 39			15 10					15 39				16 10			
Lye	d				14 13								15 13									16 13			
Stourbridge Junction 2	d				14a18					14 45			15a17					15 45				16a18			
Hagley	d									14 48								15 48							
Blakedown	d									14 51															
Kidderminster	d									14 56								15 54							
Hartlebury	d																								
University	d																								
Barnt Green	d																								
Bromsgrove	d	13 42																						16 21	
Droitwich Spa	d	13 52								15 08								16 06						16 30	
Worcester Shrub Hill 7	a	13 59																						16 38	
	d	14 14							15 10															16 45	
Worcester Foregate Street 7	a	14 16							15 12	15 16								16 14						16 47	
	d	14 17							15 13															16 48	
Malvern Link	d	14 25							15 23															16 57	
Great Malvern	a	14 28							15 26															17 01	
	d	14 29							15 27																
Colwall	d	14 34							15 33																
Ledbury	a	14 41							15 41																
	d	14 49							15 48																
Hereford 7	a	15 10							16 05																

Sundays
until 1 January

Stratford-upon-Avon, Marylebone and Leamington Spa - Birmingham - Stourbridge, Worcester and Hereford

Network Diagram - see first Page of Table 71

		GW		LM	CH	XC	CH	LM	LM	CH	XC	GW		LM	CH	XC	CH	LM	CH	LM	XC	GW		LM	CH
		◇1			◇	◇1	◇			◇	◇1	◇1				◇1	◇				◇1	◇1			
Stratford-upon-Avon	d			15 30			16 00							16 30										17 30	
Wilmcote	d			15 35			16 04							16 35										17 35	
Wootton Wawen	d																								
Henley-in-Arden	d			15 42										16 42										17 42	
Danzey	d													16x47											
Wood End	d																								
The Lakes	d			15x49										16x51										17x49	
Earlswood (West Midlands)	d																								
Wythall	d			15 53										16 55										17 53	
Whitlocks End	d			15 55										16 57										17 55	
Shirley	d			15 59										17 00										17 59	
Yardley Wood	d			16 02										17 03										18 02	
Hall Green	d			16 05										17 06										18 05	
Spring Road	d			16 07										17 08										18 07	
London Marylebone 10 ⊖	d				14 33					15 00					15 33		15 36		16 00						16 33
Banbury	d				15 31	15 54				16 10	16 25				16 30	16 54	17 00		17 11		17 25				17 30
Leamington Spa 8	a				15 49	16 11	16 26			16 28	16 41				16 47	17 11	17 19		17 28		17 41				17 47
	d				15 49	16 12				16 28	16 43				16 49	17 12	17 20		17 28		17 43				17 47
Warwick	d									16 32							17 24		17 33						
Warwick Parkway	d				15 54					16 36					16 54				17 36						17 53
Hatton	d																17a31								17 57
Lapworth	d																								18 03
Dorridge	d				16 04			16 25		16 50					17 04			17 25	17 46						18 08
Widney Manor	d							16 29										17 29							18 11
Solihull	d				16 09			16 32		16 56					17 11			17 32	17 52						18 16
Olton	d							16 36										17 36							
Acocks Green	d							16 38										17 38							
Tyseley	d			16 10										17 11										18 10	
Small Heath	d																								
Bordesley	d																								
Birmingham Moor Street	d			16 15	16a26			16 45	17 02	17 05				17 17	17a26			17 45	17 59					18 15	18a30
Birmingham Snow Hill ⇌	a			16 19				16 48	17 04	17 14				17 20				17 48	18 08					18 19	
	d			16 20				16 48	17 06					17 21				17 48						18 20	
Jewellery Quarter ⇌	d			16 22				16 51						17 24				17 51						18 22	
The Hawthorns ⇌	d			16 27				16 55						17 28				17 55						18 27	
Smethwick Galton Bridge 7	d			16 29				16 58						17 31				17 58						18 29	
Coventry	a					16 22										17 22									
Birmingham International ✈	a					16 35										17 35									
Birmingham New Street 12	a					16 48					17 12					17 48					18 09				
	d																			18 00					
Langley Green	d							17 01										18 01							
Rowley Regis	d			16 34				17 04						17 35				18 04						18 34	
Old Hill	d							17 07										18 07							
Cradley Heath	d			16 39				17 10						17 40				18 10						18 39	
Lye	d							17 13										18 13							
Stourbridge Junction 2	d			16 45				17a18	17 27					17 46				18a19						18 45	
Hagley	d			16 48					17 30					17 50										18 49	
Blakedown	d																							18 52	
Kidderminster	d			16 54					17 36					17 56										18 57	
Hartlebury	d																								
University	d																								
Barnt Green	d																								
Bromsgrove	d																			18 21					
Droitwich Spa	d			17 06					17 48					18 07						18 30				19 08	
Worcester Shrub Hill 7	a													18 15						18 38				19 16	
	d	17 10										18 08								18 43		19 10			
Worcester Foregate Street 7	a	17 12		17 14					18 01			18 10								18 45		19 13			
	d	17 13																		18 46		19 14			
Malvern Link	d	17 23																		18 55		19 23			
Great Malvern	a	17 26																		18 58		19 26			
	d	17 27																		18 58					
Colwall	d	17 33																		19 03					
Ledbury	a	17 41																		19 10					
	d	17 42																		19 10					
Hereford 7	a	17 58																		19 31					

Sundays
until 1 January

Stratford-upon-Avon, Marylebone and Leamington Spa - Birmingham - Stourbridge, Worcester and Hereford

Network Diagram - see first Page of Table 71

		XC	CH	CH	LM	XC	GW	LM		CH	XC	CH	CH	XC	LM	CH	XC	CH		CH	LM	XC	CH	XC	GW
		◇1	◇			◇1	◇1				◇1	◇		◇1			◇1	◇				◇1	◇	◇1	◇1
Stratford-upon-Avon	d		18 00					18 30							19 30			19 57							
Wilmcote	d		18 04					18 35							19 35			20 02							
Wootton Wawen	d																								
Henley-in-Arden	d							18 42							19 42										
Danzey	d																								
Wood End	d																								
The Lakes	d							18x49							19x49										
Earlswood (West Midlands)	d																								
Wythall	d							18 53							19 53										
Whitlocks End	d							18 55							19 55										
Shirley	d							18 59							19 59										
Yardley Wood	d							19 02							20 02										
Hall Green	d							19 05							20 05										
Spring Road	d							19 07							20 07										
London Marylebone 10 ⊖	d			17 00						17 33		17 36	18 00			18 33				19 00			19 33		
Banbury	d	17 54		18 11		18 25				18 30	18 54	19 00	19 11	19 25		19 29	19 54			20 10		20 25	20 31	20 54	
Leamington Spa 8	a	18 11	18 26	18 28		18 41				18 47	19 11	19 19	19 29	19 41		19 46	20 11	20 25		20 27		20 41	20 47	21 11	
	d	18 12		18 29		18 43				18 49	19 12	19 20	19 30	19 43		19 46	20 12			20 27		20 43	20 47	21 12	
Warwick	d			18 33								19 24	19 34							20 32					
Warwick Parkway	d			18 36						18 54			19 37			19 51				20 36			20 54		
Hatton	d											19a30													
Lapworth	d												19 45												
Dorridge	d			18 46						19 04			19 50			20 01				20 46			21 04		
Widney Manor	d			18 50									19 54							20 49					
Solihull	d			18 54						19 10			19 58			20 06				20 54			21 09		
Olton	d																								
Acocks Green	d																								
Tyseley	d							19 10							20 10										
Small Heath	d																								
Bordesley	d																								
Birmingham Moor Street	d			19 04				19 15		19a23			20 07		20 15	20a23				21 02			21a23		
Birmingham Snow Hill ⇌	a			19 13				19 18					20 15		20 18					21 11					
	d							19 20							20 20										
Jewellery Quarter ⇌	d							19 22							20 22										
The Hawthorns ⇌	d							19 27							20 27										
Smethwick Galton Bridge 7	d							19 29							20 29										
Coventry	a	18 22									19 22			19 53			20 22					20 53		21 22	
Birmingham International ✈	a	18 35									19 35			20 03			20 35					21 03		21 35	
Birmingham New Street 12	a	18 48				19 11					19 48			20 15			20 48					21 15		21 48	
	d				19 00																21 00				
Langley Green	d																								
Rowley Regis	d							19 34							20 34										
Old Hill	d																								
Cradley Heath	d							19 39							20 39										
Lye	d																								
Stourbridge Junction 2	d							19 45							20 45										
Hagley	d							19 48							20 49										
Blakedown	d																								
Kidderminster	d							19 55							20 57										
Hartlebury	d																								
University	d																								
Barnt Green	d																								
Bromsgrove	d				19 21																21 20				
Droitwich Spa	d				19 31			20 08							21 09						21 30				
Worcester Shrub Hill 7	a				19 41			20 16							21 16						21 37				
	d						20 12								21 22						21 42				22 11
Worcester Foregate Street 7	a						20 16								21 24						21 44				22 13
	d						20 16								21 25						21 45				22 15
Malvern Link	d						20 25								21 34						21 54				22 24
Great Malvern	a						20 29								21 37						21 57				22 27
	d						20 32														21 57				
Colwall	d						20 38														22 02				
Ledbury	a						20 45														22 09				
	d						20 47														22 10				
Hereford 7	a						21 03														22 30				

Table 71

Sundays
until 1 January

Stratford-upon-Avon, Marylebone and Leamington Spa - Birmingham - Stourbridge, Worcester and Hereford

Network Diagram - see first Page of Table 71

		LM	CH	LM		XC	CH	XC	LM	CH	XC	CH
						◇1	◇	◇1		◇	◇1	◇
Stratford-upon-Avon	d											
Wilmcote	d											
Wootton Wawen	d											
Henley-in-Arden	d											
Danzey	d											
Wood End	d											
The Lakes	d											
Earlswood (West Midlands)	d											
Wythall	d											
Whitlocks End	d											
Shirley	d											
Yardley Wood	d											
Hall Green	d											
Spring Road	d											
London Marylebone 10 ⊖	d		20 00				20 33			21 00		22 00
Banbury	d		21 11			21 24	21 44	21 54		22 10	22 24	22 55
Leamington Spa 8	a		21 29			21 41	22 01	22 11		22 28	22 40	23 12
	d		21 30			21 42	22 01	22 12		22 28	22 42	23 13
Warwick	d		21 34							22 32		23 17
Warwick Parkway	d		21 37				22 07			22 36		23 21
Hatton	d									22 40		
Lapworth	d									22 46		
Dorridge	d		21 47				22 17			22 51		23 31
Widney Manor	d									22 54		
Solihull	d		21 53				22 22			22 58		23 36
Olton	d											
Acocks Green	d											
Tyseley	d											
Small Heath	d											
Bordesley	d											
Birmingham Moor Street	d	21 35	22 01				22a36		22 52	23 06		23 45
Birmingham Snow Hill	a	21 37	22 10						22 54	23 15		23 53
	d	21 45							22 55			
Jewellery Quarter	d	21 47							22 57			
The Hawthorns	d	21 52							23 02			
Smethwick Galton Bridge 7	d	21 54							23 04			
Coventry	a					21 52		22 22			22 52	
Birmingham International ✈	a					22 02		22 32			23 02	
Birmingham New Street 12	a					22 14		22 42			23 13	
	d			22 05								
Langley Green	d											
Rowley Regis	d	21 59							23 09			
Old Hill	d											
Cradley Heath	d	22 03							23 14			
Lye	d											
Stourbridge Junction 2	d	22 09							23 19			
Hagley	d	22 12							23 23			
Blakedown	d											
Kidderminster	d	22 18							23 29			
Hartlebury	d											
University	d											
Barnt Green	d											
Bromsgrove	d											
Droitwich Spa	d	22 30		22 39					23 40			
Worcester Shrub Hill 7	a	22 37		22 48					23 48			
	d	22 41										
Worcester Foregate Street 7	a	22 43										
	d	22 44										
Malvern Link	d	22 52										
Great Malvern	a	22 55										
	d											
Colwall	d											
Ledbury	a											
	d											
Hereford 7	a											

Table 71

Sundays
8 January to 12 February

Stratford-upon-Avon, Marylebone and Leamington Spa - Birmingham - Stourbridge, Worcester and Hereford

Network Diagram - see first Page of Table 71

		LM	CH	LM	GW	LM	CH	XC	CH	CH		LM	GW	LM	CH	XC	XC	CH	CH	LM		GW	LM	CH	XC
					◇1		◇	◇1	◇				◇1		◇		◇1					◇1		◇	
			🚌							🚌						🚌			🚌						🚌
Stratford-upon-Avon	d					09 30			10 00					10 30									11 30		
Wilmcote	d					09 35			10 04					10 35									11 35		
Wootton Wawen	d																								
Henley-in-Arden	d					09 42								10 42									11 42		
Danzey	d																								
Wood End	d																								
The Lakes	d					09x49								10x49									11x49		
Earlswood (West Midlands)	d																								
Wythall	d					09 53								10 53									11 53		
Whitlocks End	d					09 55								10 55									11 55		
Shirley	d					09 59								10 59									11 59		
Yardley Wood	d					10 02								11 02									12 02		
Hall Green	d					10 05								11 05									12 05		
Spring Road	d					10 07								11 07									12 07		
London Marylebone 10 ⊖	d																								
Banbury	d									10 10						10 25			11 15						11 25
Leamington Spa 8	a		00s15						10 29	10 45						11 00			11 50						12 00
	d						09 50	10 12							10 56		11 12	11 20						11 58	
Warwick	d		00s25				09 55								11 00			11 24						12 03	
Warwick Parkway	d		00s35				09 58								11 04									12 06	
Hatton	d						10 03											11a31						12 11	
Lapworth	d						10 08																	12 16	
Dorridge	d	22p33	01s00				10 13					10 25			11 15					11 25				12 21	
Widney Manor	d	22p37										10 29								11 29					
Solihull	d	22p41	01s20				10 19					10 32			11 22					11 32				12 26	
Olton	d	22p44										10 36								11 36					
Acocks Green	d	22p47										10 38								11 38					
Tyseley	d	22p50				10 10								11 10									12 10		
Small Heath	d	22p52																							
Bordesley	d																								
Birmingham Moor Street	d	22p56		09 26		10 17	10 27					10 45		11 17	11 31					11 45			12 17	12 36	
Birmingham Snow Hill	a	22p59	01 45	09 28		10 19	10 36					10 47		11 19	11 40					11 47			12 19	12 43	
	d	23p00		09 30		10 20						10 48		11 20						11 48			12 20		
Jewellery Quarter	d	23p02		09 32		10 22						10 51		11 22						11 51			12 22		
The Hawthorns	d	23p07		09 37		10 27						10 55		11 27						11 55			12 27		
Smethwick Galton Bridge 7	d	23p10		09 39		10 29						10 58		11 29						11 58			12 29		
Coventry	a							10 22									11 22								
Birmingham International ✈	a							10 38									11 38								
Birmingham New Street 12	a							10 50									11 50								
	d																								
Langley Green	d	23p13										11 01								12 01					
Rowley Regis	d	23p16		09 44		10 34						11 04		11 34						12 04			12 34		
Old Hill	d	23p19										11 07								12 07					
Cradley Heath	d	23p23		09 49		10 39						11 10		11 39						12 10			12 39		
Lye	d	23p26										11 13								12 13					
Stourbridge Junction 2	d	23p30		09 54		10 45						11a17		11 45						12a17			12 45		
Hagley	d	23p33		09 58		10 48								11 49									12 48		
Blakedown	d	23p36												11 52									12 51		
Kidderminster	d	23p41		10 04		10 55								11 57									12 56		
Hartlebury	d																								
University	d																								
Barnt Green	d																								
Bromsgrove	d																								
Droitwich Spa	d	23p52		10 15		11 06								12 08									13 08		
Worcester Shrub Hill 7	a	00 01		10 23		11 14								12 16									13 15		
	d			10 26	10 32	11 32							12 06									13 10	13 31		
Worcester Foregate Street 7	a			10 29	10 35	11 34							12 09									13 12	13 33		
	d			10 29	10 36	11 35							12 10									13 13	13 34		
Malvern Link	d			10 38	10 47	11 43							12 19									13 24	13 42		
Great Malvern	a			10 41	10 50	11 46							12 22									13 27	13 45		
	d												12 23									13 27			
Colwall	d												12 29									13 33			
Ledbury	a												12 36									13 41			
	d												12 38									13 49			
Hereford 7	a												12 54									14 06			

Table 71

Sundays

8 January to 12 February

Stratford-upon-Avon, Marylebone and Leamington Spa - Birmingham - Stourbridge, Worcester and Hereford

Network Diagram - see first Page of Table 71

		XC	CH	CH	LM	CH		CH	XC	LM	CH	LM	XC	CH	CH	LM		CH	CH	XC	GW	LM	CH	XC	CH
		◇1 ✠	🚌	◇		◇ ✠		🚌	🚌				◇1 ✠	🚌				◇ ✠	🚌	🚌	◇1 ✠		◇	◇1 ✠	🚌
Stratford-upon-Avon	d			12 00						12 30												13 30			
Wilmcote	d			12 04						12 35												13 35			
Wootton Wawen	d																								
Henley-in-Arden	d									12 42												13 42			
Danzey	d																								
Wood End	d																								
The Lakes	d									12x49												13x49			
Earlswood (West Midlands)	d																								
Wythall	d									12 53												13 53			
Whitlocks End	d									12 55												13 55			
Shirley	d									12 59												13 59			
Yardley Wood	d									13 02												14 02			
Hall Green	d									13 05												14 05			
Spring Road	d									13 07												14 07			
London Marylebone 10 ⊖	d																								
Banbury	d		11 45					12 15	12 25					12 45					13 15	13 25					13 45
Leamington Spa 8	a		12 20	12 28				12 50	13 00					13 20					13 50	14 00					14 20
	d	12 12				12 30					13 01		13 12		13 20			13 30					14 00	14 12	
Warwick	d										13 05				13 24								14 04		
Warwick Parkway	d					12 35					13 09							13 35					14 07		
Hatton	d														13a31										
Lapworth	d																						14 15		
Dorridge	d				12 25	12 45					13 19					13 25		13 44					14 19		
Widney Manor	d				12 29											13 29									
Solihull	d				12 32	12 51					13 25					13 32		13 50					14 25		
Olton	d				12 36											13 36									
Acocks Green	d				12 38											13 38									
Tyseley	d									13 10												14 10			
Small Heath	d																								
Bordesley	d																								
Birmingham Moor Street	d				12 45	13a02				13 15	13 36					13 45		14a03				14 17	14 34		
Birmingham Snow Hill ⇌	a				12 47					13 18	13 44					13 48						14 19	14 43		
	d				12 48					13 20						13 48						14 20			
Jewellery Quarter ⇌	d				12 51					13 22						13 51						14 22			
The Hawthorns ⇌	d				12 55					13 27						13 55						14 27			
Smethwick Galton Bridge 7	d				12 58					13 29						13 58						14 29			
Coventry	a	12 22											13 22											14 22	
Birmingham International ✈	a	12 38											13 37											14 35	
Birmingham New Street 12	a	12 50											13 48											14 48	
	d											13 24													
Langley Green	d				13 01											14 01									
Rowley Regis	d				13 04					13 34						14 04						14 34			
Old Hill	d				13 07											14 07									
Cradley Heath	d				13 10					13 39						14 10						14 39			
Lye	d				13 13											14 13									
Stourbridge Junction 2	d				13a17					13 45						14a18						14 45			
Hagley	d									13 49												14 48			
Blakedown	d																					14 51			
Kidderminster	d									13 55												14 56			
Hartlebury	d																								
University	d																								
Barnt Green	d																								
Bromsgrove	d											13 42													
Droitwich Spa	d									14 07		13 52										15 08			
Worcester Shrub Hill 7	a											13 59													
	d											14 14									15 10				
Worcester Foregate Street 7	a									14 15		14 16									15 12	15 16			
	d											14 17									15 13				
Malvern Link	d											14 25									15 23				
Great Malvern	a											14 28									15 26				
	d											14 29									15 27				
Colwall	d											14 34									15 33				
Ledbury	a											14 41									15 41				
	d											14 49									15 48				
Hereford 7	a											15 10									16 05				

Table 71

Sundays

8 January to 12 February

Stratford-upon-Avon, Marylebone and Leamington Spa - Birmingham - Stourbridge, Worcester and Hereford

Network Diagram - see first Page of Table 71

		CH		LM	CH	LM	CH	XC	CH	LM	CH	LM		XC	GW	LM	CH	XC	CH	LM	LM	CH		XC	GW
					◇ ✠			◇1 ✠	◇		◇			◇1 ✠	◇1		◇	◇1 ✠	◇			◇		◇1 ✠	◇1
Stratford-upon-Avon	d	14 00				14 30										15 30			16 00						
Wilmcote	d	14 04				14 35										15 35			16 04						
Wootton Wawen	d																								
Henley-in-Arden	d					14 42										15 42									
Danzey	d																								
Wood End	d																								
The Lakes	d					14x49										15x49									
Earlswood (West Midlands)	d																								
Wythall	d					14 53										15 53									
Whitlocks End	d					14 55										15 55									
Shirley	d					14 59										15 59									
Yardley Wood	d					15 02										16 02									
Hall Green	d					15 05										16 05									
Spring Road	d					15 07										16 07									
London Marylebone 10 ⊖	d						13 33		13 36		14 00						14 33					15 00			
Banbury	d						14 35	14 54	15 00		15 10			15 25			15 31	15 54				16 10		16 25	
Leamington Spa 8	a	14 26					14 52	15 11	15 19		15 27			15 41			15 49	16 11	16 26			16 28		16 41	
	d				14 30		14 52	15 12	15 20		15 28			15 43			15 49	16 12				16 28		16 43	
Warwick	d								15 24		15 31											16 32			
Warwick Parkway	d				14 36		14 59				15 35						15 54					16 36			
Hatton	d								15a31		15 39														
Lapworth	d										15 45														
Dorridge	d			14 25	14 46		15 08			15 25	15 49						16 04			16 25		16 50			
Widney Manor	d			14 29						15 29										16 29					
Solihull	d			14 32	14 52		15 14			15 32	15 55						16 09			16 32		16 56			
Olton	d			14 36						15 36										16 36					
Acocks Green	d			14 38						15 38										16 38					
Tyseley	d					15 10										16 10									
Small Heath	d																								
Bordesley	d																								
Birmingham Moor Street	d			14 45	15a03	15 15	15a28			15 45	16 04					16 15	16a26			16 45	17 02	17 05			
Birmingham Snow Hill ⇌	a			14 47		15 19				15 48	16 12					16 19				16 48	17 04	17 14			
	d			14 48		15 20				15 48						16 20				16 48	17 06				
Jewellery Quarter ⇌	d			14 51		15 22				15 51						16 22				16 51					
The Hawthorns ⇌	d			14 55		15 27				15 55						16 27				16 55					
Smethwick Galton Bridge 7	d			14 58		15 29				15 58						16 29				16 58					
Coventry	a							15 22										16 22							
Birmingham International ✈	a							15 35										16 35							
Birmingham New Street 12	a							15 48						16 12				16 48						17 12	
	d											16 00													
Langley Green	d			15 01						16 01										17 01					
Rowley Regis	d			15 04		15 34				16 04						16 34				17 04					
Old Hill	d			15 07						16 07										17 07					
Cradley Heath	d			15 10		15 39				16 10						16 39				17 10					
Lye	d			15 13						16 13										17 13					
Stourbridge Junction 2	d			15a17		15 45				16a18						16 45				17a18	17 27				
Hagley	d					15 48										16 48					17 30				
Blakedown	d																								
Kidderminster	d					15 54										16 54					17 36				
Hartlebury	d																								
University	d																								
Barnt Green	d																								
Bromsgrove	d											16 21													
Droitwich Spa	d					16 06						16 30				17 06					17 48				
Worcester Shrub Hill 7	a											16 38													
	d											16 45			17 10										18 08
Worcester Foregate Street 7	a					16 14						16 47			17 12	17 14					18 01				18 10
	d											16 48			17 13										
Malvern Link	d											16 57			17 23										
Great Malvern	a											17 01			17 26										
	d														17 27										
Colwall	d														17 33										
Ledbury	a														17 41										
	d														17 42										
Hereford 7	a														17 58										

Table 71

Sundays
8 January to 12 February

Stratford-upon-Avon, Marylebone and Leamington Spa - Birmingham - Stourbridge, Worcester and Hereford

Network Diagram - see first Page of Table 71

		LM	CH	XC	CH	LM	CH	LM	XC	GW	LM	CH	XC	CH	CH	LM	XC	GW	LM	CH	XC	CH	CH
				◇1	◇				◇1	◇1			◇1	◇			◇1	◇1			◇1	◇	
Stratford-upon-Avon	d	16 30									17 30			18 00					18 30				
Wilmcote	d	16 35									17 35			18 04					18 35				
Wootton Wawen	d																						
Henley-in-Arden	d	16 42									17 42								18 42				
Danzey	d	16x47																					
Wood End	d																						
The Lakes	d	16x51									17x49								18x49				
Earlswood (West Midlands)	d																						
Wythall	d	16 55									17 53								18 53				
Whitlocks End	d	16 57									17 55								18 55				
Shirley	d	17 00									17 59								18 59				
Yardley Wood	d	17 03									18 02								19 02				
Hall Green	d	17 06									18 05								19 05				
Spring Road	d	17 08									18 07								19 07				
London Marylebone 10 ⊖	d		15 33		15 36		16 00					16 33			17 00					17 33		17 36	18 00
Banbury	d		16 30	16 54	17 00		17 11		17 25			17 30	17 54		18 11		18 25			18 30	18 54	19 00	19 11
Leamington Spa 8	a		16 47	17 11	17 19		17 28		17 41			17 47	18 11	18 26	18 28		18 41			18 47	19 11	19 19	19 29
	d		16 49	17 12	17 20		17 28		17 43			17 47	18 12		18 29		18 43			18 49	19 12	19 20	19 30
Warwick	d				17 24		17 33								18 33							19 24	19 34
Warwick Parkway	d		16 54				17 36					17 53			18 36					18 54			19 37
Hatton	d				17a31							17 57										19a30	
Lapworth	d											18 03											19 45
Dorridge	d		17 04			17 25	17 46					18 08			18 46					19 04			19 50
Widney Manor	d					17 29						18 11			18 50								19 54
Solihull	d		17 11			17 32	17 52					18 16			18 54					19 10			19 58
Olton	d					17 36																	
Acocks Green	d					17 38																	
Tyseley	d	17 11									18 10								19 10				
Small Heath	d																						
Bordesley	d																						
Birmingham Moor Street	d	17 17	17a26			17 45	17 59				18 15	18a30			19 04				19 15	19a23			20 07
Birmingham Snow Hill ⇌	a	17 20				17 48	18 08				18 19				19 13				19 18				20 15
	d	17 21				17 48					18 20								19 20				
Jewellery Quarter ⇌	d	17 24				17 51					18 22								19 22				
The Hawthorns ⇌	d	17 28				17 55					18 27								19 27				
Smethwick Galton Bridge 7	d	17 31				17 58					18 29								19 29				
Coventry	a			17 22									18 22								19 22		
Birmingham International ✈	a			17 35									18 35								19 35		
Birmingham New Street 12	a			17 48					18 09				18 48				19 11				19 48		
	d							18 00								19 00							
Langley Green	d					18 01																	
Rowley Regis	d	17 35				18 04					18 34								19 34				
Old Hill	d					18 07																	
Cradley Heath	d	17 40				18 10					18 39								19 39				
Lye	d					18 13																	
Stourbridge Junction 2	d	17 46				18a19					18 45								19 45				
Hagley	d	17 50									18 49								19 48				
Blakedown	d										18 52												
Kidderminster	d	17 56									18 57								19 55				
Hartlebury	d																						
University	d																						
Barnt Green	d																						
Bromsgrove	d							18 21								19 21							
Droitwich Spa	d	18 07						18 30			19 08					19 31			20 08				
Worcester Shrub Hill 7	a	18 15						18 38			19 16					19 41			20 16				
	d							18 43		19 10								20 12					
Worcester Foregate Street 7	a							18 45		19 13								20 16					
	d							18 46		19 14								20 16					
Malvern Link	d							18 55		19 23								20 25					
Great Malvern	a							18 58		19 26								20 29					
	d							18 58										20 32					
Colwall	d							19 03										20 38					
Ledbury	a							19 10										20 45					
	d							19 10										20 47					
Hereford 7	a							19 31										21 03					

Table 71

Sundays
8 January to 12 February

Stratford-upon-Avon, Marylebone and Leamington Spa - Birmingham - Stourbridge, Worcester and Hereford

Network Diagram - see first Page of Table 71

		XC	LM	CH	XC	CH	CH	LM	XC	CH	XC	GW	LM	CH	LM	XC	CH	XC	LM	CH	XC	CH
		◇1			◇1	◇			◇1	◇	◇1	◇1				◇1	◇	◇1		◇	◇1	◇
Stratford-upon-Avon	d		19 30			19 57																
Wilmcote	d		19 35			20 02																
Wootton Wawen	d																					
Henley-in-Arden	d		19 42																			
Danzey	d																					
Wood End	d																					
The Lakes	d		19x49																			
Earlswood (West Midlands)	d																					
Wythall	d		19 53																			
Whitlocks End	d		19 55																			
Shirley	d		19 59																			
Yardley Wood	d		20 02																			
Hall Green	d		20 05																			
Spring Road	d		20 07																			
London Marylebone 10 ⊖	d			18 33			19 00			19 33				20 00			20 33			21 00		22 00
Banbury	d	19 25		19 29	19 54		20 10		20 25	20 31	20 54			21 11		21 24	21 44	21 54		22 10	22 24	22 55
Leamington Spa 8	a	19 41		19 46	20 11	20 25	20 27		20 41	20 47	21 11			21 29		21 41	22 01	22 11		22 28	22 40	23 12
	d	19 43		19 46	20 12		20 27		20 43	20 47	21 12			21 30		21 42	22 01	22 12		22 28	22 42	23 13
Warwick	d						20 32							21 34						22 32		23 17
Warwick Parkway	d			19 51			20 36			20 54				21 37			22 07			22 36		23 21
Hatton	d																			22 40		
Lapworth	d																			22 46		
Dorridge	d			20 01			20 46			21 04				21 47			22 17			22 51		23 31
Widney Manor	d						20 49													22 54		
Solihull	d			20 06			20 54			21 09				21 53			22 22			22 58		23 36
Olton	d																					
Acocks Green	d																					
Tyseley	d		20 10																			
Small Heath	d																					
Bordesley	d																					
Birmingham Moor Street	d		20 15	20a23			21 02			21a23			21 35	22 01			22a36		22 52	23 06		23 45
Birmingham Snow Hill ⇌	a		20 18				21 11						21 37	22 10					22 54	23 15		23 53
	d		20 20										21 45						22 55			
Jewellery Quarter ⇌	d		20 22										21 47						22 57			
The Hawthorns ⇌	d		20 27										21 52						23 02			
Smethwick Galton Bridge 7	d		20 29										21 54						23 04			
Coventry	a	19 53			20 22				20 53		21 22					21 52		22 22			22 52	
Birmingham International ✈	a	20 03			20 35				21 03		21 35					22 02		22 32			23 02	
Birmingham New Street 12	a	20 15			20 48				21 15		21 48					22 14		22 42			23 13	
	d							21 00							22 05							
Langley Green	d																					
Rowley Regis	d		20 34										21 59						23 09			
Old Hill	d																					
Cradley Heath	d		20 39										22 03						23 14			
Lye	d																					
Stourbridge Junction 2	d		20 45										22 09						23 19			
Hagley	d		20 49										22 12						23 23			
Blakedown	d																					
Kidderminster	d		20 57										22 18						23 29			
Hartlebury	d																					
University	d																					
Barnt Green	d																					
Bromsgrove	d							21 20														
Droitwich Spa	d		21 09					21 30					22 30		22 39				23 40			
Worcester Shrub Hill 7	a		21 16					21 37					22 37		22 48				23 48			
	d		21 22					21 42				22 11	22 41									
Worcester Foregate Street 7	a		21 24					21 44				22 13	22 43									
	d		21 25					21 45				22 15	22 44									
Malvern Link	d		21 34					21 54				22 24	22 52									
Great Malvern	a		21 37					21 57				22 27	22 55									
	d							21 57														
Colwall	d							22 02														
Ledbury	a							22 09														
	d							22 10														
Hereford 7	a							22 30														

Table 71

Sundays
19 February to 25 March

Stratford-upon-Avon, Marylebone and Leamington Spa - Birmingham - Stourbridge, Worcester and Hereford

Network Diagram - see first Page of Table 71

		LM	CH	LM	GW	LM	CH	XC	CH	XC		CH	LM	GW	LM	CH	XC	CH	XC	CH		LM	GW	LM	CH
			🚌		◇1		◇	◇1 ⊼	◇	🚌		🚌		◇1 ☕		◇	◇1 ⊼		🚌	🚌			◇1 ☕		◇
Stratford-upon-Avon	d					09 30			10 00						10 30									11 30	
Wilmcote	d					09 35			10 04						10 35									11 35	
Wootton Wawen	d																								
Henley-in-Arden	d					09 42									10 42									11 42	
Danzey	d																								
Wood End	d																								
The Lakes	d					09x49									10x49									11x49	
Earlswood (West Midlands)	d																								
Wythall	d					09 53									10 53									11 53	
Whitlocks End	d					09 55									10 55									11 55	
Shirley	d					09 59									10 59									11 59	
Yardley Wood	d					10 02									11 02									12 02	
Hall Green	d					10 05									11 05									12 05	
Spring Road	d					10 07									11 07									12 07	
London Marylebone 10 ⊖	d																								
Banbury	d									10 00		10 10							11 00	11 15					
Leamington Spa 8	a		00s15						10 29	10 40		10 45							11 40	11 50					
	d						09 50	10 12								10 56	11 12	11 20							11 58
Warwick	d		00s25				09 55									11 00		11 24							12 03
Warwick Parkway	d		00s35				09 58									11 04									12 06
Hatton	d						10 03											11a31							12 11
Lapworth	d						10 08																		12 16
Dorridge	d	22p33	01s00				10 13						10 25			11 15						11 25			12 21
Widney Manor	d	22p37											10 29									11 29			
Solihull	d	22p41	01s20				10 19						10 32			11 22						11 32			12 26
Olton	d	22p44											10 36									11 36			
Acocks Green	d	22p47											10 38									11 38			
Tyseley	d	22p50				10 10									11 10									12 10	
Small Heath	d	22p52																							
Bordesley	d																								
Birmingham Moor Street	d	22p56		09 26		10 17	10 27						10 45		11 17	11 31						11 45		12 17	12 36
Birmingham Snow Hill 🚊	a	22p59	01 45	09 28		10 19	10 36						10 47		11 19	11 40						11 47		12 19	12 43
	d	23p00		09 30		10 20							10 48		11 20							11 48		12 20	
Jewellery Quarter 🚊	d	23p02		09 32		10 22							10 51		11 22							11 51		12 22	
The Hawthorns 🚊	d	23p07		09 37		10 27							10 55		11 27							11 55		12 27	
Smethwick Galton Bridge 7	d	23p10		09 39		10 29							10 58		11 29							11 58		12 29	
Coventry	a							10 22									11 22								
Birmingham International ✈	a							10 38									11 38								
Birmingham New Street 12	a							10 50									11 50								
	d																								
Langley Green	d	23p13											11 01									12 01			
Rowley Regis	d	23p16		09 44		10 34							11 04		11 34							12 04		12 34	
Old Hill	d	23p19											11 07									12 07			
Cradley Heath	d	23p23		09 49		10 39							11 10		11 39							12 10		12 39	
Lye	d	23p26											11 13									12 13			
Stourbridge Junction 2	d	23p30		09 54		10 45							11a17		11 45							12a17		12 45	
Hagley	d	23p33		09 58		10 48									11 49									12 48	
Blakedown	d	23p36													11 52									12 51	
Kidderminster	d	23p41		10 04		10 55									11 57									12 56	
Hartlebury	d																								
University	d																								
Barnt Green	d																								
Bromsgrove	d																								
Droitwich Spa	d	23p52		10 15		11 06									12 08									13 08	
Worcester Shrub Hill 7	a	00 01		10 23		11 14									12 16									13 15	
	d			10 26	10 32	11 32								12 06									13 10	13 31	
Worcester Foregate Street 7	a			10 29	10 35	11 34								12 09									13 12	13 33	
	d			10 29	10 36	11 35								12 10									13 13	13 34	
Malvern Link	d			10 38	10 47	11 43								12 19									13 23	13 42	
Great Malvern	a			10 41	10 50	11 46								12 22									13 26	13 45	
	d													12 23									13 27		
Colwall	d													12 29									13 33		
Ledbury	a													12 36									13 41		
	d													12 38									13 49		
Hereford 7	a													12 54									14 06		

Table 71

Sundays
19 February to 25 March

Stratford-upon-Avon, Marylebone and Leamington Spa - Birmingham - Stourbridge, Worcester and Hereford

Network Diagram - see first Page of Table 71

		XC	CH	CH	LM	CH		XC	CH	LM	CH	LM	XC	CH	CH	LM		CH	XC	CH	GW	LM	CH	XC	CH
		◇1 ⊼	🚌	◇		◇ ⊼		🚌	🚌				◇1 ⊼	🚌				◇ ⊼	🚌	🚌	◇1 ☕		◇	◇1 ⊼	🚌
Stratford-upon-Avon	d			12 00						12 30												13 30			
Wilmcote	d			12 04						12 35												13 35			
Wootton Wawen	d																								
Henley-in-Arden	d									12 42												13 42			
Danzey	d																								
Wood End	d																								
The Lakes	d									12x49												13x49			
Earlswood (West Midlands)	d																								
Wythall	d									12 53												13 53			
Whitlocks End	d									12 55												13 55			
Shirley	d									12 59												13 59			
Yardley Wood	d									13 02												14 02			
Hall Green	d									13 05												14 05			
Spring Road	d									13 07												14 07			
London Marylebone 10 ⊖	d																								
Banbury	d		11 45					12 00	12 15					12 45					13 00	13 15					13 45
Leamington Spa 8	a		12 20	12 28				12 40	12 50					13 20					13 40	13 50					14 20
	d	12 12				12 30					13 01		13 12		13 20			13 30					14 00	14 12	
Warwick	d										13 05				13 24								14 04		
Warwick Parkway	d					12 35					13 09							13 35					14 07		
Hatton	d														13a31										
Lapworth	d																						14 15		
Dorridge	d				12 25	12 45					13 19					13 25		13 44					14 19		
Widney Manor	d				12 29											13 29									
Solihull	d				12 32	12 51					13 25					13 32		13 50					14 25		
Olton	d				12 36											13 36									
Acocks Green	d				12 38											13 38									
Tyseley	d									13 10												14 10			
Small Heath	d																								
Bordesley	d																								
Birmingham Moor Street	d				12 45	13a02				13 15	13 36					13 45		14a03				14 17	14 34		
Birmingham Snow Hill 🚊	a				12 47					13 18	13 44					13 48						14 19	14 43		
	d				12 48					13 20						13 48						14 20			
Jewellery Quarter 🚊	d				12 51					13 22						13 51						14 22			
The Hawthorns 🚊	d				12 55					13 27						13 55						14 27			
Smethwick Galton Bridge 7	d				12 58					13 29						13 58						14 29			
Coventry	a	12 22											13 22											14 22	
Birmingham International ✈	a	12 38											13 37											14 35	
Birmingham New Street 12	a	12 50											13 48											14 48	
	d											13 24													
Langley Green	d				13 01											14 01									
Rowley Regis	d				13 04					13 34						14 04						14 34			
Old Hill	d				13 07											14 07									
Cradley Heath	d				13 10					13 39						14 10						14 39			
Lye	d				13 13											14 13									
Stourbridge Junction 2	d				13a17					13 45						14a18						14 45			
Hagley	d									13 49												14 48			
Blakedown	d																					14 51			
Kidderminster	d									13 55												14 56			
Hartlebury	d																								
University	d																								
Barnt Green	d																								
Bromsgrove	d											13 42													
Droitwich Spa	d									14 07		13 52										15 08			
Worcester Shrub Hill 7	a											13 59													
	d											14 14									15 10				
Worcester Foregate Street 7	a									14 15		14 16									15 12	15 16			
	d											14 17									15 13				
Malvern Link	d											14 25									15 23				
Great Malvern	a											14 28									15 26				
	d											14 29									15 27				
Colwall	d											14 34									15 34				
Ledbury	a											14 41									15 41				
	d											14 49									15 48				
Hereford 7	a											15 10									16 05				

Table 71

Sundays

19 February to 25 March

Stratford-upon-Avon, Marylebone and Leamington Spa - Birmingham - Stourbridge, Worcester and Hereford

Network Diagram - see first Page of Table 71

		CH	LM	CH	XC	LM	CH	XC	CH	LM	CH	LM	XC	GW	LM	CH	XC	CH	LM	LM	CH	XC
				◇ (trolley)	(bus)			◇1 (trolley)	◇		◇		◇1 (trolley)	◇1		◇	◇1 (trolley)	◇			◇	◇1 (trolley)
Stratford-upon-Avon	d	14 00				14 30									15 30			16 00				
Wilmcote	d	14 04				14 35									15 35			16 04				
Wootton Wawen	d																					
Henley-in-Arden	d					14 42									15 42							
Danzey	d																					
Wood End	d																					
The Lakes	d					14x49									15x49							
Earlswood (West Midlands)	d																					
Wythall	d					14 53									15 53							
Whitlocks End	d					14 55									15 55							
Shirley	d					14 59									15 59							
Yardley Wood	d					15 02									16 02							
Hall Green	d					15 05									16 05							
Spring Road	d					15 07									16 07							
London Marylebone 10 ⊖	d						13 33		13 36		14 00					14 33					15 00	
Banbury	d				14 00		14 35	14 54	15 00		15 10		15 25			15 31	15 54				16 10	16 25
Leamington Spa 8	a	14 26			14 40		14 52	15 11	15 19		15 27		15 41			15 49	16 11	16 26			16 28	16 41
	d			14 30			14 52	15 12	15 20		15 28		15 43			15 49	16 12				16 28	16 43
Warwick	d								15 24		15 31										16 32	
Warwick Parkway	d			14 36			14 59				15 35					15 54					16 36	
Hatton	d								15a31		15 39											
Lapworth	d										15 45											
Dorridge	d		14 25	14 46			15 08			15 25	15 49					16 04			16 25		16 50	
Widney Manor	d		14 29							15 29									16 29			
Solihull	d		14 32	14 52			15 14			15 32	15 55					16 09			16 32		16 56	
Olton	d		14 36							15 36									16 36			
Acocks Green	d		14 38							15 38									16 38			
Tyseley	d					15 10									16 10							
Small Heath	d																					
Bordesley	d																					
Birmingham Moor Street	d		14 45	15a03		15 15	15a28			15 45	16 04				16 15	16a26			16 45	17 02	17 05	
Birmingham Snow Hill (tram)	a		14 47			15 19				15 48	16 12				16 19				16 48	17 04	17 14	
	d		14 48			15 20				15 48					16 20				16 48	17 06		
Jewellery Quarter (tram)	d		14 51			15 22				15 51					16 22				16 51			
The Hawthorns (tram)	d		14 55			15 27				15 55					16 27				16 55			
Smethwick Galton Bridge 7	d		14 58			15 29				15 58					16 29				16 58			
Coventry	a							15 22									16 22					
Birmingham International ✈	a							15 35									16 35					
Birmingham New Street 12	a							15 48					16 12				16 48					17 12
	d											16 00										
Langley Green	d		15 01							16 01									17 01			
Rowley Regis	d		15 04			15 34				16 04					16 34				17 04			
Old Hill	d		15 07							16 07									17 07			
Cradley Heath	d		15 10			15 39				16 10					16 39				17 10			
Lye	d		15 13							16 13									17 13			
Stourbridge Junction 2	d		15a17			15 45				16a18					16 45				17a18	17 27		
Hagley	d					15 48									16 48					17 30		
Blakedown	d																					
Kidderminster	d					15 54									16 54					17 36		
Hartlebury	d																					
University	d																					
Barnt Green	d																					
Bromsgrove	d											16 21										
Droitwich Spa	d					16 06						16 30			17 06					17 48		
Worcester Shrub Hill 7	a											16 38										
	d											16 45		17 10								
Worcester Foregate Street 7	a					16 14						16 47		17 12	17 14					18 01		
	d											16 48		17 13								
Malvern Link	d											16 57		17 23								
Great Malvern	a											17 01		17 26								
	d													17 27								
Colwall	d													17 33								
Ledbury	a													17 41								
	d													17 42								
Hereford 7	a													17 58								

Table 71

Sundays

19 February to 25 March

Stratford-upon-Avon, Marylebone and Leamington Spa - Birmingham - Stourbridge, Worcester and Hereford

Network Diagram - see first Page of Table 71

		GW	LM	CH	XC	CH	LM	CH	LM	XC	GW	LM	CH	XC	CH	CH	LM	XC	GW	LM	CH	XC	CH
		◇1			◇1 (trolley)	◇				◇1 (trolley)	◇1			◇1 (trolley)	◇			◇1 (trolley)	◇1 (buffet)			◇1 (trolley)	◇
Stratford-upon-Avon	d		16 30									17 30			18 00					18 30			
Wilmcote	d		16 35									17 35			18 04					18 35			
Wootton Wawen	d																						
Henley-in-Arden	d		16 42									17 42								18 42			
Danzey	d		16x47																				
Wood End	d																						
The Lakes	d		16x51									17x49								18x49			
Earlswood (West Midlands)	d																						
Wythall	d		16 55									17 53								18 53			
Whitlocks End	d		16 57									17 55								18 55			
Shirley	d		17 00									17 59								18 59			
Yardley Wood	d		17 03									18 02								19 02			
Hall Green	d		17 06									18 05								19 05			
Spring Road	d		17 08									18 07								19 07			
London Marylebone 10 ⊖	d			15 33		15 36		16 00					16 33			17 00					17 33		17 36
Banbury	d			16 30	16 54	17 00		17 11		17 25			17 30	17 54		18 11		18 25			18 30	18 54	19 00
Leamington Spa 8	a			16 47	17 11	17 19		17 28		17 41			17 47	18 11	18 26	18 28		18 41			18 47	19 11	19 19
	d			16 49	17 12	17 20		17 28		17 43			17 47	18 12		18 29		18 43			18 49	19 12	19 20
Warwick	d					17 24		17 33								18 33							19 24
Warwick Parkway	d			16 54				17 36					17 53			18 36					18 54		
Hatton	d					17a31							17 57										19a30
Lapworth	d												18 03										
Dorridge	d			17 04			17 25	17 46					18 08			18 46					19 04		
Widney Manor	d						17 29						18 11			18 50							
Solihull	d			17 11			17 32	17 52					18 16			18 54					19 10		
Olton	d						17 36																
Acocks Green	d						17 38																
Tyseley	d		17 11									18 10								19 10			
Small Heath	d																						
Bordesley	d																						
Birmingham Moor Street	d		17 17	17a26			17 45	17 59				18 15	18a30			19 04				19 15	19a23		
Birmingham Snow Hill (tram)	a		17 20				17 48	18 08				18 19				19 13				19 18			
	d		17 21				17 48					18 20								19 20			
Jewellery Quarter (tram)	d		17 24				17 51					18 22								19 22			
The Hawthorns (tram)	d		17 28				17 55					18 27								19 27			
Smethwick Galton Bridge 7	d		17 31				17 58					18 29								19 29			
Coventry	a				17 22									18 22								19 22	
Birmingham International ✈	a				17 35									18 35								19 35	
Birmingham New Street 12	a				17 48					18 09				18 48				19 11				19 48	
	d								18 00								19 00						
Langley Green	d						18 01																
Rowley Regis	d		17 35				18 04					18 34								19 34			
Old Hill	d						18 07																
Cradley Heath	d		17 40				18 10					18 39								19 39			
Lye	d						18 13																
Stourbridge Junction 2	d		17 46				18a19					18 45								19 45			
Hagley	d		17 50									18 49								19 48			
Blakedown	d											18 52											
Kidderminster	d		17 56									18 57								19 55			
Hartlebury	d																						
University	d																						
Barnt Green	d																						
Bromsgrove	d								18 21								19 21						
Droitwich Spa	d		18 07						18 30			19 08					19 31			20 08			
Worcester Shrub Hill 7	a		18 15						18 38			19 16					19 41			20 16			
	d	18 08							18 43		19 11								20 12				
Worcester Foregate Street 7	a	18 10							18 45		19 12								20 16				
	d								18 46		19 15								20 16				
Malvern Link	d								18 55		19 24								20 25				
Great Malvern	a								18 58		19 28								20 29				
	d								18 58										20 32				
Colwall	d								19 03										20 38				
Ledbury	a								19 10										20 45				
	d								19 10										20 47				
Hereford 7	a								19 31										21 03				

Table 71

Sundays
19 February to 25 March

Stratford-upon-Avon, Marylebone and Leamington Spa - Birmingham - Stourbridge, Worcester and Hereford

Network Diagram - see first Page of Table 71

		CH	XC ◇1 🍴	LM		CH	XC ◇1 🍴	CH ◇	CH	LM	XC ◇1 🍴	CH ◇	XC ◇1	GW ◇1 🍽		LM	CH	LM	XC ◇1	CH ◇	XC ◇1	LM	CH ◇	XC ◇1	CH ◇
Stratford-upon-Avon	d			19 30				19 57																	
Wilmcote	d			19 35				20 02																	
Wootton Wawen	d																								
Henley-in-Arden	d			19 42																					
Danzey	d																								
Wood End	d																								
The Lakes	d			19x49																					
Earlswood (West Midlands)	d																								
Wythall	d			19 53																					
Whitlocks End	d			19 55																					
Shirley	d			19 59																					
Yardley Wood	d			20 02																					
Hall Green	d			20 05																					
Spring Road	d			20 07																					
London Marylebone 10 ⊖	d	18 00				18 33			19 00			19 33					20 00			20 33			21 00		22 00
Banbury	d	19 11	19 25			19 29	19 54		20 10		20 25	20 31	20 54				21 11		21 24	21 44	21 54		22 10	22 24	22 55
Leamington Spa 8	a	19 29	19 41			19 46	20 11	20 25	20 27		20 41	20 47	21 11				21 29		21 41	22 01	22 11		22 28	22 40	23 12
	d	19 30	19 43			19 46	20 12		20 27		20 43	20 47	21 12				21 30		21 42	22 01	22 12		22 28	22 42	23 13
Warwick	d	19 34							20 32								21 34						22 32		23 17
Warwick Parkway	d	19 37				19 51			20 36			20 54					21 37			22 07			22 36		23 21
Hatton	d																						22 40		
Lapworth	d	19 45																					22 46		
Dorridge	d	19 50				20 01			20 46			21 04					21 47			22 17			22 51		23 31
Widney Manor	d	19 54							20 49														22 54		
Solihull	d	19 58				20 06			20 54			21 09					21 53			22 22			22 58		23 36
Olton	d																								
Acocks Green	d																								
Tyseley	d			20 10																					
Small Heath	d																								
Bordesley	d																								
Birmingham Moor Street	d	20 07		20 15		20a23			21 02			21a23				21 35	22 01			22a36		22 52	23 06		23 45
Birmingham Snow Hill 🚋	a	20 15		20 18					21 11							21 37	22 10					22 54	23 15		23 53
	d			20 20												21 45						22 55			
Jewellery Quarter 🚋	d			20 22												21 47						22 57			
The Hawthorns 🚋	d			20 27												21 52						23 02			
Smethwick Galton Bridge 7	d			20 29												21 54						23 04			
Coventry	a		19 53				20 22				20 53		21 22						21 52		22 22			22 52	
Birmingham International ✈	a		20 03				20 35				21 03		21 35						22 02		22 32			23 02	
Birmingham New Street 12	a		20 15				20 48				21 15		21 48						22 14		22 42			23 13	
	d									21 00								22 05							
Langley Green	d																								
Rowley Regis	d			20 34												21 59						23 09			
Old Hill	d																								
Cradley Heath	d			20 39												22 03						23 14			
Lye	d																								
Stourbridge Junction 2	d			20 45												22 09						23 19			
Hagley	d			20 49												22 12						23 23			
Blakedown	d																								
Kidderminster	d			20 57												22 18						23 29			
Hartlebury	d																								
University	d																								
Barnt Green	d																								
Bromsgrove	d									21 20															
Droitwich Spa	d			21 09						21 30						22 30		22 39				23 40			
Worcester Shrub Hill 7	a			21 16						21 37						22 37		22 48				23 48			
	d			21 22						21 42				22 11		22 41									
Worcester Foregate Street 7	a			21 24						21 44				22 13		22 43									
	d			21 25						21 45				22 15		22 44									
Malvern Link	d			21 34						21 54				22 24		22 52									
Great Malvern	a			21 37						21 57				22 27		22 55									
	d									21 57															
Colwall	d									22 02															
Ledbury	a									22 09															
	d									22 10															
Hereford 7	a									22 30															

Table 71

Sundays
from 1 April

Stratford-upon-Avon, Marylebone and Leamington Spa - Birmingham - Stourbridge, Worcester and Hereford

Network Diagram - see first Page of Table 71

		LM	LM	GW ◇1	LM	CH ◇	XC ◇1 🍴	LM	GW ◇1 🍽	LM		CH ◇	XC ◇1 🍴	CH	LM	CH ◇	GW ◇1 🍽	LM	CH ◇	XC ◇1 🍴		LM	CH	LM	CH ◇
Stratford-upon-Avon	d				09 30					10 30								11 30						12 30	
Wilmcote	d				09 35					10 35								11 35						12 35	
Wootton Wawen	d																								
Henley-in-Arden	d				09 42					10 42								11 42						12 42	
Danzey	d																								
Wood End	d																								
The Lakes	d				09x49					10x49								11x49						12x49	
Earlswood (West Midlands)	d																								
Wythall	d				09 53					10 53								11 53						12 53	
Whitlocks End	d				09 55					10 55								11 55						12 55	
Shirley	d				09 59					10 59								11 59						12 59	
Yardley Wood	d				10 02					11 02								12 02						13 02	
Hall Green	d				10 05					11 05								12 05						13 05	
Spring Road	d				10 07					11 07								12 07						13 07	
London Marylebone 10 ⊖	d					08 25						09 23				10 03			10 33				11 03		11 33
Banbury	d					09 33	09 54					10 33	10 54			11 10			11 30	11 54			12 07		12 30
Leamington Spa 8	a					09 50	10 11					10 51	11 11			11 27			11 48	12 11			12 24		12 47
	d					09 51	10 12					10 51	11 12	11 20		11 29			11 48	12 12			12 25		12 48
Warwick	d					09 55						10 55		11 24		11 33							12 29		
Warwick Parkway	d					09 58						10 59				11 36			11 54				12 33		12 53
Hatton	d					10 03								11a31									12 37		
Lapworth	d					10 08																	12 43		
Dorridge	d	22p33				10 13		10 25				11 09			11 25	11 46			12 04			12 25	12 48		13 02
Widney Manor	d	22p37						10 29							11 29							12 29			
Solihull	d	22p41				10 19		10 32				11 13			11 32	11 52			12 09			12 32	12 53		13 08
Olton	d	22p44						10 36							11 36							12 36			
Acocks Green	d	22p47						10 38							11 38							12 38			
Tyseley	d	22p50			10 10					11 10								12 10						13 10	
Small Heath	d	22p52																							
Bordesley	d																								
Birmingham Moor Street	d	22p56	09 26		10 17	10 25		10 45		11 17		11 21			11 45	12 00		12 17	12a19			12 45	13 03	13 15	13a16
Birmingham Snow Hill 🚋	a	22p59	09 28		10 19	10 39		10 47		11 19		11 31			11 47	12 09		12 19				12 47	13 05	13 18	
	d	23p00	09 30		10 20			10 48		11 20					11 48			12 20				12 48		13 20	
Jewellery Quarter 🚋	d	23p02	09 32		10 22			10 51		11 22					11 51			12 22				12 51		13 22	
The Hawthorns 🚋	d	23p07	09 37		10 27			10 55		11 27					11 55			12 27				12 55		13 27	
Smethwick Galton Bridge 7	d	23p10	09 39		10 29			10 58		11 29					11 58			12 29				12 58		13 29	
Coventry	a						10 22						11 22							12 22					
Birmingham International ✈	a						10 38						11 38							12 38					
Birmingham New Street 12	a						10 50						11 50							12 50					
	d																								
Langley Green	d	23p13						11 01							12 01							13 01			
Rowley Regis	d	23p16	09 44		10 34			11 04		11 34					12 04			12 34				13 04		13 34	
Old Hill	d	23p19						11 07							12 07							13 07			
Cradley Heath	d	23p23	09 49		10 39			11 10		11 39					12 10			12 39				13 10		13 39	
Lye	d	23p26						11 13							12 13							13 13			
Stourbridge Junction 2	d	23p30	09 54		10 45			11a17		11 45					12a17			12 45				13a17		13 45	
Hagley	d	23p33	09 58		10 48					11 49								12 48						13 49	
Blakedown	d	23p36								11 52								12 51							
Kidderminster	d	23p41	10 04		10 55					11 57								12 56						13 55	
Hartlebury	d																								
University	d																								
Barnt Green	d																								
Bromsgrove	d																								
Droitwich Spa	d	23p52	10 15		11 06					12 08								13 08						14 07	
Worcester Shrub Hill 7	a	00 01	10 23		11 14					12 16								13 15							
	d		10 26	10 32	11 32				12 06								13 10	13 31							
Worcester Foregate Street 7	a		10 29	10 35	11 34				12 09								13 12	13 33						14 15	
	d		10 29	10 36	11 35				12 10								13 13	13 34							
Malvern Link	d		10 38	10 47	11 43				12 19								13 23	13 42							
Great Malvern	a		10 41	10 50	11 46				12 22								13 26	13 45							
	d								12 23								13 27								
Colwall	d								12 29								13 33								
Ledbury	a								12 36								13 41								
	d								12 38								13 49								
Hereford 7	a								12 54								14 06								

Table 71

Sundays
from 1 April

Stratford-upon-Avon, Marylebone and Leamington Spa - Birmingham - Stourbridge, Worcester and Hereford

Network Diagram - see first Page of Table 71

		LM	XC ◇1	CH	LM	CH ◇	XC ◇1	GW ◇1	LM	CH	XC ◇1	LM	CH ◇	CH	XC ◇1	LM	CH	XC ◇1	CH ◇	LM	CH ◇	LM	XC ◇1
Stratford-upon-Avon	d								13 30					14 00		14 30							
Wilmcote	d								13 35					14 04		14 35							
Wootton Wawen	d																						
Henley-in-Arden	d								13 42							14 42							
Danzey	d																						
Wood End	d																						
The Lakes	d								13x49							14x49							
Earlswood (West Midlands)	d																						
Wythall	d								13 53							14 53							
Whitlocks End	d								13 55							14 55							
Shirley	d								13 59							14 59							
Yardley Wood	d								14 02							15 02							
Hall Green	d								14 05							15 05							
Spring Road	d								14 07							15 07							
London Marylebone 10 ⊖	d					12 03				12 33			13 03				13 33		13 36		14 00		
Banbury	d		12 53			13 09	13 35			13 38	13 54		14 08		14 24		14 35	14 54	15 00		15 10		15 25
Leamington Spa 8	a		13 11			13 27	13 50			13 56	14 11		14 25	14 26	14 40		14 52	15 11	15 19		15 27		15 41
	d		13 12	13 20		13 28	13 52			13 56	14 12		14 25		14 42		14 52	15 12	15 20		15 28		15 43
Warwick	d			13 24		13 32							14 29						15 24		15 31		
Warwick Parkway	d					13 35				14 02			14 33				14 59				15 35		
Hatton	d			13a31									14 37						15a31		15 39		
Lapworth	d												14 43								15 45		
Dorridge	d				13 25	13 44				14 12		14 25	14 48				15 08			15 25	15 49		
Widney Manor	d				13 29							14 29								15 29			
Solihull	d				13 32	13 50				14 16		14 32	14 53				15 14			15 32	15 55		
Olton	d				13 36							14 36								15 36			
Acocks Green	d				13 38							14 38								15 38			
Tyseley	d								14 10							15 10							
Small Heath	d																						
Bordesley	d																						
Birmingham Moor Street	d				13 45	13 58			14 17	14a23		14 45	15 02			15 15	15a28			15 45	16 04		
Birmingham Snow Hill	a				13 48	14 03			14 19			14 47	15 05			15 19				15 48	16 12		
	d				13 48				14 20			14 48				15 20				15 48			
Jewellery Quarter	d				13 51				14 22			14 51				15 22				15 51			
The Hawthorns	d				13 55				14 27			14 55				15 27				15 55			
Smethwick Galton Bridge 7	d				13 58				14 29			14 58				15 29				15 58			
Coventry	a		13 22								14 22							15 22					
Birmingham International ✈	a		13 36								14 35							15 35					
Birmingham New Street 12	a		13 47				14 19				14 48				15 09			15 48					16 12
	d	13 24																				16 00	
Langley Green	d				14 01							15 01								16 01			
Rowley Regis	d				14 04				14 34			15 04				15 34				16 04			
Old Hill	d				14 07							15 07								16 07			
Cradley Heath	d				14 10				14 39			15 10				15 39				16 10			
Lye	d				14 13							15 13								16 13			
Stourbridge Junction 2	d				14a18				14 45			15a17				15 45				16a18			
Hagley	d								14 48							15 48							
Blakedown	d								14 51														
Kidderminster	d								14 56							15 54							
Hartlebury	d																						
University	d																						
Barnt Green	d																						
Bromsgrove	d	13 42																				16 21	
Droitwich Spa	d	13 52							15 08							16 06						16 30	
Worcester Shrub Hill 7	a	13 59																				16 38	
	d	14 14						15 10														16 45	
Worcester Foregate Street 7	a	14 16						15 12	15 16							16 14						16 47	
	d	14 17						15 13														16 48	
Malvern Link	d	14 25						15 23														16 57	
Great Malvern	a	14 28						15 26														17 01	
	d	14 29						15 27															
Colwall	d	14 34						15 33															
Ledbury	a	14 41						15 41															
	d	14 49						15 48															
Hereford 7	a	15 10						16 05															

Table 71

Sundays
from 1 April

Stratford-upon-Avon, Marylebone and Leamington Spa - Birmingham - Stourbridge, Worcester and Hereford

Network Diagram - see first Page of Table 71

		GW ◇1	LM	CH ◇	XC ◇1	CH ◇	LM	LM	CH ◇	XC ◇1	GW ◇1	LM	CH	XC ◇1	CH ◇	LM	CH	LM	XC ◇1	GW ◇1	LM	CH
Stratford-upon-Avon	d		15 30			16 00						16 30									17 30	
Wilmcote	d		15 35			16 04						16 35									17 35	
Wootton Wawen	d																					
Henley-in-Arden	d		15 42									16 42									17 42	
Danzey	d											16x47										
Wood End	d																					
The Lakes	d		15x49									16x51									17x49	
Earlswood (West Midlands)	d																					
Wythall	d		15 53									16 55									17 53	
Whitlocks End	d		15 55									16 57									17 55	
Shirley	d		15 59									17 00									17 59	
Yardley Wood	d		16 02									17 03									18 02	
Hall Green	d		16 05									17 06									18 05	
Spring Road	d		16 07									17 08									18 07	
London Marylebone 10 ⊖	d			14 33					15 00				15 33		15 36		16 00					16 33
Banbury	d			15 31	15 54				16 10	16 25			16 30	16 54	17 00		17 11		17 25			17 30
Leamington Spa 8	a			15 49	16 11	16 26			16 28	16 41			16 47	17 11	17 19		17 28		17 41			17 47
	d			15 49	16 12				16 28	16 43			16 49	17 12	17 20		17 28		17 43			17 47
Warwick	d								16 32						17 24		17 33					
Warwick Parkway	d			15 54					16 36				16 54				17 36					17 53
Hatton	d														17a31							17 57
Lapworth	d																					18 03
Dorridge	d			16 04			16 25		16 50				17 04			17 25	17 46					18 08
Widney Manor	d						16 29									17 29						18 11
Solihull	d			16 09			16 32		16 56				17 11			17 32	17 52					18 16
Olton	d						16 36									17 36						
Acocks Green	d						16 38									17 38						
Tyseley	d		16 10									17 11									18 10	
Small Heath	d																					
Bordesley	d																					
Birmingham Moor Street	d		16 15	16a26			16 45	17 02	17 05			17 17	17a26			17 45	17 59				18 15	18a30
Birmingham Snow Hill	a		16 19				16 48	17 04	17 14			17 20				17 48	18 08				18 19	
	d		16 20				16 48	17 06				17 21				17 48					18 20	
Jewellery Quarter	d		16 22				16 51					17 24				17 51					18 22	
The Hawthorns	d		16 27				16 55					17 28				17 55					18 27	
Smethwick Galton Bridge 7	d		16 29				16 58					17 31				17 58					18 29	
Coventry	a				16 22									17 22								
Birmingham International ✈	a				16 35									17 35								
Birmingham New Street 12	a				16 48					17 12				17 48					18 09			
	d																	18 00				
Langley Green	d						17 01									18 01						
Rowley Regis	d		16 34				17 04					17 35				18 04					18 34	
Old Hill	d						17 07									18 07						
Cradley Heath	d		16 39				17 10					17 40				18 10					18 39	
Lye	d						17 13									18 13						
Stourbridge Junction 2	d		16 45				17a18	17 27				17 46				18a19					18 45	
Hagley	d		16 48					17 30				17 50									18 49	
Blakedown	d																				18 52	
Kidderminster	d		16 54					17 36				17 56									18 57	
Hartlebury	d																					
University	d																					
Barnt Green	d																					
Bromsgrove	d																	18 21				
Droitwich Spa	d		17 06					17 48				18 07						18 30			19 08	
Worcester Shrub Hill 7	a											18 15						18 38			19 16	
	d	17 10									18 08							18 43		19 10		
Worcester Foregate Street 7	a	17 12	17 14					18 01			18 10							18 45		19 13		
	d	17 13																18 46		19 14		
Malvern Link	d	17 23																18 55		19 23		
Great Malvern	a	17 26																18 58		19 26		
	d	17 27																18 58				
Colwall	d	17 33																19 03				
Ledbury	a	17 41																19 10				
	d	17 42																19 10				
Hereford 7	a	17 58																19 31				

Table 71

Sundays from 1 April

Stratford-upon-Avon, Marylebone and Leamington Spa - Birmingham - Stourbridge, Worcester and Hereford

Network Diagram - see first Page of Table 71

		XC	CH	CH	LM	XC	GW	LM	CH	XC	CH	CH
Stratford-upon-Avon	d		18 00					18 30				
Wilmcote	d		18 04					18 35				
Wootton Wawen	d											
Henley-in-Arden	d							18 42				
Danzey	d											
Wood End	d											
The Lakes	d							18x49				
Earlswood (West Midlands)	d											
Wythall	d							18 53				
Whitlocks End	d							18 55				
Shirley	d							18 59				
Yardley Wood	d							19 02				
Hall Green	d							19 05				
Spring Road	d							19 07				
London Marylebone	d			17 00					17 33		17 36	18 00
Banbury	d	17 54		18 11		18 25			18 30	18 54	19 00	19 11
Leamington Spa	a	18 11	18 26	18 28		18 41			18 47	19 11	19 19	19 29
	d	18 12		18 29		18 43			18 49	19 12	19 20	19 30
Warwick	d			18 33							19 24	19 34
Warwick Parkway	d			18 36					18 54			19 37
Hatton	d										19a30	
Lapworth	d											19 45
Dorridge	d			18 46					19 04			19 50
Widney Manor	d			18 50								19 54
Solihull	d			18 54					19 10			19 58
Olton	d											
Acocks Green	d											
Tyseley	d							19 10				
Small Heath	d											
Bordesley	d											
Birmingham Moor Street	d			19 04				19 15	19a23			20 07
Birmingham Snow Hill	a			19 13				19 18				20 15
	d							19 20				
Jewellery Quarter	d							19 22				
The Hawthorns	d							19 27				
Smethwick Galton Bridge	d							19 29				
Coventry	a	18 22								19 22		
Birmingham International	a	18 35								19 35		
Birmingham New Street	a	18 48				19 11				19 48		
	d				19 00							
Langley Green	d											
Rowley Regis	d							19 34				
Old Hill	d											
Cradley Heath	d							19 39				
Lye	d											
Stourbridge Junction	d							19 45				
Hagley	d							19 48				
Blakedown	d											
Kidderminster	d							19 55				
Hartlebury	d											
University	d											
Barnt Green	d											
Bromsgrove	d				19 21							
Droitwich Spa	d				19 31			20 08				
Worcester Shrub Hill	a				19 41			20 16				
	d						20 13					
Worcester Foregate Street	a						20 16					
	d						20 17					
Malvern Link	d						20 25					
Great Malvern	a						20 29					
	d						20 32					
Colwall	d						20 38					
Ledbury	a						20 45					
	d						20 47					
Hereford	a						21 03					

		XC	LM	CH	XC	CH	CH	LM	XC	CH	XC	GW
Stratford-upon-Avon	d		19 30			19 57						
Wilmcote	d		19 35			20 02						
Wootton Wawen	d											
Henley-in-Arden	d		19 42									
Danzey	d											
Wood End	d											
The Lakes	d		19x49									
Earlswood (West Midlands)	d											
Wythall	d		19 53									
Whitlocks End	d		19 55									
Shirley	d		19 59									
Yardley Wood	d		20 02									
Hall Green	d		20 05									
Spring Road	d		20 07									
London Marylebone	d			18 33			19 00			19 33		
Banbury	d	19 25		19 29	19 54		20 10		20 25	20 31	20 54	
Leamington Spa	a	19 41		19 46	20 11	20 25	20 27		20 41	20 47	21 11	
	d	19 43		19 46	20 12		20 27		20 43	20 47	21 12	
Warwick	d						20 32					
Warwick Parkway	d			19 51			20 36			20 54		
Hatton	d											
Lapworth	d											
Dorridge	d			20 01			20 46			21 04		
Widney Manor	d						20 49					
Solihull	d			20 06			20 54			21 09		
Olton	d											
Acocks Green	d											
Tyseley	d		20 10									
Small Heath	d											
Bordesley	d											
Birmingham Moor Street	d		20 15	20a23			21 02			21a23		
Birmingham Snow Hill	a		20 18				21 11					
	d		20 20									
Jewellery Quarter	d		20 22									
The Hawthorns	d		20 27									
Smethwick Galton Bridge	d		20 29									
Coventry	a	19 53			20 22				20 53		21 22	
Birmingham International	a	20 03			20 35				21 03		21 35	
Birmingham New Street	a	20 15			20 48				21 15		21 48	
	d							21 00				
Langley Green	d											
Rowley Regis	d		20 34									
Old Hill	d											
Cradley Heath	d		20 39									
Lye	d											
Stourbridge Junction	d		20 45									
Hagley	d		20 49									
Blakedown	d											
Kidderminster	d		20 57									
Hartlebury	d											
University	d											
Barnt Green	d											
Bromsgrove	d							21 20				
Droitwich Spa	d		21 09					21 30				
Worcester Shrub Hill	a		21 16					21 37				
	d		21 22					21 42				22 11
Worcester Foregate Street	a		21 24					21 44				22 13
	d		21 25					21 45				22 15
Malvern Link	d		21 34					21 54				22 24
Great Malvern	a		21 37					21 57				22 27
	d							21 57				
Colwall	d							22 02				
Ledbury	a							22 09				
	d							22 10				
Hereford	a							22 30				

Table 71

Sundays from 1 April

Stratford-upon-Avon, Marylebone and Leamington Spa - Birmingham - Stourbridge, Worcester and Hereford

Network Diagram - see first Page of Table 71

		LM	CH	LM	XC	CH	XC	LM	CH	XC	CH
Stratford-upon-Avon	d										
Wilmcote	d										
Wootton Wawen	d										
Henley-in-Arden	d										
Danzey	d										
Wood End	d										
The Lakes	d										
Earlswood (West Midlands)	d										
Wythall	d										
Whitlocks End	d										
Shirley	d										
Yardley Wood	d										
Hall Green	d										
Spring Road	d										
London Marylebone	d		20 00			20 33			21 00		22 00
Banbury	d		21 11		21 24	21 44	21 54		22 10	22 24	22 55
Leamington Spa	a		21 29		21 41	22 01	22 11		22 28	22 40	23 12
	d		21 30		21 42	22 01	22 12		22 28	22 42	23 13
Warwick	d		21 34						22 32		23 17
Warwick Parkway	d		21 37			22 07			22 36		23 21
Hatton	d								22 40		
Lapworth	d								22 46		
Dorridge	d		21 47			22 17			22 51		23 31
Widney Manor	d								22 54		
Solihull	d		21 53			22 22			22 58		23 36
Olton	d										
Acocks Green	d										
Tyseley	d										
Small Heath	d										
Bordesley	d										
Birmingham Moor Street	d	21 35	22 01			22a36		22 52	23 06		23 45
Birmingham Snow Hill	a	21 37	22 10					22 54	23 15		23 53
	d	21 45						22 55			
Jewellery Quarter	d	21 47						22 57			
The Hawthorns	d	21 52						23 02			
Smethwick Galton Bridge	d	21 54						23 04			
Coventry	a				21 52		22 22			22 52	
Birmingham International	a				22 02		22 32			23 02	
Birmingham New Street	a				22 14		22 42			23 13	
	d			22 05							
Langley Green	d										
Rowley Regis	d	21 59						23 09			
Old Hill	d										
Cradley Heath	d	22 03						23 14			
Lye	d										
Stourbridge Junction	d	22 09						23 19			
Hagley	d	22 12						23 23			
Blakedown	d										
Kidderminster	d	22 18						23 29			
Hartlebury	d										
University	d										
Barnt Green	d										
Bromsgrove	d										
Droitwich Spa	d	22 30		22 39				23 40			
Worcester Shrub Hill	a	22 37		22 48				23 48			
	d	22 41									
Worcester Foregate Street	a	22 43									
	d	22 44									
Malvern Link	d	22 52									
Great Malvern	a	22 55									
	d										
Colwall	d										
Ledbury	a										
	d										
Hereford	a										

Table 72

Mondays to Saturdays

Stourbridge Junction - Stourbridge Town

Network Diagram - see first Page of Table 71

Miles			LM SX	LM	LM SX	LM	LM SX	LM SX	LM	LM SX	LM	LM	LM	LM	LM	LM	LM	LM	LM	LM	LM	LM
0	Stourbridge Junction	d	05 47	05 58	06 08	06 19	06 29	06 39	06 49	06 59	07 09	07 19	07 29	07 39	07 49	07 59	08 09	08 19	08 29	08 39	08 49	08 59
0¾	Stourbridge Town	a	05 50	06 01	06 11	06 22	06 32	06 42	06 52	07 02	07 12	07 22	07 32	07 42	07 52	08 02	08 12	08 22	08 32	08 42	08 52	09 02

		LM	LM	LM	LM	LM	LM	LM	LM	LM	LM	LM	LM	LM	LM	LM	LM	LM	LM	LM	LM	LM
Stourbridge Junction	d	09 09	09 19	09 29	09 39	09 49	09 59	10 09	10 19	10 29	10 39	10 49	10 59	11 09	11 19	11 29	11 39	11 49	11 59	12 09	12 19	12 29
Stourbridge Town	a	09 12	09 22	09 32	09 42	09 52	10 02	10 12	10 22	10 32	10 42	10 52	11 02	11 12	11 22	11 32	11 42	11 52	12 02	12 12	12 22	12 32

		LM	LM	LM	LM	LM	LM	LM	LM	LM	LM	LM	LM	LM	LM	LM	LM	LM	LM	LM	LM
Stourbridge Junction	d	12 39	12 49	12 59	13 09	13 19	13 29	13 39	13 49	13 59	14 09	14 19	14 29	14 39	14 49	14 59	15 09	15 19	15 29	15 39	15 49
Stourbridge Town	a	12 42	12 52	13 02	13 12	13 22	13 32	13 42	13 52	14 02	14 12	14 22	14 32	14 42	14 52	15 02	15 12	15 22	15 32	15 42	15 52

		LM	LM	LM	LM	LM	LM	LM	LM	LM	LM	LM	LM	LM	LM	LM	LM	LM	LM	LM	LM	LM
Stourbridge Junction	d	15 59	16 09	16 19	16 29	16 39	16 49	16 59	17 09	17 19	17 29	17 39	17 49	17 59	18 09	18 19	18 29	18 39	18 49	18 59	19 09	19 19
Stourbridge Town	a	16 02	16 12	16 22	16 32	16 42	16 52	17 02	17 12	17 22	17 32	17 42	17 52	18 02	18 12	18 22	18 32	18 42	18 52	19 02	19 12	19 22

		LM	LM	LM	LM	LM	LM	LM	LM	LM	LM	LM	LM	LM	LM	LM	LM	LM	LM	LM	LM
Stourbridge Junction	d	19 29	19 39	19 49	19 59	20 09	20 19	20 29	20 39	20 49	20 59	21 09	21 19	21 29	21 39	21 49	21 59	22 09	22 19	22 29	22 39
Stourbridge Town	a	19 32	19 42	19 52	20 02	20 12	20 22	20 32	20 42	20 52	21 02	21 12	21 22	21 32	21 42	21 52	22 02	22 12	22 22	22 32	22 42

		LM	LM	LM	LM	LM
Stourbridge Junction	d	22 50	23 00	23 15	23 30	23 54
Stourbridge Town	a	22 53	23 03	23 18	23 33	23 57

Sundays

		LM	LM	LM	LM	LM	LM	LM	LM	LM	LM	LM	LM	LM	LM	LM	LM	LM	LM	LM	LM	LM
Stourbridge Junction	d	09 43	10 00	10 11	10 21	10 41	10 54	11 11	11 21	11 41	11 54	12 11	12 21	12 41	12 54	13 11	13 21	13 41	13 54	14 11	14 21	14 41
Stourbridge Town	a	09 46	10 03	10 14	10 24	10 44	10 57	11 14	11 24	11 44	11 57	12 14	12 24	12 44	12 57	13 14	13 24	13 44	13 57	14 14	14 24	14 44

		LM	LM	LM	LM	LM	LM	LM	LM	LM	LM	LM	LM	LM	LM	LM	LM	LM	LM	LM	LM
Stourbridge Junction	d	14 54	15 11	15 21	15 41	15 54	16 11	16 21	16 41	16 54	17 11	17 21	17 41	17 54	18 11	18 21	18 41	18 54	19 11	19 21	19 47
Stourbridge Town	a	14 57	15 14	15 24	15 44	15 57	16 14	16 24	16 44	16 57	17 14	17 24	17 44	17 57	18 14	18 24	18 44	18 57	19 14	19 24	19 50

Table 72

Mondays to Saturdays

Stourbridge Town - Stourbridge Junction

Network Diagram - see first Page of Table 71

Miles			LM MX	LM SX	LM SX	LM SO	LM SX	LM SX	LM SX	LM SO	LM SX	LM	LM SX	LM	LM	LM	LM	LM	LM	LM	LM	LM
0	Stourbridge Town	d	23p59	05 52	06 03	06 10	06 13	06 24	06 34	06 40	06 44	06 54	07 04	07 14	07 24	07 34	07 44	07 54	08 04	08 14	08 24	08 34
0¾	Stourbridge Junction	a	00 02	05 55	06 06	06 13	06 16	06 27	06 37	06 43	06 47	06 57	07 07	07 17	07 27	07 37	07 47	07 57	08 07	08 17	08 27	08 37

		LM	LM	LM	LM	LM	LM	LM	LM	LM	LM	LM	LM	LM	LM	LM	LM	LM	LM	LM	LM	LM
Stourbridge Town	d	08 44	08 54	09 04	09 14	09 24	09 34	09 44	09 54	10 04	10 14	10 24	10 34	10 44	10 54	11 04	11 14	11 24	11 34	11 44	11 54	12 04
Stourbridge Junction	a	08 47	08 57	09 07	09 17	09 27	09 37	09 47	09 57	10 07	10 17	10 27	10 37	10 47	10 57	11 07	11 17	11 27	11 37	11 47	11 57	12 07

		LM	LM	LM	LM	LM	LM	LM	LM	LM	LM	LM	LM	LM	LM	LM	LM	LM	LM	LM	LM
Stourbridge Town	d	12 14	12 24	12 34	12 44	12 54	13 04	13 14	13 24	13 34	13 44	13 54	14 04	14 14	14 24	14 34	14 44	14 54	15 04	15 14	15 24
Stourbridge Junction	a	12 17	12 27	12 37	12 47	12 57	13 07	13 17	13 27	13 37	13 47	13 57	14 07	14 17	14 27	14 37	14 47	14 57	15 07	15 17	15 27

		LM	LM	LM	LM	LM	LM	LM	LM	LM	LM	LM	LM	LM	LM	LM	LM	LM	LM	LM	LM	LM
Stourbridge Town	d	15 34	15 44	15 54	16 04	16 14	16 24	16 34	16 44	16 54	17 04	17 14	17 24	17 34	17 44	17 54	18 04	18 14	18 24	18 34	18 44	18 54
Stourbridge Junction	a	15 37	15 47	15 57	16 07	16 17	16 27	16 37	16 47	16 57	17 07	17 17	17 27	17 37	17 47	17 57	18 07	18 17	18 27	18 37	18 47	18 57

		LM	LM	LM	LM	LM	LM	LM	LM	LM	LM	LM	LM	LM	LM	LM	LM	LM	LM	LM	LM
Stourbridge Town	d	19 04	19 14	19 24	19 34	19 44	19 54	20 04	20 14	20 24	20 34	20 44	20 54	21 04	21 14	21 24	21 34	21 44	21 54	22 04	22 14
Stourbridge Junction	a	19 07	19 17	19 27	19 37	19 47	19 57	20 07	20 17	20 27	20 37	20 47	20 57	21 07	21 17	21 27	21 37	21 47	21 57	22 07	22 17

		LM	LM	LM	LM	LM	LM	LM	LM
Stourbridge Town	d	22 24	22 34	22 44	22 55	23 05	23 20	23 35	23 59
Stourbridge Junction	a	22 27	22 37	22 47	22 58	23 08	23 23	23 38	00 02

Sundays

		LM A	LM	LM	LM	LM	LM	LM	LM	LM	LM	LM	LM	LM	LM	LM	LM	LM	LM	LM	LM	LM
Stourbridge Town	d	23p59	09 49	10 05	10 16	10 36	10 46	11 00	11 16	11 36	11 46	12 00	12 16	12 36	12 46	13 00	13 16	13 36	13 46	14 00	14 16	14 36
Stourbridge Junction	a	00 02	09 52	10 08	10 19	10 39	10 49	11 03	11 19	11 39	11 49	12 03	12 19	12 39	12 49	13 03	13 19	13 39	13 49	14 03	14 19	14 39

		LM	LM	LM	LM	LM	LM	LM	LM	LM	LM	LM	LM	LM	LM	LM	LM	LM	LM	LM	LM	LM
Stourbridge Town	d	14 46	15 00	15 16	15 36	15 46	16 00	16 16	16 36	16 46	17 00	17 16	17 36	17 46	18 00	18 16	18 36	18 46	19 00	19 16	19 36	19 55
Stourbridge Junction	a	14 49	15 03	15 19	15 39	15 49	16 03	16 19	16 39	16 49	17 03	17 19	17 39	17 49	18 03	18 19	18 39	18 49	19 03	19 19	19 39	19 58

A not 11 December

Network Diagram for Tables 74, 75

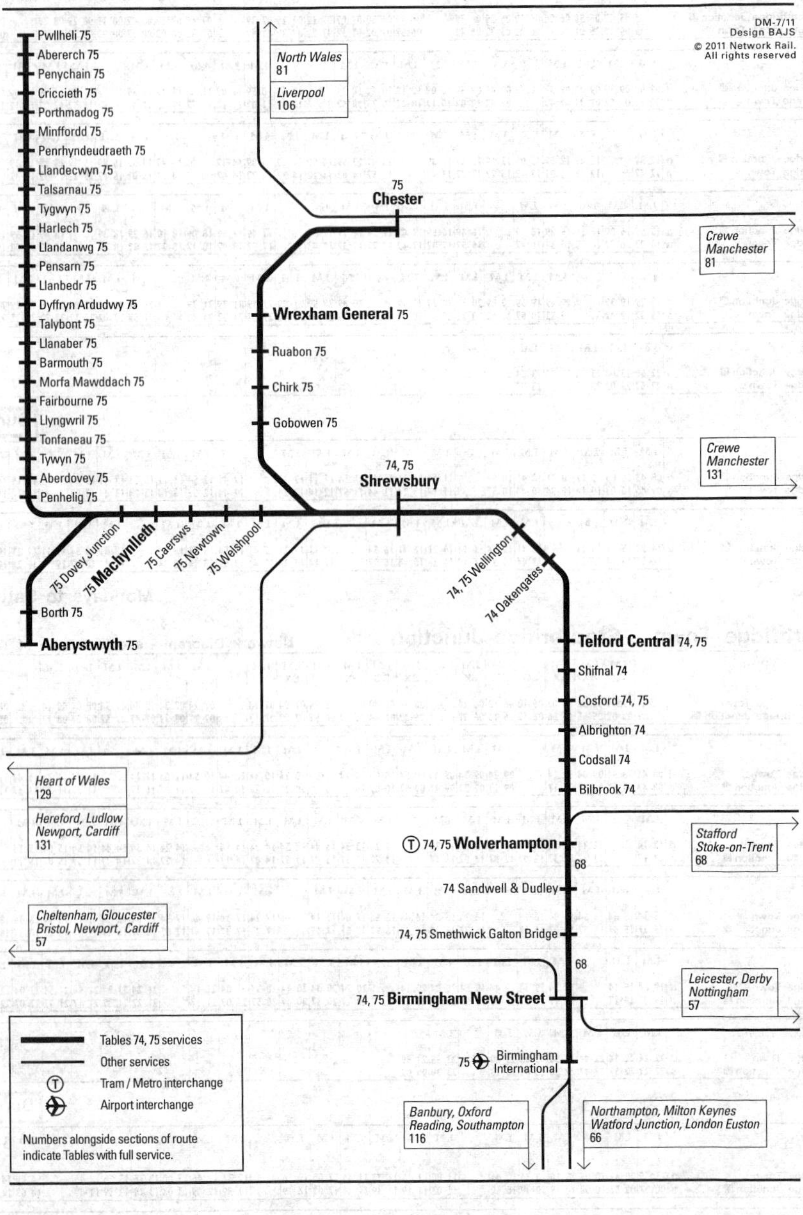

Table 74

Mondays to Fridays

until 23 March

Birmingham - Shrewsbury

Network Diagram - see first Page of Table 67

Miles			AW	AW	AW	AW	LM	AW	LM	AW	LM		LM	AW	LM	AW	LM	AW	LM	AW	LM		AW	LM	AW
			MO	TThO	WFO	MX																			
			A	B				◇ C ⚲		◇ D ⚲				◇ E ⚲		◇ D ⚲		◇ E ⚲		◇ D ⚲			◇ E ⚲		◇ D ⚲
0	**Birmingham New Street**	d	23p24	23p32	23p32		05 51	06 24		07 24	07 27		08 05	08 24	09 05	09 24	10 05	10 24	11 05	11 24	12 05		12 24	13 05	13 24
4	Smethwick Galton Bridge	d						06 30		07 30				08 30		09 30		10 30		11 30			12 30		13 30
5¼	Sandwell & Dudley	d					05 59						08 13		09 13		10 13		11 13		12 13			13 13	
13	**Wolverhampton 7**	d	23b46	00 02	00 02	00 20	06 13	06 43	06 48	07 42	07 46		08 25	08 43	09 25	09 43	10 25	10 43	11 25	11 43	12 25		12 43	13 25	13 43
17	Bilbrook	d	23p52	00 07	00 08		06 19		06 53		07 50		08 31		09 31		10 31		11 31		12 31			13 31	
17½	Codsall	d	23p54	00 10	00 11		06 21		06 56		07 53		08 33		09 33		10 33		11 33		12 33			13 33	
20¾	Albrighton	d	23p59	00 14	00 15		06 26		07 00		07 57		08 38		09 38		10 38		11 38		12 38			13 38	
22¼	Cosford	d	00 02	00 18	00 19																				
25½	Shifnal	d	00 07	00 23	00 24		06 34		07 09		08 05		08 46		09 46		10 46		11 46		12 46			13 46	
28½	Telford Central	d	00 13	00 29	00 29	00 36	06 40	06 59	07 15	07 59	08 12		08 52	08 59	09 52	09 59	10 52	10 59	11 52	11 59	12 52		12 59	13 52	13 59
29½	Oakengates	d	00 15	00 31	00 31		06 42		07 17		08 15		08 54		09 54		10 54		11 54		12 54			13 54	
32½	Wellington (Shropshire)	d	00 20	00 36	00 36	00 43	06 47	07 06	07 23	08 05	08 21		08 59	09 06	09 59	10 06	10 59	11 06	11 59	12 06	12 59		13 06	13 59	14 06
43	**Shrewsbury**	a	00 35	00 52	00 52	01 02	07 00	07 18	07 37	08 19	08 36		09 15	09 19	10 15	10 19	11 15	11 19	12 15	12 19	13 15		13 19	14 15	14 19

		LM	AW	LM	AW	LM	AW		LM	AW	LM	LM	AW	LM	AW	LM	AW		LM	AW	LM	AW	AW		
							R															MWFO			
			◇ E ⚲		◇ D ⚲		E ⚲			◇ D ⚲			◇ E ⚲		◇ F ⚲		◇ E			◇ G		H	B		
Birmingham New Street	d	14 05	14 24	15 05	15 26	16 05	16 24		17 05	17 26	17 46	18 05	18 24	19 05	19 24	20 05	20 24		21 05	21 24	22 21	23 32	23 32		
Smethwick Galton Bridge	d		14 30		15 32		16 30			17 32			18 30		19 30		20 30			21 30					
Sandwell & Dudley	d	14 13		15 13		16 13			17 13			18 13		19 13		20 13			21 13		22 29				
Wolverhampton 7	d	14 25	14 43	15 25	15 44	16 25	16 43		17 25	17 44	18 07	18 25	18 43	19 25	19 43	20 25	20 43		21 25	21 43	22 43	00 02	00 02		
Bilbrook	d	14 31		15 31		16 31			17 31		18 13	18 31		19 31		20 31			21 31		22 49	00 07	00 08		
Codsall	d	14 33		15 33		16 33			17 33		18 15	18 33		19 33		20 33			21 33		22 51	00 10	00 11		
Albrighton	d	14 38		15 38		16 38			17 38		18 20	18 38		19 38		20 38			21 38		22 56	00 14	00 15		
Cosford	d																					00 18	00 19		
Shifnal	d	14 46		15 46		16 46			17 46		18 28	18 46		19 46		20 46			21 46		23 04	00 23	00 24		
Telford Central	d	14 52	14 59	15 52	16 01	16 52	16 59		17 52	18 01	18 33	18 52	18 59	19 52	19 59	20 52	20 59		21 52	21 59	23 10	00 29	00 29		
Oakengates	d	14 54		15 54		16 54			17 54		18 35	18 54		19 54		20 54			21 54		23 12	00 31	00 31		
Wellington (Shropshire)	d	14 59	15 06	15 59	16 07	16 59	17 06		17 59	18 07	18 41	18 59	19 06	19 59	20 06	20 59	21 06		21 59	22 07	23 17	00 36	00 36		
Shrewsbury	a	15 15	15 19	16 15	16 20	17 15	17 19		18 15	18 20	18 56	19 15	19 19	20 15	20 19	21 15	21 19		22 14	22 19	23 30	00 52	00 52		

Mondays to Fridays

from 26 March

		AW	AW	AW	AW	LM	AW	LM	AW	LM		LM	AW	LM	AW	LM	AW	LM	AW	LM		AW	LM	AW	LM
		MO	TThO	WFO	MX																				
		A	B				◇ C ⚲		◇ D ⚲				◇ E ⚲		◇ D ⚲		◇ E ⚲		◇ D ⚲			◇ E ⚲		◇ D ⚲	
Birmingham New Street	d	23p24	23p32	23p32		05 51	06 24		07 24	07 27		08 05	08 24	09 05	09 24	10 05	10 24	11 05	11 24	12 05		12 24	13 05	13 24	14 05
Smethwick Galton Bridge	d						06 30		07 30				08 30		09 30		10 30		11 30			12 30		13 30	
Sandwell & Dudley	d					05 59						08 13		09 13		10 13		11 13		12 13			13 13		14 13
Wolverhampton 7	d	23b46	00 02	00 02	00 20	06 13	06 43	06 48	07 42	07 46		08 25	08 43	09 25	09 43	10 25	10 43	11 25	11 43	12 25		12 43	13 25	13 43	14 25
Bilbrook	d	23p52	00 07	00 08		06 19		06 53		07 50		08 31		09 31		10 31		11 31		12 31			13 31		14 31
Codsall	d	23p54	00 10	00 11		06 21		06 56		07 53		08 33		09 33		10 33		11 33		12 33			13 33		14 33
Albrighton	d	23p59	00 14	00 15		06 26		07 00		07 57		08 38		09 38		10 38		11 38		12 38			13 38		14 38
Cosford	d	00 02	00 18	00 19		06 29		07 04		08 01		08 41		09 41		10 41		11 41		12 41			13 41		14 41
Shifnal	d	00 07	00 23	00 24		06 34		07 09		08 05		08 46		09 46		10 46		11 46		12 46			13 46		14 46
Telford Central	d	00 13	00 29	00 29	00 36	06 40	06 59	07 15	07 59	08 12		08 52	08 59	09 52	09 59	10 52	10 59	11 52	11 59	12 52		12 59	13 52	13 59	14 52
Oakengates	d	00 15	00 31	00 31		06 42		07 17		08 15		08 54		09 54		10 54		11 54		12 54			13 54		14 54
Wellington (Shropshire)	d	00 20	00 36	00 36	00 43	06 47	07 06	07 23	08 05	08 21		08 59	09 06	09 59	10 06	10 59	11 06	11 59	12 06	12 59		13 06	13 59	14 06	14 59
Shrewsbury	a	00 35	00 52	00 52	01 02	07 00	07 18	07 37	08 19	08 36		09 15	09 19	10 15	10 19	11 15	11 19	12 15	12 19	13 15		13 19	14 15	14 19	15 15

		AW	LM	AW	LM	AW		LM	AW	LM	LM	AW	LM	AW	LM	AW		LM	AW	LM	AW	AW			
						R															MWFO				
		◇ E ⚲		◇ D ⚲		E ⚲			◇ D ⚲			◇ E ⚲		◇ F ⚲		◇ E			◇ G		H	B			
Birmingham New Street	d	14 24	15 05	15 26	16 05	16 24		17 05	17 26	17 46	18 05	18 24	19 05	19 24	20 05	20 24		21 05	21 24	22 21	23 32	23 32			
Smethwick Galton Bridge	d	14 30		15 32		16 30			17 32			18 30		19 30		20 30			21 30						
Sandwell & Dudley	d		15 13		16 13			17 13			18 13		19 13		20 13			21 13		22 29					
Wolverhampton 7	d	14 43	15 25	15 44	16 25	16 43		17 25	17 44	18 07	18 25	18 43	19 25	19 43	20 25	20 43		21 25	21 43	22 43	00 02	00 02			
Bilbrook	d		15 31		16 31			17 31		18 13	18 31		19 31		20 31			21 31		22 49	00 07	00 08			
Codsall	d		15 33		16 33			17 33		18 15	18 33		19 33		20 33			21 33		22 51	00 10	00 11			
Albrighton	d		15 38		16 38			17 38		18 20	18 38		19 38		20 38			21 38		22 56	00 14	00 15			
Cosford	d				16 41			17 41		18 23	18 41		19 41		20 41			21 41		22 59	00 18	00 19			
Shifnal	d		15 46		16 46			17 46		18 28	18 46		19 46		20 46			21 46		23 04	00 23	00 24			
Telford Central	d	14 59	15 52	16 01	16 52	16 59		17 52	18 01	18 33	18 52	18 59	19 52	19 59	20 52	20 59		21 52	21 59	23 10	00 29	00 29			
Oakengates	d		15 54		16 54			17 54		18 35	18 54		19 54		20 54			21 54		23 12	00 31	00 31			
Wellington (Shropshire)	d	15 06	15 59	16 07	16 59	17 06		17 59	18 07	18 41	18 59	19 06	19 59	20 06	20 59	21 06		21 59	22 07	23 17	00 36	00 36			
Shrewsbury	a	15 19	16 15	16 20	17 15	17 19		18 15	18 20	18 56	19 15	19 19	20 15	20 19	21 15	21 19		22 14	22 19	23 30	00 52	00 52			

A From Birmingham International
C To Aberystwyth
D From Birmingham International to Holyhead
E From Birmingham International to Aberystwyth
F From Birmingham International to Chester
G From Birmingham International to Manchester Piccadilly
b Previous night, arr. 2340

Table 74

Birmingham - Shrewsbury

Saturdays

until 24 March

Network Diagram - see first Page of Table 67

		AW	AW	AW ◇ A 🛒	LM	AW ◇ B 🛒	LM	AW ◇ C 🛒	LM	AW ◇ B 🛒		LM	AW ◇ C 🛒	LM	AW ◇ B 🛒	LM	AW ◇ C 🛒	LM	AW ◇ B 🛒	LM		AW ◇ C 🛒	LM	AW ◇ B 🛒	LM
Birmingham New Street	d	23p32		06 24	07 05	07 23	08 05	08 24	09 05	09 24		10 05	10 24	11 05	11 24	12 05	12 24	13 05	13 24	14 05		14 24	15 05	15 24	16 05
Smethwick Galton Bridge	d			06 30		07 29		08 30		09 30			10 30		11 30		12 30		13 30			14 30		15 30	
Sandwell & Dudley	d				07 13		08 13		09 13			10 13		11 13		12 13		13 13		14 13			15 13		16 13
Wolverhampton 7 ⛴	d	00 02	00 20	06 42	07 25	07 41	08 25	08 43	09 25	09 43		10 25	10 43	11 25	11 43	12 25	12 43	13 25	13 43	14 25		14 43	15 25	15 43	16 25
Bilbrook	d	00 07			07 31		08 31		09 31			10 31		11 31		12 31		13 31		14 31			15 31		16 31
Codsall	d	00 10			07 33		08 33		09 33			10 33		11 33		12 33		13 33		14 33			15 33		16 33
Albrighton	d	00 14			07 38		08 38		09 38			10 38		11 38		12 38		13 38		14 38			15 38		16 38
Cosford	d	00 18																							
Shifnal	d	00 23			07 46		08 46		09 46			10 46		11 46		12 46		13 46		14 46			15 46		16 46
Telford Central	d	00 29	00 36	06 59	07 52	07 58	08 52	08 59	09 52	09 59		10 52	10 59	11 52	11 59	12 52	12 59	13 52	13 59	14 52		14 59	15 52	15 59	16 52
Oakengates	d	00 31			07 54		08 54		09 54			10 54		11 54		12 54		13 54		14 54			15 54		16 54
Wellington (Shropshire)	d	00 36	00 43	07 05	07 59	08 04	08 59	09 06	09 59	10 06		10 59	11 06	11 59	12 06	12 59	13 06	13 59	14 06	14 59		15 06	15 59	16 06	16 59
Shrewsbury	a	00 52	01 00	07 18	08 15	08 18	09 15	09 19	10 15	10 19		11 15	11 19	12 15	12 19	13 15	13 19	14 15	14 19	15 15		15 19	16 15	16 19	17 15

		AW ■ C 🛒	LM	AW ◇ B 🛒	LM	AW ◇ C 🛒		LM	AW ◇ D 🛒	LM	AW ◇ C	LM	AW ◇ D	LM	AW E	AW
Birmingham New Street	d	16 24	17 05	17 24	18 05	18 24		19 05	19 24	20 05	20 24	21 05	21 24	22 05	22 55	23 35
Smethwick Galton Bridge	d	16 30		17 31		18 30			19 30		20 30		21 30			
Sandwell & Dudley	d		17 13		18 13			19 13		20 13		21 13		22 13		
Wolverhampton 7 ⛴	d	16 43	17 25	17 43	18 25	18 43		19 25	19 43	20 25	20 43	21 25	21 42	22 25	23 13	23 54
Bilbrook	d		17 31		18 31			19 31		20 31		21 31		22 31		00 01
Codsall	d		17 33		18 33			19 33		20 33		21 33		22 33		00 04
Albrighton	d		17 38		18 38			19 38		20 38		21 38		22 38		00 08
Cosford	d															
Shifnal	d		17 46		18 46			19 46		20 46		21 46		22 46		00 17
Telford Central	d	16 59	17 52	17 59	18 52	18 59		19 52	19 59	20 52	21 02	21 52	21 59	22 52	23 29	00 22
Oakengates	d		17 54		18 54			19 54		20 54		21 54		22 54		00 25
Wellington (Shropshire)	d	17 06	17 59	18 06	18 59	19 06		19 59	20 06	20 59	21 09	21 59	22 05	22 59	23 36	00 30
Shrewsbury	a	17 19	18 15	18 19	19 15	19 19		20 15	20 19	21 15	21 23	22 14	22 22	23 15	23 49	00 43

Saturdays

from 31 March

		AW	AW	AW ◇ A 🛒	LM	AW ◇ B 🛒	LM	AW ◇ C 🛒	LM	AW ◇ B 🛒		LM	AW ◇ C 🛒	LM	AW ◇ B 🛒	LM	AW ◇ C 🛒	LM	AW ◇ B 🛒	LM		AW ◇ C 🛒	LM	AW ◇ B 🛒	LM
Birmingham New Street	d	23p32		06 24	07 05	07 23	08 05	08 24	09 05	09 24		10 05	10 24	11 05	11 24	12 05	12 24	13 05	13 24	14 05		14 24	15 05	15 24	16 05
Smethwick Galton Bridge	d			06 30		07 29		08 30		09 30			10 30		11 30		12 30		13 30			14 30		15 30	
Sandwell & Dudley	d				07 13		08 13		09 13			10 13		11 13		12 13		13 13		14 13			15 13		16 13
Wolverhampton 7 ⛴	d	00 02	00 20	06 42	07 25	07 41	08 25	08 43	09 25	09 43		10 25	10 43	11 25	11 43	12 25	12 43	13 25	13 43	14 25		14 43	15 25	15 43	16 25
Bilbrook	d	00 07			07 31		08 31		09 31			10 31		11 31		12 31		13 31		14 31			15 31		16 31
Codsall	d	00 10			07 33		08 33		09 33			10 33		11 33		12 33		13 33		14 33			15 33		16 33
Albrighton	d	00 14			07 38		08 38		09 38			10 38		11 38		12 38		13 38		14 38			15 38		16 38
Cosford	d	00 18			07 41		08 41		09 41			10 41		11 41		12 41		13 41		14 41			15 41		16 41
Shifnal	d	00 23			07 46		08 46		09 46			10 46		11 46		12 46		13 46		14 46			15 46		16 46
Telford Central	d	00 29	00 36	06 59	07 52	07 58	08 52	08 59	09 52	09 59		10 52	10 59	11 52	11 59	12 52	12 59	13 52	13 59	14 52		14 59	15 52	15 59	16 52
Oakengates	d	00 31			07 54		08 54		09 54			10 54		11 54		12 54		13 54		14 54			15 54		16 54
Wellington (Shropshire)	d	00 36	00 43	07 05	07 59	08 04	08 59	09 06	09 59	10 06		10 59	11 06	11 59	12 06	12 59	13 06	13 59	14 06	14 59		15 06	15 59	16 06	16 59
Shrewsbury	a	00 52	01 00	07 18	08 15	08 18	09 15	09 19	10 15	10 19		11 15	11 19	12 15	12 19	13 15	13 19	14 15	14 19	15 15		15 19	16 15	16 19	17 15

		AW ■ C 🛒	LM	AW ◇ B 🛒	LM	AW ◇ C 🛒		LM	AW ◇ D 🛒	LM	AW ◇ C	LM	AW ◇ D	LM	AW E	AW
Birmingham New Street	d	16 24	17 05	17 24	18 05	18 24		19 05	19 24	20 05	20 24	21 05	21 24	22 05	22 55	23 35
Smethwick Galton Bridge	d	16 30		17 31		18 30			19 30		20 30		21 30			
Sandwell & Dudley	d		17 13		18 13			19 13		20 13		21 13		22 13		
Wolverhampton 7 ⛴	d	16 43	17 25	17 43	18 25	18 43		19 25	19 43	20 25	20 43	21 25	21 42	22 25	23 13	23 54
Bilbrook	d		17 31		18 31			19 31		20 31		21 31		22 31		00 01
Codsall	d		17 33		18 33			19 33		20 33		21 33		22 33		00 04
Albrighton	d		17 38		18 38			19 38		20 38		21 38		22 38		00 08
Cosford	d		17 41		18 41			19 41		20 41		21 41		22 41		00 12
Shifnal	d		17 46		18 46			19 46		20 46		21 46		22 46		00 17
Telford Central	d	16 59	17 52	17 59	18 52	18 59		19 52	19 59	20 52	21 02	21 52	21 59	22 52	23 29	00 22
Oakengates	d		17 54		18 54			19 54		20 54		21 54		22 54		00 25
Wellington (Shropshire)	d	17 06	17 59	18 06	18 59	19 06		19 59	20 06	20 59	21 09	21 59	22 05	22 59	23 36	00 30
Shrewsbury	a	17 19	18 15	18 19	19 15	19 19		20 15	20 19	21 15	21 23	22 14	22 22	23 15	23 49	00 43

A To Aberystwyth
B From Birmingham International to Holyhead
C From Birmingham International to Aberystwyth
D From Birmingham International to Chester
E To Crewe

Table 74

Sundays

until 25 March

Birmingham - Shrewsbury

Network Diagram - see first Page of Table 67

		AW	AW	AW	AW	AW	AW	AW	AW	AW	AW	AW	AW	AW	AW	AW	AW	AW	AW	AW	AW	AW
						◇	◇		◇	◇		◇	◇		◇	◇		◇	◇	◇		
		A		B		C	D		C	D		C	D		E	D		C	D	C	B	B
							🛒		🛒	🛒		🛒	🛒		🛒	🛒		🛒				
Birmingham New Street	d	23p35		10 05		11 05	12 24		13 25	14 24		15 24	16 24		17 24	18 24		19 24	20 24	21 24	22 24	23 24
Smethwick Galton Bridge	d																					
Sandwell & Dudley	d																					
Wolverhampton 7 🚌	d	23p54	00 18	10 22	11 06	11 27	12 42	13 06	13 42	14 43	15 06	15 43	16 43	17 06	17 43	18 43	19 06	19 43	20 43	21 43	22 42	23 46
Bilbrook	d	00 01		10 28	11 12	11 33		13 12			15 12			17 12			19 12			21 49	22 48	23 52
Codsall	d	00 04		10 31	11 15	11 35		13 15			15 15			17 15			19 15			21 51	22 50	23 54
Albrighton	d	00 08		10 35	11 19	11 40		13 19			15 19			17 19			19 19			21 56	22 55	23 59
Cosford	d																					00 02
Shifnal	d	00 17		10 44	11 28	11 48		13 28			15 28			17 28			19 28			22 04	23 03	00 07
Telford Central	d	00 22	00 36	10 49	11 34	11 54	12 59	13 34	13 58	14 59	15 34	15 59	16 59	17 34	17 59	18 59	19 34	19 59	20 59	22 10	23 09	00 13
Oakengates	d	00 25		10 51	11 37	11 56		13 37			15 37			17 37			19 37			22 12	23 11	00 15
Wellington (Shropshire)	d	00 30	00 43	10 57	11 43	12 01	13 05	13 43	14 04	15 06	15 43	16 06	17 06	17 43	18 05	19 06	19 43	20 06	21 06	22 17	23 16	00 20
Shrewsbury	a	00 43	00 59	11 10	11 58	12 15	13 18	13 58	14 18	15 19	15 58	16 26	17 19	17 59	18 19	19 19	19 58	20 19	21 19	22 30	23 32	00 35

Sundays

from 1 April

		AW	AW	AW	AW	AW	AW	AW	AW	AW	AW	AW	AW	AW	AW	AW	AW	AW	AW	AW	AW	AW
						◇	◇		◇	◇		◇	◇		◇	◇		◇	◇	◇		
				B		C	D		C	D		C	D		E	D		C	D	C	B	B
							🛒		🛒	🛒		🛒	🛒		🛒	🛒		🛒				
Birmingham New Street	d	23p35		10 05		11 05	12 24		13 25	14 24		15 24	16 24		17 24	18 24		19 24	20 24	21 24	22 24	23 24
Smethwick Galton Bridge	d																					
Sandwell & Dudley	d																					
Wolverhampton 7 🚌	d	23p54	00 18	10 22	11 06	11 27	12 42	13 06	13 42	14 43	15 06	15 43	16 43	17 06	17 43	18 43	19 06	19 43	20 43	21 43	22 42	23b46
Bilbrook	d	00 01		10 28	11 12	11 33		13 12			15 12			17 12			19 12			21 49	22 48	23 52
Codsall	d	00 04		10 31	11 15	11 35		13 15			15 15			17 15			19 15			21 51	22 50	23 54
Albrighton	d	00 08		10 35	11 19	11 40		13 19			15 19			17 19			19 19			21 56	22 55	23 59
Cosford	d	00 12		10 39	11 23	11 43		13 23			15 23			17 23			19 23			21 59	22 58	00 02
Shifnal	d	00 17		10 44	11 28	11 48		13 28			15 28			17 28			19 28			22 04	23 03	00 07
Telford Central	d	00 22	00 36	10 49	11 34	11 54	12 59	13 34	13 58	14 59	15 34	15 59	16 59	17 34	17 59	18 59	19 34	19 59	20 59	22 10	23 09	00 13
Oakengates	d	00 25		10 51	11 37	11 56		13 37			15 37			17 37			19 37			22 12	23 11	00 15
Wellington (Shropshire)	d	00 30	00 43	10 57	11 43	12 01	13 05	13 43	14 04	15 06	15 43	16 06	17 06	17 43	18 05	19 06	19 43	20 06	21 06	22 17	23 16	00 20
Shrewsbury	a	00 43	00 59	11 10	11 58	12 15	13 18	13 58	14 18	15 19	15 58	16 26	17 19	17 59	18 19	19 19	19 58	20 19	21 19	22 30	23 32	00 35

A not 11 December
B From Birmingham International
C From Birmingham International to Chester
D From Birmingham International to Aberystwyth
E From Birmingham International to Holyhead

Table 74

Shrewsbury - Birmingham

Mondays to Fridays

until 23 March

Network Diagram - see first Page of Table 67

Miles			AW	AW	LM	LM	AW	LM	LM	AW	LM		AW	LM	AW	LM	AW	LM	AW	LM	AW		LM	AW	LM
			MX ◇ A	B			B			◇ C ⊥			◇ D ⊥		◇ C ⊥		◇ D ⊥		◇ C ⊥		◇ D ⊥			◇ C ⊥	
0	**Shrewsbury**	d	23p26	05 20	05 26	05 58	06 31	06 55	07 14	07 31	07 47		08 31	08 47	09 31	09 47	10 32	10 47	11 31	11 47	12 31		12 47	13 31	13 47
10½	Wellington (Shropshire)	d	23p40	05 34	05 40	06 12	06 45	07 09	07 28	07 45	08 01		08 45	09 01	09 45	10 01	10 46	11 01	11 45	12 01	12 45		13 01	13 45	14 01
13½	Oakengates	d	23p44		05 44	06 16			07 32		08 05			09 05		10 05		11 05		12 05			13 05		14 05
14½	Telford Central	d	23p47	05 40	05 47	06 19	06 51	07 15	07 35	07 51	08 08		08 51	09 08	09 51	10 08	10 52	11 08	11 51	12 08	12 51		13 08	13 51	14 08
17½	Shifnal	d	23p52		05 52	06 24			07 40		08 13			09 13		10 13		11 13		12 13			13 13		14 13
20¾	Cosford	d																							
22¼	Albrighton	d	00 01		06 00	06 33			07 48		08 22			09 22		10 22		11 22		12 22			13 22		14 22
25½	Codsall	d	00 06		06 06	06 38			07 54		08 27			09 27		10 27		11 27		12 27			13 27		14 27
26	Bilbrook	d	00 08		06 08	06 40			07 56		08 29			09 29		10 29		11 29		12 29			13 29		14 29
30	**Wolverhampton** 7	a	00 17	05 57	06 15	06 47	07 08	07 34	08 03	08 08	08 36		09 08	09 36	10 08	10 36	11 09	11 36	12 08	12 36	13 08		13 36	14 08	14 36
37¾	Sandwell & Dudley	a				07 03		07 45			08 46			09 46		10 46		11 46		12 46			13 46		14 46
39	Smethwick Galton Bridge	a		06 10		07 06	07 21			08 20			09 20		10 19		11 21		12 20		13 20			14 20	
43	**Birmingham New Street** 12	a		06 15	06 32	07 15	07 26	07 54	08 20	08 26	08 55		09 25	09 55	10 25	10 55	11 27	11 55	12 26	12 55	13 26		13 55	14 26	14 55

		AW	LM	AW	LM	AW	LM		AW	LM	AW	LM	AW	LM	LM	AW	LM		AW	AW	AW
		◇ D ⊥		◇ C ⊥		◇ D ⊥			◇ C ⊥		◇ D ⊥		◇ C ⊥			◇ E			◇ F	◇ G	◇ A
Shrewsbury	d	14 31	14 47	15 31	15 47	16 33	16 47		17 31	17 47	18 31	18 47	19 33	19 47	20 47	21 33	21 47		22 18	22 18	23 26
Wellington (Shropshire)	d	14 45	15 01	15 45	16 01	16 47	17 01		17 45	18 01	18 45	19 01	19 47	20 01	21 01	21 47	22 01		22 32	22 32	23 40
Oakengates	d		15 05		16 05		17 05			18 05		19 05		20 05	21 05		22 05				23 44
Telford Central	d	14 51	15 08	15 51	16 08	16 53	17 08		17 51	18 08	18 51	19 08	19 53	20 08	21 08	21 53	22 08		22 38	22 38	23 47
Shifnal	d		15 13		16 13		17 13			18 13		19 13		20 13	21 13		22 13				23 52
Cosford	d																				
Albrighton	d		15 22		16 22		17 22			18 22		19 22		20 22	21 22		22 22				00 01
Codsall	d		15 27		16 27		17 27			18 27		19 27		20 27	21 27		22 27				00 06
Bilbrook	d		15 29		16 29		17 29			18 29		19 29		20 29	21 29		22 29				00 08
Wolverhampton 7	a	15 08	15 36	16 08	16 36	17 10	17 36		18 08	18 36	19 08	19 36	20 10	20 36	21 36	22 09	22 36		22 55	22 55	00 17
Sandwell & Dudley	a		15 46		16 46		17 46			18 46		19 46		20 47	21 46		22 46				
Smethwick Galton Bridge	a	15 20		16 20		17 21			18 20		19 20		20 21			22 20					
Birmingham New Street 12	a	15 26	15 55	16 26	16 55	17 27	17 55		18 26	18 55	19 26	19 55	20 26	20 56	21 55	22 32	22 55		23 27	23 28	

Mondays to Fridays

from 26 March

		AW	AW	LM	LM	AW	LM	LM	AW	LM		AW	LM	AW	LM	AW	LM	AW	LM	AW		LM	AW	LM	AW
		MX ◇ A	B			B			◇ C ⊥			◇ D ⊥		◇ C ⊥		◇ D ⊥		◇ C ⊥		◇ D ⊥			◇ C ⊥		◇ D ⊥
Shrewsbury	d	23p26	05 20	05 26	05 58	06 31	06 55	07 14	07 31	07 47		08 31	08 47	09 31	09 47	10 32	10 47	11 31	11 47	12 31		12 47	13 31	13 47	14 31
Wellington (Shropshire)	d	23p40	05 34	05 40	06 12	06 45	07 09	07 28	07 45	08 01		08 45	09 01	09 45	10 01	10 46	11 01	11 45	12 01	12 45		13 01	13 45	14 01	14 45
Oakengates	d	23p44		05 44	06 16			07 32		08 05			09 05		10 05		11 05		12 05			13 05		14 05	
Telford Central	d	23p47	05 40	05 47	06 19	06 51	07 15	07 35	07 51	08 08		08 51	09 08	09 51	10 08	10 52	11 08	11 51	12 08	12 51		13 08	13 51	14 08	14 51
Shifnal	d	23p52		05 52	06 24			07 40		08 13			09 13		10 13		11 13		12 13			13 13		14 13	
Cosford	d	23p57		05 57	06 29			07 45		08 18			09 18		10 18		11 18		12 18			13 18		14 18	
Albrighton	d	00 01		06 00	06 33			07 48		08 22			09 22		10 22		11 22		12 22			13 22		14 22	
Codsall	d	00 06		06 06	06 38			07 54		08 27			09 27		10 27		11 27		12 27			13 27		14 27	
Bilbrook	d	00 08		06 08	06 40			07 56		08 29			09 29		10 29		11 29		12 29			13 29		14 29	
Wolverhampton 7	a	00 17	05 57	06 15	06 47	07 08	07 34	08 03	08 08	08 36		09 08	09 36	10 08	10 36	11 09	11 36	12 08	12 36	13 08		13 36	14 08	14 36	15 08
Sandwell & Dudley	a				07 03		07 45			08 46			09 46		10 46		11 46		12 46			13 46		14 46	
Smethwick Galton Bridge	a		06 10		07 06	07 21			08 20			09 20		10 19		11 21		12 20		13 20			14 20		15 20
Birmingham New Street 12	a		06 15	06 32	07 15	07 26	07 54	08 20	08 26	08 55		09 25	09 55	10 25	10 55	11 27	11 55	12 26	12 55	13 26		13 55	14 26	14 55	15 26

		LM	AW	LM	AW	LM		AW	LM	AW	LM	AW	LM	LM	AW	LM		AW	AW	AW
			◇ C ⊥		◇ D ⊥			◇ C ⊥		◇ D ⊥		◇ C ⊥			◇ E			MWFO ◇ F	TThO ◇ G	◇ A
Shrewsbury	d	14 47	15 31	15 47	16 33	16 47		17 31	17 47	18 31	18 47	19 33	19 47	20 47	21 33	21 47		22 18	22 18	23 26
Wellington (Shropshire)	d	15 01	15 45	16 01	16 47	17 01		17 45	18 01	18 45	19 01	19 47	20 01	21 01	21 47	22 01		22 32	22 32	23 40
Oakengates	d	15 05		16 05		17 05			18 05		19 05		20 05	21 05		22 05				23 44
Telford Central	d	15 08	15 51	16 08	16 53	17 08		17 51	18 08	18 51	19 08	19 53	20 08	21 08	21 53	22 08		22 38	22 38	23 47
Shifnal	d	15 13		16 13		17 13			18 13		19 13		20 13	21 13		22 13				23 52
Cosford	d	15 18		16 18		17 18			18 18		19 18		20 18	21 18		22 18				23 57
Albrighton	d	15 22		16 22		17 22			18 22		19 22		20 22	21 22		22 22				00 01
Codsall	d	15 27		16 27		17 27			18 27		19 27		20 27	21 27		22 27				00 06
Bilbrook	d	15 29		16 29		17 29			18 29		19 29		20 29	21 29		22 29				00 08
Wolverhampton 7	a	15 36	16 08	16 36	17 10	17 36		18 08	18 36	19 08	19 36	20 10	20 36	21 36	22 09	22 36		22 55	22 55	00 17
Sandwell & Dudley	a	15 46		16 46		17 46			18 46		19 46		20 47	21 46		22 46				
Smethwick Galton Bridge	a		16 20		17 21			18 20		19 20		20 21			22 20					
Birmingham New Street 12	a	15 55	16 26	16 55	17 27	17 55		18 26	18 55	19 26	19 55	20 26	20 56	21 55	22 32	22 55		23 27	23 28	

A From Chester
B To Birmingham International
C From Aberystwyth to Birmingham International
D From Holyhead to Birmingham International
E From Aberystwyth
F From Holyhead
G From Holyhead

Table 74

Shrewsbury - Birmingham

Saturdays

until 24 March

Network Diagram - see first Page of Table 67

		AW ◇ A	AW B	AW B 🚲	LM	AW ◇ C 🚲	LM	AW ◇ D 🚲	LM	AW ◇ C 🚲		LM	AW ◇ D 🚲	LM	AW ◇ C 🚲	LM	AW D	LM	AW ◇ C 🚲	LM		AW ◇ D 🚲	LM	AW ◇ C 🚲	LM
Shrewsbury	d	23p26	05 24	06 31	06 47	07 31	07 47	08 31	08 47	09 31		09 47	10 32	10 47	11 31	11 47	12 31	12 47	13 31	13 47		14 31	14 47	15 31	15 47
Wellington (Shropshire)	d	23p40	05 38	06 45	07 01	07 45	08 01	08 45	09 01	09 45		10 01	10 46	11 01	11 45	12 01	12 45	13 01	13 45	14 01		14 45	15 01	15 45	16 01
Oakengates	d	23p44			07 05		08 05		09 05			10 05		11 05		12 05		13 05		14 05			15 05		16 05
Telford Central	d	23p47	05 44	06 51	07 08	07 51	08 08	08 51	09 08	09 51		10 08	10 52	11 08	11 51	12 08	12 51	13 08	13 51	14 08		14 51	15 08	15 51	16 08
Shifnal	d	23p52			07 13		08 13		09 13			10 13		11 13		12 13		13 13		14 13			15 13		16 13
Cosford	d																								
Albrighton	d	00 01			07 22		08 22		09 22			10 22		11 22		12 22		13 22		14 22			15 22		16 22
Codsall	d	00 06			07 27		08 27		09 27			10 27		11 27		12 27		13 27		14 27			15 27		16 27
Bilbrook	d	00 08			07 29		08 29		09 29			10 29		11 29		12 29		13 29		14 29			15 29		16 29
Wolverhampton 7	a	00 17	06 01	07 08	07 36	08 08	08 36	09 08	09 36	10 08		10 36	11 09	11 36	12 08	12 36	13 08	13 36	14 08	14 36		15 08	15 36	16 08	16 36
Sandwell & Dudley	a				07 46		08 46		09 46			10 46		11 46		12 46		13 46		14 46			15 46		16 46
Smethwick Galton Bridge	a		06 14	07 21		08 20		09 22		10 20			11 20		12 20		13 20		14 20			15 20		16 20	
Birmingham New Street 12	a		06 20	07 26	07 55	08 26	08 55	09 26	09 55	10 26		10 55	11 26	11 55	12 26	12 55	13 26	13 55	14 26	14 55		15 26	15 55	16 26	16 55

		AW ◇ D 🚲	LM	AW ◇ C 🚲	LM	AW ◇ D 🚲		LM	AW ◇ C 🚲	LM	LM	AW ◇ E	LM	AW ◇ F	AW ◇ A
Shrewsbury	d	16 33	16 47	17 31	17 47	18 31		18 47	19 33	19 47	20 47	21 33	21 47	22 31	23 26
Wellington (Shropshire)	d	16 47	17 01	17 45	18 01	18 45		19 01	19 47	20 01	21 01	21 47	22 01	22 45	23 40
Oakengates	d		17 05		18 05			19 05		20 05	21 05		22 05		23 44
Telford Central	d	16 53	17 08	17 51	18 08	18 51		19 08	19 53	20 08	21 08	21 53	22 08	22 51	23 47
Shifnal	d		17 13		18 13			19 13		20 13	21 13		22 13		23 52
Cosford	d														
Albrighton	d		17 22		18 22			19 22		20 22	21 22		22 22		00 02
Codsall	d		17 27		18 27			19 27		20 27	21 27		22 27		00 07
Bilbrook	d		17 29		18 29			19 29		20 29	21 29		22 29		00 09
Wolverhampton 7	a	17 10	17 36	18 08	18 36	19 08		19 36	20 09	20 36	21 36	22 08	22 36	23 07	00 16
Sandwell & Dudley	a		17 46		18 46			19 46		20 46	21 46		22 45		
Smethwick Galton Bridge	a	17 22		18 20		19 20			20 20			22 19			
Birmingham New Street 12	a	17 28	17 55	18 26	18 55	19 26		19 55	20 25	20 57	21 55	22 31	22 55	23 28	

Saturdays

from 31 March

		AW ◇ A	AW B	AW B 🚲	LM	AW ◇ C 🚲	LM	AW ◇ D 🚲	LM	AW ◇ C 🚲		LM	AW ◇ D 🚲	LM	AW ◇ C 🚲	LM	AW D	LM	AW ◇ C 🚲	LM		AW ◇ D 🚲	LM	AW ◇ C 🚲	LM
Shrewsbury	d	23p26	05 24	06 31	06 47	07 31	07 47	08 31	08 47	09 31		09 47	10 32	10 47	11 31	11 47	12 31	12 47	13 31	13 47		14 31	14 47	15 31	15 47
Wellington (Shropshire)	d	23p40	05 38	06 45	07 01	07 45	08 01	08 45	09 01	09 45		10 01	10 46	11 01	11 45	12 01	12 45	13 01	13 45	14 01		14 45	15 01	15 45	16 01
Oakengates	d	23p44			07 05		08 05		09 05			10 05		11 05		12 05		13 05		14 05			15 05		16 05
Telford Central	d	23p47	05 44	06 51	07 08	07 51	08 08	08 51	09 08	09 51		10 08	10 52	11 08	11 51	12 08	12 51	13 08	13 51	14 08		14 51	15 08	15 51	16 08
Shifnal	d	23p52			07 13		08 13		09 13			10 13		11 13		12 13		13 13		14 13			15 13		16 13
Cosford	d	23p57			07 18		08 18		09 18			10 18		11 18		12 18		13 18		14 18			15 18		16 18
Albrighton	d	00 01			07 22		08 22		09 22			10 22		11 22		12 22		13 22		14 22			15 22		16 22
Codsall	d	00 06			07 27		08 27		09 27			10 27		11 27		12 27		13 27		14 27			15 27		16 27
Bilbrook	d	00 08			07 29		08 29		09 29			10 29		11 29		12 29		13 29		14 29			15 29		16 29
Wolverhampton 7	a	00 17	06 01	07 08	07 36	08 08	08 36	09 08	09 36	10 08		10 36	11 09	11 36	12 08	12 36	13 08	13 36	14 08	14 36		15 08	15 36	16 08	16 36
Sandwell & Dudley	a				07 46		08 46		09 46			10 46		11 46		12 46		13 46		14 46			15 46		16 46
Smethwick Galton Bridge	a		06 14	07 21		08 20		09 22		10 20			11 20		12 20		13 20		14 20			15 20		16 20	
Birmingham New Street 12	a		06 20	07 26	07 55	08 26	08 55	09 26	09 55	10 26		10 55	11 26	11 55	12 26	12 55	13 26	13 55	14 26	14 55		15 26	15 55	16 26	16 55

		AW ◇ D 🚲	LM	AW ◇ C 🚲	LM	AW ◇ D 🚲		LM	AW ◇ C 🚲	LM	LM	AW ◇ E	LM	AW ◇ F	AW ◇ A
Shrewsbury	d	16 33	16 47	17 31	17 47	18 31		18 47	19 33	19 47	20 47	21 33	21 47	22 31	23 26
Wellington (Shropshire)	d	16 47	17 01	17 45	18 01	18 45		19 01	19 47	20 01	21 01	21 47	22 01	22 45	23 40
Oakengates	d		17 05		18 05			19 05		20 05	21 05		22 05		23 44
Telford Central	d	16 53	17 08	17 51	18 08	18 51		19 08	19 53	20 08	21 08	21 53	22 08	22 51	23 47
Shifnal	d		17 13		18 13			19 13		20 13	21 13		22 13		23 52
Cosford	d		17 18		18 18			19 18		20 18	21 18		22 18		23 57
Albrighton	d		17 22		18 22			19 22		20 22	21 22		22 22		00 02
Codsall	d		17 27		18 27			19 27		20 27	21 27		22 27		00 07
Bilbrook	d		17 29		18 29			19 29		20 29	21 29		22 29		00 09
Wolverhampton 7	a	17 10	17 36	18 08	18 36	19 08		19 36	20 09	20 36	21 36	22 08	22 36	23 07	00 16
Sandwell & Dudley	a		17 46		18 46			19 46		20 46	21 46		22 45		
Smethwick Galton Bridge	a	17 22		18 20		19 20			20 20			22 19			
Birmingham New Street 12	a	17 28	17 55	18 26	18 55	19 26		19 55	20 25	20 57	21 55	22 31	22 55	23 28	

A From Chester
B To Birmingham International
C From Aberystwyth to Birmingham International
D From Holyhead to Birmingham International
E From Aberystwyth
F From Holyhead

Table 74

Shrewsbury - Birmingham

Sundays
until 25 March

Network Diagram - see first Page of Table 67

		AW	AW	AW	AW	AW	AW	AW	AW	AW	AW	AW	AW	AW	AW	AW	AW	AW	AW	AW	AW	AW
		◇ A	B	B		◇ C	◇ D		◇ C	◇ D		◇ C	◇ D		◇ C	◇ D		◇ C	◇ D	C	◇ D	◇ E
Shrewsbury	d	23p26	08 10	09 09	09 55	10 20	11 40	12 10	12 31	13 31	14 10	14 31	15 33	16 10	16 40	17 33	18 10	18 31	19 31	20 23	21 31	22 23
Wellington (Shropshire)	d	23p40	08 24	09 23	10 09	10 34	11 54	12 24	12 45	13 45	14 23	14 45	15 47	16 23	16 54	17 47	18 23	18 45	19 45	20 37	21 45	22 37
Oakengates	d	23p44	08 28	09 27	10 14			12 29			14 29			16 29			18 29			20 41		22 43
Telford Central	d	23p47	08 31	09 30	10 17	10 40	12 00	12 32	12 51	13 51	14 32	14 51	15 53	16 32	17 00	17 53	18 32	18 51	19 51	20 44	21 51	22 45
Shifnal	d	23p52	08 36	09 35	10 22			12 37			14 37			16 37			18 37			20 49		22 51
Cosford	d				10 28																	
Albrighton	d	00 02	08 44	09 43	10 31			12 46			14 46			16 46			18 46			20 57		22 59
Codsall	d	00 07	08 50	09 48	10 37			12 52			14 52			16 52			18 52			21 02		23 05
Bilbrook	d	00 09	08 52	09 50	10 39			12 55			14 54			16 54			18 54			21 04		23 07
Wolverhampton 7	a	00 16	08 59	09 57	10 50	10 56	12 16	13 03	13 07	14 07	15 03	15 07	16 09	17 03	17 15	18 09	19 03	19 07	20 07	21 11	22 07	23 13
Sandwell & Dudley	a																					
Smethwick Galton Bridge	a																					
Birmingham New Street 12	a		09 15	10 14		11 13	12 32		13 23	14 23		15 24	16 24		17 35	18 27		19 26	20 23	21 29	22 27	

Sundays
from 1 April

		AW	AW	AW	AW	AW	AW	AW	AW	AW	AW	AW	AW	AW	AW	AW	AW	AW	AW	AW	AW	AW
		◇ E	B	B		◇ C	◇ D		◇ C	◇ D		◇ C	◇ D		◇ C	◇ D		◇ C	◇ D	C	◇ D	◇ E
Shrewsbury	d	23p26	08 10	09 09	09 55	10 20	11 40	12 10	12 31	13 31	14 10	14 31	15 33	16 10	16 40	17 33	18 10	18 31	19 31	20 23	21 31	22 23
Wellington (Shropshire)	d	23p40	08 24	09 23	10 09	10 34	11 54	12 24	12 45	13 45	14 23	14 45	15 47	16 23	16 54	17 47	18 23	18 45	19 45	20 37	21 45	22 37
Oakengates	d	23p44	08 28	09 27	10 14			12 29			14 29			16 29			18 29			20 41		22 43
Telford Central	d	23p47	08 31	09 30	10 17	10 40	12 00	12 32	12 51	13 51	14 32	14 51	15 53	16 32	17 00	17 53	18 32	18 51	19 51	20 44	21 51	22 45
Shifnal	d	23p52	08 36	09 35	10 22			12 37			14 37			16 37			18 37			20 49		22 51
Cosford	d	23p57	08 41	09 40	10 28			12 43			14 43			16 43			18 43			20 54		22 56
Albrighton	d	00 02	08 44	09 43	10 31			12 46			14 46			16 46			18 46			20 57		22 59
Codsall	d	00 07	08 50	09 48	10 37			12 52			14 52			16 52			18 52			21 02		23 05
Bilbrook	d	00 09	08 52	09 50	10 39			12 55			14 54			16 54			18 54			21 04		23 07
Wolverhampton 7	a	00 16	08 59	09 57	10 50	10 56	12 16	13 03	13 07	14 07	15 03	15 07	16 09	17 03	17 15	18 09	19 03	19 07	20 07	21 11	22 07	23 13
Sandwell & Dudley	a																					
Smethwick Galton Bridge	a																					
Birmingham New Street 12	a		09 15	10 14		11 13	12 32		13 23	14 23		15 24	16 24		17 35	18 27		19 26	20 23	21 29	22 27	

A not 11 December. From Chester
B To Birmingham International
C From Chester to Birmingham International
D From Aberystwyth to Birmingham International
E From Chester

Birmingham and Shrewsbury - Chester, Aberystwyth, Barmouth and Pwllheli

Network Diagram - see first Page of Table 67

Miles	Miles	Miles			AW MX	AW	AW	AW	AW	AW	AW	VT	AW		AW	AW	AW	AW	AW	AW	AW	AW	AW	AW	
							◇				◇	◇1	◇ ✠			◇ ✠	◇ ✠	◇ ✠	◇	◇ ✠	◇ ✠	◇ ✠	◇	◇ ✠	
—	—	—	Birmingham International ✈	d													07 09			08 09	09 09			10 09	
0	—	—	**Birmingham New Street** 12	d												06 24	07 24			08 24	09 24			10 24	
—	—	—	Tame Bridge Parkway	d																					
—	—	—	Smethwick Galton Bridge 4	d												06 30	07 30			08 30	09 30			10 30	
12¾	—	—	**Wolverhampton** 7	d												06 43	07 42			08 43	09 43			10 43	
22	—	—	Cosford	d																					
28¼	—	—	Telford Central	d												06 59	07 59			08 59	09 59			10 59	
32¼	—	—	Wellington (Shropshire)	d												07 06	08 05			09 06	10 06			11 06	
42¾	—	—	**Shrewsbury**	a												07 18	08 19			09 19	10 19			11 19	
—	—	—	Cardiff Central 7	d									05 10					07 21				09 21			
—	—	0	**Shrewsbury**	d	23p37			05 20	06 10				07 24			07 27	08 21	09 24		09 27	10 23	11 24		11 27	
—	—	17¾	Gobowen	d	23p57			05 39	06 30				07 43				08 40	09 43			10 42	11 43			
—	—	20¾	Chirk	d	00 03			05 45	06 35				07 48				08 46	09 48			10 48	11 48			
—	—	25	Ruabon	d	00 09			05 51	06 42				07 54				08 52	09 54			10 54	11 54			
—	—	30	Wrexham General	a	00 14			05 57	06 49				08 01				08 59	10 01			11 00	12 01			
—	—	—		d	00 15			06 04				07 00	08 02				09 00	10 02			11 01	12 02			
—	—	42	**Chester**	a	00 35			06 24				07 16	08 19				09 17	10 19			11 19	12 19			
62½	—	—	Welshpool	d												07 49				09 49				11 49	
76½	—	—	Newtown (Powys)	d												08 04				10 04				12 04	
82	—	—	Caersws	d												08 13				10 13				12 13	
103¾	0	—	**Machynlleth** 4	a												08 46				10 46				12 46	
—	—	—		d		04 35	05 15			06 35	06 49				08 07	08 48			09 03	10 48			11 00	12 48	12 56
107¾	4	—	Dovey Junction 4	d		04 42	05 22			06 42	06 56				08 14	08 55			09 10	10 55			11 07	12 55	13 03
116	—	—	Borth	d		04 53				06 53					08 25	09 06				11 06				13 06	
124¼	—	—	**Aberystwyth**	a		05 12				07 10					08 44	09 25				11 25				13 25	
—	9	—	Penhelig	d			05x30				07x04								09x18				11x15		13x11
—	10	—	Aberdovey	d			05 34				07 08								09 22				11 20		13 15
—	13½	—	Tywyn	a			05 40				07 14								09 28				11 26		13 21
—	—	—		d			05 41				07 15								09 29				11 26		13 23
—	16	—	Tonfanau	d			05x44				07x19								09x32				11x30		13x26
—	20	—	Llwyngwril	d			05x51				07x25								09x39				11x36		13x33
—	22¾	—	Fairbourne	d			05 59				07 33								09 47				11 45		13 41
—	23¾	—	Morfa Mawddach	d			06x00				07x35								09 48				11x46		13x42
—	25½	—	**Barmouth**	a			06 07				07 41								09 55				11 53		13 49
—	—	—		d			06 11				07 47								09 57				11 56		13 52
—	26¾	—	Llanaber	d			06x14				07x50								10x00				11x59		13x55
—	29¼	—	Talybont	d							07x54								10x04				12x03		13x59
—	30¼	—	Dyffryn Ardudwy	d							07x57								10x07				12x06		14x02
—	32½	—	Llanbedr	d							08x01								10x11				12x10		14x06
—	33¼	—	Pensarn	d							08x03								10x13				12x12		14x08
—	34	—	Llandanwg	d							08x05								10x15				12x14		14x10
—	35¾	—	Harlech	a			06 32				08 09								10 21				12 20		14 16
—	—	—		d			06 32				08 21								10 24				12 26		14 31
—	38½	—	Tygwyn	d							08x24								10x27				12x29		14x34
—	39¼	—	Talsarnau	d							08x27								10x30				12x32		14x37
—	40½	—	Llandecwyn	d							08x30								10x33				12x35		14x40
—	41¼	—	Penrhyndeudraeth	d							08 34								10 37				12 39		14 44
—	42½	—	Minffordd	d							08 37								10 40				12 42		14 47
—	44½	—	Porthmadog	a			06 48				08 43								10 45				12 47		14 52
—	—	—		d			06 50				08 43								10 46				12 48		14 53
—	49½	—	Criccieth	d							08 51								10 54				12 56		15 01
—	54	—	Penychain	d			07x02				08x56								10x59				13x01		15x06
—	55½	—	Abererch	d							08x59								11x02				13x04		15x09
—	57½	—	**Pwllheli**	a			07 10				09 06								11 09				13 14		15 18

For connections from London Euston please refer to Table 66

For connections from Manchester Piccadilly and Crewe please refer to Table 131

Birmingham and Shrewsbury - Chester, Aberystwyth, Barmouth and Pwllheli

Network Diagram - see first Page of Table 67

		AW ◇ 🍴	AW ◇ 🍴	AW ◇ 🍴		AW ◇ 🍴	AW ◇ 🍴	AW ◇ 🍴		AW ◇ 🍴	AW R 🍴	AW ◇ 🍴		AW ◇ 🍴	AW R 🍴	AW FO R	AW ◇ 🍴	AW R 🍴	AW ◇ 🍴	AW ◇	AW ◇
Birmingham International ✈	d	11 09		12 09		13 09		14 09		15 09		16 09		17 09			18 09		19 09		
Birmingham New Street 12	d	11 24		12 24		13 24		14 24		15 26		16 24		17 26			18 24		19 24		
Tame Bridge Parkway	d																				
Smethwick Galton Bridge 4	d	11 30		12 30		13 30		14 30		15 32		16 30		17 32			18 30		19 30		
Wolverhampton 7 🚌	d	11 43		12 43		13 43		14 43		15 44		16 43		17 44			18 43		19 43		
Cosford	d																				
Telford Central	d	11 59		12 59		13 59		14 59		16 01		16 59		18 01			18 59		19 59		
Wellington (Shropshire)	d	12 06		13 06		14 06		15 06		16 07		17 06		18 07			19 06		20 06		
Shrewsbury	a	12 19		13 19		14 19		15 19		16 20		17 19		18 20			19 19		20 19		
Cardiff Central 7	d		11 21				13 21				15 21				17 21			18 18		19 34	
Shrewsbury	d	12 22	13 24	13 27		14 22	15 24	15 27		16 24	17 24	17 27		18 24	19 24		19 30	20 05	20 24	21 39	
Gobowen	d	12 42	13 43			14 42	15 43			16 43	17 43			18 43	19 43			20 24	20 43	21 58	
Chirk	d	12 47	13 48			14 47	15 48			16 49	17 48			18 49	19 48				20 49	22 03	
Ruabon	d	12 54	13 54			14 54	15 54			16 55	17 54			18 55	19 54			20 34	20 55	22 09	
Wrexham General	a	13 00	14 01			15 00	16 01			17 01	18 01			19 01	20 01			20 39	21 01	22 13	
	d	13 00	14 02			15 00	16 02			17 02	18 02			19 02	20 02			20 41	21 02	22 14	
Chester	a	13 19	14 19			15 20	16 20			17 22	18 20			19 20	20 20			20 56	21 19	22 34	
Welshpool	d			13 49				15 49				17 49					19 52				
Newtown (Powys)	d			14 04				16 04				18 04					20 07				
Caersws	d			14 13				16 13				18 13					20 16				
Machynlleth 4	a			14 46				16 46				18 46					20 47				
	d			14 48	14 56			16 48	17 00			18 48	19 00			19 00	20 49				21 17
Dovey Junction 4	d			14 55	15 03			16 55	17 07			18 55	19 07			19 07	20 56				21 24
Borth	d			15 06				17 06				19 06					21 07				
Aberystwyth	a			15 25				17 25				19 25					21 25				
Penhelig	d				15x11				17x15				19x15			19x15					21x32
Aberdovey	d				15 15				17 19				19 20			19 20					21 36
Tywyn	a				15 21				17 25				19 26			19 26					21 42
	d				15 26				17 27				19 26			19 26					21 43
Tonfanau	d				15x29				17x30				19x30			19x30					21x46
Llwyngwril	d				15x36				17x37				19x36			19x36					21x53
Fairbourne	d				15 44				17 45				19 44			19 44					22 01
Morfa Mawddach	d				15x45				17x46				19x46			19x46					22x02
Barmouth	a				15 52				17 53				19 56			19 56					22 09
	d				15 56				17 57												22 10
Llanaber	d				15x59				18x00												22x13
Talybont	d				16x02				18x03												22x17
Dyffryn Ardudwy	d				16x05				18x06												22x20
Llanbedr	d				16x09				18x10												22x24
Pensarn	d				16x11				18x12												22x26
Llandanwg	d				16x13				18x14												22x28
Harlech	a				16 20				18 21												22 34
	d				16 22				18 26												22 37
Tygwyn	d				16x26				18x29												22x40
Talsarnau	d				16x28				18x32												22x43
Llandecwyn	d				16x31				18x35												22x46
Penrhyndeudraeth	d				16 35				18 39												22 50
Minffordd	d				16 39				18 42												22 53
Porthmadog	a				16 44				18 47												22 59
	d				16 44				18 48												22 59
Criccieth	d				16 52				18 56												23 07
Penychain	d				16x57				19x01												23x12
Abererch	d				17x00				19x04												23x15
Pwllheli	a				17 09				19 13												23 22

For connections from London Euston please refer to Table 66

For connections from Manchester Piccadilly and Crewe please refer to Table 131

Birmingham and Shrewsbury - Chester, Aberystwyth, Barmouth and Pwllheli

Network Diagram - see first Page of Table 67

		AW	AW	AW
		◇	◇	
Birmingham International	d	20 09	21 09	
Birmingham New Street 12	d	20 24	21 24	
Tame Bridge Parkway	d			
Smethwick Galton Bridge 4	d	20 30	21 30	
Wolverhampton 7	d	20 43	21 43	
Cosford	d			
Telford Central	d	20 59	21 59	
Wellington (Shropshire)	d	21 06	22 07	
Shrewsbury	a	21 19	22 19	
Cardiff Central 7	d			
Shrewsbury	d	21 42	22 24	23 37
Gobowen	d		22 43	23 57
Chirk	d		22 49	00 03
Ruabon	d		22 55	00 09
Wrexham General	a		23 01	00 14
	d		23 01	00 15
Chester	a		23 19	00 35
Welshpool	d	22 04		
Newtown (Powys)	d	22 20		
Caersws	d	22 29		
Machynlleth 4	a	23 00		
	d	23 07		
Dovey Junction 4	d	23 14		
Borth	d	23 25		
Aberystwyth	a	23 44		
Penhelig	d			
Aberdovey	d			
Tywyn	a			
	d			
Tonfanau	d			
Llwyngwril	d			
Fairbourne	d			
Morfa Mawddach	d			
Barmouth	a			
	d			
Llanaber	d			
Talybont	d			
Dyffryn Ardudwy	d			
Llanbedr	d			
Pensarn	d			
Llandanwg	d			
Harlech	a			
	d			
Tygwyn	d			
Talsarnau	d			
Llandecwyn	d			
Penrhyndeudraeth	d			
Minffordd	d			
Porthmadog	a			
	d			
Criccieth	d			
Penychain	d			
Abererch	d			
Pwllheli	a			

For connections from London Euston please refer to Table 66

For connections from Manchester Piccadilly and Crewe please refer to Table 131

Table 75

Saturdays

Birmingham and Shrewsbury - Chester, Aberystwyth, Barmouth and Pwllheli

Network Diagram - see first Page of Table 67

		AW	AW	AW	AW	AW	AW	AW	AW	AW	AW	AW	AW	AW		AW	AW	AW		AW	AW
				◇			◇		◇	◇	◇	◇	◇	◇		◇	◇	◇		◇	◇
						🚲	🚲			🚲	🚲	🚲		🚲		🚲	🚲	🚲		🚲	🚲
Birmingham International ✈	d										07 09			08 09		09 09		10 09		11 09	
Birmingham New Street 12	d									06 24	07 23			08 24		09 24		10 24		11 24	
Tame Bridge Parkway	d																				
Smethwick Galton Bridge 4	d									06 30	07 29			08 30		09 30		10 30		11 30	
Wolverhampton 7 ⛴	d									06 42	07 41			08 43		09 43		10 43		11 43	
Cosford	d																				
Telford Central	d									06 59	07 58			08 59		09 59		10 59		11 59	
Wellington (Shropshire)	d									07 05	08 04			09 06		10 06		11 06		12 06	
Shrewsbury	a									07 18	08 18			09 19		10 19		11 19		12 19	
Cardiff Central 7	d						05 20					07 21					09 21				11 21
Shrewsbury	d	23p37			05 20	06 10	07 24			07 27	08 21	09 24		09 27		10 23	11 24	11 27		12 22	13 24
Gobowen	d	23p57			05 39	06 30	07 43				08 40	09 43				10 42	11 43			12 42	13 43
Chirk	d	00 03			05 45	06 35	07 48				08 46	09 48				10 48	11 48			12 47	13 48
Ruabon	d	00 09			05 51	06 42	07 54				08 52	09 54				10 54	11 54			12 54	13 54
Wrexham General	a	00 14			05 57	06 48	08 00				08 59	10 01				11 00	12 01			13 00	14 01
	d	00 15			05 58	06 50	08 01				09 00	10 02				11 01	12 02			13 00	14 02
Chester	a	00 35			06 16	07 08	08 18				09 17	10 19				11 19	12 19			13 18	14 19
Welshpool	d									07 49				09 49				11 49			
Newtown (Powys)	d									08 04				10 04				12 04			
Caersws	d									08 13				10 13				12 13			
Machynlleth 4	a									08 46				10 46				12 46			
	d		04 35	05 15				06 35	06 49	08 48			09 03	10 48	11 00			12 48	12 56		
Dovey Junction 4	d		04 42	05 22				06 42	06 56	08 55			09 10	10 55	11 07			12 55	13 03		
Borth	d		04 53					06 53		09 06				11 06				13 06			
Aberystwyth	a		05 12					07 10		09 25				11 25				13 25			
Penhelig	d			05x30					07x04				09x18		11x15				13x11		
Aberdovey	d			05 34					07 08				09 22		11 20				13 15		
Tywyn	a			05 40					07 14				09 28		11 26				13 21		
	d			05 41					07 15				09 29		11 26				13 23		
Tonfanau	d			05x44					07x19				09x32		11x30				13x26		
Llwyngwril	d			05x51					07x25				09x39		11x36				13x33		
Fairbourne	d			05 59					07 33				09 47		11 45				13 41		
Morfa Mawddach	d			06x00					07x35				09 48		11x46				13x42		
Barmouth	a			06 09					07 41				09 55		11 53				13 49		
	d			06 11					07 47				09 57		11 56				13 52		
Llanaber	d			06x14					07x50				10x00		11x59				13x55		
Talybont	d								07x54				10x04		12x03				13x59		
Dyffryn Ardudwy	d								07x57				10x07		12x06				14x02		
Llanbedr	d								08x01				10x11		12x10				14x06		
Pensarn	d								08x03				10x13		12x12				14x08		
Llandanwg	d								08x05				10x15		12x14				14x10		
Harlech	a			06 32					08 09				10 21		12 20				14 16		
	d			06 32					08 21				10 24		12 26				14 31		
Tygwyn	d								08x24				10x27		12x29				14x34		
Talsarnau	d								08x27				10x30		12x32				14x37		
Llandecwyn	d								08x30				10x33		12x35				14x40		
Penrhyndeudraeth	d								08 34				10 37		12 39				14 44		
Minffordd	d								08 37				10 40		12 42				14 47		
Porthmadog	a			06 48					08 43				10 45		12 47				14 52		
	d			06 50					08 43				10 46		12 48				14 53		
Criccieth	d								08 51				10 54		12 56				15 01		
Penychain	d			07x02					08x56				10x59		13x01				15x06		
Abererch	d								08x59				11x02		13x04				15x09		
Pwllheli	a			07 10					09 06				11 09		13 14				15 18		

For connections from London Euston please refer to Table 66

For connections from Manchester Piccadilly and Crewe please refer to Table 131

Birmingham and Shrewsbury - Chester, Aberystwyth, Barmouth and Pwllheli

Network Diagram - see first Page of Table 67

		AW		AW	AW	AW		AW	AW	AW	AW	AW	AW	AW	AW	AW	AW	AW	AW	AW
									R	R			R							
		◇		◇	◇	◇		◇			◇			◇	◇	◇	◇	◇	◇	
													A							
		🍴		🍴	🍴	🍴		🍴	🍴	🍴	🍴		🍴	🍴	🍴					
Birmingham International ✈	d	12 09		13 09		14 09		15 09		16 09	17 09			18 09	19 09			20 09	21 09	
Birmingham New Street 12	d	12 24		13 24		14 24		15 24		16 24	17 24			18 24	19 24			20 24	21 24	
Tame Bridge Parkway	d																			
Smethwick Galton Bridge 4	d	12 30		13 30		14 30		15 30		16 30	17 31			18 30	19 30			20 30	21 30	
Wolverhampton 7 🚌	d	12 43		13 43		14 43		15 43		16 43	17 43			18 43	19 43			20 43	21 42	
Cosford	d																			
Telford Central	d	12 59		13 59		14 59		15 59		16 59	17 59			18 59	19 59			21 02	21 59	
Wellington (Shropshire)	d	13 06		14 06		15 06		16 06		17 06	18 06			19 06	20 06			21 09	22 05	
Shrewsbury	a	13 19		14 19		15 19		16 19		17 19	18 19			19 19	20 19			21 23	22 22	
Cardiff Central 7	d				13 21				15 21				17 21			19 34				
Shrewsbury	d	13 27		14 22	15 24	15 27		16 22	17 24	17 27	18 22		19 24	19 30	20 24	21 37		21 42	22 24	23 33
Gobowen	d			14 42	15 43			16 42	17 43		18 42		19 43		20 43	21 56			22 43	23 52
Chirk	d			14 47	15 48			16 47	17 48		18 47		19 48		20 49	22 01			22 49	23 58
Ruabon	d			14 54	15 54			16 54	17 54		18 54		19 54		20 55	22 07			22 55	00 04
Wrexham General	a			15 00	16 01			17 00	18 01		19 01		20 01		21 01	22 13			23 01	00 10
	d			15 00	16 02			17 02	18 02		19 02	19 46	20 02		21 02	22 13			23 02	00 14
Chester	a			15 20	16 22			17 19	18 19		19 20	20 04	20 19		21 21	22 31			23 21	00 33
Welshpool	d	13 49				15 49				17 49				19 52				22 04		
Newtown (Powys)	d	14 04				16 04				18 04				20 07				22 20		
Caersws	d	14 13				16 13				18 13				20 16				22 29		
Machynlleth 4	a	14 46				16 46				18 46				20 47				22 59		
	d	14 48	14 56			16 48	17 00			18 48				20 49			21 17	23 04		
Dovey Junction 4	d	14 55	15 03			16 55	17 07			18 55				20 56			21 24	23 11		
Borth	d	15 06				17 06				19 06				21 07				23 22		
Aberystwyth	a	15 25				17 25				19 25				21 25				23 41		
Penhelig	d		15x11				17x15										21x32			
Aberdovey	d		15 15				17 19										21 36			
Tywyn	a		15 21				17 25										21 42			
	d		15 26				17 27										21 43			
Tonfanau	d		15x29				17x30										21x46			
Llwyngwril	d		15x36				17x37										21x53			
Fairbourne	d		15 44				17 45										22 01			
Morfa Mawddach	d		15x45				17x46										22x02			
Barmouth	a		15 52				17 53										22 09			
	d		15 56				17 57										22 10			
Llanaber	d		15x59				18x00										22x13			
Talybont	d		16x02				18x03										22x17			
Dyffryn Ardudwy	d		16x05				18x06										22x20			
Llanbedr	d		16x09				18x10										22x24			
Pensarn	d		16x11				18x12										22x26			
Llandanwg	d		16x13				18x14										22x28			
Harlech	a		16 20				18 21										22 34			
	d		16 22				18 26										22 37			
Tygwyn	d		16x26				18x29										22x40			
Talsarnau	d		16x28				18x32										22x43			
Llandecwyn	d		16x31				18x35										22x46			
Penrhyndeudraeth	d		16 35				18 39										22 50			
Minffordd	d		16 39				18 42										22 53			
Porthmadog	a		16 44				18 47										22 59			
	d		16 44				18 48										22 59			
Criccieth	d		16 52				18 56										23 07			
Penychain	d		16x57				19x01										23x12			
Abererch	d		17x00				19x04										23x15			
Pwllheli	a		17 09				19 13										23 22			

A 🍴 from Shrewsbury

For connections from London Euston please refer to Table 66

For connections from Manchester Piccadilly and Crewe please refer to Table 131

Table 75

Sundays

until 12 February

Birmingham and Shrewsbury - Chester, Aberystwyth, Barmouth and Pwllheli

Network Diagram - see first Page of Table 67

		AW	AW	AW	AW	AW	AW	AW	AW	AW		AW	AW	AW		AW	AW	AW		AW	AW		AW		
										■															
						◇	◇	◇	◇			◇	◇	◇			◇	◇		◇	◇				
		A																							
				⊼				⊼	⊼			⊼	⊼	⊼		⊼	⊼	⊼		⊼					
Birmingham International ✈	d						10 48	12 08	13 12			14 07	15 07	16 07			17 07	18 07		19 07	20 07				
Birmingham New Street 12	d						11 05	12 24	13 25			14 24	15 24	16 24			17 24	18 24		19 24	20 24				
Tame Bridge Parkway	d																								
Smethwick Galton Bridge 4	d																								
Wolverhampton 7 ⛴	d						11 27	12 42	13 42			14 43	15 43	16 43			17 43	18 43		19 43	20 43				
Cosford	d																								
Telford Central	d						11 54	12 59	13 58			14 59	15 59	16 59			17 59	18 59		19 59	20 59				
Wellington (Shropshire)	d						12 01	13 05	14 04			15 06	16 06	17 06			18 05	19 06		20 06	21 06				
Shrewsbury	a						12 15	13 18	14 18			15 19	16 26	17 19			18 19	19 19		20 19	21 19				
Cardiff Central 7	d									13 22						15 22									
Shrewsbury	d	23p33		10 16		11 27	12 17	13 27	14 20	15 22		15 27	16 27	17 27		17 30	18 20	19 27		20 22	21 30				
Gobowen	d	23p52		10 35			12 37		14 39	15 42			16 47			17 49	18 40			20 42					
Chirk	d	23p58		10 41			12 42		14 45	15 47			16 52			17 55	18 45			20 47					
Ruabon	d	00 04		10 47			12 49		14 51	15 54			16 59			18 01	18 51			20 54					
Wrexham General	a	00 10		10 53			12 55		14 57	16 00			17 05			18 07	18 57			21 00					
	d	00 14		10 54			12 56		14 58	16 00			17 05			18 08	18 58			21 01			22 35		
Chester	a	00 33		11 12			13 20		15 18	16 18			17 26			18 25	19 16			21 20			22 53		
Welshpool	d					11 49		13 49				15 49		17 49				19 49			21 52				
Newtown (Powys)	d					12 05		14 04				16 04		18 04				20 04			22 07				
Caersws	d					12 14		14 13				16 13		18 13				20 13			22 16				
Machynlleth 4	a					12 46		14 46				16 46		18 46				20 46			22 47				
	d		08 50		10 50	12 48		14 48				16 48		18 48	18 55			20 48			22 49				
Dovey Junction 4	d		08 57		10 57	12 55		14 55				16 55		18 55	19 02			20 55			22 56				
Borth	d		09 08		11 08	13 06		15 06				17 06		19 06				21 06			23 07				
Aberystwyth	a		09 25		11 27	13 23		15 25				17 25		19 24				21 25			23 26				
Penhelig	d														19x10										
Aberdovey	d														19 14										
Tywyn	a														19 20										
	d														19 21										
Tonfanau	d														19x24										
Llwyngwril	d														19x31										
Fairbourne	d														19 39										
Morfa Mawddach	d														19x41										
Barmouth	a														19 48										
	d														19 49										
Llanaber	d														19x53										
Talybont	d														19x56										
Dyffryn Ardudwy	d														20x00										
Llanbedr	d														20x04										
Pensarn	d														20x07										
Llandanwg	d														20x09										
Harlech	a														20 15										
	d														20 18										
Tygwyn	d														20x21										
Talsarnau	d														20x24										
Llandecwyn	d														20x27										
Penrhyndeudraeth	d														20 31										
Minffordd	d														20 35										
Porthmadog	a														20 40										
	d														20 41										
Criccieth	d														20 48										
Penychain	d														20x54										
Abererch	d														20x57										
Pwllheli	a														21 04										

A not 11 December

For connections from London Euston please refer to Table 66

For connections from Manchester Piccadilly and Crewe please refer to Table 131

Table 75

Sundays

19 February to 25 March

Birmingham and Shrewsbury - Chester, Aberystwyth, Barmouth and Pwllheli

Network Diagram - see first Page of Table 67

		AW	AW	AW	AW	AW	AW	AW	AW	AW		AW	AW	AW		AW	AW		AW	AW	AW		AW			
										R																
						◇	◇	◇	◇			◇	◇	◇			◇		◇	◇	◇					
				⚲				⚲	⚲			⚲	⚲	⚲		⚲	⚲		⚲	⚲						
Birmingham International ✈	d						10 48	12 08	13 12			14 07	15 07	16 07			17 07		18 07	19 07	20 07					
Birmingham New Street 12	d						11 05	12 24	13 25			14 24	15 24	16 24			17 24		18 24	19 24	20 24					
Tame Bridge Parkway	d																									
Smethwick Galton Bridge 4	d																									
Wolverhampton 7	d						11 27	12 42	13 42			14 43	15 43	16 43			17 43		18 43	19 43	20 43					
Cosford	d																									
Telford Central	d						11 54	12 59	13 58			14 59	15 59	16 59			17 59		18 59	19 59	20 59					
Wellington (Shropshire)	d						12 01	13 05	14 04			15 06	16 06	17 06			18 05		19 06	20 06	21 06					
Shrewsbury	a						12 15	13 18	14 18			15 19	16 26	17 19			18 19		19 19	20 19	21 19					
Cardiff Central 7	d									13 22						15 22										
Shrewsbury	d	23p33		10 16		11 27	12 17	13 27	14 20	15 22		15 27	16 27	17 27		17 30	18 20		19 27	20 22	21 30					
Gobowen	d	23p52		10 35			12 37		14 39	15 42			16 47			17 49	18 40			20 42						
Chirk	d	23p58		10 41			12 42		14 45	15 47			16 52			17 55	18 45			20 47						
Ruabon	d	00 04		10 47			12 49		14 51	15 54			16 59			18 01	18 51			20 54						
Wrexham General	a	00 10		10 53			12 55		14 57	16 00			17 05			18 07	18 57			21 00						
	d	00 14		10 54			12 56		14 58	16 00			17 05			18 08	18 58			21 01			22 35			
Chester	a	00 33		11 12			13 20		15 18	16 18			17 26			18 25	19 16			21 20			22 53			
Welshpool	d					11 49		13 49				15 49		17 49					19 49		21 52					
Newtown (Powys)	d					12 05		14 04				16 04		18 04					20 04		22 07					
Caersws	d					12 14		14 13				16 13		18 13					20 13		22 16					
Machynlleth 4	a					12 46		14 46				16 46		18 46					20 46		22 47					
	d		08 50		10 50	12 48		14 48				16 48		18 48	18 55				20 48		22 49					
Dovey Junction 4	d		08 57		10 57	12 55		14 55				16 55		18 55	19 02				20 55		22 56					
Borth	d		09 08		11 08	13 06		15 06				17 06		19 06					21 06		23 07					
Aberystwyth	a		09 25		11 27	13 23		15 25				17 25		19 24					21 25		23 26					
Penhelig	d														19x10											
Aberdovey	d														19 14											
Tywyn	a														19 20											
	d														19 21											
Tonfanau	d														19x24											
Llwyngwril	d														19x31											
Fairbourne	d														19 39											
Morfa Mawddach	d														19x41											
Barmouth	a														19 48											
	d														19 49											
Llanaber	d														19x53											
Talybont	d														19x56											
Dyffryn Ardudwy	d														20x00											
Llanbedr	d														20x04											
Pensarn	d														20x07											
Llandanwg	d														20x09											
Harlech	a														20 15											
	d														20 18											
Tygwyn	d														20x21											
Talsarnau	d														20x24											
Llandecwyn	d														20x27											
Penrhyndeudraeth	d														20 31											
Minffordd	d														20 35											
Porthmadog	a														20 40											
	d														20 41											
Criccieth	d														20 48											
Penychain	d														20x54											
Abererch	d														20x57											
Pwllheli	a														21 04											

For connections from London Euston please refer to Table 66

For connections from Manchester Piccadilly and Crewe please refer to Table 131

Table 75

Sundays

from 1 April

Birmingham and Shrewsbury - Chester, Aberystwyth, Barmouth and Pwllheli

Network Diagram - see first Page of Table 67

		AW	AW	AW	AW	AW	AW	AW	AW	AW		AW	AW	AW		AW	AW		AW	AW	AW		AW			
										B																
						◇	◇	◇	◇			◇	◇	◇			◇		◇	◇	◇					
				🛒				🛒	🛒			🛒	🛒	🛒		🛒	🛒		🛒	🛒						
Birmingham International ✈	d						10 48	12 08	13 12			14 07	15 07	16 07			17 07		18 07	19 07	20 07					
Birmingham New Street ■12	d						11 05	12 24	13 25			14 24	15 24	16 24			17 24		18 24	19 24	20 24					
Tame Bridge Parkway	d																									
Smethwick Galton Bridge ■4	d																									
Wolverhampton ■7	d						11 27	12 42	13 42			14 43	15 43	16 43			17 43		18 43	19 43	20 43					
Cosford	d						11 43																			
Telford Central	d						11 54	12 59	13 58			14 59	15 59	16 59			17 59		18 59	19 59	20 59					
Wellington (Shropshire)	d						12 01	13 05	14 04			15 06	16 06	17 06			18 05		19 06	20 06	21 06					
Shrewsbury	a						12 15	13 18	14 18			15 19	16 26	17 19			18 19		19 19	20 19	21 19					
Cardiff Central ■7	d									13 22						15 22										
Shrewsbury	d	23p33		10 16		11 27	12 17	13 27	14 20	15 22		15 27	16 27	17 27		17 30	18 20		19 27	20 22	21 30					
Gobowen	d	23p52		10 35			12 37		14 39	15 42			16 47			17 49	18 40			20 42						
Chirk	d	23p58		10 41			12 42		14 45	15 47			16 52			17 55	18 45			20 47						
Ruabon	d	00 04		10 47			12 49		14 51	15 54			16 59			18 01	18 51			20 54						
Wrexham General	a	00 10		10 53			12 55		14 57	16 00			17 05			18 07	18 57			21 00						
	d	00 14		10 54			12 56		14 58	16 00			17 05			18 08	18 58			21 01			22 35			
Chester	a	00 33		11 12			13 20		15 18	16 18			17 26			18 25	19 16			21 20			22 53			
Welshpool	d					11 49		13 49				15 49		17 49					19 49		21 52					
Newtown (Powys)	d					12 05		14 04				16 04		18 04					20 04		22 07					
Caersws	d					12 14		14 13				16 13		18 13					20 13		22 16					
Machynlleth ■4	a					12 46		14 46				16 46		18 46					20 46		22 47					
	d		08 50		10 50	12 48		14 48				16 48		18 48	18 55				20 48		22 49					
Dovey Junction ■4	d		08 57		10 57	12 55		14 55				16 55		18 55	19 02				20 55		22 56					
Borth	d		09 08		11 08	13 06		15 06				17 06		19 06					21 06		23 07					
Aberystwyth	a		09 25		11 27	13 23		15 25				17 25		19 24					21 25		23 26					
Penhelig	d														19x10											
Aberdovey	d														19 14											
Tywyn	a														19 20											
	d														19 21											
Tonfanau	d														19x24											
Llwyngwril	d														19x31											
Fairbourne	d														19 39											
Morfa Mawddach	d														19x41											
Barmouth	a														19 48											
	d														19 49											
Llanaber	d														19x53											
Talybont	d														19x56											
Dyffryn Ardudwy	d														20x00											
Llanbedr	d														20x04											
Pensarn	d														20x07											
Llandanwg	d														20x09											
Harlech	a														20 15											
	d														20 18											
Tygwyn	d														20x21											
Talsarnau	d														20x24											
Llandecwyn	d														20x27											
Penrhyndeudraeth	d														20 31											
Minffordd	d														20 35											
Porthmadog	a														20 40											
	d														20 41											
Criccieth	d														20 48											
Penychain	d														20x54											
Abererch	d														20x57											
Pwllheli	a														21 04											

For connections from London Euston please refer to Table 66

For connections from Manchester Piccadilly and Crewe please refer to Table 131

Pwllheli, Barmouth, Aberystwyth and Chester - Shrewsbury and Birmingham

Network Diagram - see first Page of Table 67

Miles	Miles	Miles			AW MX	AW MX	AW MO	AW MX	AW	AW	AW	AW	AW		AW	AW		AW	AW		AW	AW		AW	
					◇ A	◇ B			◇	◇ 🛒		◇ 🛒	◇		◇ 🛒	◇ 🛒		◇	◇		■ 🛒	◇ 🛒		◇	
—	0	—	**Pwllheli**	d														06 25	07 25					09 36	
—	1¾	—	Abererch	d														06x28	07x28					09x39	
—	3¼	—	Penychain	d														06x31	07x31					09x42	
—	7¾	—	Criccieth	d														06 39	07 39					09 50	
—	12¾	—	Porthmadog	a														06 47	07 47					09 58	
—	—	—		d														06 52	07 49					10 00	
—	15	—	Minffordd	d														06 56	07 53					10 04	
—	16¼	—	Penrhyndeudraeth	d														07 00	07 57					10 08	
—	17	—	Llandecwyn	d														07x02	07x59					10x10	
—	18¼	—	Talsarnau	d														07x04	08x02					10x12	
—	19	—	Tygwyn	d														07x07	08x04					10x15	
—	21½	—	Harlech	a														07 12	08 09					10 20	
—	—	—		d														07 16	08 30					10 25	
—	23½	—	Llandanwg	d														07x20	08x34					10x29	
—	24¼	—	Pensarn	d														07x21	08x35					10x30	
—	30½	—	Llanbedr	d														07x24	08x38					10x33	
—	27	—	Dyffryn Ardudwy	d														07x28	08x42					10x37	
—	28¼	—	Talybont	d														07x31	08x45					10x40	
—	25	—	Llanaber	d														07x35	08x49					10x44	
—	32	—	**Barmouth**	a														07 40	08 54					10 49	
—	—	—		d									06 46					07 49	09 00					11 04	
—	33¾	—	Morfa Mawddach	d									06x50					07x53	09x04					11x08	
—	34¾	—	Fairbourne	d									06 54					07 57	09 08					11 12	
—	37¼	—	Llwyngwril	d									07x00					08x03	09x14					11x18	
—	41½	—	Tonfanau	d									07x07					08x10	09x21					11x25	
—	44¼	—	Tywyn	a									07 11					08 14	09 25					11 30	
—	—	—		d									07 16					08 18	09 30					11 31	
—	47½	—	Aberdovey	d									07 22					08 24	09 36					11 37	
—	48½	—	Penhelig	d									07x25					08x26	09x38					11x40	
0	—	—	**Aberystwyth**	d			23p30	23p53		05 14				07 30						09 30					11 30
8¼	—	—	Borth	d			23p43	00 06		05 27				07 43						09 43					11 43
16½	53½	—	Dovey Junction ■	d			23p54	00 17		05 38			07 37	07 54				08 38	09 50	09 54				11 49	11 54
20½	57½	—	**Machynlleth** ■	a			00 04	00 24		05 45			07 44	08 03				08 48	09 57	10 03				11 59	12 03
—	—	—		d						05 47			08 07						10 07					12 07	
42¼	—	—	Caersws	d						06 15			08 37						10 37					12 37	
47¾	—	—	Newtown (Powys)	d						06 25			08 46						10 46					12 46	
61¾	—	—	Welshpool	d						06 41			09 01						11 01					13 01	
—	—	0	**Chester**	d	22p28	22p28			05 15		05 45	06 18			07 19	08 19					09 26	10 20			
—	12	—	Wrexham General	a	22p44	22p44			05 31		06 03	06 35			07 35	08 34					09 42	10 35			
—	—	—		d	22p44	22p44			05 31			06 38			07 44	08 34					09 42	10 36			
—	—	17	Ruabon	d	22p51	22p51			05 38			06 45			07 51	08 41					09 49	10 42			
—	—	21¼	Chirk	d	22p57	22p57			05 44			06 51			07 57	08 47					09 56	10 48			
—	—	24¼	Gobowen	d	23p03	23p03			05 50			06 57			08 03	08 53					10 01	10 54			
81½	—	42	**Shrewsbury**	a	23p23	23p23			06 10	07 11		07 17	09 25		08 23	09 13			11 25		10 22	11 14		13 25	
—	—	—	Cardiff Central ■	a	≀	≀			08 17			09 23				11 15					12 08	13 22			
—	—	—	**Shrewsbury**	d	23p26	23p26				07 31			09 31		08 31				11 31					13 31	
92	—	—	Wellington (Shropshire)	d	23p40	23p40				07 45			09 45		08 45				11 45					13 45	
96	—	—	Telford Central	d	23p47	23p47				07 51			09 51		08 51				11 51					13 51	
122¾	—	—	Cosford	d	≀	23p57																			
111½	—	—	**Wolverhampton** ■	a	00≀17	00≀17				08 08			10 08		09 08				12 08					14 08	
120¾	—	—	Smethwick Galton Bdg L.L.	a						08 20			10 20		09 20				12 20					14 20	
—	—	—	Tame Bridge Parkway	d																					
124¾	—	—	**Birmingham New Street** ■	a						08 26			10 26		09 25				12 26					14 26	
—	—	—	Birmingham International ✈	a						08 50			10 50		09 50				12 50					14 50	

A until 23 March

B from 27 March

For connections to Crewe and Manchester Piccadilly please refer to Table 131

For connections to London Euston please refer to Table 66

Pwllheli, Barmouth, Aberystwyth and Chester - Shrewsbury and Birmingham

Network Diagram - see first Page of Table 67

		AW	AW	AW	AW		AW	AW		AW		AW	AW	AW	AW	AW	AW	AW	AW		AW	VT	AW	AW MW FO	AW TThO
			R																						
		◇		◇	◇		◇	◇		◇		◇	◇	◇	◇	◇	◇	◇	◇		◇	◇1		◇	◇
		🛒	🛒	🛒			🛒	🛒				🛒	🛒		🛒	🛒	🛒		🛒						
Pwllheli	d				11 38					13 42				15 34				17 38							
Abererch	d				11x41					13x45				15x37				17x41							
Penychain	d				11x44					13x48				15x40				17x44							
Criccieth	d				11 52					13 56				15 48				17 52							
Porthmadog	a				12 00					14 04				15 56				18 00							
	d				12 02					14 06				15 58				18 02							
Minffordd	d				12 06					14 10				16 02				18 06							
Penrhyndeudraeth	d				12 10					14 14				16 06				18 10							
Llandecwyn	d				12x12					14x16				16x08				18x12							
Talsarnau	d				12x14					14x18				16x10				18x14							
Tygwyn	d				12x17					14x21				16x13				18x17							
Harlech	a				12 22					14 26				16 18				18 22							
	d				12 25					14 30				16 23				18 24							
Llandanwg	d				12x29					14x34				16x28				18x29							
Pensarn	d				12x30					14x35				16x29				18x31							
Llanbedr	d				12x33					14x38				16x31				18x32							
Dyffryn Ardudwy	d				12x37					14x42				16x35				18x36							
Talybont	d				12x40					14x45				16x38				18x39							
Llanaber	d				12x44					14x49				16x43				18x44							
Barmouth	a				12 49					14 54				16 48				18 49							
	d				12 53					14 57				16 53				18 51							
Morfa Mawddach	d				12x57					15x01				16x57				18x55							
Fairbourne	d				13 01					15 05				17 01				18 59							
Llwyngwril	d				13x07					15x11				17x07				19x05							
Tonfanau	d				13x14					15x18				17x14				19x12							
Tywyn	a				13 18					15 22				17 18				19 17							
	d				13 24					15 24				17 28				19 27							
Aberdovey	d				13 30					15 30				17 34				19 33							
Penhelig	d				13x32					15x32				17x36				19x36							
Aberystwyth	d			11 30		13 30					15 30						17 30				19 30				
Borth	d			11 43		13 43					15 43						17 43				19 43				
Dovey Junction 4	d			11 55	13 44	13 54				15 44	15 54			17 48			17 54	19 48			19 54				
Machynlleth 4	a			12 03	13 53	14 03				15 51	16 03			17 58			18 03	19 57			20 03				
	d			12 07	14 07					16 07							18 07				20 07				
Caersws	d			12 37	14 37					16 37							18 37				20 38				
Newtown (Powys)	d			12 46	14 46					16 46							18 46				20 48				
Welshpool	d			13 01	15 01					17 01							19 01				21 04				
Chester	d	11 21	12 19				13 21	14 19				15 20	16 19		17 23	18 18			19 28			20 22		21 21	21 21
Wrexham General	a	11 36	12 34				13 37	14 34				15 36	16 35		17 39	18 36			19 44			20 38		21 37	21 37
	d	11 36	12 34				13 37	14 34				15 36	16 35		17 40	18 36			19 44				20 49	21 37	21 37
Ruabon	d	11 44	12 41				13 44	14 41				15 43	16 42		17 47	18 43			19 51				20 57	21 44	21 44
Chirk	d	11 51	12 48				13 51	14 47				15 50	16 48		17 54	18 49			19 57				21 03	21 50	21 50
Gobowen	d	11 56	12 53				13 56	14 53				15 55	16 54		17 59	18 55			20 03				21 08	21 56	21 56
Shrewsbury	a	12 27	13 14	13 25	15 25		14 27	15 13		17 25		16 28	17 14		18 24	19 15	19 25		20 26		21 28		21 28	22 16	22 16
Cardiff Central 7	a		15 19					17 15					19 21			21 19									
Shrewsbury	d	12 31		13 31	15 31		14 31			17 31		16 33			18 31		19 33				21 33			22 18	22 18
Wellington (Shropshire)	d	12 45		13 45	15 45		14 45			17 45		16 47			18 45		19 47				21 47			22 32	22 32
Telford Central	d	12 51		13 51	15 51		14 51			17 51		16 53			18 51		19 53				21 53			22 38	22 38
Cosford	d																								
Wolverhampton 7	a	13 08		14 08	16 08		15 08			18 08		17 10			19 08		20 10				22 09			22 55	22 55
Smethwick Galton Bdg L.L.	a	13 20		14 20	16 20		15 20			18 20		17 21			19 20		20 21				22 20				
Tame Bridge Parkway	d																								
Birmingham New Street 12	a	13 26		14 26	16 26		15 26			18 26		17 27			19 26		20 26				22 32			23 27	23 28
Birmingham International ✈	a	13 50		14 50	16 50		15 50			18 50		17 50			19 50		20 50								

For connections to Crewe and Manchester Piccadilly please refer to Table 131

For connections to London Euston please refer to Table 66

Table 75

Mondays to Fridays

Pwllheli, Barmouth, Aberystwyth and Chester - Shrewsbury and Birmingham

Network Diagram - see first Page of Table 67

Station		AW	AW ◇	AW FO	AW ◇ A		AW ◇ B	AW
Pwllheli	d		20 00					
Abererch	d		20x03					
Penychain	d		20x06					
Criccieth	d		20 14					
Porthmadog	a		20 22					
	d		20 24					
Minffordd	d		20 28					
Penrhyndeudraeth	d		20 32					
Llandecwyn	d		20x34					
Talsarnau	d		20x36					
Tygwyn	d		20x39					
Harlech	a		20 44					
	d		20 46					
Llandanwg	d		20x50					
Pensarn	d		20x52					
Llanbedr	d		20x54					
Dyffryn Ardudwy	d		20x58					
Talybont	d		21x01					
Llanaber	d		21x06					
Barmouth	a		21 11					
	d		21 13	22 12				
Morfa Mawddach	d		21x17	22x16				
Fairbourne	d		21 21	22 20				
Llwyngwril	d		21x27	22x26				
Tonfanau	d		21x34	22x33				
Tywyn	a		21 39	22 37				
	d		21 46	22 39				
Aberdovey	d		21 52	22 45				
Penhelig	d		21x54	22x47				
Aberystwyth	d	21 36						23 53
Borth	d	21 49						00 06
Dovey Junction 4	d	22 00	22 06	22 59				00 17
Machynlleth 4	a	22 07	22 16	23 06				00 24
	d							
Caersws	d							
Newtown (Powys)	d							
Welshpool	d							
Chester	d				22 28		22 28	
Wrexham General	a				22 44		22 44	
	d				22 44		22 44	
Ruabon	d				22 51		22 51	
Chirk	d				22 57		22 57	
Gobowen	d				23 03		23 03	
Shrewsbury	a				23 23		23 23	
Cardiff Central 7	a							
Shrewsbury	d				23 26		23 26	
Wellington (Shropshire)	d				23 40		23 40	
Telford Central	d				23 47		23 47	
Cosford	d						23 57	
Wolverhampton 7	a				00 17		00 17	
Smethwick Galton Bdg L.L.	a							
Tame Bridge Parkway	d							
Birmingham New Street 12	a							
Birmingham International	a							

A until 23 March

B from 26 March

For connections to Crewe and Manchester Piccadilly please refer to Table 131

For connections to London Euston please refer to Table 66

Table 75

Saturdays

Pwllheli, Barmouth, Aberystwyth and Chester - Shrewsbury and Birmingham

Network Diagram - see first Page of Table 67

		AW	AW	AW	AW	AW	AW	AW		AW	AW		AW	AW		AW	AW	AW		AW	AW	AW		AW	AW
																					■				
		◇	◇		◇		◇	◇		◇	◇		◇	◇		◇	◇	◇				◇		◇	◇
		A	B																						
					🛒		🛒			🛒	🛒					🛒	🛒				🛒			🛒	🛒
Pwllheli	d												06 25	07 25				09 36				11 38			
Abererch	d												06x28	07x28				09x39				11x41			
Penychain	d												06x31	07x31				09x42				11x44			
Criccieth	d												06 39	07 39				09 50				11 52			
Porthmadog	a												06 47	07 47				09 58				12 00			
	d												06 52	07 49				10 00				12 02			
Minffordd	d												06 56	07 53				10 04				12 06			
Penrhyndeudraeth	d												07 00	07 57				10 08				12 10			
Llandecwyn	d												07x02	07x59				10x10				12x12			
Talsarnau	d												07x04	08x02				10x12				12x14			
Tygwyn	d												07x07	08x04				10x15				12x17			
Harlech	a												07 12	08 09				10 20				12 22			
	d												07 16	08 30				10 25				12 25			
Llandanwg	d												07x20	08x34				10x29				12x29			
Pensarn	d												07x21	08x35				10x30				12x30			
Llanbedr	d												07x24	08x38				10x33				12x33			
Dyffryn Ardudwy	d												07x28	08x42				10x37				12x37			
Talybont	d												07x31	08x45				10x40				12x40			
Llanaber	d												07x35	08x49				10x44				12x44			
Barmouth	a												07 40	08 54				10 49				12 49			
	d							06 46					07 49	09 00				10 52				12 53			
Morfa Mawddach	d							06x50					07x53	09x04				10x56				12x57			
Fairbourne	d							06 54					07 57	09 08				11 00				13 01			
Llwyngwril	d							07x00					08x03	09x14				11x06				13x07			
Tonfanau	d							07x07					08x10	09x21				11x13				13x14			
Tywyn	a							07 11					08 14	09 25				11 17				13 18			
	d							07 16					08 18	09 30				11 27				13 24			
Aberdovey	d							07 22					08 24	09 36				11 33				13 30			
Penhelig	d							07x25					08x26	09x38				11x36				13x32			
Aberystwyth	d			23p53	05 14				07 30						09 30				11 30				13 30		
Borth	d			00 06	05 27				07 43						09 43				11 43				13 43		
Dovey Junction ■	d			00 17	05 38			07 37	07 54				08 38	09 50	09 54			11 48	11 54			13 44	13 54		
Machynlleth ■	a			00 24	05 45			07 44	08 03				08 48	09 57	10 03			11 57	12 03			13 53	14 03		
	d				05 47			08 07						10 07				12 07				14 07			
Caersws	d				06 15			08 37						10 37				12 37				14 37			
Newtown (Powys)	d				06 25			08 46						10 46				12 46				14 46			
Welshpool	d				06 41			09 01						11 01				13 01				15 01			
Chester	d	22p28	22p28			05 37	06 12			07 21	08 19					09 20	10 19			11 21	12 19			13 20	14 19
Wrexham General	a	22p44	22p44			05 55	06 35			07 37	08 34					09 36	10 34			11 37	12 34			13 36	14 34
	d	22p44	22p44				06 38			07 37	08 34					09 36	10 35			11 37	12 34			13 36	14 34
Ruabon	d	22p51	22p51				06 45			07 44	08 41					09 43	10 42			11 44	12 41			13 43	14 41
Chirk	d	22p57	22p57				06 51			07 51	08 47					09 50	10 48			11 51	12 47			13 50	14 47
Gobowen	d	23p03	23p03				06 57			07 56	08 53					09 55	10 54			11 56	12 53			13 55	14 53
Shrewsbury	a	23p23	23p23		07 11		07 17	09 25		08 20	09 13			11 25		10 29	11 14	13 25		12 27	13 13	15 25		14 27	15 13
Cardiff Central ■	a	⟆	⟆				09 22				11 15						13 15				15 26				17 08
Shrewsbury	d	23p26	23p26		07 31			09 31		08 31				11 31		10 32		13 31		12 31		15 31		14 31	
Wellington (Shropshire)	d	23p40	23p40		07 45			09 45		08 45				11 45		10 46		13 45		12 45		15 45		14 45	
Telford Central	d	23p47	23p47		07 51			09 51		08 51				11 51		10 52		13 51		12 51		15 51		14 51	
Cosford	d	⟆	23p57																						
Wolverhampton ■ ⇌	a	00⟆17	00⟆17		08 08			10 08		09 08				12 08		11 09		14 08		13 08		16 08		15 08	
Smethwick Galton Bdg L.L.	a				08 20			10 20		09 22				12 20		11 20		14 20		13 20		16 20		15 20	
Tame Bridge Parkway	d																								
Birmingham New Street ■	a				08 26			10 26		09 26				12 26		11 26		14 26		13 26		16 26		15 26	
Birmingham International ✈	a				08 50			10 50		09 50				12 50		11 50		14 50		13 50		16 50		15 50	

A until 24 March

B from 31 March

For connections to Crewe and Manchester Piccadilly please refer to Table 131

For connections to London Euston please refer to Table 66

Table 75

Saturdays

Pwllheli, Barmouth, Aberystwyth and Chester - Shrewsbury and Birmingham

Network Diagram - see first Page of Table 67

			AW		AW	AW			AW	AW	AW	AW	AW	AW	AW	AW	AW		AW	AW	AW	AW	AW		
			◇		◇	◇			◇	◇	◇	◇	◇	◇		◇	◇			◇	◇	◇			
																					A	B			
					🚲	🚲				🚲	🚲	🚲		🚲											
Pwllheli	d		13 42						15 34				17 38							20 00					
Abererch	d		13x45						15x37				17x41							20x03					
Penychain	d		13x48						15x40				17x44							20x06					
Criccieth	d		13 56						15 48				17 52							20 14					
Porthmadog	a		14 04						15 56				18 00							20 22					
	d		14 06						15 58				18 02							20 24					
Minffordd	d		14 10						16 02				18 06							20 28					
Penrhyndeudraeth	d		14 14						16 06				18 10							20 32					
Llandecwyn	d		14x16						16x08				18x12							20x34					
Talsarnau	d		14x18						16x10				18x14							20x36					
Tygwyn	d		14x21						16x13				18x17							20x39					
Harlech	a		14 26						16 18				18 22							20 44					
	d		14 30						16 23				18 24							20 46					
Llandanwg	d		14x34						16x28				18x29							20x50					
Pensarn	d		14x35						16x29				18x31							20x52					
Llanbedr	d		14x38						16x31				18x32							20x54					
Dyffryn Ardudwy	d		14x42						16x35				18x36							20x58					
Talybont	d		14x45						16x38				18x39							21x01					
Llanaber	d		14x49						16x43				18x44							21x06					
Barmouth	a		14 54						16 48				18 49							21 11					
	d		14 57						16 53				18 51							21 13					
Morfa Mawddach	d		15x01						16x57				18x55							21x17					
Fairbourne	d		15 05						17 01				18 59							21 21					
Llwyngwril	d		15x11						17x07				19x05							21x27					
Tonfanau	d		15x18						17x14				19x12							21x34					
Tywyn	a		15 22						17 18				19 17							21 39					
	d		15 24						17 28				19 27							21 46					
Aberdovey	d		15 30						17 34				19 33							21 52					
Penhelig	d		15x32						17x36				19x36							21x54					
Aberystwyth	d			15 30								17 30				19 30			21 36				23 46		
Borth	d			15 43								17 43				19 43			21 49				23 59		
Dovey Junction 4	d		15 44	15 54					17 48			17 54	19 48			19 54			22 00	22 06			00 10		
Machynlleth 4	a		15 51	16 03					17 58			18 03	19 57			20 03			22 07	22 16			00 17		
	d			16 07								18 07				20 07									
Caersws	d			16 37								18 37				20 38									
Newtown (Powys)	d			16 46								18 46				20 48									
Welshpool	d			17 01								19 01				21 04									
Chester	d				15 20	16 19				17 28	18 20			19 29	20 27		21 20				22 28	22 28			
Wrexham General	a				15 36	16 35				17 44	18 35			19 44	20 43		21 36				22 44	22 44			
	d				15 36	16 35				17 44	18 36			19 44	20 43		21 37				22 44	22 44			
Ruabon	d				15 43	16 42				17 51	18 42			19 51	20 51		21 44				22 51	22 51			
Chirk	d				15 50	16 48				17 58	18 49			19 57	20 57		21 51				22 57	22 57			
Gobowen	d				15 55	16 54				18 03	18 54			20 03	21 02		21 57				23 03	23 03			
Shrewsbury	a			17 25	16 27	17 14				18 24	19 15	19 25		20 26	21 22	21 28	22 17				23 23	23 23			
Cardiff Central 7	a					19 16					21 21														
Shrewsbury	d			17 31	16 33					18 31		19 33				21 33	22 31				23 26	23 26			
Wellington (Shropshire)	d			17 45	16 47					18 45		19 47				21 47	22 45				23 40	23 40			
Telford Central	d			17 51	16 53					18 51		19 53				21 53	22 51				23 47	23 47			
Cosford	d																					23 57			
Wolverhampton 7	a			18 08	17 10					19 08		20 09				22 08	23 07				00 16	00 16			
Smethwick Galton Bdg L.L.	a			18 20	17 22					19 20		20 20				22 19									
Tame Bridge Parkway	d																								
Birmingham New Street 12	a			18 26	17 28					19 26		20 25				22 31	23 28								
Birmingham International ✈	a			18 50	17 50					19 50		20 49													

A until 24 March

B from 31 March

For connections to Crewe and Manchester Piccadilly please refer to Table 131

For connections to London Euston please refer to Table 66

Table 75

Sundays
until 12 February

Pwllheli, Barmouth, Aberystwyth and Chester - Shrewsbury and Birmingham

Network Diagram - see first Page of Table 67

		AW	AW	AW	AW	AW	AW	AW	AW	AW		AW	AW	AW		AW		AW	AW	AW	AW	AW	AW	AW	AW
																			■						
		◇			◇	◇	◇	◇	◇	◇		◇	◇	◇		◇		◇		◇		◇	◇		
		A	A					B	C																
						🛒	🛒	🛒	🛒	🛒			🛒			🛒			🛒	🛒					
Pwllheli	d													13 48											
Abererch	d													13x51											
Penychain	d													13x54											
Criccieth	d													14 02											
Porthmadog	a													14 10											
	d													14 12											
Minffordd	d													14 16											
Penrhyndeudraeth	d													14 20											
Llandecwyn	d													14x22											
Talsarnau	d													14x24											
Tygwyn	d													14x27											
Harlech	a													14 32											
	d													14 34											
Llandanwg	d													14x38											
Pensarn	d													14x40											
Llanbedr	d													14x42											
Dyffryn Ardudwy	d													14x46											
Talybont	d													14x49											
Llanaber	d													14x54											
Barmouth	a													14 59											
	d													15 01											
Morfa Mawddach	d													15x05											
Fairbourne	d													15 09											
Llwyngwril	d													15x15											
Tonfanau	d													15x22											
Tywyn	a													15 27											
	d													15 28											
Aberdovey	d													15 35											
Penhelig	d													15x37											
Aberystwyth	d		23p46			09 30				11 30			13 30		15 30					17 30		19 30		21 30	
Borth	d		23p59			09 43				11 43			13 43		15 43					17 43		19 43		21 43	
Dovey Junction 4	d		00⟆10			09 54				11 54			13 54	15 49	15 54					17 54		19 54		21 54	
Machynlleth 4	a		00⟆17			10 03				12 03			14 03	15 56	16 03					18 03		20 03		22 04	
	d					10 07				12 07			14 07		16 07					18 07		20 07			
Caersws	d					10 35				12 37			14 37		16 35					18 37		20 37			
Newtown (Powys)	d					10 45				12 46			14 46		16 45					18 46		20 46			
Welshpool	d					11 01				13 01			15 01		17 01					19 01		21 01			
Chester	d	22p28		08 08	09 22		11 31	12⟆21	12⟆21			13 31				15 31		17 31	18 24		19 26		21 26		22 04
Wrexham General	a	22p44		08 26	09 38		11 47	12⟆38	12⟆38			13 47				15 47		17 47	18 40		19 42		21 42		22 22
	d	22p44			09 38		11 48	12⟆38	12⟆38			13 48				15 48		17 48	18 41		19 42		21 44		
Ruabon	d	22p51			09 45		11 55	12⟆45	12⟆45			13 55				15 55		17 55	18 47		19 49		21 51		
Chirk	d	22p57			09 52		12 01	12⟆52	12⟆52			14 01				16 01		18 01	18 54		19 55		21 57		
Gobowen	d	23p03			09 57		12 07	12⟆57	12⟆57			14 07				16 07		18 07	18 59		20 01		22 02		
Shrewsbury	a	23p23			10 18	11 25	12 27	13⟆18	13⟆18	13 25		14 27	15 25		17 28	16 27		18 27	19 20	19 25	20 21	21 25	22 22		
Cardiff Central 7	a	⟆						15⟆31	15⟆35										21 36						
Shrewsbury	d	23p26			10 20	11 40	12 31			13 31		14 31	15 33		17 31	16 40		18 31		19 31	20 23	21 31	22 23		
Wellington (Shropshire)	d	23p40			10 34	11 54	12 45			13 45		14 45	15 47		17 45	16 54		18 45		19 45	20 37	21 45	22 37		
Telford Central	d	23p47			10 40	12 00	12 51			13 51		14 51	15 53		17 51	17 00		18 51		19 51	20 44	21 51	22 45		
Cosford	d	⟆																							
Wolverhampton 7 ⛴	a	00⟆16			10 56	12 16	13 07			14 07		15 07	16 09		18 10	17 15		19 07		20 07	21 11	22 07	23 13		
Smethwick Galton Bdg L.L.	a																								
Tame Bridge Parkway	d																								
Birmingham New Street 12	a				11 13	12 32	13 23			14 23		15 24	16 24		18 39	17 35		19 26		20 23	21 29	22 27			
Birmingham International ✈	a				11 31	12 56	13 55			14 55		15 55	16 55			17 56		19 55		20 55	21 56	22 55			

A not 11 December **B** until 1 January **C** from 8 January until 12 February

For connections to Crewe and Manchester Piccadilly please refer to Table 131

For connections to London Euston please refer to Table 66

Table 75

Sundays
until 12 February

Pwllheli, Barmouth, Aberystwyth and Chester - Shrewsbury and Birmingham

Network Diagram - see first Page of Table 67

		AW
Pwllheli	d	
Abererch	d	
Penychain	d	
Criccieth	d	
Porthmadog	a	
	d	
Minffordd	d	
Penrhyndeudraeth	d	
Llandecwyn	d	
Talsarnau	d	
Tygwyn	d	
Harlech	a	
	d	
Llandanwg	d	
Pensarn	d	
Llanbedr	d	
Dyffryn Ardudwy	d	
Talybont	d	
Llanaber	d	
Barmouth	a	
	d	
Morfa Mawddach	d	
Fairbourne	d	
Llwyngwril	d	
Tonfanau	d	
Tywyn	a	
	d	
Aberdovey	d	
Penhelig	d	
Aberystwyth	d	23 30
Borth	d	23 43
Dovey Junction 4	d	23 54
Machynlleth 4	a	00 04
	d	
Caersws	d	
Newtown (Powys)	d	
Welshpool	d	
Chester	d	
Wrexham General	a	
	d	
Ruabon	d	
Chirk	d	
Gobowen	d	
Shrewsbury	a	
Cardiff Central 7	a	
Shrewsbury	d	
Wellington (Shropshire)	d	
Telford Central	d	
Cosford	d	
Wolverhampton 7	a	
Smethwick Galton Bdg L.L.	a	
Tame Bridge Parkway	d	
Birmingham New Street 12	a	
Birmingham International	a	

For connections to Crewe and Manchester Piccadilly please refer to Table 131

For connections to London Euston please refer to Table 66

Table 75

Sundays

19 February to 25 March

Pwllheli, Barmouth, Aberystwyth and Chester - Shrewsbury and Birmingham

Network Diagram - see first Page of Table 67

Station		AW	AW	AW	AW	AW	AW	AW	AW	AW		AW	AW		AW		AW	AW	AW	AW	AW	AW	AW	AW	AW
																		B							
		◇			◇	◇	◇	◇	◇	◇		◇	◇		◇		◇		◇		◇	◇			
						🍴	🍴	🍴	🍴			🍴			🍴			🍴	🍴						
Pwllheli	d												13 48												
Abererch	d												13x51												
Penychain	d												13x54												
Criccieth	d												14 02												
Porthmadog	a												14 10												
	d												14 12												
Minffordd	d												14 16												
Penrhyndeudraeth	d												14 20												
Llandecwyn	d												14x22												
Talsarnau	d												14x24												
Tygwyn	d												14x27												
Harlech	a												14 32												
	d												14 34												
Llandanwg	d												14x38												
Pensarn	d												14x40												
Llanbedr	d												14x42												
Dyffryn Ardudwy	d												14x46												
Talybont	d												14x49												
Llanaber	d												14x54												
Barmouth	a												14 59												
	d												15 01												
Morfa Mawddach	d												15x05												
Fairbourne	d												15 09												
Llwyngwril	d												15x15												
Tonfanau	d												15x22												
Tywyn	a												15 27												
	d												15 28												
Aberdovey	d												15 35												
Penhelig	d												15x37												
Aberystwyth	d		23p46			09 30			11 30			13 30		15 30					17 30		19 30		21 30		23 30
Borth	d		23p59			09 43			11 43			13 43		15 43					17 43		19 43		21 43		23 43
Dovey Junction 4	d		00 10			09 54			11 54			13 54	15 49	15 54					17 54		19 54		21 54		23 54
Machynlleth 4	a		00 17			10 03			12 03			14 03	15 56	16 03					18 03		20 03		22 04		00 04
	d					10 07			12 07			14 07	16 07						18 07		20 07				
Caersws	d					10 35			12 37			14 37	16 35						18 37		20 37				
Newtown (Powys)	d					10 45			12 46			14 46	16 45						18 46		20 46				
Welshpool	d					11 01			13 01			15 01	17 01						19 01		21 01				
Chester	d	22p28		08 08	09 22		11 31	12 21		13 31					15 31		17 31	18 24		19 26		21 26		22 04	
Wrexham General	a	22p44		08 26	09 38		11 47	12 38		13 47					15 47		17 47	18 40		19 42		21 42		22 22	
	d	22p44			09 38		11 48	12 38		13 48					15 48		17 48	18 41		19 42		21 44			
Ruabon	d	22p51			09 45		11 55	12 45		13 55					15 55		17 55	18 47		19 49		21 51			
Chirk	d	22p57			09 52		12 01	12 52		14 01					16 01		18 01	18 54		19 55		21 57			
Gobowen	d	23p03			09 57		12 07	12 57		14 07					16 07		18 07	18 59		20 01		22 02			
Shrewsbury	a	23p23			10 18	11 25	12 27	13 18	13 25	14 27		15 25	17 28		16 27		18 27	19 20	19 25	20 21	21 25	22 22			
Cardiff Central 7	a							15 31										21 45							
Shrewsbury	d	23p26			10 20	11 40	12 31		13 31	14 31		15 33	17 31		16 40		18 31		19 31	20 23	21 31	22 23			
Wellington (Shropshire)	d	23p40			10 34	11 54	12 45		13 45	14 45		15 47	17 45		16 54		18 45		19 45	20 37	21 45	22 37			
Telford Central	d	23p47			10 40	12 00	12 51		13 51	14 51		15 53	17 51		17 00		18 51		19 51	20 44	21 51	22 45			
Cosford	d																								
Wolverhampton 7 ⛴	a	00 16			10 56	12 16	13 07		14 07	15 07		16 09	18 10		17 15		19 07		20 07	21 11	22 07	23 13			
Smethwick Galton Bdg L.L.	a																								
Tame Bridge Parkway	d																								
Birmingham New Street 12	a				11 13	12 32	13 23		14 23	15 24		16 24	18 39		17 35		19 26		20 23	21 29	22 27				
Birmingham International ✈	a				11 31	12 56	13 55		14 55	15 55		16 55			17 56		19 55		20 55	21 56	22 55				

For connections to Crewe and Manchester Piccadilly please refer to Table 131

For connections to London Euston please refer to Table 66

Table 75

Sundays
from 1 April

Pwllheli, Barmouth, Aberystwyth and Chester - Shrewsbury and Birmingham

Network Diagram - see first Page of Table 67

		AW	AW	AW	AW	AW	AW	AW	AW	AW		AW	AW		AW		AW	AW	AW	AW	AW	AW	AW	AW	AW
		◇			◇	◇ 🛒	◇ 🛒	◇ 🛒	◇ 🛒	◇		◇ 🛒	◇		◇ 🛒		◇	■R 🛒	◇ 🛒		◇	◇			
Pwllheli	d												13 48												
Abererch	d												13x51												
Penychain	d												13x54												
Criccieth	d												14 02												
Porthmadog	a												14 10												
	d												14 12												
Minffordd	d												14 16												
Penrhyndeudraeth	d												14 20												
Llandecwyn	d												14x22												
Talsarnau	d												14x24												
Tygwyn	d												14x27												
Harlech	a												14 32												
	d												14 34												
Llandanwg	d												14x38												
Pensarn	d												14x40												
Llanbedr	d												14x42												
Dyffryn Ardudwy	d												14x46												
Talybont	d												14x49												
Llanaber	d												14x54												
Barmouth	a												14 59												
	d												15 01												
Morfa Mawddach	d												15x05												
Fairbourne	d												15 09												
Llwyngwril	d												15x15												
Tonfanau	d												15x22												
Tywyn	a												15 27												
	d												15 28												
Aberdovey	d												15 35												
Penhelig	d												15x37												
Aberystwyth	d		23p46			09 30			11 30			13 30		15 30					17 30		19 30		21 30		23 30
Borth	d		23p59			09 43			11 43			13 43		15 43					17 43		19 43		21 43		23 43
Dovey Junction 4	d		00 10			09 54			11 54			13 54	15 49	15 54					17 54		19 54		21 54		23 54
Machynlleth 4	a		00 17			10 03			12 03			14 03	15 56	16 03					18 03		20 03		22 04		00 04
	d					10 07			12 07			14 07	16 07						18 07		20 07				
Caersws	d					10 35			12 37			14 37	16 35						18 37		20 37				
Newtown (Powys)	d					10 45			12 46			14 46	16 45						18 46		20 46				
Welshpool	d					11 01			13 01			15 01	17 01						19 01		21 01				
Chester	d	22p28		08 08	09 22		11 31	12 21		13 31					15 31		17 31	18 24		19 26		21 26		22 04	
Wrexham General	a	22p44		08 26	09 38		11 47	12 38		13 47					15 47		17 47	18 40		19 42		21 42		22 22	
	d	22p44			09 38		11 48	12 38		13 48					15 48		17 48	18 41		19 42		21 44			
Ruabon	d	22p51			09 45		11 55	12 45		13 55					15 55		17 55	18 47		19 49		21 51			
Chirk	d	22p57			09 52		12 01	12 52		14 01					16 01		18 01	18 54		19 55		21 57			
Gobowen	d	23p03			09 57		12 07	12 57		14 07					16 07		18 07	18 59		20 01		22 02			
Shrewsbury	a	23p23			10 18	11 25	12 27	13 18	13 25	14 27		15 25	17 28		16 27		18 27	19 20	19 25	20 21	21 25	22 22			
Cardiff Central 7	a							15 31										21 36							
Shrewsbury	d	23p26			10 20	11 40	12 31		13 31	14 31		15 33	17 31		16 40		18 31		19 31	20 23	21 31	22 23			
Wellington (Shropshire)	d	23p40			10 34	11 54	12 45		13 45	14 45		15 47	17 45		16 54		18 45		19 45	20 37	21 45	22 37			
Telford Central	d	23p47			10 40	12 00	12 51		13 51	14 51		15 53	17 51		17 00		18 51		19 51	20 44	21 51	22 45			
Cosford	d	23p57																		20 54		22 56			
Wolverhampton 7	a	00 16			10 56	12 16	13 07		14 07	15 07		16 09	18 10		17 15		19 07		20 07	21 11	22 07	23 13			
Smethwick Galton Bdg L.L.	a																								
Tame Bridge Parkway	d																								
Birmingham New Street 12	a				11 13	12 32	13 23		14 23	15 24		16 24	18 39		17 35		19 26		20 23	21 29	22 27				
Birmingham International	a				11 31	12 56	13 55		14 55	15 55		16 55			17 56		19 55		20 55	21 56	22 55				

For connections to Crewe and Manchester Piccadilly please refer to Table 131

For connections to London Euston please refer to Table 66

Network Diagram for Tables 78, 79, 84, 85, 86

DM-22/08
Design BAJS

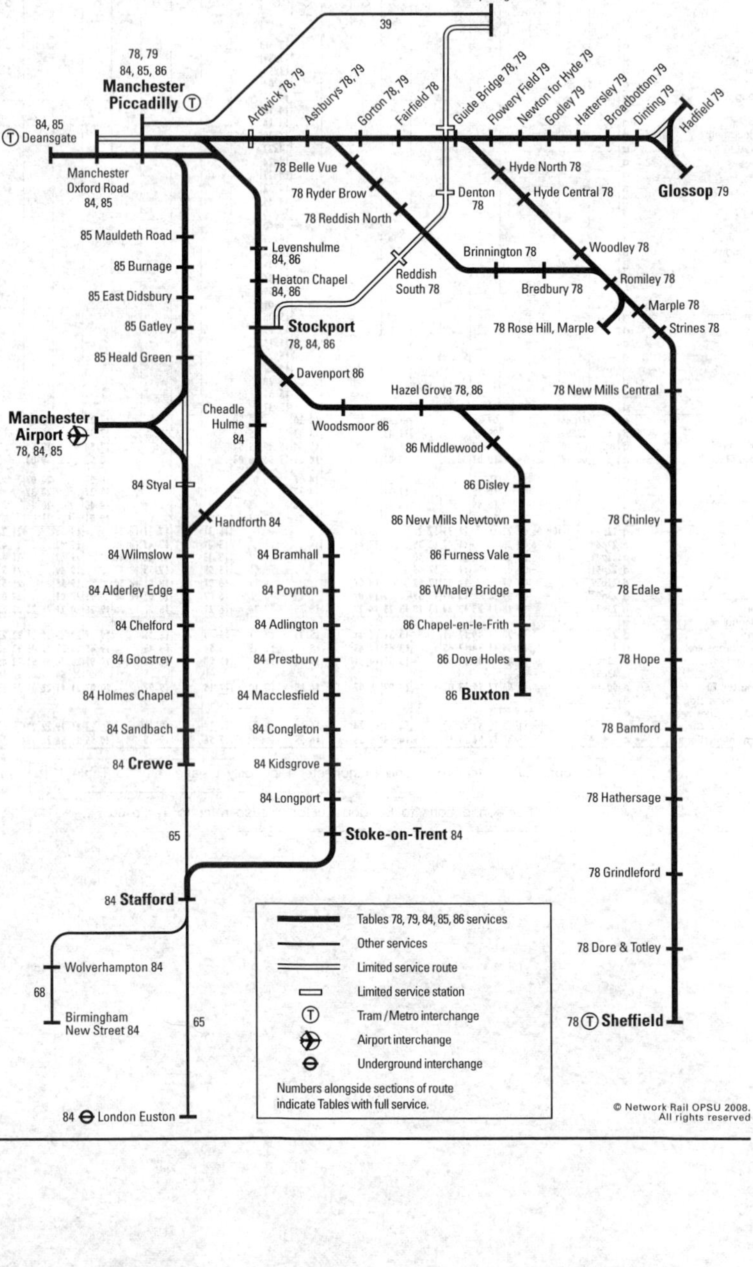

Manchester Airport and Manchester Romiley, Marple, Chinley and Sheffield

Network Diagram - see first Page of Table 78

Miles	Miles	Miles			TP MO ◇1	TP MX ◇1	TP ◇1 A	NT	NT B	NT C	NT D	NT	NT E		NT	NT B	NT	NT B	NT F	NT B	TP ◇1 A	NT E	NT		NT
—	—	—	**Manchester Airport** 85 ✈	d	22p55	23p52	05 15														06 55				
0	0	—	**Manchester Piccadilly** 10	a	23p09	00 09	05 33														07 13				
—	—	—		d	23p20	00 15	05 44	05 50	06 13	06 16	06 24	06 30			06 41	06 46	06 57	07 03	07 08	07 18	07 20		07 23		07 39
0½	0½	—	Ardwick	d																					
1½	1½	—	Ashburys	d					06 17	06 20					06 45	06 50		07 07	07 12	07 22			07 27		
2½	—	—	Belle Vue	d											06 47								07 29		
2¾	—	—	Ryder Brow	d											06 49								07 31		
3¾	—	—	Reddish North	d											06 52				07 17				07 34		
5½	—	—	Brinnington	d											06 55				07 20				07 37		
6½	—	—	Bredbury	d											06 58				07 23				07 40		
—	2½	—	Gorton	d					06 19	06 22						06 52		07 09		07 24					
—	3½	—	Fairfield	d							06 31														07 46
—	4¾	—	Guide Bridge	a					06 23	06 26	06 34					06 56		07 13		07 28					07 49
—	—	—		d							06 34														07 49
—	6½	—	Hyde North	d							06 38														07 53
—	7¾	—	Hyde Central	d							06 40														07 55
—	9¼	—	Woodley	d							06 43		←												07 58
7½	10½	—	**Romiley**	d							06 47	06 44	06 47		07 02		07 09		07 26				07 43		08 02
—	12½	—	Rose Hill Marple	d							↪		06a53												08a08
9	—	—	**Marple**	d								06 47			07 05		07 13		07 30				07a48		
11¼	—	—	Strines	d																					
12¾	—	—	New Mills Central	a								06 55			07 12		07 20		07 35						
—	—	—		d															07 39						
—	—	—	Stockport 86	d	23p28		05 52	06 00													07 28				
—	—	0	Hazel Grove 86	d				06 07																	
16½	—	8½	**Chinley**	d				06 18											07 47						
22	—	—	Edale	d				06 26											07 55						
27¼	—	—	Hope (Derbyshire)	d				06 32											08 01						
29	—	—	Bamford	d				06 35											08 04						
30¾	—	—	Hathersage	d				06 39											08 09						
32¼	—	—	Grindleford	d				06 42											08 11			←			
37¾	—	—	Dore & Totley	d				06 51											08 22		08 03	08 22			
42	—	—	**Sheffield** 7	a	00 15	01 06	06 49	07 01											↪		08 10	08 32			

		EM ◇ G	NT B	NT	NT	NT B	NT D	NT	NT E		TP ◇1 A	NT B	NT	EM ◇ G	NT	NT C	NT D	NT	NT E		NT C	NT	TP ◇1 A	NT	EM ◇ G
Manchester Airport 85 ✈	d										07 53												08 55		
Manchester Piccadilly 10	a										08 12												09 13		
	d	07 42	07 48	07 52	08 04	08 07	08 12	08 15			08 20	08 29	08 37	08 43	08 45	08 48	09 00	09 05			09 15	09 18	09 20	09 36	09 43
Ardwick	d																								
Ashburys	d		07 52		08 08	08 11						08 33				08 52		09 09			09 19	09 23			
Belle Vue	d				08 10																	09 26			
Ryder Brow	d				08 12																	09 28			
Reddish North	d				08 15										08 52			09 14							
Brinnington	d				08 18										08 56			09 17							
Bredbury	d				08 21										08 59			09 20							
Gorton	d		07 54			08 13						08 35				08 54					09 21				
Fairfield	d						08 20										09 07							09 43	
Guide Bridge	a		07 58			08 17	08 23					08 39				08 58	09 10				09 25			09 46	
	d						08 23										09 11							09 46	
Hyde North	d						08 28										09 17							09 50	
Hyde Central	d						08 30										09 20							09 52	
Woodley	d						08 33		←								09 23		←					09 55	
Romiley	d			08 05	08 24		08 37	08 29	08 37						09 02		09 26	09 23	09 26			09 35		09 59	
Rose Hill Marple	d				08a30		↪		08a45								↪		09a33					10a05	
Marple	d			08 08				08a33					08 52		09 06			09a28				09a40			
Strines	d												08 56												
New Mills Central	a			08 15									09 01		09 11										
	d														09 11										
Stockport 86	d	07 54									08 28			08 54									09 28		09 54
Hazel Grove 86	d																								
Chinley	d														09 19										
Edale	d														09 28										
Hope (Derbyshire)	d														09 34										
Bamford	d														09 37										
Hathersage	d														09 40										
Grindleford	d														09 44										
Dore & Totley	d	08 28													09 57										
Sheffield 7	a	08 34									09 08			09 35	10 07								10 08		10 35

A To Cleethorpes
B To Manchester Piccadilly
C To Hadfield
D To Rose Hill Marple
E From Manchester Piccadilly
F To Sheffield
G From Liverpool Lime Street to Norwich

Manchester Airport and Manchester Romiley, Marple, Chinley and Sheffield

Network Diagram - see first Page of Table 78

		NT	NT A	NT	NT A		NT	TP ◇1 B 🚲	NT	EM ◇ C	NT	NT A	NT	NT A	TP ◇1 B 🚲		NT	NT	EM ◇ C	NT	NT A	NT	NT A	TP ◇1 B 🚲	NT
Manchester Airport 85 ✈	d							09 55							10 55									11 55	
Manchester Piccadilly 10 🚌	a							10 13							11 13									12 13	
	d	09 45	09 48	10 03	10 15		10 18	10 20	10 36	10 43	10 45	10 48	11 03	11 18	11 20		11 23	11 36	11 43	11 45	11 48	12 03	12 18	12 20	12 23
Ardwick	d																								
Ashburys	d		09 52	10 07	10 19							10 52	11 07	11 22							11 52	12 07	12 22		
Belle Vue	d			10 09									11 09									12 09			
Ryder Brow	d			10 11									11 11									12 11			
Reddish North	d	09 52		10 14							10 52		11 14							11 52		12 14			
Brinnington	d	09 56		10 17							10 56		11 17							11 56		12 17			
Bredbury	d	09 59		10 20							10 59		11 20							11 59		12 20			
Gorton	d		09 54		10 21							10 54		11 24							11 54		12 24		
Fairfield	d								10 43									11 43							
Guide Bridge	a		09 58		10 25				10 46			10 58		11 28				11 46			11 58		12 28		
	d								10 46									11 46							
Hyde North	d								10 50									11 50							
Hyde Central	d								10 52									11 52							
Woodley	d								10 55									11 55							
Romiley	d	10 02		10 23			10 37		10 59		11 02		11 23				11 37	11 59		12 02		12 23			12 37
Rose Hill Marple	d						10a42		11a05								11a43	12a05							12a43
Marple	d	10 06		10 27							11 06		11 27							12 06		12 27			
Strines	d	10 10																		12 10					
New Mills Central	a	10 15		10 34							11 11		11 34							12 15		12 34			
	d										11 11														
Stockport 86	d							10 28		10 54					11 28				11 54					12 28	
Hazel Grove 86	d																								
Chinley	d										11 19														
Edale	d										11 28														
Hope (Derbyshire)	d										11 34														
Bamford	d										11 37														
Hathersage	d										11 40														
Grindleford	d										11 44														
Dore & Totley	d										11 53														
Sheffield 7 🚌	a							11 08		11 34	12 03				12 08				12 35					13 08	

			NT	EM ◇ C	NT	NT A	NT	NT A	TP ◇1 B 🚲	NT	NT		EM ◇ C	NT	NT A	NT	NT A	TP ◇1 B 🚲	NT	NT	EM ◇ C		NT	NT A	NT
Manchester Airport 85 ✈	d								12 55									13 55							
Manchester Piccadilly 10 🚌	a								13 13									14 13							
	d		12 36	12 43	12 45	12 48	13 03	13 18	13 20	13 23	13 36		13 43	13 45	13 48	14 03	14 18	14 20	14 23	14 36	14 43		14 45	14 48	15 03
Ardwick	d																								
Ashburys	d					12 52	13 07	13 22							13 52	14 07	14 22							14 52	15 07
Belle Vue	d						13 09									14 09									15 09
Ryder Brow	d						13 11									14 11									15 11
Reddish North	d				12 52		13 14							13 52		14 14							14 52		15 14
Brinnington	d				12 56		13 17							13 56		14 17							14 56		15 17
Bredbury	d				12 59		13 20							13 59		14 20							14 59		15 20
Gorton	d					12 54		13 24							13 54		14 24							14 54	
Fairfield	d		12 43								13 43									14 43					
Guide Bridge	a		12 46			12 58		13 28			13 46				13 58		14 28			14 46				14 58	
	d		12 46								13 46									14 46					
Hyde North	d		12 50								13 50									14 50					
Hyde Central	d		12 52								13 52									14 52					
Woodley	d		12 55								13 55									14 55					
Romiley	d		12 59		13 02		13 23			13 37	13 59			14 02		14 23			14 37	14 59			15 02		15 23
Rose Hill Marple	d		13a05							13a43	14a05								14a43	15a05					
Marple	d				13 06		13 27							14 06		14 27							15 06		15 27
Strines	d													14 10											
New Mills Central	a				13 11		13 34							14 15		14 34							15 11		15 34
	d				13 11																		15 11		
Stockport 86	d			12 54					13 28				13 54					14 28			14 54				
Hazel Grove 86	d																								
Chinley	d				13 19																		15 19		
Edale	d				13 28																		15 28		
Hope (Derbyshire)	d				13 34																		15 34		
Bamford	d				13 37																		15 37		
Hathersage	d				13 40																		15 40		
Grindleford	d				13 44																		15 44		
Dore & Totley	d				13 57																		15 58		
Sheffield 7 🚌	a			13 35	14 04				14 08				14 35					15 08			15 35		16 04		

A To Hadfield
B To Cleethorpes
C From Liverpool Lime Street to Norwich

Manchester Airport and Manchester Romiley, Marple, Chinley and Sheffield

Network Diagram - see first Page of Table 78

		NT	TP	NT	NT	EM	NT	NT	NT	NT	NT	TP	NT	NT	EM	NT	NT	NT	NT	NT	NT	TP	NT	NT
			◇■1			◇						◇■1			◇							◇■1		
		A	B			C		D			D	B		D	C			D		D		B		
			🚲									🚲										🚲		
Manchester Airport 85 ✈	d		14 55									15 55										16 55		
Manchester Piccadilly 10 🚌	a		15 13									16 13										17 13		
	d	15 18	15 20	15 23	15 36	15 43	15 45	15 48	16 03	16 06	16 15	16 20	16 23	16 36	16 43	16 45	16 48	16 59	17 03	17 15	17 18	17 20	17 21	17 23
Ardwick	d																		17 07					17 25
Ashburys	d	15 22						15 52	16 07		16 19			16 40		16 49	16 52	17 03	17 09	17 19				
Belle Vue	d								16 09										17 12					
Ryder Brow	d								16 11										17 14					
Reddish North	d						15 52		16 14				16 30			16 54			17 16					
Brinnington	d						15 56		16 17				16 34			16 57			17 20					
Bredbury	d						15 59		16 20				16 37			17 00			17 23		17 30			
Gorton	d	15 24						15 54			16 21			16 42				17 05		17 21				
Fairfield	d				15 43					16 13							16 56							
Guide Bridge	a	15 28			15 46			15 58		16 16	16 25			16 46			16 59	17 10		17 25			17 30	
	d				15 46					16 16							16 59						17 30	
Hyde North	d				15 50					16 20							17 03						17 34	
Hyde Central	d				15 52					16 22							17 05						17 36	
Woodley	d				15 55					16 25							17 08						17 39	
Romiley	d			15 37	15 59		16 02		16 23	16 29			16 40			17 03	17 13		17 27		17 33		17 43	
Rose Hill Marple	d			15a43	16a05					16a36							17a20						17a49	
Marple	d						16 06		16 27				16a44			17 07			17a31		17 38			
Strines	d						16 10																	
New Mills Central	a						16 13		16 34							17 13					17 43			
	d						16 13									17 13								
Stockport 86	d		15 28			15 54						16 28			16 54							17 28		17 36
Hazel Grove 86	d																							17 47
Chinley	d						16 21								17 09	17 19								18 00
Edale	d						16 30									17 28								
Hope (Derbyshire)	d						16 36									17 34								
Bamford	d						16 39									17 37								
Hathersage	d						16 42									17 40								
Grindleford	d						16 46									17 44								
Dore & Totley	d						16 54								17 31	17 56						18 03		
Sheffield 7 🚌	a		16 08			16 34	17 03					17 08			17 40	18 04						18 10		

		NT	NT	EM	NT	NT	NT	NT	NT	TP	NT	NT	EM	NT	NT	NT	TP	NT	NT	EM	NT	NT
				◇						◇■1			◇				◇■1			◇		
			D	E		D			A	B			C		A		B	A		E		A
										🚲												
Manchester Airport 85 ✈	d									17 55							18 55					
Manchester Piccadilly 10 🚌	a									18 13							19 13					
	d	17 32	17 37	17 43	17 48	17 59	18 03	18 06	18 15	18 20	18 22	18 36	18 43	18 45	18 48	19 00	19 18	19 18	19 23	19 43	19 45	19 48
Ardwick	d							18 09														
Ashburys	d	17 36	17 41			18 03	18 07	18 11	18 19						18 52	19 04		19 22			19 49	19 52
Belle Vue	d	17 38					18 09									19 06					19 51	
Ryder Brow	d	17 40					18 11									19 08					19 53	
Reddish North	d	17 43			17 55		18 14				18 30			18 52		19 11					19 56	
Brinnington	d	17 46			17 59		18 17							18 56		19 14					19 59	
Bredbury	d	17 49			18 02		18 20				18 36			18 59		19 17					20 02	
Gorton	d		17 43			18 05			18 21						18 54			19 24				19 54
Fairfield	d							18 15				18 43										
Guide Bridge	a		17 47			18 09		18 18	18 25			18 46			18 58			19 28				19 58
	d							18 18				18 46										
Hyde North	d							18 22				18 50										
Hyde Central	d							18 25				18 52										
Woodley	d							18 28				18 55										
Romiley	d	17 53			18 05		18 23	18 31			18 39	18 59		19 02		19 20			19 38		20 05	
Rose Hill Marple	d							18a37				19a05										
Marple	d	17 57			18 08		18a28				18 42			19 06		19a25			19a43		20 09	
Strines	d	18 01									18 46										20 13	
New Mills Central	a	18 04			18 14						18 52			19 11							20 18	
	d				18 14									19 11								
Stockport 86	d			17 54						18 28			18 54				19 26			19 54		
Hazel Grove 86	d																					
Chinley	d			18 09	18 20									19 19								
Edale	d				18 30									19 28								
Hope (Derbyshire)	d				18 36									19 34								
Bamford	d				18 39									19 37								
Hathersage	d				18 42									19 40								
Grindleford	d				18 46									19 44								
Dore & Totley	d			18 34	18 56					19 03				19 53			20 01					
Sheffield 7 🚌	a			18 41	19 06					19 09			19 33	20 03			20 08			20 36		

A To Hadfield
B To Cleethorpes
C From Liverpool Lime Street to Norwich
D To Manchester Piccadilly
E From Liverpool Lime Street to Nottingham

Manchester Airport and Manchester Romiley, Marple, Chinley and Sheffield

Network Diagram - see first Page of Table 78

			TP	NT	EM	NT	NT	TP	NT	NT		TP	EM	NT	NT	NT	NT	TP
			◇1		◇			◇1				◇1	◇					◇1
					A		B	C		B			A		B		D	
Manchester Airport	85 ✈	d	19 55					20 47				21 47						23 52
Manchester Piccadilly 10	🚌	a	20 13					21 13				22 13						00 09
		d	20 20	20 36	20 43	20 45	20 48	21 20	21 45	21 48		22 20	22 28	22 45	22 48	23 24	23 27	00 15
Ardwick		d																
Ashburys		d					20 52		21 49	21 52				22 49	22 52	23 28	23 31	
Belle Vue		d							21 51					22 51		23 30		
Ryder Brow		d							21 53					22 53		23 32		
Reddish North		d				20 52			21 56					22 56		23 35		
Brinnington		d				20 56			21 59					22 59		23 38		
Bredbury		d				20 59			22 02					23 02		23 41		
Gorton		d					20 54			21 54					22 54		23 33	
Fairfield		d		20 43														
Guide Bridge		a		20 46			20 58			21 58					22 58		23 37	
		d		20 46														
Hyde North		d		20 50														
Hyde Central		d		20 52														
Woodley		d		20 55														
Romiley		d		20 59		21 02			22 05					23 05		23 44		
Rose Hill Marple		d		21a05														
Marple		d				21 06			22 09					23 09		23 48		
Strines		d							22 13					23 13		23 52		
New Mills Central		a				21 11			22 18					23 18		23 57		
		d				21 11												
Stockport	86	d	20 28		20 54			21 28				22 28	22 37					
Hazel Grove	86	d																
Chinley		d				21 19							22 53					
Edale		d				21 28							23 02					
Hope (Derbyshire)		d				21 34							23 08					
Bamford		d				21 37							23 11					
Hathersage		d				21 41							23 15					
Grindleford		d				21 44							23 19					
Dore & Totley		d	21 03			21 52							23 28					
Sheffield 7	🚌	a	21 11		21 35	22 05		22 08				23 16	23 35					01 06

Saturdays

			TP	TP	NT	NT	NT	NT	NT	NT	TP		NT	EM	NT	NT	NT	NT	TP	NT	NT		EM	NT	NT	NT
			◇1	◇1							◇1			◇					◇1				◇			
				C		B		B		B	C			E		B		B	C				E		B	
											🍴								🍴							
Manchester Airport	85 ✈	d	23p52	05 20							06 55								07 53							
Manchester Piccadilly 10	🚌	a	00 09	05 35							07 13								08 12							
		d	00 15	05 44	05 50	06 16	06 35	06 48	07 03	07 18	07 20		07 39	07 42	07 44	07 48	08 03	08 15	08 20	08 23	08 36		08 43	08 45	08 48	09 03
Ardwick		d																								
Ashburys		d				06 20	06 39	06 52	07 07	07 22						07 52	08 07	08 19							08 52	09 07
Belle Vue		d					06 41		07 09								08 09									09 09
Ryder Brow		d					06 43		07 11								08 11									09 11
Reddish North		d					06 46		07 14						07 52		08 14							08 52		09 14
Brinnington		d					06 49		07 17						07 56		08 17							08 56		09 17
Bredbury		d					06 52		07 20						07 59		08 20							08 59		09 20
Gorton		d				06 22		06 54		07 24						07 54		08 21							08 54	
Fairfield		d											07 46								08 43					
Guide Bridge		a				06 26		06 58		07 28			07 49			07 58		08 25			08 46				08 58	
		d											07 49								08 46					
Hyde North		d											07 53								08 50					
Hyde Central		d											07 55								08 52					
Woodley		d											07 58								08 55					
Romiley		d					06 55		07 23				08 02		08 02		08 23			08 37	08 59			09 02		09 23
Rose Hill Marple		d											08a10								09a05					
Marple		d					06 59		07a28						08 06		08a28			08a43				09 06		09a28
Strines		d																						09 10		
New Mills Central		a					07 04								08 11									09 13		
		d					07 04								08 11									09 13		
Stockport	86	d		05 52	06 00						07 28			07 54					08 28				08 54			
Hazel Grove	86	d			06 07																					
Chinley		d			06 18		07 12								08 19									09 21		
Edale		d			06 26		07 21								08 28									09 30		
Hope (Derbyshire)		d			06 32		07 27								08 34									09 36		
Bamford		d			06 35		07 30								08 37									09 39		
Hathersage		d			06 39		07 33								08 40									09 42		
Grindleford		d			06 42		07 37								08 44									09 46		
Dore & Totley		d			06 51		07 47				08 03			08 28	08 53									09 57		
Sheffield 7	🚌	a	01 06	06 49	07 01		07 57				08 10			08 34	09 03				09 08				09 35	10 06		

A From Liverpool Lime Street to Nottingham
B To Hadfield
C To Cleethorpes
D To Glossop
E From Liverpool Lime Street to Norwich

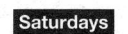

Manchester Airport and Manchester Romiley, Marple, Chinley and Sheffield

Network Diagram - see first Page of Table 78

		NT	TP	NT	NT	EM		NT	NT	NT	NT	TP	NT	NT	EM	NT		NT	NT	NT	TP	NT	NT	EM	NT
			◇1			◇						◇1			◇						◇1			◇	
		A	B			C			A		A	B			C			A		A	B			C	
Manchester Airport 85 ✈	d		08 55									09 55									10 55				
Manchester Piccadilly 10	a		09 13									10 13									11 13				
	d	09 18	09 20	09 23	09 36	09 43		09 45	09 48	10 03	10 18	10 20	10 23	10 36	10 43	10 45		10 48	11 03	11 18	11 20	11 23	11 36	11 43	11 45
Ardwick	d																								
Ashburys	d	09 22							09 52	10 07	10 22							10 52	11 07	11 22					
Belle Vue	d									10 09									11 09						
Ryder Brow	d									10 11									11 11						
Reddish North	d							09 52		10 14						10 52			11 14						11 52
Brinnington	d							09 56		10 17						10 56			11 17						11 56
Bredbury	d							09 59		10 20						10 59			11 20						11 59
Gorton	d	09 24							09 54		10 24							10 54		11 24					
Fairfield	d				09 43									10 43									11 43		
Guide Bridge	a	09 28			09 46				09 58		10 28			10 46				10 58		11 28			11 46		
	d				09 46									10 46									11 46		
Hyde North	d				09 50									10 50									11 50		
Hyde Central	d				09 52									10 52									11 52		
Woodley	d				09 55									10 55									11 55		
Romiley	d			09 37	09 59			10 02		10 23			10 37	10 59		11 02			11 23			11 37	11 59		12 02
Rose Hill Marple	d				10a05								10a43	11a05								11a43	12a05		
Marple	d			09a43				10 06		10a28						11 06			11a28						12 06
Strines	d							10 10																	12 10
New Mills Central	a							10 13								11 11									12 13
	d							10 13								11 11									12 13
Stockport 86	d		09 28			09 54						10 28			10 54						11 28			11 54	
Hazel Grove 86	d																								
Chinley	d							10 21								11 19									12 21
Edale	d							10 30								11 28									12 30
Hope (Derbyshire)	d							10 36								11 34									12 36
Bamford	d							10 39								11 37									12 39
Hathersage	d							10 42								11 40									12 42
Grindleford	d							10 46								11 44									12 46
Dore & Totley	d							10 57								11 57									12 54
Sheffield 7	a		10 08			10 35		11 04				11 08			11 35	12 04					12 08			12 35	13 03

		NT		NT	NT	TP	NT	NT	EM	NT	NT	NT		NT	TP	NT	NT	EM	NT	NT	NT	NT		TP	NT
						◇1			◇						◇1			◇						◇1	
		A			A	B			C		A			A	B			C		A		A		B	
Manchester Airport 85 ✈	d					11 55									12 55									13 55	
Manchester Piccadilly 10	a					12 13									13 13									14 13	
	d	11 48		12 03	12 18	12 20	12 23	12 36	12 43	12 45	12 48	13 03		13 18	13 20	13 23	13 36	13 43	13 45	13 48	14 03	14 18		14 20	14 23
Ardwick	d																								
Ashburys	d	11 52		12 07	12 22						12 52	13 07		13 22						13 52	14 07	14 22			
Belle Vue	d			12 09								13 09									14 09				
Ryder Brow	d			12 11								13 11									14 11				
Reddish North	d			12 14						12 52		13 14							13 52		14 14				
Brinnington	d			12 17						12 56		13 17							13 56		14 17				
Bredbury	d			12 20						12 59		13 20							13 59		14 20				
Gorton	d	11 54			12 24						12 54			13 24						13 54		14 24			
Fairfield	d							12 43									13 43								
Guide Bridge	a	11 58			12 28			12 46			12 58			13 28			13 46			13 58		14 28			
	d							12 46									13 46								
Hyde North	d							12 50									13 50								
Hyde Central	d							12 52									13 52								
Woodley	d							12 55									13 55								
Romiley	d			12 23			12 37	12 59		13 02		13 23				13 37	13 59		14 02		14 23				14 37
Rose Hill Marple	d						12a43	13a05								13a43	14a05								14a43
Marple	d			12a28						13 06		13a28							14 06		14a28				
Strines	d																		14 10						
New Mills Central	a									13 11									14 13						
	d									13 11									14 13						
Stockport 86	d					12 28			12 54						13 28			13 54						14 28	
Hazel Grove 86	d																								
Chinley	d									13 19									14 21						
Edale	d									13 28									14 30						
Hope (Derbyshire)	d									13 34									14 36						
Bamford	d									13 37									14 39						
Hathersage	d									13 40									14 42						
Grindleford	d									13 44									14 46						
Dore & Totley	d									13 57									14 57						
Sheffield 7	a					13 08			13 35	14 04					14 08			14 35	15 04					15 08	

A To Hadfield **B** To Cleethorpes **C** From Liverpool Lime Street to Norwich

Table 78

Saturdays

Manchester Airport and Manchester Romiley, Marple, Chinley and Sheffield

Network Diagram - see first Page of Table 78

		NT	EM	NT	NT	NT	NT	TP	NT	NT	EM	NT	NT	NT	NT	TP	NT	NT	EM	NT	NT	NT	NT
			◇					◇1			◇					◇1			◇				
			A		B		B	C			A		B		B	C			A		B		B
								🚲								🚲							
Manchester Airport 85 ✈	d							14 55								15 55							
Manchester Piccadilly 10	a							15 13								16 13							
	d	14 36	14 43	14 45	14 48	15 03	15 18	15 20	15 23	15 36	15 43	15 45	15 48	16 02	16 18	16 20	16 23	16 36	16 43	16 45	16 48	17 02	17 18
Ardwick	d																						
Ashburys	d				14 52	15 07	15 22						15 52	16 06	16 22						16 52	17 06	17 22
Belle Vue	d					15 09								16 08								17 08	
Ryder Brow	d					15 11								16 10								17 10	
Reddish North	d			14 52		15 14						15 52		16 13						16 52		17 13	
Brinnington	d			14 56		15 17						15 56		16 16						16 56		17 16	
Bredbury	d			14 59		15 20						15 59		16 19						16 59		17 19	
Gorton	d				14 54		15 24						15 54		16 24						16 54		17 24
Fairfield	d	14 43								15 43								16 43					
Guide Bridge	a	14 46			14 58		15 28			15 46			15 58		16 28			16 46			16 58		17 28
	d	14 46								15 46								16 46					
Hyde North	d	14 50								15 50								16 50					
Hyde Central	d	14 52								15 52								16 52					
Woodley	d	14 55								15 55								16 55					
Romiley	d	14 59		15 02		15 23			15 37	15 59		16 02		16 22			16 37	16 59		17 02		17 22	
Rose Hill Marple	d	15a05							15a43	16a05							16a43	17a05					
Marple	d			15 06		15a28						16 06		16a27						17 06		17a27	
Strines	d											16 10											
New Mills Central	a			15 11								16 13								17 11			
	d			15 11								16 13								17 11			
Stockport 86	d		14 54					15 28			15 54					16 28			16 54				
Hazel Grove 86	d																						
Chinley	d			15 19								16 21							17 09	17 19			
Edale	d			15 28								16 30								17 28			
Hope (Derbyshire)	d			15 34								16 36								17 34			
Bamford	d			15 37								16 39								17 37			
Hathersage	d			15 40								16 42								17 40			
Grindleford	d			15 44								16 46								17 44			
Dore & Totley	d			15 57								16 57							17 30	17 52			
Sheffield 7	a		15 36	16 04				16 08			16 35	17 04				17 08			17 37	18 01			

		TP	NT	NT	EM	NT	NT	NT	NT	TP	NT	NT	EM	NT	NT	TP	NT	EM	NT	NT	TP	NT
		◇1			◇					◇1			◇			◇1		◇			◇1	
		C			D		B		B	C			A		B	C		D		B		
		🚲								🚲												
Manchester Airport 85 ✈	d	16 55								17 55						18 55					19 55	
Manchester Piccadilly 10	a	17 13								18 13						19 13					20 13	
	d	17 20	17 23	17 36	17 43	17 45	17 48	18 03	18 18	18 20	18 23	18 36	18 43	18 45	18 48	19 18	19 23	19 43	19 45	19 48	20 20	20 36
Ardwick	d																					
Ashburys	d						17 52	18 07	18 22						18 52		19 28		19 49	19 52		
Belle Vue	d							18 09									19 31		19 51			
Ryder Brow	d							18 11									19 33		19 53			
Reddish North	d					17 52		18 14						18 52			19 35		19 56			
Brinnington	d					17 56		18 17						18 56			19 39		19 59			
Bredbury	d					17 59		18 20						18 59			19 42		20 02			
Gorton	d						17 54		18 24						18 54					19 54		
Fairfield	d			17 43								18 43										20 43
Guide Bridge	a			17 46			17 58		18 28			18 46			18 58					19 58		20 46
	d			17 46								18 46										20 46
Hyde North	d			17 50								18 50										20 50
Hyde Central	d			17 52								18 52										20 52
Woodley	d			17 55								18 55										20 55
Romiley	d		17 37	17 59		18 02		18 23			18 37	18 59		19 02			19 45		20 05			20 59
Rose Hill Marple	d			18a05								19a05										21a05
Marple	d		17a43			18 06		18a28			18a43			19 06			19a49		20 09			
Strines	d					18 10													20 13			
New Mills Central	a					18 13								19 11					20 18			
	d					18 13								19 11								
Stockport 86	d	17 28			17 54					18 28			18 54			19 26		19 54			20 28	
Hazel Grove 86	d																					
Chinley	d				18 08	18 21								19 19								
Edale	d					18 30								19 28								
Hope (Derbyshire)	d					18 36								19 34								
Bamford	d					18 39								19 37								
Hathersage	d					18 42								19 40								
Grindleford	d					18 46								19 44								
Dore & Totley	d	18 03				18 54				19 03				19 57		20 01					21 03	
Sheffield 7	a	18 10			18 35	19 03				19 09			19 35	20 04		20 08		20 35			21 14	

A From Liverpool Lime Street to Norwich
B To Hadfield
C To Cleethorpes
D From Liverpool Lime Street to Nottingham

Table 78

Saturdays

Manchester Airport and Manchester Romiley, Marple, Chinley and Sheffield

Network Diagram - see first Page of Table 78

		EM	NT	NT	TP	EM	NT	NT	TP	EM	NT	NT	NT	NT
		◇			◇1	◇			◇1	◇				
		A		B	C	A		B		A		B		D
Manchester Airport 85 ✈	d				20 47				21 47					
Manchester Piccadilly 10 🚢	a				21 13				22 13					
	d	20 43	20 45	20 48	21 20	21 43	21 45	21 48	22 20	22 31	22 45	22 48	23 24	23 27
Ardwick	d													
Ashburys	d			20 52			21 49	21 52			22 49	22 52	23 28	23 31
Belle Vue	d						21 51				22 51		23 30	
Ryder Brow	d						21 53				22 53		23 32	
Reddish North	d		20 52				21 56				22 56		23 35	
Brinnington	d		20 56				21 59				22 59		23 38	
Bredbury	d		20 59				22 02				23 02		23 41	
Gorton	d			20 54				21 54				22 54		23 33
Fairfield	d													
Guide Bridge	a			20 58				21 58				22 58		23 37
	d													
Hyde North	d													
Hyde Central	d													
Woodley	d													
Romiley	d		21 02				22 05				23 05		23 44	
Rose Hill Marple	d													
Marple	d		21 06				22 09				23 09		23 48	
Strines	d						22 13				23 13		23 52	
New Mills Central	a		21 11				22 18				23 18		23 57	
	d		21 11											
Stockport 86	d	20 54			21 28	21 52			22 28	22 42				
Hazel Grove 86	d													
Chinley	d		21 19							22 57				
Edale	d		21 28							23 05				
Hope (Derbyshire)	d		21 34							23 11				
Bamford	d		21 37							23 15				
Hathersage	d		21 40							23 19				
Grindleford	d		21 44							23 23				
Dore & Totley	d		21 53							23 32				
Sheffield 7 🚢	a	21 34	22 03		22 08	22 31			23 16	23 39				

Sundays

until 1 January

		NT	NT	NT	NT	NT	NT	TP	NT	NT	NT	NT	TP	EM	NT	NT	TP	EM	NT	NT	NT	TP	EM
								◇1					◇1	◇			◇1	◇				◇1	◇
			B		B	B	B	C	B		B	B	E	F	B	B	C	G		B	B	C	G
Manchester Airport 85 ✈	d							10 44									12 55					13 55	
Manchester Piccadilly 10 🚢	a							10 58									13 07					14 09	
	d	08 00	09 18	09 22	09 30	10 18	10 48	11 18	11 18	11 45	11 48	12 18	12 18	12 44	12 48	13 18	13 20	13 44	13 45	13 48	14 18	14 20	14 44
Ardwick	d																						
Ashburys	d		09 22		09 34	10 22	10 52		11 22		11 52	12 22			12 53	13 22				13 52	14 22		
Belle Vue	d																						
Ryder Brow	d																						
Reddish North	d			09 29						11 52									13 52				
Brinnington	d			09 33						11 56									13 56				
Bredbury	d			09 36						11 59									13 59				
Gorton	d		09 24		09 36	10 24	10 54		11 24		11 54	12 24			12 55	13 24				13 54	14 24		
Fairfield	d																						
Guide Bridge	a		09 28		09 40	10 28	10 58		11 28		11 58	12 28			12 59	13 28				13 58	14 28		
	d																						
Hyde North	d																						
Hyde Central	d																						
Woodley	d																						
Romiley	d			09 39						12 02									14 02				
Rose Hill Marple	d																						
Marple	d			09 43						12 06									14 06				
Strines	d			09 47						12 10									14 10				
New Mills Central	a			09 51						12 14									14 14				
	d			09 51						12 14									14 14				
Stockport 86	d	08 10						11 27					12 28	12 55			13 28	13 54				14 28	14 54
Hazel Grove 86	d																						
Chinley	d	08 23		09 59						12 23									14 23				
Edale	d	08 32		10 08						12 32									14 32				
Hope (Derbyshire)	d	08 38		10 14						12 38									14 38				
Bamford	d	08 41		10 17						12 41									14 41				
Hathersage	d	08 45		10 20						12 45									14 45				
Grindleford	d	08 48		10 24						12 48									14 48				
Dore & Totley	d	08 57		10 34						12 57									14 57				
Sheffield 7 🚢	a	09 06		10 43				12 09		13 06			13 08	13 37			14 08	14 39	15 06			15 08	15 37

A From Liverpool Lime Street to Nottingham
B To Hadfield
C To Cleethorpes
D To Glossop
E To Doncaster
F To Norwich
G From Liverpool Lime Street to Norwich

Table 78

Sundays
until 1 January

Manchester Airport and Manchester Romiley, Marple, Chinley and Sheffield

Network Diagram - see first Page of Table 78

		NT	NT	TP	EM	NT		NT	NT	TP	EM	NT	NT	TP	EM	NT		NT	NT	TP	EM	NT	NT	TP	EM
				◇1	◇					◇1	◇			◇1	◇					◇1	◇			◇1	◇
		A	A	B	C			A	A	B	C	A	A	B	D			A	A	B	C	A	A	B	D
Manchester Airport 85 ✈	d			14 55						15 55				16 55						17 55				18 55	
Manchester Piccadilly 10	a			15 09						16 09				17 09						18 09				19 09	
	d	14 48	15 18	15 20	15 44	15 45		15 48	16 18	16 20	16 44	16 48	17 18	17 20	17 44	17 45		17 48	18 18	18 20	18 44	18 48	19 18	19 20	19 44
Ardwick	d																								
Ashburys	d	14 52	15 22					15 52	16 22			16 52	17 22					17 52	18 22			18 52	19 22		
Belle Vue	d																								
Ryder Brow	d																								
Reddish North	d					15 52										17 52									
Brinnington	d					15 56										17 56									
Bredbury	d					15 59										17 59									
Gorton	d	14 54	15 24					15 54	16 24			16 54	17 24					17 54	18 24			18 54	19 24		
Fairfield	d																								
Guide Bridge	a	14 58	15 28					15 58	16 28			16 58	17 28					17 58	18 28			18 58	19 28		
	d																								
Hyde North	d																								
Hyde Central	d																								
Woodley	d																								
Romiley	d					16 02										18 02									
Rose Hill Marple	d																								
Marple	d					16 06										18 06									
Strines	d					16 10										18 10									
New Mills Central	a					16 14										18 14									
	d					16 14										18 14									
Stockport 86	d			15 28	15 54					16 28	16 54			17 28	17 54					18 28	18 54			19 28	19 54
Hazel Grove 86	d																								
Chinley	d					16 23										18 23									
Edale	d					16 32										18 32									
Hope (Derbyshire)	d					16 38										18 38									
Bamford	d					16 41										18 41									
Hathersage	d					16 45										18 45									
Grindleford	d					16 48										18 48									
Dore & Totley	d					16 57										18 57									
Sheffield 7 ⇌	a			16 09	16 36	17 06				17 08	17 36			18 08	18 37	19 06				19 08	19 34			20 08	20 34

		NT		NT	TP	EM	NT	TP	EM	TP	NT	TP
					◇1	◇		◇1	◇	◇1		◇1
				A	B	D	A		D			
Manchester Airport 85 ✈	d				19 55			20 55		21 55		22 55
Manchester Piccadilly 10	a				20 09			21 09		22 09		23 09
	d	19 45		19 48	20 18	20 44	20 48	21 20	22 11	22 15	22 20	23 20
Ardwick	d											
Ashburys	d			19 52			20 52					
Belle Vue	d											
Ryder Brow	d											
Reddish North	d	19 52									22 27	
Brinnington	d	19 56									22 31	
Bredbury	d	19 59									22 34	
Gorton	d			19 54			20 54					
Fairfield	d											
Guide Bridge	a			19 58			20 58					
	d											
Hyde North	d											
Hyde Central	d											
Woodley	d											
Romiley	d	20 02									22 37	
Rose Hill Marple	d											
Marple	d	20 06									22 40	
Strines	d	20 10									22 44	
New Mills Central	a	20 14									22 49	
	d	20 14										
Stockport 86	d				20 27	20 54		21 28	22 28	22 23		23 28
Hazel Grove 86	d											
Chinley	d	20 23							22 43			
Edale	d	20 32							22 51			
Hope (Derbyshire)	d	20 38							22 57			
Bamford	d	20 41							23 00			
Hathersage	d	20 45							23 03			
Grindleford	d	20 48							23 07			
Dore & Totley	d	20 57							23 17			
Sheffield 7 ⇌	a	21 06			21 08	21 36		22 12	23 25	23 04		00 15

A To Hadfield
B To Cleethorpes
C From Liverpool Lime Street to Norwich
D From Liverpool Lime Street to Nottingham

Table 78

Sundays

8 January to 12 February

Manchester Airport and Manchester Romiley, Marple, Chinley and Sheffield

Network Diagram - see first Page of Table 78

	NT	NT	NT	NT	NT	NT	TP	NT	NT		NT	NT	TP	EM	NT	NT	TP	EM	NT		NT	NT	TP	EM
							◇1						◇1	◇			◇1	◇					◇1	◇
		A		A	A	A		A			A	A		B	A	A		C			A	A		C
Manchester Airport 85 ✈ d							10 44										12 55						13 55	
Manchester Piccadilly 10 a							10 58										13 09						14 09	
d	08 00	09 18	09 22	09 30	10 18	10 48	11 18	11 18	11 45		11 48	12 18	12 19	12 44	12 48	13 18	13 20	13 44	13 45		13 48	14 18	14 20	14 44
Ardwick d																								
Ashburys d		09 22		09 34	10 22	10 52		11 22			11 52	12 22			12 53	13 22					13 52	14 22		
Belle Vue d																								
Ryder Brow d																								
Reddish North d			09 29						11 52										13 52					
Brinnington d			09 33						11 56										13 56					
Bredbury d			09 36						11 59										13 59					
Gorton d		09 24		09 36	10 24	10 54		11 24			11 54	12 24			12 55	13 24					13 54	14 24		
Fairfield d																								
Guide Bridge a		09 28		09 40	10 28	10 58		11 28			11 58	12 28			12 59	13 28					13 58	14 28		
d																								
Hyde North d																								
Hyde Central d																								
Woodley d																								
Romiley d			09 39						12 02										14 02					
Rose Hill Marple d																								
Marple d			09 43						12 06										14 06					
Strines d			09 47						12 10										14 10					
New Mills Central a			09 51						12 14										14 14					
d			09 51						12 14										14 14					
Stockport 86 d	08 10						11 27						12 28	12 55			13 28	13 54					14 28	14 54
Hazel Grove 86 d																								
Chinley d	08 23		09 59						12 23										14 23					
Edale d	08 32		10 08						12 32										14 32					
Hope (Derbyshire) d	08 38		10 14						12 38										14 38					
Bamford d	08 41		10 17						12 41										14 41					
Hathersage d	08 45		10 20						12 45										14 45					
Grindleford d	08 48		10 24						12 48										14 48					
Dore & Totley d	08 57		10 34						12 57										14 57					
Sheffield 7 a	09 06		10 43				12 09		13 06				13 09	13 37			14 10	14 39	15 06				15 11	15 37

	NT	NT	TP	EM	NT		NT	NT	TP	EM	NT	NT	TP	EM	NT		NT	NT	TP	EM	NT	NT	TP	EM
			◇1	◇					◇1	◇			◇1	◇					◇1	◇			◇1	◇
	A	A		C			A	A		C	A	A		D			A	A		C	A	A		D
Manchester Airport 85 ✈ d			14 55						15 55				16 55						17 55				18 55	
Manchester Piccadilly 10 a			15 09						16 09				17 09						18 09				19 09	
d	14 48	15 18	15 20	15 44	15 45		15 48	16 18	16 20	16 44	16 48	17 18	17 20	17 44	17 45		17 48	18 18	18 20	18 44	18 48	19 18	19 20	19 44
Ardwick d																								
Ashburys d	14 52	15 22					15 52	16 22			16 52	17 22					17 52	18 22			18 52	19 22		
Belle Vue d																								
Ryder Brow d																								
Reddish North d					15 52										17 52									
Brinnington d					15 56										17 56									
Bredbury d					15 59										17 59									
Gorton d	14 54	15 24					15 54	16 24			16 54	17 24					17 54	18 24			18 54	19 24		
Fairfield d																								
Guide Bridge a	14 58	15 28					15 58	16 28			16 58	17 28					17 58	18 28			18 58	19 28		
d																								
Hyde North d																								
Hyde Central d																								
Woodley d																								
Romiley d					16 02										18 02									
Rose Hill Marple d																								
Marple d					16 06										18 06									
Strines d					16 10										18 10									
New Mills Central a					16 14										18 14									
d					16 14										18 14									
Stockport 86 d			15 28	15 54					16 28	16 54			17 28	17 54					18 28	18 54			19 28	19 54
Hazel Grove 86 d																								
Chinley d					16 23										18 23									
Edale d					16 32										18 32									
Hope (Derbyshire) d					16 38										18 38									
Bamford d					16 41										18 41									
Hathersage d					16 45										18 45									
Grindleford d					16 48										18 48									
Dore & Totley d					16 57										18 57									
Sheffield 7 a			16 10	16 36	17 06				17 11	17 36			18 11	18 37	19 06				19 10	19 34			20 10	20 34

A To Hadfield
B To Norwich
C From Liverpool Lime Street to Norwich
D From Liverpool Lime Street to Nottingham

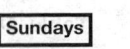

Sundays
8 January to 12 February

Manchester Airport and Manchester Romiley, Marple, Chinley and Sheffield

Network Diagram - see first Page of Table 78

		NT	NT	TP	EM	NT	TP	EM	TP	NT	TP
				◇1	◇		◇1	◇	◇1		◇1
			A		B	A		B			
Manchester Airport 85 ✈	d			19 55			20 55		21 55		22 55
Manchester Piccadilly 10 🚌	a			20 09			21 09		22 09		23 09
	d	19 45	19 48	20 18	20 44	20 48	21 20	22 11	22 15	22 20	23 20
Ardwick	d										
Ashburys	d		19 52			20 52					
Belle Vue	d										
Ryder Brow	d										
Reddish North	d	19 52								22 27	
Brinnington	d	19 56								22 31	
Bredbury	d	19 59								22 34	
Gorton	d		19 54			20 54					
Fairfield	d										
Guide Bridge	a		19 58			20 58					
	d										
Hyde North	d										
Hyde Central	d										
Woodley	d										
Romiley	d	20 02								22 37	
Rose Hill Marple	d										
Marple	d	20 06								22 40	
Strines	d	20 10								22 44	
New Mills Central	a	20 14								22 49	
	d	20 14									
Stockport 86	d			20 27	20 54		21 28	22 28	22 23		23 28
Hazel Grove 86	d										
Chinley	d	20 23						22 43			
Edale	d	20 32						22 51			
Hope (Derbyshire)	d	20 38						22 57			
Bamford	d	20 41						23 00			
Hathersage	d	20 45						23 03			
Grindleford	d	20 48						23 07			
Dore & Totley	d	20 57						23 17			
Sheffield 7 🚌	a	21 06		21 10	21 36		22 12	23 25	23 04		00 15

Sundays
19 February to 25 March

		NT	NT	NT	NT	NT	NT	TP	NT	NT	NT	NT	TP	EM	NT	NT	TP	EM	NT	NT	NT	TP	EM
								◇1					◇1	◇			◇1	◇				◇1	◇
			A		A	A	A	C	A		A	A	D	E	A	A	C	F		A	A	C	F
Manchester Airport 85 ✈	d							10 44									12 55					13 55	
Manchester Piccadilly 10 🚌	a							10 58									13 07					14 09	
	d	08 00	09 18	09 22	09 30	10 18	10 48	11 18	11 18	11 45	11 48	12 18	12 18	12 44	12 48	13 18	13 20	13 44	13 45	13 48	14 18	14 20	14 44
Ardwick	d																						
Ashburys	d		09 22		09 34	10 22	10 52		11 22		11 52	12 22			12 53	13 22				13 52	14 22		
Belle Vue	d																						
Ryder Brow	d																						
Reddish North	d			09 29						11 52									13 52				
Brinnington	d			09 33						11 56									13 56				
Bredbury	d			09 36						11 59									13 59				
Gorton	d		09 24		09 36	10 24	10 54		11 24		11 54	12 24			12 55	13 24				13 54	14 24		
Fairfield	d																						
Guide Bridge	a		09 28		09 40	10 28	10 58		11 28		11 58	12 28			12 59	13 28				13 58	14 28		
	d																						
Hyde North	d																						
Hyde Central	d																						
Woodley	d																						
Romiley	d			09 39						12 02									14 02				
Rose Hill Marple	d																						
Marple	d			09 43						12 06									14 06				
Strines	d			09 47						12 10									14 10				
New Mills Central	a			09 51						12 14									14 14				
	d			09 51						12 14									14 14				
Stockport 86	d	08 10						11 27					12 28	12 55			13 28	13 54				14 28	14 54
Hazel Grove 86	d																						
Chinley	d	08 23		09 59						12 23									14 23				
Edale	d	08 32		10 08						12 32									14 32				
Hope (Derbyshire)	d	08 38		10 14						12 38									14 38				
Bamford	d	08 41		10 17						12 41									14 41				
Hathersage	d	08 45		10 20						12 45									14 45				
Grindleford	d	08 48		10 24						12 48									14 48				
Dore & Totley	d	08 57		10 34						12 57									14 57				
Sheffield 7 🚌	a	09 06		10 43				12 09		13 06			13 08	13 37			14 08	14 39	15 06			15 08	15 37

A To Hadfield
B From Liverpool Lime Street to Nottingham
C To Cleethorpes
D To Doncaster
E To Norwich
F From Liverpool Lime Street to Norwich

Table 78

Sundays

19 February to 25 March

Manchester Airport and Manchester Romiley, Marple, Chinley and Sheffield

Network Diagram - see first Page of Table 78

		NT	NT	TP	EM	NT		NT	NT	TP	EM	NT	NT	TP	EM	NT		NT	NT	TP	EM	NT	NT	TP	EM
				◇1	◇					◇1	◇			◇1	◇					◇1	◇			◇1	◇
		A	A	B	C			A	A	B	C	A	A	B	D			A	A	B	C	A	A	B	D
Manchester Airport 85 ✈	d			14 55						15 55				16 55						17 55				18 55	
Manchester Piccadilly 10	a			15 09						16 09				17 09						18 09				19 09	
	d	14 48	15 18	15 20	15 44	15 45		15 48	16 18	16 20	16 44	16 48	17 18	17 20	17 44	17 45		17 48	18 18	18 20	18 44	18 48	19 18	19 20	19 44
Ardwick	d																								
Ashburys	d	14 52	15 22					15 52	16 22			16 52	17 22					17 52	18 22			18 52	19 22		
Belle Vue	d																								
Ryder Brow	d																								
Reddish North	d					15 52										17 52									
Brinnington	d					15 56										17 56									
Bredbury	d					15 59										17 59									
Gorton	d	14 54	15 24					15 54	16 24			16 54	17 24					17 54	18 24			18 54	19 24		
Fairfield	d																								
Guide Bridge	a	14 58	15 28					15 58	16 28			16 58	17 28					17 58	18 28			18 58	19 28		
	d																								
Hyde North	d																								
Hyde Central	d																								
Woodley	d																								
Romiley	d					16 02										18 02									
Rose Hill Marple	d																								
Marple	d					16 06										18 06									
Strines	d					16 10										18 10									
New Mills Central	a					16 14										18 14									
	d					16 14										18 14									
Stockport 86	d			15 28	15 54					16 28	16 54			17 28	17 54					18 28	18 54			19 28	19 54
Hazel Grove 86	d																								
Chinley	d					16 23										18 23									
Edale	d					16 32										18 32									
Hope (Derbyshire)	d					16 38										18 38									
Bamford	d					16 41										18 41									
Hathersage	d					16 45										18 45									
Grindleford	d					16 48										18 48									
Dore & Totley	d					16 57										18 57									
Sheffield 7	a			16 09	16 36	17 06				17 08	17 36			18 08	18 37	19 06				19 08	19 34			20 08	20 34

		NT		NT	TP	EM	NT	TP	EM	TP	NT	TP
					◇1	◇		◇1	◇	◇1		◇1
				A	B	D	A		D			
Manchester Airport 85 ✈	d				19 55			20 55		21 55		22 55
Manchester Piccadilly 10	a				20 09			21 09		22 09		23 09
	d	19 45		19 48	20 18	20 44	20 48	21 20	22 11	22 15	22 20	23 20
Ardwick	d											
Ashburys	d			19 52			20 52					
Belle Vue	d											
Ryder Brow	d											
Reddish North	d	19 52									22 27	
Brinnington	d	19 56									22 31	
Bredbury	d	19 59									22 34	
Gorton	d			19 54			20 54					
Fairfield	d											
Guide Bridge	a			19 58			20 58					
	d											
Hyde North	d											
Hyde Central	d											
Woodley	d											
Romiley	d	20 02									22 37	
Rose Hill Marple	d											
Marple	d	20 06									22 40	
Strines	d	20 10									22 44	
New Mills Central	a	20 14									22 49	
	d	20 14										
Stockport 86	d				20 27	20 54		21 28	22 28	22 23		23 28
Hazel Grove 86	d											
Chinley	d	20 23							22 43			
Edale	d	20 32							22 51			
Hope (Derbyshire)	d	20 38							22 57			
Bamford	d	20 41							23 00			
Hathersage	d	20 45							23 03			
Grindleford	d	20 48							23 07			
Dore & Totley	d	20 57							23 17			
Sheffield 7	a	21 06			21 08	21 36		22 12	23 25	23 04		00 15

A To Hadfield
B To Cleethorpes
C From Liverpool Lime Street to Norwich
D From Liverpool Lime Street to Nottingham

Table 78

Sundays
from 1 April

Manchester Airport and Manchester Romiley, Marple, Chinley and Sheffield

Network Diagram - see first Page of Table 78

		NT	TP ◇1	NT A	NT	NT A	NT A	NT A	TP ◇1 B	NT A	NT	NT A	NT A	TP ◇1 C	EM ◇ D	NT A	NT A	TP ◇1 B	EM ◇ E	NT	NT A	NT A	TP ◇1 B
Manchester Airport 85	d		08 40						10 44									12 55					13 55
Manchester Piccadilly 10	a		08 54						10 58									13 09					14 09
	d	08 00	08 58	09 18	09 22	09 48	10 18	10 48	11 18	11 18	11 45	11 48	12 18	12 20	12 44	12 48	13 18	13 20	13 44	13 45	13 48	14 18	14 20
Ardwick	d																						
Ashburys	d			09 22		09 52	10 22	10 52		11 22		11 52	12 22			12 52	13 22				13 52	14 22	
Belle Vue	d																						
Ryder Brow	d																						
Reddish North	d				09 29						11 52									13 52			
Brinnington	d				09 33						11 56									13 56			
Bredbury	d				09 36						11 59									13 59			
Gorton	d			09 24		09 54	10 24	10 54		11 24		11 54	12 24			12 54	13 24				13 54	14 24	
Fairfield	d																						
Guide Bridge	a			09 28		09 58	10 28	10 58		11 28		11 58	12 28			12 58	13 28				13 58	14 28	
	d																						
Hyde North	d																						
Hyde Central	d																						
Woodley	d																						
Romiley	d				09 39						12 02									14 02			
Rose Hill Marple	d																						
Marple	d				09 43						12 06									14 06			
Strines	d				09 47						12 10									14 10			
New Mills Central	a				09 51						12 14									14 14			
	d				09 51						12 14									14 14			
Stockport 86	d	08 10	09 07						11 27					12 28	12 55			13 29	13 54				14 28
Hazel Grove 86	d																						
Chinley	d	08 23			09 59						12 23									14 23			
Edale	d	08 32			10 08						12 32									14 32			
Hope (Derbyshire)	d	08 38			10 14						12 38									14 38			
Bamford	d	08 41			10 17						12 41									14 41			
Hathersage	d	08 45			10 20						12 45									14 45			
Grindleford	d	08 48			10 24						12 48									14 48			
Dore & Totley	d	08 57			10 34						12 57									14 57			
Sheffield 7	a	09 06	09 45		10 43				12 09		13 06			13 08	13 37			14 08	14 39	15 06			15 08

		EM ◇ E	NT	NT A	NT A	TP ◇1 B	EM ◇ E	NT	NT A	NT A	TP ◇1 B	EM ◇ E	NT A	NT A	TP ◇1 B	EM ◇ F	NT	NT A	NT A	TP ◇1 B	EM ◇ E	NT A	NT A
Manchester Airport 85	d					14 55					15 55				16 55					17 55			
Manchester Piccadilly 10	a					15 09					16 09				17 09					18 09			
	d	14 44	14 45	14 48	15 18	15 20	15 44	15 45	15 48	16 18	16 20	16 44	16 48	17 18	17 20	17 44	17 45	17 48	18 18	18 20	18 44	18 48	19 18
Ardwick	d																						
Ashburys	d			14 52	15 22				15 52	16 22			16 52	17 22				17 52	18 22			18 52	19 22
Belle Vue	d																						
Ryder Brow	d																						
Reddish North	d		14 52					15 52									17 52						
Brinnington	d		14 56					15 56									17 56						
Bredbury	d		14 59					15 59									17 59						
Gorton	d			14 54	15 24				15 54	16 24			16 54	17 24				17 54	18 24			18 54	19 24
Fairfield	d																						
Guide Bridge	a			14 58	15 28				15 58	16 28			16 58	17 28				17 58	18 28			18 58	19 28
	d																						
Hyde North	d																						
Hyde Central	d																						
Woodley	d																						
Romiley	d		15 02					16 02									18 02						
Rose Hill Marple	d																						
Marple	d		15 06					16 06									18 06						
Strines	d		15 10					16 10									18 10						
New Mills Central	a		15 14					16 14									18 14						
	d		15 14					16 14									18 14						
Stockport 86	d	14 54				15 28	15 54				16 28	16 54			17 28	17 54				18 28	18 54		
Hazel Grove 86	d																						
Chinley	d		15 23					16 23									18 23						
Edale	d		15 32					16 32									18 32						
Hope (Derbyshire)	d		15 38					16 38									18 38						
Bamford	d		15 41					16 41									18 41						
Hathersage	d		15 45					16 45									18 45						
Grindleford	d		15 48					16 48									18 48						
Dore & Totley	d		15 57					16 57									18 57						
Sheffield 7	a	15 37	16 05			16 09	16 36	17 06			17 08	17 36			18 08	18 37	19 06			19 08	19 34		

A To Hadfield
B To Cleethorpes
C To Doncaster
D To Norwich
E From Liverpool Lime Street to Norwich
F From Liverpool Lime Street to Nottingham

Table 78

Sundays
from 1 April

Manchester Airport and Manchester
Romiley, Marple, Chinley and Sheffield

Network Diagram - see first Page of Table 78

		TP	EM	NT	NT	TP	EM	NT	TP	EM	TP	NT	TP
		◇1	◇			◇1	◇		◇1	◇	◇1		◇1
		A	B		C	A	B	C		B			
Manchester Airport 85 ✈	d	18 55				19 55			20 55		21 55		22 55
Manchester Piccadilly 10 🚌	a	19 09				20 09			21 09		22 09		23 09
	d	19 20	19 44	19 45	19 48	20 18	20 44	20 48	21 20	22 11	22 15	22 20	23 20
Ardwick	d												
Ashburys	d				19 52			20 52					
Belle Vue	d												
Ryder Brow	d												
Reddish North	d			19 52								22 27	
Brinnington	d			19 56								22 31	
Bredbury	d			19 59								22 34	
Gorton	d				19 54			20 54					
Fairfield	d												
Guide Bridge	a				19 58			20 58					
	d												
Hyde North	d												
Hyde Central	d												
Woodley	d												
Romiley	d			20 02								22 37	
Rose Hill Marple	d												
Marple	d			20 06								22 40	
Strines	d			20 10								22 44	
New Mills Central	a			20 14								22 49	
	d			20 14									
Stockport 86	d	19 28	19 54			20 27	20 54		21 28	22 28	22 23		23 28
Hazel Grove 86	d												
Chinley	d			20 23						22 43			
Edale	d			20 32						22 51			
Hope (Derbyshire)	d			20 38						22 57			
Bamford	d			20 41						23 00			
Hathersage	d			20 45						23 03			
Grindleford	d			20 48						23 07			
Dore & Totley	d			20 57						23 17			
Sheffield 7 🚌	a	20 08	20 34	21 06		21 08	21 36		22 12	23 25	23 04		00 15

A To Cleethorpes
B From Liverpool Lime Street to Nottingham
C To Hadfield

Sheffield, Chinley, Marple and Romiley Manchester and Manchester Airport

Network Diagram - see first Page of Table 78

Miles	Miles	Miles			NT MX	NT MX	TP ◇[1]	TP ◇[1]	NT A	NT	TP ◇[1] B	NT	NT		NT A	EM ◇ C	NT	NT A	NT D	NT	NT	TP ◇[1] E	NT D		NT
0	—	—	**Sheffield [7]**	d	22p47		03 45	05 11			06 11					06 20						07 09			
4¾	—	—	Dore & Totley	d	22p54											06 27						07 15			
9¾	—	—	Grindleford	d	23p01											06 35									
11¼	—	—	Hathersage	d	23p05											06 39									
13	—	—	Bamford	d	23p08											06 43									
14¾	—	—	Hope (Derbyshire)	d	23p12											06 47									
20	—	—	Edale	d	23p19											06 55									
25½	—	0	**Chinley**	d	23p27											07 03									
—	—	8½	Hazel Grove 86	a																					
—	—	—	Stockport 86	a	23p47			05 53			06 53					07 22						07 53			
29¼	—	—	New Mills Central	d		23p30				06 13			06 36				07 01				07 23				
30¾	—	—	Strines	d		23p33				06 16			06 39				07 04				07 26				
33	—	—	**Marple**	d		23p36				06 19			06 42				07 07				07 29				
—	0	—	**Rose Hill Marple**	d								06 32								07 16					07 41
34¼	2	—	**Romiley**	d		23p40				06 23		06 37	06 46				07 12			07 21	07 33				07 46
—	3¼	—	Woodley	d								06 40								07 24					07 49
—	4¾	—	Hyde Central	d								06 43								07 27					07 52
—	6	—	Hyde North	d								06 46								07 30					07 55
—	7¾	—	Guide Bridge	d					06 27			06 50			06 57			07 27	07 28	07 34			07 47		07 59
—	9	—	Fairfield	d								06 53								07 37					08 02
—	10	—	Gorton	d					06 30						07 00			07 30	07 31				07 50		
35½	—	—	Bredbury	d		23p43				06 26			06 49				07 15				07 36				
36½	—	—	Brinnington	d		23p45				06 28			06 52				07 17				07 39				
38¼	—	—	Reddish North	d		23p48				06 31			06 55				07 20				07 43				
39¼	—	—	Ryder Brow	d		23p51				06 34			06 58				07 24				07 45				
39½	—	—	Belle Vue	d		23p52				06 36			07 00				07 26				07 47				
40½	11	—	Ashburys	d		23p55			06 33	06 39			07 03		07 06		07 29	07 33	07 34		07 50		07 53		
41½	12	—	Ardwick	d														07 36	07 38						
42	12½	8¾	**Manchester Piccadilly [10]**	a	00 02	00 03	04 40	06 05	06 42	06 47	07 02	07 03	07 12		07 15	07 34	07 36	07 43	07 44	07 47	07 56	08 02	08 03		08 12
—	—	—	**Manchester Airport** 85	a			05 00	06 29			07 29											08 26			

		NT	NT D	NT	NT	EM ◇ C	NT D	NT	NT		NT	TP ◇[1] E	NT D	NT	NT D	NT	NT	NT FO F	EM ◇ C	NT D		NT	TP ◇[1] E	NT D	NT A	NT
Sheffield [7]	d				07 12	07 35						08 05							08 42				09 11			
Dore & Totley	d				07 19	07 42						08 11														
Grindleford	d				07 29																					
Hathersage	d				07 32																					
Bamford	d				07 36																					
Hope (Derbyshire)	d				07 39																					
Edale	d				07 47																					
Chinley	d				07 55	08 03						08 32														
Hazel Grove 86	a					08 16																				
Stockport 86	a					08 24						08 53						09d22	09 25				09 53			
New Mills Central	d	07 39			08 02				08 22								09 04									
Strines	d	07 42							08 25								09 07									
Marple	d	07 45		07 59	08 09				08 29					08 48			09 10					09 35				09 52
Rose Hill Marple	d							08 15			08 35					08 59										
Romiley	d	07 49		08 03	08 13			08 20	08 33		08 40			08 51		09 04	09 14					09 38				09 56
Woodley	d							08 23								09 07										
Hyde Central	d							08 26								09 10										
Hyde North	d							08 29								09 13										
Guide Bridge	d		08 10				08 27	08 33					08 49		09 12	09 17		09a42		09 28				09 58	09 58	
Fairfield	d							08 36								09 20										
Gorton	d		08 13				08 31						08 52		09 15					09 31				10 01	10 01	
Bredbury	d	07 52		08 06					08 36		08 43			08 54			09 17					09 41				
Brinnington	d	07 55		08 09					08 39		08 45			08 57			09 19					09 44				
Reddish North	d	07 58		08 12					08 43		08 48			09 00			09 22					09 47				
Ryder Brow	d			08 15										09 03												10 03
Belle Vue	d			08 16										09 04												10 05
Ashburys	d		08 16	08 20			08 34		08 48				08 56	09 07	09 18					09 34				10 04	10 04	10 07
Ardwick	d			08 22							08 54															
Manchester Piccadilly [10]	a	08 09	08 25	08 30	08 33	08 36	08 43	08 47	08 55		09 00	09 02	09 04	09 15	09 27	09 30	09 34		09 36	09 42		09 57	10 02	10 11	10 12	10 15
Manchester Airport 85	a											09 33											10 26			

A From Hadfield
B From Doncaster
C From Nottingham to Liverpool Lime Street
D From Manchester Piccadilly
E From Cleethorpes
F To Stalybridge arr. 09.49. Also stops at Reddish South 09x26 and Denton 09x31 It arrives at Stalybridge a minute earlier.

Table 78

Mondays to Fridays

Sheffield, Chinley, Marple and Romiley Manchester and Manchester Airport

Network Diagram - see first Page of Table 78

		NT	NT	EM ◇ A	NT B	NT C	NT	NT	TP ◇1 D 🚲	NT B	NT C	NT	NT	EM ◇ A	NT B	NT C	NT	NT	TP ◇1 D 🚲	NT B	NT C	NT	NT
Sheffield 7 🚌	d		09 14	09 42					10 11				10 14	10 42					11 11				
Dore & Totley	d		09 21										10 21										
Grindleford	d		09 29										10 29										
Hathersage	d		09 32										10 32										
Bamford	d		09 36										10 36										
Hope (Derbyshire)	d		09 39										10 39										
Edale	d		09 47										10 47										
Chinley	d		09 55										10 55										
Hazel Grove 86	a																						
Stockport 86	a			10 25					10 53					11 25					11 53				
New Mills Central	d		10 01					10 30					11 01					11 30					12 01
Strines	d		10 04																				12 04
Marple	d		10 07					10 35					11 07					11 35					12 07
Rose Hill Marple	d	09 55					10 30					10 51					11 30					11 51	
Romiley	d	10 00	10 11				10 35	10 38				10 56	11 11				11 35	11 38				11 56	12 11
Woodley	d	10 03					10 38										11 38						
Hyde Central	d	10 06					10 41										11 41						
Hyde North	d	10 09					10 44										11 44						
Guide Bridge	d	10 13			10 28	10 28	10 48			10 58	10 58				11 28	11 28	11 48			11 58	11 58		
Fairfield	d	10 16					10 51										11 51						
Gorton	d				10 31	10 31				11 01	11 01				11 31	11 31				12 01	12 01		
Bredbury	d		10 14					10 41					11 14					11 41					12 14
Brinnington	d		10 16					10 44					11 16					11 44					12 16
Reddish North	d		10 19					10 47					11 19					11 47					12 19
Ryder Brow	d											11 03										12 03	
Belle Vue	d											11 05										12 05	
Ashburys	d				10 34	10 34				11 04	11 04	11 07			11 34	11 34				12 04	12 04	12 07	
Ardwick	d																						
Manchester Piccadilly 10 🚌	a	10 26	10 32	10 36	10 41	10 42	11 02	10 57	11 02	11 11	11 12	11 15	11 32	11 36	11 41	11 42	12 02	11 57	12 02	12 11	12 12	12 15	12 32
Manchester Airport 85 ✈	a								11 26										12 26				

		EM ◇ A	NT B	NT C	NT	NT	TP ◇1 D 🚲	NT B	NT C	NT	NT	EM ◇ A	NT B	NT C	NT	NT	TP ◇1 D 🚲	NT B	NT C	NT	NT	EM ◇ A
Sheffield 7 🚌	d	11 42					12 11				12 14	12 42					13 11					13 42
Dore & Totley	d										12 21											
Grindleford	d										12 29											
Hathersage	d										12 32											
Bamford	d										12 36											
Hope (Derbyshire)	d										12 39											
Edale	d										12 47											
Chinley	d										12 55											
Hazel Grove 86	a																					
Stockport 86	a	12 25					12 53					13 25					13 53					14 25
New Mills Central	d					12 30					13 01					13 30					14 01	
Strines	d																				14 04	
Marple	d					12 35					13 07					13 35					14 07	
Rose Hill Marple	d				12 30					12 51					13 30					13 51		
Romiley	d				12 35	12 38				12 56	13 11				13 35	13 38				13 56	14 11	
Woodley	d				12 38										13 38							
Hyde Central	d				12 41										13 41							
Hyde North	d				12 44										13 44							
Guide Bridge	d		12 28	12 28	12 48			12 58	12 58				13 28	13 28	13 48			13 58	13 58			
Fairfield	d				12 51										13 51							
Gorton	d		12 31	12 31				13 01	13 01				13 31	13 31				14 01	14 01			
Bredbury	d					12 41					13 14					13 41					14 14	
Brinnington	d					12 44					13 16					13 44					14 16	
Reddish North	d					12 47					13 19					13 47					14 19	
Ryder Brow	d									13 03										14 03		
Belle Vue	d									13 05										14 05		
Ashburys	d		12 34	12 34				13 04	13 04	13 07			13 34	13 34				14 04	14 04	14 07		
Ardwick	d																					
Manchester Piccadilly 10 🚌	a	12 36	12 41	12 42	13 02	12 57	13 02	13 11	13 12	13 15	13 32	13 36	13 41	13 42	14 02	13 57	14 02	14 11	14 12	14 15	14 32	14 36
Manchester Airport 85 ✈	a						13 26										14 26					

A From Norwich to Liverpool Lime Street
B From Manchester Piccadilly
C From Hadfield
D From Cleethorpes

Sheffield, Chinley, Marple and Romiley Manchester and Manchester Airport

Network Diagram - see first Page of Table 78

		NT	NT	NT	NT	TP	NT		NT	NT	NT	EM	NT	NT	NT	NT	TP		NT	NT	NT	NT	EM	NT	NT
						◇1						◇					◇1						◇		
		A	B			C	A		B			D	A	B			C		A	B			D	A	B
Sheffield 7	d					14 11					14 14	14 42					15 11						15 42		
Dore & Totley	d										14 21														
Grindleford	d										14 29														
Hathersage	d										14 32														
Bamford	d										14 36														
Hope (Derbyshire)	d										14 39														
Edale	d										14 47														
Chinley	d										14 55														
Hazel Grove 86	a																								
Stockport 86	a					14 53						15 25					15 53						16 25		
New Mills Central	d				14 30						15 01					15 30						16 01			
Strines	d																					16 04			
Marple	d				14 35						15 07					15 35						16 07			
Rose Hill Marple	d			14 30						14 51					15 30						15 51				
Romiley	d			14 35	14 38					14 56	15 11				15 35	15 38					15 56	16 11			
Woodley	d			14 38											15 38										
Hyde Central	d			14 41											15 41										
Hyde North	d			14 44											15 44										
Guide Bridge	d	14 28	14 28	14 48			14 58		14 58				15 28	15 28	15 48				15 58	15 58				16 28	16 28
Fairfield	d			14 51											15 51										
Gorton	d	14 31	14 31				15 01		15 01				15 31	15 31					16 01	16 01				16 31	16 31
Bredbury	d				14 41						15 14					15 41						16 14			
Brinnington	d				14 44						15 16					15 44						16 16			
Reddish North	d				14 47						15 19					15 47						16 19			
Ryder Brow	d									15 03											16 03				
Belle Vue	d									15 05											16 05				
Ashburys	d	14 34	14 34				15 04		15 04	15 07			15 34	15 34					16 04	16 04	16 07			16 34	16 34
Ardwick	d																								
Manchester Piccadilly 10	a	14 41	14 42	15 02	14 57	15 02	15 11		15 12	15 15	15 32	15 36	15 41	15 42	16 02	15 57	16 02		16 11	16 12	16 15	16 32	16 36	16 41	16 42
Manchester Airport 85	a					15 26											16 26								

		NT	TP		NT	NT	NT	NT	NT	EM	NT	NT	NT		TP	NT	NT	NT	NT	NT	EM	NT	NT		TP
			◇1							◇					◇1						◇				◇1
			C		A				A	D			A		C		A			A	D				C
Sheffield 7	d		16 11					16 14		16 42					17 11				17 14		17 40				18 11
Dore & Totley	d							16 21											17 21						
Grindleford	d							16 29											17 28						
Hathersage	d							16 32											17 31						
Bamford	d							16 36											17 35						
Hope (Derbyshire)	d							16 39											17 38						
Edale	d							16 47											17 46						
Chinley	d							16 55											17 54						
Hazel Grove 86	a																								
Stockport 86	a		16 53							17 25					17 53						18 25				18 53
New Mills Central	d					16 37		17 01										17 48	18 00						
Strines	d																		18 03						
Marple	d					16 42	16 52	17 06								17 38		17 53	18 06				18 35		
Rose Hill Marple	d	16 26									17 10	17 27										18 11			
Romiley	d	16 31				16 45	16 56	17 10			17 15	17 32				17 41		17 57	18 10			18 16	18 38		
Woodley	d					16 49					17 18											18 19			
Hyde Central	d					16 52					17 21											18 22			
Hyde North	d					16 54					17 24											18 25			
Guide Bridge	d				16 49	16 58			17 15		17 28		17 42				17 58			18 17		18 29			
Fairfield	d										17 31											18 32			
Gorton	d				16 52				17 18				17 45				18 01			18 20					
Bredbury	d	16 34						17 13								17 44			18 13				18 41		
Brinnington	d	16 37														17 47							18 44		
Reddish North	d	16 40					17 02									17 50							18 47		
Ryder Brow	d	16 42					17 04									17 52									
Belle Vue	d	16 44														17 54									
Ashburys	d	16 47			16 55	17 03	17 07		17 24				17 48			17 57	18 04	18 07		18 23					
Ardwick	d																								
Manchester Piccadilly 10	a	16 56	17 02		17 05	17 10	17 16	17 29	17 33	17 37	17 42	17 48	17 57		18 02	18 03	18 12	18 13	18 30	18 34	18 36	18 41	18 57		19 02
Manchester Airport 85	a		17 32												18 26										19 28

A From Manchester Piccadilly
B From Hadfield
C From Cleethorpes
D From Norwich to Liverpool Lime Street

Sheffield, Chinley, Marple and Romiley Manchester and Manchester Airport

Network Diagram - see first Page of Table 78

		NT	NT	NT	NT	EM	NT	TP	NT		NT	NT	NT	EM	NT	TP	NT	TP	NT		EM	NT	NT	NT	TP
																ThFO		MT WO							
						◇		◇1						◇		◇1		◇1			◇				◇1
		A		A		B	C	D				C		B	C	E		F	C		G			C	D
Sheffield 7	d				18 14	18 43		19 11					19 14	19 42		20 11		20 11			20 32		20 35		22 11
Dore & Totley	d				18 21								19 21										20 43		
Grindleford	d				18 28								19 29										20 50		
Hathersage	d				18 32								19 32										20 53		
Bamford	d												19 36										20 57		
Hope (Derbyshire)	d				18 38								19 39										21 00		
Edale	d				18 45								19 47										21 08		
Chinley	d				18 53								19 55										21 16		
Hazel Grove 86	a																								
Stockport 86	a					19 25		19 53						20 25		20 53		20 56			21 20				22 53
New Mills Central	d				19 00								20 01				20 30						21 30		
Strines	d				19 03												20 33								
Marple	d				19 07						19 37		20 07				20 36						21 36		
Rose Hill Marple	d		18 44						19 30													21 12			
Romiley	d		18 49		19 11				19 35		19 40		20 11				20 40					21 17	21 40		
Woodley	d								19 38													21 20			
Hyde Central	d								19 41													21 23			
Hyde North	d								19 44													21 26			
Guide Bridge	d	18 46		19 01			19 28		19 48			19 58			20 28				20 58			21 30		21 58	
Fairfield	d								19 51													21 33			
Gorton	d	18 49		19 04			19 31					20 01			20 31				21 01					22 01	
Bredbury	d		18 52		19 14						19 43		20 14				20 43						21 43		
Brinnington	d		18 54		19 17						19 46		20 16				20 45						21 45		
Reddish North	d		18 58		19 20						19 49		20 19				20 48						21 48		
Ryder Brow	d		19 00								19 51						20 51						21 51		
Belle Vue	d		19 02								19 53						20 52						21 52		
Ashburys	d	18 54	19 05	19 08			19 34				19 56	20 04			20 34		20 55		21 04				21 55	22 04	
Ardwick	d																								
Manchester Piccadilly 10	a	19 03	19 12	19 15	19 33	19 36	19 42	20 02	20 02		20 05	20 12	20 32	20 36	20 42	21 02	21 03	21 05	21 12		21 32	21 42	22 05	22 12	23 02
Manchester Airport 85	a							20 39								21 36		21 38							23 26

		NT	NT	NT	NT
			C		
Sheffield 7	d			22 47	
Dore & Totley	d			22 54	
Grindleford	d			23 01	
Hathersage	d			23 05	
Bamford	d			23 08	
Hope (Derbyshire)	d			23 12	
Edale	d			23 19	
Chinley	d			23 27	
Hazel Grove 86	a				
Stockport 86	a			23 47	
New Mills Central	d	22 30			23 30
Strines	d	22 33			23 33
Marple	d	22 36			23 36
Rose Hill Marple	d				
Romiley	d	22 40			23 40
Woodley	d				
Hyde Central	d				
Hyde North	d				
Guide Bridge	d		22 58		
Fairfield	d				
Gorton	d		23 01		
Bredbury	d	22 43			23 43
Brinnington	d	22 45			23 45
Reddish North	d	22 48			23 48
Ryder Brow	d	22 51			23 51
Belle Vue	d	22 52			23 52
Ashburys	d	22 55	23 04		23 55
Ardwick	d				
Manchester Piccadilly 10	a	23 03	23 12	00 02	00 03
Manchester Airport 85	a				

A From Manchester Piccadilly
B From Norwich to Liverpool Lime Street
C From Hadfield
D From Cleethorpes
E From Cleethorpes
F From Cleethorpes
G From Norwich

Table 78

Saturdays

Sheffield, Chinley, Marple and Romiley Manchester and Manchester Airport

Network Diagram - see first Page of Table 78

		NT	NT	TP	TP	TP	NT	EM	NT	NT	NT	NT	TP	NT	NT	EM	NT	NT	NT	TP	NT	NT	NT
				◇1	◇1	◇1 A	B	◇ C		B			◇1 D 🚲	B		◇ C	B			◇1 D 🚲	B		
Sheffield 7	🚢 d	22p47		03 45	05 11	06 11		06 20					07 09		07 12	07 35				08 05			08 14
Dore & Totley	d	22p54						06 27					07 15		07 19	07 42				08 11			08 21
Grindleford	d	23p01						06 35							07 29								08 29
Hathersage	d	23p05						06 39							07 32								08 32
Bamford	d	23p08						06 43							07 36								08 36
Hope (Derbyshire)	d	23p12						06 47							07 39								08 39
Edale	d	23p19						06 55							07 47								08 47
Chinley	d	23p27						07 03							07 55	08 03				08 32			08 55
Hazel Grove	86 a															08 16							
Stockport	86 a	23p47			05 53	06 53		07 22					07 53			08 24				08 53			
New Mills Central	d		23p30						06 58						08 01								09 01
Strines	d		23p33						07 01						08 04								09 04
Marple	d		23p36						07 04			07 35			08 07				08 35			08 52	09 07
Rose Hill Marple	d										07 30							08 30					
Romiley	d		23p40						07 12		07 35	07 38			08 12			08 35	08 38			08 56	09 11
Woodley	d										07 38							08 38					
Hyde Central	d										07 41							08 41					
Hyde North	d										07 44							08 44					
Guide Bridge	d						06 57			07 28	07 48			07 58			08 28	08 48			08 58		
Fairfield	d										07 51							08 51					
Gorton	d						07 00			07 31				08 01			08 31				09 01		
Bredbury	d		23p43						07 15			07 41			08 15				08 41				09 14
Brinnington	d		23p45						07 17			07 44			08 16				08 44				09 16
Reddish North	d		23p48						07 20			07 47			08 19				08 47				09 19
Ryder Brow	d		23p51						07 24													09 03	
Belle Vue	d		23p52						07 26													09 05	
Ashburys	d		23p55				07 03		07 29	07 34				08 04			08 34				09 04	09 07	
Ardwick	d																						
Manchester Piccadilly 10	🚢 a	00 02	00 03	04 40	06 05	07 02	07 12	07 34	07 36	07 42	08 02	07 59	08 02	08 12	08 32	08 36	08 42	09 02	08 57	09 02	09 12	09 15	09 32
Manchester Airport	85 ✈ a			05 00	06 29	07 29							08 26							09 26			

		EM	NT	NT	NT	TP	NT	NT	NT	EM	NT	NT	NT	TP	NT	NT	NT	EM	NT	NT	NT	TP	NT
		◇ C	B			◇1 D 🚲	B			◇ E	B			◇1 D 🚲	B			◇ E	B			◇1 D 🚲	B
Sheffield 7	🚢 d	08 42				09 11			09 14	09 42				10 11			10 14	10 42				11 11	
Dore & Totley	d								09 21								10 21						
Grindleford	d								09 29								10 29						
Hathersage	d								09 32								10 32						
Bamford	d								09 36								10 36						
Hope (Derbyshire)	d								09 39								10 39						
Edale	d								09 47								10 47						
Chinley	d								09 55								10 55						
Hazel Grove	86 a																						
Stockport	86 a	09 25				09 53				10 25				10 53				11 25				11 53	
New Mills Central	d								10 01								11 01						
Strines	d								10 04														
Marple	d				09 35			09 52	10 07				10 35				11 07				11 35		
Rose Hill Marple	d			09 30								10 30				10 51				11 30			
Romiley	d			09 35	09 38			09 56	10 11			10 35	10 38			10 56	11 11			11 35	11 38		
Woodley	d			09 38								10 38								11 38			
Hyde Central	d			09 41								10 41								11 41			
Hyde North	d			09 44								10 44								11 44			
Guide Bridge	d		09 28	09 48			09 58				10 28	10 48			10 58				11 28	11 48			11 58
Fairfield	d			09 51								10 51								11 51			
Gorton	d		09 31				10 01				10 31				11 01				11 31				12 01
Bredbury	d				09 41				10 14				10 41				11 14				11 41		
Brinnington	d				09 44				10 16				10 44				11 16				11 44		
Reddish North	d				09 47				10 19				10 47				11 19				11 47		
Ryder Brow	d							10 03								11 03							
Belle Vue	d							10 05								11 05							
Ashburys	d		09 34				10 04	10 07			10 34				11 04	11 07			11 34				12 04
Ardwick	d																						
Manchester Piccadilly 10	🚢 a	09 36	09 42	10 02	09 57	10 02	10 12	10 15	10 32	10 36	10 42	11 02	10 57	11 02	11 12	11 15	11 32	11 36	11 42	12 02	11 57	12 02	12 12
Manchester Airport	85 ✈ a					10 26								11 26								12 26	

A From Doncaster
B From Hadfield
C From Nottingham to Liverpool Lime Street
D From Cleethorpes
E From Norwich to Liverpool Lime Street

Table 78 **Saturdays**

Sheffield, Chinley, Marple and Romiley Manchester and Manchester Airport

Network Diagram - see first Page of Table 78

		NT		NT	EM	NT	NT	NT	TP	NT	NT	NT		EM	NT	NT	NT	TP	NT	NT	NT	EM		NT	NT
					◇				◇1					◇				◇1				◇			
					A	B			C	B				A	B			C	B			A		B	
Sheffield 7	d			11 14	11 42				12 11			12 14		12 42				13 11			13 14	13 42			
Dore & Totley	d			11 21								12 21									13 21				
Grindleford	d			11 29								12 29									13 29				
Hathersage	d			11 32								12 32									13 32				
Bamford	d			11 36								12 36									13 36				
Hope (Derbyshire)	d			11 39								12 39									13 39				
Edale	d			11 47								12 47									13 47				
Chinley	d			11 55								12 55									13 55				
Hazel Grove 86	a																								
Stockport 86	a				12 25				12 53					13 25				13 53				14 25			
New Mills Central	d			12 01								13 01									14 01				
Strines	d			12 04																	14 04				
Marple	d			12 07				12 35				13 07					13 35				14 07				
Rose Hill Marple	d	11 51					12 30				12 51					13 30				13 51					14 30
Romiley	d	11 56		12 11			12 35	12 38			12 56	13 11				13 35	13 38			13 56	14 11				14 35
Woodley	d						12 38									13 38									14 38
Hyde Central	d						12 41									13 41									14 41
Hyde North	d						12 44									13 44									14 44
Guide Bridge	d					12 28	12 48			12 58					13 28	13 48			13 58					14 28	14 48
Fairfield	d						12 51									13 51									14 51
Gorton	d					12 31				13 01					13 31				14 01					14 31	
Bredbury	d			12 14				12 41				13 14					13 41				14 14				
Brinnington	d			12 16				12 44				13 16					13 44				14 16				
Reddish North	d			12 19				12 47				13 19					13 47				14 19				
Ryder Brow	d	12 03									13 03									14 03					
Belle Vue	d	12 05									13 05									14 05					
Ashburys	d	12 07				12 34				13 04	13 07				13 34				14 04	14 07				14 34	
Ardwick	d																								
Manchester Piccadilly 10	a	12 15		12 32	12 36	12 42	13 02	12 57	13 02	13 12	13 15	13 32		13 36	13 42	14 02	13 57	14 02	14 12	14 15	14 32	14 36		14 42	15 02
Manchester Airport 85	a								13 26									14 26							

		NT	TP	NT	NT	NT	EM	NT		NT	NT	TP	NT	NT	NT	EM	NT	NT		NT	TP	NT	NT	NT	EM
			◇1				◇					◇1				◇					◇1				◇
			C	B			A	B				C	B			A	B				C	B			A
Sheffield 7	d		14 11			14 14	14 42					15 11			15 14	15 42					16 11			16 14	16 42
Dore & Totley	d					14 21									15 21									16 21	
Grindleford	d					14 29									15 29									16 29	
Hathersage	d					14 32									15 32									16 32	
Bamford	d					14 36									15 36									16 36	
Hope (Derbyshire)	d					14 39									15 39									16 39	
Edale	d					14 47									15 47									16 47	
Chinley	d					14 55									15 55									16 55	
Hazel Grove 86	a																								
Stockport 86	a		14 53				15 25					15 53				16 25					16 53				17 25
New Mills Central	d					15 01									16 01									17 01	
Strines	d														16 04										
Marple	d	14 35				15 07					15 35				16 07					16 34				17 07	
Rose Hill Marple	d				14 51					15 30				15 51				16 30					16 51		
Romiley	d	14 38			14 56	15 11				15 35	15 38			15 56	16 11			16 35		16 38			16 56	17 11	
Woodley	d									15 38								16 38							
Hyde Central	d									15 41								16 41							
Hyde North	d									15 44								16 44							
Guide Bridge	d			14 58				15 28		15 48			15 58				16 28	16 48				16 58			
Fairfield	d									15 51								16 51							
Gorton	d			15 01				15 31					16 01				16 31					17 01			
Bredbury	d	14 41				15 14					15 41				16 14					16 41				17 14	
Brinnington	d	14 44				15 16					15 44				16 16					16 43				17 16	
Reddish North	d	14 47				15 19					15 47				16 19					16 46				17 19	
Ryder Brow	d				15 03									16 03									17 03		
Belle Vue	d				15 05									16 05									17 05		
Ashburys	d			15 04	15 07			15 34					16 04	16 07			16 34					17 04	17 07		
Ardwick	d																								
Manchester Piccadilly 10	a	14 57	15 02	15 12	15 15	15 32	15 36	15 42		16 02	15 57	16 02	16 12	16 15	16 33	16 36	16 42	17 02		16 56	17 02	17 12	17 15	17 32	17 37
Manchester Airport 85	a		15 26									16 26									17 32				

A From Norwich to Liverpool Lime Street

B From Hadfield

C From Cleethorpes

Table 78

Saturdays

Sheffield, Chinley, Marple and Romiley Manchester and Manchester Airport

Network Diagram - see first Page of Table 78

		NT A	NT	NT		TP ◇1 B	NT A	NT	NT	EM ◇ C	NT A	NT	NT	TP ◇1 B		NT A	NT	NT	EM ◇ C	NT A	TP ◇1 B	NT	NT A	NT
Sheffield 7	d					17 11			17 14	17 40				18 11				18 14	18 42		19 11			
Dore & Totley	d								17 21									18 21						
Grindleford	d								17 29									18 28						
Hathersage	d								17 32									18 32						
Bamford	d								17 36									18 35						
Hope (Derbyshire)	d								17 39									18 39						
Edale	d								17 47									18 46						
Chinley	d								17 55									18 54						
Hazel Grove 86	a																							
Stockport 86	a					17 53				18 25				18 53					19 25		19 53			
New Mills Central	d								18 01									19 01						
Strines	d								18 04									19 04						
Marple	d			17 34				17 52	18 07				18 35				18 52	19 07						19 56
Rose Hill Marple	d		17 30									18 30										19 30		
Romiley	d		17 35	17 38				17 56	18 11			18 35	18 38				18 56	19 11				19 35		19 59
Woodley	d		17 38									18 38										19 38		
Hyde Central	d		17 41									18 41										19 41		
Hyde North	d		17 44									18 44										19 44		
Guide Bridge	d	17 28	17 48				17 58				18 28	18 48				18 58				19 28		19 48	19 58	
Fairfield	d		17 51									18 51										19 51		
Gorton	d	17 31					18 01				18 31					19 01				19 31			20 01	
Bredbury	d			17 41					18 14				18 41					19 14						20 02
Brinnington	d			17 43					18 16				18 44					19 16						20 05
Reddish North	d			17 46					18 19				18 47					19 19						20 08
Ryder Brow	d							18 03									19 03							20 10
Belle Vue	d							18 05									19 05							20 12
Ashburys	d	17 34					18 04	18 07			18 34					19 04	19 07			19 34			20 04	20 15
Ardwick	d																							
Manchester Piccadilly 10	a	17 42	18 02	17 56		18 02	18 12	18 15	18 32	18 36	18 42	19 02	18 57	19 02		19 12	19 15	19 32	19 36	19 42	20 02	20 02	20 12	20 22
Manchester Airport 85	a					18 26								19 28							20 36			

		NT	EM ◇ C	TP ◇1 B	NT	NT A	EM ◇ D	NT	NT	NT A		NT	NT A	NT	NT
Sheffield 7	d	19 14	19 42	20 11			20 31		20 35					22 24	
Dore & Totley	d	19 21							20 42					22 31	
Grindleford	d	19 29							20 50					22 38	
Hathersage	d	19 32							20 53					22 41	
Bamford	d	19 36							20 57					22 45	
Hope (Derbyshire)	d	19 39							21 00					22 48	
Edale	d	19 47							21 08					22 56	
Chinley	d	19 55							21 16					23 04	
Hazel Grove 86	a														
Stockport 86	a		20 25	20 53			21 20							23 21	
New Mills Central	d	20 01			20 30				21 30			22 30			23 30
Strines	d				20 33							22 33			23 33
Marple	d	20 07			20 36				21 36			22 36			23 36
Rose Hill Marple	d							21 12							
Romiley	d	20 11			20 40			21 17	21 40			22 40			23 40
Woodley	d							21 20							
Hyde Central	d							21 23							
Hyde North	d							21 26							
Guide Bridge	d					20 58		21 30		21 58			22 58		
Fairfield	d							21 33							
Gorton	d					21 01				22 01			23 01		
Bredbury	d	20 14			20 43				21 43			22 43			23 43
Brinnington	d	20 16			20 45				21 45			22 45			23 45
Reddish North	d	20 19			20 48				21 48			22 48			23 48
Ryder Brow	d				20 51				21 51			22 51			23 51
Belle Vue	d				20 52				21 52			22 52			23 52
Ashburys	d				20 55	21 04			21 55	22 04		22 55	23 04		23 55
Ardwick	d														
Manchester Piccadilly 10	a	20 32	20 36	21 02	21 03	21 12	21 32	21 42	22 05	22 12		23 03	23 12	23 43	00 03
Manchester Airport 85	a			21 36											

A From Hadfield
B From Cleethorpes
C From Norwich to Liverpool Lime Street
D From Norwich

Table 78

Sundays
until 1 January

Sheffield, Chinley, Marple and Romiley Manchester and Manchester Airport

Network Diagram - see first Page of Table 78

		NT A	NT	NT B	NT B	EM ◇ C	NT B	TP ◇1 D	NT B	NT	EM ◇ C	NT B	TP ◇1 D	NT B	EM ◇ C	NT B	TP ◇1 D	NT B	NT	EM ◇ C	NT B	TP ◇1 E	NT B
Sheffield 7	d		09 20			10 41		11 10		11 14	11 38		12 10		12 41		13 10		13 13	13 38		14 11	
Dore & Totley	d		09 27			10 48				11 21									13 20				
Grindleford	d		09 34							11 29									13 28				
Hathersage	d		09 38							11 32									13 31				
Bamford	d		09 41							11 36									13 35				
Hope (Derbyshire)	d		09 45							11 39									13 38				
Edale	d		09 52							11 47									13 46				
Chinley	d		10 00							11 55									13 54				
Hazel Grove 86	a																						
Stockport 86	a					11 25		11 53			12 25		12 50		13 25		13 53			14 25		14 53	
New Mills Central	d	23p30	10 07							12 01									14 00				
Strines	d	23p33	10 10							12 04									14 03				
Marple	d	23p36	10 13							12 07									14 07				
Rose Hill Marple	d																						
Romiley	d	23p40	10 17							12 11									14 10				
Woodley	d																						
Hyde Central	d																						
Hyde North	d																						
Guide Bridge	d			10 28	10 58		11 28		11 58			12 28		12 58		13 28		13 58			14 28		14 58
Fairfield	d																						
Gorton	d			10 31	11 01		11 31		12 01			12 31		13 01		13 31		14 01			14 31		15 01
Bredbury	d	23p43	10 20							12 14									14 13				
Brinnington	d	23p45	10 22							12 16									14 16				
Reddish North	d	23p48	10 25							12 19									14 19				
Ryder Brow	d	23p51																					
Belle Vue	d	23p52																					
Ashburys	d	23p55		10 34	11 04		11 34		12 04			12 34		13 04		13 34		14 04			14 34		15 04
Ardwick	d																						
Manchester Piccadilly 10	a	00 03	10 37	10 42	11 12	11 37	11 42	12 06	12 12	12 31	12 35	12 42	13 05	13 12	13 37	13 42	14 06	14 12	14 31	14 37	14 42	15 06	15 12
Manchester Airport 85	a							12 27					13 29				14 27					15 28	

		EM ◇ F	NT B	TP ◇1 D	NT B	NT	EM ◇ C	NT B	TP ◇1 D	NT B	EM ◇ C	NT B	TP ◇1 D	NT B	NT	EM ◇ F	NT B	TP ◇1 D	NT B	EM ◇ F	NT B	TP ◇1 D	NT B
Sheffield 7	d	14 39		15 11		15 14	15 38		16 11		16 44		17 11		17 14	17 44		18 11		18 37		19 11	
Dore & Totley	d					15 21									17 21								
Grindleford	d					15 29									17 29								
Hathersage	d					15 32									17 32								
Bamford	d					15 36									17 36								
Hope (Derbyshire)	d					15 39									17 39								
Edale	d					15 47									17 47								
Chinley	d					15 55									17 55								
Hazel Grove 86	a																						
Stockport 86	a	15 25		15 53			16 25		16 53		17 28		17 53			18 25		18 53		19 25		19 53	
New Mills Central	d					16 01									18 01								
Strines	d					16 04									18 04								
Marple	d					16 07									18 07								
Rose Hill Marple	d																						
Romiley	d					16 11									18 11								
Woodley	d																						
Hyde Central	d																						
Hyde North	d																						
Guide Bridge	d		15 28		15 58			16 28		16 58		17 28		17 58			18 28		18 58		19 28		19 58
Fairfield	d																						
Gorton	d		15 31		16 01			16 31		17 01		17 31		18 01			18 31		19 01		19 31		20 01
Bredbury	d					16 14									18 14								
Brinnington	d					16 16									18 16								
Reddish North	d					16 19									18 19								
Ryder Brow	d																						
Belle Vue	d																						
Ashburys	d		15 34		16 04			16 34		17 04		17 34		18 04			18 34		19 04		19 34		20 04
Ardwick	d																						
Manchester Piccadilly 10	a	15 37	15 42	16 06	16 12	16 31	16 37	16 42	17 06	17 12	17 37	17 42	18 06	18 12	18 31	18 37	18 42	19 06	19 12	19 37	19 42	20 09	20 12
Manchester Airport 85	a			16 27					17 27				18 27					19 27				20 30	

A not 11 December
B From Hadfield
C From Nottingham to Liverpool Lime Street
D From Cleethorpes
E From Doncaster
F From Norwich to Liverpool Lime Street

Table 78

Sundays
until 1 January

Sheffield, Chinley, Marple and Romiley Manchester and Manchester Airport

Network Diagram - see first Page of Table 78

	NT	EM	NT	TP	NT	EM	TP	NT	NT	NT
		◇		◇1		◇	◇1			
		A	B	C	B	A	C	B		
Sheffield 7 ⇌ d	19 14	19 35		20 11		20 35	21 11		22 17	
Dore & Totley d	19 21								22 24	
Grindleford d	19 29								22 32	
Hathersage d	19 32								22 35	
Bamford d	19 36								22 39	
Hope (Derbyshire) d	19 39								22 42	
Edale d	19 47								22 50	
Chinley d	19 55								22 58	
Hazel Grove 86 a										
Stockport 86 a		20 25		20 53		21 24	21 53		23 16	
New Mills Central d	20 01									23 01
Strines d	20 04									23 04
Marple d	20 07									23 07
Rose Hill Marple d										
Romiley d	20 11									23 11
Woodley d										
Hyde Central d										
Hyde North d										
Guide Bridge d			20 28		20 58			21 58		
Fairfield d										
Gorton d			20 31		21 01			22 01		
Bredbury d	20 14									23 14
Brinnington d	20 16									23 16
Reddish North d	20 19									23 19
Ryder Brow d										
Belle Vue d										
Ashburys d			20 34		21 04			22 04		
Ardwick d										
Manchester Piccadilly 10 ⇌ a	20 32	20 38	20 42	21 06	21 12	21 36	22 06	22 12	23 29	23 31
Manchester Airport 85 ✈ a				21 27			22 27			

Sundays
8 January to 12 February

	NT	TP	NT	NT	NT	EM	NT	TP	NT
		◇1				◇		◇1	
				B	B	D	B		B
Sheffield 7 ⇌ d		07 50	09 20			10 41		11 10	
Dore & Totley d			09 27			10 48			
Grindleford d			09 34						
Hathersage d			09 38						
Bamford d			09 41						
Hope (Derbyshire) d			09 45						
Edale d			09 52						
Chinley d			10 00						
Hazel Grove 86 a									
Stockport 86 a		08 31				11 25		11 53	
New Mills Central d	23p30		10 07						
Strines d	23p33		10 10						
Marple d	23p36		10 13						
Rose Hill Marple d									
Romiley d	23p40		10 17						
Woodley d									
Hyde Central d									
Hyde North d									
Guide Bridge d				10 28	10 58		11 28		11 58
Fairfield d									
Gorton d				10 31	11 01		11 31		12 01
Bredbury d	23p43		10 20						
Brinnington d	23p45		10 22						
Reddish North d	23p48		10 25						
Ryder Brow d	23p51								
Belle Vue d	23p52								
Ashburys d	23p55			10 34	11 04		11 34		12 04
Ardwick d									
Manchester Piccadilly 10 ⇌ a	00 03	08 42	10 37	10 42	11 12	11 37	11 42	12 06	12 12
Manchester Airport 85 ✈ a		09 07						12 34	

	NT	EM	NT	TP	NT	EM	NT	TP	NT	NT	EM	NT	TP
		◇		◇1		◇		◇1			◇		◇1
		D	B		B	D	B		B		D	B	
Sheffield 7 ⇌ d	11 14	11 38		12 10		12 41		13 10		13 13	13 38		14 11
Dore & Totley d	11 21									13 20			
Grindleford d	11 29									13 28			
Hathersage d	11 32									13 31			
Bamford d	11 36									13 35			
Hope (Derbyshire) d	11 39									13 38			
Edale d	11 47									13 46			
Chinley d	11 55									13 54			
Hazel Grove 86 a													
Stockport 86 a		12 25		12 53		13 25		13 53			14 25		14 53
New Mills Central d	12 01									14 00			
Strines d	12 04									14 03			
Marple d	12 07									14 07			
Rose Hill Marple d													
Romiley d	12 11									14 10			
Woodley d													
Hyde Central d													
Hyde North d													
Guide Bridge d			12 28		12 58		13 28		13 58			14 28	
Fairfield d													
Gorton d			12 31		13 01		13 31		14 01			14 31	
Bredbury d	12 14									14 13			
Brinnington d	12 16									14 16			
Reddish North d	12 19									14 19			
Ryder Brow d													
Belle Vue d													
Ashburys d			12 34		13 04		13 34		14 04			14 34	
Ardwick d													
Manchester Piccadilly 10 ⇌ a	12 31	12 35	12 42	13 05	13 12	13 37	13 42	14 06	14 12	14 31	14 37	14 42	15 06
Manchester Airport 85 ✈ a				13 29				14 27					15 28

A From Norwich
B From Hadfield
C From Cleethorpes
D From Nottingham to Liverpool Lime Street

Table 78

Sundays

8 January to 12 February

Sheffield, Chinley, Marple and Romiley Manchester and Manchester Airport

Network Diagram - see first Page of Table 78

		NT	EM	NT	TP	NT		NT	EM	NT	TP	NT	EM	NT	TP	NT		NT	EM	NT	TP	NT	EM	NT	TP
			◇		◇1				◇		◇1		◇		◇1				◇		◇1		◇		◇1
		A	B	A		A			C	A		A	C	A		A			B	A		A	B	A	
Sheffield 7 ⇌	d		14 39		15 11			15 14	15 38		16 11		16 44		17 11			17 14	17 44		18 11		18 37		19 11
Dore & Totley	d							15 21										17 21							
Grindleford	d							15 29										17 29							
Hathersage	d							15 32										17 32							
Bamford	d							15 36										17 36							
Hope (Derbyshire)	d							15 39										17 39							
Edale	d							15 47										17 47							
Chinley	d							15 55										17 55							
Hazel Grove 86	a																								
Stockport 86	a		15 25		15 53				16 25		16 53		17 28		17 53				18 25		18 53		19 25		19 53
New Mills Central	d							16 01										18 01							
Strines	d							16 04										18 04							
Marple	d							16 07										18 07							
Rose Hill Marple	d																								
Romiley	d							16 11										18 11							
Woodley	d																								
Hyde Central	d																								
Hyde North	d																								
Guide Bridge	d	14 58		15 28		15 58				16 28		16 58		17 28		17 58				18 28		18 58		19 28	
Fairfield	d																								
Gorton	d	15 01		15 31		16 01				16 31		17 01		17 31		18 01				18 31		19 01		19 31	
Bredbury	d							16 14										18 14							
Brinnington	d							16 16										18 16							
Reddish North	d							16 19										18 19							
Ryder Brow	d																								
Belle Vue	d																								
Ashburys	d	15 04		15 34		16 04				16 34		17 04		17 34		18 04				18 34		19 04		19 34	
Ardwick	d																								
Manchester Piccadilly 10 ⇌	a	15 12	15 37	15 42	16 06	16 12		16 31	16 37	16 42	17 06	17 12	17 37	17 42	18 06	18 12		18 31	18 37	18 42	19 06	19 12	19 37	19 42	20 09
Manchester Airport 85 ✈	a				16 27						17 27				18 27						19 27				20 30

		NT		NT	EM	NT	TP	NT	EM	TP	NT	NT		NT
					◇		◇1		◇	◇1				
		A			D	A		A	D		A			
Sheffield 7 ⇌	d			19 14	19 35		20 11		20 35	21 11		22 17		
Dore & Totley	d			19 21								22 24		
Grindleford	d			19 29								22 32		
Hathersage	d			19 32								22 35		
Bamford	d			19 36								22 39		
Hope (Derbyshire)	d			19 39								22 42		
Edale	d			19 47								22 50		
Chinley	d			19 55								22 58		
Hazel Grove 86	a													
Stockport 86	a				20 25		20 53		21 24	21 53		23 16		
New Mills Central	d			20 01										23 01
Strines	d			20 04										23 04
Marple	d			20 07										23 07
Rose Hill Marple	d													
Romiley	d			20 11										23 11
Woodley	d													
Hyde Central	d													
Hyde North	d													
Guide Bridge	d	19 58				20 28		20 58			21 58			
Fairfield	d													
Gorton	d	20 01				20 31		21 01			22 01			
Bredbury	d			20 14										23 14
Brinnington	d			20 16										23 16
Reddish North	d			20 19										23 19
Ryder Brow	d													
Belle Vue	d													
Ashburys	d	20 04				20 34		21 04			22 04			
Ardwick	d													
Manchester Piccadilly 10 ⇌	a	20 12		20 32	20 38	20 42	21 06	21 12	21 36	22 06	22 12	23 29		23 31
Manchester Airport 85 ✈	a						21 27			22 28				

A From Hadfield
B From Norwich to Liverpool Lime Street
C From Nottingham to Liverpool Lime Street
D From Norwich

Table 78

Sundays

19 February to 25 March

Sheffield, Chinley, Marple and Romiley Manchester and Manchester Airport

Network Diagram - see first Page of Table 78

		NT	NT	NT	NT	EM	NT	TP	NT	NT	EM	NT	TP	NT	EM	NT	TP	NT	NT	EM	NT	TP	NT
						◇		◇1			◇		◇1		◇		◇1			◇		◇1	
				A	A	B	A	C	A		B	A	C	A	B	A	C	A		B	A	D	A
Sheffield 7	d		09 20			10 41		11 10		11 14	11 38		12 10		12 41		13 10		13 13	13 38		14 11	
Dore & Totley	d		09 27			10 48				11 21									13 20				
Grindleford	d		09 34							11 29									13 28				
Hathersage	d		09 38							11 32									13 31				
Bamford	d		09 41							11 36									13 35				
Hope (Derbyshire)	d		09 45							11 39									13 38				
Edale	d		09 52							11 47									13 46				
Chinley	d		10 00							11 55									13 54				
Hazel Grove 86	a																						
Stockport 86	a					11 25		11 53			12 25		12 50		13 25		13 53			14 25		14 53	
New Mills Central	d	23p30	10 07							12 01									14 00				
Strines	d	23p33	10 10							12 04									14 03				
Marple	d	23p36	10 13							12 07									14 07				
Rose Hill Marple	d																						
Romiley	d	23p40	10 17							12 11									14 10				
Woodley	d																						
Hyde Central	d																						
Hyde North	d																						
Guide Bridge	d			10 28	10 58		11 28		11 58			12 28		12 58		13 28		13 58			14 28		14 58
Fairfield	d																						
Gorton	d			10 31	11 01		11 31		12 01			12 31		13 01		13 31		14 01			14 31		15 01
Bredbury	d	23p43	10 20							12 14									14 13				
Brinnington	d	23p45	10 22							12 16									14 16				
Reddish North	d	23p48	10 25							12 19									14 19				
Ryder Brow	d	23p51																					
Belle Vue	d	23p52																					
Ashburys	d	23p55		10 34	11 04		11 34		12 04			12 34		13 04		13 34		14 04			14 34		15 04
Ardwick	d																						
Manchester Piccadilly 10	a	00 03	10 37	10 42	11 12	11 37	11 42	12 06	12 12	12 31	12 35	12 42	13 05	13 12	13 37	13 42	14 06	14 12	14 31	14 37	14 42	15 06	15 12
Manchester Airport 85	a							12 27					13 29				14 27					15 28	

		EM	NT	TP	NT	NT	EM	NT	TP	NT	EM	NT	TP	NT	NT	EM	NT	TP	NT	EM	NT	TP	NT
		◇		◇1			◇		◇1		◇		◇1			◇		◇1		◇		◇1	
		E	A	C	A		B	A	C	A	B	A	C	A		E	A	C	A	E	A	C	A
Sheffield 7	d	14 39		15 11		15 14	15 38		16 11		16 44		17 11		17 14	17 44		18 11		18 37		19 11	
Dore & Totley	d					15 21									17 21								
Grindleford	d					15 29									17 29								
Hathersage	d					15 32									17 32								
Bamford	d					15 36									17 36								
Hope (Derbyshire)	d					15 39									17 39								
Edale	d					15 47									17 47								
Chinley	d					15 55									17 55								
Hazel Grove 86	a																						
Stockport 86	a	15 25		15 53			16 25		16 53		17 28		17 53			18 25		18 53		19 25		19 53	
New Mills Central	d					16 01									18 01								
Strines	d					16 04									18 04								
Marple	d					16 07									18 07								
Rose Hill Marple	d																						
Romiley	d					16 11									18 11								
Woodley	d																						
Hyde Central	d																						
Hyde North	d																						
Guide Bridge	d		15 28		15 58			16 28		16 58		17 28		17 58			18 28		18 58		19 28		19 58
Fairfield	d																						
Gorton	d		15 31		16 01			16 31		17 01		17 31		18 01			18 31		19 01		19 31		20 01
Bredbury	d					16 14									18 14								
Brinnington	d					16 16									18 16								
Reddish North	d					16 19									18 19								
Ryder Brow	d																						
Belle Vue	d																						
Ashburys	d		15 34		16 04			16 34		17 04		17 34		18 04			18 34		19 04		19 34		20 04
Ardwick	d																						
Manchester Piccadilly 10	a	15 37	15 42	16 06	16 12	16 31	16 37	16 42	17 06	17 12	17 37	17 42	18 06	18 12	18 31	18 37	18 42	19 06	19 12	19 37	19 42	20 09	20 12
Manchester Airport 85	a			16 34					17 27				18 27					19 27				20 30	

A From Hadfield
B From Nottingham to Liverpool Lime Street
C From Cleethorpes
D From Doncaster
E From Norwich to Liverpool Lime Street

Table 78

Sundays

19 February to 25 March

Sheffield, Chinley, Marple and Romiley Manchester and Manchester Airport

Network Diagram - see first Page of Table 78

		NT	EM	NT	TP	NT	EM	TP	NT	NT	NT
			◇		◇1		◇	◇1			
			A	B	C	B	A	C	B		
Sheffield 7 ⇌	d	19 14	19 35		20 11		20 35	21 11		22 17	
Dore & Totley	d	19 21								22 24	
Grindleford	d	19 29								22 32	
Hathersage	d	19 32								22 35	
Bamford	d	19 36								22 39	
Hope (Derbyshire)	d	19 39								22 42	
Edale	d	19 47								22 50	
Chinley	d	19 55								22 58	
Hazel Grove 86	a										
Stockport 86	a		20 25		20 53		21 24	21 53		23 16	
New Mills Central	d	20 01									23 01
Strines	d	20 04									23 04
Marple	d	20 07									23 07
Rose Hill Marple	d										
Romiley	d	20 11									23 11
Woodley	d										
Hyde Central	d										
Hyde North	d										
Guide Bridge	d			20 28		20 58			21 58		
Fairfield	d										
Gorton	d			20 31		21 01			22 01		
Bredbury	d	20 14									23 14
Brinnington	d	20 16									23 16
Reddish North	d	20 19									23 19
Ryder Brow	d										
Belle Vue	d										
Ashburys	d			20 34		21 04			22 04		
Ardwick	d										
Manchester Piccadilly 10 ⇌	a	20 32	20 38	20 42	21 06	21 12	21 36	22 06	22 12	23 29	23 31
Manchester Airport 85 ✈	a				21 27			22 27			

Sundays

from 1 April

		NT	TP	TP	NT	NT	TP	NT	EM	NT	TP	NT	NT	EM	NT	TP	NT	EM	NT	TP	NT	NT	EM
			◇1	◇1			◇1		◇		◇1			◇		◇1		◇		◇1			◇
				D		B		B	E	B	C	B		E	B	C	B	E	B	C	B		E
Sheffield 7 ⇌	d		07 50	09 10	09 20		10 10		10 41		11 10		11 14	11 38		12 10		12 41		13 10		13 13	13 38
Dore & Totley	d				09 27				10 48				11 21									13 20	
Grindleford	d				09 34								11 29									13 28	
Hathersage	d				09 38								11 32									13 31	
Bamford	d				09 41								11 36									13 35	
Hope (Derbyshire)	d				09 45								11 39									13 38	
Edale	d				09 52								11 47									13 46	
Chinley	d				10 00								11 55									13 54	
Hazel Grove 86	a																						
Stockport 86	a		08 31	09 53			10 53		11 25		11 53			12 25		12 53		13 25		13 53			14 25
New Mills Central	d	23p30			10 07								12 01									14 00	
Strines	d	23p33			10 10								12 04									14 03	
Marple	d	23p36			10 13								12 07									14 07	
Rose Hill Marple	d																						
Romiley	d	23p40			10 17								12 11									14 10	
Woodley	d																						
Hyde Central	d																						
Hyde North	d																						
Guide Bridge	d					10 28		10 58		11 28		11 58			12 28		12 58		13 28		13 58		
Fairfield	d																						
Gorton	d					10 31		11 01		11 31		12 01			12 31		13 01		13 31		14 01		
Bredbury	d	23p43			10 20								12 14									14 13	
Brinnington	d	23p45			10 22								12 16									14 16	
Reddish North	d	23p48			10 25								12 19									14 19	
Ryder Brow	d	23p51																					
Belle Vue	d	23p52																					
Ashburys	d	23p55				10 34		11 04		11 34		12 04			12 34		13 04		13 34		14 04		
Ardwick	d																						
Manchester Piccadilly 10 ⇌	a	00 03	08 42	10 04	10 37	10 42	11 06	11 12	11 37	11 42	12 06	12 12	12 31	12 35	12 42	13 06	13 12	13 37	13 42	14 06	14 12	14 31	14 37
Manchester Airport 85 ✈	a		09 07								12 27					13 27				14 27			

A From Norwich
B From Hadfield
C From Cleethorpes
D From Meadowhall
E From Nottingham to Liverpool Lime Street

Table 78

Sundays
from 1 April

Sheffield, Chinley, Marple and Romiley Manchester and Manchester Airport

Network Diagram - see first Page of Table 78

		NT	TP	NT	EM	NT	TP	NT	NT	EM	NT	TP	NT	NT	EM	NT	TP	NT	NT	EM	NT	TP	NT
			◇1		◇		◇1			◇		◇1			◇		◇1			◇		◇1	
		A	B	A	C	A	D	A		E	A	D	A		E	A	D	A		C	A	D	A
Sheffield 7	d		14 11		14 39		15 11		15 14	15 38		16 11		16 15	16 44		17 11		17 14	17 44		18 11	
Dore & Totley	d								15 21					16 23					17 21				
Grindleford	d								15 29					16 30					17 29				
Hathersage	d								15 32					16 33					17 32				
Bamford	d								15 36					16 37					17 36				
Hope (Derbyshire)	d								15 39					16 40					17 39				
Edale	d								15 47					16 48					17 47				
Chinley	d								15 55					16 56					17 55				
Hazel Grove 86	a																						
Stockport 86	a		14 53		15 25		15 53			16 25		16 53			17 28		17 53			18 25		18 53	
New Mills Central	d								16 01					17 02					18 01				
Strines	d								16 04					17 05					18 04				
Marple	d								16 07					17 08					18 07				
Rose Hill Marple	d																						
Romiley	d								16 11					17 12					18 11				
Woodley	d																						
Hyde Central	d																						
Hyde North	d																						
Guide Bridge	d	14 28		14 58		15 28		15 58			16 28		16 58			17 28		17 58			18 28		18 58
Fairfield	d																						
Gorton	d	14 31		15 01		15 31		16 01			16 31		17 01			17 31		18 01			18 31		19 01
Bredbury	d								16 14					17 15					18 14				
Brinnington	d								16 16					17 17					18 16				
Reddish North	d								16 19					17 20					18 19				
Ryder Brow	d																						
Belle Vue	d																						
Ashburys	d	14 34		15 04		15 34		16 04			16 34		17 04			17 34		18 04			18 34		19 04
Ardwick	d																						
Manchester Piccadilly 10	a	14 42	15 06	15 12	15 37	15 42	16 06	16 12	16 31	16 37	16 42	17 06	17 12	17 32	17 37	17 42	18 06	18 12	18 31	18 37	18 42	19 06	19 12
Manchester Airport 85	a		15 28				16 34					17 27					18 27					19 27	

		EM	NT	TP	NT	NT	EM	NT	TP	NT	EM	TP	NT	NT	NT
		◇		◇1			◇		◇1		◇	◇1			
		C	A	D	A		F	A	D	A	F	D	A		
Sheffield 7	d	18 37		19 11		19 14	19 35		20 11		20 35	21 11		22 17	
Dore & Totley	d					19 21								22 24	
Grindleford	d					19 29								22 32	
Hathersage	d					19 32								22 35	
Bamford	d					19 36								22 39	
Hope (Derbyshire)	d					19 39								22 42	
Edale	d					19 47								22 50	
Chinley	d					19 55								22 58	
Hazel Grove 86	a														
Stockport 86	a	19 25		19 53			20 25		20 53		21 24	21 53		23 16	
New Mills Central	d					20 01									23 01
Strines	d					20 04									23 04
Marple	d					20 07									23 07
Rose Hill Marple	d														
Romiley	d					20 11									23 11
Woodley	d														
Hyde Central	d														
Hyde North	d														
Guide Bridge	d		19 28		19 58			20 28		20 58			21 58		
Fairfield	d														
Gorton	d		19 31		20 01			20 31		21 01			22 01		
Bredbury	d					20 14									23 14
Brinnington	d					20 16									23 16
Reddish North	d					20 19									23 19
Ryder Brow	d														
Belle Vue	d														
Ashburys	d		19 34		20 04			20 34		21 04			22 04		
Ardwick	d														
Manchester Piccadilly 10	a	19 37	19 42	20 09	20 12	20 32	20 38	20 42	21 06	21 12	21 36	22 06	22 12	23 29	23 31
Manchester Airport 85	a			20 30					21 27			22 27			

A From Hadfield
B From Doncaster
C From Norwich to Liverpool Lime Street
D From Cleethorpes
E From Nottingham to Liverpool Lime Street
F From Norwich

Table 79

Mondays to Fridays

Manchester - Glossop and Hadfield

Network Diagram - see first Page of Table 78

Miles	Miles		NT	NT	NT	NT	NT	NT	NT	NT	NT	NT	NT	NT	NT
0	—	**Manchester Piccadilly** 10 78 ⛴ d	06 16	06 46	07 03	07 18	07 48	08 07	08 29	08 48	09 15	09 48	10 15	10 48	11 18
0½	—	Ardwick 78 d													
1½	—	Ashburys 78 d	06 20	06 50	07 07	07 22	07 52	08 11	08 33	08 52	09 19	09 52	10 19	10 52	11 22
2½	—	Gorton 78 d	06 22	06 52	07 09	07 24	07 54	08 13	08 35	08 54	09 21	09 54	10 21	10 54	11 24
4¾	—	Guide Bridge 78 d	06 26	06 56	07 13	07 28	07 58	08 17	08 39	08 58	09 25	09 58	10 25	10 58	11 28
6¾	—	Flowery Field d	06 29	06 59	07 16	07 31	08 01	08 20	08 42	09 01	09 28	10 01	10 28	11 01	11 31
7½	—	Newton for Hyde d	06 31	07 01	07 18	07 33	08 03	08 22	08 44	09 03	09 30	10 03	10 30	11 03	11 33
8½	—	Godley d	06 33	07 03	07 20	07 35	08 05	08 24	08 46	09 05	09 32	10 05	10 32	11 05	11 35
9	—	Hattersley d	06 35	07 05	07 22	07 37	08 07	08 26	08 48	09 07	09 34	10 07	10 34	11 07	11 37
10	—	Broadbottom d	06 37	07 07	07 24	07 39	08 09	08 28	08 50	09 09	09 36	10 09	10 36	11 09	11 39
12¼	0	Dinting 3 d	06 45	07 15	07 35	07 45	08 14	08 34	08 56	09 16	09 46	10 16	10 46	11 16	11 46
13¼	—	**Glossop** a	06 48	07b25	07b45	08b03	08b26	08b46	09b06	09 19	09 49	10 19	10 49	11 19	11 49
—	—	d	06 51							09 22	09 52	10 22	10 52	11 22	11 52
15	0¾	**Hadfield** a	06 59	07 17	07 37	07 47	08 17	08 38	08 58	09 28	09 58	10 28	10 58	11 28	11 58

	NT	NT	NT	NT	NT	NT	NT	NT	NT	NT	NT	NT	NT	NT
Manchester Piccadilly 10 78 ⛴ d	11 48	12 18	12 48	13 18	13 48	14 18	14 48	15 18	15 48	16 15	16 36	16 59	17 15	17 37
Ardwick 78 d														
Ashburys 78 d	11 52	12 22	12 52	13 22	13 52	14 22	14 52	15 22	15 52	16 19	16 40	17 03	17 19	17 41
Gorton 78 d	11 54	12 24	12 54	13 24	13 54	14 24	14 54	15 24	15 54	16 21	16 42	17 05	17 21	17 43
Guide Bridge 78 d	11 58	12 28	12 58	13 28	13 58	14 28	14 58	15 28	15 58	16 25	16 46	17 10	17 25	17 47
Flowery Field d	12 01	12 31	13 01	13 31	14 01	14 31	15 01	15 31	16 01	16 28	16 49	17 13	17 28	17 50
Newton for Hyde d	12 03	12 33	13 03	13 33	14 03	14 33	15 03	15 33	16 03	16 30	16 51	17 15	17 30	17 52
Godley d	12 05	12 35	13 05	13 35	14 05	14 35	15 05	15 35	16 05	16 32	16 53	17 17	17 32	17 54
Hattersley d	12 07	12 37	13 07	13 37	14 07	14 37	15 07	15 37	16 07	16 34	16 55	17 19	17 34	17 56
Broadbottom d	12 09	12 39	13 09	13 39	14 09	14 39	15 09	15 39	16 09	16 36	16 57	17 21	17 36	17 59
Dinting 3 d	12 16	12 46	13 16	13 46	14 16	14 46	15 16	15 46	16 16	16 42	17 03	17 27	17 42	18 05
Glossop a	12 19	12 49	13 19	13 49	14 19	14 49	15 19	15 49	16 19	16 45	17 06	17 31	17 45	18 08
d	12 22	12 52	13 22	13 52	14 22	14 52	15 22	15 52	16 22	16 48	17 09	17 33	17 48	18 11
Hadfield a	12 28	12 58	13 28	13 58	14 28	14 58	15 28	15 58	16 28	16 54	17 15	17 40	17 54	18 17

	NT	NT	NT	NT	NT		NT	NT
Manchester Piccadilly 10 78 ⛴ d	17 59	18 15	18 48	19 18	19 48		22 48	23 27
Ardwick 78 d								
Ashburys 78 d	18 03	18 19	18 52	19 22	19 52		22 52	23 31
Gorton 78 d	18 05	18 21	18 54	19 24	19 54		22 54	23 33
Guide Bridge 78 d	18 10	18 25	18 58	19 28	19 58	and	22 58	23 37
Flowery Field d	18 13	18 28	19 01	19 31	20 01	hourly	23 01	23 40
Newton for Hyde d	18 15	18 30	19 03	19 33	20 03	until	23 03	23 42
Godley d	18 17	18 32	19 05	19 35	20 05		23 05	23 44
Hattersley d	18 19	18 34	19 07	19 37	20 07		23 07	23 46
Broadbottom d	18 21	18 36	19 09	19 39	20 09		23 09	23 48
Dinting 3 d	18 27	18 42	19 16	19 46	20 16		23 16	23 54
Glossop a	18 30	18 45	19 19	19 49	20 19		23 19	
d	18 33	18 48	19 22	19 52	20 22		23 22	
Hadfield a	18 39	18 54	19 29	19 59	20 29		23 29	23 56

Saturdays

	NT	NT	NT	NT	NT	NT		NT	NT		NT	NT
Manchester Piccadilly 10 78 ⛴ d	06 16	06 48	07 18	07 48	08 15	08 48		18 48	19 48		22 48	23 27
Ardwick 78 d												
Ashburys 78 d	06 20	06 52	07 22	07 52	08 19	08 52		18 52	19 52		22 52	23 31
Gorton 78 d	06 22	06 54	07 24	07 54	08 21	08 54	and	18 54	19 54		22 54	23 33
Guide Bridge 78 d	06 26	06 58	07 28	07 58	08 25	08 58	every 30	18 58	19 58	and	22 58	23 37
Flowery Field d	06 29	07 01	07 31	08 01	08 28	09 01	minutes	19 01	20 01	hourly	23 01	23 40
Newton for Hyde d	06 31	07 03	07 33	08 03	08 30	09 03	until	19 03	20 03	until	23 03	23 42
Godley d	06 33	07 05	07 35	08 05	08 32	09 05		19 05	20 05		23 05	23 44
Hattersley d	06 35	07 07	07 37	08 07	08 34	09 07		19 07	20 07		23 07	23 46
Broadbottom d	06 37	07 09	07 39	08 09	08 36	09 09		19 09	20 09		23 09	23 48
Dinting 3 d	06 45	07 16	07 46	08 16	08 46	09 16		19 16	20 16		23 16	23 54
Glossop a	06 48	07 19	07 49	08 19	08 49	09 19		19 19	20 19		23 19	
d	06 51	07 22	07 52	08 22	08 52	09 22		19 22	20 22		23 22	
Hadfield a	06 59	07 29	07 59	08 29	08 59	09 29		19 29	20 29		23 29	23 56

Sundays

	NT	NT A	NT B	NT		NT	NT B	NT A	NT		NT	NT
Manchester Piccadilly 10 78 ⛴ d	09 18	09 30	09 48	10 18		12 18	12 48	12 48	13 18		19 48	20 48
Ardwick 78 d												
Ashburys 78 d	09 22	09 34	09 52	10 22		12 22	12 52	12 52	13 22		19 52	20 52
Gorton 78 d	09 24	09 36	09 54	10 24	and	12 24	12 54	12 54	13 24	and	19 54	20 54
Guide Bridge 78 d	09 28	09 58	09 58	10 28	every 30	12 28	12 58	12 58	13 28	every 30	19 58	20 58
Flowery Field d	09 31	10 01	10 01	10 31	minutes	12 31	13 01	13 02	13 31	minutes	20 01	21 01
Newton for Hyde d	09 33	10 03	10 03	10 33	until	12 33	13 03	13 03	13 33	until	20 03	21 03
Godley d	09 35	10 05	10 05	10 35		12 35	13 05	13 05	13 35		20 05	21 05
Hattersley d	09 37	10 07	10 07	10 37		12 37	13 07	13 07	13 37		20 07	21 07
Broadbottom d	09 39	10 09	10 09	10 39		12 39	13 09	13 09	13 39		20 09	21 09
Dinting 3 d	09 46	10 16	10 16	10 46		12 46	13 16	13 16	13 46		20 16	21 16
Glossop a	09 49	10 19	10 19	10 49		12 49	13 19	13 19	13 49		20 19	21 19
d	09 52	10 22	10 22	10 52		12 52	13 22	13 22	13 52		20 22	21 22
Hadfield a	09 58	10 28	10 28	10 58		12 58	13 28	13 28	13 58		20 28	21 28

A until 25 March

B from 1 April

b Via Hadfield

Hadfield and Glossop - Manchester

Network Diagram - see first Page of Table 78

Mondays to Fridays

Miles	Miles			NT MX	NT	NT	NT	NT	NT	NT	NT	NT	NT	NT	NT	NT	NT	NT	NT	NT	NT	NT	NT
0	0	**Hadfield**	d	23p59	06 00	06 30	06 55	07 00	07 20	07 40	07 58	08 21	08 41	09 01	09 24	09 31	09 54	10 01	10 24	10 31	10 54	11 01	11 24
1¾	—	**Glossop**	a	00 05	06 05	06 35	07 00	07 05	07 25	07 45	08 03	08 26	08 46	09 06	09 29	09 36	09 59	10 06	10 29	10 36	10 59	11 06	11 29
—	—		d		06 08	06 38	07 03	07 08	07 28	07 48	08 06	08 29	08 49	09 09	09 34	09 39	10 04	10 09	10 34	10 39	11 04	11 09	11 34
2¾	0¾	Dinting 3	d		06 11	06 41	07 06	07 11	07 31	07 51	08 09	08 32	08 52	09 12	09 37	09 42	10 07	10 12	10 37	10 42	11 07	11 12	11 37
5	—	Broadbottom	d		06 15	06 45	07 10	07 15	07 35	07 56	08 13	08 37	08 57	09 16	09 41	09 46	10 11	10 16	10 41	10 46	11 11	11 16	11 41
6	—	Hattersley	d		06 18	06 48	07 13	07 18	07 38	07 59	08 16	08 40	08 59	09 19	09 44	09 49	10 14	10 19	10 44	10 49	11 14	11 19	11 44
6½	—	Godley	d		06 20	06 50	07 15	07 20	07 40	08 01	08 18	08 42	09 02	09 21	09 46	09 51	10 16	10 21	10 46	10 51	11 16	11 21	11 46
7½	—	Newton for Hyde	d		06 22	06 52	07 17	07 22	07 42	08 03	08 21	08 44	09 04	09 23	09 48	09 53	10 18	10 23	10 48	10 53	11 18	11 23	11 48
8¼	—	Flowery Field	d		06 24	06 54	07 20	07 24	07 44	08 06	08 23	08 46	09 07	09 25	09 50	09 55	10 20	10 25	10 50	10 55	11 20	11 25	11 50
10¼	—	Guide Bridge 78	a		06 27	06 57	07 28	07 27	07 47	08 10	08 26	08 49	09 11	09 28	09 58	09 58	10 28	10 28	10 58	10 58	11 28	11 28	11 58
12½	—	Gorton 78	a		06 30	07 00	07 30	07 30	07 50	08 13	08 30	08 52	09 15	09 31	10 01	10 01	10 31	10 31	11 01	11 01	11 31	11 31	12 01
13½	—	Ashburys 78	a		06 33	07 06	07 34	07 33	07 53	08 16	08 34	08 56	09 18	09 34	10 04	10 04	10 34	10 34	11 04	11 04	11 34	11 34	12 04
14½	—	Ardwick 78	a				07 36	07 35															
15	—	**Manchester Piccadilly** 10 78	a		06 42	07 15	07 44	07 43	08 03	08 25	08 43	09 04	09 27	09 42	10 11	10 12	10 41	10 42	11 11	11 12	11 41	11 42	12 11

		NT	NT	NT	NT	NT	NT	NT	NT	NT	NT	NT	NT	NT	NT	NT	NT	NT	NT	NT	NT	NT	NT
Hadfield	d	11 31	11 54	12 01	12 24	12 31	13 01	13 05	13 31	13 35	14 01	14 05	14 31	14 35	15 01	15 05	15 31	15 35	16 01	16 05	16 31	16 57	17 22
Glossop	a	11 36	11 59	12 06	12 29	12 36	13 06		13 36		14 06		14 36		15 06		15 36		16 06				
	d	11 39	12 04	12 09	12 34	12 39	13 09		13 39		14 09		14 39		15 09		15 39		16 09				
Dinting 3	d	11 42	12 07	12 12	12 37	12 42	13 12	13 07	13 42	13 37	14 12	14 07	14 42	14 37	15 12	15 07	15 42	15 37	16 12	16 07	16 33	16 59	17 24
Broadbottom	d	11 46	12 11	12 16	12 41	12 46	13 16	13 11	13 46	13 41	14 16	14 11	14 46	14 41	15 16	15 11	15 46	15 41	16 16	16 11	16 37	17 03	17 28
Hattersley	d	11 49	12 14	12 19	12 44	12 49	13 19	13 14	13 49	13 44	14 19	14 14	14 49	14 44	15 19	15 14	15 49	15 44	16 19	16 14	16 40	17 06	17 31
Godley	d	11 51	12 16	12 21	12 46	12 51	13 21	13 16	13 51	13 46	14 21	14 16	14 51	14 46	15 21	15 16	15 51	15 46	16 21	16 16	16 42	17 08	17 33
Newton for Hyde	d	11 53	12 18	12 23	12 48	12 53	13 23	13 18	13 53	13 48	14 23	14 18	14 53	14 48	15 23	15 18	15 53	15 48	16 23	16 18	16 44	17 10	17 36
Flowery Field	d	11 55	12 20	12 25	12 50	12 55	13 25	13 20	13 55	13 50	14 25	14 20	14 55	14 50	15 25	15 20	15 55	15 50	16 25	16 20	16 46	17 12	17 38
Guide Bridge 78	a	11 58	12 28	12 28	12 58	12 58	13 28	13 28	13 58	13 58	14 28	14 28	14 58	14 58	15 28	15 28	15 58	15 58	16 28	16 28	16 49	17 15	17 42
Gorton 78	a	12 01	12 31	12 31	13 01	13 01	13 31	13 31	14 01	14 01	14 31	14 31	15 01	15 01	15 31	15 31	16 01	16 01	16 31	16 31	16 52	17 18	17 45
Ashburys 78	a	12 04	12 34	12 34	13 04	13 04	13 34	13 34	14 04	14 04	14 34	14 34	15 04	15 04	15 34	15 34	16 04	16 04	16 34	16 34	16 55	17 24	17 48
Ardwick 78	a																						
Manchester Piccadilly 10 78	a	12 12	12 41	12 42	13 11	13 12	13 42	13 41	14 12	14 11	14 42	14 41	15 12	15 11	15 42	15 41	16 12	16 11	16 42	16 41	17 05	17 33	17 57

		NT	NT	NT	NT	NT		NT	NT	NT	NT
Hadfield	d	17 44	17 59	18 28	18 43	19 01	and every 30 minutes until	20 31	21 31	22 31	23 59
Glossop	a					19 06		20 36	21 36	22 36	00 05
	d					19 09		20 39	21 39	22 39	
Dinting 3	d	17 46	18 01	18 30	18 45	19 12		20 42	21 42	22 42	
Broadbottom	d	17 50	18 05	18 34	18 49	19 16		20 46	21 46	22 46	
Hattersley	d		18 08	18 37	18 52	19 19		20 49	21 49	22 49	
Godley	d		18 10	18 39	18 54	19 21		20 51	21 51	22 51	
Newton for Hyde	d	17 54	18 12	18 41	18 56	19 23		20 53	21 53	22 53	
Flowery Field	d		18 14	18 43	18 58	19 25		20 55	21 55	22 55	
Guide Bridge 78	a	17 58	18 17	18 46	19 01	19 28		20 58	21 58	22 58	
Gorton 78	a	18 01	18 20	18 49	19 04	19 31		21 01	22 01	23 01	
Ashburys 78	a	18 04	18 23	18 54	19 08	19 34		21 04	22 04	23 04	
Ardwick 78	a										
Manchester Piccadilly 10 78	a	18 12	18 34	19 03	19 15	19 42		21 12	22 12	23 12	

Saturdays

		NT	NT	NT		NT	NT	NT	NT	NT
Hadfield	d	23p59	06 30	07 01	and every 30 minutes until	19 31	20 31	21 31	22 31	23 59
Glossop	a	00 05	06 35	07 06		19 36	20 36	21 36	22 36	00 05
	d		06 38	07 09		19 39	20 39	21 39	22 39	
Dinting 3	d		06 41	07 12		19 42	20 42	21 42	22 42	
Broadbottom	d		06 45	07 16		19 46	20 46	21 46	22 46	
Hattersley	d		06 48	07 19		19 49	20 49	21 49	22 49	
Godley	d		06 50	07 21		19 51	20 51	21 51	22 51	
Newton for Hyde	d		06 52	07 23		19 53	20 53	21 53	22 53	
Flowery Field	d		06 54	07 25		19 55	20 55	21 55	22 55	
Guide Bridge 78	a		06 57	07 28		19 58	20 58	21 58	22 58	
Gorton 78	a		07 00	07 31		20 01	21 01	22 01	23 01	
Ashburys 78	a		07 03	07 34		20 04	21 04	22 04	23 04	
Ardwick 78	a									
Manchester Piccadilly 10 78	a		07 12	07 42		20 12	21 12	22 12	23 12	

Sundays

		NT A	NT		NT	NT
Hadfield	d	23p59	10 01	and every 30 minutes until	20 31	21 31
Glossop	a	00§05	10 06		20 36	21 36
	d		10 09		20 39	21 39
Dinting 3	d		10 12		20 42	21 42
Broadbottom	d		10 16		20 46	21 46
Hattersley	d		10 19		20 49	21 49
Godley	d		10 21		20 51	21 51
Newton for Hyde	d		10 23		20 53	21 53
Flowery Field	d		10 25		20 55	21 55
Guide Bridge 78	a		10 28		20 58	21 58
Gorton 78	a		10 31		21 01	22 01
Ashburys 78	a		10 34		21 04	22 04
Ardwick 78	a					
Manchester Piccadilly 10 78	a		10 42		21 12	22 12

A not 11 December

Network Diagram for Tables 81, 102

DM-35/08
Design BAJS

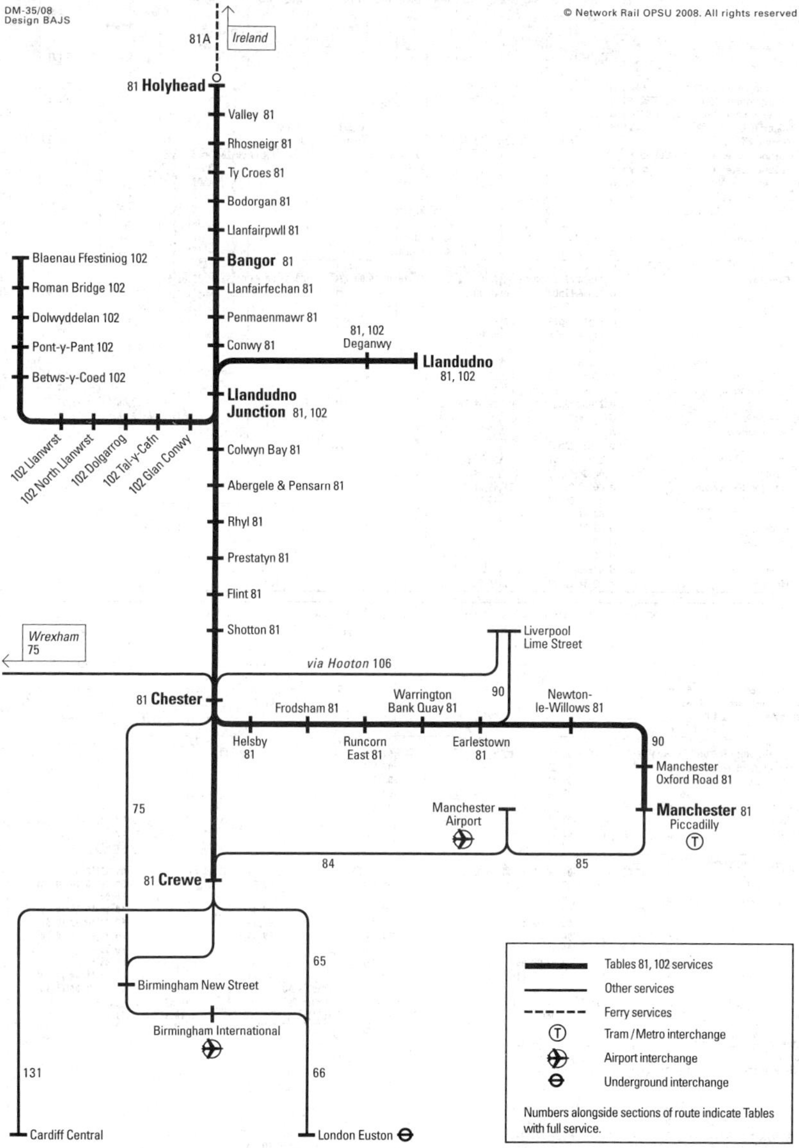

Crewe and Manchester - Chester and North Wales

Network Diagram - see first Page of Table 81

Miles	Miles																							
			AW	AW	AW	AW	AW	AW	AW	AW	AW		AW	NT	AW	AW	AW	AW	AW	AW	VT		AW	AW
			MX	MO	MO	MX	MO	MX	MO	MO	MX		MO	MX		MO								
			◇	◇		◇	◇				◇		◇								◇[1]		◇	◇
						A	B		C						D	C	E							
									🚌							🚌					⊠		⚲	⚲
—	—	London Euston [15] ⊖65 d																						
—	—	Birmingham New Street [12] 65 d				22p55	22p55														05 30			
—	—	Manchester Airport 84,85 ✈ d																					05 33	
—	—	Cardiff Central [7] 131 d	19p34								20p53		21p04											
0	—	**Crewe** [10] d		22p29	23p38	23p57	00 01				00 02		00 10				01 37				06 23			06 54
—	0	**Manchester Pic'dilly** [10] 90 ⛴ d							22p14	23p20				23p17	00 28	23p25							05 50	
—	0½	**Manchester Oxford Road** 90 d							22p19							23p30							05 53	
—	16¼	Newton-le-Willows 90 d							22p49							00 01							06 12	
—	18	Earlestown [8] 90 d							22p59							00 10							06 15	
—	22	Warrington Bank Quay 90 d						23p55	23p24							00 35							06 26	
—	27	Runcorn East d						00 02	23p44							00 55							06 33	
—	30¼	Frodsham d						00 06	23p59							01 10							06 37	
—	32¾	Helsby d						00 10	00 04							01 15							06 41	
—	—	Liverpool Lime Street [10] 106 d																						
21	40¼	**Chester** a	22p34	22p52	00 01	00 18	00 22	00 22	00 24	00 25	00 27		00 33	00 43	01 32	01 35	01 59				06 43		06 53	07 14
—	—	d	22p56	23p00		00 40	00 38														06 44		06 55	07 23
29	—	Shotton d	23p05	23p09																			07 04	
33½	—	Flint d	23p11	23p15		00 53	00 51														06 57		07 10	07 36
47½	—	Prestatyn d	23p24	23p28		01 06	01 04														07 10		07 23	07 49
51	—	Rhyl d	23p30	23p34		01 12	01 10														07 16		07 29	07 55
55¼	—	Abergele & Pensarn d	23p36																				07 35	
61½	—	Colwyn Bay d	23p44	23p45		01 23	01 21														07 26		07 43	08 06
65½	0	**Llandudno Junction** a	23p49	23p50		01 28	01 27														07 32		07 48	08 11
—	—	d	23p52	23p51		01 29	01 28											06 13	06 51	07 31	07 33		07 50	08 12
—	1¼	Deganwy d																06x16	06x54	07x34			07x54	
—	3	**Llandudno** a																06 23	07 01	07 41			08 06	
66½	—	Conwy d	23b54	23b53																				08x14
70¾	—	Penmaenmawr d	23b59	00x01																				08x20
73¼	—	Llanfairfechan d	00x04	00x03																				08x24
80¾	—	**Bangor (Gwynedd)** a	00 13	00 12		01 45	01 44														07 49			08 33
—	—	d	00 14	00 14		01 45	01 44														07 49			08 37
84½	—	Llanfairpwll d	00x21																					08x43
93½	—	Bodorgan d	00x31																					08x53
96¼	—	Ty Croes d	00x35																					08x57
98	—	Rhosneigr d	00x38																					09x00
102	—	Valley d	00x43																					09x06
105½	—	**Holyhead** a	00 58	00 49		02 15	02 20														08 23			09 20

	NT	AW	AW	AW	AW	NT	AW		AW	AW	VT	AW	AW	AW	NT	AW	AW		AW	VT	AW	NT	AW	AW
				◇	◇					◇	◇[1]	◇	◇	◇					◇	◇[1]	◇			
												F	G	B										
				⚲	⚲					⚲	⊠			⚲					⚲	⊠	⚲			
London Euston [15] ⊖65 d											07 10									08 10				
Birmingham New Street [12] 65 d														07 24										
Manchester Airport 84,85 ✈ d																								
Cardiff Central [7] 131 d					05 10																07 21			
Crewe [10] d		07 23					08 23				08 49					09 23				09 49			10 23	
Manchester Pic'dilly [10] 90 ⛴ d	06 18			06 50		07 17				07 50					08 17				08 50			09 17		
Manchester Oxford Road 90 d				06 53						07 53									08 53					
Newton-le-Willows 90 d				07 12						08 12									09 12					
Earlestown [8] 90 d				07 15						08 15									09 15					
Warrington Bank Quay 90 d				07 22						08 24									09 26					
Runcorn East d				07 29						08 31									09 33					
Frodsham d				07 34						08 35									09 37					
Helsby d				07 38						08 39									09 41					
Liverpool Lime Street [10] 106 d																								
Chester a	07 45	07 46		07 50	08 19	08 45	08 46			08 51	09 12			09 17	09 45	09 46			09 53	10 09	10 19	10 45	10 46	
d				07 55	08 22					08 55				09 23					09 55	10 16	10 24			
Shotton d				08 04						09 04									10 04					
Flint d				08 10	08 36					09 10				09 36					10 10	10 29	10 39			
Prestatyn d				08 23	08 49					09 23				09 49					10 23	10 42	10 52			
Rhyl d				08 29	08 55					09 29				09 55					10 29	10 48	10 58			
Abergele & Pensarn d				08 35						09 35									10 35					
Colwyn Bay d				08 43	09 06					09 43				10 06					10 43	10 59	11 09			
Llandudno Junction a				08 48	09 11					09 48				10 11					10 48	11 04	11 14			
d			08 28	08 50	09 12				09 28	09 50		10 03	10 03	10 12			10 28		10 50	11 06	11 15			11 26
Deganwy d			08x31	08x54					09x31	09x54		10x06	10x06				10x31		10x54					11x29
Llandudno a			08 38	09 06					09 38	10 06		10 13	10 15				10 38		11 06					11 36
Conwy d					09x14																11x17			
Penmaenmawr d					09x20																11x23			
Llanfairfechan d					09x24																11x27			
Bangor (Gwynedd) a					09 33									10 28						11 27	11 38			
d					09 35									10 29							11 40			
Llanfairpwll d														10x35										
Bodorgan d					09x49																			
Ty Croes d					09x53																			
Rhosneigr d					09x56																			
Valley d														10x53										
Holyhead a					10 14									11 07							12 14			

A until 23 March
B From Birmingham International
C from 20 February until 26 March
D from 17 January until 20 January
E from 3 January until 6 January. From Manchester Piccadilly
F not from 23 January until 27 January. From Blaenau Ffestiniog
G from 23 January until 27 January. From Blaenau Ffestiniog
b Previous night, stops on request

Crewe and Manchester - Chester and North Wales

Network Diagram - see first Page of Table 81

		AW	VT	AW		NT	AW	AW	AW	VT	AW	AW	NT	AW		AW	AW	VT	AW	NT	AW	AW	AW	VT	
		◇	◇[1]	◇					◇	◇[1]	◇	◇					◇	◇[1]	◇				◇	◇[1]	
				A							B								A						
		🛒	⊠	🛒					🛒	⊠		🛒					🛒	☕	🛒				🛒	☕	
London Euston [15] ⊖65	d		09 10							10 10								11 10						12 10	
Birmingham New Street [12] 65	d			09 24															11 24						
Manchester Airport 84,85 ✈	d																								
Cardiff Central [7] 131	d											09 21													
Crewe [10]	d		10 49				11 23			11 49				12 23				12 49			13 23			13 49	
Manchester Pic'dilly [10] 90 🚌	d	09 50				10 17			10 50				11 17				11 50			12 17			12 50		
Manchester Oxford Road 90	d	09 53							10 53								11 53						12 53		
Newton-le-Willows 90	d	10 12							11 12								12 12						13 12		
Earlestown [8] 90	d	10 15							11 15								12 15						13 15		
Warrington Bank Quay 90	d	10 26							11 26								12 26						13 26		
Runcorn East	d	10 33							11 33								12 33						13 33		
Frodsham	d	10 37							11 37								12 37						13 37		
Helsby	d	10 41							11 41								12 41						13 41		
Liverpool Lime Street [10] 106	d																								
Chester	a	10 53	11 09	11 19		11 45	11 46		11 53	12 12		12 19	12 45	12 46			12 53	13 12	13 19	13 45	13 46		13 53	14 12	
	d	10 55	11 16	11 22					11 55			12 23					12 55		13 24				13 55		
Shotton	d	11 04							12 04								13 04						14 04		
Flint	d	11 10		11 38					12 10			12 36					13 10		13 37				14 10		
Prestatyn	d	11 23		11 51					12 23			12 49					13 23		13 50				14 23		
Rhyl	d	11 29	11 43	11 57					12 29			12 55					13 29		13 56				14 29		
Abergele & Pensarn	d	11 35							12 35								13 35						14 35		
Colwyn Bay	d	11 43	11 54	12 08					12 43			13 06					13 43		14 07				14 43		
Llandudno Junction	a	11 48	12 00	12 13					12 48			13 11					13 48		14 12				14 48		
	d	11 50	12 01	12 14				12 28	12 50		13 03	13 12				13 28	13 50		14 13			14 28	14 50		
Deganwy	d	11x54						12x31	12x54		13x06					13x31	13x54					14x31	14x54		
Llandudno	a	12 06						12 38	13 06		13 13					13 38	14 06					14 38	15 06		
Conwy	d			12x16															14x15						
Penmaenmawr	d			12x22															14x21						
Llanfairfechan	d			12x26															14x25						
Bangor (Gwynedd)	a		12 16	12 35								13 28							14 34						
	d		12 17	12 37								13 29							14 36						
Llanfairpwll	d			12x43								13x36													
Bodorgan	d			12x53								13x46													
Ty Croes	d			12x57								13x50													
Rhosneigr	d			13x00								13x53													
Valley	d			13x06								13x58													
Holyhead	a		12 50	13 18								14 13							15 08						

		AW	NT	AW	AW	VT	AW	AW	NT	AW		AW	VT	AW	NT	AW	AW	VT	AW	NT		AW	AW	AW	AW
		◇			◇	◇[1]	◇	◇				◇	◇[1]	◇			◇	◇[1]	◇					◇	◇
							B	A											A					B	
		🛒			🛒	☕		🛒				🛒	☕	🛒			🛒	☕	🛒						🛒
London Euston [15] ⊖65	d					13 10							14 10					15 10							
Birmingham New Street [12] 65	d							13 24											15 26						
Manchester Airport 84,85 ✈	d																								
Cardiff Central [7] 131	d	11 21												13 21											
Crewe [10]	d			14 23		14 49				15 23			15 49			16 23		16 49				17 23			
Manchester Pic'dilly [10] 90 🚌	d		13 17		13 50				14 17			14 50			15 17		15 50			16 17					16 50
Manchester Oxford Road 90	d				13 53							14 53					15 53								16 53
Newton-le-Willows 90	d				14 12							15 12					16 12								17 12
Earlestown [8] 90	d				14 15							15 15					16 15								17 15
Warrington Bank Quay 90	d				14 26							15 26					16 26								17 26
Runcorn East	d				14 33							15 33					16 33								17 33
Frodsham	d				14 37							15 37					16 37								17 37
Helsby	d				14 41							15 41					16 41								17 41
Liverpool Lime Street [10] 106	d																								
Chester	a	14 19	14 45	14 46	14 53	15 12		15 20	15 45	15 46		15 53	16 12	16 20	16 45	16 46	16 54	17 12	17 22	17 45		17 46			17 53
	d	14 23			14 55			15 22				15 55		16 25			16 55		17 27						17 55
Shotton	d				15 04							16 04					17 04		17 36						18 04
Flint	d	14 36			15 10			15 37				16 10		16 38			17 10		17 42						18 10
Prestatyn	d	14 49			15 23			15 50				16 23		16 51			17 23		17 55						18 23
Rhyl	d	14 55			15 29			15 56				16 29		16 57			17 29		18 01						18 29
Abergele & Pensarn	d				15 35							16 35					17 35		18 07						18 35
Colwyn Bay	d	15 06			15 43			16 07				16 43		17 08			17 43		18 15						18 43
Llandudno Junction	a	15 11			15 48			16 12				16 48		17 13			17 49		18 20						18 48
	d	15 12			15 50		16 04	16 14				16 50		17 13			17 50		18 22				18 26	18 41	18 50
Deganwy	d				15x54		16x07					16x54					17x54						18x29	18x44	18x54
Llandudno	a				16 06		16 17					17 06					18 06						18 36	18 54	19 06
Conwy	d							16x16						17x15					18x24						
Penmaenmawr	d							16x22						17x21					18x30						
Llanfairfechan	d							16x26						17x25					18x34						
Bangor (Gwynedd)	a	15 28						16 35						17 34					18 43						
	d	15 30						16 36						17 36					18 44						
Llanfairpwll	d	15x38												17x42											
Bodorgan	d	15x48												17x52											
Ty Croes	d	15x52												17x56											
Rhosneigr	d	15x55												17x59											
Valley	d	16x01												18x05											
Holyhead	a	16 15						17 11						18 19					19 16						

A From Birmingham International

B From Blaenau Ffestiniog

Crewe and Manchester - Chester and North Wales

Network Diagram - see first Page of Table 81

	VT	AW	AW	NT	AW		AW	AW	AW	VT	VT	AW	NT	AW	AW		AW	VT	AW	NT	AW	AW	AW	AW
		R							R										R					R
	◇1							◇		◇1	◇1	◇						◇1					◇	
												A											B	
	☕	🛒	🛒					🛒	⊠	⊠	⊠	🛒			🛒			⊠	🛒					🛒
London Euston 15 ⊖65 d	16 10									17 10	17 10							18 10						
Birmingham New Street 12 65 d												17 26												
Manchester Airport 84,85 ✈ d																								
Cardiff Central 7 131 d		15 21							16 15										17 21					18 18
Crewe 10 d	17 49				18 23				18 43	18 56	18 56			19 23				19 56			20 23			
Manchester Pic'dilly 10 90 ⛴ d			17 19	17 09				17 50					18 17		18 50					19 17		19 50		
Manchester Oxford Road 90 d			17 22					17 53							18 53							19 53		
Newton-le-Willows 90 d			17 40					18 12							19 12							20 12		
Earlestown 8 90 d			17 44					18 15							19 16							20 15		
Warrington Bank Quay 90 d			17 53					18 24							19 26							20 26		
Runcorn East d			18 00					18 31							19 33							20 33		
Frodsham d			18 05					18 36							19 37							20 37		
Helsby d			18 09					18 40							19 41							20 41		
Liverpool Lime Street 10 106 d																								
Chester a	18 08	18 20	18 23	18 35	18 46			18 53	19 06	19 15	19 15	19 20	19 45	19 46	19 53			20 15	20 20	20 45	20 46	20 53		20 56
d	18 10	18 24						18 55	19 07		19 21	19 32						20 26	20 32					21 02
Shotton d								19 04				19 41							20 41					
Flint d	18 23	18 37						19 10	19 21		19 35	19 47							20 47					
Prestatyn d	18 36	18 50						19 23			19 48	20 00							21 02					
Rhyl d	18 42	18 56						19 29	19 39		19 54	20 06						20 53	21 08					21 28
Abergele & Pensarn d								19 35				20 12												
Colwyn Bay d	18 53	19 07						19 43			20 05	20 20						21 04	21 18					21 39
Llandudno Junction a	18 58	19 12						19 48	19 52		20 10	20 25						21 09	21 24					21 44
d	19 00	19 13					19 28	19 50	19 53		20 12	20 27					20 30	21 10	21 26				21 32	21 47
Deganwy d							19x31	19x54									20x33						21x35	
Llandudno a							19 38	20 06									20 40						21 46	
Conwy d												20x29												
Penmaenmawr d												20x35												
Llanfairfechan d												20x39												
Bangor (Gwynedd) a	19 21	19 33							20 09		20 27	20 48						21 25	21 41					22 02
d		19 35							20 11		20 28	20 49						21 27	21 43					22 04
Llanfairpwll d		19 41										20x55							21x49					
Bodorgan d		19 51										21x05							21x59					
Ty Croes d		19 55										21x10							22x03					
Rhosneigr d		19 58										21x13							22x06					
Valley d		20 04										21x18							22x12					
Holyhead a		20 18							20 49		20 59	21 31						21 59	22 25					22 35

	VT		VT	AW	AW	NT	AW	AW	VT	AW	AW		NT	AW	AW	AW	AW FO	AW FX	AW	NT	AW FX		AW FO	AW
	R		R																					
	1		1	◇					◇1		◇					◇								◇
				A												D		E						F
	☕		☕	🛒					☕															
London Euston 15 ⊖65 d	19 10		19 10						20 10															
Birmingham New Street 12 65 d				19 24												21 24								22 55
Manchester Airport 84,85 ✈ d							20 32								21 32									
Cardiff Central 7 131 d											19 34													
Crewe 10 d	20 50		20 50		21 00			21 36	21 50					22 23					23 23					23 57
Manchester Pic'dilly 10 90 ⛴ d						20 17	20 50						21 17		21 50		22 12			22 17	22 45		23 14	
Manchester Oxford Road 90 d							20 53								21 53		22 29						23 17	
Newton-le-Willows 90 d							21 12								22 12		22 47						23 36	
Earlestown 8 90 d							21 15								22 15		22 50						23 39	
Warrington Bank Quay 90 d							21 24								22 24		22 59	22 59					23 48	
Runcorn East d							21 33								22 31		23 06	23 06					23 55	
Frodsham d							21 37								22 35		23 10	23 10					23 59	
Helsby d							21 41								22 39		23 14	23 14					00 03	
Liverpool Lime Street 10 106 d																								
Chester a	21 10		21 13	21 19	21 23	21 45	21 55	21 59	22 15		22 34		22 45	22 45	22 51	23 19	23 26	23 26	23 44	23 45	23 49		00 15	00 18
d	21 17									22 04	22 56													00 40
Shotton d										22 13	23 05													
Flint d	21 30									22 19	23 11													00 53
Prestatyn d	21 43									22 32	23 24													01 06
Rhyl d	21 50									22 38	23 30													01 12
Abergele & Pensarn d										22 44	23 36													
Colwyn Bay d	22 01									22 52	23 44													01 23
Llandudno Junction a	22 06									22 57	23 49													01 28
d	22 07									22 59	23 52													01 29
Deganwy d																								
Llandudno a																								
Conwy d										23x01	23x54													
Penmaenmawr d										23x07	23x59													
Llanfairfechan d										23x11	00x04													
Bangor (Gwynedd) a	22 22									23 20	00 13													01 45
d	22 24									23 21	00 14													01 45
Llanfairpwll d											00x21													
Bodorgan d											00x31													
Ty Croes d											00x35													
Rhosneigr d											00x38													
Valley d											00x43													
Holyhead a	22 56									23 55	00 58													02 15

A From Birmingham International
B From Blaenau Ffestiniog
D From Birmingham International to Manchester Piccadilly
E Does not run from 3 January until 5 January
F until 23 March

Table 81

Mondays to Fridays

Crewe and Manchester - Chester and North Wales

Network Diagram - see first Page of Table 81

		AW FX	AW ◇	NT
London Euston 15 ⊖65	d			
Birmingham New Street 12 65	d			
Manchester Airport 84,85 ✈	d			
Cardiff Central 7 131	d		20 53	
Crewe 10	d		00 02	
Manchester Pic'dilly 10 90	d			23 17
Manchester Oxford Road 90	d			
Newton-le-Willows 90	d			
Earlestown 8 90	d			
Warrington Bank Quay 90	d	23 55		
Runcorn East	d	00 02		
Frodsham	d	00 06		
Helsby	d	00 10		
Liverpool Lime Street 10 106	d			
Chester	a	00 22	00 27	00 43
	d			
Shotton	d			
Flint	d			
Prestatyn	d			
Rhyl	d			
Abergele & Pensarn	d			
Colwyn Bay	d			
Llandudno Junction	a			
	d			
Deganwy	d			
Llandudno	a			
Conwy	d			
Penmaenmawr	d			
Llanfairfechan	d			
Bangor (Gwynedd)	a			
	d			
Llanfairpwll	d			
Bodorgan	d			
Ty Croes	d			
Rhosneigr	d			
Valley	d			
Holyhead	a			

Saturdays

		AW ◇	AW	AW ◇ A	AW ◇	NT	AW	AW	AW	AW
London Euston 15 ⊖65	d									
Birmingham New Street 12 65	d			22p55						
Manchester Airport 84,85 ✈	d									
Cardiff Central 7 131	d	19p34			20p53					
Crewe 10	d			23p57	00b02					
Manchester Pic'dilly 10 90	d		23p14			23p17	00 28			
Manchester Oxford Road 90	d		23p17				00 31			
Newton-le-Willows 90	d		23p36				00 50			
Earlestown 8 90	d		23p39				00 53			
Warrington Bank Quay 90	d		23p48				01 02			
Runcorn East	d		23p55				01 10			
Frodsham	d		23p59				01 15			
Helsby	d		00 03				01 19			
Liverpool Lime Street 10 106	d									
Chester	a	22p34	00 15	00 18	00 27	00 43	01 31			
	d	22p56		00 40						
Shotton	d	23p05								
Flint	d	23p11		00 53						
Prestatyn	d	23p24		01 06						
Rhyl	d	23p30		01 12						
Abergele & Pensarn	d	23p36								
Colwyn Bay	d	23p44		01 23						
Llandudno Junction	a	23p49		01 28						
	d	23p52		01 29				06 13	06 51	07 31
Deganwy	d							06x16	06x54	07x34
Llandudno	a							06 23	07 01	07 41
Conwy	d	23c54								
Penmaenmawr	d	23c59								
Llanfairfechan	d	00x04								
Bangor (Gwynedd)	a	00 13		01 45						
	d	00 14		01 45						
Llanfairpwll	d	00x21								
Bodorgan	d	00x31								
Ty Croes	d	00x35								
Rhosneigr	d	00x38								
Valley	d	00x43								
Holyhead	a	00 58		02 15						

		VT ◇ 1	AW ◇	AW ◇	NT	AW	AW	AW ◇	AW ◇	NT	AW	AW	AW ◇	AW ◇ B
London Euston 15 ⊖65	d													
Birmingham New Street 12 65	d	05 30												
Manchester Airport 84,85 ✈	d		05 33											
Cardiff Central 7 131	d								05 20					
Crewe 10	d	06 23		07 03		07 23					08 23			
Manchester Pic'dilly 10 90	d		05 50		06 17			06 50		07 17			07 50	
Manchester Oxford Road 90	d		05 53					06 53					07 53	
Newton-le-Willows 90	d		06 12					07 12					08 12	
Earlestown 8 90	d		06 15					07 15					08 15	
Warrington Bank Quay 90	d		06 26					07 22					08 24	
Runcorn East	d		06 33					07 29					08 31	
Frodsham	d		06 37					07 34					08 35	
Helsby	d		06 41					07 38					08 39	
Liverpool Lime Street 10 106	d													
Chester	a	06 43	06 53	07 23	07 45	07 46		07 50	08 18	08 45	08 46		08 51	
	d	06 44	06 55	07 25				07 55	08 22				08 55	
Shotton	d		07 04					08 04					09 04	
Flint	d	06 57	07 10	07 39				08 10	08 36				09 10	
Prestatyn	d	07 10	07 23	07 52				08 23	08 49				09 23	
Rhyl	d	07 16	07 29	07 58				08 29	08 55				09 29	
Abergele & Pensarn	d		07 35					08 35					09 35	
Colwyn Bay	d	07 27	07 43	08 09				08 43	09 06				09 43	
Llandudno Junction	a	07 33	07 48	08 14				08 48	09 11				09 48	
	d	07 33	07 50	08 15			08 28	08 50	09 12			09 28	09 50	10 00
Deganwy	d		07x54				08x31	08x54				09x31	09x54	10x03
Llandudno	a		08 06				08 38	09 06				09 38	10 06	10 13
Conwy	d			08x17					09x14					
Penmaenmawr	d			08x23					09x20					
Llanfairfechan	d			08x27					09x24					
Bangor (Gwynedd)	a	07 49		08 36					09 33					
	d	07 50		08 38					09 35					
Llanfairpwll	d			08x44										
Bodorgan	d			08x54					09x49					
Ty Croes	d			08x58					09x53					
Rhosneigr	d			09x01					09x56					
Valley	d			09x07										
Holyhead	a	08 23		09 21					10 14					

A until 24 March

B From Blaenau Ffestiniog

c Previous night, stops on request

Table 81

Crewe and Manchester - Chester and North Wales

Network Diagram - see first Page of Table 81

		AW	NT	AW	AW	AW		VT	AW	NT	AW	AW	AW	VT	AW	NT		AW	AW	AW	VT	AW	AW	NT	AW
		◇ A ⊥				◇ ⊥		◇1 ⊓	◇ ⊥				◇ ⊥	◇1 ⊓	◇ A ⊥					◇ ⊥	◇1 ⊓	◇ B	◇ ⊥		
London Euston 15 ⊖65	d							08 10						08 50							10 10				
Birmingham New Street 12 65	d	07 23													09 24										
Manchester Airport 84,85 ✈	d																								
Cardiff Central 7 131	d								07 21														09 21		
Crewe 10	d			09 23				09 49			10 23			10b43				11 23			11 49				12 23
Manchester Pic'dilly 10 90 ⛴	d		08 17			08 50				09 17			09 50			10 17				10 50				11 17	
Manchester Oxford Road 90	d					08 53							09 53							10 53					
Newton-le-Willows 90	d					09 12							10 12							11 12					
Earlestown 8 90	d					09 15							10 15							11 15					
Warrington Bank Quay 90	d					09 26							10 26							11 26					
Runcorn East	d					09 33							10 33							11 33					
Frodsham	d					09 37							10 37							11 37					
Helsby	d					09 41							10 41							11 41					
Liverpool Lime Street 10 106	d																								
Chester	a	09 17	09 45	09 46		09 53		10 12	10 19	10 45	10 46		10 53	11 10	11 19	11 45		11 46		11 53	12 12		12 19	12 45	12 46
	d	09 24				09 55			10 23				10 55	11 12	11 24					11 55			12 23		
Shotton	d					10 04							11 04							12 04					
Flint	d	09 37				10 10			10 36				11 10		11 39					12 10			12 36		
Prestatyn	d	09 50				10 23			10 49				11 23		11 52					12 23			12 49		
Rhyl	d	09 56				10 29			10 55				11 29	11 41	11 58					12 29			12 55		
Abergele & Pensarn	d					10 35							11 35							12 35					
Colwyn Bay	d	10 07				10 43			11 06				11 43	11 54	12 09					12 43			13 06		
Llandudno Junction	a	10 12				10 48			11 11				11 48	12 00	12 14					12 48			13 11		
	d	10 13			10 28	10 50			11 12			11 26	11 50	12 01	12 15				12 28	12 50		13 00	13 12		
Deganwy	d				10x31	10x54						11x29	11x54						12x31	12x54		13x03			
Llandudno	a				10 38	11 06						11 36	12 06						12 38	13 06		13 13			
Conwy	d								11x14						12x17										
Penmaenmawr	d								11x20						12x23										
Llanfairfechan	d								11x24						12x27										
Bangor (Gwynedd)	a	10 29							11 33					12 19	12 36								13 28		
	d	10 30							11 35					12 20	12 38								13 29		
Llanfairpwll	d	10x36													12x44								13x36		
Bodorgan	d														12x54								13x46		
Ty Croes	d														12x58								13x50		
Rhosneigr	d														13x01								13x53		
Valley	d	10x54													13x07								13x58		
Holyhead	a	11 05							12 09					12 55	13 18								14 13		

		AW		AW	VT	AW	NT	AW	AW	AW	VT	AW		NT	AW	AW	AW	VT	AW	AW	NT	AW		AW	AW
				◇ ⊥	◇1 ⊓	◇ A ⊥				◇ ⊥	◇1 ⊓	◇ ⊥					◇ ⊥	◇1 ⊓	◇ B	◇ A ⊥					◇ ⊥
London Euston 15 ⊖65	d				11 10						12 10							13 10							
Birmingham New Street 12 65	d					11 24														13 24					
Manchester Airport 84,85 ✈	d																								
Cardiff Central 7 131	d											11 21													
Crewe 10	d				12 49			13 23			13 49				14 23			14 49				15 23			
Manchester Pic'dilly 10 90 ⛴	d			11 50			12 17			12 50				13 17			13 50				14 17				14 50
Manchester Oxford Road 90	d			11 53						12 53							13 53								14 53
Newton-le-Willows 90	d			12 12						13 12							14 12								15 12
Earlestown 8 90	d			12 15						13 15							14 15								15 15
Warrington Bank Quay 90	d			12 26						13 26							14 26								15 26
Runcorn East	d			12 33						13 33							14 33								15 33
Frodsham	d			12 37						13 37							14 37								15 37
Helsby	d			12 41						13 41							14 41								15 41
Liverpool Lime Street 10 106	d																								
Chester	a			12 53	13 12	13 18	13 45	13 46		13 53	14 12	14 19		14 45	14 46		14 53	15 12		15 20	15 45	15 46			15 53
	d			12 55		13 22				13 55		14 23					14 55			15 22					15 55
Shotton	d			13 04						14 04							15 04								16 04
Flint	d			13 10		13 36				14 10		14 36					15 10			15 37					16 10
Prestatyn	d			13 23		13 49				14 23		14 49					15 23			15 50					16 23
Rhyl	d			13 29		13 55				14 29		14 55					15 29			15 56					16 29
Abergele & Pensarn	d			13 35						14 35							15 35								16 35
Colwyn Bay	d			13 43		14 06				14 43		15 06					15 43			16 07					16 43
Llandudno Junction	a			13 48		14 11				14 48		15 11					15 48			16 12					16 48
	d	13 28		13 50		14 12			14 28	14 50		15 12				15 30	15 50		16 00	16 14				16 26	16 50
Deganwy	d	13x31		13x54					14x31	14x54						15x33	15 54		16x03					16x29	16x54
Llandudno	a	13 38		14 06					14 38	15 06						15 40	16 06		16 13					16 36	17 06
Conwy	d					14x14														16x16					
Penmaenmawr	d					14x20														16x22					
Llanfairfechan	d					14x24														16x26					
Bangor (Gwynedd)	a					14 33						15 28								16 35					
	d					14 35						15 29								16 36					
Llanfairpwll	d											15x36													
Bodorgan	d											15x46													
Ty Croes	d											15x50													
Rhosneigr	d											15x53													
Valley	d											15x58													
Holyhead	a					15 08						16 13								17 11					

A From Birmingham International

B From Blaenau Ffestiniog

Table 81

Saturdays

Crewe and Manchester - Chester and North Wales

Network Diagram - see first Page of Table 81

	VT	AW	NT	AW	AW	AW	VT		AW	NT	AW	AW	AW	AW	VT	AW	NT		AW	AW	AW	VT	AW	NT
	◇1 🍴	◇ 🚲				◇ 🚲	◇1 🍴		◇ A 🚲				◇ B	◇ 🚲	◇1 🍴	R 🚲					◇ 🚲	◇1 🍴	◇ A 🚲	
London Euston 15 ⊖65 d	14 10						15 10								16 10							17 10		
Birmingham New Street 12 65 d									15 24														17 24	
Manchester Airport 84,85 ✈ d																								
Cardiff Central 7 131 d		13 21														15 21								
Crewe 10 d	15 49			16 23			16 49				17 23				17 49				18 23			18 50		
Manchester Pic'dilly 10 90 d			15 17			15 50				16 17				16 50			17 17				17 50			18 17
Manchester Oxford Road 90 d						15 53								16 53							17 53			
Newton-le-Willows 90 d						16 12								17 12							18 12			
Earlestown 8 90 d						16 15								17 15							18 15			
Warrington Bank Quay 90 d						16 26								17 26							18 25			
Runcorn East d						16 33								17 33							18 32			
Frodsham d						16 37								17 37							18 36			
Helsby d						16 41								17 41							18 40			
Liverpool Lime Street 10 106 d																								
Chester a	16 10	16 22	16 45	16 46		16 53	17 12		17 19	17 45	17 46			17 53	18 09	18 19	18 45		18 46		18 52	19 10	19 20	19 45
d	16 12	16 26				16 55			17 24					17 55	18 16	18 24					18 55	19 17	19 32	
Shotton d						17 04			17 33					18 04							19 04		19 41	
Flint d	16 25	16 39				17 10			17 39					18 10	18 29	18 39					19 10	19 30	19 47	
Prestatyn d	16 38	16 52				17 23			17 52					18 23	18 42	18 52					19 23	19 43	20 00	
Rhyl d	16 45	16 58				17 29			17 58					18 29	18 49	18 58					19 29	19 50	20 06	
Abergele & Pensarn d						17 35			18 04					18 35							19 35		20 12	
Colwyn Bay d	16 56	17 09				17 43			18 12					18 43	19 00	19 09					19 43	20 01	20 20	
Llandudno Junction a	17 01	17 14				17 48			18 17					18 48	19 05	19 14					19 48	20 06	20 25	
d	17 02	17 14			17 28	17 50			18 19			18 26	18 41	18 50	19 06	19 15				19 28	19 50	20 07	20 27	
Deganwy d					17x31	17x54						18x29	18x44	18x54						19x31	19x54			
Llandudno a					17 38	18 06						18 36	18 54	19 06						19 38	20 06			
Conwy d		17x16							18x21														20x29	
Penmaenmawr d		17x22							18x27														20x35	
Llanfairfechan d		17x26							18x31														20x39	
Bangor (Gwynedd) a	17 17	17 35							18 40						19 21	19 32						20 22	20 48	
d	17 19	17 37							18 41						19 23	19 33						20 24	20 49	
Llanfairpwll d		17x43														19 40							20x55	
Bodorgan d		17x53														19 51							21x05	
Ty Croes d		17x57														19 55							21x10	
Rhosneigr d		18x00														19 58							21x13	
Valley d		18x06														20 04							21x18	
Holyhead a	17 51	18 20							19 13						19 55	20 18						20 56	21 31	

	AW	AW	VT		AW	AW	NT	AW	AW	AW	AW	AW	NT		AW	AW	AW	NT	AW	AW	AW	AW	AW	
		🚲	◇1 🍴			R C 🚲				◇ A 🚲	◇ B	◇					◇				◇ A			
London Euston 15 ⊖65 d			18 10																					
Birmingham New Street 12 65 d										19 24											21 24			
Manchester Airport 84,85 ✈ d															20 32									
Cardiff Central 7 131 d						17 21											19 34							
Crewe 10 d	19 23		19 49					20 23				21 00				21 36			22 23				23 21	
Manchester Pic'dilly 10 90 d		18 50					19 17		19 50				20 17		20 50			21 17		21 50		22 26		
Manchester Oxford Road 90 d		18 53							19 53						20 53					21 53		22 29		
Newton-le-Willows 90 d		19 12							20 12						21 12					22 12		22 47		
Earlestown 8 90 d		19 16							20 15						21 15					22 15		22 50		
Warrington Bank Quay 90 d		19 27							20 30						21 27					22 24		22 59		
Runcorn East d		19 34							20 37						21 34					22 31		23 06		
Frodsham d		19 38							20 41						21 38					22 35		23 10		
Helsby d		19 42							20 45						21 42					22 39		23 14		
Liverpool Lime Street 10 106 d																								
Chester a	19 46	19 54	20 12			20 19	20 45	20 46	20 57	21 21		21 21	21 45		21 57	21 59	22 31	22 45	22 45	22 53	23 21	23 26	23 42	
d						20 32						21 26					22 36							
Shotton d						20 41						21 35					22 45							
Flint d						20 47						21 41					22 51							
Prestatyn d						21 00						21 54					23 05							
Rhyl d						21 06						22 00					23 11							
Abergele & Pensarn d												22 06					23 17							
Colwyn Bay d						21 17						22 14					23 25							
Llandudno Junction a						21 24						22 19					23 38							
d					20 30	21 26					21 32	22 21												
Deganwy d					20x33						21x35													
Llandudno a					20 40						21 46													
Conwy d												22 23												
Penmaenmawr d												22 29												
Llanfairfechan d												22 33												
Bangor (Gwynedd) a						21 41						22 42												
d						21 43						22 43												
Llanfairpwll d						21x49																		
Bodorgan d						21x59																		
Ty Croes d						22x03																		
Rhosneigr d						22x06																		
Valley d						22x12																		
Holyhead a						22 25						23 18												

A From Birmingham International **B** From Blaenau Ffestiniog **C** 🚲 from Chester

Table 81

Saturdays

Crewe and Manchester - Chester and North Wales

Network Diagram - see first Page of Table 81

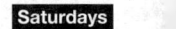

		NT	AW	AW	NT	AW
				◇		
						🚌
London Euston 15 ⊖65	d					
Birmingham New Street 12 65	d					
Manchester Airport 84,85 ✈	d					
Cardiff Central 7 131	d			20 55		
Crewe 10	d			23 58		
Manchester Pic'dilly 10 90 ⛴	d	22 17	23 14		23 17	
Manchester Oxford Road 90	d		23 17			
Newton-le-Willows 90	d		23 36			
Earlestown 8 90	d		23 39			
Warrington Bank Quay 90	d		23 48			
Runcorn East	d		23 55			
Frodsham	d		23 59			
Helsby	d		00 03			
Liverpool Lime Street 10 106	d					
Chester	a	23 45	00 15	00 24	00 43	
	d					
Shotton	d					
Flint	d					
Prestatyn	d					
Rhyl	d					
Abergele & Pensarn	d					
Colwyn Bay	d					
Llandudno Junction	a					
	d					23 48
Deganwy	d					
Llandudno	a					
Conwy	d					23 56
Penmaenmawr	d					00 08
Llanfairfechan	d					00 23
Bangor (Gwynedd)	a					00 38
	d					00 38
Llanfairpwll	d					00 47
Bodorgan	d					00 57
Ty Croes	d					01 07
Rhosneigr	d					01 27
Valley	d					01 52
Holyhead	a					02 02

Sundays

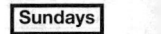

until 12 February

		AW	AW	NT	AW	AW	AW	AW	NT	AW	VT	AW	AW	AW	AW	NT	AW	AW	AW	AW	AW	AW	AW
			◇				◇				◇1		◇				◇			◇	◇		
		A	A	A	A				B							C				D			
					🚌	🚌					☕						🛒	🛒			🛒	🛒	
London Euston 15 ⊖65	d																						
Birmingham New Street 12 65	d																			11 05			
Manchester Airport 84,85 ✈	d																						
Cardiff Central 7 131	d		20p55																				
Crewe 10	d		23p58				09 24	10 07			10 42	11 05	11 27		11 57		12 27		12 54		13 27		13 57
Manchester Pic'dilly 10 90 ⛴	d	23p14		23p17		07 28			09 22	09 56				10 55		11 22		11 56				12 56	
Manchester Oxford Road 90	d	23p17				07 33				09 59				10 59				11 59				12 59	
Newton-le-Willows 90	d	23p36				08 03				10 18				11 20				12 18				13 18	
Earlestown 8 90	d	23p39				08 13				10 21				11 23				12 21				13 21	
Warrington Bank Quay 90	d	23p48				08 38				10 28				11 30				12 28				13 29	
Runcorn East	d	23p55				08 58				10 35				11 37				12 35				13 36	
Frodsham	d	23p59				09 13				10 40				11 41				12 39				13 40	
Helsby	d	00 03				09 18				10 44				11 45				12 43				13 44	
Liverpool Lime Street 10 106	d																						
Chester	a	00 15	00 24	00 43		09 38	09 46	10 30	10 46	10 59	11 02	11 30	11 50	11 57	12 20	12 43	12 52	12 55	13 19	13 20	13 51	13 56	14 20
	d						09 48				11 07		12 03				13 02				14 02		
Shotton	d						09 57						12 12				13 11				14 11		
Flint	d						10 03						12 18				13 17				14 17		
Prestatyn	d						10 16				11 30		12 31				13 30				14 30		
Rhyl	d						10 22				11 37		12 37				13 36				14 36		
Abergele & Pensarn	d						10 28										13 42				14 42		
Colwyn Bay	d						10 36				11 48		12 48				13 50				14 50		
Llandudno Junction	a						10 41				11 53		12 53				13 55				14 55		
	d				23p48		10 43				11 54		12 54				13 57				14 57		
Deganwy	d																						
Llandudno	a																						
Conwy	d				23p56		10x45										13x59						
Penmaenmawr	d				00 08		10x51										14x05						
Llanfairfechan	d				00 23		10x55										14x09						
Bangor (Gwynedd)	a				00 38		11 04				12 09		13 10				14 18				15 12		
	d				00 38		11 05				12 11		13 11				14 19				15 14		
Llanfairpwll	d				00 47		11x12														15x20		
Bodorgan	d				00 57		11x22														15x30		
Ty Croes	d				01 07		11x26														15x34		
Rhosneigr	d				01 27		11x29														15x37		
Valley	d				01 52		11x34														15x43		
Holyhead	a				02 02		11 49				12 43		13 42				14 53				15 57		

A not 11 December
B From Wigan Wallgate
C From Southport
D From Birmingham International

Table 81

Sundays
until 12 February

Crewe and Manchester - Chester and North Wales

Network Diagram - see first Page of Table 81

	NT	AW	AW	AW	AW		AW	AW	AW	NT	AW	AW	VT	AW	AW		AW	VT	AW	NT	AW	AW	VT	AW
									R															
		◇		◇			◇				◇		◇1	◇	◇			◇1	◇		◇		◇1	◇
	A			B						A				B					C	A				B
		⊥	⊥	⊥				⊥				⊥	⊐	⊥				⊐	⊥			⊥	⊐	⊥
London Euston 15 ⊖65 d													15 05					16 05					17 05	
Birmingham New Street 12 65 d				13 25										15 24										17 24
Manchester Airport 84,85 ✈ d																								
Cardiff Central 7 131 d									13 22										15 22					
Crewe 10 d		14 27			14 57		15 27				16 27		16 52		17 27			17 52			18 27		18 56	
Manchester Pic'dilly 10 90 ⇌ d	13 22		13 56					14 56		15 22		15 56					16 56			17 22		17 56		
Manchester Oxford Road 90 d			13 59					14 59				15 59					16 59					17 59		
Newton-le-Willows 90 d			14 18					15 18				16 18					17 18					18 18		
Earlestown 8 90 d			14 21					15 21				16 21					17 21					18 21		
Warrington Bank Quay 90 d			14 28					15 29				16 28					17 28					18 28		
Runcorn East d			14 35					15 36				16 35					17 35					18 35		
Frodsham d			14 39					15 40				16 39					17 39					18 39		
Helsby d			14 43					15 44				16 43					17 43					18 43		
Liverpool Lime Street 10 106 d																								
Chester a	14 46	14 51	14 55	15 18	15 20		15 49	15 56	16 18	16 46	16 49	16 55	17 14	17 26	17 49		17 55	18 14	18 25	18 46	18 49	18 55	19 14	19 16
d		15 02					16 02		16 36		17 02				18 02				18 29		18 52		19 22	19 38
Shotton d		15 11					16 11		16 45		17 11				18 11				18 38		19 01			19 47
Flint d		15 17					16 17		16 51		17 17				18 17				18 44		19 07		19 35	19 53
Prestatyn d		15 30					16 30		17 04		17 30				18 30				18 57		19 21		19 48	20 06
Rhyl d		15 36					16 36		17 10		17 36				18 36				19 03		19 27		19 55	20 12
Abergele & Pensarn d		15 42					16 42		17 16		17 42				18 42				19 09		19 33			20 18
Colwyn Bay d		15 50					16 50		17 24		17 50				18 50				19 17		19 41		20 06	20 26
Llandudno Junction a		15 55					16 55		17 29		17 55				18 55				19 22		19 46		20 11	20 31
d		15 57					16 57		17 31		17 57				18 57				19 24		19 47		20 12	20 33
Deganwy d																								
Llandudno a																								
Conwy d		15x59							17x33		17x59								19x26		19x49			20x35
Penmaenmawr d		16x05							17x39		18x05								19x32		19x55			20x41
Llanfairfechan d		16x09							17x43		18x09								19x36		19x59			20x45
Bangor (Gwynedd) a		16 18					17 12		17 52		18 18				19 12				19 45		20 08		20 27	20 54
d		16 19					17 14		17 54		18 19				19 14				19 45		20 09		20 29	20 55
Llanfairpwll d							17x20		18x00						19x20									
Bodorgan d							17x30		18x10						19x30									
Ty Croes d							17x34		18x14						19x34									
Rhosneigr d							17x37		18x17						19x37									
Valley d							17x43		18x23						19x43									
Holyhead a		16 53					17 57		18 37		18 54				19 54				20 18		20 44		20 59	21 30

	AW		AW	VT	NT	AW	AW	VT	AW	AW	AW		AW	NT	AW	AW	AW	AW	AW	AW	AW		AW	
				◇1				◇1	◇	◇						◇	◇			◇			◇	
					A				B					A			B			B				
				⊐				⊐	⊥															
London Euston 15 ⊖65 d				18 05				19 05																
Birmingham New Street 12 65 d									19 24								21 24			22 55				
Manchester Airport 84,85 ✈ d																								
Cardiff Central 7 131 d																							21 04	
Crewe 10 d	19 24			19 52		20 27		20 55		21 27			22 03			22 29	23 06		23 38	00 01			00 10	
Manchester Pic'dilly 10 90 ⇌ d			18 56		19 22		19 56				20 56			21 22	21 50			22 52			23 20			
Manchester Oxford Road 90 d			18 59				19 59				20 59													
Newton-le-Willows 90 d			19 18				20 18				21 18													
Earlestown 8 90 d			19 21				20 21				21 21													
Warrington Bank Quay 90 d			19 29				20 30				21 28													
Runcorn East d			19 36				20 37				21 35													
Frodsham d			19 40				20 41				21 39													
Helsby d			19 44				20 45				21 43													
Liverpool Lime Street 10 106 d																								
Chester a	19 45		19 56	20 11	20 46	20 50	20 57	21 14	21 20	21 50	21 55		22 26	22 46	22 52	22 52	23 31	23 54	00 01	00 22	00 25		00 33	
d				20 18				21 17		22 00						23 00				00 38				
Shotton d										22 09						23 09								
Flint d				20 31				21 30		22 15						23 15				00 51				
Prestatyn d				20 44				21 43		22 28						23 28				01 04				
Rhyl d				20 51				21 50		22 34						23 34				01 10				
Abergele & Pensarn d										22 40														
Colwyn Bay d				21 02				22 01		22 48						23 45				01 21				
Llandudno Junction a				21 07				22 06		22 53						23 50				01 27				
d				21 08				22 07		22 55						23 51				01 28				
Deganwy d																								
Llandudno a																								
Conwy d																23x53								
Penmaenmawr d																00x01								
Llanfairfechan d																00x03								
Bangor (Gwynedd) a				21 23				22 22		23 10						00 12				01 44				
d				21 25				22 24		23 12						00 14				01 44				
Llanfairpwll d										23x18														
Bodorgan d										23x28														
Ty Croes d										23x32														
Rhosneigr d										23x35														
Valley d										23x41														
Holyhead a				21 57				22 56		23 55						00 49				02 20				

A From Southport
B From Birmingham International
C ◇ from Chester

Table 81

Sundays

19 February to 25 March

Crewe and Manchester - Chester and North Wales

Network Diagram - see first Page of Table 81

		AW	AW	NT	AW	AW	AW	AW	NT	AW		AW	VT	AW	AW	AW	AW	AW	NT	AW		AW	AW	AW	AW
			◇				◇		A				◇1		◇				B			◇			◇ C
					bus	bus						bus	buffet			bus				trolley		trolley	bus		
London Euston 15 ⊖65	d																								
Birmingham New Street 12 65	d																								11 05
Manchester Airport 84,85 ✈	d																								
Cardiff Central 7 131	d		20p55																						
Crewe 10	d		23p58				09 24	10 07					10 42	11 05	11 27			11 57				12 27		12 54	
Manchester Pic'dilly 10 90	d	23p14		23p17		07 28			09 22	09 55		08 49				09 47	10 50		11 22	11 48			10 45		
Manchester Oxford Road 90	d	23p17				07 33						08 54				09 52							10 50		
Newton-le-Willows 90	d	23p36				08 03						09 24				10 22							11 20		
Earlestown 8 90	d	23p39				08 13						09 34				10 32							11 30		
Warrington Bank Quay 90	d	23p48				08 38						09 59				10 57							11 55		
Runcorn East	d	23p55				08 58						10 19				11 17							12 15		
Frodsham	d	23p59				09 13						10 34				11 32							12 30		
Helsby	d	00 03				09 18						10 39				11 37							12 35		
Liverpool Lime Street 10 106	d																								
Chester	a	00 15	00 24	00 43		09 38	09 46	10 30	10 46	10 58		10 59	11 02	11 30	11 50	11 57	11 58	12 20	12 43	12 51		12 52	12 55	13 19	13 20
	d						09 48						11 07		12 03							13 02			
Shotton	d						09 57								12 12							13 11			
Flint	d						10 03								12 18							13 17			
Prestatyn	d						10 16						11 30		12 31							13 30			
Rhyl	d						10 22						11 37		12 37							13 36			
Abergele & Pensarn	d						10 28															13 42			
Colwyn Bay	d						10 36						11 48		12 48							13 50			
Llandudno Junction	a						10 41						11 53		12 53							13 55			
	d				23p48		10 43						11 54		12 54							13 57			
Deganwy	d																								
Llandudno	a																								
Conwy	d				23p56		10x45															13x59			
Penmaenmawr	d				00 08		10x51															14x05			
Llanfairfechan	d				00 23		10x55															14x09			
Bangor (Gwynedd)	a				00 38		11 04						12 09		13 10							14 18			
	d				00 38		11 05						12 11		13 11							14 19			
Llanfairpwll	d				00 47		11x12																		
Bodorgan	d				00 57		11x22																		
Ty Croes	d				01 07		11x26																		
Rhosneigr	d				01 27		11x29																		
Valley	d				01 52		11x34																		
Holyhead	a				02 02		11 49						12 43		13 42							14 53			

		AW	AW	AW	AW	NT		AW	AW	AW	AW	AW	AW	AW	AW	AW		NT	AW	AW	AW	VT	AW	AW	AW
																R									
		◇				B		◇			◇ C		◇					B	◇			◇1	◇ C	◇	
		trolley	trolley	bus				trolley	trolley	bus	trolley			trolley	bus					trolley	bus	buffet	trolley		
London Euston 15 ⊖65	d																					15 05			
Birmingham New Street 12 65	d										13 25												15 24		
Manchester Airport 84,85 ✈	d																								
Cardiff Central 7 131	d															13 22									
Crewe 10	d	13 27			13 57			14 27				14 57	15 27						16 27			16 52		17 27	
Manchester Pic'dilly 10 90	d		12 50	11 45		13 22			13 49	12 45				14 49	13 46			15 22		15 48	14 45				16 48
Manchester Oxford Road 90	d			11 50						12 50					13 51						14 50				
Newton-le-Willows 90	d			12 20						13 20					14 21						15 20				
Earlestown 8 90	d			12 30						13 30					14 31						15 30				
Warrington Bank Quay 90	d			12 55						13 55					14 56						15 55				
Runcorn East	d			13 15						14 15					15 16						16 15				
Frodsham	d			13 30						14 30					15 31						16 30				
Helsby	d			13 35						14 35					15 36						16 35				
Liverpool Lime Street 10 106	d																								
Chester	a	13 51	13 53	13 55	14 20	14 46		14 51	14 52	14 55	15 18	15 20	15 49	15 52	15 56	16 18		16 46	16 49	16 52	16 55	17 14	17 26	17 49	17 51
	d	14 02						15 02					16 02			16 36			17 02					18 02	
Shotton	d	14 11						15 11					16 11			16 45			17 11					18 11	
Flint	d	14 17						15 17					16 17			16 51			17 17					18 17	
Prestatyn	d	14 30						15 30					16 30			17 04			17 30					18 30	
Rhyl	d	14 36						15 36					16 36			17 10			17 36					18 36	
Abergele & Pensarn	d	14 42						15 42					16 42			17 16			17 42					18 42	
Colwyn Bay	d	14 50						15 50					16 50			17 24			17 50					18 50	
Llandudno Junction	a	14 55						15 55					16 55			17 29			17 55					18 55	
	d	14 57						15 57					16 57			17 31			17 57					18 57	
Deganwy	d																								
Llandudno	a																								
Conwy	d							15x59								17x33			17x59						
Penmaenmawr	d							16x05								17x39			18x05						
Llanfairfechan	d							16x09								17x43			18x09						
Bangor (Gwynedd)	a	15 12						16 18					17 12			17 52			18 18					19 12	
	d	15 14						16 19					17 14			17 54			18 19					19 14	
Llanfairpwll	d	15x20											17x20			18x00								19x20	
Bodorgan	d	15x30											17x30			18x10								19x30	
Ty Croes	d	15x34											17x34			18x14								19x34	
Rhosneigr	d	15x37											17x37			18x17								19x37	
Valley	d	15x43											17x43			18x23								19x43	
Holyhead	a	15 57						16 53					17 57			18 37			18 54					19 54	

A From Wigan Wallgate

B From Southport

C From Birmingham International

Table 81

Sundays

19 February to 25 March

Crewe and Manchester - Chester and North Wales

Network Diagram - see first Page of Table 81

		AW		VT	AW	NT	AW	AW	AW	VT	AW	AW		AW	AW	VT	NT	AW	AW	AW	VT	AW		AW	AW
				◇1	◇		◇			◇1	◇					◇1					◇1	◇		◇	
					A	B					C						B					C			
		🚌		🍽	trolley			trolley	🚌	🍽	trolley				🚌	🍽				🚌	🍽	trolley			
London Euston [15] ⊖65	d			16 05						17 05						18 05					19 05				
Birmingham New Street [12] 65	d										17 24											19 24			
Manchester Airport 84,85 ✈	d																								
Cardiff Central [7] 131	d				15 22																				
Crewe [10]	d			17 52			18 27			18 56		19 24				19 52		20 27			20 55			21 27	
Manchester Pic'dilly [10] 90 ⛴	d	15 45				17 22		17 48	16 45					18 48	17 46		19 22		19 49	18 47					20 48
Manchester Oxford Road 90	d	15 50							16 50						17 51					18 52					
Newton-le-Willows 90	d	16 20							17 20						18 21					19 22					
Earlestown [8] 90	d	16 30							17 30						18 31					19 32					
Warrington Bank Quay 90	d	16 55							17 55						18 56					19 57					
Runcorn East	d	17 15							18 15						19 16					20 17					
Frodsham	d	17 30							18 30						19 31					20 32					
Helsby	d	17 35							18 35						19 36					20 37					
Liverpool Lime Street [10] 106	d																								
Chester	a	17 55		18 14	18 25	18 46	18 49	18 51	18 55	19 14	19 16	19 45		19 51	19 56	20 11	20 46	20 50	20 54	20 57	21 14	21 20		21 50	21 53
	d				18 29		18 52			19 22	19 38					20 18					21 17			22 00	
Shotton	d				18 38		19 01				19 47													22 09	
Flint	d				18 44		19 07			19 35	19 53					20 31					21 30			22 15	
Prestatyn	d				18 57		19 21			19 48	20 06					20 44					21 43			22 28	
Rhyl	d				19 03		19 27			19 55	20 12					20 51					21 50			22 34	
Abergele & Pensarn	d				19 09		19 33				20 18													22 40	
Colwyn Bay	d				19 17		19 41			20 06	20 26					21 02					22 01			22 48	
Llandudno Junction	a				19 22		19 46			20 11	20 31					21 07					22 06			22 53	
	d				19 24		19 47			20 12	20 33					21 08					22 07			22 55	
Deganwy	d																								
Llandudno	a																								
Conwy	d				19x26		19x49				20x35														
Penmaenmawr	d				19x32		19x55				20x41														
Llanfairfechan	d				19x36		19x59				20x45														
Bangor (Gwynedd)	a				19 45		20 08			20 27	20 54					21 23					22 22			23 10	
	d				19 45		20 09			20 29	20 55					21 25					22 24			23 12	
Llanfairpwll	d																							23x18	
Bodorgan	d																							23x28	
Ty Croes	d																							23x32	
Rhosneigr	d																							23x35	
Valley	d																							23x41	
Holyhead	a				20 18		20 44			20 59	21 30					21 57					22 56			23 55	

		AW	AW	NT	AW	AW	AW	AW		AW	AW	AW	AW	AW	AW	AW	AW
						◇		◇					◇			◇	
				B				C					C				
		🚌					🚌				🚌			🚌			🚌
London Euston [15] ⊖65	d																
Birmingham New Street [12] 65	d							21 24					22 55				
Manchester Airport 84,85 ✈	d																
Cardiff Central [7] 131	d															21 04	
Crewe [10]	d		22 03			22 29		23 06				23 38	00 01			00 10	
Manchester Pic'dilly [10] 90 ⛴	d	19 45		21 22	21 50		20 45			22 52	21 45			22 14	23 20		23 25
Manchester Oxford Road 90	d	19 50					20 50				21 50			22 19			23 30
Newton-le-Willows 90	d	20 20					21 20				22 20			22 49			00 01
Earlestown [8] 90	d	20 30					21 30				22 30			22 59			00 10
Warrington Bank Quay 90	d	20 55					21 55				22 55			23 24			00 35
Runcorn East	d	21 15					22 15				23 15			23 44			00 55
Frodsham	d	21 30					22 30				23 30			23 59			01 10
Helsby	d	21 35					22 35				23 35			00 04			01 15
Liverpool Lime Street [10] 106	d																
Chester	a	21 55	22 26	22 46	22 52	22 52	22 55	23 31		23 54	23 55	00 01	00 22	00 24	00 25	00 33	01 35
	d					23 00							00 38				
Shotton	d					23 09											
Flint	d					23 15							00 51				
Prestatyn	d					23 28							01 04				
Rhyl	d					23 34							01 10				
Abergele & Pensarn	d																
Colwyn Bay	d					23 45							01 21				
Llandudno Junction	a					23 50							01 27				
	d					23 51							01 28				
Deganwy	d																
Llandudno	a																
Conwy	d					23x53											
Penmaenmawr	d					00x01											
Llanfairfechan	d					00x03											
Bangor (Gwynedd)	a					00 12							01 44				
	d					00 14							01 44				
Llanfairpwll	d																
Bodorgan	d																
Ty Croes	d																
Rhosneigr	d																
Valley	d																
Holyhead	a					00 49							02 20				

A ◇ from Chester

B From Southport

C From Birmingham International

Table 81

Sundays

from 1 April

Crewe and Manchester - Chester and North Wales

Network Diagram - see first Page of Table 81

	AW	AW	NT	AW	AW	AW	AW	NT	AW		AW	VT	AW	AW	AW	AW	AW	NT	AW		AW	AW	AW	AW
		◇				◇						◇1			◇						◇			◇
								A			B			B				C	B					D
				🚌	🚌							☕									🍴	🍴		
London Euston 15 ⊖65 d																								
Birmingham New Street 12 65 d																								11 05
Manchester Airport 84,85 ✈ d																								
Cardiff Central 7 131 d		20p55																						
Crewe 10 d		23p58				09 24	10 07					10 42	11 05		11 27		11 57				12 27		12 54	
Manchester Pic'dilly 10 90 ⛴ d	23p14		23p17		07 28			09 22	09 56							10 55		11 22				11 56		
Manchester Oxford Road 90 d	23p17				07 33				09 59							10 59						11 59		
Newton-le-Willows 90 d	23p36				08 03				10 18							11 20						12 18		
Earlestown 8 90 d	23p39				08 13				10 21							11 23						12 21		
Warrington Bank Quay 90 d	23p48				08 38				10 28							11 30						12 28		
Runcorn East d	23p55				08 58				10 35							11 37						12 35		
Frodsham d	23p59				09 13				10 40							11 41						12 39		
Helsby d	00 03				09 18				10 44							11 45						12 43		
Liverpool Lime Street 10 106 d																								
Chester a	00 15	00 24	00 43		09 38	09 46	10 30	10 46	10 59			11 02	11 30		11 50	11 57	12 20	12 43			12 52	12 55	13 19	13 20
d						09 48						11 07			12 03						13 02			
Shotton d						09 57									12 12						13 11			
Flint d						10 03									12 18						13 17			
Prestatyn d						10 16						11 30			12 31						13 30			
Rhyl d						10 22						11 37			12 37						13 36			
Abergele & Pensarn d						10 28															13 42			
Colwyn Bay d						10 36						11 48			12 48						13 50			
Llandudno Junction a						10 41						11 53			12 53						13 55			
d				23p48		10 43					11§00	11 54		12§00	12 54				13§00		13 57			
Deganwy d											11x03			12x03					13x03					
Llandudno a											11§10			12§10					13§10					
Conwy d				23p56		10x45															13x59			
Penmaenmawr d				00 08		10x51															14x05			
Llanfairfechan d				00 23		10x55															14x09			
Bangor (Gwynedd) a				00 38		11 04						12 09			13 10						14 18			
d				00 38		11 05						12 11			13 11						14 19			
Llanfairpwll d				00 47		11x12																		
Bodorgan d				00 57		11x22																		
Ty Croes d				01 07		11x26																		
Rhosneigr d				01 27		11x29																		
Valley d				01 52		11x34																		
Holyhead a				02 02		11 49						12 43			13 42						14 53			

	AW	AW	AW	AW	NT		AW	AW	AW	AW	AW	AW	AW	AW	AW		AW	NT	AW	AW	VT	AW	AW	AW
																	R							
		◇						◇		◇			◇						◇		◇1	◇	◇	
	B				C		B			D		B			B			C				D		
		🍴	🍴					🍴	🍴	🍴				🍴						🍴	☕	🍴		
London Euston 15 ⊖65 d																					15 05			
Birmingham New Street 12 65 d										13 25												15 24		
Manchester Airport 84,85 ✈ d																								
Cardiff Central 7 131 d																	13 22							
Crewe 10 d		13 27		13 57				14 27			14 57		15 27						16 27		16 52		17 27	
Manchester Pic'dilly 10 90 ⛴ d			12 56		13 22				13 56					14 56				15 22		15 56				16 56
Manchester Oxford Road 90 d			12 59						13 59					14 59						15 59				16 59
Newton-le-Willows 90 d			13 18						14 18					15 18						16 18				17 18
Earlestown 8 90 d			13 21						14 21					15 21						16 21				17 21
Warrington Bank Quay 90 d			13 29						14 28					15 29						16 28				17 28
Runcorn East d			13 36						14 35					15 36						16 35				17 35
Frodsham d			13 40						14 39					15 40						16 39				17 39
Helsby d			13 44						14 43					15 44						16 43				17 43
Liverpool Lime Street 10 106 d																								
Chester a		13 51	13 56	14 20	14 46			14 51	14 55	15 18	15 20		15 49	15 56			16 18	16 46	16 49	16 55	17 14	17 26	17 49	17 55
d		14 02						15 02					16 02				16 36		17 02				18 02	
Shotton d		14 11						15 11					16 11				16 45		17 11				18 11	
Flint d		14 17						15 17					16 17				16 51		17 17				18 17	
Prestatyn d		14 30						15 30					16 30				17 04		17 30				18 30	
Rhyl d		14 36						15 36					16 36				17 10		17 36				18 36	
Abergele & Pensarn d		14 42						15 42					16 42				17 16		17 42				18 42	
Colwyn Bay d		14 50						15 50					16 50				17 24		17 50				18 50	
Llandudno Junction a		14 55						15 55					16 55				17 29		17 55				18 55	
d	14§00	14 57					15§00	15 57				16§00	16 57		17§00		17 31		17 57				18 57	
Deganwy d	14x03						15x03					16x03			17x03									
Llandudno a	14§10						15§10					16§10			17§10									
Conwy d								15x59									17x33		17x59					
Penmaenmawr d								16x05									17x39		18x05					
Llanfairfechan d								16x09									17x43		18x09					
Bangor (Gwynedd) a		15 12						16 18					17 12				17 52		18 18				19 12	
d		15 14						16 19					17 14				17 54		18 19				19 14	
Llanfairpwll d		15x20											17x20				18x00						19x20	
Bodorgan d		15x30											17x30				18x10						19x30	
Ty Croes d		15x34											17x34				18x14						19x34	
Rhosneigr d		15x37											17x37				18x17						19x37	
Valley d		15x43											17x43				18x23						19x43	
Holyhead a		15 57						16 53					17 57				18 37		18 54				19 54	

A From Wigan Wallgate
B not 1 April
C From Southport
D From Birmingham International

Table 81

Sundays
from 1 April

Crewe and Manchester - Chester and North Wales

Network Diagram - see first Page of Table 81

		VT		AW	NT	AW	AW	VT	AW	AW	AW	VT		NT	AW	AW	VT	AW	AW	AW	AW	NT		AW	AW
		◇1		◇		◇		◇1	◇			◇1					◇1	◇	◇						◇
				A	B				C					B				C				B			
		🍴		🛒			🛒	🍴	🛒			🍴					🍴	🛒							
London Euston 15 ⊖65	d	16 05						17 05				18 05					19 05								
Birmingham New Street 12 65	d								17 24									19 24							
Manchester Airport 84,85 ✈	d																								
Cardiff Central 7 131	d			15 22																					
Crewe 10	d	17 52				18 27		18 56		19 24		19 52			20 27		20 55		21 27		22 03				22 29
Manchester Pic'dilly 10 90 🚌	d				17 22		17 56				18 56			19 22		19 56				20 56		21 22		21 50	
Manchester Oxford Road 90	d						17 59				18 59					19 59				20 59					
Newton-le-Willows 90	d						18 18				19 18					20 18				21 18					
Earlestown 8 90	d						18 21				19 21					20 21				21 21					
Warrington Bank Quay 90	d						18 28				19 29					20 30				21 28					
Runcorn East	d						18 35				19 36					20 37				21 35					
Frodsham	d						18 39				19 40					20 41				21 39					
Helsby	d						18 43				19 44					20 45				21 43					
Liverpool Lime Street 10 106	d																								
Chester	a	18 14		18 25	18 46	18 49	18 55	19 14	19 16	19 45	19 56	20 11		20 46	20 50	20 57	21 14	21 20	21 50	21 55	22 26	22 46		22 52	22 52
	d			18 29		18 52		19 22	19 38			20 18					21 17		22 00						23 00
Shotton	d			18 38		19 01			19 47										22 09						23 09
Flint	d			18 44		19 07		19 35	19 53			20 31					21 30		22 15						23 15
Prestatyn	d			18 57		19 21		19 48	20 06			20 44					21 43		22 28						23 28
Rhyl	d			19 03		19 27		19 55	20 12			20 51					21 50		22 34						23 34
Abergele & Pensarn	d			19 09		19 33			20 18										22 40						
Colwyn Bay	d			19 17		19 41		20 06	20 26			21 02					22 01		22 48						23 45
Llandudno Junction	a			19 22		19 46		20 11	20 31			21 07					22 06		22 53						23 50
	d			19 24		19 47		20 12	20 33			21 08					22 07		22 55						23 51
Deganwy	d																								
Llandudno	a																								
Conwy	d			19x26		19x49			20x35																23x53
Penmaenmawr	d			19x32		19x55			20x41																00x01
Llanfairfechan	d			19x36		19x59			20x45																00x03
Bangor (Gwynedd)	a			19 45		20 08		20 27	20 54			21 23					22 22		23 10						00 12
	d			19 45		20 09		20 29	20 55			21 25					22 24		23 12						00 14
Llanfairpwll	d																		23x18						
Bodorgan	d																		23x28						
Ty Croes	d																		23x32						
Rhosneigr	d																		23x35						
Valley	d																		23x41						
Holyhead	a			20 18		20 44		20 59	21 30			21 57					22 56		23 55						00 49

		AW	AW	AW	AW	AW	AW
		◇			◇		◇
		C			C		
London Euston 15 ⊖65	d						
Birmingham New Street 12 65	d	21 24			22 55		
Manchester Airport 84,85 ✈	d						
Cardiff Central 7 131	d						21 04
Crewe 10	d	23 06		23 38	00 01		00 10
Manchester Pic'dilly 10 90 🚌	d		22 52			23 20	
Manchester Oxford Road 90	d						
Newton-le-Willows 90	d						
Earlestown 8 90	d						
Warrington Bank Quay 90	d						
Runcorn East	d						
Frodsham	d						
Helsby	d						
Liverpool Lime Street 10 106	d						
Chester	a	23 31	23 54	00 01	00 22	00 25	00 33
	d				00 38		
Shotton	d						
Flint	d				00 51		
Prestatyn	d				01 04		
Rhyl	d				01 10		
Abergele & Pensarn	d						
Colwyn Bay	d				01 21		
Llandudno Junction	a				01 27		
	d				01 28		
Deganwy	d						
Llandudno	a						
Conwy	d						
Penmaenmawr	d						
Llanfairfechan	d						
Bangor (Gwynedd)	a				01 44		
	d				01 44		
Llanfairpwll	d						
Bodorgan	d						
Ty Croes	d						
Rhosneigr	d						
Valley	d						
Holyhead	a				02 20		

A ◇ from Chester
B From Southport
C From Birmingham International

North Wales and Chester - Manchester and Crewe

Network Diagram - see first Page of Table 81

Miles	Miles			AW MO A	NT MX	AW	AW B	AW	AW ◇ C	AW	AW	AW	NT	AW ◇ ⊥	VT ◇1 ⊠	AW ◇	AW	NT	AW ◇ D ⊥	AW ◇ E ⊠⊥	AW ⊥	VT ◇1 ⊠	AW ◇ ⊥
0	—	**Holyhead**	d											04 25	04 48				05 11	05 32		05 51	
3½	—	Valley	d											04x31									
7½	—	Rhosneigr	d																				
9¼	—	Ty Croes	d																				
12	—	Bodorgan	d																				
21	—	Llanfairpwll	d											04x48									
24¾	—	**Bangor (Gwynedd)**	a											04 55	05 14				05 38	06 00		06 17	
—	—		d											04 57	05 14				05 40	06 02		06 18	
32¼	—	Llanfairfechan	d																05x47				
34¾	—	Penmaenmawr	d																05x51				
39	—	Conwy	d																05x57				
—	0	**Llandudno**	d																				06 34
—	1¾	Deganwy	d																				06x38
40	3	**Llandudno Junction**	a											05 13	05 32				06 01	06 19		06 35	06 42
—	—		d							04 38				05 15	05 32	05 46			06 07	06 21		06 36	06 44
44	—	Colwyn Bay	d							04 44				05 21	05 38	05 52			06 13			06 42	06 50
50¼	—	Abergele & Pensarn	d							04 51													06 57
54½	—	Rhyl	d							04 57				05 31	05 49	06 02			06 23	06 36		06 53	07 03
58	—	Prestatyn	d							05 02				05 37		06 08			06 29			06 58	07 08
72	—	Flint	d							05 16				05 50		06 21			06 42	06 52		07 12	07 21
76¼	—	Shotton	d							05 22						06 27			06 48				07 27
84¼	0	**Chester**	a							05 33				06 05	06 17	06 38			07 00	07 07		07 26	07 38
—	—		d	22p09	22p48	03 36	04 22	04 55	05 15	05 37	05 38	05 51	06 05	06 18	06 26	06 40	06 43	06 59	07 19	07 08	07 12	07 35	07 40
—	—	Liverpool Lime Street [10] 106	a																				
—	7½	Helsby	d	22p29							05 47					06 49					07 21		07 49
—	10	Frodsham	d	22p34							05 51					06 53					07 25		07 53
—	13¼	Runcorn East	d	22p49							05 56					06 59					07 31		07 59
—	18¼	Warrington Bank Quay 90	a	23p09							06 05					07 06					07 38		08 06
—	22¼	Earlestown [8] 90	a	23p34							06 12					07 14					07 46		08 15
—	24	Newton-le-Willows 90	a	23p44							06 15					07 17					07 49		08 18
—	39¾	**Manchester Oxford Road** 90	a	00 14							06 35					07 41					08 09		08 41
—	40¼	**Manchester Pic'dilly** [10] 90 ⛴	a	00 19	00 18	04 43					06 45		07 31			07 50		08 32			08 18		08 50
105½	—	**Crewe** [10]	a				04 44	05 20		05 58		06 15			06 47		07 04			07 32		07 54	
—	—	Cardiff Central [7] 131	a						08 17					09 23						09 58			
—	—	Manchester Airport 84,85 ✈	a			05 09																	
—	—	Birmingham New Street [12] 65	a				06 01												09 25				
—	—	London Euston [15] ⊖65	a												08 33							09 38	

		AW	AW	NT	AW ◇ ⊥	VT ◇1 ⊠	AW ◇ ⊥	AW	AW	NT	AW ◇ D ⊥	AW BHX [R] ⊥	VT ◇1 ⊠	AW ◇ ⊥	AW	AW	NT	AW ◇ ⊥	VT ◇1 ⊠	AW ◇ ⊥	AW	AW	NT
Holyhead	d				06 28	06 55					07 15	07 51						08 05	08 55				
Valley	d				06x34						07x21							08x11					
Rhosneigr	d				06x40						07x26							08x17					
Ty Croes	d				06x43						07x30							08x20					
Bodorgan	d				06x48						07x34							08x25					
Llanfairpwll	d				06x57						07x44							08x34					
Bangor (Gwynedd)	a				07 05	07 21					07 52	08 17						08 42	09 21				
	d				07 06	07 22					08 02	08 21						09 02	09 22				
Llanfairfechan	d										08x09							09x09					
Penmaenmawr	d										08x13							09x13					
Conwy	d										08x19							09x19					
Llandudno	d	07 08					07 45	08 08						08 45	09 08					09 45	10 08		
Deganwy	d	07x12					07x49	08x12						08x49	09x12					09x49	10x12		
Llandudno Junction	a	07 18			07 22	07 39	07 53	08 18			08 23	08 38		08 53	09 18			09 23	09 39	09 53	10 18		
	d				07 24	07 40	07 54				08 25	08 39		08 54				09 25	09 40	09 54			
Colwyn Bay	d				07 30	07 47	08 00				08 31	08 45		09 00				09 31	09 47	10 00			
Abergele & Pensarn	d						08 07							09 07						10 07			
Rhyl	d				07 40	07 58	08 13				08 41	08 56		09 13				09 41	09 58	10 13			
Prestatyn	d				07 46	08 04	08 19				08 47			09 19				09 47	10 04	10 19			
Flint	d				07 59	08 17	08 32				09 00			09 32				10 00	10 17	10 32			
Shotton	d						08 38							09 38						10 38			
Chester	a				08 14	08 31	08 50				09 14	09 23		09 50				10 15	10 31	10 50			
	d		07 55	08 07	08 19	08 35	08 52		08 55	09 07	09 19	09 26	09 35	09 52		09 55	10 07	10 20	10 35	10 52		10 55	11 07
Liverpool Lime Street [10] 106	a																						
Helsby	d						09 01							10 01						11 01			
Frodsham	d						09 05							10 05						11 05			
Runcorn East	d						09 11							10 11						11 11			
Warrington Bank Quay 90	a						09 18							10 18						11 18			
Earlestown [8] 90	a						09 26							10 26						11 26			
Newton-le-Willows 90	a						09 29							10 29						11 29			
Manchester Oxford Road 90	a						09 48							10 48						11 48			
Manchester Pic'dilly [10] 90 ⛴	a			09 36			09 57			10 36				10 57			11 36			11 57			12 36
Crewe [10]	a		08 18			08 54			09 18		09 40		09 54			10 18			10 54			11 18	
Cardiff Central [7] 131	a				11 15							12 08						13 22					
Manchester Airport 84,85 ✈	a																						
Birmingham New Street [12] 65	a										11 27												
London Euston [15] ⊖65	a					10 38							11 38						12 38				

A from 20 February until 26 March
B until 26 March and then MO from 2 April
C To Maesteg
D To Birmingham International
E ⊠ to Crewe ⊥ from Crewe

North Wales and Chester - Manchester and Crewe

Network Diagram - see first Page of Table 81

		AW	AW	VT		AW	AW	AW	NT	AW	VT	AW	AW	AW		NT	AW	VT	AW	AW	AW	NT	AW	AW	
		◇ A ☕	◇ B	◇1 🍴		◇ ☕				■ ☕	◇1 🍴	◇ ☕					◇ A ☕	◇1 🍴	◇ ☕				◇ C ☕	◇ B	
Holyhead	d	09 23								10 33							11 23						12 39		
Valley	d	09x29								10x39							11x29								
Rhosneigr	d	09x34															11x34								
Ty Croes	d	09x38															11x38								
Bodorgan	d	09x42															11x42								
Llanfairpwll	d	09x52								10x56							11x52								
Bangor (Gwynedd)	a	10 00								11 03							12 00						13 05		
	d	10 02								11 05							12 02	12 24					13 07		
Llanfairfechan	d	10x09															12x09								
Penmaenmawr	d	10x13															12x13								
Conwy	d	10x19															12x19								
Llandudno	d		10 22			10 44	11 08					11 44	12 08						12 44	13 08				13 22	
Deganwy	d		10x26			10x48	11x12					11x48	12x12						12x48	13x12				13x26	
Llandudno Junction	a	10 23	10 32			10 52	11 18			11 21		11 52	12 18				12 23	12 40	12 52	13 18			13 23	13 32	
	d	10 25				10 53				11 25		11 53					12 25	12 42	12 53				13 25		
Colwyn Bay	d	10 31				10 59				11 31		11 59					12 31	12 48	12 59				13 31		
Abergele & Pensarn	d					11 06						12 06							13 06						
Rhyl	d	10 41				11 12				11 41		12 12					12 41	12 59	13 12				13 41		
Prestatyn	d	10 47				11 18				11 47		12 18					12 47	13 05	13 18				13 47		
Flint	d	11 00				11 31				12 00		12 31					13 00	13 18	13 31				14 00		
Shotton	d					11 37						12 37							13 37						
Chester	a	11 15				11 49				12 14		12 49					13 15	13 32	13 49				14 14		
	d	11 21		11 35		11 50		11 55	12 07	12 19	12 35	12 50		12 55		13 07	13 21	13 35	13 50		13 55	14 07	14 19		
Liverpool Lime Street 10 106	a																								
Helsby	d					12 00						13 00							14 00						
Frodsham	d					12 04						13 04							14 04						
Runcorn East	d					12 09						13 09							14 09						
Warrington Bank Quay 90	a					12 18						13 18							14 18						
Earlestown 8 90	a					12 26						13 26							14 26						
Newton-le-Willows 90	a					12 29						13 29							14 29						
Manchester Oxford Road 90	a					12 48						13 48							14 48						
Manchester Pic'dilly 10 90 ⛴	a					12 57			13 36			13 57				14 36			14 57			15 36			
Crewe 10	a			11 54				12 18			12 54			13 18				13 54			14 18				
Cardiff Central 7 131	a									15 19													17 15		
Manchester Airport 84,85 ✈	a																								
Birmingham New Street 12 65	a	13 26															15 26								
London Euston 15 ⊖65	a			13 38							14 38							15 38							

		VT	AW	AW	AW	NT	AW	VT	AW	AW		NT	AW	AW	VT	AW	NT	AW	AW	AW		VT	AW	NT	AW
		◇1 🍴	◇ ☕				◇ A ☕	◇1 🍴	◇ ☕				◇ ☕	◇ ☕	◇1 🍴			◇ ☕	◇ A ☕	◇ B		◇1 ⊠			◇ ☕
Holyhead	d						13 23	13 58						14 34					15 23						
Valley	d						13x29												15x29						
Rhosneigr	d						13x34												15x34						
Ty Croes	d						13x38												15x38						
Bodorgan	d						13x42												15x42						
Llanfairpwll	d						13x52												15x52						
Bangor (Gwynedd)	a						14 00	14 24						15 01					16 00						
	d						14 02	14 25						15 04					16 02						
Llanfairfechan	d						14x09							15x11					16x09						
Penmaenmawr	d						14x13							15x15					16x13						
Conwy	d						14x19							15x21					16x19						
Llandudno	d		13 44	14 08					14 40				15 08					16 06		16 20					17 06
Deganwy	d		13x48	14x12					14x44				15x12					16x10		16x24					17x10
Llandudno Junction	a		13 52	14 18			14 23	14 42	14 48				15 16	15 26				16 14	16 23	16 28					17 14
	d		13 53				14 25	14 43	14 49				15 17	15 27				16 15	16 25						17 14
Colwyn Bay	d		13 59				14 31	14 50	14 55				15 23	15 33				16 21	16 34						17 20
Abergele & Pensarn	d		14 06						15 02				15 30					16 28							17 27
Rhyl	d		14 12				14 41	15 00	15 08				15 36	15 44				16 34	16 44						17 33
Prestatyn	d		14 18				14 47		15 14				15 42	15 49				16 39	16 50						17 38
Flint	d		14 31				15 00		15 27				15 55	16 03				16 53	17 03						17 52
Shotton	d		14 37						15 33				16 01					16 59							17 58
Chester	a		14 49				15 15	15 27	15 44				16 13	16 15				17 10	17 17						18 11
	d	14 35	14 50		14 55	15 07	15 20	15 35	15 46	15 55		16 07	16 22	16 19	16 35	16 55	17 07	17 19	17 23			17 35	17 55	18 07	18 16
Liverpool Lime Street 10 106	a																								
Helsby	d		15 00						15 55				16 31					17 28							18 25
Frodsham	d		15 04						15 59				16 35					17 33							18 30
Runcorn East	d		15 09						16 04				16 41					17 38							18 35
Warrington Bank Quay 90	a		15 18						16 12				16 51					17 49							18 45
Earlestown 8 90	a		15 26						16 26				16 59					17 57							18 57
Newton-le-Willows 90	a		15 29						16 29				17 01					17 59							18 59
Manchester Oxford Road 90	a		15 48						16 48				17 21					18 19							19 21
Manchester Pic'dilly 10 90 ⛴	a		15 57			16 36			16 57			17 36	17 30				18 36	18 28						19 35	19 29
Crewe 10	a	14 54			15 18			15 54		16 18					16 54	17 18						17 54	18 18		
Cardiff Central 7 131	a													19 21											
Manchester Airport 84,85 ✈	a																								
Birmingham New Street 12 65	a						17 27												19 26						
London Euston 15 ⊖65	a	16 38						17 38							18 38							19 38			

A To Birmingham International **B** To Blaenau Ffestiniog **C** To Maesteg

North Wales and Chester - Manchester and Crewe

Network Diagram - see first Page of Table 81

	AW	AW	AW	AW	AW		NT	VT	AW	AW	AW	AW	NT	AW	AW		AW	AW	NT	AW MW FO	AW TThO	VT	AW	AW FX
	◇		◇					◇1	◇	◇				◇	◇					◇	◇	◇1		
			A							B										C	D			
	⊤		⊤					☕	⊤					⊤								☕		
Holyhead d	16 38		17 30											18 23						19 21	19 21			
Valley d			17x36											18x29						19x27	19x27			
Rhosneigr d			17x41											18x34						19x32	19x32			
Ty Croes d			17x45											18x38						19x36	19x36			
Bodorgan d			17x49											18x42						19x40	19x40			
Llanfairpwll d			17x59											18x52						19x50	19x50			
Bangor (Gwynedd) a	17 04		18 07											19 00						19 58	19 58			
d	17 06		18 09											19 02						20 00	20 00	20 20		
Llanfairfechan d			18x16											19x09						20x07	20x07			
Penmaenmawr d			18x20											19x13						20x11	20x11			
Conwy d			18x26											19x19						20x17	20x17			
Llandudno d		18 08							18 44	19 03	19 08				19 42		20 08						20 43	
Deganwy d		18x12							18x48	19x07	19x12				19x46		20x12						20x47	
Llandudno Junction a	17 23	18 18	18 30						18 52	19 11	19 18			19 23	19 50		20 18			20 21	20 21	20 36	20 51	
d	17 25		18 32						18 53					19 25	19 51					20 23	20 23	20 38	20 52	
Colwyn Bay d	17 31		18 38						18 59					19 31	19 57					20 29	20 29	20 44	20 58	
Abergele & Pensarn d									19 06						20 04								21 05	
Rhyl d	17 41		18 48						19 12					19 41	20 10					20 39	20 39	20 55	21 11	
Prestatyn d	17 47		18 54						19 18					19 47	20 16					20 45	20 45	21 01	21 17	
Flint d	18 01		19 07						19 31					20 00	20 29					20 58	20 58	21 14	21 30	
Shotton d									19 37						20 35								21 36	
Chester a	18 16		19 24						19 49					20 15	20 47					21 15	21 15	21 28	21 47	
d	18 18			18 49	18 55		19 07	19 35	19 50			19 55	20 07	20 17	20 50			20 55	21 07	21 21	21 21	21 35		21 52
Liverpool Lime Street 10 106 a																								
Helsby d				18 59					20 00						20 59									22 01
Frodsham d				19 03					20 04						21 03									22 05
Runcorn East d				19 08					20 09						21 09									22 11
Warrington Bank Quay 90 a				19 18					20 18						21 18									22 18
Earlestown 8 90 a				19 26					20 26						21 26									
Newton-le-Willows 90 a				19 29					20 29						21 29									
Manchester Oxford Road 90 a				19 48					20 48						21 48									
Manchester Pic'dilly 10 90 ⛴ a				19 52			20 35		20 52				21 35		21 57				22 35					
Crewe 10 a					19 18			19 54				20 18		20 41				21 18				21 54		
Cardiff Central 7 131 a	21 19																							
Manchester Airport 84,85 ✈ a				20 18					21 18															
Birmingham New Street 12 65 a																				23 27	23 28	22 50		
London Euston 15 ⊖65 a								21 42																

	AW FO		AW	NT	AW	AW FO	AW FX
			◇			◇	◇
						E	E
Holyhead d			20 37				
Valley d							
Rhosneigr d							
Ty Croes d							
Bodorgan d							
Llanfairpwll d							
Bangor (Gwynedd) a			21 04				
d			21 06				
Llanfairfechan d			21x13				
Penmaenmawr d			21x17				
Conwy d			21x23				
Llandudno d					21 45		
Deganwy d					21x49		
Llandudno Junction a			21 27		21 53		
d			21 29		21 55		
Colwyn Bay d			21 35		22 01		
Abergele & Pensarn d			21 42		22 09		
Rhyl d			21 48		22 16		
Prestatyn d			21 53		22 22		
Flint d			22 07		22 37		
Shotton d			22 13		22 44		
Chester a			22 23		22 55		
d	21 52		22 26	22 48	23 01	23 22	23 22
Liverpool Lime Street 10 106 a							
Helsby d	22 01					23 31	23 31
Frodsham d	22 05					23 35	23 36
Runcorn East d	22 11					23 41	23 41
Warrington Bank Quay 90 a	22 18					23 49	23 50
Earlestown 8 90 a	22 26					23 56	
Newton-le-Willows 90 a	22 29					23 59	
Manchester Oxford Road 90 a	22 50						
Manchester Pic'dilly 10 90 ⛴ a	22 58			00 18		00 28	
Crewe 10 a			22 50		23 26		
Cardiff Central 7 131 a							
Manchester Airport 84,85 ✈ a							
Birmingham New Street 12 65 a							
London Euston 15 ⊖65 a							

A To Shrewsbury

B To Blaenau Ffestiniog

E From Birmingham International

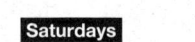

North Wales and Chester - Manchester and Crewe

Network Diagram - see first Page of Table 81

		NT	AW	AW	AW	AW	AW	AW	AW	NT		AW	AW	AW	NT	AW	VT	AW	AW	AW		AW	NT	AW	VT
			◇									◇	◇				◇1	◇						◇	◇1
			A													B		C							
												🛒				🛒	🍴	🛒	🛒					🛒	🍴
Holyhead	d											04 25						05 22						06 35	06 52
Valley	d											04x31						05x28						06x41	
Rhosneigr	d																	05x33							
Ty Croes	d																	05x37							
Bodorgan	d																	05x41							
Llanfairpwll	d											04x48						05x51						06x58	
Bangor (Gwynedd)	a											04 55						05 59						07 05	07 18
	d											04 57						06 01						07 07	07 20
Llanfairfechan	d																	06x08							
Penmaenmawr	d																	06x12							
Conwy	d																	06x18							
Llandudno	d																		06 34	07 08					
Deganwy	d																		06x38	07x12					
Llandudno Junction	a											05 13						06 22	06 42	07 18				07 23	07 36
	d						04 38					05 15		05 37				06 24	06 44					07 25	07 38
Colwyn Bay	d						04 44					05 21		05 43				06 30	06 50					07 31	07 44
Abergele & Pensarn	d						04 51							05 50					06 57						
Rhyl	d						04 57					05 31		05 56				06 40	07 03					07 41	07 55
Prestatyn	d						05 02					05 37		06 01				06 46	07 08					07 47	08 01
Flint	d						05 16					05 50		06 15				06 59	07 21					08 00	08 15
Shotton	d						05 22							06 21					07 27						
Chester	a						05 33					06 04		06 33				07 15	07 38					08 14	08 28
	d	22p48	23p22	03 36	04 22	04 55	05 37	05 38	05 51	06 05		06 12	06 13	06 35	07 03	07 12	07 17	07 21	07 40			07 55	08 07	08 19	08 35
Liverpool Lime Street 10 106	a																								
Helsby	d		23p31					05 47					06 22			07 21			07 49						
Frodsham	d		23p35					05 51					06 26			07 25			07 53						
Runcorn East	d		23p41					05 56					06 32			07 31			07 59						
Warrington Bank Quay 90	a		23p49					06 05					06 39			07 38			08 06						
Earlestown 8 90	a		23p56					06 12					06 47			07 46			08 15						
Newton-le-Willows 90	a		23p59					06 15					06 50			07 49			08 18						
Manchester Oxford Road 90	a							06 35					07 09			08 09			08 41						
Manchester Pic'dilly 10 90 ⇌	a	00 18	00 28	04 44				06 45		07 31			07 18		08 32	08 18			08 45				09 36		
Crewe 10	a				04 44	05 20	05 58		06 15					06 59			07 36					08 18			08 54
Cardiff Central 7 131	a											09 22												11 15	
Manchester Airport 84,85 ✈	a			05 19																					
Birmingham New Street 12 65	a				05 58													09 26							
London Euston 15 ⊖65	a																09 30								10 37

		AW	AW	AW	NT	AW		VT	AW	AW	AW	NT	AW	VT	AW	AW		AW	NT	AW	AW	VT	AW	AW	AW
						◇		◇1					◇	◇1							◇	◇1	◇		
						C														C	D				
		🛒				🛒		🍴	🛒				🛒	🍴	🛒							🍴	🛒		
Holyhead	d					07 15		07 55					08 20	08 55						09 23					
Valley	d					07x21							08x26							09x29					
Rhosneigr	d					07x26							08x32							09x34					
Ty Croes	d					07x30							08x35							09x38					
Bodorgan	d					07x34							08x40							09x42					
Llanfairpwll	d					07x44							08x49							09x52					
Bangor (Gwynedd)	a					07 52		08 21					08 57	09 21						10 00					
	d					08 02		08 22					09 02	09 22						10 02					
Llanfairfechan	d					08x09							09x09							10x09					
Penmaenmawr	d					08x13							09x13							10x13					
Conwy	d					08x19							09x19							10x19					
Llandudno	d	07 45	08 08						08 45	09 08					09 45	10 08					10 22		10 44	11 08	
Deganwy	d	07x49	08x12						08x49	09x12					09x49	10x12					10x26		10x48	11x12	
Llandudno Junction	a	07 53	08 18			08 23		08 39	08 53	09 18			09 23	09 39	09 53	10 18				10 23	10 32		10 52	11 18	
	d	07 54				08 25		08 40	08 54				09 25	09 40	09 54					10 25			10 53		
Colwyn Bay	d	08 00				08 31		08 47	09 00				09 31	09 47	10 00					10 31			10 59		
Abergele & Pensarn	d	08 07							09 07						10 07								11 06		
Rhyl	d	08 13				08 41		08 58	09 13				09 41	09 58	10 13					10 41			11 12		
Prestatyn	d	08 19				08 47		09 04	09 19				09 47	10 03	10 19					10 47			11 18		
Flint	d	08 32				09 00		09 17	09 32				10 00		10 32					11 00			11 31		
Shotton	d	08 38							09 38						10 38								11 37		
Chester	a	08 50				09 15		09 31	09 50				10 14	10 28	10 50					11 16			11 49		
	d	08 52		08 55	09 07	09 20		09 35	09 52		09 55	10 07	10 19	10 35	10 52			10 55	11 07	11 21		11 35	11 50		11 55
Liverpool Lime Street 10 106	a																								
Helsby	d	09 01							10 01						11 01								12 00		
Frodsham	d	09 05							10 05						11 05								12 04		
Runcorn East	d	09 11							10 11						11 11								12 09		
Warrington Bank Quay 90	a	09 18							10 18						11 18								12 18		
Earlestown 8 90	a	09 26							10 26						11 26								12 26		
Newton-le-Willows 90	a	09 29							10 29						11 29								12 29		
Manchester Oxford Road 90	a	09 48							10 48						11 48								12 48		
Manchester Pic'dilly 10 90 ⇌	a	09 52			10 36				10 52			11 36			11 52				12 36				12 52		
Crewe 10	a			09 18				09 54			10 18			10 54				11 18				11 54			12 18
Cardiff Central 7 131	a												13 15												
Manchester Airport 84,85 ✈	a																								
Birmingham New Street 12 65	a					11 26														13 26					
London Euston 15 ⊖65	a							11 38						12 38								13 38			

A From Birmingham International
B From Shrewsbury
C To Birmingham International
D To Blaenau Ffestiniog

Table 81

Saturdays

North Wales and Chester - Manchester and Crewe

Network Diagram - see first Page of Table 81

		NT		AW	VT	AW	AW	AW	NT	AW	VT	AW		AW	AW	NT	AW	AW	VT	AW	AW	AW		NT	AW
				R	◇1	◇				◇	◇1	◇					◇	◇	◇1	◇					◇
										A							B	C							A
				⊼	⊡	⊼				⊼	⊡	⊼					⊼		⊡	⊼					⊼
Holyhead	d			10 33						11 23							12 38								13 23
Valley	d			10x39						11x29															13x29
Rhosneigr	d									11x34															13x34
Ty Croes	d									11x38															13x38
Bodorgan	d									11x42															13x42
Llanfairpwll	d			10x56						11x52															13x52
Bangor (Gwynedd)	a			11 03						12 00							13 05								14 00
	d			11 05						12 02							13 07								14 02
Llanfairfechan	d									12x09															14x09
Penmaenmawr	d									12x13															14x13
Conwy	d									12x19															14x19
Llandudno	d					11 44	12 08					12 44		13 08				13 22		13 44	14 08				
Deganwy	d					11x48	12x12					12x48		13x12				13x26		13x48	14x12				
Llandudno Junction	a			11 21		11 52	12 18			12 23		12 52		13 18			13 23	13 32		13 52	14 18				14 23
	d			11 25		11 53				12 25		12 53					13 25			13 53					14 25
Colwyn Bay	d			11 31		11 59				12 31		12 59					13 31			13 59					14 31
Abergele & Pensarn	d					12 06						13 06								14 06					
Rhyl	d			11 41		12 12				12 41		13 12					13 41			14 12					14 41
Prestatyn	d			11 47		12 18				12 47		13 18					13 47			14 18					14 47
Flint	d			12 00		12 31				13 00		13 31					14 00			14 31					15 00
Shotton	d					12 37						13 37								14 37					
Chester	a			12 14		12 49				13 15		13 49					14 14			14 49					15 17
	d	12 07		12 19	12 35	12 50		12 55	13 07	13 20	13 35	13 50			13 55	14 07	14 19		14 35	14 50		14 55		15 07	15 20
Liverpool Lime Street 10 106	a																								
Helsby	d					13 00						14 00								15 00					
Frodsham	d					13 04						14 04								15 04					
Runcorn East	d					13 09						14 09								15 09					
Warrington Bank Quay 90	a					13 18						14 18								15 18					
Earlestown 8 90	a					13 26						14 26								15 26					
Newton-le-Willows 90	a					13 29						14 29								15 29					
Manchester Oxford Road 90	a					13 48						14 48								15 48					
Manchester Pic'dilly 10 90 ⛴	a	13 36				13 52			14 36			14 57				15 36				15 52				16 36	
Crewe 10	a				12 54			13 18			13 54				14 18				14 54			15 18			
Cardiff Central 7 131	a			15 26													17 08								
Manchester Airport 84,85 ✈	a																								
Birmingham New Street 12 65	a									15 26															17 28
London Euston 15 ⊖65	a				14 38						15 38								16 38						

		VT	AW	AW	NT	AW	AW	VT		AW	AW	AW	NT	AW	AW	VT	AW	AW		AW	NT	AW	AW	AW	AW
		◇1	◇			◇		◇1		◇				◇	◇	◇1	◇					◇	◇		◇
														A	C										D
		⊡	⊼			⊼		⊡		⊼				⊼		⊡	⊼					⊼	⊼		⊼
Holyhead	d					14 23		14 38						15 23								16 38			17 30
Valley	d													15x29											17x36
Rhosneigr	d													15x34											17x41
Ty Croes	d													15x38											17x45
Bodorgan	d													15x42											17x49
Llanfairpwll	d													15x52											17x59
Bangor (Gwynedd)	a					14 52		15 06						16 00								17 05			18 07
	d					14 53		15 07						16 02								17 07			18 09
Llanfairfechan	d					15x00								16x09											18x16
Penmaenmawr	d					15x04								16x13											18x20
Conwy	d					15x10								16x19											18x26
Llandudno	d		14 42				15 08			15 44	16 08				16 20		16 44	17 08					17 44	18 08	
Deganwy	d		14x46				15x12			15x48	16x12				16x24		16x48	17x12					17x48	18x12	
Llandudno Junction	a		14 50			15 15	15 18	15 25		15 52	16 18			16 23	16 30		16 52	17 18				17 23	17 52	18 18	18 30
	d		14 51			15 16		15 27		15 53				16 25			16 53					17 25	17 53		18 32
Colwyn Bay	d		14 57			15 22		15 35		15 59				16 31			16 59					17 31	17 59		18 38
Abergele & Pensarn	d		15 04							16 06							17 06						18 06		
Rhyl	d		15 10			15 33		15 48		16 12				16 41			17 12					17 41	18 12		18 48
Prestatyn	d		15 16			15 38				16 18				16 47			17 18					17 47	18 18		18 54
Flint	d		15 29			15 52				16 31				17 00			17 31					18 00	18 31		19 07
Shotton	d		15 35							16 37							17 37						18 37		
Chester	a		15 46			16 05		16 18		16 49				17 15			17 49					18 15	18 49		19 24
	d	15 35	15 48	15 55	16 07	16 19		16 24		16 50		16 55	17 07	17 28		17 35	17 50			17 55	18 07	18 20	18 50		
Liverpool Lime Street 10 106	a																								
Helsby	d		15 57							17 00							18 00						19 00		
Frodsham	d		16 02							17 04							18 04						19 04		
Runcorn East	d		16 07							17 09							18 09						19 09		
Warrington Bank Quay 90	a		16 16							17 18							18 18						19 18		
Earlestown 8 90	a		16 26							17 26							18 26						19 26		
Newton-le-Willows 90	a		16 29							17 29							18 29						19 29		
Manchester Oxford Road 90	a		16 48							17 48							18 48						19 48		
Manchester Pic'dilly 10 90 ⛴	a		16 57		17 36					17 57			18 36				18 57				19 35		19 52		
Crewe 10	a	15 54		16 18				16 47				17 18				17 54				18 18					
Cardiff Central 7 131	a					19 16																21 21			
Manchester Airport 84,85 ✈	a																						20 13		
Birmingham New Street 12 65	a													19 26											
London Euston 15 ⊖65	a	17 38						18 38																	

A To Birmingham International
B To Maesteg
C To Blaenau Ffestiniog
D To Shrewsbury

Saturdays

North Wales and Chester - Manchester and Crewe

Network Diagram - see first Page of Table 81

		AW	NT	AW ◇	AW ◇ A	AW	AW	NT	AW	VT ◇	AW ◇	AW	AW	AW ◇	AW	NT	AW	AW ◇	NT	AW	AW
Holyhead	d								18 23					19 21				20 37			
Valley	d								18x29					19x27							
Rhosneigr	d								18x34					19x32							
Ty Croes	d								18x38					19x36							
Bodorgan	d								18x42					19x40							
Llanfairpwll	d								18x52					19x50							
Bangor (Gwynedd)	a								19 00					19 58				21 05			
	d								19 02					20 00				21 06			
Llanfairfechan	d								19x09					20x07				21x13			
Penmaenmawr	d								19x13					20x11				21x17			
Conwy	d								19x19					20x17				21x23			
Llandudno	d			18 44	19 03	19 08					19 42	20 08			20 43					21 45	
Deganwy	d			18x48	19x07	19x12					19x46	20x12			20x47					21x49	
Llandudno Junction	a			18 52	19 11	19 18			19 23		19 50	20 18		20 21	20 51			21 28		21 53	
	d			18 53					19 25		19 51			20 23	20 52			21 29		21 55	
Colwyn Bay	d			18 59					19 31		19 57			20 29	20 58			21 35		22 01	
Abergele & Pensarn	d			19 06							20 04				21 05			21 42		22 09	
Rhyl	d			19 12					19 41		20 10			20 39	21 11			21 48		22 16	
Prestatyn	d			19 18					19 47		20 16			20 45	21 17			21 54		22 22	
Flint	d			19 31					20 00		20 29			20 58	21 30			22 07		22 37	
Shotton	d			19 37							20 35				21 36			22 13		22 44	
Chester	a			19 49					20 15		20 47			21 15	21 47			22 23		22 55	
	d	18 55	19 07	19 50			19 55	20 07	20 17	20 35	20 50		20 55	21 20		21 33	21 52	22 26	22 49	23 01	23 22
Liverpool Lime Street 10 106	a																				
Helsby	d			20 00							20 59						22 01				23 31
Frodsham	d			20 04							21 03						22 05				23 35
Runcorn East	d			20 09							21 09						22 11				23 41
Warrington Bank Quay 90	a			20 18							21 16						22 19				23 50
Earlestown 8 90	a			20 26							21 26						22 26				23 58
Newton-le-Willows 90	a			20 29							21 29						22 30				00 01
Manchester Oxford Road 90	a			20 48							21 48						22 50				
Manchester Pic'dilly 10 90	a		20 35	20 57				21 35			21 57					23 00	22 58		00 15		00 26
Crewe 10	a	19 18					20 18		20 41	20 54			21 18					22 50		23 26	
Cardiff Central 7 131	a																				
Manchester Airport 84,85	a																				
Birmingham New Street 12 65	a													23 28							
London Euston 15 ⊖65	a																				

Sundays

until 12 February

		NT B	AW B	AW	AW	NT C	AW ◇ D	AW	AW ◇	AW	AW ◇	NT C	VT ◇ 1	AW ◇ D	AW	AW ◇ E	AW ◇ F	AW	VT ◇ 1	AW	NT C	AW	VT ◇ 1
Holyhead	d										08 45					10 20	10 20		10 55				11 50
Valley	d															10x26	10x26						
Rhosneigr	d															10x31	10x31						
Ty Croes	d															10x35	10x35						
Bodorgan	d															10x39	10x39						
Llanfairpwll	d															10x49	10x49						
Bangor (Gwynedd)	a										09 12					10 57	10 57		11 21				12 16
	d										09 13					10 59	10 59		11 22				12 17
Llanfairfechan	d															11x06	11x06						
Penmaenmawr	d															11x10	11x10						
Conwy	d															11x16	11x16						
Llandudno	d																						
Deganwy	d																						
Llandudno Junction	a										09 29					11 20	11 20		11 39				12 34
	d										09 35					11 22	11 22		11 40				12 35
Colwyn Bay	d										09 41					11 28	11 28		11 47				12 42
Abergele & Pensarn	d										09 48					11 35	11 35						
Rhyl	d										09 54					11 41	11 41		11 58				12 53
Prestatyn	d										09 59					11 46	11 46		12 03				12 59
Flint	d										10 13					12 00	12 00		12 17				
Shotton	d										10 19					12 06	12 06						
Chester	a										10 30					12 18	12 18		12 30				13 24
	d	22p49	23p22	08 40	08 41	08 58	09 22	09 39	09 42	10 36	10 39	11 07	11 28	11 31	11 36	12 21	12 21	12 24	12 33	12 36	13 07	13 20	13 30
Liverpool Lime Street 10 106	a																						
Helsby	d		23p31		08 50				09 51	10 45					11 45					12 45			
Frodsham	d		23p35		08 54				09 55	10 49					11 49					12 49			
Runcorn East	d		23p41		08 59				10 00	10 54					11 54					12 54			
Warrington Bank Quay 90	a		23p50		09 10				10 09	11 03					12 03					13 03			
Earlestown 8 90	a		23p58		09 16				10 19	11 10					12 10					13 10			
Newton-le-Willows 90	a		00 01		09 19				10 22	11 13					12 13					13 13			
Manchester Oxford Road 90	a				09 39				10 41	11 32					12 32					13 32			
Manchester Pic'dilly 10 90	a	00 15	00 26		09 48	10 22			10 50	11 41		12 31			12 41					13 41	14 33		
Crewe 10	a			09 03				10 02			11 03		11 47					12 47	12 52			13 43	13 50
Cardiff Central 7 131	a															15 31	15 35						
Manchester Airport 84,85	a																						
Birmingham New Street 12 65	a						11 13							13 23									
London Euston 15 ⊖65	a												13 44						14 43				15 45

A To Blaenau Ffestiniog
B not 11 December
C To Southport
D To Birmingham International
E until 1 January
F from 8 January until 12 February

Table 81

Sundays
until 12 February

North Wales and Chester - Manchester and Crewe

Network Diagram - see first Page of Table 81

	AW	AW	AW	VT	AW	NT	AW	VT	AW	AW	AW	NT	AW	AW	VT	AW	AW	VT	AW	AW	NT	AW
																	■					
	◇			◇■1			◇	◇■1			◇		◇	◇	◇■1	◇		◇■1				◇
	A					B	A					B		A							B	
		bike		food	bike		bike	food			bike				food		bike	food				
Holyhead d				12 50				13 55			14 30		15 30				16 25					17 30
Valley d											14x36						16x31					
Rhosneigr d											14x42						16x36					
Ty Croes d											14x45						16x40					
Bodorgan d											14x50						16x44					
Llanfairpwll d											14x59						16x54					
Bangor (Gwynedd) a				13 16				14 21			15 07		15 56				17 02					17 57
d				13 18				14 22			15 08		15 58				17 04					17 59
Llanfairfechan d													16x05									18x06
Penmaenmawr d													16x09									18x10
Conwy d													16x15									18x16
Llandudno d																						
Deganwy d																						
Llandudno Junction a				13 34				14 39			15 25		16 19				17 20					18 20
d				13 36				14 40			15 26		16 25				17 25					18 24
Colwyn Bay d				13 42				14 46			15 32		16 31				17 31					18 30
Abergele & Pensarn d											15 39		16 38				17 38					18 37
Rhyl d				13 53				14 57			15 45		16 44				17 44					18 43
Prestatyn d				13 59				15 03			15 51		16 49				17 49					18 48
Flint d				14 13							16 04		17 03				18 03					19 02
Shotton d											16 10		17 09				18 11					19 10
Chester a				14 26				15 31			16 21		17 20				18 21					19 21
d	13 31	13 36	14 23	14 33	14 36	15 07	15 31	15 33	15 36	16 27	16 36	17 03	17 22	17 31	17 35	17 36	18 24	18 35	18 36	18 57	19 07	19 22
Liverpool Lime Street 10 106 a																						
Helsby d		13 45			14 45				15 45		16 45					17 45			18 45			
Frodsham d		13 49			14 49				15 49		16 49					17 49			18 49			
Runcorn East d		13 54			14 54				15 54		16 54					17 54			18 54			
Warrington Bank Quay 90 a		14 03			15 03				16 03		17 03					18 03			19 03			
Earlestown 8 90 a		14 10			15 10				16 10		17 10					18 10			19 10			
Newton-le-Willows 90 a		14 13			15 13				16 13		17 13					18 13			19 13			
Manchester Oxford Road 90 a		14 32			15 32				16 32		17 32					18 32			19 32			
Manchester Pic'dilly 10 90 ⇌ a		14 41			15 41	16 33			16 41		17 41	18 33				18 41			19 41		20 33	
Crewe 10 a			14 46	14 52				15 52		16 51			17 44		17 53			18 53		19 20		19 47
Cardiff Central 7 131 a																	21 36					
Manchester Airport 84,85 ✈ a																						
Birmingham New Street 12 65 a	15 24						17 35							19 26								
London Euston 15 ⊖65 a				16 44				17 44							19 43			20 44				

	AW	VT	AW	AW	AW	AW	VT	AW	NT	AW	AW	AW	AW	AW	AW	AW
		◇			◇		◇			◇				◇	◇	
	A				A				C							D
		food			bike		food									
Holyhead d					18 25					19 40				20 35	21 40	
Valley d					18x31									20x41		
Rhosneigr d					18x36									20x46		
Ty Croes d					18x40									20x50		
Bodorgan d					18x44									20x54		
Llanfairpwll d					18x54									21x04		
Bangor (Gwynedd) a					19 02					20 07				21 12	22 07	
d					19 04					20 09				21 14	22 09	
Llanfairfechan d										20x16				21x21		
Penmaenmawr d										20x20				21x25		
Conwy d										20x26				21x31		
Llandudno d																
Deganwy d																
Llandudno Junction a					19 20					20 30				21 35	22 25	
d					19 24					20 37				21 37	22 27	
Colwyn Bay d					19 30					20 43				21 43	22 33	
Abergele & Pensarn d					19 37					20 50				21 50		
Rhyl d					19 43					20 56				21 56	22 43	
Prestatyn d					19 48					21 01				22 01	22 49	
Flint d					20 02					21 15				22 15	23 02	
Shotton d					20 10					21 21				22 21		
Chester a					20 19					21 33				22 32	23 16	
d	19 26	19 35	19 36	19 57	20 27	20 36	20 37	20 50	21 07	21 35	21 36	21 50	22 09	22 35		23 00
Liverpool Lime Street 10 106 a																
Helsby d			19 45			20 45										
Frodsham d			19 49			20 49										
Runcorn East d			19 54			20 54										
Warrington Bank Quay 90 a			20 03			21 03										
Earlestown 8 90 a			20 10			21 10										
Newton-le-Willows 90 a			20 13			21 13										
Manchester Oxford Road 90 a			20 32			21 32										
Manchester Pic'dilly 10 90 ⇌ a			20 41			21 41			22 33		22 43		23 18			
Crewe 10 a		19 54		20 20	20 48		20 56	21 13		21 59		22 13		22 59		23 21
Cardiff Central 7 131 a																
Manchester Airport 84,85 ✈ a																
Birmingham New Street 12 65 a	21 29				21 52											
London Euston 15 ⊖65 a																

A To Birmingham International
B To Southport
C To Wigan Wallgate
D To Shrewsbury

Table 81

Sundays

19 February to 25 March

North Wales and Chester - Manchester and Crewe

Network Diagram - see first Page of Table 81

Station		NT	AW	AW	AW	AW (bus)	NT A	AW ◇ B	AW	AW ◇		AW (bus)	AW (trolley)	AW ◇	AW (bus)	NT A	VT ◇1 (buffet)	AW ◇ B (trolley)	AW (trolley)	AW (bus)		AW ◇ (trolley)	AW	VT ◇1 (buffet)	AW (trolley)
Holyhead	d													08 45								10 20		10 55	
Valley	d																					10x26			
Rhosneigr	d																					10x31			
Ty Croes	d																					10x35			
Bodorgan	d																					10x39			
Llanfairpwll	d																					10x49			
Bangor (Gwynedd)	a													09 12								10 57		11 21	
	d													09 13								10 59		11 22	
Llanfairfechan	d																					11x06			
Penmaenmawr	d																					11x10			
Conwy	d																					11x16			
Llandudno	d																								
Deganwy	d																								
Llandudno Junction	a													09 29								11 20		11 39	
	d													09 35								11 22		11 40	
Colwyn Bay	d													09 41								11 28		11 47	
Abergele & Pensarn	d													09 48								11 35			
Rhyl	d													09 54								11 41		11 58	
Prestatyn	d													09 59								11 46		12 03	
Flint	d													10 13								12 00		12 17	
Shotton	d													10 19								12 06			
Chester	a													10 30								12 18		12 30	
	d	22p49	23p22	08 40	08 41	08 41	08 58	09 22	09 39	09 42		09 42	10 36	10 39	10 40	11 07	11 28	11 31	11 36	11 36		12 21	12 24	12 33	12 36
Liverpool Lime Street 10 106	a																								
Helsby	d		23p31			09 01						10 02			11 00					11 56					
Frodsham	d		23p35			09 06						10 07			11 05					12 01					
Runcorn East	d		23p41			09 21						10 22			11 20					12 16					
Warrington Bank Quay 90	a		23p50			09 41						10 42			11 40					12 36					
Earlestown 8 90	a		23p58			10 06						11 07			12 05					13 01					
Newton-le-Willows 90	a		00 01			10 16						11 17			12 15					13 11					
Manchester Oxford Road 90	a					10 46						11 47			12 45					13 41					
Manchester Pic'dilly 10 90 ⛴	a	00 15	00 26		09 50	10 51	10 22			10 49		11 52	11 46		12 50	12 31			12 51	13 46					13 47
Crewe 10	a			09 03					10 02					11 03			11 47						12 47	12 52	
Cardiff Central 7 131	a																					15 31			
Manchester Airport 84,85 ✈	a																								
Birmingham New Street 12 65	a							11 13										13 23							
London Euston 15 ⊖65	a																13 44							14 43	

Station		AW (bus)	NT A	AW	VT ◇1 (buffet)	AW ◇ B		AW (trolley)	AW (bus)	AW	VT ◇1 (buffet)	AW (trolley)	AW (bus)	NT A	AW ◇ B (trolley)	VT ◇1 (buffet)		AW	AW (bus)	AW	AW ◇ (trolley)	AW (bus)	NT A	AW ◇	AW ◇ B
Holyhead	d				11 50						12 50					13 55					14 30			15 30	
Valley	d																				14x36				
Rhosneigr	d																				14x42				
Ty Croes	d																				14x45				
Bodorgan	d																				14x50				
Llanfairpwll	d																				14x59				
Bangor (Gwynedd)	a				12 16						13 16					14 21					15 07			15 56	
	d				12 17						13 18					14 22					15 08			15 58	
Llanfairfechan	d																							16x05	
Penmaenmawr	d																							16x09	
Conwy	d																							16x15	
Llandudno	d																								
Deganwy	d																								
Llandudno Junction	a				12 34						13 34					14 39					15 25			16 19	
	d				12 35						13 36					14 40					15 26			16 25	
Colwyn Bay	d				12 42						13 42					14 46					15 32			16 31	
Abergele & Pensarn	d																				15 39			16 38	
Rhyl	d				12 53						13 53					14 57					15 45			16 44	
Prestatyn	d				12 59						13 59					15 03					15 51			16 49	
Flint	d										14 13										16 04			17 03	
Shotton	d																				16 10			17 09	
Chester	a				13 24						14 26					15 31					16 21			17 20	
	d	12 36	13 07	13 20	13 30	13 31		13 36	13 36	14 23	14 33	14 36	14 36	15 07	15 31	15 33		15 36	15 36	16 27	16 36	16 36	17 03	17 22	17 31
Liverpool Lime Street 10 106	a																								
Helsby	d	12 56							13 56				14 56						15 56			16 56			
Frodsham	d	13 01							14 01				15 01						16 01			17 01			
Runcorn East	d	13 16							14 16				15 16						16 16			17 16			
Warrington Bank Quay 90	a	13 36							14 36				15 36						16 36			17 36			
Earlestown 8 90	a	14 01							15 01				16 01						17 01			18 01			
Newton-le-Willows 90	a	14 11							15 11				16 11						17 11			18 11			
Manchester Oxford Road 90	a	14 41							15 41				16 41						17 41			18 41			
Manchester Pic'dilly 10 90 ⛴	a	14 46	14 33					14 47	15 46			15 47	16 46	16 33				16 46	17 46		17 45	18 46	18 33		
Crewe 10	a			13 43	13 50					14 46	14 52					15 52				16 51				17 44	
Cardiff Central 7 131	a																								
Manchester Airport 84,85 ✈	a																								
Birmingham New Street 12 65	a					15 24									17 35										19 26
London Euston 15 ⊖65	a				15 45						16 44					17 44									

A To Southport

B To Birmingham International

Table 81

Sundays

19 February to 25 March

North Wales and Chester - Manchester and Crewe

Network Diagram - see first Page of Table 81

		VT		AW	AW	AW	VT	AW	AW	AW	NT	AW		AW	VT	AW	AW	AW	AW	AW	VT	AW		NT	AW
		◇ [1] [buffet]		◇	[bus]	[R] [trolley]	◇ [1] [buffet]		[bus]		A	◇		B	◇ [buffet]		[bus]		◇ B [trolley]	[bus]	◇ [buffet]			C	◇
Holyhead	d					16 25						17 30							18 25						19 40
Valley	d					16x31													18x31						
Rhosneigr	d					16x36													18x36						
Ty Croes	d					16x40													18x40						
Bodorgan	d					16x44													18x44						
Llanfairpwll	d					16x54													18x54						
Bangor (Gwynedd)	a					17 02						17 57							19 02						20 07
	d					17 04						17 59							19 04						20 09
Llanfairfechan	d											18x06													20x16
Penmaenmawr	d											18x10													20x20
Conwy	d											18x16													20x26
Llandudno	d																								
Deganwy	d																								
Llandudno Junction	a					17 20						18 20							19 20						20 30
	d					17 25						18 24							19 24						20 37
Colwyn Bay	d					17 31						18 30							19 30						20 43
Abergele & Pensarn	d					17 38						18 37							19 37						20 50
Rhyl	d					17 44						18 43							19 43						20 56
Prestatyn	d					17 49						18 48							19 48						21 01
Flint	d					18 03						19 02							20 02						21 15
Shotton	d					18 11						19 10							20 10						21 21
Chester	a					18 21						19 21							20 19						21 33
	d	17 35		17 36	17 36	18 24	18 35	18 36	18 36	18 57	19 07	19 22		19 26	19 35	19 36	19 36	19 57	20 27	20 36	20 37	20 50		21 07	21 35
Liverpool Lime Street [10] 106	a																								
Helsby	d				17 56				18 56								19 56			20 56					
Frodsham	d				18 01				19 01								20 01			21 01					
Runcorn East	d				18 16				19 16								20 16			21 16					
Warrington Bank Quay 90	a				18 36				19 36								20 36			21 36					
Earlestown [8] 90	a				19 01				20 01								21 01			22 01					
Newton-le-Willows 90	a				19 11				20 11								21 11			22 11					
Manchester Oxford Road 90	a				19 41				20 41								21 41			22 41					
Manchester Pic'dilly [10] 90 ⛴	a			18 47	19 46			19 45	20 46		20 33					20 47	21 46			22 46				22 33	
Crewe [10]	a	17 53					18 53			19 20		19 47			19 54			20 20	20 48		20 56	21 13			21 59
Cardiff Central [7] 131	a					21 45																			
Manchester Airport 84,85 ✈	a																								
Birmingham New Street [12] 65	a													21 29					21 52						
London Euston [15] ⊖65	a	19 43					20 44																		

		AW	AW	AW	AW	AW	AW	AW		AW
			[bus]			[bus]	◇	◇		D
Holyhead	d						20 35	21 40		
Valley	d						20x41			
Rhosneigr	d						20x46			
Ty Croes	d						20x50			
Bodorgan	d						20x54			
Llanfairpwll	d						21x04			
Bangor (Gwynedd)	a						21 12	22 07		
	d						21 14	22 09		
Llanfairfechan	d						21x21			
Penmaenmawr	d						21x25			
Conwy	d						21x31			
Llandudno	d									
Deganwy	d									
Llandudno Junction	a						21 35	22 25		
	d						21 37	22 27		
Colwyn Bay	d						21 43	22 33		
Abergele & Pensarn	d						21 50			
Rhyl	d						21 56	22 43		
Prestatyn	d						22 01	22 49		
Flint	d						22 15	23 02		
Shotton	d						22 21			
Chester	a						22 32	23 16		
	d	21 36	21 36	21 50	22 09	22 09	22 35			23 00
Liverpool Lime Street [10] 106	a									
Helsby	d		21 56			22 29				
Frodsham	d		22 01			22 34				
Runcorn East	d		22 16			22 49				
Warrington Bank Quay 90	a		22 36			23 09				
Earlestown [8] 90	a		23 01			23 34				
Newton-le-Willows 90	a		23 11			23 44				
Manchester Oxford Road 90	a		23 41			00 14				
Manchester Pic'dilly [10] 90 ⛴	a	22 43	23 46		23 18	00 19				
Crewe [10]	a			22 13			22 59			23 21
Cardiff Central [7] 131	a									
Manchester Airport 84,85 ✈	a									
Birmingham New Street [12] 65	a									
London Euston [15] ⊖65	a									

A To Southport
B To Birmingham International
C To Wigan Wallgate
D To Shrewsbury

Table 81

Sundays
from 1 April

North Wales and Chester - Manchester and Crewe

Network Diagram - see first Page of Table 81

		NT	AW	AW	AW	NT	AW	AW	AW	AW	AW	NT	VT	AW	AW	AW	AW	AW	VT	AW	AW	NT	AW
							◇		◇		◇		◇1	◇		◇			◇1				
						A	B					A		B			C			C		A	
										[trolley]			[restaurant]	[trolley]	[trolley]	[trolley]			[restaurant]		[trolley]		
Holyhead	d										08 45					10 20			10 55				
Valley	d															10x26							
Rhosneigr	d															10x31							
Ty Croes	d															10x35							
Bodorgan	d															10x39							
Llanfairpwll	d															10x49							
Bangor (Gwynedd)	a										09 12					10 57			11 21				
	d										09 13					10 59			11 22				
Llanfairfechan	d															11x06							
Penmaenmawr	d															11x10							
Conwy	d															11x16							
Llandudno	d																11ʃ19			12ʃ19			
Deganwy	d																11x23			12x23			
Llandudno Junction	a										09 29					11 20	11ʃ29		11 39	12ʃ29			
	d										09 35					11 22			11 40				
Colwyn Bay	d										09 41					11 28			11 47				
Abergele & Pensarn	d										09 48					11 35							
Rhyl	d										09 54					11 41			11 58				
Prestatyn	d										09 59					11 46			12 03				
Flint	d										10 13					12 00			12 17				
Shotton	d										10 19					12 06							
Chester	a										10 30					12 18			12 30				
	d	22p49	23p22	08 40	08 41	08 58	09 22	09 39	09 42	10 36	10 39	11 07	11 28	11 31	11 36	12 21		12 24	12 33		12 36	13 07	13 20
Liverpool Lime Street 10 106	a																						
Helsby	d		23p31		08 50				09 51	10 45					11 45						12 45		
Frodsham	d		23p35		08 54				09 55	10 49					11 49						12 49		
Runcorn East	d		23p41		08 59				10 00	10 54					11 54						12 54		
Warrington Bank Quay 90	a		23p50		09 10				10 09	11 03					12 03						13 03		
Earlestown 8 90	a		23p58		09 16				10 19	11 10					12 10						13 10		
Newton-le-Willows 90	a		00 01		09 19				10 22	11 13					12 13						13 13		
Manchester Oxford Road 90	a				09 39				10 41	11 32					12 32						13 32		
Manchester Pic'dilly 10 90	a	00 15	00 26		09 48	10 22			10 50	11 41		12 31			12 41						13 41	14 33	
Crewe 10	a			09 03				10 02			11 03		11 47					12 47	12 52				13 43
Cardiff Central 7 131	a															15 31							
Manchester Airport 84,85 ✈	a																						
Birmingham New Street 12 65	a						11 13							13 23									
London Euston 15 ⊖65	a												13 44						14 43				

		VT	AW	AW	AW	AW	VT	AW	AW	NT	AW	VT	AW	AW	AW	AW	NT	AW	AW	AW	AW	VT	AW
																							R
		◇1		◇			◇1				◇	◇1				◇		◇			◇	◇1	
			C	B				C		A	B		C				A		C	C	B		
		[restaurant]			[trolley]		[restaurant]		[trolley]		[trolley]	[restaurant]				[trolley]						[restaurant]	[trolley]
Holyhead	d	11 50					12 50					13 55				14 30		15 30					16 25
Valley	d															14x36							16x31
Rhosneigr	d															14x42							16x36
Ty Croes	d															14x45							16x40
Bodorgan	d															14x50							16x44
Llanfairpwll	d															14x59							16x54
Bangor (Gwynedd)	a	12 16					13 16					14 21				15 07		15 56					17 02
	d	12 17					13 18					14 22				15 08		15 58					17 04
Llanfairfechan	d																	16x05					
Penmaenmawr	d																	16x09					
Conwy	d																	16x15					
Llandudno	d		13ʃ19					14ʃ19					15ʃ10						16ʃ10	17ʃ10			
Deganwy	d		13x23					14x23					15x14						16x14	17x14			
Llandudno Junction	a	12 34	13ʃ29				13 34	14ʃ29				14 39	15ʃ20			15 25		16 19	16ʃ20	17ʃ20			17 20
	d	12 35					13 36					14 40				15 26		16 25					17 25
Colwyn Bay	d	12 42					13 42					14 46				15 32		16 31					17 31
Abergele & Pensarn	d															15 39		16 38					17 38
Rhyl	d	12 53					13 53					14 57				15 45		16 44					17 44
Prestatyn	d	12 59					13 59					15 03				15 51		16 49					17 49
Flint	d						14 13									16 04		17 03					18 03
Shotton	d															16 10		17 09					18 11
Chester	a	13 24					14 26					15 31				16 21		17 20					18 21
	d	13 30		13 31	13 36	14 23	14 33		14 36	15 07	15 31	15 33		15 36	16 27	16 36	17 03	17 22			17 31	17 35	18 24
Liverpool Lime Street 10 106	a																						
Helsby	d				13 45				14 45					15 45		16 45							
Frodsham	d				13 49				14 49					15 49		16 49							
Runcorn East	d				13 54				14 54					15 54		16 54							
Warrington Bank Quay 90	a				14 03				15 03					16 03		17 03							
Earlestown 8 90	a				14 10				15 10					16 10		17 10							
Newton-le-Willows 90	a				14 13				15 13					16 13		17 13							
Manchester Oxford Road 90	a				14 32				15 32					16 32		17 32							
Manchester Pic'dilly 10 90	a				14 41				15 41	16 33				16 41		17 41	18 33						
Crewe 10	a	13 50				14 46	14 52					15 52			16 51			17 44				17 53	
Cardiff Central 7 131	a																						21 36
Manchester Airport 84,85 ✈	a																						
Birmingham New Street 12 65	a			15 24							17 35										19 26		
London Euston 15 ⊖65	a	15 45					16 44					17 44										19 43	

A To Southport **B** To Birmingham International **C** not 1 April

Table 81

Sundays
from 1 April

North Wales and Chester - Manchester and Crewe

Network Diagram - see first Page of Table 81

		VT	AW	AW	NT	AW	AW	VT	AW	AW	AW	AW	VT	AW	NT	AW	AW	AW	AW	AW	AW	AW
		◇■1				◇		◇			◇		◇			◇				◇	◇	
					A		B				B				C							D
		🍴						🍴			🍴		🍴									
Holyhead	d					17 30					18 25					19 40				20 35	21 40	
Valley	d										18x31									20x41		
Rhosneigr	d										18x36									20x46		
Ty Croes	d										18x40									20x50		
Bodorgan	d										18x44									20x54		
Llanfairpwll	d										18x54									21x04		
Bangor (Gwynedd)	a					17 57					19 02					20 07				21 12	22 07	
	d					17 59					19 04					20 09				21 14	22 09	
Llanfairfechan	d					18x06										20x16				21x21		
Penmaenmawr	d					18x10										20x20				21x25		
Conwy	d					18x16										20x26				21x31		
Llandudno	d																					
Deganwy	d																					
Llandudno Junction	a					18 20					19 20					20 30				21 35	22 25	
	d					18 24					19 24					20 37				21 37	22 27	
Colwyn Bay	d					18 30					19 30					20 43				21 43	22 33	
Abergele & Pensarn	d					18 37					19 37					20 50				21 50		
Rhyl	d					18 43					19 43					20 56				21 56	22 43	
Prestatyn	d					18 48					19 48					21 01				22 01	22 49	
Flint	d					19 02					20 02					21 15				22 15	23 02	
Shotton	d					19 10					20 10					21 21				22 21		
Chester	a					19 21					20 19					21 33				22 32	23 16	
	d	18 35	18 36	18 57	19 07	19 22	19 26	19 35	19 36	19 57	20 27	20 36	20 37	20 50	21 07	21 35	21 36	21 50	22 09	22 35		23 00
Liverpool Lime Street 10 106	a																					
Helsby	d		18 45						19 45			20 45										
Frodsham	d		18 49						19 49			20 49										
Runcorn East	d		18 54						19 54			20 54										
Warrington Bank Quay 90	a		19 03						20 03			21 03										
Earlestown 8	a		19 10						20 10			21 10										
Newton-le-Willows 90	a		19 13						20 13			21 13										
Manchester Oxford Road 90	a		19 32						20 32			21 32										
Manchester Pic'dilly 10 90	a		19 41		20 33				20 41			21 41			22 33		22 43		23 18			
Crewe 10	a	18 53		19 20		19 47		19 54		20 20	20 48		20 56	21 13		21 59		22 13		22 59		23 21
Cardiff Central 7 131	a																					
Manchester Airport 84,85 ✈	a																					
Birmingham New Street 12 65	a						21 29				21 52											
London Euston 15 ⊖65	a	20 44																				

A To Southport
B To Birmingham International
C To Wigan Wallgate
D To Shrewsbury

Table 81A

Holyhead - Dublin

		AW	AW	AW	AW	AW
		[R]	[R]	[R]	[R]	[R]
Holyhead	⛴ d	02 40	10 00	12 00	14 10	17 15
Dun Laoghaire	⛴ a	.	11 39	.	.	.
Dublin Ferryport §	⛴ a	05 55		13 49	17 25	19 15

§ Bus connections to/from city centre and railway stations

Table 81A

Dublin - Holyhead

		AW	AW	AW	AW SX	AW SO	AW	AW
		[R] A	[R]	[R]	[R]	[R]	[R]	[R]
Dublin Ferryport §	⛴ d	20p55	08 45	08 05			14 30	20 55
Dun Laoghaire	⛴ d	}	.	.	13 15	13 15	.	.
Holyhead	⛴ a	00 20	10 34	11 30	14 54	15 05	16 30	00 20

§ Bus connections to/from city centre and railway stations

A not 11 December

Network Diagram for Tables 82, 83, 94

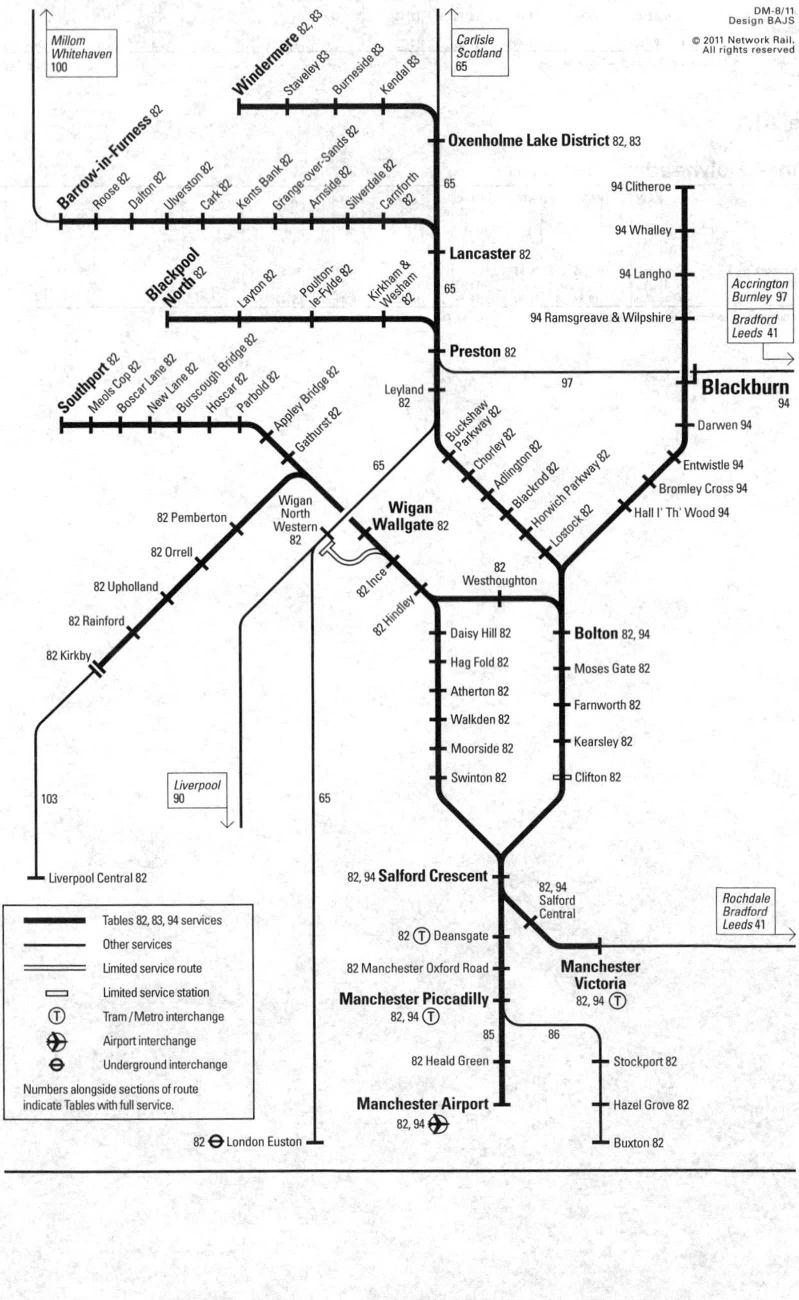

Table 82

Mondays to Fridays

Manchester - Bolton - Wigan, Kirkby, Southport, Preston, Blackpool North and Barrow-in-Furness

Network Diagram - see first Page of Table 82

Miles	Miles	Miles	Miles	Miles			TP	TP	TP	TP	TP	TP	NT	NT	TP		TP	TP	TP	TP	NT	NT	NT	TP	TP
							MX	MX	MO	MO	MX	MX	MX	MX			MX	MO			MX	MO			
							◇1	◇1	◇1	◇1	◇1	◇1			◇1		◇1	◇1	◇1	◇1				1	◇1
							A	B	C	D	A	B					E	E		F	G	G	H		
0	0	0	—	—	**Manchester Airport** 85 ✈	d	22p00	22p00	22p30	22p30	22p29	22p29			00 01		00 38	00 48	04 00	04 12	04 34	04 38			
1½	1½	1½	—	—	Heald Green 85	d					22p33	22p33													
—	—	—	—	—	Buxton 86	d																			
—	—	—	—	—	Hazel Grove 86	d																			
—	—	—	—	—	Stockport 84	d																			
9¾	9¾	9¾	—	—	**Manchester Piccadilly** 10	d	22p16	22p16	22p46	22p46	22p46	22p46			00 16		00 53	01 03	04 15	04 30	04a47	04a51			05 46
10¼	10¼	10¼	—	—	**Manchester Oxford Road**	d	22p19	22p19	22p49	22p49	22p49	22p49													
10½	10½	10½	—	—	Deansgate	d			22p51	22p51	22p51	22p51													
—	—	—	—	—	Rochdale 41	d																			
—	—	—	0	—	**Manchester Victoria**	d							23p20	23p23											
—	—	—	0¾	—	Salford Central	d																			
12	12	12	1¾	—	**Salford Crescent**	a			22p54	22p54	22p56	22p56	23p25	23p31			00 58	01 09		04 36					05 51
—	—	—	—	—		d			22p55	22p55	22p56	22p56	23p26	23p32											05 52
—	—	—	5¾	—	Swinton	d							23p33												
—	—	—	6½	—	Moorside	d							23p35												
—	—	—	8¼	—	Walkden	d							23p39												
—	—	—	11¾	—	Atherton	d							23p44												
—	—	—	13	—	Hag Fold	d							23p47												
—	—	—	13¼	—	Daisy Hill	d							23p50												
18	18	18	—	—	Kearsley	d																			
18¾	18	18¾	—	—	Farnworth	d																			
19¾	19¾	19¾	—	—	Moses Gate	d																			
21	21	21	—	—	**Bolton**	a	22p32	22p32	23p05	23p05	23p06	23p06		23p42	00s31				04s29						
—	—	—	—	—		d	22p33	22p33	23p05	23p05	23p07	23p07		23p42											
—	—	25½	—	—	Westhoughton	d																			
—	—	28	15¾	—	Hindley	d							23p54												
—	—	29½	17¼	0	Ince	d							23p57												
—	—	—	—	0¾	Wigan North Western	a	22p48	22p48											04 44						06 15
—	—	30½	18¼	—	**Wigan Wallgate**	a							00 04												
—	—	—	—	—		d																			
—	—	—	20	—	Pemberton	d																			
—	—	—	22	—	Orrell	d																			
—	—	—	23¼	—	Upholland	d																			
—	—	—	25¼	—	Rainford	d																			
—	—	—	30½	—	**Kirkby**	a																			
—	—	33¼	—	—	Gathurst	d																			
—	—	35	—	—	Appley Bridge	d																			
—	—	37¼	—	—	Parbold	d																			
—	—	38¾	—	—	Hoscar	d																			
—	—	40¼	—	—	Burscough Bridge	d																			
—	—	41½	—	—	New Lane	d																			
—	—	43½	—	—	Bescar Lane	d																			
—	—	46¾	—	—	Meols Cop	d																			
—	—	48	—	—	**Southport**	a																			
24	24	—	—	—	Lostock	d				23p10				23p47											
26	26	—	—	—	Horwich Parkway	d				23p14	23p13	23p13		23p51											
27½	27½	—	—	—	Blackrod	d				23p17				23p54											
29½	29½	—	—	—	Adlington (Lancashire)	d				23p20				23p58											
33½	33½	—	—	—	Chorley	d				23p25	23p21	23p21		00 03											
—	—	—	—	—	Buckshaw Parkway	d				23p28	23p24	23p24		00 07											
37	37	—	—	—	Leyland	d			23p34	23p34				00 14											06 27
41	41	—	—	—	**Preston** 8 65,97	a	23p09	23p12	23p42	23p42	23p33	23p34		00 19	01s05				05s04						06 35
—	—	—	—	—		d	23p13	23p15	23p47	23p47	23p35	23p37		00 21									05 22		06 37
48¾	—	—	—	—	Kirkham & Wesham 97	a			23p56	23p56				00 30											06 46
55¼	—	—	—	—	Poulton-le-Fylde 97	a			00 05	00 05	23p52	23p54		00 38											06 56
57¼	—	—	—	—	Layton 97	a								00 43											06 59
58½	—	—	—	—	**Blackpool North** 97	a			00 14	00 14	00 02	00 04		00 52	01 30				05 33						07 06
—	62	—	—	—	**Lancaster** 6 65	a	23p28	23p31															05 42		
—	—	—	—	—		d	23p29	23p31															05 42	05 46	
—	81	—	—	—	Oxenholme Lake District 65	a																		06 21	
—	91	—	—	—	Windermere 83	a																		06 41	
—	68	—	—	—	Carnforth	d	23p37	23p40															05 52		
—	71¾	—	—	—	Silverdale	d	23p43	23p46															05 58		
—	74	—	—	—	Arnside	d	23p47	23p50															06 03		
—	77¼	—	—	—	Grange-over-Sands	d	23p53	23p55															06 09		
—	79½	—	—	—	Kents Bank	d	23p56	23p59															06 12		
—	81½	—	—	—	Cark	d	00 01	00 03															06 17		
—	87½	—	—	—	Ulverston	d	00 09	00 11															06 25		
—	90¾	—	—	—	Dalton	d	00 17	00 19															06 33		
—	95	—	—	—	Roose	d	00 23	00 25															06 39		
—	96¾	—	—	—	**Barrow-in-Furness**	a	00 31	00 34															06 47		

A until 30 December and then from 27 March
B from 3 January until 23 March
C from 9 January until 13 February
D until 2 January and then from 20 February
E To York
F To Scarborough
G To Liverpool Lime Street
H To Carlisle

The Sunday service between Manchester Victoria and Wigan Wallgate via Atherton is funded by GMITA and will operate whilst funding exists

Manchester - Bolton - Wigan, Kirkby, Southport, Preston, Blackpool North and Barrow-in-Furness

Network Diagram - see first Page of Table 82

	TP ◇1 A	NT	NT B	NT	NT	TP ◇1 C	NT	NT	NT	NT B	TP ◇1 D	NT E	TP ◇1	NT F	NT	NT G	TP ◇1	NT	NT H	NT	NT
Manchester Airport 85 ✈ d	05 45					06 18											07 00				
Heald Green 85 d	05 49																				
Buxton 86 d										05 59											06 23
Hazel Grove 86 d										06 33											07 00
Stockport 84 d										06 41											07 10
Manchester Piccadilly 10 d	06 03					06 33				06 54	07 07						07 15				07 27
Manchester Oxford Road d	06 06					06 36				06 57	07a09						07 18				07 30
Deansgate d										06 59											07 32
Rochdale 41 d																					
Manchester Victoria d		05 51	05 55	06 00	06 17		06 38		06 45					07 01	07 06			07 17	07 23	07 27	
Salford Central d							06 40		06 48					07 04	07 09			07 19	07 26	07 30	
Salford Crescent a			05 59	06 04	06 23		06 44		06 51	07 03				07 07	07 12			07 24	07 29	07 33	07 37
d			06 00	06 05	06 24		06 45		06 52	07 03				07 08	07 13			07 25	07 30	07 33	07 37
Swinton d									06 58					07 14							
Moorside d														07 17							
Walkden d									07 03					07 20						07 42	
Atherton d									07 08					07 26						07 48	
Hag Fold d														07 28							
Daisy Hill d									07 12					07 31						07 51	
Kearsley d							06 52														07 45
Farnworth d							06 54														07 47
Moses Gate d							06 57														07 49
Bolton a	06 19		06 11	06 15	06 34	06 50	07 00			07 16					07 23		07 31	07 35	07 41		07 53
d	06 19			06 15	06 34	06 50	07 01								07 23		07 31	07 35			07 53
Westhoughton d				06 23											07 31	←					08 01
Hindley d				06 27					07 16					07 39	07 35	07 39					
Ince d														→		07 42					
Wigan North Western a							07 19														08 16
Wigan Wallgate a				06 32					07 21						07 40	07 45				08 03	
d				06 34				06 40	07 23						07 41	07 46					
Pemberton d				06 38												07 50					
Orrell d				06 42												07 54					
Upholland d				06 45												07 58					
Rainford d				06 49												08 01					
Kirkby a				06 59												08 11					
Gathurst d								06 44	07 27						07 46						
Appley Bridge d								06 48	07 31						07 49						
Parbold d								06 52	07 35						07 53						
Hoscar d								06 55							07 56						
Burscough Bridge d								06 58	07 39						07 59						
New Lane d								07 00							08 02						
Bescar Lane d								07 04							08 05						
Meols Cop d								07 09	07 47						08 10						
Southport a								07 18	07 56						08 20						
Lostock d					06 39													07 42			
Horwich Parkway d					06 43												07 38	07 46			
Blackrod d					06 46													07 49			
Adlington (Lancashire) d					06 50													07 53			
Chorley d	06 31				06 55												07 46	07 58			
Buckshaw Parkway d					06 59													08 01			
Leyland d					07 06													08 08			
Preston 8 65,97 a	06 42	10 32			07 11	07 11											07 57	08 14			
d	06 44	10 34			07 13	07 14							07 20				07 59	08 15			
Kirkham & Wesham 97 a					07 22												08 08	08 25			
Poulton-le-Fylde 97 a		10 50			07 30												08 18	08 33			
Layton 97 a					07 34												08 22	08 37			
Blackpool North 97 a		11 01			07 43												08 29	08 46			
Lancaster 6 65 a	06 59					07 30							07 36								
d	07 00											07 10	07 36								
Oxenholme Lake District 65 a	07 15																				
Windermere 83 a																					
Carnforth d												07a19	07 45								
Silverdale d													07 51								
Arnside d													07 55								
Grange-over-Sands d													08 00								
Kents Bank d													08 04								
Cark d													08 08								
Ulverston d													08 16								
Dalton d													08 24								
Roose d													08 30								
Barrow-in-Furness a													08 39								

A To Edinburgh
B To Clitheroe
C To Glasgow Central
D To Liverpool Lime Street
E To Leeds
F To Kirkby
G From Manchester Victoria
H To Blackburn

The Sunday service between Manchester Victoria and Wigan Wallgate via Atherton is funded by GMITA and will operate whilst funding exists

Manchester - Bolton - Wigan, Kirkby, Southport, Preston, Blackpool North and Barrow-in-Furness

Network Diagram - see first Page of Table 82

	TP	NT	NT	NT	NT	TP	NT	NT	NT	NT	TP	NT	NT	EM	NT	NT	NT	TP	NT	NT	NT
	◇1					◇1					◇1			◇				◇1			
	A	B	C		D	E		F		G				H	I	J				D	
Manchester Airport 85 ✈ d	07 25										07 56		08 01					08 25			
Heald Green 85 d	07 30												08 05					08 29			
Buxton 86 d				06 45																	
Hazel Grove 86 d				07 25										08 17					08 30		
Stockport 84 d				07 37										08 24					08 41		
Manchester Piccadilly 10 ⇌ d	07 45			07 54		08 07					08 15		08 22	08 37				08 46	08 54		
Manchester Oxford Road d				07 57		08a09					08 19		08 26	08a40				08 49	08 58		
Deansgate ⇌ d				07 59									08 28					08 51	09 00		
Rochdale 41 d																08 00					
Manchester Victoria ⇌ d		07 47			08 00			08 03	08 11			08 22			08 29	08 33	08 46			09 00	09 07
Salford Central d		07 50			08 03			08 08	08 13			08 25			08 32	08 36	08 49			09 03	09 10
Salford Crescent a		07 53		08 04	08 07			08 12	08 17			08 29	08 33		08 37	08 39	08 52	08 56	09 04	09 07	09 13
d		07 53		08 04	08 08			08 13	08 17			08 30	08 34		08 37	08 40	08 53	08 56	09 04	09 08	09 13
Swinton d		08 00						08 19									08 59				
Moorside d		08 02						08 22													
Walkden d		08 06						08 25									09 04				
Atherton d		08 11						08 31									09 09				
Hag Fold d		08 14						08 33													
Daisy Hill d		08 17						08 36									09 13				
Kearsley d																08 47					
Farnworth d																08 49					
Moses Gate d																08 52					
Bolton a	07 59			08 14	08 19				08 27		08 32	08 40	08 44		08 49	08 55		09 06	09 14	09 19	09 23
d	07 59			08 15					08 28		08 32	08 40	08 45			08 56		09 07	09 15		09 24
Westhoughton d									08 35	←			08 53								09 31
Hindley d		08 21						08 43	08 39	08 43							09 17				09 35
Ince d								→	08 42	08 46											
Wigan North Western a																					
Wigan Wallgate a		08 26							08 45	08 49			09 00			09 14	09 22				09 44
d		08 28							08 47	08 51			09 05				09 24				
Pemberton d										08 55											
Orrell d										08 59											
Upholland d										09 02											
Rainford d										09 06											
Kirkby a										09 16											
Gathurst d		08 32							08 51								09 28				
Appley Bridge d		08 36							08 55				09 11				09 32				
Parbold d									08 59				09 15				09 36				
Hoscar d																	09 39				
Burscough Bridge d		08 42							09 03				09 20				09 42				
New Lane d																	09 44				
Bescar Lane d																	09 48				
Meols Cop d									09 11								09 53				
Southport a		08 59							09 20				09 36				10 02				
Lostock d				08 20								08 45							09 20		
Horwich Parkway d				08 24							08 39	08 49						09 13	09 24		
Blackrod d												08 52									
Adlington (Lancashire) d				08 29								08 56									
Chorley d	08 11			08 34							08 47	09 01						09 21	09 32		
Buckshaw Parkway d				08 37								09 05						09 24	09 35		
Leyland d				08 43								09 12							09 42		
Preston 8 65,97 a	08 22			08 50							08 58	09 17						09 33	09 50		
d	08 24		08 38	08 51							08 59	09 19						09 38			
Kirkham & Wesham 97 a												09 28									
Poulton-le-Fylde 97 a											09 16	09 36						09 56			
Layton 97 a												09 43									
Blackpool North 97 a				09 17							09 25	09 52						10 05			
Lancaster 6 65 a	08 39		08 58																		
d	08 40		08 58				09 39														
Oxenholme Lake District 65 a	08 54																				
Windermere 83 a																					
Carnforth d			09 08				09 49														
Silverdale d			09 14				09 56														
Arnside d			09 19				10 00														
Grange-over-Sands d			09 25				10 06														
Kents Bank d			09 28				10 10														
Cark d			09 33				10 14														
Ulverston d			09 42				10 23														
Dalton d			09 50				10 31														
Roose d			09 56				10 37														
Barrow-in-Furness a			10 04				10 47														

A To Edinburgh
B From Huddersfield
C To Carlisle
D To Clitheroe
E From Hull to Liverpool Lime Street
F To Kirkby
G From Manchester Victoria
H From Nottingham to Liverpool Lime Street
I To Blackburn
J From Todmorden

The Sunday service between Manchester Victoria and Wigan Wallgate via Atherton is funded by GMITA and will operate whilst funding exists

Manchester - Bolton - Wigan, Kirkby, Southport, Preston, Blackpool North and Barrow-in-Furness

Network Diagram - see first Page of Table 82

	TP		NT	NT	NT	NT	NT	NT	TP		NT	NT	NT	TP	NT	NT	NT	NT	NT	TP	NT
	◇[1]								◇[1]					◇[1]						◇[1]	
	A							B				C		D							
	🛒								🛒					🛒						🛒	
Manchester Airport 85 ✈ d	09 00				09 03				09 29					10 00			10 03			10 29	
Heald Green 85 d									09 33											10 33	
Buxton 86 d																					
Hazel Grove 86 d											09 30										10 31
Stockport 84 d											09 41										10 41
Manchester Piccadilly [10] 🚊 d	09 16				09 22				09 46		09 54			10 16			10 22			10 46	10 54
Manchester Oxford Road d	09 19				09 26				09 49		09 58			10 19			10 26			10 49	10 58
Deansgate 🚊 d					09 28				09 51		10 00						10 28			10 51	11 00
Rochdale 41 d						09 04												10 05			
Manchester Victoria 🚊 d			09 10	09 22		09 33	09 46					10 00	10 07		10 10	10 22		10 33	10 46		
Salford Central d			09 13	09 25		09 36	09 49					10 03	10 10		10 13	10 25		10 36	10 49		
Salford Crescent a			09 16	09 29	09 33	09 39	09 52		09 56		10 04	10 07	10 13		10 16	10 29	10 33	10 39	10 52	10 56	11 04
d			09 17	09 30	09 34	09 40	09 53		09 56		10 04	10 08	10 13		10 17	10 30	10 34	10 40	10 53	10 56	11 04
Swinton d			09 23				09 59								10 23				10 59		
Moorside d			09 26												10 26						
Walkden d			09 29				10 04								10 29				11 04		
Atherton d			09 35				10 09								10 35				11 09		
Hag Fold d			09 37												10 37						
Daisy Hill d			09 40				10 13								10 40				11 13		
Kearsley d						09 47												10 47			
Farnworth d						09 49												10 49			
Moses Gate d						09 52												10 52			
Bolton a	09 32			09 40	09 45	09 55			10 06		10 14	10 19	10 23	10 32		10 40	10 45	10 55		11 06	11 14
d	09 33			09 40	09 45	09 56			10 07		10 15		10 24	10 33		10 40	10 45	10 56		11 07	11 15
Westhoughton d					09 53								10 31				10 53				
Hindley d			09 45		09 57		10 17						10 35		10 45		10 57		11 17		
Ince d			09 48												10 48						
Wigan North Western a																					
Wigan Wallgate a			09 51		10 02	10 13	10 22						10 44		10 51		11 02	11 11	11 22		
d			09 52		10 03		10 24								10 52		11 03		11 24		
Pemberton d			09 56												10 56						
Orrell d			10 00												11 00						
Upholland d			10 04												11 04						
Rainford d			10 07												11 07						
Kirkby a			10 17												11 17						
Gathurst d							10 28												11 28		
Appley Bridge d					10 10		10 32										11 10		11 32		
Parbold d					10 14		10 36										11 14		11 36		
Hoscar d																			11 39		
Burscough Bridge d					10 18		10 40										11 18		11 42		
New Lane d																			11 44		
Bescar Lane d																			11 48		
Meols Cop d							10 48												11 53		
Southport a					10 35		10 57										11 35		12 02		
Lostock d				09 45							10 20					10 45					11 20
Horwich Parkway d				09 49					10 13		10 24					10 49				11 13	11 24
Blackrod d				09 52												10 52					
Adlington (Lancashire) d				09 56												10 56					
Chorley d	09 44			10 01					10 21		10 32			10 44		11 01				11 21	11 32
Buckshaw Parkway d				10 05					10 24		10 35					11 05				11 24	11 35
Leyland d				10 12							10 42					11 12					11 42
Preston [8] 65,97 a	09 55			10 17					10 33		10 51			10 55		11 17				11 33	11 50
d	09 58	10 07		10 19					10 38	10 45				10 58		11 19				11 38	
Kirkham & Wesham 97 a				10 28												11 28					
Poulton-le-Fylde 97 a				10 36					10 56							11 36				11 56	
Layton 97 a				10 43												11 43					
Blackpool North 97 a				10 53					11 05							11 52				12 05	
Lancaster [6] 65 a	10 13	10 22								11 00				11 13							
d		10 23						10 49		11 01				11 14							
Oxenholme Lake District 65 a										11 17				11 28							
Windermere 83 a										11 39											
Carnforth d		10 32						10a58													
Silverdale d																					
Arnside d		10 41																			
Grange-over-Sands d		10 46																			
Kents Bank d																					
Cark d																					
Ulverston d		10 59																			
Dalton d																					
Roose d																					
Barrow-in-Furness a		11 17																			

A To Glasgow Central
B From Morecambe to Leeds
C To Clitheroe
D To Edinburgh

The Sunday service between Manchester Victoria and Wigan Wallgate via Atherton is funded by GMITA and will operate whilst funding exists

Table 82

Mondays to Fridays

Manchester - Bolton - Wigan, Kirkby, Southport, Preston, Blackpool North and Barrow-in-Furness

Network Diagram - see first Page of Table 82

		NT	NT	NT	NT	TP	NT	NT	NT	NT	TP	NT	NT	NT	TP	NT	TP	NT	NT	NT	NT	TP	NT
						◇1					◇1				◇1		◇1					◇1	
		A				B							A		C								
						🛒					🛒				🛒							🛒	
Manchester Airport	85 ✈ d					11 00		11 03			11 29				12 00				12 03			12 29	
Heald Green	85 d										11 33											12 33	
Buxton	86 d																						
Hazel Grove	86 d											11 31											12 31
Stockport	84 d											11 41											12 41
Manchester Piccadilly 10	🚇 d					11 16		11 22			11 46	11 54			12 16				12 22			12 46	12 54
Manchester Oxford Road	d					11 19		11 26			11 49	11 58			12 19				12 26			12 49	12 58
Deansgate	🚇 d							11 28			11 51	12 00							12 28			12 51	13 00
Rochdale	41 d								11 04											12 04			
Manchester Victoria	🚇 d	11 00	11 07	11 10			11 22		11 33	11 46			12 00	12 07		12 10		12 22		12 33	12 46		
Salford Central	d	11 03	11 10	11 13			11 25		11 36	11 49			12 03	12 10		12 13		12 25		12 36	12 49		
Salford Crescent	a	11 07	11 13	11 16			11 29	11 33	11 39	11 52	11 56	12 04	12 07	12 13		12 16		12 29	12 33	12 39	12 52	12 56	13 04
	d	11 08	11 13	11 17			11 30	11 34	11 40	11 53	11 56	12 04	12 08	12 13		12 17		12 30	12 34	12 40	12 53	12 56	13 04
Swinton	d			11 23						11 59						12 23					12 59		
Moorside	d			11 26												12 26							
Walkden	d			11 29						12 04						12 29					13 04		
Atherton	d			11 35						12 09						12 35					13 09		
Hag Fold	d			11 37												12 37							
Daisy Hill	d			11 40						12 13						12 40					13 13		
Kearsley	d								11 47											12 47			
Farnworth	d								11 49											12 49			
Moses Gate	d								11 52											12 52			
Bolton	a	11 19	11 23			11 32	11 40	11 45	11 55		12 06	12 14	12 19	12 23	12 32			12 40	12 45	12 55		13 06	13 14
	d		11 24			11 33	11 40	11 45	11 56		12 07	12 15		12 24	12 33			12 40	12 45	12 56		13 07	13 15
Westhoughton	d		11 31					11 53						12 31					12 53				
Hindley	d		11 35	11 45				11 57		12 17				12 35		12 45			12 57		13 17		
Ince	d			11 48												12 48							
Wigan North Western	a																						
Wigan Wallgate	a		11 44	11 51				12 02	12 11	12 22				12 44		12 51			13 02	13 11	13 22		
	d			11 52				12 03		12 24						12 52			13 03		13 24		
Pemberton	d			11 56												12 56							
Orrell	d			12 00												13 00							
Upholland	d			12 04												13 04							
Rainford	d			12 07												13 07							
Kirkby	a			12 17												13 17							
Gathurst	d									12 28											13 28		
Appley Bridge	d							12 10		12 32									13 10		13 32		
Parbold	d							12 14		12 36									13 14		13 36		
Hoscar	d																				13 39		
Burscough Bridge	d							12 18		12 41									13 18		13 42		
New Lane	d																				13 44		
Bescar Lane	d																				13 48		
Meols Cop	d									12 49											13 53		
Southport	a							12 35		12 59									13 35		14 02		
Lostock	d						11 45					12 20						12 45					13 20
Horwich Parkway	d						11 49				12 13	12 24						12 49				13 13	13 24
Blackrod	d						11 52											12 52					
Adlington (Lancashire)	d						11 56											12 56					
Chorley	d					11 44	12 01				12 21	12 32			12 44			13 01				13 21	13 32
Buckshaw Parkway	d						12 05				12 24	12 35						13 05				13 24	13 35
Leyland	d						12 12					12 42						13 12					13 42
Preston 8	65,97 a					11 57	12 17				12 33	12 50			12 55			13 17				13 33	13 50
	d					11 58	12 19				12 38				12 58		13 04	13 19				13 38	
Kirkham & Wesham	97 a						12 28											13 28					
Poulton-le-Fylde	97 a						12 36				12 56							13 36				13 56	
Layton	97 a						12 43											13 43					
Blackpool North	97 a						12 52				13 05							13 52				14 05	
Lancaster 6	65 a					12 13									13 13		13 19						
	d				11 32	12 14									13 14		13 20						
Oxenholme Lake District	65 a														13 28		13 36						
Windermere	83 a																13 56						
Carnforth	d				11 42	12 23																	
Silverdale	d				11 48																		
Arnside	d				11 53	12 32																	
Grange-over-Sands	d				11 59	12 38																	
Kents Bank	d				12 02																		
Cark	d				12 07																		
Ulverston	d				12 15	12 50																	
Dalton	d				12 23																		
Roose	d				12 29																		
Barrow-in-Furness	a				12 39	13 11																	

A To Clitheroe
B 🛒 to Preston
C To Edinburgh

The Sunday service between Manchester Victoria and Wigan Wallgate via Atherton is funded by GMITA and will operate whilst funding exists

Manchester - Bolton - Wigan, Kirkby, Southport, Preston, Blackpool North and Barrow-in-Furness

Network Diagram - see first Page of Table 82

	NT A	NT	NT	NT	NT B	TP ◇1 C ⚲		NT	NT	NT	NT	TP ◇1 ⚲	NT	NT A	NT	NT	TP FO ◇1	TP ◇1 D ⚲	NT	NT	NT	NT
Manchester Airport 85 ✈ d						13 00			13 03			13 29						14 00		14 03		
Heald Green 85 d												13 33										
Buxton 86 d																						
Hazel Grove 86 d													13 31									
Stockport 84 d													13 41									
Manchester Piccadilly 10 ⇌ d						13 16			13 22			13 46	13 54					14 16		14 22		
Manchester Oxford Road d						13 19			13 26			13 49	13 58					14 19		14 26		
Deansgate ⇌ d									13 28			13 51	14 00							14 28		
Rochdale 41 d										13 04											14 04	
Manchester Victoria ⇌ d	13 00	13 07	13 10					13 22		13 33	13 46			14 00	14 07	14 10			14 22		14 33	14 46
Salford Central d	13 03	13 10	13 13					13 25		13 36	13 49			14 03	14 10	14 13			14 25		14 36	14 49
Salford Crescent a	13 07	13 13	13 16					13 29	13 33	13 39	13 52	13 56	14 04	14 07	14 13	14 16			14 29	14 33	14 39	14 52
d	13 08	13 13	13 17					13 30	13 34	13 40	13 53	13 56	14 04	14 08	14 13	14 17			14 30	14 34	14 40	14 53
Swinton d			13 23								13 59					14 23						14 59
Moorside d			13 26													14 26						
Walkden d			13 29								14 04					14 29						15 04
Atherton d			13 35								14 09					14 35						15 09
Hag Fold d			13 37													14 37						
Daisy Hill d			13 40								14 13					14 40						15 13
Kearsley d										13 47											14 47	
Farnworth d										13 49											14 49	
Moses Gate d										13 52											14 52	
Bolton a	13 19	13 23				13 32		13 40	13 45	13 55		14 06	14 14	14 19	14 23			14 32	14 40	14 45	14 55	
d		13 24				13 33		13 40	13 45	13 56		14 07	14 15		14 24			14 33	14 40	14 45	14 56	
Westhoughton d		13 31							13 53						14 31					14 53		
Hindley d		13 35	13 45						13 57		14 17				14 35	14 45				14 57		15 17
Ince d			13 48													14 48						
Wigan North Western a																						
Wigan Wallgate a		13 44	13 51						14 02	14 11	14 22				14 44	14 51				15 02	15 11	15 22
d			13 52						14 03		14 24					14 52				15 03		15 24
Pemberton d			13 56													14 56						
Orrell d			14 00													15 00						
Upholland d			14 04													15 04						
Rainford d			14 07													15 07						
Kirkby a			14 17													15 17						
Gathurst d											14 28											15 28
Appley Bridge d									14 10		14 32									15 10		15 32
Parbold d									14 14		14 36									15 14		15 36
Hoscar d																						
Burscough Bridge d									14 18		14 41									15 18		15 40
New Lane d																						
Bescar Lane d																						
Meols Cop d											14 49											15 48
Southport a									14 35		14 59									15 35		15 57
Lostock d								13 45					14 20						14 45			
Horwich Parkway d								13 49				14 13	14 24						14 49			
Blackrod d								13 52											14 52			
Adlington (Lancashire) d								13 56											14 56			
Chorley d						13 44		14 01				14 21	14 32					14 44	15 01			
Buckshaw Parkway d								14 05				14 24	14 35						15 05			
Leyland d								14 12					14 42						15 12			
Preston 8 65,97 a						13 55		14 17				14 33	14 50					14 55	15 17			
d						13 58	14 04	14 19				14 38						14 58	15 19			
Kirkham & Wesham 97 a								14 28											15 28			
Poulton-le-Fylde 97 a								14 36				14 56							15 36			
Layton 97 a								14 43											15 43			
Blackpool North 97 a								14 53				15 05							15 52			
Lancaster 6 65 a						14 13	14 19											15 13				
d				13 32	13 48		14 20										14 20	15 14				
Oxenholme Lake District 65 a																		15 28				
Windermere 83 a																						
Carnforth d				13 42	13a58		14 28										14 28					
Silverdale d				13 48																		
Arnside d				13 52			14 37										14 37					
Grange-over-Sands d				13 58			14 42										14 42					
Kents Bank d				14 02																		
Cark d				14 06																		
Ulverston d				14 15			14 55										14 55					
Dalton d				14 23																		
Roose d				14 29																		
Barrow-in-Furness a				14 39			15 15										15 15					

A To Clitheroe
B From Heysham Port to Leeds
C To Glasgow Central
D To Edinburgh

The Sunday service between Manchester Victoria and Wigan Wallgate via Atherton is funded by GMITA and will operate whilst funding exists

Manchester - Bolton - Wigan, Kirkby, Southport, Preston, Blackpool North and Barrow-in-Furness

Network Diagram - see first Page of Table 82

	TP ◇1 🚲	NT	NT A	NT	NT	NT B	TP ◇1 C 🚲	NT	NT	NT	NT A	NT	TP ◇1 🚲	NT	NT	NT	NT D	NT E	TP ◇1 F 🚲		TP ◇1
Manchester Airport 85 ✈ d	14 29						15 00		15 03				15 29						16 00		
Heald Green 85 d	14 33												15 33								
Buxton 86 d																					
Hazel Grove 86 d		14 31												15 33							
Stockport 84 d		14 41												15 41							
Manchester Piccadilly 10 🚊 d	14 46	14 54					15 16		15 22				15 46	15 54					16 16		
Manchester Oxford Road d	14 49	14 58					15 19		15 26				15 49	15 58					16 19		
Deansgate 🚊 d	14 51	15 00							15 28				15 51	16 00							
Rochdale 41 d										15 04											
Manchester Victoria 🚊 d			15 00	15 07	15 10			15 22		15 33	15 40	15 46			16 07	16 10					
Salford Central d			15 03	15 10	15 13			15 25		15 36	15 43	15 49			16 10	16 13					
Salford Crescent a	14 56	15 04	15 07	15 13	15 16			15 29	15 33	15 39	15 46	15 52	15 56	16 04	16 13	16 16					
d	14 56	15 04	15 08	15 13	15 17			15 30	15 34	15 40	15 47	15 53	15 56	16 04	16 13	16 17					
Swinton d					15 23							15 59				16 23					
Moorside d					15 26											16 26					
Walkden d					15 29							16 04				16 29					
Atherton d					15 35							16 09				16 35					
Hag Fold d					15 37											16 37					
Daisy Hill d					15 40							16 13				16 40					
Kearsley d										15 47											
Farnworth d										15 49											
Moses Gate d										15 52					16 21						
Bolton a	15 06	15 14	15 19	15 23			15 32	15 40	15 45	15 55	15 59		16 06	16 19	16 25				16 32		
d	15 07	15 15		15 24			15 33	15 40	15 45	15 56			16 07		16 25				16 33		
Westhoughton d				15 31					15 53						16 33						
Hindley d				15 35	15 45				15 57			16 17			16 37	16 45					
Ince d					15 48											16 48					
Wigan North Western a																					
Wigan Wallgate a				15 44	15 51				16 02	16 11		16 22			16 46	16 51					
d					15 58				16 03			16 24				16 52					
Pemberton d					16 02											16 56					
Orrell d					16 06											17 00					
Upholland d					16 09											17 04					
Rainford d					16 13											17 07					
Kirkby a					16 23											17 17					
Gathurst d									16 08			16 28									
Appley Bridge d									16 11			16 32									
Parbold d									16 15			16 36									
Hoscar d									16 18												
Burscough Bridge d									16 21			16 40									
New Lane d									16 24												
Bescar Lane d									16 27												
Meols Cop d									16 32			16 48									
Southport a									16 42			16 57									
Lostock d		15 20						15 45					16 12								
Horwich Parkway d	15 13	15 24						15 49					16 15								
Blackrod d								15 52													
Adlington (Lancashire) d								15 56													
Chorley d	15 21	15 32					15 44	16 01					16 23						16 44		
Buckshaw Parkway d	15 24	15 36						16 05					16 26								
Leyland d		15 42						16 12													
Preston 8 65,97 a	15 33	15 50					15 57	16 19					16 35						16 55		
d	15 38						15 58						16 38						17 00	17 04	17 04
Kirkham & Wesham 97 a													16 47								
Poulton-le-Fylde 97 a	15 56												16 57								
Layton 97 a													17 00								
Blackpool North 97 a	16 05												17 07								
Lancaster 6 65 a							16 14												17 15	17 23	17 23
d						15 34	16 15										16 55	17 19	17 16	17 25	17 25
Oxenholme Lake District 65 a																			17 30	17 43	17 43
Windermere 83 a																				18 08	18 08
Carnforth d						15 44	16 23										17 05	17 28			
Silverdale d						15 51	16 29										17 12	17 35			
Arnside d						15 55	16 33										17 16	17 40			
Grange-over-Sands d						16 01	16 39										17 22	17 46			
Kents Bank d						16 05	16 42										17 26	17 49			
Cark d						16 09	16 47										17 30	17 54			
Ulverston d						16 17	16 55										17 39	18 02			
Dalton d						16 26	17 03										17 48	18 10			
Roose d						16 32	17 09										17 54	18 17			
Barrow-in-Furness a						16 39	17 18										18 02	18 25			

A To Clitheroe
B To Carlisle
C 🚲 to Preston
D To Millom
E From Morecambe
F To Edinburgh

The Sunday service between Manchester Victoria and Wigan Wallgate via Atherton is funded by GMITA and will operate whilst funding exists

Manchester - Bolton - Wigan, Kirkby, Southport, Preston, Blackpool North and Barrow-in-Furness

Network Diagram - see first Page of Table 82

Station		NT	NT	NT	NT	NT	TP	NT	NT	NT	TP		NT	NT	NT	NT	NT	NT	NT	NT	NT	TP	NT
							◇1				◇1											◇1	
			A							A	B		C			D							
							🚲				🚲											🚲	
Manchester Airport 85 ✈	d			16 03			16 29				17 00						17 03					17 29	
Heald Green 85	d						16 33															17 33	
Buxton 86	d				15 22													16 25					16 56
Hazel Grove 86	d				16 02				16 30									17 02					17 33
Stockport 84	d				16 12				16 41									17 12					17 41
Manchester Piccadilly [10] 🚊	d			16 22	16 27		16 46		16 54		17 15						17 22	17 27				17 46	17 54
Manchester Oxford Road	d			16 26	16 30		16 49		16 58		17 18						17 26	17 30				17 49	17 58
Deansgate 🚊	d			16 28	16 33				17 00									17 33				17 51	18 00
Rochdale 41	d					16 04										17 03							
Manchester Victoria 🚊	d	16 20	16 23			16 36		16 46		17 00			17 06	17 10	17 19	17 23			17 36	17 40	17 45		
Salford Central	d	16 23	16 26			16 39		16 49		17 03			17 09	17 12	17 22	17 27			17 39	17 43	17 48		
Salford Crescent	a	16 26	16 30	16 34	16 38	16 42		16 52	17 04	17 07			17 13	17 16	17 25	17 29	17 34	17 38	17 42	17 46	17 51	17 55	18 04
	d	16 27	16 31	16 34	16 38	16 43		16 53	17 04	17 08			17 14	17 17	17 27	17 30	17 34	17 38	17 43	17 47	17 52	17 55	18 04
Swinton	d							16 59						17 23							17 58		
Moorside	d							17 02						17 26							18 01		
Walkden	d							17 05						17 31							18 05		
Atherton	d							17 11					17 27	17 37						18 00	18 11		
Hag Fold	d							17 14						17 39							18 13		
Daisy Hill	d							17 17					17 31	17 43						18 04	18 17		
Kearsley	d					16 50													17 53				
Farnworth	d					16 52													17 55				
Moses Gate	d					16 55													17 57				
Bolton	a	16 37	16 42	16 45	16 48	16 58	17 05		17 14	17 19	17 31				17 37	17 42	17 45	17 48	18 01			18 06	18 14
	d	16 37		16 45	16 49	16 59	17 06		17 15		17 32				17 37		17 45	17 49	18 01			18 07	18 15
Westhoughton	d			16 53		17 06											17 53		18 09				
Hindley	d			16 57		17 10		17 21						17 48					18 13		18 22		
Ince	d							17 24						17 51							18 25		
Wigan North Western	a																						
Wigan Wallgate	a			17 02		17 19		17 31					17 39	17 54			18 01		18 22	18 12	18 28		
	d			17 03									17 40	17 55			18 02			18 15	18 29		
Pemberton	d													17 59							18 33		
Orrell	d													18 03							18 37		
Upholland	d													18 07							18 41		
Rainford	d													18 10							18 44		
Kirkby	a													18 20							18 54		
Gathurst	d			17 08									17 45							18 20			
Appley Bridge	d			17 11									17 48				18 09			18 24			
Parbold	d			17 15									17 53				18 13			18 28			
Hoscar	d																			18 31			
Burscough Bridge	d			17 20									17 58				18 17			18 35			
New Lane	d																			18 37			
Bescar Lane	d																			18 41			
Meols Cop	d			17 27									18 05				18 26			18 46			
Southport	a			17 37									18 15				18 35			18 55			
Lostock	d	16 43			16 54				17 20						17 43			17 54				18 12	18 20
Horwich Parkway	d	16 47			16 58				17 24						17 47			17 58				18 15	18 24
Blackrod	d	16 51			17 01										17 51			18 01				18 19	
Adlington (Lancashire)	d	16 55			17 05										17 55			18 05					
Chorley	d	17 00			17 10		17 19		17 32		17 44				18 00			18 10				18 26	18 32
Buckshaw Parkway	d	17 04			17 13				17 35						18 03			18 13					18 35
Leyland	d	17 11			17 21				17 42						18 11								18 42
Preston [8] 65,97	a	17 19			17 26		17 30		17 51		17 55				18 16			18 25				18 38	18 48
	d	17 21			17 28		17 32				17 58	18 08			18 18			18 26				18 40	18 49
Kirkham & Wesham 97	a	17 30					17 41								18 27							18 49	
Poulton-le-Fylde 97	a	17 38					17 51								18 35			18 43				18 59	
Layton 97	a	17 43					17 54								18 39							19 02	
Blackpool North 97	a	17 52					18 02								18 51			18 55				19 10	19 16
Lancaster [6] 65	a				17 48						18 13	18 23											
	d				17 48						18 14	18 24											
Oxenholme Lake District 65	a										18 28												
Windermere 83	a																						
Carnforth	d				18 00							18 34											
Silverdale	d				18 06							18 40											
Arnside	d				18 11							18 44											
Grange-over-Sands	d				18 19							18 50											
Kents Bank	d				18 23							18 53											
Cark	d				18 27							18 58											
Ulverston	d				18 36							19 06											
Dalton	d				18 44							19 14											
Roose	d				18 50							19 20											
Barrow-in-Furness	a				18 59							19 29											

A To Clitheroe
B To Glasgow Central
C From Stalybridge
D To Blackburn

The Sunday service between Manchester Victoria and Wigan Wallgate via Atherton is funded by GMITA and will operate whilst funding exists

Table 82

Manchester - Bolton - Wigan, Kirkby, Southport, Preston, Blackpool North and Barrow-in-Furness

Network Diagram - see first Page of Table 82

		NT A	NT	TP ◇1 B	TP ◇1 C		NT	NT D	NT	NT	NT	TP ◇1	NT	NT A	NT	NT E	TP ◇1	NT	NT	TP ◇1	NT A	TP ◇1	NT
Manchester Airport 85 ✈	d				18 00				18 03			18 29					19 00	19 03		19 29		20 00	
Heald Green 85	d											18 33								19 33			
Buxton 86	d												17 59										
Hazel Grove 86	d												18 33										
Stockport 84	d												18 41										
Manchester Piccadilly 10	d				18 16				18 22			18 46	18 54				19 16	19 20		19 46		20 16	
Manchester Oxford Road	d				18 19				18 26			18 49	18 58				19 19	19 24		19 49		20 19	
Deansgate	d								18 28			18 51	19 00					19 26		19 51			
Rochdale 41	d							18 02															
Manchester Victoria	d	18 00	18 10				18 20	18 23		18 33	18 45			19 00	19 10				19 28		20 00		20 10
Salford Central	d	18 03	18 13				18 23	18 26		18 36	18 48			19 03	19 13				19 31		20 03		20 13
Salford Crescent	a	18 07	18 16				18 26	18 30	18 34	18 39	18 51	18 56	19 04	19 07	19 16			19 29	19 34	19 56	20 07		20 16
	d	18 08	18 17				18 27	18 31	18 34	18 40	18 52	18 56	19 04	19 08	19 17			19 30	19 35	19 56	20 08		20 17
Swinton	d		18 23								18 58				19 23								20 23
Moorside	d		18 26								19 01				19 26								20 26
Walkden	d		18 29								19 04				19 29								20 29
Atherton	d		18 35								19 10				19 35								20 35
Hag Fold	d		18 37								19 12				19 37								20 37
Daisy Hill	d		18 40								19 15				19 40								20 40
Kearsley	d									18 47													
Farnworth	d									18 49													
Moses Gate	d									18 52													
Bolton	a	18 19			18 32		18 37	18 42	18 45	18 55		19 06	19 19	19 20			19 32	19 40	19 45	20 06	20 19	20 32	
	d				18 33		18 37		18 45	18 56		19 07					19 33	19 40	19 45	20 07		20 33	
Westhoughton	d								18 53	19 03								19 48					
Hindley	d		18 45						18 57	19 09	19 20				19 45			19 52					20 45
Ince	d		18 48								19 23				19 48								20 48
Wigan North Western	a		18 56																				
Wigan Wallgate	a								19 02	19 18	19 30				19 55			19 57					20 55
	d								19 03									19 59					
Pemberton	d																						
Orrell	d																						
Upholland	d																						
Rainford	d																						
Kirkby	a																						
Gathurst	d								19 08									20 03					
Appley Bridge	d								19 11									20 07					
Parbold	d								19 15									20 11					
Hoscar	d																						
Burscough Bridge	d								19 19									20 15					
New Lane	d																						
Bescar Lane	d																						
Meols Cop	d								19 27									20 23					
Southport	a								19 37									20 32					
Lostock	d						18 42					19 12							19 50				
Horwich Parkway	d						18 46					19 15							19 54	20 13		20 39	
Blackrod	d						18 49												19 57				
Adlington (Lancashire)	d						18 53												20 01				
Chorley	d				18 44		18 58					19 23					19 44		20 06	20 21		20 46	
Buckshaw Parkway	d						19 02					19 26							20 10	20 24			
Leyland	d						19 10												20 18				
Preston 8 65,97	a				18 55		19 18					19 33					19 55		20 23	20 33		20 57	
	d				19 00	19 04	19 19					19 38					19 58		20 25	20 38		20 59	
Kirkham & Wesham 97	a						19 28												20 34				
Poulton-le-Fylde 97	a						19 36					19 56							20 42	20 56			
Layton 97	a						19 43												20 46				
Blackpool North 97	a						19 52					20 06							20 56	21 06			
Lancaster 6 65	a				19 15	19 20											20 13					21 14	
	d			18 29	19 16	19 20										19 24	20 14					21 15	
Oxenholme Lake District 65	a			18 45	19 30																		
Windermere 83	a			19 08																			
Carnforth	d					19 29										19a34	20 22					21 23	
Silverdale	d					19 35											20 28					21 29	
Arnside	d					19 39											20 32					21 33	
Grange-over-Sands	d					19 44											20 38					21 39	
Kents Bank	d					19 48											20 41					21 42	
Cark	d					19 52											20 46					21 47	
Ulverston	d					20 00											20 54					21 55	
Dalton	d					20 08											21 02					22 03	
Roose	d					20 14											21 08					22 09	
Barrow-in-Furness	a					20 24											21 17					22 18	

A To Clitheroe
B From Barrow-in-Furness
C To Edinburgh
D To Blackburn
E From Morecambe to Leeds

The Sunday service between Manchester Victoria and Wigan Wallgate via Atherton is funded by GMITA and will operate whilst funding exists

Manchester - Bolton - Wigan, Kirkby, Southport, Preston, Blackpool North and Barrow-in-Furness

Network Diagram - see first Page of Table 82

	NT		NT	NT	TP	NT	NT	NT	NT	NT	NT		NT	NT	TP	NT		TP	TP	NT	NT			NT
													FO	FX										
					◇1										◇1			◇1	◇1					
				A		B					A		C	C		B		D	E	A				
Manchester Airport 85 ✈ d			20 03	20 09	20 29					21 03	21 09				21 29			22 00	22 00	22 08				
Heald Green 85 d				20 12	20 33						21 12				21 33					22 12				
Buxton 86 d																								
Hazel Grove 86 d																								
Stockport 84 d																								
Manchester Piccadilly 10 d			20 20	20 32	20 46					21 20	21 32		21 38	21 40	21 46			22 16	22 16	22 32				
Manchester Oxford Road d			20 24	20a36	20 49					21 24	21a36		21 44	21 44	21 49			22 19	22 19	22a36				
Deansgate d			20 26		20 51					21 26			21a46	21a46	21 51									
Rochdale 41 d																								
Manchester Victoria d	20 22					21 00	21 10		21 22							22 00					22 10			22 22
Salford Central d	20 25					21 03	21 13		21 25							22b04					22b13			22b25
Salford Crescent a	20 29		20 33		20 56	21 07	21 16		21 29	21 33					21 56	22 07					22 17			22 29
d	20 30		20 34		20 56	21 08	21 17		21 30	21 34					21 56	22 08					22 17			22 30
Swinton d							21 23														22 23			
Moorside d							21 26														22 26			
Walkden d							21 29														22 29			
Atherton d							21 35														22 35			
Hag Fold d							21 37														22 37			
Daisy Hill d							21 40														22 40			
Kearsley d																								
Farnworth d																								
Moses Gate d																								
Bolton a	20 40		20 45		21 06	21 19			21 40	21 45					22 06	22 19		22 32	22 32					22 40
d	20 40		20 45		21 07				21 40	21 45					22 07			22 33	22 33					22 40
Westhoughton d			20 53							21 53														
Hindley d			20 57				21 45			21 57											22 45			
Ince d							21 48														22 48			
Wigan North Western a																		22 48	22 48					
Wigan Wallgate a			21 02				21 55			22 02											22 55			
d			21 03							22 03														
Pemberton d																								
Orrell d																								
Upholland d																								
Rainford d																								
Kirkby a																								
Gathurst d			21 08							22 08														
Appley Bridge d			21 11							22 11														
Parbold d			21 15							22 15														
Hoscar d			21 18																					
Burscough Bridge d			21 21							22 20														
New Lane d			21 24																					
Bescar Lane d			21 27																					
Meols Cop d			21 32							22 27														
Southport a			21 42							22 37														
Lostock d	20 45								21 45															22 45
Horwich Parkway d	20 49				21 13				21 49						22 13									22 49
Blackrod d	20 52								21 52															22 52
Adlington (Lancashire) d	20 56								21 56															22 56
Chorley d	21 01				21 21				22 01						22 21									23 01
Buckshaw Parkway d	21 05				21 24				22 05						22 24									23 05
Leyland d	21 12								22 12															23 12
Preston 8 65,97 a	21 17				21 33				22 17						22 36			23 09	23 12					23 17
d	21 19				21 38			21 51	22 19						22 38			23 13	23 15					23 19
Kirkham & Wesham 97 a	21 28								22 28															23 28
Poulton-le-Fylde 97 a	21 36				21 56				22 36						22 55									23 36
Layton 97 a	21 40								22 43															23 40
Blackpool North 97 a	21 50				22 06				22 53						23 04									23 50
Lancaster 6 65 a								22 11										23 28	23 31					
d								22 11										23 29	23 31					
Oxenholme Lake District 65 a																								
Windermere 83 a																								
Carnforth d								22 21										23 37	23 40					
Silverdale d								22 27										23 43	23 46					
Arnside d								22 32										23 47	23 50					
Grange-over-Sands d								22 38										23 53	23 55					
Kents Bank d								22 41										23 56	23 59					
Cark d								22 46										00 01	00 03					
Ulverston d								22 54										00 09	00 11					
Dalton d								23 02										00 17	00 19					
Roose d								23 08										00 23	00 25					
Barrow-in-Furness a								23 16										00 31	00 34					

A From Wilmslow
B To Clitheroe
C To Warrington Central
D until 30 December and then from 26 March
E from 2 January until 23 March
b Fridays only

The Sunday service between Manchester Victoria and Wigan Wallgate via Atherton is funded by GMITA and will operate whilst funding exists

Table 82

Mondays to Fridays

Manchester - Bolton - Wigan, Kirkby, Southport, Preston, Blackpool North and Barrow-in-Furness

Network Diagram - see first Page of Table 82

		NT	TP	TP	NT	NT	NT	NT	TP FX
			◇1	◇1					◇1
			A	B		C			D
Manchester Airport 85 ✈	d	22 19	22 29	22 29					23 18
Heald Green 85	d		22 33	22 33					
Buxton 86	d								
Hazel Grove 86	d								
Stockport 84	d				22 34				
Manchester Piccadilly 10	d	22 36	22 46	22 46	22 50				23 38
Manchester Oxford Road	d	22 39	22 49	22 49	22 53				
Deansgate	d	22 41	22 51	22 51	22 55				
Rochdale 41	d								
Manchester Victoria	d					23 00	23 20	23 23	
Salford Central	d					23b03	23b23	23b26	
Salford Crescent	a	22 46	22 56	22 56	22 59	23 07	23 26	23 29	23 43
	d	22 46	22 56	22 56	22 59	23 08	23 26	23 30	
Swinton	d						23 33		
Moorside	d						23 35		
Walkden	d						23 39		
Atherton	d						23 44		
Hag Fold	d						23 47		
Daisy Hill	d						23 50		
Kearsley	d				23 07				
Farnworth	d				23 09				
Moses Gate	d				23 11				
Bolton	a	22 56	23 06	23 06	23 15	23 19		23 40	
	d	22 57	23 07	23 07	23 15			23 40	
Westhoughton	d	23 04			23 23				
Hindley	d	23 08			23 27		23 54		
Ince	d						23 57		
Wigan North Western	a								
Wigan Wallgate	a	23 13			23 38		00 04		
	d	23 15							
Pemberton	d								
Orrell	d								
Upholland	d								
Rainford	d								
Kirkby	a								
Gathurst	d	23 19							
Appley Bridge	d	23 23							
Parbold	d	23 27							
Hoscar	d								
Burscough Bridge	d	23 31							
New Lane	d								
Bescar Lane	d								
Meols Cop	d	23 39							
Southport	a	23 48							
Lostock	d							23 45	
Horwich Parkway	d		23 13	23 13				23 49	
Blackrod	d							23 52	
Adlington (Lancashire)	d							23 56	
Chorley	d		23 21	23 21				00 01	
Buckshaw Parkway	d		23 24	23 24				00 05	
Leyland	d							00 12	
Preston 8 65,97	a		23 33	23 34				00 17	
	d		23 35	23 37				00 19	
Kirkham & Wesham 97	a							00 28	
Poulton-le-Fylde 97	a		23 52	23 54				00 36	
Layton 97	a							00 43	
Blackpool North 97	a		00 02	00 04				00 52	
Lancaster 6 65	a								
	d								
Oxenholme Lake District 65	a								
Windermere 83	a								
Carnforth	d								
Silverdale	d								
Arnside	d								
Grange-over-Sands	d								
Kents Bank	d								
Cark	d								
Ulverston	d								
Dalton	d								
Roose	d								
Barrow-in-Furness	a								

A until 30 December and then from 26 March
B from 2 January until 23 March
C To Blackburn
D To York
b Fridays only

The Sunday service between Manchester Victoria and Wigan Wallgate via Atherton is funded by GMITA and will operate whilst funding exists

Manchester - Bolton - Wigan, Kirkby, Southport, Preston, Blackpool North and Barrow-in-Furness

Network Diagram - see first Page of Table 82

		TP ◇1 A	TP ◇1 B	TP ◇1 A	TP ◇1 B	NT	NT	TP ◇1	TP ◇1 C	TP ◇1		TP ◇1 C	NT D	TP ◇1	TP 1	NT E	NT	TP ◇1 F 🚲	NT	TP ◇1 G 🚲		NT	NT	NT	NT E
Manchester Airport 85 ✈	d	22p00	22p00	22p29	22p29			00 01	00 38	04 00		04 15	04 34					05 45		06 18					
Heald Green 85	d			22p33	22p33													05 49							
Buxton 86	d																								05 59
Hazel Grove 86	d																								06 33
Stockport 84	d																								06 41
Manchester Piccadilly 10 🚇	d	22p16	22p16	22p46	22p46			00 16	00 53	04 15		04 30	04a47	05 43				06 03		06 33					06 54
Manchester Oxford Road	d	22p19	22p19	22p49	22p49													06 06		06 36					06 57
Deansgate 🚇	d			22p51	22p51																				06 59
Rochdale 41	d																								
Manchester Victoria 🚇	d					23p20	23p23									05 55	06 00		06 17			06 38		06 45	
Salford Central	d					23p23	23p26															06 40		06 48	
Salford Crescent	a			22p56	22p56	23p26	23p29		00 58			04 36		05 48		05 59	06 04		06 23			06 44		06 51	07 03
	d			22p56	22p56	23p26	23p30							05 49		06 00	06 05		06 24			06 45		06 52	07 03
Swinton	d					23p33																		06 58	
Moorside	d					23p35																			
Walkden	d					23p39																		07 03	
Atherton	d					23p44																		07 08	
Hag Fold	d					23p47																			
Daisy Hill	d					23p50																		07 12	
Kearsley	d																					06 52			
Farnworth	d																					06 54			
Moses Gate	d																					06 57			
Bolton	a	22p32	22p32	23p06	23p06		23p40	00s31		04s29				05 59		06 11	06 15	06 19	06 34	06 50		07 00			07 16
	d	22p33	22p33	23p07	23p07		23p40							05 59			06 15	06 19	06 34	06 50		07 01			
Westhoughton	d																06 23								
Hindley	d					23p54											06 27							07 16	
Ince	d					23p57																			
Wigan North Western	a	22p48	22p48																			07 19			
Wigan Wallgate	a					00 04											06 32							07 21	
	d																06 34						06 40	07 23	
Pemberton	d																06 38								
Orrell	d																06 42								
Upholland	d																06 45								
Rainford	d																06 49								
Kirkby	a																06 59								
Gathurst	d																						06 44	07 27	
Appley Bridge	d																						06 48	07 31	
Parbold	d																						06 52	07 35	
Hoscar	d																						06 55		
Burscough Bridge	d																						06 58	07 39	
New Lane	d																						07 00		
Bescar Lane	d																						07 04		
Meols Cop	d																						07 09	07 47	
Southport	a																						07 16	07 54	
Lostock	d						23p45												06 39						
Horwich Parkway	d			23p13	23p13		23p49							06 06					06 43						
Blackrod	d						23p52												06 46						
Adlington (Lancashire)	d						23p56												06 50						
Chorley	d			23p21	23p21		00 01							06 13				06 31	06 55						
Buckshaw Parkway	d			23p24	23p24		00 05												06 59						
Leyland	d						00 12							06 22					07 06						
Preston 8 65,97	a	23p09	23p12	23p33	23p34		00 17	01s05		05s04				06 26				06 42	07 11	07 11					
	d	23p13	23p15	23p35	23p37		00 19							06 37				06 44	07 13	07 14					
Kirkham & Wesham 97	a						00 28							06 46					07 22						
Poulton-le-Fylde 97	a			23p52	23p54		00 36							06 56					07 30						
Layton 97	a						00 43							06 59					07 34						
Blackpool North 97	a			00 02	00 04		00 52	01 30		05 33				07 06					07 39						
Lancaster 6 65	a	23p28	23p31															06 59		07 30					
	d	23p29	23p31												05 46			07 00							
Oxenholme Lake District 65	a														06 21			07 15							
Windermere 83	a														06 41										
Carnforth	d	23p37	23p40																						
Silverdale	d	23p43	23p46																						
Arnside	d	23p47	23p50																						
Grange-over-Sands	d	23p53	23p55																						
Kents Bank	d	23p56	23p59																						
Cark	d	00 01	00 03																						
Ulverston	d	00 09	00 11																						
Dalton	d	00 17	00 19																						
Roose	d	00 23	00 25																						
Barrow-in-Furness	a	00 31	00 34																						

A Until 31 December and then from 31 March
B from 7 January until 24 March
C To York
D until 11 February and then from 31 March. To Liverpool Lime Street
E To Clitheroe
F To Edinburgh
G To Glasgow Central

The Sunday service between Manchester Victoria and Wigan Wallgate via Atherton is funded by GMITA and will operate whilst funding exists

Table 82

Saturdays

Manchester - Bolton - Wigan, Kirkby, Southport, Preston, Blackpool North and Barrow-in-Furness

Network Diagram - see first Page of Table 82

	TP	TP	NT	NT	NT	NT	TP	NT	NT	TP	NT	NT	NT	TP	NT	NT	NT	TP	NT	NT	EM	NT
	◇1	◇1					◇1			◇1				◇1				◇1			◇	
	A		B	C		D			E	F			G	H			I				J	E
							🛒			🛒				🛒				🛒				
Manchester Airport 85 ✈ d							07 00			07 25								07 56		08 01		
Heald Green 85 d										07 30										08 05		
Buxton 86 d																						
Hazel Grove 86 d												07 32									08 17	
Stockport 84 d												07 40									08 24	
Manchester Piccadilly 10 ⇌ d	07 07						07 15			07 45		07 54		08 07				08 15		08 22	08 37	
Manchester Oxford Road d	07a09						07 18					07 58		08a09				08 19		08 26	08a40	
Deansgate ⇌ d												08 00								08 28		
Rochdale 41 d																						
Manchester Victoria ⇌ d				07 06	07 10			07 16	07 23		07 27		08 00		08 07	08 10			08 23			08 29
Salford Central d				07 09	07 13			07 19	07 26		07 30		08 03		08 10	08 13			08 26			08 32
Salford Crescent a				07 12	07 16			07 24	07 29		07 33	08 04	08 07		08 13	08 16			08 29	08 33		08 37
d				07 13	07 16			07 25	07 30		07 33	08 04	08 08		08 13	08 17			08 30	08 34		08 37
Swinton d				07 19												08 23						
Moorside d				07 22												08 26						
Walkden d				07 25							07 43					08 29						
Atherton d				07 31							07 48					08 35						
Hag Fold d				07 33												08 37						
Daisy Hill d				07 36							07 52					08 40						
Kearsley d																						
Farnworth d																						
Moses Gate d																						
Bolton a					07 26		07 31	07 35	07 41	07 59		08 14	08 19		08 23			08 32	08 40	08 44		08 49
d					07 27		07 31	07 35		07 59		08 15			08 24			08 32	08 40	08 45		
Westhoughton d					07 34	←									08 31					08 53		
Hindley d				07 42	07 38	07 42									08 35	08 45						
Ince d				→		07 45										08 48						
Wigan North Western a																						
Wigan Wallgate a					07 43	07 48					08 02				08 42	08 51				09 00		
d					07 45	07 50										08 52				09 05		
Pemberton d						07 54										08 56						
Orrell d						07 58										09 00						
Upholland d						08 01										09 04						
Rainford d						08 05										09 07						
Kirkby a						08 19										09 17						
Gathurst d					07 49																	
Appley Bridge d					07 53															09 11		
Parbold d					07 57															09 15		
Hoscar d					08 00																	
Burscough Bridge d					08 03															09 20		
New Lane d					08 05																	
Bescar Lane d					08 09																	
Meols Cop d					08 14																	
Southport a					08 21															09 34		
Lostock d								07 42				08 20							08 45			
Horwich Parkway d							07 38	07 46				08 24						08 39	08 49			
Blackrod d								07 49											08 52			
Adlington (Lancashire) d								07 53				08 29							08 56			
Chorley d							07 46	07 58		08 11		08 34						08 47	09 01			
Buckshaw Parkway d								08 01				08 37							09 05			
Leyland d								08 08				08 43							09 12			
Preston 8 65,97 a							07 57	08 14		08 22		08 50						08 58	09 17			
d		07 20					07 59	08 15		08 24							08 42	08 59	09 19			
Kirkham & Wesham 97 a							08 08	08 25											09 28			
Poulton-le-Fylde 97 a							08 18	08 33										09 16	09 36			
Layton 97 a							08 22	08 37											09 43			
Blackpool North 97 a							08 29	08 42										09 25	09 48			
Lancaster 6 65 a		07 36								08 39							09 02					
d		07 36	08 24														09 03					
Oxenholme Lake District 65 a																						
Windermere 83 a																						
Carnforth d		07 45	08a33														09 13					
Silverdale d		07 51															09 18					
Arnside d		07 55															09 23					
Grange-over-Sands d		08 00															09 29					
Kents Bank d		08 04															09 32					
Cark d		08 08															09 37					
Ulverston d		08 16															09 45					
Dalton d		08 24															09 53					
Roose d		08 30															09 59					
Barrow-in-Furness a		08 39															10 07					

A To Liverpool Lime Street
B To Leeds
C To Kirkby
D From Manchester Victoria
E To Blackburn
F To Edinburgh
G To Clitheroe
H From Hull to Liverpool Lime Street
I To Carlisle
J From Nottingham to Liverpool Lime Street

The Sunday service between Manchester Victoria and Wigan Wallgate via Atherton is funded by GMITA and will operate whilst funding exists

Table 82

Saturdays

Manchester - Bolton - Wigan, Kirkby, Southport, Preston, Blackpool North and Barrow-in-Furness

Network Diagram - see first Page of Table 82

	NT		NT	TP	NT	NT	NT	NT	TP	TP			NT	NT	NT	NT	NT	TP	NT	NT	NT		NT	NT
				◇1					◇1	◇1								◇1						
	A			B		C			D	E					F					C				G
				🛒						🛒								🛒						
Manchester Airport 85 ✈ d				08 25						09 00				09 03				09 29						
Heald Green 85 d				08 29														09 33						
Buxton 86 d					07 51																			
Hazel Grove 86 d					08 31														09 31					
Stockport 84 d					08 41														09 41					
Manchester Piccadilly 10 d				08 46	08 54					09 16				09 22				09 46	09 54					
Manchester Oxford Road d				08 49	08 58					09 19				09 26				09 49	09 58					
Deansgate d				08 51	09 00									09 28				09 51	10 00					
Rochdale 41 d	08 00															09 04								
Manchester Victoria d	08 34		08 46			09 00	09 07	09 10					09 22		09 29	09 33	09 46			10 00	10 07		10 10	
Salford Central d	08 37		08 49			09 03	09 10	09 13					09 25		09 32	09 37	09 49			10 03	10 10		10 13	
Salford Crescent a	08 40		08 52	08 56	09 04	09 07	09 13	09 16					09 29	09 33	09 37	09 40	09 52	09 56	10 04	10 07	10 13		10 16	
d	08 41		08 53	08 56	09 04	09 08	09 13	09 17					09 30	09 34	09 37	09 41	09 53	09 56	10 04	10 08	10 13		10 17	
Swinton d			08 59					09 23									09 59						10 23	
Moorside d								09 26															10 26	
Walkden d			09 04					09 29									10 04						10 29	
Atherton d			09 09					09 35									10 09						10 35	
Hag Fold d								09 37															10 37	
Daisy Hill d			09 13					09 40									10 13						10 40	
Kearsley d	08 48															09 48								
Farnworth d	08 50															09 50								
Moses Gate d	08 53															09 53								
Bolton a	08 56			09 06	09 14	09 19	09 23			09 32			09 40	09 44	09 49	09 56		10 06	10 14	10 19	10 23			
d	08 57			09 07	09 15		09 24			09 33			09 40	09 45		09 57		10 07	10 15		10 24			
Westhoughton d							09 31							09 53							10 31			
Hindley d			09 17				09 35	09 45						09 57			10 17				10 35		10 45	
Ince d								09 48															10 48	
Wigan North Western a																								
Wigan Wallgate a	09 12		09 22				09 42	09 51						10 02		10 12	10 22				10 42		10 51	
d			09 24					09 52						10 03			10 24						10 52	
Pemberton d								09 56															10 56	
Orrell d								10 00															11 00	
Upholland d								10 04															11 04	
Rainford d								10 07															11 07	
Kirkby a								10 17															11 17	
Gathurst d			09 28														10 28							
Appley Bridge d			09 32											10 10			10 32							
Parbold d			09 36											10 14			10 36							
Hoscar d			09 39																					
Burscough Bridge d			09 42											10 18			10 40							
New Lane d			09 44																					
Bescar Lane d			09 48																					
Meols Cop d			09 53														10 48							
Southport a			10 00											10 33			10 55							
Lostock d					09 20								09 45						10 20					
Horwich Parkway d					09 24								09 49					10 13	10 24					
Blackrod d													09 52											
Adlington (Lancashire) d													09 56											
Chorley d				09 19	09 32					09 44			10 01					10 21	10 32					
Buckshaw Parkway d					09 35								10 05					10 24	10 35					
Leyland d					09 42								10 12						10 42					
Preston 8 65,97 a				09 30	09 50					09 55			10 17					10 33	10 50					
d				09 32					09 45	09 58	10 08		10 19					10 38						
Kirkham & Wesham 97 a													10 28											
Poulton-le-Fylde 97 a											10 26		10 36					10 56						
Layton 97 a													10 43											
Blackpool North 97 a											10 35		10 48					11 05						
Lancaster 6 65 a				09 47					10 00	10 13														
d				09 48					10 01															10 49
Oxenholme Lake District 65 a				10 04																				
Windermere 83 a				10 26																				
Carnforth d									10 09															10a58
Silverdale d									10 15															
Arnside d									10 19															
Grange-over-Sands d									10 25															
Kents Bank d									10 28															
Cark d									10 33															
Ulverston d									10 41															
Dalton d									10 49															
Roose d									10 55															
Barrow-in-Furness a									11 04															

A From Hebden Bridge
B 🛒 to Preston
C To Clitheroe
D From Blackpool North
E To Glasgow Central
F To Blackburn
G From Morecambe to Leeds

The Sunday service between Manchester Victoria and Wigan Wallgate via Atherton is funded by GMITA and will operate whilst funding exists

Table 82

Saturdays

Manchester - Bolton - Wigan, Kirkby, Southport, Preston, Blackpool North and Barrow-in-Furness

Network Diagram - see first Page of Table 82

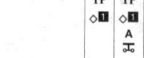

	TP	TP	NT	NT	NT	NT	TP	NT	NT	NT	NT	NT	TP	NT	NT	NT	NT	TP	NT	NT	NT	TP
	◇**1**	◇**1**					◇**1**						◇**1**					◇**1**				◇**1**
		A							B			C	D							B		A
		🛒					🛒						🛒					🛒				🛒
Manchester Airport 85 ✈ d		10 00		10 03			10 29						11 00		11 03			11 29				12 00
Heald Green 85 d							10 33											11 33				
Buxton 86 d																						
Hazel Grove 86 d								10 31											11 31			
Stockport 84 d								10 41											11 41			
Manchester Piccadilly **10** 🚊 d		10 16		10 22			10 46	10 54					11 16		11 22			11 46	11 54			12 16
Manchester Oxford Road d		10 19		10 26			10 49	10 58					11 19		11 26			11 49	11 58			12 19
Deansgate 🚊 d				10 28			10 51	11 00							11 28			11 51	12 00			
Rochdale 41 d					10 05											11 04						
Manchester Victoria 🚊 d			10 22		10 33	10 46			11 00	11 07	11 10			11 22		11 33	11 46			12 00	12 07	
Salford Central d			10 25		10 36	10 49			11 03	11 10	11 13			11 25		11 36	11 49			12 03	12 10	
Salford Crescent a			10 29	10 33	10 39	10 52	10 56	11 04	11 07	11 13	11 16			11 29	11 33	11 39	11 52	11 56	12 04	12 07	12 13	
d			10 30	10 35	10 40	10 53	10 56	11 04	11 08	11 13	11 17			11 30	11 35	11 40	11 53	11 56	12 04	12 08	12 13	
Swinton d						10 59					11 23						11 59					
Moorside d											11 26											
Walkden d						11 04					11 29						12 04					
Atherton d						11 09					11 35						12 09					
Hag Fold d											11 37											
Daisy Hill d						11 13					11 40						12 13					
Kearsley d					10 47											11 47						
Farnworth d					10 49											11 49						
Moses Gate d					10 52											11 52						
Bolton a		10 32	10 40	10 45	10 55		11 06	11 14	11 19	11 23			11 32	11 40	11 45	11 55		12 06	12 14	12 19	12 23	12 32
d		10 33	10 40	10 45	10 56		11 07	11 15		11 24			11 33	11 40	11 45	11 56		12 07	12 15		12 24	12 33
Westhoughton d				10 53						11 31					11 53						12 31	
Hindley d				10 57		11 17				11 35	11 45				11 57		12 17				12 35	
Ince d											11 48											
Wigan North Western a																						
Wigan Wallgate a				11 02	11 11	11 22				11 42	11 51				12 02	12 11	12 22				12 42	
d				11 03		11 24					11 52				12 03		12 24					
Pemberton d											11 56											
Orrell d											12 00											
Upholland d											12 04											
Rainford d											12 07											
Kirkby a											12 17											
Gathurst d						11 28											12 28					
Appley Bridge d				11 10		11 32									12 10		12 32					
Parbold d				11 14		11 36									12 14		12 36					
Hoscar d						11 39																
Burscough Bridge d				11 18		11 42									12 18		12 41					
New Lane d						11 44																
Bescar Lane d						11 48																
Meols Cop d						11 53											12 49					
Southport a				11 33		12 00									12 33		12 57					
Lostock d			10 45					11 20						11 45					12 20			
Horwich Parkway d			10 49				11 13	11 24						11 49				12 13	12 24			
Blackrod d			10 52											11 52								
Adlington (Lancashire) d			10 56											11 56								
Chorley d		10 44	11 01				11 21	11 32					11 44	12 01				12 21	12 32			12 44
Buckshaw Parkway d			11 05				11 24	11 35						12 05				12 24	12 35			
Leyland d			11 12					11 42						12 12					12 42			
Preston **8** 65,97 a		10 55	11 17				11 33	11 50					11 55	12 17				12 33	12 50			12 55
d	10 45	10 58	11 19				11 38						11 58	12 19				12 38				12 58
Kirkham & Wesham 97 a			11 28											12 28								
Poulton-le-Fylde 97 a			11 36				11 56							12 36				12 56				
Layton 97 a			11 44											12 43								
Blackpool North 97 a			11 49				12 05							12 48				13 05				
Lancaster **6** 65 a	11 00	11 13											12 13									13 13
d	11 01	11 14										11 28	12 14									13 14
Oxenholme Lake District 65 a	11 17	11 28																				13 28
Windermere 83 a	11 39																					
Carnforth d												11 37	12 23									
Silverdale d												11 43										
Arnside d												11 48	12 32									
Grange-over-Sands d												11 54	12 38									
Kents Bank d												11 57										
Cark d												12 02										
Ulverston d												12 10	12 50									
Dalton d												12 18										
Roose d												12 24										
Barrow-in-Furness a												12 32	13 11									

A To Edinburgh
B To Clitheroe
C To Carlisle
D 🛒 to Preston

The Sunday service between Manchester Victoria and Wigan Wallgate via Atherton is funded by GMITA and will operate whilst funding exists

Table 82

Saturdays

Manchester - Bolton - Wigan, Kirkby, Southport, Preston, Blackpool North and Barrow-in-Furness

Network Diagram - see first Page of Table 82

Station		NT	TP	NT		NT	NT	NT	TP	NT	NT	NT	NT	NT		NT	TP	NT	NT	NT	NT	TP	NT	NT	
			◇1						◇1								◇1					◇1			
											A			B		C	D							A	
									🛒								🛒					🛒			
Manchester Airport 85 ✈	d					12 03			12 29								13 00		13 03			13 29			
Heald Green 85	d								12 33													13 33			
Buxton 86	d																								
Hazel Grove 86	d									12 31													13 31		
Stockport 84	d									12 41													13 41		
Manchester Piccadilly 10 ⇌	d					12 22			12 46	12 54							13 16		13 22			13 46	13 54		
Manchester Oxford Road	d					12 26			12 49	12 58							13 19		13 26			13 49	13 58		
Deansgate ⇌	d					12 28			12 51	13 00									13 28			13 51	14 00		
Rochdale 41	d						12 04													13 04					
Manchester Victoria ⇌	d	12 10		12 22			12 33	12 46			13 00	13 07	13 10					13 22		13 33	13 46			14 00	
Salford Central	d	12 13		12 25			12 36	12 49			13 03	13 10	13 13					13 25		13 36	13 49			14 03	
Salford Crescent	a	12 16		12 29		12 33	12 39	12 52	12 56	13 04	13 07	13 13	13 16					13 29	13 33	13 39	13 52	13 56	14 04	14 07	
	d	12 17		12 30		12 35	12 40	12 53	12 56	13 04	13 08	13 13	13 17					13 30	13 34	13 40	13 53	13 56	14 04	14 08	
Swinton	d	12 23						12 59					13 23								13 59				
Moorside	d	12 26											13 26												
Walkden	d	12 29						13 04					13 29								14 04				
Atherton	d	12 35						13 09					13 35								14 09				
Hag Fold	d	12 37											13 37												
Daisy Hill	d	12 40						13 13					13 40								14 13				
Kearsley	d						12 47													13 47					
Farnworth	d						12 49													13 49					
Moses Gate	d						12 52													13 52					
Bolton	a			12 40		12 45	12 55		13 06	13 14	13 19	13 23					13 32	13 40	13 45	13 55		14 06	14 14	14 19	
	d			12 40		12 45	12 56		13 07	13 15		13 24					13 33	13 40	13 45	13 56		14 07	14 15		
Westhoughton	d					12 53						13 31							13 53						
Hindley	d	12 45				12 57		13 17				13 35	13 45						13 57		14 17				
Ince	d	12 48											13 48												
Wigan North Western	a																								
Wigan Wallgate	a	12 51				13 02	13 11	13 22				13 42	13 51						14 02	14 11	14 22				
	d	12 52				13 03		13 24					13 52						14 03		14 24				
Pemberton	d	12 56											13 56												
Orrell	d	13 00											14 00												
Upholland	d	13 04											14 04												
Rainford	d	13 07											14 07												
Kirkby	a	13 17											14 17												
Gathurst	d							13 28													14 28				
Appley Bridge	d					13 10		13 32											14 10		14 32				
Parbold	d					13 14		13 36											14 14		14 36				
Hoscar	d							13 39																	
Burscough Bridge	d					13 18		13 42											14 18		14 41				
New Lane	d							13 44																	
Bescar Lane	d							13 48																	
Meols Cop	d							13 53													14 49				
Southport	a					13 33		14 00											14 37		14 57				
Lostock	d			12 45						13 20								13 45					14 20		
Horwich Parkway	d			12 49					13 13	13 24								13 49				14 13	14 24		
Blackrod	d			12 52														13 52							
Adlington (Lancashire)	d			12 56														13 56							
Chorley	d			13 01					13 21	13 32							13 44	14 01				14 21	14 32		
Buckshaw Parkway	d			13 05					13 24	13 35								14 05				14 24	14 35		
Leyland	d			13 12						13 42								14 12					14 42		
Preston 8 65,97	a			13 17					13 33	13 50							13 55	14 17				14 33	14 50		
	d		13 04	13 19					13 38								13 58	14 19				14 38			
Kirkham & Wesham 97	a			13 28														14 28							
Poulton-le-Fylde 97	a			13 36					13 56									14 36				14 56			
Layton 97	a			13 43														14 43							
Blackpool North 97	a			13 51					14 05									14 48				15 05			
Lancaster 6 65	a		13 19														14 13								
	d		13 20											13 32		13 48	14 14								
Oxenholme Lake District 65	a		13 36														14 28								
Windermere 83	a		13 56																						
Carnforth	d													13 41		13a58									
Silverdale	d													13 47											
Arnside	d													13 52											
Grange-over-Sands	d													13 58											
Kents Bank	d													14 01											
Cark	d													14 06											
Ulverston	d													14 14											
Dalton	d													14 22											
Roose	d													14 28											
Barrow-in-Furness	a													14 36											

A To Clitheroe
B To Carlisle
C From Heysham Port to Leeds
D To Glasgow Central

The Sunday service between Manchester Victoria and Wigan Wallgate via Atherton is funded by GMITA and will operate whilst funding exists

Table 82

Saturdays

Manchester - Bolton - Wigan, Kirkby, Southport, Preston, Blackpool North and Barrow-in-Furness

Network Diagram - see first Page of Table 82

	NT	NT	NT	TP		NT	NT	NT	NT	TP	NT	NT	NT	TP	NT	NT	NT	NT	NT	NT	TP	NT
				◇1						◇1				◇1							◇1	
			A	B								C		D					C			
				🛒						🛒				🛒							🛒	
Manchester Airport 85 ✈ d				14 00			14 03			14 29				15 00			15 03				15 29	
Heald Green 85 d										14 33											15 33	
Buxton 86 d																						
Hazel Grove 86 d											14 31											15 33
Stockport 84 d											14 41											15 41
Manchester Piccadilly 10 🚊 d				14 16			14 22			14 46	14 54			15 16			15 22				15 46	15 54
Manchester Oxford Road d				14 19			14 26			14 49	14 58			15 19			15 26				15 49	15 58
Deansgate 🚊 d							14 28			14 51	15 00						15 28				15 51	16 00
Rochdale 41 d								14 04										15 04				
Manchester Victoria 🚊 d	14 07	14 10				14 22		14 33	14 46			15 00	15 07		15 10	15 22		15 33	15 40	15 46		
Salford Central d	14 10	14 13				14 25		14 36	14 49			15 03	15 10		15 13	15 25		15 36	15 43	15 49		
Salford Crescent a	14 13	14 16				14 29	14 33	14 39	14 52	14 56	15 04	15 08	15 13		15 16	15 29	15 33	15 39	15 46	15 52	15 56	16 04
d	14 13	14 17				14 30	14 35	14 40	14 53	14 56	15 04	15 08	15 13		15 17	15 30	15 35	15 40	15 47	15 53	15 56	16 04
Swinton d		14 23							14 59						15 23					15 59		
Moorside d		14 26													15 26							
Walkden d		14 29							15 04						15 29					16 04		
Atherton d		14 35							15 09						15 35					16 09		
Hag Fold d		14 37													15 37							
Daisy Hill d		14 40							15 13						15 40					16 13		
Kearsley d								14 47										15 47				
Farnworth d								14 49										15 49				
Moses Gate d								14 52										15 52				
Bolton a	14 23			14 32		14 40	14 45	14 55		15 06	15 14	15 19	15 23	15 32		15 40	15 45	15 55	15 59		16 06	16 14
d	14 24			14 33		14 40	14 45	14 56		15 07	15 15		15 24	15 33		15 40	15 45	15 56			16 07	16 15
Westhoughton d	14 31						14 53						15 31				15 53					
Hindley d	14 35	14 45					14 57		15 17				15 35		15 45		15 57			16 17		
Ince d		14 48													15 48							
Wigan North Western a																						
Wigan Wallgate a	14 42	14 51					15 02	15 11	15 22				15 42		15 51		16 02	16 11		16 22		
d		14 52					15 03		15 24						15 52		16 03			16 24		
Pemberton d		14 56													15 56							
Orrell d		15 00													16 00							
Upholland d		15 04													16 04							
Rainford d		15 07													16 07							
Kirkby a		15 17													16 17							
Gathurst d									15 28								16 08			16 28		
Appley Bridge d							15 10		15 32								16 11			16 32		
Parbold d							15 14		15 36								16 15			16 36		
Hoscar d																	16 18					
Burscough Bridge d							15 18		15 40								16 21			16 40		
New Lane d																	16 24					
Bescar Lane d																	16 27					
Meols Cop d									15 48								16 32			16 48		
Southport a							15 33		15 55								16 40			16 55		
Lostock d						14 45					15 20					15 45						16 20
Horwich Parkway d						14 49				15 13	15 24					15 49					16 13	16 24
Blackrod d						14 52										15 52						
Adlington (Lancashire) d						14 56										15 56						
Chorley d				14 44		15 01				15 21	15 32			15 44		16 01					16 21	16 32
Buckshaw Parkway d						15 05				15 24	15 36					16 05					16 24	16 35
Leyland d						15 12					15 42					16 12						16 42
Preston 8 65,97 a				14 55		15 17				15 33	15 50			15 57		16 19					16 33	16 50
d				14 58	15 04	15 19				15 38				15 58							16 38	
Kirkham & Wesham 97 a						15 28															16 47	
Poulton-le-Fylde 97 a						15 36				15 56											16 57	
Layton 97 a						15 43															17 00	
Blackpool North 97 a						15 48				16 05											17 07	
Lancaster 6 65 a				15 13	15 20									16 14								
d			14 22	15 14	15 20									16 15								
Oxenholme Lake District 65 a				15 28																		
Windermere 83 a																						
Carnforth d			14 32		15 28									16 23								
Silverdale d			14 38											16 29								
Arnside d			14 42		15 37									16 33								
Grange-over-Sands d			14 48		15 42									16 39								
Kents Bank d			14 52											16 42								
Cark d			14 56											16 47								
Ulverston d			15 05		15 55									16 55								
Dalton d			15 13											17 03								
Roose d			15 19											17 09								
Barrow-in-Furness a			15 26		16 15									17 18								

A To Carlisle
B To Edinburgh
C To Clitheroe
D 🛒 to Preston

The Sunday service between Manchester Victoria and Wigan Wallgate via Atherton is funded by GMITA and will operate whilst funding exists

Manchester - Bolton - Wigan, Kirkby, Southport, Preston, Blackpool North and Barrow-in-Furness

Network Diagram - see first Page of Table 82

		NT	NT	NT	NT	TP	TP	NT	NT	NT	NT	TP	NT	NT	NT	NT	NT	NT	TP	TP	TP	NT	NT
						◇1	◇1					◇1							◇1	◇1	◇1		
				A	B	C	C		D						D				E	F	G		H
Manchester Airport 85 ✈	d					16 00				16 03		16 29							17 00				
Heald Green	85 d											16 33											
Buxton	86 d																						
Hazel Grove	86 d													16 30									
Stockport	84 d													16 41									
Manchester Piccadilly 10	d					16 16				16 22		16 46		16 54					17 15				
Manchester Oxford Road	d					16 19				16 26		16 49		16 58					17 18				
Deansgate	d									16 28				17 00									
Rochdale	41 d										16 04												17 03
Manchester Victoria	d	16 07	16 10					16 20	16 23		16 36		16 46		17 00	17 07	17 10					17 19	17 23
Salford Central	d	16 10	16 13					16 23	16 26		16 39		16 49		17 03	17 10	17 13					17 22	17 26
Salford Crescent	a	16 13	16 16					16 26	16 30	16 34	16 42		16 52	17 04	17 07	17 13	17 17					17 25	17 30
	d	16 13	16 17					16 27	16 31	16 35	16 43		16 53	17 04	17 08	17 13	17 18					17 27	17 31
Swinton	d		16 23										16 59				17 24						
Moorside	d		16 26										17 02				17 27						
Walkden	d		16 29										17 05				17 30						
Atherton	d		16 35										17 11				17 36						
Hag Fold	d		16 37										17 14				17 38						
Daisy Hill	d		16 40										17 17				17 41						
Kearsley	d										16 50												
Farnworth	d										16 52												
Moses Gate	d										16 55												
Bolton	a	16 23				16 32		16 37	16 42	16 45	16 58	17 05		17 14	17 19	17 23			17 31			17 37	17 42
	d	16 24				16 33		16 37		16 46	16 59	17 06		17 15		17 24			17 32			17 37	
Westhoughton	d	16 31								16 53	17 06					17 31							
Hindley	d	16 35	16 45							16 57	17 10		17 21			17 35	17 46						
Ince	d		16 48										17 24				17 49						
Wigan North Western	a																						
Wigan Wallgate	a	16 42	16 51							17 02	17 19		17 27			17 42	17 52						
	d		16 52							17 04			17 29				17 53						
Pemberton	d		16 56														17 57						
Orrell	d		17 00														18 01						
Upholland	d		17 04														18 05						
Rainford	d		17 07														18 08						
Kirkby	a		17 17														18 18						
Gathurst	d									17 08			17 33										
Appley Bridge	d									17 12			17 37										
Parbold	d									17 16			17 41										
Hoscar	d																						
Burscough Bridge	d									17 20			17 45										
New Lane	d																						
Bescar Lane	d																						
Meols Cop	d									17 28			17 53										
Southport	a									17 35			18 00										
Lostock	d							16 43						17 20								17 43	
Horwich Parkway	d							16 47						17 24								17 47	
Blackrod	d							16 51														17 51	
Adlington (Lancashire)	d							16 55														17 55	
Chorley	d					16 44		17 00				17 19		17 32					17 44			18 00	
Buckshaw Parkway	d							17 04						17 35								18 04	
Leyland	d							17 12						17 42								18 11	
Preston 8	65,97 a					16 55		17 20				17 30		17 50					17 55			18 16	
	d					17 00	17 04	17 21				17 32							17 58	18 02	18 02	18 18	
Kirkham & Wesham	97 a							17 31				17 41										18 27	
Poulton-le-Fylde	97 a							17 39				17 51										18 35	
Layton	97 a							17 43				17 54										18 39	
Blackpool North	97 a							17 48				18 02										18 44	
Lancaster 6	65 a					17 16	17 20												18 13	18 18	18 18		
	d			16 40	17 00	17 16	17 21											17 32	18 14	18 18	18 18		
Oxenholme Lake District	65 a					17 30	17 37												18 28				
Windermere	83 a						18 00																
Carnforth	d			16a49	17 10													17 43		18 31	18 31		
Silverdale	d				17 17													17 49		18 37	18 37		
Arnside	d				17 21													17 53		18 41	18 41		
Grange-over-Sands	d				17 27													17 59		18 46	18 46		
Kents Bank	d				17 31													18 03			18 50		
Cark	d				17 35													18 07		18 53	18 54		
Ulverston	d				17 44													18 16		19 01	19 02		
Dalton	d				17 53													18 24		19 09	19 10		
Roose	d				17 59													18 30			19 16		
Barrow-in-Furness	a				18 07													18 38		19 22	19 26		

A From Morecambe to Leeds
B To Millom
C To Edinburgh
D To Clitheroe
E To Glasgow Central
F from 31 March
G until 24 March
H To Blackburn

The Sunday service between Manchester Victoria and Wigan Wallgate via Atherton is funded by GMITA and will operate whilst funding exists

Table 82

Saturdays

Manchester - Bolton - Wigan, Kirkby, Southport, Preston, Blackpool North and Barrow-in-Furness

Network Diagram - see first Page of Table 82

		NT	NT	NT	TP	NT	NT	NT	TP	NT	NT	NT	NT	NT	NT	TP	NT	NT	NT	NT	TP	NT
					◇1				◇1							◇1					◇1	
								A	B			C						A		D		
					🚲				🚲							🚲						
Manchester Airport	85 ✈ d	17 03			17 29				18 00				18 03			18 29					19 00	19 03
Heald Green	85 d				17 33											18 33						
Buxton	86 d																					
Hazel Grove	86 d						17 31										18 31					
Stockport	84 d						17 41										18 41					
Manchester Piccadilly 10	d	17 23			17 46		17 54		18 16				18 22			18 46	18 54				19 16	19 20
Manchester Oxford Road	d	17 26			17 49		17 58		18 19				18 26			18 49	18 58				19 19	19 24
Deansgate	d				17 51		18 00						18 28			18 51	19 00					19 26
Rochdale	41 d											18 02										
Manchester Victoria	d		17 36	17 40		17 50		18 00		18 08	18 20	18 23		18 33	18 45			19 00	19 10			
Salford Central	d		17 39	17 43		17 53		18 03		18 12	18 23	18 26		18 36	18 48			19 03	19 13			
Salford Crescent	a	17 34	17 42	17 46	17 55	17 58	18 04	18 07		18 16	18 26	18 30	18 34	18 39	18 51	18 56	19 04	19 08	19 16			19 29
	d	17 35	17 43	17 47	17 55	17 59	18 04	18 08		18 17	18 27	18 31	18 35	18 40	18 52	18 56	19 04	19 08	19 17			19 30
Swinton	d					18 05				18 23					18 58				19 23			
Moorside	d					18 08				18 26					19 01				19 26			
Walkden	d					18 11				18 29					19 04				19 29			
Atherton	d			18 00		18 17				18 35					19 10				19 35			
Hag Fold	d					18 19				18 37					19 12				19 37			
Daisy Hill	d			18 04		18 22				18 40					19 15				19 40			
Kearsley	d		17 53											18 47								
Farnworth	d		17 55											18 49								
Moses Gate	d		17 57											18 52								
Bolton	a	17 45	18 01		18 06		18 14	18 19	18 32		18 37	18 42	18 45	18 55		19 06	19 19	19 20			19 32	19 40
	d	17 46	18 01		18 07		18 15		18 33		18 37		18 46	18 56		19 07					19 33	19 40
Westhoughton	d	17 53	18 09										18 53	19 03								19 48
Hindley	d		18 13			18 27				18 45			18 57	19 09	19 20				19 45			19 52
Ince	d									18 48					19 23				19 48			
Wigan North Western	a									18 56												
Wigan Wallgate	a	18 01	18 20	18 12		18 32							19 02	19 16	19 28				19 53			19 57
	d	18 02		18 15		18 33							19 04									19 59
Pemberton	d					18 37																
Orrell	d					18 41																
Upholland	d					18 45																
Rainford	d					18 48																
Kirkby	a					18 58																
Gathurst	d			18 20									19 08									20 03
Appley Bridge	d	18 09		18 24									19 12									20 07
Parbold	d	18 13		18 28									19 16									20 11
Hoscar	d			18 31																		
Burscough Bridge	d	18 17		18 35									19 20									20 15
New Lane	d			18 37																		
Bescar Lane	d			18 41																		
Meols Cop	d			18 46									19 28									20 23
Southport	a	18 32		18 54									19 35									20 30
Lostock	d				18 12		18 20				18 42					19 12						
Horwich Parkway	d				18 15		18 24				18 46					19 15						
Blackrod	d				18 19						18 49											
Adlington (Lancashire)	d										18 53											
Chorley	d				18 26		18 32		18 44		18 58					19 23					19 44	
Buckshaw Parkway	d						18 35				19 02					19 26						
Leyland	d						18 42				19 11											
Preston 8	65,97 a				18 38		18 48		18 55		19 18					19 33					19 58	
	d				18 40		18 49		18 58		19 20					19 38					20 01	
Kirkham & Wesham	97 a				18 49						19 29											
Poulton-le-Fylde	97 a				18 59						19 37					19 56						
Layton	97 a				19 02						19 43											
Blackpool North	97 a				19 10		19 16				19 48					20 06						
Lancaster 6	65 a								19 13												20 17	
	d								19 15											19 24	20 17	
Oxenholme Lake District	65 a																					
Windermere	83 a																					
Carnforth	d								19 24											19a33	20 26	
Silverdale	d								19 30												20 32	
Arnside	d								19 34												20 36	
Grange-over-Sands	d								19 40												20 42	
Kents Bank	d								19 43												20 45	
Cark	d								19 48												20 50	
Ulverston	d								19 56												20 58	
Dalton	d								20 04												21 06	
Roose	d								20 10												21 12	
Barrow-in-Furness	a								20 19												21 20	

A To Clitheroe
B 🚲 to Preston
C To Blackburn
D From Morecambe to Leeds

The Sunday service between Manchester Victoria and Wigan Wallgate via Atherton is funded by GMITA and will operate whilst funding exists

Table 82

Saturdays

Manchester - Bolton - Wigan, Kirkby, Southport, Preston, Blackpool North and Barrow-in-Furness

Network Diagram - see first Page of Table 82

Station		NT	TP	NT	TP	TP	NT	TP	NT	NT	NT	NT	TP	NT	NT	NT	NT	NT	NT	NT	TP	NT	TP
			◇1		◇1	◇1		◇1					◇1								◇1		◇1
				A	B	C		B	B 🚌			D		A		C			D	E		A	B
Manchester Airport	85 ✈ d		19 29		20 00	20 00					20 03	20 09	20 29					21 03	21 09		21 29		22 00
Heald Green	85 d		19 33									20 12	20 33						21 12		21 33		
Buxton	86 d																						
Hazel Grove	86 d																						
Stockport	84 d																						
Manchester Piccadilly 10	⇌ d		19 46		20 16	20 16					20 20	20 32	20 46					21 22	21 32	21 38	21 46		22 16
Manchester Oxford Road	d		19 49		20 19	20 19					20 24	20a36	20 49					21 26	21a36	21 44	21 49		22 19
Deansgate	⇌ d		19 51								20 26		20 51					21 28		21a46	21 51		
Rochdale	41 d																						
Manchester Victoria	⇌ d	19 28		20 00			20 10			20 22				21 00	21 10		21 22					22 01	
Salford Central	d	19 31		20 03			20 13			20 25				21 03	21 13		21 25					22 04	
Salford Crescent	a	19 34	19 56	20 07			20 16			20 29	20 33		20 56	21 07	21 16		21 30	21 34			21 56	22 07	
	d	19 35	19 56	20 08			20 17			20 30	20 35		20 56	21 08	21 17		21 31	21 35			21 56	22 08	
Swinton	d						20 23								21 23								
Moorside	d						20 26								21 26								
Walkden	d						20 29								21 29								
Atherton	d						20 35								21 35								
Hag Fold	d						20 37								21 37								
Daisy Hill	d						20 40								21 40								
Kearsley	d																						
Farnworth	d																						
Moses Gate	d																						
Bolton	a	19 45	20 06	20 19	20 32	20 32				20 40	20 45		21 06	21 19			21 41	21 45			22 06	22 19	22 32
	d	19 45	20 07		20 33	20 33				20 40	20 45		21 07				21 41	21 45			22 07		22 33
Westhoughton	d										20 53							21 53					
Hindley	d						20 45				20 57				21 45			21 57					
Ince	d						20 48								21 48								
Wigan North Western	a																						
Wigan Wallgate	a						20 53				21 02				21 53			22 02					
	d										21 03							22 03					
Pemberton	d																						
Orrell	d																						
Upholland	d																						
Rainford	d																						
Kirkby	a																						
Gathurst	d										21 08							22 08					
Appley Bridge	d										21 11							22 11					
Parbold	d										21 15							22 15					
Hoscar	d										21 18												
Burscough Bridge	d										21 21							22 20					
New Lane	d										21 24												
Bescar Lane	d										21 27												
Meols Cop	d										21 32							22 27					
Southport	a										21 40							22 35					
Lostock	d	19 50								20 45							21 46						
Horwich Parkway	d	19 54	20 13		20 39	20 39				20 49			21 13				21 50				22 13		
Blackrod	d	19 57								20 52							21 53						
Adlington (Lancashire)	d	20 01								20 56							21 57						
Chorley	d	20 06	20 21		20 46	20 46				21 01			21 21				22 02				22 21		
Buckshaw Parkway	d	20 10	20 24							21 05			21 24				22 05				22 24		
Leyland	d	20 18								21 12							22 12						
Preston 8	65,97 a	20 24	20 33		20 57	20 57				21 17			21 33				22 18				22 36		22 54
	d	20 25	20 38			21 02			21 15	21 19			21 38			21 59	22 19				22 38		
Kirkham & Wesham	97 a	20 35								21 28							22 29						
Poulton-le-Fylde	97 a	20 43	20 56							21 36			21 56				22 37				22 55		
Layton	97 a	20 47								21 40							22 43						
Blackpool North	97 a	20 52	21 06							21 45			22 06				22 48				23 04		
Lancaster 6	65 a					21 17			22 05							22 19							
	d					21 18			22 05							22 19							
Oxenholme Lake District	65 a																						
Windermere	83 a																						
Carnforth	d					21 26		21 35	22a30							22 29							
Silverdale	d					21 32		21 41								22 35							
Arnside	d					21 36		21 45								22 40							
Grange-over-Sands	d					21 42		21 51								22 46							
Kents Bank	d					21 45		21 54								22 49							
Cark	d					21 50		21 59								22 54							
Ulverston	d					21 58		22 07								23 02							
Dalton	d					22 06		22 15								23 10							
Roose	d					22 12		22 21								23 16							
Barrow-in-Furness	a					22 21		22 30								23 24							

A To Clitheroe
B from 7 January
C until 31 December
D From Wilmslow
E To Warrington Central

The Sunday service between Manchester Victoria and Wigan Wallgate via Atherton is funded by GMITA and will operate whilst funding exists

Table 82

Saturdays

Manchester - Bolton - Wigan, Kirkby, Southport, Preston, Blackpool North and Barrow-in-Furness

Network Diagram - see first Page of Table 82

		NT	TP	NT	NT	NT	NT	TP	NT	NT	NT	NT	TP
			◇1					◇1					◇1
		A	B	C						D			E
Manchester Airport 85 ✈	d		22 00	22 08		22 19		22 29					23 24
Heald Green 85	d			22 12				22 33					
Buxton 86	d												
Hazel Grove 86	d												
Stockport 84	d								22 40				
Manchester Piccadilly 10 🚌	d		22 16	22 32		22 36		22 46	22 54				23 41
Manchester Oxford Road	d		22 19	22a36		22 39		22 49	22 58				
Deansgate 🚌	d					22 41		22 51	23 00				
Rochdale 41	d												
Manchester Victoria 🚌	d				22 22		22 45			23 05	23 16	23 20	
Salford Central	d				22 25		22 48			23 08	23 19	23 23	
Salford Crescent	a				22 29	22 46	22 51	22 56	23 03	23 11	23 22	23 26	23 46
	d				22 30	22 46	22 52	22 56	23 05	23 12	23 22	23 26	
Swinton	d						22 58					23 33	
Moorside	d						23 01					23 35	
Walkden	d						23 04					23 39	
Atherton	d						23 10					23 44	
Hag Fold	d						23 12					23 47	
Daisy Hill	d						23 15					23 50	
Kearsley	d								23 12				
Farnworth	d								23 14				
Moses Gate	d								23 17				
Bolton	a		22 32		22 40	22 56		23 06	23 20	23 23	23 32		
	d		22 33		22 40	22 57		23 07	23 21		23 33		
Westhoughton	d					23 04			23 28				
Hindley	d					23 08	23 20		23 32			23 54	
Ince	d						23 23					23 57	
Wigan North Western	a												
Wigan Wallgate	a					23 13	23 28		23 39			00 02	
	d					23 15							
Pemberton	d												
Orrell	d												
Upholland	d												
Rainford	d												
Kirkby	a												
Gathurst	d					23 19							
Appley Bridge	d					23 23							
Parbold	d					23 27							
Hoscar	d												
Burscough Bridge	d					23 31							
New Lane	d												
Bescar Lane	d												
Meols Cop	d					23 39							
Southport	a					23 46							
Lostock	d				22 45						23 38		
Horwich Parkway	d				22 49			23 13			23 42		
Blackrod	d				22 52						23 45		
Adlington (Lancashire)	d				22 56						23 49		
Chorley	d				23 01			23 21			23 54		
Buckshaw Parkway	d				23 05			23 24			23 57		
Leyland	d				23 12						00 04		
Preston 8 65,97	a		22 54		23 17			23 33			00 10		
	d		22 55		23 19			23 35			00 11		
Kirkham & Wesham 97	a				23 28						00 21		
Poulton-le-Fylde 97	a				23 36			23 52			00 29		
Layton 97	a				23 42						00 34		
Blackpool North 97	a				23 47			00 02			00 38		
Lancaster 6 65	a		23 11										
	d		23 11										
Oxenholme Lake District 65	a												
Windermere 83	a												
Carnforth	d	22 42	23 20										
Silverdale	d	22 48	23 26										
Arnside	d	22 53	23 30										
Grange-over-Sands	d	22 59	23 35										
Kents Bank	d	23 02	23 39										
Cark	d	23 07	23 43										
Ulverston	d	23 15	23 51										
Dalton	d	23 23	23 59										
Roose	d	23 29	00 05										
Barrow-in-Furness	a	23 37	00 15										

A from 7 January
B until 31 December
C From Wilmslow
D To Blackburn
E until 24 March. To York

The Sunday service between Manchester Victoria and Wigan Wallgate via Atherton is funded by GMITA and will operate whilst funding exists

Table 82

Sundays
until 1 January

Manchester - Bolton - Wigan, Kirkby, Southport, Preston, Blackpool North and Barrow-in-Furness

Network Diagram - see first Page of Table 82

			TP	TP	NT	NT	TP	TP	TP	NT	NT	NT	NT	TP	TP	TP	NT	NT	TP	TP		NT	TP	NT
			◇1	◇1					◇1					◇1	◇1	◇1			◇1	◇1			◇1	
			A	A	A	A				B			B		C	D						B	E	
							🚌	🚌								🚲							🚲	
Manchester Airport	85 ✈	d	22p00	22p29			00 05	05 30						08 47		09 00				09 29			10 00	
Heald Green	85	d		22p33																				
Buxton	86	d																						
Hazel Grove	86	d																						
Stockport	84	d																09 22						
Manchester Piccadilly 10	🚊	d	22p16	22p46			00 30	05 55	07 46					09 03	09 07	09 16		09 35		09 46			10 16	
Manchester Oxford Road		d	22p19	22p49					07 49					09 06	09a09	09 19		09 38		09 49			10 19	
Deansgate	🚊	d		22p51					07 51					09 08				09 40		09 51				
Rochdale	41	d																						
Manchester Victoria	🚊	d			23p16	23p20				08 01	08 25	08 39	09 00				09 25					10 00		10 09
Salford Central		d			23p19	23p23																		
Salford Crescent		a		22p56	23p22	23p26			07 54	08 06	08 29	08 44	09 06	09 11			09 29	09 44		09 54		10 06		10 16
		d		22p56	23p22	23p26			07 55	08 07	08 30	08 44	09 08	09 12			09 30	09 44		09 55		10 08		10 17
Swinton		d				23p33																		10 23
Moorside		d				23p35																		10 26
Walkden		d				23p39																		10 29
Atherton		d				23p44																		10 35
Hag Fold		d				23p47																		10 37
Daisy Hill		d				23p50																		10 40
Kearsley		d																						
Farnworth		d																						
Moses Gate		d																						
Bolton		a	22p32	23p06	23p32		00s55	06s20	08 05	08 18	08 40	08 54	09 19	09 22		09 32	09 40	09 54		10 05		10 19	10 32	
		d	22p33	23p07	23p33				08 05		08 40	08 55		09 23		09 33	09 40	09 55		10 05			10 33	
Westhoughton		d										09 02						10 02						
Hindley		d				23p54						09 06						10 06						10 45
Ince		d				23p57																		10 48
Wigan North Western		a																						
Wigan Wallgate		a				00 02						09 11						10 11						10 53
		d										09 13						10 13						
Pemberton		d																						
Orrell		d																						
Upholland		d																						
Rainford		d																						
Kirkby		a																						
Gathurst		d										09 17						10 17						
Appley Bridge		d										09 21						10 21						
Parbold		d										09 25						10 25						
Hoscar		d																						
Burscough Bridge		d										09 29						10 29						
New Lane		d																						
Bescar Lane		d																						
Meols Cop		d										09 37						10 37						
Southport		a										09 44						10 44						
Lostock		d			23p38						08 45						09 45							
Horwich Parkway		d		23p13	23p42				08 12		08 49			09 29			09 49			10 12				
Blackrod		d			23p45						08 52						09 52							
Adlington (Lancashire)		d			23p49						08 56						09 56							
Chorley		d		23p21	23p54				08 19		09 01			09 37		09 44	10 01			10 19			10 44	
Buckshaw Parkway		d		23p24	23p57				08 23		09 05			09 40			10 05			10 23				
Leyland		d			00 04						09 12						10 12							
Preston 8	65,97	a	22p54	23p33	00 10		01s30	06s55	08 32		09 18			09 50		09 57	10 18			10 33			10 57	
		d	22p55	23p35	00 11				08 33		09 20			09 52		10 00	10 20			10 35	10 41		10 58	
Kirkham & Wesham	97	a			00 21						09 29						10 29							
Poulton-le-Fylde	97	a		23p52	00 29				08 50		09 37			10 09			10 37			10 52				
Layton	97	a			00 34						09 42						10 42							
Blackpool North	97	a		00 02	00 38		02 10	07 35	08 57		09 47			10 18			10 47			11 01				
Lancaster 6	65	a	23p11													10 15					10 56		11 13	
		d	23p11													10 16			10 23		10 57		11 14	
Oxenholme Lake District	65	a														10 30			10 39				11 28	
Windermere	83	a																	10 57					
Carnforth		d	23p20																		11 05			
Silverdale		d	23p26																		11 11			
Arnside		d	23p30																		11 15			
Grange-over-Sands		d	23p35																		11 21			
Kents Bank		d	23p39																		11 24			
Cark		d	23p43																		11 29			
Ulverston		d	23p51																		11 37			
Dalton		d	23p59																		11 45			
Roose		d	00 05																		11 51			
Barrow-in-Furness		a	00 15																		12 00			

A not 11 December
B To Clitheroe
C To Liverpool Lime Street
D To Edinburgh
E To Glasgow Central

The Sunday service between Manchester Victoria and Wigan Wallgate via Atherton is funded by GMITA and will operate whilst funding exists

Table 82

Sundays
until 1 January

Manchester - Bolton - Wigan, Kirkby, Southport, Preston, Blackpool North and Barrow-in-Furness

Network Diagram - see first Page of Table 82

	NT	NT	TP	NT	TP	NT	NT	NT	NT	TP	NT	NT	NT	TP	TP	NT	NT	NT	TP	NT	TP	NT
			◇1		◇1					◇1				◇1	◇1				◇1		◇1	
		A		B	C	D					B		E		F			A		B	G	
															🚲						🚲	
Manchester Airport 85 ✈ d			10 30			11 05				11 30					12 00	12 08			12 30		12 59	
Heald Green 85 d						11 08										12 11						
Buxton 86 d																						
Hazel Grove 86 d																						
Stockport 84 d		10 12							11 15									12 21				
Manchester Piccadilly 10 🚇 d		10 24	10 46		11 07	11 27			11 33	11 46					12 16	12 29		12 33	12 46		13 16	
Manchester Oxford Road d		10 38	10 49		11a09	11a31			11 38	11 49					12 19	12a33		12 38	12 49		13 19	
Deansgate 🚇 d		10 40	10 51						11 40	11 51								12 40	12 51			
Rochdale 41 d																						
Manchester Victoria 🚇 d	10 25			11 00			11 12	11 25			12 00	12 09					12 25			13 00		13 12
Salford Central d																						
Salford Crescent a	10 29	10 44	10 54	11 06			11 16	11 29	11 44	11 54	12 06	12 13					12 29	12 44	12 54	13 06		13 16
d	10 30	10 44	10 55	11 08			11 17	11 30	11 44	11 55	12 08	12 17					12 30	12 44	12 55	13 08		13 17
Swinton d							11 23					12 23										13 23
Moorside d							11 26					12 26										13 26
Walkden d							11 29					12 29										13 29
Atherton d							11 35					12 35										13 35
Hag Fold d							11 37					12 37										13 37
Daisy Hill d							11 40					12 40										13 40
Kearsley d																						
Farnworth d																						
Moses Gate d																						
Bolton a	10 40	10 54	11 05	11 19				11 40	11 54	12 05	12 19				12 32		12 40	12 54	13 05	13 19	13 32	
d	10 40	10 55	11 05					11 40	11 55	12 05					12 33		12 40	12 55	13 05		13 33	
Westhoughton d		11 02							12 02									13 02				
Hindley d		11 06					11 45		12 06			12 45						13 06				13 45
Ince d							11 48					12 48										13 48
Wigan North Western a																						
Wigan Wallgate a		11 11					11 53		12 11			12 53						13 11				13 53
d		11 13							12 13									13 13				
Pemberton d																						
Orrell d																						
Upholland d																						
Rainford d																						
Kirkby a																						
Gathurst d		11 17							12 17									13 17				
Appley Bridge d		11 21							12 21									13 21				
Parbold d		11 25							12 25									13 25				
Hoscar d																						
Burscough Bridge d		11 29							12 29									13 29				
New Lane d																						
Bescar Lane d																						
Meols Cop d		11 37							12 37									13 37				
Southport a		11 44							12 44									13 44				
Lostock d	10 45							11 45									12 45					
Horwich Parkway d	10 49		11 12					11 49		12 12							12 49		13 12			
Blackrod d	10 52							11 52									12 52					
Adlington (Lancashire) d	10 56							11 56									12 56					
Chorley d	11 01		11 19					12 01		12 19					12 44		13 01		13 19		13 44	
Buckshaw Parkway d	11 05		11 23					12 05		12 23							13 05		13 23			
Leyland d	11 12							12 12									13 12					
Preston 8 65,97 a	11 20		11 33					12 18		12 33					12 57		13 18		13 33		13 57	
d	11 21		11 35					12 20		12 35				12 48	12 58		13 20		13 35		14 00	
Kirkham & Wesham 97 a	11 31							12 29									13 29					
Poulton-le-Fylde 97 a	11 39		11 52					12 37		12 52							13 37		13 52			
Layton 97 a	11 44							12 42									13 42					
Blackpool North 97 a	11 49		12 01					12 47		13 01							13 47		14 01			
Lancaster 6 65 a														13 03	13 13						14 15	
d													12 48	13 04	13 14						14 16	
Oxenholme Lake District 65 a															13 28						14 30	
Windermere 83 a																						
Carnforth d													12a57	13 12								
Silverdale d														13 18								
Arnside d														13 22								
Grange-over-Sands d														13 28								
Kents Bank d														13 31								
Cark d														13 36								
Ulverston d														13 44								
Dalton d														13 52								
Roose d														13 58								
Barrow-in-Furness a														14 07								

A From Chester
B To Clitheroe
C To Liverpool Lime Street
D From Alderley Edge
E From Morecambe to Leeds
F To Edinburgh
G To Glasgow Central

The Sunday service between Manchester Victoria and Wigan Wallgate via Atherton is funded by GMITA and will operate whilst funding exists

Table 82

Sundays
until 1 January

Manchester - Bolton - Wigan, Kirkby, Southport, Preston, Blackpool North and Barrow-in-Furness

Network Diagram - see first Page of Table 82

		NT	NT		TP	NT	NT	NT	TP	NT	NT	TP	NT		TP	NT	NT	NT	TP	NT	TP	NT	NT		NT
					◇■1				◇■1			◇■1			◇■1				◇■1		◇■1				
						A		B	C		D		A							A	C				D
									🛒												🛒				
Manchester Airport 85 ✈	d				13 30				14 00			14 30			15 00				15 30		16 00				
Heald Green 85	d																								
Buxton 86	d																								
Hazel Grove 86	d																								
Stockport 84	d		13 22								14 21							15 22							16 21
Manchester Piccadilly ■10 ⇌	d		13 35		13 46				14 16		14 35	14 46			15 16			15 35	15 46		16 16				16 35
Manchester Oxford Road	d		13 38		13 49				14 19		14 38	14 49			15 19			15 38	15 49		16 19				16 38
Deansgate ⇌	d		13 40		13 51						14 40	14 51						15 40	15 51						16 40
Rochdale 41	d																								
Manchester Victoria ⇌	d	13 25				14 00	14 12			14 25			15 00			15 12	15 25			16 00		16 12	16 25		
Salford Central	d																								
Salford Crescent	a	13 29	13 44		13 54	14 06	14 16			14 29	14 44	14 54	15 06			15 16	15 29	15 44	15 54	16 06		16 16	16 29		16 44
	d	13 30	13 44		13 55	14 08	14 17			14 30	14 44	14 55	15 08			15 17	15 30	15 44	15 55	16 08		16 17	16 30		16 44
Swinton	d						14 23									15 23						16 23			
Moorside	d						14 26									15 26						16 26			
Walkden	d						14 29									15 29						16 29			
Atherton	d						14 35									15 35						16 35			
Hag Fold	d						14 37									15 37						16 37			
Daisy Hill	d						14 40									15 40						16 40			
Kearsley	d																								
Farnworth	d																								
Moses Gate	d																								
Bolton	a	13 41	13 54		14 05	14 19			14 32	14 40	14 54	15 05	15 19		15 32		15 40	15 54	16 05	16 19	16 32		16 40		16 54
	d	13 41	13 55		14 05				14 33	14 40	14 55	15 05			15 33		15 40	15 55	16 05		16 33		16 40		16 55
Westhoughton	d		14 02								15 02							16 02							17 02
Hindley	d		14 06				14 45				15 06					15 45		16 06				16 45			17 06
Ince	d						14 48									15 48						16 48			
Wigan North Western	a																								
Wigan Wallgate	a		14 11				14 53				15 11					15 53		16 11				16 53			17 11
	d		14 13								15 13							16 13							17 13
Pemberton	d																								
Orrell	d																								
Upholland	d																								
Rainford	d																								
Kirkby	a																								
Gathurst	d		14 17								15 17							16 17							17 17
Appley Bridge	d		14 21								15 21							16 21							17 21
Parbold	d		14 25								15 25							16 25							17 25
Hoscar	d																								
Burscough Bridge	d		14 29								15 29							16 29							17 29
New Lane	d																								
Bescar Lane	d																								
Meols Cop	d		14 37								15 37							16 37							17 37
Southport	a		14 44								15 44							16 44							17 44
Lostock	d	13 46								14 45							15 45						16 45		
Horwich Parkway	d	13 50			14 12					14 49		15 12					15 49		16 12				16 49		
Blackrod	d	13 53								14 52							15 52						16 52		
Adlington (Lancashire)	d	13 57								14 56							15 56						16 56		
Chorley	d	14 02			14 19				14 44	15 01		15 19			15 44		16 01		16 19		16 44		17 01		
Buckshaw Parkway	d	14 06			14 23					15 05		15 23					16 05		16 23				17 05		
Leyland	d	14 13								15 13							16 12						17 12		
Preston ■8 65,97	a	14 18			14 33				14 57	15 18		15 33			15 57		16 18		16 33		16 57		17 18		
	d	14 20			14 35				15 00	15 20		15 35			16 00		16 20		16 35		17 00		17 20		
Kirkham & Wesham 97	a	14 29								15 29							16 29						17 29		
Poulton-le-Fylde 97	a	14 37			14 52					15 37		15 52					16 37		16 52				17 37		
Layton 97	a	14 42								15 43							16 42						17 42		
Blackpool North 97	a	14 47			15 01					15 48		16 01					16 47		17 01				17 47		
Lancaster ■6 65	a								15 15						16 15						17 15				
	d							14 27	15 16						16 16						17 16				
Oxenholme Lake District 65	a								15 30												17 30				
Windermere 83	a																								
Carnforth	d							14a59							16 24										
Silverdale	d														16 30										
Arnside	d														16 34										
Grange-over-Sands	d														16 40										
Kents Bank	d														16 43										
Cark	d														16 48										
Ulverston	d														16 55										
Dalton	d														17 03										
Roose	d														17 09										
Barrow-in-Furness	a														17 19										

A To Clitheroe
B To Leeds
C To Edinburgh
D From Chester

The Sunday service between Manchester Victoria and Wigan Wallgate via Atherton is funded by GMITA and will operate whilst funding exists

Table 82

Sundays
until 1 January

Manchester - Bolton - Wigan, Kirkby, Southport, Preston, Blackpool North and Barrow-in-Furness

Network Diagram - see first Page of Table 82

		TP	NT	NT	NT	NT	TP	NT	NT	TP	NT	TP		NT	NT	NT	TP	NT	NT	TP	NT	NT	TP
		◇1					◇1			◇1		◇1					◇1			◇1			◇1
			A			B	C				A	D				E		A	B				
							🛒					🛒											
Manchester Airport 85 ✈	d	16 30					17 00			17 30		18 00					18 30			19 00			19 30
Heald Green 85	d																						
Buxton 86	d																						
Hazel Grove 86	d																						
Stockport 84	d								17 22							18 21						19 22	
Manchester Piccadilly 10 🚊	d	16 46					17 16		17 35	17 46		18 16				18 35	18 46			19 16		19 35	19 46
Manchester Oxford Road	d	16 49					17 19		17 38	17 49		18 19				18 38	18 49			19 19		19 38	19 49
Deansgate 🚊	d	16 51							17 40	17 51						18 40	18 51					19 40	19 51
Rochdale 41	d																						
Manchester Victoria 🚊	d		17 00	17 12				17 25			18 00			18 12	18 25			19 00			19 25		
Salford Central	d																						
Salford Crescent	a	16 54	17 06	17 16				17 29	17 44	17 54	18 06			18 16	18 29	18 44	18 54	19 06			19 29	19 44	19 54
	d	16 55	17 08	17 17				17 30	17 44	17 55	18 08			18 17	18 30	18 44	18 55	19 08			19 30	19 44	19 55
Swinton	d			17 23										18 23									
Moorside	d			17 26										18 26									
Walkden	d			17 29										18 29									
Atherton	d			17 35										18 35									
Hag Fold	d			17 37										18 37									
Daisy Hill	d			17 40										18 40									
Kearsley	d																						
Farnworth	d																						
Moses Gate	d																						
Bolton	a	17 05	17 19				17 32	17 40	17 54	18 05	18 19	18 32			18 40	18 54	19 05	19 19		19 32	19 40	19 54	20 05
	d	17 05					17 33	17 40	17 55	18 05		18 33			18 40	18 55	19 05			19 33	19 40	19 55	20 05
Westhoughton	d								18 02							19 02						20 02	
Hindley	d			17 45					18 06					18 45		19 06						20 06	
Ince	d			17 48										18 48									
Wigan North Western	a																						
Wigan Wallgate	a			17 53					18 11					18 53		19 11						20 11	
	d								18 13							19 13						20 13	
Pemberton	d																						
Orrell	d																						
Upholland	d																						
Rainford	d																						
Kirkby	a																						
Gathurst	d								18 17							19 17						20 17	
Appley Bridge	d								18 21							19 21						20 21	
Parbold	d								18 25							19 25						20 25	
Hoscar	d																						
Burscough Bridge	d								18 29							19 29						20 29	
New Lane	d																						
Bescar Lane	d																						
Meols Cop	d								18 37							19 37						20 37	
Southport	a								18 44							19 44						20 44	
Lostock	d							17 45							18 45						19 45		
Horwich Parkway	d	17 12						17 49		18 12					18 49		19 12				19 49		20 12
Blackrod	d							17 52							18 52						19 52		
Adlington (Lancashire)	d							17 56							18 56						19 56		
Chorley	d	17 19					17 44	18 01		18 19		18 44			19 01		19 19			19 44	20 01		20 19
Buckshaw Parkway	d	17 23						18 05		18 23					19 05		19 23				20 05		20 23
Leyland	d							18 12							19 14						20 14		
Preston 8 65,97	a	17 33					17 57	18 18		18 33		18 57			19 19		19 33			19 57	20 19		20 33
	d	17 35					18 00	18 20		18 35		19 00	19 06		19 21		19 35			20 06	20 21		20 35
Kirkham & Wesham 97	a							18 29							19 30						20 30		
Poulton-le-Fylde 97	a	17 52						18 37		18 52					19 38		19 52				20 38		20 52
Layton 97	a							18 42							19 42						20 43		
Blackpool North 97	a	18 01						18 47		19 01					19 47		20 01				20 48		21 01
Lancaster 6 65	a						18 15					19 15	19 22							20 21			
	d				17 30	18 04	18 16					19 16	19 22						20 20	20 22			
Oxenholme Lake District 65	a						18 30					19 30											
Windermere 83	a																						
Carnforth	d				17 40	18a13							19 31						20a29	20 30			
Silverdale	d				17 46								19 37										
Arnside	d				17 51								19 41							20 39			
Grange-over-Sands	d				17 57								19 46							20 44			
Kents Bank	d				18 00								19 50										
Cark	d				18 04								19 54										
Ulverston	d				18 12								20 02							20 57			
Dalton	d				18 21								20 10										
Roose	d				18 27								20 16										
Barrow-in-Furness	a				18 34								20 26							21 17			

A To Clitheroe
B From Morecambe to Leeds
C To Glasgow Central
D To Edinburgh
E From Chester

The Sunday service between Manchester Victoria and Wigan Wallgate via Atherton is funded by GMITA and will operate whilst funding exists

Table 82

Sundays
until 1 January

Manchester - Bolton - Wigan, Kirkby, Southport, Preston, Blackpool North and Barrow-in-Furness

Network Diagram - see first Page of Table 82

		NT	NT	NT	TP		NT	TP	NT	NT	TP	NT	NT	NT	NT		TP
					◇1			◇1			◇1						◇1
		A		B			A	C				D		B	E		
Manchester Airport 85 ✈	d				20 30						21 30				22 27		22 30
Heald Green 85	d																
Buxton 86	d																
Hazel Grove 86	d																
Stockport 84	d			20 21						21 22				22 21			
Manchester Piccadilly 10	d			20 35	20 46					21 35	21 46			22 35	22 41		22 46
Manchester Oxford Road	d			20 38	20 49					21 38	21 49			22 38	22 45		22 49
Deansgate	d			20 40	20 51					21 40	21 51			22 40	22a47		22 51
Rochdale 41	d																
Manchester Victoria	d	20 00	20 25				21 00		21 25			22 00					
Salford Central	d																
Salford Crescent	a	20 06	20 29	20 44	20 54		21 06		21 29	21 44	21 54	22 06		22 44			22 54
	d	20 08	20 30	20 44	20 55		21 08		21 30	21 44	21 55	22 08		22 44			22 55
Swinton	d																
Moorside	d																
Walkden	d																
Atherton	d																
Hag Fold	d																
Daisy Hill	d																
Kearsley	d																
Farnworth	d																
Moses Gate	d																
Bolton	a	20 18	20 40	20 54	21 05		21 19		21 40	21 54	22 05	22 19		22 54			23 05
	d		20 40	20 55	21 05				21 40	21 55	22 05			22 55			23 05
Westhoughton	d			21 02						22 02				23 02			
Hindley	d			21 06						22 06				23 06			
Ince	d																
Wigan North Western	a																
Wigan Wallgate	a			21 11						22 13				23 13			
	d			21 13													
Pemberton	d																
Orrell	d																
Upholland	d																
Rainford	d																
Kirkby	a																
Gathurst	d			21 17													
Appley Bridge	d			21 21													
Parbold	d			21 25													
Hoscar	d																
Burscough Bridge	d			21 29													
New Lane	d																
Bescar Lane	d																
Meols Cop	d			21 37													
Southport	a			21 44													
Lostock	d		20 45						21 45								23 10
Horwich Parkway	d		20 49		21 12				21 49								23 14
Blackrod	d		20 52						21 52								23 17
Adlington (Lancashire)	d		20 56						21 56								23 20
Chorley	d		21 01		21 19				22 01		22 17						23 25
Buckshaw Parkway	d		21 05		21 23				22 05								23 28
Leyland	d		21 12						22 12								23 34
Preston 8 65,97	a		21 18		21 33				22 18		22 28						23 42
	d		21 20		21 35				22 20		22 29						23 47
Kirkham & Wesham 97	a		21 29						22 29								23 56
Poulton-le-Fylde 97	a		21 37		21 52				22 37		22 46						00 05
Layton 97	a		21 42						22 42								
Blackpool North 97	a		21 47		22 01				22 47		22 55						00 14
Lancaster 6 65	a																
	d							21 23					22 05				
Oxenholme Lake District 65	a																
Windermere 83	a																
Carnforth	d							21 31					22 15				
Silverdale	d							21 37					22 21				
Arnside	d							21 41					22 26				
Grange-over-Sands	d							21 47					22 32				
Kents Bank	d							21 50					22 35				
Cark	d							21 55					22 39				
Ulverston	d							22 02					22 47				
Dalton	d							22 10					22 56				
Roose	d							22 16					23 02				
Barrow-in-Furness	a							22 26					23 09				

A To Clitheroe
B From Chester
C From Windermere
D To Blackburn
E To Liverpool Lime Street

The Sunday service between Manchester Victoria and Wigan Wallgate via Atherton is funded by GMITA and will operate whilst funding exists

Table 82

Sundays

8 January to 12 February

Manchester - Bolton - Wigan, Kirkby, Southport, Preston, Blackpool North and Barrow-in-Furness

Network Diagram - see first Page of Table 82

		TP	NT	NT	TP	TP	TP	NT	NT	NT		TP	TP	NT	NT	NT	TP	NT	TP	TP		NT	NT	NT	TP
		◇1					◇1					◇1	◇1				◇1		◇1	◇1					◇1
								A		A			B	C		D		A	E			C	F	D	
					bus	bus								bus		bus			trolley			bus		bus	
Manchester Airport 85 ✈	d	22p29			00 05	05 30						08 47					09 29		10 00						10 30
Heald Green 85	d	22p33																							
Buxton 86	d																								
Hazel Grove 86	d																								
Stockport 84	d														09 22								10 12		
Manchester Piccadilly 10	d	22p46			00 30	05 55	07 50					09 03	09 07		09 35		09 46		10 16				10 24		10 46
Manchester Oxford Road	d	22p49					07 53					09 06	09a09		09 38		09 49		10 19				10 38		10 49
Deansgate	d	22p51					07 55					09 08			09 40		09 51						10 40		10 51
Rochdale 41	d																								
Manchester Victoria	d		23p16	23p20				08 01	08 39	09 00				09 23				10 00				10 23			
Salford Central	d		23p19	23p23																					
Salford Crescent	a	22p56	23p22	23p26			07 58	08 06	08 44	09 06		09 11		09 33	09 44		09 54	10 06				10 33	10 44		10 54
	d	22p56	23p22	23p26			07 59	08 07	08 44	09 08		09 12		09 33	09 44		09 55	10 08				10 33	10 44		10 55
Swinton	d			23p33										09 48								10 48			
Moorside	d			23p35										09 52								10 52			
Walkden	d			23p39										09 58								10 58			
Atherton	d			23p44										10 12								11 12			
Hag Fold	d			23p47										10 16								11 16			
Daisy Hill	d			23p50										10 24								11 24			
Kearsley	d																								
Farnworth	d																								
Moses Gate	d																								
Bolton	a	23p06	23p32		00s55	06s20	08 09	08 18	08 54	09 19		09 22			09 54		10 05	10 19	10 32				10 54		11 05
	d	23p07	23p33				08 09		08 55			09 23			09 55		10 05		10 33				10 55		11 05
Westhoughton	d								09 02						10 02	←							11 02	←	
Hindley	d			23p54					09 06					10 34	10 06	10 34						11 34	11 06	11 34	
Ince	d			23p57										→		10 40						→		11 40	
Wigan North Western	a											09 35							10 45						
Wigan Wallgate	a			00 02					09 11						10 11	10 52							11 11	11 52	
	d								09 13						10 13								11 13		
Pemberton	d																								
Orrell	d																								
Upholland	d																								
Rainford	d																								
Kirkby	a																								
Gathurst	d								09 17						10 17								11 17		
Appley Bridge	d								09 21						10 21								11 21		
Parbold	d								09 25						10 25								11 25		
Hoscar	d																								
Burscough Bridge	d								09 29						10 29								11 29		
New Lane	d																								
Bescar Lane	d																								
Meols Cop	d								09 37						10 37								11 37		
Southport	a								09 44						10 44								11 44		
Lostock	d		23p38																						
Horwich Parkway	d	23p13	23p42																						
Blackrod	d		23p45																						
Adlington (Lancashire)	d		23p49																						
Chorley	d	23p21	23p54																						
Buckshaw Parkway	d	23p24	23p57																						
Leyland	d		00 04																						
Preston 8 65,97	a	23p33	00 10		01s30	06s55	08 52					09 55					10 33		11 08						11 33
	d	23p35	00 11				08 53					09 56					10 35		11 10	11 14					11 35
Kirkham & Wesham 97	a		00 21																						
Poulton-le-Fylde 97	a	23p52	00 29				09 10					10 13					10 52								11 52
Layton 97	a		00 34																						
Blackpool North 97	a	00 02	00 38		02 10	07 35	09 20					10 22					11 01								12 01
Lancaster 6 65	a																		11 25	11 29					
	d																		11 26	11 30					
Oxenholme Lake District 65	a																		11 40						
Windermere 83	a																								
Carnforth	d																			11 38					
Silverdale	d																								
Arnside	d																			11 47					
Grange-over-Sands	d																			11 52					
Kents Bank	d																								
Cark	d																								
Ulverston	d																			12 05					
Dalton	d																								
Roose	d																								
Barrow-in-Furness	a																			12 25					

A To Clitheroe
B To Liverpool Lime Street
C To Wigan Wallgate
D From Manchester Victoria
E To Edinburgh
F From Chester

The Sunday service between Manchester Victoria and Wigan Wallgate via Atherton is funded by GMITA and will operate whilst funding exists

Table 82

Sundays

8 January to 12 February

Manchester - Bolton - Wigan, Kirkby, Southport, Preston, Blackpool North and Barrow-in-Furness

Network Diagram - see first Page of Table 82

			NT	TP	TP	NT	NT		NT	NT	NT	TP	NT	TP	TP	NT	NT		NT	NT	TP	NT	TP	NT	NT	NT
				◇1	◇1							◇1		◇1	◇1						◇1		◇1			
			A	B	C	D	E		F		G		A		H		F		I	G		A	C	J		E
					🚌				🚌		🚌				⚲		🚌			🚌			⚲			
Manchester Airport	85 ✈	d			11 00	11 05						11 30			12 00	12 08					12 30		13 00			
Heald Green	85	d				11 08										12 11										
Buxton	86	d																								
Hazel Grove	86	d																								
Stockport	84	d								11 15									12 21							
Manchester Piccadilly 10	⇌	d		11 07	11 16	11 27				11 33		11 46			12 16	12 29			12 33		12 46		13 16			
Manchester Oxford Road		d		11a09	11 19	11a31				11 38		11 49			12 19	12a33			12 38		12 49		13 19			
Deansgate	⇌	d								11 40		11 51							12 40		12 51					
Rochdale	41	d																								
Manchester Victoria	⇌	d	11 00						11 23				12 00				12 23					13 00				
Salford Central		d																								
Salford Crescent		a	11 06						11 33	11 44		11 54	12 06				12 33		12 44		12 54	13 06				
		d	11 08						11 33	11 44		11 55	12 08				12 33		12 44		12 55	13 08				
Swinton		d							11 48								12 48									
Moorside		d							11 52								12 52									
Walkden		d							11 58								12 58									
Atherton		d							12 12								13 12									
Hag Fold		d							12 16								13 16									
Daisy Hill		d							12 24								13 24									
Kearsley		d																								
Farnworth		d																								
Moses Gate		d																								
Bolton		a	11 19		11 32					11 54		12 05	12 19		12 32				12 54		13 05	13 19	13 32			
		d			11 33					11 55		12 05			12 33				12 55		13 05		13 33			
Westhoughton		d								12 02	←								13 02	←						
Hindley		d							12 34	12 06	12 34						13 34		13 06	13 34						
Ince		d							→		12 40						→			13 40						
Wigan North Western		a																								
Wigan Wallgate		a								12 11	12 52								13 11	13 52						
		d								12 13									13 13							
Pemberton		d																								
Orrell		d																								
Upholland		d																								
Rainford		d																								
Kirkby		a																								
Gathurst		d								12 17									13 17							
Appley Bridge		d								12 21									13 21							
Parbold		d								12 25									13 25							
Hoscar		d																								
Burscough Bridge		d								12 29									13 29							
New Lane		d																								
Bescar Lane		d																								
Meols Cop		d								12 37									13 37							
Southport		a								12 44									13 44							
Lostock		d																								
Horwich Parkway		d																								
Blackrod		d																								
Adlington (Lancashire)		d																								
Chorley		d																								
Buckshaw Parkway		d																								
Leyland		d																								
Preston 8	65,97	a			12 01							12 33			13 04						13 33		14 02			
		d			12 02							12 35		12 48	13 04						13 35		14 02			
Kirkham & Wesham	97	a																								
Poulton-le-Fylde	97	a										12 52									13 52					
Layton	97	a																								
Blackpool North	97	a										13 01									14 01					
Lancaster 6	65	a			12 17									13 03	13 19								14 18			
		d			12 18		12 48							13 04	13 20								14 18	14 27	17 30	18 04
Oxenholme Lake District	65	a			12 32										13 34								14 32			
Windermere	83	a																								
Carnforth		d					12a57							13 12										14a59	17 40	18a13
Silverdale		d												13 18											17 46	
Arnside		d												13 22											17 51	
Grange-over-Sands		d												13 28											17 57	
Kents Bank		d												13 31											18 00	
Cark		d												13 36											18 04	
Ulverston		d												13 44											18 12	
Dalton		d												13 52											18 21	
Roose		d												13 58											18 27	
Barrow-in-Furness		a												14 07											18 34	

A To Clitheroe
B To Liverpool Lime Street
C To Glasgow Central
D From Alderley Edge
E From Morecambe to Leeds
F To Wigan Wallgate
G From Manchester Victoria
H To Edinburgh
I From Chester
J To Leeds

The Sunday service between Manchester Victoria and Wigan Wallgate via Atherton is funded by GMITA and will operate whilst funding exists

Table 82

Sundays

8 January to 12 February

Manchester - Bolton - Wigan, Kirkby, Southport, Preston, Blackpool North and Barrow-in-Furness

Network Diagram - see first Page of Table 82

		NT		NT	NT	TP	NT	TP	NT	NT	NT	TP		NT	NT	NT	NT	TP	NT	TP	NT	NT		NT	TP
						◇1		◇1				◇1						◇1		◇1					◇1
		A			B		C	D	A	E	B			C	A		B		C	D	A	E		B	
		🚌			🚌			🚲	🚌		🚌				🚌		🚌			🚲	🚌			🚌	
Manchester Airport 85 ✈	d					13 30		14 00				14 30						15 30		16 00					16 30
Heald Green 85	d																								
Buxton 86	d																								
Hazel Grove 86	d																								
Stockport 84	d			13 22						14 21						15 22						16 21			
Manchester Piccadilly 10 ⇌	d			13 35		13 46		14 16		14 35		14 46				15 35		15 46		16 16		16 35			16 46
Manchester Oxford Road	d			13 38		13 49		14 19		14 38		14 49				15 38		15 49		16 19		16 38			16 49
Deansgate ⇌	d			13 40		13 51				14 40		14 51				15 40		15 51				16 40			16 51
Rochdale 41	d																								
Manchester Victoria ⇌	d	13 23					14 00		14 23					15 00	15 23				16 00		16 23				
Salford Central	d																								
Salford Crescent	a	13 33		13 44		13 54	14 06		14 33	14 44		14 54		15 06	15 33	15 44		15 54	16 06		16 33	16 44			16 54
	d	13 33		13 44		13 55	14 08		14 33	14 44		14 55		15 08	15 33	15 44		15 55	16 08		16 33	16 44			16 55
Swinton	d	13 48							14 48						15 48						16 48				
Moorside	d	13 52							14 52						15 52						16 52				
Walkden	d	13 58							14 58						15 58						16 58				
Atherton	d	14 12							15 12						16 12						17 12				
Hag Fold	d	14 16							15 16						16 16						17 16				
Daisy Hill	d	14 24							15 24						16 24						17 24				
Kearsley	d																								
Farnworth	d																								
Moses Gate	d																								
Bolton	a			13 54		14 05	14 19	14 32		14 54		15 05		15 19		15 54		16 05	16 19	16 32		16 54			17 05
	d			13 55		14 05		14 33		14 55		15 05				15 55		16 05		16 33		16 55			17 05
Westhoughton	d			14 02	←					15 02	←					16 02	←					17 02		←	
Hindley	d	14 34		14 06	14 34				15 34	15 06	15 34				16 34	16 06	16 34				17 34	17 06		17 34	
Ince	d	→			14 40				→		15 40				→		16 40				→			17 40	
Wigan North Western	a																								
Wigan Wallgate	a			14 11	14 52					15 11	15 52					16 11	16 52					17 11		17 52	
	d			14 13						15 13						16 13						17 13			
Pemberton	d																								
Orrell	d																								
Upholland	d																								
Rainford	d																								
Kirkby	a																								
Gathurst	d			14 17						15 17						16 17						17 17			
Appley Bridge	d			14 21						15 21						16 21						17 21			
Parbold	d			14 25						15 25						16 25						17 25			
Hoscar	d																								
Burscough Bridge	d			14 29						15 29						16 29						17 29			
New Lane	d																								
Bescar Lane	d																								
Meols Cop	d			14 37						15 37						16 37						17 37			
Southport	a			14 44						15 44						16 44						17 44			
Lostock	d																								
Horwich Parkway	d																								
Blackrod	d																								
Adlington (Lancashire)	d																								
Chorley	d																								
Buckshaw Parkway	d																								
Leyland	d																								
Preston 8 65,97	a					14 33		15 02				15 33						16 33		17 02					17 33
	d					14 35		15 03				15 35						16 35		17 04					17 35
Kirkham & Wesham 97	a																								
Poulton-le-Fylde 97	a					14 52						15 52						16 52							17 52
Layton 97	a																								
Blackpool North 97	a					15 01						16 01						17 02							18 01
Lancaster 6 65	a																			17 19					
	d																								
Oxenholme Lake District 65	a							15 30																	
Windermere 83	a																								
Carnforth	d																								
Silverdale	d																								
Arnside	d																								
Grange-over-Sands	d																								
Kents Bank	d																								
Cark	d																								
Ulverston	d																								
Dalton	d																								
Roose	d																								
Barrow-in-Furness	a																								

A To Wigan Wallgate
B From Manchester Victoria
C To Clitheroe
D To Edinburgh
E From Chester

The Sunday service between Manchester Victoria and Wigan Wallgate via Atherton is funded by GMITA and will operate whilst funding exists

Table 82

Sundays

8 January to 12 February

Manchester - Bolton - Wigan, Kirkby, Southport, Preston, Blackpool North and Barrow-in-Furness

Network Diagram - see first Page of Table 82

Station			NT	TP	NT	NT	NT	TP	NT		TP		NT	NT	NT	NT	TP	NT	TP		NT	TP	NT	NT	TP	NT
				◇1				◇1			◇1						◇1		◇1			◇1			◇1	
			A	B	C		D		A		E		F	C	G	D		A					A	G		A
					🚌		🚌							🚌		🚌										
				🛒							🛒															
Manchester Airport	85 ✈	d		17 00				17 30			18 00						18 30		19 00			19 30			20 30	
Heald Green	85	d																								
Buxton	86	d																								
Hazel Grove	86	d																								
Stockport	84	d				17 22									18 21						19 22			20 21		
Manchester Piccadilly 10	🚇	d		17 16		17 35		17 46			18 16				18 35		18 46		19 16		19 35	19 46		20 35	20 46	
Manchester Oxford Road		d		17 19		17 38		17 49			18 19				18 38		18 49		19 19		19 38	19 49		20 38	20 49	
Deansgate	🚇	d				17 40		17 51							18 40		18 51				19 40	19 51		20 40	20 51	
Rochdale	41	d																								
Manchester Victoria	🚇	d	17 00		17 23				18 00					18 23				19 00					20 00			21 00
Salford Central		d																								
Salford Crescent		a	17 06		17 33	17 44		17 54	18 06					18 33	18 44		18 54	19 06			19 44	19 54	20 06	20 44	20 54	21 06
		d	17 08		17 33	17 44		17 55	18 08					18 33	18 44		18 55	19 08			19 44	19 55	20 08	20 44	20 55	21 08
Swinton		d			17 48									18 48												
Moorside		d			17 52									18 52												
Walkden		d			17 58									18 58												
Atherton		d			18 12									19 12												
Hag Fold		d			18 16									19 16												
Daisy Hill		d			18 24									19 24												
Kearsley		d																								
Farnworth		d																								
Moses Gate		d																								
Bolton		a	17 19	17 32		17 54		18 05	18 19		18 32				18 54		19 05	19 19	19 32		19 54	20 05	20 18	20 54	21 05	21 19
		d		17 33		17 55		18 05			18 33				18 55		19 05		19 33		19 55	20 05		20 55	21 05	
Westhoughton		d				18 02	←								19 02	←					20 02			21 02		
Hindley		d			18 34	18 06	18 34							19 34	19 06	19 34					20 06			21 06		
Ince		d			→		18 40							→		19 40										
Wigan North Western		a																								
Wigan Wallgate		a				18 11	18 52								19 11	19 52					20 11			21 11		
		d				18 13									19 13						20 13			21 13		
Pemberton		d																								
Orrell		d																								
Upholland		d																								
Rainford		d																								
Kirkby		a																								
Gathurst		d				18 17									19 17						20 17			21 17		
Appley Bridge		d				18 21									19 21						20 21			21 21		
Parbold		d				18 25									19 25						20 25			21 25		
Hoscar		d																								
Burscough Bridge		d				18 29									19 29						20 29			21 29		
New Lane		d																								
Bescar Lane		d																								
Meols Cop		d				18 37									19 37						20 37			21 37		
Southport		a				18 44									19 44						20 44			21 44		
Lostock		d																								
Horwich Parkway		d																								
Blackrod		d																								
Adlington (Lancashire)		d																								
Chorley		d																								
Buckshaw Parkway		d																								
Leyland		d																								
Preston 8	65,97	a		18 02				18 33			19 02						19 33		20 05			20 33			21 33	
		d		18 02				18 35			19 07	19 12					19 35		20 13			20 35			21 35	
Kirkham & Wesham	97	a																								
Poulton-le-Fylde	97	a						18 52									19 52					20 52			21 52	
Layton	97	a																								
Blackpool North	97	a						19 01									20 01					21 01			22 01	
Lancaster 6	65	a		18 18							19 22	19 28							20 29							
		d		18 18							19 23	19 28	20 20						20 29							
Oxenholme Lake District	65	a		18 32							19 37															
Windermere	83	a																								
Carnforth		d										19 37	20a29						20 38							
Silverdale		d										19 43														
Arnside		d										19 47							20 46							
Grange-over-Sands		d										19 52							20 52							
Kents Bank		d										19 56														
Cark		d										20 00														
Ulverston		d										20 08							21 04							
Dalton		d										20 16														
Roose		d										20 22														
Barrow-in-Furness		a										20 32							21 25							

A To Clitheroe
B To Glasgow Central
C To Wigan Wallgate
D From Manchester Victoria
E To Edinburgh
F From Morecambe to Leeds
G From Chester

The Sunday service between Manchester Victoria and Wigan Wallgate via Atherton is funded by GMITA and will operate whilst funding exists

Table 82

Sundays

8 January to 12 February

Manchester - Bolton - Wigan, Kirkby, Southport, Preston, Blackpool North and Barrow-in-Furness

Network Diagram - see first Page of Table 82

		NT	TP ◇1 A	TP ◇1		NT B	NT	NT C	NT D	TP ◇1
Manchester Airport 85 ✈	d			21 30					22 27	22 30
Heald Green 85	d									
Buxton 86	d									
Hazel Grove 86	d									
Stockport 84	d	21 22						22 21		
Manchester Piccadilly 10 ⛴	d	21 35		21 46				22 35	22 41	22 46
Manchester Oxford Road	d	21 38		21 49				22 38	22 45	22 49
Deansgate ⛴	d	21 40		21 51				22 40	22a47	22 51
Rochdale 41	d									
Manchester Victoria ⛴	d					22 00				
Salford Central	d									
Salford Crescent	a	21 44		21 54		22 06		22 44		22 54
	d	21 44		21 55		22 08		22 44		22 55
Swinton	d									
Moorside	d									
Walkden	d									
Atherton	d									
Hag Fold	d									
Daisy Hill	d									
Kearsley	d									
Farnworth	d									
Moses Gate	d									
Bolton	a	21 54		22 05		22 19		22 54		23 05
	d	21 55		22 05				22 55		23 05
Westhoughton	d	22 02						23 02		
Hindley	d	22 06						23 06		
Ince	d									
Wigan North Western	a									
Wigan Wallgate	a	22 13						23 13		
	d									
Pemberton	d									
Orrell	d									
Upholland	d									
Rainford	d									
Kirkby	a									
Gathurst	d									
Appley Bridge	d									
Parbold	d									
Hoscar	d									
Burscough Bridge	d									
New Lane	d									
Bescar Lane	d									
Meols Cop	d									
Southport	a									
Lostock	d									
Horwich Parkway	d									
Blackrod	d									
Adlington (Lancashire)	d									
Chorley	d									
Buckshaw Parkway	d									
Leyland	d									23 34
Preston 8 65,97	a			22 33						23 42
	d			22 34						23 47
Kirkham & Wesham 97	a									23 56
Poulton-le-Fylde 97	a			22 51						00 05
Layton 97	a									
Blackpool North 97	a			23 00						00 14
Lancaster 6 65	a									
	d		21 23				22 05			
Oxenholme Lake District 65	a									
Windermere 83	a									
Carnforth	d		21 31				22 15			
Silverdale	d		21 37				22 21			
Arnside	d		21 41				22 26			
Grange-over-Sands	d		21 47				22 32			
Kents Bank	d		21 50				22 35			
Cark	d		21 55				22 39			
Ulverston	d		22 02				22 47			
Dalton	d		22 10				22 56			
Roose	d		22 16				23 02			
Barrow-in-Furness	a		22 26				23 09			

A From Windermere
B To Blackburn
C From Chester
D To Liverpool Lime Street

The Sunday service between Manchester Victoria and Wigan Wallgate via Atherton is funded by GMITA and will operate whilst funding exists

Table 82

Sundays

19 February to 25 March

Manchester - Bolton - Wigan, Kirkby, Southport, Preston, Blackpool North and Barrow-in-Furness

Network Diagram - see first Page of Table 82

		TP ◇1	NT	NT	TP 🚌	TP 🚌	TP ◇1	NT A	NT	NT	NT A	TP ◇1	TP ◇1 B	NT B	NT	NT	TP ◇1	NT A	TP ◇1 C 🚲	NT	TP ◇1	NT	NT D
Manchester Airport 85 ✈	d	22p29			00 05	05 30	07 30					08 47		08 57			09 29		10 00				
Heald Green 85	d	22p33																					
Buxton 86	d																						
Hazel Grove 86	d																						
Stockport 84	d															09 22							10 12
Manchester Piccadilly 10 🚇	d	22p46			00 30	05 55	07 46					09 03	09 07	09 11		09 35	09 46		10 16				10 24
Manchester Oxford Road	d	22p49					07 49					09 06	09a09	09 15		09 38	09 49		10 19				10 38
Deansgate 🚇	d	22p51					07 51					09 08		09a17		09 40	09 51						10 40
Rochdale 41	d																						
Manchester Victoria 🚇	d		23p16	23p20				08 01	08 25	08 39	09 00				09 25			10 00		10 09		10 25	
Salford Central	d		23p19	23p23																			
Salford Crescent	a	22p56	23p22	23p26			07 54	08 06	08 29	08 44	09 06	09 11			09 29	09 44	09 54	10 06		10 16		10 29	10 44
	d	22p56	23p22	23p26			07 55	08 07	08 30	08 44	09 08	09 12			09 30	09 44	09 55	10 08		10 17		10 30	10 44
Swinton	d			23p33																10 23			
Moorside	d			23p35																10 26			
Walkden	d			23p39																10 29			
Atherton	d			23p44																10 35			
Hag Fold	d			23p47																10 37			
Daisy Hill	d			23p50																10 40			
Kearsley	d																						
Farnworth	d																						
Moses Gate	d																						
Bolton	a	23p06	23p32		00s55	06s20	08 05	08 18	08 40	08 54	09 19	09 22			09 40	09 54	10 05	10 19	10 32			10 40	10 54
	d	23p07	23p33				08 05		08 40	08 55		09 23			09 40	09 55	10 05		10 33			10 40	10 55
Westhoughton	d									09 02						10 02							11 02
Hindley	d			23p54						09 06						10 06				10 45			11 06
Ince	d			23p57																10 48			
Wigan North Western	a																						
Wigan Wallgate	a			00 02						09 11						10 11				10 53			11 11
	d									09 13						10 13							11 13
Pemberton	d																						
Orrell	d																						
Upholland	d																						
Rainford	d																						
Kirkby	a																						
Gathurst	d									09 17						10 17							11 17
Appley Bridge	d									09 21						10 21							11 21
Parbold	d									09 25						10 25							11 25
Hoscar	d																						
Burscough Bridge	d									09 29						10 29							11 29
New Lane	d																						
Bescar Lane	d																						
Meols Cop	d									09 37						10 37							11 37
Southport	a									09 44						10 44							11 44
Lostock	d		23p38						08 45						09 45							10 45	
Horwich Parkway	d	23p13	23p42				08 12		08 49			09 29			09 49		10 12					10 49	
Blackrod	d		23p45						08 52						09 52							10 52	
Adlington (Lancashire)	d		23p49						08 56						09 56							10 56	
Chorley	d	23p21	23p54				08 19		09 01			09 37			10 01		10 20		10 44			11 01	
Buckshaw Parkway	d	23p24	23p57				08 23		09 05			09 40			10 05		10 23					11 05	
Leyland	d		00 04						09 12						10 12							11 12	
Preston 8 65,97	a	23p33	00 10		01s30	06s55	08 32		09 18			09 50			10 18		10 34		10 57			11 20	
	d	23p35	00 11				08 33		09 20			09 52			10 20		10 35		11 10		11 14	11 21	
Kirkham & Wesham 97	a		00 21						09 29						10 29							11 31	
Poulton-le-Fylde 97	a	23p52	00 29				08 50		09 37			10 09			10 37		10 52					11 39	
Layton 97	a		00 34						09 42						10 42							11 44	
Blackpool North 97	a	00 02	00 38		02 10	07 35	08 57		09 47			10 18			10 47		11 01					11 49	
Lancaster 6 65	a																		11 25		11 29		
	d																		11 26		11 30		
Oxenholme Lake District 65	a																		11 40				
Windermere 83	a																						
Carnforth	d																				11 38		
Silverdale	d																						
Arnside	d																				11 47		
Grange-over-Sands	d																				11 52		
Kents Bank	d																						
Cark	d																						
Ulverston	d																				12 05		
Dalton	d																						
Roose	d																						
Barrow-in-Furness	a																				12 25		

A To Clitheroe
B To Liverpool Lime Street
C To Edinburgh
D From Chester

The Sunday service between Manchester Victoria and Wigan Wallgate via Atherton is funded by GMITA and will operate whilst funding exists

Table 82

Sundays

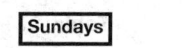

19 February to 25 March

Manchester - Bolton - Wigan, Kirkby, Southport, Preston, Blackpool North and Barrow-in-Furness

Network Diagram - see first Page of Table 82

		NT	TP	NT	TP	NT	TP	NT	NT	NT	NT	TP	NT	NT	NT	NT	TP	TP	NT	NT	NT	TP	NT
			◇1		◇1		◇1					◇1					◇1	◇1				◇1	
		A		B	A	A	C	D					A	B		E		F			G		A
Manchester Airport 85	d	10 16	10 30			10 56	11 00	11 05				11 30	11 56					12 00	12 08			12 30	12 58
Heald Green 85	d							11 08											12 11				
Buxton 86	d																						
Hazel Grove 86	d																						
Stockport 84	d										11 15										12 21		
Manchester Piccadilly 10	d	10 31	10 46		11 07	11 12	11 16	11 27			11 33	11 46	12 11					12 16	12 29		12 33	12 46	13 12
Manchester Oxford Road	d	10a34	10 49		11a09	11a14	11 19	11a31			11 38	11 49	12a13					12 19	12a33		12 38	12 49	13a14
Deansgate	d		10 51								11 40	11 51									12 40	12 51	
Rochdale 41	d																						
Manchester Victoria	d			11 00					11 12	11 25				12 00	12 09					12 25			
Salford Central	d																						
Salford Crescent	a		10 54	11 06					11 16	11 29	11 44	11 54		12 06	12 13					12 29	12 44	12 54	
	d		10 55	11 08					11 17	11 30	11 44	11 55		12 08	12 17					12 30	12 44	12 55	
Swinton	d								11 23						12 23								
Moorside	d								11 26						12 26								
Walkden	d								11 29						12 29								
Atherton	d								11 35						12 35								
Hag Fold	d								11 37						12 37								
Daisy Hill	d								11 40						12 40								
Kearsley	d																						
Farnworth	d																						
Moses Gate	d																						
Bolton	a		11 05	11 19			11 32			11 40	11 54	12 05		12 19				12 32		12 40	12 54	13 05	
	d		11 05				11 33			11 40	11 55	12 05						12 33		12 40	12 55	13 05	
Westhoughton	d										12 02										13 02		
Hindley	d								11 45		12 06				12 45						13 06		
Ince	d								11 48						12 48								
Wigan North Western	a																						
Wigan Wallgate	a								11 53		12 11				12 53						13 11		
	d										12 13										13 13		
Pemberton	d																						
Orrell	d																						
Upholland	d																						
Rainford	d																						
Kirkby	a																						
Gathurst	d										12 17										13 17		
Appley Bridge	d										12 21										13 21		
Parbold	d										12 25										13 25		
Hoscar	d																						
Burscough Bridge	d										12 29										13 29		
New Lane	d																						
Bescar Lane	d																						
Meols Cop	d										12 37										13 37		
Southport	a										12 44										13 44		
Lostock	d									11 45										12 45			
Horwich Parkway	d		11 12							11 49		12 12								12 49		13 12	
Blackrod	d									11 52										12 52			
Adlington (Lancashire)	d									11 56										12 56			
Chorley	d		11 19				11 44			12 01		12 19						12 44		13 01		13 19	
Buckshaw Parkway	d		11 23							12 05		12 23								13 05		13 23	
Leyland	d									12 12										13 12			
Preston 8 65,97	a		11 33				11 56			12 18		12 33						12 57		13 18		13 33	
	d		11 35				11 58			12 20		12 35					12 48	12 58		13 20		13 35	
Kirkham & Wesham 97	a									12 29										13 29			
Poulton-le-Fylde 97	a		11 52							12 37		12 52								13 37		13 52	
Layton 97	a									12 42										13 42			
Blackpool North 97	a		12 01							12 47		13 01								13 47		14 01	
Lancaster 6 65	a						12 13										13 03	13 13					
	d						12 14									12 48	13 04	13 14					
Oxenholme Lake District 65	a						12 28											13 28					
Windermere 83	a																						
Carnforth	d															12a57	13 12						
Silverdale	d																13 18						
Arnside	d																13 22						
Grange-over-Sands	d																13 28						
Kents Bank	d																13 31						
Cark	d																13 36						
Ulverston	d																13 44						
Dalton	d																13 52						
Roose	d																13 58						
Barrow-in-Furness	a																14 07						

A To Liverpool Lime Street
B To Clitheroe
C To Glasgow Central
D From Alderley Edge
E From Morecambe to Leeds
F To Edinburgh
G From Chester

The Sunday service between Manchester Victoria and Wigan Wallgate via Atherton is funded by GMITA and will operate whilst funding exists

Table 82

Sundays

19 February to 25 March

Manchester - Bolton - Wigan, Kirkby, Southport, Preston, Blackpool North and Barrow-in-Furness

Network Diagram - see first Page of Table 82

		NT	TP	NT	NT	NT	TP	NT	NT	NT	TP	NT	NT	NT	TP	NT	NT	TP	NT	NT	NT	TP
			◇1				◇1				◇1				◇1			◇1				◇1
		A	B					A		C	D	E		F		E	A					
			⚲								⚲											
Manchester Airport 85 ✈	d		12 59				13 30				14 00	14 06			14 30	14 58		15 00				15 30
Heald Green 85	d																					
Buxton 86	d																					
Hazel Grove 86	d																					
Stockport 84	d					13 22								14 21							15 22	
Manchester Piccadilly 10 🚇	d		13 16			13 35	13 46				14 16	14 20		14 35	14 46	15 12		15 16			15 35	15 46
Manchester Oxford Road	d		13 19			13 38	13 49				14 19	14a22		14 38	14 49	15a14		15 19			15 38	15 49
Deansgate 🚇	d					13 40	13 51							14 40	14 51						15 40	15 51
Rochdale 41	d																					
Manchester Victoria 🚇	d	13 00		13 12	13 25			14 00	14 12				14 25				15 00		15 12	15 25		
Salford Central	d																					
Salford Crescent	a	13 06		13 16	13 29	13 44	13 54	14 06	14 16				14 29	14 44	14 54		15 06		15 16	15 29	15 44	15 54
	d	13 08		13 17	13 30	13 44	13 55	14 08	14 17				14 30	14 44	14 55		15 08		15 17	15 30	15 44	15 55
Swinton	d			13 23					14 23										15 23			
Moorside	d			13 26					14 26										15 26			
Walkden	d			13 29					14 29										15 29			
Atherton	d			13 35					14 35										15 35			
Hag Fold	d			13 37					14 37										15 37			
Daisy Hill	d			13 40					14 40										15 40			
Kearsley	d																					
Farnworth	d																					
Moses Gate	d																					
Bolton	a	13 19	13 32		13 41	13 54	14 05	14 19			14 32		14 40	14 54	15 05		15 19	15 32		15 40	15 54	16 05
	d		13 33		13 41	13 55	14 05				14 33		14 40	14 55	15 05			15 33		15 40	15 55	16 05
Westhoughton	d					14 02								15 02							16 02	
Hindley	d			13 45		14 06			14 45					15 06					15 45		16 06	
Ince	d			13 48					14 48										15 48			
Wigan North Western	a																					
Wigan Wallgate	a			13 53		14 11			14 53					15 11					15 53		16 11	
	d					14 13								15 13							16 13	
Pemberton	d																					
Orrell	d																					
Upholland	d																					
Rainford	d																					
Kirkby	a																					
Gathurst	d					14 17								15 17							16 17	
Appley Bridge	d					14 21								15 21							16 21	
Parbold	d					14 25								15 25							16 25	
Hoscar	d																					
Burscough Bridge	d					14 29								15 29							16 29	
New Lane	d																					
Bescar Lane	d																					
Meols Cop	d					14 37								15 37							16 37	
Southport	a					14 44								15 44							16 44	
Lostock	d				13 46								14 45							15 45		
Horwich Parkway	d				13 50		14 12						14 49		15 12					15 49		16 12
Blackrod	d				13 53								14 52							15 52		
Adlington (Lancashire)	d				13 57								14 56							15 56		
Chorley	d		13 44		14 02		14 19				14 44		15 01		15 19			15 44		16 01		16 19
Buckshaw Parkway	d				14 06		14 23						15 05		15 23					16 05		16 23
Leyland	d				14 13								15 13							16 12		
Preston 8 65,97	a		13 57		14 18		14 33				14 57		15 18		15 33			15 57		16 18		16 33
	d		14 00		14 20		14 35				15 00		15 20		15 35			16 00		16 20		16 35
Kirkham & Wesham 97	a				14 29								15 29							16 29		
Poulton-le-Fylde 97	a				14 37		14 52						15 37		15 52					16 37		16 52
Layton 97	a				14 42								15 43							16 42		
Blackpool North 97	a				14 47		15 01						15 48		16 01					16 47		17 01
Lancaster 6 65	a		14 15								15 15							16 15				
	d		14 16							14 27	15 16							16 16				
Oxenholme Lake District 65	a		14 30								15 30											
Windermere 83	a																					
Carnforth	d									14a59								16 24				
Silverdale	d																	16 30				
Arnside	d																	16 34				
Grange-over-Sands	d																	16 40				
Kents Bank	d																	16 43				
Cark	d																	16 48				
Ulverston	d																	16 55				
Dalton	d																	17 03				
Roose	d																	17 09				
Barrow-in-Furness	a																	17 19				

A To Clitheroe
B To Glasgow Central
C To Leeds
D To Edinburgh
E To Liverpool Lime Street
F From Chester

The Sunday service between Manchester Victoria and Wigan Wallgate via Atherton is funded by GMITA and will operate whilst funding exists

Table 82

Sundays

19 February to 25 March

Manchester - Bolton - Wigan, Kirkby, Southport, Preston, Blackpool North and Barrow-in-Furness

Network Diagram - see first Page of Table 82

Station			NT A	NT B	TP ◇1 C	NT	NT	NT D	TP ◇1	NT A	NT B	NT	NT	NT E	TP ◇1 F	NT	NT	TP ◇1	NT A	NT B	TP ◇1 C		NT	NT
Manchester Airport	85	d	15 58		16 00				16 30	16 58					17 00			17 30	17 58		18 00			
Heald Green	85	d																						
Buxton	86	d																						
Hazel Grove	86	d																						
Stockport	84	d						16 21									17 22							
Manchester Piccadilly 10		d	16 12		16 16			16 35	16 46	17 12					17 16		17 35	17 46	18 12		18 16			
Manchester Oxford Road		d	16a14		16 19			16 38	16 49	17a14					17 19		17 38	17 49	18a14		18 19			
Deansgate		d						16 40	16 51								17 40	17 51						
Rochdale	41	d																						
Manchester Victoria		d		16 00		16 12	16 25				17 00	17 12				17 25				18 00			18 12	18 25
Salford Central		d																						
Salford Crescent		a		16 06		16 16	16 29	16 44	16 54		17 06	17 16				17 29	17 44	17 54		18 06			18 16	18 29
		d		16 08		16 17	16 30	16 44	16 55		17 08	17 17				17 30	17 44	17 55		18 08			18 17	18 30
Swinton		d				16 23						17 23											18 23	
Moorside		d				16 26						17 26											18 26	
Walkden		d				16 29						17 29											18 29	
Atherton		d				16 35						17 35											18 35	
Hag Fold		d				16 37						17 37											18 37	
Daisy Hill		d				16 40						17 40											18 40	
Kearsley		d																						
Farnworth		d																						
Moses Gate		d																						
Bolton		a		16 19	16 32		16 40	16 54	17 05		17 19				17 32	17 40	17 54	18 05		18 19	18 32			18 40
		d			16 33		16 40	16 55	17 05						17 33	17 40	17 55	18 05			18 33			18 40
Westhoughton		d						17 02									18 02							
Hindley		d				16 45		17 06				17 45					18 06						18 45	
Ince		d				16 48						17 48											18 48	
Wigan North Western		a																						
Wigan Wallgate		a				16 53		17 11				17 53					18 11						18 53	
		d						17 13									18 13							
Pemberton		d																						
Orrell		d																						
Upholland		d																						
Rainford		d																						
Kirkby		a																						
Gathurst		d						17 17									18 17							
Appley Bridge		d						17 21									18 21							
Parbold		d						17 25									18 25							
Hoscar		d																						
Burscough Bridge		d						17 29									18 29							
New Lane		d																						
Bescar Lane		d																						
Meols Cop		d						17 37									18 37							
Southport		a						17 44									18 44							
Lostock		d					16 45									17 45								18 45
Horwich Parkway		d					16 49		17 12							17 49		18 12						18 49
Blackrod		d					16 52									17 52								18 52
Adlington (Lancashire)		d					16 56									17 56								18 56
Chorley		d			16 44		17 01		17 19						17 44	18 01		18 19			18 44			19 01
Buckshaw Parkway		d					17 05		17 23							18 05		18 23						19 05
Leyland		d					17 12									18 12								19 14
Preston 8	65,97	a			16 57		17 18		17 33						17 57	18 18		18 33			18 57			19 19
		d			17 00		17 20		17 35						18 00	18 20		18 35			19 00	19 06		19 21
Kirkham & Wesham	97	a					17 29									18 29								19 30
Poulton-le-Fylde	97	a					17 37		17 52							18 37		18 52						19 38
Layton	97	a					17 42									18 42								19 42
Blackpool North	97	a					17 47		18 01							18 47		19 01						19 47
Lancaster 6	65	a			17 15										18 15						19 15	19 22		
		d			17 16								17 30	18 04	18 16						19 16	19 22		
Oxenholme Lake District	65	a			17 30										18 30						19 30			
Windermere	83	a																						
Carnforth		d											17 40	18a13								19 31		
Silverdale		d											17 46									19 37		
Arnside		d											17 51									19 41		
Grange-over-Sands		d											17 57									19 46		
Kents Bank		d											18 00									19 50		
Cark		d											18 04									19 54		
Ulverston		d											18 12									20 02		
Dalton		d											18 21									20 10		
Roose		d											18 27									20 16		
Barrow-in-Furness		a											18 34									20 26		

A To Liverpool Lime Street
B To Clitheroe
C To Edinburgh
D From Chester
E From Morecambe to Leeds
F To Glasgow Central

The Sunday service between Manchester Victoria and Wigan Wallgate via Atherton is funded by GMITA and will operate whilst funding exists

Table 82

Sundays

19 February to 25 March

Manchester - Bolton - Wigan, Kirkby, Southport, Preston, Blackpool North and Barrow-in-Furness

Network Diagram - see first Page of Table 82

Station		NT	TP	NT	NT	NT	TP	NT	NT	TP	NT	NT	NT	NT	TP	NT	NT	TP	NT	NT	TP	NT
			◇1				◇1			◇1					◇1			◇1			◇1	
		A		B	C	D					B	C		A		B	C	E				F
Manchester Airport 85 ✈	d		18 30	18 58			19 00			19 30	19 58				20 30	20 58					21 30	
Heald Green 85	d																					
Buxton 86	d																					
Hazel Grove 86	d																					
Stockport 84	d	18 21							19 22					20 21						21 22		
Manchester Piccadilly 10	d	18 35	18 46	19 12			19 16		19 35	19 46	20 12			20 35	20 46	21 12				21 35	21 46	
Manchester Oxford Road	d	18 38	18 49	19a14			19 19		19 38	19 49	20a14			20 38	20 49	21a14				21 38	21 49	
Deansgate	d	18 40	18 51						19 40	19 51				20 40	20 51					21 40	21 51	
Rochdale 41	d																					
Manchester Victoria	d				19 00			19 25				20 00	20 25				21 00		21 25			22 00
Salford Central	d																					
Salford Crescent	a	18 44	18 54		19 06			19 29	19 44	19 54		20 06	20 29	20 44	20 54		21 06		21 29	21 44	21 54	22 06
	d	18 44	18 55		19 08			19 30	19 44	19 55		20 08	20 30	20 44	20 55		21 08		21 30	21 44	21 55	22 08
Swinton	d																					
Moorside	d																					
Walkden	d																					
Atherton	d																					
Hag Fold	d																					
Daisy Hill	d																					
Kearsley	d																					
Farnworth	d																					
Moses Gate	d																					
Bolton	a	18 54	19 05		19 19		19 32	19 40	19 54	20 05		20 18	20 40	20 54	21 05		21 19		21 40	21 54	22 05	22 19
	d	18 55	19 05				19 33	19 40	19 55	20 05			20 40	20 55	21 05				21 40	21 55	22 05	
Westhoughton	d	19 02							20 02					21 02						22 02		
Hindley	d	19 06							20 06					21 06						22 06		
Ince	d																					
Wigan North Western	a																					
Wigan Wallgate	a	19 11							20 11					21 11						22 13		
	d	19 13							20 13					21 13								
Pemberton	d																					
Orrell	d																					
Upholland	d																					
Rainford	d																					
Kirkby	a																					
Gathurst	d	19 17							20 17					21 17								
Appley Bridge	d	19 21							20 21					21 21								
Parbold	d	19 25							20 25					21 25								
Hoscar	d																					
Burscough Bridge	d	19 29							20 29					21 29								
New Lane	d																					
Bescar Lane	d																					
Meols Cop	d	19 37							20 37					21 37								
Southport	a	19 44							20 44					21 44								
Lostock	d							19 45					20 45						21 45			
Horwich Parkway	d		19 12					19 49		20 12			20 49		21 12				21 49			
Blackrod	d							19 52					20 52						21 52			
Adlington (Lancashire)	d							19 56					20 56						21 56			
Chorley	d		19 19				19 44	20 01		20 19			21 01		21 19				22 01		22 17	
Buckshaw Parkway	d		19 23					20 05		20 23			21 05		21 23				22 05			
Leyland	d							20 14					21 12						22 12			
Preston 8 65,97	a		19 33				19 57	20 19		20 33			21 18		21 33				22 18		22 28	
	d		19 35				20 06	20 21		20 35			21 20		21 35				22 20		22 29	
Kirkham & Wesham 97	a							20 30					21 29						22 29			
Poulton-le-Fylde 97	a		19 52					20 38		20 52			21 37		21 52				22 37		22 46	
Layton 97	a							20 43					21 42						22 42			
Blackpool North 97	a		20 01					20 48		21 01			21 47		22 01				22 47		22 55	
Lancaster 6 65	a						20 21															
	d					20 20	20 22											21 23				
Oxenholme Lake District 65	a																					
Windermere 83	a																					
Carnforth	d					20a29	20 30											21 31				
Silverdale	d																	21 37				
Arnside	d						20 39											21 41				
Grange-over-Sands	d						20 44											21 47				
Kents Bank	d																	21 50				
Cark	d																	21 55				
Ulverston	d						20 57											22 02				
Dalton	d																	22 10				
Roose	d																	22 16				
Barrow-in-Furness	a						21 17											22 26				

A From Chester
B To Liverpool Lime Street
C To Clitheroe
D From Morecambe to Leeds
E From Windermere
F To Blackburn

The Sunday service between Manchester Victoria and Wigan Wallgate via Atherton is funded by GMITA and will operate whilst funding exists

Table 82

Sundays

19 February to 25 March

Manchester - Bolton - Wigan, Kirkby, Southport, Preston, Blackpool North and Barrow-in-Furness

Network Diagram - see first Page of Table 82

Station			NT	NT	NT	TP
						◇1
				A	B	
Manchester Airport	85 ✈	d			22 27	22 30
Heald Green	85	d				
Buxton	86	d				
Hazel Grove	86	d				
Stockport	84	d		22 21		
Manchester Piccadilly 10	⇌	d		22 35	22 41	22 46
Manchester Oxford Road		d		22 38	22 45	22 49
Deansgate	⇌	d		22 40	22a47	22 51
Rochdale	41	d				
Manchester Victoria	⇌	d				
Salford Central		d				
Salford Crescent		a		22 44		22 54
		d		22 44		22 55
Swinton		d				
Moorside		d				
Walkden		d				
Atherton		d				
Hag Fold		d				
Daisy Hill		d				
Kearsley		d				
Farnworth		d				
Moses Gate		d				
Bolton		a		22 54		23 05
		d		22 55		23 05
Westhoughton		d		23 02		
Hindley		d		23 06		
Ince		d				
Wigan North Western		a				
Wigan Wallgate		a		23 13		
		d				
Pemberton		d				
Orrell		d				
Upholland		d				
Rainford		d				
Kirkby		a				
Gathurst		d				
Appley Bridge		d				
Parbold		d				
Hoscar		d				
Burscough Bridge		d				
New Lane		d				
Bescar Lane		d				
Meols Cop		d				
Southport		a				
Lostock		d				23 10
Horwich Parkway		d				23 14
Blackrod		d				23 17
Adlington (Lancashire)		d				23 20
Chorley		d				23 25
Buckshaw Parkway		d				23 28
Leyland		d				23 34
Preston 8	65,97	a				23 42
		d				23 47
Kirkham & Wesham	97	a				23 56
Poulton-le-Fylde	97	a				00 05
Layton	97	a				
Blackpool North	97	a				00 14
Lancaster 6	65	a				
		d	22 05			
Oxenholme Lake District	65	a				
Windermere	83	a				
Carnforth		d	22 15			
Silverdale		d	22 21			
Arnside		d	22 26			
Grange-over-Sands		d	22 32			
Kents Bank		d	22 35			
Cark		d	22 39			
Ulverston		d	22 47			
Dalton		d	22 56			
Roose		d	23 02			
Barrow-in-Furness		a	23 09			

A From Chester

B To Liverpool Lime Street

The Sunday service between Manchester Victoria and Wigan Wallgate via Atherton is funded by GMITA and will operate whilst funding exists

Table 82

Sundays
from 1 April

Manchester - Bolton - Wigan, Kirkby, Southport, Preston, Blackpool North and Barrow-in-Furness

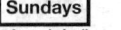

Network Diagram - see first Page of Table 82

			TP ◇1	NT	NT	TP 🚌	TP 🚌	TP A 🚌	TP ◇1 B	NT C	TP ◇1	NT	NT D	NT	NT C	TP ◇1	TP ◇1 B	NT	NT	TP ◇1	NT C	TP ◇1 E	TP ◇1 B	NT
Manchester Airport	85 ✈	d	22p29			00 05	05 30	06 05	07 50		07 55		08 34			08 47	09 03			09 30		10 00	10 03	
Heald Green	85	d	22p33																					
Buxton	86	d																						
Hazel Grove	86	d																						
Stockport	84	d																	09 22					
Manchester Piccadilly 10	🚇	d	22p46			00 30	05 55	06a30	08 05		08 11		08 49			09 03	09 20		09 35	09 46		10 16	10 21	
Manchester Oxford Road		d	22p49								08 14		08 52			09 06			09 38	09 49		10 19		
Deansgate	🚇	d	22p51								08 16		08a54			09 08			09 40	09 51				
Rochdale	41	d																						
Manchester Victoria	🚇	d		23p16	23p20				08a20	08 01		08 25		08 39	09 00		09a35	09 25			10 00		10a35	10 09
Salford Central		d		23p19	23p23																			
Salford Crescent		a	22p56	23p22	23p26					08 06	08 19	08 29		08 44	09 06	09 11		09 29	09 44	09 54	10 06			10 16
		d	22p56	23p22	23p26					08 07	08 20	08 30		08 44	09 08	09 12		09 30	09 44	09 55	10 08			10 17
Swinton		d			23p33																			10 23
Moorside		d			23p35																			10 26
Walkden		d			23p39																			10 29
Atherton		d			23p44																			10 35
Hag Fold		d			23p47																			10 37
Daisy Hill		d			23p50																			10 40
Kearsley		d																						
Farnworth		d																						
Moses Gate		d																						
Bolton		a	23p06	23p32		00s55	06s20			08 18	08 30	08 40		08 54	09 19	09 22		09 40	09 54	10 05	10 19	10 32		
		d	23p07	23p33							08 30	08 40		08 55		09 23		09 40	09 55	10 05		10 33		
Westhoughton		d												09 02					10 02					
Hindley		d			23p54									09 06					10 06					10 45
Ince		d			23p57																			10 48
Wigan North Western		a																						
Wigan Wallgate		a			00 02									09 11					10 11					10 53
		d												09 13					10 13					
Pemberton		d																						
Orrell		d																						
Upholland		d																						
Rainford		d																						
Kirkby		a																						
Gathurst		d												09 17					10 17					
Appley Bridge		d												09 21					10 21					
Parbold		d												09 25					10 25					
Hoscar		d																						
Burscough Bridge		d												09 29					10 29					
New Lane		d																						
Bescar Lane		d																						
Meols Cop		d												09 37					10 37					
Southport		a												09 44					10 44					
Lostock		d		23p38								08 45						09 45						
Horwich Parkway		d	23p13	23p42							08 37	08 49				09 29		09 49		10 12				
Blackrod		d		23p45								08 52						09 52						
Adlington (Lancashire)		d		23p49								08 56						09 56						
Chorley		d	23p21	23p54							08 44	09 01				09 37		10 01		10 19		10 44		
Buckshaw Parkway		d	23p24	23p57							08 48	09 05				09 40		10 05		10 23				
Leyland		d		00 04								09 12						10 12						
Preston 8	65,97	a	23p33	00 10		01s30	06s55				08 57	09 18				09 50		10 18		10 33		10 57		
		d	23p35	00 11							08 58	09 20				09 52		10 20		10 35		11 10		
Kirkham & Wesham	97	a		00 21								09 29						10 29						
Poulton-le-Fylde	97	a	23p52	00 29							09 15	09 37				10 09		10 37		10 52				
Layton	97	a		00 34								09 42						10 42						
Blackpool North	97	a	00 02	00 38		02 10	07 35				09 23	09 47				10 18		10 47		11 01				
Lancaster 6	65	a																				11 25		
		d																				11 26		
Oxenholme Lake District	65	a																				11 40		
Windermere	83	a																						
Carnforth		d																						
Silverdale		d																						
Arnside		d																						
Grange-over-Sands		d																						
Kents Bank		d																						
Cark		d																						
Ulverston		d																						
Dalton		d																						
Roose		d																						
Barrow-in-Furness		a																						

A To Leeds
B To Newcastle
C To Clitheroe
D To Liverpool Lime Street
E To Edinburgh

The Sunday service between Manchester Victoria and Wigan Wallgate via Atherton is funded by GMITA and will operate whilst funding exists

Table 82

Sundays
from 1 April

Manchester - Bolton - Wigan, Kirkby, Southport, Preston, Blackpool North and Barrow-in-Furness

Network Diagram - see first Page of Table 82

	TP ◇1	NT	NT A	TP ◇1	NT B	TP ◇1 C 🍴	TP ◇1 D	NT E	NT	NT	NT	TP ◇1	NT B	NT	NT F	TP ◇1	TP ◇1 G 🍴	TP ◇1 D	NT	NT	NT A	TP ◇1
Manchester Airport 85 ✈ d				10 30		11 00	11 03	11 05				11 30					12 00	12 03	12 08			12 30
Heald Green 85 d								11 08											12 11			
Buxton 86 d																						
Hazel Grove 86 d																						
Stockport 84 d			10 12								11 15										12 21	
Manchester Piccadilly 10 🚇 d			10 24	10 46		11 16	11 21	11 27			11 33	11 46					12 16	12 21	12 29		12 35	12 46
Manchester Oxford Road d			10 38	10 49		11 19		11a31			11 38	11 49					12 19		12a33		12 38	12 49
Deansgate 🚇 d			10 40	10 51							11 40	11 51									12 40	12 51
Rochdale 41 d																						
Manchester Victoria 🚇 d		10 25			11 00		11a35		11 12	11 25			12 00	12 09				12a35		12 25		
Salford Central d																						
Salford Crescent a		10 29	10 44	10 54	11 06				11 16	11 29	11 44	11 54	12 06	12 13						12 29	12 44	12 54
d		10 30	10 44	10 55	11 08				11 17	11 30	11 44	11 55	12 08	12 17						12 30	12 44	12 55
Swinton d									11 23					12 23								
Moorside d									11 26					12 26								
Walkden d									11 29					12 29								
Atherton d									11 35					12 35								
Hag Fold d									11 37					12 37								
Daisy Hill d									11 40					12 40								
Kearsley d																						
Farnworth d																						
Moses Gate d																						
Bolton a		10 40	10 54	11 05	11 19	11 32				11 40	11 54	12 05	12 19				12 32			12 40	12 54	13 05
d		10 40	10 55	11 05		11 33				11 40	11 55	12 05					12 33			12 40	12 55	13 05
Westhoughton d			11 02								12 02										13 02	
Hindley d			11 06						11 45		12 06			12 45							13 06	
Ince d									11 48					12 48								
Wigan North Western a																						
Wigan Wallgate a			11 11						11 53		12 11			12 53							13 11	
d			11 13								12 13										13 13	
Pemberton d																						
Orrell d																						
Upholland d																						
Rainford d																						
Kirkby a																						
Gathurst d			11 17								12 17										13 17	
Appley Bridge d			11 21								12 21										13 21	
Parbold d			11 25								12 25										13 25	
Hoscar d																						
Burscough Bridge d			11 29								12 29										13 29	
New Lane d																						
Bescar Lane d																						
Meols Cop d			11 37								12 37										13 37	
Southport a			11 44								12 44										13 44	
Lostock d		10 45								11 45										12 45		
Horwich Parkway d		10 49		11 12						11 49		12 12								12 49		13 12
Blackrod d		10 52								11 52										12 52		
Adlington (Lancashire) d		10 56								11 56										12 56		
Chorley d		11 01		11 19		11 44				12 01		12 19					12 44			13 01		13 19
Buckshaw Parkway d		11 05		11 23						12 05		12 23								13 05		13 23
Leyland d		11 12								12 12										13 12		
Preston 8 65,97 a		11 20		11 33		11 56				12 18		12 33					12 57			13 18		13 33
d	11 14	11 21		11 35		11 58				12 20		12 35				12 48	12 58			13 20		13 35
Kirkham & Wesham 97 a		11 31								12 29										13 29		
Poulton-le-Fylde 97 a		11 39		11 52						12 37		12 52								13 37		13 52
Layton 97 a		11 44								12 42										13 42		
Blackpool North 97 a		11 49		12 01						12 47		13 01								13 47		14 01
Lancaster 6 65 a	11 29					12 13										13 03	13 13					
d	11 30					12 14									12 48	13 04	13 14					
Oxenholme Lake District 65 a						12 28											13 28					
Windermere 83 a																						
Carnforth d	11 38														12a57	13 12						
Silverdale d																13 18						
Arnside d	11 47															13 22						
Grange-over-Sands d	11 52															13 28						
Kents Bank d																13 31						
Cark d																13 36						
Ulverston d	12 05															13 44						
Dalton d																13 52						
Roose d																13 58						
Barrow-in-Furness a	12 25															14 07						

A From Chester
B To Clitheroe
C To Glasgow Central
D To Newcastle
E From Alderley Edge
F From Morecambe to Leeds
G To Edinburgh

The Sunday service between Manchester Victoria and Wigan Wallgate via Atherton is funded by GMITA and will operate whilst funding exists

Table 82

Sundays
from 1 April

Manchester - Bolton - Wigan, Kirkby, Southport, Preston, Blackpool North and Barrow-in-Furness

Network Diagram - see first Page of Table 82

		NT		TP	TP	NT	NT	NT	TP	NT	NT	NT		TP	TP	NT	NT	TP	NT	TP	TP	NT		NT	NT
				◇1	◇1				◇1					◇1	◇1			◇1		◇1	◇1				
		A		B	C					A		D		E	C		F		A		C				
				⚲										⚲											
Manchester Airport 85 ✈	d			12 58	13 03				13 30					13 58	14 03			14 30		14 58	15 03				
Heald Green 85	d																								
Buxton 86	d																								
Hazel Grove 86	d																								
Stockport 84	d							13 22									14 21								15 22
Manchester Piccadilly 10 ⛴	d			13 16	13 21			13 35	13 46					14 16	14 21		14 35	14 46		15 16	15 21				15 35
Manchester Oxford Road	d			13 19				13 38	13 49					14 19			14 38	14 49		15 19					15 38
Deansgate ⛴	d							13 40	13 51								14 40	14 51							15 40
Rochdale 41	d																								
Manchester Victoria ⛴	d	13 00			13a35	13 12	13 25			14 00	14 12				14a35	14 25			15 00		15a35	15 12		15 25	
Salford Central	d																								
Salford Crescent	a	13 06				13 16	13 29	13 44	13 54	14 06	14 16					14 29	14 44	14 54	15 06			15 16		15 29	15 44
	d	13 08				13 17	13 30	13 44	13 55	14 08	14 17					14 30	14 44	14 55	15 08			15 17		15 30	15 44
Swinton	d					13 23					14 23											15 23			
Moorside	d					13 26					14 26											15 26			
Walkden	d					13 29					14 29											15 29			
Atherton	d					13 35					14 35											15 35			
Hag Fold	d					13 37					14 37											15 37			
Daisy Hill	d					13 40					14 40											15 40			
Kearsley	d																								
Farnworth	d																								
Moses Gate	d																								
Bolton	a	13 19		13 32			13 41	13 54	14 05	14 19				14 32		14 40	14 54	15 05	15 19	15 32				15 40	15 54
	d			13 33			13 41	13 55	14 05					14 33		14 40	14 55	15 05		15 33				15 40	15 55
Westhoughton	d							14 02									15 02								16 02
Hindley	d					13 45		14 06			14 45						15 06					15 45			16 06
Ince	d					13 48					14 48											15 48			
Wigan North Western	a																								
Wigan Wallgate	a					13 53		14 11			14 53						15 11					15 53			16 11
	d							14 13									15 13								16 13
Pemberton	d																								
Orrell	d																								
Upholland	d																								
Rainford	d																								
Kirkby	a																								
Gathurst	d							14 17									15 17								16 17
Appley Bridge	d							14 21									15 21								16 21
Parbold	d							14 25									15 25								16 25
Hoscar	d																								
Burscough Bridge	d							14 29									15 29								16 29
New Lane	d																								
Bescar Lane	d																								
Meols Cop	d							14 37									15 37								16 37
Southport	a							14 44									15 44								16 44
Lostock	d						13 46									14 45								15 45	
Horwich Parkway	d						13 50		14 12							14 49		15 12						15 49	
Blackrod	d						13 53									14 52								15 52	
Adlington (Lancashire)	d						13 57									14 56								15 56	
Chorley	d			13 44			14 02		14 19					14 44		15 01		15 19		15 44				16 01	
Buckshaw Parkway	d						14 06		14 23							15 05		15 23						16 05	
Leyland	d						14 13									15 13								16 12	
Preston 8 65,97	a			13 57			14 18		14 33					14 57		15 18		15 33		15 57				16 18	
	d			14 00			14 20		14 35					15 00		15 20		15 35		16 00				16 20	
Kirkham & Wesham 97	a						14 29									15 29								16 29	
Poulton-le-Fylde 97	a						14 37		14 52							15 37		15 52						16 37	
Layton 97	a						14 42									15 43								16 42	
Blackpool North 97	a						14 47		15 01							15 48		16 01						16 47	
Lancaster 6 65	a			14 15										15 15						16 15					
	d			14 16								14 27		15 16						16 16					
Oxenholme Lake District 65	a			14 30										15 30											
Windermere 83	a																								
Carnforth	d											14a59								16 24					
Silverdale	d																			16 30					
Arnside	d																			16 34					
Grange-over-Sands	d																			16 40					
Kents Bank	d																			16 43					
Cark	d																			16 48					
Ulverston	d																			16 56					
Dalton	d																			17 04					
Roose	d																			17 10					
Barrow-in-Furness	a																			17 19					

A To Clitheroe
B To Glasgow Central
C To Newcastle
D To Leeds
E To Edinburgh
F From Chester

The Sunday service between Manchester Victoria and Wigan Wallgate via Atherton is funded by GMITA and will operate whilst funding exists

Table 82

Sundays
from 1 April

Manchester - Bolton - Wigan, Kirkby, Southport, Preston, Blackpool North and Barrow-in-Furness

Network Diagram - see first Page of Table 82

	TP ◇1	NT A	TP ◇1 B 🍴	TP ◇1 C	NT	NT	NT D		TP ◇1	NT A	NT	NT	NT E	TP ◇1 F 🍴	TP ◇1 C	NT	NT		TP ◇1	NT A	TP ◇1 B 🍴		TP ◇1 G	NT
Manchester Airport 85 ✈ d	15 30		15 58	16 03					16 30					16 58	17 03				17 30		17 58		18 03	
Heald Green 85 d																								
Buxton 86 d																								
Hazel Grove 86 d																								
Stockport 84 d							16 21										17 22							
Manchester Piccadilly 10 ⇌ d	15 46		16 16	16 21			16 35		16 46					17 16	17 21		17 35		17 46		18 16		18 21	
Manchester Oxford Road d	15 49		16 19				16 38		16 49					17 19			17 38		17 49		18 19			
Deansgate ⇌ d	15 51						16 40		16 51								17 40		17 51					
Rochdale 41 d																								
Manchester Victoria ⇌ d		16 00		16a35	16 12	16 25				17 00	17 12				17a35	17 25				18 00			18a35	18 12
Salford Central d																								
Salford Crescent a	15 54	16 06			16 16	16 29	16 44		16 54	17 06	17 16					17 29	17 44		17 54	18 06				18 16
d	15 55	16 08			16 17	16 30	16 44		16 55	17 08	17 17					17 30	17 44		17 55	18 08				18 17
Swinton d					16 23						17 23													18 23
Moorside d					16 26						17 26													18 26
Walkden d					16 29						17 29													18 29
Atherton d					16 35						17 35													18 35
Hag Fold d					16 37						17 37													18 37
Daisy Hill d					16 40						17 40													18 40
Kearsley d																								
Farnworth d																								
Moses Gate d																								
Bolton a	16 05	16 19	16 32			16 40	16 54		17 05	17 19				17 32		17 40	17 54		18 05	18 19	18 32			
d	16 05		16 33			16 40	16 55		17 05					17 33		17 40	17 55		18 05		18 33			
Westhoughton d							17 02										18 02							
Hindley d					16 45		17 06				17 45						18 06							18 45
Ince d					16 48						17 48													18 48
Wigan North Western a																								
Wigan Wallgate a					16 53		17 11				17 53						18 11							18 53
d							17 13										18 13							
Pemberton d																								
Orrell d																								
Upholland d																								
Rainford d																								
Kirkby a																								
Gathurst d							17 17										18 17							
Appley Bridge d							17 21										18 21							
Parbold d							17 25										18 25							
Hoscar d																								
Burscough Bridge d							17 29										18 29							
New Lane d																								
Bescar Lane d																								
Meols Cop d							17 37										18 37							
Southport a							17 44										18 44							
Lostock d						16 45										17 45								
Horwich Parkway d	16 12					16 49			17 12							17 49			18 12					
Blackrod d						16 52										17 52								
Adlington (Lancashire) d						16 56										17 56								
Chorley d	16 19		16 44			17 01			17 19					17 44		18 01			18 19		18 44			
Buckshaw Parkway d	16 23					17 05			17 23							18 05			18 23					
Leyland d						17 12										18 12								
Preston 8 65,97 a	16 33		16 57			17 18			17 33					17 57		18 18			18 33		18 57			
d	16 35		17 00			17 20			17 35					18 00		18 20			18 35		19 00	19 06		
Kirkham & Wesham 97 a						17 29										18 29								
Poulton-le-Fylde 97 a	16 52					17 37			17 52							18 37			18 52					
Layton 97 a						17 42										18 42								
Blackpool North 97 a	17 01					17 47			18 01							18 47			19 01					
Lancaster 6 65 a			17 15											18 15							19 15	19 22		
d			17 16									17 30	18 04	18 16							19 16	19 22		
Oxenholme Lake District 65 a			17 30											18 30							19 30			
Windermere 83 a																								
Carnforth d												17 40	18a13									19 31		
Silverdale d												17 46										19 37		
Arnside d												17 51										19 41		
Grange-over-Sands d												17 57										19 46		
Kents Bank d												18 00										19 50		
Cark d												18 04										19 54		
Ulverston d												18 12										20 02		
Dalton d												18 21										20 10		
Roose d												18 27										20 16		
Barrow-in-Furness a												18 34										20 26		

A To Clitheroe
B To Edinburgh
C To Newcastle
D From Chester
E From Morecambe to Leeds
F To Glasgow Central
G To Middlesbrough

The Sunday service between Manchester Victoria and Wigan Wallgate via Atherton is funded by GMITA and will operate whilst funding exists

Table 82

Sundays
from 1 April

Manchester - Bolton - Wigan, Kirkby, Southport, Preston, Blackpool North and Barrow-in-Furness

Network Diagram - see first Page of Table 82

		NT	NT	TP	NT	NT	TP	TP	NT	NT	TP	NT	TP	NT	NT	TP	NT	TP	TP	NT	NT	TP
				◇1			◇1	◇1			◇1		◇1			◇1		◇1	◇1			◇1
			A		B	C		D				B	E		A		B	F	G			
Manchester Airport 85 ✈	d			18 30			18 58	19 03			19 30		20 03			20 30		21 03				21 30
Heald Green 85	d																					
Buxton 86	d																					
Hazel Grove 86	d																					
Stockport 84	d		18 21							19 22					20 21						21 22	
Manchester Piccadilly 10 🚊	d		18 35	18 46			19 16	19 21		19 35	19 46		20 21		20 35	20 46		21 21			21 35	21 46
Manchester Oxford Road	d		18 38	18 49			19 19			19 38	19 49				20 38	20 49					21 38	21 49
Deansgate 🚊	d		18 40	18 51						19 40	19 51				20 40	20 51					21 40	21 51
Rochdale 41	d																					
Manchester Victoria 🚊	d	18 25			19 00			19a35	19 25			20 00	20a35	20 25			21 00	21a35		21 25		
Salford Central	d																					
Salford Crescent	a	18 29	18 44	18 54	19 06				19 29	19 44	19 54	20 06		20 29	20 44	20 54	21 06			21 29	21 44	21 54
	d	18 30	18 44	18 55	19 08				19 30	19 44	19 55	20 08		20 30	20 44	20 55	21 08			21 30	21 44	21 55
Swinton	d																					
Moorside	d																					
Walkden	d																					
Atherton	d																					
Hag Fold	d																					
Daisy Hill	d																					
Kearsley	d																					
Farnworth	d																					
Moses Gate	d																					
Bolton	a	18 40	18 54	19 05	19 19		19 32		19 40	19 54	20 05	20 18		20 40	20 54	21 05	21 19			21 40	21 54	22 05
	d	18 40	18 55	19 05			19 33		19 40	19 55	20 05			20 40	20 55	21 05				21 40	21 55	22 05
Westhoughton	d		19 02							20 02					21 02						22 02	
Hindley	d		19 06							20 06					21 06						22 06	
Ince	d																					
Wigan North Western	a																					
Wigan Wallgate	a		19 11							20 11					21 11						22 13	
	d		19 13							20 13					21 13							
Pemberton	d																					
Orrell	d																					
Upholland	d																					
Rainford	d																					
Kirkby	a																					
Gathurst	d		19 17							20 17					21 17							
Appley Bridge	d		19 21							20 21					21 21							
Parbold	d		19 25							20 25					21 25							
Hoscar	d																					
Burscough Bridge	d		19 29							20 29					21 29							
New Lane	d																					
Bescar Lane	d																					
Meols Cop	d		19 37							20 37					21 37							
Southport	a		19 44							20 44					21 44							
Lostock	d	18 45							19 45					20 45						21 45		
Horwich Parkway	d	18 49		19 12					19 49		20 12			20 49		21 12				21 49		
Blackrod	d	18 52							19 52					20 52						21 52		
Adlington (Lancashire)	d	18 56							19 56					20 56						21 56		
Chorley	d	19 01		19 19			19 44		20 01		20 19			21 01		21 19				22 01		22 17
Buckshaw Parkway	d	19 05		19 23					20 05		20 23			21 05		21 23				22 05		
Leyland	d	19 14							20 14					21 12						22 12		
Preston 8 65,97	a	19 19		19 33			19 57		20 19		20 33			21 18		21 33				22 18		22 28
	d	19 21		19 35			20 06		20 21		20 35			21 20		21 35				22 20		22 29
Kirkham & Wesham 97	a	19 30							20 30					21 29						22 29		
Poulton-le-Fylde 97	a	19 38		19 52					20 38		20 52			21 37		21 52				22 37		22 46
Layton 97	a	19 42							20 43					21 42						22 42		
Blackpool North 97	a	19 47		20 01					20 48		21 01			21 47		22 01				22 47		22 55
Lancaster 6 65	a						20 21															
	d					20 20	20 22												21 23			
Oxenholme Lake District 65	a																					
Windermere 83	a																					
Carnforth	d					20a29	20 30												21 31			
Silverdale	d																		21 37			
Arnside	d						20 39												21 41			
Grange-over-Sands	d						20 44												21 47			
Kents Bank	d																		21 50			
Cark	d																		21 55			
Ulverston	d						20 57												22 02			
Dalton	d																		22 10			
Roose	d																		22 16			
Barrow-in-Furness	a						21 17												22 26			

A From Chester
B To Clitheroe
C From Morecambe to Leeds
D To Newcastle
E To Scarborough
F To York
G From Windermere

The Sunday service between Manchester Victoria and Wigan Wallgate via Atherton is funded by GMITA and will operate whilst funding exists

Table 82

Sundays
from 1 April

Manchester - Bolton - Wigan, Kirkby, Southport, Preston, Blackpool North and Barrow-in-Furness

Network Diagram - see first Page of Table 82

			NT	NT	NT	NT	TP	TP
							◇1	◇1
			A		B	C		D
Manchester Airport	85 ✈	d				22 27	22 30	23 22
Heald Green	85	d						
Buxton	86	d						
Hazel Grove	86	d						
Stockport	84	d			22 21			
Manchester Piccadilly 10	⇌	d			22 35	22 41	22 46	23 39
Manchester Oxford Road		d			22 38	22 45	22 49	
Deansgate	⇌	d			22 40	22a47	22 51	
Rochdale	41	d						
Manchester Victoria	⇌	d	22 00					23a52
Salford Central		d						
Salford Crescent		a	22 06		22 44		22 54	
		d	22 08		22 44		22 55	
Swinton		d						
Moorside		d						
Walkden		d						
Atherton		d						
Hag Fold		d						
Daisy Hill		d						
Kearsley		d						
Farnworth		d						
Moses Gate		d						
Bolton		a	22 19		22 54		23 05	
		d			22 55		23 05	
Westhoughton		d			23 02			
Hindley		d			23 06			
Ince		d						
Wigan North Western		a						
Wigan Wallgate		a			23 13			
		d						
Pemberton		d						
Orrell		d						
Upholland		d						
Rainford		d						
Kirkby		a						
Gathurst		d						
Appley Bridge		d						
Parbold		d						
Hoscar		d						
Burscough Bridge		d						
New Lane		d						
Bescar Lane		d						
Meols Cop		d						
Southport		a						
Lostock		d					23 10	
Horwich Parkway		d					23 14	
Blackrod		d					23 17	
Adlington (Lancashire)		d					23 20	
Chorley		d					23 25	
Buckshaw Parkway		d					23 28	
Leyland		d					23 34	
Preston 8	65,97	a					23 42	
		d					23 47	
Kirkham & Wesham	97	a					23 56	
Poulton-le-Fylde	97	a					00 05	
Layton	97	a						
Blackpool North	97	a					00 14	
Lancaster 6	65	a						
		d		22 05				
Oxenholme Lake District	65	a						
Windermere	83	a						
Carnforth		d		22 15				
Silverdale		d		22 21				
Arnside		d		22 26				
Grange-over-Sands		d		22 32				
Kents Bank		d		22 35				
Cark		d		22 39				
Ulverston		d		22 47				
Dalton		d		22 56				
Roose		d		23 02				
Barrow-in-Furness		a		23 09				

A To Blackburn
B From Chester
C To Liverpool Lime Street
D To York

The Sunday service between Manchester Victoria and Wigan Wallgate via Atherton is funded by GMITA and will operate whilst funding exists

Barrow-in-Furness, Blackpool North, Preston, Southport, Kirkby and Wigan - Bolton - Manchester

Network Diagram - see first Page of Table 82

Miles	Miles	Miles	Miles	Miles			NT	TP MX	TP MO	TP MO	NT MX	NT MX	TP	TP	NT	TP	NT	TP	NT	NT
								◇1	◇1	◇1			◇1	◇1		◇1		◇1		
							A		A	B	C	D			H					
—	0	—	—	—	**Barrow-in-Furness**	d								04 35						
—	1¾	—	—	—	Roose	d														
—	6	—	—	—	Dalton	d														
—	9¼	—	—	—	Ulverston	d								04 51						
—	15¼	—	—	—	Cark	d														
—	17¼	—	—	—	Kents Bank	d														
—	19½	—	—	—	Grange-over-Sands	d								05 03						
—	22¾	—	—	—	Arnside	d								05 10						
—	25	—	—	—	Silverdale	d														
—	28¾	—	—	—	Carnforth	d								05 19						
—	—	—	—	—	Windermere 83	d														
—	—	—	—	—	Oxenholme Lake District 65	d														
—	34¾	—	—	—	**Lancaster** 6 65	a								05 28						
—	—	—	—	—		d														
0	—	—	—	—	**Blackpool North** 97	d		22p44	23p03	23p03	23p13	23p13	03 33		04 56			05 39		
1¼	—	—	—	—	Layton 97	d					23p16	23p16								
3¼	—	—	—	—	Poulton-le-Fylde 97	d		22p50	23p09	23p09	23p21	23p21			05 02			05 45		
9¾	—	—	—	—	Kirkham & Wesham 97	d			23p17	23p17	23p30	23p30								
—	55¾	—	—	—	**Preston** 8 65,97	a		23p08	23p28	23p28	23p40	23p40			05 20			06 03		
—	—	—	—	—		d	22p14	23p10	23p28	23p28	23p42	23p42	03u58			05 16		06 05		
21½	59¾	—	—	—	Leyland	d	22p34		23p34	23p34	23p48	23p48						06 10		
—	—	—	—	—	Buckshaw Parkway	d		23p17		23p38	23p52	23p52								
26	64¼	—	—	—	Chorley	d	22p49	23p21		23p42	23p57	23p57				05 26		06 16		
29	67¼	—	—	—	Adlington (Lancashire)	d	22p55			23p46	00 03	00 03								
31	69¼	—	—	—	Blackrod	d	23p00			23p50	00 06	00 06						06 22		
32½	70¾	—	—	—	Horwich Parkway	d	23p04	23p28		23p53	00 10	00 10				05 33		06 26		
34½	72¾	—	—	—	Lostock	d	23p10			23p57	00 14	00 14						06 30		
—	—	0	—	—	**Southport**	d														
—	—	1¼	—	—	Meols Cop	d														
—	—	4½	—	—	Bescar Lane	d														
—	—	6½	—	—	New Lane	d														
—	—	7¾	—	—	Burscough Bridge	d														
—	—	9¼	—	—	Hoscar	d														
—	—	10¾	—	—	Parbold	d														
—	—	13	—	—	Appley Bridge	d														
—	—	14¾	—	—	Gathurst	d														
—	—	—	0	—	**Kirkby**	d														
—	—	—	5¼	—	Rainford	d														
—	—	—	7¼	—	Upholland	d														
—	—	—	8½	—	Orrell	d														
—	—	—	10½	—	Pemberton	d														
—	—	17½	12¼	—	**Wigan Wallgate**	a														
—	—	—	—	—		d											06 03		06 31	06 36
—	—	—	—	0	Wigan North Western	d														
—	—	18½	13¼	0¾	Ince	d											06 06			06 39
—	—	20	14¾	—	Hindley	d											06 09		06 36	06 42
—	—	22½	—	—	Westhoughton	d													06 41	
37½	75¾	27	—	—	**Bolton**	a	23p24	23p34	00 01	00 02	00 19	00 20				05 42		06 34	06 52	
—	—	—	—	—		d	23p25	23p35	00 02	00 02	00 20	00 20	04u31			05 43		06 35	06 53	
38¼	76½	27¾	—	—	Moses Gate	d														
39¾	78	29¼	—	—	Farnworth	d														
40½	78¾	30	—	—	Kearsley	d														
—	—	—	17¼	—	Daisy Hill	d											06 13			06 46
—	—	—	17½	—	Hag Fold	d											06 16			06 49
—	—	—	18¾	—	Atherton	d											06 19			06 52
—	—	—	22¼	—	Walkden	d											06 24			06 58
—	—	—	24	—	Moorside	d											06 28			07 01
—	—	—	24¾	—	Swinton	d											06 30			07 04
46½	84¾	36	28¾	—	**Salford Crescent**	a	23p49	23p47								05 55	06 38	06 47	07 05	07 11
—	—	—	—	—		d	23p50	23p47								05 55	06 38	06 47	07 08	07 11
—	—	—	29¾	—	Salford Central	d											06 41			07 14
—	—	—	30½	—	**Manchester Victoria** ⇌	a	00 01				00 37	00 39					06 46			07 20
—	—	—	—	—	Rochdale 41	a														
48	86¼	37½	—	—	Deansgate ⇌	a												06 51	07 11	
48¼	86½	37¾	—	—	**Manchester Oxford Road**	a												06 52	07 13	
48¾	87	38¼	—	—	**Manchester Piccadilly** 10 ⇌	a		23p53	00 16	00 18			04 48			06 01		06 56	07 17	
—	—	—	—	—	Stockport 84	a													07 34	
—	—	—	—	—	Hazel Grove 86	a													07 45	
—	—	—	—	—	Buxton 86	a														
57	95¼	46½	—	—	Heald Green 85	a		00 16										07 10		
58½	96¾	48	—	—	**Manchester Airport** 85 ✈	a		00 24	00 30	00 32			05 07			06 18		07 17		

A from 9 January until 13 February
B until 2 January and then from 20 February
C until 30 December and then from 27 March
D from 3 January until 23 March
H To Colne

The Sunday service between Wigan Wallgate and Manchester Victoria via Atherton is funded by GMITA and will operate whilst funding exists

Barrow-in-Furness, Blackpool North, Preston, Southport, Kirkby and Wigan - Bolton - Manchester

Network Diagram - see first Page of Table 82

		NT	TP	NT	NT	NT	NT	TP	NT	NT	NT	NT	NT	NT	NT	TP	TP	NT	NT	NT	NT
			◇1					◇1								◇1	◇1				
		A	B			C	D		E				F		D	B					D
			🛒					🛒								🛒	🛒				
Barrow-in-Furness	d		05 31													06 20					
Roose	d															06 24					
Dalton	d															06 31					
Ulverston	d		05 47													06 39					
Cark	d															06 47					
Kents Bank	d															06 51					
Grange-over-Sands	d		05 59													06 55					
Arnside	d		06 05													07 01					
Silverdale	d															07 05					
Carnforth	d		06 15			06 43										07 12					
Windermere 83	d																				
Oxenholme Lake District 65	d																				
Lancaster 6 65	a		06 23			06 52										07 21					
	d		06 23													07 22					
Blackpool North 97	d				06 19			06 40				06 53	07 02				07 10			07 18	
Layton 97	d				06 22			06 43									07 13			07 21	
Poulton-le-Fylde 97	d				06 27			06 47					07 08				07 17			07 26	
Kirkham & Wesham 97	d				06 36			06 56									07 26			07 35	
Preston 8 65,97	a		06 42		06 46			07 07				07 15	07 28			07 41	07 37			07 46	
	d		06 44		06 48			07 09				07 17	07 30			07 47				07 47	
Leyland	d				06 53							07 22	07 35							07 53	
Buckshaw Parkway	d				06 58							07 28								07 58	
Chorley	d		06 53		07 02			07 18				07 32				07 56				08 02	
Adlington (Lancashire)	d				07 07							07 37								08 07	
Blackrod	d				07 11							07 41								08 11	
Horwich Parkway	d		07 00		07 15			07 26				07 45								08 15	
Lostock	d				07 20			07 30				07 49								08 20	
Southport	d			06 23						06 53								07 21			
Meols Cop	d			06 28						06 58								07 26			
Bescar Lane	d									07 03											
New Lane	d									07 07											
Burscough Bridge	d			06 36						07 09								07 34			
Hoscar	d									07 13											
Parbold	d			06 41						07 16								07 39			
Appley Bridge	d			06 45						07 20								07 43			
Gathurst	d			06 49						07 23								07 47			
Kirkby	d													07 11							
Rainford	d													07 19							
Upholland	d													07 23							
Orrell	d													07 27							
Pemberton	d													07 30							
Wigan Wallgate	a			06 54						07 29				07 35				07 51			
	d			06 55					07 15	07 29				07 37				07 53	08 00		
Wigan North Western	d										07 22		07a50								
Ince	d								07 18		07 25			07 40							
Hindley	d								07 21		07 29			07 43				07 58			
Westhoughton	d			07 03							07 33							08 03			
Bolton	a		07 08	07 11	07 25			07 34			07 42	07 54				08 08		08 11		08 25	
	d	06 56	07 08	07 12	07 25		07 30	07 35			07 43	07 55			07 59	08 08		08 12		08 25	08 31
Moses Gate	d	06 59									07 46				08 02						
Farnworth	d	07 01									07 48				08 04						
Kearsley	d	07 03									07 50				08 06						
Daisy Hill	d								07 26	07 39				07 47					08 07		
Hag Fold	d								07 29					07 50							
Atherton	d								07 32	07 43				07 53					08 12		
Walkden	d								07 38					07 59					08 18		
Moorside	d								07 41					08 03							
Swinton	d								07 44					08 06							
Salford Crescent	a	07 15		07 24	07 38		07 43	07 47	07 51	07 59	08 02	08 07		08 13	08 17			08 24	08 29	08 38	08 43
	d	07 15		07 25	07 38		07 43	07 47	07 51	08 00	08 02	08 08		08 13	08 17			08 25	08 30	08 38	08 44
Salford Central	d	07 19			07 41		07 46		07 55	08 03	08 05			08 16	08 20				08 32	08 41	08 46
Manchester Victoria ⇌	a	07 26			07 47		07 53		08 00	08 08	08 12			08 20	08 25				08 38	08 48	08 52
Rochdale 41	a													08 51							
Deansgate ⇌	a			07 28				07 51				08 11						08 28			
Manchester Oxford Road	a		07 23	07 30				07 52				08 14				08 23		08 31			
Manchester Piccadilly 10 ⇌	a		07 27	07 34				07 56				08 18				08 27		08 35			
Stockport 84	a											08 34									
Hazel Grove 86	a											08 50									
Buxton 86	a																				
Heald Green 85	a							08 10										08 47			
Manchester Airport 85 ✈	a		07 47	07 53				08 17								08 47		08 53			

A From Blackburn
B 🛒 from Preston
C From Skipton
D From Clitheroe
E To Stalybridge
F To Liverpool Lime Street

The Sunday service between Wigan Wallgate and Manchester Victoria via Atherton is funded by GMITA and will operate whilst funding exists

Barrow-in-Furness, Blackpool North, Preston, Southport, Kirkby and Wigan - Bolton - Manchester

Network Diagram - see first Page of Table 82

		TP	TP	NT	NT	NT	NT	NT	NT	TP	NT	NT	NT	NT	NT	NT	TP	NT	NT	NT	NT	NT	TP
		◇1	◇1							◇1							◇1						◇1
			A	B					C	D	E				F	G					C		H
		[trolley]	[trolley]							[trolley]							[trolley]						[trolley]
Barrow-in-Furness	d			07 00						07 29	08 00												
Roose	d			07 04							08 04												
Dalton	d			07 10						07 38	08 10												
Ulverston	d			07 19						07 46	08 19												
Cark	d			07 26						07 54	08 27												
Kents Bank	d			07 32							08 32												
Grange-over-Sands	d			07 36						08 01	08 36												
Arnside	d			07 42						08 07	08 42												
Silverdale	d			07 47						08 11	08 47												
Carnforth	d			07 55						08 18	08 54												
Windermere 83	d																						
Oxenholme Lake District 65	d																						09 11
Lancaster 6 65	a			08 04						08 26	09 07												09 25
	d		07 47	08 05						08 27													09 26
Blackpool North 97	d	07 36												08 20			08 44						
Layton 97	d	07 39												08 23									
Poulton-le-Fylde 97	d	07 43												08 28			08 50						
Kirkham & Wesham 97	d	07 52												08 37									
Preston 8 65,97	a	08 03	08 07	08 30						08 45				08 47			09 08						09 45
	d	08 12						08 17		08 47				08 49	09 04		09 10			09 23			09 47
Leyland	d							08 23						08 54	09 09					09 29			
Buckshaw Parkway	d							08 28						08 59			09 17			09 33			
Chorley	d	08 22						08 35		08 56				09 03			09 21			09 38			09 56
Adlington (Lancashire)	d							08 39						09 08									
Blackrod	d							08 43						09 12									
Horwich Parkway	d							08 47						09 16			09 28			09 46			
Lostock	d							08 50						09 20						09 50			
Southport	d						07 58					08 25							09 02				
Meols Cop	d						08 03					08 30							09 07				
Bescar Lane	d																						
New Lane	d																						
Burscough Bridge	d						08 11					08 38							09 15				
Hoscar	d																						
Parbold	d						08 16					08 43							09 20				
Appley Bridge	d						08 20					08 47							09 24				
Gathurst	d						08 23					08 50							09 27				
Kirkby	d												08 21										
Rainford	d												08 29										
Upholland	d												08 33										
Orrell	d												08 36										
Pemberton	d												08 39										
Wigan Wallgate	a						08 28					08 55	08 45						09 32				
	d				08 13		08 29					08 56	08 50					09 20	09 32			09 46	
Wigan North Western	d					08 20									09a24								
Ince	d				08 16								08 53										
Hindley	d				08 19	08 25	08 34						08 57					09 25	09 37				
Westhoughton	d					08 29						09 04						09 29				09 54	
Bolton	a	08 34				08 38		08 55		09 08		09 12		09 25			09 34	09 38		09 55		10 02	10 08
	d	08 35				08 39		08 56	09 02	09 08		09 13		09 25		09 31	09 35	09 39		09 56	10 00	10 03	10 08
Moses Gate	d					08 42												09 42					
Farnworth	d					08 44												09 44					
Kearsley	d					08 46												09 46					
Daisy Hill	d				08 23		08 39						09 01						09 41				
Hag Fold	d				08 26								09 04										
Atherton	d				08 29		08 43						09 06						09 45				
Walkden	d				08 35		08 49						09 12						09 50				
Moorside	d				08 39								09 15										
Swinton	d				08 42		08 54						09 18						09 55				
Salford Crescent	a	08 47			08 50	08 56	09 02	09 08	09 15			09 25	09 27	09 38		09 43	09 47	09 56	10 03	10 08	10 13	10 15	
	d	08 47			08 50	08 56	09 02	09 09	09 16			09 26	09 27	09 38		09 44	09 47	09 56	10 03	10 09	10 13	10 15	
Salford Central	d				08 53	08 59	09 04		09 18				09 31	09 41		09 46		09 59	10 05		10 16	10 17	
Manchester Victoria ⇌	a				08 59	09 06	09 11		09 26				09 38	09 47		09 52		10 06	10 12		10 22	10 25	
Rochdale 41	a																					10 51	
Deansgate ⇌	a							09 12				09 29					09 51			10 12			
Manchester Oxford Road	a	08 52						09 14		09 23		09 31					09 52			10 14			10 23
Manchester Piccadilly 10 ⇌	a	08 56						09 18		09 27		09 35					09 56			10 18			10 27
Stockport 84	a							09 34												10 34			
Hazel Grove 86	a							09 47												10 47			
Buxton 86	a																						
Heald Green 85	a	09 10															10 10						
Manchester Airport 85 ✈	a	09 19								09 47		09 53					10 17						10 47

A From Edinburgh
B From Millom
C From Blackburn
D [trolley] from Preston
E From Maryport
F To L'pool Sth Pw Hl (Allertn)
G From Clitheroe
H From Glasgow Central

The Sunday service between Wigan Wallgate and Manchester Victoria via Atherton is funded by GMITA and will operate whilst funding exists

Barrow-in-Furness, Blackpool North, Preston, Southport, Kirkby and Wigan - Bolton - Manchester

Network Diagram - see first Page of Table 82

		NT	NT	NT	NT	NT	NT	TP	NT	NT	NT	NT	TP	NT	NT	NT	NT	NT	NT	TP	NT	NT
								◇1					◇1							◇1		
					A	B	C						D	E				A	C			
								⚯					⚯							⚯		
Barrow-in-Furness	d												09 23	10 16								
Roose	d												09 27	10 20								
Dalton	d												09 34	10 26								
Ulverston	d												09 42	10 35								
Cark	d												09 50	10 42								
Kents Bank	d												09 54	10 47								
Grange-over-Sands	d												09 58	10 51								
Arnside	d												10 04	10 57								
Silverdale	d												10 08	11 01								
Carnforth	d					10 02							10 15	11 08								
Windermere	83 d																					
Oxenholme Lake District	65 d																					
Lancaster 6	65 a					10 12							10 25	11 20								
	d												10 26									
Blackpool North	97 d			09 20	09 37			09 43									10 20	10 37		10 44		
Layton	97 d			09 23													10 23					
Poulton-le-Fylde	97 d			09 28				09 49									10 28			10 50		
Kirkham & Wesham	97 d			09 37	09 52												10 37	10 52				
Preston 8	65,97 a			09 47	10 02			10 07					10 45				10 47	11 02		11 08		
	d			09 49	10 04			10 12			10 23		10 47				10 49	11 04		11 10		
Leyland	d			09 54	10 09						10 29						10 54	11 09				
Buckshaw Parkway	d			09 59							10 33						10 59			11 17		
Chorley	d			10 03				10 22			10 38		10 56				11 03			11 21		
Adlington (Lancashire)	d			10 08													11 08					
Blackrod	d			10 12													11 12					
Horwich Parkway	d			10 16							10 46						11 16			11 28		
Lostock	d			10 20							10 50						11 20					
Southport	d	09 24								09 55					10 24							10 55
Meols Cop	d									10 00												11 00
Bescar Lane	d									10 05												11 05
New Lane	d									10 09												11 09
Burscough Bridge	d	09 36								10 11					10 36							11 11
Hoscar	d									10 15												11 15
Parbold	d	09 41								10 18					10 41							11 18
Appley Bridge	d	09 45								10 22					10 45							11 22
Gathurst	d									10 25												11 25
Kirkby	d		09 32													10 32						
Rainford	d		09 40													10 40						
Upholland	d		09 44													10 44						
Orrell	d		09 47													10 47						
Pemberton	d		09 50													10 50						
Wigan Wallgate	a	09 51	09 56							10 30					10 51	10 56						11 30
	d	09 53	09 58						10 20	10 32		10 48			10 53	10 58					11 20	11 32
Wigan North Western	d				10a24													11a24				
Ince	d		10 01													11 01						
Hindley	d	09 58	10 04						10 25	10 37					10 58	11 04					11 25	11 37
Westhoughton	d	10 02							10 29						11 02						11 29	
Bolton	a	10 12		10 25				10 34	10 38		10 55	11 02	11 08		11 12		11 25			11 34	11 38	
	d	10 13		10 25			10 31	10 35	10 39		10 56	11 03	11 08		11 13		11 25		11 31	11 35	11 39	
Moses Gate	d								10 42												11 42	
Farnworth	d								10 44												11 44	
Kearsley	d								10 46												11 46	
Daisy Hill	d		10 09							10 41						11 09						11 41
Hag Fold	d		10 12													11 12						
Atherton	d		10 15							10 45						11 15						11 45
Walkden	d		10 20							10 50						11 20						11 50
Moorside	d		10 24													11 24						
Swinton	d		10 26							10 55						11 26						11 55
Salford Crescent	a	10 25	10 34	10 38			10 43	10 47	10 56	11 02	11 08	11 15			11 25	11 34	11 38		11 43	11 47	11 56	12 02
	d	10 26	10 34	10 38			10 44	10 47	10 56	11 03	11 09	11 15			11 26	11 34	11 38		11 44	11 47	11 56	12 03
Salford Central	d		10 36	10 41			10 46		10 59	11 05		11 17				11 36	11 41		11 46		11 59	12 05
Manchester Victoria	⛴ a		10 43	10 47			10 52		11 06	11 11		11 25				11 43	11 47		11 52		12 06	12 11
Rochdale	41 a											11 51										
Deansgate	⛴ a	10 29						10 51			11 12				11 29					11 51		
Manchester Oxford Road	a	10 31						10 52			11 14		11 23		11 31					11 52		
Manchester Piccadilly 10	⛴ a	10 35						10 56			11 18		11 27		11 35					11 56		
Stockport	84 a										11 34											
Hazel Grove	86 a										11 45											
Buxton	86 a																					
Heald Green	85 a							11 10												12 10		
Manchester Airport	85 ✈ a	10 53						11 17					11 50		11 53					12 17		

A To L'pool Sth Pw Hl (Allertn)
B From Leeds to Morecambe
C From Clitheroe
D ⚯ from Preston
E From Sellafield

The Sunday service between Wigan Wallgate and Manchester Victoria via Atherton is funded by GMITA and will operate whilst funding exists

Barrow-in-Furness, Blackpool North, Preston, Southport, Kirkby and Wigan - Bolton - Manchester

Network Diagram - see first Page of Table 82

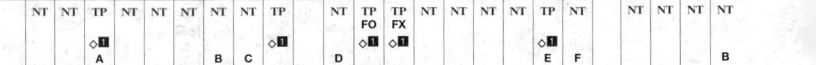

		NT	NT	TP	NT	NT	NT	NT	NT	TP	NT	TP	TP	NT	NT	NT	NT	TP	NT	NT	NT	NT	NT
												FO	FX										
				◇1						◇1		◇1	◇1					◇1					
				A				B	C		D							E	F				B
				🚲								🚲	🚲					🚲					
Barrow-in-Furness	d									11 25									12 11				
Roose	d																		12 15				
Dalton	d																		12 21				
Ulverston	d									11 41									12 29				
Cark	d																		12 37				
Kents Bank	d																		12 41				
Grange-over-Sands	d									11 53									12 45				
Arnside	d									11 59									12 51				
Silverdale	d																		12 55				
Carnforth	d								12 02	12 09									13 03				
Windermere 83	d			10 49																			
Oxenholme Lake District 65	d			11 09														12 10					
Lancaster 6 65	a			11 26					12 11	12 18								12 26	13 16				
	d			11 26						12 18								12 26					
Blackpool North 97	d						11 20	11 37				11 44	11 44									12 20	12 37
Layton 97	d						11 23															12 23	
Poulton-le-Fylde 97	d						11 28					11 50	11 50									12 28	
Kirkham & Wesham 97	d						11 37	11 52														12 37	12 52
Preston 8 65,97	a			11 45			11 47	12 02		12 37		12 08	12 08					12 45				12 47	13 02
	d	11 23		11 47			11 49	12 04				12 10	12 10			12 23		12 47				12 49	13 04
Leyland	d	11 29					11 54	12 09								12 29						12 54	13 09
Buckshaw Parkway	d	11 33					11 58					12 17	12 17			12 33						12 59	
Chorley	d	11 38		11 56			12 03					12 21	12 21			12 38		12 56				13 03	
Adlington (Lancashire)	d						12 08															13 08	
Blackrod	d						12 11															13 12	
Horwich Parkway	d	11 46					12 15					12 28	12 28			12 46						13 16	
Lostock	d	11 50					12 21									12 50						13 20	
Southport	d				11 24										12 00					12 24			
Meols Cop	d														12 05								
Bescar Lane	d																						
New Lane	d																						
Burscough Bridge	d				11 36										12 13					12 36			
Hoscar	d																						
Parbold	d				11 41										12 18					12 41			
Appley Bridge	d				11 45										12 22					12 45			
Gathurst	d														12 25								
Kirkby	d					11 32															12 32		
Rainford	d					11 40															12 40		
Upholland	d					11 44															12 44		
Orrell	d					11 47															12 47		
Pemberton	d					11 50															12 50		
Wigan Wallgate	a				11 51	11 56									12 30					12 51	12 56		
	d		11 48		11 53	11 58								12 20	12 32		12 48			12 53	12 58		
Wigan North Western	d							12a24															13a24
Ince	d					12 01															13 01		
Hindley	d				11 58	12 04								12 25	12 37					12 58	13 04		
Westhoughton	d				12 02									12 29						13 02			
Bolton	a	11 55	12 02	12 08	12 12		12 25					12 34	12 34	12 38		12 55	13 02	13 08		13 12		13 25	
	d	11 56	12 03	12 08	12 13		12 25				12 31	12 35	12 35	12 39		12 56	13 03	13 08		13 13		13 25	
Moses Gate	d													12 42									
Farnworth	d													12 44									
Kearsley	d													12 46									
Daisy Hill	d					12 09									12 41						13 09		
Hag Fold	d					12 12															13 12		
Atherton	d					12 15									12 45						13 15		
Walkden	d					12 20									12 50						13 20		
Moorside	d					12 24															13 24		
Swinton	d					12 26									12 55						13 26		
Salford Crescent	a	12 08	12 15		12 25	12 34	12 38				12 43	12 47	12 47	12 56	13 02	13 08	13 15			13 25	13 34	13 38	
	d	12 09	12 15		12 26	12 34	12 38				12 44	12 47	12 47	12 56	13 03	13 09	13 15			13 26	13 34	13 38	
Salford Central	d		12 17			12 36	12 41				12 46			12 59	13 05		13 17				13 36	13 41	
Manchester Victoria 🚋	a		12 25			12 43	12 47				12 52			13 06	13 11		13 25				13 43	13 47	
Rochdale 41	a		12 51														13 51						
Deansgate 🚋	a	12 12			12 29							12 51	12 51			13 12				13 29			
Manchester Oxford Road	a	12 14		12 23	12 31							12 52	12 52			13 14		13 23		13 31			
Manchester Piccadilly 10 🚋	a	12 18		12 27	12 35							12 56	12 56			13 18		13 27		13 35			
Stockport 84	a	12 34														13 34							
Hazel Grove 86	a	12 47														13 47							
Buxton 86	a																						
Heald Green 85	a											13 10	13 10										
Manchester Airport 85 ✈	a			12 47	12 53							13 16	13 17					13 47		13 53			

A 🚲 from Preston
B To L'pool Sth Pw Hl (Allertn)
C From Leeds to Heysham Port
D From Clitheroe
E From Edinburgh
F From Carlisle

The Sunday service between Wigan Wallgate and Manchester Victoria via Atherton is funded by GMITA and will operate whilst funding exists

Barrow-in-Furness, Blackpool North, Preston, Southport, Kirkby and Wigan - Bolton - Manchester

Network Diagram - see first Page of Table 82

		NT	TP	NT	NT	NT		NT	TP	NT	TP	TP	NT	NT	NT	NT		TP	NT	NT	NT	NT	TP	NT	NT
											FO	FX													
			◇1						◇1		◇1	◇1						◇1					◇1		
		A							B						C	A							D		
			🛒						🛒									🛒					🛒		
Barrow-in-Furness	d										13 25	13 25												14 16	
Roose	d																							14 20	
Dalton	d																							14 26	
Ulverston	d										13 41	13 41												14 35	
Cark	d																							14 42	
Kents Bank	d																							14 47	
Grange-over-Sands	d										13 53	13 53												14 51	
Arnside	d										13 59	13 59												14 57	
Silverdale	d																							15 01	
Carnforth	d										14 09	14 09												15 07	
Windermere	83 d								12 51																
Oxenholme Lake District	65 d								13 09														14 10		
Lancaster 6	65 a								13 26		14 18	14 18											14 26	15 20	
	d								13 26			14 18											14 26		
Blackpool North	97 d		12 44											13 20	13 37			13 44							
Layton	97 d													13 23											
Poulton-le-Fylde	97 d		12 50											13 28				13 50							
Kirkham & Wesham	97 d													13 37	13 52										
Preston 8	65,97 a		13 08						13 45			14 37		13 47	14 02			14 08					14 45		
	d		13 10			13 23			13 47					13 49	14 04			14 10			14 23		14 47		
Leyland	d					13 29								13 54	14 09						14 29				
Buckshaw Parkway	d		13 17			13 33								13 59				14 17			14 33				
Chorley	d		13 21			13 38			13 56					14 03				14 21			14 38		14 56		
Adlington (Lancashire)	d													14 08											
Blackrod	d													14 11											
Horwich Parkway	d		13 28			13 46								14 15				14 28			14 46				
Lostock	d					13 50								14 21							14 50				
Southport	d				12 54					13 24										14 00					14 24
Meols Cop	d				12 59															14 05					
Bescar Lane	d				13 04																				
New Lane	d				13 08																				
Burscough Bridge	d				13 11					13 36										14 13					14 36
Hoscar	d				13 15																				
Parbold	d				13 18					13 41										14 18					14 41
Appley Bridge	d				13 22					13 45										14 22					14 45
Gathurst	d				13 25															14 25					
Kirkby	d												13 32												
Rainford	d												13 40												
Upholland	d												13 44												
Orrell	d												13 47												
Pemberton	d												13 50												
Wigan Wallgate	a				13 30					13 51			13 56							14 30					14 51
	d			13 20	13 32			13 48		13 53			13 58						14 20	14 32		14 48			14 53
Wigan North Western	d														14a24										
Ince	d												14 01												
Hindley	d			13 25	13 37					13 58			14 04						14 25	14 37					14 58
Westhoughton	d			13 29						14 02									14 29						15 02
Bolton	a		13 34	13 38		13 55		14 02	14 08	14 12				14 26				14 34	14 38		14 55	15 02	15 08		15 12
	d	13 31	13 35	13 39		13 56		14 03	14 08	14 13				14 26		14 31		14 35	14 39		14 56	15 03	15 08		15 13
Moses Gate	d			13 42															14 42						
Farnworth	d			13 44															14 44						
Kearsley	d			13 46															14 46						
Daisy Hill	d				13 41								14 09							14 41					
Hag Fold	d												14 12												
Atherton	d				13 45								14 15							14 45					
Walkden	d				13 50								14 20							14 50					
Moorside	d												14 24												
Swinton	d				13 55								14 26							14 55					
Salford Crescent	a	13 43	13 47	13 56	14 02	14 08		14 15		14 25			14 34	14 38		14 43		14 47	14 56	15 02	15 08	15 15			15 25
	d	13 44	13 47	13 56	14 03	14 09		14 15		14 26			14 34	14 38		14 44		14 47	14 56	15 03	15 09	15 15			15 26
Salford Central	d	13 46		13 59	14 05			14 17					14 36	14 41		14 46			14 59	15 05		15 17			
Manchester Victoria 🚇	a	13 52		14 06	14 11			14 25					14 43	14 47		14 52			15 06	15 11		15 25			
Rochdale	41 a							14 51														15 51			
Deansgate 🚇	a		13 51			14 12				14 29								14 51			15 12				15 29
Manchester Oxford Road	a		13 52			14 14			14 23	14 31								14 52			15 14		15 23		15 31
Manchester Piccadilly 10 🚇	a		13 56			14 18			14 27	14 35								14 56			15 18		15 27		15 35
Stockport	84 a					14 34															15 34				
Hazel Grove	86 a					14 47															15 50				
Buxton	86 a																								
Heald Green	85 a		14 10															15 10							
Manchester Airport	85 ✈ a		14 17						14 47	14 53								15 17					15 47		15 53

A From Clitheroe
B 🛒 from Preston
C To L'pool Sth Pw Hl (Allertn)
D From Edinburgh

The Sunday service between Wigan Wallgate and Manchester Victoria via Atherton is funded by GMITA and will operate whilst funding exists

Barrow-in-Furness, Blackpool North, Preston, Southport, Kirkby and Wigan - Bolton - Manchester

Network Diagram - see first Page of Table 82

		NT		NT	NT	NT	TP	NT	NT	NT	NT	TP		NT	NT	TP	NT	NT	NT	NT	TP	NT		NT	NT
																FO									
							◇1					◇1				◇1					◇1				
					A	B						C			D		B			E				F	
							🛒					🛒									🛒				
Barrow-in-Furness	d															15 24									
Roose	d																								
Dalton	d																								
Ulverston	d															15 40									
Cark	d															15 47									
Kents Bank	d																								
Grange-over-Sands	d															15 54									
Arnside	d															16 00									
Silverdale	d																								
Carnforth	d														15 38	16 09									
Windermere 83	d																								
Oxenholme Lake District 65	d																								
Lancaster 6 65	a														15 47	16 18									
	d											15 22				16 18									
Blackpool North 97	d			14 20	14 37		14 44												15 20	15 37	15 44				
Layton 97	d			14 23															15 23						
Poulton-le-Fylde 97	d			14 28			14 50												15 28		15 50				
Kirkham & Wesham 97	d			14 37	14 52														15 37	15 52					
Preston 8 65,97	a			14 47	15 02		15 08					15 41				16 37			15 47	16 02	16 08				
	d			14 49	15 04		15 10			15 23		15 47							15 49	16 04	16 10				16 23
Leyland	d			14 54	15 09					15 29									15 54	16 09					16 29
Buckshaw Parkway	d			14 59			15 17			15 33									15 59		16 17				16 33
Chorley	d			15 03			15 21			15 38		15 56							16 03		16 21				16 38
Adlington (Lancashire)	d			15 08															16 08						
Blackrod	d			15 12															16 11						
Horwich Parkway	d			15 16			15 28			15 46									16 15		16 28				16 46
Lostock	d			15 20						15 50									16 21						16 50
Southport	d								14 54					15 24										15 58	
Meols Cop	d								14 59															16 03	
Bescar Lane	d								15 04																
New Lane	d								15 08																
Burscough Bridge	d								15 11					15 36										16 11	
Hoscar	d								15 15																
Parbold	d								15 18					15 41										16 16	
Appley Bridge	d								15 22					15 45										16 20	
Gathurst	d								15 25															16 24	
Kirkby	d	14 32																15 32							
Rainford	d	14 40																15 40							
Upholland	d	14 44																15 44							
Orrell	d	14 47																15 47							
Pemberton	d	14 50																15 50							
Wigan Wallgate	a	14 56							15 30					15 51				15 56						16 29	
	d	14 58						15 20	15 32		15 48			15 53				15 58				16 20		16 30	
Wigan North Western	d				15a24															16a24					
Ince	d	15 01																16 01						16 33	
Hindley	d	15 04						15 25	15 37					15 58				16 04				16 25		16 37	
Westhoughton	d							15 29						16 02								16 29			
Bolton	a			15 25			15 34	15 38		15 55	16 02	16 08		16 12					16 25		16 34	16 38			16 55
	d			15 25		15 31	15 35	15 39		15 56	16 03	16 08		16 13			16 17		16 25		16 35	16 39			16 56
Moses Gate	d							15 42														16 42			
Farnworth	d							15 44														16 44			
Kearsley	d							15 46														16 46			
Daisy Hill	d	15 09							15 41									16 09						16 41	
Hag Fold	d	15 12																16 12							
Atherton	d	15 15							15 45									16 15						16 45	
Walkden	d	15 20							15 50									16 20						16 50	
Moorside	d	15 24																16 24							
Swinton	d	15 26							15 55									16 26						16 55	
Salford Crescent	a	15 33		15 38		15 43	15 47	15 56	16 02	16 08	16 15			16 25			16 30	16 34	16 38		16 47	16 56		17 02	17 08
	d	15 34		15 38		15 44	15 47	15 56	16 03	16 09	16 15			16 26			16 30	16 34	16 38		16 47	16 56		17 03	17 09
Salford Central	d	15 36		15 41		15 46		15 59	16 05		16 17						16 33	16 36	16 41			16 59		17 05	
Manchester Victoria ⇌	a	15 43		15 47		15 54		16 06	16 11		16 23						16 41	16 43	16 47			17 06		17 13	
Rochdale 41	a										16 51														
Deansgate ⇌	a						15 51			16 12											16 51				17 15
Manchester Oxford Road	a						15 52			16 14		16 23		16 31							16 52				17 17
Manchester Piccadilly 10 ⇌	a						15 56			16 18		16 27		16 35							16 56				17 21
Stockport 84	a									16 34															17 32
Hazel Grove 86	a									16 43															17 39
Buxton 86	a									17 24															18 19
Heald Green 85	a						16 10					16 40									17 10				
Manchester Airport 85 ✈	a						16 17					16 47		16 53							17 17				

A To L'pool Sth Pw Hl (Allertn)
B From Clitheroe
C From Glasgow Central
D From Leeds to Morecambe
E To Liverpool Lime Street
F To Huddersfield

The Sunday service between Wigan Wallgate and Manchester Victoria via Atherton is funded by GMITA and will operate whilst funding exists

Barrow-in-Furness, Blackpool North, Preston, Southport, Kirkby and Wigan - Bolton - Manchester

Network Diagram - see first Page of Table 82

		NT	TP	TP	NT	NT	NT	NT		NT	NT	TP	NT	NT	NT	NT	TP	NT		NT	NT	NT	TP	TP	NT
			FX																						
			◇1	◇1								◇1					◇1						◇1	◇1	
			A	B						C	D					D						C	A	E	
			🚲	🚲								🚲					🚲						🚲		
Barrow-in-Furness	d		15 24		16 20																			17 21	
Roose	d				16 24																				
Dalton	d				16 30																			17 30	
Ulverston	d		15 40		16 38																			17 38	
Cark	d		15 47		16 46																			17 46	
Kents Bank	d				16 50																				
Grange-over-Sands	d		15 54		16 54																			17 53	
Arnside	d		16 00		17 00																			17 59	
Silverdale	d				17 04																				
Carnforth	d		16 09		17 12																			18 09	
Windermere	83 d																						17 06		
Oxenholme Lake District	65 d			16 07																			17 30		
Lancaster 6	65 a		16 18	16 21	17 26																		17 47	18 20	
	d		16 18	16 22																			17 48		
Blackpool North	97 d							16 20		16 35		16 40					17 20					17 37			
Layton	97 d							16 23				16 44					17 23								
Poulton-le-Fylde	97 d							16 28				16 48					17 27								
Kirkham & Wesham	97 d							16 37		16 52		16 57										17 52			
Preston 8	65,97 a		16 37	16 42				16 47		17 02		17 08					17 45					18 02	18 06		
	d		16 47					16 49		17 04		17 10					17 47				17 56	18 04	18 08		
Leyland	d							16 54		17 09											18 01	18 09			
Buckshaw Parkway	d							16 59				17 17									18 05		18 15		
Chorley	d		16 56					17 03				17 21					17 56				18 10		18 19		
Adlington (Lancashire)	d							17 08													18 15				
Blackrod	d							17 12													18 18				
Horwich Parkway	d							17 16				17 28									18 21		18 26		
Lostock	d							17 20															18 30		
Southport	d					16 24								16 54				17 24							
Meols Cop	d													16 59				17 29							
Bescar Lane	d													17 04											
New Lane	d													17 08											
Burscough Bridge	d					16 36								17 11				17 37							
Hoscar	d													17 15											
Parbold	d					16 41								17 18				17 42							
Appley Bridge	d					16 45								17 22				17 46							
Gathurst	d													17 25											
Kirkby	d						16 32													17 32					
Rainford	d						16 40													17 40					
Upholland	d						16 44													17 44					
Orrell	d						16 47													17 47					
Pemberton	d						16 50													17 50					
Wigan Wallgate	a					16 51	16 56							17 30				17 52		17 57					
	d	16 48				16 53	16 58						17 20	17 32	17 39			17 54		17 59					18 20
Wigan North Western	d									17a24												18a24			
Ince	d						17 01													18 02					
Hindley	d					16 58	17 04						17 25	17 37						18 05					18 25
Westhoughton	d					17 02							17 29		17 47			18 02							18 29
Bolton	a	17 02	17 08			17 12		17 25				17 34	17 38		17 55		18 08	18 12			18 31		18 34		18 38
	d	17 03	17 08			17 13		17 25			17 31	17 35	17 39		17 56	18 02	18 08	18 13			18 31		18 35		18 39
Moses Gate	d												17 42												18 42
Farnworth	d												17 44												18 44
Kearsley	d												17 46												18 46
Daisy Hill	d						17 08							17 41						18 09					
Hag Fold	d						17 11													18 12					
Atherton	d						17 14							17 45						18 15					
Walkden	d						17 19							17 50						18 20					
Moorside	d						17 23													18 24					
Swinton	d						17 25							17 55						18 26					
Salford Crescent	a	17 15				17 25	17 33	17 38			17 43	17 47	17 56	18 02	18 08	18 15		18 25		18 33	18 43		18 47		18 56
	d	17 15				17 26	17 33	17 38			17 44	17 47	17 56	18 03	18 09	18 15		18 26		18 33	18 43		18 47		18 56
Salford Central	d	17 17					17 36	17 41			17 46		17 59	18 05		18 17				18 36	18 46				18 59
Manchester Victoria	⇌ a	17 23					17 43	17 47			17 53		18 06	18 09		18 24				18 43	18 52				19 06
Rochdale	41 a	17 51														18 47									
Deansgate	⇌ a											17 51			18 12								18 51		
Manchester Oxford Road	a		17 26			17 30						17 52			18 14		18 23	18 31					18 52		
Manchester Piccadilly 10	⇌ a		17 29			17 35						17 56			18 18		18 27	18 35					18 56		
Stockport	84 a														18 34										
Hazel Grove	86 a														18 43										
Buxton	86 a														19 22										
Heald Green	85 a		17 41									18 10					18 40						19 10		
Manchester Airport	85 ✈ a		17 48			17 53						18 17					18 47	18 53					19 17		

A 🚲 from Preston
B From Edinburgh
C To Liverpool Lime Street
D From Clitheroe
E To Windermere

The Sunday service between Wigan Wallgate and Manchester Victoria via Atherton is funded by GMITA and will operate whilst funding exists

Barrow-in-Furness, Blackpool North, Preston, Southport, Kirkby and Wigan - Bolton - Manchester

Network Diagram - see first Page of Table 82

		NT	NT	TP	NT	NT	NT	NT	NT	NT	TP	TP	NT	NT	NT	TP	NT	NT	NT	NT	TP	TP ThX
				◇1							◇1	◇1				◇1					◇1	◇1
			A	B		C			D	A			E		F	G			D	A		B
Barrow-in-Furness	d												18 03									
Roose	d												18 07									
Dalton	d												18 13									
Ulverston	d												18 21									
Cark	d												18 29									
Kents Bank	d												18 33									
Grange-over-Sands	d												18 37									
Arnside	d												18 43									
Silverdale	d												18 47									
Carnforth	d					18 29							18 55									
Windermere 83	d											18 15										
Oxenholme Lake District 65	d											18 36				19 10						20 13
Lancaster 6 65	a					18 42						18 52	19 05			19 26						20 26
	d			18 26								18 52	19 06			19 26						20 26
Blackpool North 97	d							18 20	18 37		18 44							19 20	19 37		19 44	
Layton 97	d							18 23										19 23				
Poulton-le-Fylde 97	d							18 28			18 50							19 28			19 50	
Kirkham & Wesham 97	d							18 37	18 52									19 37				
Preston 8 65,97	a			18 45				18 47	19 02		19 08	19 11	19 31			19 45		19 47	20 02		20 08	20 45
	d			18 47				18 49	19 04		19 10	19 16				19 47		19 49	20 04		20 10	20 47
Leyland	d							18 54	19 09									19 54	20 09			
Buckshaw Parkway	d							18 59			19 17							19 59			20 17	
Chorley	d			18 56				19 03			19 21	19 29				19 56		20 03			20 21	20 56
Adlington (Lancashire)	d							19 08										20 08				
Blackrod	d							19 12										20 11				
Horwich Parkway	d							19 16			19 28	19 36						20 15			20 28	
Lostock	d							19 20										20 21				
Southport	d				18 17									19 00			19 23					
Meols Cop	d				18 22									19 05			19 28					
Bescar Lane	d				18 27																	
New Lane	d				18 31																	
Burscough Bridge	d				18 33									19 13			19 36					
Hoscar	d				18 37																	
Parbold	d				18 40									19 18			19 41					
Appley Bridge	d				18 44									19 22			19 45					
Gathurst	d				18 47									19 25			19 48					
Kirkby	d						18 32															
Rainford	d						18 40															
Upholland	d						18 44															
Orrell	d						18 47															
Pemberton	d						18 50															
Wigan Wallgate	a				18 52		18 56							19 30			19 53					
	d	18 32			18 53		18 58							19 32			19 55					
Wigan North Western	d								19a24										20a24			
Ince	d						19 01															
Hindley	d	18 37			18 58		19 04							19 37			20 00					
Westhoughton	d				19 02												20 04					
Bolton	a			19 08	19 12			19 25			19 33	19 42				20 08	20 12	20 25			20 34	21 08
	d		19 02	19 08	19 13			19 25		19 31	19 34	19 43			20 02	20 08	20 13	20 25		20 31	20 35	21 08
Moses Gate	d																					
Farnworth	d																					
Kearsley	d																					
Daisy Hill	d	18 41					19 08							19 41								
Hag Fold	d						19 11															
Atherton	d	18 45					19 14							19 45								
Walkden	d	18 50					19 19							19 50								
Moorside	d						19 23															
Swinton	d	18 55					19 25							19 55								
Salford Crescent	a	19 02	19 14		19 25		19 33	19 38		19 44	19 47			20 02	20 15		20 25	20 38		20 43	20 47	
	d	19 03	19 15		19 26		19 33	19 38		19 44	19 47			20 03	20 15		20 26	20 38		20 44	20 47	
Salford Central	d	19 05	19 17				19 36	19 41		19 46				20 05	20 17			20 41		20 46		
Manchester Victoria	a	19 11	19 23				19 43	19 47		19 53				20 11	20 24			20 47		20 52		
Rochdale 41	a																					
Deansgate	a				19 29						19 51						20 29				20 51	
Manchester Oxford Road	a			19 23	19 31						19 52	19 57				20 23	20 31				20 52	21 23
Manchester Piccadilly 10	a			19 27	19 35						19 56	20 01				20 27	20 35				20 56	21 27
Stockport 84	a																					
Hazel Grove 86	a																					
Buxton 86	a																					
Heald Green 85	a										20 10	20 15									21 10	
Manchester Airport 85	a			19 47	19 53						20 17	20 24				20 47	20 53				21 17	21 46

A From Clitheroe
B From Edinburgh
C From Leeds to Morecambe
D To Liverpool Lime Street
E From Carlisle
F From Blackburn
G From Glasgow Central

The Sunday service between Wigan Wallgate and Manchester Victoria via Atherton is funded by GMITA and will operate whilst funding exists

Barrow-in-Furness, Blackpool North, Preston, Southport, Kirkby and Wigan - Bolton - Manchester

Network Diagram - see first Page of Table 82

		TP ThO ◇1 A	NT	NT	NT	NT B	NT C	TP ◇1	TP ◇1	NT FO	NT FX	NT FO	NT FX	NT FX	NT FO	NT FX C	NT FO C	TP ◇1 D	TP ◇1 E	NT B	TP FO ◇1 A	NT	NT FO
Barrow-in-Furness	d								20 08													21 43	
Roose	d								20 12													21 47	
Dalton	d								20 19													21 53	
Ulverston	d								20 27													22 01	
Cark	d								20 35													22 09	
Kents Bank	d								20 39													22 13	
Grange-over-Sands	d								20 43													22 17	
Arnside	d								20 49													22 23	
Silverdale	d								20 53													22 27	
Carnforth	d								21 01													22 35	
Windermere 83	d																						
Oxenholme Lake District 65	d	20 13																			22 10		
Lancaster 6 65	a	20 26							21 10												22 26	22 45	
	d	20 26							21 10												22 26	22 46	
Blackpool North 97	d				20 20	20 37		20 44						21 20	21 20			21 44	21 44	22 14			
Layton 97	d				20 23									21 23	21 23								
Poulton-le-Fylde 97	d				20 28			20 50						21 28	21 28			21 50	21 50				
Kirkham & Wesham 97	d				20 37									21 37	21 37								
Preston 8 65,97	a	20 45			20 47	21 01		21 08	21 29					21 47	21 47			22 08	22 08	22 41	22 45	23 11	
	d	20 47			20 49	21 04		21 10	21 31					21 49	21 49			22 10	22 10	22 43	22 47		
Leyland	d				20 54	21 09								21 54	21 54					22 48			
Buckshaw Parkway	d				20 59			21 17						21 59	21 59			22 17	22 17				
Chorley	d	20 56			21 03			21 21						22 03	22 03			22 21	22 21				
Adlington (Lancashire)	d				21 08									22 08	22 08								
Blackrod	d				21 12									22 12	22 12								
Horwich Parkway	d				21 16			21 28						22 16	22 16			22 28	22 28				
Lostock	d				21 20									22 20	22 20								
Southport	d			20 23								21 23	21 23										
Meols Cop	d			20 28								21 28	21 28										
Bescar Lane	d																						
New Lane	d																						
Burscough Bridge	d			20 36								21 36	21 36										
Hoscar	d																						
Parbold	d			20 41								21 41	21 41										
Appley Bridge	d			20 45								21 45	21 45										
Gathurst	d			20 48								21 48	21 48										
Kirkby	d																						
Rainford	d																						
Upholland	d																						
Orrell	d																						
Pemberton	d																						
Wigan Wallgate	a			20 53								21 53	21 53										
	d		20 27	20 55						21 27	21 27	21 55	21 55										22 27
Wigan North Western	d					21a23			21 48											23a02			
Ince	d		20 30							21 30	21 30												22 30
Hindley	d		20 33	21 00						21 33	21 33	22 00	22 00										22 33
Westhoughton	d			21 04								22 04	22 04										
Bolton	a	21 08		21 12	21 25			21 34				22 12	22 12	22 25	22 25			22 34	22 34		23 06		
	d	21 08		21 13	21 25		21 31	21 35				22 13	22 13	22 25	22 25	22 31	22 31	22 35	22 35		23 06		
Moses Gate	d																						
Farnworth	d																						
Kearsley	d																						
Daisy Hill	d		20 37							21 37	21 37												22 37
Hag Fold	d		20 40							21 40	21 40												22 40
Atherton	d		20 43							21 43	21 43												22 43
Walkden	d		20 49							21 49	21 49												22 49
Moorside	d		20 52							21 52	21 52												22 52
Swinton	d		20 55							21 55	21 55												22 55
Salford Crescent	a		21 02	21 25	21 38		21 43	21 47		22 02	22 02	22 25	22 25	22 38	22 38	22 43	22 43	22 47	22 47				23 02
	d		21 03	21 26	21 38		21 44	21 47		22 03	22 03	22 26	22 26	22 38	22 38	22 44	22 44	22 47	22 47				23 03
Salford Central	d		21 05		21 41		21 46			22 05		22 28			22 41		22 46						23 05
Manchester Victoria	a		21 11		21 47		21 52			22 11	22 11	22 34	22 34	22 47	22 47	22 52	22 52						23 13
Rochdale 41	a																						
Deansgate	a			21 29				21 51										22 51	22 51				
Manchester Oxford Road	a	21 23		21 31				21 52	22 26									22 53	22 52		23s21		
Manchester Piccadilly 10	a	21 27		21 35				21 56	22 30									22 56	22 56		23 31		
Stockport 84	a																						
Hazel Grove 86	a																						
Buxton 86	a																						
Heald Green 85	a							22 09										23 09	23 09				
Manchester Airport 85	a	21 47		21 53				22 17	22 47									23 17	23 17				

A From Edinburgh
B To Liverpool Lime Street
C From Clitheroe
D from 2 January until 23 March
E until 30 December and then from 26 March

The Sunday service between Wigan Wallgate and Manchester Victoria via Atherton is funded by GMITA and will operate whilst funding exists

Barrow-in-Furness, Blackpool North, Preston, Southport, Kirkby and Wigan - Bolton - Manchester

Network Diagram - see first Page of Table 82

			NT FX	NT	NT	NT	TP		NT	NT	TP	NT	NT
							◇1				◇1		
					A	B	C			D		A	E
Barrow-in-Furness		d											
Roose		d											
Dalton		d											
Ulverston		d											
Cark		d											
Kents Bank		d											
Grange-over-Sands		d											
Arnside		d											
Silverdale		d											
Carnforth		d											
Windermere	83	d					22 45						
Oxenholme Lake District	65	d					23 06						
Lancaster 6	65	a					23 23						
		d				23 07	23 24						
Blackpool North	97	d			22 20						22 44	23 13	23 13
Layton	97	d			22 23							23 16	23 16
Poulton-le-Fylde	97	d			22 28						22 50	23 21	23 21
Kirkham & Wesham	97	d			22 37							23 30	23 30
Preston 8	65,97	a			22 47	23 28	23 45				23 08	23 40	23 40
		d			22 49						23 10	23 42	23 42
Leyland		d			22 54							23 48	23 48
Buckshaw Parkway		d			22 59						23 17	23 52	23 52
Chorley		d			23 03						23 21	23 57	23 57
Adlington (Lancashire)		d			23 08							00 03	00 03
Blackrod		d			23 12							00 06	00 06
Horwich Parkway		d			23 16						23 28	00 10	00 10
Lostock		d			23 20							00 14	00 14
Southport		d		22 18					23 10				
Meols Cop		d		22 23					23 15				
Bescar Lane		d		22 28									
New Lane		d		22 32									
Burscough Bridge		d		22 34					23 23				
Hoscar		d		22 38									
Parbold		d		22 41					23 28				
Appley Bridge		d		22 45					23 32				
Gathurst		d		22 48					23 35				
Kirkby		d											
Rainford		d											
Upholland		d											
Orrell		d											
Pemberton		d											
Wigan Wallgate		a		22 53					23 44				
		d	22 27	22 55									
Wigan North Western		d											
Ince		d	22 30										
Hindley		d	22 33	23 00									
Westhoughton		d		23 04									
Bolton		a		23 12	23 25						23 34	00 19	00 20
		d		23 13	23 25					23 31	23 35	00 20	00 20
Moses Gate		d											
Farnworth		d											
Kearsley		d											
Daisy Hill		d	22 37										
Hag Fold		d	22 40										
Atherton		d	22 43										
Walkden		d	22 49										
Moorside		d	22 52										
Swinton		d	22 55										
Salford Crescent		a	23 02	23 25	23 38					23 43	23 47		
		d	23 03	23 26	23 38					23 44	23 47		
Salford Central		d											
Manchester Victoria	⛴	a	23 13		23 47					23 52		00 37	00 39
Rochdale	41	a											
Deansgate	⛴	a		23 29									
Manchester Oxford Road		a		23 31									
Manchester Piccadilly 10	⛴	a		23 39							23 53		
Stockport	84	a											
Hazel Grove	86	a											
Buxton	86	a											
Heald Green	85	a									00 16		
Manchester Airport	85 ✈	a									00 24		

A until 30 December and then from 26 March
B From Morecambe
C To Blackpool North
D From Clitheroe
E from 2 January until 23 March

The Sunday service between Wigan Wallgate and Manchester Victoria via Atherton is funded by GMITA and will operate whilst funding exists

Table 82

Saturdays

Barrow-in-Furness, Blackpool North, Preston, Southport, Kirkby and Wigan - Bolton - Manchester

Network Diagram - see first Page of Table 82

Station		TP ◇1	NT A	NT B	TP ◇1 C	TP ◇1 D	TP ◇1	TP ◇1	TP ◇1 D	NT E	TP ◇1	TP ◇1	NT	NT	NT F	TP ◇1	NT	NT	TP ◇1	NT	NT	NT	NT G
Barrow-in-Furness	d							04 35								05 31							
Roose	d																						
Dalton	d																						
Ulverston	d							04 51								05 47							
Cark	d																						
Kents Bank	d																						
Grange-over-Sands	d							05 03								05 59							
Arnside	d							05 10								06 05							
Silverdale	d																						
Carnforth	d							05 19								06 15							
Windermere 83	d																						
Oxenholme Lake District 65	d																						
Lancaster 6 65	a							05 28								06 23							
	d															06 23							
Blackpool North 97	d	22p44	23p13	23p13			03 33			04 56		05 39						06 19	06 40			06 53	07 02
Layton 97	d		23p16	23p16														06 22	06 43				
Poulton-le-Fylde 97	d	22p50	23p21	23p21						05 02		05 45						06 27	06 47				07 08
Kirkham & Wesham 97	d		23p30	23p30														06 36	06 56				
Preston 8 65,97	a	23p08	23p40	23p40						05 20		06 03				06 42		06 46	07 07			07 15	07 28
	d	23p10	23p42	23p42			03u58				05 16	06 05				06 44		06 48	07 09			07 17	07 30
Leyland	d		23p48	23p48								06 10						06 53				07 22	07 35
Buckshaw Parkway	d	23p17	23p52	23p52														06 58				07 28	
Chorley	d	23p21	23p57	23p57							05 26	06 16				06 53		07 02	07 18			07 32	
Adlington (Lancashire)	d		00 03	00 03														07 07				07 37	
Blackrod	d		00 06	00 06								06 22						07 11				07 41	
Horwich Parkway	d	23p28	00 10	00 10							05 33	06 26				07 00		07 15	07 26			07 45	
Lostock	d		00 14	00 14								06 30						07 20	07 30			07 49	
Southport	d																06 23						
Meols Cop	d																06 28						
Bescar Lane	d																						
New Lane	d																						
Burscough Bridge	d																06 36						
Hoscar	d																						
Parbold	d																06 41						
Appley Bridge	d																06 45						
Gathurst	d																06 49						
Kirkby	d																						
Rainford	d																						
Upholland	d																						
Orrell	d																						
Pemberton	d																						
Wigan Wallgate	a																06 54						
	d												06 31	06 36			06 55			07 15			
Wigan North Western	d																				07 22		07a50
Ince	d													06 39						07 18	07 25		
Hindley	d												06 36	06 42						07 21	07 29		
Westhoughton	d												06 41				07 03				07 33		
Bolton	a	23p34	00 19	00 20							05 42	06 34	06 52			07 08	07 11	07 25	07 34		07 42	07 54	
	d	23p35	00 20	00 20			04u31				05 43	06 35	06 53		06 56	07 08	07 12	07 25	07 35		07 43	07 55	
Moses Gate	d														06 59						07 46		
Farnworth	d														07 01						07 48		
Kearsley	d														07 03						07 50		
Daisy Hill	d													06 46						07 26			
Hag Fold	d													06 49						07 29			
Atherton	d													06 52						07 32			
Walkden	d													06 58						07 38			
Moorside	d													07 01						07 41			
Swinton	d													07 04						07 44			
Salford Crescent	a	23p47									05 55	06 47	07 05	07 11	07 15		07 24	07 38	07 47	07 53	08 02	08 07	
	d	23p47			00 49	03 37			04 46		05 55	06 47	07 08	07 12	07 15		07 25	07 38	07 47	07 53	08 02	08 08	
Salford Central	d													07 15	07 19			07 41		07 56	08 05		
Manchester Victoria ⇌	a		00 37	00 39										07 18	07 25			07 47		07 59	08 12		
Rochdale 41	a																						
Deansgate ⇌	a											06 51	07 11				07 28		07 51			08 11	
Manchester Oxford Road	a											06 52	07 13			07 23	07 30		07 52			08 14	
Manchester Piccadilly 10 ⇌	a	23p53			00 53	03 44	04 48		04 52		06 01	06 56	07 17			07 27	07 34		07 56			08 18	
Stockport 84	a												07 34									08 34	
Hazel Grove 86	a												07 47									08 47	
Buxton 86	a																						
Heald Green 85	a	00 16										07 10							08 10				
Manchester Airport 85 ✈	a	00 24			01 10	04 00	05 07		05 10		06 18	07 17				07 47	07 53		08 17				

A until 31 December and then from 31 March
B from 7 January until 24 March
C From Newcastle
D From York
E To Colne
F From Blackburn
G To Liverpool Lime Street

The Sunday service between Wigan Wallgate and Manchester Victoria via Atherton is funded by GMITA and will operate whilst funding exists

Barrow-in-Furness, Blackpool North, Preston, Southport, Kirkby and Wigan - Bolton - Manchester

Network Diagram - see first Page of Table 82

		NT	NT	TP	NT	NT	NT	NT	TP	NT	NT	NT	NT	NT	TP	NT	NT	NT	NT	NT	TP	TP	NT
				◇1					◇1						◇1						◇1	◇1	
			A	B			C	A						D	B					A		E	
				bike					bike						bike						bike		
Barrow-in-Furness	d			06 20											07 29								
Roose	d			06 24																			
Dalton	d			06 31											07 38								
Ulverston	d			06 39											07 46								
Cark	d			06 47											07 54								
Kents Bank	d			06 51																			
Grange-over-Sands	d			06 55											08 01								
Arnside	d			07 01											08 07								
Silverdale	d			07 05											08 11								
Carnforth	d			07 12			07 43								08 18								
Windermere 83	d																						
Oxenholme Lake District 65	d																						
Lancaster 6 65	a			07 21			07 52								08 26								
	d			07 22											08 27								
Blackpool North 97	d					07 18			07 44									08 20	08 38		08 44	09 14	
Layton 97	d					07 21			07 47									08 23					
Poulton-le-Fylde 97	d					07 26			07 51									08 28			08 50	09 20	
Kirkham & Wesham 97	d					07 35			08 00									08 37					
Preston 8 65,97	a			07 41		07 46			08 11						08 45			08 47	09 02		09 08	09 41	
	d			07 47		07 47			08 12				08 17		08 47			08 49	09 04		09 10		
Leyland	d					07 53							08 23					08 54	09 09				
Buckshaw Parkway	d					07 58							08 27					08 59			09 17		
Chorley	d			07 56		08 02			08 22				08 34		08 56			09 03			09 21		
Adlington (Lancashire)	d					08 07							08 39					09 08					
Blackrod	d					08 11							08 42					09 12					
Horwich Parkway	d					08 15							08 46					09 16			09 28		
Lostock	d					08 20							08 50					09 20					
Southport	d				07 21							07 53				08 25							
Meols Cop	d				07 26							07 58				08 30							
Bescar Lane	d											08 03											
New Lane	d											08 07											
Burscough Bridge	d				07 34							08 09				08 38							
Hoscar	d											08 13											
Parbold	d				07 39							08 16				08 43							
Appley Bridge	d				07 43							08 20				08 47							
Gathurst	d				07 47							08 23				08 50							
Kirkby	d	07 11															08 21						
Rainford	d	07 19															08 29						
Upholland	d	07 23															08 33						
Orrell	d	07 27															08 36						
Pemberton	d	07 30															08 39						
Wigan Wallgate	a	07 35			07 51							08 28				08 55	08 45						
	d	07 37			07 53					08 13		08 29				08 56	08 50						09 20
Wigan North Western	d										08 20								09a27				
Ince	d	07 40								08 16							08 53						
Hindley	d	07 43			07 58					08 19	08 25	08 34					08 57						09 25
Westhoughton	d				08 03						08 29					09 04							09 29
Bolton	a			08 08	08 11	08 25			08 34		08 38		08 55		09 08	09 12		09 25			09 34		09 38
	d		07 59	08 08	08 12	08 25		08 31	08 35		08 39		08 56	09 02	09 08	09 13		09 25		09 31	09 35		09 39
Moses Gate	d		08 02								08 42												09 42
Farnworth	d		08 04								08 44												09 44
Kearsley	d		08 06								08 46												09 46
Daisy Hill	d	07 47								08 23		08 39					09 01						
Hag Fold	d	07 50								08 26							09 04						
Atherton	d	07 53								08 29		08 43					09 06						
Walkden	d	07 59								08 35		08 49					09 12						
Moorside	d	08 03								08 39							09 15						
Swinton	d	08 05								08 42		08 54					09 18						
Salford Crescent	a	08 13	08 17		08 24	08 38		08 43	08 47	08 50	08 56	09 03	09 08	09 15		09 25	09 27	09 38		09 43	09 47		09 56
	d	08 13	08 17		08 25	08 38		08 44	08 47	08 51	08 56	09 03	09 09	09 16		09 26	09 27	09 38		09 44	09 47		09 56
Salford Central	d	08 16	08 20			08 41		08 46		08 54	08 59	09 06		09 18			09 31	09 41		09 46			09 59
Manchester Victoria ⛴	a	08 20	08 25			08 47		08 52		08 57	09 06	09 11		09 26			09 38	09 47		09 52			10 06
Rochdale 41	a	08 51												09 54									
Deansgate ⛴	a				08 28								09 12			09 29					09 51		
Manchester Oxford Road	a			08 23	08 31				08 52				09 14		09 23	09 31					09 52		
Manchester Piccadilly 10 ⛴	a			08 27	08 35				08 56				09 18		09 27	09 35					09 56		
Stockport 84	a												09 34										
Hazel Grove 86	a												09 47										
Buxton 86	a																						
Heald Green 85	a				08 47				09 10												10 10		
Manchester Airport 85 ✈	a			08 47	08 52				09 19						09 47	09 51					10 17		

A From Clitheroe
B bike from Preston
C From Leeds
D From Blackburn
E To Barrow-in-Furness

The Sunday service between Wigan Wallgate and Manchester Victoria via Atherton is funded by GMITA and will operate whilst funding exists

Barrow-in-Furness, Blackpool North, Preston, Southport, Kirkby and Wigan - Bolton - Manchester

Network Diagram - see first Page of Table 82

		NT	NT	NT	NT	TP	NT	NT	NT	NT	NT	NT	TP	NT	TP	NT	NT	NT	NT	NT	TP	NT
						◇1							◇1		◇1						◇1	
				A		B	C					D		E					A		F	G
						🛒									🛒						🛒	
Barrow-in-Furness	d						08 25														09 23	10 16
Roose	d						08 29														09 27	10 20
Dalton	d						08 36														09 34	10 26
Ulverston	d						08 44														09 42	10 34
Cark	d						08 52														09 50	10 42
Kents Bank	d						08 57														09 54	10 46
Grange-over-Sands	d						09 01														09 58	10 50
Arnside	d						09 08														10 04	10 56
Silverdale	d						09 13														10 08	11 01
Carnforth	d						09 19					10 02									10 15	11 09
Windermere	83 d												09 38									
Oxenholme Lake District	65 d					09 11							09 58									
Lancaster 6	65 a					09 26	09 33					10 12	10 16								10 25	11 21
	d					09 26							10 16								10 26	
Blackpool North	97 d									09 20	09 37				09 43							
Layton	97 d									09 23												
Poulton-le-Fylde	97 d									09 28					09 49							
Kirkham & Wesham	97 d									09 37												
Preston 8	65,97 a					09 45				09 47	10 02		10 35		10 07						10 45	
	d		09 23			09 47				09 49	10 04				10 12			10 23			10 47	
Leyland	d		09 29							09 54	10 09							10 29				
Buckshaw Parkway	d		09 33							09 59								10 33				
Chorley	d		09 38			09 56				10 03					10 22			10 38			10 56	
Adlington (Lancashire)	d									10 08												
Blackrod	d									10 12												
Horwich Parkway	d		09 46							10 16								10 46				
Lostock	d		09 50							10 20								10 50				
Southport	d	09 02						09 24									09 55					
Meols Cop	d	09 07															10 00					
Bescar Lane	d																10 05					
New Lane	d																10 09					
Burscough Bridge	d	09 15						09 36									10 11					
Hoscar	d																10 15					
Parbold	d	09 20						09 41									10 18					
Appley Bridge	d	09 24						09 45									10 22					
Gathurst	d	09 27															10 25					
Kirkby	d								09 32													
Rainford	d								09 40													
Upholland	d								09 44													
Orrell	d								09 47													
Pemberton	d								09 50													
Wigan Wallgate	a	09 32						09 51	09 56								10 30					
	d	09 32			09 46			09 53	09 58							10 20	10 32			10 48		
Wigan North Western	d										10a27											
Ince	d								10 01													
Hindley	d	09 37						09 58	10 04							10 25	10 37					
Westhoughton	d				09 54			10 02								10 29						
Bolton	a		09 55		10 02	10 08		10 12		10 25					10 34	10 38		10 55		11 02	11 08	
	d		09 56	10 00	10 03	10 08		10 13		10 25				10 31	10 35	10 39		10 56	11 00	11 04	11 08	
Moses Gate	d															10 42						
Farnworth	d															10 44						
Kearsley	d															10 46						
Daisy Hill	d	09 41							10 09								10 41					
Hag Fold	d								10 12													
Atherton	d	09 45							10 15								10 45					
Walkden	d	09 50							10 20								10 50					
Moorside	d								10 24													
Swinton	d	09 55							10 26								10 55					
Salford Crescent	a	10 03	10 08	10 13	10 15			10 25	10 34	10 38				10 44	10 47	10 56	11 02	11 08	11 12	11 16		
	d	10 03	10 09	10 13	10 15			10 26	10 35	10 38				10 44	10 47	10 56	11 03	11 09	11 13	11 16		
Salford Central	d	10 05		10 16	10 17				10 37	10 41				10 47		10 59	11 05		11 15	11 18		
Manchester Victoria 🚊	a	10 12		10 22	10 25				10 41	10 47				10 52		11 06	11 11		11 23	11 25		
Rochdale	41 a				10 51															11 51		
Deansgate 🚊	a		10 12					10 29							10 51			11 12				
Manchester Oxford Road	a		10 14			10 23		10 31							10 52			11 14			11 23	
Manchester Piccadilly 10 🚊	a		10 18			10 27		10 35							10 56			11 18			11 27	
Stockport	84 a		10 34															11 34				
Hazel Grove	86 a		10 47															11 47				
Buxton	86 a																					
Heald Green	85 a														11 10							
Manchester Airport	85 ✈ a					10 47		10 53							11 17						11 47	

A From Blackburn
B From Glasgow Central
C From Maryport
D From Leeds to Morecambe
E From Clitheroe
F 🛒 from Preston
G From Sellafield

The Sunday service between Wigan Wallgate and Manchester Victoria via Atherton is funded by GMITA and will operate whilst funding exists

Table 82

Saturdays

Barrow-in-Furness, Blackpool North, Preston, Southport, Kirkby and Wigan - Bolton - Manchester

Network Diagram - see first Page of Table 82

Station	Table		NT	NT	NT	NT	NT	TP	NT	NT	NT	NT	TP	NT	NT	NT	NT	NT	TP	NT	TP	NT	NT	NT
								◇1					◇1						◇1		◇1			
							A						B					C		A				
								🚲					🚲								🚲			
Barrow-in-Furness		d																	11 25					
Roose		d																						
Dalton		d																						
Ulverston		d																	11 41					
Cark		d																						
Kents Bank		d																						
Grange-over-Sands		d																	11 53					
Arnside		d																	11 59					
Silverdale		d																						
Carnforth		d																12 02	12 09					
Windermere	83	d											10 49											
Oxenholme Lake District	65	d											11 09											
Lancaster 6	65	a											11 26					12 11	12 18					
		d											11 26						12 18					
Blackpool North	97	d			10 20	10 37		10 44								11 15	11 37				11 44			
Layton	97	d			10 23											11 18								
Poulton-le-Fylde	97	d			10 28			10 50								11 23					11 50			
Kirkham & Wesham	97	d			10 37											11 32								
Preston 8	65,97	a			10 47	11 02		11 08					11 45			11 42	12 02		12 37		12 08			
		d			10 49	11 04		11 10			11 23		11 47			11 49	12 04				12 10			12 23
Leyland		d			10 54	11 09					11 29					11 54	12 09							12 29
Buckshaw Parkway		d			10 59			11 17			11 33					11 59					12 17			12 33
Chorley		d			11 03			11 21			11 38		11 56			12 03					12 21			12 38
Adlington (Lancashire)		d			11 08											12 08								
Blackrod		d			11 12											12 12								
Horwich Parkway		d			11 16			11 28			11 46					12 16					12 28			12 46
Lostock		d			11 20						11 50					12 20								12 50
Southport		d	10 24							10 55				11 24									12 00	
Meols Cop		d								11 00													12 05	
Bescar Lane		d								11 05														
New Lane		d								11 09														
Burscough Bridge		d	10 36							11 11				11 36									12 13	
Hoscar		d								11 15														
Parbold		d	10 41							11 18				11 41									12 18	
Appley Bridge		d	10 45							11 22				11 45									12 22	
Gathurst		d								11 25													12 25	
Kirkby		d		10 32											11 32									
Rainford		d		10 40											11 40									
Upholland		d		10 44											11 44									
Orrell		d		10 47											11 47									
Pemberton		d		10 50											11 50									
Wigan Wallgate		a	10 51	10 56						11 30				11 51	11 56								12 30	
		d	10 53	10 58					11 20	11 32		11 48		11 53	11 58							12 20	12 32	
Wigan North Western		d				11a27											12a27							
Ince		d		11 01											12 01									
Hindley		d	10 58	11 04					11 25	11 37				11 58	12 04							12 25	12 37	
Westhoughton		d	11 02						11 29					12 02								12 29		
Bolton		a	11 12		11 25			11 34	11 38		11 55	12 02	12 08	12 12		12 25					12 34	12 38		12 55
		d	11 13		11 25		11 31	11 35	11 39		11 56	12 03	12 08	12 13		12 25				12 31	12 35	12 39		12 56
Moses Gate		d							11 42													12 42		
Farnworth		d							11 44													12 44		
Kearsley		d							11 46													12 46		
Daisy Hill		d		11 09						11 41					12 09								12 41	
Hag Fold		d		11 12											12 12									
Atherton		d		11 15						11 45					12 15								12 45	
Walkden		d		11 20						11 50					12 20								12 50	
Moorside		d		11 24											12 24									
Swinton		d		11 26						11 55					12 26								12 55	
Salford Crescent		a	11 25	11 34	11 38		11 43	11 47	11 56	12 02	12 08	12 15		12 25	12 34	12 38				12 43	12 47	12 56	13 02	13 08
		d	11 26	11 34	11 38		11 44	11 47	11 56	12 03	12 09	12 15		12 26	12 34	12 38				12 44	12 47	12 56	13 03	13 09
Salford Central		d		11 36	11 41		11 46		11 59	12 05		12 17			12 36	12 41				12 46		12 59	13 05	
Manchester Victoria 🚋		a		11 43	11 47		11 50		12 06	12 11		12 25			12 43	12 47				12 52		13 06	13 11	
Rochdale	41	a										12 51												
Deansgate 🚋		a	11 29					11 51			12 12			12 29							12 51			13 12
Manchester Oxford Road		a	11 31					11 52			12 14		12 23	12 31							12 52			13 14
Manchester Piccadilly 10 🚋		a	11 35					11 56			12 18		12 27	12 35							12 56			13 18
Stockport	84	a									12 34													13 34
Hazel Grove	86	a									12 47													13 47
Buxton	86	a																						
Heald Green	85	a						12 10													13 10			
Manchester Airport ✈	85	a	11 53					12 17					12 47	12 53							13 17			

A From Clitheroe

B 🚲 from Preston

C From Leeds to Heysham Port

The Sunday service between Wigan Wallgate and Manchester Victoria via Atherton is funded by GMITA and will operate whilst funding exists

Table 82

Saturdays

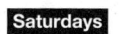

Barrow-in-Furness, Blackpool North, Preston, Southport, Kirkby and Wigan - Bolton - Manchester

Network Diagram - see first Page of Table 82

		NT	TP	NT	NT	NT	NT	NT	NT	TP	NT	NT	NT	NT	TP	NT	NT	NT	NT	NT	TP	NT
			◇1							◇1					◇1						◇1	
			A	B					C						D					C		
			🛒							🛒					🛒						🛒	
Barrow-in-Furness	d			12 11																		
Roose	d			12 15																		
Dalton	d			12 21																		
Ulverston	d			12 29																		
Cark	d			12 37																		
Kents Bank	d			12 41																		
Grange-over-Sands	d			12 45																		
Arnside	d			12 51																		
Silverdale	d			12 55																		
Carnforth	d			13 03																		
Windermere 83	d														12 51							
Oxenholme Lake District 65	d		12 10												13 09							
Lancaster 6 65	a		12 26	13 16											13 26							
	d		12 26												13 26							
Blackpool North 97	d						12 20	12 37		12 44								13 20	13 37		13 44	
Layton 97	d						12 23											13 23				
Poulton-le-Fylde 97	d						12 28			12 50								13 28			13 50	
Kirkham & Wesham 97	d						12 37											13 37				
Preston 8 65,97	a		12 45				12 47	13 02		13 08					13 45			13 47	14 02		14 08	
	d		12 47				12 49	13 04		13 10			13 23		13 47			13 49	14 04		14 10	
Leyland	d						12 54	13 09					13 29					13 54	14 09			
Buckshaw Parkway	d						12 59			13 17			13 33					13 59			14 17	
Chorley	d		12 56				13 03			13 21			13 38		13 56			14 03			14 21	
Adlington (Lancashire)	d						13 08											14 08				
Blackrod	d						13 12											14 12				
Horwich Parkway	d						13 16			13 28			13 46					14 16			14 28	
Lostock	d						13 20						13 50					14 20				
Southport	d				12 24							12 54				13 24						
Meols Cop	d											12 59										
Bescar Lane	d											13 04										
New Lane	d											13 08										
Burscough Bridge	d				12 36							13 11				13 36						
Hoscar	d											13 15										
Parbold	d				12 41							13 18				13 41						
Appley Bridge	d				12 45							13 22				13 45						
Gathurst	d											13 25										
Kirkby	d					12 32											13 32					
Rainford	d					12 40											13 40					
Upholland	d					12 44											13 44					
Orrell	d					12 47											13 47					
Pemberton	d					12 50											13 50					
Wigan Wallgate	a				12 51	12 56						13 30				13 51	13 56					
	d	12 48			12 53	12 58					13 20	13 32		13 48		13 53	13 58					14 20
Wigan North Western	d							13a27											14a27			
Ince	d					13 01											14 01					
Hindley	d				12 58	13 04					13 25	13 37				13 58	14 04					14 25
Westhoughton	d				13 02						13 29					14 02						14 29
Bolton	a	13 02	13 08		13 12		13 25			13 34	13 38		13 55	14 02	14 08	14 12		14 25			14 34	14 38
	d	13 03	13 08		13 13		13 25		13 31	13 35	13 39		13 56	14 03	14 08	14 13		14 25		14 31	14 35	14 39
Moses Gate	d										13 42											14 42
Farnworth	d										13 44											14 44
Kearsley	d										13 46											14 46
Daisy Hill	d					13 09						13 41					14 09					
Hag Fold	d					13 12											14 12					
Atherton	d					13 15						13 45					14 15					
Walkden	d					13 20						13 50					14 20					
Moorside	d					13 24											14 24					
Swinton	d					13 26						13 55					14 26					
Salford Crescent	a	13 15			13 25	13 34	13 38		13 43	13 47	13 56	14 02	14 08	14 15		14 25	14 34	14 38		14 43	14 47	14 56
	d	13 15			13 26	13 34	13 38		13 44	13 47	13 56	14 03	14 09	14 15		14 26	14 34	14 38		14 44	14 47	14 56
Salford Central	d	13 17				13 36	13 41		13 46		13 59	14 05		14 17			14 36	14 41		14 46		14 59
Manchester Victoria 🚌	a	13 25				13 43	13 47		13 52		14 06	14 11		14 25			14 43	14 47		14 52		15 06
Rochdale 41	a	13 51												14 51								
Deansgate 🚌	a				13 29					13 51			14 12			14 29					14 51	
Manchester Oxford Road	a		13 23		13 31					13 52			14 14		14 23	14 31					14 52	
Manchester Piccadilly 10 🚌	a		13 27		13 35					13 56			14 18		14 27	14 35					14 56	
Stockport 84	a												14 34									
Hazel Grove 86	a												14 47									
Buxton 86	a																					
Heald Green 85	a									14 10											15 10	
Manchester Airport 85 ✈	a		13 47		13 53					14 17					14 47	14 53					15 17	

A From Edinburgh
B From Carlisle
C From Clitheroe
D 🛒 from Preston

The Sunday service between Wigan Wallgate and Manchester Victoria via Atherton is funded by GMITA and will operate whilst funding exists

Table 82

Saturdays

Barrow-in-Furness, Blackpool North, Preston, Southport, Kirkby and Wigan - Bolton - Manchester

Network Diagram - see first Page of Table 82

			NT	NT	NT	TP	TP	NT	NT	NT	NT	NT	NT	TP	NT	NT	NT	NT	TP	NT	NT	NT	NT	NT
						◇1	◇1							◇1					◇1					
						A	B	C					D						E		F	G	D	
						🛒	🛒							🛒					🛒					
Barrow-in-Furness		d				13 25		14 16														15 18		
Roose		d						14 20														15 22		
Dalton		d						14 26														15 28		
Ulverston		d				13 41		14 35														15 36		
Cark		d						14 42														15 44		
Kents Bank		d						14 47														15 48		
Grange-over-Sands		d				13 53		14 51														15 52		
Arnside		d				13 59		14 57														15 58		
Silverdale		d						15 01														16 03		
Carnforth		d				14 09		15 08													15 36	16 11		
Windermere	83	d																						
Oxenholme Lake District	65	d					14 07												15 10					
Lancaster 6	65	a				14 18	14 21	15 20											15 26		15 45	16 24		
		d				14 18	14 22												15 26					
Blackpool North	97	d									14 20	14 37		14 44										
Layton	97	d									14 23													
Poulton-le-Fylde	97	d									14 28			14 50										
Kirkham & Wesham	97	d									14 37													
Preston 8	65,97	a				14 37	14 41				14 47	15 02		15 08					15 45					
		d		14 23			14 47				14 49	15 04		15 10			15 23		15 47					
Leyland		d		14 29							14 54	15 09					15 29							
Buckshaw Parkway		d		14 33							14 59			15 17			15 33							
Chorley		d		14 38			14 56				15 03			15 21			15 38		15 56					
Adlington (Lancashire)		d									15 08													
Blackrod		d									15 12													
Horwich Parkway		d		14 46							15 16			15 28			15 46							
Lostock		d		14 50							15 20						15 50							
Southport		d	13 56						14 24							14 54				15 24				
Meols Cop		d	14 01													14 59								
Bescar Lane		d														15 04								
New Lane		d														15 08								
Burscough Bridge		d	14 09						14 36							15 11				15 36				
Hoscar		d														15 15								
Parbold		d	14 14						14 41							15 18				15 41				
Appley Bridge		d	14 18						14 45							15 22				15 45				
Gathurst		d	14 21													15 25								
Kirkby		d								14 32														15 32
Rainford		d								14 40														15 40
Upholland		d								14 44														15 44
Orrell		d								14 47														15 47
Pemberton		d								14 50														15 50
Wigan Wallgate		a	14 28						14 51	14 56						15 30				15 51				15 56
		d	14 30		14 48				14 53	14 58					15 20	15 32		15 48		15 53				15 58
Wigan North Western		d										15a27												
Ince		d								15 01														16 01
Hindley		d	14 35						14 58	15 04					15 25	15 37				15 58				16 04
Westhoughton		d							15 02						15 29					16 02				
Bolton		a		14 55	15 02		15 08		15 12		15 25			15 34	15 40		15 55	16 02	16 08	16 12				
		d		14 56	15 03		15 08		15 13		15 25		15 31	15 35	15 41		15 56	16 03	16 08	16 13			16 17	
Moses Gate		d													15 44									
Farnworth		d													15 46									
Kearsley		d													15 48									
Daisy Hill		d	14 39							15 09						15 41								16 09
Hag Fold		d								15 12														16 12
Atherton		d	14 43							15 15						15 45								16 15
Walkden		d	14 48							15 20						15 50								16 20
Moorside		d								15 24														16 24
Swinton		d	14 53							15 26						15 55								16 26
Salford Crescent		a	15 02	15 08	15 15				15 25	15 34	15 38		15 43	15 47	15 58	16 02	16 08	16 15		16 25			16 30	16 33
		d	15 03	15 09	15 15				15 26	15 34	15 38		15 44	15 47	15 58	16 03	16 09	16 15		16 26			16 30	16 34
Salford Central		d	15 05		15 17					15 36	15 41		15 48		16 01	16 05		16 17					16 33	16 37
Manchester Victoria	🚊	a	15 11		15 25					15 43	15 47		15 54		16 08	16 11		16 23					16 41	16 43
Rochdale	41	a			15 51													16 51						
Deansgate	🚊	a		15 12					15 29					15 51			16 12							
Manchester Oxford Road		a		15 14			15 23		15 31					15 52			16 14		16 23	16 31				
Manchester Piccadilly 10	🚊	a		15 18			15 27		15 35					15 56			16 18		16 27	16 35				
Stockport	84	a		15 34													16 34							
Hazel Grove	86	a		15 47													16 47							
Buxton	86	a																						
Heald Green	85	a												16 10					16 40					
Manchester Airport	85 ✈	a					15 47		15 53					16 17					16 47	16 53				

A 🛒 from Preston
B From Edinburgh
C From Whitehaven
D From Clitheroe
E From Glasgow Central
F From Leeds to Morecambe
G From Carlisle

The Sunday service between Wigan Wallgate and Manchester Victoria via Atherton is funded by GMITA and will operate whilst funding exists

Table 82

Saturdays

Barrow-in-Furness, Blackpool North, Preston, Southport, Kirkby and Wigan - Bolton - Manchester

Network Diagram - see first Page of Table 82

		NT	NT	TP	NT	NT	NT	NT	TP	TP	NT	NT	NT	NT	NT	TP	NT	NT	NT	NT	TP	NT	NT
				◇1					◇1	◇1						◇1					◇1		
									A						B					B			
				🍴					🍴							🍴					🍴		
Barrow-in-Furness	d									16 22													
Roose	d																						
Dalton	d									16 31													
Ulverston	d									16 39													
Cark	d									16 47													
Kents Bank	d																						
Grange-over-Sands	d									16 54													
Arnside	d									17 00													
Silverdale	d									17 04													
Carnforth	d									17 11													
Windermere 83	d																						
Oxenholme Lake District 65	d								16 07														
Lancaster 6 65	a								16 26	17 19													
	d								16 26	17 20													
Blackpool North 97	d	15 20	15 37	15 44									16 20	16 35		16 40					17 20		
Layton 97	d	15 23											16 23			16 43					17 23		
Poulton-le-Fylde 97	d	15 28		15 50									16 28			16 48					17 27		
Kirkham & Wesham 97	d	15 37											16 37			16 57							
Preston 8 65,97	a	15 47	16 02	16 08					16 45	17 39			16 47	17 02		17 08					17 45		
	d	15 49	16 04	16 10			16 23		16 47				16 49	17 04		17 10			17 23		17 47		
Leyland	d	15 54	16 09				16 29						16 54	17 09					17 29				
Buckshaw Parkway	d	15 59		16 17			16 33						16 59			17 17			17 33				
Chorley	d	16 03		16 21			16 38		16 56				17 03			17 21			17 38		17 56		
Adlington (Lancashire)	d	16 08											17 08										
Blackrod	d	16 12											17 12										
Horwich Parkway	d	16 16		16 28			16 46						17 16			17 28			17 46				
Lostock	d	16 20					16 50						17 20						17 50				
Southport	d					16 00					16 24							16 54				17 24	
Meols Cop	d					16 05												16 59				17 29	
Bescar Lane	d																	17 04					
New Lane	d																	17 08					
Burscough Bridge	d					16 13					16 36							17 11				17 37	
Hoscar	d																	17 15					
Parbold	d					16 18					16 41							17 18				17 42	
Appley Bridge	d					16 22					16 45							17 22				17 46	
Gathurst	d					16 25												17 25					
Kirkby	d											16 32											17 32
Rainford	d											16 40											17 40
Upholland	d											16 44											17 44
Orrell	d											16 47											17 47
Pemberton	d											16 50											17 50
Wigan Wallgate	a					16 30					16 51	16 56						17 30				17 52	17 57
	d				16 20	16 32		16 48			16 53	16 58					17 20	17 32				17 54	17 59
Wigan North Western	d		16a27											17a27									
Ince	d											17 01											18 02
Hindley	d				16 25	16 37					16 58	17 04					17 25	17 37					18 05
Westhoughton	d				16 29						17 02						17 29					18 02	
Bolton	a	16 25		16 34	16 38		16 55	17 02	17 08		17 12		17 25			17 34	17 38		17 55		18 08	18 12	
	d	16 25		16 35	16 39		16 56	17 03	17 08		17 13		17 25		17 31	17 35	17 39		17 56	18 03	18 08	18 13	
Moses Gate	d				16 42												17 42						
Farnworth	d				16 44												17 44						
Kearsley	d				16 46												17 46						
Daisy Hill	d					16 41						17 08						17 41					18 09
Hag Fold	d											17 11											18 12
Atherton	d					16 45						17 14						17 45					18 15
Walkden	d					16 50						17 19						17 50					18 20
Moorside	d											17 23											18 24
Swinton	d					16 55						17 25						17 55					18 26
Salford Crescent	a	16 38		16 47	16 56	17 02	17 08	17 15			17 25	17 33	17 38		17 43	17 47	17 56	18 02	18 08	18 15		18 25	18 33
	d	16 38		16 47	16 56	17 03	17 09	17 15			17 26	17 33	17 38		17 44	17 47	17 56	18 03	18 09	18 16		18 26	18 33
Salford Central	d	16 41			16 59	17 05		17 17				17 36	17 41		17 47		17 59	18 05		18 18			18 36
Manchester Victoria 🚊	a	16 47			17 06	17 11		17 23				17 43	17 47		17 53		18 06	18 11		18 27			18 43
Rochdale 41	a							17 51												18 47			
Deansgate 🚊	a			16 51			17 14				17 29					17 51			18 12				
Manchester Oxford Road	a			16 52			17 16		17 23		17 31					17 52			18 14		18 23	18 31	
Manchester Piccadilly 10 🚊	a			16 56			17 20		17 27		17 35					17 56			18 18		18 27	18 35	
Stockport 84	a						17 34												18 34				
Hazel Grove 86	a						17 43												18 47				
Buxton 86	a						18 23																
Heald Green 85	a			17 10					17 41							18 10					18 40		
Manchester Airport 85 ✈	a			17 17					17 48		17 53					18 17					18 47	18 53	

A From Edinburgh

B From Clitheroe

The Sunday service between Wigan Wallgate and Manchester Victoria via Atherton is funded by GMITA and will operate whilst funding exists

Table 82

Saturdays

Barrow-in-Furness, Blackpool North, Preston, Southport, Kirkby and Wigan - Bolton - Manchester

Network Diagram - see first Page of Table 82

		NT	NT	TP	TP	NT	NT	NT	TP	NT	NT	NT	NT	NT	NT	NT	TP	NT	NT	TP	NT	NT
				◇1	◇1				◇1								◇1			◇1		
				A 🚲				B	C 🚲		D	E				B			F	G 🚲		
Barrow-in-Furness	d				17 21							18 03										
Roose	d											18 07										
Dalton	d				17 30							18 13										
Ulverston	d				17 38							18 21										
Cark	d				17 46							18 29										
Kents Bank	d											18 33										
Grange-over-Sands	d				17 53							18 37										
Arnside	d				17 59							18 43										
Silverdale	d											18 47										
Carnforth	d				18 09						18 26	18 55										
Windermere 83	d			17 06																		
Oxenholme Lake District 65	d			17 30																19 10		
Lancaster 6 65	a			17 47	18 16						18 38	19 05								19 26		
	d			17 48	18 17				18 26			19 06								19 26		
Blackpool North 97	d		17 37											18 20	18 37		18 44					19 20
Layton 97	d													18 23								19 23
Poulton-le-Fylde 97	d													18 28			18 50					19 28
Kirkham & Wesham 97	d													18 37								19 37
Preston 8 65,97	a		18 02	18 06	18 36				18 45			19 31		18 47	19 00		19 08			19 45		19 47
	d	17 56	18 04	18 08					18 47					18 49	19 04		19 10			19 47		19 49
Leyland	d	18 01	18 09											18 54	19 09							19 54
Buckshaw Parkway	d	18 05		18 15										18 59			19 17					19 59
Chorley	d	18 09		18 19					18 56					19 03			19 21			19 56		20 03
Adlington (Lancashire)	d	18 15												19 08								20 08
Blackrod	d	18 19												19 12								20 12
Horwich Parkway	d	18 21		18 26										19 16			19 28					20 16
Lostock	d			18 30										19 20								20 20
Southport	d						17 54			18 17								19 00			19 23	
Meols Cop	d						17 59			18 22								19 05			19 28	
Bescar Lane	d						18 04			18 27												
New Lane	d						18 08			18 31												
Burscough Bridge	d						18 11			18 33								19 13			19 36	
Hoscar	d						18 15			18 37												
Parbold	d						18 18			18 40								19 18			19 41	
Appley Bridge	d						18 22			18 44								19 22			19 45	
Gathurst	d						18 25			18 47								19 25			19 48	
Kirkby	d												18 32									
Rainford	d												18 40									
Upholland	d												18 44									
Orrell	d												18 47									
Pemberton	d												18 50									
Wigan Wallgate	a						18 30			18 52			18 56					19 30			19 53	
	d					18 20	18 32			18 53			18 58					19 32			19 55	
Wigan North Western	d		18a27												19a27							
Ince	d												19 01									
Hindley	d					18 25	18 37			18 58			19 04					19 37			20 00	
Westhoughton	d					18 29				19 02											20 04	
Bolton	a	18 30		18 34		18 38			19 08	19 12				19 25			19 34			20 08	20 12	20 25
	d	18 30		18 35		18 39		19 02	19 08	19 13				19 25		19 32	19 35		20 02	20 08	20 13	20 25
Moses Gate	d					18 42																
Farnworth	d					18 44																
Kearsley	d					18 46																
Daisy Hill	d						18 41						19 08					19 41				
Hag Fold	d												19 11									
Atherton	d						18 45						19 14					19 45				
Walkden	d						18 50						19 19					19 50				
Moorside	d												19 23									
Swinton	d						18 55						19 25					19 55				
Salford Crescent	a	18 43		18 47		18 56	19 02	19 14		19 25			19 33	19 38		19 44	19 47	20 02	20 15		20 25	20 38
	d	18 43		18 47		18 56	19 03	19 15		19 26			19 33	19 38		19 45	19 47	20 03	20 15		20 26	20 38
Salford Central	d	18 46				18 59	19 05	19 17					19 36	19 41		19 47		20 05	20 17			20 41
Manchester Victoria ⇌	a	18 52				19 06	19 11	19 23					19 43	19 47		19 53		20 11	20 24			20 47
Rochdale 41	a																					
Deansgate ⇌	a			18 51						19 29							19 51				20 29	
Manchester Oxford Road	a			18 52					19 23	19 31							19 52			20 23	20 31	
Manchester Piccadilly 10 ⇌	a			18 56					19 27	19 35							19 56			20 27	20 35	
Stockport 84	a																					
Hazel Grove 86	a																					
Buxton 86	a																					
Heald Green 85	a			19 10													20 10					
Manchester Airport 85 ✈	a			19 17					19 50	19 53							20 17			20 47	20 53	

A 🚲 from Preston
B From Clitheroe
C From Edinburgh
D From Leeds to Morecambe
E From Carlisle
F From Blackburn
G From Glasgow Central

The Sunday service between Wigan Wallgate and Manchester Victoria via Atherton is funded by GMITA and will operate whilst funding exists

Table 82

Saturdays

Barrow-in-Furness, Blackpool North, Preston, Southport, Kirkby and Wigan - Bolton - Manchester

Network Diagram - see first Page of Table 82

	NT	NT	TP	NT	TP	TP	NT	NT	NT	NT	TP	TP	TP	NT	NT	NT	TP	NT	NT	NT	TP	NT
			◇1		◇1	◇1					◇1	◇1	◇1				◇1				◇1	
		A			B	C				A	D	E					F	G	F	A		
Barrow-in-Furness d											19 25	19 33						21 43	21 43			
Roose d												19 37						21 47	21 47			
Dalton d											19 34	19 44						21 53	21 53			
Ulverston d											19 42	19 52						22 01	22 01			
Cark d											19 49	20 00						22 09	22 09			
Kents Bank d												20 04						22 13	22 13			
Grange-over-Sands d											19 56	20 08						22 17	22 17			
Arnside d											20 02	20 14						22 23	22 23			
Silverdale d											20 07	20 18						22 27	22 27			
Carnforth d											20 14	20 25						22a33	22 35			
Windermere 83 d																	21 40					
Oxenholme Lake District 65 d					20 12	20 13											22 01					
Lancaster 6 65 a					20 26	20 26					20 21	20 34					22 17		22 45			
d					20 27	20 26					20 22	20 35					22 17		22 46			
Blackpool North 97 d	19 37		19 44					20 20	20 37				20 42			21 20					21 44	22 14
Layton 97 d								20 23								21 23						
Poulton-le-Fylde 97 d			19 50					20 28					20 48			21 28					21 50	
Kirkham & Wesham 97 d								20 37								21 37						
Preston 8 65,97 a	20 02		20 08		20 45	20 45		20 47	21 01		20 41	20 53	21 06			21 47	22 38		23 11		22 08	22 41
d	20 04		20 10		20 47	20 47		20 49	21 04		21 10		21 10			21 49					22 10	22 43
Leyland d	20 09							20 54	21 09							21 54						22 48
Buckshaw Parkway d			20 17					20 59								21 59					22 17	
Chorley d			20 21		20 56	20 56		21 03			21 21		21 21			22 03					22 21	
Adlington (Lancashire) d								21 08								22 08						
Blackrod d								21 12								22 12						
Horwich Parkway d			20 28					21 16			21 28		21 28			22 16					22 28	
Lostock d								21 20								22 20						
Southport d							20 23								21 23							
Meols Cop d							20 28								21 28							
Bescar Lane d																						
New Lane d																						
Burscough Bridge d							20 36								21 36							
Hoscar d																						
Parbold d							20 41								21 41							
Appley Bridge d							20 45								21 45							
Gathurst d							20 48								21 48							
Kirkby d																						
Rainford d																						
Upholland d																						
Orrell d																						
Pemberton d																						
Wigan Wallgate a							20 53								21 53							
d				20 27			20 55							21 27	21 55							
Wigan North Western d	20a27								21a27													23a06
Ince d				20 30										21 30								
Hindley d				20 33			21 00							21 33	22 00							
Westhoughton d							21 04								22 04							
Bolton a			20 34		21 08	21 08	21 12	21 25			21 34		21 34		22 12	22 25					22 34	
d		20 31	20 35		21 08	21 08	21 13	21 25		21 31	21 35		21 35		22 13	22 25				22 31	22 35	
Moses Gate d																						
Farnworth d																						
Kearsley d																						
Daisy Hill d				20 37										21 37								
Hag Fold d				20 40										21 40								
Atherton d				20 43										21 43								
Walkden d				20 49										21 49								
Moorside d				20 52										21 52								
Swinton d				20 55										21 55								
Salford Crescent a		20 43	20 47	21 02			21 25	21 38		21 43	21 47		21 47	22 02	22 25	22 38				22 43	22 47	
d		20 44	20 47	21 03			21 26	21 38		21 44	21 47		21 47	22 03	22 26	22 38				22 44	22 47	
Salford Central d		20 46		21 05				21 41		21 46				22 05	22 28	22 41				22 46		
Manchester Victoria ⇌ a		20 52		21 11				21 47		21 52				22 11	22 34	22 47				22 52		
Rochdale 41 a																						
Deansgate ⇌ a			20 51				21 29				21 51		21 51								22 51	
Manchester Oxford Road a			20 52		21 23	21 23	21 31				21 52		21 52								22 52	
Manchester Piccadilly 10 ⇌ a			20 56		21 27	21 27	21 35				21 56		21 56								22 56	
Stockport 84 a																						
Hazel Grove 86 a																						
Buxton 86 a																						
Heald Green 85 a			21 10								22 09		22 09								23 09	
Manchester Airport 85 ✈ a			21 17		21 47	21 46	21 53				22 17		22 17								23 17	

A From Clitheroe
B from 31 March. From Edinburgh
C until 24 March. From Edinburgh
D from 31 March
E until 24 March
F until 31 December
G from 7 January

The Sunday service between Wigan Wallgate and Manchester Victoria via Atherton is funded by GMITA and will operate whilst funding exists

Table 82

Saturdays

Barrow-in-Furness, Blackpool North, Preston, Southport, Kirkby and Wigan - Bolton - Manchester

Network Diagram - see first Page of Table 82

Station			NT	NT	NT	NT	TP	NT	NT	NT
						A	◇1		B	
Barrow-in-Furness		d								
Roose		d								
Dalton		d								
Ulverston		d								
Cark		d								
Kents Bank		d								
Grange-over-Sands		d								
Arnside		d								
Silverdale		d								
Carnforth		d				22 42				
Windermere	83	d								
Oxenholme Lake District	65	d								
Lancaster 6	65	a				23 07				
		d				23 07				
Blackpool North	97	d			22 20		22 44			23 02
Layton	97	d			22 23					23 05
Poulton-le-Fylde	97	d			22 28		22 50			23 10
Kirkham & Wesham	97	d			22 37					23 19
Preston 8	65,97	a			22 47	23 47	23 08			23 29
		d			22 49		23 10			23 31
Leyland		d			22 54					23 36
Buckshaw Parkway		d			22 59		23 17			23 41
Chorley		d			23 03		23 21			23 45
Adlington (Lancashire)		d			23 08					23 50
Blackrod		d			23 12					23 54
Horwich Parkway		d			23 16		23 28			23 58
Lostock		d			23 20					00 02
Southport		d		22 18				23 10		
Meols Cop		d		22 23				23 15		
Bescar Lane		d		22 28						
New Lane		d		22 32						
Burscough Bridge		d		22 34				23 23		
Hoscar		d		22 38						
Parbold		d		22 41				23 28		
Appley Bridge		d		22 45				23 32		
Gathurst		d		22 48				23 35		
Kirkby		d								
Rainford		d								
Upholland		d								
Orrell		d								
Pemberton		d								
Wigan Wallgate		a		22 53				23 44		
		d	22 27	22 55						
Wigan North Western		d								
Ince		d	22 30							
Hindley		d	22 33	23 00						
Westhoughton		d		23 04						
Bolton		a		23 12	23 25		23 34			00 07
		d		23 13	23 25		23 35		23 38	00 07
Moses Gate		d								
Farnworth		d								
Kearsley		d								
Daisy Hill		d	22 37							
Hag Fold		d	22 40							
Atherton		d	22 43							
Walkden		d	22 49							
Moorside		d	22 52							
Swinton		d	22 55							
Salford Crescent		a	23 02	23 25	23 38		23 47		23 50	
		d	23 03	23 26	23 38		23 47		23 53	
Salford Central		d	23 05							
Manchester Victoria		a	23 13		23 47				00 01	00 26
Rochdale	41	a								
Deansgate		a		23 29						
Manchester Oxford Road		a		23 31						
Manchester Piccadilly 10		a		23 39			23 53			
Stockport	84	a								
Hazel Grove	86	a								
Buxton	86	a								
Heald Green	85	a					00 16			
Manchester Airport	85	a					00 23			

A from 7 January

B From Clitheroe

The Sunday service between Wigan Wallgate and Manchester Victoria via Atherton is funded by GMITA and will operate whilst funding exists

Table 82

Sundays
until 1 January

Barrow-in-Furness, Blackpool North, Preston, Southport, Kirkby and Wigan - Bolton - Manchester

Network Diagram - see first Page of Table 82

			TP ◇1 A	NT B	NT A	TP 🚌	TP 🚌	NT C	TP ◇1	NT	NT D	TP ◇1	NT E	NT	NT	NT	NT B	TP ◇1	NT E	NT	NT C	TP ◇1	NT	NT F
Barrow-in-Furness		d																				09 17		
Roose		d																				09 21		
Dalton		d																				09 28		
Ulverston		d																				09 36		
Cark		d																				09 44		
Kents Bank		d																				09 48		
Grange-over-Sands		d																				09 52		
Arnside		d																				09 58		
Silverdale		d																				10 02		
Carnforth		d																				10 09		10 31
Windermere	83	d																						
Oxenholme Lake District	65	d																						
Lancaster 6	65	a																				10 17		10 40
		d																				10 21		
Blackpool North	97	d	22p44		23p02	03 20	05 20		08 14	08 20		08 44	08 50			09 20		09 44	09 50				10 20	
Layton	97	d			23p05					08 23						09 23							10 23	
Poulton-le-Fylde	97	d	22p50		23p10				08 20	08 28		08 50	08 56			09 28		09 50	09 56				10 28	
Kirkham & Wesham	97	d			23p19					08 37						09 37							10 37	
Preston 8	65,97	a	23p08		23p29				08 38	08 47		09 08	09 14			09 47		10 07	10 14			10 40	10 47	
		d	23p10		23p31	04u00	06u00		08 42	08 49		09 10	09 15			09 49		10 10	10 15			10 47	10 49	
Leyland		d			23p36					08 54			09 21			09 54			10 21				10 54	
Buckshaw Parkway		d	23p17		23p41					08 59		09 17				09 59		10 17					10 59	
Chorley		d	23p21		23p45				08 51	09 03		09 21				10 03		10 21				10 56	11 03	
Adlington (Lancashire)		d			23p50					09 08						10 08							11 08	
Blackrod		d			23p54					09 12						10 12							11 12	
Horwich Parkway		d	23p28		23p58				08 59	09 16		09 28				10 16		10 28					11 16	
Lostock		d			00 02					09 20						10 20							11 20	
Southport		d													09 10						10 05			
Meols Cop		d													09 15						10 10			
Bescar Lane		d																						
New Lane		d																						
Burscough Bridge		d													09 23						10 18			
Hoscar		d																						
Parbold		d													09 28						10 23			
Appley Bridge		d													09 32						10 27			
Gathurst		d													09 35						10 30			
Kirkby		d																						
Rainford		d																						
Upholland		d																						
Orrell		d																						
Pemberton		d																						
Wigan Wallgate		a													09 40						10 35			
		d						08 40						09 15	09 41					10 15	10 36			
Wigan North Western		d											09a35						10a36					
Ince		d												09 18						10 18				
Hindley		d						08 45						09 22	09 46					10 22	10 41			
Westhoughton		d						08 49							09 51						10 46			
Bolton		a	23p34		00 07			08 57	09 05	09 25		09 34			09 59	10 25		10 34			10 54	11 08	11 25	
		d	23p35	23p38	00 07	04u35	06u35	08 58	09 06	09 25	09 31	09 35			09 59	10 25	10 31	10 35			10 54	11 08	11 25	
Moses Gate		d																						
Farnworth		d																						
Kearsley		d																						
Daisy Hill		d												09 26						10 26				
Hag Fold		d												09 29						10 29				
Atherton		d												09 31						10 31				
Walkden		d												09 37						10 37				
Moorside		d												09 40						10 40				
Swinton		d												09 43						10 43				
Salford Crescent		a	23p47	23p50				09 10	09 18	09 38	09 43	09 47		09 50	10 12	10 38	10 43	10 47		10 50	11 07		11 38	
		d	23p47	23p53				09 11	09 18	09 38	09 44	09 47		09 51	10 12	10 38	10 44	10 47		10 51	11 07		11 38	
Salford Central		d																						
Manchester Victoria	⇌	a		00 01	00 26					09 45	09 53			09 57		10 45	10 52			10 57			11 45	
Rochdale	41	a																						
Deansgate	⇌	a						09 14	09 23			09 51			10 16			10 51			11 11			
Manchester Oxford Road		a						09 17	09 24			09 52			10 18			10 52			11 13	11 23		
Manchester Piccadilly 10	⇌	a	23p53			05b00	07b00	09 21	09 28			09 56			10 22			10 56			11 19	11 27		
Stockport	84	a						09 31							10 33						11 30			
Hazel Grove	86	a																						
Buxton	86	a																						
Heald Green	85	a	00 16																					
Manchester Airport	85 ✈	a	00 23			05 25	07 25		09 48			10 17						11 17				11 47		

A not 11 December
B not 11 December. From Clitheroe
C To Chester
D From Blackburn
E To Liverpool Lime Street
F From Leeds to Morecambe
b Stops to pick up only

The Sunday service between Wigan Wallgate and Manchester Victoria via Atherton is funded by GMITA and will operate whilst funding exists

Table 82

Sundays
until 1 January

Barrow-in-Furness, Blackpool North, Preston, Southport, Kirkby and Wigan - Bolton - Manchester

Network Diagram - see first Page of Table 82

		NT	TP	NT	NT	NT	TP	NT	NT	TP	NT	NT	NT	TP	NT	NT	NT	TP	NT	NT	NT	TP	NT
			◇1				◇1			◇1				◇1				◇1				◇1	
		A		B					A		B		C	D		E	A		B				
										🛒				🛒									
Barrow-in-Furness	d						10 30															12 25	13 10
Roose	d																					12 29	13 14
Dalton	d																					12 36	13 20
Ulverston	d						10 46															12 44	13 29
Cark	d																					12 52	13 36
Kents Bank	d																					12 56	13 41
Grange-over-Sands	d						10 58															13 00	13 45
Arnside	d						11 04															13 06	13 51
Silverdale	d																					13 10	13 55
Carnforth	d						11 14									12 35						13 17	14 02
Windermere 83	d																						
Oxenholme Lake District 65	d													12 10									
Lancaster 6 65	a						11 22							12 26		12 44						13 26	14 15
	d						11 22							12 26								13 26	
Blackpool North 97	d		10 44	10 50				11 20		11 44	11 50				12 20			12 44	12 50				
Layton 97	d							11 23							12 23								
Poulton-le-Fylde 97	d		10 50	10 56				11 28		11 50	11 56				12 28			12 50	12 56				
Kirkham & Wesham 97	d							11 37							12 37								
Preston 8 65,97	a		11 08	11 14			11 42	11 47		12 08	12 14			12 45	12 47			13 08	13 14			13 45	
	d		11 10	11 15			11 47	11 49		12 10	12 15			12 47	12 49			13 10	13 15			13 47	
Leyland	d			11 21				11 54			12 21				12 54				13 21				
Buckshaw Parkway	d		11 17					11 59		12 17					12 59			13 17					
Chorley	d		11 21				11 56	12 03		12 21				12 56	13 03			13 21				13 56	
Adlington (Lancashire)	d							12 08							13 08								
Blackrod	d							12 12							13 12								
Horwich Parkway	d		11 28					12 16		12 28					13 16			13 28					
Lostock	d							12 20							13 20								
Southport	d					11 05							12 05								13 05		
Meols Cop	d					11 10							12 10								13 10		
Bescar Lane	d																						
New Lane	d																						
Burscough Bridge	d					11 18							12 18								13 18		
Hoscar	d																						
Parbold	d					11 23							12 23								13 23		
Appley Bridge	d					11 27							12 27								13 27		
Gathurst	d					11 30							12 30								13 30		
Kirkby	d																						
Rainford	d																						
Upholland	d																						
Orrell	d																						
Pemberton	d																						
Wigan Wallgate	a					11 35							12 35								13 35		
	d				11 15	11 36						12 15	12 36							13 15	13 36		
Wigan North Western	d			11a35							12a35								13a35				
Ince	d				11 18							12 18								13 18			
Hindley	d				11 22	11 41						12 22	12 41							13 22	13 41		
Westhoughton	d					11 46							12 46								13 46		
Bolton	a		11 34			11 54	12 08	12 25		12 34			12 54	13 08	13 25			13 34			13 54	14 08	
	d	11 31	11 35			11 54	12 08	12 25	12 31	12 35			12 54	13 08	13 25		13 31	13 35			13 54	14 08	
Moses Gate	d																						
Farnworth	d																						
Kearsley	d																						
Daisy Hill	d				11 26							12 26								13 26			
Hag Fold	d				11 29							12 29								13 29			
Atherton	d				11 31							12 31								13 31			
Walkden	d				11 37							12 37								13 37			
Moorside	d				11 40							12 40								13 40			
Swinton	d				11 43							12 43								13 43			
Salford Crescent	a	11 43	11 47		11 50	12 07		12 38	12 43	12 47		12 50	13 07		13 38		13 43	13 47		13 50	14 07		
	d	11 43	11 47		11 51	12 07		12 38	12 43	12 47		12 51	13 07		13 38		13 44	13 47		13 51	14 07		
Salford Central	d																						
Manchester Victoria ⛴	a	11 52			11 57			12 45	12 52			12 57			13 45		13 52			13 57			
Rochdale 41	a																						
Deansgate ⛴	a		11 51			12 11				12 51			13 11					13 51			14 11		
Manchester Oxford Road	a		11 52			12 13	12 23			12 52			13 13	13 23				13 52			14 13	14 23	
Manchester Piccadilly 10 ⛴	a		11 58			12 19	12 27			12 59			13 19	13 27				13 56			14 19	14 27	
Stockport 84	a					12 33							13 30								14 33		
Hazel Grove 86	a																						
Buxton 86	a																						
Heald Green 85	a																						
Manchester Airport 85 ✈	a		12 17				12 48			13 17				13 47				14 17				14 47	

A not 11 December. From Clitheroe
B To Liverpool Lime Street
C To Chester
D From Edinburgh
E From Leeds to Morecambe

The Sunday service between Wigan Wallgate and Manchester Victoria via Atherton is funded by GMITA and will operate whilst funding exists

Table 82

Sundays
until 1 January

Barrow-in-Furness, Blackpool North, Preston, Southport, Kirkby and Wigan - Bolton - Manchester

Network Diagram - see first Page of Table 82

		NT	NT	TP	NT	NT	NT	TP	NT	NT	TP	NT	NT	NT	TP	NT	NT	TP	NT	NT	NT	TP
				◇1				◇1			◇1				◇1			◇1				◇1
			A		B		C	D ✠		A		B					A		B		C	D ✠
Barrow-in-Furness	d														14 25							
Roose	d														14 29							
Dalton	d														14 36							
Ulverston	d														14 44							
Cark	d														14 52							
Kents Bank	d														14 56							
Grange-over-Sands	d														15 00							
Arnside	d														15 06							
Silverdale	d														15 10							
Carnforth	d														15 17							
Windermere	83 d																					
Oxenholme Lake District	65 d							14 10														16 10
Lancaster 6	65 a							14 26							15 26							16 26
	d							14 26							15 26							16 26
Blackpool North	97 d	13 20		13 44	13 50				14 20		14 44	14 50				15 20		15 44	15 50			
Layton	97 d	13 23							14 23							15 23						
Poulton-le-Fylde	97 d	13 28		13 50	13 56				14 28		14 50	14 56				15 28		15 50	15 56			
Kirkham & Wesham	97 d	13 37							14 37							15 37						
Preston 8	65,97 a	13 47		14 08	14 14			14 45	14 47		15 08	15 14			15 45	15 47		16 08	16 14			16 46
	d	13 49		14 10	14 15			14 47	14 49		15 10	15 15			15 47	15 49		16 10	16 15			16 47
Leyland	d	13 54			14 21				14 54			15 21				15 54			16 21			
Buckshaw Parkway	d	13 59		14 17					14 59		15 17					15 59		16 17				
Chorley	d	14 03		14 21				14 56	15 03		15 21				15 56	16 03		16 21				16 56
Adlington (Lancashire)	d	14 08							15 08							16 08						
Blackrod	d	14 12							15 11							16 11						
Horwich Parkway	d	14 16		14 28					15 15		15 28					16 15		16 28				
Lostock	d	14 20							15 20							16 20						
Southport	d						14 05							15 05							16 05	
Meols Cop	d						14 10							15 10							16 10	
Bescar Lane	d																					
New Lane	d																					
Burscough Bridge	d						14 18							15 18							16 18	
Hoscar	d																					
Parbold	d						14 23							15 23							16 23	
Appley Bridge	d						14 27							15 27							16 27	
Gathurst	d						14 30							15 30							16 30	
Kirkby	d																					
Rainford	d																					
Upholland	d																					
Orrell	d																					
Pemberton	d																					
Wigan Wallgate	a						14 35							15 35							16 35	
	d					14 15	14 36						15 15	15 36						16 15	16 36	
Wigan North Western	d				14a35							15a35							16a35			
Ince	d					14 18							15 18							16 18		
Hindley	d					14 22	14 41						15 22	15 41						16 22	16 41	
Westhoughton	d						14 46							15 46							16 46	
Bolton	a	14 25		14 34			14 54	15 08	15 25		15 34			15 54	16 08	16 25		16 34			16 54	17 08
	d	14 25	14⟆31	14 35			14 54	15 08	15 25	15⟆30	15 35			15 54	16 08	16 25	16⟆31	16 35			16 54	17 08
Moses Gate	d		⟆							⟆							⟆					
Farnworth	d		⟆							⟆							⟆					
Kearsley	d		⟆							⟆							⟆					
Daisy Hill	d		⟆			14 26				⟆			15 26				⟆			16 26		
Hag Fold	d		⟆			14 29				⟆			15 29				⟆			16 29		
Atherton	d		⟆			14 31				⟆			15 31				⟆			16 31		
Walkden	d		⟆			14 37				⟆			15 37				⟆			16 37		
Moorside	d		⟆			14 40				⟆			15 40				⟆			16 40		
Swinton	d		⟆			14 43				⟆			15 43				⟆			16 43		
Salford Crescent	a	14 38	14⟆43	14 47		14 50	15 07		15 38	15⟆42	15 47		15 50	16 07		16 38	16⟆43	16 47		16 50	17 07	
	d	14 38	14⟆43	14 47		14 51	15 07		15 38	15⟆43	15 47		15 51	16 07		16 38	16⟆44	16 47		16 51	17 07	
Salford Central	d		⟆							⟆							⟆					
Manchester Victoria	⇌ a	14 45	14⟆52			14 57			15 45	15⟆52			15 57			16 45	16⟆52			16 57		
Rochdale	41 a																					
Deansgate	⇌ a			14 51			15 11				15 51			16 11				16 51			17 11	
Manchester Oxford Road	a			14 52			15 13	15 23			15 52			16 13	16 23			16 52			17 13	17 23
Manchester Piccadilly 10	⇌ a			14 56			15 19	15 27			15 56			16 19	16 27			16 56			17 19	17 27
Stockport	84 a						15 31							16 33							17 30	
Hazel Grove	86 a																					
Buxton	86 a																					
Heald Green	85 a																					
Manchester Airport	85 ✈ a			15 17				15 47			16 17				16 46			17 17				17 47

A not 11 December. From Clitheroe
B To Liverpool Lime Street
C To Chester
D From Edinburgh

The Sunday service between Wigan Wallgate and Manchester Victoria via Atherton is funded by GMITA and will operate whilst funding exists

Table 82

Sundays
until 1 January

Barrow-in-Furness, Blackpool North, Preston, Southport, Kirkby and Wigan - Bolton - Manchester

Network Diagram - see first Page of Table 82

		NT	NT	NT	TP	NT	NT	NT		TP	NT	NT	TP	NT	NT	TP	NT	TP		NT	TP	NT	NT	TP	NT
					◇1					◇1			◇1			◇1		◇1			◇1			◇1	
			A	B		C				D		B		C	E	F	A			G		C		D	
										🚲						🚲								🚲	
Barrow-in-Furness	d																	18 17							
Roose	d																	18 21							
Dalton	d																	18 28							
Ulverston	d																	18 36							
Cark	d																	18 44							
Kents Bank	d																	18 48							
Grange-over-Sands	d																	18 52							
Arnside	d																	18 58							
Silverdale	d																	19 02							
Carnforth	d		16 37														19 04	19 08							
Windermere 83	d																								
Oxenholme Lake District 65	d									17 07						18 10								19 07	
Lancaster 6 65	a		16 46							17 22						18 26	19 13	19 17						19 22	
	d									17 22						18 26		19 17						19 22	
Blackpool North 97	d	16 20			16 44	16 50					17 20		17 44	17 50							18 44	18 50			19 20
Layton 97	d	16 23									17 23														19 23
Poulton-le-Fylde 97	d	16 28			16 50	16 56					17 28		17 50	17 56							18 50	18 56			19 28
Kirkham & Wesham 97	d	16 37									17 37														19 37
Preston 8 65,97	a	16 47			17 08	17 14				17 41	17 47		18 08	18 14		18 45		19 37			19 08	19 14		19 41	19 47
	d	16 49			17 10	17 15				17 47	17 49		18 10	18 15		18 47					19 10	19 15		19 47	19 49
Leyland	d	16 54				17 21					17 54			18 21								19 21			19 54
Buckshaw Parkway	d	16 59			17 17						17 59		18 17								19 17				19 59
Chorley	d	17 03			17 21					17 56	18 03		18 21			18 56					19 21			19 56	20 03
Adlington (Lancashire)	d	17 08									18 08														20 08
Blackrod	d	17 12									18 12														20 12
Horwich Parkway	d	17 16			17 28						18 16		18 28								19 28				20 16
Lostock	d	17 20									18 20														20 20
Southport	d							17 05							18 05								19 05		
Meols Cop	d							17 10							18 10								19 10		
Bescar Lane	d																								
New Lane	d																								
Burscough Bridge	d							17 18							18 18								19 18		
Hoscar	d																								
Parbold	d							17 23							18 23								19 23		
Appley Bridge	d							17 27							18 27								19 27		
Gathurst	d							17 30							18 30								19 30		
Kirkby	d																								
Rainford	d																								
Upholland	d																								
Orrell	d																								
Pemberton	d																								
Wigan Wallgate	a							17 35							18 35								19 35		
	d						17 15	17 36							18 36								19 36		
Wigan North Western	d					17a35								18a35								19a35			
Ince	d						17 18																		
Hindley	d						17 22	17 41							18 41								19 41		
Westhoughton	d							17 46							18 46								19 46		
Bolton	a	17 25			17 34			17 54		18 08	18 25		18 34		18 54	19 08					19 34		19 54	20 08	20 25
	d	17 25		17 30	17 35			17 54		18 08	18 25	18 31	18 35		18 54	19 08				19 31	19 35		19 54	20 08	20 25
Moses Gate	d																								
Farnworth	d																								
Kearsley	d																								
Daisy Hill	d						17 26																		
Hag Fold	d						17 29																		
Atherton	d						17 31																		
Walkden	d						17 37																		
Moorside	d						17 40																		
Swinton	d						17 43																		
Salford Crescent	a	17 38		17 42	17 47		17 50	18 07			18 38	18 43	18 47		19 07					19 44	19 47		20 07		20 38
	d	17 38		17 43	17 47		17 51	18 07			18 38	18 44	18 47		19 07					19 44	19 47		20 07		20 38
Salford Central	d																								
Manchester Victoria ⛴	a	17 45		17 52			17 57				18 45	18 52								19 52					20 45
Rochdale 41	a																								
Deansgate ⛴	a				17 51			18 11					18 51		19 11						19 51		20 11		
Manchester Oxford Road	a				17 52			18 13		18 23			18 52		19 13	19 23					19 52		20 13	20 23	
Manchester Piccadilly 10 ⛴	a				17 56			18 19		18 27			18 56		19 19	19 27					19 56		20 19	20 27	
Stockport 84	a							18 33							19 30								20 33		
Hazel Grove 86	a																								
Buxton 86	a																								
Heald Green 85	a																								
Manchester Airport 85 ✈	a				18 17					18 45			19 17			19 47					20 17			20 45	

A From Leeds to Morecambe
B not 11 December. From Clitheroe
C To Liverpool Lime Street
D From Glasgow Central
E To Chester
F From Edinburgh
G From Clitheroe

The Sunday service between Wigan Wallgate and Manchester Victoria via Atherton is funded by GMITA and will operate whilst funding exists

Table 82

Sundays
until 1 January

Barrow-in-Furness, Blackpool North, Preston, Southport, Kirkby and Wigan - Bolton - Manchester

Network Diagram - see first Page of Table 82

	NT	TP	NT	NT	TP	NT	NT	NT	TP	NT	TP	NT	NT	NT	NT	NT	TP	TP	NT	NT	NT
		◇1			◇1				◇1		◇1						◇1	◇1			
	A		B	C	D ⚒		E		F	A		B		E		B	G ⚒	D ⚒		B	H
Barrow-in-Furness d						20 02															
Roose d						20 06															
Dalton d						20 12															
Ulverston d						20 21															
Cark d						20 28															
Kents Bank d						20 33															
Grange-over-Sands d						20 37															
Arnside d						20 43															
Silverdale d						20 47															
Carnforth d						20 54															
Windermere 83 d									20 40												
Oxenholme Lake District 65 d					20 10				21 01												
Lancaster 6 65 a					20 26	21 07			21 18												
d					20 26													22 03			
Blackpool North 97 d		19 44	19 50				20 11	20 20			20 44	20 50		21 13	21 20	21 50	21 56			22 44	
Layton 97 d								20 23							21 23						
Poulton-le-Fylde 97 d		19 50	19 56				20 17	20 28			20 50	20 56		21 19	21 28	21 56	22 02			22 50	
Kirkham & Wesham 97 d								20 37							21 37						
Preston 8 65,97 a		20 08	20 14		20 45		20 34	20 47			21 08	21 14		21 36	21 47	22 14	22 20	22 23		23 08	
d		20 10	20 15		20 47			20 49			21 10	21 15			21 49	22 15	22 29			23 09	
Leyland d			20 21					20 54				21 21			21 54	22 21				23 15	
Buckshaw Parkway d		20 17						20 59			21 17				21 59						
Chorley d		20 21			20 56			21 03			21 21				22 03		22 38				
Adlington (Lancashire) d								21 08							22 08						
Blackrod d								21 12							22 12						
Horwich Parkway d		20 28						21 16			21 28				22 16						
Lostock d								21 20							22 20						
Southport d				20 05									21 05						22 05		
Meols Cop d				20 10									21 10						22 10		
Bescar Lane d																					
New Lane d																					
Burscough Bridge d				20 18									21 18						22 18		
Hoscar d																					
Parbold d				20 23									21 23						22 23		
Appley Bridge d				20 27									21 27						22 27		
Gathurst d				20 30									21 30						22 30		
Kirkby d																					
Rainford d																					
Upholland d																					
Orrell d																					
Pemberton d																					
Wigan Wallgate a				20 35									21 35						22 35		
d				20 36									21 36						22 36		
Wigan North Western d			20a35									21a35				22a35				23a29	
Ince d																					
Hindley d				20 41									21 41						22 41		
Westhoughton d				20 46									21 46						22 46		
Bolton a		20 34		20 54	21 08			21 25			21 34		21 54		22 25		22 50		22 54		
d	20 31	20 35		20 54	21 08			21 25		21 31	21 35		21 54		22 25		22 50		22 54		23 31
Moses Gate d																					
Farnworth d																					
Kearsley d																					
Daisy Hill d																					
Hag Fold d																					
Atherton d																					
Walkden d																					
Moorside d																					
Swinton d																					
Salford Crescent a	20 43	20 47		21 07				21 38		21 43	21 47		22 07		22 38		23 02		23 07		23 43
d	20 43	20 47		21 07				21 38		21 43	21 47		22 07		22 38		23 03		23 07		23 43
Salford Central d																					
Manchester Victoria ⇌ a	20 52							21 45		21 52					22 45						23 52
Rochdale 41 a																					
Deansgate ⇌ a		20 51		21 11							21 51		22 11				23 08		23 11		
Manchester Oxford Road a		20 52		21 13	21 23						21 52		22 13				23 10		23 14		
Manchester Piccadilly 10 ⇌ a		20 56		21 19	21 27						21 56		22 19				23 14		23 19		
Stockport 84 a				21 30									22 33						23 33		
Hazel Grove 86 a																					
Buxton 86 a																					
Heald Green 85 a																					
Manchester Airport 85 ✈ a		21 16			21 46						22 17						23 30				

A From Clitheroe
B To Liverpool Lime Street
C To Chester
D From Edinburgh
E To Leeds
F To Barrow-in-Furness
G ⚒ from Preston
H not 11 December. From Clitheroe

The Sunday service between Wigan Wallgate and Manchester Victoria via Atherton is funded by GMITA and will operate whilst funding exists

Table 82

Sundays
until 1 January

Barrow-in-Furness, Blackpool North, Preston, Southport, Kirkby and Wigan - Bolton - Manchester

Network Diagram - see first Page of Table 82

Station	Table		TP ◇1
Barrow-in-Furness		d	
Roose		d	
Dalton		d	
Ulverston		d	
Cark		d	
Kents Bank		d	
Grange-over-Sands		d	
Arnside		d	
Silverdale		d	
Carnforth		d	
Windermere	83	d	
Oxenholme Lake District	65	d	
Lancaster 6	65	a	
		d	
Blackpool North	97	d	23 03
Layton	97	d	
Poulton-le-Fylde	97	d	23 09
Kirkham & Wesham	97	d	23 17
Preston 8	65,97	a	23 28
		d	23 28
Leyland		d	23 34
Buckshaw Parkway		d	23 38
Chorley		d	23 42
Adlington (Lancashire)		d	23 46
Blackrod		d	23 50
Horwich Parkway		d	23 53
Lostock		d	23 57
Southport		d	
Meols Cop		d	
Bescar Lane		d	
New Lane		d	
Burscough Bridge		d	
Hoscar		d	
Parbold		d	
Appley Bridge		d	
Gathurst		d	
Kirkby		d	
Rainford		d	
Upholland		d	
Orrell		d	
Pemberton		d	
Wigan Wallgate		a	
		d	
Wigan North Western		d	
Ince		d	
Hindley		d	
Westhoughton		d	
Bolton		a	00 02
		d	00 02
Moses Gate		d	
Farnworth		d	
Kearsley		d	
Daisy Hill		d	
Hag Fold		d	
Atherton		d	
Walkden		d	
Moorside		d	
Swinton		d	
Salford Crescent		a	
		d	
Salford Central		d	
Manchester Victoria	🚊	a	
Rochdale	41	a	
Deansgate	🚊	a	
Manchester Oxford Road		a	
Manchester Piccadilly 10	🚊	a	00 18
Stockport	84	a	
Hazel Grove	86	a	
Buxton	86	a	
Heald Green	85	a	
Manchester Airport	85 ✈	a	00 32

The Sunday service between Wigan Wallgate and Manchester Victoria via Atherton is funded by GMITA and will operate whilst funding exists

Table 82

Sundays

8 January to 12 February

Barrow-in-Furness, Blackpool North, Preston, Southport, Kirkby and Wigan - Bolton - Manchester

Network Diagram - see first Page of Table 82

		TP	NT	NT	TP	TP	NT	NT	TP	TP	TP	NT	NT	TP	NT	NT	NT	NT	NT	TP	NT	NT	NT
		◇1							◇1		◇1			◇1						◇1			
			A				B			C		D					E	A			B		E
					Bus	Bus		Bus		Bus			Bus			Bus			Bus			Bus	
Barrow-in-Furness	d										09 17												
Roose	d										09 21												
Dalton	d										09 28												
Ulverston	d										09 36												
Cark	d										09 44												
Kents Bank	d										09 48												
Grange-over-Sands	d										09 52												
Arnside	d										09 58												
Silverdale	d										10 02												
Carnforth	d										10a09												
Windermere 83	d																						
Oxenholme Lake District 65	d																						
Lancaster 6 65	a																						
	d																						
Blackpool North 97	d	22p44		23p02	03 20	05 20			08 14					08 44			08 50			09 44			09 50
Layton 97	d			23p05																			
Poulton-le-Fylde 97	d	22p50		23p10					08 20					08 50			08 56			09 50			09 56
Kirkham & Wesham 97	d			23p19																			
Preston 8 65,97	a	23p08		23p29					08 38					09 08			09 14			10 07			10 14
	d	23p10		23p31	04u00	06u00		08 14	08 42	08 48				09 10		09 14	09 15			10 10		10 14	10 15
Leyland	d			23p36				08 34								09 34	09 21					10 34	10 21
Buckshaw Parkway	d	23p17		23p41																			
Chorley	d	23p21		23p45				08 49								09 49						10 49	
Adlington (Lancashire)	d			23p50				08 55								09 55						10 55	
Blackrod	d			23p54				09 00								10 00						11 00	
Horwich Parkway	d	23p28		23p58				09 04								10 04						11 04	
Lostock	d			00 02				09 10								10 10						11 10	
Southport	d														09 10						10 05		
Meols Cop	d														09 15						10 10		
Bescar Lane	d																						
New Lane	d																						
Burscough Bridge	d														09 23						10 18		
Hoscar	d																						
Parbold	d														09 28						10 23		
Appley Bridge	d														09 32						10 27		
Gathurst	d														09 35						10 30		
Kirkby	d																						
Rainford	d																						
Upholland	d																						
Orrell	d																						
Pemberton	d																						
Wigan Wallgate	a														09 40						10 35		
	d						08 40						08 26		09 41				09 26		10 36		
Wigan North Western	d																09a35						10a36
Ince	d												08 38						09 38				
Hindley	d						08 45						08 44		09 46				09 44		10 41		
Westhoughton	d						08 49								09 51						10 46		
Bolton	a	23p34		00 07			08 57	09 25	09 09	09 23				09 37	09 59	10 25				10 37	10 54	11 25	
	d	23p35	23p38	00 07	04u35	06u35	08 58		09 10			09 31		09 38	09 59			10 31		10 38	10 54		
Moses Gate	d																						
Farnworth	d																						
Kearsley	d																						
Daisy Hill	d												08 54						09 54				
Hag Fold	d												09 02						10 02				
Atherton	d												09 06						10 06				
Walkden	d												09 20						10 20				
Moorside	d												09 26						10 26				
Swinton	d												09 30						10 30				
Salford Crescent	a	23p47	23p50				09 10		09 22			09 43	09 45	09 50	10 12			10 43	10 45	10 50	11 07		
	d	23p47	23p53				09 11		09 22			09 44	09 45	09 50	10 12			10 44	10 45	10 50	11 07		
Salford Central	d																						
Manchester Victoria 🚋	a		00 01	00 26								09 53	09 55					10 52	10 55				
Rochdale 41	a																						
Deansgate 🚋	a						09 14		09 27					09 54	10 16					10 54	11 11		
Manchester Oxford Road	a						09 17		09 28					09 55	10 18					10 55	11 13		
Manchester Piccadilly 10 🚋	a	23p53			05b00	07b00	09 21		09 32					09 59	10 22					10 59	11 19		
Stockport 84	a						09 31								10 33						11 30		
Hazel Grove 86	a																						
Buxton 86	a																						
Heald Green 85	a	00 16																					
Manchester Airport 85 ✈	a	00 23			05 25	07 25			09 49					10 17						11 17			

A From Clitheroe
B To Chester
C 15 January
D From Blackburn
E To Liverpool Lime Street
b Stops to pick up only

The Sunday service between Wigan Wallgate and Manchester Victoria via Atherton is funded by GMITA and will operate whilst funding exists

Table 82

Sundays

8 January to 12 February

Barrow-in-Furness, Blackpool North, Preston, Southport, Kirkby and Wigan - Bolton - Manchester

Network Diagram - see first Page of Table 82

		TP	TP	NT	NT	TP	NT	NT	NT	TP	TP	NT	NT	TP	NT	NT	NT	TP	TP	NT	NT	NT	TP
			◇1			◇1					◇1			◇1					◇1				◇1
				A					B			A			C		B		D	E	A		
		🚌			🚌			🚌		🚌			🚌			🚌		🚌				🚌	
														🛒					🛒				
Barrow-in-Furness	d										10 22												
Roose	d										10 26												
Dalton	d										10 33												
Ulverston	d										10 41												
Cark	d										10 49												
Kents Bank	d										10 53												
Grange-over-Sands	d										10 57												
Arnside	d										11 03												
Silverdale	d										11 07												
Carnforth	d										11 14									12 35			
Windermere 83	d																						
Oxenholme Lake District 65	d																		12 04				
Lancaster 6 65	a										11 22								12 19	12 44			
	d										11 22								12 19				
Blackpool North 97	d					10 44			10 50					11 44			11 50						12 44
Layton 97	d																						
Poulton-le-Fylde 97	d					10 50			10 56					11 50			11 56						12 50
Kirkham & Wesham 97	d																						
Preston 8 65,97	a					11 08			11 14		11 42			12 08			12 14		12 38				13 08
	d	10 19	10 44			11 10		11 14	11 15	11 19	11 44			12 09		12 14	12 15	12 19	12 40				13 10
Leyland	d							11 34	11 21							12 34	12 21						
Buckshaw Parkway	d																						
Chorley	d	10 35						11 49		11 35						12 49		12 35					
Adlington (Lancashire)	d							11 55								12 55							
Blackrod	d							12 00								13 00							
Horwich Parkway	d							12 04								13 04							
Lostock	d							12 10								13 10							
Southport	d						11 05								12 05								
Meols Cop	d						11 10								12 10								
Bescar Lane	d																						
New Lane	d																						
Burscough Bridge	d						11 18								12 18								
Hoscar	d																						
Parbold	d						11 23								12 23								
Appley Bridge	d						11 27								12 27								
Gathurst	d						11 30								12 30								
Kirkby	d																						
Rainford	d																						
Upholland	d																						
Orrell	d																						
Pemberton	d																						
Wigan Wallgate	a						11 35								12 35								
	d				10 26		11 36						11 26		12 36							12 26	
Wigan North Western	d								11a35								12a35						
Ince	d				10 38								11 38									12 38	
Hindley	d				10 44		11 41						11 44		12 41							12 44	
Westhoughton	d						11 46								12 46								
Bolton	a	11 00	11 11			11 37	11 54	12 25		12 00	12 11			12 37	12 54	13 25		13 00	13 08				13 37
	d		11 12	11 31		11 38	11 54				12 12	12 31		12 37	12 54				13 08		13 31		13 38
Moses Gate	d																						
Farnworth	d																						
Kearsley	d																						
Daisy Hill	d				10 54								11 54									12 54	
Hag Fold	d				11 02								12 02									13 02	
Atherton	d				11 06								12 06									13 06	
Walkden	d				11 20								12 20									13 20	
Moorside	d				11 26								12 26									13 26	
Swinton	d				11 30								12 30									13 30	
Salford Crescent	a			11 43	11 45	11 50	12 07					12 43	12 45	12 49	13 07						13 43	13 45	13 50
	d			11 43	11 45	11 50	12 07					12 43	12 45	12 50	13 07						13 44	13 45	13 50
Salford Central	d																						
Manchester Victoria ⛴	a			11 52	11 55							12 52	12 55								13 52	13 55	
Rochdale 41	a																						
Deansgate ⛴	a					11 54	12 11							12 53	13 11								13 54
Manchester Oxford Road	a		11 26			11 55	12 13				12 26			12 55	13 13				13 23				13 55
Manchester Piccadilly 10 ⛴	a		11 30			11 59	12 19				12 30			12 58	13 19				13 27				13 59
Stockport 84	a						12 33								13 30								
Hazel Grove 86	a																						
Buxton 86	a																						
Heald Green 85	a																						
Manchester Airport 85 ✈	a		11 47			12 17					12 47			13 17					13 47				14 17

A From Clitheroe
B To Liverpool Lime Street
C To Chester
D From Edinburgh
E From Leeds to Morecambe

The Sunday service between Wigan Wallgate and Manchester Victoria via Atherton is funded by GMITA and will operate whilst funding exists

Table 82

Sundays

8 January to 12 February

Barrow-in-Furness, Blackpool North, Preston, Southport, Kirkby and Wigan - Bolton - Manchester

Network Diagram - see first Page of Table 82

		NT	NT	NT	TP	TP	NT	NT	NT	TP	NT	NT	NT	TP	TP	NT	NT	TP	NT	NT	NT	TP
						◇1				◇1					◇1			◇1				
				A				B			C		A		D	B					A	
			🚌		🚌				🚌			🚌		🚌			🚌			🚌		🚌
															🛒							
Barrow-in-Furness	d					12 30	13 10															
Roose	d						13 14															
Dalton	d						13 20															
Ulverston	d					12 46	13 29															
Cark	d						13 36															
Kents Bank	d						13 41															
Grange-over-Sands	d					12 58	13 45															
Arnside	d					13 04	13 51															
Silverdale	d						13 55															
Carnforth	d					13 13	14 02															
Windermere 83	d																					
Oxenholme Lake District 65	d														14 04							
Lancaster 6 65	a					13 20	14 15								14 20							
	d					13 20									14 20							
Blackpool North 97	d			12 50						13 44			13 50					14 44			14 50	
Layton 97	d																					
Poulton-le-Fylde 97	d			12 56						13 50			13 56					14 50			14 56	
Kirkham & Wesham 97	d																					
Preston 8 65,97	a			13 14		13 40				14 08			14 14		14 39			15 08			15 14	
	d		13 14	13 15	13 19	13 40				14 10		14 14	14 15	14 19	14 40			15 10		15 14	15 15	15 19
Leyland	d		13 34	13 21								14 34	14 21							15 34	15 21	
Buckshaw Parkway	d																					
Chorley	d		13 49		13 35							14 49		14 35						15 49		15 35
Adlington (Lancashire)	d		13 55									14 55								15 55		
Blackrod	d		14 00									15 00								16 00		
Horwich Parkway	d		14 04									15 04								16 04		
Lostock	d		14 10									15 10								16 10		
Southport	d	13 05									14 05								15 05			
Meols Cop	d	13 10									14 10								15 10			
Bescar Lane	d																					
New Lane	d																					
Burscough Bridge	d	13 18									14 18								15 18			
Hoscar	d																					
Parbold	d	13 23									14 23								15 23			
Appley Bridge	d	13 27									14 27								15 27			
Gathurst	d	13 30									14 30								15 30			
Kirkby	d																					
Rainford	d																					
Upholland	d																					
Orrell	d																					
Pemberton	d																					
Wigan Wallgate	a	13 35									14 35								15 35			
	d	13 36							13 26		14 36						14 26		15 36			
Wigan North Western	d			13a35									14a35								15a35	
Ince	d								13 38								14 38					
Hindley	d	13 41							13 44		14 41						14 44		15 41			
Westhoughton	d	13 46									14 46								15 46			
Bolton	a	13 54	14 25		14 00	14 08				14 37	14 54	15 25		15 00	15 08			15 37	15 54	16 25		16 00
	d	13 54				14 08		14 31		14 38	14 54				15 08	15 30		15 38	15 54			
Moses Gate	d																					
Farnworth	d																					
Kearsley	d																					
Daisy Hill	d								13 54								14 54					
Hag Fold	d								14 02								15 02					
Atherton	d								14 06								15 06					
Walkden	d								14 20								15 20					
Moorside	d								14 26								15 26					
Swinton	d								14 30								15 30					
Salford Crescent	a	14 07						14 43	14 45	14 50	15 07					15 42	15 45	15 50	16 07			
	d	14 07						14 43	14 45	14 50	15 07					15 43	15 45	15 50	16 07			
Salford Central	d																					
Manchester Victoria 🚇	a							14 52	14 55							15 52	15 55					
Rochdale 41	a																					
Deansgate 🚇	a	14 11								14 54	15 11							15 54	16 11			
Manchester Oxford Road	a	14 13				14 23				14 55	15 13				15 23			15 55	16 13			
Manchester Piccadilly 10 🚇	a	14 19				14 27				14 59	15 19				15 27			15 59	16 19			
Stockport 84	a	14 33									15 31								16 33			
Hazel Grove 86	a																					
Buxton 86	a																					
Heald Green 85	a																					
Manchester Airport 85 ✈	a					14 47				15 17					15 47			16 17				

A To Liverpool Lime Street
B From Clitheroe
C To Chester
D From Edinburgh

The Sunday service between Wigan Wallgate and Manchester Victoria via Atherton is funded by GMITA and will operate whilst funding exists

Table 82

Sundays

8 January to 12 February

Barrow-in-Furness, Blackpool North, Preston, Southport, Kirkby and Wigan - Bolton - Manchester

Network Diagram - see first Page of Table 82

		TP	NT	NT	TP	NT	NT	NT	TP	TP	NT	NT	NT	TP	NT	NT	NT	TP	TP	NT	NT	TP	NT
		◇1			◇1					◇1				◇1					◇1			◇1	
			A			B		C		D	E	A					C		F	A			B
				bus			bus		bus				bus			bus		bus			bus		
										trolley									trolley				
Barrow-in-Furness	d	14 18																					
Roose	d	14 22																					
Dalton	d	14 29																					
Ulverston	d	14 37																					
Cark	d	14 45																					
Kents Bank	d	14 49																					
Grange-over-Sands	d	14 53																					
Arnside	d	14 59																					
Silverdale	d	15 03																					
Carnforth	d	15 10									16 37												
Windermere 83	d																						
Oxenholme Lake District 65	d									16 04									17 04				
Lancaster 6 65	a	15 18								16 20	16 46								17 20				
	d	15 20								16 20									17 20				
Blackpool North 97	d				15 44			15 50						16 44			16 50					17 44	
Layton 97	d																						
Poulton-le-Fylde 97	d				15 50			15 56						16 50			16 56					17 50	
Kirkham & Wesham 97	d																						
Preston 8 65,97	a	15 38			16 08			16 14		16 39				17 08			17 14		17 39			18 08	
	d	15 40			16 10		16 14	16 15	16 19	16 40				17 10		17 14	17 15	17 19	17 40			18 10	
Leyland	d						16 34	16 21								17 34	17 21						
Buckshaw Parkway	d																						
Chorley	d						16 49		16 35							17 49		17 35					
Adlington (Lancashire)	d						16 55									17 55							
Blackrod	d						17 00									18 00							
Horwich Parkway	d						17 04									18 04							
Lostock	d						17 10									18 10							
Southport	d					16 05									17 05								18 05
Meols Cop	d					16 10									17 10								18 10
Bescar Lane	d																						
New Lane	d																						
Burscough Bridge	d					16 18									17 18								18 18
Hoscar	d																						
Parbold	d					16 23									17 23								18 23
Appley Bridge	d					16 27									17 27								18 27
Gathurst	d					16 30									17 30								18 30
Kirkby	d																						
Rainford	d																						
Upholland	d																						
Orrell	d																						
Pemberton	d																						
Wigan Wallgate	a					16 35									17 35								18 35
	d			15 26		16 36							16 26		17 36						17 26		18 36
Wigan North Western	d							16a35									17a35						
Ince	d			15 38									16 38								17 38		
Hindley	d			15 44		16 41							16 44		17 41						17 44		18 41
Westhoughton	d					16 46									17 46								18 46
Bolton	a	16 08			16 37	16 54	17 25		17 00	17 08				17 37	17 54	18 25		18 00	18 08			18 37	18 54
	d	16 08	16 31		16 38	16 54				17 08		17 30		17 38	17 54				18 08	18 31		18 38	18 54
Moses Gate	d																						
Farnworth	d																						
Kearsley	d																						
Daisy Hill	d			15 54									16 54								17 54		
Hag Fold	d			16 02									17 02								18 02		
Atherton	d			16 06									17 06								18 06		
Walkden	d			16 20									17 20								18 20		
Moorside	d			16 26									17 26								18 26		
Swinton	d			16 30									17 30								18 30		
Salford Crescent	a		16 43	16 45	16 50	17 07						17 42	17 45	17 50	18 07					18 43	18 45	18 50	19 07
	d		16 44	16 45	16 50	17 07						17 43	17 45	17 50	18 07					18 44	18 45	18 50	19 07
Salford Central	d																						
Manchester Victoria ⇌	a		16 52	16 55								17 52	17 55							18 52	18 55		
Rochdale 41	a																						
Deansgate ⇌	a				16 54	17 11								17 54	18 11							18 54	19 11
Manchester Oxford Road	a	16 23			16 55	17 13				17 23				17 55	18 13				18 23			18 55	19 13
Manchester Piccadilly 10 ⇌	a	16 27			16 59	17 19				17 27				17 59	18 19				18 27			18 59	19 19
Stockport 84	a					17 30									18 33								19 30
Hazel Grove 86	a																						
Buxton 86	a																						
Heald Green 85	a																						
Manchester Airport 85 ✈	a	16 47			17 17					17 47				18 17					18 47			19 17	

A From Clitheroe
B To Chester
C To Liverpool Lime Street
D From Edinburgh
E From Leeds to Morecambe
F From Glasgow Central

The Sunday service between Wigan Wallgate and Manchester Victoria via Atherton is funded by GMITA and will operate whilst funding exists

Table 82

Sundays

8 January to 12 February

Barrow-in-Furness, Blackpool North, Preston, Southport, Kirkby and Wigan - Bolton - Manchester

Network Diagram - see first Page of Table 82

		NT	NT	TP	TP	NT	TP	NT	TP	NT	NT	NT	TP	TP	NT	TP	NT	NT	NT	NT	TP	TP
					◇1		◇1		◇1					◇1		◇1						◇1
			A		B	C		D				A		E	D		F		A	G		B
		bus		bus	bike						bus		bus	bike				bus			bus	bike
Barrow-in-Furness	d						18 14															
Roose	d						18 19															
Dalton	d						18 26															
Ulverston	d						18 34															
Cark	d						18 42															
Kents Bank	d						18 46															
Grange-over-Sands	d						18 50															
Arnside	d						18 56															
Silverdale	d						19 00															
Carnforth	d					19 04	19 06															
Windermere 83	d																					
Oxenholme Lake District 65	d				18 04																	20 04
Lancaster 6 65	a				18 20	19 13	19 14															20 20
	d				18 20		19 15							19 20								20 20
Blackpool North 97	d		17 50						18 44			18 50				19 44			19 50	20 11		
Layton 97	d																					
Poulton-le-Fylde 97	d		17 56						18 50			18 56				19 50			19 56	20 17		
Kirkham & Wesham 97	d																					
Preston 8 65,97	a		18 14		18 39		19 34		19 08			19 14		19 39		20 08			20 14	20 34		20 39
	d	18 14	18 15	18 19	18 40				19 10		19 14	19 15	19 19	19 40		20 10		20 14	20 15		20 19	20 40
Leyland	d	18 34	18 21								19 34	19 21						20 34	20 21			
Buckshaw Parkway	d																					
Chorley	d	18 49		18 35							19 49		19 35					20 49			20 35	
Adlington (Lancashire)	d	18 55									19 55							20 55				
Blackrod	d	19 00									20 00							21 00				
Horwich Parkway	d	19 04									20 04							21 04				
Lostock	d	19 10									20 10							21 10				
Southport	d									19 05							20 05					
Meols Cop	d									19 10							20 10					
Bescar Lane	d																					
New Lane	d																					
Burscough Bridge	d									19 18							20 18					
Hoscar	d																					
Parbold	d									19 23							20 23					
Appley Bridge	d									19 27							20 27					
Gathurst	d									19 30							20 30					
Kirkby	d																					
Rainford	d																					
Upholland	d																					
Orrell	d																					
Pemberton	d																					
Wigan Wallgate	a									19 35							20 35					
	d									19 36							20 36					
Wigan North Western	d		18a35									19a35							20a35			
Ince	d																					
Hindley	d									19 41							20 41					
Westhoughton	d									19 46							20 46					
Bolton	a	19 25		19 00	19 08				19 37	19 54	20 25		20 00	20 08		20 37	20 54	21 25			21 00	21 08
	d				19 08			19 31	19 38	19 54				20 08	20 31	20 38	20 54					21 08
Moses Gate	d																					
Farnworth	d																					
Kearsley	d																					
Daisy Hill	d																					
Hag Fold	d																					
Atherton	d																					
Walkden	d																					
Moorside	d																					
Swinton	d																					
Salford Crescent	a							19 44	19 50	20 07					20 43	20 50	21 07					
	d							19 44	19 50	20 07					20 43	20 50	21 07					
Salford Central	d																					
Manchester Victoria (tram)	a							19 52							20 52							
Rochdale 41	a																					
Deansgate (tram)	a								19 54	20 11						20 54	21 11					
Manchester Oxford Road	a				19 23				19 55	20 13				20 23		20 55	21 13					21 23
Manchester Piccadilly 10 (tram)	a				19 27				19 59	20 19				20 27		20 59	21 19					21 27
Stockport 84	a									20 33							21 30					
Hazel Grove 86	a																					
Buxton 86	a																					
Heald Green 85	a																					
Manchester Airport 85 (plane)	a				19 47				20 17					20 47		21 17						21 47

A To Liverpool Lime Street
B From Edinburgh
C From Leeds to Morecambe
D From Clitheroe
E From Glasgow Central
F To Chester
G To Leeds

The Sunday service between Wigan Wallgate and Manchester Victoria via Atherton is funded by GMITA and will operate whilst funding exists

Table 82

Sundays

8 January to 12 February

Barrow-in-Furness, Blackpool North, Preston, Southport, Kirkby and Wigan - Bolton - Manchester

Network Diagram - see first Page of Table 82

		NT	TP	NT	TP	NT	NT	NT	NT	NT	NT	NT	TP	TP	NT	NT	TP
			◇1		◇1								◇1	◇1			◇1
			A	B				C	D			C	E	F	C	B	
							🚌				🚌						
													trolley	trolley			
Barrow-in-Furness	d	20 02															
Roose	d	20 06															
Dalton	d	20 12															
Ulverston	d	20 21															
Cark	d	20 28															
Kents Bank	d	20 33															
Grange-over-Sands	d	20 37															
Arnside	d	20 43															
Silverdale	d	20 47															
Carnforth	d	20 54															
Windermere 83	d		20 40														
Oxenholme Lake District 65	d		21 01														
Lancaster 6 65	a	21 07	21 18														
	d													22 03			
Blackpool North 97	d				20 44			20 50	21 13			21 50	21 56		22 44		23 03
Layton 97	d																
Poulton-le-Fylde 97	d				20 50			20 56	21 19			21 56	22 02		22 50		23 09
Kirkham & Wesham 97	d																23 17
Preston 8 65,97	a				21 08			21 14	21 36			22 14	22 20	22 23	23 08		23 28
	d				21 10		21 14	21 15			22 14	22 15	22 28		23 09		23 28
Leyland	d						21 34	21 21			22 34	22 21			23 15		23 34
Buckshaw Parkway	d																
Chorley	d						21 49				22 49						
Adlington (Lancashire)	d						21 55				22 55						
Blackrod	d						22 00				23 00						
Horwich Parkway	d						22 04				23 04						
Lostock	d						22 10				23 10						
Southport	d					21 05				22 05							
Meols Cop	d					21 10				22 10							
Bescar Lane	d																
New Lane	d																
Burscough Bridge	d					21 18				22 18							
Hoscar	d																
Parbold	d					21 23				22 23							
Appley Bridge	d					21 27				22 27							
Gathurst	d					21 30				22 30							
Kirkby	d																
Rainford	d																
Upholland	d																
Orrell	d																
Pemberton	d																
Wigan Wallgate	a					21 35				22 35							
	d					21 36				22 36							
Wigan North Western	d							21a35				22a35			23a29		
Ince	d																
Hindley	d					21 41				22 41							
Westhoughton	d					21 46				22 46							
Bolton	a				21 37	21 54	22 25			22 54	23 24		22 58				00 01
	d			21 31	21 38	21 54				22 54	23 25		22 58			23 31	00 02
Moses Gate	d																
Farnworth	d																
Kearsley	d																
Daisy Hill	d																
Hag Fold	d																
Atherton	d																
Walkden	d																
Moorside	d																
Swinton	d																
Salford Crescent	a			21 43	21 50	22 07				23 07	23 49		23 11			23 43	
	d			21 43	21 50	22 07				23 07	23 50		23 11			23 43	
Salford Central	d																
Manchester Victoria 🚊	a			21 52							00 01					23 52	
Rochdale 41	a																
Deansgate 🚊	a				21 54	22 11				23 11			23 15				
Manchester Oxford Road	a				21 55	22 13				23 14			23 20				
Manchester Piccadilly 10 🚊	a				21 59	22 19				23 19			23 24				00 16
Stockport 84	a					22 33				23 33							
Hazel Grove 86	a																
Buxton 86	a																
Heald Green 85	a																
Manchester Airport 85 ✈	a				22 17								23 42				00 30

A To Barrow-in-Furness
B From Clitheroe
C To Liverpool Lime Street
D To Leeds
E trolley from Preston
F From Edinburgh

The Sunday service between Wigan Wallgate and Manchester Victoria via Atherton is funded by GMITA and will operate whilst funding exists

Table 82

Sundays
19 February to 25 March

Barrow-in-Furness, Blackpool North, Preston, Southport, Kirkby and Wigan - Bolton - Manchester

Network Diagram - see first Page of Table 82

		TP	NT	NT	TP	TP	NT	TP	NT	TP		NT	TP	NT	NT	NT	NT	NT	TP	NT		NT	NT	TP	NT
		◇1						◇1		◇1			◇1						◇1					◇1	
			A				B					C						A					B		
					🚌	🚌																			
Barrow-in-Furness	d									09 17															
Roose	d									09 21															
Dalton	d									09 28															
Ulverston	d									09 36															
Cark	d									09 44															
Kents Bank	d									09 48															
Grange-over-Sands	d									09 52															
Arnside	d									09 58															
Silverdale	d									10 02															
Carnforth	d									10a09															
Windermere 83	d																								
Oxenholme Lake District 65	d																								
Lancaster 6 65	a																								
	d																								
Blackpool North 97	d	22p44		23p02	03 20	05 20		08 14	08 20				08 44	08 50			09 20		09 44	09 50					10 20
Layton 97	d			23p05					08 23								09 23								10 23
Poulton-le-Fylde 97	d	22p50		23p10				08 20	08 28				08 50	08 56			09 28		09 50	09 56					10 28
Kirkham & Wesham 97	d			23p19					08 37								09 37								10 37
Preston 8 65,97	a	23p08		23p29				08 38	08 47				09 08	09 14			09 47		10 07	10 14					10 47
	d	23p10		23p31	04u00	06u00		08 42	08 49				09 10	09 15			09 49		10 10	10 15				10 47	10 49
Leyland	d			23p36					08 54					09 21			09 54			10 21					10 54
Buckshaw Parkway	d	23p17		23p41					08 59				09 17				09 59		10 17						10 59
Chorley	d	23p21		23p45				08 51	09 03				09 21				10 03		10 21					10 56	11 03
Adlington (Lancashire)	d			23p50					09 08								10 08								11 08
Blackrod	d			23p54					09 12								10 12								11 12
Horwich Parkway	d	23p28		23p58				08 59	09 16				09 28				10 16		10 28						11 16
Lostock	d			00 02					09 20								10 20								11 20
Southport	d															09 10							10 05		
Meols Cop	d															09 15							10 10		
Bescar Lane	d																								
New Lane	d																								
Burscough Bridge	d															09 23							10 18		
Hoscar	d																								
Parbold	d															09 28							10 23		
Appley Bridge	d															09 32							10 27		
Gathurst	d															09 35							10 30		
Kirkby	d																								
Rainford	d																								
Upholland	d																								
Orrell	d																								
Pemberton	d																								
Wigan Wallgate	a															09 40							10 35		
	d						08 40								09 15	09 41						10 15	10 36		
Wigan North Western	d													09a37						10a38					
Ince	d														09 18							10 18			
Hindley	d						08 45								09 22	09 46						10 22	10 41		
Westhoughton	d						08 49									09 51							10 46		
Bolton	a	23p34		00 07			08 57	09 05	09 25				09 34			09 59	10 25		10 34				10 54	11 08	11 25
	d	23p35	23p38	00 07	04u35	06u35	08 58	09 06	09 25			09 31	09 35			09 59	10 25	10 31	10 35				10 54	11 08	11 25
Moses Gate	d																								
Farnworth	d																								
Kearsley	d																								
Daisy Hill	d														09 26							10 26			
Hag Fold	d														09 29							10 29			
Atherton	d														09 31							10 31			
Walkden	d														09 37							10 37			
Moorside	d														09 40							10 40			
Swinton	d														09 43							10 43			
Salford Crescent	a	23p47	23p50				09 10	09 18	09 38			09 43	09 47		09 50	10 12	10 38	10 43	10 47			10 50	11 07		11 38
	d	23p47	23p53				09 11	09 18	09 38			09 44	09 47		09 51	10 12	10 38	10 44	10 47			10 51	11 07		11 38
Salford Central	d																								
Manchester Victoria 🚊	a		00 01	00 26					09 45			09 53			09 57		10 45	10 52				10 57			11 45
Rochdale 41	a																								
Deansgate 🚊	a						09 14	09 23					09 51			10 16			10 51				11 11		
Manchester Oxford Road	a						09 17	09 24					09 52			10 18			10 52				11 13	11 23	
Manchester Piccadilly 10 🚊	a	23p53			05b00	07b00	09 21	09 28					09 56			10 22			10 56				11 19	11 27	
Stockport 84	a						09 31									10 33							11 30		
Hazel Grove 86	a																								
Buxton 86	a																								
Heald Green 85	a	00 16																							
Manchester Airport 85 ✈	a	00 23			05 25	07 25		09 48					10 17						11 17					11 47	

A From Clitheroe
B To Chester
C From Blackburn
b Stops to pick up only

The Sunday service between Wigan Wallgate and Manchester Victoria via Atherton is funded by GMITA and will operate whilst funding exists

Sundays

19 February to 25 March

Barrow-in-Furness, Blackpool North, Preston, Southport, Kirkby and Wigan - Bolton - Manchester

Network Diagram - see first Page of Table 82

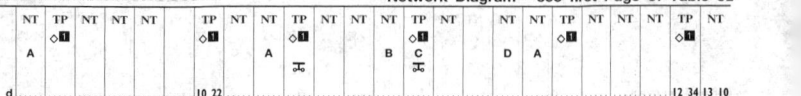

		NT	TP	NT	NT	NT	TP	NT	NT	TP	NT	NT	NT	TP	NT	NT	NT	TP	NT	NT	NT	TP	NT
			◇1				◇1			◇1				◇1				◇1				◇1	
		A							A				B	C		D	A						
										✠				✠									
Barrow-in-Furness	d						10 22															12 34	13 10
Roose	d						10 26																13 14
Dalton	d						10 33																13 20
Ulverston	d						10 41															12 50	13 29
Cark	d						10 49																13 36
Kents Bank	d						10 53																13 41
Grange-over-Sands	d						10 57															13 02	13 45
Arnside	d						11 03															13 08	13 51
Silverdale	d						11 07																13 55
Carnforth	d						11 14									12 35						13 17	14 02
Windermere 83	d																						
Oxenholme Lake District 65	d													12 10									
Lancaster 6 65	a						11 22							12 26		12 44						13 26	14 15
	d						11 22							12 26								13 26	
Blackpool North 97	d		10 44	10 50				11 20		11 44	11 50				12 20			12 44	12 50				
Layton 97	d							11 23							12 23								
Poulton-le-Fylde 97	d		10 50	10 56				11 28		11 50	11 56				12 28			12 50	12 56				
Kirkham & Wesham 97	d							11 37							12 37								
Preston 8 65,97	a		11 08	11 14			11 42	11 47		12 08	12 14			12 45	12 47			13 08	13 14			13 45	
	d		11 10	11 15			11 47	11 49		12 10	12 15			12 47	12 49			13 10	13 15			13 47	
Leyland	d			11 21				11 54			12 21				12 54				13 21				
Buckshaw Parkway	d		11 17					11 59		12 17					12 59			13 17					
Chorley	d		11 21				11 56	12 03		12 21				12 56	13 03			13 21				13 56	
Adlington (Lancashire)	d							12 08							13 08								
Blackrod	d							12 12							13 12								
Horwich Parkway	d		11 28					12 16		12 28					13 16			13 28					
Lostock	d							12 20							13 20								
Southport	d					11 05							12 05								13 05		
Meols Cop	d					11 10							12 10								13 10		
Bescar Lane	d																						
New Lane	d																						
Burscough Bridge	d					11 18							12 18								13 18		
Hoscar	d																						
Parbold	d					11 23							12 23								13 23		
Appley Bridge	d					11 27							12 27								13 27		
Gathurst	d					11 30							12 30								13 30		
Kirkby	d																						
Rainford	d																						
Upholland	d																						
Orrell	d																						
Pemberton	d																						
Wigan Wallgate	a					11 35							12 35								13 35		
	d				11 15	11 36						12 15	12 36							13 15	13 36		
Wigan North Western	d			11a38							12a38								13a39				
Ince	d				11 18							12 18								13 18			
Hindley	d				11 22	11 41						12 22	12 41							13 22	13 41		
Westhoughton	d					11 46							12 46								13 46		
Bolton	a		11 34			11 54	12 08	12 25		12 34			12 54	13 08	13 25			13 34			13 54	14 08	
	d	11 31	11 35			11 54	12 08	12 25	12 31	12 35			12 54	13 08	13 25		13 31	13 35			13 54	14 08	
Moses Gate	d																						
Farnworth	d																						
Kearsley	d																						
Daisy Hill	d				11 26							12 26								13 26			
Hag Fold	d				11 29							12 29								13 29			
Atherton	d				11 31							12 31								13 31			
Walkden	d				11 37							12 37								13 37			
Moorside	d				11 40							12 40								13 40			
Swinton	d				11 43							12 43								13 43			
Salford Crescent	a	11 43	11 47		11 50	12 07		12 38	12 43	12 47		12 50	13 07		13 38		13 43	13 47		13 50	14 07		
	d	11 43	11 47		11 51	12 07		12 38	12 43	12 47		12 51	13 07		13 38		13 44	13 47		13 51	14 07		
Salford Central	d																						
Manchester Victoria 🚋	a	11 52			11 57			12 45	12 52			12 57			13 45		13 52			13 57			
Rochdale 41	a																						
Deansgate 🚋	a		11 51			12 11				12 51			13 11					13 51			14 11		
Manchester Oxford Road	a		11 52			12 13	12 23			12 52			13 13	13 23				13 52			14 13	14 23	
Manchester Piccadilly 10 🚋	a		11 58			12 19	12 27			12 59			13 19	13 27				13 56			14 19	14 27	
Stockport 84	a					12 33							13 30								14 33		
Hazel Grove 86	a																						
Buxton 86	a																						
Heald Green 85	a																						
Manchester Airport 85 ✈	a		12 17				12 48			13 17				13 47				14 17				14 47	

A From Clitheroe
B To Chester
C From Edinburgh
D From Leeds to Morecambe

The Sunday service between Wigan Wallgate and Manchester Victoria via Atherton is funded by GMITA and will operate whilst funding exists

Table 82

Sundays

19 February to 25 March

Barrow-in-Furness, Blackpool North, Preston, Southport, Kirkby and Wigan - Bolton - Manchester

Network Diagram - see first Page of Table 82

Station		NT		NT	TP	NT	NT	NT	TP	NT	NT	TP		NT	NT	NT	TP	NT	NT	TP	NT	NT		NT	TP
					◇1				◇1			◇1					◇1			◇1					◇1
				A				B	C		A								A					B	C
									✠																✠
Barrow-in-Furness	d																14 25								
Roose	d																14 29								
Dalton	d																14 36								
Ulverston	d																14 44								
Cark	d																14 52								
Kents Bank	d																14 56								
Grange-over-Sands	d																15 00								
Arnside	d																15 06								
Silverdale	d																15 10								
Carnforth	d																15 17								
Windermere 83	d																								
Oxenholme Lake District 65	d								14 10																16 10
Lancaster 6 65	a								14 26								15 26								16 26
	d								14 26								15 26								16 26
Blackpool North 97	d	13 20			13 44	13 50				14 20		14 44		14 50				15 20		15 44	15 50				
Layton 97	d	13 23								14 23								15 23							
Poulton-le-Fylde 97	d	13 28			13 50	13 56				14 28		14 50		14 56				15 28		15 50	15 56				
Kirkham & Wesham 97	d	13 37								14 37								15 37							
Preston 8 65,97	a	13 47			14 08	14 14			14 45	14 47		15 08		15 14			15 45	15 47		16 08	16 14				16 46
	d	13 49			14 10	14 15			14 47	14 49		15 10		15 15			15 47	15 49		16 10	16 15				16 47
Leyland	d	13 54				14 21				14 54				15 21				15 54			16 21				
Buckshaw Parkway	d	13 59			14 17					14 59		15 17						15 59		16 17					
Chorley	d	14 03			14 21				14 56	15 03		15 21					15 56	16 03		16 21					16 56
Adlington (Lancashire)	d	14 08								15 08								16 08							
Blackrod	d	14 12								15 11								16 11							
Horwich Parkway	d	14 16			14 28					15 15		15 28						16 15		16 28					
Lostock	d	14 20								15 20								16 20							
Southport	d							14 05								15 05								16 05	
Meols Cop	d							14 10								15 10								16 10	
Bescar Lane	d																								
New Lane	d																								
Burscough Bridge	d							14 18								15 18								16 18	
Hoscar	d																								
Parbold	d							14 23								15 23								16 23	
Appley Bridge	d							14 27								15 27								16 27	
Gathurst	d							14 30								15 30								16 30	
Kirkby	d																								
Rainford	d																								
Upholland	d																								
Orrell	d																								
Pemberton	d																								
Wigan Wallgate	a							14 35								15 35								16 35	
	d						14 15	14 36							15 15	15 36						16 15		16 36	
Wigan North Western	d					14a38								15a38							16a38				
Ince	d						14 18								15 18							16 18			
Hindley	d						14 22	14 41							15 22	15 41						16 22		16 41	
Westhoughton	d							14 46								15 46								16 46	
Bolton	a	14 25			14 34			14 54	15 08	15 25		15 34				15 54	16 08	16 25		16 34				16 54	17 08
	d	14 25		14 31	14 35			14 54	15 08	15 25	15 30	15 35				15 54	16 08	16 25	16 31	16 35				16 54	17 08
Moses Gate	d																								
Farnworth	d																								
Kearsley	d																								
Daisy Hill	d						14 26								15 26							16 26			
Hag Fold	d						14 29								15 29							16 29			
Atherton	d						14 31								15 31							16 31			
Walkden	d						14 37								15 37							16 37			
Moorside	d						14 40								15 40							16 40			
Swinton	d						14 43								15 43							16 43			
Salford Crescent	a	14 38		14 43	14 47		14 50	15 07		15 38	15 42	15 47			15 50	16 07		16 38	16 43	16 47		16 50		17 07	
	d	14 38		14 43	14 47		14 51	15 07		15 38	15 43	15 47			15 51	16 07		16 38	16 44	16 47		16 51		17 07	
Salford Central	d																								
Manchester Victoria ⇌	a	14 45		14 52			14 57			15 45	15 52				15 57			16 45	16 52			16 57			
Rochdale 41	a																								
Deansgate ⇌	a				14 51			15 11				15 51				16 11				16 51				17 11	
Manchester Oxford Road	a				14 52			15 13	15 23			15 52				16 13	16 23			16 52				17 13	17 23
Manchester Piccadilly 10 ⇌	a				14 56			15 19	15 27			15 56				16 19	16 27			16 56				17 19	17 27
Stockport 84	a							15 31								16 33								17 30	
Hazel Grove 86	a																								
Buxton 86	a																								
Heald Green 85	a																								
Manchester Airport 85 ✈	a				15 17				15 47			16 17					16 46			17 17					17 47

A From Clitheroe **B** To Chester **C** From Edinburgh

The Sunday service between Wigan Wallgate and Manchester Victoria via Atherton is funded by GMITA and will operate whilst funding exists

Table 82

Sundays

19 February to 25 March

Barrow-in-Furness, Blackpool North, Preston, Southport, Kirkby and Wigan - Bolton - Manchester

Network Diagram - see first Page of Table 82

		NT	NT	NT	TP	NT	NT	NT	TP	NT	NT	TP	NT	NT	TP	NT	TP	NT	TP	NT	NT	TP	NT
					◇1				◇1			◇1			◇1		◇1		◇1			◇1	
			A	B					C 🍴		B			D	E 🍴	A		B				C 🍴	
Barrow-in-Furness	d																18 17						
Roose	d																18 21						
Dalton	d																18 28						
Ulverston	d																18 36						
Cark	d																18 44						
Kents Bank	d																18 48						
Grange-over-Sands	d																18 52						
Arnside	d																18 58						
Silverdale	d																19 02						
Carnforth	d		16 37													19 04	19 08						
Windermere 83	d																						
Oxenholme Lake District 65	d								17 07						18 10							19 07	
Lancaster 6 65	a		16 46						17 22						18 26	19 13	19 17					19 22	
	d								17 22						18 26		19 17					19 22	
Blackpool North 97	d	16 20			16 44	16 50				17 20		17 44	17 50						18 44	18 50			19 20
Layton 97	d	16 23								17 23													19 23
Poulton-le-Fylde 97	d	16 28			16 50	16 56				17 28		17 50	17 56						18 50	18 56			19 28
Kirkham & Wesham 97	d	16 37								17 37													19 37
Preston 8 65,97	a	16 47			17 08	17 14			17 41	17 47		18 08	18 14		18 45		19 37		19 08	19 14		19 41	19 47
	d	16 49			17 10	17 15			17 47	17 49		18 10	18 15		18 47				19 10	19 15		19 47	19 49
Leyland	d	16 54				17 21				17 54			18 21							19 21			19 54
Buckshaw Parkway	d	16 59			17 17					17 59		18 17							19 17				19 59
Chorley	d	17 03			17 21				17 56	18 03		18 21			18 56				19 21			19 56	20 03
Adlington (Lancashire)	d	17 08								18 08													20 08
Blackrod	d	17 12								18 12													20 12
Horwich Parkway	d	17 16			17 28					18 16		18 28							19 28				20 16
Lostock	d	17 20								18 20													20 20
Southport	d							17 05						18 05							19 05		
Meols Cop	d							17 10						18 10							19 10		
Bescar Lane	d																						
New Lane	d																						
Burscough Bridge	d							17 18						18 18							19 18		
Hoscar	d																						
Parbold	d							17 23						18 23							19 23		
Appley Bridge	d							17 27						18 27							19 27		
Gathurst	d							17 30						18 30							19 30		
Kirkby	d																						
Rainford	d																						
Upholland	d																						
Orrell	d																						
Pemberton	d																						
Wigan Wallgate	a							17 35						18 35							19 35		
	d						17 15	17 36						18 36							19 36		
Wigan North Western	d					17a38							18a38							19a38			
Ince	d						17 18																
Hindley	d						17 22	17 41						18 41							19 41		
Westhoughton	d							17 46						18 46							19 46		
Bolton	a	17 25			17 34			17 54	18 08	18 25		18 34		18 54	19 08				19 34		19 54	20 08	20 25
	d	17 25		17 30	17 35			17 54	18 08	18 25	18 31	18 35		18 54	19 08			19 31	19 35		19 54	20 08	20 25
Moses Gate	d																						
Farnworth	d																						
Kearsley	d																						
Daisy Hill	d						17 26																
Hag Fold	d						17 29																
Atherton	d						17 31																
Walkden	d						17 37																
Moorside	d						17 40																
Swinton	d						17 43																
Salford Crescent	a	17 38		17 42	17 47		17 50	18 07		18 38	18 43	18 47		19 07				19 44	19 47		20 07		20 38
	d	17 38		17 43	17 47		17 51	18 07		18 38	18 44	18 47		19 07				19 44	19 47		20 07		20 38
Salford Central	d																						
Manchester Victoria ⛴	a	17 45		17 52			17 57			18 45	18 52							19 52					20 45
Rochdale 41	a																						
Deansgate ⛴	a				17 51			18 11				18 51		19 11					19 51		20 11		
Manchester Oxford Road	a				17 52			18 13	18 23			18 52		19 13	19 23				19 52		20 13	20 23	
Manchester Piccadilly 10 ⛴	a				17 56			18 19	18 27			18 56		19 19	19 27				19 56		20 19	20 27	
Stockport 84	a							18 33						19 30							20 33		
Hazel Grove 86	a																						
Buxton 86	a																						
Heald Green 85	a																						
Manchester Airport 85 ✈	a				18 17				18 45			19 17			19 47				20 17			20 45	

A From Leeds to Morecambe
B From Clitheroe
C From Glasgow Central
D To Chester
E From Edinburgh

The Sunday service between Wigan Wallgate and Manchester Victoria via Atherton is funded by GMITA and will operate whilst funding exists

Table 82

Sundays
19 February to 25 March

Barrow-in-Furness, Blackpool North, Preston, Southport, Kirkby and Wigan - Bolton - Manchester

Network Diagram - see first Page of Table 82

		NT	TP	NT	NT	TP	NT	NT	NT	TP	NT	TP	NT	NT	NT	NT	NT	TP	TP	NT	NT	NT
			◇1			◇1				◇1		◇1						◇1	◇1			
		A			B	C		D		E	A				D			F	C			A
						🛒												🛒	🛒			
Barrow-in-Furness	d						20 02															
Roose	d						20 06															
Dalton	d						20 12															
Ulverston	d						20 21															
Cark	d						20 28															
Kents Bank	d						20 33															
Grange-over-Sands	d						20 37															
Arnside	d						20 43															
Silverdale	d						20 47															
Carnforth	d						20 54															
Windermere 83	d									20 40												
Oxenholme Lake District 65	d					20 10				21 01												
Lancaster 6 65	a					20 26	21 07			21 18												
	d					20 26													22 03			
Blackpool North 97	d		19 44	19 50				20 11	20 20			20 44	20 50		21 13	21 20	21 50	21 56			22 44	
Layton 97	d								20 23							21 23						
Poulton-le-Fylde 97	d		19 50	19 56				20 17	20 28			20 50	20 56		21 19	21 28	21 56	22 02			22 50	
Kirkham & Wesham 97	d								20 37							21 37						
Preston 8 65,97	a		20 08	20 14		20 45		20 34	20 47			21 08	21 14		21 36	21 47	22 14	22 20	22 23		23 08	
	d		20 10	20 15		20 47			20 49			21 10	21 15			21 49	22 15	22 29			23 09	
Leyland	d			20 21					20 54				21 21			21 54	22 21				23 15	
Buckshaw Parkway	d		20 17						20 59			21 17				21 59						
Chorley	d		20 21			20 56			21 03			21 21				22 03		22 38				
Adlington (Lancashire)	d								21 08							22 08						
Blackrod	d								21 12							22 12						
Horwich Parkway	d		20 28						21 16			21 28				22 16						
Lostock	d								21 20							22 20						
Southport	d				20 05									21 05						22 05		
Meols Cop	d				20 10									21 10						22 10		
Bescar Lane	d																					
New Lane	d																					
Burscough Bridge	d				20 18									21 18						22 18		
Hoscar	d																					
Parbold	d				20 23									21 23						22 23		
Appley Bridge	d				20 27									21 27						22 27		
Gathurst	d				20 30									21 30						22 30		
Kirkby	d																					
Rainford	d																					
Upholland	d																					
Orrell	d																					
Pemberton	d																					
Wigan Wallgate	a				20 35									21 35						22 35		
	d				20 36									21 36						22 36		
Wigan North Western	d			20a38									21a38				22a38				23a32	
Ince	d																					
Hindley	d				20 41									21 41						22 41		
Westhoughton	d				20 46									21 46						22 46		
Bolton	a		20 34		20 54	21 08			21 25			21 34		21 54		22 25		22 50		22 54		
	d	20 31	20 35		20 54	21 08			21 25		21 31	21 35		21 54		22 25		22 50		22 54		23 31
Moses Gate	d																					
Farnworth	d																					
Kearsley	d																					
Daisy Hill	d																					
Hag Fold	d																					
Atherton	d																					
Walkden	d																					
Moorside	d																					
Swinton	d																					
Salford Crescent	a	20 43	20 47		21 07				21 38		21 43	21 47		22 07		22 38		23 02		23 07		23 43
	d	20 43	20 47		21 07				21 38		21 43	21 47		22 07		22 38		23 03		23 07		23 43
Salford Central	d																					
Manchester Victoria 🚊	a	20 52							21 45		21 52					22 45						23 52
Rochdale 41	a																					
Deansgate 🚊	a		20 51		21 11							21 51		22 11				23 08		23 11		
Manchester Oxford Road	a		20 52		21 13	21 23						21 52		22 13				23 10		23 14		
Manchester Piccadilly 10 🚊	a		20 56		21 19	21 27						21 56		22 19				23 14		23 19		
Stockport 84	a				21 30									22 33						23 33		
Hazel Grove 86	a																					
Buxton 86	a																					
Heald Green 85	a																					
Manchester Airport 85 ✈	a		21 16			21 46						22 17						23 30				

A From Clitheroe
B To Chester
C From Edinburgh
D To Leeds
E To Barrow-in-Furness
F 🛒 from Preston

The Sunday service between Wigan Wallgate and Manchester Victoria via Atherton is funded by GMITA and will operate whilst funding exists

Table 82

Sundays

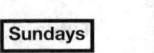

19 February to 25 March

Barrow-in-Furness, Blackpool North, Preston, Southport, Kirkby and Wigan - Bolton - Manchester

Network Diagram - see first Page of Table 82

Station	Table		TP ◇1
Barrow-in-Furness		d	
Roose		d	
Dalton		d	
Ulverston		d	
Cark		d	
Kents Bank		d	
Grange-over-Sands		d	
Arnside		d	
Silverdale		d	
Carnforth		d	
Windermere	83	d	
Oxenholme Lake District	65	d	
Lancaster 6	65	a	
		d	
Blackpool North	97	d	23 03
Layton	97	d	
Poulton-le-Fylde	97	d	23 09
Kirkham & Wesham	97	d	23 17
Preston 8	65,97	a	23 28
		d	23 28
Leyland		d	23 34
Buckshaw Parkway		d	23 38
Chorley		d	23 42
Adlington (Lancashire)		d	23 46
Blackrod		d	23 50
Horwich Parkway		d	23 53
Lostock		d	23 57
Southport		d	
Meols Cop		d	
Bescar Lane		d	
New Lane		d	
Burscough Bridge		d	
Hoscar		d	
Parbold		d	
Appley Bridge		d	
Gathurst		d	
Kirkby		d	
Rainford		d	
Upholland		d	
Orrell		d	
Pemberton		d	
Wigan Wallgate		a	
		d	
Wigan North Western		d	
Ince		d	
Hindley		d	
Westhoughton		d	
Bolton		a	00 02
		d	00 02
Moses Gate		d	
Farnworth		d	
Kearsley		d	
Daisy Hill		d	
Hag Fold		d	
Atherton		d	
Walkden		d	
Moorside		d	
Swinton		d	
Salford Crescent		a	
		d	
Salford Central		d	
Manchester Victoria	🚋	a	
Rochdale	41	a	
Deansgate	🚋	a	
Manchester Oxford Road		a	
Manchester Piccadilly 10	🚋	a	00 18
Stockport	84	a	
Hazel Grove	86	a	
Buxton	86	a	
Heald Green	85	a	
Manchester Airport	85 ✈	a	00 32

The Sunday service between Wigan Wallgate and Manchester Victoria via Atherton is funded by GMITA and will operate whilst funding exists

Table 82

Sundays
from 1 April

Barrow-in-Furness, Blackpool North, Preston, Southport, Kirkby and Wigan - Bolton - Manchester

Network Diagram - see first Page of Table 82

		TP	NT	NT	TP	TP	TP	NT	NT	NT	TP	NT	TP	NT	NT	NT	NT	TP	NT	TP	NT	NT	NT
		◇1					◇1				◇1		◇1							◇1			
			A					B		C		D		E					A		E		B
					🚌	🚌				🚲								🚌					
Barrow-in-Furness	d										09 17												
Roose	d										09 21												
Dalton	d										09 28												
Ulverston	d										09 36												
Cark	d										09 44												
Kents Bank	d										09 48												
Grange-over-Sands	d										09 52												
Arnside	d										09 58												
Silverdale	d										10 02												
Carnforth	d										10a09							10 20					
Windermere 83	d																						
Oxenholme Lake District 65	d																						
Lancaster 6 65	a																	10 45					
	d																	10 45					
Blackpool North 97	d	22p44		23p02	03 20	05 20	07 48		08 20	08 36			08 44	08 50			09 20			09 44	09 50		
Layton 97	d			23p05					08 23								09 23						
Poulton-le-Fylde 97	d	22p50		23p10			07 54		08 28	08 42			08 50	08 56			09 28			09 50	09 56		
Kirkham & Wesham 97	d			23p19					08 37	08 51							09 37						
Preston 8 65,97	a	23p08		23p29			08 12		08 47	09 02			09 08	09 14			09 47	11 35		10 08	10 14		
	d	23p10		23p31	04u00	06u00	08 14		08 49				09 10	09 15			09 49			10 10	10 15		
Leyland	d			23p36					08 54					09 21			09 54				10 21		
Buckshaw Parkway	d	23p17		23p41					08 59				09 17				09 59			10 17			
Chorley	d	23p21		23p45			08 23		09 03				09 21				10 03			10 21			
Adlington (Lancashire)	d			23p50					09 08								10 08						
Blackrod	d			23p54					09 12								10 12						
Horwich Parkway	d	23p28		23p58			08 30		09 16				09 28				10 16			10 28			
Lostock	d			00 02					09 20								10 20						
Southport	d															09 10							10 05
Meols Cop	d															09 15							10 10
Bescar Lane	d																						
New Lane	d																						
Burscough Bridge	d															09 23							10 18
Hoscar	d																						
Parbold	d															09 28							10 23
Appley Bridge	d															09 32							10 27
Gathurst	d															09 35							10 30
Kirkby	d																						
Rainford	d																						
Upholland	d																						
Orrell	d																						
Pemberton	d																						
Wigan Wallgate	a															09 40							10 35
	d							08 40							09 15	09 41						10 15	10 36
Wigan North Western	d													09a35							10a36		
Ince	d														09 18							10 18	
Hindley	d							08 45							09 22	09 46						10 22	10 41
Westhoughton	d							08 49								09 51							10 46
Bolton	a	23p34		00 07			08 37	08 57	09 25				09 34			09 59	10 25			10 34			10 54
	d	23p35	23p38	00 07	04u35	06u35	08 37	08 58	09 25			09 31	09 35			09 59	10 25		10 31	10 35			10 54
Moses Gate	d																						
Farnworth	d																						
Kearsley	d																						
Daisy Hill	d														09 26							10 26	
Hag Fold	d														09 29							10 29	
Atherton	d														09 31							10 31	
Walkden	d														09 37							10 37	
Moorside	d														09 40							10 40	
Swinton	d														09 43							10 43	
Salford Crescent	a	23p47	23p50				08 49	09 10	09 38			09 43	09 47		09 50	10 12	10 38		10 43	10 47		10 50	11 07
	d	23p47	23p53				08 50	09 11	09 38			09 44	09 47		09 51	10 12	10 38		10 44	10 47		10 51	11 07
Salford Central	d																						
Manchester Victoria 🚊	a		00 01	00 26					09 45			09 53			09 57		10 45		10 52			10 57	
Rochdale 41	a																						
Deansgate 🚊	a						08 53	09 14					09 51			10 16				10 51			11 11
Manchester Oxford Road	a						08 55	09 17					09 52			10 18				10 52			11 13
Manchester Piccadilly 10 🚊	a	23p53			05b00	07b00	08 59	09 21					09 56			10 22				10 56			11 19
Stockport 84	a							09 31								10 33							11 30
Hazel Grove 86	a																						
Buxton 86	a																						
Heald Green 85	a	00 16																					
Manchester Airport 85 ✈	a	00 23			05 25	07 25	09 17						10 17							11 17			

A From Clitheroe
B To Chester
C To Carlisle
D From Blackburn
E To Liverpool Lime Street
b Stops to pick up only

The Sunday service between Wigan Wallgate and Manchester Victoria via Atherton is funded by GMITA and will operate whilst funding exists

Table 82

Sundays
from 1 April

Barrow-in-Furness, Blackpool North, Preston, Southport, Kirkby and Wigan - Bolton - Manchester

Network Diagram - see first Page of Table 82

	TP ◇1	NT	NT A	TP ◇1	NT B		NT	NT	TP ◇1	NT	NT A	TP ◇1	NT B	NT	NT C		TP ◇1	NT	NT D	NT A	TP ◇1	NT B	NT	NT
Barrow-in-Furness d																	11 22							
Roose d																	11 26							
Dalton d																	11 32							
Ulverston d																	11 41							
Cark d																	11 48							
Kents Bank d																	11 52							
Grange-over-Sands d																	11 56							
Arnside d																	12 02							
Silverdale d																	12 07							
Carnforth d																	12 13		12 35					
Windermere 83 d																								
Oxenholme Lake District 65 d																								
Lancaster 6 65 a																	12 22		12 44					
d																	12 22							
Blackpool North 97 d		10 20		10 44	10 50					11 20		11 44	11 50					12 20			12 44	12 50		
Layton 97 d		10 23								11 23								12 23						
Poulton-le-Fylde 97 d		10 28		10 50	10 56					11 28		11 50	11 56					12 28			12 50	12 56		
Kirkham & Wesham 97 d		10 37								11 37								12 37						
Preston 8 65,97 a		10 47		11 08	11 14					11 47		12 08	12 14				12 41	12 47			13 08	13 14		
d	10 47	10 49		11 10	11 15				11 47	11 49		12 10	12 15				12 47	12 49			13 10	13 15		
Leyland d		10 54			11 21					11 54			12 21					12 54				13 21		
Buckshaw Parkway d		10 59		11 17						11 59		12 17						12 59			13 17			
Chorley d	10 56	11 03		11 21					11 56	12 03		12 21					12 56	13 03			13 21			
Adlington (Lancashire) d		11 08								12 08								13 08						
Blackrod d		11 12								12 12								13 12						
Horwich Parkway d		11 16		11 28						12 16		12 28						13 16			13 28			
Lostock d		11 20								12 20								13 20						
Southport d								11 05							12 05									13 05
Meols Cop d								11 10							12 10									13 10
Bescar Lane d																								
New Lane d																								
Burscough Bridge d								11 18							12 18									13 18
Hoscar d																								
Parbold d								11 23							12 23									13 23
Appley Bridge d								11 27							12 27									13 27
Gathurst d								11 30							12 30									13 30
Kirkby d																								
Rainford d																								
Upholland d																								
Orrell d																								
Pemberton d																								
Wigan Wallgate a								11 35							12 35									13 35
d							11 15	11 36						12 15	12 36								13 15	13 36
Wigan North Western d					11a35								12a35									13a35		
Ince d							11 18							12 18									13 18	
Hindley d							11 22	11 41						12 22	12 41								13 22	13 41
Westhoughton d								11 46							12 46									13 46
Bolton a	11 08	11 25		11 34				11 54	12 08	12 25		12 34			12 54		13 08	13 25			13 34			13 54
d	11 08	11 25	11 31	11 35				11 54	12 08	12 25	12 31	12 35			12 54		13 08	13 25		13 31	13 35			13 54
Moses Gate d																								
Farnworth d																								
Kearsley d																								
Daisy Hill d							11 26							12 26									13 26	
Hag Fold d							11 29							12 29									13 29	
Atherton d							11 31							12 31									13 31	
Walkden d							11 37							12 37									13 37	
Moorside d							11 40							12 40									13 40	
Swinton d							11 43							12 43									13 43	
Salford Crescent a		11 38	11 43	11 47			11 50	12 07		12 38	12 43	12 47		12 50	13 07			13 38		13 43	13 47		13 50	14 07
d		11 38	11 43	11 47			11 51	12 07		12 38	12 43	12 47		12 51	13 07			13 38		13 44	13 47		13 51	14 07
Salford Central d																								
Manchester Victoria ⛴ a		11 45	11 52				11 57			12 45	12 52			12 57				13 45		13 52			13 57	
Rochdale 41 a																								
Deansgate ⛴ a				11 51				12 11				12 51			13 11						13 51			14 11
Manchester Oxford Road a	11 23			11 52				12 13	12 23			12 52			13 13		13 23				13 52			14 13
Manchester Piccadilly 10 ⛴ a	11 27			11 56				12 19	12 27			12 59			13 19		13 27				13 56			14 19
Stockport 84 a								12 33							13 30									14 33
Hazel Grove 86 a																								
Buxton 86 a																								
Heald Green 85 a																								
Manchester Airport 85 ✈ a	11 47			12 17					12 47			13 17					13 47				14 17			

A From Clitheroe
B To Liverpool Lime Street
C To Chester
D From Leeds to Morecambe

The Sunday service between Wigan Wallgate and Manchester Victoria via Atherton is funded by GMITA and will operate whilst funding exists

Table 82

Sundays
from 1 April

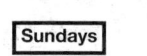

Barrow-in-Furness, Blackpool North, Preston, Southport, Kirkby and Wigan - Bolton - Manchester

Network Diagram - see first Page of Table 82

		TP		NT	NT	NT	TP	NT	NT	NT	TP	NT		NT	TP	NT	NT	NT	TP	NT	NT	TP		NT	NT
		◇1					◇1				◇1				◇1				◇1			◇1			
						A		B		C	D			A		B					A			B	
Barrow-in-Furness	d	12 34		13 10															14 25						
Roose	d			13 14															14 29						
Dalton	d			13 20															14 36						
Ulverston	d	12 50		13 29															14 44						
Cark	d			13 36															14 52						
Kents Bank	d			13 41															14 56						
Grange-over-Sands	d	13 02		13 45															15 00						
Arnside	d	13 08		13 51															15 06						
Silverdale	d			13 55															15 10						
Carnforth	d	13 17		14 02															15 17						
Windermere 83	d																								
Oxenholme Lake District 65	d										14 10														
Lancaster 6 65	a	13 26		14 15							14 26								15 26						
	d	13 26									14 26								15 26						
Blackpool North 97	d				13 20		13 44	13 50				14 20			14 44	14 50				15 20		15 44		15 50	
Layton 97	d				13 23							14 23								15 23					
Poulton-le-Fylde 97	d				13 28		13 50	13 56				14 28			14 50	14 56				15 28		15 50		15 56	
Kirkham & Wesham 97	d				13 37							14 37								15 37					
Preston 8 65,97	a	13 45			13 47		14 08	14 14			14 45	14 47			15 08	15 14			15 45	15 47		16 08		16 14	
	d	13 47			13 49		14 10	14 15			14 47	14 49			15 10	15 15			15 47	15 49		16 10		16 15	
Leyland	d				13 54			14 21				14 54				15 21				15 54				16 21	
Buckshaw Parkway	d				13 59		14 17					14 59			15 17					15 59		16 17			
Chorley	d	13 56			14 03		14 21				14 56	15 03			15 21				15 56	16 03		16 21			
Adlington (Lancashire)	d				14 08							15 08								16 08					
Blackrod	d				14 12							15 11								16 11					
Horwich Parkway	d				14 16		14 28					15 15			15 28					16 15		16 28			
Lostock	d				14 20							15 20								16 20					
Southport	d									14 05								15 05							
Meols Cop	d									14 10								15 10							
Bescar Lane	d																								
New Lane	d																								
Burscough Bridge	d									14 18								15 18							
Hoscar	d																								
Parbold	d									14 23								15 23							
Appley Bridge	d									14 27								15 27							
Gathurst	d									14 30								15 30							
Kirkby	d																								
Rainford	d																								
Upholland	d																								
Orrell	d																								
Pemberton	d																								
Wigan Wallgate	a									14 35								15 35							
	d								14 15	14 36							15 15	15 36							16 15
Wigan North Western	d							14a35								15a35								16a35	
Ince	d								14 18								15 18								16 18
Hindley	d								14 22	14 41							15 22	15 41							16 22
Westhoughton	d									14 46								15 46							
Bolton	a	14 08			14 25		14 34			14 54	15 08	15 25			15 34			15 54	16 08	16 25		16 34			
	d	14 08			14 25	14 31	14 35			14 54	15 08	15 25		15 30	15 35			15 54	16 08	16 25	16 31	16 35			
Moses Gate	d																								
Farnworth	d																								
Kearsley	d																								
Daisy Hill	d								14 26								15 26								16 26
Hag Fold	d								14 29								15 29								16 29
Atherton	d								14 31								15 31								16 31
Walkden	d								14 37								15 37								16 37
Moorside	d								14 40								15 40								16 40
Swinton	d								14 43								15 43								16 43
Salford Crescent	a				14 38	14 43	14 47		14 50	15 07		15 38		15 42	15 47		15 50	16 07		16 38	16 43	16 47			16 50
	d				14 38	14 43	14 47		14 51	15 07		15 38		15 43	15 47		15 51	16 07		16 38	16 44	16 47			16 51
Salford Central	d																								
Manchester Victoria ⇌	a				14 45	14 52			14 57			15 45		15 52			15 57			16 45	16 52				16 57
Rochdale 41	a																								
Deansgate ⇌	a						14 51			15 11					15 51			16 11				16 51			
Manchester Oxford Road	a	14 23					14 52			15 13	15 23				15 52			16 13	16 23			16 52			
Manchester Piccadilly 10 ⇌	a	14 27					14 56			15 19	15 27				15 56			16 19	16 27			16 56			
Stockport 84	a									15 31								16 33							
Hazel Grove 86	a																								
Buxton 86	a																								
Heald Green 85	a																								
Manchester Airport 85 ✈	a	14 47					15 17				15 47				16 17				16 46			17 17			

A From Clitheroe
B To Liverpool Lime Street
C To Chester
D From Edinburgh

The Sunday service between Wigan Wallgate and Manchester Victoria via Atherton is funded by GMITA and will operate whilst funding exists

Table 82

Sundays
from 1 April

Barrow-in-Furness, Blackpool North, Preston, Southport, Kirkby and Wigan - Bolton - Manchester

Network Diagram - see first Page of Table 82

		NT	TP	NT	NT	NT	TP	NT		NT	NT	TP	NT	NT	TP	NT	NT	TP		NT	TP	NT	TP	NT	NT
			◇1				◇1					◇1			◇1			◇1			◇1		◇1		
		A	B		C	D		E				F		D		E	A	B		C		D		E	
			🚲									🚲						🚲							
Barrow-in-Furness	d																				18 17				
Roose	d																				18 21				
Dalton	d																				18 28				
Ulverston	d																				18 36				
Cark	d																				18 44				
Kents Bank	d																				18 48				
Grange-over-Sands	d																				18 52				
Arnside	d																				18 58				
Silverdale	d																				19 02				
Carnforth	d				16 37															19 04	19 08				
Windermere 83	d																								
Oxenholme Lake District 65	d		16 10									17 07						18 10							
Lancaster 6 65	a		16 26		16 46							17 22						18 26		19 13	19 17				
	d		16 26									17 22						18 26			19 17				
Blackpool North 97	d			16 20			16 44	16 50					17 20		17 44	17 50							18 44	18 50	
Layton 97	d			16 23									17 23												
Poulton-le-Fylde 97	d			16 28			16 50	16 56					17 28		17 50	17 56							18 50	18 56	
Kirkham & Wesham 97	d			16 37									17 37												
Preston 8 65,97	a		16 46	16 47			17 08	17 14				17 41	17 47		18 08	18 14		18 45			19 37		19 08	19 14	
	d		16 47	16 49			17 10	17 15				17 47	17 49		18 10	18 15		18 47					19 10	19 15	
Leyland	d			16 54				17 21					17 54			18 21								19 21	
Buckshaw Parkway	d			16 59			17 17						17 59		18 17								19 17		
Chorley	d		16 56	17 03			17 21					17 56	18 03		18 21			18 56					19 21		
Adlington (Lancashire)	d			17 08									18 08												
Blackrod	d			17 12									18 12												
Horwich Parkway	d			17 16			17 28						18 16		18 28								19 28		
Lostock	d			17 20									18 20												
Southport	d	16 05									17 05						18 05								19 05
Meols Cop	d	16 10									17 10						18 10								19 10
Bescar Lane	d																								
New Lane	d																								
Burscough Bridge	d	16 18									17 18						18 18								19 18
Hoscar	d																								
Parbold	d	16 23									17 23						18 23								19 23
Appley Bridge	d	16 27									17 27						18 27								19 27
Gathurst	d	16 30									17 30						18 30								19 30
Kirkby	d																								
Rainford	d																								
Upholland	d																								
Orrell	d																								
Pemberton	d																								
Wigan Wallgate	a	16 35									17 35						18 35								19 35
	d	16 36								17 15	17 36						18 36								19 36
Wigan North Western	d							17a35								18a35								19a35	
Ince	d									17 18															
Hindley	d	16 41								17 22	17 41						18 41								19 41
Westhoughton	d	16 46									17 46						18 46								19 46
Bolton	a	16 54	17 08	17 25			17 34				17 54	18 08	18 25		18 34		18 54	19 08					19 34		19 54
	d	16 54	17 08	17 25		17 30	17 35				17 54	18 08	18 25	18 31	18 35		18 54	19 08				19 31	19 35		19 54
Moses Gate	d																								
Farnworth	d																								
Kearsley	d																								
Daisy Hill	d									17 26															
Hag Fold	d									17 29															
Atherton	d									17 31															
Walkden	d									17 37															
Moorside	d									17 40															
Swinton	d									17 43															
Salford Crescent	a	17 07		17 38		17 42	17 47			17 50	18 07		18 38	18 43	18 47		19 08					19 44	19 47		20 07
	d	17 07		17 38		17 43	17 47			17 51	18 07		18 38	18 44	18 47		19 09					19 44	19 47		20 07
Salford Central	d																								
Manchester Victoria 🚊	a			17 45		17 52				17 57			18 45	18 52								19 52			
Rochdale 41	a																								
Deansgate 🚊	a	17 11					17 51				18 11				18 51		19 12						19 51		20 11
Manchester Oxford Road	a	17 13	17 23				17 52				18 13	18 23			18 52		19 15	19 23					19 52		20 13
Manchester Piccadilly 10 🚊	a	17 19	17 27				17 56				18 19	18 27			18 56		19 19	19 27					19 56		20 19
Stockport 84	a	17 30									18 33						19 30								20 33
Hazel Grove 86	a																								
Buxton 86	a																								
Heald Green 85	a																								
Manchester Airport 85 ✈	a		17 47				18 17					18 45			19 17			19 47					20 17		

A To Chester
B From Edinburgh
C From Leeds to Morecambe
D From Clitheroe
E To Liverpool Lime Street
F From Glasgow Central

The Sunday service between Wigan Wallgate and Manchester Victoria via Atherton is funded by GMITA and will operate whilst funding exists

Table 82

Sundays
from 1 April

Barrow-in-Furness, Blackpool North, Preston, Southport, Kirkby and Wigan - Bolton - Manchester

Network Diagram - see first Page of Table 82

		TP	NT	NT	TP	NT	NT	TP	NT	NT	NT	TP	NT	TP	NT	NT	NT	NT	NT	TP	NT	NT
		◇[1]			◇[1]			◇[1]				◇[1]		◇[1]						◇[1]		
		A		B		C	D	E		F		G	B		C		F		C	E		C
Barrow-in-Furness	d								20 02													
Roose	d								20 06													
Dalton	d								20 12													
Ulverston	d								20 21													
Cark	d								20 28													
Kents Bank	d								20 33													
Grange-over-Sands	d								20 37													
Arnside	d								20 43													
Silverdale	d								20 47													
Carnforth	d								20 54													
Windermere 83	d											20 40										
Oxenholme Lake District 65	d	19 07						20 10				21 01										
Lancaster [6] 65	a	19 22						20 26	21 07			21 18										
	d	19 22						20 26												22 03		
Blackpool North 97	d		19 20		19 44	19 50				20 11	20 20			20 44	20 50		21 13	21 20	21 50			22 44
Layton 97	d		19 23								20 23							21 23				
Poulton-le-Fylde 97	d		19 28		19 50	19 56				20 17	20 28			20 50	20 56		21 19	21 28	21 56			22 50
Kirkham & Wesham 97	d		19 37								20 37							21 37				
Preston [8] 65,97	a	19 41	19 47		20 08	20 14		20 45		20 34	20 47			21 08	21 14		21 36	21 47	22 14	22 23		23 08
	d	19 47	19 49		20 10	20 15		20 47			20 49			21 10	21 15			21 49	22 15	22 29		23 09
Leyland	d		19 54			20 21					20 54				21 21			21 54	22 21			23 15
Buckshaw Parkway	d		19 59		20 17						20 59			21 17				21 59				
Chorley	d	19 56	20 03		20 21			20 56			21 03			21 21				22 03		22 38		
Adlington (Lancashire)	d		20 08								21 08							22 08				
Blackrod	d		20 12								21 12							22 12				
Horwich Parkway	d		20 16		20 28						21 16			21 28				22 16				
Lostock	d		20 20								21 20							22 20				
Southport	d						20 05									21 05					22 05	
Meols Cop	d						20 10									21 10					22 10	
Bescar Lane	d																					
New Lane	d																					
Burscough Bridge	d						20 18									21 18					22 18	
Hoscar	d																					
Parbold	d						20 23									21 23					22 23	
Appley Bridge	d						20 27									21 27					22 27	
Gathurst	d						20 30									21 30					22 30	
Kirkby	d																					
Rainford	d																					
Upholland	d																					
Orrell	d																					
Pemberton	d																					
Wigan Wallgate	a						20 35									21 35					22 35	
	d						20 36									21 36					22 36	
Wigan North Western	d					20a35									21a35				22a35			23a29
Ince	d																					
Hindley	d						20 41									21 41					22 41	
Westhoughton	d						20 46									21 46					22 46	
Bolton	a	20 08	20 25		20 34		20 54	21 08			21 25			21 34		21 54		22 25		22 50	22 54	
	d	20 08	20 25	20 31	20 35		20 54	21 08			21 25		21 31	21 35		21 54		22 25		22 50	22 54	
Moses Gate	d																					
Farnworth	d																					
Kearsley	d																					
Daisy Hill	d																					
Hag Fold	d																					
Atherton	d																					
Walkden	d																					
Moorside	d																					
Swinton	d																					
Salford Crescent	a		20 38	20 43	20 47		21 07				21 38		21 43	21 47		22 07		22 38		23 02	23 07	
	d		20 38	20 43	20 47		21 07				21 38		21 43	21 47		22 07		22 38		23 05	23 07	
Salford Central	d																					
Manchester Victoria 🚋	a		20 45	20 52							21 45		21 52					22 45				
Rochdale 41	a																					
Deansgate 🚋	a				20 51		21 11							21 51		22 11				23 08	23 11	
Manchester Oxford Road	a	20 23			20 52		21 13	21 23						21 52		22 13				23 10	23 14	
Manchester Piccadilly [10] 🚋	a	20 27			20 56		21 19	21 27						21 56		22 19				23 14	23 19	
Stockport 84	a						21 30									22 33					23 33	
Hazel Grove 86	a																					
Buxton 86	a																					
Heald Green 85	a																					
Manchester Airport 85 ✈	a	20 45			21 16			21 46						22 17						23 30		

A From Glasgow Central
B From Clitheroe
C To Liverpool Lime Street
D To Chester
E From Edinburgh
F To Leeds
G To Barrow-in-Furness

The Sunday service between Wigan Wallgate and Manchester Victoria via Atherton is funded by GMITA and will operate whilst funding exists

Table 82

Sundays
from 1 April

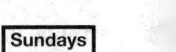

Barrow-in-Furness, Blackpool North, Preston, Southport, Kirkby and Wigan - Bolton - Manchester

Network Diagram - see first Page of Table 82

			NT	TP
				◇**1**
			A	
Barrow-in-Furness		d		
Roose		d		
Dalton		d		
Ulverston		d		
Cark		d		
Kents Bank		d		
Grange-over-Sands		d		
Arnside		d		
Silverdale		d		
Carnforth		d		
Windermere	83	d		
Oxenholme Lake District	65	d		
Lancaster 6	65	a		
		d		
Blackpool North	97	d		23 03
Layton	97	d		
Poulton-le-Fylde	97	d		23 09
Kirkham & Wesham	97	d		23 17
Preston 8	65,97	a		23 28
		d		23 28
Leyland		d		23 34
Buckshaw Parkway		d		23 38
Chorley		d		23 42
Adlington (Lancashire)		d		23 46
Blackrod		d		23 50
Horwich Parkway		d		23 53
Lostock		d		23 57
Southport		d		
Meols Cop		d		
Bescar Lane		d		
New Lane		d		
Burscough Bridge		d		
Hoscar		d		
Parbold		d		
Appley Bridge		d		
Gathurst		d		
Kirkby		d		
Rainford		d		
Upholland		d		
Orrell		d		
Pemberton		d		
Wigan Wallgate		a		
		d		
Wigan North Western		d		
Ince		d		
Hindley		d		
Westhoughton		d		
Bolton		a		00 02
		d	23 31	00 02
Moses Gate		d		
Farnworth		d		
Kearsley		d		
Daisy Hill		d		
Hag Fold		d		
Atherton		d		
Walkden		d		
Moorside		d		
Swinton		d		
Salford Crescent		a	23 43	
		d	23 43	
Salford Central		d		
Manchester Victoria	⇌	a	23 52	
Rochdale	41	a		
Deansgate	⇌	a		
Manchester Oxford Road		a		
Manchester Piccadilly 10	⇌	a		00 18
Stockport	84	a		
Hazel Grove	86	a		
Buxton	86	a		
Heald Green	85	a		
Manchester Airport	85 ✈	a		00 32

A From Clitheroe

The Sunday service between Wigan Wallgate and Manchester Victoria via Atherton is funded by GMITA and will operate whilst funding exists

Table 83

Mondays to Fridays

Oxenholme - Lake District - Windermere

Network Diagram - see first Page of Table 82

Miles			TP	TP	TP	TP	TP	TP	TP	TP	TP	TP	TP	TP	TP	TP	TP	TP	TP
			1	1	1	1	1	◇1	1	◇1	1	1	1	◇1	◇1	1	1	1	1
			A					B		C				B	D				
0	**Oxenholme Lake District**	d	06 21	07 21	08 27	09 14	10 27	11 18	12 28	13 37	14 27	15 38	16 28	17 49	18 46	19 37	20 27	21 15	22 20
2¼	Kendal	d	06 26	07 25	08 31	09 18	10 31	11 22	12 32	13 41	14 31	15 43	16 32	17 53	18 50	19 41	20 31	21 19	22 24
4	Burneside	d		07x29	08x35	09x22		11 26	12x36		14x35	15x46	16x36	17x57	18x54	19x45	20x35	21x23	22x28
6½	Staveley	d		07x34	08x40	09x27		11 31	12x41		14x40	15x51	16x41	18x02	18x59	19x50	20x40	21x28	22x33
10	**Windermere**	a	06 41	07 40	08 46	09 33	10 44	11 39	12 47	13 56	14 46	15 59	16 48	18 08	19 08	19 56	20 46	21 34	22 39

Saturdays

		TP	TP	TP	TP	TP	TP	TP	TP	TP	TP	TP	TP	TP	TP	TP	TP	TP
		1	1	1	1	◇1	◇1	1	◇1	1	1	1	◇1	1	1	1	1	1
		A				B	C		C				B		E	F	F	G
Oxenholme Lake District	d	06 21	07 21	08 27	09 11	10 05	11 18	12 28	13 37	14 33	15 38	16 28	17 38	18 37	19ʃ27	19ʃ37	20ʃ23	21ʃ15
Kendal	d	06 26	07 25	08 31	09 15	10 09	11 22	12 32	13 41	14 37	15 43	16 32	17 42	18 41	19ʃ31	19ʃ41	20ʃ27	21ʃ19
Burneside	d		07x29	08x35	09x19	10x13	11x26	12x36		14x41	15x46	16x36	17x46	18x45	19x35	19x45	20x31	21x23
Staveley	d		07x34	08x40	09x24	10x18	11x31	12x41		14x46	15x51	16x41	17x51	18x50	19x40	19x50	20x36	21x28
Windermere	a	06 41	07 40	08 46	09 30	10 26	11 39	12 47	13 56	14 52	15 59	16 48	18 00	18 56	19ʃ46	19ʃ56	20ʃ42	21ʃ34

Sundays

		TP	TP	TP	TP	TP	TP	TP	TP	TP	TP	TP	TP	TP
		◇1	1	1	1	1	1	1	1	1	1	1	1	1
		H	I	J	I	J								
Oxenholme Lake District	d	10ʃ40	11ʃ35	11ʃ50	12ʃ29	12ʃ38	13 35	14 37	15 35	16 29	17 37	18 37	19 29	20 16
Kendal	d	10ʃ44	11ʃ39	11ʃ54	12ʃ33	12ʃ42	13 39	14 41	15 39	16 33	17 41	18 41	19 33	20 20
Burneside	d	ʃ	11x43	11x58	12x37	ʃ	13x43	14x45	15x43	16x37	17x45	18x45		20x24
Staveley	d	ʃ	11x48	12x03	12x42	ʃ	13x48	14x50	15x48	16x42	17x50	18x50		20x29
Windermere	a	10ʃ57	11ʃ54	12ʃ09	12ʃ48	12ʃ55	13 54	14 56	15 54	16 48	17 56	18 56	19 45	20 35

- **A** From Lancaster
- **B** From Manchester Airport
- **C** From Preston
- **D** From Barrow-in-Furness
- **F** until 24 March
- **G** until 31 December
- **E** from 31 March
- **H** until 25 March. From Lancaster
- **I** until 25 March
- **J** from 1 April

Table 83

Mondays to Fridays

Windermere - Oxenholme - Lake District

Network Diagram - see first Page of Table 82

Miles			TP	TP	TP	TP	TP	TP	TP	TP	TP	TP	TP	TP	TP	TP	TP	TP	TP
			1	1	1	1	◇1	1	◇1	1	1	1	◇1	◇1	1	1	1	1	◇1
							A		A				A	A					B
0	**Windermere**	d	06 50	07 55	08 50	09 59	10 49	11 59	12 51	14 00	14 59	16 02	17 06	18 15	19 10	20 00	20 50	21 40	22 45
3½	Staveley	d	06x55	08x01		10x04	10x54	12x04		14x05	15x04		17x11	18x20		20x05	20x55	21x45	22x50
6	Burneside	d	07x00	08x06		10x09	10x59	12x09		14x10	15x09		17x16	18x25		20x10	21x00	21x50	22x55
7¾	Kendal	d	07 04	08 11	09 01	10 13	11 03	12 13	13 02	14 14	15 13	16 14	17 20	18 29	19 21	20 14	21 04	21 54	22 59
10	**Oxenholme Lake District**	a	07 09	08 16	09 06	10 18	11 08	12 18	13 07	14 19	15 18	16 19	17 25	18 34	19 27	20 19	21 09	21 59	23 04

Saturdays

		TP	TP	TP	TP	TP	TP	TP	TP	TP	TP	TP	TP	TP	TP	TP	TP	TP	TP	TP
		1	1	1	◇1	◇1	1	◇1	1	1	1	◇1	1	1	1	1	1	1	◇1
					C	A		A				A			D	E	F	G	H
Windermere	d	06 50	07 55	08 50	09 38	10 49	11 59	12 51	14 00	14 59	16 02	17 06	18 02	19 00	19ʃ50	20ʃ00	20ʃ47	20ʃ47	21ʃ40
Staveley	d	06x55	08x01		09x43	10x54	12x04		14x05	15x04		17x11	18x07	19x05	ʃ	20x05	ʃ	20ʃ52	21x45
Burneside	d	07x00	08x06		09x48	10x59	12x09		14x10	15x09		17x16	18x12	19x10	ʃ	20x10	ʃ	20ʃ57	21x50
Kendal	d	07 04	08 11	09 01	09 52	11 03	12 13	13 02	14 14	15 13	16 14	17 20	18 16	19 14	20ʃ01	20ʃ14	20ʃ58	21ʃ00	21ʃ54
Oxenholme Lake District	a	07 09	08 16	09 06	09 57	11 08	12 18	13 07	14 19	15 18	16 19	17 25	18 21	19 19	20ʃ06	20ʃ19	21ʃ04	21ʃ06	21ʃ59

Sundays

		TP	TP	TP	TP	TP	TP	TP	TP	TP	TP	TP	TP	TP
		1	1	1	1	1	1	1	1	1	1	1	1	◇1
		I	I	J	I	J								K
Windermere	d	11ʃ01	11ʃ59	12ʃ14	12ʃ58	13ʃ00	13 58	15 00	15 58	16 58	18 04	19 00	19 49	20 40
Staveley	d	ʃ	12x03	12x19	13x03	ʃ	14x03		16x03	17x03	18x09	19x05		20x45
Burneside	d	ʃ	12x08	12x24	13x08	ʃ	14x08		16x08	17x08	18x14	19x10		20x50
Kendal	d	11ʃ13	12ʃ12	12ʃ28	13ʃ12	13ʃ12	14 12	15 12	16 12	17 12	18 18	19 14	20 00	20 54
Oxenholme Lake District	a	11ʃ18	12ʃ18	12ʃ33	13ʃ17	13ʃ17	14 17	15 17	16 17	17 17	18 23	19 19	20 05	20 59

- **A** To Manchester Airport
- **B** To Blackpool North
- **C** To Preston
- **D** from 31 March
- **E** until 24 March
- **F** from 18 February until 24 March
- **G** until 11 February
- **H** until 31 December. To Preston
- **I** until 25 March
- **J** from 1 April
- **K** To Barrow-in-Furness

Stoke-on-Trent and Crewe - Manchester Airport, Stockport and Manchester

Network Diagram - see first Page of Table 78

Miles	Miles	Miles			NT	NT	XC	VT	NT	VT	VT	NT	TP		NT	NT	VT	NT	NT	TP	AW	NT	NT		NT
					MX	MX	MX	MO	MX	MX	MO	MX													
							◇1	◇1		◇1	◇1		◇1				◇1			◇1					
					A				B				C					D		E		F	G		
								🚌		🚌	🚌														
—	—	—	London Euston 15 ⊖65	d				21p25		22p00	21p51														
—	—	—	Birmingham New Street 12 68	d			22p30																		
—	—	—	Wolverhampton 7 68 ⇌	d			22p48																		
—	—	—	Stafford 65,68	d			23p01			23b38	23b53														
0	—	—	**Stoke-on-Trent** 50,68	d			23p21	23p29																	
3	—	—	Longport 50	d																					
6¼	—	—	Kidsgrove 50	d																					
—	0	—	**Crewe** 10 65	d		23p12				00s03	00s21	00 44				05 48	06 11				06 27				
—	4¾	—	Sandbach	d		23p19										05 55									
—	8½	—	Holmes Chapel	d		23p24										06 00									
—	10½	—	Goostrey	d		23p27										06 03									
—	14¼	—	Chelford	d		23p31										06 07									
—	17¼	—	Alderley Edge	d		23p35										06 11									06 49
—	19	0	**Wilmslow**	d		23p39									05 46	06 15	06 27				06 45				06 52
—	—	2	Styal	d																					
—	—	4¼	**Manchester Airport** ✈	a								01 16			05 53										
—	20½	—	Handforth	d		23p42										06 18									06 55
11¾	—	—	Congleton	d																					
19¾	—	—	**Macclesfield**	a				23p45																	
—	—	—		d				23p46											06 22						
22½	—	—	Prestbury	d															06 26						
24½	—	—	Adlington (Cheshire)	d															06 29						
26½	—	—	Poynton	d															06 33						
28	—	—	Bramhall	d															06 35						
29½	22¾	—	Cheadle Hulme	d		23p46										06 22			06 38						06 59
31¾	25	—	**Stockport**	a		23p51		23p59		00s26	00s50					06 27	06 36		06 43		06 55				07 04
—	—	—		d	23p48	23p51		00 01	00 02				05 53			06 27	06 37	06 41	06 43	06 53	06 55		06 58		07 04
31¾	26½	—	Heaton Chapel	d		23p55										06 31			06 46						07 08
34¾	28	—	Levenshulme	d		23p58										06 34			06 49						07 11
37¾	31	—	**Manchester Piccadilly** 10 ⇌	a	00 02	00 07	00 12	00 12	00 18	00 35	01 00	01 36	06 05		06 25	06 42	06 49	06 52	06 58	07 02	07 07		07 10		07 21
—	—	—		d														06 54				06 58			
38¼	31½	—	**Manchester Oxford Road**	a														06 56				07 00			
38¾	32	—	Deansgate ⇌	a														06 59							

		NT	NT	NT	EM	XC	NT	NT	NT		NT	XC	NT	TP	NT	AW	NT	NT	TP		NT		NT	VT	NT
					◇	◇1						◇1		◇1		◇			◇1					◇1	
		H		B	I				G					J	G	K		F	L		M				B
						🛒						🛒		🛒					🛒					⊠	
London Euston 15 ⊖65	d																							06 17	
Birmingham New Street 12 68	d					05 57						06 22													
Wolverhampton 7 68 ⇌	d					06 16						06 40													
Stafford 65,68	d					06 30						06 55													
Stoke-on-Trent 50,68	d		06 30			06 51						07 14					07 17							07 45	
Longport 50	d		06 34														07 21								
Kidsgrove 50	d		06 38														07 25								
Crewe 10 65	d						06 33	06 49								07 27							07 22		
Sandbach	d						06 40	06 56															07 35		
Holmes Chapel	d						06 44	07 00															07 41		
Goostrey	d							07 03															07 45		
Chelford	d							07 08															07 51		
Alderley Edge	d						06 53	07 12					07 30										07 56		
Wilmslow	d						06 57	07 16					07 33			07 44							08 00		
Styal	d																								
Manchester Airport ✈	a						07 04																		
Handforth	d							07 19					07 37										08 03		
Congleton	d		06 45			07 03											07 32								
Macclesfield	a		06 52			07 11						07 30					07 39							08 01	
	d		06 53			07 12					07 15	07 31					07 40							08 02	
Prestbury	d		06 57								07 21						07 44								
Adlington (Cheshire)	d		07 00								07 24						07 47								
Poynton	d		07 04								07 27						07 51								
Bramhall	d		07 07								07 31						07 54								
Cheadle Hulme	d		07 11					07 24			07 34		07 42				07 59						08 09		
Stockport	a		07 15			07 27		07 29			07 41	07 45	07 47			07 54	08 03						08 14	08 16	
	d	07 10	07 16	07 19	07 22	07 28		07 29	07 31		07 42	07 50	07 48	07 53	07 57	07 54	08 04				08 10		08 14	08 17	08 19
Heaton Chapel	d	07 15						07 33									08 07						08 18		
Levenshulme	d	07 18						07 36									08 10						08 21		
Manchester Piccadilly 10 ⇌	a	07 26	07 27	07 28	07 34	07 37	07 42	07 44	07 45		07 56	07 59	07 59	08 02	08 09	08 10	08 21				08 25		08 27	08 28	08 32
	d	07 27			07 34													07 59	08 07				08 29		
Manchester Oxford Road	a	07 29			07 37													08 01	08 09				08 33		
Deansgate ⇌	a	07 32																							

A From Sheffield
B From Chester
C From Sheffield to Manchester Airport
D From Buxton to Clitheroe
E From Doncaster to Manchester Airport
F From Manchester Airport to Liverpool Lime Street
G From Hazel Grove
H From Buxton to Wigan North Western
I From Nottingham to Liverpool Lime Street
J From Cleethorpes to Manchester Airport
K From Cardiff Central
L From Hull to Liverpool Lime Street
M From Buxton
b Previous night, stops to set down only

Stoke-on-Trent and Crewe - Manchester Airport, Stockport and Manchester

Network Diagram - see first Page of Table 78

		XC	EM	NT	NT		NT	VT	NT	NT	XC	TP	VT	AW	NT		NT	TP	NT	VT	TP	NT		EM	XC
		◇1	◇					◇1			◇1	◇1	◇1	◇				◇1		◇1	◇1			◇	◇1
			A						B			C		D			E	F	G		H	I		A	K
		🛒						⊠			🛒	🛒	⊠	🛒				🛒		⊠	🛒				🛒
London Euston 15 ⊖65	d							06 36					06 55							07 20					
Birmingham New Street 12 68	d	06 57									07 31														07 57
Wolverhampton 7 68 🚢	d	07 15									07 49														08 15
Stafford 65,68	d	07 30									08 01														08 30
Stoke-on-Trent 50,68	d									07 57	08 20		08 25							08 48					08 55
Longport 50	d																								
Kidsgrove 50	d									08 04															
Crewe 10 65	d	07 52		07 50				08 11						08 28											
Sandbach	d			07 57																					
Holmes Chapel	d			08 01																					
Goostrey	d																								
Chelford	d																								
Alderley Edge	d			08 10	07 53										08 49										
Wilmslow	d	08 09		08 13	07 56			08 27						08 45	08 52										
Styal	d				07 59																				
Manchester Airport ✈	a				08 04																				
Handforth	d			08 16											08 55										
Congleton	d									08 11															
Macclesfield	a									08 18	08 36		08 41												09 11
	d						08 06			08 19	08 37		08 41												09 12
Prestbury	d						08 10			08 23															
Adlington (Cheshire)	d									08 26															
Poynton	d						08 15			08 30															
Bramhall	d						08 17			08 33															
Cheadle Hulme	d			08 21			08 20			08 37					08 59										
Stockport	a	08 20		08 25			08 27	08 37		08 41	08 50		08 55	08 58	09 04					09 16					09 27
	d	08 21	08 24	08 25			08 28	08 38	08 41	08 42	08 50	08 53	08 56	08 59	09 04				09 12	09 17		09 21		09 25	09 28
Heaton Chapel	d			08 30						08 45					09 08				09 16						
Levenshulme	d						08 32			08 48					09 11				09 19						
Manchester Piccadilly 10 🚢	a	08 34	08 36	08 40	08 42		08 42	08 49	08 52	08 56	08 59	09 02	09 07	09 15	09 20				09 28	09 28		09 36		09 36	09 39
	d		08 37						08 54								09 01	09 07			09 16			09 37	
Manchester Oxford Road	a		08 40						08 56								09 03	09 09			09 18			09 40	
Deansgate 🚢	a								09 00																

			NT	NT	VT	TP	NT	NT	XC	TP	VT		AW	NT	NT	TP	NT	VT	NT		EM		XC	NT	NT
					◇1	◇1			◇1	◇1	◇1		◇			◇1		◇1			◇		◇1		
						L	B		M	C			N		E	O	G		I		P		K		
					⊠	🛒			🛒	🛒	⊠		🛒			🛒		⊠					🛒		
London Euston 15 ⊖65	d				07 35						08 00							08 20							
Birmingham New Street 12 68	d								08 31														08 57		
Wolverhampton 7 68 🚢	d								08 49														09 15		
Stafford 65,68	d								09 01														09 30		
Stoke-on-Trent 50,68	d							08 58	09 20		09 25							09 48					09 55		
Longport 50	d																								
Kidsgrove 50	d							09 05																	
Crewe 10 65	d		08 31	08 50	09 11								09 31											09 33	09 50
Sandbach	d		08 38	08 57																				09 40	09 57
Holmes Chapel	d		08 42	09 02																				09 44	10 02
Goostrey	d		08 45	09 05																					10 05
Chelford	d		08 50	09 09																					10 09
Alderley Edge	d		08 54	09 13										09 48										09 53	10 13
Wilmslow	d		08 57	09 17	09 27								09 48	09 51										09 57	10 17
Styal	d																								
Manchester Airport ✈	a		09 04																					10 04	
Handforth	d			09 20										09 54											10 20
Congleton	d							09 12																	
Macclesfield	a							09 19			09 41												10 11		
	d							09 20			09 41												10 12		
Prestbury	d							09 24																	
Adlington (Cheshire)	d							09 27																	
Poynton	d							09 30																	
Bramhall	d							09 33																	
Cheadle Hulme	d			09 24				09 37						09 59											10 24
Stockport	a			09 29	09 36			09 41	09 49		09 55		09 58	10 04				10 16					10 27		10 29
	d			09 29	09 37		09 41	09 42	09 50	09 53	09 56		09 58	10 04			10 12	10 17	10 21		10 26		10 28		10 29
Heaton Chapel	d			09 33				09 45						10 08			10 16								10 33
Levenshulme	d			09 36				09 48						10 11			10 19								10 36
Manchester Piccadilly 10 🚢	a		09 42	09 44	09 49		09 52	09 56	09 59	10 02	10 07		10 15	10 20			10 28	10 28	10 36		10 36		10 39	10 42	10 44
	d					09 46	09 54								10 01	10 07					10 37				
Manchester Oxford Road	a					09 48	09 56								10 03	10 09					10 40				
Deansgate 🚢	a					09 51	10 00																		

A From Nottingham to Liverpool Lime Street
B From Hazel Grove to Preston
C From Cleethorpes to Manchester Airport
D From Cardiff Central
E From Manchester Airport to Liverpool Lime Street
F From Newcastle to Liverpool Lime Street
G From Buxton
H From Manchester Airport to Barrow-in-Furness
I From Chester
K From Southampton Central
L From Manchester Airport to Windermere
M From Bristol Temple Meads
N From Carmarthen
O From Scarborough to Liverpool Lime Street
P From Norwich to Liverpool Lime Street

Stoke-on-Trent and Crewe - Manchester Airport, Stockport and Manchester

Network Diagram - see first Page of Table 78

		VT	NT	NT	XC	TP	VT		AW	NT	NT	TP	NT	VT	TP	NT			EM	XC	NT	NT	VT	NT	NT
		◇1 ⊠	A		◇1 B 🍴	◇1 C 🍴	◇1 ⊠		◇ D 🍴		E	◇1 F 🍴	G	◇1 ⊠	◇1 H 🍴	I			◇ K	◇1 L 🍴			◇1 ⊠	A	
London Euston 15 ⊖65	d	08 40					09 00							09 20									09 40		
Birmingham New Street 12 68	d				09 31															09 57					
Wolverhampton 7 68 ⛴	d				09 49															10 15					
Stafford 65,68	d				10 01															10 30					
Stoke-on-Trent 50,68	d			09 58	10 20		10 25							10 48						10 55					10 58
Longport 50	d																								
Kidsgrove 50	d			10 05																					11 05
Crewe 10 65	d	10 11							10 31												10 34	10 50	11 11		
Sandbach	d																				10 41	10 57			
Holmes Chapel	d																				10 45	11 02			
Goostrey	d																					11 05			
Chelford	d																					11 09			
Alderley Edge	d									10 49											10 54	11 13			
Wilmslow	d	10 27							10 49	10 52											10 57	11 17	11 27		
Styal	d																								
Manchester Airport ✈	a																				11 04				
Handforth	d									10 55												11 20			
Congleton	d			10 12																					11 12
Macclesfield	a			10 19			10 41													11 11					11 19
	d			10 20			10 41													11 12					11 20
Prestbury	d			10 24																					11 24
Adlington (Cheshire)	d			10 27																					11 27
Poynton	d			10 30																					11 30
Bramhall	d			10 33																					11 33
Cheadle Hulme	d			10 37						10 59												11 24			11 37
Stockport	a	10 36		10 41	10 49		10 55		10 58	11 04				11 16						11 27		11 29	11 36		11 41
	d	10 37	10 41	10 42	10 50	10 53	10 56		10 58	11 04			11 12	11 17		11 21			11 26	11 28		11 29	11 37	11 41	11 42
Heaton Chapel	d			10 45						11 08			11 16									11 33			11 45
Levenshulme	d			10 48						11 11			11 19									11 36			11 48
Manchester Piccadilly 10 ⛴	a	10 49	10 52	10 56	10 59	11 02	11 07		11 15	11 20			11 28	11 28		11 36			11 36	11 39	11 42	11 44	11 49	11 52	11 56
	d		10 54								11 01	11 07			11 16				11 37					11 54	
Manchester Oxford Road	a		10 56								11 03	11 09			11 18				11 40					11 56	
Deansgate ⛴	a		11 00																					12 00	

		XC	TP		VT	AW	NT	NT	TP	NT	VT	NT			EM	XC	NT	NT	VT	NT	NT	XC	TP		VT
		◇1 M 🍴	◇1 C 🍴		◇1 ⊠	◇ N 🍴		E	◇1 F 🍴	G	◇1 ⊠	I			◇ K	◇1 L 🍴			◇1 ⊠	A		◇1 O 🍴	◇1 C 🍴		◇1 ☕
London Euston 15 ⊖65	d				10 00						10 20								10 40						11 00
Birmingham New Street 12 68	d	10 31														10 57						11 31			
Wolverhampton 7 68 ⛴	d	10 49														11 15						11 49			
Stafford 65,68	d	11 01														11 30						12 01			
Stoke-on-Trent 50,68	d	11 20			11 25						11 48					11 55					11 58	12 20			12 25
Longport 50	d																								
Kidsgrove 50	d																				12 05				
Crewe 10 65	d					11 31											11 34	11 50	12 11						
Sandbach	d																11 41	11 57							
Holmes Chapel	d																11 45	12 02							
Goostrey	d																	12 05							
Chelford	d																	12 09							
Alderley Edge	d						11 48										11 54	12 13							
Wilmslow	d					11 48	11 51										11 57	12 17	12 27						
Styal	d																								
Manchester Airport ✈	a																12 04								
Handforth	d						11 54											12 20							
Congleton	d																				12 12				
Macclesfield	a				11 41											12 11					12 19				12 41
	d				11 41											12 12					12 20				12 41
Prestbury	d																				12 24				
Adlington (Cheshire)	d																				12 27				
Poynton	d																				12 30				
Bramhall	d																				12 33				
Cheadle Hulme	d						11 59											12 24			12 37				
Stockport	a	11 49			11 55	11 58	12 04				12 16					12 27		12 29	12 36		12 41	12 49			12 55
	d	11 50	11 53		11 56	11 58	12 04			12 12	12 17	12 21			12 26	12 28		12 29	12 37	12 41	12 42	12 50	12 53		12 56
Heaton Chapel	d						12 08			12 16								12 33			12 45				
Levenshulme	d						12 11			12 19								12 36			12 48				
Manchester Piccadilly 10 ⛴	a	11 59	12 02		12 07	12 15	12 20			12 28	12 28	12 36			12 36	12 39	12 42	12 44	12 49	12 52	12 56	12 59	13 02		13 07
	d							12 01	12 07						12 37					12 54					
Manchester Oxford Road	a							12 03	12 09						12 40					12 56					
Deansgate ⛴	a																			13 00					

A From Hazel Grove to Preston
B From Cardiff Central
C From Cleethorpes to Manchester Airport
D From Carmarthen
E From Manchester Airport to Liverpool Lime Street
F From Scarborough to Liverpool Lime Street
G From Buxton
H From Manchester Airport to Barrow-in-Furness
I From Chester
K From Norwich to Liverpool Lime Street
L From Bournemouth
M From Paignton
N From Milford Haven
O From Bristol Temple Meads

Stoke-on-Trent and Crewe - Manchester Airport, Stockport and Manchester

Network Diagram - see first Page of Table 78

		AW	NT	NT	TP	NT	VT	TP FX	NT			EM	XC	NT	NT	VT	NT	NT	XC		TP	VT	AW	NT	NT
		◇			◇1		◇1	◇1				◇	◇1			◇1			◇1		◇1	◇1	◇		
		A		B	C	D		E	F			H	I				J		K		L		M		B
London Euston 15 ⊖65	d						11 20									11 40						12 00			
Birmingham New Street 12 68	d												11 57						12 31						
Wolverhampton 7 68	d												12 15						12 49						
Stafford 65,68	d												12 30						13 01						
Stoke-on-Trent 50,68	d						12 48						12 55					12 58	13 20			13 25			
Longport 50	d																								
Kidsgrove 50	d																	13 05							
Crewe 10 65	d	12 31												12 34	12 50	13 11							13 31		
Sandbach	d													12 41	12 57										
Holmes Chapel	d													12 45	13 02										
Goostrey	d														13 05										
Chelford	d														13 09										
Alderley Edge	d		12 49											12 54	13 13									13 48	
Wilmslow	d	12 49	12 52											12 57	13 17	13 27							13 48	13 51	
Styal	d																								
Manchester Airport	a													13 04											
Handforth	d		12 55												13 20									13 54	
Congleton	d																	13 12							
Macclesfield	a												13 11					13 19				13 41			
	d												13 12					13 20				13 41			
Prestbury	d																	13 24							
Adlington (Cheshire)	d																	13 27							
Poynton	d																	13 30							
Bramhall	d																	13 33							
Cheadle Hulme	d		12 59												13 24			13 37						13 59	
Stockport	a	12 58	13 04				13 16						13 27		13 29	13 36		13 41	13 49			13 55	13 58	14 04	
	d	12 58	13 04			13 12	13 17		13 21			13 26	13 28		13 29	13 37	13 41	13 42	13 50		13 53	13 56	13 58	14 04	
Heaton Chapel	d		13 08			13 16									13 33			13 45						14 08	
Levenshulme	d		13 11			13 19									13 36			13 48						14 11	
Manchester Piccadilly 10	a	13 15	13 20			13 28	13 28		13 36			13 36	13 39	13 42	13 44	13 49	13 52	13 56	13 59		14 02	14 07	14 15	14 20	
	d			13 01	13 07			13 16				13 37					13 54								14 01
Manchester Oxford Road	a			13 03	13 09			13 18				13 40					13 56								14 03
Deansgate	a																14 00								

		TP	NT	VT	NT			EM	XC	NT	NT	VT	NT	NT	XC		TP	VT	AW	NT	NT	TP	NT	VT	TP
		◇1		◇1				◇	◇1			◇1			◇1		◇1	◇1	◇			◇1		◇1	◇1
		C	D		F			H	I				J		N		L		A		B	C	D		E
London Euston 15 ⊖65	d			12 20								12 40						13 00						13 20	
Birmingham New Street 12 68	d								12 57						13 31										
Wolverhampton 7 68	d								13 15						13 49										
Stafford 65,68	d								13 30						14 01										
Stoke-on-Trent 50,68	d			13 48					13 55					13 58	14 20			14 25						14 48	
Longport 50	d																								
Kidsgrove 50	d													14 05											
Crewe 10 65	d									13 34	13 50	14 11							14 31						
Sandbach	d									13 41	13 57														
Holmes Chapel	d									13 45	14 02														
Goostrey	d										14 05														
Chelford	d										14 09														
Alderley Edge	d									13 54	14 13									14 49					
Wilmslow	d									13 57	14 17	14 27							14 49	14 52					
Styal	d																								
Manchester Airport	a									14 04															
Handforth	d										14 20									14 55					
Congleton	d													14 12											
Macclesfield	a								14 11					14 19				14 41							
	d								14 12					14 20				14 41							
Prestbury	d													14 24											
Adlington (Cheshire)	d													14 27											
Poynton	d													14 30											
Bramhall	d													14 33											
Cheadle Hulme	d										14 24			14 37						14 59					
Stockport	a			14 16					14 27		14 29	14 36		14 41	14 49			14 55	14 58	15 04				15 16	
	d		14 12	14 17	14 21			14 26	14 28		14 29	14 37	14 41	14 42	14 50		14 53	14 56	14 58	15 04			15 12	15 17	
Heaton Chapel	d		14 16								14 33			14 45						15 08			15 16		
Levenshulme	d		14 19								14 36			14 48						15 11			15 19		
Manchester Piccadilly 10	a		14 28	14 28	14 36			14 36	14 39	14 42	14 44	14 49	14 52	14 56	14 59		15 02	15 07	15 15	15 20			15 28	15 28	
	d	14 07						14 37					14 54								15 01	15 07			15 16
Manchester Oxford Road	a	14 09						14 40					14 56								15 03	15 09			15 18
Deansgate	a												15 00												

- **A** From Milford Haven
- **B** From Manchester Airport to Liverpool Lime Street
- **C** From Scarborough to Liverpool Lime Street
- **D** From Buxton
- **E** From Manchester Airport to Barrow-in-Furness
- **F** From Chester
- **H** From Norwich to Liverpool Lime Street
- **I** From Bournemouth
- **J** From Hazel Grove to Preston
- **K** From Bristol Temple Meads
- **L** From Cleethorpes to Manchester Airport
- **M** From Fishguard Harbour
- **N** From Paignton

Stoke-on-Trent and Crewe - Manchester Airport, Stockport and Manchester

Network Diagram - see first Page of Table 78

		NT		EM	XC	NT	NT	VT	NT	NT		XC	TP	VT	AW	NT	NT	TP	TP FX			NT	VT	NT
				◇	◇1			◇1				◇1	◇1	◇1	◇			◇1	◇1				◇1	
		A		C	D				E			F	G		H		I	J	K			L		A
					⊥			⊏P				⊥	⊥	⊏P	⊥			⊥	⊥				⊏P	
London Euston 15 ⊖65	d							13 40						14 00									14 20	
Birmingham New Street 12 68	d				13 57							14 31												
Wolverhampton 7 68	d				14 15							14 49												
Stafford 65,68	d				14 30							15 01												
Stoke-on-Trent 50,68	d				14 55					14 58		15 20		15 25									15 48	
Longport 50	d																							
Kidsgrove 50	d									15 05														
Crewe 10 65	d					14 34	14 50	15 11							15 29									
Sandbach	d					14 41	14 57																	
Holmes Chapel	d					14 45	15 02																	
Goostrey	d						15 05																	
Chelford	d						15 09																	
Alderley Edge	d					14 54	15 13									15 48								
Wilmslow	d					14 57	15 17	15 27							15 47	15 51								
Styal	d																							
Manchester Airport	a					15 04																		
Handforth	d						15 20									15 54								
Congleton	d									15 12														
Macclesfield	a				15 11					15 19				15 41										
	d				15 12					15 20				15 41										
Prestbury	d									15 24														
Adlington (Cheshire)	d									15 27														
Poynton	d									15 30														
Bramhall	d									15 33														
Cheadle Hulme	d						15 24			15 37						15 59								
Stockport	a				15 27		15 29	15 36		15 41		15 49		15 55	15 58	16 04							16 16	
	d	15 21		15 26	15 28		15 29	15 37	15 41	15 42		15 50	15 53	15 56	15 58	16 04						16 12	16 17	16 21
Heaton Chapel	d						15 33			15 45						16 08						16 16		
Levenshulme	d						15 36			15 48						16 11						16 19		
Manchester Piccadilly 10	a	15 36		15 36	15 39	15 41	15 44	15 49	15 52	15 56		16 00	16 02	16 07	16 15	16 20						16 25	16 28	16 36
	d			15 37		15 42			15 54								16 01	16 07	16 16			16 27		
Manchester Oxford Road	a			15 40		15 46			15 56								16 03	16 09	16 18			16 29		
Deansgate	a								16 00													16 32		

		EM	XC	NT	NT	VT	NT		NT	XC	TP	VT	AW	NT	VT	NT	TP		TP	NT	NT	EM	XC	NT	NT
		◇	◇1			◇1				◇1	◇1	◇1	◇		◇1		◇1		◇1			◇	◇1		
		C	D				M			N	G		O			I	J		P	A	B	C	D		
			⊥			⊏P				⊥	⊥	⊏P	⊥		⊏P		⊥		⊥				⊥		
London Euston 15 ⊖65	d					14 40						15 00			15 20										
Birmingham New Street 12 68	d		14 57							15 31													15 57		
Wolverhampton 7 68	d		15 15							15 50													16 15		
Stafford 65,68	d		15 30							16 02													16 31		
Stoke-on-Trent 50,68	d		15 55						15 58	16 21		16 25			16 48								16 55		
Longport 50	d																								
Kidsgrove 50	d								16 05																
Crewe 10 65	d			15 33	15 50	16 12							16 31											16 34	16 50
Sandbach	d			15 40	15 57																			16 41	16 57
Holmes Chapel	d			15 44	16 02																			16 45	17 02
Goostrey	d				16 05																				17 05
Chelford	d				16 09																				17 09
Alderley Edge	d			15 53	16 13									16 49										16 54	17 13
Wilmslow	d			15 56	16 17	16 27							16 48	16 52										16 57	17 17
Styal	d			15 59																					
Manchester Airport	a			16 04																				17 04	
Handforth	d				16 20									16 55											17 20
Congleton	d								16 12																
Macclesfield	a		16 11						16 19			16 41											17 11		
	d		16 12						16 20			16 41											17 12		
Prestbury	d								16 24																
Adlington (Cheshire)	d								16 27																
Poynton	d								16 30																
Bramhall	d								16 33																
Cheadle Hulme	d				16 24				16 37					16 59											17 24
Stockport	a		16 27		16 29	16 36			16 41	16 49		16 54	16 58	17 04	17 16								17 27		17 29
	d	16 26	16 28		16 29	16 37	16 41		16 42	16 50	16 53	16 55	16 58	17 04	17 17					17 21		17 26	17 28		17 29
Heaton Chapel	d				16 33				16 45					17 08											17 33
Levenshulme	d				16 36				16 48					17 11											17 36
Manchester Piccadilly 10	a	16 36	16 39	16 42	16 44	16 49	16 52		16 56	16 59	17 02	17 07	17 14	17 20	17 28					17 36		17 37	17 39	17 42	17 44
	d	16 37					16 54									17 01	17 07		17 15		17 22	17 37			
Manchester Oxford Road	a	16 40					16 56									17 03	17 09		17 17		17 25	17 40			
Deansgate	a						17 00																		

A From Chester
B From Manchester Airport to Southport
C From Norwich to Liverpool Lime Street
D From Bournemouth
E From Hazel Grove to Bolton
F From Bristol Temple Meads
G From Cleethorpes to Manchester Airport
H From Carmarthen
I From Manchester Airport to Liverpool Lime Street
J From Scarborough to Liverpool Lime Street
K From Manchester Airport to Windermere
L From Buxton to Barrow-in-Furness
M From Hazel Grove to Preston
N From Penzance
O From Milford Haven
P From Manchester Airport to Barrow-in-Furness

Stoke-on-Trent and Crewe - Manchester Airport, Stockport and Manchester

Network Diagram - see first Page of Table 78

	VT	NT		XC	TP	VT	AW	NT	NT	TP	NT	VT		TP	NT		EM	XC	NT	NT	VT	NT		NT
	◇1 ☕			◇1 A 🛒	◇1 B 🛒	◇1 ☕	◇ C 🛒		D	◇1 E 🛒	F	◇1 ☕		◇1 G 🛒	H		◇ J	◇1 K 🛒			◇1 ☕	L		
London Euston [15] ⊖65 d	15 40					16 00						16 20									16 40			
Birmingham New Street [12] 68 d				16 31														16 57						
Wolverhampton [7] 68 🚌 d				16 49														17 15						
Stafford 65,68 d				17 01														17 30						
Stoke-on-Trent 50,68 d		16 58		17 20		17 25						17 48						17 55						17 58
Longport 50 d																								
Kidsgrove 50 d		17 05																						18 05
Crewe [10] 65 d	17 11						17 30												17 33	17 50	18 11			
Sandbach d																			17 40	17 57				
Holmes Chapel d																			17 44	18 02				
Goostrey d																				18 05				
Chelford d																				18 09				
Alderley Edge d								17 48											17 53	18 13				
Wilmslow d	17 27						17 47	17 51											17 56	18 17	18 27			
Styal d																			17 59					
Manchester Airport ✈ a																			18 04					
Handforth d								17 54												18 20				
Congleton d		17 12																						18 12
Macclesfield a		17 19				17 41												18 11						18 19
d		17 20				17 41												18 12						18 20
Prestbury d		17 24																						18 24
Adlington (Cheshire) d		17 27																						18 27
Poynton d		17 30																						18 30
Bramhall d		17 33																						18 33
Cheadle Hulme d		17 36						17 59												18 24				18 37
Stockport a	17 36	17 41		17 49		17 55	17 57	18 04				18 16						18 27		18 29	18 37			18 41
d	17 37	17 42		17 50	17 53	17 56	17 58	18 04			18 12	18 17			18 21		18 26	18 28		18 29	18 38	18 41		18 42
Heaton Chapel d		17 45						18 08			18 16									18 33				18 45
Levenshulme d		17 48						18 11			18 19									18 36				18 48
Manchester Piccadilly [10] 🚌 a	17 49	17 56		17 59	18 02	18 07	18 13	18 20			18 28	18 28			18 36		18 36	18 39	18 42	18 44	18 49	18 52		18 56
d									18 01	18 07				18 16			18 37					18 54		
Manchester Oxford Road a									18 03	18 09				18 18			18 40					18 56		
Deansgate 🚌 a																						19 00		

	XC	TP	VT	AW	NT	TP	NT	VT		TP		NT	NT	EM	XC	NT	VT	NT		XC	TP	VT	AW	NT
	◇1 M 🛒	◇1 B 🛒	◇1 ⊠	R N 🛒	D	◇1 E 🛒	F	◇1 ⊠		◇1 G			H	◇ J	◇1 K 🛒		◇1 ⊠			◇1 A 🛒	◇1 B 🛒	◇1 ⊠	R C 🛒	D
London Euston [15] ⊖65 d			17 00					17 20									17 40					18 00		
Birmingham New Street [12] 68 d	17 31														17 57					18 31				
Wolverhampton [7] 68 🚌 d	17 50														18 15					18 49				
Stafford 65,68 d	18 02														18 30					19 01				
Stoke-on-Trent 50,68 d	18 21		18 25					18 49							18 55			18 58		19 20		19 25		
Longport 50 d																								
Kidsgrove 50 d																		19 05						
Crewe [10] 65 d				18 31								18 34				18 50	19 11						19 31	
Sandbach d												18 41				18 57								
Holmes Chapel d												18 45				19 02								
Goostrey d																19 05								
Chelford d																19 09								
Alderley Edge d												18 54				19 13								
Wilmslow d				18 48								18 57				19 17	19 27						19 48	
Styal d																								
Manchester Airport ✈ a												19 05												
Handforth d																19 20								
Congleton d																		19 12						
Macclesfield a			18 41												19 11			19 19				19 41		
d			18 41												19 12			19 20				19 41		
Prestbury d																		19 24						
Adlington (Cheshire) d																		19 27						
Poynton d																		19 30						
Bramhall d																		19 33						
Cheadle Hulme d																19 24		19 37						
Stockport a	18 49		18 55	18 58				19 16							19 27	19 29	19 36	19 41		19 48		19 55	19 58	
d	18 50	18 53	18 56	18 58			19 12	19 17					19 21	19 26	19 28	19 29	19 37	19 42		19 50	19 53	19 56	19 58	
Heaton Chapel d							19 16											19 45						
Levenshulme d							19 19											19 48						
Manchester Piccadilly [10] 🚌 a	18 59	19 02	19 07	19 15			19 28	19 28				19 31	19 35	19 36	19 39	19 43	19 49	19 56		20 00	20 02	20 07	20 15	
d					19 01	19 07				19 16		19 32		19 37										20 01
Manchester Oxford Road a					19 03	19 09				19 18		19 36		19 40										20 03
Deansgate 🚌 a																								

A From Bristol Temple Meads
B From Cleethorpes to Manchester Airport
C From Carmarthen
D From Manchester Airport to Liverpool Lime Street
E From Scarborough to Liverpool Lime Street
F From Buxton
G From Manchester Airport to Barrow-in-Furness
H From Chester
J From Norwich to Liverpool Lime Street
K From Bournemouth
L From Buxton to Bolton
M From Paignton
N From Milford Haven

Stoke-on-Trent and Crewe - Manchester Airport, Stockport and Manchester

Network Diagram - see first Page of Table 78

		TP	NT	VT	TP			NT	NT	EM	XC	NT	VT	NT	XC		AW	TP TH FO	AW	TP MT WO	VT	VT FO	TP	NT	VT
		◇1 A	B	◇1 ⊠	◇1 C				E	◇ F	◇1 G 🛒		◇1 ⊠		◇1 H 🛒		I	◇1 J	R K 🛒	◇1 L	R 1 🍴	◇ 🍴	◇1 A	B	R 1 🍴
London Euston 15	⊖65 d			18 20									18 40								19 00	18 57			19 20
Birmingham New Street 12	68 d										18 57				19 31										
Wolverhampton 7	68 ⛴ d										19 15				19 49										
Stafford	65,68 d										19 29				20 01										
Stoke-on-Trent	50,68 d			19 48							19 55			19 58	20 20						20 25				20 48
Longport	50 d																								
Kidsgrove	50 d													20 05											
Crewe 10	65 d											19 50	20 12						20 23			20s33			
Sandbach	d											19 57													
Holmes Chapel	d											20 02													
Goostrey	d											20 05													
Chelford	d											20 09													
Alderley Edge	d											20 13													
Wilmslow	d							19 56				20 17	20 27						20 40						
Styal	d																								
Manchester Airport	✈ a							20 04																	
Handforth	d											20 20													
Congleton	d													20 12											
Macclesfield	a										20 11			20 19							20 41				
	d										20 12			20 20							20 41				
Prestbury	d													20 24											
Adlington (Cheshire)	d													20 27											
Poynton	d													20 30											
Bramhall	d													20 33											
Cheadle Hulme	d											20 24		20 37											
Stockport	a			20 16							20 27	20 29	20 36	20 41	20 48				20 50		20 55				21 16
	d		20 12	20 17					20 21	20 26	20 28	20 29	20 37	20 42	20 50			20 53	20 50	20 56	20 56			21 12	21 17
Heaton Chapel	d		20 16											20 45										21 16	
Levenshulme	d		20 19											20 48										21 19	
Manchester Piccadilly 10	⛴ a		20 28	20 28				20 32	20 35	20 36	20 39	20 43	20 49	20 56	20 58			21 02	21 05	21 05	21 07	21 09		21 28	21 28
	d	20 07			20 16			20 32		20 37							20 50						21 07		
Manchester Oxford Road	a	20 09			20 18			20 36		20 40							20 52						21 09		
Deansgate	⛴ a																								

			EM		NT	NT	XC	NT	VT	NT	XC		VT	AW	AW	NT FO	TP	NT	TP	NT	NT		XC	NT
			◇ M			E	◇1 G		◇1 🍴		◇1 N		◇1 🍴	◇ O 🛒	I	P	◇1 A	B	◇1 C		E		◇1 G	
London Euston 15	⊖65 d								19 40				20 00											
Birmingham New Street 12	68 d						19 57				20 31												20 57	
Wolverhampton 7	68 ⛴ d						20 16				20 49												21 16	
Stafford	65,68 d						20 30		21 04														21 32	
Stoke-on-Trent	50,68 d						20 55			20 58	21 18		21 24										21 55	
Longport	50 d																							
Kidsgrove	50 d									21 05														
Crewe 10	65 d							20 50	21 23					21 31										21 45
Sandbach	d							20 57																21 52
Holmes Chapel	d							21 02																21 58
Goostrey	d							21 05																22 01
Chelford	d							21 09																22 07
Alderley Edge	d							21 13																22 12
Wilmslow	d				20 56			21 17	21 38					21 48						21 55				22 15
Styal	d																							
Manchester Airport	✈ a				21 04															22 04				
Handforth	d							21 20																22 19
Congleton	d									21 12														
Macclesfield	a						21 11			21 19			21 40										22 11	
	d						21 12			21 20			21 40										22 12	
Prestbury	d									21 24														
Adlington (Cheshire)	d									21 27														
Poynton	d									21 30														
Bramhall	d									21 33														
Cheadle Hulme	d							21 24		21 37														22 24
Stockport	a						21 27	21 29		21 41	21 46		21 55	21 58									22 25	22 29
	d		21 20			21 21	21 28	21 29		21 42	21 49		21 56	21 59				22 12			22 21		22 26	22 29
Heaton Chapel	d									21 45								22 16						
Levenshulme	d									21 48								22 19						
Manchester Piccadilly 10	⛴ a		21 32		21 32	21 35	21 39	21 43	21 57	21 57	21 59		22 07	22 13				22 28		22 31	22 35		22 35	22 43
	d				21 32										21 50	22 01	22 07		22 16	22 32				
Manchester Oxford Road	a				21 36										21 52	22 03	22 09		22 18	22 36				
Deansgate	⛴ a																							

A From Scarborough to Liverpool Lime Street
B From Buxton
C From Manchester Airport to Barrow-in-Furness
E From Chester
F From Norwich to Liverpool Lime Street
G From Bournemouth
H From Exeter St Davids
I From Manchester Airport to Chester
J From Cleethorpes to Manchester Airport
K From Milford Haven
L From Cleethorpes to Manchester Airport
M From Norwich
N From Bristol Temple Meads
O From Carmarthen
P From Manchester Airport to Liverpool Lime Street

Stoke-on-Trent and Crewe - Manchester Airport, Stockport and Manchester

Network Diagram - see first Page of Table 78

		NT	VT	TP	VT	NT	NT		XC	VT	AW	NT	NT	NT	XC	AW FO	VT
			◇1	◇1	◇1				◇1	◇1	◇				◇1		◇1
		A		B					C		D	E	F			G	
			🍴		🍴					🍴							🍴
London Euston 15 ⊖65	d		20 40		21 00					21 40							22 00
Birmingham New Street 12 68	d								21 57						22 30	21 24	
Wolverhampton 7 68	d								22 16						22 48	21 43	
Stafford 65,68	d								22 30						23 01		23s38
Stoke-on-Trent 50,68	d				22 28	22 18			22 55	23 07					23 21		
Longport 50	d																
Kidsgrove 50	d					22 25											
Crewe 10 65	d		22 13								23 04			23 12			00s03
Sandbach	d													23 19			
Holmes Chapel	d													23 24			
Goostrey	d													23 27			
Chelford	d													23 31			
Alderley Edge	d													23 35			
Wilmslow	d		22 29				22 56				23 22			23 39			
Styal	d																
Manchester Airport ✈	a						23 04										
Handforth	d													23 42			
Congleton	d					22 32											
Macclesfield	a				22 44	22 40			23 11	23 23							
	d				22 44	22 48			23 12	23 23							
Prestbury	d					22 53											
Adlington (Cheshire)	d					22 56											
Poynton	d					22 59											
Bramhall	d					23 02											
Cheadle Hulme	d					23 05								23 46			
Stockport	a		22 38		22 58	23 10			23 25	23 37	23 30			23 51			00s26
	d	22 34	22 39	22 53	22 59	23 10			23 26	23 38	23 31	23 41	23 48	23 51			
Heaton Chapel	d	22 38				23 14								23 55			
Levenshulme	d	22 41				23 17								23 58			
Manchester Piccadilly 10	a	22 48	22 48	23 02	23 11	23 25	23 33		23 37	23 46	23 48	23 54	00 02	00 07	00 12	00 28	00 35
	d	22 50															
Manchester Oxford Road	a	22 52															
Deansgate	a	22 55															

Saturdays

		NT	NT	XC	NT	AW	VT	NT	TP	NT		NT	TP	AW	NT	NT	NT	NT	EM	XC		NT	NT	NT	NT
				◇1			◇1		◇1				◇1						◇	◇1					
		F			H	G			I			J	K			L	E	H	M					N	
							🍴													🛒					
London Euston 15 ⊖65	d						22p00																		
Birmingham New Street 12 68	d			22p30		21p24														05 57					
Wolverhampton 7 68	d			22p48		21p43														06 16					
Stafford 65,68	d			23p01			23b38													06 30					
Stoke-on-Trent 50,68	d			23p21																06 51					06 57
Longport 50	d																								
Kidsgrove 50	d																								07 04
Crewe 10 65	d		23p12				00s03	00 44						06 27								06 33	06 49		
Sandbach	d		23p19																			06 40	06 56		
Holmes Chapel	d		23p24																			06 44	07 00		
Goostrey	d		23p27																				07 03		
Chelford	d		23p31																				07 08		
Alderley Edge	d		23p35												06 49							06 53	07 12		
Wilmslow	d		23p39							05 46				06 45	06 52							06 57	07 16		
Styal	d																								
Manchester Airport ✈	a							01 16		05 53												07 04			
Handforth	d		23p42												06 55								07 19		
Congleton	d																			07 03					07 11
Macclesfield	a																			07 11					07 18
	d																			07 12					07 19
Prestbury	d																								07 23
Adlington (Cheshire)	d																								07 26
Poynton	d																								07 29
Bramhall	d																								07 32
Cheadle Hulme	d		23p46												06 59								07 24		07 36
Stockport	a		23p51				00s26							06 55	07 04					07 27			07 29		07 40
	d	23p48	23p51		00 02				05 53			06 41	06 53	06 55	07 04		07 13	07 19	07 22	07 28			07 29	07 40	07 41
Heaton Chapel	d		23p55												07 08		07 16						07 33		07 44
Levenshulme	d		23p58												07 11		07 19						07 36		07 47
Manchester Piccadilly 10	a	00 02	00 07	00 12	00 18	00 28	00 35	01 36	06 05	06 25		06 52	07 02	07 07	07 21		07 26	07 31	07 34	07 38		07 42	07 44	07 52	07 56
	d											06 54				06 58			07 34					07 54	
Manchester Oxford Road	a											06 56				07 00			07 37					07 56	
Deansgate	a											06 59												08 00	

A To Wigan Wallgate
B From Cleethorpes to Manchester Airport
C From Bournemouth
D From Cardiff Central
E From Buxton
F From Sheffield
G From Birmingham International
H From Chester
I From Sheffield to Manchester Airport
J From Buxton to Clitheroe
K From Doncaster to Manchester Airport
L until 11 February and then from 31 March. From Manchester Airport to Liverpool Lime Street
M From Nottingham to Liverpool Lime Street
N From Hazel Grove to Preston
b Previous night, stops to set down only

Table 84

Saturdays

Stoke-on-Trent and Crewe - Manchester Airport, Stockport and Manchester

Network Diagram - see first Page of Table 78

		XC	TP	NT	AW	NT		NT	TP	NT	NT	XC		EM	NT	NT		VT		NT	NT	XC	TP	VT	AW
		◇1	◇1		◇				◇1			◇1		◇				◇1				◇1	◇1	◇1	◇
			A	B	C			D	E	F	G			I						K			A		C
		🛒	🛒						🛒			🛒						🍽				🛒	🛒	🍽	🛒
London Euston 15 ⊖65	d																	06 36						06 55	
Birmingham New Street 12 68	d	06 31										06 57										07 31			
Wolverhampton 7 68 ⛴	d	06 49										07 15										07 49			
Stafford 65,68	d	07 01										07 30										08 01			
Stoke-on-Trent 50,68	d	07 19																			07 57	08 20		08 25	
Longport 50	d																								
Kidsgrove 50	d																				08 04				
Crewe 10 65	d				07 27							07 53			07 30	07 55		08 11							08 28
Sandbach	d														07 37	08 02									
Holmes Chapel	d														07 41	08 07									
Goostrey	d														07 44										
Chelford	d														07 49										
Alderley Edge	d					07 49									07 53	08 15									
Wilmslow	d				07 44	07 52						08 10			07 56	08 19		08 27							08 45
Styal	d														07 59										
Manchester Airport ✈	a														08 05										
Handforth	d					07 55										08 22									
Congleton	d																				08 11				
Macclesfield	a	07 36																			08 18	08 36		08 41	
	d	07 37																			08 19	08 37		08 41	
Prestbury	d																				08 23				
Adlington (Cheshire)	d																				08 26				
Poynton	d																				08 30				
Bramhall	d																				08 33				
Cheadle Hulme	d					07 59										08 26					08 37				
Stockport	a	07 49			08 01	08 04						08 20				08 31		08 36			08 41	08 49		08 55	08 58
	d	07 50	07 53	07 57	08 01	08 04				08 13	08 19	08 20		08 24		08 31		08 37		08 41	08 42	08 50	08 53	08 56	08 59
Heaton Chapel	d					08 08				08 16						08 35					08 45				
Levenshulme	d					08 11				08 19											08 48				
Manchester Piccadilly 10 ⛴	a	07 59	08 02	08 09	08 20	08 20				08 26	08 32	08 35		08 36	08 42	08 45		08 49		08 52	08 56	08 59	09 02	09 07	09 15
	d							07 59	08 07					08 37						08 54					
Manchester Oxford Road	a							08 01	08 09					08 40						08 56					
Deansgate ⛴	a																			09 00					

		NT		NT	TP	NT	VT	NT		EM	XC	NT		NT	VT	NT	NT	XC	TP	VT	AW	NT		NT	TP
					◇1		◇1			◇	◇1				◇1			◇1	◇1	◇1	◇				◇1
				D	L	F		G		I	M					N		O	A		P			D	Q
					🛒		🍽				🛒				🍽			🍽	🛒	🍽	🛒				🛒
London Euston 15 ⊖65	d						07 20								07 35					08 00					
Birmingham New Street 12 68	d										07 57							08 31							
Wolverhampton 7 68 ⛴	d										08 15							08 49							
Stafford 65,68	d										08 30							09 01							
Stoke-on-Trent 50,68	d						08 48				08 55						08 58	09 20		09 25					
Longport 50	d																								
Kidsgrove 50	d																09 05								
Crewe 10 65	d											08 31		08 50	09 11						09 30				
Sandbach	d											08 38		08 57											
Holmes Chapel	d											08 42		09 02											
Goostrey	d											08 45		09 05											
Chelford	d											08 50		09 09											
Alderley Edge	d	08 49										08 54		09 13								09 49			
Wilmslow	d	08 52										08 57		09 17	09 27						09 47	09 52			
Styal	d																								
Manchester Airport ✈	a											09 04													
Handforth	d	08 55												09 20								09 55			
Congleton	d																09 12								
Macclesfield	a										09 11						09 19			09 41					
	d										09 12						09 20			09 41					
Prestbury	d																09 24								
Adlington (Cheshire)	d																09 27								
Poynton	d																09 30								
Bramhall	d																09 33								
Cheadle Hulme	d	08 59												09 24			09 37					09 59			
Stockport	a	09 04					09 16				09 27			09 29	09 36		09 41	09 49		09 55	09 57	10 04			
	d	09 04				09 13	09 17	09 21		09 25	09 28			09 29	09 37	09 41	09 42	09 50	09 53	09 56	09 58	10 04			
Heaton Chapel	d	09 08				09 16								09 33			09 45					10 08			
Levenshulme	d	09 11				09 19								09 36			09 48					10 11			
Manchester Piccadilly 10 ⛴	a	09 20				09 26	09 28	09 36		09 36	09 39	09 42		09 44	09 49	09 52	09 56	09 59	10 02	10 07	10 14	10 20			
	d			09 01	09 07					09 37						09 54								10 01	10 07
Manchester Oxford Road	a			09 03	09 09					09 40						09 56								10 03	10 09
Deansgate ⛴	a															10 00									

A From Cleethorpes to Manchester Airport
B From Hazel Grove
C From Cardiff Central
D until 11 February and then from 31 March. From Manchester Airport to Liverpool Lime Street
E From Hull to Liverpool Lime Street
F From Buxton
G From Chester
I From Nottingham to Liverpool Lime Street
K From Buxton to Preston
L From Newcastle to Liverpool Lime Street
M From Southampton Central
N From Hazel Grove to Preston
O From Bristol Temple Meads
P From Carmarthen
Q From Scarborough to Liverpool Lime Street

Table 84

Saturdays

Stoke-on-Trent and Crewe - Manchester Airport, Stockport and Manchester

Network Diagram - see first Page of Table 78

		NT A	VT ◇1	NT B		EM ◇ D	XC ◇1 E	NT		NT	VT ◇1	NT F	NT	XC ◇1 G	TP ◇1 H	VT ◇1	AW ◇ I	NT		NT J	TP ◇1 K	NT A	VT ◇1	TP ◇1 L	NT B
London Euston 15 ⊖65	d		08 20								08 40					09 00							09 20		
Birmingham New Street 12 68	d						08 57							09 31											
Wolverhampton 7 68	d						09 15							09 49											
Stafford 65,68	d						09 30							10 01											
Stoke-on-Trent 50,68	d		09 48				09 55						09 58	10 20		10 25							10 48		
Longport 50	d																								
Kidsgrove 50	d												10 05												
Crewe 10 65	d							09 33		09 50	10 11						10 31								
Sandbach	d							09 40		09 57															
Holmes Chapel	d							09 44		10 02															
Goostrey	d									10 05															
Chelford	d									10 09															
Alderley Edge	d							09 53		10 13								10 49							
Wilmslow	d							09 57		10 17	10 27						10 49	10 52							
Styal	d																								
Manchester Airport ✈	a							10 04																	
Handforth	d									10 20								10 55							
Congleton	d												10 12												
Macclesfield	a						10 11						10 19			10 41									
	d						10 12						10 20			10 41									
Prestbury	d												10 24												
Adlington (Cheshire)	d												10 27												
Poynton	d												10 30												
Bramhall	d												10 33												
Cheadle Hulme	d									10 24			10 37					10 59							
Stockport	a		10 16				10 27			10 29	10 36		10 41	10 49		10 55	10 58	11 04					11 16		
	d	10 13	10 17	10 21		10 26	10 28			10 29	10 37	10 41	10 42	10 50	10 53	10 56	10 58	11 04				11 13	11 17		11 21
Heaton Chapel	d	10 16								10 33			10 45					11 08				11 16			
Levenshulme	d	10 19								10 36			10 48					11 11				11 19			
Manchester Piccadilly 10	a	10 26	10 28	10 36		10 36	10 39	10 42		10 44	10 49	10 52	10 56	10 59	11 02	11 07	11 15	11 20				11 26	11 28		11 36
	d					10 37						10 54								11 01	11 07			11 16	
Manchester Oxford Road	a					10 40						10 56								11 03	11 09			11 18	
Deansgate	a											11 00													

			EM ◇ D	XC ◇1 M		NT	NT	VT ◇1	NT F	NT	XC ◇1 N	TP ◇1 H	VT ◇1	AW ◇ O		NT	NT J	TP ◇1 K	NT A	VT ◇1	NT B		EM ◇ D	XC ◇1 M	
London Euston 15 ⊖65	d							09 40					10 00							10 20					
Birmingham New Street 12 68	d			09 57							10 31													10 57	
Wolverhampton 7 68	d			10 15							10 49													11 15	
Stafford 65,68	d			10 30							11 01													11 30	
Stoke-on-Trent 50,68	d			10 55						10 58	11 20		11 25							11 48				11 55	
Longport 50	d																								
Kidsgrove 50	d									11 05															
Crewe 10 65	d					10 34	10 50	11 11						11 31											
Sandbach	d					10 41	10 57																		
Holmes Chapel	d					10 45	11 02																		
Goostrey	d						11 05																		
Chelford	d						11 09																		
Alderley Edge	d					10 54	11 13									11 49									
Wilmslow	d					10 57	11 17	11 27						11 48		11 52									
Styal	d																								
Manchester Airport ✈	a					11 04																			
Handforth	d						11 20									11 55									
Congleton	d									11 12															
Macclesfield	a			11 11						11 19			11 41											12 11	
	d			11 12						11 20			11 41											12 12	
Prestbury	d									11 24															
Adlington (Cheshire)	d									11 27															
Poynton	d									11 30															
Bramhall	d									11 33															
Cheadle Hulme	d						11 24			11 37						11 59									
Stockport	a			11 27			11 29	11 36		11 41	11 49		11 55	11 58		12 04				12 16				12 27	
	d		11 26	11 28			11 29	11 37	11 41	11 42	11 50	11 53	11 56	11 58		12 04			12 13	12 17	12 21		12 26	12 28	
Heaton Chapel	d						11 33			11 45						12 08			12 16						
Levenshulme	d						11 36			11 48						12 11			12 19						
Manchester Piccadilly 10	a		11 36	11 39		11 42	11 44	11 49	11 52	11 56	11 59	12 02	12 07	12 15		12 20			12 26	12 28	12 36		12 36	12 39	
	d		11 37						11 54								12 01	12 07					12 37		
Manchester Oxford Road	a		11 40						11 56								12 03	12 09					12 40		
Deansgate	a								12 00																

A From Buxton
B From Chester
D From Norwich to Liverpool Lime Street
E From Southampton Central
F From Hazel Grove to Preston
G From Cardiff Central
H From Cleethorpes to Manchester Airport
I From Carmarthen
J until 11 February and then from 31 March. From Manchester Airport to Liverpool Lime Street
K From Scarborough to Liverpool Lime Street
L From Manchester Airport to Barrow-in-Furness
M From Bournemouth
N From Paignton
O From Milford Haven

Stoke-on-Trent and Crewe - Manchester Airport, Stockport and Manchester

Network Diagram - see first Page of Table 78

	NT	NT	VT	NT	NT	XC	TP	VT	AW		NT	NT	TP	NT	VT	NT		EM	XC		NT	NT	VT	NT
			◇1			◇1	◇1	◇1	◇				◇1		◇1			◇	◇1				◇1	
				A		B	C		D			E	F	G		H		J	K					A
			⊥P			⊥P	⊥o	⊥P	⊥o				⊥o		⊥P				⊥o				⊥P	
London Euston 15 ⊖65 d			10 40					11 00							11 20								11 40	
Birmingham New Street 12 68 d						11 31													11 57					
Wolverhampton 7 68 ⇌ d						11 49													12 15					
Stafford 65,68 d						12 01													12 30					
Stoke-on-Trent 50,68 d					11 58	12 20		12 25							12 48				12 55					
Longport 50 d																								
Kidsgrove 50 d					12 05																			
Crewe 10 65 d	11 34	11 50	12 11						12 31												12 34	12 50	13 11	
Sandbach d	11 41	11 57																			12 41	12 57		
Holmes Chapel d	11 45	12 02																			12 45	13 02		
Goostrey d		12 05																				13 05		
Chelford d		12 09																				13 09		
Alderley Edge d	11 54	12 13									12 49										12 54	13 13		
Wilmslow d	11 57	12 17	12 27						12 49		12 52										12 57	13 17	13 27	
Styal d																								
Manchester Airport ✈ a	12 04																				13 04			
Handforth d		12 20									12 55											13 20		
Congleton d					12 12																			
Macclesfield a					12 19			12 41											13 11					
d					12 20			12 41											13 12					
Prestbury d					12 24																			
Adlington (Cheshire) d					12 27																			
Poynton d					12 30																			
Bramhall d					12 33																			
Cheadle Hulme d		12 24			12 37						12 59											13 24		
Stockport a		12 29	12 36		12 41	12 49		12 55	12 58		13 04				13 16				13 27			13 29	13 36	
d		12 29	12 37	12 41	12 42	12 50	12 53	12 56	12 58		13 04			13 13	13 17	13 21		13 26	13 28			13 29	13 37	13 41
Heaton Chapel d		12 33			12 45						13 08			13 16								13 33		
Levenshulme d		12 36			12 48						13 11			13 19								13 36		
Manchester Piccadilly 10 ⇌ a	12 42	12 44	12 49	12 52	12 56	12 59	13 02	13 07	13 15		13 20			13 26	13 28	13 36		13 36	13 39		13 42	13 44	13 49	13 52
d				12 54								13 01	13 07					13 37						13 54
Manchester Oxford Road a				12 56								13 03	13 09					13 40						13 56
Deansgate ⇌ a				13 00																				14 00

	NT	XC	TP	VT	AW		NT	NT	TP	NT	VT	TP	NT		EM		XC	NT	NT	VT	NT	NT	XC	TP
		◇1	◇1	◇1	◇				◇1		◇1	◇1			◇		◇1			◇1			◇1	◇1
		B	C		L			E	F	G		M	H		J		K				A		N	C
		⊥P	⊥o	⊥P	⊥o						⊥P	⊥o					⊥o			⊥P			⊥P	⊥o
London Euston 15 ⊖65 d				12 00							12 20									12 40				
Birmingham New Street 12 68 d		12 31															12 57						13 31	
Wolverhampton 7 68 ⇌ d		12 49															13 15						13 49	
Stafford 65,68 d		13 01															13 30						14 01	
Stoke-on-Trent 50,68 d	12 58	13 20		13 25							13 48						13 55					13 58	14 20	
Longport 50 d																								
Kidsgrove 50 d	13 05																					14 05		
Crewe 10 65 d					13 31													13 34	13 50	14 11				
Sandbach d																		13 41	13 57					
Holmes Chapel d																		13 45	14 02					
Goostrey d																			14 05					
Chelford d																			14 09					
Alderley Edge d							13 49											13 54	14 13					
Wilmslow d					13 48		13 52											13 57	14 17	14 27				
Styal d																								
Manchester Airport ✈ a																		14 04						
Handforth d							13 55												14 20					
Congleton d	13 12																					14 12		
Macclesfield a	13 19			13 41													14 11					14 19		
d	13 20			13 41													14 12					14 20		
Prestbury d	13 24																					14 24		
Adlington (Cheshire) d	13 27																					14 27		
Poynton d	13 30																					14 30		
Bramhall d	13 33																					14 33		
Cheadle Hulme d	13 37						13 59												14 24			14 37		
Stockport a	13 41	13 49		13 55	13 58		14 04				14 16						14 27		14 29	14 36		14 41	14 49	
d	13 42	13 50	13 53	13 56	13 58		14 04			14 13	14 17		14 21		14 26		14 28		14 29	14 37	14 41	14 42	14 50	14 53
Heaton Chapel d	13 45						14 08			14 16									14 33			14 45		
Levenshulme d	13 48						14 11			14 19									14 36			14 48		
Manchester Piccadilly 10 ⇌ a	13 56	13 59	14 02	14 07	14 15		14 20			14 26	14 28		14 36		14 36		14 39	14 42	14 44	14 49	14 52	14 56	14 59	15 02
d								14 01	14 07			14 16			14 37						14 54			
Manchester Oxford Road a								14 03	14 09			14 18			14 40						14 56			
Deansgate ⇌ a																					15 00			

A From Hazel Grove to Preston
B From Bristol Temple Meads
C From Cleethorpes to Manchester Airport
D From Milford Haven
E until 11 February and then from 31 March. From Manchester Airport to Liverpool Lime Street
F From Scarborough to Liverpool Lime Street
G From Buxton
H From Chester
J From Norwich to Liverpool Lime Street
K From Bournemouth
L From Fishguard Harbour
M From Manchester Airport to Barrow-in-Furness
N From Paignton

Table 84

Saturdays

Stoke-on-Trent and Crewe - Manchester Airport, Stockport and Manchester

Network Diagram - see first Page of Table 78

		VT ◇1 🍴		AW ◇ A 🛒	NT	NT B	TP ◇1 C 🛒	NT D	VT ◇1 🍴	TP ◇1 E 🛒	NT F			EM ◇ H	XC ◇1 I 🛒	NT	NT	VT ◇1 🍴	NT J	NT	XC ◇1 K 🍴	TP ◇1 L 🛒		VT ◇1 🍴	AW ◇ M 🛒
London Euston [15] ⊖65	d	13 00							13 20									13 40						14 00	
Birmingham New Street [12] 68	d														13 57						14 31				
Wolverhampton [7] 68	d														14 15						14 49				
Stafford 65,68	d														14 30						15 01				
Stoke-on-Trent 50,68	d	14 25							14 48						14 55					14 58	15 20			15 25	
Longport 50	d																								
Kidsgrove 50	d																			15 05					
Crewe [10] 65	d			14 31												14 34	14 50	15 11							15 28
Sandbach	d															14 41	14 57								
Holmes Chapel	d															14 45	15 02								
Goostrey	d																15 05								
Chelford	d																15 09								
Alderley Edge	d				14 49											14 54	15 13								
Wilmslow	d			14 49	14 52											14 57	15 17	15 27							15 45
Styal	d																								
Manchester Airport ✈	a															15 04									
Handforth	d				14 55												15 20								
Congleton	d																			15 12					
Macclesfield	a	14 41													15 11					15 19				15 41	
	d	14 41													15 12					15 20				15 41	
Prestbury	d																			15 24					
Adlington (Cheshire)	d																			15 27					
Poynton	d																			15 30					
Bramhall	d																			15 33					
Cheadle Hulme	d				14 59												15 24			15 37					
Stockport	a	14 55		14 58	15 04				15 16						15 27		15 29	15 36		15 41	15 49			15 55	15 58
	d	14 56		14 58	15 04			15 13	15 17		15 21			15 26	15 28		15 29	15 37	15 41	15 42	15 50	15 53		15 56	15 58
Heaton Chapel	d				15 08			15 16									15 33			15 45					
Levenshulme	d				15 11			15 19									15 36			15 48					
Manchester Piccadilly [10]	a	15 07		15 15	15 20			15 26	15 28		15 36			15 36	15 39	15 42	15 44	15 49	15 52	15 56	15 59	16 02		16 07	16 15
	d					15 01	15 07			15 16				15 37					15 54						
Manchester Oxford Road	a					15 03	15 09			15 18				15 40					15 56						
Deansgate	a																		16 00						

		NT	NT B	TP ◇1 C 🛒	NT D	VT ◇1 🍴	TP ◇1 N 🛒	NT F			EM ◇ H	XC ◇1 I 🛒	NT	NT	VT ◇1 🍴	NT J	NT	XC ◇1 O 🍴		TP ◇1 L 🛒	VT ◇1 🍴	AW ◇ A 🛒	NT	NT B	TP ◇1 C 🛒
London Euston [15] ⊖65	d					14 20									14 40						15 00				
Birmingham New Street [12] 68	d											14 57						15 31							
Wolverhampton [7] 68	d											15 15						15 49							
Stafford 65,68	d											15 30						16 01							
Stoke-on-Trent 50,68	d					15 48						15 55					15 58	16 20			16 25				
Longport 50	d																								
Kidsgrove 50	d																16 05								
Crewe [10] 65	d												15 33	15 50	16 11							16 31			
Sandbach	d												15 40	15 57											
Holmes Chapel	d												15 44	16 02											
Goostrey	d													16 05											
Chelford	d													16 09											
Alderley Edge	d	15 49											15 53	16 13									16 49		
Wilmslow	d	15 52											15 56	16 17	16 27							16 48	16 52		
Styal	d												15 59												
Manchester Airport ✈	a												16 04												
Handforth	d	15 55												16 20									16 55		
Congleton	d																16 12								
Macclesfield	a											16 11					16 19				16 41				
	d											16 12					16 20				16 41				
Prestbury	d																16 24								
Adlington (Cheshire)	d																16 27								
Poynton	d																16 30								
Bramhall	d																16 33								
Cheadle Hulme	d	15 59												16 24			16 37						16 59		
Stockport	a	16 04				16 16						16 27		16 29	16 36		16 41	16 49			16 54	16 58	17 04		
	d	16 04			16 13	16 17		16 21			16 26	16 28		16 29	16 37	16 41	16 42	16 50		16 53	16 55	16 58	17 04		
Heaton Chapel	d	16 08			16 16									16 33			16 45						17 08		
Levenshulme	d	16 11			16 19									16 36			16 48						17 11		
Manchester Piccadilly [10]	a	16 20			16 26	16 28		16 36			16 36	16 39	16 42	16 44	16 49	16 52	16 56	16 59		17 02	17 07	17 14	17 20		
	d		16 01	16 07			16 16				16 37					16 54								17 01	17 07
Manchester Oxford Road	a		16 03	16 09			16 18				16 40					16 56								17 03	17 09
Deansgate	a															17 00									

A From Milford Haven
B until 11 February and then from 31 March. From Manchester Airport to Liverpool Lime Street
C From Scarborough to Liverpool Lime Street
D From Buxton
E From Manchester Airport to Barrow-in-Furness
F From Chester
H From Norwich to Liverpool Lime Street
I From Bournemouth
J From Hazel Grove to Preston
K From Bristol Temple Meads
L From Cleethorpes to Manchester Airport
M From Carmarthen
N From Manchester Airport to Windermere
O From Penzance

Table 84

Stoke-on-Trent and Crewe - Manchester Airport, Stockport and Manchester

Network Diagram - see first Page of Table 78

		NT	VT	NT		NT	EM	XC	NT	NT	VT	NT	XC	TP		VT	AW	NT	NT	TP	NT	VT	TP	NT	
			◇1				◇	◇1			◇1		◇1	◇1		◇1	◇			◇1		◇1	◇1		
		A		B		C	D	E					F	G			H		I	J	A		K	B	
			🍽					🛒			🍽		🍽	🛒		🍽	🛒			🛒		🍽	🛒		
London Euston 15 ⊖65	d		15 20								15 40					16 00						16 20			
Birmingham New Street 12 68	d							15 57					16 31												
Wolverhampton 7 68 ⛴	d							16 15					16 49												
Stafford 65,68	d							16 30					17 01												
Stoke-on-Trent 50,68	d		16 48					16 55				16 58	17 20			17 25						17 48			
Longport 50	d																								
Kidsgrove 50	d											17 05													
Crewe 10 65	d								16 34	16 50	17 11						17 28								
Sandbach	d								16 41	16 57															
Holmes Chapel	d								16 45	17 02															
Goostrey	d									17 05															
Chelford	d									17 09															
Alderley Edge	d								16 54	17 13								17 49							
Wilmslow	d								16 57	17 17	17 27						17 45	17 52							
Styal	d																								
Manchester Airport ✈	a								17 04																
Handforth	d									17 20								17 55							
Congleton	d											17 12													
Macclesfield	a							17 11				17 19				17 41									
	d							17 12				17 20				17 41									
Prestbury	d											17 24													
Adlington (Cheshire)	d											17 27													
Poynton	d											17 30													
Bramhall	d											17 33													
Cheadle Hulme	d									17 24		17 37						17 59							
Stockport	a		17 16					17 27		17 29	17 36	17 41	17 49			17 55	17 58	18 04				18 16			
	d	17 13	17 17	17 21			17 26	17 28		17 29	17 37	17 42	17 50	17 53		17 56	17 58	18 04			18 13	18 17		18 21	
Heaton Chapel	d	17 16								17 33		17 45						18 08			18 16				
Levenshulme	d	17 19								17 36		17 48						18 11			18 19				
Manchester Piccadilly 10 ⛴	a	17 26	17 28	17 36			17 37	17 39	17 42	17 44	17 49	17 56	17 59	18 02		18 07	18 15	18 20			18 26	18 28		18 36	
	d					17 23	17 37												18⟆01	18 07			18 16		
Manchester Oxford Road	a					17 25	17 40												18⟆03	18 09			18 18		
Deansgate ⛴	a																								

			EM	XC	NT	NT	VT	NT	NT	XC		TP	VT	AW	NT	TP	NT	VT	TP			NT	NT	EM	XC
														R											
			◇	◇1			◇1			◇1		◇1	◇1			◇1		◇1	◇1					◇	◇1
			D	E				L		M		G		N	I	J	A		K				B	D	E
				🛒			🍽			🛒		🛒	🍽	🛒				🍽							🛒
London Euston 15 ⊖65	d						16 40						17 00					17 20							
Birmingham New Street 12 68	d			16 57						17 31															17 57
Wolverhampton 7 68 ⛴	d			17 15						17 49															18 15
Stafford 65,68	d			17 30						18 01															18 30
Stoke-on-Trent 50,68	d			17 55					17 58	18 20			18 25					18 48							18 55
Longport 50	d																								
Kidsgrove 50	d								18 05																
Crewe 10 65	d				17 33	17 50	18 11							18 31								18 34			
Sandbach	d				17 40	17 57																18 41			
Holmes Chapel	d				17 44	18 02																18 45			
Goostrey	d					18 05																			
Chelford	d					18 09																			
Alderley Edge	d				17 53	18 13																18 54			
Wilmslow	d				17 56	18 17	18 27							18 48								18 57			
Styal	d				17 59																				
Manchester Airport ✈	a				18 04																	19 05			
Handforth	d					18 20																			
Congleton	d								18 12																
Macclesfield	a			18 11					18 19				18 41												19 11
	d			18 12					18 20				18 41												19 12
Prestbury	d								18 24																
Adlington (Cheshire)	d								18 27																
Poynton	d								18 30																
Bramhall	d								18 33																
Cheadle Hulme	d					18 24			18 37																
Stockport	a			18 27		18 29	18 36		18 41	18 49			18 55	18 58				19 16							19 27
	d		18 26	18 28		18 29	18 37	18 41	18 42	18 50		18 53	18 56	18 58			19 13	19 17					19 21	19 26	19 28
Heaton Chapel	d					18 33			18 45								19 16								
Levenshulme	d					18 36			18 48								19 19								
Manchester Piccadilly 10 ⛴	a		18 36	18 39	18 42	18 44	18 49	18 52	18 56	18 59		19 02	19 07	19 15			19 26	19 28				19 31	19 35	19 36	19 40
	d		18 37					18 54							19⟆01	19 07			19 16			19 32		19 37	
Manchester Oxford Road	a		18 40					18 56							19⟆03	19 09			19 18			19 36		19 40	
Deansgate ⛴	a							19 00																	

- **A** From Buxton
- **B** From Chester
- **C** From Manchester Airport to Southport
- **D** From Norwich to Liverpool Lime Street
- **E** From Bournemouth
- **F** From Bristol Temple Meads
- **G** From Cleethorpes to Manchester Airport
- **H** From Carmarthen
- **I** until 11 February and then from 31 March. From Manchester Airport to Liverpool Lime Street
- **J** From Scarborough to Liverpool Lime Street
- **K** From Manchester Airport to Barrow-in-Furness
- **L** From Hazel Grove to Bolton
- **M** From Paignton
- **N** From Milford Haven

Table 84

Saturdays

Stoke-on-Trent and Crewe - Manchester Airport, Stockport and Manchester

Network Diagram - see first Page of Table 78

		NT	VT	NT	XC	TP		VT	AW	NT	TP	NT	VT	TP		NT		NT	EM	XC	NT	VT	NT	XC	AW
			◇1		◇1	◇1		◇1	R		◇1		◇1	◇1					◇	◇1		◇1		◇1	
					A	B			C	D	E	F		G				I	J	K				L	M
			🍴		🍴	🍴		🍴	🍴				🍴							🍴		🍴		🍴	
London Euston 15 ⊖65	d		17 40					18 00					18 20									18 40			
Birmingham New Street 12 68	d				18 31															18 57				19 31	
Wolverhampton 7 68	d				18 49															19 15				19 49	
Stafford 65,68	d				19 01															19 30				20 01	
Stoke-on-Trent 50,68	d			18 58	19 20			19 25					19 48							19 55			19 58	20 20	
Longport 50	d																								
Kidsgrove 50	d			19 05																			20 05		
Crewe 10 65	d	18 50	19 11						19 31												19 50	20 11			
Sandbach	d	18 57																			19 57				
Holmes Chapel	d	19 02																			20 02				
Goostrey	d	19 05																			20 05				
Chelford	d	19 09																			20 09				
Alderley Edge	d	19 13																			20 13				
Wilmslow	d	19 17	19 27						19 48							19 56					20 17	20 27			
Styal	d																								
Manchester Airport ✈	a															20 04									
Handforth	d	19 20																			20 20				
Congleton	d			19 12																			20 12		
Macclesfield	a			19 19				19 41												20 11			20 19	20 36	
	d			19 20				19 41												20 12			20 20	20 37	
Prestbury	d			19 24																			20 24		
Adlington (Cheshire)	d			19 27																			20 27		
Poynton	d			19 30																			20 30		
Bramhall	d			19 33																			20 33		
Cheadle Hulme	d	19 24		19 37																	20 24		20 37		
Stockport	a	19 29	19 36	19 41	19 49			19 55	19 58				20 16							20 27	20 29	20 36	20 41	20 49	
	d	19 29	19 37	19 42	19 50	19 53		19 56	19 58			20 13	20 17					20 21	20 26	20 28	20 29	20 37	20 42	20 50	
Heaton Chapel	d			19 45								20 16											20 45		
Levenshulme	d			19 48								20 19											20 48		
Manchester Piccadilly 10	a	19 43	19 49	19 56	19 59	20 02		20 07	20 15			20 26	20 28			20 31		20 35	20 36	20 39	20 43	20 49	20 56	20 59	
	d									20⟆01	20 07			20 16		20 32			20 37						20 50
Manchester Oxford Road	a									20⟆03	20 09			20 18		20 36			20 40						20 52
Deansgate	a																								

		TP		VT	AW	TP	NT	VT		NT	EM	NT		XC	NT	VT	NT	XC	AW	NT	TP	NT		NT	XC
		◇1		◇1	R	◇1		◇1			◇			◇1		◇1		◇1	◇		◇1				◇1
		B			N	E	F				O	I		K				A	C	D	E	F			K
				🍴	🍴			🍴								🍴		🍴	🍴						
London Euston 15 ⊖65	d			19 00				19 20								19 40									
Birmingham New Street 12 68	d													19 57				20 31							20 57
Wolverhampton 7 68	d													20 15				20 49							21 15
Stafford 65,68	d													20 30				21 01							21 30
Stoke-on-Trent 50,68	d			20 25				20 48						20 55			20 58	21 21							21 53
Longport 50	d																								
Kidsgrove 50	d																21 05								
Crewe 10 65	d				20 28										20 50	21 19			21 33						
Sandbach	d														20 57										
Holmes Chapel	d														21 02										
Goostrey	d														21 05										
Chelford	d														21 09										
Alderley Edge	d														21 13										
Wilmslow	d				20 45					20 56					21 17	21 34			21 50					21 55	
Styal	d																								
Manchester Airport ✈	a									21 05														22 04	
Handforth	d														21 20										
Congleton	d																21 12								
Macclesfield	a			20 41										21 11			21 19	21 38							22 11
	d			20 41										21 12			21 20	21 39							22 12
Prestbury	d																21 24								
Adlington (Cheshire)	d																21 27								
Poynton	d																21 30								
Bramhall	d																21 33								
Cheadle Hulme	d														21 24		21 37								
Stockport	a			20 55	20 58			21 16						21 27	21 29	21 44	21 41	21 53	22 00						22 27
	d	20 53		20 56	20 59		21 13	21 17			21 20	21 21		21 28	21 29	21 45	21 42	21 54	22 00			22 13			22 28
Heaton Chapel	d						21 16										21 45					22 16			
Levenshulme	d						21 19										21 48					22 19			
Manchester Piccadilly 10	a	21 02		21 07	21 15		21 26	21 28		21 31	21 32	21 35		21 39	21 43	21 53	21 57	22 04	22 15			22 26		22 31	22 39
	d					21 07				21 32										22⟆01	22 07			22 32	
Manchester Oxford Road	a					21 09				21 36										22⟆03	22 09			22 36	
Deansgate	a																								

A From Bristol Temple Meads
B From Cleethorpes to Manchester Airport
C From Carmarthen
D until 11 February, from 31 March. From Manchester Airport to Liverpool Lime Street
E From Scarborough to Liverpool Lime Street
F From Buxton
G From Manchester Airport to Preston
I From Chester
J From Norwich to Liverpool Lime Street
K From Bournemouth
L From Exeter St Davids
M From Manchester Airport to Chester
N From Milford Haven
O From Norwich

Stoke-on-Trent and Crewe - Manchester Airport, Stockport and Manchester

Network Diagram - see first Page of Table 78

		NT	VT	NT	NT	NT	XC	VT	NT	AW	NT	NT	NT	XC
			◇1				◇1	◇1		◇				◇1
				B	C		D		E	F		G		
			🍴					🍴						
London Euston 15 ⊖65	d		20 20					21 00						
Birmingham New Street 12 68	d						21 57							22 31
Wolverhampton 7 68 ⛴	d						22 16							22 49
Stafford 65,68	d						22 30	22 34						23 02
Stoke-on-Trent 50,68	d		22 05			22 18	22 51							23 21
Longport 50	d													
Kidsgrove 50	d					22 25								
Crewe 10 65	d	21 50						22 59		23 06			23 12	
Sandbach	d	21 57											23 19	
Holmes Chapel	d	22 02											23 24	
Goostrey	d	22 05											23 27	
Chelford	d	22 09											23 31	
Alderley Edge	d	22 13											23 35	
Wilmslow	d	22 17						23 15		23 24	23 15		23 39	
Styal	d													
Manchester Airport ✈	a										23 23			
Handforth	d	22 20											23 42	
Congleton	d					22 32								
Macclesfield	a		22 21			22 39	23 07							23 38
	d		22 21			22 40	23 08							23 39
Prestbury	d					22 44								
Adlington (Cheshire)	d					22 47								
Poynton	d					22 50								
Bramhall	d					22 53								
Cheadle Hulme	d	22 24				22 56							23 46	
Stockport	a	22 29	22 35			23 01	23 21	23 25		23 32			23 51	23 53
	d	22 29	22 36	22 40	22 48	23 01	23 22	23 26	23 22	23 33		23 42	23 51	23 54
Heaton Chapel	d			22 44		23 05							23 55	
Levenshulme	d			22 47		23 08							23 58	
Manchester Piccadilly 10 ⛴	a	22 43	22 51	22 53	23 00	23 16	23 32	23 38	23 43	23 50	23 51	23 52	00 07	00 10
	d			22 54										
Manchester Oxford Road	a			22 56										
Deansgate ⛴	a			23 00										

Sundays

until 1 January

		NT	XC	NT	AW	NT	NT	NT	AW	NT	NT	TP	NT	XC	VT	NT	VT	AW	NT	NT	NT	NT
			◇1									◇1		◇1	◇1		◇1	◇				
		H	H	I		G	J			L	G	M	N					O	L	G		J
														🛒	🍴		🍴					
London Euston 15 ⊖65	d														08 10		08 20					
Birmingham New Street 12 68	d		22p31											09 01								
Wolverhampton 7 68 ⛴	d		22p49											09 19								
Stafford 65,68	d		23p02											09 33								
Stoke-on-Trent 50,68	d		23p21														10 21					
Longport 50	d																					
Kidsgrove 50	d																					
Crewe 10 65	d	23p12			08 28				09 28					09 56	10 19			10 28				
Sandbach	d	23p19																				
Holmes Chapel	d	23p24																				
Goostrey	d	23p27																				
Chelford	d	23p31																				
Alderley Edge	d	23p35						09 19								10 19					10 40	
Wilmslow	d	23p39			08 48			09 23	09 47					10 13	10 34	10 23		10 47			10 43	
Styal	d																				10 47	
Manchester Airport ✈	a																				10 56	
Handforth	d	23p42						09 26								10 26						
Congleton	d																					
Macclesfield	a		23p38														10 36					
	d		23p39														10 38					
Prestbury	d																					
Adlington (Cheshire)	d																					
Poynton	d																					
Bramhall	d																					
Cheadle Hulme	d	23p46						09 30								10 30						
Stockport	a	23p51	23p53					09 38						10 21	10 43	10 35	10 50	10 58				
	d	23p51	23p54	00 02		09 09	09 22	09 40			10 04		10 12	10 22	10 44	10 39	10 52	10 58		11 12		11 15
Heaton Chapel	d	23p55				09 12		09 44			10 08					10 43						11 19
Levenshulme	d	23p58				09 15		09 47			10 11					10 46						11 22
Manchester Piccadilly 10 ⛴	a	00 07	00 10	00 15	09 11	09 23	09 33	09 54	10 11		10 20		10 22	10 37	10 55	10 56	11 03	11 12		11 23	11 25	11 28
	d						09 35			09 50		10 12	10 24						10 50		11 27	11 33
Manchester Oxford Road	a						09 37			09 52		10 14	10 26						10 52		11 31	11 35
Deansgate ⛴	a						09 40						10 40									11 40

B To Wigan Wallgate
C From Chester
D From Bournemouth
E From Sheffield
F From Maesteg
G From Buxton
H not 11 December
I not 11 December. From Chester
J To Southport
L From Manchester Airport to Liverpool Lime Street
M From York to Liverpool Lime Street
N From Chester to Southport
O From Shrewsbury

Table 84

Sundays
until 1 January

Stoke-on-Trent and Crewe - Manchester Airport, Stockport and Manchester

Network Diagram - see first Page of Table 78

		XC	EM	NT	AW	VT		NT	TP	TP	NT	NT	NT	EM	XC	NT		TP	VT	AW	NT	TP	NT	NT	NT
		◇1	◇		◇	◇1			◇1	◇1				◇	◇1			◇1	◇1	◇		◇1			
			A		B			C	D	E	F	G	H	A	I			D		B	C	J	F		K
		🛒			🛒	🍴									🛒				🍴	🛒					
London Euston [15] ⊖65	d					09 20													10 20						
Birmingham New Street [12] 68	d	10 01													11 01										
Wolverhampton [7] 68 🚌	d	10 19													11 19										
Stafford 65,68	d	10 33													11 32										
Stoke-on-Trent 50,68	d	10 52				11 22									11 52				12 25						
Longport 50	d																								
Kidsgrove 50	d																								
Crewe [10] 65	d			10 56	11 23															12 28					
Sandbach	d			11 03																					
Holmes Chapel	d			11 08																					
Goostrey	d			11 11																					
Chelford	d			11 15																					
Alderley Edge	d			11 19												12 19								12 51	
Wilmslow	d			11 23	11 42											12 23				12 47				12 54	
Styal	d																							12 58	
Manchester Airport ✈	a																							13 05	
Handforth	d			11 26												12 26									
Congleton	d																								
Macclesfield	a	11 08				11 37									12 09				12 40						
	d	11 09				11 38									12 10				12 42						
Prestbury	d																								
Adlington (Cheshire)	d																								
Poynton	d																								
Bramhall	d																								
Cheadle Hulme	d			11 30												12 30									
Stockport	a	11 22		11 37		11 51									12 22	12 37			12 55	12 58					
	d	11 23	11 26	11 37		11 53			11 53		12 11		12 21	12 26	12 27	12 37		12 50	12 56	12 58			13 13		13 22
Heaton Chapel	d			11 41							12 15					12 41							13 16		
Levenshulme	d			11 44							12 18					12 44							13 19		
Manchester Piccadilly [10] 🚌	a	11 31	11 37	11 53	12 02	12 04			12 06		12 25		12 31	12 35	12 40	12 57		13 05	13 08	13 15			13 27	13 31	13 33
	d		11 38					11 50		12 07		12 29	12 33	12 38							12 50	13 07			13 35
Manchester Oxford Road	a		11 41					11 52		12 09		12 33	12 35	12 41							12 52	13 09			13 37
Deansgate 🚌	a												12 40												13 40

		EM		XC	VT	NT	NT	TP	AW	TP	NT	VT		NT	EM	XC	VT	NT	XC	NT	TP	VT		AW	TP
		◇		◇1	◇1			◇1	◇	◇1		◇1			◇	◇1	◇1		◇1		◇1	◇1		◇	◇1
		A		L			C	D	B	J	F			H	A	M				C	N			B	O
				🛒	🍴				🛒			🍴				🛒	🍴		🛒			🍴		🛒	
London Euston [15] ⊖65	d				11 20							12 15					12 35					12 55			
Birmingham New Street [12] 68	d			12 01												13 01			13 31						
Wolverhampton [7] 68 🚌	d			12 19												13 19			13 49						
Stafford 65,68	d			12 33												13 34									
Stoke-on-Trent 50,68	d			12 54	13 11							13 50				13 57			14 21			14 26			
Longport 50	d																								
Kidsgrove 50	d																								
Crewe [10] 65	d					12 56			13 29								14 13							14 28	
Sandbach	d					13 03																			
Holmes Chapel	d					13 08																			
Goostrey	d					13 11																			
Chelford	d					13 15																			
Alderley Edge	d					13 19												14 19							
Wilmslow	d					13 23			13 49								14 29	14 23						14 47	
Styal	d																								
Manchester Airport ✈	a																								
Handforth	d					13 26												14 26							
Congleton	d																								
Macclesfield	a			13 10	13 26											14 14						14 42			
	d			13 11	13 28											14 15						14 42			
Prestbury	d																								
Adlington (Cheshire)	d																								
Poynton	d																								
Bramhall	d																								
Cheadle Hulme	d					13 30												14 30							
Stockport	a			13 28	13 41	13 37			14 00			14 18				14 28	14 38	14 37				14 56		14 58	
	d	13 26		13 29	13 42	13 37		13 53	14 00		14 13	14 19		14 21	14 26	14 29	14 39	14 37			14 53	14 57		14 58	
Heaton Chapel	d					13 41					14 16							14 41							
Levenshulme	d					13 44					14 19							14 44							
Manchester Piccadilly [10] 🚌	a	13 37		13 40	13 53	13 55		14 06	14 19		14 27	14 29		14 33	14 37	14 40	14 50	14 53	14 57		15 06	15 09		15 15	
	d	13 38					13 50			14 07				14 35	14 38					14 50					15 07
Manchester Oxford Road	a	13 41					13 52			14 09				14 37	14 41					14 52					15 09
Deansgate 🚌	a													14 40											

A From Nottingham to Liverpool Lime Street
B From Cardiff Central
C From Manchester Airport to Liverpool Lime Street
D From Cleethorpes to Manchester Airport
E From Newcastle to Liverpool Lime Street
F From Buxton
G From Manchester Airport
H From Chester to Southport
I From Reading
J From Scarborough to Liverpool Lime Street
K To Southport
L From Southampton Central
M From Bournemouth
N From Doncaster to Manchester Airport
O From Middlesbrough to Liverpool Lime Street

Table 84

Sundays
until 1 January

Stoke-on-Trent and Crewe - Manchester Airport, Stockport and Manchester

Network Diagram - see first Page of Table 78

		NT	VT	NT	TP	NT	EM	XC		VT	NT	XC	NT	TP	VT	TP	NT	VT		NT	EM	XC	VT	NT	NT
			◇1		◇1		◇	◇1		◇1		◇1		◇1	◇1	◇1		◇1			◇	◇1	◇1		
		A			B	C	D	E				F	G	H		I	A			J	K	E			
			⊥P					⊥o		⊥P		⊥o			⊥P			⊥P				⊥o	⊥P		
London Euston 15 ⊖65	d		13 15							13 35					13 55			14 15					14 35		
Birmingham New Street 12 68	d							14 01				14 31										15 01			
Wolverhampton 7 68	d							14 19				14 49										15 19			
Stafford 65,68	d							14 34														15 34			
Stoke-on-Trent 50,68	d		14 50					14 57				15 21			15 26			15 50				15 57			16 01
Longport 50	d																								
Kidsgrove 50	d																								16 08
Crewe 10 65	d									15 13	14 56												16 13		
Sandbach	d										15 03														
Holmes Chapel	d										15 08														
Goostrey	d										15 11														
Chelford	d										15 15														
Alderley Edge	d			14 51							15 19													16 19	
Wilmslow	d			14 54						15 29	15 23												16 29	16 23	
Styal	d			14 58																					
Manchester Airport ✈	a			15 04																					
Handforth	d										15 26													16 26	
Congleton	d																								16 15
Macclesfield	a							15 14							15 42							16 14			16 22
	d							15 15							15 42							16 15			16 23
Prestbury	d																								16 27
Adlington (Cheshire)	d																								16 30
Poynton	d																								16 33
Bramhall	d																								16 36
Cheadle Hulme	d										15 30													16 30	16 39
Stockport	a		15 18					15 28		15 38	15 37				15 56			16 18				16 28	16 38	16 37	16 44
	d	15 13	15 19			15 22	15 26	15 29		15 39	15 37			15 53	15 57		16 13	16 19		16 21	16 26	16 29	16 39	16 37	16 44
Heaton Chapel	d	15 16									15 41						16 16							16 41	
Levenshulme	d	15 19									15 44						16 19							16 44	
Manchester Piccadilly 10	a	15 27	15 29	15 32		15 33	15 37	15 40		15 50	15 53	15 59		16 06	16 09		16 27	16 29		16 33	16 37	16 40	16 50	16 53	16 58
	d				15 16	15 35	15 38						15 50			16 07				16 35	16 38				
Manchester Oxford Road	a				15 18	15 37	15 41						15 52			16 09				16 37	16 41				
Deansgate	a					15 40														16 40					

		XC	NT	TP		VT	AW	TP	NT	VT	NT	NT	EM	XC		VT	NT	XC	NT	TP	VT	TP	NT	VT	
		◇1		◇1		◇1	R	◇1		◇1			◇	◇1		◇1		◇1		◇1	◇1	◇1		◇1	
		L	G	H			M	N	A			C	K	E				L	G	H		I	A		
		⊥o				⊥P	⊥o			⊥P				⊥o		⊥P		⊥o			⊥P			⊥P	
London Euston 15 ⊖65	d					14 55				15 15						15 35					15 55			16 15	
Birmingham New Street 12 68	d	15 31												16 01				16 31							
Wolverhampton 7 68	d	15 49												16 19				16 49							
Stafford 65,68	d													16 34											
Stoke-on-Trent 50,68	d	16 21				16 25				16 50				16 57				17 21			17 26			17 50	
Longport 50	d																								
Kidsgrove 50	d																								
Crewe 10 65	d						16 28									17 13	16 56								
Sandbach	d																17 03								
Holmes Chapel	d																17 08								
Goostrey	d																17 11								
Chelford	d																17 15								
Alderley Edge	d										16 51						17 19								
Wilmslow	d						16 47				16 54					17 29	17 23								
Styal	d										16 58														
Manchester Airport ✈	a										17 05														
Handforth	d																17 26								
Congleton	d																								
Macclesfield	a					16 42								17 14							17 42				
	d					16 42								17 15							17 42				
Prestbury	d																								
Adlington (Cheshire)	d																								
Poynton	d																								
Bramhall	d																								
Cheadle Hulme	d																17 30								
Stockport	a					16 56	16 58			17 18				17 28		17 38	17 37				17 56			18 18	
	d			16 53		16 57	16 58		17 13	17 19		17 22	17 29	17 29		17 39	17 37			17 53	17 57		18 13	18 19	
Heaton Chapel	d								17 16								17 41						18 16		
Levenshulme	d								17 19								17 44						18 19		
Manchester Piccadilly 10	a	16 59		17 06		17 09	17 15		17 27	17 29	17 31	17 33	17 37	17 40		17 50	17 53	17 56		18 06	18 09		18 27	18 29	
	d		16 50					17 07				17 35	17 38						17 50			18 07			
Manchester Oxford Road	a		16 52					17 09				17 37	17 41						17 52			18 09			
Deansgate	a											17 40													

- **A** From Buxton
- **B** From Manchester Airport to Barrow-in-Furness
- **C** To Southport
- **D** From Norwich to Liverpool Lime Street
- **E** From Bournemouth
- **F** From Paignton
- **G** From Manchester Airport to Liverpool Lime Street
- **H** From Cleethorpes to Manchester Airport
- **I** From Scarborough to Liverpool Lime Street
- **J** From Chester to Southport
- **K** From Nottingham to Liverpool Lime Street
- **L** From Plymouth
- **M** From Cardiff Central
- **N** From Middlesbrough to Liverpool Lime Street

Table 84

Sundays
until 1 January

Stoke-on-Trent and Crewe - Manchester Airport, Stockport and Manchester

Network Diagram - see first Page of Table 78

	TP	NT	EM	XC	VT	NT	XC	NT	TP	VT	AW	TP	NT	VT	NT	TP	NT	EM	XC	VT	NT	XC
	◇1		◇	◇1	◇1		◇1		◇1	◇1	R	◇1		◇1		◇1		◇	◇1	◇1		◇1
	A	B	C	D			E	F	G		H	I	J			A	K	C	D			L
	⊤			⊤	☕		⊤			☕	⊤			☕					⊤	☕		
London Euston 15 ⊖65 d					16 35					16 55				17 15						17 35		
Birmingham New Street 12 68 d				17 01			17 31												18 01			18 31
Wolverhampton 7 68 ⇌ d				17 19			17 49												18 19			18 49
Stafford 65,68 d				17 36															18 36			
Stoke-on-Trent 50,68 d				17 57			18 21			18 26				18 50					18 57			19 21
Longport 50 d																						
Kidsgrove 50 d																						
Crewe 10 65 d					18 13						18 28									19 13	18 56	
Sandbach d																					19 03	
Holmes Chapel d																					19 08	
Goostrey d																					19 11	
Chelford d																					19 15	
Alderley Edge d						18 19									18 51						19 19	
Wilmslow d					18 29	18 23					18 47				18 54					19 29	19 23	
Styal d															18 58							
Manchester Airport ✈ a															19 05							
Handforth d						18 26															19 26	
Congleton d																						
Macclesfield a				18 14						18 42									19 15			
d				18 15						18 42									19 15			
Prestbury d																						
Adlington (Cheshire) d																						
Poynton d																						
Bramhall d																						
Cheadle Hulme d						18 30															19 30	
Stockport a				18 28	18 38	18 37				18 56	18 58			19 18					19 28	19 38	19 37	
d		18 21	18 26	18 29	18 39	18 37			18 53	18 57	18 58		19 13	19 19			19 22	19 26	19 29	19 39	19 37	
Heaton Chapel d						18 41							19 16								19 41	
Levenshulme d						18 44							19 19								19 44	
Manchester Piccadilly 10 ⇌ a		18 33	18 37	18 40	18 50	18 53	18 56		19 06	19 09	19 15		19 27	19 29	19 31		19 33	19 37	19 40	19 50	19 53	19 58
d	18 16	18 35	18 38					18 50				19 07				19 16	19 35	19 38				
Manchester Oxford Road a	18 18	18 37	18 41					18 52				19 09				19 18	19 37	19 41				
Deansgate ⇌ a		18 40															19 40					

	NT	TP	VT	TP	NT	VT	NT	EM	XC	VT	NT	NT	XC	NT	TP	VT	AW	TP	NT	VT	NT	NT
		◇1	◇1	◇1		◇1		◇	◇1	◇1			◇1		◇1	◇1	R	◇1		◇1		
	F	G		M	J		B	N	D				E	F	G		H	I	J			O
			☕			☕			⊤	☕			⊤			☕				☕		
London Euston 15 ⊖65 d			17 55			18 15				18 35						18 55				19 15		
Birmingham New Street 12 68 d									19 01				19 31									
Wolverhampton 7 68 ⇌ d									19 19				19 49									
Stafford 65,68 d									19 38													
Stoke-on-Trent 50,68 d			19 26			19 50			19 57			20 01	20 21			20 26				20 50		
Longport 50 d																						
Kidsgrove 50 d												20 08										
Crewe 10 65 d										20 13							20 28					
Sandbach d																						
Holmes Chapel d																						
Goostrey d																						
Chelford d																						
Alderley Edge d											20 19										20 51	
Wilmslow d										20 29	20 23						20 46				20 54	
Styal d																					20 58	
Manchester Airport ✈ a																					21 05	
Handforth d											20 26											
Congleton d												20 15										
Macclesfield a			19 42						20 14			20 22				20 42						
d			19 42						20 15			20 23				20 42						
Prestbury d												20 27										
Adlington (Cheshire) d												20 30										
Poynton d												20 33										
Bramhall d												20 36										
Cheadle Hulme d											20 30	20 39										
Stockport a			19 56			20 18			20 28	20 38	20 37	20 44				20 56	20 57			21 18		
d		19 53	19 57		20 13	20 19	20 21	20 26	20 29	20 39	20 37	20 44			20 53	20 57	20 57		21 13	21 19		21 22
Heaton Chapel d					20 16						20 41								21 16			
Levenshulme d					20 19						20 44								21 19			
Manchester Piccadilly 10 ⇌ a		20 09	20 09		20 27	20 29	20 33	20 38	20 40	20 50	20 53	20 58	21 00		21 06	21 09	21 14		21 27	21 29	21 31	21 33
d	19 50			20 07			20 35							20 50				21 07				21 35
Manchester Oxford Road a	19 52			20 09			20 37							20 52				21 09				21 37
Deansgate ⇌ a							20 40															21 40

A From Manchester Airport to Barrow-in-Furness
B From Chester to Southport
C From Norwich to Liverpool Lime Street
D From Bournemouth
E From Bristol Temple Meads
F From Manchester Airport to Liverpool Lime Street
G From Cleethorpes to Manchester Airport
H From Cardiff Central
I From Middlesbrough to Liverpool Lime Street
J From Buxton
K To Southport
L From Penzance
M From Scarborough to Liverpool Lime Street
N From Norwich
O To Wigan Wallgate

Table 84

Sundays

until 1 January

Stoke-on-Trent and Crewe - Manchester Airport, Stockport and Manchester

Network Diagram - see first Page of Table 78

		EM		XC	VT	NT	XC	NT	TP	VT	TP	NT		VT	NT	XC	NT	VT		NT	NT	NT		NT	XC
		◇		◇1	◇1		◇1		◇1	◇1	◇1			◇1		◇1		◇1							◇1
		A		B			C	D	E		F	G			H	B				G		I			B
London Euston 15 ⊖65	d				19 35					19 55				20 15				20 35							
Birmingham New Street 12 68	d			20 01			20 31									21 01									22 01
Wolverhampton 7 68 ⛴	d			20 19			20 52									21 19									22 19
Stafford 65,68	d			20 37												21 37		22 00							22 37
Stoke-on-Trent 50,68	d			20 57			21 21			21 26				21 50		21 57								22 39	22 57
Longport 50	d																								
Kidsgrove 50	d																							22 46	
Crewe 10 65	d				21 14	20 56												22 21							
Sandbach	d					21 03																			
Holmes Chapel	d					21 08																			
Goostrey	d					21 11																			
Chelford	d					21 15																			
Alderley Edge	d					21 19											22 19				22 51				
Wilmslow	d				21 30	21 23											22 23	22 36			22 54				
Styal	d																				22 58				
Manchester Airport ✈	a																				23 05				
Handforth	d					21 26											22 26								
Congleton	d																							22 53	
Macclesfield	a			21 15						21 42						22 14								23 00	23 12
	d			21 15						21 42						22 15								23 01	23 13
Prestbury	d																							23 05	
Adlington (Cheshire)	d																							23 08	
Poynton	d																							23 11	
Bramhall	d																							23 14	
Cheadle Hulme	d					21 30											22 30							23 17	
Stockport	a			21 28	21 39	21 37				21 56				22 18		22 28	22 37	22 45						23 22	23 27
	d	21 24		21 29	21 40	21 37			21 53	21 57		22 13		22 19	22 21	22 29	22 37	22 46		23 13		23 16		23 23	23 28
Heaton Chapel	d					21 41						22 16					22 41			23 16					
Levenshulme	d					21 44						22 19					22 44			23 19					
Manchester Piccadilly 10 ⛴	a	21 36		21 40	21 50	21 53	21 56		22 06	22 09		22 27		22 29	22 33	22 40	22 53	22 57		23 27	23 29	23 29		23 37	23 41
	d							21 50			22 07				22 35										
Manchester Oxford Road	a							21 52			22 09				22 37										
Deansgate ⛴	a														22 40										

		NT	VT	VT
			◇1	◇1
London Euston 15 ⊖65	d		21 25	21 51
Birmingham New Street 12 68	d			
Wolverhampton 7 68 ⛴	d			
Stafford 65,68	d			23s53
Stoke-on-Trent 50,68	d		23 29	
Longport 50	d			
Kidsgrove 50	d			
Crewe 10 65	d	22 56		00s21
Sandbach	d	23 03		
Holmes Chapel	d	23 08		
Goostrey	d	23 11		
Chelford	d	23 15		
Alderley Edge	d	23 19		
Wilmslow	d	23 23		
Styal	d			
Manchester Airport ✈	a			
Handforth	d	23 26		
Congleton	d			
Macclesfield	a		23 45	
	d		23 46	
Prestbury	d			
Adlington (Cheshire)	d			
Poynton	d			
Bramhall	d			
Cheadle Hulme	d	23 30		
Stockport	a	23 35	23 59	00s50
	d	23 37	00 01	
Heaton Chapel	d	23 41		
Levenshulme	d	23 44		
Manchester Piccadilly 10 ⛴	a	23 53	00 12	01 00
	d			
Manchester Oxford Road	a			
Deansgate ⛴	a			

A From Norwich
B From Bournemouth
C From Bristol Temple Meads
E From Cleethorpes to Manchester Airport
F From Scarborough to Liverpool Lime Street
G From Buxton
H From Chester to Wigan Wallgate
I From Sheffield

Table 84

Sundays

8 January to 12 February

Stoke-on-Trent and Crewe - Manchester Airport, Stockport and Manchester

Network Diagram - see first Page of Table 78

		NT	XC	NT	TP	AW	NT	NT	NT	AW		NT	NT	TP	NT	XC	VT	NT	VT	AW		NT	NT	NT	NT
			◇1		◇1									◇1		◇1	◇1		◇1	◇					
				A	B		C	D				E	C	F	G					H		E	C		D
																⊼	⊡		⊡						
London Euston 15 ⊖65	d																08 10		08 20						
Birmingham New Street 12 68	d		22p31													09 01									
Wolverhampton 7 68 ⛴	d		22p49													09 19									
Stafford 65,68	d		23p02													09 33									
Stoke-on-Trent 50,68	d		23p21																10 21						
Longport 50	d																								
Kidsgrove 50	d																								
Crewe 10 65	d	23p12				08 28				09 28						09 56	10 19			10 28					
Sandbach	d	23p19																							
Holmes Chapel	d	23p24																							
Goostrey	d	23p27																							
Chelford	d	23p31																							
Alderley Edge	d	23p35							09 19									10 19						10 40	
Wilmslow	d	23p39				08 48			09 23	09 47						10 13	10 34	10 23		10 47				10 43	
Styal	d																							10 47	
Manchester Airport ✈	a																							10 56	
Handforth	d	23p42							09 26									10 26							
Congleton	d																								
Macclesfield	a		23p38																10 36						
	d		23p39																10 38						
Prestbury	d																								
Adlington (Cheshire)	d																								
Poynton	d																								
Bramhall	d																								
Cheadle Hulme	d	23p46							09 30									10 30							
Stockport	a	23p51	23p53						09 38							10 21	10 43	10 35	10 50	10 58					
	d	23p51	23p54	00 02	08 31		09 09	09 22	09 40				10 04		10 12	10 22	10 44	10 39	10 52	10 58			11 12		11 15
Heaton Chapel	d	23p55					09 12		09 44				10 08					10 43							11 19
Levenshulme	d	23p58					09 15		09 47				10 11					10 46							11 22
Manchester Piccadilly 10 ⛴	a	00 07	00 10	00 15	08 42	09 11	09 23	09 33	09 54	10 11			10 20		10 22	10 37	10 55	10 56	11 03	11 12			11 23	11 25	11 28
	d							09 35				09 50		10 12	10 24							10 50		11 27	11 33
Manchester Oxford Road	a							09 37				09 52		10 14	10 26							10 52		11 31	11 35
Deansgate ⛴	a							09 40							10 40										11 40

		XC	EM	NT	AW	VT		NT	TP	TP	NT	NT	NT	EM	XC	NT		NT	TP	VT	AW	TP	NT	NT	NT
		◇1	◇		◇	◇1			◇1	◇1				◇	◇1				◇1	◇1	◇	◇1			
			I		J			E	B	K	C	L	G	I	M			E	B		J	N	C		D
		⊼			⊼	⊡									⊼					⊡	⊼				
London Euston 15 ⊖65	d					09 20														10 20					
Birmingham New Street 12 68	d	10 01													11 01										
Wolverhampton 7 68 ⛴	d	10 19													11 19										
Stafford 65,68	d	10 33													11 32										
Stoke-on-Trent 50,68	d	10 52				11 22									11 52					12 25					
Longport 50	d																								
Kidsgrove 50	d																								
Crewe 10 65	d			10 56	11 23																12 28				
Sandbach	d			11 03																					
Holmes Chapel	d			11 08																					
Goostrey	d			11 11																					
Chelford	d			11 15																					
Alderley Edge	d			11 19												12 19								12 51	
Wilmslow	d			11 23	11 42											12 23					12 47			12 54	
Styal	d																							12 58	
Manchester Airport ✈	a																							13 05	
Handforth	d			11 26												12 26									
Congleton	d																								
Macclesfield	a	11 08				11 37									12 09					12 40					
	d	11 09				11 38									12 10					12 42					
Prestbury	d																								
Adlington (Cheshire)	d																								
Poynton	d																								
Bramhall	d																								
Cheadle Hulme	d			11 30												12 30									
Stockport	a	11 22		11 37		11 51									12 22	12 37				12 55	12 58				
	d	11 23	11 26	11 37		11 53			11 53		12 11		12 21	12 26	12 27	12 37			12 53	12 56	12 58		13 13		13 22
Heaton Chapel	d			11 41							12 15					12 41							13 16		
Levenshulme	d			11 44							12 18					12 44							13 19		
Manchester Piccadilly 10 ⛴	a	11 31	11 37	11 53	12 02	12 04			12 06		12 25		12 31	12 35	12 40	12 57			13 05	13 08	13 15		13 27	13 31	13 33
	d		11 38					11 50		12 07		12 29	12 33	12 38				12 50				13 07			13 35
Manchester Oxford Road	a		11 41					11 52		12 09		12 33	12 35	12 41				12 52				13 09			13 37
Deansgate ⛴	a												12 40												13 40

A From Chester
B From Sheffield to Manchester Airport
C From Buxton
D To Southport
E From Manchester Airport to Liverpool Lime Street
F From York to Liverpool Lime Street
G From Chester to Southport
H From Shrewsbury
I From Nottingham to Liverpool Lime Street
J From Cardiff Central
K From Newcastle to Liverpool Lime Street
L From Manchester Airport
M From Leamington Spa
N From Scarborough to Liverpool Lime Street

Table 84

Sundays

8 January to 12 February

Stoke-on-Trent and Crewe - Manchester Airport, Stockport and Manchester

Network Diagram - see first Page of Table 78

Station	Table		EM		XC	VT	NT	NT	TP	AW	TP	NT	VT		NT	EM	XC	VT	NT	XC	NT	TP	VT		TP	NT
			◇		◇1	◇1			◇1	◇	◇1		◇1			◇	◇1	◇1		◇1		◇1	◇1		◇1	
			A		B			C	D	E	F	G			H	A	B				C	D			I	G
					⊥	⊡				⊥			⊡				⊥	⊡		⊥			⊡			
London Euston 15	⊖65	d				11 20							12 15					12 35					12 55			
Birmingham New Street 12	68	d			12 01												13 01			13 31						
Wolverhampton 7	68 ⛴	d			12 19												13 19			13 49						
Stafford	65,68	d			12 33												13 34									
Stoke-on-Trent	50,68	d			12 54	13 11							13 50				13 57			14 21			14 26			
Longport	50	d																								
Kidsgrove	50	d																								
Crewe 10	65	d					12 56			13 29								14 13								
Sandbach		d					13 03																			
Holmes Chapel		d					13 08																			
Goostrey		d					13 11																			
Chelford		d					13 15																			
Alderley Edge		d					13 19												14 19							
Wilmslow		d					13 23			13 49								14 29	14 23							
Styal		d																								
Manchester Airport	✈	a																								
Handforth		d					13 26												14 26							
Congleton		d																								
Macclesfield		a			13 10	13 26											14 14						14 42			
		d			13 11	13 28											14 15						14 42			
Prestbury		d																								
Adlington (Cheshire)		d																								
Poynton		d																								
Bramhall		d																								
Cheadle Hulme		d					13 30												14 30							
Stockport		a			13 28	13 41	13 37			14 00			14 18				14 28	14 38	14 37				14 56			
		d	13 26		13 29	13 42	13 37		13 53	14 00		14 13	14 19		14 21	14 26	14 29	14 39	14 37			14 53	14 57			15 13
Heaton Chapel		d					13 41					14 16							14 41							15 16
Levenshulme		d					13 44					14 19							14 44							15 19
Manchester Piccadilly 10	⛴	a	13 37		13 40	13 53	13 55		14 06	14 19		14 27	14 29		14 33	14 37	14 40	14 50	14 53	14 57		15 06	15 09			15 27
		d	13 38					13 50			14 07				14 35	14 38					14 50				15 07	
Manchester Oxford Road		a	13 41					13 52			14 09				14 37	14 41					14 52				15 09	
Deansgate	⛴	a													14 40											

Station	Table		VT	NT	NT	EM	XC	VT	NT		XC	NT	TP	VT	TP	NT	VT	NT	EM		XC	VT	NT	NT	XC	NT
			◇1			◇	◇1	◇1			◇1		◇1	◇1	◇1		◇1		◇		◇1	◇1			◇1	
					J	K	B				L	C	D		F	G		H	A		B				M	C
			⊡				⊥	⊡			⊥			⊡			⊡				⊥	⊡			⊥	
London Euston 15	⊖65	d	13 15					13 35						13 55			14 15					14 35				
Birmingham New Street 12	68	d					14 01				14 31										15 01				15 31	
Wolverhampton 7	68 ⛴	d					14 19				14 49										15 19				15 49	
Stafford	65,68	d					14 34														15 34					
Stoke-on-Trent	50,68	d	14 50				14 57				15 21			15 26			15 50				15 57			16 01	16 21	
Longport	50	d																								
Kidsgrove	50	d																						16 08		
Crewe 10	65	d						15 13	14 56													16 13				
Sandbach		d							15 03																	
Holmes Chapel		d							15 08																	
Goostrey		d							15 11																	
Chelford		d							15 15																	
Alderley Edge		d		14 51					15 19														16 19			
Wilmslow		d		14 54				15 29	15 23													16 29	16 23			
Styal		d		14 58																						
Manchester Airport	✈	a		15 04																						
Handforth		d							15 26														16 26			
Congleton		d																						16 15		
Macclesfield		a					15 14							15 42							16 14			16 22		
		d					15 15							15 42							16 15			16 23		
Prestbury		d																						16 27		
Adlington (Cheshire)		d																						16 30		
Poynton		d																						16 33		
Bramhall		d																						16 36		
Cheadle Hulme		d							15 30														16 30	16 39		
Stockport		a	15 18				15 28	15 38	15 37					15 56			16 18				16 28	16 38	16 37	16 44		
		d	15 19		15 22	15 26	15 29	15 39	15 37				15 53	15 57		16 13	16 19	16 21	16 26		16 29	16 39	16 37	16 44		
Heaton Chapel		d							15 41							16 16							16 41			
Levenshulme		d							15 44							16 19							16 44			
Manchester Piccadilly 10	⛴	a	15 29	15 32	15 33	15 37	15 40	15 50	15 53		15 59		16 06	16 09		16 27	16 29	16 33	16 37		16 40	16 50	16 53	16 58	16 59	
		d			15 35	15 38						15 50			16 07			16 35	16 38							16 50
Manchester Oxford Road		a			15 37	15 41						15 52			16 09			16 37	16 41							16 52
Deansgate	⛴	a			15 40													16 40								

A From Nottingham to Liverpool Lime Street
B From Leamington Spa
C From Manchester Airport to Liverpool Lime Street
D From Sheffield to Manchester Airport
E From Cardiff Central
F From Scarborough to Liverpool Lime Street
G From Buxton
H From Chester to Southport
I From Middlesbrough to Liverpool Lime Street
J To Southport
K From Norwich to Liverpool Lime Street
L From Paignton
M From Plymouth

Table 84

Sundays

8 January to 12 February

Stoke-on-Trent and Crewe - Manchester Airport, Stockport and Manchester

Network Diagram - see first Page of Table 78

		TP	VT	AW		TP	NT	VT	NT	NT	EM	XC	VT	NT		XC	NT	TP	VT	TP	NT	VT	TP	NT
		◇1	◇1			◇1		◇1			◇	◇1	◇1			◇1		◇1	◇1	◇1		◇1	◇1	
		A		B		C	D			E	F	G				H	I	A		J	D		K	L
London Euston 15 ⊖65	d		14 55					15 15					15 35						15 55			16 15		
Birmingham New Street 12 68	d											16 01				16 31								
Wolverhampton 7 68	d											16 19				16 49								
Stafford 65,68	d											16 34												
Stoke-on-Trent 50,68	d		16 25					16 50				16 57				17 21			17 26			17 50		
Longport 50	d																							
Kidsgrove 50	d																							
Crewe 10 65	d			16 28									17 13	16 56										
Sandbach	d													17 03										
Holmes Chapel	d													17 08										
Goostrey	d													17 11										
Chelford	d													17 15										
Alderley Edge	d								16 51					17 19										
Wilmslow	d			16 47					16 54				17 29	17 23										
Styal	d								16 58															
Manchester Airport ✈	a								17 05															
Handforth	d													17 26										
Congleton	d																							
Macclesfield	a		16 42									17 14							17 42					
	d		16 42									17 15							17 42					
Prestbury	d																							
Adlington (Cheshire)	d																							
Poynton	d																							
Bramhall	d																							
Cheadle Hulme	d													17 30										
Stockport	a		16 56	16 58				17 18				17 28	17 38	17 37					17 56			18 18		
	d	16 53	16 57	16 58			17 13	17 19		17 22	17 29	17 29	17 39	17 37				17 53	17 57		18 13	18 19		18 21
Heaton Chapel	d						17 16							17 41							18 16			
Levenshulme	d						17 19							17 44							18 19			
Manchester Piccadilly 10	a	17 06	17 09	17 15			17 27	17 29	17 31	17 33	17 37	17 40	17 50	17 53		17 56		18 06	18 09		18 27	18 29		18 33
	d					17 07				17 35	17 38						17 50			18 07			18 16	18 35
Manchester Oxford Road	a					17 09				17 37	17 41						17 52			18 09			18 18	18 37
Deansgate	a									17 40														18 40

		EM	XC	VT	NT	XC	NT	TP	VT	TP		NT	VT	NT	NT	EM	XC	VT	NT	XC		NT	TP	VT	TP
		◇	◇1	◇1		◇1		◇1	◇1	◇1			◇1			◇	◇1	◇1		◇1			◇1	◇1	◇1
		M	G			N	I	A		C		D			E	M	G			O		I	A		J
London Euston 15 ⊖65	d			16 35					16 55				17 15					17 35						17 55	
Birmingham New Street 12 68	d		17 01			17 31											18 01			18 31					
Wolverhampton 7 68	d		17 19			17 49											18 19			18 49					
Stafford 65,68	d		17 36														18 36								
Stoke-on-Trent 50,68	d		17 57			18 21			18 26				18 50				18 57			19 21				19 26	
Longport 50	d																								
Kidsgrove 50	d																								
Crewe 10 65	d			18 13														19 13	18 56						
Sandbach	d																		19 03						
Holmes Chapel	d																		19 08						
Goostrey	d																		19 11						
Chelford	d																		19 15						
Alderley Edge	d				18 19									18 51					19 19						
Wilmslow	d			18 29	18 23									18 54				19 29	19 23						
Styal	d													18 58											
Manchester Airport ✈	a													19 05											
Handforth	d				18 26														19 26						
Congleton	d																								
Macclesfield	a		18 14						18 42								19 15							19 42	
	d		18 15						18 42								19 15							19 42	
Prestbury	d																								
Adlington (Cheshire)	d																								
Poynton	d																								
Bramhall	d																								
Cheadle Hulme	d				18 30														19 30						
Stockport	a		18 28	18 38	18 37				18 56				19 18				19 28	19 38	19 37					19 56	
	d	18 26	18 29	18 39	18 37			18 53	18 57			19 13	19 19		19 22	19 26	19 29	19 39	19 37				19 53	19 57	
Heaton Chapel	d				18 41							19 16							19 41						
Levenshulme	d				18 44							19 19							19 44						
Manchester Piccadilly 10	a	18 37	18 40	18 50	18 53	18 56		19 06	19 09			19 27	19 29	19 31	19 33	19 37	19 40	19 50	19 53	19 58			20 09	20 09	
	d	18 38					18 50			19 07					19 35	19 38						19 50			20 07
Manchester Oxford Road	a	18 41					18 52			19 09					19 37	19 41						19 52			20 09
Deansgate	a														19 40										

A From Sheffield to Manchester Airport
B From Cardiff Central
C From Middlesbrough to Liverpool Lime Street
D From Buxton
E To Southport
F From Nottingham to Liverpool Lime Street
G From Bournemouth
H From Plymouth
I From Manchester Airport to Liverpool Lime Street
J From Scarborough to Liverpool Lime Street
K From Manchester Airport to Barrow-in-Furness
L From Chester to Southport
M From Norwich to Liverpool Lime Street
N From Bristol Temple Meads
O From Penzance

Table 84

Sundays

8 January to 12 February

Stoke-on-Trent and Crewe - Manchester Airport, Stockport and Manchester

Network Diagram - see first Page of Table 78

		NT	VT	NT	EM	XC		VT	NT	NT	XC	NT	TP	VT	AW	TP		NT	VT	NT	NT	EM	XC	VT	NT
			◇1		◇	◇1		◇1			◇1		◇1	◇1	■	◇1			◇1			◇	◇1	◇1	
		A		B	C	D					E	F	G		H	I		A			J	C	D		
			🍴			🛒		🍴			🛒			🍴					🍴					🍴	
London Euston 15 ⊖65	d		18 15					18 35						18 55					19 15					19 35	
Birmingham New Street 12 68	d					19 01					19 31												20 01		
Wolverhampton 7 68 ⛴	d					19 19					19 49												20 19		
Stafford 65,68	d					19 38																	20 37		
Stoke-on-Trent 50,68	d		19 50			19 57				20 01	20 21			20 26					20 50				20 57		
Longport 50	d																								
Kidsgrove 50	d									20 08															
Crewe 10 65	d							20 13							20 28									21 14	20 56
Sandbach	d																								21 03
Holmes Chapel	d																								21 08
Goostrey	d																								21 11
Chelford	d																								21 15
Alderley Edge	d								20 19											20 51					21 19
Wilmslow	d							20 29	20 23						20 46					20 54				21 30	21 23
Styal	d																			20 58					
Manchester Airport ✈	a																			21 05					
Handforth	d								20 26																21 26
Congleton	d									20 15															
Macclesfield	a					20 14				20 22				20 42									21 15		
	d					20 15				20 23				20 42									21 15		
Prestbury	d									20 27															
Adlington (Cheshire)	d									20 30															
Poynton	d									20 33															
Bramhall	d									20 36															
Cheadle Hulme	d								20 30	20 39															21 30
Stockport	a		20 18			20 28		20 38	20 37	20 44				20 56	20 57				21 18				21 28	21 39	21 37
	d	20 13	20 19	20 21	20 26	20 29		20 39	20 37	20 44			20 53	20 57	20 57			21 13	21 19		21 22	21 24	21 29	21 40	21 37
Heaton Chapel	d	20 16							20 41									21 16							21 41
Levenshulme	d	20 19							20 44									21 19							21 44
Manchester Piccadilly 10 ⛴	a	20 27	20 29	20 33	20 38	20 40		20 50	20 53	20 58	21 00		21 06	21 09	21 14			21 27	21 29	21 31	21 33	21 36	21 40	21 50	21 53
	d			20 35								20 50				21 07					21 35				
Manchester Oxford Road	a			20 37								20 52				21 09					21 37				
Deansgate ⛴	a			20 40																	21 40				

		XC		NT	TP	VT	TP	NT	VT	NT	XC	NT		VT		NT	NT	NT	NT	XC	NT	VT		VT	
		◇1			◇1	◇1	◇1		◇1		◇1			◇1						◇1		◇1		◇1	
		E		F	G		K	A		L	D					A		M		D					
		🛒				🍴			🍴					🍴								🍴		🍴	
London Euston 15 ⊖65	d					19 55			20 15					20 35								21 25		21 51	
Birmingham New Street 12 68	d	20 31									21 01									22 01					
Wolverhampton 7 68 ⛴	d	20 52									21 19									22 19					
Stafford 65,68	d										21 37			22 00						22 37				23s53	
Stoke-on-Trent 50,68	d	21 21				21 26			21 50		21 57								22 39	22 57		23 29			
Longport 50	d																								
Kidsgrove 50	d																		22 46						
Crewe 10 65	d													22 21							22 56			00s21	
Sandbach	d																				23 03				
Holmes Chapel	d																				23 08				
Goostrey	d																				23 11				
Chelford	d																				23 15				
Alderley Edge	d											22 19					22 51				23 19				
Wilmslow	d											22 23		22 36			22 54				23 23				
Styal	d																22 58								
Manchester Airport ✈	a																23 05								
Handforth	d											22 26									23 26				
Congleton	d																		22 53						
Macclesfield	a					21 42					22 14								23 00	23 12		23 45			
	d					21 42					22 15								23 01	23 13		23 46			
Prestbury	d																		23 05						
Adlington (Cheshire)	d																		23 08						
Poynton	d																		23 11						
Bramhall	d																		23 14						
Cheadle Hulme	d											22 30							23 17		23 30				
Stockport	a					21 56			22 18		22 28	22 37		22 45					23 22	23 27	23 35	23 59		00s50	
	d				21 53	21 57		22 13	22 19	22 21	22 29	22 37		22 46		23 13		23 16	23 23	23 28	23 37	00 01			
Heaton Chapel	d							22 16				22 41				23 16					23 41				
Levenshulme	d							22 19				22 44				23 19					23 44				
Manchester Piccadilly 10 ⛴	a	21 56			22 06	22 09		22 27	22 29	22 33	22 40	22 53		22 57		23 27	23 29	23 29	23 37	23 41	23 53	00 12		01 00	
	d			21 50			22 07			22 35															
Manchester Oxford Road	a			21 52			22 09			22 37															
Deansgate ⛴	a									22 40															

A From Buxton
B From Chester to Southport
C From Norwich
D From Bournemouth
E From Bristol Temple Meads
F From Manchester Airport to Liverpool Lime Street
G From Sheffield to Manchester Airport
H From Cardiff Central
I From Middlesbrough to Liverpool Lime Street
J To Wigan Wallgate
K From Scarborough to Liverpool Lime Street
L From Chester to Wigan Wallgate
M From Sheffield

Table 84

Sundays

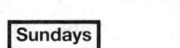

19 February to 25 March

Stoke-on-Trent and Crewe - Manchester Airport, Stockport and Manchester

Network Diagram - see first Page of Table 78

		NT	XC	NT	AW	NT	NT	NT	NT	AW		NT	TP	NT	XC	VT	NT	VT	AW	NT		NT	NT	NT	NT
			◇1										◇1		◇1	◇1		◇1	◇						
				A		B	C	D				B	E	F					G	H		B	H		D
															🛒	🍴		🍴							
London Euston 15 ⊖65	d															08 10		08 20							
Birmingham New Street 12 68	d		22p31												09 01										
Wolverhampton 7 68 ⛴	d		22p49												09 19										
Stafford 65,68	d		23p02												09 33										
Stoke-on-Trent 50,68	d		23p21															10 21							
Longport 50	d																								
Kidsgrove 50	d																								
Crewe 10 65	d	23p12			08 28					09 28					09 56	10 19			10 28						
Sandbach	d	23p19																							
Holmes Chapel	d	23p24																							
Goostrey	d	23p27																							
Chelford	d	23p31																							
Alderley Edge	d	23p35							09 19								10 19							10 40	
Wilmslow	d	23p39			08 48				09 23	09 47					10 13	10 34	10 23		10 47					10 43	
Styal	d																							10 47	
Manchester Airport ✈	a																							10 56	
Handforth	d	23p42							09 26								10 26								
Congleton	d																								
Macclesfield	a		23p38															10 36							
	d		23p39															10 38							
Prestbury	d																								
Adlington (Cheshire)	d																								
Poynton	d																								
Bramhall	d																								
Cheadle Hulme	d	23p46							09 30								10 30								
Stockport	a	23p51	23p53						09 38						10 21	10 43	10 35	10 50	10 58						
	d	23p51	23p54	00 02		09 09		09 22	09 40			10 04		10 12	10 22	10 44	10 39	10 52	10 58			11 12			11 15
Heaton Chapel	d	23p55				09 12			09 44			10 08					10 43								11 19
Levenshulme	d	23p58				09 15			09 47			10 11					10 46								11 22
Manchester Piccadilly 10 ⛴	a	00 07	00 10	00 15	09 11	09 23		09 33	09 54	10 11		10 20		10 22	10 37	10 55	10 56	11 03	11 12			11 23		11 25	11 28
	d						09 11	09 35					10 12	10 24						10 31			11 12	11 27	11 33
Manchester Oxford Road	a						09 11	09 37					10 14	10 26						10 34			11 14	11 31	11 35
Deansgate ⛴	a							09 40						10 40											11 40

		XC	EM	NT	AW	VT		TP	TP	NT	NT	NT	NT	EM	XC	NT		TP	VT	AW	TP	NT	NT	NT	NT
		◇1	◇		◇	◇1		◇1	◇1					◇	◇1			◇1	◇1	◇	◇1				
			I		J			K	L	B	H	C	F	I	M			K		J	N	H	B		D
		🛒			🛒	🍴									🛒				🍴	🛒					
London Euston 15 ⊖65	d					09 20													10 20						
Birmingham New Street 12 68	d	10 01													11 01										
Wolverhampton 7 68 ⛴	d	10 19													11 19										
Stafford 65,68	d	10 33													11 32										
Stoke-on-Trent 50,68	d	10 52				11 22									11 52				12 25						
Longport 50	d																								
Kidsgrove 50	d																								
Crewe 10 65	d			10 56	11 23															12 28					
Sandbach	d			11 03																					
Holmes Chapel	d			11 08																					
Goostrey	d			11 11																					
Chelford	d			11 15																					
Alderley Edge	d			11 19												12 19								12 51	
Wilmslow	d			11 23	11 42											12 23				12 47				12 54	
Styal	d																							12 58	
Manchester Airport ✈	a																							13 05	
Handforth	d			11 26												12 26									
Congleton	d																								
Macclesfield	a	11 08				11 37									12 09				12 40						
	d	11 09				11 38									12 10				12 42						
Prestbury	d																								
Adlington (Cheshire)	d																								
Poynton	d																								
Bramhall	d																								
Cheadle Hulme	d			11 30												12 30									
Stockport	a	11 22		11 37		11 51									12 22	12 37			12 55	12 58					
	d	11 23	11 26	11 37		11 53		11 53		12 11			12 21	12 26	12 27	12 37		12 50	12 56	12 58			13 13		13 22
Heaton Chapel	d			11 41						12 15						12 41							13 16		
Levenshulme	d			11 44						12 18						12 44							13 19		
Manchester Piccadilly 10 ⛴	a	11 31	11 37	11 53	12 02	12 04		12 06		12 25			12 31	12 35	12 40	12 57		13 05	13 08	13 15			13 27	13 31	13 33
	d		11 38						12 07		12 11	12 29	12 33	12 38							13 07	13 12			13 35
Manchester Oxford Road	a		11 41						12 09		12 13	12 33	12 35	12 41							13 09	13 14			13 37
Deansgate ⛴	a												12 40												13 40

A From Chester
B From Buxton
C From Manchester Airport
D To Southport
E From York to Liverpool Lime Street
F From Chester to Southport
G From Shrewsbury
H From Manchester Airport to Liverpool Lime Street
I From Nottingham to Liverpool Lime Street
J From Cardiff Central
K From Cleethorpes to Manchester Airport
L From Newcastle to Liverpool Lime Street
M From Leamington Spa
N From Scarborough to Liverpool Lime Street

Table 84

Sundays

19 February to 25 March

Stoke-on-Trent and Crewe - Manchester Airport, Stockport and Manchester

Network Diagram - see first Page of Table 78

	EM		XC	VT	NT	TP	AW	TP	NT	VT	NT		NT	EM	XC	VT	NT	XC	TP	VT	AW		TP	NT
	◇		◇1	◇1		◇1	◇	◇1		◇1				◇	◇1	◇1		◇1	◇1	◇1	◇		◇1	
	A		B			C	D	E	F		G		H	A	B				I		D		J	G
			🛒	🍴			🛒			🍴					🛒	🍴		🛒		🍴	🛒			
London Euston 15 ⊖65 d				11 20						12 15						12 35				12 55				
Birmingham New Street 12 68 d			12 01												13 01			13 31						
Wolverhampton 7 68 ⛴ d			12 19												13 19			13 49						
Stafford 65,68 d			12 33												13 34									
Stoke-on-Trent 50,68 d			12 54	13 11						13 50					13 57			14 21		14 26				
Longport 50 d																								
Kidsgrove 50 d																								
Crewe 10 65 d					12 56		13 29									14 13					14 28			
Sandbach d					13 03																			
Holmes Chapel d					13 08																			
Goostrey d					13 11																			
Chelford d					13 15																			
Alderley Edge d					13 19												14 19							
Wilmslow d					13 23		13 49									14 29	14 23				14 47			
Styal d																								
Manchester Airport ✈ a																								
Handforth d					13 26												14 26							
Congleton d																								
Macclesfield a			13 10	13 26											14 14					14 42				
d			13 11	13 28											14 15					14 42				
Prestbury d																								
Adlington (Cheshire) d																								
Poynton d																								
Bramhall d																								
Cheadle Hulme d					13 30												14 30							
Stockport a			13 28	13 41	13 37		14 00			14 18					14 28	14 38	14 37			14 56	14 58			
d	13 26		13 29	13 42	13 37	13 53	14 00		14 13	14 19			14 21	14 26	14 29	14 39	14 37		14 53	14 57	14 58			
Heaton Chapel d					13 41				14 16								14 41							
Levenshulme d					13 44				14 19								14 44							
Manchester Piccadilly 10 ⛴ a	13 37		13 40	13 53	13 55	14 06	14 19		14 27	14 29			14 33	14 37	14 40	14 50	14 53	14 57	15 06	15 09	15 15			
d	13 38							14 07			14 20		14 35	14 38									15 07	15 12
Manchester Oxford Road a	13 41							14 09			14 22		14 37	14 41									15 09	15 14
Deansgate ⛴ a													14 40											

	NT	VT	NT	TP	NT	EM	XC		VT	NT	XC	TP	VT	TP	NT	NT	VT		NT	EM	XC	VT	NT	NT
		◇1		◇1		◇	◇1		◇1		◇1	◇1	◇1	◇1			◇1			◇	◇1	◇1		
	F			K	L	M	B				N	C		E	G	F			H	A	B			
		🍴					🛒		🍴		🛒		🍴				🍴				🛒	🍴		
London Euston 15 ⊖65 d		13 15							13 35				13 55				14 15					14 35		
Birmingham New Street 12 68 d							14 01				14 31										15 01			
Wolverhampton 7 68 ⛴ d							14 19				14 49										15 19			
Stafford 65,68 d							14 34														15 34			
Stoke-on-Trent 50,68 d		14 50					14 57				15 21		15 26				15 50				15 57			16 01
Longport 50 d																								
Kidsgrove 50 d																								16 08
Crewe 10 65 d									15 13	14 56												16 13		
Sandbach d										15 03														
Holmes Chapel d										15 08														
Goostrey d										15 11														
Chelford d										15 15														
Alderley Edge d			14 51							15 19													16 19	
Wilmslow d			14 54						15 29	15 23												16 29	16 23	
Styal d			14 58																					
Manchester Airport ✈ a			15 04																					
Handforth d										15 26													16 26	
Congleton d																								16 15
Macclesfield a							15 14						15 42								16 14			16 22
d							15 15						15 42								16 15			16 23
Prestbury d																								16 27
Adlington (Cheshire) d																								16 30
Poynton d																								16 33
Bramhall d																								16 36
Cheadle Hulme d										15 30													16 30	16 39
Stockport a		15 18					15 28		15 38	15 37			15 56				16 18				16 28	16 38	16 37	16 44
d	15 13	15 19			15 22	15 26	15 29		15 39	15 37		15 53	15 57			16 13	16 19		16 21	16 26	16 29	16 39	16 37	16 44
Heaton Chapel d	15 16									15 41						16 16							16 41	
Levenshulme d	15 19									15 44						16 19							16 44	
Manchester Piccadilly 10 ⛴ a	15 27	15 29	15 32		15 33	15 37	15 40		15 50	15 53	16 00	16 06	16 09			16 27	16 29		16 33	16 37	16 40	16 50	16 53	16 58
d				15 16	15 35	15 38								16 07	16 12				16 35	16 38				
Manchester Oxford Road a				15 18	15 37	15 41								16 09	16 14				16 37	16 41				
Deansgate ⛴ a					15 40														16 40					

A From Nottingham to Liverpool Lime Street
B From Leamington Spa
C From Cleethorpes to Manchester Airport
D From Cardiff Central
E From Scarborough to Liverpool Lime Street
F From Buxton
G From Manchester Airport to Liverpool Lime Street
H From Chester to Southport
I From Doncaster to Manchester Airport
J From Middlesbrough to Liverpool Lime Street
K From Manchester Airport to Barrow-in-Furness
L To Southport
M From Norwich to Liverpool Lime Street
N From Paignton

Table 84

Sundays

19 February to 25 March

Stoke-on-Trent and Crewe - Manchester Airport, Stockport and Manchester

Network Diagram - see first Page of Table 78

	XC	TP	VT		AW	TP	NT	NT	VT	NT	NT	EM	XC		VT	NT	XC	TP	VT	TP	NT	NT	VT
					R																		
	◇1	◇1	◇1			◇1			◇1			◇	◇1		◇1		◇1	◇1	◇1	◇1			◇1
	A	B			C	D	E	F			G	H	I				A	B		J	E	F	
	🛒		☕		🛒				☕				🛒		☕		🛒		☕				☕
London Euston 15 ⊖65 d			14 55						15 15						15 35				15 55				16 15
Birmingham New Street 12 68 d	15 31												16 01				16 31						
Wolverhampton 7 68 ⛴ d	15 49												16 19				16 49						
Stafford 65,68 d													16 34										
Stoke-on-Trent 50,68 d	16 21		16 25						16 50				16 57				17 21		17 26				17 50
Longport 50 d																							
Kidsgrove 50 d																							
Crewe 10 65 d					16 28										17 13	16 56							
Sandbach d																17 03							
Holmes Chapel d																17 08							
Goostrey d																17 11							
Chelford d																17 15							
Alderley Edge d										16 51						17 19							
Wilmslow d					16 47					16 54					17 29	17 23							
Styal d										16 58													
Manchester Airport ✈ a										17 05													
Handforth d																17 26							
Congleton d																							
Macclesfield a			16 42										17 14						17 42				
d			16 42										17 15						17 42				
Prestbury d																							
Adlington (Cheshire) d																							
Poynton d																							
Bramhall d																							
Cheadle Hulme d																17 30							
Stockport a			16 56		16 58				17 18				17 28		17 38	17 37			17 56				18 18
d		16 53	16 57		16 58			17 13	17 19		17 22	17 29	17 29		17 39	17 37		17 53	17 57			18 13	18 19
Heaton Chapel d								17 16								17 41						18 16	
Levenshulme d								17 19								17 44						18 19	
Manchester Piccadilly 10 ⛴ a	16 59	17 06	17 09		17 15			17 27	17 29	17 31	17 33	17 37	17 40		17 50	17 53	17 56	18 06	18 09			18 27	18 29
d						17 07	17 12				17 35	17 38								18 07	18 12		
Manchester Oxford Road a						17 09	17 14				17 37	17 41								18 09	18 14		
Deansgate ⛴ a											17 40												

	TP	NT	EM	XC	VT	NT	XC	TP	VT		AW	TP	NT	NT	VT	NT	TP	NT	EM		XC	VT	NT	XC
											R													
	◇1		◇	◇1	◇1		◇1	◇1	◇1			◇1			◇1		◇1		◇		◇1	◇1		◇1
	K	L	M	I			A	B			C	D	E	F			K	G	M		I			A
	🛒			🛒	☕		🛒		☕		🛒				☕						🛒	☕		
London Euston 15 ⊖65 d					16 35				16 55						17 15							17 35		
Birmingham New Street 12 68 d				17 01			17 31														18 01			18 31
Wolverhampton 7 68 ⛴ d				17 19			17 49														18 19			18 49
Stafford 65,68 d				17 36																	18 36			
Stoke-on-Trent 50,68 d				17 57			18 21		18 26						18 50						18 57			19 21
Longport 50 d																								
Kidsgrove 50 d																								
Crewe 10 65 d					18 13						18 28											19 13	18 56	
Sandbach d																							19 03	
Holmes Chapel d																							19 08	
Goostrey d																							19 11	
Chelford d																							19 15	
Alderley Edge d						18 19										18 51							19 19	
Wilmslow d					18 29	18 23					18 47					18 54						19 29	19 23	
Styal d																18 58								
Manchester Airport ✈ a																19 05								
Handforth d						18 26																	19 26	
Congleton d																								
Macclesfield a				18 14					18 42												19 15			
d				18 15					18 42												19 15			
Prestbury d																								
Adlington (Cheshire) d																								
Poynton d																								
Bramhall d																								
Cheadle Hulme d						18 30																	19 30	
Stockport a				18 28	18 38	18 37			18 56		18 58				19 18						19 28	19 38	19 37	
d		18 21	18 26	18 29	18 39	18 37		18 53	18 57		18 58			19 13	19 19			19 22	19 26		19 29	19 39	19 37	
Heaton Chapel d						18 41								19 16									19 41	
Levenshulme d						18 44								19 19									19 44	
Manchester Piccadilly 10 ⛴ a		18 33	18 37	18 40	18 50	18 53	18 56	19 06	19 09		19 15			19 27	19 29	19 31		19 33	19 37		19 40	19 50	19 53	19 58
d	18 16	18 35	18 38									19 07	19 12				19 16	19 35	19 38					
Manchester Oxford Road a	18 18	18 37	18 41									19 09	19 14				19 18	19 37	19 41					
Deansgate ⛴ a		18 40																19 40						

A From Bristol Temple Meads
B From Cleethorpes to Manchester Airport
C From Cardiff Central
D From Middlesbrough to Liverpool Lime Street
E From Manchester Airport to Liverpool Lime Street
F From Buxton
G To Southport
H From Nottingham to Liverpool Lime Street
I From Bournemouth
J From Scarborough to Liverpool Lime Street
K From Manchester Airport to Barrow-in-Furness
L From Chester to Southport
M From Norwich to Liverpool Lime Street

Table 84

Sundays

19 February to 25 March

Stoke-on-Trent and Crewe - Manchester Airport, Stockport and Manchester

Network Diagram - see first Page of Table 78

		TP	VT	TP	NT	NT		VT	NT	EM	XC	VT	NT	NT	XC	TP		VT	AW	TP	NT	NT	VT	NT	NT
																			R						
		◇1	◇1	◇1				◇1		◇	◇1	◇1			◇1	◇1		◇1		◇1			◇1		
		A		B	C	D			E	F	G				H	A			I	J	C	D			K
			☕					☕			🛒	☕			🛒			☕					☕		
London Euston 15 ⊖65	d		17 55					18 15				18 35						18 55					19 15		
Birmingham New Street 12 68	d										19 01				19 31										
Wolverhampton 7 68 ⛴	d										19 19				19 49										
Stafford 65,68	d										19 38														
Stoke-on-Trent 50,68	d		19 26					19 50			19 57			20 01	20 21			20 26					20 50		
Longport 50	d																								
Kidsgrove 50	d													20 08											
Crewe 10 65	d											20 13							20 28						
Sandbach	d																								
Holmes Chapel	d																								
Goostrey	d																								
Chelford	d																								
Alderley Edge	d												20 19											20 51	
Wilmslow	d											20 29	20 23						20 46					20 54	
Styal	d																							20 58	
Manchester Airport ✈	a																							21 05	
Handforth	d												20 26												
Congleton	d													20 15											
Macclesfield	a		19 42								20 14			20 22				20 42							
	d		19 42								20 15			20 23				20 42							
Prestbury	d													20 27											
Adlington (Cheshire)	d													20 30											
Poynton	d													20 33											
Bramhall	d													20 36											
Cheadle Hulme	d												20 30	20 39											
Stockport	a		19 56					20 18			20 28	20 38	20 37	20 44				20 56	20 57				21 18		
	d	19 53	19 57			20 13		20 19	20 21	20 26	20 29	20 39	20 37	20 44		20 53		20 57	20 57			21 13	21 19		21 22
Heaton Chapel	d					20 16							20 41									21 16			
Levenshulme	d					20 19							20 44									21 19			
Manchester Piccadilly 10 ⛴	a	20 09	20 09			20 27		20 29	20 33	20 38	20 40	20 50	20 53	20 58	21 00	21 06		21 09	21 14			21 27	21 29	21 31	21 33
	d			20 07	20 12				20 35											21 07	21 12				21 35
Manchester Oxford Road	a			20 09	20 14				20 37											21 09	21 14				21 37
Deansgate ⛴	a								20 40																21 40

		EM		XC	VT	NT	XC	TP	VT	TP	NT	VT		NT	XC	NT	VT		NT	NT	NT	NT		XC	NT
		◇		◇1	◇1		◇1	◇1	◇1	◇1		◇1			◇1		◇1							◇1	
		F		G			H	A		B	D			L	G				D		M			G	
					☕		🛒		☕			☕					☕								
London Euston 15 ⊖65	d				19 35				19 55			20 15					20 35								
Birmingham New Street 12 68	d			20 01			20 31								21 01									22 01	
Wolverhampton 7 68 ⛴	d			20 19			20 52								21 19									22 19	
Stafford 65,68	d			20 37											21 37		22 00							22 37	
Stoke-on-Trent 50,68	d			20 57			21 21		21 26			21 50			21 57							22 39		22 57	
Longport 50	d																								
Kidsgrove 50	d																					22 46			
Crewe 10 65	d				21 14	20 56											22 21								22 56
Sandbach	d					21 03																			23 03
Holmes Chapel	d					21 08																			23 08
Goostrey	d					21 11																			23 11
Chelford	d					21 15																			23 15
Alderley Edge	d					21 19										22 19				22 51					23 19
Wilmslow	d				21 30	21 23										22 23	22 36			22 54					23 23
Styal	d																			22 58					
Manchester Airport ✈	a																			23 05					
Handforth	d					21 26										22 26									23 26
Congleton	d																					22 53			
Macclesfield	a			21 15					21 42						22 14							23 00		23 12	
	d			21 15					21 42						22 15							23 01		23 13	
Prestbury	d																					23 05			
Adlington (Cheshire)	d																					23 08			
Poynton	d																					23 11			
Bramhall	d																					23 14			
Cheadle Hulme	d					21 30										22 30						23 17			23 30
Stockport	a			21 28	21 39	21 37			21 56			22 18			22 28	22 37	22 45					23 22		23 27	23 35
	d	21 24		21 29	21 40	21 37		21 53	21 57		22 13	22 19		22 21	22 29	22 37	22 46		23 13		23 16	23 23		23 28	23 37
Heaton Chapel	d					21 41					22 16					22 41			23 16						23 41
Levenshulme	d					21 44					22 19					22 44			23 19						23 44
Manchester Piccadilly 10 ⛴	a	21 36		21 40	21 50	21 53	21 56	22 06	22 09		22 27	22 29		22 33	22 40	22 53	22 57		23 27	23 29	23 29	23 37		23 41	23 53
	d									22 07				22 35											
Manchester Oxford Road	a									22 09				22 37											
Deansgate ⛴	a													22 40											

A From Cleethorpes to Manchester Airport
B From Scarborough to Liverpool Lime Street
C From Manchester Airport to Liverpool Lime Street
D From Buxton
E From Chester to Southport
F From Norwich
G From Bournemouth
H From Bristol Temple Meads
I From Cardiff Central
J From Middlesbrough to Liverpool Lime Street
K To Wigan Wallgate
L From Chester to Wigan Wallgate
M From Sheffield

Table 84

Sundays

19 February to 25 March

Stoke-on-Trent and Crewe - Manchester Airport, Stockport and Manchester

Network Diagram - see first Page of Table 78

		VT	VT
		◇1	◇1
		🍴	🍴
London Euston 15 ⊖65	d	21 25	21 51
Birmingham New Street 12 68	d		
Wolverhampton 7 68	d		
Stafford 65,68	d		23s53
Stoke-on-Trent 50,68	d	23 29	
Longport 50	d		
Kidsgrove 50	d		
Crewe 10 65	d		00s21
Sandbach	d		
Holmes Chapel	d		
Goostrey	d		
Chelford	d		
Alderley Edge	d		
Wilmslow	d		
Styal	d		
Manchester Airport ✈	a		
Handforth	d		
Congleton	d		
Macclesfield	a	23 45	
	d	23 46	
Prestbury	d		
Adlington (Cheshire)	d		
Poynton	d		
Bramhall	d		
Cheadle Hulme	d		
Stockport	a	23 59	00s50
	d	00 01	
Heaton Chapel	d		
Levenshulme	d		
Manchester Piccadilly 10	a	00 12	01 00
	d		
Manchester Oxford Road	a		
Deansgate	a		

Sundays

from 1 April

		NT	XC	NT	TP	AW	NT	NT	NT	NT		TP	AW	NT	NT	XC	VT	NT	VT	NT		TP	AW	NT	NT
			◇1		◇1							◇1				◇1	◇1		◇1			◇1	◇		
				A	B		C	D		E		F		C	G					E		H	I	C	
																🚲	🍴		🍴						
London Euston 15 ⊖65	d																08 10		08 20						
Birmingham New Street 12 68	d		22p31													09 01									
Wolverhampton 7 68	d		22p49													09 19									
Stafford 65,68	d		23p02													09 33									
Stoke-on-Trent 50,68	d		23p21																10 21						
Longport 50	d																								
Kidsgrove 50	d																								
Crewe 10 65	d	23p12				08 28							09 28			09 56	10 19						10 28		
Sandbach	d	23p19																							
Holmes Chapel	d	23p24																							
Goostrey	d	23p27																							
Chelford	d	23p31																							
Alderley Edge	d	23p35							09 19									10 19							10 40
Wilmslow	d	23p39				08 48			09 23				09 47			10 13	10 34	10 23					10 47		10 43
Styal	d																								10 47
Manchester Airport ✈	a																								10 56
Handforth	d	23p42							09 26									10 26							
Congleton	d																								
Macclesfield	a		23p38																10 36						
	d		23p39																10 38						
Prestbury	d																								
Adlington (Cheshire)	d																								
Poynton	d																								
Bramhall	d																								
Cheadle Hulme	d	23p46							09 30									10 30							
Stockport	a	23p51	23p53						09 38							10 21	10 43	10 35	10 50				10 58		
	d	23p51	23p54	00 02	08 31		09 09	09 22	09 40			09 53		10 04	10 12	10 22	10 44	10 39	10 52			10 53	10 58	11 12	
Heaton Chapel	d	23p55					09 12		09 44					10 08				10 43							
Levenshulme	d	23p58					09 15		09 47					10 11				10 46							
Manchester Piccadilly 10	a	00 07	00 10	00 15	08 42	09 11	09 23	09 33	09 54			10 04	10 17	10 20	10 22	10 37	10 55	10 56	11 03			11 06	11 12	11 23	11 25
	d							09 35		09 50					10 24					10 50					11 27
Manchester Oxford Road	a							09 37		09 52					10 26					10 52					11 31
Deansgate	a							09 40							10 40										

A From Chester
B From Sheffield to Manchester Airport
C From Buxton
D To Southport
E From Manchester Airport to Liverpool Lime Street
F From Meadowhall
G From Chester to Southport
H From Sheffield
I From Shrewsbury

Table 84

Sundays
from 1 April

Stoke-on-Trent and Crewe - Manchester Airport, Stockport and Manchester

Network Diagram - see first Page of Table 78

	NT	XC	EM	NT	VT		NT	TP	NT	NT	NT	EM	XC	NT	NT		TP	VT	AW	NT	NT	NT	EM	XC
		◇1	◇		◇1			◇1				◇	◇1				◇1	◇1	◇				◇	◇1
	A		B				C	D	E	F	G	B	H		C		D		I	E		A	B	J
London Euston 15 ⊖65 d					09 20													10 20						
Birmingham New Street 12 68 d		10 01											11 01											12 01
Wolverhampton 7 68 d		10 19											11 19											12 19
Stafford 65,68 d		10 33											11 32											12 33
Stoke-on-Trent 50,68 d		10 52			11 22								11 52					12 25						12 54
Longport 50 d																								
Kidsgrove 50 d																								
Crewe 10 65 d				10 56															12 28					
Sandbach d				11 03																				
Holmes Chapel d				11 08																				
Goostrey d				11 11																				
Chelford d				11 15																				
Alderley Edge d				11 19										12 19							12 51			
Wilmslow d				11 23										12 23					12 47		12 54			
Styal d																					12 58			
Manchester Airport a																					13 05			
Handforth d				11 26										12 26										
Congleton d																								
Macclesfield a		11 08			11 37								12 09					12 40						13 10
d		11 09			11 38								12 10					12 42						13 11
Prestbury d																								
Adlington (Cheshire) d																								
Poynton d																								
Bramhall d																								
Cheadle Hulme d				11 30										12 30										
Stockport a		11 22		11 37	11 51								12 22	12 37				12 55	12 58					13 28
d	11 15	11 23	11 26	11 37	11 53			11 53	12 11		12 21	12 26	12 27	12 37			12 53	12 56	12 58	13 13		13 22	13 26	13 29
Heaton Chapel d	11 19			11 41					12 15					12 41						13 16				
Levenshulme d	11 22			11 44					12 18					12 44						13 19				
Manchester Piccadilly 10 a	11 28	11 31	11 37	11 53	12 04			12 06	12 25		12 31	12 35	12 40	12 57			13 06	13 08	13 15	13 27	13 31	13 33	13 37	13 40
d	11 33		11 38				11 50			12 29	12 35	12 38			12 50							13 35	13 38	
Manchester Oxford Road a	11 35		11 41				11 52			12 33	12 37	12 41			12 52							13 37	13 41	
Deansgate a	11 40										12 40											13 40		

	VT		NT	NT	TP	AW	NT	VT	NT	EM	XC		VT	NT	XC	NT	TP	VT	AW	NT	VT		NT	NT
	◇1				◇1	◇		◇1		◇	◇1		◇1		◇1		◇1	◇1	◇		◇1			
				C	D	I	E		G	B	K					C	L		I	E				A
London Euston 15 ⊖65 d	11 20							12 15					12 35					12 55			13 15			
Birmingham New Street 12 68 d											13 01				13 31									
Wolverhampton 7 68 d											13 19				13 49									
Stafford 65,68 d											13 34													
Stoke-on-Trent 50,68 d	13 11							13 50			13 57				14 21			14 26			14 50			
Longport 50 d																								
Kidsgrove 50 d																								
Crewe 10 65 d			12 56			13 29							14 13						14 28					
Sandbach d			13 03																					
Holmes Chapel d			13 08																					
Goostrey d			13 11																					
Chelford d			13 15																					
Alderley Edge d			13 19											14 19									14 51	
Wilmslow d			13 23			13 49							14 29	14 23					14 47				14 54	
Styal d																							14 58	
Manchester Airport a																							15 04	
Handforth d			13 26											14 26										
Congleton d																								
Macclesfield a	13 26										14 14							14 42						
d	13 28										14 15							14 42						
Prestbury d																								
Adlington (Cheshire) d																								
Poynton d																								
Bramhall d																								
Cheadle Hulme d			13 30											14 30										
Stockport a	13 41		13 37			14 00		14 18			14 28		14 38	14 37				14 56	14 58		15 18			
d	13 42		13 37		13 53	14 00	14 13	14 19	14 21	14 26	14 29		14 39	14 37			14 53	14 57	14 58	15 13	15 19			15 22
Heaton Chapel d			13 41				14 16							14 41						15 16				
Levenshulme d			13 44				14 19							14 44						15 19				
Manchester Piccadilly 10 a	13 53		13 55		14 06	14 19	14 27	14 29	14 33	14 37	14 40		14 50	14 53	14 57		15 06	15 09	15 15	15 27	15 29		15 32	15 33
d				13 50					14 35	14 38						14 50								15 35
Manchester Oxford Road a				13 52					14 37	14 41						14 52								15 37
Deansgate a									14 40															15 40

A To Southport
B From Nottingham to Liverpool Lime Street
C From Manchester Airport to Liverpool Lime Street
D From Cleethorpes to Manchester Airport
E From Buxton
F From Manchester Airport
G From Chester to Southport
H From Reading
I From Cardiff Central
J From Southampton Central
K From Bournemouth
L From Doncaster to Manchester Airport

Table 84

Sundays

from 1 April

Stoke-on-Trent and Crewe - Manchester Airport, Stockport and Manchester

Network Diagram - see first Page of Table 78

		EM	XC	VT	NT	XC	NT	TP		VT	NT	VT	NT	EM	XC	VT	NT	NT		XC	NT	TP	VT	AW	NT
																								R	
		◇	◇1	◇1		◇1		◇1		◇1		◇1		◇	◇1	◇1				◇1		◇1	◇1		
		A	B			C	D	E			F		G	H	B					I	D	E		J	F
			🛒	☕		🛒				☕		☕			🛒	☕				🛒			☕	🛒	
London Euston [15] ⊖65	d			13 35						13 55		14 15				14 35							14 55		
Birmingham New Street [12] 68	d		14 00			14 31									15 01					15 31					
Wolverhampton [7] 68 🚌	d		14 18			14 49									15 19					15 49					
Stafford 65,68	d		14 33												15 34										
Stoke-on-Trent 50,68	d		14 56			15 21				15 26		15 50			15 57			16 01		16 21			16 25		
Longport 50	d																								
Kidsgrove 50	d																	16 08							
Crewe [10] 65	d			15 13	14 56											16 13								16 28	
Sandbach	d				15 03																				
Holmes Chapel	d				15 08																				
Goostrey	d				15 11																				
Chelford	d				15 15																				
Alderley Edge	d				15 19												16 19								
Wilmslow	d			15 29	15 23											16 29	16 23							16 47	
Styal	d																								
Manchester Airport ✈	a																								
Handforth	d				15 26												16 26								
Congleton	d																	16 15							
Macclesfield	a		15 13							15 42					16 14			16 22					16 42		
	d		15 14							15 42					16 15			16 23					16 42		
Prestbury	d																	16 27							
Adlington (Cheshire)	d																	16 30							
Poynton	d																	16 33							
Bramhall	d																	16 36							
Cheadle Hulme	d				15 30												16 30	16 39							
Stockport	a		15 27	15 38	15 37					15 56		16 18			16 28	16 38	16 37	16 44					16 56	16 58	
	d	15 26	15 28	15 39	15 37			15 53		15 57	16 13	16 19	16 21	16 26	16 29	16 39	16 37	16 44				16 53	16 57	16 58	17 13
Heaton Chapel	d				15 41						16 16						16 41								17 16
Levenshulme	d				15 44						16 19						16 44								17 19
Manchester Piccadilly [10] 🚌	a	15 37	15 39	15 50	15 53	15 59		16 06		16 09	16 27	16 29	16 33	16 37	16 40	16 50	16 53	16 58		16 59		17 06	17 09	17 15	17 27
	d	15 38					15 50						16 35	16 38							16 50				
Manchester Oxford Road	a	15 41					15 52						16 37	16 41							16 52				
Deansgate 🚌	a												16 40												

		VT	NT	NT		EM	XC	VT	NT	XC	NT	TP	VT	NT		VT	TP	NT	EM	XC	VT	NT	XC	NT	
		◇1				◇	◇1	◇1		◇1		◇1	◇1			◇1	◇1		◇	◇1	◇1		◇1		
				K		H	B			I	D	E		F			L	G	A	B			M	D	
		☕					🛒	☕		🛒			☕			☕	🛒			🛒	☕		🛒		
London Euston [15] ⊖65	d	15 15						15 35					15 55			16 15					16 35				
Birmingham New Street [12] 68	d						16 01			16 31										17 01			17 31		
Wolverhampton [7] 68 🚌	d						16 19			16 49										17 19			17 49		
Stafford 65,68	d						16 34													17 36					
Stoke-on-Trent 50,68	d	16 50					16 57			17 21			17 26			17 50				17 57			18 21		
Longport 50	d																								
Kidsgrove 50	d																								
Crewe [10] 65	d							17 13	16 56												18 13				
Sandbach	d								17 03																
Holmes Chapel	d								17 08																
Goostrey	d								17 11																
Chelford	d								17 15																
Alderley Edge	d		16 51						17 19													18 19			
Wilmslow	d		16 54					17 29	17 23												18 29	18 23			
Styal	d		16 58																						
Manchester Airport ✈	a		17 05																						
Handforth	d								17 26													18 26			
Congleton	d																								
Macclesfield	a						17 14						17 42							18 14					
	d						17 15						17 42							18 15					
Prestbury	d																								
Adlington (Cheshire)	d																								
Poynton	d																								
Bramhall	d																								
Cheadle Hulme	d								17 30													18 30			
Stockport	a	17 18					17 28	17 38	17 37				17 56			18 18				18 28	18 38	18 37			
	d	17 19		17 22		17 29	17 29	17 39	17 37			17 53	17 57	18 13		18 19		18 21	18 26	18 29	18 39	18 37			
Heaton Chapel	d								17 41					18 16								18 41			
Levenshulme	d								17 44					18 19								18 44			
Manchester Piccadilly [10] 🚌	a	17 29	17 31	17 33		17 37	17 40	17 50	17 53	17 56		18 06	18 09	18 27		18 29		18 33	18 37	18 40	18 50	18 53	18 56		
	d			17 35		17 38					17 50						18 16	18 35	18 38					18 50	
Manchester Oxford Road	a			17 37		17 41					17 52						18 18	18 37	18 41					18 52	
Deansgate 🚌	a			17 40														18 40							

A From Norwich to Liverpool Lime Street
B From Bournemouth
C From Paignton
D From Manchester Airport to Liverpool Lime Street
E From Cleethorpes to Manchester Airport
F From Buxton
G From Chester to Southport
H From Nottingham to Liverpool Lime Street
I From Plymouth
J From Cardiff Central
K To Southport
L From Manchester Airport to Barrow-in-Furness
M From Bristol Temple Meads

Table 84

Sundays
from 1 April

Stoke-on-Trent and Crewe - Manchester Airport, Stockport and Manchester

Network Diagram - see first Page of Table 78

	TP	VT	AW	NT	VT	NT	NT	EM	XC		VT	NT	XC	NT	TP	VT	NT	VT	NT		EM	XC	VT	NT
			R																					
	◇1	◇1			◇1			◇	◇1		◇1		◇1		◇1	◇1		◇1			◇	◇1	◇1	
	A		B	C			D	E	F				G	H	A		C		I		J	F		
		☕	🛒		☕				🛒		☕					☕		☕				🛒	☕	
London Euston [15] ⊖65 d		16 55			17 15						17 35					17 55		18 15					18 35	
Birmingham New Street [12] 68 d									18 01				18 31									19 01		
Wolverhampton [7] 68 ⛴ d									18 19				18 49									19 19		
Stafford 65,68 d									18 36													19 38		
Stoke-on-Trent 50,68 d		18 26			18 50				18 57				19 21			19 26		19 50				19 57		
Longport 50 d																								
Kidsgrove 50 d																								
Crewe [10] 65 d			18 28								19 13	18 56											20 13	
Sandbach d												19 03												
Holmes Chapel d												19 08												
Goostrey d												19 11												
Chelford d												19 15												
Alderley Edge d						18 51						19 19												20 19
Wilmslow d			18 47			18 54					19 29	19 23											20 29	20 23
Styal d						18 58																		
Manchester Airport ✈ a						19 05																		
Handforth d												19 26												20 26
Congleton d																								
Macclesfield a		18 42							19 15							19 42						20 14		
d		18 42							19 15							19 42						20 15		
Prestbury d																								
Adlington (Cheshire) d																								
Poynton d																								
Bramhall d																								
Cheadle Hulme d												19 30												20 30
Stockport a		18 56	18 58		19 18				19 28		19 38	19 37				19 56		20 18				20 28	20 38	20 37
d	18 53	18 57	18 58	19 13	19 19		19 22	19 26	19 29		19 39	19 37			19 53	19 57	20 13	20 19	20 21		20 26	20 29	20 39	20 37
Heaton Chapel d				19 16								19 41					20 16							20 41
Levenshulme d				19 19								19 44					20 19							20 44
Manchester Piccadilly [10] ⛴ a	19 06	19 09	19 15	19 27	19 29	19 31	19 33	19 37	19 40		19 50	19 53	19 58		20 09	20 09	20 27	20 29	20 33		20 38	20 40	20 50	20 53
d							19 35	19 38						19 50					20 35					
Manchester Oxford Road a							19 37	19 41						19 52					20 37					
Deansgate ⛴ a							19 40												20 40					

	NT	XC	NT	TP	VT		AW	NT	VT	NT	NT	EM	XC	VT	NT		XC	NT	TP	VT	NT	VT	NT	XC
							R																	
		◇1		◇1	◇1				◇1			◇	◇1	◇1			◇1		◇1	◇1		◇1		◇1
		K	H	A			B	C			L	J	F				K	H	A		C		M	F
		🛒			☕				☕					☕			🛒			☕		☕		
London Euston [15] ⊖65 d					18 55				19 15					19 35						19 55		20 15		
Birmingham New Street [12] 68 d		19 31											20 01				20 31							21 01
Wolverhampton [7] 68 ⛴ d		19 49											20 19				20 52							21 19
Stafford 65,68 d													20 37											21 37
Stoke-on-Trent 50,68 d	20 01	20 21			20 26				20 50				20 57				21 21			21 26		21 50		21 57
Longport 50 d																								
Kidsgrove 50 d	20 08																							
Crewe [10] 65 d							20 28							21 14	20 56									
Sandbach d															21 03									
Holmes Chapel d															21 08									
Goostrey d															21 11									
Chelford d															21 15									
Alderley Edge d										20 51					21 19									
Wilmslow d							20 46			20 54				21 30	21 23									
Styal d										20 58														
Manchester Airport ✈ a										21 05														
Handforth d															21 26									
Congleton d	20 15																							
Macclesfield a	20 22				20 42								21 15							21 42				22 14
d	20 23				20 42								21 15							21 42				22 15
Prestbury d	20 27																							
Adlington (Cheshire) d	20 30																							
Poynton d	20 33																							
Bramhall d	20 36																							
Cheadle Hulme d	20 39														21 30									
Stockport a	20 44				20 56		20 57		21 18				21 28	21 39	21 37					21 56		22 18		22 28
d	20 44			20 53	20 57		20 57	21 13	21 19		21 22	21 24	21 29	21 40	21 37				21 53	21 57	22 13	22 19	22 21	22 29
Heaton Chapel d								21 16							21 41						22 16			
Levenshulme d								21 19							21 44						22 19			
Manchester Piccadilly [10] ⛴ a	20 58	21 00		21 06	21 09		21 14	21 27	21 29	21 31	21 33	21 36	21 40	21 50	21 53		21 56		22 06	22 09	22 27	22 29	22 33	22 40
d			20 50								21 35							21 50					22 35	
Manchester Oxford Road a			20 52								21 37							21 52					22 37	
Deansgate ⛴ a											21 40												22 40	

A From Cleethorpes to Manchester Airport
B From Cardiff Central
C From Buxton
D To Southport
E From Norwich to Liverpool Lime Street
F From Bournemouth
G From Penzance
H From Manchester Airport to Liverpool Lime Street
I From Chester to Southport
J From Norwich
K From Bristol Temple Meads
L To Wigan Wallgate
M From Chester to Wigan Wallgate

Table 84

Sundays
from 1 April

Stoke-on-Trent and Crewe - Manchester Airport, Stockport and Manchester

Network Diagram - see first Page of Table 78

		NT	VT	NT	NT	NT	NT	XC	NT	VT	VT
			◇1					◇1		◇1	◇1
				B		C		D			
			☕							☕	☕
London Euston 15 ⊖65	d		20 35							21 25	21 51
Birmingham New Street 12 68	d							22 01			
Wolverhampton 7 68 🚢	d							22 19			
Stafford 65,68	d		22 00					22 37			23s53
Stoke-on-Trent 50,68	d						22 39	22 57		23 29	
Longport 50	d										
Kidsgrove 50	d						22 46				
Crewe 10 65	d		22 21						22 56		00s21
Sandbach	d								23 03		
Holmes Chapel	d								23 08		
Goostrey	d								23 11		
Chelford	d								23 15		
Alderley Edge	d	22 19			22 51				23 19		
Wilmslow	d	22 23	22 36		22 54				23 23		
Styal	d				22 58						
Manchester Airport ✈	a				23 05						
Handforth	d	22 26							23 26		
Congleton	d						22 53				
Macclesfield	a						23 00	23 12		23 45	
	d						23 01	23 13		23 46	
Prestbury	d						23 05				
Adlington (Cheshire)	d						23 08				
Poynton	d						23 11				
Bramhall	d						23 14				
Cheadle Hulme	d	22 30					23 17		23 30		
Stockport	a	22 37	22 45				23 22	23 27	23 35	23 59	00s50
	d	22 37	22 46	23 13		23 16	23 23	23 28	23 37	00 01	
Heaton Chapel	d	22 41		23 16					23 41		
Levenshulme	d	22 44		23 19					23 44		
Manchester Piccadilly 10 🚢	a	22 53	22 57	23 27	23 29	23 29	23 37	23 41	23 53	00 12	01 00
	d										
Manchester Oxford Road	a										
Deansgate 🚢	a										

B From Buxton

C From Sheffield

D From Bournemouth

Table 84

Manchester, Stockport and Manchester Airport - Crewe and Stoke-on-Trent

Network Diagram - see first Page of Table 78

Miles	Miles	Miles	Station		NT MX	VT ◇1 ⊠	XC ◇1 D 🛒	NT	TP ◇1 E	NT F	VT ◇1 ⊠	XC ◇1 G 🛒	NT	NT	VT ◇1 ⊠	NT H	NT I
0	0	—	Deansgate	d													
0½	0½	—	**Manchester Oxford Road**	d													
1	1	—	**Manchester Piccadilly 10**	a													
—	—	—		d	23p38	05 05	05 11	05 35	05 44	05 50	05 55	06 00		06 06	06 10	06 18	06 21
4	4	—	Levenshulme	d	23p43									06 11			06 28
5½	5½	—	Heaton Chapel	d	23p46									06 14			06 31
7	7	—	**Stockport**	a	23p50	05 12			05 52	05 59	06 02	06 07		06 18	06 17	06 27	06 34
—	—	—		d	23p50	05 13					06 03	06 08		06 19	06 18		
9¼	9¼	—	Cheadle Hulme	d	23p54									06 26			
9¾	—	—	Bramhall	d													
12¼	—	—	Poynton	d													
14¼	—	—	Adlington (Cheshire)	d													
16¼	—	—	Prestbury	d													
19	—	—	**Macclesfield**	a											06 30		
—	—	—		d									06 03		06 31		
27	—	—	Congleton	d									06 10				
—	11½	—	Handforth	d	23p58									06 30			
—	—	0	**Manchester Airport**	d				06 05									
—	—	2¼	Styal	d													
—	13	4	**Wilmslow**	d	00 01			06 17			06 11			06 34			
—	14¾	—	Alderley Edge	d	00 04			06 20						06 37			
—	17¾	—	Chelford	d	00 08			06 24									
—	21½	—	Goostrey	d	00 12			06 29									
—	23½	—	Holmes Chapel	d	00 15			06 32						06 47			
—	27¼	—	Sandbach	d	00 20			06 36						06 53			
—	32	—	**Crewe 10**	65 a	00 30	05 34	05 44	06 46			06 27	06 32		07 04			
32½	—	—	Kidsgrove	50 a									06 16				
35¾	—	—	Longport	50 a													
38¾	—	—	**Stoke-on-Trent**	50,68 a			06 06						06 26		06 46		
—	—	—	Stafford	68 a		05 53	06 24					06 57					
—	—	—	Wolverhampton 7	68 a			06 39					07 12					
—	—	—	Birmingham New Street 12	68 a			06 58					07 31					
—	—	—	London Euston 15	⊖65 a		07 28					08 07				08 22		

Station		VT ◇1 ⊠	AW ◇ J 🛒	NT	VT ◇1 ⊠	VT ◇1 ⊠	NT	NT K	VT ◇1 ⊠	NT	TP ◇1 M 🛒	XC ◇1 G 🛒	VT ◇1 ⊠	NT H	TP ◇1 E 🛒	NT N	XC ◇1 D 🛒	AW ◇ O 🛒	VT ◇1 ⊠
Deansgate	d															07 11			
Manchester Oxford Road	d										07 07					07 15			
Manchester Piccadilly 10	a										07 09					07 17			
	d	06 27	06 30	06 32	06 35	06 43	06 46	06 49	07 00	07 03		07 07	07 15	07 17	07 20	07 21	07 26	07 30	07 35
Levenshulme	d			06 37				06 55		07 09						07 28			
Heaton Chapel	d			06 40				06 58		07 12						07 31			
Stockport	a	06 34	06 38	06 44	06 43	06 50		07 01		07 16		07 15	07 22	07 26	07 28	07 34	07 34	07 38	07 43
	d	06 35	06 39	06 45	06 43	06 51			07u07	07 18		07 16	07 23				07 35	07 39	07 43
Cheadle Hulme	d			06 51						07 24									
Bramhall	d			06 54															
Poynton	d			06 57															
Adlington (Cheshire)	d			07 01															
Prestbury	d			07 04															
Macclesfield	a	06 47		07 07	06 55												07 47		07 56
	d	06 48		07 08	06 56												07 49		07 56
Congleton	d			07 15															
Handforth	d									07 28									
Manchester Airport	d						07 11												
Styal	d																		
Wilmslow	d		06 46			06 59	07 21			07 31								07 46	
Alderley Edge	d						07 24			07 34									
Chelford	d									07 38									
Goostrey	d									07 43									
Holmes Chapel	d						07 32			07 46									
Sandbach	d						07 36			07 51									
Crewe 10	65 a		07 05			07 15	07 46			08 01								08 05	
Kidsgrove	50 a																		
Longport	50 a																		
Stoke-on-Trent	50,68 a	07 04		07 30	07 11							07 43	07 48				08 06		08 12
Stafford	68 a	07 27				07 34						08 01					08 24		
Wolverhampton 7	68 a	07 43										08 15					08 39		
Birmingham New Street 12	68 a	08 06										08 32					08 58		
London Euston 15	⊖65 a	09 34			08 45	08 52			08 58				09 23						09 52

- **D** To Bournemouth
- **E** From Manchester Airport to Cleethorpes
- **F** To Sheffield
- **G** To Bristol Temple Meads
- **H** To Chester
- **I** To Hazel Grove
- **J** To Milford Haven
- **K** To Buxton
- **M** From Liverpool Lime Street to Scarborough
- **N** From Wigan Wallgate to Hazel Grove
- **O** To Carmarthen

Manchester, Stockport and Manchester Airport - Crewe and Stoke-on-Trent

Network Diagram - see first Page of Table 78

		NT	EM ◇ A	NT	NT	NT B	VT ◇1 ⊠	NT	TP ◇1 E ⊥	XC ◇1 F ⊥	VT ◇1 ⊠	NT G	TP ◇1 H ⊥	XC ◇1 I ⊥	AW ◇ J ⊥	VT ◇1 ⊠	NT	EM ◇ A	NT
Deansgate ⇌	d																		
Manchester Oxford Road	d		07 38						08 06									08 39	
Manchester Piccadilly 10 ⇌	a		07 41						08 08									08 41	
	d	07 38	07 42	07 46	07 48	07 52	07 55	08 04		08 07	08 15	08 17	08 20	08 27	08 30	08 35	08 38	08 43	08 46
Levenshulme	d	07 43						08 09									08 43		
Heaton Chapel	d	07 46						08 12									08 46		
Stockport	a	07 50	07 53		07 57	08 01	08 03	08 16		08 15	08 22	08 27	08 28	08 34	08 38	08 42	08 50	08 53	
	d	07 51			07 58		08 04	08 17		08 16	08 23			08 35	08 39	08 43	08 51		
Cheadle Hulme	d	07 55			08 02			08 24									08 55		
Bramhall	d				08 05														
Poynton	d				08 08														
Adlington (Cheshire)	d				08 11														
Prestbury	d				08 14														
Macclesfield	a				08 18									08 47		08 55			
	d				08 18									08 49		08 56			
Congleton	d				08 26														
Handforth	d	07 59						08 28									08 59		
Manchester Airport ✈	d			08 11															09 11
Styal	d			08 18															
Wilmslow	d	08 02		08 22			08 11	08 31							08 46		09 02		09 21
Alderley Edge	d	08a08		08 25				08 34									09 05		09 24
Chelford	d							08 38											
Goostrey	d							08 43											
Holmes Chapel	d			08 33				08 46											09 32
Sandbach	d			08 37				08 52											09 36
Crewe 10 65	a			08 47			08 27	09 04							09 07		09 23		09 46
Kidsgrove 50	a				08 32														
Longport 50	a																		
Stoke-on-Trent 50,68	a				08 42					08 43	08 48			09 06		09 11			
Stafford 68	a									09 02				09 24					
Wolverhampton 7 68 ⇌	a									09 15				09 39					
Birmingham New Street 12 68	a									09 32				09 58					
London Euston 15 ⊖65	a						10 04				10 23					10 42			

		NT	NT B	VT ◇1 ⊠	NT	TP ◇1 E ⊥	XC ◇1 L ⊥	VT ◇1 ⊠	NT G	TP ◇1 H ⊥	XC ◇1 I ⊥	AW ◇ M ⊥	VT ◇1 ⊠	NT	EM ◇ A	NT	NT	NT B
Deansgate ⇌	d																	
Manchester Oxford Road	d					09 07									09 39			
Manchester Piccadilly 10 ⇌	a					09 09									09 41			
	d	08 48	08 52	08 55	09 04		09 07	09 15	09 17	09 20	09 27	09 30	09 35	09 38	09 43	09 46	09 48	09 52
Levenshulme	d		08 58		09 09									09 43				09 58
Heaton Chapel	d		09 01		09 12									09 46				10 01
Stockport	a	08 57	09 04	09 03	09 16		09 15	09 22	09 27	09 28	09 34	09 38	09 42	09 50	09 53		09 57	10 04
	d	08 58		09 04	09 17		09 16	09 23			09 35	09 39	09 43	09 51			09 58	
Cheadle Hulme	d	09 02			09 24									09 55			10 02	
Bramhall	d	09 05															10 05	
Poynton	d	09 08															10 08	
Adlington (Cheshire)	d	09 11															10 11	
Prestbury	d	09 14															10 14	
Macclesfield	a	09 18									09 47		09 55				10 18	
	d	09 18									09 49		09 56				10 18	
Congleton	d	09 26															10 26	
Handforth	d				09 28									09 59				
Manchester Airport ✈	d															10 11		
Styal	d																	
Wilmslow	d			09 11	09 31							09 46		10 02		10 21		
Alderley Edge	d				09 34									10a08		10 24		
Chelford	d				09 38													
Goostrey	d				09 43													
Holmes Chapel	d				09 46											10 32		
Sandbach	d				09 51											10 36		
Crewe 10 65	a			09 27	10 01							10 05				10 46		
Kidsgrove 50	a	09 32															10 32	
Longport 50	a																	
Stoke-on-Trent 50,68	a	09 42					09 43	09 48			10 06		10 11				10 42	
Stafford 68	a						10 02				10 24							
Wolverhampton 7 68 ⇌	a						10 15				10 39							
Birmingham New Street 12 68	a						10 39				10 58							
London Euston 15 ⊖65	a			11 04				11 23					11 42					

A From Liverpool Lime Street to Norwich
B To Buxton
E From Liverpool Lime Street to Scarborough
F To Paignton
G To Chester
H From Manchester Airport to Cleethorpes
I To Bournemouth
J To Milford Haven
L To Bristol Temple Meads
M To Carmarthen

Manchester, Stockport and Manchester Airport - Crewe and Stoke-on-Trent

Network Diagram - see first Page of Table 78

Station			VT	NT	TP	XC	VT	NT	TP	XC	AW	VT	NT	EM	NT	NT	NT	VT	NT
			◇1		◇1	◇1	◇1		◇1	◇1	◇	◇1		◇				◇1	
					C	D		E	F	G	H			J			K		
			☒		🛒	🛒	☒		🛒	🛒	🛒	☒						☒	
Deansgate 🚊		d																	
Manchester Oxford Road		d			10 07									10 39					
Manchester Piccadilly 10 🚊		a			10 09									10 41					
		d	09 55	10 04		10 07	10 15	10 17	10 20	10 27	10 30	10 35	10 38	10 43	10 46	10 48	10 52	10 55	11 04
Levenshulme		d		10 09									10 43				10 58		11 09
Heaton Chapel		d		10 12									10 46				11 01		11 12
Stockport		a	10 03	10 16		10 15	10 22	10 27	10 28	10 34	10 38	10 42	10 50	10 53		10 57	11 04	11 03	11 16
		d	10 04	10 17		10 16	10 23			10 35	10 39	10 43	10 51			10 58		11 04	11 17
Cheadle Hulme		d		10 24									10 55			11 02			11 24
Bramhall		d														11 05			
Poynton		d														11 08			
Adlington (Cheshire)		d														11 11			
Prestbury		d														11 14			
Macclesfield		a								10 47		10 55				11 18			
		d								10 49		10 56				11 18			
Congleton		d														11 26			
Handforth		d		10 28									10 59						11 28
Manchester Airport ✈		d													11 11				
Styal		d													11 18				
Wilmslow		d	10 11	10 31							10 46		11 02		11 22			11 11	11 31
Alderley Edge		d		10 34									11a08		11 25				11 34
Chelford		d		10 38															11 38
Goostrey		d		10 43															11 43
Holmes Chapel		d		10 46											11 33				11 46
Sandbach		d		10 51											11 37				11 51
Crewe 10	65	a	10 27	11 01							11 05				11 47			11 27	12 01
Kidsgrove	50	a														11 32			
Longport	50	a																	
Stoke-on-Trent	50,68	a				10 43	10 48			11 06		11 11				11 42			
Stafford	68	a				11 01				11 24									
Wolverhampton 7 🚊	68	a				11 15				11 39									
Birmingham New Street 12	68	a				11 32				11 58									
London Euston 15 ⊖	65	a	12 04				12 23					12 42						13 03	

Station			TP	XC	VT	NT	TP	XC	AW	VT	NT	EM	NT	NT	NT	VT	NT	TP
			◇1	◇1	◇1		◇1	◇1	◇	◇1		◇				◇1		◇1
			C	D		E	F	G	L			J			K			C
			🛒	🛒	🍽		🛒	🛒	🛒	🍽						🍽		🛒
Deansgate 🚊		d																
Manchester Oxford Road		d	11 07									11 39						12 07
Manchester Piccadilly 10 🚊		a	11 09									11 41						12 09
		d		11 07	11 15	11 17	11 20	11 27	11 30	11 35	11 38	11 43	11 46	11 48	11 52	11 55	12 04	
Levenshulme		d									11 43				11 58		12 09	
Heaton Chapel		d									11 46				12 01		12 12	
Stockport		a		11 15	11 22	11 27	11 28	11 34	11 38	11 42	11 50	11 53		11 57	12 04	12 03	12 16	
		d		11 16	11 23			11 35	11 39	11 43	11 51			11 58		12 04	12 17	
Cheadle Hulme		d									11 55			12 02			12 24	
Bramhall		d												12 05				
Poynton		d												12 08				
Adlington (Cheshire)		d												12 11				
Prestbury		d												12 14				
Macclesfield		a						11 47		11 55				12 18				
		d						11 49		11 56				12 18				
Congleton		d												12 26				
Handforth		d									11 59						12 28	
Manchester Airport ✈		d											12 11					
Styal		d																
Wilmslow		d							11 46		12 02		12 21			12 11	12 31	
Alderley Edge		d									12a08		12 24				12 34	
Chelford		d															12 38	
Goostrey		d															12 43	
Holmes Chapel		d											12 32				12 46	
Sandbach		d											12 36				12 51	
Crewe 10	65	a							12 05				12 46			12 27	13 01	
Kidsgrove	50	a												12 32				
Longport	50	a																
Stoke-on-Trent	50,68	a		11 43	11 48			12 06		12 11				12 42				
Stafford	68	a		12 02				12 24										
Wolverhampton 7 🚊	68	a		12 15				12 39										
Birmingham New Street 12	68	a		12 39				12 58										
London Euston 15 ⊖	65	a			13 23					13 42						14 04		

C From Liverpool Lime Street to Scarborough
D To Bristol Temple Meads
E To Chester
F From Manchester Airport to Cleethorpes
G To Bournemouth
H To Milford Haven
J From Liverpool Lime Street to Norwich
K To Buxton
L To Carmarthen

Manchester, Stockport and Manchester Airport - Crewe and Stoke-on-Trent

Network Diagram - see first Page of Table 78

	XC		VT	NT	TP	XC	AW	VT			NT	EM	NT	NT	NT	VT		NT			TP	XC		VT
							R																	
	◇1		◇1		◇1	◇1		◇1				◇				◇1					◇1	◇1		◇1
	A			B	C	D	E					G			H						K	L		
	🛒		☕		🛒	🛒	🛒	☕								☕					🛒	🛒		☕
Deansgate d																								
Manchester Oxford Road d												12 39									13 07			
Manchester Piccadilly 10 a												12 41									13 09			
d	12 07		12 15	12 17	12 20	12 27	12 30	12 35			12 38	12 43	12 46	12 48	12 52	12 55		13 04				13 07		13 15
Levenshulme d											12 43				12 58			13 09						
Heaton Chapel d											12 46				13 01			13 12						
Stockport a	12 15		12 22	12 27	12 28	12 34	12 38	12 42			12 50	12 53		12 57	13 04	13 03		13 16				13 15		13 22
d	12 16		12 23			12 35	12 39	12 43			12 51			12 58		13 04		13 17				13 16		13 23
Cheadle Hulme d											12 55			13 02				13 24						
Bramhall d														13 05										
Poynton d														13 08										
Adlington (Cheshire) d														13 11										
Prestbury d														13 14										
Macclesfield a						12 47		12 55						13 18										
d						12 49		12 56						13 18										
Congleton d														13 26										
Handforth d											12 59							13 28						
Manchester Airport ✈ d													13 11											
Styal d													13 18											
Wilmslow d							12 46				13 02		13 22			13 11		13 31						
Alderley Edge d											13a08		13 25					13 34						
Chelford d																		13 38						
Goostrey d																		13 43						
Holmes Chapel d													13 33					13 46						
Sandbach d													13 37					13 51						
Crewe 10 65 a							13 05						13 47			13 27		14 01						
Kidsgrove 50 a														13 32										
Longport 50 a																								
Stoke-on-Trent 50,68 a	12 43		12 48			13 06		13 11						13 42								13 43		13 48
Stafford 68 a	13 01					13 24																14 01		
Wolverhampton 7 68 a	13 15					13 39																14 15		
Birmingham New Street 12 68 a	13 39					13 58																14 32		
London Euston 15 ⊖65 a			14 23					14 42								15 04								15 23

	NT	TP	XC	AW		VT		NT	EM	NT	NT	NT	VT			NT		TP	XC		VT	NT	TP	XC
				R																				
		◇1	◇1			◇1			◇				◇1					◇1	◇1		◇1		◇1	◇1
	B	C	D	M					G			H						K	N			B	C	D
		🛒	🛒	🛒		☕							☕					🛒	🛒		☕		🛒	🛒
Deansgate d																								
Manchester Oxford Road d									13 39									14 07						
Manchester Piccadilly 10 a									13 41									14 09						
d	13 17	13 20	13 27	13 30		13 35		13 38	13 43	13 46	13 48	13 52	13 55			14 04			14 07		14 15	14 17	14 20	14 27
Levenshulme d								13 43				13 58				14 09								
Heaton Chapel d								13 46				14 01				14 12								
Stockport a	13 27	13 28	13 34	13 38		13 42		13 50	13 53		13 57	14 04	14 03			14 16			14 15		14 22	14 27	14 28	14 34
d			13 35	13 39		13 43		13 51			13 58		14 04			14 17			14 16		14 23			14 35
Cheadle Hulme d								13 55			14 02					14 24								
Bramhall d											14 05													
Poynton d											14 08													
Adlington (Cheshire) d											14 11													
Prestbury d											14 14													
Macclesfield a			13 47			13 55					14 18													14 47
d			13 49			13 56					14 18													14 49
Congleton d											14 26													
Handforth d								13 59								14 28								
Manchester Airport ✈ d										14 11														
Styal d																								
Wilmslow d				13 46				14 02		14 21			14 11			14 31								
Alderley Edge d								14a08		14 24						14 34								
Chelford d																14 38								
Goostrey d																14 43								
Holmes Chapel d										14 32						14 46								
Sandbach d										14 36						14 51								
Crewe 10 65 a				14 05						14 46			14 27			15 01								
Kidsgrove 50 a											14 32													
Longport 50 a																								
Stoke-on-Trent 50,68 a			14 06			14 11					14 42								14 43		14 48			15 06
Stafford 68 a			14 24																15 02					15 24
Wolverhampton 7 68 a			14 39																15 15					15 39
Birmingham New Street 12 68 a			14 58																15 39					15 58
London Euston 15 ⊖65 a						15 42							16 04								16 23			

A To Exeter St Davids
B To Chester
C From Manchester Airport to Cleethorpes
D To Bournemouth
E To Milford Haven
G From Liverpool Lime Street to Norwich
H To Buxton
K From Liverpool Lime Street to Scarborough
L To Bristol Temple Meads
M To Tenby
N To Paignton

Manchester, Stockport and Manchester Airport - Crewe and Stoke-on-Trent

Network Diagram - see first Page of Table 78

Station		AW ■ A ⊥	VT ◇1 ⊡	NT	EM ◇ C	NT	NT	NT D	VT ◇1 ⊡	NT	TP ◇1 G ⊥	XC ◇1 H ⊥	VT ◇1 ⊡	NT I	TP ◇1 J ⊥	XC ◇1 K ⊥	AW ■ L ⊥	VT ◇1 ⊡
Deansgate 🚊	d																	
Manchester Oxford Road	d				14 39						15 07							
Manchester Piccadilly 10 🚊	a				14 41						15 09							
	d	14 30	14 35	14 38	14 43	14 46	14 48	14 52	14 55	15 04		15 07	15 15	15 17	15 20	15 27	15 30	15 35
Levenshulme	d			14 43				14 58		15 09								
Heaton Chapel	d			14 46				15 01		15 12								
Stockport	a	14 38	14 42	14 50	14 53		14 57	15 04	15 03	15 16		15 15	15 22	15 27	15 28	15 34	15 38	15 42
	d	14 39	14 43	14 51			14 58		15 04	15 17		15 16	15 23			15 35	15 39	15 43
Cheadle Hulme	d			14 55			15 02			15 24								
Bramhall	d						15 05											
Poynton	d						15 08											
Adlington (Cheshire)	d						15 11											
Prestbury	d						15 14											
Macclesfield	a		14 55				15 18									15 47		15 55
	d		14 56				15 18									15 49		15 56
Congleton	d						15 26											
Handforth	d			14 59						15 28								
Manchester Airport ✈	d					15 11												
Styal	d																	
Wilmslow	d	14 46		15 02		15 21			15 11	15 31							15 46	
Alderley Edge	d			15a08		15 24				15 34								
Chelford	d									15 38								
Goostrey	d									15 43								
Holmes Chapel	d					15 32				15 46								
Sandbach	d					15 36				15 51								
Crewe 10 65	a	15 05				15 46			15 27	16 01							16 05	
Kidsgrove 50	a						15 32											
Longport 50	a																	
Stoke-on-Trent 50,68	a		15 11				15 42					15 43	15 48			16 06		16 11
Stafford 68	a											16 02				16 24		
Wolverhampton 7 68 🚊	a											16 15				16 39		
Birmingham New Street 12 68	a											16 39				16 58		
London Euston 15 ⊖65	a		16 42						17 04				17 23					17 42

Station		NT	EM ◇ C	NT	NT	NT D	VT ◇1 ⊡	NT	TP ◇1 M ⊥	XC ◇1 H ⊥	VT ◇1 ⊡	NT I	TP ◇1 J ⊥	XC ◇1 K ⊥	AW ■ A ⊥	VT ◇1 ⊡	NT	EM ◇ C
Deansgate 🚊	d																	
Manchester Oxford Road	d		15 39						16 07									16 39
Manchester Piccadilly 10 🚊	a		15 41						16 09									16 41
	d	15 38	15 43	15 46	15 48	15 52	15 55	16 04		16 07	16 15	16 17	16 20	16 27	16 30	16 35	16 38	16 43
Levenshulme	d	15 43				15 58		16 09									16 43	
Heaton Chapel	d	15 46				16 01		16 12									16 46	
Stockport	a	15 50	15 53		15 57	16 04	16 03	16 16		16 15	16 22	16 27	16 28	16 34	16 38	16 42	16 50	16 53
	d	15 51			15 58		16 04	16 17		16 16	16 23			16 35	16 39	16 43	16 51	
Cheadle Hulme	d	15 55			16 02			16 24									16 55	
Bramhall	d				16 05													
Poynton	d				16 08													
Adlington (Cheshire)	d				16 11													
Prestbury	d				16 14													
Macclesfield	a				16 18									16 47		16 55		
	d				16 18									16 49		16 56		
Congleton	d				16 26													
Handforth	d	15 59						16 28									16 59	
Manchester Airport ✈	d			16 11														
Styal	d																	
Wilmslow	d	16 02		16 21			16 11	16 31							16 46		17 03	
Alderley Edge	d	16a08		16 24				16 34									17a09	
Chelford	d							16 38										
Goostrey	d							16 43										
Holmes Chapel	d			16 32				16 46										
Sandbach	d			16 36				16 51										
Crewe 10 65	a			16 46			16 27	17 01							17 05			
Kidsgrove 50	a				16 32													
Longport 50	a																	
Stoke-on-Trent 50,68	a				16 42					16 43	16 49			17 06		17 11		
Stafford 68	a									17 02				17 24				
Wolverhampton 7 68 🚊	a									17 15				17 39				
Birmingham New Street 12 68	a									17 32				17 58				
London Euston 15 ⊖65	a						18 03				18 23					18 42		

A To Milford Haven
C From Liverpool Lime Street to Norwich
D To Buxton
G From Liverpool Lime Street to Scarborough
H To Bristol Temple Meads
I To Chester
J From Manchester Airport to Cleethorpes
K To Bournemouth
L To Pembroke Dock
M From Liverpool Lime Street to Middlesbrough

Manchester, Stockport and Manchester Airport - Crewe and Stoke-on-Trent

Network Diagram - see first Page of Table 78

	NT	NT		NT	VT	NT		NT	XC		TP	NT			VT	NT	TP	NT	XC	AW	VT			NT
																				R				
					◇1				◇1		◇1				◇1		◇1		◇1		◇1			
				A		B			D		F	G					H	I	J	D				
					☕				🛒		🛒				⊠		🛒		🛒	🛒	⊠			
Deansgate 🚢 d																17 10								
Manchester Oxford Road d											17 07					17 13								
Manchester Piccadilly 10 🚢 a											17 09					17 15								
d	16 46	16 48		16 51	16 55	16 58		17 03	17 05			17 09			17 15	17 17	17 20	17 23	17 27	17 30	17 35			17 38
Levenshulme d						17 03		17 08										17 28						17 43
Heaton Chapel d						17 06		17 11										17 31						17 46
Stockport a		16 58		17 02	17 03	17 10		17 15	17 12			17 17			17 22	17 27	17 28	17 35	17 35	17 38	17 42			17 50
d		16 58			17 04			17 16	17 13						17 23	17 28			17 35	17 39	17 43			17 51
Cheadle Hulme d		17 02						17 24								17 32								17 55
Bramhall d		17 05														17 35								
Poynton d		17 08														17 38								
Adlington (Cheshire) d		17 11														17 41								
Prestbury d		17 14														17 44								
Macclesfield a		17 18							17 25							17 48					17 55			
d		17 18							17 27							17 48					17 56			
Congleton d		17 26														17 56								
Handforth d								17 28																17 59
Manchester Airport ✈ d	17 11																							
Styal d	17 18																							
Wilmslow d	17 22				17 11			17 31											17 44	17 46				18 02
Alderley Edge d	17 25							17 34																18 05
Chelford d								17 38																
Goostrey d								17 43																
Holmes Chapel d	17 33							17 46																
Sandbach d	17 37							17 51																18 16
Crewe 10 65 a	17 47				17 27			18 01											18 04	18 07				18 26
Kidsgrove 50 a		17 32																						
Longport 50 a																								
Stoke-on-Trent 50,68 a		17 42							17 43						17 49	18 10					18 11			
Stafford 68 a									18 03										18 27					
Wolverhampton 7 68 🚢 a									18 15										18 39					
Birmingham New Street 12 68 a									18 38										18 58					
London Euston 15 ⊖65 a					19 08										19 23						19 42			

	EM	NT	NT	NT	VT		XC			TP	NT		VT	NT	TP	NT	XC	AW		VT		NT	EM	NT
	◇				◇1		◇1			◇1			◇1		◇1		◇1	◇		◇1			◇	
	L			A			M			F				G	H	N	J	O					P	
					⊠		🛒			🛒			⊠		🛒		🛒	🛒		⊠				
Deansgate 🚢 d																18 12								
Manchester Oxford Road d	17 39									18 07						18 16							18 39	
Manchester Piccadilly 10 🚢 a	17 41									18 09						18 18							18 41	
d	17 43	17 46	17 48	17 52	17 55		18 05				18 08		18 15	18 17	18 20	18 21	18 27	18 30		18 35		18 38	18 43	18 46
Levenshulme d				17 58							18 13					18 28						18 43		
Heaton Chapel d				18 01							18 16					18 31						18 46		
Stockport a	17 53		17 57	18 04	18 03		18 12				18 20		18 22	18 27	18 28	18 34	18 34	18 38		18 42		18 50	18 53	
d			17 58		18 04		18 13				18 21		18 23				18 35	18 39		18 43		18 51		
Cheadle Hulme d			18 02								18 25											18 55		
Bramhall d			18 05																					
Poynton d			18 08																					
Adlington (Cheshire) d			18 11																					
Prestbury d			18 14																					
Macclesfield a			18 18				18 25													18 55				
d			18 18				18 26													18 56				
Congleton d			18 26														18 54							
Handforth d											18 29											18 59		
Manchester Airport ✈ d		18 11																						19 14
Styal d		18 18																						
Wilmslow d		18 22			18 11						18 31							18 46				19 02		19 26
Alderley Edge d		18 25									18 34											19a08		19a32
Chelford d											18 38													
Goostrey d											18 43													
Holmes Chapel d		18 33									18 46													
Sandbach d		18 37									18 50													
Crewe 10 65 a		18 47			18 27						19 00							19 05						
Kidsgrove 50 a			18 32																					
Longport 50 a																								
Stoke-on-Trent 50,68 a			18 42				18 43						18 48				19 06			19 11				
Stafford 68 a							19 01										19 24							
Wolverhampton 7 68 🚢 a							19 15										19 39							
Birmingham New Street 12 68 a							19 32										19 58							
London Euston 15 ⊖65 a					20 06								20 23							20 42				

A To Buxton
B To Hazel Grove
D To Cardiff Central
F From Liverpool Lime Street to Scarborough
G To Chester
H From Manchester Airport to Cleethorpes
I To Chinley
J To Bournemouth
L From Liverpool Lime Street to Nottingham
M To Plymouth
N From Wigan Wallgate to Buxton
O To Carmarthen
P From Liverpool Lime Street to Norwich

Table 84

Mondays to Fridays

Manchester, Stockport and Manchester Airport - Crewe and Stoke-on-Trent

Network Diagram - see first Page of Table 78

	NT	NT	VT	NT	TP	XC	VT	NT	TP	NT	XC	AW	EM	NT	NT	NT	VT
			◇1		◇1	◇1	◇1		◇1		◇1	◇	◇				◇1
		A			D	E		F	G	H	I	J	L			A	
			☒			🛒	☕				🛒						☕
Deansgate ⇌ d																	
Manchester Oxford Road d					19 07								19 39	19 43			
Manchester Piccadilly 10 ⇌ a					19 09								19 41	19 45			
d	18 48	18 52	18 55	19 04		19 07	19 15	19 17	19 18	19 22	19 27	19 30	19 43	19 46	19 48	19 51	19 55
Levenshulme d		18 58		19 09						19 28						19 58	
Heaton Chapel d		19 01		19 12						19 31						20 01	
Stockport a	18 57	19 04	19 03	19 16		19 15	19 22	19 27	19 26	19 34	19 34	19 38	19 53		19 57	20 04	20 03
d	18 58		19 04	19 17		19 16	19 23				19 35	19 39			19 58		20 04
Cheadle Hulme d	19 02			19 24											20 02		
Bramhall d	19 05														20 05		
Poynton d	19 08														20 08		
Adlington (Cheshire) d	19 11														20 11		
Prestbury d	19 14														20 14		
Macclesfield a	19 18						19 35				19 47				20 18		
d	19 18						19 36				19 49				20 18		
Congleton d	19 26														20 26		
Handforth d				19 28													
Manchester Airport ✈ d														20 14			
Styal d																	
Wilmslow d			19 11	19 31								19 46		20a24			20 11
Alderley Edge d				19 34													
Chelford d				19 38													
Goostrey d				19 43													
Holmes Chapel d				19 46													
Sandbach d				19 51													
Crewe 10 65 a			19 27	20 01								20 05					20 27
Kidsgrove 50 a	19 32														20 32		
Longport 50 a																	
Stoke-on-Trent 50,68 a	19 42					19 43	19 51				20 06				20 42		
Stafford 68 a						20 03					20 25						20 47
Wolverhampton 7 68 ⇌ a						20 16					20 40						
Birmingham New Street 12 68 a						20 33					21 00						
London Euston 15 ⊖65 a			21 06				21 26										22 12

	NT	TP	XC	VT	NT	TP	XC	AW	EM	NT	NT	NT	NT	TP	VT
		◇1	◇1	◇1		◇1	◇1	◇	◇					◇1	◇1
		N			F	O		J	L			A		R	
				☕											☕
Deansgate ⇌ d															
Manchester Oxford Road d		20 07							20 39	20 43				21 07	
Manchester Piccadilly 10 ⇌ a		20 09							20 41	20 45				21 09	
d	20 04		20 07	20 15	20 17	20 20	20 27	20 30	20 43	20 46	20 48	20 51	21 04		21 15
Levenshulme d	20 09											20 58	21 09		
Heaton Chapel d	20 12											21 01	21 12		
Stockport a	20 15		20 15	20 22	20 27	20 28	20 34	20 38	20 53		20 58	21 04	21 16		21 22
d	20 17		20 16	20 23			20 35	20 39			20 58		21 17		21 23
Cheadle Hulme d	20 23										21 02		21 24		
Bramhall d											21 05				
Poynton d											21 08				
Adlington (Cheshire) d											21 11				
Prestbury d											21 14				
Macclesfield a				20 35			20 47				21 18				21 35
d				20 36			20 49				21 18				21 36
Congleton d											21 26				
Handforth d	20 27												21 28		
Manchester Airport ✈ d										21 15					
Styal d															
Wilmslow d	20 30							20 46		21a25			21 31		
Alderley Edge d	20 33												21 34		
Chelford d	20 37												21 38		
Goostrey d	20 42												21 43		
Holmes Chapel d	20 45												21 46		
Sandbach d	20 51												21 51		
Crewe 10 65 a	21 03							21 04					22 01		
Kidsgrove 50 a											21 32				
Longport 50 a															
Stoke-on-Trent 50,68 a			20 43	20 51			21 06				21 42				21 51
Stafford 68 a			21 02				21 24								
Wolverhampton 7 68 ⇌ a			21 15				21 39								
Birmingham New Street 12 68 a			21 32				22 00								
London Euston 15 ⊖65 a				22 33											23 48

A To Buxton
D From Liverpool Lime Street to Scarborough
E To Bristol Temple Meads
F To Chester
G From Manchester Airport to Cleethorpes
H To Hazel Grove
I To Southampton Central
J To Cardiff Central
L From Liverpool Lime Street to Nottingham
N From Liverpool Lime Street to Hull
O From Manchester Airport to Sheffield
R From Liverpool Lime Street to York

Table 84

Manchester, Stockport and Manchester Airport - Crewe and Stoke-on-Trent

Network Diagram - see first Page of Table 78

		NT	TP	XC	AW	NT	NT	NT	NT	XC	NT	TP	EM	AW	NT	NT	NT	NT	NT	TP
			◇1	◇1						◇1		◇1	◇	◇						◇1
		A	B		C			E			A	F	G	C				E		J
Deansgate	d																			
Manchester Oxford Road	d					21 43							22 24		22 43					23 17
Manchester Piccadilly 10	a					21 45							22 26		22 45					23 19
	d	21 17	21 20	21 27	21 35	21 46	21 48	21 52	22 04	22 07	22 17	22 20	22 28	22 35	22 46	22 48	23 04	23 10	23 14	
Levenshulme	d							21 58	22 09								23 09			
Heaton Chapel	d							22 01	22 12								23 12			
Stockport	a	21 27	21 28	21 34	21 43		21 57	22 04	22 16	22 15	22 27	22 28	22 37	22 43		22 57	23 16	23 19	23 23	
	d			21 35	21 44		21 58		22 17	22 16				22 44		22 58	23 16		23 23	
Cheadle Hulme	d						22 02		22 24							23 02	23 23		23 27	
Bramhall	d						22 05									23 05			23 30	
Poynton	d						22 08									23 08			23 33	
Adlington (Cheshire)	d						22 11									23 11			23 37	
Prestbury	d						22 14									23 14			23 40	
Macclesfield	a			21 47			22 18			22 28						23 20			23 46	
	d			21 49			22 18			22 29										
Congleton	d						22 26													
Handforth	d								22 28								23 27			
Manchester Airport	d					22 14									23 14					
Styal	d																			
Wilmslow	d				21 51	22a22			22 31					22 52	23a22		23 31			
Alderley Edge	d								22 34								23a37			
Chelford	d								22 38											
Goostrey	d								22 43											
Holmes Chapel	d								22 46											
Sandbach	d								22 51											
Crewe 10 65	a				22 11				23 01					23 10						
Kidsgrove 50	a						22 32													
Longport 50	a																			
Stoke-on-Trent 50,68	a			22 07			22 42			22 46										
Stafford 68	a			22 25						23 06										
Wolverhampton 7 68	a			22 39						23 19										
Birmingham New Street 12 68	a			22 58						23 39										
London Euston 15 ⊖65	a																			

		NT	NT
		A	
Deansgate	d		
Manchester Oxford Road	d		
Manchester Piccadilly 10	a		
	d	23 17	23 38
Levenshulme	d		23 43
Heaton Chapel	d		23 46
Stockport	a	23 26	23 50
	d		23 50
Cheadle Hulme	d		23 54
Bramhall	d		
Poynton	d		
Adlington (Cheshire)	d		
Prestbury	d		
Macclesfield	a		
	d		
Congleton	d		
Handforth	d		23 58
Manchester Airport	d		
Styal	d		
Wilmslow	d		00 01
Alderley Edge	d		00 04
Chelford	d		00 08
Goostrey	d		00 12
Holmes Chapel	d		00 15
Sandbach	d		00 20
Crewe 10 65	a		00 30
Kidsgrove 50	a		
Longport 50	a		
Stoke-on-Trent 50,68	a		
Stafford 68	a		
Wolverhampton 7 68	a		
Birmingham New Street 12 68	a		
London Euston 15 ⊖65	a		

A To Chester
B From Manchester Airport to Cleethorpes
C To Shrewsbury
E To Buxton
F From Manchester Airport to Sheffield
G From Liverpool Lime Street to Nottingham
J From Liverpool Lime Street to York

Table 84

Saturdays

Manchester, Stockport and Manchester Airport - Crewe and Stoke-on-Trent

Network Diagram - see first Page of Table 78

	NT				XC	VT	NT	TP	NT		VT		NT	XC	NT	VT			NT		AW	VT	NT	NT
					◇1	◇1		◇1			◇1			◇1		◇1					◇	◇1		
					D			E	F					H					I		J			
Deansgate d																								
Manchester Oxford Road d																								
Manchester Piccadilly 10 a																								
d	23p38				05 11	05 25	05 35	05 44	05 50		05 55			06 00	06 06	06 10			06 17		06 30	06 35	06 44	06 46
Levenshulme d	23p43														06 11									
Heaton Chapel d	23p46														06 14									
Stockport a	23p50					05 33		05 52	05 59		06 02			06 07	06 18	06 17			06 27		06 38	06 43	06 52	
d	23p50					05 34					06 03			06 08	06 19	06 18					06 39	06 43	06 53	
Cheadle Hulme d	23p54														06 26								06 57	
Bramhall d																							07 00	
Poynton d																							07 03	
Adlington (Cheshire) d																							07 06	
Prestbury d																							07 09	
Macclesfield a														06 20		06 30						06 55	07 13	
d													06 03	06 21		06 31						06 56	07 13	
Congleton d													06 10										07 21	
Handforth d	23p58														06 30									
Manchester Airport d							06 05																	07 11
Styal d																								
Wilmslow d	00 01					05 41	06 14				06 11				06 33						06 46			07 21
Alderley Edge d	00 04						06 17								06 36									07 24
Chelford d	00 08						06 21																	
Goostrey d	00 12						06 25																	
Holmes Chapel d	00 15						06 28								06 44									07 32
Sandbach d	00 20						06 33								06 49									07 36
Crewe 10 65 a	00 30				05 41	05 57	06 43				06 27				06 59						07 05			07 46
Kidsgrove 50 a													06 16										07 28	
Longport 50 a																								
Stoke-on-Trent 50,68 a					06 07								06 26	06 38		06 46						07 11	07 40	
Stafford 68 a					06 25	06 17								06 57										
Wolverhampton 7 68 a					06 39									07 12										
Birmingham New Street 12 68 a					06 57									07 31										
London Euston 15 ⊖65 a						07 52					08 09					08 27						08 46		

	NT	VT		NT			TP	XC		VT	NT	TP	NT	XC	AW		VT		NT	EM	NT	NT	NT	VT
		◇1					◇1	◇1		◇1		◇1		◇1	◇		◇1			◇				◇1
	K						M	H			I	E	N	D	O					Q			K	
Deansgate d													07 11											
Manchester Oxford Road d							07 07						07 15							07 38				
Manchester Piccadilly 10 a							07 09						07 17							07 41				
d	06 49	06 55		07 03				07 07		07 15	07 17	07 20	07 21	07 27	07 30		07 35		07 38	07 42	07 46	07 48	07 52	07 55
Levenshulme d	06 55			07 09									07 28						07 43				07 58	
Heaton Chapel d	06 58			07 12									07 31						07 46					
Stockport a	07 01	07 03		07 16				07 15		07 22	07 27	07 28	07 34	07 34	07 38		07 43		07 50	07 53		07 57	08 02	08 03
d		07 04		07 18				07 16		07 23				07 35	07 39		07 43		07 51			07 58		08 04
Cheadle Hulme d				07 24															07 55			08 02		
Bramhall d																						08 05		
Poynton d																						08 08		
Adlington (Cheshire) d																						08 11		
Prestbury d																						08 14		
Macclesfield a														07 47			07 55					08 18		
d														07 49			07 56					08 18		
Congleton d																						08 26		
Handforth d				07 28															07 59					
Manchester Airport d																					08 11			
Styal d																					08 18			
Wilmslow d		07 11		07 31											07 46				08 01		08 22			08 11
Alderley Edge d				07 34															08a07		08 25			
Chelford d				07 38																				
Goostrey d				07 43																				
Holmes Chapel d				07 46																	08 33			
Sandbach d				07 51																	08 37			
Crewe 10 65 a		07 27		08 01											08 05						08 47			08 27
Kidsgrove 50 a																						08 32		
Longport 50 a																								
Stoke-on-Trent 50,68 a								07 43		07 48				08 06			08 11					08 42		
Stafford 68 a								08 02						08 25										
Wolverhampton 7 68 a								08 16						08 39										
Birmingham New Street 12 68 a								08 38						08 58										
London Euston 15 ⊖65 a		09 04								09 23							09 42							10 04

- **D** To Bournemouth
- **E** From Manchester Airport to Cleethorpes
- **F** To Sheffield
- **H** To Bristol Temple Meads
- **I** To Chester
- **J** To Milford Haven
- **K** To Buxton
- **M** From Liverpool Lime Street to Scarborough
- **N** From Wigan Wallgate to Hazel Grove
- **O** To Carmarthen
- **Q** From Liverpool Lime Street to Norwich

Table 84

Saturdays

Manchester, Stockport and Manchester Airport - Crewe and Stoke-on-Trent

Network Diagram - see first Page of Table 78

		NT	TP	XC	VT	NT	TP	XC	AW	VT	NT	EM	NT	NT	NT	VT	NT
			◇1	◇1	◇1		◇1	◇1	◇	◇1		◇				◇1	
			C	D		E	F	G	H			J			K		
			🍴	🍴	🍽		🍴	🍴	🍴	🍽						🍽	
Deansgate	d																
Manchester Oxford Road	d		08 06									08 39					
Manchester Piccadilly 10	a		08 08									08 41					
	d	08 04		08 07	08 15	08 17	08 20	08 27	08 30	08 35	08 38	08 43	08 46	08 48	08 52	08 55	09 04
Levenshulme	d	08 09									08 43				08 58		09 09
Heaton Chapel	d	08 12									08 46				09 01		09 12
Stockport	a	08 16		08 15	08 22	08 27	08 28	08 34	08 38	08 43	08 50	08 53		08 57	09 04	09 03	09 16
	d	08 17		08 16	08 23			08 35	08 39	08 43	08 51			08 58		09 04	09 17
Cheadle Hulme	d	08 24									08 55			09 02			09 24
Bramhall	d													09 05			
Poynton	d													09 08			
Adlington (Cheshire)	d													09 11			
Prestbury	d													09 14			
Macclesfield	a							08 47		08 55				09 18			
	d							08 49		08 56				09 18			
Congleton	d													09 26			
Handforth	d	08 28									08 59						09 28
Manchester Airport ✈	d												09 11				
Styal	d																
Wilmslow	d	08 31							08 46		09 02		09 21			09 11	09 31
Alderley Edge	d	08 34									09a08		09 24				09 34
Chelford	d	08 38															09 38
Goostrey	d	08 43															09 43
Holmes Chapel	d	08 46											09 32				09 46
Sandbach	d	08 51											09 36				09 51
Crewe 10 65	a	09 01							09 05				09 46			09 27	10 01
Kidsgrove 50	a													09 32			
Longport 50	a																
Stoke-on-Trent 50,68	a			08 43	08 48			09 06		09 11				09 42			
Stafford 68	a			09 02				09 25									
Wolverhampton 7 68	a			09 15				09 39									
Birmingham New Street 12 68	a			09 39				09 58									
London Euston 15 ⊖65	a				10 23					10 42						11 04	

		TP	XC	VT	NT	TP	XC	AW	VT	NT	EM	NT	NT	NT	VT	NT	TP	XC
		◇1	◇1	◇1		◇1	◇1	◇	◇1		◇				◇1		◇1	◇1
		C	L		E	F	G	M			J			K			C	L
		🍴	🍴	🍽		🍴	🍴	🍴	🍽						🍽		🍴	🍴
Deansgate	d																	
Manchester Oxford Road	d	09 07									09 39						10 07	
Manchester Piccadilly 10	a	09 09									09 41						10 09	
	d		09 07	09 15	09 17	09 20	09 27	09 30	09 35	09 38	09 43	09 46	09 48	09 52	09 55	10 04		10 07
Levenshulme	d									09 43				09 58		10 09		
Heaton Chapel	d									09 46				10 01		10 12		
Stockport	a		09 15	09 22	09 27	09 28	09 34	09 38	09 42	09 50	09 53		09 57	10 04	10 03	10 16		10 15
	d		09 16	09 23			09 35	09 39	09 43	09 51			09 58		10 04	10 17		10 16
Cheadle Hulme	d									09 55			10 02			10 24		
Bramhall	d												10 05					
Poynton	d												10 08					
Adlington (Cheshire)	d												10 11					
Prestbury	d												10 14					
Macclesfield	a						09 47		09 55				10 18					
	d						09 49		09 56				10 18					
Congleton	d												10 26					
Handforth	d									09 59						10 28		
Manchester Airport ✈	d											10 11						
Styal	d																	
Wilmslow	d							09 46		10 02		10 21			10 11	10 31		
Alderley Edge	d									10a08		10 24				10 34		
Chelford	d															10 38		
Goostrey	d															10 43		
Holmes Chapel	d											10 32				10 46		
Sandbach	d											10 36				10 51		
Crewe 10 65	a							10 05				10 46			10 27	11 01		
Kidsgrove 50	a												10 32					
Longport 50	a																	
Stoke-on-Trent 50,68	a		09 43	09 48			10 06		10 11				10 42					10 43
Stafford 68	a		10 02				10 25											11 02
Wolverhampton 7 68	a		10 15				10 39											11 16
Birmingham New Street 12 68	a		10 39				10 58											11 39
London Euston 15 ⊖65	a			11 23					11 42						12 04			

C From Liverpool Lime Street to Scarborough
D To Paignton
E To Chester
F From Manchester Airport to Cleethorpes
G To Bournemouth
H To Milford Haven
J From Liverpool Lime Street to Norwich
K To Buxton
L To Bristol Temple Meads
M To Carmarthen

Manchester, Stockport and Manchester Airport - Crewe and Stoke-on-Trent

Network Diagram - see first Page of Table 78

		VT	NT	TP	XC	AW	VT	NT	EM	NT	NT	NT	VT	NT	TP	XC	VT
		◇1		◇1	◇1	◇	◇1		◇				◇1		◇1	◇1	◇1
			A	B	C	D			F			G			J	K	
		⊐		⊥	⊥	⊥	⊐						⊐		⊥	⊥	⊐
Deansgate 🚊	d																
Manchester Oxford Road	d								10 39						11 07		
Manchester Piccadilly 10 🚊	a								10 41						11 09		
	d	10 15	10 17	10 20	10 27	10 30	10 35	10 38	10 43	10 46	10 48	10 52	10 55	11 04		11 07	11 15
Levenshulme	d							10 43				10 58		11 09			
Heaton Chapel	d							10 46				11 01		11 12			
Stockport	a	10 22	10 27	10 28	10 34	10 38	10 42	10 50	10 53		10 57	11 04	11 03	11 16		11 15	11 22
	d	10 23			10 35	10 39	10 43	10 51			10 58		11 04	11 17		11 16	11 23
Cheadle Hulme	d							10 55			11 02			11 24			
Bramhall	d										11 05						
Poynton	d										11 08						
Adlington (Cheshire)	d										11 11						
Prestbury	d										11 14						
Macclesfield	a				10 47		10 55				11 18						
	d				10 49		10 56				11 18						
Congleton	d										11 26						
Handforth	d							10 59						11 28			
Manchester Airport ✈	d									11 11							
Styal	d									11 18							
Wilmslow	d					10 46		11 02		11 22			11 11	11 31			
Alderley Edge	d							11a08		11 25				11 34			
Chelford	d													11 38			
Goostrey	d													11 43			
Holmes Chapel	d									11 33				11 46			
Sandbach	d									11 37				11 51			
Crewe 10 65	a					11 05				11 47			11 27	12 01			
Kidsgrove 50	a										11 32						
Longport 50	a																
Stoke-on-Trent 50,68	a	10 48			11 06		11 11				11 42					11 43	11 48
Stafford 68	a				11 25											12 02	
Wolverhampton 7 68 🚊	a				11 39											12 16	
Birmingham New Street 12 68	a				11 58											12 39	
London Euston 15 ⊖65	a	12 23					12 42						13 04				13 23

		NT	TP	XC	AW	VT	NT	EM	NT	NT	NT	VT	NT	TP	XC	VT	NT	TP	XC
			◇1	◇1	◇	◇1		◇				◇1		◇1	◇1	◇1		◇1	◇1
		A	B	C	L			F			G			J	M		A	B	C
			⊥	⊥	⊥	⊐						⊐		⊥	⊥	⊐		⊥	⊥
Deansgate 🚊	d																		
Manchester Oxford Road	d							11 39						12 07					
Manchester Piccadilly 10 🚊	a							11 41						12 09					
	d	11 17	11 20	11 27	11 30	11 35	11 38	11 43	11 46	11 48	11 52	11 55	12 04		12 07	12 15	12 17	12 20	12 27
Levenshulme	d						11 43				11 58		12 09						
Heaton Chapel	d						11 46				12 01		12 12						
Stockport	a	11 27	11 28	11 34	11 38	11 42	11 50	11 53		11 57	12 04	12 03	12 16		12 15	12 22	12 27	12 28	12 34
	d			11 35	11 39	11 43	11 51			11 58		12 04	12 17		12 16	12 23			12 35
Cheadle Hulme	d						11 55			12 02			12 24						
Bramhall	d									12 05									
Poynton	d									12 08									
Adlington (Cheshire)	d									12 11									
Prestbury	d									12 14									
Macclesfield	a			11 47		11 55				12 18									12 47
	d			11 49		11 56				12 18									12 49
Congleton	d									12 26									
Handforth	d						11 59						12 28						
Manchester Airport ✈	d								12 11										
Styal	d																		
Wilmslow	d				11 46		12 02		12 21			12 11	12 31						
Alderley Edge	d						12a08		12 24				12 34						
Chelford	d												12 38						
Goostrey	d												12 43						
Holmes Chapel	d								12 32				12 46						
Sandbach	d								12 36				12 51						
Crewe 10 65	a				12 05				12 46			12 27	13 01						
Kidsgrove 50	a									12 32									
Longport 50	a																		
Stoke-on-Trent 50,68	a			12 06		12 11				12 42					12 43	12 48			13 06
Stafford 68	a			12 24											13 02				13 25
Wolverhampton 7 68 🚊	a			12 39											13 15				13 39
Birmingham New Street 12 68	a			12 58											13 39				13 58
London Euston 15 ⊖65	a					13 42						14 04				14 23			

A To Chester
B From Manchester Airport to Cleethorpes
C To Bournemouth
D To Milford Haven
F From Liverpool Lime Street to Norwich
G To Buxton
J From Liverpool Lime Street to Scarborough
K To Bristol Temple Meads
L To Carmarthen
M To Exeter St Davids

Table 84

Saturdays

Manchester, Stockport and Manchester Airport - Crewe and Stoke-on-Trent

Network Diagram - see first Page of Table 78

Station		VT	NT	EM	NT	NT	NT	VT	NT	TP	XC	VT	NT	TP	XC	AW	VT	NT
																R		
		◇1		◇				◇1		◇1	◇1	◇1		◇1	◇1		◇1	
				B			C			F	G		H	I	J	K		
Deansgate	d																	
Manchester Oxford Road	d			12 39						13 07								
Manchester Piccadilly 10	a			12 41						13 09								
	d	12 35	12 38	12 43	12 46	12 48	12 52	12 55	13 04		13 07	13 15	13 17	13 20	13 27	13 30	13 35	13 38
Levenshulme	d		12 43				12 58		13 09									13 43
Heaton Chapel	d		12 46				13 01		13 12									13 46
Stockport	a	12 42	12 50	12 53		12 57	13 04	13 03	13 16		13 15	13 22	13 27	13 28	13 34	13 38	13 42	13 50
	d	12 43	12 51			12 58		13 04	13 17		13 16	13 23			13 35	13 39	13 43	13 51
Cheadle Hulme	d		12 55			13 02			13 24									13 55
Bramhall	d					13 05												
Poynton	d					13 08												
Adlington (Cheshire)	d					13 11												
Prestbury	d					13 14												
Macclesfield	a	12 55				13 18									13 47		13 55	
	d	12 56				13 18									13 49		13 56	
Congleton	d					13 26												
Handforth	d		12 59						13 28									13 59
Manchester Airport	d				13 11													
Styal	d				13 18													
Wilmslow	d		13 02		13 22			13 11	13 31							13 46		14 02
Alderley Edge	d		13a08		13 25				13 34									14a08
Chelford	d								13 38									
Goostrey	d								13 43									
Holmes Chapel	d				13 33				13 46									
Sandbach	d				13 37				13 51									
Crewe 10 65	a				13 47			13 27	14 01							14 05		
Kidsgrove 50	a					13 32												
Longport 50	a																	
Stoke-on-Trent 50,68	a	13 11				13 42					13 43	13 48			14 06		14 11	
Stafford 68	a										14 02				14 25			
Wolverhampton 7 68	a										14 16				14 39			
Birmingham New Street 12 68	a										14 39				14 58			
London Euston 15 ⊖65	a	14 42						15 04				15 23					15 42	

Station		EM	NT	NT	NT	VT	NT	TP	XC	VT	NT	TP	XC	AW	VT	NT	EM	NT
														R				
		◇				◇1		◇1	◇1	◇1		◇1	◇1		◇1		◇	
		B			C			F	L		H	I	J	M			B	
Deansgate	d																	
Manchester Oxford Road	d	13 39						14 07									14 39	
Manchester Piccadilly 10	a	13 41						14 09									14 41	
	d	13 43	13 46	13 48	13 52	13 55	14 04		14 07	14 15	14 17	14 20	14 27	14 30	14 35	14 38	14 43	14 46
Levenshulme	d				13 58		14 09									14 43		
Heaton Chapel	d				14 01		14 12									14 46		
Stockport	a	13 53		13 57	14 04	14 03	14 16		14 15	14 22	14 27	14 28	14 34	14 38	14 42	14 50	14 53	
	d			13 58		14 04	14 17		14 16	14 23			14 35	14 39	14 43	14 51		
Cheadle Hulme	d			14 02			14 24									14 55		
Bramhall	d			14 05														
Poynton	d			14 08														
Adlington (Cheshire)	d			14 11														
Prestbury	d			14 14														
Macclesfield	a			14 18									14 47		14 55			
	d			14 18									14 49		14 56			
Congleton	d			14 26														
Handforth	d						14 28									14 59		
Manchester Airport	d		14 11															15 11
Styal	d																	
Wilmslow	d		14 21			14 11	14 31							14 46		15 02		15 21
Alderley Edge	d		14 24				14 34									15a08		15 24
Chelford	d						14 38											
Goostrey	d						14 43											
Holmes Chapel	d		14 32				14 46											15 32
Sandbach	d		14 36				14 51											15 36
Crewe 10 65	a		14 46			14 27	15 01							15 05				15 46
Kidsgrove 50	a			14 32														
Longport 50	a																	
Stoke-on-Trent 50,68	a			14 42					14 43	14 48			15 06		15 11			
Stafford 68	a								15 02				15 25					
Wolverhampton 7 68	a								15 16				15 39					
Birmingham New Street 12 68	a								15 39				15 58					
London Euston 15 ⊖65	a					16 04				16 23					16 42			

B From Liverpool Lime Street to Norwich
C To Buxton
F From Liverpool Lime Street to Scarborough
G To Bristol Temple Meads
H To Chester
I From Manchester Airport to Cleethorpes
J To Bournemouth
K To Pembroke Dock
L To Paignton
M To Milford Haven

Manchester, Stockport and Manchester Airport - Crewe and Stoke-on-Trent

Network Diagram - see first Page of Table 78

Station		NT	NT A	VT ◇1 ⌸		NT		TP ◇1 D ⍑		XC ◇1 E ⍑		VT ◇1 ⌸	NT F	TP ◇1 G ⍑	XC ◇1 H ⍑	AW R I ⍑	VT ◇1 ⌸			NT	EM ◇ K	NT	NT	NT A	VT ◇1 ⌸
Deansgate	d																								
Manchester Oxford Road	d							15 07													15 39				
Manchester Piccadilly 10	a							15 09													15 41				
	d	14 48	14 52	14 55		15 04				15 07		15 15	15 17	15 20	15 27	15 30	15 35			15 38	15 43	15 46	15 48	15 52	15 55
Levenshulme	d		14 58			15 09														15 43				15 58	
Heaton Chapel	d		15 01			15 12														15 46				16 01	
Stockport	a	14 57	15 04	15 03		15 16				15 15		15 22	15 27	15 28	15 34	15 38	15 42			15 50	15 53		15 57	16 04	16 03
	d	14 58		15 04		15 17				15 16		15 23			15 35	15 39	15 43			15 51			15 58		16 04
Cheadle Hulme	d	15 02				15 24														15 55			16 02		
Bramhall	d	15 05																					16 05		
Poynton	d	15 08																					16 08		
Adlington (Cheshire)	d	15 11																					16 11		
Prestbury	d	15 14																					16 14		
Macclesfield	a	15 18													15 47		15 55						16 18		
	d	15 18													15 49		15 56						16 18		
Congleton	d	15 26																					16 26		
Handforth	d					15 28														15 59					
Manchester Airport ✈	d																					16 11			
Styal	d																								
Wilmslow	d			15 11		15 31										15 46				16 02		16 21			16 11
Alderley Edge	d					15 34														16a08		16 24			
Chelford	d					15 38																			
Goostrey	d					15 43																			
Holmes Chapel	d					15 46																16 32			
Sandbach	d					15 51																16 36			
Crewe 10 65	a			15 27		16 01										16 05						16 46			16 27
Kidsgrove 50	a	15 32																					16 32		
Longport 50	a																								
Stoke-on-Trent 50,68	a	15 42								15 43		15 48			16 06		16 11						16 42		
Stafford 68	a									16 02					16 24										
Wolverhampton 7 68	a									16 16					16 39										
Birmingham New Street 12 68	a									16 39					16 58										
London Euston 15 ⊖65	a			17 04								17 23					17 42								18 04

Station			NT			TP ◇1 D	XC ◇1 E ⍑		VT ◇1 ⌸	NT F	TP ◇1 G ⍑	XC ◇1 H ⍑	AW R L ⍑	VT ◇1 ⌸			NT	EM ◇ K	NT	NT	NT A	VT ◇1 ⌸		NT	
Deansgate	d																								
Manchester Oxford Road	d					16 07												16 39							
Manchester Piccadilly 10	a					16 09												16 41							
	d		16 04				16 07		16 15	16 17	16 20	16 27	16 30	16 35			16 38	16 43	16 46	16 48	16 51	16 55		17 03	
Levenshulme	d		16 09														16 43				16 58			17 08	
Heaton Chapel	d		16 12														16 46				17 01			17 11	
Stockport	a		16 16				16 15		16 22	16 27	16 28	16 34	16 38	16 42			16 50	16 53		16 58	17 04	17 03		17 15	
	d		16 17				16 16		16 23			16 35	16 39	16 43			16 51			16 58		17 04		17 16	
Cheadle Hulme	d		16 24														16 55			17 02				17 24	
Bramhall	d																			17 05					
Poynton	d																			17 08					
Adlington (Cheshire)	d																			17 11					
Prestbury	d																			17 14					
Macclesfield	a											16 47		16 55						17 18					
	d											16 49		16 56						17 18					
Congleton	d																			17 26					
Handforth	d		16 28														16 59							17 28	
Manchester Airport ✈	d																		17 11						
Styal	d																		17 18						
Wilmslow	d		16 31										16 46				17 02		17 22			17 11		17 31	
Alderley Edge	d		16 34														17a08		17 25					17 34	
Chelford	d		16 38																					17 38	
Goostrey	d		16 43																					17 43	
Holmes Chapel	d		16 46																17 33					17 46	
Sandbach	d		16 51																17 37					17 51	
Crewe 10 65	a		17 01										17 05						17 47			17 27		18 01	
Kidsgrove 50	a																			17 32					
Longport 50	a																								
Stoke-on-Trent 50,68	a						16 43		16 48			17 06		17 11						17 42					
Stafford 68	a						17 02					17 25													
Wolverhampton 7 68	a						17 16					17 39													
Birmingham New Street 12 68	a						17 39					17 58													
London Euston 15 ⊖65	a								18 23					18 42								19 04			

A To Buxton
D From Liverpool Lime Street to Scarborough
E To Bristol Temple Meads
F To Chester
G From Manchester Airport to Cleethorpes
H To Bournemouth
I To Pembroke Dock
K From Liverpool Lime Street to Norwich
L To Milford Haven

Table 84

Saturdays

Manchester, Stockport and Manchester Airport - Crewe and Stoke-on-Trent

Network Diagram - see first Page of Table 78

		XC	TP	NT	VT	NT	TP	XC	AW	VT	NT	EM	NT	NT	NT	VT	XC	TP
		◇1 B	◇1 C	D	◇1	E	◇1 F	◇1 G	R B	◇1		◇ I			J	◇1	◇1 L	◇1 C
Deansgate	d																	
Manchester Oxford Road	d		17 07									17 39						18 07
Manchester Piccadilly 10	a		17 09									17 41						18 09
	d	17 06		17 09	17 15	17 17	17 20	17 27	17 30	17 35	17 38	17 43	17 46	17 48	17 52	17 55	18 05	
Levenshulme	d			17 14							17 43				17 58			
Heaton Chapel	d			17 17							17 46				18 01			
Stockport	a			17 21	17 22	17 27	17 28	17 35	17 38	17 42	17 50	17 53		17 57	18 04	18 03	18 12	
	d				17 23			17 36	17 39	17 43	17 51			17 58		18 04	18 13	
Cheadle Hulme	d										17 55			18 02				
Bramhall	d													18 05				
Poynton	d													18 08				
Adlington (Cheshire)	d													18 11				
Prestbury	d													18 14				
Macclesfield	a	17 25								17 55				18 18			18 25	
	d	17 26								17 56				18 18			18 26	
Congleton	d							17 54						18 26				
Handforth	d										17 59							
Manchester Airport	d												18 11					
Styal	d												18 18					
Wilmslow	d								17 46		18 02		18 22			18 11		
Alderley Edge	d										18a08		18 25					
Chelford	d																	
Goostrey	d																	
Holmes Chapel	d												18 33					
Sandbach	d												18 37					
Crewe 10 65	a								18 05				18 47			18 27		
Kidsgrove 50	a													18 32				
Longport 50	a																	
Stoke-on-Trent 50,68	a	17 43			17 49			18 07		18 11				18 42			18 43	
Stafford 68	a	18 03						18 26									19 02	
Wolverhampton 7 68	a	18 16						18 40									19 16	
Birmingham New Street 12 68	a	18 38						18 58									19 33	
London Euston 15 ⊖65	a				19 23					19 42						20 04		

		NT	VT	NT	TP	XC	AW	VT	NT	EM	NT	NT	NT	VT	NT	TP	XC	NT
			◇1	E	◇1 F	◇1 G	◇ M	◇1		◇ N			J	◇1		◇1 C	◇1 L	E
Deansgate	d																	
Manchester Oxford Road	d									18 39						19 07		
Manchester Piccadilly 10	a									18 41						19 09		
	d	18 08	18 15	18 17	18 20	18 27	18 30	18 35	18 38	18 43	18 46	18 48	18 52	18 55	19 04		19 07	19 17
Levenshulme	d	18 13							18 43				18 58		19 09			
Heaton Chapel	d	18 16							18 46				19 01		19 12			
Stockport	a	18 20	18 22	18 27	18 28	18 34	18 38	18 42	18 50	18 53		18 57	19 04	19 03	19 16		19 15	19 27
	d	18 22	18 23			18 35	18 39	18 43	18 51			18 58		19 04	19 17		19 16	
Cheadle Hulme	d	18 30							18 55			19 02			19 24			
Bramhall	d											19 05						
Poynton	d											19 08						
Adlington (Cheshire)	d											19 11						
Prestbury	d											19 14						
Macclesfield	a							18 55				19 18						
	d							18 56				19 18						
Congleton	d					18 54						19 26						
Handforth	d	18 34							18 59						19 28			
Manchester Airport	d										19 14							
Styal	d																	
Wilmslow	d	18 37					18 46		19 02		19 26			19 11	19 31			
Alderley Edge	d	18 40							19a08		19a32				19 34			
Chelford	d	18 44													19 38			
Goostrey	d	18 48													19 43			
Holmes Chapel	d	18 51													19 46			
Sandbach	d	18 56													19 51			
Crewe 10 65	a	19 06					19 08							19 27	20 01			
Kidsgrove 50	a											19 32						
Longport 50	a																	
Stoke-on-Trent 50,68	a		18 48			19 06		19 11				19 42					19 43	
Stafford 68	a					19 25											20 02	
Wolverhampton 7 68	a					19 39											20 16	
Birmingham New Street 12 68	a					19 58											20 33	
London Euston 15 ⊖65	a		20 24					20 59						21 18				

B To Cardiff Central
C From Liverpool Lime Street to Scarborough
D To Hazel Grove
E To Chester
F From Manchester Airport to Cleethorpes
G To Bournemouth
I From Liverpool Lime Street to Nottingham
J To Buxton
L To Bristol Temple Meads
M To Carmarthen
N From Liverpool Lime Street to Norwich

Table 84

Saturdays

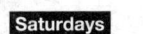

Manchester, Stockport and Manchester Airport - Crewe and Stoke-on-Trent

Network Diagram - see first Page of Table 78

		TP		NT	XC	AW	VT		EM	NT	NT	NT			NT		TP	XC	NT	TP	XC	AW		VT	
		◇1			◇1		◇1		◇								◇1	◇1		◇1	◇1			◇1	
		A		B	C	D			F			G					J		K	L		D			
Deansgate	d																								
Manchester Oxford Road	d								19 39	19 43							20 07								
Manchester Piccadilly 10	a								19 41	19 45							20 09								
	d	19 18		19 22	19 27	19 30	19 35		19 43	19 46	19 48	19 51			20 04			20 07	20 17	20 20	20 27	20 30		20 35	
Levenshulme	d			19 28								19 58			20 09										
Heaton Chapel	d			19 31								20 01			20 12										
Stockport	a	19 26		19 34	19 34	19 38	19 42		19 53		19 57	20 04			20 16			20 15	20 27	20 28	20 34	20 38		20 42	
	d				19 35	19 39	19 43				19 58				20 17			20 16			20 35	20 39		20 43	
Cheadle Hulme	d										20 02				20 24										
Bramhall	d										20 05														
Poynton	d										20 08														
Adlington (Cheshire)	d										20 11														
Prestbury	d										20 14														
Macclesfield	a				19 47		19 55				20 18										20 47			20 55	
	d				19 49		19 56				20 18										20 49			20 56	
Congleton	d										20 26														
Handforth	d														20 28										
Manchester Airport	d									20 14															
Styal	d																								
Wilmslow	d					19 46				20a24					20 31							20 46			
Alderley Edge	d														20 34										
Chelford	d														20 38										
Goostrey	d														20 43										
Holmes Chapel	d														20 46										
Sandbach	d														20 51										
Crewe 10 65	a					20 05									21 01							21 05			
Kidsgrove 50	a										20 32														
Longport 50	a																								
Stoke-on-Trent 50,68	a				20 06		20 11				20 42							20 43			21 06			21 11	
Stafford 68	a				20 25													21 02			21 26				
Wolverhampton 7 68	a				20 39													21 15			21 39				
Birmingham New Street 12 68	a				20 58													21 32			21 58				
London Euston 15 ⊖65	a						22 00																	23 02	

		EM	NT	NT	NT		NT			TP	XC	NT	TP	XC	AW		EM	NT		NT	NT	NT	NT	TP	EM
		◇								◇1	◇1		◇1	◇1			◇							◇1	◇
		F			G					J		K	A		N		F				G		K	L	F
Deansgate	d																								
Manchester Oxford Road	d	20 39	20 43							21 07							21 39	21 43							22 27
Manchester Piccadilly 10	a	20 41	20 45							21 09							21 41	21 45							22 29
	d	20 43	20 46	20 48	20 52		21 04				21 07	21 17	21 20	21 27	21 35		21 43	21 46		21 48	21 54	22 04	22 17	22 20	22 31
Levenshulme	d				20 58		21 09														22 00	22 09			
Heaton Chapel	d				21 01		21 12														22 03	22 12			
Stockport	a	20 53		20 57	21 04		21 16					21 27	21 28	21 35	21 43		21 52			21 58	22 06	22 16	22 27	22 28	22 41
	d			20 58			21 17							21 36	21 44					21 58		22 17			
Cheadle Hulme	d			21 02			21 24													22 02		22 24			
Bramhall	d			21 05																22 05					
Poynton	d			21 08																22 08					
Adlington (Cheshire)	d			21 11																22 11					
Prestbury	d			21 14																22 14					
Macclesfield	a			21 18										21 48						22 18					
	d			21 18										21 50						22 18					
Congleton	d			21 26																22 26					
Handforth	d						21 28															22 28			
Manchester Airport	d		21 14															22 14							
Styal	d																								
Wilmslow	d		21a24				21 31								21 51			22a22				22 31			
Alderley Edge	d						21 34															22 34			
Chelford	d						21 38															22 38			
Goostrey	d						21 43															22 43			
Holmes Chapel	d						21 46															22 46			
Sandbach	d						21 51															22 51			
Crewe 10 65	a						22 01								22 11							23 01			
Kidsgrove 50	a			21 32																22 32					
Longport 50	a																								
Stoke-on-Trent 50,68	a			21 42							21 43			22 07						22 42					
Stafford 68	a										22 02			22 32											
Wolverhampton 7 68	a										22 14			22 45											
Birmingham New Street 12 68	a										22 32			23 02											
London Euston 15 ⊖65	a																								

A From Manchester Airport to Cleethorpes
B To Hazel Grove
C To Southampton Central
D To Cardiff Central
F From Liverpool Lime Street to Nottingham
G To Buxton
J From Liverpool Lime Street to York
K To Chester
L From Manchester Airport to Sheffield
N To Shrewsbury

Table 84

Saturdays

Manchester, Stockport and Manchester Airport - Crewe and Stoke-on-Trent

Network Diagram - see first Page of Table 78

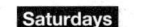

		AW	NT	NT	NT	NT	NT	TP	NT	NT
								◇■1		
		A				B		C	D	
Deansgate ⇌	d									
Manchester Oxford Road	d		22 43					23 17		
Manchester Piccadilly 10 ⇌	a		22 45					23 19		
	d	22 35	22 46	22 48	23 04	23 10	23 14		23 17	23 37
Levenshulme	d				23 09					23 42
Heaton Chapel	d				23 12					23 45
Stockport	a	22 43		22 57	23 16	23 19	23 23		23 26	23 49
	d	22 44		22 58	23 16		23 23			23 50
Cheadle Hulme	d			23 02	23 21		23 27			23 54
Bramhall	d			23 05			23 30			
Poynton	d			23 08			23 33			
Adlington (Cheshire)	d			23 11			23 37			
Prestbury	d			23 14			23 40			
Macclesfield	a			23 20			23 46			
	d									
Congleton	d									
Handforth	d				23 25					23 58
Manchester Airport ✈	d		23 14							
Styal	d									
Wilmslow	d	22 52	23a22		23 28					00 01
Alderley Edge	d				23 31					00a07
Chelford	d				23 35					
Goostrey	d				23 40					
Holmes Chapel	d				23 43					
Sandbach	d				23 48					
Crewe 10 65	a	23 10			23 58					
Kidsgrove 50	a									
Longport 50	a									
Stoke-on-Trent 50,68	a									
Stafford 68	a									
Wolverhampton 7 68 ⇌	a									
Birmingham New Street 12 68	a									
London Euston 15 ⊖65	a									

Sundays

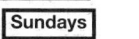

until 1 January

		NT	NT	VT	VT	XC	NT	NT	NT	TP	VT	NT	XC	AW	NT	NT	TP
				◇■1	◇■1	◇■1				◇■1	◇■1		◇■1	◇			◇■1
		E	F			G		B		I		J	G	K		B	L
				🍴	🍴	🍴					🍴		🍴	🍴			
Deansgate ⇌	d											09 15					
Manchester Oxford Road	d									09 10		09 18					10 07
Manchester Piccadilly 10 ⇌	a									09 11		09 21					10 09
	d	23p37	08 00	08 05	08 20	08 27	08 41	08 55	09 04		09 20	09 22	09 27	09 30	09 51	10 03	
Levenshulme	d	23p42						09 00	09 09						09 58	10 08	
Heaton Chapel	d	23p45						09 03	09 12						10 01	10 11	
Stockport	a	23p49	08 09	08 13	08 28	08 34		09 07	09 17		09 27	09 31	09 35	09 39	10 04	10 15	
	d	23p50		08 14	08 28	08 36			09 17		09 27		09 36	09 39		10 17	
Cheadle Hulme	d	23p54							09 21							10 23	
Bramhall	d																
Poynton	d																
Adlington (Cheshire)	d																
Prestbury	d																
Macclesfield	a				08 41						09 40		09 48				
	d				08 42						09 40		09 49				
Congleton	d																
Handforth	d	23p58							09 25							10 27	
Manchester Airport ✈	d						09 06										
Styal	d						09 10										
Wilmslow	d	00 01		08 22		08 43	09 15		09 28					09 47		10 30	
Alderley Edge	d	00a07					09a22		09 31							10a36	
Chelford	d								09 35								
Goostrey	d								09 40								
Holmes Chapel	d								09 43								
Sandbach	d								09 48								
Crewe 10 65	a			08 39		09 01			09 58					10 06			
Kidsgrove 50	a																
Longport 50	a																
Stoke-on-Trent 50,68	a				08 59						09 57		10 05				
Stafford 68	a			09 01		09 25							10 26				
Wolverhampton 7 68 ⇌	a					09 40							10 42				
Birmingham New Street 12 68	a					09 58							10 59				
London Euston 15 ⊖65	a			10 57	11 02						12 08						

A To Shrewsbury
B To Buxton
C From Liverpool Lime Street to York
D To Chester
E not 11 December
F To Sheffield
G To Bournemouth
I From Liverpool Lime Street to Hull
J From Wigan Wallgate to Chester
K To Cardiff Central
L From Liverpool Lime Street to Scarborough

Table 84

Sundays
until 1 January

Manchester, Stockport and Manchester Airport - Crewe and Stoke-on-Trent

Network Diagram - see first Page of Table 78

		VT	NT	XC	VT	NT		NT	NT		TP	VT	TP	NT	AW	XC		VT		NT	VT	NT		TP
															R									
		◇1		◇1	◇1						◇1	◇1	◇1			◇1		◇1			◇1			◇1
			A	B				C			E		F	G	H	B				C				I
		⊡		⊥	⊡							⊡			⊥	⊥		⊡			⊡			
Deansgate	d		10 16											11 11										
Manchester Oxford Road	d		10 19								11 07			11 17										12 07
Manchester Piccadilly 10	a		10 22								11 09			11 19										12 09
	d	10 20	10 22	10 27	10 35	10 41		10 53	11 04			11 15	11 18	11 22	11 24	11 27		11 35		11 52	11 55	12 04		
Levenshulme	d							10 59	11 10											11 58		12 09		
Heaton Chapel	d							11 02	11 13											12 01		12 12		
Stockport	a	10 28	10 33	10 34	10 42			11 05	11 17			11 23	11 27	11 30	11 34	11 34		11 43		12 04	12 04	12 16		
	d	10 29		10 36	10 42				11 17			11 23			11 40	11 36		11 43			12 05	12 16		
Cheadle Hulme	d								11 22													12 22		
Bramhall	d																							
Poynton	d																							
Adlington (Cheshire)	d																							
Prestbury	d																							
Macclesfield	a			10 48	10 55											11 49		11 56						
	d			10 49	10 55											11 49		11 56						
Congleton	d																							
Handforth	d								11 26													12 26		
Manchester Airport ✈	d					11 08																		
Styal	d					11 12																		
Wilmslow	d	10 36				11 16			11 29						11 47						12 12	12 29		
Alderley Edge	d					11a21			11 32													12a35		
Chelford	d								11 36															
Goostrey	d								11 41															
Holmes Chapel	d								11 44															
Sandbach	d								11 49															
Crewe 10 65	a	10 53							11 59						12 07						12 28			
Kidsgrove 50	a																							
Longport 50	a																							
Stoke-on-Trent 50,68	a			11 06	11 12							11 50				12 06		12 13						
Stafford 68	a			11 27												12 24								
Wolverhampton 7 68	a			11 41												12 40								
Birmingham New Street 12 68	a			12 00												12 58								
London Euston 15 ⊖65	a	12 56			12 59							13 28						13 47			14 09			

		VT		TP	NT	XC	VT	EM	NT	NT	VT			NT	TP	XC		VT	TP	NT	XC	AW		VT
																						R		
		◇1		◇1		◇1	◇1	◇			◇1				◇1	◇1		◇1	◇1		◇1			◇1
				K	A	B		L		C					E	M			F	G	B	H		
		⊡				⊥	⊡				⊡					⊥		⊡			⊥	⊥		⊡
Deansgate	d				12 11															13 11				
Manchester Oxford Road	d				12 17				12 43						13 07					13 17				
Manchester Piccadilly 10	a				12 19				12 45						13 09					13 19				
	d	12 15		12 18	12 22	12 26	12 35	12 44	12 47	12 52	12 55			13 04		13 07		13 15	13 20	13 22	13 27	13 30		13 35
Levenshulme	d									12 58				13 09										
Heaton Chapel	d									13 01				13 12										
Stockport	a	12 23		12 28	12 33	12 35	12 44	12 53		13 04	13 04			13 16				13 22	13 28	13 30	13 35	13 39		13 42
	d	12 23				12 35	12 44				13 05			13 17				13 22			13 36	13 40		13 42
Cheadle Hulme	d													13 21										
Bramhall	d																							
Poynton	d																							
Adlington (Cheshire)	d																							
Prestbury	d																							
Macclesfield	a					12 48	12 57														13 48			13 55
	d					12 49	12 57														13 49			13 55
Congleton	d																							
Handforth	d													13 25										
Manchester Airport ✈	d								13 12															
Styal	d								13 16															
Wilmslow	d								13 23		13 12			13 28								13 47		
Alderley Edge	d								13a29					13 31										
Chelford	d													13 35										
Goostrey	d													13 40										
Holmes Chapel	d													13 43										
Sandbach	d													13 48										
Crewe 10 65	a										13 28			13 58								14 07		
Kidsgrove 50	a																							
Longport 50	a																							
Stoke-on-Trent 50,68	a	12 50				13 06	13 14									13 42		13 49			14 06			14 12
Stafford 68	a					13 24															14 24			
Wolverhampton 7 68	a					13 40										14 13					14 40			
Birmingham New Street 12 68	a					13 58										14 31					14 58			
London Euston 15 ⊖65	a	14 27					14 47				15 09							15 27						15 47

A From Southport
B To Bournemouth
C To Buxton
E From Liverpool Lime Street to Middlesbrough
F From Manchester Airport to Cleethorpes
G From Southport to Chester
H To Cardiff Central
I From Liverpool Lime Street to Scarborough
K To Doncaster
L To Norwich
M To Paignton

Table 84

Sundays
until 1 January

Manchester, Stockport and Manchester Airport - Crewe and Stoke-on-Trent

Network Diagram - see first Page of Table 78

		EM	NT	VT	NT	TP	XC	VT	TP	NT	XC	VT	NT	NT	EM	NT	VT	NT	TP	XC
		◇		◇1		◇1	◇1	◇1	◇1		◇1	◇1			◇		◇1		◇1	◇1
		A	B			D	E		G	H	I				A	B			J	E
Deansgate	d									14 11										
Manchester Oxford Road	d	13 39				14 07				14 17					14 39				15 07	
Manchester Piccadilly 10	a	13 41				14 09				14 19					14 41				15 09	
	d	13 44	13 52	13 55	14 04		14 07	14 15	14 20	14 22	14 27	14 35	14 41	14 41	14 44	14 52	14 55	15 04		15 07
Levenshulme	d		13 58		14 09											14 58		15 09		
Heaton Chapel	d		14 01		14 12											15 01		15 12		
Stockport	a	13 53	14 04	14 03	14 16			14 22	14 28	14 33	14 34	14 42		14 49	14 53	15 04	15 03	15 16		
	d			14 04	14 17			14 22			14 36	14 42		14 51			15 04	15 17		
Cheadle Hulme	d				14 22									14 56				15 22		
Bramhall	d													14 59						
Poynton	d													15 02						
Adlington (Cheshire)	d													15 04						
Prestbury	d													15 07						
Macclesfield	a										14 48	14 55		15 11						
	d										14 49	14 55		15 11						
Congleton	d													15 19						
Handforth	d				14 26													15 26		
Manchester Airport	d												15 06							
Styal	d												15 10							
Wilmslow	d			14 11	14 29								15 14				15 11	15 29		
Alderley Edge	d				14a35								15a20					15 32		
Chelford	d																	15 36		
Goostrey	d																	15 40		
Holmes Chapel	d																	15 43		
Sandbach	d																	15 48		
Crewe 10 65	a			14 27													15 27	15 58		
Kidsgrove 50	a													15 25						
Longport 50	a																			
Stoke-on-Trent 50,68	a						14 42	14 49			15 06	15 12		15 37						15 42
Stafford 68	a										15 24									
Wolverhampton 7 68	a						15 13				15 40									16 13
Birmingham New Street 12 68	a						15 31				15 58									16 31
London Euston 15 ⊖65	a			16 09				16 27				16 47					17 09			

		VT	TP	NT	XC	AW	VT	EM	NT	VT	NT	TP	XC	VT	TP	NT	XC	AW
						R												R
		◇1	◇1		◇1		◇1	◇		◇1		◇1	◇1	◇1	◇1		◇1	
			G	L	I	M		A	B			D	E		G	H	I	M
Deansgate	d			15 11												16 11		
Manchester Oxford Road	d			15 17				15 39				16 07				16 17		
Manchester Piccadilly 10	a			15 19				15 41				16 09				16 19		
	d	15 15	15 20	15 22	15 27	15 30	15 35	15 44	15 52	15 55	16 04		16 07	16 15	16 20	16 22	16 27	16 30
Levenshulme	d								15 58		16 09							
Heaton Chapel	d								16 01		16 12							
Stockport	a	15 22	15 28	15 31	15 35	15 39	15 42	15 53	16 04	16 03	16 16			16 22	16 28	16 33	16 34	16 39
	d	15 22			15 36	15 39	15 42			16 04	16 17			16 23			16 36	16 39
Cheadle Hulme	d										16 22							
Bramhall	d																	
Poynton	d																	
Adlington (Cheshire)	d																	
Prestbury	d																	
Macclesfield	a				15 48		15 55										16 48	
	d				15 49		15 55										16 49	
Congleton	d																	
Handforth	d										16 26							
Manchester Airport	d																	
Styal	d																	
Wilmslow	d					15 47				16 11	16 29							16 47
Alderley Edge	d										16a35							
Chelford	d																	
Goostrey	d																	
Holmes Chapel	d																	
Sandbach	d																	
Crewe 10 65	a					16 06				16 27								17 06
Kidsgrove 50	a																	
Longport 50	a																	
Stoke-on-Trent 50,68	a	15 49			16 06		16 12						16 42	16 48			17 06	
Stafford 68	a				16 24												17 25	
Wolverhampton 7 68	a				16 40								17 13				17 40	
Birmingham New Street 12 68	a				16 58								17 31				17 58	
London Euston 15 ⊖65	a	17 27					17 47			18 09				18 27				

A From Liverpool Lime Street to Norwich
B To Buxton
D From Liverpool Lime Street to Scarborough
E To Bristol Temple Meads
G From Manchester Airport to Cleethorpes
H From Southport
I To Bournemouth
J From Liverpool Lime Street to Middlesbrough
L From Southport to Chester
M To Cardiff Central

Table 84

Sundays
until 1 January

Manchester, Stockport and Manchester Airport - Crewe and Stoke-on-Trent

Network Diagram - see first Page of Table 78

		VT	NT	EM	NT	VT		NT	TP	XC			VT	TP	NT	XC	AW	VT		EM		NT	VT		NT
		◇1 🍴		◇ A	B	◇1 🍴			◇1 D	◇1 E 🛒			◇1 🍴	◇1 G	H	◇1 I 🛒	R J 🛒	◇1 🍴		◇ K		B	◇1 🍴		
Deansgate 🚊	d														17 11										
Manchester Oxford Road	d			16 39					17 07						17 17					17 39					
Manchester Piccadilly 10 🚊	a			16 41					17 09						17 19					17 41					
	d	16 35	16 41	16 44	16 52	16 55		17 04		17 07			17 15	17 20	17 22	17 27	17 30	17 35		17 44		17 52	17 55		18 04
Levenshulme	d				16 58			17 09														17 58			18 09
Heaton Chapel	d				17 01			17 12														18 01			18 12
Stockport	a	16 42		16 53	17 04	17 03		17 16					17 22	17 28	17 30	17 34	17 39	17 42		17 53		18 04	18 03		18 16
	d	16 42				17 04		17 17					17 22			17 36	17 39	17 42					18 04		18 17
Cheadle Hulme	d							17 22																	18 22
Bramhall	d																								
Poynton	d																								
Adlington (Cheshire)	d																								
Prestbury	d																								
Macclesfield	a	16 55														17 48		17 55							
	d	16 55														17 49		17 55							
Congleton	d																								
Handforth	d							17 26																	18 26
Manchester Airport ✈	d		17 06																						
Styal	d		17 10																						
Wilmslow	d		17 15			17 11		17 29									17 47						18 11		18 29
Alderley Edge	d		17a21					17 32																	18a35
Chelford	d							17 36																	
Goostrey	d							17 40																	
Holmes Chapel	d							17 43																	
Sandbach	d							17 48																	
Crewe 10 65	a					17 27		17 58									18 07						18 27		
Kidsgrove 50	a																								
Longport 50	a																								
Stoke-on-Trent 50,68	a	17 12								17 42			17 49			18 06		18 12							
Stafford 68	a															18 25									
Wolverhampton 7 68 🚊	a									18 13						18 40									
Birmingham New Street 12 68	a									18 31						18 58									
London Euston 15 ⊖65	a	18 47				19 09							19 27					19 47					20 09		

		TP	XC		VT	TP		NT	XC	AW	VT	NT	NT	EM	NT	VT			NT	TP	XC		VT	TP	NT
		◇1 L	◇1 M 🛒		◇1 🍴	◇1 G		N	◇1 O 🛒	R J 🛒	◇1 🍴			◇ A	B	◇1 🍴				◇1 L	◇1 M 🛒		◇1 🍴	◇1 G	H
Deansgate 🚊	d							18 11																	19 11
Manchester Oxford Road	d	18 07						18 17						18 39						19 07					19 17
Manchester Piccadilly 10 🚊	a	18 09						18 19						18 41						19 09					19 19
	d		18 07		18 15	18 20		18 22	18 27	18 30	18 35	18 41	18 42	18 44	18 52	18 55			19 04		19 07		19 15	19 20	19 22
Levenshulme	d														18 58				19 09						
Heaton Chapel	d														19 01				19 12						
Stockport	a				18 22	18 28		18 33	18 34	18 39	18 42		18 50	18 53	19 04	19 03			19 16				19 22	19 28	19 30
	d				18 22				18 36	18 39	18 42		18 52			19 04			19 17				19 22		
Cheadle Hulme	d												18 57						19 22						
Bramhall	d												19 00												
Poynton	d												19 03												
Adlington (Cheshire)	d												19 06												
Prestbury	d												19 09												
Macclesfield	a								18 48		18 55		19 13												
	d								18 49		18 55		19 13												
Congleton	d												19 21												
Handforth	d																		19 26						
Manchester Airport ✈	d											19 06													
Styal	d											19 10													
Wilmslow	d									18 47		19 15				19 11			19 29						
Alderley Edge	d											19a21							19 32						
Chelford	d																		19 36						
Goostrey	d																		19 40						
Holmes Chapel	d																		19 43						
Sandbach	d																		19 48						
Crewe 10 65	a									19 06						19 27			19 58						
Kidsgrove 50	a												19 28												
Longport 50	a																								
Stoke-on-Trent 50,68	a		18 42		18 49				19 06		19 12		19 40								19 42		19 49		
Stafford 68	a								19 24																
Wolverhampton 7 68 🚊	a		19 13						19 40												20 13				
Birmingham New Street 12 68	a		19 31						19 58												20 31				
London Euston 15 ⊖65	a				20 27						20 47					21 09							21 31		

A From Liverpool Lime Street to Norwich
B To Buxton
D From Liverpool Lime Street to Middlesbrough
E To Plymouth
G From Manchester Airport to Cleethorpes
H From Southport to Chester
I To Bournemouth
J To Cardiff Central
K From Liverpool Lime Street to Nottingham
L From Liverpool Lime Street to Scarborough
M To Bristol Temple Meads
N From Southport
O To Southampton Central

Table 84

Sundays
until 1 January

Manchester, Stockport and Manchester Airport - Crewe and Stoke-on-Trent

Network Diagram - see first Page of Table 78

		XC ◇1 A		AW ◇ B	VT ◇1		EM ◇ C	NT D		NT	TP ◇1 F	XC ◇1 G			TP ◇1 I	VT ◇1	NT J	AW ◇ B	NT	EM ◇ C	NT D	VT ◇1			NT
Deansgate	d																20 11								
Manchester Oxford Road	d						19 39				20 07						20 17			20 39					
Manchester Piccadilly 10	a						19 41				20 09						20 19			20 41					
	d	19 27		19 30	19 35		19 44	19 52		20 04		20 07			20 18	20 20	20 22	20 30	20 41	20 44	20 52	20 55			21 04
Levenshulme	d							19 58		20 09											20 58				21 09
Heaton Chapel	d							20 01		20 12											21 01				21 12
Stockport	a	19 34		19 39	19 41		19 53	20 04		20 16		20 15			20 26	20 27	20 33	20 38		20 53	21 04	21 03			21 16
	d	19 36		19 39	19 41					20 17		20 16				20 27		20 39				21 03			21 17
Cheadle Hulme	d									20 22															21 22
Bramhall	d																								
Poynton	d																								
Adlington (Cheshire)	d																								
Prestbury	d																								
Macclesfield	a	19 48			19 54							20 28				20 40						21 15			
	d	19 49			19 54							20 29				20 40						21 15			
Congleton	d																								
Handforth	d									20 26															21 26
Manchester Airport	d																		21 06						
Styal	d																		21 10						
Wilmslow	d			19 47						20 29								20 47	21 14						21 29
Alderley Edge	d									20a37									21a20						21 32
Chelford	d																								21 36
Goostrey	d																								21 40
Holmes Chapel	d																								21 43
Sandbach	d																								21 48
Crewe 10 65	a			20 07														21 07							21 58
Kidsgrove 50	a																								
Longport 50	a																								
Stoke-on-Trent 50,68	a	20 06			20 11							20 46				20 57						21 32			
Stafford 68	a	20 26										21 08													
Wolverhampton 7 68	a	20 39										21 21													
Birmingham New Street 12 68	a	20 58										21 39													
London Euston 15 ⊖65	a				21 58											22 56						23 49			

		TP ◇1 K	XC ◇1		TP ◇1 L	NT M	AW			NT	NT D		NT	XC ◇1	EM ◇ C		TP ◇1 L	NT J		AW	TP ◇1 F			NT D	NT
Deansgate	d					21 11												22 11							
Manchester Oxford Road	d	21 07				21 17									22 07			22 17			22 37				
Manchester Piccadilly 10	a	21 09				21 19									22 09			22 19			22 39				
	d		21 07		21 20	21 22	21 34			21 41	21 52		22 04	22 07	22 11		22 15	22 22		22 35				22 52	23 04
Levenshulme	d										21 58		22 09											22 58	23 09
Heaton Chapel	d										22 01		22 12											23 01	23 12
Stockport	a		21 15		21 28	21 30				21 49	22 04		22 16	22 15	22 20		22 23	22 33						23 04	23 16
	d		21 16							21 52			22 17	22 16											23 17
Cheadle Hulme	d									21 56			22 22												23 21
Bramhall	d									21 59															
Poynton	d									22 02															
Adlington (Cheshire)	d									22 05															
Prestbury	d									22 08															
Macclesfield	a		21 28							22 12				22 28											
	d		21 29							22 13				22 29											
Congleton	d									22 20															
Handforth	d												22 26												23 25
Manchester Airport	d																								
Styal	d																								
Wilmslow	d						21 50						22 29							22 50					23 28
Alderley Edge	d												22a35												23a35
Chelford	d																								
Goostrey	d																								
Holmes Chapel	d																								
Sandbach	d																								
Crewe 10 65	a						22 13													23 10					
Kidsgrove 50	a									22 26															
Longport 50	a																								
Stoke-on-Trent 50,68	a		21 46							22 36				22 46											
Stafford 68	a		22 06											23 04											
Wolverhampton 7 68	a		22 20											23 18											
Birmingham New Street 12 68	a		22 39											23 36											
London Euston 15 ⊖65	a																								

A To Reading
B To Cardiff Central
C From Liverpool Lime Street to Nottingham
D To Buxton
F From Liverpool Lime Street to York
G To Bristol Temple Meads
I From Manchester Airport to Cleethorpes
J From Southport
K From Liverpool Lime Street to Newcastle
L From Manchester Airport to Sheffield
M From Southport to Chester

Table 84

Sundays
until 1 January

Manchester, Stockport and Manchester Airport - Crewe and Stoke-on-Trent

Network Diagram - see first Page of Table 78

		TP	NT
		◇1	
		A	B
Deansgate	d		23 11
Manchester Oxford Road	d		23 17
Manchester Piccadilly 10	a		23 19
	d	23 20	23 22
Levenshulme	d		
Heaton Chapel	d		
Stockport	a	23 28	23 33
	d		
Cheadle Hulme	d		
Bramhall	d		
Poynton	d		
Adlington (Cheshire)	d		
Prestbury	d		
Macclesfield	a		
	d		
Congleton	d		
Handforth	d		
Manchester Airport	d		
Styal	d		
Wilmslow	d		
Alderley Edge	d		
Chelford	d		
Goostrey	d		
Holmes Chapel	d		
Sandbach	d		
Crewe 10 65	a		
Kidsgrove 50	a		
Longport 50	a		
Stoke-on-Trent 50,68	a		
Stafford 68	a		
Wolverhampton 7 68	a		
Birmingham New Street 12 68	a		
London Euston 15 ⊖65	a		

Sundays
8 January to 12 February

		NT	NT	NT	VT	NT	VT	XC	NT			NT	NT		TP	VT	NT	XC	AW			NT	NT		TP
					◇1		◇1	◇1							◇1	◇1		◇1	◇						◇1
				D				E				G			H		I	E	J			G			K
Deansgate	d																09 15								
Manchester Oxford Road	d														09 10		09 18								10 07
Manchester Piccadilly 10	a														09 11		09 21								10 09
	d	23p37	07 25	08 00	08 05	08 10	08 20	08 27	08 41			08 55	09 04			09 20	09 22	09 27	09 30			09 51	10 03		
Levenshulme	d	23p42										09 00	09 09									09 58	10 08		
Heaton Chapel	d	23p45										09 03	09 12									10 01	10 11		
Stockport	a	23p49		08 09	08 13		08 28	08 34				09 07	09 17			09 27	09 31	09 34	09 39			10 04	10 15		
	d	23p50			08 14		08 28	08 36					09 17			09 27		09 36	09 39				10 17		
Cheadle Hulme	d	23p54											09 21										10 23		
Bramhall	d																								
Poynton	d																								
Adlington (Cheshire)	d																								
Prestbury	d																								
Macclesfield	a						08 41									09 40									
	d						08 42									09 40									
Congleton	d																								
Handforth	d	23p58											09 25										10 27		
Manchester Airport	d		08a05			08a35			09 06																
Styal	d								09 10																
Wilmslow	d	00 01			08 22			08 43	09 15				09 28					09 43	09 47				10 30		
Alderley Edge	d	00a07							09a22				09 31										10a36		
Chelford	d												09 35												
Goostrey	d												09 40												
Holmes Chapel	d												09 43												
Sandbach	d												09 48												
Crewe 10 65	a				08 39			09 01					09 58					10 01	10 06						
Kidsgrove 50	a																								
Longport 50	a																								
Stoke-on-Trent 50,68	a						08 59									09 57									
Stafford 68	a				09 01			09 25										10 26							
Wolverhampton 7 68	a							09 40										10 42							
Birmingham New Street 12 68	a							09 58										10 59							
London Euston 15 ⊖65	a				10 57		11 02									12 08									

A From Manchester Airport to Sheffield
B From Southport
D To Sheffield
E To Leamington Spa
G To Buxton
H From Liverpool Lime Street to Hull
I From Wigan Wallgate to Chester
J To Cardiff Central
K From Liverpool Lime Street to Scarborough

Table 84

Sundays

8 January to 12 February

Manchester, Stockport and Manchester Airport - Crewe and Stoke-on-Trent

Network Diagram - see first Page of Table 78

		VT	NT	XC	VT	NT	NT	NT	TP	VT	TP	NT	AW	XC	VT	NT	VT	NT	TP
		◇1	A	◇1 B	◇1		C		◇1 E	◇1	◇1 F	G	H	◇1 B	◇1	C	◇1		◇1 I
Deansgate	d		10 16									11 11							
Manchester Oxford Road	d		10 19						11 07			11 17							12 07
Manchester Piccadilly	a		10 22						11 09			11 19							12 09
	d	10 20	10 22	10 27	10 35	10 41	10 53	11 04		11 15	11 18	11 22	11 24	11 27	11 35	11 52	11 55	12 04	
Levenshulme	d						10 59	11 10								11 58		12 09	
Heaton Chapel	d						11 02	11 13								12 01		12 12	
Stockport	a	10 28	10 33	10 34	10 42		11 05	11 17		11 23	11 27	11 30	11 34	11 34	11 43	12 04	12 04	12 16	
	d	10 29		10 36	10 42			11 17		11 23			11 40	11 36	11 43		12 05	12 16	
Cheadle Hulme	d							11 22										12 22	
Bramhall	d																		
Poynton	d																		
Adlington (Cheshire)	d																		
Prestbury	d																		
Macclesfield	a			10 48	10 55									11 49	11 56				
	d			10 49	10 55									11 49	11 56				
Congleton	d																		
Handforth	d							11 26										12 26	
Manchester Airport	d					11 08													
Styal	d					11 12													
Wilmslow	d	10 36				11 16		11 29					11 47				12 12	12 29	
Alderley Edge	d					11a21		11 32										12a35	
Chelford	d							11 36											
Goostrey	d							11 41											
Holmes Chapel	d							11 44											
Sandbach	d							11 49											
Crewe 65	a	10 53						11 59					12 07				12 28		
Kidsgrove 50	a																		
Longport 50	a																		
Stoke-on-Trent 50,68	a			11 06	11 12					11 50				12 06	12 13				
Stafford 68	a			11 27										12 24					
Wolverhampton 68	a			11 41										12 40					
Birmingham New Street 68	a			12 00										12 58					
London Euston ⊖65	a	12 56			12 59					13 28					13 47		14 09		

		VT	TP	NT	XC	VT	EM	NT	NT	VT	NT	TP	XC	VT	TP	NT	XC	AW	VT
		◇1	◇1 K	A	◇1 L	◇1	◇ M		C	◇1		◇1 E	◇1 N	◇1	◇1 F	G	◇1 L	H	◇1
Deansgate	d			12 11												13 11			
Manchester Oxford Road	d			12 17				12 43				13 07				13 17			
Manchester Piccadilly	a			12 19				12 45				13 09				13 19			
	d	12 15	12 19	12 22	12 26	12 35	12 44	12 47	12 52	12 55	13 04		13 07	13 15	13 20	13 22	13 27	13 30	13 35
Levenshulme	d								12 58		13 09								
Heaton Chapel	d								13 01		13 12								
Stockport	a	12 23	12 28	12 33	12 35	12 44	12 53		13 04	13 04	13 16			13 22	13 28	13 30	13 35	13 39	13 42
	d	12 23			12 35	12 44				13 05	13 17			13 22			13 36	13 40	13 42
Cheadle Hulme	d										13 21								
Bramhall	d																		
Poynton	d																		
Adlington (Cheshire)	d																		
Prestbury	d																		
Macclesfield	a				12 48	12 57											13 48		13 55
	d				12 49	12 57											13 49		13 55
Congleton	d																		
Handforth	d										13 25								
Manchester Airport	d							13 12											
Styal	d							13 16											
Wilmslow	d							13 23		13 12	13 28							13 47	
Alderley Edge	d							13a29			13 31								
Chelford	d										13 35								
Goostrey	d										13 40								
Holmes Chapel	d										13 43								
Sandbach	d										13 48								
Crewe 65	a									13 28	13 58							14 07	
Kidsgrove 50	a																		
Longport 50	a																		
Stoke-on-Trent 50,68	a	12 50			13 06	13 14							13 42	13 49			14 06		14 12
Stafford 68	a				13 24												14 24		
Wolverhampton 68	a				13 40								14 13				14 40		
Birmingham New Street 68	a				13 58								14 31				14 58		
London Euston ⊖65	a	14 27				14 47				15 09				15 27					15 47

A From Southport
B To Leamington Spa
C To Buxton
E From Liverpool Lime Street to Middlesbrough
F From Manchester Airport to Sheffield
G From Southport to Chester
H To Cardiff Central
I From Liverpool Lime Street to Scarborough
K To Sheffield
L To Bournemouth
M To Norwich
N To Paignton

Table 84

Sundays

8 January to 12 February

Manchester, Stockport and Manchester Airport - Crewe and Stoke-on-Trent

Network Diagram - see first Page of Table 78

	EM	NT	VT	NT	TP	XC	VT	TP	NT	XC	VT	NT	NT	EM	NT	VT	NT	TP	XC
	◇		◇1		◇1	◇1	◇1	◇1		◇1	◇1			◇		◇1		◇1	◇1
	A	B			D	E		G	H	I				A	B			J	E
Deansgate d									14 11										
Manchester Oxford Road d	13 39				14 07				14 17					14 39				15 07	
Manchester Piccadilly 10 a	13 41				14 09				14 19					14 41				15 09	
d	13 44	13 52	13 55	14 04		14 07	14 15	14 20	14 22	14 27	14 35	14 41	14 41	14 44	14 52	14 55	15 04		15 07
Levenshulme d		13 58		14 09											14 58		15 09		
Heaton Chapel d		14 01		14 12											15 01		15 12		
Stockport a	13 53	14 04	14 03	14 16			14 22	14 28	14 33	14 34	14 42		14 49	14 53	15 04	15 03	15 16		
d			14 04	14 17			14 22			14 36	14 42		14 51			15 04	15 17		
Cheadle Hulme d				14 22									14 56				15 22		
Bramhall d													14 59						
Poynton d													15 02						
Adlington (Cheshire) d													15 04						
Prestbury d													15 07						
Macclesfield a										14 48	14 55		15 11						
d										14 49	14 55		15 11						
Congleton d													15 19						
Handforth d				14 26													15 26		
Manchester Airport d												15 06							
Styal d												15 10							
Wilmslow d			14 11	14 29								15 14				15 11	15 29		
Alderley Edge d				14a35								15a20					15 32		
Chelford d																	15 36		
Goostrey d																	15 40		
Holmes Chapel d																	15 43		
Sandbach d																	15 48		
Crewe 10 65 a			14 27													15 27	15 58		
Kidsgrove 50 a													15 25						
Longport 50 a																			
Stoke-on-Trent 50,68 a						14 42	14 49			15 06	15 12		15 37						15 42
Stafford 68 a										15 24									
Wolverhampton 7 68 a						15 13				15 40									16 13
Birmingham New Street 12 68 a						15 31				15 58									16 31
London Euston 15 ⊖65 a			16 09				16 27				16 47					17 09			

	VT	TP	NT	XC	AW	VT	EM	NT	VT	NT	TP	XC	VT	TP	NT	XC	VT
	◇1	◇1		◇1	R	◇1	◇		◇1		◇1	◇1	◇1	◇1		◇1	◇1
		G	K	I	L		A	B			D	E		G	H	I	
Deansgate d			15 11												16 11		
Manchester Oxford Road d			15 17				15 39				16 07				16 17		
Manchester Piccadilly 10 a			15 19				15 41				16 09				16 19		
d	15 15	15 20	15 22	15 27	15 30	15 35	15 44	15 52	15 55	16 04		16 07	16 15	16 20	16 22	16 27	16 35
Levenshulme d								15 58		16 09							
Heaton Chapel d								16 01		16 12							
Stockport a	15 22	15 28	15 31	15 35	15 39	15 42	15 53	16 04	16 03	16 16			16 22	16 28	16 33	16 34	16 42
d	15 22			15 36	15 39	15 42			16 04	16 17			16 23			16 36	16 42
Cheadle Hulme d										16 22							
Bramhall d																	
Poynton d																	
Adlington (Cheshire) d																	
Prestbury d																	
Macclesfield a				15 48		15 55										16 48	16 55
d				15 49		15 55										16 49	16 55
Congleton d																	
Handforth d										16 26							
Manchester Airport d																	
Styal d																	
Wilmslow d					15 47				16 11	16 29							
Alderley Edge d										16a35							
Chelford d																	
Goostrey d																	
Holmes Chapel d																	
Sandbach d																	
Crewe 10 65 a					16 06				16 27								
Kidsgrove 50 a																	
Longport 50 a																	
Stoke-on-Trent 50,68 a	15 49			16 06		16 12						16 42	16 48			17 06	17 12
Stafford 68 a				16 24												17 25	
Wolverhampton 7 68 a				16 40								17 13				17 40	
Birmingham New Street 12 68 a				16 58								17 31				17 58	
London Euston 15 ⊖65 a	17 27					17 47			18 09				18 27				18 47

A From Liverpool Lime Street to Norwich
B To Buxton
D From Liverpool Lime Street to Scarborough
E To Bristol Temple Meads
G From Manchester Airport to Sheffield
H From Southport
I To Bournemouth
J From Liverpool Lime Street to Middlesbrough
K From Southport to Chester
L To Cardiff Central

Table 84

Sundays

8 January to 12 February

Manchester, Stockport and Manchester Airport - Crewe and Stoke-on-Trent

Network Diagram - see first Page of Table 78

	NT	EM	NT	VT	NT	TP	XC	VT	TP	NT	XC	AW	VT	EM	NT	VT	NT	TP
												R						
		◇		◇1		◇1	◇1	◇1	◇1		◇1		◇1	◇		◇1		◇1
		A	B			D	E		G	H	I	J		K	B			L
				☕			🛒	☕			🛒	🛒	☕			☕		
Deansgate d										17 11								
Manchester Oxford Road d		16 39				17 07				17 17				17 39				18 07
Manchester Piccadilly [10] a		16 41				17 09				17 19				17 41				18 09
d	16 41	16 44	16 52	16 55	17 04		17 07	17 15	17 20	17 22	17 27	17 30	17 35	17 44	17 52	17 55	18 04	
Levenshulme d			16 58		17 09										17 58		18 09	
Heaton Chapel d			17 01		17 12										18 01		18 12	
Stockport a		16 53	17 04	17 03	17 16			17 22	17 28	17 30	17 34	17 39	17 42	17 53	18 04	18 03	18 16	
d				17 04	17 17			17 22			17 36	17 39	17 42			18 04	18 17	
Cheadle Hulme d					17 22												18 22	
Bramhall d																		
Poynton d																		
Adlington (Cheshire) d																		
Prestbury d																		
Macclesfield a											17 48		17 55					
d											17 49		17 55					
Congleton d																		
Handforth d					17 26												18 26	
Manchester Airport ✈ d	17 06																	
Styal d	17 10																	
Wilmslow d	17 15			17 11	17 29							17 47				18 11	18 29	
Alderley Edge d	17a21				17 32												18a35	
Chelford d					17 36													
Goostrey d					17 40													
Holmes Chapel d					17 43													
Sandbach d					17 48													
Crewe [10] 65 a				17 27	17 58							18 07				18 27		
Kidsgrove 50 a																		
Longport 50 a																		
Stoke-on-Trent 50,68 a							17 42	17 49			18 06		18 12					
Stafford 68 a											18 25							
Wolverhampton [7] 68 a							18 13				18 40							
Birmingham New Street [12] 68 a							18 31				18 58							
London Euston [15] ⊖65 a				19 09				19 27					19 47			20 09		

	XC	VT	TP	NT	XC	AW	VT	NT	NT	EM	NT	VT	NT	TP	XC	VT	TP	NT	XC
						R													
	◇1	◇1	◇1		◇1		◇1			◇		◇1		◇1	◇1	◇1	◇1		◇1
	M		G	N	O	J				A	B			L	M		G	H	P
	🛒	☕			🛒	🛒	☕					☕			🛒	☕			🛒
Deansgate d				18 11														19 11	
Manchester Oxford Road d				18 17						18 39				19 07				19 17	
Manchester Piccadilly [10] a				18 19						18 41				19 09				19 19	
d	18 07	18 15	18 20	18 22	18 27	18 30	18 35	18 41	18 42	18 44	18 52	18 55	19 04		19 07	19 15	19 20	19 22	19 27
Levenshulme d											18 58		19 09						
Heaton Chapel d											19 01		19 12						
Stockport a		18 22	18 28	18 33	18 34	18 39	18 42		18 50	18 53	19 04	19 03	19 16			19 22	19 28	19 30	19 34
d		18 22			18 36	18 39	18 42		18 52			19 04	19 17			19 22			19 36
Cheadle Hulme d									18 57				19 22						
Bramhall d									19 00										
Poynton d									19 03										
Adlington (Cheshire) d									19 06										
Prestbury d									19 09										
Macclesfield a					18 48		18 55		19 13										19 48
d					18 49		18 55		19 13										19 49
Congleton d									19 21										
Handforth d													19 26						
Manchester Airport ✈ d								19 06											
Styal d								19 10											
Wilmslow d						18 47		19 15				19 11	19 29						
Alderley Edge d								19a21					19 32						
Chelford d													19 36						
Goostrey d													19 40						
Holmes Chapel d													19 43						
Sandbach d													19 48						
Crewe [10] 65 a						19 06						19 27	19 58						
Kidsgrove 50 a									19 28										
Longport 50 a																			
Stoke-on-Trent 50,68 a	18 42	18 49			19 06		19 12		19 40						19 42	19 49			20 06
Stafford 68 a					19 24														20 26
Wolverhampton [7] 68 a	19 13				19 40										20 13				20 39
Birmingham New Street [12] 68 a	19 31				19 58										20 31				20 58
London Euston [15] ⊖65 a		20 27					20 47					21 09				21 31			

A From Liverpool Lime Street to Norwich
B To Buxton
D From Liverpool Lime Street to Middlesbrough
E To Plymouth
G From Manchester Airport to Sheffield
H From Southport to Chester
I To Bournemouth
J To Cardiff Central
K From Liverpool Lime Street to Nottingham
L From Liverpool Lime Street to Scarborough
M To Bristol Temple Meads
N From Southport
O To Southampton Central
P To Reading

Table 84

Sundays

8 January to 12 February

Manchester, Stockport and Manchester Airport - Crewe and Stoke-on-Trent

Network Diagram - see first Page of Table 78

		AW	VT	EM	NT	NT	TP	XC	TP	VT	NT	AW	NT	EM	NT	VT	NT	TP
		◇	◇1	◇			◇1	◇1	◇1	◇1		◇		◇		◇1		◇1
		A		B	C		E	F	H		I	A		B	C			J
			🍴							🍴						🍴		
Deansgate 🚊	d										20 11							
Manchester Oxford Road	d			19 39			20 07				20 17			20 39				21 07
Manchester Piccadilly 10 🚊	a			19 41			20 09				20 19			20 41				21 09
	d	19 30	19 35	19 44	19 52	20 04		20 07	20 18	20 20	20 22	20 30	20 41	20 44	20 52	20 55	21 04	
Levenshulme	d				19 58	20 09									20 58		21 09	
Heaton Chapel	d				20 01	20 12									21 01		21 12	
Stockport	a	19 39	19 41	19 53	20 04	20 16		20 15	20 26	20 27	20 33	20 38		20 53	21 04	21 03	21 16	
	d	19 39	19 41			20 17		20 16		20 27		20 39				21 03	21 17	
Cheadle Hulme	d					20 22											21 22	
Bramhall	d																	
Poynton	d																	
Adlington (Cheshire)	d																	
Prestbury	d																	
Macclesfield	a		19 54					20 28		20 40						21 15		
	d		19 54					20 29		20 40						21 15		
Congleton	d																	
Handforth	d					20 26											21 26	
Manchester Airport ✈	d												21 06					
Styal	d												21 10					
Wilmslow	d	19 47				20 29						20 47	21 14				21 29	
Alderley Edge	d					20a37							21a20				21 32	
Chelford	d																21 36	
Goostrey	d																21 40	
Holmes Chapel	d																21 43	
Sandbach	d																21 48	
Crewe 10 65	a	20 07										21 07					21 58	
Kidsgrove 50	a																	
Longport 50	a																	
Stoke-on-Trent 50,68	a		20 11					20 46		20 57						21 32		
Stafford 68	a							21 08										
Wolverhampton 7 68 🚊	a							21 21										
Birmingham New Street 12 68	a							21 39										
London Euston 15 ⊖65	a		21 58							22 56						23 49		

		XC	TP	NT	AW	NT	NT	NT	XC	EM	TP	NT	AW	TP	NT	NT	TP
		◇1	◇1						◇1	◇	◇1			◇1			◇1
			H	K			C			B	H	I		E	C		H
Deansgate 🚊	d			21 11								22 11					
Manchester Oxford Road	d			21 17						22 07		22 17		22 37			
Manchester Piccadilly 10 🚊	a			21 19						22 09		22 19		22 39			
	d	21 07	21 20	21 22	21 34	21 41	21 52	22 04	22 07	22 11	22 15	22 22	22 35		22 52	23 04	23 20
Levenshulme	d						21 58	22 09							22 58	23 09	
Heaton Chapel	d						22 01	22 12							23 01	23 12	
Stockport	a	21 15	21 28	21 30		21 49	22 04	22 16	22 15	22 20	22 23	22 33			23 04	23 16	23 28
	d	21 16				21 52		22 17	22 16							23 17	
Cheadle Hulme	d					21 56		22 22								23 21	
Bramhall	d					21 59											
Poynton	d					22 02											
Adlington (Cheshire)	d					22 05											
Prestbury	d					22 08											
Macclesfield	a	21 28				22 12			22 28								
	d	21 29				22 13			22 29								
Congleton	d					22 20											
Handforth	d							22 26								23 25	
Manchester Airport ✈	d																
Styal	d																
Wilmslow	d				21 50			22 29					22 50			23 28	
Alderley Edge	d							22a35								23a35	
Chelford	d																
Goostrey	d																
Holmes Chapel	d																
Sandbach	d																
Crewe 10 65	a				22 13								23 10				
Kidsgrove 50	a					22 26											
Longport 50	a																
Stoke-on-Trent 50,68	a	21 46				22 36			22 46								
Stafford 68	a	22 06							23 04								
Wolverhampton 7 68 🚊	a	22 20							23 18								
Birmingham New Street 12 68	a	22 39							23 36								
London Euston 15 ⊖65	a																

- **A** To Cardiff Central
- **B** From Liverpool Lime Street to Nottingham
- **C** To Buxton
- **E** From Liverpool Lime Street to York
- **F** To Bristol Temple Meads
- **H** From Manchester Airport to Sheffield
- **I** From Southport
- **J** From Liverpool Lime Street to Newcastle
- **K** From Southport to Chester

Table 84

Manchester, Stockport and Manchester Airport - Crewe and Stoke-on-Trent

Sundays

8 January to 12 February

Network Diagram - see first Page of Table 78

		NT
		A
Deansgate	d	23 11
Manchester Oxford Road	d	23 17
Manchester Piccadilly 10	a	23 19
	d	23 22
Levenshulme	d	
Heaton Chapel	d	
Stockport	a	23 33
	d	
Cheadle Hulme	d	
Bramhall	d	
Poynton	d	
Adlington (Cheshire)	d	
Prestbury	d	
Macclesfield	a	
	d	
Congleton	d	
Handforth	d	
Manchester Airport	d	
Styal	d	
Wilmslow	d	
Alderley Edge	d	
Chelford	d	
Goostrey	d	
Holmes Chapel	d	
Sandbach	d	
Crewe 10 65	a	
Kidsgrove 50	a	
Longport 50	a	
Stoke-on-Trent 50,68	a	
Stafford 68	a	
Wolverhampton 7 68	a	
Birmingham New Street 12 68	a	
London Euston 15 ⊖65	a	

Sundays

19 February to 25 March

		NT	NT	VT	VT	XC	NT	NT	NT	TP	VT	NT	XC	AW	NT	NT	TP	VT
				◇1	◇1	◇1				◇1	◇1		◇1	◇			◇1	◇1
			C			D		E		F		G	D	H	E		I	
Deansgate	d											09 15						
Manchester Oxford Road	d									09 10		09 18					10 07	
Manchester Piccadilly 10	a									09 11		09 21					10 09	
	d	23p37	08 00	08 05	08 20	08 27	08 41	08 55	09 04		09 20	09 22	09 27	09 30	09 47	10 03		10 20
Levenshulme	d	23p42						09 00	09 09						09 54	10 08		
Heaton Chapel	d	23p45						09 03	09 12						09 57	10 11		
Stockport	a	23p49	08 09	08 13	08 28	08 34		09 07	09 17		09 27	09 31	09 34	09 39	10 00	10 15		10 28
	d	23p50		08 14	08 28	08 36			09 17		09 27		09 36	09 39		10 17		10 29
Cheadle Hulme	d	23p54							09 21							10 23		
Bramhall	d																	
Poynton	d																	
Adlington (Cheshire)	d																	
Prestbury	d																	
Macclesfield	a				08 41						09 40							
	d				08 42						09 40							
Congleton	d																	
Handforth	d	23p58							09 25							10 27		
Manchester Airport	d						09 06											
Styal	d						09 10											
Wilmslow	d	00 01		08 22		08 43	09 15		09 28				09 43	09 47		10 30		10 36
Alderley Edge	d	00a07					09a22		09 31							10a36		
Chelford	d								09 35									
Goostrey	d								09 40									
Holmes Chapel	d								09 43									
Sandbach	d								09 48									
Crewe 10 65	a			08 39		09 01			09 58				10 01	10 06				10 53
Kidsgrove 50	a																	
Longport 50	a																	
Stoke-on-Trent 50,68	a				08 59						09 57							
Stafford 68	a			09 01		09 25							10 26					
Wolverhampton 7 68	a					09 40							10 42					
Birmingham New Street 12 68	a					09 58							10 59					
London Euston 15 ⊖65	a			10 57	11 02						12 08							12 56

A From Southport
C To Sheffield
D To Leamington Spa
E To Buxton
F From Liverpool Lime Street to Hull
G From Wigan Wallgate to Chester
H To Cardiff Central
I From Liverpool Lime Street to Scarborough

Table 84

Sundays

19 February to 25 March

Manchester, Stockport and Manchester Airport - Crewe and Stoke-on-Trent

Network Diagram - see first Page of Table 78

		NT	XC	VT	NT	NT			NT	TP	VT	TP	NT	AW	XC	VT			NT	VT		NT	TP		VT
			◇1	◇1						◇1	◇1	◇1		R	◇1	◇1				◇1			◇1		◇1
		A	B			C				E		F	G	H	B				C				I		
Deansgate	d	10 16											11 11												
Manchester Oxford Road	d	10 19								11 07			11 17										12 07		
Manchester Piccadilly 10	a	10 22								11 09			11 19										12 09		
	d	10 22	10 27	10 35	10 41	10 53			11 04		11 15	11 18	11 22	11 24	11 27	11 35			11 52	11 55		12 04			12 15
Levenshulme	d					10 59			11 10										11 58			12 09			
Heaton Chapel	d					11 02			11 13										12 01			12 12			
Stockport	a	10 33	10 34	10 42		11 05			11 17		11 23	11 27	11 30	11 34	11 34	11 43			12 04	12 04		12 16			12 23
	d		10 36	10 42					11 17		11 23			11 40	11 36	11 43				12 05		12 16			12 23
Cheadle Hulme	d								11 22													12 22			
Bramhall	d																								
Poynton	d																								
Adlington (Cheshire)	d																								
Prestbury	d																								
Macclesfield	a		10 48	10 55											11 49	11 56									
	d		10 49	10 55											11 49	11 56									
Congleton	d																								
Handforth	d								11 26													12 26			
Manchester Airport	d				11 08																				
Styal	d				11 12																				
Wilmslow	d				11 16				11 29					11 47						12 12		12 29			
Alderley Edge	d				11a21				11 32													12a35			
Chelford	d								11 36																
Goostrey	d								11 41																
Holmes Chapel	d								11 44																
Sandbach	d								11 49																
Crewe 10 65	a								11 59					12 07						12 28					
Kidsgrove 50	a																								
Longport 50	a																								
Stoke-on-Trent 50,68	a		11 06	11 12							11 50				12 06	12 13									12 50
Stafford 68	a		11 27												12 24										
Wolverhampton 7 68	a		11 41												12 40										
Birmingham New Street 12 68	a		12 00												12 58										
London Euston 15 ⊖65	a			12 59							13 28					13 47				14 09					14 27

		TP		NT	XC	VT	EM	NT	NT	VT		NT		TP	XC		VT	TP	NT	XC	AW	VT			EM
																					R				
		◇1			◇1	◇1	◇			◇1				◇1	◇1		◇1	◇1		◇1		◇1			◇
		K		A	L		M		C					E	N			F	G	L	H				O
Deansgate	d			12 11															13 11						
Manchester Oxford Road	d			12 17				12 43						13 07					13 17						13 39
Manchester Piccadilly 10	a			12 19				12 45						13 09					13 19						13 41
	d	12 18		12 22	12 26	12 35	12 44	12 47	12 52	12 55		13 04			13 07		13 15	13 20	13 22	13 27	13 30	13 35			13 44
Levenshulme	d								12 58			13 09													
Heaton Chapel	d								13 01			13 12													
Stockport	a	12 28		12 33	12 35	12 44	12 53		13 04	13 04		13 16					13 22	13 28	13 30	13 35	13 39	13 42			13 53
	d				12 35	12 44				13 05		13 17					13 22			13 36	13 40	13 42			
Cheadle Hulme	d											13 21													
Bramhall	d																								
Poynton	d																								
Adlington (Cheshire)	d																								
Prestbury	d																								
Macclesfield	a				12 48	12 57														13 48		13 55			
	d				12 49	12 57														13 49		13 55			
Congleton	d																								
Handforth	d											13 25													
Manchester Airport	d							13 12																	
Styal	d							13 16																	
Wilmslow	d							13 23		13 12		13 28									13 47				
Alderley Edge	d							13a29				13 31													
Chelford	d											13 35													
Goostrey	d											13 40													
Holmes Chapel	d											13 43													
Sandbach	d											13 48													
Crewe 10 65	a									13 28		13 58									14 07				
Kidsgrove 50	a																								
Longport 50	a																								
Stoke-on-Trent 50,68	a				13 06	13 14									13 42		13 49			14 06		14 12			
Stafford 68	a				13 24															14 24					
Wolverhampton 7 68	a				13 40										14 13					14 40					
Birmingham New Street 12 68	a				13 58										14 31					14 58					
London Euston 15 ⊖65	a					14 47				15 09							15 27					15 47			

A From Southport
B To Leamington Spa
C To Buxton
E From Liverpool Lime Street to Middlesbrough
F From Manchester Airport to Cleethorpes
G From Southport to Chester
H To Cardiff Central
I From Liverpool Lime Street to Scarborough
K To Doncaster
L To Bournemouth
M To Norwich
N To Bristol Temple Meads
O From Liverpool Lime Street to Norwich

Table 84

Sundays
19 February to 25 March

Manchester, Stockport and Manchester Airport - Crewe and Stoke-on-Trent

Network Diagram - see first Page of Table 78

		NT	VT	NT	TP	XC	VT	TP	NT	XC	VT	NT	NT	EM	NT	VT	NT	TP	XC
			◇1		◇1	◇1	◇1	◇1		◇1	◇1			◇		◇1		◇1	◇1
		A			C	D		F	G	H				I	A			J	D
Deansgate	d								14 11										
Manchester Oxford Road	d				14 07				14 17					14 39				15 07	
Manchester Piccadilly 10	a				14 09				14 19					14 41				15 09	
	d	13 52	13 55	14 04		14 07	14 15	14 20	14 22	14 27	14 35	14 41	14 41	14 44	14 52	14 55	15 04		15 07
Levenshulme	d	13 58		14 09											14 58		15 09		
Heaton Chapel	d	14 01		14 12											15 01		15 12		
Stockport	a	14 04	14 03	14 16			14 22	14 28	14 33	14 34	14 42		14 49	14 53	15 04	15 03	15 16		
	d		14 04	14 17			14 22			14 36	14 42		14 51			15 04	15 17		
Cheadle Hulme	d			14 22									14 56				15 22		
Bramhall	d												14 59						
Poynton	d												15 02						
Adlington (Cheshire)	d												15 04						
Prestbury	d												15 07						
Macclesfield	a									14 48	14 55		15 11						
	d									14 49	14 55		15 11						
Congleton	d												15 19						
Handforth	d			14 26													15 26		
Manchester Airport	d											15 06							
Styal	d											15 10							
Wilmslow	d		14 11	14 29								15 14				15 11	15 29		
Alderley Edge	d			14a35								15a20					15 32		
Chelford	d																15 36		
Goostrey	d																15 40		
Holmes Chapel	d																15 43		
Sandbach	d																15 48		
Crewe 10 65	a		14 27													15 27	15 58		
Kidsgrove 50	a												15 25						
Longport 50	a																		
Stoke-on-Trent 50,68	a					14 42	14 49			15 06	15 12		15 37						15 42
Stafford 68	a									15 24									
Wolverhampton 7 68	a					15 13				15 40									16 13
Birmingham New Street 12 68	a					15 31				15 58									16 31
London Euston 15 ⊖65	a		16 09				16 27				16 47					17 09			

		VT	TP	NT	XC	AW	VT	EM	NT	VT	NT	TP	XC	VT	TP	NT	XC	AW	VT
		◇1	◇1		◇1	R	◇1	◇		◇1		◇1	◇1	◇1	◇1		◇1	R	◇1
			F	L	H	M		I	A			C	D		F	G	H	M	
Deansgate	d			15 11												16 11			
Manchester Oxford Road	d			15 17				15 39				16 07				16 17			
Manchester Piccadilly 10	a			15 19				15 41				16 09				16 19			
	d	15 15	15 20	15 22	15 27	15 30	15 35	15 44	15 52	15 55	16 04		16 07	16 15	16 20	16 22	16 27	16 30	16 35
Levenshulme	d								15 58		16 09								
Heaton Chapel	d								16 01		16 12								
Stockport	a	15 22	15 28	15 31	15 35	15 39	15 42	15 53	16 04	16 03	16 16			16 22	16 28	16 33	16 34	16 39	16 42
	d	15 22			15 36	15 39	15 42			16 04	16 17			16 23			16 36	16 39	16 42
Cheadle Hulme	d										16 22								
Bramhall	d																		
Poynton	d																		
Adlington (Cheshire)	d																		
Prestbury	d																		
Macclesfield	a				15 48		15 55										16 48		16 55
	d				15 49		15 55										16 49		16 55
Congleton	d																		
Handforth	d										16 26								
Manchester Airport	d																		
Styal	d																		
Wilmslow	d					15 47				16 11	16 29							16 47	
Alderley Edge	d										16a35								
Chelford	d																		
Goostrey	d																		
Holmes Chapel	d																		
Sandbach	d																		
Crewe 10 65	a					16 06				16 27								17 06	
Kidsgrove 50	a																		
Longport 50	a																		
Stoke-on-Trent 50,68	a	15 49			16 06		16 12						16 42	16 48			17 06		17 12
Stafford 68	a				16 24												17 25		
Wolverhampton 7 68	a				16 40								17 13				17 40		
Birmingham New Street 12 68	a				16 58								17 31				17 58		
London Euston 15 ⊖65	a	17 27					17 47			18 09				18 27					18 47

A To Buxton
C From Liverpool Lime Street to Scarborough
D To Bristol Temple Meads
F From Manchester Airport to Cleethorpes
G From Southport
H To Bournemouth
I From Liverpool Lime Street to Norwich
J From Liverpool Lime Street to Middlesbrough
L From Southport to Chester
M To Cardiff Central

Table 84

Sundays

19 February to 25 March

Manchester, Stockport and Manchester Airport - Crewe and Stoke-on-Trent

Network Diagram - see first Page of Table 78

		NT	EM	NT		VT	NT	TP	XC			VT	TP	NT	XC	AW	VT		EM	NT			VT	NT	TP
			◇			◇1		◇1	◇1			◇1	◇1		◇1	R	◇1		◇				◇1		◇1
			A	B				D	E				G	H	I	J			K	B					L
						[buffet]			[trolley]			[buffet]			[trolley]	[trolley]	[buffet]						[buffet]		
Deansgate	d													17 11											
Manchester Oxford Road	d		16 39					17 07						17 17					17 39						18 07
Manchester Piccadilly 10	a		16 41					17 09						17 19					17 41						18 09
	d	16 41	16 44	16 52		16 55	17 04		17 07			17 15	17 20	17 22	17 27	17 30	17 35		17 44	17 52			17 55	18 04	
Levenshulme	d			16 58			17 09													17 58				18 09	
Heaton Chapel	d			17 01			17 12													18 01				18 12	
Stockport	a		16 53	17 04		17 03	17 16					17 22	17 28	17 30	17 34	17 39	17 42		17 53	18 04			18 03	18 16	
	d					17 04	17 17					17 22			17 36	17 39	17 42						18 04	18 17	
Cheadle Hulme	d						17 22																	18 22	
Bramhall	d																								
Poynton	d																								
Adlington (Cheshire)	d																								
Prestbury	d																								
Macclesfield	a														17 48		17 55								
	d														17 49		17 55								
Congleton	d																								
Handforth	d						17 26																	18 26	
Manchester Airport ✈	d	17 06																							
Styal	d	17 10																							
Wilmslow	d	17 15				17 11	17 29									17 47							18 11	18 29	
Alderley Edge	d	17a21					17 32																	18a35	
Chelford	d						17 36																		
Goostrey	d						17 40																		
Holmes Chapel	d						17 43																		
Sandbach	d						17 48																		
Crewe 10 65	a					17 27	17 58									18 07							18 27		
Kidsgrove 50	a																								
Longport 50	a																								
Stoke-on-Trent 50,68	a								17 42			17 49			18 06		18 12								
Stafford 68	a														18 25										
Wolverhampton 7 68	a								18 13						18 40										
Birmingham New Street 12 68	a								18 31						18 58										
London Euston 15 ⊖65	a					19 09						19 27					19 47						20 09		

		XC		VT	TP	NT		XC	AW	VT	NT	NT	EM	NT		VT		NT	TP	XC		VT	TP	NT	XC
		◇1		◇1	◇1			◇1	R	◇1			◇			◇1			◇1	◇1		◇1	◇1		◇1
		E			G	M		N	J				A	B					L	E			G	H	O
		[trolley]		[buffet]				[trolley]	[trolley]	[buffet]						[buffet]				[trolley]		[buffet]			[trolley]
Deansgate	d					18 11																		19 11	
Manchester Oxford Road	d					18 17							18 39						19 07					19 17	
Manchester Piccadilly 10	a					18 19							18 41						19 09					19 19	
	d	18 07		18 15	18 20	18 22		18 27	18 30	18 35	18 41	18 42	18 44	18 52		18 55		19 04		19 07		19 15	19 20	19 22	19 27
Levenshulme	d													18 58				19 09							
Heaton Chapel	d													19 01				19 12							
Stockport	a			18 22	18 28	18 33		18 34	18 39	18 42		18 50	18 53	19 04		19 03		19 16				19 22	19 28	19 30	19 34
	d			18 22				18 36	18 39	18 42		18 52				19 04		19 17				19 22			19 36
Cheadle Hulme	d											18 57						19 22							
Bramhall	d											19 00													
Poynton	d											19 03													
Adlington (Cheshire)	d											19 06													
Prestbury	d											19 09													
Macclesfield	a							18 48		18 55		19 13													19 48
	d							18 49		18 55		19 13													19 49
Congleton	d											19 21													
Handforth	d																	19 26							
Manchester Airport ✈	d										19 06														
Styal	d										19 10														
Wilmslow	d								18 47		19 15					19 11		19 29							
Alderley Edge	d										19a21							19 32							
Chelford	d																	19 36							
Goostrey	d																	19 40							
Holmes Chapel	d																	19 43							
Sandbach	d																	19 48							
Crewe 10 65	a								19 06							19 27		19 58							
Kidsgrove 50	a											19 28													
Longport 50	a																								
Stoke-on-Trent 50,68	a	18 42		18 49				19 06		19 12		19 40								19 42		19 49			20 06
Stafford 68	a							19 24																	20 26
Wolverhampton 7 68	a	19 13						19 40												20 13					20 39
Birmingham New Street 12 68	a	19 31						19 58												20 31					20 58
London Euston 15 ⊖65	a			20 27						20 47						21 09						21 31			

A From Liverpool Lime Street to Norwich
B To Buxton
D From Liverpool Lime Street to Middlesbrough
E To Bristol Temple Meads
G From Manchester Airport to Cleethorpes
H From Southport to Chester
I To Bournemouth
J To Cardiff Central
K From Liverpool Lime Street to Nottingham
L From Liverpool Lime Street to Scarborough
M From Southport
N To Southampton Central
O To Reading

Table 84

Sundays

19 February to 25 March

Manchester, Stockport and Manchester Airport - Crewe and Stoke-on-Trent

Network Diagram - see first Page of Table 78

		VT			EM	NT		NT	TP	XC		TP		VT	NT	AW	NT	EM	NT		VT	NT		TP	XC
		◇1			◇				◇1	◇1		◇1		◇1		◇		◇			◇1			◇1	◇1
					A	B			D			F			G	H		A	B					I	
Deansgate	d														20 11										
Manchester Oxford Road	d				19 39				20 07						20 17			20 39						21 07	
Manchester Piccadilly 10	a				19 41				20 09						20 19			20 41						21 09	
	d	19 35			19 44	19 52		20 04		20 07		20 18		20 20	20 22	20 30	20 41	20 44	20 52		20 55	21 04			21 07
Levenshulme	d					19 58		20 09											20 58			21 09			
Heaton Chapel	d					20 01		20 12											21 01			21 12			
Stockport	a	19 41			19 53	20 04		20 16		20 15		20 26		20 27	20 33	20 38		20 53	21 04		21 03	21 16			21 15
	d	19 41						20 17		20 16				20 27		20 39					21 03	21 17			21 16
Cheadle Hulme	d							20 22														21 22			
Bramhall	d																								
Poynton	d																								
Adlington (Cheshire)	d																								
Prestbury	d																								
Macclesfield	a	19 54								20 28				20 40							21 15				21 28
	d	19 54								20 29				20 40							21 15				21 29
Congleton	d																								
Handforth	d							20 26														21 26			
Manchester Airport	d																21 06								
Styal	d																21 10								
Wilmslow	d							20 29								20 47	21 14					21 29			
Alderley Edge	d							20a37									21a20					21 32			
Chelford	d																					21 36			
Goostrey	d																					21 40			
Holmes Chapel	d																					21 43			
Sandbach	d																					21 48			
Crewe 10 65	a															21 07						21 58			
Kidsgrove 50	a																								
Longport 50	a																								
Stoke-on-Trent 50,68	a	20 11								20 46				20 57							21 32				21 46
Stafford 68	a									21 08															22 06
Wolverhampton 7 68	a									21 21															22 20
Birmingham New Street 12 68	a									21 39															22 39
London Euston 15 ⊖65	a	21 58												22 56							23 49				

			TP	NT	AW		NT	NT			NT	XC	EM		TP	NT	AW	TP				NT	NT	TP	NT
			◇1									◇1	◇		◇1			◇1						◇1	
			J	K				B					A		J	G		D				B		J	G
Deansgate	d			21 11												22 11									23 11
Manchester Oxford Road	d			21 17									22 07			22 17		22 37							23 17
Manchester Piccadilly 10	a			21 19									22 09			22 19		22 39							23 19
	d		21 20	21 22	21 34		21 41	21 52			22 04	22 07	22 11		22 15	22 22	22 35					22 52	23 04	23 20	23 22
Levenshulme	d							21 58			22 09											22 58	23 09		
Heaton Chapel	d							22 01			22 12											23 01	23 12		
Stockport	a		21 28	21 30			21 49	22 04			22 16	22 15	22 20		22 23	22 33						23 04	23 16	23 28	23 33
	d						21 52				22 17	22 16											23 17		
Cheadle Hulme	d						21 56				22 22												23 21		
Bramhall	d						21 59																		
Poynton	d						22 02																		
Adlington (Cheshire)	d						22 05																		
Prestbury	d						22 08																		
Macclesfield	a						22 12					22 28													
	d						22 13					22 29													
Congleton	d						22 20																		
Handforth	d										22 26												23 25		
Manchester Airport	d																								
Styal	d																								
Wilmslow	d				21 50						22 29						22 50						23 28		
Alderley Edge	d										22a35												23a35		
Chelford	d																								
Goostrey	d																								
Holmes Chapel	d																								
Sandbach	d																								
Crewe 10 65	a				22 13												23 10								
Kidsgrove 50	a						22 26																		
Longport 50	a																								
Stoke-on-Trent 50,68	a						22 36					22 46													
Stafford 68	a											23 04													
Wolverhampton 7 68	a											23 18													
Birmingham New Street 12 68	a											23 36													
London Euston 15 ⊖65	a																								

A From Liverpool Lime Street to Nottingham
B To Buxton
D From Liverpool Lime Street to York
F From Manchester Airport to Cleethorpes
G From Southport
H To Cardiff Central
I From Liverpool Lime Street to Newcastle
J From Manchester Airport to Sheffield
K From Southport to Chester

Table 84

Sundays
From 1 April

Manchester, Stockport and Manchester Airport - Crewe and Stoke-on-Trent

Network Diagram - see first Page of Table 78

		NT	NT	VT	VT	XC	NT	NT	TP	NT	VT	NT	XC	AW	NT	NT
				◇1	◇1	◇1			◇1		◇1		◇1	◇		
			B			C		E	F			G	C	H	E	
Deansgate ⇌	d											09 15				
Manchester Oxford Road	d											09 18				
Manchester Piccadilly 10 ⇌	a											09 21				
	d	23p37	08 00	08 05	08 20	08 27	08 41	08 55	08 58	09 04	09 20	09 22	09 27	09 30	09 51	10 03
Levenshulme	d	23p42						09 00		09 09					09 58	10 08
Heaton Chapel	d	23p45						09 03		09 12					10 01	10 11
Stockport	a	23p49	08 09	08 13	08 28	08 34		09 07	09 06	09 17	09 27	09 31	09 35	09 39	10 04	10 15
	d	23p50		08 14	08 28	08 36				09 17	09 27		09 36	09 39		10 17
Cheadle Hulme	d	23p54								09 21						10 23
Bramhall	d															
Poynton	d															
Adlington (Cheshire)	d															
Prestbury	d															
Macclesfield	a				08 41						09 40		09 48			
	d				08 42						09 40		09 49			
Congleton	d															
Handforth	d	23p58								09 25						10 27
Manchester Airport ✈	d						09 06									
Styal	d						09 10									
Wilmslow	d	00 01		08 22		08 43	09 15			09 28				09 47		10 30
Alderley Edge	d	00a07					09a22			09 31						10a36
Chelford	d									09 35						
Goostrey	d									09 40						
Holmes Chapel	d									09 43						
Sandbach	d									09 48						
Crewe 10 65	a			08 39		09 01				09 58				10 06		
Kidsgrove 50	a															
Longport 50	a															
Stoke-on-Trent 50,68	a				08 59						09 57		10 05			
Stafford 68	a			09 01		09 25							10 26			
Wolverhampton 7 68 ⇌	a					09 40							10 42			
Birmingham New Street 12 68	a					09 58							10 59			
London Euston 15 ⊖65	a			10 57	11 02						12 08					

B To Sheffield
C To Bournemouth
E To Buxton
F From Manchester Airport to Sheffield
G From Wigan Wallgate to Chester
H To Cardiff Central

Table 84

Sundays
from 1 April

Manchester, Stockport and Manchester Airport - Crewe and Stoke-on-Trent

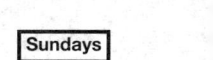

Network Diagram - see first Page of Table 78

		VT	NT	XC	VT	NT	NT	NT	VT	TP	NT	AW	XC	VT	NT	VT	NT
		◇1		◇1	◇1				◇1	◇1		R	◇1	◇1		◇1	
			B	C			D			E	F	G	C		D		
		🍴		☕	🍴				🍴			☕	☕	🍴		🍴	
Deansgate	d		10 16								11 11						
Manchester Oxford Road	d		10 19								11 17						
Manchester Piccadilly 10	a		10 22								11 19						
	d	10 20	10 22	10 27	10 35	10 41	10 53	11 04	11 15	11 18	11 22	11 24	11 27	11 35	11 52	11 55	12 04
Levenshulme	d						10 59	11 10							11 58		12 09
Heaton Chapel	d						11 02	11 13							12 01		12 12
Stockport	a	10 28	10 33	10 34	10 42		11 05	11 17	11 23	11 27	11 30	11 34	11 34	11 43	12 04	12 04	12 16
	d	10 29		10 36	10 42			11 17	11 23			11 40	11 36	11 43		12 05	12 16
Cheadle Hulme	d							11 22									12 22
Bramhall	d																
Poynton	d																
Adlington (Cheshire)	d																
Prestbury	d																
Macclesfield	a			10 48	10 55								11 49	11 56			
	d			10 49	10 55								11 49	11 56			
Congleton	d																
Handforth	d							11 26									12 26
Manchester Airport ✈	d					11 08											
Styal	d					11 12											
Wilmslow	d	10 36				11 16		11 29				11 47				12 12	12 29
Alderley Edge	d					11a21		11 32									12a35
Chelford	d							11 36									
Goostrey	d							11 41									
Holmes Chapel	d							11 44									
Sandbach	d							11 49									
Crewe 10 65	a	10 53						11 59				12 07				12 28	
Kidsgrove 50	a																
Longport 50	a																
Stoke-on-Trent 50,68	a			11 06	11 12				11 50				12 06	12 13			
Stafford 68	a			11 27									12 24				
Wolverhampton 7 68	a			11 41									12 40				
Birmingham New Street 12 68	a			12 00									12 58				
London Euston 15 ⊖65	a	12 56			12 59				13 28					13 47		14 09	

		VT	TP	NT	XC	VT	EM	NT	NT	VT	NT	XC	VT	TP	NT	XC	AW	VT	EM
		◇1	◇1		◇1	◇1	◇			◇1		◇1	◇1	◇1		◇1	R	◇1	◇
			I	B	C		J		D			K		E	F	C	G		L
		🍴			☕	🍴				🍴		☕	🍴			☕	☕	🍴	
Deansgate	d			12 11											13 11				
Manchester Oxford Road	d			12 17				12 43							13 17				13 39
Manchester Piccadilly 10	a			12 19				12 45							13 19				13 41
	d	12 15	12 20	12 22	12 26	12 35	12 44	12 47	12 52	12 55	13 04	13 07	13 15	13 20	13 22	13 27	13 30	13 35	13 44
Levenshulme	d								12 58		13 09								
Heaton Chapel	d								13 01		13 12								
Stockport	a	12 23	12 28	12 33	12 35	12 44	12 53		13 04	13 04	13 16		13 22	13 29	13 30	13 35	13 39	13 42	13 53
	d	12 23			12 35	12 44				13 05	13 17		13 22			13 36	13 40	13 42	
Cheadle Hulme	d										13 21								
Bramhall	d																		
Poynton	d																		
Adlington (Cheshire)	d																		
Prestbury	d																		
Macclesfield	a				12 48	12 57										13 48		13 55	
	d				12 49	12 57										13 49		13 55	
Congleton	d																		
Handforth	d										13 25								
Manchester Airport ✈	d							13 12											
Styal	d							13 16											
Wilmslow	d							13 23		13 12	13 28						13 47		
Alderley Edge	d							13a29			13 31								
Chelford	d										13 35								
Goostrey	d										13 40								
Holmes Chapel	d										13 43								
Sandbach	d										13 48								
Crewe 10 65	a									13 28	13 58						14 07		
Kidsgrove 50	a																		
Longport 50	a																		
Stoke-on-Trent 50,68	a	12 50			13 06	13 14						13 42	13 49			14 06		14 12	
Stafford 68	a				13 24											14 24			
Wolverhampton 7 68	a				13 40							14 13				14 40			
Birmingham New Street 12 68	a				13 58							14 31				14 58			
London Euston 15 ⊖65	a	14 27				14 47				15 09			15 27					15 47	

B From Southport
C To Bournemouth
D To Buxton
E From Manchester Airport to Cleethorpes
F From Southport to Chester
G To Cardiff Central
I To Doncaster
J To Norwich
K To Paignton
L From Liverpool Lime Street to Norwich

Table 84

Sundays from 1 April

Manchester, Stockport and Manchester Airport - Crewe and Stoke-on-Trent

Network Diagram - see first Page of Table 78

		NT	VT		NT	XC		VT		TP	NT	XC	VT	NT	NT	EM	NT	VT			NT	XC		VT	TP
			◇1			◇1		◇1		◇1		◇1	◇1			◇		◇1				◇1		◇1	◇1
		A				C				E	F	G				H	A					C			E
Deansgate	d										14 11														
Manchester Oxford Road	d										14 17					14 39									
Manchester Piccadilly 10	a										14 19					14 41									
	d	13 52	13 55		14 04	14 07		14 15		14 20	14 22	14 27	14 35	14 41	14 41	14 44	14 52	14 55			15 04	15 07		15 15	15 20
Levenshulme	d	13 58			14 09												14 58				15 09				
Heaton Chapel	d	14 01			14 12												15 01				15 12				
Stockport	a	14 04	14 03		14 16			14 22		14 28	14 33	14 34	14 42		14 49	14 53	15 04	15 03			15 16			15 22	15 28
	d		14 04		14 17			14 22				14 36	14 42		14 51			15 04			15 17			15 22	
Cheadle Hulme	d				14 22										14 56						15 22				
Bramhall	d														14 59										
Poynton	d														15 02										
Adlington (Cheshire)	d														15 04										
Prestbury	d														15 07										
Macclesfield	a											14 48	14 55		15 11										
	d											14 49	14 55		15 11										
Congleton	d														15 19										
Handforth	d				14 26																15 26				
Manchester Airport	d													15 06											
Styal	d													15 10											
Wilmslow	d		14 11		14 29									15 14				15 11			15 29				
Alderley Edge	d				14a35									15a20							15 32				
Chelford	d																				15 36				
Goostrey	d																				15 40				
Holmes Chapel	d																				15 43				
Sandbach	d																				15 48				
Crewe 10 65	a		14 27															15 27			15 58				
Kidsgrove 50	a														15 25										
Longport 50	a																								
Stoke-on-Trent 50,68	a					14 42		14 49				15 06	15 12		15 37							15 42		15 49	
Stafford 68	a											15 24													
Wolverhampton 7 68	a					15 13						15 40										16 13			
Birmingham New Street 12 68	a					15 31						15 58										16 31			
London Euston 15 ⊖65	a		16 09					16 27					16 47					17 09						17 27	

		NT	XC	AW		VT		EM	NT	VT		NT	XC			VT	TP	NT	XC	AW	VT	NT	EM	NT	
			◇1	R		◇1		◇		◇1			◇1			◇1	◇1		◇1	R	◇1		◇		
		J	G	K				H	A				C				E	F	G	K			H	A	
Deansgate	d	15 11																16 11							
Manchester Oxford Road	d	15 17						15 39										16 17					16 39		
Manchester Piccadilly 10	a	15 19						15 41										16 19					16 41		
	d	15 22	15 27	15 30		15 35		15 44	15 52	15 55		16 04	16 07			16 15	16 20	16 22	16 27	16 30	16 35	16 41	16 44	16 52	
Levenshulme	d								15 58			16 09												16 58	
Heaton Chapel	d								16 01			16 12												17 01	
Stockport	a	15 31	15 35	15 39		15 42		15 53	16 04	16 03		16 16				16 22	16 28	16 33	16 34	16 39	16 42		16 53	17 04	
	d		15 36	15 39		15 42				16 04		16 17				16 23			16 36	16 39	16 42				
Cheadle Hulme	d											16 22													
Bramhall	d																								
Poynton	d																								
Adlington (Cheshire)	d																								
Prestbury	d																								
Macclesfield	a		15 48			15 55													16 48		16 55				
	d		15 49			15 55													16 49		16 55				
Congleton	d																								
Handforth	d											16 26													
Manchester Airport	d																					17 06			
Styal	d																					17 10			
Wilmslow	d			15 47						16 11		16 29								16 47		17 15			
Alderley Edge	d											16a35										17a21			
Chelford	d																								
Goostrey	d																								
Holmes Chapel	d																								
Sandbach	d																								
Crewe 10 65	a			16 06						16 27										17 06					
Kidsgrove 50	a																								
Longport 50	a																								
Stoke-on-Trent 50,68	a		16 06			16 12							16 42			16 48			17 06		17 12				
Stafford 68	a		16 24																17 25						
Wolverhampton 7 68	a		16 40										17 13						17 40						
Birmingham New Street 12 68	a		16 58										17 31						17 58						
London Euston 15 ⊖65	a					17 47				18 09						18 27					18 47				

A To Buxton
C To Bristol Temple Meads
E From Manchester Airport to Cleethorpes
F From Southport
G To Bournemouth
H From Liverpool Lime Street to Norwich
I From Doncaster
J From Southport to Chester
K To Cardiff Central

Table 84

Sundays
from 1 April

Manchester, Stockport and Manchester Airport - Crewe and Stoke-on-Trent

Network Diagram - see first Page of Table 78

		VT	NT	XC	VT	TP	NT	XC	AW	VT	EM	NT	VT	NT	XC	VT	TP	NT
									R									
		◇1		◇1	◇1	◇1		◇1		◇1	◇		◇1		◇1	◇1	◇1	
				B		D	E	F	G		H	I			J		D	K
Deansgate	d						17 11											18 11
Manchester Oxford Road	d						17 17				17 39							18 17
Manchester Piccadilly 10	a						17 19				17 41							18 19
	d	16 55	17 04	17 07	17 15	17 20	17 22	17 27	17 30	17 35	17 44	17 52	17 55	18 04	18 07	18 15	18 20	18 22
Levenshulme	d		17 09									17 58		18 09				
Heaton Chapel	d		17 12									18 01		18 12				
Stockport	a	17 03	17 16		17 22	17 28	17 30	17 34	17 39	17 42	17 53	18 04	18 03	18 16		18 22	18 28	18 33
	d	17 04	17 17		17 22			17 36	17 39	17 42			18 04	18 17		18 22		
Cheadle Hulme	d		17 22											18 22				
Bramhall	d																	
Poynton	d																	
Adlington (Cheshire)	d																	
Prestbury	d																	
Macclesfield	a							17 48		17 55								
	d							17 49		17 55								
Congleton	d																	
Handforth	d		17 26											18 26				
Manchester Airport	d																	
Styal	d																	
Wilmslow	d	17 11	17 29						17 47				18 11	18 29				
Alderley Edge	d		17 32											18a35				
Chelford	d		17 36															
Goostrey	d		17 40															
Holmes Chapel	d		17 43															
Sandbach	d		17 48															
Crewe 10 65	a	17 27	17 58						18 07				18 27					
Kidsgrove 50	a																	
Longport 50	a																	
Stoke-on-Trent 50,68	a			17 42	17 49			18 06		18 12					18 42	18 49		
Stafford 68	a							18 25										
Wolverhampton 7 68	a			18 13				18 40							19 13			
Birmingham New Street 12 68	a			18 31				18 58							19 31			
London Euston 15 ⊖65	a	19 09			19 27					19 47			20 09			20 27		

		XC	VT	NT	NT	EM	NT	VT	NT	XC	VT	TP	NT	XC	AW	VT	EM	NT	NT
		◇1	◇1			◇		◇1		◇1	◇1	◇1		◇1	◇	◇1	◇		
		L				M	I			J		D	E	N	G		H	I	
Deansgate	d												19 13						
Manchester Oxford Road	d					18 39							19 17				19 39		
Manchester Piccadilly 10	a					18 41							19 19				19 41		
	d	18 27	18 35	18 41	18 42	18 44	18 52	18 55	19 04	19 07	19 15	19 20	19 22	19 27	19 30	19 35	19 44	19 52	20 04
Levenshulme	d						18 58		19 09									19 58	20 09
Heaton Chapel	d						19 01		19 12									20 01	20 12
Stockport	a	18 34	18 42		18 50	18 53	19 04	19 03	19 16		19 22	19 28	19 30	19 34	19 39	19 41	19 53	20 04	20 16
	d	18 36	18 42		18 52			19 04	19 17		19 22			19 36	19 39	19 41			20 17
Cheadle Hulme	d				18 57				19 22										20 22
Bramhall	d				19 00														
Poynton	d				19 03														
Adlington (Cheshire)	d				19 06														
Prestbury	d				19 09														
Macclesfield	a	18 48	18 55		19 13									19 48		19 54			
	d	18 49	18 55		19 13									19 49		19 54			
Congleton	d				19 21														
Handforth	d								19 26										20 26
Manchester Airport	d			19 06															
Styal	d			19 10															
Wilmslow	d			19 15				19 11	19 29						19 47				20 29
Alderley Edge	d			19a21					19 32										20a37
Chelford	d								19 36										
Goostrey	d								19 40										
Holmes Chapel	d								19 43										
Sandbach	d								19 48										
Crewe 10 65	a							19 27	19 58						20 07				
Kidsgrove 50	a				19 28														
Longport 50	a																		
Stoke-on-Trent 50,68	a	19 06	19 12		19 40					19 42	19 49			20 06		20 11			
Stafford 68	a	19 24												20 26					
Wolverhampton 7 68	a	19 40								20 13				20 39					
Birmingham New Street 12 68	a	19 58								20 31				20 58					
London Euston 15 ⊖65	a		20 47					21 09			21 31					21 58			

B To Plymouth
D From Manchester Airport to Cleethorpes
E From Southport to Chester
F To Bournemouth
G To Cardiff Central
H From Liverpool Lime Street to Nottingham
I To Buxton
J To Bristol Temple Meads
K From Southport
L To Southampton Central
M From Liverpool Lime Street to Norwich
N To Reading

Table 84

Sundays
from 1 April

Manchester, Stockport and Manchester Airport - Crewe and Stoke-on-Trent

Network Diagram - see first Page of Table 78

		XC ◇1 A			TP ◇1 C	VT ◇1	NT D	AW ◇ E	NT	EM ◇ F	NT G	VT ◇1			NT	XC ◇1		TP ◇1 I	NT J	AW		NT		NT G
Deansgate	d						20 11												21 11					
Manchester Oxford Road	d						20 17			20 39									21 17					
Manchester Piccadilly 10	a						20 19			20 41									21 19					
	d	20 07			20 18	20 20	20 22	20 30	20 41	20 44	20 52	20 55			21 04	21 07		21 20	21 22	21 34		21 41		21 52
Levenshulme	d										20 58				21 09									21 58
Heaton Chapel	d										21 01				21 12									22 01
Stockport	a	20 15			20 26	20 27	20 33	20 38		20 53	21 04	21 03			21 16	21 15		21 28	21 30			21 49		22 04
	d	20 16				20 27		20 39				21 03			21 17	21 16						21 52		
Cheadle Hulme	d														21 22							21 56		
Bramhall	d																					21 59		
Poynton	d																					22 02		
Adlington (Cheshire)	d																					22 05		
Prestbury	d																					22 08		
Macclesfield	a	20 28				20 40						21 15				21 28						22 12		
	d	20 29				20 40						21 15				21 29						22 13		
Congleton	d																					22 20		
Handforth	d														21 26									
Manchester Airport ✈	d								21 06															
Styal	d								21 10															
Wilmslow	d							20 47	21 14						21 29					21 50				
Alderley Edge	d								21a20						21 32									
Chelford	d														21 36									
Goostrey	d														21 40									
Holmes Chapel	d														21 43									
Sandbach	d														21 48									
Crewe 10 65	a							21 07							21 58					22 13				
Kidsgrove 50	a																					22 26		
Longport 50	a																							
Stoke-on-Trent 50,68	a	20 46				20 57						21 32				21 46						22 36		
Stafford 68	a	21 08														22 06								
Wolverhampton 7 68	a	21 21														22 20								
Birmingham New Street 12 68	a	21 39														22 39								
London Euston 15 ⊖65	a					22 56						23 49												

		NT	XC ◇1	EM ◇ F		TP ◇1 I	NT D	AW				NT G	NT	TP ◇1 I	NT D
Deansgate	d						22 11								23 11
Manchester Oxford Road	d			22 07			22 17								23 17
Manchester Piccadilly 10	a			22 09			22 19								23 19
	d	22 04	22 07	22 11		22 15	22 22	22 35				22 52	23 04	23 20	23 22
Levenshulme	d	22 09										22 58	23 09		
Heaton Chapel	d	22 12										23 01	23 12		
Stockport	a	22 16	22 15	22 20		22 23	22 33					23 04	23 16	23 28	23 33
	d	22 17	22 16										23 17		
Cheadle Hulme	d	22 22											23 21		
Bramhall	d														
Poynton	d														
Adlington (Cheshire)	d														
Prestbury	d														
Macclesfield	a		22 28												
	d		22 29												
Congleton	d														
Handforth	d	22 26											23 25		
Manchester Airport ✈	d														
Styal	d														
Wilmslow	d	22 29						22 50					23 28		
Alderley Edge	d	22a35											23a35		
Chelford	d														
Goostrey	d														
Holmes Chapel	d														
Sandbach	d														
Crewe 10 65	a							23 10							
Kidsgrove 50	a														
Longport 50	a														
Stoke-on-Trent 50,68	a		22 46												
Stafford 68	a		23 04												
Wolverhampton 7 68	a		23 18												
Birmingham New Street 12 68	a		23 36												
London Euston 15 ⊖65	a														

A To Bristol Temple Meads
C From Manchester Airport to Cleethorpes
D From Southport
E To Cardiff Central
F From Liverpool Lime Street to Nottingham
G To Buxton
I From Manchester Airport to Sheffield
J From Southport to Chester

Manchester - Manchester Airport

Network Diagram - see first Page of Table 78

Miles		NT MO	TP MX ◇1	TP MO ◇1 A	TP MO ◇1 B	AW C	TP MX ◇1	TP MO ◇1 D	TP ◇1	NT MO		NT MX	TP ◇1	AW	TP ◇1	TP ◇1	NT	NT	TP ◇1	TP ◇1		TP ◇1	NT	NT
—	Deansgate d																							
—	Manchester Oxford Road d	23p47																						
0	Manchester Piccadilly 10 a	23p50																						
—	d	23p52	23p55	00 16	00 44	00 50	00 54	01 10	03 44	04 14		04 14	04 44	04 49	04 50	05 00	05 35	05 58	06 03	06 08		06 12	06 15	06 46
3½	Mauldeth Road d		00 04														05 42						06 22	06 53
4½	Burnage d		00 07														05 44						06 24	06 55
5½	East Didsbury d		00 10														05 46						06 26	06 57
6¾	Gatley d		00 13														05 49						06 29	06 59
8¼	Heald Green d		00 17														05 52						06 32	07 02
9¾	Manchester Airport a	00 07	00 24	00 30	00 57		01 10	01 23	04 00	04 27		04 29	05 00	05 09	05 07	05 19	05 57	06 14	06 18	06 24		06 29	06 39	07 07
—	Wilmslow 84 a																06 11							07 20
—	Crewe 10 84 a					01 31											06 46							07 46

	TP ◇1	NT	TP ◇1	NT	NT	TP ◇1		TP ◇1 🚲	NT	NT	TP ◇1 🚲	NT	TP ◇1 🚲	NT	TP ◇1 🚲	TP ◇1 🚲		NT	NT	TP ◇1 🚲	TP ◇1 🚲	NT	TP ◇1 🚲	NT
Deansgate d				07 11					07 28									08 29						
Manchester Oxford Road d		06 58		07 15				07 24	07 32			07 58				08 24		08 33			08 54	08 58		
Manchester Piccadilly 10 a		07 01		07 17				07 27	07 34			08 01				08 27		08 35			08 56	09 01		
d	06 54	07 03	07 06		07 14	07 23		07 29	07 36	07 46	07 54	08 03	08 06	08 14	08 24	08 29		08 37	08 46	08 54	08 58	09 03	09 06	09 14
Mauldeth Road d					07 21					07 53				08 21					08 53					09 21
Burnage d					07 23					07 55				08 23					08 55					09 23
East Didsbury d					07 25					07 57				08 25					08 57				09 16	09 25
Gatley d					07 27					07 59				08 27					08 59					09 27
Heald Green d					07 30					08 02				08 30				08 47	09 02		09 10			09 30
Manchester Airport a	07 12	07 22	07 29		07 38	07 42		07 47	07 53	08 07	08 12	08 22	08 26	08 38	08 42	08 47		08 53	09 07	09 12	09 19	09 22	09 33	09 38
Wilmslow 84 a										08 21									09 20					
Crewe 10 84 a										08 47									09 46					

	TP ◇1 🚲	TP ◇1 🚲		NT	NT	TP ◇1 🚲	TP ◇1 🚲	NT	TP ◇1 🚲	NT	TP ◇1 🚲	TP ◇1 🚲		NT	NT	TP ◇1 🚲	TP ◇1 🚲	NT	TP ◇1 🚲	NT	TP ◇1 🚲	TP ◇1 🚲		NT
Deansgate d				09 29			09 51							10 29			10 51							11 29
Manchester Oxford Road d		09 24		09 33			09 54	09 58				10 24		10 33			10 54	10 58				11 24		11 33
Manchester Piccadilly 10 a		09 27		09 35			09 56	10 01				10 27		10 35			10 56	11 01				11 27		11 35
d	09 24	09 29		09 37	09 46	09 54	09 58	10 03	10 06	10 14	10 24	10 29		10 37	10 46	10 54	10 58	11 03	11 06	11 14	11 24	11 29		11 37
Mauldeth Road d					09 53					10 21					10 53					11 21				
Burnage d					09 55					10 23					10 55					11 23				
East Didsbury d					09 57					10 25					10 57					11 25				
Gatley d					09 59					10 27					10 59					11 27				
Heald Green d					10 02		10 10			10 30					11 02		11 10			11 30				
Manchester Airport a	09 42	09 47		09 53	10 07	10 12	10 17	10 22	10 26	10 38	10 42	10 47		10 53	11 08	11 12	11 17	11 22	11 26	11 38	11 45	11 50		11 53
Wilmslow 84 a					10 20										11 21									
Crewe 10 84 a					10 46										11 47									

	NT	TP ◇1 🚲	TP ◇1 🚲	NT	TP ◇1 🚲	NT	TP ◇1 🚲	TP ◇1 🚲		NT	NT	TP FO ◇1 🚲	TP FX ◇1 🚲	TP FO ◇1 🚲	TP FX ◇1 🚲	NT	TP ◇1 🚲	NT		TP ◇1 🚲	TP ◇1 🚲	NT	NT	TP ◇1 🚲
Deansgate d			11 51							12 29				12 51	12 51							13 29		
Manchester Oxford Road d			11 54	11 58				12 24		12 33				12 54	12 54	12 58					13 24	13 33		
Manchester Piccadilly 10 a			11 56	12 01				12 27		12 35				12 56	12 56	13 01					13 27	13 35		
d	11 46	11 54	11 58	12 03	12 06	12 14	12 24	12 29		12 37	12 46	12 54	12 54	12 58	12 58	13 03	13 06	13 14		13 24	13 29	13 37	13 46	13 54
Mauldeth Road d	11 53					12 21					12 53							13 21					13 53	
Burnage d	11 55					12 23					12 55							13 23					13 55	
East Didsbury d	11 57					12 25					12 57							13 25					13 57	
Gatley d	11 59					12 27					12 59							13 27					13 59	
Heald Green d	12 02		12 10			12 30					13 02			13 10	13 10			13 30					14 02	
Manchester Airport a	12 07	12 12	12 17	12 22	12 26	12 38	12 42	12 47		12 53	13 07	13 11	13 12	13 16	13 17	13 22	13 26	13 38		13 42	13 47	13 53	14 07	14 12
Wilmslow 84 a	12 20										13 21												14 20	
Crewe 10 84 a	12 46										13 47												14 46	

	TP ◇1 🚲	NT	TP ◇1 🚲	NT		TP ◇1 🚲	TP ◇1 🚲	NT	NT	TP ◇1 🚲	TP ◇1 🚲	NT	TP ◇1 🚲	NT		TP ◇1 🚲	TP ◇1 🚲	NT	NT	TP ◇1 🚲	TP ◇1 🚲	NT	TP ◇1 🚲	NT
Deansgate d	13 51							14 29			14 51							15 29			15 51			
Manchester Oxford Road d	13 54	13 58					14 24	14 33			14 54	14 58					15 24	15 33			15 54	15 58		
Manchester Piccadilly 10 a	13 56	14 01					14 27	14 35			14 56	15 01					15 27	15 35			15 56	16 01		
d	13 58	14 03	14 06	14 14		14 24	14 29	14 37	14 46	14 54	14 58	15 03	15 06	15 14		15 24	15 29	15 37	15 46	15 54	15 58	16 03	16 06	16 14
Mauldeth Road d				14 21					14 53					15 21					15 53					16 21
Burnage d				14 23					14 55					15 23					15 55					16 23
East Didsbury d				14 25					14 57					15 25					15 57					16 25
Gatley d				14 27					14 59					15 27					15 59					16 27
Heald Green d	14 10			14 30					15 02		15 10			15 30					16 02		16 10			16 30
Manchester Airport a	14 17	14 22	14 26	14 38		14 42	14 47	14 53	15 07	15 12	15 17	15 22	15 26	15 38		15 42	15 47	15 53	16 07	16 12	16 17	16 22	16 26	16 38
Wilmslow 84 a									15 20										16 20					
Crewe 10 84 a									15 46										16 46					

A from 9 January until 13 February
B until 26 March
C from 3 January until 6 January
D from 2 April

Manchester - Manchester Airport

Network Diagram - see first Page of Table 78

			TP	TP	NT	NT	TP	TP	NT	TP	NT		TP	NT	NT	TP	TP	NT	TP	NT	NT		TP FX	TP	NT
			◇1 🛒	◇1 🛒			◇1 🛒	◇1 🛒		◇1 🛒			◇1 🛒			◇1 🛒	◇1 🛒		◇1 🛒				◇1 🛒	◇1 🛒	
Deansgate 🚊	d							16 51									17 51			18 12					
Manchester Oxford Road	d			16 24	16 33			16 54	16 58				17 27	17 33			17 54	17 58		18 16				18 24	18 33
Manchester Piccadilly [10] 🚊	a			16 27	16 35			16 56	17 01				17 29	17 35			17 56	18 01		18 18				18 27	18 35
	d		16 24	16 29	16 37	16 46	16 54	16 58	17 03	17 06	17 14		17 31	17 37	17 46	17 54	17 58	18 03	18 06		18 14		18 24	18 29	18 37
Mauldeth Road	d					16 53					17 21				17 53						18 21				
Burnage	d					16 55					17 23				17 55						18 23				
East Didsbury	d					16 57				17 17	17 25				17 57						18 25				
Gatley	d					16 59				17 20	17 27				17 59						18 27				
Heald Green	d			16 40		17 02		17 10		17 23	17 30		17 41		18 02		18 10				18 30			18 40	
Manchester Airport ✈	a		16 42	16 47	16 53	17 07	17 12	17 17	17 22	17 32	17 39		17 48	17 53	18 07	18 12	18 17	18 22	18 26		18 38		18 42	18 47	18 53
Wilmslow 84	a					17 21									18 21										
Crewe [10] 84	a					17 47									18 47										

		NT	TP	NT	TP	NT	TP		NT	TP	NT	AW	TP	TP	TP	TP	NT		TP	NT	AW	TP	NT	TP ThFO	TP MT WO
			◇1 🛒		◇1 🛒		◇1 🛒			◇1 🛒			◇1 🛒	◇1	◇1 🛒	◇1 🛒			◇1		◇ 🛒	◇1		◇1 A	◇1 B
Deansgate 🚊	d								19 29				19 51				20 29					20 51			
Manchester Oxford Road	d			18 58			19 24		19 33		19 43	19 49	19 54	19 59		20 24	20 33			20 43	20 49	20 54	20 58		
Manchester Piccadilly [10] 🚊	a			19 01			19 27		19 35		19 45	19 52	19 56	20 01		20 27	20 35			20 45	20 52	20 56	21 01		
	d	18 46	18 54	19 03	19 06	19 14	19 29		19 37	19 40	19 46	19 54	19 58	20 03	20 13	20 29	20 37		20 40	20 46	20 54	20 58	21 03	21 06	21 09
Mauldeth Road	d	18 53				19 21					19 53				20 21					20 53				21 15	21 15
Burnage	d	18 55				19 23					19 55				20 23					20 55				21 17	21 17
East Didsbury	d	18 57				19 25					19 57				20 26					20 57				21 20	21 20
Gatley	d	18 59				19 27					19 59				20 29					20 59				21 23	21 23
Heald Green	d	19 02				19 30					20 02		20 10	20 15	20 32					21 02		21 10		21 26	21 26
Manchester Airport ✈	a	19 08	19 13	19 24	19 28	19 38	19 47		19 53	19 59	20 07	20 18	20 17	20 24	20 39	20 47	20 53		20 57	21 07	21 18	21 17	21 20	21 36	21 38
Wilmslow 84	a	19 23									20 24									21 25					
Crewe [10] 84	a																								

		TP ThX	TP ThO		NT	TP	NT	TP	TP	TP	NT	TP	TP		TP
		◇1 🛒	◇1 🛒			◇1		◇1	◇1	◇1		◇1	◇1		◇1
Deansgate 🚊	d				21 29			21 51				22 51			
Manchester Oxford Road	d	21 24	21 24		21 33		21 43	21 54	22 27		22 43	22 54			
Manchester Piccadilly [10] 🚊	a	21 27	21 27		21 35		21 45	21 56	22 30		22 45	22 56			
	d	21 29	21 29		21 37	21 40	21 46	21 58	22 32	22 40	22 46	22 58	23 06		23 55
Mauldeth Road	d						21 53				22 53				00 04
Burnage	d						21 55				22 55				00 07
East Didsbury	d						21 57				22 57				00 10
Gatley	d						21 59				22 59				00 13
Heald Green	d						22 02	22 09			23 02	23 09			00 17
Manchester Airport ✈	a	21 46	21 47		21 53	21 57	22 10	22 17	22 47	22 57	23 08	23 17	23 26		00 24
Wilmslow 84	a						22 22				23 22				
Crewe [10] 84	a														

Saturdays

until 11 February

		TP	TP	TP	NT	TP	TP	TP	AW	NT		NT	TP	TP	TP	NT	NT	TP	NT	TP		NT	NT	TP	TP
		◇1	◇1	◇1		◇1	◇1	◇1					◇1	◇1	◇1			◇1		◇1				◇1	◇1
Deansgate 🚊	d																					07 11			
Manchester Oxford Road	d																		06 58			07 15			07 24
Manchester Piccadilly [10] 🚊	a																		07 01			07 17			07 27
	d	23p55	00 54	03 44	04 15	04 44	04 50	04 54	05 00	05 35		05 58	06 03	06 08	06 12	06 15	06 46	06 54	07 03	07 06			07 14	07 23	07 29
Mauldeth Road	d	00 04								05 42						06 22	06 53						07 21		
Burnage	d	00 07								05 44						06 24	06 55						07 23		
East Didsbury	d	00 10								05 46						06 26	06 57						07 25		
Gatley	d	00 13								05 49						06 29	06 59						07 27		
Heald Green	d	00 17								05 52						06 32	07 02						07 30		
Manchester Airport ✈	a	00 24	01 10	04 00	04 30	05 00	05 07	05 10	05 19	05 57		06 14	06 18	06 24	06 29	06 39	07 07	07 12	07 22	07 29			07 38	07 42	07 47
Wilmslow 84	a									06 11							07 20								
Crewe [10] 84	a									06 43							07 46								

		NT	NT	TP	NT	TP		NT	TP	TP	NT	NT	TP	TP	NT	TP		NT	TP	TP	NT	NT	TP	TP	NT
				◇1		◇1 🛒			◇1	◇1 🛒			◇1	◇1 🛒		◇1 🛒			◇1 🛒	◇1 🛒			◇1 🛒	◇1 🛒	
Deansgate 🚊	d	07 28									08 29										09 29			09 51	
Manchester Oxford Road	d	07 32			07 58					08 24	08 33			08 54	08 58					09 24	09 33			09 54	09 58
Manchester Piccadilly [10] 🚊	a	07 34			08 01					08 27	08 35			08 56	09 01					09 27	09 35			09 56	10 01
	d	07 36	07 46	07 54	08 03	08 06		08 14	08 24	08 29	08 37	08 46	08 54	08 58	09 03	09 06		09 14	09 24	09 29	09 37	09 46	09 54	09 58	10 03
Mauldeth Road	d		07 53					08 21				08 53						09 21				09 53			
Burnage	d		07 55					08 23				08 55						09 23				09 55			
East Didsbury	d		07 57					08 25				08 57				09 16		09 25				09 57			
Gatley	d		07 59					08 27				08 59						09 27				09 59			
Heald Green	d		08 02					08 30			08 47	09 02		09 10				09 30				10 02		10 10	
Manchester Airport ✈	a	07 53	08 07	08 12	08 22	08 26		08 38	08 42	08 47	08 52	09 08	09 12	09 19	09 22	09 26		09 38	09 42	09 47	09 51	10 07	10 12	10 17	10 22
Wilmslow 84	a		08 21									09 21										10 20			
Crewe [10] 84	a		08 47									09 46										10 46			

Table 85

Saturdays

until 11 February

Manchester - Manchester Airport

Network Diagram - see first Page of Table 78

		TP ◇1 🛒		NT	TP ◇1 🛒	TP ◇1 🛒	NT	NT	TP ◇1 🛒	TP ◇1 🛒	NT	TP ◇1 🛒		NT	TP ◇1 🛒	TP ◇1 🛒	NT	NT	TP ◇1 🛒	TP ◇1 🛒	NT	TP ◇1 🛒		NT	TP ◇1 🛒
Deansgate	d						10 29			10 51							11 29			11 51					
Manchester Oxford Road	d					10 24	10 33			10 54	10 58					11 24	11 33			11 54	11 58				
Manchester Piccadilly 10	a					10 27	10 35			10 56	11 01					11 27	11 35			11 56	12 01				
	d	10 06		10 14	10 24	10 29	10 37	10 46	10 54	10 58	11 03	11 06		11 14	11 24	11 29	11 37	11 46	11 54	11 58	12 03	12 06		12 14	12 24
Mauldeth Road	d			10 21				10 53						11 21				11 53						12 21	
Burnage	d			10 23				10 55						11 23				11 55						12 23	
East Didsbury	d			10 25				10 57						11 25				11 57						12 25	
Gatley	d			10 27				10 59						11 27				11 59						12 27	
Heald Green	d			10 30				11 02		11 10				11 30				12 02		12 10				12 30	
Manchester Airport	a	10 26		10 38	10 42	10 47	10 53	11 07	11 12	11 17	11 22	11 26		11 38	11 42	11 47	11 53	12 07	12 12	12 17	12 22	12 26		12 38	12 42
Wilmslow 84	a							11 21										12 20							
Crewe 10 84	a							11 47										12 46							

		TP ◇1 🛒	NT	NT	TP ◇1 🛒	TP ◇1 🛒	NT	TP ◇1 🛒		NT	TP ◇1 🛒	TP ◇1 🛒	NT	NT	TP ◇1 🛒	TP ◇1 🛒	NT	TP ◇1 🛒		NT	TP ◇1 🛒	TP ◇1 🛒	NT	NT	TP ◇1 🛒
Deansgate	d		12 29			12 51							13 29			13 51							14 29		
Manchester Oxford Road	d	12 24	12 33			12 54	12 58					13 24	13 33			13 54	13 58					14 24	14 33		
Manchester Piccadilly 10	a	12 27	12 35			12 56	13 01					13 27	13 35			13 56	14 01					14 27	14 35		
	d	12 29	12 37	12 46	12 54	12 58	13 03	13 06		13 14	13 24	13 29	13 37	13 46	13 54	13 58	14 03	14 06		14 14	14 24	14 29	14 37	14 46	14 54
Mauldeth Road	d			12 53						13 21				13 53						14 21				14 53	
Burnage	d			12 55						13 23				13 55						14 23				14 55	
East Didsbury	d			12 57						13 25				13 57						14 25				14 57	
Gatley	d			12 59						13 27				13 59						14 27				14 59	
Heald Green	d			13 02		13 10				13 30				14 02		14 10				14 30				15 02	
Manchester Airport	a	12 47	12 53	13 07	13 12	13 17	13 22	13 26		13 38	13 42	13 47	13 53	14 07	14 12	14 17	14 22	14 26		14 38	14 42	14 47	14 53	15 07	15 12
Wilmslow 84	a			13 21										14 20										15 20	
Crewe 10 84	a			13 47										14 46										15 46	

		TP ◇1 🛒	NT	TP ◇1 🛒		NT	TP ◇1 🛒	TP ◇1 🛒	NT	NT	TP ◇1 🛒	TP ◇1 🛒	NT	TP ◇1 🛒		NT	TP ◇1 🛒	TP ◇1 🛒	NT	NT	TP ◇1 🛒	TP ◇1 🛒	NT	TP ◇1 🛒	
Deansgate	d	14 51							15 29			15 51										16 51			
Manchester Oxford Road	d	14 54	14 58					15 24	15 33			15 54	15 58					16 24	16 33			16 54	16 58		
Manchester Piccadilly 10	a	14 56	15 01					15 27	15 35			15 56	16 01					16 27	16 35			16 56	17 01		
	d	14 58	15 03	15 06		15 14	15 24	15 29	15 37	15 46	15 54	15 58	16 03	16 06		16 14	16 24	16 29	16 37	16 46	16 54	16 58	17 03	17 06	
Mauldeth Road	d					15 21				15 53						16 21				16 53					
Burnage	d					15 23				15 55						16 23				16 55					
East Didsbury	d					15 25				15 57						16 25				16 57				17 17	
Gatley	d					15 27				15 59						16 27				16 59				17 20	
Heald Green	d	15 10				15 30				16 02		16 10				16 30		16 40		17 02		17 10		17 23	
Manchester Airport	a	15 17	15 22	15 26		15 38	15 42	15 47	15 53	16 07	16 12	16 17	16 22	16 26		16 38	16 42	16 47	16 53	17 07	17 12	17 17	17 22	17 32	
Wilmslow 84	a									16 20										17 21					
Crewe 10 84	a									16 46										17 47					

		NT	TP ◇1 🛒	NT	NT	TP ◇1 🛒	TP ◇1 🛒	NT	TP ◇1 🛒	NT		TP ◇1 🛒	TP ◇1 🛒	NT	NT	TP ◇1 🛒	NT	TP ◇1 🛒	NT	TP ◇1 🛒		NT	TP ◇1	NT	AW ◇ 🛒
Deansgate	d			17 29			17 51															19 29			
Manchester Oxford Road	d		17 24	17 33			17 54	17 58					18 24	18 33			18 58			19 24		19 33		19 43	19 49
Manchester Piccadilly 10	a		17 27	17 35			17 56	18 01					18 27	18 35			19 01			19 27		19 35		19 45	19 52
	d	17 14	17 29	17 37	17 46	17 54	17 58	18 03	18 06	18 14		18 24	18 29	18 37	18 46	18 54	19 03	19 06	19 14	19 32		19 37	19 40	19 46	19 54
Mauldeth Road	d	17 21			17 53					18 21					18 53				19 21					19 53	
Burnage	d	17 23			17 55					18 23					18 55				19 23					19 55	
East Didsbury	d	17 25			17 57					18 25					18 57				19 25					19 57	
Gatley	d	17 27			17 59					18 27					18 59				19 27					19 59	
Heald Green	d	17 30	17 41		18 02		18 10			18 30			18 40		19 02				19 30					20 02	
Manchester Airport	a	17 38	17 48	17 53	18 07	18 12	18 17	18 22	18 26	18 38		18 42	18 47	18 53	19 08	19 13	19 24	19 28	19 38	19 50		19 53	19 59	20 07	20 13
Wilmslow 84	a				18 21										19 23									20 24	
Crewe 10 84	a				18 47																				

		TP ◇1	TP ◇1 🛒	TP ◇1 🛒	NT	TP ◇1		NT	TP ◇1	NT	TP ◇1	TP ◇1 🛒	NT	TP ◇1	NT	TP ◇1		TP ◇1	NT	TP ◇1	TP ◇1				
Deansgate	d	19 51			20 29				20 51				21 29			21 51				22 51					
Manchester Oxford Road	d	19 54		20 24	20 33			20 43	20 54	20 58		21 24	21 33		21 43	21 54			22 43	22 54					
Manchester Piccadilly 10	a	19 56		20 27	20 35			20 45	20 56	21 01		21 27	21 35		21 45	21 56			22 45	22 56					
	d	19 58	20 06	20 32	20 37	20 40		20 46	20 58	21 03	21 06	21 29	21 37	21 40	21 46	21 58		22 40	22 46	22 58	23 55				
Mauldeth Road	d		20 15					20 53			21 15				21 53				22 53		00 04				
Burnage	d		20 17					20 55			21 17				21 55				22 55		00 07				
East Didsbury	d		20 20					20 57			21 20				21 57				22 57		00 10				
Gatley	d		20 23					20 59			21 23				21 59				22 59		00 13				
Heald Green	d	20 10	20 26					21 02	21 10		21 26				22 02	22 09			23 02	23 09	00 17				
Manchester Airport	a	20 17	20 36	20 47	20 53	20 57		21 07	21 17	21 24	21 36	21 46	21 53	21 57	22 08	22 17		22 57	23 08	23 17	00 23				
Wilmslow 84	a							21 24							22 22				23 22						
Crewe 10 84	a																								

Table 85

Saturdays

18 February to 24 March

Manchester - Manchester Airport

Network Diagram - see first Page of Table 78

		TP	TP	TP	NT	TP	TP	TP	AW	NT		TP	TP	TP	NT	NT	TP	TP	NT	NT		TP	TP	NT	NT
		◇1	◇1	◇1		◇1	◇1	◇1				◇1	◇1	◇1			◇1	◇1				◇1	◇1		
Deansgate (tram)	d																		07 11					07 28	
Manchester Oxford Road	d																		07 15				07 24	07 32	
Manchester Piccadilly 10 (tram)	a																		07 17				07 27	07 34	
	d	23p55	00 54	03 44	04 15	04 44	04 50	04 54	05 00	05 35		06 03	06 08	06 12	06 15	06 46	06 54	07 06		07 14		07 23	07 29	07 36	07 46
Mauldeth Road	d	00 04								05 42					06 22	06 53				07 21					07 53
Burnage	d	00 07								05 44					06 24	06 55				07 23					07 55
East Didsbury	d	00 10								05 46					06 26	06 57				07 25					07 57
Gatley	d	00 13								05 49					06 29	06 59				07 27					07 59
Heald Green	d	00 17								05 52					06 32	07 02				07 30					08 02
Manchester Airport (air)	a	00 24	01 10	04 00	04 30	05 00	05 07	05 10	05 19	05 57		06 18	06 24	06 29	06 39	07 07	07 12	07 29		07 38		07 42	07 47	07 53	08 07
Wilmslow 84	a									06 11						07 20									08 21
Crewe 10 84	a									06 43						07 46									08 47

		TP	TP	NT	TP	TP		NT	NT	TP	TP	TP	NT	TP	TP	NT		NT	TP	TP	TP	NT	TP	TP	NT
		◇1	◇1		◇1	◇1				◇1	◇1	◇1		◇1	◇1				◇1	◇1	◇1		◇1	◇1	
			trolley			trolley					trolley	trolley		trolley	trolley				trolley	trolley	trolley		trolley	trolley	
Deansgate (tram)	d							08 29								09 29				09 51					10 29
Manchester Oxford Road	d					08 24		08 33			08 54				09 24	09 33				09 54				10 24	10 33
Manchester Piccadilly 10 (tram)	a					08 27		08 35			08 56				09 27	09 35				09 56				10 27	10 35
	d	07 54	08 06	08 14	08 24	08 29		08 37	08 46	08 54	08 58	09 06	09 14	09 24	09 29	09 37		09 46	09 54	09 58	10 06	10 14	10 24	10 29	10 37
Mauldeth Road	d			08 21					08 53				09 21					09 53				10 21			
Burnage	d			08 23					08 55				09 23					09 55				10 23			
East Didsbury	d			08 25					08 57			09 16	09 25					09 57				10 25			
Gatley	d			08 27					08 59				09 27					09 59				10 27			
Heald Green	d			08 30				08 47	09 02		09 10		09 30					10 02		10 10		10 30			
Manchester Airport (air)	a	08 12	08 26	08 38	08 42	08 47		08 52	09 08	09 12	09 19	09 26	09 38	09 42	09 47	09 51		10 07	10 12	10 17	10 26	10 38	10 42	10 47	10 53
Wilmslow 84	a								09 21									10 20							
Crewe 10 84	a								09 46									10 46							

		NT		TP	TP	TP	NT	TP	TP	NT	NT	TP		TP	TP	NT	TP	TP	NT	NT	TP	TP		TP	NT
				◇1	◇1	◇1		◇1	◇1			◇1		◇1	◇1		◇1	◇1			◇1	◇1		◇1	
				trolley	trolley	trolley		trolley	trolley			trolley		trolley	trolley		trolley	trolley			trolley	trolley		trolley	
Deansgate (tram)	d				10 51					11 29				11 51					12 29			12 51			
Manchester Oxford Road	d				10 54				11 24	11 33				11 54				12 24	12 33			12 54			
Manchester Piccadilly 10 (tram)	a				10 56				11 27	11 35				11 56				12 27	12 35			12 56			
	d	10 46		10 54	10 58	11 06	11 14	11 24	11 29	11 37	11 46	11 54		11 58	12 06	12 14	12 24	12 29	12 37	12 46	12 54	12 58		13 06	13 14
Mauldeth Road	d	10 53					11 21				11 53					12 21				12 53					13 21
Burnage	d	10 55					11 23				11 55					12 23				12 55					13 23
East Didsbury	d	10 57					11 25				11 57					12 25				12 57					13 25
Gatley	d	10 59					11 27				11 59					12 27				12 59					13 27
Heald Green	d	11 02			11 10		11 30				12 02			12 10		12 30				13 02		13 10			13 30
Manchester Airport (air)	a	11 07		11 12	11 17	11 26	11 38	11 42	11 47	11 53	12 07	12 12		12 17	12 26	12 38	12 42	12 47	12 53	13 07	13 12	13 17		13 26	13 38
Wilmslow 84	a	11 21									12 20									13 21					
Crewe 10 84	a	11 47									12 46									13 47					

		TP	TP	NT	NT	TP	TP	TP		NT	TP	TP	NT	NT	TP	TP	TP	NT		TP	TP	NT	NT	TP	TP
		◇1	◇1			◇1	◇1	◇1			◇1	◇1			◇1	◇1	◇1			◇1	◇1			◇1	◇1
		trolley	trolley			trolley	trolley	trolley			trolley	trolley			trolley	trolley	trolley			trolley	trolley			trolley	trolley
Deansgate (tram)	d			13 29			13 51						14 29			14 51						15 29			15 51
Manchester Oxford Road	d		13 24	13 33			13 54					14 24	14 33			14 54					15 24	15 33			15 54
Manchester Piccadilly 10 (tram)	a		13 27	13 35			13 56					14 27	14 35			14 56					15 27	15 35			15 56
	d	13 24	13 29	13 37	13 46	13 54	13 58	14 06		14 14	14 24	14 29	14 37	14 46	14 54	14 58	15 06	15 14		15 24	15 29	15 37	15 46	15 54	15 58
Mauldeth Road	d				13 53					14 21				14 53				15 21					15 53		
Burnage	d				13 55					14 23				14 55				15 23					15 55		
East Didsbury	d				13 57					14 25				14 57				15 25					15 57		
Gatley	d				13 59					14 27				14 59				15 27					15 59		
Heald Green	d				14 02		14 10			14 30				15 02		15 10		15 30					16 02		16 10
Manchester Airport (air)	a	13 42	13 47	13 53	14 07	14 12	14 17	14 26		14 38	14 42	14 47	14 53	15 07	15 12	15 17	15 26	15 38		15 42	15 47	15 53	16 07	16 12	16 17
Wilmslow 84	a				14 20									15 20									16 20		
Crewe 10 84	a				14 46									15 46									16 46		

		TP	NT	TP		TP	NT	NT	TP	TP	TP	NT	TP	NT		NT	TP	TP	TP	NT	TP	TP	NT	NT	
		◇1		◇1		◇1			◇1	◇1	◇1		◇1				◇1	◇1	◇1		◇1	◇1			
		trolley		trolley		trolley			trolley	trolley	trolley		trolley				trolley	trolley	trolley		trolley	trolley			
Deansgate (tram)	d									16 51				17 29				17 51							
Manchester Oxford Road	d					16 24	16 33			16 54			17 24	17 33				17 54				18 24	18 33		
Manchester Piccadilly 10 (tram)	a					16 27	16 35			16 56			17 27	17 35				17 56				18 27	18 35		
	d	16 06	16 14	16 24		16 29	16 37	16 46	16 54	16 58	17 06	17 14	17 29	17 37		17 46	17 54	17 58	18 06	18 14	18 24	18 29	18 37	18 46	
Mauldeth Road	d		16 21					16 53				17 21				17 53				18 21				18 53	
Burnage	d		16 23					16 55				17 23				17 55				18 23				18 55	
East Didsbury	d		16 25					16 57			17 17	17 25				17 57				18 25				18 57	
Gatley	d		16 27					16 59			17 20	17 27				17 59				18 27				18 59	
Heald Green	d		16 30			16 40		17 02		17 10	17 23	17 30	17 41			18 02		18 10		18 30		18 40		19 02	
Manchester Airport (air)	a	16 26	16 38	16 42		16 47	16 53	17 07	17 12	17 17	17 32	17 38	17 48	17 53		18 07	18 12	18 17	18 26	18 38	18 42	18 47	18 53	19 08	
Wilmslow 84	a							17 21								18 21								19 23	
Crewe 10 84	a							17 47								18 47									

Table 85

Saturdays

18 February to 24 March

Manchester - Manchester Airport

Network Diagram - see first Page of Table 78

		TP	TP	NT	TP	NT	TP	NT	AW	TP		TP	TP	NT	TP	NT	TP	TP	TP	NT		TP	NT	TP	TP
		◇1	◇1		◇1		◇1		◇	◇1		◇1	◇1		◇1		◇1	◇1	◇1			◇1		◇1	◇1
		🛒	🛒		🛒				🛒			🛒	🛒						🛒						
Deansgate 🚊	d					19 29				19 51				20 29			20 51			21 29				21 51	
Manchester Oxford Road	d				19 24	19 33		19 43	19 49	19 54			20 24	20 33		20 43	20 54		21 24	21 33			21 43	21 54	
Manchester Piccadilly 10 🚊	a				19 27	19 35		19 45	19 52	19 56			20 27	20 35		20 45	20 56		21 27	21 35			21 45	21 56	
	d	18 54	19 06	19 14	19 32	19 37	19 40	19 46	19 54	19 58		20 06	20 32	20 37	20 40	20 46	20 58	21 06	21 29	21 37		21 40	21 46	21 58	22 40
Mauldeth Road	d			19 21				19 53				20 15				20 53		21 15					21 53		
Burnage	d			19 23				19 55				20 17				20 55		21 17					21 55		
East Didsbury	d			19 25				19 57				20 20				20 57		21 20					21 57		
Gatley	d			19 27				19 59				20 23				20 59		21 23					21 59		
Heald Green	d			19 30				20 02		20 10		20 26				21 02	21 10	21 26					22 02	22 09	
Manchester Airport ✈	a	19 13	19 28	19 38	19 50	19 53	19 59	20 07	20 13	20 17		20 36	20 47	20 53	20 57	21 07	21 17	21 36	21 46	21 53		21 57	22 08	22 17	22 57
Wilmslow 84	a							20 24								21 24							22 22		
Crewe 10 84	a																								

		NT	TP	TP
			◇1	◇1
Deansgate 🚊	d		22 51	
Manchester Oxford Road	d	22 43	22 54	
Manchester Piccadilly 10 🚊	a	22 45	22 56	
	d	22 46	22 58	23 55
Mauldeth Road	d	22 53		00 04
Burnage	d	22 55		00 07
East Didsbury	d	22 57		00 10
Gatley	d	22 59		00 13
Heald Green	d	23 02	23 09	00 17
Manchester Airport ✈	a	23 08	23 17	00 23
Wilmslow 84	a	23 22		
Crewe 10 84	a			

Saturdays

from 31 March

		TP	TP	TP	NT	TP	TP	TP	AW	NT		NT	TP	TP	TP	NT	NT	TP	NT	TP		NT	NT	TP	TP
		◇1	◇1	◇1		◇1	◇1	◇1					◇1	◇1	◇1			◇1		◇1				◇1	◇1
Deansgate 🚊	d																					07 11			
Manchester Oxford Road	d																		06 58			07 15			07 24
Manchester Piccadilly 10 🚊	a																		07 01			07 17			07 27
	d	23p55	00 54	03 44	04 15	04 44	04 50	04 54	05 00	05 35		05 58	06 03	06 08	06 12	06 15	06 46	06 54	07 03	07 06			07 14	07 23	07 29
Mauldeth Road	d	00 04								05 42						06 22	06 53						07 21		
Burnage	d	00 07								05 44						06 24	06 55						07 23		
East Didsbury	d	00 10								05 46						06 26	06 57						07 25		
Gatley	d	00 13								05 49						06 29	06 59						07 27		
Heald Green	d	00 17								05 52						06 32	07 02						07 30		
Manchester Airport ✈	a	00 24	01 10	04 00	04 30	05 00	05 07	05 10	05 19	05 57		06 14	06 18	06 24	06 29	06 39	07 07	07 12	07 22	07 29			07 38	07 42	07 47
Wilmslow 84	a									06 11							07 20								
Crewe 10 84	a									06 43							07 46								

		NT	NT	TP	NT	TP		NT	TP	TP	NT	NT	TP	TP	NT	TP		NT	TP	TP	NT	NT	TP	TP	NT
				◇1		◇1			◇1	◇1			◇1	◇1		◇1			◇1	◇1			◇1	◇1	
						🛒				🛒				🛒		🛒			🛒	🛒			🛒	🛒	
Deansgate 🚊	d	07 28									08 29										09 29			09 51	
Manchester Oxford Road	d	07 32			07 58					08 24	08 33			08 54	08 58					09 24	09 33			09 54	09 58
Manchester Piccadilly 10 🚊	a	07 34			08 01					08 27	08 35			08 56	09 01					09 27	09 35			09 56	10 01
	d	07 36	07 46	07 54	08 03	08 06		08 14	08 24	08 29	08 37	08 46	08 54	08 58	09 03	09 06		09 14	09 24	09 29	09 37	09 46	09 54	09 58	10 03
Mauldeth Road	d		07 53					08 21				08 53						09 21				09 53			
Burnage	d		07 55					08 23				08 55						09 23				09 55			
East Didsbury	d		07 57					08 25				08 57				09 16		09 25				09 57			
Gatley	d		07 59					08 27				08 59						09 27				09 59			
Heald Green	d		08 02					08 30			08 47	09 02		09 10				09 30				10 02		10 10	
Manchester Airport ✈	a	07 53	08 07	08 12	08 22	08 26		08 38	08 42	08 47	08 52	09 08	09 12	09 19	09 22	09 26		09 38	09 42	09 47	09 51	10 07	10 12	10 17	10 22
Wilmslow 84	a		08 21									09 21										10 20			
Crewe 10 84	a		08 47									09 46										10 46			

		TP		NT	TP	TP	NT	NT	TP	TP	NT	TP		NT	TP	TP	NT	NT	TP	TP	NT	TP		NT	TP
		◇1			◇1	◇1			◇1	◇1		◇1			◇1	◇1			◇1	◇1		◇1			◇1
		🛒			🛒	🛒			🛒	🛒		🛒			🛒	🛒			🛒	🛒		🛒			🛒
Deansgate 🚊	d						10 29			10 51							11 29			11 51					
Manchester Oxford Road	d					10 24	10 33			10 54	10 58					11 24	11 33			11 54	11 58				
Manchester Piccadilly 10 🚊	a					10 27	10 35			10 56	11 01					11 27	11 35			11 56	12 01				
	d	10 06		10 14	10 24	10 29	10 37	10 46	10 54	10 58	11 03	11 06		11 14	11 24	11 29	11 37	11 46	11 54	11 58	12 03	12 06		12 14	12 24
Mauldeth Road	d			10 21				10 53						11 21				11 53						12 21	
Burnage	d			10 23				10 55						11 23				11 55						12 23	
East Didsbury	d			10 25				10 57						11 25				11 57						12 25	
Gatley	d			10 27				10 59						11 27				11 59						12 27	
Heald Green	d			10 30				11 02		11 10				11 30				12 02		12 10				12 30	
Manchester Airport ✈	a	10 26		10 38	10 42	10 47	10 53	11 07	11 12	11 17	11 22	11 26		11 38	11 42	11 47	11 53	12 07	12 12	12 17	12 22	12 26		12 38	12 42
Wilmslow 84	a							11 21										12 20							
Crewe 10 84	a							11 47										12 46							

Table 85

Saturdays

from 31 March

Manchester - Manchester Airport

Network Diagram - see first Page of Table 78

		TP	NT	NT	TP	TP	NT	TP		NT	TP	TP	NT	NT	TP	TP	NT	TP		NT	TP	TP	NT	NT	TP
		◇1 🚲			◇1 🚲	◇1 🚲		◇1 🚲			◇1 🚲	◇1 🚲			◇1 🚲	◇1 🚲		◇1 🚲			◇1 🚲	◇1 🚲			◇1 🚲
Deansgate	d		12 29			12 51							13 29			13 51							14 29		
Manchester Oxford Road	d	12 24	12 33			12 54	12 58					13 24	13 33			13 54	13 58					14 24	14 33		
Manchester Piccadilly 10	a	12 27	12 35			12 56	13 01					13 27	13 35			13 56	14 01					14 27	14 35		
	d	12 29	12 37	12 46	12 54	12 58	13 03	13 06		13 14	13 24	13 29	13 37	13 46	13 54	13 58	14 03	14 06		14 14	14 24	14 29	14 37	14 46	14 54
Mauldeth Road	d			12 53						13 21				13 53						14 21				14 53	
Burnage	d			12 55						13 23				13 55						14 23				14 55	
East Didsbury	d			12 57						13 25				13 57						14 25				14 57	
Gatley	d			12 59						13 27				13 59						14 27				14 59	
Heald Green	d			13 02		13 10				13 30				14 02		14 10				14 30				15 02	
Manchester Airport	a	12 47	12 53	13 07	13 12	13 17	13 22	13 26		13 38	13 42	13 47	13 53	14 07	14 12	14 17	14 22	14 26		14 38	14 42	14 47	14 53	15 07	15 12
Wilmslow 84	a			13 21										14 20										15 20	
Crewe 10 84	a			13 47										14 46										15 46	

		TP	NT	TP		NT	TP	TP	NT	NT	TP	TP	NT	TP		NT	TP	TP	NT	NT	TP	TP	NT	TP	
		◇1 🚲		◇1 🚲			◇1 🚲	◇1 🚲			◇1 🚲	◇1 🚲		◇1 🚲			◇1 🚲	◇1 🚲			◇1 🚲	◇1 🚲		◇1 🚲	
Deansgate	d	14 51							15 29			15 51										16 51			
Manchester Oxford Road	d	14 54	14 58					15 24	15 33			15 54	15 58					16 24	16 33			16 54	16 58		
Manchester Piccadilly 10	a	14 56	15 01					15 27	15 35			15 56	16 01					16 27	16 35			16 56	17 01		
	d	14 58	15 03	15 06		15 14	15 24	15 29	15 37	15 46	15 54	15 58	16 03	16 06		16 14	16 24	16 29	16 37	16 46	16 54	16 58	17 03	17 06	
Mauldeth Road	d					15 21				15 53						16 21				16 53					
Burnage	d					15 23				15 55						16 23				16 55					
East Didsbury	d					15 25				15 57						16 25				16 57				17 17	
Gatley	d					15 27				15 59						16 27				16 59				17 20	
Heald Green	d	15 10				15 30				16 02		16 10				16 30		16 40		17 02		17 10		17 23	
Manchester Airport	a	15 17	15 22	15 26		15 38	15 42	15 47	15 53	16 07	16 12	16 17	16 22	16 26		16 38	16 42	16 47	16 53	17 07	17 12	17 17	17 22	17 32	
Wilmslow 84	a									16 20										17 21					
Crewe 10 84	a									16 46										17 47					

		NT	TP	NT	NT	TP	TP	NT	TP	NT		TP	TP	NT	NT	TP	NT	TP	NT	TP		NT	TP	NT	AW
			◇1 🚲			◇1 🚲	◇1 🚲		◇1 🚲			◇1 🚲	◇1 🚲			◇1 🚲		◇1 🚲		◇1 🚲			◇1		◇ 🚲
Deansgate	d			17 29			17 51															19 29			
Manchester Oxford Road	d		17 24	17 33			17 54	17 58					18 24	18 33			18 58			19 24		19 33		19 43	19 49
Manchester Piccadilly 10	a		17 27	17 35			17 56	18 01					18 27	18 35			19 01			19 27		19 35		19 45	19 52
	d	17 14	17 29	17 37	17 46	17 54	17 58	18 03	18 06	18 14		18 24	18 29	18 37	18 46	18 54	19 03	19 06	19 14	19 32		19 37	19 40	19 46	19 54
Mauldeth Road	d	17 21			17 53					18 21					18 53				19 21					19 53	
Burnage	d	17 23			17 55					18 23					18 55				19 23					19 55	
East Didsbury	d	17 25			17 57					18 25					18 57				19 25					19 57	
Gatley	d	17 27			17 59					18 27					18 59				19 27					19 59	
Heald Green	d	17 30	17 41		18 02		18 10			18 30			18 40		19 02				19 30					20 02	
Manchester Airport	a	17 38	17 48	17 53	18 07	18 12	18 17	18 22	18 26	18 38		18 42	18 47	18 53	19 08	19 13	19 24	19 28	19 38	19 50		19 53	19 59	20 07	20 13
Wilmslow 84	a				18 21										19 23									20 24	
Crewe 10 84	a				18 47																				

		TP	TP	TP	NT	TP		NT	TP	NT	TP	TP	NT	TP	NT	TP		TP	NT	TP	TP				
		◇1	◇1 🚲	◇1 🚲		◇1			◇1		◇1	◇1 🚲		◇1		◇1		◇1		◇1	◇1				
Deansgate	d	19 51			20 29				20 51				21 29			21 51				22 51					
Manchester Oxford Road	d	19 54		20 24	20 33			20 43	20 54	20 58		21 24	21 33		21 43	21 54			22 43	22 54					
Manchester Piccadilly 10	a	19 56		20 27	20 35			20 45	20 56	21 01		21 27	21 35		21 45	21 56			22 45	22 56					
	d	19 58	20 06	20 32	20 37	20 40		20 46	20 58	21 03	21 06	21 29	21 37	21 40	21 46	21 58		22 40	22 46	22 58	23 55				
Mauldeth Road	d		20 15					20 53			21 15				21 53				22 53		00 04				
Burnage	d		20 17					20 55			21 17				21 55				22 55		00 07				
East Didsbury	d		20 20					20 57			21 20				21 57				22 57		00 10				
Gatley	d		20 23					20 59			21 23				21 59				22 59		00 13				
Heald Green	d	20 10	20 26					21 02	21 10		21 26				22 02	22 09			23 02	23 09	00 17				
Manchester Airport	a	20 17	20 36	20 47	20 53	20 57		21 07	21 17	21 24	21 36	21 47	21 53	21 57	22 08	22 17		22 57	23 08	23 17	00 23				
Wilmslow 84	a							21 24							22 22				23 22						
Crewe 10 84	a																								

Sundays

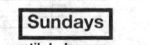

until 1 January

		TP	TP	NT	NT	TP	NT	TP	TP	NT		TP	NT	NT	TP	TP	NT	TP	NT	NT		TP	TP	NT	TP
		◇1 A	🚌			🚌		◇1	◇1			◇1			◇1	◇1		◇1				◇1	◇1		◇1
Deansgate	d													09 15	09 23			09 51		10 16					10 51
Manchester Oxford Road	d												09 05	09 18	09 26			09 54	10 00	10 19					10 54
Manchester Piccadilly 10	a												09 08	09 21	09 28			09 56	10 03	10 22					10 56
	d	23p55	05u00	05 41	06 41	07u00	07 41	07 50	08 38	08 41		08 47	09 10		09 32	09 38	09 41	09 58	10 07			10 16	10 38	10 41	10 58
Mauldeth Road	d	00 04		05 48	06 50		07 48			08 48							09 48							10 48	
Burnage	d	00 07		05 50	06 52		07 50			08 50							09 50							10 50	
East Didsbury	d	00 10		05 52	06 54		07 52			08 52							09 52							10 52	
Gatley	d	00 13		05 54	06 56		07 54			08 54							09 54							10 54	
Heald Green	d	00 17		05 57	06 59		07 57			08 57							09 57							10 57	
Manchester Airport	a	00 23	05 25	06 03	07 05	07 25	08 02	08 05	08 55	09 04		09 07	09 25		09 48	09 55	10 03	10 17	10 24			10 29	10 55	11 01	11 17
Wilmslow 84	a									09 15														11 16	
Crewe 10 84	a																								

A not 11 December

Table 85

Sundays

until 1 January

Manchester - Manchester Airport

Network Diagram - see first Page of Table 78

	NT	NT	TP	TP	NT		TP	NT	NT	TP	TP	TP	NT	TP	NT		NT	TP	TP	TP	NT	TP	NT	NT
			◇1	◇1			◇1			◇1	◇1	◇1		◇1 trolley				◇1	◇1 trolley	◇1		◇1		
Deansgate d		11 11					11 51		12 11					12 51			13 11					13 51		14 11
Manchester Oxford Road d	11 03	11 17	11 24		11 38		11 56	12 00	12 17		12 24		12 43	12 54	13 00		13 17		13 24			13 54	14 01	14 17
Manchester Piccadilly 10 a	11 06	11 19	11 27		11 40		11 58	12 03	12 19		12 27		12 45	12 59	13 03		13 19		13 27			13 56	14 03	14 19
d	11 08		11 29	11 38	11 41		11 58	12 07		12 13	12 29	12 38	12 47	13 01	13 04			13 15	13 30	13 38	13 41	13 58	14 04	
Mauldeth Road d					11 48								12 54								13 48			
Burnage d					11 50								12 56								13 50			
East Didsbury d					11 52								12 58								13 52			
Gatley d					11 54								13 00								13 54			
Heald Green d					11 57								13 03								13 57			
Manchester Airport a	11 24		11 47	11 55	12 04		12 17	12 21		12 27	12 48	12 55	13 08	13 17	13 19			13 29	13 47	13 55	14 03	14 17	14 21	
Wilmslow 84 a													13 19											
Crewe 10 84 a																								

	TP		TP	TP	NT	TP	NT	NT	TP	TP	TP		NT	TP	NT	NT	TP	TP	TP	NT	TP		NT	NT
	◇1		◇1	◇1		◇1			◇1	◇1 trolley	◇1			◇1			◇1	◇1	◇1		◇1			
Deansgate d						14 51		15 11						15 51		16 11					16 51			17 11
Manchester Oxford Road d			14 24			14 54	15 00	15 17		15 24				15 54	16 00	16 17		16 24			16 54		17 00	17 17
Manchester Piccadilly 10 a			14 27			14 56	15 02	15 19		15 27				15 56	16 02	16 19		16 27			16 56		17 02	17 19
d	14 13		14 29	14 38	14 41	14 58	15 04		15 13	15 29	15 38		15 41	15 58	16 04		16 13	16 29	16 38	16 41	16 58		17 04	
Mauldeth Road d					14 48								15 48							16 48				
Burnage d					14 50								15 50							16 50				
East Didsbury d					14 52								15 52							16 52				
Gatley d					14 54								15 54							16 54				
Heald Green d					14 57								15 57							16 57				
Manchester Airport a	14 27		14 47	14 55	15 01	15 17	15 20		15 28	15 47	15 55		16 03	16 17	16 21		16 27	16 46	16 55	17 02	17 17		17 21	
Wilmslow 84 a					15 13															17 13				
Crewe 10 84 a																								

	TP	TP	TP	NT	TP	NT	NT		TP	TP	TP	NT	TP	NT	NT	TP	TP		TP	NT	TP	NT	NT	TP
	◇1	◇1 trolley	◇1		◇1				◇1	◇1 trolley	◇1		◇1			◇1	◇1 trolley		◇1		◇1			◇1
Deansgate d					17 51		18 11						18 51		19 11						19 51		20 11	
Manchester Oxford Road d		17 24			17 54	18 00	18 17			18 24			18 54	19 00	19 17		19 24				19 54	20 00	20 17	
Manchester Piccadilly 10 a		17 27			17 56	18 02	18 19			18 27			18 56	19 02	19 19		19 27				19 56	20 02	20 19	
d	17 13	17 29	17 38	17 41	17 58	18 04			18 13	18 29	18 38	18 41	18 58	19 04		19 13	19 29		19 38	19 41	19 58	20 04		20 13
Mauldeth Road d				17 48								18 48								19 48				
Burnage d				17 50								18 50								19 50				
East Didsbury d				17 52								18 52								19 52				
Gatley d				17 54								18 54								19 54				
Heald Green d				17 57								18 57								19 57				
Manchester Airport a	17 27	17 47	17 55	18 03	18 17	18 21			18 27	18 45	18 55	19 02	19 17	19 21		19 27	19 47		19 55	20 02	20 17	20 26		20 30
Wilmslow 84 a												19 13												
Crewe 10 84 a																								

	TP	TP	NT		TP	NT	NT	TP	TP	AW	NT	TP	NT		NT	TP	AW	TP	NT	NT	TP	NT	NT	
	◇1 trolley	◇1	1		◇1			◇1	◇1 trolley		1	◇1				◇1		◇1	1		◇1 trolley			
Deansgate d					20 51		21 11					21 51			22 11						23 08	23 11		
Manchester Oxford Road d	20 24				20 54	21 00	21 17		21 24			21 54	22 00		22 17					22 47	23 11	23 17	23 47	
Manchester Piccadilly 10 a	20 27				20 56	21 02	21 19		21 27			21 56	22 02		22 19					22 50	23 14	23 19	23 50	
d	20 29	20 38	20 41		20 58	21 04		21 13	21 29	21 34	21 41	21 58	22 04			22 13	22 35	22 38	22 46	22 52	23 15		23 52	
Mauldeth Road d			20 48								21 48								22 53					
Burnage d			20 50								21 50								22 55					
East Didsbury d			20 52								21 52								22 57					
Gatley d			20 54								21 54								22 59					
Heald Green d			20 57								21 57								23 02					
Manchester Airport a	20 45	20 55	21 01		21 16	21 20		21 27	21 46		22 03	22 17	22 21			22 27		22 55	23 09	23 15	23 30		00 07	
Wilmslow 84 a			21 12							21 50							22 50							
Crewe 10 84 a										22 13							23 10							

Sundays

8 January to 12 February

	TP	TP	TP	TP	NT	TP	NT	TP	TP		NT	TP	NT	TP	NT	TP	NT	NT	TP		TP	NT	TP	NT
	◇1	bus	bus	bus	bus	bus	bus	bus	bus		bus	bus	bus	◇1		◇1			◇1		◇1		◇1	
Deansgate d																		09 15	09 27				09 54	
Manchester Oxford Road d																	09 05	09 18	09 30				09 56	10 00
Manchester Piccadilly 10 a																	09 08	09 21	09 32				09 59	10 03
d	23p55	00 37	04 12	05u00	05 25	05 27	06 25	06 45	07u00		07 25	07 45	08 10	08 38	08 41	08 47	09 10		09 34		09 38	09 41	09 59	10 07
Mauldeth Road d	00 04				05 36		06 36				07 36				08 48							09 48		
Burnage d	00 07				05 41		06 41				07 41				08 50							09 50		
East Didsbury d	00 10				05 47		06 47				07 47				08 52							09 52		
Gatley d	00 13				05 52		06 52				07 52				08 54							09 54		
Heald Green d	00 17				06 00		07 00				08 00				08 57							09 57		
Manchester Airport a	00 23	01 02	04 37	05 25	06 05	05 52	07 05	07 10	07 25		08 05	08 10	08 35	08 55	09 04	09 07	09 25		09 49		09 55	10 03	10 17	10 24
Wilmslow 84 a															09 15									
Crewe 10 84 a																								

Table 85

Sundays

8 January to 12 February

Manchester - Manchester Airport

Network Diagram - see first Page of Table 78

		NT	TP ◇1	TP ◇1	NT	TP ◇1		NT	NT	TP ◇1	TP ◇1	NT	TP ◇1	NT	NT	TP ◇1		TP ◇1	TP ◇1	NT	TP ◇1 trolley	NT	NT	TP ◇1	TP ◇1 trolley
Deansgate	d	10 16				10 54			11 11				11 54		12 11						12 53		13 11		
Manchester Oxford Road	d	10 19				10 56		11 03	11 17	11 27		11 38	11 56	12 00	12 17			12 28		12 43	12 56	13 00	13 17		13 24
Manchester Piccadilly 10	a	10 22				10 59		11 06	11 19	11 30		11 40	11 59	12 03	12 19			12 30		12 45	12 58	13 03	13 19		13 27
	d		10 16	10 38	10 41	10 59		11 08		11 31	11 38	11 41	12 01	12 07		12 13		12 31	12 38	12 47	13 00	13 04		13 15	13 30
Mauldeth Road	d				10 48							11 48								12 54					
Burnage	d				10 50							11 50								12 56					
East Didsbury	d				10 52							11 52								12 58					
Gatley	d				10 54							11 54								13 00					
Heald Green	d				10 57							11 57								13 03					
Manchester Airport ✈	a		10 29	10 55	11 01	11 17		11 24		11 47	11 55	12 04	12 17	12 21		12 34		12 47	12 55	13 08	13 17	13 19		13 29	13 47
Wilmslow	84 a				11 16															13 19					
Crewe 10	84 a																								

		TP ◇1		NT	TP ◇1	NT	NT	TP ◇1	TP ◇1	TP ◇1	NT	TP ◇1		NT	NT	TP ◇1	TP ◇1 trolley	TP ◇1	NT	TP ◇1	NT	NT		TP ◇1	TP ◇1
Deansgate	d				13 54		14 11					14 54			15 11					15 54		16 11			
Manchester Oxford Road	d				13 56	14 01	14 17		14 24			14 56		15 00	15 17		15 24			15 56	16 00	16 17			16 24
Manchester Piccadilly 10	a				13 59	14 03	14 19		14 27			14 59		15 02	15 19		15 27			15 59	16 02	16 19			16 27
	d	13 38		13 41	13 59	14 04		14 13	14 29	14 38	14 41	14 59		15 04		15 14	15 29	15 38	15 41	15 59	16 04			16 13	16 29
Mauldeth Road	d			13 48							14 48								15 48						
Burnage	d			13 50							14 50								15 50						
East Didsbury	d			13 52							14 52								15 52						
Gatley	d			13 54							14 54								15 54						
Heald Green	d			13 57							14 57								15 57						
Manchester Airport ✈	a	13 55		14 03	14 17	14 21		14 27	14 47	14 55	15 01	15 17		15 20		15 28	15 47	15 55	16 03	16 17	16 21			16 27	16 47
Wilmslow	84 a										15 13														
Crewe 10	84 a																								

		TP ◇1	NT	TP ◇1	NT	NT	TP ◇1	TP ◇1 trolley		TP ◇1	NT	TP ◇1	NT	NT	TP ◇1	TP ◇1 trolley	TP ◇1	NT		TP ◇1	NT	NT	TP ◇1	TP ◇1 trolley	TP ◇1
Deansgate	d			16 54		17 11						17 54		18 11						18 54		19 11			
Manchester Oxford Road	d			16 56	17 00	17 17		17 24				17 56	18 00	18 17		18 24				18 56	19 00	19 17		19 24	
Manchester Piccadilly 10	a			16 59	17 02	17 19		17 27				17 59	18 02	18 19		18 27				18 59	19 02	19 19		19 27	
	d	16 38	16 41	16 59	17 04		17 13	17 29		17 38	17 41	17 59	18 04		18 13	18 29	18 38	18 41		18 59	19 04		19 13	19 29	19 38
Mauldeth Road	d		16 48								17 48							18 48							
Burnage	d		16 50								17 50							18 50							
East Didsbury	d		16 52								17 52							18 52							
Gatley	d		16 54								17 54							18 54							
Heald Green	d		16 57								17 57							18 57							
Manchester Airport ✈	a	16 55	17 02	17 17	17 21		17 27	17 47		17 55	18 03	18 17	18 21		18 27	18 47	18 55	19 02		19 17	19 21		19 27	19 47	19 55
Wilmslow	84 a		17 13															19 13							
Crewe 10	84 a																								

		NT	TP ◇1	NT		NT	TP ◇1	TP ◇1 trolley	TP ◇1	NT	TP ◇1	NT	NT	TP ◇1		TP ◇1 trolley	AW	NT	TP ◇1	NT	NT	TP ◇1	AW	TP ◇1	
Deansgate	d		19 54			20 11					20 54		21 11						21 54		22 11				
Manchester Oxford Road	d		19 56	20 00		20 17		20 24			20 56	21 00	21 17			21 24			21 56	22 00	22 17				
Manchester Piccadilly 10	a		19 59	20 02		20 19		20 27			20 59	21 02	21 19			21 27			21 59	22 02	22 19				
	d	19 41	19 59	20 04			20 13	20 29	20 38	20 41	20 59	21 04		21 13		21 29	21 34	21 41	21 59	22 04		22 13	22 35	22 38	
Mauldeth Road	d	19 48								20 48								21 48							
Burnage	d	19 50								20 50								21 50							
East Didsbury	d	19 52								20 52								21 52							
Gatley	d	19 54								20 54								21 54							
Heald Green	d	19 57								20 57								21 57							
Manchester Airport ✈	a	20 02	20 17	20 26			20 30	20 47	20 55	21 01	21 17	21 20		21 27		21 47		22 03	22 17	22 21		22 28		22 55	
Wilmslow	84 a									21 12							21 50						22 50		
Crewe 10	84 a																22 13						23 10		

		NT	NT	NT	TP ◇1 trolley	NT
Deansgate	d			23 11	23 15	
Manchester Oxford Road	d		22 47	23 17	23 22	23 47
Manchester Piccadilly 10	a		22 50	23 19	23 24	23 50
	d	22 46	22 52		23 26	23 52
Mauldeth Road	d	22 53				
Burnage	d	22 55				
East Didsbury	d	22 57				
Gatley	d	22 59				
Heald Green	d	23 02				
Manchester Airport ✈	a	23 09	23 15		23 42	00 07
Wilmslow	84 a					
Crewe 10	84 a					

Table 85

Sundays

19 February to 25 March

Manchester - Manchester Airport

Network Diagram - see first Page of Table 78

	TP	TP	TP	TP	TP	NT	TP	NT	TP		TP	TP	NT	TP	TP	NT	TP	NT	TP		TP	NT	NT	TP
	◇1	◇1	◇1	🚌	◇1		◇1	1	🚌		◇1	◇1		◇1	◇1		◇1		◇1		◇1			◇1
Deansgate 🚊 d																		09 15	09 23					09 51
Manchester Oxford Road d																		09 18	09 26				09 47	09 54
Manchester Piccadilly 10 🚊 a																		09 21	09 28				09 49	09 56
d	23p55	00 31	04 06	05u00	05 21	05 41	06 38	06 41	07u00		07 08	07 38	07 41	07 50	08 38	08 41	08 47		09 32		09 38	09 41	09 51	09 58
Mauldeth Road d	00 04					05 48		06 50					07 48			08 48						09 48		
Burnage d	00 07					05 50		06 52					07 50			08 50						09 50		
East Didsbury d	00 10					05 52		06 54					07 52			08 52						09 52		
Gatley d	00 13					05 54		06 56					07 54			08 54						09 54		
Heald Green d	00 17					05 57		06 59					07 57			08 57						09 57		
Manchester Airport ✈ a	00 23	00 46	04 23	05 25	05 38	06 03	06 55	07 05	07 25		07 22	07 55	08 02	08 05	08 55	09 04	09 07		09 48		09 55	10 03	10 05	10 17
Wilmslow 84 a																09 15								
Crewe 10 84 a																								

	NT	TP	TP	NT	NT		TP	NT	TP	TP	NT	NT	TP	NT	TP		TP	TP	NT	NT	TP	NT	TP	TP
		◇1	◇1				◇1		◇1	◇1			◇1		◇1		◇1	◇1			◇1 🛒		◇1	◇1 🛒
Deansgate 🚊 d	10 16						10 51	11 11					11 51	12 11							12 51	13 11		
Manchester Oxford Road d	10 19				10 50		10 54	11 17	11 24		11 38	11 49	11 56	12 17			12 24		12 43	12 52	12 54	13 17		13 24
Manchester Piccadilly 10 🚊 a	10 22				10 52		10 56	11 19	11 27		11 40	11 52	11 58	12 19			12 27		12 45	12 54	12 59	13 19		13 27
d		10 16	10 38	10 41	10 56		10 58		11 29	11 38	11 41	11 56	11 58		12 13		12 29	12 38	12 47	12 57	13 01		13 15	13 30
Mauldeth Road d				10 48							11 48								12 54					
Burnage d				10 50							11 50								12 56					
East Didsbury d				10 52							11 52								12 58					
Gatley d				10 54							11 54								13 00					
Heald Green d				10 57							11 57								13 03					
Manchester Airport ✈ a		10 29	10 55	11 01	11 09		11 17		11 47	11 55	12 04	12 11	12 17		12 27		12 48	12 55	13 08	13 11	13 17		13 29	13 47
Wilmslow 84 a				11 16															13 19					
Crewe 10 84 a																								

	TP		NT	NT	TP	NT	TP	TP	TP	NT	NT		TP	NT	TP	TP	TP	NT	NT	TP	NT		TP	TP
	◇1				◇1		◇1	◇1	◇1				◇1		◇1	◇1 🛒	◇1			◇1			◇1	◇1
Deansgate 🚊 d					13 51	14 11							14 51	15 11						15 51	16 11			
Manchester Oxford Road d				13 49	13 54	14 17		14 24			14 50		14 54	15 17		15 24			15 50	15 54	16 17			16 24
Manchester Piccadilly 10 🚊 a				13 51	13 56	14 19		14 27			14 52		14 56	15 19		15 27			15 52	15 56	16 19			16 27
d	13 38		13 41	13 54	13 58		14 13	14 29	14 38	14 41	14 54		14 58		15 13	15 29	15 38	15 41	15 54	15 58			16 13	16 29
Mauldeth Road d			13 48							14 48								15 48						
Burnage d			13 50							14 50								15 50						
East Didsbury d			13 52							14 52								15 52						
Gatley d			13 54							14 54								15 54						
Heald Green d			13 57							14 57								15 57						
Manchester Airport ✈ a	13 55		14 03	14 07	14 17		14 27	14 47	14 55	15 01	15 08		15 17		15 28	15 47	15 55	16 03	16 08	16 17			16 34	16 46
Wilmslow 84 a										15 13														
Crewe 10 84 a																								

	TP	NT	NT	TP	NT	TP	TP		TP	NT	NT	TP	NT	TP	TP	TP	NT		NT	TP	NT	TP	TP	TP
	◇1			◇1		◇1	◇1 🛒		◇1			◇1		◇1	◇1 🛒	◇1				◇1		◇1	◇1 🛒	◇1
Deansgate 🚊 d				16 51	17 11							17 51	18 11							18 51	19 11			
Manchester Oxford Road d			16 50	16 54	17 17		17 24				17 50	17 54	18 17		18 24				18 50	18 54	19 17		19 24	
Manchester Piccadilly 10 🚊 a			16 52	16 56	17 19		17 27				17 52	17 56	18 19		18 27				18 52	18 56	19 19		19 27	
d	16 38	16 41	16 54	16 58		17 13	17 29		17 38	17 41	17 54	17 58		18 13	18 29	18 38	18 41		18 54	18 58		19 13	19 29	19 38
Mauldeth Road d		16 48								17 48							18 48							
Burnage d		16 50								17 50							18 50							
East Didsbury d		16 52								17 52							18 52							
Gatley d		16 54								17 54							18 54							
Heald Green d		16 57								17 57							18 57							
Manchester Airport ✈ a	16 55	17 02	17 08	17 17		17 27	17 47		17 55	18 03	18 08	18 17		18 27	18 45	18 55	19 02		19 08	19 17		19 27	19 47	19 55
Wilmslow 84 a		17 13															19 13							
Crewe 10 84 a																								

	NT	NT	TP		NT	TP	TP	TP	NT	NT	TP	NT	TP		TP	AW	NT	NT	TP	NT	TP	AW	TP	
			◇1			◇1	◇1 🛒	◇1			◇1		◇1		◇1 🛒				◇1		◇1		◇1	
Deansgate 🚊 d			19 51		20 11						20 51	21 11							21 51	22 11				
Manchester Oxford Road d		19 50	19 54		20 17		20 24			20 50	20 54	21 17			21 24			21 50	21 54	22 17				
Manchester Piccadilly 10 🚊 a		19 52	19 56		20 19		20 27			20 52	20 56	21 19			21 27			21 52	21 56	22 19				
d	19 41	19 54	19 58			20 13	20 29	20 38	20 41	20 54	20 58		21 13		21 29	21 34	21 41	21 54	21 58		22 13	22 35	22 38	
Mauldeth Road d	19 48								20 48								21 48							
Burnage d	19 50								20 50								21 50							
East Didsbury d	19 52								20 52								21 52							
Gatley d	19 54								20 54								21 54							
Heald Green d	19 57								20 57								21 57							
Manchester Airport ✈ a	20 02	20 08	20 17			20 30	20 45	20 55	21 01	21 08	21 16		21 27		21 46		22 03	22 08	22 17		22 27		22 55	
Wilmslow 84 a									21 12							21 50						22 50		
Crewe 10 84 a																22 13						23 10		

Table 85 **Sundays**

19 February to 25 March

Manchester - Manchester Airport

Network Diagram - see first Page of Table 78

		NT	NT	TP	NT	NT
				◇1 🛒		
Deansgate 🚊	d			23 08	23 11	
Manchester Oxford Road	d		22 47	23 11	23 17	23 47
Manchester Piccadilly 10 🚊	a		22 50	23 14	23 19	23 50
	d	22 46	22 52	23 15		23 52
Mauldeth Road	d	22 53				
Burnage	d	22 55				
East Didsbury	d	22 57				
Gatley	d	22 59				
Heald Green	d	23 02				
Manchester Airport ✈	a	23 09	23 15	23 30		00 07
Wilmslow 84	a					
Crewe 10 84	a					

Sundays

from 1 April

		TP	TP	TP	TP	TP	TP	TP	NT	TP		TP	TP	NT	TP	TP	NT	NT	NT	TP		NT	NT	TP	TP
		◇1	🚌	🚌	🚌	🚌	◇1	🚌		◇1		◇1	🚌		◇1	◇1				◇1				◇1	◇1
Deansgate 🚊	d															08 53		09 15		09 51			10 16		
Manchester Oxford Road	d															08 56	09 05	09 18		09 54		10 00	10 19		
Manchester Piccadilly 10 🚊	a															08 59	09 08	09 21		09 56		10 03	10 22		
	d	23p55	03 55	05u00	05 55	07u00	07 38	07 40	07 41	08 13		08 38	08 40	08 41	08 47	09 00	09 10		09 41	09 58		10 07		10 16	10 38
Mauldeth Road	d	00 04							07 48					08 48					09 48						
Burnage	d	00 07							07 50					08 50					09 50						
East Didsbury	d	00 10							07 52					08 52					09 52						
Gatley	d	00 13							07 54					08 54					09 54						
Heald Green	d	00 17							07 57					08 57					09 57						
Manchester Airport ✈	a	00 23	04 20	05 25	06 20	07 25	07 55	08 05	08 02	08 26		08 55	09 05	09 04	09 07	09 17	09 25		10 03	10 17		10 24		10 29	10 55
Wilmslow 84	a													09 15											
Crewe 10 84	a																								

		NT	TP	NT	TP	NT		TP	NT	TP	NT	TP	NT	TP	TP	NT		TP	NT	TP	NT	TP	TP	NT	TP
			◇1		◇1			◇1		◇1		◇1		◇1	◇1			◇1 🛒		◇1		◇1	◇1		◇1
Deansgate 🚊	d		10 51			11 11				11 51			12 11					12 51			13 11				13 51
Manchester Oxford Road	d		10 54	11 03		11 17		11 24	11 38	11 54	12 00		12 17		12 24	12 43		12 54	13 00		13 17		13 24		13 54
Manchester Piccadilly 10 🚊	a		10 56	11 06		11 19		11 27	11 40	11 56	12 03		12 19		12 27	12 45		12 59	13 03		13 19		13 27		13 56
	d	10 41	10 58	11 08	11 10			11 29	11 41	11 58	12 07	12 10		12 13	12 29	12 47		13 01	13 04	13 10		13 13	13 29	13 41	13 58
Mauldeth Road	d	10 48							11 48							12 54								13 48	
Burnage	d	10 50							11 50							12 56								13 50	
East Didsbury	d	10 52							11 52							12 58								13 52	
Gatley	d	10 54							11 54							13 00								13 54	
Heald Green	d	10 57							11 57							13 03								13 57	
Manchester Airport ✈	a	11 01	11 17	11 24	11 24			11 47	12 04	12 17	12 21	12 24		12 27	12 47	13 08		13 17	13 19	13 24		13 27	13 47	14 03	14 17
Wilmslow 84	a	11 16														13 19									
Crewe 10 84	a																								

		NT		TP	NT	TP	TP	NT	TP	NT	TP	NT		TP	TP	NT	TP	NT	TP	NT	TP	TP		NT	TP
				◇1		◇1	◇1		◇1		◇1			◇1	◇1 🛒		◇1		◇1		◇1	◇1			◇1
Deansgate 🚊	d				14 11				14 51			15 11					15 51			16 11					16 51
Manchester Oxford Road	d	14 01			14 17		14 24		14 54	15 00		15 17			15 24		15 54	16 00		16 17		16 24			16 54
Manchester Piccadilly 10 🚊	a	14 03			14 19		14 27		14 56	15 02		15 19			15 27		15 56	16 02		16 19		16 27			16 56
	d	14 04		14 10		14 13	14 29	14 41	14 58	15 04	15 10			15 13	15 29	15 41	15 58	16 04	16 10		16 13	16 29		16 41	16 58
Mauldeth Road	d							14 48								15 48								16 48	
Burnage	d							14 50								15 50								16 50	
East Didsbury	d							14 52								15 52								16 52	
Gatley	d							14 54								15 54								16 54	
Heald Green	d							14 57								15 57								16 57	
Manchester Airport ✈	a	14 21		14 24		14 27	14 47	15 01	15 17	15 20	15 24			15 28	15 47	16 03	16 17	16 21	16 24		16 34	16 46		17 02	17 17
Wilmslow 84	a							15 13																17 13	
Crewe 10 84	a																								

		NT	TP	NT	TP	TP	NT	TP		NT	TP	NT	TP	TP	NT	TP	NT	TP		TP	NT	TP	NT	TP	NT
			◇1		◇1	◇1 🛒		◇1			◇1		◇1	◇1 🛒		◇1		◇1		◇1		◇1 🛒		◇1	
Deansgate 🚊	d			17 11				17 51				18 11				18 51					19 13			19 51	
Manchester Oxford Road	d	17 00		17 17		17 24		17 54		18 00		18 17		18 24		18 54	19 00				19 17	19 24		19 54	20 00
Manchester Piccadilly 10 🚊	a	17 02		17 19		17 27		17 56		18 02		18 19		18 27		18 56	19 02				19 19	19 27		19 56	20 02
	d	17 04	17 10		17 13	17 29	17 41	17 58		18 04	18 10		18 13	18 29	18 41	18 58	19 04	19 10		19 13		19 29	19 41	19 58	20 04
Mauldeth Road	d						17 48								18 48								19 48		
Burnage	d						17 50								18 50								19 50		
East Didsbury	d						17 52								18 52								19 52		
Gatley	d						17 54								18 54								19 54		
Heald Green	d						17 57								18 57								19 57		
Manchester Airport ✈	a	17 21	17 24		17 27	17 47	18 03	18 17		18 21	18 24		18 27	18 45	19 02	19 17	19 21	19 26		19 27		19 47	20 02	20 17	20 26
Wilmslow 84	a														19 13										
Crewe 10 84	a																								

Table 85

Sundays

from 1 April

Manchester - Manchester Airport

Network Diagram - see first Page of Table 78

		TP ◇1	NT	TP ◇1	TP ◇1 🚲	NT	TP ◇1	NT	TP ◇1	NT	TP ◇1	TP ◇1 🚲	AW	NT	TP ◇1	NT	NT	TP ◇1	AW	NT	NT	TP ◇1
Deansgate	d		20 11				20 51			21 11					21 51		22 11					
Manchester Oxford Road	d		20 17		20 24		20 54	21 00		21 17		21 24			21 54	22 00	22 17				22 47	
Manchester Piccadilly 10	a		20 19		20 27		20 56	21 02		21 19		21 27			21 56	22 02	22 19				22 50	
	d	20 10		20 13	20 29	20 41	20 58	21 04	21 09		21 13	21 29	21 34	21 41	21 58	22 04		22 13	22 35	22 46	22 52	23 09
Mauldeth Road	d					20 48								21 48						22 53		
Burnage	d					20 50								21 50						22 55		
East Didsbury	d					20 52								21 52						22 57		
Gatley	d					20 54								21 54						22 59		
Heald Green	d					20 57								21 57						23 02		
Manchester Airport ✈	a	20 24		20 30	20 45	21 01	21 16	21 20	21 24		21 27	21 46		22 03	22 17	22 21		22 27		23 09	23 15	23 24
Wilmslow 84	a					21 12							21 50						22 50			
Crewe 10 84	a												22 13						23 10			

		TP ◇1 🚲	NT	NT
Deansgate	d	23 08	23 11	
Manchester Oxford Road	d	23 11	23 17	23 47
Manchester Piccadilly 10	a	23 14	23 19	23 50
	d	23 15		23 52
Mauldeth Road	d			
Burnage	d			
East Didsbury	d			
Gatley	d			
Heald Green	d			
Manchester Airport ✈	a	23 30		00 07
Wilmslow 84	a			
Crewe 10 84	a			

Manchester Airport - Manchester

Network Diagram - see first Page of Table 78

Miles		TP	TP	TP	TP	NT	TP	TP	NT	NT		TP	AW	TP	TP	NT	TP	TP	NT	NT		TP	TP	TP
		MX		MX	MO	MX			MX	MO														
		◇1	◇1	◇1	◇1		◇1	◇1				◇1	◇ 🛒	◇1	◇1 🛒		◇1 🛒	◇1 🛒				◇1 🛒	◇1 🛒	◇1 🛒
—	Crewe 10 84 d					00 44																		
—	Wilmslow 84 d															05 46								
0	**Manchester Airport** ✈ d	23p52	00 01	00 38	00 48	01 20	04 00	04 12	04 34	04 38		05 15	05 33	05 37	05 45	06 01	06 18	06 23	06 41	06 46		06 55	07 00	07 05
1½	Heald Green d														05 49	06 04				06 49				
4	Gatley d															06 07				06 52				
5¼	East Didsbury d															06 10				06 55				
6¼	Burnage d															06 12				06 57				
7¼	Mauldeth Road d															06 14				06 59				
—	**Manchester Piccadilly** 10 🚊 a	00 09	00 15	00 51	01 01	01 36	04 14	04 27	04 47	04 51		05 33	05 48	05 51	06 00	06 25	06 31	06 39	06 56	07 11		07 13	07 14	07 22
—	d												05 50		06 03		06 33		06 58				07 15	
—	**Manchester Oxford Road** a												05 52		06 05		06 35		07 00				07 17	
—	Deansgate 🚊 a																							

	NT	TP	TP	NT	NT	TP		TP	NT	TP	NT	TP	TP	NT	NT	TP		TP	NT	TP	NT	TP	TP	NT
		◇1 🛒	◇1 🛒			◇1 🛒		◇1 🛒		◇1 🛒		◇1 🛒	◇1 🛒			◇1 🛒		◇1 🛒		◇1 🛒		◇1 🛒	◇1 🛒	
Crewe 10 84 d	06 33																				08 31			
Wilmslow 84 d	06 57										07 56										08 57			
Manchester Airport ✈ d	07 17	07 25	07 35	07 38	07 46	07 53		07 56	08 01	08 05	08 17	08 25	08 35	08 41	08 46	08 55		09 00	09 03	09 05	09 17	09 29	09 35	09 41
Heald Green d	07 20	07 30		07 42	07 49				08 05		08 20	08 29			08 49						09 20	09 33		
Gatley d	07 23			07 45	07 52			08 02			08 23	08 32			08 52						09 23			
East Didsbury d	07 26			07 48	07 55			08 05			08 26	08 35			08 55						09 26			
Burnage d	07 28				07 57						08 28				08 57						09 28			
Mauldeth Road d	07 30				07 59						08 30				08 59						09 30			
Manchester Piccadilly 10 🚊 a	07 42	07 43	07 49	07 57	08 11	08 12		08 14	08 21	08 22	08 42	08 44	08 49	08 58	09 11	09 13		09 14	09 18	09 22	09 42	09 44	09 52	09 59
d				07 59				08 15	08 22			08 46		09 01				09 16	09 22			09 46		10 01
Manchester Oxford Road a				08 01				08 17	08 24			08 48		09 03				09 18	09 24			09 48		10 03
Deansgate 🚊 a									08 28			08 51							09 28			09 51		

	NT	TP		TP	NT	TP	NT	TP	TP	NT	NT	TP		TP	NT	TP	NT	TP	TP	NT	NT	TP		TP
		◇1 🛒		◇1 🛒		◇1 🛒		◇1 🛒	◇1 🛒			◇1 🛒		◇1 🛒		◇1 🛒		◇1 🛒	◇1 🛒			◇1 🛒		◇1 🛒
Crewe 10 84 d							09 33										10 34							
Wilmslow 84 d							09 57										10 57							
Manchester Airport ✈ d	09 46	09 55		10 00	10 03	10 05	10 17	10 29	10 35	10 41	10 46	10 55		11 00	11 03	11 05	11 17	11 29	11 35	11 41	11 46	11 55		12 00
Heald Green d	09 49						10 20	10 33			10 49						11 20	11 33			11 49			
Gatley d	09 52						10 23				10 52						11 23				11 52			
East Didsbury d	09 55						10 26				10 55						11 26				11 55			
Burnage d	09 57						10 28				10 57						11 28				11 57			
Mauldeth Road d	09 59						10 30				10 59						11 30				11 59			
Manchester Piccadilly 10 🚊 a	10 11	10 13		10 14	10 18	10 22	10 42	10 44	10 52	10 59	11 11	11 13		11 14	11 18	11 22	11 42	11 44	11 52	11 59	12 11	12 13		12 14
d				10 16	10 22			10 46		11 01				11 16	11 22			11 46		12 01				12 16
Manchester Oxford Road a				10 18	10 24			10 48		11 03				11 18	11 24			11 48		12 03				12 18
Deansgate 🚊 a					10 28			10 51							11 28			11 51						

	NT	TP	NT	TP	TP	NT	NT	TP		TP	NT	TP	NT	TP	TP	NT	NT	TP		TP	NT	TP	NT	TP
		◇1 🛒		◇1 🛒	◇1 🛒			◇1 🛒		◇1 🛒		◇1 🛒		◇1 🛒	◇1 🛒			◇1 🛒		◇1 🛒		◇1 🛒		◇1 🛒
Crewe 10 84 d			11 34										12 34										13 34	
Wilmslow 84 d			11 57										12 57										13 57	
Manchester Airport ✈ d	12 03	12 05	12 17	12 29	12 35	12 41	12 46	12 55		13 00	13 03	13 05	13 17	13 29	13 35	13 41	13 46	13 55		14 00	14 03	14 05	14 17	14 29
Heald Green d			12 20	12 33			12 49						13 20	13 33			13 49						14 20	14 33
Gatley d			12 23				12 52						13 23				13 52						14 23	
East Didsbury d			12 26				12 55						13 26				13 55						14 26	
Burnage d			12 28				12 57						13 28				13 57						14 28	
Mauldeth Road d			12 30				12 59						13 30				13 59						14 30	
Manchester Piccadilly 10 🚊 a	12 18	12 22	12 42	12 44	12 52	12 59	13 11	13 13		13 14	13 18	13 22	13 42	13 44	13 52	13 59	14 11	14 13		14 14	14 18	14 22	14 42	14 44
d	12 22			12 46		13 01				13 16	13 22			13 46		14 01				14 16	14 22			14 46
Manchester Oxford Road a	12 24			12 48		13 03				13 18	13 24			13 48		14 03				14 18	14 24			14 48
Deansgate 🚊 a	12 28			12 51							13 28			13 51							14 28			14 51

	TP	NT	NT	TP		TP	NT	TP	NT	TP	NT	NT	TP	TP		NT	TP	NT	TP	TP	NT	NT	TP	TP
	◇1 🛒			◇1 🛒		◇1 🛒		◇1 🛒		◇1 🛒			◇1 🛒	◇1 🛒			◇1 🛒		◇1 🛒	◇1 🛒			◇1 🛒	◇1 🛒
Crewe 10 84 d									14 34									15 33						
Wilmslow 84 d									14 57									15 56						
Manchester Airport ✈ d	14 35	14 41	14 46	14 55		15 00	15 03	15 05	15 17	15 35	15 41	15 46	15 55	16 00		16 03	16 05	16 17	16 29	16 35	16 41	16 46	16 55	17 00
Heald Green d			14 49						15 20			15 49						16 20	16 33			16 49		
Gatley d			14 52						15 23			15 52						16 23				16 52		
East Didsbury d			14 55						15 26			15 55						16 26				16 55		
Burnage d			14 57						15 28			15 57						16 28				16 57		
Mauldeth Road d			14 59						15 30			15 59						16 30				16 59		
Manchester Piccadilly 10 🚊 a	14 52	14 59	15 11	15 13		15 14	15 18	15 22	15 41	15 52	15 59	16 11	16 13	16 14		16 18	16 22	16 42	16 44	16 52	16 59	17 11	17 13	17 14
d		15 01				15 16	15 22		15 42		16 01			16 16		16 22			16 46		17 01			17 15
Manchester Oxford Road a		15 03				15 18	15 24		15 46		16 03			16 18		16 24			16 48		17 03			17 17
Deansgate 🚊 a							15 28									16 28								

Manchester Airport - Manchester

Network Diagram - see first Page of Table 78

			NT	TP FX	NT	TP	NT	NT	TP	TP	NT		NT	TP	NT	NT	TP	TP	NT	NT	TP		TP	NT	NT
				◇1		◇1			◇1	◇1				◇1			◇1	◇1			◇1		◇1		
				🛒		🛒			🛒	🛒															
Crewe 10	84 d				16 34								17 33							18 34					
Wilmslow	84 d				16 57								17 56							18 57					
Manchester Airport	d		17 03	17 05	17 17	17 35	17 41	17 46	17 55	18 00	18 03		18 17	18 35	18 41	18 46	18 55	19 00	19 03	19 09	19 20		19 29	19 41	19 46
Heald Green	d				17 20			17 49					18 20			18 49				19 12			19 33		19 49
Gatley	d				17 23			17 52					18 23			18 52				19 15					19 52
East Didsbury	d				17 26			17 55					18 26			18 55				19 18					19 55
Burnage	d				17 28			17 57					18 28			18 57				19 20					19 57
Mauldeth Road	d				17 30			17 59					18 30			18 59				19 22					19 59
Manchester Piccadilly 10	a		17 21	17 22	17 42	17 52	17 59	18 11	18 13	18 14	18 18		18 42	18 52	18 59	19 11	19 13	19 14	19 18	19 31	19 36		19 44	19 59	20 11
	d		17 22				18 01			18 16	18 22				19 01			19 16	19 20	19 32			19 46	20 01	
Manchester Oxford Road	a		17 25				18 03			18 18	18 24				19 03			19 18	19 22	19 36			19 48	20 03	
Deansgate	a										18 28								19 26				19 51		

		TP	TP	NT	NT	TP	TP		AW	TP	NT	NT	TP	NT FX	TP	AW	NT FO		TP	TP	NT	NT	TP	TP	NT
		◇1	◇1			◇1	◇1			◇1			◇1		◇1				◇1	◇1			◇1	◇1	
Crewe 10	84 d																								
Wilmslow	84 d				19 56							20 56									21 55				22 56
Manchester Airport	d	19 55	20 00	20 03	20 09	20 20	20 29		20 32	20 47	21 03	21 09	21 20	21 24	21 29	21 32	21 42		21 47	22 00	22 08	22 19	22 22	22 29	23 09
Heald Green	d				20 12		20 33			20 51		21 12			21 33				21 51		22 12			22 33	23 12
Gatley	d				20 15					20 54		21 15							21 54		22 15				23 15
East Didsbury	d				20 18					20 57		21 18							21 57		22 17				23 18
Burnage	d				20 20					20 59		21 20							21 59		22 19				23 20
Mauldeth Road	d				20 22					21 02		21 22							22 02		22 21				23 22
Manchester Piccadilly 10	a	20 13	20 14	20 18	20 32	20 36	20 44		20 48	21 13	21 18	21 32	21 36	21 38	21 44	21 48	21 59		22 13	22 14	22 31	22 34	22 36	22 44	23 33
	d		20 16	20 20	20 32		20 46		20 50		21 20	21 32			21 46	21 50	22 01			22 16	22 32	22 36		22 46	
Manchester Oxford Road	a		20 18	20 22	20 36		20 48		20 52		21 22	21 36			21 48	21 52	22 03			22 18	22 36	22 38		22 48	
Deansgate	a			20 26			20 51				21 26				21 51							22 41		22 51	

		TP	TP
		◇1	◇1
Crewe 10	84 d		
Wilmslow	84 d		
Manchester Airport	d	23 18	23 52
Heald Green	d		
Gatley	d		
East Didsbury	d		
Burnage	d		
Mauldeth Road	d		
Manchester Piccadilly 10	a	23 34	00 09
	d		
Manchester Oxford Road	a		
Deansgate	a		

Saturdays

until 11 February

		TP	TP	TP	NT	TP	TP	NT	TP	AW		TP	TP	NT	TP	TP	NT	NT	TP	TP		TP	NT	TP	TP
		◇1	◇1	◇1		◇1	◇🚌		◇1	◇		◇1	◇1		◇1	◇1			◇1	◇1		◇1		◇1	◇1
										🛒			🛒		🛒	🛒			🛒	🛒		🛒		🛒	🛒
Crewe 10	84 d				00 44																		06 33		
Wilmslow	84 d													05 46									06 57		
Manchester Airport	d	23p52	00 01	00 38	01 20	04 00	04 15	04 34	05 20	05 33		05 37	05 45	06 01	06 18	06 23	06 41	06 46	06 55	07 00		07 05	07 17	07 25	07 33
Heald Green	d												05 49	06 04				06 49					07 20	07 30	
Gatley	d													06 07				06 52					07 23		
East Didsbury	d													06 10				06 55					07 26		
Burnage	d													06 12				06 57					07 28		
Mauldeth Road	d													06 14				06 59					07 30		
Manchester Piccadilly 10	a	00 09	00 15	00 51	01 36	04 14	04 29	04 47	05 35	05 48		05 51	06 00	06 25	06 31	06 39	06 56	07 11	07 13	07 14		07 22	07 42	07 43	07 48
	d									05 50			06 03		06 33		06 58			07 15					
Manchester Oxford Road	a									05 52			06 05		06 35		07 00			07 17					
Deansgate	a																								

		NT	NT	TP	TP	NT		TP	NT	TP	TP	NT	NT	TP	TP	NT		TP	NT	TP	TP	NT	NT	TP	TP
				◇1	◇1			◇1		◇1	◇1			◇1	◇1			◇1		◇1	◇1			◇1	◇1
				🛒	🛒			🛒		🛒	🛒			🛒	🛒			🛒		🛒	🛒			🛒	🛒
Crewe 10	84 d								07 30										08 31						
Wilmslow	84 d								07 56										08 57						
Manchester Airport	d	07 38	07 46	07 53	07 56	08 01		08 05	08 17	08 25	08 35	08 41	08 46	08 55	09 00	09 03		09 05	09 17	09 29	09 35	09 41	09 46	09 55	10 00
Heald Green	d	07 42	07 49			08 05			08 20	08 29			08 49						09 20	09 33			09 49		
Gatley	d	07 45	07 52		08 02				08 23	08 32			08 52						09 23				09 52		
East Didsbury	d	07 48	07 55		08 05				08 26	08 35			08 55						09 26				09 55		
Burnage	d		07 57						08 28				08 57						09 28				09 57		
Mauldeth Road	d		07 59						08 30				08 59						09 30				09 59		
Manchester Piccadilly 10	a	07 57	08 11	08 12	08 14	08 21		08 22	08 42	08 44	08 49	08 59	09 11	09 13	09 14	09 18		09 22	09 42	09 44	09 52	09 59	10 11	10 13	10 14
	d	07 59			08 15	08 22				08 46		09 01			09 16	09 22				09 46		10 01			10 16
Manchester Oxford Road	a	08 01			08 17	08 24				08 48		09 03			09 18	09 24				09 48		10 03			10 18
Deansgate	a					08 28				08 51						09 28				09 51					

Table 85

Saturdays

until 11 February

Manchester Airport - Manchester

Network Diagram - see first Page of Table 78

	NT		TP	NT	TP	TP	NT	NT	TP	TP	NT		TP	NT	TP	TP	NT	NT	TP	TP	NT		TP	NT
			◇1		◇1	◇1			◇1	◇1			◇1		◇1	◇1			◇1	◇1			◇1	
					🛒	🛒			🛒	🛒			🛒		🛒	🛒			🛒	🛒			🛒	
Crewe 10 84 d				09 33										10 34										11 34
Wilmslow 84 d				09 57										10 57										11 57
Manchester Airport ✈ d	10 03		10 05	10 17	10 29	10 35	10 41	10 46	10 55	11 00	11 03		11 05	11 17	11 29	11 35	11 41	11 46	11 55	12 00	12 03		12 05	12 17
Heald Green d				10 20	10 33			10 49						11 20	11 33			11 49						12 20
Gatley d				10 23				10 52						11 23				11 52						12 23
East Didsbury d				10 26				10 55						11 26				11 55						12 26
Burnage d				10 28				10 57						11 28				11 57						12 28
Mauldeth Road d				10 30				10 59						11 30				11 59						12 30
Manchester Piccadilly 10 a	10 18		10 22	10 42	10 44	10 52	10 59	11 11	11 13	11 14	11 18		11 22	11 42	11 44	11 52	11 59	12 11	12 13	12 14	12 18		12 22	12 42
d	10 22				10 46		11 01			11 16	11 22				11 46		12 01			12 16	12 22			
Manchester Oxford Road a	10 24				10 48		11 03			11 18	11 24				11 48		12 03			12 18	12 24			
Deansgate a	10 28				10 51						11 28				11 51						12 28			

	TP	TP	NT	NT	TP	TP	NT		TP	NT	TP	TP	NT	NT	TP	TP	NT		TP	NT	TP	TP	NT	NT
	◇1	◇1			◇1	◇1			◇1		◇1	◇1			◇1	◇1			◇1		◇1	◇1		
	🛒	🛒			🛒	🛒			🛒		🛒	🛒			🛒	🛒			🛒		🛒			
Crewe 10 84 d										12 34										13 34				
Wilmslow 84 d										12 57										13 57				
Manchester Airport ✈ d	12 29	12 35	12 41	12 46	12 55	13 00	13 03		13 05	13 17	13 29	13 35	13 41	13 46	13 55	14 00	14 03		14 05	14 17	14 29	14 35	14 41	14 46
Heald Green d	12 33			12 49						13 20	13 33			13 49						14 20	14 33			14 49
Gatley d				12 52						13 23				13 52						14 23				14 52
East Didsbury d				12 55						13 26				13 55						14 26				14 55
Burnage d				12 57						13 28				13 57						14 28				14 57
Mauldeth Road d				12 59						13 30				13 59						14 30				14 59
Manchester Piccadilly 10 a	12 44	12 52	12 59	13 11	13 13	13 14	13 18		13 22	13 42	13 44	13 52	13 59	14 11	14 13	14 14	14 18		14 22	14 42	14 44	14 52	14 59	15 11
d	12 46		13 01			13 16	13 22				13 46		14 01			14 16	14 22				14 46		15 01	
Manchester Oxford Road a	12 48		13 03			13 18	13 24				13 48		14 03			14 18	14 24				14 48		15 03	
Deansgate a	12 51						13 28				13 51						14 28				14 51			

	TP	TP	NT		TP	NT	TP	TP	NT	NT	TP	TP	NT		TP	NT	TP	TP	NT	NT	TP	TP	NT	
	◇1	◇1			◇1		◇1	◇1			◇1	◇1			◇1		◇1	◇1			◇1	◇1		
	🛒	🛒			🛒		🛒	🛒			🛒	🛒					🛒				🛒	🛒		
Crewe 10 84 d						14 34										15 33								
Wilmslow 84 d						14 57										15 56								
Manchester Airport ✈ d	14 55	15 00	15 03		15 05	15 17	15 29	15 35	15 41	15 46	15 55	16 00	16 03		16 05	16 17	16 29	16 35	16 41	16 46	16 55	17 00	17 03	
Heald Green d						15 20	15 33			15 49						16 20	16 33			16 49				
Gatley d						15 23				15 52						16 23				16 52				
East Didsbury d						15 26				15 55						16 26				16 55				
Burnage d						15 28				15 57						16 28				16 57				
Mauldeth Road d						15 30				15 59						16 30				16 59				
Manchester Piccadilly 10 a	15 13	15 14	15 18		15 22	15 42	15 44	15 52	15 59	16 11	16 13	16 14	16 18		16 22	16 42	16 44	16 52	16 59	17 11	17 13	17 14	17 21	
d		15 16	15 22				15 46		16 01			16 16	16 22				16 46		17 01			17 15	17 23	
Manchester Oxford Road a		15 18	15 24				15 48		16 03			16 18	16 24				16 48		17 03			17 17	17 25	
Deansgate a			15 28				15 51						16 28											

	TP	NT	TP	NT	NT	TP	TP	NT	NT		TP	NT	NT	TP	TP	NT	NT	TP	TP		NT	NT	TP	TP
	◇1		◇1			◇1	◇1				◇1			◇1	◇1			◇1	◇1				◇1	◇1
						🛒	🛒																	
Crewe 10 84 d		16 34							17 33								18 34							
Wilmslow 84 d		16 57							17 56								18 57							
Manchester Airport ✈ d	17 05	17 17	17 35	17 41	17 46	17 55	18 00	18 03	18 17		18 35	18 41	18 46	18 55	19 00	19 03	19 09	19 20	19 29		19 41	19 46	19 55	20 00
Heald Green d		17 20			17 49				18 20				18 49				19 12		19 33			19 49		
Gatley d		17 23			17 52				18 23				18 52				19 15					19 52		
East Didsbury d		17 26			17 55				18 26				18 55				19 18					19 55		
Burnage d		17 28			17 57				18 28				18 57				19 20					19 57		
Mauldeth Road d		17 30			17 59				18 30				18 59				19 22					19 59		
Manchester Piccadilly 10 a	17 22	17 42	17 52	17 59	18 11	18 13	18 14	18 18	18 42		18 52	18 59	19 11	19 13	19 14	19 18	19 31	19 36	19 44		19 59	20 11	20 13	20 14
d				18 01			18 16	18 22				19 01			19 16	19 20	19 32		19 46		20 01			20 16
Manchester Oxford Road a				18 03			18 18	18 24				19 03			19 18	19 22	19 36		19 48		20 03			20 18
Deansgate a								18 28								19 26			19 51					

	NT	NT	TP	TP	AW		TP	NT	NT	TP	TP	NT	TP	TP	NT		NT	TP	TP	TP	NT			
			◇1	◇1			◇1			◇1	◇1		◇1	◇1				◇1	◇1	◇1				
Crewe 10 84 d																								
Wilmslow 84 d		19 56							20 56						21 55						23 15			
Manchester Airport ✈ d	20 03	20 09	20 20	20 29	20 32		20 47	21 03	21 09	21 20	21 29	21 41	21 47	22 00	22 08		22 19	22 22	22 29	23 24	23 27			
Heald Green d		20 12		20 33			20 51		21 12		21 33		21 51		22 12				22 33		23 30			
Gatley d		20 15					20 54		21 15				21 54		22 15						23 33			
East Didsbury d		20 18					20 57		21 18				21 57		22 17						23 36			
Burnage d		20 20					20 59		21 20				21 59		22 19						23 38			
Mauldeth Road d		20 22					21 02		21 22				22 02		22 21						23 40			
Manchester Piccadilly 10 a	20 18	20 31	20 36	20 44	20 48		21 13	21 18	21 31	21 36	21 44	22 00	22 13	22 14	22 31		22 34	22 36	22 44	23 39	23 51			
d	20 20	20 32		20 46	20 50			21 22	21 32		21 46	22 01		22 16	22 32		22 36		22 46					
Manchester Oxford Road a	20 22	20 36		20 48	20 52			21 24	21 36		21 48	22 03		22 18	22 36		22 38		22 48					
Deansgate a	20 26			20 51				21 28			21 51						22 41		22 51					

Table 85

18 February to 24 March

Manchester Airport - Manchester

Network Diagram - see first Page of Table 78

			TP ◇1	TP ◇1	TP ◇1	NT	TP ◇1	TP ◇1	TP ◇1	AW ◇ 🛒	TP ◇1		TP ◇1 🛒	NT	TP ◇1 🛒	TP ◇1 🛒	NT	TP ◇1 🛒	TP ◇1 🛒	TP ◇1 🛒	NT		TP ◇1 🛒	TP ◇1 🛒	NT	TP ◇1 🛒
Crewe 10	84	d				00 44															06 33					
Wilmslow	84	d												05 46							06 57					
Manchester Airport	✈	d	23p52	00 01	00 38	01 20	04 00	04 15	05 20	05 33	05 37		05 45	06 01	06 18	06 23	06 46	06 55	07 00	07 05	07 17		07 25	07 33	07 46	07 53
Heald Green		d											05 49	06 04			06 49				07 20		07 30		07 49	
Gatley		d												06 07			06 52				07 23				07 52	
East Didsbury		d												06 10			06 55				07 26				07 55	
Burnage		d												06 12			06 57				07 28				07 57	
Mauldeth Road		d												06 14			06 59				07 30				07 59	
Manchester Piccadilly 10		a	00 09	00 15	00 51	01 36	04 14	04 29	05 35	05 48	05 51		06 00	06 25	06 31	06 39	07 11	07 13	07 14	07 22	07 42		07 43	07 48	08 11	08 12
		d								05 50			06 03		06 33				07 15							
Manchester Oxford Road		a								05 52			06 05		06 35				07 17							
Deansgate		a																								

			TP ◇1 🛒	NT	TP ◇1 🛒	NT	TP ◇1 🛒		TP ◇1 🛒	NT	TP ◇1 🛒	TP ◇1 🛒	NT	TP ◇1 🛒	NT	TP ◇1 🛒	TP ◇1 🛒		NT	TP ◇1 🛒	TP ◇1 🛒	NT	TP ◇1	NT	TP ◇1 🛒	TP ◇1 🛒
Crewe 10	84	d				07 30									08 31									09 33		
Wilmslow	84	d				07 56									08 57									09 57		
Manchester Airport	✈	d	07 56	08 01	08 05	08 17	08 25		08 35	08 46	08 55	09 00	09 03	09 05	09 17	09 29	09 35		09 46	09 55	10 00	10 03	10 05	10 17	10 29	10 35
Heald Green		d		08 05		08 20	08 29			08 49					09 20	09 33			09 49					10 20	10 33	
Gatley		d	08 02			08 23	08 32			08 52					09 23				09 52					10 23		
East Didsbury		d	08 05			08 26	08 35			08 55					09 26				09 55					10 26		
Burnage		d				08 28				08 57					09 28				09 57					10 28		
Mauldeth Road		d				08 30				08 59					09 30				09 59					10 30		
Manchester Piccadilly 10		a	08 14	08 21	08 22	08 42	08 44		08 49	09 11	09 13	09 14	09 18	09 22	09 42	09 44	09 52		10 11	10 13	10 14	10 18	10 22	10 42	10 44	10 52
		d	08 15	08 22			08 46					09 16	09 22			09 46					10 16	10 22			10 46	
Manchester Oxford Road		a	08 17	08 24			08 48					09 18	09 24			09 48					10 18	10 24			10 48	
Deansgate		a		08 28			08 51						09 28			09 51						10 28			10 51	

			NT		TP ◇1 🛒	TP ◇1 🛒	NT	TP ◇1 🛒	NT	TP ◇1 🛒	TP ◇1 🛒	NT	TP ◇1 🛒		TP ◇1 🛒	NT	TP ◇1 🛒	NT	TP ◇1 🛒	TP ◇1 🛒	NT	TP ◇1 🛒	TP ◇1 🛒		NT	TP ◇1 🛒
Crewe 10	84	d							10 34									11 34								
Wilmslow	84	d							10 57									11 57								
Manchester Airport	✈	d	10 46		10 55	11 00	11 03	11 05	11 17	11 29	11 35	11 46	11 55		12 00	12 03	12 05	12 17	12 29	12 35	12 46	12 55	13 00		13 03	13 05
Heald Green		d	10 49						11 20	11 33		11 49						12 20	12 33		12 49					
Gatley		d	10 52						11 23			11 52						12 23			12 52					
East Didsbury		d	10 55						11 26			11 55						12 26			12 55					
Burnage		d	10 57						11 28			11 57						12 28			12 57					
Mauldeth Road		d	10 59						11 30			11 59						12 30			12 59					
Manchester Piccadilly 10		a	11 11		11 13	11 14	11 18	11 22	11 42	11 44	11 52	12 11	12 13		12 14	12 18	12 22	12 42	12 44	12 52	13 11	13 13	13 14		13 18	13 22
		d				11 16	11 22			11 46					12 16	12 22			12 46				13 16		13 22	
Manchester Oxford Road		a				11 18	11 24			11 48					12 18	12 24			12 48				13 18		13 24	
Deansgate		a					11 28			11 51						12 28			12 51						13 28	

			NT	TP ◇1 🛒	TP ◇1 🛒	NT	TP ◇1 🛒	TP ◇1 🛒	NT		TP ◇1 🛒	NT	TP ◇1 🛒	TP ◇1	NT	TP ◇1 🛒	TP ◇1 🛒	NT	TP ◇1 🛒		NT	TP ◇1 🛒	TP ◇1 🛒	NT	TP ◇1 🛒	TP ◇1 🛒
Crewe 10	84	d	12 34									13 34									14 34					
Wilmslow	84	d	12 57									13 57									14 57					
Manchester Airport	✈	d	13 17	13 29	13 35	13 46	13 55	14 00	14 03		14 05	14 17	14 29	14 35	14 46	14 55	15 00	15 03	15 05		15 17	15 29	15 35	15 46	15 55	16 00
Heald Green		d	13 20	13 33		13 49						14 20	14 33		14 49						15 20	15 33		15 49		
Gatley		d	13 23			13 52						14 23			14 52						15 23			15 52		
East Didsbury		d	13 26			13 55						14 26			14 55						15 26			15 55		
Burnage		d	13 28			13 57						14 28			14 57						15 28			15 57		
Mauldeth Road		d	13 30			13 59						14 30			14 59						15 30			15 59		
Manchester Piccadilly 10		a	13 42	13 44	13 52	14 11	14 13	14 14	14 18		14 22	14 42	14 44	14 52	15 11	15 13	15 14	15 18	15 22		15 42	15 44	15 52	16 11	16 13	16 14
		d		13 46				14 16	14 22				14 46				15 16	15 22				15 46				16 16
Manchester Oxford Road		a		13 48				14 18	14 24				14 48				15 18	15 24				15 48				16 18
Deansgate		a		13 51					14 28				14 51					15 28				15 51				

			NT	TP ◇1	NT		TP ◇1 🛒	TP ◇1	NT	TP ◇1 🛒	TP ◇1 🛒	NT	TP ◇1	NT	TP ◇1		NT	TP ◇1 🛒	TP ◇1 🛒	NT	NT	TP ◇1	NT	TP ◇1	TP ◇1	
Crewe 10	84	d			15 33									16 34							17 33					
Wilmslow	84	d			15 56									16 57							17 56					
Manchester Airport	✈	d	16 03	16 05	16 17		16 29	16 35	16 46	16 55	17 00	17 03	17 05	17 17	17 35		17 46	17 55	18 00	18 03	18 17	18 35	18 46	18 55	19 00	
Heald Green		d			16 20		16 33		16 49					17 20			17 49				18 20		18 49			
Gatley		d			16 23				16 52					17 23			17 52				18 23		18 52			
East Didsbury		d			16 26				16 55					17 26			17 55				18 26		18 55			
Burnage		d			16 28				16 57					17 28			17 57				18 28		18 57			
Mauldeth Road		d			16 30				16 59					17 30			17 59				18 30		18 59			
Manchester Piccadilly 10		a	16 18	16 22	16 42		16 44	16 52	17 11	17 13	17 14	17 21	17 22	17 42	17 52		18 11	18 13	18 14	18 18	18 42	18 52	19 11	19 13	19 14	
		d	16 22				16 46				17 15	17 23							18 16	18 22					19 16	
Manchester Oxford Road		a	16 24				16 48				17 17	17 25							18 18	18 24					19 18	
Deansgate		a	16 28																	18 28						

Table 85

Saturdays

18 February to 24 March

Manchester Airport - Manchester

Network Diagram - see first Page of Table 78

	NT	NT	TP	TP	NT	TP	TP	NT	NT		TP	TP	AW	TP	NT	NT	TP	TP	TP		TP	NT	NT	TP
			◇1	◇1		◇1	◇1				◇1	◇1		◇1			◇1	◇1	◇1		◇1			◇1
Crewe 10 84 d		18 34																						
Wilmslow 84 d		18 57							19 56							20 56						21 55		
Manchester Airport ✈ d	19 03	19 09	19 20	19 29	19 46	19 55	20 00	20 03	20 09		20 20	20 29	20 32	20 47	21 03	21 09	21 20	21 29	21 47		22 00	22 08	22 19	22 22
Heald Green d		19 12		19 33	19 49				20 12			20 33		20 51		21 12		21 33	21 51			22 12		
Gatley d		19 15			19 52				20 15					20 54		21 15			21 54			22 15		
East Didsbury d		19 18			19 55				20 18					20 57		21 18			21 57			22 17		
Burnage d		19 20			19 57				20 20					20 59		21 20			21 59			22 19		
Mauldeth Road d		19 22			19 59				20 22					21 02		21 22			22 02			22 21		
Manchester Piccadilly 10 🚊 a	19 18	19 31	19 36	19 44	20 11	20 13	20 14	20 18	20 31		20 36	20 44	20 48	21 13	21 18	21 31	21 36	21 44	22 13		22 14	22 31	22 34	22 36
d	19 20	19 32		19 46			20 16	20 20	20 32			20 46	20 50		21 22	21 32		21 46			22 16	22 32	22 36	
Manchester Oxford Road a	19 22	19 36		19 48			20 18	20 22	20 36			20 48	20 52		21 24	21 36		21 48			22 18	22 36	22 38	
Deansgate 🚊 a	19 26			19 51				20 26				20 51			21 28			21 51					22 41	

	TP	TP	NT
	◇1	◇1	
Crewe 10 84 d			
Wilmslow 84 d			23 15
Manchester Airport ✈ d	22 29	23 24	23 27
Heald Green d	22 33		23 30
Gatley d			23 33
East Didsbury d			23 36
Burnage d			23 38
Mauldeth Road d			23 40
Manchester Piccadilly 10 🚊 a	22 44	23 39	23 51
d	22 46		
Manchester Oxford Road a	22 48		
Deansgate 🚊 a	22 51		

Saturdays

from 31 March

	TP	TP	TP	NT	TP	TP	NT	TP	AW		TP	TP	NT	TP	TP	NT	NT	TP	TP		TP	NT	TP	TP
	◇1	◇1	◇1		◇1	◇1		◇1	◇ trolley		◇1	◇1 trolley		◇1 trolley	◇1 trolley			◇1 trolley	◇1 trolley		◇1 trolley		◇1 trolley	◇1 trolley
Crewe 10 84 d				00 44																		06 33		
Wilmslow 84 d													05 46									06 57		
Manchester Airport ✈ d	23p52	00 01	00 38	01 20	04 00	04 15	04 34	05 20	05 33		05 37	05 45	06 01	06 18	06 23	06 41	06 46	06 55	07 00		07 05	07 17	07 25	07 33
Heald Green d												05 49	06 04				06 49					07 20	07 30	
Gatley d													06 07				06 52					07 23		
East Didsbury d													06 10				06 55					07 26		
Burnage d													06 12				06 57					07 28		
Mauldeth Road d													06 14				06 59					07 30		
Manchester Piccadilly 10 🚊 a	00 09	00 15	00 51	01 36	04 14	04 29	04 47	05 35	05 48		05 51	06 00	06 25	06 31	06 39	06 56	07 11	07 13	07 14		07 22	07 42	07 43	07 48
d									05 50			06 03		06 33		06 58			07 15					
Manchester Oxford Road a									05 52			06 05		06 35		07 00			07 17					
Deansgate 🚊 a																								

	NT	NT	TP	TP	NT		TP	NT	TP	TP	NT	NT	TP	TP	NT		TP	NT	TP	TP	NT	NT	TP	TP
			◇1 trolley	◇1 trolley			◇1 trolley		◇1 trolley	◇1 trolley			◇1 trolley	◇1 trolley			◇1 trolley		◇1 trolley	◇1 trolley			◇1 trolley	◇1 trolley
Crewe 10 84 d								07 30										08 31						
Wilmslow 84 d								07 56										08 57						
Manchester Airport ✈ d	07 38	07 46	07 53	07 56	08 01		08 05	08 17	08 25	08 35	08 41	08 46	08 55	09 00	09 03		09 05	09 17	09 29	09 35	09 41	09 46	09 55	10 00
Heald Green d	07 42	07 49			08 05			08 20	08 29			08 49						09 20	09 33			09 49		
Gatley d	07 45	07 52		08 02				08 23	08 32			08 52						09 23				09 52		
East Didsbury d	07 48	07 55		08 05				08 26	08 35			08 55						09 26				09 55		
Burnage d		07 57						08 28				08 57						09 28				09 57		
Mauldeth Road d		07 59						08 30				08 59						09 30				09 59		
Manchester Piccadilly 10 🚊 a	07 57	08 11	08 12	08 14	08 21		08 22	08 42	08 44	08 49	08 59	09 11	09 13	09 14	09 18		09 22	09 42	09 44	09 52	09 59	10 11	10 13	10 14
d	07 59			08 15	08 22				08 46		09 01			09 16	09 22				09 46		10 01			10 16
Manchester Oxford Road a	08 01			08 17	08 24				08 48		09 03			09 18	09 24				09 48		10 03			10 18
Deansgate 🚊 a					08 28				08 51						09 28				09 51					

	NT		TP	NT	TP	TP	NT	NT	TP	TP	NT		TP	NT	TP	TP	NT	NT	TP	TP	NT		TP	NT
			◇1		◇1 trolley	◇1 trolley			◇1 trolley	◇1 trolley			◇1 trolley		◇1 trolley	◇1 trolley			◇1 trolley	◇1 trolley			◇1 trolley	
Crewe 10 84 d				09 33										10 34										11 34
Wilmslow 84 d				09 57										10 57										11 57
Manchester Airport ✈ d	10 03		10 05	10 17	10 29	10 35	10 41	10 46	10 55	11 00	11 03		11 05	11 17	11 29	11 35	11 41	11 46	11 55	12 00	12 03		12 05	12 17
Heald Green d				10 20	10 33			10 49						11 20	11 33			11 49						12 20
Gatley d				10 23				10 52						11 23				11 52						12 23
East Didsbury d				10 26				10 55						11 26				11 55						12 26
Burnage d				10 28				10 57						11 28				11 57						12 28
Mauldeth Road d				10 30				10 59						11 30				11 59						12 30
Manchester Piccadilly 10 🚊 a	10 18		10 22	10 42	10 44	10 52	10 59	11 11	11 13	11 14	11 18		11 22	11 42	11 44	11 52	11 59	12 11	12 13	12 14	12 18		12 22	12 42
d	10 22				10 46		11 01			11 16	11 22				11 46		12 01			12 16	12 22			
Manchester Oxford Road a	10 24				10 48		11 03			11 18	11 24				11 48		12 03			12 18	12 24			
Deansgate 🚊 a	10 28				10 51						11 28				11 51						12 28			

Table 85

Saturdays
from 31 March

Manchester Airport - Manchester

Network Diagram - see first Page of Table 78

		TP ◇1 🛒	TP ◇1 🛒	NT	NT	TP ◇1 🛒	TP ◇1 🛒	NT		TP ◇1 🛒	NT	TP ◇1 🛒	TP ◇1 🛒	NT	NT	TP ◇1 🛒	TP ◇1 🛒	NT		TP ◇1 🛒	NT	TP ◇1 🛒	TP ◇1	NT	NT
Crewe 10	84 d										12 34										13 34				
Wilmslow	84 d										12 57										13 57				
Manchester Airport ✈	d	12 29	12 35	12 41	12 46	12 55	13 00	13 03		13 05	13 17	13 29	13 35	13 41	13 46	13 55	14 00	14 03		14 05	14 17	14 29	14 35	14 41	14 46
Heald Green	d	12 33			12 49						13 20	13 33			13 49						14 20	14 33			14 49
Gatley	d				12 52						13 23				13 52						14 23				14 52
East Didsbury	d				12 55						13 26				13 55						14 26				14 55
Burnage	d				12 57						13 28				13 57						14 28				14 57
Mauldeth Road	d				12 59						13 30				13 59						14 30				14 59
Manchester Piccadilly 10 🚊	a	12 44	12 52	12 59	13 11	13 13	13 14	13 18		13 22	13 42	13 44	13 52	13 59	14 11	14 13	14 14	14 18		14 22	14 42	14 44	14 52	14 59	15 11
	d	12 46		13 01			13 16	13 22				13 46		14 01			14 16	14 22				14 46		15 01	
Manchester Oxford Road	a	12 48		13 03			13 18	13 24				13 48		14 03			14 18	14 24				14 48		15 03	
Deansgate 🚊	a	12 51						13 28				13 51						14 28				14 51			

		TP ◇1 🛒	TP ◇1 🛒	NT		TP ◇1 🛒	NT	TP ◇1 🛒	TP ◇1 🛒	NT	NT	TP ◇1 🛒	TP ◇1 🛒	NT		TP ◇1	NT	TP ◇1 🛒	TP ◇1	NT	NT	TP ◇1 🛒	TP ◇1 🛒	NT	
Crewe 10	84 d						14 34										15 33								
Wilmslow	84 d						14 57										15 56								
Manchester Airport ✈	d	14 55	15 00	15 03		15 05	15 17	15 29	15 35	15 41	15 46	15 55	16 00	16 03		16 05	16 17	16 29	16 35	16 41	16 46	16 55	17 00	17 03	
Heald Green	d						15 20	15 33			15 49						16 20	16 33			16 49				
Gatley	d						15 23				15 52						16 23				16 52				
East Didsbury	d						15 26				15 55						16 26				16 55				
Burnage	d						15 28				15 57						16 28				16 57				
Mauldeth Road	d						15 30				15 59						16 30				16 59				
Manchester Piccadilly 10 🚊	a	15 13	15 14	15 18		15 22	15 42	15 44	15 52	15 59	16 11	16 13	16 14	16 18		16 22	16 42	16 44	16 52	16 59	17 11	17 13	17 14	17 21	
	d		15 16	15 22				15 46		16 01			16 16	16 22				16 46		17 01			17 15	17 23	
Manchester Oxford Road	a		15 18	15 24				15 48		16 03			16 18	16 24				16 48		17 03			17 17	17 25	
Deansgate 🚊	a			15 28				15 51						16 28											

		TP ◇1	NT	TP ◇1	NT	NT	TP ◇1 🛒	TP ◇1 🛒	NT	NT		TP ◇1	NT	NT	TP ◇1	TP ◇1	NT	NT	TP ◇1	TP ◇1		NT	NT	TP ◇1	TP ◇1
Crewe 10	84 d		16 34							17 33								18 34							
Wilmslow	84 d		16 57							17 56								18 57							
Manchester Airport ✈	d	17 05	17 17	17 35	17 41	17 46	17 55	18 00	18 03	18 17		18 35	18 41	18 46	18 55	19 00	19 03	19 09	19 20	19 29		19 41	19 46	19 55	20 00
Heald Green	d		17 20			17 49				18 20				18 49				19 12		19 33			19 49		
Gatley	d		17 23			17 52				18 23				18 52				19 15					19 52		
East Didsbury	d		17 26			17 55				18 26				18 55				19 18					19 55		
Burnage	d		17 28			17 57				18 28				18 57				19 20					19 57		
Mauldeth Road	d		17 30			17 59				18 30				18 59				19 22					19 59		
Manchester Piccadilly 10 🚊	a	17 22	17 42	17 52	17 59	18 11	18 13	18 14	18 18	18 42		18 52	18 59	19 11	19 13	19 14	19 18	19 31	19 36	19 44		19 59	20 11	20 13	20 14
	d				18 01			18 16	18 22				19 01			19 16	19 20	19 32		19 46		20 01			20 16
Manchester Oxford Road	a				18 03			18 18	18 24				19 03			19 18	19 22	19 36		19 48		20 03			20 18
Deansgate 🚊	a								18 28								19 26			19 51					

		NT	NT	TP ◇1	TP ◇1	AW		TP ◇1	NT	NT	TP ◇1	TP ◇1	NT	TP ◇1	TP ◇1	NT		NT	TP ◇1	TP ◇1	TP ◇1	TP 🚌	NT		
Crewe 10	84 d																								
Wilmslow	84 d		19 56							20 56						21 55							23 15		
Manchester Airport ✈	d	20 03	20 09	20 20	20 29	20 32		20 47	21 03	21 09	21 20	21 29	21 41	21 47	22 00	22 08		22 19	22 22	22 29	22 55	23 25	23 27		
Heald Green	d		20 12		20 33			20 51		21 12		21 33		21 51		22 12				22 33			23 30		
Gatley	d		20 15					20 54		21 15				21 54		22 15							23 33		
East Didsbury	d		20 18					20 57		21 18				21 57		22 17							23 36		
Burnage	d		20 20					20 59		21 20				21 59		22 19							23 38		
Mauldeth Road	d		20 22					21 02		21 22				22 02		22 21							23 40		
Manchester Piccadilly 10 🚊	a	20 18	20 31	20 36	20 44	20 48		21 13	21 18	21 31	21 36	21 44	22 00	22 13	22 14	22 31		22 34	22 36	22 44	23 09	23 50	23 51		
	d	20 20	20 32		20 46	20 50			21 22	21 32		21 46	22 01		22 16	22 32		22 36		22 46					
Manchester Oxford Road	a	20 22	20 36		20 48	20 52			21 24	21 36		21 48	22 03		22 18	22 36		22 38		22 48					
Deansgate 🚊	a	20 26			20 51				21 28			21 51						22 41		22 51					

Sundays
until 1 January

		TP 🚌	TP 🚌	NT	NT	NT	TP ◇1	TP ◇1 🛒	TP ◇1	NT		TP ◇1	NT	TP ◇1 🛒	NT	TP ◇1	TP ◇1	NT	TP ◇1	NT		TP ◇1	TP ◇1	NT	TP ◇1 🛒
Crewe 10	84 d																								
Wilmslow	84 d																			10 43					
Manchester Airport ✈	d	00 05	05 30	06 09	07 09	08 24	08 47	09 00	09 03	09 06		09 29	09 35	10 00	10 06	10 20	10 30	10 35	10 44	11 05		11 20	11 30	11 33	12 00
Heald Green	d			06 12	07 12	08 27				09 09					10 09					11 08					
Gatley	d			06 15	07 15	08 30				09 12					10 12					11 11					
East Didsbury	d			06 18	07 18	08 33				09 15					10 15					11 14					
Burnage	d			06 20	07 20	08 35				09 17					10 17					11 16					
Mauldeth Road	d			06 22	07 22	08 37				09 19					10 19					11 18					
Manchester Piccadilly 10 🚊	a	00 30	05 55	06 31	07 31	08 47	09 01	09 14	09 17	09 26		09 42	09 48	10 14	10 26	10 37	10 44	10 48	10 58	11 25		11 35	11 44	11 48	12 14
	d						09 03	09 16				09 46	09 50	10 16			10 46	10 50		11 27			11 46	11 50	12 16
Manchester Oxford Road	a						09 05	09 18				09 48	09 52	10 18			10 48	10 52		11 31			11 48	11 52	12 18
Deansgate 🚊	a						09 08					09 51					10 51						11 51		

Table 85

Sundays

until 1 January

Manchester Airport - Manchester

Network Diagram - see first Page of Table 78

			NT	TP	TP	NT	TP		TP	NT	TP	TP	NT	TP	TP	NT	TP		TP	NT	TP	TP	NT	TP	TP	NT
				◇1	◇1		◇1		◇1 🛒		◇1	◇1		◇1	◇1 🛒		◇1		◇1		◇1	◇1		◇1	◇1	
Crewe 10	84	d																								
Wilmslow	84	d								12 54													14 54			
Manchester Airport ✈		d	12 08	12 19	12 30	12 35	12 55		12 59	13 09	13 20	13 30	13 35	13 55	14 00	14 09	14 20		14 30	14 35	14 55	15 00	15 09	15 20	15 30	15 35
Heald Green		d	12 11							13 12						14 12							15 11			
Gatley		d	12 14							13 15						14 15							15 14			
East Didsbury		d	12 17							13 18						14 18							15 18			
Burnage		d	12 19							13 20						14 20							15 20			
Mauldeth Road		d	12 21							13 22						14 22							15 22			
Manchester Piccadilly 10		a	12 29	12 38	12 44	12 49	13 07		13 14	13 31	13 37	13 44	13 48	14 09	14 14	14 31	14 37		14 44	14 48	15 09	15 14	15 32	15 37	15 44	15 48
		d	12 29		12 46	12 50			13 16			13 46	13 50		14 16				14 46	14 50		15 16			15 46	15 50
Manchester Oxford Road		a	12 33		12 48	12 52			13 18			13 48	13 52		14 18				14 48	14 52		15 18			15 48	15 52
Deansgate		a			12 51							13 51							14 51						15 51	

			TP		TP	NT	TP	TP	NT	TP	TP	NT	TP		TP	NT	TP	TP	NT	TP	TP	NT	TP		TP	NT
			◇1		◇1 🛒		◇1	◇1		◇1	◇1 🛒		◇1		◇1		◇1	◇1 🛒		◇1	◇1		◇1		◇1	
Crewe 10	84	d																								
Wilmslow	84	d										16 54														18 54
Manchester Airport ✈		d	15 55		16 00	16 09	16 20	16 30	16 35	16 55	17 00	17 09	17 20		17 30	17 35	17 55	18 00	18 09	18 20	18 30	18 35	18 55		19 00	19 09
Heald Green		d				16 12						17 12							18 12							19 12
Gatley		d				16 15						17 15							18 15							19 15
East Didsbury		d				16 18						17 18							18 18							19 18
Burnage		d				16 20						17 20							18 20							19 20
Mauldeth Road		d				16 22						17 22							18 22							19 22
Manchester Piccadilly 10		a	16 09		16 14	16 31	16 37	16 44	16 48	17 09	17 14	17 31	17 37		17 44	17 48	18 09	18 14	18 31	18 37	18 44	18 48	19 09		19 14	19 31
		d			16 16			16 46	16 50		17 16				17 46	17 50		18 16			18 46	18 50			19 16	
Manchester Oxford Road		a			16 18			16 48	16 52		17 18				17 48	17 52		18 18			18 48	18 52			19 18	
Deansgate		a						16 51							17 51						18 51					

			TP	TP	NT	TP	NT	TP	TP		NT	TP	NT	TP	TP	NT	TP	NT	TP		NT	TP				
			◇1	◇1		◇1		◇1	◇1			◇1		◇1	◇1		◇1		◇1			◇1				
Crewe 10	84	d																								
Wilmslow	84	d											20 54								22 54					
Manchester Airport ✈		d	19 20	19 30	19 35	19 55	20 09	20 20	20 30		20 35	20 55	21 09	21 20	21 30	21 35	21 55	22 09	22 55		23 09	23 20				
Heald Green		d					20 12						21 12					22 12			23 12					
Gatley		d					20 15						21 15					22 15			23 15					
East Didsbury		d					20 18						21 18					22 18			23 18					
Burnage		d					20 20						21 20					22 20			23 20					
Mauldeth Road		d					20 22						21 22					22 22			23 22					
Manchester Piccadilly 10		a	19 37	19 44	19 48	20 09	20 31	20 37	20 44		20 48	21 09	21 31	21 37	21 44	21 48	22 09	22 31	23 09		23 29	23 37				
		d		19 46	19 50				20 46		20 50				21 46	21 50										
Manchester Oxford Road		a		19 48	19 52				20 48		20 52				21 48	21 52										
Deansgate		a		19 51					20 51						21 51											

Sundays

8 January to 12 February

			TP	TP	TP	TP	TP	NT	TP	NT	TP		NT	TP	TP	TP	NT	TP	NT	TP	NT		TP	TP	NT	TP
			🚌	🚌	🚌	🚌	🚌	🚌	🚌	🚌	🚌		🚌	🚌	◇1	◇1		◇1		◇1 🛒			◇1	◇1		◇1
Crewe 10	84	d																								
Wilmslow	84	d																								
Manchester Airport ✈		d	00 05	01 07	04 25	05 30	06 05	06 10	07 07	07 10	07 52		08 10	08 20	08 47	09 03	09 06	09 29	09 35	10 00	10 06		10 20	10 30	10 35	10 44
Heald Green		d						06 15		07 15			08 15				09 09				10 09					
Gatley		d						06 23		07 23			08 23				09 12				10 12					
East Didsbury		d						06 31		07 31			08 31				09 15				10 15					
Burnage		d						06 36		07 36			08 36				09 17				10 17					
Mauldeth Road		d						06 41		07 41			08 41				09 19				10 19					
Manchester Piccadilly 10		a	00 30	01 32	04 50	05 55	06 30	06 52	07 32	07 52	08 17		08 52	08 45	09 01	09 17	09 29	09 42	09 48	10 14	10 26		10 37	10 44	10 48	10 58
		d													09 03			09 46	09 50	10 16				10 46	10 50	
Manchester Oxford Road		a													09 05			09 48	09 52	10 18				10 48	10 52	
Deansgate		a													09 08			09 51						10 51		

			TP	NT	TP	TP	NT		TP	NT	TP	TP	NT	TP	TP	NT	TP		TP	NT	TP	TP	NT	TP	TP	NT
			◇1 🛒		◇1	◇1			◇1 🛒		◇1	◇1		◇1	◇1 🛒		◇1		◇1		◇1	◇1 🛒		◇1	◇1	
Crewe 10	84	d																								
Wilmslow	84	d		10 43												12 54										
Manchester Airport ✈		d	11 00	11 05	11 20	11 30	11 33		12 00	12 08	12 19	12 30	12 35	12 55	13 00	13 09	13 20		13 30	13 35	13 55	14 00	14 09	14 20	14 30	14 35
Heald Green		d		11 08						12 11						13 12							14 12			
Gatley		d		11 11						12 14						13 15							14 15			
East Didsbury		d		11 14						12 17						13 18							14 18			
Burnage		d		11 16						12 19						13 20							14 20			
Mauldeth Road		d		11 18						12 21						13 22							14 22			
Manchester Piccadilly 10		a	11 14	11 25	11 35	11 44	11 48		12 14	12 29	12 38	12 44	12 49	13 09	13 14	13 31	13 37		13 44	13 48	14 09	14 14	14 31	14 37	14 44	14 48
		d	11 16	11 27		11 46	11 50		12 16	12 29		12 46	12 50		13 16				13 46	13 50		14 16			14 46	14 50
Manchester Oxford Road		a	11 18	11 31		11 48	11 52		12 18	12 33		12 48	12 52		13 18				13 48	13 52		14 18			14 48	14 52
Deansgate		a				11 51						12 51							13 51						14 51	

Table 85

Sundays

8 January to 12 February

Manchester Airport - Manchester

Network Diagram - see first Page of Table 78

Station		TP		NT	TP	TP	NT	TP	TP	NT	TP	TP		NT	TP	TP	NT	TP	TP	NT	TP	TP		NT	TP
		◇1			◇1	◇1		◇1	◇1 trolley		◇1	◇1			◇1	◇1 trolley		◇1	◇1		◇1	◇1 trolley			◇1
Crewe 10	84 d																								
Wilmslow	84 d			14 54													16 54								
Manchester Airport ✈	d	14 55		15 09	15 20	15 30	15 35	15 55	16 00	16 09	16 20	16 30		16 35	16 55	17 00	17 09	17 20	17 30	17 35	17 55	18 00		18 09	18 20
Heald Green	d			15 11						16 12							17 12							18 12	
Gatley	d			15 14						16 15							17 15							18 15	
East Didsbury	d			15 18						16 18							17 18							18 18	
Burnage	d			15 20						16 20							17 20							18 20	
Mauldeth Road	d			15 22						16 22							17 22							18 22	
Manchester Piccadilly 10	a	15 09		15 32	15 37	15 44	15 48	16 09	16 14	16 31	16 37	16 44		16 48	17 09	17 14	17 31	17 37	17 44	17 48	18 09	18 14		18 31	18 37
	d					15 46	15 50		16 16			16 46		16 50		17 16			17 46	17 50		18 16			
Manchester Oxford Road	a					15 48	15 52		16 18			16 48		16 52		17 18			17 48	17 52		18 18			
Deansgate	a					15 51						16 51							17 51						

Station		TP	NT	TP	TP	NT	TP	TP		NT	TP	NT	TP	TP	NT	TP	NT	TP		TP	NT	TP	NT	TP	TP
		◇1		◇1	◇1		◇1	◇1			◇1		◇1	◇1		◇1		◇1		◇1		◇1		◇1	◇1
Crewe 10	84 d																								
Wilmslow	84 d					18 54											20 54								
Manchester Airport ✈	d	18 30	18 35	18 55	19 00	19 09	19 20	19 30		19 35	19 55	20 09	20 20	20 30	20 35	20 55	21 09	21 20		21 30	21 35	21 55	22 09	22 30	22 55
Heald Green	d					19 12						20 12					21 12						22 12		
Gatley	d					19 15						20 15					21 15						22 15		
East Didsbury	d					19 18						20 18					21 18						22 18		
Burnage	d					19 20						20 20					21 20						22 20		
Mauldeth Road	d					19 22						20 22					21 22						22 22		
Manchester Piccadilly 10	a	18 44	18 48	19 09	19 14	19 31	19 37	19 44		19 48	20 09	20 31	20 37	20 44	20 48	21 09	21 31	21 37		21 44	21 48	22 09	22 31	22 44	23 09
	d	18 46	18 50		19 16			19 46		19 50				20 46	20 50					21 46	21 50			22 46	
Manchester Oxford Road	a	18 48	18 52		19 18			19 48		19 52				20 48	20 52					21 48	21 52			22 48	
Deansgate	a	18 51						19 51						20 51						21 51				22 51	

Station		NT	TP
			◇1
Crewe 10	84 d		
Wilmslow	84 d	22 54	
Manchester Airport ✈	d	23 09	23 20
Heald Green	d	23 12	
Gatley	d	23 15	
East Didsbury	d	23 18	
Burnage	d	23 20	
Mauldeth Road	d	23 22	
Manchester Piccadilly 10	a	23 29	23 37
	d		
Manchester Oxford Road	a		
Deansgate	a		

Sundays

19 February to 25 March

Station		TP	TP	TP	TP	NT	TP	NT	TP	TP		TP	NT	TP	TP	TP	NT	TP	TP	NT		NT	TP	TP	TP
		bus	◇1	◇1	bus		◇1		◇1	◇1		◇1		◇1	◇1	◇1		◇1	◇1 trolley				◇1	◇1	◇1
Crewe 10	84 d																								
Wilmslow	84 d																								
Manchester Airport ✈	d	00 05	01 22	04 43	05 30	06 09	06 24	07 09	07 24	07 30		07 50	08 24	08 40	08 47	09 03	09 06	09 29	10 00	10 06		10 16	10 20	10 30	10 44
Heald Green	d					06 12		07 12					08 27				09 09			10 09					
Gatley	d					06 15		07 15					08 30				09 12			10 12					
East Didsbury	d					06 18		07 18					08 33				09 15			10 15					
Burnage	d					06 20		07 20					08 35				09 17			10 17					
Mauldeth Road	d					06 22		07 22					08 37				09 19			10 19					
Manchester Piccadilly 10	a	00 30	01 36	04 57	05 55	06 31	06 38	07 31	07 37	07 44		08 04	08 47	08 54	09 01	09 17	09 26	09 42	10 14	10 26		10 30	10 37	10 44	10 58
	d									07 46					09 03			09 46	10 16			10 31		10 46	
Manchester Oxford Road	a									07 48					09 05			09 48	10 18			10 34		10 48	
Deansgate	a									07 51					09 08			09 51						10 51	

Station		NT	TP	NT	TP	TP		NT	TP	NT	TP	TP	TP	NT	TP	NT		TP	TP	TP	TP	NT	NT	TP	TP
			◇1 trolley		◇1	◇1			◇1 trolley		◇1	◇1	◇1		◇1 trolley			◇1	◇1	◇1	◇1 trolley			◇1	◇1
Crewe 10	84 d																								
Wilmslow	84 d			10 43												12 54									
Manchester Airport ✈	d	10 56	11 00	11 05	11 20	11 30		11 56	12 00	12 08	12 19	12 30	12 55	12 58	12 59	13 09		13 20	13 30	13 55	14 00	14 06	14 09	14 20	14 30
Heald Green	d			11 08						12 11						13 12							14 12		
Gatley	d			11 11						12 14						13 15							14 15		
East Didsbury	d			11 14						12 17						13 18							14 18		
Burnage	d			11 16						12 19						13 20							14 20		
Mauldeth Road	d			11 18						12 21						13 22							14 22		
Manchester Piccadilly 10	a	11 10	11 14	11 25	11 35	11 44		12 09	12 14	12 29	12 38	12 44	13 07	13 11	13 14	13 31		13 37	13 44	14 09	14 14	14 18	14 31	14 37	14 44
	d	11 12	11 16	11 27		11 46		12 11	12 16	12 29		12 46		13 12	13 16				13 46		14 16	14 20			14 46
Manchester Oxford Road	a	11 14	11 18	11 31		11 48		12 13	12 18	12 33		12 48		13 14	13 18				13 48		14 18	14 22			14 48
Deansgate	a					11 51						12 51							13 51						14 51

Table 85

Sundays

19 February to 25 March

Manchester Airport - Manchester

Network Diagram - see first Page of Table 78

		TP		NT	TP	NT	TP	TP	TP	NT	TP	NT		TP	TP	TP	NT	TP	NT	TP	TP	TP		NT	TP
		◇1			◇1		◇1	◇1	◇1		◇1 (trolley)			◇1	◇1	◇1		◇1 (trolley)		◇1	◇1	◇1			◇1 (trolley)
Crewe 10	84 d																								
Wilmslow	84 d					14 54													16 54						
Manchester Airport ✈	d	14 55		14 58	15 00	15 09	15 20	15 30	15 55	15 58	16 00	16 09		16 20	16 30	16 55	16 58	17 00	17 09	17 20	17 30	17 55		17 58	18 00
Heald Green	d					15 11						16 12							17 12						
Gatley	d					15 14						16 15							17 15						
East Didsbury	d					15 18						16 18							17 18						
Burnage	d					15 20						16 20							17 20						
Mauldeth Road	d					15 22						16 22							17 22						
Manchester Piccadilly 10	a	15 09		15 11	15 14	15 32	15 37	15 44	16 09	16 11	16 14	16 31		16 37	16 44	17 09	17 11	17 14	17 31	17 37	17 44	18 09		18 11	18 14
	d			15 12	15 16			15 46		16 12	16 16				16 46		17 12	17 16			17 46			18 12	18 16
Manchester Oxford Road	a			15 14	15 18			15 48		16 14	16 18				16 48		17 14	17 18			17 48			18 14	18 18
Deansgate	a							15 51							16 51						17 51				

		NT	TP	TP	TP	NT	TP	NT		TP	TP	TP	NT	NT	TP	TP	TP	NT		NT	TP	TP	TP	NT	TP
			◇1	◇1	◇1		◇1			◇1	◇1	◇1			◇1	◇1	◇1				◇1	◇1	◇1		◇1
Crewe 10	84 d																								
Wilmslow	84 d							18 54												20 54					
Manchester Airport ✈	d	18 09	18 20	18 30	18 55	18 58	19 00	19 09		19 20	19 30	19 55	19 58	20 09	20 20	20 30	20 55	20 58		21 09	21 20	21 30	21 55	22 09	22 55
Heald Green	d	18 12						19 12						20 12						21 12				22 12	
Gatley	d	18 15						19 15						20 15						21 15				22 15	
East Didsbury	d	18 18						19 18						20 18						21 18				22 18	
Burnage	d	18 20						19 20						20 20						21 20				22 20	
Mauldeth Road	d	18 22						19 22						20 22						21 22				22 22	
Manchester Piccadilly 10	a	18 31	18 37	18 44	19 09	19 11	19 14	19 31		19 37	19 44	20 09	20 11	20 31	20 37	20 44	21 09	21 11		21 31	21 37	21 44	22 09	22 31	23 09
	d			18 46		19 12	19 16				19 46		20 12			20 46		21 12				21 46			
Manchester Oxford Road	a			18 48		19 14	19 18				19 48		20 14			20 48		21 14				21 48			
Deansgate	a			18 51							19 51					20 51						21 51			

		NT	TP
			◇1
Crewe 10	84 d		
Wilmslow	84 d	22 54	
Manchester Airport ✈	d	23 09	23 20
Heald Green	d	23 12	
Gatley	d	23 15	
East Didsbury	d	23 18	
Burnage	d	23 20	
Mauldeth Road	d	23 22	
Manchester Piccadilly 10	a	23 29	23 37
	d		
Manchester Oxford Road	a		
Deansgate	a		

Sundays

from 1 April

		TP	TP	TP	TP	TP	TP	TP	NT	NT		TP	TP	TP	NT	TP	NT	TP	TP	NT		TP	NT	TP	TP
		🚌	🚌	🚌	🚌	🚌	◇1	◇1				◇1	◇1	◇1		◇1		◇1 (trolley)	◇1			◇1		◇1	◇1 (trolley)
Crewe 10	84 d																								
Wilmslow	84 d																								
Manchester Airport ✈	d	00 05	01 20	05 05	05 30	06 05	07 50	07 55	08 24	08 34		08 40	08 47	09 03	09 06	09 30	09 35	10 00	10 03	10 06		10 30	10 35	10 44	11 00
Heald Green	d								08 27						09 09					10 09					
Gatley	d								08 30						09 12					10 12					
East Didsbury	d								08 33						09 15					10 15					
Burnage	d								08 35						09 17					10 17					
Mauldeth Road	d								08 37						09 19					10 19					
Manchester Piccadilly 10	a	00 30	01 45	05 30	05 55	06 30	08 03	08 08	08 47	08 47		08 54	09 01	09 19	09 29	09 44	09 48	10 14	10 18	10 26		10 44	10 48	10 58	11 14
	d							08 11		08 49			09 03			09 46	09 50	10 16				10 46	10 50		11 16
Manchester Oxford Road	a							08 13		08 51			09 05			09 48	09 52	10 18				10 48	10 52		11 18
Deansgate	a							08 16		08 54			09 08			09 51						10 51			

		TP	NT	TP	NT	TP		TP	NT	TP	NT	TP	TP	TP	NT	TP		NT	TP	TP	TP	NT	TP	NT	TP
		◇1		◇1		◇1 (trolley)		◇1		◇1		◇1	◇1 (trolley)	◇1		◇1			◇1	◇1 (trolley)	◇1		◇1		◇1
Crewe 10	84 d																								
Wilmslow	84 d		10 43												12 54										
Manchester Airport ✈	d	11 03	11 05	11 30	11 33	12 00		12 03	12 08	12 30	12 35	12 55	12 58	13 03	13 09	13 30		13 35	13 55	13 58	14 03	14 09	14 30	14 35	14 55
Heald Green	d		11 08						12 11						13 12							14 12			
Gatley	d		11 11						12 14						13 15							14 15			
East Didsbury	d		11 14						12 17						13 18							14 18			
Burnage	d		11 16						12 19						13 20							14 20			
Mauldeth Road	d		11 18						12 21						13 22							14 22			
Manchester Piccadilly 10	a	11 18	11 25	11 44	11 48	12 14		12 18	12 29	12 44	12 49	13 09	13 14	13 18	13 31	13 44		13 48	14 09	14 14	14 18	14 31	14 44	14 48	15 09
	d		11 27	11 46	11 50	12 16			12 29	12 46	12 50		13 16			13 46		13 50		14 16			14 46	14 50	
Manchester Oxford Road	a		11 31	11 48	11 52	12 18			12 33	12 48	12 52		13 18			13 48		13 52		14 18			14 48	14 52	
Deansgate	a			11 51						12 51						13 51							14 51		

Table 85

Sundays

from 1 April

Manchester Airport - Manchester

Network Diagram - see first Page of Table 78

	TP		TP	NT	TP	NT	TP	TP	TP	NT	TP		NT	TP	TP	TP	NT	TP	NT	TP	TP		TP	NT
	◇1		◇1		◇1		◇1	◇1	◇1		◇1			◇1	◇1	◇1		◇1		◇1	◇1		◇1	
								🚲							🚲						🚲			
Crewe 10 84 d																								
Wilmslow 84 d				14 54													16 54							
Manchester Airport ✈ d	14 58		15 03	15 09	15 30	15 35	15 55	15 58	16 03	16 09	16 30		16 35	16 55	16 58	17 03	17 09	17 30	17 35	17 55	17 58		18 03	18 09
Heald Green d				15 11						16 12							17 12							18 12
Gatley d				15 14						16 15							17 15							18 15
East Didsbury d				15 18						16 18							17 18							18 18
Burnage d				15 20						16 20							17 20							18 20
Mauldeth Road d				15 22						16 22							17 22							18 22
Manchester Piccadilly 10 a	15 14		15 18	15 32	15 44	15 48	16 09	16 14	16 18	16 31	16 44		16 48	17 09	17 14	17 18	17 31	17 44	17 48	18 09	18 14		18 18	18 31
d	15 16				15 46	15 50		16 16			16 46		16 50		17 16			17 46	17 50		18 16			
Manchester Oxford Road a	15 18				15 48	15 52		16 18			16 48		16 52		17 18			17 48	17 52		18 18			
Deansgate a					15 51						16 51							17 51						

	TP	NT	TP	TP	TP	NT	TP		NT	TP	TP	NT	TP	NT	TP	TP	NT		TP	NT	TP	NT	TP	NT
	◇1		◇1	◇1	◇1		◇1			◇1	◇1		◇1		◇1	◇1			◇1		◇1		◇1	
Crewe 10 84 d																								
Wilmslow 84 d						18 54											20 54							22 54
Manchester Airport ✈ d	18 30	18 35	18 55	18 58	19 03	19 09	19 30		19 35	19 55	20 03	20 09	20 30	20 35	20 55	21 03	21 09		21 30	21 35	21 55	22 09	22 55	23 09
Heald Green d						19 12						20 12					21 12					22 12		23 12
Gatley d						19 15						20 15					21 15					22 15		23 15
East Didsbury d						19 18						20 18					21 18					22 18		23 18
Burnage d						19 20						20 20					21 20					22 20		23 20
Mauldeth Road d						19 22						20 22					21 22					22 22		23 22
Manchester Piccadilly 10 a	18 44	18 48	19 09	19 14	19 18	19 31	19 44		19 48	20 09	20 18	20 31	20 44	20 48	21 09	21 18	21 31		21 44	21 48	22 09	22 31	23 09	23 29
d	18 46	18 50		19 16			19 46		19 50				20 46	20 50					21 46	21 50				
Manchester Oxford Road a	18 48	18 52		19 18			19 48		19 52				20 48	20 52					21 48	21 52				
Deansgate a	18 51						19 51						20 51						21 51					

	TP
	◇1
Crewe 10 84 d	
Wilmslow 84 d	
Manchester Airport ✈ d	23 22
Heald Green d	
Gatley d	
East Didsbury d	
Burnage d	
Mauldeth Road d	
Manchester Piccadilly 10 a	23 35
d	
Manchester Oxford Road a	
Deansgate a	

Manchester - Hazel Grove and Buxton

Network Diagram - see first Page of Table 78

Miles		NT MX	NT A	NT	NT	NT B	NT	NT C	NT	NT D		NT	NT D	NT	NT D	NT	NT D	NT	NT D	NT		NT D	NT	NT D
—	Deansgate d					07 11		08 12		09 12			10 12		11 12		12 12		13 12			14 12		15 12
—	Manchester Oxford Road d					07 15		08 15		09 16			10 16		11 16		12 16		13 16			14 16		15 16
0	**Manchester Picc.** 10 84 d	23p10	05 50	06 21	06 49	07 21	07 52	08 20	08 52	09 21		09 52	10 21	10 52	11 21	11 52	12 21	12 52	13 21	13 52		14 21	14 52	15 21
3	Levenshulme 84 d			06 28	06 55	07 28		08 28	08 58	09 28		09 58	10 28	10 58	11 28	11 58	12 28	12 58	13 28	13 58		14 28	14 58	15 28
4½	Heaton Chapel 84 d			06 31	06 58	07 31		08 31	09 01	09 31		10 01	10 31	11 01	11 31	12 01	12 31	13 01	13 31	14 01		14 31	15 01	15 31
6	**Stockport** 84 d	23p20	06 00	06 35	07 02	07 35	08 01	08 35	09 05	09 35		10 05	10 35	11 05	11 35	12 05	12 35	13 05	13 35	14 05		14 35	15 05	15 35
7	Davenport d	23p23		06 39	07 06	07 39	08 05	08 39	09 09	09 39		10 09	10 39	11 09	11 39	12 09	12 39	13 09	13 39	14 09		14 39	15 09	15 39
7¾	Woodsmoor d	23p25		06 41	07 08	07 41	08 07	08 41	09 11	09 41		10 11	10 41	11 11	11 41	12 11	12 41	13 11	13 41	14 11		14 41	15 11	15 41
8¾	**Hazel Grove** a	23p27	06 06	06 45	07 10	07 45	08 09	08 50	09 13	09 47		10 13	10 47	11 13	11 45	12 13	12 47	13 13	13 47	14 13		14 47	15 13	15 50
—	d	23p28			07 10		08 10		09 13			10 13		11 13		12 13		13 13		14 13			15 13	
11	Middlewood d	23p32			07 15				09 18			10 18				12 18				14 18				
12½	Disley d	23p36			07 19		08 17		09 22			10 22		11 20		12 22		13 20		14 22			15 20	
14¼	New Mills Newtown d	23p40			07 22		08 20		09 25			10 25		11 24		12 25		13 24		14 25			15 24	
15¼	Furness Vale d	23p42			07 25		08 23		09 28			10 28		11 26		12 28		13 26		14 28			15 26	
16¼	Whaley Bridge d	23p45			07 28		08 26		09 31			10 31		11 29		12 31		13 29		14 31			15 29	
20½	Chapel-en-le-Frith d	23p52			07 35		08 33		09 38			10 38		11 36		12 38		13 36		14 38			15 36	
22¾	Dove Holes d	23p57			07 40				09 43			10 43				12 43				14 43				
25¾	**Buxton** a	00 07			07 50		08 44		09 53			10 53		11 50		12 53		13 50		14 53			15 50	

	NT	NT D	NT	NT	NT D	NT E		NT	NT B	NT	NT	NT	NT	NT	NT
Deansgate d		16 12			17 15				18 12						
Manchester Oxford Road d		16 16			17 19				18 16						
Manchester Picc. 10 84 d	15 52	16 21	16 51	16 58	17 23	17 23		17 52	18 21	18 52	19 22	19 51	20 51	21 52	23 10
Levenshulme 84 d	15 58	16 28		17 03		17 28		17 58	18 28	18 58	19 28	19 58	20 58	21 58	
Heaton Chapel 84 d	16 01	16 31		17 06		17 31		18 01	18 31	19 01	19 31	20 01	21 01	22 01	
Stockport 84 d	16 05	16 35	17 03	17 10	17 32	17 35		18 05	18 35	19 05	19 35	20 05	21 05	22 05	23 20
Davenport d	16 09	16 39	17 06	17 14		17 39		18 09	18 39	19 09	19 39	20 09	21 09	22 09	23 23
Woodsmoor d	16 11	16 41	17 08	17 16		17 41		18 11	18 41	19 11	19 41	20 11	21 11	22 11	23 25
Hazel Grove a	16 13	16 43	17 10	17 20	17 39	17 43		18 13	18 43	19 13	19 45	20 13	21 13	22 13	23 27
d	16 13	16 46	17 11		17 39			18 13	18 46	19 13		20 13	21 13	22 13	23 28
Middlewood d	16 18		17 15					18 18		19 18		20 18	21 18	22 18	23 32
Disley d	16 22	16 53	17 19		17 46			18 22	18 53	19 22		20 22	21 22	22 22	23 36
New Mills Newtown d	16 25	16 56	17 23		17 50			18 25	18 56	19 25		20 25	21 25	22 25	23 40
Furness Vale d	16 28	16 59	17 26		17 52			18 28	18 59	19 28		20 28	21 28	22 28	23 42
Whaley Bridge d	16 31	17 02	17 29		17 55			18 31	19 02	19 31		20 31	21 31	22 31	23 45
Chapel-en-le-Frith d	16 38	17 09	17 36		18 03			18 38	19 09	19 38		20 38	21 38	22 38	23 52
Dove Holes d	16 43		17 41					18 43		19 43		20 43	21 43	22 43	23 57
Buxton a	16 53	17 24	17 51		18 19			18 54	19 22	19 53		20 53	21 53	22 53	00 07

Saturdays

	NT	NT A	NT	NT B	NT	NT C	NT	NT D	NT		NT D	NT	NT D	NT	NT D	NT	NT D	NT	NT D		NT	NT D	NT	NT D
Deansgate d				07 11		08 12		09 12			10 12		11 12		12 12		13 12		14 12			15 12		16 12
Manchester Oxford Road d				07 15		08 15		09 16			10 16		11 16		12 16		13 16		14 16			15 16		16 16
Manchester Picc. 10 84 d	23p10	05 50	06 49	07 21	07 52	08 20	08 52	09 21	09 52		10 21	10 52	11 21	11 52	12 21	12 52	13 21	13 52	14 21		14 52	15 21	15 52	16 21
Levenshulme 84 d			06 55	07 28	07 58	08 28	08 58	09 28	09 58		10 28	10 58	11 28	11 58	12 28	12 58	13 28	13 58	14 28		14 58	15 28	15 58	16 28
Heaton Chapel 84 d			06 58	07 31		08 31	09 01	09 31	10 01		10 31	11 01	11 31	12 01	12 31	13 01	13 31	14 01	14 31		15 01	15 31	16 01	16 31
Stockport 84 d	23p20	06 00	07 02	07 35	08 03	08 35	09 05	09 35	10 05		10 35	11 05	11 35	12 05	12 35	13 05	13 35	14 05	14 35		15 05	15 35	16 05	16 35
Davenport d	23p23		07 06	07 39	08 07	08 39	09 09	09 39	10 09		10 39	11 09	11 39	12 09	12 39	13 09	13 39	14 09	14 39		15 09	15 39	16 09	16 39
Woodsmoor d	23p25		07 08	07 41	08 09	08 41	09 11	09 41	10 11		10 41	11 11	11 41	12 11	12 41	13 11	13 41	14 11	14 41		15 11	15 41	16 11	16 41
Hazel Grove a	23p27	06 06	07 10	07 47	08 11	08 47	09 13	09 47	10 13		10 47	11 13	11 47	12 13	12 47	13 13	13 47	14 13	14 47		15 13	15 47	16 13	16 47
d	23p28		07 10		08 11		09 13		10 13			11 13		12 13		13 13		14 13			15 13		16 13	
Middlewood d	23p32		07 15				09 18		10 18					12 18				14 18					16 18	
Disley d	23p36		07 19		08 18		09 22		10 22			11 20		12 22		13 20		14 22			15 20		16 22	
New Mills Newtown d	23p40		07 22		08 22		09 25		10 25			11 24		12 25		13 24		14 25			15 24		16 25	
Furness Vale d	23p42		07 25		08 24		09 28		10 28			11 26		12 28		13 26		14 28			15 26		16 28	
Whaley Bridge d	23p45		07 28		08 27		09 31		10 31			11 29		12 31		13 29		14 31			15 29		16 31	
Chapel-en-le-Frith d	23p52		07 35		08 34		09 38		10 38			11 36		12 38		13 36		14 38			15 36		16 38	
Dove Holes d	23p57		07 40				09 43		10 43					12 43				14 43					16 43	
Buxton a	00 07		07 48		08 46		09 51		10 51			11 48		12 51		13 48		14 51			15 48		16 51	

	NT	NT	NT D	NT	NT D		NT	NT	NT	NT	NT	NT
Deansgate d			17 14		18 12							
Manchester Oxford Road d			17 18		18 16							
Manchester Picc. 10 84 d	16 51	17 09	17 22	17 52	18 21		18 52	19 22	19 51	20 52	21 54	23 10
Levenshulme 84 d	16 58	17 14	17 28	17 58	18 28		18 58	19 28	19 58	20 58	22 00	
Heaton Chapel 84 d	17 01	17 17	17 31	18 01	18 31		19 01	19 31	20 01	21 01	22 03	
Stockport 84 d	17 05	17 32	17 35	18 05	18 35		19 05	19 35	20 05	21 05	22 07	23 20
Davenport d	17 09		17 39	18 09	18 39		19 09	19 39	20 09	21 09	22 11	23 23
Woodsmoor d	17 11		17 41	18 11	18 41		19 11	19 41	20 11	21 11	22 13	23 25
Hazel Grove a	17 13	17 41	17 43	18 13	18 47		19 13	19 47	20 13	21 13	22 15	23 27
d	17 13		17 46	18 13			19 13		20 13	21 13	22 15	23 28
Middlewood d			17 50				19 18		20 18	21 18	22 20	23 32
Disley d	17 20		17 54	18 20			19 22		20 22	21 22	22 24	23 36
New Mills Newtown d	17 24		17 58	18 24			19 25		20 25	21 25	22 27	23 40
Furness Vale d	17 26		18 00	18 26			19 28		20 28	21 28	22 30	23 42
Whaley Bridge d	17 29		18 03	18 29			19 31		20 31	21 31	22 33	23 45
Chapel-en-le-Frith d	17 36		18 10	18 36			19 38		20 38	21 38	22 40	23 52
Dove Holes d			18 15				19 43		20 43	21 43	22 45	23 57
Buxton a	17 48		18 23	18 48			19 51		20 51	21 51	22 53	00 05

A To Sheffield
B From Wigan Wallgate
C From Blackpool North
D From Preston
E To Chinley

Table 86

Sundays

Manchester - Hazel Grove and Buxton

Network Diagram - see first Page of Table 78

		NT A	NT	NT B	NT C	NT	NT	NT	NT	NT	NT	NT	NT	NT	NT	NT	NT	NT
Deansgate	d																	
Manchester Oxford Road	d																	
Manchester Picc. 10 84	d	23p10	08 55	09 47	09 51	10 53	11 52	12 52	13 52	14 52	15 52	16 52	17 52	18 52	19 52	20 52	21 52	22 52
Levenshulme 84	d		09 00	09 54	09 58	10 59	11 58	12 58	13 58	14 58	15 58	16 58	17 58	18 58	19 58	20 58	21 58	22 58
Heaton Chapel 84	d		09 03	09 57	10 01	11 02	12 01	13 01	14 01	15 01	16 01	17 01	18 01	19 01	20 01	21 01	22 01	23 01
Stockport 84	d	23p20	09 10	10 02	10 06	11 06	12 05	13 05	14 05	15 05	16 05	17 05	18 05	19 05	20 05	21 05	22 05	23 05
Davenport	d	23p23	09 13	10 06	10 10	11 10	12 09	13 09	14 09	15 09	16 09	17 09	18 09	19 09	20 09	21 09	22 09	23 09
Woodsmoor	d	23p25	09 15	10 08	10 12	11 12	12 11	13 11	14 11	15 11	16 11	17 11	18 11	19 11	20 11	21 11	22 11	23 11
Hazel Grove	a	23p27	09 17	10 10	10 14	11 14	12 13	13 13	14 13	15 13	16 13	17 13	18 13	19 13	20 13	21 13	22 13	23 13
	d	23p28	09 18	10 11	10 15	11 14	12 13	13 13	14 13	15 13	16 13	17 13	18 13	19 13	20 13	21 13	22 13	23 13
Middlewood	d	23p32	09 22	10 15	10 19	11 19	12 18	13 18	14 18	15 18	16 18	17 18	18 18	19 18	20 18	21 18	22 18	23 18
Disley	d	23p36	09 26	10 19	10 23	11 23	12 22	13 22	14 22	15 22	16 22	17 22	18 22	19 22	20 22	21 22	22 22	23 22
New Mills Newtown	d	23p40	09 30	10 23	10 27	11 26	12 25	13 25	14 25	15 25	16 25	17 25	18 25	19 25	20 25	21 25	22 25	23 25
Furness Vale	d	23p42	09 32	10 25	10 29	11 29	12 28	13 28	14 28	15 28	16 28	17 28	18 28	19 28	20 28	21 28	22 28	23 28
Whaley Bridge	d	23p45	09 35	10 28	10 32	11 32	12 31	13 31	14 31	15 31	16 31	17 31	18 31	19 31	20 31	21 31	22 31	23 31
Chapel-en-le-Frith	d	23p52	09 42	10 35	10 39	11 39	12 38	13 38	14 38	15 38	16 38	17 38	18 38	19 38	20 38	21 38	22 38	23 38
Dove Holes	d	23p57	09 47	10 40	10 44	11 44	12 43	13 43	14 43	15 43	16 43	17 43	18 43	19 43	20 43	21 43	22 43	23 43
Buxton	a	00 05	09 55	10 48	10 52	11 52	12 51	13 51	14 51	15 51	16 51	17 51	18 51	19 51	20 51	21 51	22 51	23 51

A not 11 December
B from 19 February until 25 March
C until 12 February and then from 1 April

Buxton and Hazel Grove - Manchester

Network Diagram - see first Page of Table 78

Miles		NT	NT	NT	NT	NT	NT	NT		NT		NT	NT	NT	NT	NT	NT	NT	NT	NT		NT	NT	NT
		A		B		C						E		E		E		E		E			E	
0	**Buxton** d	05 59		06 23		06 45		07 24		07 48			08 27		09 27		10 30		11 27			12 30		13 25
3	Dove Holes d			06 29		06 51		07 30					08 33		09 33				11 33					13 31
5¼	Chapel-en-le-Frith d	06 08		06 34		06 56		07 35		07 57			08 38		09 38		10 39		11 38			12 39		13 36
9½	Whaley Bridge d	06 14		06 40		07 02		07 41		08 03			08 44		09 44		10 45		11 44			12 45		13 42
10½	Furness Vale d	06 17		06 43		07 05		07 44		08 06			08 47		09 47		10 48		11 47			12 48		13 45
11½	New Mills Newtown d	06 20		06 46		07 08		07 47		08 10			08 50		09 50		10 51		11 50			12 51		13 48
13¼	Disley d	06 24		06 49		07 12		07 51		08 14			08 53		09 53		10 55		11 53			12 55		13 51
14¾	Middlewood d			06 53		07 16		07 55					08 57		09 57				11 57					13 55
17	**Hazel Grove** a	06 32		06 59		07 25		08 00		08 22			09 03		10 03		11 03		12 03			13 03		14 01
—	d	06 33	06 50	07 00	07 22	07 25	07 48	08 01		08 22		08 30	09 04	09 30	10 04	10 31	11 04	11 31	12 04	12 31		13 04	13 31	14 01
18	Woodsmoor d	06 35	06 52	07 02	07 24	07 28	07 50	08 03				08 32	09 06	09 32	10 06	10 33	11 06	11 33	12 06	12 33		13 06	13 33	14 03
18¾	Davenport d	06 37	06 54	07 04	07 27	07 30	07 53	08 06				08 35	09 08	09 35	10 08	10 35	11 08	11 35	12 08	12 35		13 08	13 35	14 05
19¾	**Stockport** 84 a	06 41	06 58	07 08	07 31	07 37	07 57	08 10				08 41	09 12	09 41	10 12	10 41	11 12	11 41	12 12	12 41		13 12	13 41	14 09
21¼	Heaton Chapel 84 a			07 15		07 41							09 16		10 16		11 16		12 16			13 16		14 16
22¾	Levenshulme 84 a			07 18		07 44							09 19		10 19		11 19		12 19			13 19		14 19
25¾	**Manchester Picc.** 10 84 a	06 52	07 10	07 26	07 45	07 52	08 09	08 25		08 39		08 52	09 28	09 52	10 28	10 52	11 28	11 52	12 28	12 52		13 28	13 52	14 28
—	Manchester Oxford Road a	06 56		07 29		07 56						08 56		09 56		10 56		11 56		12 56			13 56	
—	Deansgate a	06 59		07 32		07 59						09 00		10 00		11 00		12 00		13 00			14 00	

	NT	NT	NT	NT	NT	NT		NT	NT	NT	NT	NT	NT	NT	NT
	E		F	G	E	C		C		F					
Buxton d		14 30		15 22		16 25		16 56	17 27	17 59	18 27	19 27	20 27	21 27	22 56
Dove Holes d				15 28					17 33		18 33	19 33	20 33	21 33	23 02
Chapel-en-le-Frith d		14 39		15 33		16 34		17 05	17 38	18 08	18 38	19 38	20 38	21 38	23 07
Whaley Bridge d		14 45		15 39		16 40		17 11	17 44	18 14	18 44	19 44	20 44	21 44	23 13
Furness Vale d		14 48		15 42		16 43		17 14	17 47	18 17	18 47	19 47	20 47	21 47	23 16
New Mills Newtown d		14 51		15 45		16 46		17 17	17 50	18 20	18 50	19 50	20 50	21 50	23 19
Disley d		14 55		15 48		16 50		17 21	17 53	18 24	18 53	19 53	20 53	21 53	23 22
Middlewood d				15 52					17 57		18 57	19 57	20 57	21 57	23 26
Hazel Grove a		15 03		16 01		17 01		17 32	18 03	18 32	19 03	20 03	21 03	22 03	23 31
d	14 31	15 04	15 33	16 02	16 30	17 02		17 33	18 04	18 33	19 04	20 04	21 04	22 04	23 32
Woodsmoor d	14 33	15 06	15 35	16 04	16 32	17 04		17 35	18 06	18 35	19 06	20 06	21 06	22 06	23 34
Davenport d	14 35	15 08	15 37	16 06	16 35	17 06		17 37	18 08	18 37	19 08	20 08	21 08	22 08	23 36
Stockport 84 a	14 41	15 12	15 41	16 12	16 40	17 12		17 41	18 12	18 41	19 12	20 12	21 12	22 12	23 40
Heaton Chapel 84 a		15 16		16 16		17 16			18 16		19 16	20 16	21 16	22 16	
Levenshulme 84 a		15 19		16 19		17 19			18 19		19 19	20 19	21 19	22 19	
Manchester Picc. 10 84 a	14 52	15 28	15 52	16 25	16 52	17 25		17 52	18 28	18 52	19 28	20 28	21 28	22 28	23 54
Manchester Oxford Road a	14 56		15 56	16 29	16 56	17 29		17 56		18 56					
Deansgate a	15 00		16 00	16 32	17 00	17 32		18 00		19 00					

Saturdays

	NT	NT	NT	NT	NT		NT	NT	NT		NT	NT	NT	NT	NT	NT	NT	NT	NT		NT	NT	NT	NT
	A		E				E		E			E		E		E		E			E		E	
Buxton d	05 59	06 22			07 22		07 51	08 22			09 22		10 25		11 22		12 25		13 22			14 25		15 22
Dove Holes d		06 28			07 28		07 57	08 28			09 28				11 28				13 28					15 28
Chapel-en-le-Frith d	06 08	06 33			07 33		08 02	08 33			09 33		10 34		11 33		12 34		13 33			14 34		15 33
Whaley Bridge d	06 14	06 39			07 39		08 08	08 39			09 39		10 40		11 39		12 40		13 39			14 40		15 39
Furness Vale d	06 17	06 42			07 42		08 11	08 42			09 42		10 43		11 42		12 43		13 42			14 43		15 42
New Mills Newtown d	06 20	06 45			07 45		08 14	08 45			09 45		10 46		11 45		12 46		13 45			14 46		15 45
Disley d	06 24	06 48			07 48		08 17	08 48			09 48		10 50		11 48		12 50		13 48			14 50		15 48
Middlewood d		06 52			07 52		08 21	08 52			09 52				11 52				13 52					15 52
Hazel Grove a	06 32	07 01			08 01		08 30	09 01			10 01		11 01		12 01		13 01		14 01			15 01		16 01
d	06 33	07 01	07 32	07 48	08 01		08 31	09 02	09 31		10 02	10 31	11 02	11 31	12 02	12 31	13 02	13 31	14 02		14 31	15 02	15 33	16 02
Woodsmoor d	06 35	07 03	07 34	07 50	08 03		08 33	09 04	09 33		10 04	10 33	11 04	11 33	12 04	12 33	13 04	13 33	14 04		14 33	15 04	15 35	16 04
Davenport d	06 37	07 05	07 36	07 53	08 05		08 35	09 06	09 35		10 06	10 35	11 06	11 35	12 06	12 35	13 06	13 35	14 06		14 35	15 06	15 37	16 06
Stockport 84 a	06 41	07 12	07 40	07 57	08 12		08 41	09 12	09 41		10 12	10 41	11 12	11 41	12 12	12 41	13 12	13 41	14 12		14 41	15 12	15 41	16 12
Heaton Chapel 84 a		07 16			08 16			09 16			10 16		11 16		12 16		13 16		14 16			15 16		16 16
Levenshulme 84 a		07 19			08 19			09 19			10 19		11 19		12 19		13 19		14 19			15 19		16 19
Manchester Picc. 10 84 a	06 52	07 26	07 52	08 09	08 26		08 52	09 26	09 52		10 26	10 52	11 26	11 52	12 26	12 52	13 26	13 52	14 26		14 52	15 26	15 52	16 26
Manchester Oxford Road a	06 56		07 56				08 56		09 56			10 56		11 56		12 56		13 56			14 56		15 56	
Deansgate a	06 59		08 00				09 00		10 00			11 00		12 00		13 00		14 00			15 00		16 00	

	NT	NT	NT	NT	NT		NT	NT	NT	NT	NT
	E		C		F						
Buxton d		16 25		17 22			18 22	19 22	20 22	21 27	22 51
Dove Holes d				17 28			18 28	19 28	20 28	21 33	22 57
Chapel-en-le-Frith d		16 34		17 33			18 33	19 33	20 33	21 38	23 02
Whaley Bridge d		16 40		17 39			18 39	19 39	20 39	21 44	23 08
Furness Vale d		16 43		17 42			18 42	19 42	20 42	21 47	23 11
New Mills Newtown d		16 46		17 45			18 45	19 45	20 45	21 50	23 14
Disley d		16 50		17 48			18 48	19 48	20 48	21 53	23 17
Middlewood d				17 52			18 52	19 52	20 52	21 57	23 21
Hazel Grove a		17 01		18 01			19 01	20 01	21 01	22 03	23 30
d	16 30	17 02	17 31	18 02	18 31		19 02	20 02	21 02	22 04	23 31
Woodsmoor d	16 32	17 04	17 33	18 04	18 33		19 04	20 04	21 04	22 06	23 33
Davenport d	16 34	17 06	17 35	18 06	18 35		19 06	20 06	21 06	22 08	23 35
Stockport 84 a	16 40	17 12	17 41	18 12	18 41		19 12	20 12	21 12	22 12	23 41
Heaton Chapel 84 a		17 16		18 16			19 16	20 16	21 16	22 16	
Levenshulme 84 a		17 19		18 19			19 19	20 19	21 19	22 19	
Manchester Picc. 10 84 a	16 52	17 26	17 52	18 26	18 52		19 26	20 26	21 26	22 26	23 52
Manchester Oxford Road a	16 56		17 56		18 56						
Deansgate a	17 00		18 00		19 00						

A To Clitheroe
B To Wigan North Western
C To Blackpool North
E To Preston
F To Bolton
G To Barrow-in-Furness

Table 86

Sundays

Buxton and Hazel Grove - Manchester

Network Diagram - see first Page of Table 78

			NT	NT	NT	NT	NT	NT	NT	NT	NT	NT	NT	NT	NT	NT	NT
Buxton		d	08 21	09 14	10 22	11 21	12 22	13 22	14 22	15 22	16 22	17 22	18 22	19 22	20 22	21 27	22 22
Dove Holes		d	08 27	09 20	10 28	11 27	12 28	13 28	14 28	15 28	16 28	17 28	18 28	19 28	20 28	21 33	22 28
Chapel-en-le-Frith		d	08 32	09 25	10 33	11 32	12 33	13 33	14 33	15 33	16 33	17 33	18 33	19 33	20 33	21 38	22 33
Whaley Bridge		d	08 38	09 31	10 39	11 38	12 39	13 39	14 39	15 39	16 39	17 39	18 39	19 39	20 39	21 44	22 39
Furness Vale		d	08 41	09 34	10 42	11 41	12 42	13 42	14 42	15 42	16 42	17 42	18 42	19 42	20 42	21 47	22 42
New Mills Newtown		d	08 44	09 37	10 45	11 44	12 45	13 45	14 45	15 45	16 45	17 45	18 45	19 45	20 45	21 50	22 45
Disley		d	08 47	09 40	10 48	11 47	12 48	13 48	14 48	15 48	16 48	17 48	18 48	19 48	20 48	21 53	22 48
Middlewood		d	08 51	09 44	10 52	11 51	12 52	13 52	14 52	15 52	16 52	17 52	18 52	19 52	20 52	21 57	22 52
Hazel Grove		a	08 57	09 53	11 00	12 00	13 01	14 01	15 01	16 01	17 01	18 01	19 01	20 01	21 01	22 03	23 01
		d	08 58	09 53	11 01	12 00	13 02	14 02	15 02	16 02	17 02	18 02	19 02	20 02	21 02	22 04	23 02
Woodsmoor		d	09 00	09 55	11 03	12 02	13 04	14 04	15 04	16 04	17 04	18 04	19 04	20 04	21 04	22 06	23 04
Davenport		d	09 02	09 57	11 05	12 04	13 06	14 06	15 06	16 06	17 06	18 06	19 06	20 06	21 06	22 08	23 06
Stockport	84	a	09 08	10 04	11 11	12 11	13 12	14 12	15 12	16 12	17 12	18 12	19 12	20 12	21 12	22 12	23 12
Heaton Chapel	84	a	09 12	10 08		12 15	13 16	14 16	15 16	16 16	17 16	18 16	19 16	20 16	21 16	22 16	23 16
Levenshulme	84	a	09 15	10 11		12 18	13 19	14 19	15 19	16 19	17 19	18 19	19 19	20 19	21 19	22 19	23 19
Manchester Picc. 10	84 ⇌	a	09 23	10 20	11 23	12 25	13 27	14 27	15 27	16 27	17 27	18 27	19 27	20 27	21 27	22 27	23 27
Manchester Oxford Road		a															
Deansgate	⇌	a															

Network Diagram for Tables 88, 89, 90, 91

DM-12/06(2)
Design BAJS

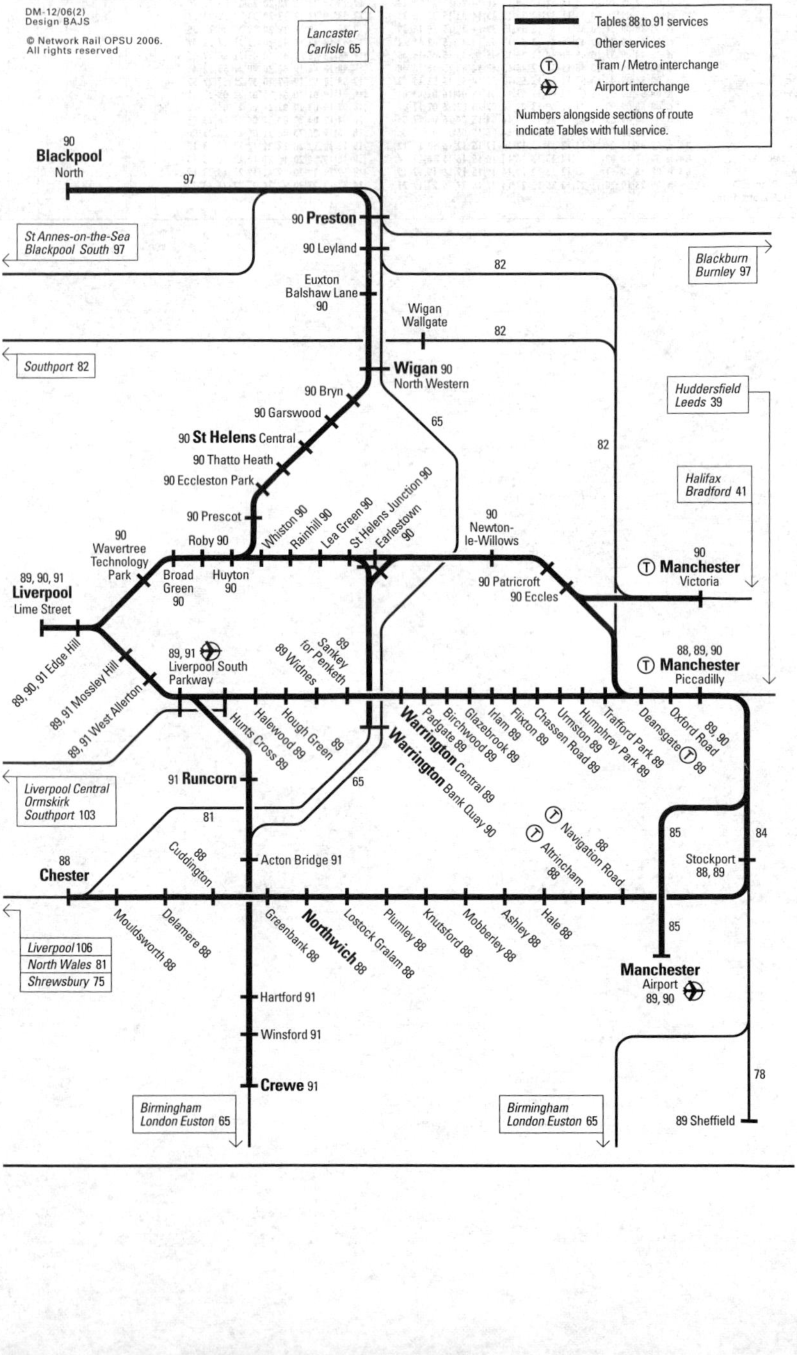

Manchester - Northwich and Chester

Network Diagram - see first Page of Table 88

Miles	Station			NT MX	NT	NT	NT	NT	NT	NT	NT	NT	NT	NT	NT	NT	NT	NT	NT	NT	NT	NT	NT	NT
0	**Manchester Picc.** 10	84	d	23p17	06 18	07 17	08 17	09 17	10 17	11 17	12 17	13 17	14 17	15 17	16 17		17 09		18 17	19 17	20 17	21 17	22 17	23 17
6½	**Stockport**	84	d	23p27	06 30	07 30	08 30	09 30	10 30	11 30	12 30	13 30	14 30	15 30	16 30	16 58	17 19	17 58	18 30	19 30	20 30	21 30	22 30	23 27
14¾	Navigation Road		d	23p41	06 44	07 44	08 44	09 44	10 44	11 44	12 44	13 44	14 44	15 44	16 44	17 12	17 33	18 12	18 44	19 44	20 44	21 44	22 44	23 41
15¼	**Altrincham**		a	23p43	06 46	07 46	08 46	09 46	10 46	11 46	12 46	13 46	14 46	15 46	16 46	17 14	17 35	18 14	18 46	19 46	20 46	21 46	22 46	23 43
—			d	23p43	06 46	07 46	08 46	09 46	10 46	11 46	12 46	13 46	14 46	15 46	16 46	17 14	17 35	18 14	18 46	19 46	20 46	21 46	22 46	23 43
16	Hale		d	23p46	06 49	07 49	08 49	09 49	10 49	11 49	12 49	13 49	14 49	15 49	16 49	17 17	17 38	18 17	18 49	19 49	20 49	21 49	22 49	23 46
17¾	Ashley		d	23p49	06 52	07 52	08 52	09 52	10 52	11 52	12 52	13 52	14 52	15 52	16 52	17 20	17 41	18 20	18 52	19 52	20 52	21 52	22 52	23 49
18½	Mobberley		d	23p52	06 55	07 55	08 55	09 55	10 55	11 55	12 55	13 55	14 55	15 55	16 55	17 23	17 44	18 23	18 55	19 55	20 55	21 55	22 55	23 52
22¼	Knutsford		d	23p57	06 59	07 59	08 59	09 59	10 59	11 59	12 59	13 59	14 59	15 59	16 59	17 27	17 49	18 27	18 59	19 59	20 59	21 59	22 59	23 57
24¾	Plumley		d	00 01	07 03	08 03	09 03	10 03	11 03	12 03	13 03	14 03	15 03	16 03	17 03	17 31	17 53	18 31	19 03	20 03	21 03	22 03	23 03	00 01
26¾	Lostock Gralam		d	00 04	07 07	08 07	09 07	10 07	11 07	12 07	13 07	14 07	15 07	16 07	17 07	17 35	17 56	18 35	19 07	20 07	21 07	22 07	23 07	00 04
28¼	**Northwich**		d	00 10	07 12	08 12	09 12	10 12	11 12	12 12	13 12	14 12	15 12	16 12	17 12	17 40	18 02	18 40	19 12	20 12	21 12	22 12	23 12	00 10
30	Greenbank		d	00 14	07 17	08 17	09 17	10 17	11 17	12 17	13 17	14 17	15 17	16 17	17 17	17 45	18 06	18 45	19 17	20 17	21 17	22 17	23 17	00 14
32¾	Cuddington		d	00 19	07 22	08 22	09 22	10 22	11 22	12 22	13 22	14 22	15 22	16 22	17 22	17 50	18 11	18 50	19 22	20 22	21 22	22 22	23 22	00 19
35¾	Delamere		d	00 24	07 26	08 26	09 26	10 26	11 26	12 26	13 26	14 26	15 26	16 26	17 26	17 54	18 16	18 54	19 26	20 26	21 26	22 26	23 26	00 24
38¾	Mouldsworth		d	00 28	07 31	08 31	09 31	10 31	11 31	12 31	13 31	14 31	15 31	16 31	17 31	17 59	18 21	18 59	19 31	20 31	21 31	22 31	23 31	00 28
45¼	**Chester**	81	a	00 43	07 44	08 44	09 43	10 45	11 42	12 45	13 42	14 45	15 42	16 45	17 42	18 10	18 35	19 13	19 42	20 45	21 42	22 45	23 44	00 43

Saturdays

Station			NT	NT	NT	NT	NT	NT	NT	NT	NT	NT	NT	NT	NT	NT	NT	NT	NT	NT	NT
Manchester Picc. 10	84	d	23p17	06 17	07 17	08 17	09 17	10 17	11 17	12 17	13 17	14 17	15 17	16 17	17 17	18 17	19 17	20 17	21 17	22 17	23 17
Stockport	84	d	23p27	06 30	07 30	08 30	09 30	10 30	11 30	12 30	13 30	14 30	15 30	16 30	17 30	18 30	19 30	20 30	21 30	22 30	23 27
Navigation Road		d	23p41	06 44	07 44	08 44	09 44	10 44	11 44	12 44	13 44	14 44	15 44	16 44	17 44	18 44	19 44	20 44	21 44	22 44	23 41
Altrincham		a	23p43	06 46	07 46	08 46	09 46	10 46	11 46	12 46	13 46	14 46	15 46	16 46	17 46	18 46	19 46	20 46	21 46	22 46	23 43
		d	23p43	06 46	07 46	08 46	09 46	10 46	11 46	12 46	13 46	14 46	15 46	16 46	17 46	18 46	19 46	20 46	21 46	22 46	23 43
Hale		d	23p46	06 49	07 49	08 49	09 49	10 49	11 49	12 49	13 49	14 49	15 49	16 49	17 49	18 49	19 49	20 49	21 49	22 49	23 46
Ashley		d	23p49	06 52	07 52	08 52	09 52	10 52	11 52	12 52	13 52	14 52	15 52	16 52	17 52	18 52	19 52	20 52	21 52	22 52	23 49
Mobberley		d	23p52	06 55	07 55	08 55	09 55	10 55	11 55	12 55	13 55	14 55	15 55	16 55	17 55	18 55	19 55	20 55	21 55	22 55	23 52
Knutsford		d	23p57	06 59	07 59	08 59	09 59	10 59	11 59	12 59	13 59	14 59	15 59	16 59	17 59	18 59	19 59	20 59	21 59	22 59	23 57
Plumley		d	00 01	07 03	08 03	09 03	10 03	11 03	12 03	13 03	14 03	15 03	16 03	17 03	18 03	19 03	20 03	21 03	22 03	23 03	00 01
Lostock Gralam		d	00 04	07 07	08 07	09 07	10 07	11 07	12 07	13 07	14 07	15 07	16 07	17 07	18 07	19 07	20 07	21 07	22 07	23 07	00 04
Northwich		d	00 10	07 12	08 12	09 12	10 12	11 12	12 12	13 12	14 12	15 12	16 12	17 12	18 12	19 12	20 12	21 12	22 12	23 12	00 10
Greenbank		d	00 14	07 17	08 17	09 17	10 17	11 17	12 17	13 17	14 17	15 17	16 17	17 17	18 17	19 17	20 17	21 17	22 17	23 17	00 14
Cuddington		d	00 19	07 22	08 22	09 22	10 22	11 22	12 22	13 22	14 22	15 22	16 22	17 22	18 22	19 22	20 22	21 22	22 22	23 22	00 19
Delamere		d	00 24	07 26	08 26	09 26	10 26	11 26	12 26	13 26	14 26	15 26	16 26	17 26	18 26	19 26	20 26	21 26	22 26	23 26	00 24
Mouldsworth		d	00 28	07 31	08 31	09 31	10 31	11 31	12 31	13 31	14 31	15 31	16 31	17 31	18 31	19 31	20 31	21 31	22 31	23 31	00 28
Chester	81	a	00 43	07 47	08 47	09 47	10 47	11 47	12 47	13 47	14 47	15 47	16 47	17 47	18 47	19 47	20 47	21 47	22 47	23 47	00 45

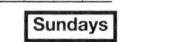

Sundays

Station			NT A	NT	NT	NT	NT	NT	NT B	NT C	NT
Manchester Picc. 10	84	d	23p17	09 22	11 22	13 22	15 22	17 22	19 22	19 22	21 22
Stockport	84	d	23p27	09 31	11 31	13 31	15 32	17 31	19 31	19 31	21 31
Navigation Road		d	23p41	09 45	11 45	13 45	15 45	17 45	19 45	19 45	21 45
Altrincham		a	23p43	09 47	11 47	13 47	15 47	17 47	19 47	19 47	21 47
		d	23p43	09 47	11 47	13 47	15 48	17 47	19 47	19 47	21 47
Hale		d	23p46	09 50	11 50	13 50	15 50	17 50	19 50	19 50	21 50
Ashley		d	23p49	09 53	11 53	13 53	15 53	17 53	19 53	19 53	21 53
Mobberley		d	23p52	09 56	11 56	13 56	15 56	17 56	19 56	19 56	21 56
Knutsford		d	23p57	10 00	12 00	14 00	16 01	18 00	20 00	20 00	22 00
Plumley		d	00 01	10 05	12 04	14 04	16 05	18 04	20 04	20 04	22 04
Lostock Gralam		d	00 04	10 08	12 08	14 08	16 08	18 08	20 08	20 08	22 08
Northwich		d	00 10	10 13	12 13	14 13	16 14	18 13	20 13	20 13	22 13
Greenbank		d	00 14	10 18	12 18	14 18	16 18	18 18	20 18	20 18	22 18
Cuddington		d	00 19	10 23	12 23	14 23	16 23	18 23	20 23	20 23	22 23
Delamere		d	00 24	10 27	12 27	14 27	16 28	18 27	20 27	20 27	22 27
Mouldsworth		d	00 28	10 32	12 32	14 32	16 32	18 32	20 32	20 32	22 32
Chester	81	a	00 45	10 46	12 43	14 43	16 44	18 43	20 43	20 48	22 43

A not 11 December

B from 1 April

C until 25 March

On Sundays only, National Rail Tickets to stations between Hale and Mouldsworth inclusive are valid for travel on Metrolink services between Manchester City Centre and Altrincham

Table 88

Mondays to Fridays

Chester and Northwich - Manchester

Network Diagram - see first Page of Table 88

Miles				NT MX	NT	NT	NT	NT	NT	NT	NT	NT	NT	NT	NT	NT	NT	NT	NT	NT	NT	NT	NT
0	**Chester**	81	d	22p48	06 05	06 35	07 03	07 35	08 07	09 07	10 07	11 07	12 07	13 07	14 07	15 07	16 07	17 07	18 07	19 07	20 07	21 07	22 48
6½	Mouldsworth		d	22p59	06 16	06 46	07 14	07 46	08 18	09 18	10 18	11 18	12 18	13 18	14 18	15 18	16 18	17 18	18 18	19 18	20 18	21 18	22 59
9½	Delamere		d	23p04	06 21	06 51	07 19	07 51	08 23	09 23	10 23	11 23	12 23	13 23	14 23	15 23	16 23	17 23	18 23	19 23	20 23	21 23	23 04
12½	Cuddington		d	23p08	06 25	06 55	07 23	07 55	08 27	09 27	10 27	11 27	12 27	13 27	14 27	15 27	16 27	17 27	18 27	19 27	20 27	21 27	23 08
15¼	Greenbank		d	23p13	06 30	07 00	07 28	08 00	08 32	09 32	10 32	11 32	12 32	13 32	14 32	15 32	16 32	17 32	18 32	19 32	20 32	21 32	23 13
17	**Northwich**		d	23p17	06 35	07 05	07 33	08 05	08 37	09 37	10 37	11 37	12 37	13 37	14 37	15 37	16 37	17 37	18 37	19 37	20 37	21 37	23 17
18½	Lostock Gralam		d	23p20	06 38	07 08	07 36	08 08	08 40	09 40	10 40	11 40	12 40	13 40	14 40	15 40	16 40	17 40	18 40	19 40	20 40	21 40	23 20
20½	Plumley		d	23p24	06 41	07 11	07 40	08 11	08 43	09 43	10 43	11 43	12 43	13 43	14 43	15 43	16 43	17 43	18 43	19 43	20 43	21 43	23 24
23	Knutsford		d	23p29	06 46	07 17	07 45	08 17	08 49	09 49	10 49	11 49	12 49	13 49	14 49	15 49	16 49	17 49	18 49	19 49	20 49	21 49	23 29
26¾	Mobberley		d	23p33	06 50	07 21	07 49	08 21	08 53	09 53	10 53	11 53	12 53	13 53	14 53	15 53	16 53	17 53	18 53	19 53	20 53	21 53	23 33
27½	Ashley		d	23p36	06 54	07 24	07 53	08 24	08 56	09 56	10 56	11 56	12 56	13 56	14 56	15 56	16 56	17 56	18 56	19 56	20 56	21 56	23 36
29¼	Hale		d	23p39	06 57	07 28	07 57	08 28	08 59	09 59	10 59	11 59	12 59	13 59	14 59	15 59	16 59	17 59	18 59	19 59	20 59	21 59	23 39
30	**Altrincham**	🚋	a	23p44	07 01	07 32	08 01	08 32	09 04	10 04	11 04	12 04	13 04	14 04	15 04	16 04	17 04	18 04	19 04	20 04	21 04	22 04	23 44
—			d	23p44	07 02	07 33	08 02	08 33	09 04	10 04	11 04	12 04	13 04	14 04	15 04	16 04	17 04	18 04	19 04	20 04	21 04	22 04	23 44
30½	Navigation Road	🚋	d	23p46	07 04	07 35	08 04	08 35	09 06	10 06	11 06	12 06	13 06	14 06	15 06	16 06	17 06	18 06	19 06	20 06	21 06	22 06	23 46
38¾	**Stockport**	84	a	00 02	07 18	07 56	08 19	08 56	09 21	10 21	11 21	12 21	13 21	14 21	15 21	16 21	17 21	18 21	19 21	20 21	21 21	22 21	00 02
44¾	**Manchester Picc.** 10	81 🚋	a	00 18	07 28		08 32		09 36	10 36	11 36	12 36	13 36	14 36	15 36	16 36	17 36	18 36	19 35	20 35	21 35	22 35	00 18

Saturdays

			NT	NT	NT	NT	NT	NT	NT	NT	NT	NT	NT	NT	NT	NT	NT	NT	NT	NT
Chester	81	d	22p48	06 01	06 59	08 03	09 03	10 03	11 03	12 03	13 03	14 03	15 03	16 03	17 03	18 03	19 03	20 03	21 33	22 45
Mouldsworth		d	22p59	06 12	07 10	08 14	09 14	10 14	11 14	12 14	13 14	14 14	15 14	16 14	17 14	18 14	19 14	20 14	21 45	22 56
Delamere		d	23p04	06 17	07 15	08 19	09 19	10 19	11 19	12 19	13 19	14 19	15 19	16 19	17 19	18 19	19 19	20 19	21 49	23 01
Cuddington		d	23p08	06 21	07 19	08 23	09 23	10 23	11 23	12 23	13 23	14 23	15 23	16 23	17 23	18 23	19 23	20 23	21 54	23 05
Greenbank		d	23p13	06 26	07 24	08 28	09 28	10 28	11 28	12 28	13 28	14 28	15 28	16 28	17 28	18 28	19 28	20 28	21 58	23 10
Northwich		d	23p17	06 31	07 29	08 33	09 33	10 33	11 33	12 33	13 33	14 33	15 33	16 33	17 33	18 33	19 33	20 33	22 03	23 14
Lostock Gralam		d	23p20	06 34	07 32	08 36	09 36	10 36	11 36	12 36	13 36	14 36	15 36	16 36	17 36	18 36	19 36	20 36	22 06	23 17
Plumley		d	23p24	06 37	07 36	08 39	09 39	10 39	11 39	12 39	13 39	14 39	15 39	16 39	17 39	18 39	19 39	20 39	22 10	23 21
Knutsford		d	23p29	06 42	07 41	08 45	09 45	10 45	11 45	12 45	13 45	14 45	15 45	16 45	17 45	18 45	19 45	20 45	22 15	23 26
Mobberley		d	23p33	06 46	07 45	08 49	09 49	10 49	11 49	12 49	13 49	14 49	15 49	16 49	17 49	18 49	19 49	20 49	22 19	23 30
Ashley		d	23p36	06 50	07 49	08 52	09 52	10 52	11 52	12 52	13 52	14 52	15 52	16 52	17 52	18 52	19 52	20 52	22 23	23 33
Hale		d	23p39	06 53	07 53	08 55	09 55	10 55	11 55	12 55	13 55	14 55	15 55	16 55	17 55	18 55	19 55	20 55	22 26	23 36
Altrincham	🚋	a	23p44	06 57	07 57	09 00	10 00	11 00	12 00	13 00	14 00	15 00	16 00	17 00	18 00	19 00	20 00	21 00	22 30	23 41
		d	23p44	06 58	07 58	09 00	10 00	11 00	12 00	13 00	14 00	15 00	16 00	17 00	18 00	19 00	20 00	21 00	22 31	23 41
Navigation Road	🚋	d	23p46	07 00	08 00	09 02	10 02	11 02	12 02	13 02	14 02	15 02	16 02	17 02	18 02	19 02	20 02	21 02	22 33	23 43
Stockport	84	a	00 02	07 18	08 19	09 21	10 21	11 21	12 21	13 21	14 21	15 21	16 21	17 21	18 21	19 21	20 21	21 21	22 47	00 02
Manchester Picc. 10	81 🚋	a	00 18	07 31	08 32	09 36	10 36	11 36	12 36	13 36	14 36	15 36	16 36	17 36	18 36	19 35	20 35	21 35	23 00	00 15

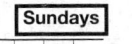

Sundays

			NT A	NT	NT	NT	NT	NT	NT	NT
Chester	81	d	22p45	08 58	11 07	13 07	15 07	17 03	19 07	21 07
Mouldsworth		d	22p56	09 09	11 18	13 18	15 18	17 14	19 18	21 18
Delamere		d	23p01	09 14	11 23	13 23	15 23	17 19	19 23	21 23
Cuddington		d	23p05	09 18	11 27	13 27	15 27	17 23	19 27	21 27
Greenbank		d	23p10	09 23	11 32	13 32	15 32	17 28	19 32	21 32
Northwich		d	23p14	09 28	11 37	13 37	15 37	17 33	19 37	21 37
Lostock Gralam		d	23p17	09 31	11 40	13 40	15 40	17 36	19 40	21 40
Plumley		d	23p21	09 34	11 43	13 43	15 43	17 39	19 43	21 43
Knutsford		d	23p26	09 40	11 49	13 49	15 49	17 45	19 49	21 49
Mobberley		d	23p30	09 44	11 53	13 53	15 53	17 49	19 53	21 53
Ashley		d	23p33	09 47	11 56	13 56	15 56	17 52	19 56	21 56
Hale		d	23p36	09 50	11 59	13 59	15 59	17 55	19 59	21 59
Altrincham	🚋	a	23p41	09 55	12 04	14 04	16 04	18 00	20 04	22 04
		d	23p41	09 55	12 04	14 04	16 04	18 00	20 04	22 04
Navigation Road	🚋	d	23p43	09 57	12 06	14 06	16 06	18 02	20 06	22 06
Stockport	84	a	00 02	10 12	12 21	14 21	16 21	18 21	20 21	22 21
Manchester Picc. 10	81 🚋	a	00 15	10 22	12 31	14 33	16 33	18 33	20 33	22 33

A not 11 December

On Sundays only, National Rail Tickets from stations between Mouldsworth and Hale inclusive are valid for travel on Metrolink services between Altrincham and Manchester City Centre

Liverpool - Warrington Central - Manchester and Manchester Airport

Network Diagram - see first Page of Table 88

Miles	Station		NT MO	NT MO	NT MO	NT MX	NT MO	NT MX	NT	NT	NT		NT	TP	NT	EM	NT	NT	NT	TP	NT		EM	NT	NT
			🚌		🚌									◇[1] A 🛒		◇ B				◇[1] A 🛒			◇ B		
0	**Liverpool Lime Street [10] 90,91**	d	22p01	23p01	23p01	23p38	03 31	03 31	05 13	05 49			06 13	06 15	06 21	06 47	06 50	07 13		07 15	07 26		07 42	07 45	08 13
1¾	Edge Hill 90,91	d				23p42				05 53							06 54				07 30				
3¾	Mossley Hill 91	d				23p47				05 58					06 29		06 59				07 35			07 53	
4½	West Allerton 91	d				23p50				06 00					06 31		07 01				07 37			07 56	
—	Liverpool Central [10] 103	d																							
5½	L'pool Sth Parkway [7] 91,103 ✈	d				23p53				06 03				06 25	06 34	06 57	07 04			07 25	07 40		07 53	07 59	
7¼	Hunts Cross 103	d				23p56				06 07							07 08						07 59	08 04	
8¼	Halewood	d				23p59				06 09							07 10							08 07	
10½	Hough Green	d				00 03				06 13					06 41		07 14				07 47			08 11	
12¼	Widnes	d				00 06				06 17					06 44	07 07	07 18			07 33			08 05	08 15	
16	Sankey for Penketh	d				00 11				06 22							07 23							08 20	
18½	**Warrington Central**	a				00 16				06 28				06 37	06 52	07 15	07 29			07 39	07 56		08 13	08 25	
—		d				00 17					06 02			06 38	06 53	07 15			07 22	07 40	07 57		08 13	08 25	
20¼	Padgate	d									06 05				06 56				07 25		08 00				
21¾	Birchwood	d									06 08			06 43	06 59	07 20			07 28	07 45	08 03		08 18	08 30	
24½	Glazebrook	d									06 13				07 04				07 33		08 08				
25¾	Irlam	d									06 16				07 07				07 36	07 50	08 11			08 37	
28	Flixton	d									06 20				07 11				07 40		08 15			08 41	
28½	Chassen Road	d									06 22				07 13				07 42		08 17			08 43	
29	Urmston	d									06 24				07 15				07 44		08 19			08 46	
30¼	Humphrey Park	d									06 26				07 17				07 46		08 21			08 49	
31	Trafford Park	d									06 29				07 20				07 49		08 24			08 52	
34	Deansgate 84,85 🚊	a									06 36				07 29				07 58		08 32			09 00	
34½	**Manchester Oxford Road 84,85**	a	00 12	23p47	01 12						06 41		06 57	07 00	07 36	07 38		07 57	08 03	08 04	08 36		08 38	09 04	08 57
35	**Manchester Piccadilly [10] 78,84,85 🚊**	a		23p50		00 40	04 13	04 13	05 57				07 01	07 09		07 41		08 01		08 08			08 41		09 01
—	Stockport 84	a														07 53							08 53		
—	Sheffield [7] 78 🚊	a														08 34							09 35		
44¾	**Manchester Airport 85 ✈**	a		00 07			04 27	04 29	06 14				07 22					08 22							09 22

Station		TP	NT	EM	NT	NT	TP		NT	EM	NT	NT		TP	NT	EM	NT		NT		TP	NT	EM	NT	NT
		◇[1] A 🛒		◇ B			◇[1] A 🛒			◇ B				◇[1] A 🛒		◇ B					◇[1] A 🛒		◇ B		
Liverpool Lime Street [10] 90,91	d	08 22	08 26	08 52	08 55	09 13	09 22		09 27	09 52	09 55	10 13		10 22	10 27	10 52	10 55		11 13		11 22	11 27	11 52	11 55	12 13
Edge Hill 90,91	d		08 30		08 59						09 59						10 59							11 59	
Mossley Hill 91	d		08 35		09 04				09 35		10 04				10 35		11 04					11 35		12 04	
West Allerton 91	d		08 37		09 06				09 37		10 06				10 37		11 06					11 37		12 06	
Liverpool Central [10] 103	d																								
L'pool Sth Parkway [7] 91,103 ✈	d	08 32	08 40	09 03	09 09		09 32		09 40	10 03	10 09			10 32	10 40	11 03	11 09				11 32	11 40	12 03	12 09	
Hunts Cross 103	d				09 13						10 13						11 13							12 13	
Halewood	d				09 16						10 16						11 16							12 16	
Hough Green	d		08 47		09 20				09 47		10 20				10 47		11 20					11 47		12 20	
Widnes	d		08 50	09 11	09 23				09 50	10 11	10 23				10 50	11 11	11 23					11 50	12 11	12 23	
Sankey for Penketh	d				09 28						10 28						11 28							12 28	
Warrington Central	a	08 44	08 58	09 18	09 33		09 44		09 58	10 18	10 33			10 44	10 58	11 18	11 33				11 44	11 58	12 18	12 33	
	d	08 45	08 59	09 19	09 34		09 45		09 59	10 19	10 34			10 45	10 59	11 19	11 34				11 45	11 59	12 19	12 34	
Padgate	d		09 02						10 02						11 02							12 02			
Birchwood	d	08 50	09 05		09 38		09 50		10 05		10 38			10 50	11 05		11 38				11 50	12 05		12 38	
Glazebrook	d								10 10													12 10			
Irlam	d		09 11		09 44				10 13		10 44				11 11		11 44					12 13		12 44	
Flixton	d		09 15						10 17						11 15							12 17			
Chassen Road	d								10 19													12 19			
Urmston	d		09 18		09 49				10 21		10 49				11 18		11 49					12 21		12 49	
Humphrey Park	d		09 20												11 20										
Trafford Park	d		09 23												11 23										
Deansgate 84,85 🚊	a		09 31		09 59				10 31		10 59				11 31		11 59					12 31		12 59	
Manchester Oxford Road 84,85	a	09 05	09 36	09 39	10 04	09 57	10 05		10 36	10 39	11 04	10 57		11 05	11 36	11 39	12 04		11 57		12 05	12 36	12 39	13 04	12 57
Manchester Piccadilly [10] 78,84,85 🚊	a	09 09		09 41		10 01	10 09			10 41		11 01		11 09		11 41			12 01		12 09		12 41		13 01
Stockport 84	a			09 53						10 53						11 53							12 53		
Sheffield [7] 78 🚊	a			10 35						11 34						12 35							13 35		
Manchester Airport 85 ✈	a					10 22						11 22							12 22						13 22

A To Scarborough

B To Norwich

Liverpool - Warrington Central - Manchester and Manchester Airport

Network Diagram - see first Page of Table 88

		TP	NT	EM	NT	NT	TP	NT	EM	NT		NT	TP	NT	EM	NT	NT	TP	NT	EM		NT	NT	TP	NT
		◇1 B 🛒		◇ C			◇1 B 🛒		◇ C				◇1 B 🛒		◇ C			◇1 D 🛒		◇ C				◇1 B 🛒	
Liverpool Lime Street [10] 90,91	d	12 22	12 27	12 52	12 55	13 13	13 22	13 27	13 52	13 55		14 13	14 22	14 27	14 52	14 55	15 13	15 22	15 27	15 52		15 55	16 13	16 22	16 27
Edge Hill 90,91	d				12 59					13 59						14 59						15 59			
Mossley Hill 91	d		12 35		13 04			13 35		14 04				14 35		15 04			15 35			16 04			16 35
West Allerton 91	d		12 37		13 06			13 37		14 06				14 37		15 06			15 37			16 06			16 37
Liverpool Central [10] 103	d																								
L'pool Sth Parkway [7] 91,103 ✈	d	12 32	12 40	13 03	13 09		13 32	13 40	14 03	14 09			14 32	14 40	15 03	15 09		15 32	15 40	16 03		16 09		16 32	16 40
Hunts Cross 103	d				13 13					14 13						15 13						16 13			
Halewood	d				13 16					14 16						15 16						16 16			
Hough Green	d		12 47		13 20			13 47		14 20				14 47		15 20			15 47			16 20			16 47
Widnes	d		12 50	13 11	13 23			13 50	14 11	14 23				14 50	15 11	15 23			15 50	16 11		16 23			16 50
Sankey for Penketh	d				13 28					14 28						15 28						16 28			
Warrington Central	a	12 44	12 58	13 18	13 33		13 44	13 58	14 18	14 33			14 44	14 58	15 18	15 33		15 44	15 58	16 18		16 33		16 44	16 58
	d	12 45	12 59	13 19	13 34		13 45	13 59	14 19	14 34			14 45	14 59	15 19	15 34		15 45	15 59	16 19		16 34		16 45	16 59
Padgate	d		13 02					14 02						15 02					16 02						17 02
Birchwood	d	12 50	13 05		13 38		13 50	14 05		14 38			14 50	15 05		15 38		15 50	16 05			16 38		16 50	17 05
Glazebrook	d							14 10											16 10						
Irlam	d		13 11		13 44			14 13		14 44				15 11		15 44			16 13			16 44			17 11
Flixton	d		13 15					14 17						15 15					16 17						17 15
Chassen Road	d							14 19											16 19						
Urmston	d		13 18		13 49			14 21		14 49				15 18		15 49			16 21			16 49			17 18
Humphrey Park	d		13 20											15 20											17 20
Trafford Park	d		13 23											15 23											17 23
Deansgate 84,85 ⛴	a		13 31		13 59			14 31		14 59				15 31		15 59			16 30			16 59			17 31
Manchester Oxford Road 84,85	a	13 05	13 36	13 39	14 04	13 57	14 05	14 36	14 39	15 04		14 57	15 05	15 36	15 39	16 04	15 57	16 05	16 36	16 38		17 04	16 57	17 05	17 36
Manchester Piccadilly [10] 78,84,85 ⛴	a	13 09		13 41		14 01	14 09		14 41			15 01	15 09		15 41		16 01	16 09		16 41			17 01	17 09	
Stockport 84	a			13 53					14 53						15 53					16 53					
Sheffield [7] 78 ⛴	a			14 35					15 35						16 34					17 40					
Manchester Airport 85 ✈	a					14 22						15 22					16 22						17 22		

		EM	NT	NT	TP	NT	EM	NT	NT		TP	NT	EM	NT	TP	NT	EM	NT	NT
		◇ E			◇1 B 🛒		◇ C				◇1 B		◇ E		◇1 F		◇ E		
Liverpool Lime Street [10] 90,91	d	16 52	16 55	17 06	17 22	17 25	17 52	17 55	18 13		18 22	18 25	18 52	18 55	19 22		19 52	19 55	20 09
Edge Hill 90,91	d		16 59			17 29		17 59				18 29		18 59				19 59	
Mossley Hill 91	d		17 04			17 34		18 04				18 34		19 04				20 04	
West Allerton 91	d		17 06			17 36		18 06				18 36		19 06				20 06	
Liverpool Central [10] 103	d																		
L'pool Sth Parkway [7] 91,103 ✈	d	17 03	17 09		17 32	17 39	18 03	18 09			18 32	18 39	19 03	19 09	19 32		20 03	20 09	
Hunts Cross 103	d		17 13			17 43		18 13				18 43		19 13				20 13	
Halewood	d		17 16			17 46		18 16				18 46		19 16				20 16	
Hough Green	d		17 20			17 50		18 20				18 50		19 20				20 20	
Widnes	d	17 11	17 23			17 53	18 11	18 23				18 53	19 11	19 23			20 11	20 23	
Sankey for Penketh	d		17 28			17 58		18 28				18 58		19 28				20 28	
Warrington Central	a	17 18	17 33		17 44	18 03	18 18	18 33			18 44	19 03	19 18	19 34	19 44		20 18	20 34	
	d	17 19	17 34		17 45	18 04	18 19	18 34			18 45	19 04	19 19		19 45	19 56	20 19		
Padgate	d					18 07						19 07				19 59			
Birchwood	d		17 38		17 50	18 10		18 38			18 50	19 10			19 50	20 02			
Glazebrook	d											19 15				20 07			
Irlam	d		17 44			18 16		18 44				19 18				20 10			
Flixton	d					18 20										20 14			
Chassen Road	d															20 16			
Urmston	d		17 49			18 23		18 49				19 23				20 18			
Humphrey Park	d															20 20			
Trafford Park	d															20 23			
Deansgate 84,85 ⛴	a		17 59			18 31		18 59				19 31				20 31			
Manchester Oxford Road 84,85	a	17 38	18 04	17 57	18 05	18 36	18 39	19 04	18 57		19 05	19 36	19 39		20 05	20 36	20 39		20 57
Manchester Piccadilly [10] 78,84,85 ⛴	a	17 41		18 01	18 09		18 41		19 01		19 09		19 41		20 09		20 41		21 01
Stockport 84	a	17 53					18 53						19 53				20 53		
Sheffield [7] 78 ⛴	a	18 41					19 33						20 36				21 35		
Manchester Airport 85 ✈	a			18 22					19 24										21 20

B To Scarborough
C To Norwich
D To Middlesbrough
E To Nottingham
F To Hull

Table 89

Mondays to Fridays

Liverpool - Warrington Central - Manchester and Manchester Airport

Network Diagram - see first Page of Table 88

	TP	NT	EM	NT	TP	LM	LM	NT
	◇1		◇		◇1	◇1	◇1	
	A		B		A	D	D	
Liverpool Lime Street 10 90,91 d	20 22	20 55	21 37	21 55	22 30	22 34	23 34	23 38
Edge Hill 90,91 d		20 59		21 59				23 42
Mossley Hill 91 d		21 04		22 04				23 47
West Allerton 91 d		21 06		22 06				23 50
Liverpool Central 10 103 d								
L'pool Sth Parkway 7 91,103 ✈ d	20 32	21 09	21 47	22 09	22 40	22a44	23a44	23 53
Hunts Cross 103 d		21 13		22 13				23 56
Halewood d		21 16		22 16				23 59
Hough Green d		21 20		22 20				00 03
Widnes d		21 23	21 55	22 23				00 06
Sankey for Penketh d		21 28		22 28				00 11
Warrington Central a	20 44	21 33	22 03	22 33	22 52			00 16
d	20 45	21 34	22 03	22 34	22 53			00 17
Padgate d		21 37		22 37				
Birchwood d	20 50	21 40		22 40	22 58			
Glazebrook d		21 45		22 45				
Irlam d		21 48		22 48				
Flixton d		21 52		22 52				
Chassen Road d		21 54		22 54				
Urmston d		21 56		22 56				
Humphrey Park d		21 58		22 58				
Trafford Park d		22 01		23 01				
Deansgate 84,85 🚊 a		22 08		23 08				
Manchester Oxford Road 84,85 a	21 06	22 13	22 23	23 13	23 14			
Manchester Piccadilly 10 78,84,85 🚊 a	21 09		22 26		23 19			00 40
Stockport 84 a			22 37					
Sheffield 7 78 🚊 a			23 35					
Manchester Airport 85 ✈ a								

Saturdays

	NT	NT	NT	NT	NT	NT	NT	NT	NT	TP	NT	NT	EM	NT	NT	NT	TP	NT	NT	EM	NT	NT
										◇1			◇				◇1			◇		
		E	F	G 🚌	F	G 🚌		F	G 🚌	H 🛒		G 🚌	I		G 🚌	F	H 🛒		G 🚌	I		G 🚌
Liverpool Lime Street 10 90,91 d	23p38	03§31	03§38	04§40	05§13	05§40	05 49	06§13	06§15	06 15	06 25	06§40	06 49	06 55	07§10	07§13	07 15	07 26	07§40	07 42	07 45	08§10
Edge Hill 90,91 d	23p42			04a47		05a47	05 53		06a22			06a47		06 59	07a17			07 30	07a47			08a17
Mossley Hill 91 d	23p47						05 58				06 33			07 04				07 35			07 53	
West Allerton 91 d	23p50						06 00				06 35			07 06				07 37			07 56	
Liverpool Central 10 103 d																						
L'pool Sth Parkway 7 91,103 ✈ d	23p53						06 03			06 25	06 38		06 59	07 09			07 25	07 40		07 52	07 59	
Hunts Cross 103 d	23p56						06 07							07 13						07 59	08 04	
Halewood d	23p59						06 09							07 16							08 07	
Hough Green d	00 03						06 13				06 46			07 20				07 47			08 11	
Widnes d	00 06						06 17				06 49		07 07	07 23			07 33			08 05	08 15	
Sankey for Penketh d	00 11						06 22							07 28							08 20	
Warrington Central a	00 16						06 28			06 37	06 57		07 15	07 34			07 39	07 56		08 13	08 25	
d	00 17									06 38	06 58		07 15				07 40	07 57		08 13	08 25	
Padgate d											07 01							08 00				
Birchwood d										06 43	07 04		07 20				07 45	08 03		08 18	08 30	
Glazebrook d											07 09							08 08				
Irlam d											07 12						07 50	08 11			08 37	
Flixton d											07 16							08 15			08 41	
Chassen Road d											07 18							08 17			08 43	
Urmston d											07 20							08 19			08 46	
Humphrey Park d											07 22							08 21			08 49	
Trafford Park d											07 25							08 24			08 52	
Deansgate 84,85 🚊 a											07 32							08 32			09 00	
Manchester Oxford Road 84,85 a								06§57		07 00	07 37		07 38			07§57	08 04	08 36		08 38	09 04	
Manchester Piccadilly 10 78,84,85 🚊 a	00 40	04§14	04§14		05§57			07§01		07 09			07 41			08§01	08 08			08 41		
Stockport 84 a													07 53							08 53		
Sheffield 7 78 🚊 a													08 34							09 35		
Manchester Airport 85 ✈ a		04§30	04§30		06§14			07§22								08§22						

A To York
B To Nottingham
D To Crewe
E from 18 February until 24 March
F until 11 February and then from 31 March
G from 18 February until 24 March. To Earlestown
H To Scarborough
I To Norwich

Table 89

Saturdays

Liverpool - Warrington Central - Manchester and Manchester Airport

Network Diagram - see first Page of Table 88

	NT A	TP ◇1 B 🚲	NT	NT C 🚌	EM ◇ D	NT	NT C 🚌	NT A	TP ◇1 B 🚲	NT	NT C 🚌	EM ◇ D	NT	NT C 🚌	NT A	NT E	TP ◇1 B 🚲	NT	NT C 🚌	EM ◇ D	NT	NT C 🚌
Liverpool Lime Street [10] 90,91 d	08 13	08 22	08 26	08 40	08 52	08 55	09 10	09 13	09 22	09 27	09 40	09 52	09 55	10 10	10 13	10 16	10 22	10 27	10 40	10 52	10 55	11 10
Edge Hill 90,91 d			08 30	08a47		08 59	09a17				09a47		09 59	10a17					10a47		10 59	11a17
Mossley Hill 91 d			08 35			09 04				09 35			10 04					10 35			11 04	
West Allerton 91 d			08 37			09 06				09 37			10 06					10 37			11 06	
Liverpool Central [10] 103 d																						
L'pool Sth Parkway [7] 91,103 ✈ d		08 32	08 40		09 03	09 09			09 32	09 40		10 03	10 09			10a27	10 32	10 40		11 03	11 09	
Hunts Cross 103 d						09 13							10 13								11 13	
Halewood d						09 16							10 16								11 16	
Hough Green d			08 47			09 20				09 47			10 20					10 47			11 20	
Widnes d			08 50		09 11	09 23				09 50		10 11	10 23					10 50		11 11	11 23	
Sankey for Penketh d						09 28							10 28								11 28	
Warrington Central a		08 44	08 58		09 18	09 33			09 44	09 58		10 18	10 33				10 44	10 58		11 18	11 33	
d		08 45	08 59		09 19	09 34			09 45	09 59		10 19	10 34				10 45	10 59		11 19	11 34	
Padgate d			09 02							10 02								11 02				
Birchwood d		08 50	09 05			09 38			09 50	10 05			10 38				10 50	11 05			11 38	
Glazebrook d										10 10												
Irlam d			09 11			09 44				10 13			10 44					11 11			11 44	
Flixton d			09 15							10 17								11 15				
Chassen Road d										10 19												
Urmston d			09 18			09 49				10 21			10 49					11 18			11 49	
Humphrey Park d			09 20															11 20				
Trafford Park d			09 23															11 23				
Deansgate 84,85 🚊 a			09 31			09 59				10 31			10 59					11 31			11 59	
Manchester Oxford Road 84,85 a	08 57	09 05	09 36		09 39	10 04		09 57	10 05	10 36		10 39	11 04		10 57		11 05	11 36		11 39	12 04	
Manchester Piccadilly [10] 78,84,85 🚊 a	09 01	09 09			09 41			10 01	10 09			10 41			11 01		11 09			11 41		
Stockport 84 a					09 53							10 53								11 53		
Sheffield [7] 78 🚊 a					10 35							11 35								12 35		
Manchester Airport 85 ✈ a	09 22							10 22							11 22							

	NT A	TP ◇1 B 🚲	NT	NT C 🚌	EM ◇ D	NT	NT C 🚌	NT A	TP ◇1 B 🚲	NT	NT C 🚌	EM ◇ D	NT	NT C 🚌	NT A	TP ◇1 B 🚲	NT	NT C 🚌
Liverpool Lime Street [10] 90,91 d	11 13	11 22	11 27	11 40	11 52	11 55	12 10	12 13	12 22	12 27	12 40	12 52	12 55	13 10	13 13	13 22	13 27	13 40
Edge Hill 90,91 d				11a47		11 59	12a17				12a47		12 59	13a17				13a47
Mossley Hill 91 d			11 35			12 04				12 35			13 04				13 35	
West Allerton 91 d			11 37			12 06				12 37			13 06				13 37	
Liverpool Central [10] 103 d																		
L'pool Sth Parkway [7] 91,103 ✈ d		11 32	11 40		12 03	12 09			12 32	12 40		13 03	13 09			13 32	13 40	
Hunts Cross 103 d						12 13							13 13					
Halewood d						12 16							13 16					
Hough Green d			11 47			12 20				12 47			13 20				13 47	
Widnes d			11 50		12 11	12 23				12 50		13 11	13 23				13 50	
Sankey for Penketh d						12 28							13 28					
Warrington Central a		11 44	11 58		12 18	12 33			12 44	12 58		13 18	13 33			13 44	13 58	
d		11 45	11 59		12 19	12 34			12 45	12 59		13 19	13 34			13 45	13 59	
Padgate d			12 02							13 02							14 02	
Birchwood d		11 50	12 05			12 38			12 50	13 05			13 38			13 50	14 05	
Glazebrook d			12 10														14 10	
Irlam d			12 13			12 44				13 11			13 44				14 13	
Flixton d			12 17							13 15							14 17	
Chassen Road d			12 19														14 19	
Urmston d			12 21			12 49				13 18			13 49				14 21	
Humphrey Park d										13 20								
Trafford Park d										13 23								
Deansgate 84,85 🚊 a			12 31			12 59				13 31			13 59				14 31	
Manchester Oxford Road 84,85 a	11 57	12 05	12 36		12 39	13 04		12 57	13 05	13 36		13 39	14 04		13 57	14 05	14 36	
Manchester Piccadilly [10] 78,84,85 🚊 a	12 01	12 09			12 41			13 01	13 09			13 41			14 01	14 09		
Stockport 84 a					12 53							13 53						
Sheffield [7] 78 🚊 a					13 35							14 35						
Manchester Airport 85 ✈ a	12 22							13 22							14 22			

A until 11 February and then from 31 March
B To Scarborough
C from 18 February until 24 March. To Earlestown
D To Norwich

Liverpool - Warrington Central - Manchester and Manchester Airport

Network Diagram - see first Page of Table 88

		EM	NT	NT	NT	TP	NT	NT	EM	NT	NT	NT	TP	NT	NT	EM	NT	NT	NT	TP
		◇				◇1			◇				◇1			◇				◇1
		A		B	C	E		B	A		B	C	E		B	A		B	C	E
				🚌				🚌			🚌				🚌			🚌		
						⚲														
Liverpool Lime Street [10] 90,91	d	13 52	13 55	14ʃ10	14ʃ13	14 22	14 27	14ʃ40	14 52	14 55	15ʃ10	15ʃ13	15 22	15 27	15ʃ40	15 52	15 55	16ʃ05	16ʃ13	16 22
Edge Hill 90,91	d		13 59	14a17				14a47		14 59	15a17				15a47		15 59	16a12		
Mossley Hill 91	d		14 04				14 35			15 04				15 35			16 04			
West Allerton 91	d		14 06				14 37			15 06				15 37			16 06			
Liverpool Central [10] 103	d																			
L'pool Sth Parkway [7] 91,103 ✈	d	14 03	14 09			14 32	14 40		15 03	15 09			15 32	15 40		16 03	16 09			16 32
Hunts Cross 103	d		14 13							15 13							16 13			
Halewood	d		14 16							15 16							16 16			
Hough Green	d		14 20				14 47			15 20				15 47			16 20			
Widnes	d	14 11	14 23				14 50		15 11	15 23				15 50		16 11	16 23			
Sankey for Penketh	d		14 28							15 28							16 28			
Warrington Central	a	14 18	14 33			14 44	14 58		15 18	15 33			15 44	15 58		16 18	16 33			16 44
	d	14 19	14 34			14 45	14 59		15 19	15 34			15 45	15 59		16 19	16 34			16 45
Padgate	d						15 02							16 02						
Birchwood	d		14 38			14 50	15 05			15 38			15 50	16 05			16 38			16 50
Glazebrook	d													16 10						
Irlam	d		14 44				15 11			15 44				16 13			16 44			
Flixton	d						15 15							16 17						
Chassen Road	d													16 19						
Urmston	d		14 49				15 18			15 49				16 21			16 49			
Humphrey Park	d						15 20													
Trafford Park	d						15 23													
Deansgate 84,85	a		14 59				15 31			15 59				16 30			16 59			
Manchester Oxford Road 84,85	a	14 39	15 04		14ʃ57	15 05	15 36		15 39	16 04		15ʃ57	16 05	16 36		16 38	17 04		16ʃ57	17 05
Manchester Piccadilly [10] 78,84,85	a	14 41			15ʃ01	15 09			15 41			16ʃ01	16 09			16 41			17ʃ01	17 09
Stockport 84	a	14 53							15 53							16 53				
Sheffield [7] 78	a	15 36							16 35							17 37				
Manchester Airport 85 ✈	a				15ʃ22							16ʃ22							17ʃ22	

		NT	NT	EM	NT	NT	NT	TP	NT	NT	EM	NT	NT	NT	TP	NT	NT	EM	NT	NT	TP	NT
				◇				◇1			◇				◇1			◇			◇1	
			B	F		B	C	E		B	A		B	C	E		B	F		B	G	
			🚌			🚌				🚌			🚌				🚌			🚌		
Liverpool Lime Street [10] 90,91	d	16 27	16ʃ40	16 52	16 55	17ʃ05	17ʃ06	17 22	17 25	17ʃ40	17 52	17 55	18ʃ05	18ʃ13	18 22	18 25	18ʃ40	18 52	18 55	19ʃ05	19 22	
Edge Hill 90,91	d		16a47		16 59	17a12			17 29	17a47		17 59	18a12			18 29	18a47		18 59	19a12		
Mossley Hill 91	d	16 35			17 04				17 34			18 04				18 34			19 04			
West Allerton 91	d	16 37			17 06				17 36			18 06				18 36			19 06			
Liverpool Central [10] 103	d																					
L'pool Sth Parkway [7] 91,103 ✈	d	16 40		17 03	17 09			17 32	17 39		18 03	18 09			18 32	18 39		19 03	19 09		19 32	
Hunts Cross 103	d				17 13				17 43			18 13				18 43			19 13			
Halewood	d				17 16				17 46			18 16				18 46			19 16			
Hough Green	d	16 47			17 20				17 50			18 20				18 50			19 20			
Widnes	d	16 50		17 11	17 23				17 54		18 11	18 23				18 53		19 11	19 23			
Sankey for Penketh	d				17 28				17 58			18 28				18 58			19 28			
Warrington Central	a	16 58		17 18	17 33			17 44	18 03		18 18	18 33			18 44	19 03		19 18	19 34		19 44	
	d	16 59		17 19	17 34			17 45	18 04		18 19	18 34			18 45	19 04		19 19			19 45	19 56
Padgate	d	17 02							18 07							19 07						19 59
Birchwood	d	17 05			17 38			17 50	18 10			18 38			18 50	19 10					19 50	20 02
Glazebrook	d															19 15						20 07
Irlam	d	17 11			17 44				18 16			18 44				19 18						20 10
Flixton	d	17 15							18 20													20 14
Chassen Road	d																					20 16
Urmston	d	17 18			17 49				18 23			18 49				19 23						20 18
Humphrey Park	d	17 20																				20 20
Trafford Park	d	17 23																				20 23
Deansgate 84,85	a	17 31			17 59				18 31			18 59				19 31						20 31
Manchester Oxford Road 84,85	a	17 36		17 38	18 04		17ʃ57	18 05	18 36		18 39	19 04		18ʃ57	19 05	19 36		19 39			20 05	20 36
Manchester Piccadilly [10] 78,84,85	a			17 41			18ʃ01	18 09			18 41			19ʃ01	19 09			19 41			20 09	
Stockport 84	a			17 53							18 53							19 53				
Sheffield [7] 78	a			18 35							19 35							20 35				
Manchester Airport 85 ✈	a						18ʃ22							19ʃ24								

A To Norwich
B from 18 February until 24 March. To Earlestown
C until 11 February and then from 31 March
E To Scarborough
F To Nottingham
G To York

Saturdays

Liverpool - Warrington Central - Manchester and Manchester Airport

Network Diagram - see first Page of Table 88

		EM	NT	NT	NT	TP	EM	NT	NT	EM	NT	LM	NT	TP	NT
		◇				◇■1	◇			◇		■1		◇■1	
		A		B	C	D	A		B	A		E	B	D	
				🚌					🚌				🚌		
Liverpool Lime Street ■10 90,91	d	19 52	19 55	20§05	20§09	20 22	20 52	20 55	21§05	21 37	21 55	22 04	22§10	22 30	23 38
Edge Hill 90,91	d		19 59	20a12	§			20 59	21a12		21 59		22a17		23 42
Mossley Hill 91	d		20 04		§			21 04			22 04				23 47
West Allerton 91	d		20 06		§			21 06			22 06				23 49
Liverpool Central ■10 103	d				§										
L'pool Sth Parkway ■7 91,103 ✈	d	20 03	20 09		§	20 32	21 03	21 09		21 47	22 09	22a14		22 40	23 52
Hunts Cross 103	d		20 13		§			21 13			22 13				23 56
Halewood	d		20 16		§			21 16			22 16				23 59
Hough Green	d		20 20		§			21 20			22 20				00 03
Widnes	d	20 11	20 23		§		21 11	21 23		21 55	22 23				00 06
Sankey for Penketh	d		20 28		§			21 28			22 28				00 11
Warrington Central	a	20 18	20 34		§	20 44	21 18	21 33		22 03	22 33			22 52	00 16
	d	20 19			§	20 45	21 19	21 34		22 03	22 34			22 53	00 17
Padgate	d				§			21 37			22 37				
Birchwood	d				§	20 50		21 40			22 40			22 58	
Glazebrook	d				§			21 45			22 45				
Irlam	d				§			21 48			22 48				
Flixton	d				§			21 52			22 52				
Chassen Road	d				§			21 54			22 54				
Urmston	d				§			21 56			22 56				
Humphrey Park	d				§			21 58			22 58				
Trafford Park	d				§			22 01			23 01				
Deansgate 84,85 🚊	a				§			22 08			23 08				
Manchester Oxford Road 84,85	a	20 39			20§57	21 06	21 38	22 13		22 26	23 13			23 14	
Manchester Piccadilly ■10 78,84,85 🚊	a	20 41			21§01	21 09	21 41			22 29				23 19	00 39
Stockport 84	a	20 53			§		21 52			22 41					
Sheffield ■7 78 🚊	a	21 34			§		22 31			23 39					
Manchester Airport 85 ✈	a				21§24										

Sundays

until 12 February

		NT	NT	TP	NT	NT	TP	NT	NT	TP	NT	NT	TP	NT	NT	TP	NT	EM	NT	TP	NT	EM	NT
				◇■1			◇■1			◇■1			◇■1			◇■1		◇		◇■1		◇	
		F		G			H			I			H			I		J		H		J	
Liverpool Lime Street ■10 90,91	d	23p38	08 07	08 22	08 26	09 01	09 22	09 26	10 01	10 22	10 26	11 01	11 22	11 26	12 01	12 22	12 26	12 52	13 01	13 22	13 26	13 52	14 01
Edge Hill 90,91	d	23p42																					
Mossley Hill 91	d	23p47			08 34			09 34			10 34			11 34			12 34				13 34		
West Allerton 91	d	23p49			08 36			09 36			10 36			11 36			12 36				13 36		
Liverpool Central ■10 103	d	§																					
L'pool Sth Parkway ■7 91,103 ✈	d	23p52		08 32	08 39		09 32	09 39		10 32	10 39		11 32	11 39		12 32	12 39	13 03		13 32	13 39	14 03	
Hunts Cross 103	d	23p56			08 43			09 43			10 43			11 43			12 43				13 43		
Halewood	d	23p59			08 46			09 46			10 46			11 46			12 46				13 46		
Hough Green	d	00§03			08 50			09 50			10 50			11 50			12 50				13 50		
Widnes	d	00§06			08 53			09 53			10 53			11 53			12 53	13 11			13 53	14 11	
Sankey for Penketh	d	00§11																					
Warrington Central	a	00§16		08 44	09 01		09 44	10 01		10 44	11 01		11 44	12 01		12 44	13 01	13 18		13 44	14 01	14 18	
	d	00§17		08 45	09 02		09 45	10 02		10 45	11 02		11 45	12 02		12 45	13 02	13 19		13 45	14 02	14 19	
Padgate	d	§																					
Birchwood	d	§		08 50	09 06		09 50	10 06		10 50	11 06		11 50	12 06		12 50	13 06			13 50	14 06		
Glazebrook	d	§																					
Irlam	d	§			09 12			10 12			11 12			12 12			13 12				14 12		
Flixton	d	§																					
Chassen Road	d	§																					
Urmston	d	§			09 17			10 17			11 17			12 17			13 17				14 17		
Humphrey Park	d	§																					
Trafford Park	d	§																					
Deansgate 84,85 🚊	a	§			09 29			10 27			11 27			12 27			13 27				14 27		
Manchester Oxford Road 84,85	a	§	09 05	09 06	09 33	09 59	10 05	10 31	10 59	11 05	11 31	11 59	12 05	12 30	12 59	13 05	13 31	13 39	13 57	14 05	14 31	14 39	14 59
Manchester Piccadilly ■10 78,84,85 🚊	a	00§39	09 08	09 11		10 03	10 09		11 06	11 09		12 03	12 09		13 03	13 09		13 41	14 03	14 09		14 41	15 02
Stockport 84	a																	13 53				14 53	
Sheffield ■7 78 🚊	a																	14 39				15 37	
Manchester Airport 85 ✈	a		09 25			10 24			11 24			12 21			13 19				14 21				15 20

A To Nottingham
B from 18 February until 24 March. To Earlestown
C until 11 February and then from 31 March
D To York
E To Crewe
F not 11 December
G To Hull
H To Scarborough
I To Middlesbrough
J To Norwich

Table 89

Sundays
until 12 February

Liverpool - Warrington Central - Manchester and Manchester Airport

Network Diagram - see first Page of Table 88

		TP	NT	EM	NT	TP	NT	EM	NT	TP	NT	EM	NT	TP	NT	EM	NT	TP	NT	EM	NT	TP	NT
		◇1		◇		◇1		◇		◇1		◇		◇1		◇		◇1		◇		◇1	
		A		B		C		B		A		D		C		B		C		D		E	
Liverpool Lime Street 10 90,91	d	14 22	14 26	14 52	15 01	15 22	15 26	15 52	16 01	16 22	16 26	16 52	17 01	17 22	17 26	17 52	18 01	18 22	18 26	18 52	19 01	19 22	19 26
Edge Hill 90,91	d																						
Mossley Hill 91	d		14 34				15 34				16 34				17 34				18 34				19 34
West Allerton 91	d		14 36				15 36				16 36				17 36				18 36				19 36
Liverpool Central 10 103	d																						
L'pool Sth Parkway 7 91,103 ✈	d	14 32	14 39	15 03		15 32	15 39	16 03		16 32	16 39	17 03		17 32	17 39	18 03		18 32	18 39	19 03		19 32	19 39
Hunts Cross 103	d		14 43				15 43				16 43				17 43				18 43				19 43
Halewood	d		14 46				15 46				16 46				17 46				18 46				19 46
Hough Green	d		14 50				15 50				16 50				17 50				18 50				19 50
Widnes	d		14 53	15 11			15 53	16 11			16 53	17 11			17 53	18 11			18 53	19 11			19 53
Sankey for Penketh	d																						
Warrington Central	a	14 44	15 01	15 18		15 44	16 01	16 18		16 44	17 01	17 18		17 44	18 01	18 18		18 44	19 01	19 18		19 44	20 01
	d	14 45	15 02	15 19		15 45	16 02	16 19		16 45	17 02	17 19		17 45	18 02	18 19		18 45	19 02	19 19		19 45	20 02
Padgate	d																						
Birchwood	d	14 50	15 06			15 50	16 06			16 50	17 06			17 50	18 06			18 50	19 06			19 50	20 06
Glazebrook	d																						
Irlam	d		15 12				16 12				17 12				18 12				19 12				20 12
Flixton	d																						
Chassen Road	d																						
Urmston	d		15 17				16 17				17 17				18 17				19 17				20 17
Humphrey Park	d																						
Trafford Park	d																						
Deansgate 84,85 🚋	a		15 27				16 27				17 27				18 27				19 27				20 27
Manchester Oxford Road 84,85	a	15 05	15 31	15 39	15 59	16 05	16 31	16 38	16 59	17 05	17 31	17 38	17 59	18 05	18 31	18 39	18 59	19 05	19 31	19 39	19 59	20 05	20 31
Manchester Piccadilly 10 78,84,85 🚋	a	15 09		15 41	16 02	16 09		16 41	17 02	17 09		17 41	18 02	18 09		18 41	19 02	19 09		19 41	20 02	20 09	
Stockport 84	a			15 53				16 53				17 53				18 53				19 53			
Sheffield 7 78 🚋	a			16 36				17 36				18 37				19 34				20 34			
Manchester Airport 85 ✈	a				16 21				17 21				18 21				19 21				20 26		

		EM	NT	TP	NT	NT	EM	NT	TP	NT	NT	NT	NT	NT
		◇		◇1			◇		◇1					
		D		F			D		E					
											(bus)			(bus)
Liverpool Lime Street 10 90,91	d	19 52	20 01	20 22	20 26	21 01	21 21	21 26	21 52	22 01	22 01	22 26	23 01	23 01
Edge Hill 90,91	d													
Mossley Hill 91	d				20 34			21 34				22 34		
West Allerton 91	d				20 36			21 36				22 36		
Liverpool Central 10 103	d													
L'pool Sth Parkway 7 91,103 ✈	d	20 03		20 32	20 39		21 31	21 39	22 02			22 39		
Hunts Cross 103	d				20 43			21 43				22 43		
Halewood	d				20 46			21 46				22 46		
Hough Green	d				20 50			21 50				22 50		
Widnes	d	20 11			20 53		21 39	21 53				22 53		
Sankey for Penketh	d													
Warrington Central	a	20 18		20 44	21 01		21 47	22 01	22 14			23 01		
	d	20 19		20 45	21 02		21 47	22 02	22 15			23 02		
Padgate	d													
Birchwood	d			20 50	21 06			22 06	22 20			23 06		
Glazebrook	d													
Irlam	d				21 12			22 12				23 12		
Flixton	d													
Chassen Road	d													
Urmston	d				21 17			22 17				23 17		
Humphrey Park	d													
Trafford Park	d													
Deansgate 84,85 🚋	a				21 27			22 27				23 27		
Manchester Oxford Road 84,85	a	20 39	20 59	21 05	21 31	21 59	22 06	22 31	22 35	22 47	00 12	23 32	23 47	01 12
Manchester Piccadilly 10 78,84,85 🚋	a	20 41	21 02	21 09		22 02	22 09		22 39	22 50			23 50	
Stockport 84	a	20 53					22 20							
Sheffield 7 78 🚋	a	21 36					23 25							
Manchester Airport 85 ✈	a		21 20			22 21				23 15			00 07	

A To Middlesbrough
B To Norwich
C To Scarborough
D To Nottingham
E To York
F To Newcastle

Table 89

Sundays

19 February to 25 March

Liverpool - Warrington Central - Manchester and Manchester Airport

Network Diagram - see first Page of Table 88

	NT	NT (bus)	TP ◇[1] A	NT	NT (bus)	NT	TP ◇[1] B	NT	NT (bus)	NT	TP ◇[1] C	NT	NT (bus)	NT	TP ◇[1] B	NT	NT (bus)	NT	TP ◇[1] C	NT	EM ◇ D	NT (bus)
Liverpool Lime Street [10] 90,91 d	23p38	08 01	08 22	08 26	09 01	09 04	09 22	09 26	10 01	10 06	10 22	10 26	11 01	11 06	11 22	11 26	12 01	12 06	12 22	12 26	12 52	13 01
Edge Hill 90,91 d	23p42																					
Mossley Hill 91 d	23p47			08 34				09 34				10 34				11 34				12 34		
West Allerton 91 d	23p49			08 36				09 36				10 36				11 36				12 36		
Liverpool Central [10] 103 d																						
L'pool Sth Parkway [7] 91,103 ✈ d	23p52		08 32	08 39			09 32	09 39			10 32	10 39			11 32	11 39			12 32	12 39	13 03	
Hunts Cross 103 d	23p56			08 43				09 43				10 43				11 43				12 43		
Halewood d	23p59			08 46				09 46				10 46				11 46				12 46		
Hough Green d	00 03			08 50				09 50				10 50				11 50				12 50		
Widnes d	00 06			08 53				09 53				10 53				11 53				12 53	13 11	
Sankey for Penketh d	00 11																					
Warrington Central a	00 16		08 44	09 01			09 44	10 01			10 44	11 01			11 44	12 01			12 44	13 01	13 18	
d	00 17		08 45	09 02			09 45	10 02			10 45	11 02			11 45	12 02			12 45	13 02	13 19	
Padgate d																						
Birchwood d			08 50	09 06			09 50	10 06			10 50	11 06			11 50	12 06			12 50	13 06		
Glazebrook d																						
Irlam d				09 12				10 12				11 12				12 12				13 12		
Flixton d																						
Chassen Road d																						
Urmston d				09 17				10 17				11 17				12 17				13 17		
Humphrey Park d																						
Trafford Park d																						
Deansgate 84,85 ⛴ a				09 27				10 27				11 27				12 27				13 27		
Manchester Oxford Road 84,85 a		10 12	09 06	09 31	11 12	09 45	10 05	10 31	12 12	10 47	11 05	11 31	13 12	11 48	12 05	12 30	14 12	12 47	13 05	13 31	13 39	15 12
Manchester Piccadilly [10] 78,84,85 ⛴ a	00 39		09 11			09 49	10 09			10 52	11 09			11 52	12 09			12 54	13 09		13 41	
Stockport 84 a																					13 53	
Sheffield [7] 78 ⛴ a																					14 39	
Manchester Airport 85 ✈ a						10 05				11 09				12 11				13 11				

	NT	TP ◇[1] B	NT	EM ◇ D	NT (bus)	NT	TP ◇[1] C	NT	EM ◇ D	NT (bus)	NT	TP ◇[1] B	NT	EM ◇ D	NT (bus)	NT	TP ◇[1] C	NT	EM ◇ E	NT (bus)	NT	TP ◇[1] B
Liverpool Lime Street [10] 90,91 d	13 06	13 22	13 26	13 52	14 01	14 06	14 22	14 26	14 52	15 01	15 06	15 22	15 26	15 52	16 01	16 06	16 22	16 26	16 52	17 01	17 06	17 22
Edge Hill 90,91 d																						
Mossley Hill 91 d			13 34					14 34					15 34					16 34				
West Allerton 91 d			13 36					14 36					15 36					16 36				
Liverpool Central [10] 103 d																						
L'pool Sth Parkway [7] 91,103 ✈ d		13 32	13 39	14 03			14 32	14 39	15 03			15 32	15 39	16 03			16 32	16 39	17 03			17 32
Hunts Cross 103 d			13 43					14 43					15 43					16 43				
Halewood d			13 46					14 46					15 46					16 46				
Hough Green d			13 50					14 50					15 50					16 50				
Widnes d			13 53	14 11				14 53	15 11				15 53	16 11				16 53	17 11			
Sankey for Penketh d																						
Warrington Central a		13 44	14 01	14 18			14 44	15 01	15 18			15 44	16 01	16 18			16 44	17 01	17 18			17 44
d		13 45	14 02	14 19			14 45	15 02	15 19			15 45	16 02	16 19			16 45	17 02	17 19			17 45
Padgate d																						
Birchwood d		13 50	14 06				14 50	15 06				15 50	16 06				16 50	17 06				17 50
Glazebrook d																						
Irlam d			14 12					15 12					16 12					17 12				
Flixton d																						
Chassen Road d																						
Urmston d			14 17					15 17					16 17					17 17				
Humphrey Park d																						
Trafford Park d																						
Deansgate 84,85 ⛴ a			14 27					15 27					16 27					17 27				
Manchester Oxford Road 84,85 a	13 47	14 05	14 31	14 39	16 12	14 48	15 05	15 31	15 39	17 12	15 48	16 05	16 31	16 38	18 12	16 48	17 05	17 31	17 38	19 12	17 48	18 05
Manchester Piccadilly [10] 78,84,85 ⛴ a	13 51	14 09		14 41		14 52	15 09		15 41		15 52	16 09		16 41		16 52	17 09		17 41		17 52	18 09
Stockport 84 a				14 53					15 53					16 53					17 53			
Sheffield [7] 78 ⛴ a				15 37					16 36					17 36					18 37			
Manchester Airport 85 ✈ a	14 07					15 08					16 08					17 08					18 08	

A To Hull
B To Scarborough
C To Middlesbrough
D To Norwich
E To Nottingham

Liverpool - Warrington Central - Manchester and Manchester Airport

Network Diagram - see first Page of Table 88

		NT	EM	NT	NT	TP	NT	EM	NT	NT	TP	NT	EM	NT	NT	TP	NT	NT	NT	EM	NT	TP
			◇			◇1		◇			◇1		◇			◇1				◇		◇1
			A			B		C			D		C			E				C		D
				🚌					🚌					🚌				🚌				
Liverpool Lime Street 10 90,91	d	17 26	17 52	18 01	18 06	18 22	18 26	18 52	19 01	19 06	19 22	19 26	19 52	20 01	20 06	20 22	20 26	21 01	21 06	21 21	21 26	21 52
Edge Hill 90,91	d																					
Mossley Hill 91	d	17 34					18 34					19 34					20 34				21 34	
West Allerton 91	d	17 36					18 36					19 36					20 36				21 36	
Liverpool Central 10 103	d																					
L'pool Sth Parkway 7 91,103 ✈	d	17 39	18 03			18 32	18 39	19 03			19 32	19 39	20 03			20 32	20 39			21 31	21 39	22 02
Hunts Cross 103	d	17 43					18 43					19 43					20 43				21 43	
Halewood	d	17 46					18 46					19 46					20 46				21 46	
Hough Green	d	17 50					18 50					19 50					20 50				21 50	
Widnes	d	17 53	18 11				18 53	19 11				19 53	20 11				20 53			21 39	21 53	
Sankey for Penketh	d																					
Warrington Central	a	18 01	18 18			18 44	19 01	19 18			19 44	20 01	20 18			20 44	21 01			21 47	22 01	22 14
	d	18 02	18 19			18 45	19 02	19 19			19 45	20 02	20 19			20 45	21 02			21 47	22 02	22 15
Padgate	d																					
Birchwood	d	18 06				18 50	19 06				19 50	20 06				20 50	21 06				22 06	22 20
Glazebrook	d																					
Irlam	d	18 12					19 12					20 12					21 12				22 12	
Flixton	d																					
Chassen Road	d																					
Urmston	d	18 17					19 17					20 17					21 17				22 17	
Humphrey Park	d																					
Trafford Park	d																					
Deansgate 84,85 ⛴	a	18 27					19 27					20 27					21 27				22 27	
Manchester Oxford Road 84,85	a	18 31	18 39	20 12	18 48	19 05	19 31	19 39	21 12	19 48	20 05	20 31	20 39	22 12	20 48	21 05	21 31	23 12	21 48	22 06	22 31	22 35
Manchester Piccadilly 10 78,84,85 ⛴	a		18 41		18 52	19 09		19 41		19 52	20 09		20 41		20 52	21 09			21 52	22 09		22 39
Stockport 84	a		18 53					19 53					20 53							22 20		
Sheffield 7 78 ⛴	a		19 34					20 34					21 36							23 25		
Manchester Airport 85 ✈	a				19 08					20 08					21 08				22 08			

		NT	NT	NT	NT	NT
			🚌			🚌
Liverpool Lime Street 10 90,91	d	22 01	22 01	22 26	23 01	23 01
Edge Hill 90,91	d					
Mossley Hill 91	d			22 34		
West Allerton 91	d			22 36		
Liverpool Central 10 103	d					
L'pool Sth Parkway 7 91,103 ✈	d			22 39		
Hunts Cross 103	d			22 43		
Halewood	d			22 46		
Hough Green	d			22 50		
Widnes	d			22 53		
Sankey for Penketh	d					
Warrington Central	a			23 01		
	d			23 02		
Padgate	d					
Birchwood	d			23 06		
Glazebrook	d					
Irlam	d			23 12		
Flixton	d					
Chassen Road	d					
Urmston	d			23 17		
Humphrey Park	d					
Trafford Park	d					
Deansgate 84,85 ⛴	a			23 27		
Manchester Oxford Road 84,85	a	22 47	00 12	23 32	23 47	01 12
Manchester Piccadilly 10 78,84,85 ⛴	a	22 50			23 50	
Stockport 84	a					
Sheffield 7 78 ⛴	a					
Manchester Airport 85 ✈	a	23 15			00 07	

A To Norwich
B To Scarborough
C To Nottingham
D To York
E To Newcastle

Table 89

Sundays
from 1 April

Liverpool - Warrington Central - Manchester and Manchester Airport

Network Diagram - see first Page of Table 88

		NT	NT	NT	NT	NT	NT	NT	NT	NT		NT	NT	EM	NT	NT	EM	NT	NT	EM		NT	NT	EM	NT
														◇ A			◇ A			◇ A				◇ A	
Liverpool Lime Street [10] 90,91	d	23p38	08 07	08 26	09 01	09 26	10 01	10 26	11 01	11 26		12 01	12 26	12 52	13 01	13 26	13 52	14 01	14 26	14 52		15 01	15 26	15 52	16 01
Edge Hill 90,91	d	23p42																							
Mossley Hill 91	d	23p47		08 34		09 34		10 34		11 34			12 34			13 34			14 34				15 34		
West Allerton 91	d	23p49		08 36		09 36		10 36		11 36			12 36			13 36			14 36				15 36		
Liverpool Central [10] 103	d																								
L'pool Sth Parkway [7] 91,103	d	23p52		08 39		09 39		10 39		11 39			12 39	13 03		13 39	14 03		14 39	15 03			15 39	16 03	
Hunts Cross 103	d	23p56		08 43		09 43		10 43		11 43			12 43			13 43			14 43				15 43		
Halewood	d	23p59		08 46		09 46		10 46		11 46			12 46			13 46			14 46				15 46		
Hough Green	d	00 03		08 50		09 50		10 50		11 50			12 50			13 50			14 50				15 50		
Widnes	d	00 06		08 53		09 53		10 53		11 53			12 53	13 11		13 53	14 11		14 53	15 11			15 53	16 11	
Sankey for Penketh	d	00 11																							
Warrington Central	a	00 16		09 01		10 01		11 01		12 01			13 01	13 18		14 01	14 18		15 01	15 18			16 01	16 18	
	d	00 17		09 02		10 02		11 02		12 02			13 02	13 19		14 02	14 19		15 02	15 19			16 02	16 19	
Padgate	d																								
Birchwood	d			09 06		10 06		11 06		12 06			13 06			14 06			15 06				16 06		
Glazebrook	d																								
Irlam	d			09 12		10 12		11 12		12 12			13 12			14 12			15 12				16 12		
Flixton	d																								
Chassen Road	d																								
Urmston	d			09 17		10 17		11 17		12 17			13 17			14 17			15 17				16 17		
Humphrey Park	d																								
Trafford Park	d																								
Deansgate 84,85	a			09 29		10 27		11 27		12 27			13 27			14 27			15 27				16 27		
Manchester Oxford Road 84,85	a		09 05	09 33	09 59	10 31	10 59	11 31	11 59	12 30		12 59	13 31	13 39	13 57	14 31	14 39	14 59	15 31	15 39		15 59	16 31	16 38	16 59
Manchester Piccadilly [10] 78,84,85	a	00 39	09 08		10 03		11 06		12 03			13 03		13 41	14 03		14 41	15 02		15 41		16 02		16 41	17 02
Stockport 84	a													13 53			14 53			15 53				16 53	
Sheffield [7] 78	a													14 39			15 37			16 36				17 36	
Manchester Airport 85	a		09 25		10 24		11 24		12 21			13 19			14 21			15 20				16 21			17 21

		NT	EM	NT	NT	EM		NT	NT	EM	NT	NT	EM	NT	NT	NT		EM	NT	NT	NT	NT	NT	NT	
			◇ B			◇ A				◇ B			◇ B					◇ B			Bus			Bus	
Liverpool Lime Street [10] 90,91	d	16 26	16 52	17 01	17 26	17 52		18 01	18 26	18 52	19 01	19 26	19 52	20 01	20 26	21 01		21 21	21 26	22 01	22 01	22 26	23 01	23 01	
Edge Hill 90,91	d																								
Mossley Hill 91	d	16 34			17 34				18 34			19 34			20 34				21 34			22 34			
West Allerton 91	d	16 36			17 36				18 36			19 36			20 36				21 36			22 36			
Liverpool Central [10] 103	d																								
L'pool Sth Parkway [7] 91,103	d	16 39	17 03		17 39	18 03			18 39	19 03		19 39	20 03		20 39			21 31	21 39			22 39			
Hunts Cross 103	d	16 43			17 43				18 43			19 43			20 43				21 43			22 43			
Halewood	d	16 46			17 46				18 46			19 46			20 46				21 46			22 46			
Hough Green	d	16 50			17 50				18 50			19 50			20 50				21 50			22 50			
Widnes	d	16 53	17 11		17 53	18 11			18 53	19 11		19 53	20 11		20 53			21 39	21 53			22 53			
Sankey for Penketh	d																								
Warrington Central	a	17 01	17 18		18 01	18 18			19 01	19 18		20 01	20 18		21 01			21 47	22 01			23 01			
	d	17 02	17 19		18 02	18 19			19 02	19 19		20 02	20 19		21 02			21 47	22 02			23 02			
Padgate	d																								
Birchwood	d	17 06			18 06				19 06			20 06			21 06				22 06			23 06			
Glazebrook	d																								
Irlam	d	17 12			18 12				19 12			20 12			21 12				22 12			23 12			
Flixton	d																								
Chassen Road	d																								
Urmston	d	17 17			18 17				19 17			20 17			21 17				22 17			23 17			
Humphrey Park	d																								
Trafford Park	d																								
Deansgate 84,85	a	17 27			18 27				19 27			20 27			21 27				22 27			23 27			
Manchester Oxford Road 84,85	a	17 31	17 38	17 59	18 31	18 39		18 59	19 31	19 39	19 59	20 31	20 39	20 59	21 31	21 59		22 06	22 31	22 47	00 12	23 32	23 47	01 12	
Manchester Piccadilly [10] 78,84,85	a		17 41	18 02		18 41		19 02		19 41	20 02		20 41	21 02		22 02		22 09		22 50			23 50		
Stockport 84	a		17 53			18 53				19 53			20 53					22 20							
Sheffield [7] 78	a		18 37			19 34				20 34			21 36					23 25							
Manchester Airport 85	a			18 21				19 21			20 26			21 20		22 21				23 15			00 07		

A To Norwich

B To Nottingham

Manchester Airport and Manchester - Warrington Central - Liverpool

Network Diagram - see first Page of Table 88

Miles		NT MO A (bus)	NT MO (bus)	NT MX	NT MX	NT MO	NT	NT	NT	NT	NT	TP ◇1	NT	EM ◇ D	NT	NT
0	**Manchester Airport** 85 ✈ d				04 34	04 38					06 41					07 38
—	Sheffield 7 78 🚆 d													06 20		
—	Stockport 84 d													07 22		
9¾	**Manchester Piccadilly** 10 78,84,85 🚆 d				04 49	04 53					06 58	07 07		07 34		07 59
10¼	**Manchester Oxford Road** 84,85 d	21p55	23p00	23p27					06 22	06 46	07 01	07 10		07 37	07 39	08 03
10¾	Deansgate 84,85 🚆 d			23p29					06 24						07 41	
13¾	Trafford Park d			23p34					06 29						07 46	
14½	Humphrey Park d			23p36					06 31							
15¾	Urmston d			23p38					06 33	06 53					07 49	
16¼	Chassen Road d			23p40					06 35							
16¾	Flixton d			23p43					06 38						07 52	
19	Irlam d			23p47					06 42	06 58					07 56	
20¼	Glazebrook d			23p50					06 45						07 59	
23	Birchwood d			23p54					06 49	07 04		07 23			08 04	
24½	Padgate d			23p57					06 52						08 07	
26¼	**Warrington Central** a			00 01					06 56	07 12		07 27		07 53	08 10	
—	d			00 02			06 03	06 37	06 56			07 28	07 35	07 53	08 11	
28¾	Sankey for Penketh d			00 05			06 07	06 41	07 00				07 39		08 15	
32½	Widnes d			00 11			06 12	06 46	07 06				07 44	08 01	08 20	
34¼	Hough Green d			00 13			06 15	06 49	07 09				07 47	08 05	08 24	
36½	Halewood d			00 18			06 20	06 54	07 13				07 52		08 28	
37½	Hunts Cross 89 d			00 21			06 23	06 57	07 17				07 55	08s10	08 32	
39¼	L'pool Sth Parkway 7 91,103 ✈ d			00 27			06 27	07 01	07 22				07 59	08 18	08 37	
—	Liverpool Central 10 103 a															
40¼	West Allerton 91 a						06 31	07 05	07 25				08 03		08 40	
41	Mossley Hill 91 a						06 33	07 07	07 28				08 06		08 43	
43	Edge Hill 90,91 a						06 39	07 13	07 32				08 11		08 48	
44¾	**Liverpool Lime Street** 10 90,91 a	00 06	01 11	00 41	05 33	05 36	06 45	07 19	07 40		07 49	07 53	08 18	08 31	08 55	08 59

	TP ◇1 E 🍴	NT	EM ◇ D	LM 1 G	NT	NT	TP ◇1 H 🍴	NT	EM ◇ D	NT	NT	TP ◇1 J 🍴	NT	EM ◇ K	NT	NT
Manchester Airport 85 ✈ d						08 41					09 41					10 41
Sheffield 7 78 🚆 d			07 35						08 42					09 42		
Stockport 84 d			08 24						09 25					10 26		
Manchester Piccadilly 10 78,84,85 🚆 d	08 07		08 37			09 01	09 07		09 37		10 01	10 07		10 37		11 01
Manchester Oxford Road 84,85 d	08 12	08 15	08 41		08 44	09 04	09 12	09 15	09 41	09 44	10 04	10 12	10 16	10 41	10 44	11 04
Deansgate 84,85 🚆 d		08 17			08 46			09 17		09 46			10 18		10 46	
Trafford Park d								09 22								
Humphrey Park d								09 24								
Urmston d		08 24			08 52			09 27		09 52			10 24		10 52	
Chassen Road d		08 26											10 26			
Flixton d		08 28						09 30					10 29			
Irlam d		08 32			08 57			09 34		09 57			10 33		10 57	
Glazebrook d		08 35											10 36			
Birchwood d	08 25	08 40			09 03		09 25	09 40		10 03		10 25	10 40		11 03	
Padgate d					09 06					10 06					11 06	
Warrington Central a	08 30	08 45	08 57		09 09		09 30	09 45	09 57	10 09		10 30	10 45	10 57	11 09	
d	08 30	08 45	08 57		09 10		09 30	09 45	09 57	10 10		10 30	10 46	10 57	11 10	
Sankey for Penketh d					09 14					10 14					11 14	
Widnes d		08 53	09 05		09 19			09 53	10 05	10 19			10 54	11 05	11 19	
Hough Green d		08 56			09 23			09 56		10 23			10 57		11 23	
Halewood d					09 27					10 27					11 27	
Hunts Cross 89 d					09 30					10 30					11 30	
L'pool Sth Parkway 7 91,103 ✈ d	08 47	09 06	09 15	09 31	09 36		09 47	10 06	10 15	10 36		10 47	11 06	11 15	11 36	
Liverpool Central 10 103 a																
West Allerton 91 a		09 09			09 39			10 10		10 39			11 10		11 39	
Mossley Hill 91 a		09 12			09 41			10 12		10 41			11 13		11 41	
Edge Hill 90,91 a					09 47					10 47					11 47	
Liverpool Lime Street 10 90,91 a	08 58	09 24	09 31	09 43	09 53	09 48	09 58	10 24	10 31	10 53	10 48	10 58	11 24	11 31	11 53	11 48

A from 20 February until 26 March
D From Nottingham
E From Hull
G From Walsall
H From Newcastle
J From Scarborough
K From Norwich

Manchester Airport and Manchester - Warrington Central - Liverpool

Network Diagram - see first Page of Table 88

	TP	NT	EM	NT	NT	TP	NT	EM		NT	NT	TP	NT	EM
	◇1		◇			◇1		◇				◇1		◇
	B		D			B		D				B		D
	🍴					🍴						🍴		
Manchester Airport 85 ✈ d					11 41						12 41			
Sheffield 7 78 🚌 d			10 42					11 42						12 42
Stockport 84 d			11 26					12 26						13 26
Manchester Piccadilly 10 78,84,85 🚌 d	11 07		11 37		12 01	12 07		12 37			13 01	13 07		13 37
Manchester Oxford Road 84,85 d	11 12	11 16	11 41	11 44	12 04	12 12	12 16	12 41		12 44	13 04	13 12	13 16	13 41
Deansgate 84,85 🚌 d		11 18		11 46			12 18			12 46			13 18	
Trafford Park d		11 23											13 23	
Humphrey Park d		11 25											13 25	
Urmston d		11 27		11 52			12 24			12 52			13 27	
Chassen Road d							12 26							
Flixton d		11 30					12 29						13 30	
Irlam d		11 34		11 57			12 33			12 57			13 34	
Glazebrook d							12 36							
Birchwood d	11 25	11 40		12 03		12 25	12 40			13 03		13 25	13 40	
Padgate d				12 06						13 06				
Warrington Central a	11 30	11 45	11 57	12 09		12 30	12 45	12 57		13 09		13 30	13 45	13 57
d	11 30	11 46	11 57	12 10		12 30	12 46	12 57		13 10		13 30	13 46	13 57
Sankey for Penketh d				12 14						13 14				
Widnes d		11 54	12 05	12 19			12 54	13 05		13 19			13 54	14 05
Hough Green d		11 57		12 23			12 57			13 23			13 57	
Halewood d				12 27						13 27				
Hunts Cross 89 d				12 30						13 30				
L'pool Sth Parkway 7 91,103 ✈ d	11 47	12 06	12 15	12 36		12 47	13 06	13 15		13 36		13 47	14 06	14 15
Liverpool Central 10 103 a														
West Allerton 91 a		12 10		12 39			13 10			13 39			14 10	
Mossley Hill 91 a		12 13		12 41			13 13			13 41			14 13	
Edge Hill 90,91 a				12 47						13 47				
Liverpool Lime Street 10 90,91 a	11 58	12 24	12 31	12 53	12 48	12 58	13 24	13 31		13 53	13 48	13 58	14 24	14 31

	NT	NT	TP	NT	EM	NT	NT		TP	NT	EM	NT	NT	TP
			◇1		◇				◇1		◇			◇1
			B		D				B		D			B
			🍴						🍴					🍴
Manchester Airport 85 ✈ d		13 41					14 41						15 41	
Sheffield 7 78 🚌 d					13 42						14 42			
Stockport 84 d					14 26						15 26			
Manchester Piccadilly 10 78,84,85 🚌 d		14 01	14 07		14 37		15 01		15 07		15 37		16 01	16 07
Manchester Oxford Road 84,85 d	13 44	14 04	14 12	14 16	14 41	14 44	15 04		15 12	15 16	15 41	15 44	16 04	16 12
Deansgate 84,85 🚌 d	13 46			14 18		14 46				15 18		15 46		
Trafford Park d										15 23				
Humphrey Park d										15 25				
Urmston d	13 52			14 24		14 52				15 27		15 52		
Chassen Road d				14 26										
Flixton d				14 29						15 30				
Irlam d	13 57			14 33		14 57				15 34		15 57		
Glazebrook d				14 36										
Birchwood d	14 03		14 25	14 40		15 03			15 25	15 40		16 03		16 25
Padgate d	14 06					15 06						16 06		
Warrington Central a	14 09		14 30	14 45	14 57	15 09			15 30	15 45	15 57	16 09		16 30
d	14 10		14 30	14 46	14 57	15 10			15 30	15 45	15 57	16 10		16 30
Sankey for Penketh d	14 14					15 14						16 14		
Widnes d	14 19			14 54	15 05	15 19				15 53	16 05	16 19		
Hough Green d	14 23			14 57		15 23				15 56		16 23		
Halewood d	14 27					15 27				16 01		16 27		
Hunts Cross 89 d	14 30					15 30						16 30		
L'pool Sth Parkway 7 91,103 ✈ d	14 36		14 47	15 06	15 15	15 36			15 47	16 07	16 15	16 36		16 47
Liverpool Central 10 103 a														
West Allerton 91 a	14 39			15 10		15 39				16 11		16 39		
Mossley Hill 91 a	14 41			15 13		15 41				16 13		16 42		
Edge Hill 90,91 a	14 47					15 47						16 47		
Liverpool Lime Street 10 90,91 a	14 53	14 48	14 58	15 24	15 31	15 53	15 48		15 58	16 25	16 31	16 54	16 48	16 58

B From Scarborough

D From Norwich

Manchester Airport and Manchester - Warrington Central - Liverpool

Network Diagram - see first Page of Table 88

		NT	EM	NT	NT	TP	NT	EM		NT	NT	TP	NT	EM	NT	NT	TP	NT
			◇			◇1		◇				◇1		◇			◇1	
			A			C		A				C		A			C	
Manchester Airport 85 ✈	d				16 41						17 41					18 41		
Sheffield 7 78	d		15 42					16 42						17 40				
Stockport 84	d		16 26					17 26						18 26				
Manchester Piccadilly 10 78,84,85	d		16 37		17 01	17 07		17 37			18 01	18 07		18 37		19 01	19 07	
Manchester Oxford Road 84,85	d	16 16	16 41	16 43	17 04	17 11	17 13	17 42		17 44	18 04	18 12	18 16	18 41	18 44	19 04	19 12	
Deansgate 84,85	d	16 18		16 45			17 15			17 46			18 18		18 46			
Trafford Park	d			16 51			17 20			17 51			18 23		18 51			
Humphrey Park	d						17 22			17 53			18 25		18 53			
Urmston	d	16 24		16 54			17 25			17 55			18 27		18 55			
Chassen Road	d	16 26					17 27			17 57			18 29		18 57			
Flixton	d	16 29		16 57			17 29			18 00			18 32		19 00			
Irlam	d	16 33		17 01			17 33	17 52		18 04			18 36		19 04			
Glazebrook	d	16 36					17 36			18 07					19 07			
Birchwood	d	16 40		17 07		17 25	17 41	17 58		18 11		18 25	18 41		19 11		19 25	
Padgate	d	16 43		17 10			17 44			18 14					19 14			
Warrington Central	a	16 47	16 57	17 13		17 30	17 48	18 03		18 18		18 30	18 46	18 57	19 20		19 30	
	d	16 47	16 57	17 14		17 30	17 48	18 03		18 18		18 30	18 47	18 57			19 30	19 49
Sankey for Penketh	d			17 18			17 52						18 51					19 53
Widnes	d	16 55	17 05	17 23			17 58	18 11					18 56	19 05				19 58
Hough Green	d	16 58		17 27			18 01			18 28			18 59					20 02
Halewood	d			17 31			18 06						19 04					20 06
Hunts Cross 89	d			17 34			18 09			18 33			19 07	19 12				20 09
L'pool Sth Parkway 7 91,103 ✈	d	17 07	17 15	17 39		17 47	18 14	18 22		18 38		18 47	19 13	19 18			19 47	20 13
Liverpool Central 10 103	a																	
West Allerton 91	a	17 11		17 42			18 18			18 41			19 16					20 16
Mossley Hill 91	a	17 13		17 45			18 20			18 44			19 18					20 18
Edge Hill 90,91	a			17 50			18 30			18 49			19 26					20 24
Liverpool Lime Street 10 90,91	a	17 25	17 31	17 58	17 48	18 01	18 38	18 35		18 57	19 00	19 01	19 35	19 35		19 48	20 01	20 30

		EM	NT	NT	TP	NT	EM	NT	TP		NT	NT	NT	NT	TP	NT	NT
											FX	FO		FO			
		◇			◇1		◇		◇1						◇1		
		A			C		A		C						C		
Manchester Airport 85 ✈	d			19 41										21 42			
Sheffield 7 78	d	18 43					19 42										
Stockport 84	d	19 26					20 26										
Manchester Piccadilly 10 78,84,85	d	19 37		20 01	20 07		20 37		21 07		21 40	21 38		22 01	22 07		
Manchester Oxford Road 84,85	d	19 41	19 44	20 04	20 12		20 41	20 44	21 12		21 44	21 44		22 04	22 12		23 27
Deansgate 84,85	d		19 46					20 46			21 46	21 46					23 29
Trafford Park	d		19 51					20 51			21 51	21 51					23 34
Humphrey Park	d		19 53					20 53			21 53	21 53					23 36
Urmston	d		19 55					20 55			21 55	21 55					23 38
Chassen Road	d		19 57					20 57			21 57	21 57					23 40
Flixton	d		20 00					21 00			22 00	22 00					23 43
Irlam	d		20 04					21 04			22 04	22 04					23 47
Glazebrook	d		20 07					21 07			22 07	22 07					23 50
Birchwood	d		20 11		20 25			21 11	21 25		22 11	22 11			22 25		23 54
Padgate	d		20 14					21 14			22 14	22 14					23 57
Warrington Central	a	19 57	20 18		20 30		20 57	21 20	21 30		22 19	22 20			22 30		00 01
	d	19 57	20 18		20 30	20 49	20 57		21 30				21 49		22 30	22 58	00 02
Sankey for Penketh	d					20 53							21 53			23 02	00 05
Widnes	d	20 05				20 58	21 05						21 58			23 07	00 11
Hough Green	d		20 28			21 01							22 01			23 10	00 13
Halewood	d					21 06							22 06			23 15	00 18
Hunts Cross 89	d		20 33			21 09							22 09			23 18	00 21
L'pool Sth Parkway 7 91,103 ✈	d	20 16	20 38		20 47	21 12	21 20		21 47				22 12		22 47	23 22	00 27
Liverpool Central 10 103	a																
West Allerton 91	a		20 41			21 15							22 15			23 25	
Mossley Hill 91	a		20 44			21 18							22 18			23 27	
Edge Hill 90,91	a					21 23							22 23			23 32	
Liverpool Lime Street 10 90,91	a	20 35	20 56	20 48	21 01	21 30	21 35		22 01				22 30	22 48	23 01	23 39	00 41

A From Norwich

C From Scarborough

Table 89

Saturdays

Manchester Airport and Manchester - Warrington Central - Liverpool

Network Diagram - see first Page of Table 88

	NT	NT	NT	NT	NT	NT	TP	NT	EM	NT	NT	TP	NT	EM
							◇1		◇			◇1		◇
		A				A			D		A	E		D
Manchester Airport 85 d		04 34				06 41					07 38			
Sheffield 7 78 d									06 20					07 35
Stockport 84 d									07 22					08 24
Manchester Piccadilly 10 78,84,85 d		04 49				06 58	07 07		07 34		07 59	08 07		08 37
Manchester Oxford Road 84,85 d	23p27				06 22	07 01	07 10		07 37	07 39	08 03	08 12	08 15	08 41
Deansgate 84,85 d	23p29				06 24					07 41			08 17	
Trafford Park d	23p34				06 29					07 46				
Humphrey Park d	23p36				06 31									
Urmston d	23p38				06 33					07 49			08 24	
Chassen Road d	23p40				06 35								08 26	
Flixton d	23p43				06 38					07 52			08 28	
Irlam d	23p47				06 42					07 56			08 32	
Glazebrook d	23p50				06 45					07 59			08 35	
Birchwood d	23p54				06 49		07 23			08 04		08 25	08 40	
Padgate d	23p57				06 52					08 07				
Warrington Central a	00 01				06 56		07 27		07 53	08 10		08 30	08 45	08 57
d	00 02		06 03	06 37	06 56		07 28	07 40	07 53	08 11		08 30	08 45	08 57
Sankey for Penketh d	00 05		06 07	06 41	07 00			07 44		08 15				
Widnes d	00 11		06 12	06 46	07 06			07 49	08 01	08 20			08 53	09 05
Hough Green d	00 13		06 15	06 49	07 09			07 52	08 05	08 24			08 56	
Halewood d	00 18		06 20	06 54	07 13			07 57		08 28				
Hunts Cross 89 d	00 21		06 23	06 57	07 17			08 00	08s10	08 32				
L'pool Sth Parkway 7 91,103 d	00 27		06 27	07 01	07 22			08 03	08 18	08 37		08 47	09 06	09 15
Liverpool Central 10 103 a														
West Allerton 91 a			06 31	07 05	07 25			08 06		08 40			09 09	
Mossley Hill 91 a			06 33	07 07	07 28			08 09		08 43			09 12	
Edge Hill 90,91 a			06 39	07 13	07 34			08 14		08 48				
Liverpool Lime Street 10 90,91 a	00 41	05 32	06 45	07 20	07 40	07 49	07 53	08 21	08 31	08 55	08 59	08 58	09 24	09 31

	NT	NT	TP	NT	EM	NT	NT	TP	NT	EM	NT	NT	TP	NT	EM
			◇1		◇			◇1		◇			◇1		◇
		A	F		D		A	H		I		A	H		I
Manchester Airport 85 d		08 41					09 41					10 41			
Sheffield 7 78 d					08 42					09 42					10 42
Stockport 84 d					09 25					10 26					11 26
Manchester Piccadilly 10 78,84,85 d		09 01	09 07		09 37		10 01	10 07		10 37		11 01	11 07		11 37
Manchester Oxford Road 84,85 d	08 44	09 04	09 12	09 16	09 41	09 44	10 04	10 12	10 16	10 41	10 44	11 04	11 12	11 16	11 41
Deansgate 84,85 d	08 46			09 18		09 46			10 18		10 46			11 18	
Trafford Park d				09 23										11 23	
Humphrey Park d				09 25										11 25	
Urmston d	08 52			09 27		09 52			10 24		10 52			11 27	
Chassen Road d									10 26						
Flixton d				09 30					10 29					11 30	
Irlam d	08 57			09 34		09 57			10 33		10 57			11 34	
Glazebrook d									10 36						
Birchwood d	09 03		09 25	09 40		10 03		10 25	10 40		11 03		11 25	11 40	
Padgate d	09 06					10 06					11 06				
Warrington Central a	09 09		09 30	09 45	09 57	10 09		10 30	10 45	10 57	11 09		11 30	11 45	11 57
d	09 10		09 30	09 46	09 57	10 10		10 30	10 46	10 57	11 10		11 30	11 46	11 57
Sankey for Penketh d	09 14					10 14					11 14				
Widnes d	09 19			09 54	10 05	10 19			10 54	11 05	11 19			11 54	12 05
Hough Green d	09 23			09 57		10 23			10 57		11 23			11 57	
Halewood d	09 27					10 27					11 27				
Hunts Cross 89 d	09 30					10 30					11 30				
L'pool Sth Parkway 7 91,103 d	09 36		09 47	10 06	10 15	10 36		10 47	11 06	11 15	11 36		11 47	12 06	12 15
Liverpool Central 10 103 a															
West Allerton 91 a	09 39			10 10		10 39			11 10		11 39			12 10	
Mossley Hill 91 a	09 41			10 12		10 41			11 13		11 41			12 13	
Edge Hill 90,91 a	09 47					10 47					11 47				
Liverpool Lime Street 10 90,91 a	09 53	09 48	09 58	10 23	10 31	10 53	10 48	10 58	11 24	11 31	11 53	11 48	11 58	12 24	12 31

A until 11 February and then from 31 March
D From Nottingham
E From Hull
F From Newcastle
H From Scarborough
I From Norwich

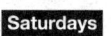

Manchester Airport and Manchester - Warrington Central - Liverpool

Network Diagram - see first Page of Table 88

	NT	NT B	TP ◇1 D	NT	EM ◇ E	NT	NT B	TP ◇1 D	NT	EM ◇ E	NT	NT B	TP ◇1 D
Manchester Airport 85 d		11 41					12 41					13 41	
Sheffield 7 78 d					11 42					12 42			
Stockport 84 d					12 26					13 26			
Manchester Piccadilly 10 78,84,85 d		12 01	12 07		12 37		13 01	13 07		13 37		14 01	14 07
Manchester Oxford Road 84,85 d	11 44	12 04	12 12	12 16	12 41	12 44	13 04	13 12	13 16	13 41	13 44	14 04	14 12
Deansgate 84,85 d	11 46			12 18		12 46			13 18		13 46		
Trafford Park d									13 23				
Humphrey Park d									13 25				
Urmston d	11 52			12 24		12 52			13 27		13 52		
Chassen Road d				12 26									
Flixton d				12 29					13 30				
Irlam d	11 57			12 33		12 57			13 34		13 57		
Glazebrook d				12 36									
Birchwood d	12 03		12 25	12 40		13 03		13 25	13 40		14 03		14 25
Padgate d	12 06					13 06					14 06		
Warrington Central a	12 09		12 30	12 45	12 57	13 09		13 30	13 45	13 57	14 09		14 30
d	12 10		12 30	12 46	12 57	13 10		13 30	13 46	13 57	14 10		14 30
Sankey for Penketh d	12 14					13 14					14 14		
Widnes d	12 19			12 54	13 05	13 19			13 54	14 05	14 19		
Hough Green d	12 23			12 57		13 23			13 57		14 23		
Halewood d	12 27					13 27					14 27		
Hunts Cross 89 d	12 30					13 30					14 30		
L'pool Sth Parkway 7 91,103 d	12 36		12 47	13 06	13 15	13 36		13 47	14 06	14 15	14 36		14 47
Liverpool Central 10 103 a													
West Allerton 91 a	12 39			13 10		13 39			14 10		14 39		
Mossley Hill 91 a	12 41			13 13		13 41			14 13		14 41		
Edge Hill 90,91 a	12 47					13 47					14 47		
Liverpool Lime Street 10 90,91 a	12 53	12 48	12 58	13 24	13 31	13 53	13 48	13 58	14 24	14 31	14 53	14 48	14 58

	NT	EM ◇ E	NT	NT B	TP ◇1 D	LM ◇1 A	NT	EM ◇ E	NT	NT B	TP ◇1 D	NT	EM ◇ E	NT	NT B
Manchester Airport 85 d				14 41						15 41					16 41
Sheffield 7 78 d		13 42						14 42					15 42		
Stockport 84 d		14 26						15 26					16 26		
Manchester Piccadilly 10 78,84,85 d		14 37		15 01	15 07			15 37		16 01	16 07		16 37		17 01
Manchester Oxford Road 84,85 d	14 16	14 41	14 44	15 04	15 12		15 16	15 41	15 44	16 04	16 12	16 16	16 41	16 43	17 04
Deansgate 84,85 d	14 18		14 46				15 18		15 46			16 18		16 45	
Trafford Park d							15 23							16 51	
Humphrey Park d							15 25								
Urmston d	14 24		14 52				15 27		15 52			16 24		16 54	
Chassen Road d	14 26											16 26			
Flixton d	14 29						15 30					16 29		16 57	
Irlam d	14 33		14 57				15 34		15 57			16 33		17 01	
Glazebrook d	14 36											16 36			
Birchwood d	14 40		15 03		15 25		15 40		16 03		16 25	16 40		17 07	
Padgate d			15 06						16 06			16 43		17 10	
Warrington Central a	14 45	14 57	15 09		15 30		15 45	15 57	16 09		16 30	16 47	16 57	17 13	
d	14 46	14 57	15 10		15 30		15 45	15 57	16 10		16 30	16 47	16 57	17 14	
Sankey for Penketh d			15 14						16 14					17 18	
Widnes d	14 54	15 05	15 19				15 53	16 05	16 19			16 55	17 05	17 23	
Hough Green d	14 57		15 23				15 56		16 23			16 58		17 27	
Halewood d			15 27				16 01		16 27					17 31	
Hunts Cross 89 d			15 30						16 30					17 34	
L'pool Sth Parkway 7 91,103 d	15 06	15 15	15 36		15 47	15 59	16 07	16 15	16 36		16 47	17 07	17 15	17 39	
Liverpool Central 10 103 a															
West Allerton 91 a	15 10		15 39				16 11		16 39			17 11		17 42	
Mossley Hill 91 a	15 13		15 41				16 13		16 41			17 13		17 45	
Edge Hill 90,91 a			15 47						16 47					17 50	
Liverpool Lime Street 10 90,91 a	15 24	15 31	15 53	15 48	15 58	16 10	16 25	16 31	16 54	16 48	16 58	17 25	17 31	17 58	17 48

B until 11 February and then from 31 March

D From Scarborough

E From Norwich

Manchester Airport and Manchester - Warrington Central - Liverpool

Network Diagram - see first Page of Table 88

		TP	NT	EM	NT	NT	TP	NT	EM	NT	NT	TP	NT	EM	NT	NT	TP
		◇1		◇			◇1		◇			◇1		◇			◇1
		A		C		D	A		C		D	A		C		D	A
Manchester Airport 85 ✈	d					17 41					18 41					19 41	
Sheffield 7 78 🚌	d			16 42					17 40					18 42			
Stockport 84	d			17 26					18 26					19 26			
Manchester Piccadilly 10 78,84,85 🚌	d	17 07		17 37		18 01	18 07		18 37		19 01	19 07		19 37		20 01	20 07
Manchester Oxford Road 84,85	d	17 11	17 13	17 42	17 44	18 04	18 12	18 16	18 41	18 44	19 04	19 12		19 41	19 44	20 04	20 12
Deansgate 84,85 🚌	d		17 15		17 46			18 18		18 46					19 46		
Trafford Park	d		17 20		17 51			18 23		18 51					19 51		
Humphrey Park	d		17 22		17 53			18 25		18 53					19 53		
Urmston	d		17 25		17 55			18 27		18 55					19 55		
Chassen Road	d		17 27		17 57			18 29		18 57					19 57		
Flixton	d		17 29		18 00			18 32		19 00					20 00		
Irlam	d		17 33	17 52	18 04			18 36		19 04					20 04		
Glazebrook	d		17 36		18 07					19 07					20 07		
Birchwood	d	17 25	17 41	17 58	18 11		18 25	18 41		19 11		19 25			20 11		20 25
Padgate	d		17 44		18 14					19 14					20 14		
Warrington Central	a	17 30	17 48	18 03	18 18		18 30	18 46	18 57	19 20		19 30		19 57	20 18		20 30
	d	17 30	17 48	18 03	18 18		18 30	18 47	18 57			19 30	19 34	19 57	20 18		20 30
Sankey for Penketh	d		17 52					18 51					19 38				
Widnes	d		17 58	18 11				18 56	19 05				19 43	20 05			
Hough Green	d		18 01		18 28			18 59					19 46		20 28		
Halewood	d		18 06					19 04					19 51				
Hunts Cross 89	d		18 09		18 33			19 07	19 12				19 54		20 33		
L'pool Sth Parkway 7 91,103 ✈	d	17 47	18 14	18 22	18 38		18 47	19 11	19 18			19 47	19 59	20 15	20 38		20 47
Liverpool Central 10 103	a																
West Allerton 91	a		18 18		18 41			19 15					20 03		20 41		
Mossley Hill 91	a		18 20		18 44			19 18					20 05		20 44		
Edge Hill 90,91	a		18 30		18 50			19 26					20 11				
Liverpool Lime Street 10 90,91	a	18 01	18 38	18 35	18 57	19 00	19 01	19 35	19 35		19 48	20 01	20 18	20 30	20 55	20 48	21 01

		NT	EM	NT	TP	NT	NT	NT	TP	NT	NT
			◇		◇1				◇1		
			C		A			D	A		
Manchester Airport 85 ✈	d							21 41			
Sheffield 7 78 🚌	d		19 42								
Stockport 84	d		20 26								
Manchester Piccadilly 10 78,84,85 🚌	d		20 37		21 07	21 38		22 01	22 07		
Manchester Oxford Road 84,85	d		20 41	20 44	21 12	21 44		22 04	22 12		23 20
Deansgate 84,85 🚌	d			20 46		21 46					23 22
Trafford Park	d			20 51		21 51					23 27
Humphrey Park	d			20 53		21 53					23 29
Urmston	d			20 55		21 55					23 31
Chassen Road	d			20 57		21 57					23 33
Flixton	d			21 00		22 00					23 36
Irlam	d			21 04		22 04					23 40
Glazebrook	d			21 07		22 07					23 43
Birchwood	d			21 11	21 25	22 11			22 25		23 47
Padgate	d			21 14		22 14					23 50
Warrington Central	a		20 57	21 20	21 30	22 20			22 30		23 54
	d	20 49	20 57		21 30		21 49		22 30	22 49	23 54
Sankey for Penketh	d	20 53					21 53			22 53	23 58
Widnes	d	20 58	21 05				21 58			22 58	00 04
Hough Green	d	21 01					22 01			23 01	00 06
Halewood	d	21 06					22 06			23 06	00 11
Hunts Cross 89	d	21 09					22 09			23 09	00 14
L'pool Sth Parkway 7 91,103 ✈	d	21 15	21 20		21 47		22 12		22 47	23 12	00 20
Liverpool Central 10 103	a										
West Allerton 91	a	21 19					22 15			23 15	
Mossley Hill 91	a	21 21					22 18			23 18	
Edge Hill 90,91	a	21 27					22 23			23 23	
Liverpool Lime Street 10 90,91	a	21 34	21 35		22 01		22 30	22 48	23 01	23 30	00 34

A From Scarborough
C From Norwich
D until 11 February and then from 31 March

Table 89

Sundays
until 12 February

Manchester Airport and Manchester - Warrington Central - Liverpool

Network Diagram - see first Page of Table 88

		NT	NT	TP	NT	NT	NT	TP		NT	NT	TP	EM	NT	NT	TP	EM		NT	NT	TP
				◇1				◇1				◇1	◇			◇1	◇				◇1
		A						B					D			E	D				F
Manchester Airport 85 ✈	d						09 35				10 35				11 33					12 35	
Sheffield 7 78	d												10 41				11 38				
Stockport 84	d												11 26				12 26				
Manchester Piccadilly 10 78,84,85	d			09 07			09 50	10 12			10 50	11 07	11 38		11 50	12 07	12 38			12 50	13 07
Manchester Oxford Road 84,85	d	23p20	07 45	09 12	09 15	09 45	09 53	10 15		10 45	10 53	11 12	11 42	11 45	11 53	12 12	12 42		12 45	12 53	13 12
Deansgate 84,85	d	23p22	07 47		09 17	09 47				10 47				11 47					12 47		
Trafford Park	d	23p27																			
Humphrey Park	d	23p29																			
Urmston	d	23p31	07 53		09 23	09 53				10 53				11 53					12 53		
Chassen Road	d	23p33																			
Flixton	d	23p36																			
Irlam	d	23p40	07 58		09 28	09 58				10 58				11 58					12 58		
Glazebrook	d	23p43																			
Birchwood	d	23p47	08 04	09 25	09 34	10 04		10 29		11 04		11 25		12 04		12 25			13 04		13 25
Padgate	d	23p50																			
Warrington Central	a	23p54	08 09	09 30	09 39	10 09		10 33		11 09		11 30	11 58	12 09		12 30	12 58		13 09		13 30
	d	23p54	08 30	09 30	09 39	10 09		10 34		11 09		11 30	11 59	12 09		12 30	12 58		13 09		13 30
Sankey for Penketh	d	23p58																			
Widnes	d	00 04	08 38		09 47	10 17				11 17			12 06	12 17			13 06		13 17		
Hough Green	d	00 06	08 42		09 51	10 21				11 21				12 21					13 21		
Halewood	d	00 11	08 46		09 55	10 25				11 25				12 25					13 25		
Hunts Cross 89	d	00 14	08 49		09 58	10 28				11 28				12 28					13 28		
L'pool Sth Parkway 7 91,103 ✈	d	00 20	08 54	09 47	10 03	10 33		10 49		11 33		11 47	12 17	12 33		12 47	13 17		13 33		13 47
Liverpool Central 10 103	a																				
West Allerton 91	a		08 57		10 06	10 36				11 36				12 36					13 36		
Mossley Hill 91	a		09 00		10 09	10 39				11 39				12 39					13 39		
Edge Hill 90,91	a																				
Liverpool Lime Street 10 90,91	a	00 34	09 11	10 00	10 20	10 50	10 54	11 00		11 50	11 54	11 59	12 30	12 50	12 54	12 58	13 30		13 50	13 54	13 58

		EM	NT	NT	TP	EM	NT	NT	TP		EM	NT	NT	TP	EM	NT	NT	TP		EM	NT
		◇			◇1	◇			◇1		◇			◇1	◇			◇1		◇	
		D			F	D			G		H			F	D			G		D	
Manchester Airport 85 ✈	d			13 35				14 35					15 35				16 35				
Sheffield 7 78	d	12 41				13 38					14 39				15 38					16 44	
Stockport 84	d	13 26				14 26					15 26				16 26					17 29	
Manchester Piccadilly 10 78,84,85	d	13 38		13 50	14 07	14 38		14 50	15 07		15 38		15 50	16 07	16 38		16 50	17 07		17 38	
Manchester Oxford Road 84,85	d	13 42	13 45	13 53	14 12	14 42	14 45	14 53	15 12		15 42	15 45	15 53	16 12	16 42	16 45	16 53	17 12		17 42	17 45
Deansgate 84,85	d		13 47				14 47					15 47				16 47					17 47
Trafford Park	d																				
Humphrey Park	d																				
Urmston	d		13 53				14 53					15 53				16 53					17 53
Chassen Road	d																				
Flixton	d																				
Irlam	d		13 58				14 58					15 58				16 58					17 58
Glazebrook	d																				
Birchwood	d		14 04		14 25		15 04		15 25			16 04		16 25		17 04		17 25			18 04
Padgate	d																				
Warrington Central	a	13 58	14 09		14 30	14 58	15 09		15 30		15 58	16 09		16 30	16 58	17 09		17 30		17 58	18 09
	d	13 58	14 09		14 30	14 58	15 09		15 30		15 58	16 09		16 30	16 58	17 09		17 30		17 58	18 09
Sankey for Penketh	d																				
Widnes	d	14 06	14 17			15 06	15 17				16 06	16 17			17 06	17 17				18 06	18 17
Hough Green	d		14 21				15 21					16 21				17 21					18 21
Halewood	d		14 25				15 25					16 25				17 25					18 25
Hunts Cross 89	d		14 28				15 28					16 28				17 28					18 28
L'pool Sth Parkway 7 91,103 ✈	d	14 16	14 33		14 47	15 16	15 33		15 47		16 16	16 33		16 47	17 16	17 33		17 47		18 16	18 33
Liverpool Central 10 103	a																				
West Allerton 91	a		14 36				15 36					16 36				17 36					18 36
Mossley Hill 91	a		14 39				15 39					16 39				17 39					18 39
Edge Hill 90,91	a																				
Liverpool Lime Street 10 90,91	a	14 30	14 50	14 54	14 58	15 30	15 50	15 54	15 58		16 30	16 50	16 54	16 58	17 30	17 50	17 54	17 58		18 30	18 50

A not 11 December
B From York
D From Nottingham
E From Newcastle
F From Scarborough
G From Middlesbrough
H From Norwich

Table 89

Sundays

until 12 February

Manchester Airport and Manchester - Warrington Central - Liverpool

Network Diagram - see first Page of Table 88

		NT	TP	EM	NT	NT	TP	EM	NT	NT	TP	NT	NT	TP	NT	NT	TP	NT	NT
			◇1	◇			◇1	◇			◇1			◇1			◇1		
			A	C			D	C			A			D			A		
																			bus
Manchester Airport 85 ✈	d	17 35				18 35				19 35			20 35			21 35		22 27	
Sheffield 7 78	d			17 44				18 37											
Stockport 84	d			18 26				19 26											
Manchester Piccadilly 10 78,84,85	d	17 50	18 07	18 38		18 50	19 07	19 38		19 50	20 07		20 50	21 07		21 50	22 07	22 41	
Manchester Oxford Road 84,85	d	17 53	18 12	18 42	18 45	18 53	19 12	19 42	19 45	19 53	20 12	20 45	20 53	21 12	21 45	21 53	22 12	22 45	23 00
Deansgate 84,85	d				18 47				19 47			20 47			21 47			22 47	
Trafford Park	d																		
Humphrey Park	d																		
Urmston	d				18 53				19 53			20 53			21 53			22 53	
Chassen Road	d																		
Flixton	d																		
Irlam	d				18 58				19 58			20 58			21 58			22 58	
Glazebrook	d																		
Birchwood	d		18 25		19 04		19 25		20 04		20 25	21 04		21 25	22 04		22 25	23 04	
Padgate	d																		
Warrington Central	a		18 30	18 58	19 09		19 30	19 58	20 09		20 30	21 09		21 30	22 09		22 30	23 09	
	d		18 30	18 58	19 09		19 30	19 58	20 09		20 30	21 09		21 30	22 09		22 30	23 09	
Sankey for Penketh	d																		
Widnes	d			19 06	19 17			20 06	20 17			21 17			22 17			23 17	
Hough Green	d				19 21				20 21			21 21			22 21			23 21	
Halewood	d				19 25				20 25			21 25			22 25			23 25	
Hunts Cross 89	d				19 28				20 28			21 28			22 28			23 28	
L'pool Sth Parkway 7 91,103 ✈	d		18 47	19 17	19 33		19 47	20 16	20 33		20 47	21 33		21 47	22 33		22 47	23 33	
Liverpool Central 10 103	a																		
West Allerton 91	a				19 36				20 36			21 36			22 36			23 36	
Mossley Hill 91	a				19 39				20 39			21 39			22 39			23 39	
Edge Hill 90,91	a																		
Liverpool Lime Street 10 90,91	a	18 54	18 58	19 30	19 50	19 54	19 58	20 30	20 50	20 54	20 58	21 50	21 54	21 58	22 50	22 54	22 58	23 50	01 11

Sundays

19 February to 25 March

		NT	NT	NT	TP	NT	NT	NT	NT	TP	NT	NT	NT	TP	NT	EM	NT	NT	TP	NT
					◇1					◇1				◇1		◇			◇1	
										E						F			G	
				bus					bus				bus					bus		
Manchester Airport 85 ✈	d					08 57					10 16				10 56					11 56
Sheffield 7 78	d															10 41				
Stockport 84	d															11 26				
Manchester Piccadilly 10 78,84,85	d				09 07	09 11				10 12	10 31			11 07	11 12	11 38			12 07	12 11
Manchester Oxford Road 84,85	d	23p20	07 45	08 55	09 12	09 15	09 35	09 45	09 55	10 15	10 36	10 45	10 55	11 12	11 22	11 42	11 45	11 55	12 12	12 22
Deansgate 84,85	d	23p22	07 47			09 17		09 47				10 47					11 47			
Trafford Park	d	23p27																		
Humphrey Park	d	23p29																		
Urmston	d	23p31	07 53			09 23		09 53				10 53					11 53			
Chassen Road	d	23p33																		
Flixton	d	23p36																		
Irlam	d	23p40	07 58			09 28		09 58				10 58					11 58			
Glazebrook	d	23p43																		
Birchwood	d	23p47	08 04		09 25	09 34		10 04		10 29		11 04		11 25			12 04		12 25	
Padgate	d	23p50																		
Warrington Central	a	23p54	08 09		09 30	09 39		10 09		10 33		11 09		11 30		11 58	12 09		12 30	
	d	23p54	08 30		09 30	09 39		10 09		10 34		11 09		11 30		11 59	12 09		12 30	
Sankey for Penketh	d	23p58																		
Widnes	d	00 04	08 38			09 47		10 17				11 17				12 06	12 17			
Hough Green	d	00 06	08 42			09 51		10 21				11 21					12 21			
Halewood	d	00 11	08 46			09 55		10 25				11 25					12 25			
Hunts Cross 89	d	00 14	08 49			09 58		10 28				11 28					12 28			
L'pool Sth Parkway 7 91,103 ✈	d	00 20	08 54		09 47	10 03		10 33		10 49		11 33		11 47		12 17	12 33		12 47	
Liverpool Central 10 103	a																			
West Allerton 91	a		08 57			10 06		10 36				11 36					12 36			
Mossley Hill 91	a		09 00			10 09		10 39				11 39					12 39			
Edge Hill 90,91	a																			
Liverpool Lime Street 10 90,91	a	00 34	09 11	11 06	10 00	10 20	10 21	10 50	12 06	11 00	11 16	11 50	13 06	11 59	12 02	12 30	12 50	14 06	12 58	13 02

A From Scarborough
C From Norwich
D From Middlesbrough
E From York
F From Nottingham
G From Newcastle

Table 89

Sundays

19 February to 25 March

Manchester Airport and Manchester - Warrington Central - Liverpool

Network Diagram - see first Page of Table 88

		EM	NT	NT	TP	NT	EM	NT	NT	TP	NT	EM	NT	NT	TP	NT	EM	NT	NT	TP
		◇			◇[1]		◇			◇[1]		◇			◇[1]		◇			◇[1]
		A		🚌	B		A		🚌	B		A		🚌	D		E		🚌	B
Manchester Airport 85 ✈	d					12 58					14 06					14 58				
Sheffield [7] 78 🚌	d	11 38					12 41					13 38					14 39			
Stockport 84	d	12 26					13 26					14 26					15 26			
Manchester Piccadilly [10] 78,84,85 🚌	d	12 38			13 07	13 12	13 38			14 07	14 20	14 38			15 07	15 12	15 38			16 07
Manchester Oxford Road 84,85	d	12 42	12 45	12 55	13 12	13 22	13 42	13 45	13 55	14 12	14 23	14 42	14 45	14 55	15 12	15 22	15 42	15 45	15 55	16 12
Deansgate 84,85 🚌	d		12 47					13 47					14 47					15 47		
Trafford Park	d																			
Humphrey Park	d																			
Urmston	d		12 53					13 53					14 53					15 53		
Chassen Road	d																			
Flixton	d																			
Irlam	d		12 58					13 58					14 58					15 58		
Glazebrook	d																			
Birchwood	d		13 04		13 25			14 04		14 25			15 04		15 25			16 04		16 25
Padgate	d																			
Warrington Central	a	12 58	13 09		13 30		13 58	14 09		14 30		14 58	15 09		15 30		15 58	16 09		16 30
	d	12 58	13 09		13 30		13 58	14 09		14 30		14 58	15 09		15 30		15 58	16 09		16 30
Sankey for Penketh	d																			
Widnes	d	13 06	13 17				14 06	14 17				15 06	15 17				16 06	16 17		
Hough Green	d		13 21					14 21					15 21					16 21		
Halewood	d		13 25					14 25					15 25					16 25		
Hunts Cross 89	d		13 28					14 28					15 28					16 28		
L'pool Sth Parkway [7] 91,103 ✈	d	13 17	13 33		13 47		14 16	14 33		14 47		15 16	15 33		15 47		16 16	16 33		16 47
Liverpool Central [10] 103	a																			
West Allerton 91	a		13 36					14 36					15 36					16 36		
Mossley Hill 91	a		13 39					14 39					15 39					16 39		
Edge Hill 90,91	a																			
Liverpool Lime Street [10] 90,91	a	13 30	13 50	15 06	13 58	14 02	14 30	14 50	16 06	14 58	15 04	15 30	15 50	17 05	15 58	16 02	16 30	16 50	18 06	16 58

		NT	EM	NT	NT	TP	NT	EM	NT	NT	TP	NT	EM	NT	NT	TP	NT	EM
			◇			◇[1]		◇			◇[1]		◇			◇[1]		◇
			A		🚌	D		A		🚌	B		E		🚌	D		E
Manchester Airport 85 ✈	d	15 58					16 58					17 58					18 58	
Sheffield [7] 78 🚌	d		15 38					16 44					17 44					18 37
Stockport 84	d		16 26					17 29					18 26					19 26
Manchester Piccadilly [10] 78,84,85 🚌	d	16 12	16 38			17 07	17 12	17 38			18 07	18 12	18 38			19 07	19 12	19 38
Manchester Oxford Road 84,85	d	16 22	16 42	16 45	16 55	17 12	17 22	17 42	17 45	17 55	18 12	18 22	18 42	18 45	18 55	19 12	19 22	19 42
Deansgate 84,85 🚌	d			16 47					17 47					18 47				
Trafford Park	d																	
Humphrey Park	d																	
Urmston	d			16 53					17 53					18 53				
Chassen Road	d																	
Flixton	d																	
Irlam	d			16 58					17 58					18 58				
Glazebrook	d																	
Birchwood	d			17 04		17 25			18 04		18 25			19 04		19 25		
Padgate	d																	
Warrington Central	a		16 58	17 09		17 30		17 58	18 09		18 30		18 58	19 09		19 30		19 58
	d		16 58	17 09		17 30		17 58	18 09		18 30		18 58	19 09		19 30		19 58
Sankey for Penketh	d																	
Widnes	d		17 06	17 17				18 06	18 17				19 06	19 17				20 06
Hough Green	d			17 21					18 21					19 21				
Halewood	d			17 25					18 25					19 25				
Hunts Cross 89	d			17 28					18 28					19 28				
L'pool Sth Parkway [7] 91,103 ✈	d		17 16	17 33		17 47		18 16	18 33		18 47		19 17	19 33		19 47		20 16
Liverpool Central [10] 103	a																	
West Allerton 91	a			17 36					18 36					19 36				
Mossley Hill 91	a			17 39					18 39					19 39				
Edge Hill 90,91	a																	
Liverpool Lime Street [10] 90,91	a	17 02	17 30	17 50	19 06	17 58	18 02	18 30	18 50	20 06	18 58	19 02	19 30	19 50	21 06	19 58	20 02	20 30

A From Nottingham
B From Scarborough
D From Middlesbrough
E From Norwich

Table 89

Sundays

19 February to 25 March

Manchester Airport and Manchester - Warrington Central - Liverpool

Network Diagram - see first Page of Table 88

	NT	NT	TP	NT	NT	NT		TP	NT	NT	NT	TP	NT	NT
			◇1					◇1				◇1		
			A					C				A		
		🚌				🚌					🚌			🚌
Manchester Airport 85 ✈ d				19 58					20 58				22 27	
Sheffield 7 78 🚌 d														
Stockport 84 d														
Manchester Piccadilly 10 78,84,85 🚌 d			20 07	20 12				21 07	21 12			22 07	22 41	
Manchester Oxford Road 84,85 d	19 45	19 55	20 12	20 22	20 45	20 55		21 12	21 22	21 45	21 55	22 12	22 45	23 00
Deansgate 84,85 🚌 d	19 47				20 47					21 47			22 47	
Trafford Park d														
Humphrey Park d														
Urmston d	19 53				20 53					21 53			22 53	
Chassen Road d														
Flixton d														
Irlam d	19 58				20 58					21 58			22 58	
Glazebrook d														
Birchwood d	20 04		20 25		21 04			21 25		22 04		22 25	23 04	
Padgate d														
Warrington Central a	20 09		20 30		21 09			21 30		22 09		22 30	23 09	
d	20 09		20 30		21 09			21 30		22 09		22 30	23 09	
Sankey for Penketh d														
Widnes d	20 17				21 17					22 17			23 17	
Hough Green d	20 21				21 21					22 21			23 21	
Halewood d	20 25				21 25					22 25			23 25	
Hunts Cross 89 d	20 28				21 28					22 28			23 28	
L'pool Sth Parkway 7 91,103 ✈ d	20 33		20 47		21 33			21 47		22 33		22 47	23 33	
Liverpool Central 10 103 a														
West Allerton 91 a	20 36				21 36					22 36			23 36	
Mossley Hill 91 a	20 39				21 39					22 39			23 39	
Edge Hill 90,91 a														
Liverpool Lime Street 10 90,91 a	20 50	22 06	20 58	21 02	21 50	23 06		21 58	22 02	22 50	00 06	22 58	23 50	01 11

Sundays

from 1 April

	NT	NT	NT	NT	NT	NT		NT	NT	EM	NT	NT		EM	NT	NT	EM	NT	NT
										◇				◇			◇		
										D				D			D		
Manchester Airport 85 ✈ d			08 34			09 35			10 35			11 33				12 35			13 35
Sheffield 7 78 🚌 d										10 41				11 38			12 41		
Stockport 84 d										11 26				12 26			13 26		
Manchester Piccadilly 10 78,84,85 🚌 d			08 49			09 50			10 50	11 38		11 50		12 38		12 50	13 38		13 50
Manchester Oxford Road 84,85 d	23p20	08 06	08 52	09 15	09 45	09 53		10 45	10 53	11 42	11 45	11 53		12 42	12 45	12 53	13 42	13 45	13 53
Deansgate 84,85 🚌 d	23p22	08 08	08 54	09 17	09 47			10 47			11 47				12 47			13 47	
Trafford Park d	23p27																		
Humphrey Park d	23p29																		
Urmston d	23p31	08 14		09 23	09 53			10 53			11 53				12 53			13 53	
Chassen Road d	23p33																		
Flixton d	23p36																		
Irlam d	23p40	08 19		09 28	09 58			10 58			11 58				12 58			13 58	
Glazebrook d	23p43																		
Birchwood d	23p47	08 25		09 34	10 04			11 04			12 04				13 04			14 04	
Padgate d	23p50																		
Warrington Central a	23p54	08 30		09 39	10 09			11 09		11 58	12 09			12 58	13 09		13 58	14 09	
d	23p54	08 30		09 39	10 09			11 09		11 59	12 09			12 58	13 09		13 58	14 09	
Sankey for Penketh d	23p58																		
Widnes d	00 04	08 37		09 47	10 17			11 17		12 06	12 17			13 06	13 17		14 06	14 17	
Hough Green d	00 06	08 42		09 51	10 21			11 21			12 21				13 21			14 21	
Halewood d	00 11	08 46		09 55	10 25			11 25			12 25				13 25			14 25	
Hunts Cross 89 d	00 14	08 49		09 58	10 28			11 28			12 28				13 28			14 28	
L'pool Sth Parkway 7 91,103 ✈ d	00 20	08 53		10 03	10 33			11 33		12 17	12 33			13 17	13 33		14 16	14 33	
Liverpool Central 10 103 a																			
West Allerton 91 a		08 56		10 06	10 36			11 36			12 36				13 36			14 36	
Mossley Hill 91 a		09 00		10 09	10 39			11 39			12 39				13 39			14 39	
Edge Hill 90,91 a																			
Liverpool Lime Street 10 90,91 a	00 34	09 11	09 52	10 20	10 50	10 54		11 50	11 54	12 30	12 50	12 54		13 30	13 50	13 54	14 30	14 50	14 54

A From Scarborough
C From Middlesbrough
D From Nottingham

Table 89

Sundays
from 1 April

Manchester Airport and Manchester - Warrington Central - Liverpool

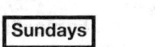

Network Diagram - see first Page of Table 88

	EM ◇ A	NT	NT	EM ◇ C	NT	NT	EM ◇ A	NT	NT	EM ◇ A	NT	NT	EM ◇ C	NT	NT	EM ◇ C	NT
Manchester Airport 85 ✈ d			14 35			15 35			16 35			17 35			18 35		
Sheffield 7 78 🚌 d	13 38			14 39			15 38			16 44			17 44			18 37	
Stockport 84 d	14 26			15 26			16 26			17 29			18 26			19 26	
Manchester Piccadilly 10 78,84,85 🚌 d	14 38		14 50	15 38		15 50	16 38		16 50	17 38		17 50	18 38		18 50	19 38	
Manchester Oxford Road 84,85 d	14 42	14 45	14 53	15 42	15 45	15 53	16 42	16 45	16 53	17 42	17 45	17 53	18 42	18 45	18 53	19 42	19 45
Deansgate 84,85 🚌 d		14 47			15 47			16 47			17 47			18 47			19 47
Trafford Park d																	
Humphrey Park d																	
Urmston d		14 53			15 53			16 53			17 53			18 53			19 53
Chassen Road d																	
Flixton d																	
Irlam d		14 58			15 58			16 58			17 58			18 58			19 58
Glazebrook d																	
Birchwood d		15 04			16 04			17 04			18 04			19 04			20 04
Padgate d																	
Warrington Central a	14 58	15 09		15 58	16 09		16 58	17 09		17 58	18 09		18 58	19 09		19 58	20 09
d	14 58	15 09		15 58	16 09		16 58	17 09		17 58	18 09		18 58	19 09		19 58	20 09
Sankey for Penketh d																	
Widnes d	15 06	15 17		16 06	16 17		17 06	17 17		18 06	18 17		19 06	19 17		20 06	20 17
Hough Green d		15 21			16 21			17 21			18 21			19 21			20 21
Halewood d		15 25			16 25			17 25			18 25			19 25			20 25
Hunts Cross 89 d		15 28			16 28			17 28			18 28			19 28			20 28
L'pool Sth Parkway 7 91,103 ✈ d	15 16	15 33		16 16	16 33		17 16	17 33		18 16	18 33		19 17	19 33		20 16	20 33
Liverpool Central 10 103 a																	
West Allerton 91 a		15 36			16 36			17 36			18 36			19 36			20 36
Mossley Hill 91 a		15 39			16 39			17 39			18 39			19 39			20 39
Edge Hill 90,91 a																	
Liverpool Lime Street 10 90,91 a	15 30	15 50	15 54	16 30	16 50	16 54	17 30	17 50	17 54	18 30	18 50	18 54	19 30	19 50	19 54	20 30	20 50

	NT	NT	NT	NT	NT	NT	NT 🚌
Manchester Airport 85 ✈ d	19 35		20 35		21 35	22 27	
Sheffield 7 78 🚌 d							
Stockport 84 d							
Manchester Piccadilly 10 78,84,85 🚌 d	19 50		20 50		21 50	22 41	
Manchester Oxford Road 84,85 d	19 53	20 45	20 53	21 45	21 53	22 45	23 00
Deansgate 84,85 🚌 d		20 47		21 47		22 47	
Trafford Park d							
Humphrey Park d							
Urmston d		20 53		21 53		22 53	
Chassen Road d							
Flixton d							
Irlam d		20 58		21 58		22 58	
Glazebrook d							
Birchwood d		21 04		22 04		23 04	
Padgate d							
Warrington Central a		21 09		22 09		23 09	
d		21 09		22 09		23 09	
Sankey for Penketh d							
Widnes d		21 17		22 17		23 17	
Hough Green d		21 21		22 21		23 21	
Halewood d		21 25		22 25		23 25	
Hunts Cross 89 d		21 28		22 28		23 28	
L'pool Sth Parkway 7 91,103 ✈ d		21 33		22 33		23 33	
Liverpool Central 10 103 a							
West Allerton 91 a		21 36		22 36		23 36	
Mossley Hill 91 a		21 39		22 39		23 39	
Edge Hill 90,91 a							
Liverpool Lime Street 10 90,91 a	20 54	21 50	21 54	22 50	22 54	23 50	01 11

A From Nottingham
C From Norwich

Liverpool and St Helens - Newton-le-Willows, Wigan, Preston and Manchester

Network Diagram - see first Page of Table 88

Miles	Miles	Miles	Miles			NT MO (bus)	NT MO A	NT MO B	NT MO C (bus)	NT MO	AW MO D (bus)	NT MO (bus)	NT MX	NT A (bus)	AW MX (bus)	NT MO	NT MX	TP ◇1 E	NT	NT	AW F	NT	NT
0	0	0	—	**Liverpool Lime Street** 10 89,91	d	22p01	22p31	22p31	22p31	23p01		23p01	23p02			03 31	03 31		05 13	05 31		05 46	06 01
1¾	1¾	1¾	—	Edge Hill 89,91	d								23p06							05 35		05 50	06 05
2½	2½	2½	—	Wavertree Technology Park	d	22p16	22p37	22p37	22p46			23p16	23p08						05 19	05 37		05 52	06 07
3½	3½	3½	—	Broad Green	d	22p26	22p40	22p40	22p56			23p26	23p11							05 40		05 55	06 10
5	5	5	—	Roby	d	22p33	22p43	22p43	23p03			23p33	23p15							05 44		05 59	06 14
5½	5½	5½	—	Huyton	d	22p37	22p46	22p46	23p07			23p37	23p17	22p52						05 46		06 01	06 16
—	7¾	—	—	Prescot	d			22p50	23p17				23p22	23p02						05 51			06 21
—	8¾	—	—	Eccleston Park	d								23p24							05 53			06 23
—	9¾	—	—	Thatto Heath	d			22p54	23p27				23p27	23p12						05 56			06 26
—	11¼	—	—	**St Helens Central**	a			22p57	23p37				23p30	23p22						05 59			06 29
—	—	—	—		d			22p58	23p37				23p31	23p22						06 00			06 30
—	15	—	—	Garswood	d			23p05	23p57				23p38	23p42						06 07			06 37
—	16¼	—	—	Bryn	d								23p41							06 10			06 40
7½	—	7½	—	Whiston	d	22p47						23p47										06 05	
9	—	9	—	Rainhill	d	22p57						23p57										06 08	
10¾	—	10¾	—	Lea Green	d	23p05						00 05										06 11	
12	—	12	—	**St Helens Junction**	d	23p12						00 12							05 29			06 14	
—	—	—	—	Warrington Bank Quay	d						23p09				23p59						06 06		
14¾	—	14¾	—	Earlestown 8	d	23p24					23p34	00 24			00 24						06 12	06 19	
—	—	—	—	Warrington Bank Quay	a																		
16¼	—	16¼	0	**Newton-le-Willows**	d	23p32					23p44	00 32			00 34				05 35		06 15	06 22	
—	20	23¼	—	**Wigan North Western** 65	a		23p08	23p13	00 17				23p48	00 02						06 21			06 51
—	—	—	—		d		23p14	23p14					23p48					04 44					
—	28¼	31½	—	Euxton Balshaw Lane	d								23p59										
—	31	34¼	—	Leyland 82	a		23p27	23p27					00 04										
—	35	38¼	—	**Preston** 8 65,82	a		23p35	23p35					00 13					05s04					
—	52½	—	—	Blackpool North 97	a		00 05	00 05										05 33					
26¾	—	—	10½	Patricroft	d																	06 34	
27¾	—	—	11½	Eccles	d	23p57						00 57										06 36	
31¾	—	—	—	**Manchester Victoria**	a																	06 47	
—	—	—	15¾	**Manchester Oxford Road**	a	00 12				23p47	00 14	01 12									06 35		
—	—	—	16¼	**Manchester Piccadilly** 10	a					23p50	00 19				01 09	04 13	04 13		05 57		06 45		
—	—	—	26	**Manchester Airport** 85	a					00 07						04 27	04 29		06 14				

		NT	TP ◇1 G	NT	NT	AW ◇ H	NT	NT	NT	NT	AW F	NT I	NT	AW ◇ J	NT	NT	NT	NT	NT	NT
Liverpool Lime Street 10 89,91	d	06 13		06 16	06 31		06 46	06 57	07 01	07 13		07 16	07 31		07 46	07 57	08 01	08 13	08 16	08 31
Edge Hill 89,91	d			06 20	06 35		06 50		07 05			07 20	07 35		07 50		08 05		08 20	08 35
Wavertree Technology Park	d	06 19		06 22	06 37		06 52		07 07	07 19		07 22	07 37		07 52		08 07	08 19	08 22	08 37
Broad Green	d			06 25	06 40		06 55		07 10			07 25	07 40		07 55		08 10		08 25	08 40
Roby	d			06 29	06 44		06 59		07 14			07 29	07 44		07 59		08 14		08 29	08 44
Huyton	d			06 31	06 46		07 01	07 06	07 16			07 31	07 46		08 01	08 06	08 16		08 31	08 46
Prescot	d				06 51				07 21				07 51				08 21			08 51
Eccleston Park	d				06 53				07 23				07 53				08 23			08 53
Thatto Heath	d				06 56				07 26				07 56				08 26			08 56
St Helens Central	a				06 59			07 15	07 29				07 59			08 15	08 29			08 59
	d				07 00			07 15	07 30				08 00			08 15	08 30			09 00
Garswood	d				07 07				07 37				08 07				08 37			09 07
Bryn	d				07 10				07 40				08 10				08 40			09 10
Whiston	d			06 35			07 05					07 35			08 05				08 35	
Rainhill	d			06 38			07 08					07 38			08 08				08 38	
Lea Green	d			06 41			07 11			07 28		07 41			08 11				08 41	
St Helens Junction	d	06 29		06 44			07 14			07 31		07 44			08 14			08 29	08 44	
Warrington Bank Quay	d					07 07					07 39			08 08						
Earlestown 8	d			06 50		07 14	07 19				07 46	07 49		08 16	08 19				08 50	
Warrington Bank Quay	a			07 01															09 01	
Newton-le-Willows	d	06 35				07 17	07 22			07 37	07 49	07 52		08 19	08 22			08 35		
Wigan North Western 65	a				07 21			07 30	07 51				08 21			08 30	08 51			09 21
	d		06 15					07 31								08 31				
Euxton Balshaw Lane	d							07 41								08 41				
Leyland 82	a		06 27					07 46								08 46				
Preston 8 65,82	a		06 35					07 56								08 56				
Blackpool North 97	a		07 06																	
Patricroft	d						07 34					08 04			08 34					
Eccles	d						07 36					08 06			08 36					
Manchester Victoria	a						07 49					08 19			08 50					
Manchester Oxford Road	a	06 57				07 41				07 57	08 09			08 41				08 57		
Manchester Piccadilly 10	a	07 01				07 50				08 01	08 18			08 50				09 01		
Manchester Airport 85	a	07 22								08 22								09 22		

A from 2 April
B until 13 February
C from 20 February until 26 March
D from 20 February until 26 March. From Chester
E From Manchester Airport
F From Chester
G From Manchester Piccadilly
H From Llandudno Junction
I To Huddersfield
J From Llandudno

Liverpool and St Helens - Newton-le-Willows, Wigan, Preston and Manchester

Network Diagram - see first Page of Table 88

		NT	NT	NT	AW	NT	NT	NT	NT	NT	NT	NT	NT	AW	NT	NT	NT	NT	NT	NT	NT
		A			◇ B 🚲		C			D	E			◇ B 🚲		C			A	F	
Liverpool Lime Street 10 89,91	d	08 44	08 57	09 01		09 13		09 16	09 31	09 46	09 46	09 57	10 02		10 13		10 16	10 31	10 46	10 57	11 02
Edge Hill 89,91	d	08 50		09 05				09 20	09 35	09 50	09 50		10 05				10 20	10 35	10 50		11 05
Wavertree Technology Park	d	08 52		09 07		09 19		09 22	09 37	09 52	09 52		10 07		10 19		10 22	10 37	10 52		11 07
Broad Green	d	08 55		09 10				09 25	09 40	09 55	09 55		10 10				10 25	10 40	10 55		11 10
Roby	d	08 59		09 14				09 29	09 44	09 59	09 59		10 14				10 29	10 44	10 59		11 14
Huyton	d	09 01	09 06	09 16				09 31	09 46	10 01	10 01	10 06	10 16				10 31	10 46	11 01	11 06	11 16
Prescot	d			09 21					09 51				10 21					10 51			11 21
Eccleston Park	d			09 23					09 53				10 23					10 53			11 23
Thatto Heath	d			09 26					09 56				10 26					10 56			11 26
St Helens Central	a		09 15	09 29					09 59			10 15	10 29					10 59		11 15	11 29
	d		09 15	09 30					10 00			10 15	10 30					11 00		11 15	11 30
Garswood	d			09 37					10 07				10 37					11 07			11 37
Bryn	d			09 40					10 10				10 40					11 10			11 40
Whiston	d	09 05						09 35		10 05	10 05						10 35		11 05		
Rainhill	d	09 08						09 38		10 08	10 08						10 38		11 08		
Lea Green	d	09 11						09 41		10 11	10 11						10 41		11 11		
St Helens Junction	d	09 14				09 29		09 44		10 14	10 14				10 29		10 44		11 14		
Warrington Bank Quay	d				09 19		09 22							10 19		10 22					
Earlestown 8	d	09 19			09 26		09a33	09 50		10 19	10 19			10 26		10a33	10 50		11 19		
Warrington Bank Quay	a							10 01									11 02				
Newton-le-Willows	d	09 22			09 29	09 35				10 22	10 22			10 29	10 35				11 22		
Wigan North Western 65	a		09 30	09 51					10 21			10 30	10 51					11 19		11 30	11 51
	d		09 31									10 31								11 31	
Euxton Balshaw Lane	d		09 41									10 41								11 41	
Leyland 82	a		09 46									10 46								11 46	
Preston 8 65,82	a		09 54									10 54								11 54	
Blackpool North 97	a		10 21									11 21								12 21	
Patricroft	d	09 34								10 34	10 34								11 34		
Eccles	d	09 36								10 36	10 36								11 36		
Manchester Victoria 🚊	a	09 47								10 47	10 49								11 49		
Manchester Oxford Road	a				09 48	09 57								10 48	10 57						
Manchester Piccadilly 10 🚊	a				09 57	10 01								10 57	11 01						
Manchester Airport 85 ✈	a					10 22									11 22						

		AW	NT	NT	NT	NT	NT	NT	NT	AW	NT	NT	NT	NT	NT	NT	NT	AW	NT	NT
		◇ B 🚲		C			A	F		◇ B 🚲		C			A	F		◇ B 🚲		C
Liverpool Lime Street 10 89,91	d		11 13		11 16	11 31	11 46	11 57	12 02		12 13		12 16	12 31	12 46	12 57	13 02		13 13	
Edge Hill 89,91	d				11 20	11 35	11 50		12 05				12 20	12 35	12 50		13 05			
Wavertree Technology Park	d		11 19		11 22	11 37	11 52		12 07		12 19		12 22	12 37	12 52		13 07		13 19	
Broad Green	d				11 25	11 40	11 55		12 10				12 25	12 40	12 55		13 10			
Roby	d				11 29	11 44	11 59		12 14				12 29	12 44	12 59		13 14			
Huyton	d				11 31	11 46	12 01	12 06	12 16				12 31	12 46	13 01	13 06	13 16			
Prescot	d					11 51			12 21					12 51			13 21			
Eccleston Park	d					11 53			12 23					12 53			13 23			
Thatto Heath	d					11 56			12 26					12 56			13 26			
St Helens Central	a					11 59		12 15	12 29					12 59		13 15	13 29			
	d					12 00		12 15	12 30					13 00		13 15	13 30			
Garswood	d					12 07			12 37					13 07			13 37			
Bryn	d					12 10			12 40					13 10			13 40			
Whiston	d				11 35		12 05						12 35		13 05					
Rainhill	d				11 38		12 08						12 38		13 08					
Lea Green	d				11 41		12 11						12 41		13 11					
St Helens Junction	d		11 29		11 44		12 14				12 29		12 44		13 14				13 29	
Warrington Bank Quay	d	11 19		11 22						12 19		12 22						13 19		13 22
Earlestown 8	d	11 26		11a33	11 50		12 19			12 26		12a33	12 50		13 19			13 26		13a33
Warrington Bank Quay	a				12 01								13 01							
Newton-le-Willows	d	11 29	11 35				12 22			12 29	12 35				13 22			13 29	13 35	
Wigan North Western 65	a					12 21		12 30	12 51					13 21		13 30	13 51			
	d							12 31								13 31				
Euxton Balshaw Lane	d							12 41								13 41				
Leyland 82	a							12 46								13 46				
Preston 8 65,82	a							12 54								13 54				
Blackpool North 97	a							13 21								14 21				
Patricroft	d						12 34								13 34					
Eccles	d						12 36								13 36					
Manchester Victoria 🚊	a						12 50								13 47					
Manchester Oxford Road	a	11 48	11 57							12 48	12 57							13 48	13 57	
Manchester Piccadilly 10 🚊	a	11 57	12 01							12 57	13 01							13 57	14 01	
Manchester Airport 85 ✈	a		12 22								13 22								14 22	

A To Stalybridge
B From Llandudno
C To Liverpool Lime Street
D from 26 March
E until 23 March. To Stalybridge
F From Liverpool South Parkway

Liverpool and St Helens - Newton-le-Willows, Wigan, Preston and Manchester

Network Diagram - see first Page of Table 88

		NT		NT	NT	NT	NT	AW		NT	NT	NT		NT	NT	NT	NT	AW		NT	NT	NT		NT	NT
					A	B		◇ C			D				A	B		◇ C			D				E
Liverpool Lime Street 10 89,91	d	13 16		13 31	13 46	13 57	14 01			14 13		14 16		14 31	14 46	14 57	15 02			15 13		15 16		15 31	15 46
Edge Hill 89,91	d	13 20		13 35	13 50		14 05					14 20		14 35	14 50		15 05					15 20		15 35	15 50
Wavertree Technology Park	d	13 22		13 37	13 52		14 07			14 19		14 22		14 37	14 52		15 07			15 19		15 22		15 37	15 52
Broad Green	d	13 25		13 40	13 55		14 10					14 25		14 40	14 55		15 10					15 25		15 40	15 55
Roby	d	13 29		13 44	13 59		14 14					14 29		14 44	14 59		15 14					15 29		15 44	15 59
Huyton	d	13 31		13 46	14 01	14 06	14 16					14 31		14 46	15 01	15 06	15 16					15 31		15 46	16 01
Prescot	d			13 51			14 21							14 51			15 21							15 51	
Eccleston Park	d			13 53			14 23							14 53			15 23							15 53	
Thatto Heath	d			13 56			14 26							14 56			15 26							15 56	
St Helens Central	a			13 59		14 15	14 29							14 59		15 15	15 29							15 59	
	d			14 00		14 15	14 30							15 00		15 15	15 30							16 00	
Garswood	d			14 07			14 37							15 07			15 37							16 07	
Bryn	d			14 10			14 40							15 10			15 40							16 10	
Whiston	d	13 35			14 05							14 35			15 05							15 35			16 05
Rainhill	d	13 38			14 08							14 38			15 08							15 38			16 08
Lea Green	d	13 41			14 11							14 41			15 11							15 41			16 11
St Helens Junction	d	13 44			14 14					14 29		14 44			15 14					15 29		15 44			16 14
Warrington Bank Quay	d							14 19			14 22							15 19			15 22				
Earlestown 8	d	13 50			14 19			14 26			14a33	14 50			15 19			15 26			15a33	15 50			16 19
Warrington Bank Quay	a	14 01										15 01										16 01			
Newton-le-Willows	d				14 22			14 29		14 35					15 22			15 29		15 35					16 22
Wigan North Western 65	a			14 21		14 30	14 51							15 21		15 30	15 51							16 19	
	d					14 31										15 31									
Euxton Balshaw Lane	d					14 41										15 41									
Leyland 82	a					14 46										15 46									
Preston 8 65,82	a					14 54										15 54									
Blackpool North 97	a					15 21										16 21									
Patricroft	d				14 34										15 34										16 34
Eccles	d				14 36										15 36										16 36
Manchester Victoria	a				14 50										15 49										16 49
Manchester Oxford Road	a							14 48		14 57								15 48		15 57					
Manchester Piccadilly 10	a							14 57		15 01								15 57		16 01					
Manchester Airport 85	a									15 22										16 22					

		NT	NT	AW		NT	NT	NT	AW		NT	NT	NT	NT		NT	NT	NT	NT	AW	NT	NT	NT	NT	
		B		◇ C			D		◇ C			E	B							◇ C					
Liverpool Lime Street 10 89,91	d	15 57	16 02			16 13		16 16			16 31	16 46	16 57	17 01		17 06	17 10	17 19	17 27		17 35	17 44	17 48	18 01	
Edge Hill 89,91	d		16 05					16 20			16 35	16 50		17 05			17 14		17 31		17 39		17 52	18 05	
Wavertree Technology Park	d		16 07			16 19		16 22			16 37	16 52		17 07		17 12	17 16		17 33		17 41	17 49	17 54	18 07	
Broad Green	d		16 10					16 25			16 40	16 55		17 10			17 19		17 36		17 44	17 52	17 57	18 10	
Roby	d		16 14					16 29			16 44	16 59		17 14			17 23		17 40		17 48		18 01	18 14	
Huyton	d	16 06	16 16					16 31			16 46	17 01	17 06	17 16		17 19	17 25	17 29	17 42		17 50	17 57	18 03	18 16	
Prescot	d		16 21								16 51			17 21				17 33				18 02		18 21	
Eccleston Park	d		16 23								16 53			17 23				17 36				18 05		18 23	
Thatto Heath	d		16 26								16 56			17 26				17 38				18 07		18 26	
St Helens Central	a	16 15	16 29								16 59		17 15	17 29				17 42	17 51			18 11		18 29	
	d	16 15	16 30								17 00		17 15	17 30				17 42	17 51			18 11		18 30	
Garswood	d		16 37								17 07			17 37				17 49				18 19		18 37	
Bryn	d		16 40								17 10			17 40				17 52				18 22		18 40	
Whiston	d							16 35				17 05					17 28				17 54		18 07		
Rainhill	d							16 38				17 08					17 32				17 57		18 10		
Lea Green	d							16 41				17 11				17 26	17 35				18 00		18 13		
St Helens Junction	d					16 29		16 44				17 14				17 29	17 39				18 03		18 16		
Warrington Bank Quay	d			16 19			16 22		16 51											17 49					
Earlestown 8	d			16 26			16a33	16 49	16 59			17 19					17 44			17 57	18 08		18 21		
Warrington Bank Quay	a																								
Newton-le-Willows	d			16 29		16 35		16 52	17 02			17 22				17 35	17 47			18 00	18 11		18 24		
Wigan North Western 65	a	16 30	16 51								17 21		17 30	17 52				18 04	18 04			18 30		18 49	
	d	16 30											17 31						18 05			18 31		18 49	
Euxton Balshaw Lane	d	16 40											17 41						18 16			18 41		19 01	
Leyland 82	a	16 45											17 46						18 21			18 46		19 06	
Preston 8 65,82	a	16 54											17 54						18 31			18 54		19 15	
Blackpool North 97	a	17 21											18 24									19 23			
Patricroft	d							17 04				17 34					17 59				18 23				
Eccles	d							17 06				17 36					18 01				18 25		18 36		
Manchester Victoria	a							17 20				17 47					18 14				18 41		18 49		
Manchester Oxford Road	a			16 48		16 57			17 21							17 57				18 19					
Manchester Piccadilly 10	a			16 57		17 01			17 30							18 01				18 28					
Manchester Airport 85	a					17 22										18 22									

A To Stalybridge
B From Liverpool South Parkway
C From Llandudno
D To Liverpool Lime Street
E To Huddersfield

Table 90

Mondays to Fridays

Liverpool and St Helens - Newton-le-Willows, Wigan, Preston and Manchester

Network Diagram - see first Page of Table 88

		NT	NT	NT	AW	NT	NT	AW	NT	NT	NT	NT	AW	NT	NT	NT	NT	AW	NT	NT	TP	AW	NT
																						FO	FO
					◇								◇					◇			◇[1]		
					A			B	C				A					A			D	B	
					Trolley								Trolley										
Liverpool Lime Street [10] 89,91	d	18 13	18 16	18 31		18 46	19 02			19 12	19 23	19 42		20 09	20 12	20 25	20 42		21 12	21 42			22 12
Edge Hill 89,91	d		18 20	18 35		18 50	19 05			19 16		19 46			20 16		20 46		21 16	21 46			22 16
Wavertree Technology Park	d	18 19	18 22	18 37		18 52	19 07			19 18		19 48		20 15	20 18		20 48		21 18	21 48			22 18
Broad Green	d		18 25	18 40		18 55	19 10			19 21		19 51			20 21		20 51		21 21	21 51			22 21
Roby	d		18 29	18 44		18 59	19 14			19 25		19 55			20 25		20 55		21 25	21 55			22 25
Huyton	d		18 31	18 46		19 01	19 16			19 27	19 32	19 57			20 27	20 34	20 57		21 27	21 57			22 27
Prescot	d			18 51			19 21					20 02					21 02			22 02			
Eccleston Park	d			18 53			19 23					20 04					21 04			22 04			
Thatto Heath	d			18 56			19 26					20 07					21 07			22 07			
St Helens Central	a			18 59			19 29				19 40	20 10				20 42	21 10			22 10			
	d			19 00			19 30				19 41	20 11				20 43	21 11			22 11			
Garswood	d			19 07			19 37					20 18					21 18			22 18			
Bryn	d			19 10			19 40					20 21					21 21			22 21			
Whiston	d		18 35			19 05				19 31					20 31				21 31				22 31
Rainhill	d		18 38			19 08				19 34					20 34				21 34				22 34
Lea Green	d		18 41			19 11				19 37					20 37				21 37				22 37
St Helens Junction	d	18 29	18 44			19 14				19 40				20 25	20 40				21 40				22 40
Warrington Bank Quay	d				18 46			19 19	19 22				20 19					21 19				22 19	
Earlestown [8]	d		18 50		18 57	19 19		19 26	19a33	19 45			20 26		20 45			21 26	21 45			22 26	22 45
Warrington Bank Quay	a		19 01																				
Newton-le-Willows	d	18 35			19 00	19 22		19 29		19 48			20 29	20 35	20 48			21 29	21 48			22 29	22 48
Wigan North Western 65	a			19 21			19 51				19 54	20 32				20 57	21 32			22 28			
	d										19 55					20 57				22 28	21 48		
Euxton Balshaw Lane	d										20 05					21 08				22 39			
Leyland 82	a										20 10					21 16				22 44			
Preston [8] 65,82	a										20 18					21 22				22 55			
Blackpool North 97	a										20 44					21 53				23 22			
Patricroft	d					19 34				20 00					21 00				22 00				23 00
Eccles	d					19 36				20 02					21 02				22 02				23 02
Manchester Victoria	a					19 49				20 16					21 15				22 15				23 15
Manchester Oxford Road	a	18 57			19 21			19 48					20 48	20 57				21 48			22 26	22 50	
Manchester Piccadilly [10]	a	19 01			19 29			19 52					20 52	21 01				21 57			22 30	22 58	
Manchester Airport 85 ✈	a	19 24						20 18					21 18	21 20							22 47		

		NT	NT	AW	NT	NT	NT	NT	AW
		MX	FX	FX	FX		FO	FX	FX
		Bus		Bus	Bus				Bus
Liverpool Lime Street [10] 89,91	d		22 12			23 02	23 16	23 16	
Edge Hill 89,91	d		22 16			23 06	23 20	23 20	
Wavertree Technology Park	d		22 18			23 08	23 22	23 22	
Broad Green	d		22 21			23 11	23 26	23 26	
Roby	d		22 25			23 15	23 30	23 30	
Huyton	d		22 27			23 17	23 32	23 32	
Prescot	d					23 22			
Eccleston Park	d					23 24			
Thatto Heath	d					23 27			
St Helens Central	a					23 30			
	d					23 31			
Garswood	d					23 38			
Bryn	d					23 41			
Whiston	d		22 31				23 36	23 36	
Rainhill	d		22 34				23 39	23 39	
Lea Green	d		22 37				23 42	23 42	
St Helens Junction	d		22 40				23 45	23 45	
Warrington Bank Quay	d			22 28					23 59
Earlestown [8]	d	00 05	22a47	22 53	23 00		23 50	23a52	00 24
Warrington Bank Quay	a								
Newton-le-Willows	d	00 13		23 03	23 08		23 53		00 34
Wigan North Western 65	a					23 48			
	d					23 48			
Euxton Balshaw Lane	d					23 59			
Leyland 82	a					00 04			
Preston [8] 65,82	a					00 13			
Blackpool North 97	a								
Patricroft	d	00 43			23 38		00 05		
Eccles	d	00 53			23 48		00 08		
Manchester Victoria	a	01 12			00 07		00 21		
Manchester Oxford Road	a			23 33					
Manchester Piccadilly [10]	a			23 38					01 09
Manchester Airport 85 ✈	a								

A From Llandudno
B From Chester
C To Liverpool Lime Street
D From Barrow-in-Furness

Table 90

Saturdays

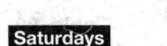

until 11 February

Liverpool and St Helens - Newton-le-Willows, Wigan, Preston and Manchester

Network Diagram - see first Page of Table 88

		NT	NT	NT	NT	NT	AW	NT	NT	NT	AW	NT	NT	NT	NT	NT	NT	AW	NT	NT	NT	AW
							A				◇ A			B				C	D			E
Liverpool Lime Street [10] 89,91	d	23p02	23p16	03 38	05 13	05 31		05 46	06 01	06 13		06 16	06 31	06 46	06 57	07 01	07 13		07 16	07 26	07 31	
Edge Hill 89,91	d	23p06	23p20			05 35		05 50	06 05			06 20	06 35	06 50		07 05			07 20	07 30	07 35	
Wavertree Technology Park	d	23p08	23p22		05 19	05 37		05 52	06 07	06 19		06 22	06 37	06 52		07 07	07 19		07 22		07 37	
Broad Green	d	23p11	23p26			05 40		05 55	06 10			06 25	06 40	06 55		07 10			07 25		07 40	
Roby	d	23p15	23p30			05 44		05 59	06 14			06 29	06 44	06 59		07 14			07 29		07 44	
Huyton	d	23p17	23p32			05 46		06 01	06 16			06 31	06 46	07 01	07 06	07 16			07 31		07 46	
Prescot	d	23p22				05 51			06 21				06 51			07 21					07 51	
Eccleston Park	d	23p24				05 53			06 23				06 53			07 23					07 53	
Thatto Heath	d	23p27				05 56			06 26				06 56			07 26					07 56	
St Helens Central	a	23p30				05 59			06 29				06 59		07 15	07 29					07 59	
	d	23p31				06 00			06 30				07 00		07 15	07 30					08 00	
Garswood	d	23p38				06 07			06 37				07 07			07 37					08 07	
Bryn	d	23p41				06 10			06 40				07 10			07 40					08 10	
Whiston	d		23p36					06 05				06 35		07 05					07 35			
Rainhill	d		23p39					06 08				06 38		07 08					07 38			
Lea Green	d		23p42					06 11				06 41		07 11			07 28		07 41			
St Helens Junction	d		23p45		05 29			06 14		06 29		06 44		07 14			07 31		07 44			
Warrington Bank Quay	d						06 06				06 40							07 39				08 08
Earlestown [8]	d		23p50				06 12	06 19			06 47	06 50		07 19				07 46	07 49			08 16
Warrington Bank Quay	a											07 01										
Newton-le-Willows	d		23p53		05 35		06 15	06 22		06 35	06 50			07 22			07 37	07 49	07 52			08 19
Wigan North Western 65	a	23p48				06 21			06 51				07 21		07 30	07 51					08 21	
	d	23p48													07 31							
Euxton Balshaw Lane	d	23p59													07 41							
Leyland 82	a	00 04													07 46							
Preston [8] 65,82	a	00 13													07 54							
Blackpool North 97	a														08 21							
Patricroft	d		00 05					06 34						07 34					08 04			
Eccles	d		00 08					06 36						07 36					08 06			
Manchester Victoria	a		00 21					06 49						07 49					08 19			
Manchester Oxford Road	a						06 35			06 57	07 09						07 57	08 09		08 36		08 41
Manchester Piccadilly [10]	a			04 14	05 57		06 45			07 01	07 18						08 01	08 18				08 45
Manchester Airport 85 ✈	a			04 30	06 14					07 22							08 22					

		NT	NT	NT	NT	NT	NT	NT	NT	NT	AW	NT	NT	NT	NT	NT	NT	NT	NT	AW	NT	NT	NT
								B			E		F				B			E		F	
Liverpool Lime Street [10] 89,91	d	07 46	08 01	08 13	08 16	08 26	08 31	08 44	08 57	09 01		09 13		09 16	09 27	09 31	09 46	09 57	10 01		10 13		10 16
Edge Hill 89,91	d	07 50	08 05		08 20	08 30	08 35	08 50		09 05				09 20		09 35	09 50		10 05				10 20
Wavertree Technology Park	d	07 52	08 07	08 19	08 22		08 37	08 52		09 07		09 19		09 22		09 37	09 52		10 07		10 19		10 22
Broad Green	d	07 55	08 10		08 25		08 40	08 55		09 10				09 25		09 40	09 55		10 10				10 25
Roby	d	07 59	08 14		08 29		08 44	08 59		09 14				09 29		09 44	09 59		10 14				10 29
Huyton	d	08 01	08 16		08 31		08 46	09 01	09 06	09 16				09 31		09 46	10 01	10 06	10 16				10 31
Prescot	d		08 21				08 51			09 21						09 51			10 21				
Eccleston Park	d		08 23				08 53			09 23						09 53			10 23				
Thatto Heath	d		08 26				08 56			09 26						09 56			10 26				
St Helens Central	a		08 29				08 59		09 15	09 29						09 59		10 15	10 29				
	d		08 30				09 00		09 15	09 30						10 00		10 15	10 30				
Garswood	d		08 37				09 07			09 37						10 07			10 37				
Bryn	d		08 40				09 10			09 40						10 10			10 40				
Whiston	d	08 05			08 35			09 05						09 35			10 05						10 35
Rainhill	d	08 08			08 38			09 08						09 38			10 08						10 38
Lea Green	d	08 11			08 41			09 11						09 41			10 11						10 41
St Helens Junction	d	08 14		08 29	08 44			09 14				09 29		09 44			10 14				10 29		10 44
Warrington Bank Quay	d										09 19		09 22							10 19		10 22	
Earlestown [8]	d	08 19			08 50			09 19			09 26		09a33	09 50			10 19			10 26		10a33	10 50
Warrington Bank Quay	a				09 01									10 01									11 01
Newton-le-Willows	d	08 22		08 35				09 22			09 29	09 35					10 22			10 29	10 35		
Wigan North Western 65	a		08 51				09 21		09 30	09 51						10 21		10 30	10 51				
	d								09 31									10 31					
Euxton Balshaw Lane	d								09 41									10 41					
Leyland 82	a								09 46									10 46					
Preston [8] 65,82	a								09 54									10 54					
Blackpool North 97	a								10 21									11 21					
Patricroft	d	08 34						09 34									10 34						
Eccles	d	08 36						09 36									10 36						
Manchester Victoria	a	08 50						09 47									10 49						
Manchester Oxford Road	a			08 57		09 36					09 48	09 57			10 36					10 48	10 57		
Manchester Piccadilly [10]	a			09 01							09 52	10 01								10 52	11 01		
Manchester Airport 85 ✈	a			09 22								10 22									11 22		

A From Chester
B To Stalybridge
C From Shrewsbury
D To Huddersfield
E From Llandudno
F To Liverpool Lime Street

Table 90

Saturdays
until 11 February

Liverpool and St Helens - Newton-le-Willows, Wigan, Preston and Manchester

Network Diagram - see first Page of Table 88

		NT	NT	NT	NT	NT	AW	NT	NT	NT	NT
			A	B		C		D		
Liverpool Lime Street [10] 89,91	d	10 27	10 31	10 46	10 57	11 01		11 13		11 16	11 27
Edge Hill 89,91	d		10 35	10 50		11 05				11 20	
Wavertree Technology Park	d		10 37	10 52		11 07		11 19		11 22	
Broad Green	d		10 40	10 55		11 10				11 25	
Roby	d		10 44	10 59		11 14				11 29	
Huyton	d		10 46	11 01	11 06	11 16				11 31	
Prescot	d		10 51			11 21					
Eccleston Park	d		10 53			11 23					
Thatto Heath	d		10 56			11 26					
St Helens Central	a		10 59		11 15	11 29					
	d		11 00		11 15	11 30					
Garswood	d		11 07			11 37					
Bryn	d		11 10			11 40					
Whiston	d			11 05						11 35	
Rainhill	d			11 08						11 38	
Lea Green	d			11 11						11 41	
St Helens Junction	d			11 14				11 29		11 44	
Warrington Bank Quay	d						11 19		11 22		
Earlestown [8]	d			11 19			11 26		11a33	11 50	
Warrington Bank Quay	a									12 01	
Newton-le-Willows	d			11 22			11 29	11 35			
Wigan North Western 65	a		11 21		11 30	11 51					
	d				11 31						
Euxton Balshaw Lane	d				11 41						
Leyland 82	a				11 46						
Preston [8] 65,82	a				11 54						
Blackpool North 97	a				12 21						
Patricroft	d			11 34							
Eccles	d			11 36							
Manchester Victoria	a			11 49							
Manchester Oxford Road	a	11 36					11 48	11 57			12 36
Manchester Piccadilly [10]	a						11 52	12 01			
Manchester Airport 85	a							12 22			

		NT	NT	NT	NT	AW	NT	NT	NT	NT	NT	NT
			A	B		◇ C		D				A
Liverpool Lime Street [10] 89,91	d	11 31	11 46	11 57	12 01		12 13		12 16	12 27	12 31	12 46
Edge Hill 89,91	d	11 35	11 50		12 05				12 20		12 35	12 50
Wavertree Technology Park	d	11 37	11 52		12 07		12 19		12 22		12 37	12 52
Broad Green	d	11 40	11 55		12 10				12 25		12 40	12 55
Roby	d	11 44	11 59		12 14				12 29		12 44	12 59
Huyton	d	11 46	12 01	12 06	12 16				12 31		12 46	13 01
Prescot	d	11 51			12 21						12 51	
Eccleston Park	d	11 53			12 23						12 53	
Thatto Heath	d	11 56			12 26						12 56	
St Helens Central	a	11 59		12 15	12 29						12 59	
	d	12 00		12 15	12 30						13 00	
Garswood	d	12 07			12 37						13 07	
Bryn	d	12 10			12 40						13 10	
Whiston	d		12 05						12 35			13 05
Rainhill	d		12 08						12 38			13 08
Lea Green	d		12 11						12 41			13 11
St Helens Junction	d		12 14				12 29		12 44			13 14
Warrington Bank Quay	d					12 19		12 22				
Earlestown [8]	d		12 19			12 26		12a33	12 50			13 19
Warrington Bank Quay	a								13 01			
Newton-le-Willows	d		12 22			12 29	12 35					13 22
Wigan North Western 65	a	12 21		12 30	12 51						13 21	
	d			12 31								
Euxton Balshaw Lane	d			12 41								
Leyland 82	a			12 46								
Preston [8] 65,82	a			12 54								
Blackpool North 97	a			13 21								
Patricroft	d		12 34									13 34
Eccles	d		12 36									13 36
Manchester Victoria	a		12 49									13 49
Manchester Oxford Road	a					12 48	12 57			13 36		
Manchester Piccadilly [10]	a					12 52	13 01					
Manchester Airport 85	a						13 22					

		NT	NT	AW	NT	NT	NT	NT	NT	NT	NT	NT
		B		◇ C		D				A	B	
Liverpool Lime Street [10] 89,91	d	12 57	13 01		13 13		13 16	13 27	13 31	13 46	13 57	14 01
Edge Hill 89,91	d		13 05				13 20		13 35	13 50		14 05
Wavertree Technology Park	d		13 07		13 19		13 22		13 37	13 52		14 07
Broad Green	d		13 10				13 25		13 40	13 55		14 10
Roby	d		13 14				13 29		13 44	13 59		14 14
Huyton	d	13 06	13 16				13 31		13 46	14 01	14 06	14 16
Prescot	d		13 21						13 51			14 21
Eccleston Park	d		13 23						13 53			14 23
Thatto Heath	d		13 26						13 56			14 26
St Helens Central	a	13 15	13 29						13 59		14 15	14 29
	d	13 15	13 30						14 00		14 15	14 30
Garswood	d		13 37						14 07			14 37
Bryn	d		13 40						14 10			14 40
Whiston	d						13 35			14 05		
Rainhill	d						13 38			14 08		
Lea Green	d						13 41			14 11		
St Helens Junction	d				13 29		13 44			14 14		
Warrington Bank Quay	d			13 19		13 22						
Earlestown [8]	d			13 26		13a33	13 50			14 19		
Warrington Bank Quay	a						14 01					
Newton-le-Willows	d			13 29	13 35					14 22		
Wigan North Western 65	a	13 30	13 51						14 21		14 30	14 51
	d	13 31									14 31	
Euxton Balshaw Lane	d	13 41									14 41	
Leyland 82	a	13 46									14 46	
Preston [8] 65,82	a	13 54									14 54	
Blackpool North 97	a	14 21									15 21	
Patricroft	d									14 34		
Eccles	d									14 36		
Manchester Victoria	a									14 50		
Manchester Oxford Road	a			13 48	13 57			14 36				
Manchester Piccadilly [10]	a			13 52	14 01							
Manchester Airport 85	a				14 22							

		AW	NT	NT	NT	NT	NT	NT	NT	NT	AW	NT
		◇ C		D				A	B		◇ C	
Liverpool Lime Street [10] 89,91	d		14 13		14 16	14 27	14 31	14 46	14 57	15 01		15 13
Edge Hill 89,91	d				14 20		14 35	14 50		15 05		
Wavertree Technology Park	d		14 19		14 22		14 37	14 52		15 07		15 19
Broad Green	d				14 25		14 40	14 55		15 10		
Roby	d				14 29		14 44	14 59		15 14		
Huyton	d				14 31		14 46	15 01	15 06	15 16		
Prescot	d						14 51			15 21		
Eccleston Park	d						14 53			15 23		
Thatto Heath	d						14 56			15 26		
St Helens Central	a						14 59		15 15	15 29		
	d						15 00		15 15	15 30		
Garswood	d						15 07			15 37		
Bryn	d						15 10			15 40		
Whiston	d				14 35			15 05				
Rainhill	d				14 38			15 08				
Lea Green	d				14 41			15 11				
St Helens Junction	d		14 29		14 44			15 14				15 29
Warrington Bank Quay	d	14 19		14 22							15 19	
Earlestown [8]	d	14 26		14a33	14 50			15 19			15 26	
Warrington Bank Quay	a				15 01							
Newton-le-Willows	d	14 29	14 35					15 22			15 29	15 35
Wigan North Western 65	a						15 21		15 30	15 51		
	d								15 31			
Euxton Balshaw Lane	d								15 41			
Leyland 82	a								15 46			
Preston [8] 65,82	a								15 54			
Blackpool North 97	a								16 21			
Patricroft	d							15 34				
Eccles	d							15 36				
Manchester Victoria	a							15 49				
Manchester Oxford Road	a	14 48	14 57			15 36					15 48	15 57
Manchester Piccadilly [10]	a	14 57	15 01								15 52	16 01
Manchester Airport 85	a		15 22									16 22

A To Stalybridge
B From Liverpool South Parkway
C From Llandudno
D To Liverpool Lime Street

Table 90

Saturdays
until 11 February

Liverpool and St Helens - Newton-le-Willows, Wigan, Preston and Manchester

Network Diagram - see first Page of Table 88

		NT	NT	NT	NT	NT	NT	NT	AW	NT	NT	NT	NT	NT	NT	NT	NT	AW	NT	NT	NT	NT
		A				B	C		◇ D		A				B	C		◇ D				
Liverpool Lime Street 10 89,91	d		15 16	15 27	15 31	15 46	15 57	16 01		16 13		16 16	16 27	16 31	16 46	16 57	17 01		17 06	17 10	17 19	17 27
Edge Hill 89,91	d		15 20		15 35	15 50		16 05				16 20		16 35	16 50		17 05			17 14		17 31
Wavertree Technology Park	d		15 22		15 37	15 52		16 07		16 19		16 22		16 37	16 52		17 07		17 12	17 16		17 33
Broad Green	d		15 25		15 40	15 55		16 10				16 25		16 40	16 55		17 10			17 19		17 36
Roby	d		15 29		15 44	15 59		16 14				16 29		16 44	16 59		17 14			17 23		17 40
Huyton	d		15 31		15 46	16 01	16 06	16 16				16 31		16 46	17 01	17 06	17 16		17 19	17 25	17 29	17 42
Prescot	d				15 51			16 21						16 51			17 21				17 33	
Eccleston Park	d				15 53			16 23						16 53			17 23				17 36	
Thatto Heath	d				15 56			16 26						16 56			17 26				17 38	
St Helens Central	a				15 59		16 15	16 29						16 59		17 15	17 29				17 42	17 51
	d				16 00		16 15	16 30						17 00		17 15	17 30				17 42	17 51
Garswood	d				16 07			16 37						17 07			17 37				17 49	
Bryn	d				16 10			16 40						17 10			17 40				17 52	
Whiston	d		15 35			16 05						16 35			17 05					17 28		
Rainhill	d		15 38			16 08						16 38			17 08					17 32		
Lea Green	d		15 41			16 11						16 41			17 11				17 26	17 35		
St Helens Junction	d		15 44			16 14				16 29		16 44			17 14				17 29	17 39		
Warrington Bank Quay	d	15 22							16 19		16 22							17 19				
Earlestown 8	d	15a33	15 50			16 19			16 26		16a33	16 49			17 19			17 26		17 44		
Warrington Bank Quay	a		16 01																			
Newton-le-Willows	d					16 22			16 29	16 35		16 52			17 22			17 29	17 35	17 47		
Wigan North Western 65	a				16 21		16 30	16 51						17 21		17 30	17 52				18 04	18 05
	d						16 31									17 31						18 05
Euxton Balshaw Lane	d						16 41									17 41						18 16
Leyland 82	a						16 46									17 46						18 21
Preston 8 65,82	a						16 54									17 54						18 31
Blackpool North 97	a						17 21									18 24						
Patricroft	d					16 34						17 04			17 34					17 59		
Eccles	d					16 36						17 06			17 36					18 01		
Manchester Victoria	a					16 49						17 20			17 47					18 15		
Manchester Oxford Road	a			16 36					16 48	16 57			17 36					17 48	17 57			
Manchester Piccadilly 10	a								16 57	17 01								17 57	18 01			
Manchester Airport 85	a									17 22									18 22			

		NT	NT	NT	NT	AW	NT	NT	NT	NT	NT	AW	NT	NT	NT	NT	AW	NT	NT	NT	NT	AW	NT
						◇ D						◇ D	A				◇ D					◇ D	
Liverpool Lime Street 10 89,91	d	17 35	17 44	17 48	18 01		18 13	18 16	18 31	18 46	19 01			19 12	19 23	19 42		20 09	20 12	20 25	20 42		21 12
Edge Hill 89,91	d	17 39		17 52	18 05			18 20	18 35	18 50	19 05			19 16		19 46			20 16		20 46		21 16
Wavertree Technology Park	d	17 41	17 49	17 54	18 07		18 19	18 22	18 37	18 52	19 07			19 18		19 48		20 15	20 18		20 48		21 18
Broad Green	d	17 44	17 52	17 57	18 10			18 25	18 40	18 55	19 10			19 21		19 51			20 21		20 51		21 21
Roby	d	17 48		18 01	18 14			18 29	18 44	18 59	19 14			19 25		19 55			20 25		20 55		21 25
Huyton	d	17 50	17 57	18 03	18 16			18 31	18 46	19 01	19 16			19 27	19 32	19 57			20 27	20 34	20 57		21 27
Prescot	d		18 02		18 21				18 51		19 21					20 02					21 02		
Eccleston Park	d		18 05		18 23				18 53		19 23					20 04					21 04		
Thatto Heath	d		18 07		18 26				18 56		19 26					20 07					21 07		
St Helens Central	a		18 11		18 29				18 59		19 29				19 40	20 10				20 42	21 10		
	d		18 11		18 30				19 00		19 30				19 41	20 11				20 43	21 11		
Garswood	d		18 19		18 37				19 07		19 37					20 18					21 18		
Bryn	d		18 22		18 40				19 10		19 40					20 21					21 21		
Whiston	d	17 54		18 07				18 35		19 05				19 31					20 31				21 31
Rainhill	d	17 57		18 10				18 38		19 08				19 34					20 34				21 34
Lea Green	d	18 00		18 13				18 41		19 11				19 37					20 37				21 37
St Helens Junction	d	18 03		18 16			18 29	18 44		19 14				19 40				20 25	20 40				21 40
Warrington Bank Quay	d					18 19						19 19	19 22				20 19					21 19	
Earlestown 8	d	18 08		18 21		18 26		18 50		19 19		19 26	19a33	19 45			20 26		20 45			21 26	21 45
Warrington Bank Quay	a							19 01															
Newton-le-Willows	d	18 11		18 24		18 29	18 35			19 22		19 29		19 48			20 29	20 35	20 48			21 29	21 48
Wigan North Western 65	a		18 30		18 49				19 21		19 51				19 54	20 32				20 57	21 32		
	d		18 31		18 49										19 55					20 57			
Euxton Balshaw Lane	d		18 41		19 01										20 05					21 08			
Leyland 82	a		18 46		19 06										20 10					21 16			
Preston 8 65,82	a		18 54		19 15										20 18					21 22			
Blackpool North 97	a		19 21												20 44					21 53			
Patricroft	d	18 23								19 34				20 00					21 00				22 00
Eccles	d	18 25		18 36						19 36				20 02					21 02				22 02
Manchester Victoria	a	18 41		18 49						19 49				20 15					21 15				22 15
Manchester Oxford Road	a					18 48	18 57					19 48					20 48	20 57				21 48	
Manchester Piccadilly 10	a					18 57	19 01					19 52					20 57	21 01				21 57	
Manchester Airport 85	a						19 24					20 13						21 24					

A To Liverpool Lime Street
B To Stalybridge
C From Liverpool South Parkway
D From Llandudno

Table 90

Saturdays

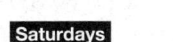

until 11 February

Liverpool and St Helens - Newton-le-Willows, Wigan, Preston and Manchester

Network Diagram - see first Page of Table 88

		NT	AW A	NT	NT	NT	AW A
Liverpool Lime Street 10 89,91	d	21 42		22 12	23 02	23 16	
Edge Hill 89,91	d	21 46		22 16	23 06	23 20	
Wavertree Technology Park	d	21 48		22 18	23 08	23 22	
Broad Green	d	21 51		22 21	23 11	23 26	
Roby	d	21 55		22 25	23 15	23 30	
Huyton	d	21 57		22 27	23 17	23 32	
Prescot	d	22 02			23 22		
Eccleston Park	d	22 04			23 24		
Thatto Heath	d	22 07			23 27		
St Helens Central	a	22 10			23 30		
	d	22 11			23 31		
Garswood	d	22 18			23 38		
Bryn	d	22 21			23 41		
Whiston	d			22 31		23 36	
Rainhill	d			22 34		23 39	
Lea Green	d			22 37		23 42	
St Helens Junction	d			22 40		23 45	
Warrington Bank Quay	d		22 19				23 50
Earlestown 8	d		22 27	22 45		23 50	23 58
Warrington Bank Quay	a						
Newton-le-Willows	d		22 30	22 48		23 53	00 02
Wigan North Western 65	a	22 28			23 48		
	d	22 28			23 48		
Euxton Balshaw Lane	d	22 39			23 59		
Leyland 82	a	22 44			00 04		
Preston 8 65,82	a	22 55			00 13		
Blackpool North 97	a	23 22					
Patricroft	d			23 00		00 05	
Eccles	d			23 02		00 08	
Manchester Victoria 🚇	a			23 15		00 21	
Manchester Oxford Road	a		22 50				
Manchester Piccadilly 10 🚇	a		22 58				00 26
Manchester Airport 85 ✈	a						

Saturdays

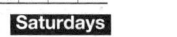

18 February to 24 March

		NT	NT	NT	NT 🚌	NT 🚌	AW A	AW ◇ A	NT 🚌	NT 🚌	NT 🚌	NT 🚌	NT 🚌	AW B 🍴	NT 🚌	NT 🚌	AW C 🍴	NT 🚌	NT 🚌	NT	NT 🚌	NT
Liverpool Lime Street 10 89,91	d	23p02	23p16	03 31	04 40	05 26			05 40	05 56	06 15	06 20	06 26		06 40	06 56		07 10	07 20	07 26	07 26	07 31
Edge Hill 89,91	d	23p06	23p20		04 47	05 33			05 47	06 03	06 22		06 33		06 47	07 03		07 17		07 30	07 33	07 35
Wavertree Technology Park	d	23p08	23p22		04 57	05 43			05 57	06 13	06 32		06 43		06 57	07 13		07 27			07 43	07 37
Broad Green	d	23p11	23p26		05 07	05 53			06 07	06 23	06 42		06 53		07 07	07 23		07 37			07 53	07 40
Roby	d	23p15	23p30		05 14	06 00			06 14	06 30	06 49		07 00		07 14	07 30		07 44			08 00	07 44
Huyton	d	23p17	23p32		05 18	06 04			06 18	06 34	06 53		07 04		07 18	07 34		07 48			08 04	07 46
Prescot	d	23p22				06 14				06 44			07 14			07 44					08 14	
Eccleston Park	d	23p24				06 20				06 50			07 20			07 50					08 20	
Thatto Heath	d	23p27				06 30				07 00			07 30			08 00					08 30	
St Helens Central	a	23p30				06 40				07 10			07 40			08 10					08 40	
	d	23p31				06 40				07 10			07 40			08 10					08 40	
Garswood	d	23p38				07 00				07 30			08 00			08 30					09 00	
Bryn	d	23p41				07 07				07 37			08 07			08 37					09 07	
Whiston	d		23p36		05 28				06 28		07 03				07 28			07 58				
Rainhill	d		23p39		05 38				06 38		07 13				07 38			08 08				
Lea Green	d		23p42		05 46				06 46		07 21				07 46			08 16				
St Helens Junction	d		23p45		05 53				06 53		07 28				07 53			08 23				
Warrington Bank Quay	d						06 06	06 40						07 39			08 08					
Earlestown 8	d		23p50		06a05		06 12	06 47	07a05		07a40			07 46	08a05		08 16	08a35				
Warrington Bank Quay	a																					
Newton-le-Willows	d		23p53				06 15	06 50						07 49			08 19					
Wigan North Western 65	a	23p48				07 20				07 50		07 20	08 20			08 50			08 20		09 20	08 14
	d	23p48																				08 30
Euxton Balshaw Lane	d	23p59																				08 41
Leyland 82	a	00 04																				08 46
Preston 8 65,82	a	00 13																				08 54
Blackpool North 97	a																					09 21
Patricroft	d		00 05																			
Eccles	d		00 08																			
Manchester Victoria 🚇	a		00 21																			
Manchester Oxford Road	a						06 35	07 09						08 09			08 41			08 36		
Manchester Piccadilly 10 🚇	a			04 14			06 45	07 18						08 18			08 45					
Manchester Airport 85 ✈	a			04 30																		

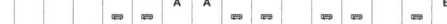

A From Chester   **B** From Shrewsbury   **C** From Llandudno

Table 90

Saturdays

18 February to 24 March

Liverpool and St Helens - Newton-le-Willows, Wigan, Preston and Manchester

Network Diagram - see first Page of Table 88

		NT	NT	AW	NT	NT		NT	NT	NT	NT	AW	NT	NT	NT	NT		NT	NT	AW	NT	NT	NT	NT	NT
				A								A								A					
		🚌	🚌		🚌	🚌			🚌	🚌	🚌		🚌	🚌	🚌			🚌	🚌		🚌	🚌	🚌		🚌
				🛒								🛒								🛒					
Liverpool Lime Street 10 89,91	d	07 40	07 56		08 10	08 20		08 26	08 26	08 40	08 56		09 10	09 20	09 26	09 27		09 40	09 56		10 10	10 20	10 26	10 27	10 40
Edge Hill 89,91	d	07 47	08 03		08 17			08 30	08 33	08 47	09 03		09 17		09 33			09 47	10 03		10 17		10 33		10 47
Wavertree Technology Park	d	07 57	08 13		08 27				08 43	08 57	09 13		09 27		09 43			09 57	10 13		10 27		10 43		10 57
Broad Green	d	08 07	08 23		08 37				08 53	09 07	09 23		09 37		09 53			10 07	10 23		10 37		10 53		11 07
Roby	d	08 14	08 30		08 44				09 00	09 14	09 30		09 44		10 00			10 14	10 30		10 44		11 00		11 14
Huyton	d	08 18	08 34		08 48				09 04	09 18	09 34		09 48		10 04			10 18	10 34		10 48		11 04		11 18
Prescot	d		08 44						09 14		09 44				10 14				10 44				11 14		
Eccleston Park	d		08 50						09 20		09 50				10 20				10 50				11 20		
Thatto Heath	d		09 00						09 30		10 00				10 30				11 00				11 30		
St Helens Central	a		09 10						09 40		10 10				10 40				11 10				11 40		
	d		09 10						09 40		10 10				10 40				11 10				11 40		
Garswood	d		09 30						10 00		10 30				11 00				11 30				12 00		
Bryn	d		09 37						10 07		10 37				11 07				11 37				12 07		
Whiston	d	08 28			08 58					09 28			09 58					10 28			10 58				11 28
Rainhill	d	08 38			09 08					09 38			10 08					10 38			11 08				11 38
Lea Green	d	08 46			09 16					09 46			10 16					10 46			11 16				11 46
St Helens Junction	d	08 53			09 23					09 53			10 23					10 53			11 23				11 53
Warrington Bank Quay	d			09 19								10 19								11 19					
Earlestown 8	d	09a05		09 26	09a35					10a05		10 26	10a35					11a05		11 26	11a35				12a05
Warrington Bank Quay	a																								
Newton-le-Willows	d			09 29								10 29								11 29					
Wigan North Western 65	a		09 50			09 20			10 20		10 50			10 20	11 20				11 50			11 20	12 20		
	d																								
Euxton Balshaw Lane	d																								
Leyland 82	a																								
Preston 8 65,82	a																								
Blackpool North 97	a																								
Patricroft	d																								
Eccles	d																								
Manchester Victoria	a																								
Manchester Oxford Road	a			09 48				09 36				10 48				10 36				11 48				11 36	
Manchester Piccadilly 10	a			09 52								10 52								11 52					
Manchester Airport 85 ✈	a																								

		NT		AW	NT	NT	NT	NT	NT	NT	AW	NT		NT	NT	NT	NT	NT	AW	NT	NT	NT		NT	NT
				◇							◇								◇						
				A							A								A						
		🚌			🚌	🚌	🚌		🚌	🚌		🚌		🚌	🚌		🚌	🚌		🚌	🚌	🚌			🚌
				🛒							🛒								🛒						
Liverpool Lime Street 10 89,91	d	10 56			11 10	11 20	11 26	11 27	11 40	11 56		12 10		12 20	12 26	12 27	12 40	12 56		13 10	13 20	13 26		13 27	13 40
Edge Hill 89,91	d	11 03			11 17		11 33		11 47	12 03		12 17			12 33		12 47	13 03		13 17		13 33			13 47
Wavertree Technology Park	d	11 13			11 27		11 43		11 57	12 13		12 27			12 43		12 57	13 13		13 27		13 43			13 57
Broad Green	d	11 23			11 37		11 53		12 07	12 23		12 37			12 53		13 07	13 23		13 37		13 53			14 07
Roby	d	11 30			11 44		12 00		12 14	12 30		12 44			13 00		13 14	13 30		13 44		14 00			14 14
Huyton	d	11 34			11 48		12 04		12 18	12 34		12 48			13 04		13 18	13 34		13 48		14 04			14 18
Prescot	d	11 44					12 14			12 44					13 14			13 44				14 14			
Eccleston Park	d	11 50					12 20			12 50					13 20			13 50				14 20			
Thatto Heath	d	12 00					12 30			13 00					13 30			14 00				14 30			
St Helens Central	a	12 10					12 40			13 10					13 40			14 10				14 40			
	d	12 10					12 40			13 10					13 40			14 10				14 40			
Garswood	d	12 30					13 00			13 30					14 00			14 30				15 00			
Bryn	d	12 37					13 07			13 37					14 07			14 37				15 07			
Whiston	d				11 58				12 28			12 58					13 28			13 58					14 28
Rainhill	d				12 08				12 38			13 08					13 38			14 08					14 38
Lea Green	d				12 16				12 46			13 16					13 46			14 16					14 46
St Helens Junction	d				12 23				12 53			13 23					13 53			14 23					14 53
Warrington Bank Quay	d			12 19							13 19								14 19						
Earlestown 8	d			12 26	12a35				13a05		13 26	13a35					14a05		14 26	14a35					15a05
Warrington Bank Quay	a																								
Newton-le-Willows	d			12 29							13 29								14 29						
Wigan North Western 65	a	12 50				12 20	13 20			13 50				13 20	14 20			14 50			14 20	15 20			
	d																								
Euxton Balshaw Lane	d																								
Leyland 82	a																								
Preston 8 65,82	a																								
Blackpool North 97	a																								
Patricroft	d																								
Eccles	d																								
Manchester Victoria	a																								
Manchester Oxford Road	a			12 48				12 36			13 48					13 36			14 48					14 36	
Manchester Piccadilly 10	a			12 52							13 52								14 57						
Manchester Airport 85 ✈	a																								

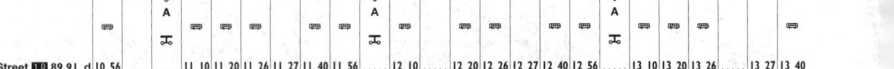

A From Llandudno

Table 90

Saturdays

18 February to 24 March

Liverpool and St Helens - Newton-le-Willows, Wigan, Preston and Manchester

Network Diagram - see first Page of Table 88

		NT	AW	NT	NT	NT	NT	NT		NT	AW	NT	NT	NT	NT	NT	NT	AW		NT	NT	NT	NT	NT	NT
			◇								◇							◇							
			A								A							A							
Liverpool Lime Street 10 89,91	d	13 56		14 10	14 20	14 26	14 27	14 40		14 56		15 10	15 20	15 26	15 27	15 40	15 56			16 05	16 20	16 26	16 27	16 40	16 56
Edge Hill 89,91	d	14 03		14 17		14 33		14 47		15 03		15 17		15 33		15 47	16 03			16 12		16 33		16 47	17 03
Wavertree Technology Park	d	14 13		14 27		14 43		14 57		15 13		15 27		15 43		15 57	16 13			16 22		16 43		16 57	17 13
Broad Green	d	14 23		14 37		14 53		15 07		15 23		15 37		15 53		16 07	16 23			16 32		16 53		17 07	17 23
Roby	d	14 30		14 44		15 00		15 14		15 30		15 44		16 00		16 14	16 30			16 39		17 00		17 14	17 30
Huyton	d	14 34		14 48		15 04		15 18		15 34		15 48		16 04		16 18	16 34			16 43		17 04		17 18	17 34
Prescot	d	14 44				15 14				15 44				16 14			16 44					17 14			17 44
Eccleston Park	d	14 50				15 20				15 50				16 20			16 50					17 20			17 50
Thatto Heath	d	15 00				15 30				16 00				16 30			17 00					17 30			18 00
St Helens Central	a	15 10				15 40				16 10				16 40			17 10					17 40			18 10
	d	15 10				15 40				16 10				16 40			17 10					17 40			18 10
Garswood	d	15 30				16 00				16 30				17 00			17 30					18 00			18 30
Bryn	d	15 37				16 07				16 37				17 07			17 37					18 07			18 37
Whiston	d			14 58				15 28				15 58				16 28				16 53				17 28	
Rainhill	d			15 08				15 38				16 08				16 38				17 03				17 38	
Lea Green	d			15 16				15 46				16 16				16 46				17 11				17 46	
St Helens Junction	d			15 23				15 53				16 23				16 53				17 18				17 53	
Warrington Bank Quay	d		15 19								16 19							17 19							
Earlestown 8	d		15 26	15a35				16a05			16 26	16a35				17a05		17 26		17a30				18a05	
Warrington Bank Quay	a																								
Newton-le-Willows	d		15 29								16 29							17 29							
Wigan North Western 65	a	15 50			15 20	16 20				16 50			16 20	17 20			17 50				17 20	18 20			18 50
	d																								
Euxton Balshaw Lane	d																								
Leyland 82	a																								
Preston 8 65,82	a																								
Blackpool North 97	a																								
Patricroft	d																								
Eccles	d																								
Manchester Victoria	a																								
Manchester Oxford Road	a		15 48				15 36				16 48				16 36			17 48					17 36		
Manchester Piccadilly 10	a		15 52								16 57							17 57							
Manchester Airport 85	a																								

		AW	NT	NT		NT	NT	NT	AW	NT	NT	NT	NT	NT		AW	NT	NT	NT	AW	NT	NT	AW	NT	
		◇							◇							◇				◇					
		A							A							A				A			B		
Liverpool Lime Street 10 89,91	d		17 05	17 20		17 26	17 40	17 56		18 05	18 26	18 40	18 40	18 56			19 05	19 40	19 42		20 05	20 42		21 05	
Edge Hill 89,91	d		17 12			17 33	17 47	18 03		18 12	18 33		18 47	19 03			19 12		19 49		20 12	20 49		21 12	
Wavertree Technology Park	d		17 22			17 43	17 57	18 13		18 22	18 43		18 57	19 13			19 22		19 59		20 22	20 59		21 22	
Broad Green	d		17 32			17 53	18 07	18 23		18 32	18 53		19 07	19 23			19 32		20 09		20 32	21 09		21 32	
Roby	d		17 39			18 00	18 14	18 30		18 39	19 00		19 14	19 30			19 39		20 16		20 39	21 16		21 39	
Huyton	d		17 43			18 04	18 18	18 34		18 43	19 04		19 18	19 34			19 43		20 20		20 43	21 20		21 43	
Prescot	d					18 14		18 44			19 14			19 44					20 30			21 30			
Eccleston Park	d					18 20		18 50			19 20			19 50					20 36			21 36			
Thatto Heath	d					18 30		19 00			19 30			20 00					20 46			21 46			
St Helens Central	a					18 40		19 10			19 40			20 10					20 56			21 56			
	d					18 40		19 10			19 40			20 10					20 56			21 56			
Garswood	d					19 00		19 30			20 00			20 30					21 16			22 16			
Bryn	d					19 07		19 37			20 07			20 37					21 23			22 23			
Whiston	d		17 53				18 28			18 53			19 28				19 53				20 53			21 53	
Rainhill	d		18 03				18 38			19 03			19 38				20 03				21 03			22 03	
Lea Green	d		18 11				18 46			19 11			19 46				20 11				21 11			22 11	
St Helens Junction	d		18 18				18 53			19 18			19 53				20 18				21 18			22 18	
Warrington Bank Quay	d	18 19							19 19							20 19				21 19			22 19		
Earlestown 8	d	18 26	18a30				19a05		19 26	19a30			20a05			20 26	20a30			21 26	21a30		22 27	22a30	
Warrington Bank Quay	a																								
Newton-le-Willows	d	18 29							19 29							20 29				21 29			22 30		
Wigan North Western 65	a			18 20		19 20		19 50			20 20	19 40		20 50				20 40	21 36			22 36			
	d																								
Euxton Balshaw Lane	d																								
Leyland 82	a																								
Preston 8 65,82	a																								
Blackpool North 97	a																								
Patricroft	d																								
Eccles	d																								
Manchester Victoria	a																								
Manchester Oxford Road	a	18 48							19 48							20 48				21 48			22 50		
Manchester Piccadilly 10	a	18 57							19 52							20 57				21 57			22 58		
Manchester Airport 85	a								20 13																

A From Llandudno

B From Chester

Table 90

Saturdays
18 February to 24 March

Liverpool and St Helens - Newton-le-Willows, Wigan, Preston and Manchester

Network Diagram - see first Page of Table 88

		NT	NT	NT	NT	NT	NT	AW	NT
								A	
		🚌	🚌	🚌	🚌	🚌	🚌		🚌
Liverpool Lime Street 10 89,91	d	21 15	21 42	22 10	22 35	22 42	23 02		23 16
Edge Hill 89,91	d		21 49	22 17		22 49	23 09		23 22
Wavertree Technology Park	d		21 59	22 27		22 59	23 19		23 32
Broad Green	d		22 09	22 37		23 09	23 29		23 42
Roby	d		22 16	22 44		23 16	23 36		23 49
Huyton	d		22 20	22 48		23 20	23 40		23 53
Prescot	d		22 30			23 30	23 50		
Eccleston Park	d		22 36			23 36	23 56		
Thatto Heath	d		22 46			23 46	00 06		
St Helens Central	a		22 56			23 56	00 16		
	d		22 56			23 56	00 16		
Garswood	d		23 16			00 16	00 36		
Bryn	d		23 23			00 23	00 43		
Whiston	d			22 58					00 03
Rainhill	d			23 08					00 13
Lea Green	d			23 16					00 20
St Helens Junction	d			23 23					00 25
Warrington Bank Quay	d							23 50	
Earlestown 8	d			23a35				23 58	00 37
Warrington Bank Quay	a								
Newton-le-Willows	d							00 02	00 45
Wigan North Western 65	a	22 15	23 36		23 35	00 36	00 56		
	d								
Euxton Balshaw Lane	d								
Leyland 82	a								
Preston 8 65,82	a								
Blackpool North 97	a								
Patricroft	d								01 15
Eccles	d								01 25
Manchester Victoria ⛴	a								01 44
Manchester Oxford Road	a								
Manchester Piccadilly 10 ⛴	a							00 26	
Manchester Airport 85 ✈	a								

Saturdays
from 31 March

		NT	NT	NT	NT	NT	AW	NT	NT	NT		NT	AW	NT	NT	NT	NT	NT	NT	NT		NT	AW	NT	NT
													◇												
							A						A					B					C	D	
										🚌							🚌			🚌					
																							🚲		
Liverpool Lime Street 10 89,91	d	23p02	23p16	03 38	05 13	05 31		05 46	06 01			06 13		06 16	06 25	06 31		06 46	07 01			07 13		07 16	07 26
Edge Hill 89,91	d	23p06	23p20			05 35		05 50	06 05					06 20		06 35		06 50	07 05					07 20	07 30
Wavertree Technology Park	d	23p08	23p22		05 19	05 37		05 52	06 07			06 19		06 22		06 37		06 52	07 07			07 19		07 22	
Broad Green	d	23p11	23p26			05 40		05 55	06 10					06 25		06 40		06 55	07 10					07 25	
Roby	d	23p15	23p30			05 44		05 59	06 14					06 29		06 44		06 59	07 14					07 29	
Huyton	d	23p17	23p32			05 46		06 01	06 16	05 55				06 31		06 46	06 25	07 01	07 16	06 55				07 31	
Prescot	d	23p22								06 05							06 35			07 05					
Eccleston Park	d	23p24								06 11							06 41			07 11					
Thatto Heath	d	23p27								06 21							06 51			07 21					
St Helens Central	a	23p30								06 31							07 01			07 31					
	d	23p31								06 31							07 01			07 31					
Garswood	d	23p38								06 51							07 21			07 51					
Bryn	d	23p41								06 58							07 28			07 58					
Whiston	d		23p36					06 05						06 35				07 05						07 35	
Rainhill	d		23p39					06 08						06 38				07 08						07 38	
Lea Green	d		23p42					06 11						06 41				07 11				07 28		07 41	
St Helens Junction	d		23p45		05 29			06 14				06 29		06 44				07 14				07 31		07 44	
Warrington Bank Quay	d						06 06						06 40										07 39		
Earlestown 8	d		23p50				06 12	06 19					06 47	06 50				07 19					07 46	07 49	
Warrington Bank Quay	a													07 01											
Newton-le-Willows	d		23p53		05 35		06 15	06 22				06 35	06 50					07 22				07 37	07 49	07 52	
Wigan North Western 65	a	23p48				06 19			06 49	07 11						07 19	07 41		07 49	08 11					
	d	23p48														07 30									
Euxton Balshaw Lane	d	23p59														07 41									
Leyland 82	a	00 04														07 46									
Preston 8 65,82	a	00 13														07 54									
Blackpool North 97	a															08 21									
Patricroft	d		00 05					06 34										07 34						08 04	
Eccles	d		00 08					06 36										07 36						08 06	
Manchester Victoria ⛴	a		00 21					06 49										07 49						08 19	
Manchester Oxford Road	a						06 35					06 57	07 09		07 37							07 57	08 09		08 36
Manchester Piccadilly 10 ⛴	a			04 14	05 57		06 45					07 01	07 18									08 01	08 18		
Manchester Airport 85 ✈	a			04 30	06 14							07 22										08 22			

A From Chester
B To Stalybridge
C From Shrewsbury
D To Huddersfield

Table 90

Saturdays
from 31 March

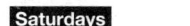

Liverpool and St Helens - Newton-le-Willows, Wigan, Preston and Manchester

Network Diagram - see first Page of Table 88

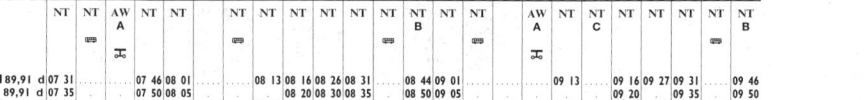

		NT	NT 🚌	AW A	NT	NT		NT 🚌	NT	NT	NT	NT	NT 🚌	NT B	NT	NT 🚌		AW A	NT	NT C	NT	NT	NT	NT 🚌	NT B
Liverpool Lime Street [10] 89,91	d	07 31			07 46	08 01			08 13	08 16	08 26	08 31		08 44	09 01				09 13		09 16	09 27	09 31		09 46
Edge Hill 89,91	d	07 35			07 50	08 05				08 20	08 30	08 35		08 50	09 05						09 20		09 35		09 50
Wavertree Technology Park	d	07 37			07 52	08 07			08 19	08 22		08 37		08 52	09 07				09 19		09 22		09 37		09 52
Broad Green	d	07 40			07 55	08 10				08 25		08 40		08 55	09 10						09 25		09 40		09 55
Roby	d	07 44			07 59	08 14				08 29		08 44		08 59	09 14						09 29		09 44		09 59
Huyton	d	07 46	07 25		08 01	08 16		07 55		08 31		08 46	08 25	09 01	09 16	08 55					09 31		09 46	09 25	10 01
Prescot	d		07 35					08 05					08 35			09 05								09 35	
Eccleston Park	d		07 41					08 11					08 41			09 11								09 41	
Thatto Heath	d		07 51					08 21					08 51			09 21								09 51	
St Helens Central	a		08 01					08 31					09 01			09 31								10 01	
	d		08 01					08 31					09 01			09 31								10 01	
Garswood	d		08 21					08 51					09 21			09 51								10 21	
Bryn	d		08 28					08 58					09 28			09 58								10 28	
Whiston	d				08 05					08 35				09 05							09 35				10 05
Rainhill	d				08 08					08 38				09 08							09 38				10 08
Lea Green	d				08 11					08 41				09 11							09 41				10 11
St Helens Junction	d				08 14				08 29	08 44				09 14					09 29		09 44				10 14
Warrington Bank Quay	d			08 08														09 19		09 22					
Earlestown [8]	d			08 16	08 19					08 50				09 19				09 26		09a33	09 50				10 19
Warrington Bank Quay	a									09 01											10 01				
Newton-le-Willows	d			08 19	08 22				08 35					09 22				09 29	09 35						10 22
Wigan North Western 65	a	08 14	08 41			08 43		09 11				09 17	09 41		09 49	10 11							10 17	10 41	
	d	08 30										09 30											10 30		
Euxton Balshaw Lane	d	08 41										09 41											10 41		
Leyland 82	a	08 46										09 46											10 46		
Preston [8] 65,82	a	08 54										09 54											10 54		
Blackpool North 97	a	09 21										10 23											11 21		
Patricroft	d				08 34									09 34											10 34
Eccles	d				08 36									09 36											10 36
Manchester Victoria	a				08 50									09 47											10 49
Manchester Oxford Road	a			08 41					08 57		09 36							09 48	09 57			10 36			
Manchester Piccadilly [10]	a			08 45					09 01									09 52	10 01						
Manchester Airport 85 ✈	a								09 22										10 22						

		NT		NT 🚌	AW A	NT	NT C	NT	NT	NT	NT 🚌	NT B		NT	NT 🚌	AW A	NT	NT C	NT	NT	NT	NT 🚌		NT B	NT
Liverpool Lime Street [10] 89,91	d	10 02				10 13		10 16	10 27	10 31		10 46		11 01			11 13		11 16	11 27	11 31			11 46	12 01
Edge Hill 89,91	d	10 05						10 20		10 35		10 50		11 05					11 20		11 35			11 50	12 05
Wavertree Technology Park	d	10 07				10 19		10 22		10 37		10 52		11 07			11 19		11 22		11 37			11 52	12 07
Broad Green	d	10 10						10 25		10 40		10 55		11 10					11 25		11 40			11 55	12 10
Roby	d	10 14						10 29		10 44		10 59		11 14					11 29		11 44			11 59	12 14
Huyton	d	10 16		09 55				10 31		10 46	10 25	11 01		11 16	10 55				11 31		11 46	11 25		12 01	12 16
Prescot	d			10 05							10 35				11 05							11 35			
Eccleston Park	d			10 11							10 41				11 11							11 41			
Thatto Heath	d			10 21							10 51				11 21							11 51			
St Helens Central	a			10 31							11 01				11 31							12 01			
	d			10 31							11 01				11 31							12 01			
Garswood	d			10 51							11 21				11 51							12 21			
Bryn	d			10 58							11 28				11 58							12 28			
Whiston	d							10 35				11 05							11 35					12 05	
Rainhill	d							10 38				11 08							11 38					12 08	
Lea Green	d							10 41				11 11							11 41					12 11	
St Helens Junction	d					10 29		10 44				11 14					11 29		11 44					12 14	
Warrington Bank Quay	d				10 19		10 22									11 19		11 22							
Earlestown [8]	d				10 26		10a33	10 50				11 19				11 26		11a33	11 50					12 19	
Warrington Bank Quay	a							11 01											12 01						
Newton-le-Willows	d				10 29	10 35						11 22				11 29	11 35							12 22	
Wigan North Western 65	a	10 49		11 11						11 17	11 41			11 48	12 11						12 17	12 41			12 53
	d									11 30											12 30				
Euxton Balshaw Lane	d									11 41											12 41				
Leyland 82	a									11 46											12 46				
Preston [8] 65,82	a									11 54											12 54				
Blackpool North 97	a									12 21											13 21				
Patricroft	d											11 34												12 34	
Eccles	d											11 36												12 36	
Manchester Victoria	a											11 49												12 49	
Manchester Oxford Road	a				10 48	10 57			11 36							11 48	11 57			12 36					
Manchester Piccadilly [10]	a				10 52	11 01										11 52	12 01								
Manchester Airport 85 ✈	a					11 22											12 22								

A From Llandudno

B To Stalybridge

C To Liverpool Lime Street

Table 90

Saturdays
from 31 March

Liverpool and St Helens - Newton-le-Willows, Wigan, Preston and Manchester

Network Diagram - see first Page of Table 88

		NT	AW	NT	NT	NT	NT	NT		NT	NT	NT	NT	AW	NT	NT	NT	NT		NT	NT	NT	NT	NT	AW
		[bus]	◇ A [trolley]		B					[bus]	C		[bus]	◇ A [trolley]		B					[bus]	C		[bus]	◇ A [trolley]
Liverpool Lime Street [10] 89,91	d			12 13		12 16	12 27	12 31			12 46	13 02			13 13		13 16	13 27		13 31		13 46	14 01		
Edge Hill 89,91	d					12 20		12 35			12 50	13 06					13 20			13 35		13 50	14 05		
Wavertree Technology Park	d			12 19		12 22		12 37			12 52	13 07			13 19		13 22			13 37		13 52	14 07		
Broad Green	d					12 25		12 40			12 55	13 10					13 25			13 40		13 55	14 10		
Roby	d					12 29		12 44			12 59	13 14					13 29			13 44		13 59	14 14		
Huyton	d	11 55				12 31		12 46		12 25	13 01	13 16	12 55				13 31			13 46	13 25	14 01	14 16	13 55	
Prescot	d	12 05								12 35			13 05								13 35			14 05	
Eccleston Park	d	12 11								12 41			13 11								13 41			14 11	
Thatto Heath	d	12 21								12 51			13 21								13 51			14 21	
St Helens Central	a	12 31								13 01			13 31								14 01			14 31	
	d	12 31								13 01			13 31								14 01			14 31	
Garswood	d	12 51								13 21			13 51								14 21			14 51	
Bryn	d	12 58								13 28			13 58								14 28			14 58	
Whiston	d					12 35					13 05						13 35					14 05			
Rainhill	d					12 38					13 08						13 38					14 08			
Lea Green	d					12 41					13 11						13 41					14 11			
St Helens Junction	d			12 29		12 44					13 14				13 29		13 44					14 14			
Warrington Bank Quay	d		12 19		12 22									13 19		13 22									14 19
Earlestown [8]	d		12 26		12a33	12 50					13 19			13 26		13a33	13 50					14 19			14 26
Warrington Bank Quay	a					13 01											14 01								
Newton-le-Willows	d		12 29	12 35							13 22			13 29	13 35							14 22			14 29
Wigan North Western 65	a	13 11						13 17		13 41		13 48	14 11							14 17	14 41		14 48	15 11	
	d							13 30												14 30					
Euxton Balshaw Lane	d							13 41												14 41					
Leyland 82	a							13 46												14 46					
Preston [8] 65,82	a							13 54												14 54					
Blackpool North 97	a							14 21												15 23					
Patricroft	d										13 34											14 34			
Eccles	d										13 36											14 36			
Manchester Victoria [tram]	a										13 49											14 50			
Manchester Oxford Road	a		12 48	12 57			13 36							13 48	13 57			14 36							14 48
Manchester Piccadilly [10] [tram]	a		12 52	13 01										13 52	14 01										14 57
Manchester Airport 85 [plane]	a			13 22											14 22										

		NT	NT	NT		NT	NT	NT	NT	NT	NT	AW	NT	NT		NT	NT	NT	NT	NT	NT	NT	AW	NT	
			B					[bus]	C		[bus]	◇ A [trolley]		B					[bus]	C		[bus]	◇ A [trolley]		
Liverpool Lime Street [10] 89,91	d	14 13		14 16		14 27	14 31		14 46	15 01			15 13			15 16	15 27	15 31		15 46	16 01			16 13	
Edge Hill 89,91	d			14 20			14 35		14 50	15 05						15 20		15 35		15 50	16 05				
Wavertree Technology Park	d	14 19		14 22			14 37		14 52	15 07			15 19			15 22		15 37		15 52	16 07			16 19	
Broad Green	d			14 25			14 40		14 55	15 10						15 25		15 40		15 55	16 10				
Roby	d			14 29			14 44		14 59	15 14						15 29		15 44		15 59	16 14				
Huyton	d			14 31			14 46	14 25	15 01	15 16	14 55					15 31		15 46	15 25	16 01	16 16	15 55			
Prescot	d							14 35			15 05								15 35			16 05			
Eccleston Park	d							14 41			15 11								15 41			16 11			
Thatto Heath	d							14 51			15 21								15 51			16 21			
St Helens Central	a							15 01			15 31								16 01			16 31			
	d							15 01			15 31								16 01			16 31			
Garswood	d							15 21			15 51								16 21			16 51			
Bryn	d							15 28			15 58								16 28			16 58			
Whiston	d			14 35					15 05							15 35				16 05					
Rainhill	d			14 38					15 08							15 38				16 08					
Lea Green	d			14 41					15 11							15 41				16 11					
St Helens Junction	d	14 29		14 44					15 14				15 29			15 44				16 14				16 29	
Warrington Bank Quay	d		14 22									15 19		15 22									16 19		
Earlestown [8]	d		14a33	14 50					15 19			15 26		15a33		15 50				16 19			16 26		
Warrington Bank Quay	a			15 01												16 01									
Newton-le-Willows	d	14 35							15 22			15 29	15 35							16 22			16 29	16 35	
Wigan North Western 65	a						15 17	15 41		15 48	16 11							16 17	16 41		16 48	17 11			
	d						15 30											16 30							
Euxton Balshaw Lane	d						15 41											16 41							
Leyland 82	a						15 46											16 46							
Preston [8] 65,82	a						15 54											16 54							
Blackpool North 97	a						16 22											17 23							
Patricroft	d								15 34											16 34					
Eccles	d								15 36											16 36					
Manchester Victoria [tram]	a								15 49											16 49					
Manchester Oxford Road	a	14 57				15 36						15 48	15 57				16 36						16 48	16 57	
Manchester Piccadilly [10] [tram]	a	15 01										15 52	16 01										16 57	17 01	
Manchester Airport 85 [plane]	a	15 22											16 22											17 22	

A From Llandudno
B To Liverpool Lime Street
C To Stalybridge

Table 90

Saturdays
from 31 March

Liverpool and St Helens - Newton-le-Willows, Wigan, Preston and Manchester

Network Diagram - see first Page of Table 88

	NT	NT	NT	NT	NT	NT	NT	NT	AW	NT	NT	NT	NT	NT	NT	NT	AW	NT	NT	NT	NT	NT
	A				🚌			🚌	◇ B 🚲				🚌		🚌		◇ B 🚲				🚌	
Liverpool Lime Street [10] 89,91 d		16 16	16 27	16 31		16 46	17 01			17 06	17 10	17 31		17 35		17 48		18 13	18 16	18 31		18 46
Edge Hill 89,91 d		16 20		16 35		16 50	17 05				17 14			17 39		17 52			18 20	18 35		18 50
Wavertree Technology Park d		16 22		16 37		16 52	17 07			17 12	17 16			17 41		17 54		18 19	18 22	18 37		18 52
Broad Green d		16 25		16 40		16 55	17 10				17 19			17 44		17 57			18 25	18 40		18 55
Roby d		16 29		16 44		16 59	17 14				17 23			17 48		18 01			18 29	18 44		18 59
Huyton d		16 31		16 46	16 25	17 01	17 16	16 55		17 19	17 25	17 41	17 25	17 50	17 55	18 03			18 31	18 46	18 25	19 01
Prescot d					16 35			17 05					17 35		18 05						18 35	
Eccleston Park d					16 41			17 11					17 41		18 11						18 41	
Thatto Heath d					16 51			17 21					17 51		18 21						18 51	
St Helens Central a					17 01			17 31					18 01		18 31						19 01	
d					17 01			17 31					18 01		18 31						19 01	
Garswood d					17 21			17 51					18 21		18 51						19 21	
Bryn d					17 28			17 58					18 28		18 58						19 28	
Whiston d		16 35				17 05					17 28			17 54		18 07			18 35			19 05
Rainhill d		16 38				17 08					17 32			17 57		18 10			18 38			19 08
Lea Green d		16 41				17 11				17 26	17 35			18 00		18 13			18 41			19 11
St Helens Junction d		16 44				17 14				17 29	17 39			18 03		18 16		18 29	18 44			19 14
Warrington Bank Quay d	16 22								17 19								18 19					
Earlestown [8] d	16a33	16 49				17 19			17 26		17 44			18 08		18 21	18 26		18 50			19 19
Warrington Bank Quay a																			19 01			
Newton-le-Willows d		16 52				17 22			17 29	17 35	17 47			18 11		18 24	18 29	18 35				19 22
Wigan North Western 65 a				17 17	17 41		17 49	18 11				18 17	18 41		19 11					19 13	19 41	
d				17 30								18 30										
Euxton Balshaw Lane d				17 41								18 41										
Leyland 82 a				17 46								18 46										
Preston [8] 65,82 a				17 54								18 54										
Blackpool North 97 a				18 24								19 21										
Patricroft d		17 04				17 34					17 59			18 23								19 34
Eccles d		17 06				17 36					18 01			18 25		18 36						19 36
Manchester Victoria 🚊 a		17 20				17 47					18 15			18 41		18 49						19 49
Manchester Oxford Road a			17 36						17 48	17 57							18 48	18 57				
Manchester Piccadilly [10] 🚊 a									17 57	18 01							18 57	19 01				
Manchester Airport 85 ✈ a										18 22								19 24				

	NT	NT	AW	NT	NT	NT	NT	NT	AW	NT	NT	NT	AW	NT	NT	NT	NT	AW	NT	TP	NT	NT
		🚌	◇ B 🚲	A			🚌	🚌	◇ B 🚲				◇ B			🚌	🚌	C		◇[1] D	🚌	🚌
Liverpool Lime Street [10] 89,91 d	19 02				19 12	19 42				20 09	20 12	20 42		21 12	21 42				22 12	22 30		
Edge Hill 89,91 d	19 05				19 16	19 46					20 16	20 46		21 16	21 46				22 16			
Wavertree Technology Park d	19 07				19 18	19 48				20 15	20 18	20 48		21 18	21 48				22 18			
Broad Green d	19 10				19 21	19 51					20 21	20 51		21 21	21 51				22 21			
Roby d	19 14				19 25	19 55					20 25	20 55		21 25	21 55				22 25			
Huyton d	19 16	18 55			19 27	19 57	19 25	20 08			20 27	20 57		21 27	21 57	21 08	22 08		22 27		23 08	23 28
Prescot d		19 05					19 35	20 18								21 18	22 18				23 18	23 38
Eccleston Park d		19 11					19 41	20 24								21 24	22 24				23 24	23 44
Thatto Heath d		19 21					19 51	20 34								21 34	22 34				23 34	23 54
St Helens Central a		19 31					20 01	20 44								21 44	22 44				23 44	00 04
d		19 31					20 01	20 44								21 44	22 44				23 44	00 04
Garswood d		19 51					20 21	21 04								22 04	23 04				00 04	00 24
Bryn d		19 58					20 28	21 11								22 11	23 11				00 11	00 31
Whiston d					19 31						20 31			21 31					22 31			
Rainhill d					19 34						20 34			21 34					22 34			
Lea Green d					19 37						20 37			21 37					22 37			
St Helens Junction d					19 40					20 25	20 40			21 40					22 40			
Warrington Bank Quay d			19 19	19 22					20 19				21 19					22 19				
Earlestown [8] d			19 26	19a33	19 45				20 26		20 45		21 26	21 45				22 27	22 45			
Warrington Bank Quay a																						
Newton-le-Willows d			19 29		19 48				20 29	20 35	20 48		21 29	21 48				22 30	22 48			
Wigan North Western 65 a	19 47	20 11				20 24	20 41	21 24				21 24			22 22	22 24	23 24				00 24	00 44
d	19 54														22 27							
Euxton Balshaw Lane d	20 05														22 39							
Leyland 82 a	20 10														22 44							
Preston [8] 65,82 a	20 18														22 55							
Blackpool North 97 a	20 44														23 22							
Patricroft d					20 00						21 00			22 00					23 00			
Eccles d					20 02						21 02			22 02					23 02			
Manchester Victoria 🚊 a					20 15						21 15			22 15					23 15			
Manchester Oxford Road a			19 48						20 48	20 57			21 48					22 50		23 14		
Manchester Piccadilly [10] 🚊 a			19 52						20 57	21 01			21 57					22 58		23 19		
Manchester Airport 85 ✈ a			20 13							21 24												

A To Liverpool Lime Street
B From Llandudno
C From Chester
D To Huddersfield

Table 90

Saturdays from 31 March

Liverpool and St Helens - Newton-le-Willows, Wigan, Preston and Manchester

Network Diagram - see first Page of Table 88

		NT	AW
			A
Liverpool Lime Street 10 89,91	d	23 16	
Edge Hill 89,91	d	23 20	
Wavertree Technology Park	d	23 22	
Broad Green	d	23 26	
Roby	d	23 30	
Huyton	d	23 32	
Prescot	d		
Eccleston Park	d		
Thatto Heath	d		
St Helens Central	a		
	d		
Garswood	d		
Bryn	d		
Whiston	d	23 36	
Rainhill	d	23 39	
Lea Green	d	23 42	
St Helens Junction	d	23 45	
Warrington Bank Quay	d		23 50
Earlestown 8	d	23 50	23 58
Warrington Bank Quay	a		
Newton-le-Willows	d	23 53	00 02
Wigan North Western 65	a		
	d		
Euxton Balshaw Lane	d		
Leyland 82	a		
Preston 8 65,82	a		
Blackpool North 97	a		
Patricroft	d	00 05	
Eccles	d	00 08	
Manchester Victoria ⇌	a	00 21	
Manchester Oxford Road	a		
Manchester Piccadilly 10 ⇌	a		00 26
Manchester Airport 85 ✈	a		

Sundays until 12 February

		NT	NT	AW	NT	NT	AW	NT	TP	NT	AW	NT	NT	AW	NT	NT	AW	NT	NT	AW	NT
									◇1		◇										
		B	B	C			A		D		A			A ⚲			A ⚲			A ⚲	
Liverpool Lime Street 10 89,91	d	23p02	23p16		08 07	08 31		09 01		09 31		10 01	10 31		11 01	11 31		12 01	12 31		13 01
Edge Hill 89,91	d	23p06	23p20																		
Wavertree Technology Park	d	23p08	23p22		08 13	08 37		09 07		09 37		10 07	10 37		11 07	11 37		12 07	12 37		13 07
Broad Green	d	23p11	23p26		08 16	08 40		09 10		09 40		10 10	10 40		11 10	11 40		12 10	12 40		13 10
Roby	d	23p15	23p30		08 19	08 43		09 13		09 43		10 13	10 43		11 13	11 43		12 13	12 43		13 13
Huyton	d	23p17	23p32		08 22	08 46		09 16		09 46		10 16	10 46		11 16	11 46		12 16	12 46		13 16
Prescot	d	23p22				08 50				09 50			10 50			11 50					
Eccleston Park	d	23p24																			
Thatto Heath	d	23p27				08 54				09 54			10 54			11 54					
St Helens Central	a	23p30				08 57				09 57			10 57			11 57					
	d	23p31				08 58				09 58			10 58			11 58					
Garswood	d	23p38				09 05				10 05			11 05			12 05					
Bryn	d	23p41																			
Whiston	d		23p36		08 25			09 19				10 19			11 19			12 19			13 19
Rainhill	d		23p39		08 28			09 22				10 22			11 22			12 22			13 22
Lea Green	d		23p42		08 32			09 26				10 26			11 26			12 26			13 26
St Helens Junction	d		23p45		08 35			09 29				10 29			11 29			12 29			13 29
Warrington Bank Quay	d			23p50			09 10				10 12			11 03			12 03			13 03	
Earlestown 8	d		23p50	23p58	08 39		09 16	09 33			10 19	10 33		11 10	11 33		12 10	12 33		13 10	13 33
Warrington Bank Quay	a																				
Newton-le-Willows	d		23p53	00 02	08 42		09 19	09 36			10 22	10 36		11 13	11 36		12 13	12 36		13 13	13 36
Wigan North Western 65	a	23p48				09 13				10 13			11 13			12 13			13 08		
	d	23p48				09 14			09 39	10 14			11 14			12 14			13 14		
Euxton Balshaw Lane	d	23p59				09 24				10 26			11 24			12 24			13 24		
Leyland 82	a	00 04				09 29				10 31			11 29			12 29			13 29		
Preston 8 65,82	a	00 13				09 37			09 55	10 39			11 37			12 37			13 37		
Blackpool North 97	a					10 07			10 22	11 09			12 07			13 07			14 07		
Patricroft	d		00 05																		
Eccles	d		00 08		08 55			09 49				10 49			11 49			12 49			13 49
Manchester Victoria ⇌	a		00 21																		
Manchester Oxford Road	a				09 05		09 39	09 59			10 41	10 59		11 32	11 59		12 32	12 59		13 32	13 57
Manchester Piccadilly 10 ⇌	a			00 26	09 08		09 48	10 03			10 50	11 06		11 41	12 03		12 41	13 03		13 41	14 03
Manchester Airport 85 ✈	a				09 25			10 24				11 24			12 21			13 19			14 21

A From Chester
B not 11 December
C not 11 December. From Chester
D from 8 January until 12 February. From Manchester Airport

Table 90

Sundays
until 12 February

Liverpool and St Helens - Newton-le-Willows, Wigan, Preston and Manchester

Network Diagram - see first Page of Table 88

		NT	AW	NT	NT	AW	NT	NT	AW	NT	NT	AW	NT	NT	AW	NT	NT	AW	NT	NT	AW	NT	NT
			A 🛒			A 🛒			A			◇ B 🛒			◇ A			A			A		
Liverpool Lime Street [10] 89,91	d	13 31		14 01	14 31		15 01	15 31		16 01	16 31		17 01	17 31		18 01	18 31		19 01	19 31		20 01	20 31
Edge Hill 89,91	d																						
Wavertree Technology Park	d	13 37		14 07	14 37		15 07	15 37		16 07	16 37		17 07	17 37		18 07	18 37		19 07	19 37		20 07	20 37
Broad Green	d	13 40		14 10	14 40		15 10	15 40		16 10	16 40		17 10	17 40		18 10	18 40		19 10	19 40		20 10	20 40
Roby	d	13 43		14 13	14 43		15 13	15 43		16 13	16 43		17 13	17 43		18 13	18 43		19 13	19 43		20 13	20 43
Huyton	d	13 46		14 16	14 46		15 16	15 46		16 16	16 46		17 16	17 46		18 16	18 46		19 16	19 46		20 16	20 46
Prescot	d	13 50			14 50			15 50			16 50			17 50			18 50			19 50			20 50
Eccleston Park	d																						
Thatto Heath	d	13 54			14 54			15 54			16 54			17 54			18 54			19 54			20 54
St Helens Central	a	13 57			14 57			15 57			16 57			17 57			18 57			19 57			20 57
	d	13 58			14 58			15 58			16 58			17 58			18 58			19 58			20 58
Garswood	d	14 05			15 05			16 05			17 05			18 05			19 05			20 05			21 05
Bryn	d																						
Whiston	d			14 19			15 19			16 19			17 19			18 19			19 19			20 19	
Rainhill	d			14 22			15 22			16 22			17 22			18 22			19 22			20 22	
Lea Green	d			14 26			15 26			16 26			17 26			18 26			19 26			20 26	
St Helens Junction	d			14 29			15 29			16 29			17 29			18 29			19 29			20 29	
Warrington Bank Quay	d		14 03			15 03			16 03			17 03			18 03			19 03			20 03		
Earlestown [8]	d		14 10	14 33		15 10	15 33		16 10	16 33		17 10	17 33		18 10	18 33		19 10	19 33		20 10	20 33	
Warrington Bank Quay	a																						
Newton-le-Willows	d		14 13	14 36		15 13	15 36		16 13	16 36		17 13	17 36		18 13	18 36		19 13	19 36		20 13	20 36	
Wigan North Western 65	a	14 13			15 13			16 13			17 13			18 13			19 13			20 13			21 13
	d	14 14			15 14			16 14			17 14			18 14			19 14			20 14			21 14
Euxton Balshaw Lane	d	14 24			15 24			16 24			17 24			18 24			19 24			20 24			21 24
Leyland 82	a	14 29			15 29			16 29			17 29			18 29			19 29			20 29			21 29
Preston [8] 65,82	a	14 37			15 37			16 37			17 37			18 37			19 37			20 37			21 37
Blackpool North 97	a	15 07			16 07			17 07			18 07			19 07			20 07			21 07			22 07
Patricroft	d																						
Eccles	d			14 49			15 49			16 49			17 49			18 49			19 49			20 49	
Manchester Victoria 🚊	a																						
Manchester Oxford Road	a		14 32	14 59		15 32	15 59		16 32	16 59		17 32	17 59		18 32	18 59		19 32	19 59		20 32	20 59	
Manchester Piccadilly [10] 🚊	a		14 41	15 02		15 41	16 02		16 41	17 02		17 41	18 02		18 41	19 02		19 41	20 02		20 41	21 02	
Manchester Airport 85 ✈	a			15 20			16 21			17 21			18 21			19 21			20 26			21 20	

		AW	NT	NT	NT	NT	NT	NT	NT
		A				🚌			🚌
Liverpool Lime Street [10] 89,91	d		21 01	21 31	22 01	22 01	22 31	23 01	23 01
Edge Hill 89,91	d								
Wavertree Technology Park	d		21 07	21 37		22 16	22 37		23 16
Broad Green	d		21 10	21 40		22 26	22 40		23 26
Roby	d		21 13	21 43		22 33	22 43		23 33
Huyton	d		21 16	21 46		22 37	22 46		23 37
Prescot	d			21 50			22 50		
Eccleston Park	d								
Thatto Heath	d			21 54			22 54		
St Helens Central	a			21 57			22 57		
	d			21 58			22 58		
Garswood	d			22 05			23 05		
Bryn	d								
Whiston	d		21 19			22 47			23 47
Rainhill	d		21 22			22 57			23 57
Lea Green	d		21 26			23 05			00 05
St Helens Junction	d		21 29			23 12			00 12
Warrington Bank Quay	d	21 03							
Earlestown [8]	d	21 10	21 33			23 24			00 24
Warrington Bank Quay	a								
Newton-le-Willows	d	21 13	21 36			23 32			00 32
Wigan North Western 65	a			22 13			23 13		
	d			22 14			23 14		
Euxton Balshaw Lane	d			22 24					
Leyland 82	a			22 29			23 27		
Preston [8] 65,82	a			22 37			23 35		
Blackpool North 97	a			23 07			00 05		
Patricroft	d								
Eccles	d		21 49			23 57			00 57
Manchester Victoria 🚊	a								
Manchester Oxford Road	a	21 32	21 59		22 47	00 12		23 47	01 12
Manchester Piccadilly [10] 🚊	a	21 41	22 02		22 50			23 50	
Manchester Airport 85 ✈	a		22 21		23 15			00 07	

A From Chester

B From Holyhead

Table 90

Sundays

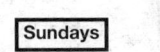

19 February to 25 March

Liverpool and St Helens - Newton-le-Willows, Wigan, Preston and Manchester

Network Diagram - see first Page of Table 88

		NT	NT	AW	NT	NT	NT	NT	AW	NT		NT		NT	AW	NT	NT	NT	AW	NT		NT	NT	AW	NT
				A					A						A				A					A	
		🚌	🚌		🚌	🚌	🚌	🚌	🚌	🚌				🚌	🚌	🚌		🚌	🚌	🚌			🚌	🚌	🚌
Liverpool Lime Street 10 89,91	d	22p42	23p02		23p16	07 14	08 01	08 14		09 01		09 04		09 14		10 01	10 06	10 14		11 01		11 06	11 14		12 01
Edge Hill 89,91	d	22p49	23p09		23p22																				
Wavertree Technology Park	d	22p59	23p19		23p32	07 30	08 16	08 30		09 16				09 29		10 16		10 29		11 16			11 29		12 16
Broad Green	d	23p09	23p29		23p42	07 39	08 26	08 39		09 26				09 39		10 26		10 39		11 26			11 39		12 26
Roby	d	23p16	23p36		23p49	07 46	08 33	08 46		09 33				09 46		10 33		10 46		11 33			11 46		12 33
Huyton	d	23p20	23p40		23p53	07 50	08 37	08 50		09 37				09 50		10 37		10 50		11 37			11 50		12 37
Prescot	d	23p30	23p50			08 00		09 00						10 00				11 00					12 00		
Eccleston Park	d	23p36	23p56																						
Thatto Heath	d	23p46	00 06			08 10		09 10						10 10				11 10					12 10		
St Helens Central	a	23p56	00 16			08 20		09 20						10 20				11 20					12 20		
	d	23p56	00 16			08 20		09 20						10 20				11 20					12 20		
Garswood	d	00 16	00 36			08 40		09 40						10 40				11 40					12 40		
Bryn	d	00 23	00 43																						
Whiston	d				00 03		08 47			09 47						10 47				11 47					12 47
Rainhill	d				00 13		08 57			09 57						10 57				11 57					12 57
Lea Green	d				00 20		09 05			10 05						11 05				12 05					13 05
St Helens Junction	d				00 25		09 12			10 12						11 12				12 12					13 12
Warrington Bank Quay	d			23p50					09 41						10 42				11 40					12 36	
Earlestown 8	d			23p58	00 37		09 24		10 06	10 24					11 07	11 24			12 05	12 24				13 01	13 24
Warrington Bank Quay	a																								
Newton-le-Willows	d			00 02	00 45		09 32		10 16	10 32					11 17	11 32			12 15	12 32				13 11	13 32
Wigan North Western 65	a	00 36	00 56			09 00		10 00						11 00				12 00					13 00		
	d																								
Euxton Balshaw Lane	d																								
Leyland 82	a																								
Preston 8 65,82	a																								
Blackpool North 97	a																								
Patricroft	d				01 15																				
Eccles	d				01 25		09 57			10 57						11 57				12 57					13 57
Manchester Victoria ⛴	a				01 44																				
Manchester Oxford Road	a						10 12		10 46	11 12		09 45			11 47	12 12	10 47		12 45	13 12		11 48		13 41	14 12
Manchester Piccadilly 10 ⛴	a			00 26					10 51			09 49			11 52		10 52		12 50			11 52		13 46	
Manchester Airport 85 ✈	a											10 05					11 09					12 11			

		NT	NT	AW	NT	NT		NT	AW	NT	NT	NT	AW	NT	NT	NT		AW	NT	NT	NT	AW	NT	NT	NT
				A					A				A					A				A			
			🚌	🚌	🚌			🚌	🚌	🚌		🚌	🚌	🚌		🚌		🚌	🚌		🚌	🚌	🚌		🚌
Liverpool Lime Street 10 89,91	d	12 06	12 14		13 01	13 06		13 14		14 01	14 06	14 14		15 01	15 06	15 14			16 01	16 06	16 14		17 01	17 06	17 14
Edge Hill 89,91	d																								
Wavertree Technology Park	d		12 29		13 16			13 29		14 16		14 29		15 16		15 29			16 16		16 29		17 16		17 29
Broad Green	d		12 39		13 26			13 39		14 26		14 39		15 26		15 39			16 26		16 39		17 26		17 39
Roby	d		12 46		13 33			13 46		14 33		14 46		15 33		15 46			16 33		16 46		17 33		17 46
Huyton	d		12 50		13 37			13 50		14 37		14 50		15 37		15 50			16 37		16 50		17 37		17 50
Prescot	d		13 00					14 00				15 00				16 00					17 00				18 00
Eccleston Park	d																								
Thatto Heath	d		13 10					14 10				15 10				16 10					17 10				18 10
St Helens Central	a		13 20					14 20				15 20				16 20					17 20				18 20
	d		13 20					14 20				15 20				16 20					17 20				18 20
Garswood	d		13 40					14 40				15 40				16 40					17 40				18 40
Bryn	d																								
Whiston	d				13 47					14 47				15 47					16 47				17 47		
Rainhill	d				13 57					14 57				15 57					16 57				17 57		
Lea Green	d				14 05					15 05				16 05					17 05				18 05		
St Helens Junction	d				14 12					15 12				16 12					17 12				18 12		
Warrington Bank Quay	d			13 36					14 36				15 36					16 36				17 36			
Earlestown 8	d			14 01	14 24				15 01	15 24			16 01	16 24				17 01	17 24			18 01	18 24		
Warrington Bank Quay	a																								
Newton-le-Willows	d			14 11	14 32				15 11	15 32			16 11	16 32				17 11	17 32			18 11	18 32		
Wigan North Western 65	a		14 00					15 00				16 00				17 00					18 00				19 00
	d																								
Euxton Balshaw Lane	d																								
Leyland 82	a																								
Preston 8 65,82	a																								
Blackpool North 97	a																								
Patricroft	d																								
Eccles	d				14 57					15 57				16 57					17 57				18 57		
Manchester Victoria ⛴	a																								
Manchester Oxford Road	a	12 47		14 41	15 12	13 47			15 41	16 12	14 48		16 41	17 12	15 48			17 41	18 12	16 48		18 41	19 12	17 48	
Manchester Piccadilly 10 ⛴	a	12 54		14 46		13 51			15 46		14 52		16 46		15 52			17 46		16 52		18 46		17 52	
Manchester Airport 85 ✈	a	13 11				14 07					15 08				16 08					17 08				18 08	

A From Chester

Table 90

Sundays

19 February to 25 March

Liverpool and St Helens - Newton-le-Willows, Wigan, Preston and Manchester

Network Diagram - see first Page of Table 88

		AW		NT	NT	NT	AW	NT	NT	NT	AW	NT		NT	NT	AW	NT	NT	NT	NT	AW	NT		NT	NT
		A					A				A					A					A				
		🚌		🚌		🚌	🚌	🚌		🚌	🚌	🚌			🚌	🚌	🚌		🚌		🚌	🚌		🚌	
Liverpool Lime Street 10 89,91	d			18 01	18 06	18 14		19 01	19 06	19 14		20 01		20 06	20 14		21 01	21 06	21 14	22 01		22 01		22 31	23 01
Edge Hill 89,91	d																								
Wavertree Technology Park	d			18 16		18 29		19 16		19 29		20 16			20 29		21 16		21 29			22 16		22 46	
Broad Green	d			18 26		18 39		19 26		19 39		20 26			20 39		21 26		21 39			22 26		22 56	
Roby	d			18 33		18 46		19 33		19 46		20 33			20 46		21 33		21 46			22 33		23 03	
Huyton	d			18 37		18 50		19 37		19 50		20 37			20 50		21 37		21 50			22 37		23 07	
Prescot	d					19 00				20 00					21 00				22 00					23 17	
Eccleston Park	d																								
Thatto Heath	d					19 10				20 10					21 10				22 10					23 27	
St Helens Central	a					19 20				20 20					21 20				22 20					23 37	
	d					19 20				20 20					21 20				22 20					23 37	
Garswood	d					19 40				20 40					21 40				22 40					23 57	
Bryn	d																								
Whiston	d			18 47				19 47				20 47					21 47					22 47			
Rainhill	d			18 57				19 57				20 57					21 57					22 57			
Lea Green	d			19 05				20 05				21 05					22 05					23 05			
St Helens Junction	d			19 12				20 12				21 12					22 12					23 12			
Warrington Bank Quay	d	18 36					19 36				20 36					21 36					22 36				
Earlestown 8	d	19 01		19 24			20 01	20 24			21 01	21 24				22 01	22 24				23 01	23 24			
Warrington Bank Quay	a																								
Newton-le-Willows	d	19 11		19 32			20 11	20 32			21 11	21 32				22 11	22 32				23 11	23 32			
Wigan North Western 65	a					20 00				21 00					22 00				23 00					00 17	
	d																								
Euxton Balshaw Lane	d																								
Leyland 82	a																								
Preston 8 65,82	a																								
Blackpool North 97	a																								
Patricroft	d																								
Eccles	d			19 57				20 57				21 57					22 57					23 57			
Manchester Victoria ⇌	a																								
Manchester Oxford Road	a	19 41		20 12	18 48		20 41	21 12	19 48		21 41	22 12		20 48		22 41	23 12	21 48		22 47	23 41	00 12			23 47
Manchester Piccadilly 10 ⇌	a	19 46			18 52		20 46		19 52		21 46			20 52		22 46		21 52		22 50	23 46				23 50
Manchester Airport 85 ✈	a				19 08				20 08					21 08				22 08		23 15					00 07

		AW	NT
		A	
		🚌	🚌
Liverpool Lime Street 10 89,91	d		23 01
Edge Hill 89,91	d		
Wavertree Technology Park	d		23 16
Broad Green	d		23 26
Roby	d		23 33
Huyton	d		23 37
Prescot	d		
Eccleston Park	d		
Thatto Heath	d		
St Helens Central	a		
	d		
Garswood	d		
Bryn	d		
Whiston	d		23 47
Rainhill	d		23 57
Lea Green	d		00 05
St Helens Junction	d		00 12
Warrington Bank Quay	d	23 09	
Earlestown 8	d	23 34	00 24
Warrington Bank Quay	a		
Newton-le-Willows	d	23 44	00 32
Wigan North Western 65	a		
	d		
Euxton Balshaw Lane	d		
Leyland 82	a		
Preston 8 65,82	a		
Blackpool North 97	a		
Patricroft	d		
Eccles	d		00 57
Manchester Victoria ⇌	a		
Manchester Oxford Road	a	00 14	01 12
Manchester Piccadilly 10 ⇌	a	00 19	
Manchester Airport 85 ✈	a		

A From Chester

Liverpool and St Helens - Newton-le-Willows, Wigan, Preston and Manchester

Network Diagram - see first Page of Table 88

		NT	NT	NT	AW	NT	NT	NT	NT	AW		NT	NT	AW	VT	NT	NT	NT	NT	AW		NT	NT	NT	AW
														◇	◇1										
					A					A				A	B					A					A
		🚌	🚌			🚌			🚌						🍴	🚌			🚌	⊥				🚌	⊥
Liverpool Lime Street 10 89,91	d			23p16			08 07	08 31				09 01	09 31				10 01	10 31				11 01	11 31		
Edge Hill 89,91	d			23p20																					
Wavertree Technology Park	d			23p22			08 13	08 37				09 07	09 37				10 07	10 37				11 07	11 37		
Broad Green	d			23p26			08 16	08 40				09 10	09 40				10 10	10 40				11 10	11 40		
Roby	d			23p30			08 19	08 43				09 13	09 43				10 13	10 43				11 13	11 43		
Huyton	d	23p08	23p28	23p32		07 52	08 22	08 46	08 52			09 16	09 46			09 52	10 16	10 46	10 52			11 16	11 46	11 52	
Prescot	d	23p18	23p38			08 02			09 02							10 02			11 02					12 02	
Eccleston Park	d	23p24	23p44																						
Thatto Heath	d	23p34	23p54			08 12			09 12							10 12			11 12					12 12	
St Helens Central	a	23p44	00 04			08 22			09 22							10 22			11 22					12 22	
	d	23p44	00 04			08 22			09 22							10 22			11 22					12 22	
Garswood	d	00 04	00 24			08 42			09 42							10 42			11 42					12 42	
Bryn	d	00 11	00 31																						
Whiston	d			23p36			08 25					09 19					10 19					11 19			
Rainhill	d			23p39			08 28					09 22					10 22					11 22			
Lea Green	d			23p42			08 32					09 26					10 26					11 26			
St Helens Junction	d			23p45			08 35					09 29					10 29					11 29			
Warrington Bank Quay	d				23p50					09 10				10 12						11 03					12 03
Earlestown 8	d			23p50	23p58		08 39			09 16		09 33		10 19			10 33			11 10		11 33			12 10
Warrington Bank Quay	a														10d37										
Newton-le-Willows	d			23p53	00 02		08 42			09 19		09 36		10 22			10 36			11 13		11 36			12 13
Wigan North Western 65	a	00 24	00 44			09 02		09 08	10 02				10 08		10 48	11 02		11 08	12 02				12 08	13 02	
	d							09 14					10 14		10 48			11 14					12 14		
Euxton Balshaw Lane	d							09 24					10 26					11 24					12 24		
Leyland 82	a							09 29					10 31					11 29					12 29		
Preston 8 65,82	a							09 37					10 39		11 02			11 37					12 37		
Blackpool North 97	a							10 07					11 09					12 07					13 07		
Patricroft	d			00 05																					
Eccles	d			00 08			08 55					09 49					10 49					11 49			
Manchester Victoria	a			00 21																					
Manchester Oxford Road	a						09 05			09 39		09 59		10 41			10 59			11 32		11 59			12 32
Manchester Piccadilly 10	a				00 26		09 08			09 48		10 03		10 50			11 06			11 41		12 03			12 41
Manchester Airport 85 ✈	a						09 25					10 24					11 24					12 21			

		NT	NT	NT	AW	NT		NT	NT	AW	NT	NT	NT	AW	NT	NT		NT	AW	NT	NT	NT	AW	NT	NT
																							◇		
					A					A				A					A				C		
				🚌	⊥				🚌	⊥			🚌	⊥				🚌				🚌	⊥		
Liverpool Lime Street 10 89,91	d	12 01	12 31			13 01		13 31			14 01	14 31			15 01	15 31				16 01	16 31			17 01	17 31
Edge Hill 89,91	d																								
Wavertree Technology Park	d	12 07	12 37			13 07		13 37			14 07	14 37			15 07	15 37				16 07	16 37			17 07	17 37
Broad Green	d	12 10	12 40			13 10		13 40			14 10	14 40			15 10	15 40				16 10	16 40			17 10	17 40
Roby	d	12 13	12 43			13 13		13 43			14 13	14 43			15 13	15 43				16 13	16 43			17 13	17 43
Huyton	d	12 16	12 46	12 52		13 16		13 46	13 52		14 16	14 46	14 52		15 16	15 46		15 52		16 16	16 46	16 52		17 16	17 46
Prescot	d			13 02					14 02				15 02					16 02				17 02			
Eccleston Park	d																								
Thatto Heath	d			13 12					14 12				15 12					16 12				17 12			
St Helens Central	a			13 22					14 22				15 22					16 22				17 22			
	d			13 22					14 22				15 22					16 22				17 22			
Garswood	d			13 42					14 42				15 42					16 42				17 42			
Bryn	d																								
Whiston	d	12 19				13 19					14 19				15 19					16 19				17 19	
Rainhill	d	12 22				13 22					14 22				15 22					16 22				17 22	
Lea Green	d	12 26				13 26					14 26				15 26					16 26				17 26	
St Helens Junction	d	12 29				13 29					14 29				15 29					16 29				17 29	
Warrington Bank Quay	d				13 03					14 03				15 03					16 03				17 03		
Earlestown 8	d	12 33			13 10	13 33				14 10	14 33			15 10	15 33				16 10	16 33			17 10	17 33	
Warrington Bank Quay	a																								
Newton-le-Willows	d	12 36			13 13	13 36				14 13	14 36			15 13	15 36				16 13	16 36			17 13	17 36	
Wigan North Western 65	a		13 08	14 02				14 08	15 02			15 08	16 02			16 08		17 02			17 08	18 02			18 08
	d		13 14					14 14				15 14				16 14					17 14				18 14
Euxton Balshaw Lane	d		13 24					14 24				15 24				16 24					17 24				18 24
Leyland 82	a		13 29					14 29				15 29				16 29					17 29				18 29
Preston 8 65,82	a		13 37					14 37				15 37				16 37					17 37				18 37
Blackpool North 97	a		14 07					15 07				16 07				17 07					18 07				19 07
Patricroft	d																								
Eccles	d	12 49				13 49					14 49				15 49					16 49				17 49	
Manchester Victoria	a																								
Manchester Oxford Road	a	12 59			13 32	13 57				14 32	14 59			15 32	15 59				16 32	16 59			17 32	17 59	
Manchester Piccadilly 10	a	13 03			13 41	14 03				14 41	15 02			15 41	16 02				16 41	17 02			17 41	18 02	
Manchester Airport 85 ✈	a	13 19				14 21					15 20				16 21					17 21				18 21	

A From Chester

B From Crewe

C From Holyhead

Table 90

Sundays
from 1 April

Liverpool and St Helens - Newton-le-Willows, Wigan, Preston and Manchester

Network Diagram - see first Page of Table 88

		NT		NT	NT	NT	AW	NT	NT	NT	AW	NT		NT	NT	AW	NT	NT	NT	NT	NT	NT		NT	NT
							A				A					A									
		🚌				🚌				🚌					🚌				🚌		🚌			🚌	
Liverpool Lime Street 10 89,91	d			18 01	18 31			19 01	19 31			20 01		20 31			21 01	21 31		22 01	22 01	22 31			23 01
Edge Hill 89,91	d																								
Wavertree Technology Park	d			18 07	18 37			19 07	19 37			20 07		20 37			21 07	21 37			22 16	22 37			
Broad Green	d			18 10	18 40			19 10	19 40			20 10		20 40			21 10	21 40			22 26	22 40			
Roby	d			18 13	18 43			19 13	19 43			20 13		20 43			21 13	21 43			22 33	22 43			
Huyton	d	17 52		18 16	18 46	18 52		19 16	19 46	19 52		20 16		20 46	20 52		21 16	21 46	21 52		22 37	22 46		22 52	
Prescot	d	18 02				19 02				20 02					21 02				22 02					23 02	
Eccleston Park	d																								
Thatto Heath	d	18 12				19 12				20 12					21 12				22 12					23 12	
St Helens Central	a	18 22				19 22				20 22					21 22				22 22					23 22	
	d	18 22				19 22				20 22					21 22				22 22					23 22	
Garswood	d	18 42				19 42				20 42					21 42				22 42					23 42	
Bryn	d																								
Whiston	d			18 19				19 19				20 19					21 19				22 47				
Rainhill	d			18 22				19 22				20 22					21 22				22 57				
Lea Green	d			18 26				19 26				20 26					21 26				23 05				
St Helens Junction	d			18 29				19 29				20 29					21 29				23 12				
Warrington Bank Quay	d						19 03				20 03					21 03									
Earlestown 8	d			18 33			19 10	19 33			20 10	20 33				21 10	21 33				23 24				
Warrington Bank Quay	a																								
Newton-le-Willows	d			18 36			19 13	19 36			20 13	20 36				21 13	21 36				23 32				
Wigan North Western 65	a	19 02			19 08	20 02			20 08	21 02				21 08	22 02			22 08	23 02			23 08		00 02	
	d				19 14				20 14					21 14				22 14				23 14			
Euxton Balshaw Lane	d				19 24				20 24					21 24				22 24							
Leyland 82	a				19 29				20 29					21 29				22 29				23 27			
Preston 8 65,82	a				19 37				20 37					21 37				22 37				23 35			
Blackpool North 97	a				20 07				21 07					22 07				23 07				00 05			
Patricroft	d																								
Eccles	d			18 49				19 49				20 49					21 49				23 57				
Manchester Victoria 🚊	a																								
Manchester Oxford Road	a			18 59			19 32	19 59			20 32	20 59				21 32	21 59			22 47	00 12				23 47
Manchester Piccadilly 10 🚊	a			19 02			19 41	20 02			20 41	21 02				21 41	22 02			22 50					23 50
Manchester Airport 85 ✈	a			19 21				20 26				21 20					22 21			23 15					00 07

		NT
		🚌
Liverpool Lime Street 10 89,91	d	23 01
Edge Hill 89,91	d	
Wavertree Technology Park	d	23 16
Broad Green	d	23 26
Roby	d	23 33
Huyton	d	23 37
Prescot	d	
Eccleston Park	d	
Thatto Heath	d	
St Helens Central	a	
	d	
Garswood	d	
Bryn	d	
Whiston	d	23 47
Rainhill	d	23 57
Lea Green	d	00 05
St Helens Junction	d	00 12
Warrington Bank Quay	d	
Earlestown 8	d	00 24
Warrington Bank Quay	a	
Newton-le-Willows	d	00 32
Wigan North Western 65	a	
	d	
Euxton Balshaw Lane	d	
Leyland 82	a	
Preston 8 65,82	a	
Blackpool North 97	a	
Patricroft	d	
Eccles	d	00 57
Manchester Victoria 🚊	a	
Manchester Oxford Road	a	01 12
Manchester Piccadilly 10 🚊	a	
Manchester Airport 85 ✈	a	

A From Chester

Manchester, Preston, Wigan and Newton-le-Willows - St Helens and Liverpool

Network Diagram - see first Page of Table 88

Miles	Miles	Miles	Miles		NT MO A	NT MO A	NT MO B	NT MO C	NT MO	AW MO D	NT MO E	AW MX	NT MX		NT MO		NT	NT	AW G	AW ◇ H	NT	NT		
—	—	—	0	**Manchester Airport** 85 d									04 34		04 38					05 33				
—	—	—	9¾	**Manchester Piccadilly** 10 d						23p25		23p50	04 49		04 53					05 50				
—	—	—	10¼	**Manchester Oxford Road** d	21p55				23p00	23p30		23p55								05 53				
0	—	—	—	**Manchester Victoria** d														05 39				06 09		
4	—	—	14½	Eccles d	22p10				23p15									05 46				06 16		
5	—	—	15½	Patricroft d														05 49				06 19		
—	—	—	—	Blackpool North 97 d			22p44	22p44																
—	0	0	—	**Preston** 8 65,82 d			23p09	23p09																
—	4	4	—	Leyland 82 d			23p15	23p15																
—	6¾	6¾	—	Euxton Balshaw Lane d			23p19	23p19																
—	15	15	—	**Wigan North Western** 65 a			23p29	23p29																
—	—	—	—	d		22p50	23p30	23p30			23p42										06 08			
15½	—	22	26	**Newton-le-Willows** d	22p35				23p40	00 01		00 25						06 01		06 12		06 31		
—	—	—	—	Warrington Bank Quay d															06 06					
17	—	23½	27½	Earlestown 8 d	22p43				23p48	00 10		00 35						06 04	06a12	06 15		06 34		
—	—	—	—	Warrington Bank Quay a						00 35		01 00								06 25				
19¾	—	26¼	30¼	**St Helens Junction** d	22p55				00 01									06 09				06 39		
21	—	27½	31½	Lea Green d	23p02				00 07									06 12				06 42		
22¾	—	29¼	33¼	Rainhill d	23p10				00 15									06 16				06 46		
24¼	—	30¾	34¾	Whiston d	23p20				00 25									06 19				06 49		
—	18¾	—	—	Bryn d																	06 15			
—	20	—	—	Garswood d		23p10		23p40			00 02										06 19			
—	23¾	—	—	**St Helens Central** a		23p30		23p46			00 22										06 25			
—	—	—	—	d		23p30		23p47			00 22						05 56				06 26			
—	25¼	—	—	Thatto Heath d		23p40		23p50			00 32						05 59				06 29			
—	26¼	—	—	Eccleston Park d													06 02				06 32			
—	27¼	—	—	Prescot d		23p51		23p54			00 43						06 04				06 34			
26¼	29½	32¾	36¾	Huyton d	23p30	00 01	23p59	23p59	00 35		00 53						06 08	06 23			06 38	06 53		
26¾	30	33¼	37¼	Roby d	23p34	00 05	00 01	00 01	00 39		00 57						06 10	06 25			06 40	06 55		
28¼	31½	34¾	38¾	Broad Green d	23p41	00 12	00 04	00 04	00 46		01 04						06 13	06 28			06 43	06 58		
29¼	32½	35¾	39¾	Wavertree Technology Park d	23p51	00 22	00 07	00 07	00 56		01 14						06 16	06 31			06 46	07 01		
30	33¼	36½	40½	Edge Hill 89,91 d													06 19	06 34			06 49	07 04		
31¾	35	38¼	42¼	**Liverpool Lime Street** 10 89,91 a	00 06	00 37	00 18	00 18	01 11		01 29		05 33		05 36		06 28	06 43			06 58	07 13		

	NT	NT J	NT	AW ◇ K	AW ◇ H	NT	NT	NT	NT		NT	AW G	NT	AW ◇ H	NT	AW ◇ L	NT	NT	NT J		NT	NT M	AW ◇ H	NT
Manchester Airport 85 d						06 41																		08 41
Manchester Piccadilly 10 d					06 50	06 58								07 50									08 50	09 01
Manchester Oxford Road d					06 53	07 01								07 53									08 53	09 04
Manchester Victoria d								07 09					07 39				08 09					08 39		
Eccles d								07 16					07 46				08 16					08 46		
Patricroft d								07 19					07 49				08 19					08 49		
Blackpool North 97 d											07 02													
Preston 8 65,82 d											07 30													
Leyland 82 d											07 35													
Euxton Balshaw Lane d											07 40													
Wigan North Western 65 a											07 50													
d	06 38		06 47				07 08		07 38		07 50				07 58			08 28						
Newton-le-Willows d			07 00		07 12	07 19		07 31					08 01	08 12			08 31					09 01	09 12	09 22
Warrington Bank Quay d				07 07								07 39				08 08								
Earlestown 8 d		06 50	07 03	07a14	07 15			07 34				07a46	08 04	08 15		08a15	08 34		08 50			09 04	09 15	
Warrington Bank Quay a		07 01			07 22									08 23					09 01				09 25	
St Helens Junction d			07 09			07 24		07 39					08 09				08 39					09 09		09 27
Lea Green d			07 12					07 42					08 12				08 42					09 12		
Rainhill d			07 16			07 29		07 46					08 16				08 46					09 16		
Whiston d			07 19					07 49					08 19				08 49					09 19		
Bryn d	06 45						07 15		07 45						08 05			08 35						
Garswood d	06 49						07 19		07 49		07 59				08 09			08 39						
St Helens Central a	06 55						07 25		07 55		08 06				08 15			08 45						
d	06 56						07 26		07 56		08 06				08 16			08 46			08 56			
Thatto Heath d	06 59						07 29		07 59						08 19			08 49			08 59			
Eccleston Park d	07 02						07 32		08 02						08 22			08 52			09 02			
Prescot d	07 04						07 34		08 04		08 12				08 24			08 54			09 04			
Huyton d	07 08		07 23			07 34	07 38	07 53	08 08		08 16		08 23		08 28		08 53	08 58			09 08	09 23		
Roby d	07 10		07 25				07 40	07 55	08 10				08 25		08 30		08 55	09 00			09 10	09 25		
Broad Green d	07 13		07 28				07 43	07 58	08 13		08 20		08 28		08 33		08 58	09 03			09 13	09 28		
Wavertree Technology Park d	07 16		07 31			07 39	07 46	08 01	08 16		08 24		08 31		08 36		09 01	09 06			09 16	09 31		09 38
Edge Hill 89,91 d	07 19		07 34				07 49	08 04	08 19				08 34		08 39		09 04	09 09			09 19	09 34		
Liverpool Lime Street 10 89,91 a	07 28		07 43			07 49	07 58	08 13	08 28		08 35		08 43		08 50		09 13	09 18			09 28	09 43		09 48

A from 20 February until 26 March
B from 2 April
C until 13 February
D from 20 February until 26 March. To Chester
E from 20 February

G From Chester to Manchester Piccadilly
H To Llandudno
J From Liverpool Lime Street
K From Llandudno Junction to Manchester Piccadilly

L From Llandudno to Manchester Piccadilly
M From Stalybridge

Manchester, Preston, Wigan and Newton-le-Willows - St Helens and Liverpool

Network Diagram - see first Page of Table 88

	NT	NT	AW	NT	NT		NT	NT	AW	NT	NT	NT	AW	NT	NT			NT	NT	AW	NT	NT	NT	AW
		A	◇ B				C	D	◇ E			A	◇ B					C	D	◇ E			A	◇ B
Manchester Airport 85 d										09 41											10 41			
Manchester Piccadilly 10 d									09 50	10 01										10 50	11 01			
Manchester Oxford Road d									09 53	10 04										10 53	11 04			
Manchester Victoria d								09 39											10 39					
Eccles d								09 46											10 46					
Patricroft d								09 49											10 49					
Blackpool North 97 d												09 37											10 37	
Preston 8 65,82 d		09 04										10 04											11 04	
Leyland 82 d		09 09										10 09											11 09	
Euxton Balshaw Lane d		09 14										10 14											11 14	
Wigan North Western 65 a		09 24										10 24											11 24	
d	09 08	09 24			09 38						10 08	10 24			10 38							11 08	11 24	
Newton-le-Willows d								10 01	10 12	10 22									11 01	11 12	11 22			
Warrington Bank Quay d			09 19	09 22									10 19	10 22										11 19
Earlestown 8 d			09a26	09 34			09 50	10 04	10 15				10a26	10 34				10 50	11 04	11 15				11a26
Warrington Bank Quay a							10 01		10 25									11 02		11 25				
St Helens Junction d				09 39				10 09		10 27				10 39					11 09		11 27			
Lea Green d				09 42				10 12						10 42					11 12					
Rainhill d				09 46				10 16						10 46					11 16					
Whiston d				09 49				10 19						10 49					11 19					
Bryn d	09 15				09 45						10 15				10 45							11 15		
Garswood d	09 19				09 49						10 19				10 49							11 19		
St Helens Central a	09 25	09 39			09 55						10 25	10 39			10 55							11 25	11 39	
d	09 26	09 39			09 56						10 26	10 39			10 56							11 26	11 39	
Thatto Heath d	09 29				09 59						10 29				10 59							11 29		
Eccleston Park d	09 32				10 02						10 32				11 02							11 32		
Prescot d	09 34				10 04						10 34				11 04							11 34		
Huyton d	09 38	09 48		09 53	10 08			10 23			10 38	10 48		10 53	11 08				11 23			11 38	11 48	
Roby d	09 40			09 55	10 10			10 25			10 40			10 55	11 10				11 25			11 40		
Broad Green d	09 43			09 58	10 13			10 28			10 43			10 58	11 13				11 28			11 43		
Wavertree Technology Park d	09 46			10 01	10 16			10 31		10 38	10 46			11 01	11 16				11 31		11 38	11 46		
Edge Hill 89,91 d	09 49			10 04	10 19			10 34			10 49			11 04	11 19				11 34			11 49		
Liverpool Lime Street 10 89,91 a	09 58	10 02		10 13	10 28			10 43		10 48	10 58	11 02		11 13	11 28				11 43		11 48	11 58	12 02	

	NT		NT	NT	NT	AW	NT	NT	NT	AW	NT		NT	NT	NT	AW	NT	NT	NT	AW	NT		NT	NT
				C	D	◇ E			A	◇ B				C	D	◇ E			A	◇ B				C
Manchester Airport 85 d							11 41										12 41							
Manchester Piccadilly 10 d						11 50	12 01									12 50	13 01							
Manchester Oxford Road d						11 53	12 04									12 53	13 04							
Manchester Victoria d					11 39										12 39									
Eccles d					11 46										12 46									
Patricroft d					11 49										12 49									
Blackpool North 97 d									11 37										12 37					
Preston 8 65,82 d									12 04										13 04					
Leyland 82 d									12 09										13 09					
Euxton Balshaw Lane d									12 14										13 14					
Wigan North Western 65 a									12 24										13 24					
d			11 38					12 08	12 24				12 38					13 08	13 24				13 38	
Newton-le-Willows d					12 01	12 12	12 22								13 01	13 12	13 22							
Warrington Bank Quay d	11 22									12 19	12 22									13 19	13 22			
Earlestown 8 d	11 34			11 50	12 04	12 15				12a26	12 34			12 50	13 04	13 15				13a26	13 34			13 50
Warrington Bank Quay a				12 01		12 25								13 01		13 25								14 01
St Helens Junction d	11 39				12 09		12 27				12 39				13 09		13 27				13 39			
Lea Green d	11 42				12 12						12 42				13 12						13 42			
Rainhill d	11 46				12 16						12 46				13 16						13 46			
Whiston d	11 49				12 19						12 49				13 19						13 49			
Bryn d			11 45					12 15					12 45					13 15					13 45	
Garswood d			11 49					12 19					12 49					13 19					13 49	
St Helens Central a			11 55					12 25	12 39				12 55					13 25	13 39				13 55	
d			11 56					12 26	12 39				12 56					13 26	13 39				13 56	
Thatto Heath d			11 59					12 29					12 59					13 29					13 59	
Eccleston Park d			12 02					12 32					13 02					13 32					14 02	
Prescot d			12 04					12 34					13 04					13 34					14 04	
Huyton d	11 53		12 08		12 23			12 38	12 48		12 53		13 08		13 23			13 38	13 48		13 53		14 08	
Roby d	11 55		12 10		12 25			12 40			12 55		13 10		13 25			13 40			13 55		14 10	
Broad Green d	11 58		12 13		12 28			12 43			12 58		13 13		13 28			13 43			13 58		14 13	
Wavertree Technology Park d	12 01		12 16		12 31		12 38	12 46			13 01		13 16		13 31		13 38	13 46			14 01		14 16	
Edge Hill 89,91 d	12 04		12 19		12 34			12 49			13 04		13 19		13 34			13 49			14 04		14 19	
Liverpool Lime Street 10 89,91 a	12 13		12 28		12 43		12 48	12 58	13 02		13 13		13 28		13 43		13 48	13 58	14 02		14 13		14 28	

A To Liverpool South Parkway
B From Llandudno to Manchester Piccadilly
C From Liverpool Lime Street
D From Stalybridge
E To Llandudno

Manchester, Preston, Wigan and Newton-le-Willows - St Helens and Liverpool

Network Diagram - see first Page of Table 88

		NT	AW	NT	NT	NT	AW	NT		NT	NT	NT	AW	NT	NT	NT	AW	NT		NT	NT	NT	AW	NT	NT
		A	◇ B			C	◇ D				E	A	◇ B			C	◇ D				E	A	◇ B		
Manchester Airport 85 ✈	d			13 41										14 41										15 41	
Manchester Piccadilly 10	d		13 50	14 01									14 50	15 01									15 50	16 01	
Manchester Oxford Road	d		13 53	14 04									14 53	15 04									15 53	16 04	
Manchester Victoria	d	13 39										14 39										15 39			
Eccles	d	13 46										14 46										15 46			
Patricroft	d	13 49										14 49										15 49			
Blackpool North 97	d					13 37										14 37									
Preston 8 65,82	d					14 04										15 04									
Leyland 82	d					14 09										15 09									
Euxton Balshaw Lane	d					14 14										15 14									
Wigan North Western 65	a					14 24										15 24									
	d				14 08	14 24				14 38					15 08	15 24				15 38					16 08
Newton-le-Willows	d	14 01	14 12	14 22								15 01	15 12	15 22								16 01	16 12	16 22	
Warrington Bank Quay	d						14 19	14 22									15 19	15 22							
Earlestown 8	d	14 04	14 15				14a26	14 34			14 50	15 04	15 15				15a26	15 34			15 50	16 04	16 15		
Warrington Bank Quay	a		14 25								15 01		15 25								16 01		16 26		
St Helens Junction	d	14 09		14 27				14 39				15 09		15 27				15 39				16 09		16 27	
Lea Green	d	14 12						14 42				15 12						15 42				16 12			
Rainhill	d	14 16						14 46				15 16						15 46				16 16			
Whiston	d	14 19						14 49				15 19						15 49				16 19			
Bryn	d				14 15					14 45					15 15					15 45					16 15
Garswood	d				14 19					14 49					15 19					15 49					16 19
St Helens Central	a				14 25	14 39				14 55					15 25	15 39				15 55					16 25
	d				14 26	14 39				14 56					15 26	15 39				15 56					16 26
Thatto Heath	d				14 29					14 59					15 29					15 59					16 29
Eccleston Park	d				14 32					15 02					15 32					16 02					16 32
Prescot	d				14 34					15 04					15 34					16 04					16 34
Huyton	d	14 23			14 38	14 48		14 53		15 08		15 23			15 38	15 48		15 53		16 08		16 23			16 38
Roby	d	14 25			14 40			14 55		15 10		15 25			15 40			15 55		16 10		16 25			16 40
Broad Green	d	14 28			14 43			14 58		15 13		15 28			15 43			15 58		16 13		16 28			16 43
Wavertree Technology Park	d	14 31		14 38	14 46			15 01		15 16		15 31		15 38	15 46			16 01		16 16		16 31		16 38	16 46
Edge Hill 89,91	d	14 34			14 49			15 04		15 19		15 34			15 49			16 04		16 19		16 34			16 49
Liverpool Lime Street 10 89,91	a	14 43		14 48	14 58	15 02		15 13		15 28		15 43		15 48	15 58	16 02		16 13		16 28		16 43		16 48	16 58

		NT	AW	NT		NT	AW	NT	AW	NT	NT	NT	NT	AW		NT	AW	NT	AW	NT	NT	NT	NT	NT	
			◇ D				◇ D	A	◇ B					F			◇ D		◇ B						
Manchester Airport 85 ✈	d									16 41											17 41				
Manchester Piccadilly 10	d								16 50	17 01				17 19					17 50		18 01				
Manchester Oxford Road	d								16 53	17 04				17 22					17 53		18 04				
Manchester Victoria	d							16 39					17 09					17 37							
Eccles	d							16 46					17 16					17 46			18 11				
Patricroft	d							16 49					17 19					17 49							
Blackpool North 97	d	15 37										16 35											17 37		
Preston 8 65,82	d	16 04										17 04											18 04		
Leyland 82	d	16 09										17 09											18 09		
Euxton Balshaw Lane	d	16 14										17 14											18 14		
Wigan North Western 65	a	16 24										17 24											18 24		
	d	16 24				16 38					17 08	17 24				17 38				18 08		18 21	18 24	18 35	
Newton-le-Willows	d							17 01	17 12	17 22			17 31	17 40				18 01	18 12		18 24	18 33			
Warrington Bank Quay	d		16 19	16 22			16 51										17 49								
Earlestown 8	d		16a26	16 34			16a59	17 04	17 15				17 34	17 44			17a57	18 04	18 15			18 36			
Warrington Bank Quay	a								17 25					17 52					18 23						
St Helens Junction	d			16 39				17 09		17 27			17 39					18 09			18 29	18 41			
Lea Green	d			16 42				17 12					17 42					18 12			18 32	18 44			
Rainhill	d			16 46				17 16					17 46					18 16			18 36	18 48			
Whiston	d			16 49				17 19					17 49					18 19				18 51			
Bryn	d					16 45					17 15					17 45				18 15				18 45	
Garswood	d					16 49					17 19					17 49				18 19				18 49	
St Helens Central	a	16 39				16 55					17 25	17 39				17 55				18 25			18 39	18 55	
	d	16 39				16 56					17 26	17 39				17 56				18 26			18 39	18 56	
Thatto Heath	d					16 59					17 29					17 59				18 29				18 59	
Eccleston Park	d					17 02					17 32					18 02				18 32				19 02	
Prescot	d					17 04					17 34					18 04				18 34				19 04	
Huyton	d	16 48		16 53		17 08		17 23			17 38	17 48	17 53			18 08		18 23		18 38	18 41	18 55	18 48	19 08	
Roby	d			16 55		17 10		17 25			17 40		17 55			18 10		18 25			18 43	18 57		19 10	
Broad Green	d			16 58		17 13		17 28			17 43		17 58			18 13		18 28			18 47	19 00		19 13	
Wavertree Technology Park	d			17 01		17 16		17 31		17 38	17 46		18 01			18 16		18 31		18 43	18 50	19 03		19 16	
Edge Hill 89,91	d			17 04		17 19		17 34			17 49		18 04			18 19		18 34		18 46		19 06		19 19	
Liverpool Lime Street 10 89,91	a	17 05		17 13		17 28		17 43		17 48	17 58	18 02	18 13			18 28		18 43		18 54	19 00	19 15	19 03	19 28	

A From Stalybridge
B To Llandudno
C To Liverpool South Parkway
D From Llandudno to Manchester Piccadilly
E From Liverpool Lime Street
F To Chester

Manchester, Preston, Wigan and Newton-le-Willows - St Helens and Liverpool

Network Diagram - see first Page of Table 88

		NT	AW	NT	AW	NT	NT	NT	AW	NT		NT	AW	NT	NT	NT	AW	NT	NT	AW		NT	AW	NT	NT
																								FX	
		A	◇ B 🛒		C 🛒				D				C				◇ E 🛒			C			◇ B		
Manchester Airport 85 ✈	d					18 41								19 41						20 32				21 24	
Manchester Piccadilly 10 🚊	d				18 50	19 01							19 50	20 01						20 50				21a38	
Manchester Oxford Road	d				18 53	19 04							19 53	20 04						20 53					
Manchester Victoria 🚊	d			18 39								19 39							20 39						21 39
Eccles	d			18 46								19 46							20 46						21 46
Patricroft	d			18 49								19 49							20 49						21 49
Blackpool North 97	d							18 37								19 37						20 37			
Preston 8 65,82	d							19 04								20 04						21 04			
Leyland 82	d							19 09								20 09						21 09			
Euxton Balshaw Lane	d							19 14								20 14						21 14			
Wigan North Western 65	a							19 24								20 24						21 23			
	d						19 08	19 24							20 08	20 24		20 38				21 23			
Newton-le-Willows	d			19 01	19 12	19 22						20 01	20 12	20 22					21 01	21 12					22 01
Warrington Bank Quay	d		18 46						19 19	19 22							20 19						21 19		
Earlestown 8	d	18 50	18a57	19 04	19 16				19a26	19 34		20 04	20 15				20a26		21 04	21 15			21a26		22 04
Warrington Bank Quay	a	19 01			19 24								20 25							21 24					
St Helens Junction	d			19 09		19 27				19 39		20 09		20 27					21 09						22 09
Lea Green	d			19 12						19 42		20 12							21 12						22 12
Rainhill	d			19 16						19 46		20 16							21 16						22 16
Whiston	d			19 19						19 49		20 19							21 19						22 19
Bryn	d						19 15								20 15			20 45				21 30			
Garswood	d						19 19								20 19			20 49				21 34			
St Helens Central	a						19 25	19 39							20 25	20 39		20 55				21 40			
	d						19 26	19 39							20 26	20 39		20 56				21 41			
Thatto Heath	d						19 29								20 29			20 59				21 44			
Eccleston Park	d						19 32								20 32			21 02				21 47			
Prescot	d						19 34								20 34			21 04				21 49			
Huyton	d			19 23			19 38	19 48		19 53		20 23			20 38	20 48		21 08	21 23			21 53			22 23
Roby	d			19 25			19 40			19 55		20 25			20 40			21 10	21 25			21 55			22 25
Broad Green	d			19 28			19 43			19 58		20 28			20 43			21 13	21 28			21 58			22 28
Wavertree Technology Park	d			19 31		19 38	19 46			20 01		20 31		20 38	20 46			21 16	21 31			22 03			22 31
Edge Hill 89,91	d			19 35			19 49			20 04		20 34			20 49			21 19	21 34			22 06			22 34
Liverpool Lime Street 10 89,91	a			19 43		19 48	19 58	20 02		20 13		20 43		20 48	20 58	21 02		21 28	21 43			22 16			22 43

		AW	NT	AW	AW	NT		AW	NT		NT	NT	AW	NT	AW	AW		AW
			FO	FO	FO			FX	FO				FX	FO	FO	FX		FX
		C		F	C			G 🚌			I	J	🚌		C	G 🚌		🚌
Manchester Airport 85 ✈	d	21 32	21 42															
Manchester Piccadilly 10 🚊	d	21 50	22 01		22 12								22 35		23 14			23 50
Manchester Oxford Road	d	21 53	22 04		22 29								22 40		23 17			23 55
Manchester Victoria 🚊	d								22 39					23 09				
Eccles	d								22 46					23 16				
Patricroft	d								22 49					23 19				
Blackpool North 97	d										22 14	22 14						
Preston 8 65,82	d										22 43	22 43						
Leyland 82	d										22 48	22 48						
Euxton Balshaw Lane	d										22 53	22 53						
Wigan North Western 65	a										23 02	23 03						
	d					22 25					23 03	23 03						
Newton-le-Willows	d	22 12	22 22		22 47				23 01				23 10	23 31	23 36			00 25
Warrington Bank Quay	d			22 19				22 28								23 59		
Earlestown 8	d	22 15		22a26	22 50			22a53	23 04				23 20	23 34	23 39	00a24		00 35
Warrington Bank Quay	a	22 23			22 58								23 45		23 47			01 00
St Helens Junction	d		22 27						23 09					23 39				
Lea Green	d								23 12					23 42				
Rainhill	d								23 16					23 46				
Whiston	d								23 19					23 49				
Bryn	d					22 32					23 10	23 10						
Garswood	d					22 36					23 14	23 14						
St Helens Central	a					22 42					23 20	23 21						
	d					22 43					23 21	23 21						
Thatto Heath	d					22 46					23 24	23 24						
Eccleston Park	d					22 49					23 27	23 27						
Prescot	d					22 51					23 29	23 29						
Huyton	d					22 55			23 23		23 33	23 33		23 53				
Roby	d					22 57			23 25		23 35	23 35		23 55				
Broad Green	d					23 00			23 28		23 38	23 38		23 58				
Wavertree Technology Park	d		22 38			23 03			23 31		23 41	23 41		00 01				
Edge Hill 89,91	d					23 06			23 34		23 46	23 46		00 04				
Liverpool Lime Street 10 89,91	a		22 48			23 15			23 43		23 54	23 56		00 13				

A From Liverpool Lime Street
B From Llandudno to Manchester Piccadilly
C To Chester
D From Chester to Manchester Airport
E From Llandudno to Manchester Airport
F From Chester to Manchester Piccadilly
G To Manchester Piccadilly
I until 30 December and then from 26 March
J from 2 January until 23 March

Table 90

Saturdays until 11 February

Manchester, Preston, Wigan and Newton-le-Willows - St Helens and Liverpool

Network Diagram - see first Page of Table 88

		NT	AW	NT	NT	NT	AW	AW	NT	NT		VT	NT	AW	NT	NT	AW	NT	NT	NT		NT	NT	AW	NT
			A				B	◇ C				◇1 D		◇ B	E		◇ C							F	
Manchester Airport 85 ✈	d			04 34				05 33										06 41							
Manchester Piccadilly 10	d		00 28	04 49				05 50									06 50	06 58							
Manchester Oxford Road	d		00 31					05 53									06 53	07 01							
Manchester Victoria	d	23p09				05 39				06 09										07 09					07 39
Eccles	d	23p16				05 46				06 16										07 16					07 46
Patricroft	d	23p19				05 49				06 19										07 19					07 49
Blackpool North 97	d																						07 02		
Preston 8 65,82	d											06 17											07 30		
Leyland 82	d																						07 35		
Euxton Balshaw Lane	d																						07 40		
Wigan North Western 65	a											06 28											07 50		
	d								06 08			06 28	06 38			06 47			07 08			07 38	07 50		
Newton-le-Willows	d	23p31	00 50			06 01		06 12		06 31						07 00	07 12	07 19		07 31					08 01
Warrington Bank Quay	d						06 06					06a39		06 40										07 39	
Earlestown 8	d	23p34	00 53			06 04	06a12	06 15		06 34				06a47	06 50	07 03	07 15			07 34				07a46	08 04
Warrington Bank Quay	a		01 02					06 25							07 01		07 22								
St Helens Junction	d	23p39				06 09				06 39						07 09		07 24		07 39					08 09
Lea Green	d	23p42				06 12				06 42						07 12				07 42					08 12
Rainhill	d	23p46				06 16				06 46						07 16		07 29		07 46					08 16
Whiston	d	23p49				06 19				06 49						07 19				07 49					08 19
Bryn	d								06 15				06 45						07 15			07 45			
Garswood	d								06 19				06 49						07 19			07 49	07 59		
St Helens Central	a								06 25				06 55						07 25			07 55	08 06		
	d				05 56				06 26				06 56						07 26			07 56	08 06		
Thatto Heath	d				05 59				06 29				06 59						07 29			07 59			
Eccleston Park	d				06 02				06 32				07 02						07 32			08 02			
Prescot	d				06 04				06 34				07 04						07 34			08 04	08 12		
Huyton	d	23p53			06 08	06 23			06 38	06 53			07 08			07 23		07 34	07 38	07 53		08 08	08 16		08 23
Roby	d	23p55			06 10	06 25			06 40	06 55			07 10			07 25			07 40	07 55		08 10			08 25
Broad Green	d	23p58			06 13	06 28			06 43	06 58			07 13			07 28			07 43	07 58		08 13	08 20		08 28
Wavertree Technology Park	d	00 01			06 16	06 31			06 46	07 01			07 16			07 31		07 39	07 46	08 01		08 16	08 24		08 31
Edge Hill 89,91	d	00 04			06 19	06 34			06 49	07 04			07 19			07 34			07 49	08 04		08 19			08 34
Liverpool Lime Street 10 89,91	a	00 13		05 32	06 28	06 43			06 58	07 13			07 28			07 43		07 49	07 58	08 13		08 28	08 34		08 43

		AW	NT	AW	NT	NT		NT	NT	NT	AW	NT	NT	NT	AW	NT		NT	NT	NT	AW	NT	NT	NT	AW
		◇ C		G				E		H	◇ C			I	G				E	H	◇ C			I	G
Manchester Airport 85 ✈	d											08 41										09 41			
Manchester Piccadilly 10	d	07 50									08 50	09 01									09 50	10 01			
Manchester Oxford Road	d	07 53									08 53	09 04									09 53	10 04			
Manchester Victoria	d				08 09					08 39										09 39					
Eccles	d				08 16					08 46										09 46					
Patricroft	d				08 19					08 49										09 49					
Blackpool North 97	d													08 38										09 37	
Preston 8 65,82	d													09 04										10 04	
Leyland 82	d													09 09										10 09	
Euxton Balshaw Lane	d													09 14										10 14	
Wigan North Western 65	a													09 24										10 24	
	d		07 58			08 28							09 08	09 24				09 38					10 08	10 24	
Newton-le-Willows	d	08 12			08 31					09 01	09 12	09 22								10 01	10 12	10 22			
Warrington Bank Quay	d			08 08											09 19	09 22									10 19
Earlestown 8	d	08 15		08a15	08 34			08 50		09 04	09 15				09a26	09 34			09 50	10 04	10 15				10a26
Warrington Bank Quay	a	08 23						09 01			09 25								10 01		10 25				
St Helens Junction	d				08 39					09 09		09 27				09 39				10 09		10 27			
Lea Green	d				08 42					09 12						09 42				10 12					
Rainhill	d				08 46					09 16						09 46				10 16					
Whiston	d				08 49					09 19						09 49				10 19					
Bryn	d		08 05			08 35							09 15					09 45					10 15		
Garswood	d		08 09			08 39							09 19					09 49					10 19		
St Helens Central	a		08 15			08 45							09 25	09 39				09 55					10 25	10 39	
	d		08 16			08 46			08 56				09 26	09 39				09 56					10 26	10 39	
Thatto Heath	d		08 19			08 49			08 59				09 29					09 59					10 29		
Eccleston Park	d		08 22			08 52			09 02				09 32					10 02					10 32		
Prescot	d		08 24			08 54			09 04				09 34					10 04					10 34		
Huyton	d		08 28		08 53	08 58			09 08	09 23			09 38	09 48		09 53		10 08		10 23			10 38	10 48	
Roby	d		08 30		08 55	09 00			09 10	09 25			09 40			09 55		10 10		10 25			10 40		
Broad Green	d		08 33		08 58	09 03			09 13	09 28			09 43			09 58		10 13		10 28			10 43		
Wavertree Technology Park	d		08 36		09 01	09 06			09 16	09 31		09 38	09 46			10 01		10 16		10 31		10 38	10 46		
Edge Hill 89,91	d		08 39		09 04	09 09			09 19	09 34			09 49			10 04		10 21		10 34			10 49		
Liverpool Lime Street 10 89,91	a		08 48		09 13	09 18			09 28	09 43		09 48	09 58	10 02		10 13		10 29		10 43		10 48	10 58	11 02	

A To Chester
B From Chester to Manchester Piccadilly
C To Llandudno
D To Birmingham New Street
E From Liverpool Lime Street
F From Shrewsbury to Manchester Piccadilly
G From Llandudno to Manchester Piccadilly
H From Stalybridge
I To Liverpool South Parkway

Table 90

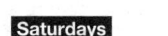

Saturdays
until 11 February

Manchester, Preston, Wigan and Newton-le-Willows - St Helens and Liverpool

Network Diagram - see first Page of Table 88

	NT		NT	NT	NT	AW	NT	NT	NT	AW	NT		NT	NT	NT	AW	NT	NT	NT	AW	NT		NT	NT
				A	B	◇ C			D	E				A	B	◇ C			D	◇ E				A
Manchester Airport 85 ✈ d							10 41										11 41							
Manchester Piccadilly 10 d						10 50	11 01									11 50	12 01							
Manchester Oxford Road d						10 53	11 04									11 53	12 04							
Manchester Victoria d					10 39										11 39									
Eccles d					10 46										11 46									
Patricroft d					10 49										11 49									
Blackpool North 97 d									10 37										11 37					
Preston 8 65,82 d									11 04										12 04					
Leyland 82 d									11 09										12 09					
Euxton Balshaw Lane d									11 14										12 14					
Wigan North Western 65 a									11 24										12 24					
d			10 38					11 08	11 24				11 38					12 08	12 24				12 38	
Newton-le-Willows d					11 01	11 12	11 22								12 01	12 12	12 22							
Warrington Bank Quay d	10 22									11 19	11 22									12 19	12 22			
Earlestown 8 d	10 34			10 50	11 04	11 15				11a26	11 34			11 50	12 04	12 15				12a26	12 34			12 50
Warrington Bank Quay a				11 01		11 25								12 01		12 25								13 01
St Helens Junction d	10 39				11 09		11 27				11 39				12 09		12 27				12 39			
Lea Green d	10 42				11 12						11 42				12 12						12 42			
Rainhill d	10 46				11 16						11 46				12 16						12 46			
Whiston d	10 49				11 19						11 49				12 19						12 49			
Bryn d			10 45					11 15					11 45					12 15					12 45	
Garswood d			10 49					11 19					11 49					12 19					12 49	
St Helens Central a			10 55					11 25	11 39				11 55					12 25	12 39				12 55	
d			10 56					11 26	11 39				11 56					12 26	12 39				12 56	
Thatto Heath d			10 59					11 29					11 59					12 29					12 59	
Eccleston Park d			11 02					11 32					12 02					12 32					13 02	
Prescot d			11 04					11 34					12 04					12 34					13 04	
Huyton d	10 53		11 08		11 23			11 38	11 48		11 53		12 08		12 23			12 38	12 48		12 53		13 08	
Roby d	10 55		11 10		11 25			11 40			11 55		12 10		12 25			12 40			12 55		13 10	
Broad Green d	10 58		11 13		11 28			11 43			11 58		12 13		12 28			12 43			12 58		13 13	
Wavertree Technology Park d	11 01		11 16		11 31		11 38	11 46			12 01		12 16		12 31		12 38	12 46			13 01		13 16	
Edge Hill 89,91 d	11 04		11 19		11 34			11 49			12 04		12 19		12 34			12 49			13 04		13 19	
Liverpool Lime Street 10 89,91 a	11 13		11 28		11 43		11 48	11 58	12 02		12 13		12 28		12 43		12 48	12 58	13 02		13 13		13 28	

	NT	AW	NT	NT	NT	AW	NT		NT	NT	NT	AW	NT	NT	NT	AW	NT		NT	NT	NT	AW	NT	NT
	B	◇ C			D	◇ E				A	B	◇ C			D	◇ E				A	B	◇ C		
Manchester Airport 85 ✈ d			12 41										13 41										14 41	
Manchester Piccadilly 10 d		12 50	13 01									13 50	14 01									14 50	15 01	
Manchester Oxford Road d		12 53	13 04									13 53	14 04									14 53	15 04	
Manchester Victoria d	12 39										13 39										14 39			
Eccles d	12 46										13 46										14 46			
Patricroft d	12 49										13 49										14 49			
Blackpool North 97 d					12 37										13 37									
Preston 8 65,82 d					13 04										14 04									
Leyland 82 d					13 09										14 09									
Euxton Balshaw Lane d					13 14										14 14									
Wigan North Western 65 a					13 24										14 24									
d				13 08	13 24				13 38					14 08	14 24				14 38					15 08
Newton-le-Willows d	13 01	13 12	13 22								14 01	14 12	14 22								15 01	15 12	15 22	
Warrington Bank Quay d						13 19	13 22									14 19	14 22							
Earlestown 8 d	13 04	13 15				13a26	13 34			13 50	14 04	14 15				14a26	14 34			14 50	15 04	15 15		
Warrington Bank Quay a		13 25								14 01		14 25								15 01		15 25		
St Helens Junction d	13 09		13 27				13 39				14 09		14 27				14 39				15 09		15 27	
Lea Green d	13 12						13 42				14 12						14 42				15 12			
Rainhill d	13 16						13 46				14 16						14 46				15 16			
Whiston d	13 19						13 49				14 19						14 49				15 19			
Bryn d				13 15					13 45					14 15					14 45					15 15
Garswood d				13 19					13 49					14 19					14 49					15 19
St Helens Central a				13 25	13 39				13 55					14 25	14 39				14 55					15 25
d				13 26	13 39				13 56					14 26	14 39				14 56					15 26
Thatto Heath d				13 29					13 59					14 29					14 59					15 29
Eccleston Park d				13 32					14 02					14 32					15 02					15 32
Prescot d				13 34					14 04					14 34					15 04					15 34
Huyton d	13 23			13 38	13 48		13 53		14 08		14 23			14 38	14 48		14 53		15 08		15 23			15 38
Roby d	13 25			13 40			13 55		14 10		14 25			14 40			14 55		15 10		15 25			15 40
Broad Green d	13 28			13 43			13 58		14 13		14 28			14 43			14 58		15 13		15 28			15 43
Wavertree Technology Park d	13 31		13 38	13 46			14 01		14 16		14 31		14 38	14 46			15 01		15 16		15 31		15 38	15 46
Edge Hill 89,91 d	13 34			13 49			14 04		14 19		14 34			14 49			15 04		15 19		15 34			15 49
Liverpool Lime Street 10 89,91 a	13 43		13 48	13 58	14 02		14 13		14 28		14 43		14 48	14 58	15 02		15 13		15 28		15 43		15 48	15 58

A From Liverpool Lime Street
B From Stalybridge
C To Llandudno
D To Liverpool South Parkway
E From Llandudno to Manchester Piccadilly

Table 90

Saturdays
until 11 February

Manchester, Preston, Wigan and Newton-le-Willows - St Helens and Liverpool

Network Diagram - see first Page of Table 88

		NT A	AW ◇ B	NT		NT	NT C	NT D	AW ◇ E	NT	NT	NT	AW ◇ B	NT		NT	NT D	AW ◇ E	NT	NT	NT	AW ◇ B	NT	NT	
Manchester Airport 85	d									15 41									16 41						
Manchester Piccadilly 10	d								15 50	16 01								16 50	17 01						
Manchester Oxford Road	d								15 53	16 04								16 53	17 04						
Manchester Victoria	d							15 39									16 39						17 09		
Eccles	d							15 46									16 46						17 16		
Patricroft	d							15 49									16 49						17 19		
Blackpool North 97	d	14 37										15 37									16 35				
Preston 8 65,82	d	15 04										16 04									17 04				
Leyland 82	d	15 09										16 09									17 09				
Euxton Balshaw Lane	d	15 14										16 14									17 14				
Wigan North Western 65	a	15 24										16 24									17 24				
	d	15 24				15 38					16 08	16 24				16 38				17 08	17 24			17 38	
Newton-le-Willows	d							16 01	16 12	16 22							17 01	17 12	17 22				17 31		
Warrington Bank Quay	d		15 19	15 22									16 19	16 22								17 19			
Earlestown 8	d		15a26	15 34			15 50	16 04	16 15				16a26	16 34			17 04	17 15				17a26	17 34		
Warrington Bank Quay	a						16 01		16 25									17 25							
St Helens Junction	d			15 39				16 09		16 27				16 39			17 09		17 27				17 39		
Lea Green	d			15 42				16 12						16 42			17 12						17 42		
Rainhill	d			15 46				16 16						16 46			17 16						17 46		
Whiston	d			15 49				16 19						16 49			17 19						17 49		
Bryn	d					15 45					16 15					16 45				17 15				17 45	
Garswood	d					15 49					16 19					16 49				17 19				17 49	
St Helens Central	a	15 39				15 55					16 25	16 39				16 55				17 25	17 39			17 55	
	d	15 39				15 56					16 26	16 39				16 56				17 26	17 39			17 56	
Thatto Heath	d					15 59					16 29					16 59				17 29				17 59	
Eccleston Park	d					16 02					16 32					17 02				17 32				18 02	
Prescot	d					16 04					16 34					17 04				17 34				18 04	
Huyton	d	15 48		15 53		16 08		16 23			16 38	16 48		16 53		17 08	17 23			17 38	17 48		17 53	18 08	
Roby	d			15 55		16 10		16 25			16 40			16 55		17 10	17 25			17 40			17 55	18 10	
Broad Green	d			15 58		16 13		16 28			16 43			16 58		17 13	17 28			17 43			17 58	18 13	
Wavertree Technology Park	d			16 01		16 16		16 31		16 38	16 46			17 01		17 16	17 31		17 38	17 46			18 01	18 16	
Edge Hill 89,91	d			16 04		16 19		16 34			16 49			17 04		17 19	17 34			17 49			18 04	18 19	
Liverpool Lime Street 10 89,91	a	16 02		16 13		16 28		16 43		16 48	16 58	17 05		17 13		17 28	17 43		17 48	17 58	18 02		18 13	18 28	

		NT D	AW ◇ E	NT	NT	AW ◇ B	NT	NT	NT	NT C		NT D	AW F	NT	NT	NT	AW ◇ G	NT	NT	AW F		NT	NT	NT	AW ◇ B
Manchester Airport 85	d				17 41									18 41								19 41			
Manchester Piccadilly 10	d		17 50		18 01								18 50	19 01						19 50		20 01			
Manchester Oxford Road	d		17 53		18 04								18 53	19 04						19 53		20 04			
Manchester Victoria	d	17 39										18 39							19 39						
Eccles	d	17 46			18 11							18 46							19 46						
Patricroft	d	17 49										18 49							19 49						
Blackpool North 97	d							17 37								18 37								19 37	
Preston 8 65,82	d							18 04								19 04								20 04	
Leyland 82	d							18 09								19 09								20 09	
Euxton Balshaw Lane	d							18 14								19 14								20 14	
Wigan North Western 65	a							18 24								19 24								20 24	
	d			18 08			18 21	18 24	18 35						19 08	19 24							20 08	20 24	
Newton-le-Willows	d	18 01	18 12		18 24		18 33					19 01	19 12	19 22					20 01	20 12		20 22			
Warrington Bank Quay	d					18 19											19 19	19 22							20 19
Earlestown 8	d	18 04	18 15			18a26	18 36			18 50		19 04	19 16				19a26	19 34	20 04	20 15					20a26
Warrington Bank Quay	a		18 24							19 01			19 26							20 29					
St Helens Junction	d	18 09			18 29		18 41					19 09		19 27				19 39	20 09			20 27			
Lea Green	d	18 12			18 32		18 44					19 12						19 42	20 12						
Rainhill	d	18 16			18 36		18 48					19 16						19 46	20 16						
Whiston	d	18 19					18 51					19 19						19 49	20 19						
Bryn	d			18 15					18 45						19 15								20 15		
Garswood	d			18 19					18 49						19 19								20 19		
St Helens Central	a			18 25				18 39	18 55						19 25	19 39							20 25	20 39	
	d			18 26				18 39	18 56						19 26	19 39							20 26	20 39	
Thatto Heath	d			18 29					18 59						19 29								20 29		
Eccleston Park	d			18 32					19 02						19 32								20 32		
Prescot	d			18 34					19 04						19 34								20 34		
Huyton	d	18 23		18 38	18 41		18 55	18 48	19 08			19 23			19 38	19 48		19 53	20 23				20 38	20 48	
Roby	d	18 25			18 43		18 57		19 10			19 25			19 40			19 55	20 25				20 40		
Broad Green	d	18 28			18 47		19 00		19 13			19 28			19 43			19 58	20 28				20 43		
Wavertree Technology Park	d	18 31		18 43	18 50		19 03		19 16			19 31		19 38	19 46			20 01	20 31			20 38	20 46		
Edge Hill 89,91	d	18 34		18 46			19 06		19 19			19 34			19 49			20 04	20 34				20 49		
Liverpool Lime Street 10 89,91	a	18 43		18 54	19 00		19 15	19 02	19 28			19 43		19 48	19 58	20 02		20 13	20 43			20 48	20 58	21 02	

A To Liverpool South Parkway
B From Llandudno to Manchester Piccadilly
C From Liverpool Lime Street
D From Stalybridge
E To Llandudno
F To Chester
G From Llandudno to Manchester Airport

Table 90

Saturdays
until 11 February

Manchester, Preston, Wigan and Newton-le-Willows - St Helens and Liverpool

Network Diagram - see first Page of Table 88

		NT	NT	AW	NT	AW	NT	AW	NT	AW	NT	AW	NT	NT	NT	AW	AW
						◇											
				A		B		A		C		A				A	C
Manchester Airport 85 ✈	d			20 32					21 41								
Manchester Piccadilly 10	d			20 50				21 50	22 01			22 26				23 14	
Manchester Oxford Road	d			20 53				21 53	22 04			22 29				23 17	
Manchester Victoria	d		20 39				21 39						22 39		23 09		
Eccles	d		20 46				21 46						22 46		23 16		
Patricroft	d		20 49				21 49						22 49		23 19		
Blackpool North 97	d				20 37									22 14			
Preston 8 65,82	d				21 04									22 43			
Leyland 82	d				21 09									22 48			
Euxton Balshaw Lane	d				21 14									22 53			
Wigan North Western 65	a				21 23									23 02			
	d	20 38			21 23						22 25			23 03			
Newton-le-Willows	d		20 59	21 12			22 01	22 12	22 22			22 47	23 01		23 31	23 36	
Warrington Bank Quay	d					21 19				22 19							23 50
Earlestown 8	d		21 04	21 15		21a26	22 04	22 15		22a26		22 50	23 04		23 34	23 39	23a58
Warrington Bank Quay	a			21 26				22 23				22 58				23 47	
St Helens Junction	d		21 09				22 09		22 27				23 09		23 39		
Lea Green	d		21 12				22 12						23 12		23 42		
Rainhill	d		21 16				22 16						23 16		23 46		
Whiston	d		21 19				22 19						23 19		23 49		
Bryn	d	20 45			21 30						22 32			23 10			
Garswood	d	20 49			21 34						22 36			23 14			
St Helens Central	a	20 55			21 40						22 42			23 20			
	d	20 56			21 41						22 43			23 21			
Thatto Heath	d	20 59			21 44						22 46			23 24			
Eccleston Park	d	21 02			21 47						22 49			23 27			
Prescot	d	21 04			21 49						22 51			23 29			
Huyton	d	21 08	21 23		21 53		22 23				22 55		23 23	23 33	23 53		
Roby	d	21 10	21 25		21 55		22 25				22 57		23 25	23 35	23 55		
Broad Green	d	21 13	21 28		21 58		22 28				23 00		23 28	23 38	23 57		
Wavertree Technology Park	d	21 16	21 31		22 03		22 31		22 38		23 03		23 31	23 41	00 01		
Edge Hill 89,91	d	21 19	21 34		22 06		22 34				23 06		23 34	23 46	00 04		
Liverpool Lime Street 10 89,91	a	21 28	21 43		22 14		22 43		22 48		23 15		23 43	23 54	00 13		

Saturdays
18 February to 24 March

		NT	AW	NT	NT	AW	AW	VT	NT	AW	NT	AW	NT	NT	NT	NT	AW	NT	AW	NT	NT	AW	NT
							◇	◇1		◇		◇							◇				
			A			C	D	E		C		D					F		D			B	
					🚌				🚌				🚌		🚌					🚌	🚌		🚌
							🛒	☕				🛒					🛒		🛒			🛒	
Manchester Airport 85 ✈	d						05 33																
Manchester Piccadilly 10	d		00 28				05 50					06 50							07 50				
Manchester Oxford Road	d		00 31				05 53					06 53							07 53				
Manchester Victoria	d	23p09		05 39							06 39			07 09				07 39					
Eccles	d	23p16		05 44							06 46			07 16				07 46					
Patricroft	d	23p19		05 47							06 49			07 19				07 49					
Blackpool North 97	d															07 02							
Preston 8 65,82	d							06 17								07 30							
Leyland 82	d															07 35							
Euxton Balshaw Lane	d															07 40							
Wigan North Western 65	a							06 28								07 50							
	d				06 05			06 28	06 35				07 05		07 35	07 50				08 05	08 05		08 35
Newton-le-Willows	d	23p31	00 50	05 59			06 12				07 01	07 12		07 31				08 01	08 12				
Warrington Bank Quay	d					06 06		06a39		06 40							07 39					08 08	
Earlestown 8	d	23p34	00 53	06a03		06a12	06 15			06a47	07a05	07 15		07a35			07a46	08a04	08 15			08a15	
Warrington Bank Quay	a		01 02				06 25					07 22							08 23				
St Helens Junction	d	23p39																					
Lea Green	d	23p42																					
Rainhill	d	23p46																					
Whiston	d	23p49																					
Bryn	d				06 18				06 48				07 18		07 48						08 18		08 48
Garswood	d				06 25				06 55				07 25		07 55	07 59					08 25		08 55
St Helens Central	a				06 45				07 15				07 45		08 15	08 06					08 45		09 15
	d				06 45				07 15				07 45		08 15	08 06					08 45		09 15
Thatto Heath	d				06 55				07 25				07 55		08 25						08 55		09 25
Eccleston Park	d				07 05				07 35				08 05		08 35						09 05		09 35
Prescot	d				07 11				07 41				08 11		08 41	08 12					09 11		09 41
Huyton	d	23p53			07 21				07 51				08 21		08 51	08 16					09 21		09 51
Roby	d	23p55			07 25				07 55				08 25		08 55						09 25		09 55
Broad Green	d	23p58			07 32				08 02				08 32		09 02	08 20					09 32		10 02
Wavertree Technology Park	d	00 01			07 42				08 12				08 42		09 12	08 24					09 42		10 12
Edge Hill 89,91	d	00 04			07 52				08 22				08 52		09 22						09 52		10 22
Liverpool Lime Street 10 89,91	a	00 13			07 59				08 29				08 59		09 29	08 34				09 05	09 59		10 29

A To Chester
B From Llandudno to Manchester Piccadilly
C From Chester to Manchester Piccadilly
D To Llandudno
E To Birmingham New Street
F From Shrewsbury to Manchester Piccadilly

Table 90

Saturdays

18 February to 24 March

Manchester, Preston, Wigan and Newton-le-Willows - St Helens and Liverpool

Network Diagram - see first Page of Table 88

		NT	AW	NT	AW	NT		NT	NT	AW	NT	AW	NT	NT	NT	AW		NT	AW	NT	NT	NT	AW	NT	AW
			◇							◇						◇							◇		◇
		A	B		C				A	B		C			A	B			C			A	B		C
				🚌		🚌		🚌			🚌		🚌	🚌				🚌		🚌	🚌			🚌	
			🛒		🛒					🛒		🛒				🛒			🛒				🛒		🛒
Manchester Airport 85 ✈	d																								
Manchester Piccadilly 10	d		08 50							09 50						10 50							11 50		
Manchester Oxford Road	d		08 53							09 53						10 53							11 53		
Manchester Victoria	d	08 39							09 39						10 39							11 39			
Eccles	d	08 46							09 46						10 46							11 46			
Patricroft	d	08 49							09 49						10 49							11 49			
Blackpool North 97	d																								
Preston 8 65,82	d																								
Leyland 82	d																								
Euxton Balshaw Lane	d																								
Wigan North Western 65	a																								
	d			09 05		09 35		09 35			10 05		10 35	10 35				11 05		11 35	11 35			12 05	
Newton-le-Willows	d	09 01	09 12						10 01	10 12					11 01	11 12						11 59	12 12		
Warrington Bank Quay	d				09 19							10 19							11 19						12 19
Earlestown 8	d	09a06	09 15		09a26				10a05	10 15		10a26			11a06	11 15			11a26			12a06	12 15		12a26
Warrington Bank Quay	a		09 25							10 25						11 25							12 25		
St Helens Junction	d																								
Lea Green	d																								
Rainhill	d																								
Whiston	d																								
Bryn	d			09 18				09 48			10 18			10 48				11 18			11 48			12 18	
Garswood	d			09 25				09 55			10 25			10 55				11 25			11 55			12 25	
St Helens Central	a			09 45				10 15			10 45			11 15				11 45			12 15			12 45	
	d			09 45				10 15			10 45			11 15				11 45			12 15			12 45	
Thatto Heath	d			09 55				10 25			10 55			11 25				11 55			12 25			12 55	
Eccleston Park	d			10 05				10 35			11 05			11 35				12 05			12 35			13 05	
Prescot	d			10 11				10 41			11 11			11 41				12 11			12 41			13 11	
Huyton	d			10 21				10 51			11 21			11 51				12 21			12 51			13 21	
Roby	d			10 25				10 55			11 25			11 55				12 25			12 55			13 25	
Broad Green	d			10 32				11 02			11 32			12 02				12 32			13 02			13 32	
Wavertree Technology Park	d			10 42				11 12			11 42			12 12				12 42			13 12			13 42	
Edge Hill 89,91	d			10 52				11 22			11 52			12 22				12 52			13 22			13 52	
Liverpool Lime Street 10 89,91	a			10 59		10 35		11 29			11 59		11 35	12 29				12 59		12 35	13 29			13 59	

		NT		NT	NT	AW	NT	AW	NT	NT	NT	AW		NT	AW	NT	NT	NT	AW	NT	AW	NT		NT	NT
						◇		◇				◇			◇				◇		◇				
					A	B		C			A	B			C			A	B		C				A
		🚌		🚌			🚌		🚌	🚌				🚌		🚌	🚌			🚌		🚌		🚌	
						🛒		🛒				🛒			🛒				🛒		🛒				
Manchester Airport 85 ✈	d																								
Manchester Piccadilly 10	d					12 50						13 50							14 50						
Manchester Oxford Road	d					12 53						13 53							14 53						
Manchester Victoria	d				12 39						13 39							14 39							15 39
Eccles	d				12 46						13 46							14 46							15 46
Patricroft	d				12 49						13 49							14 49							15 49
Blackpool North 97	d																								
Preston 8 65,82	d																								
Leyland 82	d																								
Euxton Balshaw Lane	d																								
Wigan North Western 65	a																								
	d	12 35		12 35			13 05		13 35	13 35				14 05		14 35	14 35			15 05		15 35		15 35	
Newton-le-Willows	d				12 59	13 12					13 59	14 12						14 59	15 12						15 59
Warrington Bank Quay	d							13 19							14 19						15 19				
Earlestown 8	d				13a05	13 15		13a26			14a05	14 15			14a26			15a05	15 15		15a26				16a05
Warrington Bank Quay	a					13 25						14 25							15 25						
St Helens Junction	d																								
Lea Green	d																								
Rainhill	d																								
Whiston	d																								
Bryn	d			12 48			13 18			13 48				14 18			14 48			15 18				15 48	
Garswood	d			12 55			13 25			13 55				14 25			14 55			15 25				15 55	
St Helens Central	a			13 15			13 45			14 15				14 45			15 15			15 45				16 15	
	d			13 15			13 45			14 15				14 45			15 15			15 45				16 15	
Thatto Heath	d			13 25			13 55			14 25				14 55			15 25			15 55				16 25	
Eccleston Park	d			13 35			14 05			14 35				15 05			15 35			16 05				16 35	
Prescot	d			13 41			14 11			14 41				15 11			15 41			16 11				16 41	
Huyton	d			13 51			14 21			14 51				15 21			15 51			16 21				16 51	
Roby	d			13 55			14 25			14 55				15 25			15 55			16 25				16 55	
Broad Green	d			14 02			14 32			15 02				15 32			16 02			16 32				17 02	
Wavertree Technology Park	d			14 12			14 42			15 12				15 42			16 12			16 42				17 12	
Edge Hill 89,91	d			14 22			14 52			15 22				15 52			16 22			16 52				17 22	
Liverpool Lime Street 10 89,91	a	13 35		14 29			14 59		14 35	15 29				15 59		15 35	16 29			16 59		16 35		17 29	

A From Stalybridge
B To Llandudno
C From Llandudno to Manchester Piccadilly

Table 90

Saturdays

18 February to 24 March

Manchester, Preston, Wigan and Newton-le-Willows - St Helens and Liverpool

Network Diagram - see first Page of Table 88

	AW ◇ A 🚲	NT 🚌	AW ◇ B 🚲	NT 🚌	NT 🚌	NT C	AW ◇ A 🚲		NT 🚌	AW ◇ B 🚲	NT	NT 🚌	NT 🚌	NT C	AW ◇ A 🚲	NT 🚌	AW ◇ B 🚲		NT	NT 🚌	NT 🚌	NT C	AW D 🚲	NT 🚌
Manchester Airport 85 ✈ d																								
Manchester Piccadilly 10 🚇 d	15 50						16 50								17 50								18 50	
Manchester Oxford Road d	15 53						16 53								17 53								18 53	
Manchester Victoria 🚇 d						16 39					17 09			17 39					18 10			18 39		
Eccles d						16 46					17 16			17 46					18 17			18 46		
Patricroft d						16 49					17 19			17 49					18 20			18 49		
Blackpool North 97 d																								
Preston 8 65,82 d																								
Leyland 82 d																								
Euxton Balshaw Lane d																								
Wigan North Western 65 a																								
d		16 05		16 35	16 35				17 05			17 35	17 35			18 05				18 35	18 35			19 05
Newton-le-Willows d	16 12					16 59	17 12				17 30			17 59	18 12				18 30			18 59	19 12	
Warrington Bank Quay d			16 19							17 19							18 19							
Earlestown 8 d	16 15		16a26			17a05	17 15			17a26	17a38			18a06	18 15		18a26		18a37			19a06	19 16	
Warrington Bank Quay a	16 25						17 25								18 24								19 26	
St Helens Junction d																								
Lea Green d																								
Rainhill d																								
Whiston d																								
Bryn d		16 18			16 48				17 18				17 48			18 18					18 48			19 18
Garswood d		16 25			16 55				17 25				17 55			18 25					18 55			19 25
St Helens Central a		16 45			17 15				17 45				18 15			18 45					19 15			19 45
d		16 45			17 15				17 45				18 15			18 45					19 15			19 45
Thatto Heath d		16 55			17 25				17 55				18 25			18 55					19 25			19 55
Eccleston Park d		17 05			17 35				18 05				18 35			19 05					19 35			20 05
Prescot d		17 11			17 41				18 11				18 41			19 11					19 41			20 11
Huyton d		17 21			17 51				18 21				18 51			19 21					19 51			20 21
Roby d		17 25			17 55				18 25				18 55			19 25					19 55			20 25
Broad Green d		17 32			18 02				18 32				19 02			19 32					20 02			20 32
Wavertree Technology Park d		17 42			18 12				18 42				19 12			19 42					20 12			20 42
Edge Hill 89,91 d		17 52			18 22				18 52				19 22			19 52					20 22			20 52
Liverpool Lime Street 10 89,91 a		17 59		17 35	18 29				18 59			18 35	19 29			19 59				19 35	20 29			20 59

	AW ◇ E 🚲	NT 🚌	NT		AW D	NT 🚌	AW ◇ B 🚲	NT 🚌	NT 🚌	NT	AW D	AW ◇ B	NT 🚌		NT 🚌	NT	AW D	AW F	AW D	NT 🚌	NT	NT	AW D	
Manchester Airport 85 ✈ d											20 32													
Manchester Piccadilly 10 🚇 d					19 50						20 50						21 50		22 26				23 14	
Manchester Oxford Road d					19 53						20 53						21 53		22 29				23 17	
Manchester Victoria 🚇 d			19 39							20 39						21 39					22 39	23 09		
Eccles d			19 46							20 46						21 46					22 46	23 16		
Patricroft d			19 49							20 49						21 49					22 49	23 19		
Blackpool North 97 d																								
Preston 8 65,82 d																								
Leyland 82 d																								
Euxton Balshaw Lane d																								
Wigan North Western 65 a																								
d		19 35				20 05		20 35	20 35				21 35		21 35					22 35				
Newton-le-Willows d			19 59		20 12					21 01	21 12					21 59	22 12		22 47		22 59	23 29	23 36	
Warrington Bank Quay d	19 19						20 19					21 19						22 19						
Earlestown 8 d	19a26		20a06		20 15		20a26			21a05	21 15	21a26				22a06	22 15	22a26	22 50		23a06	23a36	23 39	
Warrington Bank Quay a					20 29						21 26						22 23		22 58				23 47	
St Helens Junction d																								
Lea Green d																								
Rainhill d																								
Whiston d																								
Bryn d						20 18			20 48						21 48					22 48				
Garswood d						20 25			20 55						21 55					22 55				
St Helens Central a						20 45			21 15						22 15					23 15				
d						20 45			21 15						22 15					23 15				
Thatto Heath d						20 55			21 25						22 25					23 25				
Eccleston Park d						21 05			21 35						22 35					23 35				
Prescot d						21 11			21 41						22 41					23 41				
Huyton d						21 21			21 51						22 51					23 51				
Roby d						21 25			21 55						22 55					23 55				
Broad Green d						21 32			22 02						23 02					00 02				
Wavertree Technology Park d						21 42			22 12						23 12					00 12				
Edge Hill 89,91 d						21 52			22 22						23 22					00 22				
Liverpool Lime Street 10 89,91 a		20 35				21 59		21 35	22 29				22 35		23 29					00 29				

A To Llandudno
B From Llandudno to Manchester Piccadilly
C From Stalybridge
D To Chester
E From Llandudno to Manchester Airport
F From Chester to Manchester Piccadilly

Table 90

Saturdays

18 February to 24 March

Manchester, Preston, Wigan and Newton-le-Willows - St Helens and Liverpool

Network Diagram - see first Page of Table 88

Station		NT 🚌	AW A
Manchester Airport 85 ✈	d		
Manchester Piccadilly 10	d		
Manchester Oxford Road	d		
Manchester Victoria	d		
Eccles	d		
Patricroft	d		
Blackpool North 97	d		
Preston 8 65,82	d		
Leyland 82	d		
Euxton Balshaw Lane	d		
Wigan North Western 65	a		
	d	23 15	
Newton-le-Willows	d		
Warrington Bank Quay	d		23 50
Earlestown 8	d		23a58
Warrington Bank Quay	a		
St Helens Junction	d		
Lea Green	d		
Rainhill	d		
Whiston	d		
Bryn	d		
Garswood	d		
St Helens Central	a		
	d		
Thatto Heath	d		
Eccleston Park	d		
Prescot	d		
Huyton	d		
Roby	d		
Broad Green	d		
Wavertree Technology Park	d		
Edge Hill 89,91	d		
Liverpool Lime Street 10 89,91	a	00 15	

Saturdays

from 31 March

Station		NT	AW B	NT	NT	NT 🚌	NT 🚌	AW A	AW ◇ C	NT	NT	NT 🚌	VT ◇1 D	NT	AW ◇ A	NT 🚌	NT E	NT	AW ◇ C	NT	NT 🚌	NT	NT
Manchester Airport 85 ✈	d			04 34					05 33											06 41			
Manchester Piccadilly 10	d		00 28	04 49					05 50										06 50	06 58			
Manchester Oxford Road	d		00 31						05 53										06 53	07 01			
Manchester Victoria	d	23p09			05 39						06 09												07 09
Eccles	d	23p16			05 46						06 16												07 16
Patricroft	d	23p19			05 49						06 19												07 19
Blackpool North 97	d																						
Preston 8 65,82	d												06 17										
Leyland 82	d																						
Euxton Balshaw Lane	d																						
Wigan North Western 65	a												06 28										
	d					05 14	05 44			06 08		06 14	06 28	06 38		06 44		06 47			07 04	07 08	
Newton-le-Willows	d	23p31	00 50		06 01				06 12		06 31							07 01	07 12	07 19			07 31
Warrington Bank Quay	d							06 06					06a39		06 40								
Earlestown 8	d	23p34	00 53		06 04			06a12	06 15		06 34				06a47		06 50	07 04	07 15				07 34
Warrington Bank Quay	a		01 02						06 25								07 01		07 22				
St Helens Junction	d	23p39			06 09						06 39							07 10		07 24			07 39
Lea Green	d	23p42			06 12						06 42							07 13					07 42
Rainhill	d	23p46			06 16						06 46							07 17		07 29			07 46
Whiston	d	23p49			06 19						06 49							07 20					07 49
Bryn	d					05 27	05 57					06 27				06 57					07 17		
Garswood	d					05 34	06 04					06 34				07 04					07 24		
St Helens Central	a					05 54	06 24					06 54				07 24					07 44		
	d					05 54	06 24					06 54				07 24					07 44		
Thatto Heath	d					06 04	06 34					07 04				07 34					07 54		
Eccleston Park	d					06 14	06 44					07 14				07 44					08 04		
Prescot	d					06 20	06 50					07 20				07 50					08 10		
Huyton	d	23p53			06 23	06a30	07a00			06 29	06 53	07a30		07 03		08a00		07 24		07 34	08a20	07 42	07 53
Roby	d	23p55			06 25					06 31	06 55			07 05				07 26				07 44	07 55
Broad Green	d	23p58			06 28					06 35	06 58			07 09				07 29				07 48	07 58
Wavertree Technology Park	d	00 01			06 31					06 38	07 01			07 12				07 32		07 39		07 51	08 01
Edge Hill 89,91	d	00 04			06 34					06 45	07 04			07 18				07 35				07 54	08 04
Liverpool Lime Street 10 89,91	a	00 13		05 32	06 43					06 53	07 13			07 26				07 44		07 49		08 02	08 13

A From Chester to Manchester Piccadilly
B To Chester
C To Llandudno
D To Birmingham New Street
E From Liverpool Lime Street

Table 90

Saturdays
from 31 March

Manchester, Preston, Wigan and Newton-le-Willows - St Helens and Liverpool

Network Diagram - see first Page of Table 88

		NT 🚌	NT	AW A 🚲	NT	NT		AW ◇ B 🚲	AW C 🚲	NT	NT 🚌	NT	NT D	NT	NT 🚌	AW ◇ B 🚲		NT	NT	AW C 🚲	NT	NT 🚌	NT	NT D	NT E
Manchester Airport 85 ✈	d																	08 41							
Manchester Piccadilly 10	d							07 50								08 50		09 01							
Manchester Oxford Road	d							07 53								08 53		09 04							
Manchester Victoria	d				07 39					08 09				08 39											09 39
Eccles	d				07 46					08 16				08 46											09 46
Patricroft	d				07 49					08 19				08 49											09 49
Blackpool North 97	d					07 02																	08 38		
Preston 8 65,82	d					07 30																	09 04		
Leyland 82	d					07 35																	09 09		
Euxton Balshaw Lane	d					07 40																	09 14		
Wigan North Western 65	a					07 53																	09 26		
	d	07 34	07 38			07 58					08 14	08 28			08 44				09 08			09 14	09 38		
Newton-le-Willows	d				08 01			08 12		08 31				09 01		09 12		09 22							10 01
Warrington Bank Quay	d			07 39					08 08											09 19	09 22				
Earlestown 8	d			07a46	08 04			08 15	08a15	08 34			08 50	09 04		09 15				09a26	09 34			09 50	10 04
Warrington Bank Quay	a							08 23					09 01			09 25								10 01	
St Helens Junction	d				08 09					08 39				09 09				09 27			09 39				10 09
Lea Green	d				08 12					08 42				09 12							09 42				10 12
Rainhill	d				08 16					08 46				09 16							09 46				10 16
Whiston	d				08 19					08 49				09 19							09 49				10 19
Bryn	d	07 47									08 27				08 57							09 27			
Garswood	d	07 54									08 34				09 04							09 34			
St Helens Central	a	08 14									08 54				09 24							09 54			
	d	08 14									08 54				09 24							09 54			
Thatto Heath	d	08 24									09 04				09 34							10 04			
Eccleston Park	d	08 34									09 14				09 44							10 14			
Prescot	d	08 40									09 20				09 50							10 20			
Huyton	d	08a50	08 08		08 23	08 27				08 53	09a30	08 58		09 23	10a00				09 39		09 53	10a30	09 59		10 23
Roby	d		08 10		08 25	08 29				08 55		09 00		09 25					09 41		09 55		10 01		10 25
Broad Green	d		08 13		08 28	08 33				08 58		09 03		09 28					09 44		09 58		10 04		10 28
Wavertree Technology Park	d		08 16		08 31	08 36				09 01		09 06		09 31				09 38	09 47		10 01		10 07		10 31
Edge Hill 89,91	d		08 19		08 34	08 39				09 04		09 09		09 34					09 50		10 04		10 08		10 34
Liverpool Lime Street 10 89,91	a		08 28		08 43	08 44				09 13		09 18		09 43				09 48	09 59		10 13		10 17		10 43

		NT 🚌		AW ◇ B 🚲	NT	NT	AW C 🚲	NT	NT 🚌	NT	NT D	NT E		NT 🚌	AW ◇ B 🚲	NT	NT	AW C 🚲	NT	NT 🚌	NT	NT D		NT E	NT 🚌
Manchester Airport 85 ✈	d				09 41											10 41									
Manchester Piccadilly 10	d			09 50	10 01										10 50	11 01									
Manchester Oxford Road	d			09 53	10 04										10 53	11 04									
Manchester Victoria	d											10 39												11 39	
Eccles	d											10 46												11 46	
Patricroft	d											10 49												11 49	
Blackpool North 97	d									09 37											10 37				
Preston 8 65,82	d									10 04											11 04				
Leyland 82	d									10 09											11 09				
Euxton Balshaw Lane	d									10 14											11 14				
Wigan North Western 65	a									10 26											11 26				
	d	09 44				10 08			10 14	10 38				10 44			11 08			11 14	11 38				11 44
Newton-le-Willows	d			10 12	10 22							11 01			11 12	11 22								12 01	
Warrington Bank Quay	d						10 19	10 22										11 19	11 22						
Earlestown 8	d			10 15			10a26	10 34			10 50	11 04			11 15			11a26	11 34			11 50		12 04	
Warrington Bank Quay	a			10 25							11 01				11 25							12 01			
St Helens Junction	d				10 27			10 39				11 09				11 27			11 39					12 09	
Lea Green	d							10 42				11 12							11 42					12 12	
Rainhill	d							10 46				11 16							11 46					12 16	
Whiston	d							10 49				11 19							11 49					12 19	
Bryn	d	09 57							10 27					10 57						11 27					11 57
Garswood	d	10 04							10 34					11 04						11 34					12 04
St Helens Central	a	10 24							10 54					11 24						11 54					12 24
	d	10 24							10 54					11 24						11 54					12 24
Thatto Heath	d	10 34							11 04					11 34						12 04					12 34
Eccleston Park	d	10 44							11 14					11 44						12 14					12 44
Prescot	d	10 50							11 20					11 50						12 20					12 50
Huyton	d	11a00				10 39		10 53	11a30	11 01		11 23		12a00			11 39		11 53	12a30	12 00			12 23	13a00
Roby	d					10 41		10 55		11 03		11 25					11 41		11 55		12 02			12 25	
Broad Green	d					10 44		10 58		11 07		11 28					11 44		11 58		12 06			12 28	
Wavertree Technology Park	d				10 38	10 47		11 01		11 10		11 31				11 38	11 47		12 01		12 09			12 31	
Edge Hill 89,91	d					10 50		11 04		11 13		11 34					11 50		12 04		12 12			12 34	
Liverpool Lime Street 10 89,91	a				10 48	10 59		11 13		11 21		11 43				11 48	11 59		12 13		12 21			12 43	

A From Shrewsbury to Manchester Piccadilly
B To Llandudno
C From Llandudno to Manchester Piccadilly
D From Liverpool Lime Street
E From Stalybridge

Table 90

Saturdays
from 31 March

Manchester, Preston, Wigan and Newton-le-Willows - St Helens and Liverpool

Network Diagram - see first Page of Table 88

		AW	NT	NT	AW	NT	NT	NT		NT	NT	NT	AW	NT	NT	AW	NT	NT		NT	NT	NT	NT	AW	NT
		◇ A			◇ B					C	D		◇ A			◇ B					C	D		◇ A	
		🛒			🛒		🚌					🚌	🛒			🛒		🚌					🚌	🛒	
Manchester Airport 85 ✈	d		11 41											12 41											13 41
Manchester Piccadilly 10 🚇	d	11 50	12 01										12 50	13 01										13 50	14 01
Manchester Oxford Road	d	11 53	12 04										12 53	13 04										13 53	14 04
Manchester Victoria 🚇	d										12 39											13 39			
Eccles	d										12 46											13 46			
Patricroft	d										12 49											13 49			
Blackpool North 97	d							11 37												12 37					
Preston 8 65,82	d							12 04												13 04					
Leyland 82	d							12 09												13 09					
Euxton Balshaw Lane	d							12 14												13 14					
Wigan North Western 65	a							12 26												13 26					
	d			12 08			12 14	12 38				12 44			13 08			13 14		13 38			13 44		
Newton-le-Willows	d	12 12	12 22								13 01		13 12	13 22								14 01		14 12	14 22
Warrington Bank Quay	d				12 19	12 22										13 19	13 22								
Earlestown 8	d	12 15			12a26	12 34				12 50	13 04		13 15			13a26	13 34				13 50	14 04		14 15	
Warrington Bank Quay	a	12 25								13 01			13 25								14 01			14 25	
St Helens Junction	d		12 27			12 39					13 09			13 27			13 39					14 09			14 27
Lea Green	d					12 42					13 12						13 42					14 12			
Rainhill	d					12 46					13 16						13 46					14 16			
Whiston	d					12 49					13 19						13 49					14 19			
Bryn	d						12 27					12 57						13 27					13 57		
Garswood	d						12 34					13 04						13 34					14 04		
St Helens Central	a						12 54					13 24						13 54					14 24		
	d						12 54					13 24						13 54					14 24		
Thatto Heath	d						13 04					13 34						14 04					14 34		
Eccleston Park	d						13 14					13 44						14 14					14 44		
Prescot	d						13 20					13 50						14 20					14 50		
Huyton	d			12 39		12 53	13a30	13 01			13 23	14a00			13 39		13 53	14a30		14 01		14 23	15a00		
Roby	d			12 41		12 55		13 03			13 25				13 41		13 55			14 03		14 25			
Broad Green	d			12 44		12 58		13 07			13 28				13 44		13 58			14 07		14 28			
Wavertree Technology Park	d		12 38	12 47		13 01		13 10			13 31			13 38	13 47		14 01			14 10		14 31			14 38
Edge Hill 89,91	d			12 50		13 04		13 13			13 34				13 50		14 04			14 13		14 34			
Liverpool Lime Street 10 89,91	a		12 48	12 59		13 13		13 21			13 43			13 48	13 59		14 13			14 21		14 43			14 48

		NT	AW	NT		NT	NT	NT	NT	NT	AW	NT	NT	AW		NT	NT	NT	NT	NT	NT	AW	NT	NT
			◇ B					C	D		◇ A			◇ B					C	D		◇ A		
			🛒			🚌				🚌	🛒			🛒			🚌				🚌	🛒		
Manchester Airport 85 ✈	d											14 41											15 41	
Manchester Piccadilly 10 🚇	d										14 50	15 01										15 50	16 01	
Manchester Oxford Road	d										14 53	15 04										15 53	16 04	
Manchester Victoria 🚇	d								14 39											15 39				
Eccles	d								14 46											15 46				
Patricroft	d								14 49											15 49				
Blackpool North 97	d						13 37											14 37						
Preston 8 65,82	d						14 04											15 04						
Leyland 82	d						14 09											15 09						
Euxton Balshaw Lane	d						14 14											15 14						
Wigan North Western 65	a						14 26											15 26						
	d	14 08				14 14	14 38			14 44			15 08				15 14	15 38			15 44			16 08
Newton-le-Willows	d								15 01		15 12	15 22								16 01		16 12	16 22	
Warrington Bank Quay	d		14 19	14 22										15 19		15 22								
Earlestown 8	d		14a26	14 34				14 50	15 04		15 15			15a26		15 34			15 50	16 04		16 15		
Warrington Bank Quay	a							15 01			15 25								16 01			16 25		
St Helens Junction	d			14 39					15 09			15 27				15 39				16 09			16 27	
Lea Green	d			14 42					15 12							15 42				16 12				
Rainhill	d			14 46					15 16							15 46				16 16				
Whiston	d			14 49					15 19							15 49				16 19				
Bryn	d					14 27				14 57							15 27				15 57			
Garswood	d					14 34				15 04							15 34				16 04			
St Helens Central	a					14 54				15 24							15 54				16 24			
	d					14 54				15 24							15 54				16 24			
Thatto Heath	d					15 04				15 34							16 04				16 34			
Eccleston Park	d					15 14				15 44							16 14				16 44			
Prescot	d					15 20				15 50							16 20				16 50			
Huyton	d	14 39		14 53		15a30	15 01		15 23	16a00			15 39			15 53	16a30	16 00		16 23	17a00			16 39
Roby	d	14 41		14 55			15 03		15 25				15 41			15 55		16 02		16 25				16 41
Broad Green	d	14 44		14 58			15 07		15 28				15 44			15 58		16 06		16 28				16 44
Wavertree Technology Park	d	14 47		15 01			15 10		15 31			15 38	15 47			16 01		16 09		16 31			16 38	16 47
Edge Hill 89,91	d	14 50		15 04			15 13		15 34				15 50			16 04		16 12		16 34				16 50
Liverpool Lime Street 10 89,91	a	14 59		15 13			15 21		15 43			15 48	15 59			16 13		16 20		16 43			16 48	16 59

A To Llandudno
B From Llandudno to Manchester Piccadilly
C From Liverpool Lime Street
D From Stalybridge

Table 90

Saturdays
from 31 March

Manchester, Preston, Wigan and Newton-le-Willows - St Helens and Liverpool

Network Diagram - see first Page of Table 88

Station		AW ◇ A [trolley]	NT	NT [bus]	NT	NT B	NT [bus]	AW ◇ C [trolley]	NT	NT		AW ◇ A [trolley]	NT	NT [bus]	NT	NT B	AW ◇ C [trolley]	NT	NT [bus]	NT		NT [bus]	AW ◇ A [trolley]	NT	NT
Manchester Airport 85 ✈	d								16 41									17 41							
Manchester Piccadilly 10	d							16 50	17 01								17 50	18 01							
Manchester Oxford Road	d							16 53	17 04								17 53	18 04							
Manchester Victoria	d					16 39							17 09			17 39									
Eccles	d					16 46							17 16			17 46		18 11							
Patricroft	d					16 49							17 19			17 49									
Blackpool North 97	d				15 37										16 35										17 37
Preston 8 65,82	d				16 04										17 04										18 04
Leyland 82	d				16 09										17 09										18 09
Euxton Balshaw Lane	d				16 14										17 14										18 14
Wigan North Western 65	a				16 26										17 26										18 26
	d			16 14	16 38		16 44			17 08				17 14	17 38				17 44	18 08		18 14		18 21	18 38
Newton-le-Willows	d					17 01		17 12	17 22				17 31			18 01	18 12	18 24						18 33	
Warrington Bank Quay	d	16 19	16 22									17 19											18 19		
Earlestown 8	d	16a26	16 34			17 04		17 15				17a26	17 34			18 04	18 15						18a26	18 36	
Warrington Bank Quay	a							17 25									18 24								
St Helens Junction	d		16 39			17 09			17 27				17 39			18 09		18 29						18 41	
Lea Green	d		16 42			17 12							17 42			18 12		18 32						18 44	
Rainhill	d		16 46			17 16							17 46			18 16		18 36						18 48	
Whiston	d		16 49			17 19							17 49			18 19								18 51	
Bryn	d			16 27			16 57							17 27					17 57			18 27			
Garswood	d			16 34			17 04							17 34					18 04			18 34			
St Helens Central	a			16 54			17 24							17 54					18 24			18 54			
	d			16 54			17 24							17 54					18 24			18 54			
Thatto Heath	d			17 04			17 34							18 04					18 34			19 04			
Eccleston Park	d			17 14			17 44							18 14					18 44			19 14			
Prescot	d			17 20			17 50							18 20					18 50			19 20			
Huyton	d		16 53	17a30	17 02	17 23	18a00			17 39			17 53	18a30	18 01	18 23		18 41	19a00	18 46		19a30		18 55	19 00
Roby	d		16 55		17 04	17 25				17 41			17 55		18 03	18 25		18 43						18 57	19 02
Broad Green	d		16 58		17 07	17 28				17 44			17 58		18 07	18 28		18 47						19 00	19 06
Wavertree Technology Park	d		17 01		17 10	17 31			17 38	17 47			18 01		18 10	18 31		18 50		18 54				19 03	19 09
Edge Hill 89,91	d		17 04		17 13	17 34				17 50			18 04		18 13	18 34				18 57				19 06	19 12
Liverpool Lime Street 10 89,91	a		17 13		17 22	17 43			17 48	17 59			18 13		18 21	18 43		19 00		19 08				19 15	19 19

Station		NT D	NT B	AW E [trolley]	NT	NT		AW ◇ F [trolley]	NT	NT [bus]	NT	NT	NT [bus]	AW E	NT	AW ◇ A [trolley]		NT	NT	NT	AW E	NT [bus]	NT	AW ◇ A	NT
Manchester Airport 85 ✈	d				18 41										19 41						20 32				
Manchester Piccadilly 10	d			18 50	19 01									19 50	20 01						20 50				
Manchester Oxford Road	d			18 53	19 04									19 53	20 04						20 53				
Manchester Victoria	d		18 39									19 39								20 39					21 39
Eccles	d		18 46									19 46								20 46					21 46
Patricroft	d		18 49									19 49								20 49					21 49
Blackpool North 97	d										18 37								19 37				20 37		
Preston 8 65,82	d										19 04								20 04				21 04		
Leyland 82	d										19 09								20 09				21 09		
Euxton Balshaw Lane	d										19 14								20 14				21 14		
Wigan North Western 65	a										19 26								20 26				21 25		
	d					19 08				19 14	19 37		19 44					20 19	20 37			20 44	21 32		
Newton-le-Willows	d		19 01	19 12	19 22							20 01		20 12	20 22					20 59	21 12				22 01
Warrington Bank Quay	d							19 19	19 22							20 19								21 19	
Earlestown 8	d	18 50	19 04	19 16				19a26	19 34			20 04		20 15		20a26				21 04	21 15			21a26	22 04
Warrington Bank Quay	a	19 01		19 26										20 29							21 26				
St Helens Junction	d		19 09		19 27				19 39			20 09			20 27					21 09					22 09
Lea Green	d		19 12						19 42			20 12								21 12					22 12
Rainhill	d		19 16						19 46			20 16								21 16					22 16
Whiston	d		19 19						19 49			20 19								21 19					22 19
Bryn	d									19 27			19 57									20 57			
Garswood	d									19 34			20 04									21 04			
St Helens Central	a									19 54			20 24									21 24			
	d									19 54			20 24									21 24			
Thatto Heath	d									20 04			20 34									21 34			
Eccleston Park	d									20 14			20 44									21 44			
Prescot	d									20 20			20 50									21 50			
Huyton	d		19 23			19 39			19 53	20a30	19 59	20 23	21a00					20 39	20 57	21 23		22a00	21 54		22 23
Roby	d		19 25			19 41			19 55		20 01	20 25						20 41	20 59	21 25			21 56		22 25
Broad Green	d		19 28			19 44			19 58		20 05	20 28						20 44	21 02	21 28			21 59		22 28
Wavertree Technology Park	d		19 31		19 38	19 47			20 01		20 08	20 31			20 38			20 47	21 05	21 31			22 02		22 31
Edge Hill 89,91	d		19 34			19 50			20 04		20 11	20 34						20 50	21 08	21 34			22 05		22 34
Liverpool Lime Street 10 89,91	a		19 43		19 48	19 59			20 13		20 18	20 43			20 48			20 59	21 17	21 43			22 13		22 43

A From Llandudno to Manchester Piccadilly
B From Stalybridge
C To Llandudno
D From Liverpool Lime Street
E To Chester
F From Llandudno to Manchester Airport

Table 90

Saturdays
from 31 March

Manchester, Preston, Wigan and Newton-le-Willows - St Helens and Liverpool

Network Diagram - see first Page of Table 88

		NT		AW	NT	AW	NT	AW	NT	NT	VT	NT		TP	NT	AW	NT	AW
											◇1			◇1				
				A		B		A			C					A		B
		🚌								🚌							🚌	
											☕							
Manchester Airport 85 ✈	d				21 41									22 55				
Manchester Piccadilly 10 🚊	d			21 50	22 01			22 26						23a09		23 14		
Manchester Oxford Road	d			21 53	22 04			22 29								23 17		
Manchester Victoria 🚊	d								22 39						23 09			
Eccles	d								22 46						23 16			
Patricroft	d								22 49						23 19			
Blackpool North 97	d											22 14						
Preston 8 65,82	d										22 26	22 43						
Leyland 82	d											22 48						
Euxton Balshaw Lane	d											22 53						
Wigan North Western 65	a										22 37	23 01						
	d	21 34					22 25			22 35	22 37	23 05					23 15	
Newton-le-Willows	d			22 12	22 22			22 47	23 01						23 31	23 36		
Warrington Bank Quay	d					22 19					22a48							23 50
Earlestown 8	d			22 15		22a26		22 50	23 04						23 34	23 39		23a58
Warrington Bank Quay	a			22 23				22 58								23 47		
St Helens Junction	d				22 27				23 09						23 39			
Lea Green	d								23 12						23 42			
Rainhill	d								23 16						23 46			
Whiston	d								23 19						23 49			
Bryn	d	21 47								22 48								
Garswood	d	21 54								22 55								
St Helens Central	a	22 14								23 15								
	d	22 14								23 15								
Thatto Heath	d	22 24								23 25								
Eccleston Park	d	22 34								23 35								
Prescot	d	22 40								23 41								
Huyton	d	22a50					22 45		23 23	23 51		23 28			23 53			
Roby	d						22 47		23 25	23 55		23 30			23 55			
Broad Green	d						22 50		23 28	00 02		23 34			23 57			
Wavertree Technology Park	d				22 38		22 53		23 31	00 12		23 37			00 01			
Edge Hill 89,91	d						22 58		23 34	00 22		23 40			00 04			
Liverpool Lime Street 10 89,91	a				22 48		23 06		23 43	00 29		23 47			00 13		00 15	

Sundays
until 12 February

		NT	TP	TP	TP	AW	TP	TP	TP	NT		NT	VT	NT	AW	NT	VT	AW	AW	VT		NT	VT	AW	NT
													◇1				◇1	◇		◇1			◇1		
		D	E	E	E	A	E	E	E				F		B		F	B	A	G			F	B	
			🚌	🚌	🚌	🚌	🚌	🚌	🚌																
													☕				☕			☕			☕	trolley	
Manchester Airport 85 ✈	d		01∫07	04∫25	06∫05		07∫07	07∫52	08∫20							09 35									10 35
Manchester Piccadilly 10 🚊	d		01a32	04a50	06a30	07 28	07a32	08a17	08a45							09 50			09 56						10 50
Manchester Oxford Road	d					07 33										09 53			09 59						10 53
Manchester Victoria 🚊	d	23p09										08 53													
Eccles	d	23p16										09 00				10 00									11 00
Patricroft	d	23p19																							
Blackpool North 97	d													08 50								09 50			
Preston 8 65,82	d												09 00	09 15			10 00			10 17		10 15	10 58		
Leyland 82	d													09 21								10 21			
Euxton Balshaw Lane	d													09 25								10 25			
Wigan North Western 65	a												09 10	09 35			10 10			10 28		10 36	11 09		
	d									08 36			09 11	09 36			10 11			10 28		10 36	11 09		
Newton-le-Willows	d	23p31				08 03						09 13				10 13			10 18						11 13
Warrington Bank Quay	d												09a21		09 10		10a21	10 12		10a39			11a20	11 03	
Earlestown 8	d	23p34				08 13						09 16			09a16	10 16		10a19	10 21					11a10	11 16
Warrington Bank Quay	a					08 38													10 27						
St Helens Junction	d	23p39										09 21				10 21									11 21
Lea Green	d	23p42										09 24				10 24									11 24
Rainhill	d	23p46										09 28				10 28									11 28
Whiston	d	23p49										09 31				10 31									11 31
Bryn	d																								
Garswood	d									08 46				09 46								10 46			
St Helens Central	a									08 52				09 52								10 52			
	d									08 53				09 53								10 53			
Thatto Heath	d									08 56				09 56								10 56			
Eccleston Park	d																								
Prescot	d									09 00				10 00								11 00			
Huyton	d	23p53								09 05		09 35		10 05		10 35						11 05			11 35
Roby	d	23p55								09 07		09 37		10 07		10 37						11 07			11 37
Broad Green	d	23p57								09 10		09 40		10 10		10 40						11 10			11 40
Wavertree Technology Park	d	00∫01								09 13		09 43		10 13		10 43						11 13			11 43
Edge Hill 89,91	d	00∫04																							
Liverpool Lime Street 10 89,91	a	00∫13								09 26		09 52		10 24		10 54						11 24			11 54

A To Chester
B From Chester to Manchester Piccadilly
C From Edinburgh to Crewe
D not 11 December
E from 8 January until 12 February
F To London Euston
G To Birmingham New Street

Table 90

Sundays
until 12 February

Manchester, Preston, Wigan and Newton-le-Willows - St Helens and Liverpool

Network Diagram - see first Page of Table 88

		AW	VT	NT	AW	NT		AW	VT	NT	AW	NT	NT	AW	AW	NT		NT	AW	AW	NT	NT	AW	AW	NT
			◇1						◇1																
		A	B ☕		C 🛒			A 🛒	D ☕		C 🛒			A 🛒	C 🛒				A 🛒	C 🛒			A 🛒	C	
Manchester Airport 85 ✈	d					11 33						12 35				13 35					14 35				15 35
Manchester Piccadilly 10 🚊	d	10 55				11 50		11 56				12 50		12 56		13 50			13 56		14 50		14 56		15 50
Manchester Oxford Road	d	10 59				11 53		11 59				12 53		12 59		13 53			13 59		14 53		14 59		15 53
Manchester Victoria 🚊	d																								
Eccles	d					12 00						13 00				14 00					15 00				16 00
Patricroft	d																								
Blackpool North 97	d			10 50						11 50			12 50					13 50				14 50			
Preston 8 65,82	d		11 17	11 15					12 17	12 15			13 15					14 15				15 15			
Leyland 82	d			11 21						12 21			13 21					14 21				15 21			
Euxton Balshaw Lane	d			11 25						12 25			13 25					14 25				15 25			
Wigan North Western 65	a		11 28	11 35					12 28	12 35			13 35					14 35				15 35			
	d		11 28	11 36					12 28	12 36			13 36					14 36				15 36			
Newton-le-Willows	d	11 20				12 13		12 18				13 13		13 18		14 13			14 18		15 13		15 18		16 13
Warrington Bank Quay	d		11a39		12 03				12a39		13 03				14 03					15 03				16 03	
Earlestown 8	d	11 23			12a10	12 16		12 21			13a10	13 16		13 21	14a10	14 16			14 21	15a10	15 16		15 21	16a10	16 16
Warrington Bank Quay	a	11 29						12 27						13 28					14 27				15 28		
St Helens Junction	d					12 21						13 21				14 21					15 21				16 21
Lea Green	d					12 24						13 24				14 24					15 24				16 24
Rainhill	d					12 28						13 28				14 28					15 28				16 28
Whiston	d					12 31						13 31				14 31					15 31				16 31
Bryn	d																								
Garswood	d			11 46						12 46			13 46					14 46				15 46			
St Helens Central	a			11 52						12 52			13 52					14 52				15 52			
	d			11 53						12 53			13 53					14 53				15 53			
Thatto Heath	d			11 56						12 56			13 56					14 56				15 56			
Eccleston Park	d																								
Prescot	d			12 00						13 00			14 00					15 00				16 00			
Huyton	d			12 05		12 35				13 05		13 35	14 05			14 35		15 05			15 35	16 05			16 35
Roby	d			12 07		12 37				13 07		13 37	14 07			14 37		15 07			15 37	16 07			16 37
Broad Green	d			12 10		12 40				13 10		13 40	14 10			14 40		15 10			15 40	16 10			16 40
Wavertree Technology Park	d			12 13		12 43				13 13		13 43	14 13			14 43		15 13			15 43	16 13			16 43
Edge Hill 89,91	d																								
Liverpool Lime Street 10 89,91	a			12 24		12 54				13 24		13 54	14 24			14 54		15 24			15 54	16 24			16 54

		NT		AW	AW	NT	NT	AW	AW	NT	NT	AW		AW	NT	NT	AW	AW	NT	NT	AW	AW		NT	NT
					◇				◇																
				A 🛒	E 🛒			A	C			A 🛒		C			A	C			A	C			
Manchester Airport 85 ✈	d					16 35				17 35					18 35				19 35					20 35	
Manchester Piccadilly 10 🚊	d			15 56		16 50		16 56		17 50		17 56			18 50		18 56		19 50		19 56			20 50	
Manchester Oxford Road	d			15 59		16 53		16 59		17 53		17 59			18 53		18 59		19 53		19 59			20 53	
Manchester Victoria 🚊	d																								
Eccles	d					17 00				18 00					19 00				20 00					21 00	
Patricroft	d																								
Blackpool North 97	d	15 50					16 50				17 50					18 50				19 50					20 50
Preston 8 65,82	d	16 15					17 15				18 15					19 15				20 15					21 15
Leyland 82	d	16 21					17 21				18 21					19 21				20 21					21 21
Euxton Balshaw Lane	d	16 25					17 25				18 25					19 25				20 25					21 25
Wigan North Western 65	a	16 35					17 35				18 35					19 35				20 35					21 35
	d	16 36					17 36				18 36					19 36				20 36					21 36
Newton-le-Willows	d			16 18		17 13		17 18		18 13		18 18			19 13		19 18		20 13		20 18			21 13	
Warrington Bank Quay	d				17 03				18 03					19 03				20 03				21 03			
Earlestown 8	d			16 21	17a10	17 16		17 21	18a10	18 16		18 21		19a10	19 16		19 21	20a10	20 16		20 21	21a10		21 16	
Warrington Bank Quay	a			16 27				17 27				18 27					19 28				20 29				
St Helens Junction	d					17 21				18 21					19 21				20 21					21 21	
Lea Green	d					17 24				18 24					19 24				20 24					21 24	
Rainhill	d					17 28				18 28					19 28				20 28					21 28	
Whiston	d					17 31				18 31					19 31				20 31					21 31	
Bryn	d																								
Garswood	d	16 46					17 46				18 46					19 46				20 46					21 46
St Helens Central	a	16 52					17 52				18 52					19 52				20 52					21 52
	d	16 53					17 53				18 53					19 53				20 53					21 53
Thatto Heath	d	16 56					17 56				18 56					19 56				20 56					21 56
Eccleston Park	d																								
Prescot	d	17 00					18 00				19 00					20 00				21 00					22 00
Huyton	d	17 05				17 35	18 05			18 35	19 05				19 35	20 05			20 35	21 05				21 35	22 05
Roby	d	17 07				17 37	18 07			18 37	19 07				19 37	20 07			20 37	21 07				21 37	22 07
Broad Green	d	17 10				17 40	18 10			18 40	19 10				19 40	20 10			20 40	21 10				21 40	22 10
Wavertree Technology Park	d	17 13				17 43	18 13			18 43	19 13				19 43	20 13			20 43	21 13				21 43	22 13
Edge Hill 89,91	d																								
Liverpool Lime Street 10 89,91	a	17 24				17 54	18 24			18 54	19 24				19 54	20 24			20 54	21 24				21 54	22 24

A To Chester
B To Birmingham New Street
C From Chester to Manchester Piccadilly
D from 8 January until 12 February. To Birmingham New Street
E From Holyhead to Manchester Piccadilly

Table 90

Sundays
until 12 February

Manchester, Preston, Wigan and Newton-le-Willows - St Helens and Liverpool

Network Diagram - see first Page of Table 88

		AW	NT	NT	NT	NT
		A				🚌
Manchester Airport 85 ✈	d		21 35			
Manchester Piccadilly 10 🚆	d	20 56	21 50			
Manchester Oxford Road	d	20 59	21 53			23 00
Manchester Victoria 🚆	d					
Eccles	d		22 00			23 15
Patricroft	d					
Blackpool North 97	d			21 50	22 44	
Preston 8 65,82	d			22 15	23 09	
Leyland 82	d			22 21	23 15	
Euxton Balshaw Lane	d			22 25	23 19	
Wigan North Western 65	a			22 35	23 29	
	d			22 36	23 30	
Newton-le-Willows	d	21 18	22 13			23 40
Warrington Bank Quay	d					
Earlestown 8	d	21 21	22 16			23 48
Warrington Bank Quay	a	21 27				
St Helens Junction	d		22 21			00 01
Lea Green	d		22 24			00 07
Rainhill	d		22 28			00 15
Whiston	d		22 31			00 25
Bryn	d					
Garswood	d			22 46	23 40	
St Helens Central	a			22 53	23 46	
	d			22 53	23 47	
Thatto Heath	d			22 56	23 50	
Eccleston Park	d					
Prescot	d			23 00	23 54	
Huyton	d		22 35	23 05	23 59	00 35
Roby	d		22 37	23 07	00 01	00 39
Broad Green	d		22 40	23 10	00 04	00 46
Wavertree Technology Park	d		22 43	23 13	00 07	00 56
Edge Hill 89,91	d					
Liverpool Lime Street 10 89,91	a		22 54	23 24	00 18	01 11

Sundays
19 February to 25 March

		NT	NT	AW	NT	AW	NT	NT	VT	AW		AW	NT
									◇1				
				A		A			B	C		A	
		🚌	🚌	🚌	🚌	🚌	🚌	🚌		🚌		🚌	
									☕				
Manchester Airport 85 ✈	d												10 16
Manchester Piccadilly 10 🚆	d			07 28		08 49						09 47	10 31
Manchester Oxford Road	d			07 33		08 54		08 55				09 52	10 36
Manchester Victoria 🚆	d												
Eccles	d							09 10					
Patricroft	d												
Blackpool North 97	d												
Preston 8 65,82	d								09 00				
Leyland 82	d												
Euxton Balshaw Lane	d												
Wigan North Western 65	a								09 10				
	d	22p35	23p15		07 50		08 50		09 11				
Newton-le-Willows	d			08 03		09 24		09 35				10 22	
Warrington Bank Quay	d								09a21	09 41			
Earlestown 8	d			08 13		09 34		09 43		10a06		10 32	
Warrington Bank Quay	a			08 38		09 59						10 57	
St Helens Junction	d							09 55					
Lea Green	d							10 02					
Rainhill	d							10 10					
Whiston	d							10 20					
Bryn	d	22p48											
Garswood	d	22p55			08 10		09 10						
St Helens Central	a	23p15			08 30		09 30						
	d	23p15			08 30		09 30						
Thatto Heath	d	23p25			08 40		09 40						
Eccleston Park	d	23p35											
Prescot	d	23p41			08 50		09 50						
Huyton	d	23p51			09 00		10 00	10 30					
Roby	d	23p55			09 04		10 04	10 34					
Broad Green	d	00 02			09 11		10 11	10 41					
Wavertree Technology Park	d	00 12			09 21		10 21	10 51					
Edge Hill 89,91	d	00 22											
Liverpool Lime Street 10 89,91	a	00 29	00 15		09 36		10 36	11 06					11 16

		NT	VT	VT	NT	NT	AW	AW		NT	VT	VT	NT
			◇1	◇1							◇1	◇1	
			B	D			C	A			B	D	
		🚌				🚌	🚌	🚌		🚌			
			☕	☕							☕	☕	
Manchester Airport 85 ✈	d				10 56								11 56
Manchester Piccadilly 10 🚆	d				11 12			10 45					12 11
Manchester Oxford Road	d				11 22	09 55		10 50					12 22
Manchester Victoria 🚆	d												
Eccles	d					10 10							
Patricroft	d												
Blackpool North 97	d												
Preston 8 65,82	d		10 00	10 17							10 58	11 17	
Leyland 82	d												
Euxton Balshaw Lane	d												
Wigan North Western 65	a		10 10	10 28							11 09	11 28	
	d	09 50	10 11	10 28						10 50	11 09	11 28	
Newton-le-Willows	d					10 35		11 20					
Warrington Bank Quay	d		10a21	10a39			10 42				11a20	11a39	
Earlestown 8	d					10 43	11a07	11 30					
Warrington Bank Quay	a							11 55					
St Helens Junction	d					10 55							
Lea Green	d					11 02							
Rainhill	d					11 10							
Whiston	d					11 20							
Bryn	d												
Garswood	d	10 10								11 10			
St Helens Central	a	10 30								11 30			
	d	10 30								11 30			
Thatto Heath	d	10 40								11 40			
Eccleston Park	d												
Prescot	d	10 50								11 50			
Huyton	d	11 00				11 30				12 00			
Roby	d	11 04				11 34				12 04			
Broad Green	d	11 11				11 41				12 11			
Wavertree Technology Park	d	11 21				11 51				12 21			
Edge Hill 89,91	d												
Liverpool Lime Street 10 89,91	a	11 36			12 02	12 06				12 36			13 02

A To Chester
B To London Euston
C From Chester to Manchester Piccadilly
D To Birmingham New Street

Table 90

Sundays

19 February to 25 March

Manchester, Preston, Wigan and Newton-le-Willows - St Helens and Liverpool

Network Diagram - see first Page of Table 88

		NT	AW	AW	NT	VT		NT	NT	AW	AW	NT	NT	NT	AW	AW		NT	NT	NT	AW	AW	NT	NT	NT
						◇1																			
			A	B		C				A	B				A	B					A	B			
		🚌	🚌	🚌	🚌				🚌	🚌	🚌	🚌		🚌	🚌	🚌		🚌		🚌	🚌	🚌	🚌		🚌
						🍴																			
Manchester Airport 85 ✈	d							12 58					14 06						14 58					15 58	
Manchester Piccadilly 10	d			11 45				13 12			12 45		14 20			13 46			15 12			14 45		16 12	
Manchester Oxford Road	d	10 55		11 50				13 22	11 55		12 50		14 23	12 55		13 51			15 22	13 55		14 50		16 22	14 55
Manchester Victoria	d																								
Eccles	d	11 10							12 10					13 10						14 10					15 10
Patricroft	d																								
Blackpool North 97	d																								
Preston 8 65,82	d					12 17																			
Leyland 82	d																								
Euxton Balshaw Lane	d																								
Wigan North Western 65	a					12 28																			
	d				11 50	12 28						12 50						13 50					14 50		
Newton-le-Willows	d	11 35		12 20					12 35		13 20			13 35		14 21				14 35		15 20			15 35
Warrington Bank Quay	d		11 40			12a39				12 36					13 36						14 36				
Earlestown 8	d	11 43	12a05	12 30					12 43	13a01	13 30			13 43	14a01	14 31				14 43	15a01	15 30			15 43
Warrington Bank Quay	a			12 55							13 55					14 56						15 55			
St Helens Junction	d	11 55							12 55					13 55						14 55					15 55
Lea Green	d	12 02							13 02					14 02						15 02					16 02
Rainhill	d	12 10							13 10					14 10						15 10					16 10
Whiston	d	12 20							13 20					14 20						15 20					16 20
Bryn	d																								
Garswood	d				12 10							13 10						14 10					15 10		
St Helens Central	a				12 30							13 30						14 30					15 30		
	d				12 30							13 30						14 30					15 30		
Thatto Heath	d				12 40							13 40						14 40					15 40		
Eccleston Park	d																								
Prescot	d				12 50							13 50						14 50					15 50		
Huyton	d	12 30			13 00				13 30			14 00		14 30				15 00		15 30			16 00		16 30
Roby	d	12 34			13 04				13 34			14 04		14 34				15 04		15 34			16 04		16 34
Broad Green	d	12 41			13 11				13 41			14 11		14 41				15 11		15 41			16 11		16 41
Wavertree Technology Park	d	12 51			13 21				13 51			14 21		14 51				15 21		15 51			16 21		16 50
Edge Hill 89,91	d																								
Liverpool Lime Street 10 89,91	a	13 06			13 36			14 02	14 06			14 36	15 04	15 06				15 36	16 02	16 06			16 36	17 02	17 05

		AW		AW	NT	NT	NT	AW	AW	NT	NT	NT		AW	AW	NT	NT	NT	AW	AW	NT	NT		NT	AW
		A		B				A	B					A	B				A	B					A
		🚌		🚌	🚌		🚌	🚌	🚌	🚌		🚌		🚌	🚌	🚌		🚌	🚌	🚌	🚌			🚌	🚌
Manchester Airport 85 ✈	d					16 58					17 58						18 58					19 58			
Manchester Piccadilly 10	d			15 45		17 12			16 45		18 12				17 46		19 12			18 47		20 12			
Manchester Oxford Road	d			15 50		17 22	15 55		16 50		18 22	16 55			17 51		19 22	17 55		18 52		20 22		18 55	
Manchester Victoria	d																								
Eccles	d						16 10					17 10						18 10						19 10	
Patricroft	d																								
Blackpool North 97	d																								
Preston 8 65,82	d																								
Leyland 82	d																								
Euxton Balshaw Lane	d																								
Wigan North Western 65	a																								
	d				15 50					16 50						17 50					18 50				
Newton-le-Willows	d			16 20			16 35		17 20			17 35			18 21			18 35		19 22				19 35	
Warrington Bank Quay	d	15 36						16 36						17 36					18 36						19 36
Earlestown 8	d	16a01		16 30			16 43	17a01	17 30			17 43		18a01	18 31			18 43	19a01	19 32				19 43	20a01
Warrington Bank Quay	a			16 55					17 55						18 56					19 57					
St Helens Junction	d						16 55					17 55						18 55						19 55	
Lea Green	d						17 02					18 02						19 02						20 02	
Rainhill	d						17 10					18 10						19 10						20 10	
Whiston	d						17 20					18 20						19 20						20 20	
Bryn	d																								
Garswood	d				16 10					17 10						18 10					19 10				
St Helens Central	a				16 30					17 30						18 30					19 30				
	d				16 30					17 30						18 30					19 30				
Thatto Heath	d				16 40					17 40						18 40					19 40				
Eccleston Park	d																								
Prescot	d				16 50					17 50						18 50					19 50				
Huyton	d				17 00		17 30			18 00		18 30				19 00		19 30			20 00			20 30	
Roby	d				17 04		17 34			18 04		18 34				19 04		19 34			20 04			20 34	
Broad Green	d				17 11		17 41			18 11		18 41				19 11		19 41			20 11			20 41	
Wavertree Technology Park	d				17 21		17 51			18 21		18 51				19 21		19 51			20 21			20 51	
Edge Hill 89,91	d																								
Liverpool Lime Street 10 89,91	a				17 36	18 02	18 06			18 36	19 02	19 06				19 36	20 02	20 06			20 36	21 02		21 06	

A From Chester to Manchester Piccadilly
B To Chester
C To Birmingham New Street

Table 90

Sundays

19 February to 25 March

Manchester, Preston, Wigan and Newton-le-Willows - St Helens and Liverpool

Network Diagram - see first Page of Table 88

		AW	NT	NT	NT	AW	AW	NT		NT	AW	AW	NT	NT	AW	AW	NT	AW		NT	AW	NT			
		A				B	A				B	A			A	B		B			A				
		🚌	🚌		🚌	🚌	🚌	🚌		🚌	🚌	🚌	🚌	🚌	🚌	🚌	🚌	🚌		🚌	🚌	🚌			
Manchester Airport 85 ✈	d			20 58																					
Manchester Piccadilly 10	d	19 45		21 12			20 45					21 45			22 14						23 25				
Manchester Oxford Road	d	19 50		21 22	19 55		20 50			20 55		21 50		21 55	22 19					23 00	23 30				
Manchester Victoria	d																								
Eccles	d				20 10					21 10				22 10						23 15					
Patricroft	d																								
Blackpool North 97	d																								
Preston 8 65,82	d																								
Leyland 82	d																								
Euxton Balshaw Lane	d																								
Wigan North Western 65	a																								
	d		19 50					20 50					21 50				22 50					23 42			
Newton-le-Willows	d	20 20			20 35		21 20			21 35		22 20		22 35	22 49					23 40	00 01				
Warrington Bank Quay	d					20 36					21 36					22 36		23 09							
Earlestown 8	d	20 30			20 43	21a01	21 30			21 43	22a01	22 30		22 43	22 59	23a01		23a34		23 48	00 10				
Warrington Bank Quay	a	20 55					21 55					22 55			23 24						00 35				
St Helens Junction	d				20 55					21 55				22 55						00 01					
Lea Green	d				21 02					22 02				23 02						00 07					
Rainhill	d				21 10					22 10				23 10						00 15					
Whiston	d				21 20					22 20				23 20						00 25					
Bryn	d																								
Garswood	d		20 10					21 10					22 10				23 10					00 02			
St Helens Central	a		20 30					21 30					22 30				23 30					00 22			
	d		20 30					21 30					22 30				23 30					00 22			
Thatto Heath	d		20 40					21 40					22 40				23 40					00 32			
Eccleston Park	d																								
Prescot	d		20 50					21 50					22 50				23 51					00 43			
Huyton	d		21 00		21 30			22 00		22 30			23 00	23 30			00 01			00 35		00 53			
Roby	d		21 04		21 34			22 04		22 34			23 04	23 34			00 05			00 39		00 57			
Broad Green	d		21 11		21 41			22 11		22 41			23 11	23 41			00 12			00 46		01 04			
Wavertree Technology Park	d		21 21		21 51			22 21		22 51			23 21	23 51			00 22			00 56		01 14			
Edge Hill 89,91	d																								
Liverpool Lime Street 10 89,91	a		21 36	22 02	22 06			22 36		23 06			23 36	00 06			00 37			01 11		01 29			

Sundays

from 1 April

		NT	NT	NT	TP	AW	NT	NT	NT	NT		VT	AW	TP	NT	NT	NT	VT	AW	AW		VT	NT	AW	NT
												◇1		◇1				◇1	◇			◇1			
					C	A						D	B					D	B	A		E		B	
			🚌	🚌	🚌	🚌	🚌			🚌							🚌								
												🍴						🍴				🍴		🛒	
Manchester Airport 85 ✈	d				06 05				08 34							09 35									10 35
Manchester Piccadilly 10	d				06a30	07 28			08 49							09 50				09 56					10 50
Manchester Oxford Road	d					07 33			08 52							09 53				09 59					10 53
Manchester Victoria	d	23p09												09 15											
Eccles	d	23p16							09 00							10 00									11 00
Patricroft	d	23p19																							
Blackpool North 97	d														08 50								09 50		
Preston 8 65,82	d											09 00			09 15			10 00				10 17	10 15		
Leyland 82	d														09 21								10 21		
Euxton Balshaw Lane	d														09 25								10 25		
Wigan North Western 65	a											09 10			09 35			10 10				10 28	10 36		
	d		22p35	23p15			07 42	08 36		08 42		09 11			09 36		09 42	10 11				10 28	10 36		
Newton-le-Willows	d	23p31				08 03			09 13					09 33		10 13				10 18					11 13
Warrington Bank Quay	d											09a21	09 10					10a21	10 12			10a39		11 03	
Earlestown 8	d	23p34				08 13			09 16				09a16			10 16			10a19	10 21				11a10	11 16
Warrington Bank Quay	a					08 38														10 27					
St Helens Junction	d	23p39							09 21							10 21									11 21
Lea Green	d	23p42							09 24							10 24									11 24
Rainhill	d	23p46							09 28							10 28									11 28
Whiston	d	23p49							09 31							10 31									11 31
Bryn	d		22p48																						
Garswood	d		22p55				08 02			09 02							10 02								
St Helens Central	a		23p15				08 22			09 22							10 22								
	d		23p15				08 22			09 22							10 22								
Thatto Heath	d		23p25				08 32			09 32							10 32								
Eccleston Park	d		23p35																						
Prescot	d		23p41				08 42			09 42							10 42								
Huyton	d	23p53	23p51				08a52	09 05	09 35	09a52					10 05	10 35	10a52						11 05		11 35
Roby	d	23p55	23p55					09 07	09 37						10 07	10 37							11 07		11 37
Broad Green	d	23p57	00 02					09 10	09 40						10 10	10 40							11 10		11 40
Wavertree Technology Park	d	00 01	00 12					09 13	09 43						10 13	10 43							11 13		11 43
Edge Hill 89,91	d	00 04	00 22																						
Liverpool Lime Street 10 89,91	a	00 13	00 29	00 15				09 26	09 52					09 56	10 24	10 54							11 24		11 54

A To Chester
B From Chester to Manchester Piccadilly
C To Leeds
D To London Euston
E To Birmingham New Street

Table 90

Sundays
from 1 April

Manchester, Preston, Wigan and Newton-le-Willows - St Helens and Liverpool

Network Diagram - see first Page of Table 88

		NT	AW	VT	VT	NT	AW	NT	NT	AW	VT	VT	NT	AW	NT	NT	NT	AW	AW	NT	NT	NT	AW
				◇1	◇1						◇1	◇1											
			A	B	C		D			A	B	C		D				A	D				A
Manchester Airport 85	d							11 33							12 35					13 35			
Manchester Piccadilly 10	d		10 55					11 50		11 56					12 50			12 56		13 50			13 56
Manchester Oxford Road	d		10 59					11 53		11 59					12 53			12 59		13 53			13 59
Manchester Victoria	d																						
Eccles	d							12 00							13 00					14 00			
Patricroft	d																						
Blackpool North 97	d					10 50							11 50				12 50					13 50	
Preston 8 65,82	d			10 58	11 17	11 15					11 58	12 17	12 15				13 15					14 15	
Leyland 82	d					11 21							12 21				13 21					14 21	
Euxton Balshaw Lane	d					11 25							12 25				13 25					14 25	
Wigan North Western 65	a			11 09	11 28	11 35					12 09	12 28	12 35				13 35					14 35	
	d	10 42		11 09	11 28	11 36			11 42		12 09	12 28	12 36			12 42	13 36				13 42	14 36	
Newton-le-Willows	d		11 20					12 13		12 18					13 13			13 18		14 13			14 18
Warrington Bank Quay	d			11a20	11a39		12 03				12a20	12a39		13 03					14 03				
Earlestown 8	d		11 23				12a10	12 16		12 21				13a10	13 16			13 21	14a10	14 16			14 21
Warrington Bank Quay	a		11 29							12 27								13 28					14 27
St Helens Junction	d							12 21							13 21					14 21			
Lea Green	d							12 24							13 24					14 24			
Rainhill	d							12 28							13 28					14 28			
Whiston	d							12 31							13 31					14 31			
Bryn	d																						
Garswood	d	11 02							12 02							13 02					14 02		
St Helens Central	a	11 22							12 22							13 22					14 22		
	d	11 22							12 22							13 22					14 22		
Thatto Heath	d	11 32							12 32							13 32					14 32		
Eccleston Park	d																						
Prescot	d	11 42							12 42							13 42					14 42		
Huyton	d	11a52				12 05		12 35	12a52				13 05		13 35	13a52	14 05			14 35	14a52	15 05	
Roby	d					12 07		12 37					13 07		13 37		14 07			14 37		15 07	
Broad Green	d					12 10		12 40					13 10		13 40		14 10			14 40		15 10	
Wavertree Technology Park	d					12 13		12 43					13 13		13 43		14 13			14 43		15 13	
Edge Hill 89,91	d																						
Liverpool Lime Street 10 89,91	a					12 24		12 54					13 24		13 54		14 24			14 54		15 24	

		AW	NT	NT	NT	AW	AW	NT	NT	NT	AW	AW	NT	NT	NT	AW	NT	NT	NT	AW	AW	NT
												◇										
		D				A	D				A	E				A				A	D	
Manchester Airport 85	d		14 35					15 35					16 35				17 35					18 35
Manchester Piccadilly 10	d		14 50			14 56		15 50			15 56		16 50			16 56	17 50			17 56		18 50
Manchester Oxford Road	d		14 53			14 59		15 53			15 59		16 53			16 59	17 53			17 59		18 53
Manchester Victoria	d																					
Eccles	d		15 00					16 00					17 00				18 00					19 00
Patricroft	d																					
Blackpool North 97	d				14 50					15 50					16 50				17 50			
Preston 8 65,82	d				15 15					16 15					17 15				18 15			
Leyland 82	d				15 21					16 21					17 21				18 21			
Euxton Balshaw Lane	d				15 25					16 25					17 25				18 25			
Wigan North Western 65	a				15 35					16 35					17 35				18 35			
	d			14 42	15 36				15 42	16 36				16 42	17 36			17 42	18 36			
Newton-le-Willows	d		15 13			15 18		16 13			16 18		17 13			17 18	18 13			18 18		19 13
Warrington Bank Quay	d	15 03					16 03					17 03									19 03	
Earlestown 8	d	15a10	15 16			15 21	16a10	16 16			16 21	17a10	17 16			17 21	18 16			18 21	19a10	19 16
Warrington Bank Quay	a					15 28					16 27					17 27				18 27		
St Helens Junction	d		15 21					16 21					17 21				18 21					19 21
Lea Green	d		15 24					16 24					17 24				18 24					19 24
Rainhill	d		15 28					16 28					17 28				18 28					19 28
Whiston	d		15 31					16 31					17 31				18 31					19 31
Bryn	d																					
Garswood	d			15 02					16 02					17 02				18 02				
St Helens Central	a			15 22					16 22					17 22				18 22				
	d			15 22					16 22					17 22				18 22				
Thatto Heath	d			15 32					16 32					17 32				18 32				
Eccleston Park	d																					
Prescot	d			15 42					16 42					17 42				18 42				
Huyton	d		15 35	15a52	16 05			16 35	16a52	17 05			17 35	17a52	18 05		18 35	18a52	19b05			19 35
Roby	d		15 37		16 07			16 37		17 07			17 37		18 07		18 37		19 07			19 37
Broad Green	d		15 40		16 10			16 40		17 10			17 40		18 10		18 40		19 10			19 40
Wavertree Technology Park	d		15 43		16 13			16 43		17 13			17 43		18 13		18 43		19 13			19 43
Edge Hill 89,91	d																					
Liverpool Lime Street 10 89,91	a		15 54		16 24			16 54		17 24			17 54		18 24		18 54		19 24			19 54

A To Chester
B To London Euston
C To Birmingham New Street
D From Chester to Manchester Piccadilly
E From Holyhead to Manchester Piccadilly

Table 90

Sundays
from 1 April

Manchester, Preston, Wigan and Newton-le-Willows - St Helens and Liverpool

Network Diagram - see first Page of Table 88

		NT	NT	AW	AW	NT	NT	NT		AW	AW	NT	NT	NT	AW	NT	NT	NT		NT	NT	NT	NT		
				A	B					A	B				A										
		🚌					🚌						🚌				🚌			🚌		🚌	🚌		
Manchester Airport 85 ✈	d					19 35						20 35				21 35									
Manchester Piccadilly 10	d			18 56		19 50				19 56		20 50			20 56	21 50									
Manchester Oxford Road	d			18 59		19 53				19 59		20 53			20 59	21 53						23 00			
Manchester Victoria	d																								
Eccles	d					20 00						21 00				22 00						23 15			
Patricroft	d																								
Blackpool North 97	d		18 50					19 50						20 50				21 50			22 44				
Preston 8 65,82	d		19 15					20 15						21 15				22 15			23 09				
Leyland 82	d		19 21					20 21						21 21				22 21			23 15				
Euxton Balshaw Lane	d		19 25					20 25						21 25				22 25			23 19				
Wigan North Western 65	a		19 35					20 35						21 35				22 35			23 29				
	d	18 42	19 36				19 42	20 36					20 42	21 36			21 42	22 36		22 42	23 30		23 42		
Newton-le-Willows	d			19 18		20 13				20 18		21 13			21 18	22 13						23 40			
Warrington Bank Quay	d				20 03						21 03														
Earlestown 8	d			19 21	20a10	20 16				20 21	21a10	21 16			21 21	22 16						23 48			
Warrington Bank Quay	a			19 28						20 29					21 27										
St Helens Junction	d					20 21						21 21				22 21						00 01			
Lea Green	d					20 24						21 24				22 24						00 07			
Rainhill	d					20 28						21 28				22 28						00 15			
Whiston	d					20 31						21 31				22 31						00 25			
Bryn	d																								
Garswood	d	19 02					20 02						21 02				22 02			23 02			00 02		
St Helens Central	a	19 22					20 22						21 22				22 22			23 22			00 22		
	d	19 22					20 22						21 22				22 22			23 22			00 22		
Thatto Heath	d	19 32					20 32						21 32				22 32			23 32			00 32		
Eccleston Park	d																								
Prescot	d	19 42					20 42						21 42				22 42			23 42			00 43		
Huyton	d	19a52	20 05			20 35	20a52	21 05				21 35	21a52	22 05		22 35	22a52	23 05		23a52	23 59	00 35	00 53		
Roby	d		20 07			20 37		21 07				21 37		22 07		22 37		23 07			00 01	00 39	00 57		
Broad Green	d		20 10			20 40		21 10				21 40		22 10		22 40		23 10			00 04	00 46	01 04		
Wavertree Technology Park	d		20 13			20 43		21 13				21 43		22 13		22 43		23 13			00 07	00 56	01 14		
Edge Hill 89,91	d																								
Liverpool Lime Street 10 89,91	a		20 24			20 54		21 24				21 54		22 24		22 54		23 24			00 18	01 11	01 29		

A To Chester

B From Chester to Manchester Piccadilly

Liverpool - Runcorn and Crewe

Network Diagram - see first Page of Table 88

Miles		LM MX	VT	NT	VT	TP	NT	LM	EM	NT		VT	LM	TP	NT	LM	EM	NT	VT	LM		TP	NT	LM
		◇1	◇1		◇1	◇1		◇1	◇			◇1	◇1	◇1		◇1	◇		◇1	◇1		◇1		◇1
				A		B	C		D	A				B	C		D	C				B	C	
			⊠		⊠	🛒						⊠		🛒					⊠			🛒		
0	**Liverpool Lime Street** 10 90 d	23p34	05 27	05 49	06 05	06 15	06 21	06 30	06 47	06 50		07 00	07 04	07 15	07 26	07 34	07 42	07 45	07 48	08 04		08 22	08 26	08 34
1¾	Edge Hill 90 d			05 53						06 54					07 30								08 30	
3¾	Mossley Hill d			05 58			06 29			06 59					07 35			07 53					08 35	
4½	West Allerton d			06 00			06 31			07 01					07 37			07 56					08 37	
5½	**Liverpool South Parkway** 7 ⇐ a	23p44		06 03		06 25	06 34	06 39	06 57	07 04			07 13	07 25	07 40	07 43	07 52	07 59		08 15		08 32	08 40	08 43
—	d	23p45						06 40					07 14			07 44				08 15				08 44
13	**Runcorn** a	23p53	05 42		06 20			06 47					07 21			07 51			08 03	08 24				08 51
—	d	23p53	05 43		06 21			06 48				07u15	07 22			07 52			08 04	08 24				08 52
21	Acton Bridge d	00 02						06 57					07 32							08 34				09 02
23¾	Hartford d	00 07						07 02					07 36			08 04								09 06
28	Winsford d	00 11						07 06								08 08								
35½	**Crewe** 10 65 a	00 22	06 00					07 14					07 48			08 19				08 47				09 20
—	Birmingham New Street 12 65 a							08 17					08 47			09 18				09 47				10 17
—	London Euston ⊖65 a		07 50		08 22							09 01							09 56					

	VT	EM	NT	LM	TP	NT		LM	VT	EM	NT	LM	NT	TP	NT	LM		VT	EM	NT	LM	NT	TP	NT
	◇1	◇		◇1	◇1			◇1	◇1	◇		◇1		◇1		◇1		◇1	◇		◇1		◇1	
		D	C		B	C				D	C		E	B	C				D	C		F	B	C
	⊠				🛒				⊠					🛒				⊠					🛒	
Liverpool Lime Street 10 90 d	08 48	08 52	08 55	09 04	09 22	09 27		09 34	09 48	09 52	09 55	10 04	10 16	10 22	10 27	10 34		10 48	10 52	10 55	11 04	11 16	11 22	11 27
Edge Hill 90 d			08 59								09 59									10 59				
Mossley Hill d			09 04			09 35					10 04				10 35					11 04				11 35
West Allerton d			09 06			09 37					10 06				10 37					11 06				11 37
Liverpool South Parkway 7 ⇐ a		09 02	09 09	09 15	09 32	09 40		09 43		10 02	10 09	10 15	10 27	10 32	10 40	10 43			11 02	11 09	11 15	11 27	11 32	11 40
d				09 15				09 44				10 15				10 44					11 15			
Runcorn a	09 03			09 24				09 51	10 03			10 24				10 51		11 03			11 24			
d	09 04			09 25				09 52	10 04			10 25				10 52		11 04			11 25			
Acton Bridge d																								
Hartford d								10 04								11 04								
Winsford d								10 08								11 08								
Crewe 10 65 a				09 44				10 19				10 45				11 19					11 45			
Birmingham New Street 12 65 a				10 47				11 18				11 47				12 17					12 47			
London Euston ⊖65 a	10 56								11 56									12 56						

	LM	VT		EM	NT	LM	NT	TP	NT	LM	VT	EM		NT	LM	NT	TP	NT	LM	VT	EM	NT		LM
	◇1	◇1		◇		◇1		◇1		◇1	◇1	◇			◇1		◇1		◇1	◇1	◇			1
				D	C		F	B	C			D		C		F	B	C			D	C		
		☕						🛒			☕						🛒			☕				
Liverpool Lime Street 10 90 d	11 34	11 48		11 52	11 55	12 04	12 16	12 22	12 27	12 34	12 48	12 52		12 55	13 04	13 16	13 22	13 27	13 34	13 48	13 52	13 55		14 04
Edge Hill 90 d					11 59									12 59								13 59		
Mossley Hill d					12 04				12 35					13 04				13 35				14 04		
West Allerton d					12 06				12 37					13 06				13 37				14 06		
Liverpool South Parkway 7 ⇐ a	11 43			12 02	12 09	12 15	12 27	12 32	12 40	12 43		13 02		13 09	13 15	13 27	13 32	13 40	13 43		14 02	14 09		14 15
d	11 44					12 15				12 44					13 15				13 44					14 15
Runcorn a	11 51	12 03				12 24				12 51	13 03				13 24				13 51	14 03				14 24
d	11 52	12 04				12 25				12 52	13 04				13 25				13 52	14 04				14 25
Acton Bridge d										13 02														
Hartford d	12 04									13 06									14 04					
Winsford d	12 08																		14 08					
Crewe 10 65 a	12 19					12 45				13 20					13 45				14 19					14 45
Birmingham New Street 12 65 a	13 17					13 47				14 17					14 47				15 20					15 47
London Euston ⊖65 a		13 56									14 56									15 56				

	NT	TP	NT	LM	VT	EM	NT	LM		NT	TP	NT	LM	VT	EM	NT	LM	NT		TP	NT	LM	VT	EM
		◇1		◇1	◇1	◇		◇1			◇1		◇1	◇1	◇		◇1			◇1		◇1	◇1	◇
	F	B	C			D	C			F	G	C			D	C		F		B	C			H
		🛒			☕						🛒			☕						🛒			☕	
Liverpool Lime Street 10 90 d	14 16	14 22	14 27	14 34	14 48	14 52	14 55	15 04		15 16	15 22	15 27	15 34	15 48	15 52	15 55	16 04	16 16		16 22	16 27	16 34	16 48	16 52
Edge Hill 90 d							14 59									15 59								
Mossley Hill d			14 35				15 04					15 35				16 04					16 35			
West Allerton d			14 37				15 06					15 37				16 06					16 37			
Liverpool South Parkway 7 ⇐ a	14 27	14 32	14 40	14 43		15 02	15 09	15 15		15 27	15 32	15 40	15 43		16 02	16 09	16 15	16 27		16 32	16 40	16 43		17 02
d				14 44				15 15					15 44				16 15					16 44		
Runcorn a				14 51	15 03			15 24					15 51	16 03			16 24					16 52	17 03	
d				14 52	15 04			15 25					15 52	16 04			16 25					16 52	17 04	
Acton Bridge d																						17 01		
Hartford d				15 04									16 04									17 06		
Winsford d				15 08									16 08											
Crewe 10 65 a				15 19				15 45					16 19				16 45					17 19		
Birmingham New Street 12 65 a				16 17				16 47					17 20				17 47					18 17		
London Euston ⊖65 a					16 59									17 56									18 59	

A To Warrington Central
B To Scarborough
C To Manchester Oxford Road
D To Norwich
E From Preston
F From Blackpool North
G To Middlesbrough
H To Nottingham

Liverpool - Runcorn and Crewe

Network Diagram - see first Page of Table 88

Mondays to Fridays

	NT	LM	TP	NT	LM	VT	EM	NT	LM	TP	NT	LM	VT	EM	NT	LM	TP	LM	VT	EM	NT	LM
		◇1	◇1		◇1	◇1	◇		◇1	◇1		◇1	◇1	◇		◇1	◇1	◇1	◇1	◇		◇1
	A		B	A			C	A		B	A			D	E		F			D	E	
			🛒			⊠							⊠						☕			
Liverpool Lime Street 10 90 d	16 55	17 04	17 22	17 25	17 34	17 48	17 52	17 55	18 04	18 22	18 25	18 34	18 48	18 52	18 55	19 11	19 22	19 34	19 48	19 52	19 55	20 04
Edge Hill 90 d	16 59			17 29				17 59			18 29				18 59						19 59	
Mossley Hill d	17 04			17 34				18 04			18 34				19 04						20 04	
West Allerton d	17 06			17 36				18 06			18 36				19 06						20 06	
Liverpool South Parkway 7 ✈ a	17 09	17 15	17 32	17 39	17 43		18 02	18 09	18 14	18 32	18 39	18 43		19 02	19 09	19 20	19 32	19 43		20 02	20 09	20 15
d		17 15			17 44				18 15			18 44				19 21		19 44				20 15
Runcorn a		17 24			17 51	18 03			18 24			18 51	19 03			19 28		19 51	20 03			20 24
d		17 25			17 52	18 04			18 24			18 52	19 04			19 29		19 52	20 04			20 24
Acton Bridge d					18 01											19 40						
Hartford d					18 06							19 04						20 04				
Winsford d		17 39							18 38			19 08						20 08				
Crewe 10 65 a		17 47			18 20				18 47			19 16	19 21			19 53		20 16	20 21			20 45
Birmingham New Street 12 65 a		18 48			19 17				19 47			20 18				20 47		21 18				21 47
London Euston ⊖65 a						20 02							21 05						22 09			

	TP	LM	VT	NT	LM	EM	NT	NT FX	TP	LM	NT FX	LM	NT
	◇1	◇1	◇1		◇1	◇			◇1	◇1		◇1	
	G			A		D	A	H	G		H		I
			☕										
Liverpool Lime Street 10 90 d	20 22	20 34	20 48	20 55	21 34	21 37	21 55	22 12	22 30	22 34	23 16	23 34	23 38
Edge Hill 90 d				20 59			21 59	22a16			23a20		23 42
Mossley Hill d				21 04			22 04						23 47
West Allerton d				21 06			22 06						23 50
Liverpool South Parkway 7 ✈ a	20 32	20 43		21 09	21 43	21 47	22 09		22 40	22 44		23 44	23 53
d		20 44			21 44					22 45		23 45	
Runcorn a		20 51	21 03		21 51					22 54		23 53	
d		20 52	21 04		21 52					22 54		23 53	
Acton Bridge d										23 03		00 02	
Hartford d		21 04			22 04					23 08		00 07	
Winsford d		21 08			22 08					23 12		00 11	
Crewe 10 65 a		21 16	21 21		22 18					23 21		00 22	
Birmingham New Street 12 65 a		22 17			23 18								
London Euston ⊖65 a			23 56										

Saturdays

	LM	VT	NT	TP	NT	LM	VT	EM	NT	LM	TP	VT	NT	LM	EM	NT
	◇1	◇1		◇1		◇1	◇1	◇		◇1	◇1	◇1		◇1	◇	
			E	B	A			C	E		B		A		C	A
		☕		🛒			☕				🛒	☕				
Liverpool Lime Street 10 90 d	23p34	05 47	05 49	06 15	06 25	06 32	06 45	06 49	06 55	07 04	07 15	07 19	07 26	07 34	07 42	07 45
Edge Hill 90 d			05 53						06 59				07 30			
Mossley Hill d			05 58		06 33				07 04				07 35			07 53
West Allerton d			06 00		06 35				07 06				07 37			07 56
Liverpool South Parkway 7 ✈ a	23p44		06 03	06 25	06 38	06 41		06 59	07 09	07 14	07 25		07 40	07 43	07 52	07 59
d	23p45					06 42				07 14				07 44		
Runcorn a	23p53	06 02				06 49	07 00			07 22		07 35		07 51		
d	23p53	06 03				06 50	07 01			07 22		07 36		07 52		
Acton Bridge d	00 02									07 32						
Hartford d	00 07					07 02				07 36				08 04		
Winsford d	00 11					07 06								08 08		
Crewe 10 65 a	00 22					07 14	07 18			07 47		07 52		08 19		
Birmingham New Street 12 65 a						08 17				08 47				09 18		
London Euston ⊖65 a		08 05					08 59					09 46				

	VT	LM	TP	NT	LM	VT	EM	NT	LM	TP	NT	LM	VT	EM	NT	LM	NT
	◇1	◇1	◇1		◇1	◇1	◇		◇1	◇1		◇1	◇1	◇		◇1	
			B	A			C	A		B	A			C	A		K
	☕		🛒			☕				🛒			☕				
Liverpool Lime Street 10 90 d	07 48	08 04	08 22	08 26	08 34	08 48	08 52	08 55	09 04	09 22	09 27	09 34	09 48	09 52	09 55	10 04	10 16
Edge Hill 90 d				08 30				08 59							09 59		
Mossley Hill d				08 35				09 04			09 35				10 04		
West Allerton d				08 37				09 06			09 37				10 06		
Liverpool South Parkway 7 ✈ a		08 14	08 32	08 40	08 43		09 02	09 09	09 15	09 32	09 40	09 43		10 02	10 09	10 15	10 27
d		08 15			08 44				09 15			09 44				10 15	
Runcorn a	08 03	08 24			08 51	09 03			09 24			09 51	10 03			10 24	
d	08 04	08 24			08 52	09 04			09 24			09 52	10 04			10 25	
Acton Bridge d		08 34			09 02												
Hartford d					09 06							10 04					
Winsford d												10 08					
Crewe 10 65 a		08 47			09 20				09 44			10 19				10 45	
Birmingham New Street 12 65 a		09 47			10 17				10 47			11 17				11 47	
London Euston ⊖65 a	10 00					11 01							11 56				

A To Manchester Oxford Road
B To Scarborough
C To Norwich
D To Nottingham
E To Warrington Central
F To Hull
G To York
H To Earlestown
I To Manchester Piccadilly
K until 11 February. From Blackpool North

Table 91

Saturdays

Liverpool - Runcorn and Crewe

Network Diagram - see first Page of Table 88

		TP ◇1 A	NT B	LM ◇1	VT ◇1	EM ◇ D	NT B	LM ◇1	NT E	TP ◇1 A	NT B	LM ◇1	VT ◇1	EM ◇ D	NT B	LM ◇1	NT E	TP ◇1 A
Liverpool Lime Street 10 90	d	10 22	10 27	10 34	10 48	10 52	10 55	11 04	11 16	11 22	11 27	11 34	11 48	11 52	11 55	12 04	12 16	12 22
Edge Hill 90	d						10 59								11 59			
Mossley Hill	d		10 35				11 04				11 35				12 04			
West Allerton	d		10 37				11 06				11 37				12 06			
Liverpool South Parkway 7 ✈	a	10 32	10 40	10 43		11 02	11 09	11 15	11 27	11 32	11 40	11 43		12 02	12 09	12 15	12 27	12 32
	d			10 44				11 15				11 44				12 15		
Runcorn	a			10 51	11 03			11 24				11 51	12 03			12 24		
	d			10 52	11 04			11 25				11 52	12 04			12 25		
Acton Bridge	d																	
Hartford	d			11 04								12 04						
Winsford	d			11 08								12 08						
Crewe 10 65	a			11 19				11 45				12 19				12 45		
Birmingham New Street 12 65	a			12 17				12 47				13 17				13 47		
London Euston ⊖65	a				12 56								13 56					

		NT B	LM ◇1	VT ◇1	EM ◇ D	NT B	LM ◇1	NT E	TP ◇1 A	NT B	LM ◇1	VT ◇1	EM ◇ D	NT B	LM ◇1	NT E	TP ◇1 A	NT B	LM ◇1
Liverpool Lime Street 10 90	d	12 27	12 34	12 48	12 52	12 55	13 04	13 16	13 22	13 27	13 34	13 48	13 52	13 55	14 04	14 16	14 22	14 27	14 34
Edge Hill 90	d					12 59								13 59					
Mossley Hill	d	12 35				13 04				13 35				14 04				14 35	
West Allerton	d	12 37				13 06				13 37				14 06				14 37	
Liverpool South Parkway 7 ✈	a	12 40	12 43		13 02	13 09	13 15	13 27	13 32	13 40	13 43		14 02	14 09	14 15	14 27	14 32	14 40	14 43
	d		12 44				13 15				13 44				14 15				14 44
Runcorn	a		12 51	13 03			13 24				13 51	14 03			14 24				14 51
	d		12 52	13 04			13 25				13 52	14 04			14 25				14 52
Acton Bridge	d		13 02																
Hartford	d		13 06								14 04								15 04
Winsford	d										14 08								15 08
Crewe 10 65	a		13 20				13 45				14 19				14 45				15 19
Birmingham New Street 12 65	a		14 17				14 47				15 18				15 47				16 17
London Euston ⊖65	a			14 56								15 56							

		VT ◇1	EM ◇ D	NT B	LM ◇1	NT E	TP ◇1 A	NT B	LM ◇1	VT ◇1	EM ◇ D	NT B	LM ◇1	NT E	TP ◇1 A	NT B	LM ◇1
Liverpool Lime Street 10 90	d	14 48	14 52	14 55	15 04	15 16	15 22	15 27	15 34	15 48	15 52	15 55	16 04	16 16	16 22	16 27	16 34
Edge Hill 90	d			14 59								15 59					
Mossley Hill	d			15 04				15 35				16 04				16 35	
West Allerton	d			15 06				15 37				16 06				16 37	
Liverpool South Parkway 7 ✈	a		15 02	15 09	15 15	15 27	15 32	15 40	15 43		16 02	16 09	16 15	16 27	16 32	16 40	16 43
	d				15 15				15 44				16 15				16 44
Runcorn	a	15 03			15 24				15 51	16 03			16 24				16 51
	d	15 04			15 25				15 52	16 04			16 25				16 52
Acton Bridge	d																17 02
Hartford	d								16 04								17 06
Winsford	d								16 08								
Crewe 10 65	a				15 45				16 19				16 45				17 20
Birmingham New Street 12 65	a				16 47				17 18				17 47				18 17
London Euston ⊖65	a	16 56								17 56							

		VT ◇1	EM ◇ F	NT B	LM ◇1	TP ◇1 A	NT B	LM ◇1	VT ◇1	EM ◇ D	NT B	LM ◇1	TP ◇1 A	NT B	LM ◇1	VT ◇1	EM ◇ F	NT G	LM ◇1
Liverpool Lime Street 10 90	d	16 48	16 52	16 55	17 04	17 22	17 25	17 34	17 48	17 52	17 55	18 04	18 22	18 25	18 34	18 48	18 52	18 55	19 04
Edge Hill 90	d			16 59			17 29				17 59			18 29				18 59	
Mossley Hill	d			17 04			17 34				18 04			18 34				19 04	
West Allerton	d			17 06			17 36				18 06			18 36				19 06	
Liverpool South Parkway 7 ✈	a		17 02	17 09	17 15	17 32	17 39	17 43		18 02	18 09	18 14	18 32	18 39	18 43		19 02	19 09	19 14
	d				17 15			17 44				18 15			18 44				19 14
Runcorn	a	17 03			17 24			17 51	18 03			18 24			18 51	19 03			19 23
	d	17 04			17 25			17 52	18 04			18 24			18 52	19 04			19 23
Acton Bridge	d							18 02											19 36
Hartford	d							18 06							19 04				
Winsford	d				17 39							18 38			19 08				
Crewe 10 65	a				17 47			18 20				18 46			19 19				19 49
Birmingham New Street 12 65	a				18 47			19 17				19 47			20 17				20 47
London Euston ⊖65	a	18 56							19 56							21 15			

A To Scarborough
B To Manchester Oxford Road
D To Norwich
E until 11 February. From Blackpool North
F To Nottingham
G To Warrington Central

Table 91

Liverpool - Runcorn and Crewe

Network Diagram - see first Page of Table 88

	TP	LM	VT	EM	NT	TP	LM	EM	NT	LM	EM	NT	LM	TP	NT
	◇1	◇1	◇1	◇		◇1	◇1	◇		◇1	◇		1	◇1	
	B			C	D	B		C	E		C	E		B	F
			🍴												
Liverpool Lime Street 10 .. 90 d	19 22	19 34	19 48	19 52	19 55	20 22	20 34	20 52	20 55	21 34	21 37	21 55	22 04	22 30	23 38
Edge Hill 90 d					19 59				20 59			21 59			23 42
Mossley Hill d					20 04				21 04			22 04			23 47
West Allerton d					20 06				21 06			22 06			23 49
Liverpool South Parkway 7 ✈ a	19 32	19 43		20 02	20 09	20 32	20 43	21 02	21 09	21 43	21 47	22 09	22 14	22 40	23 52
d		19 44					20 44			21 44			22 14		
Runcorn a		19 51	20 03				20 51			21 51			22 22		
d		19 52	20 04				20 52			21 52			22 23		
Acton Bridge d															
Hartford d		20 04					21 03			22 04			22 34		
Winsford d		20 08					21 08			22 08			22 39		
Crewe 10 65 a		20 16					21 16			22 21			22 48		
Birmingham New Street 12 65 a		21 19					22 20			23 21					
London Euston ⊖65 a			22 14												

Sundays

	VT	TP	NT	VT	TP	NT	VT	TP	NT	VT	TP	NT	LM	VT	TP	NT	LM	VT	EM	TP	NT	LM
	◇1	◇1		◇1	◇1		◇1	◇1		◇1	◇1		◇1	◇1	◇1		◇1	◇1	◇	◇1		◇1
		G	E		H	E		I	E		H	E			I	E			J	H	E	
	🍴			🍴			🍴			🍴				🍴				🍴				
Liverpool Lime Street 10 .. 90 d	08 15	08 22	08 26	08 38	09 22	09 26	09 38	10 22	10 26	10 38	11 22	11 26	11 34	11 48	12 22	12 26	12 34	12 48	12 52	13 22	13 26	13 34
Edge Hill 90 d																						
Mossley Hill d			08 34			09 34			10 34			11 34				12 34					13 34	
West Allerton d			08 36			09 36			10 36			11 36				12 36					13 36	
Liverpool South Parkway 7 ✈ a		08 32	08 39		09 32	09 39		10 32	10 39		11 32	11 39	11 43		12 32	12 39	12 43		13 02	13 32	13 39	13 43
d													11 44				12 44					13 44
Runcorn a	08 34			08 53			09 53			10 53			11 51	12 03			12 51	13 03				13 51
d	08 35			08 54			09 54			10 54			11 52	12 04			12 52	13 04				13 52
Acton Bridge d																						
Hartford d													12 03				13 03					14 03
Winsford d													12 08				13 08					14 08
Crewe 10 65 a	08 52			09 11			10 12			11 12			12 20				13 19					14 18
Birmingham New Street 12 65 a													13 16				14 15					15 15
London Euston ⊖65 a	11 06			11 37			12 32			13 11				14 01				15 01				

	VT	EM	TP	NT	LM	VT	EM	TP	NT	LM	VT	EM	VT	TP	NT	LM	VT	EM	TP	NT	LM	VT
	◇1	◇	◇1		◇1	◇1	◇	◇1		◇1	◇1	◇	◇1	◇1		◇1	◇1	◇	◇1		◇1	◇1
		J	I	E			J	H	E			J		I	E			C	H	E		
	🍴					🍴					🍴		🍴				🍴					🍴
Liverpool Lime Street 10 .. 90 d	13 48	13 52	14 22	14 26	14 34	14 48	14 52	15 22	15 26	15 34	15 48	15 52	16 18	16 22	16 26	16 34	16 48	16 52	17 22	17 26	17 34	17 48
Edge Hill 90 d																						
Mossley Hill d				14 34					15 34						16 34					17 34		
West Allerton d				14 36					15 36						16 36					17 36		
Liverpool South Parkway 7 ✈ a		14 02	14 32	14 39	14 43		15 02	15 32	15 39	15 43		16 02		16 32	16 39	16 43		17 02	17 32	17 39	17 43	
d					14 44					15 44						16 44					17 44	
Runcorn a	14 03				14 51	15 03				15 51	16 03		16 33			16 51	17 03				17 51	18 03
d	14 04				14 52	15 04				15 52	16 04		16 34			16 52	17 04				17 52	18 04
Acton Bridge d																						
Hartford d					15 03					16 03						17 03					18 03	
Winsford d					15 08					16 08						17 08					18 08	
Crewe 10 65 a					15 20					16 18			16 51			17 18					18 20	
Birmingham New Street 12 65 a					16 15					17 15						18 15					19 15	
London Euston ⊖65 a	16 01					17 01					18 01		18 44				19 01					20 01

	EM	TP	NT	LM	VT	EM	TP	NT	LM	VT	EM	TP	NT	LM	VT	EM	NT	LM	TP	NT
	◇	◇1		◇1	◇1	◇	◇1		◇1	◇1	◇	◇1		◇1	◇1	◇		◇1	◇1	
	J	H	E			C	K	E			C	L	E			C	E		K	E
					🍴					🍴					🍴					
Liverpool Lime Street 10 .. 90 d	17 52	18 22	18 26	18 34	18 48	18 52	19 22	19 26	19 34	19 48	19 52	20 22	20 26	20 34	20 48	21 21	21 26	21 34	21 52	22 26
Edge Hill 90 d																				
Mossley Hill d			18 34					19 34					20 34				21 34			22 34
West Allerton d			18 36					19 36					20 36				21 36			22 36
Liverpool South Parkway 7 ✈ a	18 02	18 32	18 39	18 43		19 02	19 32	19 39	19 43		20 02	20 32	20 39	20 43		21 31	21 39	21 43	22 02	22 39
d				18 44					19 44					20 44				21 44		
Runcorn a				18 51	19 03				19 51	20 03				20 51	21 03			21 51		
d				18 52	19 04				19 52	20 04				20 52	21 04			21 52		
Acton Bridge d																				
Hartford d				19 03					20 03					21 03				22 03		
Winsford d				19 08					20 08					21 08				22 08		
Crewe 10 65 a				19 20					20 16	20 22				21 16	21 21			22 18		
Birmingham New Street 12 65 a				20 15					21 15					22 15				23 17		
London Euston ⊖65 a					21 01					22 27					23 54					

B To York
C To Nottingham
D To Warrington Central
E To Manchester Oxford Road
F To Manchester Piccadilly
G until 25 March. To Hull
H until 25 March. To Scarborough
I until 25 March. To Middlesbrough
J To Norwich
K until 25 March. To York
L until 25 March. To Newcastle

Crewe and Runcorn - Liverpool

Network Diagram - see first Page of Table 88

Miles			VT	NT	LM	NT	LM	NT	LM	NT	LM		VT	NT	LM	EM	LM	NT	TP	LM	VT		NT	EM	LM
			MO	MX																					
			◇1		◇1		◇1		◇1		1		◇1		◇1	◇	◇1		◇1	◇1	◇1			◇	1
				A		B		B		A				B		C		A	D	E			A	C	F
			☕										⊠						🛒		⊠				
—	London Euston ⊖65	d	21p21										05 27								07 07				
—	Birmingham New Street 12 65	d									06 01				06 36		07 01			07 36					08 01
0	**Crewe 10** 65	d	23p45		05 40		06 02		06 32		06 57		07 24		07 34		07 57			08 31					08 57
7½	Winsford	d					06 10		06 41		07 05				07 43		08 05								09 06
11¾	Hartford	d					06 15		06 46		07 10				07 48		08 10								09 12
14½	Acton Bridge	d					06 19		06 51		07 14				07 52		08 14								
22½	**Runcorn**	a	00 07		05 58		06 27		06 59		07 22		07 41		08 00		08 22			08 50	08 55				09 22
—		d	00 07		06 01		06 28		06 59		07 22		07 41		08 01		08 22			08 50	08 55				09 22
30	**Liverpool South Parkway 7** ✈	a			06 10		06 36		07 08		07 31				08 09		08 31			08 59					09 31
—		d		00 27	06 10	06 27	06 37	07 01	07 08	07 22	07 31			07 59	08 10	08 18	08 31	08 37	08 47	08 59			09 06	09 15	09 31
31	West Allerton	d				06 31		07 05		07 25				08 03				08 40					09 09		
31¾	Mossley Hill	d				06 33		07 07		07 28				08 06				08 43					09 12		
33¾	Edge Hill 90	d				06 39		07 13		07 32				08 11				08 48							
35½	**Liverpool Lime Street 10** 90	a	00 30	00 41	06 22	06 45	06 49	07 19	07 22	07 40	07 43		08 01	08 18	08 21	08 31	08 44	08 55	08 58	09 10	09 15		09 24	09 31	09 43

		NT	TP	LM	VT	NT	EM		LM	NT	NT	TP	LM	VT	NT	EM	LM		NT	NT	TP	LM	VT	NT	EM
			◇1	◇1	◇1		◇		◇1			◇1	◇1	◇1		◇	◇1				◇1	◇1	◇1		◇
		A	G			A	C			H	A	I			A	J			H	A	I			A	J
			🛒		⊠							🛒		⊠							🛒		⊠		
London Euston ⊖65	d				08 07									09 07									10 07		
Birmingham New Street 12 65	d			08 36					09 01				09 36				10 01					10 36			
Crewe 10 65	d			09 31					09 57				10 31				10 57					11 31			
Winsford	d																11 06								
Hartford	d								10 10								11 12								
Acton Bridge	d								10 14																
Runcorn	a			09 50	09 55				10 22				10 50	10 55			11 21					11 50	11 55		
	d			09 50	09 55				10 22				10 50	10 55			11 22					11 50	11 55		
Liverpool South Parkway 7 ✈	a			09 59					10 31				10 59				11 30					11 59			
	d	09 36	09 47	09 59		10 06	10 15		10 31	10 36	10 36	10 47	10 59		11 06	11 15	11 31		11 36	11 36	11 47	11 59		12 06	12 15
West Allerton	d	09 39				10 10					10 39				11 10					11 39				12 10	
Mossley Hill	d	09 41				10 12					10 41				11 13					11 41				12 13	
Edge Hill 90	d	09 47									10 47									11 47					
Liverpool Lime Street 10 90	a	09 53	09 58	10 10	10 15	10 24	10 31		10 43	10 49	10 53	10 58	11 10	11 15	11 24	11 31	11 43		11 49	11 53	11 58	12 10	12 15	12 24	12 31

		LM	NT		NT	TP	LM	VT	NT	EM	LM	NT	NT		TP	LM	VT	NT	EM	LM	NT	NT	TP		LM
		◇1				◇1	◇1	◇1		◇	◇1				◇1	◇1	◇1		◇	◇1			◇1		◇1
			H		A	I			A	J		H	A		I			A	J		H	A	I		
						🛒		☕							🛒		☕						🛒		
London Euston ⊖65	d							11 07									12 07								
Birmingham New Street 12 65	d	11 01					11 36				12 01					12 36				13 01					13 36
Crewe 10 65	d	11 57					12 31				12 57					13 31				13 57					14 31
Winsford	d										13 06									14 06					
Hartford	d	12 10									13 12									14 12					
Acton Bridge	d	12 14																							
Runcorn	a	12 22					12 50	12 55			13 21					13 50	13 55			14 21					14 50
	d	12 22					12 50	12 55			13 22					13 50	13 55			14 22					14 50
Liverpool South Parkway 7 ✈	a	12 31					12 59				13 30					13 59				14 30					14 59
	d	12 31	12 36		12 36	12 47	12 59		13 06	13 15	13 31	13 36	13 36		13 47	13 59		14 06	14 15	14 31	14 36	14 36	14 47		14 59
West Allerton	d				12 39				13 10				13 39					14 10				14 39			
Mossley Hill	d				12 41				13 13				13 41					14 13				14 41			
Edge Hill 90	d				12 47								13 47									14 47			
Liverpool Lime Street 10 90	a	12 43	12 49		12 53	12 58	13 10	13 15	13 24	13 31	13 43	13 49	13 53		13 58	14 10	14 15	14 24	14 31	14 43	14 49	14 53	14 58		15 10

		VT	NT	EM	LM	NT	NT	TP	LM		VT	NT	EM	LM	NT	NT	TP	LM	VT		NT	EM	LM	NT	TP
		◇1		◇	◇1			◇1	◇1		◇1		◇	◇1			◇1	◇1	◇1			◇	◇1		◇1
			A	J		H	A	I				A	J		H	A	I				A	J		A	I
		☕						🛒			☕						🛒		☕						🛒
London Euston ⊖65	d	13 07									14 07								15 07						
Birmingham New Street 12 65	d				14 01				14 36					15 01				15 36					16 01		
Crewe 10 65	d				14 57				15 31					15 57				16 31					16 57		
Winsford	d				15 06																		17 06		
Hartford	d				15 12									16 10									17 12		
Acton Bridge	d													16 14											
Runcorn	a	14 55			15 21				15 50		15 55			16 22				16 50	16 55				17 21		
	d	14 55			15 22				15 50		15 55			16 22				16 50	16 55				17 22		
Liverpool South Parkway 7 ✈	a				15 30				15 59					16 31				16 59					17 30		
	d		15 06	15 15	15 31	15 36	15 36	15 47	15 59			16 07	16 15	16 31	16 36	16 36	16 47	16 59			17 07	17 15	17 31	17 39	17 47
West Allerton	d		15 10				15 39					16 11				16 39					17 11			17 42	
Mossley Hill	d		15 13				15 41					16 13				16 42					17 13			17 45	
Edge Hill 90	d						15 47									16 47								17 50	
Liverpool Lime Street 10 90	a	15 15	15 24	15 31	15 43	15 49	15 53	15 58	16 10		16 15	16 25	16 31	16 44	16 49	16 54	16 58	17 10	17 15		17 25	17 31	17 43	17 58	18 01

A From Manchester Oxford Road
B From Warrington Central
C From Nottingham
D From Hull
E From Birmingham International
F From Walsall
G From Newcastle
H To Blackpool North
I From Scarborough
J From Norwich

Crewe and Runcorn - Liverpool

Network Diagram - see first Page of Table 88

	LM	VT	NT	EM		LM	NT	TP	LM	VT	NT	EM	LM	VT		TP	LM	VT	NT	EM	VT	NT	TP	LM
	◇1	◇1		◇		◇1		◇1	1	◇1		◇	◇1	◇1		◇1	◇1	◇1		◇	◇1		◇1	◇1
			A	B			A	C			A	B				C			D	B		A	C	
		☕						🛒		⊠				⊠		🛒		⊠			⊠			
London Euston ⊖65 d		16 07								17 07				17 33				18 07			18 33			
Birmingham New Street 12 65 d	16 36					17 01			17 36				18 01				18 36							19 36
Crewe 10 65 d	17 31					17 57			18 31	18 44			19 02	19 16			19 31	19 44			20 17			20 31
Winsford d						18 06							19 10				19 42							20 40
Hartford d						18 12			18 44								19 47							20 45
Acton Bridge d									18 48															
Runcorn a	17 50	17 55				18 21			18 56	19 02			19 22	19 33			19 57	20 01			20 34			20 56
d	17 50	17 55				18 22			18 57	19 02			19 23	19 33			19 57	20 01			20 34			20 56
Liverpool South Parkway 7 ⇜ a	17 59					18 30			19 05				19 31				20 06							21 05
d	17 59		18 14	18 22		18 31	18 38	18 47	19 06		19 13	19 18	19 32			19 47	20 06		20 13	20 16		20 38	20 47	21 05
West Allerton d			18 18				18 41				19 16								20 16			20 41		
Mossley Hill d			18 20				18 44				19 18								20 18			20 44		
Edge Hill 90 d			18 30				18 49				19 26								20 24					
Liverpool Lime Street 10 90 a	18 10	18 15	18 38	18 35		18 43	18 57	19 01	19 16	19 22	19 35	19 35	19 44	19 51		20 01	20 18	20 19	20 30	20 35	20 53	20 56	21 01	21 16

		VT	NT	EM	TP	LM	VT	NT	TP	LM		VT	NT
		R 1		◇	◇1	◇1	◇1		◇1	◇1		◇1	
			D	B	C			D	C				D
		☕					☕					☕	
London Euston ⊖65 d		19 07					20 07					21 07	
Birmingham New Street 12 65 d						20 36				21 36			
Crewe 10 65 d						21 31				22 31		22 48	
Winsford d						21 39				22 39			
Hartford d						21 44				22 44			
Acton Bridge d										22 48			
Runcorn a		21 01				21 54	21 59			22 56		23 05	
d		21 01				21 54	21 59			22 57		23 05	
Liverpool South Parkway 7 ⇜ a						22 05				23 07			
d			21 12	21 20	21 47	22 05		22 12	22 47	23 08			23 22
West Allerton d			21 15					22 15					23 25
Mossley Hill d			21 18					22 18					23 27
Edge Hill 90 d			21 23					22 23					23 32
Liverpool Lime Street 10 90 a		21 21	21 30	21 35	22 01	22 15	22 20	22 30	23 01	23 23		23 29	23 39

Saturdays

	NT	LM	NT	LM	NT	LM	NT	LM	NT		LM	EM	LM	NT	TP	LM	VT	NT	EM		LM	NT	TP	LM
		1		1		◇1		◇1			◇1	◇	◇1		◇1	◇1	◇1		◇		◇1		◇1	◇1
	A		D		D		A		D			E		A	F			A	E			A	G	
															🛒		☕						🛒	
London Euston ⊖65 d																	07 07							
Birmingham New Street 12 65 d								06 01			06 36		07 01			07 36					08 01			08 36
Crewe 10 65 d		05 48		06 12		06 32		06 57			07 35		08 00			08 31	08 43				08 57			09 31
Winsford d						06 41		07 05			07 44		08 07								09 07			
Hartford d						06 46		07 10			07 49		08 12								09 12			
Acton Bridge d						06 51					07 53		08 16											
Runcorn a		06 07		06 31		06 59		07 20			08 02		08 24			08 50	09 00				09 21			09 50
d		06 08		06 31		06 59		07 21			08 03		08 25			08 50	09 00				09 22			09 50
Liverpool South Parkway 7 ⇜ a		06 15		06 39		07 08		07 30			08 11		08 33			08 59					09 30			09 59
d	00 27	06 15	06 27	06 39	07 01	07 08	07 22	07 30	08 03		08 12	08 18	08 34	08 37	08 47	08 59		09 06	09 15		09 31	09 36	09 47	09 59
West Allerton d			06 31		07 05		07 25		08 06					08 40				09 09				09 39		
Mossley Hill d			06 33		07 07		07 28		08 09					08 43				09 12				09 41		
Edge Hill 90 d			06 39		07 13		07 34		08 14					08 48								09 47		
Liverpool Lime Street 10 90 a	00 41	06 26	06 45	06 53	07 20	07 22	07 40	07 42	08 21		08 24	08 31	08 46	08 55	08 58	09 12	09 21	09 24	09 31		09 43	09 53	09 58	10 10

	VT	NT	EM	LM	NT		NT	TP	LM	VT	NT	EM	LM	NT	NT		TP	LM	VT	NT	EM	LM	NT	NT
	◇1		◇	◇1				◇1	◇1	◇1		◇	◇1				◇1	◇1	◇1		◇	◇1		
		A	E		H		A	C			A	B		H	A		C			A	B		H	A
	☕							🛒		☕									☕					
London Euston ⊖65 d	08 07									09 07									10 07					
Birmingham New Street 12 65 d				09 01					09 36				10 01					10 36				11 01		
Crewe 10 65 d				09 57					10 31				10 57					11 31				11 57		
Winsford d													11 07											
Hartford d				10 10									11 12									12 10		
Acton Bridge d				10 14																		12 14		
Runcorn a	09 55			10 22					10 50	10 55			11 21					11 50	11 55			12 22		
d	09 55			10 23					10 50	10 55			11 22					11 50	11 55			12 23		
Liverpool South Parkway 7 ⇜ a				10 31					10 59				11 30					11 59				12 31		
d		10 06	10 15	10 32	10 36		10 36	10 47	10 59		11 06	11 15	11 31	11 36	11 36		11 47	11 59		12 06	12 15	12 32	12 36	12 36
West Allerton d		10 10					10 39				11 10				11 39					12 10				12 39
Mossley Hill d		10 12					10 41				11 13				11 41					12 13				12 41
Edge Hill 90 d							10 47								11 47									12 47
Liverpool Lime Street 10 90 a	10 15	10 23	10 31	10 44	10 49		10 53	10 58	11 10	11 15	11 24	11 31	11 43	11 49	11 53		11 58	12 10	12 15	12 24	12 31	12 44	12 49	12 53

A From Manchester Oxford Road
B From Norwich
C From Scarborough
D From Warrington Central
E From Nottingham
F From Hull
G From Newcastle
H until 11 February. To Blackpool North

Crewe and Runcorn - Liverpool

Network Diagram - see first Page of Table 88

		TP ◇1 A 🛒		LM ◇1	VT ◇1 ☕	NT B	EM ◇ C	LM ◇1	NT D	NT B	TP ◇1 A 🛒	LM ◇1		VT ◇1 ☕	NT B	EM ◇ C	LM ◇1	NT D	NT B	TP ◇1 A	LM ◇1	VT ◇1 ☕		NT B	EM ◇ C
London Euston ⊖65	d				11 07									12 07								13 07			
Birmingham New Street 12 65	d			11 36				12 01				12 36					13 01				13 36				
Crewe 10 65	d			12 31				12 57				13 31					13 57				14 31				
Winsford	d							13 07									14 07								
Hartford	d							13 12									14 12								
Acton Bridge	d																								
Runcorn	a			12 50	12 55			13 21				13 50		13 55			14 21				14 50	14 55			
	d			12 50	12 55			13 22				13 50		13 55			14 22				14 50	14 55			
Liverpool South Parkway 7 ⇐	a			12 59				13 30				13 59					14 30				14 59				
	d	12 47		12 59		13 06	13 15	13 31	13 36	13 36	13 47	13 59			14 06	14 15	14 31	14 36	14 36	14 47	14 59			15 06	15 15
West Allerton	d					13 10				13 39					14 10				14 39					15 10	
Mossley Hill	d					13 13				13 41					14 13				14 41					15 13	
Edge Hill 90	d									13 47									14 47						
Liverpool Lime Street 10 90	a	12 58		13 10	13 15	13 24	13 31	13 43	13 49	13 53	13 58	14 10		14 15	14 24	14 31	14 43	14 49	14 53	14 58	15 10	15 15		15 24	15 31

		LM ◇1	NT D	NT B	TP ◇1 A 🛒	LM ◇1	VT ◇1 ☕	NT B		EM ◇ C	LM ◇1	NT D	NT B	TP ◇1 A 🛒	LM ◇1	VT ◇1 ☕	NT B	EM ◇ C		LM ◇1	NT B	TP ◇1 A 🛒	LM ◇1	VT ◇1 ☕	NT B
London Euston ⊖65	d						14 07									15 07								16 07	
Birmingham New Street 12 65	d	14 01				14 36					15 01				15 36					16 01			16 36		
Crewe 10 65	d	14 57				15 31					15 57				16 31					16 57			17 31		
Winsford	d	15 07																		17 07					
Hartford	d	15 12									16 10									17 12					
Acton Bridge	d										16 14														
Runcorn	a	15 21				15 50	15 55				16 22				16 50	16 55				17 21			17 50	17 55	
	d	15 22				15 50	15 55				16 23				16 50	16 55				17 22			17 50	17 55	
Liverpool South Parkway 7 ⇐	a	15 30				15 59					16 31				16 59					17 30			17 59		
	d	15 31	15 36	15 36	15 47	15 59		16 07		16 15	16 32	16 36	16 36	16 47	16 59		17 07	17 15		17 31	17 39	17 47	17 59		18 14
West Allerton	d			15 39				16 11					16 39				17 11				17 42				18 18
Mossley Hill	d			15 41				16 13					16 41				17 13				17 45				18 20
Edge Hill 90	d			15 47									16 47								17 50				18 30
Liverpool Lime Street 10 90	a	15 43	15 49	15 53	15 58	16 10	16 15	16 25		16 31	16 44	16 49	16 54	16 58	17 10	17 15	17 25	17 31		17 43	17 58	18 01	18 10	18 15	18 38

		EM ◇ C	LM ◇1	VT ◇1 ☕		NT B	TP ◇1 A 🛒	LM ◇1	VT ◇1 ☕	NT B	EM ◇ C	LM ◇1	TP ◇1 A	VT ◇1 ☕		NT E	EM ◇ C	LM ◇1	VT ◇1 ☕	NT B	TP ◇1 A	VT ◇1 ☕	NT E	EM ◇ C	
London Euston ⊖65	d			16 33					17 07					18 07					18 33			19 07			
Birmingham New Street 12 65	d		17 01					17 36				18 01						19 01							
Crewe 10 65	d		17 57					18 33				18 59						19 58				20 47			
Winsford	d		18 07									19 08						20 07							
Hartford	d		18 12					18 44				19 13						20 12							
Acton Bridge	d																	20 16							
Runcorn	a		18 21	18 31				18 52	18 59			19 22		19 55				20 24	20 31			21 05			
	d		18 22	18 31				18 53	18 59			19 23		19 55				20 25	20 32			21 05			
Liverpool South Parkway 7 ⇐	a		18 30					19 02				19 31						20 33							
	d	18 22	18 31			18 38	18 47	19 02		19 11	19 18	19 32	19 47			19 59	20 15	20 34		20 38	20 47		21 15	21 20	
West Allerton	d					18 41				19 15						20 03				20 41			21 19		
Mossley Hill	d					18 44				19 18						20 05				20 44			21 21		
Edge Hill 90	d					18 50				19 26						20 11							21 27		
Liverpool Lime Street 10 90	a	18 35	18 43	18 52		18 57	19 01	19 14	19 17	19 35	19 35	19 44	20 01	20 15		20 18	20 30	20 46	20 52	20 55	21 01	21 25	21 34	21 35	

		LM ◇1	TP ◇1 A	NT E	VT ◇1 ☕	TP ◇1 A	NT E
London Euston ⊖65	d				20 11		
Birmingham New Street 12 65	d	20 01					
Crewe 10 65	d	21 06			22 06		
Winsford	d	21 14					
Hartford	d	21 19					
Acton Bridge	d						
Runcorn	a	21 29			22 24		
	d	21 29			22 24		
Liverpool South Parkway 7 ⇐	a	21 38					
	d	21 38	21 47	22 12		22 47	23 12
West Allerton	d			22 15			23 15
Mossley Hill	d			22 18			23 18
Edge Hill 90	d			22 23			23 23
Liverpool Lime Street 10 90	a	21 50	22 01	22 30	22 46	23 01	23 30

A From Scarborough
B From Manchester Oxford Road
C From Norwich
D until 11 February. To Blackpool North
E From Warrington Central

Table 91

Sundays

Crewe and Runcorn - Liverpool

Network Diagram - see first Page of Table 88

	NT	NT	TP	NT	NT	TP	VT	LM	NT		TP	VT	LM	EM	NT	TP	VT	LM	EM		NT	VT	TP	LM
			◇1			◇1	◇1	◇1			◇1	◇1	◇1	◇		◇1	◇1	◇1	◇			◇1	◇1	◇1
	A	B	C	B	B	D			B		C			E	B	F			E		B		G	
							🍴					🍴					🍴					🍴		
London Euston ⊖65 d							08 15					09 15					10 15					11 15		
Birmingham New Street 12 65 d								09 42					10 42					11 42						12 35
Crewe 10 65 d							10 30	10 38				11 32	11 38				12 34	12 38				13 15		13 31
Winsford d								10 45					11 45					12 45						13 38
Hartford d								10 50					11 50					12 50						13 43
Acton Bridge d																								
Runcorn a							10 47	11 00				11 49	12 01				12 51	13 01				13 32		13 54
d							10 47	11 01				11 49	12 01				12 51	13 01				13 32		13 54
Liverpool South Parkway 7 ✈ a								11 09					12 10					13 10						14 03
d	00 20	08 54	09 47	10 03	10 33	10 49		11 10	11 33		11 47		12 10	12 17	12 33	12 47		13 10	13 17		13 33		13 47	14 03
West Allerton d		08 57		10 06	10 36				11 36						12 36						13 36			
Mossley Hill d		09 00		10 09	10 39				11 39						12 39						13 39			
Edge Hill 90 d																								
Liverpool Lime Street 10 90 a	00 34	09 11	10 00	10 20	10 50	11 00	11 09	11 21	11 50		11 59	12 10	12 21	12 30	12 50	12 58	13 12	13 21	13 30		13 50	13 54	13 58	14 14

	VT	EM	NT	TP	LM		VT	EM	NT	TP	LM	VT	EM	NT	TP		LM	VT	EM	NT	TP	LM	VT	EM
	◇1	◇		◇1	◇1		◇1	◇		◇1	◇1	◇1	◇		◇1		◇1	◇1	◇		◇1	◇1	◇1	◇
		E	B	G				E	B	H			I	B	G				E	B	H			E
	🍴						🍴					🍴						🍴					🍴	
London Euston ⊖65 d	12 02						13 02					14 02						15 02					16 02	
Birmingham New Street 12 65 d					13 35						14 35						15 35					16 35		
Crewe 10 65 d	13 45				14 31		14 45				15 31	15 45					16 31					17 31		
Winsford d					14 38						15 38						16 38					17 38		
Hartford d					14 43						15 43						16 43					17 43		
Acton Bridge d																								
Runcorn a	14 02				14 53		15 02				15 53	16 02					16 54	16 57				17 54	17 57	
d	14 02				14 54		15 02				15 54	16 02					16 54	16 57				17 54	17 57	
Liverpool South Parkway 7 ✈ a					15 02						16 02						17 03					18 03		
d		14 16	14 33	14 47	15 03			15 16	15 33	15 47	16 03		16 16	16 33	16 47		17 03		17 16	17 33	17 47	18 03		18 16
West Allerton d			14 36						15 36					16 36						17 36				
Mossley Hill d			14 39						15 39					16 39						17 39				
Edge Hill 90 d																								
Liverpool Lime Street 10 90 a	14 24	14 30	14 50	14 58	15 14		15 24	15 30	15 50	15 58	16 14	16 24	16 30	16 50	16 58		17 14	17 16	17 30	17 50	17 58	18 14	18 16	18 30

	NT		TP	LM	VT	EM	NT	TP	LM	VT	EM		NT	TP	LM	VT	NT	TP	VT	VT	NT		TP	NT
			◇1	◇1	◇1	◇		◇1	◇1	◇1	◇			◇1	◇1	◇1		◇1	◇1	◇1			◇1	
	B		G			I	B	H			I		B	G			B	H			B		G	J
					🍴					🍴						🍴			🍴	🍴				
London Euston ⊖65 d					17 02					18 02						19 02			20 02	20 05				
Birmingham New Street 12 65 d				17 35					18 35						19 35									
Crewe 10 65 d				18 31					19 31						20 31	20 50			21 46	21 55				
Winsford d				18 38					19 38						20 38									
Hartford d				18 43					19 43						20 43									
Acton Bridge d																								
Runcorn a				18 54	18 57				19 53	19 58					20 54	21 07			22 03	22 12				
d				18 54	18 57				19 54	19 58					20 54	21 07			22 03	22 12				
Liverpool South Parkway 7 ✈ a				19 03					20 02						21 03									
d	18 33		18 47	19 03		19 17	19 33	19 47	20 03		20 16		20 33	20 47	21 03		21 33	21 47			22 33		22 47	23 33
West Allerton d	18 36						19 36						20 36				21 36				22 36			23 36
Mossley Hill d	18 39						19 39						20 39				21 39				22 39			23 39
Edge Hill 90 d																								
Liverpool Lime Street 10 90 a	18 50		18 58	19 14	19 19	19 30	19 50	19 58	20 14	20 16	20 30		20 50	20 58	21 14	21 28	21 50	21 58	22 23	22 33	22 50		22 58	23 50

	VT
	◇1
	🍴
London Euston ⊖65 d	21 21
Birmingham New Street 12 65 d	
Crewe 10 65 d	23 45
Winsford d	
Hartford d	
Acton Bridge d	
Runcorn a	00 07
d	00 07
Liverpool South Parkway 7 ✈ a	
d	
West Allerton d	
Mossley Hill d	
Edge Hill 90 d	
Liverpool Lime Street 10 90 a	00 30

A not 11 December. From Manchester Oxford Road
B From Manchester Oxford Road
C until 25 March. From Manchester Piccadilly
D until 25 March. From York
E From Nottingham
F until 25 March. From Newcastle
G until 25 March. From Scarborough
H until 25 March. From Middlesbrough
I From Norwich
J From Manchester Airport

Manchester and Bolton - Blackburn - Clitheroe

Network Diagram - see first page of Table 94

Miles			NT	NT	NT	NT	NT	NT	NT	NT	NT		NT	NT	NT	NT	NT	NT	NT	NT	NT		NT	NT	NT
0	**Manchester Victoria**	82 d	05 51		05 55		07 23	08 00	08 29	09 00	10 00		11 00	12 00	13 00	14 00	15 00	15 40	16 23	17 00	17 23		18 00	18 23	19 00
0¾	Salford Central	82 d					07 26	08 03	08 32	09 03	10 03		11 03	12 03	13 03	14 03	15 03	15 43	16 26	17 03	17 27		18 03	18 26	19 03
—	Manchester Piccadilly 10	82 d				06 54																			
1¾	Salford Crescent	82 d			06 00	07 03	07 30	08 08	08 37	09 08	10 08		11 08	12 08	13 08	14 08	15 08	15 47	16 31	17 08	17 30		18 08	18 31	19 08
10¾	**Bolton**	82 d			06 12	07 19	07 42	08 20	08 49	09 20	10 20		11 20	12 20	13 20	14 20	15 20	16 00	16 43	17 20	17 43		18 20	18 43	19 20
12½	Hall I' Th' Wood	d			06 17	07 24	07 47	08 25	08 54	09 25	10 25		11 25	12 25	13 25	14 25	15 25	16 05	16 48	17 25	17 48		18 25	18 48	19 25
13½	Bromley Cross	d			06 20	07 27	07 53	08 28	08 57	09 28	10 28		11 28	12 28	13 28	14 28	15 28	16 10	16 51	17 28	17 55		18 28	18 54	19 28
16½	Entwistle	d					07x59	08x34		09x34	10x34		11x34	12x34	13x34	14x34	15x34	16x16	16x57	17x34			18x34		19x34
20¼	Darwen	a			06 31	07 39	08 06	08 41	09 09	09 41	10 41		11 41	12 41	13 41	14 41	15 41	16 23	17 04	17 41	18 07		18 41	19 06	19 41
—		d			06 42	07 39	08 11	08 41	09 11	09 41	10 41		11 41	12 41	13 41	14 41	15 41	16 23	17 11	17 41	18 07		18 41	19 11	19 41
—	Blackpool North	97 d																							
—	Preston 8	97 d																							
24½	**Blackburn**	a	10 14		06 49	07 46	08 20	08 51	09 20	09 50	10 50		11 50	12 50	13 50	14 50	15 50	16 30	17 20	17 51	18 16		18 48	19 21	19 51
—		d		06 25	06 52	07 47		08 52		09 52	10 52		11 52	12 52	13 52	14 52	15 52	16 31	17 20	17 53			18 49		19 52
27¼	Ramsgreave & Wilpshire	d		06 31	06 58	07 53		08 58		09 58	10 58		11 58	12 58	13 58	14 58	15 58	16 37	17 26	17 59			18 55		19 58
29¾	Langho	d		06 35	07 02	07 57		09 02		10 02	11 02		12 02	13 02	14 02	15 02	16 02	16 41	17 31	18 03			18 59		20 02
31¾	Whalley	d		06 39	07 06	08 01		09 06		10 06	11 06		12 06	13 06	14 06	15 06	16 06	16 45	17 35	18 07			19 03		20 06
34¼	**Clitheroe**	a		06 50	07 17	08 12		09 17		10 17	11 17		12 17	13 17	14 17	15 17	16 17	16 56	17 45	18 18			19 14		20 17

		NT	NT	NT FO	NT FX	NT FO	NT FX
Manchester Victoria	82 d	20 00	21 00	22 00	22 00	23 00	23 00
Salford Central	82 d	20 03	21 03	22 04		23 03	
Manchester Piccadilly 10	82 d						
Salford Crescent	82 d	20 08	21 08	22 08	22 08	23 08	23 08
Bolton	82 d	20 20	21 20	22 20	22 20	23 20	23 20
Hall I' Th' Wood	d	20 25	21 25	22 25	22 25	23 25	23 25
Bromley Cross	d	20 28	21 28	22 28	22 28	23 28	23 28
Entwistle	d	20x34	21x34	22x34	22x34	23x34	23x34
Darwen	a	20 41	21 41	22 41	22 41	23 41	23 41
	d	20 41	21 41	22 41	22 41	23 41	23 41
Blackpool North	97 d						
Preston 8	97 d						
Blackburn	a	20 50	21 50	22 50	22 50	23 51	23 51
	d	20 52	21 52	22 51	22 51		
Ramsgreave & Wilpshire	d	20 58	21 58	22 57	22 57		
Langho	d	21 02	22 02	23 01	23 01		
Whalley	d	21 06	22 06	23 05	23 05		
Clitheroe	a	21 17	22 17	23 16	23 16		

Saturdays

		NT	NT	NT	NT	NT	NT	NT	NT	NT		NT	NT	NT	NT	NT	NT	NT	NT	NT		NT	NT	NT	NT
Manchester Victoria	82 d		05 55		07 23	08 00	08 29	09 00	09 29	10 00		11 00	12 00	13 00	14 00	15 00	15 40	16 23	17 00	17 23		18 00	18 23	19 00	20 00
Salford Central	82 d				07 26	08 03	08 32	09 03	09 32	10 03		11 03	12 03	13 03	14 03	15 03	15 43	16 26	17 03	17 26		18 03	18 26	19 03	20 03
Manchester Piccadilly 10	82 d			06 54																					
Salford Crescent	82 d		06 00	07 03	07 30	08 08	08 37	09 08	09 37	10 08		11 08	12 08	13 08	14 08	15 08	15 47	16 31	17 08	17 31		18 08	18 31	19 08	20 08
Bolton	82 d		06 12	07 19	07 42	08 20	08 49	09 20	09 49	10 20		11 20	12 20	13 20	14 20	15 20	16 00	16 43	17 20	17 43		18 20	18 43	19 20	20 20
Hall I' Th' Wood	d		06 17	07 24	07 47	08 25	08 54	09 25	09 54	10 25		11 25	12 25	13 25	14 25	15 25	16 05	16 48	17 25	17 48		18 25	18 48	19 25	20 25
Bromley Cross	d		06 20	07 27	07 53	08 28	08 57	09 28	09 57	10 28		11 28	12 28	13 28	14 28	15 28	16 10	16 51	17 28	17 55		18 28	18 54	19 28	20 28
Entwistle	d				07x59	08x34		09x34		10x34		11x34	12x34	13x34	14x34	15x34	16x16	16x57	17x34			18x34		19x34	20x34
Darwen	a		06 31	07 39	08 06	08 41	09 09	09 41	10 09	10 41		11 41	12 41	13 41	14 41	15 41	16 23	17 04	17 41	18 07		18 41	19 06	19 41	20 41
	d		06 42	07 39	08 11	08 41	09 11	09 41	10 11	10 41		11 41	12 41	13 41	14 41	15 41	16 23	17 11	17 41	18 07		18 41	19 11	19 41	20 41
Blackpool North	97 d																								
Preston 8	97 d																								
Blackburn	a		06 49	07 46	08 20	08 51	09 20	09 50	10 20	10 50		11 50	12 50	13 50	14 50	15 49	16 30	17 19	17 51	18 21		18 48	19 21	19 51	20 50
	d	06 25	06 52	07 47		08 52		09 52		10 52		11 52	12 52	13 52	14 52	15 52	16 31	17 19	17 53			18 49		19 52	20 52
Ramsgreave & Wilpshire	d	06 31	06 58	07 53		08 58		09 58		10 58		11 58	12 58	13 58	14 58	15 58	16 37	17 25	17 59			18 55		19 58	20 58
Langho	d	06 35	07 02	07 57		09 03		10 02		11 02		12 02	13 02	14 02	15 02	16 02	16 41	17 30	18 03			18 59		20 02	21 02
Whalley	d	06 39	07 06	08 01		09 07		10 06		11 06		12 06	13 06	14 06	15 06	16 06	16 45	17 34	18 07			19 03		20 06	21 06
Clitheroe	a	06 50	07 17	08 12		09 17		10 17		11 17		12 17	13 17	14 17	15 17	16 17	16 56	17 44	18 18			19 14		20 17	21 17

		NT	NT	NT
Manchester Victoria	82 d	21 00	22 01	23 05
Salford Central	82 d	21 03	22 04	23 08
Manchester Piccadilly 10	82 d			
Salford Crescent	82 d	21 08	22 08	23 12
Bolton	82 d	21 20	22 20	23 24
Hall I' Th' Wood	d	21 25	22 25	23 29
Bromley Cross	d	21 28	22 28	23 32
Entwistle	d	21x34	22x34	23x38
Darwen	a	21 41	22 41	23 45
	d	21 41	22 41	23 45
Blackpool North	97 d			
Preston 8	97 d			
Blackburn	a	21 50	22 50	23 54
	d	21 52	22 51	
Ramsgreave & Wilpshire	d	21 58	22 57	
Langho	d	22 02	23 01	
Whalley	d	22 06	23 05	
Clitheroe	a	22 17	23 14	

Table 94

Sundays
until 26 February

Manchester and Bolton - Blackburn - Clitheroe

Network Diagram - see first page of Table 94

		NT	NT	NT	NT	NT	NT	NT	NT	NT	NT	NT	NT	NT	NT	NT
Manchester Victoria 82	d	08 01	09 00	10 00	11 00	12 00	13 00	14 00	15 00	16 00	17 00	18 00	19 00	20 00	21 00	22 00
Salford Central 82	d															
Manchester Piccadilly 10 82	d															
Salford Crescent 82	d	08 07	09 08	10 08	11 08	12 08	13 08	14 08	15 08	16 08	17 08	18 08	19 08	20 08	21 08	22 08
Bolton 82	d	08 19	09 20	10 20	11 20	12 20	13 20	14 20	15 20	16 20	17 20	18 20	19 20	20 18	21 20	22 20
Hall I' Th' Wood	d	08 24	09 25	10 25	11 25	12 25	13 25	14 25	15 25	16 25	17 25	18 25	19 25	20 23	21 25	22 25
Bromley Cross	d	08 27	09 28	10 28	11 28	12 28	13 28	14 28	15 28	16 28	17 28	18 28	19 28	20 26	21 28	22 28
Entwistle	d	08x33	09x34	10x34	11x34	12x34	13x34	14x34	15x34	16x34	17x34	18x34	19x34	20x33	21x34	22x34
Darwen	a	08 40	09 41	10 41	11 41	12 41	13 41	14 41	15 41	16 41	17 41	18 41	19 41	20 39	21 41	22 41
	d	08 40	09 41	10 41	11 41	12 41	13 41	14 41	15 41	16 41	17 41	18 41	19 41	20 39	21 41	22 41
Blackpool North 97	d															
Preston 8 97	d															
Blackburn	a	08 47	09 48	10 48	11 48	12 48	13 48	14 48	15 48	16 48	17 48	18 48	19 48	20 46	21 48	22 50
	d	08 52	09 50	10 50	11 50	12 50	13 50	14 50	15 50	16 50	17 50	18 50	19 50	20 49	21 50	
Ramsgreave & Wilpshire	d	08 58	09 56	10 56	11 56	12 56	13 56	14 56	15 56	16 56	17 56	18 56	19 56	20 55	21 56	
Langho	d	09 02	10 00	11 00	12 00	13 00	14 00	15 00	16 00	17 00	18 00	19 00	20 00	20 58	22 00	
Whalley	d	09 06	10 04	11 04	12 04	13 04	14 04	15 04	16 04	17 04	18 04	19 04	20 04	21 02	22 04	
Clitheroe	a	09 17	10 15	11 15	12 15	13 15	14 15	15 15	16 15	17 15	18 15	19 15	20 15	21 14	22 15	

Sundays
4 March to 1 April

		NT	NT A	NT	NT	NT	NT	NT	NT	NT	NT	NT	NT	NT	NT	NT	NT
Manchester Victoria 82	d	08 01		09 00	10 00	11 00	12 00	13 00	14 00	15 00	16 00	17 00	18 00	19 00	20 00	21 00	22 00
Salford Central 82	d																
Manchester Piccadilly 10 82	d																
Salford Crescent 82	d	08 07		09 08	10 08	11 08	12 08	13 08	14 08	15 08	16 08	17 08	18 08	19 08	20 08	21 08	22 08
Bolton 82	d	08 19		09 20	10 20	11 20	12 20	13 20	14 20	15 20	16 20	17 20	18 20	19 20	20 18	21 20	22 20
Hall I' Th' Wood	d	08 24		09 25	10 25	11 25	12 25	13 25	14 25	15 25	16 25	17 25	18 25	19 25	20 23	21 25	22 25
Bromley Cross	d	08 27		09 28	10 28	11 28	12 28	13 28	14 28	15 28	16 28	17 28	18 28	19 28	20 26	21 28	22 28
Entwistle	d	08x33		09x34	10x34	11x34	12x34	13x34	14x34	15x34	16x34	17x34	18x34	19x34	20x33	21x34	22x34
Darwen	a	08 40		09 41	10 41	11 41	12 41	13 41	14 41	15 41	16 41	17 41	18 41	19 41	20 39	21 41	22 41
	d	08 40		09 41	10 41	11 41	12 41	13 41	14 41	15 41	16 41	17 41	18 41	19 41	20 39	21 41	22 41
Blackpool North 97	d		08 36														
Preston 8 97	d		09 05														
Blackburn	a	08 47	09 25	09 48	10 48	11 48	12 48	13 48	14 48	15 48	16 48	17 48	18 48	19 48	20 46	21 48	22 50
	d	08 52	09 27	09 50	10 50	11 50	12 50	13 50	14 50	15 50	16 50	17 50	18 50	19 50	20 49	21 50	
Ramsgreave & Wilpshire	d	08 58	09 34	09 56	10 56	11 56	12 56	13 56	14 56	15 56	16 56	17 56	18 56	19 56	20 55	21 56	
Langho	d	09 02	09 39	10 00	11 00	12 00	13 00	14 00	15 00	16 00	17 00	18 00	19 00	20 00	20 58	22 00	
Whalley	d	09 06	09 43	10 04	11 04	12 04	13 04	14 04	15 04	16 04	17 04	18 04	19 04	20 04	21 02	22 04	
Clitheroe	a	09 17	09 50	10 15	11 15	12 15	13 15	14 15	15 15	16 15	17 15	18 15	19 15	20 15	21 14	22 15	

Sundays
from 8 April

		NT	NT	NT	NT	NT	NT	NT	NT	NT	NT	NT	NT	NT	NT	NT	NT
Manchester Victoria 82	d	08 01		09 00	10 00	11 00	12 00	13 00	14 00	15 00	16 00	17 00	18 00	19 00	20 00	21 00	22 00
Salford Central 82	d																
Manchester Piccadilly 10 82	d																
Salford Crescent 82	d	08 07		09 08	10 08	11 08	12 08	13 08	14 08	15 08	16 08	17 08	18 08	19 08	20 08	21 08	22 08
Bolton 82	d	08 19		09 20	10 20	11 20	12 20	13 20	14 20	15 20	16 20	17 20	18 20	19 20	20 18	21 20	22 20
Hall I' Th' Wood	d	08 24		09 25	10 25	11 25	12 25	13 25	14 25	15 25	16 25	17 25	18 25	19 25	20 23	21 25	22 25
Bromley Cross	d	08 27		09 28	10 28	11 28	12 28	13 28	14 28	15 28	16 28	17 28	18 28	19 28	20 26	21 28	22 28
Entwistle	d	08x33		09x34	10x34	11x34	12x34	13x34	14x34	15x34	16x34	17x34	18x34	19x34	20x33	21x34	22x34
Darwen	a	08 40		09 41	10 41	11 41	12 41	13 41	14 41	15 41	16 41	17 41	18 41	19 41	20 39	21 41	22 41
	d	08 40		09 41	10 41	11 41	12 41	13 41	14 41	15 41	16 41	17 41	18 41	19 41	20 39	21 41	22 41
Blackpool North 97	d		08 36														
Preston 8 97	d		09 05														
Blackburn	a	08 47	09 25	09 48	10 48	11 48	12 48	13 48	14 48	15 48	16 48	17 48	18 48	19 48	20 46	21 48	22 50
	d	08 52	09 27	09 50	10 50	11 50	12 50	13 50	14 50	15 50	16 50	17 50	18 50	19 50	20 49	21 50	
Ramsgreave & Wilpshire	d	08 58	09 34	09 56	10 56	11 56	12 56	13 56	14 56	15 56	16 56	17 56	18 56	19 56	20 55	21 56	
Langho	d	09 02	09 39	10 00	11 00	12 00	13 00	14 00	15 00	16 00	17 00	18 00	19 00	20 00	20 58	22 00	
Whalley	d	09 06	09 43	10 04	11 04	12 04	13 04	14 04	15 04	16 04	17 04	18 04	19 04	20 04	21 02	22 04	
Clitheroe	a	09 17	09 50	10 15	11 15	12 15	13 15	14 15	15 15	16 15	17 15	18 15	19 15	20 15	21 14	22 15	

A 1 April

Clitheroe - Blackburn - Bolton and Manchester

Network Diagram - see first page of Table 94

Mondays to Fridays

Miles			NT	NT	NT	NT	NT	NT	NT	NT	NT	NT
0	**Clitheroe**	d		06 40	07 07	07 40		08 26		09 40	10 40	11 40
2½	Whalley	d		06 46	07 13	07 46		08 32		09 46	10 46	11 46
4½	Langho	d		06 50	07 17	07 50		08 36		09 50	10 50	11 50
7	Ramsgreave & Wilpshire	d		06 55	07 22	07 55		08 41		09 55	10 55	11 55
9¾	**Blackburn**	a		07 01	07 29	08 01		08 47		10 01	11 01	12 01
—		d	06 28	07 02	07 30	08 03	08 32	09 03	09 31	10 03	11 03	12 03
—	Preston 8 97	a										
—	Blackpool North 97	a										
14	Darwen	a	06 35	07 09	07 37	08 10	08 39	09 11	09 38	10 10	11 10	12 10
—		d	06 35	07 09	07 40	08 10	08 42	09 11	09 41	10 10	11 10	12 10
17¾	Entwistle	d	06x42	07x16		08x17				10x17	11x17	12x17
20¾	Bromley Cross	d	06 48	07 22	07 51	08 23	08 52	09 22	09 52	10 23	11 23	12 23
21¾	Hall I' Th' Wood	d	06 50	07 24	07 53	08 25	08 55	09 25	09 55	10 25	11 25	12 25
23½	**Bolton** 82	a	06 55	07 30	07 58	08 30	09 02	09 30	10 00	10 30	11 30	12 30
32½	Salford Crescent 82	a	07 15	07 43	08 17	08 43	09 15	09 43	10 13	10 43	11 43	12 43
—	Manchester Piccadilly 10 82 ⇌	a										
33½	Salford Central 82	a	07 18	07 46	08 20	08 46	09 18	09 46	10 16	10 46	11 46	12 46
34¼	**Manchester Victoria** 82 ⇌	a	07 26	07 53	08 25	08 52	09 26	09 52	10 22	10 52	11 52	12 52

		NT	NT	NT	NT	NT	NT	NT
Clitheroe	d	12 40	13 40	14 40	15 26	16 40	17 09	18 09
Whalley	d	12 46	13 46	14 46	15 32	16 46	17 15	18 15
Langho	d	12 50	13 50	14 50	15 36	16 49	17 19	18 19
Ramsgreave & Wilpshire	d	12 55	13 55	14 55	15 41	16 55	17 24	18 24
Blackburn	a	13 01	14 01	15 01	15 47	17 01	17 30	18 30
	d	13 03	14 03	15 03	15 51	17 03	17 31	18 31
Preston 8 97	a							
Blackpool North 97	a							
Darwen	a	13 10	14 10	15 10	15 58	17 10	17 38	18 38
	d	13 10	14 10	15 10	15 58	17 10	17 41	18 41
Entwistle	d	13x17	14x17	15x17		17x17	17x48	18x48
Bromley Cross	d	13 23	14 23	15 23	16 09	17 23	17 54	18 54
Hall I' Th' Wood	d	13 25	14 25	15 25	16 12	17 25	17 56	18 56
Bolton 82	a	13 30	14 30	15 30	16 17	17 30	18 01	19 01
Salford Crescent 82	a	13 43	14 43	15 43	16 30	17 43	18 15	19 14
Manchester Piccadilly 10 82 ⇌	a							
Salford Central 82	a	13 46	14 46	15 46	16 33	17 46	18 17	19 17
Manchester Victoria 82 ⇌	a	13 52	14 52	15 54	16 41	17 53	18 24	19 23

		NT	NT	NT	NT	NT FX	NT FO	NT
Clitheroe	d	18 40		19 40	20 40	21 40	21 40	22 40
Whalley	d	18 46		19 46	20 46	21 46	21 46	22 46
Langho	d	18 50		19 50	20 50	21 50	21 50	22 50
Ramsgreave & Wilpshire	d	18 55		19 55	20 55	21 55	21 55	22 55
Blackburn	a	19 01		20 01	21 01	22 01	22 01	23 01
	d	19 03	19 31	20 03	21 03	22 03	22 03	23 03
Preston 8 97	a							
Blackpool North 97	a							
Darwen	a	19 10	19 38	20 10	21 10	22 10	22 10	23 10
	d	19 10	19 42	20 10	21 10	22 10	22 10	23 10
Entwistle	d	19x17	19x49	20x17	21x17	22x17	22x17	23x17
Bromley Cross	d	19 23	19 54	20 23	21 23	22 23	22 23	23 23
Hall I' Th' Wood	d	19 25	19 57	20 25	21 25	22 25	22 25	23 25
Bolton 82	a	19 31	20 02	20 30	21 30	22 30	22 30	23 30
Salford Crescent 82	a	19 44	20 15	20 43	21 43	22 43	22 43	23 43
Manchester Piccadilly 10 82 ⇌	a							
Salford Central 82	a	19 46	20 17	20 46	21 46		22 46	
Manchester Victoria 82 ⇌	a	19 53	20 24	20 52	21 52	22 52	22 52	23 52

Saturdays

		NT	NT	NT	NT	NT	NT	NT	NT	NT	NT
Clitheroe	d		07 07	07 41		08 26		09 40		10 40	11 40
Whalley	d		07 13	07 47		08 32		09 46		10 46	11 46
Langho	d		07 17	07 51		08 36		09 50		10 50	11 50
Ramsgreave & Wilpshire	d		07 22	07 56		08 41		09 55		10 55	11 55
Blackburn	a		07 28	08 02		08 47		10 01		11 01	12 01
	d	06 28	07 29	08 03	08 32	09 03	09 31	10 03	10 31	11 03	12 03
Preston 8 97	a										
Blackpool North 97	a										
Darwen	a	06 35	07 37	08 10	08 39	09 11	09 38	10 11	10 38	11 10	12 10
	d	06 35	07 40	08 10	08 42	09 11	09 41	10 11	10 39	11 10	12 10
Entwistle	d	06x42		08x17				10x18	10x46	11x17	12x17
Bromley Cross	d	06 48	07 51	08 23	08 52	09 22	09 52	10 23	10 51	11 23	12 23
Hall I' Th' Wood	d	06 50	07 53	08 25	08 55	09 25	09 55	10 26	10 54	11 25	12 25
Bolton 82	a	06 55	07 58	08 30	09 02	09 30	10 00	10 31	10 59	11 30	12 30
Salford Crescent 82	a	07 15	08 17	08 43	09 15	09 43	10 13	10 44	11 12	11 43	12 43
Manchester Piccadilly 10 82 ⇌	a										
Salford Central 82	a	07 19	08 20	08 46	09 18	09 46	10 16	10 47	11 15	11 46	12 46
Manchester Victoria 82 ⇌	a	07 25	08 25	08 52	09 26	09 52	10 22	10 52	11 23	11 50	12 52

Table 94

Saturdays

Clitheroe - Blackburn - Bolton and Manchester

Network Diagram - see first page of Table 94

		NT	NT	NT	NT	NT	NT	NT	NT
Clitheroe	d	12 40	13 40	14 40	15 26	16 40	17 09	18 09	18 40
Whalley	d	12 46	13 46	14 46	15 32	16 46	17 15	18 15	18 46
Langho	d	12 50	13 50	14 50	15 36	16 50	17 19	18 19	18 50
Ramsgreave & Wilpshire	d	12 55	13 55	14 55	15 41	16 55	17 24	18 24	18 55
Blackburn	a	13 01	14 01	15 01	15 47	17 01	17 30	18 30	19 01
	d	13 03	14 03	15 03	15 51	17 03	17 31	18 31	19 03
Preston 8 97	a								
Blackpool North 97	a								
Darwen	a	13 10	14 10	15 10	15 58	17 10	17 38	18 38	19 10
	d	13 10	14 10	15 10	15 58	17 10	17 41	18 41	19 10
Entwistle	d	13x17	14x17	15x17		17x17	17x48	18x48	19x17
Bromley Cross	d	13 23	14 23	15 23	16 09	17 23	17 54	18 54	19 23
Hall I' Th' Wood	d	13 25	14 25	15 25	16 12	17 25	17 56	18 56	19 26
Bolton 82	a	13 30	14 30	15 30	16 17	17 30	18 01	19 01	19 31
Salford Crescent 82	a	13 43	14 43	15 43	16 30	17 43	18 15	19 14	19 44
Manchester Piccadilly 10 82 ⛴	a								
Salford Central 82	a	13 46	14 46	15 46	16 33	17 46	18 18	19 17	19 47
Manchester Victoria 82 ⛴	a	13 52	14 52	15 54	16 41	17 53	18 27	19 23	19 53

		NT	NT	NT	NT	NT
Clitheroe	d		19 40	20 40	21 40	22 46
Whalley	d		19 46	20 46	21 46	22 52
Langho	d		19 50	20 50	21 50	22 56
Ramsgreave & Wilpshire	d		19 55	20 55	21 55	23 01
Blackburn	a		20 01	21 01	22 01	23 07
	d	19 31	20 03	21 03	22 03	23 09
Preston 8 97	a					
Blackpool North 97	a					
Darwen	a	19 38	20 10	21 10	22 10	23 16
	d	19 42	20 10	21 10	22 10	23 16
Entwistle	d	19x49	20x17	21x17	22x17	23x23
Bromley Cross	d	19 54	20 23	21 23	22 23	23 29
Hall I' Th' Wood	d	19 57	20 25	21 25	22 25	23 31
Bolton 82	a	20 02	20 30	21 30	22 30	23 36
Salford Crescent 82	a	20 15	20 43	21 43	22 43	23 50
Manchester Piccadilly 10 82 ⛴	a					
Salford Central 82	a	20 17	20 46	21 46	22 46	
Manchester Victoria 82 ⛴	a	20 24	20 52	21 52	22 52	00 01

Sundays

until 26 February

		NT A	NT	NT A	NT A	NT A	NT A	NT A	NT A	NT A	NT A
Clitheroe	d	22p46		09 40	10 40	11 40	12 40	13 40	14 40	15 40	16 40
Whalley	d	22p52		09 46	10 46	11 46	12 46	13 46	14 46	15 46	16 46
Langho	d	22p56		09 50	10 50	11 50	12 50	13 50	14 50	15 50	16 50
Ramsgreave & Wilpshire	d	23p01		09 55	10 55	11 55	12 55	13 55	14 55	15 55	16 55
Blackburn	a	23p07		10 01	11 01	12 01	13 01	14 01	15 01	16 01	17 01
	d	23p09	09 03	10 03	11 03	12 03	13 03	14 03	15 02	16 05	17 02
Preston 8 97	a										
Blackpool North 97	a										
Darwen	a	23p16	09 10	10 10	11 10	12 10	13 10	14 10	15 10	16 12	17 10
	d	23p16	09 10	10 10	11 10	12 10	13 10	14 10	15 10	16 12	17 10
Entwistle	d	23b23	09x17	10x17	11x17	12x17	13x17	14x17	15x17		17x17
Bromley Cross	d	23p29	09 23	10 23	11 23	12 23	13 23	14 23	15 22	16 23	17 22
Hall I' Th' Wood	d	23p31	09 25	10 25	11 25	12 25	13 25	14 25	15 25	16 26	17 25
Bolton 82	a	23p36	09 30	10 31	11 30	12 30	13 30	14 30	15 30	16 31	17 30
Salford Crescent 82	a	23p50	09 43	10 43	11 43	12 43	13 43	14 43	15 42	16 43	17 42
Manchester Piccadilly 10 82 ⛴	a										
Salford Central 82	a										
Manchester Victoria 82 ⛴	a	00 01	09 53	10 52	11 52	12 52	13 52	14 52	15 52	16 52	17 52

		NT A	NT	NT	NT	NT	NT A
Clitheroe	d	17 40	18 40	19 40	20 40	21 40	22 40
Whalley	d	17 46	18 46	19 46	20 46	21 46	22 46
Langho	d	17 50	18 50	19 50	20 50	21 50	22 50
Ramsgreave & Wilpshire	d	17 55	18 55	19 55	20 55	21 55	22 55
Blackburn	a	18 01	19 01	20 01	21 01	22 01	23 01
	d	18 03	19 03	20 03	21 03	22 03	23 03
Preston 8 97	a						
Blackpool North 97	a						
Darwen	a	18 10	19 10	20 10	21 10	22 10	23 10
	d	18 10	19 10	20 10	21 10	22 10	23 10
Entwistle	d	18x17	19x17	20x17	21x17	22x17	23x17
Bromley Cross	d	18 23	19 23	20 23	21 23	22 23	23 23
Hall I' Th' Wood	d	18 25	19 25	20 25	21 25	22 25	23 25
Bolton 82	a	18 30	19 31	20 30	21 30	22 30	23 30
Salford Crescent 82	a	18 43	19 44	20 43	21 43		23 43
Manchester Piccadilly 10 82 ⛴	a						
Salford Central 82	a					22 44	
Manchester Victoria 82 ⛴	a	18 52	19 52	20 52	21 52	22 52	23 52

A not 11 December

b Previous night, stops on request

Table 94

Sundays

4 March to 1 April

Clitheroe - Blackburn - Bolton and Manchester

Network Diagram - see first page of Table 94

		NT	NT	NT	NT	NT	NT	NT	NT	NT	NT
Clitheroe	d	22p46		09 40	10 40	11 40	12 40	13 40	14 40	15 40	16 40
Whalley	d	22p52		09 46	10 46	11 46	12 46	13 46	14 46	15 46	16 46
Langho	d	22p56		09 50	10 50	11 50	12 50	13 50	14 50	15 50	16 50
Ramsgreave & Wilpshire	d	23p01		09 55	10 55	11 55	12 55	13 55	14 55	15 55	16 55
Blackburn	a	23p07		10 01	11 01	12 01	13 01	14 01	15 01	16 01	17 01
	d	23p09	09 03	10 03	11 03	12 03	13 03	14 03	15 02	16 05	17 02
Preston 8 97	a										
Blackpool North 97	a										
Darwen	a	23p16	09 10	10 10	11 10	12 10	13 10	14 10	15 10	16 12	17 10
	d	23p16	09 10	10 10	11 10	12 10	13 10	14 10	15 10	16 12	17 10
Entwistle	d	23b23	09x17	10x17	11x17	12x17	13x17	14x17	15x17		17x17
Bromley Cross	d	23p29	09 23	10 23	11 23	12 23	13 23	14 23	15 22	16 23	17 22
Hall I' Th' Wood	d	23p31	09 25	10 25	11 25	12 25	13 25	14 25	15 25	16 26	17 25
Bolton 82	a	23p36	09 30	10 31	11 30	12 30	13 30	14 30	15 30	16 31	17 30
Salford Crescent 82	a	23p50	09 43	10 43	11 43	12 43	13 43	14 43	15 42	16 43	17 42
Manchester Piccadilly 10 82	a										
Salford Central 82	a										
Manchester Victoria 82	a	00 01	09 53	10 52	11 52	12 52	13 52	14 52	15 52	16 52	17 52

		NT	NT	NT	NT A	NT	NT	NT
Clitheroe	d	17 40	18 40	19 40	19 57	20 40	21 40	22 40
Whalley	d	17 46	18 46	19 46	20 04	20 46	21 46	22 46
Langho	d	17 50	18 50	19 50	20 09	20 50	21 50	22 50
Ramsgreave & Wilpshire	d	17 55	18 55	19 55	20 14	20 55	21 55	22 55
Blackburn	a	18 01	19 01	20 01	20 22	21 01	22 01	23 01
	d	18 03	19 03	20 03	20 25	21 03	22 03	23 03
Preston 8 97	a				20 47			
Blackpool North 97	a				21 16			
Darwen	a	18 10	19 10	20 10		21 10	22 10	23 10
	d	18 10	19 10	20 10		21 10	22 10	23 10
Entwistle	d	18x17	19x17	20x17		21x17	22x17	23x17
Bromley Cross	d	18 23	19 23	20 23		21 23	22 23	23 23
Hall I' Th' Wood	d	18 25	19 25	20 25		21 25	22 25	23 25
Bolton 82	a	18 30	19 31	20 30		21 30	22 30	23 30
Salford Crescent 82	a	18 43	19 44	20 43		21 43		23 43
Manchester Piccadilly 10 82	a							
Salford Central 82	a							
Manchester Victoria 82	a	18 52	19 52	20 52		21 52	22 52	23 52

Sundays

from 8 April

		NT	NT	NT	NT	NT	NT	NT	NT	NT	NT
Clitheroe	d	22p46		09 40	10 40	11 40	12 40	13 40	14 40	15 40	16 40
Whalley	d	22p52		09 46	10 46	11 46	12 46	13 46	14 46	15 46	16 46
Langho	d	22p56		09 50	10 50	11 50	12 50	13 50	14 50	15 50	16 50
Ramsgreave & Wilpshire	d	23p01		09 55	10 55	11 55	12 55	13 55	14 55	15 55	16 55
Blackburn	a	23p07		10 01	11 01	12 01	13 01	14 01	15 01	16 01	17 01
	d	23p09	09 03	10 03	11 03	12 03	13 03	14 03	15 02	16 05	17 02
Preston 8 97	a										
Blackpool North 97	a										
Darwen	a	23p16	09 10	10 10	11 10	12 10	13 10	14 10	15 10	16 12	17 10
	d	23p16	09 10	10 10	11 10	12 10	13 10	14 10	15 10	16 12	17 10
Entwistle	d	23b23	09x17	10x17	11x17	12x17	13x17	14x17	15x17		17x17
Bromley Cross	d	23p29	09 23	10 23	11 23	12 23	13 23	14 23	15 22	16 23	17 22
Hall I' Th' Wood	d	23p31	09 25	10 25	11 25	12 25	13 25	14 25	15 25	16 26	17 25
Bolton 82	a	23p36	09 30	10 31	11 30	12 30	13 30	14 30	15 30	16 31	17 30
Salford Crescent 82	a	23p50	09 43	10 43	11 43	12 43	13 43	14 43	15 42	16 43	17 42
Manchester Piccadilly 10 82	a										
Salford Central 82	a										
Manchester Victoria 82	a	00 01	09 53	10 52	11 52	12 52	13 52	14 52	15 52	16 52	17 52

		NT	NT	NT	NT	NT	NT	NT
Clitheroe	d	17 40	18 40	19 40	19 57	20 40	21 40	22 40
Whalley	d	17 46	18 46	19 46	20 04	20 46	21 46	22 46
Langho	d	17 50	18 50	19 50	20 09	20 50	21 50	22 50
Ramsgreave & Wilpshire	d	17 55	18 55	19 55	20 14	20 55	21 55	22 55
Blackburn	a	18 01	19 01	20 01	20 22	21 01	22 01	23 01
	d	18 03	19 03	20 03	20 25	21 03	22 03	23 03
Preston 8 97	a				20 47			
Blackpool North 97	a				21 16			
Darwen	a	18 10	19 10	20 10		21 10	22 10	23 10
	d	18 10	19 10	20 10		21 10	22 10	23 10
Entwistle	d	18x17	19x17	20x17		21x17	22x17	23x17
Bromley Cross	d	18 23	19 23	20 23		21 23	22 23	23 23
Hall I' Th' Wood	d	18 25	19 25	20 25		21 25	22 25	23 25
Bolton 82	a	18 30	19 31	20 30		21 30	22 30	23 30
Salford Crescent 82	a	18 43	19 44	20 43		21 43		23 43
Manchester Piccadilly 10 82	a							
Salford Central 82	a							
Manchester Victoria 82	a	18 52	19 52	20 52		21 52	22 52	23 52

A 1 April

b Previous night, stops on request

Network Diagram for Tables 97, 98, 99, 100

DM-15/08
Design BAJS

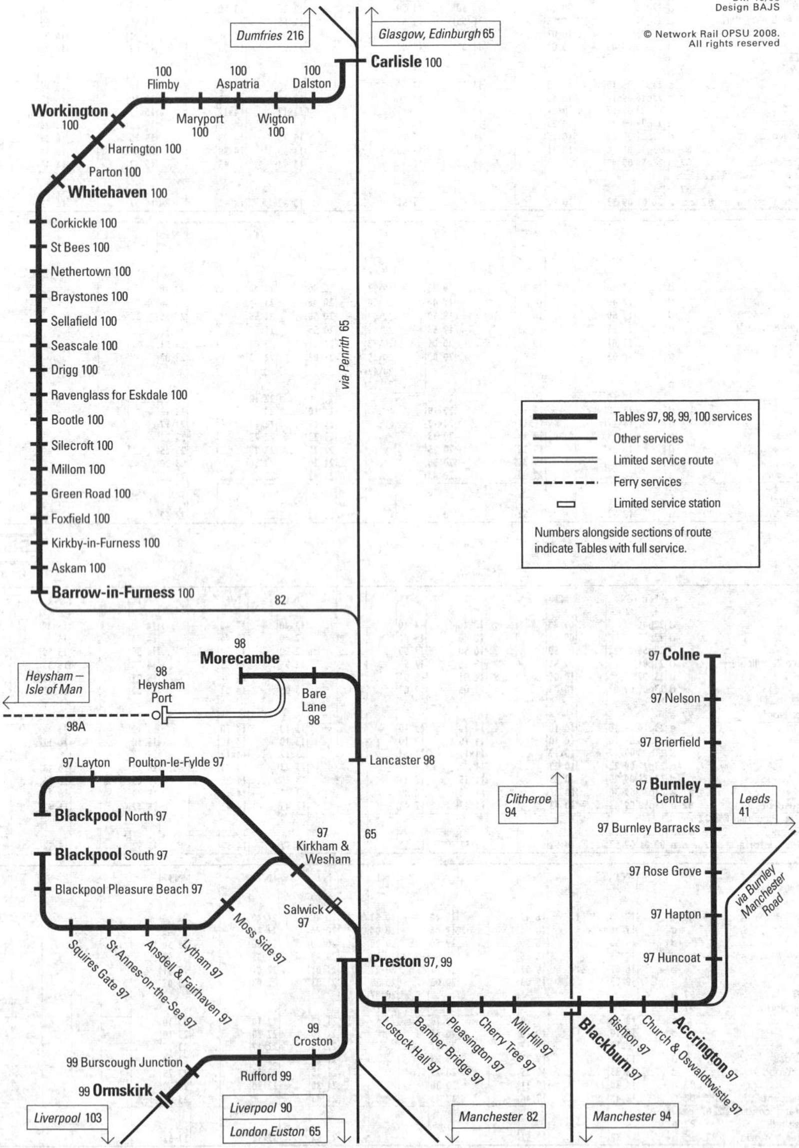

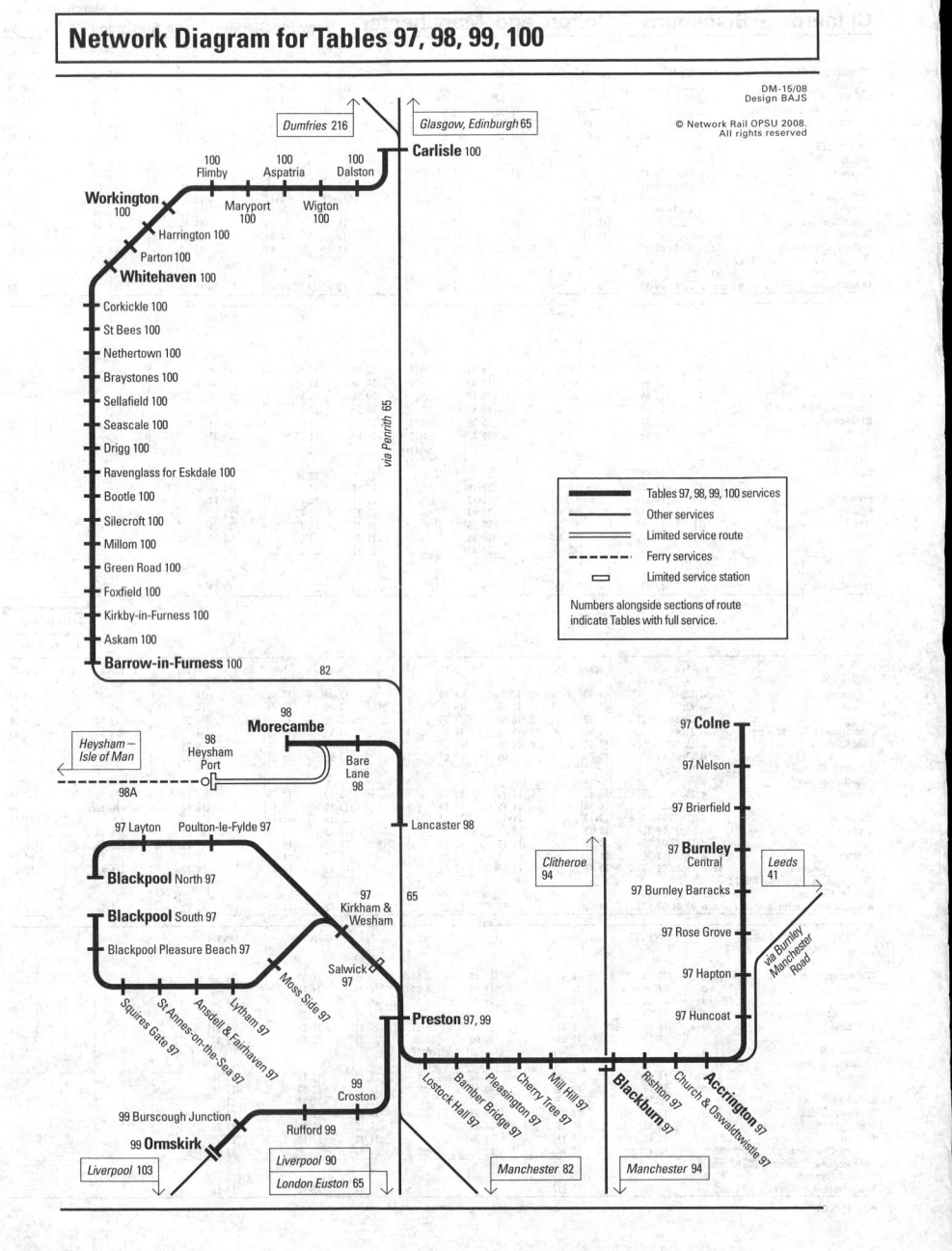

Blackpool - Preston - Blackburn, Accrington, Burnley and Colne

Network Diagram - see first Page of Table 97

Miles	Miles			NT MX		NT B	NT MX C	NT D	NT E	NT F	TP ◇1 A	NT		NT G	NT F	TP ◇1 A	NT H	NT	NT I	TP ◇1	NT G	NT F		TP ◇1	NT
—	0	**Blackpool North**	d					04 56	04 56	05 29	05 39			06 19	06 28	06 40	06 53		07 02	07 10	07 18	07 29		07 36	
—	1¼	Layton	d											06 22		06 43				07 13	07 21			07 39	
—	3¼	Poulton-le-Fylde	d					05 02	05 02	05 35	05 45			06 27	06 34	06 47			07 08	07 17	07 26	07 35		07 43	
0	—	**Blackpool South**	d	23p30								05 42						06 42							07 42
0½	—	Blackpool Pleasure Beach	d	23p32								05 44						06 44							07 44
1¾	—	Squires Gate	d	23p34								05 46						06 46							07 46
3¼	—	St Annes-on-the-Sea	d	23p38								05 50						06 50							07 50
5¼	—	Ansdell & Fairhaven	d	23p41								05 53						06 53							07 53
6½	—	Lytham	d	23p44								05 56						06 56							07 56
9	—	Moss Side	d	23p49								06 01						07 01							08 01
12¼	9¾	Kirkham & Wesham	d	23p56								06 08		06 36		06 56		07 09		07 26	07 35			07 52	08 09
14¾	12¼	Salwick	d															07 13							08 13
20	17½	**Preston** 8	a	00 08				05 20	05 20	05 52	06 03	06 19		06 46	06 52	07 07	07 15	07 20	07 28	07 37	07 46	07 52		08 03	08 20
—	—		d			04 47	04 47	05 22	05 22	05 54		06 21			06 54			07 22				07 54			08 22
22¾	—	Lostock Hall	d									06 26						07 27							08 27
24	—	Bamber Bridge	d									06 29						07 30							08 30
29	—	Pleasington	d									06 37						07 38							08 38
30	—	Cherry Tree	d									06 40						07 41							08 41
30¾	—	Mill Hill (Lancashire)	d									06 42						07 43							08 43
32	—	**Blackburn**	a			05 03	05 07	05 38	05 42	06 09		06 45			07 09			07 50				08 09			08 47
—	—	Clitheroe 94	a																						
—	—	**Blackburn**	d			05 04	05 08	05 39	05 43	06 10		06 48			07 10			07 51				08 10			08 48
35¾	—	Rishton	d					05 44	05 48			06 53						07 56							08 53
37½	—	Church & Oswaldtwistle	d					05 47	05 51			06 56						07 59							08 56
38¼	—	**Accrington**	d			05 11	05 14	05 50	05 54	06 17		06 59			07 17			08 02				08 17			08 59
40	—	Huncoat	d					05 54	05 58			07 03						08 06							09 03
41½	—	Hapton	d					05 57	06 01			07 06						08 09							09 06
43	—	Rose Grove	d					06 00	06 04			07 09						08 12							09 09
—	—	Burnley Manchester Road 41	a							06 26					07 26							08 26			
—	—	Leeds 10 41	a							07 39					08 39							09 39			
44	—	Burnley Barracks	d									07 12						08 15							09 12
44½	—	**Burnley Central**	d			05 21	05 25	06 05	06 09			07 15						08 18							09 15
46¾	—	Brierfield	d					06 09	06 13			07 19						08 22							09 19
48	—	Nelson	d					06 12	06 16			07 22						08 25							09 22
50	—	**Colne**	a			05 35	05 38	06 22	06 26			07 32						08 35							09 32

		NT G	NT F	TP ◇1 A	NT	NT G	NT F	NT J		TP ◇1 A	NT	NT G	NT F	NT J	TP ◇1 A	NT	NT G	NT F		NT J	TP ◇1 A	NT	NT G	NT K	NT J
Blackpool North	d	08 20	08 29	08 44		09 20	09 29	09 37		09 43		10 20	10 29	10 37	10 44		11 20	11 29		11 37	11 44		12 20	12 29	12 37
Layton	d	08 23				09 23						10 23					11 23						12 23		
Poulton-le-Fylde	d	08 28	08 35	08 50		09 28	09 35			09 49		10 28	10 35		10 50		11 28	11 35			11 50		12 28	12 35	
Blackpool South	d				08 44						09 44					10 44						11 44			
Blackpool Pleasure Beach	d				08 46						09 46					10 46						11 46			
Squires Gate	d				08 48						09 48					10 48						11 48			
St Annes-on-the-Sea	d				08 52						09 52					10 52						11 52			
Ansdell & Fairhaven	d				08 55						09 55					10 55						11 55			
Lytham	d				08 58						09 58					10 58						11 58			
Moss Side	d				09 03						10 03					11 03						12 03			
Kirkham & Wesham	d	08 37			09 10	09 37		09 52			10 10	10 37		10 52		11 10	11 37			11 52		12 10	12 37		12 52
Salwick	d																								
Preston 8	a	08 47	08 52	09 08	09 20	09 47	09 52	10 02		10 07	10 20	10 47	10 52	11 02	11 08	11 20	11 47	11 52		12 02	12 08	12 20	12 47	12 52	13 02
	d		08 54		09 22		09 54				10 22		10 54			11 22		11 54				12 22		12 54	
Lostock Hall	d				09 27						10 27					11 27						12 27			
Bamber Bridge	d				09 30						10 30					11 30						12 30			
Pleasington	d				09 38						10 38					11 38						12 38			
Cherry Tree	d				09 41						10 41					11 41						12 41			
Mill Hill (Lancashire)	d				09 43						10 43					11 43						12 43			
Blackburn	a		09 09		09 46		10 09				10 46		11 09			11 46		12 09				12 46		13 09	
Clitheroe 94	a																								
Blackburn	d		09 10		09 48		10 10				10 48		11 10			11 48		12 10				12 48		13 10	
Rishton	d				09 53						10 53					11 53						12 53			
Church & Oswaldtwistle	d				09 56						10 56					11 56						12 56			
Accrington	d		09 17		09 59		10 17				10 59		11 17			11 59		12 17				12 59		13 17	
Huncoat	d				10 03						11 03					12 03						13 03			
Hapton	d				10 06						11 06					12 06						13 06			
Rose Grove	d				10 09						11 09					12 09						13 09			
Burnley Manchester Road 41	a		09 26				10 26						11 27					12 26						13 26	
Leeds 10 41	a		10 38				11 39						12 39					13 40						14 39	
Burnley Barracks	d				10 12						11 12					12 12						13 12			
Burnley Central	d				10 15						11 15					12 15						13 15			
Brierfield	d				10 19						11 19					12 19						13 19			
Nelson	d				10 22						11 22					12 22						13 22			
Colne	a				10 32						11 32					12 32						13 32			

A To Manchester Airport
B until 2 January then from 9 January until 19 March, and then from 26 March
C from 3 January until 23 March
D until 30 December and then from 26 March
E from 2 January until 23 March
F To Blackpool North
G To Manchester Victoria
H To Hazel Grove
I To Liverpool Lime Street
J To Liverpool South Parkway
K To York

Blackpool - Preston - Blackburn, Accrington, Burnley and Colne

Network Diagram - see first Page of Table 97

		TP ◇1 A	NT	NT B		NT C	NT D	TP ◇1 A	NT	NT B	NT C	NT D	TP ◇1 A	NT		NT B	NT C	NT E	TP ◇1 A	NT	NT B	NT F	NT E	TP ◇1 A	
Blackpool North	d	12 44		13 20		13 29	13 37	13 44		14 20	14 29	14 37	14 44			15 20	15 29	15 37	15 44		16 20	16 29	16 35	16 40	
Layton	d			13 23						14 23						15 23					16 23			16 44	
Poulton-le-Fylde	d	12 50		13 28		13 35		13 50		14 28	14 35		14 50			15 28	15 35		15 50		16 28	16 35		16 48	
Blackpool South	d		12 44						13 44					14 44						15 44					
Blackpool Pleasure Beach	d		12 46						13 46					14 46						15 46					
Squires Gate	d		12 48						13 48					14 48						15 48					
St Annes-on-the-Sea	d		12 52						13 52					14 52						15 52					
Ansdell & Fairhaven	d		12 55						13 55					14 55						15 55					
Lytham	d		12 58						13 58					14 58						15 58					
Moss Side	d		13 03						14 03					15 03						16 02					
Kirkham & Wesham	d		13 10	13 37			13 52		14 10	14 37		14 52		15 10		15 37		15 52		16 10	16 37		16 52	16 57	
Salwick	d																			16 15					
Preston 8	a	13 08	13 20	13 47		13 52	14 02	14 08	14 20	14 47	14 52	15 02	15 08	15 20		15 47	15 52	16 02	16 08	16 22	16 47	16 52	17 02	17 08	
	d		13 22			13 54			14 22		14 54			15 22			15 54			16 22		16 54			
Lostock Hall	d		13 27						14 27					15 27						16 27					
Bamber Bridge	d		13 30						14 30					15 30						16 30					
Pleasington	d		13 38						14 38					15 38						16 38					
Cherry Tree	d		13 41						14 41					15 41						16 41					
Mill Hill (Lancashire)	d		13 43						14 43					15 43						16 43					
Blackburn	a		13 46			14 10			14 46		15 09			15 47			16 09			16 48		17 09			
Clitheroe 94	a																								
Blackburn	d		13 48			14 10			14 48		15 10			15 48			16 10			16 50		17 10			
Rishton	d		13 53						14 53					15 53						16 55					
Church & Oswaldtwistle	d		13 56						14 56					15 56						16 58					
Accrington	d		13 59			14 17			14 59		15 17			15 59			16 17			17 01		17 17			
Huncoat	d		14 03						15 03					16 03						17 05					
Hapton	d		14 06						15 06					16 06						17 08					
Rose Grove	d		14 09						15 09					16 09						17 11					
Burnley Manchester Road 41	a					14 26					15 26						16 26					17 26			
Leeds 10 41	a					15 39					16 39						17 39					18 39			
Burnley Barracks	d		14 12						15 12					16 12						17 14					
Burnley Central	d		14 15						15 15					16 15						17 18					
Brierfield	d		14 19						15 19					16 19						17 21					
Nelson	d		14 22						15 22					16 22						17 24					
Colne	a		14 32						15 32					16 32						17 34					

		NT	NT G	TP ◇1 A	NT E	NT	NT B	NT G	NT E	TP ◇1 A		NT	NT B	NT E	TP ◇1 A	NT	NT B	NT G	NT E	TP ◇1 A		NT	NT B	TP ◇1 A	NT H
Blackpool North	d		17 14	17 20	17 37		18 20	18 29	18 37	18 44			19 20	19 37	19 44		20 20	20 29	20 37	20 44			21 20	21 44	
Layton	d			17 23			18 23						19 23				20 23						21 23		
Poulton-le-Fylde	d		17 20	17 27			18 28	18 35		18 50			19 28		19 50		20 28	20 35		20 50			21 28	21 50	
Blackpool South	d	16 44				17 44						18 44				19 44						20 44			22 00
Blackpool Pleasure Beach	d	16 46				17 46						18 46				19 46						20 46			22 02
Squires Gate	d	16 48				17 48						18 48				19 48						20 48			22 04
St Annes-on-the-Sea	d	16 52				17 52						18 52				19 52						20 52			22 08
Ansdell & Fairhaven	d	16 55				17 55						18 55				19 55						20 55			22 11
Lytham	d	16 58				17 58						18 58				19 58						20 58			22 14
Moss Side	d	17 03				18 03						19 03				20 03						21 03			22 19
Kirkham & Wesham	d	17 10	17 29		17 52	18 10	18 37		18 52			19 10	19 37			20 10	20 37					21 10	21 37		22 26
Salwick	d																								
Preston 8	a	17 20	17 44	17 45	18 02	18 20	18 47	18 52	19 02	19 08		19 20	19 47	20 02	20 08	20 20	20 47	20 53	21 01	21 08		21 20	21 47	22 08	22 36
	d	17 22	17 44			18 24		18 54				19 22				20 22		20 54				21 22			22 38
Lostock Hall	d	17 27	17 51			18 30						19 27				20 27						21 27			22 43
Bamber Bridge	d	17 30	17 54			18 33						19 30				20 30						21 30			22 46
Pleasington	d	17 38	18 01			18 41						19 38				20 38						21 38			22 54
Cherry Tree	d	17 41	18 05			18 44						19 41				20 41						21 41			22 57
Mill Hill (Lancashire)	d	17 44	18 08			18 46						19 43				20 43						21 43			22 59
Blackburn	a	17 48	18 11			18 52		19 09				19 46				20 46		21 09				21 46			23 04
Clitheroe 94	a																								
Blackburn	d	17 58	18 11			18 53		19 10				19 48				20 48		21 10				21 48			23 05
Rishton	d	18 03				18 58						19 53				20 53						21 53			23 10
Church & Oswaldtwistle	d	18 06				19 01						19 56				20 56						21 56			23 13
Accrington	d	18 09	18 19			19 04		19 17				19 59				20 59		21 17				21 59			23 16
Huncoat	d	18 13				19 08						20 03				21 03						22 03			23 20
Hapton	d	18 16				19 11						20 06				21 06						22 06			23 23
Rose Grove	d	18 19				19 14						20 09				21 09						22 09			23 26
Burnley Manchester Road 41	a		18 27					19 26										21 28							
Leeds 10 41	a		19 39					20 38										22 41							
Burnley Barracks	d	18 22				19 17						20 12				21 12						22 12			23 29
Burnley Central	d	18 25				19 20						20 15				21 15						22 15			23 32
Brierfield	d	18 29				19 24						20 19				21 19						22 19			23 36
Nelson	d	18 32				19 27						20 22				21 22						22 22			23 39
Colne	a	18 42				19 37						20 32				21 32						22 32			23 49

A To Manchester Airport
B To Manchester Victoria
C To Blackpool North
D To Liverpool South Parkway
E To Liverpool Lime Street
F To Selby
G To York
H until 30 December and then from 26 March

Table 97

Mondays to Fridays

Blackpool - Preston - Blackburn, Accrington, Burnley and Colne

Network Diagram - see first Page of Table 97

		NT A	NT B	NT C	TP ◇1 D	NT E		NT
Blackpool North	d		22 14	22 20	22 44	23 13		
Layton	d			22 23		23 16		
Poulton-le-Fylde	d			22 28	22 50	23 21		
Blackpool South	d	22 00						23 30
Blackpool Pleasure Beach	d	22 02						23 32
Squires Gate	d	22 04						23 34
St Annes-on-the-Sea	d	22 08						23 38
Ansdell & Fairhaven	d	22 11						23 41
Lytham	d	22 14						23 44
Moss Side	d	22 19						23 49
Kirkham & Wesham	d	22 26		22 37		23 30		23 56
Salwick	d							
Preston 8	a	22 36	22 41	22 47	23 08	23 40		00 08
	d	22 38						
Lostock Hall	d	22 43						
Bamber Bridge	d	22 46						
Pleasington	d	22 54						
Cherry Tree	d	22 57						
Mill Hill (Lancashire)	d	22 59						
Blackburn	a	23 05						
Clitheroe 94	a							
Blackburn	d	23 05						
Rishton	d	23 10						
Church & Oswaldtwistle	d	23 13						
Accrington	d	23 16						
Huncoat	d	23 20						
Hapton	d	23 23						
Rose Grove	d	23 26						
Burnley Manchester Road 41	a							
Leeds 10 41	a							
Burnley Barracks	d	23 29						
Burnley Central	d	23 32						
Brierfield	d	23 36						
Nelson	d	23 39						
Colne	a	23 49						

Saturdays

		NT		NT F	NT G	NT F	NT G	NT H	TP ◇1 D	NT		NT E	NT H	TP ◇1 D	NT I	NT	NT B	NT E	NT H	TP ◇1 D		NT	NT E	NT H	NT J
Blackpool North	d					04 56	04 56	05 29	05 39			06 19	06 28	06 40	06 53		07 02	07 18	07 29	07 44			08 20	08 29	08 38
Layton	d											06 22		06 43				07 21		07 47			08 23		
Poulton-le-Fylde	d					05 02	05 02	05 35	05 45			06 27	06 34	06 47			07 08	07 26	07 35	07 51			08 28	08 35	
Blackpool South	d	23p30								05 42						06 42						07 42			
Blackpool Pleasure Beach	d	23p32								05 44						06 44						07 44			
Squires Gate	d	23p34								05 46						06 46						07 46			
St Annes-on-the-Sea	d	23p38								05 50						06 50						07 50			
Ansdell & Fairhaven	d	23p41								05 53						06 53						07 53			
Lytham	d	23p44								05 56						06 56						07 56			
Moss Side	d	23p49								06 01						07 01						08 01			
Kirkham & Wesham	d	23p56								06 08		06 36		06 56		07 09		07 35		08 00		08 09	08 37		
Salwick	d															07 13						08 13			
Preston 8	a	00 08				05 20	05 20	05 52	06 03	06 19		06 46	06 52	07 07	07 15	07 20	07 28	07 46	07 52	08 11		08 20	08 47	08 52	09 02
	d			04 47	04 47	05 22	05 22	05 54		06 21			06 54			07 22			07 54			08 22		08 54	
Lostock Hall	d									06 26						07 27						08 27			
Bamber Bridge	d									06 29						07 30						08 30			
Pleasington	d									06 37						07 38						08 38			
Cherry Tree	d									06 40						07 41						08 41			
Mill Hill (Lancashire)	d									06 42						07 43						08 43			
Blackburn	a			05 03	05 07	05 38	05 42	06 09		06 45			07 09			07 50			08 09			08 46		09 09	
Clitheroe 94	a																								
Blackburn	d			05 04	05 08	05 39	05 43	06 10		06 48			07 10			07 51			08 10			08 48		09 10	
Rishton	d					05 44	05 48			06 53						07 56						08 53			
Church & Oswaldtwistle	d					05 47	05 51			06 56						07 59						08 56			
Accrington	d			05 11	05 15	05 50	05 54	06 17		06 59			07 17			08 02			08 17			08 59		09 17	
Huncoat	d					05 54	05 58			07 03						08 06						09 03			
Hapton	d					05 57	06 01			07 06						08 09						09 06			
Rose Grove	d					06 00	06 04			07 09						08 12						09 09			
Burnley Manchester Road 41	a							06 26					07 26						08 26					09 26	
Leeds 10 41	a							07 39					08 39						09 39					10 38	
Burnley Barracks	d									07 12						08 15						09 12			
Burnley Central	d			05 21	05 25	06 05	06 09			07 15						08 18						09 15			
Brierfield	d					06 09	06 13			07 19						08 22						09 19			
Nelson	d					06 12	06 16			07 22						08 25						09 22			
Colne	a			05 35	05 39	06 22	06 26			07 32						08 35						09 32			

A from 2 January until 23 March
B To Liverpool Lime Street
C until 30 December and then from 26 March. To Manchester Victoria
D To Manchester Airport
E To Manchester Victoria
F until 31 December and then from 31 March
G from 7 January until 24 March
H To Blackpool North
I To Hazel Grove
J To Wigan North Western

Blackpool - Preston - Blackburn, Accrington, Burnley and Colne

Network Diagram - see first Page of Table 97

		TP ◇1 A	NT	TP ◇1 B	NT C	NT D	NT E	TP ◇1 A	NT	NT C	NT D	NT E	TP ◇1 A	NT	NT C	NT D	NT E	TP ◇1 A	NT	NT C	NT F	NT E	TP ◇1 A
Blackpool North	d	08 44		09 14	09 20	09 29	09 37	09 43		10 20	10 29	10 37	10 44		11 15	11 29	11 37	11 44		12 20	12 29	12 37	12 44
Layton	d				09 23					10 23					11 18					12 23			
Poulton-le-Fylde	d	08 50		09 20	09 28	09 35		09 49		10 28	10 35		10 50		11 23	11 35		11 50		12 28	12 35		12 50
Blackpool South	d		08 44						09 44					10 44					11 44				
Blackpool Pleasure Beach	d		08 46						09 46					10 46					11 46				
Squires Gate	d		08 48						09 48					10 48					11 48				
St Annes-on-the-Sea	d		08 52						09 52					10 52					11 52				
Ansdell & Fairhaven	d		08 55						09 55					10 55					11 55				
Lytham	d		08 58						09 58					10 58					11 58				
Moss Side	d		09 03						10 03					11 03					12 03				
Kirkham & Wesham	d		09 10		09 37				10 10	10 37				11 10	11 32				12 10	12 37			
Salwick	d																						
Preston 8	a	09 08	09 20	09 41	09 47	09 52	10 02	10 07	10 20	10 47	10 52	11 02	11 08	11 20	11 42	11 52	12 02	12 08	12 20	12 47	12 51	13 02	13 08
	d		09 22			09 54			10 22		10 54			11 22		11 54			12 22		12 53		
Lostock Hall	d		09 27						10 27					11 27					12 27				
Bamber Bridge	d		09 30						10 30					11 30					12 30				
Pleasington	d		09 38						10 38					11 38					12 38				
Cherry Tree	d		09 41						10 41					11 41					12 41				
Mill Hill (Lancashire)	d		09 43						10 43					11 43					12 43				
Blackburn	a		09 46			10 09			10 46		11 09			11 46		12 09			12 46		13 08		
Clitheroe 94	a																						
Blackburn	d		09 48			10 10			10 48		11 10			11 48		12 10			12 48		13 09		
Rishton	d		09 53						10 53					11 53					12 53				
Church & Oswaldtwistle	d		09 56						10 56					11 56					12 56				
Accrington	d		09 59			10 18			10 59		11 17			11 59		12 17			12 59		13 16		
Huncoat	d		10 03						11 03					12 03					13 03				
Hapton	d		10 06						11 06					12 06					13 06				
Rose Grove	d		10 09						11 09					12 09					13 09				
Burnley Manchester Road 41	a					10 26					11 27					12 26					13 25		
Leeds 10 41	a					11 39					12 39					13 39					14 39		
Burnley Barracks	d		10 12						11 12					12 12					13 12				
Burnley Central	d		10 15						11 15					12 15					13 15				
Brierfield	d		10 19						11 19					12 19					13 19				
Nelson	d		10 22						11 22					12 22					13 22				
Colne	a		10 32						11 32					12 32					13 32				

		NT	NT C	NT D	NT E	TP ◇1 A	NT	NT C	NT D	NT E	TP ◇1 A	NT	NT C	NT D	NT E	TP ◇1 A	NT	NT C	NT G	NT E	TP ◇1 A	NT
Blackpool North	d		13 20	13 29	13 37	13 44		14 20	14 29	14 37	14 44		15 20	15 29	15 37	15 44		16 20	16 29	16 35	16 40	
Layton	d		13 23					14 23					15 23					16 23			16 43	
Poulton-le-Fylde	d		13 28	13 35		13 50		14 28	14 35		14 50		15 28	15 35		15 50		16 28	16 35		16 48	
Blackpool South	d	12 44					13 44					14 44					15 44					16 44
Blackpool Pleasure Beach	d	12 46					13 46					14 46					15 46					16 46
Squires Gate	d	12 48					13 48					14 48					15 48					16 48
St Annes-on-the-Sea	d	12 52					13 52					14 52					15 52					16 52
Ansdell & Fairhaven	d	12 55					13 55					14 55					15 55					16 55
Lytham	d	12 58					13 58					14 58					15 58					16 58
Moss Side	d	13 03					14 03					15 03					16 03					17 03
Kirkham & Wesham	d	13 10	13 37				14 10	14 37				15 10	15 37				16 10	16 37			16 57	17 10
Salwick	d																16 15					
Preston 8	a	13 20	13 47	13 52	14 02	14 08	14 20	14 47	14 52	15 02	15 08	15 20	15 47	15 52	16 02	16 08	16 22	16 47	16 52	17 02	17 08	17 20
	d	13 22		13 54			14 22		14 54			15 22		15 54			16 22		16 54			17 22
Lostock Hall	d	13 27					14 27					15 27					16 27					17 27
Bamber Bridge	d	13 30					14 30					15 30					16 30					17 30
Pleasington	d	13 38					14 38					15 38					16 38					17 38
Cherry Tree	d	13 41					14 41					15 41					16 41					17 41
Mill Hill (Lancashire)	d	13 43					14 43					15 43					16 43					17 43
Blackburn	a	13 46		14 09			14 46		15 09			15 46		16 09			16 48		17 09			17 47
Clitheroe 94	a																					
Blackburn	d	13 48		14 10			14 48		15 10			15 48		16 10			16 50		17 10			17 48
Rishton	d	13 53					14 53					15 53					16 55					17 53
Church & Oswaldtwistle	d	13 56					14 56					15 56					16 58					17 56
Accrington	d	13 59		14 17			14 59		15 17			15 59		16 17			17 01		17 17			17 59
Huncoat	d	14 03					15 03					16 03					17 05					18 03
Hapton	d	14 06					15 06					16 06					17 08					18 06
Rose Grove	d	14 09					15 09					16 09					17 11					18 09
Burnley Manchester Road 41	a			14 26					15 26					16 26					17 26			
Leeds 10 41	a			15 39					16 39					17 39					18 39			
Burnley Barracks	d	14 12					15 12					16 12					17 14					18 12
Burnley Central	d	14 15					15 15					16 15					17 16					18 15
Brierfield	d	14 19					15 19					16 19					17 21					18 19
Nelson	d	14 22					15 22					16 22					17 24					18 22
Colne	a	14 32					15 32					16 32					17 34					18 32

A To Manchester Airport
B To Barrow-in-Furness
C To Manchester Victoria
D To Blackpool North
E To Wigan North Western
F To York
G To Hull

Table 97

Saturdays

Blackpool - Preston - Blackburn, Accrington, Burnley and Colne

Network Diagram - see first Page of Table 97

		NT	TP	NT	NT	NT	NT	NT		TP	NT	NT	NT	TP	NT	NT	NT	NT		TP	NT	NT	TP	NT	NT
			◇1							◇1				◇1						◇1			◇1		
		A	B (trolley)	C		D	A	C		B		D	C	B		D	A	C		B		D	B		C
Blackpool North	d	17 14	17 20	17 37		18 20	18 29	18 37		18 44		19 20	19 37	19 44		20 20	20 29	20 37		20 42		21 20	21 44		22 14
Layton	d		17 23			18 23						19 23				20 23						21 23			
Poulton-le-Fylde	d	17 20	17 27			18 28	18 35			18 50		19 28		19 50		20 28	20 35			20 48		21 28	21 50		
Blackpool South	d				17 44						18 44				19 44						20 44			22 00	
Blackpool Pleasure Beach	d				17 46						18 46				19 46						20 46			22 02	
Squires Gate	d				17 48						18 48				19 48						20 48			22 04	
St Annes-on-the-Sea	d				17 52						18 52				19 52						20 52			22 08	
Ansdell & Fairhaven	d				17 55						18 55				19 55						20 55			22 11	
Lytham	d				17 58						18 58				19 58						20 58			22 14	
Moss Side	d				18 03						19 03				20 03						21 03			22 19	
Kirkham & Wesham	d	17 29			18 10	18 37					19 10	19 37			20 10	20 37					21 10	21 37		22 26	
Salwick	d																								
Preston 8	a	17 42	17 45	18 02	18 22	18 47	18 52	19 00		19 08	19 20	19 47	20 02	20 08	20 20	20 47	20 53	21 01		21 06	21 20	21 47	22 08	22 36	22 41
	d	17 44			18 24		18 54				19 22				20 22		20 54				21 22			22 38	
Lostock Hall	d	17 51			18 30						19 27				20 27						21 27			22 43	
Bamber Bridge	d	17 54			18 33						19 30				20 30						21 30			22 46	
Pleasington	d	18 01			18 41						19 38				20 38						21 38			22 54	
Cherry Tree	d	18 05			18 44						19 41				20 41						21 41			22 57	
Mill Hill (Lancashire)	d	18 08			18 46						19 43				20 43						21 43			22 59	
Blackburn	a	18 11			18 52		19 09				19 46				20 46		21 09				21 46			23 06	
Clitheroe 94	a																								
Blackburn	d	18 11			18 53		19 10				19 48				20 48		21 10				21 48				
Rishton	d				18 58						19 53				20 53						21 53				
Church & Oswaldtwistle	d				19 01						19 56				20 56						21 56				
Accrington	d	18 19			19 04		19 17				19 59				20 59		21 17				21 59				
Huncoat	d				19 08						20 03				21 03						22 03				
Hapton	d				19 11						20 06				21 06						22 06				
Rose Grove	d				19 14						20 09				21 09						22 09				
Burnley Manchester Road 41	a	18 27					19 26										21 28								
Leeds 10 41	a	19 39					20 38										22 37								
Burnley Barracks	d				19 17						20 12				21 12						22 12				
Burnley Central	d				19 20						20 15				21 15						22 15				
Brierfield	d				19 24						20 19				21 19						22 19				
Nelson	d				19 27						20 22				21 22						22 22				
Colne	a				19 37						20 32				21 32						22 32				

		NT	TP	NT		NT	NT
			◇1				
		D	B	D		(bus)	
Blackpool North	d	22 20	22 44	23 02			
Layton	d	22 23		23 05			
Poulton-le-Fylde	d	22 28	22 50	23 10			
Blackpool South	d						23 30
Blackpool Pleasure Beach	d						23 32
Squires Gate	d						23 34
St Annes-on-the-Sea	d						23 38
Ansdell & Fairhaven	d						23 41
Lytham	d						23 44
Moss Side	d						23 49
Kirkham & Wesham	d	22 37		23 19			23 56
Salwick	d						
Preston 8	a	22 47	23 08	23 29			00 08
	d						
Lostock Hall	d						
Bamber Bridge	d						
Pleasington	d						
Cherry Tree	d						
Mill Hill (Lancashire)	d						
Blackburn	a						
Clitheroe 94	a						
Blackburn	d					23 14	
Rishton	d					23 24	
Church & Oswaldtwistle	d					23 36	
Accrington	d					23 40	
Huncoat	d					23 46	
Hapton	d					23 52	
Rose Grove	d					23 58	
Burnley Manchester Road 41	a						
Leeds 10 41	a						
Burnley Barracks	d					00 02	
Burnley Central	d					00 07	
Brierfield	d					00 15	
Nelson	d					00 20	
Colne	a					00 28	

A To York
B To Manchester Airport
C To Wigan North Western
D To Manchester Victoria

Table 97

Sundays
until 1 January

Blackpool - Preston - Blackburn, Accrington, Burnley and Colne

Network Diagram - see first Page of Table 97

		NT	NT	TP	TP	NT	TP	NT	TP	NT	NT	NT	NT	TP	NT	NT	NT	TP	NT	NT	NT	NT	TP
							◇1		◇1					◇1				◇1					◇1
		A	A	B	B		B	C	B	D	E	C		B	D	E	C	B	D	E	C		B
Blackpool North	d			03 20	05 20		08 14	08 20	08 44	08 50	09 01	09 20		09 44	09 50	10 11	10 20	10 44	10 50	11 13	11 20		11 44
Layton	d							08 23				09 23					10 23				11 23		
Poulton-le-Fylde	d						08 20	08 28	08 50	08 56	09 07	09 28		09 50	09 56	10 17	10 28	10 50	10 56	11 19	11 28		11 50
Blackpool South	d		23p30																				
Blackpool Pleasure Beach	d		23p32																				
Squires Gate	d		23p34																				
St Annes-on-the-Sea	d		23p38																				
Ansdell & Fairhaven	d		23p41																				
Lytham	d		23p44																				
Moss Side	d		23p49																				
Kirkham & Wesham	d		23p56					08 37				09 37					10 37				11 37		
Salwick	d																						
Preston 8	a		00 08				08 38	08 47	09 08	09 14	09 24	09 47		10 07	10 14	10 34	10 47	11 08	11 14	11 36	11 47		12 08
	d					08 16					09 27		10 05			10 37				11 37		12 05	
Lostock Hall	d					08 21							10 11									12 11	
Bamber Bridge	d					08 24							10 14									12 14	
Pleasington	d												10 21									12 21	
Cherry Tree	d												10 24									12 24	
Mill Hill (Lancashire)	d												10 27									12 27	
Blackburn	a					08 35					09 42		10 30			10 53				11 53		12 30	
Clitheroe 94	a																						
Blackburn	d	23p14				08 37					09 44		10 31			10 54				11 54		12 31	
Rishton	d	23p24											10 36									12 36	
Church & Oswaldtwistle	d	23p36											10 39									12 39	
Accrington	d	23p40				08 44					09 51		10 42			11 01				12 01		12 42	
Huncoat	d	23p46											10 47									12 47	
Hapton	d	23p52											10 50									12 50	
Rose Grove	d	23p58				08 51							10 53									12 53	
Burnley Manchester Road 41	a										10 00					11 10				12 10			
Leeds 10 41	a										11 21					12 22				13 22			
Burnley Barracks	d	00 02											10 56									12 56	
Burnley Central	d	00 07				08 56							10 58									12 58	
Brierfield	d	00 15				09 00							11 03									13 03	
Nelson	d	00 20				09 03							11 06									13 06	
Colne	a	00 28				09 13							11 15									13 15	

		NT	NT	NT	TP	NT	NT	NT	NT	TP	NT	NT	NT	TP	NT	NT	NT	NT	TP	NT	NT	NT	TP
					◇1					◇1				◇1					◇1				◇1
		D	E	C	B	D	E	C		B	D	E	C	B	D	E	C		B	D	E	C	B
Blackpool North	d	11 50	12 11	12 20	12 44	12 50	13 13	13 20		13 44	13 50	14 11	14 20	14 44	14 50	15 13	15 20		15 44	15 50	16 11	16 20	16 44
Layton	d			12 23				13 23					14 23				15 23					16 23	
Poulton-le-Fylde	d	11 56	12 17	12 28	12 50	12 56	13 19	13 28		13 50	13 56	14 17	14 28	14 50	14 56	15 19	15 28		15 50	15 56	16 17	16 28	16 50
Blackpool South	d																						
Blackpool Pleasure Beach	d																						
Squires Gate	d																						
St Annes-on-the-Sea	d																						
Ansdell & Fairhaven	d																						
Lytham	d																						
Moss Side	d																						
Kirkham & Wesham	d			12 37				13 37					14 37				15 37					16 37	
Salwick	d																						
Preston 8	a	12 14	12 34	12 47	13 08	13 14	13 36	13 47		14 08	14 14	14 34	14 47	15 08	15 14	15 36	15 47		16 08	16 14	16 34	16 47	17 08
	d		12 37				13 37		14 05			14 37				15 37		16 05			16 37		
Lostock Hall	d								14 11									16 11					
Bamber Bridge	d								14 14									16 14					
Pleasington	d								14 21									16 21					
Cherry Tree	d								14 24									16 24					
Mill Hill (Lancashire)	d								14 27									16 27					
Blackburn	a		12 52				13 53		14 30			14 52				15 53		16 30			16 52		
Clitheroe 94	a																						
Blackburn	d		12 54				13 54		14 31			14 54				15 54		16 31			16 54		
Rishton	d								14 36									16 36					
Church & Oswaldtwistle	d								14 39									16 39					
Accrington	d		13 01				14 01		14 42			15 01				16 01		16 42			17 01		
Huncoat	d								14 47									16 47					
Hapton	d								14 50									16 50					
Rose Grove	d								14 53									16 53					
Burnley Manchester Road 41	a		13 10				14 10					15 10				16 10					17 10		
Leeds 10 41	a		14 22				15 22					16 22				17 21					18 21		
Burnley Barracks	d								14 56									16 56					
Burnley Central	d								14 58									16 58					
Brierfield	d								15 03									17 03					
Nelson	d								15 06									17 06					
Colne	a								15 15									17 15					

A not 11 December
B To Manchester Airport
C To Manchester Victoria
D To Liverpool Lime Street
E To York

Table 97

Sundays

until 1 January

Blackpool - Preston - Blackburn, Accrington, Burnley and Colne

Network Diagram - see first Page of Table 97

		NT		NT	NT	NT	TP	NT	NT	TP	NT	NT		NT	NT	TP	NT	NT	NT	TP	NT	NT		NT	NT
							◇1			◇1						◇1				◇1					
		A		B	C		D	A	B	D	A	B		C		D	A		C	D	A			C	
Blackpool North	d	16 50		17 11	17 20		17 44	17 50	18 11	18 44	18 50	19 13		19 20		19 44	19 50	20 11	20 20	20 44	20 50	21 13		21 20	
Layton	d				17 23									19 23					20 23					21 23	
Poulton-le-Fylde	d	16 56		17 17	17 28		17 50	17 56	18 17	18 50	18 56	19 19		19 28		19 50	19 56	20 17	20 28	20 50	20 56	21 19		21 28	
Blackpool South	d																								
Blackpool Pleasure Beach	d																								
Squires Gate	d																								
St Annes-on-the-Sea	d																								
Ansdell & Fairhaven	d																								
Lytham	d																								
Moss Side	d																								
Kirkham & Wesham	d				17 37									19 37					20 37					21 37	
Salwick	d																								
Preston 8	a	17 14		17 34	17 47		18 08	18 14	18 34	19 08	19 14	19 36		19 47		20 08	20 14	20 34	20 47	21 08	21 14	21 36		21 47	
	d			17 37		18 05			18 37			19 37			20 05			20 37				21 39			22 05
Lostock Hall	d					18 11									20 11										22 11
Bamber Bridge	d					18 14									20 14										22 14
Pleasington	d					18 21									20 21										22 21
Cherry Tree	d					18 24									20 24										22 24
Mill Hill (Lancashire)	d					18 27									20 27										22 27
Blackburn	a			17 52		18 30			18 52			19 53			20 30			20 52				21 54			22 30
Clitheroe 94	a																								
Blackburn	d			17 54		18 31			18 54			19 54			20 31			20 54				21 55			22 31
Rishton	d					18 36									20 36										22 36
Church & Oswaldtwistle	d					18 39									20 39										22 39
Accrington	d			18 01		18 42			19 01			20 01			20 42			21 01				22 02			22 42
Huncoat	d					18 47									20 47										22 47
Hapton	d					18 50									20 50										22 50
Rose Grove	d					18 53									20 53										22 53
Burnley Manchester Road 41	a			18 10					19 10			20 10						21 10				22 12			
Leeds 10 41	a			19 22					20 22			21 22						22 21				23 23			
Burnley Barracks	d					18 56									20 56										22 56
Burnley Central	d					18 58									20 58										22 58
Brierfield	d					19 03									21 03										23 03
Nelson	d					19 06									21 06										23 06
Colne	a					19 15									21 15										23 15

		NT	TP	NT	TP
			◇1		◇1
		A		A	D
Blackpool North	d	21 50	21 56	22 44	23 03
Layton	d				
Poulton-le-Fylde	d	21 56	22 02	22 50	23 09
Blackpool South	d				
Blackpool Pleasure Beach	d				
Squires Gate	d				
St Annes-on-the-Sea	d				
Ansdell & Fairhaven	d				
Lytham	d				
Moss Side	d				
Kirkham & Wesham	d				23 17
Salwick	d				
Preston 8	a	22 14	22 20	23 08	23 28
	d				
Lostock Hall	d				
Bamber Bridge	d				
Pleasington	d				
Cherry Tree	d				
Mill Hill (Lancashire)	d				
Blackburn	a				
Clitheroe 94	a				
Blackburn	d				
Rishton	d				
Church & Oswaldtwistle	d				
Accrington	d				
Huncoat	d				
Hapton	d				
Rose Grove	d				
Burnley Manchester Road 41	a				
Leeds 10 41	a				
Burnley Barracks	d				
Burnley Central	d				
Brierfield	d				
Nelson	d				
Colne	a				

A To Liverpool Lime Street
B To York
C To Manchester Victoria
D To Manchester Airport

Table 97

Sundays

8 January to 12 February

Blackpool - Preston - Blackburn, Accrington, Burnley and Colne

Network Diagram - see first Page of Table 97

		NT	NT	TP	TP	NT	TP	TP	NT	NT		NT	TP	NT	NT	TP	NT	NT	NT	TP		NT	NT	TP	NT
							◇1	◇1					◇1			◇1				◇1				◇1	
				A	A		A	A	B	C			A	B	C	A	B	C		A		B	C	A	B
		bus		bus	bus															trolley					
Blackpool North	d			03 20	05 20		08 14	08 44	08 50	09 01			09 44	09 50	10 11	10 44	10 50	11 13		11 44		11 50	12 11	12 44	12 50
Layton	d																								
Poulton-le-Fylde	d						08 20	08 50	08 56	09 07			09 50	09 56	10 17	10 50	10 56	11 19		11 50		11 56	12 17	12 50	12 56
Blackpool South	d		23p30																						
Blackpool Pleasure Beach	d		23p32																						
Squires Gate	d		23p34																						
St Annes-on-the-Sea	d		23p38																						
Ansdell & Fairhaven	d		23p41																						
Lytham	d		23p44																						
Moss Side	d		23p49																						
Kirkham & Wesham	d		23p56																						
Salwick	d																								
Preston 8	a		00 08				08 38	09 08	09 14	09 24			10 07	10 14	10 34	11 08	11 14	11 36		12 08		12 14	12 34	13 08	13 14
	d					08 16				09 27		10 05			10 37			11 37	12 05				12 37		
Lostock Hall	d					08 21						10 11							12 11						
Bamber Bridge	d					08 24						10 14							12 14						
Pleasington	d											10 21							12 21						
Cherry Tree	d											10 24							12 24						
Mill Hill (Lancashire)	d											10 27							12 27						
Blackburn	a					08 35				09 42		10 30			10 53			11 53	12 30				12 52		
Clitheroe 94	a																								
Blackburn	d	23p14				08 37				09 44		10 31			10 54			11 54	12 31				12 54		
Rishton	d	23p24										10 36							12 36						
Church & Oswaldtwistle	d	23p36										10 39							12 39						
Accrington	d	23p40				08 44				09 51		10 42			11 01			12 01	12 42				13 01		
Huncoat	d	23p46										10 47							12 47						
Hapton	d	23p52										10 50							12 50						
Rose Grove	d	23p58				08 51						10 53							12 53						
Burnley Manchester Road 41	a									10 00					11 10			12 10					13 10		
Leeds 10 41	a									11 21					12 22			13 22					14 22		
Burnley Barracks	d	00 02										10 56							12 56						
Burnley Central	d	00 07				08 56						10 58							12 58						
Brierfield	d	00 15				09 00						11 03							13 03						
Nelson	d	00 20				09 03						11 06							13 06						
Colne	a	00 28				09 13						11 15							13 15						

		NT	NT	TP	NT	NT		TP	NT	NT	NT	TP	NT	NT	TP	NT		NT	NT	TP	NT	NT	TP	NT	NT
				◇1				◇1				◇1			◇1					◇1			◇1		
		C		A	B	C		A	B	C		A	B	C	A	B		C		A	B	C	A	B	C
Blackpool North	d	13 13		13 44	13 50	14 11		14 44	14 50	15 13		15 44	15 50	16 11	16 44	16 50		17 11		17 44	17 50	18 11	18 44	18 50	19 13
Layton	d																								
Poulton-le-Fylde	d	13 19		13 50	13 56	14 17		14 50	14 56	15 19		15 50	15 56	16 17	16 50	16 56		17 17		17 50	17 56	18 17	18 50	18 56	19 19
Blackpool South	d																								
Blackpool Pleasure Beach	d																								
Squires Gate	d																								
St Annes-on-the-Sea	d																								
Ansdell & Fairhaven	d																								
Lytham	d																								
Moss Side	d																								
Kirkham & Wesham	d																								
Salwick	d																								
Preston 8	a	13 36		14 08	14 14	14 34		15 08	15 14	15 36		16 08	16 14	16 34	17 08	17 14		17 34		18 08	18 14	18 34	19 08	19 14	19 36
	d	13 37	14 05			14 37				15 37	16 05			16 37				17 37	18 05			18 37			19 37
Lostock Hall	d		14 11								16 11								18 11						
Bamber Bridge	d		14 14								16 14								18 14						
Pleasington	d		14 21								16 21								18 21						
Cherry Tree	d		14 24								16 24								18 24						
Mill Hill (Lancashire)	d		14 27								16 27								18 27						
Blackburn	a	13 53	14 30			14 52				15 53	16 30			16 52				17 52	18 30			18 52			19 53
Clitheroe 94	a																								
Blackburn	d	13 54	14 31			14 54				15 54	16 31			16 54				17 54	18 31			18 54			19 54
Rishton	d		14 36								16 36								18 36						
Church & Oswaldtwistle	d		14 39								16 39								18 39						
Accrington	d	14 01	14 42			15 01				16 01	16 42			17 01				18 01	18 42			19 01			20 01
Huncoat	d		14 47								16 47								18 47						
Hapton	d		14 50								16 50								18 50						
Rose Grove	d		14 53								16 53								18 53						
Burnley Manchester Road 41	a	14 10				15 10				16 10				17 10				18 10				19 10			20 10
Leeds 10 41	a	15 22				16 22				17 21				18 21				19 22				20 22			21 22
Burnley Barracks	d		14 56								16 56								18 56						
Burnley Central	d		14 58								16 58								18 58						
Brierfield	d		15 03								17 03								19 03						
Nelson	d		15 06								17 06								19 06						
Colne	a		15 15								17 15								19 15						

A To Manchester Airport

B To Liverpool Lime Street

C To York

Table 97

Sundays

8 January to 12 February

Blackpool - Preston - Blackburn, Accrington, Burnley and Colne

Network Diagram - see first Page of Table 97

		NT		TP	NT	NT	TP	NT	NT	NT	NT	TP		NT	TP
				◇1			◇1					◇1			◇1
				A	B		A	B			B			B	A
Blackpool North	d			19 44	19 50	20 11	20 44	20 50	21 13		21 50	21 56		22 44	23 03
Layton	d														
Poulton-le-Fylde	d			19 50	19 56	20 17	20 50	20 56	21 19		21 56	22 02		22 50	23 09
Blackpool South	d														
Blackpool Pleasure Beach	d														
Squires Gate	d														
St Annes-on-the-Sea	d														
Ansdell & Fairhaven	d														
Lytham	d														
Moss Side	d														
Kirkham & Wesham	d														23 17
Salwick	d														
Preston 8	a			20 08	20 14	20 34	21 08	21 14	21 36		22 14	22 20		23 08	23 28
	d	20 05				20 37			21 39	22 05					
Lostock Hall	d	20 11								22 11					
Bamber Bridge	d	20 14								22 14					
Pleasington	d	20 21								22 21					
Cherry Tree	d	20 24								22 24					
Mill Hill (Lancashire)	d	20 27								22 27					
Blackburn	a	20 30				20 52			21 54	22 30					
Clitheroe 94	a														
Blackburn	d	20 31				20 54			21 55	22 31					
Rishton	d	20 36								22 36					
Church & Oswaldtwistle	d	20 39								22 39					
Accrington	d	20 42				21 01			22 02	22 42					
Huncoat	d	20 47								22 47					
Hapton	d	20 50								22 50					
Rose Grove	d	20 53								22 53					
Burnley Manchester Road 41	a					21 10			22 12						
Leeds 10 41	a					22 21			23 23						
Burnley Barracks	d	20 56								22 56					
Burnley Central	d	20 58								22 58					
Brierfield	d	21 03								23 03					
Nelson	d	21 06								23 06					
Colne	a	21 15								23 15					

Sundays

19 February to 26 February

		NT	NT	TP	TP	NT	TP	NT	TP	NT		NT	NT	NT	TP	NT	NT	NT	TP	NT		NT	NT	NT	TP
							◇1		◇1						◇1				◇1						◇1
				A	A		A	C	A	D		E	C		A	D	E	C	A	D		E	C		A
		🚌		🚌	🚌																				🛒
Blackpool North	d			03 20	05 20		08 14	08 20	08 44	08 50		09 01	09 20		09 44	09 50	10 11	10 20	10 44	10 50		11 13	11 20		11 44
Layton	d							08 23					09 23					10 23					11 23		
Poulton-le-Fylde	d						08 20	08 28	08 50	08 56		09 07	09 28		09 50	09 56	10 17	10 28	10 50	10 56		11 19	11 28		11 50
Blackpool South	d		23p30																						
Blackpool Pleasure Beach	d		23p32																						
Squires Gate	d		23p34																						
St Annes-on-the-Sea	d		23p38																						
Ansdell & Fairhaven	d		23p41																						
Lytham	d		23p44																						
Moss Side	d		23p49																						
Kirkham & Wesham	d		23p56					08 37					09 37					10 37					11 37		
Salwick	d																								
Preston 8	a		00 08				08 38	08 47	09 08	09 14		09 24	09 47		10 07	10 14	10 34	10 47	11 08	11 14		11 36	11 47		12 08
	d					08 16						09 27		10 05			10 37					11 37		12 05	
Lostock Hall	d					08 21								10 11										12 11	
Bamber Bridge	d					08 24								10 14										12 14	
Pleasington	d													10 21										12 21	
Cherry Tree	d													10 24										12 24	
Mill Hill (Lancashire)	d													10 27										12 27	
Blackburn	a					08 35						09 42		10 30			10 53					11 53		12 30	
Clitheroe 94	a																								
Blackburn	d	23p14				08 37						09 44		10 31			10 54					11 54		12 31	
Rishton	d	23p24												10 36										12 36	
Church & Oswaldtwistle	d	23p36												10 39										12 39	
Accrington	d	23p40				08 44						09 51		10 42			11 01					12 01		12 42	
Huncoat	d	23p46												10 47										12 47	
Hapton	d	23p52												10 50										12 50	
Rose Grove	d	23p58				08 51								10 53										12 53	
Burnley Manchester Road 41	a											10 00					11 10					12 10			
Leeds 10 41	a											11 21					12 22					13 22			
Burnley Barracks	d	00 02												10 56										12 56	
Burnley Central	d	00 07				08 56								10 58										12 58	
Brierfield	d	00 15				09 00								11 03										13 03	
Nelson	d	00 20				09 03								11 06										13 06	
Colne	a	00 28				09 13								11 15										13 15	

A To Manchester Airport
B To Liverpool Lime Street
C To Manchester Victoria
D To Wigan North Western
E To York

Table 97

Sundays

19 February to 26 February

Blackpool - Preston - Blackburn, Accrington, Burnley and Colne

Network Diagram - see first Page of Table 97

		NT A	NT B	NT C	TP ◇1 D	NT A		NT B	NT C	NT	TP ◇1 D	NT A	NT B	NT C	TP ◇1 D	NT A		NT B	NT C	NT	TP ◇1 D	NT A	NT B	NT C	TP ◇1 D
Blackpool North	d	11 50	12 11	12 20	12 44	12 50		13 13	13 20		13 44	13 50	14 11	14 20	14 44	14 50		15 13	15 20		15 44	15 50	16 11	16 20	16 44
Layton	d			12 23					13 23					14 23					15 23					16 23	
Poulton-le-Fylde	d	11 56	12 17	12 28	12 50	12 56		13 19	13 28		13 50	13 56	14 17	14 28	14 50	14 56		15 19	15 28		15 50	15 56	16 17	16 28	16 50
Blackpool South	d																								
Blackpool Pleasure Beach	d																								
Squires Gate	d																								
St Annes-on-the-Sea	d																								
Ansdell & Fairhaven	d																								
Lytham	d																								
Moss Side	d																								
Kirkham & Wesham	d			12 37					13 37					14 37					15 37					16 37	
Salwick	d																								
Preston 8	a	12 14	12 34	12 47	13 08	13 14		13 36	13 47		14 08	14 14	14 34	14 47	15 08	15 14		15 36	15 47		16 08	16 14	16 34	16 47	17 08
	d		12 37					13 37		14 05			14 37					15 37		16 05			16 37		
Lostock Hall	d									14 11										16 11					
Bamber Bridge	d									14 14										16 14					
Pleasington	d									14 21										16 21					
Cherry Tree	d									14 24										16 24					
Mill Hill (Lancashire)	d									14 27										16 27					
Blackburn	a		12 52					13 53		14 30			14 52					15 53		16 30			16 52		
Clitheroe 94	a																								
Blackburn	d		12 54					13 54		14 31			14 54					15 54		16 31			16 54		
Rishton	d									14 36										16 36					
Church & Oswaldtwistle	d									14 39										16 39					
Accrington	d		13 01					14 01		14 42			15 01					16 01		16 42			17 01		
Huncoat	d									14 47										16 47					
Hapton	d									14 50										16 50					
Rose Grove	d									14 53										16 53					
Burnley Manchester Road 41	a		13 10					14 10					15 10					16 10					17 10		
Leeds 10 41	a		14 22					15 22					16 22					17 21					18 21		
Burnley Barracks	d									14 56										16 56					
Burnley Central	d									14 58										16 58					
Brierfield	d									15 03										17 03					
Nelson	d									15 06										17 06					
Colne	a									15 15										17 15					

		NT A		NT B	NT C	NT	TP ◇1 D	NT A	NT B	TP ◇1 D	NT A	NT B		NT C	NT	TP ◇1 D	NT A	NT	NT C	TP ◇1 D	NT A	NT		NT C	NT
Blackpool North	d	16 50		17 11	17 20		17 44	17 50	18 11	18 44	18 50	19 13		19 20		19 44	19 50	20 11	20 20	20 44	20 50	21 13		21 20	
Layton	d				17 23									19 23					20 23					21 23	
Poulton-le-Fylde	d	16 56		17 17	17 28		17 50	17 56	18 17	18 50	18 56	19 19		19 28		19 50	19 56	20 17	20 28	20 50	20 56	21 19		21 28	
Blackpool South	d																								
Blackpool Pleasure Beach	d																								
Squires Gate	d																								
St Annes-on-the-Sea	d																								
Ansdell & Fairhaven	d																								
Lytham	d																								
Moss Side	d																								
Kirkham & Wesham	d				17 37									19 37					20 37					21 37	
Salwick	d																								
Preston 8	a	17 14		17 34	17 47		18 08	18 14	18 34	19 08	19 14	19 36		19 47		20 08	20 14	20 34	20 47	21 08	21 14	21 36		21 47	
	d			17 37		18 05			18 37			19 37			20 05			20 37				21 39			22 05
Lostock Hall	d					18 11									20 11										22 11
Bamber Bridge	d					18 14									20 14										22 14
Pleasington	d					18 21									20 21										22 21
Cherry Tree	d					18 24									20 24										22 24
Mill Hill (Lancashire)	d					18 27									20 27										22 27
Blackburn	a			17 52		18 30			18 52			19 53			20 30			20 52				21 54			22 30
Clitheroe 94	a																								
Blackburn	d			17 54		18 31			18 54			19 54			20 31			20 54				21 55			22 31
Rishton	d					18 36									20 36										22 36
Church & Oswaldtwistle	d					18 39									20 39										22 39
Accrington	d			18 01		18 42			19 01			20 01			20 42			21 01				22 02			22 42
Huncoat	d					18 47									20 47										22 47
Hapton	d					18 50									20 50										22 50
Rose Grove	d					18 53									20 53										22 53
Burnley Manchester Road 41	a			18 10					19 10			20 10						21 10				22 12			
Leeds 10 41	a			19 22					20 22			21 22						22 21				23 23			
Burnley Barracks	d					18 56									20 56										22 56
Burnley Central	d					18 58									20 58										22 58
Brierfield	d					19 03									21 03										23 03
Nelson	d					19 06									21 06										23 06
Colne	a					19 15									21 15										23 15

A To Wigan North Western
B To York
C To Manchester Victoria
D To Manchester Airport

Table 97

Sundays

19 February to 26 February

Blackpool - Preston - Blackburn, Accrington, Burnley and Colne

Network Diagram - see first Page of Table 97

		NT	TP	NT	TP
			◇1		◇1
		A		A	B
Blackpool North	d	21 50	21 56	22 44	23 03
Layton	d				
Poulton-le-Fylde	d	21 56	22 02	22 50	23 09
Blackpool South	d				
Blackpool Pleasure Beach	d				
Squires Gate	d				
St Annes-on-the-Sea	d				
Ansdell & Fairhaven	d				
Lytham	d				
Moss Side	d				
Kirkham & Wesham	d				23 17
Salwick	d				
Preston 8	a	22 14	22 20	23 08	23 28
	d				
Lostock Hall	d				
Bamber Bridge	d				
Pleasington	d				
Cherry Tree	d				
Mill Hill (Lancashire)	d				
Blackburn	a				
Clitheroe 94	a				
Blackburn	d				
Rishton	d				
Church & Oswaldtwistle	d				
Accrington	d				
Huncoat	d				
Hapton	d				
Rose Grove	d				
Burnley Manchester Road 41	a				
Leeds 10 41	a				
Burnley Barracks	d				
Burnley Central	d				
Brierfield	d				
Nelson	d				
Colne	a				

Sundays

4 March to 25 March

		NT	NT	TP	TP	NT	TP	NT	TP	NT		NT	NT	NT	TP	NT	NT	NT	TP	NT		NT	NT	NT	TP
							◇1		◇1						◇1				◇1						◇1
				B	B		B	C	B	A		D	C		B	A	D	C	B	A		D	C		B
		🚌		🚌	🚌																				🚲
Blackpool North	d			03 20	05 20		08 14	08 20	08 44	08 50		09 01	09 20		09 44	09 50	10 11	10 20	10 44	10 50		11 13	11 20		11 44
Layton	d							08 23					09 23					10 23					11 23		
Poulton-le-Fylde	d						08 20	08 28	08 50	08 56		09 07	09 28		09 50	09 56	10 17	10 28	10 50	10 56		11 19	11 28		11 50
Blackpool South	d		23p30											09 28										11 27	
Blackpool Pleasure Beach	d		23p32											09 30										11 29	
Squires Gate	d		23p34											09 32										11 31	
St Annes-on-the-Sea	d		23p38											09 36										11 35	
Ansdell & Fairhaven	d		23p41											09 39										11 38	
Lytham	d		23p44											09 42										11 41	
Moss Side	d		23p49											09 47										11 46	
Kirkham & Wesham	d		23p56					08 37					09 37	09 54				10 37					11 37	11 53	
Salwick	d																								
Preston 8	a		00 08				08 38	08 47	09 08	09 14		09 24	09 47	10 04	10 07	10 14	10 34	10 47	11 08	11 14		11 36	11 47	12 03	12 08
	d					08 16						09 27		10 05			10 37					11 37		12 05	
Lostock Hall	d					08 21								10 11										12 11	
Bamber Bridge	d					08 24								10 14										12 14	
Pleasington	d													10 21										12 21	
Cherry Tree	d													10 24										12 24	
Mill Hill (Lancashire)	d													10 27										12 27	
Blackburn	a					08 35						09 42		10 30			10 53					11 53		12 30	
Clitheroe 94	a																								
Blackburn	d	23p14				08 37						09 44		10 31			10 54					11 54		12 31	
Rishton	d	23p24												10 36										12 36	
Church & Oswaldtwistle	d	23p36												10 39										12 39	
Accrington	d	23p40				08 44						09 51		10 42			11 01					12 01		12 42	
Huncoat	d	23p46												10 47										12 47	
Hapton	d	23p52												10 50										12 50	
Rose Grove	d	23p58				08 51								10 53										12 53	
Burnley Manchester Road 41	a											10 00					11 10					12 10			
Leeds 10 41	a											11 21					12 22					13 22			
Burnley Barracks	d	00 02												10 56										12 56	
Burnley Central	d	00 07				08 56								10 58										12 58	
Brierfield	d	00 15				09 00								11 03										13 03	
Nelson	d	00 20				09 03								11 06										13 06	
Colne	a	00 28				09 13								11 15										13 15	

A To Wigan North Western
B To Manchester Airport
C To Manchester Victoria
D To York

Table 97

Sundays

4 March to 25 March

Blackpool - Preston - Blackburn, Accrington, Burnley and Colne

Network Diagram - see first Page of Table 97

		NT A	NT B	NT C	NT	TP ◇1 D		NT A	NT B	NT C	NT	TP ◇1 D	NT A	NT B	NT C	NT		TP ◇1 D	NT A	NT B	NT C	NT	TP ◇1 D	NT A	NT B
Blackpool North	d	11 50	12 11	12 20		12 44		12 50	13 13	13 20		13 44	13 50	14 11	14 20			14 44	14 50	15 13	15 20		15 44	15 50	16 11
Layton	d			12 23						13 23					14 23						15 23				
Poulton-le-Fylde	d	11 56	12 17	12 28		12 50		12 56	13 19	13 28		13 50	13 56	14 17	14 28			14 50	14 56	15 19	15 28		15 50	15 56	16 17
Blackpool South	d				12 24						13 27					14 27						15 27			
Blackpool Pleasure Beach	d				12 26						13 29					14 29						15 29			
Squires Gate	d				12 28						13 31					14 31						15 31			
St Annes-on-the-Sea	d				12 32						13 35					14 35						15 35			
Ansdell & Fairhaven	d				12 35						13 38					14 38						15 38			
Lytham	d				12 38						13 41					14 41						15 41			
Moss Side	d				12 43						13 46					14 46						15 46			
Kirkham & Wesham	d			12 37	12 50					13 37	13 53				14 37	14 53					15 37	15 53			
Salwick	d																								
Preston 8	a	12 14	12 34	12 47	13 01	13 08		13 14	13 36	13 47	14 03	14 08	14 14	14 34	14 47	15 04		15 08	15 14	15 36	15 47	16 03	16 08	16 14	16 34
	d		12 37						13 37		14 05			14 37						15 37		16 05			16 37
Lostock Hall	d										14 11											16 11			
Bamber Bridge	d										14 14											16 14			
Pleasington	d										14 21											16 21			
Cherry Tree	d										14 24											16 24			
Mill Hill (Lancashire)	d										14 27											16 27			
Blackburn	a		12 52						13 53		14 30			14 52						15 53		16 30			16 52
Clitheroe 94	a																								
Blackburn	d		12 54						13 54		14 31			14 54						15 54		16 31			16 54
Rishton	d										14 36											16 36			
Church & Oswaldtwistle	d										14 39											16 39			
Accrington	d		13 01						14 01		14 42			15 01						16 01		16 42			17 01
Huncoat	d										14 47											16 47			
Hapton	d										14 50											16 50			
Rose Grove	d										14 53											16 53			
Burnley Manchester Road 41	a		13 10						14 10					15 10						16 10					17 10
Leeds 10 41	a		14 22						15 22					16 22						17 21					18 21
Burnley Barracks	d										14 56											16 56			
Burnley Central	d										14 58											16 58			
Brierfield	d										15 03											17 03			
Nelson	d										15 06											17 06			
Colne	a										15 15											17 15			

		NT C		NT	TP ◇1 D	NT A	NT B	NT C	NT	TP ◇1 D	NT A	NT B		NT	TP ◇1 D	NT A	NT B	NT C	NT	TP ◇1 D	NT A	NT		NT C	NT
Blackpool North	d	16 20			16 44	16 50	17 11	17 20		17 44	17 50	18 11			18 44	18 50	19 13	19 20		19 44	19 50	20 11		20 20	
Layton	d	16 23						17 23										19 23						20 23	
Poulton-le-Fylde	d	16 28			16 50	16 56	17 17	17 28		17 50	17 56	18 17			18 50	18 56	19 19	19 28		19 50	19 56	20 17		20 28	
Blackpool South	d			16 27					17 24					18 27					19 27						20 27
Blackpool Pleasure Beach	d			16 29					17 26					18 29					19 29						20 29
Squires Gate	d			16 31					17 28					18 31					19 31						20 31
St Annes-on-the-Sea	d			16 35					17 32					18 35					19 35						20 35
Ansdell & Fairhaven	d			16 38					17 35					18 38					19 38						20 38
Lytham	d			16 41					17 38					18 41					19 41						20 41
Moss Side	d			16 46					17 43					18 46					19 46						20 46
Kirkham & Wesham	d	16 37		16 53				17 37	17 50					18 53				19 37	19 53					20 37	20 53
Salwick	d																								
Preston 8	a	16 47		17 04	17 08	17 14	17 34	17 47	18 00	18 08	18 14	18 34		19 04	19 08	19 14	19 36	19 47	20 03	20 08	20 14	20 34		20 47	21 03
	d						17 37		18 05			18 37					19 37		20 05			20 37			21 05
Lostock Hall	d								18 11										20 11						21 10
Bamber Bridge	d								18 14										20 14						21 13
Pleasington	d								18 21										20 21						21 20
Cherry Tree	d								18 24										20 24						21 23
Mill Hill (Lancashire)	d								18 27										20 27						21 26
Blackburn	a						17 52		18 30			18 52					19 53		20 30			20 52			21 29
Clitheroe 94	a																								
Blackburn	d						17 54		18 31			18 54					19 54		20 31			20 54			21 29
Rishton	d								18 36										20 36						21 34
Church & Oswaldtwistle	d								18 39										20 39						21 37
Accrington	d						18 01		18 42			19 01					20 01		20 42			21 01			21 40
Huncoat	d								18 47										20 47						21 45
Hapton	d								18 50										20 50						21 48
Rose Grove	d								18 53										20 53						21 51
Burnley Manchester Road 41	a						18 10					19 10					20 10					21 10			
Leeds 10 41	a						19 22					20 22					21 22					22 21			
Burnley Barracks	d								18 56										20 56						21 54
Burnley Central	d								18 58										20 58						21a57
Brierfield	d								19 03										21 03						
Nelson	d								19 06										21 06						
Colne	a								19 15										21 15						

A To Wigan North Western
B To York
C To Manchester Victoria
D To Manchester Airport

Table 97

Blackpool - Preston - Blackburn, Accrington, Burnley and Colne

Sundays
4 March to 25 March

Network Diagram - see first Page of Table 97

		TP	NT	NT	NT	NT	NT	TP		NT	TP
		◇1						◇1			◇1
		A	B		C		B			B	A
Blackpool North	d	20 44	20 50	21 13	21 20		21 50	21 56		22 44	23 03
Layton	d				21 23						
Poulton-le-Fylde	d	20 50	20 56	21 19	21 28		21 56	22 02		22 50	23 09
Blackpool South	d					21 27					
Blackpool Pleasure Beach	d					21 29					
Squires Gate	d					21 31					
St Annes-on-the-Sea	d					21 35					
Ansdell & Fairhaven	d					21 38					
Lytham	d					21 41					
Moss Side	d					21 46					
Kirkham & Wesham	d				21 37	21 53					23 17
Salwick	d										
Preston 8	a	21 08	21 14	21 36	21 47	22 03	22 14	22 20		23 08	23 28
	d			21 39		22 05					
Lostock Hall	d					22 11					
Bamber Bridge	d					22 14					
Pleasington	d					22 21					
Cherry Tree	d					22 24					
Mill Hill (Lancashire)	d					22 27					
Blackburn	a			21 54		22 30					
Clitheroe 94	a										
Blackburn	d			21 55		22 31					
Rishton	d					22 36					
Church & Oswaldtwistle	d					22 39					
Accrington	d			22 02		22 42					
Huncoat	d					22 47					
Hapton	d					22 50					
Rose Grove	d					22 53					
Burnley Manchester Road 41	a			22 12							
Leeds 10 41	a			23 23							
Burnley Barracks	d					22 56					
Burnley Central	d					22 58					
Brierfield	d					23 03					
Nelson	d					23 06					
Colne	a					23 15					

Sundays
from 1 April

		NT	NT	TP	TP	TP	NT	NT	NT	TP		NT	NT	NT	NT	TP	NT	NT	NT	TP		NT	NT	NT	NT
						◇1				◇1						◇1				◇1					
				A	A	A		C	D	A		E	F	C		A	E	F	C	A		E	F	C	
		🚌		🚌	🚌																				
Blackpool North	d			03 20	05 20	07 48		08 20	08 36	08 44		08 50	09 01	09 20		09 44	09 50	10 11	10 20	10 44		10 50	11 13	11 20	
Layton	d							08 23						09 23					10 23					11 23	
Poulton-le-Fylde	d					07 54		08 28	08 42	08 50		08 56	09 07	09 28		09 50	09 56	10 17	10 28	10 50		10 56	11 19	11 28	
Blackpool South	d		23p30												09 28										11 27
Blackpool Pleasure Beach	d		23p32												09 30										11 29
Squires Gate	d		23p34												09 32										11 31
St Annes-on-the-Sea	d		23p38												09 36										11 35
Ansdell & Fairhaven	d		23p41												09 39										11 38
Lytham	d		23p44												09 42										11 41
Moss Side	d		23p49												09 47										11 46
Kirkham & Wesham	d		23p56					08 37	08 51					09 37	09 54				10 37					11 37	11 53
Salwick	d																								
Preston 8	a		00 08			08 12		08 47	09 02	09 08		09 14	09 24	09 47	10 04	10 08	10 14	10 34	10 47	11 08		11 14	11 36	11 47	12 03
	d						08 16		09 05				09 27		10 05			10 37					11 37		12 05
Lostock Hall	d						08 21		09 11						10 11										12 11
Bamber Bridge	d						08 24		09 14						10 14										12 14
Pleasington	d														10 21										12 21
Cherry Tree	d														10 24										12 24
Mill Hill (Lancashire)	d														10 27										12 27
Blackburn	a						08 35		09 25				09 42		10 30			10 53					11 53		12 30
Clitheroe 94	a								09 50																
Blackburn	d	23p14					08 37						09 44		10 31			10 54					11 54		12 31
Rishton	d	23p24													10 36										12 36
Church & Oswaldtwistle	d	23p36													10 39										12 39
Accrington	d	23p40					08 44						09 51		10 42			11 01					12 01		12 42
Huncoat	d	23p46													10 47										12 47
Hapton	d	23p52													10 50										12 50
Rose Grove	d	23p58					08 51								10 53										12 53
Burnley Manchester Road 41	a												10 00					11 10					12 10		
Leeds 10 41	a												11 21					12 22					13 22		
Burnley Barracks	d	00 02													10 56										12 56
Burnley Central	d	00 07					08 56								10 58										12 58
Brierfield	d	00 15					09 00								11 03										13 03
Nelson	d	00 20					09 03								11 06										13 06
Colne	a	00 28					09 13								11 15										13 15

A To Manchester Airport
B To Wigan North Western
C To Manchester Victoria
D To Carlisle
E To Liverpool Lime Street
F To York

Table 97

Sundays

from 1 April

Blackpool - Preston - Blackburn, Accrington, Burnley and Colne

Network Diagram - see first Page of Table 97

		TP	NT	NT	NT	NT		TP	NT	NT	NT	NT	TP	NT	NT	NT		NT	TP	NT	NT	NT	NT	TP	NT
		◇1						◇1					◇1						◇1					◇1	
		A	B	C	D			A	B	C	D		A	B	C	D			A	B	C	D		A	B
Blackpool North	d	11 44	11 50	12 11	12 20			12 44	12 50	13 13	13 20		13 44	13 50	14 11	14 20			14 44	14 50	15 13	15 20		15 44	15 50
Layton	d				12 23						13 23					14 23						15 23			
Poulton-le-Fylde	d	11 50	11 56	12 17	12 28			12 50	12 56	13 19	13 28		13 50	13 56	14 17	14 28			14 50	14 56	15 19	15 28		15 50	15 56
Blackpool South	d					12 24						13 27						14 27					15 27		
Blackpool Pleasure Beach	d					12 26						13 29						14 29					15 29		
Squires Gate	d					12 28						13 31						14 31					15 31		
St Annes-on-the-Sea	d					12 32						13 35						14 35					15 35		
Ansdell & Fairhaven	d					12 35						13 38						14 38					15 38		
Lytham	d					12 38						13 41						14 41					15 41		
Moss Side	d					12 43						13 46						14 46					15 46		
Kirkham & Wesham	d				12 37	12 50					13 37	13 53				14 37		14 53				15 37	15 53		
Salwick	d																								
Preston 8	a	12 08	12 14	12 34	12 47	13 01		13 08	13 14	13 36	13 47	14 03	14 08	14 14	14 34	14 47		15 04	15 08	15 14	15 36	15 47	16 03	16 08	16 14
	d			12 37						13 37		14 05			14 37						15 37		16 05		
Lostock Hall	d											14 11											16 11		
Bamber Bridge	d											14 14											16 14		
Pleasington	d											14 21											16 21		
Cherry Tree	d											14 24											16 24		
Mill Hill (Lancashire)	d											14 27											16 27		
Blackburn	a			12 52						13 53		14 30			14 52						15 53		16 30		
Clitheroe 94	a																								
Blackburn	d			12 54						13 54		14 31			14 54						15 54		16 31		
Rishton	d											14 36											16 36		
Church & Oswaldtwistle	d											14 39											16 39		
Accrington	d			13 01						14 01		14 42			15 01						16 01		16 42		
Huncoat	d											14 47											16 47		
Hapton	d											14 50											16 50		
Rose Grove	d											14 53											16 53		
Burnley Manchester Road 41	a			13 10						14 10					15 10						16 10				
Leeds 10 41	a			14 22						15 22					16 22						17 21				
Burnley Barracks	d											14 56											16 56		
Burnley Central	d											14 58											16 58		
Brierfield	d											15 03											17 03		
Nelson	d											15 06											17 06		
Colne	a											15 15											17 15		

		NT		NT	NT	TP	NT	NT	NT	NT	TP	NT		NT	NT	TP	NT	NT	NT	NT	TP	NT		NT	NT
						◇1					◇1					◇1					◇1				
		C		D		A	B	C	D		A	B		C		A	B	C	D		A	B			D
Blackpool North	d	16 11		16 20		16 44	16 50	17 11	17 20		17 44	17 50		18 11		18 44	18 50	19 13	19 20		19 44	19 50		20 11	20 20
Layton	d			16 23					17 23										19 23						20 23
Poulton-le-Fylde	d	16 17		16 28		16 50	16 56	17 17	17 28		17 50	17 56		18 17		18 50	18 56	19 19	19 28		19 50	19 56		20 17	20 28
Blackpool South	d				16 27					17 24					18 27					19 27					
Blackpool Pleasure Beach	d				16 29					17 26					18 29					19 29					
Squires Gate	d				16 31					17 28					18 31					19 31					
St Annes-on-the-Sea	d				16 35					17 32					18 35					19 35					
Ansdell & Fairhaven	d				16 38					17 35					18 38					19 38					
Lytham	d				16 41					17 38					18 41					19 41					
Moss Side	d				16 46					17 43					18 46					19 46					
Kirkham & Wesham	d			16 37	16 53				17 37	17 50					18 53				19 37	19 53					20 37
Salwick	d																								
Preston 8	a	16 34		16 47	17 04	17 08	17 14	17 34	17 47	18 00	18 08	18 14		18 34	19 04	19 08	19 14	19 36	19 47	20 03	20 08	20 14		20 34	20 47
	d	16 37						17 37		18 05				18 37				19 37		20 05				20 37	
Lostock Hall	d									18 11										20 11					
Bamber Bridge	d									18 14										20 14					
Pleasington	d									18 21										20 21					
Cherry Tree	d									18 24										20 24					
Mill Hill (Lancashire)	d									18 27										20 27					
Blackburn	a	16 52						17 52		18 30				18 52				19 53		20 30				20 52	
Clitheroe 94	a																								
Blackburn	d	16 54						17 54		18 31				18 54				19 54		20 31				20 54	
Rishton	d									18 36										20 36					
Church & Oswaldtwistle	d									18 39										20 39					
Accrington	d	17 01						18 01		18 42				19 01				20 01		20 42				21 01	
Huncoat	d									18 47										20 47					
Hapton	d									18 50										20 50					
Rose Grove	d									18 53										20 53					
Burnley Manchester Road 41	a	17 10						18 10						19 10				20 10						21 10	
Leeds 10 41	a	18 21						19 22						20 22				21 22						22 21	
Burnley Barracks	d									18 56										20 56					
Burnley Central	d									18 58										20 58					
Brierfield	d									19 03										21 03					
Nelson	d									19 06										21 06					
Colne	a									19 15										21 15					

A To Manchester Airport
B To Liverpool Lime Street
C To York
D To Manchester Victoria

Table 97

Sundays
from 1 April

Blackpool - Preston - Blackburn, Accrington, Burnley and Colne

Network Diagram - see first Page of Table 97

		NT	TP	NT	NT	NT	NT	NT	TP	NT	TP
			◇1						◇1		◇1
			A	B		C		B		B	A
Blackpool North	d		20 44	20 50	21 13	21 20		21 50	21 56	22 44	23 03
Layton	d					21 23					
Poulton-le-Fylde	d		20 50	20 56	21 19	21 28		21 56	22 02	22 50	23 09
Blackpool South	d	20 27					21 27				
Blackpool Pleasure Beach	d	20 29					21 29				
Squires Gate	d	20 31					21 31				
St Annes-on-the-Sea	d	20 35					21 35				
Ansdell & Fairhaven	d	20 38					21 38				
Lytham	d	20 41					21 41				
Moss Side	d	20 46					21 46				
Kirkham & Wesham	d	20 53				21 37	21 53				23 17
Salwick	d										
Preston 8	a	21 03	21 08	21 14	21 36	21 47	22 03	22 14	22 20	23 08	23 28
	d	21 05			21 39		22 05				
Lostock Hall	d	21 10					22 11				
Bamber Bridge	d	21 13					22 14				
Pleasington	d	21 20					22 21				
Cherry Tree	d	21 23					22 24				
Mill Hill (Lancashire)	d	21 26					22 27				
Blackburn	a	21 29			21 54		22 30				
Clitheroe 94	a										
Blackburn	d	21 29			21 55		22 31				
Rishton	d	21 34					22 36				
Church & Oswaldtwistle	d	21 37					22 39				
Accrington	d	21 40			22 02		22 42				
Huncoat	d	21 45					22 47				
Hapton	d	21 48					22 50				
Rose Grove	d	21 51					22 53				
Burnley Manchester Road 41	a				22 12						
Leeds 10 41	a				23 23						
Burnley Barracks	d	21 54					22 56				
Burnley Central	d	21a57					22 58				
Brierfield	d						23 03				
Nelson	d						23 06				
Colne	a						23 15				

A To Manchester Airport **B** To Liverpool Lime Street **C** To Manchester Victoria

Colne, Burnley, Accrington and Blackburn - Preston - Blackpool

Network Diagram - see first Page of Table 97

Miles	Miles			TP	TP	NT	NT	TP	TP	NT	TP	TP		TP	NT	NT	NT	TP	NT	NT	NT	NT		NT	TP
				MX	MX	MO	MO	MO	MX	MX															
				◇1	◇1			◇1	◇1		◇1	◇1		◇1				◇1							◇1
				A	B	C	D	E	F	G	E	E		H		G		E		G	I			J	E
0	—	**Colne**	d												05 40				06 46			07 47			
2	—	Nelson	d												05 45				06 51			07 52			
3¼	—	Brierfield	d												05 48				06 54			07 55			
5½	—	**Burnley Central**	d												05 53				06 59			08 00			
—	—	Burnley Barracks	d												05 55				07 01			08 02			
—	—	Leeds 10 41	d														05 51				06 51				
—	—	Burnley Manchester Road 41	d														06 57				07 57				
7	—	Rose Grove	d												05 58				07 05			08 05			
8½	—	Hapton	d												06 01							08 08			
10	—	Huncoat	d												06 04				07 09			08 11			
11¾	—	Accrington	d												06 09		07 06		07 14		08 06	08 16			
12½	—	Church & Oswaldtwistle	d												06 11				07 16			08 18			
14¼	—	Rishton	d												06 14				07 19			08 21			
18	—	**Blackburn**	a												06 23		07 16		07 24		08 14	08 27			
—	—	Clitheroe 94	d																						
—	—	**Blackburn**	d												06 25		07 16		07 35		08 15	08 35			
19¼	—	Mill Hill (Lancashire)	d												06 28				07 38		08 18	08 38			
20	—	Cherry Tree	d												06 30				07 40			08 40			
21	—	Pleasington	d												06 32				07 42			08 42			
26	—	Bamber Bridge	d												06 39		07 26		07 49		08 27	08 49			
27¼	—	Lostock Hall	d												06 42		07 28		07 52		08 30	08 52			
30	—	**Preston 8**	a												06 50		07 36		08 00		08 38	09 00			
—	—		d	23p35	23p37	23p36	23p39	23p47	23p51	00 21				06 37	07 00	07 13	07 38	07 59	08 02	08 15	08 40	09 02		08 51	08 59
35¼	5¼	Salwick	d												07 07				08 09						
37¾	7¾	Kirkham & Wesham	d					23p56		00 30				06 46	07 11	07 22		08 09	08 13	08 25		09 11			
41	—	Moss Side	d												07 17				08 19			09 17			
43½	—	Lytham	d												07 21				08 23			09 21			
44¾	—	Ansdell & Fairhaven	d												07 24				08 26			09 24			
46¾	—	St Annes-on-the-Sea	d												07 28				08 30			09 28			
48¼	—	Squires Gate	d												07 32				08 34			09 32			
49½	—	Blackpool Pleasure Beach	d												07 34				08 36			09 34			
50	—	**Blackpool South**	a												07 38				08 41			09 39			
—	14¼	Poulton-le-Fylde	d	23p52	23p54	23p54	23p56	00 05	00 08	00 38				06 56		07 30	07 54	08 18		08 33	08 56				09 16
—	16¼	Layton	d							00 43				06 59		07 34		08 22		08 37					
—	17½	**Blackpool North**	a	00 02	00 04	00 05	00 05	00 14	00 16	00 52	01 30	05 33		07 06		07 43	08 05	08 29		08 46	09 05			09 17	09 25

		NT	NT	TP	NT	NT	NT	NT		TP	NT	NT	NT	NT	TP	NT	NT	NT		NT	TP	NT	NT	NT	NT
				◇1						◇1					◇1						◇1				
		G	I	E	K		G	G		E	K		G	L	E	M		G		L	E	M		G	L
Colne	d					08 40						09 50					10 50						11 50		
Nelson	d					08 45						09 55					10 55						11 55		
Brierfield	d					08 48						09 58					10 58						11 58		
Burnley Central	d					09 03						10 03					11 03						12 03		
Burnley Barracks	d					09 05						10 05					11 05						12 05		
Leeds 10 41	d		07 51					08 51						09 53						10 53					11 53
Burnley Manchester Road 41	d		08 57					09 57						10 57						11 57					12 57
Rose Grove	d					09 08						10 08					11 08						12 08		
Hapton	d					09 11						10 11					11 11						12 11		
Huncoat	d					09 14						10 14					11 14						12 14		
Accrington	d		09 06			09 19		10 06				10 19		11 06			11 19			12 06			12 19		13 06
Church & Oswaldtwistle	d					09 21						10 21					11 21						12 21		
Rishton	d					09 24						10 24					11 24						12 24		
Blackburn	a		09 14			09 33		10 14				10 34		11 14			11 33			12 14			12 33		13 14
Clitheroe 94	d																								
Blackburn	d		09 15			09 35		10 15				10 35		11 15			11 35			12 15			12 35		13 15
Mill Hill (Lancashire)	d					09 38						10 38					11 38						12 38		
Cherry Tree	d					09 40						10 40					11 40						12 40		
Pleasington	d					09 42						10 42					11 42						12 42		
Bamber Bridge	d					09 49						10 49					11 49						12 49		
Lostock Hall	d					09 52						10 52					11 52						12 52		
Preston 8	a		09 32			10 00		10 32				11 00		11 32			12 00			12 32			13 00		13 32
	d	09 19	09 34	09 38	09 55	10 02	10 19	10 34		10 38	10 55	11 02	11 19	11 34	11 38	11 55	12 02	12 19		12 34	12 38	12 55	13 02	13 19	13 34
Salwick	d																12 09								
Kirkham & Wesham	d	09 28			10 05	10 11	10 28				11 05	11 11	11 28			12 05	12 13	12 28				13 05	13 11	13 28	
Moss Side	d					10 17						11 17					12 19						13 17		
Lytham	d					10 21						11 21					12 23						13 21		
Ansdell & Fairhaven	d					10 24						11 24					12 26						13 24		
St Annes-on-the-Sea	d					10 28						11 28					12 30						13 28		
Squires Gate	d					10 32						11 32					12 34						13 32		
Blackpool Pleasure Beach	d					10 34						11 34					12 36						13 34		
Blackpool South	a					10 39						11 39					12 41						13 39		
Poulton-le-Fylde	d	09 36	09 51	09 56			10 36	10 51		10 56			11 36	11 50	11 56			12 36		12 50	12 56			13 36	13 50
Layton	d	09 43					10 43						11 43					12 43						13 43	
Blackpool North	a	09 52	10 01	10 05	10 21		10 53	11 01		11 05	11 21		11 52	12 00	12 05	12 21		12 52		13 00	13 05	13 21		13 52	14 00

A until 30 December and then from 27 March. From Manchester Airport
B from 3 January until 23 March. From Manchester Airport
C from 20 February until 26 March. From Wigan North Western
D until 13 February and then from 2 April. From Liverpool Lime Street
E From Manchester Airport
F From Windermere
G From Manchester Victoria
H From Manchester Piccadilly
I From York
J From Buxton
K From Liverpool Lime Street
L From Blackpool North
M From Liverpool South Parkway

Colne, Burnley, Accrington and Blackburn - Preston - Blackpool

Network Diagram - see first Page of Table 97

		TP ◇1 A 🚲	NT B	NT		NT C	NT D	TP ◇1 A 🚲	NT B	NT	NT C	NT D	TP ◇1 A 🚲	NT B		NT	NT D	TP ◇1 A 🚲	NT B	NT	NT C	TP ◇1 A 🚲	NT D	NT B	
Colne	d			12 50						13 50						14 50				15 50					
Nelson	d			12 55						13 55						14 55				15 55					
Brierfield	d			12 58						13 58						14 58				15 58					
Burnley Central	d			13 03						14 03						15 03				16 03					
Burnley Barracks	d			13 05						14 05						15 05				16 05					
Leeds 10 41	d						12 53					13 53					14 53						15 52		
Burnley Manchester Road 41	d						13 57					14 57					15 57						16 58		
Rose Grove	d			13 08						14 08						15 08				16 08					
Hapton	d			13 11						14 11						15 11				16 11					
Huncoat	d			13 14						14 14						15 14				16 14					
Accrington	d			13 19			14 06			14 19		15 06				15 19	16 06			16 19			17 06		
Church & Oswaldtwistle	d			13 21						14 21						15 21				16 21					
Rishton	d			13 24						14 24						15 24				16 24					
Blackburn	a			13 33			14 14			14 33		15 14				15 33	16 14			16 33			17 14		
Clitheroe 94	d																								
Blackburn	d			13 35			14 15			14 35		15 15				15 35	16 15			16 35			17 15		
Mill Hill (Lancashire)	d			13 38						14 38						15 38				16 38					
Cherry Tree	d			13 40						14 40						15 40				16 40					
Pleasington	d			13 42						14 42						15 42				16 42					
Bamber Bridge	d			13 49						14 49						15 49				16 49					
Lostock Hall	d			13 52						14 52						15 52				16 52					
Preston 8	a			14 00			14 32			15 00		15 32				16 00	16 32			17 00			17 32		
	d	13 38	13 55	14 02		14 19	14 34	14 38	14 55	15 02	15 19	15 34	15 38	15 55		16 02	16 34	16 38	16 56	17 02	17 21	17 32	17 35	17 55	
Salwick	d															16 09									
Kirkham & Wesham	d		14 05	14 11		14 28			15 05	15 11	15 28			16 05		16 13		16 47	17 05	17 11	17 30	17 41		18 05	
Moss Side	d			14 17						15 17						16 19				17 17					
Lytham	d			14 21						15 21						16 23				17 21					
Ansdell & Fairhaven	d			14 24						15 24						16 26				17 24					
St Annes-on-the-Sea	d			14 28						15 28						16 30				17 28					
Squires Gate	d			14 32						15 32						16 34				17 32					
Blackpool Pleasure Beach	d			14 34						15 34						16 36				17 34					
Blackpool South	a			14 39						15 39						16 41				17 39					
Poulton-le-Fylde	d	13 56				14 36	14 50	14 56			15 36	15 50	15 56				16 50	16 57	17 13		17 38	17 51	17 56	18 13	
Layton	d					14 43					15 43							17 00			17 43	17 54			
Blackpool North	a	14 05	14 21			14 53	15 00	15 05	15 21		15 52	16 00	16 05	16 21			17 00	17 07	17 21		17 52	18 02	18 06	18 24	

		NT	NT C	NT E	NT F	TP ◇1 A 🚲	NT E	NT G	NT	NT		NT C	NT D	NT	TP ◇1 A 🚲	NT G	NT C	NT D	NT	TP ◇1 A		NT	NT C	NT G	TP ◇1 A
Colne	d	16 50							17 50					18 54					19 50			20 50			
Nelson	d	16 55							17 55					18 59					19 55			20 55			
Brierfield	d	16 58							17 58					19 02					19 58			20 58			
Burnley Central	d	17 03							18 03					19 07					20 03			21 03			
Burnley Barracks	d	17 05							18 05					19 09					20 05			21 05			
Leeds 10 41	d				16 51								17 51					18 51							
Burnley Manchester Road 41	d				17 57								18 57					19 57							
Rose Grove	d	17 08							18 08					19 12					20 08			21 08			
Hapton	d	17 11							18 11					19 15					20 11			21 11			
Huncoat	d	17 14							18 14					19 18					20 14			21 14			
Accrington	d	17 19			18 06				18 19				19 06	19 23				20 06	20 19			21 19			
Church & Oswaldtwistle	d	17 21							18 21					19 25					20 21			21 21			
Rishton	d	17 24							18 24					19 28					20 24			21 24			
Blackburn	a	17 33			18 14				18 33				19 14	19 33				20 14	20 33			21 33			
Clitheroe 94	d																								
Blackburn	d	17 35			18 15				18 35	18 44			19 15	19 35				20 15	20 35			21 35			
Mill Hill (Lancashire)	d	17 38							18 38					19 38					20 38			21 38			
Cherry Tree	d	17 40							18 40					19 40					20 40			21 40			
Pleasington	d	17 42							18 42					19 42					20 42			21 42			
Bamber Bridge	d	17 49							18 49					19 49					20 49			21 49			
Lostock Hall	d	17 52							18 52					19 52					20 52			21 52			
Preston 8	a	18 00			18 33				19 00	19 05			19 32	20 00				20 32	21 00			22 02			
	d	18 02	18 18	18 26	18 34	18 40	18 49	18 55	19 02	19 08		19 19	19 34	20 02	19 38	20 19	20 25	20 34	21 02	20 38			21 19	21 24	21 38
Salwick	d																								
Kirkham & Wesham	d	18 11	18 27			18 49		19 05	19 11			19 28		20 11			20 34		21 11				21 28		
Moss Side	d	18 17							19 17					20 17					21 17						
Lytham	d	18 21							19 21					20 21					21 21						
Ansdell & Fairhaven	d	18 24							19 24					20 24					21 24						
St Annes-on-the-Sea	d	18 28							19 28					20 28					21 28						
Squires Gate	d	18 32							19 32					20 32					21 32						
Blackpool Pleasure Beach	d	18 34							19 34					20 34					21 34						
Blackpool South	a	18 39							19 39					20 39					21 39						
Poulton-le-Fylde	d		18 35	18 43	18 50	18 59						19 36	19 50		19 56		20 42	20 50		20 56			21 36		21 56
Layton	d		18 39			19 02						19 43					20 47						21 40		
Blackpool North	a		18 51	18 55	18 58	19 10	19 16	19 23		19 33		19 52	20 00		20 06	20 44	20 56	21 00		21 06			21 50	21 53	22 06

A From Manchester Airport
B From Liverpool South Parkway
C From Manchester Victoria
D From Blackpool North
E From Buxton
F From York
G From Liverpool Lime Street

Colne, Burnley, Accrington and Blackburn - Preston - Blackpool

Network Diagram - see first Page of Table 97

Station		NT A	NT B	NT	TP ◇1 C	NT		NT D	NT A	TP ◇1 E	TP ◇1 F	TP ◇1 G
Colne	d			21 45		22 55						
Nelson	d			21 50		23 00						
Brierfield	d			21 53		23 03						
Burnley Central	d			21 58		23 08						
Burnley Barracks	d			22 00		23 10						
Leeds 10 41	d		20 51									
Burnley Manchester Road 41	d		21 56									
Rose Grove	d			22 03		23 13						
Hapton	d			22 06								
Huncoat	d			22 09								
Accrington	d		22 05	22 14		23 20						
Church & Oswaldtwistle	d			22 16								
Rishton	d			22 19								
Blackburn	a		22 13	22 24		23 28						
Clitheroe 94	d											
Blackburn	d		22 14	22 25		23 30						
Mill Hill (Lancashire)	d			22 28		23 33						
Cherry Tree	d			22 30								
Pleasington	d			22 32								
Bamber Bridge	d			22 39		23 41						
Lostock Hall	d			22 42		23 43						
Preston 8	a		22 31	22 50		23 54						
	d	22 19	22 32	22 51	22 38			22 57	23 19	23 35	23 37	23 51
Salwick	d											
Kirkham & Wesham	d	22 28		23 01					23 28			
Moss Side	d			23 07								
Lytham	d			23 11								
Ansdell & Fairhaven	d			23 14								
St Annes-on-the-Sea	d			23 18								
Squires Gate	d			23 21								
Blackpool Pleasure Beach	d			23 24								
Blackpool South	a			23 28								
Poulton-le-Fylde	d	22 36	22 49		22 55				23 36	23 52	23 54	00 08
Layton	d	22 43							23 40			
Blackpool North	a	22 53	22 59		23 04			23 22	23 50	00 02	00 04	00 16

Saturdays

Station		TP ◇1 H	TP ◇1 I	TP ◇1 G	NT A	TP ◇1 C	TP ◇1 C	TP ◇1 J	NT	NT A		NT	NT D	TP ◇1 C 🚲	NT	NT A	NT K	NT	NT D	TP ◇1 C 🚲		NT A	NT K	NT	NT L
Colne	d								05 40						06 50			07 50						08 50	
Nelson	d								05 45						06 55			07 55						08 55	
Brierfield	d								05 48						06 58			07 58						08 58	
Burnley Central	d								05 53						07 03			08 03						09 03	
Burnley Barracks	d								05 55						07 05			08 05						09 05	
Leeds 10 41	d											05 51					06 51						07 51		
Burnley Manchester Road 41	d											06 57					07 57						08 57		
Rose Grove	d								05 58						07 08			08 08						09 08	
Hapton	d								06 01						07 11			08 11						09 11	
Huncoat	d								06 04						07 14			08 14						09 14	
Accrington	d								06 09			07 06			07 19		08 06	08 19					09 06	09 19	
Church & Oswaldtwistle	d								06 11						07 21			08 21						09 21	
Rishton	d								06 14						07 24			08 24						09 24	
Blackburn	a								06 23			07 16			07 33		08 14	08 33					09 14	09 33	
Clitheroe 94	d																								
Blackburn	d								06 25			07 16			07 35		08 15	08 35					09 15	09 35	
Mill Hill (Lancashire)	d								06 28						07 38		08 18	08 38						09 38	
Cherry Tree	d								06 30						07 40			08 40						09 40	
Pleasington	d								06 32						07 42			08 42						09 42	
Bamber Bridge	d								06 39			07 26			07 49		08 27	08 49						09 49	
Lostock Hall	d								06 42			07 28			07 52		08 30	08 52						09 52	
Preston 8	a								06 50			07 36			08 00		08 38	09 00					09 32	10 00	
	d	23p35	23p37	23p51	00 19			06 37	07 00	07 13		07 38	07 55	07 59	08 02	08 15	08 40	09 02	08 55	08 59		09 19	09 34	10 02	09 55
Salwick	d								07 07						08 09										
Kirkham & Wesham	d				00 28			06 46	07 11	07 22				08 09	08 13	08 25		09 11				09 28		10 11	
Moss Side	d								07 17						08 19			09 17						10 17	
Lytham	d								07 21						08 23			09 21						10 21	
Ansdell & Fairhaven	d								07 24						08 26			09 24						10 24	
St Annes-on-the-Sea	d								07 28						08 30			09 28						10 28	
Squires Gate	d								07 32						08 34			09 32						10 32	
Blackpool Pleasure Beach	d								07 34						08 36			09 34						10 34	
Blackpool South	a								07 38						08 41			09 39						10 39	
Poulton-le-Fylde	d	23p52	23p54	00 08	00 36			06 56		07 30		07 54		08 18		08 33	08 56			09 16		09 36	09 51		
Layton	d				00 43			06 59		07 34				08 22		08 37						09 43			
Blackpool North	a	00 02	00 04	00 16	00 52	01 30	05 33	07 06		07 39		08 05	08 21	08 29		08 42	09 05		09 21	09 25		09 48	10 01		10 21

A From Manchester Victoria
B From Blackpool North
C From Manchester Airport
D From Liverpool Lime Street
E until 30 December and then from 26 March.From Manchester Airport
F from 2 January until 23 March. From Manchester Airport
G From Windermere
H until 31 December and then from 31 March. From Manchester Airport
I from 7 January until 24 March. From Manchester Airport
J From Manchester Piccadilly
K From York
L until 24 March. From Liverpool Lime Street

Table 97

Saturdays

Colne, Burnley, Accrington and Blackburn - Preston - Blackpool

Network Diagram - see first Page of Table 97

		NT	TP	NT	NT	NT	TP	NT	NT	NT	NT	TP	NT	NT	NT	NT	TP	NT	NT	NT	NT	NT	TP
			◇1				◇1					◇1					◇1						◇1
		A	B	C			B	D	C	E		B	D	C	E		B	F	A	C	E		B
Colne	d					09 50					10 50					11 50						12 50	
Nelson	d					09 55					10 55					11 55						12 55	
Brierfield	d					09 58					10 58					11 58						12 58	
Burnley Central	d					10 03					11 03					12 03						13 03	
Burnley Barracks	d					10 05					11 05					12 05						13 05	
Leeds 10 41	d				08 51					09 53					10 53						11 53		
Burnley Manchester Road 41	d				09 57					10 57					11 57						12 57		
Rose Grove	d					10 08					11 08					12 08						13 08	
Hapton	d					10 11					11 11					12 11						13 11	
Huncoat	d					10 14					11 14					12 14						13 14	
Accrington	d				10 06	10 19				11 06	11 19				12 06	12 19					13 06	13 19	
Church & Oswaldtwistle	d					10 21					11 21					12 21						13 21	
Rishton	d					10 24					11 24					12 24						13 24	
Blackburn	a				10 14	10 33				11 14	11 33				12 14	12 33					13 14	13 33	
Clitheroe 94	d																						
Blackburn	d				10 15	10 35				11 15	11 35				12 15	12 35					13 15	13 35	
Mill Hill (Lancashire)	d					10 38					11 38					12 38						13 38	
Cherry Tree	d					10 40					11 40					12 40						13 40	
Pleasington	d					10 42					11 42					12 42						13 42	
Bamber Bridge	d					10 49					11 49					12 49						13 49	
Lostock Hall	d					10 52					11 52					12 52						13 52	
Preston 8	a				10 32	11 00				11 32	12 00				12 32	13 00					13 32	14 00	
	d	09 55	10 08	10 19	10 34	11 02	10 38	10 55	11 19	11 34	12 02	11 38	11 55	12 19	12 34	13 02	12 38	12 55	12 56	13 19	13 34	14 02	13 38
Salwick	d										12 09												
Kirkham & Wesham	d			10 28		11 11			11 28		12 13			12 28		13 11				13 28		14 11	
Moss Side	d					11 17					12 19					13 17						14 17	
Lytham	d					11 21					12 23					13 21						14 21	
Ansdell & Fairhaven	d					11 24					12 26					13 24						14 24	
St Annes-on-the-Sea	d					11 28					12 30					13 28						14 28	
Squires Gate	d					11 32					12 34					13 32						14 32	
Blackpool Pleasure Beach	d					11 34					12 36					13 34						14 34	
Blackpool South	a					11 39					12 41					13 39						14 39	
Poulton-le-Fylde	d		10 26	10 36	10 51		10 56		11 36	11 50		11 56		12 36	12 50		12 56			13 36	13 50		13 56
Layton	d			10 43					11 44					12 43						13 45			
Blackpool North	a	10 23	10 35	10 48	11 01		11 05	11 21	11 49	12 00		12 05	12 21	12 48	13 00		13 05	13 21	13 21	13 51	14 00		14 05

		NT	NT	NT	NT	TP	NT	NT	NT	NT	NT	TP	NT	NT	NT	TP	NT	NT	NT	NT	NT	TP
						◇1						◇1				◇1						◇1
		D	C	E		B	F	A	C	E		B	F	A	E	B		G	H	A	C	B
Colne	d				13 50						14 50						15 50					
Nelson	d				13 55						14 55						15 55					
Brierfield	d				13 58						14 58						15 58					
Burnley Central	d				14 03						15 03						16 03					
Burnley Barracks	d				14 05						15 05						16 05					
Leeds 10 41	d			12 53						13 53					14 53							
Burnley Manchester Road 41	d			13 57						14 57					15 57							
Rose Grove	d				14 08						15 08						16 08					
Hapton	d				14 11						15 11						16 11					
Huncoat	d				14 14						15 14						16 14					
Accrington	d			14 06	14 19					15 06	15 19				16 06		16 19					
Church & Oswaldtwistle	d				14 21						15 21						16 21					
Rishton	d				14 24						15 24						16 24					
Blackburn	a			14 14	14 33					15 14	15 33				16 14		16 33					
Clitheroe 94	d																					
Blackburn	d			14 15	14 35					15 15	15 35				16 15		16 35					
Mill Hill (Lancashire)	d				14 38						15 38						16 38					
Cherry Tree	d				14 40						15 40						16 40					
Pleasington	d				14 42						15 42						16 42					
Bamber Bridge	d				14 49						15 49						16 49					
Lostock Hall	d				14 52						15 52						16 52					
Preston 8	a			14 32	15 00					15 32	16 00				16 32		17 00					
	d	13 55	14 19	14 34	15 02	14 38	14 55	14 55	15 19	15 34	16 02	15 38	15 55	15 56	16 34	16 38	17 02	16 55	16 55	16 55	17 21	17 32
Salwick	d										16 09											
Kirkham & Wesham	d		14 28		15 11				15 28		16 13					16 47	17 11				17 31	17 41
Moss Side	d				15 17						16 19						17 17					
Lytham	d				15 21						16 23						17 21					
Ansdell & Fairhaven	d				15 24						16 26						17 24					
St Annes-on-the-Sea	d				15 28						16 30						17 28					
Squires Gate	d				15 32						16 34						17 32					
Blackpool Pleasure Beach	d				15 34						16 36						17 34					
Blackpool South	a				15 39						16 41						17 39					
Poulton-le-Fylde	d		14 36	14 50		14 56			15 36	15 50		15 56			16 50	16 57		17 12		17 12	17 39	17 51
Layton	d		14 43						15 43							17 00					17 43	17 54
Blackpool North	a	14 21	14 48	15 00		15 05	15 21	15 23	15 48	16 00		16 05	16 21	16 22	17 00	17 07		17 21	17 21	17 23	17 48	18 02

A from 31 March. From Liverpool Lime Street
B From Manchester Airport
C From Manchester Victoria
D From Liverpool Lime Street
E From Blackpool North
F until 24 March. From Liverpool South Parkway
G until 11 February. From Liverpool South Parkway
H from 18 February until 24 March. From Wigan North Western

Colne, Burnley, Accrington and Blackburn - Preston - Blackpool

Network Diagram - see first Page of Table 97

		NT	NT	NT	NT	NT	NT	TP		NT	NT	NT	NT	NT	NT	TP	NT	NT		NT	NT	TP	NT	NT	NT
								◇1								◇1						◇1			
		A		B	C	D	A	E			F	G	D	A		E	G	D		A		E		D	G
Colne	d		16 50							17 50					18 50						19 50		20 50		
Nelson	d		16 55							17 55					18 55						19 55		20 55		
Brierfield	d		16 58							17 58					18 58						19 58		20 58		
Burnley Central	d		17 03							18 03					19 03						20 03		21 03		
Burnley Barracks	d		17 05							18 05					19 05						20 05		21 05		
Leeds 10 41	d	15 52					16 51							17 51						18 51					
Burnley Manchester Road 41	d	16 58					17 57							18 57						19 57					
Rose Grove	d		17 08							18 08					19 08						20 08		21 08		
Hapton	d		17 11							18 11					19 11						20 11		21 11		
Huncoat	d		17 14							18 14					19 14						20 14		21 14		
Accrington	d	17 06	17 19				18 06			18 19				19 06	19 19					20 06	20 19		21 19		
Church & Oswaldtwistle	d		17 21							18 21					19 21						20 21		21 21		
Rishton	d		17 24							18 24					19 24						20 24		21 24		
Blackburn	a	17 14	17 34				18 14			18 34				19 14	19 33					20 14	20 33		21 33		
Clitheroe 94	d																								
Blackburn	d	17 15	17 35				18 15			18 35				19 15	19 35					20 15	20 35		21 35		
Mill Hill (Lancashire)	d		17 38							18 38					19 38						20 38		21 38		
Cherry Tree	d		17 40							18 40					19 40						20 40		21 40		
Pleasington	d		17 42							18 42					19 42						20 42		21 42		
Bamber Bridge	d		17 49							18 49					19 49						20 49		21 49		
Lostock Hall	d		17 52							18 52					19 52						20 52		21 52		
Preston 8	a	17 32	18 00				18 33			19 00				19 32	20 00					20 32	21 00		22 02		
	d	17 35	18 02	17 55	17 56	18 18	18 34	18 40		19 02	18 49	18 55	19 20	19 34	20 02	19 38	20 19	20 25		20 34	21 02	20 38		21 19	21 24
Salwick	d																								
Kirkham & Wesham	d		18 11			18 27		18 49		19 11			19 29		20 11			20 35			21 11			21 28	
Moss Side	d		18 17							19 17					20 17						21 17				
Lytham	d		18 21							19 21					20 21						21 21				
Ansdell & Fairhaven	d		18 24							19 24					20 24						21 24				
St Annes-on-the-Sea	d		18 28							19 28					20 28						21 28				
Squires Gate	d		18 32							19 32					20 32						21 32				
Blackpool Pleasure Beach	d		18 34							19 34					20 34						21 34				
Blackpool South	a		18 39							19 39					20 39						21 39				
Poulton-le-Fylde	d	17 56				18 35	18 50	18 59					19 37	19 50		19 56		20 43		20 50		20 56		21 36	
Layton	d					18 39		19 02					19 43					20 47						21 40	
Blackpool North	a	18 06		18 24	18 24	18 44	19 00	19 10			19 16	19 21	19 48	20 00		20 06	20 44	20 52		21 00		21 06		21 45	21 53

		TP	NT	NT		NT	TP	NT	NT	NT	TP
		◇1					◇1				◇1
		E	D	A			E		G	D	E
Colne	d					21 45		22 55			
Nelson	d					21 50		23 00			
Brierfield	d					21 53		23 03			
Burnley Central	d					21 58		23 08			
Burnley Barracks	d					22 00		23 10			
Leeds 10 41	d			20 51							
Burnley Manchester Road 41	d			21 56							
Rose Grove	d					22 03		23 13			
Hapton	d					22 06					
Huncoat	d					22 09					
Accrington	d			22 05		22 14		23 20			
Church & Oswaldtwistle	d					22 16					
Rishton	d					22 19					
Blackburn	a			22 13		22 24		23 28			
Clitheroe 94	d										
Blackburn	d			22 14		22 25		23 30			
Mill Hill (Lancashire)	d					22 28		23 33			
Cherry Tree	d					22 30					
Pleasington	d					22 32					
Bamber Bridge	d					22 39		23 41			
Lostock Hall	d					22 42		23 43			
Preston 8	a			22 31		22 50		23 54			
	d	21 38	22 19	22 32		22 51	22 38		22 57	23 19	23 35
Salwick	d										
Kirkham & Wesham	d		22 29			23 01				23 28	
Moss Side	d					23 07					
Lytham	d					23 11					
Ansdell & Fairhaven	d					23 14					
St Annes-on-the-Sea	d					23 18					
Squires Gate	d					23 21					
Blackpool Pleasure Beach	d					23 24					
Blackpool South	a					23 28					
Poulton-le-Fylde	d	21 56	22 37	22 49			22 55			23 36	23 52
Layton	d		22 43							23 42	
Blackpool North	a	22 06	22 48	22 59			23 04		23 22	23 47	00 02

A From Blackpool North
B until 24 March. From Liverpool South Parkway
C from 31 March. From Liverpool Lime Street
D From Manchester Victoria
E From Manchester Airport
F From Hazel Grove
G From Liverpool Lime Street

Table 97

Sundays until 1 January

Colne, Burnley, Accrington and Blackburn - Preston - Blackpool

Network Diagram - see first Page of Table 97

		TP	NT	TP	TP	TP	NT	NT	NT	TP		NT	NT	TP	NT	NT	NT	TP	NT	NT		NT	NT	TP	NT
		◇1				◇1				◇1				◇1				◇1						◇1	
		A	B	C	C	D		E	F	C		E		C	F	G	E	C	F	G			E	C	F
				🚌	🚌																				
Colne	d						09 16															11 35			
Nelson	d						09 21															11 40			
Brierfield	d						09 24															11 43			
Burnley Central	d						09 29															11 48			
Burnley Barracks	d						09 31															11 50			
Leeds 10 41	d												08 45			09 35				10 35					
Burnley Manchester Road 41	d												09 50			10 39				11 39					
Rose Grove	d						09 34															11 53			
Hapton	d						09 37															11 56			
Huncoat	d						09 40															11 59			
Accrington	d						09 45						09 59			10 48				11 47		12 04			
Church & Oswaldtwistle	d						09 47															12 06			
Rishton	d						09 50															12 09			
Blackburn	a						09 55						10 07			10 56				11 55		12 14			
Clitheroe 94	d																								
Blackburn	d						09 57						10 07			10 56				11 56		12 16			
Mill Hill (Lancashire)	d						10 00															12 19			
Cherry Tree	d						10 02															12 21			
Pleasington	d						10 04															12 23			
Bamber Bridge	d						10 11															12 30			
Lostock Hall	d						10 14															12 33			
Preston 8	a						10 22						10 27			11 13				12 13		12 42			
	d	23p35	00 11			08 33		09 20	09 39	09 52		10 20	10 29	10 35	10 40	11 15	11 21	11 35	11 39	12 14			12 20	12 35	12 39
Salwick	d																								
Kirkham & Wesham	d		00 21					09 29				10 29					11 31						12 29		
Moss Side	d																								
Lytham	d																								
Ansdell & Fairhaven	d																								
St Annes-on-the-Sea	d																								
Squires Gate	d																								
Blackpool Pleasure Beach	d																								
Blackpool South	a																								
Poulton-le-Fylde	d	23p52	00 29			08 50		09 37	09 57	10 09		10 37	10 46	10 52	10 57	11 32	11 39	11 52	11 57	12 31			12 37	12 52	12 57
Layton	d		00 34					09 42				10 42					11 44						12 42		
Blackpool North	a	00 02	00 38	02 10	07 35	08 57		09 47	10 07	10 18		10 47	10 53	11 01	11 09	11 39	11 49	12 01	12 07	12 38			12 47	13 01	13 07

		NT	NT	TP	NT	NT		NT	NT	TP	NT	NT	NT	TP	NT	NT		NT	NT	TP	NT	NT	NT	TP	NT
				◇1						◇1				◇1						◇1				◇1	
		G	E	C	F	G			E	C	F	G	E	C	F	G			E	C	F	G	E	C	F
Colne	d							13 35										15 35							
Nelson	d							13 40										15 40							
Brierfield	d							13 43										15 43							
Burnley Central	d							13 48										15 48							
Burnley Barracks	d							13 50										15 50							
Leeds 10 41	d	11 35				12 35						13 35				14 35						15 35			
Burnley Manchester Road 41	d	12 39				13 39						14 39				15 39						16 39			
Rose Grove	d							13 53										15 53							
Hapton	d							13 56										15 56							
Huncoat	d							13 59										15 59							
Accrington	d	12 47				13 47		14 04				14 47				15 47		16 04				16 47			
Church & Oswaldtwistle	d							14 06										16 06							
Rishton	d							14 09										16 09							
Blackburn	a	12 55				13 55		14 14				14 55				15 55		16 14				16 55			
Clitheroe 94	d																								
Blackburn	d	12 56				13 56		14 16				14 56				15 56		16 16				16 56			
Mill Hill (Lancashire)	d							14 19										16 19							
Cherry Tree	d							14 21										16 21							
Pleasington	d							14 23										16 23							
Bamber Bridge	d							14 30										16 30							
Lostock Hall	d							14 33										16 33							
Preston 8	a	13 13				14 13		14 42				15 13				16 13		16 42				17 13			
	d	13 14	13 20	13 35	13 39	14 14			14 20	14 35	14 39	15 14	15 20	15 35	15 39	16 14			16 20	16 35	16 39	17 14	17 20	17 35	17 39
Salwick	d																								
Kirkham & Wesham	d		13 29						14 29				15 29						16 29				17 29		
Moss Side	d																								
Lytham	d																								
Ansdell & Fairhaven	d																								
St Annes-on-the-Sea	d																								
Squires Gate	d																								
Blackpool Pleasure Beach	d																								
Blackpool South	a																								
Poulton-le-Fylde	d	13 31	13 37	13 52	13 57	14 30			14 37	14 52	14 57	15 32	15 37	15 52	15 57	16 31			16 37	16 52	16 57	17 31	17 37	17 52	17 57
Layton	d		13 42						14 42				15 43						16 42				17 42		
Blackpool North	a	13 38	13 47	14 01	14 07	14 38			14 47	15 01	15 07	15 39	15 48	16 01	16 07	16 38			16 47	17 01	17 07	17 38	17 47	18 01	18 07

A not 11 December. From Manchester Airport
B not 11 December. From Manchester Victoria
C From Manchester Airport
D From Manchester Piccadilly
E From Manchester Victoria
F From Liverpool Lime Street
G From York

Table 97

Sundays

until 1 January

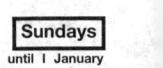

Colne, Burnley, Accrington and Blackburn - Preston - Blackpool

Network Diagram - see first Page of Table 97

			NT		NT	NT	TP	NT	NT	NT	TP	NT	NT	
							◇**1**				◇**1**			
			A			B	C	D	A	B	C	D	A	
Colne		d			17 35									
Nelson		d			17 40									
Brierfield		d			17 43									
Burnley Central		d			17 48									
Burnley Barracks		d			17 50									
Leeds **10**	41	d	16 35						17 35				18 35	
Burnley Manchester Road	41	d	17 39						18 39				19 39	
Rose Grove		d			17 53									
Hapton		d			17 56									
Huncoat		d			17 59									
Accrington		d	17 47		18 04				18 47				19 47	
Church & Oswaldtwistle		d			18 06									
Rishton		d			18 09									
Blackburn		a	17 55		18 14				18 55				19 56	
Clitheroe	94	d												
Blackburn		d	17 56		18 16				18 56				19 57	
Mill Hill (Lancashire)		d			18 19									
Cherry Tree		d			18 21									
Pleasington		d			18 23									
Bamber Bridge		d			18 30									
Lostock Hall		d			18 33									
Preston 8		a	18 13		18 42				19 13				20 14	
		d	18 14			18 20	18 35	18 39	19 14	19 21	19 35	19 39	20 15	
Salwick		d												
Kirkham & Wesham		d				18 29				19 30				
Moss Side		d												
Lytham		d												
Ansdell & Fairhaven		d												
St Annes-on-the-Sea		d												
Squires Gate		d												
Blackpool Pleasure Beach		d												
Blackpool South		a												
Poulton-le-Fylde		d	18 31			18 37	18 52	18 57	19 31	19 38	19 52	19 57	20 32	
Layton		d				18 42				19 42				
Blackpool North		a	18 38			18 47	19 01	19 07	19 38	19 47	20 01	20 07	20 39	

			NT	NT	TP	NT	NT	NT	TP	NT	NT		NT	NT
					◇**1**				◇**1**					
				B	C	D	A	B	C	D	A			B
Colne		d	19 35										21 35	
Nelson		d	19 40										21 40	
Brierfield		d	19 43										21 43	
Burnley Central		d	19 48										21 48	
Burnley Barracks		d	19 50										21 50	
Leeds **10**	41	d					19 35				20 35			
Burnley Manchester Road	41	d					20 39				21 39			
Rose Grove		d	19 53										21 53	
Hapton		d	19 56										21 56	
Huncoat		d	19 59										21 59	
Accrington		d	20 04				20 47				21 47		22 04	
Church & Oswaldtwistle		d	20 06										22 06	
Rishton		d	20 09										22 09	
Blackburn		a	20 14				20 55				21 55		22 14	
Clitheroe	94	d												
Blackburn		d	20 16				20 56				21 56		22 16	
Mill Hill (Lancashire)		d	20 19										22 19	
Cherry Tree		d	20 21										22 21	
Pleasington		d	20 23										22 23	
Bamber Bridge		d	20 30										22 30	
Lostock Hall		d	20 33										22 33	
Preston 8		a	20 42				21 13				22 13		22 44	
		d		20 21	20 35	20 39	21 14	21 20	21 35	21 39	22 14			22 20
Salwick		d												
Kirkham & Wesham		d		20 30				21 29						22 29
Moss Side		d												
Lytham		d												
Ansdell & Fairhaven		d												
St Annes-on-the-Sea		d												
Squires Gate		d												
Blackpool Pleasure Beach		d												
Blackpool South		a												
Poulton-le-Fylde		d		20 38	20 52	20 57	21 31	21 37	21 52	21 57	22 31			22 37
Layton		d		20 43				21 42						22 42
Blackpool North		a		20 48	21 01	21 07	21 38	21 47	22 01	22 07	22 38			22 47

			TP	NT	NT	TP
			◇**1**			◇**1**
			C	D	D	C
Colne		d				
Nelson		d				
Brierfield		d				
Burnley Central		d				
Burnley Barracks		d				
Leeds **10**	41	d				
Burnley Manchester Road	41	d				
Rose Grove		d				
Hapton		d				
Huncoat		d				
Accrington		d				
Church & Oswaldtwistle		d				
Rishton		d				
Blackburn		a				
Clitheroe	94	d				
Blackburn		d				
Mill Hill (Lancashire)		d				
Cherry Tree		d				
Pleasington		d				
Bamber Bridge		d				
Lostock Hall		d				
Preston 8		a				
		d	22 29	22 39	23 39	23 47
Salwick		d				
Kirkham & Wesham		d				23 56
Moss Side		d				
Lytham		d				
Ansdell & Fairhaven		d				
St Annes-on-the-Sea		d				
Squires Gate		d				
Blackpool Pleasure Beach		d				
Blackpool South		a				
Poulton-le-Fylde		d	22 46	22 57	23 56	00 05
Layton		d				
Blackpool North		a	22 55	23 07	00 05	00 14

A From York
B From Manchester Victoria
C From Manchester Airport
D From Liverpool Lime Street

Table 97

Sundays

8 January to 12 February

Colne, Burnley, Accrington and Blackburn - Preston - Blackpool

Network Diagram - see first Page of Table 97

		TP ◇1 A	NT B	TP A [bus]	TP A [bus]	TP ◇1 C	NT	NT D	TP ◇1 A	NT		TP ◇1 A	NT D	NT E	TP ◇1 A	NT D	NT E	NT	TP ◇1 A	NT D		NT E	TP ◇1 A	NT D	NT E
Colne	d						09 16											11 35							
Nelson	d						09 21											11 40							
Brierfield	d						09 24											11 43							
Burnley Central	d						09 29											11 48							
Burnley Barracks	d						09 31											11 50							
Leeds 10 41	d									08 45				09 35			10 35					11 35			12 35
Burnley Manchester Road 41	d									09 50				10 39			11 39					12 39			13 39
Rose Grove	d						09 34											11 53							
Hapton	d						09 37											11 56							
Huncoat	d						09 40											11 59							
Accrington	d						09 45			09 59				10 48			11 47	12 04				12 47			13 47
Church & Oswaldtwistle	d						09 47											12 06							
Rishton	d						09 50											12 09							
Blackburn	a						09 55			10 07				10 56			11 55	12 14				12 55			13 55
Clitheroe 94	d																								
Blackburn	d						09 57			10 07				10 56			11 56	12 16				12 56			13 56
Mill Hill (Lancashire)	d						10 00											12 19							
Cherry Tree	d						10 02											12 21							
Pleasington	d						10 04											12 23							
Bamber Bridge	d						10 11											12 30							
Lostock Hall	d						10 14											12 33							
Preston 8	a						10 22			10 27				11 13			12 13	12 42				13 13			14 13
	d	23p35	00 11			08 53		09 39	09 56	10 29		10 35	10 40	11 15	11 35	11 39	12 14		12 35	12 39		13 14	13 35	13 39	14 14
Salwick	d																								
Kirkham & Wesham	d		00 21																						
Moss Side	d																								
Lytham	d																								
Ansdell & Fairhaven	d																								
St Annes-on-the-Sea	d																								
Squires Gate	d																								
Blackpool Pleasure Beach	d																								
Blackpool South	a																								
Poulton-le-Fylde	d	23p52	00 29			09 10		09 57	10 13	10 46		10 52	10 57	11 32	11 52	11 57	12 31		12 52	12 57		13 31	13 52	13 57	14 30
Layton	d		00 34																						
Blackpool North	a	00 02	00 38	02 10	07 35	09 20		10 07	10 22	10 53		11 01	11 09	11 39	12 01	12 07	12 38		13 01	13 07		13 38	14 01	14 07	14 38

		NT	TP ◇1 A	NT D	NT E	TP ◇1 A		NT D	NT E	NT	TP ◇1 A	NT D	NT E	TP ◇1 A	NT D	NT E		NT	TP ◇1 A	NT D	NT E	TP ◇1 A	NT D	NT E	NT
Colne	d	13 35								15 35								17 35							19 35
Nelson	d	13 40								15 40								17 40							19 40
Brierfield	d	13 43								15 43								17 43							19 43
Burnley Central	d	13 48								15 48								17 48							19 48
Burnley Barracks	d	13 50								15 50								17 50							19 50
Leeds 10 41	d				13 35				14 35				15 35			16 35					17 35			18 35	
Burnley Manchester Road 41	d				14 39				15 39				16 39			17 39					18 39			19 39	
Rose Grove	d	13 53								15 53								17 53							19 53
Hapton	d	13 56								15 56								17 56							19 56
Huncoat	d	13 59								15 59								17 59							19 59
Accrington	d	14 04			14 47				15 47	16 04			16 47			17 47		18 04			18 47			19 47	20 04
Church & Oswaldtwistle	d	14 06								16 06								18 06							20 06
Rishton	d	14 09								16 09								18 09							20 09
Blackburn	a	14 14			14 55				15 55	16 14			16 55			17 55		18 14			18 55			19 56	20 14
Clitheroe 94	d																								
Blackburn	d	14 16			14 56				15 56	16 16			16 56			17 56		18 16			18 56			19 57	20 16
Mill Hill (Lancashire)	d	14 19								16 19								18 19							20 19
Cherry Tree	d	14 21								16 21								18 21							20 21
Pleasington	d	14 23								16 23								18 23							20 23
Bamber Bridge	d	14 30								16 30								18 30							20 30
Lostock Hall	d	14 33								16 33								18 33							20 33
Preston 8	a	14 42			15 13				16 13	16 42			17 13			18 13		18 42			19 13			20 14	20 42
	d		14 35	14 39	15 14	15 35		15 39	16 14		16 35	16 39	17 14	17 35	17 39	18 14			18 35	18 39	19 14	19 35	19 39	20 15	
Salwick	d																								
Kirkham & Wesham	d																								
Moss Side	d																								
Lytham	d																								
Ansdell & Fairhaven	d																								
St Annes-on-the-Sea	d																								
Squires Gate	d																								
Blackpool Pleasure Beach	d																								
Blackpool South	a																								
Poulton-le-Fylde	d		14 52	14 57	15 32	15 52		15 57	16 31		16 52	16 57	17 31	17 52	17 57	18 31			18 52	18 57	19 31	19 52	19 57	20 32	
Layton	d																								
Blackpool North	a		15 01	15 07	15 39	16 01		16 07	16 38		17 02	17 07	17 38	18 01	18 07	18 38			19 01	19 07	19 38	20 01	20 07	20 39	

A From Manchester Airport
B From Manchester Victoria
C From Manchester Piccadilly
D From Liverpool Lime Street
E From York

Table 97

Sundays

8 January to 12 February

Colne, Burnley, Accrington and Blackburn - Preston - Blackpool

Network Diagram - see first Page of Table 97

		TP		NT	NT	TP	NT	NT	NT	TP	NT	NT		TP
		◇1				◇1				◇1				◇1
		A		B	C	A	B	C		A	B	B		A
Colne	d								21 35					
Nelson	d								21 40					
Brierfield	d								21 43					
Burnley Central	d								21 48					
Burnley Barracks	d								21 50					
Leeds 10 41	d				19 35			20 35						
Burnley Manchester Road 41	d				20 39			21 39						
Rose Grove	d								21 53					
Hapton	d								21 56					
Huncoat	d								21 59					
Accrington	d				20 47			21 47	22 04					
Church & Oswaldtwistle	d								22 06					
Rishton	d								22 09					
Blackburn	a				20 55			21 55	22 14					
Clitheroe 94	d													
Blackburn	d				20 56			21 56	22 16					
Mill Hill (Lancashire)	d								22 19					
Cherry Tree	d								22 21					
Pleasington	d								22 23					
Bamber Bridge	d								22 30					
Lostock Hall	d								22 33					
Preston 8	a				21 13			22 13	22 44					
	d	20 35		20 39	21 14	21 35	21 39	22 14		22 34	22 39	23 39		23 47
Salwick	d													
Kirkham & Wesham	d													23 56
Moss Side	d													
Lytham	d													
Ansdell & Fairhaven	d													
St Annes-on-the-Sea	d													
Squires Gate	d													
Blackpool Pleasure Beach	d													
Blackpool South	a													
Poulton-le-Fylde	d	20 52		20 57	21 31	21 52	21 57	22 31		22 51	22 57	23 56		00 05
Layton	d													
Blackpool North	a	21 01		21 07	21 38	22 01	22 07	22 38		23 00	23 07	00 05		00 14

Sundays

19 February to 26 February

		TP	NT	TP	TP	TP	NT	NT	NT	TP		NT	NT	TP	NT	NT	NT	TP	NT	NT		NT	NT	TP	NT
		◇1				◇1				◇1				◇1				◇1						◇1	
		A	D	A	A	A		D	E	A		D		A	E	C	D	A	E	C			D	A	E
				🚌	🚌																				
Colne	d						09 16															11 35			
Nelson	d						09 21															11 40			
Brierfield	d						09 24															11 43			
Burnley Central	d						09 29															11 48			
Burnley Barracks	d						09 31															11 50			
Leeds 10 41	d												08 45			09 35				10 35					
Burnley Manchester Road 41	d												09 50			10 39				11 39					
Rose Grove	d						09 34															11 53			
Hapton	d						09 37															11 56			
Huncoat	d						09 40															11 59			
Accrington	d						09 45						09 59			10 48				11 47		12 04			
Church & Oswaldtwistle	d						09 47															12 06			
Rishton	d						09 50															12 09			
Blackburn	a						09 55						10 07			10 56				11 55		12 14			
Clitheroe 94	d																								
Blackburn	d						09 57						10 07			10 56				11 56		12 16			
Mill Hill (Lancashire)	d						10 00															12 19			
Cherry Tree	d						10 02															12 21			
Pleasington	d						10 04															12 23			
Bamber Bridge	d						10 11															12 30			
Lostock Hall	d						10 14															12 33			
Preston 8	a						10 22						10 27			11 13				12 13		12 42			
	d	23p35	00 11			08 33		09 20	09 39	09 52		10 20	10 29	10 35	10 40	11 15	11 21	11 35	11 39	12 14			12 20	12 35	12 39
Salwick	d																								
Kirkham & Wesham	d		00 21					09 29				10 29					11 31						12 29		
Moss Side	d																								
Lytham	d																								
Ansdell & Fairhaven	d																								
St Annes-on-the-Sea	d																								
Squires Gate	d																								
Blackpool Pleasure Beach	d																								
Blackpool South	a																								
Poulton-le-Fylde	d	23p52	00 29			08 50		09 37	09 57	10 09		10 37	10 46	10 52	10 57	11 32	11 39	11 52	11 57	12 31			12 37	12 52	12 57
Layton	d		00 34					09 42				10 42					11 44						12 42		
Blackpool North	a	00 02	00 38	02 10	07 35	08 57		09 47	10 07	10 18		10 47	10 53	11 01	11 07	11 39	11 49	12 01	12 07	12 38			12 47	13 01	13 07

A From Manchester Airport
B From Liverpool Lime Street
C From York
D From Manchester Victoria
E From Wigan North Western

Table 97

Sundays

19 February to 26 February

Colne, Burnley, Accrington and Blackburn - Preston - Blackpool

Network Diagram - see first Page of Table 97

		NT A	NT B	TP ◇1 C	NT D	NT A		NT	NT B	TP ◇1 C	NT D	NT A	NT B	TP ◇1 C	NT D	NT A		NT	NT B	TP ◇1 C	NT D	NT A	NT B	TP ◇1 C	NT A
Colne	d							13 35										15 35							
Nelson	d							13 40										15 40							
Brierfield	d							13 43										15 43							
Burnley Central	d							13 48										15 48							
Burnley Barracks	d							13 50										15 50							
Leeds 10 — 41	d	11 35				12 35						13 35				14 35						15 35			16 35
Burnley Manchester Road — 41	d	12 39				13 39						14 39				15 39						16 39			17 39
Rose Grove	d							13 53										15 53							
Hapton	d							13 56										15 56							
Huncoat	d							13 59										15 59							
Accrington	d	12 47				13 47		14 04				14 47				15 47		16 04				16 47			17 47
Church & Oswaldtwistle	d							14 06										16 06							
Rishton	d							14 09										16 09							
Blackburn	a	12 55				13 55		14 14				14 55				15 55		16 14				16 55			17 55
Clitheroe — 94	d																								
Blackburn	d	12 56				13 56		14 16				14 56				15 56		16 16				16 56			17 56
Mill Hill (Lancashire)	d							14 19										16 19							
Cherry Tree	d							14 21										16 21							
Pleasington	d							14 23										16 23							
Bamber Bridge	d							14 30										16 30							
Lostock Hall	d							14 33										16 33							
Preston 8	a	13 13				14 13		14 42				15 13				16 13		16 42				17 13			18 13
	d	13 14	13 20	13 35	13 39	14 14			14 20	14 35	14 39	15 14	15 20	15 35	15 39	16 14			16 20	16 35	16 39	17 14	17 20	17 35	18 14
Salwick	d																								
Kirkham & Wesham	d		13 29						14 29				15 29						16 29				17 29		
Moss Side	d																								
Lytham	d																								
Ansdell & Fairhaven	d																								
St Annes-on-the-Sea	d																								
Squires Gate	d																								
Blackpool Pleasure Beach	d																								
Blackpool South	a																								
Poulton-le-Fylde	d	13 31	13 37	13 52	13 57	14 30			14 37	14 52	14 57	15 32	15 37	15 52	15 57	16 31			16 37	16 52	16 57	17 31	17 37	17 52	18 31
Layton	d		13 42						14 42				15 43						16 42				17 42		
Blackpool North	a	13 38	13 47	14 01	14 09	14 38			14 47	15 01	15 07	15 39	15 48	16 01	16 07	16 38			16 47	17 01	17 07	17 38	17 47	18 01	18 38

		NT		NT B	TP ◇1 C	NT D	NT A	NT B	TP ◇1 C	NT D	NT A	NT		NT B	TP ◇1 C	NT D	NT A	NT B	TP ◇1 C	NT D	NT A	NT		NT B	TP ◇1 C
Colne	d	17 35										19 35										21 35			
Nelson	d	17 40										19 40										21 40			
Brierfield	d	17 43										19 43										21 43			
Burnley Central	d	17 48										19 48										21 48			
Burnley Barracks	d	17 50										19 50										21 50			
Leeds 10 — 41	d						17 35				18 35						19 35				20 35				
Burnley Manchester Road — 41	d						18 39				19 39						20 39				21 39				
Rose Grove	d	17 53										19 53										21 53			
Hapton	d	17 56										19 56										21 56			
Huncoat	d	17 59										19 59										21 59			
Accrington	d	18 04					18 47				19 47	20 04					20 47				21 47	22 04			
Church & Oswaldtwistle	d	18 06										20 06										22 06			
Rishton	d	18 09										20 09										22 09			
Blackburn	a	18 14					18 55				19 56	20 14					20 55				21 55	22 14			
Clitheroe — 94	d																								
Blackburn	d	18 16					18 56				19 57	20 16					20 56				21 56	22 16			
Mill Hill (Lancashire)	d	18 19										20 19										22 19			
Cherry Tree	d	18 21										20 21										22 21			
Pleasington	d	18 23										20 23										22 23			
Bamber Bridge	d	18 30										20 30										22 30			
Lostock Hall	d	18 33										20 33										22 33			
Preston 8	a	18 42					19 13				20 14	20 42					21 13				22 13	22 44			
	d			18 20	18 35	18 39	19 14	19 21	19 35	19 39	20 15			20 21	20 35	20 39	21 14	21 20	21 35	21 39	22 14			22 20	22 29
Salwick	d																								
Kirkham & Wesham	d			18 29				19 30						20 30				21 29						22 29	
Moss Side	d																								
Lytham	d																								
Ansdell & Fairhaven	d																								
St Annes-on-the-Sea	d																								
Squires Gate	d																								
Blackpool Pleasure Beach	d																								
Blackpool South	a																								
Poulton-le-Fylde	d			18 37	18 52	18 57	19 31	19 38	19 52	19 57	20 32			20 38	20 52	20 57	21 31	21 37	21 52	21 57	22 31			22 37	22 46
Layton	d			18 42				19 42						20 43				21 42						22 42	
Blackpool North	a			18 47	19 01	19 07	19 38	19 47	20 01	20 07	20 39			20 48	21 01	21 07	21 38	21 47	22 01	22 07	22 38			22 47	22 55

A From York
B From Manchester Victoria
C From Manchester Airport
D From Wigan North Western

Table 97

Sundays

19 February to 26 February

Colne, Burnley, Accrington and Blackburn - Preston - Blackpool

Network Diagram - see first Page of Table 97

		NT	NT	TP
				◇1
		A	A	B
Colne	d			
Nelson	d			
Brierfield	d			
Burnley Central	d			
Burnley Barracks	d			
Leeds 10 41	d			
Burnley Manchester Road 41	d			
Rose Grove	d			
Hapton	d			
Huncoat	d			
Accrington	d			
Church & Oswaldtwistle	d			
Rishton	d			
Blackburn	a			
Clitheroe 94	d			
Blackburn	d			
Mill Hill (Lancashire)	d			
Cherry Tree	d			
Pleasington	d			
Bamber Bridge	d			
Lostock Hall	d			
Preston 8	a			
	d	22 39	23 36	23 47
Salwick	d			
Kirkham & Wesham	d			23 56
Moss Side	d			
Lytham	d			
Ansdell & Fairhaven	d			
St Annes-on-the-Sea	d			
Squires Gate	d			
Blackpool Pleasure Beach	d			
Blackpool South	a			
Poulton-le-Fylde	d	22 57	23 54	00 05
Layton	d			
Blackpool North	a	23 07	00 05	00 14

Sundays

4 March to 25 March

		TP	NT	TP	TP	TP	NT	NT	NT	TP	NT	NT	NT	TP	NT	NT	NT	TP	NT	NT	NT	NT	NT
		◇1				◇1				◇1				◇1				◇1					
		B	C	B	B	B		C	A	B	C			B	A	D	C	B	A	D		C	
				(bus)	(bus)																		
Colne	d											09 16											11 35
Nelson	d											09 21											11 40
Brierfield	d											09 24											11 43
Burnley Central	d											09 29											11 48
Burnley Barracks	d											09 31											11 50
Leeds 10 41	d												08 45			09 35				10 35			
Burnley Manchester Road 41	d												09 50			10 39				11 39			
Rose Grove	d											09 34											11 53
Hapton	d											09 37											11 56
Huncoat	d											09 40											11 59
Accrington	d											09 45	09 59			10 48				11 47			12 04
Church & Oswaldtwistle	d											09 47											12 06
Rishton	d											09 50											12 09
Blackburn	a											09 55	10 07			10 56				11 55			12 14
Clitheroe 94	d																						
Blackburn	d											09 57	10 07			10 56				11 56			12 16
Mill Hill (Lancashire)	d											10 00											12 19
Cherry Tree	d											10 02											12 21
Pleasington	d											10 04											12 23
Bamber Bridge	d											10 11											12 30
Lostock Hall	d											10 14											12 33
Preston 8	a											10 22	10 27			11 13				12 13			12 41
	d	23p35	00 11			08 33	08 49	09 20	09 39	09 52	10 20	10 23	10 29	10 35	10 40	11 15	11 21	11 35	11 39	12 14	11 44	12 20	12 42
Salwick	d																						
Kirkham & Wesham	d		00 21				08 58	09 29			10 29	10 33					11 31				11 53	12 29	12 52
Moss Side	d						09 06					10 39									12 01		12 58
Lytham	d						09 10					10 43									12 05		13 02
Ansdell & Fairhaven	d						09 13					10 46									12 08		13 05
St Annes-on-the-Sea	d						09 17					10 50									12 12		13 09
Squires Gate	d						09 20					10 54									12 15		13 13
Blackpool Pleasure Beach	d						09 23					10 56									12 18		13 15
Blackpool South	a						09 26					10 59									12 21		13 18
Poulton-le-Fylde	d	23p52	00 29			08 50		09 37	09 57	10 09	10 37		10 46	10 52	10 57	11 32	11 39	11 52	11 57	12 31		12 37	
Layton	d		00 34					09 42			10 42						11 44					12 42	
Blackpool North	a	00 02	00 38	02 10	07 35	08 57		09 47	10 07	10 18	10 47		10 53	11 01	11 07	11 39	11 49	12 01	12 07	12 38		12 47	

A From Wigan North Western
B From Manchester Airport
C From Manchester Victoria
D From York

Table 97

Sundays

4 March to 25 March

Colne, Burnley, Accrington and Blackburn - Preston - Blackpool

Network Diagram - see first Page of Table 97

		TP ◇1 A	NT B	NT C	NT D	TP ◇1 A		NT B	NT C	NT	NT D	NT	TP ◇1 A	NT B	NT C	NT D		TP ◇1 A	NT B	NT C	NT	NT D	NT	TP ◇1 A	NT B
Colne	d											13 35											15 35		
Nelson	d											13 40											15 40		
Brierfield	d											13 43											15 43		
Burnley Central	d											13 48											15 48		
Burnley Barracks	d											13 50											15 50		
Leeds 10 41	d			11 35					12 35						13 35					14 35					
Burnley Manchester Road 41	d			12 39					13 39						14 39					15 39					
Rose Grove	d											13 53											15 53		
Hapton	d											13 56											15 56		
Huncoat	d											13 59											15 59		
Accrington	d			12 47					13 47			14 04			14 47					15 47			16 04		
Church & Oswaldtwistle	d											14 06											16 06		
Rishton	d											14 09											16 09		
Blackburn	a			12 55					13 55			14 14			14 55					15 55			16 14		
Clitheroe 94	d																								
Blackburn	d			12 56					13 56			14 16			14 56					15 56			16 16		
Mill Hill (Lancashire)	d											14 19											16 19		
Cherry Tree	d											14 21											16 21		
Pleasington	d											14 23											16 23		
Bamber Bridge	d											14 30											16 30		
Lostock Hall	d											14 33											16 33		
Preston 8	a			13 13					14 13			14 41			15 13					16 13			16 41		
	d	12 35	12 39	13 14	13 20	13 35		13 39	14 14	13 44	14 20	14 42	14 35	14 39	15 14	15 20		15 35	15 39	16 14	15 44	16 20	16 41	16 35	16 39
Salwick	d																								
Kirkham & Wesham	d				13 29					13 53	14 29	14 52				15 29					15 53	16 29	16 52		
Moss Side	d									14 01		14 59									16 01		16 58		
Lytham	d									14 05		15 03									16 05		17 02		
Ansdell & Fairhaven	d									14 08		15 06									16 08		17 05		
St Annes-on-the-Sea	d									14 12		15 10									16 12		17 09		
Squires Gate	d									14 15		15 13									16 15		17 13		
Blackpool Pleasure Beach	d									14 18		15 16									16 18		17 15		
Blackpool South	a									14 21		15 19									16 21		17 18		
Poulton-le-Fylde	d	12 52	12 57	13 31	13 37	13 52		13 57	14 30		14 37		14 52	14 57	15 32	15 37		15 52	15 57	16 31		16 37		16 52	16 57
Layton	d				13 42						14 42					15 43						16 42			
Blackpool North	a	13 01	13 07	13 38	13 47	14 01		14 09	14 38		14 47		15 01	15 07	15 39	15 48		16 01	16 07	16 38		16 47		17 01	17 07

		NT C		NT D	TP ◇1 A	NT C	NT	NT D	NT	TP ◇1 A	NT B	NT C		NT D	TP ◇1 A	NT B	NT C	NT	NT D	NT	TP ◇1 A	NT B		NT C	NT D
Colne	d								17 35											19 35					
Nelson	d								17 40											19 40					
Brierfield	d								17 43											19 43					
Burnley Central	d								17 48											19 48					
Burnley Barracks	d								17 50											19 50					
Leeds 10 41	d	15 35				16 35						17 35					18 35							19 35	
Burnley Manchester Road 41	d	16 39				17 39						18 39					19 39							20 39	
Rose Grove	d								17 53											19 53					
Hapton	d								17 56											19 56					
Huncoat	d								17 59											19 59					
Accrington	d	16 47				17 47			18 04			18 47					19 47			20 04				20 47	
Church & Oswaldtwistle	d								18 06											20 06					
Rishton	d								18 09											20 09					
Blackburn	a	16 55				17 55			18 14			18 55					19 56			20 14				20 55	
Clitheroe 94	d																								
Blackburn	d	16 56				17 56			18 16			18 56					19 57			20 16				20 56	
Mill Hill (Lancashire)	d								18 19											20 19					
Cherry Tree	d								18 21											20 21					
Pleasington	d								18 23											20 23					
Bamber Bridge	d								18 30											20 30					
Lostock Hall	d								18 33											20 33					
Preston 8	a	17 13				18 13			18 41			19 13					20 14			20 41				21 13	
	d	17 14		17 20	17 35	18 14	17 44	18 20	18 41	18 35	18 39	19 14		19 21	19 35	19 39	20 15	19 44	20 21	20 41	20 35	20 39		21 14	21 20
Salwick	d																								
Kirkham & Wesham	d			17 29			17 53	18 29	18 52					19 30				19 53	20 30	20 52					21 29
Moss Side	d						18 01		18 58									20 01		20 58					
Lytham	d						18 05		19 02									20 05		21 02					
Ansdell & Fairhaven	d						18 08		19 05									20 08		21 05					
St Annes-on-the-Sea	d						18 12		19 09									20 12		21 09					
Squires Gate	d						18 15		19 13									20 15		21 13					
Blackpool Pleasure Beach	d						18 18		19 15									20 18		21 15					
Blackpool South	a						18 21		19 18									20 21		21 18					
Poulton-le-Fylde	d	17 31		17 37	17 52	18 31		18 37		18 52	18 57	19 31		19 38	19 52	19 57	20 32		20 38		20 52	20 57		21 31	21 37
Layton	d			17 42				18 42						19 42					20 43						21 42
Blackpool North	a	17 38		17 47	18 01	18 38		18 47		19 01	19 07	19 38		19 47	20 01	20 07	20 39		20 48		21 01	21 07		21 38	21 47

A From Manchester Airport
B From Wigan North Western
C From York
D From Manchester Victoria

Table 97

Sundays

4 March to 25 March

Colne, Burnley, Accrington and Blackburn - Preston - Blackpool

Network Diagram - see first Page of Table 97

		TP	NT	NT	NT	NT	TP	NT		NT	TP
		◇1					◇1				◇1
		A	B	C		D	A	B		B	A
Colne	d				21 35						
Nelson	d				21 40						
Brierfield	d				21 43						
Burnley Central	d				21 48						
Burnley Barracks	d				21 50						
Leeds 10 41	d			20 35							
Burnley Manchester Road 41	d			21 39							
Rose Grove	d				21 53						
Hapton	d				21 56						
Huncoat	d				21 59						
Accrington	d			21 47	22 04						
Church & Oswaldtwistle	d				22 06						
Rishton	d				22 09						
Blackburn	a			21 55	22 14						
Clitheroe 94	d										
Blackburn	d			21 56	22 16						
Mill Hill (Lancashire)	d				22 19						
Cherry Tree	d				22 21						
Pleasington	d				22 23						
Bamber Bridge	d				22 30						
Lostock Hall	d				22 33						
Preston 8	a			22 13	22 44						
	d	21 35	21 39	22 14		22 20	22 29	22 39		23 36	23 47
Salwick	d										
Kirkham & Wesham	d					22 29					23 56
Moss Side	d										
Lytham	d										
Ansdell & Fairhaven	d										
St Annes-on-the-Sea	d										
Squires Gate	d										
Blackpool Pleasure Beach	d										
Blackpool South	a										
Poulton-le-Fylde	d	21 52	21 57	22 31		22 37	22 46	22 57		23 54	00 05
Layton	d					22 42					
Blackpool North	a	22 01	22 07	22 38		22 47	22 55	23 07		00 05	00 14

Sundays

from 1 April

		TP	NT	TP	TP	NT	TP	NT	NT	TP		NT	NT	NT	TP	NT	NT	NT	TP	NT		NT	NT	NT	NT
		◇1					◇1			◇1					◇1				◇1						
		A	D	A	A		A	D	E	A		D			A	E	C	D	A	E		C		D	
				Bus	Bus																				
Colne	d												09 16												11 35
Nelson	d												09 21												11 40
Brierfield	d												09 24												11 43
Burnley Central	d												09 29												11 48
Burnley Barracks	d												09 31												11 50
Leeds 10 41	d													08 45			09 35					10 35			
Burnley Manchester Road 41	d													09 50			10 39					11 39			
Rose Grove	d												09 34												11 53
Hapton	d												09 37												11 56
Huncoat	d												09 40												11 59
Accrington	d												09 45	09 59			10 48					11 47			12 04
Church & Oswaldtwistle	d												09 47												12 06
Rishton	d												09 50												12 09
Blackburn	a												09 55	10 07			10 56					11 55			12 14
Clitheroe 94	d																								
Blackburn	d												09 57	10 07			10 56					11 56			12 16
Mill Hill (Lancashire)	d												10 00												12 19
Cherry Tree	d												10 02												12 21
Pleasington	d												10 04												12 23
Bamber Bridge	d												10 11												12 30
Lostock Hall	d												10 14												12 33
Preston 8	a												10 22	10 27			11 13					12 13			12 41
	d	23p35	00 11			08 49	08 58	09 20	09 39	09 52		10 20	10 23	10 29	10 35	10 40	11 15	11 21	11 35	11 39		12 14	11 44	12 20	12 42
Salwick	d																								
Kirkham & Wesham	d		00 21			08 58		09 29				10 29	10 33					11 31					11 53	12 29	12 52
Moss Side	d					09 06							10 39										12 01		12 58
Lytham	d					09 10							10 43										12 05		13 02
Ansdell & Fairhaven	d					09 13							10 46										12 08		13 05
St Annes-on-the-Sea	d					09 17							10 50										12 12		13 09
Squires Gate	d					09 20							10 54										12 15		13 13
Blackpool Pleasure Beach	d					09 23							10 56										12 18		13 15
Blackpool South	a					09 26							10 59										12 21		13 18
Poulton-le-Fylde	d	23p52	00 29				09 15	09 37	09 57	10 09		10 37		10 46	10 52	10 57	11 32	11 39	11 52	11 57		12 31		12 37	
Layton	d		00 34					09 42				10 42						11 44						12 42	
Blackpool North	a	00 02	00 38	02 10	07 35		09 23	09 47	10 07	10 18		10 47		10 53	11 01	11 09	11 39	11 49	12 01	12 07		12 38		12 47	

A From Manchester Airport
B From Wigan North Western
C From York
D From Manchester Victoria
E From Liverpool Lime Street

Table 97

Sundays
from 1 April

Colne, Burnley, Accrington and Blackburn - Preston - Blackpool

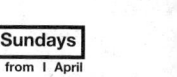

Network Diagram - see first Page of Table 97

		TP ◇1 A	NT B	NT C	NT D	TP ◇1 A	NT B	NT C	NT	NT D	NT	TP ◇1 A	NT B	NT C	NT D	TP ◇1 A	NT B	NT C	NT	NT D	NT	TP ◇1 A	NT B
Colne	d										13 35										15 35		
Nelson	d										13 40										15 40		
Brierfield	d										13 43										15 43		
Burnley Central	d										13 48										15 48		
Burnley Barracks	d										13 50										15 50		
Leeds 10 41	d			11 35				12 35						13 35				14 35					
Burnley Manchester Road 41	d			12 39				13 39						14 39				15 39					
Rose Grove	d										13 53										15 53		
Hapton	d										13 56										15 56		
Huncoat	d										13 59										15 59		
Accrington	d			12 47				13 47			14 04			14 47				15 47			16 04		
Church & Oswaldtwistle	d										14 06										16 06		
Rishton	d										14 09										16 09		
Blackburn	a			12 55				13 55			14 14			14 55				15 55			16 14		
Clitheroe 94	d																						
Blackburn	d			12 56				13 56			14 16			14 56				15 56			16 16		
Mill Hill (Lancashire)	d										14 19										16 19		
Cherry Tree	d										14 21										16 21		
Pleasington	d										14 23										16 23		
Bamber Bridge	d										14 30										16 30		
Lostock Hall	d										14 33										16 33		
Preston 8	a			13 13				14 13			14 41			15 13				16 13			16 41		
	d	12 35	12 39	13 14	13 20	13 35	13 39	14 14	13 44	14 20	14 42	14 35	14 39	15 14	15 20	15 35	15 39	16 14	15 44	16 20	16 41	16 35	16 39
Salwick	d																						
Kirkham & Wesham	d				13 29				13 53	14 29	14 52				15 29				15 53	16 29	16 52		
Moss Side	d								14 01		14 59								16 01		16 58		
Lytham	d								14 05		15 03								16 05		17 02		
Ansdell & Fairhaven	d								14 08		15 06								16 08		17 05		
St Annes-on-the-Sea	d								14 12		15 10								16 12		17 09		
Squires Gate	d								14 15		15 13								16 15		17 13		
Blackpool Pleasure Beach	d								14 18		15 16								16 18		17 15		
Blackpool South	a								14 21		15 19								16 21		17 18		
Poulton-le-Fylde	d	12 52	12 57	13 31	13 37	13 52	13 57	14 30		14 37		14 52	14 57	15 32	15 37	15 52	15 57	16 31		16 37		16 52	16 57
Layton	d				13 42					14 42					15 43					16 42			
Blackpool North	a	13 01	13 07	13 38	13 47	14 01	14 07	14 38		14 47		15 01	15 07	15 39	15 48	16 01	16 07	16 38		16 47		17 01	17 07

		NT C	NT D	TP ◇1 A	NT B	NT C	NT	NT D	NT	TP ◇1 A	NT B	NT C	NT D	TP ◇1 A	NT B	NT C	NT	NT D	NT	TP ◇1 A	NT B	NT E 🚲
Colne	d								17 35										19 35			
Nelson	d								17 40										19 40			
Brierfield	d								17 43										19 43			
Burnley Central	d								17 48										19 48			
Burnley Barracks	d								17 50										19 50			
Leeds 10 41	d	15 35				16 35						17 35				18 35						
Burnley Manchester Road 41	d	16 39				17 39						18 39				19 39						
Rose Grove	d								17 53										19 53			
Hapton	d								17 56										19 56			
Huncoat	d								17 59										19 59			
Accrington	d	16 47				17 47			18 04			18 47				19 47			20 04			
Church & Oswaldtwistle	d								18 06										20 06			
Rishton	d								18 09										20 09			
Blackburn	a	16 55				17 55			18 14			18 55				19 56			20 14			
Clitheroe 94	d																					19 57
Blackburn	d	16 56				17 56			18 16			18 56				19 57			20 16			20 25
Mill Hill (Lancashire)	d								18 19										20 19			
Cherry Tree	d								18 21										20 21			
Pleasington	d								18 23										20 23			
Bamber Bridge	d								18 30										20 30			20 34
Lostock Hall	d								18 33										20 33			20 38
Preston 8	a	17 13				18 13			18 41			19 13				20 14			20 41			20 47
	d	17 14	17 20	17 35	17 39	18 14	17 44	18 20	18 41	18 35	18 39	19 14	19 21	19 35	19 39	20 15	19 44	20 21	20 41	20 35	20 39	20 49
Salwick	d																					
Kirkham & Wesham	d		17 29				17 53	18 29	18 52				19 30				19 53	20 30	20 52			20 59
Moss Side	d						18 01		18 58								20 01		20 58			
Lytham	d						18 05		19 02								20 05		21 02			
Ansdell & Fairhaven	d						18 08		19 05								20 08		21 05			
St Annes-on-the-Sea	d						18 12		19 09								20 12		21 09			
Squires Gate	d						18 15		19 13								20 15		21 13			
Blackpool Pleasure Beach	d						18 18		19 15								20 18		21 15			
Blackpool South	a						18 21		19 18								20 21		21 18			
Poulton-le-Fylde	d	17 31	17 37	17 52	17 57	18 31		18 37		18 52	18 57	19 31	19 38	19 52	19 57	20 32		20 38		20 52	20 57	21 07
Layton	d		17 42					18 42					19 42					20 43				
Blackpool North	a	17 38	17 47	18 01	18 07	18 38		18 47		19 01	19 07	19 38	19 47	20 01	20 07	20 39		20 48		21 01	21 07	21 16

A From Manchester Airport
B From Liverpool Lime Street
C From York
D From Manchester Victoria
E From Carlisle

Sundays
from 1 April

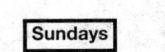

Colne, Burnley, Accrington and Blackburn - Preston - Blackpool

Network Diagram - see first Page of Table 97

		NT	NT	TP	NT	NT	NT	NT	TP	NT	NT	TP
				◇1					◇1			◇1
		A	B	C	D	A		B	C	D	D	C
Colne	d						21 35					
Nelson	d						21 40					
Brierfield	d						21 43					
Burnley Central	d						21 48					
Burnley Barracks	d						21 50					
Leeds 10 41	d	19 35				20 35						
Burnley Manchester Road 41	d	20 39				21 39						
Rose Grove	d						21 53					
Hapton	d						21 56					
Huncoat	d						21 59					
Accrington	d	20 47				21 47	22 04					
Church & Oswaldtwistle	d						22 06					
Rishton	d						22 09					
Blackburn	a	20 55				21 55	22 14					
Clitheroe 94	d											
Blackburn	d	20 56				21 56	22 16					
Mill Hill (Lancashire)	d						22 19					
Cherry Tree	d						22 21					
Pleasington	d						22 23					
Bamber Bridge	d						22 30					
Lostock Hall	d						22 33					
Preston 8	a	21 13				22 13	22 44					
	d	21 14	21 20	21 35	21 39	22 14		22 20	22 29	22 39	23 39	23 47
Salwick	d											
Kirkham & Wesham	d		21 29					22 29				23 56
Moss Side	d											
Lytham	d											
Ansdell & Fairhaven	d											
St Annes-on-the-Sea	d											
Squires Gate	d											
Blackpool Pleasure Beach	d											
Blackpool South	a											
Poulton-le-Fylde	d	21 31	21 37	21 52	21 57	22 31		22 37	22 46	22 57	23 56	00 05
Layton	d		21 42					22 42				
Blackpool North	a	21 38	21 47	22 01	22 07	22 38		22 47	22 55	23 07	00 05	00 14

A From York
B From Manchester Victoria
C From Manchester Airport
D From Liverpool Lime Street

Table 98

Mondays to Fridays

Lancaster - Morecambe and Heysham

Network Diagram - see first Page of Table 97

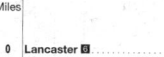

Miles			TP ■1	NT	NT	NT	NT	NT	NT	NT	NT	NT	NT	NT	NT	NT	NT	NT	NT	NT	NT	NT	NT
0	**Lancaster** ■6	82 d	05 46	06 38	07 25	07 58	08 35	09 15	10 04	10 19	11 22	12 02	12 28	13 44	14 27	15 25	16 03	16 19	16 49	17 38	18 33	18 49	19 40
2½	Bare Lane	d	05 52	06 44	07 31	08 04	08 41	09 21	10 10	10 27	11 28	12 08	12 34	13 50	14 33	15 31	16 09	16 26	16 55	17 44	18 39	18 55	19 46
4¼	**Morecambe**	a	05 56	06 49	07 36	08 09	08 46	09 26	10 15	10 33	11 33	12 13	12 39	13 55	14 38	15 36	16 13	16 30	17 00	17 49	18 44	19 01	19 50
—		d											12 42										
8½	**Heysham Port**	a											12 57										

		NT	NT	NT	NT
Lancaster ■6	82 d	20 22	21 03	22 06	22 35
Bare Lane	d	20 28	21 09	22 12	22 41
Morecambe	a	20 32	21 13	22 16	22 45
	d				
Heysham Port	a				

Saturdays

		TP ■1	NT	NT	NT	NT	NT	NT	NT	NT	NT	NT	NT	NT	NT	NT	NT	NT	NT	NT	NT	NT	NT B
Lancaster ■6	82 d	05 46	06 38	07 25	07 57	08 35	09 15	10 05	10 19	11 23	12 02	12 25	13 24	14 27	15 25	15 49	16 03	17 04	17 37	18 21	18 47	19 40	20 22
Bare Lane	d	05 52	06 44	07 31	08 03	08 41	09 21	10 11	10 26	11 29	12 08	12 31	13 30	14 33	15 31	15 56	16 09	17 10	17 43	18 27	18 53	19 46	20 28
Morecambe	a	05 56	06 49	07 36	08 08	08 46	09 26	10 16	10 32	11 34	12 13	12 36	13 35	14 38	15 36	16 02	16 14	17 15	17 48	18 32	18 59	19 50	20 32
	d											12 39											
Heysham Port	a											12 54											

		NT C	NT D	NT C	NT C	NT D
Lancaster ■6	82 d	21 03	21 55	22 06	22 35	22 55
Bare Lane	d	21 09	22 10	22 12	22 41	23 10
Morecambe	a	21 13	22 20	22 16	22 46	23 20
	d					
Heysham Port	a					

Sundays
until 1 January

		NT	NT	NT	NT	NT	NT	NT	NT
Lancaster ■6	82 d	10 45	12 05	13 01	14 27	15 05	16 51	19 23	21 18
Bare Lane	d	10 51	12 11	13 07	14 34	15 11	16 56	19 29	21 24
Morecambe	a	10 57	12 16	13 13	14 38	15 16	17 03	19 35	21 29
	d								
Heysham Port	a								

Sundays
8 January to 12 February

		NT	NT	NT	NT	NT	NT	NT
Lancaster ■6	82 d	12 05	13 01	14 27	15 05	16 51	19 18	21 18
Bare Lane	d	12 11	13 07	14 34	15 11	16 56	19 25	21 24
Morecambe	a	12 16	13 13	14 38	15 16	17 03	19 31	21 29
	d							
Heysham Port	a							

Sundays
19 February to 25 March

		NT	NT	NT	NT	NT	NT	NT
Lancaster ■6	82 d	12 05	13 01	14 27	15 05	16 51	19 23	21 18
Bare Lane	d	12 11	13 07	14 34	15 11	16 56	19 29	21 24
Morecambe	a	12 16	13 13	14 38	15 16	17 03	19 35	21 29
	d							
Heysham Port	a							

Sundays
from 1 April

		NT	NT	NT	NT	NT	NT
Lancaster ■6	82 d	13 01	14 27	15 05	16 51	19 23	21 18
Bare Lane	d	13 07	14 34	15 11	16 56	19 29	21 24
Morecambe	a	13 13	14 38	15 16	17 03	19 35	21 29
	d						
Heysham Port	a						

B until 24 March
C Runs until 31 December
D from 7 January

Table 98

Mondays to Fridays

Heysham and Morecambe - Lancaster

Network Diagram - see first Page of Table 97

Miles			TP 1	NT	NT	NT	NT	NT	NT	NT	NT
0	Heysham Port	d									
4¼	Morecambe	a									
—		d	05 59	06 19	07 03	07 42	08 11	08 51	09 32	10 34	10 55
6	Bare Lane	d	06a03	06 23	07 07	07 46	08 15	08 55	09 36	10 38	10 59
8½	Lancaster 6	82 a		06 30	07 14	07 53	08 21	09 03	09 43	10 45	11 06

Miles			NT	NT	NT	NT	NT	NT	NT	NT	NT	NT	NT	NT
0	Heysham Port	d			13 15									
4¼	Morecambe	a			13 25									
—		d	11 39	12 32	13 29	13 58	14 42	15 45	16 19	16 34	17 03	17 56	19 00	19 08
6	Bare Lane	d	11 43	12 36	13 36	14 02	14 46	15 49	16a23	16 38	17 07	18 00	19 04	19 12
8½	Lancaster 6	82 a	11 50	12 43	13 42	14 09	14 53	15 56		16 45	17 14	18 07	19 11	19 19

		NT	NT	NT	NT	NT
Heysham Port	d					
Morecambe	a					
	d	19 55	20 40	21 36	22 20	22 55
Bare Lane	d	19 59	20 44	21 40	22 24	22 59
Lancaster 6	82 a	20 06	20 51	21 47	22 31	23 05

Saturdays

		TP 1	NT	NT	NT	NT	NT	NT	NT	NT
Heysham Port	d									
Morecambe	a									
	d	05 59	06 19	07 03	07 38	08 11	08 51	09 41	10 34	10 54
Bare Lane	d	06a03	06 23	07 07	07 42	08 15	08 55	09 45	10 38	10 58
Lancaster 6	82 a		06 30	07 14	07 49	08 22	09 03	09 52	10 45	11 05

		NT	NT	NT	NT	NT	NT	NT	NT	NT	NT	NT	NT	NT
Heysham Port	d			13 15										
Morecambe	a			13 25										
	d	11 40	12 32	13 29	13 58	14 42	15 44	16 19	16 40	17 20	17 56	18 58	19 09	19 55
Bare Lane	d	11 44	12 36	13 36	14 02	14 46	15 48	16 24	16 44	17 24	18 00	19 02	19 13	19 59
Lancaster 6	82 a	11 51	12 43	13 42	14 09	14 53	15 55	16 30	16 50	17 31	18 07	19 09	19 20	20 06

		NT A	NT B	NT A	NT B	NT B	NT A
Heysham Port	d						
Morecambe	a						
	d	20 25	20 40	21 25	21 36	22 20	22 25
Bare Lane	d	20 35	20 44	21 35	21 40	22 24	22 35
Lancaster 6	82 a	20 51	20 51	21 50	21 47	22 31	22 50

Sundays

until 1 January

		NT	NT	NT	NT	NT	NT	NT	NT
Heysham Port	d								
Morecambe	a								
	d	11 20	12 20	13 23	14 46	15 21	17 45	20 00	21 41
Bare Lane	d	11 24	12 24	13 27	14a50	15 25	17 49	20 04	21 45
Lancaster 6	82 a	11 31	12 30	13 34		15 32	17 55	20 11	21 51

Sundays

8 January to 12 February

		NT	NT	NT	NT	NT	NT	NT	NT
Heysham Port	d								
Morecambe	a								
	d	11 43	12 20	13 23	14 46	15 21	17 45	20 00	21 41
Bare Lane	d	11 47	12 24	13 27	14a50	15 25	17 49	20 04	21 45
Lancaster 6	82 a	11 54	12 30	13 34		15 32	17 55	20 11	21 51

Sundays

19 February to 25 March

		NT	NT	NT	NT	NT	NT	NT	NT
Heysham Port	d								
Morecambe	a								
	d	11 43	12 20	13 23	14 46	15 21	17 45	20 00	21 41
Bare Lane	d	11 47	12 24	13 27	14a50	15 25	17 49	20 04	21 45
Lancaster 6	82 a	11 54	12 30	13 34		15 32	17 55	20 11	21 51

Sundays

from 1 April

		NT	NT	NT	NT	NT	NT	NT	NT
Heysham Port	d								
Morecambe	a								
	d	11 20	12 31	13 23	14 46	15 21	17 45	20 00	21 41
Bare Lane	d	11 24	12 35	13 27	14a50	15 25	17 49	20 04	21 45
Lancaster 6	82 a	11 31	12 41	13 34		15 32	17 55	20 11	21 51

A from 7 January

B Runs until 31 December

Table 98A

Mondays to Fridays

To and from The Isle of Man via Heysham and Liverpool

One Class only on ship

		VT	VT	VT	VT	VT
					TX	
		A	B		C	D
Liverpool Landing Stage	⛴ d		11 15		18 45	19 00
Heysham Port	⛴ d	02 15		14 15		
Douglas (Isle of Man)	⛴ a	05 45	14 00	17 45	21 30	21 45

Saturdays

		VT	VT	VT	VT	VT
		E	F	G	H	G
Liverpool Landing Stage	⛴ d		11 15		18 45	19 00
Heysham Port	⛴ d	02 15		14 15		
Douglas (Isle of Man)	⛴ a	05 45	14 00	17 45	21 30	21 45

Sundays

		VT	VT	VT	VT
		I	J	K	L
Liverpool Landing Stage	⛴ d		14 00		19 00
Heysham Port	⛴ d	02 15		14 15	
Douglas (Isle of Man)	⛴ a	05 45	16 45	17 45	21 45

Mondays to Fridays

		VT	VT	VT	VT	VT
		M		N	D	O
Douglas (Isle of Man)	⛴ d	07 30	08 15	08 45	15 00	19 45
Heysham Port	⛴ a		11 45	12 15		23 15
Liverpool Landing Stage	⛴ a	10 15			17 45	

Saturdays

		VT	VT	VT	VT	VT
		G	P	G	F	Q
Douglas (Isle of Man)	⛴ d	07 30	08 00	08 45	15 00	20 00
Heysham Port	⛴ a			12 15		23 30
Liverpool Landing Stage	⛴ a	10 15	10 45		17 45	

Sundays

		VT	VT	VT	VT
		R	K	L	S
Douglas (Isle of Man)	⛴ d	07 30	08 45	15 00	19 45
Heysham Port	⛴ a		12 15		23 15
Liverpool Landing Stage	⛴ a	10 15		17 45	

A until 2 March, and then from 26 March
B from 2 January until 23 March, MX from 27 March, (not 30 March), 9 April, and then from 30 April until 7 May
C from 2 January
D from 26 March, not 6 April
E until 25 February and then from 24 March
F from 31 March
G from 24 March
H from 7 January
I 11 December
J from 4 March until 18 March
K from 25 March
L from 25 March
M 23 March, 5, 6, 9, 10, 12, 13, 20, 27, 30, and also 04, 07, 11 May
N until 30 December
O not from 2 March until 22 March
P 3 to 17 March
Q from 14 January until 25 February, not 11 February, also 24 and 31 March, 5 May
R 15 April
S until 26 February and then from 25 March

Table 99

Mondays to Saturdays

Ormskirk - Preston

Network Diagram - see first Page of Table 97

Miles			NT	NT	NT	NT	NT	NT	NT	NT	NT		NT	NT	NT
0	**Ormskirk**	d	06 58	08 06	09 17	10 36	12 17	13 36	15 17	16 36	17 52		19 06	20 47	22 47
2½	Burscough Junction	d	07 02	08 10	09 21	10 40	12 21	13 40	15 21	16 40	17 56		19 10	20 51	22 51
5½	Rufford	d	07 07	08 15	09 25	10 45	12 25	13 45	15 25	16 45	18 01		19 15	20 55	22 55
8	Croston	d	07 11	08 19	09 30	10 49	12 30	13 50	15 30	16 49	18 06		19 19	21 00	23 00
15	**Preston** 8	a	07 29	08 36	09 47	11 08	12 47	14 08	15 47	17 08	18 23		19 38	21 17	23 17

For connections from Liverpool Central please refer to Table 103

No Sunday Service

Table 99

Mondays to Saturdays

Preston - Ormskirk

Network Diagram - see first Page of Table 97

Miles			NT	NT	NT	NT	NT	NT	NT	NT	NT		NT	NT	NT SX	NT SO
0	**Preston** 8	d	06 25	07 33	08 41	09 59	11 29	12 59	14 29	15 59	17 10		18 34	20 08	22 03	22 08
7	Croston	d	06 36	07 45	08 52	10 11	11 41	13 11	14 41	16 11	17 22		18 47	20 19	22 15	22 20
9½	Rufford	d	06 41	07 50	08 57	10 16	11 46	13 16	14 46	16 16	17 27		18 51	20 24	22 19	22 24
12½	Burscough Junction	d	06 46	07 55	09 02	10 21	11 51	13 21	14 51	16 21	17 32		18 56	20 29	22 24	22 29
15	**Ormskirk**	a	06 55	08 04	09 11	10 30	12 00	13 30	15 00	16 30	17 41		19 05	20 38	22 33	22 38

For connections to Liverpool Central please refer to Table 103

No Sunday Service

Barrow-in-Furness - Whitehaven and Carlisle

Network Diagram - see first Page of Table 97

Miles			NT	NT	NT	NT	NT	NT	NT	NT	NT	NT	NT	NT	NT	NT	NT	NT	NT	NT	NT
—	Lancaster 6	82 d			05 42				08 58					15 34		16 55					
0	**Barrow-in-Furness**	d		06 00	06 50	08 01		09 10	10 11	11 22	12 31	13 31	14 54	16 41	17 28	18 05		19 35		21 25	
6	Askam	d		06 10	07 00	08 11		09 20	10 21	11 32	12 41	13 41	15 04	16 51	17 40	18 15		19 45		21 35	
9¼	Kirkby-in-Furness	d		06 14	07x04	08x15		09x24	10x25	11x36	12x45	13x45	15x08	16x55	17x44	18x19		19x49		21x39	
11¼	Foxfield	d		06x18	07x08	08x18		09x27	10x29	11x39	12x48	13x48	15x11	16x58	17x48	18x22		19x52		21x42	
13½	Green Road	d		06x22	07x12	08x22		09x31	10x32	11x43	12x52	13x52	15x15	17x02	17x51	18x26		19x56		21x46	
16	Millom	a		06 29	07 19	08 28		09 37	10 39	11 49	12 58	13 58	15 21	17 08	17 58	18 35		20 05		21 55	
—		d		06 29	07 19	08 29		09 38	10 39	11 49	12 59	13 58	15 22	17 09	17 58						
19	Silecroft	d		06x34	07x24			09x42	10x44	11x54	13x03	14x03	15x26	17x13	18x03						
24½	Bootle	d		06x41	07x31			09x49	10x50	12x00	13x10	14x09	15x33	17x20	18x09						
29¼	Ravenglass for Eskdale	d		06 47	07 37	08 44		09 55	10 56	12 06	13 15	14 15	15 39	17 26	18 15						
31	Drigg	d		06x51	07x41			09x58	10x59	12x09	13x18	14x18	15x42	17x29	18x18						
33¼	Seascale	d		06x54	07x44	08x49		10x01	11x02	12x12	13x21	14x21	15x45	17x32	18x21						
35	Sellafield	d		07 02	07 51	08a58		10 10	11 07	12 18	13 28	14 27	15 51	17 39	18 27						
37	Braystones	d		07x05	07x54							14x31			18x31						
38¼	Nethertown	d		07x08	07x57							14x33			18x33						
41¼	St Bees	d		07 12	08 01			10 20	11 20	12 27	13 38	14 38	16 00	17 49	18 45						
44¾	Corkickle	d		07x17	08x06			10x25	11x25	12x32	13x43	14x43	16x05	17x54	18x50						
45¾	**Whitehaven**	a		07 20	08 10			10 27	11 27	12 36	13 45	14 46	16 09	17 57	18 53						
—		d	06 30	07 25	08 11		09 02	10 28	11 29	12 37	13 47	14 48	16 11	17 58	18 55		19 31		20 30		21 50
47	Parton	d	06x33	07x29	08x15		09x05	10x31	11x32	12x41	13x50	14x51	16x15	18x02	18x58		19x34		20x33		21x53
50½	Harrington	d	06x41	07x37	08x23		09x13	10x40	11x40	12x49	13x58	14x59	16x23	18x10	19x06		19x42		20x41		22x01
52¼	**Workington**	d	06 48	07 43	08 29		09 20	10 46	11 47	12 55	14 05	15 06	16 29	18 16	19 12		19 49		20 48		22a10
56	Flimby	d	06x52	07x48	08x34		09x24	10x50	11x51	13x00	14x09	15x10	16x34	18x21	19x17		19x53		20x52		
58	Maryport	d	06 56	07 51	08 37		09 28	10 54	11 55	13 03	14 13	15 14	16 37	18 26	19 20		19 57		20 56		
65½	Aspatria	d	07x05	08x01	08x47		09x37	11x03	12x04	13x13	14x22	15x23	16x47	18x36	19x30		20x06		21x05		
71¾	Wigton	d	07 15	08 11	08 57		09 47	11 13	12 14	13 23	14 32	15 33	16 57	18 46	19 40		20 16		21 15		
81¼	Dalston	d	07x24	08x19	09x05		09x56	11x22	12x23	13x31	14x41	15x42	17x05	18x54	19x48		20x25		21x24		
85¼	**Carlisle** 8	a	07 38	08 35	09 22		10 13	11 37	12 39	13 47	14 57	15 58	17 21	19 08	20 04		20 41		21 39		

Saturdays

		NT	NT	NT	NT	NT	NT	NT	NT	NT	NT	NT	NT	NT	NT	NT	NT	NT	NT	NT
Lancaster 6	82 d							09 03			11 28		13 32	14 22		17 00				
Barrow-in-Furness	d		06 00	07 05	08 01		09 07	10 11	11 22		12 34	13 50	14 50	15 33	17 25	18 10		19 35		21 25
Askam	d		06 10	07 15	08 11		09 17	10 21	11 32		12 44	14 00	15 00	15 43	17 35	18 20		19 45		21 35
Kirkby-in-Furness	d		06x14	07x19	08x15		09x21	10x25	11x36		12x48	14x04	15x04	15x47	17x39	18x24		19x49		21x39
Foxfield	d		06x17	07x23	08x18		09x24	10x28	11x39		12x51	14x07	15x07	15x50	17x42	18x27		19x52		21x42
Green Road	d		06x21	07x27	08x22		09x28	10x32	11x43		12x55	14x11	15x11	15x54	17x46	18x31		19x56		21x46
Millom	a		06 25	07 34	08 28		09 34	10 38	11 49		13 01	14 17	15 17	16 00	17 52	18 40		20 05		21 55
	d		06 26	07 34	08 29		09 35	10 39	11 50		13 02	14 18	15 18	16 01	17 53					
Silecroft	d		06x30	07x39			09x39	10x43	11x54		13x06	14x22	15x22	16x05	17x57					
Bootle	d		06x37	07x46			09x46	10x50	12x01		13x13	14x29	15x29	16x12	18x04					
Ravenglass for Eskdale	d		06 42	07 52	08 44		09 52	10 56	12 07		13 19	14 35	15 35	16 18	18 10					
Drigg	d		06x45	07x56			09x55	10x59	12x10		13x22	14x38	15x38	16x21	18x13					
Seascale	d		06x50	07x59	08x49		09x58	11x04	12x13		13x25	14x41	15x41	16x24	18x16					
Sellafield	d		06 55	08 06	08a58		10 04	11 10	12 19		13 31	14 47	15 51	16 30	18 22					
Braystones	d		06x59	08x09										16x34	18x26					
Nethertown	d		07x01	08x12										16x36	18x28					
St Bees	d		07 06	08 16			10 14	11 19	12 29		13 40	14 56	16 01	16 46	18 33					
Corkickle	d		07x11	08x21			10x19	11x24	12x34		13x45	15x01	16x06	16x51	18x38					
Whitehaven	a		07 15	08 25			10 22	11 27	12 41		13 49	15 05	16 09	16 54	18 41					
	d	06 30	07 19	08 26		09 15	10 24	11 29		12 54	13 50	15 06	16 11	16 56	18 43		19 31		20 30	
Parton	d	06x33	07x23	08x30		09x18	10x27	11x32		12x57	13x54	15x10	16x15	17x00	18x46		19x34		20x33	
Harrington	d	06x41	07x31	08x38		09x26	10x35	11x40		13x05	14x02	15x18	16x23	17x08	18x54		19x42		20x41	
Workington	d	06 48	07 37	08 44		09 33	10 42	11 47		13 12	14 09	15 24	16 29	17 14	19 01		19 49		20 48	
Flimby	d	06x52	07x42	08x49		09x37	10x46	11x51		13x16	14x13	15x29	16x34	17x19	19x05		19x53		20x52	
Maryport	d	06 56	07 45	08 52		09 41	10 50	11 55		13 20	14 17	15 32	16 37	17 22	19 09		19 57		20 56	
Aspatria	d	07x05	07x55	09x02		09x50	10x59	12x04		13x29	14x26	15x42	16x47	17x32	19x18		20x06		21x05	
Wigton	d	07 15	08 05	09 12		10 00	11 09	12 14		13 39	14 36	15 52	16 57	17 42	19 28		20 16		21 15	
Dalston	d	07x24	08x13	09x20		10x08	11x18	12x23		13x48	14x45	16x00	17x05	17x50	19x37		20x25		21x24	
Carlisle 8	a	07 38	08 27	09 36		10 24	11 34	12 39		14 04	15 01	16 16	17 21	18 06	19 53		20 41		21 39	

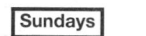

Sundays

		NT	NT	NT
Lancaster 6	82 d			
Barrow-in-Furness	d			
Askam	d			
Kirkby-in-Furness	d			
Foxfield	d			
Green Road	d			
Millom	a			
	d			
Silecroft	d			
Bootle	d			
Ravenglass for Eskdale	d			
Drigg	d			
Seascale	d			
Sellafield	d			
Braystones	d			
Nethertown	d			
St Bees	d			
Corkickle	d			
Whitehaven	a			
	d	12 57	16 28	20 28
Parton	d	13x00	16x31	20x31
Harrington	d	13x08	16x39	20x39
Workington	d	13 15	16 46	20 46
Flimby	d	13x19	16x50	20x50
Maryport	d	13 23	16 54	20 54
Aspatria	d	13x32	17x03	21x03
Wigton	d	13 42	17 13	21 13
Dalston	d	13x50	17x21	21x21
Carlisle 8	a	14 07	17 37	21 38

No Sunday Service Barrow-in-Furness to Whitehaven

Carlisle and Whitehaven - Barrow-in-Furness

Network Diagram - see first Page of Table 97

Mondays to Fridays

Miles			NT	NT	NT	NT	NT	NT	NT	NT	NT		NT	NT	NT	NT	NT	NT	NT	NT	NT		NT	NT	
0	**Carlisle** 8	d				07 44		08 44	09 40	10 43	11 50		12 47	14 20	15 12	16 31	17 27	18 13	19 15		20 33		21 50		
4	Dalston	d				07x52		08x52	09x48	10x51	11x58		12x55	14x28	15x20	16x39	17x35	18x21	19x23		20x41		21x58		
11½	Wigton	d				08 01		09 01	09 57	11 00	12 07		13 04	14 37	15 29	16 48	17 44	18 30	19 32		20 50		22 07		
19¾	Aspatria	d				08x11		09x11	10x07	11x10	12x17		13x14	14x47	15x39	16x58	17x54	18x40	19x42		21x00		22x17		
27¼	Maryport	d		06 00		08 21		09 21	10 17	11 20	12 27		13 24	14 57	15 49	17 08	18 04	18 50	19 52		21 10		22 27		
29¼	Flimby	d		06x03		08x24		09x24	10x20	11x23	12x30		13x27	15x00	15x52	17x11	18x07	18x53	19x55		21x13		22x30		
33	**Workington**	d		06 09		08 33		09 33	10 29	11 32	12 39		13 36	15 09	16 01	17 20	18 16	19 02	20 04		21 22		22 39		
34¾	Harrington	d		06x13		08x36		09x36	10x32	11x35	12x42		13x39	15x12	16x04	17x23	18x19	19x05	20x07		21x25		22x42		
38¼	Parton	d		06x21		08x45		09x45	10x42	11x44	12x52		13x48	15x21	16x13	17x32	18x28	19x14	20x16		21x34		22x51		
39½	**Whitehaven**	a		06 26		08 54		09 49	10 47	11 50	13 00		13 54	15 27	16 19	17 38	18 34	19 23	20 25		21 43		23 00		
—		d		06 28	07 28			09 51	10 48	11 51			13 56	15 28	16 20	17 39	18 35								
40½	Corkickle	d		06x30	07x30			09x53	10x50	11x53			13x58	15x30	16x22	17x41	18x37								
44	St Bees	d		06 35	07 35			09 58	10 56	11 59			14 03	15 36	16 28	17 50	18 43								
47	Nethertown	d		06x39						12x03				15x40		17x54									
48¼	Braystones	d		06x42						12x05				15x42		17x57									
50¼	Sellafield	d		06 48	07 48		09 07	10 09	11 08	12 11			14 14	15 54	16 42	18 03	18 54								
52	Seascale	d		06x51	07x51		09x10	10x14	11x11	12x14			14x17	15x57	16x45	18x07	18x57								
54¼	Drigg	d		06x54	07x54		09x13	10x17	11x14	12x17			14x20	16x01	16x49	18x11	19x00								
56	Ravenglass for Eskdale	d		06 57	07 57		09 16	10 20	11 18	12 21			14 23	16 04	16 52	18 14	19 03								
60¾	Bootle	d		07x03	08x03		09x22	10x26	11x23	12x26			14x29	16x10	16x58	18x20	19x09								
66¼	Silecroft	d		07x09	08x09		09x28	10x32	11x30	12x33			14x35	16x17	17x05	18x27	19x15								
69¼	Millom	a		07 16	08 14		09 35	10 39	11 37	12 40			14 42	16 24	17 12	18 34	19 22								
—		d	06 10	07 17	08 15		09 36	10 40	11 37	12 40			14 43	16 25	17 13	18 34	19 23			20 12				22 02	
71¾	Green Road	d	06x14	07x21	08x19		09x40	10x44	11x41	12x44			14x47	16x29	17x17	18x39	19x27			20x16				22x06	
73¾	Foxfield	d	06x17	07x24	08x22		09x43	10x47	11x44	12x47			14x50	16x33	17x21	18x43	19x30			20x19				22x09	
76	Kirkby-in-Furness	d	06x21	07x28	08x26		09x47	10x51	11x48	12x51			14x54	16x38	17x26	18x47	19x34			20x23				22x13	
79¼	Askam	d	06 26	07 33	08 31		09 52	10 56	11 53	12 56			14 59	16 43	17 31	18 52	19 39			20 28				22 18	
85¼	**Barrow-in-Furness**	a	06 42	07 49	08 49		10 07	11 14	12 09	13 12			15 17	17 01	17 47	19 10	19 57			20 45				22 35	
—	Lancaster 6 82	a	08 04	09 07			11 20		13 16						19 05										

Saturdays

		NT	NT	NT	NT	NT	NT	NT	NT	NT		NT	NT	NT	NT	NT	NT	NT	NT	NT		NT	NT		
Carlisle 8	d			07 44		08 37	09 40	10 43	11 39			12 48	14 21	15 25	16 30	17 40	18 15	19 00	20 05			21 45			
Dalston	d			07x52		08x45	09x48	10x51	11x47			12x56	14x29	15x33	16x38	17x48	18 24	19x08	20x13			21x53			
Wigton	d			08 01		08 54	09 57	11 00	11 56			13 05	14 38	15 42	16 47	17 57	18 33	19 17	20 22			22 02			
Aspatria	d			08x11		09x04	10x07	11x10	12x06			13x15	14x48	15x52	16x57	18x07	18 43	19x27	20x32			22x12			
Maryport	d		06 26	08 21		09 14	10 17	11 20	12 16			13 25	14 58	16 02	17 07	18 17	18 54	19 37	20 42			22 22			
Flimby	d		06x29	08x24		09x17	10x20	11x23	12x19			13x28	15x01	16x05	17x10	18x20	18 57	19x40	20x45			22x25			
Workington	d		06 37	08 33		09 26	10 29	11 32	12 28			13 37	15 10	16 14	17 19	18 29	19 06	19 49	20 54			22 34			
Harrington	d		06x41	08x36		09x29	10x32	11x35	12x31			13x40	15x14	16x18	17x23	18x32	19 10	19x52	20x57			22x37			
Parton	d		06x49	08x45		09x38	10x40	11x44	12x40			13x49	15x22	16x26	17x31	18x41	19x19	20x01	21x06			22x46			
Whitehaven	a		06 55	08 54		09 44	10 47	11 50	12 49			13 55	15 28	16 32	17 37	18 47	19 28	20 10	21 15			22 55			
	d		06 57			09 45	10 48	11 51		12 54		13 57	15 30	16 34	17 39	18 48									
Corkickle	d		06x59			09x47	10x50	11x53		12x56		13x59	15x32	16x36	17x41	18x50									
St Bees	d		07 10			09 53	10 56	11 59		13 01		14 04	15 37	16 43	17 46	18 56									
Nethertown	d		07x14				11x00						15x41		17x50										
Braystones	d		07x16				11x02						15x44		17x53										
Sellafield	d		07 22		09 07	10 03	11 08	12 10		13 12		14 15	15 50	16 53	17 59	19 06									
Seascale	d		07x25		09x10	10x06	11x11	12x13		13x15		14x18	15x53	16x56	18x02	19x09									
Drigg	d		07x28		09x13	10x09	11x14	12x16		13x18		14x21	15x56	16x59	18x05	19x12									
Ravenglass for Eskdale	d		07 32		09 16	10 13	11 18	12 20		13 21		14 24	15 59	17 03	18 08	19 16									
Bootle	d		07x37		09x22	10x18	11x23	12x25		13x27		14x30	16x05	17x08	18x14	19x21									
Silecroft	d		07x44		09x28	10x25	11x30	12x32		13x33		14x36	16x11	17x15	18x20	19x28									
Millom	a		07 51		09 35	10 32	11 37	12 39		13 40		14 43	16 18	17 22	18 27	19 35									
	d	06 10	07 51		09 36	10 32	11 37	12 39		13 41		14 44	16 19	17 22	18 28	19 36				20 12			22 02		
Green Road	d	06x14	07x55		09x40	10x36	11x41	12x43		13x45		14x48	16x23	17x26	18x32	19x40				20x16			22x06		
Foxfield	d	06x17	07x59		09x43	10x40	11x44	12x47		13x48		14x51	16x26	17x30	18x35	19x43				20x19			22x09		
Kirkby-in-Furness	d	06x21	08x03		09x47	10x44	11x48	12x51		13x52		14x55	16x30	17x34	18x39	19x47				20x23			22x13		
Askam	d	06 26	08 08		09 52	10 49	11 53	12 56		13 57		15 00	16 35	17 39	18 44	19 52				20 28			22 18		
Barrow-in-Furness	a	06 42	08 24		10 07	11 07	12 09	13 14		14 13		15 16	16 53	17 55	19 02	20 10				20 45			22 35		
Lancaster 6 82	a		09 33		11 21		13 16			15 20		16 24		19 05											

Sundays

		NT	NT	NT
Carlisle 8	d	15 00	19 00	21 50
Dalston	d	15x08	19x08	21x58
Wigton	d	15 17	19 17	22 07
Aspatria	d	15x27	19x27	22x17
Maryport	d	15 37	19 37	22 27
Flimby	d	15x40	19x40	22x30
Workington	d	15 49	19 49	22 39
Harrington	d	15x52	19x52	22x42
Parton	d	16x01	20x01	22x51
Whitehaven	a	16 10	20 10	23 00
	d			
Corkickle	d			
St Bees	d			
Nethertown	d			
Braystones	d			
Sellafield	d			
Seascale	d			
Drigg	d			
Ravenglass for Eskdale	d			
Bootle	d			
Silecroft	d			
Millom	a			
	d			
Green Road	d			
Foxfield	d			
Kirkby-in-Furness	d			
Askam	d			
Barrow-in-Furness	a			
Lancaster 6 82	a			

No Sunday Service Whitehaven to Barrow-in-Furness

Network Diagram for Tables 101, 103, 106, 109

DM-14/06(2)
Design BAJS

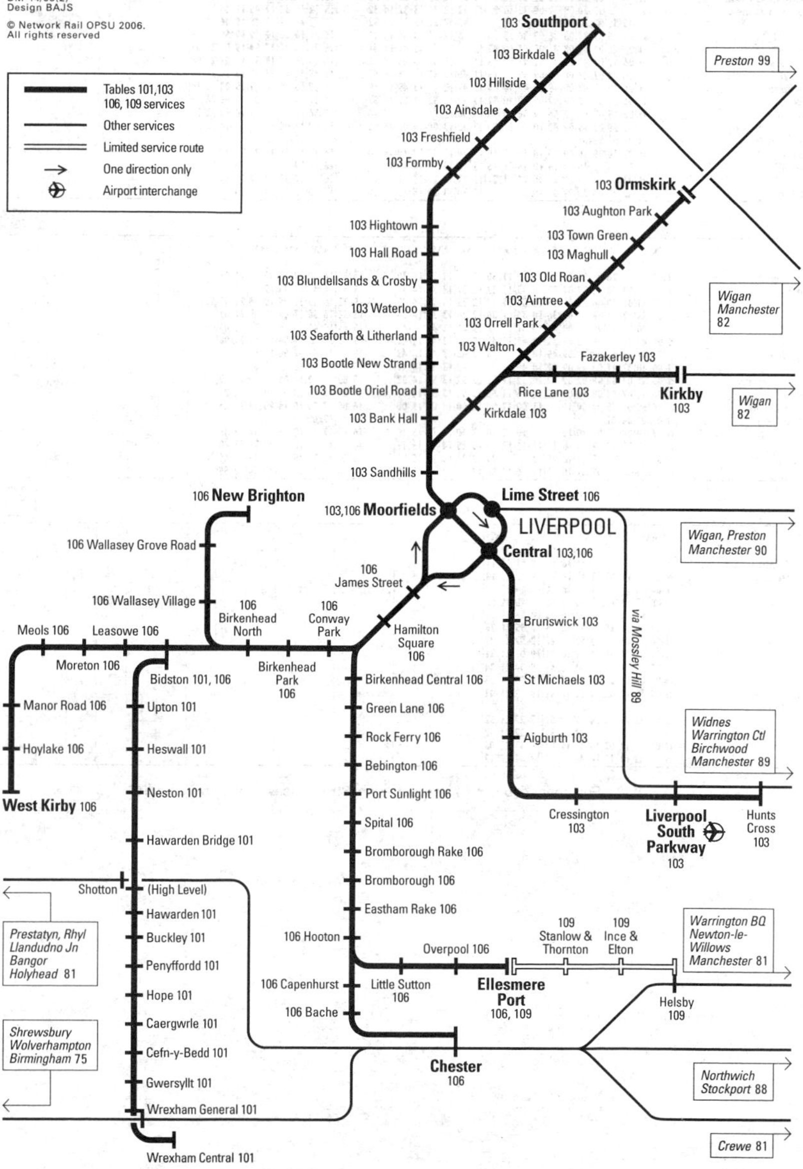

Wrexham - Bidston

Network Diagram - see first Page of Table 101

Miles			AW	AW BHX	AW	AW BHX	AW	AW BHX	AW	AW BHX	AW		AW BHX	AW	AW BHX	AW	AW
0	**Wrexham Central**	d		07 28	08 30	09 30	10 30	11 30	12 30	13 30	14 30		15 30	16 30	17 43	19 44	21 55
0½	**Wrexham General**	a		07 30	08 32	09 32	10 32	11 32	12 32	13 32	14 32		15 32	16 32	17 45	19 46	21 57
—		d	06 31	07 30	08 32	09 32	10 32	11 32	12 32	13 32	14 32		15 32	16 32	17 45	19 46	21 57
2¼	Gwersyllt	d	06 35	07 34	08 36	09 36	10 36	11 36	12 36	13 36	14 36		15 36	16 36	17 49	19 50	22 01
4	Cefn-y-Bedd	d	06 40	07 39	08 41	09 41	10 41	11 41	12 41	13 41	14 41		15 41	16 41	17 54	19 55	22 06
4¾	Caergwrle	d	06 42	07 41	08 43	09 43	10 43	11 43	12 43	13 43	14 43		15 43	16 43	17 56	19 57	22 08
5¼	Hope (Flintshire)	d	06 44	07 43	08 45	09 45	10 45	11 45	12 45	13 45	14 45		15 45	16 45	17 58	19 59	22 10
7¼	Penyffordd	d	06 48	07 47	08 49	09 49	10 49	11 49	12 49	13 49	14 49		15 49	16 49	18 02	20 03	22 14
8½	Buckley	d	06 51	07 50	08 52	09 52	10 52	11 52	12 52	13 52	14 52		15 52	16 52	18 05	20 06	22 17
10½	Hawarden	d	06 55	07 54	08 56	09 56	10 56	11 56	12 56	13 56	14 56		15 56	16 56	18 09	20 10	22 21
12¾	Shotton High Level	d	06 59	07 59	09 00	10 00	11 00	12 00	13 00	14 00	15 00		16 00	17 00	18 13	20 14	22 25
13¼	Hawarden Bridge	d	07x01	08x01										17x02			
18¾	Neston	d	07 10	08 10	09 10	10 10	11 10	12 10	13 10	14 10	15 10		16 10	17 11	18 23	20 24	22 35
21¼	Heswall	d	07 15	08 15	09 15	10 15	11 15	12 15	13 15	14 15	15 15		16 15	17 16	18 28	20 29	22 40
25½	Upton	d	07 21	08 21	09 21	10 21	11 21	12 21	13 21	14 21	15 21		16 21	17 22	18 34	20 35	22 46
27½	**Bidston**	a	07 30	08 30	09 31	10 30	11 30	12 30	13 30	14 30	15 30		16 30	17 31	18 45	20 44	22 55

Saturdays

		AW	AW	AW	AW	AW	AW	AW	AW	AW		AW	AW	AW	AW	AW
Wrexham Central	d		07 28	08 30	09 30	10 30	11 30	12 30	13 30	14 30		15 30	16 30	17 43	19 44	21 55
Wrexham General	a		07 30	08 32	09 32	10 32	11 32	12 32	13 32	14 32		15 32	16 32	17 45	19 46	21 57
	d	06 31	07 30	08 32	09 32	10 32	11 32	12 32	13 32	14 32		15 32	16 32	17 45	19 46	21 57
Gwersyllt	d	06 35	07 34	08 36	09 36	10 36	11 36	12 36	13 36	14 36		15 36	16 36	17 49	19 50	22 01
Cefn-y-Bedd	d	06 40	07 39	08 41	09 41	10 41	11 41	12 41	13 41	14 41		15 41	16 41	17 54	19 55	22 06
Caergwrle	d	06 42	07 41	08 43	09 43	10 43	11 43	12 43	13 43	14 43		15 43	16 43	17 56	19 57	22 08
Hope (Flintshire)	d	06 44	07 43	08 45	09 45	10 45	11 45	12 45	13 45	14 45		15 45	16 45	17 58	19 59	22 10
Penyffordd	d	06 48	07 47	08 49	09 49	10 49	11 49	12 49	13 49	14 49		15 49	16 49	18 02	20 03	22 14
Buckley	d	06 51	07 50	08 52	09 52	10 52	11 52	12 52	13 52	14 52		15 52	16 52	18 05	20 06	22 17
Hawarden	d	06 55	07 54	08 56	09 56	10 56	11 56	12 56	13 56	14 56		15 56	16 56	18 09	20 10	22 21
Shotton High Level	d	06 59	07 59	09 00	10 00	11 00	12 00	13 00	14 00	15 00		16 00	17 00	18 13	20 14	22 25
Hawarden Bridge	d	07x01	08x01										17x02			
Neston	d	07 10	08 10	09 10	10 10	11 10	12 10	13 10	14 10	15 10		16 10	17 11	18 23	20 24	22 35
Heswall	d	07 15	08 15	09 15	10 15	11 15	12 15	13 15	14 15	15 15		16 15	17 16	18 28	20 29	22 40
Upton	d	07 21	08 21	09 21	10 21	11 21	12 21	13 21	14 21	15 21		16 21	17 22	18 34	20 35	22 46
Bidston	a	07 30	08 30	09 31	10 30	11 30	12 30	13 30	14 30	15 30		16 30	17 31	18 45	20 44	22 55

Sundays

		AW	AW	AW	AW	AW	AW
Wrexham Central	d		11 11	13 41	16 11	18 41	21 11
Wrexham General	a		11 13	13 43	16 13	18 43	21 13
	d	08 44	11 14	13 44	16 14	18 44	21 14
Gwersyllt	d	08 48	11 18	13 48	16 18	18 48	21 18
Cefn-y-Bedd	d	08 53	11 23	13 53	16 23	18 53	21 23
Caergwrle	d	08 55	11 25	13 55	16 25	18 55	21 25
Hope (Flintshire)	d	08 57	11 27	13 57	16 27	18 57	21 27
Penyffordd	d	09 01	11 31	14 01	16 31	19 01	21 31
Buckley	d	09 04	11 34	14 04	16 34	19 04	21 34
Hawarden	d	09 08	11 38	14 08	16 38	19 08	21 38
Shotton High Level	d	09 12	11 42	14 12	16 42	19 12	21 42
Hawarden Bridge	d						
Neston	d	09 22	11 52	14 22	16 52	19 22	21 52
Heswall	d	09 27	11 57	14 27	16 57	19 27	21 57
Upton	d	09 33	12 03	14 33	17 03	19 33	22 03
Bidston	a	09 42	12 12	14 42	17 12	19 42	22 12

For connections to Liverpool Lime Street please refer to Table 106

Bidston - Wrexham

Network Diagram - see first Page of Table 101

Mondays to Fridays

Miles			AW BHX	AW	AW BHX	AW	AW BHX	AW	AW BHX	AW	AW BHX	AW	AW BHX	AW	AW BHX	AW	AW
0	**Bidston**	d		07 31	08 31	09 32	10 32	11 32	12 32	13 32	14 32	15 32	16 31	17 45	18 46	20 56	22 56
2	Upton	d		07 32	08 32	09 33	10 33	11 33	12 33	13 33	14 33	15 33	16 32	17 46	18 47	20 57	22 57
6¼	Heswall	d		07 39	08 39	09 40	10 40	11 40	12 40	13 40	14 40	15 40	16 39	17 53	18 54	21 04	23 04
8¾	Neston	d		07 44	08 44	09 45	10 45	11 45	12 45	13 45	14 45	15 45	16 44	17 58	18 59	21 09	23 09
14¼	Hawarden Bridge	d		07x53	08x53								16x53	18x07			
14¾	Shotton High Level	d		07 55	08 55	09 55	10 55	11 55	12 55	13 55	14 55	15 55	16 55	18 09	19 09	21 19	23 20
17½	Hawarden	d		08 00	09 00	10 00	11 00	12 00	13 00	14 00	15 00	16 00	17 00	18 14	19 14	21 24	23 25
19	Buckley	d		08 05	09 05	10 05	11 05	12 05	13 05	14 05	15 05	16 05	17 05	18 19	19 19	21 29	23 30
20¼	Penyffordd	d		08 08	09 08	10 08	11 08	12 08	13 08	14 08	15 08	16 08	17 08	18 22	19 22	21 32	23 33
22¼	Hope (Flintshire)	d		08 12	09 12	10 12	11 12	12 12	13 12	14 12	15 12	16 12	17 12	18 26	19 26	21 36	23 37
22¾	Caergwrle	d		08 14	09 14	10 14	11 14	12 14	13 14	14 14	15 14	16 14	17 14	18 28	19 28	21 38	23 39
23½	Cefn-y-Bedd	d		08 16	09 16	10 16	11 16	12 16	13 16	14 16	15 16	16 16	17 16	18 30	19 30	21 40	23 41
25¼	Gwersyllt	d		08 20	09 20	10 20	11 20	12 20	13 20	14 20	15 20	16 20	17 20	18 34	19 34	21 44	23 47
27	**Wrexham General**	a		08 27	09 27	10 27	11 27	12 27	13 27	14 27	15 27	16 27	17 27	18 41	19 41	21 51	23 54
—		d	07 10	08 27	09 27	10 27	11 27	12 27	13 27	14 27	15 27	16 27	17 27	18 41	19 41	21 51	
27½	**Wrexham Central**	a	07 13	08 32	09 32	10 32	11 32	12 32	13 32	14 32	15 32	16 32	17 32	18 46	19 46	21 56	

Saturdays

		AW	AW	AW	AW	AW	AW	AW	AW	AW	AW	AW	AW	AW	AW	AW
Bidston	d		07 31	08 31	09 32	10 32	11 32	12 32	13 32	14 32	15 32	16 31	17 45	18 46	20 56	22 56
Upton	d		07 32	08 32	09 33	10 33	11 33	12 33	13 33	14 33	15 33	16 32	17 46	18 47	20 57	22 57
Heswall	d		07 39	08 39	09 40	10 40	11 40	12 40	13 40	14 40	15 40	16 39	17 53	18 54	21 04	23 04
Neston	d		07 44	08 44	09 45	10 45	11 45	12 45	13 45	14 45	15 45	16 44	17 58	18 59	21 09	23 09
Hawarden Bridge	d		07x53	08x53								16x53	18x07			
Shotton High Level	d		07 55	08 55	09 55	10 55	11 55	12 55	13 55	14 55	15 55	16 55	18 09	19 09	21 19	23 20
Hawarden	d		08 00	09 00	10 00	11 00	12 00	13 00	14 00	15 00	16 00	17 00	18 14	19 14	21 24	23 25
Buckley	d		08 05	09 05	10 05	11 05	12 05	13 05	14 05	15 05	16 05	17 05	18 19	19 19	21 29	23 30
Penyffordd	d		08 08	09 08	10 08	11 08	12 08	13 08	14 08	15 08	16 08	17 08	18 22	19 22	21 32	23 33
Hope (Flintshire)	d		08 12	09 12	10 12	11 12	12 12	13 12	14 12	15 12	16 12	17 12	18 26	19 26	21 36	23 37
Caergwrle	d		08 14	09 14	10 14	11 14	12 14	13 14	14 14	15 14	16 14	17 14	18 28	19 28	21 38	23 39
Cefn-y-Bedd	d		08 16	09 16	10 16	11 16	12 16	13 16	14 16	15 16	16 16	17 16	18 30	19 30	21 40	23 41
Gwersyllt	d		08 20	09 20	10 20	11 20	12 20	13 20	14 20	15 20	16 20	17 20	18 34	19 34	21 44	23 47
Wrexham General	a		08 27	09 27	10 27	11 27	12 27	13 27	14 27	15 27	16 27	17 27	18 41	19 41	21 51	23 54
	d	07 10	08 27	09 27	10 27	11 27	12 27	13 27	14 27	15 27	16 27	17 27	18 41	19 41	21 51	
Wrexham Central	a	07 13	08 32	09 32	10 32	11 32	12 32	13 32	14 32	15 32	16 32	17 32	18 46	19 46	21 56	

Sundays

		AW	AW	AW	AW	AW	AW
Bidston	d	09 57	12 27	14 57	17 27	19 57	22 27
Upton	d	09 58	12 28	14 58	17 28	19 58	22 28
Heswall	d	10 05	12 35	15 05	17 35	20 05	22 35
Neston	d	10 10	12 40	15 10	17 40	20 10	22 40
Hawarden Bridge	d						
Shotton High Level	d	10 20	12 50	15 20	17 50	20 20	22 50
Hawarden	d	10 25	12 55	15 25	17 55	20 25	22 55
Buckley	d	10 30	13 00	15 30	18 00	20 30	23 00
Penyffordd	d	10 33	13 03	15 33	18 03	20 33	23 03
Hope (Flintshire)	d	10 37	13 07	15 37	18 07	20 37	23 07
Caergwrle	d	10 39	13 09	15 39	18 09	20 39	23 09
Cefn-y-Bedd	d	10 41	13 11	15 41	18 11	20 41	23 11
Gwersyllt	d	10 45	13 15	15 45	18 15	20 45	23 15
Wrexham General	a	10 52	13 22	15 52	18 22	20 52	23 25
	d	10 53	13 23	15 53	18 23	20 53	
Wrexham Central	a	10 58	13 28	15 58	18 28	20 58	

For connections from Liverpool Lime Street please refer to Table 106

Table 102

Llandudno - Blaenau Ffestiniog

Mondays to Fridays

until 30 December

Network Diagram - see first Page of Table 81

Miles			AW ◇	AW ◇	AW ◇	AW ◇	AW ◇	AW ◇
0	**Llandudno**	81 d			10 22	13 22	16 20	19 03
1¾	Deganwy	81 d			10x26	13x26	16x24	19x07
3	**Llandudno Junction**	81 d	05 35	07 39	10 34	13 34	16 33	19b20
5	Glan Conwy	d		07x42	10x37	13x37	16x36	19x23
8½	Tal-y-Cafn	d		07 48	10 43	13 43	16 42	19 29
11½	Dolgarrog	d		07x53	10x48	13x48	16x47	19x34
14½	North Llanrwst	d		08x00	10x54	13x54	16x53	19x40
15	Llanrwst	d	05 53	08 02	10 56	13 56	16 55	19 42
18½	Betws-y-Coed	d	05 59	08 08	11 02	14 02	17 01	19 48
22¾	Pont-y-Pant	d		08x16	11x10	14x10	17x09	19x56
24¼	Dolwyddelan	d		08x19	11x13	14x13	17x12	19x59
26	Roman Bridge	d		08x23	11x17	14x17	17x16	20x03
31	**Blaenau Ffestiniog**	a	06 29	08 42	11 36	14 36	17 35	20 20

Mondays to Fridays

2 January to 23 March

		AW ◇	AW ◇	AW ◇	AW ◇	AW ◇	AW ◇
Llandudno	81 d			10 22	13 22	16 20	19 03
Deganwy	81 d			10x26	13x26	16x24	19x07
Llandudno Junction	81 d	05 35	07 39	10 34	13 34	16 33	19b20
Glan Conwy	d		07x42	10x37	13x37	16x36	19x23
Tal-y-Cafn	d		07 48	10 43	13 43	16 42	19 29
Dolgarrog	d		07x53	10x48	13x48	16x47	19x34
North Llanrwst	d		08x00	10x54	13x54	16x53	19x40
Llanrwst	d	05 53	08 02	10 56	13 56	16 55	19 42
Betws-y-Coed	d	05 59	08 08	11 02	14 02	17 01	19 48
Pont-y-Pant	d		08x16	11x10	14x10	17x09	19x56
Dolwyddelan	d		08x19	11x13	14x13	17x12	19x59
Roman Bridge	d						
Blaenau Ffestiniog	a	06 29	08 42	11 36	14 36	17 35	20 20

Mondays to Fridays

from 26 March

		AW ◇	AW ◇	AW ◇	AW ◇	AW ◇	AW ◇
Llandudno	81 d			10 22	13 22	16 20	19 03
Deganwy	81 d			10x26	13x26	16x24	19x07
Llandudno Junction	81 d	05 35	07 39	10 34	13 34	16 33	19b20
Glan Conwy	d		07x42	10x37	13x37	16x36	19x23
Tal-y-Cafn	d		07 48	10 43	13 43	16 42	19 29
Dolgarrog	d		07x53	10x48	13x48	16x47	19x34
North Llanrwst	d		08x00	10x54	13x54	16x53	19x40
Llanrwst	d	05 53	08 02	10 56	13 56	16 55	19 42
Betws-y-Coed	d	05 59	08 08	11 02	14 02	17 01	19 48
Pont-y-Pant	d		08x16	11x10	14x10	17x09	19x56
Dolwyddelan	d		08x19	11x13	14x13	17x12	19x59
Roman Bridge	d		08x23	11x17	14x17	17x16	20x03
Blaenau Ffestiniog	a	06 29	08 42	11 36	14 36	17 35	20 20

Saturdays

until 31 December

		AW ◇	AW ◇	AW ◇	AW ◇	AW ◇	AW ◇
Llandudno	81 d			10 22	13 22	16 20	19 03
Deganwy	81 d			10x26	13x26	16x24	19x07
Llandudno Junction	81 d	05 35	07 39	10 34	13 34	16 33	19b20
Glan Conwy	d		07x42	10x37	13x37	16x36	19x23
Tal-y-Cafn	d		07 48	10 43	13 43	16 42	19 29
Dolgarrog	d		07x53	10x48	13x48	16x47	19x34
North Llanrwst	d		08x00	10x54	13x54	16x53	19x40
Llanrwst	d	05 53	08 02	10 56	13 56	16 55	19 42
Betws-y-Coed	d	05 59	08 08	11 02	14 02	17 01	19 48
Pont-y-Pant	d		08x16	11x10	14x10	17x09	19x56
Dolwyddelan	d		08x19	11x13	14x13	17x12	19x59
Roman Bridge	d		08x23	11x17	14x17	17x16	20x03
Blaenau Ffestiniog	a	06 29	08 42	11 36	14 36	17 35	20 20

For connections from Crewe, Chester, Rhyl and Bangor (Gwynedd) please refer to Table 81

Table 102

Saturdays

7 January to 24 March

Llandudno - Blaenau Ffestiniog

Network Diagram - see first Page of Table 81

			AW	AW	AW	AW	AW	AW
			◇	◇	◇	◇	◇	◇
Llandudno	81	d			10 22	13 22	16 20	19 03
Deganwy	81	d			10x26	13x26	16x24	19x07
Llandudno Junction	81	d	05 35	07 39	10 34	13 34	16 33	19 20
Glan Conwy		d		07x42	10x37	13x37	16x36	19x23
Tal-y-Cafn		d		07 48	10 43	13 43	16 42	19 29
Dolgarrog		d		07x53	10x48	13x48	16x47	19x34
North Llanrwst		d		08x00	10x54	13x54	16x53	19x40
Llanrwst		d	05 53	08 02	10 56	13 56	16 55	19 42
Betws-y-Coed		d	05 59	08 08	11 02	14 02	17 01	19 48
Pont-y-Pant		d		08x16	11x10	14x10	17x09	19x56
Dolwyddelan		d		08x19	11x13	14x13	17x12	19x59
Roman Bridge		d						
Blaenau Ffestiniog		a	06 29	08 42	11 36	14 36	17 35	20 20

Saturdays

from 31 March

			AW	AW	AW	AW	AW	AW
			◇	◇	◇	◇	◇	◇
Llandudno	81	d			10 22	13 22	16 20	19 03
Deganwy	81	d			10x26	13x26	16x24	19x07
Llandudno Junction	81	d	05 35	07 39	10 34	13 34	16 33	19b20
Glan Conwy		d		07x42	10x37	13x37	16x36	19x23
Tal-y-Cafn		d		07 48	10 43	13 43	16 42	19 29
Dolgarrog		d		07x53	10x48	13x48	16x47	19x34
North Llanrwst		d		08x00	10x54	13x54	16x53	19x40
Llanrwst		d	05 53	08 02	10 56	13 56	16 55	19 42
Betws-y-Coed		d	05 59	08 08	11 02	14 02	17 01	19 48
Pont-y-Pant		d		08x16	11x10	14x10	17x09	19x56
Dolwyddelan		d		08x19	11x13	14x13	17x12	19x59
Roman Bridge		d		08x23	11x17	14x17	17x16	20x03
Blaenau Ffestiniog		a	06 29	08 42	11 36	14 36	17 35	20 20

Sundays

			AW	AW	AW
			◇	◇	◇
Llandudno	81	d	10 22	13 30	
Deganwy	81	d	10x26	13x34	
Llandudno Junction	81	d	10 32	13 40	16 15
Glan Conwy		d	10x35	13x43	16x18
Tal-y-Cafn		d	10 41	13 49	16 24
Dolgarrog		d	10x46	13x54	16x29
North Llanrwst		d	10x52	14x00	16x35
Llanrwst		d	10 54	14 02	16 37
Betws-y-Coed		d	11 00	14 08	16 43
Pont-y-Pant		d	11x08	14x16	16x51
Dolwyddelan		d	11x11	14x19	16x54
Roman Bridge		d	11x15	14x23	16x58
Blaenau Ffestiniog		a	11 32	14 40	17 15

For connections from Crewe, Chester, Rhyl and Bangor (Gwynedd) please refer to Table 81

On Sundays a bus service is available at Llandudno Junction station to various destinations between Blaenau Ffestiniog - Llandudno, please contact Traveline 0871 200 22 33 for further information on these services or contact a staff member at Llandudno Junction upon Arrival.

Table 102

Blaenau Ffestiniog - Llandudno

Mondays to Fridays

until 30 December

Network Diagram - see first Page of Table 81

Miles			AW ◇	AW ◇	AW ◇	AW ◇	AW ◇	AW ◇
—	**Blaenau Ffestiniog**	d	06 30	08 46	11 46	14 57	17 37	20 23
—	Roman Bridge	d	06x40	08x56	11x56	15x07	17x47	20x33
6¾	Dolwyddelan	d	06x43	09x00	12x00	15x11	17x51	20x37
8¼	Pont-y-Pant	d	06x46	09x03	12x03	15x14	17x54	20x40
12½	Betws-y-Coed	d	06 56	09 13	12 13	15 24	18 04	20 50
16	Llanrwst	d	07 02	09 19	12 19	15 30	18 10	20 56
16½	North Llanrwst	d	07x03	09x20	12x20	15x31	18x11	20x57
19½	Dolgarrog	d	07x09	09x27	12x27	15x38	18x18	21x04
22½	Tal-y-Cafn	d	07x15	09x33	12x33	15x44	18x24	21x10
26	Glan Conwy	d	07x21	09x39	12x39	15x50	18x30	21x16
28	**Llandudno Junction**	81 a	07 31	09 44	12 44	15 56	18 35	21 21
29¼	Deganwy	81 a		10x06	13x06	16x07	18x44	21x35
31	**Llandudno**	81 a		10 13	13 13	16 17	18 54	21 46

Mondays to Fridays

2 January to 23 March

		AW ◇	AW ◇ A	AW ◇ B	AW ◇	AW ◇	AW ◇	AW ◇
Blaenau Ffestiniog	d	06 30	08∫46	08∫46	11 46	14 57	17 37	20 23
Roman Bridge	d		∫	08x56				
Dolwyddelan	d	06x43	09x00	09x00	12x00	15x11	17x51	20x37
Pont-y-Pant	d	06x46	09x03	09x03	12x03	15x14	17x54	20x40
Betws-y-Coed	d	06 56	09∫13	09∫13	12 13	15 24	18 04	20 50
Llanrwst	d	07 02	09∫19	09∫19	12 19	15 30	18 10	20 56
North Llanrwst	d	07x03	09x20	09x20	12x20	15x31	18x11	20x57
Dolgarrog	d	07x09	09x27	09x27	12x27	15x38	18x18	21x04
Tal-y-Cafn	d	07x15	09x33	09x33	12x33	15x44	18x24	21x10
Glan Conwy	d	07x21	09x39	09x39	12x39	15x50	18x30	21x16
Llandudno Junction	81 a	07 31	09∫44	09∫44	12 44	15 56	18 35	21 21
Deganwy	81 a		10x06	10x06	13x06	16x07	18x44	21x35
Llandudno	81 a		10∫13	10∫15	13 13	16 17	18 54	21 46

Mondays to Fridays

from 26 March

		AW ◇	AW ◇	AW ◇	AW ◇	AW ◇	AW ◇
Blaenau Ffestiniog	d	06 30	08 46	11 46	14 57	17 37	20 23
Roman Bridge	d	06x40	08x56	11x56	15x07	17x47	20x33
Dolwyddelan	d	06x43	09x00	12x00	15x11	17x51	20x37
Pont-y-Pant	d	06x46	09x03	12x03	15x14	17x54	20x40
Betws-y-Coed	d	06 56	09 13	12 13	15 24	18 04	20 50
Llanrwst	d	07 02	09 19	12 19	15 30	18 10	20 56
North Llanrwst	d	07x03	09x20	12x20	15x31	18x11	20x57
Dolgarrog	d	07x09	09x27	12x27	15x38	18x18	21x04
Tal-y-Cafn	d	07x15	09x33	12x33	15x44	18x24	21x10
Glan Conwy	d	07x21	09x39	12x39	15x50	18x30	21x16
Llandudno Junction	81 a	07 31	09 44	12 44	15 56	18 35	21 21
Deganwy	81 a		10x06	13x06	16x07	18x44	21x35
Llandudno	81 a		10 13	13 13	16 17	18 54	21 46

Saturdays

until 31 December

		AW ◇	AW ◇	AW ◇	AW ◇	AW ◇	AW ◇
Blaenau Ffestiniog	d	06 30	08 46	11 46	14 57	17 37	20 23
Roman Bridge	d	06x40	08x56	11x56	15x07	17x47	20x33
Dolwyddelan	d	06x43	09x00	12x00	15x11	17x51	20x37
Pont-y-Pant	d	06x46	09x03	12x03	15x14	17x54	20x40
Betws-y-Coed	d	06 56	09 13	12 13	15 24	18 04	20 50
Llanrwst	d	07 02	09 19	12 19	15 30	18 10	20 56
North Llanrwst	d	07x03	09x20	12x20	15x31	18x11	20x57
Dolgarrog	d	07x09	09x27	12x27	15x38	18x18	21x04
Tal-y-Cafn	d	07x15	09x33	12x33	15x44	18x24	21x10
Glan Conwy	d	07x21	09x39	12x39	15x50	18x30	21x16
Llandudno Junction	81 a	07 31	09 45	12 45	15 56	18 35	21 21
Deganwy	81 a		10x03	13x03	16x03	18x44	21x35
Llandudno	81 a		10 13	13 13	16 13	18 54	21 46

A not from 23 January until 27 January

B from 23 January until 27 January

For connections to Bangor (Gwynedd), Rhyl, Chester and Crewe please refer to Table 81

Table 102

Saturdays

7 January to 24 March

Blaenau Ffestiniog - Llandudno

Network Diagram - see first Page of Table 81

			AW	AW		AW	AW		AW	AW
			◇	◇		◇	◇		◇	◇
Blaenau Ffestiniog		d	06 30	08 46		11 46	14 57		17 37	20 23
Roman Bridge		d								
Dolwyddelan		d	06x43	09x00		12x00	15x11		17x51	20x37
Pont-y-Pant		d	06x46	09x03		12x03	15x14		17x54	20x40
Betws-y-Coed		d	06 56	09 13		12 13	15 24		18 04	20 50
Llanrwst		d	07 02	09 19		12 19	15 30		18 10	20 56
North Llanrwst		d	07x03	09x20		12x20	15x31		18x11	20x57
Dolgarrog		d	07x09	09x27		12x27	15x38		18x18	21x04
Tal-y-Cafn		d	07x15	09x33		12x33	15x44		18x24	21x10
Glan Conwy		d	07x21	09x39		12x39	15x50		18x30	21x16
Llandudno Junction	81	a	07 31	09 45		12 45	15 56		18 35	21 21
Deganwy	81	a		10x03		13x03	16x03		18x44	21x35
Llandudno	81	a		10 13		13 13	16 13		18 54	21 46

Saturdays

from 31 March

			AW	AW		AW	AW		AW	AW
			◇	◇		◇	◇		◇	◇
Blaenau Ffestiniog		d	06 30	08 46		11 46	14 57		17 37	20 23
Roman Bridge		d	06x40	08x56		11x56	15x07		17x47	20x33
Dolwyddelan		d	06x43	09x00		12x00	15x11		17x51	20x37
Pont-y-Pant		d	06x46	09x03		12x03	15x14		17x54	20x40
Betws-y-Coed		d	06 56	09 13		12 13	15 24		18 04	20 50
Llanrwst		d	07 02	09 19		12 19	15 30		18 10	20 56
North Llanrwst		d	07x03	09x20		12x20	15x31		18x11	20x57
Dolgarrog		d	07x09	09x27		12x27	15x38		18x18	21x04
Tal-y-Cafn		d	07x15	09x33		12x33	15x44		18x24	21x10
Glan Conwy		d	07x21	09x39		12x39	15x50		18x30	21x16
Llandudno Junction	81	a	07 31	09 45		12 45	15 56		18 35	21 21
Deganwy	81	a		10x03		13x03	16x03		18x44	21x35
Llandudno	81	a		10 13		13 13	16 13		18 54	21 46

Sundays

			AW	AW	AW
			◇	◇	◇
Blaenau Ffestiniog		d	11 45	15 03	17 30
Roman Bridge		d	11x55	15x13	17x40
Dolwyddelan		d	11x58	15x16	17x44
Pont-y-Pant		d	12x01	15x19	17x48
Betws-y-Coed		d	12 11	15 29	17 57
Llanrwst		d	12 17	15 35	18 03
North Llanrwst		d	12x18	15x36	18x05
Dolgarrog		d	12x24	15x42	18x11
Tal-y-Cafn		d	12x29	15x48	18x17
Glan Conwy		d	12x35	15x54	18x23
Llandudno Junction	81	a	12 40	15 59	18 29
Deganwy	81	a	12x45		18x34
Llandudno	81	a	12 55		18 44

For connections to Bangor (Gwynedd), Rhyl, Chester and Crewe please refer to Table 81

On Sundays a bus service is available at Llandudno Junction station to various destinations between Blaenau Ffestiniog - Llandudno, please contact Traveline 0871 200 22 33 for further information on these services or contact a staff member at Llandudno Junction upon Arrival.

Hunts Cross and Liverpool - Kirkby, Ormskirk and Southport

Network Diagram - see first Page of Table 101

Miles	Miles	Miles		ME	ME MX	ME MO	ME	ME	ME SX	ME SO	ME	ME SX		ME SO	ME	ME SX	ME SO	ME	ME SX	ME SO	ME	ME		ME
0	—	—	**Hunts Cross** 89 d	23p06	23p21											06 06	06 06		06 21	06 21				06 36
1½	—	—	**Liverpool Sth Parkway** 7 89 ⇋ d	23p09	23p24											06 09	06 09		06 24	06 24				06 39
2½	—	—	Cressington d	23p12	23p27											06 12	06 12		06 27	06 27				06 42
3¼	—	—	Aigburth d	23p14	23p29											06 14	06 14		06 29	06 29				06 44
4½	—	—	St Michaels d	23p16	23p31											06 16	06 16		06 31	06 31				06 46
5¾	—	—	Brunswick d	23p19	23p34											06 19	06 19		06 34	06 34				06 49
7¼	0	0	**Liverpool Central** 10 a	23p23	23p38											06 23	06 23		06 38	06 38				06 53
—	—	—	d	23p23	23p38	23p38	23p40	23p55			05 55	06 08		06 08	06 10	06 23	06 23	06 25	06 38	06 38	06 40	06 50		06 53
7¾	0½	0½	**Moorfields** 10 d	23p25	23p40	23p40	23p42	23p57			05 57	06 10		06 10	06 12	06 25	06 25	06 27	06 40	06 40	06 42	06 52		06 55
9¼	2	2	Sandhills d	23p29	23p44	23p44	23p46	00 01	05 59	05 59	06 01	06 14		06 14	06 16	06 29	06 29	06 31	06 44	06 44	06 46	06 56		06 59
—	3	3	Kirkdale d				23p49	00 04			06 04				06 19			06 34			06 49	06 59		
—	—	4¼	Rice Lane d					00 07			06 07							06 37				07 02		
—	—	5¾	Fazakerley d					00 10			06 10							06 40				07 03		
—	—	7½	**Kirkby** a					00 13			06 13							06 43				07 08		
—	4¼	—	Walton (Merseyside) d				23p52								06 22						06 52			
—	4½	—	Orrell Park d				23p53								06 23						06 53			
—	5½	—	Aintree d				23p56								06 26						06 56			
—	6¼	—	Old Roan d				23p58								06 28						06 58			
—	8	—	Maghull d				00 01								06 31						07 01			
—	10½	—	Town Green d				00 05								06 35						07 05			
—	11½	—	Aughton Park d				00 07								06 37						07 07			
—	12¾	—	**Ormskirk** a				00 12								06 43						07 12			
10	—	—	Bank Hall d	23p31	23p46	23p46			06 01	06 01		06 16		06 16		06 31	06 31		06 46	06 46				07 01
10¾	—	—	Bootle Oriel Road d	23p33	23p48	23p48			06 03	06 03		06 18		06 18		06 33	06 33		06 48	06 48				07 03
11	—	—	Bootle New Strand d	23p35	23p50	23p50			06 05	06 05		06 20		06 20		06 35	06 35		06 50	06 50				07 05
12	—	—	Seaforth & Litherland d	23p37	23p52	23p52			06 07	06 07		06 22		06 22		06 37	06 37		06 52	06 52				07 07
13¼	—	—	Waterloo (Merseyside) d	23p39	23p54	23p54			06 09	06 09		06 24		06 24		06 39	06 39		06 54	06 54				07 09
14¼	—	—	Blundellsands & Crosby d	23p42	23p57	23p57			06 12	06 12		06 27		06 27		06 42	06 42		06 57	06 57				07 12
15	—	—	Hall Road d	23p44	23p59	23p59			06 14	06 14		06 29		06 29		06 44	06 44		06 59	06 59				07 14
17	—	—	Hightown d	23p47	00 02	00 02			06 17	06 17		06 32		06 32		06 47	06 47		07 02	07 02				07 17
19	—	—	Formby d	23p51	00 06	00 06			06 21	06 21		06 36		06 36		06 51	06 51		07 06	07 06				07 21
20	—	—	Freshfield d	23p53	00 08	00 08			06 23	06 23		06 38		06 38		06 53	06 53		07 08	07 08				07 23
22¾	—	—	Ainsdale d	23p57	00 12	00 12			06 27	06 27		06 42		06 42		06 57	06 57		07 12	07 12				07 27
24½	—	—	Hillside d	23p59	00 15	00 15			06 30	06 30		06 45		06 45		07 00	07 00		07 15	07 15				07 30
25¼	—	—	Birkdale d	00 02	00 17	00 17			06 32	06 32		06 47		06 47		07 02	07 02		07 17	07 17				07 32
26¼	—	—	**Southport** a	00 09	00 24	00 24			06 37	06 39		06 52		06 54		07 07	07 09		07 22	07 24				07 39

	ME	ME SX	ME SO	ME	ME	ME SX	ME SO	ME		ME	ME SX	ME SO	ME	ME	ME SX	ME SO	ME	ME		ME SX	ME SO	ME	ME	ME SX
Hunts Cross 89 d		06 51	06 51			07 06	07 06				07 21	07 21			07 36	07 36				07 51	07 51			08 06
Liverpool Sth Parkway 7 89 ⇋ d		06 54	06 54			07 09	07 09				07 24	07 24			07 39	07 39				07 54	07 54			08 09
Cressington d		06 57	06 57			07 12	07 12				07 27	07 27			07 42	07 42				07 57	07 57			08 12
Aigburth d		06 59	06 59			07 14	07 14				07 29	07 29			07 44	07 44				07 59	07 59			08 14
St Michaels d		07 01	07 01			07 16	07 16				07 31	07 31			07 46	07 46				08 01	08 01			08 16
Brunswick d		07 04	07 04			07 19	07 19				07 34	07 34			07 49	07 49				08 04	08 04			08 19
Liverpool Central 10 a		07 08	07 08			07 23	07 23				07 38	07 38			07 53	07 53				08 08	08 08			08 23
d	06 55	07 08	07 08	07 10	07 20	07 23	07 23	07 25		07 35	07 38	07 38	07 40	07 50	07 53	07 53	07 55	08 05		08 08	08 08	08 10	08 20	08 23
Moorfields 10 d	06 57	07 10	07 10	07 12	07 22	07 25	07 25	07 27		07 37	07 40	07 40	07 42	07 52	07 55	07 55	07 57	08 07		08 10	08 10	08 12	08 22	08 25
Sandhills d	07 01	07 14	07 14	07 16	07 26	07 29	07 29	07 31		07 41	07 44	07 44	07 46	07 56	07 59	07 59	08 01	08 11		08 14	08 14	08 16	08 26	08 29
Kirkdale d	07 04			07 19	07 29			07 34		07 44			07 49	07 59			08 04	08 14				08 19	08 29	
Rice Lane d					07 32					07 47				08 02				08 17					08 32	
Fazakerley d					07 34					07 49				08 04				08 19					08 34	
Kirkby a					07 38					07 53				08 08				08 23					08 38	
Walton (Merseyside) d	07 07			07 22				07 37					07 52				08 07					08 22		
Orrell Park d	07 08			07 23				07 38					07 53				08 08					08 23		
Aintree d	07 11			07 26				07 41					07 56				08 11					08 26		
Old Roan d	07 13			07 28				07 43					07 58				08 13					08 28		
Maghull d	07 16			07 31				07 46					08 01				08 16					08 31		
Town Green d	07 20			07 35				07 50					08 05				08 20					08 35		
Aughton Park d	07 22			07 37				07 52					08 07				08 22					08 37		
Ormskirk a	07 28			07 43				07 58					08 13				08 28					08 43		
Bank Hall d		07 16	07 16			07 31	07 31				07 46	07 46			08 01	08 01				08 16	08 16			08 31
Bootle Oriel Road d		07 18	07 18			07 33	07 33				07 48	07 48			08 03	08 03				08 18	08 18			08 33
Bootle New Strand d		07 20	07 20			07 35	07 35				07 50	07 50			08 05	08 05				08 20	08 20			08 35
Seaforth & Litherland d		07 22	07 22			07 37	07 37				07 52	07 52			08 07	08 07				08 22	08 22			08 37
Waterloo (Merseyside) d		07 24	07 24			07 39	07 39				07 54	07 54			08 09	08 09				08 24	08 24			08 39
Blundellsands & Crosby d		07 27	07 27			07 42	07 42				07 57	07 57			08 12	08 12				08 27	08 27			08 42
Hall Road d		07 29	07 29			07 44	07 44				07 59	07 59			08 14	08 14				08 29	08 29			08 44
Hightown d		07 32	07 32			07 47	07 47				08 02	08 02			08 17	08 17				08 32	08 32			08 47
Formby d		07 36	07 36			07 51	07 51				08 06	08 06			08 21	08 21				08 36	08 36			08 51
Freshfield d		07 38	07 38			07 53	07 53				08 08	08 08			08 23	08 23				08 38	08 38			08 53
Ainsdale d		07 42	07 42			07 57	07 57				08 12	08 12			08 27	08 27				08 42	08 42			08 57
Hillside d		07 45	07 45			08 00	08 00				08 15	08 15			08 30	08 30				08 45	08 45			09 00
Birkdale d		07 47	07 47			08 02	08 02				08 17	08 17			08 32	08 32				08 47	08 47			09 02
Southport a		07 52	07 54			08 07	08 09				08 22	08 24			08 37	08 39				08 52	08 54			09 07

Hunts Cross and Liverpool - Kirkby, Ormskirk and Southport

Network Diagram - see first Page of Table 101

	ME SO	ME	ME	ME SX		ME SO	ME	ME	ME SX	ME SO	ME	ME	ME	ME		ME	ME	ME	ME	ME	ME	ME	ME	ME
Hunts Cross 89 d	08 06			08 21		08 21			08 36	08 36			08 51				09 06			09 21			09 36	
Liverpool Sth Parkway 7 89 ⇚ d	08 09			08 24		08 24			08 39	08 39			08 54				09 09			09 24			09 39	
Cressington d	08 12			08 27		08 27			08 42	08 42			08 57				09 12			09 27			09 42	
Aigburth d	08 14			08 29		08 29			08 44	08 44			08 59				09 14			09 29			09 44	
St Michaels d	08 16			08 31		08 31			08 46	08 46			09 01				09 16			09 31			09 46	
Brunswick d	08 19			08 34		08 34			08 49	08 49			09 04				09 19			09 34			09 49	
Liverpool Central 10 a	08 23			08 38		08 38			08 53	08 53			09 08				09 23			09 38			09 53	
d	08 23	08 25	08 35	08 38		08 38	08 40	08 50	08 53	08 53	08 55	09 05	09 08	09 10		09 20	09 23	09 25	09 35	09 38	09 40	09 50	09 53	09 55
Moorfields 10 d	08 25	08 27	08 37	08 40		08 40	08 42	08 52	08 55	08 55	08 57	09 07	09 10	09 12		09 22	09 25	09 27	09 37	09 40	09 42	09 52	09 55	09 57
Sandhills d	08 29	08 31	08 41	08 44		08 44	08 46	08 56	08 59	08 59	09 01	09 11	09 14	09 16		09 26	09 29	09 31	09 41	09 44	09 46	09 56	09 59	10 01
Kirkdale d		08 34	08 44				08 49	08 59			09 04	09 14		09 19		09 29		09 34	09 44		09 49	09 59		10 04
Rice Lane d			08 47					09 02				09 17				09 32			09 47			10 02		
Fazakerley d			08 49					09 05				09 19				09 34			09 49			10 04		
Kirkby a			08 53					09 08				09 23				09 38			09 53			10 08		
Walton (Merseyside) d		08 37					08 52				09 07			09 22				09 37			09 52			10 07
Orrell Park d		08 38					08 53				09 08			09 23				09 38			09 53			10 08
Aintree d		08 41					08 56				09 11			09 26				09 41			09 56			10 11
Old Roan d		08 43					08 58				09 13			09 28				09 43			09 58			10 13
Maghull d		08 46					09 01				09 16			09 31				09 46			10 01			10 16
Town Green d		08 50					09 05				09 20			09 35				09 50			10 05			10 20
Aughton Park d		08 52					09 07				09 22			09 37				09 52			10 07			10 22
Ormskirk a		08 58					09 13				09 28			09 43				09 58			10 13			10 28
Bank Hall d	08 31			08 46		08 46			09 01	09 01			09 16				09 31			09 46			10 01	
Bootle Oriel Road d	08 33			08 48		08 48			09 03	09 03			09 18				09 33			09 48			10 03	
Bootle New Strand d	08 35			08 50		08 50			09 05	09 05			09 20				09 35			09 50			10 05	
Seaforth & Litherland d	08 37			08 52		08 52			09 07	09 07			09 22				09 37			09 52			10 07	
Waterloo (Merseyside) d	08 39			08 54		08 54			09 09	09 09			09 24				09 39			09 54			10 09	
Blundellsands & Crosby d	08 42			08 57		08 57			09 12	09 12			09 27				09 42			09 57			10 12	
Hall Road d	08 44			08 59		08 59			09 14	09 14			09 29				09 44			09 59			10 14	
Hightown d	08 47			09 02		09 02			09 17	09 17			09 32				09 47			10 02			10 17	
Formby d	08 51			09 06		09 06			09 21	09 21			09 36				09 51			10 06			10 21	
Freshfield d	08 53			09 08		09 08			09 23	09 23			09 38				09 53			10 08			10 23	
Ainsdale d	08 57			09 12		09 12			09 27	09 27			09 42				09 57			10 12			10 27	
Hillside d	09 00			09 15		09 15			09 30	09 30			09 45				10 00			10 15			10 30	
Birkdale d	09 02			09 17		09 17			09 32	09 32			09 47				10 02			10 17			10 32	
Southport a	09 09			09 22		09 24			09 37	09 39			09 54				10 09			10 24			10 39	

		ME	ME	ME	ME	ME	ME	ME	ME	ME		ME	ME	ME	ME	ME	ME	ME	ME	ME		ME	ME	ME
Hunts Cross 89 d			09 51			10 06			10 21				10 36			10 51			11 06				11 21	
Liverpool Sth Parkway 7 89 ⇚ d			09 54			10 09			10 24				10 39			10 54			11 09				11 24	
Cressington d			09 57			10 12			10 27				10 42			10 57			11 12				11 27	
Aigburth d			09 59			10 14			10 29				10 44			10 59			11 14				11 29	
St Michaels d			10 01			10 16			10 31				10 46			11 01			11 16				11 31	
Brunswick d			10 04			10 19			10 34				10 49			11 04			11 19				11 34	
Liverpool Central 10 a			10 08			10 23			10 38				10 53			11 08			11 23				11 38	
d		10 05	10 08	10 10	10 20	10 23	10 25	10 35	10 38	10 40		10 50	10 53	10 55	11 05	11 08	11 10	11 20	11 23	11 25		11 35	11 38	11 40
Moorfields 10 d		10 07	10 10	10 12	10 22	10 25	10 27	10 37	10 40	10 42		10 52	10 55	10 57	11 07	11 10	11 12	11 22	11 25	11 27		11 37	11 40	11 42
Sandhills d		10 11	10 14	10 16	10 26	10 29	10 31	10 41	10 44	10 46		10 56	10 59	11 01	11 11	11 14	11 16	11 26	11 29	11 31		11 41	11 44	11 46
Kirkdale d		10 14		10 19	10 29		10 34	10 44		10 49		10 59		11 04	11 14		11 19	11 29		11 34		11 44		11 49
Rice Lane d		10 17			10 32			10 47				11 02			11 17			11 32				11 47		
Fazakerley d		10 19			10 34			10 49				11 04			11 19			11 34				11 49		
Kirkby a		10 23			10 38			10 53				11 08			11 23			11 38				11 53		
Walton (Merseyside) d				10 22			10 37			10 52				11 07			11 22			11 37				11 52
Orrell Park d				10 23			10 38			10 53				11 08			11 23			11 38				11 53
Aintree d				10 26			10 41			10 56				11 11			11 26			11 41				11 56
Old Roan d				10 28			10 43			10 58				11 13			11 28			11 43				11 58
Maghull d				10 31			10 46			11 01				11 16			11 31			11 46				12 01
Town Green d				10 35			10 50			11 05				11 20			11 35			11 50				12 05
Aughton Park d				10 37			10 52			11 07				11 22			11 37			11 52				12 07
Ormskirk a				10 43			10 58			11 13				11 28			11 43			11 58				12 13
Bank Hall d			10 16			10 31			10 46				11 01			11 16			11 31				11 46	
Bootle Oriel Road d			10 18			10 33			10 48				11 03			11 18			11 33				11 48	
Bootle New Strand d			10 20			10 35			10 50				11 05			11 20			11 35				11 50	
Seaforth & Litherland d			10 22			10 37			10 52				11 07			11 22			11 37				11 52	
Waterloo (Merseyside) d			10 24			10 39			10 54				11 09			11 24			11 39				11 54	
Blundellsands & Crosby d			10 27			10 42			10 57				11 12			11 27			11 42				11 57	
Hall Road d			10 29			10 44			10 59				11 14			11 29			11 44				11 59	
Hightown d			10 32			10 47			11 02				11 17			11 32			11 47				12 02	
Formby d			10 36			10 51			11 06				11 21			11 36			11 51				12 06	
Freshfield d			10 38			10 53			11 08				11 23			11 38			11 53				12 08	
Ainsdale d			10 42			10 57			11 12				11 27			11 42			11 57				12 12	
Hillside d			10 45			11 00			11 15				11 30			11 45			12 00				12 15	
Birkdale d			10 47			11 02			11 17				11 32			11 47			12 02				12 17	
Southport a			10 54			11 09			11 24				11 39			11 54			12 09				12 24	

Hunts Cross and Liverpool - Kirkby, Ormskirk and Southport

Network Diagram - see first Page of Table 101

		ME	ME	ME	ME	ME	ME		ME	ME	ME	ME	ME	ME	ME	ME	ME		ME	ME	ME	ME	ME	ME	ME
Hunts Cross 89	d		11 36			11 51				12 06			12 21			12 36				12 51			13 06		
Liverpool Sth Parkway 7 89 ⇆	d		11 39			11 54				12 09			12 24			12 39				12 54			13 09		
Cressington	d		11 42			11 57				12 12			12 27			12 42				12 57			13 12		
Aigburth	d		11 44			11 59				12 14			12 29			12 44				12 59			13 14		
St Michaels	d		11 46			12 01				12 16			12 31			12 46				13 01			13 16		
Brunswick	d		11 49			12 04				12 19			12 34			12 49				13 04			13 19		
Liverpool Central 10	a		11 53			12 08				12 23			12 38			12 53				13 08			13 23		
	d	11 50	11 53	11 55	12 05	12 08	12 10		12 20	12 23	12 25	12 35	12 38	12 40	12 50	12 53	12 55		13 05	13 08	13 10	13 20	13 23	13 25	13 35
Moorfields 10	d	11 52	11 55	11 57	12 07	12 10	12 12		12 22	12 25	12 27	12 37	12 40	12 42	12 52	12 55	12 57		13 07	13 10	13 12	13 22	13 25	13 27	13 37
Sandhills	d	11 56	11 59	12 01	12 11	12 14	12 16		12 26	12 29	12 31	12 41	12 44	12 46	12 56	12 59	13 01		13 11	13 14	13 16	13 26	13 29	13 31	13 41
Kirkdale	d	11 59		12 04	12 14		12 19		12 29		12 34	12 44		12 49	12 59		13 04		13 14		13 19	13 29		13 34	13 44
Rice Lane	d	12 02			12 17				12 32			12 47			13 02				13 17			13 32			13 47
Fazakerley	d	12 04			12 19				12 34			12 49			13 04				13 19			13 34			13 49
Kirkby	a	12 08			12 23				12 38			12 53			13 08				13 23			13 38			13 53
Walton (Merseyside)	d			12 07			12 22				12 37			12 52			13 07				13 22			13 37	
Orrell Park	d			12 08			12 23				12 38			12 53			13 08				13 23			13 38	
Aintree	d			12 11			12 26				12 41			12 56			13 11				13 26			13 41	
Old Roan	d			12 13			12 28				12 43			12 58			13 13				13 28			13 43	
Maghull	d			12 16			12 31				12 46			13 01			13 16				13 31			13 46	
Town Green	d			12 20			12 35				12 50			13 05			13 20				13 35			13 50	
Aughton Park	d			12 22			12 37				12 52			13 07			13 22				13 37			13 52	
Ormskirk	a			12 28			12 43				12 58			13 13			13 28				13 43			13 58	
Bank Hall	d		12 01			12 16				12 31			12 46			13 01				13 16			13 31		
Bootle Oriel Road	d		12 03			12 18				12 33			12 48			13 03				13 18			13 33		
Bootle New Strand	d		12 05			12 20				12 35			12 50			13 05				13 20			13 35		
Seaforth & Litherland	d		12 07			12 22				12 37			12 52			13 07				13 22			13 37		
Waterloo (Merseyside)	d		12 09			12 24				12 39			12 54			13 09				13 24			13 39		
Blundellsands & Crosby	d		12 12			12 27				12 42			12 57			13 12				13 27			13 42		
Hall Road	d		12 14			12 29				12 44			12 59			13 14				13 29			13 44		
Hightown	d		12 17			12 32				12 47			13 02			13 17				13 32			13 47		
Formby	d		12 21			12 36				12 51			13 06			13 21				13 36			13 51		
Freshfield	d		12 23			12 38				12 53			13 08			13 23				13 38			13 53		
Ainsdale	d		12 27			12 42				12 57			13 12			13 27				13 42			13 57		
Hillside	d		12 30			12 45				13 00			13 15			13 30				13 45			14 00		
Birkdale	d		12 32			12 47				13 02			13 17			13 32				13 47			14 02		
Southport	a		12 39			12 54				13 09			13 24			13 39				13 54			14 09		

		ME	ME		ME	ME	ME	ME	ME	ME	ME	ME SX	ME SO		ME	ME	ME SX	ME SO	ME	ME	ME	ME SX	ME SO		ME
Hunts Cross 89	d	13 21				13 36			13 51			14 06	14 06				14 21	14 21			14 36				
Liverpool Sth Parkway 7 89 ⇆	d	13 24				13 39			13 54			14 09	14 09				14 24	14 24			14 39				
Cressington	d	13 27				13 42			13 57			14 12	14 12				14 27	14 27			14 42				
Aigburth	d	13 29				13 44			13 59			14 14	14 14				14 29	14 29			14 44				
St Michaels	d	13 31				13 46			14 01			14 16	14 16				14 31	14 31			14 46				
Brunswick	d	13 34				13 49			14 04			14 19	14 19				14 34	14 34			14 49				
Liverpool Central 10	a	13 38				13 53			14 08			14 23	14 23				14 38	14 38			14 53				
	d	13 38	13 40		13 50	13 53	13 55	14 05	14 08	14 10	14 20	14 23	14 23		14 25	14 35	14 38	14 38	14 40	14 50	14 53	14 55	14 55		15 05
Moorfields 10	d	13 40	13 42		13 52	13 55	13 57	14 07	14 10	14 12	14 22	14 25	14 25		14 27	14 37	14 40	14 40	14 42	14 52	14 55	14 57	14 57		15 07
Sandhills	d	13 44	13 46		13 56	13 59	14 01	14 11	14 14	14 16	14 26	14 29	14 29		14 31	14 41	14 44	14 44	14 46	14 56	14 59	15 01	15 01		15 11
Kirkdale	d		13 49		13 59		14 04	14 14		14 19	14 29				14 34	14 44			14 49	14 59		15 04	15 04		15 14
Rice Lane	d				14 02			14 17			14 32					14 47				15 02					15 17
Fazakerley	d				14 04			14 19			14 34					14 49				15 04					15 19
Kirkby	a				14 08			14 23			14 38					14 53				15 08					15 23
Walton (Merseyside)	d		13 52				14 07			14 22					14 37				14 52			15 07	15 07		
Orrell Park	d		13 53				14 08			14 23					14 38				14 53			15 08	15 08		
Aintree	d		13 56				14 11			14 26					14 41				14 56			15 11	15 11		
Old Roan	d		13 58				14 13			14 28					14 43				14 58			15 13	15 13		
Maghull	d		14 01				14 16			14 31					14 46				15 01			15 16	15 16		
Town Green	d		14 05				14 20			14 35					14 50				15 05			15 20	15 20		
Aughton Park	d		14 07				14 22			14 37					14 52				15 07			15 22	15 22		
Ormskirk	a		14 13				14 28			14 43					14 58				15 13			15 27	15 28		
Bank Hall	d	13 46				14 01			14 16			14 31	14 31				14 46	14 46			15 01				
Bootle Oriel Road	d	13 48				14 03			14 18			14 33	14 33				14 48	14 48			15 03				
Bootle New Strand	d	13 50				14 05			14 20			14 35	14 35				14 50	14 50			15 05				
Seaforth & Litherland	d	13 52				14 07			14 22			14 37	14 37				14 52	14 52			15 07				
Waterloo (Merseyside)	d	13 54				14 09			14 24			14 39	14 39				14 54	14 54			15 09				
Blundellsands & Crosby	d	13 57				14 12			14 27			14 42	14 42				14 57	14 57			15 12				
Hall Road	d	13 59				14 14			14 29			14 44	14 44				14 59	14 59			15 14				
Hightown	d	14 02				14 17			14 32			14 47	14 47				15 02	15 02			15 17				
Formby	d	14 06				14 21			14 36			14 51	14 51				15 06	15 06			15 21				
Freshfield	d	14 08				14 23			14 38			14 53	14 53				15 08	15 08			15 23				
Ainsdale	d	14 12				14 27			14 42			14 57	14 57				15 12	15 12			15 27				
Hillside	d	14 15				14 30			14 45			15 00	15 00				15 15	15 15			15 30				
Birkdale	d	14 17				14 32			14 47			15 02	15 02				15 17	15 17			15 32				
Southport	a	14 24				14 39			14 54			15 07	15 09				15 22	15 24			15 39				

Hunts Cross and Liverpool - Kirkby, Ormskirk and Southport

Network Diagram - see first Page of Table 101

		ME	ME	ME	ME SX	ME SO	ME	ME	ME SX		ME SO	ME	ME	ME SX	ME SO	ME	ME	ME SX	ME SO		ME	ME	ME SX	ME SO	ME
Hunts Cross 89	d	14 51			15 06	15 06			15 21		15 21			15 36	15 36			15 51	15 51				16 06	16 06	
Liverpool Sth Parkway 7 89 ✈	d	14 54			15 09	15 09			15 24		15 24			15 39	15 39			15 54	15 54				16 09	16 09	
Cressington	d	14 57			15 12	15 12			15 27		15 27			15 42	15 42			15 57	15 57				16 12	16 12	
Aigburth	d	14 59			15 14	15 14			15 29		15 29			15 44	15 44			15 59	15 59				16 14	16 14	
St Michaels	d	15 01			15 16	15 16			15 31		15 31			15 46	15 46			16 01	16 01				16 16	16 16	
Brunswick	d	15 04			15 19	15 19			15 34		15 34			15 49	15 49			16 04	16 04				16 19	16 19	
Liverpool Central 10	a	15 08			15 23	15 23			15 38		15 38			15 53	15 53			16 08	16 08				16 23	16 23	
	d	15 08	15 10	15 20	15 23	15 23	15 25	15 35	15 38		15 38	15 40	15 50	15 53	15 53	15 55	16 05	16 08	16 08		16 10	16 20	16 23	16 23	16 25
Moorfields 10	d	15 10	15 12	15 22	15 25	15 25	15 27	15 37	15 40		15 40	15 42	15 52	15 55	15 55	15 57	16 07	16 10	16 10		16 12	16 22	16 25	16 25	16 27
Sandhills	d	15 14	15 16	15 26	15 29	15 29	15 31	15 41	15 44		15 44	15 46	15 56	15 59	15 59	16 01	16 11	16 14	16 14		16 16	16 26	16 29	16 29	16 31
Kirkdale	d		15 19	15 29			15 34	15 44				15 49	15 59			16 04	16 14				16 19	16 29			16 34
Rice Lane	d			15 32				15 47					16 02				16 17					16 32			
Fazakerley	d			15 34				15 49					16 04				16 19					16 34			
Kirkby	a			15 38				15 53					16 08				16 23					16 38			
Walton (Merseyside)	d		15 22				15 37					15 52				16 07					16 22				16 37
Orrell Park	d		15 23				15 38					15 53				16 08					16 23				16 38
Aintree	d		15 26				15 41					15 56				16 11					16 26				16 41
Old Roan	d		15 28				15 43					15 58				16 13					16 28				16 43
Maghull	d		15 31				15 46					16 01				16 16					16 31				16 46
Town Green	d		15 35				15 50					16 05				16 20					16 35				16 50
Aughton Park	d		15 37				15 52					16 07				16 22					16 37				16 52
Ormskirk	a		15 43				15 58					16 13				16 28					16 43				16 58
Bank Hall	d	15 16			15 31	15 31			15 46		15 46			16 01	16 01			16 16	16 16				16 31	16 31	
Bootle Oriel Road	d	15 18			15 33	15 33			15 48		15 48			16 03	16 03			16 18	16 18				16 33	16 33	
Bootle New Strand	d	15 20			15 35	15 35			15 50		15 50			16 05	16 05			16 20	16 20				16 35	16 35	
Seaforth & Litherland	d	15 22			15 37	15 37			15 52		15 52			16 07	16 07			16 22	16 22				16 37	16 37	
Waterloo (Merseyside)	d	15 24			15 39	15 39			15 54		15 54			16 09	16 09			16 24	16 24				16 39	16 39	
Blundellsands & Crosby	d	15 27			15 42	15 42			15 57		15 57			16 12	16 12			16 27	16 27				16 42	16 42	
Hall Road	d	15 29			15 44	15 44			15 59		15 59			16 14	16 14			16 29	16 29				16 44	16 44	
Hightown	d	15 32			15 47	15 47			16 02		16 02			16 17	16 17			16 32	16 32				16 47	16 47	
Formby	d	15 36			15 51	15 51			16 06		16 06			16 21	16 21			16 36	16 36				16 51	16 51	
Freshfield	d	15 38			15 53	15 53			16 08		16 08			16 23	16 23			16 38	16 38				16 53	16 53	
Ainsdale	d	15 42			15 57	15 57			16 12		16 12			16 27	16 27			16 42	16 42				16 57	16 57	
Hillside	d	15 45			16 00	16 00			16 15		16 15			16 30	16 30			16 45	16 45				17 00	17 00	
Birkdale	d	15 47			16 02	16 02			16 17		16 17			16 32	16 32			16 47	16 47				17 02	17 02	
Southport	a	15 54			16 07	16 09			16 22		16 24			16 37	16 39			16 52	16 54				17 07	17 09	

		ME	ME SX	ME SO	ME		ME	ME SX	ME SO	ME	ME	ME SX	ME SO	ME	ME SX		ME	ME	ME	ME	ME	ME	ME	ME	ME
Hunts Cross 89	d		16 21	16 21				16 36	16 36			16 51	16 51					17 06			17 21			17 36	
Liverpool Sth Parkway 7 89 ✈	d		16 24	16 24				16 39	16 39			16 54	16 54					17 09			17 24			17 39	
Cressington	d		16 27	16 27				16 42	16 42			16 57	16 57					17 12			17 27			17 42	
Aigburth	d		16 29	16 29				16 44	16 44			16 59	16 59					17 14			17 29			17 44	
St Michaels	d		16 31	16 31				16 46	16 46			17 01	17 01					17 16			17 31			17 46	
Brunswick	d		16 34	16 34				16 49	16 49			17 04	17 04					17 19			17 34			17 49	
Liverpool Central 10	a		16 38	16 38				16 53	16 53			17 08	17 08					17 23			17 38			17 53	
	d	16 35	16 38	16 38	16 40		16 50	16 53	16 53	16 55	17 05	17 08	17 08	17 10	17 13		17 20	17 23	17 25	17 35	17 38	17 40	17 50	17 53	17 55
Moorfields 10	d	16 37	16 40	16 40	16 42		16 52	16 55	16 55	16 57	17 07	17 10	17 10	17 12	17 15		17 22	17 25	17 27	17 37	17 40	17 42	17 52	17 55	17 57
Sandhills	d	16 41	16 44	16 44	16 46		16 56	16 59	16 59	17 01	17 11	17 14	17 14	17 16	17 19		17 26	17 29	17 31	17 41	17 44	17 46	17 56	17 59	18 01
Kirkdale	d	16 44			16 49		16 59			17 04	17 14			17 19			17 29		17 34	17 44		17 49	17 59		18 04
Rice Lane	d	16 47					17 02				17 17						17 32			17 47			18 02		
Fazakerley	d	16 49					17 04				17 19						17 34			17 49			18 04		
Kirkby	a	16 53					17 08				17 23						17 38			17 53			18 08		
Walton (Merseyside)	d				16 52					17 07				17 22					17 37			17 52			18 07
Orrell Park	d				16 53					17 08				17 23					17 38			17 53			18 08
Aintree	d				16 56					17 11				17 26					17 41			17 56			18 11
Old Roan	d				16 58					17 13				17 28					17 43			17 58			18 13
Maghull	d				17 01					17 16				17 31					17 46			18 01			18 16
Town Green	d				17 05					17 20				17 35					17 50			18 05			18 20
Aughton Park	d				17 07					17 22				17 37					17 52			18 07			18 22
Ormskirk	a				17 13					17 28				17 43					17 58			18 13			18 28
Bank Hall	d		16 46	16 46				17 01	17 01			17 16	17 16		17 21			17 31			17 46			18 01	
Bootle Oriel Road	d		16 48	16 48				17 03	17 03			17 18	17 18		17 23			17 33			17 48			18 03	
Bootle New Strand	d		16 50	16 50				17 05	17 05			17 20	17 20		17 25			17 35			17 50			18 05	
Seaforth & Litherland	d		16 52	16 52				17 07	17 07			17 22	17 22		17 27			17 37			17 52			18 07	
Waterloo (Merseyside)	d		16 54	16 54				17 09	17 09			17 24	17 24		17 29			17 39			17 54			18 09	
Blundellsands & Crosby	d		16 57	16 57				17 12	17 12			17 27	17 27		17 32			17 42			17 57			18 12	
Hall Road	d		16 59	16 59				17 14	17 14			17 29	17 29		17 34			17 44			17 59			18 14	
Hightown	d		17 02	17 02				17 17	17 17			17 32	17 32		17 37			17 47			18 02			18 17	
Formby	d		17 06	17 06				17 21	17 21			17 36	17 36		17 41			17 51			18 06			18 21	
Freshfield	d		17 08	17 08				17 23	17 23			17 38	17 38		17 43			17 53			18 08			18 23	
Ainsdale	d		17 12	17 12				17 27	17 27			17 42	17 42		17 47			17 57			18 12			18 27	
Hillside	d		17 15	17 15				17 30	17 30			17 45	17 45		17 50			18 00			18 15			18 30	
Birkdale	d		17 17	17 17				17 32	17 32			17 47	17 47		17 52			18 02			18 17			18 32	
Southport	a		17 22	17 24				17 37	17 39			17 52	17 54		17 59			18 09			18 24			18 39	

Hunts Cross and Liverpool - Kirkby, Ormskirk and Southport

Network Diagram - see first Page of Table 101

Station		ME	ME	ME	ME	ME	ME	ME	ME	ME	ME	ME	ME	ME	ME	ME	ME	ME SO	ME SX	ME	ME	ME
Hunts Cross 89	d		17 51			18 06			18 21			18 36			18 51		19 06			19 21		19 36
Liverpool Sth Parkway 7 89 ✈	d		17 54			18 09			18 24			18 39			18 54		19 09			19 24		19 39
Cressington	d		17 57			18 12			18 27			18 42			18 57		19 12			19 27		19 42
Aigburth	d		17 59			18 14			18 29			18 44			18 59		19 14			19 29		19 44
St Michaels	d		18 01			18 16			18 31			18 46			19 01		19 16			19 31		19 46
Brunswick	d		18 04			18 19			18 34			18 49			19 04		19 19			19 34		19 49
Liverpool Central 10	a		18 08			18 23			18 38			18 53			19 08		19 23			19 38		19 53
	d	18 05	18 08	18 10	18 20	18 23	18 25	18 35	18 38	18 40	18 50	18 53	18 55	19 05	19 08	19 10	19 23	19 25	19 25	19 38	19 40	19 53
Moorfields 10	d	18 07	18 10	18 12	18 22	18 25	18 27	18 37	18 40	18 42	18 52	18 55	18 57	19 07	19 10	19 12	19 25	19 27	19 27	19 40	19 42	19 55
Sandhills	d	18 11	18 14	18 16	18 26	18 29	18 31	18 41	18 44	18 46	18 56	18 59	19 01	19 11	19 14	19 16	19 29	19 31	19 31	19 44	19 46	19 59
Kirkdale	d	18 14		18 19	18 29		18 34	18 44		18 49	18 59		19 04	19 14		19 19		19 34	19 34		19 49	
Rice Lane	d	18 17			18 32			18 47			19 02			19 17				19 37	19 37			
Fazakerley	d	18 19			18 34			18 49			19 04			19 19				19 40	19 40			
Kirkby	a	18 23			18 38			18 53			19 08			19 23				19 43	19 45			
Walton (Merseyside)	d			18 22			18 37			18 52			19 07			19 22					19 52	
Orrell Park	d			18 23			18 38			18 53			19 08			19 23					19 53	
Aintree	d			18 26			18 41			18 56			19 11			19 26					19 56	
Old Roan	d			18 28			18 43			18 58			19 13			19 28					19 58	
Maghull	d			18 31			18 46			19 01			19 16			19 31					20 01	
Town Green	d			18 35			18 50			19 05			19 20			19 35					20 05	
Aughton Park	d			18 37			18 52			19 07			19 22			19 37					20 07	
Ormskirk	a			18 43			18 58			19 13			19 28			19 43					20 13	
Bank Hall	d		18 16			18 31			18 46			19 01			19 16		19 31			19 46		20 01
Bootle Oriel Road	d		18 18			18 33			18 48			19 03			19 18		19 33			19 48		20 03
Bootle New Strand	d		18 20			18 35			18 50			19 05			19 20		19 35			19 50		20 05
Seaforth & Litherland	d		18 22			18 37			18 52			19 07			19 22		19 37			19 52		20 07
Waterloo (Merseyside)	d		18 24			18 39			18 54			19 09			19 24		19 39			19 54		20 09
Blundellsands & Crosby	d		18 27			18 42			18 57			19 12			19 27		19 42			19 57		20 12
Hall Road	d		18 29			18 44			18 59			19 14			19 29		19 44			19 59		20 14
Hightown	d		18 32			18 47			19 02			19 17			19 32		19 47			20 02		20 17
Formby	d		18 36			18 51			19 06			19 21			19 36		19 51			20 06		20 21
Freshfield	d		18 38			18 53			19 08			19 23			19 38		19 53			20 08		20 23
Ainsdale	d		18 42			18 57			19 12			19 27			19 42		19 57			20 12		20 27
Hillside	d		18 45			19 00			19 15			19 30			19 45		20 00			20 15		20 30
Birkdale	d		18 47			19 02			19 17			19 32			19 47		20 02			20 17		20 32
Southport	a		18 54			19 09			19 24			19 39			19 54		20 09			20 24		20 39

Station		ME SO	ME SX	ME	ME	ME	ME	ME	ME	ME	ME	ME	ME	ME	ME	ME	ME	ME	ME	ME	ME	ME	ME
Hunts Cross 89	d			19 51		20 06		20 21		20 36		20 51		21 06		21 21		21 36		21 51		22 06	
Liverpool Sth Parkway 7 89 ✈	d			19 54		20 09		20 24		20 39		20 54		21 09		21 24		21 39		21 54		22 09	
Cressington	d			19 57		20 12		20 27		20 42		20 57		21 12		21 27		21 42		21 57		22 12	
Aigburth	d			19 59		20 14		20 29		20 44		20 59		21 14		21 29		21 44		21 59		22 14	
St Michaels	d			20 01		20 16		20 31		20 46		21 01		21 16		21 31		21 46		22 01		22 16	
Brunswick	d			20 04		20 19		20 34		20 49		21 04		21 19		21 34		21 49		22 04		22 19	
Liverpool Central 10	a			20 08		20 23		20 38		20 53		21 08		21 23		21 38		21 53		22 08		22 23	
	d	19 55	19 55	20 08	20 10	20 23	20 25	20 38	20 40	20 53	20 55	21 08	21 10	21 23	21 25	21 38	21 40	21 53	21 55	22 08	22 10	22 23	22 25
Moorfields 10	d	19 57	19 57	20 10	20 12	20 25	20 27	20 40	20 42	20 55	20 57	21 10	21 12	21 25	21 27	21 40	21 42	21 55	21 57	22 10	22 12	22 25	22 27
Sandhills	d	20 01	20 01	20 14	20 16	20 29	20 31	20 44	20 46	20 59	21 01	21 14	21 16	21 29	21 31	21 44	21 46	21 59	22 01	22 14	22 16	22 29	22 31
Kirkdale	d	20 04	20 04		20 19		20 34		20 49		21 04		21 19		21 34		21 49		22 04		22 19		22 34
Rice Lane	d	20 07	20 07				20 37				21 07				21 37				22 07				22 37
Fazakerley	d	20 10	20 10				20 40				21 10				21 40				22 10				22 40
Kirkby	a	20 13	20 15				20 43				21 13				21 43				22 13				22 43
Walton (Merseyside)	d				20 22				20 52				21 22				21 52				22 22		
Orrell Park	d				20 23				20 53				21 23				21 53				22 23		
Aintree	d				20 26				20 56				21 26				21 56				22 26		
Old Roan	d				20 28				20 58				21 28				21 58				22 28		
Maghull	d				20 31				21 01				21 31				22 01				22 31		
Town Green	d				20 35				21 05				21 35				22 05				22 35		
Aughton Park	d				20 37				21 07				21 37				22 07				22 37		
Ormskirk	a				20 43				21 13				21 43				22 13				22 43		
Bank Hall	d			20 16		20 31		20 46		21 01		21 16		21 31		21 46		22 01		22 16		22 31	
Bootle Oriel Road	d			20 18		20 33		20 48		21 03		21 18		21 33		21 48		22 03		22 18		22 33	
Bootle New Strand	d			20 20		20 35		20 50		21 05		21 20		21 35		21 50		22 05		22 20		22 35	
Seaforth & Litherland	d			20 22		20 37		20 52		21 07		21 22		21 37		21 52		22 07		22 22		22 37	
Waterloo (Merseyside)	d			20 24		20 39		20 54		21 09		21 24		21 39		21 54		22 09		22 24		22 39	
Blundellsands & Crosby	d			20 27		20 42		20 57		21 12		21 27		21 42		21 57		22 12		22 27		22 42	
Hall Road	d			20 29		20 44		20 59		21 14		21 29		21 44		21 59		22 14		22 29		22 44	
Hightown	d			20 32		20 47		21 02		21 17		21 32		21 47		22 02		22 17		22 32		22 47	
Formby	d			20 36		20 51		21 06		21 21		21 36		21 51		22 06		22 21		22 36		22 51	
Freshfield	d			20 38		20 53		21 08		21 23		21 38		21 53		22 08		22 23		22 38		22 53	
Ainsdale	d			20 42		20 57		21 12		21 27		21 42		21 57		22 12		22 27		22 42		22 57	
Hillside	d			20 45		21 00		21 15		21 30		21 45		22 00		22 15		22 30		22 45		23 00	
Birkdale	d			20 47		21 02		21 17		21 32		21 47		22 02		22 17		22 32		22 47		23 02	
Southport	a			20 54		21 09		21 24		21 39		21 54		22 09		22 24		22 39		22 54		23 09	

Hunts Cross and Liverpool - Kirkby, Ormskirk and Southport

Network Diagram - see first Page of Table 101

		ME	ME		ME	ME	ME	ME	ME	ME	ME	ME	ME
Hunts Cross 89	d	22 21			22 36		22 51		23 06		23 21		
Liverpool Sth Parkway 7 89 ✈	d	22 24			22 39		22 54		23 09		23 24		
Cressington	d	22 27			22 42		22 57		23 12		23 27		
Aigburth	d	22 29			22 44		22 59		23 14		23 29		
St Michaels	d	22 31			22 46		23 01		23 16		23 31		
Brunswick	d	22 34			22 49		23 04		23 19		23 34		
Liverpool Central 10	a	22 38			22 53		23 08		23 23		23 38		
	d	22 38	22 40		22 53	22 55	23 08	23 10	23 23	23 25	23 38	23 40	23 55
Moorfields 10	d	22 40	22 42		22 55	22 57	23 10	23 12	23 25	23 27	23 40	23 42	23 57
Sandhills	d	22 44	22 46		22 59	23 01	23 14	23 16	23 29	23 31	23 44	23 46	00 01
Kirkdale	d		22 49			23 04		23 19		23 34		23 49	00 04
Rice Lane	d					23 07				23 37			00 07
Fazakerley	d					23 10				23 40			00 10
Kirkby	a					23 13				23 43			00 13
Walton (Merseyside)	d		22 52					23 22				23 52	
Orrell Park	d		22 53					23 23				23 53	
Aintree	d		22 56					23 26				23 56	
Old Roan	d		22 58					23 28				23 58	
Maghull	d		23 01					23 31				00 01	
Town Green	d		23 05					23 35				00 05	
Aughton Park	d		23 07					23 37				00 07	
Ormskirk	a		23 13					23 42				00 12	
Bank Hall	d	22 46			23 01		23 16		23 31		23 46		
Bootle Oriel Road	d	22 48			23 03		23 18		23 33		23 48		
Bootle New Strand	d	22 50			23 05		23 20		23 35		23 50		
Seaforth & Litherland	d	22 52			23 07		23 22		23 37		23 52		
Waterloo (Merseyside)	d	22 54			23 09		23 24		23 39		23 54		
Blundellsands & Crosby	d	22 57			23 12		23 27		23 42		23 57		
Hall Road	d	22 59			23 14		23 29		23 44		23 59		
Hightown	d	23 02			23 17		23 32		23 47		00 02		
Formby	d	23 06			23 21		23 36		23 51		00 06		
Freshfield	d	23 08			23 23		23 38		23 53		00 08		
Ainsdale	d	23 12			23 27		23 42		23 57		00 12		
Hillside	d	23 15			23 30		23 45		23 59		00 15		
Birkdale	d	23 17			23 32		23 47		00 02		00 17		
Southport	a	23 24			23 39		23 54		00 09		00 24		

Sundays

		ME A	ME A	ME A	ME A	ME	ME	ME	ME	ME		ME	ME	ME	ME	ME	ME	ME	ME	ME		ME	ME	ME
Hunts Cross 89	d	23p06	23p21					08 06				08 36			09 06			09 36					10 06	
Liverpool Sth Parkway 7 89 ✈	d	23p09	23p24					08 09				08 39			09 09			09 39					10 09	
Cressington	d	23p12	23p27					08 12				08 42			09 12			09 42					10 12	
Aigburth	d	23p14	23p29					08 14				08 44			09 14			09 44					10 14	
St Michaels	d	23p16	23p31					08 16				08 46			09 16			09 46					10 16	
Brunswick	d	23p19	23p34					08 19				08 49			09 19			09 49					10 19	
Liverpool Central 10	a	23p23	23p38					08 23				08 53			09 23			09 53					10 23	
	d	23p23	23p38	23p40	23p55	08 08	08 10	08 23	08 25	08 40		08 53	08 55	09 10	09 23	09 25	09 40	09 53	09 55	10 08		10 10	10 23	10 25
Moorfields 10	d	23p25	23p40	23p42	23p57	08 10	08 12	08 25	08 27	08 42		08 55	08 57	09 12	09 25	09 27	09 42	09 55	09 57	10 10		10 12	10 25	10 27
Sandhills	d	23p29	23p44	23p46	00 01	08 14	08 16	08 29	08 31	08 46		08 59	09 01	09 16	09 29	09 31	09 46	09 59	10 01	10 14		10 16	10 29	10 31
Kirkdale	d			23p49	00 04		08 19		08 34	08 49			09 04	09 19		09 34	09 49		10 04			10 19		10 34
Rice Lane	d				00 07				08 37				09 07			09 37			10 07					10 37
Fazakerley	d				00 10				08 40				09 10			09 40			10 10					10 40
Kirkby	a				00 13				08 43				09 13			09 43			10 13					10 43
Walton (Merseyside)	d			23p52			08 22			08 52				09 22			09 52					10 22		
Orrell Park	d			23p53			08 23			08 53				09 23			09 53					10 23		
Aintree	d			23p56			08 26			08 56				09 26			09 56					10 26		
Old Roan	d			23p58			08 28			08 58				09 28			09 58					10 28		
Maghull	d			00 01			08 31			09 01				09 31			10 01					10 31		
Town Green	d			00 05			08 35			09 05				09 35			10 05					10 35		
Aughton Park	d			00 07			08 37			09 07				09 37			10 07					10 37		
Ormskirk	a			00 12			08 43			09 13				09 43			10 13					10 43		
Bank Hall	d	23p31	23p46			08 16		08 31				09 01			09 31			10 01		10 16			10 31	
Bootle Oriel Road	d	23p33	23p48			08 18		08 33				09 03			09 33			10 03		10 18			10 33	
Bootle New Strand	d	23p35	23p50			08 20		08 35				09 05			09 35			10 05		10 20			10 35	
Seaforth & Litherland	d	23p37	23p52			08 22		08 37				09 07			09 37			10 07		10 22			10 37	
Waterloo (Merseyside)	d	23p39	23p54			08 24		08 39				09 09			09 39			10 09		10 24			10 39	
Blundellsands & Crosby	d	23p42	23p57			08 27		08 42				09 12			09 42			10 12		10 27			10 42	
Hall Road	d	23p44	23p59			08 29		08 44				09 14			09 44			10 14		10 29			10 44	
Hightown	d	23p47	00 02			08 32		08 47				09 17			09 47			10 17		10 32			10 47	
Formby	d	23p51	00 06			08 36		08 51				09 21			09 51			10 21		10 36			10 51	
Freshfield	d	23p53	00 08			08 38		08 53				09 23			09 53			10 23		10 38			10 53	
Ainsdale	d	23p57	00 12			08 42		08 57				09 27			09 57			10 27		10 42			10 57	
Hillside	d	23p59	00 15			08 45		09 00				09 30			10 00			10 30		10 45			11 00	
Birkdale	d	00 02	00 17			08 47		09 02				09 32			10 02			10 32		10 47			11 02	
Southport	a	00 09	00 24			08 52		09 09				09 39			10 09			10 39		10 52			11 09	

A not 11 December

Hunts Cross and Liverpool - Kirkby, Ormskirk and Southport

Network Diagram - see first Page of Table 101

		ME		ME	ME	ME		ME	ME	ME	ME	ME	ME	ME	ME	ME
Hunts Cross 89	d					22 36					23 06	23 06				
Liverpool Sth Parkway 7 89 ✈	d					22 39					23 09	23 09				
Cressington	d					22 42					23 12	23 12				
Aigburth	d					22 44					23 14	23 14				
St Michaels	d					22 46					23 16	23 16				
Brunswick	d					22 49					23 19	23 19				
Liverpool Central 10	a					22 53					23 23	23 23				
	d	10 38		22 38	22 40	22 53		22 55	23 08	23 10	23 23	23 23	23 25	23 38	23 40	23 55
Moorfields 10	d	10 40		22 40	22 42	22 55		22 57	23 10	23 12	23 25	23 25	23 27	23 40	23 42	23 57
Sandhills	d	10 44		22 44	22 46	22 59		23 01	23 14	23 16	23 29	23a29	23 31	23 44	23 46	00 01
Kirkdale	d				22 49			23 04		23 19			23 34		23 49	00 04
Rice Lane	d							23 07					23 37			00 07
Fazakerley	d							23 10					23 40			00 10
Kirkby	a							23 13					23 43			00 13
Walton (Merseyside)	d		and at		22 52					23 22					23 52	
Orrell Park	d		the same		22 53					23 23					23 53	
Aintree	d		minutes		22 56					23 26					23 56	
Old Roan	d		past		22 58					23 28					23 58	
Maghull	d		each		23 01					23 31					00 01	
Town Green	d		hour until		23 05					23 35					00 05	
Aughton Park	d				23 07					23 37					00 07	
Ormskirk	a				23 13					23 42					00 12	
Bank Hall	d	10 46		22 46		23 01			23 16		23 31			23 46		
Bootle Oriel Road	d	10 48		22 48		23 03			23 18		23 33			23 48		
Bootle New Strand	d	10 50		22 50		23 05			23 20		23 35			23 50		
Seaforth & Litherland	d	10 52		22 52		23 07			23 22		23 37			23 52		
Waterloo (Merseyside)	d	10 54		22 54		23 09			23 24		23 39			23 54		
Blundellsands & Crosby	d	10 57		22 57		23 12			23 27		23 42			23 57		
Hall Road	d	10 59		22 59		23 14			23 29		23 44			23 59		
Hightown	d	11 02		23 02		23 17			23 32		23 47			00 02		
Formby	d	11 06		23 06		23 21			23 36		23 51			00 06		
Freshfield	d	11 08		23 08		23 23			23 38		23 53			00 08		
Ainsdale	d	11 12		23 12		23 27			23 42		23 57			00 12		
Hillside	d	11 15		23 15		23 30			23 45		23 59			00 15		
Birkdale	d	11 17		23 17		23 32			23 47		00 02			00 17		
Southport	a	11 22		23 22		23 39			23 52		00 09			00 24		

Southport, Ormskirk and Kirby - Liverpool and Hunts Cross

Network Diagram - see first Page of Table 101

Miles	Miles	Miles			ME	ME	ME	ME	ME	ME	ME	ME	ME		ME	ME	ME	ME	ME	ME	ME	ME SX	ME SO		ME
0	—	—	**Southport**	d	22p58	23p16				05 38		05 53			06 08		06 23		06 43			06 58	06 58		
1	—	—	Birkdale	d	23p02	23p20				05 42		05 57			06 12		06 27		06 47			07 02	07 02		
2	—	—	Hillside	d	23p04	23p22				05 44		05 59			06 14		06 29		06 49			07 04	07 04		
3½	—	—	Ainsdale	d	23p07	23p25				05 47		06 02			06 17		06 32		06 52			07 07	07 07		
6¼	—	—	Freshfield	d	23p11	23p29				05 51		06 06			06 21		06 36		06 56			07 11	07 11		
7¼	—	—	Formby	d	23p13	23p31				05 53		06 08			06 23		06 38		06 58			07 13	07 13		
9¼	—	—	Hightown	d	23p17	23p35				05 57		06 12			06 27		06 42		07 02			07 17	07 17		
11¼	—	—	Hall Road	d	23p20	23p38				06 00		06 15			06 30		06 45		07 05			07 20	07 20		
12	—	—	Blundellsands & Crosby	d	23p22	23p40				06 02		06 17			06 32		06 47		07 07			07 22	07 22		
13	—	—	Waterloo (Merseyside)	d	23p25	23p43				06 05		06 20			06 35		06 50		07 10			07 25	07 25		
14¼	—	—	Seaforth & Litherland	d	23p27	23p45				06 07		06 22			06 37		06 52		07 12			07 27	07 27		
15¼	—	—	Bootle New Strand	d	23p30	23p48				06 10		06 25			06 40		06 55		07 15			07 30	07 30		
15½	—	—	Bootle Oriel Road	d	23p31	23p49				06 11		06 26			06 41		06 56		07 16			07 31	07 31		
16¼	—	—	Bank Hall	d	23p33	23p51				06 18		06 33			06 48		07 03		07 18			07 33	07 33		
—	0	—	**Ormskirk**	d					05 50				06 20					06 50			07 05				
—	1¼	—	Aughton Park	d					05 53				06 23					06 53			07 08				
—	2¼	—	Town Green	d					05 55				06 25					06 55			07 10				
—	4¾	—	Maghull	d					06 00				06 30					07 00			07 15				
—	6½	—	Old Roan	d					06 03				06 33					07 03			07 18				
—	7¼	—	Aintree	d					06 05				06 35					07 05			07 20				
—	8¼	—	Orrell Park	d					06 07				06 37					07 07			07 22				
—	8½	—	Walton (Merseyside)	d					06 09				06 39					07 09			07 24				
—	—	0	**Kirkby**	d			05 48				06 18					06 48				07 13					07 28
—	—	1¾	Fazakerley	d			05 51				06 21					06 51				07 16					07 31
—	—	3¼	Rice Lane	d			05 54				06 24					06 54				07 19					07 34
—	9¾	4½	Kirkdale	d			05 57		06 12		06 27		06 42			06 57		07 12		07 22	07 27				07 37
17	10¾	5½	Sandhills	d	23p36	23p55	06 00	06 06	06 14	06 21	06 30	06 36	06 44		06 51	07 00	07 06	07 14	07 21	07 25	07 29	07 36	07 36		07 40
18½	12¼	7	**Moorfields** [10]	d	23p40	23p58	06 03	06 10	06 18	06 25	06 33	06 40	06 48		06 55	07 03	07 10	07 18	07 25	07 28	07 33	07 40	07 40		07 43
19	12¾	7½	**Liverpool Central** [10]	a	23p43	00 01	06 06	06 13	06 20	06 28	06 36	06 43	06 50		06 58	07 06	07 13	07 20	07 28	07 31	07 35	07 43	07 43		07 46
—	—	—		d	23p44			06 14		06 29		06 43			06 59		07 14		07 29			07 44	07 44		
20½	—	—	Brunswick	d	23p47			06 17		06 32		06 47			07 02		07 17		07 32			07 47	07 47		
21¾	—	—	St Michaels	d	23p50			06 20		06 35		06 49			07 05		07 20		07 35			07 50	07 50		
23	—	—	Aigburth	d	23p52			06 22		06 37		06 52			07 07		07 22		07 37			07 52	07 52		
23¾	—	—	Cressington	d	23p54			06 24		06 39		06 54			07 09		07 24		07 39			07 54	07 54		
24¾	—	—	**Liverpool Sth Parkway** [7] 89 ✈	d	23p57			06 27		06 42		06 56			07 12		07 27		07 42			07 57	07 57		
26¼	—	—	**Hunts Cross** 89	a	00 02			06 32		06 47		07 02			07 17		07 32		07 47			08 01	08 02		

		ME	ME	ME	ME	ME	ME	ME	ME SX		ME SO	ME	ME SX	ME	ME	ME	ME SX	ME	ME		ME	ME	ME	ME	ME
Southport	d		07 13			07 28			07 38		07 43		07 48		07 58		08 03		08 13				08 28		
Birkdale	d		07 17			07 32			07 42		07 47		07 52		08 02		08 07		08 17				08 32		
Hillside	d		07 19			07 34			07 44		07 49		07 54		08 04		08 09		08 19				08 34		
Ainsdale	d		07 22			07 37			07 47		07 52		07 57		08 07		08 12		08 22				08 37		
Freshfield	d		07 26			07 41			07 51		07 56		08 01		08 11		08 16		08 26				08 41		
Formby	d		07 28			07 43			07 53		07 58		08 03		08 13		08 18		08 28				08 43		
Hightown	d		07 32			07 47			07 57		08 02		08 07		08 17		08 22		08 32				08 47		
Hall Road	d		07 35			07 50			08 00		08 05		08 10		08 20		08 25		08 35				08 50		
Blundellsands & Crosby	d		07 37			07 52			08 02		08 07		08 12		08 22		08 27		08 37				08 52		
Waterloo (Merseyside)	d		07 40			07 55			08 05		08 10		08 15		08 25		08 30		08 40				08 55		
Seaforth & Litherland	d		07 42			07 57			08 07		08 12		08 17		08 27		08 32		08 42				08 57		
Bootle New Strand	d		07 45			08 00			08 10		08 15		08 20		08 30		08 35		08 45				09 00		
Bootle Oriel Road	d		07 46			08 01			08 11		08 16		08 21		08 31		08 36		08 46				09 01		
Bank Hall	d		07 48			08 03			08 18		08 18		08 23		08 33		08 38		08 48				09 03		
Ormskirk	d	07 20			07 35			07 50						08 05				08 20				08 35			08 50
Aughton Park	d	07 23			07 38			07 53						08 08				08 23				08 38			08 53
Town Green	d	07 25			07 40			07 55						08 10				08 25				08 40			08 55
Maghull	d	07 30			07 45			08 00						08 15				08 30				08 45			09 00
Old Roan	d	07 33			07 48			08 03						08 18				08 33				08 48			09 03
Aintree	d	07 35			07 50			08 05						08 20				08 35				08 50			09 05
Orrell Park	d	07 37			07 52			08 07						08 22				08 37				08 52			09 07
Walton (Merseyside)	d	07 39			07 54			08 09						08 24				08 39				08 54			09 09
Kirkby	d			07 43			07 58					08 13				08 28					08 43			08 58	
Fazakerley	d			07 46			08 01					08 16				08 31					08 46			09 01	
Rice Lane	d			07 49			08 04					08 19				08 34					08 49			09 04	
Kirkdale	d	07 42		07 52	07 57		08 07	08 12				08 22		08 27		08 37		08 42			08 52	08 57		09 07	09 12
Sandhills	d	07 44	07 51	07 55	07 59	08 06	08 10	08 14	08 21		08 21	08 25	08 27	08 29	08 36	08 40	08 42	08 44	08 51		08 55	08 59	09 06	09 10	09 14
Moorfields [10]	d	07 48	07 55	07 58	08 03	08 10	08 13	08 18	08 25		08 25	08 28	08 31	08 33	08 40	08 43	08 46	08 48	08 55		08 58	09 03	09 10	09 13	09 18
Liverpool Central [10]	a	07 50	07 58	08 01	08 05	08 13	08 16	08 20	08 28		08 28	08 31	08 33	08 35	08 43	08 46	08 48	08 50	08 58		09 01	09 05	09 13	09 16	09 20
	d		07 59			08 14			08 29		08 29				08 44				08 59				09 14		
Brunswick	d		08 02			08 17			08 32		08 32				08 47				09 02				09 17		
St Michaels	d		08 05			08 20			08 35		08 35				08 50				09 05				09 20		
Aigburth	d		08 07			08 22			08 37		08 37				08 52				09 07				09 22		
Cressington	d		08 09			08 24			08 39		08 39				08 54				09 09				09 24		
Liverpool Sth Parkway [7] 89 ✈	d		08 12			08 27			08 42		08 42				08 57				09 12				09 27		
Hunts Cross 89	a		08 17			08 32			08 47		08 47				09 02				09 17				09 32		

Southport, Ormskirk and Kirby - Liverpool and Hunts Cross

Network Diagram - see first Page of Table 101

		ME	ME	ME	ME		ME	ME	ME	ME	ME	ME	ME	ME	ME		ME	ME	ME	ME	ME	ME	ME	ME	ME
Southport	d	08 43			08 58				09 13			09 28			09 43				09 58			10 13			10 28
Birkdale	d	08 47			09 02				09 17			09 32			09 47				10 02			10 17			10 32
Hillside	d	08 49			09 04				09 19			09 34			09 49				10 04			10 19			10 34
Ainsdale	d	08 52			09 07				09 22			09 37			09 52				10 07			10 22			10 37
Freshfield	d	08 56			09 11				09 26			09 41			09 56				10 11			10 26			10 41
Formby	d	08 58			09 13				09 28			09 43			09 58				10 13			10 28			10 43
Hightown	d	09 02			09 17				09 32			09 47			10 02				10 17			10 32			10 47
Hall Road	d	09 05			09 20				09 35			09 50			10 05				10 20			10 35			10 50
Blundellsands & Crosby	d	09 07			09 22				09 37			09 52			10 07				10 22			10 37			10 52
Waterloo (Merseyside)	d	09 10			09 25				09 40			09 55			10 10				10 25			10 40			10 55
Seaforth & Litherland	d	09 12			09 27				09 42			09 57			10 12				10 27			10 42			10 57
Bootle New Strand	d	09 15			09 30				09 45			10 00			10 15				10 30			10 45			11 00
Bootle Oriel Road	d	09 16			09 31				09 46			10 01			10 16				10 31			10 46			11 01
Bank Hall	d	09 18			09 33				09 48			10 03			10 18				10 33			10 48			11 03
Ormskirk	d			09 05				09 20			09 35			09 50				10 05			10 20			10 35	
Aughton Park	d			09 08				09 23			09 38			09 53				10 08			10 23			10 38	
Town Green	d			09 10				09 25			09 40			09 55				10 10			10 25			10 40	
Maghull	d			09 15				09 30			09 45			10 00				10 15			10 30			10 45	
Old Roan	d			09 18				09 33			09 48			10 03				10 18			10 33			10 48	
Aintree	d			09 20				09 35			09 50			10 05				10 20			10 35			10 50	
Orrell Park	d			09 22				09 37			09 52			10 07				10 22			10 37			10 52	
Walton (Merseyside)	d			09 24				09 39			09 54			10 09				10 24			10 39			10 54	
Kirkby	d		09 13				09 28			09 43			09 58				10 13			10 28			10 43		
Fazakerley	d		09 16				09 31			09 46			10 01				10 16			10 31			10 46		
Rice Lane	d		09 19				09 34			09 49			10 04				10 19			10 34			10 49		
Kirkdale	d		09 22	09 27			09 37	09 42		09 52	09 57		10 07	10 12			10 22	10 27		10 37	10 42		10 52	10 57	
Sandhills	d	09 21	09 25	09 29	09 36		09 40	09 44	09 51	09 55	09 59	10 06	10 10	10 14	10 21		10 25	10 29	10 36	10 40	10 44	10 51	10 55	10 59	11 06
Moorfields [10]	d	09 25	09 28	09 33	09 40		09 43	09 48	09 55	09 58	10 03	10 10	10 13	10 18	10 25		10 28	10 33	10 40	10 43	10 48	10 55	10 58	11 03	11 10
Liverpool Central [10]	a	09 28	09 31	09 35	09 43		09 46	09 50	09 58	10 01	10 05	10 13	10 16	10 20	10 28		10 31	10 35	10 43	10 46	10 50	10 58	11 01	11 05	11 13
	d	09 29			09 44				09 59			10 14			10 29				10 44			10 59			11 14
Brunswick	d	09 32			09 47				10 02			10 17			10 32				10 47			11 02			11 17
St Michaels	d	09 35			09 50				10 05			10 20			10 35				10 50			11 05			11 20
Aigburth	d	09 37			09 52				10 07			10 22			10 37				10 52			11 07			11 22
Cressington	d	09 39			09 54				10 09			10 24			10 39				10 54			11 09			11 24
Liverpool Sth Parkway [7] 89 ✈	d	09 42			09 57				10 12			10 27			10 42				10 57			11 12			11 27
Hunts Cross 89	a	09 47			10 02				10 17			10 32			10 47				11 02			11 17			11 32

			ME	ME	ME	ME	ME	ME	ME	ME	ME		ME	ME	ME	ME	ME	ME	ME	ME	ME		ME	ME	ME
Southport	d				10 43			10 58			11 13				11 28			11 43			11 58				12 13
Birkdale	d				10 47			11 02			11 17				11 32			11 47			12 02				12 17
Hillside	d				10 49			11 04			11 19				11 34			11 49			12 04				12 19
Ainsdale	d				10 52			11 07			11 22				11 37			11 52			12 07				12 22
Freshfield	d				10 56			11 11			11 26				11 41			11 56			12 11				12 26
Formby	d				10 58			11 13			11 28				11 43			11 58			12 13				12 28
Hightown	d				11 02			11 17			11 32				11 47			12 02			12 17				12 32
Hall Road	d				11 05			11 20			11 35				11 50			12 05			12 20				12 35
Blundellsands & Crosby	d				11 07			11 22			11 37				11 52			12 07			12 22				12 37
Waterloo (Merseyside)	d				11 10			11 25			11 40				11 55			12 10			12 25				12 40
Seaforth & Litherland	d				11 12			11 27			11 42				11 57			12 12			12 27				12 42
Bootle New Strand	d				11 15			11 30			11 45				12 00			12 15			12 30				12 45
Bootle Oriel Road	d				11 16			11 31			11 46				12 01			12 16			12 31				12 46
Bank Hall	d				11 18			11 33			11 48				12 03			12 18			12 33				12 48
Ormskirk	d			10 50			11 05			11 20				11 35			11 50			12 05				12 20	
Aughton Park	d			10 53			11 08			11 23				11 38			11 53			12 08				12 23	
Town Green	d			10 55			11 10			11 25				11 40			11 55			12 10				12 25	
Maghull	d			11 00			11 15			11 30				11 45			12 00			12 15				12 30	
Old Roan	d			11 03			11 18			11 33				11 48			12 03			12 18				12 33	
Aintree	d			11 05			11 20			11 35				11 50			12 05			12 20				12 35	
Orrell Park	d			11 07			11 22			11 37				11 52			12 07			12 22				12 37	
Walton (Merseyside)	d			11 09			11 24			11 39				11 54			12 09			12 24				12 39	
Kirkby	d		10 58			11 13			11 28				11 43			11 58			12 13				12 28		
Fazakerley	d		11 01			11 16			11 31				11 46			12 01			12 16				12 31		
Rice Lane	d		11 04			11 19			11 34				11 49			12 04			12 19				12 34		
Kirkdale	d		11 07	11 12		11 22	11 27		11 37	11 42			11 52	11 57		12 07	12 12		12 22	12 27			12 37	12 42	
Sandhills	d		11 10	11 14	11 21	11 25	11 29	11 36	11 40	11 44	11 51		11 55	11 59	12 06	12 10	12 14	12 21	12 25	12 29	12 36		12 40	12 44	12 51
Moorfields [10]	d		11 13	11 18	11 25	11 28	11 33	11 40	11 43	11 48	11 55		11 58	12 03	12 10	12 13	12 18	12 25	12 28	12 33	12 40		12 43	12 48	12 55
Liverpool Central [10]	a		11 16	11 20	11 28	11 31	11 35	11 43	11 46	11 50	11 58		12 01	12 05	12 13	12 16	12 20	12 28	12 31	12 35	12 43		12 46	12 50	12 58
	d				11 29			11 44			11 59				12 14			12 29			12 44				12 59
Brunswick	d				11 32			11 47			12 02				12 17			12 32			12 47				13 02
St Michaels	d				11 35			11 50			12 05				12 20			12 35			12 50				13 05
Aigburth	d				11 37			11 52			12 07				12 22			12 37			12 52				13 07
Cressington	d				11 39			11 54			12 09				12 24			12 39			12 54				13 09
Liverpool Sth Parkway [7] 89 ✈	d				11 42			11 57			12 12				12 27			12 42			12 57				13 12
Hunts Cross 89	a				11 47			12 02			12 17				12 32			12 47			13 02				13 17

Table 103

Mondays to Saturdays

Southport, Ormskirk and Kirby - Liverpool and Hunts Cross

Network Diagram - see first Page of Table 101

		ME	ME	ME	ME	ME	ME		ME	ME	ME	ME	ME	ME	ME	ME	ME		ME	ME	ME	ME	ME	ME	ME
Southport	d			12 28			12 43				12 58			13 13			13 28				13 43			13 58	
Birkdale	d			12 32			12 47				13 02			13 17			13 32				13 47			14 02	
Hillside	d			12 34			12 49				13 04			13 19			13 34				13 49			14 04	
Ainsdale	d			12 37			12 52				13 07			13 22			13 37				13 52			14 07	
Freshfield	d			12 41			12 56				13 11			13 26			13 41				13 56			14 11	
Formby	d			12 43			12 58				13 13			13 28			13 43				13 58			14 13	
Hightown	d			12 47			13 02				13 17			13 32			13 47				14 02			14 17	
Hall Road	d			12 50			13 05				13 20			13 35			13 50				14 05			14 20	
Blundellsands & Crosby	d			12 52			13 07				13 22			13 37			13 52				14 07			14 22	
Waterloo (Merseyside)	d			12 55			13 10				13 25			13 40			13 55				14 10			14 25	
Seaforth & Litherland	d			12 57			13 12				13 27			13 42			13 57				14 12			14 27	
Bootle New Strand	d			13 00			13 15				13 30			13 45			14 00				14 15			14 30	
Bootle Oriel Road	d			13 01			13 16				13 31			13 46			14 01				14 16			14 31	
Bank Hall	d			13 03			13 18				13 33			13 48			14 03				14 18			14 33	
Ormskirk	d		12 35			12 50				13 05			13 20			13 35				13 50			14 05		
Aughton Park	d		12 38			12 53				13 08			13 23			13 38				13 53			14 08		
Town Green	d		12 40			12 55				13 10			13 25			13 40				13 55			14 10		
Maghull	d		12 45			13 00				13 15			13 30			13 45				14 00			14 15		
Old Roan	d		12 48			13 03				13 18			13 33			13 48				14 03			14 18		
Aintree	d		12 50			13 05				13 20			13 35			13 50				14 05			14 20		
Orrell Park	d		12 52			13 07				13 22			13 37			13 52				14 07			14 22		
Walton (Merseyside)	d		12 54			13 09				13 24			13 39			13 54				14 09			14 24		
Kirkby	d	12 43			12 58				13 13			13 28			13 43				13 58			14 13			14 28
Fazakerley	d	12 46			13 01				13 16			13 31			13 46				14 01			14 16			14 31
Rice Lane	d	12 49			13 04				13 19			13 34			13 49				14 04			14 19			14 34
Kirkdale	d	12 52	12 57		13 07	13 12			13 22	13 27		13 37	13 42		13 52	13 57			14 07	14 12		14 22	14 27		14 37
Sandhills	d	12 55	12 59	13 06	13 10	13 14	13 21		13 25	13 29	13 36	13 40	13 44	13 51	13 55	13 59	14 06		14 10	14 14	14 21	14 25	14 29	14 36	14 40
Moorfields [10]	d	12 58	13 03	13 10	13 13	13 18	13 25		13 28	13 33	13 40	13 43	13 48	13 55	13 58	14 03	14 10		14 13	14 18	14 25	14 28	14 33	14 40	14 43
Liverpool Central [10]	a	13 01	13 05	13 13	13 16	13 20	13 28		13 31	13 35	13 43	13 46	13 50	13 58	14 01	14 05	14 13		14 16	14 20	14 28	14 31	14 35	14 43	14 46
	d			13 14			13 29				13 44			13 59			14 14				14 29			14 44	
Brunswick	d			13 17			13 32				13 47			14 02			14 17				14 32			14 47	
St Michaels	d			13 20			13 35				13 50			14 05			14 20				14 35			14 50	
Aigburth	d			13 22			13 37				13 52			14 07			14 22				14 37			14 52	
Cressington	d			13 24			13 39				13 54			14 09			14 24				14 39			14 54	
Liverpool Sth Parkway [7] 89 ✈	d			13 27			13 42				13 57			14 12			14 27				14 42			14 57	
Hunts Cross 89	a			13 32			13 47				14 02			14 17			14 32				14 47			15 02	

		ME	ME		ME	ME	ME	ME	ME	ME	ME	ME	ME		ME	ME	ME	ME	ME	ME	ME	ME	ME		ME
Southport	d		14 13				14 28			14 43			14 58				15 13			15 28			15 43		
Birkdale	d		14 17				14 32			14 47			15 02				15 17			15 32			15 47		
Hillside	d		14 19				14 34			14 49			15 04				15 19			15 34			15 49		
Ainsdale	d		14 22				14 37			14 52			15 07				15 22			15 37			15 52		
Freshfield	d		14 26				14 41			14 56			15 11				15 26			15 41			15 56		
Formby	d		14 28				14 43			14 58			15 13				15 28			15 43			15 58		
Hightown	d		14 32				14 47			15 02			15 17				15 32			15 47			16 02		
Hall Road	d		14 35				14 50			15 05			15 20				15 35			15 50			16 05		
Blundellsands & Crosby	d		14 37				14 52			15 07			15 22				15 37			15 52			16 07		
Waterloo (Merseyside)	d		14 40				14 55			15 10			15 25				15 40			15 55			16 10		
Seaforth & Litherland	d		14 42				14 57			15 12			15 27				15 42			15 57			16 12		
Bootle New Strand	d		14 45				15 00			15 15			15 30				15 45			16 00			16 15		
Bootle Oriel Road	d		14 46				15 01			15 16			15 31				15 46			16 01			16 16		
Bank Hall	d		14 48				15 03			15 18			15 33				15 48			16 03			16 18		
Ormskirk	d	14 20				14 35			14 50			15 05				15 20			15 35			15 50			
Aughton Park	d	14 23				14 38			14 53			15 08				15 23			15 38			15 53			
Town Green	d	14 25				14 40			14 55			15 10				15 25			15 40			15 55			
Maghull	d	14 30				14 45			15 00			15 15				15 30			15 45			16 00			
Old Roan	d	14 33				14 48			15 03			15 18				15 33			15 48			16 03			
Aintree	d	14 35				14 50			15 05			15 20				15 35			15 50			16 05			
Orrell Park	d	14 37				14 52			15 07			15 22				15 37			15 52			16 07			
Walton (Merseyside)	d	14 39				14 54			15 09			15 24				15 39			15 54			16 09			
Kirkby	d				14 43			14 58			15 13				15 28			15 43			15 58				16 13
Fazakerley	d				14 46			15 01			15 16				15 31			15 46			16 01				16 16
Rice Lane	d				14 49			15 04			15 19				15 34			15 49			16 04				16 19
Kirkdale	d	14 42			14 52	14 57		15 07	15 12		15 22	15 27			15 37	15 42		15 52	15 57		16 07	16 12			16 22
Sandhills	d	14 44	14 51		14 55	14 59	15 06	15 10	15 14	15 21	15 25	15 29	15 36		15 40	15 44	15 51	15 55	15 59	16 06	16 10	16 14	16 21		16 25
Moorfields [10]	d	14 48	14 55		14 58	15 03	15 10	15 13	15 18	15 25	15 28	15 33	15 40		15 43	15 48	15 55	15 58	16 03	16 10	16 13	16 18	16 25		16 28
Liverpool Central [10]	a	14 50	14 58		15 01	15 05	15 13	15 16	15 20	15 28	15 31	15 35	15 43		15 46	15 50	15 58	16 01	16 05	16 13	16 16	16 20	16 28		16 31
	d		14 59				15 14			15 29			15 44				15 59			16 14			16 29		
Brunswick	d		15 02				15 17			15 32			15 47				16 02			16 17			16 32		
St Michaels	d		15 05				15 20			15 35			15 50				16 05			16 20			16 35		
Aigburth	d		15 07				15 22			15 37			15 52				16 07			16 22			16 37		
Cressington	d		15 09				15 24			15 39			15 54				16 09			16 24			16 39		
Liverpool Sth Parkway [7] 89 ✈	d		15 12				15 27			15 42			15 57				16 12			16 27			16 42		
Hunts Cross 89	a		15 17				15 32			15 47			16 02				16 17			16 32			16 47		

Southport, Ormskirk and Kirby - Liverpool and Hunts Cross

Network Diagram - see first Page of Table 101

		ME	ME	ME	ME	ME	ME	ME	ME		ME	ME	ME	ME	ME	ME	ME	ME	ME		ME	ME	ME	ME	ME
Southport	d		15 58			16 13			16 28				16 43			16 58			17 13				17 28		
Birkdale	d		16 02			16 17			16 32				16 47			17 02			17 17				17 32		
Hillside	d		16 04			16 19			16 34				16 49			17 04			17 19				17 34		
Ainsdale	d		16 07			16 22			16 37				16 52			17 07			17 22				17 37		
Freshfield	d		16 11			16 26			16 41				16 56			17 11			17 26				17 41		
Formby	d		16 13			16 28			16 43				16 58			17 13			17 28				17 43		
Hightown	d		16 17			16 32			16 47				17 02			17 17			17 32				17 47		
Hall Road	d		16 20			16 35			16 50				17 05			17 20			17 35				17 50		
Blundellsands & Crosby	d		16 22			16 37			16 52				17 07			17 22			17 37				17 52		
Waterloo (Merseyside)	d		16 25			16 40			16 55				17 10			17 25			17 40				17 55		
Seaforth & Litherland	d		16 27			16 42			16 57				17 12			17 27			17 42				17 57		
Bootle New Strand	d		16 30			16 45			17 00				17 15			17 30			17 45				18 00		
Bootle Oriel Road	d		16 31			16 46			17 01				17 16			17 31			17 46				18 01		
Bank Hall	d		16 33			16 48			17 03				17 18			17 33			17 48				18 03		
Ormskirk	d	16 05			16 20			16 35				16 50			17 05			17 20				17 35			17 50
Aughton Park	d	16 08			16 23			16 38				16 53			17 08			17 23				17 38			17 53
Town Green	d	16 10			16 25			16 40				16 55			17 10			17 25				17 40			17 55
Maghull	d	16 15			16 30			16 45				17 00			17 15			17 30				17 45			18 00
Old Roan	d	16 18			16 33			16 48				17 03			17 18			17 33				17 48			18 03
Aintree	d	16 20			16 35			16 50				17 05			17 20			17 35				17 50			18 05
Orrell Park	d	16 22			16 37			16 52				17 07			17 22			17 37				17 52			18 07
Walton (Merseyside)	d	16 24			16 39			16 54				17 09			17 24			17 39				17 54			18 09
Kirkby	d			16 28			16 43				16 58			17 13			17 28				17 43			17 58	
Fazakerley	d			16 31			16 46				17 01			17 16			17 31				17 46			18 01	
Rice Lane	d			16 34			16 49				17 04			17 19			17 34				17 49			18 04	
Kirkdale	d	16 27		16 37	16 42		16 52	16 57			17 07	17 12		17 22	17 27		17 37	17 42			17 52	17 57		18 07	18 12
Sandhills	d	16 29	16 36	16 40	16 44	16 51	16 55	16 59	17 06		17 10	17 14	17 21	17 25	17 29	17 36	17 40	17 44	17 51		17 55	17 59	18 06	18 10	18 14
Moorfields 10	d	16 33	16 40	16 43	16 48	16 55	16 58	17 03	17 10		17 13	17 18	17 25	17 28	17 33	17 40	17 43	17 48	17 55		17 58	18 03	18 10	18 13	18 18
Liverpool Central 10	a	16 35	16 43	16 46	16 50	16 58	17 01	17 05	17 13		17 16	17 20	17 28	17 31	17 35	17 43	17 46	17 50	17 58		18 01	18 05	18 13	18 16	18 20
	d		16 44			16 59			17 14				17 29			17 44			17 59				18 14		
Brunswick	d		16 47			17 02			17 17				17 32			17 47			18 02				18 17		
St Michaels	d		16 50			17 05			17 20				17 35			17 50			18 05				18 20		
Aigburth	d		16 52			17 07			17 22				17 37			17 52			18 07				18 22		
Cressington	d		16 54			17 09			17 24				17 39			17 54			18 09				18 24		
Liverpool Sth Parkway 7 89 ✈	d		16 57			17 12			17 27				17 42			17 57			18 12				18 27		
Hunts Cross 89	a		17 02			17 17			17 32				17 47			18 02			18 17				18 32		

		ME	ME	ME	ME		ME	ME	ME	ME	ME	ME	ME	ME	ME		ME	ME	ME	ME	ME	ME	ME	ME	ME
Southport	d	17 43			17 58				18 13			18 28			18 43				18 58			19 13		19 28	
Birkdale	d	17 47			18 02				18 17			18 32			18 47				19 02			19 17		19 32	
Hillside	d	17 49			18 04				18 19			18 34			18 49				19 04			19 19		19 34	
Ainsdale	d	17 52			18 07				18 22			18 37			18 52				19 07			19 22		19 37	
Freshfield	d	17 56			18 11				18 26			18 41			18 56				19 11			19 26		19 41	
Formby	d	17 58			18 13				18 28			18 43			18 58				19 13			19 28		19 43	
Hightown	d	18 02			18 17				18 32			18 47			19 02				19 17			19 32		19 47	
Hall Road	d	18 05			18 20				18 35			18 50			19 05				19 20			19 35		19 50	
Blundellsands & Crosby	d	18 07			18 22				18 37			18 52			19 07				19 22			19 37		19 52	
Waterloo (Merseyside)	d	18 10			18 25				18 40			18 55			19 10				19 25			19 40		19 55	
Seaforth & Litherland	d	18 12			18 27				18 42			18 57			19 12				19 27			19 42		19 57	
Bootle New Strand	d	18 15			18 30				18 45			19 00			19 15				19 30			19 45		20 00	
Bootle Oriel Road	d	18 16			18 31				18 46			19 01			19 16				19 31			19 46		20 01	
Bank Hall	d	18 18			18 33				18 48			19 03			19 18				19 33			19 48		20 03	
Ormskirk	d			18 05				18 20			18 35			18 50				19 05			19 20				19 50
Aughton Park	d			18 08				18 23			18 38			18 53				19 08			19 23				19 53
Town Green	d			18 10				18 25			18 40			18 55				19 10			19 25				19 55
Maghull	d			18 15				18 30			18 45			19 00				19 15			19 30				20 00
Old Roan	d			18 18				18 33			18 48			19 03				19 18			19 33				20 03
Aintree	d			18 20				18 35			18 50			19 05				19 20			19 35				20 05
Orrell Park	d			18 22				18 37			18 52			19 07				19 22			19 37				20 07
Walton (Merseyside)	d			18 24				18 39			18 54			19 09				19 24			19 39				20 09
Kirkby	d		18 13				18 28			18 43			18 58				19 13			19 28			19 48		
Fazakerley	d		18 16				18 31			18 46			19 01				19 16			19 31			19 51		
Rice Lane	d		18 19				18 34			18 49			19 04				19 19			19 34			19 54		
Kirkdale	d		18 22	18 27			18 37	18 42		18 52	18 57		19 07	19 12			19 22	19 27		19 37	19 42		19 57		20 12
Sandhills	d	18 21	18 25	18 29	18 36		18 40	18 44	18 51	18 55	18 59	19 06	19 10	19 14	19 21		19 25	19 29	19 36	19 40	19 44	19 51	20 00	20 06	20 14
Moorfields 10	d	18 25	18 28	18 33	18 40		18 43	18 48	18 55	18 58	19 03	19 10	19 13	19 18	19 25		19 28	19 33	19 40	19 43	19 48	19 55	20 03	20 10	20 18
Liverpool Central 10	a	18 28	18 31	18 35	18 43		18 46	18 50	18 58	19 01	19 05	19 13	19 16	19 20	19 28		19 31	19 35	19 43	19 46	19 50	19 58	20 06	20 13	20 20
	d	18 29			18 44				18 59			19 14			19 29				19 44			19 59		20 14	
Brunswick	d	18 32			18 47				19 02			19 17			19 32				19 47			20 02		20 17	
St Michaels	d	18 35			18 50				19 05			19 20			19 35				19 50			20 05		20 20	
Aigburth	d	18 37			18 52				19 07			19 22			19 37				19 52			20 07		20 22	
Cressington	d	18 39			18 54				19 09			19 24			19 39				19 54			20 09		20 24	
Liverpool Sth Parkway 7 89 ✈	d	18 42			18 57				19 12			19 27			19 42				19 57			20 12		20 27	
Hunts Cross 89	a	18 47			19 02				19 16			19 32			19 47				20 02			20 16		20 32	

Southport, Ormskirk and Kirby - Liverpool and Hunts Cross

Network Diagram - see first Page of Table 101

		ME	ME	ME	ME	ME	ME	ME	ME	ME	ME	ME	ME	ME	ME	ME	ME	ME	ME	ME	ME	ME
Southport	d	19 43		19 58		20 13		20 28		20 43		20 58		21 13		21 28		21 43		21 58		22 13
Birkdale	d	19 47		20 02		20 17		20 32		20 47		21 02		21 17		21 32		21 47		22 02		22 17
Hillside	d	19 49		20 04		20 19		20 34		20 49		21 04		21 19		21 34		21 49		22 04		22 19
Ainsdale	d	19 52		20 07		20 22		20 37		20 52		21 07		21 22		21 37		21 52		22 07		22 22
Freshfield	d	19 56		20 11		20 26		20 41		20 56		21 11		21 26		21 41		21 56		22 11		22 26
Formby	d	19 58		20 13		20 28		20 43		20 58		21 13		21 28		21 43		21 58		22 13		22 28
Hightown	d	20 02		20 17		20 32		20 47		21 02		21 17		21 32		21 47		22 02		22 17		22 32
Hall Road	d	20 05		20 20		20 35		20 50		21 05		21 20		21 35		21 50		22 05		22 20		22 35
Blundellsands & Crosby	d	20 07		20 22		20 37		20 52		21 07		21 22		21 37		21 52		22 07		22 22		22 37
Waterloo (Merseyside)	d	20 10		20 25		20 40		20 55		21 10		21 25		21 40		21 55		22 10		22 25		22 40
Seaforth & Litherland	d	20 12		20 27		20 42		20 57		21 12		21 27		21 42		21 57		22 12		22 27		22 42
Bootle New Strand	d	20 15		20 30		20 45		21 00		21 15		21 30		21 45		22 00		22 15		22 30		22 45
Bootle Oriel Road	d	20 16		20 31		20 46		21 01		21 16		21 31		21 46		22 01		22 16		22 31		22 46
Bank Hall	d	20 18		20 33		20 48		21 03		21 18		21 33		21 48		22 03		22 18		22 33		22 48
Ormskirk	d				20 20				20 50				21 20				21 50				22 20	
Aughton Park	d				20 23				20 53				21 23				21 53				22 23	
Town Green	d				20 25				20 55				21 25				21 55				22 25	
Maghull	d				20 30				21 00				21 30				22 00				22 30	
Old Roan	d				20 33				21 03				21 33				22 03				22 33	
Aintree	d				20 35				21 05				21 35				22 05				22 35	
Orrell Park	d				20 37				21 07				21 37				22 07				22 37	
Walton (Merseyside)	d				20 39				21 09				21 39				22 09				22 39	
Kirkby	d		20 18				20 48				21 18				21 48				22 18			
Fazakerley	d		20 21				20 51				21 21				21 51				22 21			
Rice Lane	d		20 24				20 54				21 24				21 54				22 24			
Kirkdale	d		20 27		20 42		20 57		21 12		21 27		21 42		21 57		22 12		22 27		22 42	
Sandhills	d	20 21	20 30	20 36	20 44	20 51	21 00	21 06	21 14	21 21	21 30	21 36	21 44	21 51	22 00	22 06	22 14	22 21	22 30	22 36	22 44	22 51
Moorfields 10	d	20 25	20 33	20 40	20 48	20 55	21 03	21 10	21 18	21 25	21 33	21 40	21 48	21 55	22 03	22 10	22 18	22 25	22 33	22 40	22 48	22 55
Liverpool Central 10	a	20 28	20 36	20 43	20 50	20 58	21 06	21 13	21 20	21 28	21 36	21 43	21 50	21 58	22 06	22 13	22 20	22 28	22 36	22 43	22 50	22 58
	d	20 29		20 44		20 59		21 14		21 29		21 44		21 59		22 14		22 29		22 44		22 59
Brunswick	d	20 32		20 47		21 02		21 17		21 32		21 47		22 02		22 17		22 32		22 47		23 02
St Michaels	d	20 35		20 50		21 05		21 20		21 35		21 50		22 05		22 20		22 35		22 50		23 05
Aigburth	d	20 37		20 52		21 07		21 22		21 37		21 52		22 07		22 22		22 37		22 52		23 07
Cressington	d	20 39		20 54		21 09		21 24		21 39		21 54		22 09		22 24		22 39		22 54		23 09
Liverpool Sth Parkway 7 89 ✈	d	20 42		20 57		21 12		21 27		21 42		21 57		22 12		22 27		22 42		22 57		23 12
Hunts Cross 89	a	20 47		21 02		21 17		21 32		21 47		22 01		22 17		22 32		22 47		23 02		23 18

		ME	ME	ME	ME	ME	ME	ME	ME
Southport	d		22 28		22 43		22 58		23 16
Birkdale	d		22 32		22 47		23 02		23 20
Hillside	d		22 34		22 49		23 04		23 22
Ainsdale	d		22 37		22 52		23 07		23 25
Freshfield	d		22 41		22 56		23 11		23 29
Formby	d		22 43		22 58		23 13		23 31
Hightown	d		22 47		23 02		23 17		23 35
Hall Road	d		22 50		23 05		23 20		23 38
Blundellsands & Crosby	d		22 52		23 07		23 22		23 40
Waterloo (Merseyside)	d		22 55		23 10		23 25		23 43
Seaforth & Litherland	d		22 57		23 12		23 27		23 45
Bootle New Strand	d		23 00		23 15		23 30		23 48
Bootle Oriel Road	d		23 01		23 16		23 31		23 49
Bank Hall	d		23 03		23 18		23 33		23 51
Ormskirk	d			22 50				23 20	
Aughton Park	d			22 53				23 23	
Town Green	d			22 55				23 25	
Maghull	d			23 00				23 30	
Old Roan	d			23 03				23 33	
Aintree	d			23 05				23 35	
Orrell Park	d			23 07				23 37	
Walton (Merseyside)	d			23 09				23 39	
Kirkby	d	22 48				23 18			
Fazakerley	d	22 51				23 21			
Rice Lane	d	22 54				23 24			
Kirkdale	d	22 57		23 12		23 27		23 42	
Sandhills	d	23 00	23 06	23 14	23 21	23 30	23 36	23 44	23 55
Moorfields 10	d	23 03	23 10	23 18	23 25	23 33	23 40	23 48	23 58
Liverpool Central 10	a	23 06	23 13	23 20	23 28	23 36	23 43	23 50	00 01
	d		23 14		23 29		23 44		
Brunswick	d		23 17		23 32		23 47		
St Michaels	d		23 20		23 35		23 50		
Aigburth	d		23 22		23 37		23 52		
Cressington	d		23 24		23 39		23 54		
Liverpool Sth Parkway 7 89 ✈	d		23 27		23 42		23 57		
Hunts Cross 89	a		23 32		23 47		00 02		

Table 103

Sundays

Southport, Ormskirk and Kirby - Liverpool and Hunts Cross

Network Diagram - see first Page of Table 101

		ME A	ME A	ME	ME	ME	ME	ME	ME	ME		ME	ME	ME	ME	ME	ME	ME	ME	ME		ME	ME	ME	ME
Southport	d	22p58	23p16			07 58			08 28				08 58			09 28			09 58			10 13		10 28	
Birkdale	d	23p02	23p20			08 02			08 32				09 02			09 32			10 02			10 17		10 32	
Hillside	d	23p04	23p22			08 04			08 34				09 04			09 34			10 04			10 19		10 34	
Ainsdale	d	23p07	23p25			08 07			08 37				09 07			09 37			10 07			10 22		10 37	
Freshfield	d	23p11	23p29			08 11			08 41				09 11			09 41			10 11			10 26		10 41	
Formby	d	23p13	23p31			08 13			08 43				09 13			09 43			10 13			10 28		10 43	
Hightown	d	23p17	23p35			08 17			08 47				09 17			09 47			10 17			10 32		10 47	
Hall Road	d	23p20	23p38			08 20			08 50				09 20			09 50			10 20			10 35		10 50	
Blundellsands & Crosby	d	23p22	23p40			08 22			08 52				09 22			09 52			10 22			10 37		10 52	
Waterloo (Merseyside)	d	23p25	23p43			08 25			08 55				09 25			09 55			10 25			10 40		10 55	
Seaforth & Litherland	d	23p27	23p45			08 27			08 57				09 27			09 57			10 27			10 42		10 57	
Bootle New Strand	d	23p30	23p48			08 30			09 00				09 30			10 00			10 30			10 45		11 00	
Bootle Oriel Road	d	23p31	23p49			08 31			09 01				09 31			10 01			10 31			10 46		11 01	
Bank Hall	d	23p33	23p51			08 33			09 03				09 33			10 03			10 33			10 48		11 03	
Ormskirk	d						08 20			08 50				09 20			09 50			10 20					10 50
Aughton Park	d						08 23			08 53				09 23			09 53			10 23					10 53
Town Green	d						08 25			08 55				09 25			09 55			10 25					10 55
Maghull	d						08 30			09 00				09 30			10 00			10 30					11 00
Old Roan	d						08 33			09 03				09 33			10 03			10 33					11 03
Aintree	d						08 35			09 05				09 35			10 05			10 35					11 05
Orrell Park	d						08 37			09 07				09 37			10 07			10 37					11 07
Walton (Merseyside)	d						08 39			09 09				09 39			10 09			10 39					11 09
Kirkby	d				08 18			08 48				09 18			09 48			10 18					10 48		
Fazakerley	d				08 21			08 51				09 21			09 51			10 21					10 51		
Rice Lane	d				08 24			08 54				09 24			09 54			10 24					10 54		
Kirkdale	d				08 27		08 42	08 57		09 12		09 27		09 42	09 57		10 12	10 27		10 42			10 57		11 12
Sandhills	d	23p36	23p55		08 30	08 36	08 44	09 00	09 06	09 14		09 30	09 36	09 44	10 00	10 06	10 14	10 30	10 36	10 44		10 51	11 00	11 06	11 14
Moorfields 10	d	23p40	23p58		08 33	08 40	08 48	09 03	09 10	09 18		09 33	09 40	09 48	10 03	10 10	10 18	10 33	10 40	10 48		10 55	11 03	11 10	11 18
Liverpool Central 10	a	23p43	00 01		08 36	08 43	08 50	09 06	09 13	09 20		09 36	09 43	09 50	10 06	10 13	10 20	10 36	10 43	10 50		10 58	11 06	11 13	11 20
	d	23p44		08 14		08 44			09 14				09 44			10 14			10 44					11 14	
Brunswick	d	23p47		08 17		08 47			09 17				09 47			10 17			10 47					11 17	
St Michaels	d	23p50		08 20		08 50			09 20				09 50			10 20			10 50					11 20	
Aigburth	d	23p52		08 22		08 52			09 22				09 52			10 22			10 52					11 22	
Cressington	d	23p54		08 24		08 54			09 24				09 54			10 24			10 54					11 24	
Liverpool Sth Parkway 7 89	d	23p57		08 27		08 57			09 27				09 57			10 27			10 57					11 27	
Hunts Cross 89	a	00 02		08 32		09 02			09 32				10 02			10 32			11 02					11 32	

		ME		ME	ME		ME	ME	ME
Southport	d	10 43		22 43			22 58		23 16
Birkdale	d	10 47		22 47			23 02		23 20
Hillside	d	10 49		22 49			23 04		23 22
Ainsdale	d	10 52		22 52			23 07		23 25
Freshfield	d	10 56		22 56			23 11		23 29
Formby	d	10 58		22 58			23 13		23 31
Hightown	d	11 02		23 02			23 17		23 35
Hall Road	d	11 05		23 05			23 20		23 38
Blundellsands & Crosby	d	11 07		23 07			23 22		23 40
Waterloo (Merseyside)	d	11 10		23 10			23 25		23 43
Seaforth & Litherland	d	11 12		23 12			23 27		23 45
Bootle New Strand	d	11 15		23 15			23 30		23 48
Bootle Oriel Road	d	11 16		23 16			23 31		23 49
Bank Hall	d	11 18		23 18			23 33		23 51
Ormskirk	d		and at the same minutes past each hour until					23 20	
Aughton Park	d							23 23	
Town Green	d							23 25	
Maghull	d							23 30	
Old Roan	d							23 33	
Aintree	d							23 35	
Orrell Park	d							23 37	
Walton (Merseyside)	d							23 39	
Kirkby	d				23 18				
Fazakerley	d				23 21				
Rice Lane	d				23 24				
Kirkdale	d				23 27			23 42	
Sandhills	d	11 21		23 21	23 30		23 36	23 44	23 55
Moorfields 10	d	11 25		23 25	23 33		23 40	23 48	23 58
Liverpool Central 10	a	11 28		23 28	23 36		23 43	23 50	00 01
	d						23 44		
Brunswick	d						23 47		
St Michaels	d						23 50		
Aigburth	d						23 52		
Cressington	d						23 54		
Liverpool Sth Parkway 7 89	d						23 57		
Hunts Cross 89	a						00 02		

A not 11 December

Liverpool and Birkenhead - New Brighton, West Kirby, Ellesmere Port and Chester

Network Diagram - see first Page of Table 101

Miles	Miles	Miles	Miles			ME	ME	ME	ME	ME	ME	ME	ME	ME	ME	ME	ME	ME	ME	ME	ME	ME	ME
0	—	0	0	Moorfields 10	d	23p26	23p31	23p41	23p46	23p56	05 36	05 56	06 06	06 16	06 21	06 26	06 41	06 46	06 51	06 56	07 11	07 16	07 21
0½	—	0½	0½	Liverpool Lime Street 10	d	23p28	23p33	23p43	23p48	23p58	05 38	05 58	06 08	06 18	06 23	06 28	06 43	06 48	06 53	06 58	07 13	07 18	07 23
1	—	1	1	Liverpool Central 10	d	23p30	23p35	23p45	23p50	23p59	05 40	06 00	06 10	06 20	06 25	06 30	06 45	06 50	06 55	07 00	07 15	07 20	07 25
1½	—	1½	1½	James Street	d	23p32	23p37	23p47	23p52	00 02	05 42	06 02	06 12	06 22	06 27	06 32	06 47	06 52	06 57	07 02	07 17	07 22	07 27
2¾	—	2¾	2¾	Hamilton Square	d	23p35	23p40	23p50	23p55	00a05	05 45	06 05	06 15	06 25	06 30	06 35	06 50	06 55	07 00	07 05	07 20	07 25	07 30
—	—	3¼	3¼	Conway Park	d		23p42		23p57					06 27	06 32			06 57	07 02			07 27	07 32
—	—	4	4	Birkenhead Park	d		23p44		23p59					06 29	06 34			06 59	07 04			07 29	07 34
—	—	4¾	4¾	Birkenhead North	d		23p47		00 02					06 32	06 37			07 02	07 07			07 32	07 37
—	—	—	6¼	Wallasey Village	d				00 07					06 37				07 07				07 37	
—	—	—	6½	Wallasey Grove Road	d				00 08					06 38				07 08				07 38	
—	—	—	7¾	**New Brighton**	a				00 13					06 43				07 13				07 43	
—	—	5¼	—	Bidston	d		23p50								06 40				07 10				07 40
—	—	6½	—	Leasowe	d		23p52								06 42				07 12				07 42
—	—	7	—	Moreton (Merseyside)	d		23p54								06 44				07 14				07 44
—	—	8¼	—	Meols	d		23p58								06 48				07 18				07 48
—	—	9½	—	Manor Road	d		23p59								06 50				07 20				07 50
—	—	10	—	Hoylake	d		00 02								06 52				07 22				07 52
—	—	11¼	—	**West Kirby**	a		00 07								06 57				07 27				07 57
3	—	—	—	Birkenhead Central	d	23p37		23p52			05 47	06 07	06 17			06 37	06 52			07 07	07 22		
3¾	—	—	—	Green Lane	d	23p39		23p54			05 49	06 09	06 19			06 39	06 54			07 09	07 24		
4½	—	—	—	Rock Ferry	d	23p42		23p57			05 52	06 12	06 22			06 42	06 57			07 12	07 27		
5½	—	—	—	Bebington	d	23p44		23p59			05 54	06 14	06 24			06 44	06 59			07 14	07 29		
6½	—	—	—	Port Sunlight	d	23p46		00 01			05 56	06 16	06 26			06 46	07 01			07 16	07 31		
7	—	—	—	Spital	d	23p48		00 03			05 58	06 18	06 28			06 48	07 03			07 18	07 33		
7¾	—	—	—	Bromborough Rake	d	23p50		00 05			06 00	06 20	06 30			06 50	07 05			07 20	07 35		
8½	—	—	—	Bromborough	d	23p52		00 07			06 02	06 22	06 32			06 52	07 07			07 22	07 37		
9	—	—	—	Eastham Rake	d	23p55		00 10			06 05	06 25	06 35			06 55	07 10			07 25	07 40		
10	0	—	—	Hooton	d	23p57		00 12			06 07	06 27	06 37			06 57	07 12			07 27	07 42		
—	1½	—	—	Little Sutton	d	00 01						06 31				07 01				07 31			
—	2½	—	—	Overpool	d	00 03						06 33				07 03				07 33			
—	4	—	—	**Ellesmere Port**	a	00 07						06 38				07 08				07 38			
13	—	—	—	Capenhurst	d			00 17			06 12		06 42				07 17				07 47		
16¾	—	—	—	Bache	d			00 22			06 17		06 47				07 22				07 52		
18¼	—	—	—	**Chester**	a			00 26			06 26		06 56				07 26				07 56		

		ME	ME	ME	ME	ME	ME	ME SX	ME SO	ME	ME SX	ME	ME	ME	ME SX	ME	ME	ME	ME SX	ME	ME SO	ME SX	ME
Moorfields 10	d	07 26	07 31	07 36	07 41	07 46	07 51	07 53	07 56	08 01	08 03	08 06	08 11	08 16	08 18	08 21	08 26	08 31	08 33	08 36	08 41	08 41	08 46
Liverpool Lime Street 10	d	07 28	07 33	07 38	07 43	07 48	07 53	07 55	07 58	08 03	08 05	08 08	08 13	08 18	08 20	08 23	08 28	08 33	08 35	08 38	08 43	08 43	08 48
Liverpool Central 10	d	07 30	07 35	07 40	07 45	07 50	07 55	07 57	08 00	08 05	08a07	08 10	08 15	08 20	08 22	08 25	08 30	08 35	08 37	08 40	08 45	08 45	08 50
James Street	d	07 32	07 37	07 42	07 47	07 52	07 57	07 59	08 02	08 07		08 12	08 17	08 22	08 24	08 27	08 32	08 37	08 39	08 42	08 47	08 47	08 52
Hamilton Square	d	07 35	07 40	07 45	07 50	07 55	08 00	08 02	08 05	08 10		08 15	08 20	08 25	08 27	08 30	08 35	08 40	08 42	08 45	08 50	08 50	08 55
Conway Park	d		07 42	07 47		07 57	08 02			08 12		08 17		08 27		08 32		08 42		08 47			08 57
Birkenhead Park	d		07 44	07 49		07 59	08 04			08 14		08 19		08 29		08 34		08 44		08 49			08 59
Birkenhead North	d		07 47	07 52		08 02	08 07			08 17		08 22		08 32		08 37		08 47		08 52			09 02
Wallasey Village	d		07 52			08 07				08 22				08 37				08 52					09 07
Wallasey Grove Road	d		07 53			08 08				08 23				08 38				08 53					09 08
New Brighton	a		07 58			08 13				08 28				08 43				08 58					09 13
Bidston	d			07 55			08 10					08 25				08 40				08 55			
Leasowe	d			07 57			08 12					08 27				08 42				08 57			
Moreton (Merseyside)	d			07 59			08 14					08 29				08 44				08 59			
Meols	d			08 03			08 18					08 33				08 48				09 03			
Manor Road	d			08 05			08 20					08 35				08 50				09 05			
Hoylake	d			08 07			08 22					08 37				08 52				09 07			
West Kirby	a			08 12			08 27					08 42				08 57				09 12			
Birkenhead Central	d	07 37			07 52			08 05	08 07				08 22		08 30		08 37		08a44		08 52	08 53	
Green Lane	d	07 39			07 54			08 07	08 09				08 24		08 32		08 39				08 54	08 55	
Rock Ferry	d	07 42			07 57			08 09	08 12				08 27		08 34		08 42				08 57	08 57	
Bebington	d	07 44			07 59			08 12	08 14				08 29		08 37		08 44				08 59	09 00	
Port Sunlight	d	07 46			08 01			08 14	08 16				08 31		08 39		08 46				09 01	09 02	
Spital	d	07 48			08 03			08 16	08 18				08 33		08 41		08 48				09 03	09 04	
Bromborough Rake	d	07 50			08 05			08 18	08 20				08 35		08 43		08 50				09 05	09 06	
Bromborough	d	07 52			08 07			08 20	08 22				08 37		08 45		08 52				09 07	09 08	
Eastham Rake	d	07 55			08 10			08 22	08 25				08 40		08 47		08 55				09 10	09 10	
Hooton	d	07 57			08 12			08 24	08 27				08 42		08 49		08 57				09 12	09 12	
Little Sutton	d	08 01						08 29	08 31								09 01						
Overpool	d	08 03						08 31	08 33								09 03						
Ellesmere Port	a	08 08						08 34	08 38								09 08						
Capenhurst	d				08 17								08 47		08 54						09 17	09 17	
Bache	d				08 22								08 52		09 00						09 22	09 23	
Chester	a				08 27								08 57		09 06						09 27	09 27	

Liverpool and Birkenhead - New Brighton, West Kirby, Ellesmere Port and Chester

Network Diagram - see first Page of Table 101

		ME SX	ME SO	ME	ME SO	ME SX	ME	ME	ME	ME	ME SO	ME SX	ME	ME	ME	ME	ME	ME	ME	ME	ME	ME	ME
Moorfields 10	d	08 48	08 48	08 51	08 56	08 56	09 01	09 06	09 11	09 16	09 18	09 19	09 21	09 26	09 31	09 36	09 41	09 46	09 48	09 51	09 56	10 01	10 06
Liverpool Lime Street 10	d	08 50	08 50	08 53	08 58	08 58	09 03	09 08	09 13	09 18	09 20	09 21	09 23	09 28	09 33	09 38	09 43	09 48	09 50	09 53	09 58	10 03	10 08
Liverpool Central 10	d	08 52	08 52	08 55	09 00	09 00	09 05	09 10	09 15	09 20	09 22	09 23	09 25	09 30	09 35	09 40	09 45	09 50	09 52	09 55	10 00	10 05	10 10
James Street	d	08 54	08 54	08 57	09 02	09 02	09 07	09 12	09 17	09 22	09 24	09 25	09 27	09 32	09 37	09 42	09 47	09 52	09 54	09 57	10 02	10 07	10 12
Hamilton Square	d	08 57	08 57	09 00	09 05	09 05	09 10	09 15	09 20	09 25	09 27	09 28	09 30	09 35	09 40	09 45	09 50	09 55	09 57	10 00	10 05	10 10	10 15
Conway Park	d	09 00		09 02			09 12	09 17		09 27			09 32		09 42	09 47		09 57		10 02		10 12	10 17
Birkenhead Park	d	09 02		09 04			09 14	09 19		09 29			09 34		09 44	09 49		09 59		10 04		10 14	10 19
Birkenhead North	d	09a05		09 07			09 17	09 22		09 32			09 37		09 47	09 52		10 02		10 07		10 17	10 22
Wallasey Village	d						09 22			09 37					09 52			10 07				10 22	
Wallasey Grove Road	d						09 23			09 38					09 53			10 08				10 23	
New Brighton	a						09 28			09 43					09 58			10 13				10 28	
Bidston	d			09 10				09 25					09 40			09 55				10 10			10 25
Leasowe	d			09 12				09 27					09 42			09 57				10 12			10 27
Moreton (Merseyside)	d			09 14				09 29					09 44			09 59				10 14			10 29
Meols	d			09 18				09 33					09 48			10 03				10 18			10 33
Manor Road	d			09 20				09 35					09 50			10 05				10 20			10 35
Hoylake	d			09 22				09 37					09 52			10 07				10 22			10 37
West Kirby	a			09 27				09 42					09 57			10 12				10 27			10 42
Birkenhead Central	d		09 00		09 07	09 07			09 22		09 30	09 30		09 37			09 52		10 00		10 07		
Green Lane	d		09 02		09 09	09 09			09 24		09 32	09 32		09 39			09 54		10 02		10 09		
Rock Ferry	d		09 04		09 12	09 12			09 27		09 34	09 35		09 42			09 57		10 04		10 12		
Bebington	d		09 07		09 14	09 14			09 29		09 37	09 37		09 44			09 59		10 07		10 14		
Port Sunlight	d		09 09		09 16	09 16			09 31		09 39	09 39		09 46			10 01		10 09		10 16		
Spital	d		09 11		09 18	09 18			09 33		09 41	09 41		09 48			10 03		10 11		10 18		
Bromborough Rake	d		09 13		09 20	09 20			09 35		09 43	09 43		09 50			10 05		10 13		10 20		
Bromborough	d		09 15		09 22	09 22			09 37		09 45	09 45		09 52			10 07		10 15		10 22		
Eastham Rake	d		09 17		09 25	09 25			09 40		09 47	09 48		09 55			10 10		10 17		10 25		
Hooton	d		09 19		09 27	09 27			09 42		09 49	09 50		09 57			10 12		10 19		10 27		
Little Sutton	d		09 24			09 31					09 54	09 54							10 24				
Overpool	d		09 26			09 33					09 56	09 56							10 26				
Ellesmere Port	a		09 32			09 38					10 00	10 00							10 30				
Capenhurst	d								09 47								10 17						
Bache	d				09 36				09 52					10 06			10 22				10 36		
Chester	a				09 41				09 57					10 11			10 27				10 41		

		ME	ME	ME	ME	ME	ME	ME	ME	ME	ME	ME	ME	ME	ME	ME	ME	ME	ME	ME	ME	ME
Moorfields 10	d	10 11	10 16	10 18	10 21	10 26	10 31	10 36	10 41	10 46	10 48	10 51	10 56	11 01	11 06	11 11	11 16	11 18	11 21	11 26	11 31	11 36
Liverpool Lime Street 10	d	10 13	10 18	10 20	10 23	10 28	10 33	10 38	10 43	10 48	10 50	10 53	10 58	11 03	11 08	11 13	11 18	11 20	11 23	11 28	11 33	11 38
Liverpool Central 10	d	10 15	10 20	10 22	10 25	10 30	10 35	10 40	10 45	10 50	10 52	10 55	11 00	11 05	11 10	11 15	11 20	11 22	11 25	11 30	11 35	11 40
James Street	d	10 17	10 22	10 24	10 27	10 32	10 37	10 42	10 47	10 52	10 54	10 57	11 02	11 07	11 12	11 17	11 22	11 24	11 27	11 32	11 37	11 42
Hamilton Square	d	10 20	10 25	10 27	10 30	10 35	10 40	10 45	10 50	10 55	10 57	11 00	11 05	11 10	11 15	11 20	11 25	11 27	11 30	11 35	11 40	11 45
Conway Park	d		10 27		10 32		10 42	10 47		10 57		11 02		11 12	11 17		11 27		11 32		11 42	11 47
Birkenhead Park	d		10 29		10 34		10 44	10 49		10 59		11 04		11 14	11 19		11 29		11 34		11 44	11 49
Birkenhead North	d		10 32		10 37		10 47	10 52		11 02		11 07		11 17	11 22		11 32		11 37		11 47	11 52
Wallasey Village	d		10 37				10 52			11 07				11 22			11 37				11 52	
Wallasey Grove Road	d		10 38				10 53			11 08				11 23			11 38				11 53	
New Brighton	a		10 43				10 58			11 13				11 28			11 43				11 58	
Bidston	d				10 40			10 55				11 10			11 25				11 40			11 55
Leasowe	d				10 42			10 57				11 12			11 27				11 42			11 57
Moreton (Merseyside)	d				10 44			10 59				11 14			11 29				11 44			11 59
Meols	d				10 48			11 03				11 18			11 33				11 48			12 03
Manor Road	d				10 50			11 05				11 20			11 35				11 50			12 05
Hoylake	d				10 52			11 07				11 22			11 37				11 52			12 07
West Kirby	a				10 57			11 12				11 27			11 42				11 57			12 12
Birkenhead Central	d	10 22		10 30		10 37			10 52		11 00		11 07			11 22		11 30		11 37		
Green Lane	d	10 24		10 32		10 39			10 54		11 02		11 09			11 24		11 32		11 39		
Rock Ferry	d	10 27		10 34		10 42			10 57		11 04		11 12			11 27		11 34		11 42		
Bebington	d	10 29		10 37		10 44			10 59		11 07		11 14			11 29		11 37		11 44		
Port Sunlight	d	10 31		10 39		10 46			11 01		11 09		11 16			11 31		11 39		11 46		
Spital	d	10 33		10 41		10 48			11 03		11 11		11 18			11 33		11 41		11 48		
Bromborough Rake	d	10 35		10 43		10 50			11 05		11 13		11 20			11 35		11 43		11 50		
Bromborough	d	10 37		10 45		10 52			11 07		11 15		11 22			11 37		11 45		11 52		
Eastham Rake	d	10 40		10 47		10 55			11 10		11 17		11 25			11 40		11 47		11 55		
Hooton	d	10 42		10 49		10 57			11 12		11 19		11 27			11 42		11 49		11 57		
Little Sutton	d			10 54							11 24							11 54				
Overpool	d			10 56							11 26							11 56				
Ellesmere Port	a			11 00							11 30							12 00				
Capenhurst	d	10 47							11 17							11 47						
Bache	d	10 52				11 06			11 22				11 36			11 52				12 06		
Chester	a	10 57				11 11			11 27				11 41			11 57				12 11		

Liverpool and Birkenhead - New Brighton, West Kirby, Ellesmere Port and Chester

Network Diagram - see first Page of Table 101

		ME	ME	ME	ME	ME	ME	ME		ME	ME	ME	ME	ME	ME	ME	ME	ME		ME	ME	ME	ME	ME	ME
Moorfields 10	d	11 41	11 46	11 48	11 51	11 56	12 01	12 06		12 11	12 16	12 18	12 21	12 26	12 31	12 36	12 41	12 46		12 48	12 51	12 56	13 01	13 06	13 11
Liverpool Lime Street 10	d	11 43	11 48	11 50	11 53	11 58	12 03	12 08		12 13	12 18	12 20	12 23	12 28	12 33	12 38	12 43	12 48		12 50	12 53	12 58	13 03	13 08	13 13
Liverpool Central 10	d	11 45	11 50	11 52	11 55	12 00	12 05	12 10		12 15	12 20	12 22	12 25	12 30	12 35	12 40	12 45	12 50		12 52	12 55	13 00	13 05	13 10	13 15
James Street	d	11 47	11 52	11 54	11 57	12 02	12 07	12 12		12 17	12 22	12 24	12 27	12 32	12 37	12 42	12 47	12 52		12 54	12 57	13 02	13 07	13 12	13 17
Hamilton Square	d	11 50	11 55	11 57	12 00	12 05	12 10	12 15		12 20	12 25	12 27	12 30	12 35	12 40	12 45	12 50	12 55		12 57	13 00	13 05	13 10	13 15	13 20
Conway Park	d		11 57		12 02		12 12	12 17			12 27		12 32		12 42	12 47		12 57			13 02		13 12	13 17	
Birkenhead Park	d		11 59		12 04		12 14	12 19			12 29		12 34		12 44	12 49		12 59			13 04		13 14	13 19	
Birkenhead North	d		12 02		12 07		12 17	12 22			12 32		12 37		12 47	12 52		13 02			13 07		13 17	13 22	
Wallasey Village	d		12 07				12 22				12 37				12 52			13 07					13 22		
Wallasey Grove Road	d		12 08				12 23				12 38				12 53			13 08					13 23		
New Brighton	a		12 13				12 28				12 43				12 58			13 13					13 28		
Bidston	d				12 10			12 25					12 40			12 55					13 10			13 25	
Leasowe	d				12 12			12 27					12 42			12 57					13 12			13 27	
Moreton (Merseyside)	d				12 14			12 29					12 44			12 59					13 14			13 29	
Meols	d				12 18			12 33					12 48			13 03					13 18			13 33	
Manor Road	d				12 20			12 35					12 50			13 05					13 20			13 35	
Hoylake	d				12 22			12 37					12 52			13 07					13 22			13 37	
West Kirby	a				12 27			12 42					12 57			13 12					13 27			13 42	
Birkenhead Central	d	11 52		12 00		12 07				12 22		12 30		12 37			12 52			13 00		13 07			13 22
Green Lane	d	11 54		12 02		12 09				12 24		12 32		12 39			12 54			13 02		13 09			13 24
Rock Ferry	d	11 57		12 04		12 12				12 27		12 34		12 42			12 57			13 04		13 12			13 27
Bebington	d	11 59		12 07		12 14				12 29		12 37		12 44			12 59			13 07		13 14			13 29
Port Sunlight	d	12 01		12 09		12 16				12 31		12 39		12 46			13 01			13 09		13 16			13 31
Spital	d	12 03		12 11		12 18				12 33		12 41		12 48			13 03			13 11		13 18			13 33
Bromborough Rake	d	12 05		12 13		12 20				12 35		12 43		12 50			13 05			13 13		13 20			13 35
Bromborough	d	12 07		12 15		12 22				12 37		12 45		12 52			13 07			13 15		13 22			13 37
Eastham Rake	d	12 10		12 17		12 25				12 40		12 47		12 55			13 10			13 17		13 25			13 40
Hooton	d	12 12		12 19		12 27				12 42		12 49		12 57			13 12			13 19		13 27			13 42
Little Sutton	d			12 24								12 54								13 24					
Overpool	d			12 26								12 56								13 26					
Ellesmere Port	a			12 31								13 00								13 30					
Capenhurst	d	12 17								12 47							13 17								13 47
Bache	d	12 22				12 36				12 52				13 06			13 22					13 36			13 52
Chester	a	12 27				12 41				12 57				13 11			13 27					13 41			13 57

		ME	ME	ME		ME	ME	ME	ME	ME	ME	ME	ME	ME		ME	ME	ME	ME	ME	ME	ME	ME	ME	
Moorfields 10	d	13 16	13 18	13 21		13 26	13 31	13 36	13 41	13 46	13 48	13 51	13 56	14 01		14 06	14 11	14 16	14 18	14 21	14 26	14 31	14 36	14 41	
Liverpool Lime Street 10	d	13 18	13 20	13 23		13 28	13 33	13 38	13 43	13 48	13 50	13 53	13 58	14 03		14 08	14 13	14 18	14 20	14 23	14 28	14 33	14 38	14 43	
Liverpool Central 10	d	13 20	13 22	13 25		13 30	13 35	13 40	13 45	13 50	13 52	13 55	14 00	14 05		14 10	14 15	14 20	14 22	14 25	14 30	14 35	14 40	14 45	
James Street	d	13 22	13 24	13 27		13 32	13 37	13 42	13 47	13 52	13 54	13 57	14 02	14 07		14 12	14 17	14 22	14 24	14 27	14 32	14 37	14 42	14 47	
Hamilton Square	d	13 25	13 27	13 30		13 35	13 40	13 45	13 50	13 55	13 57	14 00	14 05	14 10		14 15	14 20	14 25	14 27	14 30	14 35	14 40	14 45	14 50	
Conway Park	d	13 27		13 32			13 42	13 47		13 57		14 02		14 12		14 17		14 27		14 32		14 42	14 47		
Birkenhead Park	d	13 29		13 34			13 44	13 49		13 59		14 04		14 14		14 19		14 29		14 34		14 44	14 49		
Birkenhead North	d	13 32		13 37			13 47	13 52		14 02		14 07		14 17		14 22		14 32		14 37		14 47	14 52		
Wallasey Village	d	13 37					13 52			14 07				14 22				14 37				14 52			
Wallasey Grove Road	d	13 38					13 53			14 08				14 23				14 38				14 53			
New Brighton	a	13 43					13 58			14 13				14 28				14 43				14 58			
Bidston	d			13 40				13 55				14 10				14 25				14 40			14 55		
Leasowe	d			13 42				13 57				14 12				14 27				14 42			14 57		
Moreton (Merseyside)	d			13 44				13 59				14 14				14 29				14 44			14 59		
Meols	d			13 48				14 03				14 18				14 33				14 48			15 03		
Manor Road	d			13 50				14 05				14 20				14 35				14 50			15 05		
Hoylake	d			13 52				14 07				14 22				14 37				14 52			15 07		
West Kirby	a			13 57				14 12				14 27				14 42				14 57			15 12		
Birkenhead Central	d		13 30			13 37			13 52		14 00		14 07				14 22		14 30		14 37			14 52	
Green Lane	d		13 32			13 39			13 54		14 02		14 09				14 24		14 32		14 39			14 54	
Rock Ferry	d		13 34			13 42			13 57		14 04		14 12				14 27		14 34		14 42			14 57	
Bebington	d		13 37			13 44			13 59		14 07		14 14				14 29		14 37		14 44			14 59	
Port Sunlight	d		13 39			13 46			14 01		14 09		14 16				14 31		14 39		14 46			15 01	
Spital	d		13 41			13 48			14 03		14 11		14 18				14 33		14 41		14 48			15 03	
Bromborough Rake	d		13 43			13 50			14 05		14 13		14 20				14 35		14 43		14 50			15 05	
Bromborough	d		13 45			13 52			14 07		14 15		14 22				14 37		14 45		14 52			15 07	
Eastham Rake	d		13 47			13 55			14 10		14 17		14 25				14 40		14 47		14 55			15 10	
Hooton	d		13 49			13 57			14 12		14 19		14 27				14 42		14 49		14 57			15 12	
Little Sutton	d		13 54								14 24								14 54						
Overpool	d		13 56								14 26								14 56						
Ellesmere Port	a		14 00								14 30								15 00						
Capenhurst	d								14 17								14 47							15 17	
Bache	d					14 06			14 22				14 36				14 52				15 06			15 22	
Chester	a					14 11			14 27				14 41				14 57				15 11			15 27	

Liverpool and Birkenhead - New Brighton, West Kirby, Ellesmere Port and Chester

Network Diagram - see first Page of Table 101

		ME	ME	ME	ME	ME	ME	ME	ME	ME	ME	ME	ME	ME	ME	ME	ME	ME	ME	ME	ME	ME	ME
																					SX		
Moorfields 10	d	14 46	14 48	14 51	14 56	15 01	15 06	15 11	15 16	15 18	15 21	15 26	15 31	15 36	15 41	15 46	15 48	15 51	15 56	16 01	16 03	16 06	16 11
Liverpool Lime Street 10	d	14 48	14 50	14 53	14 58	15 03	15 08	15 13	15 18	15 20	15 23	15 28	15 33	15 38	15 43	15 48	15 50	15 53	15 58	16 03	16 05	16 08	16 13
Liverpool Central 10	d	14 50	14 52	14 55	15 00	15 05	15 10	15 15	15 20	15 22	15 25	15 30	15 35	15 40	15 45	15 50	15 52	15 55	16 00	16 05	16 07	16 10	16 15
James Street	d	14 52	14 54	14 57	15 02	15 07	15 12	15 17	15 22	15 24	15 27	15 32	15 37	15 42	15 47	15 52	15 54	15 57	16 02	16 07	16 09	16 12	16 17
Hamilton Square	d	14 55	14 57	15 00	15 05	15 10	15 15	15 20	15 25	15 27	15 30	15 35	15 40	15 45	15 50	15 55	15 57	16 00	16 05	16 10	16a12	16 15	16 20
Conway Park	d	14 57		15 02		15 12	15 17		15 27		15 32		15 42	15 47		15 57		16 02		16 12		16 17	
Birkenhead Park	d	14 59		15 04		15 14	15 19		15 29		15 34		15 44	15 49		15 59		16 04		16 14		16 19	
Birkenhead North	d	15 02		15 07		15 17	15 22		15 32		15 37		15 47	15 52		16 02		16 07		16 17		16 22	
Wallasey Village	d	15 07				15 22			15 37				15 52			16 07				16 22			
Wallasey Grove Road	d	15 08				15 23			15 38				15 53			16 08				16 23			
New Brighton	a	15 13				15 28			15 43				15 58			16 13				16 28			
Bidston	d			15 10			15 25				15 40			15 55				16 10				16 25	
Leasowe	d			15 12			15 27				15 42			15 57				16 12				16 27	
Moreton (Merseyside)	d			15 14			15 29				15 44			15 59				16 14				16 29	
Meols	d			15 18			15 33				15 48			16 03				16 18				16 33	
Manor Road	d			15 20			15 35				15 50			16 05				16 20				16 35	
Hoylake	d			15 22			15 37				15 52			16 07				16 22				16 37	
West Kirby	a			15 27			15 42				15 57			16 12				16 27				16 42	
Birkenhead Central	d		15 00		15 07			15 22		15 30		15 37			15 52		16 00		16 07		16 15		16 22
Green Lane	d		15 02		15 09			15 24		15 32		15 39			15 54		16 02		16 09		16 17		16 24
Rock Ferry	d		15 04		15 12			15 27		15 34		15 42			15 57		16 04		16 12		16 19		16 27
Bebington	d		15 07		15 14			15 29		15 37		15 44			15 59		16 07		16 14		16 22		16 29
Port Sunlight	d		15 09		15 16			15 31		15 39		15 46			16 01		16 09		16 16		16 24		16 31
Spital	d		15 11		15 18			15 33		15 41		15 48			16 03		16 11		16 18		16 26		16 33
Bromborough Rake	d		15 13		15 20			15 35		15 43		15 50			16 05		16 13		16 20		16 28		16 35
Bromborough	d		15 15		15 22			15 37		15 45		15 52			16 07		16 15		16 22		16 30		16 37
Eastham Rake	d		15 17		15 25			15 40		15 47		15 55			16 10		16 17		16 25		16 32		16 40
Hooton	d		15 19		15 27			15 42		15 49		15 57			16 12		16 19		16 27		16a34		16 42
Little Sutton	d		15 24							15 54							16 24						
Overpool	d		15 26							15 56							16 26						
Ellesmere Port	a		15 30							16 00							16 30						
Capenhurst	d							15 47							16 17								16 47
Bache	d				15 36			15 52				16 06			16 22				16 36				16 52
Chester	a				15 41			15 57				16 11			16 27				16 41				16 57

		ME	ME	ME	ME	ME	ME	ME	ME	ME	ME	ME	ME	ME	ME	ME	ME	ME	ME	ME	ME	ME	ME
							SX						SO	SX		SX						SO	SX
Moorfields 10	d	16 16	16 18	16 21	16 26	16 31	16 33	16 36	16 41	16 46	16 48	16 51	16 56	16 56	17 01	17 03	17 06	17 11	17 16	17 18	17 21	17 26	17 26
Liverpool Lime Street 10	d	16 18	16 20	16 23	16 28	16 33	16 35	16 38	16 43	16 48	16 50	16 53	16 58	16 58	17 03	17 05	17 08	17 13	17 18	17 20	17 23	17 28	17 28
Liverpool Central 10	d	16 20	16 22	16 25	16 30	16 35	16 37	16 40	16 45	16 50	16 52	16 55	17 00	17 00	17 05	17 07	17 10	17 15	17 20	17 22	17 25	17 30	17 30
James Street	d	16 22	16 24	16 27	16 32	16 37	16 39	16 42	16 47	16 52	16 54	16 57	17 02	17 02	17 07	17 09	17 12	17 17	17 22	17 24	17 27	17 32	17 32
Hamilton Square	d	16 25	16 27	16 30	16 35	16 40	16 42	16 45	16 50	16 55	16 57	17 00	17 05	17 05	17 10	17 12	17 15	17 20	17 25	17 27	17 30	17 35	17 35
Conway Park	d	16 27		16 32		16 42		16 47		16 57		17 02			17 12		17 17		17 27		17 32		
Birkenhead Park	d	16 29		16 34		16 44		16 49		16 59		17 04			17 14		17 19		17 29		17 34		
Birkenhead North	d	16 32		16 37		16 47		16 52		17 02		17 07			17 17		17 22		17 32		17 37		
Wallasey Village	d	16 37				16 52				17 07					17 22				17 37				
Wallasey Grove Road	d	16 38				16 53				17 08					17 23				17 38				
New Brighton	a	16 43				16 58				17 13					17 28				17 43				
Bidston	d			16 40				16 55				17 10					17 25				17 40		
Leasowe	d			16 42				16 57				17 12					17 27				17 42		
Moreton (Merseyside)	d			16 44				16 59				17 14					17 29				17 44		
Meols	d			16 48				17 03				17 18					17 33				17 48		
Manor Road	d			16 50				17 05				17 20					17 35				17 50		
Hoylake	d			16 52				17 07				17 22					17 37				17 52		
West Kirby	a			16 57				17 12				17 27					17 42				17 57		
Birkenhead Central	d		16 30		16 37		16 45		16 52		17 00		17 07	17 07		17 15		17 22		17 30		17 37	17 37
Green Lane	d		16 32		16 39		16 47		16 54		17 02		17 09	17 09		17 17		17 24		17 32		17 39	17 39
Rock Ferry	d		16 34		16 42		16 49		16 57		17 04		17 12	17 12		17 19		17 27		17 34		17 42	17 42
Bebington	d		16 37		16 44		16 52		16 59		17 07		17 14	17 14		17 22		17 29		17 37		17 44	17 44
Port Sunlight	d		16 39		16 46		16 54		17 01		17 09		17 16	17 16		17 24		17 31		17 39		17 46	17 46
Spital	d		16 41		16 48		16 56		17 03		17 11		17 18	17 18		17 26		17 33		17 41		17 48	17 48
Bromborough Rake	d		16 43		16 50		16 58		17 05		17 13		17 20	17 20		17 28		17 35		17 43		17 50	17 50
Bromborough	d		16 45		16 52		17 00		17 07		17 15		17 22	17 22		17 30		17 37		17 45		17 52	17 52
Eastham Rake	d		16 47		16 55		17 02		17 10		17 17		17 25	17 25		17 32		17 40		17 47		17 55	17 55
Hooton	d		16 49		16 57		17 04		17 12		17 19		17 27	17 27		17 34		17 42		17 49		17 57	17 57
Little Sutton	d		16 54				17 09				17 24					17 39				17 54			
Overpool	d		16 56				17 11				17 26					17 41				17 56			
Ellesmere Port	a		17 00				17 16				17 30					17 46				18 00			
Capenhurst	d								17 17					17 32				17 47					18 02
Bache	d				17 06				17 22				17 36	17 37				17 52				18 06	18 07
Chester	a				17 11				17 27				17 41	17 41				17 57				18 11	18 11

Liverpool and Birkenhead - New Brighton, West Kirby, Ellesmere Port and Chester

Network Diagram - see first Page of Table 101

		ME	ME SX	ME	ME	ME	ME	ME	ME	ME	ME	ME	ME	ME	ME	ME	ME	ME	ME	ME	ME	ME
Moorfields 10	d	17 31	17 33	17 36	17 41	17 46	17 48	17 51	17 56	18 01	18 06	18 11	18 16	18 18	18 21	18 26	18 31	18 36	18 41	18 46	18 48	18 51
Liverpool Lime Street 10	d	17 33	17 35	17 38	17 43	17 48	17 50	17 53	17 58	18 03	18 08	18 13	18 18	18 20	18 23	18 28	18 33	18 38	18 43	18 48	18 50	18 53
Liverpool Central 10	d	17 35	17 37	17 40	17 45	17 50	17 52	17 55	18 00	18 05	18 10	18 15	18 20	18 22	18 25	18 30	18 35	18 40	18 45	18 50	18 52	18 55
James Street	d	17 37	17 39	17 42	17 47	17 52	17 54	17 57	18 02	18 07	18 12	18 17	18 22	18 24	18 27	18 32	18 37	18 42	18 47	18 52	18 54	18 57
Hamilton Square	d	17 40	17 42	17 45	17 50	17 55	17 57	18 00	18 05	18 10	18 15	18 20	18 25	18 27	18 30	18 35	18 40	18 45	18 50	18 55	18 57	19 00
Conway Park	d	17 42		17 47		17 57		18 02		18 12	18 17		18 27		18 32		18 42	18 47		18 57		19 02
Birkenhead Park	d	17 44		17 49		17 59		18 04		18 14	18 19		18 29		18 34		18 44	18 49		18 59		19 04
Birkenhead North	d	17 47		17 52		18 02		18 07		18 17	18 22		18 32		18 37		18 47	18 52		19 02		19 07
Wallasey Village	d	17 52				18 07				18 22			18 37				18 52			19 07		
Wallasey Grove Road	d	17 53				18 08				18 23			18 38				18 53			19 08		
New Brighton	a	17 58				18 13				18 28			18 43				18 58			19 13		
Bidston	d			17 55				18 10			18 25				18 40			18 55				19 10
Leasowe	d			17 57				18 12			18 27				18 42			18 57				19 12
Moreton (Merseyside)	d			17 59				18 14			18 29				18 44			18 59				19 14
Meols	d			18 03				18 18			18 33				18 48			19 03				19 18
Manor Road	d			18 05				18 20			18 35				18 50			19 05				19 20
Hoylake	d			18 07				18 22			18 37				18 52			19 07				19 22
West Kirby	a			18 12				18 27			18 42				18 57			19 12				19 27
Birkenhead Central	d		17 45		17 52		18 00		18 07			18 22		18 30		18 37			18 52		19 00	
Green Lane	d		17 47		17 54		18 02		18 09			18 24		18 32		18 39			18 54		19 02	
Rock Ferry	d		17 49		17 57		18 04		18 12			18 27		18 34		18 42			18 57		19 04	
Bebington	d		17 52		17 59		18 07		18 14			18 29		18 37		18 44			18 59		19 07	
Port Sunlight	d		17 54		18 01		18 09		18 16			18 31		18 39		18 46			19 01		19 09	
Spital	d		17 56		18 03		18 11		18 18			18 33		18 41		18 48			19 03		19 11	
Bromborough Rake	d		17 58		18 05		18 13		18 20			18 35		18 43		18 50			19 05		19 13	
Bromborough	d		18 00		18 07		18 15		18 22			18 37		18 45		18 52			19 07		19 15	
Eastham Rake	d		18 02		18 10		18 17		18 25			18 40		18 47		18 55			19 10		19 17	
Hooton	d		18 04		18 12		18 19		18 27			18 42		18 49		18 57			19 12		19 19	
Little Sutton	d		18 09				18 24							18 54							19 24	
Overpool	d		18 11				18 26							18 56							19 26	
Ellesmere Port	a		18 16				18 30							19 00							19 30	
Capenhurst	d				18 17							18 47							19 17			
Bache	d				18 22				18 36			18 52				19 06			19 22			
Chester	a				18 26				18 39			18 56				19 10			19 26			

		ME	ME	ME	ME	ME	ME	ME	ME	ME	ME	ME	ME	ME	ME	ME	ME	ME	ME	ME	ME	ME	ME
Moorfields 10	d	18 56	19 01	19 06	19 11	19 16	19 26	19 31	19 41	19 46	19 56	20 01	20 11	20 16	20 26	20 31	20 41	20 46	20 56	21 01	21 11	21 16	21 26
Liverpool Lime Street 10	d	18 58	19 03	19 08	19 13	19 18	19 28	19 33	19 43	19 48	19 58	20 03	20 13	20 18	20 28	20 33	20 43	20 48	20 58	21 03	21 13	21 18	21 28
Liverpool Central 10	d	19 00	19 05	19 10	19 15	19 20	19 30	19 35	19 45	19 50	20 00	20 05	20 15	20 20	20 30	20 35	20 45	20 50	21 00	21 05	21 15	21 20	21 30
James Street	d	19 02	19 07	19 12	19 17	19 22	19 32	19 37	19 47	19 52	20 02	20 07	20 17	20 22	20 32	20 37	20 47	20 52	21 02	21 07	21 17	21 22	21 32
Hamilton Square	d	19 05	19 10	19 15	19 20	19 25	19 35	19 40	19 50	19 55	20 05	20 10	20 20	20 25	20 35	20 40	20 50	20 55	21 05	21 10	21 20	21 25	21 35
Conway Park	d		19 12	19 17		19 27		19 42		19 57		20 12		20 27		20 42		20 57		21 12		21 27	
Birkenhead Park	d		19 14	19 19		19 29		19 44		19 59		20 14		20 29		20 44		20 59		21 14		21 29	
Birkenhead North	d		19 17	19 22		19 32		19 47		20 02		20 17		20 32		20 47		21 02		21 17		21 32	
Wallasey Village	d		19 22			19 37				20 07				20 37				21 07				21 37	
Wallasey Grove Road	d		19 23			19 38				20 08				20 38				21 08				21 38	
New Brighton	a		19 28			19 43				20 13				20 43				21 13				21 43	
Bidston	d			19 25				19 50				20 20				20 50				21 20			
Leasowe	d			19 27				19 52				20 22				20 52				21 22			
Moreton (Merseyside)	d			19 29				19 54				20 24				20 54				21 24			
Meols	d			19 33				19 58				20 28				20 58				21 28			
Manor Road	d			19 35				20 00				20 30				21 00				21 30			
Hoylake	d			19 37				20 02				20 32				21 02				21 32			
West Kirby	a			19 42				20 07				20 37				21 07				21 37			
Birkenhead Central	d	19 07			19 22		19 37		19 52		20 07		20 22		20 37		20 52		21 07		21 22		21 37
Green Lane	d	19 09			19 24		19 39		19 54		20 09		20 24		20 39		20 54		21 09		21 24		21 39
Rock Ferry	d	19 12			19 27		19 42		19 57		20 12		20 27		20 42		20 57		21 12		21 27		21 42
Bebington	d	19 14			19 29		19 44		19 59		20 14		20 29		20 44		20 59		21 14		21 29		21 44
Port Sunlight	d	19 16			19 31		19 46		20 01		20 16		20 31		20 46		21 01		21 16		21 31		21 46
Spital	d	19 18			19 33		19 48		20 03		20 18		20 33		20 48		21 03		21 18		21 33		21 48
Bromborough Rake	d	19 20			19 35		19 50		20 05		20 20		20 35		20 50		21 05		21 20		21 35		21 50
Bromborough	d	19 22			19 37		19 52		20 07		20 22		20 37		20 52		21 07		21 22		21 37		21 52
Eastham Rake	d	19 25			19 40		19 55		20 10		20 25		20 40		20 55		21 10		21 25		21 40		21 55
Hooton	d	19 27			19 42		19 57		20 12		20 27		20 42		20 57		21 12		21 27		21 42		21 57
Little Sutton	d						20 01				20 31				21 01				21 31				22 01
Overpool	d						20 03				20 33				21 03				21 33				22 03
Ellesmere Port	a						20 08				20 38				21 08				21 38				22 08
Capenhurst	d				19 47				20 17				20 47				21 17				21 47		
Bache	d	19 36			19 52				20 22				20 52				21 22				21 52		
Chester	a	19 41			19 56				20 26				20 56				21 26				21 56		

Liverpool and Birkenhead - New Brighton, West Kirby, Ellesmere Port and Chester

Network Diagram - see first Page of Table 101

		ME	ME	ME		ME	ME	ME	ME	ME	ME	ME	ME	ME		ME	ME	ME	ME	ME	ME	ME	ME		
Moorfields 10	d	21 31	21 41	21 46		21 56	22 01	22 11	22 16	22 26	22 31	22 41	22 46	22 56		23 01	23 11	23 16	23 26	23 31	23 41	23 46	23 56		
Liverpool Lime Street 10	d	21 33	21 43	21 48		21 58	22 03	22 13	22 18	22 28	22 33	22 43	22 48	22 58		23 03	23 13	23 18	23 28	23 33	23 43	23 48	23 58		
Liverpool Central 10	d	21 35	21 45	21 50		22 00	22 05	22 15	22 20	22 30	22 35	22 45	22 50	23 00		23 05	23 15	23 20	23 30	23 35	23 45	23 50	23 59		
James Street	d	21 37	21 47	21 52		22 02	22 07	22 17	22 22	22 32	22 37	22 47	22 52	23 02		23 07	23 17	23 22	23 32	23 37	23 47	23 52	00 02		
Hamilton Square	d	21 40	21 50	21 55		22 05	22 10	22 20	22 25	22 35	22 40	22 50	22 55	23 05		23 10	23 20	23 25	23 35	23 40	23 50	23 55	00a05		
Conway Park	d	21 42		21 57			22 12		22 27		22 42		22 57			23 12		23 27		23 42		23 57			
Birkenhead Park	d	21 44		21 59			22 14		22 29		22 44		22 59			23 14		23 29		23 44		23 59			
Birkenhead North	d	21 47		22 02			22 17		22 32		22 47		23 02			23 17		23 32		23 47		00 02			
Wallasey Village	d			22 07					22 37				23 07					23 37				00 07			
Wallasey Grove Road	d			22 08					22 38				23 08					23 38				00 08			
New Brighton	a			22 13					22 43				23 13					23 43				00 13			
Bidston	d	21 50					22 20				22 50					23 20				23 50					
Leasowe	d	21 52					22 22				22 52					23 22				23 52					
Moreton (Merseyside)	d	21 54					22 24				22 54					23 24				23 54					
Meols	d	21 58					22 28				22 58					23 28				23 58					
Manor Road	d	22 00					22 30				23 00					23 30				23 59					
Hoylake	d	22 02					22 32				23 02					23 32				00 02					
West Kirby	a	22 07					22 37				23 07					23 37				00 07					
Birkenhead Central	d		21 52			22 07		22 22		22 37		22 52		23 07			23 22		23 37		23 52				
Green Lane	d		21 54			22 09		22 24		22 39		22 54		23 09			23 24		23 39		23 54				
Rock Ferry	d		21 57			22 12		22 27		22 42		22 57		23 12			23 27		23 42		23 57				
Bebington	d		21 59			22 14		22 29		22 44		22 59		23 14			23 29		23 44		23 59				
Port Sunlight	d		22 01			22 16		22 31		22 46		23 01		23 16			23 31		23 46		00 01				
Spital	d		22 03			22 18		22 33		22 48		23 03		23 18			23 33		23 48		00 03				
Bromborough Rake	d		22 05			22 20		22 35		22 50		23 05		23 20			23 35		23 50		00 05				
Bromborough	d		22 07			22 22		22 37		22 52		23 07		23 22			23 37		23 52		00 07				
Eastham Rake	d		22 10			22 25		22 40		22 55		23 10		23 25			23 40		23 55		00 10				
Hooton	d		22 12			22 27		22 42		22 57		23 12		23 27			23 42		23 57		00 12				
Little Sutton	d					22 31				23 01				23 31					00 01						
Overpool	d					22 33				23 03				23 33					00 03						
Ellesmere Port	a					22 38				23 08				23 37					00 07						
Capenhurst	d		22 17					22 47				23 17					23 47				00 17				
Bache	d		22 22					22 52				23 22					23 52				00 22				
Chester	a		22 26					22 56				23 26					23 56				00 26				

Sundays

		ME A	ME A	ME A	ME A	ME A	ME	ME	ME	ME		ME	ME	ME	ME		ME	ME	ME		ME	ME	ME	ME
Moorfields 10	d	23p26	23p31	23p41	23p46	23p56	07 56	08 01	08 11	08 16		08 26	08 31	08 41	08 46		22 46	22 56	23 11		23 16	23 26	23 31	23 41
Liverpool Lime Street 10	d	23p28	23p33	23p43	23p48	23p58	07 58	08 03	08 13	08 18		08 28	08 33	08 43	08 48		22 48	22 58	23 13		23 18	23 28	23 33	23 43
Liverpool Central 10	d	23p30	23p35	23p45	23p50	23p59	08 00	08 05	08 15	08 20		08 30	08 35	08 45	08 50		22 50	23 00	23 15		23 20	23 30	23 35	23 45
James Street	d	23p32	23p37	23p47	23p52	00 02	08 02	08 07	08 17	08 22		08 32	08 37	08 47	08 52		22 52	23 02	23 17		23 22	23 32	23 37	23 47
Hamilton Square	d	23p35	23p40	23p50	23p55	00a05	08 05	08 10	08 20	08 25		08 35	08 40	08 50	08 55		22 55	23 05	23 20		23 25	23 35	23 40	23 50
Conway Park	d		23p42		23p57			08 12		08 27			08 42		08 57		22 57				23 27		23 42	
Birkenhead Park	d		23p44		23p59			08 14		08 29			08 44		08 59		22 59				23 29		23 44	
Birkenhead North	d		23p47		00 02			08 17		08 32			08 47		09 02		23 02				23 32		23 47	
Wallasey Village	d				00 07					08 37					09 07		23 07				23 37			
Wallasey Grove Road	d				00 08					08 38					09 08		23 08				23 38			
New Brighton	a				00 13					08 43					09 13		23 13				23 43			
Bidston	d		23p50					08 20					08 50										23 50	
Leasowe	d		23p52					08 22					08 52			and at							23 52	
Moreton (Merseyside)	d		23p54					08 24					08 54			the same							23 54	
Meols	d		23p58					08 28					08 58			minutes							23 58	
Manor Road	d		23p59					08 30					09 00			past							23 59	
Hoylake	d		00 02					08 32					09 02			each							00 02	
West Kirby	a		00 07					08 37					09 07			hour until							00 07	
Birkenhead Central	d	23p37		23p52			08 07		08 22			08 37		08 52				23 07	23 22			23 37		23 52
Green Lane	d	23p39		23p54			08 09		08 24			08 39		08 54				23 09	23 24			23 39		23 54
Rock Ferry	d	23p42		23p57			08 12		08 27			08 42		08 57				23 12	23 27			23 42		23 57
Bebington	d	23p44		23p59			08 14		08 29			08 44		08 59				23 14	23 29			23 44		23 59
Port Sunlight	d	23p46		00 01			08 16		08 31			08 46		09 01				23 16	23 31			23 46		00 01
Spital	d	23p48		00 03			08 18		08 33			08 48		09 03				23 18	23 33			23 48		00 03
Bromborough Rake	d	23p50		00 05			08 20		08 35			08 50		09 05				23 20	23 35			23 50		00 05
Bromborough	d	23p52		00 07			08 22		08 37			08 52		09 07				23 22	23 37			23 52		00 07
Eastham Rake	d	23p55		00 10			08 25		08 40			08 55		09 10				23 25	23 40			23 55		00 10
Hooton	d	23p57		00 12			08 27		08 42			08 57		09 12				23 27	23 42			23 57		00 12
Little Sutton	d	00 01					08 31					09 01						23 31				00 01		
Overpool	d	00 03					08 33					09 03						23 33				00 03		
Ellesmere Port	a	00 07					08 38					09 08						23 37				00 07		
Capenhurst	d			00 17					08 47					09 17					23 47					00 17
Bache	d			00 22					08 52					09 22					23 52					00 22
Chester	a			00 26					08 56					09 26					23 56					00 26

A not 11 December

Table 106

Sundays

Liverpool and Birkenhead - New Brighton, West Kirby, Ellesmere Port and Chester

Network Diagram - see first Page of Table 101

		ME	ME
Moorfields 10	d	23 46	23 56
Liverpool Lime Street 10	d	23 48	23 58
Liverpool Central 10	d	23 50	23 59
James Street	d	23 52	00 02
Hamilton Square	d	23 55	00a05
Conway Park	d	23 57	
Birkenhead Park	d	23 59	
Birkenhead North	d	00 02	
Wallasey Village	d	00 07	
Wallasey Grove Road	d	00 08	
New Brighton	a	00 13	
Bidston	d		
Leasowe	d		
Moreton (Merseyside)	d		
Meols	d		
Manor Road	d		
Hoylake	d		
West Kirby	a		
Birkenhead Central	d		
Green Lane	d		
Rock Ferry	d		
Bebington	d		
Port Sunlight	d		
Spital	d		
Bromborough Rake	d		
Bromborough	d		
Eastham Rake	d		
Hooton	d		
Little Sutton	d		
Overpool	d		
Ellesmere Port	a		
Capenhurst	d		
Bache	d		
Chester	a		

Chester, Ellesmere Port, West Kirby and New Brighton - Birkenhead and Liverpool

Network Diagram - see first Page of Table 101

Miles	Miles	Miles	Miles			ME	ME	ME	ME	ME	ME	ME	ME	ME		ME	ME	ME	ME	ME	ME	ME	ME	ME
0	—	—	—	**Chester**	d						05 55					06 30						07 00		
1½	—	—	—	Bache	d						05 58					06 33						07 03		
5¼	—	—	—	Capenhurst	d						06 04					06 39						07 09		
—	0	—	—	**Ellesmere Port**	d									06 17					06 47					
—	1½	—	—	Overpool	d									06 20					06 50					
—	2½	—	—	Little Sutton	d									06 22					06 52					
8¼	4	—	—	Hooton	d		05 39			05 59	06 09			06 26		06 44			06 56			07 14		
9¼	—	—	—	Eastham Rake	d		05 41			06 01	06 11			06 28		06 46			06 58			07 16		
9¾	—	—	—	Bromborough	d		05 43			06 03	06 13			06 31		06 48			07 01			07 18		
10½	—	—	—	Bromborough Rake	d		05 45			06 05	06 15			06 33		06 50			07 03			07 20		
11¼	—	—	—	Spital	d		05 47			06 07	06 17			06 35		06 52			07 05			07 22		
11¾	—	—	—	Port Sunlight	d		05 49			06 09	06 19			06 37		06 54			07 07			07 24		
12¾	—	—	—	Bebington	d		05 51			06 11	06 21			06 39		06 56			07 09			07 26		
13¾	—	—	—	Rock Ferry	d	05 44	05 54			06 14	06 24			06 42		06 59			07 12			07 29		
14½	—	—	—	Green Lane	d	05 47	05 57			06 17	06 27			06 44		07 02			07 14			07 32		
15	—	—	—	Birkenhead Central	d	05 49	05 59			06 19	06 34			06 49		07 04			07 19			07 34		
—	—	0	—	**West Kirby**	d				05 51				06 21					06 51			07 06			07 21
—	—	1	—	Hoylake	d				05 54				06 24					06 54			07 09			07 24
—	—	1¾	—	Manor Road	d				05 56				06 26					06 56			07 11			07 26
—	—	3	—	Meols	d				05 58				06 28					06 58			07 13			07 28
—	—	4¼	—	Moreton (Merseyside)	d				06 01				06 31					07 01			07 16			07 31
—	—	4¾	—	Leasowe	d				06 03				06 33					07 03			07 18			07 33
—	—	5¾	—	Bidston	d				06 06				06 36					07 06			07 21			07 36
—	—	—	0	**New Brighton**	d			05 53				06 23					06 53			07 08			07 23	
—	—	—	1¼	Wallasey Grove Road	d			05 57				06 27					06 57			07 12			07 27	
—	—	—	1½	Wallasey Village	d			05 59				06 29					06 59			07 14			07 29	
—	—	6½	3	Birkenhead North	d			06 04	06 09			06 34	06 39				07 04	07 09		07 19	07 24		07 34	07 39
—	—	7½	3¾	Birkenhead Park	d			06 06	06 11			06 36	06 41				07 06	07 11		07 21	07 26		07 36	07 41
—	—	8¼	4½	Conway Park	d			06 09	06 14			06 39	06 44				07 09	07 14		07 24	07 29		07 39	07 44
15½	—	8¾	5	Hamilton Square	d	05 51	06 01	06 11	06 16	06 21	06 36	06 41	06 46	06 51		07 06	07 11	07 16	07 21	07 26	07 31	07 36	07 41	07 46
16¾	—	8¾	6¼	James Street	d	05 54	06 04	06 14	06 19	06 24	06 39	06 44	06 49	06 54		07 09	07 14	07 19	07 24	07 29	07 34	07 39	07 44	07 49
17¼	—	10¼	7¾	Moorfields [10]	a	05 56	06 06	06 16	06 21	06 26	06 41	06 46	06 51	06 56		07 11	07 16	07 21	07 26	07 31	07 36	07 41	07 46	07 51
17¾	—	10¾	8¼	Liverpool Lime Street [10]	a	05 58	06 08	06 18	06 23	06 28	06 43	06 48	06 53	06 58		07 13	07 18	07 23	07 28	07 33	07 38	07 43	07 48	07 53
18½	—	11¼	8¾	**Liverpool Central** [10]	a	06 00	06 10	06 20	06 25	06 30	06 45	06 50	06 55	07 00		07 15	07 20	07 25	07 30	07 35	07 40	07 45	07 50	07 55

		ME SX	ME SO	ME	ME SX	ME	ME SO	ME SX	ME	ME SX		ME	ME	ME	ME SX	ME	ME SO	ME SX	ME	ME SX		ME SO	ME	ME SO	ME SX
Chester	d				07 22		07 30			07 37					07 52		08 00			08 07				08 15	
Bache	d				07 26		07 33			07 41					07 56		08 03			08 11				08 18	
Capenhurst	d				07 32		07 39			07 47					08 02		08 09			08 17				08 24	
Ellesmere Port	d	07 17	07 19					07 31					07 49					08 01				08 12			08 17
Overpool	d	07 20	07 22					07 34					07 52					08 04				08 15			08 20
Little Sutton	d	07 22	07 24					07 36					07 54					08 06				08 17			08 22
Hooton	d	07 26	07 29		07 36		07 44	07 44		07 51			07 59		08 06		08 14	08 14		08 21		08 21		08 29	08 29
Eastham Rake	d	07 28	07 31		07 38		07 46	07 46		07 53			08 01		08 08		08 16	08 16		08 23		08 23		08 31	08 31
Bromborough	d	07 31	07 33		07 41		07 48	07 48		07 56			08 03		08 11		08 18	08 18		08 26		08 26		08 33	08 33
Bromborough Rake	d	07 33	07 35		07 43		07 50	07 50		07 58			08 05		08 13		08 20	08 20		08 28		08 28		08 35	08 35
Spital	d	07 35	07 37		07 45		07 52	07 52		08 00			08 07		08 15		08 22	08 22		08 30		08 30		08 37	08 37
Port Sunlight	d	07 37	07 39		07 47		07 54	07 54		08 02			08 09		08 17		08 24	08 24		08 32		08 32		08 39	08 39
Bebington	d	07 39	07 41		07 49		07 56	07 56		08 04			08 11		08 19		08 26	08 26		08 34		08 34		08 41	08 41
Rock Ferry	d	07 42	07 44		07 52		07 59	07 59		08 07			08 14		08 22		08 29	08 29		08 37		08 37		08 44	08 44
Green Lane	d	07 44	07 47		07 54		08 02	08 02		08 09			08 17		08 24		08 32	08 32		08 39		08 39		08 47	08 47
Birkenhead Central	d	07 47	07 49		07 57		08 04	08 04		08 12			08 19		08 27		08 34	08 34		08 42		08 42		08 49	08 49
West Kirby	d					07 36						07 51				08 06							08 21		
Hoylake	d					07 39						07 54				08 09							08 24		
Manor Road	d					07 41						07 56				08 11							08 26		
Meols	d					07 43						07 58				08 13							08 28		
Moreton (Merseyside)	d					07 46						08 01				08 16							08 31		
Leasowe	d					07 48						08 03				08 18							08 33		
Bidston	d					07 51						08 06				08 21							08 36		
New Brighton	d			07 38					07 53					08 08					08 23						
Wallasey Grove Road	d			07 42					07 57					08 12					08 27						
Wallasey Village	d			07 44					07 59					08 14					08 29						
Birkenhead North	d			07 49		07 54			08 04			08 09		08 19		08 24			08 34				08 39		
Birkenhead Park	d			07 51		07 56			08 06			08 11		08 21		08 26			08 36				08 41		
Conway Park	d			07 54		07 59			08 09			08 14		08 24		08 29			08 39				08 44		
Hamilton Square	d	07 49	07 51	07 56	07 59	08 01	08 06	08 06	08 11	08 14		08 16	08 21	08 26	08 29	08 31	08 36	08 36	08 41	08 44		08 44	08 46	08 51	08 51
James Street	d	07 52	07 54	07 59	08 02	08 04	08 09	08 09	08 14	08 17		08 19	08 24	08 29	08 32	08 34	08 39	08 39	08 44	08 47		08 47	08 49	08 54	08 54
Moorfields [10]	a	07 53	07 56	08 01	08 03	08 06	08 11	08 11	08 16	08 18		08 21	08 26	08 31	08 33	08 36	08 41	08 41	08 46	08 48		08 48	08 51	08 56	08 56
Liverpool Lime Street [10]	a	07 55	07 58	08 03	08 05	08 08	08 13	08 13	08 18	08 20		08 23	08 28	08 33	08 35	08 38	08 43	08 43	08 48	08 50		08 50	08 53	08 58	08 58
Liverpool Central [10]	a	07 57	08 00	08 05	08 07	08 10	08 15	08 15	08 20	08 22		08 25	08 30	08 35	08 37	08 40	08 45	08 45	08 50	08 52		08 52	08 55	09 00	09 00

Chester, Ellesmere Port, West Kirby and New Brighton - Birkenhead and Liverpool

Network Diagram - see first Page of Table 101

		ME	ME	ME	ME	ME SO		ME SX	ME	ME	ME	ME	ME	ME	ME	ME		ME	ME	ME	ME	ME	ME	ME	ME
Chester	d			08 31						08 45			09 01					09 15			09 31				09 45
Bache	d			08 35						08 48			09 05					09 18			09 35				09 48
Capenhurst	d									08 54								09 24							09 54
Ellesmere Port	d					08 42		08 42							09 12								09 42		
Overpool	d					08 45		08 45							09 15								09 45		
Little Sutton	d					08 47		08 47							09 17								09 47		
Hooton	d			08 44		08 51		08 52		08 59			09 14		09 21			09 29			09 44		09 51		09 59
Eastham Rake	d			08 46		08 53		08 54		09 01			09 16		09 23			09 31			09 46		09 53		10 01
Bromborough	d			08 48		08 56		08 56		09 03			09 18		09 26			09 33			09 48		09 56		10 03
Bromborough Rake	d			08 50		08 58		08 58		09 05			09 20		09 28			09 35			09 50		09 58		10 05
Spital	d			08 52		09 00		09 00		09 07			09 22		09 30			09 37			09 52		10 00		10 07
Port Sunlight	d			08 54		09 02		09 02		09 09			09 24		09 32			09 39			09 54		10 02		10 09
Bebington	d			08 56		09 04		09 04		09 11			09 26		09 34			09 41			09 56		10 04		10 11
Rock Ferry	d			08 59		09 07		09 07		09 14			09 29		09 37			09 44			09 59		10 07		10 14
Green Lane	d			09 02		09 09		09 10		09 17			09 32		09 39			09 47			10 02		10 09		10 17
Birkenhead Central	d			09 04		09 12		09 12		09 19			09 34		09 42			09 49			10 04		10 12		10 19
West Kirby	d		08 36						08 51			09 06				09 21				09 36				09 51	
Hoylake	d		08 39						08 54			09 09				09 24				09 39				09 54	
Manor Road	d		08 41						08 56			09 11				09 26				09 41				09 56	
Meols	d		08 43						08 58			09 13				09 28				09 43				09 58	
Moreton (Merseyside)	d		08 46						09 01			09 16				09 31				09 46				10 01	
Leasowe	d		08 48						09 03			09 18				09 33				09 48				10 03	
Bidston	d		08 51						09 06			09 21				09 36				09 51				10 06	
New Brighton	d	08 38			08 53						09 08			09 23					09 38			09 53			
Wallasey Grove Road	d	08 42			08 57						09 12			09 27					09 42			09 57			
Wallasey Village	d	08 44			08 59						09 14			09 29					09 44			09 59			
Birkenhead North	d	08 49	08 54		09 04				09 09		09 19	09 24		09 34		09 39			09 49	09 54		10 04		10 09	
Birkenhead Park	d	08 51	08 56		09 06				09 11		09 21	09 26		09 36		09 41			09 51	09 56		10 06		10 11	
Conway Park	d	08 54	08 59		09 09				09 14		09 24	09 29		09 39		09 44			09 54	09 59		10 09		10 14	
Hamilton Square	d	08 56	09 01	09 06	09 11	09 14		09 14	09 16	09 21	09 26	09 31	09 36	09 41	09 44	09 46		09 51	09 56	10 01	10 06	10 11	10 14	10 16	10 21
James Street	d	08 59	09 04	09 09	09 14	09 17		09 17	09 19	09 24	09 29	09 34	09 39	09 44	09 47	09 49		09 54	09 59	10 04	10 09	10 14	10 17	10 19	10 24
Moorfields 10	a	09 01	09 06	09 11	09 16	09 18		09 19	09 21	09 26	09 31	09 36	09 41	09 46	09 48	09 51		09 56	10 01	10 06	10 11	10 16	10 18	10 21	10 26
Liverpool Lime Street 10	a	09 03	09 08	09 13	09 18	09 20		09 21	09 23	09 28	09 33	09 38	09 43	09 48	09 50	09 53		09 58	10 03	10 08	10 13	10 18	10 20	10 23	10 28
Liverpool Central 10	a	09 05	09 10	09 15	09 20	09 22		09 23	09 25	09 30	09 35	09 40	09 45	09 50	09 52	09 55		10 00	10 05	10 10	10 15	10 20	10 22	10 25	10 30

		ME		ME	ME	ME	ME	ME	ME	ME	ME	ME		ME	ME	ME	ME	ME	ME	ME	ME	ME		ME	ME
Chester	d				10 01				10 15			10 31					10 45			11 01					11 15
Bache	d				10 05				10 18			10 35					10 48			11 05					11 18
Capenhurst	d								10 24								10 54								11 24
Ellesmere Port	d						10 12								10 42							11 12			
Overpool	d						10 15								10 45							11 15			
Little Sutton	d						10 17								10 47							11 17			
Hooton	d				10 14		10 21		10 29			10 44			10 51		10 59			11 14		11 21			11 29
Eastham Rake	d				10 16		10 23		10 31			10 46			10 53		11 01			11 16		11 23			11 31
Bromborough	d				10 18		10 26		10 33			10 48			10 56		11 03			11 18		11 26			11 33
Bromborough Rake	d				10 20		10 28		10 35			10 50			10 58		11 05			11 20		11 28			11 35
Spital	d				10 22		10 30		10 37			10 52			11 00		11 07			11 22		11 30			11 37
Port Sunlight	d				10 24		10 32		10 39			10 54			11 02		11 09			11 24		11 32			11 39
Bebington	d				10 26		10 34		10 41			10 56			11 04		11 11			11 26		11 34			11 41
Rock Ferry	d				10 29		10 37		10 44			10 59			11 07		11 14			11 29		11 37			11 44
Green Lane	d				10 32		10 39		10 47			11 02			11 09		11 17			11 32		11 39			11 47
Birkenhead Central	d				10 34		10 42		10 49			11 04			11 12		11 19			11 34		11 42			11 49
West Kirby	d			10 06				10 21			10 36					10 51			11 06					11 21	
Hoylake	d			10 09				10 24			10 39					10 54			11 09					11 24	
Manor Road	d			10 11				10 26			10 41					10 56			11 11					11 26	
Meols	d			10 13				10 28			10 43					10 58			11 13					11 28	
Moreton (Merseyside)	d			10 16				10 31			10 46					11 01			11 16					11 31	
Leasowe	d			10 18				10 33			10 48					11 03			11 18					11 33	
Bidston	d			10 21				10 36			10 51					11 06			11 21					11 36	
New Brighton	d	10 08				10 23				10 38				10 53				11 08			11 23				
Wallasey Grove Road	d	10 12				10 27				10 42				10 57				11 12			11 27				
Wallasey Village	d	10 14				10 29				10 44				10 59				11 14			11 29				
Birkenhead North	d	10 19		10 24		10 34		10 39		10 49	10 54			11 04		11 09		11 19	11 24		11 34			11 39	
Birkenhead Park	d	10 21		10 26		10 36		10 41		10 51	10 56			11 06		11 11		11 21	11 26		11 36			11 41	
Conway Park	d	10 24		10 29		10 39		10 44		10 54	10 59			11 09		11 14		11 24	11 29		11 39			11 44	
Hamilton Square	d	10 26		10 31	10 36	10 41	10 44	10 46	10 51	10 56	11 01	11 06		11 11	11 14	11 16	11 21	11 26	11 31	11 36	11 41	11 44		11 46	11 51
James Street	d	10 29		10 34	10 39	10 44	10 47	10 49	10 54	10 59	11 04	11 09		11 14	11 17	11 19	11 24	11 29	11 34	11 39	11 44	11 47		11 49	11 54
Moorfields 10	a	10 31		10 36	10 41	10 46	10 48	10 51	10 56	11 01	11 06	11 11		11 16	11 18	11 21	11 26	11 31	11 36	11 41	11 46	11 48		11 51	11 56
Liverpool Lime Street 10	a	10 33		10 38	10 43	10 48	10 50	10 53	10 58	11 03	11 08	11 13		11 18	11 20	11 23	11 28	11 33	11 38	11 43	11 48	11 50		11 53	11 58
Liverpool Central 10	a	10 35		10 40	10 45	10 50	10 52	10 55	11 00	11 05	11 10	11 15		11 20	11 22	11 25	11 30	11 35	11 40	11 45	11 50	11 52		11 55	12 00

Chester, Ellesmere Port, West Kirby and New Brighton - Birkenhead and Liverpool

Network Diagram - see first Page of Table 101

		ME	ME	ME	ME	ME	ME	ME		ME	ME	ME	ME	ME	ME	ME	ME	ME		ME	ME	ME	ME	ME	ME
Chester	d			11 31				11 45				12 01				12 15				12 31				12 45	
Bache	d			11 35				11 48				12 05				12 18				12 35				12 48	
Capenhurst	d							11 54								12 24								12 54	
Ellesmere Port	d					11 42								12 12								12 42			
Overpool	d					11 45								12 15								12 45			
Little Sutton	d					11 47								12 17								12 47			
Hooton	d			11 44		11 51		11 59				12 14		12 21		12 29				12 44		12 51		12 59	
Eastham Rake	d			11 46		11 53		12 01				12 16		12 23		12 31				12 46		12 53		13 01	
Bromborough	d			11 48		11 56		12 03				12 18		12 26		12 33				12 48		12 56		13 03	
Bromborough Rake	d			11 50		11 58		12 05				12 20		12 28		12 35				12 50		12 58		13 05	
Spital	d			11 52		12 00		12 07				12 22		12 30		12 37				12 52		13 00		13 07	
Port Sunlight	d			11 54		12 02		12 09				12 24		12 32		12 39				12 54		13 02		13 09	
Bebington	d			11 56		12 04		12 11				12 26		12 34		12 41				12 56		13 04		13 11	
Rock Ferry	d			11 59		12 07		12 14				12 29		12 37		12 44				12 59		13 07		13 14	
Green Lane	d			12 02		12 09		12 17				12 32		12 39		12 47				13 02		13 09		13 17	
Birkenhead Central	d			12 04		12 12		12 19				12 34		12 42		12 49				13 04		13 12		13 19	
West Kirby	d		11 36				11 51				12 06				12 21			12 36					12 51		
Hoylake	d		11 39				11 54				12 09				12 24			12 39					12 54		
Manor Road	d		11 41				11 56				12 11				12 26			12 41					12 56		
Meols	d		11 43				11 58				12 13				12 28			12 43					12 58		
Moreton (Merseyside)	d		11 46				12 01				12 16				12 31			12 46					13 01		
Leasowe	d		11 48				12 03				12 18				12 33			12 48					13 03		
Bidston	d		11 51				12 06				12 21				12 36			12 51					13 06		
New Brighton	d	11 38			11 53					12 08			12 23				12 38				12 53				13 08
Wallasey Grove Road	d	11 42			11 57					12 12			12 27				12 42				12 57				13 12
Wallasey Village	d	11 44			11 59					12 14			12 29				12 44				12 59				13 14
Birkenhead North	d	11 49	11 54		12 04		12 09			12 19	12 24		12 34		12 39		12 49	12 54			13 04		13 09		13 19
Birkenhead Park	d	11 51	11 56		12 06		12 11			12 21	12 26		12 36		12 41		12 51	12 56			13 06		13 11		13 21
Conway Park	d	11 54	11 59		12 09		12 14			12 24	12 29		12 39		12 44		12 54	12 59			13 09		13 14		13 24
Hamilton Square	d	11 56	12 01	12 06	12 11	12 14	12 16	12 21		12 26	12 31	12 36	12 41	12 44	12 46	12 51	12 56	13 01		13 06	13 11	13 14	13 16	13 21	13 26
James Street	d	11 59	12 04	12 09	12 14	12 17	12 19	12 24		12 29	12 34	12 39	12 44	12 47	12 49	12 54	12 59	13 04		13 09	13 14	13 17	13 19	13 24	13 29
Moorfields 10	a	12 01	12 06	12 11	12 16	12 18	12 21	12 26		12 31	12 36	12 41	12 46	12 48	12 51	12 56	13 01	13 06		13 11	13 16	13 18	13 21	13 26	13 31
Liverpool Lime Street 10	a	12 03	12 08	12 13	12 18	12 20	12 23	12 28		12 33	12 38	12 43	12 48	12 50	12 53	12 58	13 03	13 08		13 13	13 18	13 20	13 23	13 28	13 33
Liverpool Central 10	a	12 05	12 10	12 15	12 20	12 22	12 25	12 30		12 35	12 40	12 45	12 50	12 52	12 55	13 00	13 05	13 10		13 15	13 20	13 22	13 25	13 30	13 35

		ME	ME	ME		ME	ME	ME	ME	ME	ME	ME	ME	ME		ME	ME	ME	ME	ME	ME	ME	ME	ME	
Chester	d		13 01					13 15			13 31					13 45			14 01				14 15		
Bache	d		13 05					13 18			13 35					13 48			14 05				14 18		
Capenhurst	d							13 24								13 54							14 24		
Ellesmere Port	d					13 12							13 42								14 12				
Overpool	d					13 15							13 45								14 15				
Little Sutton	d					13 17							13 47								14 17				
Hooton	d		13 14			13 21		13 29			13 44		13 51			13 59			14 14		14 21		14 29		
Eastham Rake	d		13 16			13 23		13 31			13 46		13 53			14 01			14 16		14 23		14 31		
Bromborough	d		13 18			13 26		13 33			13 48		13 56			14 03			14 18		14 26		14 33		
Bromborough Rake	d		13 20			13 28		13 35			13 50		13 58			14 05			14 20		14 28		14 35		
Spital	d		13 22			13 30		13 37			13 52		14 00			14 07			14 22		14 30		14 37		
Port Sunlight	d		13 24			13 32		13 39			13 54		14 02			14 09			14 24		14 32		14 39		
Bebington	d		13 26			13 34		13 41			13 56		14 04			14 11			14 26		14 34		14 41		
Rock Ferry	d		13 29			13 37		13 44			13 59		14 07			14 14			14 29		14 37		14 44		
Green Lane	d		13 32			13 39		13 47			14 02		14 09			14 17			14 32		14 39		14 47		
Birkenhead Central	d		13 34			13 42		13 49			14 04		14 12			14 19			14 34		14 42		14 49		
West Kirby	d	13 06					13 21			13 36				13 51				14 06				14 21			
Hoylake	d	13 09					13 24			13 39				13 54				14 09				14 24			
Manor Road	d	13 11					13 26			13 41				13 56				14 11				14 26			
Meols	d	13 13					13 28			13 43				13 58				14 13				14 28			
Moreton (Merseyside)	d	13 16					13 31			13 46				14 01				14 16				14 31			
Leasowe	d	13 18					13 33			13 48				14 03				14 18				14 33			
Bidston	d	13 21					13 36			13 51				14 06				14 21				14 36			
New Brighton	d			13 23					13 38			13 53					14 08			14 23				14 38	
Wallasey Grove Road	d			13 27					13 42			13 57					14 12			14 27				14 42	
Wallasey Village	d			13 29					13 44			13 59					14 14			14 29				14 44	
Birkenhead North	d	13 24		13 34			13 39		13 49	13 54		14 04		14 09			14 19	14 24		14 34		14 39		14 49	
Birkenhead Park	d	13 26		13 36			13 41		13 51	13 56		14 06		14 11			14 21	14 26		14 36		14 41		14 51	
Conway Park	d	13 29		13 39			13 44		13 54	13 59		14 09		14 14			14 24	14 29		14 39		14 44		14 54	
Hamilton Square	d	13 31	13 36	13 41		13 44	13 46	13 51	13 56	14 01	14 06	14 11	14 14	14 16		14 21	14 26	14 31	14 36	14 41	14 44	14 46	14 51	14 56	
James Street	d	13 34	13 39	13 44		13 47	13 49	13 54	13 59	14 04	14 09	14 14	14 17	14 19		14 24	14 29	14 34	14 39	14 44	14 47	14 49	14 54	14 59	
Moorfields 10	a	13 36	13 41	13 46		13 48	13 51	13 56	14 01	14 06	14 11	14 16	14 18	14 21		14 26	14 31	14 36	14 41	14 46	14 48	14 51	14 56	15 01	
Liverpool Lime Street 10	a	13 38	13 43	13 48		13 50	13 53	13 58	14 03	14 08	14 13	14 18	14 20	14 23		14 28	14 33	14 38	14 43	14 48	14 50	14 53	14 58	15 03	
Liverpool Central 10	a	13 40	13 45	13 50		13 52	13 55	14 00	14 05	14 10	14 15	14 20	14 22	14 25		14 30	14 35	14 40	14 45	14 50	14 52	14 55	15 00	15 05	

Chester, Ellesmere Port, West Kirby and New Brighton - Birkenhead and Liverpool

Network Diagram - see first Page of Table 101

		ME	ME	ME	ME	ME	ME	ME	ME	ME		ME	ME	ME	ME	ME	ME	ME	ME	ME		ME	ME	ME	ME
Chester	d		14 31				14 45			15 01					15 15			15 31					15 45		
Bache	d		14 35				14 48			15 05					15 18			15 35					15 48		
Capenhurst	d						14 54								15 24								15 54		
Ellesmere Port	d				14 42								15 12							15 42					
Overpool	d				14 45								15 15							15 45					
Little Sutton	d				14 47								15 17							15 47					
Hooton	d		14 44		14 51		14 59			15 14			15 21		15 29			15 44		15 51			15 59		
Eastham Rake	d		14 46		14 53		15 01			15 16			15 23		15 31			15 46		15 53			16 01		
Bromborough	d		14 48		14 56		15 03			15 18			15 26		15 33			15 48		15 56			16 03		
Bromborough Rake	d		14 50		14 58		15 05			15 20			15 28		15 35			15 50		15 58			16 05		
Spital	d		14 52		15 00		15 07			15 22			15 30		15 37			15 52		16 00			16 07		
Port Sunlight	d		14 54		15 02		15 09			15 24			15 32		15 39			15 54		16 02			16 09		
Bebington	d		14 56		15 04		15 11			15 26			15 34		15 41			15 56		16 04			16 11		
Rock Ferry	d		14 59		15 07		15 14			15 29			15 37		15 44			15 59		16 07			16 14		
Green Lane	d		15 02		15 09		15 17			15 32			15 39		15 47			16 02		16 09			16 17		
Birkenhead Central	d		15 04		15 12		15 19			15 34			15 42		15 49			16 04		16 12			16 19		
West Kirby	d	14 36				14 51			15 06					15 21			15 36					15 51			16 06
Hoylake	d	14 39				14 54			15 09					15 24			15 39					15 54			16 09
Manor Road	d	14 41				14 56			15 11					15 26			15 41					15 56			16 11
Meols	d	14 43				14 58			15 13					15 28			15 43					15 58			16 13
Moreton (Merseyside)	d	14 46				15 01			15 16					15 31			15 46					16 01			16 16
Leasowe	d	14 48				15 03			15 18					15 33			15 48					16 03			16 18
Bidston	d	14 51				15 06			15 21					15 36			15 51					16 06			16 21
New Brighton	d			14 53				15 08				15 23				15 38			15 53					16 08	
Wallasey Grove Road	d			14 57				15 12				15 27				15 42			15 57					16 12	
Wallasey Village	d			14 59				15 14				15 29				15 44			15 59					16 14	
Birkenhead North	d	14 54		15 04		15 09		15 19	15 24			15 34		15 39		15 49	15 54		16 04			16 09		16 19	16 24
Birkenhead Park	d	14 56		15 06		15 11		15 21	15 26			15 36		15 41		15 51	15 56		16 06			16 11		16 21	16 26
Conway Park	d	14 59		15 09		15 14		15 24	15 29			15 39		15 44		15 54	15 59		16 09			16 14		16 24	16 29
Hamilton Square	d	15 01	15 06	15 11	15 14	15 16	15 21	15 26	15 31	15 36		15 41	15 44	15 46	15 51	15 56	16 01	16 06	16 11	16 14		16 16	16 21	16 26	16 31
James Street	d	15 04	15 09	15 14	15 17	15 19	15 24	15 29	15 34	15 39		15 44	15 47	15 49	15 54	15 59	16 04	16 09	16 14	16 17		16 19	16 24	16 29	16 34
Moorfields 10	a	15 06	15 11	15 16	15 18	15 21	15 26	15 31	15 36	15 41		15 46	15 48	15 51	15 56	16 01	16 06	16 11	16 16	16 18		16 21	16 26	16 31	16 36
Liverpool Lime Street 10	a	15 08	15 13	15 18	15 20	15 23	15 28	15 33	15 38	15 43		15 48	15 50	15 53	15 58	16 03	16 08	16 13	16 18	16 20		16 23	16 28	16 33	16 38
Liverpool Central 10	a	15 10	15 15	15 20	15 22	15 25	15 30	15 35	15 40	15 45		15 50	15 52	15 55	16 00	16 05	16 10	16 15	16 20	16 22		16 25	16 30	16 35	16 40

		ME	ME	ME	ME	ME		ME	ME	ME	ME	ME	ME	ME	ME	ME		ME	ME	ME	ME	ME	ME	ME	ME
Chester	d	16 01				16 15				16 31				16 45				17 01				17 15			17 31
Bache	d	16 05				16 18				16 35				16 48				17 05				17 18			17 35
Capenhurst	d					16 24								16 54								17 24			
Ellesmere Port	d			16 12								16 42								17 12					
Overpool	d			16 15								16 45								17 15					
Little Sutton	d			16 17								16 47								17 17					
Hooton	d	16 14		16 21		16 29				16 44		16 51		16 59				17 14		17 21		17 29			17 44
Eastham Rake	d	16 16		16 23		16 31				16 46		16 53		17 01				17 16		17 23		17 31			17 46
Bromborough	d	16 18		16 26		16 33				16 48		16 56		17 03				17 18		17 26		17 33			17 48
Bromborough Rake	d	16 20		16 28		16 35				16 50		16 58		17 05				17 20		17 28		17 35			17 50
Spital	d	16 22		16 30		16 37				16 52		17 00		17 07				17 22		17 30		17 37			17 52
Port Sunlight	d	16 24		16 32		16 39				16 54		17 02		17 09				17 24		17 32		17 39			17 54
Bebington	d	16 26		16 34		16 41				16 56		17 04		17 11				17 26		17 34		17 41			17 56
Rock Ferry	d	16 29		16 37		16 44				16 59		17 07		17 14				17 29		17 37		17 44			17 59
Green Lane	d	16 32		16 39		16 47				17 02		17 09		17 17				17 32		17 39		17 47			18 02
Birkenhead Central	d	16 34		16 42		16 49				17 04		17 12		17 19				17 34		17 42		17 49			18 04
West Kirby	d				16 21				16 36				16 51			17 06					17 21			17 36	
Hoylake	d				16 24				16 39				16 54			17 09					17 24			17 39	
Manor Road	d				16 26				16 41				16 56			17 11					17 26			17 41	
Meols	d				16 28				16 43				16 58			17 13					17 28			17 43	
Moreton (Merseyside)	d				16 31				16 46				17 01			17 16					17 31			17 46	
Leasowe	d				16 33				16 48				17 03			17 18					17 33			17 48	
Bidston	d				16 36				16 51				17 06			17 21					17 36			17 51	
New Brighton	d		16 23					16 38			16 53				17 08				17 23				17 38		
Wallasey Grove Road	d		16 27					16 42			16 57				17 12				17 27				17 42		
Wallasey Village	d		16 29					16 44			16 59				17 14				17 29				17 44		
Birkenhead North	d		16 34		16 39			16 49	16 54		17 04		17 09		17 19	17 24			17 34		17 39		17 49	17 54	
Birkenhead Park	d		16 36		16 41			16 51	16 56		17 06		17 11		17 21	17 26			17 36		17 41		17 51	17 56	
Conway Park	d		16 39		16 44			16 54	16 59		17 09		17 14		17 24	17 29			17 39		17 44		17 54	17 59	
Hamilton Square	d	16 36	16 41	16 44	16 46	16 51		16 56	17 01	17 06	17 11	17 14	17 16	17 21	17 26	17 31		17 36	17 41	17 44	17 46	17 51	17 56	18 01	18 06
James Street	d	16 39	16 44	16 47	16 49	16 54		16 59	17 04	17 09	17 14	17 17	17 19	17 24	17 29	17 34		17 39	17 44	17 47	17 49	17 54	17 59	18 04	18 09
Moorfields 10	a	16 41	16 46	16 48	16 51	16 56		17 01	17 06	17 11	17 16	17 18	17 21	17 26	17 31	17 36		17 41	17 46	17 48	17 51	17 56	18 01	18 06	18 11
Liverpool Lime Street 10	a	16 43	16 48	16 50	16 53	16 58		17 03	17 08	17 13	17 18	17 20	17 23	17 28	17 33	17 38		17 43	17 48	17 50	17 53	17 58	18 03	18 08	18 13
Liverpool Central 10	a	16 45	16 50	16 52	16 55	17 00		17 05	17 10	17 15	17 20	17 22	17 25	17 30	17 35	17 40		17 45	17 50	17 52	17 55	18 00	18 05	18 10	18 15

Chester, Ellesmere Port, West Kirby and New Brighton - Birkenhead and Liverpool

Network Diagram - see first Page of Table 101

		ME		ME	ME	ME	ME	ME	ME	ME	ME	ME		ME	ME	ME	ME	ME	ME	ME	ME	ME		ME	ME
Chester	d					17 45			18 01					18 15			18 30				19 00				
Bache	d					17 48			18 05					18 18			18 33				19 03				
Capenhurst	d					17 54								18 24			18 39				19 09				
Ellesmere Port	d			17 42							18 12								18 46					19 16	
Overpool	d			17 45							18 15								18 49					19 19	
Little Sutton	d			17 47							18 17								18 51					19 21	
Hooton	d			17 51		17 59			18 14		18 21			18 29			18 44		18 59		19 14			19 29	
Eastham Rake	d			17 53		18 01			18 16		18 23			18 31			18 46		19 01		19 16			19 31	
Bromborough	d			17 56		18 03			18 18		18 26			18 33			18 48		19 03		19 18			19 33	
Bromborough Rake	d			17 58		18 05			18 20		18 28			18 35			18 50		19 05		19 20			19 35	
Spital	d			18 00		18 07			18 22		18 30			18 37			18 52		19 07		19 22			19 37	
Port Sunlight	d			18 02		18 09			18 24		18 32			18 39			18 54		19 09		19 24			19 39	
Bebington	d			18 04		18 11			18 26		18 34			18 41			18 56		19 11		19 26			19 41	
Rock Ferry	d			18 07		18 14			18 29		18 37			18 44			18 59		19 14		19 29			19 44	
Green Lane	d			18 09		18 17			18 32		18 39			18 47			19 02		19 17		19 32			19 47	
Birkenhead Central	d			18 12		18 19			18 34		18 42			18 49			19 04		19 19		19 34			19 49	
West Kirby	d				17 51			18 06				18 21				18 36				19 01					19 31
Hoylake	d				17 54			18 09				18 24				18 39				19 04					19 34
Manor Road	d				17 56			18 11				18 26				18 41				19 06					19 36
Meols	d				17 58			18 13				18 28				18 43				19 08					19 38
Moreton (Merseyside)	d				18 01			18 16				18 31				18 46				19 11					19 41
Leasowe	d				18 03			18 18				18 33				18 48				19 13					19 43
Bidston	d				18 06			18 21				18 36				18 51				19 16					19 46
New Brighton	d	17 53					18 08			18 23					18 38			18 53				19 23			
Wallasey Grove Road	d	17 57					18 12			18 27					18 42			18 57				19 27			
Wallasey Village	d	17 59					18 14			18 29					18 44			18 59				19 29			
Birkenhead North	d	18 04			18 09		18 19	18 24		18 34		18 39			18 49	18 54		19 04		19 19		19 34			19 49
Birkenhead Park	d	18 06			18 11		18 21	18 26		18 36		18 41			18 51	18 56		19 06		19 21		19 36			19 51
Conway Park	d	18 09			18 14		18 24	18 29		18 39		18 44			18 54	18 59		19 09		19 24		19 39			19 54
Hamilton Square	d	18 11		18 14	18 16	18 21	18 26	18 31	18 36	18 41	18 44	18 46		18 51	18 56	19 01	19 06	19 11	19 21	19 26	19 36	19 41		19 51	19 56
James Street	d	18 14		18 17	18 19	18 24	18 29	18 34	18 39	18 44	18 47	18 49		18 54	18 59	19 04	19 09	19 14	19 24	19 29	19 39	19 44		19 54	19 59
Moorfields 10	a	18 16		18 18	18 21	18 26	18 31	18 36	18 41	18 46	18 48	18 51		18 56	19 01	19 06	19 11	19 16	19 26	19 31	19 41	19 46		19 56	20 01
Liverpool Lime Street 10	a	18 18		18 20	18 23	18 28	18 33	18 38	18 43	18 48	18 50	18 53		18 58	19 03	19 08	19 13	19 18	19 28	19 33	19 43	19 48		19 58	20 03
Liverpool Central 10	a	18 20		18 22	18 25	18 30	18 35	18 40	18 45	18 50	18 52	18 55		19 00	19 05	19 10	19 15	19 20	19 30	19 35	19 45	19 50		20 00	20 05

		ME	ME	ME	ME	ME	ME	ME		ME	ME	ME	ME	ME	ME	ME	ME	ME		ME	ME	ME	ME	ME	ME
Chester	d	19 30				20 00					20 30				21 00					21 30				22 00	
Bache	d	19 33				20 03					20 33				21 03					21 33				22 03	
Capenhurst	d	19 39				20 09					20 39				21 09					21 39				22 09	
Ellesmere Port	d			19 49				20 19					20 49				21 19					21 49			
Overpool	d			19 52				20 22					20 52				21 22					21 52			
Little Sutton	d			19 54				20 24					20 54				21 24					21 54			
Hooton	d	19 44		19 59		20 14		20 29			20 44		20 59		21 14		21 29			21 44		21 59		22 14	
Eastham Rake	d	19 46		20 01		20 16		20 31			20 46		21 01		21 16		21 31			21 46		22 01		22 16	
Bromborough	d	19 48		20 03		20 18		20 33			20 48		21 03		21 18		21 33			21 48		22 03		22 18	
Bromborough Rake	d	19 50		20 05		20 20		20 35			20 50		21 05		21 20		21 35			21 50		22 05		22 20	
Spital	d	19 52		20 07		20 22		20 37			20 52		21 07		21 22		21 37			21 52		22 07		22 22	
Port Sunlight	d	19 54		20 09		20 24		20 39			20 54		21 09		21 24		21 39			21 54		22 09		22 24	
Bebington	d	19 56		20 11		20 26		20 41			20 56		21 11		21 26		21 41			21 56		22 11		22 26	
Rock Ferry	d	19 59		20 14		20 29		20 44			20 59		21 14		21 29		21 44			21 59		22 14		22 29	
Green Lane	d	20 02		20 17		20 32		20 47			21 02		21 17		21 32		21 47			22 02		22 17		22 32	
Birkenhead Central	d	20 04		20 19		20 34		20 49			21 04		21 19		21 34		21 49			22 04		22 19		22 34	
West Kirby	d				20 01					20 31				21 01				21 31					22 01		
Hoylake	d				20 04					20 34				21 04				21 34					22 04		
Manor Road	d				20 06					20 36				21 06				21 36					22 06		
Meols	d				20 08					20 38				21 08				21 38					22 08		
Moreton (Merseyside)	d				20 11					20 41				21 11				21 41					22 11		
Leasowe	d				20 13					20 43				21 13				21 43					22 13		
Bidston	d				20 16					20 46				21 16				21 46					22 16		
New Brighton	d		19 53				20 23					20 53				21 23					21 53				22 23
Wallasey Grove Road	d		19 57				20 27					20 57				21 27					21 57				22 27
Wallasey Village	d		19 59				20 29					20 59				21 29					21 59				22 29
Birkenhead North	d		20 04		20 19		20 34			20 49		21 04		21 19		21 34		21 49			22 04		22 19		22 34
Birkenhead Park	d		20 06		20 21		20 36			20 51		21 06		21 21		21 36		21 51			22 06		22 21		22 36
Conway Park	d		20 09		20 24		20 39			20 54		21 09		21 24		21 39		21 54			22 09		22 24		22 39
Hamilton Square	d	20 06	20 11	20 21	20 26	20 36	20 41	20 51		20 56	21 06	21 11	21 21	21 26	21 36	21 41	21 51	21 56		22 06	22 11	22 21	22 26	22 36	22 41
James Street	d	20 09	20 14	20 24	20 29	20 39	20 44	20 54		20 59	21 09	21 14	21 24	21 29	21 39	21 44	21 54	21 59		22 09	22 14	22 24	22 29	22 39	22 44
Moorfields 10	a	20 11	20 16	20 26	20 31	20 41	20 46	20 56		21 01	21 11	21 16	21 26	21 31	21 41	21 46	21 56	22 01		22 11	22 16	22 26	22 31	22 41	22 46
Liverpool Lime Street 10	a	20 13	20 18	20 28	20 33	20 43	20 48	20 58		21 03	21 13	21 18	21 28	21 33	21 43	21 48	21 58	22 03		22 13	22 18	22 28	22 33	22 43	22 48
Liverpool Central 10	a	20 15	20 20	20 30	20 35	20 45	20 50	21 00		21 05	21 15	21 20	21 30	21 35	21 45	21 50	22 00	22 05		22 15	22 20	22 30	22 35	22 45	22 50

Table 106

Mondays to Saturdays

Chester, Ellesmere Port, West Kirby and New Brighton - Birkenhead and Liverpool

Network Diagram - see first Page of Table 101

		ME	ME	ME		ME	ME	ME	ME	ME	ME
Chester	d			22 30					23 00		
Bache	d			22 33					23 03		
Capenhurst	d			22 39					23 09		
Ellesmere Port	d	22 19					22 49				23 19
Overpool	d	22 22					22 52				23 22
Little Sutton	d	22 24					22 54				23 24
Hooton	d	22 29		22 44			22 59		23 14		23 29
Eastham Rake	d	22 31		22 46			23 01		23 16		23 31
Bromborough	d	22 33		22 48			23 03		23 18		23 33
Bromborough Rake	d	22 35		22 50			23 05		23 20		23 35
Spital	d	22 37		22 52			23 07		23 22		23 37
Port Sunlight	d	22 39		22 54			23 09		23 24		23 39
Bebington	d	22 41		22 56			23 11		23 26		23 41
Rock Ferry	d	22 44		22 59			23 14		23 29		23 44
Green Lane	d	22 47		23 02			23 17		23 32		23 47
Birkenhead Central	d	22 49		23 04			23 19		23 34		23 49
West Kirby	d		22 31					23 01			
Hoylake	d		22 34					23 04			
Manor Road	d		22 36					23 06			
Meols	d		22 38					23 08			
Moreton (Merseyside)	d		22 41					23 11			
Leasowe	d		22 43					23 13			
Bidston	d		22 46					23 16			
New Brighton	d					22 53				23 23	
Wallasey Grove Road	d					22 57				23 27	
Wallasey Village	d					22 59				23 29	
Birkenhead North	d		22 49			23 04		23 19		23 34	
Birkenhead Park	d		22 51			23 06		23 21		23 36	
Conway Park	d		22 54			23 09		23 24		23 39	
Hamilton Square	d	22 51	22 56	23 06		23 11	23 21	23 26	23 36	23 41	23 51
James Street	d	22 54	22 59	23 09		23 14	23 24	23 29	23 39	23 44	23 54
Moorfields 10	a	22 56	23 01	23 11		23 16	23 26	23 31	23 41	23 46	23 56
Liverpool Lime Street 10	a	22 58	23 03	23 13		23 18	23 28	23 33	23 43	23 48	23 58
Liverpool Central 10	a	23 00	23 05	23 15		23 20	23 30	23 35	23 45	23 50	23 59

Sundays

		ME	ME	ME	ME	ME	ME	ME	ME	ME		ME	ME		ME	ME	ME	ME	ME		ME	ME	ME	ME
Chester	d							08 00					08 30		21 30				22 00				22 30	
Bache	d							08 03					08 33		21 33				22 03				22 33	
Capenhurst	d							08 09					08 39		21 39				22 09				22 39	
Ellesmere Port	d					07 49				08 19							21 49					22 19		
Overpool	d					07 52				08 22							21 52					22 22		
Little Sutton	d					07 54				08 24							21 54					22 24		
Hooton	d			07 44		07 59		08 14		08 29			08 44		21 44		21 59		22 14			22 29	22 44	
Eastham Rake	d			07 46		08 01		08 16		08 31			08 46		21 46		22 01		22 16			22 31	22 46	
Bromborough	d			07 48		08 03		08 18		08 33			08 48		21 48		22 03		22 18			22 33	22 48	
Bromborough Rake	d			07 50		08 05		08 20		08 35			08 50		21 50		22 05		22 20			22 35	22 50	
Spital	d			07 52		08 07		08 22		08 37			08 52		21 52		22 07		22 22			22 37	22 52	
Port Sunlight	d			07 54		08 09		08 24		08 39			08 54		21 54		22 09		22 24			22 39	22 54	
Bebington	d			07 56		08 11		08 26		08 41			08 56		21 56		22 11		22 26			22 41	22 56	
Rock Ferry	d	07 44	07 49	07 59		08 14		08 29		08 44			08 59	and at the same minutes past each hour until	21 59		22 14		22 29			22 44	22 59	
Green Lane	d	07 47	07 52	08 02		08 17		08 32		08 47			09 02		22 02		22 17		22 32			22 47	23 02	
Birkenhead Central	d	07 49	07 54	08 04		08 19		08 34		08 49			09 04		22 04		22 19		22 34			22 49	23 04	
West Kirby	d						08 01					08 31						22 01						
Hoylake	d						08 04					08 34						22 04						
Manor Road	d						08 06					08 36						22 06						
Meols	d						08 08					08 38						22 08						
Moreton (Merseyside)	d						08 11					08 41						22 11						
Leasowe	d						08 13					08 43						22 13						
Bidston	d						08 16					08 46						22 16						
New Brighton	d				07 53				08 23							21 53					22 23			22 53
Wallasey Grove Road	d				07 57				08 27							21 57					22 27			22 57
Wallasey Village	d				07 59				08 29							21 59					22 29			22 59
Birkenhead North	d				08 04		08 19		08 34			08 49				22 04		22 19			22 34			23 04
Birkenhead Park	d				08 06		08 21		08 36			08 51				22 06		22 21			22 36			23 06
Conway Park	d				08 09		08 24		08 39			08 54				22 09		22 24			22 39			23 09
Hamilton Square	d	07 51	07 56	08 06	08 11	08 21	08 26	08 36	08 41	08 51		08 56	09 06		22 06	22 11	22 21	22 26	22 36		22 41	22 51	23 06	23 11
James Street	d	07 54	07 59	08 09	08 14	08 24	08 29	08 39	08 44	08 54		08 59	09 09		22 09	22 14	22 24	22 29	22 39		22 44	22 54	23 09	23 14
Moorfields 10	a	07 56	08 01	08 11	08 16	08 26	08 31	08 41	08 46	08 56		09 01	09 11		22 11	22 16	22 26	22 31	22 41		22 46	22 56	23 11	23 16
Liverpool Lime Street 10	a	07 58	08 03	08 13	08 18	08 28	08 33	08 43	08 48	08 58		09 03	09 13		22 13	22 18	22 28	22 33	22 43		22 48	22 58	23 13	23 18
Liverpool Central 10	a	08 00	08 05	08 15	08 20	08 30	08 35	08 45	08 50	09 00		09 05	09 15		22 15	22 20	22 30	22 35	22 45		22 50	23 00	23 15	23 20

Table 106

Sundays

Chester, Ellesmere Port, West Kirby and New Brighton - Birkenhead and Liverpool

Network Diagram - see first Page of Table 101

		ME	ME	ME	ME	ME
Chester	d			23 00		
Bache	d			23 03		
Capenhurst	d			23 09		
Ellesmere Port	d	22 49				23 19
Overpool	d	22 52				23 22
Little Sutton	d	22 54				23 24
Hooton	d	22 59		23 14		23 29
Eastham Rake	d	23 01		23 16		23 31
Bromborough	d	23 03		23 18		23 33
Bromborough Rake	d	23 05		23 20		23 35
Spital	d	23 07		23 22		23 37
Port Sunlight	d	23 09		23 24		23 39
Bebington	d	23 11		23 26		23 41
Rock Ferry	d	23 14		23 29		23 44
Green Lane	d	23 17		23 32		23 47
Birkenhead Central	d	23 19		23 34		23 49
West Kirby	d		23 01			
Hoylake	d		23 04			
Manor Road	d		23 06			
Meols	d		23 08			
Moreton (Merseyside)	d		23 11			
Leasowe	d		23 13			
Bidston	d		23 16			
New Brighton	d				23 23	
Wallasey Grove Road	d				23 27	
Wallasey Village	d				23 29	
Birkenhead North	d		23 19		23 34	
Birkenhead Park	d		23 21		23 36	
Conway Park	d		23 24		23 39	
Hamilton Square	d	23 21	23 26	23 36	23 41	23 51
James Street	d	23 24	23 29	23 39	23 44	23 54
Moorfields 10	a	23 26	23 31	23 41	23 46	23 56
Liverpool Lime Street 10	a	23 28	23 33	23 43	23 48	23 58
Liverpool Central 10	a	23 30	23 35	23 45	23 50	23 59

Table 109

Mondays to Fridays

Helsby - Ellesmere Port

Network Diagram - see first Page of Table 101

Miles			NT	NT	NT	NT
—	Warrington Bank Quay 81	d	05 49			
0	**Helsby**	d	06 03	06 33	15 17	15 48
2	Ince & Elton	d	06 06	06 36	15 20	15 51
2¾	Stanlow & Thornton	d	06 08	06 38	15 22	15 53
5¼	**Ellesmere Port**	a	06 18	06 48	15 28	15 59

Saturdays

		NT B	NT C	NT B	NT B	NT C	NT B
Warrington Bank Quay 81	d	05 49	05 49				
Helsby	d	06 03	06 29	06 33	15 17	15 17	15 48
Ince & Elton	d	06 06	06 39	06 36	15 20	15 27	15 51
Stanlow & Thornton	d	06 08	06 44	06 38	15 22	15 32	15 53
Ellesmere Port	a	06 18	06 54	06 48	15 28	15 42	15 59

B until 11 February and then from 31 March **C** from 18 February until 24 March

No Sunday Service

Table 109

Mondays to Fridays

Ellesmere Port - Helsby

Network Diagram - see first Page of Table 101

Miles			NT	NT	NT	NT
0	**Ellesmere Port**	d	06 19	06 53	15 34	16 04
2½	Stanlow & Thornton	d	06 23	06 57	15 38	16 08
3¼	Ince & Elton	d	06 26	07 00	15 41	16 11
5¼	**Helsby**	a	06 32	07 03	15 45	16 14
—	Warrington Bank Quay 81	a		07 23		16 34

Saturdays

		NT A	NT A	NT B	NT A	NT A	NT B
Ellesmere Port	d	06 19	06 56	07 00	15 34	16 04	16 04
Stanlow & Thornton	d	06 23	07 00	07 10	15 38	16 08	16 14
Ince & Elton	d	06 26	07 03	07 15	15 41	16 11	16 19
Helsby	a	06 32	07 07	07 25	15 45	16 14	16 29
Warrington Bank Quay 81	a					16 34	17 19

A until 11 February and then from 31 March **B** from 18 February until 24 March

No Sunday Service

Network Diagram for Tables 114, 115

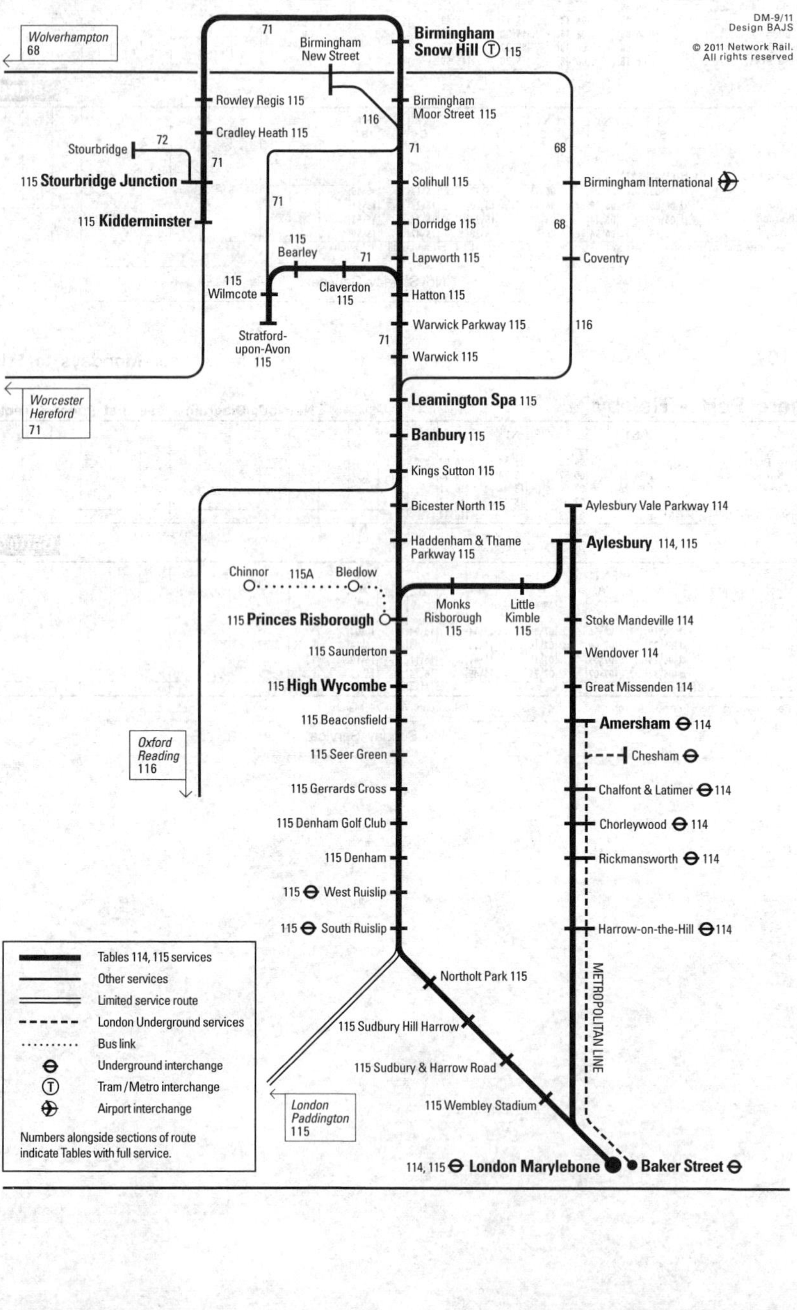

London - Amersham and Aylesbury

Network Diagram - see first Page of Table 114

Miles			CH MX	CH ◇	CH MX	CH	CH ◇	CH	CH	CH	CH ◇	CH ◇	CH ◇	CH	CH ◇	CH	CH	CH	CH	CH ◇	CH	CH	CH ◇
0	**London Marylebone [10]**	⊖ d	22p57	23p27	23p57	06 32	07 03	07 24	07 57	08 27	08 57	09 27	09 57	10 27	10 57	11 27	11 57	12 27	12 57	13 27	13 57	14 27	14 57
9	Harrow-on-the-Hill [3] §	⊖ d	23p09	23p39	00 09	06 45	07 15	07 36	08 09	08 39	09 09	09 39	10 09	10 39	11 09	11 39	12 09	12 39	13 09	13 39	14 09	14 39	15 09
17	Rickmansworth §	⊖ d	23p19	23p49	00 19	06 55	07 25	07 46	08 19	08 49	09 19	09 49	10 19	10 49	11 19	11 49	12 19	12 49	13 19	13 49	14 19	14 49	15 19
19¼	Chorleywood §	⊖ d	23p24	23p54	00 24	07 00	07 30	07 51	08 24	08 54	09 24	09 54	10 24	10 54	11 24	11 54	12 24	12 54	13 24	13 54	14 24	14 54	15 24
21½	Chalfont & Latimer §	⊖ d	23p28	23p58	00 28	07 04	07 34	07 55	08 28	08 58	09 28	09 58	10 28	10 58	11 28	11 58	12 28	12 58	13 28	13 58	14 28	14 58	15 28
23½	**Amersham §**	⊖ d	23p32	00 02	00 32	07 08	07 38	07 59	08 32	09 02	09 32	10 02	10 32	11 02	11 32	12 02	12 32	13 02	13 32	14 02	14 32	15 02	15 32
28¾	Great Missenden	d	23p38	00 08	00 38	07 14	07 44	08 05	08 38	09 08	09 38	10 08	10 38	11 08	11 38	12 08	12 38	13 08	13 38	14 08	14 38	15 08	15 38
33¼	Wendover	d	23p44	00 14	00 44	07 20	07 50	08 11	08 44	09 14	09 44	10 14	10 44	11 14	11 44	12 14	12 44	13 14	13 44	14 14	14 44	15 14	15 44
35¼	Stoke Mandeville	d	23p48	00 18	00 48	07 24	07 54	08 15	08 48	09 18	09 48	10 18	10 48	11 18	11 48	12 18	12 48	13 18	13 48	14 18	14 48	15 18	15 48
37¾	**Aylesbury**	d	23p53	00a26	00a56	07 44	08a02	08 20	09 05	09a26	09 59	10a26	10 53	11a26	11 53	12a26	12 53	13a26	13 53	14a26	14 53	15a26	15 53
40½	**Aylesbury Vale Parkway**	a	00 01			07 53		08 29	09 15		10 07		11 01		12 04		13 04		14 01		15 01		16 01

		CH	CH	CH	CH	CH	CH	CH	CH	CH	CH	CH	CH	CH	CH	CH	CH	CH ◇	CH	CH	CH	CH	CH ◇
London Marylebone [10]	⊖ d	15 27	15 56	16 26	16 43	16 53	17 16	17 27	17 46	17 59	18 19	18 33	18 50	19 04	19 27	19 57	20 27	20 57	21 27	21 57	22 27	22 57	23 27
Harrow-on-the-Hill [3] §	⊖ d	15 39	16 09	16 39		17 07		17 40		18 13		18 45	19 03		19 39	20 09	20 39	21 09	21 39	22 09	22 39	23 09	23 39
Rickmansworth §	⊖ d	15 49	16 19	16 49		17 17		17 50							19 49	20 19	20 49	21 19	21 49	22 19	22 49	23 19	23 49
Chorleywood §	⊖ d	15 54	16 24	16 54		17 22		17 55		18 27		18 59	19 17		19 54	20 24	20 54	21 24	21 54	22 24	22 54	23 24	23 54
Chalfont & Latimer §	⊖ d	15 58	16 28	16 58		17 26		17 59		18 31		19 03	19 21		19 58	20 28	20 58	21 28	21 58	22 28	22 58	23 28	23 58
Amersham §	⊖ d	16 02	16 32	17 02	17 15	17 30		18 03	18 18	18 35		19 07	19 25		20 02	20 32	21 02	21 32	22 02	22 32	23 02	23 32	00 02
Great Missenden	d	16 08	16 38	17 08	17 22	17 36	17 51	18 09	18 25	18 41	18 57	19 13	19 31	19 44	20 08	20 38	21 08	21 38	22 08	22 38	23 08	23 38	00 08
Wendover	d	16 14	16 44	17 14	17 28	17 42	17 57	18 15	18 31	18 47	19 03	19 19	19 37	19 51	20 14	20 44	21 14	21 44	22 14	22 44	23 14	23 44	00 14
Stoke Mandeville	d	16 18	16 48	17 18	17 32	17 46	18 01	18 19	18 35	18 51	19 07	19 23	19 41	19 55	20 18	20 48	21 18	21 48	22 18	22 48	23 18	23 48	00 18
Aylesbury	d	16a26	16 53	17a25	17 37	17a52	18 06	18a26	18 40	18a58	19 12	19a32	19a49	20 09	20a26	20 53	21a26	21 53	22a26	22 53	23a26	23 53	00a26
Aylesbury Vale Parkway	a		17 04		17 45		18 15		18 48		19 20			20 17		21 01		22 01		23 01		00 01	

		CH
London Marylebone [10]	⊖ d	23 57
Harrow-on-the-Hill [3] §	⊖ d	00 09
Rickmansworth §	⊖ d	00 19
Chorleywood §	⊖ d	00 24
Chalfont & Latimer §	⊖ d	00 28
Amersham §	⊖ d	00 32
Great Missenden	d	00 38
Wendover	d	00 44
Stoke Mandeville	d	00 48
Aylesbury	d	00a56
Aylesbury Vale Parkway	a	

Saturdays

		CH	CH ◇	CH	CH	CH ◇	CH	CH	CH ◇	CH	CH	CH	CH	CH ◇	CH	CH	CH	CH ◇	CH	CH	CH ◇	CH	CH
London Marylebone [10]	⊖ d	22p57	23p27	23p57		07 27	07 57	08 27	08 57	09 27	09 57	10 27	10 57	11 27	11 57	12 27	12 57	13 27	13 57	14 27	14 57	15 27	15 57
Harrow-on-the-Hill [3] §	⊖ d	23p09	23p39	00 09		07 39	08 09	08 39	09 09	09 39	10 09	10 39	11 09	11 39	12 09	12 39	13 09	13 39	14 09	14 39	15 09	15 39	16 09
Rickmansworth §	⊖ d	23p19	23p49	00 19		07 49	08 19	08 49	09 19	09 49	10 19	10 49	11 19	11 49	12 19	12 49	13 19	13 49	14 19	14 49	15 19	15 49	16 19
Chorleywood §	⊖ d	23p24	23p54	00 24		07 54	08 24	08 54	09 24	09 54	10 24	10 54	11 24	11 54	12 24	12 54	13 24	13 54	14 24	14 54	15 24	15 54	16 24
Chalfont & Latimer §	⊖ d	23p28	23p58	00 28		07 58	08 28	08 58	09 28	09 58	10 28	10 58	11 28	11 58	12 28	12 58	13 28	13 58	14 28	14 58	15 28	15 58	16 28
Amersham §	⊖ d	23p32	00 02	00 32	07 05	08 02	08 32	09 02	09 32	10 02	10 32	11 02	11 32	12 02	12 32	13 02	13 32	14 02	14 32	15 02	15 32	16 02	16 32
Great Missenden	d	23p38	00 08	00 38	07 11	08 08	08 38	09 08	09 38	10 08	10 38	11 08	11 38	12 08	12 38	13 08	13 38	14 08	14 38	15 08	15 38	16 08	16 38
Wendover	d	23p44	00 14	00 44	07 17	08 14	08 44	09 14	09 44	10 14	10 44	11 14	11 44	12 14	12 44	13 14	13 44	14 14	14 44	15 14	15 44	16 14	16 44
Stoke Mandeville	d	23p48	00 18	00 48	07 21	08 18	08 48	09 18	09 48	10 18	10 48	11 18	11 48	12 18	12 48	13 18	13 48	14 18	14 48	15 18	15 48	16 18	16 48
Aylesbury	d	23p53	00a26	00a56	07a29	08a26	08 53	09a26	09 53	10a26	10 53	11a26	11 53	12a26	12 53	13a26	13 53	14a26	14 53	15a26	15 53	16a26	16 53
Aylesbury Vale Parkway	a	00 01					09 01		10 01		11 01		12 01		13 01		14 01		15 01		16 01		17 01

		CH	CH	CH	CH	CH	CH	CH	CH	CH ◇	CH	CH	CH
London Marylebone [10]	⊖ d	16 27	16 57	17 27	17 57	18 27	18 57	19 27	19 57	20 57	21 57	22 57	23 57
Harrow-on-the-Hill [3] §	⊖ d	16 39	17 09	17 39	18 09	18 39	19 09	19 39	20 09	21 09	22 09	23 09	00 09
Rickmansworth §	⊖ d	16 49	17 19	17 49	18 19	18 49	19 19	19 49	20 19	21 19	22 19	23 19	00 19
Chorleywood §	⊖ d	16 54	17 24	17 54	18 24	18 54	19 24	19 54	20 24	21 24	22 24	23 24	00 24
Chalfont & Latimer §	⊖ d	16 58	17 28	17 58	18 28	18 58	19 28	19 58	20 28	21 28	22 28	23 28	00 28
Amersham §	⊖ d	17 02	17 32	18 02	18 32	19 02	19 32	20 02	20 32	21 32	22 32	23 32	00 32
Great Missenden	d	17 08	17 38	18 08	18 38	19 08	19 38	20 08	20 38	21 38	22 38	23 38	00 38
Wendover	d	17 14	17 44	18 14	18 44	19 14	19 44	20 14	20 44	21 44	22 44	23 44	00 44
Stoke Mandeville	d	17 18	17 48	18 18	18 48	19 18	19 48	20 18	20 48	21 48	22 48	23 48	00 48
Aylesbury	d	17a26	17 53	18a26	18 53	19a26	19 53	20a26	20 53	21 53	22 53	23 53	00a56
Aylesbury Vale Parkway	a		18 01		19 01		20 01		21 01	22 01	23 01	00 01	

§ London Underground Limited (Metropolitan Line) services operate between Harrow-on-the-Hill, Rickmansworth, Chorleywood, Chalfont & Latimer and Amersham

Table 114

Sundays

London - Amersham and Aylesbury

Network Diagram - see first Page of Table 114

			CH	CH	CH	CH	CH	CH	CH	CH	CH	CH	CH
							◇				◇		
			A		A								
London Marylebone 10	⊖	d	22p57		23p57		08 27	09 27	10 27	11 27	12 27	13 27	14 27
Harrow-on-the-Hill 3 §	⊖	d	23p09		00 09		08 39	09 39	10 39	11 39	12 39	13 39	14 39
Rickmansworth §	⊖	d	23p19		00 19		08 49	09 49	10 49	11 49	12 49	13 49	14 49
Chorleywood §	⊖	d	23p24		00 24		08 54	09 54	10 54	11 54	12 54	13 54	14 54
Chalfont & Latimer §	⊖	d	23p28		00 28		08 58	09 58	10 58	11 58	12 58	13 58	14 58
Amersham §	⊖	d	23p32	00 02	00 32	08 32	09 02	10 02	11 02	12 02	13 02	14 02	15 02
Great Missenden		d	23p38	00 08	00 38	08 38	09 08	10 08	11 08	12 08	13 08	14 08	15 08
Wendover		d	23p44	00 14	00 44	08 44	09 14	10 14	11 14	12 14	13 14	14 14	15 14
Stoke Mandeville		d	23p48	00 18	00 48	08 48	09 18	10 18	11 18	12 18	13 18	14 18	15 18
Aylesbury		d	23p53	00a26	00a56	08a56	09 23	10 23	11 23	12 23	13 23	14 23	15 23
Aylesbury Vale Parkway		a	00 01				09 31	10 31	11 31	12 31	13 31	14 31	15 31

			CH	CH	CH	CH	CH	CH	CH	CH	CH	CH	CH
				◇									
London Marylebone 10	⊖	d		15 27		16 27		17 27		18 27		19 27	
Harrow-on-the-Hill 3 §	⊖	d		15 39		16 39		17 39		18 39		19 39	
Rickmansworth §	⊖	d		15 49		16 49		17 49		18 49		19 49	
Chorleywood §	⊖	d		15 54		16 54		17 54		18 54		19 54	
Chalfont & Latimer §	⊖	d		15 58		16 58		17 58		18 58		19 58	
Amersham §	⊖	d	15 32	16 02	16 32	17 02	17 32	18 02	18 32	19 02	19 32	20 02	20 32
Great Missenden		d	15 38	16 08	16 38	17 08	17 38	18 08	18 38	19 08	19 38	20 08	20 38
Wendover		d	15 44	16 14	16 44	17 14	17 44	18 14	18 44	19 14	19 44	20 14	20 44
Stoke Mandeville		d	15 48	16 18	16 48	17 18	17 48	18 18	18 48	19 18	19 48	20 18	20 48
Aylesbury		d	15a56	16 23	16a56	17 23	17a56	18 23	18a56	19 23	19a56	20 23	20a56
Aylesbury Vale Parkway		a		16 31		17 31		18 31		19 31		20 31	

			CH	CH	CH	CH	CH
							◇
London Marylebone 10	⊖	d	20 27		21 27	22 27	23 27
Harrow-on-the-Hill 3 §	⊖	d	20 39		21 39	22 39	23 39
Rickmansworth §	⊖	d	20 49		21 49	22 49	23 49
Chorleywood §	⊖	d	20 54		21 54	22 54	23 54
Chalfont & Latimer §	⊖	d	20 58		21 58	22 58	23 58
Amersham §	⊖	d	21 02	21 32	22 02	23 02	00 02
Great Missenden		d	21 08	21 38	22 08	23 08	00 08
Wendover		d	21 14	21 44	22 14	23 14	00 14
Stoke Mandeville		d	21 18	21 48	22 18	23 18	00 18
Aylesbury		d	21 23	21a56	22 23	23 23	00a26
Aylesbury Vale Parkway		a	21 31		22 31	23 31	

§ London Underground Limited (Metropolitan Line) services operate between Harrow-on-the-Hill, Rickmansworth, Chorleywood, Chalfont & Latimer and Amersham

A not 11 December

Aylesbury and Amersham - London

Network Diagram - see first Page of Table 114

Miles			CH	CH	CH	CH	CH	CH	CH	CH	CH		CH	CH	CH	CH	CH	CH	CH	CH	CH		CH	CH	CH
															◇						◇		◇		◇
0	**Aylesbury Vale Parkway**	d	05 30	06 00		06 34		07 06		07 39			08 09		09 00	09 30		10 30		11 30			12 30		13 30
2¾	**Aylesbury**	d	05 35	06 05	06 23	06 39	06 55	07 11	07 27	07 44	07 58		08 14	08 30	09 05	09 35	10 05	10 35	11 05	11 35	12 05		12 35	13 05	13 35
5¼	Stoke Mandeville	d	05 39	06 09	06 27	06 43	06 59	07 15	07 31	07 48	08 02		08 18	08 34	09 09	09 39	10 09	10 39	11 09	11 39	12 09		12 39	13 09	13 39
7¼	Wendover	d	05 43	06 13	06 31	06 47	07 03	07 19	07 35	07 52	08 06		08 22	08 38	09 13	09 43	10 13	10 43	11 13	11 43	12 13		12 43	13 13	13 43
11¾	Great Missenden	d	05 49	06 19	06 37	06 53	07 09	07 25	07 41	07 58	08 12		08 28	08 44	09 19	09 49	10 19	10 49	11 19	11 49	12 19		12 49	13 19	13 49
17	**Amersham** §	⊖ d	05 56	06 26	06 44	07 00	07 16	07 32	07 48	08 05	08 19		08 35	08 51	09 26	09 56	10 26	10 56	11 26	11 56	12 26		12 56	13 26	13 56
19	Chalfont & Latimer §	⊖ d		06 30	06 48		07 20		07 52		08 23			08 55	09 30	10 00	10 30	11 00	11 30	12 00	12 30		13 00	13 30	14 00
21¼	Chorleywood §	⊖ d		06 33	06 51		07 23		07 55		08 27			08 58	09 33	10 03	10 33	11 03	11 33	12 03	12 33		13 03	13 33	14 03
23½	Rickmansworth §	⊖ d			06 56				08 00		08 31			09 03	09 38	10 08	10 38	11 08	11 38	12 08	12 38		13 08	13 38	14 08
31½	Harrow-on-the-Hill 3 §	⊖ d	06 18	06 48	07 07		07 39		08 11		08 42			09 14	09 49	10 19	10 49	11 19	11 49	12 19	12 49		13 19	13 49	14 19
40½	**London Marylebone 10**	⊖ a	06 32	07 05	07 23	07 39	07 55	08 11	08 30	08 44	08 58		09 14	09 30	10 05	10 35	11 05	11 35	12 05	12 35	13 05		13 35	14 05	14 35

		CH	CH	CH	CH	CH	CH		CH	CH	CH	CH	CH	CH	CH	CH	CH		CH	CH	CH
				◇			◇							◇	◇		◇				
Aylesbury Vale Parkway	d		14 30		15 30		16 30			17 27		18 18			19 30		20 30			21 30	22 30
Aylesbury	d	14 05	14 35	15 05	15 35	16 05	16 35		17 03	17 32	17 52	18 23	18 52	19 11	19 35	20 05	20 35		21 05	21 35	22 35
Stoke Mandeville	d	14 09	14 39	15 09	15 39	16 09	16 39		17 07	17 36	17 56	18 27	18 56	19 15	19 39	20 09	20 39		21 09	21 39	22 39
Wendover	d	14 13	14 43	15 13	15 43	16 13	16 43		17 11	17 40	18 00	18 31	19 00	19 19	19 43	20 13	20 43		21 13	21 43	22 43
Great Missenden	d	14 19	14 49	15 19	15 49	16 19	16 49		17 17	17 46	18 06	18 37	19 06	19 25	19 49	20 19	20 49		21 19	21 49	22 49
Amersham §	⊖ d	14 26	14 56	15 26	15 56	16 26	16 56		17 24	17 53	18 13	18 44	19 13	19 32	19 56	20 26	20 56		21 26	21 56	22 56
Chalfont & Latimer §	⊖ d	14 30	15 00	15 30	16 00	16 30	17 00		17 28	17 57	18 17	18 48	19 17	19 36	20 00	20 30	21 00		21 30	22 00	23 00
Chorleywood §	⊖ d	14 33	15 03	15 33	16 03	16 33	17 03		17 31	18 00	18 20	18 52	19 20	19 40	20 03	20 33	21 03		21 33	22 03	23 03
Rickmansworth §	⊖ d	14 38	15 08	15 38	16 08	16 38	17 08		17 36	18 05	18 25	18 56	19 25	19 44	20 08	20 38	21 08		21 38	22 08	23 08
Harrow-on-the-Hill 3 §	⊖ d	14 49	15 19	15 49	16 19	16 49	17 19		17 49	18 17	18 36	19 08	19 36	19 56	20 19	20 49	21 19		21 49	22 19	23 19
London Marylebone 10	⊖ a	15 05	15 35	16 05	16 35	17 05	17 35		18 05	18 39	18 53	19 23	19 52	20 11	20 35	21 05	21 35		22 05	22 35	23 35

Saturdays

		CH	CH	CH	CH	CH	CH	CH	CH	CH		CH	CH	CH	CH	CH	CH	CH	CH	CH		CH	CH	CH	CH
		◇																◇		◇				◇	
Aylesbury Vale Parkway	d			07 00	07 30		08 30		09 30			10 30		11 30		12 30		13 30		14 30			15 30		16 30
Aylesbury	d	06 05	06 35	07 05	07 35	08 05	08 35	09 05	09 35	10 05		10 35	11 05	11 35	12 05	12 35	13 05	13 35	14 05	14 35		15 05	15 35	16 05	16 35
Stoke Mandeville	d	06 09	06 39	07 09	07 39	08 09	08 39	09 09	09 39	10 09		10 39	11 09	11 39	12 09	12 39	13 09	13 39	14 09	14 39		15 09	15 39	16 09	16 39
Wendover	d	06 13	06 43	07 13	07 43	08 13	08 43	09 13	09 43	10 13		10 43	11 13	11 43	12 13	12 43	13 13	13 43	14 13	14 43		15 13	15 43	16 13	16 43
Great Missenden	d	06 19	06 49	07 19	07 49	08 19	08 49	09 19	09 49	10 19		10 49	11 19	11 49	12 19	12 49	13 19	13 49	14 19	14 49		15 19	15 49	16 19	16 49
Amersham §	⊖ d	06 26	06a58	07 26	07 56	08 26	08 56	09 26	09 56	10 26		10 56	11 26	11 56	12 26	12 56	13 26	13 56	14 26	14 56		15 26	15 56	16 26	16 56
Chalfont & Latimer §	⊖ d	06 30		07 30	08 00	08 30	09 00	09 30	10 00	10 30		11 00	11 30	12 00	12 30	13 00	13 30	14 00	14 30	15 00		15 30	16 00	16 30	17 00
Chorleywood §	⊖ d	06 33		07 33	08 03	08 33	09 03	09 33	10 03	10 33		11 03	11 33	12 03	12 33	13 03	13 33	14 03	14 33	15 03		15 33	16 03	16 33	17 03
Rickmansworth §	⊖ d	06 38		07 38	08 08	08 38	09 08	09 38	10 08	10 38		11 08	11 38	12 08	12 38	13 08	13 38	14 08	14 38	15 08		15 38	16 08	16 38	17 08
Harrow-on-the-Hill 3 §	⊖ d	06 49		07 49	08 19	08 49	09 19	09 49	10 19	10 49		11 19	11 49	12 19	12 49	13 19	13 49	14 19	14 49	15 19		15 49	16 19	16 49	17 19
London Marylebone 10	⊖ a	07 05		08 04	08 35	09 05	09 34	10 03	10 33	11 04		11 33	12 03	12 33	13 03	13 33	14 03	14 33	15 04	15 33		16 04	16 33	17 04	17 33

		CH	CH	CH	CH	CH		CH	CH	CH	CH
				◇					◇		
Aylesbury Vale Parkway	d		17 30		18 30			19 46	20 46	21 46	
Aylesbury	d	17 05	17 35	18 05	18 35	19 05		20 05	21 05	22 05	23 20
Stoke Mandeville	d	17 09	17 39	18 09	18 39	19 09		20 09	21 09	22 09	23 24
Wendover	d	17 13	17 43	18 13	18 43	19 13		20 13	21 13	22 13	23 28
Great Missenden	d	17 19	17 49	18 19	18 49	19 19		20 19	21 19	22 19	23 34
Amersham §	⊖ d	17 26	17 56	18 26	18 56	19 26		20 26	21 26	22 26	23a43
Chalfont & Latimer §	⊖ d	17 30	18 00	18 30	19 00	19 30		20 30	21 30	22 30	
Chorleywood §	⊖ d	17 33	18 03	18 33	19 03	19 33		20 33	21 33	22 33	
Rickmansworth §	⊖ d	17 38	18 08	18 38	19 08	19 38		20 38	21 38	22 38	
Harrow-on-the-Hill 3 §	⊖ d	17 49	18 19	18 49	19 19	19 49		20 49	21 49	22 49	
London Marylebone 10	⊖ a	18 04	18 33	19 03	19 33	20 04		21 04	22 03	23 03	

Sundays

		CH	CH	CH	CH	CH	CH	CH	CH	CH		CH	CH	CH	CH	CH	CH	CH	CH	CH		CH	CH	CH	CH
		◇							◇										◇						
Aylesbury Vale Parkway	d	07 30	08 30	09 00	10 00	11 00	12 00	13 00	14 00	15 00			16 00		17 00		18 00		19 00			20 00		21 00	
Aylesbury	d	07 35	08 35	09 05	10 05	11 05	12 05	13 05	14 05	15 05		15 35	16 05	16 35	17 05	17 35	18 05	18 35	19 05	19 35		20 05	20 35	21 05	21 35
Stoke Mandeville	d	07 39	08 39	09 09	10 09	11 09	12 09	13 09	14 09	15 09		15 39	16 09	16 39	17 09	17 39	18 09	18 39	19 09	19 39		20 09	20 39	21 09	21 39
Wendover	d	07 43	08 43	09 13	10 13	11 13	12 13	13 13	14 13	15 13		15 43	16 13	16 43	17 13	17 43	18 13	18 43	19 13	19 43		20 13	20 43	21 13	21 43
Great Missenden	d	07 49	08 49	09 19	10 19	11 19	12 19	13 19	14 19	15 19		15 49	16 19	16 49	17 19	17 49	18 19	18 49	19 19	19 49		20 19	20 49	21 19	21 49
Amersham §	⊖ d	07 56	08 56	09 26	10 26	11 26	12 26	13 26	14 26	15 26		15a58	16 26	16a58	17 26	17a58	18 26	18a58	19 26	19a58		20 26	20a58	21 26	21a58
Chalfont & Latimer §	⊖ d	08 00	09 00	09 30	10 30	11 30	12 30	13 30	14 30	15 30			16 30		17 30		18 30		19 30			20 30		21 30	
Chorleywood §	⊖ d	08 03	09 03	09 33	10 33	11 33	12 33	13 33	14 33	15 33			16 33		17 33		18 33		19 33			20 33		21 33	
Rickmansworth §	⊖ d	08 08	09 08	09 38	10 38	11 38	12 38	13 38	14 38	15 38			16 38		17 38		18 38		19 38			20 38		21 38	
Harrow-on-the-Hill 3 §	⊖ d	08 19	09 19	09 49	10 49	11 49	12 49	13 49	14 49	15 49			16 49		17 49		18 49		19 49			20 49		21 49	
London Marylebone 10	⊖ a	08 33	09 33	10 03	11 03	12 03	13 03	14 03	15 03	16 03			17 04		18 04		19 03		20 04			21 03		22 03	

§ London Underground Limited (Metropolitan Line) services operate between Harrow-on-the-Hill, Rickmansworth, Chorleywood, Chalfont & Latimer and Amersham

Aylesbury and Amersham - London

Network Diagram - see first Page of Table 114

			CH	CH
				◇
Aylesbury Vale Parkway		d	22 00	
Aylesbury		d	22 05	22 35
Stoke Mandeville		d	22 09	22 39
Wendover		d	22 13	22 43
Great Missenden		d	22 19	22 49
Amersham §	⊖	d	22a28	22 56
Chalfont & Latimer §	⊖	d		23 00
Chorleywood §	⊖	d		23 03
Rickmansworth §	⊖	d		23 08
Harrow-on-the-Hill 3 §	⊖	d		23 19
London Marylebone 10	⊖	a		23 34

§ London Underground Limited (Metropolitan Line) services operate between Harrow-on-the-Hill, Rickmansworth, Chorleywood, Chalfont & Latimer and Amersham

London - High Wycombe, Aylesbury, Banbury, Stratford-upon-Avon, Birmingham Snow Hill and Kidderminster

Network Diagram - see first Page of Table 114

Miles	Miles	Miles			CH MX ◇	CH MX ◇	CH MO	CH MO	CH MX	CH MX	CH MX	CH MO	CH ◇	CH MO	CH MO 🚌	CH MX	LM	CH	CH	CH	CH	CH	CH		CH ◇ 🛒
—	—	—	**London Marylebone** 10 ⊖	d	22p37	23p07	22p45		23p00	23p20	23p30	23p45	00 05			00 10				06 00	06 12	06 20	06 40		07 00
—	—	0	**London Paddington** 15 ⊖	d																					
6½	—	—	Wembley Stadium	d			22p53		23p08	23p28	23p39	23p53				00 18				06 08		06 28	06 48		
8	—	—	Sudbury & Harrow Road	d																					
8¾	—	—	Sudbury Hill Harrow	d																					
9¾	—	—	Northolt Park	d			22p58				23p44	23p58				00 23				06 13		06 33			
11½	—	—	South Ruislip § ⊖	d			23p02		23p20		23p47	00 03				00 27				06 17		06 37			
13¼	—	—	West Ruislip 3 § ⊖	d			23p05				23p51	00 06				00 30					06 26		06 56		
16	—	—	Denham	d			23p10		23p25		23p55	00 11				00 35				06 22	06 30	06 42	07 01		
17	—	—	Denham Golf Club	d							23p58	00 13				00 37							07 03		
18¾	—	—	Gerrards Cross 1	d			23p14		23p30	23p42	00 01	00 17	00 23			00 41				06 27	06 35	06 47	07 07		
21¼	—	—	Seer Green	d			23p19		23p34		00 06	00 21				00 45				06 31			07 11		
23	—	—	Beaconsfield	d			23p22		23p37	23p48	00 09	00 24	00 29			00 48				06 34	06 42	06 53	07 14		
27¾	—	—	**High Wycombe** 1	d			23p28		23p43	23p54	00 15	00 30	00 35			00 54			06 10	06 40	06 48	07a05	07a24		07 25
32¾	—	—	Saunderton	d			23p34				00 21	00 37				01 01			06 17	06 47					
36	—	—	**Princes Risborough** 2	d			23p39	23p48	23p52	00 03	00 26	00a44	00 44	00 48	00 50	01 06			06 22	06 52	06 58				07 34
—	1½	—	Monks Risborough	d				23p51			00 30			00 51		01 09				06 55					
—	3	—	Little Kimble	d				23p55			00 33			00 55		01 13				06 59					
—	7½	—	**Aylesbury**	a				00 06			00 47			01 06		01 26				07 12					
4¾	—	—	Haddenham & Thame Parkway	d			23p46		23p59	00 09			00 51		01 05				06 30		07 04				07 40
54¾	—	—	**Bicester North** 3	d	23p20	23p50	23p59		00 12	00 23			01 03		01 35				06 45		07 17				07 51
65¼	—	—	Kings Sutton	d			00 09			00 32									06 56		07 28				
68¾	—	—	**Banbury**	d	23p39	00 04	00a19		00a33	00a45			01a24		02 05				07 02		07a41				08 04
88¾	—	—	**Leamington Spa** 8	d	23p56	00 22												06 52	07 22						08 26
90¾	—	—	Warwick	d	00 01	00 26												06 56	07 26						08 30
92	—	—	Warwick Parkway	d	00 04	00 29												06 59	07 29						08 33
94¾	—	—	Hatton	d														07 04	07 34						
—	—	7¾	Claverdon	d													06x34	07 10							
—	—	10	Bearley	d													06x38	07 15							
—	—	11½	Wilmcote	d													06 42	07 20							
—	—	15¼	**Stratford-upon-Avon**	a													06 48	07 27							
99	—	—	Lapworth	a																					
101½	—	—	Dorridge	a	00 13														07 41						08 43
104¾	—	—	Solihull	a	00 18	00 41													07 49						08 48
111¼	—	—	**Birmingham Moor Street**	a	00 32	00 55													08 01						08 59
112	—	—	**Birmingham Snow Hill** ⛴	a															08 10						09 07
—	—	—	Rowley Regis	a																					
—	—	—	Cradley Heath	a																					
—	—	—	**Stourbridge Junction** 2	a																					
—	—	—	**Kidderminster**	a																					

		CH	CH	CH ◇	CH	CH	CH	CH	CH ◇		CH ◇	CH	CH	CH ◇ 🛒	CH ◇	CH		CH ◇ 🛒	CH		CH ◇	CH ◇	CH	CH ◇ 🛒	CH
London Marylebone 10 ⊖	d	07 08	07 12	07 33		07 43	07 46	08 00	08 03		08 06	08 10	08 30	08 37	08 41	08 45		09 07			09 10	09 14	09 17	09 37	09 40
London Paddington 15 ⊖	d																								
Wembley Stadium	d		07 20				07 54					08 19	08 38			08 53							09 25		
Sudbury & Harrow Road	d																								
Sudbury Hill Harrow	d		07 24					08 10					08 42										09 29		
Northolt Park	d		07 27			07 54						08 24				08 58						09 25			
South Ruislip § ⊖	d		07 30				08 01	08a19				08 28	08 54										09 34		
West Ruislip 3 § ⊖	d					07 59										09 03									
Denham	d		07 36				08 06					08 34	09 00			09 08							09 40		
Denham Golf Club	d						08 09						09 02												
Gerrards Cross 1	d	07 27	07 40			08 06	08 12				08 26	08 39	09a08			09 13						09 36	09 44		09 58
Seer Green	d	07 31					08 17					08 43				09 18						09 41			
Beaconsfield	d	07 35	07 46			08 12	08 20				08 32	08 47				09 21						09 44	09 50		10 04
High Wycombe 1	d	07 41	07 52	07 57		08 18	08a28		08 29		08 38	08a59			09 07	09a30		09 31			09 35	09 50	10a02		10 10
Saunderton	d	07 47									08 44				09 14							09 56			
Princes Risborough 2	d	07 53	08a05	08 06	08 16	08 27			08 39		08 49				09 19				09 24		09 44	10a08			10 19
Monks Risborough	d				08 19														09 27						
Little Kimble	d				08 23														09 31						
Aylesbury	a				08 34														09 42						
Haddenham & Thame Parkway	d	08 00		08 12		08 33									09 25						09 50				10 26
Bicester North 3	d	08 13		08 23		08 46			08 52		09a13				09 39			09 52			10 01				10a48
Kings Sutton	d	08 25													09 50										
Banbury	d	08 32		08 38		09a07			09 05					09 30	10a05			10 05			10 16			10 30	
Leamington Spa 8	d	08 51		08 57					09 23					09 47				10 23			10 33			10 48	
Warwick	d	08 55		09 01					09 27									10 27			10 37				
Warwick Parkway	d			09 04					09 30					09 53				10 31						10 54	
Hatton	d	09 02		09 09																					
Claverdon	d	09 09																							
Bearley	d	09 14																							
Wilmcote	d	09 19																							
Stratford-upon-Avon	a	09 31																			11 09				
Lapworth	a			09 14																					
Dorridge	a			09 19					09 40									10 40							
Solihull	a			09 25					09 46					10 04				10 46						11 05	
Birmingham Moor Street	a			09 38					09 54					10 17				10 54						11 19	
Birmingham Snow Hill ⛴	a								10 05									11 04							
Rowley Regis	a																								
Cradley Heath	a																								
Stourbridge Junction 2	a																								
Kidderminster	a																								

§ London Underground Limited (Central Line) also operate services between South Ruislip and West Ruislip at frequent intervals

Table 115

Mondays to Fridays

London - High Wycombe, Aylesbury, Banbury, Stratford-upon-Avon, Birmingham Snow Hill and Kidderminster

Network Diagram - see first Page of Table 114

		CH	CH ◇ ⊼	CH	CH ◇		CH ◇	CH	CH ◇ ⊼	CH ◇	CH	CH ◇ ⊼	CH	CH ◇	CH ◇		CH	CH ⊼	CH	CH	CH	CH	CH ◇ ⊼	CH ◇	CH
London Marylebone 10 ⊖	d	09 43	10 07		10 10		10 13	10 16	10 37	10 40	10 43	11 07		11 10	11 13		11 16	11 37		11 40		11 43	12 07	12 10	12 13
London Paddington 15 ⊖	d																				11 36				
Wembley Stadium	d	09 51						10 24			10 51						11 25					11 51			
Sudbury & Harrow Road	d																								
Sudbury Hill Harrow	d	09 55									10 55											11 55			
Northolt Park	d	09 58						10 29			10 58						11 30					11 58			
South Ruislip § ⊖	d							10 33									11 33								
West Ruislip 3 § ⊖	d	10 03									11 03											12 04			
Denham	d	10 07						10 38			11 07						11 39					12 09			
Denham Golf Club	d	10 10									11 10														
Gerrards Cross 1	d	10 13					10 31	10 43		10 58	11 13				11 34		11 43			11 58	12a08	12 13			12 31
Seer Green	d	10 18						10 47			11 18						11 48					12 18			
Beaconsfield	d	10 21					10 37	10 50		11 04	11 21				11 40		11 51			12 04		12 21			12 37
High Wycombe 1	d	10a30	10 31		10 36		10 43	11a02		11 10	11a30	11 31		11 35	11 46		12a03			12 10		12a30	12 31	12 35	12 44
Saunderton	d						10 50								11 52										12 50
Princes Risborough 2	d			10 24	10 45		10 55			11 19			11 24	11 44	12a07				12 17	12 19				12 44	13a02
Monks Risborough	d			10 27									11 27						12 20						
Little Kimble	d			10 31									11 31						12 24						
Aylesbury	a			10 42									11 43						12 38						
Haddenham & Thame Parkway	d				10 52		11 01			11 26				11 50						12 26				12 50	
Bicester North 3	d		10 52		11a12		11 14			11 40		11 52		12 01						12a45			12 52	13 01	
Kings Sutton	d									11 54														13 12	
Banbury	d		11 05				11a35		11 33	11 59		12 06		12a21				12 29					13 06	13a24	
Leamington Spa 8	d		11 23						11 50	12 18		12 23						12 47					13 23		
Warwick	d		11 27							12 22		12 27											13 27		
Warwick Parkway	d		11 31						11 56			12 31						12 52					13 31		
Hatton	d									12 29															
Claverdon	d									12 34															
Bearley	d									12 39															
Wilmcote	d																								
Stratford-upon-Avon	a									12 52															
Lapworth	a																								
Dorridge	a		11 40									12 40											13 40		
Solihull	a		11 46						12 07			12 46						13 05					13 46		
Birmingham Moor Street	a		11 54						12 25			12 54						13 19					13 54		
Birmingham Snow Hill ⛴	a		12 04									13 04											14 04		
Rowley Regis	a																								
Cradley Heath	a																								
Stourbridge Junction 2	a																								
Kidderminster	a																								

§ London Underground Limited (Central Line) also operate services between South Ruislip and West Ruislip at frequent intervals

r

London - High Wycombe, Aylesbury, Banbury, Stratford-upon-Avon, Birmingham Snow Hill and Kidderminster

Network Diagram - see first Page of Table 114

		CH	CH	CH	CH	CH	CH	CH	CH	CH	CH	CH	CH	CH	CH	CH	CH	CH	CH	CH	CH	CH
						◇		◇			◇				◇		◇					
				🚲		🚲						🚲			🚲					🚲		
London Marylebone	d	12 16	12 37	12 40	12 43	13 07		13 10	13 13	13 16		13 37	13 40	13 43	14 07		14 10	14 13	14 16	14 37	14 40	14 43
London Paddington	d																					
Wembley Stadium	d	12 24			12 51					13 24				13 51					14 24			14 51
Sudbury & Harrow Road	d																					
Sudbury Hill Harrow	d				12 55									13 55								14 55
Northolt Park	d	12 29			12 58					13 29				13 58					14 29			14 58
South Ruislip §	d	12 33								13 33									14 33			
West Ruislip §	d				13 03									14 03								15 03
Denham	d	12 38			13 07					13 38				14 07					14 38			15 07
Denham Golf Club	d				13 10									14 10								15 10
Gerrards Cross	d	12 43		12 58	13 13				13 31	13 43			13 58	14 13				14 31	14 43		14 58	15 13
Seer Green	d	12 47			13 18					13 47				14 18					14 47			15 18
Beaconsfield	d	12 50		13 04	13 21				13 37	13 50			14 04	14 21				14 37	14 50		15 04	15 21
High Wycombe	d	13a02		13 10	13a30	13 31		13 36	13 44	14a02			14 10	14a30	14 31		14 36	14 44	15a02		15 10	15a30
Saunderton	d								13 50									14 50				
Princes Risborough	d			13 19			13 24	13 45	14a02				14 19			14 24	14 45	15a02			15 19	
Monks Risborough	d						13 27									14 27						
Little Kimble	d						13 31									14 31						
Aylesbury	a						13 42									14 42						
Haddenham & Thame Parkway	d			13 26				13 52					14 26				14 52				15 26	
Bicester North	d			13a45		13 52		14 05					14a45		14 52		15 05				15a47	
Kings Sutton	d																					
Banbury	d		13 29			14 06		14a25				14 30			15 06		15a24			15 29		
Leamington Spa	d		13 47			14 23					14 34	14 47			15 23					15 47		
Warwick	d					14 27					14 38				15 27							
Warwick Parkway	d		13 52			14 31						14 53			15 31					15 52		
Hatton	d										14 45											
Claverdon	d										14 51											
Bearley	d										14 56											
Wilmcote	d										15 01											
Stratford-upon-Avon	a										15 09											
Lapworth	a																					
Dorridge	a					14 40									15 40							
Solihull	a		14 04			14 46						15 04			15 46					16 04		
Birmingham Moor Street	a		14 18			14 54						15 19			15 54					16 13		
Birmingham Snow Hill	a					15 04									16 04					16 21		
Rowley Regis	a																					
Cradley Heath	a																					
Stourbridge Junction	a																					
Kidderminster	a																					

§ London Underground Limited (Central Line) also operate services between South Ruislip and West Ruislip at frequent intervals

London - High Wycombe, Aylesbury, Banbury, Stratford-upon-Avon, Birmingham Snow Hill and Kidderminster

Network Diagram - see first Page of Table 114

		CH	CH	CH	CH	CH	CH	CH	CH	CH	CH	CH	CH	CH	CH	CH	CH	CH	CH	CH	CH	CH	CH
		◇									◇									🚲		◇	
London Marylebone 10 ⊖	d	15 07		15 10	15 13	15 16	15 37	15 40	15 43	16 00	16 07		16 10	16 13	16 30	16 33	16 36	16 40	16 43	16 46		16 49	16 56
London Paddington 15 ⊖	d																						
Wembley Stadium	d					15 24			15 51	16 08								16 48				16 59	
Sudbury & Harrow Road	d																	16 51					
Sudbury Hill Harrow	d								15 55									16 54					
Northolt Park	d					15 29			15 58	16 13								16 56					
South Ruislip § ⊖	d					15 33				16 26								17 09					
West Ruislip 3 § ⊖	d								16 03	16 31								17 13					
Denham	d					15 38			16 07	16 35				16 29									17 12
Denham Golf Club	d								16 10					16 31									
Gerrards Cross 1	d				15 31	15 43		15 58	16 13	16a46				16 35			16 54	17a26					17 17
Seer Green	d					15 47			16 18					16 39			16 59						
Beaconsfield	d				15 37	15 50		16 04	16 21				16 30	16 42			17 02						17 23
High Wycombe 1	d	15 31		15 35	15 44	16a02		16 10	16a32				16 36	16a54		16 59	17a14					17 16	17a34
Saunderton	d				15 50								16 42									17 22	
Princes Risborough 2	d		15 24	15 44	16a02			16 19				16 24	16 47			17 08					17 16	17 27	
Monks Risborough	d		15 27									16 27									17 19		
Little Kimble	d		15 31									16 31									17 23		
Aylesbury	a		15 42									16 42							17 36		17 37		
Haddenham & Thame Parkway	d			15 50				16 26					16 53			17 15						17 33	
Bicester North 3	d	15 52		16 01				16a45			16 49		17a12			17a31						17 45	
Kings Sutton	d			16 12																			
Banbury	d	16 06		16 17			16 30				17 03									17 43		18a02	
Leamington Spa 8	d	16 24		16 35			16 47				17 21									18 01			
Warwick	d	16 28		16 39							17 25												
Warwick Parkway	d	16 31					16 53				17 29				17 39					18 07			
Hatton	d			16 46																			
Claverdon	d			16 53																			
Bearley	d			16 58																			
Wilmcote	d			17 02																			
Stratford-upon-Avon	a			17 14																			
Lapworth	a																						
Dorridge	a	16 41									17 38									18 16			
Solihull	a	16 46					17 04				17 44				17 51					18 22			
Birmingham Moor Street	a	17 01					17 13				17 55				18 00					18 35			
Birmingham Snow Hill 🚌	a						17 21				18 03				18 12								
Rowley Regis	a																						
Cradley Heath	a																						
Stourbridge Junction 2	a																						
Kidderminster	a																						

§ London Underground Limited (Central Line) also operate services between South Ruislip and West Ruislip at frequent intervals

Table 115

Mondays to Fridays

London - High Wycombe, Aylesbury, Banbury, Stratford-upon-Avon, Birmingham Snow Hill and Kidderminster

Network Diagram - see first Page of Table 114

		CH	CH		CH	CH	CH	CH	CH	CH	CH	CH	CH		CH	CH	CH	CH	CH	CH	CH	CH	CH		CH
		◇														◇ 🚌	◇ B	◇							
London Marylebone 10 ⊖	d	17 07	17 10		17 13	17 16	17 19	17 23	17 37	17 40	17 43	17 46	17 50		17 56	18 07	18 10	18 13		18 16	18 19	18 22	18 25		18 29
London Paddington 15 ⊖	d																								
Wembley Stadium	d				17 21			17 32			17 52									18 24					18 37
Sudbury & Harrow Road	d							17 35																	18 40
Sudbury Hill Harrow	d							17 38																	18 43
Northolt Park	d						17 30	17 41							18 07										18 45
South Ruislip § ⊖	d							17 51							18 11										19 00
West Ruislip 3 § ⊖	d						17 36	17a59					18 04										18 39		19a07
Denham	d						17 41						18 09										18 43		
Denham Golf Club	d				17 33								18 11												
Gerrards Cross 1	d				17 36						18 06		18 15		18a23							18 40	18 48		
Seer Green	d				17 41						18 11												18 52		
Beaconsfield	d				17 44		17 50				18 14		18 21							18 41		18 47	18 55		
High Wycombe 1	d		17 36		17 50		18a01			18 03	18 21		18a33							18 47		18 53	19a06		
Saunderton	d				17 56						18 27											19 00			
Princes Risborough 2	d		17 45		18 01					18 12	18a38							18 48	18 50	18 56		19 05			
Monks Risborough	d				18 05														18 53						
Little Kimble	d				18 08														18 57						
Aylesbury	a				18 23	18 05						18 39							19 08		19 11	19 23			
Haddenham & Thame Parkway	d		17 51							18 19								18 56		19 02					
Bicester North 3	d		18 03						18 22	18a39								19 10		19a21					
Kings Sutton	d		18 13																						
Banbury	d	18 04	18 19						18 35								19 05	19a30							
Leamington Spa 8	d	18 21	18 36						18 54								19 23								
Warwick	d		18 40						18 58								19 27								
Warwick Parkway	d	18 27							19 01							19 20	19 31								
Hatton	d		18 47																						
Claverdon	d		18 53																						
Bearley	d																								
Wilmcote	d		19 00																						
Stratford-upon-Avon	a		19 12																						
Lapworth	a																								
Dorridge	a	18 39							19 11								19 40								
Solihull	a	18 44							19 16							19 31	19 46								
Birmingham Moor Street	a	19 01							19 25							19 40	19 57								
Birmingham Snow Hill	a	19 04							19 36							19 43	20 00								
Rowley Regis	a	19 24														20 01	20 24								
Cradley Heath	a	19 29															20 29								
Stourbridge Junction 2	a	19 35														20 14	20 40								
Kidderminster	a	19 48														20 30									

§ London Underground Limited (Central Line) also operate services between South Ruislip and West Ruislip at frequent intervals

B 🚌 to Birmingham Snow Hill

Table 115

Mondays to Fridays

London - High Wycombe, Aylesbury, Banbury, Stratford-upon-Avon, Birmingham Snow Hill and Kidderminster

Network Diagram - see first Page of Table 114

		CH	CH	CH	CH	CH	CH	CH	CH	CH	CH	CH	CH	CH	CH	CH	CH	CH	CH	CH	CH	CH	CH
									◇				◇				◇		◇		◇		
London Marylebone [10] ⊖	d	18 40	18 44	18 47	18 53	18 56	18 59	19 04	19 15	19 18	19 21	19 37	19 40	19 43	19 46	20 10	20 15	20 18	20 37	20 40	21 07	21 13	
London Paddington [15] ⊖	d																						
Wembley Stadium	d						19 07				19 29				19 54			20 26		20 48		21 21	
Sudbury & Harrow Road	d														19 57					20 51			
Sudbury Hill Harrow	d														20 00					20 54			
Northolt Park	d					19 07					19 34				20 02			20 31		20 56		21 26	
South Ruislip § ⊖	d						19 14				19 38				20 06					21 00			
West Ruislip [3] § ⊖	d					19 12								19 57				20 36				21 31	
Denham	d						19 19				19 43			20 02				20 41		21 05		21 36	
Denham Golf Club	d						19 22							20 05						21 08		21 38	
Gerrards Cross [1]	d			19 06		19 19	19 25			19 37	19 48			20 09	20 14		20 34	20 45		21 11		21 42	
Seer Green	d					19 23				19 41					20 18			20 50		21 16		21 46	
Beaconsfield	d			19 12		19 26				19 44				20 16	20 22		20 40	20 53		21 19		21 49	
High Wycombe [1]	d		19 10	19a21	19 22	19 33	19a42			19 50	20a04		20 06	20 24	20a34		20 46	20 59	21 03	21 25	21 31	21 55	
Saunderton	d				19 28									20 30						21 31		22 02	
Princes Risborough [2]	d		19 20		19 33	19 42				19 59			20 16	20 36			20 56	21 08	21 12	21a40	21 42	22 10	
Monks Risborough	d					19 45								20 39				21 11				22 13	
Little Kimble	d					19 49								20 43				21 15				22 17	
Aylesbury	a					20 02		20 08						20 56				21 28				22 30	
Haddenham & Thame Parkway	d		19 26		19 40					20 06		20 13	20 24				21 03		21 18		21 48		
Bicester North [3]	d	19 24	19 41		19a56				20 00	20 19		20 25	20 39			20 52	21 17		21 29		21 59		
Kings Sutton	d		19 55														21 28						
Banbury	d	19 37	20 00						20 13	20a39		20 40	20 57			21 06	21a40		21 45		22 14		
Leamington Spa [8]	d	19 55	20a24						20 31			20 57	21 17			21 24			22 04		22 32		22 40
Warwick	d	19 59										21 01	21 21						22 08		22 36		22 44
Warwick Parkway	d	20 02							20 36			21 05				21 30			22 12		22 40		
Hatton	d												21 28										
Claverdon	d												21 34										
Bearley	d												21 39										
Wilmcote	d												21 43										
Stratford-upon-Avon	a												21 54										23 11
Lapworth	a																						
Dorridge	a	20 13							20 46			21 14				21 39			22 21		22 49		
Solihull	a	20 18							20 51			21 20				21 45			22 27		22 55		
Birmingham Moor Street	a	20 27							21 00			21 28				21 57			22 42		23 04		
Birmingham Snow Hill ⛴	a	20 37							21 04			21 37				22 00					23 11		
Rowley Regis	a								21 19							22 24					23 38		
Cradley Heath	a								21 25							22 29					23 44		
Stourbridge Junction [2]	a								21 32							22 35					23 52		
Kidderminster	a								21 49							22 50							

		CH	CH	CH	CH	CH	CH	CH	CH	CH	CH	CH	CH	CH
		◇			◇			◇	◇		◇			
London Marylebone [10] ⊖	d	21 37	21 40	21 43	22 07	22 10	22 13	22 37	22 40	22 43	23 07	23 00	23 20	23 30
London Paddington [15] ⊖	d													
Wembley Stadium	d			21 51			22 21			22 51		23 08	23 28	23 39
Sudbury & Harrow Road	d													
Sudbury Hill Harrow	d													
Northolt Park	d			21 56			22 26			22 56				23 44
South Ruislip § ⊖	d			22 00						23 00		23 20		23 47
West Ruislip [3] § ⊖	d						22 31							23 51
Denham	d			22 05			22 36			23 05		23 25		23 55
Denham Golf Club	d						22 38			23 08				23 58
Gerrards Cross [1]	d		21 59	22 10		22 28	22 42		22 58	23 11		23 30	23 42	00 01
Seer Green	d			22 14			22 46					23 34		00 06
Beaconsfield	d		22 05	22 17		22 34	22 49		23 04	23 17		23 37	23 48	00 09
High Wycombe [1]	d	22 01	22 11	22 23		22 40	23a01		23 10	23 23		23 43	23 54	00 15
Saunderton	d			22 30						23 30				00 21
Princes Risborough [2]	d		22 20	22 35		22 49			23 19	23 35		23 52	00 03	00 26
Monks Risborough	d			22 38						23 38				00 30
Little Kimble	d			22 42						23 42				00 33
Aylesbury	a			22 55						23 56				00 47
Haddenham & Thame Parkway	d	22 17	22 26			22 56			23 26			23 59	00 09	
Bicester North [3]	d	22 28	22a45		22 50	23a15		23 20	23a45		23 50	00 12	00 23	
Kings Sutton	d												00 32	
Banbury	d	22 43			23 04			23 39			00 04	00a33	00a45	
Leamington Spa [8]	d	23 00			23 22			23 56			00 22			
Warwick	d	23 04			23 26			00 01			00 26			
Warwick Parkway	d	23 08			23 30			00 04			00 29			
Hatton	d													
Claverdon	d													
Bearley	d													
Wilmcote	d													
Stratford-upon-Avon	a													
Lapworth	a													
Dorridge	a	23 18			23 40			00 13						
Solihull	a	23 24			23 45			00 18			00 41			
Birmingham Moor Street	a	23 37			23 59			00 32			00 55			
Birmingham Snow Hill ⛴	a													
Rowley Regis	a													
Cradley Heath	a													
Stourbridge Junction [2]	a													
Kidderminster	a													

§ London Underground Limited (Central Line) also operate services between South Ruislip and West Ruislip at frequent intervals

Table 115

Saturdays

London - High Wycombe, Aylesbury, Banbury, Stratford-upon-Avon, Birmingham Snow Hill and Kidderminster

Network Diagram - see first Page of Table 114

		CH	CH	CH	CH	CH	CH	CH	CH	CH		CH	CH	CH	CH	CH	CH	CH	CH	CH		CH	CH	CH	CH
		◇	◇				◇					◇			◇	◇		◇	◇				◇	◇	
London Marylebone 10 ⊖	d	22p37	23p07	23p00	23p20	23p30	00 05	00 10		06 30		07 00	07 30		08 00	08 20	08 30	08 54	09 00			09 03	09 30	09 33	09 36
London Paddington 15 ⊖	d																								
Wembley Stadium	d			23p08	23p28	23p39		00 18		06 38			07 38				08 38					09 11			09 44
Sudbury & Harrow Road	d																								
Sudbury Hill Harrow	d																								
Northolt Park	d					23p44		00 23		06 43			07 43				08 43					09 16			09 49
South Ruislip § ⊖	d			23p20		23p47		00 27		06 47			07 47				08 47					09 20			
West Ruislip 3 § ⊖	d					23p51		00 30		06 50			07 50				08 50								09 54
Denham	d			23p25		23p55		00 35		06 55			07 55				08 55					09 25			09 59
Denham Golf Club	d					23p58		00 37		06 57			07 57				08 57								10 01
Gerrards Cross 1	d			23p30	23p42	00 01	00 23	00 41		07 01			08 01			08 37	09 01					09 30		09 51	10 05
Seer Green	d			23p34		00 06		00 45		07 05			08 05				09 05					09 34			10 09
Beaconsfield	d			23p37	23p48	00 09	00 29	00 48		07 08			08 08			08 43	09 08					09 37		09 57	10 12
High Wycombe 1	d			23p43	23p54	00 15	00 35	00 54	06 18	07 14		07 23	08 14		08 23	08 52	09a17		09 23			09 43		10 04	10a23
Saunderton	d					00 21		01 01	06 24	07 21			08 21			08 58						09 50		10 11	
Princes Risborough 2	d			23p52	00 03	00 26	00 44	01 06	06 30	07 26		07 33	08 27		08 33	09 04			09 33	09 38		09a58		10 16	
Monks Risborough	d					00 30		01 09		07 29			08 30							09 41					
Little Kimble	d					00 33		01 13		07 33			08 34							09 45					
Aylesbury	a					00 47		01 26		07 46			08 47							09 55					
Haddenham & Thame Parkway	d			23p59	00 09		00 51		06 36			07 39			08 39	09 10			09 39					10 22	
Bicester North 3	d	23p20	23p50	00 12	00 23		01 03		06 48			07 50			08 50	09 22		09 38	09 50				10 12	10 40	
Kings Sutton	d				00 32				07 00						09 02									10 51	
Banbury	d	23p39	00 04	00a33	00a45		01 19		07 07			08 04			09 08	09 36		09 51	10 05				10 28	11a02	
Leamington Spa 8	d	23p56	00 22				01a50		07 26			08 22		08 31	09 26	09 55		10 09	10 23				10 46		
Warwick	d	00 01	00 26						07 30			08 26		08 35	09 30	09 59		10 14	10 27						
Warwick Parkway	d	00 04	00 29						07 33			08 29		08 38	09 34	10 02			10 31				10 51		
Hatton	d											08 34		08 44		10 07									
Claverdon	d													08 50											
Bearley	d													08 55											
Wilmcote	d													09 00											
Stratford-upon-Avon	a													09 11				10 40							
Lapworth	a											08 39				10 12									
Dorridge	a	00 13							07 43			08 44			09 43	10 17			10 40						
Solihull	a	00 18	00 41						07 50			08 50			09 49	10 22			10 46				11 04		
Birmingham Moor Street	a	00 32	00 55						07 59			08 59			10 01	10 35			10 54				11 17		
Birmingham Snow Hill	a								08 07			09 07			10 09				11 02						
Rowley Regis	a																								
Cradley Heath	a																								
Stourbridge Junction 2	a																								
Kidderminster	a																								

		CH	CH	CH	CH	CH		CH	CH	CH	CH	CH	CH	CH	CH	CH		CH	CH	CH	CH	CH	CH	CH	CH
		◇			◇	◇						◇	◇			◇			◇			◇			◇
London Marylebone 10 ⊖	d	10 00		10 03	10 30	10 33		10 36	11 00		11 03	11 30	11 37	12 00	12 03	12 30			12 37	13 00	13 03	13 30		13 37	14 00
London Paddington 15 ⊖	d																								
Wembley Stadium	d			10 11				10 44			11 11		11 45		12 11				12 45		13 11			13 45	
Sudbury & Harrow Road	d																								
Sudbury Hill Harrow	d																								
Northolt Park	d			10 16				10 49			11 16				12 16						13 16				
South Ruislip § ⊖	d			10 20							11 20				12 20						13 20				
West Ruislip 3 § ⊖	d							10 54			11 23				12 23						13 23				
Denham	d			10 25				10 59			11 28				12 28						13 28				
Denham Golf Club	d							11 01			11 30				12 30						13 30				
Gerrards Cross 1	d			10 30		10 52		11 05			11 34		11 58		12 34				12 58		13 34			13 58	
Seer Green	d			10 34				11 09			11 38				12 38						13 38				
Beaconsfield	d			10 37		10 58		11 12			11 41		12 04		12 41				13 04		13 41			14 04	
High Wycombe 1	d	10 24		10 43		11 04		11a21	11 23		11 47		12 10	12 23	12a50				13 10	13 23	13a50			14 10	14 23
Saunderton	d					11 10							12 16						13 16					14 16	
Princes Risborough 2	d	10 34	10 38	10a55		11 16			11 33	11 38	11a59		12 22	12 33				12 38	13 22	13 33			13 38	14 22	14 33
Monks Risborough	d		10 41							11 41								12 41					13 41		
Little Kimble	d		10 45							11 45								12 45					13 45		
Aylesbury	a		11 00							11 59								12 55					13 55		
Haddenham & Thame Parkway	d	10 40				11 23			11 39				12 29	12 39					13 29	13 39				14 29	14 39
Bicester North 3	d	10 51			11 12	11 40			11 50			12 13	12 42	12 50		13 12			13 42	13 50		14 12		14 42	14 50
Kings Sutton	d												12 54											14 54	
Banbury	d	11 05			11 29	11 58			12 04			12 28	13a01	13 05		13 29			13 58	14 05		14 29		15a02	15 05
Leamington Spa 8	d	11 22			11 47	12 17			12 22			12 47		13 22		13 47			14 17	14 23		14 47			15 23
Warwick	d	11 27				12 21			12 26					13 26					14 21	14 27					15 27
Warwick Parkway	d	11 31			11 53				12 30			12 52		13 30		13 53				14 31		14 53			15 31
Hatton	d					12 27													14 28						
Claverdon	d					12 33													14 33						
Bearley	d					12 38																			
Wilmcote	d					12 42																			
Stratford-upon-Avon	a					12 52													14 49						
Lapworth	a																								
Dorridge	a	11 40							12 39					13 39						14 40					15 40
Solihull	a	11 46			12 04				12 45			13 04		13 45		14 04				14 46		15 04			15 46
Birmingham Moor Street	a	11 54			12 17				12 54			13 17		13 53		14 17				14 54		15 17			15 54
Birmingham Snow Hill	a	12 02							13 02					14 02						15 02					16 02
Rowley Regis	a																								
Cradley Heath	a																								
Stourbridge Junction 2	a																								
Kidderminster	a																								

§ London Underground Limited (Central Line) also operate services between South Ruislip and West Ruislip at frequent intervals

Table 115

Saturdays

London - High Wycombe, Aylesbury, Banbury, Stratford-upon-Avon, Birmingham Snow Hill and Kidderminster

Network Diagram - see first Page of Table 114

	CH		CH	CH ◇	CH	CH	CH	CH	CH	CH	CH		CH	CH	CH	CH	CH	CH	CH	CH	CH		CH	CH ◇
London Marylebone 10 ⊖ d			14 03	14 30	14 33	14 36	15 00		15 03	15 30	15 33		15 36	16 00		16 03	16 30	16 33	16 36	17 00			17 03	17 30
London Paddington 15 ⊖ d																								
Wembley Stadium d			14 11			14 44			15 11				15 44			16 11			16 44				17 11	
Sudbury & Harrow Road d																								
Sudbury Hill Harrow d																								
Northolt Park d			14 16			14 49			15 16				15 49			16 16			16 49				17 16	
South Ruislip § ⊖ d			14 20						15 20							16 20							17 20	
West Ruislip 3 § ⊖ d			14 23			14 54							15 54						16 54					
Denham d			14 28			14 59			15 25				15 59			16 25			16 59				17 25	
Denham Golf Club d			14 30						15 28							16 28							17 28	
Gerrards Cross 1 d			14 34		14 50	15 03			15 31		15 52		16 03			16 31		16 51	17 03				17 31	
Seer Green d			14 38			15 08			15 36				16 08			16 36			17 08				17 36	
Beaconsfield d			14 41		14 56	15 11			15 39		15 58		16 11			16 39		16 57	17 11				17 39	
High Wycombe 1 d			14 47		15 02	15a19	15 23		15 45		16 04		16a19	16 23		16 45		17 03	17a19	17 23			17 45	
Saunderton d					15 08						16 10							17 10						
Princes Risborough 2 d	14 38		14a59		15 14		15 33	15 38	15a58		16 16			16 33	16 38	16a58		17 16		17 33	17 38		17a58	
Monks Risborough d	14 41							15 41							16 41						17 41			
Little Kimble d	14 45							15 45							16 45						17 45			
Aylesbury a	14 55							15 55							16 55						17 55			
Haddenham & Thame Parkway d					15 20		15 39				16 23			16 39				17 22		17 39				
Bicester North 3 d				15 13	15 32		15 50			16 12	16 40			16 50			17 12	17 40		17 50				18 12
Kings Sutton d											16 51							17 51						
Banbury d				15 28	15 46		16 05			16 28	17a02			17 05			17 28	17 59		18 05				18 28
Leamington Spa 8 d				15 47	16 05		16 23			16 47				17 23			17 47	18 19		18 23				18 46
Warwick d					16 09		16 27							17 27				18 23		18 27				
Warwick Parkway d				15 52			16 31			16 52				17 31			17 52			18 31				18 51
Hatton d					16 16													18 30						
Claverdon d					16 22													18 36						
Bearley d					16 27													18 41						
Wilmcote d					16 31													18 45						
Stratford-upon-Avon a					16 42													18 59						
Lapworth a																								
Dorridge a							16 40							17 40						18 40				
Solihull a				16 04			16 46			17 05				17 46			18 06			18 46				19 04
Birmingham Moor Street a				16 17			16 54			17 17				17 54			18 17			18 55				19 17
Birmingham Snow Hill a							17 02							18 02						19 03				
Rowley Regis a																								
Cradley Heath a																								
Stourbridge Junction 2 a																								
Kidderminster a																								

	CH	CH	CH	CH	CH ◇	CH	CH		CH	CH	CH	CH ◇	CH	CH	CH ◇	CH	CH		CH ◇ A	CH ◇ B	CH	CH	CH ◇ B	CH ◇ A
London Marylebone 10 ⊖ d	17 33	17 36	18 00	18 03	18 30		18 33		18 36	19 00	19 03	19 30	19 33	19 36	20 00	20 05	20 35		21 00	21 00	21 03	21 35	22 10	22 10
London Paddington 15 ⊖ d																								
Wembley Stadium d		17 44		18 11					18 44		19 11			19 45		20 13					21 11			
Sudbury & Harrow Road d																								
Sudbury Hill Harrow d																								
Northolt Park d		17 49		18 16					18 49		19 16			19 50		20 18					21 16			
South Ruislip § ⊖ d				18 20							19 20					20 22					21 20			
West Ruislip 3 § ⊖ d		17 54							18 54					19 55		20 25					21 23			
Denham d		17 59		18 25					18 59		19 25			20 00		20 30					21 28			
Denham Golf Club d				18 28							19 28					20 32					21 30			
Gerrards Cross 1 d	17 50	18 03		18 31			18 51		19 03		19 31		19 52	20 04		20 36	20 53				21 34	21 53		
Seer Green d		18 08		18 36					19 08		19 36			20 09		20 40					21 38			
Beaconsfield d	17 56	18 11		18 39			18 57		19 11		19 39		19 58	20 12		20 43	20 59				21 41	21 59		
High Wycombe 1 d	18 02	18a19	18 22	18a49			19 03		19 17	19 23	19 45		20 04	20a20	20 23	20 49	21 05		21 23	21 23	21 47	22 05		
Saunderton d	18 08						19 10						20 11				21 12				21 54			
Princes Risborough 2 d	18 14		18 33			18 38	19 16		19 29	19 33	19 54		20 17		20 33	20 58	21 18		21 33	21 33	21 59	22 15		
Monks Risborough d						18 41			19 32		19 57					21 02					22 02			
Little Kimble d						18 45			19 36		20 01					21 05					22 06			
Aylesbury a						18 55			19 48		20 14					21 19					22 19			
Haddenham & Thame Parkway d	18 20		18 39				19 22			19 39			20 23		20 39		21 24		21 39	21 39		22 22		
Bicester North 3 d	18a33		18 50		19 12		19 40			19 50		20 13	20a39		20 51		21 40		21 50	21 50		22a40	22 52	22a58
Kings Sutton d							19 51										21 51							
Banbury d			19 05		19 28		20 08			20 05		20 33			21 04		22a02		22a07	22 05			23 06	
Leamington Spa 8 d			19 23		19 47		20 29			20 23		20 52			21 23					22 23			23 25	
Warwick d			19 27				20 33			20 27					21 27					22 27			23 29	
Warwick Parkway d			19 31		19 52					20 31		20 57			21 30					22 31			23 32	
Hatton d							20 39																	
Claverdon d							20 45																	
Bearley d							20 50																	
Wilmcote d							20 55																	
Stratford-upon-Avon a							21 05																	
Lapworth a																								
Dorridge a			19 41							20 40					21 40					22 40			23 42	
Solihull a			19 47		20 04					20 46		21 09			21 45					22 46			23 49	
Birmingham Moor Street a			19 55		20 17					20 55		21 22			21 55					23 01			00 01	
Birmingham Snow Hill a			20 03							21 03					22 03					23 09				
Rowley Regis a																								
Cradley Heath a																								
Stourbridge Junction 2 a																								
Kidderminster a																								

§ London Underground Limited (Central Line) also operate services between South Ruislip and West Ruislip at frequent intervals

A from 7 January until 24 March

B Runs until 31 December and then from 31 March

Table 115

Saturdays

London - High Wycombe, Aylesbury, Banbury, Stratford-upon-Avon, Birmingham Snow Hill and Kidderminster

Network Diagram - see first Page of Table 114

		CH	CH A (bus)	CH B		CH A	CH A (bus)	CH B	CH A	CH	CH B	CH A
London Marylebone 10 ⊖	d	22 13		22 40		22 40		23 10	23 10	23 13	23 45	23 45
London Paddington 15 ⊖	d											
Wembley Stadium	d	22 21		22 48		22 48		23 18	23 18	23 21	23 53	23 53
Sudbury & Harrow Road	d											
Sudbury Hill Harrow	d											
Northolt Park	d	22 26								23 26		
South Ruislip § ⊖	d	22 30								23 30		
West Ruislip 3 § ⊖	d	22 33								23 33		
Denham	d	22 38								23 38		
Denham Golf Club	d	22 40								23 40		
Gerrards Cross 1	d	22 44		23 01		23 01		23 31	23 31	23 43	00 06	00 06
Seer Green	d	22 48								23 48		
Beaconsfield	d	22 51		23 07		23 07		23 37	23 37	23 51	00 12	00 12
High Wycombe 1	d	22 57		23 13		23 13		23 42	23 42	23 59	00 18	00 18
Saunderton	d	23 04								00 06		
Princes Risborough 2	d	23 10		23 24		23 24		23 53	23 53	00 10	00 29	00 29
Monks Risborough	d	23 13								00 15		
Little Kimble	d	23 17								00 17		
Aylesbury	a	23 30								00 33		
Haddenham & Thame Parkway	d			23 29		23 29		00 02	00 02		00 35	00 35
Bicester North 3	d		23 10	23 43		23a46	23 55	00 14	00a17		00 49	00a51
Kings Sutton	d			23 53							00 59	
Banbury	d		23s35	00a04			00a20	00a31			01a09	
Leamington Spa 8	d		00s15									
Warwick	d		00s25									
Warwick Parkway	d		00s35									
Hatton	d											
Claverdon	d											
Bearley	d											
Wilmcote	d											
Stratford-upon-Avon	a											
Lapworth	a											
Dorridge	a		01s00									
Solihull	a		01s20									
Birmingham Moor Street	a											
Birmingham Snow Hill	a		01 45									
Rowley Regis	a											
Cradley Heath	a											
Stourbridge Junction 2	a											
Kidderminster	a											

§ London Underground Limited (Central Line) also operate services between South Ruislip and West Ruislip at frequent intervals

A from 7 January until 24 March

B Runs until 31 December and then from 31 March

Table 115

Sundays
until 1 January

London - High Wycombe, Aylesbury, Banbury, Stratford-upon-Avon, Birmingham Snow Hill and Kidderminster

Network Diagram - see first Page of Table 114

		CH	CH	CH	CH	CH	CH	CH	CH	CH	CH	CH	CH	CH	CH	CH	CH	CH	CH	CH	CH	CH	CH
		◇							◇		◇		◇			◇			◇			◇	
		A	A	A	A																		
London Marylebone 10 ⊖	d	22p10	23p10	23p13	23p45	00 10	07 35	08 00	08 25	09 00	09 23		10 03	09 50	10 08	10 33	11 03	10 50	11 33	11 38		12 03	11 50
London Paddington 15 ⊖	d																						
Wembley Stadium	d		23p18	23p21	23p53	00 18	07 43	08 08		09 08				09 58				10 58					11 58
Sudbury & Harrow Road	d																						
Sudbury Hill Harrow	d																						
Northolt Park	d			23p26		00 23		08 13		09 13				10 03				11 03					12 03
South Ruislip § ⊖	d			23p30		00 27	07 50	08 17		09 17				10 07				11 07					12 07
West Ruislip 3 § ⊖	d			23p33		00 30		08 20		09 20				10 10				11 10					12 10
Denham	d			23p38		00 35	07 55	08 25		09 25				10 15				11 15					12 15
Denham Golf Club	d			23p40		00 37		08 27		09 27								11 17					
Gerrards Cross 1	d		23p31	23p43	00 06	00 41	08 00	08 31		09 30	09 40			10 19	10 26			11 21		11 56			12 19
Seer Green	d			23p48		00 45		08 35		09 35				10 24				11 25					12 24
Beaconsfield	d		23p37	23p51	00 12	00 48	08 06	08 38		09 37	09 46			10 27	10 32			11 28		12 02			12 27
High Wycombe 1	d		23p42	23p59	00 18	00 54	08 12	08 44	08 49	09 43	09 53		10 26	10 33	10 38		11 26	11 34		12 08		12 26	12 33
Saunderton	d			00 06		01 01		08 51		09 50				10 39				11 41					12 39
Princes Risborough 2	d		23p53	00 10	00 29	01 06	08 22	08 56	08 59	09 55	10 02		10 36	10 45	10 48		11 36	11 46		12 17		12 35	12 45
Monks Risborough	d			00 15		01 09		08 59		09 58				10 48				11 49					12 48
Little Kimble	d			00 17		01 13		09 03		10 02				10 52				11 53					12 52
Aylesbury	a			00 33		01 26		09 16		10 16				11 05				12 06					13 05
Haddenham & Thame Parkway	d		00 02		00 35		08 28		09 05		10 08		10 42		10 55		11 42			12 24		12 41	
Bicester North 3	d	22p52	00 14		00 49		08a44		09 16		10 19		10 53		11a10	11 16	11 53		12 16	12a40		12 51	
Kings Sutton	d				00 59				09 27				11 05									13 04	
Banbury	d	23p06	00a31		01a09				09 33		10 33		11 10			11 30	12 07		12 30			13 09	
Leamington Spa 8	d	23p25							09 51		10 51	11 20	11 29			11 48	12 25		12 48		13 20	13 28	
Warwick	d	23p29							09 55		10 55	11 24	11 33				12 29				13 24	13 32	
Warwick Parkway	d	23p32							09 58		10 59		11 36			11 54	12 33		12 53			13 35	
Hatton	d								10 03			11 31					12 37				13 31		
Claverdon	d																						
Bearley	d																						
Wilmcote	d											11 42									13 42		
Stratford-upon-Avon	a											11 54									13 54		
Lapworth	a								10 08								12 43						
Dorridge	a	23p42							10 13		11 08		11 45			12 03	12 46		13 02			13 44	
Solihull	a	23p49							10 18		11 13		11 51			12 09	12 53		13 07			13 49	
Birmingham Moor Street	a	00 01							10 25		11 20		11 59			12 21	13 01		13 20			13 58	
Birmingham Snow Hill ⛴	a								10 39		11 31		12 09				13 05					14 03	
Rowley Regis	a																						
Cradley Heath	a																						
Stourbridge Junction 2	a																						
Kidderminster	a																						

		CH	CH	CH	CH	CH	CH	CH	CH	CH	CH	CH	CH	CH	CH	CH	CH	CH	CH	CH	CH	CH	CH
				◇			◇	◇		◇		◇			◇								◇
London Marylebone 10 ⊖	d	12 33	12 38	13 03	12 50	13 33	13 36	14 00	14 03	14 33	14 36	15 00	15 03	15 33	15 36	16 00	16 03	16 33	16 36	17 00	17 03	17 33	17 36
London Paddington 15 ⊖	d																						
Wembley Stadium	d				12 58		13 44		14 11		14 44		15 11		15 44		16 11		16 44		17 11		17 44
Sudbury & Harrow Road	d																						
Sudbury Hill Harrow	d																						
Northolt Park	d				13 03				14 16				15 16				16 16				17 16		
South Ruislip § ⊖	d				13 07				14 20				15 20				16 20				17 20		
West Ruislip 3 § ⊖	d				13 10				14 23				15 23				16 23				17 23		
Denham	d				13 15				14 28				15 28				16 28				17 28		
Denham Golf Club	d				13 17								15 30								17 30		
Gerrards Cross 1	d		12 56		13 21		13 57	14 17	14 32		14 57	15 17	15 34		15 57	16 17	16 32		16 57	17 17	17 34		17 57
Seer Green	d				13 25				14 37				15 38				16 37				17 38		
Beaconsfield	d		13 02		13 28		14 03	14 23	14 40		15 03	15 23	15 41		16 03	16 23	16 40		17 03	17 23	17 41		18 03
High Wycombe 1	d		13 08	13 26	13 34		14 09	14 29	14 46		15 09	15 29	15 47		16 09	16 29	16 46		17 09	17 29	17 47		18 10
Saunderton	d				13 41				14 52				15 54				16 52				17 54		
Princes Risborough 2	d		13 18	13 36	13 46		14 18	14 39	14 57		15 18	15 39	15 59		16 18	16 39	16 57		17 18	17 39	17 59		18 19
Monks Risborough	d				13 49				15 01				16 02				17 01				18 02		
Little Kimble	d				13 53				15 04				16 06				17 04				18 06		
Aylesbury	a				14 06				15 18				16 19				17 18				18 19		
Haddenham & Thame Parkway	d		13 25	13 42			14 24	14 45			15 24	15 45			16 24	16 45			17 24	17 45			18 25
Bicester North 3	d	13 17	13a40	13 53		14 15	14 38	14 56		15 17	15a40	15 56		16 16	16 39	16 57		17 16	17a40	17 56		18 16	18 39
Kings Sutton	d						14 53								16 53								18 53
Banbury	d	13 38		14 08		14 35	15 00	15 10		15 31		16 10		16 30	17 00	17 11		17 30		18 11		18 30	19 00
Leamington Spa 8	d	13 56		14 25		14 52	15 20	15 28		15 49		16 28		16 49	17 20	17 28		17 47		18 29		18 49	19 20
Warwick	d			14 29			15 24	15 31				16 32			17 24	17 33				18 33			19 24
Warwick Parkway	d	14 02		14 33		14 59		15 35		15 54		16 36		16 54		17 36		17 53		18 36		18 54	
Hatton	d			14 37			15 31	15 39							17 31			17 57					19 30
Claverdon	d																						
Bearley	d																						
Wilmcote	d						15 42								17 42								19 42
Stratford-upon-Avon	a						15 54								17 54								19 54
Lapworth	a			14 43				15 45										18 03					
Dorridge	a	14 11		14 47		15 07		15 49		16 03		16 49		17 03		17 45		18 07		18 46		19 03	
Solihull	a	14 16		14 53		15 14		15 54		16 09		16 56		17 10		17 52		18 15		18 54		19 09	
Birmingham Moor Street	a	14 23		15 00		15 28		16 04		16 26		17 05		17 26		17 59		18 30		19 03		19 23	
Birmingham Snow Hill ⛴	a			15 05				16 12				17 14				18 08				19 13			
Rowley Regis	a																						
Cradley Heath	a																						
Stourbridge Junction 2	a																						
Kidderminster	a																						

§ London Underground Limited (Central Line) also operate services between South Ruislip and West Ruislip at frequent intervals

A not 11 December

Table 115

Sundays
until 1 January

London - High Wycombe, Aylesbury, Banbury, Stratford-upon-Avon, Birmingham Snow Hill and Kidderminster

Network Diagram - see first Page of Table 114

		CH		CH	CH	CH	CH	CH	CH ◇	CH	CH	CH		CH ◇	CH ◇	CH	CH	CH ◇	CH	CH	CH	CH		
London Marylebone [10] ⊖	d	18 00		18 03	18 33	18 36	19 00	19 03	19 33	19 36	20 00	20 03		20 33	21 00	21 03	21 33	22 00	22 03	22 45		23 45		
London Paddington [15] ⊖	d																							
Wembley Stadium	d			18 11		18 44		19 11		19 44		20 11				21 11			22 11	22 53		23 53		
Sudbury & Harrow Road	d																							
Sudbury Hill Harrow	d																							
Northolt Park	d			18 16				19 16				20 16				21 16			22 16	22 58		23 58		
South Ruislip § ⊖	d			18 20				19 20				20 20				21 20			22 20	23 02		00 03		
West Ruislip [3] § ⊖	d			18 23				19 23				20 23				21 23			22 23	23 05		00 06		
Denham	d			18 28				19 28				20 28				21 28			22 28	23 10		00 11		
Denham Golf Club	d							19 30								21 30						00 13		
Gerrards Cross [1]	d	18 17		18 32		18 57	19 18	19 34		19 57	20 17	20 32		20 50	21 17	21 34	21 51		22 32	23 14		00 13		
Seer Green	d			18 37				19 38				20 37				21 38			22 37	23 19		00 21		
Beaconsfield	d	18 23		18 40		19 03	19 24	19 41		20 03	20 23	20 40		20 56	21 23	21 41	21 57		22 40	23 22		00 24		
High Wycombe [1]	d	18 29		18 46		19 09	19 30	19 47		20 09	20 29	20 46		21 02	21 29	21 47	22 03		22 46	23 28		00 30		
Saunderton	d			18 52				19 54				20 52				21 54			22 52	23 34		00 37		
Princes Risborough [2]	d	18 39		18 57		19 18	19 39	19 59		20 18	20 39	20 57		21 12	21 39	21 59	22 12		22 57	23 39	23 48	00a44		
Monks Risborough	d			19 01				20 02				21 01				22 02			23 01		23 51			
Little Kimble	d			19 04				20 06				21 04				22 06			23 04		23 55			
Aylesbury	a			19 18				20 19				21 18				22 19			23 18		00 06			
Haddenham & Thame Parkway	d	18 45				19 24	19 45			20 24	20 45			21 18	21 45		22 19			23 46				
Bicester North [3]	d	18 56			19 15	19 37	19 56		20 17	20 38	20 57			21 29	21 56		22a35	22 41		23 59				
Kings Sutton	d									20 52										00 09				
Banbury	d	19 11			19 29	20a00	20 10		20 31	21a01	21 11			21 44	22 10			22 55		00a19				
Leamington Spa [8]	d	19 30			19 46		20 27		20 47		21 30			22 01	22 28			23 13						
Warwick	d	19 34					20 32				21 34				22 32			23 17						
Warwick Parkway	d	19 37			19 51		20 36		20 54		21 37			22 07	22 36			23 21						
Hatton	d														22 40									
Claverdon	d																							
Bearley	d																							
Wilmcote	d																							
Stratford-upon-Avon	a																							
Lapworth	a	19 45													22 46									
Dorridge	a	19 50			20 00		20 45		21 03		21 47			22 16	22 50			23 30						
Solihull	a	19 58			20 06		20 53		21 09		21 52			22 22	22 57			23 36						
Birmingham Moor Street	a	20 07			20 23		21 01		21 23		22 01			22 36	23 06			23 45						
Birmingham Snow Hill 🚢	a	20 15					21 11				22 10				23 15			23 53						
Rowley Regis	a																							
Cradley Heath	a																							
Stourbridge Junction [2]	a																							
Kidderminster	a																							

Sundays
8 January to 12 February

		CH 🚌	CH	CH	CH 🚌	CH	CH	CH 🚌	CH	CH		CH 🚌	CH	CH	CH 🚌	CH	CH	CH	CH 🚌	CH 🚌		CH	CH 🚌	CH	CH
London Marylebone [10] ⊖	d		23p10	23p13		23p45	00 10		07 35	08 00			08 33	09 00		09 38	09 50					10 08		10 38	10 50
London Paddington [15] ⊖	d																								
Wembley Stadium	d		23p18	23p21		23p53	00 18		07 43	08 08				09 08			09 58								10 58
Sudbury & Harrow Road	d																								
Sudbury Hill Harrow	d																								
Northolt Park	d			23p26			00 23			08 13				09 13			10 03								11 03
South Ruislip § ⊖	d			23p30			00 27		07 50	08 17				09 17			10 07								11 07
West Ruislip [3] § ⊖	d			23p33			00 30			08 20				09 20			10 10								11 10
Denham	d			23p38			00 35		07 55	08 25				09 25			10 15								11 15
Denham Golf Club	d			23p40			00 37			08 27				09 27											11 17
Gerrards Cross [1]	d		23p31	23p43		00 06	00 41		08 00	08 31			08 51	09 30		09 56	10 19					10 26		10 56	11 21
Seer Green	d			23p48			00 45			08 35				09 35			10 24								11 25
Beaconsfield	d		23p37	23p51		00 12	00 48		08 06	08 38			08 57	09 37		10 02	10 27					10 32		11 02	11 28
High Wycombe [1]	d		23p42	23p59		00 18	00 54		08 12	08 44			09 03	09 43		10 08	10 33					10 38		11 08	11 34
Saunderton	d			00 06			01 01			08 51				09 50			10 39								11 41
Princes Risborough [2]	d		23p53	00 10		00 29	01 06		08 22	08 56			09 12	09 55		10 17	10 45					10 48		11 17	11 46
Monks Risborough	d			00 15			01 09			08 59				09 58			10 48								11 49
Little Kimble	d			00 17			01 13			09 03				10 02			10 52								11 53
Aylesbury	a			00 33			01 26			09 16				10 16			11 05								12 06
Haddenham & Thame Parkway	d		00 02			00 35			08 28				09 19			10 24						10 55		11 24	
Bicester North [3]	d	23p10	00a17		00 25	00a51		01 00	08a44			08 50	09a35		09 40	10a40			10 45	10 45		11a10	11 15	11a40	
Kings Sutton	d																								
Banbury	d	23b35			00a55			01a30				09 20			10 10				11 15	11 15			11 45		
Leamington Spa [8]	d	00s15										09a55			10a45			11 20	11a50				12a20		
Warwick	d	00s25																11 24							
Warwick Parkway	d	00s35																							
Hatton	d																	11 31							
Claverdon	d																								
Bearley	d																								
Wilmcote	d																	11 42							
Stratford-upon-Avon	a																	11 54		11 55					
Lapworth	a																								
Dorridge	a	01s00																							
Solihull	a	01s20																							
Birmingham Moor Street	a																								
Birmingham Snow Hill 🚢	a	01 45																							
Rowley Regis	a																								
Cradley Heath	a																								
Stourbridge Junction [2]	a																								
Kidderminster	a																								

§ London Underground Limited (Central Line) also operate services between South Ruislip and West Ruislip at frequent intervals

b Previous night, stops to set down only

Table 115 | **Sundays**

8 January to 12 February

London - High Wycombe, Aylesbury, Banbury, Stratford-upon-Avon, Birmingham Snow Hill and Kidderminster

Network Diagram - see first Page of Table 114

		CH	CH	CH	CH	CH		CH	CH	CH	CH	CH	CH	CH	CH	CH		CH	CH	CH	CH	CH	CH	CH	CH
																		◇	◇		◇		◇		
		🚌		🚌					🚌	🚌		🚌													
London Marylebone [10] ⊖	d		11 08		11 38	11 50					12 08		12 38	12 50	13 08	13 33		13 36	14 00	14 03	14 33	14 36	15 00	15 03	15 33
London Paddington [15] ⊖	d																								
Wembley Stadium	d					11 58								12 58				13 44		14 11		14 44		15 11	
Sudbury & Harrow Road	d																								
Sudbury Hill Harrow	d																								
Northolt Park	d					12 03								13 03						14 16				15 16	
South Ruislip § ⊖	d					12 07								13 07						14 20				15 20	
West Ruislip [3] § ⊖	d					12 10								13 10						14 23				15 23	
Denham	d					12 15								13 15						14 28				15 28	
Denham Golf Club	d													13 17										15 30	
Gerrards Cross [1]	d		11 26		11 56	12 19					12 26		12 56	13 21	13 26			13 57	14 17	14 32		14 57	15 17	15 34	
Seer Green	d					12 24								13 25						14 37				15 38	
Beaconsfield	d		11 32		12 02	12 27					12 32		13 02	13 28	13 32			14 03	14 23	14 40		15 03	15 23	15 41	
High Wycombe [1]	d		11 38		12 08	12 33					12 38		13 08	13 34	13 38			14 09	14 29	14 46		15 09	15 29	15 47	
Saunderton	d					12 39								13 41						14 52				15 54	
Princes Risborough [2]	d		11 49		12 17	12 45					12 48		13 18	13 46	13 49			14 18	14 39	14 57		15 18	15 39	15 59	
Monks Risborough	d					12 48								13 49						15 01				16 02	
Little Kimble	d					12 52								13 53						15 04				16 06	
Aylesbury	a					13 05								14 06						15 18				16 19	
Haddenham & Thame Parkway	d		11 55		12 24						12 55		13 25		13 55			14 24	14 45			15 24	15 45		
Bicester North [3]	d	11 45	12a10	12 15	12a40				12 45	12 45	13a10	13 15	13a40		14a10	14 15		14 38	14 56		15 17	15a40	15 56		16 16
Kings Sutton	d																	14 53							
Banbury	d	12 15		12 45					13 15	13 15		13 45				14 35		15 00	15 10		15 31		16 10		16 30
Leamington Spa [8]	d	12a50		13a20				13 20	13a50			14a20				14 52		15 20	15 28		15 49		16 28		16 49
Warwick	d							13 24										15 24	15 31				16 32		
Warwick Parkway	d															14 59			15 35		15 54		16 36		16 54
Hatton	d							13 31										15 31	15 39						
Claverdon	d																								
Bearley	d																								
Wilmcote	d							13 42										15 42							
Stratford-upon-Avon	a							13 54		13 55								15 54							
Lapworth	a																		15 45						
Dorridge	a															15 07			15 49		16 03		16 49		17 03
Solihull	a															15 14			15 54		16 09		16 56		17 10
Birmingham Moor Street	a															15 28			16 04		16 26		17 05		17 26
Birmingham Snow Hill	a																		16 12				17 14		
Rowley Regis	a																								
Cradley Heath	a																								
Stourbridge Junction [2]	a																								
Kidderminster	a																								

		CH		CH	CH	CH	CH	CH	CH	CH	CH	CH		CH	CH	CH	CH	CH	CH	CH	CH	CH		CH	CH
		◇									◇								◇					◇	◇
London Marylebone [10] ⊖	d	15 36		16 00	16 03	16 33	16 36	17 00	17 03	17 33	17 36	18 00		18 03	18 33	18 36	19 00	19 03	19 33	19 36	20 00	20 03		20 33	21 00
London Paddington [15] ⊖	d																								
Wembley Stadium	d	15 44			16 11		16 44		17 11		17 44			18 11		18 44		19 11		19 44		20 11			
Sudbury & Harrow Road	d																								
Sudbury Hill Harrow	d																								
Northolt Park	d				16 16				17 16					18 16				19 16				20 16			
South Ruislip § ⊖	d				16 20				17 20					18 20				19 20				20 20			
West Ruislip [3] § ⊖	d				16 23				17 23					18 23				19 23				20 23			
Denham	d				16 28				17 28					18 28				19 28				20 28			
Denham Golf Club	d								17 30									19 30							
Gerrards Cross [1]	d	15 57		16 17	16 32		16 57	17 17	17 34		17 57	18 17		18 32		18 57	19 18	19 34		19 57	20 17	20 32		20 50	21 17
Seer Green	d				16 37				17 38					18 37				19 38				20 37			
Beaconsfield	d	16 03		16 23	16 40		17 03	17 23	17 41		18 03	18 23		18 40		19 03	19 24	19 41		20 03	20 23	20 40		20 56	21 23
High Wycombe [1]	d	16 09		16 29	16 46		17 09	17 29	17 47		18 10	18 29		18 46		19 09	19 30	19 47		20 09	20 29	20 46		21 02	21 29
Saunderton	d				16 52				17 54					18 52				19 54				20 52			
Princes Risborough [2]	d	16 18		16 39	16 57		17 18	17 39	17 59		18 19	18 39		18 57		19 18	19 39	19 59		20 18	20 39	20 57		21 12	21 39
Monks Risborough	d				17 01				18 02					19 01				20 02				21 01			
Little Kimble	d				17 04				18 06					19 04				20 06				21 04			
Aylesbury	a				17 18				18 19					19 18				20 19				21 18			
Haddenham & Thame Parkway	d	16 24		16 45			17 24	17 45			18 25	18 45				19 24	19 45			20 24	20 45			21 18	21 45
Bicester North [3]	d	16 39		16 57		17 16	17a40	17 56		18 16	18 39	18 56			19 15	19 37	19 56		20 17	20 38	20 57			21 29	21 56
Kings Sutton	d	16 53									18 53									20 52					
Banbury	d	17 00		17 11		17 30		18 11		18 30	19 00	19 11			19 29	20a00	20 10		20 31	21a01	21 11			21 44	22 10
Leamington Spa [8]	d	17 20		17 28		17 47		18 29		18 49	19 20	19 30			19 46		20 27		20 47		21 30			22 01	22 28
Warwick	d	17 24		17 33				18 33			19 24	19 34					20 32				21 34				22 32
Warwick Parkway	d			17 36		17 53		18 36		18 54		19 37			19 51		20 36		20 54		21 37			22 07	22 36
Hatton	d	17 31				17 57					19 30														22 40
Claverdon	d																								
Bearley	d																								
Wilmcote	d	17 42									19 42														
Stratford-upon-Avon	a	17 54									19 54														
Lapworth	a					18 03						19 45													22 46
Dorridge	a			17 45		18 07		18 46		19 03		19 50			20 00		20 45		21 03		21 47			22 16	22 50
Solihull	a			17 52		18 15		18 54		19 09		19 58			20 06		20 53		21 09		21 52			22 22	22 57
Birmingham Moor Street	a			17 59		18 30		19 03		19 23		20 07			20 23		21 01		21 23		22 01			22 36	23 06
Birmingham Snow Hill	a			18 08				19 13				20 15					21 11				22 10				23 15
Rowley Regis	a																								
Cradley Heath	a																								
Stourbridge Junction [2]	a																								
Kidderminster	a																								

§ London Underground Limited (Central Line) also operate services between South Ruislip and West Ruislip at frequent intervals

Table 115

Sundays

8 January to 12 February

London - High Wycombe, Aylesbury, Banbury, Stratford-upon-Avon, Birmingham Snow Hill and Kidderminster

Network Diagram - see first Page of Table 114

		CH	CH	CH ◇	CH	CH	CH	CH
London Marylebone [10] ⊖	d	21 03	21 33	22 00	22 03	22 45		23 45
London Paddington [15] ⊖	d							
Wembley Stadium	d	21 11			22 11	22 53		23 53
Sudbury & Harrow Road	d							
Sudbury Hill Harrow	d							
Northolt Park	d	21 16			22 16	22 58		23 58
South Ruislip § ⊖	d	21 20			22 20	23 02		00 03
West Ruislip [3] § ⊖	d	21 23			22 23	23 05		00 06
Denham	d	21 28			22 28	23 10		00 11
Denham Golf Club	d	21 30						00 13
Gerrards Cross [1]	d	21 34	21 51		22 32	23 14		00 17
Seer Green	d	21 38			22 37	23 19		00 21
Beaconsfield	d	21 41	21 57		22 40	23 22		00 24
High Wycombe [1]	d	21 47	22 03		22 46	23 28		00 30
Saunderton	d	21 54			22 52	23 34		00 37
Princes Risborough [2]	d	21 59	22 12		22 57	23 39	23 48	00a44
Monks Risborough	d	22 02			23 01		23 51	
Little Kimble	d	22 06			23 04		23 55	
Aylesbury	a	22 19			23 18		00 06	
Haddenham & Thame Parkway	d		22 19			23 46		
Bicester North [3]	d		22a35	22 41		23 59		
Kings Sutton	d					00 09		
Banbury	d			22 55		00a19		
Leamington Spa [8]	d			23 13				
Warwick	d			23 17				
Warwick Parkway	d			23 21				
Hatton	d							
Claverdon	d							
Bearley	d							
Wilmcote	d							
Stratford-upon-Avon	a							
Lapworth	a							
Dorridge	a			23 30				
Solihull	a			23 36				
Birmingham Moor Street	a			23 45				
Birmingham Snow Hill ⛴	a			23 53				
Rowley Regis	a							
Cradley Heath	a							
Stourbridge Junction [2]	a							
Kidderminster	a							

Sundays

19 February to 25 March

		CH 🚌	CH	CH	CH 🚌	CH	CH	CH 🚌	CH	CH	CH 🚌	CH	CH	CH 🚌	CH	CH	CH	CH 🚌	CH 🚌	CH	CH 🚌	CH	CH
London Marylebone [10] ⊖	d		23p10	23p13		23p45	00 10		07 35	08 00		08 33	09 00		09 38	09 50				10 08		10 38	10 50
London Paddington [15] ⊖	d																						
Wembley Stadium	d		23p18	23p21		23p53	00 18		07 43	08 08			09 08			09 58							10 58
Sudbury & Harrow Road	d																						
Sudbury Hill Harrow	d																						
Northolt Park	d			23p26			00 23			08 13			09 13			10 03							11 03
South Ruislip § ⊖	d			23p30			00 27		07 50	08 17			09 17			10 07							11 07
West Ruislip [3] § ⊖	d			23p33			00 30			08 20			09 20			10 10							11 10
Denham	d			23p38			00 35		07 55	08 25			09 25			10 15							11 15
Denham Golf Club	d			23p40			00 37			08 27			09 27										11 17
Gerrards Cross [1]	d		23p31	23p43		00 06	00 41		08 00	08 31		08 51	09 30		09 56	10 19				10 26		10 56	11 21
Seer Green	d			23p48			00 45			08 35			09 35			10 24							11 25
Beaconsfield	d		23p37	23p51		00 12	00 48		08 06	08 38		08 57	09 37		10 02	10 27				10 32		11 02	11 28
High Wycombe [1]	d		23p42	23p59		00 18	00 54		08 12	08 44		09 03	09 43		10 08	10 33				10 38		11 08	11 34
Saunderton	d			00 06			01 01			08 51			09 50			10 39							11 41
Princes Risborough [2]	d		23p53	00 10		00 29	01 06		08 22	08 56		09 12	09 55		10 17	10 45				10 48		11 17	11 46
Monks Risborough	d			00 15			01 09			08 59			09 58			10 48							11 49
Little Kimble	d			00 17			01 13			09 03			10 02			10 52							11 53
Aylesbury	a			00 33			01 26			09 16			10 16			11 05							12 06
Haddenham & Thame Parkway	d		00 02			00 35			08 28			09 19			10 24					10 55		11 24	
Bicester North [3]	d	23p10	00a17		00 25	00a51		01 00	08a44		08 50	09a35		09 40	10a40			10 45	10 45	11a10	11 15	11a40	
Kings Sutton	d																						
Banbury	d	23b35			00a55			01a30			09 20			10 10				11 15	11 15		11 45		
Leamington Spa [8]	d	00s15									09a55			10a45			11 20	11a50			12a20		
Warwick	d	00s25															11 24						
Warwick Parkway	d	00s35																					
Hatton	d																11 31						
Claverdon	d																						
Bearley	d																						
Wilmcote	d																11 42						
Stratford-upon-Avon	a																11 54		11 55				
Lapworth	a																						
Dorridge	a	01s00																					
Solihull	a	01s20																					
Birmingham Moor Street	a																						
Birmingham Snow Hill ⛴	a	01 45																					
Rowley Regis	a																						
Cradley Heath	a																						
Stourbridge Junction [2]	a																						
Kidderminster	a																						

§ London Underground Limited (Central Line) also operate services between South Ruislip and West Ruislip at frequent intervals

b Previous night, stops to set down only

Table 115

Sundays

19 February to 25 March

London - High Wycombe, Aylesbury, Banbury, Stratford-upon-Avon, Birmingham Snow Hill and Kidderminster

Network Diagram - see first Page of Table 114

		CH	CH	CH	CH	CH		CH	CH	CH	CH	CH	CH	CH	CH	CH		CH	CH	CH	CH	CH	CH	CH	CH
																		◇	◇		◇		◇		
		🚌		🚌					🚌	🚌		🚌													
London Marylebone 10 ⊖	d		11 08		11 38	11 50					12 08		12 38	12 50	13 08	13 33		13 36	14 00	14 03	14 33	14 36	15 00	15 03	15 33
London Paddington 15 ⊖	d																								
Wembley Stadium	d					11 58								12 58				13 44		14 11		14 44		15 11	
Sudbury & Harrow Road	d																								
Sudbury Hill Harrow	d																								
Northolt Park	d					12 03								13 03						14 16				15 16	
South Ruislip § ⊖	d					12 07								13 07						14 20				15 20	
West Ruislip 3 § ⊖	d					12 10								13 10						14 23				15 23	
Denham	d					12 15								13 15						14 28				15 28	
Denham Golf Club	d													13 17										15 30	
Gerrards Cross 1	d		11 26		11 56	12 19					12 26		12 56	13 21	13 26			13 57	14 17	14 32		14 57	15 17	15 34	
Seer Green	d					12 24								13 25						14 37				15 38	
Beaconsfield	d		11 32		12 02	12 27					12 32		13 02	13 28	13 32			14 03	14 23	14 40		15 03	15 23	15 41	
High Wycombe 1	d		11 38		12 08	12 33					12 38		13 08	13 34	13 38			14 09	14 29	14 46		15 09	15 29	15 47	
Saunderton	d					12 39								13 41						14 52				15 54	
Princes Risborough 2	d		11 49		12 17	12 45					12 48		13 18	13 46	13 49			14 18	14 39	14 57		15 18	15 39	15 59	
Monks Risborough	d					12 48								13 49						15 01				16 02	
Little Kimble	d					12 52								13 53						15 04				16 06	
Aylesbury	a					13 05								14 06						15 18				16 19	
Haddenham & Thame Parkway	d		11 55		12 24						12 55		13 25		13 55			14 24	14 45			15 24	15 45		
Bicester North 3	d	11 45	12a10	12 15	12a40				12 45	12 45	13a10	13 15	13a40		14a10	14 15		14 38	14 56		15 17	15a40	15 56		16 16
Kings Sutton	d																	14 53							
Banbury	d	12 15		12 45					13 15	13 15		13 45				14 35		15 00	15 10		15 31		16 10		16 30
Leamington Spa 8	d	12a50		13a20				13 20	13a50			14a20				14 52		15 20	15 28		15 49		16 28		16 49
Warwick	d							13 24										15 24	15 31				16 32		
Warwick Parkway	d															14 59			15 35		15 54		16 36		16 54
Hatton	d							13 31										15 31	15 39						
Claverdon	d																								
Bearley	d																								
Wilmcote	d							13 42										15 42							
Stratford-upon-Avon	a							13 54		13 55								15 54							
Lapworth	a																		15 45						
Dorridge	a															15 07			15 49		16 03		16 49		17 03
Solihull	a															15 14			15 54		16 09		16 56		17 10
Birmingham Moor Street	a															15 28			16 04		16 26		17 05		17 26
Birmingham Snow Hill 🚊	a																		16 12				17 14		
Rowley Regis	a																								
Cradley Heath	a																								
Stourbridge Junction 2	a																								
Kidderminster	a																								

		CH		CH	CH	CH	CH	CH	CH	CH	CH	CH		CH	CH	CH	CH	CH	CH	CH	CH	CH		CH	CH
		◇									◇								◇					◇	◇
London Marylebone 10 ⊖	d	15 36		16 00	16 03	16 33	16 36	17 00	17 03	17 33	17 36	18 00		18 03	18 33	18 36	19 00	19 03	19 33	19 36	20 00	20 03		20 33	21 00
London Paddington 15 ⊖	d																								
Wembley Stadium	d	15 44			16 11		16 44		17 11		17 44			18 11		18 44		19 11		19 44		20 11			
Sudbury & Harrow Road	d																								
Sudbury Hill Harrow	d																								
Northolt Park	d				16 16				17 16					18 16				19 16				20 16			
South Ruislip § ⊖	d				16 20				17 20					18 20				19 20				20 20			
West Ruislip 3 § ⊖	d				16 23				17 23					18 23				19 23				20 23			
Denham	d				16 28				17 28					18 28				19 28				20 28			
Denham Golf Club	d								17 30									19 30							
Gerrards Cross 1	d	15 57		16 17	16 32		16 57	17 17	17 34		17 57	18 17		18 32		18 57	19 18	19 34		19 57	20 17	20 32		20 50	21 17
Seer Green	d				16 37				17 38					18 37				19 38				20 37			
Beaconsfield	d	16 03		16 23	16 40		17 03	17 23	17 41		18 03	18 23		18 40		19 03	19 24	19 41		20 03	20 23	20 40		20 56	21 23
High Wycombe 1	d	16 09		16 29	16 46		17 09	17 29	17 47		18 10	18 29		18 46		19 09	19 30	19 47		20 09	20 29	20 46		21 02	21 29
Saunderton	d				16 52				17 54					18 52				19 54				20 52			
Princes Risborough 2	d	16 18		16 39	16 57		17 18	17 39	17 59		18 19	18 39		18 57		19 18	19 39	19 59		20 18	20 39	20 57		21 12	21 39
Monks Risborough	d				17 01				18 02					19 01				20 02				21 01			
Little Kimble	d				17 04				18 06					19 04				20 06				21 04			
Aylesbury	a				17 18				18 19					19 18				20 19				21 18			
Haddenham & Thame Parkway	d	16 24		16 45			17 24	17 45			18 25	18 45				19 24	19 45			20 24	20 45			21 18	21 45
Bicester North 3	d	16 39		16 57		17 16	17a40	17 56		18 16	18 39	18 56			19 15	19 37	19 56		20 17	20 38	20 57			21 29	21 56
Kings Sutton	d	16 53									18 53									20 52					
Banbury	d	17 00		17 11		17 30		18 11		18 30	19 00	19 11			19 29	20a00	20 10		20 31	21a01	21 11			21 44	22 10
Leamington Spa 8	d	17 20		17 28		17 47		18 29		18 49	19 20	19 30			19 46		20 27		20 47		21 30			22 01	22 28
Warwick	d	17 24		17 33				18 33			19 24	19 34					20 32				21 34				22 32
Warwick Parkway	d			17 36		17 53		18 36		18 54		19 37			19 51		20 36		20 54		21 37			22 07	22 36
Hatton	d	17 31				17 57					19 30														22 40
Claverdon	d																								
Bearley	d																								
Wilmcote	d	17 42									19 42														
Stratford-upon-Avon	a	17 54									19 54														
Lapworth	a					18 03						19 45													22 46
Dorridge	a			17 45		18 07		18 46		19 03		19 50			20 00		20 45		21 03		21 47			22 16	22 50
Solihull	a			17 52		18 15		18 54		19 09		19 58			20 06		20 53		21 09		21 52			22 22	22 57
Birmingham Moor Street	a			17 59		18 30		19 03		19 23		20 07			20 23		21 01		21 23		22 01			22 36	23 06
Birmingham Snow Hill 🚊	a			18 08				19 13				20 15					21 11				22 10				23 15
Rowley Regis	a																								
Cradley Heath	a																								
Stourbridge Junction 2	a																								
Kidderminster	a																								

§ London Underground Limited (Central Line) also operate services between South Ruislip and West Ruislip at frequent intervals

Table 115

Sundays

19 February to 25 March

London - High Wycombe, Aylesbury, Banbury, Stratford-upon-Avon, Birmingham Snow Hill and Kidderminster

Network Diagram - see first Page of Table 114

		CH	CH	CH	CH	CH	CH	CH
				◇				
London Marylebone 10 ⊖	d	21 03	21 33	22 00	22 03	22 45		23 45
London Paddington 15 ⊖	d							
Wembley Stadium	d	21 11			22 11	22 53		23 53
Sudbury & Harrow Road	d							
Sudbury Hill Harrow	d							
Northolt Park	d	21 16			22 16	22 58		23 58
South Ruislip § ⊖	d	21 20			22 20	23 02		00 03
West Ruislip 3 § ⊖	d	21 23			22 23	23 05		00 06
Denham	d	21 28			22 28	23 10		00 11
Denham Golf Club	d	21 30						00 13
Gerrards Cross 1	d	21 34	21 51		22 32	23 14		00 17
Seer Green	d	21 38			22 37	23 19		00 21
Beaconsfield	d	21 41	21 57		22 40	23 22		00 24
High Wycombe 1	d	21 47	22 03		22 46	23 28		00 30
Saunderton	d	21 54			22 52	23 34		00 37
Princes Risborough 2	d	21 59	22 12		22 57	23 39	23 48	00a44
Monks Risborough	d	22 02			23 01		23 51	
Little Kimble	d	22 06			23 04		23 55	
Aylesbury	a	22 19			23 18		00 06	
Haddenham & Thame Parkway	d		22 19			23 46		
Bicester North 3	d		22a35	22 41		23 59		
Kings Sutton	d					00 09		
Banbury	d			22 55		00a19		
Leamington Spa 8	d			23 13				
Warwick	d			23 17				
Warwick Parkway	d			23 21				
Hatton	d							
Claverdon	d							
Bearley	d							
Wilmcote	d							
Stratford-upon-Avon	a							
Lapworth	a							
Dorridge	a			23 30				
Solihull	a			23 36				
Birmingham Moor Street	a			23 45				
Birmingham Snow Hill	a			23 53				
Rowley Regis	a							
Cradley Heath	a							
Stourbridge Junction 2	a							
Kidderminster	a							

Sundays

from 1 April

		CH	CH	CH	CH	CH	CH	CH	CH	CH	CH	CH	CH	CH	CH	CH	CH	CH	CH	CH	CH	CH	CH
		◇							◇		◇		◇			◇			◇			◇	
London Marylebone 10 ⊖	d	22p10	23p10	23p13	23p45	00 10	07 35	08 00	08 25	09 00	09 23		10 03	09 50	10 08	10 33	11 03	10 50	11 33	11 38		12 03	11 50
London Paddington 15 ⊖	d																						
Wembley Stadium	d		23p18	23p21	23p53	00 18	07 43	08 08		09 08				09 58				10 58					11 58
Sudbury & Harrow Road	d																						
Sudbury Hill Harrow	d																						
Northolt Park	d			23p26		00 23		08 13		09 13				10 03				11 03					12 03
South Ruislip § ⊖	d			23p30		00 27	07 50	08 17		09 17				10 07				11 07					12 07
West Ruislip 3 § ⊖	d			23p33		00 30		08 20		09 20				10 10				11 10					12 10
Denham	d			23p38		00 35	07 55	08 25		09 25				10 15				11 15					12 15
Denham Golf Club	d			23p40		00 37		08 27		09 27								11 17					
Gerrards Cross 1	d		23p31	23p43	00 06	00 41	08 00	08 31		09 30	09 40			10 19	10 26			11 21		11 56			12 19
Seer Green	d			23p48		00 45		08 35		09 35				10 24				11 25					12 24
Beaconsfield	d		23p37	23p51	00 12	00 48	08 06	08 38		09 37	09 46			10 27	10 32			11 28		12 02			12 27
High Wycombe 1	d		23p42	23p59	00 18	00 54	08 12	08 44	08 49	09 43	09 53		10 26	10 33	10 38		11 26	11 34		12 08		12 26	12 33
Saunderton	d			00 06		01 01		08 51		09 50				10 39				11 41					12 39
Princes Risborough 2	d		23p53	00 10	00 29	01 06	08 22	08 56	08 59	09 55	10 02		10 36	10 45	10 48		11 36	11 46		12 17		12 35	12 45
Monks Risborough	d			00 15		01 09		08 59		09 58				10 48				11 49					12 48
Little Kimble	d			00 17		01 13		09 03		10 02				10 52				11 53					12 52
Aylesbury	a			00 33		01 26		09 16		10 16				11 05				12 06					13 05
Haddenham & Thame Parkway	d		00 02		00 35		08 28		09 05		10 08		10 42		10 55		11 42			12 24		12 41	
Bicester North 3	d	22p52	00 14		00 49		08a44		09 16		10 19		10 53		11a10	11 16	11 53		12 16	12a40		12 51	
Kings Sutton	d				00 59				09 27				11 05									13 04	
Banbury	d	23p06	00a31		01a09				09 33		10 33		11 10			11 30	12 07		12 30			13 09	
Leamington Spa 8	d	23p25							09 51		10 51	11 20	11 29			11 48	12 25		12 48		13 20	13 28	
Warwick	d	23p29							09 55		10 55	11 24	11 33				12 29				13 24	13 32	
Warwick Parkway	d	23p32							09 58		10 59		11 36			11 54	12 33		12 53			13 35	
Hatton	d								10 03			11 31					12 37				13 31		
Claverdon	d																						
Bearley	d																						
Wilmcote	d											11 42									13 42		
Stratford-upon-Avon	a											11 54									13 54		
Lapworth	a								10 08								12 43						
Dorridge	a	23p42							10 13		11 08		11 45			12 03	12 46		13 02			13 44	
Solihull	a	23p49							10 18		11 13		11 51			12 09	12 53		13 07			13 49	
Birmingham Moor Street	a	00 01							10 25		11 20		11 59			12 19	13 01		13 16			13 58	
Birmingham Snow Hill	a								10 39		11 31		12 09				13 05					14 03	
Rowley Regis	a																						
Cradley Heath	a																						
Stourbridge Junction 2	a																						
Kidderminster	a																						

§ London Underground Limited (Central Line) also operate services between South Ruislip and West Ruislip at frequent intervals

Table 115

Sundays
from 1 April

London - High Wycombe, Aylesbury, Banbury, Stratford-upon-Avon, Birmingham Snow Hill and Kidderminster

Network Diagram - see first Page of Table 114

		CH	CH	CH	CH	CH		CH	CH	CH	CH	CH	CH	CH	CH	CH		CH	CH	CH	CH	CH	CH	CH	CH
				◇				◇	◇		◇		◇			◇									◇
London Marylebone 10 ⊖	d	12 33	12 38	13 03	12 50	13 33		13 36	14 00	14 03	14 33	14 36	15 00	15 03	15 33	15 36		16 00	16 03	16 33	16 36	17 00	17 03	17 33	17 36
London Paddington 15 ⊖	d																								
Wembley Stadium	d				12 58			13 44		14 11		14 44		15 11		15 44			16 11		16 44		17 11		17 44
Sudbury & Harrow Road	d																								
Sudbury Hill Harrow	d																								
Northolt Park	d				13 03					14 16				15 16					16 16				17 16		
South Ruislip § ⊖	d				13 07					14 20				15 20					16 20				17 20		
West Ruislip 3 § ⊖	d				13 10					14 23				15 23					16 23				17 23		
Denham	d				13 15					14 28				15 28					16 28				17 28		
Denham Golf Club	d				13 17									15 30									17 30		
Gerrards Cross 1	d		12 56		13 21			13 57	14 17	14 32		14 57	15 17	15 34		15 57		16 17	16 32		16 57	17 17	17 34		17 57
Seer Green	d				13 25					14 37				15 38					16 37				17 38		
Beaconsfield	d		13 02		13 28			14 03	14 23	14 40		15 03	15 23	15 41		16 03		16 23	16 40		17 03	17 23	17 41		18 03
High Wycombe 1	d		13 08	13 26	13 34			14 09	14 29	14 46		15 09	15 29	15 47		16 09		16 29	16 46		17 09	17 29	17 47		18 10
Saunderton	d				13 41					14 52				15 54					16 52				17 54		
Princes Risborough 2	d		13 18	13 36	13 46			14 18	14 39	14 57		15 18	15 39	15 59		16 18		16 39	16 57		17 18	17 39	17 59		18 19
Monks Risborough	d				13 49					15 01				16 02					17 01				18 02		
Little Kimble	d				13 53					15 04				16 06					17 04				18 06		
Aylesbury	a				14 06					15 18				16 19					17 18				18 19		
Haddenham & Thame Parkway	d		13 25	13 42				14 24	14 45			15 24	15 45			16 24		16 45			17 24	17 45			18 25
Bicester North 3	d	13 17	13a40	13 53		14 15		14 38	14 56		15 17	15a40	15 56		16 16	16 39		16 57		17 16	17a40	17 56		18 16	18 39
Kings Sutton	d							14 53								16 53									18 53
Banbury	d	13 38		14 08		14 35		15 00	15 10		15 31		16 10		16 30	17 00		17 11		17 30		18 11		18 30	19 00
Leamington Spa 8	d	13 56		14 25		14 52		15 20	15 28		15 49		16 28		16 49	17 20		17 28		17 47		18 29		18 49	19 20
Warwick	d			14 29				15 24	15 31				16 32			17 24		17 33				18 33			19 24
Warwick Parkway	d	14 02		14 33		14 59			15 35		15 54		16 36		16 54			17 36		17 53		18 36		18 54	
Hatton	d			14 37				15 31	15 39							17 31				17 57					19 30
Claverdon	d																								
Bearley	d																								
Wilmcote	d							15 42								17 42									19 42
Stratford-upon-Avon	a							15 54								17 54									19 54
Lapworth	a			14 43					15 45											18 03					
Dorridge	a	14 11		14 47		15 07			15 49		16 03		16 49		17 03			17 45		18 07		18 46		19 03	
Solihull	a	14 16		14 53		15 14			15 54		16 09		16 56		17 10			17 52		18 15		18 54		19 09	
Birmingham Moor Street	a	14 23		15 00		15 28			16 04		16 26		17 05		17 26			17 59		18 30		19 03		19 23	
Birmingham Snow Hill	a			15 05					16 12				17 14					18 08				19 13			
Rowley Regis	a																								
Cradley Heath	a																								
Stourbridge Junction 2	a																								
Kidderminster	a																								

		CH		CH	CH	CH	CH	CH	CH	CH	CH	CH		CH	CH	CH	CH	CH	CH	CH	CH	CH			
									◇					◇	◇			◇							
London Marylebone 10 ⊖	d	18 00		18 03	18 33	18 36	19 00	19 03	19 33	19 36	20 00	20 03		20 33	21 00	21 03	21 33	22 00	22 03	22 45		23 45			
London Paddington 15 ⊖	d																								
Wembley Stadium	d			18 11		18 44		19 11		19 44		20 11				21 11			22 11	22 53		23 53			
Sudbury & Harrow Road	d																								
Sudbury Hill Harrow	d																								
Northolt Park	d			18 16				19 16				20 16				21 16			22 16	22 58		23 58			
South Ruislip § ⊖	d			18 20				19 20				20 20				21 20			22 20	23 02		00 03			
West Ruislip 3 § ⊖	d			18 23				19 23				20 23				21 23			22 23	23 05		00 06			
Denham	d			18 28				19 28				20 28				21 28			22 28	23 10		00 11			
Denham Golf Club	d							19 30								21 30						00 13			
Gerrards Cross 1	d	18 17		18 32		18 57	19 18	19 34		19 57	20 17	20 32		20 50	21 17	21 34	21 51		22 32	23 14		00 17			
Seer Green	d			18 37				19 38				20 37				21 38			22 37	23 19		00 21			
Beaconsfield	d	18 23		18 40		19 03	19 24	19 41		20 03	20 23	20 40		20 56	21 23	21 41	21 57		22 40	23 22		00 24			
High Wycombe 1	d	18 29		18 46		19 09	19 30	19 47		20 09	20 29	20 46		21 02	21 29	21 47	22 03		22 46	23 28		00 30			
Saunderton	d			18 52				19 54				20 52				21 54			22 52	23 34		00 37			
Princes Risborough 2	d	18 39		18 57		19 18	19 39	19 59		20 18	20 39	20 57		21 12	21 39	21 59	22 12		22 57	23 39	23 48	00a44			
Monks Risborough	d			19 01				20 02				21 01				22 02			23 01		23 51				
Little Kimble	d			19 04				20 06				21 04				22 06			23 04		23 55				
Aylesbury	a			19 18				20 19				21 18				22 19			23 18		00 06				
Haddenham & Thame Parkway	d	18 45				19 24	19 45			20 24	20 45			21 18	21 45		22 19			23 46					
Bicester North 3	d	18 56			19 15	19 37	19 56		20 17	20 38	20 57			21 29	21 56		22a35	22 41		23 59					
Kings Sutton	d									20 52										00 09					
Banbury	d	19 11			19 29	20a00	20 10		20 31	21a01	21 11			21 44	22 10			22 55		00a19					
Leamington Spa 8	d	19 30			19 46		20 27		20 47		21 30			22 01	22 28			23 13							
Warwick	d	19 34					20 32				21 34				22 32			23 17							
Warwick Parkway	d	19 37			19 51		20 36		20 54		21 37			22 07	22 36			23 21							
Hatton	d														22 40										
Claverdon	d																								
Bearley	d																								
Wilmcote	d																								
Stratford-upon-Avon	a																								
Lapworth	a	19 45													22 46										
Dorridge	a	19 50			20 00		20 45		21 03		21 47			22 16	22 50			23 30							
Solihull	a	19 58			20 06		20 53		21 09		21 52			22 22	22 57			23 36							
Birmingham Moor Street	a	20 07			20 23		21 01		21 23		22 01			22 36	23 06			23 45							
Birmingham Snow Hill	a	20 15					21 11				22 10				23 15			23 53							
Rowley Regis	a																								
Cradley Heath	a																								
Stourbridge Junction 2	a																								
Kidderminster	a																								

§ London Underground Limited (Central Line) also operate services between South Ruislip and West Ruislip at frequent intervals

Table 115

Mondays to Fridays

Kidderminster, Birmingham Snow Hill, Stratford-upon-Avon, Banbury, Aylesbury and High Wycombe - London

Network Diagram - see first Page of Table 114

Miles	Miles	Miles			CH MX	CH MX	CH	CH	CH	CH	CH	CH	CH		CH	CH	CH	CH ◇	CH	CH	CH	CH	CH		CH
—	—	—	**Kidderminster**	d																					
—	—	—	**Stourbridge Junction** 2	d																					
—	—	—	Cradley Heath	d																					
—	—	—	Rowley Regis	d																					
0	—	—	**Birmingham Snow Hill**	d																					
0¾	—	—	**Birmingham Moor Street**	d														05 46							
7¼	—	—	Solihull	d														05 54							
10½	—	—	Dorridge	d														05 59							
13	—	—	Lapworth	d																					
—	—	0	**Stratford-upon-Avon**	d															06 10						
—	—	2¾	Wilmcote	d															06 16						
—	—	4¼	Bearley	d															06 20						
—	—	7¼	Claverdon	d															06 26						
17¼	—	9¼	Hatton	d															06 31						
20	—	12	Warwick Parkway	d									05 40					06 09							
21¼	—	13¼	Warwick	d														06 12	06 39						
23¼	—	15¼	**Leamington Spa** 8	d									05 45					06 17	06a45						
43¼	—	—	**Banbury**	d						05 24		05 42	06 03				06 12	06 36							06 53
46¾	—	—	Kings Sutton	d						05 29							06 16								
57¼	—	—	**Bicester North** 3	d						05 41		05 57	06 15				06 27	06 48					06 54		07 07
70¼	—	—	Haddenham & Thame Parkway	d						05 53		06 09	06 26				06 39						07 06		07 19
—	0	—	**Aylesbury**	d		23p01	05 05	05 15	05 25		05 48					06 20				06 39					
—	4½	—	Little Kimble	d		23p09	05 13				05 56					06 28									
—	6	—	Monks Risborough	d		23p13	05 17				06 00					06 32									
76	7½	—	**Princes Risborough** 2	d		23p17	05 20	05 28	05 38	06 00	06 04	06 16	06 33			06 37	06 46						07 14		07 28
79¾	—	—	Saunderton	d		23p22	05 25				06 09						06 51								
84¼	—	—	**High Wycombe** 1	d	23p25	23p30	05 32	05 38	05 54	06 10	06 16	06 26				06 47	06 58					07 10	07 25		
89	—	—	Beaconsfield	d	23p31	23p36	05 38	05 44	06 01	06 16	06 22	06 32				06 53	07 04					07 17	07 32		
90¾	—	—	Seer Green	d		23p39	05 41		06 04			06 35				06 56						07 20			
93¼	—	—	Gerrards Cross 1	d	23p36	23p43	05 45	05 50	06 09	06 21	06 28	06 40			06 52	07 00	07 10				07 19	07 25	07 38		
95	—	—	Denham Golf Club	d		23p46	05 48								06 55							07 28			
96	—	—	Denham	d		23p49	05 51	05 55	06 14		06 33					07 05						07 31			
98¾	—	—	West Ruislip 3 § ⊖	d		23p53	06 00				06 37					07 09						07 36			
100½	—	—	South Ruislip § ⊖	d		23p57	06 03		06 20						07 02						07 27				
102¼	—	—	Northolt Park	d		23p59	06 07				06 42				07 05						07 30				
103¼	—	—	Sudbury Hill Harrow	d											07 08						07 33				
104	—	—	Sudbury & Harrow Road	d											07 10						07 35				
105½	—	—	Wembley Stadium	d	23p48	00 05	06 12		06 27		06 47					07 17						07 44			
—	—	12	**London Paddington** 15 ⊖	a																					
112	—	—	**London Marylebone** 10 ⊖	a	00 06	00 20	06 28	06 18	06 42	06 46	07 00	07 03	07 09		07 25	07 30	07 33	07 38		07 39	07 51	07 57	08 02		08 04

§ London Underground Limited (Central Line) also operate services between South Ruislip and West Ruislip at frequent intervals

Kidderminster, Birmingham Snow Hill, Stratford-upon-Avon, Banbury, Aylesbury and High Wycombe - London

Network Diagram - see first Page of Table 114

Station		CH	CH	CH	CH	CH	CH	CH	CH	CH	CH	CH	CH	CH	CH	CH	CH	CH	CH	CH	CH	CH	CH
								◇												◇			
		🛒						🛒												🛒			
Kidderminster	d																		06 10				
Stourbridge Junction [2]	d																		06 18				
Cradley Heath	d																		06 23				
Rowley Regis	d																		06 29				
Birmingham Snow Hill	d																		06 46				
Birmingham Moor Street	d	06 19						06 55											06 59	07 33			
Solihull	d	06 29						07 03											07 09	07 41			
Dorridge	d	06 35																	07 14				
Lapworth	d																						
Stratford-upon-Avon	d											06§47											
Wilmcote	d																						
Bearley	d																						
Claverdon	d																						
Hatton	d																		07 22				
Warwick Parkway	d	06 45						07 15				07 07							07 27	07 52			
Warwick	d											07 11							07 30				
Leamington Spa [8]	d	06 52										07 22							07 34	07 58			
Banbury	d	07 11					07 17					07 40							07 52	08 16			08 01
Kings Sutton	d																						08 05
Bicester North [3]	d						07 29					07 52							08 06				08 17
Haddenham & Thame Parkway	d						07 39					08 02							08 18				
Aylesbury	d		07 11			07 20				07 40	07 50		07 50								08 14		
Little Kimble	d					07 28							07 58										
Monks Risborough	d					07 32							08 02										
Princes Risborough [2]	d					07 37	07 46			07 58			08a08			08 12			08 26				08f42
Saunderton	d					07 42										08 17							08 47
High Wycombe [1]	d				07 42	07 48	07 55			08 08					08 18	08 23			08 35			08 48	08 53
Beaconsfield	d				07 48	07 54	08 01			08 15						08 29			08 41			08 54	09 00
Seer Green	d				07 51										08 25								09 03
Gerrards Cross [1]	d			07 50	07 56	08 00			08 13						08 29	08 35	08 40	08 40	08 47			08 59	09 08
Denham Golf Club	d														08 32							09 02	
Denham	d			07 54					08 18						08 35		08 44	08 44				09 05	
West Ruislip [3] §	⊖ d					08a08								08 29			08a51	08 58					09 14
South Ruislip §	⊖ d				08 04											08 44						09 11	
Northolt Park	d			08 01										08 34				09 03					
Sudbury Hill Harrow	d													08 36				09 05					
Sudbury & Harrow Road	d													08 39				09 08					
Wembley Stadium	d			08 06											08 46			09 11					09 22
London Paddington [15]	⊖ a																						
London Marylebone [10]	⊖ a	08 06	08 11	08 18	08 21		08 24	08 25	08 38	08 42	08 47	08 48		08 54	09 00	09 03		09 25	09 07	09 07	09 14	09 28	09 36

§ London Underground Limited (Central Line) also operate services between South Ruislip and West Ruislip at frequent intervals

Kidderminster, Birmingham Snow Hill, Stratford-upon-Avon, Banbury, Aylesbury and High Wycombe - London

Network Diagram - see first Page of Table 114

		CH	CH	CH	CH		CH ◇	CH ◇ 🛒	CH	CH	CH	CH	CH ◇ 🛒	CH ◇ 🛒	CH		CH	CH	CH ◇	CH ◇ 🛒	CH	CH	CH ◇	CH ◇ 🛒	CH
Kidderminster	d						06 59	07 30						08 09											
Stourbridge Junction [2]	d						07 07	07 40						08 23											
Cradley Heath	d						07 14	07 45						08 28											
Rowley Regis	d						07 22	07 53						08 34											
Birmingham Snow Hill 🚌	d						07 44	08 12					08 22	08 52						09 12					
Birmingham Moor Street	d						07 47	08 15					08 25	08 55						09 15				09 55	
Solihull	d						07 55	08 24					08 37	09 03						09 23				10 03	
Dorridge	d						08 00	08 29					08 50							09 28					
Lapworth	d						08 04						08 54							09 32					
Stratford-upon-Avon	d	07 35																							
Wilmcote	d	07 41																							
Bearley	d	07 45																							
Claverdon	d	07 51																							
Hatton	d	08 00					08 10						09 00												
Warwick Parkway	d	08 06					08 16	08 39						09 15						09 40				10 14	
Warwick	d						08 19	08 43					09 06							09 44					
Leamington Spa [8]	d	08 12					08 24	08 47					09 10							09 49				10 21	
Banbury	d	08 31					08 43	09 06					09 29						09 45	10 07				10 38	
Kings Sutton	d																		09 51						
Bicester North [3]	d	08 43					08 56	09 18				09 24	09 41						10 02	10 21			10 28		
Haddenham & Thame Parkway	d	08 55					09 06					09 36							10 14				10 40		
Aylesbury	d		08 50												09 50										
Little Kimble	d		08 58												09 58										
Monks Risborough	d		09 02												10 02										
Princes Risborough [2]	d		09a08				09 13					09 43			10a08			10 10	10 21				10 47		
Saunderton	d						09 18					09 48						10 15							
High Wycombe [1]	d				09 12		09 25				09 41	09 55					10 10	10 21	10 31	10 41		10 46	10 57		11 10
Beaconsfield	d				09 18		09 32				09 47						10 16	10 27				10 52	11 03		11 16
Seer Green	d				09 21						09 50							10 30				10 55			11 19
Gerrards Cross [1]	d			09 21	09 26		09 38			09 48	09 55						10 21	10 35			10 44	10 59	11 09		11 23
Denham Golf Club	d									09 51											10 47				
Denham	d				09 31					09 54							10 26				10 49				11 28
West Ruislip [3] § ⊖	d				09 35				09 49												10 59	11 06			
South Ruislip § ⊖	d			09 29							10 03						10 32								11 34
Northolt Park	d			09 32					09 54								10 35					11 11			11 37
Sudbury Hill Harrow	d								09 57								10 38								
Sudbury & Harrow Road	d																								
Wembley Stadium	d			09 37	09 43					10 04							10 42					11 16			11 42
London Paddington [15] ⊖	a																				11 32				
London Marylebone [10] ⊖	a	09 40		09 50	09 55		09 58	09 59	10 15	10 18	10 25	10 27	10 28	10 29			10 58	10 59	11 00	11 14		11 30	11 31	11 32	11 58

			CH	CH	CH ◇ 🛒	CH ◇ 🛒	CH	CH	CH ◇ 🛒	CH	CH		CH ◇	CH	CH ◇ 🛒	CH	CH	CH 🛒	CH	CH	CH		CH	CH ◇	CH
Kidderminster	d																								
Stourbridge Junction [2]	d																								
Cradley Heath	d																								
Rowley Regis	d																								
Birmingham Snow Hill 🚌	d					10 12									11 12									12 12	
Birmingham Moor Street	d					10 15			10 55						11 15			11 55						12 15	
Solihull	d					10 23			11 03						11 23			12 03						12 23	
Dorridge	d					10 28									11 28									12 28	
Lapworth	d																								
Stratford-upon-Avon	d				09 55												11 20								
Wilmcote	d				10 00												11 25								
Bearley	d				10 04																				
Claverdon	d				10 09												11 32								
Hatton	d				10 16												11 39								
Warwick Parkway	d					10 39			11 14						11 39			12 14						12 39	
Warwick	d				10 23	10 42									11 42		11 46							12 42	
Leamington Spa [8]	d				10 27	10 46			11 21						11 46		11 50	12 20						12 46	
Banbury	d				10 48	11 04			11 38					11 45	12 04		12 10	12 38					12 47	13 04	
Kings Sutton	d													11 51											
Bicester North [3]	d		10 54		11 02	11 16		11 26						12 02	12 16		12 26						13 02	13 16	
Haddenham & Thame Parkway	d		11 06		11 14			11 38						12 14			12 38						13 14		
Aylesbury	d			10 59						11 54									12 50						
Little Kimble	d			11 07						12 02									12 58						
Monks Risborough	d			11 11						12 06									13 02						
Princes Risborough [2]	d		11 13	11a17	11 21			11 45		12a10			12 12	12 21			12 45		13a08		13 12		13 21		
Saunderton	d		11 18										12 17								13 17				
High Wycombe [1]	d		11 24		11 31	11 36	11 40	11 55			12 10		12 23	12 31	12 36	12 40	12 55			13 10	13 23		13 31	13 36	13 40
Beaconsfield	d		11 30				11 46	12 01			12 16		12 29			12 46	13 01			13 16	13 29				13 46
Seer Green	d						11 49				12 19					12 49				13 19					13 49
Gerrards Cross [1]	d		11 36				11 53	12 06			12 23		12 35			12 53	13 06			13 23	13 35				13 53
Denham Golf Club	d						11 56									12 56									13 56
Denham	d						11 59				12 28					12 59				13 28					13 59
West Ruislip [3] § ⊖	d						12 03									13 03									14 03
South Ruislip § ⊖	d										12 34									13 34					
Northolt Park	d						12 08				12 37					13 08				13 37					14 08
Sudbury Hill Harrow	d						12 11									13 11									14 11
Sudbury & Harrow Road	d																								
Wembley Stadium	d						12 15				12 42					13 15				13 42					14 15
London Paddington [15] ⊖	a																								
London Marylebone [10] ⊖	a		11 59		12 00	12 09	12 30	12 31	12 32		12 58		12 59	13 00	13 07	13 30	13 31	13 32		13 58	13 59		14 00	14 09	14 30

§ London Underground Limited (Central Line) also operate services between South Ruislip and West Ruislip at frequent intervals

Kidderminster, Birmingham Snow Hill, Stratford-upon-Avon, Banbury, Aylesbury and High Wycombe - London

Network Diagram - see first Page of Table 114

		CH	CH	CH	CH	CH	CH		CH	CH	CH	CH	CH	CH	CH	CH	CH		CH	CH	CH	CH	CH	CH	CH
			◇						◇	◇			◇				◇		◇			◇			
Kidderminster	d																								
Stourbridge Junction [2]	d																								
Cradley Heath	d																								
Rowley Regis	d																								
Birmingham Snow Hill	d									13 12									14 12						
Birmingham Moor Street	d		12 55							13 15			13 55						14 15			14 55			
Solihull	d		13 03							13 23			14 03						14 23			15 03			
Dorridge	d									13 28									14 28						
Lapworth	d																								
Stratford-upon-Avon	d			13 06																					
Wilmcote	d			13 11																					
Bearley	d			13 15																					
Claverdon	d			13 20																					
Hatton	d			13 28																					
Warwick Parkway	d		13 14							13 39			14 14						14 39			15 14			
Warwick	d			13 36						13 42									14 42						
Leamington Spa [8]	d		13 20	13a41						13 46			14 21						14 46			15 20			
Banbury	d		13 38						13 45	14 04			14 38				14 47		15 04			15 38			
Kings Sutton	d								13 51																
Bicester North [3]	d	13 26							14 02	14 16		14 26					15 02		15 16		15 26				
Haddenham & Thame Parkway	d	13 38							14 14			14 38					15 14				15 38				
Aylesbury	d				13 50									14 50									15 50		
Little Kimble	d				13 58									14 58									15 58		
Monks Risborough	d				14 02									15 02									16 02		
Princes Risborough [2]	d	13 45			14a08		14 12		14 21			14 45		15a08		15 12	15 21				15 45		16a08		16 10
Saunderton	d						14 17									15 17									16 15
High Wycombe [1]	d	13 55				14 10	14 23		14 31	14 36	14 40	14 55			15 10	15 23	15 31		15 36	15 40	15 55			16 10	16 21
Beaconsfield	d	14 01				14 16	14 29				14 46	15 01			15 16	15 29				15 46	16 01			16 16	16 27
Seer Green	d					14 19					14 49				15 19					15 49					16 30
Gerrards Cross [1]	d	14 06				14 23	14 35				14 53	15 06			15 23	15 35				15 53	16 06			16 21	16 35
Denham Golf Club	d										14 56									15 56					
Denham	d					14 28					14 59				15 28					15 59				16 26	
West Ruislip [3] § ⊖	d										15 03									16 03					
South Ruislip § ⊖	d					14 34									15 34									16 32	
Northolt Park	d					14 37					15 08				15 37					16 08				16 35	
Sudbury Hill Harrow	d										15 11									16 11					
Sudbury & Harrow Road	d																								
Wembley Stadium	d					14 42					15 15				15 42					16 15				16 40	
London Paddington [15] ⊖	a																								
London Marylebone [10] ⊖	a	14 31	14 32			14 58	14 59		15 00	15 07	15 30	15 31	15 32		15 58	15 59	16 00		16 11	16 30	16 31	16 32		16 57	16 59

		CH	CH		CH	CH	CH	CH	CH	CH	CH	CH	CH		CH	CH	CH	CH	CH	CH	CH	CH	CH		CH
		◇	◇		◇					◇			◇							◇					◇
Kidderminster	d																								
Stourbridge Junction [2]	d																								
Cradley Heath	d																								
Rowley Regis	d																								
Birmingham Snow Hill	d		15 12												16 12						16 52				
Birmingham Moor Street	d		15 15							15 55					16 15						16 55				17 10
Solihull	d		15 23							16 03					16 23						17 03				17 18
Dorridge	d		15 28												16 28										17 26
Lapworth	d																								
Stratford-upon-Avon	d				15 37																				
Wilmcote	d				15 42																				
Bearley	d				15 46																				
Claverdon	d				15 51																				
Hatton	d				15 57																				
Warwick Parkway	d		15 39							16 15					16 39						17 14				17 35
Warwick	d		15 42		16 04										16 42						17 18				17 39
Leamington Spa [8]	d		15 46		16a12					16 22					16 46						17 23				17 43
Banbury	d	15 45	16 04							16 40					17 05						17 41				18 00
Kings Sutton	d	15 51																							
Bicester North [3]	d	16 02	16 16				16 24			16 52		16 57	17 03		17 18				17 24		17 53		17 58		18 13
Haddenham & Thame Parkway	d	16 14					16 36					17 09	17 15						17 36				18 10		18 24
Aylesbury	d							16 53												17 34					
Little Kimble	d							17 01												17 42					
Monks Risborough	d							17 05												17 46					
Princes Risborough [2]	d	16 21					16 43	17a11				17 16	17 22						17 43	17 49			18 17		
Saunderton	d												17 27						17 48						
High Wycombe [1]	d	16 31	16 36			16 40	16 53		17 01	17 12	17 19	17 26	17 33		17 39		17 46		17 55	18 00		18 15	18 27		18 37
Beaconsfield	d					16 46	16 59		17 07			17 32					17 52			18 06		18 21	18 33		
Seer Green	d					16 49			17 10								17 55					18 24			
Gerrards Cross [1]	d					16 53	17 04		17 14		17 29	17 38				17 51	18 00		18 06			18 29	18 38		
Denham Golf Club	d					16 56										17 54									
Denham	d					16 59			17 19		17 34					17 57						18 33			
West Ruislip [3] § ⊖	d					17 03			17 28									18 08				18 38			
South Ruislip § ⊖	d						17 12				17 40					18 03				18 18					
Northolt Park	d					17 08					17 43								18 16						
Sudbury Hill Harrow	d					17 11			17 35									18 14							
Sudbury & Harrow Road	d																								
Wembley Stadium	d					17 15			17 39			17 51				18 09				18 25		18 46			
London Paddington [15] ⊖	a																								
London Marylebone [10] ⊖	a	17 00	17 11			17 30	17 33		17 55	17 46	18 04	18 12	18 15		18 19	18 27	18 30	18 34	18 38	18 45	18 47	19 03	19 04		19 09

§ London Underground Limited (Central Line) also operate services between South Ruislip and West Ruislip at frequent intervals

Kidderminster, Birmingham Snow Hill, Stratford-upon-Avon, Banbury, Aylesbury and High Wycombe - London

Network Diagram - see first Page of Table 114

Station		CH	CH	CH	CH ◇	CH	CH	CH	CH
Kidderminster	d								
Stourbridge Junction 2	d								
Cradley Heath	d								
Rowley Regis	d								
Birmingham Snow Hill	d				17 10			17 52	
Birmingham Moor Street	d				17 13			17 55	
Solihull	d				17 23			18 04	
Dorridge	d				17 30			18 11	
Lapworth	d				17 34				
Stratford-upon-Avon	d					17 40			
Wilmcote	d					17 46			
Bearley	d					17 50			
Claverdon	d					17 56			
Hatton	d				17 39	18 01			
Warwick Parkway	d				17 44			18 21	
Warwick	d				17 47	18 08			
Leamington Spa 8	d				17 51	18 12		18 28	
Banbury	d				18 12	18 30		18 45	
Kings Sutton	d				18 17				
Bicester North 3	d				18 30	18 43		18 57	
Haddenham & Thame Parkway	d				18 42				
Aylesbury	d	18 20							
Little Kimble	d	18 28							
Monks Risborough	d	18 32							
Princes Risborough 2	d	18a38		18 43	18 52				
Saunderton	d				18 57				
High Wycombe 1	d		18 42	18 53	19 05		19 11	19 20	19 28
Beaconsfield	d		18 48	18 59			19 17		19 34
Seer Green	d			19 02					19 37
Gerrards Cross 1	d		18 53	19 06			19 22		19 41
Denham Golf Club	d						19 25		
Denham	d		18 58				19 28		
West Ruislip 3 § ⊖	d						19 39		
South Ruislip § ⊖	d		19 04						
Northolt Park	d		19 07				19 44		
Sudbury Hill Harrow	d		19 10				19 46		
Sudbury & Harrow Road	d								
Wembley Stadium	d		19 14				19 50		19 55
London Paddington 15 ⊖	a								
London Marylebone 10 ⊖	a		19 30	19 35	19 38	19 39	20 06	19 56	20 10

Station		CH	CH	CH ◇	CH	CH	CH	CH ◇	CH	CH ◇	CH ◇	CH	CH	CH	CH
Kidderminster	d														
Stourbridge Junction 2	d														
Cradley Heath	d														
Rowley Regis	d														
Birmingham Snow Hill	d			18 12	18 40						19 48				
Birmingham Moor Street	d			18 15	18 43						19 51				
Solihull	d			18 24	18 51						19 59				
Dorridge	d			18 29	18 56						20 04				
Lapworth	d			18 33											
Stratford-upon-Avon	d									19 20					
Wilmcote	d									19 25					
Bearley	d														
Claverdon	d									19 32					
Hatton	d			18 39						19 37					
Warwick Parkway	d			18 44	19 06						20 14				
Warwick	d			18 47						19 44	20 17				
Leamington Spa 8	d			18 52	19 11					19 48	20 21				
Banbury	d			19 12	19 30					20 07	20 41				
Kings Sutton	d			19 16						20 11					
Bicester North 3	d	19 04		19 27	19 42	19 48		20 04		20 21	20 54		21 04		
Haddenham & Thame Parkway	d	19 16		19 39	19 52	20 00				20 32	21 06		21 16		
Aylesbury	d		19 20						20 16					21 25	
Little Kimble	d		19 28						20 24					21 33	
Monks Risborough	d		19 32						20 28					21 37	
Princes Risborough 2	d	19 23	19 35	19 47	19 59				20 31	20 40			21 23	21a43	21 48
Saunderton	d	19 28							20 36						21 53
High Wycombe 1	d	19 34	19 45	19 57	20 08	20 14	20 19	20 28	20 43	20 49	21 19	21 25	21 33		21 59
Beaconsfield	d	19 40				20 20	20 25		20 49	20 55		21 31	21 39		22 05
Seer Green	d	19 43					20 28			20 58		21 34			22 08
Gerrards Cross 1	d	19 48	19 56			20 25	20 32		20 54	21 03		21 38	21 44		22 13
Denham Golf Club	d						20 35					21 41			22 16
Denham	d	19 52					20 38					21 44			22 18
West Ruislip 3 § ⊖	d		20 11				20 42					21 54			22 23
South Ruislip § ⊖	d	19 58							21 02			21 57			22 26
Northolt Park	d		20 16				20 47					22 01			22 30
Sudbury Hill Harrow	d						20 50								
Sudbury & Harrow Road	d														
Wembley Stadium	d		20 21				20 54			21 12	21 34	22 06	21 58		22 35
London Paddington 15 ⊖	a														
London Marylebone 10 ⊖	a	20 19	20 37	20 27	20 43	20 53	21 11	21 15	21 23	21 28	21 51	22 22	22 15		22 51

Station		CH ◇	CH ◇	CH ◇	CH	CH	CH	CH
Kidderminster	d							
Stourbridge Junction 2	d							
Cradley Heath	d							
Rowley Regis	d							
Birmingham Snow Hill	d	20 42		21 42				
Birmingham Moor Street	d	20 45		21 45				
Solihull	d	20 53		21 53				
Dorridge	d	20 58		21 58				
Lapworth	d							
Stratford-upon-Avon	d				22 00	23 15		
Wilmcote	d				22 05			
Bearley	d							
Claverdon	d							
Hatton	d				22 17			
Warwick Parkway	d	21 08		22 08				
Warwick	d	21 11		22 11	22 24	23 34		
Leamington Spa 8	d	21 16		22 16	22a28	23 38		
Banbury	d	21 34	22 02	22 34		23a56		
Kings Sutton	d			22 38				
Bicester North 3	d	21 46	22 19	22 49				
Haddenham & Thame Parkway	d	21 56	22 31	23 01				
Aylesbury	d							23 01
Little Kimble	d							23 09
Monks Risborough	d							23 13
Princes Risborough 2	d	22 03	22 39	23 08				23 17
Saunderton	d		22 44					23 22
High Wycombe 1	d	22 12	22 51	23 18			23 25	23 30
Beaconsfield	d	22 18	22 57				23 31	23 36
Seer Green	d		23 00					23 39
Gerrards Cross 1	d	22 24	23 05				23 36	23 43
Denham Golf Club	d		23 08					23 46
Denham	d		23 11					23 49
West Ruislip 3 § ⊖	d		23 16					23 53
South Ruislip § ⊖	d		23 20					23 57
Northolt Park	d		23 24					23 59
Sudbury Hill Harrow	d							
Sudbury & Harrow Road	d							
Wembley Stadium	d		23 29	23 34			23 48	00 05
London Paddington 15 ⊖	a							
London Marylebone 10 ⊖	a	22 52	23 45	23 50			00 06	00 20

§ London Underground Limited (Central Line) also operate services between South Ruislip and West Ruislip at frequent intervals

Table 115

Saturdays

Kidderminster, Birmingham Snow Hill, Stratford-upon-Avon, Banbury, Aylesbury and High Wycombe - London

Network Diagram - see first Page of Table 114

		CH	CH	CH	CH	CH	CH	CH	CH	CH		CH	CH	CH	CH	CH	CH	CH	CH	CH		CH	CH	CH	CH
									◇	◇				◇			◇		◇			◇			
Kidderminster	d													06 37	07 14							08 13			
Stourbridge Junction 2	d													06 45	07 22							08 26			
Cradley Heath	d													06 50	07 27							08 32			
Rowley Regis	d													06 56	07 33							08 37			
Birmingham Snow Hill	d													07 12	07 52				08 12			08 52			
Birmingham Moor Street	d								06 15	06 44				07 15	07 55				08 15			08 55			
Solihull	d								06 24	06 52				07 24	08 04				08 25			09 05			
Dorridge	d								06 29	06 57				07 29					08 30						
Lapworth	d								06 33																
Stratford-upon-Avon	d																08 00								
Wilmcote	d																								
Bearley	d																								
Claverdon	d																08 10								
Hatton	d								06 39								08 17								
Warwick Parkway	d								06 44	07 07				07 39	08 18				08 39			09 19			
Warwick	d								06 47					07 43			08 24		08 43						
Leamington Spa 8	d								06 52	07 13				07 47	08 23		08 28		08 47			09 24			
Banbury	d					06 05	06 29		07 09	07 31				08 05	08 44		08 48		09 10			09 44	09 25		
Kings Sutton	d						06 33										08 52						09 29		
Bicester North 3	d					06 17	06 44		07 22	07 44				08 17			09 03		09 21				09 40		
Haddenham & Thame Parkway	d					06 29	06 56		07 33	07 54				08 28			09 15		09 32				09 53		
Aylesbury	d		23p01	05 15	05 57			06 56				07 53	08 10			08 53		09 10							10 10
Little Kimble	d		23p09	05 23	06 05			07 04				08 01				09 01		09 18							10 18
Monks Risborough	d		23p13	05 27	06 09			07 08				08 05				09 05		09 22							10 22
Princes Risborough 2	d		23p17	05 30	06 12	06 37		07 11	07 41			08 08	08 23	08 36		09 09	09 23	09a28	09 39				10 01	10 12	10a28
Saunderton	d		23p22	05 35	06 17			07 16				08 13	08 28				09 28						10 06		
High Wycombe 1	d	23p25	23p30	05 42	06 24	06 46	07 11	07 23	07 50			08 20	08 48	08 45		09 19	09 35		09 48	09 53			10 18	10 22	
Beaconsfield	d	23p31	23p36	05 48	06 30	06 52		07 29	07 56			08 26	08 54			09 25	09 41			09 59			10 24	10 28	
Seer Green	d		23p39	05 51	06 33			07 32				08 29	08 57			09 28				10 02				10 31	
Gerrards Cross 1	d	23p36	23p43	05 55	06 37	06 57		07 36	08 01			08 33	09 01			09 32	09 46			10 06			10 29	10 35	
Denham Golf Club	d		23p46	05 58	06 40			07 39				08 36				09 35								10 38	
Denham	d		23p49	06 01	06 43			07 42				08 39	09 06			09 38				10 11				10 41	
West Ruislip 3 § ⊖	d		23p53	06 05	06 47			07 46				08 43				09 42								10 46	
South Ruislip § ⊖	d		23p57	06 09	06 51			07 50				08 47	09 12							10 17					
Northolt Park	d		23p59	06 12	06 54			07 53				08 50	09 15			09 47				10 20				10 51	
Sudbury Hill Harrow	d																								
Sudbury & Harrow Road	d																								
Wembley Stadium	d	23p48	00 05	06 17	06 59			07 58				08 55	09 20			09 52				10 25				10 56	
London Paddington 15 ⊖	a																								
London Marylebone 10 ⊖	a	00 06	00 20	06 30	07 12	07 18	07 40	08 11	08 21	08 31		09 08	09 31	09 11	09 37	10 06	10 09		10 14	10 38		10 41	10 51	11 08	

		CH	CH	CH	CH	CH		CH	CH	CH	CH	CH	CH	CH	CH	CH		CH	CH	CH	CH	CH	CH	CH	CH
		◇			◇				◇			◇			◇										
Kidderminster	d				09 03																				
Stourbridge Junction 2	d				09 16																				
Cradley Heath	d				09 21																				
Rowley Regis	d				09 27																				
Birmingham Snow Hill	d	09 12			09 52				10 12						11 12						12 12				
Birmingham Moor Street	d	09 15			09 55				10 15			10 55			11 15			11 55			12 15		12 55		
Solihull	d	09 23			10 05				10 24			11 03			11 23			12 04			12 23		13 05		
Dorridge	d	09 28							10 30						11 28						12 28				
Lapworth	d																								
Stratford-upon-Avon	d			09 37												11 34									
Wilmcote	d			09 43												11 40									
Bearley	d			09 47												11 44									
Claverdon	d			09 53												11 50									
Hatton	d			09 58												11 56									
Warwick Parkway	d	09 38			10 19				10 39			11 14			11 38			12 20			12 38		13 18		
Warwick	d	09 41		10 04					10 43						11 41	12 03					12 41				
Leamington Spa 8	d	09 46		10 08	10 25				10 48			11 20			11 46	12 07		12 26			12 46		13 24		
Banbury	d	10 05		10 26	10 46				11 09		11 13	11 39			12 04	12 25		12 48			13 08	13 13	13 44		
Kings Sutton	d										11 18											13 18			
Bicester North 3	d	10 18		10 39	10 58				11 22		11 34	11 53			12 21	12 38		13 00			13 21	13 29	13 56		
Haddenham & Thame Parkway	d	10 28		10 49					11 33		11 46				12 32	12 48					13 32	13 41			
Aylesbury	d							11 10						12 10					13 10					14 10	
Little Kimble	d							11 18						12 18					13 18					14 18	
Monks Risborough	d							11 22						12 22					13 22					14 22	
Princes Risborough 2	d	10 36		10 58		11 15		11a30	11 40		11 54		12 14	12a28	12 38	12 56			13a28		13 38	13 49		14a28	
Saunderton	d			11 03							11 59					13 01						13 54			
High Wycombe 1	d	10 45	10 53	11 10		11 25			11 49	11 53	12 05		12 24		12 49	13 08				13 24	13 49	14 01			14 24
Beaconsfield	d		10 59	11 16		11 31				11 59	12 11		12 30			13 14				13 30		14 07			14 30
Seer Green	d		11 02			11 34				12 02			12 33							13 33					14 33
Gerrards Cross 1	d		11 06	11 22		11 38				12 06	12 17		12 37			13 20				13 37		14 12			14 37
Denham Golf Club	d					11 41							12 40							13 40					14 40
Denham	d		11 11			11 44				12 11			12 43							13 43					14 43
West Ruislip 3 § ⊖	d					11 48							12 47							13 47					14 47
South Ruislip § ⊖	d		11 17							12 17			12 51							13 51					14 51
Northolt Park	d		11 20			11 53				12 20			12 54							13 54					14 54
Sudbury Hill Harrow	d																								
Sudbury & Harrow Road	d																								
Wembley Stadium	d		11 25			11 58				12 25			12 59			13 29				13 59		14 24			14 59
London Paddington 15 ⊖	a																								
London Marylebone 10 ⊖	a	11 11	11 37	11 41	11 45	12 10			12 14	12 37	12 41	12 44	13 11		13 14	13 41		13 45		14 11	14 14	14 36	14 41		15 11

§ London Underground Limited (Central Line) also operate services between South Ruislip and West Ruislip at frequent intervals

Table 115

Saturdays

Kidderminster, Birmingham Snow Hill, Stratford-upon-Avon, Banbury, Aylesbury and High Wycombe - London

Network Diagram - see first Page of Table 114

		CH		CH	CH	CH	CH	CH	CH	CH	CH	CH		CH	CH	CH	CH	CH	CH	CH	CH	CH		CH	CH
		◇		◇	◇						◇							◇							◇
Kidderminster	d																								
Stourbridge Junction 2	d																								
Cradley Heath	d																								
Rowley Regis	d																								
Birmingham Snow Hill ⛴	d	13 12						14 12							15 12						16 12				
Birmingham Moor Street	d	13 15			13 55			14 15			14 55				15 15			15 55			16 15				16 55
Solihull	d	13 23			14 03			14 23			15 03				15 23			16 03			16 23				17 02
Dorridge	d	13 28						14 28							15 28						16 28				
Lapworth	d																								
Stratford-upon-Avon	d			13 18													15 19								
Wilmcote	d			13 23													15 24								
Bearley	d			13 27																					
Claverdon	d			13 32													15 31								
Hatton	d			13 42													15 44								
Warwick Parkway	d	13 38			14 14			14 38			15 14				15 38			16 14			16 38				17 14
Warwick	d	13 41		13 50				14 41							15 41		15 51				16 41				
Leamington Spa 8	d	13 46		13 55	14 21			14 46			15 21				15 46		15 56	16 21			16 46				17 21
Banbury	d	14 08		14 14	14 44			15 08		15 13	15 45				16 08		16 15	16 45			17i08			17 13	17 44
Kings Sutton	d									15 18														17 18	
Bicester North 3	d	14 21		14 29	14 57			15 22		15 34	15 58				16 21		16 34	16 58			17 21			17 34	17 57
Haddenham & Thame Parkway	d	14 32		14 41				15 33		15 46					16 32		16 46				17 32			17 46	
Aylesbury	d						15 10							16 10						17 10					
Little Kimble	d						15 18							16 18						17 18					
Monks Risborough	d						15 22							16 22						17 22					
Princes Risborough 2	d	14 38		14 49		15 14	15a28	15 38		15 53		16 15		16a28	16 38		16 53		17 15	17a28	17 38			17 53	
Saunderton	d			14 54						15 59							16 59							17 59	
High Wycombe 1	d	14 49		15 01		15 24		15 49	15 53	16 05		16 25			16 49	16 53	17 05		17 25		17 49	17 53		18 05	
Beaconsfield	d			15 07		15 30			15 59	16 11		16 31				16 59	17 11		17 31			17 59		18 11	
Seer Green	d					15 33			16 02			16 34				17 02			17 34			18 02			
Gerrards Cross 1	d			15 12		15 37			16 06	16 17		16 38				17 06	17 17		17 38			18 06		18 17	
Denham Golf Club	d					15 40						16 41							17 41						
Denham	d					15 43			16 11			16 44				17 11			17 44			18 11			
West Ruislip 3 §	⊖ d					15 47						16 48							17 49						
South Ruislip §	⊖ d					15 51			16 17							17 17						18 17			
Northolt Park	d					15 54			16 20			16 53				17 20			17 54			18 20			
Sudbury Hill Harrow	d																								
Sudbury & Harrow Road	d																								
Wembley Stadium	d			15 24		15 59			16 25			16 58				17 25			17 59			18 25			
London Paddington 15	⊖ a																								
London Marylebone 10	⊖ a	15 15		15 36	15 41	16 11		16 14	16 37	16 40	16 44	17 10			17 14	17 37	17 40	17 44	18 11		18 14	18 37		18 41	18 44

§ London Underground Limited (Central Line) also operate services between South Ruislip and West Ruislip at frequent intervals

Table 115

Saturdays

Kidderminster, Birmingham Snow Hill, Stratford-upon-Avon, Banbury, Aylesbury and High Wycombe - London

Network Diagram - see first Page of Table 114

		CH	CH	CH	CH	CH	CH	CH		CH	CH	CH	CH	CH	CH	CH	CH	CH		CH	CH	CH	CH	CH	CH
												◇		◇	◇		◇	A 🚌				◇ B	A		A 🚌
Kidderminster	d																								
Stourbridge Junction 2	d																								
Cradley Heath	d																								
Rowley Regis	d																								
Birmingham Snow Hill	d			17 12								18 42			19 42		20 42					21 20			
Birmingham Moor Street	d			17 15				17 55				18 45			19 45		20 45					21 23			
Solihull	d			17 23				18 03				18 53			19 53		20 53					21 31			
Dorridge	d			17 28								18 58			19 58		20 58					21 38			
Lapworth	d																21 02					21 42			
Stratford-upon-Avon	d				17 40									19 16						21 15					
Wilmcote	d													19 22											
Bearley	d													19 26											
Claverdon	d													19 32											
Hatton	d													19 37			21 08					21 48			
Warwick Parkway	d			17 38				18 14				19 08			20 08		21 13					21 53			
Warwick	d			17 41	18 01			18 18				19 11		19 45	20 11		21 16			21 35		21 56			
Leamington Spa 8	d			17 46	18 06			18 23				19 16		19 51	20 16		21 21	21 30		21a45		22 02			22 10
Banbury	d			18 06	18 23			18 45				19 34		20 10	20 34		21 39	22 10				22 19			22 40
Kings Sutton	d													20 14								22 24			
Bicester North 3	d			18 18			18 41	18 58				19 47		20 25	20 49		21 52	22a35				22 34	22 45		
Haddenham & Thame Parkway	d			18 29			18 51					19 57		20 37	20 59		22 02					22 46	22 56		
Aylesbury	d		18 10								19 10					21 16					22 16			22 48	
Little Kimble	d		18 18								19 18					21 24					22 24			22 56	
Monks Risborough	d		18 22								19 22					21 28					22 28			23 00	
Princes Risborough 2	d	18 13	18a30	18 37			18 58				19 25	20 05		20 44	21 07	21 31	22 10				22 31	22 55	23 03	23 06	
Saunderton	d						19 03				19 30			20 50		21 36					22 36			23 11	
High Wycombe 1	d	18 23		18 46		18 55	19 10			19 25	19 48	20 14	20 25	20 57	21 16	21 43	22 19				22 43	23 05	23 12	23 18	
Beaconsfield	d	18 29				19 01	19 16			19 31	19 54		20 31	21 03	21 22	21 49	22 25				22 49			23 24	
Seer Green	d	18 32				19 04				19 34	19 57		20 34	21 06		21 52					22 52			23 27	
Gerrards Cross 1	d	18 36				19 08	19 22			19 38	20 01		20 38	21 10	21 28	21 56	22 30				22 56			23 31	
Denham Golf Club	d	18 39								19 41			20 41	21 13		21 59					22 59			23 34	
Denham	d	18 42				19 13				19 44	20 06		20 44	21 16		22 02					23 02			23 37	
West Ruislip 3 § ⊖	d	18 46								19 48			20 48	21 20		22 06					23 06			23 41	
South Ruislip § ⊖	d					19 19					20 12			21 24		22 10					23 10			23 45	
Northolt Park	d	18 51				19 22				19 53	20 15		20 53	21 27		22 13					23 13			23 48	
Sudbury Hill Harrow	d																								
Sudbury & Harrow Road	d																								
Wembley Stadium	d	18 56				19 27				19 58	20 20		20 58	21 32		22 18					23 18	23 21	23 27	23 53	
London Paddington 15 ⊖	a																								
London Marylebone 10 ⊖	a	19 08		19 11	19 17	19 39	19 42	19 45		20 11	20 33	20 40	21 13	21 44	21 47	22 31	22 58				23 30	23 33	23 39	00 05	00 10

		CH
		A 🚌
Kidderminster	d	
Stourbridge Junction 2	d	
Cradley Heath	d	
Rowley Regis	d	
Birmingham Snow Hill	d	
Birmingham Moor Street	d	
Solihull	d	
Dorridge	d	
Lapworth	d	
Stratford-upon-Avon	d	
Wilmcote	d	
Bearley	d	
Claverdon	d	
Hatton	d	
Warwick Parkway	d	
Warwick	d	
Leamington Spa 8	d	22 10
Banbury	d	22 40
Kings Sutton	d	
Bicester North 3	d	23s10
Haddenham & Thame Parkway	d	23s40
Aylesbury	d	
Little Kimble	d	
Monks Risborough	d	
Princes Risborough 2	d	23s55
Saunderton	d	23s59
High Wycombe 1	d	00s20
Beaconsfield	d	00s40
Seer Green	d	
Gerrards Cross 1	d	00s55
Denham Golf Club	d	
Denham	d	01s15
West Ruislip 3 § ⊖	d	01s30
South Ruislip § ⊖	d	
Northolt Park	d	
Sudbury Hill Harrow	d	
Sudbury & Harrow Road	d	
Wembley Stadium	d	
London Paddington 15 ⊖	a	
London Marylebone 10 ⊖	a	01 55

§ London Underground Limited (Central Line) also operate services between South Ruislip and West Ruislip at frequent intervals

A from 7 January until 24 March

B Runs until 31 December and then from 31 March

Table 115

Sundays
until 1 January

Kidderminster, Birmingham Snow Hill, Stratford-upon-Avon, Banbury, Aylesbury and High Wycombe - London

Network Diagram - see first Page of Table 114

		CH A	CH	CH	CH	CH	CH	CH	CH ◇	CH		CH ◇	CH	CH		CH	CH ◇	CH	CH ◇	CH ◇	CH	CH	CH	CH	CH ◇
Kidderminster	d																								
Stourbridge Junction 2	d																								
Cradley Heath	d																								
Rowley Regis	d																								
Birmingham Snow Hill	d													09 40					10 40				11 40		
Birmingham Moor Street	d								08 55			09 13		09 43			10 13		10 43	11 13			11 43	12 13	
Solihull	d								09 04			09 22		09 52			10 21		10 52	11 21			11 51	12 21	
Dorridge	d								09 09			09 27		09 57			10 26		10 57	11 26			11 56	12 26	
Lapworth	d																		11 01						
Stratford-upon-Avon	d																								
Wilmcote	d																								
Bearley	d																								
Claverdon	d																								
Hatton	d																		11 06						
Warwick Parkway	d								09 18			09 35		10 06			10 35		11 11	11 35			12 06	12 35	
Warwick	d								09 22			09 40					10 39			11 39				12 39	
Leamington Spa 8	d								09 27			09 45		10 14			10 44		11 18	11 43			12 13	12 43	
Banbury	d								09 44	09 50		10 02		10 31			11 06		11 35	12 01			12 30	13 01	
Kings Sutton	d													10 36									12 35		
Bicester North 3	d				08 24	09 15		09 45	09 57	10 04		10 24		10 48		11 15	11 28		11 48	12 27	12 15		12 45	13 28	13 15
Haddenham & Thame Parkway	d				08 36	09 27		09 57		10 16				10 59		11 27			11 59		12 27		12 56		13 27
Aylesbury	d	22p48	07 26	08 20			09 30						10 25					11 25				12 25			
Little Kimble	d	22p56	07 34	08 28			09 38						10 33					11 33				12 33			
Monks Risborough	d	23p00	07 38	08 32			09 42						10 37					11 37				12 37			
Princes Risborough 2	d	23p06	07 41	08 35	08 43	09 34	09 45	10 04		10 21			10 40	11 07		11 34		11 40	12 06		12 34	12 40	13 03		13 34
Saunderton	d	23p11	07 46		08 48		09 50						10 45					11 45				12 45			
High Wycombe 1	d	23p18	07 53	08 45	08 54	09 44	09 57	10 14		10 31			10 52	11 16		11 44		11 52	12 15		12 44	12 52	13 12		13 44
Beaconsfield	d	23p24	07 59	08 51	09 00	09 50	10 03	10 20		10 37			10 58			11 50		11 58			12 50	12 58			13 50
Seer Green	d	23p27	08 02		09 03		10 06						11 01					12 01				13 01			
Gerrards Cross 1	d	23p31	08 06	08 57	09 08	09 55	10 10	10 25		10 42			11 05			11 55		12 05			12 55	13 05			13 55
Denham Golf Club	d	23p34	08 09				10 13											12 08							
Denham	d	23p37	08 12		09 12		10 16						11 10					12 11				13 10			
West Ruislip 3 §	d	23p41	08 17		09 17		10 20						11 14					12 15				13 14			
South Ruislip §	d	23p45	08 20		09 20		10 24						11 18					12 19				13 18			
Northolt Park	d	23p48	08 24		09 24		10 27						11 21					12 22				13 21			
Sudbury Hill Harrow	d																								
Sudbury & Harrow Road	d																								
Wembley Stadium	d	23p53	08 29		09 29		10 32						11 26					12 27				13 26			
London Paddington 15	a																								
London Marylebone 10	a	00 05	08 42	09 20	09 41	10 19	10 44	10 48	10 47	11 06		11 09	11 38	11 44		12 18	12 12	12 39	12 40	13 12	13 18	13 38	13 37	14 12	14 18

		CH	CH	CH	CH ◇	CH		CH	CH ◇	CH ◇	CH	CH	CH	CH	CH	CH		CH ◇	CH	CH	CH	CH	CH	CH	CH
Kidderminster	d																								
Stourbridge Junction 2	d																								
Cradley Heath	d																								
Rowley Regis	d																								
Birmingham Snow Hill	d		12 40					13 40				14 40				15 40					16 40				17 40
Birmingham Moor Street	d		12 43		13 11			13 43		14 13		14 43		15 13		15 43			16 13		16 43		17 13		17 43
Solihull	d		12 50		13 20			13 51		14 21		14 51		15 21		15 51			16 21		16 51		17 21		17 51
Dorridge	d		12 56		13 25			13 56		14 26		14 56		15 26		15 56			16 26		16 56		17 26		17 56
Lapworth	d							14 00								16 00									18 00
Stratford-upon-Avon	d								14 00									16 00							
Wilmcote	d								14 04									16 04							
Bearley	d																								
Claverdon	d																								
Hatton	d							14 06	14 15							16 06		16 14							18 06
Warwick Parkway	d		13 06		13 34			14 11		14 37		15 05		15 37		16 11			16 37		17 05		17 36		18 11
Warwick	d				13 39				14 22	14 39				15 40				16 23	16 40				17 40		
Leamington Spa 8	d		13 11		13 43			14 17	14 26	14 44		15 11		15 45		16 17		16 27	16 45		17 12		17 45		18 17
Banbury	d		13 29		14 05			14 35	14 45	15 04		15 30		16 05		16 35		16 46	17 05		17 30		18 05		18 35
Kings Sutton	d								14 50									16 50							
Bicester North 3	d		13 42	14 15	14 27			14 47	15 02	15 19		15 43	15 56	16 19		16 47		17 01	17 19		17 47	18 00	18 20		18 46
Haddenham & Thame Parkway	d		13 52	14 27				14 58	15 14			15 53	16 08			16 57		17 13			17 57	18 12			18 56
Aylesbury	d	13 25				14 25					15 25				16 25					17 25				18 25	
Little Kimble	d	13 33				14 33					15 33				16 33					17 33				18 33	
Monks Risborough	d	13 37				14 37					15 37				16 37					17 37				18 37	
Princes Risborough 2	d	13 40	13 59	14 34		14 40		15 05	15 22		15 40	16 02	16 15		16 40	17 06		17 20		17 40	18 05	18 19		18 40	19 05
Saunderton	d	13 45				14 45					15 45				16 45					17 45				18 45	
High Wycombe 1	d	13 52	14 08	14 44		14 52		15 14	15 32		15 52	16 11	16 25		16 52	17 15		17 30		17 52	18 14	18 29		18 52	19 14
Beaconsfield	d	13 58		14 50		14 58		15 20	15 38		15 58	16 17	16 31		16 58	17 21		17 36		17 58	18 20	18 35		18 58	19 20
Seer Green	d	14 01				15 01					16 01				17 01					18 01				19 01	
Gerrards Cross 1	d	14 05		14 55		15 05		15 26	15 43		16 05	16 22	16 35		17 05	17 26		17 42		18 05	18 26	18 40		19 05	19 25
Denham Golf Club	d	14 08									16 08									18 08					
Denham	d	14 11				15 10					16 11				17 10					18 11				19 10	
West Ruislip 3 §	d	14 15				15 14					16 15				17 14					18 15				19 14	
South Ruislip §	d	14 19				15 18					16 19				17 18					18 19				19 18	
Northolt Park	d	14 22				15 21					16 22				17 21					18 22				19 21	
Sudbury Hill Harrow	d																								
Sudbury & Harrow Road	d																								
Wembley Stadium	d	14 27				15 26			15 55		16 27		16 49		17 26					18 27		18 52		19 26	
London Paddington 15	a																								
London Marylebone 10	a	14 39	14 38	15 18	15 12	15 39		15 46	16 08	16 12	16 39	16 45	17 01	17 13	17 39	17 46		18 08	18 12	18 41	18 45	19 06	19 13	19 39	19 45

§ London Underground Limited (Central Line) also operate services between South Ruislip and West Ruislip at frequent intervals

A not 11 December

Table 115

Sundays
until 1 January

Kidderminster, Birmingham Snow Hill, Stratford-upon-Avon, Banbury, Aylesbury and High Wycombe - London

Network Diagram - see first Page of Table 114

		CH		CH	CH	CH	CH	CH	CH	CH	CH
		◇		◇				◇	◇		◇
Kidderminster	d										
Stourbridge Junction 2	d										
Cradley Heath	d										
Rowley Regis	d										
Birmingham Snow Hill	d					18 40	19 15		20 15		21 15
Birmingham Moor Street	d			18 13		18 43	19 18		20 18		21 18
Solihull	d			18 21		18 51	19 26		20 28		21 28
Dorridge	d			18 26		18 56	19 33		20 35		21 35
Lapworth	d						19 37				
Stratford-upon-Avon	d	18 00						19 57			
Wilmcote	d	18 04						20 02			
Bearley	d										
Claverdon	d										
Hatton	d	18 14					19 43	20 15			
Warwick Parkway	d			18 36		19 05	19 47		20 45		21 45
Warwick	d	18 22		18 40			19 51	20 21	20 48		21 48
Leamington Spa 8	d	18 26		18 45		19 11	19 56	20 26	20 53		21 53
Banbury	d	18 45		19 05		19 29	20 14	20 46	21 12		22 15
Kings Sutton	d	18 50					20 18				22 19
Bicester North 3	d	19 01		19 20		19 45	20 29	21 01	21 28		22 31
Haddenham & Thame Parkway	d	19 13				19 55	20 40		21 41		22 43
Aylesbury	d				19 25					22 28	
Little Kimble	d				19 33					22 36	
Monks Risborough	d				19 37					22 40	
Princes Risborough 2	d	19 20			19 40	20 03	20 47		21 49	22a46	22 51
Saunderton	d				19 45		20 52		21 54		22 56
High Wycombe 1	d	19 30			19 52	20 12	20 59		22 02		23 03
Beaconsfield	d	19 36			19 58	20 18	21 05		22 08		23 09
Seer Green	d				20 01		21 08		22 11		23 12
Gerrards Cross 1	d	19 41			20 05	20 24	21 12		22 15		23 16
Denham Golf Club	d				20 08				22 18		
Denham	d				20 11		21 17		22 21		23 21
West Ruislip 3 § ⊖	d				20 15		21 21		22 25		23 25
South Ruislip § ⊖	d				20 19		21 25		22 29		23 29
Northolt Park	d				20 22		21 28		22 32		23 32
Sudbury Hill Harrow	d										
Sudbury & Harrow Road	d										
Wembley Stadium	d	19 53			20 27		21 33		22 36		23 37
London Paddington 15 ⊖	a										
London Marylebone 10 ⊖	a	20 08		20 12	20 39	20 45	21 46	21 53	22 50		23 50

Sundays
8 January to 12 February

		CH	CH	CH	CH	CH	CH	CH	CH	CH	CH	CH	CH	CH	CH	CH	CH	CH	CH	CH		CH	CH	CH	CH
																							◇		◇
			🚌	🚌				🚌		🚌		🚌			🚌			🚌	🚌			🚌			
Kidderminster	d																								
Stourbridge Junction 2	d																								
Cradley Heath	d																								
Rowley Regis	d																								
Birmingham Snow Hill	d																								
Birmingham Moor Street	d																								
Solihull	d																								
Dorridge	d																								
Lapworth	d																								
Stratford-upon-Avon	d																		10 00				10 00		
Wilmcote	d																						10 04		
Bearley	d																								
Claverdon	d																								
Hatton	d																						10 15		
Warwick Parkway	d									08 10															
Warwick	d									08 20													10 23		
Leamington Spa 8	d		22p10	22p10						08 30		09 20			09 30			09 55				10 25	10a29		
Banbury	d		22p40	22p40				08 35		09 05					10 05			10 30	10 40			11 00			
Kings Sutton	d																								
Bicester North 3	d			23b10			08 24	09a05	09 15	09a35	09 45	10a05		10 15	10a35		10 45	11a00	11a10	11 15		11a30			11 45
Haddenham & Thame Parkway	d			23b40			08 36		09 27		09 57			10 27			10 57			11 27					11 57
Aylesbury	d	22p48			07 26	08 20							09 30			10 25								11 25	
Little Kimble	d	22p56			07 34	08 28							09 38			10 33								11 33	
Monks Risborough	d	23p00			07 38	08 32							09 42			10 37								11 37	
Princes Risborough 2	d	23p06		23b55	07 41	08 35	08 43		09 34		10 04		09 45	10 34		10 40	11 04			11 34				11 40	12 04
Saunderton	d	23p11		23b59	07 46		08 48						09 50			10 45								11 45	
High Wycombe 1	d	23p18		00s20	07 53	08 45	08 54		09 44		10 14		09 57	10 44		10 52	11 14			11 44				11 52	12 14
Beaconsfield	d	23p24		00s40	07 59	08 51	09 00		09 50		10 20		10 03	10 50		10 58	11 20			11 50				11 58	12 20
Seer Green	d	23p27			08 02		09 03						10 06			11 01								12 01	
Gerrards Cross 1	d	23p31		00s55	08 06	08 57	09 08		09 55		10 25		10 10	10 55		11 05	11 25			11 55				12 05	12 25
Denham Golf Club	d	23p34			08 09								10 13											12 08	
Denham	d	23p37		01s15	08 12		09 12						10 16			11 10								12 11	
West Ruislip 3 § ⊖	d	23p41		01s30	08 17		09 17						10 20			11 14								12 15	
South Ruislip § ⊖	d	23p45			08 20		09 20						10 24			11 18								12 19	
Northolt Park	d	23p48			08 24		09 24						10 27			11 21								12 22	
Sudbury Hill Harrow	d																								
Sudbury & Harrow Road	d																								
Wembley Stadium	d	23p53			08 29		09 29						10 32			11 26								12 27	
London Paddington 15 ⊖	a																								
London Marylebone 10 ⊖	a	00 05	00 10	01 55	08 42	09 20	09 41		10 19		10 48		10 44	11 18		11 38	11 48			12 18				12 39	12 48

§ London Underground Limited (Central Line) also operate services between South Ruislip and West Ruislip at frequent intervals

b Previous night, stops to set down only

Table 115

Sundays

8 January to 12 February

Kidderminster, Birmingham Snow Hill, Stratford-upon-Avon, Banbury, Aylesbury and High Wycombe - London

Network Diagram - see first Page of Table 114

		CH	CH	CH	CH	CH	CH	CH	CH	CH	CH	CH	CH	CH	CH	CH		CH	CH	CH	CH	CH	CH	CH	CH
									◇		◇									◇	◇				
		🚌		🚌		🚌	🚌			🚌				🚌	🚌										
Kidderminster	d																								
Stourbridge Junction 2	d																								
Cradley Heath	d																								
Rowley Regis	d																								
Birmingham Snow Hill	d																		13 40				14 40		
Birmingham Moor Street	d																		13 43		14 13		14 43		15 13
Solihull	d																		13 51		14 21		14 51		15 21
Dorridge	d																		13 56		14 26		14 56		15 26
Lapworth	d																		14 00						
Stratford-upon-Avon	d						12 00				12 00									14 00					
Wilmcote	d										12 04									14 04					
Bearley	d																								
Claverdon	d																								
Hatton	d										12 15								14 06	14 15					
Warwick Parkway	d																		14 11		14 37		15 05		15 37
Warwick	d										12 22									14 22	14 39				15 40
Leamington Spa 8	d	10 55		11 30		11 55				12 25	12a28			12 55	13 20				14 17	14 26	14 44		15 11		15 45
Banbury	d	11 30		12 05		12 30	12 40			13 00				13 30					14 35	14 45	15 04		15 30		16 05
Kings Sutton	d																			14 50					
Bicester North 3	d	12a00	12 15	12a35	12 45	13a00	13a10		13 15	13a30			13 45	14a00	14a05	14 15			14 47	15 02	15 19		15 43	15 56	16 19
Haddenham & Thame Parkway	d		12 27		12 57				13 27				13 57			14 27			14 58	15 14			15 53	16 08	
Aylesbury	d							12 25				13 25						14 25				15 25			
Little Kimble	d							12 33				13 33						14 33				15 33			
Monks Risborough	d							12 37				13 37						14 37				15 37			
Princes Risborough 2	d		12 34		13 04			12 40	13 34			13 40	14 04			14 34		14 40	15 05	15 22		15 40	16 02	16 15	
Saunderton	d							12 45				13 45						14 45				15 45			
High Wycombe 1	d		12 44		13 14			12 52	13 44			13 52	14 14			14 44		14 52	15 14	15 32		15 52	16 11	16 25	
Beaconsfield	d		12 50		13 20			12 58	13 50			13 58	14 20			14 50		14 58	15 20	15 38		15 58	16 17	16 31	
Seer Green	d							13 01				14 01						15 01				16 01			
Gerrards Cross 1	d		12 55		13 25			13 05	13 55			14 05	14 25			14 55		15 05	15 26	15 43		16 05	16 22	16 35	
Denham Golf Club	d											14 08										16 08			
Denham	d							13 10				14 11						15 10				16 11			
West Ruislip 3 § ⊖	d							13 14				14 15						15 14				16 15			
South Ruislip § ⊖	d							13 18				14 19						15 18				16 19			
Northolt Park	d							13 21				14 22						15 21				16 22			
Sudbury Hill Harrow	d																								
Sudbury & Harrow Road	d																								
Wembley Stadium	d							13 26				14 27						15 26		15 55		16 27		16 49	
London Paddington 15 ⊖	a																								
London Marylebone 10 ⊖	a		13 18		13 48			13 38	14 18			14 39	14 48			15 18		15 39	15 46	16 08	16 12	16 39	16 45	17 01	17 13

		CH		CH	CH	CH	CH	CH	CH	CH	CH	CH		CH	CH	CH	CH	CH	CH	CH	CH	CH			
					◇									◇	◇				◇	◇		◇			
Kidderminster	d																								
Stourbridge Junction 2	d																								
Cradley Heath	d																								
Rowley Regis	d																								
Birmingham Snow Hill	d			15 40				16 40				17 40					18 40	19 15		20 15		21 15			
Birmingham Moor Street	d			15 43		16 13		16 43		17 13		17 43			18 13		18 43	19 18		20 18		21 18			
Solihull	d			15 51		16 21		16 51		17 21		17 51			18 21		18 51	19 26		20 28		21 28			
Dorridge	d			15 56		16 26		16 56		17 26		17 56			18 26		18 56	19 33		20 35		21 35			
Lapworth	d			16 00								18 00						19 37							
Stratford-upon-Avon	d				16 00									18 00					19 57						
Wilmcote	d				16 04									18 04					20 02						
Bearley	d																								
Claverdon	d																								
Hatton	d			16 06	16 14							18 06		18 14				19 43	20 15						
Warwick Parkway	d			16 11		16 37		17 05		17 36		18 11			18 36		19 05	19 47		20 45		21 45			
Warwick	d				16 23	16 40				17 40				18 22	18 40			19 51	20 21	20 48		21 48			
Leamington Spa 8	d			16 17	16 27	16 45		17 12		17 45		18 17		18 26	18 45		19 11	19 56	20 26	20 53		21 53			
Banbury	d			16 35	16 46	17 05		17 30		18 05		18 35		18 45	19 05		19 29	20 14	20 46	21 12		22 15			
Kings Sutton	d				16 50									18 50				20 18				22 19			
Bicester North 3	d			16 47	17 01	17 19		17 47	18 00	18 20		18 46		19 01	19 20		19 45	20 29	21 01	21 28		22 31			
Haddenham & Thame Parkway	d			16 57	17 13			17 57	18 12			18 56		19 13			19 55	20 40		21 41		22 43			
Aylesbury	d	16 25					17 25				18 25					19 25					22 28				
Little Kimble	d	16 33					17 33				18 33					19 33					22 36				
Monks Risborough	d	16 37					17 37				18 37					19 37					22 40				
Princes Risborough 2	d	16 40		17 06	17 20		17 40	18 05	18 19		18 40	19 05		19 20		19 40	20 03	20 47		21 49	22a46	22 51			
Saunderton	d	16 45					17 45				18 45					19 45		20 52		21 54		22 56			
High Wycombe 1	d	16 52		17 15	17 30		17 52	18 14	18 29		18 52	19 14		19 30		19 52	20 12	20 59		22 02		23 03			
Beaconsfield	d	16 58		17 21	17 36		17 58	18 20	18 35		18 58	19 20		19 36		19 58	20 18	21 05		22 08		23 09			
Seer Green	d	17 01					18 01				19 01					20 01		21 08		22 11		23 12			
Gerrards Cross 1	d	17 05		17 26	17 42		18 05	18 26	18 40		19 05	19 25		19 41		20 05	20 24	21 12		22 15		23 16			
Denham Golf Club	d						18 08									20 08				22 18					
Denham	d	17 10					18 11				19 10					20 11		21 17		22 21		23 21			
West Ruislip 3 § ⊖	d	17 14					18 15				19 14					20 15		21 21		22 25		23 25			
South Ruislip § ⊖	d	17 18					18 19				19 18					20 19		21 25		22 29		23 29			
Northolt Park	d	17 21					18 22				19 21					20 22		21 28		22 32		23 32			
Sudbury Hill Harrow	d																								
Sudbury & Harrow Road	d																								
Wembley Stadium	d	17 26					18 27		18 52		19 26			19 53		20 27		21 33		22 36		23 37			
London Paddington 15 ⊖	a																								
London Marylebone 10 ⊖	a	17 39		17 46	18 08	18 12	18 41	18 45	19 06	19 13	19 39	19 45		20 08	20 12	20 39	20 45	21 46	21 53	22 50		23 50			

§ London Underground Limited (Central Line) also operate services between South Ruislip and West Ruislip at frequent intervals

Table 115

Sundays

19 February to 25 March

Kidderminster, Birmingham Snow Hill, Stratford-upon-Avon, Banbury, Aylesbury and High Wycombe - London

Network Diagram - see first Page of Table 114

		CH	CH	CH	CH	CH	CH	CH	CH	CH		CH	CH	CH	CH	CH	CH	CH	CH	CH		CH	CH	CH	CH
			🚌	🚌				🚌		🚌				🚌		🚌			🚌	🚌			🚌	◇	
Kidderminster	d																								
Stourbridge Junction 2	d																								
Cradley Heath	d																								
Rowley Regis	d																								
Birmingham Snow Hill	d																								
Birmingham Moor Street	d																								
Solihull	d																								
Dorridge	d																								
Lapworth	d																								
Stratford-upon-Avon	d																			10 00				10 00	
Wilmcote	d																							10 04	
Bearley	d																								
Claverdon	d																								
Hatton	d																							10 15	
Warwick Parkway	d									08 10															
Warwick	d									08 20														10 23	
Leamington Spa 8	d		22p10	22p10						08 30				09 20		09 30			09 55				10 25	10a29	
Banbury	d		22p40	22p40				08 35		09 05						10 05			10 30	10 40			11 00		
Kings Sutton	d																								
Bicester North 3	d			23b10			08 24	09a05	09 15	09a35			09 45	10a05	10 15	10a35		10 45	11a00	11a10		11 15	11a30		
Haddenham & Thame Parkway	d			23b40			08 36		09 27				09 57		10 27			10 57				11 27			
Aylesbury	d	22p48			07 26	08 20						09 30					10 25								11 25
Little Kimble	d	22p56			07 34	08 28						09 38					10 33								11 33
Monks Risborough	d	23p00			07 38	08 32						09 42					10 37								11 37
Princes Risborough 2	d	23p06		23b55	07 41	08 35	08 43		09 34			09 45	10 04		10 34		10 40	11 04				11 34			11 40
Saunderton	d	23p11		23b59	07 46		08 48					09 50					10 45								11 45
High Wycombe 1	d	23p18		00s20	07 53	08 45	08 54		09 44			09 57	10 14		10 44		10 52	11 14				11 44			11 52
Beaconsfield	d	23p24		00s40	07 59	08 51	09 00		09 50			10 03	10 20		10 50		10 58	11 20				11 50			11 58
Seer Green	d	23p27			08 02		09 03					10 06					11 01								12 01
Gerrards Cross 1	d	23p31		00s55	08 06	08 57	09 08		09 55			10 10	10 25		10 55		11 05	11 25				11 55			12 05
Denham Golf Club	d	23p34			08 09							10 13													12 08
Denham	d	23p37		01s15	08 12		09 12					10 16					11 10								12 11
West Ruislip 3 §	⊖ d	23p41		01s30	08 17		09 17					10 20					11 14								12 15
South Ruislip §	⊖ d	23p45			08 20		09 20					10 24					11 18								12 19
Northolt Park	d	23p48			08 24		09 24					10 27					11 21								12 22
Sudbury Hill Harrow	d																								
Sudbury & Harrow Road	d																								
Wembley Stadium	d	23p53			08 29		09 29					10 32					11 26								12 27
London Paddington 15	⊖ a																								
London Marylebone 10	⊖ a	00 05	00 10	01 55	08 42	09 20	09 41		10 19			10 44	10 48		11 18		11 38	11 48				12 18			12 39

		CH	CH	CH	CH	CH		CH	CH	CH	CH	CH	CH	CH	CH	CH		CH	CH	CH	CH	CH	CH	CH	CH
		◇									◇		◇									◇	◇		
			🚌		🚌				🚌	🚌		🚌				🚌		🚌							
Kidderminster	d																								
Stourbridge Junction 2	d																								
Cradley Heath	d																								
Rowley Regis	d																								
Birmingham Snow Hill	d																				13 40				14 40
Birmingham Moor Street	d																				13 43		14 13		14 43
Solihull	d																				13 51		14 21		14 51
Dorridge	d																				13 56		14 26		14 56
Lapworth	d																				14 00				
Stratford-upon-Avon	d									12 00			12 00									14 00			
Wilmcote	d												12 04									14 04			
Bearley	d																								
Claverdon	d																								
Hatton	d												12 15								14 06	14 15			
Warwick Parkway	d																				14 11		14 37		15 05
Warwick	d												12 22									14 22	14 39		
Leamington Spa 8	d		10 55		11 30				11 55			12 25	12a28			12 55		13 20			14 17	14 26	14 44		15 11
Banbury	d		11 30		12 05				12 30	12 40		13 00				13 30					14 35	14 45	15 04		15 30
Kings Sutton	d																					14 50			
Bicester North 3	d	11 45	12a00	12 15	12a35			12 45	13a00	13a10	13 15	13a30			13 45	14a00		14a05	14 15		14 47	15 02	15 19		15 43
Haddenham & Thame Parkway	d	11 57		12 27				12 57			13 27				13 57				14 27		14 58	15 14			15 53
Aylesbury	d					12 25								13 25						14 25				15 25	
Little Kimble	d					12 33								13 33						14 33				15 33	
Monks Risborough	d					12 37								13 37						14 37				15 37	
Princes Risborough 2	d	12 04		12 34		12 40		13 04			13 34			13 40	14 04				14 34	14 40	15 05	15 22		15 40	16 02
Saunderton	d					12 45								13 45						14 45				15 45	
High Wycombe 1	d	12 14		12 44		12 52		13 14			13 44			13 52	14 14				14 44	14 52	15 14	15 32		15 52	16 11
Beaconsfield	d	12 20		12 50		12 58		13 20			13 50			13 58	14 20				14 50	14 58	15 20	15 38		15 58	16 17
Seer Green	d					13 01								14 01						15 01				16 01	
Gerrards Cross 1	d	12 25		12 55		13 05		13 25			13 55			14 05	14 25				14 55	15 05	15 26	15 43		16 05	16 22
Denham Golf Club	d													14 08										16 08	
Denham	d					13 10								14 11						15 10				16 11	
West Ruislip 3 §	⊖ d					13 14								14 15						15 14				16 15	
South Ruislip §	⊖ d					13 18								14 19						15 18				16 19	
Northolt Park	d					13 21								14 22						15 21				16 22	
Sudbury Hill Harrow	d																								
Sudbury & Harrow Road	d																								
Wembley Stadium	d					13 26								14 27						15 26		15 55		16 27	
London Paddington 15	⊖ a																								
London Marylebone 10	⊖ a	12 48		13 18		13 38		13 48			14 18			14 39	14 48				15 18	15 39	15 46	16 08	16 12	16 39	16 45

§ London Underground Limited (Central Line) also operate services between South Ruislip and West Ruislip at frequent intervals

b Previous night, stops to set down only

Table 115

Sundays

19 February to 25 March

Kidderminster, Birmingham Snow Hill, Stratford-upon-Avon, Banbury, Aylesbury and High Wycombe - London

Network Diagram - see first Page of Table 114

		CH		CH	CH	CH	CH	CH	CH	CH	CH	CH		CH	CH	CH	CH	CH	CH	CH	CH	CH		CH	CH
							◇									◇	◇				◇	◇			◇
Kidderminster	d																								
Stourbridge Junction [2]	d																								
Cradley Heath	d																								
Rowley Regis	d																								
Birmingham Snow Hill	d					15 40				16 40					17 40				18 40	19 15		20 15			21 15
Birmingham Moor Street	d			15 13		15 43		16 13		16 43		17 13			17 43		18 13		18 43	19 18		20 18			21 18
Solihull	d			15 21		15 51		16 21		16 51		17 21			17 51		18 21		18 51	19 26		20 28			21 28
Dorridge	d			15 26		15 56		16 26		16 56		17 26			17 56		18 26		18 56	19 33		20 35			21 35
Lapworth	d					16 00									18 00					19 37					
Stratford-upon-Avon	d						16 00									18 00					19 57				
Wilmcote	d						16 04									18 04					20 02				
Bearley	d																								
Claverdon	d																								
Hatton	d					16 06	16 14								18 06	18 14				19 43	20 15				
Warwick Parkway	d			15 37		16 11		16 37		17 05		17 36			18 11		18 36		19 05	19 47		20 45			21 45
Warwick	d			15 40			16 23	16 40				17 40				18 22	18 40			19 51	20 21	20 48			21 48
Leamington Spa [8]	d			15 45		16 17	16 27	16 45		17 12		17 45			18 17	18 26	18 45		19 11	19 56	20 26	20 53			21 53
Banbury	d			16 05		16 35	16 46	17 05		17 30		18 05			18 35	18 45	19 05		19 29	20 14	20 46	21 12			22 15
Kings Sutton	d						16 50									18 50				20 18					22 19
Bicester North [3]	d	15 56		16 19		16 47	17 01	17 19		17 47	18 00	18 20			18 46	19 01	19 20		19 45	20 29	21 01	21 28			22 31
Haddenham & Thame Parkway	d	16 08				16 57	17 13			17 57	18 12				18 56	19 13			19 55	20 40		21 41			22 43
Aylesbury	d				16 25				17 25					18 25				19 25						22 28	
Little Kimble	d				16 33				17 33					18 33				19 33						22 36	
Monks Risborough	d				16 37				17 37					18 37				19 37						22 40	
Princes Risborough [2]	d	16 15			16 40	17 06	17 20		17 40	18 05	18 19			18 40	19 05	19 20		19 40	20 03	20 47		21 49		22a46	22 51
Saunderton	d				16 45				17 45					18 45				19 45		20 52		21 54			22 56
High Wycombe [1]	d	16 25			16 52	17 15	17 30		17 52	18 14	18 29			18 52	19 14	19 30		19 52	20 12	20 59		22 02			23 03
Beaconsfield	d	16 31			16 58	17 21	17 36		17 58	18 20	18 35			18 58	19 20	19 36		19 58	20 18	21 05		22 08			23 09
Seer Green	d				17 01				18 01					19 01				20 01		21 08		22 11			23 12
Gerrards Cross [1]	d	16 35			17 05	17 26	17 42		18 05	18 26	18 40			19 05	19 25	19 41		20 05	20 24	21 12		22 15			23 16
Denham Golf Club	d								18 08									20 08				22 18			
Denham	d				17 10				18 11					19 10				20 11		21 17		22 21			23 21
West Ruislip [3] § ⊖	d				17 14				18 15					19 14				20 15		21 21		22 25			23 25
South Ruislip § ⊖	d				17 18				18 19					19 18				20 19		21 25		22 29			23 29
Northolt Park	d				17 21				18 22					19 21				20 22		21 28		22 32			23 32
Sudbury Hill Harrow	d																								
Sudbury & Harrow Road	d																								
Wembley Stadium	d	16 49			17 26				18 27		18 52			19 26		19 53		20 27		21 33		22 36			23 37
London Paddington [15] ⊖	a																								
London Marylebone [10] ⊖	a	17 01		17 13	17 39	17 46	18 08	18 12	18 41	18 45	19 06	19 13		19 39	19 45	20 08	20 12	20 39	20 45	21 46	21 53	22 50			23 50

Sundays

from 1 April

		CH	CH	CH	CH	CH	CH	CH	CH	CH		CH	CH	CH	CH	CH	CH	CH	CH	CH		CH	CH	CH	CH
									◇			◇				◇		◇	◇						◇
Kidderminster	d																								
Stourbridge Junction [2]	d																								
Cradley Heath	d																								
Rowley Regis	d																								
Birmingham Snow Hill	d													09 40				10 40					11 40		
Birmingham Moor Street	d								08 55			09 13		09 43		10 13		10 43	11 13				11 43	12 13	
Solihull	d								09 04			09 22		09 52		10 21		10 52	11 21				11 51	12 21	
Dorridge	d								09 09			09 27		09 57		10 26		10 57	11 26				11 56	12 26	
Lapworth	d																	11 01							
Stratford-upon-Avon	d																								
Wilmcote	d																								
Bearley	d																								
Claverdon	d																								
Hatton	d																	11 06							
Warwick Parkway	d								09 18			09 35		10 06		10 35		11 11	11 35				12 06	12 35	
Warwick	d								09 22			09 40				10 39			11 39					12 39	
Leamington Spa [8]	d								09 27			09 45		10 14		10 44		11 18	11 43				12 13	12 43	
Banbury	d								09 44	09 50		10 02		10 31		11 06		11 35	12 01				12 30	13 01	
Kings Sutton	d													10 36									12 35		
Bicester North [3]	d				08 24	09 15		09 45	09 57	10 04		10 24		10 48	11 15	11 28		11 48	12 27	12 15			12 45	13 28	13 15
Haddenham & Thame Parkway	d				08 36	09 27		09 57		10 16				10 59	11 27			11 59		12 27			12 56		13 27
Aylesbury	d	22p48	07 26	08 20			09 30						10 25				11 25					12 25			
Little Kimble	d	22p56	07 34	08 28			09 38						10 33				11 33					12 33			
Monks Risborough	d	23p00	07 38	08 32			09 42						10 37				11 37					12 37			
Princes Risborough [2]	d	23p06	07 41	08 35	08 43	09 34	09 45	10 04		10 21			10 40	11 07	11 34		11 40	12 06		12 34		12 40	13 03		13 34
Saunderton	d	23p11	07 46		08 48		09 50						10 45				11 45					12 45			
High Wycombe [1]	d	23p18	07 53	08 45	08 54	09 44	09 57	10 14		10 31			10 52	11 16	11 44		11 52	12 15		12 44		12 52	13 12		13 44
Beaconsfield	d	23p24	07 59	08 51	09 00	09 50	10 03	10 20		10 37			10 58		11 50		11 58			12 50		12 58			13 50
Seer Green	d	23p27	08 02		09 03		10 06						11 01				12 01					13 01			
Gerrards Cross [1]	d	23p31	08 06	08 57	09 08	09 55	10 10	10 25		10 42			11 05		11 55		12 05			12 55		13 05			13 55
Denham Golf Club	d	23p34	08 09				10 13										12 08								
Denham	d	23p37	08 12		09 12		10 16						11 10				12 11					13 10			
West Ruislip [3] § ⊖	d	23p41	08 17		09 17		10 20						11 14				12 15					13 14			
South Ruislip § ⊖	d	23p45	08 20		09 20		10 24						11 18				12 19					13 18			
Northolt Park	d	23p48	08 24		09 24		10 27						11 21				12 22					13 21			
Sudbury Hill Harrow	d																								
Sudbury & Harrow Road	d																								
Wembley Stadium	d	23p53	08 29		09 29		10 32						11 26				12 27					13 26			
London Paddington [15] ⊖	a																								
London Marylebone [10] ⊖	a	00 05	08 42	09 20	09 41	10 19	10 44	10 48	10 47	11 06		11 09	11 38	11 44	12 18	12 12	12 39	12 40	13 12	13 18		13 38	13 37	14 12	14 18

§ London Underground Limited (Central Line) also operate services between South Ruislip and West Ruislip at frequent intervals

Table 115

Sundays
from 1 April

Kidderminster, Birmingham Snow Hill, Stratford-upon-Avon, Banbury, Aylesbury and High Wycombe - London

Network Diagram - see first Page of Table 114

		CH	CH	CH	CH ◇	CH	CH	CH ◇	CH ◇	CH	CH	CH	CH	CH	CH	CH ◇	CH	CH	CH	CH	CH	CH	CH
Kidderminster	d																						
Stourbridge Junction 2	d																						
Cradley Heath	d																						
Rowley Regis	d																						
Birmingham Snow Hill	d		12 40				13 40				14 40				15 40				16 40				17 40
Birmingham Moor Street	d		12 43		13 11		13 43		14 13		14 43		15 13		15 43		16 13		16 43		17 13		17 43
Solihull	d		12 50		13 20		13 51		14 21		14 51		15 21		15 51		16 21		16 51		17 21		17 51
Dorridge	d		12 56		13 25		13 56		14 26		14 56		15 26		15 56		16 26		16 56		17 26		17 56
Lapworth	d						14 00								16 00								18 00
Stratford-upon-Avon	d							14 00								16 00							
Wilmcote	d							14 04								16 04							
Bearley	d																						
Claverdon	d																						
Hatton	d						14 06	14 15							16 06	16 14							18 06
Warwick Parkway	d		13 06		13 34		14 11		14 37		15 05		15 37		16 11		16 37		17 05		17 36		18 11
Warwick	d				13 39			14 22	14 39				15 40			16 23	16 40				17 40		
Leamington Spa 8	d		13 11		13 43		14 17	14 26	14 44		15 11		15 45		16 17	16 27	16 45		17 12		17 45		18 17
Banbury	d		13 29		14 05		14 35	14 45	15 04		15 30		16 05		16 35	16 46	17 05		17 30		18 05		18 35
Kings Sutton	d							14 50								16 50							
Bicester North 3	d		13 42	14 15	14 27		14 47	15 02	15 19		15 43	15 56	16 19		16 47	17 01	17 19		17 47	18 00	18 20		18 46
Haddenham & Thame Parkway	d		13 52	14 27			14 58	15 14			15 53	16 08			16 57	17 13			17 57	18 12			18 56
Aylesbury	d	13 25				14 25				15 25				16 25				17 25				18 25	
Little Kimble	d	13 33				14 33				15 33				16 33				17 33				18 33	
Monks Risborough	d	13 37				14 37				15 37				16 37				17 37				18 37	
Princes Risborough 2	d	13 40	13 59	14 34		14 40	15 05	15 22		15 40	16 02	16 15		16 40	17 06	17 20		17 40	18 05	18 19		18 40	19 05
Saunderton	d	13 45				14 45				15 45				16 45				17 45				18 45	
High Wycombe 1	d	13 52	14 08	14 44		14 52	15 14	15 32		15 52	16 11	16 25		16 52	17 15	17 30		17 52	18 14	18 29		18 52	19 14
Beaconsfield	d	13 58		14 50		14 58	15 20	15 38		15 58	16 17	16 31		16 58	17 21	17 36		17 58	18 20	18 35		18 58	19 20
Seer Green	d	14 01				15 01				16 01				17 01				18 01				19 01	
Gerrards Cross 1	d	14 05		14 55		15 05	15 26	15 43		16 05	16 22	16 35		17 05	17 26	17 42		18 05	18 26	18 40		19 05	19 25
Denham Golf Club	d	14 08								16 08								18 08					
Denham	d	14 11				15 10				16 11				17 10				18 11				19 10	
West Ruislip 3 § ⊖	d	14 15				15 14				16 15				17 14				18 15				19 14	
South Ruislip § ⊖	d	14 19				15 18				16 19				17 18				18 19				19 18	
Northolt Park	d	14 22				15 21				16 22				17 21				18 22				19 21	
Sudbury Hill Harrow	d																						
Sudbury & Harrow Road	d																						
Wembley Stadium	d	14 27				15 26		15 55		16 27		16 49		17 26				18 27		18 52		19 26	
London Paddington 15 ⊖	a																						
London Marylebone 10 ⊖	a	14 39	14 38	15 18	15 12	15 39	15 46	16 08	16 12	16 39	16 45	17 01	17 13	17 39	17 46	18 08	18 12	18 41	18 45	19 06	19 13	19 39	19 45

		CH ◇	CH ◇	CH	CH	CH	CH ◇	CH ◇	CH	CH ◇
Kidderminster	d									
Stourbridge Junction 2	d									
Cradley Heath	d									
Rowley Regis	d									
Birmingham Snow Hill	d				18 40	19 15		20 15		21 15
Birmingham Moor Street	d		18 13		18 43	19 18		20 18		21 18
Solihull	d		18 21		18 51	19 26		20 28		21 28
Dorridge	d		18 26		18 56	19 33		20 35		21 35
Lapworth	d					19 37				
Stratford-upon-Avon	d	18 00					19 57			
Wilmcote	d	18 04					20 02			
Bearley	d									
Claverdon	d									
Hatton	d	18 14				19 43	20 15			
Warwick Parkway	d		18 36		19 05	19 47		20 45		21 45
Warwick	d	18 22	18 40			19 51	20 21	20 48		21 48
Leamington Spa 8	d	18 26	18 45		19 11	19 56	20 26	20 53		21 53
Banbury	d	18 45	19 05		19 29	20 14	20 46	21 12		22 15
Kings Sutton	d	18 50				20 18				22 19
Bicester North 3	d	19 01	19 20		19 45	20 29	21 01	21 28		22 31
Haddenham & Thame Parkway	d	19 13			19 55	20 40		21 41		22 43
Aylesbury	d			19 25					22 28	
Little Kimble	d			19 33					22 36	
Monks Risborough	d			19 37					22 40	
Princes Risborough 2	d	19 20		19 40	20 03	20 47		21 49	22a46	22 51
Saunderton	d			19 45		20 52		21 54		22 56
High Wycombe 1	d	19 30		19 52	20 12	20 59		22 02		23 03
Beaconsfield	d	19 36		19 58	20 18	21 05		22 08		23 09
Seer Green	d			20 01		21 08		22 11		23 12
Gerrards Cross 1	d	19 41		20 05	20 24	21 12		22 15		23 16
Denham Golf Club	d			20 08				22 18		
Denham	d			20 11		21 17		22 21		23 21
West Ruislip 3 § ⊖	d			20 15		21 21		22 25		23 25
South Ruislip § ⊖	d			20 19		21 25		22 29		23 29
Northolt Park	d			20 22		21 28		22 32		23 32
Sudbury Hill Harrow	d									
Sudbury & Harrow Road	d									
Wembley Stadium	d	19 53		20 27		21 33		22 36		23 37
London Paddington 15 ⊖	a									
London Marylebone 10 ⊖	a	20 08	20 12	20 39	20 45	21 46	21 53	22 50		23 50

§ London Underground Limited (Central Line) also operate services between South Ruislip and West Ruislip at frequent intervals

Table 115A

Mondays to Fridays

Chinnor - Princes Risborough

Bus Service

		CH	CH	CH	CH	CH A	CH	CH	CH	CH	CH	CH	CH	CH	CH
Chinnor, Lower Road	d	06 08	06 48	07 22	07 56	08 30	09 16	09 42	17 01	17 28	18 20	19 04	19 37	20 14	21 12
Chinnor, Estover Way	d	06 10	06 50	07 24	07 58	08 32	09 18	09 44	17 03	17 32	18 22	19 06	19 39	20 16	21 14
Chinnor, The Wheatsheaf	d	06 11	06 51	07 25	07 59	08 33	09 19	09 45	17 04	17 33	18 23	19 07	19 40	20 17	21 15
Chinnor, The Red Lion	d	06 14	06 54	07 28	08 02	08a36	09 22	09 48	17a07	17a36	18a26	19a10	19a43	20a20	21a17
Bledlow, Village Hall	d	06 17	06 57	07 31	08 05		09 25	09 51		17 38					
Princes Risborough	a	06 24	07 04	07 38	08 12		09 32	09 58		17 50					

No Saturday or Sunday service

Table 115A

Mondays to Fridays

Princes Risborough - Chinnor

Bus Service

		CH	CH	CH	CH	CH	CH	CH	CH	CH	CH	CH	CH	CH	CH
Princes Risborough	d				07 38	08 12			16 51	17 18	18 10	18 54	19 27	20 04	21 02
Bledlow, Village Hall	d				07 52	08 27			16 58	17 25	18 17	19 01	19 34	20 11	21 09
Chinnor, Lower Road	d	06 08	06 48	07 22	07 56	08 30	09 16	09 42	17 01	17 28	18 20	19 04	19 37	20 14	21 12
Chinnor, Estover Way	d	06 10	06 50	07 24	07 58	08 32	09 18	09 44	17 03	17 32	18 22	19 06	19 39	20 16	21 14
Chinnor, The Wheatsheaf	d	06 11	06 51	07 25	07 59	08 33	09 19	09 45	17 04	17 33	18 23	19 07	19 40	20 17	21 15
Chinnor, The Red Lion	a	06 14	06 54	07 28	08 02	08 36	09 22	09 48	17 07	17 36	18 26	19 10	19 43	20 20	21 17

No Saturday or Sunday service

Network Diagram for Tables 116, 117, 118, 119, 120, 121, 122, 126

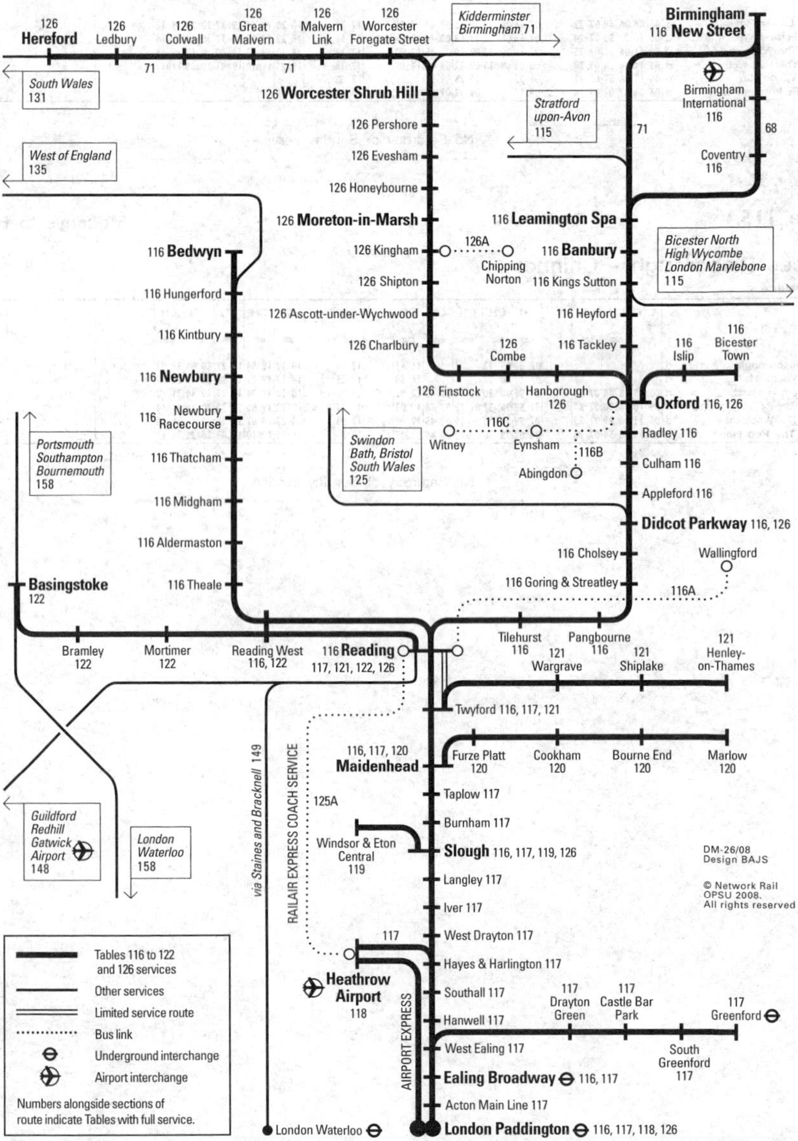

London and Reading - Bedwyn, Oxford, Bicester, Banbury and Birmingham

Network Diagram - see first Page of Table 116

Miles	Miles			GW MO A 🚌	GW MO 🚌	GW 1 B	GW 1 C	GW MX 1	GW MO ◇1 B ☕	GW MO ◇1 C ☕	GW MO 1 B	GW MO 1 C		GW MX ◇1	CH MX	GW MO 🚌	GW MX 1	GW MX ◇1 ☕	GW MO ◇1 D ☕	GW MO ◇1 E ☕	GW MX 1	GW MO 🚌		GW MX 1	GW MX ◇1
0	—	**London Paddington** 15 ⊖	d			22p43	22p43	22p45	23p03	23p03				23p18			23p29	23p30	23p37	23p37					00 22
5¾	—	Ealing Broadway ⊖	d			22p50	22p50	22p54									23p37								
18½	—	Slough 3	d			23p16	23p16	23p12						23p36			23p54		00 01	00 02					00 39
24¼	—	Maidenhead 3	d			23p24	23p25	23p24						23p44			00 01								
31	—	Twyford 3	d			23p32	23p32	23p32			←	←					00 09							←	
36	0	**Reading** 7	d	23p13		23b51	23b53	23p41	23p47	23p46	23p51	23p53		23p58			00 24	00 08	00 15	00 15	00 20			00 24	01 00
—	1	Reading West	d	23p29		→	→										→				00s23				
—	5¼	Theale	d	23p44																	00s29				
—	8¾	Aldermaston	d	23p50																	00s34				
—	10¾	Midgham	d	23p58																	00s37				
—	13½	Thatcham	d	00 05																	00s42				
—	16½	Newbury Racecourse	d	00 15																	00s47				
—	17	**Newbury**	a	00 25																	00 52				
—	—		d																						
—	22½	Kintbury	d																						
—	25½	Hungerford	d																						
—	30½	**Bedwyn**	a																						
38¾	—	Tilehurst	d					23p45			23p55	23p57												00 29	
41½	—	Pangbourne	d					23p49				00 01												00 33	
44¾	—	Goring & Streatley	d					23p53			00 04	00 07												00 37	
48½	—	Cholsey	d					23p57			00 09	00 12												00 42	
53¼	—	**Didcot Parkway**	a					00 07	00s01	00s02	00 16	00 20						00 25	00s30	00s31				00 51	01 19
—	—		d		23p45			00 07								00 25						00 40		00 51	01 19
55¼	—	Appleford	d																					00 56	
56¼	—	Culham	d																					00 58	
58½	—	Radley	d					00 15								00 40								01 02	
63½	0	**Oxford**	a		00 10			00 26						00 28		00 55						01 05		01 17	01 34
—	—		d												00 38										
—	5¾	Islip	d																						
—	11¾	**Bicester Town**	a																						
72½	—	Tackley	d												00 48										
75¼	—	Heyford	d												00 53										
82¾	—	Kings Sutton	d												01 01										
86¼	—	**Banbury**	a												01 10										
106¼	—	Leamington Spa 8	a																						
115¾	—	Coventry	a																						
126½	—	Birmingham International	a																						
135	—	**Birmingham New Street** 12	a																						

		GW 1	GW 1	CH	GW 1	GW 1	GW 1	GW ◇1 ☕		XC ◇1 trolley	GW 1	GW 1	GW ◇1	GW 1	XC ◇1 trolley	GW 1	GW 1	GW 1		CH	GW 1	GW ◇1 ☕	XC ◇1 trolley	GW 1	GW 1
London Paddington 15 ⊖	d					05 17	05 22	05 36					05 48			05 57	06 20					06 30			06 48
Ealing Broadway ⊖	d						05 30									06 05									
Slough 3	d					05 34	05 54	05 52					06 05			06 29	06 35								07 04
Maidenhead 3	d						06 02									06 37									
Twyford 3	d						06 10							←		06 45					←				
Reading 7	d	05 18			05 49	05 52	06 21	06 07		06 11		06 15	06 22	06 21	06 41	06 53	06 51	06 52			06 53	06 56	07 09	07 12	07 22
Reading West	d	05 20					→					06 17				→		06 54						07 14	
Theale	d	05 26										06 23						07 00						07 20	
Aldermaston	d	05 31										06 28						07 05						07 25	
Midgham	d	05 35										06 32						07 09						07 29	
Thatcham	d	05 40										06 37						07 14						07 34	
Newbury Racecourse	d	05 44										06 41						07 18						07 38	
Newbury	a	05 47										06 47						07 21						07 44	
	d	05 47																07 21							
Kintbury	d	05 54																07 28							
Hungerford	d	05 58																07 32							
Bedwyn	a	06 08																07 42							
Tilehurst	d				05 54									06 25							06 57				07 27
Pangbourne	d				05 58									06 29							07 01				07 31
Goring & Streatley	d				06 03									06 34							07 06				07 36
Cholsey	d				06 08						←			06 39							07 11				07 41
Didcot Parkway	a				06 18	06 08		06 20			06 18		06 39	06 47			07 06				07 19	07 10			07 49
	d				06 25	06 09					06 25		06 39	06 47			07 08				07 25				07 49
Appleford	d				→																07 30				
Culham	d										06 31										07 32				
Radley	d												06 48								07 36				
Oxford	a					06 22				06 34	06 41		06 56	07 02	07 05		07 22				07 46		07 35		08 02
	d		05 45	05 51						06 36	06 41				07 07					07 27			07 36		
Islip	d			06 04																07 40					
Bicester Town	a			06 16																07 53					
Tackley	d		05 54								06 49														
Heyford	d		05 58								06 55														
Kings Sutton	d		06 07								07 02														
Banbury	a		06 14							06 52	07 10				07 24								07 53		
Leamington Spa 8	a									07 10					07 42								08 11		
Coventry	a									07 22													08 23		
Birmingham International	a									07 37													08 37		
Birmingham New Street 12	a									07 48					08 15								08 48		

A from 2 April
B from 9 January
C until 2 January
D from 20 February until 26 March
E until 13 February, MO from 2 April
b Previous night, arr. 2343

London and Reading - Bedwyn, Oxford, Bicester, Banbury and Birmingham

Network Diagram - see first Page of Table 116

		GW	GW	GW		GW	GW	XC	GW	GW	CH	GW	XC	GW		GW	GW	GW	GW	GW	GW	GW	GW	XC	
		1	◇1	◇1		1	◇1	◇1	1	1		1	◇1	1		1	◇1	1	1	1	◇1	1	◇1	◇1	
				A																					
			🛒	🛒			🛒	🍴					🍴				🛒				🛒		🛒	🍴	
London Paddington 15 ⊖	d	06 57	07 00	07 06			07 15		07 18	07 21						07 27	07 48	07 50		07 57	08 00		08 15		
Ealing Broadway ⊖	d	07 05														07 35				08 05					
Slough 3	d	07 29								07 36						07 59		08 06		08 29					
Maidenhead 3	d	07 37														08 07				08 38					
Twyford 3	d	07 45										←				08 15			←	08 46					
Reading 7	d	07 53	07 26	07 33		07 34	07 42	07 40	07 48	07 52		07 53	08 11	08 12		08 23	08 16	08 22	08 23	08 55	08 27	08 34	08 42	08 41	
Reading West	d	→												08 14		→				→					
Theale	d								07 56					08 20								08 41			
Aldermaston	d								08 01					08 25								08 46			
Midgham	d													08 29											
Thatcham	d								08 08					08 34								08 53			
Newbury Racecourse	d													08 38											
Newbury	a			07 47					08 13					08 44								08 59			
	d								08 13													08 59			
Kintbury	d								08 20													09 05			
Hungerford	d								08 24													09 09			
Bedwyn	a								08 34													09 20			
Tilehurst	d											07 57							08 27						
Pangbourne	d											08 01							08 31						
Goring & Streatley	d											08 06							08 36						
Cholsey	d											08 11							08 41						
Didcot Parkway	a		07 40			07 57	07 56					08 20					08 32		08 50		08 40		08 56		
	d					08 08						08 25							08 55						
Appleford	d					08 13													09 00						
Culham	d					08 15													09 01						
Radley	d					08 19						08 33							09 06						
Oxford	a					08 30		08 05		08 19		08 43	08 34					08 49	09 15					09 04	
	d							08 07			08 35		08 36					08 53						09 07	
Islip	d										08 48														
Bicester Town	a										09 01														
Tackley	d																	09 01							
Heyford	d																	09 06							
Kings Sutton	d																	09 15							
Banbury	a							08 26					08 52					09 22						09 25	
Leamington Spa 8	a							08 43					09 10											09 42	
Coventry	a												09 22												
Birmingham International	a												09 37												
Birmingham New Street 12	a							09 18					09 48											10 18	

		GW	GW	GW	GW	GW	XC	GW	GW	CH		GW	XC	GW	GW	GW	GW	GW	GW	GW		XC	GW	GW	GW
		1	◇1	1	1	◇1	◇1	1	1			1	◇1	1	◇1	1	◇1	1	1	◇1		◇1	1	◇1	◇1
			🛒			🛒	🍴						🍴		🛒		🍴			🛒		🍴		🛒	
London Paddington 15 ⊖	d	08 18	08 22		08 27	08 30			08 51					08 55	09 15	09 18	09 21		09 27	09 30				09 48	09 50
Ealing Broadway ⊖	d				08 35									09 03					09 35						
Slough 3	d		08 36		08 59				09 06					09 27			09 36		09 57						10 06
Maidenhead 3	d				09 06									09 35					10 04						
Twyford 3	d			←	09 16							←		09 43				←	10 12						
Reading 7	d	08 48	08 52	08 55	09 23	08 57	09 11	09 12	09 22			09 23	09 40	09 53	09 42	09 48	09 52	09 53	10 23	09 57		10 11	10 12	10 16	10 22
Reading West	d				→			09 14						→					→				10 14		
Theale	d	08 56						09 20								09 56							10 20		
Aldermaston	d							09 25															10 25		
Midgham	d							09 29															10 29		
Thatcham	d	09 04						09 34								10 04							10 34		
Newbury Racecourse	d							09 38															10 38		
Newbury	a	09 13						09 44								10 10							10 44		
	d															10 10									
Kintbury	d															10 17									
Hungerford	d															10 21									
Bedwyn	a															10 31									
Tilehurst	d			09 00								09 27						09 57							
Pangbourne	d			09 04								09 31						10 01							
Goring & Streatley	d			09 09								09 36						10 06							
Cholsey	d			09 14								09 41						10 11							
Didcot Parkway	a			09 22		09 11			09 37			09 50			09 56			10 18		10 11				10 32	
	d			09 25					09 38			09 55						10 25							
Appleford	d																								
Culham	d											10 01													
Radley	d			09 33								10 03													
Oxford	a		09 20	09 46			09 34		09 53			10 14	10 01				10 18	10 41				10 34			10 47
	d						09 36			10 00			10 07									10 36			
Islip	d									10 13															
Bicester Town	a									10 25															
Tackley	d																								
Heyford	d																								
Kings Sutton	d																								
Banbury	a						09 53						10 24									10 52			
Leamington Spa 8	a						10 11						10 41									11 10			
Coventry	a						10 23															11 22			
Birmingham International	a						10 37															11 37			
Birmingham New Street 12	a						10 48						11 18									11 48			

A The Devon Express

London and Reading - Bedwyn, Oxford, Bicester, Banbury and Birmingham

Network Diagram - see first Page of Table 116

		CH	GW	XC	GW	GW	GW	GW	GW	GW	GW	GW	XC	GW	GW	GW	XC	GW	GW	GW	GW	GW	GW
			1	◇1	1	◇1	1	◇1	1	1	1	◇1	◇1	1	◇1	1	◇1	1	◇1	1	◇1	1	1
				🚲		☕		☕				☕	🚲				🚲		☕		🚲		
London Paddington 15 ⊖	d				09 57	10 15	10 18	10 22			10 27	10 30			10 50			10 57	11 15	11 18	11 20		11 27
Ealing Broadway ⊖	d				10 05						10 35							11 05					11 35
Slough 3	d				10 27			10 36			10 57				11 06			11 27			11 36		11 57
Maidenhead 3	d				10 34						11 04							11 34					12 04
Twyford 3	d		←		10 42					←	11 12					←		11 42				←	12 12
Reading 7	d		10 23	10 41	10 53	10 42	10 48	10 52		10 53	11 23	10 57	11 11	11 12	11 21	11 23	11 40	11 53	11 42	11 48	11 52	11 53	12 23
Reading West	d				→						→			11 14				→					→
Theale	d						10 56							11 20						11 56			
Aldermaston	d													11 25									
Midgham	d													11 29									
Thatcham	d						11 04							11 34						12 04			
Newbury Racecourse	d													11 38									
Newbury	a						11 10							11 44						12 10			
	d						11 10													12 10			
Kintbury	d						11 17													12 17			
Hungerford	d						11 21													12 21			
Bedwyn	a						11 31													12 31			
Tilehurst	d		10 27							10 57						11 27						11 57	
Pangbourne	d		10 31							11 01						11 31						12 01	
Goring & Streatley	d		10 36							11 06						11 36						12 06	
Cholsey	d		10 41							11 11						11 41						12 11	
Didcot Parkway	a		10 49			10 56				11 19		11 11			11 37	11 50			11 56			12 20	
	d		10 55							11 25					11 38	11 55						12 25	
Appleford	d		11 00																				
Culham	d																						
Radley	d		11 03													12 03							
Oxford	a		11 14	11 04				11 18		11 41			11 34		11 50	12 14	12 01				12 18	12 41	
	d	11 00		11 07					11 23				11 36				12 07						
Islip	d	11 13																					
Bicester Town	a	11 25																					
Tackley	d								11 32														
Heyford	d								11 36														
Kings Sutton	d								11 45														
Banbury	a			11 24					11 51				11 52				12 24						
Leamington Spa 8	a			11 41									12 11				12 42						
Coventry	a												12 24										
Birmingham International	a												12 37										
Birmingham New Street 12	a			12 18									12 48				13 18						

		GW	XC	GW	GW	GW	GW	XC	GW	GW	GW	GW	CH	GW	GW	GW	XC	GW	GW	GW	XC	GW
		◇1	◇1	1	◇1	◇1	1	◇1	1	◇1	◇1	◇1		1	1	◇1	◇1	1	◇1	1	◇1	1
					A																	
		☕	🚲		☕	🚲		🚲		☕	☕	🚲				☕	🚲		🚲		🚲	
London Paddington 15 ⊖	d	11 30			11 48	11 50			11 57	12 15	12 18	12 21			12 27	12 30			12 50			12 57
Ealing Broadway ⊖	d								12 05						12 35							13 05
Slough 3	d					12 06			12 27			12 36			12 57				13 06			13 27
Maidenhead 3	d								12 34						13 04							13 34
Twyford 3	d						←		12 42					←	13 12					←		13 42
Reading 7	d	11 57	12 11	12 12	12 16	12 22	12 23	12 41	12 53	12 42	12 48	12 52		12 53	13 23	12 57	13 11	13 12	13 22	13 23	13 40	13 53
Reading West	d			12 14					→						→			13 14				→
Theale	d			12 20							12 56							13 20				
Aldermaston	d			12 25														13 25				
Midgham	d			12 29														13 29				
Thatcham	d			12 34							13 04							13 34				
Newbury Racecourse	d			12 38														13 38				
Newbury	a			12 44							13 12							13 44				
	d										13 12											
Kintbury	d																					
Hungerford	d										13 21											
Bedwyn	a										13 30											
Tilehurst	d						12 27							12 57						13 27		
Pangbourne	d						12 31							13 01						13 31		
Goring & Streatley	d						12 36							13 06						13 36		
Cholsey	d						12 41							13 11						13 41		
Didcot Parkway	a	12 11			12 32		12 49			12 56				13 19		13 11			13 37	13 49		
	d						12 55							13 25					13 38	13 55		
Appleford	d						13 00															
Culham	d																			14 01		
Radley	d						13 03													14 03		
Oxford	a		12 34			12 48	13 14	13 02				13 18		13 41			13 34		13 50	14 14	14 02	
	d		12 36					13 07					13 30				13 36				14 07	
Islip	d												13 43									
Bicester Town	a												13 55									
Tackley	d																					
Heyford	d																					
Kings Sutton	d																					
Banbury	a		12 52					13 24									13 52				14 25	
Leamington Spa 8	a		13 10					13 42									14 10				14 41	
Coventry	a		13 22														14 22					
Birmingham International	a		13 37														14 37					
Birmingham New Street 12	a		13 48					14 18									14 48				15 18	

A The Cheltenham Spa Express

London and Reading - Bedwyn, Oxford, Bicester, Banbury and Birmingham

Network Diagram - see first Page of Table 116

Station		GW ◇1 ⊡	GW 1	GW ◇1 trolley	GW 1	GW 1	GW 1	GW ◇1 ⊡		XC ◇1 trolley	GW 1	GW ◇1 ⊡	GW ◇1 trolley	CH	GW 1	XC ◇1 trolley	GW 1	GW ◇1 ⊡		GW 1	GW ◇1 trolley	GW 1	GW 1	GW ◇1 ⊡	XC ◇1 trolley
London Paddington 15 ⊖	d	13 15	13 18	13 21			13 27	13 30				13 48	13 50				13 57	14 15		14 18	14 21		14 27	14 30	
Ealing Broadway ⊖	d						13 35										14 05						14 35		
Slough 3	d			13 36			13 57						14 06				14 27				14 36		14 57		
Maidenhead 3	d						14 04										14 34						15 04		
Twyford 3	d					←	14 12								←		14 42					←	15 12		
Reading 7	d	13 42	13 48	13 52		13 53	14 23	13 57		14 11	14 12	14 16	14 22		14 23	14 41	14 53	14 42		14 48	14 52	14 53	15 23	14 57	15 11
Reading West	d						→				14 14						→						→		
Theale	d		13 56								14 20									14 56					
Aldermaston	d										14 25														
Midgham	d										14 29														
Thatcham	d		14 04								14 34									15 04					
Newbury Racecourse	d										14 38														
Newbury	a		14 10								14 44									15 10					
	d		14 10																	15 10					
Kintbury	d		14 17																	15 17					
Hungerford	d		14 21																	15 21					
Bedwyn	a		14 31																	15 31					
Tilehurst	d					13 57									14 27							14 57			
Pangbourne	d					14 01									14 31							15 01			
Goring & Streatley	d					14 06									14 36							15 06			
Cholsey	d					14 11									14 41							15 11			
Didcot Parkway	a	13 56				14 20		14 11				14 32			14 49			14 56				15 21		15 11	
	d					14 25									14 55							15 25			
Appleford	d														15 00										
Culham	d																								
Radley	d														15 03										
Oxford	a			14 18		14 42				14 34			14 48		15 14	15 02					15 18	15 41			15 34
	d				14 24					14 36				15 00		15 07									15 36
Islip	d													15 13											
Bicester Town	a													15 25											
Tackley	d				14 33																				
Heyford	d				14 37																				
Kings Sutton	d				14 46																				
Banbury	a				14 52					14 53						15 24									15 52
Leamington Spa 8	a									15 11						15 42									16 10
Coventry	a									15 24															16 22
Birmingham International	a									15 37															16 37
Birmingham New Street 12	a									15 48						16 18									16 48

Station		GW 1	GW ◇1 trolley	GW 1		XC ◇1 trolley	GW 1	GW ◇1 ⊡	GW 1	GW ◇1 trolley	GW 1	CH	GW 1	GW 1		GW ◇1 ⊡	XC ◇1 trolley	GW 1	GW ◇1 ⊡	GW ◇1 ⊡	GW 1	XC ◇1 trolley	GW 1	GW 1	
London Paddington 15 ⊖	d		14 50				14 57	15 15	15 18	15 22				15 27		15 30			15 48	15 51				15 57	
Ealing Broadway ⊖	d						15 05							15 35										16 05	
Slough 3	d		15 06				15 27			15 36				15 59						16 06				16 27	
Maidenhead 3	d						15 34							16 07										16 34	
Twyford 3	d			←			15 42						←	16 15							←			16 42	
Reading 7	d	15 12	15 22	15 23		15 40	15 53	15 42	15 48	15 52			15 53	16 25		15 57	16 11	16 12	16 16	16 22	16 25	16 40		16 53	
Reading West	d	15 14					→							→				16 14						→	
Theale	d	15 20							15 56									16 20							
Aldermaston	d	15 25																16 25							
Midgham	d	15 29																16 29							
Thatcham	d	15 34							16 04									16 34							
Newbury Racecourse	d	15 38																16 38							
Newbury	a	15 44							16 10									16 44							
	d								16 10														17 08		
Kintbury	d								16 17														17 14		
Hungerford	d								16 21														17 19		
Bedwyn	a								16 31														17 28		
Tilehurst	d			15 27									15 57								16 29				
Pangbourne	d			15 31									16 01								16 34				
Goring & Streatley	d			15 36									16 06								16 39				
Cholsey	d			15 41									16 11								16 43				
Didcot Parkway	a		15 37	15 49				15 56					16 19			16 11			16 32		16 50				
	d		15 38	15 55									16 25								16 55				
Appleford	d																				17 00				
Culham	d			16 01																	17 02				
Radley	d			16 03									16 33								17 06				
Oxford	a		15 50	16 14		16 05				16 18			16 43				16 34			16 47	17 15	17 03			
	d					16 07					16 23	16 26					16 36					17 07			
Islip	d											16 39													
Bicester Town	a											16 51													
Tackley	d										16 32														
Heyford	d										16 36														
Kings Sutton	d										16 45														
Banbury	a					16 25					16 51						16 52					17 27			
Leamington Spa 8	a					16 43											17 11					17 47			
Coventry	a																17 23								
Birmingham International	a																17 37								
Birmingham New Street 12	a					17 18											17 48					18 18			

London and Reading - Bedwyn, Oxford, Bicester, Banbury and Birmingham

Network Diagram - see first Page of Table 116

		GW	GW	GW	GW	GW	GW	GW	GW	XC		GW	CH	GW	GW	GW	GW	GW	GW	XC		GW	GW	GW	GW
		◇1	1	◇1	1	1	◇1	◇1	1	◇1		1		◇1	1	◇1	◇1	◇1	◇1	◇1		1	◇1	1	◇1
																			A						
		☕		🛒			☕	☕		🛒						☕	☕	☕	☕	🛒			☕		☕
London Paddington 15 ⊖	d	16 15	16 18	16 22		16 27	16 30	16 36						16 49		17 00	17 03	17 06	17 15			17 18	17 22	17 25	17 30
Ealing Broadway ⊖	d					16 35																		17 33	
Slough 3	d			16 38		16 57								17 04										17 58	
Maidenhead 3	d					17 04																17 40		18 10	
Twyford 3	d				←	17 12									←			17 28				17 48		18 17	
Reading 7	d	16 41	16 48	16 52	16 53	17 23	16 57	17 04		17 11		17 12		17 20	17 23	17 26	17 32	17 36	17 41	17 41		17 57	17 50	18 28	17 56
Reading West	d					↳						17 14										↳		↳	
Theale	d		16 56									17 20						17 45							
Aldermaston	d		17 01									17 25													
Midgham	d											17 29													
Thatcham	d		17 08									17 34						17 55							
Newbury Racecourse	d								←			17 38													
Newbury	a		17 14					17 18	17 14			17 44					17 47	18 02							
	d		17 24					17 19	17 24									18 02							
Kintbury	d		↳						17 31									18 10							
Hungerford	d							17a28	17 35									18 16							
Bedwyn	a								17 45									18 24							
Tilehurst	d				16 57										17 27										
Pangbourne	d				17 01										17 31										
Goring & Streatley	d				17 06										17 36										
Cholsey	d				17 11										17 41										
Didcot Parkway	a	16 54		17 08	17 20		17 11							17 35	17 49	17 40			17 56						18 09
	d			17 09	17 25									17 37	17 55										
Appleford	d				17 30																				
Culham	d				17 32																				
Radley	d				17 36										18 03										
Oxford	a			17 24	17 44					17 34				17 50	18 12					18 05			18 15		
	d				17 45					17 36			17 45							18 07					
Islip	d												17 58												
Bicester Town	a												18 10												
Tackley	d				17 54																				
Heyford	d				17 58																				
Kings Sutton	d				18 07																				
Banbury	a				18 15					17 53										18 25					
Leamington Spa 8	a									18 11										18 45					
Coventry	a									18 22															
Birmingham International	a									18 37															
Birmingham New Street 12	a									18 48										19 18					

		GW	GW	XC	GW	GW		GW	GW	GW	GW	GW	GW	GW	GW	XC		GW	GW	GW	CH	GW	GW	GW	GW
																						FX	FO		
		1	◇1	◇1	1	1		1	◇1	1	◇1	◇1	1	◇1	◇1	◇1		1	1	◇1		1	1	◇1	1
												B								C					
			☕	🛒					☕		☕	☕		☕	☕	🛒				☕				☕	
London Paddington 15 ⊖	d		17 33					17 36	17 48		17 50	18 00		18 06	18 15			18 15	18 18	18 22		18 25	18 25	18 30	
Ealing Broadway ⊖	d																	18 23				18 33	18 33		
Slough 3	d																	18 47				18 59	18 59		
Maidenhead 3	d							17 58			18 09							18 57	18 40			19 10	19 10		
Twyford 3	d	←						18 07		←			←	18 28				19 05	18 48			19 18	19 18		←
Reading 7	d	17 57	18 04	18 11		18 12		18 18	18 16	18 18	18 22	18 27	18 28	18 37	18 41	18 41		19 18	18 57	18 50		19 27	19 27	18 56	18 57
Reading West	d					18 14		↳										↳	↳			↳	↳		
Theale	d					18 20								18 45											
Aldermaston	d					18 25																			
Midgham	d					18 29																			
Thatcham	d					18 34								18 55											
Newbury Racecourse	d					18 38																			
Newbury	a		18 18			18 44								19 02											
	d				18 26									19 02											
Kintbury	d				18 32									19 10											
Hungerford	d				18 37									19 16											
Bedwyn	a				18 46									19 24											
Tilehurst	d	18 01								18 24			18 33												19 01
Pangbourne	d	18 06								18 29			18 38												19 06
Goring & Streatley	d	18 11								18 34			18 43												19 11
Cholsey	d	18 16								18 40			18 49												19 16
Didcot Parkway	a	18 22							18 32	18 46		18 40	18 57		18 56									19 10	19 22
	d	18 25								18 46			18 58												19 25
Appleford	d												19 03												
Culham	d	18 31																							
Radley	d	18 35								18 54															19 33
Oxford	a	18 45		18 34						19 04	18 47		19 16			19 11				19 19					19 43
	d			18 36									19 17			19 12					19 30				
Islip	d																				19 43				
Bicester Town	a																				19 55				
Tackley	d												19 27												
Heyford	d												19 31												
Kings Sutton	d												19 40												
Banbury	a			18 53									19 48			19 30									
Leamington Spa 8	a			19 10												19 49									
Coventry	a			19 22																					
Birmingham International	a			19 37																					
Birmingham New Street 12	a			19 48												20 18									

A The Red Dragon

B The Bristolian

C The Cathedrals Express

London and Reading - Bedwyn, Oxford, Bicester, Banbury and Birmingham

Network Diagram - see first Page of Table 116

		GW	XC	GW	GW	GW	GW	GW	GW	GW	GW	GW	GW	GW	XC	GW	GW	GW	GW	GW	GW	GW
											FO	FX	R									
		◇1	◇1	1	1	◇1	1	1	◇1	◇1	1	1	1	◇1	◇1	1	1	◇1	1	◇1	1	◇1
		☕	🛒			☕			🛒	☕			✕	☕				☕		☕		☕
London Paddington 15 ⊖	d	18 33				18 47			18 51	19 00			19 03	19 15			19 18	19 22	19 27	19 30		19 45
Ealing Broadway ⊖	d																		19 35			
Slough 3	d								19 06									19 36	19 59			
Maidenhead 3	d																19 40		20 09			
Twyford 3	d					19 09	←				←	←					19 48		20 17		←	
Reading 7	d	19 02	19 11		19 12	19 18	19 18	19 21	19 22	19 27	19 27	19 27	19u33	19 41	19 40	19 42	19 57	19 52	20 23	19 57	19 57	20 12
Reading West	d				19 15											19 44	→		→			
Theale	d				19 20			19 28								19 50						
Aldermaston	d				19 25											19 55						
Midgham	d				19 29											19 59						
Thatcham	d				19 34			19 39								20 04						
Newbury Racecourse	d				19 39			19 52								20 08						
Newbury	a	19 16			19 44			19 56					19 50			20 17						20 27
	d	19 17		19 27				19 56								20 32						
Kintbury	d			19 33				20 03								20 38						
Hungerford	d	19 27		19 38				20 08								20 42						
Bedwyn	a	19 35		19 47				20 17								20 52						
Tilehurst	d						19 24				19 31	19 31									20 01	
Pangbourne	d						19 28				19 35	19 35									20 06	
Goring & Streatley	d						19 33				19 40	19 40									20 11	
Cholsey	d						19 38				19 46	19 46									20 16	
Didcot Parkway	a					19 32	19 47			19 41	19 53	19 53		19 56						20 11	20 22	
	d						19 55				20 08	20 08									20 25	
Appleford	d										20 13	20 13										
Culham	d						20 03														20 31	
Radley	d										20 18	20 18									20 35	
Oxford	a		19 34				20 13		19 48		20 26	20 27			20 05			20 18			20 45	
	d		19 36												20 07							
Islip	d																					
Bicester Town	a																					
Tackley	d																					
Heyford	d																					
Kings Sutton	d																					
Banbury	a		19 52												20 27							
Leamington Spa 8	a		20 10												20 45							
Coventry	a		20 22																			
Birmingham International	a		20 37																			
Birmingham New Street 12	a		20 48												21 22							

		XC	GW	GW	CH	GW	GW	GW	GW	XC	GW	GW	GW	GW	GW	GW	XC	GW	GW	GW	GW	GW	XC
		◇1	◇1	◇1		1	1	◇1	◇1	◇1	1	◇1	1	1	◇1	◇1	◇1	1	◇1	1	1	◇1	◇1
			☕	🛒				☕	☕			🛒			☕	☕						☕	
London Paddington 15 ⊖	d		19 48	19 50			19 57	20 00	20 15			20 20		20 27	20 35	20 45			20 48		20 57	21 15	
Ealing Broadway ⊖	d						20 05							20 35							21 05		
Slough 3	d			20 06			20 27					20 36		20 57					21 05		21 27		
Maidenhead 3	d		20 06				20 34							21 04							21 34		
Twyford 3	d					←	20 42						←	21 12						←	21 42		
Reading 7	d	20 11	20 18	20 22		20 23	20 53	20 27	20 41	20 40	20 41	20 52	20 53	21 23	21 02	21 11	21 11		21 20	21 23	21 58	21 41	21 46
Reading West	d						→				20 44			→							→		
Theale	d										20 50												
Aldermaston	d										20 55												
Midgham	d										20 58												
Thatcham	d										21 03												
Newbury Racecourse	d										21 08												
Newbury	a										21 11				21 17								
	d										21 22												
Kintbury	d										21 29												
Hungerford	d										21 33												
Bedwyn	a										21 43												
Tilehurst	d					20 27							20 57							21 27			
Pangbourne	d					20 31							21 01							21 31			
Goring & Streatley	d					20 36							21 06							21 36			
Cholsey	d					20 41							21 11							21 41			
Didcot Parkway	a		20 32			20 51		20 41	20 56				21 19			21 25				21 52		22 00	
	d					20 55							21 25							21 52			
Appleford	d					20 59														21 56			
Culham	d																			21 59			
Radley	d					21 04							21 33							22 03			
Oxford	a	20 34		20 47		21 13				21 05		21 16	21 43				21 34		21 51	22 14			22 28
	d	20 36		20 55	21 00					21 08							21 36	21 41					22 30
Islip	d				21 13																		
Bicester Town	a				21 25																		
Tackley	d			21 04														21 50					
Heyford	d			21 08														21 54					
Kings Sutton	d			21 17														22 03					
Banbury	a	20 52		21 23						21 31							21 52	22 09					22 53
Leamington Spa 8	a	21 10								21 51							22 10						23 12
Coventry	a	21 22															22 22						23 25
Birmingham International	a	21 37															22 33						23 36
Birmingham New Street 12	a	21 48								22 17							22 45						23 57

London and Reading - Bedwyn, Oxford, Bicester, Banbury and Birmingham

Network Diagram - see first Page of Table 116

		GW	GW	GW	GW	GW	GW	GW	GW	CH	GW	GW	GW	GW	GW	GW	GW	GW	GW	GW	GW	GW
							FO	FX		FO			FO	FX				FO	FX			
		◇1	1	1	1	◇1	◇1	◇1	1		1	1	◇1	◇1	◇1	1	1	◇1	◇1	1	◇1	1
						☕	trolley	☕					☕	☕				☕	☕			
London Paddington 15 ⊖	d	21 18			21 27	21 45	21 48	21 48				21 58	22 15	22 15	22 18			22 45	22 45	22 45	22 48	
Ealing Broadway ⊖	d				21 35							22 06								22 54		
Slough 3	d	21 35			22 07		22 03	22 03				22 39			22 36					23 12	23 06	
Maidenhead 3	d				22 14							22 47			22 44					23 24	23 14	
Twyford 3	d		←		22 22						←	22 55					←			23 32		←
Reading 7	d	21 50	21 58	22 01	22 32	22 11	22 22	22 22			22 32	23 04	22 41	22 49	22 58	23 00	23 04	23 11	23 19	23 41	23 28	23 41
Reading West	d			22 03	→							→				23 02				→		
Theale	d			22 10												23 08						
Aldermaston	d			22 15												23 13						
Midgham	d			22 18												23 17						
Thatcham	d			22 23												23 22						
Newbury Racecourse	d			22 28												23 26						
Newbury	a			22 31												23 29						
	d			22 31												23 29						
Kintbury	d			22 37												23 36						
Hungerford	d			22 42												23 40						
Bedwyn	a			22 52												23 50						
Tilehurst	d		22 02								22 35						23 08					23 45
Pangbourne	d		22 06								22 40						23 12					23 49
Goring & Streatley	d		22 10								22 43						23 16					23 53
Cholsey	d		22 15								22 48						23 21					23 57
Didcot Parkway	a		22 25			22 31					22 58		23 01	23 08			23 31	23 29	23 38			00 07
	d		22 25								22 58						23 31					00 07
Appleford	d										23 03											
Culham	d										23 05											
Radley	d										23 09											00 15
Oxford	a	22 18	22 41				22 47	22 47			23 21				23 28		23 48				23 56	00 26
	d								23 06	23 12												
Islip	d									23 25												
Bicester Town	a									23 37												
Tackley	d								23 15													
Heyford	d								23 19													
Kings Sutton	d								23 28													
Banbury	a								23 34													
Leamington Spa 8	a																					
Coventry	a																					
Birmingham International	a																					
Birmingham New Street 12	a																					

		GW	GW	GW	GW	GW	GW	GW
			FX	FO		FO	FX	FO
		◇1	1	1	◇1	1	1	1
					☕			
London Paddington 15 ⊖	d	23 18	23 29	23 29	23 30	23 42		
Ealing Broadway ⊖	d		23 37	23 37				
Slough 3	d	23 36	23 54	23 54		23 58		
Maidenhead 3	d	23 44	00 01	00 01		00 08		
Twyford 3	d		00 09	00 09			←	←
Reading 7	d	23 58	00 24	00 24	00 08	00 21	00 24	00 25
Reading West	d		→	→				
Theale	d							
Aldermaston	d							
Midgham	d							
Thatcham	d							
Newbury Racecourse	d							
Newbury	a							
	d							
Kintbury	d							
Hungerford	d							
Bedwyn	a							
Tilehurst	d						00 29	00 29
Pangbourne	d						00 33	00 33
Goring & Streatley	d						00 37	00 37
Cholsey	d						00 42	00 42
Didcot Parkway	a				00 25	00 43	00 51	00 51
	d					00 44	00 51	00 51
Appleford	d						00 56	00 56
Culham	d						00 58	00 58
Radley	d						01 02	01 02
Oxford	a	00 28				01 02	01 16	01 16
	d							
Islip	d							
Bicester Town	a							
Tackley	d							
Heyford	d							
Kings Sutton	d							
Banbury	a							
Leamington Spa 8	a							
Coventry	a							
Birmingham International	a							
Birmingham New Street 12	a							

Table 116

Saturdays
until 31 December

London and Reading - Bedwyn, Oxford, Bicester, Banbury and Birmingham

Network Diagram - see first Page of Table 116

		GW	GW	CH	GW	GW	GW	GW	GW	GW	GW	GW	GW	GW	GW	GW	XC	GW	GW	GW	CH	GW	XC
		1	◇1		1	◇1 ⊡	1	1	1	◇1	1	1	1	1	◇1	1	◇1 ⚲	1	1	◇1		1	◇1 ⚲
London Paddington 15 ⊖	d	22p45	23p18		23p29	23p30		23p42		00 22					05 21				05 25	05 50			
Ealing Broadway ⊖	d	22p54			23p37														05 33				
Slough 3	d	23p12	23p36		23p54			23p58		00 39					05 38				05 51	06 06			
Maidenhead 3	d	23p24	23p44		00 01			00 08											06 02				
Twyford 3	d	23p32			00 09				←										06 10				
Reading 7	d	23p41	23p58		00 25	00 08	00 20	00 21	00 25	00 56	05 08	05 41		05 46	05 54		06 11	06 12	06 21	06 22			06 46
Reading West	d				→		00s23				05 11	05 44						06 14					
Theale	d						00s29				05 17	05 50						06 20					
Aldermaston	d						00s34				05 22	05 55						06 25					
Midgham	d						00s37				05 25	05 58						06 29					
Thatcham	d						00s42				05 30	06 03						06 34					
Newbury Racecourse	d						00s47				05 35	06 08						06 38					
Newbury	a						00 52				05 37	06 10						06 44					
	d										05 37	06 10											
Kintbury	d										05 44	06 17											
Hungerford	d										05 48	06 21											
Bedwyn	a										05 57	06 30											
Tilehurst	d	23p45							00 29					05 50					06 25				
Pangbourne	d	23p49							00 34					05 54					06 29				
Goring & Streatley	d	23p53							00 37					05 59					06 34				
Cholsey	d	23p57							00 42					06 04		←			06 39			←	
Didcot Parkway	a	00 07				00 25		00 43	00 50	01 13				06 12	06 07	06 12			06 46	06 37		06 46	
	d	00 07						00 44	00 52	01 14				06 13	06 08	06 13			06 47	06 38		06 47	
Appleford	d								00 57					→		06 17			→				
Culham	d								00 59							06 20							
Radley	d	00 15							01 03							06 24						06 54	
Oxford	a	00 26	00 28					01 02	01 16	01 28					06 22	06 32	06 36			06 52		07 03	07 10
	d			00 38									06 16				06 38				07 00		07 12
Islip	d																				07 13		
Bicester Town	a																				07 25		
Tackley	d			00 48									06 25										
Heyford	d			00 53									06 29										
Kings Sutton	d			01 01									06 38										
Banbury	a			01 10									06 46				06 54						07 32
Leamington Spa 8	a																07 12						07 50
Coventry	a																07 24						
Birmingham International	a																07 37						
Birmingham New Street 12	a																07 48						08 17

		GW	GW	GW	GW	GW	GW	XC	GW	GW	GW	CH	GW	XC	GW	GW	GW	GW	GW	XC	GW	GW	GW
		1	1	◇1	1	1	◇1 ⊡	◇1 ⚲	1	◇1	1		1	◇1 ⚲	1	1	◇1	1	R 1 ⊡	◇1 ⚲	1	◇1	1
London Paddington 15 ⊖	d		05 57	06 21		06 27	06 30			06 50						06 57	07 21	07 27	07 30			07 50	
Ealing Broadway ⊖	d		06 05			06 35										07 05		07 35					
Slough 3	d		06 31	06 38		06 57				07 06						07 27	07 38	07 57				08 06	
Maidenhead 3	d		06 42			07 04										07 34		08 04					
Twyford 3	d		06 50		←	07 12							←			07 42		08 12					←
Reading 7	d	06 48	06 56	06 54	06 56	07 23	06 59	07 11	07 11	07 22			07 23	07 47	07 48	07 53	07 53	08 23	07 57	08 11	08 18	08 22	08 23
Reading West	d		→			→			07 14									→			08 20		
Theale	d	06 55							07 20						07 57						08 27		
Aldermaston	d								07 25												08 32		
Midgham	d								07 29												08 36		
Thatcham	d	07 04							07 34						08 05						08 41		
Newbury Racecourse	d								07 38												08 45		
Newbury	a	07 09							07 43						08 11						08 50		
	d	07 09													08 11								
Kintbury	d	07 16													08 17								
Hungerford	d	07 20													08 22								
Bedwyn	a	07 29													08 31								
Tilehurst	d				07 00								07 27			07 57							08 27
Pangbourne	d				07 04								07 31			08 01							08 31
Goring & Streatley	d				07 09								07 36			08 06							08 36
Cholsey	d				07 14								07 41			08 11							08 41
Didcot Parkway	a				07 30		07 12						07 49			08 19			08 12				08 48
	d				07 30								07 51			08 25							08 55
Appleford	d																						09 00
Culham	d												07 56										
Radley	d												08 00										09 03
Oxford	a			07 18	07 43			07 34		07 48			08 09	08 13		08 40	08 19			08 34		08 48	09 14
	d							07 36			07 53	08 07		08 15						08 36			
Islip	d											08 20											
Bicester Town	a											08 32											
Tackley	d										08 02												
Heyford	d										08 06												
Kings Sutton	d										08 15												
Banbury	a							07 52			08 23			08 32						08 52			
Leamington Spa 8	a							08 10						08 49						09 10			
Coventry	a							08 22												09 22			
Birmingham International	a							08 37												09 37			
Birmingham New Street 12	a							08 48						09 19						09 48			

Table 116

Saturdays

until 31 December

London and Reading - Bedwyn, Oxford, Bicester, Banbury and Birmingham

Network Diagram - see first Page of Table 116

		XC		GW	GW	GW	GW	GW	GW	CH	GW	GW		XC	GW	GW	GW	XC	GW	GW	GW	GW		GW	GW
		◇1 🚲		1	1	◇1 ☕	◇1 ☕	1	◇1 ☕		1	◇1 ☕		◇1 🚲	1	◇1	1	◇1 🚲	1	1	1	1		◇1	1
London Paddington 15 ⊖	d				07 57	08 15	08 18		08 21		08 27	08 30				08 50				08 57	09 18			09 21	09 27
Ealing Broadway ⊖	d				08 05						08 35									09 05					09 35
Slough 3	d				08 27				08 39		08 57					09 06				09 27				09 39	09 57
Maidenhead 3	d				08 34						09 04									09 34					10 04
Twyford 3	d				08 42			←			09 12						←			09 42		←			10 12
Reading 7	d	08 40			08 53	08 42	08 48	08 53	08 54		09 23	08 57		09 11	09 12	09 22	09 23	09 40		09 53	09 48	09 53		09 54	10 23
Reading West	d				↪						↪				09 14					↪					↪
Theale	d						08 58								09 20						09 56				
Aldermaston	d														09 25										
Midgham	d														09 29										
Thatcham	d						09 07								09 34						10 04				
Newbury Racecourse	d														09 38										
Newbury	a						09 13								09 44						10 10				
	d			08 58			09 14														10 10				
Kintbury	d			09 04																	10 17				
Hungerford	d			09 09			09 23														10 21				
Bedwyn	a			09 17			09 30														10 31				
Tilehurst	d							08 57									09 27					09 57			
Pangbourne	d							09 01									09 31					10 01			
Goring & Streatley	d							09 06									09 36					10 06			
Cholsey	d							09 11									09 41					10 11			
Didcot Parkway	a					08 55		09 19				09 12					09 48					10 18			
	d							09 25									09 55					10 25			
Appleford	d																								
Culham	d																10 01								
Radley	d																10 03								
Oxford	a	09 04						09 40	09 18					09 34		09 48	10 14	10 04				10 40		10 19	
	d	09 07								09 28				09 36				10 07	10 16						
Islip	d									09 41															
Bicester Town	a									09 53															
Tackley	d																		10 25						
Heyford	d																		10 29						
Kings Sutton	d																		10 38						
Banbury	a	09 23												09 52				10 23	10 46						
Leamington Spa 8	a	09 41												10 12				10 41							
Coventry	a													10 22											
Birmingham International	a													10 37											
Birmingham New Street 12	a	10 18												10 48				11 18							

		GW	XC	GW	GW	CH	GW	XC		GW	GW	GW	GW	GW	GW	GW	XC	GW		GW	GW	XC	GW	GW	GW
		◇1 ☕	◇1 🚲	1	◇1		1	◇1 🚲		1	◇1 ☕	1	1	◇1 ☕	1	◇1 ☕	◇1 🚲	1		◇1 🚲	1	◇1 🚲	1	1	1
London Paddington 15 ⊖	d	09 30			09 50					09 57	10 15	10 18		10 21	10 27	10 30				10 50				10 57	11 18
Ealing Broadway ⊖	d									10 05					10 35									11 05	
Slough 3	d				10 06					10 27				10 39	10 57					11 06				11 27	
Maidenhead 3	d									10 34					11 04									11 34	
Twyford 3	d						←			10 42			←		11 12						←			11 42	
Reading 7	d	09 57	10 11	10 12	10 22		10 23	10 40		10 53	10 42	10 48	10 53	10 54	11 23	10 57	11 11	11 12		11 22	11 23	11 40		11 53	11 48
Reading West	d			10 14						↪					↪			11 14						↪	
Theale	d			10 20								10 56						11 20							11 56
Aldermaston	d			10 25														11 25							
Midgham	d			10 29														11 29							
Thatcham	d			10 34								11 04						11 34							12 04
Newbury Racecourse	d			10 38														11 38							
Newbury	a			10 44								11 10						11 44							12 10
	d											11 10													12 10
Kintbury	d											11 17													12 17
Hungerford	d											11 21													12 21
Bedwyn	a											11 31													12 31
Tilehurst	d						10 27						10 57								11 27				
Pangbourne	d						10 31						11 01								11 31				
Goring & Streatley	d						10 36						11 06								11 36				
Cholsey	d						10 41						11 11								11 41				
Didcot Parkway	a	10 12					10 48				10 55		11 19			11 12					11 49				
	d						10 55						11 25								11 55				
Appleford	d						11 00																		
Culham	d																								
Radley	d						11 03														12 03				
Oxford	a		10 34		10 48		11 14	11 04					11 40	11 19			11 34			11 48	12 14	12 04			
	d		10 36			11 00		11 07									11 36					12 07	12 16		
Islip	d					11 13																			
Bicester Town	a					11 25																			
Tackley	d																						12 25		
Heyford	d																						12 29		
Kings Sutton	d																						12 38		
Banbury	a		10 52					11 23									11 52					12 23	12 46		
Leamington Spa 8	a		11 10					11 41									12 10					12 41			
Coventry	a		11 22														12 22								
Birmingham International	a		11 37														12 37								
Birmingham New Street 12	a		11 48					12 18									12 48					13 18			

Table 116

Saturdays
until 31 December

London and Reading - Bedwyn, Oxford, Bicester, Banbury and Birmingham

Network Diagram - see first Page of Table 116

		GW	GW	CH		GW	GW	XC	GW	GW	GW	XC	GW	GW		GW	GW	GW	GW	GW	XC	GW	CH	GW	
		1	◇1			1	◇1	◇1	1	◇1	1	◇1	1	◇1		◇1	1	◇1	1	◇1	◇1	1		◇1	
			🚲				Ø	🚲				🚲		🍴		🍴				🍴	🚲			🚲	
London Paddington 15 ⊖	d		11 21			11 27	11 30			11 50			11 57	12 15		12 18		12 21	12 27	12 30				12 50	
Ealing Broadway ⊖	d					11 35							12 05						12 35						
Slough 3	d		11 39			11 57				12 06			12 27					12 39	12 57					13 06	
Maidenhead 3	d					12 04							12 34						13 04						
Twyford 3	d	←				12 12					←		12 42				←		13 12						
Reading 7	d	11 53	11 54			12 23	11 58	12 11	12 12	12 22	12 23	12 40	12 53	12 42		12 48	12 53	12 54	13 23	12 57	13 11	13 12		13 22	
Reading West	d					→			12 14				→						→			13 14			
Theale	d								12 20							12 57						13 20			
Aldermaston	d								12 25													13 25			
Midgham	d								12 29													13 29			
Thatcham	d								12 34							13 05						13 34			
Newbury Racecourse	d								12 38													13 38			
Newbury	a								12 44							13 12						13 44			
	d															13 13									
Kintbury	d																								
Hungerford	d															13 21									
Bedwyn	a															13 29									
Tilehurst	d	11 57									12 27						12 57								
Pangbourne	d	12 01									12 31						13 01								
Goring & Streatley	d	12 06									12 36						13 06								
Cholsey	d	12 11									12 41						13 11								
Didcot Parkway	a	12 19					12 12				12 48			12 55			13 19			13 12					
	d	12 25									12 55						13 25								
Appleford	d										13 00														
Culham	d																								
Radley	d										13 03														
Oxford	a	12 40	12 20					12 34		12 48	13 14	13 04					13 40	13 19			13 34			13 48	
	d			12 30				12 36				13 07									13 36		13 41		
Islip	d			12 43																			13 54		
Bicester Town	a			12 55																			14 06		
Tackley	d																								
Heyford	d																								
Kings Sutton	d																								
Banbury	a							12 52				13 23									13 52				
Leamington Spa 8	a							13 10				13 41									14 10				
Coventry	a							13 22													14 22				
Birmingham International	a							13 37													14 37				
Birmingham New Street 12	a							13 48				14 18									14 48				

		GW	XC	GW	GW	GW	GW	GW	GW	GW		XC	GW	GW	CH	GW	XC	GW	GW	GW		GW	GW	GW	GW
		1	◇1	1	1	1	1	◇1	1	◇1		◇1	1	◇1		1	◇1	1	◇1	1		1	◇1	1	◇1
			🚲					🚲		🍴		🚲		🚲			🚲		🍴				🚲		🍴
London Paddington 15 ⊖	d				12 57	13 18		13 21	13 27	13 30				13 50				13 57	14 15	14 18			14 21	14 27	14 30
Ealing Broadway ⊖	d				13 05				13 35									14 05						14 35	
Slough 3	d				13 27			13 39	13 57					14 06				14 27					14 39	14 57	
Maidenhead 3	d				13 34				14 04									14 34						15 04	
Twyford 3	d	←			13 42		←		14 12							←		14 42				←		15 12	
Reading 7	d	13 23	13 40		13 53	13 48	13 53	13 54	14 23	13 59		14 11	14 12	14 22		14 23	14 40	14 53	14 42	14 48		14 53	14 54	15 23	14 57
Reading West	d				→				→				14 14					→						→	
Theale	d					13 56							14 20							14 56					
Aldermaston	d												14 25												
Midgham	d												14 29												
Thatcham	d					14 04							14 34							15 04					
Newbury Racecourse	d												14 38												
Newbury	a					14 10							14 44							15 10					
	d					14 10														15 10					
Kintbury	d					14 17														15 17					
Hungerford	d					14 21														15 21					
Bedwyn	a					14 31														15 31					
Tilehurst	d	13 27					13 57									14 27						14 57			
Pangbourne	d	13 31					14 01									14 31						15 01			
Goring & Streatley	d	13 36					14 06									14 36						15 06			
Cholsey	d	13 41					14 11									14 41						15 11			
Didcot Parkway	a	13 48					14 19			14 12						14 48			14 55			15 19			15 12
	d	13 55					14 25									14 55						15 25			
Appleford	d															15 00									
Culham	d	14 01																							
Radley	d	14 03														15 03									
Oxford	a	14 14	14 04				14 40	14 19				14 34		14 48		15 14	15 04					15 40	15 18		
	d		14 07	14 16								14 36			14 57		15 07								
Islip	d														15 10										
Bicester Town	a														15 22										
Tackley	d			14 25																					
Heyford	d			14 29																					
Kings Sutton	d			14 38																					
Banbury	a		14 23	14 46								14 52					15 23								
Leamington Spa 8	a		14 41									15 10					15 41								
Coventry	a											15 22													
Birmingham International	a											15 37													
Birmingham New Street 12	a		15 18									15 48					16 18								

Table 116

Saturdays

until 31 December

London and Reading - Bedwyn, Oxford, Bicester, Banbury and Birmingham

Network Diagram - see first Page of Table 116

		XC	GW	GW	CH	GW		XC	GW	GW	GW	GW	GW	GW	GW	XC		GW	GW	GW	XC	CH	GW	GW	GW
		◇1	1	◇1		1		◇1	1	1	1	1	◇1	1	◇1	◇1		1	◇1	1	◇1		1	◇1	1
		[trolley]						[trolley]					[trolley]		[cup]	[trolley]					[trolley]			[cup]	
London Paddington 15 ⊖	d			14 50						14 57	15 18		15 21	15 27	15 30				15 50				15 57	16 15	16 18
Ealing Broadway ⊖	d									15 05				15 35									16 05		
Slough 3	d			15 06						15 27			15 39	15 57					16 06				16 27		
Maidenhead 3	d									15 34				16 04									16 34		
Twyford 3	d					←				15 42		←		16 12						←			16 42		
Reading 7	d	15 11	15 12	15 22		15 23		15 40		15 53	15 48	15 53	15 54	16 23	15 59	16 11		16 12	16 22	16 23	16 40		16 53	16 42	16 48
Reading West	d		15 14							→				→				16 14					→		
Theale	d		15 20								15 56							16 20							16 56
Aldermaston	d		15 25															16 25							
Midgham	d		15 29															16 29							
Thatcham	d		15 34								16 04							16 34							17 04
Newbury Racecourse	d		15 38															16 38							
Newbury	a		15 44								16 10							16 44							17 10
	d										16 10														17 10
Kintbury	d										16 17														17 17
Hungerford	d										16 21														17 21
Bedwyn	a										16 31														17 31
Tilehurst	d					15 27						15 57								16 27					
Pangbourne	d					15 31						16 01								16 31					
Goring & Streatley	d					15 36						16 06								16 36					
Cholsey	d					15 41						16 11								16 41					
Didcot Parkway	a					15 48						16 19			16 12					16 48				16 55	
	d					15 55						16 25								16 55					
Appleford	d																			17 00					
Culham	d					16 01																			
Radley	d					16 03														17 03					
Oxford	a	15 34		15 48		16 14		16 04				16 40	16 19			16 34			16 48	17 14	17 04				
	d	15 36			16 00			16 07	16 16							16 36					17 07	17 10			
Islip	d				16 14																	17 23			
Bicester Town	a				16 26																	17 35			
Tackley	d								16 25																
Heyford	d								16 29																
Kings Sutton	d								16 38																
Banbury	a	15 52						16 23	16 46							16 52					17 23				
Leamington Spa 8	a	16 10						16 41								17 10					17 41				
Coventry	a	16 22														17 22									
Birmingham International	a	16 37														17 37									
Birmingham New Street 12	a	16 48						17 18								17 48					18 18				

		GW		GW	GW	GW	XC	GW	GW	GW	XC	GW		GW	GW	GW	GW	GW	GW	XC	GW	CH		GW	GW
		1		◇1	1	◇1	◇1	1	◇1	1	◇1	1		1	1	1	◇1	1	◇1	◇1	1			◇1	1
				[cup]		[cup]	[trolley]		[trolley]		[trolley]						[cup]		[cup]	[trolley]				[trolley]	
London Paddington 15 ⊖	d			16 21	16 27	16 30			16 50					16 57	17 18		17 21	17 27	17 30					17 50	
Ealing Broadway ⊖	d				16 35									17 05				17 35							
Slough 3	d			16 39	16 57				17 06					17 27			17 39	17 57						18 06	
Maidenhead 3	d				17 04									17 34				18 04							
Twyford 3	d	←			17 12					←				17 42		←		18 12							←
Reading 7	d	16 53		16 54	17 23	16 57	17 11	17 12	17 22	17 23	17 40			17 53	17 48	17 53	17 54	18 23	17 57	18 11	18 12			18 22	18 23
Reading West	d				→			17 14						→				→			18 14				
Theale	d							17 20							17 56						18 20				
Aldermaston	d							17 25													18 25				
Midgham	d							17 29													18 29				
Thatcham	d							17 34							18 04						18 34				
Newbury Racecourse	d							17 38													18 38				
Newbury	a							17 44							18 10						18 44				
	d														18 10										
Kintbury	d														18 17										
Hungerford	d														18 21										
Bedwyn	a														18 31										
Tilehurst	d	16 57								17 27						17 57									18 27
Pangbourne	d	17 01								17 31						18 01									18 31
Goring & Streatley	d	17 06								17 36						18 06									18 36
Cholsey	d	17 11								17 41						18 11									18 41
Didcot Parkway	a	17 19				17 12				17 48						18 19			18 12						18 48
	d	17 25								17 55						18 25									18 55
Appleford	d																								19 00
Culham	d									18 01															
Radley	d									18 03															19 03
Oxford	a	17 40		17 18			17 34		17 48	18 14	18 04					18 40	18 18			18 34				18 48	19 14
	d						17 36				18 07	18 16								18 36		18 41			
Islip	d																					18 54			
Bicester Town	a																					19 06			
Tackley	d											18 25													
Heyford	d											18 29													
Kings Sutton	d											18 38													
Banbury	a						17 52				18 23	18 46								18 52					
Leamington Spa 8	a						18 10				18 41									19 10					
Coventry	a						18 22													19 22					
Birmingham International	a						18 37													19 37					
Birmingham New Street 12	a						18 48				19 18									19 48					

Table 116

Saturdays
until 31 December

London and Reading - Bedwyn, Oxford, Bicester, Banbury and Birmingham

Network Diagram - see first Page of Table 116

		XC ◇1 ⚲	GW 1	GW ◇1 ⊡	GW 1	GW 1	GW ◇1 ⊡	GW 1		GW ◇1 ⊡	XC ◇1 ⚲	GW ◇1	CH	GW 1	GW 1	GW 1	GW ◇1 ⊡	GW ◇1 ⊡		XC ◇1	GW 1	GW ◇1	GW 1	GW 1	GW ◇1 ⊡
London Paddington [15] ⊖	d		17 57	18 15	18 18		18 21	18 27		18 30		18 50				18 57	19 06	19 15				19 21		19 27	19 30
Ealing Broadway ⊖	d		18 05					18 35								19 05								19 35	
Slough [3]	d		18 27				18 39	18 57				19 06				19 27						19 38		19 57	
Maidenhead [3]	d		18 34					19 04								19 34								20 04	
Twyford [3]	d		18 42			←		19 12							←	19 42							←	20 12	
Reading [7]	d	18 40	18 53	18 42	18 48	18 53	18 54	19 23		18 57	19 11	19 23			19 23	19 53	19 32	19 42		19 40	19 49	19 52	19 53	20 23	19 57
Reading West	d		↪					↪								↪					19 52			↪	
Theale	d				18 56																19 58				
Aldermaston	d																				20 03				
Midgham	d																				20 06				
Thatcham	d				19 04																20 11				
Newbury Racecourse	d																				20 16				
Newbury	a				19 10												19 48				20 18				
	d				19 10																20 18				
Kintbury	d				19 17																20 25				
Hungerford	d				19 21																20 29				
Bedwyn	a				19 31																20 38				
Tilehurst	d					18 57									19 27								19 57		
Pangbourne	d					19 01									19 31								20 01		
Goring & Streatley	d					19 06									19 36								20 06		
Cholsey	d					19 11									19 41								20 11		
Didcot Parkway	a			18 55		19 19				19 12					19 48			19 55					20 19		20 11
	d					19 25									19 55								20 25		
Appleford	d																								
Culham	d														20 01										
Radley	d														20 03										
Oxford	a	19 04				19 40	19 18				19 34	19 48			20 14					20 04		20 20	20 40		
	d	19 07									19 36		19 48	19 56						20 07					
Islip	d												20 01												
Bicester Town	a												20 13												
Tackley	d													20 05											
Heyford	d													20 09											
Kings Sutton	d													20 18											
Banbury	a	19 23									19 52			20 25						20 28					
Leamington Spa [8]	a	19 41									20 10									20 45					
Coventry	a										20 22														
Birmingham International	a										20 37														
Birmingham New Street [12]	a	20 18									20 48									21 18					

		XC ◇1	GW ◇1 ⚲	CH		GW 1	GW 1	GW ◇1 ⊡	GW ◇1 ⊡	GW ◇1 ⊡	XC ◇1	GW 1	GW ◇1	GW 1		GW 1	GW 1	GW ◇1 ⊡	XC ◇1	GW ◇1 ⚲	GW 1	GW 1	GW ◇1	CH	
London Paddington [15] ⊖	d		19 50				19 57	20 00	20 06	20 15			20 20				20 27	20 30		20 50		20 57	21 17		
Ealing Broadway ⊖	d						20 05										20 35					21 05			
Slough [3]	d		20 06				20 27						20 35				20 57			21 06		21 27	21 35		
Maidenhead [3]	d						20 34										21 04					21 34			
Twyford [3]	d					←	20 42									←	21 12				←	21 42			
Reading [7]	d	20 11	20 22			20 23	20 53	20 27	20 33	20 42	20 40	20 49	20 51			20 53	21 23	20 57	21 11	21 22	21 23	21 53	21 52		
Reading West	d						↪					20 52					↪					↪			
Theale	d											20 58													
Aldermaston	d											21 03													
Midgham	d											21 06													
Thatcham	d											21 11													
Newbury Racecourse	d											21 16													
Newbury	a								20 47			21 18													
	d											21 32													
Kintbury	d											21 39													
Hungerford	d											21 43													
Bedwyn	a											21 52													
Tilehurst	d					20 27										20 57					21 27				
Pangbourne	d					20 31										21 01					21 31				
Goring & Streatley	d					20 37										21 06					21 36				
Cholsey	d					20 41										21 11					21 41				
Didcot Parkway	a					20 49		20 41		20 55						21 19		21 12		21 39	21 48		22 07		
	d					20 55										21 25				21 40	21 55		22 08		
Appleford	d					21 00																			
Culham	d																				22 01				
Radley	d					21 03															22 03				
Oxford	a	20 34	20 47			21 14					21 04		21 19			21 40			21 34	21 53	22 14		22 20		
	d	20 36		21 00							21 07			21 20					21 36					22 25	
Islip	d			21 13																				22 38	
Bicester Town	a			21 25																				22 50	
Tackley	d													21 29											
Heyford	d													21 33											
Kings Sutton	d													21 42											
Banbury	a	20 52									21 23			21 49					21 52						
Leamington Spa [8]	a	21 10									21 44								22 10						
Coventry	a	21 22									21 55								22 22						
Birmingham International	a	21 37									22 10								22 36						
Birmingham New Street [12]	a	21 48									22 21								22 48						

Table 116

Saturdays

until 31 December

London and Reading - Bedwyn, Oxford, Bicester, Banbury and Birmingham

Network Diagram - see first Page of Table 116

		GW	GW	GW	GW	GW	GW	GW	GW	GW	GW	GW	GW	GW	GW	GW	GW	GW	GW
		1	◇1	1	◇1	1	◇1	◇1	1	◇1	1		1	◇1	1	1	◇1	◇1	1
												🚌							
			☕				☕			☕							☕		
London Paddington 15 ⊖	d		21 30		21 50	21 57	22 00	22 15		22 35			22 45	23 00		23 20	23 30	23 33	
Ealing Broadway ⊖	d					22 05							22 55			23 28			
Slough 3	d				22 06	22 27		22 32					23 21	23 17		23 54		23 50	
Maidenhead 3	d					22 34							23 32			00 05			
Twyford 3	d	←				22 42			←				23 39		←	00 13			←
Reading 7	d	21 53	21 57	22 03	22 23	22 53	22 27	22 51	22 53	23 02	23 12		23 49	23 34	23 49	00 20	23 59	00 08	00 20
Reading West	d			22 06		→					23 14		→			→			
Theale	d			22 12							23 20								
Aldermaston	d			22 17							23 25								
Midgham	d			22 20							23 29								
Thatcham	d			22 25							23 34								
Newbury Racecourse	d			22 30							23 38								
Newbury	a			22 32							23 41								
	d			22 32							23 41								
Kintbury	d			22 39							23 48								
Hungerford	d			22 43							23 52								
Bedwyn	a			22 51							00 01								
Tilehurst	d	21 57							22 57						23 53				00 24
Pangbourne	d	22 01							23 01						23 58				
Goring & Streatley	d	22 06							23 06						00 03				00 31
Cholsey	d	22 11							23 11						00 08				00 36
Didcot Parkway	a	22 19	22 12		22 37		22 41	23 06	23 19	23 21				23 51	00 14		00 18	00 22	00 44
	d	22 25			22 38			23 07	23 20					23 51	00 15			00 24	00 45
Appleford	d																		00s49
Culham	d																		00s51
Radley	d	22 34							23 27						00s22				00s55
Oxford	a	22 43			22 50			23 20	23 38					00 04	00 32			00 38	01 05
	d											23 47							
Islip	d																		
Bicester Town	a																		
Tackley	d											00s06							
Heyford	d											00s20							
Kings Sutton	d																		
Banbury	a											00 45							
Leamington Spa 8	a																		
Coventry	a																		
Birmingham International	a																		
Birmingham New Street 12	a																		

Saturdays

7 January to 24 March

		GW	GW	CH	GW	GW	GW	GW	GW	GW	GW	GW	GW	GW	GW	GW	XC	GW	GW	GW	CH	GW	XC
		1	◇1		1	◇1	1	1	1	◇1	1	1	1	1	◇1	1	◇1	1	1	◇1		1	◇1
						☕											🛒						🛒
London Paddington 15 ⊖	d	22p45	23p18		23p29	23p30		23p42		00 22					05 21				05 25	05 50			
Ealing Broadway ⊖	d	22p54			23p37														05 33				
Slough 3	d	23p12	23p36		23p54			23p58		00 39					05 38				05 51	06 06			
Maidenhead 3	d	23p24	23p44		00 01			00 08											06 02				
Twyford 3	d	23p32			00 09				←										06 10				
Reading 7	d	23p41	23p58		00 25	00 08	00 20	00 21	00 25	00 56	05 08	05 41		05 46	05 54		06 11	06 12	06 21	06 22			06 46
Reading West	d				→		00s23				05 11	05 44						06 14					
Theale	d						00s29				05 17	05 50						06 20					
Aldermaston	d						00s34				05 22	05 55						06 25					
Midgham	d						00s37				05 25	05 58						06 29					
Thatcham	d						00s42				05 30	06 03						06 34					
Newbury Racecourse	d						00s47				05 35	06 08						06 38					
Newbury	a						00 52				05 37	06 10						06 44					
	d										05 37	06 10											
Kintbury	d										05 44	06 17											
Hungerford	d										05 48	06 21											
Bedwyn	a										05 57	06 30											
Tilehurst	d	23p45							00 29					05 50					06 25				
Pangbourne	d	23p49							00 34					05 54					06 29				
Goring & Streatley	d	23p53							00 37					05 59					06 34				
Cholsey	d	23p57							00 42					06 04		←			06 39			←	
Didcot Parkway	a	00 07				00 25		00 43	00 50	01 13				06 12	06 07	06 12			06 46	06 37		06 46	
	d	00 07						00 44	00 52	01 14				06 13	06 08	06 13			06 47	06 38		06 47	
Appleford	d								00 57					→		06 17			→				
Culham	d								00 59							06 20							
Radley	d	00 15							01 03							06 24						06 54	
Oxford	a	00 26	00 28					01 02	01 16	01 28					06 22	06 32	06 36			06 52		07 03	07 10
	d			00 38									06 16				06 38				07 00		07 12
Islip	d																				07 13		
Bicester Town	a																				07 25		
Tackley	d			00 48									06 25										
Heyford	d			00 53									06 29										
Kings Sutton	d			01 01									06 38										
Banbury	a			01 10									06 46				06 54						07 32
Leamington Spa 8	a																07 12						07 50
Coventry	a																07 24						
Birmingham International	a																07 37						
Birmingham New Street 12	a																07 48						08 17

Table 116

Saturdays

7 January to 24 March

London and Reading - Bedwyn, Oxford, Bicester, Banbury and Birmingham

Network Diagram - see first Page of Table 116

Station		GW	GW	GW	GW	GW	GW	XC	GW	GW	GW	CH	GW	XC	GW	GW	GW	GW	GW	XC	GW	GW	GW
		1	1	◇1	1	1	◇1	◇1	1	◇1	1		1	◇1	1	1	◇1	1	R 1	◇1	1	◇1	1
							☕	🛒						🛒					☕	🛒			
London Paddington 15 ⊖	d		05 57	06 21		06 27	06 30			06 50						06 57	07 21	07 27	07 30			07 50	
Ealing Broadway ⊖	d		06 05			06 35										07 05		07 35					
Slough 3	d		06 31	06 38		06 57				07 06						07 27	07 38	07 57				08 06	
Maidenhead 3	d		06 42			07 04										07 34		08 04					
Twyford 3	d		06 50		←	07 12							←			07 42		08 12					←
Reading 7	d	06 48	06 56	06 54	06 56	07 23	06 59	07 11	07 11	07 22			07 23	07 47	07 48	07 53	07 53	08 23	07 57	08 11	08 18	08 22	08 23
Reading West	d		→			→			07 14									→			08 20		
Theale	d	06 55							07 20						07 57						08 27		
Aldermaston	d								07 25												08 32		
Midgham	d								07 29												08 36		
Thatcham	d	07 04							07 34						08 05						08 41		
Newbury Racecourse	d								07 38												08 45		
Newbury	a	07 09							07 43						08 11						08 50		
	d	07 09													08 11								
Kintbury	d	07 16													08 17								
Hungerford	d	07 20													08 22								
Bedwyn	a	07 29													08 31								
Tilehurst	d				07 00								07 27			07 57							08 27
Pangbourne	d				07 04								07 31			08 01							08 31
Goring & Streatley	d				07 09								07 36			08 06							08 36
Cholsey	d				07 14								07 41			08 11							08 41
Didcot Parkway	a				07 30		07 12						07 49			08 19			08 12				08 48
	d				07 30								07 51			08 25							08 55
Appleford	d																						09 00
Culham	d												07 56										
Radley	d												08 00										09 03
Oxford	a			07 18	07 43			07 34		07 48			08 09	08 13		08 40	08 19			08 34		08 48	09 14
	d							07 36			07 53	08 07		08 15						08 36			
Islip	d											08 20											
Bicester Town	a											08 32											
Tackley	d										08 02												
Heyford	d										08 06												
Kings Sutton	d										08 15												
Banbury	a							07 52			08 23			08 32						08 52			
Leamington Spa 8	a							08 10						08 49						09 10			
Coventry	a							08 22												09 22			
Birmingham International	a							08 37												09 37			
Birmingham New Street 12	a							08 48						09 19						09 48			

Station		XC	GW	GW	GW	GW	GW	GW	CH	GW	GW	XC	GW	GW	GW	XC	GW	GW	GW	GW	GW	GW
		◇1	1	1	◇1	◇1	1	◇1		1	◇1	◇1	1	◇1	1	◇1	1	1	1	1	◇1	1
		🛒			☕	☕		☕			☕	🛒				🛒						
London Paddington 15 ⊖	d			07 57	08 15	08 18		08 21		08 27	08 30			08 50				08 57	09 18		09 21	09 27
Ealing Broadway ⊖	d			08 05						08 35								09 05				09 35
Slough 3	d			08 27				08 39		08 57				09 06				09 27			09 39	09 57
Maidenhead 3	d			08 34						09 04								09 34				10 04
Twyford 3	d			08 42			←			09 12					←			09 42		←		10 12
Reading 7	d	08 40		08 53	08 42	08 48	08 53	08 54		09 23	08 57	09 11	09 12	09 22	09 23	09 40		09 53	09 48	09 53	09 54	10 23
Reading West	d			→						→			09 14					→				→
Theale	d					08 58							09 20						09 56			
Aldermaston	d												09 25									
Midgham	d												09 29									
Thatcham	d					09 07							09 34						10 04			
Newbury Racecourse	d												09 38									
Newbury	a					09 13							09 44						10 10			
	d		08 58			09 14													10 10			
Kintbury	d		09 04																10 17			
Hungerford	d		09 09			09 23													10 21			
Bedwyn	a		09 17			09 30													10 31			
Tilehurst	d						08 57								09 27					09 57		
Pangbourne	d						09 01								09 31					10 01		
Goring & Streatley	d						09 06								09 36					10 06		
Cholsey	d						09 11								09 41					10 11		
Didcot Parkway	a				08 55		09 19				09 12				09 48					10 18		
	d						09 25								09 55					10 25		
Appleford	d																					
Culham	d														10 01							
Radley	d														10 03							
Oxford	a	09 04					09 40	09 18				09 34		09 48	10 14	10 04				10 40	10 19	
	d	09 07							09 28			09 36				10 07	10 16					
Islip	d								09 41													
Bicester Town	a								09 53													
Tackley	d																10 25					
Heyford	d																10 29					
Kings Sutton	d																10 38					
Banbury	a	09 23										09 52				10 23	10 46					
Leamington Spa 8	a	09 41										10 12				10 41						
Coventry	a											10 22										
Birmingham International	a											10 37										
Birmingham New Street 12	a	10 18										10 48				11 18						

Table 116

Saturdays

7 January to 24 March

London and Reading - Bedwyn, Oxford, Bicester, Banbury and Birmingham

Network Diagram - see first Page of Table 116

		GW	XC	GW	GW	CH	GW	XC	GW	GW	GW	GW	GW	GW	GW	XC	GW	GW	GW	XC	GW	GW	GW
		◇1 ☕	◇1 🛒	1	◇1		1	◇1 🛒	1	◇1 ☕	1	1	◇1 ☕	1	◇1 ☕	◇1 🛒	1	◇1 🛒	1	◇1 🛒	1	1	1
London Paddington 15 ⊖	d	09 30			09 50				09 57	10 15	10 18		10 21	10 27	10 30			10 50				10 57	11 18
Ealing Broadway ⊖	d								10 05					10 35								11 05	
Slough 3	d				10 06				10 27				10 39	10 57				11 06				11 27	
Maidenhead 3	d								10 34					11 04								11 34	
Twyford 3	d						←		10 42			←		11 12					←			11 42	
Reading 7	d	09 57	10 11	10 12	10 22		10 23	10 40	10 53	10 42	10 48	10 53	10 54	11 23	10 57	11 11	11 12	11 22	11 23	11 40		11 53	11 48
Reading West	d			10 14					→					→			11 14					→	
Theale	d			10 20							10 56						11 20						11 56
Aldermaston	d			10 25													11 25						
Midgham	d			10 29													11 29						
Thatcham	d			10 34							11 04						11 34						12 04
Newbury Racecourse	d			10 38													11 38						
Newbury	a			10 44							11 10						11 44						12 10
	d										11 10												12 10
Kintbury	d										11 17												12 17
Hungerford	d										11 21												12 21
Bedwyn	a										11 31												12 31
Tilehurst	d						10 27					10 57							11 27				
Pangbourne	d						10 31					11 01							11 31				
Goring & Streatley	d						10 36					11 06							11 36				
Cholsey	d						10 41					11 11							11 41				
Didcot Parkway	a	10 12					10 48			10 55		11 19			11 12				11 49				
	d						10 55					11 25							11 55				
Appleford	d						11 00																
Culham	d																						
Radley	d						11 03												12 03				
Oxford	a		10 34		10 48		11 14	11 04				11 40	11 19			11 34		11 48	12 14	12 04			
	d		10 36			11 00		11 07								11 36				12 07	12 16		
Islip	d					11 13																	
Bicester Town	a					11 25																	
Tackley	d																				12 25		
Heyford	d																				12 29		
Kings Sutton	d																				12 38		
Banbury	a		10 52					11 23								11 52				12 23	12 46		
Leamington Spa 8	a		11 10					11 41								12 10				12 41			
Coventry	a		11 22													12 22							
Birmingham International	a		11 37													12 37							
Birmingham New Street 12	a		11 48					12 18								12 48				13 18			

		GW	GW	CH	GW	GW	XC	GW	GW	GW	XC	GW	GW	GW	GW	GW	GW	GW	XC	GW	CH	GW
		1	◇1 🛒		1	◇1 ⊘	◇1 🛒	1	◇1	1	◇1 🛒	1	◇1 ☕	◇1 ☕	1	◇1	1	◇1 ☕	◇1 🛒	1		◇1 🛒
London Paddington 15 ⊖	d		11 21		11 27	11 30			11 50			11 57	12 15	12 18		12 21	12 27	12 30				12 50
Ealing Broadway ⊖	d				11 35							12 05					12 35					
Slough 3	d		11 39		11 57				12 06			12 27				12 39	12 57					13 06
Maidenhead 3	d				12 04							12 34					13 04					
Twyford 3	d	←			12 12					←		12 42			←		13 12					
Reading 7	d	11 53	11 54		12 23	11 58	12 11	12 12	12 22	12 23	12 40	12 53	12 42	12 48	12 53	12 54	13 23	12 57	13 11	13 12		13 22
Reading West	d				→			12 14				→					→			13 14		
Theale	d							12 20						12 57						13 20		
Aldermaston	d							12 25												13 25		
Midgham	d							12 29												13 29		
Thatcham	d							12 34						13 05						13 34		
Newbury Racecourse	d							12 38												13 38		
Newbury	a							12 44						13 12						13 44		
	d													13 13								
Kintbury	d																					
Hungerford	d													13 21								
Bedwyn	a													13 29								
Tilehurst	d	11 57								12 27					12 57							
Pangbourne	d	12 01								12 31					13 01							
Goring & Streatley	d	12 06								12 36					13 06							
Cholsey	d	12 11								12 41					13 11							
Didcot Parkway	a	12 19				12 12				12 48			12 55		13 19			13 12				
	d	12 25								12 55					13 25							
Appleford	d									13 00												
Culham	d																					
Radley	d									13 03												
Oxford	a	12 40	12 20				12 34		12 48	13 14	13 04				13 40	13 19			13 34			13 48
	d			12 30			12 36				13 07								13 36		13 41	
Islip	d			12 43																	13 54	
Bicester Town	a			12 55																	14 06	
Tackley	d																					
Heyford	d																					
Kings Sutton	d																					
Banbury	a						12 52				13 23								13 52			
Leamington Spa 8	a						13 10				13 41								14 10			
Coventry	a						13 22												14 22			
Birmingham International	a						13 37												14 37			
Birmingham New Street 12	a						13 48				14 18								14 48			

Table 116

Saturdays

7 January to 24 March

London and Reading - Bedwyn, Oxford, Bicester, Banbury and Birmingham

Network Diagram - see first Page of Table 116

		GW	XC	GW	GW	GW	GW	GW	GW	GW		XC	GW	GW	CH	GW	XC	GW	GW	GW		GW	GW	GW	GW
		1	◇1	1	1	1	1	◇1	1	◇1		◇1	1	◇1		1	◇1	1	◇1	1		1	◇1	1	◇1
			trolley					trolley		restaurant		trolley		trolley			trolley		restaurant				trolley		restaurant
London Paddington 15 ⊖	d				12 57	13 18		13 21	13 27	13 30				13 50				13 57	14 15	14 18			14 21	14 27	14 30
Ealing Broadway ⊖	d				13 05				13 35									14 05						14 35	
Slough 3	d				13 27			13 39	13 57					14 06				14 27					14 39	14 57	
Maidenhead 3	d				13 34				14 04									14 34						15 04	
Twyford 3	d	←			13 42		←		14 12							←		14 42				←		15 12	
Reading 7	d	13 23	13 40		13 53	13 48	13 53	13 54	14 23	13 59		14 11	14 12	14 22		14 23	14 40	14 53	14 42	14 48		14 53	14 54	15 23	14 57
Reading West	d				→				→				14 14					→						→	
Theale	d					13 56							14 20							14 56					
Aldermaston	d												14 25												
Midgham	d												14 29												
Thatcham	d					14 04							14 34							15 04					
Newbury Racecourse	d												14 38												
Newbury	a					14 10							14 44							15 10					
	d					14 10														15 10					
Kintbury	d					14 17														15 17					
Hungerford	d					14 21														15 21					
Bedwyn	a					14 31														15 31					
Tilehurst	d	13 27					13 57									14 27						14 57			
Pangbourne	d	13 31					14 01									14 31						15 01			
Goring & Streatley	d	13 36					14 06									14 36						15 06			
Cholsey	d	13 41					14 11									14 41						15 11			
Didcot Parkway	a	13 48					14 19			14 12						14 48			14 55			15 19			15 12
	d	13 55					14 25									14 55						15 25			
Appleford	d															15 00									
Culham	d	14 01																							
Radley	d	14 03														15 03									
Oxford	a	14 14	14 04				14 40	14 19				14 34		14 48		15 14	15 04					15 40	15 18		
	d		14 07	14 16								14 36			14 57		15 07								
Islip	d														15 10										
Bicester Town	a														15 22										
Tackley	d			14 25																					
Heyford	d			14 29																					
Kings Sutton	d			14 38																					
Banbury	a		14 23	14 46								14 52					15 23								
Leamington Spa 8	a		14 41									15 10					15 41								
Coventry	a											15 22													
Birmingham International	a											15 37													
Birmingham New Street 12	a		15 18									15 48					16 18								

		XC	GW	GW	CH	GW		XC	GW	GW	GW	GW	GW	GW	GW	XC		GW	GW	GW	XC	CH	GW	GW	GW
		◇1	1	◇1		1		◇1	1	1	1	1	◇1	1	◇1	◇1		1	◇1	1	◇1		1	◇1	1
																								A	
		trolley						trolley					trolley		restaurant	trolley					trolley			restaurant	
London Paddington 15 ⊖	d			14 50						14 57	15 18		15 21	15 27	15 30				15 50				15 57	16 15	16 18
Ealing Broadway ⊖	d									15 05				15 35									16 05		
Slough 3	d			15 06						15 27			15 39	15 57					16 06				16 27		
Maidenhead 3	d									15 34				16 04									16 34		
Twyford 3	d					←				15 42		←		16 12						←			16 42		
Reading 7	d	15 11	15 12	15 22		15 23		15 40		15 53	15 48	15 53	15 54	16 23	15 59	16 11		16 12	16 22	16 23	16 40		16 53	16 42	16 48
Reading West	d		15 14							→				→				16 14					→		
Theale	d		15 20								15 56							16 20							16 56
Aldermaston	d		15 25															16 25							
Midgham	d		15 29															16 29							
Thatcham	d		15 34								16 04							16 34							17 04
Newbury Racecourse	d		15 38															16 38							
Newbury	a		15 44								16 10							16 44							17 10
	d										16 10														17 10
Kintbury	d										16 17														17 17
Hungerford	d										16 21														17 21
Bedwyn	a										16 31														17 31
Tilehurst	d					15 27						15 57								16 27					
Pangbourne	d					15 31						16 01								16 31					
Goring & Streatley	d					15 36						16 06								16 36					
Cholsey	d					15 41						16 11								16 41					
Didcot Parkway	a					15 48						16 19			16 12					16 48				16 55	
	d					15 55						16 25								16 55					
Appleford	d																			17 00					
Culham	d					16 01																			
Radley	d					16 03														17 03					
Oxford	a	15 34		15 48		16 14		16 04				16 40	16 19			16 34			16 48	17 14	17 04				
	d	15 36			16 00			16 07	16 16							16 36					17 07	17 10			
Islip	d				16 14																	17 23			
Bicester Town	a				16 26																	17 35			
Tackley	d								16 25																
Heyford	d								16 29																
Kings Sutton	d								16 38																
Banbury	a	15 52						16 23	16 46							16 52					17 23				
Leamington Spa 8	a	16 10						16 41								17 10					17 41				
Coventry	a	16 22														17 22									
Birmingham International	a	16 37														17 37									
Birmingham New Street 12	a	16 48						17 18								17 48					18 18				

A from 7 January until 11 February

Table 116

Saturdays

7 January to 24 March

London and Reading - Bedwyn, Oxford, Bicester, Banbury and Birmingham

Network Diagram - see first Page of Table 116

Station		GW 1		GW ◇1 ⊡	GW 1	GW ◇1 ⊡	XC ◇1 ⊼	GW 1	GW ◇1 ⊼	GW 1	XC ◇1 ⊼	GW 1		GW 1	GW 1	GW 1	GW ◇1 ⊡	GW 1	GW ◇1 ⊡	XC ◇1 ⊼	GW 1	CH		GW ◇1 ⊼	GW 1
London Paddington 15 ⊖	d			16 21	16 27	16 30			16 50					16 57	17 18		17 21	17 27	17 30					17 50	
Ealing Broadway ⊖	d				16 35									17 05				17 35							
Slough 3	d			16 39	16 57				17 06					17 27			17 39	17 57						18 06	
Maidenhead 3	d				17 04									17 34				18 04							
Twyford 3	d	←			17 12					←				17 42		←		18 12							←
Reading 7	d	16 53		16 54	17 23	16 57	17 11	17 12	17 22	17 23	17 40			17 53	17 48	17 53	17 54	18 23	17 57	18 11	18 12			18 22	18 23
Reading West	d				→			17 14						→				→			18 14				
Theale	d							17 20							17 56						18 20				
Aldermaston	d							17 25													18 25				
Midgham	d							17 29													18 29				
Thatcham	d							17 34							18 04						18 34				
Newbury Racecourse	d							17 38													18 38				
Newbury	a							17 44							18 10						18 44				
	d														18 10										
Kintbury	d														18 17										
Hungerford	d														18 21										
Bedwyn	a														18 31										
Tilehurst	d	16 57								17 27						17 57									18 27
Pangbourne	d	17 01								17 31						18 01									18 31
Goring & Streatley	d	17 06								17 36						18 06									18 36
Cholsey	d	17 11								17 41						18 11									18 41
Didcot Parkway	a	17 19				17 12				17 48						18 19			18 12						18 48
	d	17 25								17 55						18 25									18 55
Appleford	d																								19 00
Culham	d									18 01															
Radley	d									18 03															19 03
Oxford	a	17 40		17 18			17 34		17 48	18 14	18 04					18 40	18 18			18 34				18 48	19 14
	d						17 36				18 07	18 16								18 36		18 41			
Islip	d																					18 54			
Bicester Town	a																					19 06			
Tackley	d											18 25													
Heyford	d											18 29													
Kings Sutton	d											18 38													
Banbury	a						17 52				18 23	18 46								18 52					
Leamington Spa 8	a						18 10				18 41									19 10					
Coventry	a						18 22													19 22					
Birmingham International	a						18 37													19 37					
Birmingham New Street 12	a						18 48				19 18									19 48					

Station		XC ◇1 ⊼	GW 1	GW ◇1 ⊡	GW 1	GW 1	GW ◇1 ⊡	GW 1		GW ◇1 ⊡	XC ◇1 ⊼	GW ◇1	CH	GW 1	GW 1	GW 1	GW ◇1 A ⊡	GW ◇1 ⊡		XC ◇1	GW 1	GW ◇1	GW 1	GW 1	GW ◇1 A ⊡
London Paddington 15 ⊖	d		17 57	18 15	18 18		18 21	18 27		18 30		18 50				18 57	19 06	19 15				19 21		19 27	19 30
Ealing Broadway ⊖	d		18 05					18 35								19 05								19 35	
Slough 3	d		18 27				18 39	18 57				19 06				19 27						19 38		19 57	
Maidenhead 3	d		18 34					19 04								19 34								20 04	
Twyford 3	d		18 42			←		19 12							←	19 42							←	20 12	
Reading 7	d	18 40	18 53	18 42	18 48	18 53	18 54	19 23		18 57	19 11	19 23			19 23	19 53	19 32	19 42		19 40	19 49	19 52	19 53	20 23	19 57
Reading West	d		→					→								→					19 52			→	
Theale	d				18 56																19 58				
Aldermaston	d																				20 03				
Midgham	d																				20 06				
Thatcham	d				19 04																20 11				
Newbury Racecourse	d																				20 16				
Newbury	a				19 10												19 48				20 18				
	d				19 10																20 18				
Kintbury	d				19 17																20 25				
Hungerford	d				19 21																20 29				
Bedwyn	a				19 31																20 38				
Tilehurst	d					18 57									19 27								19 57		
Pangbourne	d					19 01									19 31								20 01		
Goring & Streatley	d					19 06									19 36								20 06		
Cholsey	d					19 11									19 41								20 11		
Didcot Parkway	a			18 55		19 19				19 12					19 48			19 55					20 19		20 11
	d					19 25									19 55								20 25		
Appleford	d																								
Culham	d														20 01										
Radley	d														20 03										
Oxford	a	19 04				19 40	19 18				19 34	19 48			20 14					20 04		20 20	20 40		
	d	19 07									19 36		19 48	19 56						20 07					
Islip	d												20 01												
Bicester Town	a												20 13												
Tackley	d													20 05											
Heyford	d													20 09											
Kings Sutton	d													20 18											
Banbury	a	19 23									19 52			20 25						20 28					
Leamington Spa 8	a	19 41									20 10									20 45					
Coventry	a										20 22														
Birmingham International	a										20 37														
Birmingham New Street 12	a	20 18									20 48									21 18					

A from 7 January until 11 February

Table 116

Saturdays

7 January to 24 March

London and Reading - Bedwyn, Oxford, Bicester, Banbury and Birmingham

Network Diagram - see first Page of Table 116

		XC	GW	CH	GW	GW	GW	GW	GW	XC	GW	GW	GW	GW	GW	GW	XC	GW	GW	GW	GW	GW
		◇1	◇1		1	1	◇1	◇1	◇1	◇1	◇1	1	1	1	1	◇1	◇1	◇1	1	1	◇1	◇1
			A																			
			🚲				☕	☕	☕							☕		🚲				☕
London Paddington 15 ⊖	d		19 50			19 57	20 00	20 06	20 15		20 17				20 27	20 30		20 50		20 57	21 17	21 30
Ealing Broadway ⊖	d					20 05									20 35					21 05		
Slough 3	d		20 06			20 27					20 32				20 57			21 06		21 27	21 35	
Maidenhead 3	d					20 34									21 04					21 34		
Twyford 3	d				←	20 42								←	21 12				←	21 47		
Reading 7	d	20 11	20 22		20 23	20 53	20 27	20 33	20 42	20 40	20 48	20 49		20 53	21 29	20 59	21 11	21 22	21 29	22 04	21 52	21 57
Reading West	d					→						20 52			→					→		
Theale	d											20 58										
Aldermaston	d											21 03										
Midgham	d											21 06										
Thatcham	d											21 11										
Newbury Racecourse	d											21 16										
Newbury	a							20 47				21 18										
	d											21 32										
Kintbury	d											21 39										
Hungerford	d											21 43										
Bedwyn	a											21 52										
Tilehurst	d				20 27									20 57					21 33			
Pangbourne	d				20 31																	
Goring & Streatley	d				20 37									21 06					21 42			
Cholsey	d				20 41									21 11					21 47			
Didcot Parkway	a				20 49		20 41		20 55					21 19		21 22		21 39	21 54		22 07	22 12
	d				20 55									21 27				21 40	21 55		22 08	
Appleford	d				21 00																	
Culham	d																		22 01			
Radley	d				21 03														22 03			
Oxford	a	20 34	20 47		21 14					21 04	21 19			21 40			21 34	21 53	22 14		22 20	
	d	20 36		21 00						21 07			21 20				21 36					
Islip	d			21 13																		
Bicester Town	a			21 25																		
Tackley	d												21 29									
Heyford	d												21 33									
Kings Sutton	d												21 42									
Banbury	a	20 52								21 23			21 49				21 52					
Leamington Spa 8	a	21 10								21 44							22 10					
Coventry	a	21 22								21 55							22 22					
Birmingham International	a	21 37								22 10							22 36					
Birmingham New Street 12	a	21 48								22 21							22 48					

		GW	CH	GW	GW	GW	GW	GW	GW	GW	GW	GW	GW	GW	GW	GW	GW
		1		1	◇1	1	◇1	◇1	1	◇1	1		1	◇1	1	◇1	◇1
												🚌					
							☕			☕						☕	
London Paddington 15 ⊖	d				21 50	21 57	22 00	22 15		22 35			22 45	23 00		23 30	23 33
Ealing Broadway ⊖	d					22 05							22 55				
Slough 3	d				22 06	22 27		22 32					23 21	23 17			23 50
Maidenhead 3	d					22 34							23 32				
Twyford 3	d			←		22 45			←				23 39		←		
Reading 7	d	22 03		22 04	22 23	22 55	22 27	22 51	22 55	23 02	23 12		23 49	23 34	23 49	23 59	00 08
Reading West	d	22 06				→					23 14		→				
Theale	d	22 12									23 20						
Aldermaston	d	22 17									23 25						
Midgham	d	22 20									23 29						
Thatcham	d	22 25									23 34						
Newbury Racecourse	d	22 30									23 38						
Newbury	a	22 32									23 41						
	d	22 32									23 41						
Kintbury	d	22 39									23 48						
Hungerford	d	22 43									23 52						
Bedwyn	a	22 51									00 01						
Tilehurst	d			22 09					22 59						23 53		
Pangbourne	d																
Goring & Streatley	d			22 15					23 06						00 03		
Cholsey	d			22 20					23 11						00 08		
Didcot Parkway	a			22 28	22 37		22 41	23 05	23 19	23 23				23 51	00 14	00 18	00 22
	d			22 28	22 38			23 07	23 20					23 51	00 15		00 24
Appleford	d																
Culham	d																
Radley	d			22 37					23 27						00s22		
Oxford	a			22 46	22 50			23 20	23 38					00 04	00 32		00 38
	d		22 25									23 47					
Islip	d		22 38														
Bicester Town	a		22 50														
Tackley	d											00s06					
Heyford	d											00s20					
Kings Sutton	d																
Banbury	a											00 45					
Leamington Spa 8	a																
Coventry	a																
Birmingham International	a																
Birmingham New Street 12	a																

A from 7 January until 11 February

Table 116

Saturdays
from 31 March

London and Reading - Bedwyn, Oxford, Bicester, Banbury and Birmingham

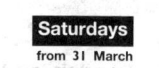

Network Diagram - see first Page of Table 116

		GW	GW	CH	GW	GW	GW	GW	GW	GW		GW	GW	GW	GW	GW	GW	XC	GW	GW		GW	CH	GW	XC
		1	◇1		1	◇1 🍴	1	1	1	◇1		1	1	1	1	◇1	1	◇1 trolley	1	1		◇1		1	◇1 trolley
London Paddington 15 ⊖	d	22p45	23p18		23p29	23p30		23p42		00 22						05 21				05 25		05 50			
Ealing Broadway ⊖	d	22p54			23p37															05 33					
Slough 3	d	23p12	23p36		23p54			23p58		00 39						05 38				05 51		06 06			
Maidenhead 3	d	23p24	23p44		00 01			00 08												06 02					
Twyford 3	d	23p32			00 09				←											06 10					
Reading 7	d	23p41	23p58		00 25	00 08	00 20	00 21	00 25	00 56		05 08	05 41		05 46	05 54		06 11	06 12	06 21		06 22			06 46
Reading West	d				→		00s23					05 11	05 44						06 14						
Theale	d						00s29					05 17	05 50						06 20						
Aldermaston	d						00s34					05 22	05 55						06 25						
Midgham	d						00s37					05 25	05 58						06 29						
Thatcham	d						00s42					05 30	06 03						06 34						
Newbury Racecourse	d						00s47					05 35	06 08						06 38						
Newbury	a						00 52					05 37	06 10						06 44						
	d											05 37	06 10												
Kintbury	d											05 44	06 17												
Hungerford	d											05 48	06 21												
Bedwyn	a											05 57	06 30												
Tilehurst	d	23p45							00 29						05 50					06 25					
Pangbourne	d	23p49							00 34						05 54					06 29					
Goring & Streatley	d	23p53							00 37						05 59					06 34					
Cholsey	d	23p57							00 42						06 04		←			06 39				←	
Didcot Parkway	a	00 07				00 25		00 43	00 50	01 13					06 12	06 07	06 12			06 46		06 37		06 46	
	d	00 07						00 44	00 52	01 14					06 13	06 08	06 13			06 47		06 38		06 47	
Appleford	d								00 57						→		06 17			→					
Culham	d								00 59								06 20								
Radley	d	00 15							01 03								06 24							06 54	
Oxford	a	00 26	00 28					01 02	01 16	01 28						06 22	06 32	06 36				06 52		07 03	07 10
	d			00 38										06 16				06 38					07 00		07 12
Islip	d																						07 13		
Bicester Town	a																						07 25		
Tackley	d			00 48										06 25											
Heyford	d			00 53										06 29											
Kings Sutton	d			01 01										06 38											
Banbury	a			01 10										06 46				06 54							07 32
Leamington Spa 8	a																	07 12							07 50
Coventry	a																	07 24							
Birmingham International	a																	07 37							
Birmingham New Street 12	a																	07 48							08 17

		GW	GW	GW	GW	GW		GW	XC	GW	GW	GW	CH	GW	XC	GW		GW	GW	GW	GW	XC	GW	GW	GW
		1	1	◇1	1	1		◇1 🍴	◇1 trolley	1	◇1	1		1	◇1 trolley	1		1	◇1	1	R 1 🍴	◇1 trolley	1	◇1	1
London Paddington 15 ⊖	d		05 57	06 21		06 27		06 30			06 50							06 57	07 21	07 27	07 30			07 50	
Ealing Broadway ⊖	d		06 05			06 35												07 05		07 35					
Slough 3	d		06 31	06 38		06 57					07 06							07 27	07 38	07 57				08 06	
Maidenhead 3	d		06 42			07 04												07 34		08 04					
Twyford 3	d		06 50		←	07 12								←				07 42		08 12					←
Reading 7	d	06 48	06 56	06 54	06 56	07 23		06 59	07 11	07 11	07 22			07 23	07 47	07 48		07 53	07 53	08 23	07 57	08 11	08 18	08 22	08 23
Reading West	d		→			→				07 14										→			08 20		
Theale	d	06 55								07 20						07 57							08 27		
Aldermaston	d									07 25													08 32		
Midgham	d									07 29													08 36		
Thatcham	d	07 04								07 34						08 05							08 41		
Newbury Racecourse	d									07 38													08 45		
Newbury	a	07 09								07 43						08 11							08 50		
	d	07 09														08 11									
Kintbury	d	07 16														08 17									
Hungerford	d	07 20														08 22									
Bedwyn	a	07 29														08 31									
Tilehurst	d				07 00									07 27				07 57							08 27
Pangbourne	d				07 04									07 31				08 01							08 31
Goring & Streatley	d				07 09									07 36				08 06							08 36
Cholsey	d				07 14									07 41				08 11							08 41
Didcot Parkway	a				07 30			07 12						07 49				08 19			08 12				08 48
	d				07 30									07 51				08 25							08 55
Appleford	d																								09 00
Culham	d													07 56											
Radley	d													08 00											09 03
Oxford	a			07 18	07 43				07 34		07 48			08 09	08 13			08 40	08 19			08 34		08 48	09 14
	d								07 36			07 53	08 07		08 15							08 36			
Islip	d												08 20												
Bicester Town	a												08 32												
Tackley	d											08 02													
Heyford	d											08 06													
Kings Sutton	d											08 15													
Banbury	a								07 52			08 23			08 32							08 52			
Leamington Spa 8	a								08 10						08 49							09 10			
Coventry	a								08 22													09 22			
Birmingham International	a								08 37													09 37			
Birmingham New Street 12	a								08 48						09 19							09 48			

Table 116

Saturdays
from 31 March

London and Reading - Bedwyn, Oxford, Bicester, Banbury and Birmingham

Network Diagram - see first Page of Table 116

		XC ◇1 ⌶		GW 1	GW 1	GW ◇1 ▭	GW ◇1 ▭	GW 1	GW ◇1 ▭	CH	GW 1	GW ◇1 ▭		XC ◇1 ⌶	GW 1	GW ◇1	GW 1	XC ◇1 ⌶	GW 1	GW 1	GW 1	GW 1		GW ◇1	GW 1
London Paddington 15 ⊖	d				07 57	08 15	08 18		08 21		08 27	08 30				08 50				08 57	09 18			09 21	09 27
Ealing Broadway ⊖	d				08 05						08 35									09 05					09 35
Slough 3	d				08 27				08 39		08 57					09 06				09 27				09 39	09 57
Maidenhead 3	d				08 34						09 04									09 34					10 04
Twyford 3	d				08 42			←			09 12						←			09 42		←			10 12
Reading 7	d	08 40			08 53	08 42	08 48	08 53	08 54		09 23	08 57		09 11	09 12	09 22	09 23	09 40		09 53	09 48	09 53		09 54	10 23
Reading West	d				→						→				09 14					→					→
Theale	d						08 58								09 20						09 56				
Aldermaston	d														09 25										
Midgham	d														09 29										
Thatcham	d						09 07								09 34						10 04				
Newbury Racecourse	d														09 38										
Newbury	a						09 13								09 44						10 10				
	d			08 58			09 14														10 10				
Kintbury	d			09 04																	10 17				
Hungerford	d			09 09			09 23														10 21				
Bedwyn	a			09 17			09 30														10 31				
Tilehurst	d							08 57									09 27					09 57			
Pangbourne	d							09 01									09 31					10 01			
Goring & Streatley	d							09 06									09 36					10 06			
Cholsey	d							09 11									09 41					10 11			
Didcot Parkway	a					08 55		09 19				09 12					09 48					10 18			
	d							09 25									09 55					10 25			
Appleford	d																								
Culham	d																10 01								
Radley	d																10 03								
Oxford	a	09 04						09 40	09 18					09 34		09 48	10 14	10 04				10 40		10 19	
	d	09 07								09 28				09 36				10 07	10 16						
Islip	d									09 41															
Bicester Town	a									09 53															
Tackley	d																		10 25						
Heyford	d																		10 29						
Kings Sutton	d																		10 38						
Banbury	a	09 23												09 52				10 23	10 46						
Leamington Spa 8	a	09 41												10 12				10 41							
Coventry	a													10 22											
Birmingham International	a													10 37											
Birmingham New Street 12	a	10 18												10 48				11 18							

		GW ◇1 ▭	XC ◇1 ⌶	GW 1	GW ◇1	CH	GW 1	XC ◇1 ⌶		GW 1	GW ◇1 ▭	GW 1	GW 1	GW ◇1 ▭	GW 1	GW ◇1 ▭	XC ◇1 ⌶	GW 1		GW ◇1 ⌶	GW 1	XC ◇1 ⌶	GW 1	GW 1	GW 1
London Paddington 15 ⊖	d	09 30			09 50					09 57	10 15	10 18		10 21	10 27	10 30				10 50				10 57	11 18
Ealing Broadway ⊖	d									10 05					10 35									11 05	
Slough 3	d				10 06					10 27				10 39	10 57					11 06				11 27	
Maidenhead 3	d									10 34					11 04									11 34	
Twyford 3	d						←			10 42			←		11 12						←			11 42	
Reading 7	d	09 57	10 11	10 12	10 22		10 23	10 40		10 53	10 42	10 48	10 53	10 54	11 23	10 57	11 11	11 12		11 22	11 23	11 40		11 53	11 48
Reading West	d			10 14						→					→			11 14						→	
Theale	d			10 20								10 56						11 20							11 56
Aldermaston	d			10 25														11 25							
Midgham	d			10 29														11 29							
Thatcham	d			10 34								11 04						11 34							12 04
Newbury Racecourse	d			10 38														11 38							
Newbury	a			10 44								11 10						11 44							12 10
	d											11 10													12 10
Kintbury	d											11 17													12 17
Hungerford	d											11 21													12 21
Bedwyn	a											11 31													12 31
Tilehurst	d						10 27						10 57								11 27				
Pangbourne	d						10 31						11 01								11 31				
Goring & Streatley	d						10 36						11 06								11 36				
Cholsey	d						10 41						11 11								11 41				
Didcot Parkway	a	10 12					10 48				10 55		11 19			11 12					11 49				
	d						10 55						11 25								11 55				
Appleford	d						11 00																		
Culham	d																								
Radley	d						11 03														12 03				
Oxford	a		10 34		10 48		11 14	11 04					11 40	11 19			11 34			11 48	12 14	12 04			
	d		10 36			11 00		11 07									11 36					12 07	12 16		
Islip	d					11 13																			
Bicester Town	a					11 25																			
Tackley	d																						12 25		
Heyford	d																						12 29		
Kings Sutton	d																						12 38		
Banbury	a		10 52					11 23									11 52					12 23	12 46		
Leamington Spa 8	a		11 10					11 41									12 10					12 41			
Coventry	a		11 22														12 22								
Birmingham International	a		11 37														12 37								
Birmingham New Street 12	a		11 48					12 18									12 48					13 18			

Table 116

Saturdays
from 31 March

London and Reading - Bedwyn, Oxford, Bicester, Banbury and Birmingham

Network Diagram - see first Page of Table 116

		GW	GW	CH		GW	GW	XC	GW	GW	GW	XC	GW	GW		GW	GW	GW	GW	GW	XC	GW	CH	GW
		1	◇1			1	◇1	◇1	1	◇1	1	◇1	1	◇1		◇1	1	◇1	1	◇1	◇1	1		◇1
			⊥				Ø	⊥				⊥		⊡		⊡				⊡	⊥			⊥
London Paddington 15 ⊖	d		11 21			11 27	11 30			11 50			11 57	12 15		12 18		12 21	12 27	12 30				12 50
Ealing Broadway ⊖	d					11 35							12 05						12 35					
Slough 3	d		11 39			11 57				12 06			12 27					12 39	12 57					13 06
Maidenhead 3	d					12 04							12 34						13 04					
Twyford 3	d	←				12 12					←		12 42				←		13 12					
Reading 7	d	11 53	11 54			12 23	11 58	12 11	12 12	12 22	12 23	12 40	12 53	12 42		12 48	12 53	12 54	13 23	12 57	13 11	13 12		13 22
Reading West	d					→			12 14				→						→			13 14		
Theale	d								12 20							12 57						13 20		
Aldermaston	d								12 25													13 25		
Midgham	d								12 29													13 29		
Thatcham	d								12 34							13 05						13 34		
Newbury Racecourse	d								12 38													13 38		
Newbury	a								12 44							13 12						13 44		
	d															13 13								
Kintbury	d																							
Hungerford	d															13 21								
Bedwyn	a															13 29								
Tilehurst	d	11 57									12 27						12 57							
Pangbourne	d	12 01									12 31						13 01							
Goring & Streatley	d	12 06									12 36						13 06							
Cholsey	d	12 11									12 41						13 11							
Didcot Parkway	a	12 19					12 12				12 48			12 55			13 19			13 12				
	d	12 25									12 55						13 25							
Appleford	d										13 00													
Culham	d																							
Radley	d										13 03													
Oxford	a	12 40	12 20					12 34		12 48	13 14	13 04					13 40	13 19			13 34			13 48
	d			12 30				12 36				13 07									13 36		13 41	
Islip	d			12 43																			13 54	
Bicester Town	a			12 55																			14 06	
Tackley	d																							
Heyford	d																							
Kings Sutton	d																							
Banbury	a							12 52				13 23									13 52			
Leamington Spa 8	a							13 10				13 41									14 10			
Coventry	a							13 22													14 22			
Birmingham International	a							13 37													14 37			
Birmingham New Street 12	a							13 48				14 18									14 48			

		GW	XC	GW	GW	GW	GW	GW	GW	GW		XC	GW	GW	CH	GW	XC	GW	GW	GW		GW	GW	GW	GW
		1	◇1	1	1	1	1	◇1	1	◇1		◇1	1	◇1		1	◇1	1	◇1	1		1	◇1	1	◇1
			⊥					⊥		⊡		⊥		⊥			⊥		⊡				⊥		⊡
London Paddington 15 ⊖	d				12 57	13 18		13 21	13 27	13 30				13 50				13 57	14 15	14 18			14 21	14 27	14 30
Ealing Broadway ⊖	d				13 05				13 35									14 05						14 35	
Slough 3	d				13 27			13 39	13 57					14 06				14 27					14 39	14 57	
Maidenhead 3	d				13 34				14 04									14 34						15 04	
Twyford 3	d	←			13 42		←		14 12							←		14 42				←		15 12	
Reading 7	d	13 23	13 40		13 53	13 48	13 53	13 54	14 23	13 59		14 11	14 12	14 22		14 23	14 40	14 53	14 42	14 48		14 53	14 54	15 23	14 57
Reading West	d				→				→				14 14					→						→	
Theale	d					13 56							14 20							14 56					
Aldermaston	d												14 25												
Midgham	d												14 29												
Thatcham	d					14 04							14 34							15 04					
Newbury Racecourse	d												14 38												
Newbury	a					14 10							14 44							15 10					
	d					14 10														15 10					
Kintbury	d					14 17														15 17					
Hungerford	d					14 21														15 21					
Bedwyn	a					14 31														15 31					
Tilehurst	d	13 27					13 57									14 27						14 57			
Pangbourne	d	13 31					14 01									14 31						15 01			
Goring & Streatley	d	13 36					14 06									14 36						15 06			
Cholsey	d	13 41					14 11									14 41						15 11			
Didcot Parkway	a	13 48					14 19			14 12						14 48			14 55			15 19			15 12
	d	13 55					14 25									14 55						15 25			
Appleford	d															15 00									
Culham	d	14 01																							
Radley	d	14 03														15 03									
Oxford	a	14 14	14 04				14 40	14 19				14 34		14 48		15 14	15 04					15 40	15 18		
	d		14 07	14 16								14 36			14 57		15 07								
Islip	d														15 10										
Bicester Town	a														15 22										
Tackley	d			14 25																					
Heyford	d			14 29																					
Kings Sutton	d			14 38																					
Banbury	a		14 23	14 46								14 52					15 23								
Leamington Spa 8	a		14 41									15 10					15 41								
Coventry	a											15 22													
Birmingham International	a											15 37													
Birmingham New Street 12	a		15 18									15 48					16 18								

Table 116

Saturdays
from 31 March

London and Reading - Bedwyn, Oxford, Bicester, Banbury and Birmingham

Network Diagram - see first Page of Table 116

		XC	GW	GW	CH	GW		XC	GW	GW	GW	GW	GW	GW	GW	XC		GW	GW	GW	XC	CH	GW	GW	GW
		◇1	1	◇1		1		◇1	1	1	1	1	◇1	1	◇1	◇1		1	◇1	1	◇1		1	◇1	1
London Paddington 15 ⊖	d			14 50						14 57	15 18		15 21	15 27	15 30				15 50				15 57	16 15	16 18
Ealing Broadway ⊖	d									15 05				15 35									16 05		
Slough 3	d			15 06						15 27			15 39	15 57					16 06				16 27		
Maidenhead 3	d									15 34				16 04									16 34		
Twyford 3	d					←				15 42		←		16 12						←			16 42		
Reading 7	d	15 11	15 12	15 22		15 23		15 40		15 53	15 48	15 53	15 54	16 23	15 59	16 11		16 12	16 22	16 23	16 40		16 53	16 42	16 48
Reading West	d		15 14							→				→				16 14					→		
Theale	d		15 20								15 56							16 20							16 56
Aldermaston	d		15 25															16 25							
Midgham	d		15 29															16 29							
Thatcham	d		15 34								16 04							16 34							17 04
Newbury Racecourse	d		15 38															16 38							
Newbury	a		15 44								16 10							16 44							17 10
	d										16 10														17 10
Kintbury	d										16 17														17 17
Hungerford	d										16 21														17 21
Bedwyn	a										16 31														17 31
Tilehurst	d					15 27						15 57								16 27					
Pangbourne	d					15 31						16 01								16 31					
Goring & Streatley	d					15 36						16 06								16 36					
Cholsey	d					15 41						16 11								16 41					
Didcot Parkway	a					15 48						16 19			16 12					16 48				16 55	
	d					15 55						16 25								16 55					
Appleford	d																			17 00					
Culham	d					16 01																			
Radley	d					16 03														17 03					
Oxford	a	15 34		15 48		16 14		16 04				16 40	16 19			16 34			16 48	17 14	17 04				
	d	15 36			16 00			16 07	16 16							16 36					17 07	17 10			
Islip	d				16 14																	17 23			
Bicester Town	a				16 26																	17 35			
Tackley	d								16 25																
Heyford	d								16 29																
Kings Sutton	d								16 38																
Banbury	a	15 52						16 23	16 46							16 52					17 23				
Leamington Spa 8	a	16 10						16 41								17 10					17 41				
Coventry	a	16 22														17 22									
Birmingham International	a	16 37														17 37									
Birmingham New Street 12	a	16 48						17 18								17 48					18 18				

		GW		GW	GW	GW	XC	GW	GW	GW	XC	GW		GW	GW	GW	GW	GW	GW	XC	GW	CH		GW	GW
		1		◇1	1	◇1	◇1	1	◇1	1	◇1	1		1	1	1	◇1	1	◇1	◇1	1			◇1	1
London Paddington 15 ⊖	d			16 21	16 27	16 30			16 50					16 57	17 18		17 21	17 27	17 30					17 50	
Ealing Broadway ⊖	d				16 35									17 05				17 35							
Slough 3	d			16 39	16 57				17 06					17 27			17 39	17 57						18 06	
Maidenhead 3	d				17 04									17 34				18 04							
Twyford 3	d	←			17 12					←				17 42		←		18 12							←
Reading 7	d	16 53		16 54	17 23	16 57	17 11	17 12	17 22	17 23	17 40			17 53	17 48	17 53	17 54	18 23	17 57	18 11	18 12			18 22	18 23
Reading West	d				→			17 14						→				→			18 14				
Theale	d							17 20							17 56						18 20				
Aldermaston	d							17 25													18 25				
Midgham	d							17 29													18 29				
Thatcham	d							17 34							18 04						18 34				
Newbury Racecourse	d							17 38													18 38				
Newbury	a							17 44							18 10						18 44				
	d														18 10										
Kintbury	d														18 17										
Hungerford	d														18 21										
Bedwyn	a														18 31										
Tilehurst	d	16 57								17 27						17 57									18 27
Pangbourne	d	17 01								17 31						18 01									18 31
Goring & Streatley	d	17 06								17 36						18 06									18 36
Cholsey	d	17 11								17 41						18 11									18 41
Didcot Parkway	a	17 19				17 12				17 48						18 19			18 12						18 48
	d	17 25								17 55						18 25									18 55
Appleford	d																								19 00
Culham	d									18 01															
Radley	d									18 03															19 03
Oxford	a	17 40		17 18			17 34		17 48	18 14	18 04					18 40	18 18			18 34				18 48	19 14
	d						17 36				18 07	18 16								18 36		18 41			
Islip	d																					18 54			
Bicester Town	a																					19 06			
Tackley	d											18 25													
Heyford	d											18 29													
Kings Sutton	d											18 38													
Banbury	a						17 52				18 23	18 46								18 52					
Leamington Spa 8	a						18 10				18 41									19 10					
Coventry	a						18 22													19 22					
Birmingham International	a						18 37													19 37					
Birmingham New Street 12	a						18 48				19 18									19 48					

Table 116

Saturdays
from 31 March

London and Reading - Bedwyn, Oxford, Bicester, Banbury and Birmingham

Network Diagram - see first Page of Table 116

		XC ◇1 🛒	GW 1	GW ◇1 ☕	GW 1	GW 1	GW ◇1 ☕	GW 1	GW ◇1 ☕	XC ◇1 🛒	GW ◇1	CH	GW 1	GW 1	GW 1	GW ◇1 ☕	GW ◇1 ☕	XC ◇1	GW 1	GW ◇1	GW 1	GW 1	GW ◇1 ☕
London Paddington 15 ⊖	d		17 57	18 15	18 18		18 21	18 27	18 30		18 50				18 57	19 06	19 15			19 21		19 27	19 30
Ealing Broadway ⊖	d		18 05					18 35							19 05							19 35	
Slough 3	d		18 27				18 39	18 57			19 06				19 27					19 38		19 57	
Maidenhead 3	d		18 34					19 04							19 34							20 04	
Twyford 3	d		18 42			←		19 12						←	19 42						←	20 12	
Reading 7	d	18 40	18 53	18 42	18 48	18 53	18 54	19 23	18 57	19 11	19 23			19 23	19 53	19 32	19 42	19 40	19 49	19 52	19 53	20 23	19 57
Reading West	d		↪					↪							↪				19 52			↪	
Theale	d				18 56														19 58				
Aldermaston	d																		20 03				
Midgham	d																		20 06				
Thatcham	d				19 04														20 11				
Newbury Racecourse	d																		20 16				
Newbury	a				19 10											19 48			20 18				
	d				19 10														20 18				
Kintbury	d				19 17														20 25				
Hungerford	d				19 21														20 29				
Bedwyn	a				19 31														20 38				
Tilehurst	d					18 57								19 27							19 57		
Pangbourne	d					19 01								19 31							20 01		
Goring & Streatley	d					19 06								19 36							20 06		
Cholsey	d					19 11								19 41							20 11		
Didcot Parkway	a			18 55		19 19			19 12					19 48			19 55				20 19		20 11
	d					19 25								19 55							20 25		
Appleford	d																						
Culham	d													20 01									
Radley	d													20 03									
Oxford	a	19 04				19 40	19 18			19 34	19 48			20 14				20 04		20 20	20 40		
	d	19 07								19 36		19 48	19 56					20 07					
Islip	d											20 01											
Bicester Town	a											20 13											
Tackley	d												20 05										
Heyford	d												20 09										
Kings Sutton	d												20 18										
Banbury	a	19 23								19 52			20 25					20 28					
Leamington Spa 8	a	19 41								20 10								20 45					
Coventry	a									20 22													
Birmingham International	a									20 37													
Birmingham New Street 12	a	20 18								20 48								21 18					

		XC ◇1	GW ◇1 🛒	CH	GW 1	GW 1	GW ◇1 ☕	GW ◇1 ☕	GW ◇1 ☕	XC ◇1	GW 1	GW ◇1	GW 1	GW 1	GW 1	GW ◇1 ☕	XC ◇1	GW ◇1 🛒	GW 1	GW 1	GW ◇1	CH
London Paddington 15 ⊖	d		19 50			19 57	20 00	20 06	20 15			20 20			20 27	20 30		20 50		20 57	21 17	
Ealing Broadway ⊖	d					20 05									20 35					21 05		
Slough 3	d		20 06			20 27						20 35			20 57			21 06		21 27	21 35	
Maidenhead 3	d					20 34									21 04					21 34		
Twyford 3	d				←	20 42								←	21 12				←	21 42		
Reading 7	d	20 11	20 22		20 23	20 53	20 27	20 33	20 42	20 40	20 49	20 51		20 53	21 23	20 57	21 11	21 22	21 23	21 53	21 52	
Reading West	d					↪					20 52				↪					↪		
Theale	d										20 58											
Aldermaston	d										21 03											
Midgham	d										21 06											
Thatcham	d										21 11											
Newbury Racecourse	d										21 16											
Newbury	a							20 47			21 18											
	d										21 32											
Kintbury	d										21 39											
Hungerford	d										21 43											
Bedwyn	a										21 52											
Tilehurst	d				20 27									20 57					21 27			
Pangbourne	d				20 31									21 01					21 31			
Goring & Streatley	d				20 37									21 06					21 36			
Cholsey	d				20 41									21 11					21 41			
Didcot Parkway	a				20 49		20 41		20 55					21 19		21 12		21 39	21 48		22 07	
	d				20 55									21 25				21 40	21 55		22 08	
Appleford	d				21 00																	
Culham	d																		22 01			
Radley	d				21 03														22 03			
Oxford	a	20 34	20 47		21 14					21 04		21 19		21 40			21 34	21 53	22 14		22 20	
	d	20 36		21 00						21 07			21 20				21 36					22 25
Islip	d			21 13																		22 38
Bicester Town	a			21 25																		22 50
Tackley	d												21 29									
Heyford	d												21 33									
Kings Sutton	d												21 42									
Banbury	a	20 52								21 23			21 49				21 52					
Leamington Spa 8	a	21 10								21 44							22 10					
Coventry	a	21 22								21 55							22 22					
Birmingham International	a	21 37								22 10							22 36					
Birmingham New Street 12	a	21 48								22 21							22 48					

Table 116

Saturdays
from 31 March

London and Reading - Bedwyn, Oxford, Bicester, Banbury and Birmingham

Network Diagram - see first Page of Table 116

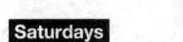

		GW	GW	GW	GW	GW	GW	GW	GW	GW	GW	GW	GW	GW	GW	GW	GW
		■1	◇■1	■1	◇■1	■1	◇■1	◇■1	■1	◇■1	■1		■1	◇■1	■1	◇■1	◇■1
												🚌					
			🍴				🍴			🍴						🍴	
London Paddington ■15 ⊖	d		21 30		21 50	21 57	22 00	22 15		22 35			22 45	23 00		23 30	23 33
Ealing Broadway ⊖	d					22 05							22 55				
Slough ■3	d				22 06	22 27		22 32					23 21	23 17			23 50
Maidenhead ■3	d					22 34							23 32				
Twyford ■3	d	←				22 42			←				23 39		←		
Reading ■7	d	21 53	21 57	22 03	22 23	22 55	22 27	22 51	22 55	23 02	23 12		23 49	23 34	23 49	23 59	00 08
Reading West	d			22 06		↦					23 14		↦				
Theale	d			22 12							23 20						
Aldermaston	d			22 17							23 25						
Midgham	d			22 20							23 29						
Thatcham	d			22 25							23 34						
Newbury Racecourse	d			22 30							23 38						
Newbury	a			22 32							23 41						
	d			22 32							23 41						
Kintbury	d			22 39							23 48						
Hungerford	d			22 43							23 52						
Bedwyn	a			22 51							00 01						
Tilehurst	d	21 57							22 59						23 53		
Pangbourne	d	22 01															
Goring & Streatley	d	22 06							23 06						00 03		
Cholsey	d	22 11							23 11						00 08		
Didcot Parkway	a	22 19	22 12		22 37		22 41	23 06	23 18	23 22				23 51	00 14	00 18	00 22
	d	22 25			22 38			23 07	23 20					23 51	00 15		00 24
Appleford	d																
Culham	d																
Radley	d	22 34							23 27						00s22		
Oxford	a	22 43			22 50			23 20	23 38					00 04	00 32		00 38
	d											23 47					
Islip	d																
Bicester Town	a																
Tackley	d											00s06					
Heyford	d											00s20					
Kings Sutton	d																
Banbury	a											00 45					
Leamington Spa ■8	a																
Coventry	a																
Birmingham International	a																
Birmingham New Street ■12	a																

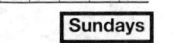

Sundays
until 1 January

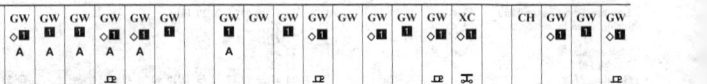

		GW	GW	GW	GW	GW	GW	GW	GW	GW	GW	GW	GW	GW	GW	GW	GW	GW	XC	CH	GW	GW	GW
		■1		■1	◇■1	■1	■1	◇■1	◇■1	■1	■1		■1	◇■1		◇■1	■1	◇■1	◇■1		◇■1	■1	◇■1
		A	A	A	A	A	A	A	A		A												
			🚌					🍴						🍴				🍴	🛒				🍴
London Paddington ■15 ⊖	d			22p45	23p00		23p20	23p30	23p33				07 29	08 00		08 03		08 30			08 42	08 43	08 57
Ealing Broadway ⊖	d			22p55			23p28						07 36									08 50	
Slough ■3	d			23p21	23p17		23p54		23p50				07 58			08 26					09 04	09 14	
Maidenhead ■3	d			23p32			00 05						08 08			08 33						09 27	
Twyford ■3	d			23p39		←	00 13				←		08 16				←					09 35	
Reading ■7	d	23p12		23p49	23p34	23p49	00 20	23p59	00 08	00 15	00 20	08 14	08 48	08 34	08 44	08 45	08 48	09 06	09 11		09 21	09 43	09 33
Reading West	d	23p14		↦			↦			00s18		08 17	↦									↦	
Theale	d	23p20								00s24		08 23			08 51								
Aldermaston	d	23p25								00s29		08 28											
Midgham	d	23p29								00s32		08 31											
Thatcham	d	23p34								00s37		08 36			09 00								
Newbury Racecourse	d	23p38								00s42													
Newbury	a	23p41								00 45		08 43			09 05								09 48
	d	23p41													09 06								
Kintbury	d	23p48													09 12								
Hungerford	d	23p52													09 17								
Bedwyn	a	00 01													09 24								
Tilehurst	d					23p53					00 24						08 52						
Pangbourne	d					23p58											08 57						
Goring & Streatley	d					00 03					00 31						09 02						
Cholsey	d					00 08					00 36						09 07						
Didcot Parkway	a				23p51	00 14		00 18	00 22		00 44			08 49		09 00	09 12	09 22			09 36		
	d				23p51	00 15			00 24		00 45					09 02	09 14				09 37		
Appleford	d										00s49												
Culham	d										00s51												
Radley	d					00s22					00s55						09 21						
Oxford	a				00 04	00 32			00 38		01 05					09 13	09 30		09 34		09 51		
	d		23p47																09 37	09 36			
Islip	d																			09 49			
Bicester Town	a																			10 01			
Tackley	d		00s06																				
Heyford	d		00s20																				
Kings Sutton	d																						
Banbury	a		00 45																09 53				
Leamington Spa ■8	a																		10 11				
Coventry	a																		10 22				
Birmingham International	a																		10 38				
Birmingham New Street ■12	a																		10 50				

A not 11 December

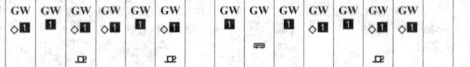

Table 116

Sundays
until 1 January

London and Reading - Bedwyn, Oxford, Bicester, Banbury and Birmingham

Network Diagram - see first Page of Table 116

		GW	GW	GW	GW	GW		XC	GW	CH	GW	GW	GW	GW	GW	XC		GW	GW	GW	GW	GW	GW	CH	XC
		◇1 ☕	1	1	1	◇1 ☕		◇1 🛒	◇1 ☕		1	◇1 ☕	1	1	◇1 ☕	◇1 🛒		◇1 ☕	1	◇1 ☕	1	1	◇1 ☕		◇1 🛒
London Paddington 15 ⊖	d	09 03				09 30			09 35		09 43	10 03			10 37			10 42	10 43	11 03			11 37		
Ealing Broadway ⊖	d										09 50								10 50						
Slough 3	d								09 58		10 16							11 05	11 16						
Maidenhead 3	d										10 27								11 27						
Twyford 3	d		←								10 35		←						11 35		←				
Reading 7	d	09 38	09 43	09 44	10 00	10 06		10 11	10 11		10 43	10 38	10 43	10 44	11 12	11 11		11 21	11 43	11 38	11 43	11 44	12 12		12 11
Reading West	d			09 47							↦			10 47					↦						
Theale	d			09 53										10 53								11 51			
Aldermaston	d			09 58										10 58											
Midgham	d			10 01										11 01											
Thatcham	d			10 06										11 06								12 00			
Newbury Racecourse	d													11 11											
Newbury	a			10 12										11 15								12 05			
	d			10 12																		12 06			
Kintbury	d			10 18																		12 12			
Hungerford	d			10 23																		12 17			
Bedwyn	a			10 31																		12 25			
Tilehurst	d		09 47										10 47								11 47				
Pangbourne	d		09 52										10 52								11 52				
Goring & Streatley	d		09 57										10 57								11 57				
Cholsey	d		10 02										11 02								12 02				
Didcot Parkway	a	09 51	10 09			10 19			10 28			10 51	11 09		11 25			11 36		11 51	12 09		12 25		
	d		10 09						10 28				11 10					11 37			12 10				
Appleford	d		10 14																						
Culham	d																								
Radley	d		10 19										11 17								12 17				
Oxford	a		10 28		10 30			10 35	10 43				11 27			11 35		11 50			12 27				12 35
	d							10 37		10 56						11 37								12 33	12 37
Islip	d									11 09														12 46	
Bicester Town	a									11 21														12 58	
Tackley	d																								
Heyford	d																								
Kings Sutton	d																								
Banbury	a							10 53								11 53									12 53
Leamington Spa 8	a							11 11								12 11									13 11
Coventry	a							11 22								12 22									13 22
Birmingham International	a							11 38								12 38									13 37
Birmingham New Street 12	a							11 50								12 50									13 48

		GW		GW	GW	GW	GW	GW	XC	GW	XC	GW		CH	GW	GW	XC	GW	GW	GW	XC	GW		GW	GW
		◇1		1	◇1 ☕	◇1 ☕	1	1	◇1 🛒	◇1 ☕	◇1 🛒	◇1 ☕			1	◇1 ☕	◇1 🛒	1	1	◇1 ☕	◇1 🛒	◇1 ☕		1	◇1 ☕
London Paddington 15 ⊖	d	11 42		11 43	11 57	12 03				12 37		12 42			12 43	13 03				13 37		13 42		13 43	13 57
Ealing Broadway ⊖	d			11 50											12 50									13 50	
Slough 3	d	12 04		12 16								13 07			13 16							14 06		14 16	
Maidenhead 3	d			12 27											13 27									14 27	
Twyford 3	d			12 35			←								13 35			←						14 36	
Reading 7	d	12 21		12 43	12 33	12 38	12 43	12 44	12 54	13 12	13 11	13 23			13 43	13 38	13 40	13 43	13 44	14 12	14 11	14 21		14 43	14 33
Reading West	d			↦				12 47							↦									↦	
Theale	d							12 53											13 51						
Aldermaston	d							12 58																	
Midgham	d							13 01																	
Thatcham	d							13 06											14 00						
Newbury Racecourse	d							13 11																	
Newbury	a				12 48			13 15											14 05						14 48
	d																		14 06						
Kintbury	d																		14 12						
Hungerford	d																		14 17						
Bedwyn	a																		14 25						
Tilehurst	d						12 47											13 47							
Pangbourne	d						12 52											13 52							
Goring & Streatley	d						12 57											13 57							
Cholsey	d						13 02											14 02							
Didcot Parkway	a	12 36				12 51	13 09			13 25		13 37				13 51		14 09		14 25		14 36			
	d	12 37					13 10					13 38						14 10				14 37			
Appleford	d						13 15																		
Culham	d																								
Radley	d						13 19											14 17							
Oxford	a	12 49					13 28		13 15		13 35	13 50					14 03	14 27			14 35	14 50			
	d								13 17		13 37			13 56			14 05				14 37				
Islip	d													14 09											
Bicester Town	a													14 21											
Tackley	d																								
Heyford	d																								
Kings Sutton	d																								
Banbury	a								13 33		13 53						14 22				14 53				
Leamington Spa 8	a								13 50		14 11						14 40				15 11				
Coventry	a										14 22										15 22				
Birmingham International	a										14 35										15 35				
Birmingham New Street 12	a								14 19		14 48						15 09				15 48				

Table 116

Sundays

until 1 January

London and Reading - Bedwyn, Oxford, Bicester, Banbury and Birmingham

Network Diagram - see first Page of Table 116

		GW	XC	GW	GW	GW	CH	XC		GW	GW	GW	XC	GW	GW	XC	GW	GW		GW	GW	CH	GW	GW	GW
		◇1	◇1	1	1	◇1		◇1		◇1	1	◇1	◇1	1	1	◇1	◇1	◇1		◇1	◇1		1	◇1	◇1
		⊡	⊤			⊡		⊤				⊡	⊤			⊤		⊡						⊡	⊡
London Paddington [15] ⊖	d	14 03				14 37				14 42	14 43	15 03					15 27	15 37			15 42		15 43	15 57	16 03
Ealing Broadway ⊖	d										14 50												15 50		
Slough [3]	d									15 05	15 16						15 50				16 05		16 16		
Maidenhead [3]	d										15 27						16 01						16 27		
Twyford [3]	d			←							15 35			←			16 10			←			16 35		
Reading [7]	d	14 38	14 40	14 43	14 44	15 12		15 11		15 21	15 43	15 38	15 40	15 43	15 44	16 11	16 16	16 12		16 16	16 21		16 43	16 33	16 38
Reading West	d				14 47						→						→						→		
Theale	d				14 53										15 51										
Aldermaston	d				14 58																				
Midgham	d				15 01																				
Thatcham	d				15 06										16 00										
Newbury Racecourse	d				15 11																				
Newbury	a				15 15										16 05									16 47	
	d														16 06										
Kintbury	d														16 12										
Hungerford	d														16 17										
Bedwyn	a														16 25										
Tilehurst	d			14 47										15 47											
Pangbourne	d			14 52										15 52											
Goring & Streatley	d			14 57										15 57											
Cholsey	d			15 02										16 02											
Didcot Parkway	a	14 51		15 09		15 25				15 35		15 51		16 09				16 25			16 36				16 51
	d			15 10						15 36				16 10							16 37				
Appleford	d			15 14																					
Culham	d																								
Radley	d			15 19										16 17											
Oxford	a		15 04	15 27				15 35		15 50			16 04	16 27		16 35				16 41	16 50				
	d		15 06				15 33	15 37					16 06			16 37						16 56			
Islip	d						15 46															17 09			
Bicester Town	a						15 58															17 21			
Tackley	d																								
Heyford	d																								
Kings Sutton	d																								
Banbury	a		15 23					15 53					16 23			16 53									
Leamington Spa [8]	a		15 41					16 11					16 41			17 11									
Coventry	a							16 22								17 22									
Birmingham International	a							16 35								17 35									
Birmingham New Street [12]	a		16 12					16 48					17 12			17 48									

		XC	GW	GW		GW	XC	GW	GW	GW	XC	GW	GW	GW		XC	CH	GW	GW	GW	GW	XC	GW	GW	
		◇1	1	1		◇1	◇1	◇1	1	◇1	◇1	1	1	◇1		◇1		◇1	1	◇1	◇1	◇1	1	1	
		⊤				⊡	⊤			⊡	⊤			⊡		⊤		⊡		⊡	⊡	⊤			
London Paddington [15] ⊖	d					16 37		16 42	16 43	17 03				17 37				17 42	17 43	17 57	18 03				
Ealing Broadway ⊖	d								16 50										17 50						
Slough [3]	d							17 04	17 16									18 04	18 16						
Maidenhead [3]	d							17 11	17 27									18 13	18 27						
Twyford [3]	d		←						17 35			←							18 35				←		
Reading [7]	d	16 41	16 43	16 44		17 12	17 11	17 24	17 43	17 38	17 40	17 43	17 44	18 12		18 11		18 25	18 43	18 33	18 38	18 41	18 43	18 44	
Reading West	d			16 47					→										→					18 47	
Theale	d			16 53									17 51											18 53	
Aldermaston	d			16 58																				18 58	
Midgham	d			17 01																				19 01	
Thatcham	d			17 06									18 00											19 06	
Newbury Racecourse	d			17 11																				19 11	
Newbury	a			17 15									18 05							18 49				19 15	
	d												18 06												
Kintbury	d												18 12												
Hungerford	d												18 17												
Bedwyn	a												18 25												
Tilehurst	d		16 47									17 47											18 47		
Pangbourne	d		16 52									17 52											18 52		
Goring & Streatley	d		16 57									17 57											18 57		
Cholsey	d		17 02									18 02											19 02		
Didcot Parkway	a		17 09			17 25		17 39		17 51		18 09		18 26				18 39			18 51		19 09		
	d		17 10					17 39				18 10						18 39					19 10		
Appleford	d											18 14													
Culham	d																								
Radley	d		17 17									18 19											19 17		
Oxford	a	17 04	17 27				17 35	17 50			18 04	18 27				18 35		18 51				19 03	19 27		
	d	17 06					17 37				18 06					18 37	18 37					19 06			
Islip	d																18 50								
Bicester Town	a																19 02								
Tackley	d																								
Heyford	d																								
Kings Sutton	d																								
Banbury	a	17 23					17 53				18 23					18 53						19 23			
Leamington Spa [8]	a	17 41					18 11				18 41					19 11						19 41			
Coventry	a						18 22									19 22						19 53			
Birmingham International	a						18 35									19 35						20 03			
Birmingham New Street [12]	a	18 09					18 48				19 11					19 48						20 15			

Table 116

Sundays
until 1 January

London and Reading - Bedwyn, Oxford, Bicester, Banbury and Birmingham

Network Diagram - see first Page of Table 116

		GW	XC	GW	CH	GW	GW	XC	GW	GW		GW	XC	GW	GW	GW	GW	XC	GW	GW		GW	CH	XC	GW
		◇1	◇1	◇1		1	◇1	◇1	1	1		◇1	◇1	◇1	1	◇1	◇1	◇1	1	1		◇1		◇1	◇1
		☕	🛒				☕	🛒				☕		☕		☕	☕					☕			
London Paddington 15 ⊖	d	18 37		18 42		18 43	19 03					19 37		19 42	19 43	19 57	20 03					20 37			20 42
Ealing Broadway ⊖	d					18 50									19 50										
Slough 3	d			19 07		19 16								20 06	20 16										21 04
Maidenhead 3	d			19 14		19 27									20 27										
Twyford 3	d					19 35			↩						20 35				↩						
Reading 7	d	19 12	19 11	19 27		19 43	19 38	19 40	19 43	19 44		20 13	20 10	20 21	20 43	20 33	20 38	20 41	20 43	20 44		21 12		21 11	21 21
Reading West	d					↪									↪					20 47					
Theale	d									19 51										20 53					
Aldermaston	d																			20 58					
Midgham	d																			21 01					
Thatcham	d									20 00										21 06					
Newbury Racecourse	d																			21 11					
Newbury	a									20 05						20 49				21 16					
	d									20 06															
Kintbury	d									20 12															
Hungerford	d									20 17															
Bedwyn	a									20 25															
Tilehurst	d								19 47										20 47						
Pangbourne	d								19 52										20 52						
Goring & Streatley	d								19 57										20 57						
Cholsey	d								20 02										21 02						
Didcot Parkway	a	19 25		19 43			19 51		20 09			20 26		20 36			20 50		21 11			21 25			21 36
	d			19 43					20 10					20 37					21 13						21 37
Appleford	d																								
Culham	d																								
Radley	d								20 17										21 21						
Oxford	a		19 35	19 55				20 03	20 27				20 35	20 50				21 04	21 30					21 35	21 49
	d		19 37		19 56			20 06					20 37					21 06					21 33	21 37	
Islip	d				20 09																		21 46		
Bicester Town	a				20 21																		21 58		
Tackley	d																								
Heyford	d																								
Kings Sutton	d																								
Banbury	a		19 53					20 24					20 53					21 23						21 53	
Leamington Spa 8	a		20 11					20 41					21 11					21 41						22 11	
Coventry	a		20 22					20 53					21 22					21 52						22 22	
Birmingham International	a		20 35					21 03					21 35					22 02						22 32	
Birmingham New Street 12	a		20 48					21 15					21 48					22 14						22 42	

		GW	GW	XC	GW	GW		GW	GW	GW	GW	GW	GW	GW	GW	GW		GW	GW	GW	GW	GW	GW		
		1	◇1	◇1	1	1		◇1	◇1	1	1	◇1	1	1		◇1		◇1		1	◇1	1	◇1		
														A											
															🚌				🚌						
			☕					☕				☕				☕					☕		☕		
London Paddington 15 ⊖	d	20 43	21 03					21 37	21 42		21 43	22 03		22 15		22 37		22 42		22 43	23 03		23 37		
Ealing Broadway ⊖	d	20 50									21 50			22 24						22 50					
Slough 3	d	21 16							22 06		22 16			22 46				23 02		23 16			00 02		
Maidenhead 3	d	21 27									22 31			22 56						23 25					
Twyford 3	d	21 35			↩						22 39		↩	23 04						23 32		↩			
Reading 7	d	21 47	21 38	21 40	21 47	21 44		22 14	22 22	22 44	22 54	22 50	22 54	23 12		23 15		23 21		23 53	23 46	23 53	00 15		
Reading West	d	↪								22 47	↪			23 15						↪					
Theale	d					21 51				22 53				23 21											
Aldermaston	d									22 58															
Midgham	d									23 01															
Thatcham	d					22 00				23 06				23 30											
Newbury Racecourse	d									23 11															
Newbury	a					22 05				23 15				23 37											
	d					22 06																			
Kintbury	d					22 12																			
Hungerford	d					22 17																			
Bedwyn	a					22 25																			
Tilehurst	d				21 52								22 58									23 57			
Pangbourne	d				21 56								23 03									00 01			
Goring & Streatley	d				22 01								23 07									00 07			
Cholsey	d				22 06								23 12									00 12			
Didcot Parkway	a		21 51		22 13			22 29	22 38			23 05	23 21			23s30		23 36			00s02	00 20	00s31		
	d				22 14				22 38						23 27				23 45						
Appleford	d																								
Culham	d																								
Radley	d				22 21										23 42										
Oxford	a			22 04	22 29				22 50						23 57				00 10						
	d			22 06																					
Islip	d																								
Bicester Town	a																								
Tackley	d																								
Heyford	d																								
Kings Sutton	d																								
Banbury	a			22 22																					
Leamington Spa 8	a			22 40																					
Coventry	a			22 52																					
Birmingham International	a			23 02																					
Birmingham New Street 12	a			23 13																					

A 1 to Reading

Table 116

Sundays

8 January to 12 February

London and Reading - Bedwyn, Oxford, Bicester, Banbury and Birmingham

Network Diagram - see first Page of Table 116

		GW 1	GW 🚌	GW 1	GW ◇1	GW 1	GW ◇1 ☕	GW ◇1	GW 1	GW		GW 1	GW ◇1 ☕	GW ◇1	GW 1	GW	GW ◇1 ☕	XC ◇1 🛒	CH	XC 🚌		GW ◇1	GW 1	GW ◇1 ☕	GW ◇1 ☕
London Paddington 15 Θ	d			22p45	23p00		23p30	23p33				07 29	08 00	08 03			08 30					08 42	08 43	08 57	09 03
Ealing Broadway Θ	d			22p55								07 36											08 50		
Slough 3	d			23p21	23p17			23p50				07 58		08 26								09 04	09 16		
Maidenhead 3	d			23p32								08 08		08 33									09 27		
Twyford 3	d			23p39		←						08 17			←								09 35		
Reading 7	d	23p12		23p49	23p34	23p49	23p59	00 08	00 15	08 14		08 48	08 38	08 44	08 48	08 44	09 06	09 11				09 21	09 42	09 33	09 38
Reading West	d	23p14		→					00s18	08 17		→											→		
Theale	d	23p20							00s24	08 23						08 51									
Aldermaston	d	23p25							00s29	08 28															
Midgham	d	23p29							00s32	08 31															
Thatcham	d	23p34							00s37	08 36						09 00									
Newbury Racecourse	d	23p38							00s42																
Newbury	a	23p41							00 45	08 43						09 05								09 48	
	d	23p41														09 06									
Kintbury	d	23p48														09 12									
Hungerford	d	23p52														09 17									
Bedwyn	a	00 01														09 24									
Tilehurst	d					23p53									08 52										
Pangbourne	d																								
Goring & Streatley	d					00 03									09 01										
Cholsey	d					00 08									09 06										
Didcot Parkway	a				23p51	00 14	00 18	00 22					08 51	08 59	09 11		09 19					09 36			09 51
	d				23p51	00 15		00 24						09 02	09 14							09 37			
Appleford	d																								
Culham	d																								
Radley	d					00s22									09 21										
Oxford	a				00 04	00 32		00 38						09 13	09 30			09 34				09 51			
	d		23p47																09 36	09 40					
Islip	d																		09 49						
Bicester Town	a																		10 01						
Tackley	d		00s06																						
Heyford	d		00s20																						
Kings Sutton	d																								
Banbury	a		00 45																	10 25					
Leamington Spa 8	a																			11 00					
Coventry	a																								
Birmingham International	a																								
Birmingham New Street 12	a																								

		GW 1	GW 1	GW 1	GW ◇1 ☕	XC ◇1 🛒		XC 🚌	GW ◇1 ☕	CH	GW 1	GW ◇1 ☕	GW 1	GW 1	GW ◇1 ☕	XC ◇1 🛒		XC 🚌	GW ◇1 ☕	GW 1	GW ◇1 ☕	GW 1	GW 1	GW ◇1 ☕	CH
London Paddington 15 Θ	d				09 30				09 35		09 43	10 03			10 37				10 42	10 43	11 03			11 37	
Ealing Broadway Θ	d										09 50									10 50					
Slough 3	d								09 58		10 16								11 05	11 16					
Maidenhead 3	d										10 27									11 27					
Twyford 3	d	←									10 35		←							11 35		←			
Reading 7	d	09 42	09 44	10 00	10 06	10 11			10 11		10 43	10 38	10 43	10 44	11 12	11 11			11 21	11 42	11 38	11 42	11 44	12 12	
Reading West	d		09 47								→			10 47						→					
Theale	d		09 53											10 53									11 51		
Aldermaston	d		09 58											10 58											
Midgham	d		10 01											11 01											
Thatcham	d		10 06											11 06									12 00		
Newbury Racecourse	d													11 11											
Newbury	a		10 12											11 15									12 05		
	d		10 12																				12 06		
Kintbury	d		10 18																				12 12		
Hungerford	d		10 23																				12 17		
Bedwyn	a		10 31																				12 25		
Tilehurst	d	09 46											10 47									11 46			
Pangbourne	d																								
Goring & Streatley	d	09 55											10 57									11 55			
Cholsey	d	10 00											11 02									12 00			
Didcot Parkway	a	10 07			10 19				10 28			10 51	11 09		11 26				11 36		11 51	12 08		12 25	
	d	10 08							10 28				11 10						11 37			12 09			
Appleford	d	10 12																							
Culham	d																								
Radley	d	10 17											11 17									12 16			
Oxford	a	10 27		10 30		10 35			10 43				11 27			11 35			11 50			12 26			
	d							10 40		10 56								11 40							12 33
Islip	d									11 09															12 46
Bicester Town	a									11 21															12 58
Tackley	d																								
Heyford	d																								
Kings Sutton	d																								
Banbury	a							11 25										12 25							
Leamington Spa 8	a							12 00										13 00							
Coventry	a																								
Birmingham International	a																								
Birmingham New Street 12	a																								

Table 116

Sundays

8 January to 12 February

London and Reading - Bedwyn, Oxford, Bicester, Banbury and Birmingham

Network Diagram - see first Page of Table 116

		XC ◇1	XC	GW ◇1	GW 1	GW ◇1	GW ◇1	GW 1	GW 1	GW ◇1	XC ◇1	XC	GW ◇1	CH	GW 1	GW ◇1	GW 1	GW 1	GW ◇1	XC ◇1	GW ◇1	GW 1
London Paddington 15 ⊖	d			11 42	11 43	11 57	12 03			12 37			12 42		12 43	13 03			13 37		13 42	13 43
Ealing Broadway ⊖	d				11 50										12 50							13 50
Slough 3	d			12 03	12 16								13 07		13 16						14 06	14 16
Maidenhead 3	d				12 27										13 27							14 27
Twyford 3	d				12 35			←							13 35		←					14 36
Reading 7	d	12 11		12 20	12 45	12 33	12 38	12 45	12 44	13 12	13 11		13 23		13 45	13 38	13 45	13 44	14 12	14 11	14 21	14 43
Reading West	d				→				12 47						→							→
Theale	d								12 53									13 51				
Aldermaston	d								12 58													
Midgham	d								13 01													
Thatcham	d								13 06									14 00				
Newbury Racecourse	d								13 11													
Newbury	a					12 48			13 15									14 05				
	d																	14 06				
Kintbury	d																	14 12				
Hungerford	d																	14 17				
Bedwyn	a																	14 25				
Tilehurst	d							12 49									13 49					
Pangbourne	d																					
Goring & Streatley	d							12 59									13 58					
Cholsey	d							13 04									14 03					
Didcot Parkway	a			12 35			12 51	13 10		13 25			13 37			13 51	14 10		14 25		14 38	
	d			12 36				13 12					13 38				14 12				14 39	
Appleford	d							13 16														
Culham	d																					
Radley	d							13 20									14 18					
Oxford	a	12 35		12 48				13 29			13 35		13 50				14 28			14 35	14 50	
	d		12 40									13 40		13 56						14 37		
Islip	d													14 09								
Bicester Town	a													14 21								
Tackley	d																					
Heyford	d																					
Kings Sutton	d																					
Banbury	a		13 25									14 25								14 53		
Leamington Spa 8	a		14 00																	15 11		
Coventry	a																			15 22		
Birmingham International	a																			15 35		
Birmingham New Street 12	a																			15 48		

		GW ◇1	GW ◇1	XC ◇1	GW 1	GW 1	GW ◇1	CH	XC ◇1	GW ◇1	GW 1	GW ◇1	XC ◇1	GW 1	GW 1	XC ◇1	GW ◇1	GW ◇1	GW ◇1	GW ◇1	CH	GW 1	GW ◇1
London Paddington 15 ⊖	d	13 57	14 03				14 37			14 42	14 43	15 03					15 27	15 37		15 42		15 43	15 57
Ealing Broadway ⊖	d										14 50											15 50	
Slough 3	d									15 03	15 16						15 50			16 04		16 16	
Maidenhead 3	d										15 27						16 01					16 27	
Twyford 3	d				←						15 35				←		16 09		←			16 35	
Reading 7	d	14 33	14 38	14 40	14 43	14 44	15 12		15 11	15 21	15 46	15 38	15 40	15 44	15 46	16 09	16 17	16 12	16 17	16 21		16 43	16 33
Reading West	d					14 47					→						→					→	
Theale	d					14 53								15 51									
Aldermaston	d					14 58																	
Midgham	d					15 01																	
Thatcham	d					15 06								16 00									
Newbury Racecourse	d					15 11																	
Newbury	a	14 48				15 15								16 05									16 47
	d													16 06									
Kintbury	d													16 12									
Hungerford	d													16 17									
Bedwyn	a													16 25									
Tilehurst	d				14 49										15 49								
Pangbourne	d																						
Goring & Streatley	d				14 59										15 59								
Cholsey	d				15 04										16 04								
Didcot Parkway	a		14 51		15 11		15 25			15 35		15 51			16 11			16 25		16 36			
	d				15 12					15 36					16 12					16 37			
Appleford	d				15 16																		
Culham	d																						
Radley	d				15 21										16 19								
Oxford	a			15 03	15 29				15 35	15 50			16 04		16 27	16 35			16 42	16 50			
	d			15 06				15 33	15 37				16 06			16 37					16 56		
Islip	d							15 46													17 09		
Bicester Town	a							15 58													17 21		
Tackley	d																						
Heyford	d																						
Kings Sutton	d																						
Banbury	a			15 23					15 53				16 23			16 53							
Leamington Spa 8	a			15 41					16 11				16 41			17 11							
Coventry	a								16 22							17 22							
Birmingham International	a								16 35							17 35							
Birmingham New Street 12	a			16 12					16 48				17 12			17 48							

Table 116

Sundays

8 January to 12 February

London and Reading - Bedwyn, Oxford, Bicester, Banbury and Birmingham

Network Diagram - see first Page of Table 116

		GW	XC	GW		GW	XC	GW	GW	GW	GW	XC	GW	GW		XC	GW	CH	GW	GW	GW	GW	XC	GW	
		◇1 ☕	◇1 🛒	1		1	◇1 🛒	◇1 ☕	◇1	1	◇1 ☕	◇1 🛒	1	1		◇1 🛒	◇1 ☕		◇1 ☕	1	◇1 ☕	◇1 ☕	◇1 🛒	1	
London Paddington 15 ⊖	d	16 03						16 37	16 42	16 43	17 03						17 37		17 42	17 43	17 57	18 03			
Ealing Broadway ⊖	d									16 50										17 51					
Slough 3	d								17 03	17 16									18 04	18 16					
Maidenhead 3	d								17 10	17 27									18 13	18 27					
Twyford 3	d			←						17 37			←							18 36				←	
Reading 7	d	16 38	16 41	16 43		16 44	17 09	17 12	17 26	17 43	17 38	17 40	17 43	17 44		18 09	18 12		18 24	18 43	18 33	18 37	18 41	18 43	
Reading West	d					16 47				→										→					
Theale	d					16 53								17 51											
Aldermaston	d					16 58																			
Midgham	d					17 01																			
Thatcham	d					17 06								18 00											
Newbury Racecourse	d					17 11																			
Newbury	a					17 15								18 05							18 49				
	d													18 06											
Kintbury	d													18 12											
Hungerford	d													18 17											
Bedwyn	a													18 25											
Tilehurst	d			16 47									17 49											18 49	
Pangbourne	d																								
Goring & Streatley	d			16 57									17 59											18 59	
Cholsey	d			17 02									18 04											19 04	
Didcot Parkway	a	16 51		17 10				17 25	17 40		17 51		18 11				18 25		18 39			18 50		19 11	
	d			17 13					17 41				18 12						18 39					19 12	
Appleford	d												18 16												
Culham	d																								
Radley	d			17 20									18 21											19 19	
Oxford	a		17 04	17 28			17 35		17 50			18 04	18 29			18 35			18 50				19 03	19 27	
	d		17 06				17 37					18 06				18 37		18 37					19 06		
Islip	d																	18 50							
Bicester Town	a																	19 02							
Tackley	d																								
Heyford	d																								
Kings Sutton	d																								
Banbury	a		17 23				17 53					18 23				18 53							19 23		
Leamington Spa 8	a		17 41				18 11					18 41				19 11							19 41		
Coventry	a						18 22									19 22							19 53		
Birmingham International	a						18 35									19 35							20 03		
Birmingham New Street 12	a		18 09				18 48					19 11				19 48							20 15		

		GW	XC	GW	GW	CH	GW	GW	XC	GW		GW	XC	GW	GW	GW	GW	GW	XC	GW		GW	CH	XC	GW
		1	◇1 🛒	◇1 ☕	◇1		1	◇1 ☕	◇1 🛒	1		1	◇1	◇1 ☕	◇1 ☕	1	◇1 ☕	◇1 ☕	◇1	1		1		◇1	◇1 ☕
London Paddington 15 ⊖	d			18 37	18 42		18 43	19 03						19 37	19 42	19 43	19 57	20 03							20 37
Ealing Broadway ⊖	d						18 50									19 50									
Slough 3	d				19 08		19 16								20 06	20 16									
Maidenhead 3	d				19 15		19 27									20 27									
Twyford 3	d						19 35			←						20 35				←					
Reading 7	d	18 44	19 09	19 13	19 27		19 43	19 38	19 40	19 43		19 44	20 09	20 13	20 21	20 43	20 33	20 37	20 41	20 43		20 44		21 09	21 13
Reading West	d	18 47					→									→						20 47			
Theale	d	18 53										19 51										20 53			
Aldermaston	d	18 58																				20 58			
Midgham	d	19 01																				21 01			
Thatcham	d	19 06										20 00										21 06			
Newbury Racecourse	d	19 11																				21 11			
Newbury	a	19 15										20 05					20 49					21 16			
	d											20 06													
Kintbury	d											20 12													
Hungerford	d											20 17													
Bedwyn	a											20 25													
Tilehurst	d									19 49										20 47					
Pangbourne	d																								
Goring & Streatley	d									19 58										20 59					
Cholsey	d									20 03										21 02					
Didcot Parkway	a			19 25	19 43			19 51		20 11				20 26	20 36			20 50		21 10					21 25
	d				19 43					20 12					20 37					21 14					
Appleford	d																								
Culham	d																								
Radley	d									20 19										21 22					
Oxford	a		19 35		19 55				20 03	20 27			20 35		20 50				21 03	21 30				21 35	
	d		19 37			19 56			20 06				20 37						21 06				21 33	21 37	
Islip	d					20 09																	21 46		
Bicester Town	a					20 21																	21 58		
Tackley	d																								
Heyford	d																								
Kings Sutton	d																								
Banbury	a		19 53						20 24				20 53						21 23					21 53	
Leamington Spa 8	a		20 11						20 41				21 11						21 41					22 11	
Coventry	a		20 22						20 53				21 22						21 52					22 22	
Birmingham International	a		20 35						21 03				21 35						22 02					22 32	
Birmingham New Street 12	a		20 48						21 15				21 48						22 14					22 42	

Table 116

Sundays
8 January to 12 February

London and Reading - Bedwyn, Oxford, Bicester, Banbury and Birmingham

Network Diagram - see first Page of Table 116

		GW ◇1	GW 1	GW ◇1 ☕	XC ◇1	GW 1	GW 1	GW ◇1 ☕	GW ◇1	GW 1	GW 1	GW ◇1 ☕	GW 1	GW 1 A	GW 🚌	GW ◇1 ☕	GW ◇1	GW 🚌	GW 1	GW ◇1 ☕	GW 1	GW ◇1 ☕
London Paddington 15 ⊖	d	20 42	20 43	21 03				21 37	21 42		21 43	22 03		22 15		22 37	22 42		22 43	23 03		23 37
Ealing Broadway ⊖	d		20 50								21 50			22 24					22 50			
Slough 3	d	21 02	21 16						22 06		22 16			22 46			23 02		23 16			00 02
Maidenhead 3	d		21 27								22 31			22 56					23 24			
Twyford 3	d		21 35			←					22 41		←	23 04					23 32		←	
Reading 7	d	21 25	21 45	21 38	21 40	21 45	21 44	22 12	22 22	22 44	22 50	22 45	22 50	23 12		23 15	23 21		23 51	23 47	23 51	00 15
Reading West	d		↪							22 47	↪			23 15					↪			
Theale	d						21 51			22 53				23 21								
Aldermaston	d									22 58												
Midgham	d									23 01												
Thatcham	d						22 00			23 06				23 30								
Newbury Racecourse	d									23 11												
Newbury	a						22 05			23 15				23 37								
	d						22 06															
Kintbury	d						22 12															
Hungerford	d						22 17															
Bedwyn	a						22 25															
Tilehurst	d					21 49							22 53								23 55	
Pangbourne	d																					
Goring & Streatley	d					21 58							23 02								00 04	
Cholsey	d					22 03							23 07								00 09	
Didcot Parkway	a	21 40		21 50		22 10		22 28	22 38			22 59	23 18			23s30	23 36			00s01	00 16	00s31
	d	21 41				22 11			22 38						23 27			23 45				
Appleford	d																					
Culham	d																					
Radley	d					22 18									23 42							
Oxford	a	21 53			22 04	22 26			22 50						23 57			00 10				
	d				22 06																	
Islip	d																					
Bicester Town	a																					
Tackley	d																					
Heyford	d																					
Kings Sutton	d																					
Banbury	a				22 22																	
Leamington Spa 8	a				22 40																	
Coventry	a				22 52																	
Birmingham International	a				23 02																	
Birmingham New Street 12	a				23 13																	

Sundays
19 February to 25 March

		GW 1	GW 🚌	GW 1	GW ◇1	GW 1	GW ◇1 ☕	GW ◇1	GW 1	GW	GW 1	GW ◇1 ☕	GW ◇1 ☕	GW ◇1	GW 1	GW	XC ◇1 🛒	CH	GW ◇1	GW 1	GW ◇1 ☕	GW ◇1 ☕	GW 1
London Paddington 15 ⊖	d			22p45	23p00		23p30	23p33			07 29	07 57	08 00	08 03					08 42	08 43	08 57	09 03	
Ealing Broadway ⊖	d			22p55							07 36									08 50			
Slough 3	d			23p21	23p17			23p50			07 58			08 26					09 04	09 16			
Maidenhead 3	d			23p32							08 08			08 33						09 27			
Twyford 3	d			23p39		←					08 17				←					09 35			←
Reading 7	d	23p12		23p49	23p34	23p49	23p59	00 08	00 15	08 14	08 48	08 32	08 38	08 44	08 48	08 44	09 11		09 21	09 43	09 33	09 38	09 43
Reading West	d	23p14		↪					00s18	08 17	↪									↪			
Theale	d	23p20							00s24	08 23						08 51							
Aldermaston	d	23p25							00s29	08 28													
Midgham	d	23p29							00s32	08 31													
Thatcham	d	23p34							00s37	08 36						09 00							
Newbury Racecourse	d	23p38							00s42														
Newbury	a	23p41							00 45	08 43						09 05					09 49		
	d	23p41														09 06							
Kintbury	d	23p48														09 12							
Hungerford	d	23p52														09 17							
Bedwyn	a	00 01														09 24							
Tilehurst	d					23p53									08 52								09 47
Pangbourne	d																						
Goring & Streatley	d					00 03									09 01								09 56
Cholsey	d					00 08									09 06								10 01
Didcot Parkway	a				23p51	00 14	00 18	00 22				08 46	08 51	08 59	09 11				09 36			09 51	10 07
	d				23p51	00 15		00 24						09 02	09 14				09 37				10 08
Appleford	d																						10 12
Culham	d																						
Radley	d					00s22									09 21								10 17
Oxford	a				00 04	00 32		00 38						09 13	09 30		09 34		09 51				10 27
	d		23p47														09 37	09 36					
Islip	d																	09 49					
Bicester Town	a																	10 01					
Tackley	d		00s06																				
Heyford	d		00s20																				
Kings Sutton	d																						
Banbury	a		00 45														09 53						
Leamington Spa 8	a																						
Coventry	a																						
Birmingham International	a																						
Birmingham New Street 12	a																						

A 1 to Reading

Table 116

Sundays

19 February to 25 March

London and Reading - Bedwyn, Oxford, Bicester, Banbury and Birmingham

Network Diagram - see first Page of Table 116

		GW	GW	GW	XC	GW		CH	GW	GW	GW	GW	GW	XC	GW	GW		GW	GW	GW	GW	CH	XC	GW	GW
		1	1	◇1 ☕	◇1 🛒	◇1 ☕			1	◇1 ☕	1	1	◇1 ☕	◇1 🛒	◇1 ☕	1		◇1 ☕	1	1	◇1 ☕		◇1 🛒	◇1	1
London Paddington 15 ⊖	d			09 30		09 35			09 43	10 03			10 30		10 42	10 43		11 03			11 30			11 42	11 43
Ealing Broadway ⊖	d								09 50							10 50									11 50
Slough 3	d					09 58			10 16						11 05	11 16								12 03	12 16
Maidenhead 3	d								10 27							11 27									12 27
Twyford 3	d								10 35		←					11 35			←						12 35
Reading 7	d	09 44	10 00	10 06	10 11	10 11			10 43	10 39	10 43	10 44	11 06	11 11	11 21	11 42		11 38	11 42	11 44	12 06		12 11	12 20	12 45
Reading West	d	09 47							→			10 47				→									→
Theale	d	09 53										10 53								11 51					
Aldermaston	d	09 58										10 58													
Midgham	d	10 01										11 01													
Thatcham	d	10 06										11 06								12 00					
Newbury Racecourse	d											11 11													
Newbury	a	10 12										11 15								12 05					
	d	10 12																		12 06					
Kintbury	d	10 18																		12 12					
Hungerford	d	10 23																		12 17					
Bedwyn	a	10 31																		12 25					
Tilehurst	d										10 47								11 46						
Pangbourne	d																								
Goring & Streatley	d										10 57								11 55						
Cholsey	d										11 02								12 00						
Didcot Parkway	a			10 18		10 28				10 51	11 09		11 18		11 36			11 52	12 08		12 18			12 35	
	d					10 28					11 10				11 37				12 09					12 36	
Appleford	d																								
Culham	d																								
Radley	d										11 17								12 16						
Oxford	a		10 30		10 35	10 43					11 27			11 35	11 50				12 26				12 35	12 48	
	d				10 37			10 56						11 37								12 33	12 37		
Islip	d							11 09														12 46			
Bicester Town	a							11 21														12 58			
Tackley	d																								
Heyford	d																								
Kings Sutton	d																								
Banbury	a				10 53									11 53									12 53		
Leamington Spa 8	a																								
Coventry	a																								
Birmingham International	a																								
Birmingham New Street 12	a																								

		GW		GW	GW	GW	GW	XC	GW	CH	GW	GW		GW	GW	GW	XC	GW	GW	GW	GW	XC		GW	GW
		◇1 ☕		◇1 ☕	1	1	◇1 ☕	◇1 🛒	◇1 ☕		1	◇1 ☕		1	1	◇1 ☕	◇1 🛒	◇1 ☕	1	◇1 ☕	◇1 ☕	◇1 🛒		1	1
London Paddington 15 ⊖	d	11 57		12 03			12 30		12 42		12 43	13 03				13 30		13 42	13 43	13 57	14 03				
Ealing Broadway ⊖	d										12 50								13 50						
Slough 3	d								13 07		13 16							14 06	14 16						
Maidenhead 3	d										13 27								14 27						
Twyford 3	d				←						13 35			←					14 36					←	
Reading 7	d	12 33		12 38	12 45	12 44	13 06	13 11	13 23		13 45	13 38		13 45	13 44	14 04	14 11	14 21	14 43	14 33	14 38	14 40		14 43	14 44
Reading West	d					12 47					→								→						14 47
Theale	d					12 53									13 51										14 53
Aldermaston	d					12 58																			14 58
Midgham	d					13 01																			15 01
Thatcham	d					13 06									14 00										15 06
Newbury Racecourse	d					13 11																			15 11
Newbury	a	12 48				13 15									14 05					14 48					15 15
	d														14 06										
Kintbury	d														14 12										
Hungerford	d														14 17										
Bedwyn	a														14 25										
Tilehurst	d				12 49									13 49										14 49	
Pangbourne	d																								
Goring & Streatley	d				12 59									13 58										14 59	
Cholsey	d				13 04									14 03										15 04	
Didcot Parkway	a			12 51	13 10		13 18		13 37			13 50		14 10		14 18		14 36			14 51			15 11	
	d				13 12				13 38					14 12				14 37						15 12	
Appleford	d				13 16																			15 16	
Culham	d																								
Radley	d				13 20									14 18										15 21	
Oxford	a				13 29			13 35	13 49					14 28			14 35	14 50				15 03		15 29	
	d							13 37		13 56							14 37					15 06			
Islip	d									14 09															
Bicester Town	a									14 21															
Tackley	d																								
Heyford	d																								
Kings Sutton	d																								
Banbury	a							13 53									14 53					15 23			
Leamington Spa 8	a																15 11					15 41			
Coventry	a																15 22								
Birmingham International	a																15 35								
Birmingham New Street 12	a																15 48					16 12			

Table 116

Sundays

19 February to 25 March

London and Reading - Bedwyn, Oxford, Bicester, Banbury and Birmingham

Network Diagram - see first Page of Table 116

		GW	CH	XC	GW	GW	GW	XC	GW	GW	GW	GW	XC	GW	GW	CH	GW	GW	GW	XC	GW	GW	GW
		◇1 ⊐P		◇1 🛒	◇1	1	◇1 ⊐P	◇1 🛒	1	1	◇1	◇1 ⊐P	◇1 🛒	◇1	◇1		1	◇1 ⊐P	◇1 ⊐P	◇1 🛒	1	1	◇1 ⊐P
London Paddington 15 ⊖	d	14 30			14 42	14 43	15 03				15 27	15 30			15 42		15 43	15 57	16 03				16 30
Ealing Broadway ⊖	d					14 50											15 50						
Slough 3	d				15 03	15 16					15 50				16 04		16 16						
Maidenhead 3	d					15 27					16 01						16 27						
Twyford 3	d					15 35				←	16 09			←			16 35				←		
Reading 7	d	15 05		15 11	15 21	15 46	15 37	15 40	15 44	15 46	16 17	16 06	16 09	16 17	16 21		16 43	16 33	16 38	16 41	16 43	16 44	17 06
Reading West	d					→					→						→					16 47	
Theale	d								15 51													16 53	
Aldermaston	d																					16 58	
Midgham	d																					17 01	
Thatcham	d								16 00													17 06	
Newbury Racecourse	d																					17 11	
Newbury	a								16 05									16 48				17 15	
	d								16 06														
Kintbury	d								16 12														
Hungerford	d								16 17														
Bedwyn	a								16 25														
Tilehurst	d									15 49											16 47		
Pangbourne	d																						
Goring & Streatley	d									15 59											16 57		
Cholsey	d									16 04											17 02		
Didcot Parkway	a	15 17			15 35		15 49			16 11		16 17			16 36				16 51		17 10		17 18
	d				15 36					16 12					16 37						17 13		
Appleford	d																						
Culham	d																						
Radley	d									16 19											17 20		
Oxford	a			15 35	15 50			16 04		16 27			16 35	16 42	16 50					17 04	17 28		
	d		15 33	15 37				16 06					16 37			16 56				17 06			
Islip	d		15 46													17 09							
Bicester Town	a		15 58													17 21							
Tackley	d																						
Heyford	d																						
Kings Sutton	d																						
Banbury	a			15 53				16 23					16 53							17 23			
Leamington Spa 8	a			16 11				16 41					17 11							17 41			
Coventry	a			16 22									17 22										
Birmingham International	a			16 35									17 35										
Birmingham New Street 12	a			16 48				17 12					17 48							18 09			

		XC	GW	GW	GW	XC	GW	GW	GW	XC	CH	GW	GW	GW	GW	XC	GW	GW	GW	XC	CH	GW
		◇1 🛒	◇1	1	◇1 ⊐P	◇1 🛒	1	1	◇1 ⊐P	◇1 🛒		◇1 ⊐P	1	◇1 ⊐P	◇1 ⊐P	◇1 🛒	1	1	◇1 ⊐P	◇1 🛒		◇1
London Paddington 15 ⊖	d		16 42	16 43	17 03				17 30			17 42	17 43	17 55	18 03				18 30			18 42
Ealing Broadway ⊖	d			16 50									17 51									
Slough 3	d		17 03	17 16								18 05	18 16									19 08
Maidenhead 3	d		17 10	17 27								18 13	18 27									19 15
Twyford 3	d			17 37			←						18 36				←					
Reading 7	d	17 09	17 26	17 43	17 38	17 40	17 43	17 44	18 06	18 09		18 25	18 43	18 32	18 37	18 41	18 43	18 44	19 05	19 09		19 27
Reading West	d			→									→					18 47				
Theale	d							17 51										18 53				
Aldermaston	d																	18 58				
Midgham	d																	19 01				
Thatcham	d							18 00										19 06				
Newbury Racecourse	d																	19 11				
Newbury	a							18 05						18 49				19 15				
	d							18 06														
Kintbury	d							18 12														
Hungerford	d							18 17														
Bedwyn	a							18 25														
Tilehurst	d						17 49										18 49					
Pangbourne	d																					
Goring & Streatley	d						17 59										18 59					
Cholsey	d						18 04										19 04					
Didcot Parkway	a		17 40		17 51		18 11		18 19			18 40			18 49		19 11		19 17			19 43
	d		17 41				18 12					18 40					19 12					19 43
Appleford	d						18 16															
Culham	d																					
Radley	d						18 21										19 19					
Oxford	a	17 35	17 51			18 04	18 29			18 35		18 51				19 03	19 27			19 35		19 58
	d	17 37				18 06				18 37	18 37					19 06				19 37	19 56	
Islip	d										18 50										20 09	
Bicester Town	a										19 02										20 21	
Tackley	d																					
Heyford	d																					
Kings Sutton	d																					
Banbury	a	17 53				18 23				18 53						19 23				19 53		
Leamington Spa 8	a	18 11				18 41				19 11						19 41				20 11		
Coventry	a	18 22								19 22						19 53				20 22		
Birmingham International	a	18 35								19 35						20 03				20 35		
Birmingham New Street 12	a	18 48				19 11				19 48						20 15				20 48		

Table 116

Sundays

19 February to 25 March

London and Reading - Bedwyn, Oxford, Bicester, Banbury and Birmingham

Network Diagram - see first Page of Table 116

		GW	GW	XC	GW	GW	XC	GW	GW	GW		GW	GW	XC	GW	GW	CH	XC	GW	GW		GW	GW	XC	GW
		1	◇1	◇1	1	1	◇1	◇1	◇1	1		◇1	◇1	◇1	1	1		◇1	◇1	◇1		1	◇1	◇1	1
			☕	trolley				☕	☕			☕	☕						☕				☕		
London Paddington 15 ⊖	d	18 43	19 03					19 37	19 42	19 43		19 57	20 03						20 37	20 42		20 43	21 03		
Ealing Broadway ⊖	d	18 50								19 50												20 50			
Slough 3	d	19 16							20 06	20 16										21 03		21 16			
Maidenhead 3	d	19 27								20 27												21 27			
Twyford 3	d	19 35			←					20 35					←							21 35			←
Reading 7	d	19 43	19 38	19 40	19 43	19 44	20 09	20 13	20 21	20 43		20 32	20 37	20 41	20 43	20 44		21 09	21 14	21 20		21 45	21 37	21 40	21 45
Reading West	d	↦								↦						20 47						↦			
Theale	d					19 51										20 53									
Aldermaston	d															20 58									
Midgham	d															21 01									
Thatcham	d					20 00										21 06									
Newbury Racecourse	d															21 11									
Newbury	a					20 05						20 49				21 16									
	d					20 06																			
Kintbury	d					20 12																			
Hungerford	d					20 17																			
Bedwyn	a					20 25																			
Tilehurst	d				19 49										20 47										21 49
Pangbourne	d																								
Goring & Streatley	d				19 58										20 59										21 58
Cholsey	d				20 03										21 02										22 03
Didcot Parkway	a		19 51		20 11			20 27	20 36				20 50		21 10				21 27	21 36			21 49		22 10
	d				20 12				20 37						21 14					21 36					22 11
Appleford	d																								
Culham	d																								
Radley	d				20 19										21 22										22 18
Oxford	a			20 03	20 27		20 35		20 50					21 03	21 30			21 35		21 49				22 04	22 26
	d			20 06			20 37							21 06			21 33	21 37						22 06	
Islip	d																21 46								
Bicester Town	a																21 58								
Tackley	d																								
Heyford	d																								
Kings Sutton	d																								
Banbury	a			20 24			20 53							21 23				21 53						22 22	
Leamington Spa 8	a			20 41			21 11							21 41				22 11						22 40	
Coventry	a			20 53			21 22							21 52				22 22						22 52	
Birmingham International	a			21 03			21 35							22 02				22 32						23 02	
Birmingham New Street 12	a			21 15			21 48							22 14				22 42						23 13	

		GW	GW	GW	GW	GW		GW	GW	GW	GW	GW	GW	GW	GW	GW		GW	GW
		1	◇1	◇1	1	1		◇1	1	1		◇1	◇1		1	◇1		1	◇1
										A									
											bus			bus					
			☕					☕				☕				☕			☕
London Paddington 15 ⊖	d		21 37	21 42		21 43		22 03		22 15		22 37	22 42		22 43	23 03			23 37
Ealing Broadway ⊖	d					21 50				22 24					22 50				
Slough 3	d			22 06		22 16				22 46			23 02		23 16				00 01
Maidenhead 3	d					22 31				22 56					23 24				
Twyford 3	d					22 41			←	23 04					23 32			←	
Reading 7	d	21 44	22 15	22 22	22 44	22 50		22 45	22 50	23 12		23 15	23 20		23 51	23 47		23 51	00 15
Reading West	d				22 47	↦				23 15					↦				
Theale	d	21 51			22 53					23 21									
Aldermaston	d				22 58														
Midgham	d				23 01														
Thatcham	d	22 00			23 06					23 30									
Newbury Racecourse	d				23 11														
Newbury	a	22 05			23 15					23 37									
	d	22 06																	
Kintbury	d	22 12																	
Hungerford	d	22 17																	
Bedwyn	a	22 25																	
Tilehurst	d								22 53									23 55	
Pangbourne	d																		
Goring & Streatley	d								23 02									00 04	
Cholsey	d								23 07									00 09	
Didcot Parkway	a		22 28	22 38				22 59	23 18			23s30	23 36			00s01		00 16	00s30
	d			22 38							23 27			23 45					
Appleford	d																		
Culham	d																		
Radley	d										23 42								
Oxford	a			22 50							23 57			00 10					
	d																		
Islip	d																		
Bicester Town	a																		
Tackley	d																		
Heyford	d																		
Kings Sutton	d																		
Banbury	a																		
Leamington Spa 8	a																		
Coventry	a																		
Birmingham International	a																		
Birmingham New Street 12	a																		

A 1 to Reading

Table 116

Sundays
from 1 April

London and Reading - Bedwyn, Oxford, Bicester, Banbury and Birmingham

Network Diagram - see first Page of Table 116

		GW	GW	GW	GW	GW	GW	GW	GW	GW	GW	GW	GW	GW	XC	CH	GW	GW	GW	GW	GW	GW	XC
		1		◇1	◇1	◇1	1		1	◇1		◇1	1	◇1	◇1		◇1	1	◇1	1		1	◇1
			🚌		☕			🚌		☕	🚌			☕	🛒				☕		🚌		🛒
London Paddington 15 ⊖	d			23p00	23p30	23p33			07 29	08 00		08 03		08 30			08 42	08 43	09 03				
Ealing Broadway ⊖	d								07 36									08 50					
Slough 3	d			23p17		23p50			07 58			08 26					09 04	09 16					
Maidenhead 3	d								08 08			08 33						09 27					
Twyford 3	d								08 17				←					09 35		←			
Reading 7	d	23p12		23p34	23p59	00 08	00 15	08 00	08 48	08 35	08 36	08 44	08 48	09 06	09 11		09 21	09 43	09 38	09 43	09 52	09 59	10 10
Reading West	d	23p14					00s18	08 16	↪									↪			10 08		
Theale	d	23p20					00s24	08 31			09 02										10 23		
Aldermaston	d	23p25					00s29	08 37													10 29		
Midgham	d	23p29					00s32	08 45													10 37		
Thatcham	d	23p34					00s37	08 52			09 17										10 44		
Newbury Racecourse	d	23p38					00s42																
Newbury	a	23p41					00 45	09 05			09 30										10 57		
	d	23p41									09 30										10 57		
Kintbury	d	23p48									09 50										11 17		
Hungerford	d	23p52									10 00										11 27		
Bedwyn	a	00 01									10 15										11 42		
Tilehurst	d												08 52							09 47			
Pangbourne	d																						
Goring & Streatley	d												09 01							09 57			
Cholsey	d												09 06							10 02			
Didcot Parkway	a			23p51	00 18	00 22				08 48		08 59	09 11	09 20			09 36		09 51	10 09			
	d			23p51		00 24						09 02	09 14				09 37			10 09			
Appleford	d																			10 14			
Culham	d																						
Radley	d												09 21							10 19			
Oxford	a			00 04		00 38						09 13	09 30		09 34		09 51			10 28		10 30	10 35
	d		23p47												09 37	09 36							10 37
Islip	d															09 49							
Bicester Town	a															10 01							
Tackley	d		00s06																				
Heyford	d		00s20																				
Kings Sutton	d																						
Banbury	a		00 45												09 53								10 53
Leamington Spa 8	a														10 11								11 11
Coventry	a														10 22								11 22
Birmingham International	a														10 38								11 38
Birmingham New Street 12	a														10 50								11 50

		GW	GW	CH	GW	GW	GW	GW	GW	XC	GW	GW	GW	GW	GW	CH	XC	GW	GW	GW	GW	GW	GW
		◇1	◇1		1	◇1	1		◇1	◇1	◇1	1	◇1	1			◇1	◇1	◇1	1	◇1	1	
		☕	☕			☕		🚌	☕	🛒	☕		☕		🚌		🛒	☕			☕		🚌
London Paddington 15 ⊖	d	09 35	09 42		09 43	10 03			10 37		10 42	10 43	11 03					11 37	11 42	11 43	12 03		
Ealing Broadway ⊖	d				09 50							10 50								11 50			
Slough 3	d	09 58			10 16						11 05	11 16							12 03	12 16			
Maidenhead 3	d				10 27							11 27								12 25			
Twyford 3	d				10 35		←					11 35		←						12 33		←	
Reading 7	d	10 11	10 18		10 43	10 39	10 43	10 52	11 12	11 11	11 21	11 43	11 38	11 43	11 52		12 11	12 12	12 20	12 44	12 38	12 44	12 52
Reading West	d				↪			11 08				↪								↪			13 08
Theale	d							11 23							12 18								13 23
Aldermaston	d							11 29															13 29
Midgham	d							11 37															13 37
Thatcham	d							11 44							12 33								13 44
Newbury Racecourse	d							11 54															13 54
Newbury	a							12 04							12 46								14 04
	d														12 46								
Kintbury	d														13 06								
Hungerford	d														13 16								
Bedwyn	a														13 31								
Tilehurst	d						10 47							11 47								12 47	
Pangbourne	d																						
Goring & Streatley	d						10 57							11 57								12 55	
Cholsey	d						11 02							12 02								13 00	
Didcot Parkway	a	10 28	10 31			10 51	11 09		11 25		11 36		11 51	12 09				12 26	12 35		12 51	13 06	
	d	10 28					11 10				11 37			12 10					12 36			13 09	
Appleford	d																					13 14	
Culham	d																						
Radley	d						11 17							12 17								13 18	
Oxford	a	10 43					11 27			11 35	11 50			12 27			12 34		12 48			13 27	
	d			10 56						11 37						12 33	12 36						
Islip	d			11 09												12 46							
Bicester Town	a			11 21												12 58							
Tackley	d																						
Heyford	d																						
Kings Sutton	d																						
Banbury	a									11 53							12 52						
Leamington Spa 8	a									12 11							13 11						
Coventry	a									12 22							13 22						
Birmingham International	a									12 38							13 36						
Birmingham New Street 12	a									12 50							13 47						

Table 116

Sundays
from 1 April

London and Reading - Bedwyn, Oxford, Bicester, Banbury and Birmingham

Network Diagram - see first Page of Table 116

		XC		XC	GW	GW	CH	GW	GW	XC	GW	GW		XC	GW	GW	GW	GW	XC	GW	GW	CH		XC	GW
		◇1		◇1	◇1	◇1		1	◇1	◇1	1			◇1	◇1	◇1	1	◇1	◇1	1				◇1	◇1
												🚌									🚌				
		🛒		🛒	☕	☕			☕	🛒				🛒	☕	☕		☕	🛒					🛒	☕
London Paddington 15 ⊖	d				12 37	12 42		12 43	13 03						13 37	13 42	13 43	14 03							14 37
Ealing Broadway ⊖	d							12 50									13 50								
Slough 3	d					13 07		13 16								14 06	14 16								
Maidenhead 3	d							13 27									14 27								
Twyford 3	d							13 35			←						14 35			←					
Reading 7	d	12 54		13 11	13 13	13 23		13 45	13 38	13 40	13 45	13 52		14 09	14 13	14 21	14 43	14 38	14 40	14 43	14 52			15 09	15 13
Reading West	d							→									→				15 08				
Theale	d											14 18									15 23				
Aldermaston	d																				15 29				
Midgham	d																				15 37				
Thatcham	d											14 33									15 44				
Newbury Racecourse	d																				15 54				
Newbury	a											14 46									16 04				
	d											14 46													
Kintbury	d											15 06													
Hungerford	d											15 16													
Bedwyn	a											15 31													
Tilehurst	d										13 49									14 48					
Pangbourne	d																								
Goring & Streatley	d										13 58									14 57					
Cholsey	d										14 03									15 02					
Didcot Parkway	a				13 25	13 37			13 51		14 10				14 26	14 38		14 52		15 09					15 26
	d					13 38					14 12					14 39				15 10					
Appleford	d																			15 14					
Culham	d																								
Radley	d										14 18									15 19					
Oxford	a	13 15		13 35		13 50				14 03	14 28			14 35		14 50			15 03	15 27				15 35	
	d	13 17		13 37			13 56			14 05				14 37					15 06			15 33		15 37	
Islip	d						14 09															15 46			
Bicester Town	a						14 21															15 58			
Tackley	d																								
Heyford	d																								
Kings Sutton	d																								
Banbury	a	13 33		13 53						14 22				14 53					15 23					15 53	
Leamington Spa 8	a	13 50		14 11						14 40				15 11					15 41					16 11	
Coventry	a			14 22										15 22										16 22	
Birmingham International	a			14 35										15 35										16 35	
Birmingham New Street 12	a	14 19		14 48						15 09				15 48					16 12					16 48	

		GW	GW	GW	XC	GW	GW	XC		GW	GW	GW	GW	CH	GW	GW	XC	GW		GW	GW	XC	GW	GW	GW
		◇1	1	◇1	◇1	1		◇1		◇1	◇1	◇1	◇1		1	◇1	◇1	1			◇1	◇1	◇1	1	◇1
							🚌													🚌					
				☕	🛒			🛒			☕					☕	🛒				☕	🛒			☕
London Paddington 15 ⊖	d	14 42	14 43	15 03						15 27	15 37		15 42		15 43	16 03					16 37		16 42	16 43	16 57
Ealing Broadway ⊖	d		14 50												15 50									16 50	
Slough 3	d	15 03	15 16							15 50			16 04		16 16								17 04	17 16	
Maidenhead 3	d		15 27							16 01					16 27								17 11	17 27	
Twyford 3	d		15 35			←				16 10		←			16 35			←						17 35	
Reading 7	d	15 21	15 46	15 38	15 40	15 46	15 52	16 09		16 16	16 13	16 16	16 21		16 44	16 38	16 41	16 44		16 52	17 13	17 09	17 24	17 45	17 32
Reading West	d		→							→					→					17 08				→	
Theale	d						16 18													17 23					
Aldermaston	d																			17 29					
Midgham	d																			17 37					
Thatcham	d						16 33													17 44					
Newbury Racecourse	d																			17 54					
Newbury	a						16 46													18 04					
	d						16 46																		
Kintbury	d						17 06																		
Hungerford	d						17 16																		
Bedwyn	a						17 31																		
Tilehurst	d					15 48												16 48							
Pangbourne	d																								
Goring & Streatley	d					15 57												16 58							
Cholsey	d					16 02												17 03							
Didcot Parkway	a	15 35		15 51		16 09					16 26		16 36			16 51		17 12			17 26		17 39		17 45
	d	15 36				16 10							16 37					17 13					17 39		
Appleford	d																								
Culham	d																								
Radley	d					16 17												17 20							
Oxford	a	15 50			16 03	16 27		16 35				16 41	16 50				17 04	17 30				17 35	17 50		
	d				16 06			16 37						16 56			17 06					17 37			
Islip	d													17 09											
Bicester Town	a													17 21											
Tackley	d																								
Heyford	d																								
Kings Sutton	d																								
Banbury	a				16 23			16 53									17 23					17 53			
Leamington Spa 8	a				16 41			17 11									17 41					18 11			
Coventry	a							17 22														18 22			
Birmingham International	a							17 35														18 35			
Birmingham New Street 12	a				17 12			17 48									18 09					18 48			

Table 116

Sundays

from 1 April

London and Reading - Bedwyn, Oxford, Bicester, Banbury and Birmingham

Network Diagram - see first Page of Table 116

		GW	XC	GW		GW	XC	GW	CH	GW	GW	GW	XC	GW		GW	XC	GW	CH	GW	GW	GW	XC	GW
		◇1	◇1	1			◇1	◇1		◇1	1	◇1	◇1	1			◇1	◇1		◇1	1	◇1	◇1	1
		☕	🛒			🚌	🛒	☕		☕		☕	🛒			🚌	🛒	☕				☕	🛒	
London Paddington 15 ⊖	d	17 03						17 37		17 42	17 43	18 03						18 37		18 42	18 43	19 03		
Ealing Broadway ⊖	d										17 51										18 50			
Slough 3	d									18 05	18 16									19 07	19 16			
Maidenhead 3	d									18 14	18 27									19 14	19 27			
Twyford 3	d			←							18 35			←							19 35			←
Reading 7	d	17 38	17 40	17 45		17 52	18 09	18 13		18 26	18 43	18 37	18 41	18 43		18 58	19 09	19 12		19 27	19 45	19 38	19 40	19 45
Reading West	d										→					19 14					→			
Theale	d					18 18										19 29								
Aldermaston	d															19 35								
Midgham	d															19 43								
Thatcham	d					18 33										19 50								
Newbury Racecourse	d															20 00								
Newbury	a					18 46										20 10								
	d					18 46																		
Kintbury	d					19 06																		
Hungerford	d					19 16																		
Bedwyn	a					19 31																		
Tilehurst	d			17 50										18 48										19 50
Pangbourne	d																							
Goring & Streatley	d			17 59										18 57										19 59
Cholsey	d			18 04										19 02										20 04
Didcot Parkway	a	17 51		18 11				18 26		18 40		18 50		19 09				19 25		19 43		19 51		20 11
	d			18 12						18 40				19 10						19 43				20 12
Appleford	d			18 16																				
Culham	d																							
Radley	d			18 21										19 17										20 19
Oxford	a		18 03	18 29			18 35			18 50			19 03	19 25			19 35			19 58			20 03	20 27
	d		18 06				18 37		18 37				19 06				19 37		19 56				20 06	
Islip	d								18 50										20 09					
Bicester Town	a								19 02										20 21					
Tackley	d																							
Heyford	d																							
Kings Sutton	d																							
Banbury	a		18 23				18 53						19 23				19 53						20 24	
Leamington Spa 8	a		18 41				19 11						19 41				20 11						20 41	
Coventry	a						19 22						19 53				20 22						20 53	
Birmingham International	a						19 35						20 03				20 35						21 03	
Birmingham New Street 12	a		19 11				19 48						20 15				20 48						21 15	

		GW	GW	XC	GW	GW	GW	XC	GW	GW		CH	XC	GW	GW	GW	GW	GW	XC	GW		GW	GW	GW	GW
			◇1	◇1	◇1	1	◇1	◇1	1				◇1	◇1	◇1		1	◇1	◇1	1		◇1	◇1		1
		🚌	☕		☕		☕			🚌				☕		🚌		☕				☕		🚌	
London Paddington 15 ⊖	d		19 37		19 42	19 43	20 03							20 37	20 42		20 43	21 03				21 37	21 42		21 43
Ealing Broadway ⊖	d					19 50											20 50								21 50
Slough 3	d				20 06	20 16									21 02		21 16						22 06		22 16
Maidenhead 3	d					20 27											21 27								22 25
Twyford 3	d					20 35			←								21 35			←					22 41
Reading 7	d	19 52	20 14	20 10	20 21	20 43	20 37	20 41	20 43	20 44			21 09	21 13	21 25	21 36	21 52	21 37	21 40	21 52		22 12	22 22	22 36	22 50
Reading West	d					→				20 52							→							22 52	→
Theale	d	20 18								21 07						22 02								23 07	
Aldermaston	d									21 13														23 13	
Midgham	d									21 21														23 21	
Thatcham	d	20 33								21 28						22 17								23 28	
Newbury Racecourse	d									21 38														23 38	
Newbury	a	20 46								21 48						22 30								23 48	
	d	20 46														22 30									
Kintbury	d	21 06														22 50									
Hungerford	d	21 16														23 00									
Bedwyn	a	21 31														23 15									
Tilehurst	d								20 47											21 55					
Pangbourne	d																								
Goring & Streatley	d								20 59											22 04					
Cholsey	d								21 02											22 09					
Didcot Parkway	a		20 27		20 36		20 50		21 10					21 26	21 40			21 50		22 16		22 27	22 38		
	d				20 37				21 14						21 41					22 17			22 38		
Appleford	d																								
Culham	d																								
Radley	d								21 22											22 24					
Oxford	a			20 35	20 50			21 03	21 30				21 35		21 53				22 04	22 32			22 50		
	d			20 37				21 05				21 33	21 37						22 06						
Islip	d											21 46													
Bicester Town	a											21 58													
Tackley	d																								
Heyford	d																								
Kings Sutton	d																								
Banbury	a			20 53				21 23					21 53						22 22						
Leamington Spa 8	a			21 11				21 41					22 11						22 40						
Coventry	a			21 22				21 52					22 22						22 52						
Birmingham International	a			21 35				22 02					22 32						23 02						
Birmingham New Street 12	a			21 48				22 14					22 42						23 13						

Table 116

Sundays
from 1 April

London and Reading - Bedwyn, Oxford, Bicester, Banbury and Birmingham

Network Diagram - see first Page of Table 116

		GW	GW	GW	GW	GW		GW	GW	GW	GW	GW	GW
		◇1	1			◇1		◇1		1	◇1	1	◇1
				🚌	🚌				🚌				
		☕				☕					☕		☕
London Paddington 15 ⊖	d	22 03				22 37		22 42		22 43	23 03		23 37
Ealing Broadway ⊖	d									22 50			
Slough 3	d							23 02		23 16			00 02
Maidenhead 3	d									23 24			
Twyford 3	d		←							23 32		←	
Reading 7	d	22 45	22 50	23 13		23 15		23 21		23 51	23 47	23 51	00 15
Reading West	d			23 29						→			
Theale	d			23 44									
Aldermaston	d			23 50									
Midgham	d			23 58									
Thatcham	d			00 05									
Newbury Racecourse	d			00 15									
Newbury	a			00 25									
	d												
Kintbury	d												
Hungerford	d												
Bedwyn	a												
Tilehurst	d		22 53									23 55	
Pangbourne	d												
Goring & Streatley	d		23 02									00 04	
Cholsey	d		23 07									00 09	
Didcot Parkway	a	22 59	23 18			23s30		23 37			00s01	00 16	00s31
	d				23 27				23 45				
Appleford	d												
Culham	d												
Radley	d				23 42								
Oxford	a				23 57				00 10				
	d												
Islip	d												
Bicester Town	a												
Tackley	d												
Heyford	d												
Kings Sutton	d												
Banbury	a												
Leamington Spa 8	a												
Coventry	a												
Birmingham International	a												
Birmingham New Street 12	a												

Table 116

Birmingham, Banbury, Bicester, Oxford and Bedwyn - Reading and London

Network Diagram - see first Page of Table 116

Miles	Miles			GW MO 1 A	GW MO ◇1 B	GW MO ◇1 C	GW MO ◇1 D	GW MO ◇1 E ☕	GW MO ◇1 F ☕	GW MX ◇1	GW MX ◇1 ☕	GW MO C 🚌		GW MO 1 C	GW MO 1 G	GW MO 1 G	GW MO 🚌	GW MX ◇1	GW MO ◇1	GW MO C 🚌	GW MX 1	CH MX		GW MO 🚌	GW MX 1
0	—	**Birmingham New Street 12**	d																						
8½	—	Birmingham International	d																						
19¼	—	Coventry	d																						
28¾	—	Leamington Spa 8	d																				23p38			
48¾	—	**Banbury**	d																			23p45	23p57			
52¼	—	Kings Sutton	d																			23p50				
59¾	—	Heyford	d																			23p58				
62½	—	Tackley	d																			00 03				
—	0	**Bicester Town**	d																						
—	6	Islip	d																						
71½	11¾	**Oxford**	a																			00 13	00 22			
—	—		d	22p21	22p46	22p46	22p50			23p09							00 05	00 07			00 27			03 38	04 00
76½	—	Radley	d	22p27																	00 33				
78¾	—	Culham	d																		00 37				
79¾	—	Appleford	d																		00 39				
81½	—	**Didcot Parkway**	a	22p36	22p58	22p58	23p01			23p23							00 30	00 20			00 46			04 03	04 12
—	—		d	22p44	22p59	22p59	23p03	23p11	23p13	23p23	23p35			23p50	23p50			00 21	00 35		00 46				04 12
86¾	—	Cholsey	d	22p50										23p56	23p56						00 52				04 18
90¼	—	Goring & Streatley	d	22p55										00 01	00 01						00 57				04 23
93½	—	Pangbourne	d																		01 01				04 28
96¼	—	Tilehurst	d	23p04										00 08	00 09						01 06				04 32
—	0	**Bedwyn**	d									22p35													
—	5	Hungerford	d									22p50													
—	8	Kintbury	d									23p00													
—	13½	**Newbury**	a									23p19													
—	—		d									23p19				23p45				23p50					
—	14	Newbury Racecourse	d													23p47				23p55					
—	17	Thatcham	d									23p30				23p52				00 05					
—	19¾	Midgham	d													23p57				00 15					
—	21¾	Aldermaston	d													00 01				00 22					
—	25¾	Theale	d									23p48				00 06				00 34					
—	29½	Reading West	d													00s13				00 49					
99	30½	**Reading 7**	a	23p09	23p15	23p15	23p17	23p28	23p28	23p40	23p53	00 14		00 14	00 15	00 17		00 38	00 51	01 05	01 12				04 38
—	—		d	23p10	23p22	23p22	23p24	23p30	23p30	23p45	23p55			00 15	00 15			00 39	00 53		01 12				04 39
104	—	Twyford 3	a	23p16										00 21	00 21				00 59		01 18				04 45
110¾	—	Maidenhead 3	a	23p24						23p58				00 29	00 29				01 06		01 26				04 53
116½	—	Slough 3	a	23p31	23p40	23p42	23p41			00 05				00 36	00 36			00 55	01 14		01 34				05 00
129¼	—	Ealing Broadway ⊖	a	23p55										00 59	00 59				01 30		01 50				05 25
135	—	**London Paddington 15** ⊖	a	00 04	00 02	00 04	00 04	00 13	00 12	00 29	00 33			01 09	01 11			01 17	01 39		02 02				05 41

		GW MO 1	GW 1	GW ◇1 ☕	GW 1	GW 1	GW 1	GW 1		GW ◇1	GW 1	GW 1	GW ◇1 ☕	GW 1	GW 1	GW 1	GW ◇1 ☕	GW ◇1 ☕		GW 1	GW 1	GW 1	GW ◇1 ☕	GW ◇1 ☕	GW 1
Birmingham New Street 12	d																								
Birmingham International	d																								
Coventry	d																								
Leamington Spa 8	d																								
Banbury	d																								06 07
Kings Sutton	d																								06 11
Heyford	d																								06 21
Tackley	d																								06 25
Bicester Town	d																								
Islip	d																								
Oxford	a																								06 35
	d		05 03		05 24		05 43			05 59					06 07		06 27								06 36
Radley	d		05 09				05 49								06 13										06 42
Culham	d														06 17										06 46
Appleford	d														06 19										06 48
Didcot Parkway	a		05 17		05 36		05 58			06 12					06 25		06 39								06 56
	d	04 12	05 18	05 41	05 46		06 00			06 13		06 20	06 30		06 31	06 37	06 39	06 47					06 59		07 01
Cholsey	d	04 18	05 23		05 52							06 25			06 37	06 43									07 07
Goring & Streatley	d	04 23	05 28		05 57							06 30			06 42	06 48									07 12
Pangbourne	d	04 28	05 33		06 02							06 35			06 47	06 53									07 17
Tilehurst	d	04 32	05 37		06 06							06 40			06 51	06 58									07 21
Bedwyn	d										05 55									06 13					
Hungerford	d										06 01									06 18				06 40	
Kintbury	d										06 05									06 23					
Newbury	a										06 12									06 30				06 49	
	d					05 40		05 58			06 12									06 30				06 50	
Newbury Racecourse	d					05 42														06 32					
Thatcham	d					05 47		06 02			06 17									06 37				06 57	
Midgham	d					05 51														06 42					
Aldermaston	d					05 55														06 45					
Theale	d					06 00		06 10			06 25									06 50				07 07	
Reading West	d					06 07		06 17			06 32			←						06 57	←	←			
Reading 7	a	04 38	05 43	05 56	06 12	06 12	06 16	06 21		06 30	06 36	06 46	06 43	06 46	06 58	07 05	06 54	07 00		07 02	07 05	06 58	07 14	07 19	07 28
	d	04 39	05 44	05 57	06 15		06 16	06 22		06 31	06 36	06 46	06 44	06 46	07 10	07 07	06 56	07 01			07 07	07 10	07 16	07 21	07 30
Twyford 3	a	04 45	05 50		06 21		06 23				06 43	→		06 53	→	→						07 16			→
Maidenhead 3	a	04 53	05 58		06 28		06 31			06 42				07 02			07 07				07 18	07 24			
Slough 3	a	05 00	06 10		06 40			06 40		06 50			06 58									07 36			
Ealing Broadway ⊖	a	05 25	06 35		07 05																	08 03			
London Paddington 15 ⊖	a	05 41	06 46	06 24	07 17		06 54	07 01		07 08	07 14		07 16	07 29			07 30	07 32			07 43	08 16	07 44	07 53	

A from 9 January until 13 February
B until 2 January
C from 2 April
D from 9 January until 26 March
E until 13 February, MO from 2 April
F from 20 February until 26 March
G until 26 March

Birmingham, Banbury, Bicester, Oxford and Bedwyn - Reading and London

Network Diagram - see first Page of Table 116

		CH	GW	GW		GW	GW	GW	GW	GW	XC	GW	GW	GW		GW	GW	GW	GW	XC	GW	GW	GW	GW	
			◇1	1		◇1	1	◇1	◇1	1	◇1	◇1	1	1		1	◇1	◇1	◇1	◇1	◇1	◇1	1	◇1	
																			A					A	
			⊡					⊡	⊡		🛒	⊡					🛒	⊡	⊡⊘		⊡	⊡		⊡⊘	
Birmingham New Street 12	d										06 04									06 33					
Birmingham International	d										06 14														
Coventry	d										06 25														
Leamington Spa 8	d										06 38									07 00					
Banbury	d									06 27	06 57									07 22					
Kings Sutton	d									06 33															
Heyford	d									06 41															
Tackley	d									06 46															
Bicester Town	d	06 21																							
Islip	d	06 32																							
Oxford	a	06 47								06 58	07 14									07 41					
	d		06 56							07 00	07 16					07 21	07 31			07 43				07 52	
Radley	d									07 06						07 27									
Culham	d									07 10						07 31									
Appleford	d									07 12						07 33									
Didcot Parkway	a		07 07							07 19						07 40									
	d		07 09			07 14		07 20		07 28		07 29				07 49		07 47			07 55	08 01			
Cholsey	d					07 20				07 34						07 55									
Goring & Streatley	d					07 26				07 39						08 00									
Pangbourne	d					07 33				07 44						08 04									
Tilehurst	d					07 40				07 48						08 09									
Bedwyn	d								06 47					07 07											
Hungerford	d								06 54					07 12					07 34						
Kintbury	d								07 00					07 17											
Newbury	a								07 08					07 24					07 46						
	d			06 56					07 09					07 24					07 49						
Newbury Racecourse	d			06 58										07 26											
Thatcham	d			07 03					07 16					07 32											
Midgham	d			07 07										07 36											
Aldermaston	d			07 11										07 40											
Theale	d			07 16					07 25					07 45											
Reading West	d			07 23			←		07 34				←	07 52									←		
Reading 7	a		07 25	07 29			07 28	07 34	07 37	07 53	07 39	07 43	07 53	07 56		08 17	07 57	08 00	08 06	08 10	08 12	08 16	08 17	08 21	
	d		07 27				07 30	07 36	07 39	07 55		07 45	07 55			08 19	07 58	08 02	08 08		08 14	08 17	08 19	08 23	
Twyford 3	a						07 37			→			08 02			→							08 25		
Maidenhead 3	a					07 59	07 45						08 10										08 33		
Slough 3	a						07 55						08 20												
Ealing Broadway ⊖	a						08 18																		
London Paddington 15 ⊖	a		07 59			08 26	08 32	08 07	08 09			08 14	08 48				08 31	08 33	08 38		08 40	08 44	08 58	08 51	

		GW	GW	GW	GW	XC	GW	GW	GW	GW		CH	GW	GW	GW	GW	GW	XC	GW	GW		GW	GW	GW	GW
		1	1	1	1	◇1	◇1	1	◇1	1			◇1	1	1	◇1	1	◇1	◇1	◇1		1	1	◇1	1
							B						A							C					
						🛒	⊡		⊡				⊡⊘			⊡			⊡	⊡⊘					
Birmingham New Street 12	d					07 04												07 33							
Birmingham International	d					07 14																			
Coventry	d					07 25																			
Leamington Spa 8	d					07 38												08 04							
Banbury	d			07 27		07 55												08 21							
Kings Sutton	d			07 31																					
Heyford	d			07 40																					
Tackley	d			07 44																					
Bicester Town	d											07 57													
Islip	d											08 08													
Oxford	a			07 55		08 14						08 23						08 41							
	d			07 56	08 06	08 16				08 21							08 36	08 44		08 51				09 01	09 07
Radley	d			08 02						08 27															09 13
Culham	d			08 06																					09 17
Appleford	d			08 09													08 45								
Didcot Parkway	a			08 15	08 18					08 36							08 51							09 14	09 24
	d			08 15	08 20		08 29			08 37			08 47			08 53	09 01		08 59					09 15	09 31
Cholsey	d			08 22						08 43							09 07								09 37
Goring & Streatley	d			08 27						08 48							09 12								09 42
Pangbourne	d			08 32						08 53							09 17								09 47
Tilehurst	d			08 37						08 57							09 21								09 51
Bedwyn	d		07 56																			08 41			
Hungerford	d		08 01																			08 46			
Kintbury	d		08 06																			08 51			
Newbury	a		08 14																			08 58			
	d	07 55							08 29						08 36							08 58			
Newbury Racecourse	d	07 57													08 38										
Thatcham	d	08 02													08 43							09 03			
Midgham	d	08 07													08 47										
Aldermaston	d	08 10													08 51										
Theale	d	08 16													08 56							09 11			
Reading West	d	08 23						←						←	09 03								←		
Reading 7	a	08 27		08 46	08 35	08 39	08 44	08 46	08 50	09 03			09 01	09 03	09 08	09 07	09 27	09 11	09 14	09 14		09 20	09 27	09 32	09 57
	d			08 48	08 35		08 45	08 48	08 52	09 03			09 02	09 03		09 08	09 33		09 16	09 18		09 21	09 33	09 37	10 03
Twyford 3	a			→				08 54		→				09 09			→						09 39		→
Maidenhead 3	a							09 02						09 17									09 47		
Slough 3	a													09 29									09 54	09 52	
Ealing Broadway ⊖	a													09 54									10 19		
London Paddington 15 ⊖	a				09 06		09 14	09 27	09 21				09 29	10 03		09 39			09 44	09 47		09 56	10 31	10 12	

A ⊡ from Reading ⊘ to Reading

B The Bristolian

C The Cathedrals Express. ⊡ from Reading ⊘ to Reading

Birmingham, Banbury, Bicester, Oxford and Bedwyn - Reading and London

Network Diagram - see first Page of Table 116

		XC	GW	GW	GW	GW		CH	GW	GW	XC	GW	GW	GW	GW	GW		XC	GW	GW	GW	GW	GW	GW	XC
		◇1	◇1	1	◇1	1			◇1	1	◇1	1	◇1	◇1	1	1		◇1	1	◇1	◇1	◇1	1	1	◇1
																						A			
		🚲	☕						☕		🚲		🚲	☕				🚲		☕		☕			🚲
Birmingham New Street 12	d	08 04									08 33							09 04							09 33
Birmingham International	d	08 14																09 14							
Coventry	d	08 25																09 25							
Leamington Spa 8	d	08 38									09 00							09 38							10 00
Banbury	d	08 55									09 19					09 39		09 55							10 19
Kings Sutton	d															09 45									
Heyford	d															09 53									
Tackley	d															09 58									
Bicester Town	d							09 07																	
Islip	d							09 18																	
Oxford	a	09 14						09 32			09 41					10 08		10 14							10 41
	d	09 16			09 31					09 36	09 43		10 01			10 08		10 16			10 31			10 36	10 43
Radley	d															10 14									
Culham	d																								
Appleford	d									09 44														10 44	
Didcot Parkway	a									09 50						10 23								10 51	
	d		09 29						09 53	10 01				10 16		10 31				10 29		10 47		11 01	
Cholsey	d									10 07						10 37								11 07	
Goring & Streatley	d									10 12						10 42								11 12	
Pangbourne	d									10 17						10 47								11 17	
Tilehurst	d									10 21						10 51								11 21	
Bedwyn	d											09 36													
Hungerford	d											09 41													
Kintbury	d											09 46													
Newbury	a											09 53													
	d			09 22								09 53							10 13						
Newbury Racecourse	d			09 25															10 15						
Thatcham	d			09 30								09 58							10 20						
Midgham	d			09 34															10 24						
Aldermaston	d			09 38															10 28						
Theale	d			09 43								10 06							10 33						
Reading West	d			09 50		←									←				10 40				←		
Reading 7	a	09 39	09 44	09 54	09 54	09 57			10 06	10 28	10 10	10 16	10 25	10 31	10 28	10 58		10 39	10 45	10 44	10 54	11 00	10 58	11 27	11 07
	d		09 46		09 55	10 03			10 08	10 33		10 18	10 26	10 32	10 33	11 03				10 45	10 55	11 02	11 03	11 33	
Twyford 3	a					10 09				→					10 39	→							11 09	→	
Maidenhead 3	a					10 17									10 47								11 17		
Slough 3	a				10 10	10 24							10 39		10 54						11 09		11 24		
Ealing Broadway ⊖	a					10 49									11 18								11 49		
London Paddington 15 ⊖	a		10 15		10 30	11 01			10 37			10 56	11 00	11 07	11 32					11 14	11 29	11 32	12 01		

		CH		GW	GW	GW	GW	GW	XC	GW	GW	GW		GW	GW	GW	XC	CH	GW	GW	GW	GW		GW	XC
				1	◇1	◇1	1	1	◇1	◇1	1	◇1		1	◇1	1	◇1		1	◇1	◇1	1		1	◇1
					🚲	☕			🚲	☕		🚲			☕		🚲			🚲	☕				🚲
Birmingham New Street 12	d								10 04								10 33								11 04
Birmingham International	d								10 14																11 14
Coventry	d								10 25																11 25
Leamington Spa 8	d								10 38								11 00								11 38
Banbury	d								10 55								11 19								11 55
Kings Sutton	d																								
Heyford	d																								
Tackley	d																								
Bicester Town	d	10 30																11 30							
Islip	d	10 41																11 41							
Oxford	a	10 56							11 14								11 40	11 56							12 14
	d				11 01			11 07	11 16			11 31				11 37	11 43			12 01				12 07	12 16
Radley	d							11 13																12 13	
Culham	d																								
Appleford	d																							12 17	
Didcot Parkway	a							11 22								11 51								12 24	
	d					11 16		11 31		11 29					11 53	12 01					12 16			12 31	
Cholsey	d							11 37								12 07								12 37	
Goring & Streatley	d							11 42								12 12								12 42	
Pangbourne	d							11 47								12 17								12 47	
Tilehurst	d							11 51								12 21								12 51	
Bedwyn	d			10 38															11 38						
Hungerford	d			10 43															11 43						
Kintbury	d			10 48															11 48						
Newbury	a			10 55															11 55						
	d			10 55							11 13								11 55						
Newbury Racecourse	d										11 15														
Thatcham	d			11 00							11 20								12 00						
Midgham	d										11 24														
Aldermaston	d										11 28														
Theale	d			11 08							11 33								12 08						
Reading West	d						←				11 40			←								←			
Reading 7	a			11 20	11 24	11 30	11 27	11 58	11 39	11 43	11 45	11 54		11 58	12 06	12 27	12 10		12 17	12 24	12 30	12 27		12 57	12 39
	d			11 20	11 26	11 32	11 33	12 03		11 44		11 55		12 03	12 08	12 33			12 18	12 26	12 32	12 33		13 03	
Twyford 3	a						11 39	→						12 09		→						12 39		→	
Maidenhead 3	a						11 47							12 17								12 47			
Slough 3	a				11 39		11 54					12 09		12 24						12 39		12 54			
Ealing Broadway ⊖	a						12 19							12 49								13 19			
London Paddington 15 ⊖	a			11 55	11 59	12 02	12 31			12 14		12 29		13 02	12 37				12 52	13 06	13 00	13 31			

A The Red Dragon

Birmingham, Banbury, Bicester, Oxford and Bedwyn - Reading and London

Network Diagram - see first Page of Table 116

		GW	GW	GW	GW	GW	GW	XC		GW	GW	GW	GW	GW	GW	XC	GW	GW		GW	GW	GW	GW	XC	GW
		1	◇1	◇1	◇1	1	1	◇1		◇1	1	◇1	1	1	1	◇1	◇1	1		◇1	1	◇1	1	◇1	◇1
			🍴	☕	🍴			☕		☕		🍴				☕	🍴			☕		🍴		☕	🍴
Birmingham New Street 12	d							11 33								12 04								12 33	
Birmingham International	d															12 14									
Coventry	d															12 25									
Leamington Spa 8	d							12 00								12 38								13 00	
Banbury	d							12 19							12 42	12 55								13 21	
Kings Sutton	d														12 48										
Heyford	d														12 56										
Tackley	d														13 01										
Bicester Town	d																								
Islip	d																								
Oxford	a							12 40							13 11	13 14								13 40	
	d			12 31			12 37	12 43		13 01				13 07		13 16				13 31			13 37	13 43	
Radley	d													13 13											
Culham	d													13 17											
Appleford	d																								
Didcot Parkway	a						12 49							13 24									13 49		
	d		12 29		12 47		13 01					13 16		13 31			13 29					13 53	14 01		
Cholsey	d						13 07							13 37									14 07		
Goring & Streatley	d						13 12							13 42									14 12		
Pangbourne	d						13 17							13 47									14 17		
Tilehurst	d						13 21							13 51									14 21		
Bedwyn	d										12 38														13 32
Hungerford	d										12 43														13 39
Kintbury	d										12 48														
Newbury	a										12 55														13 48
	d	12 13									13 04							13 13							13 48
Newbury Racecourse	d	12 15																13 15							
Thatcham	d	12 20									13 09							13 20							13 55
Midgham	d	12 24																13 24							
Aldermaston	d	12 28																13 28							
Theale	d	12 33									13 17							13 33							14 04
Reading West	d	12 40				←							←					13 40			←				
Reading 7	a	12 45	12 44	12 54	13 00	12 57	13 29	13 07		13 24	13 27	13 31	13 29	13 58		13 39	13 43	13 45		13 54	13 58	14 06	14 27	14 10	14 15
	d		12 45	12 55	13 02	13 03	13 33			13 26	13 29	13 32	13 33	14 03			13 44			13 55	14 03	14 08	14 33		14 17
Twyford 3	a					13 09	→						13 39	→							14 09		→		
Maidenhead 3	a					13 17							13 47								14 17				
Slough 3	a			13 09		13 24				13 39			13 54							14 09	14 24				
Ealing Broadway ⊖	a					13 49							14 19								14 49				
London Paddington 15 ⊖	a		13 14	13 29	13 32	14 01				14 01	14 09	14 06	14 31				14 14			14 29	15 01	14 37			14 44

		GW	GW	GW		GW	XC	CH	GW	GW	GW	GW	GW	GW		XC	GW	GW	GW	GW	GW	XC	GW	GW	
		◇1	◇1	1		1	◇1		◇1	1	◇1	◇1	1	1		◇1	1	◇1	◇1	1	1	◇1	◇1	1	
												A													
		☕	🍴				☕		🍴			🍴⌀				☕		☕	🍴			☕	🍴		
Birmingham New Street 12	d						13 04									13 33						14 04			
Birmingham International	d						13 14															14 14			
Coventry	d						13 25															14 25			
Leamington Spa 8	d						13 38									14 00						14 38			
Banbury	d						13 55									14 19						14 55			
Kings Sutton	d																								
Heyford	d																								
Tackley	d																								
Bicester Town	d							14 00																	
Islip	d							14 11																	
Oxford	a						14 14	14 28								14 40						15 14			
	d	14 01				14 07	14 16				14 31			14 37		14 43		15 01			15 07	15 16			
Radley	d					14 13															15 13				
Culham	d																				15 17				
Appleford	d					14 17																			
Didcot Parkway	a					14 24								14 51							15 24				
	d		14 16			14 31			14 29			14 47		15 01					15 16		15 31		15 29		
Cholsey	d					14 37								15 07							15 37				
Goring & Streatley	d					14 42								15 12							15 42				
Pangbourne	d					14 47								15 17							15 47				
Tilehurst	d					14 51								15 21							15 51				
Bedwyn	d																14 38								
Hungerford	d																14 43								
Kintbury	d																14 48								
Newbury	a																14 55								
	d									14 13							14 55							15 13	
Newbury Racecourse	d									14 15														15 15	
Thatcham	d									14 20							15 00							15 20	
Midgham	d									14 24														15 24	
Aldermaston	d									14 28														15 28	
Theale	d									14 33							15 08							15 33	
Reading West	d			←						14 40			←							←				15 40	
Reading 7	a	14 24	14 31	14 27		14 58	14 39		14 43	14 45	14 54	15 00	14 58	15 27		15 07	15 20	15 24	15 31	15 27	15 58	15 39	15 43	15 45	
	d	14 26	14 32	14 33		15 03			14 44		14 55	15 02	15 03	15 33			15 20	15 26	15 32	15 33	16 03		15 44		
Twyford 3	a			14 39		→							15 09	→						15 39	→				
Maidenhead 3	a			14 47									15 17							15 47					
Slough 3	a	14 39		14 54							15 09		15 24					15 39		15 54					
Ealing Broadway ⊖	a			15 19									15 49							16 19					
London Paddington 15 ⊖	a	15 00	15 08	15 32					15 14		15 29	15 32	16 02				15 54	16 01	16 09	16 31			16 14		

A 🍴 from Reading ⌀ to Reading

Birmingham, Banbury, Bicester, Oxford and Bedwyn - Reading and London

Network Diagram - see first Page of Table 116

		GW ◇1 ☕	GW 1	GW ◇1 A ☕	GW 1	GW 1	XC ◇1 🛒	CH	GW 1	GW ◇1 🛒		GW 1	GW ◇1 ☕	GW 1	XC ◇1 🛒	GW ◇1 ☕	GW 1	GW ◇1	GW ◇1 ☕	GW 1		GW 1	XC ◇1 🛒	GW ◇1 ☕	GW 1
Birmingham New Street 12	d						14 33								15 04								15 33		
Birmingham International	d														15 14										
Coventry	d														15 25										
Leamington Spa 8	d						15 00								15 38								16 00		
Banbury	d					15 08	15 19								15 55								16 19		
Kings Sutton	d					15 14																			
Heyford	d					15 22																			
Tackley	d					15 27																			
Bicester Town	d							15 30																	
Islip	d							15 41																	
Oxford	a					15 39	15 41	15 56							16 14								16 40		
	d	15 31			15 37		15 43			16 01				16 07	16 16			16 31				16 37	16 43		
Radley	d				15 43									16 13								16 43			
Culham	d																								
Appleford	d													16 17											
Didcot Parkway	a				15 51									16 24								16 51			
	d			15 53	16 01								16 16	16 31		16 29			16 47			17 05			
Cholsey	d				16 07									16 37								17 11			
Goring & Streatley	d				16 12									16 42								17 16			
Pangbourne	d				16 17									16 47								17 20			
Tilehurst	d				16 21									16 51								17 25			
Bedwyn	d								15 36																16 44
Hungerford	d								15 41															16 39	16 49
Kintbury	d								15 46																16 54
Newbury	a								15 53															16 48	17 03
	d								15 53								16 13							16 48	
Newbury Racecourse	d																16 15								
Thatcham	d								15 58								16 20							16 55	
Midgham	d																16 24								
Aldermaston	d																16 28								
Theale	d								16 06								16 33							17 04	
Reading West	d		←									←					16 40			←					
Reading 7	a	15 54	15 58	16 06	16 27		16 10		16 16	16 24		16 27	16 31	16 59	16 39	16 43	16 45	16 54	17 00	16 59		17 31	17 07	17 15	
	d	15 55	16 03	16 08	16 33				16 19	16 26		16 33	16 34	17 03		16 44		16 55	17 02	17 03		17 33		17 17	
Twyford 3	a		16 09		→							16 39		→						17 09		→			
Maidenhead 3	a		16 17									16 47								17 17				17 28	
Slough 3	a	16 09	16 24							16 39		16 54						17 09		17 24					
Ealing Broadway ⊖	a		16 49									17 21								17 49					
London Paddington 15 ⊖	a	16 27	17 02	16 39					16 57	17 00		17 31	17 09			17 14		17 34	17 30	18 01				17 54	

		GW 1	GW 1 🛒	GW ◇1 ☕	GW 1	GW 1		XC ◇1 🛒	CH	GW 1	GW ◇1 ☕	GW ◇1 ☕	GW 1	GW ◇1 ☕	GW 1	XC ◇1 🛒		GW 1	GW 1	GW 1 🛒	GW ◇1 ☕	GW 1	GW 1	XC ◇1 🛒	GW 1
Birmingham New Street 12	d							16 04								16 33								17 04	
Birmingham International	d							16 14																17 14	
Coventry	d							16 25																17 25	
Leamington Spa 8	d							16 38								17 00								17 38	
Banbury	d							16 55								17 19		17 23						17 55	
Kings Sutton	d																	17 27							
Heyford	d																	17 36							
Tackley	d																	17 40							
Bicester Town	d								16 57																
Islip	d								17 08																
Oxford	a							17 14	17 23							17 39		17 52						18 14	
	d	16 47	17 01			17 07		17 16				17 31			17 37	17 43				18 01			18 07	18 16	
Radley	d					17 13									17 43								18 13		
Culham	d					17 17																	18 17		
Appleford	d														17 47										
Didcot Parkway	a	17 04				17 24									17 54								18 24		
	d			17 16		17 31					17 29			17 53	18 01						18 16		18 31		
Cholsey	d					17 37									18 07								18 37		
Goring & Streatley	d					17 42									18 12								18 42		
Pangbourne	d					17 47									18 17								18 47		
Tilehurst	d					17 51									18 21								18 51		
Bedwyn	d																		17 36						17 55
Hungerford	d																		17 41						18 00
Kintbury	d																		17 46						18 05
Newbury	a																		17 53						18 12
	d									17 13									17 53						18 13
Newbury Racecourse	d									17 15															18 15
Thatcham	d									17 20									17 58						18 20
Midgham	d									17 24															18 24
Aldermaston	d									17 28									18 04						18 28
Theale	d									17 33									18 09						18 33
Reading West	d				←					17 40			←									←			18 40
Reading 7	a		17 24	17 31	17 31	17 57		17 39		17 45	17 44	17 54	17 57	18 06	18 27	18 09			18 21	18 24	18 31	18 27	19 00	18 39	18 45
	d		17 26	17 32	17 33	18 00					17 46	17 56	18 00	18 08	18 33				18 22	18 26	18 32	18 33	19 03		
Twyford 3	a				17 39	→							18 06		→							18 39	→		
Maidenhead 3	a				17 47								18 17									18 47			
Slough 3	a		17 39		17 54							18 10	18 24							18 39		18 54			
Ealing Broadway ⊖	a				18 19								18 49									19 19			
London Paddington 15 ⊖	a		17 59	18 02	18 31						18 14	18 28	19 00	18 39					18 54	18 59	19 02	19 31			

A The Cheltenham Spa Express

Birmingham, Banbury, Bicester, Oxford and Bedwyn - Reading and London

Network Diagram - see first Page of Table 116

		GW		GW	GW	GW	GW	XC	CH	GW	GW	GW		GW	GW	GW	XC	GW	GW FO	GW FX	GW	GW		GW	GW
		◇1		1	◇1	1	1	◇1		1	1	1		◇1	1	1	◇1	◇1	◇1	◇1	1	◇1		◇1	1
		☕			☕			🛒						🛒			🛒	☕				☕		☕	
Birmingham New Street 12	d							17 33									18 04								
Birmingham International	d																18 14								
Coventry	d																18 25								
Leamington Spa 8	d							18 00									18 38								
Banbury	d							18 19								18 37	18 55								
Kings Sutton	d															18 43									
Heyford	d															18 51									
Tackley	d															18 56									
Bicester Town	d								18 18																
Islip	d								18 29																
Oxford	a							18 40	18 44							19 08	19 14								
	d			18 31			18 37	18 43				19 01		19 06			19 16		19 31	19 31					19 37
Radley	d						18 43					19 07													
Culham	d																								
Appleford	d						18 47																		
Didcot Parkway	a						18 56					19 16													19 49
	d	18 29			18 47		19 01					19 32						19 29				19 47			20 01
Cholsey	d						19 07					19 37													20 07
Goring & Streatley	d						19 12					19 42													20 12
Pangbourne	d						19 17					19 47													20 17
Tilehurst	d						19 21					19 51													20 21
Bedwyn	d										19 03														
Hungerford	d										19 08														
Kintbury	d										19 13														
Newbury	a										19 22														
	d									18 53														19 49	
Newbury Racecourse	d																								
Thatcham	d									18 58															
Midgham	d																								
Aldermaston	d																								
Theale	d									19 06															
Reading West	d					←									←						←				
Reading 7	a	18 46		18 55	19 01	19 00	19 27	19 07		19 16		19 57		19 32	19 27		19 39	19 44	19 54	19 54	19 57	20 00		20 06	20 27
	d	18 47		18 57	19 02	19 03	19 33			19 18		19 58		19 32	19 33			19 45	19 55	19 55	19 58	20 02		20 08	20 33
Twyford 3	a					19 09	→					→			19 42						20 04				→
Maidenhead 3	a					19 21									19 50						20 12				
Slough 3	a			19 09		19 29								19 47	19 57				20 09	20 09	20 19				
Ealing Broadway ⊖	a					19 53									20 22						20 49				
London Paddington 15 ⊖	a	19 14		19 31	19 32	20 02				19 54				20 06	20 31			20 14	20 30	20 31	20 59	20 32		20 39	

		XC	GW	GW	GW	GW	GW	GW		XC	CH	GW	GW	GW	GW	GW	GW	XC		GW	GW FX	GW FO	GW	XC	GW
		◇1	◇1	◇1	1	1	1	1		◇1		◇1	◇1	1	◇1	1	1	◇1		1	◇1	◇1	1	◇1	◇1
		🛒	☕							🛒		☕	☕		☕			🛒							☕
Birmingham New Street 12	d	18 33								19 04								19 33						20 04	
Birmingham International	d									19 14														20 14	
Coventry	d									19 25														20 25	
Leamington Spa 8	d	19 00								19 38								20 05						20 38	
Banbury	d	19 19								19 55				20 01				20 23						20 55	
Kings Sutton	d													20 07											
Heyford	d													20 15											
Tackley	d													20 20											
Bicester Town	d										20 00														
Islip	d										20 11														
Oxford	a	19 39								20 14	20 26			20 32				20 40						21 14	
	d	19 42		20 01				20 07		20 16			20 31				20 37	20 42			21 01	21 01		21 16	
Radley	d							20 13																	
Culham	d							20 17																	
Appleford	d																20 45								
Didcot Parkway	a							20 24									20 51								
	d		20 00					20 31				20 29			20 47		21 01								21 29
Cholsey	d							20 37									21 08								
Goring & Streatley	d							20 42									21 13								
Pangbourne	d							20 47									21 19								
Tilehurst	d							20 51									21 22								
Bedwyn	d						19 55													20 33					
Hungerford	d						20 00													20 38					
Kintbury	d						20 05													20 43					
Newbury	a						20 12													20 50					
	d					19 55	20 12													20 50					
Newbury Racecourse	d					19 57														20 52					
Thatcham	d					20 02	20 17													20 57					
Midgham	d					20 06														21 02					
Aldermaston	d					20 10														21 05					
Theale	d					20 15	20 25													21 10					
Reading West	d				←	20 21										←				21 17			←		
Reading 7	a	20 10	20 14	20 24	20 27	20 27	20 34	20 58		20 39		20 44	20 54		21 00	20 58	21 29	21 07		21 22	21 24	21 24	21 29	21 40	21 43
	d		20 15	20 26	20 33		20 34	21 14				20 45	20 55		21 02	21 14	21 33				21 26	21 26	21 33		21 44
Twyford 3	a				20 39			→								21 20	→						21 39		
Maidenhead 3	a				20 47											21 28							21 47		
Slough 3	a			20 39	20 54								21 09			21 40					21 39	21 39	21 58		
Ealing Broadway ⊖	a				21 19											22 04							22 21		
London Paddington 15 ⊖	a		20 46	21 01	21 31		21 08					21 14	21 29		21 32	22 16					22 00	22 01	22 33		22 14

Birmingham, Banbury, Bicester, Oxford and Bedwyn - Reading and London

Network Diagram - see first Page of Table 116

		GW	GW	GW	GW	GW FX	GW FO	XC	GW	CH	GW	XC	GW	GW FO	GW FX	GW FX	GW FO	GW	GW	GW	GW	XC
		1	1	◇1	◇1 ☕	◇1 ☕	◇1 ☕	◇1	1		◇	◇1	1	◇1	◇1	◇1 ☕	◇1 ☕	1	1	◇1	1	◇1
Birmingham New Street 12	d							20 33				21 04										22 04
Birmingham International	d											21 14										22 14
Coventry	d											21 25										22 25
Leamington Spa 8	d							21 00				21 38										22 38
Banbury	d							21 19			21 38	21 55							22 25			22 55
Kings Sutton	d										21 42								22 31			
Heyford	d										21 51								22 39			
Tackley	d										21 55								22 44			
Bicester Town	d									21 30												
Islip	d									21 41												
Oxford	a							21 40		21 56	22 05	22 14							22 56			23 14
	d		21 21	21 32				21 43	21 51		22 11	22 16		22 34	22 34			22 52		23 09		23 15
Radley	d		21 27						21 57									22 58				
Culham	d		21 31															23 02				
Appleford	d																	23 04				
Didcot Parkway	a		21 38						22 06		22 24							23 11		23 23		
	d		21 44			21 53	21 53		22 08		22 27					22 52	22 52	23 11		23 23		
Cholsey	d		21 50						22 14									23 18				
Goring & Streatley	d		21 55						22 19									23 23				
Pangbourne	d		21 59						22 24									23 26				
Tilehurst	d		22 02						22 27									23 30				
Bedwyn	d	21 06											21 55								23 00	
Hungerford	d	21 11											22 00								23 05	
Kintbury	d	21 16											22 05								23 10	
Newbury	a	21 23											22 12								23 17	
	d	21 23			21 42								22 13								23 17	
Newbury Racecourse	d	21 25											22 15								23 19	
Thatcham	d	21 30											22 20								23 24	
Midgham	d	21 35											22 24								23 29	
Aldermaston	d	21 38											22 28								23 32	
Theale	d	21 43											22 33								23 37	
Reading West	d	21 50											22 40								23 44	
Reading 7	a	21 55	22 12	21 55	21 59	22 11	22 11	22 17	22 37		22 44	22 41	22 45	22 58	22 58	23 06	23 06	23 40		23 40	23 49	23 52
	d			21 56	22 01	22 12	22 12				22 44			22 59	22 59	23 08	23 08			23 45		
Twyford 3	a																					
Maidenhead 3	a																			23 58		
Slough 3	a			22 13							23 01			23 12	23 15					00 05		
Ealing Broadway ⊖	a																					
London Paddington 15 ⊖	a			22 39	22 30	22 44	22 45				23 25			23 36	23 36	23 41	23 41			00 29		

		GW	CH FO	GW	CH
		◇1 ☕		1	
Birmingham New Street 12	d				
Birmingham International	d				
Coventry	d				
Leamington Spa 8	d				23 38
Banbury	d			23 45	23 57
Kings Sutton	d			23 50	
Heyford	d			23 58	
Tackley	d			00 03	
Bicester Town	d		23 42		
Islip	d		23 53		
Oxford	a		00 08	00 13	00 22
	d			00 27	
Radley	d			00 33	
Culham	d			00 37	
Appleford	d			00 39	
Didcot Parkway	a			00 46	
	d	23 35		00 46	
Cholsey	d			00 52	
Goring & Streatley	d			00 57	
Pangbourne	d			01 01	
Tilehurst	d			01 06	
Bedwyn	d				
Hungerford	d				
Kintbury	d				
Newbury	a				
	d				
Newbury Racecourse	d				
Thatcham	d				
Midgham	d				
Aldermaston	d				
Theale	d				
Reading West	d				
Reading 7	a	23 53		01 12	
	d	23 55		01 12	
Twyford 3	a			01 18	
Maidenhead 3	a			01 26	
Slough 3	a			01 34	
Ealing Broadway ⊖	a			01 50	
London Paddington 15 ⊖	a	00 33		02 02	

Table 116

Saturdays
until 31 December

Birmingham, Banbury, Bicester, Oxford and Bedwyn - Reading and London

Network Diagram - see first Page of Table 116

		GW ◇1	GW ◇1 ☕	GW ◇1	CH	GW 1	CH	GW 1	GW 1	GW 1		GW ◇1 ☕	GW 1	GW 1	GW ◇1	GW 1	GW ◇1 ☕	GW 1	GW 1	GW ◇1		GW ◇1 ☕	GW 1	GW 1	XC ◇1 🛒
Birmingham New Street 12	d																								06 04
Birmingham International	d																								06 14
Coventry	d																								06 25
Leamington Spa 8	d						23p38																		06 38
Banbury	d					23p45	23p57																		06 55
Kings Sutton	d					23p50																			
Heyford	d					23p58																			
Tackley	d					00 03																			
Bicester Town	d				23p42																				
Islip	d				23p53																				
Oxford	a				00 08	00 13	00 22																		07 14
	d	23p09		00 07		00 27		03 59	05 14	05 49				06 07	06 31				06 42	07 01				07 07	07 16
Radley	d					00 33			05 20					06 13										07 13	
Culham	d					00 37			05 24															07 17	
Appleford	d					00 39								06 17											
Didcot Parkway	a	23p23		00 20		00 46		04 10	05 31	06 01				06 24					06 54					07 24	
	d	23p23	23p35	00 22		00 46		04 10	05 31	06 01		06 29		06 31			06 59		07 01			07 17		07 31	
Cholsey	d					00 52			05 37	06 07				06 37					07 07					07 37	
Goring & Streatley	d					00 57			05 42	06 12				06 42					07 12					07 42	
Pangbourne	d					01 01			05 47	06 17				06 47					07 17					07 47	
Tilehurst	d					01 06			05 51	06 21				06 51					07 21					07 51	
Bedwyn	d												06 05					06 39							
Hungerford	d												06 11					06 43							
Kintbury	d												06 15					06 48							
Newbury	a												06 22					06 55							
	d												06 22					06 55							
Newbury Racecourse	d												06 24												
Thatcham	d												06 29					07 00							
Midgham	d												06 34												
Aldermaston	d												06 37												
Theale	d												06 42					07 08							
Reading West	d												06 49			←							←		
Reading 7	a	23p40	23p53	00 38		01 12		04 27	05 57	06 27		06 43	06 52	06 57	07 00	06 57	07 14	07 20	07 27	07 27		07 31	07 27	07 59	07 39
	d	23p45	23p55	00 38		01 12		04 40	06 03	06 33		06 45	06 52	07 03	07 00	07 03	07 15	07 21	07 33	07 27		07 32	07 33	08 03	
Twyford 3	a					01 18		04 46	06 09	06 39				→		07 09			→				07 39	→	
Maidenhead 3	a	23p58				01 26		04 54	06 17	06 47						07 17							07 47		
Slough 3	a	00 05		00 55		01 34		05 01	06 24	06 54					07 16	07 24				07 42			07 54		
Ealing Broadway ⊖	a					01 50		05 19	06 49	07 19						07 49							08 19		
London Paddington 15 ⊖	a	00 29	00 33	01 17		02 02		05 31	07 01	07 31		07 14	07 22		07 37	08 01	07 44	07 54		08 01		08 07	08 31		

		GW 1	GW ◇1 ☕	GW ◇1 ☕	GW 1	GW ◇1 ☕		GW 1	GW 1	XC ◇1	GW ◇1 ☕	GW 1	GW ◇1	CH	GW ◇1 ☕	GW 1		GW 1	XC ◇1 🛒	GW 1	GW ◇1 ☕	GW ◇1 ☕	GW ◇1 ☕	GW ◇1 ☕	GW 1
Birmingham New Street 12	d									06 33									07 04						
Birmingham International	d																		07 14						
Coventry	d																		07 25						
Leamington Spa 8	d									07 00									07 38						
Banbury	d				07 02					07 19									07 55						
Kings Sutton	d				07 08																				
Heyford	d				07 17																				
Tackley	d				07 21																				
Bicester Town	d													07 36											
Islip	d													07 47											
Oxford	a				07 32					07 40				08 02					08 14						
	d			07 31					07 37	07 43			08 01					08 07	08 16				08 31		
Radley	d																	08 13							
Culham	d																								
Appleford	d																	08 17							
Didcot Parkway	a								07 49									08 24							
	d		07 29			07 47			08 01		07 59				08 17			08 31			08 29			08 47	
Cholsey	d								08 07									08 37							
Goring & Streatley	d								08 12									08 42							
Pangbourne	d								08 17									08 47							
Tilehurst	d								08 21									08 51							
Bedwyn	d											07 37													
Hungerford	d											07 41													
Kintbury	d											07 46													
Newbury	a											07 53													
	d	07 13										07 53								08 13		08 34			
Newbury Racecourse	d	07 15																		08 15					
Thatcham	d	07 20										07 58								08 20					
Midgham	d	07 24																		08 24					
Aldermaston	d	07 28																		08 28					
Theale	d	07 33										08 06								08 33					
Reading West	d	07 42						←								←				08 40					←
Reading 7	a	07 45	07 44	07 54		08 00		07 59	08 27	08 06	08 14	08 19	08 25		08 31	08 27		08 57	08 39	08 44	08 44	08 52	08 54	09 00	08 57
	d		07 46	07 54		08 02		08 03	08 33		08 16	08 20	08 26		08 32	08 33		09 03			08 46	08 52	08 55	09 02	09 03
Twyford 3	a							08 09	→							08 39		→							09 09
Maidenhead 3	a							08 17								08 47									09 17
Slough 3	a			08 09				08 24					08 40			08 54							09 09		09 24
Ealing Broadway ⊖	a							08 49								09 19									09 49
London Paddington 15 ⊖	a		08 14	08 29		08 32		09 01			08 44	08 52	08 59		09 02	09 31					09 14	09 21	09 29	09 32	10 01

Table 116

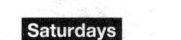

Saturdays
until 31 December

Birmingham, Banbury, Bicester, Oxford and Bedwyn - Reading and London

Network Diagram - see first Page of Table 116

		GW	GW	XC	GW	GW	GW	GW	GW	GW	GW	CH	XC	GW	GW	GW	GW	GW	GW	XC	GW	GW
		◇1	1	◇1	◇1	1	◇1	◇1	1	1	1		◇1	◇1	◇1	1	◇1	1	1	◇1	1	◇1
								A							A		A					
		☕		🛒	☕		🛒	☕⊘					🛒	☕	☕⊘		☕⊘			🛒		🛒
Birmingham New Street 12	d			07 33									08 04							08 33		
Birmingham International	d												08 14									
Coventry	d												08 25									
Leamington Spa 8	d			08 00									08 38							09 00		
Banbury	d			08 19									08 55			09 02				09 19		
Kings Sutton	d															09 08						
Heyford	d															09 17						
Tackley	d															09 21						
Bicester Town	d											08 45										
Islip	d											08 56										
Oxford	a			08 40								09 11	09 14			09 32				09 40		
	d		08 37	08 43			09 01				09 07		09 16		09 31				09 37	09 43		10 01
Radley	d										09 13											
Culham	d										09 17											
Appleford	d																					
Didcot Parkway	a		08 49								09 24								09 49			
	d	08 52	09 01		08 59			09 17			09 31			09 29			09 47		10 01			
Cholsey	d		09 07								09 37								10 07			
Goring & Streatley	d		09 12								09 42								10 12			
Pangbourne	d		09 17								09 47								10 17			
Tilehurst	d		09 21								09 51								10 21			
Bedwyn	d					08 38															09 37	
Hungerford	d					08 43															09 41	
Kintbury	d					08 48															09 46	
Newbury	a					08 55															09 53	
	d					08 55				09 03											09 53	
Newbury Racecourse	d									09 06												
Thatcham	d					09 00				09 11											09 58	
Midgham	d									09 16												
Aldermaston	d									09 19												
Theale	d					09 08				09 24											10 06	
Reading West	d								←	09 31								←				
Reading 7	a	09 07	09 27	09 11	09 14	09 20	09 24	09 32	09 27	09 35	09 57		09 39	09 45	09 54		10 00	09 57	10 27	10 07	10 17	10 25
	d	09 09	09 33		09 16	09 20	09 24	09 33	09 33		10 03			09 46	09 55		10 02	10 03	10 33		10 18	10 25
Twyford 3	a		→						09 39		→							10 09	→			
Maidenhead 3	a								09 47									10 17				
Slough 3	a						09 40		09 54						10 09			10 24				10 40
Ealing Broadway ⊖	a								10 19									10 49				
London Paddington 15 ⊖	a	09 37			09 44	09 52	09 59	10 02	10 31					10 14	10 29		10 32	11 01			10 52	10 59

		GW	GW	GW	GW	XC	CH	GW	GW	GW	GW	GW	GW	XC	GW	GW	GW	GW	XC	GW	GW	GW	GW
		◇1	1	◇1	1	◇1		1	◇1	◇1	◇1	1	1	◇1	1	◇1	1	1	◇1	1	◇1	◇1	1
		☕		☕		🛒			☕	☕	☕			🛒					🛒		☕	🛒	
Birmingham New Street 12	d					09 04								09 33					10 04				
Birmingham International	d					09 14													10 14				
Coventry	d					09 25													10 25				
Leamington Spa 8	d					09 38								10 00					10 38				
Banbury	d					09 55								10 19					10 55				11 02
Kings Sutton	d																						11 08
Heyford	d																						11 17
Tackley	d																						11 21
Bicester Town	d						09 57																
Islip	d						10 08																
Oxford	a					10 14	10 23							10 40					11 14				11 32
	d				10 07	10 16				10 31			10 37	10 43		11 01		11 07	11 16			11 31	
Radley	d				10 13													11 13					
Culham	d																						
Appleford	d				10 17																		
Didcot Parkway	a				10 23								10 49					11 24					
	d	10 17		10 22	10 31				10 29		10 47		11 01					11 31			11 29		
Cholsey	d				10 37								11 07					11 37					
Goring & Streatley	d				10 42								11 12					11 42					
Pangbourne	d				10 47								11 17					11 47					
Tilehurst	d				10 51								11 21					11 51					
Bedwyn	d														10 40								
Hungerford	d														10 46								
Kintbury	d														10 50								
Newbury	a														10 57								
	d							10 13							10 57					11 13			
Newbury Racecourse	d							10 15												11 15			
Thatcham	d							10 20							11 02					11 20			
Midgham	d							10 24												11 24			
Aldermaston	d							10 28												11 28			
Theale	d							10 33							11 10					11 33			
Reading West	d		←					10 40				←					←			11 40			
Reading 7	a	10 32	10 27	10 36	10 58	10 39		10 44	10 45	10 54	11 01	10 58	11 27	11 09	11 21	11 24	11 27	11 58	11 39	11 44	11 44	11 54	
	d	10 33	10 33	10 39	11 03				10 46	10 55	11 02	11 03	11 33		11 21	11 25	11 33	12 03			11 45	11 55	
Twyford 3	a		10 39		→							11 09	→				11 39	→					
Maidenhead 3	a		10 47									11 17					11 47						
Slough 3	a		10 54							11 09		11 24				11 39	11 54					12 09	
Ealing Broadway ⊖	a		11 19									11 49					12 19						
London Paddington 15 ⊖	a	11 02	11 31	11 08					11 14	11 29	11 33	12 01			11 52	11 59	12 31				12 14	12 29	

A ☕ from Reading ⊘ to Reading

Table 116

Saturdays
until 31 December

Birmingham, Banbury, Bicester, Oxford and Bedwyn - Reading and London

Network Diagram - see first Page of Table 116

		GW ◇1 ☕	GW 1	GW 1		XC ◇1 🛒	CH	GW 1	GW ◇1 🛒	GW 1	GW ◇1 ☕	GW 1	XC ◇1 🛒	GW 1		GW ◇1 ☕	GW ◇1 🛒	GW ◇1 ☕	GW 1	GW 1	XC ◇1 🛒	GW ◇1 🛒	GW 1	GW 1	
Birmingham New Street 12	d					10 33							11 04								11 33				
Birmingham International	d												11 14												
Coventry	d												11 25												
Leamington Spa 8	d					11 00							11 38								12 00				
Banbury	d					11 19							11 55								12 19				
Kings Sutton	d																								
Heyford	d																								
Tackley	d																								
Bicester Town	d						11 30																		
Islip	d						11 41																		
Oxford	a					11 40	11 56						12 14								12 40				
	d			11 37		11 43			12 01			12 07	12 16				12 31			12 37	12 43	13 01		13 07	
Radley	d											12 13												13 13	
Culham	d																							13 17	
Appleford	d											12 17													
Didcot Parkway	a			11 49								12 24								12 49				13 24	
	d	11 47		12 01							12 22	12 31				12 29		12 47		13 01				13 31	
Cholsey	d			12 07								12 37								13 07				13 37	
Goring & Streatley	d			12 12								12 42								13 12				13 42	
Pangbourne	d			12 17								12 47								13 17				13 47	
Tilehurst	d			12 21								12 51								13 21				13 51	
Bedwyn	d							11 38																	
Hungerford	d							11 43																	
Kintbury	d							11 48																	
Newbury	a							11 55																	
	d							11 55						12 13											
Newbury Racecourse	d													12 15											
Thatcham	d							12 00						12 20											
Midgham	d													12 24											
Aldermaston	d													12 28											
Theale	d							12 08						12 33											
Reading West	d		←							←				12 40					←				←		
Reading 7	a	12 00	11 58	12 28		12 07		12 17	12 25	12 28	12 37	12 57	12 39	12 44		12 44	12 53	13 00	12 57	13 27	13 06	13 25	13 27	13 59	
	d	12 02	12 03	12 33				12 18	12 25	12 33	12 39	13 03				12 45	12 55	13 02	13 03	13 33		13 25	13 33	14 03	
Twyford 3	a		12 09	→						12 39		→							13 09	→			13 39	→	
Maidenhead 3	a		12 17							12 47									13 17				13 47		
Slough 3	a		12 24						12 40	12 54							13 09		13 24			13 40	13 54		
Ealing Broadway ⊖	a		12 49							13 19									13 49				14 19		
London Paddington 15 ⊖	a	12 32	13 01					12 52	12 59	13 31	13 07					13 12	13 30	13 33	14 01			13 59	14 31		

		XC ◇1 🛒	CH	GW 1	GW ◇1 ☕	GW 1	GW ◇1	GW 1	GW ◇1 ☕	GW 1		GW 1	XC ◇1 🛒	GW ◇1 ☕	GW ◇1 🛒	GW 1	GW ◇1 ☕	GW 1	XC ◇1 🛒	GW 1		GW ◇1 ☕	GW ◇1 ☕	GW ◇1 ☕	GW 1
Birmingham New Street 12	d	12 04											12 33						13 04						
Birmingham International	d	12 14																	13 14						
Coventry	d	12 25																	13 25						
Leamington Spa 8	d	12 38											13 02						13 38						
Banbury	d	12 55						13 02					13 21						13 55						
Kings Sutton	d							13 08																	
Heyford	d							13 17																	
Tackley	d							13 21																	
Bicester Town	d		13 00																						
Islip	d		13 11																						
Oxford	a	13 14	13 26					13 32					13 40						14 14						
	d	13 16					13 31					13 37	13 43		14 01			14 07	14 16				14 31		
Radley	d																	14 13							
Culham	d																								
Appleford	d																	14 17							
Didcot Parkway	a											13 51						14 24							
	d				13 29				13 47			14 01					14 22	14 31				14 29		14 47	
Cholsey	d											14 07						14 37							
Goring & Streatley	d											14 12						14 42							
Pangbourne	d											14 17						14 47							
Tilehurst	d											14 21						14 51							
Bedwyn	d					13 07								13 33											
Hungerford	d					13 13								13 40											
Kintbury	d					13 17																			
Newbury	a					13 24								13 49											
	d			13 13		13 28								13 50						14 13					
Newbury Racecourse	d			13 15																14 15					
Thatcham	d			13 20		13 33								13 57						14 20					
Midgham	d			13 24																14 24					
Aldermaston	d			13 28																14 28					
Theale	d			13 33		13 41								14 06						14 33					
Reading West	d			13 40						←						←				14 40					←
Reading 7	a	13 39		13 44	13 44	13 51	13 54		14 00	13 59		14 27	14 07	14 19	14 25	14 27	14 38	14 58	14 39	14 44		14 44	14 53	15 00	14 58
	d				13 45	13 51	13 55		14 02	14 03		14 33		14 19	14 25	14 33	14 39	15 03				14 45	14 55	15 02	15 03
Twyford 3	a									14 09		→				14 39		→							15 09
Maidenhead 3	a									14 17						14 47									15 17
Slough 3	a						14 09			14 24					14 40	14 54							15 10		15 24
Ealing Broadway ⊖	a									14 49						15 19									15 49
London Paddington 15 ⊖	a				14 14	14 23	14 29		14 32	15 01				14 45	14 59	15 31	15 09					15 14	15 29	15 32	16 01

Table 116

Saturdays
until 31 December

Birmingham, Banbury, Bicester, Oxford and Bedwyn - Reading and London

Network Diagram - see first Page of Table 116

		GW	XC	CH	GW	GW		GW	GW	XC	GW	GW	GW	GW	GW	GW		GW	XC	CH	GW	GW	GW	GW	GW
		1	◇1		1	◇1		1	1	◇1	1	◇1	◇1	1	◇1	1		1	◇1		1	◇1	1	◇1	1
			🚲							🚲		☕	🚲		☕				🚲					☕	
Birmingham New Street 12	d		13 33							14 04									14 33						
Birmingham International	d									14 14															
Coventry	d									14 25															
Leamington Spa 8	d		14 00							14 38									15 00						
Banbury	d		14 19							14 55				15 02					15 20						
Kings Sutton	d													15 08											
Heyford	d													15 17											
Tackley	d													15 21											
Bicester Town	d			14 18																15 28					
Islip	d			14 29																15 39					
Oxford	a		14 40	14 44						15 14				15 32					15 41	15 54					
	d	14 37	14 43			15 01			15 07	15 16			15 31					15 37	15 43			16 01			16 07
Radley	d								15 13																16 13
Culham	d								15 17																
Appleford	d																								16 17
Didcot Parkway	a	14 49							15 24									15 49							16 24
	d	15 01							15 31			15 29			15 47			16 01						16 22	16 31
Cholsey	d	15 07							15 37									16 07							16 37
Goring & Streatley	d	15 12							15 42									16 12							16 42
Pangbourne	d	15 17							15 47									16 17							16 47
Tilehurst	d	15 21							15 51									16 21							16 51
Bedwyn	d				14 38																15 38				
Hungerford	d				14 43																15 43				
Kintbury	d				14 48																15 48				
Newbury	a				14 55																15 55				
	d				14 55						15 13										15 55				
Newbury Racecourse	d										15 15														
Thatcham	d				15 00						15 20										16 00				
Midgham	d										15 24														
Aldermaston	d										15 28														
Theale	d				15 08						15 33										16 08				
Reading West	d							←			15 40					←							←		
Reading 7	a	15 27	15 07		15 17	15 25		15 27	15 59	15 39	15 44	15 44	15 54		16 00	15 59		16 29	16 08		16 17	16 25	16 29	16 38	16 58
	d	15 33			15 19	15 25		15 33	16 03			15 45	15 55		16 01	16 03		16 33			16 18	16 26	16 33	16 39	17 03
Twyford 3	a	→						15 39	→							16 09		→					16 39		→
Maidenhead 3	a							15 47								16 17							16 47		
Slough 3	a					15 40		15 54					16 10			16 24						16 40	16 54		
Ealing Broadway ⊖	a							16 19								16 49							17 19		
London Paddington 15 ⊖	a				15 54	15 59		16 31				16 14	16 29		16 32	17 01					16 52	16 59	17 31	17 07	

		XC		GW	GW	GW	GW	GW	GW	XC	CH	GW		GW	GW	GW	XC	GW	GW	GW	GW	GW		GW	XC
		◇1		1	◇1	◇1	◇1	1	1	◇1		◇1		◇1	1	1	◇1	1	◇1	◇1	◇1	1		1	◇1
		🚲			☕	🚲	☕			🚲		☕					🚲		☕	☕	☕				🚲
Birmingham New Street 12	d	15 04								15 33							16 04								16 33
Birmingham International	d	15 14															16 14								
Coventry	d	15 25															16 25								
Leamington Spa 8	d	15 38								16 02							16 38								17 00
Banbury	d	15 55								16 20							16 55								17 19
Kings Sutton	d																								
Heyford	d																								
Tackley	d																								
Bicester Town	d										16 30														
Islip	d										16 41														
Oxford	a	16 14								16 40	16 56						17 14								17 41
	d	16 16				16 31			16 37	16 43				17 01		17 07	17 16			17 31				17 37	17 43
Radley	d															17 13									
Culham	d															17 17									
Appleford	d																								
Didcot Parkway	a								16 49							17 24								17 49	
	d				16 29		16 47		17 01							17 31			17 29		17 47			18 01	
Cholsey	d								17 07							17 37								18 07	
Goring & Streatley	d								17 12							17 42								18 12	
Pangbourne	d								17 17							17 47								18 17	
Tilehurst	d								17 21							17 51								18 21	
Bedwyn	d											16 35						16 56							
Hungerford	d											16 42						17 00							
Kintbury	d																	17 05							
Newbury	a											16 52						17 13							
	d			16 13								16 53						17 13							
Newbury Racecourse	d			16 15														17 15							
Thatcham	d			16 20								16 59						17 20							
Midgham	d			16 24														17 25							
Aldermaston	d			16 28														17 28							
Theale	d			16 33								17 08						17 33							
Reading West	d			16 40				←							←			17 40				←			
Reading 7	a	16 39		16 44	16 44	16 55	17 00	16 58	17 27	17 07		17 17		17 26	17 27	17 57	17 39	17 44	17 44	17 55	18 00	17 57		18 27	18 07
	d				16 45	16 55	17 02	17 03	17 33			17 18		17 27	17 33	18 03			17 45	17 57	18 02	18 03		18 33	
Twyford 3	a							17 09	→						17 39	→						18 09		→	
Maidenhead 3	a							17 17							17 47							18 17			
Slough 3	a					17 10		17 24						17 41	17 54					18 10		18 24			
Ealing Broadway ⊖	a							17 49							18 19							18 49			
London Paddington 15 ⊖	a				17 14	17 29	17 32	18 01				17 51		18 00	18 31				18 14	18 29	18 32	19 01			

Table 116

Saturdays
until 31 December

Birmingham, Banbury, Bicester, Oxford and Bedwyn - Reading and London

Network Diagram - see first Page of Table 116

		GW	GW	GW	GW	GW	GW	XC		CH	GW	GW	GW	GW	GW	GW	XC	GW		GW	GW	GW	XC	GW	GW
		1	1	◇1	1	◇1	1	◇1			1	◇1	◇1	◇1	1	1	◇1	1		◇1	1	1	◇1	1	◇1
						☕		🛒				☕	🛒	☕			🛒						🛒		☕
Birmingham New Street 12	d							17 04									17 33						18 04		
Birmingham International	d							17 14															18 14		
Coventry	d							17 25															18 25		
Leamington Spa 8	d							17 38									18 02						18 38		
Banbury	d	17 23						17 55									18 19						18 55		
Kings Sutton	d	17 29																							
Heyford	d	17 38																							
Tackley	d	17 42																							
Bicester Town	d									18 04															
Islip	d									18 15															
Oxford	a	17 53						18 14		18 30							18 40						19 14		
	d			18 01			18 07	18 16					18 31			18 37	18 43			19 01		19 07	19 16		
Radley	d						18 13															19 13			
Culham	d																					19 17			
Appleford	d						18 17																		
Didcot Parkway	a						18 24									18 49						19 24			
	d					18 22	18 31					18 29		18 47		19 01						19 31			19 29
Cholsey	d						18 37									19 07						19 37			
Goring & Streatley	d						18 42									19 12						19 42			
Pangbourne	d						18 47									19 17						19 47			
Tilehurst	d						18 51									19 21						19 51			
Bedwyn	d		17 38															18 38							
Hungerford	d		17 43															18 43							
Kintbury	d		17 48															18 48							
Newbury	a		17 55															18 55							
	d		17 55								18 13							18 55						19 13	
Newbury Racecourse	d										18 15													19 15	
Thatcham	d		18 00								18 20							19 00						19 20	
Midgham	d										18 24													19 24	
Aldermaston	d										18 28													19 28	
Theale	d		18 08								18 33							19 08						19 33	
Reading West	d				←						18 40				←						←			19 40	
Reading 7	a		18 18	18 25	18 27	18 38	18 58	18 39			18 44	18 44	18 55	19 00	18 58	19 29	19 07	19 17		19 25	19 29	19 57	19 39	19 44	19 44
	d		18 19	18 25	18 33	18 39	19 03					18 45	18 56	19 02	19 03	19 33		19 20		19 25	19 33	20 03			19 45
Twyford 3	a				18 39		→								19 09	→					19 39	→			
Maidenhead 3	a				18 47										19 17						19 47				
Slough 3	a			18 40	18 54								19 10		19 24					19 40	19 54				
Ealing Broadway ⊖	a				19 19										19 49						20 19				
London Paddington 15 ⊖	a		18 52	18 59	19 31	19 08						19 14	19 29	19 32	20 01			19 52		19 59	20 31				20 14

		GW	GW	GW		GW	GW	GW	XC	CH	GW	GW	GW	GW		GW	XC	GW	GW	GW	GW	GW	XC	CH	
		◇1	1	◇1		1	◇1	1	◇1		◇1	1	1	◇1		1	◇1	◇1	◇1	1	◇1	1	◇1		
		🛒		☕			☕		🛒					☕			🛒	☕			☕		🛒		
Birmingham New Street 12	d								18 33								19 04						19 33		
Birmingham International	d																19 14								
Coventry	d																19 25								
Leamington Spa 8	d								19 00								19 38						20 03		
Banbury	d		19 02						19 19								19 55						20 21		
Kings Sutton	d		19 08																						
Heyford	d		19 17																						
Tackley	d		19 21																						
Bicester Town	d									19 17														20 28	
Islip	d									19 28														20 39	
Oxford	a		19 32						19 40	19 43							20 14						20 40	20 54	
	d	19 31						19 37	19 43		20 01					20 07	20 16		20 31			20 37	20 43		
Radley	d															20 13									
Culham	d																								
Appleford	d															20 17									
Didcot Parkway	a							19 49								20 24						20 49			
	d			19 47				20 01						20 23		20 31		20 29			20 47	21 01			
Cholsey	d							20 07								20 37						21 07			
Goring & Streatley	d							20 12								20 42						21 12			
Pangbourne	d							20 17								20 47						21 17			
Tilehurst	d							20 21								20 51						21 21			
Bedwyn	d											19 41													
Hungerford	d											19 47													
Kintbury	d											19 51													
Newbury	a											19 58													
	d						19 46					19 58													
Newbury Racecourse	d											20 00													
Thatcham	d											20 05													
Midgham	d											20 10													
Aldermaston	d											20 13													
Theale	d											20 18													
Reading West	d					←						20 25	←							←					
Reading 7	a	19 55		20 00		19 57	20 07	20 29	20 10		20 25	20 28	20 29	20 38		20 57	20 39	20 44	20 54	20 57	21 06	21 27	21 10		
	d	19 55		20 03		20 03	20 09	20 33			20 25		20 33	20 39		21 03		20 45	20 54	21 03	21 08	21 33			
Twyford 3	a					20 09		→					20 39			→				21 09		→			
Maidenhead 3	a					20 17							20 47							21 17					
Slough 3	a	20 10				20 24					20 40		20 54						21 09	21 24					
Ealing Broadway ⊖	a					20 49							21 19							21 49					
London Paddington 15 ⊖	a	20 29		20 32		21 01	20 37				20 59		21 31	21 07				21 14	21 29	22 02	21 36				

Table 116

Saturdays
until 31 December

Birmingham, Banbury, Bicester, Oxford and Bedwyn - Reading and London

Network Diagram - see first Page of Table 116

		GW	GW	GW	GW	XC	GW	GW	GW	GW	GW	GW	CH	XC	GW	GW	GW	GW	GW	GW	GW	GW	CH
		◇1	1	1	1	◇1	◇1	◇1	◇1	1	◇1	1		◇1	1	1	◇1	◇1	◇1	1	◇1	1	
						trolley	buffet		buffet									buffet			buffet		
Birmingham New Street 12	d					20 04								21 04									
Birmingham International	d					20 14								21 14									
Coventry	d					20 25								21 25									
Leamington Spa 8	d					20 38								21 38									
Banbury	d			20 38		20 55								21 55	22 00								
Kings Sutton	d			20 44											22 06								
Heyford	d			20 53											22 15								
Tackley	d			20 57											22 19								
Bicester Town	d												21 37										22 55
Islip	d												21 48										23 06
Oxford	a			21 08		21 14							22 03	22 16	22 30								23 21
	d	21 01				21 16		21 31		21 50	22 01			22 18			22 35		23 01			23 07	
Radley	d									21 56												23 13	
Culham	d																					23 17	
Appleford	d																					23 20	
Didcot Parkway	a							21 43		22 04	22 12						22 47		23 13			23 25	
	d						21 34	21 45	21 47	22 04	22 13						22 48	22 49	23 14		23 30	23 36	
Cholsey	d									22 10												23 42	
Goring & Streatley	d									22 15												23 47	
Pangbourne	d									22 21												23 51	
Tilehurst	d									22 24												23 56	
Bedwyn	d				20 48											22 00				23 00			
Hungerford	d				20 54											22 06				23 06			
Kintbury	d				20 58											22 10				23 10			
Newbury	a				21 05											22 17				23 17			
	d				21 05											22 17				23 17			
Newbury Racecourse	d				21 07											22 19				23 19			
Thatcham	d				21 12											22 24				23 24			
Midgham	d				21 17											22 29				23 29			
Aldermaston	d				21 20											22 32				23 32			
Theale	d				21 25											22 37				23 37			
Reading West	d		←		21 32							←				22 44				23 44			
Reading 7	a	21 25	21 27		21 36	21 40	21 48	21 59	21 59	22 31	22 28	22 31		22 41		22 48	23 04	23 04	23 29	23 48	23 51	00 01	
	d	21 25	21 33				21 50	22 01	22 03	22 33	22 29	22 33					23 05	23 05	23 29		23 51	00 03	
Twyford 3	a		21 39							↪		22 39										00 09	
Maidenhead 3	a		21 47									22 47										00 17	
Slough 3	a	21 40	21 54					22 14			22 43	22 54					23 23		23 44			00 28	
Ealing Broadway ⊖	a		22 19									23 19										00 52	
London Paddington 15 ⊖	a	21 59	22 31				22 16	22 32	22 37		23 02	23 28					23 43	23 36	00 10		00 34	01 02	

Saturdays
7 January to 24 March

		GW	GW	GW	CH	GW	CH	GW	GW	GW	GW	GW	GW	GW	GW	GW	GW	GW	GW	GW	GW	GW	XC
		◇1	◇1	◇1		1		1	1	1	◇1	1	1	◇1	1	◇1	1	1	◇1	◇1	1	1	◇1
			buffet								buffet					buffet				buffet			trolley
Birmingham New Street 12	d																						06 04
Birmingham International	d																						06 14
Coventry	d																						06 25
Leamington Spa 8	d						23p38																06 38
Banbury	d					23p45	23p57																06 55
Kings Sutton	d					23p50																	
Heyford	d					23p58																	
Tackley	d					00 03																	
Bicester Town	d				23p42																		
Islip	d				23p53																		
Oxford	a				00 08	00 13	00 22																07 14
	d	23p09		00 07		00 27		03 59	05 14	05 49			06 07	06 31				06 42	07 01			07 07	07 16
Radley	d					00 33			05 20				06 13									07 13	
Culham	d					00 37			05 24													07 17	
Appleford	d					00 39							06 17										
Didcot Parkway	a	23p23		00 20		00 46		04 10	05 31	06 01			06 24					06 54				07 24	
	d	23p23	23p35	00 22		00 46		04 10	05 31	06 01	06 29		06 31			06 59		07 01		07 17		07 31	
Cholsey	d					00 52			05 37	06 07			06 37					07 07				07 37	
Goring & Streatley	d					00 57			05 42	06 12			06 42					07 12				07 42	
Pangbourne	d					01 01			05 47	06 17			06 47					07 17				07 47	
Tilehurst	d					01 06			05 51	06 21			06 51					07 21				07 51	
Bedwyn	d											06 05					06 39						
Hungerford	d											06 11					06 43						
Kintbury	d											06 15					06 48						
Newbury	a											06 22					06 55						
	d											06 22					06 55						
Newbury Racecourse	d											06 24											
Thatcham	d											06 29					07 00						
Midgham	d											06 34											
Aldermaston	d											06 37											
Theale	d											06 42					07 08						
Reading West	d											06 49			←						←		
Reading 7	a	23p40	23p53	00 38		01 12		04 27	05 57	06 27	06 43	06 52	06 57	07 00	06 57	07 14	07 20	07 27	07 27	07 31	07 27	07 59	07 39
	d	23p45	23p55	00 38		01 12		04 40	06 03	06 33	06 45	06 52	07 03	07 00	07 03	07 15	07 21	07 33	07 27	07 32	07 33	08 03	
Twyford 3	a					01 18		04 46	06 09	06 39			↪		07 09			↪			07 39	↪	
Maidenhead 3	a	23p58				01 26		04 54	06 17	06 47					07 17						07 47		
Slough 3	a	00 05		00 55		01 34		05 01	06 24	06 54				07 16	07 24				07 42		07 54		
Ealing Broadway ⊖	a					01 50		05 19	06 49	07 19					07 49						08 19		
London Paddington 15 ⊖	a	00 29	00 33	01 17		02 02		05 31	07 01	07 31	07 14	07 22		07 37	08 01	07 44	07 54		08 01	08 07	08 31		

Table 116

Saturdays

7 January to 24 March

Birmingham, Banbury, Bicester, Oxford and Bedwyn - Reading and London

Network Diagram - see first Page of Table 116

		GW	GW	GW	GW	GW		GW	GW	XC	GW	GW	GW	CH	GW	GW		GW	XC	GW	GW	GW	GW	GW	GW
		1	◇1	◇1	1	◇1		1	1	◇1	◇1	1	◇1		◇1	1		1	◇1	1	◇1	◇1	◇1	◇1	1
			☕	☕		☕					☕				☕				🛒		☕	☕	☕	☕	
Birmingham New Street 12	d									06 33									07 04						
Birmingham International	d																		07 14						
Coventry	d																		07 25						
Leamington Spa 8	d									07 00									07 38						
Banbury	d				07 02					07 19									07 55						
Kings Sutton	d				07 08																				
Heyford	d				07 17																				
Tackley	d				07 21																				
Bicester Town	d													07 36											
Islip	d													07 47											
Oxford	a				07 32					07 40				08 02					08 14						
	d			07 31					07 37	07 43			08 01					08 07	08 16				08 31		
Radley	d																	08 13							
Culham	d																								
Appleford	d																	08 17							
Didcot Parkway	a								07 49									08 24							
	d		07 29			07 47			08 01		07 59				08 17			08 31			08 29			08 47	
Cholsey	d								08 07									08 37							
Goring & Streatley	d								08 12									08 42							
Pangbourne	d								08 17									08 47							
Tilehurst	d								08 21									08 51							
Bedwyn	d											07 37													
Hungerford	d											07 41													
Kintbury	d											07 46													
Newbury	a											07 53													
	d	07 13										07 53								08 13		08 34			
Newbury Racecourse	d	07 15																		08 15					
Thatcham	d	07 20										07 58								08 20					
Midgham	d	07 24																		08 24					
Aldermaston	d	07 28																		08 28					
Theale	d	07 33										08 06								08 33					
Reading West	d	07 42						←								←				08 40					←
Reading 7	a	07 45	07 44	07 54		08 00		07 59	08 27	08 06	08 14	08 19	08 25		08 31	08 27		08 57	08 39	08 44	08 44	08 52	08 54	09 00	08 57
	d		07 46	07 54		08 02		08 03	08 33		08 16	08 20	08 26		08 32	08 33		09 03			08 46	08 52	08 55	09 02	09 03
Twyford 3	a							08 09	→							08 39		→							09 09
Maidenhead 3	a							08 17								08 47									09 17
Slough 3	a			08 09				08 24					08 40			08 54							09 09		09 24
Ealing Broadway ⊖	a							08 49								09 19									09 49
London Paddington 15 ⊖	a		08 14	08 29		08 32		09 01			08 44	08 52	08 59		09 02	09 31					09 14	09 21	09 29	09 32	10 01

		GW		GW	XC	GW	GW	GW	GW	GW	GW	GW		CH	XC	GW	GW	GW	GW	GW	GW	XC		GW	GW
		◇1		1	◇1	◇1	1	◇1	◇1	1	1	1			◇1	◇1	◇1	1	◇1	1	1	◇1		1	◇1
									A								A		A						
		☕			🛒	☕		🛒	☕∅						🛒	☕	☕∅		☕∅			🛒			🛒
Birmingham New Street 12	d				07 33										08 04							08 33			
Birmingham International	d														08 14										
Coventry	d														08 25										
Leamington Spa 8	d				08 00										08 38							09 00			
Banbury	d				08 19										08 55			09 02				09 19			
Kings Sutton	d																	09 08							
Heyford	d																	09 17							
Tackley	d																	09 21							
Bicester Town	d													08 45											
Islip	d													08 56											
Oxford	a				08 40									09 11	09 14			09 32				09 40			
	d			08 37	08 43			09 01				09 07			09 16		09 31				09 37	09 43			10 01
Radley	d											09 13													
Culham	d											09 17													
Appleford	d																								
Didcot Parkway	a			08 49								09 24									09 49				
	d	08 52		09 01		08 59			09 17			09 31				09 29			09 47		10 01				
Cholsey	d			09 07								09 37									10 07				
Goring & Streatley	d			09 12								09 42									10 12				
Pangbourne	d			09 17								09 47									10 17				
Tilehurst	d			09 21								09 51									10 21				
Bedwyn	d						08 38																	09 37	
Hungerford	d						08 43																	09 41	
Kintbury	d						08 48																	09 46	
Newbury	a						08 55																	09 53	
	d						08 55				09 03													09 53	
Newbury Racecourse	d										09 06														
Thatcham	d						09 00				09 11													09 58	
Midgham	d										09 16														
Aldermaston	d										09 19														
Theale	d						09 08				09 24													10 06	
Reading West	d									←	09 31									←					
Reading 7	a	09 07		09 27	09 11	09 14	09 20	09 24	09 32	09 27	09 35	09 57			09 39	09 45	09 54		10 00	09 57	10 27	10 07		10 17	10 25
	d	09 09		09 33		09 16	09 20	09 24	09 33	09 33		10 03				09 46	09 55		10 02	10 03	10 33			10 18	10 25
Twyford 3	a			→						09 39		→								10 09	→				
Maidenhead 3	a									09 47										10 17					
Slough 3	a							09 40		09 54							10 09			10 24					10 40
Ealing Broadway ⊖	a									10 19										10 49					
London Paddington 15 ⊖	a	09 37				09 44	09 52	09 59	10 02	10 31						10 14	10 29		10 32	11 01				10 52	10 59

A ☕ from Reading ∅ to Reading

Table 116

Saturdays

7 January to 24 March

Birmingham, Banbury, Bicester, Oxford and Bedwyn - Reading and London

Network Diagram - see first Page of Table 116

		GW ◇1 ☕	GW 1	GW ◇1 ☕	GW 1	XC ◇1 🛒	CH	GW 1		GW ◇1 ☕	GW ◇1 ☕	GW ◇1 ☕	GW 1	GW 1	XC ◇1 🛒	GW 1	GW ◇1	GW 1		GW 1	XC ◇1 🛒	GW 1	GW ◇1 ☕	GW ◇1 🛒	GW 1
Birmingham New Street 12	d					09 04									09 33						10 04				
Birmingham International	d					09 14															10 14				
Coventry	d					09 25															10 25				
Leamington Spa 8	d					09 38									10 00						10 38				
Banbury	d					09 55									10 19						10 55				11 02
Kings Sutton	d																								11 08
Heyford	d																								11 17
Tackley	d																								11 21
Bicester Town	d						09 57																		
Islip	d						10 08																		
Oxford	a					10 14	10 23								10 40						11 14				11 32
	d				10 07	10 16					10 31			10 37	10 43		11 01			11 07	11 16			11 31	
Radley	d				10 13															11 13					
Culham	d																								
Appleford	d				10 17																				
Didcot Parkway	a				10 23									10 49						11 24					
	d	10 17		10 22	10 31					10 29		10 47		11 01						11 31			11 29		
Cholsey	d				10 37									11 07						11 37					
Goring & Streatley	d				10 42									11 12						11 42					
Pangbourne	d				10 47									11 17						11 47					
Tilehurst	d				10 51									11 21						11 51					
Bedwyn	d															10 40									
Hungerford	d															10 46									
Kintbury	d															10 50									
Newbury	a															10 57									
	d							10 13								10 57						11 13			
Newbury Racecourse	d							10 15														11 15			
Thatcham	d							10 20								11 02						11 20			
Midgham	d							10 24														11 24			
Aldermaston	d							10 28														11 28			
Theale	d							10 33								11 10						11 33			
Reading West	d		←					10 40					←					←				11 40			
Reading 7	a	10 32	10 27	10 36	10 58	10 39		10 44		10 45	10 54	11 01	10 58	11 27	11 09	11 21	11 24	11 27		11 58	11 39	11 44	11 44	11 54	
	d	10 33	10 33	10 39	11 03					10 46	10 55	11 02	11 03	11 33		11 21	11 25	11 33		12 03			11 45	11 55	
Twyford 3	a		10 39		→								11 09	→				11 39		→					
Maidenhead 3	a		10 47										11 17					11 47							
Slough 3	a		10 54								11 09		11 24				11 39	11 54						12 09	
Ealing Broadway ⊖	a		11 19										11 49					12 19							
London Paddington 15 ⊖	a	11 02	11 31	11 08						11 14	11 29	11 33	12 01			11 52	11 59	12 31					12 14	12 29	

		GW ◇1 ☕	GW 1	GW 1		XC ◇1 🛒	CH	GW 1	GW ◇1 🛒	GW 1	GW ◇1 ☕	GW 1	XC ◇1 🛒	GW 1		GW ◇1 ☕	GW ◇1 🛒	GW ◇1 ☕	GW 1	GW 1	XC ◇1 🛒	GW ◇1 🛒	GW 1	GW 1	
Birmingham New Street 12	d					10 33							11 04								11 33				
Birmingham International	d												11 14												
Coventry	d												11 25												
Leamington Spa 8	d					11 00							11 38								12 00				
Banbury	d					11 19							11 55								12 19				
Kings Sutton	d																								
Heyford	d																								
Tackley	d																								
Bicester Town	d						11 30																		
Islip	d						11 41																		
Oxford	a					11 40	11 56						12 14								12 40				
	d			11 37		11 43			12 01			12 07	12 16				12 31			12 37	12 43	13 01		13 07	
Radley	d											12 13												13 13	
Culham	d																							13 17	
Appleford	d											12 17													
Didcot Parkway	a			11 49								12 24								12 49				13 24	
	d	11 47		12 01							12 22	12 31				12 29		12 47		13 01				13 31	
Cholsey	d			12 07								12 37								13 07				13 37	
Goring & Streatley	d			12 12								12 42								13 12				13 42	
Pangbourne	d			12 17								12 47								13 17				13 47	
Tilehurst	d			12 21								12 51								13 21				13 51	
Bedwyn	d							11 38																	
Hungerford	d							11 43																	
Kintbury	d							11 48																	
Newbury	a							11 55																	
	d							11 55						12 13											
Newbury Racecourse	d													12 15											
Thatcham	d							12 00						12 20											
Midgham	d													12 24											
Aldermaston	d													12 28											
Theale	d							12 08						12 33											
Reading West	d		←							←				12 40					←				←		
Reading 7	a	12 00	11 58	12 28		12 07		12 17	12 25	12 28	12 37	12 57	12 39	12 44		12 44	12 53	13 00	12 57	13 27	13 06	13 25	13 27	13 59	
	d	12 02	12 03	12 33				12 18	12 25	12 33	12 39	13 03				12 45	12 55	13 02	13 03	13 33		13 25	13 33	14 03	
Twyford 3	a		12 09	→						12 39		→							13 09	→			13 39	→	
Maidenhead 3	a		12 17							12 47									13 17				13 47		
Slough 3	a		12 24						12 40	12 54							13 09		13 24			13 40	13 54		
Ealing Broadway ⊖	a		12 49							13 19									13 49				14 19		
London Paddington 15 ⊖	a	12 32	13 01					12 52	12 59	13 31	13 07					13 12	13 30	13 33	14 01			13 59	14 31		

Table 116

Saturdays

7 January to 24 March

Birmingham, Banbury, Bicester, Oxford and Bedwyn - Reading and London

Network Diagram - see first Page of Table 116

		XC	CH	GW	GW	GW	GW	GW	GW	GW		GW	XC	GW	GW	GW	GW	GW	XC	GW		GW	GW	GW	GW
		◇1		1	◇1	1	◇1	1	◇1	1		1	◇1	◇1	◇1	1	◇1	1	◇1	1		◇1	◇1	◇1	1
																							A	A	
		🛒			☕				☕				🛒	☕	🛒		☕		🛒			☕	☕	☕	
Birmingham New Street 12	d	12 04											12 33						13 04						
Birmingham International	d	12 14																	13 14						
Coventry	d	12 25																	13 25						
Leamington Spa 8	d	12 38											13 02						13 38						
Banbury	d	12 55						13 02					13 21						13 55						
Kings Sutton	d							13 08																	
Heyford	d							13 17																	
Tackley	d							13 21																	
Bicester Town	d		13 00																						
Islip	d		13 11																						
Oxford	a	13 14	13 26					13 32					13 40						14 14						
	d	13 16					13 31					13 37	13 43		14 01			14 07	14 16				14 31		
Radley	d																	14 13							
Culham	d																								
Appleford	d																	14 17							
Didcot Parkway	a											13 51						14 24							
	d				13 29				13 47			14 01					14 22	14 31				14 29		14 47	
Cholsey	d											14 07						14 37							
Goring & Streatley	d											14 12						14 42							
Pangbourne	d											14 17						14 47							
Tilehurst	d											14 21						14 51							
Bedwyn	d					13 07								13 33											
Hungerford	d					13 13								13 40											
Kintbury	d					13 17																			
Newbury	a					13 24								13 49											
	d			13 13		13 28								13 50						14 13					
Newbury Racecourse	d			13 15																14 15					
Thatcham	d			13 20		13 33								13 57						14 20					
Midgham	d			13 24																14 24					
Aldermaston	d			13 28																14 28					
Theale	d			13 33		13 41								14 06						14 33					
Reading West	d			13 40						←						←				14 40					←
Reading 7	a	13 39		13 44	13 44	13 51	13 54		14 00	13 59		14 27	14 07	14 19	14 25	14 27	14 38	14 58	14 39	14 44		14 44	14 53	15 00	14 58
	d				13 45	13 51	13 55		14 02	14 03		14 33		14 19	14 25	14 33	14 39	15 03				14 45	14 55	15 02	15 03
Twyford 3	a									14 09		→				14 39		→							15 09
Maidenhead 3	a									14 17						14 47									15 17
Slough 3	a						14 09			14 24					14 40	14 54							15 10		15 24
Ealing Broadway ⊖	a									14 49						15 19									15 49
London Paddington 15 ⊖	a				14 14	14 23	14 29		14 32	15 01				14 45	14 59	15 31	15 09					15 14	15 29	15 32	16 01

		GW	XC	CH	GW	GW		GW	GW	XC	GW	GW	GW	GW	GW	GW		GW	XC	CH	GW	GW	GW	GW	GW
		1	◇1		1	◇1		1	1	◇1	1	◇1	◇1	1	◇1	1		1	◇1		1	◇1	1	◇1	1
			🛒							🛒		☕	🛒		☕				🛒					☕	
Birmingham New Street 12	d		13 33							14 04									14 33						
Birmingham International	d									14 14															
Coventry	d									14 25															
Leamington Spa 8	d		14 00							14 38									15 00						
Banbury	d		14 19							14 55				15 02					15 20						
Kings Sutton	d													15 08											
Heyford	d													15 17											
Tackley	d													15 21											
Bicester Town	d			14 18																15 28					
Islip	d			14 29																15 39					
Oxford	a		14 40	14 44						15 14				15 32					15 41	15 54					
	d	14 37	14 43			15 01			15 07	15 16			15 31					15 37	15 43			16 01			16 07
Radley	d								15 13																16 13
Culham	d								15 17																
Appleford	d																								16 17
Didcot Parkway	a	14 49							15 24									15 49							16 24
	d	15 01							15 31			15 29			15 47			16 01						16 22	16 31
Cholsey	d	15 07							15 37									16 07							16 37
Goring & Streatley	d	15 12							15 42									16 12							16 42
Pangbourne	d	15 17							15 47									16 17							16 47
Tilehurst	d	15 21							15 51									16 21							16 51
Bedwyn	d				14 38																15 38				
Hungerford	d				14 43																15 43				
Kintbury	d				14 48																15 48				
Newbury	a				14 55																15 55				
	d				14 55						15 13										15 55				
Newbury Racecourse	d										15 15														
Thatcham	d				15 00						15 20										16 00				
Midgham	d										15 24														
Aldermaston	d										15 28														
Theale	d				15 08						15 33										16 08				
Reading West	d							←			15 40					←							←		
Reading 7	a	15 27	15 07		15 17	15 25		15 27	15 59	15 39	15 44	15 44	15 54		16 00	15 59		16 29	16 08		16 17	16 25	16 29	16 38	16 58
	d	15 33			15 19	15 25		15 33	16 03			15 45	15 55		16 01	16 03		16 33			16 18	16 26	16 33	16 39	17 03
Twyford 3	a	→						15 39	→							16 09		→					16 39		→
Maidenhead 3	a							15 47								16 17							16 47		
Slough 3	a					15 40		15 54					16 10			16 24						16 40	16 54		
Ealing Broadway ⊖	a							16 19								16 49							17 19		
London Paddington 15 ⊖	a				15 54	15 59		16 31				16 14	16 29		16 32	17 01					16 52	16 59	17 31	17 07	

A from 7 January until 11 February

Table 116

Saturdays

7 January to 24 March

Birmingham, Banbury, Bicester, Oxford and Bedwyn - Reading and London

Network Diagram - see first Page of Table 116

		XC	GW	GW	GW	GW	GW	GW	XC	CH	GW	GW	GW	GW	XC	GW	GW	GW	GW	GW	GW	XC
		◇1	1	◇1	◇1	◇1	1	1	◇1		◇1	◇1	1	1	◇1	1	◇1	◇1	◇1	1	1	◇1
																			A			
		🛒		☕	🛒	☕			🛒		☕				🛒		☕	☕	☕			🛒
Birmingham New Street 12	d	15 04							15 33						16 04							16 33
Birmingham International	d	15 14													16 14							
Coventry	d	15 25													16 25							
Leamington Spa 8	d	15 38							16 02						16 38							17 00
Banbury	d	15 55							16 20						16 55							17 19
Kings Sutton	d																					
Heyford	d																					
Tackley	d																					
Bicester Town	d									16 30												
Islip	d									16 41												
Oxford	a	16 14							16 40	16 56					17 14							17 41
	d	16 16			16 31			16 37	16 43			17 01		17 07	17 16			17 31			17 37	17 43
Radley	d													17 13								
Culham	d													17 17								
Appleford	d																					
Didcot Parkway	a							16 49						17 24							17 49	
	d			16 29		16 47		17 01						17 31			17 29		17 47		18 01	
Cholsey	d							17 07						17 37							18 07	
Goring & Streatley	d							17 12						17 42							18 12	
Pangbourne	d							17 17						17 47							18 17	
Tilehurst	d							17 21						17 51							18 21	
Bedwyn	d										16 35					16 56						
Hungerford	d										16 42					17 00						
Kintbury	d															17 05						
Newbury	a										16 52					17 13						
	d		16 13								16 53					17 13						
Newbury Racecourse	d		16 15													17 15						
Thatcham	d		16 20								16 59					17 20						
Midgham	d		16 24													17 25						
Aldermaston	d		16 28													17 28						
Theale	d		16 33								17 08					17 33						
Reading West	d		16 40				←						←			17 40				←		
Reading 7	a	16 39	16 44	16 44	16 55	17 00	16 58	17 27	17 07		17 17	17 26	17 27	17 57	17 39	17 44	17 44	17 55	18 00	17 57	18 27	18 07
	d			16 45	16 55	17 02	17 03	17 33			17 18	17 27	17 33	18 03			17 45	17 57	18 02	18 03	18 33	
Twyford 3	a						17 09	→					17 39	→						18 09	→	
Maidenhead 3	a						17 17						17 47							18 17		
Slough 3	a				17 10		17 24					17 41	17 54					18 10		18 24		
Ealing Broadway ⊖	a						17 49						18 19							18 49		
London Paddington 15 ⊖	a			17 14	17 29	17 32	18 01				17 51	18 00	18 31				18 14	18 29	18 32	19 01		

		GW	GW	GW	GW	GW	GW	XC	CH	GW	GW	GW	GW	GW	GW	XC	GW	GW	GW	GW	XC	GW	GW
		1	1	◇1	1	◇1	1	◇1		1	◇1	◇1	◇1	1	1	◇1	1	◇1	1	1	◇1	1	◇1
												A					A						A
						☕		🛒			☕	🛒	☕			🛒					🛒		☕
Birmingham New Street 12	d							17 04								17 33					18 04		
Birmingham International	d							17 14													18 14		
Coventry	d							17 25													18 25		
Leamington Spa 8	d							17 38								18 02					18 38		
Banbury	d	17 23						17 55								18 19					18 55		
Kings Sutton	d	17 29																					
Heyford	d	17 38																					
Tackley	d	17 42																					
Bicester Town	d								18 04														
Islip	d								18 15														
Oxford	a	17 53						18 14	18 30							18 40					19 14		
	d			18 01			18 07	18 16				18 31			18 37	18 43		19 01		19 07	19 16		
Radley	d						18 13													19 13			
Culham	d																			19 17			
Appleford	d						18 17																
Didcot Parkway	a						18 24								18 49					19 24			
	d					18 22	18 31				18 29		18 47		19 01					19 31			19 29
Cholsey	d						18 37								19 07					19 37			
Goring & Streatley	d						18 42								19 12					19 42			
Pangbourne	d						18 47								19 17					19 47			
Tilehurst	d						18 51								19 21					19 51			
Bedwyn	d		17 38														18 38						
Hungerford	d		17 43														18 43						
Kintbury	d		17 48														18 48						
Newbury	a		17 55														18 55						
	d		17 55							18 13							18 55					19 13	
Newbury Racecourse	d									18 15												19 15	
Thatcham	d		18 00							18 20							19 00					19 20	
Midgham	d									18 24												19 24	
Aldermaston	d									18 28												19 28	
Theale	d		18 08							18 33							19 08					19 33	
Reading West	d				←					18 40				←					←			19 40	
Reading 7	a		18 18	18 25	18 27	18 38	18 58	18 39		18 44	18 44	18 55	19 00	18 58	19 29	19 07	19 17	19 25	19 29	19 57	19 39	19 44	19 44
	d		18 19	18 25	18 33	18 39	19 03				18 45	18 56	19 02	19 03	19 33		19 20	19 25	19 33	20 03			19 45
Twyford 3	a				18 39		→							19 09	→				19 39	→			
Maidenhead 3	a				18 47									19 17					19 47				
Slough 3	a			18 40	18 54							19 10		19 24				19 40	19 54				
Ealing Broadway ⊖	a				19 19									19 49					20 19				
London Paddington 15 ⊖	a		18 52	18 59	19 31	19 08					19 14	19 29	19 32	20 01			19 52		19 59	20 31			20 14

A from 7 January until 11 February

Saturdays

7 January to 24 March

Birmingham, Banbury, Bicester, Oxford and Bedwyn - Reading and London

Network Diagram - see first Page of Table 116

		GW	GW	GW		GW	GW	GW	XC	CH	GW	GW	GW	GW		GW	XC	GW	GW	GW	GW	XC	GW	CH
		◇1	1	◇1		1	◇1	1	◇1		◇1	1	1	◇1		1	◇1	◇1	◇1	1	◇1	◇1	1	
		[trolley]		[buffet]			[buffet]		[trolley]					[buffet]			[trolley]	[buffet]			[buffet]	[trolley]		
Birmingham New Street 12	d								18 33								19 04					19 33		
Birmingham International	d																19 14							
Coventry	d																19 25							
Leamington Spa 8	d								19 00								19 38					20 03		
Banbury	d		19 02						19 19								19 55					20 21		
Kings Sutton	d		19 08																					
Heyford	d		19 17																					
Tackley	d		19 21																					
Bicester Town	d									19 17														20 28
Islip	d									19 28														20 39
Oxford	a		19 32						19 40	19 43							20 14					20 40		20 54
	d	19 31						19 37	19 43		20 01					20 07	20 16		20 31			20 43	20 53	
Radley	d															20 13								
Culham	d																							
Appleford	d															20 17								
Didcot Parkway	a							19 49								20 24							21 05	
	d			19 47				20 01						20 23		20 31		20 29			20 47		21 09	
Cholsey	d							20 07								20 37							21 15	
Goring & Streatley	d							20 12								20 42							21 20	
Pangbourne	d							20 17								20 47								
Tilehurst	d							20 21								20 51							21 29	
Bedwyn	d											19 41												
Hungerford	d											19 47												
Kintbury	d											19 51												
Newbury	a											19 58												
	d						19 46					19 58												
Newbury Racecourse	d											20 00												
Thatcham	d											20 05												
Midgham	d											20 10												
Aldermaston	d											20 13												
Theale	d											20 18												
Reading West	d					←						20 25	←							←				
Reading 7	a	19 55		20 00		19 57	20 07	20 29	20 10		20 25	20 28	20 29	20 38		20 57	20 39	20 44	20 54	20 57	21 06	21 10	21 36	
	d	19 55		20 03		20 03	20 09	20 33			20 25		20 33	20 39		20 59		20 45	20 54	20 59	21 08		21 37	
Twyford 3	a					20 09		→					20 39			→				21 05			→	
Maidenhead 3	a					20 17							20 47							21 13				
Slough 3	a	20 10				20 24					20 40		20 54						21 09	21 20				
Ealing Broadway ⊖	a					20 49							21 19							21 49				
London Paddington 15 ⊖	a	20 29		20 32		21 01	20 37				20 59		21 31	21 07				21 14	21 29	22 02	21 36			

		GW	GW	GW	GW	XC	GW	GW	GW	GW		CH	GW	XC	GW	GW	GW	GW	GW	GW		GW	GW	CH
		◇1	1	1	1	◇1	◇1	◇1	◇1	1			◇1	◇1	1	1	◇1	◇1	◇1	1		◇1	1	
						[trolley]	[buffet]		[buffet]								[buffet]					[buffet]		
Birmingham New Street 12	d					20 04								21 04										
Birmingham International	d					20 14								21 14										
Coventry	d					20 25								21 25										
Leamington Spa 8	d					20 38								21 38										
Banbury	d			20 38		20 55								21 55	22 00									
Kings Sutton	d			20 44											22 06									
Heyford	d			20 53											22 15									
Tackley	d			20 57											22 19									
Bicester Town	d											21 37												22 55
Islip	d											21 48												23 06
Oxford	a			21 08		21 14						22 03		22 16	22 30									23 21
	d	20 59				21 16		21 31		21 50			22 10	22 18				22 35	23 01				23 13	
Radley	d									21 56													23 19	
Culham	d																						23 23	
Appleford	d																						23 26	
Didcot Parkway	a							21 43		22 04			22 21					22 47	23 13				23 31	
	d						21 34	21 45	21 47	22 04			22 22				22 49	22 51	23 14			23 30	23 40	
Cholsey	d									22 10													23 46	
Goring & Streatley	d									22 15													23 51	
Pangbourne	d																							
Tilehurst	d									22 24													23 58	
Bedwyn	d				20 48											22 00				23 00				
Hungerford	d				20 54											22 06				23 06				
Kintbury	d				20 58											22 10				23 10				
Newbury	a				21 05											22 17				23 17				
	d				21 05											22 17				23 17				
Newbury Racecourse	d				21 07											22 19				23 19				
Thatcham	d				21 12											22 24				23 24				
Midgham	d				21 17											22 29				23 29				
Aldermaston	d				21 20											22 32				23 32				
Theale	d				21 25											22 37				23 37				
Reading West	d		←		21 32											22 44				23 44				
Reading 7	a	21 23	21 36		21 36	21 40	21 52	21 58	21 59	22 31			22 37	22 41		22 48	23 04	23 08	23 29	23 48		23 51	00 04	
	d	21 25	21 37				21 54	22 00	22 03	22 33			22 38				23 05	23 09	23 29			23 51	00 06	
Twyford 3	a		21 43							22 40													00 13	
Maidenhead 3	a		21 51							22 47													00 21	
Slough 3	a	21 40	21 58					22 13		22 54			22 52					23 26	23 44				00 32	
Ealing Broadway ⊖	a		22 23							23 19													00 58	
London Paddington 15 ⊖	a	21 59	22 32				22 22	22 31	22 38	23 29			23 11				23 36	23 46	00 10			00 34	01 08	

Table 116

Saturdays
from 31 March

Birmingham, Banbury, Bicester, Oxford and Bedwyn - Reading and London

Network Diagram - see first Page of Table 116

		GW	GW	GW	CH	GW	CH	GW	GW	GW		GW	GW	GW	GW	GW	GW	GW	GW	GW		GW	GW	GW	XC
		◇1	◇1 ☕	◇1		1		1	1	1		◇1 ☕	1	1	◇1	1	◇1 ☕	1	1	◇1		◇1 ☕	1	1	◇1 🛒
Birmingham New Street 12	d																								06 04
Birmingham International	d																								06 14
Coventry	d																								06 25
Leamington Spa 8	d						23p38																		06 38
Banbury	d					23p45	23p57																		06 55
Kings Sutton	d					23p50																			
Heyford	d					23p58																			
Tackley	d					00 03																			
Bicester Town	d				23p42																				
Islip	d				23p53																				
Oxford	a				00 08	00 13	00 22																		07 14
	d	23p09		00 07		00 27		03 59	05 14	05 49				06 07	06 31				06 42	07 01				07 07	07 16
Radley	d					00 33			05 20					06 13										07 13	
Culham	d					00 37			05 24															07 17	
Appleford	d					00 39								06 17											
Didcot Parkway	a	23p23		00 20		00 46		04 10	05 31	06 01				06 24					06 54					07 24	
	d	23p23	23p35	00 22		00 46		04 10	05 31	06 01		06 29		06 31			06 59		07 01			07 17		07 31	
Cholsey	d					00 52			05 37	06 07				06 37					07 07					07 37	
Goring & Streatley	d					00 57			05 42	06 12				06 42					07 12					07 42	
Pangbourne	d					01 01			05 47	06 17				06 47					07 17					07 47	
Tilehurst	d					01 06			05 51	06 21				06 51					07 21					07 51	
Bedwyn	d												06 05					06 39							
Hungerford	d												06 11					06 43							
Kintbury	d												06 15					06 48							
Newbury	a												06 22					06 55							
	d												06 22					06 55							
Newbury Racecourse	d												06 24												
Thatcham	d												06 29					07 00							
Midgham	d												06 34												
Aldermaston	d												06 37												
Theale	d												06 42					07 08							
Reading West	d												06 49			←							←		
Reading 7	a	23p40	23p53	00 38		01 12		04 27	05 57	06 27		06 43	06 52	06 57	07 00	06 57	07 14	07 20	07 27	07 27		07 31	07 27	07 59	07 39
	d	23p45	23p55	00 38		01 12		04 40	06 03	06 33		06 45	06 52	07 03	07 00	07 03	07 15	07 21	07 33	07 27		07 32	07 33	08 03	
Twyford 3	a					01 18		04 46	06 09	06 39				→		07 09			→				07 39	→	
Maidenhead 3	a	23p58				01 26		04 54	06 17	06 47						07 17							07 47		
Slough 3	a	00 05		00 55		01 34		05 01	06 24	06 54					07 16	07 24				07 42			07 54		
Ealing Broadway ⊖	a					01 50		05 19	06 49	07 19						07 49							08 19		
London Paddington 15 ⊖	a	00 29	00 33	01 17		02 02		05 31	07 01	07 31		07 14	07 22		07 37	08 01	07 44	07 54		08 01		08 07	08 31		

		GW	GW	GW	GW	GW		GW	GW	XC	GW	GW	GW	CH	GW	GW		GW	XC	GW	GW	GW	GW	GW	GW
		1	◇1 ☕	◇1 ☕	1	◇1 ☕		1	1	◇1	◇1 ☕	1	◇1		◇1 ☕	1		1	◇1 🛒	1	◇1 ☕	◇1 ☕	◇1 ☕	◇1 ☕	1
Birmingham New Street 12	d									06 33									07 04						
Birmingham International	d																		07 14						
Coventry	d																		07 25						
Leamington Spa 8	d									07 00									07 38						
Banbury	d				07 02					07 19									07 55						
Kings Sutton	d				07 08																				
Heyford	d				07 17																				
Tackley	d				07 21																				
Bicester Town	d													07 36											
Islip	d													07 47											
Oxford	a				07 32					07 40				08 02					08 14						
	d			07 31					07 37	07 43			08 01					08 07	08 16				08 31		
Radley	d																	08 13							
Culham	d																								
Appleford	d																	08 17							
Didcot Parkway	a								07 49									08 24							
	d		07 29			07 47			08 01		07 59				08 17			08 31			08 29			08 47	
Cholsey	d								08 07									08 37							
Goring & Streatley	d								08 12									08 42							
Pangbourne	d								08 17									08 47							
Tilehurst	d								08 21									08 51							
Bedwyn	d											07 37													
Hungerford	d											07 41													
Kintbury	d											07 46													
Newbury	a											07 53													
	d	07 13										07 53								08 13		08 34			
Newbury Racecourse	d	07 15																		08 15					
Thatcham	d	07 20										07 58								08 20					
Midgham	d	07 24																		08 24					
Aldermaston	d	07 28																		08 28					
Theale	d	07 33										08 06								08 33					
Reading West	d	07 42						←								←				08 40					←
Reading 7	a	07 45	07 44	07 54		08 00		07 59	08 27	08 06	08 14	08 19	08 25		08 31	08 27		08 57	08 39	08 44	08 44	08 52	08 54	09 00	08 57
	d		07 46	07 54		08 02		08 03	08 33		08 16	08 20	08 26		08 32	08 33		09 03			08 46	08 52	08 55	09 02	09 03
Twyford 3	a							08 09	→							08 39		→							09 09
Maidenhead 3	a							08 17								08 47									09 17
Slough 3	a			08 09				08 24					08 40			08 54							09 09		09 24
Ealing Broadway ⊖	a							08 49								09 19									09 49
London Paddington 15 ⊖	a		08 14	08 29		08 32		09 01			08 44	08 52	08 59		09 02	09 31					09 14	09 21	09 29	09 32	10 01

Table 116

Saturdays
from 31 March

Birmingham, Banbury, Bicester, Oxford and Bedwyn - Reading and London

Network Diagram - see first Page of Table 116

		GW		GW	XC	GW	GW	GW	GW	GW	GW	GW		CH	XC	GW	GW	GW	GW	GW	GW	XC		GW	GW
		◇1		1	◇1	◇1	1	◇1	◇1	1	1	1			◇1	◇1	◇1	1	◇1	1	1	◇1		1	◇1
									A								A		A						
		☕			🛒	☕		🛒	☕⊘						🛒	☕	☕⊘		☕⊘			🛒			🛒
Birmingham New Street 12	d				07 33										08 04							08 33			
Birmingham International	d														08 14										
Coventry	d														08 25										
Leamington Spa 8	d				08 00										08 38							09 00			
Banbury	d				08 19										08 55			09 02				09 19			
Kings Sutton	d																	09 08							
Heyford	d																	09 17							
Tackley	d																	09 21							
Bicester Town	d													08 45											
Islip	d													08 56											
Oxford	a				08 40									09 11	09 14			09 32				09 40			
	d			08 37	08 43			09 01				09 07			09 16		09 31				09 37	09 43			10 01
Radley	d											09 13													
Culham	d											09 17													
Appleford	d																								
Didcot Parkway	a			08 49								09 24									09 49				
	d	08 52		09 01		08 59			09 17			09 31				09 29			09 47		10 01				
Cholsey	d			09 07								09 37									10 07				
Goring & Streatley	d			09 12								09 42									10 12				
Pangbourne	d			09 17								09 47									10 17				
Tilehurst	d			09 21								09 51									10 21				
Bedwyn	d						08 38																	09 37	
Hungerford	d						08 43																	09 41	
Kintbury	d						08 48																	09 46	
Newbury	a						08 55																	09 53	
	d						08 55				09 03													09 53	
Newbury Racecourse	d										09 06														
Thatcham	d						09 00				09 11													09 58	
Midgham	d										09 16														
Aldermaston	d										09 19														
Theale	d						09 08				09 24													10 06	
Reading West	d									←	09 31									←					
Reading 7	a	09 07		09 27	09 11	09 14	09 20	09 24	09 32	09 27	09 35	09 57			09 39	09 45	09 54		10 00	09 57	10 27	10 07		10 17	10 25
	d	09 09		09 33		09 16	09 20	09 24	09 33	09 33		10 03				09 46	09 55		10 02	10 03	10 33			10 18	10 25
Twyford 3	a			→						09 39		→								10 09	→				
Maidenhead 3	a									09 47										10 17					
Slough 3	a							09 40		09 54							10 09			10 24					10 40
Ealing Broadway ⊖	a									10 19										10 49					
London Paddington 15 ⊖	a	09 37				09 44	09 52	09 59	10 02	10 31						10 14	10 29		10 32	11 01				10 52	10 59

		GW	GW	GW	GW	XC	CH	GW		GW	GW	GW	GW	GW	XC	GW	GW	GW		GW	XC	GW	GW	GW	GW
		◇1	1	◇1	1	◇1		1		◇1	◇1	◇1	1	1	◇1	1	◇1	1		1	◇1	1	◇1	◇1	1
		☕		☕		🛒				☕	☕	☕			🛒						🛒		☕	🛒	
Birmingham New Street 12	d					09 04									09 33						10 04				
Birmingham International	d					09 14															10 14				
Coventry	d					09 25															10 25				
Leamington Spa 8	d					09 38									10 00						10 38				
Banbury	d					09 55									10 19						10 55				11 02
Kings Sutton	d																								11 08
Heyford	d																								11 17
Tackley	d																								11 21
Bicester Town	d						09 57																		
Islip	d						10 08																		
Oxford	a					10 14	10 23								10 40						11 14				11 32
	d				10 07	10 16					10 31			10 37	10 43		11 01			11 07	11 16			11 31	
Radley	d				10 13															11 13					
Culham	d																								
Appleford	d				10 17																				
Didcot Parkway	a				10 23									10 49						11 24					
	d	10 17		10 22	10 31					10 29		10 47		11 01						11 31			11 29		
Cholsey	d				10 37									11 07						11 37					
Goring & Streatley	d				10 42									11 12						11 42					
Pangbourne	d				10 47									11 17						11 47					
Tilehurst	d				10 51									11 21						11 51					
Bedwyn	d															10 40									
Hungerford	d															10 46									
Kintbury	d															10 50									
Newbury	a															10 57									
	d							10 13								10 57						11 13			
Newbury Racecourse	d							10 15														11 15			
Thatcham	d							10 20								11 02						11 20			
Midgham	d							10 24														11 24			
Aldermaston	d							10 28														11 28			
Theale	d							10 33								11 10						11 33			
Reading West	d		←					10 40					←					←				11 40			
Reading 7	a	10 32	10 27	10 36	10 58	10 39		10 44		10 45	10 54	11 01	10 58	11 27	11 09	11 21	11 24	11 27		11 58	11 39	11 44	11 44	11 54	
	d	10 33	10 33	10 39	11 03					10 46	10 55	11 02	11 03	11 33		11 21	11 25	11 33		12 03			11 45	11 55	
Twyford 3	a		10 39		→								11 09	→				11 39		→					
Maidenhead 3	a		10 47										11 17					11 47							
Slough 3	a		10 54								11 09		11 24				11 39	11 54						12 09	
Ealing Broadway ⊖	a		11 19										11 49					12 19							
London Paddington 15 ⊖	a	11 02	11 31	11 08						11 14	11 29	11 33	12 01			11 52	11 59	12 31					12 14	12 29	

A ☕ from Reading ⊘ to Reading

Table 116

Saturdays
from 31 March

Birmingham, Banbury, Bicester, Oxford and Bedwyn - Reading and London

Network Diagram - see first Page of Table 116

		GW	GW	GW		XC	CH	GW	GW	GW	GW	GW	XC	GW		GW	GW	GW	GW	GW	XC	GW	GW	GW	
		◇1	1	1		◇1		1	◇1	1	◇1	1	◇1	1		◇1	◇1	◇1	1	1	◇1	◇1	1	1	
		⊡				⊞			⊞		⊡		⊞			⊡	⊞	⊡			⊞	⊞			
Birmingham New Street 12	d					10 33							11 04								11 33				
Birmingham International	d												11 14												
Coventry	d												11 25												
Leamington Spa 8	d					11 00							11 38								12 00				
Banbury	d					11 19							11 55								12 19				
Kings Sutton	d																								
Heyford	d																								
Tackley	d																								
Bicester Town	d						11 30																		
Islip	d						11 41																		
Oxford	a					11 40	11 56						12 14								12 40				
	d			11 37		11 43			12 01			12 07	12 16				12 31			12 37	12 43	13 01		13 07	
Radley	d											12 13												13 13	
Culham	d																							13 17	
Appleford	d											12 17													
Didcot Parkway	a			11 49								12 24								12 49				13 24	
	d	11 47		12 01							12 22	12 31				12 29		12 47		13 01				13 31	
Cholsey	d			12 07								12 37								13 07				13 37	
Goring & Streatley	d			12 12								12 42								13 12				13 42	
Pangbourne	d			12 17								12 47								13 17				13 47	
Tilehurst	d			12 21								12 51								13 21				13 51	
Bedwyn	d							11 38																	
Hungerford	d							11 43																	
Kintbury	d							11 48																	
Newbury	a							11 55																	
	d							11 55						12 13											
Newbury Racecourse	d													12 15											
Thatcham	d							12 00						12 20											
Midgham	d													12 24											
Aldermaston	d													12 28											
Theale	d							12 08						12 33											
Reading West	d		←							←				12 40					←				←		
Reading 7	a	12 00	11 58	12 28		12 07		12 17	12 25	12 28	12 37	12 57	12 39	12 44		12 44	12 53	13 00	12 57	13 27	13 06	13 25	13 27	13 59	
	d	12 02	12 03	12 33				12 18	12 25	12 33	12 39	13 03				12 45	12 55	13 02	13 03	13 33		13 25	13 33	14 03	
Twyford 3	a		12 09	→						12 39		→							13 09	→			13 39	→	
Maidenhead 3	a		12 17							12 47									13 17				13 47		
Slough 3	a		12 24						12 40	12 54							13 09		13 24			13 40	13 54		
Ealing Broadway ⊖	a		12 49							13 19									13 49				14 19		
London Paddington 15 ⊖	a	12 32	13 01					12 52	12 59	13 31	13 07					13 12	13 30	13 33	14 01			13 59	14 31		

		XC	CH	GW	GW	GW	GW	GW	GW	GW		GW	XC	GW	GW	GW	GW	GW	XC	GW		GW	GW	GW	GW
		◇1		1	◇1	1	◇1	1	◇1	1		1	◇1	◇1	◇1	1	◇1	1	◇1	1		◇1	◇1	◇1	1
		⊞			⊡				⊡				⊞	⊡	⊞		⊡		⊞			⊡	⊡	⊡	
Birmingham New Street 12	d	12 04											12 33						13 04						
Birmingham International	d	12 14																	13 14						
Coventry	d	12 25																	13 25						
Leamington Spa 8	d	12 38											13 02						13 38						
Banbury	d	12 55						13 02					13 21						13 55						
Kings Sutton	d							13 08																	
Heyford	d							13 17																	
Tackley	d							13 21																	
Bicester Town	d		13 00																						
Islip	d		13 11																						
Oxford	a	13 14	13 26					13 32					13 40						14 14						
	d	13 16					13 31					13 37	13 43		14 01			14 07	14 16				14 31		
Radley	d																	14 13							
Culham	d																								
Appleford	d																	14 17							
Didcot Parkway	a											13 51						14 24							
	d				13 29				13 47			14 01					14 22	14 31				14 29		14 47	
Cholsey	d											14 07						14 37							
Goring & Streatley	d											14 12						14 42							
Pangbourne	d											14 17						14 47							
Tilehurst	d											14 21						14 51							
Bedwyn	d					13 07								13 33											
Hungerford	d					13 13								13 40											
Kintbury	d					13 17																			
Newbury	a					13 24								13 49											
	d			13 13		13 28								13 50						14 13					
Newbury Racecourse	d			13 15																14 15					
Thatcham	d			13 20		13 33								13 57						14 20					
Midgham	d			13 24																14 24					
Aldermaston	d			13 28																14 28					
Theale	d			13 33		13 41								14 06						14 33					
Reading West	d			13 40						←						←				14 40					←
Reading 7	a	13 39		13 44	13 44	13 51	13 54		14 00	13 59		14 27	14 07	14 19	14 25	14 27	14 38	14 58	14 39	14 44		14 44	14 53	15 00	14 58
	d				13 45	13 51	13 55		14 02	14 03		14 33		14 19	14 25	14 33	14 39	15 03				14 45	14 55	15 02	15 03
Twyford 3	a									14 09		→				14 39		→							15 09
Maidenhead 3	a									14 17						14 47									15 17
Slough 3	a						14 09			14 24					14 40	14 54							15 10		15 24
Ealing Broadway ⊖	a									14 49						15 19									15 49
London Paddington 15 ⊖	a				14 14	14 23	14 29		14 32	15 01				14 45	14 59	15 31	15 09					15 14	15 29	15 32	16 01

Table 116

Saturdays

from 31 March

Birmingham, Banbury, Bicester, Oxford and Bedwyn - Reading and London

Network Diagram - see first Page of Table 116

		GW 1	XC ◇1 ⊼	CH	GW 1	GW ◇1		GW 1	GW 1	XC ◇1 ⊼	GW 1	GW ◇1 ⊡	GW ◇1 ⊼	GW 1	GW ◇1 ⊡	GW 1		GW 1	XC ◇1 ⊼	CH	GW 1	GW ◇1	GW 1	GW ◇1 ⊡	GW 1
Birmingham New Street 12	d		13 33							14 04									14 33						
Birmingham International	d									14 14															
Coventry	d									14 25															
Leamington Spa 8	d		14 00							14 38									15 00						
Banbury	d		14 19							14 55				15 02					15 20						
Kings Sutton	d													15 08											
Heyford	d													15 17											
Tackley	d													15 21											
Bicester Town	d			14 18																15 28					
Islip	d			14 29																15 39					
Oxford	a		14 40	14 44						15 14				15 32					15 41	15 54					
	d	14 37	14 43			15 01			15 07	15 16			15 31					15 37	15 43			16 01			16 07
Radley	d								15 13																16 13
Culham	d								15 17																
Appleford	d																								16 17
Didcot Parkway	a	14 49							15 24									15 49							16 24
	d	15 01							15 31			15 29			15 47			16 01						16 22	16 31
Cholsey	d	15 07							15 37									16 07							16 37
Goring & Streatley	d	15 12							15 42									16 12							16 42
Pangbourne	d	15 17							15 47									16 17							16 47
Tilehurst	d	15 21							15 51									16 21							16 51
Bedwyn	d				14 38																15 38				
Hungerford	d				14 43																15 43				
Kintbury	d				14 48																15 48				
Newbury	a				14 55																15 55				
	d				14 55						15 13										15 55				
Newbury Racecourse	d										15 15														
Thatcham	d				15 00						15 20										16 00				
Midgham	d										15 24														
Aldermaston	d										15 28														
Theale	d				15 08						15 33										16 08				
Reading West	d							←			15 40					←							←		
Reading 7	a	15 27	15 07		15 17	15 25		15 27	15 59	15 39	15 44	15 44	15 54		16 00	15 59		16 29	16 08		16 17	16 25	16 29	16 38	16 58
	d	15 33			15 19	15 25		15 33	16 03			15 45	15 55		16 01	16 03		16 33			16 18	16 26	16 33	16 39	17 03
Twyford 3	a	→						15 39	→							16 09		→					16 39		→
Maidenhead 3	a							15 47								16 17							16 47		
Slough 3	a					15 40		15 54					16 10			16 24						16 40	16 54		
Ealing Broadway ⊖	a							16 19								16 49							17 19		
London Paddington 15 ⊖	a				15 54	15 59		16 31				16 14	16 29		16 32	17 01					16 52	16 59	17 31	17 07	

		XC ◇1 ⊼		GW 1	GW ◇1 ⊡	GW ◇1 ⊼	GW ◇1 ⊡	GW 1	GW 1	XC ◇1 ⊼	CH	GW ◇1 ⊡		GW ◇1	GW 1	GW 1	XC ◇1 ⊼	GW 1	GW ◇1 ⊡	GW ◇1 ⊡	GW ◇1 ⊡	GW 1		GW 1	XC ◇1 ⊼
Birmingham New Street 12	d	15 04								15 33							16 04								16 33
Birmingham International	d	15 14															16 14								
Coventry	d	15 25															16 25								
Leamington Spa 8	d	15 38								16 02							16 38								17 00
Banbury	d	15 55								16 20							16 55								17 19
Kings Sutton	d																								
Heyford	d																								
Tackley	d																								
Bicester Town	d										16 30														
Islip	d										16 41														
Oxford	a	16 14								16 40	16 56						17 14								17 41
	d	16 16				16 31			16 37	16 43				17 01		17 07	17 16			17 31				17 37	17 43
Radley	d															17 13									
Culham	d															17 17									
Appleford	d																								
Didcot Parkway	a								16 49							17 24								17 49	
	d				16 29		16 47		17 01							17 31			17 29		17 47			18 01	
Cholsey	d								17 07							17 37								18 07	
Goring & Streatley	d								17 12							17 42								18 12	
Pangbourne	d								17 17							17 47								18 17	
Tilehurst	d								17 21							17 51								18 21	
Bedwyn	d											16 35						16 56							
Hungerford	d											16 42						17 00							
Kintbury	d																	17 05							
Newbury	a											16 52						17 13							
	d			16 13								16 53						17 13							
Newbury Racecourse	d			16 15														17 15							
Thatcham	d			16 20								16 59						17 20							
Midgham	d			16 24														17 25							
Aldermaston	d			16 28														17 28							
Theale	d			16 33								17 08						17 33							
Reading West	d			16 40				←							←			17 40				←			
Reading 7	a	16 39		16 44	16 44	16 55	17 00	16 58	17 27	17 07		17 17		17 26	17 27	17 57	17 39	17 44	17 44	17 55	18 00	17 57		18 27	18 07
	d				16 45	16 55	17 02	17 03	17 33			17 18		17 27	17 33	18 03			17 45	17 57	18 02	18 03		18 33	
Twyford 3	a							17 09	→						17 39	→						18 09		→	
Maidenhead 3	a							17 17							17 47							18 17			
Slough 3	a					17 10		17 24						17 41	17 54					18 10		18 24			
Ealing Broadway ⊖	a							17 49							18 19							18 49			
London Paddington 15 ⊖	a				17 14	17 29	17 32	18 01				17 51		18 00	18 31				18 14	18 29	18 32	19 01			

Table 116

Saturdays

from 31 March

Birmingham, Banbury, Bicester, Oxford and Bedwyn - Reading and London

Network Diagram - see first Page of Table 116

		GW	GW	GW	GW	GW	GW	XC		CH	GW	GW	GW	GW	GW	GW	XC	GW		GW	GW	GW	XC	GW	GW
		1	1	◇1	1	◇1	1	◇1			1	◇1	◇1	◇1	1	1	◇1	1		◇1	1	1	◇1	1	◇1
						☕		🛒				☕	🛒	☕			🛒						🛒		☕
Birmingham New Street 12	d							17 04									17 33						18 04		
Birmingham International	d							17 14															18 14		
Coventry	d							17 25															18 25		
Leamington Spa 8	d							17 38									18 02						18 38		
Banbury	d	17 23						17 55									18 19						18 55		
Kings Sutton	d	17 29																							
Heyford	d	17 38																							
Tackley	d	17 42																							
Bicester Town	d									18 04															
Islip	d									18 15															
Oxford	a	17 53						18 14		18 30							18 40						19 14		
	d			18 01			18 07	18 16					18 31			18 37	18 43			19 01		19 07	19 16		
Radley	d						18 13															19 13			
Culham	d																					19 17			
Appleford	d						18 17																		
Didcot Parkway	a						18 24									18 49						19 24			
	d					18 22	18 31					18 29		18 47		19 01						19 31			19 29
Cholsey	d						18 37									19 07						19 37			
Goring & Streatley	d						18 42									19 12						19 42			
Pangbourne	d						18 47									19 17						19 47			
Tilehurst	d						18 51									19 21						19 51			
Bedwyn	d		17 38															18 38							
Hungerford	d		17 43															18 43							
Kintbury	d		17 48															18 48							
Newbury	a		17 55															18 55							
	d		17 55								18 13							18 55						19 13	
Newbury Racecourse	d										18 15													19 15	
Thatcham	d		18 00								18 20							19 00						19 20	
Midgham	d										18 24													19 24	
Aldermaston	d										18 28													19 28	
Theale	d		18 08								18 33							19 08						19 33	
Reading West	d				←						18 40				←						←			19 40	
Reading 7	a		18 18	18 25	18 27	18 38	18 58	18 39			18 44	18 44	18 55	19 00	18 58	19 29	19 07	19 17		19 25	19 29	19 57	19 39	19 44	19 44
	d		18 19	18 25	18 33	18 39	19 03					18 45	18 56	19 02	19 03	19 33		19 20		19 25	19 33	20 03			19 45
Twyford 3	a				18 39		→								19 09	→					19 39	→			
Maidenhead 3	a				18 47										19 17						19 47				
Slough 3	a			18 40	18 54								19 10		19 24					19 40	19 54				
Ealing Broadway ⊖	a				19 19										19 49						20 19				
London Paddington 15 ⊖	a		18 52	18 59	19 31	19 08						19 14	19 29	19 32	20 01			19 52		19 59	20 31				20 14

		GW	GW	GW		GW	GW	GW	XC	CH	GW	GW	GW	GW		GW	XC	GW	GW	GW	GW	GW	XC	CH	
		◇1	1	◇1		1	◇1	1	◇1		◇1	1	1	◇1		1	◇1	◇1	◇1	1	◇1	1	◇1		
		🛒		☕			☕		🛒					☕			🛒	☕			☕		🛒		
Birmingham New Street 12	d								18 33								19 04						19 33		
Birmingham International	d																19 14								
Coventry	d																19 25								
Leamington Spa 8	d								19 00								19 38						20 03		
Banbury	d		19 02						19 19								19 55						20 21		
Kings Sutton	d		19 08																						
Heyford	d		19 17																						
Tackley	d		19 21																						
Bicester Town	d									19 17														20 28	
Islip	d									19 28														20 39	
Oxford	a		19 32						19 40	19 43							20 14						20 40	20 54	
	d	19 31						19 37	19 43		20 01					20 07	20 16		20 31			20 37	20 43		
Radley	d															20 13									
Culham	d																								
Appleford	d															20 17									
Didcot Parkway	a							19 49								20 24						20 49			
	d			19 47				20 01						20 23		20 31		20 29			20 47	21 01			
Cholsey	d							20 07								20 37						21 07			
Goring & Streatley	d							20 12								20 42						21 12			
Pangbourne	d							20 17								20 47						21 17			
Tilehurst	d							20 21								20 51						21 21			
Bedwyn	d											19 41													
Hungerford	d											19 47													
Kintbury	d											19 51													
Newbury	a											19 58													
	d						19 46					19 58													
Newbury Racecourse	d											20 00													
Thatcham	d											20 05													
Midgham	d											20 10													
Aldermaston	d											20 13													
Theale	d											20 18													
Reading West	d					←						20 25	←							←					
Reading 7	a	19 55		20 00		19 57	20 07	20 29	20 10		20 25	20 28	20 29	20 38		20 57	20 39	20 44	20 54	20 57	21 06	21 27	21 10		
	d	19 55		20 03		20 03	20 09	20 33			20 25		20 33	20 39		21 03		20 45	20 54	21 03	21 08	21 33			
Twyford 3	a					20 09		→					20 39			→				21 09		→			
Maidenhead 3	a					20 17							20 47							21 17					
Slough 3	a	20 10				20 24					20 40		20 54						21 09	21 24					
Ealing Broadway ⊖	a					20 49							21 19							21 49					
London Paddington 15 ⊖	a	20 29		20 32		21 01	20 37				20 59		21 31	21 07				21 14	21 29	22 02	21 36				

Table 116

Saturdays
from 31 March

Birmingham, Banbury, Bicester, Oxford and Bedwyn - Reading and London

Network Diagram - see first Page of Table 116

		GW	GW	GW	GW	XC	GW	GW	GW	GW		GW	GW	CH	XC	GW	GW	GW	GW	GW		GW	GW	GW	GW
		◇1	1	1	1	◇1	◇1	◇1	◇1	1		◇1	1		◇1	1	1	◇1	◇1	◇1		◇1	1	◇1	1
						🛒	☕		☕										☕					☕	
Birmingham New Street 12	d					20 04									21 04										
Birmingham International	d					20 14									21 14										
Coventry	d					20 25									21 25										
Leamington Spa 8	d					20 38									21 38										
Banbury	d			20 38		20 55									21 55	22 00									
Kings Sutton	d			20 44												22 06									
Heyford	d			20 53												22 15									
Tackley	d			20 57												22 19									
Bicester Town	d													21 37											
Islip	d													21 48											
Oxford	a			21 08		21 14								22 03	22 16	22 30									
	d	21 01				21 16		21 31		21 50		22 01			22 18			22 35				23 01			23 07
Radley	d									21 56															23 13
Culham	d																								23 17
Appleford	d																								23 20
Didcot Parkway	a							21 43		22 04		22 12						22 47				23 13			23 25
	d						21 34	21 45	21 47	22 04		22 13						22 48	22 49			23 14		23 30	23 36
Cholsey	d									22 10															23 42
Goring & Streatley	d									22 15															23 49
Pangbourne	d									22 21															
Tilehurst	d									22 24															23 56
Bedwyn	d				20 48												22 00						23 00		
Hungerford	d				20 54												22 06						23 06		
Kintbury	d				20 58												22 10						23 10		
Newbury	a				21 05												22 17						23 17		
	d				21 05												22 17						23 17		
Newbury Racecourse	d				21 07												22 19						23 19		
Thatcham	d				21 12												22 24						23 24		
Midgham	d				21 17												22 29						23 29		
Aldermaston	d				21 20												22 32						23 32		
Theale	d				21 25												22 37						23 37		
Reading West	d		←		21 32								←				22 44			←			23 44		
Reading 7	a	21 25	21 27		21 36	21 40	21 48	21 59	21 59	22 31		22 28	22 31		22 41		22 48	23 08	23 04	23 08		23 29	23 48	23 49	00 02
	d	21 25	21 33				21 50	22 01	22 03	22 33		22 29	22 33					23 09	23 05	23 09		23 29		23 51	00 03
Twyford 3	a		21 39							↪			22 39					↪							00 10
Maidenhead 3	a		21 47										22 47												00 18
Slough 3	a	21 40	21 54					22 14				22 43	22 54							23 26		23 44			00 29
Ealing Broadway ⊖	a		22 19										23 19												00 53
London Paddington 15 ⊖	a	21 59	22 31				22 16	22 32	22 37			23 02	23 28						23 36	23 46		00 10		00 33	01 03

		CH
Birmingham New Street 12	d	
Birmingham International	d	
Coventry	d	
Leamington Spa 8	d	
Banbury	d	
Kings Sutton	d	
Heyford	d	
Tackley	d	
Bicester Town	d	22 55
Islip	d	23 06
Oxford	a	23 21
	d	
Radley	d	
Culham	d	
Appleford	d	
Didcot Parkway	a	
	d	
Cholsey	d	
Goring & Streatley	d	
Pangbourne	d	
Tilehurst	d	
Bedwyn	d	
Hungerford	d	
Kintbury	d	
Newbury	a	
	d	
Newbury Racecourse	d	
Thatcham	d	
Midgham	d	
Aldermaston	d	
Theale	d	
Reading West	d	
Reading 7	a	
	d	
Twyford 3	a	
Maidenhead 3	a	
Slough 3	a	
Ealing Broadway ⊖	a	
London Paddington 15 ⊖	a	

Table 116

Sundays

until 1 January

Birmingham, Banbury, Bicester, Oxford and Bedwyn - Reading and London

Network Diagram - see first Page of Table 116

		GW	GW	GW	GW	GW	GW	GW	GW	GW		GW	GW	GW	GW	GW	XC	CH	GW	GW		GW	GW	GW	GW
		◇1	◇1	1	1		1	◇1	1	◇1		1	◇1	◇1	1	1	◇1		◇1	◇1		◇1	1	◇1	1
		A	A	A																					
			☕			🚌		☕					☕				🛒		☕	☕					
Birmingham New Street 12	d																09 04								
Birmingham International	d																09 14								
Coventry	d																09 25								
Leamington Spa 8	d																09 38								
Banbury	d																09 55								
Kings Sutton	d																								
Heyford	d																								
Tackley	d																								
Bicester Town	d																	10 04							
Islip	d																	10 15							
Oxford	a																10 14	10 31							
	d	23p01		23p07		07 45				08 50		09 01		09 50		10 05	10 16					10 44		10 55	11 05
Radley	d			23p13								09 07				10 11									11 11
Culham	d			23p17																					
Appleford	d			23p20												10 16									
Didcot Parkway	a	23p13		23p25		08 10				09 02		09 16		10 02		10 21						10 58		11 07	11 20
	d	23p14	23p30	23p36	07 45		08 20	08 43		09 03		09 16	09 45	10 03		10 21				10 46		10 58		11 07	11 21
Cholsey	d			23p42			08 26					09 22				10 27									11 27
Goring & Streatley	d			23p47	07 53		08 32					09 27				10 33									11 33
Pangbourne	d			23p51			08 36					09 32				10 37									11 37
Tilehurst	d			23p56			08 41					09 36				10 42									11 42
Bedwyn	d														09 35								10 42		
Hungerford	d														09 41								10 48		
Kintbury	d														09 46								10 52		
Newbury	a														09 52								10 59		
	d								08 46						09 53				10 32				11 00		
Newbury Racecourse	d								08 48						09 55										
Thatcham	d								08 53						10 00								11 05		
Midgham	d								08 58						10 05										
Aldermaston	d								09 01						10 08										
Theale	d								09 06						10 13								11 13		
Reading West	d								09 14						10 21										
Reading 7	a	23p29	23p51	00 01	08 03		08 47	09 01	09 17	09 22		09 42	09 59	10 18	10 24	10 49	10 38		10 48	11 00		11 13	11 21	11 23	11 49
	d	23p29	23p51	00 03	08 03		08 52	09 03		09 23		09 52	10 00	10 20		10 52			10 49	11 02		11 14		11 23	11 52
Twyford 3	a			00 09			08 58					09 58				10 58						11 20			↦
Maidenhead 3	a			00 17			09 06					10 06				11 06						11 28			
Slough 3	a	23p44		00 28	08 20		09 14			09 38		10 14		10 35		11 14						11 35		11 42	
Ealing Broadway ⊖	a			00 52			09 42					10 42				11 42									
London Paddington 15 ⊖	a	00 10	00 34	01 02	08 44		09 51	09 44		10 00		10 51	10 44	10 59		11 50			11 29	11 44		11 58		12 06	

		XC	GW	GW	GW	GW		GW	CH	GW	GW	XC	GW	GW	GW	GW		GW	GW	GW	XC	CH	GW	GW	GW
		◇1	◇1	◇1	1	◇1		◇1		1	1	◇1	◇1	1	◇1	◇1		◇1	1	1	◇1		◇1	◇1	1
		☕	☕	☕		☕						☕	☕		☕	☕					☕		☕	☕	
Birmingham New Street 12	d	10 04										11 04									12 04				
Birmingham International	d	10 14										11 14									12 14				
Coventry	d	10 25										11 25									12 25				
Leamington Spa 8	d	10 38										11 38									12 38				
Banbury	d	10 55										11 55									12 55				
Kings Sutton	d																								
Heyford	d																								
Tackley	d																								
Bicester Town	d								11 33													13 03			
Islip	d								11 44													13 14			
Oxford	a	11 14							12 00			12 14									13 14	13 30			
	d	11 16						11 50			12 05	12 16						12 50		13 05	13 16				
Radley	d										12 11									13 11					
Culham	d																								
Appleford	d										12 16														
Didcot Parkway	a							12 02			12 21							13 01		13 20					
	d		11 29			11 47		12 03			12 21		12 29		12 47	12 59		13 02		13 21			13 29		
Cholsey	d										12 27									13 27					
Goring & Streatley	d										12 33									13 33					
Pangbourne	d										12 37									13 37					
Tilehurst	d										12 42									13 42					
Bedwyn	d																		12 42						
Hungerford	d																		12 48						
Kintbury	d																		12 52						
Newbury	a																		12 59						
	d			11 26						11 53									13 00					13 31	
Newbury Racecourse	d									11 55															
Thatcham	d									12 00									13 05						
Midgham	d									12 05															
Aldermaston	d									12 08															
Theale	d									12 13									13 13						
Reading West	d				↤					12 21				↤											↤
Reading 7	a	11 43	11 42	11 49	11 49	12 01		12 21		12 24	12 47	12 40	12 42	12 47	13 00	13 14		13 20	13 21	13 49	13 42		13 47	13 51	13 49
	d		11 44	11 51	11 52	12 02		12 23			12 52		12 44	12 52	13 02	13 15		13 20		13 52			13 49	13 51	13 52
Twyford 3	a				11 58						↦			12 58						↦					13 58
Maidenhead 3	a				12 06									13 06											14 06
Slough 3	a				12 14			12 38						13 14				13 36							14 14
Ealing Broadway ⊖	a				12 42									13 42											14 42
London Paddington 15 ⊖	a		12 21	12 29	12 50	12 44		13 03					13 22	13 51	13 44	13 59		14 02					14 22	14 29	14 50

A not 11 December

Table 116

Sundays
until 1 January

Birmingham, Banbury, Bicester, Oxford and Bedwyn - Reading and London

Network Diagram - see first Page of Table 116

		GW	XC	GW	GW	GW	XC	GW	GW	GW	XC	GW	GW	CH	GW	GW	XC	GW	GW	XC	GW	GW
		◇1	◇1	◇1	1	1	◇1	◇1	1	◇1	◇1	1	◇1		1	◇1	◇1	1	◇1	◇1	◇1	1
		☕	🛒				☕	☕		☕	🛒					☕	☕		☕	🛒	☕	
Birmingham New Street 12	d		12 33				13 04				13 33						14 04			14 33		
Birmingham International	d						13 14										14 14					
Coventry	d						13 25										14 25					
Leamington Spa 8	d		13 00				13 38				14 00						14 38			15 00		
Banbury	d		13 19				13 55				14 19						14 55			15 19		
Kings Sutton	d																					
Heyford	d																					
Tackley	d																					
Bicester Town	d													14 33								
Islip	d													14 44								
Oxford	a		13 41				14 14				14 38			15 00			15 14			15 41		
	d		13 43	13 50		14 05	14 17				14 43		14 50		15 05		15 16			15 43	15 50	
Radley	d					14 11									15 11							
Culham	d																					
Appleford	d					14 16																
Didcot Parkway	a			14 02		14 20							15 03		15 20						16 02	
	d	13 47		14 03		14 21		14 29		14 47			15 04		15 21	15 29			15 47		16 03	
Cholsey	d					14 27									15 27							
Goring & Streatley	d					14 33									15 33							
Pangbourne	d					14 37									15 37							
Tilehurst	d					14 42									15 42							
Bedwyn	d											14 42										
Hungerford	d											14 48										
Kintbury	d											14 52										
Newbury	a											14 59										
	d				13 53							15 00										15 53
Newbury Racecourse	d				13 55																	15 55
Thatcham	d				14 00							15 05										16 00
Midgham	d				14 05																	16 05
Aldermaston	d				14 08																	16 08
Theale	d				14 13							15 13										16 13
Reading West	d				14 21				←									←				16 21
Reading 7	a	14 00	14 09	14 21	14 24	14 49	14 43	14 42	14 49	15 00	15 07	15 21	15 21		15 49	15 42	15 45	15 49	16 00	16 07	16 20	16 24
	d	14 02		14 21		14 52		14 44	14 52	15 02			15 22		15 52	15 44		15 52	16 02		16 20	
Twyford 3	a					→			14 58						→			15 58				
Maidenhead 3	a								15 06									16 06				
Slough 3	a			14 37					15 14				15 36					16 14			16 33	
Ealing Broadway ⊖	a								15 42									16 42				
London Paddington 15 ⊖	a	14 44		14 59				15 21	15 50	15 44			15 59			16 22		16 51	16 44		16 59	

		GW	XC	CH	GW	GW	GW	GW	GW	XC	GW	GW	GW	GW	XC	GW	GW	GW	XC	GW	GW	CH	GW
		1	◇1		◇1	◇1	1	◇1	◇1	◇1	◇1	1	◇1	1	◇1	◇1	1	◇1	◇1	◇1	◇1		1
			☕		☕	☕		☕		🛒	☕		☕		☕	☕		☕	🛒	☕	☕		
Birmingham New Street 12	d		15 04							15 33					16 04				16 33				
Birmingham International	d		15 14												16 14								
Coventry	d		15 25												16 25								
Leamington Spa 8	d		15 38							16 00					16 38				17 00				
Banbury	d		15 55							16 19					16 55				17 19				
Kings Sutton	d																						
Heyford	d																						
Tackley	d																						
Bicester Town	d			16 03																		17 33	
Islip	d			16 14																		17 44	
Oxford	a		16 14	16 30						16 41					17 14				17 38			18 00	
	d	16 05	16 16						16 37	16 43			16 50	17 05	17 16				17 43		17 50		
Radley	d	16 11												17 11									
Culham	d																						
Appleford	d	16 16																					
Didcot Parkway	a	16 20							16 50				17 02	17 20							18 02		
	d	16 21			16 32			16 47	16 55		16 59		17 04	17 21		17 29		17 47		17 59	18 03		
Cholsey	d	16 27												17 27									
Goring & Streatley	d	16 33												17 33									
Pangbourne	d	16 37												17 37									
Tilehurst	d	16 42												17 42									
Bedwyn	d											16 42											
Hungerford	d											16 48											
Kintbury	d											16 52											
Newbury	a											16 59											
	d					16 31						17 00											17 53
Newbury Racecourse	d																						17 55
Thatcham	d											17 05											18 00
Midgham	d																						18 05
Aldermaston	d																						18 08
Theale	d											17 13											18 13
Reading West	d						←										←						18 21
Reading 7	a	16 49	16 40		16 46	16 48	16 49	17 00	17 12	17 11	17 13	17 21	17 21	17 49	17 38	17 42	17 49	18 01	18 13	18 14	18 21		18 24
	d	16 52			16 47	16 51	16 52	17 02	17 12		17 15		17 21	17 52		17 44	17 52	18 03		18 16	18 21		
Twyford 3	a	→					16 58		17 18					→			17 58						
Maidenhead 3	a						17 06		17 26								18 06						
Slough 3	a						17 14		17 35				17 40				18 14				18 36		
Ealing Broadway ⊖	a						17 42										18 42						
London Paddington 15 ⊖	a				17 22	17 30	17 51	17 43	18 03		17 58		18 06			18 22	18 51	18 44		18 59	19 02		

Table 116

Sundays

until 1 January

Birmingham, Banbury, Bicester, Oxford and Bedwyn - Reading and London

Network Diagram - see first Page of Table 116

		GW	XC	GW		GW	XC	GW	GW	GW	GW	GW	XC	CH		XC	GW	GW	GW	GW	GW	XC	GW	XC	
		1	◇1	◇1		◇1	◇1	◇1	1	◇1	◇1	1	◇1			◇1	◇1	◇1	1	◇1	1	◇1	◇1	◇1	
			☕	☕		☕	🛒	☕		☕	☕		☕			🛒	☕			☕		☕	☕	🛒	
Birmingham New Street 12	d		17 04				17 33						18 04			18 33						19 04		19 33	
Birmingham International	d		17 14										18 14									19 14			
Coventry	d		17 25										18 25									19 25			
Leamington Spa 8	d		17 38				18 01						18 38			19 00						19 38		20 00	
Banbury	d		17 55				18 20						18 55			19 19						19 55		20 19	
Kings Sutton	d																								
Heyford	d																								
Tackley	d																								
Bicester Town	d													19 07											
Islip	d													19 18											
Oxford	a		18 14				18 41						19 14	19 34		19 38						20 14		20 40	
	d	18 05	18 16				18 42			18 50		19 05	19 16			19 43		19 50			20 05	20 16		20 43	
Radley	d	18 11										19 11									20 11				
Culham	d																								
Appleford	d	18 16																							
Didcot Parkway	a	18 20								19 02		19 20						20 04			20 20				
	d	18 21				18 47		18 59		19 10	19 17	19 21					19 59	20 06		20 17	20 21				
Cholsey	d	18 27										19 27									20 27				
Goring & Streatley	d	18 33										19 33									20 33				
Pangbourne	d	18 37										19 37									20 37				
Tilehurst	d	18 42										19 42									20 42				
Bedwyn	d								18 42																
Hungerford	d								18 48																
Kintbury	d								18 52																
Newbury	a								18 59																
	d			18 34					19 00										19 53				20 19		
Newbury Racecourse	d																		19 55						
Thatcham	d								19 05										20 00						
Midgham	d																		20 05						
Aldermaston	d																		20 08						
Theale	d								19 13										20 13						
Reading West	d																		20 21						
Reading 7	a	18 49	18 40	18 51		19 00	19 07	19 12	19 21	19 28	19 32	19 49	19 40			20 13	20 21	20 23	20 24	20 32	20 46	20 42	20 45	21 11	
	d	18 52		18 53		19 02		19 14		19 28	19 34	19 52					20 23	20 23		20 32	20 52		20 47		
Twyford 3	a	18 58										19 58									20 58				
Maidenhead 3	a	19 06										20 06									21 06				
Slough 3	a	19 15								19 42		20 14						20 42			21 14				
Ealing Broadway ⊖	a	19 42										20 42									21 42				
London Paddington 15 ⊖	a	19 51		19 29		19 44		19 59		20 06	20 14	20 51					20 59	21 03		21 13	21 51		21 29		

		GW	GW	CH	GW	GW	XC	GW	GW	XC		GW	GW	GW	XC	GW	GW	CH	GW	GW	GW	GW	GW	GW	GW
		◇1	◇1		◇1	1	◇1	◇1	1	◇1		◇1	◇1	1	◇1	◇1	1		1	◇1	◇1			1	1
		☕			☕		☕	☕		🛒		☕				☕					☕	🚌			
Birmingham New Street 12	d						20 04			20 33					21 04										
Birmingham International	d						20 14								21 14										
Coventry	d						20 25								21 24										
Leamington Spa 8	d						20 38			21 00					21 35										
Banbury	d						20 55			21 19															
Kings Sutton	d																								
Heyford	d																								
Tackley	d																								
Bicester Town	d			20 33														22 03							
Islip	d			20 44														22 14							
Oxford	a			21 00			21 14			21 38					22 08			22 30							
	d		20 50				21 16		21 21	21 40			21 50		22 10		22 21			22 46		23 00			
Radley	d								21 27								22 27					23 15			
Culham	d																								
Appleford	d																								
Didcot Parkway	a		21 00						21 35				22 00				22 35			22 58		23 25			
	d	20 59	21 01		21 17			21 31	21 35			22 01	22 02				22 35			22 59	23 11			23 50	
Cholsey	d								21 41								22 41							23 56	
Goring & Streatley	d								21 46								22 46							00 01	
Pangbourne	d								21 51								22 51								
Tilehurst	d								21 55								22 55							00 09	
Bedwyn	d					20 54													22 35						
Hungerford	d					21 00													22 41						
Kintbury	d					21 04													22 45						
Newbury	a					21 11													22 52						
	d					21 12								21 53		22 19			22 53				23 23		23 45
Newbury Racecourse	d													21 55											23 47
Thatcham	d					21 17								22 00					22 58				23 28		23 52
Midgham	d													22 05											23 57
Aldermaston	d													22 08											00 01
Theale	d					21 25								22 13					23 06				23 36		00 06
Reading West	d													22 21											00s13
Reading 7	a	21 16	21 21		21 32	21 33	21 43	21 45	22 02	22 07		22 17	22 19	22 24	22 33	22 36	23 00		23 15	23 15	23 28		23 44	00 15	00 17
	d	21 18	21 22		21 32			21 47	22 10			22 18	22 22			22 37	23 00			23 22	23 30			00 15	
Twyford 3	a								22 16								23 06							00 21	
Maidenhead 3	a		21 35						22 24								23 14							00 29	
Slough 3	a		21 42						22 33				22 43				23 22			23 40				00 36	
Ealing Broadway ⊖	a								22 56								23 44							00 59	
London Paddington 15 ⊖	a	22 02	22 04		22 14			22 29	23 05			23 07	23 13			23 16	23 53			00 02	00 13			01 11	

Table 116

Sundays

8 January to 12 February

Birmingham, Banbury, Bicester, Oxford and Bedwyn - Reading and London

Network Diagram - see first Page of Table 116

		GW ◇1	GW ◇1 🍴	GW 1	GW 1	GW 🚌	GW 1	GW ◇1 🍴	GW 1	GW ◇1	GW 1	GW ◇1 🍴	GW ◇1	GW 1	GW 1	XC ◇1 trolley	CH	GW ◇1 🍴	GW ◇1 🍴	GW 1	GW ◇1	GW 1	GW ◇1
Birmingham New Street 12	d																						
Birmingham International	d																						
Coventry	d																						
Leamington Spa 8	d																						
Banbury	d																						
Kings Sutton	d																						
Heyford	d																						
Tackley	d																						
Bicester Town	d																10 04						
Islip	d																10 15						
Oxford	a																10 31						
	d	23p01		23p13		07 45				08 50	09 00		09 48		09 53	10 16				10 39	10 44		10 55
Radley	d			23p19							09 06				09 59					10 45			
Culham	d			23p23																			
Appleford	d			23p26											10 04								
Didcot Parkway	a	23p13		23p31		08 10				09 02	09 15		10 00		10 08					10 53	10 58		11 07
	d	23p14	23p30	23p40	08 00		08 25	08 42		09 03	09 15	09 45	10 01		10 09				10 46	11 13	10 58		11 07
Cholsey	d			23p46			08 31				09 21				10 15					↪			
Goring & Streatley	d			23p51	08 07		08 37				09 26				10 20								
Pangbourne	d																						
Tilehurst	d			23p58			08 47				09 36				10 30								
Bedwyn	d													09 35								10 42	
Hungerford	d													09 41								10 48	
Kintbury	d													09 46								10 52	
Newbury	a													09 52								10 59	
	d								08 46					09 53				10 32				11 00	
Newbury Racecourse	d								08 48					09 55									
Thatcham	d								08 53					10 00								11 05	
Midgham	d								08 58					10 05									
Aldermaston	d								09 01					10 08									
Theale	d								09 06					10 13								11 13	
Reading West	d								09 14					10 21									
Reading 7	a	23p29	23p51	00 04	08 17		08 51	09 01	09 17	09 22	09 42	09 59	10 21	10 24	10 34	10 38		10 48	11 00		11 13	11 21	11 23
	d	23p29	23p51	00 06	08 19		08 52	09 06		09 23	09 43	10 04	10 22		10 36			10 49	11 02		11 14		11 23
Twyford 3	a			00 13			08 58				09 49				10 46						11 20		
Maidenhead 3	a			00 21			09 06				09 57				10 54						11 28		
Slough 3	a	23p44		00 32	08 35		09 14			09 38	10 14		10 37		11 15						11 35		11 37
Ealing Broadway ⊖	a			00 58			09 42				10 41				11 42								
London Paddington 15 ⊖	a	00 10	00 34	01 08	08 59		09 52	09 44		10 00	10 51	10 44	10 59		11 51			11 29	11 44		11 56		12 01

		GW 1	XC 🚌	XC ◇1 🍴	GW ◇1 🍴	GW ◇1 🍴	GW ◇1 🍴	GW ◇1	GW 1	GW 1	CH	XC 🚌	XC ◇1 🍴	GW ◇1 🍴	GW ◇1 🍴	GW 1	GW ◇1 🍴	GW ◇1	GW 1	XC 🚌	XC ◇1 🍴	CH	GW ◇1 🍴
Birmingham New Street 12	d																						
Birmingham International	d																						
Coventry	d																						
Leamington Spa 8	d		09 45									10 45								11 45			
Banbury	d		10 25									11 25								12 25			
Kings Sutton	d																						
Heyford	d																						
Tackley	d																						
Bicester Town	d										11 33											13 03	
Islip	d										11 44											13 14	
Oxford	a		11 10								12 00	12 10								13 10		13 30	
	d			11 16				11 50		11 56			12 16					12 50	12 56		13 16		
Radley	d									12 02									13 02				
Culham	d																						
Appleford	d	←								12 07									13 07				
Didcot Parkway	a	10 53						12 02		12 12								13 02	13 12				
	d	11 13			11 29		11 47	12 03		12 12				12 29	12 47		12 59	13 03	13 13				13 29
Cholsey	d	11 19								12 17									13 19				
Goring & Streatley	d	11 24								12 23									13 25				
Pangbourne	d																						
Tilehurst	d	11 34								12 33									13 35				
Bedwyn	d															12 42							
Hungerford	d															12 48							
Kintbury	d															12 52							
Newbury	a															12 59							
	d					11 26			11 53							13 00							
Newbury Racecourse	d								11 55														
Thatcham	d								12 00							13 05							
Midgham	d								12 05														
Aldermaston	d								12 08														
Theale	d								12 13							13 13							
Reading West	d								12 21														
Reading 7	a	11 37		11 42	11 45	11 49	12 01	12 21	12 24	12 38			12 42	12 44	13 00	13 21	13 21	13 25	13 38		13 42		13 47
	d	11 42			11 47	11 51	12 02	12 23		12 42				12 44	13 02		13 23	13 25	13 42				13 49
Twyford 3	a	11 49								12 48									13 50				
Maidenhead 3	a	11 57								12 56									13 58				
Slough 3	a	12 15						12 38		13 15								13 41	14 15				
Ealing Broadway ⊖	a	12 42								13 42									14 42				
London Paddington 15 ⊖	a	12 51			12 22	12 29	12 44	13 03		13 51				13 22	13 44		13 59	14 04	14 51				14 22

Table 116

Sundays

8 January to 12 February

Birmingham, Banbury, Bicester, Oxford and Bedwyn - Reading and London

Network Diagram - see first Page of Table 116

		GW		GW	GW	GW	GW	XC	XC	GW	GW	XC		GW	GW	GW	CH	XC	GW	GW	XC	GW		GW	GW
		◇1		◇1	◇1	1	1		◇1	◇1	◇1	◇1		1	◇1	1		◇1	◇1	◇1	◇1	◇1		1	1
		☕		☕				🚌	☕	☕	☕	🛒						☕	☕	☕	🛒	☕			
Birmingham New Street 12	d											13 33						14 04			14 33				
Birmingham International	d																	14 14							
Coventry	d																	14 25							
Leamington Spa 8	d							12 45				14 00						14 38			15 00				
Banbury	d							13 25				14 19						14 55			15 19				
Kings Sutton	d																								
Heyford	d																								
Tackley	d																								
Bicester Town	d																14 33								
Islip	d																14 44								
Oxford	a							14 10				14 38					15 00	15 14			15 41				
	d				13 50		13 56		14 17			14 43			14 50	14 58		15 16			15 43	15 50			15 56
Radley	d						14 02									15 04									16 02
Culham	d																								
Appleford	d						14 07																		16 07
Didcot Parkway	a				14 02		14 11								15 03	15 12						16 02			16 11
	d			13 47	14 03		14 12			14 32	14 47				15 04	15 13			15 32	15 47		16 03			16 12
Cholsey	d						14 18									15 19									16 18
Goring & Streatley	d						14 24									15 25									16 24
Pangbourne	d																								
Tilehurst	d						14 34									15 35									16 34
Bedwyn	d													14 42											
Hungerford	d													14 48											
Kintbury	d													14 52											
Newbury	a													14 59											
	d	13 31				13 53								15 00										15 53	
Newbury Racecourse	d					13 55																		15 55	
Thatcham	d					14 00								15 05										16 00	
Midgham	d					14 05																		16 05	
Aldermaston	d					14 08																		16 08	
Theale	d					14 13								15 13										16 13	
Reading West	d					14 21																		16 21	
Reading 7	a	13 51		14 00	14 21	14 24	14 36		14 46	14 47	15 00	15 07		15 21	15 21	15 38		15 42	15 47	16 00	16 13	16 23		16 24	16 38
	d	13 51		14 06	14 21		14 42			14 49	15 06				15 22	15 44			15 49	16 06		16 24			16 44
Twyford 3	a						14 48									15 50									16 50
Maidenhead 3	a						14 58									15 58									16 58
Slough 3	a				14 37		15 15								15 36	16 14						16 37			17 16
Ealing Broadway ⊖	a						15 42									16 43									17 42
London Paddington 15 ⊖	a	14 29		14 44	14 59		15 51			15 22	15 44				15 59	16 51			16 22	16 44		17 02			17 51

		XC	CH	GW	GW	GW	GW	XC		GW	GW	GW	GW	XC	GW	GW	XC	GW		GW	GW	GW	CH	XC	GW
		◇1		◇1	◇1	◇1	◇1	◇1		◇1	1	◇1	1	◇1	◇1	◇1	◇1	◇1		◇1	1	1	1	◇1	◇1
		☕		☕	☕	☕		🛒		☕		☕		☕	☕	☕	🛒	☕		☕				☕	☕
Birmingham New Street 12	d	15 04						15 33						16 04			16 33							17 04	
Birmingham International	d	15 14												16 14										17 14	
Coventry	d	15 25												16 25										17 25	
Leamington Spa 8	d	15 38						16 00						16 38			17 00							17 38	
Banbury	d	15 55						16 19						16 55			17 19							17 55	
Kings Sutton	d																								
Heyford	d																								
Tackley	d																								
Bicester Town	d		16 03																				17 33		
Islip	d		16 14																				17 44		
Oxford	a	16 14	16 30					16 41						17 14			17 38						18 00	18 14	
	d	16 16					16 37	16 43				16 50	16 56	17 16			17 43			17 50		17 55		18 16	
Radley	d												17 02									18 02			
Culham	d																								
Appleford	d												17 07									18 07			
Didcot Parkway	a						16 49					17 02	17 12							18 02		18 10			
	d			16 32		16 47	16 51			17 00		17 10	17 14		17 29	17 47		17 59		18 03		18 12			
Cholsey	d												17 20									18 18			
Goring & Streatley	d												17 25									18 24			
Pangbourne	d																								
Tilehurst	d												17 35									18 33			
Bedwyn	d										16 42														
Hungerford	d										16 48														
Kintbury	d										16 52														
Newbury	a										16 59														
	d				16 31						17 00										17 53				18 34
Newbury Racecourse	d																				17 55				
Thatcham	d										17 05										18 00				
Midgham	d																				18 05				
Aldermaston	d																				18 08				
Theale	d										17 13										18 13				
Reading West	d																				18 21				
Reading 7	a	16 43		16 47	16 48	17 04	17 11	17 13		17 15	17 21	17 25	17 38	17 43	17 46	18 00	18 13	18 17		18 21	18 24	18 40		18 43	18 51
	d			16 49	16 51	17 06	17 12			17 17		17 27	17 42		17 49	18 06		18 19		18 21		18 44			18 53
Twyford 3	a						17 18						17 48									18 50			
Maidenhead 3	a						17 26						17 58									18 58			
Slough 3	a						17 34					17 43	18 15							18 36		19 16			
Ealing Broadway ⊖	a												18 42									19 42			
London Paddington 15 ⊖	a			17 22	17 30	17 43	17 58			18 01		18 06	18 51		18 22	18 44		18 58		19 03		19 51			19 29

Table 116

Sundays

8 January to 12 February

Birmingham, Banbury, Bicester, Oxford and Bedwyn - Reading and London

Network Diagram - see first Page of Table 116

		GW	XC	GW	GW	GW	GW	GW	GW	XC	CH	XC	GW	GW	GW	GW	GW	XC	GW	XC	GW	GW
		◇1	◇1	◇1	1	◇1	1	◇1	1	◇1		◇1	◇1	1	◇1	◇1	1	◇1	◇1	◇1	◇1	◇1
		⊡	⊥	⊡		⊡		⊡		⊡		⊥	⊡			⊡		⊡	⊡	⊥	⊡	
Birmingham New Street 12	d		17 33							18 04		18 33						19 04		19 33		
Birmingham International	d									18 14								19 14				
Coventry	d									18 25								19 25				
Leamington Spa 8	d		18 01							18 38		19 00						19 38		20 00		
Banbury	d		18 20							18 55		19 19						19 55		20 19		
Kings Sutton	d																					
Heyford	d																					
Tackley	d																					
Bicester Town	d										19 07											
Islip	d										19 18											
Oxford	a		18 41							19 14	19 34	19 38						20 14		20 40		
	d		18 43			18 50	18 56			19 16		19 43			19 50		20 05	20 16		20 43		20 50
Radley	d						19 02										20 11					
Culham	d																					
Appleford	d																					
Didcot Parkway	a					19 02	19 10								20 02		20 19					21 00
	d	18 47		18 59		19 10	19 14	19 17					19 59		20 04	20 17	20 29				20 59	21 01
Cholsey	d						19 20										20 35					
Goring & Streatley	d						19 25										20 40					
Pangbourne	d																					
Tilehurst	d						19 35										20 50					
Bedwyn	d				18 42																	
Hungerford	d				18 48																	
Kintbury	d				18 52																	
Newbury	a				18 59																	
	d				19 00									19 53					20 19			
Newbury Racecourse	d													19 55								
Thatcham	d				19 05									20 00								
Midgham	d													20 05								
Aldermaston	d													20 08								
Theale	d				19 13									20 13								
Reading West	d								←					20 21								
Reading 7	a	19 00	19 13	19 17	19 21	19 28	19 38	19 33	19 38	19 43		20 13	20 21	20 24	20 25	20 31	20 53	20 42	20 50	21 11	21 21	21 26
	d	19 05		19 19		19 28	19 44	19 35	19 44				20 23		20 25	20 32	20 55		20 51		21 23	21 27
Twyford 3	a						→		19 50								21 01					
Maidenhead 3	a								19 59								21 10					21 39
Slough 3	a					19 44			20 14						20 44		21 19					21 45
Ealing Broadway ⊖	a								20 42								21 42					
London Paddington 15 ⊖	a	19 43		19 59		20 07		20 13	20 51				20 59		21 04	21 13	21 51		21 29		22 01	22 07

		CH	GW	GW	GW	XC	GW	XC	GW	GW	GW	GW	XC	GW	CH	GW	GW	GW	GW	GW	GW	GW
			◇1	1	1	◇1	◇1	◇1	◇1	◇1	1	◇1	◇1	1		1	◇1	◇1			1	1
			⊡			⊡	⊡	⊥	⊡			⊡						⊡	🚌			
Birmingham New Street 12	d					20 04		20 33					21 04									
Birmingham International	d					20 14							21 14									
Coventry	d					20 25							21 24									
Leamington Spa 8	d					20 38		21 00					21 35									
Banbury	d					20 55		21 19														
Kings Sutton	d																					
Heyford	d																					
Tackley	d																					
Bicester Town	d	20 33													22 03							
Islip	d	20 44													22 14							
Oxford	a	21 00				21 14		21 38					22 08		22 30							
	d				21 05	21 16		21 40		21 50			22 10	22 21			22 50		23 00			
Radley	d				21 11									22 27					23 15			
Culham	d																					
Appleford	d																					
Didcot Parkway	a				21 19					22 00				22 36			23 01		23 25			
	d		21 17		21 31		21 29		22 00	22 02				22 44			23 03	23 11			23 50	
Cholsey	d				21 37									22 50							23 56	
Goring & Streatley	d				21 42									22 55							00 01	
Pangbourne	d																					
Tilehurst	d				21 49									23 04							00 09	
Bedwyn	d			20 54												22 35						
Hungerford	d			21 00												22 41						
Kintbury	d			21 04												22 45						
Newbury	a			21 11												22 52						
	d			21 12							21 53	22 19				22 53				23 23		23 45
Newbury Racecourse	d										21 55											23 47
Thatcham	d			21 17							22 00					22 58				23 28		23 52
Midgham	d										22 05											23 57
Aldermaston	d										22 08											00 01
Theale	d			21 25							22 13					23 06				23 36		00 06
Reading West	d										22 21											00s13
Reading 7	a		21 32	21 33	21 56	21 43	21 47	22 11	22 16	22 23	22 24	22 40	22 45	23 09		23 15	23 17	23 28		23 44	00 15	00 17
	d		21 32		21 56		21 49		22 21	22 23		22 41		23 10			23 24	23 30			00 15	
Twyford 3	a				22 02									23 16							00 21	
Maidenhead 3	a				22 10									23 24							00 29	
Slough 3	a				22 21					22 40				23 31			23 41				00 36	
Ealing Broadway ⊖	a				22 43									23 55							00 59	
London Paddington 15 ⊖	a		22 13		22 51		22 27		22 58	23 01		23 18		00 04			00 04	00 13			01 11	

Table 116

Sundays

19 February to 25 March

Birmingham, Banbury, Bicester, Oxford and Bedwyn - Reading and London

Network Diagram - see first Page of Table 116

		GW ◇1	GW ◇1 ☕	GW 1	GW 1	GW 🚌	GW 1	GW ◇1 ☕	GW 1	GW ◇1	GW 1	GW ◇1 ☕	GW ◇1	GW 1	GW ◇1 ☕	GW 1	XC ◇1 🛒	CH	GW ◇1 ☕	GW ◇1 ☕	GW 1	GW ◇1	GW 1
Birmingham New Street 12	d																						
Birmingham International	d																						
Coventry	d																						
Leamington Spa 8	d																						
Banbury	d																						
Kings Sutton	d																						
Heyford	d																						
Tackley	d																						
Bicester Town	d																	10 04					
Islip	d																	10 15					
Oxford	a																	10 31					
	d	23p01		23p13		07 45				08 50	09 10		09 48			09 53	10 16				10 39	10 44	
Radley	d			23p19							09 16					09 59					10 45		
Culham	d			23p23																			
Appleford	d			23p26												10 04							
Didcot Parkway	a	23p13		23p31		08 10				09 02	09 25		10 00			10 08					10 53	10 58	
	d	23p14	23p30	23p40	08 00		08 25	08 43		09 03	09 26	09 45	10 01		10 08	10 09				10 46	11 13	10 58	
Cholsey	d			23p46			08 31				09 32					10 15					↦		
Goring & Streatley	d			23p51	08 07		08 37				09 37					10 20							
Pangbourne	d																						
Tilehurst	d			23p58			08 47				09 47					10 30							
Bedwyn	d													09 35									10 42
Hungerford	d													09 41									10 48
Kintbury	d													09 46									10 52
Newbury	a													09 52									10 59
	d								08 46					09 53					10 32				11 00
Newbury Racecourse	d								08 48					09 55									
Thatcham	d								08 53					10 00									11 05
Midgham	d								08 58					10 05									
Aldermaston	d								09 01					10 08									
Theale	d								09 06					10 13									11 13
Reading West	d								09 14					10 21									
Reading 7	a	23p29	23p51	00 04	08 17		08 51	09 01	09 17	09 22	09 53	09 58	10 21	10 24	10 25	10 34	10 38		10 48	11 00		11 13	11 21
	d	23p29	23p51	00 06	08 19		08 52	09 03		09 23	09 54	10 00	10 22		10 27	10 36			10 49	11 02		11 14	
Twyford 3	a			00 13			08 58				10 00					10 46						11 20	
Maidenhead 3	a			00 21			09 06				10 08					10 54						11 28	
Slough 3	a	23p44		00 32	08 35		09 14			09 38	10 17		10 37			11 15						11 35	
Ealing Broadway ⊖	a			00 58			09 42				10 42					11 42							
London Paddington 15 ⊖	a	00 10	00 34	01 08	08 59		09 52	09 44		10 00	10 51	10 44	10 58		11 06	11 51			11 29	11 44		11 56	

		GW ◇1	GW 1	XC ◇1 ☕	GW ◇1 ☕	GW ◇1 ☕	GW ◇1	GW 1	GW ◇1 ☕	GW 1	CH	XC ◇1 ☕	GW ◇1 ☕	GW 1	GW ◇1 ☕	GW ◇1	GW 1	XC ◇1 ☕	CH	GW ◇1 ☕	GW ◇1 ☕	GW ◇1 ☕	GW ◇1
Birmingham New Street 12	d																						
Birmingham International	d																						
Coventry	d																						
Leamington Spa 8	d																						
Banbury	d			10 55								11 55						12 55					
Kings Sutton	d																						
Heyford	d																						
Tackley	d																						
Bicester Town	d										11 33								13 03				
Islip	d										11 44								13 14				
Oxford	a			11 14							12 00	12 14						13 14	13 30				
	d	10 55		11 16			11 50			11 56		12 16				12 50	12 56	13 16					13 50
Radley	d									12 02							13 02						
Culham	d																						
Appleford	d		↤							12 07							13 07						
Didcot Parkway	a	11 07	10 53				12 02			12 12						13 02	13 12						14 02
	d	11 07	11 13		11 29		12 03		12 09	12 12			12 29		12 59	13 03	13 15			13 29		13 46	14 03
Cholsey	d		11 19							12 17							13 21						
Goring & Streatley	d		11 24							12 23							13 26						
Pangbourne	d																						
Tilehurst	d		11 34							12 33							13 35						
Bedwyn	d													12 42									
Hungerford	d													12 48									
Kintbury	d													12 52									
Newbury	a													12 59									
	d					11 26		11 53						13 00							13 31		
Newbury Racecourse	d							11 55															
Thatcham	d							12 00						13 05									
Midgham	d							12 05															
Aldermaston	d							12 08															
Theale	d							12 13						13 13									
Reading West	d							12 21															
Reading 7	a	11 23	11 37	11 42	11 45	11 49	12 21	12 24	12 26	12 38		12 42	12 44	13 21	13 21	13 25	13 42	13 42		13 47	13 51	13 59	14 21
	d	11 23	11 42		11 47	11 53	12 23		12 27	12 42			12 44		13 23	13 25	13 44			13 49	13 52	14 04	14 21
Twyford 3	a		11 49							12 48							13 50						
Maidenhead 3	a		11 57							12 56							13 58						
Slough 3	a	11 37	12 15				12 38			13 15						13 41	14 15						14 37
Ealing Broadway ⊖	a		12 42							13 42							14 42						
London Paddington 15 ⊖	a	12 01	12 51		12 22	12 29	13 07		13 03	13 51			13 22		13 59	14 04	14 51			14 22	14 29	14 44	14 59

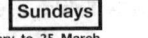

Birmingham, Banbury, Bicester, Oxford and Bedwyn - Reading and London

Network Diagram - see first Page of Table 116

		GW	GW	XC	GW	GW	XC	GW	GW	GW	CH	XC	GW	GW	XC	GW	GW	GW	GW	XC	CH	GW
		1	1	◇1	◇1	◇1	◇1	1	◇1	1		◇1	◇1	◇1	◇1	◇1	1	◇1	1	◇1		◇1
				☕	☕	☕	🍴					☕	☕	☕	🍴	☕		☕		☕		☕
Birmingham New Street 12	d											14 04			14 33					15 04		
Birmingham International	d											14 14								15 14		
Coventry	d											14 25								15 25		
Leamington Spa 8	d											14 38			15 00					15 38		
Banbury	d			13 55			14 19					14 55			15 19					15 55		
Kings Sutton	d																					
Heyford	d																					
Tackley	d																					
Bicester Town	d										14 33										16 03	
Islip	d										14 44										16 14	
Oxford	a			14 16			14 38				15 00	15 14			15 41					16 14	16 30	
	d		13 56	14 17			14 43		14 49	14 58		15 16			15 43			15 50	15 56	16 16		
Radley	d		14 02							15 04									16 02			
Culham	d																					
Appleford	d		14 07																16 07			
Didcot Parkway	a		14 11						15 03	15 12								16 02	16 11			
	d		14 12		14 32	14 47			15 04	15 13			15 32	15 47		15 59		16 03	16 12			16 32
Cholsey	d		14 18							15 19									16 18			
Goring & Streatley	d		14 24							15 25									16 24			
Pangbourne	d																					
Tilehurst	d		14 34							15 35									16 34			
Bedwyn	d							14 42														
Hungerford	d							14 48														
Kintbury	d							14 52														
Newbury	a							14 59														
	d	13 53						15 00									15 53					
Newbury Racecourse	d	13 55															15 55					
Thatcham	d	14 00						15 05									16 00					
Midgham	d	14 05															16 05					
Aldermaston	d	14 08															16 08					
Theale	d	14 13						15 13									16 13					
Reading West	d	14 21															16 21					
Reading 7	a	14 24	14 36	14 46	14 47	15 00	15 15	15 21	15 21	15 38		15 42	15 47	16 00	16 13	16 20	16 24	16 27	16 38	16 43		16 47
	d		14 39		14 49	15 05			15 22	15 44			15 49	16 05		16 22		16 28	16 44			16 49
Twyford 3	a		14 50							15 50									16 50			
Maidenhead 3	a		14 58							15 58									16 58			
Slough 3	a		15 15						15 37	16 14								16 41	17 16			
Ealing Broadway ⊖	a		15 42							16 43									17 42			
London Paddington 15 ⊖	a		15 51		15 22	15 44			15 59	16 51			16 22	16 44		16 58		17 06	17 51			17 22

		GW	GW	GW	XC	GW	GW	GW	GW	XC	GW	GW	XC	GW	GW	GW	CH	XC	GW	XC	GW	GW	GW
		◇1	◇1	◇1	◇1	◇1	1	◇1	1	◇1	◇1	◇1	◇1	◇1	1	1		◇1	◇1	◇1	◇1	1	◇1
		☕	☕		🍴	☕		☕		☕	☕	☕	🍴	☕				☕	☕	🍴	☕		☕
Birmingham New Street 12	d				15 33					16 04			16 33					17 04		17 33			
Birmingham International	d									16 14								17 14					
Coventry	d									16 25								17 25					
Leamington Spa 8	d				16 00					16 38			17 00					17 38		18 01			
Banbury	d				16 19					16 55			17 19					17 55		18 20			
Kings Sutton	d																						
Heyford	d																						
Tackley	d																						
Bicester Town	d																17 33						
Islip	d																17 44						
Oxford	a				16 41					17 14			17 38				18 00	18 14		18 41			
	d			16 37	16 43			16 50	16 56	17 16			17 43	17 50		17 55		18 16		18 43			18 50
Radley	d								17 02							18 02							
Culham	d																						
Appleford	d								17 07							18 07							
Didcot Parkway	a			16 49				17 02	17 12					18 02		18 10							19 02
	d		16 47	16 51		17 00		17 10	17 14		17 29	17 46		18 03		18 12					18 59		19 10
Cholsey	d								17 20							18 18							
Goring & Streatley	d								17 25							18 24							
Pangbourne	d																						
Tilehurst	d								17 35							18 33							
Bedwyn	d						16 42															18 42	
Hungerford	d						16 48															18 48	
Kintbury	d						16 52															18 52	
Newbury	a						16 59															18 59	
	d	16 31					17 00								17 53				18 34			19 00	
Newbury Racecourse	d														17 55								
Thatcham	d						17 05								18 00							19 05	
Midgham	d														18 05								
Aldermaston	d														18 08								
Theale	d						17 13								18 13							19 13	
Reading West	d														18 21								
Reading 7	a	16 48	17 03	17 11	17 13	17 15	17 21	17 24	17 38	17 43	17 46	17 59	18 13	18 23	18 24	18 40		18 43	18 51	19 13	19 17	19 21	19 29
	d	16 51	17 05	17 12		17 17		17 24	17 42		17 49	18 04		18 23		18 44			18 53		19 19		19 30
Twyford 3	a			17 18					17 48							18 50							
Maidenhead 3	a			17 26					17 58							18 58							
Slough 3	a			17 34				17 44	18 15					18 38		19 16							19 44
Ealing Broadway ⊖	a								18 42							19 42							
London Paddington 15 ⊖	a	17 30	17 43	17 56		18 01		18 07	18 51		18 22	18 45		19 03		19 51			19 29		19 59		20 07

Table 116

Sundays

19 February to 25 March

Birmingham, Banbury, Bicester, Oxford and Bedwyn - Reading and London

Network Diagram - see first Page of Table 116

		GW 1	XC ◇1 ☕	CH		XC ◇1 🛒	GW ◇1 ☕	GW ◇1	GW 1	GW ◇1 ☕	GW 1	XC ◇1 ☕	GW ◇1 ☕	XC ◇1 🛒		GW ◇1 ☕	GW ◇1	CH	GW 1	GW ◇1 ☕	GW 1	XC ◇1 ☕	XC ◇1 🛒	GW ◇1 ☕
Birmingham New Street 12	d		18 04			18 33						19 04		19 33								20 04	20 33	
Birmingham International	d		18 14									19 14										20 14		
Coventry	d		18 25									19 25										20 25		
Leamington Spa 8	d		18 38			19 00						19 38		20 00								20 38	21 00	
Banbury	d		18 55			19 19						19 55		20 19								20 55	21 19	
Kings Sutton	d																							
Heyford	d																							
Tackley	d																							
Bicester Town	d			19 07														20 33						
Islip	d			19 18														20 44						
Oxford	a		19 14	19 34		19 38						20 14		20 40				21 00				21 14	21 38	
	d	18 56	19 16			19 43		19 49			20 05	20 16		20 43			20 50				21 05	21 16	21 40	
Radley	d	19 02									20 11										21 11			
Culham	d																							
Appleford	d																							
Didcot Parkway	a	19 10						20 02			20 19						21 00				21 19			
	d	19 14					19 59	20 04		20 19	20 29					20 59	21 01			21 16	21 28			22 00
Cholsey	d	19 20									20 35										21 34			
Goring & Streatley	d	19 25									20 40										21 39			
Pangbourne	d																							
Tilehurst	d	19 35									20 50										21 48			
Bedwyn	d																		20 54					
Hungerford	d																		21 00					
Kintbury	d																		21 04					
Newbury	a																		21 11					
	d								19 53				20 28						21 12					
Newbury Racecourse	d								19 55															
Thatcham	d								20 00										21 17					
Midgham	d								20 05															
Aldermaston	d								20 08															
Theale	d								20 13										21 25					
Reading West	d								20 21															
Reading 7	a	19 38	19 43			20 13	20 21	20 23	20 24	20 32	20 53	20 42	20 50	21 11		21 21	21 26		21 33	21 31	21 55	21 43	22 11	22 16
	d	19 44					20 23	20 25		20 34	20 55		20 51			21 23	21 27			21 35	21 56			22 18
Twyford 3	a	19 50									21 01										22 02			
Maidenhead 3	a	19 59									21 10						21 39				22 10			
Slough 3	a	20 14						20 42			21 19						21 45				22 19			
Ealing Broadway ⊖	a	20 42									21 42										22 42			
London Paddington 15 ⊖	a	20 51					20 59	21 04		21 13	21 51		21 30			22 00	22 07			22 14	22 51			22 58

		GW ◇1	GW 1	GW ◇1 ☕	GW ◇1 ☕	XC ◇1	GW 1	CH	GW 1	GW ◇1		GW ◇1 ☕	GW 🚌	GW	GW 1	GW 1
Birmingham New Street 12	d					21 04										
Birmingham International	d					21 14										
Coventry	d					21 24										
Leamington Spa 8	d					21 35										
Banbury	d															
Kings Sutton	d															
Heyford	d															
Tackley	d															
Bicester Town	d							22 03								
Islip	d							22 14								
Oxford	a					22 08		22 30								
	d	21 50				22 10	22 17			22 50			23 00			
Radley	d						22 23						23 15			
Culham	d															
Appleford	d															
Didcot Parkway	a	22 00					22 32			23 01			23 25			
	d	22 02		22 14			22 32			23 03		23 13			23 50	
Cholsey	d						22 38								23 56	
Goring & Streatley	d						22 43								00 01	
Pangbourne	d															
Tilehurst	d						22 53								00 09	
Bedwyn	d								22 35							
Hungerford	d								22 41							
Kintbury	d								22 45							
Newbury	a								22 52							
	d		21 53		22 19				22 53					23 23		23 45
Newbury Racecourse	d		21 55													23 47
Thatcham	d		22 00						22 58					23 28		23 52
Midgham	d		22 05													23 57
Aldermaston	d		22 08													00 01
Theale	d		22 13						23 06					23 36		00 06
Reading West	d		22 21													00s13
Reading 7	a	22 21	22 24	22 31	22 38	22 45	22 58		23 15	23 17		23 28		23 44	00 15	00 17
	d	22 23		22 34	22 39		22 58			23 24		23 30			00 15	
Twyford 3	a						23 04								00 21	
Maidenhead 3	a						23 12								00 29	
Slough 3	a	22 40					23 20			23 41					00 36	
Ealing Broadway ⊖	a						23 43								00 59	
London Paddington 15 ⊖	a	23 01		23 13	23 16		23 52			00 04		00 12			01 11	

Table 116

Sundays
from 1 April

Birmingham, Banbury, Bicester, Oxford and Bedwyn - Reading and London

Network Diagram - see first Page of Table 116

		GW	GW	GW	GW	GW	GW	GW	GW	GW		GW	GW	GW	GW	GW	XC	CH	GW	GW		GW	GW	GW	GW
		◇1	◇1	1	1		1	◇1	◇1			1	◇1	◇1		1	◇1		◇1	1		◇1	◇1		1
			☕			🚌		☕		🚌			☕		🚌		trolley		☕					🚌	
Birmingham New Street 12	d																09 04								
Birmingham International	d																09 14								
Coventry	d																09 25								
Leamington Spa 8	d																09 38								
Banbury	d																09 55								
Kings Sutton	d																								
Heyford	d																								
Tackley	d																								
Bicester Town	d																	10 04							
Islip	d																	10 15							
Oxford	a																10 14	10 31							
	d	23p01		23p07		07 45	08 05		08 50			09 00		09 48		09 54	10 16			10 39		10 44	10 55		
Radley	d			23p13			08 11					09 06				10 00				10 45					
Culham	d			23p17																					
Appleford	d			23p20												10 05									←
Didcot Parkway	a	23p13		23p25		08 10	08 19		09 02			09 15		10 00		10 09				10 53		10 58	11 07		10 53
	d	23p14	23p30	23p36	07 45		08 20	08 43	09 03			09 15	09 45	10 01		10 10			10 46	11 13		10 58	11 07		11 13
Cholsey	d			23p42			08 27					09 21				10 16				→					11 19
Goring & Streatley	d			23p49	07 53		08 32					09 26				10 22									11 24
Pangbourne	d																								
Tilehurst	d			23p56			08 42					09 36				10 29									11 34
Bedwyn	d																							09 35	
Hungerford	d																							09 50	
Kintbury	d																							10 00	
Newbury	a																							10 19	
	d									08 35					09 15									10 19	
Newbury Racecourse	d														09 20									10 24	
Thatcham	d									08 46					09 30									10 34	
Midgham	d														09 40									10 44	
Aldermaston	d														09 47									10 51	
Theale	d									09 04					09 59									11 03	
Reading West	d														10 14									11 18	
Reading 7	a	23p29	23p49	00 02	08 03		08 51	09 01	09 22	09 30		09 42	09 58	10 21	10 30	10 34	10 38		11 00			11 13	11 23	11 34	11 37
	d	23p29	23p51	00 03	08 03		08 52	09 03	09 23			09 43	10 00	10 22		10 39			11 02			11 14	11 23		11 42
Twyford 3	a			00 10			08 58					09 49				10 46						11 26			11 49
Maidenhead 3	a			00 18			09 06					09 57				10 54						11 34			11 57
Slough 3	a	23p44		00 29	08 22		09 14		09 38			10 14		10 37		11 17						11 43	11 37		12 15
Ealing Broadway ⊖	a			00 53			09 42					10 42				11 42									12 42
London Paddington 15 ⊖	a	00 10	00 33	01 03	08 44		09 52	09 44	10 00			10 51	10 44	10 58		11 51			11 44			12 03	12 01		12 51

		XC	GW	GW	GW	GW		GW	CH	XC	GW	GW	GW	GW	GW	GW		XC	CH	GW	GW	XC	GW	GW	GW
		◇1	◇1	◇1	◇1			1		◇1	◇1	◇1	◇1	◇1		1		◇1		◇1	◇1	◇1	◇1		1
		☕	☕	☕		🚌				☕	☕	☕	☕		🚌			☕		☕	☕	trolley		🚌	
Birmingham New Street 12	d	10 04								11 04								12 04				12 33			
Birmingham International	d	10 14								11 14								12 14							
Coventry	d	10 25								11 25								12 25							
Leamington Spa 8	d	10 38								11 38								12 38				13 00			
Banbury	d	10 55								11 55								12 55				13 19			
Kings Sutton	d																								
Heyford	d																								
Tackley	d																								
Bicester Town	d								11 33										13 03						
Islip	d								11 44										13 14						
Oxford	a	11 14							12 00	12 14								13 14	13 30			13 41			
	d	11 16			11 50			11 54		12 16				12 50		12 55		13 16				13 43	13 50		13 54
Radley	d							12 00								13 01									14 00
Culham	d																								
Appleford	d							12 05								13 06									14 05
Didcot Parkway	a				12 02			12 10						13 02		13 12							14 02		14 09
	d		11 29	11 50	12 03			12 10			12 29	12 47	12 59	13 10		13 14				13 29	13 51		14 03		14 10
Cholsey	d							12 15								13 20									14 16
Goring & Streatley	d							12 22								13 25									14 22
Pangbourne	d																								
Tilehurst	d							12 29								13 32									14 29
Bedwyn	d					10 54																		12 54	
Hungerford	d					11 09																		13 09	
Kintbury	d					11 19																		13 19	
Newbury	a					11 38																		13 38	
	d					11 38									12 19									13 38	
Newbury Racecourse	d														12 24										
Thatcham	d					11 49									12 34									13 49	
Midgham	d														12 44										
Aldermaston	d														12 51										
Theale	d					12 07									13 03									14 07	
Reading West	d														13 18										
Reading 7	a	11 42	11 45	12 04	12 21	12 33		12 34		12 43	12 44	13 00	13 14	13 25	13 34	13 36		13 42		13 47	14 05	14 13	14 21	14 33	14 33
	d		11 47	12 05	12 23			12 41			12 44	13 02	13 15	13 25		13 39				13 49	14 06		14 21		14 36
Twyford 3	a							12 48								13 48									14 43
Maidenhead 3	a							12 56								13 56									14 51
Slough 3	a				12 38			13 15						13 40		14 15							14 37		15 15
Ealing Broadway ⊖	a							13 42								14 42									15 42
London Paddington 15 ⊖	a		12 22	12 42	13 03			13 51			13 22	13 42	13 59	14 05		14 51				14 22	14 43		14 59		15 51

Table 116

Sundays
from 1 April

Birmingham, Banbury, Bicester, Oxford and Bedwyn - Reading and London

Network Diagram - see first Page of Table 116

		XC		GW	GW	XC	GW	GW	GW	CH	XC	GW		GW	XC	GW	GW	GW	XC	CH	GW	GW		GW	XC
		◇1		◇1	◇1	◇1	◇1		1		◇1	◇1		◇1	◇1	◇1		1	◇1		◇1	◇1		◇1	◇1
								🚌									🚌								
		☕		☕	☕	🛒					☕	☕		☕	🛒	☕			☕		☕	☕			🛒
Birmingham New Street 12	d	13 04				13 33					14 04				14 33				15 04						15 33
Birmingham International	d	13 14									14 14								15 14						
Coventry	d	13 25									14 25								15 25						
Leamington Spa 8	d	13 38				14 00					14 38				15 00				15 38						16 00
Banbury	d	13 55				14 19					14 55				15 19				15 55						16 19
Kings Sutton	d																								
Heyford	d																								
Tackley	d																								
Bicester Town	d									14 33										16 03					
Islip	d									14 44										16 14					
Oxford	a	14 14				14 38				15 00	15 14				15 41				16 14	16 30					16 41
	d	14 17				14 43	14 50		14 58		15 16				15 43	15 50		15 56	16 16					16 37	16 43
Radley	d								15 04									16 02							
Culham	d																								
Appleford	d																	16 07							
Didcot Parkway	a						15 04		15 12							16 02		16 11							
	d			14 34	14 52		15 08		15 13			15 32		15 47		16 03		16 12			16 32	16 51			
Cholsey	d								15 19									16 18							
Goring & Streatley	d								15 25									16 24							
Pangbourne	d																								
Tilehurst	d								15 35									16 31							
Bedwyn	d																14 54								
Hungerford	d																15 09								
Kintbury	d																15 19								
Newbury	a																15 38								
	d							14 19									15 38								
Newbury Racecourse	d							14 24																	
Thatcham	d							14 34									15 49								
Midgham	d							14 44																	
Aldermaston	d							14 51																	
Theale	d							15 03									16 07								
Reading West	d							15 18																	
Reading 7	a	14 46		14 45	15 05	15 13	15 25	15 34	15 38		15 42	15 47		16 00	16 13	16 25	16 33	16 35	16 43		16 47	17 04		17 10	17 10
	d			14 47	15 07		15 26		15 44			15 49		16 02		16 26		16 43			16 49	17 06		17 10	
Twyford 3	a								15 50									16 49						17 17	
Maidenhead 3	a								15 58									16 57						17 25	
Slough 3	a						15 41		16 14							16 40		17 16						17 33	
Ealing Broadway ⊖	a								16 42									17 42							
London Paddington 15 ⊖	a			15 23	15 43		16 03		16 51			16 22		16 42		17 05		17 51			17 22	17 44		17 57	

		GW	GW	GW	GW	XC	GW	GW		XC	GW	GW	GW	GW	CH	XC	GW	XC		GW	GW	GW	GW	GW	XC
		◇1	◇1		1	◇1	◇1	◇1		◇1	◇1	◇1		1		◇1	◇1	◇1		◇1	◇1		◇1	1	◇1
				🚌									🚌									🚌			
		☕	☕			☕	☕	☕		🛒	☕	☕				☕	☕	🛒		☕	☕		☕		☕
Birmingham New Street 12	d					16 04				16 33						17 04		17 33							18 04
Birmingham International	d					16 14										17 14									18 14
Coventry	d					16 25										17 25									18 25
Leamington Spa 8	d					16 38				17 00						17 38		18 01							18 38
Banbury	d					16 55				17 19						17 55		18 20							18 55
Kings Sutton	d																								
Heyford	d																								
Tackley	d																								
Bicester Town	d														17 33										
Islip	d														17 44										
Oxford	a					17 14				17 38					18 00	18 14		18 41							19 14
	d		16 50		16 56	17 16				17 43		17 50		17 55		18 16		18 42			18 50			19 05	19 16
Radley	d				17 02									18 02										19 11	
Culham	d																								
Appleford	d				17 07									18 07											
Didcot Parkway	a		17 02		17 12							18 02		18 10							19 02			19 21	
	d	17 01	17 10		17 13		17 29	17 47			17 59	18 05		18 12			18 49			18 59	19 11		19 19	19 31	
Cholsey	d				17 19									18 18										19 37	
Goring & Streatley	d				17 25									18 24										19 42	
Pangbourne	d																								
Tilehurst	d				17 32									18 33										19 50	
Bedwyn	d												16 54												
Hungerford	d												17 09												
Kintbury	d												17 19												
Newbury	a												17 38												
	d			16 19									17 38									18 19			
Newbury Racecourse	d			16 24																		18 24			
Thatcham	d			16 34									17 49									18 34			
Midgham	d			16 44																		18 44			
Aldermaston	d			16 51																		18 51			
Theale	d			17 03									18 07									19 03			
Reading West	d			17 18																		19 18			
Reading 7	a	17 16	17 26	17 34	17 35	17 43	17 46	18 00		18 13	18 19	18 25	18 33	18 39		18 43	19 02	19 13		19 12	19 30	19 34	19 36	19 53	19 43
	d	17 18	17 27		17 44		17 49	18 02			18 21	18 26		18 43			19 05			19 14	19 30		19 38	19 56	
Twyford 3	a				17 50									18 50										20 02	
Maidenhead 3	a				17 58									18 58										20 11	
Slough 3	a		17 47		18 15							18 41		19 16							19 44			20 19	
Ealing Broadway ⊖	a				18 43									19 42										20 42	
London Paddington 15 ⊖	a	18 03	18 13		18 51		18 22	18 43			18 59	19 06		19 51			19 44			19 59	20 07		20 14	20 51	

Table 116

Sundays
from 1 April

Birmingham, Banbury, Bicester, Oxford and Bedwyn - Reading and London

Network Diagram - see first Page of Table 116

		CH	XC	GW		GW	GW	GW	XC	GW	XC	GW	GW	CH		GW	GW	GW	XC	GW	XC	GW	GW	GW
			◇1	◇1		◇1		1	◇1	◇1	◇1	◇1	◇1			◇1		1	◇1	◇1	◇1	◇1	◇1	
							🚌										🚌							🚌
			🛒	☕					☕	☕	🛒	☕				☕			☕	☕	🛒	☕		
Birmingham New Street 12	d		18 33						19 04		19 33								20 04		20 33			
Birmingham International	d								19 14										20 14					
Coventry	d								19 25										20 25					
Leamington Spa 8	d		19 00						19 38		20 00								20 38		21 00			
Banbury	d		19 19						19 55		20 19								20 55		21 19			
Kings Sutton	d																							
Heyford	d																							
Tackley	d																							
Bicester Town	d	19 07												20 33										
Islip	d	19 18												20 44										
Oxford	a	19 34	19 38						20 14		20 40			21 00					21 14		21 38			
	d		19 43			19 50		19 58	20 16		20 43		20 50					21 05	21 16		21 40		21 50	
Radley	d							20 04										21 11						
Culham	d																							
Appleford	d																							
Didcot Parkway	a					20 04		20 12					21 00					21 19					22 00	
	d			19 59		20 05		20 14		20 17		20 59	21 04			21 17		21 31		21 29		22 00	22 02	
Cholsey	d							20 20										21 37						
Goring & Streatley	d							20 25										21 42						
Pangbourne	d																							
Tilehurst	d							20 33										21 49						
Bedwyn	d						18 47																	20 54
Hungerford	d						19 02																	21 09
Kintbury	d						19 12																	21 19
Newbury	a						19 31																	21 38
	d						19 31										20 19							21 38
Newbury Racecourse	d																20 24							
Thatcham	d						19 42										20 34							21 49
Midgham	d																20 44							
Aldermaston	d																20 51							
Theale	d						20 00										21 03							22 07
Reading West	d																21 18							
Reading 7	a		20 13	20 16		20 24	20 26	20 36	20 42	20 42	21 11	21 18	21 26			21 32	21 34	21 56	21 43	21 47	22 07	22 16	22 20	22 33
	d			20 18		20 24		20 38		20 43		21 20	21 28			21 32		21 56		21 49		22 18	22 23	
Twyford 3	a							20 44										22 02						
Maidenhead 3	a							20 53					21 40					22 10						
Slough 3	a					20 42		21 19					21 46					22 21					22 40	
Ealing Broadway ⊖	a							21 43										22 43						
London Paddington 15 ⊖	a			20 58		21 05		21 51		21 19		21 59	22 07			22 14		22 51		22 27		22 58	23 01	

		XC	GW	GW	CH	GW	GW	GW	GW	GW		GW
		◇1	1			◇1	◇1			1		
				🚌				🚌	🚌			🚌
							☕					
Birmingham New Street 12	d	21 04										
Birmingham International	d	21 14										
Coventry	d	21 24										
Leamington Spa 8	d	21 35										
Banbury	d											
Kings Sutton	d											
Heyford	d											
Tackley	d											
Bicester Town	d				22 03							
Islip	d				22 14							
Oxford	a	22 08			22 30							
	d	22 10	22 21			22 46			23 00			
Radley	d		22 27						23 15			
Culham	d											
Appleford	d											
Didcot Parkway	a		22 35			22 58			23 25			
	d		22 35			22 59	23 11			23 50		
Cholsey	d		22 41							23 56		
Goring & Streatley	d		22 46							00 01		
Pangbourne	d											
Tilehurst	d		22 53							00 08		
Bedwyn	d							22 35				
Hungerford	d							22 50				
Kintbury	d							23 00				
Newbury	a							23 19				
	d			21 53				23 19				23 50
Newbury Racecourse	d			21 58								23 55
Thatcham	d			22 08				23 30				00 05
Midgham	d			22 18								00 15
Aldermaston	d			22 25								00 22
Theale	d			22 37				23 48				00 34
Reading West	d			22 52								00 49
Reading 7	a	22 33	22 58	23 08		23 15	23 28	00 14		00 14		01 05
	d		23 00			23 22	23 30			00 15		
Twyford 3	a		23 06							00 21		
Maidenhead 3	a		23 14							00 29		
Slough 3	a		23 21			23 42				00 36		
Ealing Broadway ⊖	a		23 44							00 59		
London Paddington 15 ⊖	a		23 53			00 04	00 13			01 09		

London - Greenford and Reading

Network Diagram - see first Page of Table 116

Miles	Miles	Miles			GW MX 1	GW MO 1	GW MX ◇1	GW MO 1	GW MX 1	GW MX 1	GW MX ◇1 ☕	GW MO ◇1 A ☕	GW MO ◇1 B ☕		GW MO ◇1	GW MX 1	GW MO 1	GW MX 1	GW MX ◇1	GW MO 1	GW MX 1	GW 1	GW 1		HC
0	0	0	**London Paddington** 15 ⊖	d	22p45	23p15	23p18			23p29	23p30	23p37	23p37		23p47	23p48	23p53		00 22	00 34	00 34	01 34	03 34		04 42
4¼	4¼	4¼	Acton Main Line	d	22p51											23p54									
5¾	5¾	5¾	**Ealing Broadway** ⊖	d	22p54	23p24				23p37					23p55	23p57	00 02			00 42	00 42	01 42	03 42		04 50
6½	6½	6½	West Ealing	d												23p59									
—	7¼	—	Drayton Green	d																					
—	7½	—	Castle Bar Park	d																					
—	8¼	—	South Greenford	d																					
—	9¼	—	**Greenford** ⊖	a																					
7¼	—	7¼	Hanwell	d												00 02									
9	—	9	Southall	d		23p29										00 06	00 07			00 47	00 47	01 47	03 48		04 54
10¾	—	10¾	Hayes & Harlington	d	23p01	23p33				23p44						00 10	00 11			00 51	00 51	01 51	03 52		04 58
—	—	14¾	**Heathrow Terminal 1-2-3** 2 ✈	a																					05 04
—	—	16½	**Heathrow Terminal 4** ✈	a																					05 10
13¼	—	—	West Drayton	d		23p37										00 14	00 15			00 55	00 55	01 55	03 56		
14¾	—	—	Iver	d												00 17									
16¼	—	—	Langley	d		23p42		←								00 21	00 20	←		01 00	01 00				
18½	—	—	**Slough** 3	a	23p11	23p46	23p36	23p46		23p53		00 01	00 01		00 09	00 26	00 24	00 26	00 39	01 05	01 05	02 04	04 04		
—	—	—		d	23p12	23p46	23p36	23p46		23p54		00 01	00 02		00 10	00 26	00 24	00 26	00 39	01 05	01 05	02 04	04 05		
21	—	—	Burnham	d	23p16	→		23p51								→	00 28	00 30		01 09	01 09				
22½	—	—	Taplow	d	23p20													00 34			01 13				
24¼	—	—	**Maidenhead** 3	d	23p24		23p44	23p56		00 01					00 17		00 34	00 41		01 15	01 16	02 11	04 12		
31	—	—	**Twyford** 3	d	23p32			00 04	00 07	00 09							00 42	00 48		01 23	01 24	02 19	04 20		
36	—	—	**Reading** 7	a	23p41		23p58	00 14	00 16	00 19	00 04	00 15	00 15		00 29		00 49	00 57	01 00	01 32	01 35	02 29	04 30		
—	—	—	Oxford	a	00 26		00 28			01 17									01 34						

		HC	GW 1	GW 1	GW ◇1 ☕	HC	GW ◇1 ☕	GW 1	GW 1		GW 1	GW ◇1	GW 1	GW 1	HC	GW 1	GW 1	GW 1	GW 1		GW 1	GW ◇1 ☕	HC	GW 1	GW 1
London Paddington 15 ⊖	d	05 13	05 17	05 22	05 27	05 33	05 36		05 42		05 45	05 48		05 57	06 03	06 12	06 15	06 20			06 27	06 30	06 33	06 42	06 45
Acton Main Line	d										05 51						06 21								06 51
Ealing Broadway ⊖	d	05 21		05 30		05 41			05 50		05 54			06 05	06 11	06 20	06 24				06 35		06 41	06 50	06 54
West Ealing	d					05 43					05 57				06 13		06 27						06 43		06 57
Drayton Green	d										05 59						06 29								06 59
Castle Bar Park	d										06 01						06 31								07 01
South Greenford	d										06 04						06 34								07 04
Greenford ⊖	a										06 09						06 39								07 09
Hanwell	d					05 45									06 15								06 45		
Southall	d	05 25		05 35		05 49			05 58					06 10	06 19	06 28					06 41		06 49	06 58	
Hayes & Harlington	d	05 29		05 39		05 53			06 02					06 14	06 23	06 32					06 45		06 53	07 02	
Heathrow Terminal 1-2-3 2 ✈	a	05 35				06 05									06 35								07 05		
Heathrow Terminal 4 ✈	a	05 41																							
West Drayton	d			05 43					06 06					06 18		06 40					06 49			07 06	
Iver	d			05 46										06 21							06 52				
Langley	d			05 50				←					←	06 25					←		06 56				
Slough 3	a		05 33	05 54			05 51	05 54	06 13			06 05	06 13	06 29		06 47		06 34	06 47		07 00			07 13	
	d		05 33	05 54			05 52	05 54	06 13			06 05	06 13	06 29		06 47		06 35	06 47		07 00			07 13	
Burnham	d			→					→				06 17			→			06 51					→	
Taplow	d												06 21						06 54						
Maidenhead 3	d							06 02					06 28	06 37					06 58		07 08				
Twyford 3	d							06 10					06 35	06 45					07 06		07 16				
Reading 7	a		05 51		05 55		06 05	06 20				06 20	06 45	06 53				06 49	07 15		07 27	06 54			
Oxford	a		06 22					07 02				06 56		07 46				07 22							

		GW ◇1 ☕	GW 1	GW 1	GW 1		GW ◇1 ☕	HC	GW ◇1 C ☕	GW 1	GW 1	GW 1	GW ◇1 ☕	GW 1	GW 1		GW 1	GW 1	GW ◇1 D Ø	HC	GW 1	GW 1	GW ◇1 E ☕	GW ◇1 ☕	GW 1
London Paddington 15 ⊖	d	06 45	06 48		06 57		07 00	07 03	07 06	07 12	07 12	07 15	07 15	07 18	07 21			07 27	07 30	07 33	07 42	07 45	07 45	07 48	07 50
Acton Main Line	d											07 21										07 51			
Ealing Broadway ⊖	d				07 05			07 11			07 20	07 24						07 35		07 41	07 50	07 54			
West Ealing	d							07 13				07 27								07 43		07 57			
Drayton Green	d											07 29										07 59			
Castle Bar Park	d											07 31										08 01			
South Greenford	d											07 34										08 04			
Greenford ⊖	a											07 39										08 09			
Hanwell	d							07 15												07 45					
Southall	d				07 10			07 19			07 28							07 40		07 49	07 59				
Hayes & Harlington	d				07 14			07 23			07 32							07 44		07 53	08 02				
Heathrow Terminal 1-2-3 2 ✈	a							07 35												08 05					
Heathrow Terminal 4 ✈	a																								
West Drayton	d				07 18						07 36							07 48			08 06				
Iver	d				07 21													07 51							
Langley	d			←	07 25												←	07 55							
Slough 3	a		07 04	07 13	07 29						07 43				07 36		07 43	07 59			08 13				08 06
	d		07 04	07 13	07 29						07 43				07 36		07 43	07 59			08 13				08 06
Burnham	d			07 17							→						07 47				→				
Taplow	d			07 21													07 51								
Maidenhead 3	d			07 25	07 37					07 41							07 55	08 07							
Twyford 3	d			07 33	07 45					07 49							08 03	08 15							
Reading 7	a	07 09	07 19	07 45	07 52		07 24		07 30	08 02			07 40	07 47	07 51		08 14	08 23	07 57				08 09	08 14	08 21
Oxford	a		08 02		08 43										08 19			09 15							08 49

A from 20 February until 26 March
B until 13 February, MO from 2 April
C The Devon Express
D The Merchant Venturer
E The St. David

London - Greenford and Reading

Network Diagram - see first Page of Table 116

Station			GW	GW	GW	HC	GW	GW	GW	GW	GW		GW	GW	GW	GW	GW	HC	GW	GW	GW		GW	GW	GW
			1	◇1 ⊡	1		1	1	1	◇1 ⊡	1		1	◇1 ⊡	1	1	◇1 ⊡		1	1	◇1 ⊘		1	1	1
London Paddington 15 ⊖	d		07 57	08 00		08 03	08 06	08 12	08 15	08 15	08 18			08 22		08 27	08 30	08 33	08 38	08 45	08 45		08 47	08 51	
Acton Main Line	d								08 21											08 51					
Ealing Broadway ⊖	d		08 05			08 11		08 20	08 24							08 35		08 41	08 47	08 54			08 59		
West Ealing	d					08 13			08 27									08 43		08 57			09 01		
Drayton Green	d								08 29											08 59					
Castle Bar Park	d								08 31											09 01					
South Greenford	d								08 34											09 04					
Greenford ⊖	a								08 39											09 09					
Hanwell	d					08 15												08 45	08 50						
Southall	d		08 10			08 19		08 28								08 40		08 49							
Hayes & Harlington	d		08 14			08 23		08 32								08 44		08 53	08 56				09 08		
Heathrow Terminal 1-2-3 2 ✈	a					08 35												09 05							
Heathrow Terminal 4 ✈	a																								
West Drayton	d		08 18					08 36								08 48			09 00						
Iver	d		08 21													08 51			09 03						
Langley	d		08 25		←								←		←	08 55			09 06						←
Slough 3	a		08 29		08 13		08 24	08 43					08 29	08 36	08 43	08 59			09 11				09 16	09 06	09 11
	d		08 29		08 13		08 24	08 43					08 29	08 36	08 43	08 59			09 11				09 16	09 06	09 11
Burnham	d		→		08 17			→							08 47				→				→		
Taplow	d				08 21										08 51										
Maidenhead 3	d				08 25		08 32						08 38		08 55	09 06									09 18
Twyford 3	d				08 33		08a42						08 46		09 03	09 16									09a29
Reading 7	a			08 25	08 44					08 39	08 48		08 55	08 51	09 13	09 23	08 56				09 09			09 20	
Oxford	a												09 46	09 20		10 14								09 53	

Station		GW	GW	GW	HC	GW			GW	GW	GW	GW	GW	GW	GW	GW	HC		GW	GW	GW	GW	GW	GW	GW
		1	1	◇1 ⊡		◇1 ⊡			1	1	◇1 ⊡	1	◇1 ⊼	1	1	◇1 ⊡			1	1	◇1 ⊘	◇1 ⊡	◇1	1	1
London Paddington 15 ⊖	d		08 55	09 00	09 03	09 06			09 12	09 15	09 15	09 18	09 21		09 27	09 30	09 33		09 42	09 45	09 45	09 48	09 50		09 57
Acton Main Line	d									09 21										09 51					
Ealing Broadway ⊖	d		09 03		09 11				09 20	09 24					09 35		09 41		09 50	09 54					10 05
West Ealing	d				09 13					09 27							09 43			09 57					
Drayton Green	d									09 29										09 59					
Castle Bar Park	d									09 31										10 01					
South Greenford	d									09 34										10 04					
Greenford ⊖	a									09 39										10 09					
Hanwell	d				09 15												09 45								
Southall	d		09 08		09 19				09 28								09 49		09 58						
Hayes & Harlington	d		09 12		09 23				09 32						09 42		09 53		10 02						10 12
Heathrow Terminal 1-2-3 2 ✈	a				09 35												10 05								
Heathrow Terminal 4 ✈	a																								
West Drayton	d		09 16						09 36						09 46				10 06						10 16
Iver	d		09 19												09 49										10 19
Langley	d	←	09 23											←	09 52									←	10 22
Slough 3	a	09 16	09 27						09 43				09 36	09 43	09 57				10 13				10 06	10 13	10 27
	d	09 16	09 27						09 43				09 36	09 43	09 57				10 13				10 06	10 13	10 27
Burnham	d	09 20							→					09 45					→					10 17	
Taplow	d	09 24												09 51										10 21	
Maidenhead 3	d	09 28	09 35											09 55	10 04									10 25	10 34
Twyford 3	d	09 36	09 43											10 03	10 12									10 33	10 42
Reading 7	a	09 46	09 52	09 25		09 30					09 39	09 48	09 52	10 17	10 22	09 56					10 09	10 14	10 21	10 45	10 52
Oxford	a		10 41										10 18		11 14								10 47		11 41

Station		GW	HC			GW	GW	GW	GW	GW	GW	GW	GW		GW	HC	GW	GW	GW	GW	GW	GW	GW		HC
		◇1 A ⊡				◇1 B ⊘	1	1	◇1 ⊡	1	◇1 ⊡	1	1		◇1 ⊡		1	1	◇1 ⊘	◇1	1	1	◇1 ⊡		
London Paddington 15 ⊖	d	10 00	10 03			10 06	10 12	10 15	10 15	10 18	10 22		10 27		10 30	10 33	10 42	10 45	10 45	10 50		10 57	11 00		11 03
Acton Main Line	d							10 21										10 51							
Ealing Broadway ⊖	d		10 11				10 20	10 24					10 35			10 41	10 50	10 54				11 05			11 11
West Ealing	d		10 13					10 27								10 43		10 57							11 13
Drayton Green	d							10 29										10 59							
Castle Bar Park	d							10 31										11 01							
South Greenford	d							10 34										11 04							
Greenford ⊖	a							10 39										11 09							
Hanwell	d		10 15													10 45									11 15
Southall	d		10 19				10 28									10 49	10 58								11 19
Hayes & Harlington	d		10 23				10 32						10 42			10 53	11 02					11 12			11 23
Heathrow Terminal 1-2-3 2 ✈	a		10 35													11 05									11 35
Heathrow Terminal 4 ✈	a																								
West Drayton	d						10 36						10 46				11 06					11 16			
Iver	d												10 49									11 19			
Langley	d											←	10 52								←	11 22			
Slough 3	a						10 43				10 36	10 43	10 57				11 13			11 06	11 13	11 27			
	d						10 43				10 36	10 43	10 57				11 13			11 06	11 13	11 27			
Burnham	d						→					10 47					→				11 17				
Taplow	d											10 51									11 21				
Maidenhead 3	d											10 55	11 04								11 25	11 34			
Twyford 3	d											11 03	11 12								11 33	11 42			
Reading 7	a	10 25				10 30			10 39	10 48	10 51	11 13	11 22		10 56				11 09	11 21	11 45	11 52	11 25		
Oxford	a										11 18		12 14							11 50		12 41			

A The Torbay Express

B The Cornish Riveira

Table 117

Mondays to Fridays

London - Greenford and Reading

Network Diagram - see first Page of Table 116

		GW		GW	GW	GW	GW	GW	GW		GW	GW	HC	GW	GW	GW	GW	GW	GW		GW	GW	HC	GW	
		◇1		1	1	◇1	1	◇1	1		1	◇1		1	1	◇1	◇1	◇1	1		1	◇1		◇1	
		A Ø				☕		🛒				☕				Ø	B ☕	🛒				☕		C Ø	
London Paddington 15 ⊖	d	11 06		11 12	11 15	11 15	11 18	11 20			11 27	11 30	11 33	11 42	11 45	11 45	11 48	11 50			11 57	12 00	12 03	12 06	
Acton Main Line	d				11 21										11 51										
Ealing Broadway ⊖	d			11 20	11 24						11 35		11 41	11 50	11 54						12 05		12 11		
West Ealing	d				11 27								11 43		11 57								12 13		
Drayton Green	d				11 29										11 59										
Castle Bar Park	d				11 31										12 01										
South Greenford	d				11 34										12 04										
Greenford ⊖	a				11 39										12 09										
Hanwell	d												11 45										12 15		
Southall	d			11 28									11 49	11 58									12 19		
Hayes & Harlington	d			11 32							11 42		11 53	12 02							12 12		12 23		
Heathrow Terminal 1-2-3 2 ✈	a												12 05										12 35		
Heathrow Terminal 4 ✈	a																								
West Drayton	d			11 36							11 46			12 06							12 16				
Iver	d										11 49										12 19				
Langley	d								←		11 52								←		12 22				
Slough 3	a			11 43				11 36	11 43		11 57			12 13				12 06	12 13		12 27				
	d			11 43				11 36	11 43		11 57			12 13				12 06	12 13		12 27				
Burnham	d			→					11 47					→					12 17						
Taplow	d								11 51										12 21						
Maidenhead 3	d								11 55		12 04								12 25		12 34				
Twyford 3	d								12 03		12 12								12 33		12 42				
Reading 7	a	11 30				11 39	11 47	11 52	12 17		12 22	11 56				12 09	12 14	12 22	12 45		12 50	12 25		12 30	
Oxford	a							12 18			13 14							12 48			13 41				

		GW	GW	GW	GW		GW	GW	GW	GW	HC	GW	GW	GW	GW		GW	GW	GW	HC	GW		GW	GW	GW
		1	1	◇1	◇1		◇1	1	1	◇1		1	1	◇1	◇1		1	1	◇1		◇1		1	1	◇1
				☕	☕		🛒			☕				Ø	🛒				☕		Ø				☕
London Paddington 15 ⊖	d	12 12	12 15	12 15	12 18		12 21		12 27	12 30	12 33	12 42	12 45	12 45	12 50			12 57	13 00	13 03	13 06		13 12	13 15	13 15
Acton Main Line	d		12 21										12 51											13 21	
Ealing Broadway ⊖	d	12 20	12 24						12 35		12 41	12 50	12 54					13 05		13 11			13 20	13 24	
West Ealing	d		12 27								12 43		12 57							13 13				13 27	
Drayton Green	d		12 29										12 59											13 29	
Castle Bar Park	d		12 31										13 01											13 31	
South Greenford	d		12 34										13 04											13 34	
Greenford ⊖	a		12 39										13 10											13 39	
Hanwell	d										12 45									13 15					
Southall	d	12 28									12 49	12 58								13 19			13 28		
Hayes & Harlington	d	12 32							12 42		12 53	13 02						13 12		13 23			13 32		
Heathrow Terminal 1-2-3 2 ✈	a										13 05									13 35					
Heathrow Terminal 4 ✈	a																								
West Drayton	d	12 36							12 46			13 06						13 16					13 36		
Iver	d								12 49									13 19							
Langley	d							←	12 52								←	13 22							
Slough 3	a	12 43					12 36	12 43	12 57			13 13			13 06		13 13	13 27					13 43		
	d	12 43					12 36	12 43	12 57			13 13			13 06		13 13	13 27					13 43		
Burnham	d	→						12 47				→					13 17						→		
Taplow	d							12 51									13 21								
Maidenhead 3	d							12 55	13 04								13 25	13 34							
Twyford 3	d							13 03	13 12								13 33	13 42							
Reading 7	a			12 39	12 46		12 51	13 14	13 22	12 56				13 09	13 22		13 45	13 51	13 25		13 30				13 39
Oxford	a						13 18		14 14						13 50			14 42							

			GW	GW	GW	GW	GW	HC	GW	GW	GW		GW	GW	GW	GW	GW	HC	GW		GW		GW	GW	GW
			1	◇1	1	1	◇1		1	1	◇1		◇1	◇1	1	1	◇1		◇1		1		1	◇1	1
				🛒			☕				☕		☕	🛒			☕		Ø					☕	
London Paddington 15 ⊖	d		13 18	13 21		13 27	13 30	13 33	13 42	13 45	13 45		13 48	13 50		13 57	14 00	14 03	14 06		14 12		14 15	14 15	14 18
Acton Main Line	d									13 51													14 21		
Ealing Broadway ⊖	d					13 35		13 41	13 50	13 54						14 05		14 11			14 20		14 24		
West Ealing	d							13 43		13 57								14 13					14 27		
Drayton Green	d									13 59													14 29		
Castle Bar Park	d									14 01													14 31		
South Greenford	d									14 04													14 34		
Greenford ⊖	a									14 09													14 39		
Hanwell	d							13 45										14 15							
Southall	d							13 49	13 58									14 19			14 28				
Hayes & Harlington	d					13 42		13 53	14 02							14 12		14 23			14 32				
Heathrow Terminal 1-2-3 2 ✈	a							14 05										14 35							
Heathrow Terminal 4 ✈	a																								
West Drayton	d					13 46			14 06							14 16					14 36				
Iver	d					13 49										14 19									
Langley	d				←	13 52									←	14 22									
Slough 3	a			13 36	13 43	13 57			14 13					14 06	14 13	14 27					14 43				
	d			13 36	13 43	13 57			14 13					14 06	14 13	14 27					14 43				
Burnham	d				13 47				→						14 17						→				
Taplow	d				13 51										14 21										
Maidenhead 3	d				13 55	14 04									14 25	14 34									
Twyford 3	d				14 03	14 12									14 33	14 42									
Reading 7	a		13 47	13 52	14 17	14 21	13 56				14 09		14 14	14 21	14 45	14 52	14 25		14 30					14 39	14 47
Oxford	a			14 18		15 14								14 48		15 41									

A The Mayflower

B The Cheltenham Spa Express

C The Royal Duchy

London - Greenford and Reading

Network Diagram - see first Page of Table 116

	GW	GW	GW	GW	HC	GW		GW	GW	GW	GW	GW	GW	HC	GW			GW	GW	GW	GW	GW	GW	GW
	◇1 🚲	1	1	◇1 ☕		1		1	◇1 ☕	◇1 🚲	1	1	◇1 ☕		◇1 ∅			1	1	◇1 ☕	1	◇1 🚲	1	1
London Paddington 15 ⊖ d	14 21		14 27	14 30	14 33	14 42		14 45	14 45	14 50		14 57	15 00	15 03	15 06			15 12	15 15	15 15	15 18	15 22		15 27
Acton Main Line d								14 51											15 21					
Ealing Broadway ⊖ d			14 35		14 41	14 50		14 54				15 05		15 11				15 20	15 24					15 35
West Ealing d					14 43			14 57						15 13					15 27					
Drayton Green d								14 59											15 29					
Castle Bar Park d								15 01											15 31					
South Greenford d								15 04											15 34					
Greenford ⊖ a								15 09											15 39					
Hanwell d					14 45									15 15										
Southall d					14 49	14 58								15 19				15 28						15 40
Hayes & Harlington d			14 42		14 53	15 02						15 12		15 23				15 32						15 44
Heathrow Terminal 1-2-3 2 ✈ a					15 05									15 35										
Heathrow Terminal 4 ✈ a																								
West Drayton d			14 46			15 06						15 16						15 36						15 48
Iver d			14 49									15 19												15 51
Langley d		←	14 52								←	15 22											←	15 55
Slough 3 a	14 36	14 43	14 57			15 13				15 06	15 13	15 27						15 43				15 36	15 43	15 59
d	14 36	14 43	14 57			15 13				15 06	15 13	15 27						15 43				15 36	15 43	15 59
Burnham d		14 47				→					15 17							→					15 47	
Taplow d		14 51									15 21												15 51	
Maidenhead 3 d		14 55	15 04								15 25	15 34											15 55	16 07
Twyford 3 d		15 03	15 12								15 33	15 42											16 03	16 15
Reading 7 a	14 52	15 13	15 22	14 56					15 09	15 22	15 44	15 52	15 25		15 30					15 39	15 47	15 51	16 13	16 23
Oxford a	15 18		16 14							15 50		16 43										16 18		17 15

	GW	HC		GW	GW	GW	GW	GW	GW	GW	GW	HC		GW		GW	GW	GW	GW	GW	GW	GW		GW
	◇1 ☕			1	1	◇1 ☕	◇1 ☕	◇1 ☕	1	1	◇1 ☕			◇1 ☕		1	1	◇1 ☕	1	◇1 🚲	1	1		◇1 ☕
London Paddington 15 ⊖ d	15 30	15 33		15 42	15 45	15 45	15 48	15 51		15 57	16 00	16 03		16 06		16 12	16 15	16 15	16 18	16 22		16 27		16 30
Acton Main Line d					15 51												16 21							
Ealing Broadway ⊖ d		15 41		15 50	15 54					16 05		16 11				16 20	16 24					16 35		
West Ealing d		15 43			15 57							16 13					16 27							
Drayton Green d					15 59												16 29							
Castle Bar Park d					16 01												16 31							
South Greenford d					16 04												16 34							
Greenford ⊖ a					16 09												16 39							
Hanwell d		15 45										16 15												
Southall d		15 49		15 58								16 19				16 28						16 40		
Hayes & Harlington d		15 53		16 02						16 11		16 23				16 32						16 44		
Heathrow Terminal 1-2-3 2 ✈ a		16 05										16 35												
Heathrow Terminal 4 ✈ a																								
West Drayton d				16 06						16 16						16 36								
Iver d										16 19												16 49		
Langley d									←	16 22											←	16 52		
Slough 3 a				16 13				16 06	16 13	16 27						16 43				16 37	16 43	16 57		
d				16 13				16 06	16 13	16 27						16 43				16 38	16 43	16 57		
Burnham d				→					16 17							→					16 47			
Taplow d									16 21												16 51			
Maidenhead 3 d									16 25	16 34											16 55	17 04		
Twyford 3 d									16 33	16 42											17 03	17 12		
Reading 7 a	15 56					16 09	16 14	16 20	16 44	16 52	16 25			16 30				16 39	16 47	16 52	17 14	17 21		16 56
Oxford a								16 47		17 44										17 24		18 12		

	HC	GW	GW	GW	GW	GW	GW	GW		GW	HC	GW		GW	GW	GW	GW	GW		GW	GW	GW	GW	GW
		◇1 ☕	1	1	◇1 A ☕	◇1	1	1		◇1 ☕		◇1 ☕		◇1 ☕	1	1	1	◇1 B ☕		1	1	◇1 ☕	1	◇1 ☕
London Paddington 15 ⊖ d	16 33	16 36	16 42	16 45	16 45	16 49		16 55		17 00	17 03	17 03		17 06		17 12	17 15	17 15		17 18	17 18	17 22	17 25	17 30
Acton Main Line d				16 51																17 24				
Ealing Broadway ⊖ d	16 41		16 50	16 54				17 04			17 11						17 23			17 27			17 33	
West Ealing d	16 43			16 57							17 13									17 30				
Drayton Green d				16 59																17 32				
Castle Bar Park d				17 01																17 34				
South Greenford d				17 04																17 37				
Greenford ⊖ a				17 09																17 42				
Hanwell d	16 45										17 15													
Southall d	16 49		16 58								17 19						17 29						17 38	
Hayes & Harlington d	16 53		17 02					17 11			17 23						17 33						17 42	
Heathrow Terminal 1-2-3 2 ✈ a	17 05										17 35													
Heathrow Terminal 4 ✈ a																								
West Drayton d			17 07					17 16									17 38						17 47	
Iver d			17 10					17 20									17 41						17 50	
Langley d			17 14				←	17 24									17 44						17 54	
Slough 3 a			17 18			17 04	17 18	17 27								17 32	17 49						17 58	
d			17 18			17 04	17 18	17 28								17 35	17 49						17 58	
Burnham d			→				17 22	17 33								17 40	17 53						18 02	
Taplow d							17 26	17 36								17 43	17 57						18 06	
Maidenhead 3 d							17 30	17 43							←	17 47	18a05				17 40		18 10	
Twyford 3 d							17 38	17 51						17 28	17 38	17a57					17 48		18 17	
Reading 7 a		17 01			17 09	17 19	→	→		17 24		17 29		17 35	17 46			17 40			17 56	17 49	→	17 54
Oxford a						17 50															18 45	18 15		

A The Capitals United

B The Red Dragon

London - Greenford and Reading

Network Diagram - see first Page of Table 116

		HC	GW	GW	GW		GW	GW	GW	GW	GW	GW	GW	GW	GW		HC	GW		GW	GW	GW	GW	GW	GW
			◇1	1	1		1	◇1	1	1	◇1	◇1	1	◇1	1			◇1		◇1	1	1	◇1	1	1
														A				B							
			☕					☕			☕	☕		☕				✕		☕			☕		
London Paddington 15 ⊖	d	17 33	17 33		17 36		17 42	17 45	17 45	17 48	17 48	17 50	17 57	18 00			18 03	18 03		18 06		18 12	18 15	18 15	18 18
Acton Main Line	d									17 54															18 24
Ealing Broadway ⊖	d	17 41							17 53	17 57			18 05				18 11							18 23	18 27
West Ealing	d	17 43								18 00							18 13								18 30
Drayton Green	d									18 02															18 32
Castle Bar Park	d									18 04															18 34
South Greenford	d									18 07															18 37
Greenford ⊖	a									18 12															18 42
Hanwell	d	17 45															18 15								
Southall	d	17 49							17 59				18 10				18 19							18 29	
Hayes & Harlington	d	17 53							18 03				18 14				18 23							18 33	
Heathrow Terminal 1-2-3 2 ✈	a	18 05															18 35								
Heathrow Terminal 4 ✈	a																								
West Drayton	d								18 08				18 19											18 38	
Iver	d												18 22												
Langley	d								18 12				18 26											18 42	
Slough 3	a						18 04		18 16				18 30									18 35		18 47	
	d						18 05		18 16				18 30									18 36		18 47	
Burnham	d								18 21				18 35											18 51	
Taplow	d												18 39												
Maidenhead 3	d			←	17 58		18a13		18 26			18 09	18 45		←						←	18 49		18 57	
Twyford 3	d			17 51	18 07				18 34				18 52		18 17					18 28	18 34	18a58		19 05	
Reading 7	a		17 59	18 00	18 15			18 09	→		18 14	18 20	→	18 25	18 26			18 30		18 35	18 44		18 40	→	
Oxford	a				19 04							18 47			19 16										

			GW	GW	GW	GW	GW	HC	GW	GW	GW		GW	GW	GW	GW	GW	GW	GW	GW	GW		GW	GW	
					FX	FO											FO	FX							
			1	◇1	1	1	◇1		◇1	1	1		◇1	1	1	◇1	1	1	1	◇1	1		1	◇1	
				C																					
				☕			☕		☕				☕			☕				trolley				☕	
London Paddington 15 ⊖	d		18 18	18 22	18 25	18 25	18 30	18 33	18 33		18 36		18 45		18 45	18 47			18 48	18 51			18 57	19 00	
Acton Main Line	d																		18 54						
Ealing Broadway ⊖	d				18 33	18 33		18 41							18 53				18 57				19 05		
West Ealing	d							18 43											19 00						
Drayton Green	d																		19 02						
Castle Bar Park	d																		19 04						
South Greenford	d																		19 07						
Greenford ⊖	a																		19 12						
Hanwell	d							18 45																	
Southall	d				18 38	18 38		18 49							18 59								19 10		
Hayes & Harlington	d				18 42	18 42		18 53							19 03								19 14		
Heathrow Terminal 1-2-3 2 ✈	a							19 05																	
Heathrow Terminal 4 ✈	a																								
West Drayton	d				18 46	18 46																	19 19		
Iver	d				18 49	18 49																	19 22		
Langley	d				18 52	18 52											←	←			←		19 26		
Slough 3	a				18 59	18 59					18 54				19 11		18 59	18 59		19 06	19 11		19 30		
	d				18 59	18 59					18 55				19 11		18 59	18 59		19 06	19 11		19 30		
Burnham	d				→	→									→		19 03	19 03			19 15		19 34		
Taplow	d																19 06	19 06					19 38		
Maidenhead 3	d		18 40							←	19a03			←			19 10	19 10			19 21		19 43		
Twyford 3	d		18 48							18 52				19 05		19 09	19 18	19 18			19 38		19 51		
Reading 7	a		18 56	18 49			18 54		18 59	19 01			19 09	19 13		19 17	19 26	19 26		19 22	19 47		→	19 27	
Oxford	a		19 43	19 19										20 13			20 26	20 27		19 48					

A The Bristolian

B The Golden Hind

C The Cathedrals Express

London - Greenford and Reading

Network Diagram - see first Page of Table 116

		HC	GW	GW	GW	GW	GW		GW	GW	GW	GW	GW	GW	HC	GW	GW		GW	GW	GW	GW	GW	GW	HC
			R 1	1	1	1	◇1		1	◇1	1	1	1	◇1		1	1		◇1	◇1	◇1	1	1	◇1	
			✕				☕			☕				☕					☕	☕	🛒			☕	
London Paddington 15 ⊖	d	19 03	19 03	19 06	19 12	19 15	19 15		19 18	19 22			19 27	19 30	19 33	19 42	19 45		19 45	19 48	19 50		19 57	20 00	20 03
Acton Main Line	d					19 21											19 51								
Ealing Broadway ⊖	d	19 11			19 20	19 24							19 35		19 41	19 50	19 54						20 05		20 11
West Ealing	d	19 13				19 27									19 43		19 57								20 13
Drayton Green	d					19 29											19 59								
Castle Bar Park	d					19 31											20 01								
South Greenford	d					19 34											20 04								
Greenford ⊖	a					19 39											20 09								
Hanwell	d	19 15													19 45										20 15
Southall	d	19 19			19 28								19 40		19 49	19 58									20 19
Hayes & Harlington	d	19 23			19 32								19 44		19 53	20 02							20 12		20 23
Heathrow Terminal 1-2-3 2 ✈	a	19 35													20 05										20 35
Heathrow Terminal 4 ✈	a																								
West Drayton	d												19 48			20 06							20 16		
Iver	d												19 51			20 09							20 19		
Langley	d											←	19 55			20 13						←	20 22		
Slough 3	a				19 41					19 36		19 41	19 59			20 17					20 06	20 17	20 27		
	d				19 41					19 36		19 41	19 59			20 17					20 06	20 17	20 27		
Burnham	d				↪							19 45	20 03			↪						20 20			
Taplow	d											19 48										20 25			
Maidenhead 3	d			19 27					19 40		←	19 52	20 09							20 06		20 29	20 34		
Twyford 3	d			19a38					19 48		19 51	20 00	20 17									20 37	20 42		
Reading 7	a		19 32				19 39		19 56	19 51	20 00	20 11	20 23	19 56					20 09	20 17	20 22	20 45	20 52	20 25	
Oxford	a								20 45	20 18			21 13								20 47		21 43		

		GW	GW		GW	GW	GW	GW	HC	GW	GW	GW	GW		GW	GW	GW	HC	GW	GW	GW	GW	GW		HC
		1	1		◇1	◇1	1	1		◇1	1	1	◇1		◇1	1	1		1	◇1	1	◇1	1		
					☕	🛒				☕			☕							☕					
London Paddington 15 ⊖	d	20 12	20 15		20 15	20 20		20 27	20 33	20 35	20 42	20 45	20 45		20 48		20 57	21 03	21 12	21 15	21 15	21 18	21 27		21 33
Acton Main Line	d		20 21									20 51									21 21				
Ealing Broadway ⊖	d	20 20	20 24					20 35	20 41		20 50	20 54					21 05	21 11	21 20		21 24		21 35		21 41
West Ealing	d		20 27						20 43			20 57						21 13			21 27				21 43
Drayton Green	d		20 29									20 59									21 29				
Castle Bar Park	d		20 31									21 01									21 31				
South Greenford	d		20 34									21 04									21 34				
Greenford ⊖	a		20 39									21 09									21 39				
Hanwell	d								20 45									21 15							21 45
Southall	d	20 28							20 49		20 58							21 19	21 28				21 42		21 49
Hayes & Harlington	d	20 32						20 42	20 53		21 02						21 12	21 23	21 32				21 46		21 53
Heathrow Terminal 1-2-3 2 ✈	a								21 05									21 35							22 05
Heathrow Terminal 4 ✈	a																								
West Drayton	d	20 36						20 46			21 06						21 16		21 36				21 50		
Iver	d							20 49									21 19						21 53		
Langley	d						←	20 52								←	21 22						21 57		
Slough 3	a	20 43				20 35	20 43	20 57			21 13				21 04	21 13	21 27		21 43			21 34	22 02		
	d	20 43				20 36	20 43	20 57			21 13				21 05	21 13	21 27		21 43			21 35	22 07		
Burnham	d	↪					20 47				↪					21 17			↪				↪		
Taplow	d						20 51									21 21									
Maidenhead 3	d						20 55	21 04								21 25	21 34								
Twyford 3	d						21 03	21 12								21 33	21 42								
Reading 7	a				20 39	20 50	21 13	21 20		20 59			21 09		21 20	21 45	21 51			21 39		21 50			
Oxford	a					21 16		22 14							21 51		22 41					22 18			

		GW	GW	GW	GW	GW	GW	GW	HC		GW	GW	GW	GW	GW	GW	GW	HC	GW		GW	GW	GW	GW	GW
					FO	FX					FO		FX	FO	FX				FO		FO	FX	FX		
		1	◇1	1	◇1	◇1	1	1			◇1	1	◇1	1	1	◇1	1		◇1		1	1	◇1	1	◇1
			☕		🛒	☕					☕		☕						☕				☕		
London Paddington 15 ⊖	d	21 42	21 45		21 48	21 48		21 58	22 03		22 15		22 15	22 16	22 16	22 18		22 33	22 45				22 45	22 45	22 48
Acton Main Line	d	21 48																						22 51	
Ealing Broadway ⊖	d	21 51						22 06	22 11					22 24	22 24			22 41						22 54	
West Ealing	d								22 13									22 43							
Drayton Green	d																								
Castle Bar Park	d																								
South Greenford	d																								
Greenford ⊖	a																								
Hanwell	d								22 15									22 45							
Southall	d	21 58							22 19					22 29	22 29			22 49							
Hayes & Harlington	d	22 02						22 13	22 23					22 33	22 33			22 53						23 01	
Heathrow Terminal 1-2-3 2 ✈	a								22 35									23 05							
Heathrow Terminal 4 ✈	a																								
West Drayton	d	22 06						22 17						22 37	22 37										
Iver	d							22 20																	
Langley	d			←			←	22 23				←					←				←	←			
Slough 3	a	22 14		21 43	22 03	22 03	22 02	22 28				22 14		22 45	22 45	22 35	22 28				22 45	22 45		23 11	23 06
	d	22 15		21 43	22 03	22 03	22 07	22 39				22 15		22 45	22 45	22 36	22 39				22 45	22 45		23 12	23 06
Burnham	d	↪		21 47				↪				22 18		↪	↪						22 49	22 49		↪	
Taplow	d			21 51								22 22									22 53	22 53			
Maidenhead 3	d			21 55			22 14					22 26				22 44	22 47				22 57	22 57			23 14
Twyford 3	d			22 03			22 22					22 34					22 55				23 05	23 05			
Reading 7	a		22 09	22 16	22 22	22 22	22 30				22 39	22 46	22 48			22 58	23 04		23 09		23 14	23 16	23 18		23 28
Oxford	a				22 47	22 47	23 21									23 28	23 48								23 56

Table 117

London - Greenford and Reading

Network Diagram - see first Page of Table 116

		GW	GW	HC	GW	GW	GW	GW	GW	GW	GW
						FO	FX		FO		
		1	1		◇1	1	1	◇1	1	B A 🛏 ☕	1
								☕			
London Paddington 15 ⊖	d		22 59	23 03	23 18	23 29	23 29	23 30	23 42	23 45	23 48
Acton Main Line	d										23 54
Ealing Broadway ⊖	d		23 07	23 11		23 37	23 37				23 57
West Ealing	d			23 13							23 59
Drayton Green	d										
Castle Bar Park	d										
South Greenford	d										
Greenford ⊖	a										
Hanwell	d			23 15							00 02
Southall	d		23 12	23 19							00 06
Hayes & Harlington	d		23 16	23 23		23 44	23 44				00 10
Heathrow Terminal 1-2-3 2 ✈	a			23 35							
Heathrow Terminal 4 ✈	a			23 41							
West Drayton	d		23 20								00 14
Iver	d		23 23								00 17
Langley	d	←	23 27								00 21
Slough 3	a	23 11	23 32		23 36	23 53	23 53		23 58		00 26
	d	23 12	23 32		23 36	23 54	23 54		23 58		00 26
Burnham	d	23 16									00 30
Taplow	d	23 20									00 34
Maidenhead 3	d	23 24	23 40		23 44	00 01	00 01		00 08		00 41
Twyford 3	d	23 32	23 48			00 09	00 09				00 48
Reading 7	a	23 41	23 58		23 58	00 24	00 24	00 04	00 21		00 57
Oxford	a	00 26			00 28	01 16	01 16		01 02		

Saturdays

until 31 December

		GW	GW	GW	GW	GW	GW	GW	GW	GW	GW	GW
		1	◇1	1	1	◇1 ☕	1	1	◇1	1	1	1
London Paddington 15 ⊖	d	22p45	23p18		23p29	23p30	23p42	23p48	00 22	00 34	01 44	03 34
Acton Main Line	d	22p51						23p54				
Ealing Broadway ⊖	d	22p54			23p37			23p57		00 42	01 52	03 42
West Ealing	d							23p59				
Drayton Green	d											
Castle Bar Park	d											
South Greenford	d											
Greenford ⊖	a											
Hanwell	d							00 02				
Southall	d							00 06		00 47	01 57	03 47
Hayes & Harlington	d	23p01			23p44			00 10		00 51	02 01	03 51
Heathrow Terminal 1-2-3 2 ✈	a											
Heathrow Terminal 4 ✈	a											
West Drayton	d							00 14		00 55	02 05	03 55
Iver	d							00 17				
Langley	d							00 21		01 00		
Slough 3	a	23p11	23p36		23p53		23p58	00 26	00 38	01 05	02 13	04 03
	d	23p12	23p36		23p54		23p58	00 26	00 39	01 05	02 13	04 03
Burnham	d	23p16						00 30		01 09		
Taplow	d	23p20						00 34		01 13		
Maidenhead 3	d	23p24	23p44		00 01		00 08	00 41		01 16	02 21	04 11
Twyford 3	d	23p32		00 07	00 09			00 48		01 24	02 29	04 19
Reading 7	a	23p41	23p58	00 16	00 19	00 04	00 21	00 57	00 55	01 35	02 38	04 30
Oxford	a	00 26	00 28		01 16		01 02		01 28			

		HC	HC	GW	GW	HC	GW	GW	GW	HC	GW	GW
				◇1	1		1	◇1	1		1	1
London Paddington 15 ⊖	d	04 42	05 13	05 21	05 25	05 33	05 45	05 50	05 57	06 03	06 12	06 15
Acton Main Line	d						05 51					06 21
Ealing Broadway ⊖	d	04 50	05 21		05 33	05 41	05 54		06 05	06 11	06 20	06 24
West Ealing	d					05 43	05 57			06 13		06 27
Drayton Green	d						05 59					06 29
Castle Bar Park	d						06 01					06 31
South Greenford	d						06 04					06 34
Greenford ⊖	a						06 09					06 39
Hanwell	d					05 45				06 15		
Southall	d	04 54	05 25		05 38	05 49			06 10	06 19	06 28	
Hayes & Harlington	d	04 58	05 29		05 42	05 53			06 14	06 23	06 32	
Heathrow Terminal 1-2-3 2 ✈	a	05 04	05 35			06 05				06 35		
Heathrow Terminal 4 ✈	a	05 10	05 41									
West Drayton	d								06 18		06 36	
Iver	d								06 21			
Langley	d								06 25			
Slough 3	a			05 37	05 50			06 06	06 30		06 43	
	d			05 38	05 51			06 06	06 31		06 43	
Burnham	d				05 55				06 35		→	
Taplow	d				05 58				06 38			
Maidenhead 3	d				06 02				06 42			
Twyford 3	d				06 10				06 50			
Reading 7	a			05 52	06 17			06 22	06 56			
Oxford	a			06 22	07 03			06 52	07 43			

A The Night Riviera

Table 117

Saturdays

until 31 December

London - Greenford and Reading

Network Diagram - see first Page of Table 116

		GW	GW	GW	GW	HC		GW	GW	GW	GW	GW	GW	HC	GW	GW		GW	GW	GW	GW	HC	GW	GW	GW
		◇1	1	1	◇1 ☕			1	1	◇1	1	1	◇1 ☕		1	1		◇1	1	1	R 1 ☕		1	1	◇1 ☕
London Paddington 15 ⊖	d	06 21		06 27	06 30	06 33		06 42	06 45	06 50		06 57	07 00	07 03	07 12	07 15		07 21		07 27	07 30	07 33	07 42	07 45	07 45
Acton Main Line	d								06 51							07 21								07 51	
Ealing Broadway ⊖	d			06 35		06 41		06 50	06 54			07 05		07 11	07 20	07 24				07 35		07 41	07 50	07 54	
West Ealing	d					06 43			06 57					07 13		07 27						07 43		07 57	
Drayton Green	d								06 59							07 29								07 59	
Castle Bar Park	d								07 01							07 31								08 01	
South Greenford	d								07 04							07 34								08 04	
Greenford ⊖	a								07 09							07 39								08 09	
Hanwell	d					06 45								07 15								07 45			
Southall	d					06 49		06 58						07 19	07 28							07 49	07 58		
Hayes & Harlington	d			06 42		06 53		07 02				07 12		07 23	07 32					07 42		07 53	08 02		
Heathrow Terminal 1-2-3 2 ✈	a					07 05								07 35								08 05			
Heathrow Terminal 4 ✈	a																								
West Drayton	d			06 46				07 06				07 16			07 36					07 46			08 06		
Iver	d			06 49								07 19								07 49					
Langley	d		←	06 52							←	07 22							←	07 52					
Slough 3	a	06 37	06 43	06 57				07 13		07 06	07 13	07 27			07 43			07 37	07 43	07 57			08 13		
	d	06 38	06 43	06 57				07 13		07 06	07 13	07 27			07 43			07 38	07 43	07 57			08 13		
Burnham	d		06 47					→			07 17				→				07 47				→		
Taplow	d		06 51								07 21								07 51						
Maidenhead 3	d		06 55	07 04							07 25	07 34							07 55	08 04					
Twyford 3	d		07 03	07 12							07 33	07 42							08 03	08 12					
Reading 7	a	06 53	07 13	07 20	06 57					07 22	07 43	07 52	07 26					07 53	08 13	08 22	07 57				08 09
Oxford	a	07 18		08 09						07 48		08 40						08 19		09 14					

		GW		GW	GW	GW	HC	GW	GW	GW	GW	GW		GW	GW	GW	HC	GW	GW	GW	GW	GW		GW	GW
		◇1		1	1	◇1 ☕		1	1	◇1 ☕	◇1 ☕	◇1 ☕		1	1	◇1 ☕		1	1	◇1 ☕	◇1	1		1	◇1 ☕
London Paddington 15 ⊖	d	07 50			07 57	08 00	08 03	08 12	08 15	08 15	08 18	08 21			08 27	08 30	08 33	08 42	08 45	08 45	08 50			08 57	09 00
Acton Main Line	d								08 21										08 51						
Ealing Broadway ⊖	d				08 05		08 11	08 20	08 24						08 35		08 41	08 50	08 54					09 05	
West Ealing	d						08 13		08 27								08 43		08 57						
Drayton Green	d								08 29										08 59						
Castle Bar Park	d								08 31										09 01						
South Greenford	d								08 34										09 04						
Greenford ⊖	a								08 39										09 09						
Hanwell	d						08 15										08 45								
Southall	d						08 19	08 28									08 49	08 58							
Hayes & Harlington	d				08 12		08 23	08 32							08 42		08 53	09 02						09 12	
Heathrow Terminal 1-2-3 2 ✈	a						08 35										09 05								
Heathrow Terminal 4 ✈	a																								
West Drayton	d				08 16			08 36							08 46			09 06						09 16	
Iver	d				08 19										08 49									09 19	
Langley	d			←	08 22									←	08 52							←		09 22	
Slough 3	a	08 06		08 13	08 27			08 43				08 38		08 43	08 57			09 13			09 06	09 13		09 27	
	d	08 06		08 13	08 27			08 43				08 39		08 43	08 57			09 13			09 06	09 13		09 27	
Burnham	d			08 17				→						08 47				→				09 17			
Taplow	d			08 21										08 51								09 21			
Maidenhead 3	d			08 25	08 34									08 55	09 04							09 25		09 34	
Twyford 3	d			08 33	08 42									09 03	09 12							09 33		09 42	
Reading 7	a	08 22		08 43	08 52	08 26				08 40	08 46	08 53		09 13	09 23	08 56				09 09	09 22	09 43		09 52	09 26
Oxford	a	08 48			09 40							09 18			10 14						09 48			10 40	

		HC	GW	GW	GW	GW	GW	GW		GW	GW	HC	GW	GW	GW	GW	GW	GW		GW	HC	GW	GW	GW	GW
			◇1 Ø	1	1	1	◇1	1		1	◇1 ☕		1	1	◇1 ☕	◇1	1	1		◇1 ☕		◇1 Ø	1	1	◇1 ☕
London Paddington 15 ⊖	d	09 03	09 06	09 12	09 15	09 18	09 21			09 27	09 30	09 33	09 42	09 45	09 45	09 50		09 57		10 00	10 03	10 06	10 12	10 15	10 15
Acton Main Line	d				09 21									09 51										10 21	
Ealing Broadway ⊖	d	09 11		09 20	09 24					09 35		09 41	09 50	09 54				10 05			10 11		10 20	10 24	
West Ealing	d	09 13			09 27							09 43		09 57							10 13			10 27	
Drayton Green	d				09 29									09 59										10 29	
Castle Bar Park	d				09 31									10 01										10 31	
South Greenford	d				09 34									10 04										10 34	
Greenford ⊖	a				09 39									10 09										10 39	
Hanwell	d	09 15										09 45									10 15				
Southall	d	09 19		09 28								09 49	09 58								10 19		10 28		
Hayes & Harlington	d	09 23		09 32						09 42		09 53	10 02					10 12			10 23		10 32		
Heathrow Terminal 1-2-3 2 ✈	a	09 35										10 05									10 35				
Heathrow Terminal 4 ✈	a																								
West Drayton	d			09 36						09 46			10 06					10 16					10 36		
Iver	d									09 49								10 19							
Langley	d							←		09 52							←	10 22							
Slough 3	a			09 43			09 38	09 43		09 57			10 13			10 06	10 13	10 27					10 43		
	d			09 43			09 39	09 43		09 57			10 13			10 06	10 13	10 27					10 43		
Burnham	d			→				09 47					→				10 17						→		
Taplow	d							09 51									10 21								
Maidenhead 3	d							09 55		10 04							10 25	10 34							
Twyford 3	d							10 03		10 12							10 33	10 42							
Reading 7	a		09 30			09 48	09 54	10 13		10 22	09 57				10 09	10 22	10 43	10 52		10 26		10 30			10 40
Oxford	a						10 19			11 14						10 48		11 40							

Table 117

Saturdays

until 31 December

London - Greenford and Reading

Network Diagram - see first Page of Table 116

	GW 1	GW ◇1 🍴	GW 1		GW 1	GW ◇1 🍴	HC	GW 1	GW 1	GW ◇1 Ø	GW ◇1 🛒	GW 1	GW 1		GW ◇1 🍴	HC	GW ◇1 Ø	GW 1	GW 1	GW 1	GW ◇1 🛒	GW 1	GW 1	
London Paddington 15 ⊖ d	10 18	10 21			10 27	10 30	10 33	10 42	10 45	10 45	10 50		10 57		11 00	11 03	11 06	11 12	11 15	11 18	11 21		11 27	
Acton Main Line d									10 51										11 21					
Ealing Broadway ⊖ d					10 35		10 41	10 52	10 54				11 05			11 11		11 20	11 24				11 35	
West Ealing d							10 43		10 57							11 13			11 27					
Drayton Green d									10 59										11 29					
Castle Bar Park d									11 01										11 31					
South Greenford d									11 04										11 34					
Greenford ⊖ a									11 09										11 39					
Hanwell d							10 45									11 15								
Southall d							10 49	10 58								11 19		11 28						
Hayes & Harlington d					10 42		10 53	11 02					11 12			11 23		11 32					11 42	
Heathrow Terminal 1-2-3 2 ✈ a							11 05									11 35								
Heathrow Terminal 4 ✈ a																								
West Drayton d					10 46			11 06					11 16					11 36					11 46	
Iver d					10 49								11 19										11 49	
Langley d			←		10 52							←	11 22									←	11 52	
Slough 3 a		10 38	10 43		10 57			11 13			11 06	11 13	11 27					11 43			11 38	11 43	11 57	
d		10 39	10 43		10 57			11 13			11 06	11 13	11 27					11 43			11 39	11 43	11 57	
Burnham d			10 47					→				11 17						→				11 47		
Taplow d			10 51									11 21										11 51		
Maidenhead 3 d			10 55		11 04							11 25	11 34									11 55	12 04	
Twyford 3 d			11 03		11 12							11 33	11 42									12 03	12 12	
Reading 7 a	10 48	10 53	11 13		11 22	10 57				11 09	11 22	11 43	11 52		11 26		11 30			11 48	11 54	12 13	12 22	
Oxford a		11 19			12 14						11 48		12 40								12 20		13 14	

	GW ◇1 Ø	HC	GW 1	GW 1	GW ◇1 Ø	GW ◇1	GW 1	GW 1	GW ◇1 🍴		HC	GW ◇1 Ø	GW 1	GW 1	GW ◇1 🍴	GW ◇1 🍴	GW ◇1	GW 1	GW 1		GW ◇1 🍴	HC	GW 1	GW 1
London Paddington 15 ⊖ d	11 30	11 33	11 42	11 45	11 45	11 50		11 57	12 00		12 03	12 06	12 12	12 15	12 15	12 18	12 21		12 27		12 30	12 33	12 42	12 45
Acton Main Line d				11 51										12 21										12 51
Ealing Broadway ⊖ d		11 41	11 50	11 54				12 05			12 11		12 20	12 24					12 35			12 41	12 50	12 54
West Ealing d		11 43		11 57							12 13			12 27								12 43		12 57
Drayton Green d				11 59										12 29										12 59
Castle Bar Park d				12 01										12 31										13 01
South Greenford d				12 04										12 34										13 04
Greenford ⊖ a				12 09										12 39										13 09
Hanwell d		11 45									12 15											12 45		
Southall d		11 49	11 58								12 19		12 28									12 49	12 58	
Hayes & Harlington d		11 53	12 02					12 12			12 23		12 32						12 42			12 53	13 02	
Heathrow Terminal 1-2-3 2 ✈ a		12 05									12 35											13 05		
Heathrow Terminal 4 ✈ a																								
West Drayton d			12 06					12 16					12 36						12 46				13 06	
Iver d								12 19											12 49					
Langley d							←	12 22										←	12 52					
Slough 3 a			12 13			12 06	12 13	12 27					12 43				12 38	12 43	12 57				13 13	
d			12 13			12 06	12 13	12 27					12 43				12 39	12 43	12 57				13 13	
Burnham d			→				12 17						→					12 47					→	
Taplow d							12 21											12 51						
Maidenhead 3 d							12 25	12 34										12 55	13 04					
Twyford 3 d							12 33	12 42										13 03	13 12					
Reading 7 a	11 57				12 09	12 22	12 43	12 52	12 26			12 30			12 40	12 45	12 54	13 13	13 22		12 57			
Oxford a						12 48		13 40									13 19		14 14					

	GW ◇1 🍴	GW ◇1 🛒	GW 1	GW 1	GW ◇1 🍴		HC	GW R 1 🍴	GW 1	GW 1	GW 1	GW ◇1 🛒	GW 1	GW 1	GW ◇1 🍴		HC	GW 1	GW 1	GW ◇1 🍴	GW ◇1 🛒	GW 1	GW 1	GW ◇1 🍴
London Paddington 15 ⊖ d	12 45	12 50		12 57	13 00		13 03	13 06	13 12	13 15	13 18	13 21		13 27	13 30		13 33	13 42	13 45	13 45	13 50		13 57	14 00
Acton Main Line d										13 21									13 51					
Ealing Broadway ⊖ d				13 05			13 11		13 20	13 24				13 35			13 41	13 50	13 54				14 05	
West Ealing d							13 13			13 27							13 43		13 57					
Drayton Green d										13 29									13 59					
Castle Bar Park d										13 31									14 01					
South Greenford d										13 34									14 04					
Greenford ⊖ a										13 39									14 09					
Hanwell d							13 15										13 45							
Southall d							13 19		13 28								13 49	13 58						
Hayes & Harlington d				13 12			13 23		13 32					13 42			13 53	14 02					14 12	
Heathrow Terminal 1-2-3 2 ✈ a							13 35										14 05							
Heathrow Terminal 4 ✈ a																								
West Drayton d				13 16					13 36					13 46				14 06					14 16	
Iver d				13 19										13 49									14 19	
Langley d			←	13 22									←	13 52								←	14 22	
Slough 3 a		13 06	13 13	13 27					13 43			13 38	13 43	13 57				14 13			14 06	14 13	14 27	
d		13 06	13 13	13 27					13 43			13 39	13 43	13 57				14 13			14 06	14 13	14 27	
Burnham d			13 17						→				13 47					→				14 17		
Taplow d			13 21										13 51									14 21		
Maidenhead 3 d			13 25	13 34									13 55	14 04								14 25	14 34	
Twyford 3 d			13 33	13 42									14 03	14 12								14 33	14 42	
Reading 7 a	13 09	13 22	13 43	13 52	13 26			13 30			13 48	13 54	14 13	14 22	13 58					14 09	14 22	14 43	14 52	14 26
Oxford a		13 48		14 40								14 19		15 14							14 48		15 40	

Table 117

Saturdays

until 31 December

London - Greenford and Reading

Network Diagram - see first Page of Table 116

		HC		GW	GW	GW	GW	GW	GW	GW	GW	GW		HC	GW	GW	GW	GW	GW	GW	GW	HC		GW	GW
				◇1	1	1	◇1	1	◇1	1	1	◇1			1	1	◇1	◇1	1	1	◇1			◇1	1
				☕			☕		🛒			☕					☕				☕			☕	
London Paddington 15 ⊖	d	14 03		14 06	14 12	14 15	14 15	14 18	14 21		14 27	14 30		14 33	14 42	14 45	14 45	14 50		14 57	15 00	15 03		15 06	15 12
Acton Main Line	d					14 21										14 51									
Ealing Broadway ⊖	d	14 11			14 20	14 24					14 35			14 41	14 50	14 54				15 05		15 11			15 20
West Ealing	d	14 13				14 27								14 43		14 57						15 13			
Drayton Green	d					14 29										14 59									
Castle Bar Park	d					14 31										15 01									
South Greenford	d					14 34										15 04									
Greenford ⊖	a					14 39										15 09									
Hanwell	d	14 15												14 45								15 15			
Southall	d	14 19			14 28									14 49	14 58							15 19			15 28
Hayes & Harlington	d	14 23			14 32						14 42			14 53	15 02					15 12		15 23			15 32
Heathrow Terminal 1-2-3 2 ✈	a	14 35												15 05								15 35			
Heathrow Terminal 4 ✈	a																								
West Drayton	d				14 36						14 46				15 06					15 16					15 36
Iver	d										14 49									15 19					
Langley	d									←	14 52								←	15 22					
Slough 3	a				14 43				14 38	14 43	14 57				15 13			15 06	15 13	15 27					15 43
	d				14 43				14 39	14 43	14 57				15 13			15 06	15 13	15 27					15 43
Burnham	d				→					14 47					→				15 17						→
Taplow	d									14 51									15 21						
Maidenhead 3	d									14 55	15 04								15 25	15 34					
Twyford 3	d									15 03	15 12								15 33	15 42					
Reading 7	a			14 30			14 40	14 48	14 53	15 13	15 22	14 57					15 09	15 22	15 43	15 52	15 26			15 29	
Oxford	a								15 18		16 14							15 48		16 40					

		GW	GW	GW	GW	GW	GW	HC		GW	GW	GW	GW	GW	GW	GW	HC	GW		GW	GW	GW	GW	GW	GW
		1	1	◇1	1	1	◇1			1	1	◇1	◇1	1	1	◇1		◇1		1	1	◇1	1	◇1	1
				🛒			☕					☕				☕		☕				☕		☕	
London Paddington 15 ⊖	d	15 15	15 18	15 21		15 27	15 30	15 33		15 42	15 45	15 45	15 50		15 57	16 00	16 03	16 06		16 12	16 15	16 15	16 18	16 21	
Acton Main Line	d	15 21									15 51										16 21				
Ealing Broadway ⊖	d	15 24				15 35		15 41		15 50	15 54				16 05		16 11			16 20	16 24				
West Ealing	d	15 27						15 43			15 57						16 13				16 27				
Drayton Green	d	15 29									15 59										16 29				
Castle Bar Park	d	15 31									16 01										16 31				
South Greenford	d	15 34									16 04										16 34				
Greenford ⊖	a	15 39									16 09										16 39				
Hanwell	d							15 45									16 15								
Southall	d							15 49		15 58							16 19			16 28					
Hayes & Harlington	d					15 42		15 53		16 02					16 12		16 23			16 32					
Heathrow Terminal 1-2-3 2 ✈	a							16 05									16 35								
Heathrow Terminal 4 ✈	a																								
West Drayton	d					15 46				16 06					16 16					16 36					
Iver	d					15 49									16 19										
Langley	d				←	15 52								←	16 22										←
Slough 3	a			15 38	15 43	15 57				16 13			16 06	16 13	16 27					16 43				16 38	16 43
	d			15 39	15 43	15 57				16 13			16 06	16 13	16 27					16 43				16 39	16 43
Burnham	d				15 47					→				16 17						→					16 47
Taplow	d				15 51									16 21											16 51
Maidenhead 3	d				15 55	16 04								16 25	16 34										16 55
Twyford 3	d				16 03	16 12								16 33	16 42										17 03
Reading 7	a		15 48	15 54	16 13	16 22	15 58					16 09	16 22	16 43	16 52	16 26		16 31				16 40	16 48	16 53	17 13
Oxford	a			16 19		17 14							16 48		17 40									17 18	

		GW	GW	HC		GW	GW	GW	GW	GW	GW	GW	HC	GW		GW	GW	GW	GW	GW	GW	GW	HC	GW	
		1	◇1			1	1	◇1	◇1	1	1	◇1		◇1		1	1	1	◇1	1	1	◇1		1	
			☕					☕	🛒			☕		☕					☕			☕			
London Paddington 15 ⊖	d	16 27	16 30	16 33		16 42	16 45	16 45	16 50		16 57	17 00	17 03	17 06		17 12	17 15	17 18	17 21		17 27	17 30	17 33	17 42	
Acton Main Line	d						16 51										17 21								
Ealing Broadway ⊖	d	16 35		16 41		16 50	16 54				17 05		17 11			17 20	17 24				17 35		17 41	17 50	
West Ealing	d			16 43			16 57						17 13				17 27						17 43		
Drayton Green	d						16 59										17 29								
Castle Bar Park	d						17 01										17 31								
South Greenford	d						17 04										17 34								
Greenford ⊖	a						17 09										17 39								
Hanwell	d			16 45									17 15										17 45		
Southall	d			16 49		16 58							17 19			17 28							17 49	17 58	
Hayes & Harlington	d	16 42		16 53		17 02					17 12		17 23			17 32					17 42		17 53	18 02	
Heathrow Terminal 1-2-3 2 ✈	a			17 05									17 35										18 05		
Heathrow Terminal 4 ✈	a																								
West Drayton	d	16 46				17 06					17 16					17 36					17 46			18 06	
Iver	d	16 49									17 19										17 49				
Langley	d	16 52								←	17 22									←	17 52				
Slough 3	a	16 57				17 13			17 06	17 13	17 27					17 43			17 38	17 43	17 57			18 13	
	d	16 57				17 13			17 06	17 13	17 27					17 43			17 39	17 43	17 57			18 13	
Burnham	d					→				17 17						→				17 47				→	
Taplow	d									17 21										17 51					
Maidenhead 3	d	17 04								17 25	17 34									17 55	18 04				
Twyford 3	d	17 12								17 33	17 42									18 03	18 12				
Reading 7	a	17 22	16 57					17 09	17 22	17 43	17 52	17 26		17 30				17 48	17 53	18 13	18 22	17 57			
Oxford	a	18 14							17 48		18 40								18 18		19 14				

Table 117

Saturdays

until 31 December

London - Greenford and Reading

Network Diagram - see first Page of Table 116

		GW	GW	GW	GW	GW	GW	HC	GW	GW		GW	GW	GW	GW	GW	GW	GW	HC	GW		GW	GW	GW	GW
		1	◇1	◇1	1	1	◇1		◇1	1		1	◇1	1	◇1	1	1	◇1		1		1	◇1	◇1	1
			☕	🛒			☕		☕				☕		☕			☕					☕		
London Paddington 15 ⊖	d	17 45	17 45	17 50		17 57	18 00	18 03	18 06	18 12		18 15	18 15	18 18	18 21		18 27	18 30	18 33	18 42		18 45	18 45	18 50	
Acton Main Line	d	17 51										18 21										18 51			
Ealing Broadway ⊖	d	17 54				18 05		18 11		18 20		18 24					18 35		18 41	18 50		18 54			
West Ealing	d	17 57						18 13				18 27							18 43			18 57			
Drayton Green	d	17 59										18 29										18 59			
Castle Bar Park	d	18 01										18 31										19 01			
South Greenford	d	18 04										18 34										19 04			
Greenford ⊖	a	18 09										18 39										19 09			
Hanwell	d							18 15											18 45						
Southall	d							18 19		18 28									18 49	18 58					
Hayes & Harlington	d					18 12		18 23		18 32							18 42		18 53	19 02					
Heathrow Terminal 1-2-3 2 ✈	a							18 35											19 05						
Heathrow Terminal 4 ✈	a																								
West Drayton	d					18 16				18 36							18 46			19 06					
Iver	d					18 19											18 49								
Langley	d				←	18 22										←	18 52								←
Slough 3	a			18 06	18 13	18 27				18 43					18 38	18 43	18 57			19 13				19 06	19 13
	d			18 06	18 13	18 27				18 43					18 39	18 43	18 57			19 13				19 06	19 13
Burnham	d				18 17					→						18 47				→					19 17
Taplow	d				18 21											18 51									19 21
Maidenhead 3	d				18 25	18 34										18 55	19 04								19 25
Twyford 3	d				18 33	18 42										19 03	19 12								19 33
Reading 7	a		18 09	18 22	18 43	18 52	18 27		18 30				18 40	18 48	18 53	19 13	19 22	18 57					19 09	19 22	19 43
Oxford	a			18 48		19 40									19 18		20 14							19 48	

		GW	GW	HC	GW	GW		GW	GW	GW	GW	GW	GW	HC	GW	GW		GW	GW	GW	GW	GW	HC	GW	GW
		1	◇1		◇1	1		1	◇1	◇1	1	1	◇1		1	1		◇1	◇1	1	1	◇1		◇1	1
			☕		☕				☕				☕					☕	🛒			☕		☕	
London Paddington 15 ⊖	d	18 57	19 00	19 03	19 06	19 12		19 15	19 15	19 21		19 27	19 30	19 33	19 42	19 45		19 45	19 50		19 57	20 00	20 03	20 06	20 12
Acton Main Line	d							19 21								19 51									
Ealing Broadway ⊖	d	19 05		19 11		19 20		19 24				19 35		19 41	19 50	19 54					20 05		20 11		20 20
West Ealing	d			19 13				19 27						19 43		19 57							20 13		
Drayton Green	d							19 29								19 59									
Castle Bar Park	d							19 31								20 01									
South Greenford	d							19 34								20 04									
Greenford ⊖	a							19 39								20 09									
Hanwell	d			19 15										19 45									20 15		
Southall	d			19 19		19 28								19 49	19 58								20 19		20 28
Hayes & Harlington	d	19 12		19 23		19 32						19 42		19 53	20 02						20 12		20 23		20 32
Heathrow Terminal 1-2-3 2 ✈	a			19 35										20 05									20 35		
Heathrow Terminal 4 ✈	a																								
West Drayton	d	19 16				19 36						19 46			20 06						20 16				20 36
Iver	d	19 19										19 49									20 19				
Langley	d	19 22									←	19 52								←	20 22				
Slough 3	a	19 27				19 43				19 37	19 43	19 57			20 13				20 06	20 13	20 27				20 43
	d	19 27				19 43				19 38	19 43	19 57			20 13				20 06	20 13	20 27				20 43
Burnham	d					→					19 47				→					20 17					→
Taplow	d										19 51									20 21					
Maidenhead 3	d	19 34									19 55	20 04								20 25	20 34				
Twyford 3	d	19 42									20 03	20 12								20 33	20 42				
Reading 7	a	19 52	19 26		19 30				19 39	19 52	20 13	20 20	19 57					20 09	20 21	20 43	20 52	20 27		20 31	
Oxford	a	20 40								20 20		21 14							20 47		21 40				

		GW		GW	GW	GW	GW	GW	HC	GW	GW	GW		GW	GW	GW	HC	GW	GW	GW	GW	GW		HC	GW
		1		◇1	◇1	1	1	◇1		1	◇1	1		◇1	1	1		1	1	◇1	◇1	1			1
				☕				☕			☕			🛒							☕				
London Paddington 15 ⊖	d	20 15		20 15	20 20		20 27	20 30	20 33	20 42	20 45	20 45		20 50		20 57	21 03	21 12	21 15	21 17	21 30			21 33	21 42
Acton Main Line	d	20 21										20 51							21 21						21 48
Ealing Broadway ⊖	d	20 24					20 35		20 41	20 50		20 54				21 05	21 11	21 20	21 24					21 41	21 52
West Ealing	d	20 27							20 43			20 57					21 13		21 27					21 43	
Drayton Green	d	20 29										20 59							21 29						
Castle Bar Park	d	20 31										21 01							21 31						
South Greenford	d	20 34										21 04							21 34						
Greenford ⊖	a	20 39										21 09							21 39						
Hanwell	d								20 45								21 15							21 45	
Southall	d								20 49	20 58							21 19	21 28						21 49	21 58
Hayes & Harlington	d						20 42		20 53	21 02						21 12	21 23	21 32						21 53	22 02
Heathrow Terminal 1-2-3 2 ✈	a								21 05								21 35							22 05	
Heathrow Terminal 4 ✈	a																								
West Drayton	d						20 46			21 06						21 16		21 36							22 06
Iver	d						20 49									21 19									
Langley	d					←	20 52								←	21 22						←			
Slough 3	a				20 35	20 43	20 57			21 13				21 06	21 13	21 27		21 43		21 34		21 43			22 13
	d				20 35	20 43	20 57			21 13				21 06	21 13	21 27		21 43		21 35		21 43			22 13
Burnham	d					20 47				→					21 17			→				21 47			→
Taplow	d					20 51									21 21							21 51			
Maidenhead 3	d					20 55	21 04								21 25	21 34						21 55			
Twyford 3	d					21 06	21 12								21 33	21 42						22 03			
Reading 7	a			20 40	20 51	21 14	21 22	20 57			21 09			21 22	21 43	21 52				21 51	21 55	22 13			
Oxford	a				21 19		22 14							21 53		22 43				22 20					

Table 117

London - Greenford and Reading

Saturdays

until 31 December

Network Diagram - see first Page of Table 116

		GW ◇1	GW 1	GW 1	GW ◇1 ☕	HC	GW 1	GW ◇1		HC	GW ◇1 ☕	GW 1	GW 1	GW ◇1	GW 1	HC	GW 1	GW ◇1 ☕		GW ◇1	GW 1	GW 1			
London Paddington 15 ⊖	d	21 50		21 57	22 00	22 03	22 12	22 15		22 33	22 35		22 45	23 00		23 03	23 20	23 30		23 33		23 42			
Acton Main Line	d												22 51												
Ealing Broadway ⊖	d			22 05		22 11	22 20			22 41			22 55			23 11	23 28					23 50			
West Ealing	d					22 13				22 43						23 13									
Drayton Green	d																								
Castle Bar Park	d																								
South Greenford	d																								
Greenford ⊖	a																								
Hanwell	d					22 15				22 45						23 15									
Southall	d					22 19	22 28			22 49			23 00			23 19	23 33					23 56			
Hayes & Harlington	d			22 12		22 23	22 32			22 53			23 04			23 23	23 37					00 01			
Heathrow Terminal 1-2-3 2 ✈	a					22 35				23 05						23 35									
Heathrow Terminal 4 ✈	a															23 41									
West Drayton	d			22 16			22 36						23 08				23 41					00 06			
Iver	d			22 19									23 11				23 44								
Langley	d		←	22 22								←	23 14		←		23 48				←				
Slough 3	a	22 06	22 13	22 27			22 43	22 31				22 43	23 19	23 16	23 19		23 53			23 49	23 53	00 13			
	d	22 06	22 13	22 27			22 43	22 32				22 43	23 21	23 17	23 21		23 54			23 50	23 54	00 14			
Burnham	d		22 17				→					22 47	→		23 25		→				23 57	00 18			
Taplow	d		22 21									22 51									00 01	00 21			
Maidenhead 3	d		22 25	22 34								22 55			23 32						00 05	00 25			
Twyford 3	d		22 33	22 42								23 03			23 39						00 13	00 33			
Reading 7	a	22 22	22 41	22 52	22 27			22 48			23 00	23 13		23 33	23 46			23 59		00 06	00 20	00 43			
Oxford	a	22 50		23 38				23 20						00 04	00 32					00 38	01 05				

Saturdays

7 January to 24 March

		GW 1	GW ◇1	GW 1	GW 1	GW ◇1 ☕	GW 1	GW 1	GW ◇1	GW 1		GW 1	GW 1	HC	HC	GW ◇1	GW 1	HC	GW 1	GW ◇1		GW 1	HC	GW 1	GW 1
London Paddington 15 ⊖	d	22p45	23p18		23p29	23p30	23p42	23p48	00 22	00 34		01 44	03 34	04 42	05 13	05 21	05 25	05 33	05 45	05 50		05 57	06 03	06 12	06 15
Acton Main Line	d	22p51						23p54											05 51						06 21
Ealing Broadway ⊖	d	22p54			23p37			23p57		00 42		01 52	03 42	04 50	05 21		05 33	05 41	05 54			06 05	06 11	06 20	06 24
West Ealing	d							23p59										05 43	05 57				06 13		06 27
Drayton Green	d																		05 59						06 29
Castle Bar Park	d																		06 01						06 31
South Greenford	d																		06 04						06 34
Greenford ⊖	a																		06 09						06 39
Hanwell	d							00 02										05 45					06 15		
Southall	d							00 06		00 47		01 57	03 47	04 54	05 25		05 38	05 49				06 10	06 19	06 28	
Hayes & Harlington	d	23p01			23p44			00 10		00 51		02 01	03 51	04 58	05 29		05 42	05 53				06 14	06 23	06 32	
Heathrow Terminal 1-2-3 2 ✈	a													05 04	05 35			06 05					06 35		
Heathrow Terminal 4 ✈	a													05 10	05 41										
West Drayton	d							00 14		00 55		02 05	03 55									06 18		06 36	
Iver	d							00 17														06 21			
Langley	d							00 21		01 00												06 25			
Slough 3	a	23p11	23p36		23p53		23p58	00 26	00 38	01 05		02 13	04 03			05 37	05 50			06 06		06 30		06 43	
	d	23p12	23p36		23p54		23p58	00 26	00 39	01 05		02 13	04 03			05 38	05 51			06 06		06 31		06 43	
Burnham	d	23p16						00 30		01 09							05 55					06 35		→	
Taplow	d	23p20						00 34		01 13							05 58					06 38			
Maidenhead 3	d	23p24	23p44		00 01		00 08	00 41		01 16		02 21	04 11				06 02					06 42			
Twyford 3	d	23p32		00 07	00 09			00 48		01 24		02 29	04 19				06 10					06 50			
Reading 7	a	23p41	23p58	00 16	00 19	00 04	00 21	00 57	00 55	01 35		02 38	04 30			05 52	06 17			06 22		06 56			
Oxford	a	00 26	00 28		01 16		01 02		01 28							06 22	07 03			06 52		07 43			

		GW ◇1	GW 1	GW 1	GW ◇1 ☕	HC		GW 1	GW 1	GW ◇1	GW 1	GW 1	GW ◇1 ☕	HC	GW 1	GW 1		GW ◇1	GW 1	GW 1	GW R 1 ☕	HC	GW 1	GW 1	GW ◇1 ☕
London Paddington 15 ⊖	d	06 21		06 27	06 30	06 33		06 42	06 45	06 50		06 57	07 00	07 03	07 12	07 15		07 21		07 27	07 30	07 33	07 42	07 45	07 45
Acton Main Line	d								06 51							07 21								07 51	
Ealing Broadway ⊖	d			06 35		06 41		06 50	06 54			07 05		07 11	07 20	07 24				07 35		07 41	07 50	07 54	
West Ealing	d					06 43			06 57					07 13		07 27						07 43		07 57	
Drayton Green	d								06 59							07 29								07 59	
Castle Bar Park	d								07 01							07 31								08 01	
South Greenford	d								07 04							07 34								08 04	
Greenford ⊖	a								07 09							07 39								08 09	
Hanwell	d					06 45								07 15								07 45			
Southall	d					06 49		06 58						07 19	07 28							07 49	07 58		
Hayes & Harlington	d			06 42		06 53		07 02				07 12		07 23	07 32					07 42		07 53	08 02		
Heathrow Terminal 1-2-3 2 ✈	a					07 05								07 35								08 05			
Heathrow Terminal 4 ✈	a																								
West Drayton	d			06 46				07 06				07 16			07 36					07 46			08 06		
Iver	d			06 49								07 19								07 49					
Langley	d		←	06 52							←	07 22							←	07 52					
Slough 3	a	06 37	06 43	06 57				07 13		07 06	07 13	07 27			07 43			07 37	07 43	07 57			08 13		
	d	06 38	06 43	06 57				07 13		07 06	07 13	07 27			07 43			07 38	07 43	07 57			08 13		
Burnham	d		06 47					→			07 17				→				07 47				→		
Taplow	d		06 51								07 21								07 51						
Maidenhead 3	d		06 55	07 04							07 25	07 34							07 55	08 04					
Twyford 3	d		07 03	07 12							07 33	07 42							08 03	08 12					
Reading 7	a	06 53	07 13	07 20	06 57					07 22	07 43	07 52	07 26					07 53	08 13	08 22	07 57				08 09
Oxford	a	07 18		08 09						07 48		08 40						08 19		09 14					

Table 117

Saturdays

7 January to 24 March

London - Greenford and Reading

Network Diagram - see first Page of Table 116

		GW ◇1		GW 1	GW 1	GW ◇1 ☕	HC	GW 1	GW 1	GW ◇1 ☕	GW ◇1 ☕	GW ◇1 ☕		GW 1	GW 1	GW ◇1 ☕	HC	GW 1	GW 1	GW ◇1 ☕	GW ◇1	GW 1		GW 1	GW ◇1 ☕
London Paddington 15 ⊖	d	07 50			07 57	08 00	08 03	08 12	08 15	08 15	08 18	08 21			08 27	08 30	08 33	08 42	08 45	08 45	08 50			08 57	09 00
Acton Main Line	d								08 21										08 51						
Ealing Broadway ⊖	d				08 05		08 11	08 20	08 24						08 35		08 41	08 50	08 54					09 05	
West Ealing	d						08 13		08 27								08 43		08 57						
Drayton Green	d								08 29										08 59						
Castle Bar Park	d								08 31										09 01						
South Greenford	d								08 34										09 04						
Greenford ⊖	a								08 39										09 09						
Hanwell	d						08 15										08 45								
Southall	d						08 19	08 28									08 49	08 58							
Hayes & Harlington	d				08 12		08 23	08 32							08 42		08 53	09 02						09 12	
Heathrow Terminal 1-2-3 2 ✈	a						08 35										09 05								
Heathrow Terminal 4 ✈	a																								
West Drayton	d				08 16			08 36							08 46			09 06						09 16	
Iver	d				08 19										08 49									09 19	
Langley	d			←	08 22									←	08 52							←		09 22	
Slough 3	a	08 06		08 13	08 27			08 43				08 38		08 43	08 57			09 13			09 06	09 13		09 27	
	d	08 06		08 13	08 27			08 43				08 39		08 43	08 57			09 13			09 06	09 13		09 27	
Burnham	d			08 17				↪						08 47				↪				09 17			
Taplow	d			08 21										08 51								09 21			
Maidenhead 3	d			08 25	08 34									08 55	09 04							09 25		09 34	
Twyford 3	d			08 33	08 42									09 03	09 12							09 33		09 42	
Reading 7	a	08 22		08 43	08 52	08 26				08 40	08 46	08 53		09 13	09 23	08 56				09 09	09 22	09 43		09 52	09 26
Oxford	a	08 48			09 40							09 18			10 14						09 48			10 40	

		HC	GW ◇1 Ø	GW 1	GW 1	GW 1	GW ◇1	GW 1		GW 1	GW ◇1 ☕	HC	GW 1	GW 1	GW ◇1 ☕	GW ◇1	GW 1	GW 1		GW ◇1 ☕	HC	GW ◇1 Ø	GW 1	GW 1	GW ◇1 ☕
London Paddington 15 ⊖	d	09 03	09 06	09 12	09 15	09 18	09 21			09 27	09 30	09 33	09 42	09 45	09 45	09 50		09 57		10 00	10 03	10 06	10 12	10 15	10 15
Acton Main Line	d				09 21									09 51										10 21	
Ealing Broadway ⊖	d	09 11		09 20	09 24					09 35		09 41	09 50	09 54				10 05			10 11		10 20	10 24	
West Ealing	d	09 13			09 27							09 43		09 57							10 13			10 27	
Drayton Green	d				09 29									09 59										10 29	
Castle Bar Park	d				09 31									10 01										10 31	
South Greenford	d				09 34									10 04										10 34	
Greenford ⊖	a				09 39									10 09										10 39	
Hanwell	d	09 15										09 45									10 15				
Southall	d	09 19		09 28								09 49	09 58								10 19		10 28		
Hayes & Harlington	d	09 23		09 32						09 42		09 53	10 02					10 12			10 23		10 32		
Heathrow Terminal 1-2-3 2 ✈	a	09 35										10 05									10 35				
Heathrow Terminal 4 ✈	a																								
West Drayton	d			09 36						09 46			10 06					10 16					10 36		
Iver	d									09 49								10 19							
Langley	d							←		09 52							←	10 22							
Slough 3	a			09 43			09 38	09 43		09 57			10 13			10 06	10 13	10 27					10 43		
	d			09 43			09 39	09 43		09 57			10 13			10 06	10 13	10 27					10 43		
Burnham	d			↪				09 47					↪				10 17						↪		
Taplow	d							09 51									10 21								
Maidenhead 3	d							09 55		10 04							10 25	10 34							
Twyford 3	d							10 03		10 12							10 33	10 42							
Reading 7	a		09 30			09 48	09 54	10 13		10 22	09 57				10 09	10 22	10 43	10 52		10 26		10 30			10 40
Oxford	a						10 19			11 14						10 48		11 40							

		GW 1	GW ◇1 ☕	GW 1		GW 1	GW ◇1 ☕	HC	GW 1	GW 1	GW ◇1 Ø	GW ◇1 🛒	GW 1	GW 1		GW ◇1 ☕	HC	GW ◇1 Ø	GW 1	GW 1	GW 1	GW ◇1 🛒	GW 1	GW 1	
London Paddington 15 ⊖	d	10 18	10 21			10 27	10 30	10 33	10 42	10 45	10 45	10 50		10 57		11 00	11 03	11 06	11 12	11 15	11 18	11 21		11 27	
Acton Main Line	d									10 51										11 21					
Ealing Broadway ⊖	d					10 35		10 41	10 52	10 54				11 05			11 11		11 20	11 24				11 35	
West Ealing	d							10 43		10 57							11 13			11 27					
Drayton Green	d									10 59										11 29					
Castle Bar Park	d									11 01										11 31					
South Greenford	d									11 04										11 34					
Greenford ⊖	a									11 09										11 39					
Hanwell	d							10 45									11 15								
Southall	d							10 49	10 58								11 19		11 28						
Hayes & Harlington	d					10 42		10 53	11 02					11 12			11 23		11 32					11 42	
Heathrow Terminal 1-2-3 2 ✈	a							11 05									11 35								
Heathrow Terminal 4 ✈	a																								
West Drayton	d					10 46			11 06					11 16					11 36					11 46	
Iver	d					10 49								11 19										11 49	
Langley	d			←		10 52							←	11 22									←	11 52	
Slough 3	a		10 38	10 43		10 57			11 13			11 06	11 13	11 27					11 43			11 38	11 43	11 57	
	d		10 39	10 43		10 57			11 13			11 06	11 13	11 27					11 43			11 39	11 43	11 57	
Burnham	d			10 47					↪				11 17						↪				11 47		
Taplow	d			10 51									11 21										11 51		
Maidenhead 3	d			10 55		11 04							11 25	11 34									11 55	12 04	
Twyford 3	d			11 03		11 12							11 33	11 42									12 03	12 12	
Reading 7	a	10 48	10 53	11 13		11 22	10 57				11 09	11 22	11 43	11 52		11 26		11 30			11 48	11 54	12 13	12 22	
Oxford	a		11 19			12 14						11 48		12 40								12 20		13 14	

Table 117

London - Greenford and Reading

Saturdays

7 January to 24 March

Network Diagram - see first Page of Table 116

		GW	HC	GW	GW	GW	GW	GW	GW	GW		HC	GW	GW	GW	GW	GW	GW	GW	GW		GW	HC	GW	GW
		◇1 Ø		1	1	◇1 Ø	◇1	1	1	◇1 ☕			◇1 Ø	1	1	◇1 ☕	◇1 ☕	◇1	1	1		◇1 ☕		1	1
London Paddington 15 ⊖	d	11 30	11 33	11 42	11 45	11 45	11 50		11 57	12 00		12 03	12 06	12 12	12 15	12 15	12 18	12 21		12 27		12 30	12 33	12 42	12 45
Acton Main Line	d				11 51										12 21										12 51
Ealing Broadway ⊖	d		11 41	11 50	11 54				12 05			12 11		12 20	12 24					12 35			12 41	12 50	12 54
West Ealing	d		11 43		11 57							12 13			12 27								12 43		12 57
Drayton Green	d				11 59										12 29										12 59
Castle Bar Park	d				12 01										12 31										13 01
South Greenford	d				12 04										12 34										13 04
Greenford ⊖	a				12 09										12 39										13 09
Hanwell	d		11 45									12 15											12 45		
Southall	d		11 49	11 58								12 19		12 28									12 49	12 58	
Hayes & Harlington	d		11 53	12 02					12 12			12 23		12 32						12 42			12 53	13 02	
Heathrow Terminal 1-2-3 2 ✈	a		12 05									12 35											13 05		
Heathrow Terminal 4 ✈	a																								
West Drayton	d			12 06					12 16					12 36						12 46				13 06	
Iver	d								12 19											12 49					
Langley	d							←	12 22										←	12 52					
Slough 3	a			12 13			12 06	12 13	12 27					12 43				12 38	12 43	12 57				13 13	
	d			12 13			12 06	12 13	12 27					12 43				12 39	12 43	12 57				13 13	
Burnham	d			→				12 17						→					12 47					→	
Taplow	d							12 21											12 51						
Maidenhead 3	d							12 25	12 34										12 55	13 04					
Twyford 3	d							12 33	12 42										13 03	13 12					
Reading 7	a	11 57				12 09	12 22	12 43	12 52	12 26			12 30			12 40	12 45	12 54	13 13	13 22		12 57			
Oxford	a						12 48		13 40									13 19		14 14					

		GW	GW	GW	GW	GW		HC	GW	GW	GW	GW	GW	GW	GW	GW		HC	GW	GW	GW	GW	GW	GW	GW
		◇1 ☕	◇1 🍴	1	1	◇1 ☕			R 1 ☕	1	1	1	◇1 🍴	1	1	◇1 ☕			1	1	◇1 ☕	◇1 🍴	1	1	◇1 ☕
London Paddington 15 ⊖	d	12 45	12 50		12 57	13 00		13 03	13 06	13 12	13 15	13 18	13 21		13 27	13 30		13 33	13 42	13 45	13 45	13 50		13 57	14 00
Acton Main Line	d										13 21									13 51					
Ealing Broadway ⊖	d				13 05			13 11		13 20	13 24				13 35			13 41	13 50	13 54				14 05	
West Ealing	d							13 13			13 27							13 43		13 57					
Drayton Green	d										13 29									13 59					
Castle Bar Park	d										13 31									14 01					
South Greenford	d										13 34									14 04					
Greenford ⊖	a										13 39									14 09					
Hanwell	d							13 15										13 45							
Southall	d							13 19		13 28								13 49	13 58						
Hayes & Harlington	d				13 12			13 23		13 32					13 42			13 53	14 02					14 12	
Heathrow Terminal 1-2-3 2 ✈	a							13 35										14 05							
Heathrow Terminal 4 ✈	a																								
West Drayton	d				13 16					13 36					13 46				14 06					14 16	
Iver	d				13 19										13 49									14 19	
Langley	d			←	13 22									←	13 52								←	14 22	
Slough 3	a		13 06	13 13	13 27					13 43			13 38	13 43	13 57				14 13			14 06	14 13	14 27	
	d		13 06	13 13	13 27					13 43			13 39	13 43	13 57				14 13			14 06	14 13	14 27	
Burnham	d			13 17						→				13 47					→				14 17		
Taplow	d			13 21										13 51									14 21		
Maidenhead 3	d			13 25	13 34									13 55	14 04								14 25	14 34	
Twyford 3	d			13 33	13 42									14 03	14 12								14 33	14 42	
Reading 7	a	13 09	13 22	13 43	13 52	13 26			13 30			13 48	13 54	14 13	14 22	13 58					14 09	14 22	14 43	14 52	14 26
Oxford	a		13 48		14 40								14 19		15 14							14 48		15 40	

		HC		GW	GW	GW	GW	GW	GW	GW	GW	GW		HC	GW	GW	GW	GW	GW	GW	GW	HC		GW	GW
				◇1 ☕	1	1	◇1 ☕	1	◇1 🍴	1	1	◇1 ☕			1	1	◇1 ☕	◇1	1	1	◇1 ☕			◇1 ☕	1
London Paddington 15 ⊖	d	14 03		14 06	14 12	14 15	14 15	14 18	14 21		14 27	14 30		14 33	14 42	14 45	14 45	14 50		14 57	15 00	15 03		15 06	15 12
Acton Main Line	d					14 21										14 51									
Ealing Broadway ⊖	d	14 11			14 20	14 24					14 35			14 41	14 50	14 54				15 05		15 11			15 20
West Ealing	d	14 13				14 27								14 43		14 57						15 13			
Drayton Green	d					14 29										14 59									
Castle Bar Park	d					14 31										15 01									
South Greenford	d					14 34										15 04									
Greenford ⊖	a					14 39										15 09									
Hanwell	d	14 15												14 45								15 15			
Southall	d	14 19			14 28									14 49	14 58							15 19			15 28
Hayes & Harlington	d	14 23			14 32						14 42			14 53	15 02					15 12		15 23			15 32
Heathrow Terminal 1-2-3 2 ✈	a	14 35												15 05								15 35			
Heathrow Terminal 4 ✈	a																								
West Drayton	d				14 36						14 46				15 06					15 16					15 36
Iver	d										14 49									15 19					
Langley	d									←	14 52								←	15 22					
Slough 3	a				14 43				14 38	14 43	14 57				15 13			15 06	15 13	15 27					15 43
	d				14 43				14 39	14 43	14 57				15 13			15 06	15 13	15 27					15 43
Burnham	d				→					14 47					→				15 17						→
Taplow	d									14 51									15 21						
Maidenhead 3	d									14 55	15 04								15 25	15 34					
Twyford 3	d									15 03	15 12								15 33	15 42					
Reading 7	a			14 30			14 40	14 48	14 53	15 13	15 22	14 57					15 09	15 22	15 43	15 52	15 26			15 29	
Oxford	a								15 18		16 14							15 48		16 40					

Table 117

7 January to 24 March

London - Greenford and Reading

Network Diagram - see first Page of Table 116

		GW	GW	GW	GW	GW	GW	HC		GW	GW	GW	GW	GW	GW	GW	HC	GW		GW	GW	GW	GW	GW	GW
		1	1	◇1	1	1	◇1			1	1	◇1	◇1	1	1	◇1		◇1		1	1	◇1	1	◇1	1
																		A				A			
				🛒			☕					☕				☕		☕				☕		☕	
London Paddington 15 ⊖	d	15 15	15 18	15 21		15 27	15 30	15 33		15 42	15 45	15 45	15 50		15 57	16 00	16 03	16 06		16 12	16 15	16 15	16 18	16 21	
Acton Main Line	d	15 21									15 51										16 21				
Ealing Broadway ⊖	d	15 24				15 35		15 41		15 50	15 54				16 05		16 11			16 20	16 24				
West Ealing	d	15 27						15 43			15 57						16 13				16 27				
Drayton Green	d	15 29									15 59										16 29				
Castle Bar Park	d	15 31									16 01										16 31				
South Greenford	d	15 34									16 04										16 34				
Greenford ⊖	a	15 39									16 09										16 39				
Hanwell	d							15 45									16 15								
Southall	d							15 49		15 58							16 19			16 28					
Hayes & Harlington	d					15 42		15 53		16 02					16 12		16 23			16 32					
Heathrow Terminal 1-2-3 2 ✈	a							16 05									16 35								
Heathrow Terminal 4 ✈	a																								
West Drayton	d					15 46				16 06					16 16					16 36					
Iver	d					15 49									16 19										
Langley	d				←	15 52								←	16 22										←
Slough 3	a			15 38	15 43	15 57				16 13			16 06	16 13	16 27					16 43				16 38	16 43
	d			15 39	15 43	15 57				16 13			16 06	16 13	16 27					16 43				16 39	16 43
Burnham	d				15 47					→				16 17						→					16 47
Taplow	d				15 51									16 21											16 51
Maidenhead 3	d				15 55	16 04								16 25	16 34										16 55
Twyford 3	d				16 03	16 12								16 33	16 42										17 03
Reading 7	a		15 48	15 54	16 13	16 22	15 58					16 09	16 22	16 43	16 52	16 26		16 31				16 40	16 48	16 53	17 13
Oxford	a			16 19		17 14							16 48		17 40									17 18	

		GW	GW	HC		GW	GW	GW	GW	GW	GW	GW	HC	GW		GW	GW	GW	GW	GW	GW	GW	HC	GW	
		1	◇1			1	1	◇1	◇1	1	1	◇1		◇1		1	1	1	◇1	1	1	◇1		1	
			☕					☕	🛒			☕		☕					☕			☕			
London Paddington 15 ⊖	d	16 27	16 30	16 33		16 42	16 45	16 45	16 50		16 57	17 00	17 03	17 06		17 12	17 15	17 18	17 21		17 27	17 30	17 33	17 42	
Acton Main Line	d						16 51										17 21								
Ealing Broadway ⊖	d	16 35		16 41		16 50	16 54				17 05		17 11			17 20	17 24				17 35		17 41	17 50	
West Ealing	d			16 43			16 57						17 13				17 27						17 43		
Drayton Green	d						16 59										17 29								
Castle Bar Park	d						17 01										17 31								
South Greenford	d						17 04										17 34								
Greenford ⊖	a						17 09										17 39								
Hanwell	d			16 45									17 15										17 45		
Southall	d			16 49		16 58							17 19			17 28							17 49	17 58	
Hayes & Harlington	d	16 42		16 53		17 02					17 12		17 23			17 32					17 42		17 53	18 02	
Heathrow Terminal 1-2-3 2 ✈	a			17 05									17 35										18 05		
Heathrow Terminal 4 ✈	a																								
West Drayton	d	16 46				17 06					17 16					17 36					17 46			18 06	
Iver	d	16 49									17 19										17 49				
Langley	d	16 52								←	17 22									←	17 52				
Slough 3	a	16 57				17 13			17 06	17 13	17 27					17 43			17 38	17 43	17 57			18 13	
	d	16 57				17 13			17 06	17 13	17 27					17 43			17 39	17 43	17 57			18 13	
Burnham	d					→				17 17						→				17 47				→	
Taplow	d									17 21										17 51					
Maidenhead 3	d	17 04								17 25	17 34									17 55	18 04				
Twyford 3	d	17 12								17 33	17 42									18 03	18 12				
Reading 7	a	17 22	16 57					17 09	17 22	17 43	17 52	17 26		17 30				17 48	17 53	18 13	18 22	17 57			
Oxford	a	18 14							17 48		18 40								18 18		19 14				

		GW	GW	GW	GW	GW	GW	HC	GW	GW		GW	GW	GW	GW	GW	GW	GW	HC	GW		GW	GW	GW	GW
		1	◇1	◇1	1	1	◇1		◇1	1		1	◇1	1	◇1	1	1	◇1		1		1	◇1	◇1	1
			☕	🛒			☕		☕				☕		☕			☕					☕		
London Paddington 15 ⊖	d	17 45	17 45	17 50		17 57	18 00	18 03	18 06	18 12		18 15	18 15	18 18	18 21		18 27	18 30	18 33	18 42		18 45	18 45	18 50	
Acton Main Line	d	17 51										18 21										18 51			
Ealing Broadway ⊖	d	17 54				18 05		18 11		18 20		18 24					18 35		18 41	18 50		18 54			
West Ealing	d	17 57						18 13				18 27							18 43			18 57			
Drayton Green	d	17 59										18 29										18 59			
Castle Bar Park	d	18 01										18 31										19 01			
South Greenford	d	18 04										18 34										19 04			
Greenford ⊖	a	18 09										18 39										19 09			
Hanwell	d							18 15											18 45						
Southall	d							18 19		18 28									18 49	18 58					
Hayes & Harlington	d					18 12		18 23		18 32							18 42		18 53	19 02					
Heathrow Terminal 1-2-3 2 ✈	a							18 35											19 05						
Heathrow Terminal 4 ✈	a																								
West Drayton	d					18 16				18 36							18 46			19 06					
Iver	d					18 19											18 49								
Langley	d				←	18 22										←	18 52								←
Slough 3	a			18 06	18 13	18 27				18 43					18 38	18 43	18 57			19 13				19 06	19 13
	d			18 06	18 13	18 27				18 43					18 39	18 43	18 57			19 13				19 06	19 13
Burnham	d				18 17					→						18 47				→					19 17
Taplow	d				18 21											18 51									19 21
Maidenhead 3	d				18 25	18 34										18 55	19 04								19 25
Twyford 3	d				18 33	18 42										19 03	19 12								19 33
Reading 7	a		18 09	18 22	18 43	18 52	18 27		18 30				18 40	18 48	18 53	19 13	19 22	18 57					19 09	19 22	19 43
Oxford	a			18 48		19 40									19 18		20 14							19 48	

A from 7 January until 11 February

Table 117

Saturdays

7 January to 24 March

London - Greenford and Reading

Network Diagram - see first Page of Table 116

Station		GW 1	GW ◇1 ☕	HC	GW ◇1 A ☕	GW 1	GW 1	GW ◇1 ☕	GW ◇1	GW 1	GW 1	GW ◇1 A ☕	HC	GW 1	GW 1	GW ◇1 ☕	GW ◇1 A 🚲	GW 1	GW 1	GW ◇1 ☕	HC	GW ◇1 ☕	GW 1
London Paddington 15 ⊖	d	18 57	19 00	19 03	19 06	19 12	19 15	19 15	19 21		19 27	19 30	19 33	19 42	19 45	19 45	19 50		19 57	20 00	20 03	20 06	20 12
Acton Main Line	d						19 21								19 51								
Ealing Broadway ⊖	d	19 05		19 11		19 20	19 24				19 35		19 41	19 50	19 54				20 05		20 11		20 20
West Ealing	d			19 13			19 27						19 43		19 57						20 13		
Drayton Green	d						19 29								19 59								
Castle Bar Park	d						19 31								20 01								
South Greenford	d						19 34								20 04								
Greenford ⊖	a						19 39								20 09								
Hanwell	d			19 15									19 45								20 15		
Southall	d			19 19		19 28							19 49	19 58							20 19		20 28
Hayes & Harlington	d	19 12		19 23		19 32					19 42		19 53	20 02					20 12		20 23		20 32
Heathrow Terminal 1-2-3 2 ✈	a			19 35									20 05								20 35		
Heathrow Terminal 4 ✈	a																						
West Drayton	d	19 16				19 36					19 46			20 06					20 16				20 36
Iver	d	19 19									19 49								20 19				
Langley	d	19 22								←	19 52							←	20 22				
Slough 3	a	19 27				19 43			19 37	19 43	19 57			20 13			20 06	20 13	20 27				20 43
	d	19 27				19 43			19 38	19 43	19 57			20 13			20 06	20 13	20 27				20 43
Burnham	d					→				19 47				→				20 17					→
Taplow	d									19 51								20 21					
Maidenhead 3	d	19 34								19 55	20 04							20 25	20 34				
Twyford 3	d	19 42								20 03	20 12							20 33	20 42				
Reading 7	a	19 52	19 26		19 30			19 39	19 52	20 13	20 20	19 57				20 09	20 21	20 43	20 51	20 27		20 31	
Oxford	a	20 40							20 20		21 14						20 47		21 40				

Station		GW 1	GW ◇1 ☕	GW ◇1	GW 1	GW 1	GW ◇1 ☕	HC	GW 1	GW ◇1 A ☕	GW 1	GW ◇1 🚲	GW 1	GW 1	HC	GW 1	GW 1	GW ◇1	GW ◇1 ☕	GW 1	HC	GW 1
London Paddington 15 ⊖	d	20 15	20 15	20 17		20 27	20 30	20 33	20 42	20 45	20 45	20 50		20 57	21 03	21 12	21 15	21 17	21 30		21 33	21 42
Acton Main Line	d	20 21									20 51						21 21					21 48
Ealing Broadway ⊖	d	20 24				20 35		20 41	20 50		20 54			21 05	21 11	21 20	21 24				21 41	21 52
West Ealing	d	20 27						20 43			20 57				21 13		21 27				21 43	
Drayton Green	d	20 29									20 59						21 29					
Castle Bar Park	d	20 31									21 01						21 31					
South Greenford	d	20 34									21 04						21 34					
Greenford ⊖	a	20 39									21 09						21 39					
Hanwell	d							20 45							21 15						21 45	
Southall	d							20 49	20 58						21 19	21 28					21 49	21 58
Hayes & Harlington	d					20 42		20 53	21 02					21 12	21 23	21 32					21 53	22 02
Heathrow Terminal 1-2-3 2 ✈	a							21 05							21 35						22 05	
Heathrow Terminal 4 ✈	a																					
West Drayton	d					20 46			21 06					21 16		21 36						22 06
Iver	d					20 49								21 19								
Langley	d				←	20 52							←	21 22						←		
Slough 3	a			20 32	20 43	20 57			21 13			21 06	21 13	21 27		21 43		21 34		21 43		22 13
	d			20 32	20 43	20 57			21 13			21 06	21 13	21 27		21 43		21 35		21 43		22 13
Burnham	d				20 47				→				21 17			→				21 47		→
Taplow	d				20 51								21 21							21 51		
Maidenhead 3	d				20 55	21 04							21 25	21 34						21 55		
Twyford 3	d				21 03	21 12							21 33	21 47						22 03		
Reading 7	a		20 40	20 48	21 13	21 29	20 58			21 09		21 22	21 43	22 03				21 51	21 55	22 18		
Oxford	a			21 19		22 14						21 53		22 46				22 20				

Station		GW ◇1	GW 1	GW 1	GW ◇1 ☕	HC	GW 1	GW ◇1	HC	GW ◇1 ☕	GW 1	GW 1	GW ◇1	GW 1	HC	GW ◇1 ☕	GW ◇1
London Paddington 15 ⊖	d	21 50		21 57	22 00	22 03	22 12	22 15	22 33	22 35		22 45	23 00		23 03	23 30	23 33
Acton Main Line	d											22 51					
Ealing Broadway ⊖	d			22 05		22 11	22 20		22 41			22 55			23 11		
West Ealing	d					22 13			22 43						23 13		
Drayton Green	d																
Castle Bar Park	d																
South Greenford	d																
Greenford ⊖	a																
Hanwell	d					22 15			22 45						23 15		
Southall	d					22 19	22 28		22 49			23 00			23 19		
Hayes & Harlington	d			22 12		22 23	22 32		22 53			23 04			23 23		
Heathrow Terminal 1-2-3 2 ✈	a					22 35			23 05						23 35		
Heathrow Terminal 4 ✈	a														23 41		
West Drayton	d			22 16			22 36					23 08					
Iver	d			22 19								23 11					
Langley	d		←	22 22							←	23 14		←			
Slough 3	a	22 06	22 13	22 27			22 43	22 31			22 43	23 19	23 16	23 19			23 49
	d	22 06	22 13	22 27			22 43	22 32			22 43	23 21	23 17	23 21			23 50
Burnham	d		22 17				→				22 47	→		23 25			
Taplow	d		22 21								22 51						
Maidenhead 3	d		22 25	22 34							22 55			23 32			
Twyford 3	d		22 33	22 45							23 03			23 39			
Reading 7	a	22 22	22 41	22 54	22 27			22 49		23 00	23 13		23 33	23 46		23 59	00 06
Oxford	a	22 50		23 38				23 20					00 04	00 32			00 38

A from 7 January until 11 February

Table 117

Saturdays
from 31 March

London - Greenford and Reading

Network Diagram - see first Page of Table 116

		GW	GW	GW	GW	GW	GW	GW	GW	GW		GW	GW	HC	HC	GW	GW	HC	GW	GW		GW	HC	GW	GW
		1	◇1	1	1	◇1 🍴	1	1	◇1	1		1	1			◇1	1		1	◇1		1		1	1
London Paddington 15 ⊖	d	22p45	23p18		23p29	23p30	23p42	23p48	00 22	00 34		01 44	03 34	04 42	05 13	05 21	05 25	05 33	05 45	05 50		05 57	06 03	06 12	06 15
Acton Main Line	d	22p51						23p54											05 51						06 21
Ealing Broadway ⊖	d	22p54			23p37			23p57		00 42		01 52	03 42	04 50	05 21		05 33	05 41	05 54			06 05	06 11	06 20	06 24
West Ealing	d							23p59										05 43	05 57				06 13		06 27
Drayton Green	d																		05 59						06 29
Castle Bar Park	d																		06 01						06 31
South Greenford	d																		06 04						06 34
Greenford ⊖	a																		06 09						06 39
Hanwell	d							00 02										05 45					06 15		
Southall	d							00 06		00 47		01 57	03 47	04 54	05 25		05 38	05 49				06 10	06 19	06 28	
Hayes & Harlington	d	23p01			23p44			00 10		00 51		02 01	03 51	04 58	05 29		05 42	05 53				06 14	06 23	06 32	
Heathrow Terminal 1-2-3 2 ✈	a													05 04	05 35			06 05					06 35		
Heathrow Terminal 4 ✈	a													05 10	05 41										
West Drayton	d							00 14		00 55		02 05	03 55									06 18		06 36	
Iver	d							00 17														06 21			
Langley	d							00 21		01 00												06 25			
Slough 3	a	23p11	23p36		23p53		23p58	00 26	00 38	01 05		02 13	04 03			05 37	05 50			06 06		06 30		06 43	
	d	23p12	23p36		23p54		23p58	00 26	00 39	01 05		02 13	04 03			05 38	05 51			06 06		06 31		06 43	
Burnham	d	23p16						00 30		01 09							05 55					06 35		→	
Taplow	d	23p20						00 34		01 13							05 58					06 38			
Maidenhead 3	d	23p24	23p44		00 01		00 08	00 41		01 16		02 21	04 11				06 02					06 42			
Twyford 3	d	23p32		00 07	00 09			00 48		01 24		02 29	04 19				06 10					06 50			
Reading 7	a	23p41	23p58	00 16	00 19	00 04	00 21	00 57	00 55	01 35		02 38	04 30			05 52	06 17			06 22		06 56			
Oxford	a	00 26	00 28		01 16		01 02		01 28							06 22	07 03			06 52		07 43			

		GW	GW	GW	GW	HC		GW	GW	GW	GW	GW	GW	HC	GW	GW		GW	GW	GW	GW	HC	GW	GW	GW
		◇1	1	1	◇1 🍴			1	1	◇1	1	1	◇1 🍴		1	1		◇1	1	1	R 1 🍴		1	1	◇1 🍴
London Paddington 15 ⊖	d	06 21		06 27	06 30	06 33		06 42	06 45	06 50		06 57	07 00	07 03	07 12	07 15		07 21		07 27	07 30	07 33	07 42	07 45	07 45
Acton Main Line	d								06 51							07 21								07 51	
Ealing Broadway ⊖	d			06 35		06 41		06 50	06 54			07 05		07 11	07 20	07 24				07 35		07 41	07 50	07 54	
West Ealing	d					06 43			06 57					07 13		07 27						07 43		07 57	
Drayton Green	d								06 59							07 29								07 59	
Castle Bar Park	d								07 01							07 31								08 01	
South Greenford	d								07 04							07 34								08 04	
Greenford ⊖	a								07 09							07 39								08 09	
Hanwell	d					06 45								07 15								07 45			
Southall	d					06 49		06 58						07 19	07 28							07 49	07 58		
Hayes & Harlington	d			06 42		06 53		07 02				07 12		07 23	07 32					07 42		07 53	08 02		
Heathrow Terminal 1-2-3 2 ✈	a					07 05								07 35								08 05			
Heathrow Terminal 4 ✈	a																								
West Drayton	d			06 46				07 06				07 16			07 36					07 46			08 06		
Iver	d			06 49								07 19								07 49					
Langley	d		←	06 52							←	07 22							←	07 52					
Slough 3	a	06 37	06 43	06 57				07 13		07 06	07 13	07 27			07 43			07 37	07 43	07 57			08 13		
	d	06 38	06 43	06 57				07 13		07 06	07 13	07 27			07 43			07 38	07 43	07 57			08 13		
Burnham	d		06 47					→			07 17				→				07 47				→		
Taplow	d		06 51								07 21								07 51						
Maidenhead 3	d		06 55	07 04							07 25	07 34							07 55	08 04					
Twyford 3	d		07 03	07 12							07 33	07 42							08 03	08 12					
Reading 7	a	06 53	07 13	07 20	06 57					07 22	07 43	07 52	07 26					07 53	08 13	08 22	07 57				08 09
Oxford	a	07 18		08 09						07 48		08 40						08 19		09 14					

		GW		GW	GW	GW	HC	GW	GW	GW	GW	GW		GW	GW	GW	HC	GW	GW	GW	GW	GW		GW	GW
		◇1		1	1	◇1 🍴		1	1	◇1 🍴	◇1 🍴	◇1 🍴		1	1	◇1 🍴		1	1	◇1 🍴	◇1	1		1	◇1 🍴
London Paddington 15 ⊖	d	07 50			07 57	08 00	08 03	08 12	08 15	08 15	08 18	08 21			08 27	08 30	08 33	08 42	08 45	08 45	08 50			08 57	09 00
Acton Main Line	d								08 21										08 51						
Ealing Broadway ⊖	d				08 05		08 11	08 20	08 24						08 35		08 41	08 50	08 54					09 05	
West Ealing	d						08 13		08 27								08 43		08 57						
Drayton Green	d								08 29										08 59						
Castle Bar Park	d								08 31										09 01						
South Greenford	d								08 34										09 04						
Greenford ⊖	a								08 39										09 09						
Hanwell	d						08 15										08 45								
Southall	d						08 19	08 28									08 49	08 58							
Hayes & Harlington	d				08 12		08 23	08 32							08 42		08 53	09 02						09 12	
Heathrow Terminal 1-2-3 2 ✈	a						08 35										09 05								
Heathrow Terminal 4 ✈	a																								
West Drayton	d				08 16			08 36							08 46			09 06						09 16	
Iver	d				08 19										08 49									09 19	
Langley	d			←	08 22									←	08 52							←		09 22	
Slough 3	a	08 06		08 13	08 27			08 43				08 38		08 43	08 57			09 13			09 06	09 13		09 27	
	d	08 06		08 13	08 27			08 43				08 39		08 43	08 57			09 13			09 06	09 13		09 27	
Burnham	d			08 17				→						08 47				→				09 17			
Taplow	d			08 21										08 51								09 21			
Maidenhead 3	d			08 25	08 34									08 55	09 04							09 25		09 34	
Twyford 3	d			08 33	08 42									09 03	09 12							09 33		09 42	
Reading 7	a	08 22		08 43	08 52	08 26				08 40	08 46	08 53		09 13	09 23	08 56				09 09	09 22	09 43		09 52	09 26
Oxford	a	08 48			09 40							09 18			10 14						09 48			10 40	

London - Greenford and Reading

Network Diagram - see first Page of Table 116

		HC	GW ◇1 Ø	GW 1	GW 1	GW 1	GW ◇1	GW 1		GW 1	GW ◇1 ☕	HC	GW 1	GW 1	GW ◇1 ☕	GW ◇1	GW 1	GW 1		GW ◇1 ☕	HC	GW ◇1 Ø	GW 1	GW 1	GW ◇1 ☕
London Paddington 15 ⊖	d	09 03	09 06	09 12	09 15	09 18	09 21			09 27	09 30	09 33	09 42	09 45	09 45	09 50		09 57		10 00	10 03	10 06	10 12	10 15	10 15
Acton Main Line	d				09 21									09 51										10 21	
Ealing Broadway ⊖	d	09 11		09 20	09 24					09 35		09 41	09 50	09 54				10 05			10 11		10 20	10 24	
West Ealing	d	09 13			09 27							09 43		09 57							10 13			10 27	
Drayton Green	d				09 29									09 59										10 29	
Castle Bar Park	d				09 31									10 01										10 31	
South Greenford	d				09 34									10 04										10 34	
Greenford ⊖	a				09 39									10 09										10 39	
Hanwell	d	09 15										09 45									10 15				
Southall	d	09 19		09 28								09 49	09 58								10 19		10 28		
Hayes & Harlington	d	09 23		09 32						09 42		09 53	10 02					10 12			10 23		10 32		
Heathrow Terminal 1-2-3 2 ✈	a	09 35										10 05									10 35				
Heathrow Terminal 4 ✈	a																								
West Drayton	d			09 36						09 46			10 06					10 16					10 36		
Iver	d									09 49								10 19							
Langley	d							←		09 52							←	10 22							
Slough 3	a			09 43			09 38	09 43		09 57			10 13			10 06	10 13	10 27					10 43		
	d			09 43			09 39	09 43		09 57			10 13			10 06	10 13	10 27					10 43		
Burnham	d			→				09 47					→				10 17						→		
Taplow	d							09 51									10 21								
Maidenhead 3	d							09 55		10 04							10 25	10 34							
Twyford 3	d							10 03		10 12							10 33	10 42							
Reading 7	a		09 30			09 48	09 54	10 13		10 22	09 57				10 09	10 22	10 43	10 52		10 26		10 30			10 40
Oxford	a						10 19			11 14						10 48		11 40							

		GW 1	GW ◇1 ☕	GW 1		GW 1	GW ◇1 ☕	HC	GW 1	GW 1	GW ◇1 Ø	GW ◇1 trolley	GW 1	GW 1		GW ◇1 ☕	HC	GW ◇1 Ø	GW 1	GW 1	GW 1	GW ◇1 trolley	GW 1	GW 1	
London Paddington 15 ⊖	d	10 18	10 21			10 27	10 30	10 33	10 42	10 45	10 45	10 50		10 57		11 00	11 03	11 06	11 12	11 15	11 18	11 21		11 27	
Acton Main Line	d									10 51										11 21					
Ealing Broadway ⊖	d					10 35		10 41	10 52	10 54				11 05			11 11		11 20	11 24				11 35	
West Ealing	d							10 43		10 57							11 13			11 27					
Drayton Green	d									10 59										11 29					
Castle Bar Park	d									11 01										11 31					
South Greenford	d									11 04										11 34					
Greenford ⊖	a									11 09										11 39					
Hanwell	d							10 45									11 15								
Southall	d							10 49	10 58								11 19		11 28						
Hayes & Harlington	d					10 42		10 53	11 02					11 12			11 23		11 32					11 42	
Heathrow Terminal 1-2-3 2 ✈	a							11 05									11 35								
Heathrow Terminal 4 ✈	a																								
West Drayton	d					10 46			11 06					11 16					11 36					11 46	
Iver	d					10 49								11 19										11 49	
Langley	d			←		10 52							←	11 22									←	11 52	
Slough 3	a		10 38	10 43		10 57			11 13			11 06	11 13	11 27					11 43			11 38	11 43	11 57	
	d		10 39	10 43		10 57			11 13			11 06	11 13	11 27					11 43			11 39	11 43	11 57	
Burnham	d			10 47					→				11 17						→				11 47		
Taplow	d			10 51									11 21										11 51		
Maidenhead 3	d			10 55		11 04							11 25	11 34									11 55	12 04	
Twyford 3	d			11 03		11 12							11 33	11 42									12 03	12 12	
Reading 7	a	10 48	10 53	11 13		11 22	10 57				11 09	11 22	11 43	11 52		11 26		11 30			11 48	11 54	12 13	12 22	
Oxford	a		11 19			12 14						11 48		12 40								12 20		13 14	

		GW ◇1 Ø	HC	GW 1	GW 1	GW ◇1 Ø	GW ◇1	GW 1	GW 1	GW ◇1 ☕		HC	GW ◇1 Ø	GW 1	GW 1	GW ◇1 ☕	GW ◇1 ☕	GW ◇1	GW 1	GW 1		GW ◇1 ☕	HC	GW 1	GW 1
London Paddington 15 ⊖	d	11 30	11 33	11 42	11 45	11 45	11 50		11 57	12 00		12 03	12 06	12 12	12 15	12 15	12 18	12 21		12 27		12 30	12 33	12 42	12 45
Acton Main Line	d				11 51										12 21										12 51
Ealing Broadway ⊖	d		11 41	11 50	11 54				12 05			12 11		12 20	12 24					12 35			12 41	12 50	12 54
West Ealing	d		11 43		11 57							12 13			12 27								12 43		12 57
Drayton Green	d				11 59										12 29										12 59
Castle Bar Park	d				12 01										12 31										13 01
South Greenford	d				12 04										12 34										13 04
Greenford ⊖	a				12 09										12 39										13 09
Hanwell	d		11 45									12 15											12 45		
Southall	d		11 49	11 58								12 19		12 28									12 49	12 58	
Hayes & Harlington	d		11 53	12 02					12 12			12 23		12 32						12 42			12 53	13 02	
Heathrow Terminal 1-2-3 2 ✈	a		12 05									12 35											13 05		
Heathrow Terminal 4 ✈	a																								
West Drayton	d			12 06					12 16					12 36						12 46				13 06	
Iver	d								12 19											12 49					
Langley	d							←	12 22										←	12 52					
Slough 3	a			12 13			12 06	12 13	12 27					12 43				12 38	12 43	12 57				13 13	
	d			12 13			12 06	12 13	12 27					12 43				12 39	12 43	12 57				13 13	
Burnham	d			→				12 17						→					12 47					→	
Taplow	d							12 21											12 51						
Maidenhead 3	d							12 25	12 34										12 55	13 04					
Twyford 3	d							12 33	12 42										13 03	13 12					
Reading 7	a	11 57				12 09	12 22	12 43	12 52	12 26			12 30			12 40	12 45	12 54	13 13	13 22		12 57			
Oxford	a						12 48		13 40									13 19		14 14					

Table 117

London - Greenford and Reading

Network Diagram - see first Page of Table 116

		GW	GW	GW	GW	GW		HC	GW	GW	GW	GW	GW	GW	GW	GW		HC	GW	GW	GW	GW	GW	GW	GW
		◇1 ☕	◇1 🛒	1	1	◇1 ☕			R 1 ☕	1	1	1	◇1 🛒	1	1	◇1 ☕			1	1	◇1 ☕	◇1 🛒	1	1	◇1 ☕
London Paddington 15 ⊖	d	12 45	12 50		12 57	13 00		13 03	13 06	13 12	13 15	13 18	13 21		13 27	13 30		13 33	13 42	13 45	13 45	13 50		13 57	14 00
Acton Main Line	d										13 21									13 51					
Ealing Broadway ⊖	d				13 05			13 11		13 20	13 24				13 35			13 41	13 50	13 54				14 05	
West Ealing	d							13 13			13 27							13 43		13 57					
Drayton Green	d										13 29									13 59					
Castle Bar Park	d										13 31									14 01					
South Greenford	d										13 34									14 04					
Greenford ⊖	a										13 39									14 09					
Hanwell	d							13 15										13 45							
Southall	d							13 19		13 28								13 49	13 58						
Hayes & Harlington	d				13 12			13 23		13 32					13 42			13 53	14 02					14 12	
Heathrow Terminal 1-2-3 2 ✈	a							13 35										14 05							
Heathrow Terminal 4 ✈	a																								
West Drayton	d				13 16					13 36					13 46				14 06					14 16	
Iver	d				13 19										13 49									14 19	
Langley	d			←	13 22									←	13 52								←	14 22	
Slough 3	a		13 06	13 13	13 27					13 43			13 38	13 43	13 57				14 13			14 06	14 13	14 27	
	d		13 06	13 13	13 27					13 43			13 39	13 43	13 57				14 13			14 06	14 13	14 27	
Burnham	d			13 17						↪				13 47					↪				14 17		
Taplow	d			13 21										13 51									14 21		
Maidenhead 3	d			13 25	13 34									13 55	14 04								14 25	14 34	
Twyford 3	d			13 33	13 42									14 03	14 12								14 33	14 42	
Reading 7	a	13 09	13 22	13 43	13 52	13 26			13 30			13 48	13 54	14 13	14 22	13 58					14 09	14 22	14 43	14 52	14 26
Oxford	a		13 48		14 40								14 19		15 14							14 48		15 40	

		HC		GW	GW	GW	GW	GW	GW	GW	GW	GW		HC	GW	GW	GW	GW	GW	GW	GW	HC		GW	GW
				◇1 ☕	1	1	◇1 ☕	1	◇1 🛒	1	1	◇1 ☕			1	1	◇1 ☕	◇1	1	1	◇1 ☕			◇1 ☕	1
London Paddington 15 ⊖	d	14 03		14 06	14 12	14 15	14 15	14 18	14 21		14 27	14 30		14 33	14 42	14 45	14 45	14 50		14 57	15 00	15 03		15 06	15 12
Acton Main Line	d					14 21										14 51									
Ealing Broadway ⊖	d	14 11			14 20	14 24					14 35			14 41	14 50	14 54				15 05		15 11			15 20
West Ealing	d	14 13				14 27								14 43		14 57						15 13			
Drayton Green	d					14 29										14 59									
Castle Bar Park	d					14 31										15 01									
South Greenford	d					14 34										15 04									
Greenford ⊖	a					14 39										15 09									
Hanwell	d	14 15												14 45								15 15			
Southall	d	14 19			14 28									14 49	14 58							15 19			15 28
Hayes & Harlington	d	14 23			14 32						14 42			14 53	15 02					15 12		15 23			15 32
Heathrow Terminal 1-2-3 2 ✈	a	14 35												15 05								15 35			
Heathrow Terminal 4 ✈	a																								
West Drayton	d				14 36						14 46				15 06					15 16					15 36
Iver	d										14 49									15 19					
Langley	d									←	14 52								←	15 22					
Slough 3	a				14 43				14 38	14 43	14 57				15 13			15 06	15 13	15 27					15 43
	d				14 43				14 39	14 43	14 57				15 13			15 06	15 13	15 27					15 43
Burnham	d				↪					14 47					↪				15 17						↪
Taplow	d									14 51									15 21						
Maidenhead 3	d									14 55	15 04								15 25	15 34					
Twyford 3	d									15 03	15 12								15 33	15 42					
Reading 7	a			14 30			14 40	14 48	14 53	15 13	15 22	14 57					15 09	15 22	15 43	15 52	15 26			15 29	
Oxford	a								15 18		16 14							15 48		16 40					

		GW	GW	GW	GW	GW	GW	HC		GW	GW	GW	GW	GW	GW	GW	HC	GW		GW	GW	GW	GW	GW	GW
		1	1	◇1 🛒	1	1	◇1 ☕			1	1	◇1 ☕	◇1	1	1	◇1 ☕		◇1 ☕		1	1	◇1 ☕	1	◇1 ☕	1
London Paddington 15 ⊖	d	15 15	15 18	15 21		15 27	15 30	15 33		15 42	15 45	15 45	15 50		15 57	16 00	16 03	16 06		16 12	16 15	16 15	16 18	16 21	
Acton Main Line	d	15 21									15 51										16 21				
Ealing Broadway ⊖	d	15 24				15 35		15 41		15 50	15 54				16 05		16 11			16 20	16 24				
West Ealing	d	15 27						15 43			15 57						16 13				16 27				
Drayton Green	d	15 29									15 59										16 29				
Castle Bar Park	d	15 31									16 01										16 31				
South Greenford	d	15 34									16 04										16 34				
Greenford ⊖	a	15 39									16 09										16 39				
Hanwell	d							15 45									16 15								
Southall	d							15 49		15 58							16 19			16 28					
Hayes & Harlington	d					15 42		15 53		16 02					16 12		16 23			16 32					
Heathrow Terminal 1-2-3 2 ✈	a							16 05									16 35								
Heathrow Terminal 4 ✈	a																								
West Drayton	d					15 46				16 06					16 16					16 36					
Iver	d					15 49									16 19										
Langley	d				←	15 52								←	16 22										←
Slough 3	a			15 38	15 43	15 57				16 13			16 06	16 13	16 27					16 43				16 38	16 43
	d			15 39	15 43	15 57				16 13			16 06	16 13	16 27					16 43				16 39	16 43
Burnham	d				15 47					↪				16 17						↪					16 47
Taplow	d				15 51									16 21											16 51
Maidenhead 3	d				15 55	16 04								16 25	16 34										16 55
Twyford 3	d				16 03	16 12								16 33	16 42										17 03
Reading 7	a		15 48	15 54	16 13	16 22	15 58					16 09	16 22	16 43	16 52	16 26		16 31				16 40	16 48	16 53	17 13
Oxford	a			16 19		17 14							16 48		17 40									17 18	

Table 117

Saturdays

from 31 March

London - Greenford and Reading

Network Diagram - see first Page of Table 116

		GW ■1	GW ◇■1 ☕	HC		GW ■1	GW ■1	GW ◇■1 ☕	GW ◇■1 🛒	GW ■1	GW ■1	GW ◇■1 ☕	HC	GW ◇■1 ☕		GW ■1	GW ■1	GW ■1	GW ◇■1 ☕	GW ■1	GW ■1	GW ◇■1 ☕	HC	GW ■1	
London Paddington 15 ⊖	d	16 27	16 30	16 33		16 42	16 45	16 45	16 50		16 57	17 00	17 03	17 06		17 12	17 15	17 18	17 21		17 27	17 30	17 33	17 42	
Acton Main Line	d						16 51										17 21								
Ealing Broadway ⊖	d	16 35		16 41		16 50	16 54				17 05		17 11			17 20	17 24				17 35		17 41	17 50	
West Ealing	d			16 43			16 57						17 13				17 27						17 43		
Drayton Green	d						16 59										17 29								
Castle Bar Park	d						17 01										17 31								
South Greenford	d						17 04										17 34								
Greenford ⊖	a						17 09										17 39								
Hanwell	d			16 45									17 15										17 45		
Southall	d			16 49		16 58							17 19			17 28							17 49	17 58	
Hayes & Harlington	d	16 42		16 53		17 02					17 12		17 23			17 32					17 42		17 53	18 02	
Heathrow Terminal 1-2-3 2 ✈	a			17 05									17 35										18 05		
Heathrow Terminal 4 ✈	a																								
West Drayton	d	16 46				17 06					17 16					17 36					17 46			18 06	
Iver	d	16 49									17 19										17 49				
Langley	d	16 52								←	17 22									←	17 52				
Slough 3	a	16 57				17 13			17 06	17 13	17 27					17 43			17 38	17 43	17 57			18 13	
	d	16 57				17 13			17 06	17 13	17 27					17 43			17 39	17 43	17 57			18 13	
Burnham	d					→				17 17						→				17 47				→	
Taplow	d									17 21										17 51					
Maidenhead 3	d	17 04								17 25	17 34									17 55	18 04				
Twyford 3	d	17 12								17 33	17 42									18 03	18 12				
Reading 7	a	17 22	16 57					17 09	17 22	17 43	17 52	17 26		17 30				17 48	17 53	18 13	18 22	17 57			
Oxford	a	18 14							17 48		18 40								18 18		19 14				

		GW ■1	GW ◇■1 ☕	GW ◇■1 🛒	GW ■1	GW ■1	GW ◇■1 ☕	HC	GW ◇■1 ☕	GW ■1		GW ■1	GW ◇■1 ☕	GW ■1	GW ◇■1 ☕	GW ■1	GW ■1	GW ◇■1 ☕	HC	GW ■1		GW ■1	GW ◇■1 ☕	GW ◇■1	GW ■1
London Paddington 15 ⊖	d	17 45	17 45	17 50		17 57	18 00	18 03	18 06	18 12		18 15	18 15	18 18	18 21		18 27	18 30	18 33	18 42		18 45	18 45	18 50	
Acton Main Line	d	17 51										18 21										18 51			
Ealing Broadway ⊖	d	17 54				18 05		18 11		18 20		18 24					18 35		18 41	18 50		18 54			
West Ealing	d	17 57						18 13				18 27							18 43			18 57			
Drayton Green	d	17 59										18 29										18 59			
Castle Bar Park	d	18 01										18 31										19 01			
South Greenford	d	18 04										18 34										19 04			
Greenford ⊖	a	18 09										18 39										19 09			
Hanwell	d							18 15											18 45						
Southall	d							18 19		18 28									18 49	18 58					
Hayes & Harlington	d					18 12		18 23		18 32							18 42		18 53	19 02					
Heathrow Terminal 1-2-3 2 ✈	a							18 35											19 05						
Heathrow Terminal 4 ✈	a																								
West Drayton	d					18 16				18 36							18 46			19 06					
Iver	d					18 19											18 49								
Langley	d				←	18 22										←	18 52								←
Slough 3	a			18 06	18 13	18 27				18 43					18 38	18 43	18 57			19 13				19 06	19 13
	d			18 06	18 13	18 27				18 43					18 39	18 43	18 57			19 13				19 06	19 13
Burnham	d				18 17					→						18 47				→					19 17
Taplow	d				18 21											18 51									19 21
Maidenhead 3	d				18 25	18 34										18 55	19 04								19 25
Twyford 3	d				18 33	18 42										19 03	19 12								19 33
Reading 7	a		18 09	18 22	18 43	18 52	18 27		18 30				18 40	18 48	18 53	19 13	19 22	18 57					19 09	19 22	19 43
Oxford	a			18 48		19 40									19 18		20 14							19 48	

		GW ■1	GW ◇■1 ☕	HC	GW ◇■1 ☕	GW ■1		GW ■1	GW ◇■1 ☕	GW ◇■1	GW ■1	GW ■1	GW ◇■1 ☕	HC	GW ■1	GW ■1		GW ◇■1 ☕	GW ◇■1 🛒	GW ■1	GW ■1	GW ◇■1 ☕	HC	GW ◇■1 ☕	GW ■1
London Paddington 15 ⊖	d	18 57	19 00	19 03	19 06	19 12		19 15	19 15	19 21		19 27	19 30	19 33	19 42	19 45		19 45	19 50		19 57	20 00	20 03	20 06	20 12
Acton Main Line	d							19 21								19 51									
Ealing Broadway ⊖	d	19 05		19 11		19 20		19 24				19 35		19 41	19 50	19 54					20 05		20 11		20 20
West Ealing	d			19 13				19 27						19 43		19 57							20 13		
Drayton Green	d							19 29								19 59									
Castle Bar Park	d							19 31								20 01									
South Greenford	d							19 34								20 04									
Greenford ⊖	a							19 39								20 09									
Hanwell	d			19 15										19 45									20 15		
Southall	d			19 19		19 28								19 49	19 58								20 19		20 28
Hayes & Harlington	d	19 12		19 23		19 32						19 42		19 53	20 02						20 12		20 23		20 32
Heathrow Terminal 1-2-3 2 ✈	a			19 35										20 05									20 35		
Heathrow Terminal 4 ✈	a																								
West Drayton	d	19 16				19 36						19 46			20 06						20 16				20 36
Iver	d	19 19										19 49									20 19				
Langley	d	19 22									←	19 52								←	20 22				
Slough 3	a	19 27				19 43				19 37	19 43	19 57			20 13				20 06	20 13	20 27				20 43
	d	19 27				19 43				19 38	19 43	19 57			20 13				20 06	20 13	20 27				20 43
Burnham	d					→					19 47				→					20 17					→
Taplow	d										19 51									20 21					
Maidenhead 3	d	19 34									19 55	20 04								20 25	20 34				
Twyford 3	d	19 42									20 03	20 12								20 33	20 42				
Reading 7	a	19 52	19 26		19 30				19 39	19 52	20 13	20 20	19 57					20 09	20 21	20 43	20 52	20 27		20 31	
Oxford	a	20 40								20 20		21 14							20 47		21 40				

Table 117

Saturdays
from 31 March

London - Greenford and Reading

Network Diagram - see first Page of Table 116

	GW		GW	GW	GW	GW	GW	HC	GW	GW	GW		GW	GW	GW	HC	GW	GW	GW	GW	GW		HC	GW
	1		◇1 ☕	◇1	1	1	◇1 ☕		1	◇1 ☕	1		◇1 🛒	1	1		1	1	◇1	◇1 ☕	1			1
London Paddington 15 ⊖ d	20 15		20 15	20 20		20 27	20 30	20 33	20 42	20 45	20 45		20 50		20 57	21 03	21 12	21 15	21 17	21 30			21 33	21 42
Acton Main Line d	20 21										20 51							21 21						21 48
Ealing Broadway ⊖ d	20 24					20 35		20 41	20 50		20 54				21 05	21 11	21 20	21 24					21 41	21 52
West Ealing d	20 27							20 43			20 57					21 13		21 27					21 43	
Drayton Green d	20 29										20 59							21 29						
Castle Bar Park d	20 31										21 01							21 31						
South Greenford d	20 34										21 04							21 34						
Greenford ⊖ a	20 39										21 09							21 39						
Hanwell d								20 45								21 15							21 45	
Southall d								20 49	20 58							21 19	21 28						21 49	21 58
Hayes & Harlington d						20 42		20 53	21 02						21 12	21 23	21 32						21 53	22 02
Heathrow Terminal 1-2-3 2 ✈ a								21 05								21 35							22 05	
Heathrow Terminal 4 ✈ a																								
West Drayton d						20 46			21 06						21 16		21 36							22 06
Iver d						20 49									21 19									
Langley d					←	20 52								←	21 22						←			
Slough 3 a				20 35	20 43	20 57			21 13				21 06	21 13	21 27		21 43		21 34		21 43			22 13
d				20 35	20 43	20 57			21 13				21 06	21 13	21 27		21 43		21 35		21 43			22 13
Burnham d					20 47				→					21 17			→				21 47			→
Taplow d					20 51									21 21							21 51			
Maidenhead 3 d					20 55	21 04								21 25	21 34						21 55			
Twyford 3 d					21 06	21 12								21 33	21 42						22 03			
Reading 7 a			20 40	20 51	21 14	21 22	20 57			21 09			21 22	21 43	21 52				21 51	21 55	22 13			
Oxford a				21 19		22 14							21 53		22 43				22 20					

	GW	GW	GW	GW	HC	GW	GW		HC	GW	GW	GW	HC	GW	GW	GW
	◇1	1	1	◇1 ☕		1	◇1			◇1 ☕	1	◇1		◇1 ☕	◇1	1
London Paddington 15 ⊖ d	21 50		21 57	22 00	22 03	22 12	22 15		22 33	22 35		23 00	23 03	23 30	23 33	23 42
Acton Main Line d																
Ealing Broadway ⊖ d			22 05		22 11	22 20			22 41				23 11			23 50
West Ealing d					22 13				22 43				23 13			
Drayton Green d																
Castle Bar Park d																
South Greenford d																
Greenford ⊖ a																
Hanwell d					22 15				22 45				23 15			
Southall d					22 19	22 28			22 49				23 19			23 56
Hayes & Harlington d			22 12		22 23	22 32			22 53				23 23			00 01
Heathrow Terminal 1-2-3 2 ✈ a					22 35				23 05				23 35			
Heathrow Terminal 4 ✈ a													23 41			
West Drayton d			22 16			22 36										00 06
Iver d			22 19													
Langley d		←	22 22								←					
Slough 3 a	22 06	22 13	22 27			22 43	22 31				22 43	23 16			23 49	00 13
d	22 06	22 13	22 27			22 43	22 32				22 43	23 17			23 50	00 14
Burnham d		22 17				→					22 47					00 18
Taplow d		22 21									22 51					00 21
Maidenhead 3 d		22 25	22 34								22 55					00 25
Twyford 3 d		22 33	22 42								23 03					00 33
Reading 7 a	22 22	22 41	22 54	22 27			22 48			23 00	23 13	23 33		23 59	00 06	00 43
Oxford a	22 50		23 38				23 20					00 04			00 38	

Sundays
until 1 January

	GW	GW	GW	GW	GW	GW	GW	GW	GW		GW	HC	HC	GW	HC	GW	GW	GW	HC		GW	GW	GW	GW
	1	◇1	1	1	◇1	1	1	1	1		1			1		1	◇1	◇1			1	◇1	◇1	1
	A	A	A	A	A	A	A										☕					☕		
London Paddington 15 ⊖ d	22p45	23p00		23p20	23p33		23p42	00 05	00 30		01 00		06 12	06 43	07 12	07 29	08 00	08 03	08 12		08 15	08 30	08 42	08 43
Acton Main Line d	22p51																							
Ealing Broadway ⊖ d	22p55			23p28			23p50	00 13	00 38		01 08	05 20	06 20	06 52	07 20	07 36			08 20		08 24			08 50
West Ealing d																								
Drayton Green d																								
Castle Bar Park d																								
South Greenford d																								
Greenford ⊖ a																								
Hanwell d																								
Southall d	23p00			23p33			23p56	00 19	00 44		01 13	05 24	06 24	06 58	07 24	07 42			08 24		08 29			08 56
Hayes & Harlington d	23p04			23p37			00 01	00 23	00 48		01 17	05 28	06 28	07 02	07 28	07 46			08 28		08 33			09 01
Heathrow Terminal 1-2-3 2 ✈ a												05 34	06 34		07 34				08 34					
Heathrow Terminal 4 ✈ a												05 40	06 41		07 41				08 41					
West Drayton d	23p08			23p41			00 06	00 27	00 52					07 06		07 50					08 37			09 06
Iver d	23p11			23p44				00 30																
Langley d	23p14		←	23p48		←		00 33	00 56					07 11		07 55					08 42			09 10
Slough 3 a	23p19	23p16	23p19	23p53	23p49	23p53	00 13	00 37	01 00		01 25			07 16		07 58		08 26			08 46		09 03	09 14
d	23p21	23p17	23p21	23p54	23p50	23p54	00 14	00 38	01 01		01 26			07 16		07 58		08 26			08 46		09 04	09 14
Burnham d	→		23p25	→		23p57	00 18	00 42						07 20		08 03								09 20
Taplow d						00 01	00 21	00 45																
Maidenhead 3 d			23p32			00 05	00 25	00 49	01 08		01 33			07 25		08 08		08 33			08 54			09 27
Twyford 3 d			23p39			00 13	00 33	00 57	01 16		01 41			07 33		08 16					09 02			09 35
Reading 7 a		23p33	23p46		00 06	00 20	00 43	01 05	01 23		01 50			07 42		08 25	08 33	08 45			09 10	09 05	09 20	09 42
Oxford a		00 04	00 32		00 38	01 05										09 30		09 13					09 51	10 28

A not 11 December

Table 117

Sundays

until 1 January

London - Greenford and Reading

Network Diagram - see first Page of Table 116

		GW	GW	HC	GW	GW		GW	GW	GW	GW	HC	GW	GW	GW	GW		GW	GW	HC	GW	GW	GW	GW	GW
		◇1	◇1		1	◇1		◇1	1	◇1	◇1		1	◇1	◇1	1		◇1	◇1		1	◇1	◇1	◇1	1
		⊡	⊡			⊡		⊡		⊡	⊡			⊡	⊡			⊡	⊡			⊡	⊡		
London Paddington 15 ⊖	d	08 57	09 03	09 12	09 15	09 30		09 35	09 43	09 57	10 03	10 12	10 15	10 37	10 42	10 43		10 57	11 03	11 12	11 15	11 27	11 37	11 42	11 43
Acton Main Line	d																								
Ealing Broadway ⊖	d			09 20	09 24				09 50			10 20	10 24			10 50				11 20	11 24				11 50
West Ealing	d																								
Drayton Green	d																								
Castle Bar Park	d																								
South Greenford	d																								
Greenford ⊖	a																								
Hanwell	d																								
Southall	d			09 24	09 29				09 56			10 24	10 29			10 56				11 24	11 29				11 56
Hayes & Harlington	d			09 28	09 33				10 02			10 28	10 33			11 02				11 28	11 33				12 02
Heathrow Terminal 1-2-3 2 ✈	a			09 34								10 34								11 34					
Heathrow Terminal 4 ✈	a			09 41								10 41								11 41					
West Drayton	d				09 37				10 06				10 37			11 06					11 37				12 06
Iver	d																								
Langley	d				09 42				10 10				10 42			11 10					11 42				12 10
Slough 3	a				09 46			09 57	10 14				10 46		11 05	11 14					11 46			12 03	12 14
	d				09 46			09 58	10 16				10 46		11 05	11 16					11 46			12 04	12 16
Burnham	d								10 20							11 20									12 20
Taplow	d																								
Maidenhead 3	d				09 54				10 27				10 54			11 27					11 54				12 27
Twyford 3	d				10 02				10 35				11 02			11 35					12 02				12 35
Reading 7	a	09 31	09 36		10 10	10 02		10 11	10 42	10 31	10 36		11 10	11 11	11 20	11 42		11 32	11 36		12 10	12 01	12 11	12 19	12 42
Oxford	a							10 43	11 27						11 50	12 27								12 49	13 28

		GW		GW	HC	GW	GW	GW	GW	GW	GW	HC		GW	GW	GW	GW	GW	GW	HC	GW	GW		GW	GW
		◇1		◇1		1	◇1	◇1	1	◇1	◇1			1	◇1	◇1	1	◇1	◇1		1	◇1		◇1	1
		⊡		⊡			⊡	⊡		⊡	⊡				⊡	⊡		⊡	⊡			⊡			
London Paddington 15 ⊖	d	11 57		12 03	12 12	12 15	12 37	12 42	12 43	12 57	13 03	13 12		13 15	13 37	13 42	13 43	13 57	14 03	14 12	14 15	14 37		14 42	14 43
Acton Main Line	d																								
Ealing Broadway ⊖	d				12 20	12 24			12 50			13 20		13 24			13 50			14 20	14 24				14 50
West Ealing	d																								
Drayton Green	d																								
Castle Bar Park	d																								
South Greenford	d																								
Greenford ⊖	a																								
Hanwell	d																								
Southall	d				12 24	12 29			12 56			13 24		13 29			13 56			14 24	14 29				14 56
Hayes & Harlington	d				12 28	12 33			13 02			13 28		13 33			14 02			14 28	14 33				15 02
Heathrow Terminal 1-2-3 2 ✈	a				12 34							13 34								14 34					
Heathrow Terminal 4 ✈	a				12 41							13 41								14 41					
West Drayton	d					12 37			13 06					13 37			14 06				14 37				15 06
Iver	d																								
Langley	d					12 42			13 10					13 42			14 10				14 42				15 10
Slough 3	a					12 46		13 06	13 14					13 46		14 05	14 14				14 46			15 04	15 14
	d					12 46		13 07	13 16					13 46		14 06	14 16				14 46			15 05	15 16
Burnham	d								13 20								14 20								15 20
Taplow	d																								
Maidenhead 3	d					12 54			13 27					13 54			14 27				14 54				15 27
Twyford 3	d					13 02			13 35					14 02			14 36				15 02				15 35
Reading 7	a	12 31		12 36		13 10	13 11	13 22	13 42	13 31	13 36			14 10	14 11	14 21	14 42	14 31	14 36		15 10	15 11		15 19	15 42
Oxford	a							13 50	14 27							14 50	15 27							15 50	16 27

		GW	GW	HC	GW	GW	GW	GW		GW	GW	GW	HC	GW	GW	GW	GW	GW		GW	GW	HC	GW	GW	GW
		◇1	◇1		1	◇1	◇1	◇1		1	◇1	◇1		1	◇1	◇1	◇1	1		◇1	◇1		1	◇1	◇1
		⊡	⊡				⊡				⊡	⊡			⊡	⊡				⊡	⊡			⊡	⊡
London Paddington 15 ⊖	d	14 57	15 03	15 12	15 15	15 27	15 37	15 42		15 43	15 57	16 03	16 12	16 15	16 30	16 37	16 42	16 43		16 57	17 03	17 12	17 15	17 30	17 37
Acton Main Line	d																								
Ealing Broadway ⊖	d			15 20	15 24					15 50			16 20	16 24				16 50				17 20	17 24		
West Ealing	d																								
Drayton Green	d																								
Castle Bar Park	d																								
South Greenford	d																								
Greenford ⊖	a																								
Hanwell	d																								
Southall	d			15 24	15 29					15 56			16 24	16 29				16 56				17 24	17 29		
Hayes & Harlington	d			15 28	15 33					16 02			16 28	16 33				17 02				17 28	17 33		
Heathrow Terminal 1-2-3 2 ✈	a			15 34									16 34									17 34			
Heathrow Terminal 4 ✈	a			15 41									16 41									17 41			
West Drayton	d				15 37					16 06				16 37				17 06					17 37		
Iver	d																								
Langley	d				15 42					16 10				16 42				17 10					17 42		
Slough 3	a				15 46	15 49		16 04		16 14				16 46			17 03	17 14					17 46		
	d				15 46	15 50		16 05		16 16				16 46			17 04	17 16					17 46		
Burnham	d				15 51					16 20				16 51				17 20					17 51		
Taplow	d																								
Maidenhead 3	d				15 56	16 01				16 27				16 56			17 11	17 27					17 56		
Twyford 3	d				16 04	16 10				16 35				17 04				17 35					18 04		
Reading 7	a	15 30	15 36		16 12	16 16	16 10	16 19		16 42	16 30	16 36		17 12	17 03	17 09	17 22	17 42		17 30	17 36		18 12	18 03	18 10
Oxford	a					16 41		16 50		17 27							17 50	18 27							

Table 117

Sundays

until 1 January

London - Greenford and Reading

Network Diagram - see first Page of Table 116

		GW	GW	GW		GW	HC	GW	GW	GW	GW	GW	GW	GW		HC	GW	GW	GW	GW	GW	GW	GW	HC	
		◇1	1	◇1		◇1		1	◇1	◇1	◇1	1	◇1	◇1			1	◇1	◇1	◇1	1	◇1	◇1		
		☕		☕		☕			☕	☕			☕	☕				☕	☕	☕		☕	☕		
London Paddington 15 ⊖	d	17 42	17 43	17 57		18 03	18 12	18 15	18 30	18 37	18 42	18 43	18 57	19 03		19 12	19 15	19 30	19 37	19 42	19 43	19 57	20 03	20 12	
Acton Main Line	d																								
Ealing Broadway ⊖	d		17 50				18 20	18 24				18 50				19 20	19 24				19 50			20 20	
West Ealing	d																								
Drayton Green	d																								
Castle Bar Park	d																								
South Greenford	d																								
Greenford ⊖	a																								
Hanwell	d																								
Southall	d		17 56				18 24	18 29				18 56				19 24	19 29				19 56			20 24	
Hayes & Harlington	d		18 02				18 28	18 33				19 02				19 28	19 33				20 02			20 28	
Heathrow Terminal 1-2-3 2 ✈	a						18 34									19 34								20 34	
Heathrow Terminal 4 ✈	a						18 41									19 41								20 41	
West Drayton	d		18 06					18 37				19 06					19 37				20 06				
Iver	d																								
Langley	d		18 10					18 42				19 10					19 42				20 10				
Slough 3	a	18 03	18 14					18 46			19 07	19 14					19 46			20 05	20 14				
	d	18 04	18 16					18 46			19 07	19 16					19 46			20 06	20 16				
Burnham	d		18 20					18 51				19 20					19 51				20 20				
Taplow	d																								
Maidenhead 3	d	18 13	18 27					18 56			19 14	19 27					19 56				20 27				
Twyford 3	d		18 35					19 04				19 35					20 04				20 35				
Reading 7	a	18 23	18 42	18 30		18 36		19 12	19 04	19 10	19 26	19 42	19 31	19 36			20 12	20 06	20 10	20 20	20 42	20 30	20 36		
Oxford	a	18 51	19 27								19 55	20 27								20 50	21 30				

		GW	GW	GW	GW	GW	GW	GW	HC	GW		GW	GW	GW	GW	HC	GW	GW	GW	GW		GW	HC	GW	GW
		1	◇1	◇1	◇1	1	◇1	◇1		1		◇1	◇1	1	◇1		1	◇1	◇1	1		◇1		1	◇1
			☕	☕			☕	☕				☕			☕			☕				☕			☕
London Paddington 15 ⊖	d	20 15	20 30	20 37	20 42	20 43	20 57	21 03	21 12	21 15		21 37	21 42	21 43	22 03	22 12	22 15	22 37	22 42	22 43		23 03	23 12	23 15	23 37
Acton Main Line	d																								
Ealing Broadway ⊖	d	20 24				20 50			21 20	21 24				21 50		22 20	22 24			22 50			23 20	23 24	
West Ealing	d																								
Drayton Green	d																								
Castle Bar Park	d																								
South Greenford	d																								
Greenford ⊖	a																								
Hanwell	d																								
Southall	d	20 29				20 56			21 24	21 29				21 56		22 24	22 29			22 56			23 24	23 29	
Hayes & Harlington	d	20 33				21 02			21 28	21 33				22 02		22 28	22 33			23 02			23 28	23 33	
Heathrow Terminal 1-2-3 2 ✈	a								21 34							22 34							23 34		
Heathrow Terminal 4 ✈	a								21 41							22 41							23 41		
West Drayton	d	20 37				21 06				21 37				22 06			22 37			23 06				23 37	
Iver	d																								
Langley	d	20 42				21 10				21 42				22 10			22 42			23 10				23 42	
Slough 3	a	20 46			21 03	21 14				21 46			22 05	22 14			22 46		23 02	23 14				23 46	00 01
	d	20 46			21 04	21 16				21 46			22 06	22 16			22 46		23 02	23 16				23 46	00 02
Burnham	d	20 51				21 20				21 51				22 20			22 51			23 20				23 51	
Taplow	d																								
Maidenhead 3	d	20 56				21 27				21 56				22 31			22 56			23 25				23 56	
Twyford 3	d	21 04				21 35				22 04				22 39			23 04			23 32				00 04	
Reading 7	a	21 12	21 04	21 10	21 19	21 42	21 30	21 36		22 11		22 12	22 20	22 46	22 47		23 11	23 14	23 19	23 43		23 45		00 14	00 15
Oxford	a				21 49	22 29							22 50												

		GW		GW
		◇1		1
London Paddington 15 ⊖	d	23 47		23 53
Acton Main Line	d			
Ealing Broadway ⊖	d	23 55		00 02
West Ealing	d			
Drayton Green	d			
Castle Bar Park	d			
South Greenford	d			
Greenford ⊖	a			
Hanwell	d			
Southall	d			00 07
Hayes & Harlington	d			00 11
Heathrow Terminal 1-2-3 2 ✈	a			
Heathrow Terminal 4 ✈	a			
West Drayton	d			00 15
Iver	d			
Langley	d			00 20
Slough 3	a	00 09		00 24
	d	00 10		00 24
Burnham	d			00 28
Taplow	d			
Maidenhead 3	d	00 17		00 34
Twyford 3	d			00 42
Reading 7	a	00 29		00 49
Oxford	a			

Table 117 | **Sundays**

8 January to 12 February

London - Greenford and Reading

Network Diagram - see first Page of Table 116

		GW	GW	GW	GW	GW	GW	GW	GW	GW		GW	GW	HC	HC	GW	HC	GW	GW	GW		GW	HC	GW	GW
		1	◇1	1	◇1	🚌	1	🚌	1	🚌		1	🚌			1		🚌	1	◇1 ☕		◇1		1	◇1 ☕
London Paddington [15] ⊖	d	22p45	23p00		23p33		00 05		00 30			01 00			06 12	06 43	07 12		07 29	08 00		08 03	08 12	08 15	08 30
Acton Main Line	d	22p51																							
Ealing Broadway ⊖	d	22p55					00 13		00 38			01 08		05 20	06 20	06 52	07 20		07 36				08 20	08 24	
West Ealing	d																								
Drayton Green	d																								
Castle Bar Park	d																								
South Greenford	d																								
Greenford ⊖	a																								
Hanwell	d																								
Southall	d	23p00					00 19		00 44			01 13		05 24	06 24	06 58	07 24		07 42				08 24	08 29	
Hayes & Harlington	d	23p04					00 23		00 48			01 17		05 28	06 28	07 02	07 28		07 46				08 28	08 33	
Heathrow Terminal 1-2-3 [2] ✈	a													05 34	06 34		07 34						08 34		
Heathrow Terminal 4 ✈	a													05 40	06 41		07 41						08 41		
West Drayton	d	23p08					00 27		00 52							07 06			07 50					08 37	
Iver	d	23p11					00 30																		
Langley	d	23p14		←			00 33		00 56							07 11			07 55					08 42	
Slough [3]	a	23p19	23p16	23p19	23p49		00 37		01 00			01 25				07 16			07 58			08 25		08 46	
	d	23p21	23p17	23p21	23p50		00 38		01 01			01 26				07 16			07 58			08 26		08 46	
Burnham	d	→		23p25			00 42									07 20			08 03						
Taplow	d						00 45																		
Maidenhead [3]	d			23p32			00 49		01 08			01 33				07 25			08 08			08 33		08 54	
Twyford [3]	d			23p39		00 42	00a57	01 04	01a16	01 23		01a42	01 49			07a34		07 45	08 17					09 02	
Reading [7]	a		23p33	23p46	00 06	01 15		01 37		01 56			02 22					08 18	08 25	08 33		08 44		09 10	09 05
Oxford	a		00 04	00 32	00 38														09 30			09 13			

		GW	GW	GW	GW	HC		GW	GW	GW	GW	GW	GW	HC	GW	GW		GW	GW	GW	GW	HC	GW	GW	GW
		◇1	1	◇1 ☕	◇1 ☕			1	◇1 ☕	◇1 ☕	1	◇1 ☕	◇1 ☕		1	◇1 ☕		◇1 ☕	1	◇1 ☕	◇1 ☕		1	◇1 ☕	◇1 ☕
London Paddington [15] ⊖	d	08 42	08 43	08 57	09 03	09 12		09 15	09 30	09 35	09 43	09 57	10 03	10 12	10 15	10 37		10 42	10 43	10 57	11 03	11 12	11 15	11 27	11 37
Acton Main Line	d																								
Ealing Broadway ⊖	d		08 50			09 20		09 24			09 50			10 20	10 24				10 50			11 20	11 24		
West Ealing	d																								
Drayton Green	d																								
Castle Bar Park	d																								
South Greenford	d																								
Greenford ⊖	a																								
Hanwell	d																								
Southall	d		08 56			09 24		09 29			09 56			10 24	10 29				10 56			11 24	11 29		
Hayes & Harlington	d		09 02			09 28		09 33			10 02			10 28	10 33				11 02			11 28	11 33		
Heathrow Terminal 1-2-3 [2] ✈	a					09 34								10 34								11 34			
Heathrow Terminal 4 ✈	a					09 41								10 41								11 41			
West Drayton	d		09 06					09 37			10 06				10 37				11 06				11 37		
Iver	d																								
Langley	d		09 10					09 42			10 10				10 42				11 10				11 43		
Slough [3]	a	09 03	09 14					09 46		09 57	10 14				10 46			11 04	11 14				11 47		
	d	09 04	09 16					09 46		09 58	10 16				10 46			11 05	11 16				11 48		
Burnham	d		09 20								10 20								11 20						
Taplow	d																								
Maidenhead [3]	d		09 27					09 54			10 27				10 54				11 27				11 55		
Twyford [3]	d		09 35					10 03			10 35				11 16				11 35				12 03		
Reading [7]	a	09 20	09 42	09 31	09 36			10 11	10 02	10 11	10 42	10 31	10 36		11 24	11 11		11 19	11 42	11 30	11 36		12 11	12 01	12 11
Oxford	a	09 51	10 27							10 43	11 27							11 50	12 26						

		GW		GW	GW	GW	HC	GW	GW	GW	GW	GW		GW	HC	GW	GW	GW	GW	GW	GW	HC		GW	GW
		◇1		1	◇1 ☕	◇1 ☕		1	◇1 ☕	◇1 ☕	1	◇1 ☕		◇1 ☕		1	◇1 ☕	◇1 ☕	1	◇1 ☕	◇1 ☕			1	◇1 ☕
London Paddington [15] ⊖	d	11 42		11 43	11 57	12 03	12 12	12 15	12 37	12 42	12 43	12 57		13 03	13 12	13 15	13 37	13 42	13 43	13 57	14 03	14 12		14 15	14 37
Acton Main Line	d																								
Ealing Broadway ⊖	d			11 50			12 20	12 24			12 50				13 20	13 24			13 50			14 20		14 24	
West Ealing	d																								
Drayton Green	d																								
Castle Bar Park	d																								
South Greenford	d																								
Greenford ⊖	a																								
Hanwell	d																								
Southall	d			11 56			12 24	12 29			12 56				13 24	13 29			13 56			14 24		14 29	
Hayes & Harlington	d			12 02			12 28	12 33			13 02				13 28	13 33			14 02			14 28		14 33	
Heathrow Terminal 1-2-3 [2] ✈	a						12 34								13 34							14 34			
Heathrow Terminal 4 ✈	a						12 41								13 41							14 41			
West Drayton	d			12 06				12 37			13 06					13 37			14 06					14 37	
Iver	d																								
Langley	d			12 10				12 42			13 10					13 42			14 10					14 42	
Slough [3]	a	12 02		12 14				12 46		13 06	13 14					13 47		14 05	14 14					14 46	
	d	12 03		12 16				12 46		13 07	13 16					13 48		14 06	14 16					14 46	
Burnham	d			12 20							13 20								14 20						
Taplow	d																								
Maidenhead [3]	d			12 27				12 54			13 27					13 55			14 27					14 54	
Twyford [3]	d			12 35				13 02			13 35					14 03			14 36					15 02	
Reading [7]	a	12 18		12 42	12 31	12 36		13 10	13 11	13 22	13 42	13 30		13 36		14 11	14 11	14 21	14 42	14 30	14 36			15 11	15 11
Oxford	a	12 48		13 29						13 50	14 28							14 50	15 29						

Table 117

Sundays

8 January to 12 February

London - Greenford and Reading

Network Diagram - see first Page of Table 116

		GW	GW	GW	GW	HC	GW	GW		GW	GW	GW	GW	GW	HC	GW	GW	GW		GW	GW	GW	GW	HC	GW
		◇1	1	◇1	◇1		1	◇1		◇1	◇1	1	◇1	◇1		1	◇1	◇1		◇1	1	◇1	◇1		1
				☕	☕					☕			☕	☕			☕	☕				☕	☕		
London Paddington 15 ⊖	d	14 42	14 43	14 57	15 03	15 12	15 15	15 27		15 37	15 42	15 43	15 57	16 03	16 12	16 15	16 30	16 37		16 42	16 43	16 57	17 03	17 12	17 15
Acton Main Line	d																								
Ealing Broadway ⊖	d		14 50			15 20	15 24					15 50			16 20	16 24					16 50			17 20	17 24
West Ealing	d																								
Drayton Green	d																								
Castle Bar Park	d																								
South Greenford	d																								
Greenford ⊖	a																								
Hanwell	d																								
Southall	d		14 56			15 24	15 29					15 56			16 24	16 29					16 56			17 24	17 29
Hayes & Harlington	d		15 02			15 28	15 33					16 02			16 28	16 33					17 02			17 28	17 33
Heathrow Terminal 1-2-3 2 ✈	a					15 34									16 34									17 34	
Heathrow Terminal 4 ✈	a					15 41									16 41									17 41	
West Drayton	d		15 06				15 37					16 06				16 37					17 06				17 37
Iver	d																								
Langley	d		15 10				15 42					16 10				16 42					17 10				17 42
Slough 3	a	15 02	15 14				15 46	15 49			16 03	16 14				16 46				17 03	17 14				17 46
	d	15 03	15 16				15 46	15 50			16 04	16 16				16 46				17 03	17 16				17 46
Burnham	d		15 20				15 51					16 20				16 51					17 20				17 51
Taplow	d																								
Maidenhead 3	d		15 27				15 56	16 01				16 27				16 56				17 10	17 27				17 56
Twyford 3	d		15 35				16 04	16 09				16 35				17 09					17 37				18 04
Reading 7	a	15 19	15 45	15 30	15 36		16 12	16 16		16 10	16 19	16 42	16 30	16 36		17 17	17 03	17 11		17 24	17 42	17 30	17 36		18 12
Oxford	a	15 50	16 27					16 42			16 50	17 28								17 50	18 29				

		GW	GW	GW		GW	GW	GW	HC	GW	GW	GW	GW	GW		GW	GW	HC	GW	GW	GW	GW	GW	GW	
		◇1	◇1	◇1		1	◇1	◇1		1	◇1	◇1	◇1	1		◇1	◇1		1	◇1	◇1	◇1	1	◇1	
		☕	☕	☕			☕	☕			☕	☕				☕	☕			☕	☕	☕		☕	
London Paddington 15 ⊖	d	17 30	17 37	17 42		17 43	17 57	18 03	18 12	18 15	18 30	18 37	18 42	18 43		18 57	19 03	19 12	19 15	19 30	19 37	19 42	19 43	19 57	
Acton Main Line	d																								
Ealing Broadway ⊖	d					17 51			18 20	18 24				18 50				19 20	19 24				19 50		
West Ealing	d																								
Drayton Green	d																								
Castle Bar Park	d																								
South Greenford	d																								
Greenford ⊖	a																								
Hanwell	d																								
Southall	d					17 57			18 24	18 29				18 56				19 24	19 29				19 56		
Hayes & Harlington	d					18 02			18 28	18 33				19 02				19 28	19 33				20 02		
Heathrow Terminal 1-2-3 2 ✈	a								18 34									19 34							
Heathrow Terminal 4 ✈	a								18 41									19 41							
West Drayton	d					18 06				18 37				19 06					19 37				20 06		
Iver	d																								
Langley	d					18 11				18 42				19 10					19 42				20 10		
Slough 3	a			18 03		18 15				18 46			19 07	19 14					19 46			20 05	20 14		
	d			18 04		18 16				18 46			19 08	19 16					19 46			20 06	20 16		
Burnham	d					18 20				18 51				19 20					19 51				20 20		
Taplow	d																								
Maidenhead 3	d			18 13		18 27				18 56			19 15	19 27					19 56				20 27		
Twyford 3	d					18 36				19 04				19 35					20 04				20 35		
Reading 7	a	18 01	18 10	18 23		18 42	18 30	18 35		19 12	19 04	19 11	19 26	19 42		19 31	19 36		20 12	20 04	20 10	20 20	20 42	20 30	
Oxford	a			18 50		19 27							19 55	20 27								20 50	21 30		

		GW	HC	GW	GW	GW	GW	GW	GW	GW		HC	GW	GW	GW	GW	GW	HC	GW	GW		GW	GW	GW	HC
		◇1		1	◇1	◇1	◇1	1	◇1	◇1			1	◇1	◇1	1	◇1		1	◇1		◇1	1	◇1	
		☕			☕	☕			☕	☕				☕			☕			☕				☕	
London Paddington 15 ⊖	d	20 03	20 12	20 15	20 30	20 37	20 42	20 43	20 57	21 03		21 12	21 15	21 37	21 42	21 43	22 03	22 12	22 15	22 37		22 42	22 43	23 03	23 12
Acton Main Line	d																								
Ealing Broadway ⊖	d		20 20	20 24				20 50				21 20	21 24			21 50		22 20	22 24				22 50		23 20
West Ealing	d																								
Drayton Green	d																								
Castle Bar Park	d																								
South Greenford	d																								
Greenford ⊖	a																								
Hanwell	d																								
Southall	d		20 24	20 29				20 56				21 24	21 29			21 56		22 24	22 29				22 56		23 24
Hayes & Harlington	d		20 28	20 33				21 02				21 28	21 33			22 02		22 28	22 33				23 02		23 28
Heathrow Terminal 1-2-3 2 ✈	a		20 34									21 34						22 34							23 34
Heathrow Terminal 4 ✈	a		20 41									21 41						22 41							23 41
West Drayton	d			20 37				21 06					21 37			22 06			22 37				23 06		
Iver	d																								
Langley	d			20 42				21 10					21 42			22 10			22 42				23 10		
Slough 3	a			20 46			21 01	21 14					21 46		22 05	22 14			22 46			23 02	23 14		
	d			20 46			21 02	21 16					21 46		22 06	22 16			22 46			23 02	23 16		
Burnham	d			20 50				21 20					21 51			22 20			22 51				23 20		
Taplow	d																								
Maidenhead 3	d			20 56				21 27					21 56			22 31			22 56				23 24		
Twyford 3	d			21 04				21 35					22 15			22 41			23 04				23 32		
Reading 7	a	20 35		21 11	21 04	21 11	21 23	21 42	21 30	21 36			22 25	22 11	22 20	22 48	22 42		23 11	23 14		23 19	23 43	23 45	
Oxford	a						21 53	22 26							22 50										

Table 117

Sundays

8 January to 12 February

London - Greenford and Reading

Network Diagram - see first Page of Table 116

		GW 1	GW ◇1 ⊡	GW ◇1		GW 1
London Paddington 15 ⊖	d	23 15	23 37	23 47		23 53
Acton Main Line	d					
Ealing Broadway ⊖	d	23 24		23 55		00 02
West Ealing	d					
Drayton Green	d					
Castle Bar Park	d					
South Greenford	d					
Greenford ⊖	a					
Hanwell	d					
Southall	d	23 29				00 07
Hayes & Harlington	d	23 33				00 11
Heathrow Terminal 1-2-3 2 ✈	a					
Heathrow Terminal 4 ✈	a					
West Drayton	d	23 37				00 15
Iver	d					
Langley	d	23 42				00 20
Slough 3	a	23 46	00 01	00 09		00 24
	d	23 46	00 02	00 10		00 24
Burnham	d	23 51				00 28
Taplow	d					
Maidenhead 3	d	23 56		00 17		00 34
Twyford 3	d	00 04				00 42
Reading 7	a	00 14	00 15	00 29		00 49
Oxford	a					

Sundays

19 February to 25 March

		GW 1	GW ◇1	GW 1	GW ◇1	GW 🚌	GW 1	GW 🚌	GW 1	GW 🚌		GW 1	GW 🚌	HC	HC	GW 1	HC	GW 🚌	GW 1	GW ◇1 ⊡		GW ◇1 ⊡	GW ◇1	HC	GW 1
London Paddington 15 ⊖	d	22p45	23p00		23p33		00 05		00 30			01 00			06 12	06 43	07 12		07 29	07 57		08 00	08 03	08 12	08 15
Acton Main Line	d	22p51																							
Ealing Broadway ⊖	d	22p55					00 13		00 38			01 08		05 20	06 20	06 52	07 20		07 36					08 20	08 24
West Ealing	d																								
Drayton Green	d																								
Castle Bar Park	d																								
South Greenford	d																								
Greenford ⊖	a																								
Hanwell	d																								
Southall	d	23p00					00 19		00 44			01 13		05 24	06 24	06 58	07 24		07 42					08 24	08 29
Hayes & Harlington	d	23p04					00 23		00 48			01 17		05 28	06 28	07 02	07 28		07 46					08 28	08 33
Heathrow Terminal 1-2-3 2 ✈	a													05 34	06 34		07 34							08 34	
Heathrow Terminal 4 ✈	a													05 40	06 41		07 41							08 41	
West Drayton	d	23p08					00 27		00 52							07 06			07 50						08 37
Iver	d	23p11					00 30																		
Langley	d	23p14		←			00 33		00 56							07 11			07 55						08 42
Slough 3	a	23p19	23p16	23p19	23p49		00 37		01 00			01 25				07 16			07 58				08 25		08 46
	d	23p21	23p17	23p21	23p50		00 38		01 01			01 26				07 16			07 58				08 26		08 46
Burnham	d	→		23p25			00 42									07 20			08 03						
Taplow	d						00 45																		
Maidenhead 3	d			23p32			00 49		01 08			01 33				07 25			08 08				08 33		08 54
Twyford 3	d			23p39		00 42	00a57	01 04	01a16	01 23		01a42	01 49			07a34		07 45	08 17						09 02
Reading 7	a		23p33	23p46	00 06	01 15		01 37		01 56			02 22					08 18	08 25	08 31		08 35	08 44		09 10
Oxford	a		00 04	00 32	00 38														09 30				09 13		

		GW ◇1	GW 1	GW ◇1 ⊡	GW ◇1 ⊡	HC		GW 1	GW ◇1 ⊡	GW ◇1 ⊡	GW 1	GW ◇1 ⊡	GW ◇1 ⊡	HC	GW 1	GW ◇1 ⊡		GW ◇1 ⊡	GW 1	GW ◇1 ⊡	GW ◇1 ⊡	HC	GW 1	GW ◇1 ⊡	GW ◇1 ⊡
London Paddington 15 ⊖	d	08 42	08 43	08 57	09 03	09 12		09 15	09 30	09 35	09 43	09 57	10 03	10 12	10 15	10 30		10 42	10 43	10 55	11 03	11 12	11 15	11 27	11 30
Acton Main Line	d																								
Ealing Broadway ⊖	d		08 50			09 20		09 24			09 50			10 20	10 24				10 50			11 20	11 24		
West Ealing	d																								
Drayton Green	d																								
Castle Bar Park	d																								
South Greenford	d																								
Greenford ⊖	a																								
Hanwell	d																								
Southall	d		08 56			09 24		09 29			09 56			10 24	10 29				10 56			11 24	11 29		
Hayes & Harlington	d		09 02			09 28		09 33			10 02			10 28	10 33				11 02			11 28	11 33		
Heathrow Terminal 1-2-3 2 ✈	a					09 34								10 34								11 34			
Heathrow Terminal 4 ✈	a					09 41								10 41								11 41			
West Drayton	d		09 06					09 37			10 06				10 37				11 06				11 37		
Iver	d																								
Langley	d		09 10					09 42			10 10				10 42				11 10				11 43		
Slough 3	a	09 03	09 14					09 46		09 57	10 14				10 46			11 04	11 14				11 47		
	d	09 04	09 16					09 46		09 58	10 16				10 46			11 05	11 16				11 48		
Burnham	d		09 20								10 20								11 20						
Taplow	d																								
Maidenhead 3	d		09 27					09 54			10 27				10 54				11 27				11 55		
Twyford 3	d		09 35					10 03			10 35				11 16				11 35				12 03		
Reading 7	a	09 20	09 42	09 32	09 36			10 11	10 04	10 11	10 42	10 31	10 37		11 24	11 04		11 19	11 42	11 30	11 37		12 11	12 01	12 06
Oxford	a	09 51	10 27							10 43	11 27							11 50	12 26						

Table 117

Sundays

19 February to 25 March

London - Greenford and Reading

Network Diagram - see first Page of Table 116

Station		GW		GW	GW	GW	HC	GW	GW	GW	GW	GW		GW	HC	GW	GW	GW	GW	GW	GW	HC		GW	GW
		◇1		1	◇1 ᗑ	◇1 ᗑ		1	◇1 ᗑ	◇1 ᗑ	1	◇1 ᗑ		◇1 ᗑ		1	◇1 ᗑ	◇1 ᗑ	1	◇1 ᗑ	◇1 ᗑ			1	◇1 ᗑ
London Paddington 15 ⊖	d	11 42		11 43	11 57	12 03	12 12	12 15	12 30	12 42	12 43	12 57		13 03	13 12	13 15	13 30	13 42	13 43	13 57	14 03	14 12		14 15	14 30
Acton Main Line	d																								
Ealing Broadway ⊖	d			11 50			12 20	12 24			12 50				13 20	13 24			13 50			14 20		14 24	
West Ealing	d																								
Drayton Green	d																								
Castle Bar Park	d																								
South Greenford	d																								
Greenford ⊖	a																								
Hanwell	d																								
Southall	d			11 56			12 24	12 29			12 56				13 24	13 29			13 56			14 24		14 29	
Hayes & Harlington	d			12 02			12 28	12 33			13 02				13 28	13 33			14 02			14 28		14 33	
Heathrow Terminal 1-2-3 2 ✈	a						12 34								13 34							14 34			
Heathrow Terminal 4 ✈	a						12 41								13 41							14 41			
West Drayton	d			12 06				12 37			13 06					13 37			14 06					14 37	
Iver	d																								
Langley	d			12 10				12 42			13 10					13 42			14 10					14 42	
Slough 3	a	12 02		12 14				12 46		13 06	13 14					13 47		14 05	14 14					14 46	
	d	12 03		12 16				12 46		13 07	13 16					13 48		14 06	14 16					14 46	
Burnham	d			12 20							13 20								14 20						
Taplow	d																								
Maidenhead 3	d			12 27				12 54			13 27					13 55			14 27					14 54	
Twyford 3	d			12 35				13 02			13 35					14 03			14 36					15 02	
Reading 7	a	12 18		12 42	12 31	12 36		13 10	13 04	13 22	13 42	13 30		13 36		14 11	14 03	14 21	14 42	14 30	14 36			15 11	15 03
Oxford	a	12 48		13 29						13 49	14 28							14 50	15 29						

Station		GW	GW	GW	GW	HC	GW	GW		GW	GW	GW	GW	GW	HC	GW	GW	GW		GW	GW	GW	GW	HC	GW
		◇1	1	◇1 ᗑ	◇1 ᗑ		1	◇1		◇1 ᗑ	◇1	1	◇1 ᗑ	◇1 ᗑ		1	◇1 ᗑ	◇1 ᗑ		◇1	1	◇1 ᗑ	◇1 ᗑ		1
London Paddington 15 ⊖	d	14 42	14 43	14 57	15 03	15 12	15 15	15 27		15 30	15 42	15 43	15 57	16 03	16 12	16 15	16 30	16 37		16 42	16 43	16 57	17 03	17 12	17 15
Acton Main Line	d																								
Ealing Broadway ⊖	d		14 50			15 20	15 24					15 50			16 20	16 24					16 50			17 20	17 24
West Ealing	d																								
Drayton Green	d																								
Castle Bar Park	d																								
South Greenford	d																								
Greenford ⊖	a																								
Hanwell	d																								
Southall	d		14 56			15 24	15 29					15 56			16 24	16 29					16 56			17 24	17 29
Hayes & Harlington	d		15 02			15 28	15 33					16 02			16 28	16 33					17 02			17 28	17 33
Heathrow Terminal 1-2-3 2 ✈	a					15 34									16 34									17 34	
Heathrow Terminal 4 ✈	a					15 41									16 41									17 41	
West Drayton	d		15 06				15 37					16 06				16 37					17 06				17 37
Iver	d																								
Langley	d		15 10				15 42					16 10				16 42					17 10				17 42
Slough 3	a	15 02	15 14				15 46	15 49			16 03	16 14				16 46				17 03	17 14				17 46
	d	15 03	15 16				15 46	15 50			16 04	16 16				16 46				17 03	17 16				17 46
Burnham	d		15 20				15 51					16 20				16 51					17 20				17 51
Taplow	d																								
Maidenhead 3	d		15 27				15 56	16 01				16 27				16 56				17 10	17 27				17 56
Twyford 3	d		15 35				16 04	16 09				16 35				17 09					17 37				18 04
Reading 7	a	15 19	15 45	15 30	15 35		16 12	16 16		16 03	16 19	16 42	16 30	16 36		17 17	17 05	17 10		17 24	17 42	17 30	17 36		18 12
Oxford	a	15 50	16 27					16 42			16 50	17 28								17 51	18 29				

Station		GW	GW	GW		GW	GW	GW	HC	GW	GW	GW	GW	GW		GW	GW	HC	GW	GW	GW	GW	GW	GW	
		◇1 ᗑ	◇1 ᗑ	◇1 ᗑ		1	◇1 ᗑ	◇1 ᗑ		1	◇1 ᗑ	◇1 ᗑ	◇1	1		◇1 ᗑ	◇1 ᗑ		1	◇1 ᗑ	◇1 ᗑ	◇1 ᗑ	1	◇1 ᗑ	
London Paddington 15 ⊖	d	17 30	17 37	17 42		17 43	17 55	18 03	18 12	18 15	18 30	18 37	18 42	18 43		18 57	19 03	19 12	19 15	19 30	19 37	19 42	19 43	19 57	
Acton Main Line	d																								
Ealing Broadway ⊖	d					17 51			18 20	18 24				18 50				19 20	19 24				19 50		
West Ealing	d																								
Drayton Green	d																								
Castle Bar Park	d																								
South Greenford	d																								
Greenford ⊖	a																								
Hanwell	d																								
Southall	d					17 57			18 24	18 29				18 56				19 24	19 29				19 56		
Hayes & Harlington	d					18 02			18 28	18 33				19 02				19 28	19 33				20 02		
Heathrow Terminal 1-2-3 2 ✈	a								18 34									19 34							
Heathrow Terminal 4 ✈	a								18 41									19 41							
West Drayton	d					18 06				18 37				19 06					19 37				20 06		
Iver	d																								
Langley	d					18 11				18 42				19 10					19 42				20 10		
Slough 3	a			18 04		18 15				18 46			19 07	19 14					19 46			20 05	20 14		
	d			18 05		18 16				18 46			19 08	19 16					19 46			20 06	20 16		
Burnham	d					18 20				18 51				19 20					19 51				20 20		
Taplow	d																								
Maidenhead 3	d			18 13		18 27				18 56			19 15	19 27					19 56				20 27		
Twyford 3	d					18 36				19 04				19 35					20 04				20 35		
Reading 7	a	18 05	18 11	18 24		18 42	18 30	18 34		19 12	19 03	19 10	19 26	19 42		19 30	19 36		20 12	20 04	20 10	20 20	20 42	20 30	
Oxford	a			18 51		19 27							19 58	20 27								20 50	21 30		

Table 117

Sundays

19 February to 25 March

London - Greenford and Reading

Network Diagram - see first Page of Table 116

		GW ◇1 ☕	HC	GW 1	GW ◇1 ☕	GW ◇1	GW 1	GW ◇1 ☕	GW ◇1 ☕	HC	GW 1	GW ◇1 ☕	GW ◇1	GW 1	GW ◇1 ☕	HC	GW 1	GW ◇1 ☕	GW ◇1	GW 1	GW ◇1 ☕	HC	GW 1
London Paddington 15 ⊖	d	20 03	20 12	20 15	20 37	20 42	20 43	20 57	21 03	21 12	21 15	21 37	21 42	21 43	22 03	22 12	22 15	22 37	22 42	22 43	23 03	23 12	23 15
Acton Main Line	d																						
Ealing Broadway ⊖	d		20 20	20 24			20 50			21 20	21 24			21 50		22 20	22 24			22 50		23 20	23 24
West Ealing	d																						
Drayton Green	d																						
Castle Bar Park	d																						
South Greenford	d																						
Greenford ⊖	a																						
Hanwell	d																						
Southall	d		20 24	20 29			20 56			21 24	21 29			21 56		22 24	22 29			22 56		23 24	23 29
Hayes & Harlington	d		20 28	20 33			21 02			21 28	21 33			22 02		22 28	22 33			23 02		23 28	23 33
Heathrow Terminal 1-2-3 2 ✈	a		20 34							21 34						22 34						23 34	
Heathrow Terminal 4 ✈	a		20 41							21 41						22 41						23 41	
West Drayton	d			20 37			21 06				21 37			22 06			22 37			23 06			23 37
Iver	d																						
Langley	d			20 42			21 10				21 42			22 10			22 42			23 10			23 42
Slough 3	a			20 46		21 03	21 14				21 46		22 05	22 14			22 46		23 01	23 14			23 46
	d			20 46		21 03	21 16				21 46		22 06	22 16			22 46		23 02	23 16			23 46
Burnham	d			20 50			21 20				21 51			22 20			22 51			23 20			23 51
Taplow	d																						
Maidenhead 3	d			20 56			21 27				21 56			22 31			22 56			23 24			23 56
Twyford 3	d			21 04			21 35				22 15			22 41			23 04			23 32			00 04
Reading 7	a	20 35		21 11	21 10	21 18	21 42	21 30	21 35		22 25	22 13	22 20	22 48	22 42		23 11	23 14	23 19	23 43	23 45		00 14
Oxford	a					21 49	22 26						22 50										

		GW ◇1 ☕	GW ◇1	GW 1
London Paddington 15 ⊖	d	23 37	23 47	23 53
Acton Main Line	d			
Ealing Broadway ⊖	d		23 55	00 02
West Ealing	d			
Drayton Green	d			
Castle Bar Park	d			
South Greenford	d			
Greenford ⊖	a			
Hanwell	d			
Southall	d			00 07
Hayes & Harlington	d			00 11
Heathrow Terminal 1-2-3 2 ✈	a			
Heathrow Terminal 4 ✈	a			
West Drayton	d			00 15
Iver	d			
Langley	d			00 20
Slough 3	a	00 01	00 09	00 24
	d	00 01	00 10	00 24
Burnham	d			00 28
Taplow	d			
Maidenhead 3	d		00 17	00 34
Twyford 3	d			00 42
Reading 7	a	00 15	00 29	00 49
Oxford	a			

Sundays

from 1 April

		GW ◇1	GW ◇1	GW 1	GW 1	GW 1	GW 1	HC	HC	GW 1	HC	GW 1	GW ◇1 ☕	GW ◇1	HC	GW 1	GW ◇1 ☕	GW ◇1 ☕	GW ◇1	GW 1	GW ◇1 ☕	HC	GW 1
London Paddington 15 ⊖	d	23p00	23p33	23p42	00 05	00 30	01 00		06 12	06 43	07 12	07 29	08 00	08 03	08 12	08 15	08 30	08 37	08 42	08 43	09 03	09 12	09 15
Acton Main Line	d																						
Ealing Broadway ⊖	d			23p50	00 13	00 38	01 08	05 20	06 20	06 52	07 20	07 36			08 20	08 24				08 50		09 20	09 24
West Ealing	d																						
Drayton Green	d																						
Castle Bar Park	d																						
South Greenford	d																						
Greenford ⊖	a																						
Hanwell	d																						
Southall	d			23p56	00 19	00 44	01 13	05 24	06 24	06 58	07 24	07 42			08 24	08 29				08 56		09 24	09 29
Hayes & Harlington	d			00 01	00 23	00 48	01 17	05 28	06 28	07 02	07 28	07 46			08 28	08 33				09 02		09 28	09 33
Heathrow Terminal 1-2-3 2 ✈	a							05 34	06 34		07 34				08 34							09 34	
Heathrow Terminal 4 ✈	a							05 40	06 41		07 41				08 41							09 41	
West Drayton	d			00 06	00 27	00 52				07 06		07 50				08 37				09 06			09 37
Iver	d				00 30																		
Langley	d				00 33	00 56				07 11		07 55				08 42				09 10			09 42
Slough 3	a	23p16	23p49	00 13	00 37	01 00	01 25			07 16		07 58		08 25		08 46			09 03	09 14			09 46
	d	23p17	23p50	00 14	00 38	01 01	01 26			07 16		07 58		08 26		08 46			09 04	09 16			09 46
Burnham	d			00 18	00 42					07 20		08 03								09 20			
Taplow	d			00 21	00 45																		
Maidenhead 3	d			00 25	00 49	01 08	01 33			07 25		08 08		08 33		08 54				09 27			09 54
Twyford 3	d			00 33	00 57	01 16	01 41			07 33		08 17				09 02				09 35			10 06
Reading 7	a	23p33	00 06	00 43	01 05	01 24	01 50			07 42		08 25	08 33	08 44		09 10	09 05	09 14	09 20	09 42	09 36		10 21
Oxford	a	00 04	00 38									09 30		09 13					09 51	10 28			

Table 117

Sundays

from 1 April

London - Greenford and Reading

Network Diagram - see first Page of Table 116

	GW	GW	GW	GW	GW		HC	GW	GW	GW	GW	GW	GW	HC	GW		GW	GW	GW	GW	GW	HC	GW	GW
	◇1 🍴	◇1 🍴	◇1 🍴	1	◇1 🍴			1	◇1 🍴	◇1 🍴	◇1 🍴	1	◇1 🍴		1		◇1 🍴	◇1 🍴	◇1	1	◇1 🍴		1	◇1 🍴
London Paddington 15 ⊖ d	09 30	09 35	09 42	09 43	10 03		10 12	10 15	10 30	10 37	10 42	10 43	11 03	11 12	11 15		11 30	11 37	11 42	11 43	12 03	12 12	12 15	12 30
Acton Main Line d																								
Ealing Broadway ⊖ d				09 50			10 20	10 24				10 50		11 20	11 24					11 50		12 20	12 24	
West Ealing d																								
Drayton Green d																								
Castle Bar Park d																								
South Greenford d																								
Greenford ⊖ a																								
Hanwell d																								
Southall d				09 56			10 24	10 29				10 56		11 24	11 29					11 56		12 24	12 29	
Hayes & Harlington d				10 02			10 28	10 33				11 02		11 28	11 33					12 02		12 28	12 33	
Heathrow Terminal 1-2-3 2 ✈ a							10 34							11 34								12 34		
Heathrow Terminal 4 ✈ a							10 41							11 41								12 41		
West Drayton d				10 06				10 37				11 06			11 37					12 06			12 37	
Iver d																								
Langley d				10 10				10 42				11 10			11 43					12 10			12 42	
Slough 3 a		09 57		10 14				10 46			11 04	11 14			11 47				12 02	12 14			12 46	
d		09 58		10 16				10 46			11 05	11 16			11 48				12 03	12 16			12 46	
Burnham d				10 20								11 20								12 20				
Taplow d																								
Maidenhead 3 d				10 27				10 54				11 27			11 55					12 25			12 54	
Twyford 3 d				10 35				11 16				11 35			12 03					12 33			13 02	
Reading 7 a	10 02	10 11	10 14	10 42	10 36			11 24	11 03	11 10	11 19	11 42	11 36		12 11		12 03	12 12	12 18	12 43	12 36		13 10	13 03
Oxford a		10 43		11 27							11 50	12 27							12 48	13 27				

	GW		GW	GW	GW	HC	GW	GW	GW	GW	GW		GW	HC	GW	GW	GW	GW	GW	GW	HC		GW	GW
	◇1 🍴		◇1 🍴	1	◇1 🍴		1	◇1 🍴	◇1 🍴	◇1 🍴	1		◇1 🍴		1	◇1 🍴	◇1 🍴	◇1	1	◇1 🍴			1	◇1
London Paddington 15 ⊖ d	12 37		12 42	12 43	13 03	13 12	13 15	13 30	13 37	13 42	13 43		14 03	14 12	14 15	14 30	14 37	14 42	14 43	15 03	15 12		15 15	15 27
Acton Main Line d																								
Ealing Broadway ⊖ d				12 50		13 20	13 24				13 50			14 20	14 24				14 50		15 20		15 24	
West Ealing d																								
Drayton Green d																								
Castle Bar Park d																								
South Greenford d																								
Greenford ⊖ a																								
Hanwell d																								
Southall d				12 56		13 24	13 29				13 56			14 24	14 29				14 56		15 24		15 29	
Hayes & Harlington d				13 02		13 28	13 33				14 02			14 28	14 33				15 02		15 28		15 33	
Heathrow Terminal 1-2-3 2 ✈ a						13 34								14 34							15 34			
Heathrow Terminal 4 ✈ a						13 41								14 41							15 41			
West Drayton d				13 06			13 37				14 06				14 37				15 06				15 37	
Iver d																								
Langley d				13 10			13 42				14 10				14 42				15 10				15 42	
Slough 3 a			13 06	13 14			13 47			14 05	14 14				14 46			15 02	15 14				15 46	15 49
d			13 07	13 16			13 48			14 06	14 16				14 46			15 03	15 16				15 46	15 50
Burnham d				13 20							14 20								15 20				15 51	
Taplow d																								
Maidenhead 3 d				13 27			13 55				14 27				14 54				15 27				15 56	16 01
Twyford 3 d				13 35			14 03				14 35				15 02				15 35				16 04	16 10
Reading 7 a	13 12		13 22	13 42	13 36		14 11	14 03	14 10	14 21	14 42		14 36		15 11	15 02	15 10	15 19	15 46	15 36			16 12	16 16
Oxford a			13 50	14 28						14 50	15 27							15 50	16 27					16 41

	GW	GW	GW	GW	GW	HC	GW		GW	GW	GW	GW	GW	GW	HC	GW	GW		GW	GW	GW	GW	GW	HC
	◇1 🍴	◇1 🍴	◇1	1	◇1 🍴		1		◇1 🍴	◇1 🍴	◇1	1	◇1 🍴	◇1 🍴		1	◇1 🍴		◇1 🍴	◇1 🍴	1	◇1 🍴	◇1 🍴	
London Paddington 15 ⊖ d	15 30	15 37	15 42	15 43	16 03	16 12	16 15		16 30	16 37	16 42	16 43	16 57	17 03	17 12	17 15	17 30		17 37	17 42	17 43	17 57	18 03	18 12
Acton Main Line d																								
Ealing Broadway ⊖ d				15 50		16 20	16 24					16 50			17 20	17 24					17 51			18 20
West Ealing d																								
Drayton Green d																								
Castle Bar Park d																								
South Greenford d																								
Greenford ⊖ a																								
Hanwell d																								
Southall d				15 56		16 24	16 29					16 56			17 24	17 29					17 56			18 24
Hayes & Harlington d				16 02		16 28	16 33					17 02			17 28	17 33					18 02			18 28
Heathrow Terminal 1-2-3 2 ✈ a						16 34									17 34									18 34
Heathrow Terminal 4 ✈ a						16 41									17 41									18 41
West Drayton d				16 06			16 37					17 06				17 37					18 06			
Iver d																								
Langley d				16 10			16 42					17 10				17 42					18 10			
Slough 3 a			16 03	16 14			16 46				17 03	17 14				17 46				18 04	18 14			
d			16 04	16 16			16 46				17 04	17 16				17 46				18 05	18 16			
Burnham d				16 20			16 51					17 20				17 51					18 20			
Taplow d																								
Maidenhead 3 d				16 27			16 56				17 11	17 27				17 56				18 14	18 27			
Twyford 3 d				16 35			17 09					17 35				18 04					18 35			
Reading 7 a	16 02	16 10	16 19	16 42	16 36		17 17		17 02	17 09	17 22	17 42	17 30	17 36		18 17	18 01		18 10	18 24	18 42	18 30	18 35	
Oxford a			16 50	17 30							17 50	18 29								18 50	19 25			

Table 117

Sundays

from 1 April

London - Greenford and Reading

Network Diagram - see first Page of Table 116

		GW	GW	GW		GW	GW	GW	GW	HC	GW	GW	GW	GW		GW	GW	GW	HC	GW	GW	GW	GW	GW	
		1	◇1	◇1		◇1	1	◇1	◇1		1	◇1	◇1	◇1		1	◇1	◇1		1	◇1	◇1	◇1	1	
			☕	☕				☕	☕			☕	☕	☕			☕	☕			☕	☕			
London Paddington 15 ⊖	d	18 15	18 30	18 37		18 42	18 43	18 57	19 03	19 12	19 15	19 30	19 37	19 42		19 43	19 57	20 03	20 12	20 15	20 30	20 37	20 42	20 43	
Acton Main Line	d																								
Ealing Broadway ⊖	d	18 24					18 50			19 20	19 24					19 50			20 20	20 24				20 50	
West Ealing	d																								
Drayton Green	d																								
Castle Bar Park	d																								
South Greenford	d																								
Greenford ⊖	a																								
Hanwell	d																								
Southall	d	18 29					18 56			19 24	19 29					19 56			20 24	20 29				20 56	
Hayes & Harlington	d	18 33					19 02			19 28	19 33					20 02			20 28	20 33				21 02	
Heathrow Terminal 1-2-3 2 ✈	a									19 34									20 34						
Heathrow Terminal 4 ✈	a									19 41									20 41						
West Drayton	d	18 37					19 06				19 37					20 06				20 37				21 06	
Iver	d																								
Langley	d	18 42					19 10				19 43					20 10				20 42				21 10	
Slough 3	a	18 48				19 07	19 14				19 47			20 05		20 14				20 46			21 01	21 14	
	d	18 48				19 07	19 16				19 48			20 06		20 16				20 46			21 02	21 16	
Burnham	d	18 53					19 20				19 52					20 20				20 50				21 20	
Taplow	d																								
Maidenhead 3	d	18 58				19 14	19 27				19 58					20 27				20 56				21 27	
Twyford 3	d	19 06					19 35				20 15					20 35				21 04				21 35	
Reading 7	a	19 14	19 04	19 10		19 26	19 42	19 29	19 36		20 26	20 04	20 10	20 20		20 42	20 30	20 35		21 11	21 04	21 11	21 23	21 42	
Oxford	a					19 58	20 27							20 50		21 30							21 53	22 32	

		GW	GW	HC	GW	GW	GW	GW	GW	HC		GW	GW	GW	GW	HC	GW	GW	GW			GW			
		◇1	◇1		1	◇1	◇1	1	◇1			◇1	◇1	1	◇1		1	◇1	◇1			1			
		☕	☕			☕			☕			☕			☕			☕							
London Paddington 15 ⊖	d	20 57	21 03	21 12	21 15	21 37	21 42	21 43	22 03	22 12		22 37	22 42	22 43	23 03	23 12	23 15	23 37	23 47			23 53			
Acton Main Line	d																								
Ealing Broadway ⊖	d			21 20	21 24			21 50		22 20				22 50		23 20	23 24		23 55			00 02			
West Ealing	d																								
Drayton Green	d																								
Castle Bar Park	d																								
South Greenford	d																								
Greenford ⊖	a																								
Hanwell	d																								
Southall	d			21 24	21 29			21 56		22 24				22 56		23 24	23 29					00 07			
Hayes & Harlington	d			21 28	21 33			22 02		22 28				23 02		23 28	23 33					00 11			
Heathrow Terminal 1-2-3 2 ✈	a			21 34						22 34						23 34									
Heathrow Terminal 4 ✈	a			21 41						22 41						23 41									
West Drayton	d				21 37			22 06						23 06			23 37					00 15			
Iver	d																								
Langley	d				21 42			22 10						23 10			23 42					00 20			
Slough 3	a				21 46		22 05	22 14					23 02	23 14			23 46	00 01	00 09			00 24			
	d				21 46		22 06	22 16					23 02	23 16			23 46	00 02	00 10			00 24			
Burnham	d				21 51			22 20						23 20			23 51					00 28			
Taplow	d																								
Maidenhead 3	d				21 56			22 25						23 24			23 56		00 17			00 34			
Twyford 3	d				22 15			22 41						23 32			00 04					00 42			
Reading 7	a	21 29	21 35		22 25	22 12	22 20	22 48	22 42			23 14	23 19	23 43	23 45		00 14	00 15	00 29			00 49			
Oxford	a						22 50																		

Reading and Greenford - London

Network Diagram - see first Page of Table 116

Miles	Miles	Miles			GW	GW	GW	GW	GW	GW	GW	GW	GW		GW	HC	HC	GW	GW	GW	GW	GW	GW		GW
					MX	MO	MX	MO	MO	MO	MO	MO	MO		MO	MX	MO	MO	MO	MX	MX	MO	MO		MO
					1	1	1	◇1	◇1	◇1	◇1	◇1	◇1		◇1			1	1	◇1	◇1	1	1		1
						A		B	C	D	E	D	B		F			C	G			H	D		D
								☕					☕		☕						☕				
—	—	—	Oxford	d		22p21			22p46	22p46	22p50									23p09					
0	—	—	**Reading 7**	d	22p48	23p10	23p15	23p21	23b22	23b22	23c24		23p30		23p30			23p35	23p36	23p45	23p55	00 15	00 15		00 15
5	—	—	**Twyford 3**	d	22p54	23p16	23p22											23p41	23p42			00 21	00 21		00 21
11¾	—	—	**Maidenhead 3**	d	23p02	23p24	23p29											23p49	23p50	23p58		00 29	00 29		00 29
13½	—	—	Taplow	d	23p05		23p33																		
15	—	—	Burnham	d	23p08		23p36					←						23p54	23p55						
17½	—	—	**Slough 3**	a	23p13	23p31	23p41		23p40	23p42	23p41	23p42						23p58	23p59	00 05		00 36	00 36		00 36
—	—	—		d	23p27	23p32	23p41		23p41	23p43	23p42	23p43						23p59	00 01	00 05		00 36	00 37		00 40
19¾	—	—	Langley	d	23p31	23p36	23p45			→								00 03	00 05			00 40	00 41		00 44
21¼	—	—	Iver	d	23p34		23p48																		
22¾	—	—	West Drayton	d	23p38	23p41	23p51											00 08	00 10			00 45	00 45		00 49
—	—	0	**Heathrow Terminal 4** ✈	d												00 01	00 01								
—	—	1¾	**Heathrow Terminal 1-2-3 2** ✈	d												00 07	00 07								
25¼	—	5¾	Hayes & Harlington	d	23p43	23p47	23p56									00 13	00 13	00 16	00 16			00 50	00 51		00 54
27	—	7½	Southall	d	23p47	23p50	23p59									00 16	00 16	00 20	00 20			00 53	00 54		00 57
28¾	—	9¼	Hanwell	d																					
—	0	—	**Greenford** ⊖	d																					
—	1	—	South Greenford	d																					
—	1¾	—	Castle Bar Park	d																					
—	2	—	Drayton Green	d																					
29½	2¾	10	West Ealing	d																					
30¼	3½	11	**Ealing Broadway** ⊖	d	23p52	23p55	00 06									00 22	00 21	00 25	00 25			00 59	01 00		01 03
31¾	5	12¼	Acton Main Line	d																					
36	9¼	16½	**London Paddington 15** ⊖	a	00 02	00 04	00 17	00 01	00 02		00 04	00 04	00 12		00 13	00 30	00 30	00 34	00 34	00 29	00 33	01 11	01 09		01 14

		GW	GW	GW	GW	GW	GW	GW	GW		GW	GW	HC	GW	GW	HC	GW	GW	GW		GW	GW	HC	GW	GW
		MX	MX	MO	MX			MO	MX		MX	MO		MO											
								R	R					R											
		1	◇1	◇1	1	1	1				1	1			1		1	1	1		◇1	1		1	1
								F	I					B											
								🛏	🛏					🛏											
								☕	☕					☕							☕				
Oxford	d		00 07		00 27						04 00								05 03						
Reading 7	d	00 15	00 39	00 53	01 12	02 24	03 54				04 39	04 39			05 14		05 39		05 44		05 57	05 59		06 07	
Twyford 3	d	00 21		00 59	01 18	02 30	04 00				04 45	04 45			05 20		05 45		05 50					06 13	
Maidenhead 3	d	00 29		01 07	01 26	02 38	04 08				04 53	04 53			05 28		05 53		05 58			06 10		06 21	
Taplow	d	00 32													05 32				06 02					06 24	
Burnham	d	00 35													05 35				06 05					06 27	
Slough 3	a	00 40	00 55	01 14	01 34	02 45	04 15				05 00	05 00			05 40		06 01		06 10			06 17		06 32	
	d	00 40	00 56	01 14	01 34	02 45	04 15				05 00	05 00			05 40		06 01		06 10			06 17		06 32	
Langley	d	00 44									05 04	05 04			05 44				06 14					06 36	
Iver	d										05 07	05 07			05 47				06 17						
West Drayton	d	00 49				02 52	04 22				05 11	05 11			05 51				06 21					06 41	
Heathrow Terminal 4 ✈	d												05 23			05 51									
Heathrow Terminal 1-2-3 2 ✈	d												05 29			05 57							06 27		
Hayes & Harlington	d	00 54		01 23	01 43	02 57	04 27				05 16	05 16	05 35		05 56	06 03	06 10		06 26				06 33	06 46	
Southall	d	00 57				03 00	04 30				05 19	05 19	05 38		05 59	06 06	06 13		06 29				06 36	06 50	
Hanwell	d												05 41			06 09							06 39		
Greenford ⊖	d																	06 16							06 46
South Greenford	d																	06 19							06 49
Castle Bar Park	d																	06 22							06 52
Drayton Green	d																	06 24							06 54
West Ealing	d												05 43			06 11		06 26					06 41		06 56
Ealing Broadway ⊖	d	01 03		01 30	01 50	03 06	04 36				05 28	05 28	05 46		06 05	06 14	06 19	06 29	06 35				06 44	06 55	06 59
Acton Main Line	d										05 31	05 31			06 08			06 33	06 38						07 03
London Paddington 15 ⊖	a	01 16	01 17	01 39	02 02	03 18	04 47	05 05	05 25		05 41	05 41	05 56	06 09	06 16	06 24	06 31	06 42	06 46		06 24	06 36	06 54	07 09	07 12

A from 9 January until 13 February
B from 20 February until 26 March
C until 2 January
D from 2 April
E from 9 January until 26 March
F until 13 February, MO from 2 April
G from 9 January
H until 26 March
I **The Night Riviera**
b Previous night, arr. 2315
c Previous night, arr. 2317

Reading and Greenford - London

Network Diagram - see first Page of Table 116

		GW	GW	GW	GW		HC	GW	GW	GW	GW	GW	GW	GW	GW		GW	GW	HC	GW	GW	GW	GW	GW	GW
		1	1	1	◇1			1	1	1	◇1 ☕	1	◇1 ☕	1	1		1	◇1 ☕		1	1	1	1	◇1 ☕	◇1 ☕
Oxford	d	05 24	05 43		05 59								06 27										06 07		
Reading 7	d	06 15	06 16	06 22	06 31			06 31	06 36	06 36	06 44	06 46	06 56				06 57	07 01		07 02	07 07		07 10	07 16	07 21
Twyford 3	d	06 21	06 23					06 37	06 42	06 44		06 53					07 03			07 08			07 16		
Maidenhead 3	d	06 29	06 31		06 43			06 46	06 53			07 03	07 08				07 11			07 16	07 18		07 24		
Taplow	d	06 32							06 57														07 28		
Burnham	d	06 35						06 50	07 01						←					07 21			07 31		
Slough 3	a	06 40		06 40	06 50			06 55	07 06		06 58				07 06		07 19			07 26			07 36		
	d	06 40		06 41	06 50			06 56	07 06		06 59				07 06		07 20			07 26			07 36		
Langley	d	06 44						06 59	→						07 11					07 31			07 41		
Iver	d	06 47						07 03							07 14								07 44		
West Drayton	d	06 51						07 07							07 18					07 35			07 48		
Heathrow Terminal 4 ✈	d																								
Heathrow Terminal 1-2-3 2 ✈	d						06 57												07 27						
Hayes & Harlington	d	06 56					07 03	07 11							07 23				07 33	07 41			07 53		
Southall	d	07 00					07 06	07 15							07 27				07 36	07 45			07 57		
Hanwell	d						07 09												07 39						
Greenford ⊖	d													07 16								07 46			
South Greenford	d													07 19								07 49			
Castle Bar Park	d													07 22								07 52			
Drayton Green	d													07 24								07 54			
West Ealing	d						07 11							07 26					07 41			07 56			
Ealing Broadway ⊖	d	07 05					07 14	07 21						07 29	07 33				07 44	07 52		07 59	08 03		
Acton Main Line	d													07 33								08 03			
London Paddington 15 ⊖	a	07 17	06 54	07 01	07 08		07 24	07 32		07 14	07 16	07 29	07 30	07 42	07 44		07 49	07 32	07 54	08 04	07 43	08 12	08 16	07 44	07 53

			GW	GW	GW	HC	GW	GW	GW	GW	GW		GW	GW	GW	GW		GW	GW	GW	GW		GW	HC	GW
			1	◇1 ☕	1		1	◇1 ☕	1	◇1 ☕	◇1 ☕		◇1 ☕	◇1	1	1		◇1 ⊼	◇1 ☕	1	◇1 ☕		1		1
Oxford	d			06 56			06 36									07 00		07 31							
Reading 7	d			07 27			07 30	07 33	07 34	07 36	07 39		07 45			07 55		07 58	08 02	08 06	08 08				
Twyford 3	d		07 22				07 37		07 41						07 56	08 02				08a12					
Maidenhead 3	d		07 31		07 41		07 45		07 49					08 00	08 04	08 11									
Taplow	d								07 53																
Burnham	d						07 51		07 56							08 15									
Slough 3	a				07 49		07 55		08 01							08 20									
	d				07 50		07 56		08 01							08 20									08 26
Langley	d						08 00		08 06																08 30
Iver	d								08 09																
West Drayton	d						08 04		08 13																08 35
Heathrow Terminal 4 ✈	d																								
Heathrow Terminal 1-2-3 2 ✈	d					07 57																		08 27	
Hayes & Harlington	d					08 03	08 10		08 17															08 33	08 39
Southall	d					08 06	08 13									08 30								08 36	08 43
Hanwell	d					08 09																		08 39	
Greenford ⊖	d																						08 16		
South Greenford	d																						08 19		
Castle Bar Park	d																						08 22		
Drayton Green	d																						08 24		
West Ealing	d					08 11																	08 26	08 41	
Ealing Broadway ⊖	d					08 14	08 18		08 24														08 29	08 44	08 49
Acton Main Line	d																						08 33		
London Paddington 15 ⊖	a		07 57	07 59	08 21	08 24	08 32	08 02	08 36	08 07	08 09		08 14	08 26	08 28	08 48		08 31	08 33		08 38		08 42	08 54	09 03

		GW	GW	GW	GW	GW			GW	GW	HC	GW	GW	GW	GW	GW			GW	GW	GW	GW	HC	GW	GW
		1	1	◇1 ☕	◇1 ☕	1			◇1 A ☕⊘	1		1	◇1 ☕	1	◇1 B ☕	1			◇1 ☕	◇1 ☕	1	1		1	◇1 ☕
Oxford	d					07 21			07 52					08 06		07 56								08 21	
Reading 7	d		08 12	08 14	08 17	08 19			08 23			08 31	08 34	08 35	08 45	08 48			08 52	09 02				09 03	09 08
Twyford 3	d		08 18			08 26						08 37				08 54								09 09	
Maidenhead 3	d		08 26			08 34				08 41		08 45				09 03								09 17	
Taplow	d		08 29									08 49												09 21	
Burnham	d		08 32									08 50												09 24	
Slough 3	a		08 38							08 49		08 57												09 29	
	d		08 38							08 50		08 57										09 14		09 29	
Langley	d		08 42									09 01												09 33	
Iver	d		08 45									09 04												09 36	
West Drayton	d		08 49									09 08										09 21		09 40	
Heathrow Terminal 4 ✈	d																								
Heathrow Terminal 1-2-3 2 ✈	d										08 57												09 27		
Hayes & Harlington	d		08 53								09 03	09 13										09 26	09 33	09 45	
Southall	d									09 00	09 06	09 17										09 30	09 36	09 48	
Hanwell	d										09 09												09 39		
Greenford ⊖	d	08 46																			09 16				
South Greenford	d	08 49																			09 19				
Castle Bar Park	d	08 52																			09 22				
Drayton Green	d	08 54																			09 24				
West Ealing	d	08 56									09 11										09 26		09 41		
Ealing Broadway ⊖	d	08 59	09 04								09 14	09 23									09 29	09 36	09 44	09 54	
Acton Main Line	d	09 03																			09 33				
London Paddington 15 ⊖	a	09 12	09 16	08 40	08 44	08 58			08 51	09 21	09 24	09 35	09 00	09 06	09 14	09 27			09 21	09 29	09 42	09 48	09 54	10 03	09 39

A ☕ from Reading ⊘ to Reading

B The Bristolian

Reading and Greenford - London

Network Diagram - see first Page of Table 116

		GW ◇1 ☕	GW 1		GW 1	GW ◇1 A ☕⊘	GW 1	GW ◇1 ☕	GW 1	GW ◇1 B ☕	GW ◇1	GW ◇1 ☕	HC		GW 1	GW 1	GW ◇1	GW ◇1 ☕	GW 1	GW 1	HC	GW 1			GW ◇1 ☕
Oxford	d					08 51			08 36		09 01						09 31					09 07			
Reading 7	d	09 16			09 17	09 18	09 21	09 27	09 33	09 34	09 37	09 46				09 48	09 55	10 02				10 03			10 08
Twyford 3	d				09 24				09 39							09 54						10 09			
Maidenhead 3	d				09 35				09 47							10 02						10 17			
Taplow	d				09 36											10 06									
Burnham	d				09 39										←	10 09				←					
Slough 3	a				09 44				09 54		09 52				09 54	10 14	10 10			10 14		10 24			
	d				09 44				09 54		09 52				09 54	10 14	10 11			10 14		10 24			
Langley	d								→						09 58	→						10 28			
Iver	d														10 01							10 31			
West Drayton	d				09 51										10 05					10 21		10 35			
Heathrow Terminal 4 ✈	d																								
Heathrow Terminal 1-2-3 2 ✈	d												09 57								10 27				
Hayes & Harlington	d				09 56								10 03		10 10					10 26	10 33	10 40			
Southall	d												10 06		10 13						10 36	10 43			
Hanwell	d												10 09								10 39				
Greenford ⊖	d		09 46																10 16						
South Greenford	d		09 49																10 19						
Castle Bar Park	d		09 52																10 22						
Drayton Green	d		09 54																10 24						
West Ealing	d		09 56										10 11						10 26		10 41				
Ealing Broadway ⊖	d		09 59		10 03								10 14		10 19				10 29	10 33	10 44	10 49			
Acton Main Line	d		10 03																10 33						
London Paddington 15 ⊖	a	09 44	10 12		10 16	09 47	09 56	09 59		10 02	10 12	10 15	10 24		10 31		10 30	10 32	10 42	10 46	10 54	11 01			10 37

		GW ◇1 ☕	GW 1	GW 1	GW ◇1 🛒	GW ◇1 ☕	GW 1	GW 1	HC		GW 1		GW ◇1 ☕	GW 1	GW ◇1 ☕	GW ◇1	GW ◇1 C ☕	GW 1	GW 1		HC	GW 1		GW ◇1 ☕	GW 1
Oxford	d				10 01						09 36					10 31						10 08			
Reading 7	d	10 12	10 18	10 18	10 26	10 32					10 33		10 45	10 48	10 52	10 55	11 02					11 03		11 11	11 18
Twyford 3	d			10 24							10 39			10 54								11 09			11 24
Maidenhead 3	d			10 32							10 47			11 02								11 17			11 32
Taplow	d			10 36										11 06											11 36
Burnham	d			10 39				←						11 09					←						11 39
Slough 3	a			10 44	10 39			10 44			10 54			11 14		11 09			11 14			11 24			11 44
	d			10 44	10 40			10 44			10 54			11 14		11 10			11 14			11 24			11 44
Langley	d			→							10 58			→								11 28			→
Iver	d										11 01											11 31			
West Drayton	d							10 51			11 05								11 21			11 35			
Heathrow Terminal 4 ✈	d																								
Heathrow Terminal 1-2-3 2 ✈	d								10 57												11 27				
Hayes & Harlington	d							10 56	11 03		11 10								11 26		11 33	11 40			
Southall	d								11 06		11 13										11 36	11 43			
Hanwell	d								11 09												11 39				
Greenford ⊖	d						10 46											11 16							
South Greenford	d						10 49											11 19							
Castle Bar Park	d						10 52											11 22							
Drayton Green	d						10 54											11 24							
West Ealing	d						10 56		11 11									11 26			11 41				
Ealing Broadway ⊖	d						10 59	11 03	11 14		11 19							11 29	11 33		11 44	11 49			
Acton Main Line	d						11 03											11 33							
London Paddington 15 ⊖	a	10 39	10 56		11 00	11 07	11 12	11 16	11 24		11 32		11 14		11 24	11 29	11 32	11 42	11 46		11 54	12 01		11 38	

		GW 1	GW ◇1 🛒	GW ◇1 ☕	GW 1		GW 1	HC	GW 1	GW ◇1 ☕	GW 1	GW ◇1 ☕	GW ◇1 🛒	GW ◇1 ☕	GW 1		GW 1	HC	GW 1		GW ◇1 ☕	GW ◇1 ☕	GW 1	GW 1	GW ◇1 🛒
Oxford	d		11 01						10 36				11 31						11 07						12 01
Reading 7	d	11 20	11 26	11 32					11 33	11 44	11 48	11 52	11 55	12 02					12 03		12 08	12 12	12 18	12 18	12 26
Twyford 3	d								11 39		11 54								12 09					12 24	
Maidenhead 3	d								11 47		12 02								12 17					12 32	
Taplow	d										12 06													12 36	
Burnham	d						←				12 09						←							12 39	
Slough 3	a		11 39				11 44		11 54		12 14		12 09				12 14		12 24					12 44	12 39
	d		11 40				11 44		11 54		12 14		12 10				12 14		12 24					12 44	12 40
Langley	d								11 58		→								12 28					→	
Iver	d								12 01										12 31						
West Drayton	d						11 51		12 05								12 21		12 35						
Heathrow Terminal 4 ✈	d																								
Heathrow Terminal 1-2-3 2 ✈	d							11 57										12 27							
Hayes & Harlington	d						11 56	12 03	12 10								12 26	12 33	12 40						
Southall	d							12 06	12 13									12 36	12 43						
Hanwell	d							12 09										12 39							
Greenford ⊖	d				11 46										12 16										
South Greenford	d				11 49										12 19										
Castle Bar Park	d				11 52										12 22										
Drayton Green	d				11 54										12 24										
West Ealing	d				11 56			12 11							12 26			12 41							
Ealing Broadway ⊖	d				11 59		12 03	12 14	12 19						12 29		12 33	12 44	12 49						
Acton Main Line	d				12 03										12 33										
London Paddington 15 ⊖	a	11 55	11 59	12 02	12 12		12 16	12 24	12 31	12 14		12 23	12 29	12 32	12 42		12 46	12 54	13 02		12 37	12 40	12 52		13 06

A The Cathedrals Express. ☕ from Reading ⊘ to Reading

B The Golden Hind

C The Red Dragon

Reading and Greenford - London

Network Diagram - see first Page of Table 116

			GW	GW	GW	HC	GW		GW	GW	GW		GW	GW	GW	HC	GW		GW	GW	GW		GW	GW	GW
			◇1 ☕	1	1		1		◇1 ☕	1	◇1 🛒		◇1 ☕	1	1		1		◇1 ☕	R 1 A ☕	1		◇1 🛒	1	◇1 ☕
Oxford	d						11 37				12 31						12 07						13 01		
Reading 7	d		12 32				12 33		12 45	12 48	12 55		13 02				13 03		13 11	13 17	13 18		13 26	13 29	13 32
Twyford 3	d						12 39			12 54							13 09				13 24				
Maidenhead 3	d						12 47			13 02							13 17				13 32				
Taplow	d									13 06											13 36				
Burnham	d				←					13 09					←						13 39				
Slough 3	a				12 44		12 54			13 14	13 09				13 14		13 24				13 44		13 39		
	d				12 44		12 54			13 14	13 10				13 14		13 24				13 44		13 40		
Langley	d						12 58			→							13 28				→				
Iver	d						13 01										13 31								
West Drayton	d				12 51		13 05								13 21		13 35								
Heathrow Terminal 4 ✈	d																								
Heathrow Terminal 1-2-3 2 ✈	d					12 57										13 27									
Hayes & Harlington	d				12 56	13 03	13 10								13 26	13 33	13 40								
Southall	d					13 06	13 13									13 36	13 43								
Hanwell	d					13 09										13 39									
Greenford ⊖	d			12 46										13 16											
South Greenford	d			12 49										13 19											
Castle Bar Park	d			12 52										13 22											
Drayton Green	d			12 54										13 24											
West Ealing	d			12 56		13 11								13 26		13 41									
Ealing Broadway ⊖	d			12 59	13 03	13 14	13 19							13 29	13 33	13 44	13 49								
Acton Main Line	d			13 03										13 33											
London Paddington 15 ⊖	a		13 00	13 12	13 16	13 24	13 31		13 14		13 29		13 32	13 42	13 46	13 54	14 01		13 38	13 44			14 01	14 09	14 06

		GW	GW	HC	GW	GW	GW		GW	GW	GW	GW	HC	GW		GW	GW		GW	GW	GW	GW	GW	GW	HC
		1	1		1	◇1 ☕	1		◇1 🛒	◇1 B ☕	1	1		1		◇1 ☕	◇1 ☕		◇1 ☕	1	◇1 🛒	◇1 ☕	1	1	
Oxford	d				12 37				13 31					13 07							14 01				
Reading 7	d				13 33	13 44	13 48		13 55	14 01				14 03		14 08	14 12		14 17	14 18	14 26	14 32			
Twyford 3	d				13 39		13 54							14 09						14 24					
Maidenhead 3	d				13 47		14 02							14 17						14 32					
Taplow	d						14 06													14 36					
Burnham	d		←				14 09					←								14 39				←	
Slough 3	a		13 44		13 54		14 14		14 09			14 14		14 24						14 44	14 39			14 44	
	d		13 44		13 54		14 14		14 10			14 14		14 24						14 44	14 40			14 44	
Langley	d				13 58		→							14 28						→					
Iver	d				14 01									14 31											
West Drayton	d		13 51		14 05							14 21		14 35										14 51	
Heathrow Terminal 4 ✈	d																								
Heathrow Terminal 1-2-3 2 ✈	d			13 57									14 27												14 57
Hayes & Harlington	d		13 56	14 03	14 10							14 26	14 33	14 40										14 56	15 03
Southall	d			14 06	14 13								14 36	14 43											15 06
Hanwell	d			14 09									14 39												15 09
Greenford ⊖	d	13 46									14 16												14 46		
South Greenford	d	13 49									14 19												14 49		
Castle Bar Park	d	13 52									14 22												14 52		
Drayton Green	d	13 54									14 24												14 54		
West Ealing	d	13 56		14 11							14 26		14 41										14 56		15 11
Ealing Broadway ⊖	d	13 59	14 03	14 14	14 19						14 29	14 33	14 44	14 49									14 59	15 03	15 14
Acton Main Line	d	14 03									14 33												15 03		
London Paddington 15 ⊖	a	14 12	14 16	14 24	14 31	14 14			14 29	14 32	14 42	14 46	14 54	15 01		14 37	14 40		14 44		15 00	15 08	15 12	15 16	15 24

		GW			GW	GW	GW	GW	GW	GW	GW	HC	GW			GW	GW	GW	GW	GW	GW	GW	HC		GW
		1			◇1 ☕	1	R 1 ☕	◇1	◇1 ☕	1	1		1			◇1 ☕	1	1	◇1 🛒	◇1 ☕	1	1			1
Oxford	d	13 37						14 31					14 07						15 01						14 37
Reading 7	d	14 33			14 44	14 48	14 52	14 55	15 02				15 03			15 11	15 18	15 20	15 26	15 32					15 33
Twyford 3	d	14 39				14 54							15 09				15 24								15 39
Maidenhead 3	d	14 47				15 02							15 17				15 32								15 47
Taplow	d					15 06											15 36								
Burnham	d					15 09					←						15 39					←			
Slough 3	a	14 54				15 14		15 09			15 14		15 24				15 44		15 39			15 44			15 54
	d	14 54				15 14		15 10			15 14		15 24				15 44		15 40			15 44			15 54
Langley	d	14 58				→							15 28				→								15 58
Iver	d	15 01											15 31												16 01
West Drayton	d	15 05									15 21		15 35									15 51			16 05
Heathrow Terminal 4 ✈	d																								
Heathrow Terminal 1-2-3 2 ✈	d											15 27											15 57		
Hayes & Harlington	d	15 10									15 26	15 33	15 40									15 56	16 03		16 10
Southall	d	15 13										15 36	15 43										16 06		16 13
Hanwell	d											15 39											16 09		
Greenford ⊖	d									15 16											15 46				
South Greenford	d									15 19											15 49				
Castle Bar Park	d									15 22											15 52				
Drayton Green	d									15 24											15 54				
West Ealing	d									15 26		15 41									15 56		16 11		
Ealing Broadway ⊖	d	15 19								15 29	15 33	15 44	15 49								15 59	16 03	16 14		16 19
Acton Main Line	d									15 33											16 03				
London Paddington 15 ⊖	a	15 32			15 14		15 24	15 29	15 32	15 42	15 46	15 54	16 02			15 38		15 54	16 01	16 09	16 12	16 17	16 24		16 31

A The Cornish Riviera

B The St. David

Reading and Greenford - London

Network Diagram - see first Page of Table 116

	GW ◇1 ☕	GW 1	GW ◇1 ☕	GW ◇1 ☕	GW ◇1 ☕	GW 1	GW 1	HC	GW 1	GW ◇1 B ☕	GW ◇1 ☕	GW 1	GW 1	GW ◇1 🛒	GW 1	GW 1	HC	GW 1	GW ◇1 ☕	GW ◇1 ☕
Oxford d				15 31					15 07					16 01				15 37		
Reading 7 d	15 44	15 48	15 52	15 55	16 02				16 03	16 08	16 15	16 18	16 19	16 26				16 33	16 34	16 44
Twyford 3 d		15 54							16 09			16 24						16 39		
Maidenhead 3 d		16 02							16 17			16 32						16 47		
Taplow d		16 06										16 36								
Burnham d		16 09					↤					16 39				↤				
Slough 3 a		16 14		16 09			16 14		16 24			16 44		16 39		16 44		16 54		
d		16 14		16 10			16 14		16 24			16 44		16 40		16 44		16 54		
Langley d		↦							16 28			↦						16 58		
Iver d									16 31									17 01		
West Drayton d							16 21		16 35							16 51		17 05		
Heathrow Terminal 4 ✈ d																				
Heathrow Terminal 1-2-3 2 ✈ d								16 27									16 57			
Hayes & Harlington d							16 26	16 33	16 40							16 56	17 03	17 10		
Southall d								16 36	16 43								17 06	17 13		
Hanwell d								16 39									17 09			
Greenford ⊖ d						16 16									16 46					
South Greenford d						16 19									16 49					
Castle Bar Park d						16 22									16 52					
Drayton Green d						16 24									16 54					
West Ealing d						16 26		16 41							16 56		17 11			
Ealing Broadway ⊖ d						16 29	16 33	16 44	16 49						16 59	17 03	17 14	17 21		
Acton Main Line d						16 33									17 03					
London Paddington 15 ⊖ a	16 14		16 22	16 27	16 30	16 42	16 46	16 54	17 02	16 39	16 44		16 57	17 00	17 12	17 19	17 24	17 31	17 09	17 14

	GW 1	GW ◇1 C ☕	GW ◇1	GW ◇1 ☕	GW 1	GW 1	HC	GW 1	GW ◇1 D ☕	GW ◇1 ☕	GW 1	GW 1 🛒	GW ◇1 ☕	GW 1	GW 1	HC	GW 1	GW 1	GW ◇1 ☕	GW ◇1 E ☕	GW 1
Oxford d			16 31					16 07				17 01					16 37				
Reading 7 d	16 48	16 51	16 55	17 02				17 03	17 11	17 17	17 17	17 26	17 32				17 33	17 42	17 46	17 51	17 54
Twyford 3 d	16 54							17 09			17 24						17 39	17 48			
Maidenhead 3 d	17 02							17 17		17 29	17 32						17 47	17 56			18 08
Taplow d	17 06										17 36							18 00			
Burnham d	17 09					↤					17 39				↤			18 02			
Slough 3 a	17 14		17 09			17 14		17 24			17 44	17 39			17 44		17 54	18 07			18 14
d	17 14		17 10			17 14		17 24			17 44	17 40			17 44		17 54	18 07			18 14
Langley d	↦							17 28			↦						17 58				↦
Iver d								17 31									18 01				
West Drayton d						17 21		17 35							17 51		18 05	18 14			
Heathrow Terminal 4 ✈ d																					
Heathrow Terminal 1-2-3 2 ✈ d							17 27									17 57					
Hayes & Harlington d						17 26	17 33	17 40							17 56	18 03	18 10	18 19			
Southall d							17 36	17 43								18 06	18 13				
Hanwell d							17 39									18 09					
Greenford ⊖ d					17 16									17 46							
South Greenford d					17 19									17 49							
Castle Bar Park d					17 22									17 52							
Drayton Green d					17 24									17 54							
West Ealing d					17 26		17 41							17 56		18 11					
Ealing Broadway ⊖ d					17 29	17 33	17 44	17 49						17 59	18 03	18 14	18 19	18 26			
Acton Main Line d					17 33									18 03							
London Paddington 15 ⊖ a		17 24	17 34	17 30	17 42	17 48	17 54	18 01	17 39	17 54		17 59	18 02	18 12	18 14	18 24	18 31	18 37	18 14	18 21	

	GW ◇1 ☕	GW 1	GW 1	HC	GW 1	GW ◇1 ☕	GW ◇1 ☕	GW ◇1 ☕	GW 1	GW 1	GW 1	GW 1 🛒	GW ◇1 ☕	GW 1	GW 1	HC	GW 1	GW ◇1 ☕	GW 1
Oxford d	17 31				17 07							18 01					17 37		
Reading 7 d	17 56				18 00	18 01	18 08	18 12		18 18	18 22	18 26	18 32				18 33	18 47	18 48
Twyford 3 d					18 10					18 24							18 39		18 54
Maidenhead 3 d					18 17				18 26	18 32							18 48		19 05
Taplow d										18 35									19 09
Burnham d			↤							18 39					↤				19 12
Slough 3 a	18 10		18 14		18 24				18 33	18 44		18 39			18 44		18 54		19 17
d	18 11		18 14		18 24				18 33	18 44		18 40			18 44		18 54		19 17
Langley d					18 28					↦							18 58		↦
Iver d					18 32												19 01		
West Drayton d					18 35										18 51		19 05		
Heathrow Terminal 4 ✈ d																			
Heathrow Terminal 1-2-3 2 ✈ d				18 27												18 57			
Hayes & Harlington d			18 26	18 33	18 40				18 45						18 56	19 03	19 10		
Southall d				18 36	18 43											19 06	19 13		
Hanwell d				18 39												19 09			
Greenford ⊖ d		18 16												18 46					
South Greenford d		18 19												18 49					
Castle Bar Park d		18 22												18 52					
Drayton Green d		18 24												18 54					
West Ealing d		18 26		18 41										18 56		19 11			
Ealing Broadway ⊖ d		18 29	18 33	18 44	18 49				18 54					18 59	19 05	19 14	19 19		
Acton Main Line d		18 33												19 03					
London Paddington 15 ⊖ a	18 28	18 42	18 46	18 54	19 00	18 30	18 39	18 44	19 04		18 54	18 59	19 02	19 12	19 18	19 24	19 31	19 14	

B The Cheltenham Spa Express
C The Torbay Express
D The Merchant Venturer
E The Mayflower

Reading and Greenford - London

Network Diagram - see first Page of Table 116

		GW	GW	GW	GW	GW	HC		GW		GW	GW	GW	GW	GW	GW	HC		GW	GW	GW	GW FO	GW FX	GW	GW
		◇1 A 🍽	1	◇1 🍽	1	1			1		◇1 🍽	1	1	1	◇1 🍽	◇1 🛒			1	◇1 🍽	1	◇1	◇1	1	1
Oxford	d		18 31						18 07							19 06			18 37			19 31	19 31		
Reading 7	d	18 51	18 57	19 02					19 03		19 11	19 18		19 18	19 25	19 32			19 33	19 45	19 48	19 55	19 55		
Twyford 3	d								19 09					19 24					19 42		19 54				
Maidenhead 3	d								19 21					19 32					19 50		20 02				
Taplow	d													19 36							20 05				
Burnham	d					←								19 39							20 09				←
Slough 3	a		19 09			19 17			19 29					19 44		19 47			19 57		20 14	20 09	20 09		20 14
	d		19 10			19 17			19 29					19 44		19 47			19 57		20 14	20 10	20 10		20 14
Langley	d								19 33										20 01		→				
Iver	d								19 36										20 04						
West Drayton	d					19 24			19 39					19 51					20 08						20 21
Heathrow Terminal 4 ✈	d																								
Heathrow Terminal 1-2-3 2 ✈	d						19 27										19 57								
Hayes & Harlington	d					19 29	19 33		19 44					19 56			20 03		20 13						20 26
Southall	d						19 36		19 47								20 06		20 16						
Hanwell	d						19 39										20 09								
Greenford ⊖	d				19 16								19 46											20 16	
South Greenford	d				19 19								19 49											20 19	
Castle Bar Park	d				19 22								19 52											20 22	
Drayton Green	d				19 24								19 54											20 24	
West Ealing	d				19 26		19 41						19 56				20 11							20 26	
Ealing Broadway ⊖	d				19 29	19 36	19 44		19 53				19 59	20 03			20 14		20 22					20 29	20 33
Acton Main Line	d				19 33								20 03											20 33	
London Paddington 15 ⊖	a	19 24	19 31	19 32	19 42	19 45	19 54		20 02		19 38	19 54	20 12	20 16	19 54	20 06	20 24		20 31	20 14		20 30	20 31	20 42	20 49

		HC	GW			GW	GW	GW	GW	GW	GW	GW	HC		GW	GW	GW	GW	GW	GW	GW	GW	GW		HC
			1			◇1 🍽	◇1 🍽	◇1 🍽	1	◇1	1	1			1	1	◇1 🍽	1	◇1 🍽	◇1 🍽	◇1 🍽	1	1		
Oxford	d		19 01							20 01					19 37					20 31					
Reading 7	d		19 58			20 02	20 08	20 15	20 18	20 26					20 33	20 34	20 45	20 48	20 52	20 55	21 02				
Twyford 3	d		20 04						20 24						20 39			20 54							
Maidenhead 3	d		20 12						20 32						20 47			21 02							
Taplow	d								20 36									21 06							
Burnham	d								20 39			←						21 09					←		
Slough 3	a		20 19						20 44	20 39		20 44			20 54			21 13		21 09			21 13		
	d		20 24						20 44	20 40		20 44			20 54			21 14		21 10			21 14		
Langley	d		20 28						→						20 58			→					21 17		
Iver	d		20 31												21 01								21 20		
West Drayton	d		20 35									20 51			21 05								21 24		
Heathrow Terminal 4 ✈	d																								
Heathrow Terminal 1-2-3 2 ✈	d	20 27											20 57												21 27
Hayes & Harlington	d	20 33	20 40									20 56	21 03		21 10								21 28		21 33
Southall	d	20 36	20 43										21 06		21 13										21 36
Hanwell	d	20 39											21 09												21 39
Greenford ⊖	d										20 46											21 16			
South Greenford	d										20 49											21 19			
Castle Bar Park	d										20 52											21 22			
Drayton Green	d										20 54											21 24			
West Ealing	d	20 41									20 56		21 11									21 26			21 41
Ealing Broadway ⊖	d	20 44	20 49								20 59	21 03	21 14		21 19							21 29	21 35		21 44
Acton Main Line	d										21 03											21 33			
London Paddington 15 ⊖	a	20 54	20 59			20 32	20 39	20 46		21 01	21 12	21 15	21 24		21 31	21 08	21 14		21 21	21 29	21 32	21 42	21 48		21 54

		GW	GW		GW FX	GW FO	HC	GW			GW	GW		GW	GW FX	GW FO	HC	GW	HC		GW		GW	GW FX	GW FO
		1	1		◇1	◇1		1			◇1 🍽	◇1		◇1 🍽	◇1 🍽	◇1 🍽		1			◇		1	◇1	◇1
Oxford	d		20 07		21 01	21 01		20 37				21 31									22 11			22 34	22 34
Reading 7	d		21 14		21 26	21 26		21 33			21 44	21 56		22 01	22 12	22 12		22 16			22 44		22 48	22 59	22 59
Twyford 3	d		21 20					21 39										22 22					22 54		
Maidenhead 3	d		21 28					21 47										22 31					23 02		
Taplow	d		21 32					21 50										22 34					23 05		
Burnham	d		21 35					21 53										22 37					23 08		
Slough 3	a		21 40		21 39	21 39		21 58				22 13						22 42			23 01		23 13	23 15	23 12
	d		21 40		21 40	21 40		21 59				22 13						22 42			23 01		23 27	23 16	23 16
Langley	d		21 44					22 02										22 46					→		
Iver	d		21 47					22 05										22 49							
West Drayton	d		21 51					22 09										22 53							
Heathrow Terminal 4 ✈	d																								
Heathrow Terminal 1-2-3 2 ✈	d						21 57										22 27		22 57						
Hayes & Harlington	d		21 56				22 03	22 14									22 33	22 57	23 03						
Southall	d		21 59				22 06										22 36	23 01	23 06						
Hanwell	d						22 09										22 39		23 09						
Greenford ⊖	d	21 46																							
South Greenford	d	21 49																							
Castle Bar Park	d	21 52																							
Drayton Green	d	21 54																							
West Ealing	d	21 56					22 11										22 41		23 11						
Ealing Broadway ⊖	d	21 59	22 05				22 14	22 21									22 44	23 06	23 14						
Acton Main Line	d	22 03																							
London Paddington 15 ⊖	a	22 13	22 16		22 00	22 01	22 24	22 33			22 14	22 39		22 30	22 44	22 45	22 54	23 18	23 24		23 25			23 36	23 36

A The Royal Duchy

Table 117

Reading and Greenford - London

Network Diagram - see first Page of Table 116

		GW	GW FX	GW FO	HC		GW	GW	GW	GW
		◇1 ⊏P	◇1 ⊏P	◇1 ⊏P			1	1	◇1	◇1 ⊏P
Oxford	d								23 09	
Reading 7	d	23 04	23 08	23 09				23 15	23 45	23 55
Twyford 3	d							23 22		
Maidenhead 3	d							23 29	23 58	
Taplow	d							23 33		
Burnham	d						←	23 36		
Slough 3	a						23 13	23 41	00 05	
	d						23 27	23 41	00 05	
Langley	d						23 31	23 45		
Iver	d						23 34	23 48		
West Drayton	d						23 38	23 51		
Heathrow Terminal 4 ✈	d									
Heathrow Terminal 1-2-3 2 ✈	d				23 27					
Hayes & Harlington	d				23 33		23 43	23 56		
Southall	d				23 36		23 47	23 59		
Hanwell	d				23 39					
Greenford ⊖	d									
South Greenford	d									
Castle Bar Park	d									
Drayton Green	d									
West Ealing	d				23 41					
Ealing Broadway ⊖	d				23 44		23 52	00 06		
Acton Main Line	d									
London Paddington 15 ⊖	a	23 38	23 41	23 41	23 54		00 02	00 17	00 29	00 33

Saturdays

until 31 December

		GW	GW	GW	HC	GW	GW	GW	GW	GW		
		1	1	◇1		◇1 ⊏P	1	◇1	1	1		
Oxford	d			23p09				00 07	00 27			
Reading 7	d	22p48	23p15	23p45		23p55	00 15	00 38	01 12	04 10		
Twyford 3	d	22p54	23p22				00 21		01 18	04 16		
Maidenhead 3	d	23p02	23p29	23p58			00 29		01 26	04 24		
Taplow	d	23p05	23p33				00 32					
Burnham	d	23p08	23p36				00 35					
Slough 3	a	23p13	23p41	00 05			00 40	00 55	01 34	04 31		
	d	23p27	23p41	00 05			00 40	00 56	01 34	04 32		
Langley	d	23p31	23p45				00 44					
Iver	d	23p34	23p48									
West Drayton	d	23p38	23p51				00 49			04 38		
Heathrow Terminal 4 ✈	d				00 01							
Heathrow Terminal 1-2-3 2 ✈	d				00 07							
Hayes & Harlington	d	23p43	23p56		00 13		00 54		01 43	04 43		
Southall	d	23p47	23p59		00 16		00 57			04 46		
Hanwell	d											
Greenford ⊖	d											
South Greenford	d											
Castle Bar Park	d											
Drayton Green	d											
West Ealing	d											
Ealing Broadway ⊖	d	23p52	00 06		00 21		01 03		01 50	04 52		
Acton Main Line	d											
London Paddington 15 ⊖	a	00 02	00 17	00 29	00 30	00 33	01 14	01 17	02 02	05 01		

		GW	HC	GW	HC	GW	GW	GW	HC		GW	GW	GW	HC
		1		1		1	1	1			1	1	1	
Oxford	d	03 59									05 14			
Reading 7	d	04 40		05 10		05 33		05 48			06 03		06 18	
Twyford 3	d	04 46		05 16		05 39		05 54			06 09		06 24	
Maidenhead 3	d	04 54		05 24		05 47		06 02			06 17		06 32	
Taplow	d			05 28				06 06					06 36	
Burnham	d			05 31				06 09					06 39	
Slough 3	a	05 01		05 35		05 54		06 14			06 24		06 44	
	d	05 02		05 36		05 54		06 14			06 24		06 44	
Langley	d			05 40		05 58					06 28			
Iver	d			05 43		06 01					06 31			
West Drayton	d			05 45		06 05		06 21			06 35		06 51	
Heathrow Terminal 4 ✈	d		05 23		05 51									
Heathrow Terminal 1-2-3 2 ✈	d		05 29		05 57				06 27					06 57
Hayes & Harlington	d	05 11	05 35	05 51	06 03	06 10		06 26	06 33		06 40		06 56	07 03
Southall	d	05 13	05 38	05 54	06 06	06 13			06 36		06 43			07 06
Hanwell	d		05 41		06 09				06 39					07 09
Greenford ⊖	d						06 16					06 46		
South Greenford	d						06 19					06 49		
Castle Bar Park	d						06 22					06 52		
Drayton Green	d						06 24					06 54		
West Ealing	d		05 43		06 11		06 26		06 41			06 56		07 11
Ealing Broadway ⊖	d	05 19	05 46	06 00	06 14	06 19	06 29	06 33	06 44		06 49	06 59	07 03	07 14
Acton Main Line	d	05 23		06 03			06 33					07 03		
London Paddington 15 ⊖	a	05 31	05 56	06 11	06 24	06 31	06 42	06 46	06 54		07 01	07 12	07 16	07 24

A The Night Riviera

Table 117

Saturdays

until 31 December

Reading and Greenford - London

Network Diagram - see first Page of Table 116

		GW	GW	GW	GW	GW		GW	HC	GW	GW	GW	GW	GW	GW	GW		GW	HC	GW	GW	GW	GW	GW	GW
		1	◇1 🍴	1	1	1		◇1		1	◇1 🍴	1	1	◇1	◇1 🍴	1		1		1	◇1 🍴	1	◇1 🍴	◇1 🍴	1
Oxford	d	05 49						06 31		06 07				07 01						06 42			07 31		
Reading 7	d	06 33	06 45		06 48	06 52		07 00		07 03	07 15	07 18	07 21	07 27	07 32					07 33	07 46	07 48	07 54	08 02	
Twyford 3	d	06 39			06 54					07 09		07 24								07 39		07 54			
Maidenhead 3	d	06 47			07 02					07 17		07 32								07 47		08 02			
Taplow	d				07 06							07 36										08 06			
Burnham	d				07 09							07 39						←				08 09			
Slough 3	a	06 54			07 14			07 16		07 24		07 44		07 42				07 44		07 54		08 14	08 09		
	d	06 54			07 14			07 17		07 24		07 44		07 42				07 44		07 54		08 14	08 09		
Langley	d	06 58								07 28		→								07 58		→			
Iver	d	07 01								07 31										08 01					
West Drayton	d	07 05			07 21					07 35								07 51		08 05					
Heathrow Terminal 4 ✈	d																								
Heathrow Terminal 1-2-3 2 ✈	d								07 27										07 57						
Hayes & Harlington	d	07 10			07 26				07 33	07 40								07 56	08 03	08 10					
Southall	d	07 13							07 36	07 43									08 06	08 13					
Hanwell	d								07 39										08 09						
Greenford ⊖	d			07 16												07 46									08 16
South Greenford	d			07 19												07 49									08 19
Castle Bar Park	d			07 22												07 52									08 22
Drayton Green	d			07 24												07 54									08 24
West Ealing	d			07 26					07 41							07 56			08 11						08 26
Ealing Broadway ⊖	d	07 19		07 29	07 33				07 44	07 49						07 59		08 03	08 14	08 19					08 29
Acton Main Line	d			07 33												08 03									08 33
London Paddington 15 ⊖	a	07 31	07 14	07 42	07 46	07 22		07 37	07 54	08 01	07 44		07 54	08 01	08 07	08 12		08 16	08 24	08 31	08 14		08 29	08 32	08 42

		GW		HC	GW		GW	GW	GW	GW	GW	GW		GW	HC	GW		GW	GW	GW	GW	GW		GW	GW
		1			1		◇1 🍴	1	1	◇1	◇1 🍴	1		1		1		◇1 🍴	1	◇1 🍴	◇1 🍴	◇1 🍴		1	1
Oxford	d				07 07					08 01						07 37					08 31				
Reading 7	d				08 03		08 16	08 18	08 20	08 26	08 32					08 33		08 46	08 48	08 52	08 55	09 02			
Twyford 3	d				08 09			08 24								08 39			08 54						
Maidenhead 3	d				08 17			08 32								08 47			09 02						
Taplow	d							08 36											09 06						
Burnham	d	←						08 39						←					09 09						←
Slough 3	a	08 14			08 24			08 44		08 40				08 44		08 54			09 14		09 09				09 14
	d	08 14			08 24			08 44		08 41				08 44		08 54			09 14		09 11				09 14
Langley	d				08 28			→								08 58			→						
Iver	d				08 31											09 01									
West Drayton	d	08 21			08 35									08 51		09 05									09 21
Heathrow Terminal 4 ✈	d																								
Heathrow Terminal 1-2-3 2 ✈	d			08 27											08 57										
Hayes & Harlington	d	08 26		08 33	08 40									08 56	09 03	09 10									09 26
Southall	d			08 36	08 43										09 06	09 13									
Hanwell	d			08 39											09 09										
Greenford ⊖	d											08 46												09 16	
South Greenford	d											08 49												09 19	
Castle Bar Park	d											08 52												09 22	
Drayton Green	d											08 54												09 24	
West Ealing	d			08 41								08 56			09 11									09 26	
Ealing Broadway ⊖	d	08 33		08 44	08 49							08 59		09 03	09 14	09 19								09 29	09 33
Acton Main Line	d											09 03												09 33	
London Paddington 15 ⊖	a	08 46		08 54	09 01		08 44		08 52	08 59	09 02	09 12		09 16	09 24	09 31		09 14		09 21	09 29	09 32		09 42	09 46

		HC	GW		GW	GW	GW	GW		GW	GW	GW	GW	HC	GW	GW	GW	GW		GW	GW	GW	GW	HC	GW
			1		◇1 🍴	◇1 🍴	1	1		◇1 🛒	◇1 🍴	1	1		1	◇1 🍴	◇1 🍴	1		◇1 A 🍴Ø	◇1 🍴	1	1		1
Oxford	d		08 07							09 01					08 37					09 31					09 07
Reading 7	d		09 03		09 09	09 16	09 18	09 20		09 24	09 33				09 33	09 42	09 46	09 48		09 55	10 02				10 03
Twyford 3	d		09 09				09 24								09 39			09 54							10 09
Maidenhead 3	d		09 17				09 32								09 47			10 02							10 17
Taplow	d						09 36											10 06							
Burnham	d						09 39						←					10 09					←		
Slough 3	a		09 24				09 44			09 40			09 44		09 54			10 14		10 09			10 14		10 24
	d		09 24				09 44			09 40			09 44		09 54			10 14		10 10			10 14		10 24
Langley	d		09 28				→								09 58			→							10 28
Iver	d		09 31												10 01										10 31
West Drayton	d		09 35										09 51		10 05								10 21		10 35
Heathrow Terminal 4 ✈	d																								
Heathrow Terminal 1-2-3 2 ✈	d	09 27												09 57										10 27	
Hayes & Harlington	d	09 33	09 40										09 56	10 03	10 10								10 26	10 33	10 40
Southall	d	09 36	09 43											10 06	10 13									10 36	10 43
Hanwell	d	09 39												10 09										10 39	
Greenford ⊖	d											09 46										10 16			
South Greenford	d											09 49										10 19			
Castle Bar Park	d											09 52										10 22			
Drayton Green	d											09 54										10 24			
West Ealing	d	09 41										09 56		10 11								10 26		10 41	
Ealing Broadway ⊖	d	09 44	09 49									09 59	10 03	10 14	10 19							10 29	10 33	10 44	10 49
Acton Main Line	d											10 03										10 33			
London Paddington 15 ⊖	a	09 54	10 01		09 37	09 44		09 52		09 59	10 02	10 12	10 16	10 24	10 31	10 11	10 14			10 29	10 32	10 42	10 46	10 54	11 01

A 🍴 from Reading Ø to Reading

Table 117

Saturdays

until 31 December

Reading and Greenford - London

Network Diagram - see first Page of Table 116

			GW	GW		GW	GW	GW	GW	GW	HC	GW		GW		GW	GW	GW	GW	GW	GW	GW	HC	GW	
			◇1 ☕	1		1	◇1 🍴	◇1 ☕	1	1		1		◇1 ☕		◇1 ☕	1	◇1 ☕	◇1 ☕	◇1 ☕	1	1		1	
Oxford	d						10 01					09 37							10 31					10 07	
Reading 7	d		10 13	10 18		10 18	10 25	10 33				10 33		10 39		10 46	10 48	10 53	10 55	11 02				11 03	
Twyford 3	d					10 24						10 39					10 54							11 09	
Maidenhead 3	d					10 32						10 47					11 02							11 17	
Taplow	d					10 36											11 06								
Burnham	d					10 39				←							11 09					←			
Slough 3	a					10 44	10 40			10 44		10 54					11 14		11 09			11 14		11 24	
	d					10 44	10 40			10 44		10 54					11 14		11 10			11 14		11 24	
Langley	d					→						10 58					→							11 28	
Iver	d											11 01												11 31	
West Drayton	d									10 51		11 05										11 21		11 35	
Heathrow Terminal 4 ✈	d																								
Heathrow Terminal 1-2-3 2 ✈	d										10 57												11 27		
Hayes & Harlington	d									10 56	11 03	11 10										11 26	11 33	11 40	
Southall	d										11 06	11 13											11 36	11 43	
Hanwell	d										11 09												11 39		
Greenford ⊖	d								10 46												11 16				
South Greenford	d								10 49												11 19				
Castle Bar Park	d								10 52												11 22				
Drayton Green	d								10 54												11 24				
West Ealing	d								10 56		11 11										11 26		11 41		
Ealing Broadway ⊖	d								10 59	11 03	11 14	11 19									11 29	11 33	11 44	11 49	
Acton Main Line	d								11 03												11 33				
London Paddington 15 ⊖	a		10 39	10 52			10 59	11 02	11 12	11 16	11 24	11 31		11 08		11 14		11 24	11 29	11 33	11 42	11 46	11 54	12 01	

			GW	GW	GW	GW	GW	GW	HC	GW		GW	GW	GW	GW	GW	GW	GW	HC	GW			GW	GW	GW
			◇1 ☕	1	1	◇1	1	1		1		◇1 ☕	1	R 1 ☕	◇1 🍴	◇1 ☕	1	1		1			◇1 ☕	1	1
Oxford	d					11 01				10 37					11 31					11 07					
Reading 7	d		11 14	11 18	11 21	11 25				11 33		11 45	11 48	11 53	11 55	12 02				12 03			12 13	12 18	12 18
Twyford 3	d			11 24						11 39			11 54							12 09					12 24
Maidenhead 3	d			11 32						11 47			12 02							12 17					12 32
Taplow	d			11 36									12 06												12 36
Burnham	d			11 39				←					12 09					←							12 39
Slough 3	a			11 44		11 39		11 44		11 54			12 14		12 09			12 14		12 24					12 44
	d			11 44		11 40		11 44		11 54			12 14		12 11			12 14		12 24					12 44
Langley	d			→						11 58			→							12 28					→
Iver	d									12 01										12 31					
West Drayton	d							11 51		12 05								12 21		12 35					
Heathrow Terminal 4 ✈	d																								
Heathrow Terminal 1-2-3 2 ✈	d								11 57										12 27						
Hayes & Harlington	d							11 56	12 03	12 10								12 26	12 33	12 40					
Southall	d								12 06	12 13									12 36	12 43					
Hanwell	d								12 09										12 39						
Greenford ⊖	d						11 46										12 16								
South Greenford	d						11 49										12 19								
Castle Bar Park	d						11 52										12 22								
Drayton Green	d						11 54										12 24								
West Ealing	d						11 56		12 11								12 26		12 41						
Ealing Broadway ⊖	d						11 59	12 03	12 14	12 19							12 29	12 33	12 44	12 49					
Acton Main Line	d						12 03										12 33								
London Paddington 15 ⊖	a		11 40		11 52	11 59	12 12	12 16	12 24	12 31		12 14		12 23	12 29	12 32	12 42	12 46	12 54	13 01			12 39	12 52	

		GW	GW	GW	HC	GW			GW	GW	GW	GW	GW	GW	GW	GW		HC	GW		GW	GW	GW	GW	GW
		◇1 🍴	1	1		1			◇1 ☕	◇1 ☕	1	◇1 ☕	◇1 🍴	◇1 ☕	1	1			1		◇1 ☕	1	◇1 ☕	◇1 🍴	1
Oxford	d	12 01				11 37							12 31						12 07					13 01	
Reading 7	d	12 25				12 33			12 39	12 45	12 48	12 54	12 55	13 02					13 03		13 12	13 18	13 20	13 25	
Twyford 3	d					12 39					12 54								13 09			13 24			
Maidenhead 3	d					12 47					13 02								13 17			13 32			
Taplow	d										13 06											13 36			
Burnham	d			←							13 09					←						13 39			
Slough 3	a	12 40		12 44		12 54					13 14		13 09			13 14			13 24			13 44		13 40	
	d	12 40		12 44		12 54					13 14		13 11			13 14			13 24			13 44		13 40	
Langley	d					12 58					→								13 28			→			
Iver	d					13 01													13 31						
West Drayton	d			12 51		13 05										13 21			13 35						
Heathrow Terminal 4 ✈	d																								
Heathrow Terminal 1-2-3 2 ✈	d				12 57													13 27							
Hayes & Harlington	d			12 56	13 03	13 10										13 26		13 33	13 40						
Southall	d				13 06	13 13												13 36	13 43						
Hanwell	d				13 09													13 39							
Greenford ⊖	d		12 46												13 16										13 46
South Greenford	d		12 49												13 19										13 49
Castle Bar Park	d		12 52												13 22										13 52
Drayton Green	d		12 54												13 24										13 54
West Ealing	d		12 56		13 11										13 26			13 41							13 56
Ealing Broadway ⊖	d		12 59	13 03	13 14	13 19									13 29	13 33		13 44	13 49						13 59
Acton Main Line	d		13 03												13 33										14 03
London Paddington 15 ⊖	a	12 59	13 12	13 16	13 24	13 31			13 07	13 12		13 21	13 30	13 33	13 42	13 46		13 54	14 01		13 41		13 46	13 59	14 12

Table 117

Saturdays

until 31 December

Reading and Greenford - London

Network Diagram - see first Page of Table 116

		GW 1		HC	GW 1	GW ◇1 ☕	GW 1	GW 1	GW ◇1	GW ◇1 ☕	GW 1	GW 1		HC	GW 1		GW ◇1 ☕	GW 1	GW ◇1 ☕	GW ◇1 🛒	GW 1	GW 1		HC	GW 1
Oxford	d				12 37				13 31						13 07					14 01					13 37
Reading 7	d				13 33	13 45	13 48	13 51	13 55	14 02					14 03		14 13	14 18	14 19	14 25					14 33
Twyford 3	d				13 39		13 54								14 09			14 24							14 39
Maidenhead 3	d				13 47		14 02								14 17			14 32							14 47
Taplow	d						14 06											14 36							
Burnham	d	←					14 09					←						14 39				←			
Slough 3	a	13 44			13 54		14 14		14 09			14 14			14 24			14 44		14 40		14 44			14 54
	d	13 44			13 54		14 14		14 10			14 14			14 24			14 44		14 40		14 44			14 54
Langley	d				13 58		→								14 28			→							14 58
Iver	d				14 01										14 31										15 01
West Drayton	d	13 51			14 05							14 21			14 35							14 51			15 05
Heathrow Terminal 4 ✈	d																								
Heathrow Terminal 1-2-3 2 ✈	d			13 57										14 27										14 57	
Hayes & Harlington	d	13 56		14 03	14 10							14 26		14 33	14 40							14 56		15 03	15 10
Southall	d			14 06	14 13									14 36	14 43									15 06	15 13
Hanwell	d			14 09										14 39										15 09	
Greenford ⊖	d										14 16										14 46				
South Greenford	d										14 19										14 49				
Castle Bar Park	d										14 22										14 52				
Drayton Green	d										14 24										14 54				
West Ealing	d			14 11							14 26			14 41							14 56			15 11	
Ealing Broadway ⊖	d	14 03		14 14	14 19						14 29	14 33		14 44	14 49						14 59	15 03		15 14	15 19
Acton Main Line	d										14 33										15 03				
London Paddington 15 ⊖	a	14 16		14 24	14 31	14 14		14 23	14 29	14 32	14 42	14 46		14 54	15 01		14 39		14 45	14 59	15 12	15 16		15 24	15 31

			GW ◇1 ☕	GW ◇1 ☕	GW 1	GW ◇1 ☕	GW ◇1 ☕	GW ◇1 ☕		GW 1	GW 1	HC	GW 1		GW ◇1 ☕	GW 1	GW 1	GW ◇1		GW 1	GW 1	HC	GW 1	GW ◇1 ☕	GW 1
Oxford	d						14 31						14 07					15 01					14 37		
Reading 7	d		14 39	14 45	14 48	14 53	14 55	15 02					15 03		15 12	15 18	15 19	15 25					15 33	15 45	15 48
Twyford 3	d				14 54								15 09			15 24							15 39		15 54
Maidenhead 3	d				15 02								15 17			15 32							15 47		16 02
Taplow	d				15 06											15 36									16 06
Burnham	d				15 09						←					15 39					←				16 09
Slough 3	a				15 14		15 10				15 14		15 24			15 44		15 40			15 44		15 54		16 14
	d				15 14		15 11				15 14		15 24			15 44		15 40			15 44		15 54		16 14
Langley	d				→								15 28			→							15 58		→
Iver	d												15 31										16 01		
West Drayton	d										15 21		15 35								15 51		16 05		
Heathrow Terminal 4 ✈	d																								
Heathrow Terminal 1-2-3 2 ✈	d											15 27										15 57			
Hayes & Harlington	d										15 26	15 33	15 40								15 56	16 03	16 10		
Southall	d											15 36	15 43									16 06	16 13		
Hanwell	d											15 39										16 09			
Greenford ⊖	d									15 16										15 46					
South Greenford	d									15 19										15 49					
Castle Bar Park	d									15 22										15 52					
Drayton Green	d									15 24										15 54					
West Ealing	d									15 26		15 41								15 56		16 11			
Ealing Broadway ⊖	d									15 29	15 33	15 44	15 49							15 59	16 03	16 14	16 19		
Acton Main Line	d									15 33										16 03					
London Paddington 15 ⊖	a		15 09	15 14		15 22	15 29	15 32		15 42	15 46	15 54	16 01		15 39		15 54	15 59		16 12	16 16	16 24	16 31	16 14	

		GW ◇1 ☕	GW ◇1 🛒	GW ◇1 ☕		GW 1	GW 1	HC	GW 1		GW ◇1 ☕	GW 1	GW 1	GW ◇1		GW 1	GW 1	HC	GW 1		GW ◇1 ☕	GW ◇1 ☕	GW 1	GW ◇1 ☕	
Oxford	d		15 31						15 07					16 01					15 37						
Reading 7	d	15 53	15 55	16 01					16 03		16 13	16 18	16 18	16 26					16 33		16 39	16 45	16 48	16 51	
Twyford 3	d								16 09				16 24						16 39				16 54		
Maidenhead 3	d								16 17				16 32						16 47				17 02		
Taplow	d												16 36										17 06		
Burnham	d						←						16 39				←						17 09		
Slough 3	a		16 10				16 14		16 24				16 44	16 40			16 44		16 54				17 14		
	d		16 11				16 14		16 24				16 44	16 41			16 44		16 54				17 14		
Langley	d								16 28				→						16 58				→		
Iver	d								16 31										17 01						
West Drayton	d						16 21		16 35								16 51		17 05						
Heathrow Terminal 4 ✈	d																								
Heathrow Terminal 1-2-3 2 ✈	d							16 27										16 57							
Hayes & Harlington	d						16 26	16 33	16 40								16 56	17 03	17 10						
Southall	d							16 36	16 43									17 06	17 13						
Hanwell	d							16 39										17 09							
Greenford ⊖	d					16 16										16 46									
South Greenford	d					16 19										16 49									
Castle Bar Park	d					16 22										16 52									
Drayton Green	d					16 24										16 54									
West Ealing	d					16 26		16 41								16 56		17 11							
Ealing Broadway ⊖	d					16 29	16 33	16 44	16 49							16 59	17 03	17 14	17 19						
Acton Main Line	d					16 33										17 03									
London Paddington 15 ⊖	a	16 23	16 29	16 32		16 42	16 46	16 54	17 01		16 39	16 52		16 59		17 12	17 16	17 24	17 31		17 07	17 14		17 21	

Table 117

Saturdays

until 31 December

Reading and Greenford - London

Network Diagram - see first Page of Table 116

		GW	GW	GW	GW	HC	GW		GW	GW		GW	GW	GW	GW	HC	GW	GW	GW	GW		GW	GW	GW	GW
		◇1 🍴	◇1 ☕	1	1		1		◇1 ☕	◇1 ☕		1	◇1	1	1		1	◇1 ☕	1	◇1 ☕		◇1 ☕	◇1 ☕	1	1
Oxford	d	16 31					16 07						17 01				16 37					17 31			
Reading 7	d	16 55	17 02				17 03		17 12	17 18		17 18	17 27				17 33	17 45	17 48	17 54		17 57	18 02		
Twyford 3	d						17 09					17 24					17 39		17 54						
Maidenhead 3	d						17 17					17 32					17 47		18 02						
Taplow	d											17 36							18 06						
Burnham	d				←							17 39			←				18 09						←
Slough 3	a	17 10			17 14		17 24					17 44	17 41		17 44		17 54		18 14			18 10			18 14
	d	17 11			17 14		17 24					17 44	17 42		17 44		17 54		18 14			18 11			18 14
Langley	d						17 28					→					17 58		→						
Iver	d						17 31										18 01								
West Drayton	d				17 21		17 35								17 51		18 05								18 21
Heathrow Terminal 4 ✈	d																								
Heathrow Terminal 1-2-3 2 ✈	d					17 27										17 57									
Hayes & Harlington	d				17 26	17 33	17 40								17 56	18 03	18 10								18 26
Southall	d					17 36	17 43									18 06	18 13								
Hanwell	d					17 39										18 09									
Greenford ⊖	d			17 16										17 46										18 16	
South Greenford	d			17 19										17 49										18 19	
Castle Bar Park	d			17 22										17 52										18 22	
Drayton Green	d			17 24										17 54										18 24	
West Ealing	d			17 26		17 41								17 56		18 11								18 26	
Ealing Broadway ⊖	d			17 29	17 33	17 44	17 49							17 59	18 03	18 14	18 19							18 29	18 33
Acton Main Line	d			17 33										18 03										18 33	
London Paddington 15 ⊖	a	17 29	17 32	17 42	17 46	17 54	18 01		17 38	17 51			18 00	18 12	18 16	18 24	18 31	18 14		18 21		18 29	18 32	18 42	18 46

		HC	GW		GW	GW		GW	GW	GW	GW	HC	GW		GW	GW		GW	GW	GW	GW	GW	GW	HC	GW
			1		◇1 ☕	1		1	◇1	1	1		1		◇1 ☕	◇1 ☕		1	◇1 ☕	◇1 🍴	◇1 ☕	1	1		1
Oxford	d		17 07						18 01				17 37							18 31					18 07
Reading 7	d		18 03		18 13	18 18		18 19	18 25				18 33		18 39	18 45		18 48	18 50	18 56	19 02				19 03
Twyford 3	d		18 09			18 24							18 39					18 54							19 09
Maidenhead 3	d		18 17			18 32							18 47					19 02							19 17
Taplow	d					18 36												19 06							
Burnham	d					18 39					←							19 09					←		
Slough 3	a		18 24			18 44			18 40		18 44		18 54					19 14		19 10			19 14		19 24
	d		18 24			18 44			18 40		18 44		18 54					19 14		19 11			19 14		19 24
Langley	d		18 28			→							18 58					→							19 28
Iver	d		18 31										19 01												19 31
West Drayton	d		18 35								18 51		19 05										19 21		19 35
Heathrow Terminal 4 ✈	d																								
Heathrow Terminal 1-2-3 2 ✈	d	18 27										18 57												19 27	
Hayes & Harlington	d	18 33	18 40								18 56	19 03	19 10										19 26	19 33	19 40
Southall	d	18 36	18 43									19 06	19 13											19 36	19 43
Hanwell	d	18 39										19 09												19 39	
Greenford ⊖	d									18 46												19 16			
South Greenford	d									18 49												19 19			
Castle Bar Park	d									18 52												19 22			
Drayton Green	d									18 54												19 24			
West Ealing	d	18 41								18 56		19 11										19 26		19 41	
Ealing Broadway ⊖	d	18 44	18 49							18 59	19 03	19 14	19 19									19 29	19 33	19 44	19 49
Acton Main Line	d									19 03												19 33			
London Paddington 15 ⊖	a	18 54	19 01		18 39			18 52	18 59	19 12	19 16	19 24	19 31		19 08	19 14			19 22	19 29	19 32	19 42	19 46	19 54	20 01

				GW	GW	GW	GW	GW	GW	HC	GW	GW		GW	GW	GW	GW	GW	HC	GW		GW		GW	GW
				◇1 ☕	1	1	◇1	1	1		1	◇1 ☕		1	◇1 🍴	◇1 ☕	1	1		1		◇1 ☕		1	◇1
Oxford	d						19 01				18 37				19 31					19 07					20 01
Reading 7	d			19 12	19 18	19 20	19 25				19 33	19 45		19 48	19 55	20 03				20 03		20 09		20 18	20 25
Twyford 3	d				19 24						19 39			19 54						20 09				20 24	
Maidenhead 3	d				19 32						19 47			20 02						20 17				20 32	
Taplow	d				19 36									20 06										20 36	
Burnham	d				19 39				←					20 09				←						20 39	
Slough 3	a				19 44		19 40		19 44		19 54			20 14	20 10			20 14		20 24				20 44	20 40
	d				19 44		19 40		19 44		19 54			20 14	20 10			20 14		20 24				20 44	20 40
Langley	d				→						19 58			→						20 28				→	
Iver	d										20 01									20 31					
West Drayton	d								19 51		20 05							20 21		20 35					
Heathrow Terminal 4 ✈	d																								
Heathrow Terminal 1-2-3 2 ✈	d									19 57									20 27						
Hayes & Harlington	d								19 56	20 03	20 10							20 26	20 33	20 40					
Southall	d									20 06	20 13								20 36	20 43					
Hanwell	d									20 09									20 39						
Greenford ⊖	d							19 46									20 16								
South Greenford	d							19 49									20 19								
Castle Bar Park	d							19 52									20 22								
Drayton Green	d							19 54									20 24								
West Ealing	d							19 56		20 11							20 26		20 41						
Ealing Broadway ⊖	d							19 59	20 03	20 14	20 19						20 29	20 33	20 44	20 49					
Acton Main Line	d							20 03									20 33								
London Paddington 15 ⊖	a			19 39		19 52	19 59	20 12	20 16	20 24	20 31	20 14			20 29	20 32	20 42	20 46	20 54	21 01		20 37			20 59

Table 117

Reading and Greenford - London

Saturdays

until 31 December

Network Diagram - see first Page of Table 116

		GW	GW	HC	GW	GW	GW	GW	GW	GW	GW	GW	HC	GW	GW	GW	GW	GW	GW	HC	GW
		1	1		1	◇1 ☕	◇1 ☕	1	◇1	◇1 ☕	1	1		1	◇1 ☕	1	◇1	1	1		1
Oxford	d				19 37				20 31					20 07			21 01				20 37
Reading 7	d				20 33	20 39	20 45	20 48	20 54	21 01				21 03	21 08	21 18	21 25				21c33
Twyford 3	d				20 39			20 54						21 09		21 24					21 39
Maidenhead 3	d				20 47			21 02						21 17		21 32					21 47
Taplow	d							21 06								21 36					
Burnham	d		←					21 09				←				21 39			←		
Slough 3	a		20 44		20 54			21 14	21 09			21 14		21 24		21 44	21 40		21 44		21 54
	d		20 44		20 54			21 14	21 09			21 14		21 24		21 44	21 40		21 44		21 54
Langley	d				20 58			↦						21 28		↦					21 58
Iver	d				21 01									21 31							22 01
West Drayton	d		20 51		21 05							21 21		21 35					21 51		22 05
Heathrow Terminal 4 ✈	d																				
Heathrow Terminal 1-2-3 2 ✈	d			20 57									21 27							21 57	
Hayes & Harlington	d		20 56	21 03	21 10							21 26	21 33	21 40					21 56	22 03	22 10
Southall	d			21 06	21 13								21 36	21 43						22 06	22 13
Hanwell	d			21 09									21 39							22 09	
Greenford ⊖	d	20 46									21 16							21 46			
South Greenford	d	20 49									21 19							21 49			
Castle Bar Park	d	20 52									21 22							21 52			
Drayton Green	d	20 54									21 24							21 54			
West Ealing	d	20 56		21 11							21 26		21 41					21 56		22 11	
Ealing Broadway ⊖	d	20 59	21 03	21 14	21 19						21 29	21 33	21 44	21 49				21 59	22 03	22 14	22 19
Acton Main Line	d	21 03									21 33							22 03			
London Paddington 15 ⊖	a	21 12	21 16	21 24	21 31	21 07	21 14		21 29	21 32	21 42	21 46	21 54	22 02	21 36		21 59	22 12	22 16	22 24	22 31

		GW	GW	GW	GW	HC	GW	GW	HC	GW	GW	GW	GW	HC	GW	GW	GW	GW
		1	◇1 ☕	◇1	◇1 ☕		1	◇1		1	1	◇1 ☕	◇1		1	◇1	◇1 ☕	1
Oxford	d			21 31				22 01		21 50			22 35			23 01		23 07
Reading 7	d	21 48	21 50	22 01	22 03		22 18	22 29		22 33	22 48	23 05	23 05		23 18	23 29	23 51	00 03
Twyford 3	d	21 54					22 24			22 39	22 54				23 24			00 09
Maidenhead 3	d	22 02					22 32			22 47	23 02				23 32			00 17
Taplow	d	22 06					22 36				23 06				23 36			00 21
Burnham	d	22 09					22 39				23 09				23 39			00 24
Slough 3	a	22 14		22 14			22 44	22 43		22 54	23 14		23 23		23 44	23 44		00 28
	d	22 14		22 15			22 44	22 44		22 54	23 14		23 24		23 44	23 44		00 29
Langley	d									22 58								00 33
Iver	d									23 01								00 36
West Drayton	d	22 21					22 51			23 05	23 21				23 51			00 39
Heathrow Terminal 4 ✈	d																	
Heathrow Terminal 1-2-3 2 ✈	d					22 27			22 57					23 27				
Hayes & Harlington	d	22 26				22 33	22 56		23 03	23 10	23 26			23 33	23 56			00 44
Southall	d					22 36			23 06	23 13				23 36				00 47
Hanwell	d					22 39			23 09					23 39				
Greenford ⊖	d																	
South Greenford	d																	
Castle Bar Park	d																	
Drayton Green	d																	
West Ealing	d					22 41			23 11					23 41				
Ealing Broadway ⊖	d	22 33				22 44	23 03		23 14	23 19	23 33			23 44	00 03			00 53
Acton Main Line	d																	
London Paddington 15 ⊖	a	22 46	22 16	22 32	22 37	22 54	23 16	23 02	23 24	23 28	23 46	23 36	23 43	23 54	00 16	00 10	00 34	01 02

Saturdays

7 January to 24 March

		GW	GW	GW	HC	GW	GW	GW	GW	GW	GW	HC	GW	HC	GW	GW	GW	HC	GW	GW	GW	HC
		1	1	◇1		◇1 ☕	1	◇1	1	1	1		1		1	1	1		1	1	1	
Oxford	d			23p09				00 07	00 27		03 59								05 14			
Reading 7	d	22p48	23p15	23p45		23p55	00 15	00 38	01 12	04 10	04 40		05 10		05 33		05 48		06 03		06 18	
Twyford 3	d	22p54	23p22				00 21		01 18	04 16	04 46		05 16		05 39		05 54		06 09		06 24	
Maidenhead 3	d	23p02	23p29	23p58			00 29		01 26	04 24	04 54		05 24		05 47		06 02		06 17		06 32	
Taplow	d	23p05	23p33				00 32						05 28				06 06				06 36	
Burnham	d	23p08	23p36				00 35						05 31				06 09				06 39	
Slough 3	a	23p13	23p41	00 05			00 40	00 55	01 34	04 31	05 01		05 35		05 54		06 14		06 24		06 44	
	d	23p27	23p41	00 05			00 40	00 56	01 34	04 32	05 02		05 36		05 54		06 14		06 24		06 44	
Langley	d	23p31	23p45				00 44						05 40		05 58				06 28			
Iver	d	23p34	23p48										05 43		06 01				06 31			
West Drayton	d	23p38	23p51				00 49			04 38			05 45		06 05		06 21		06 35		06 51	
Heathrow Terminal 4 ✈	d				00 01							05 23		05 51								
Heathrow Terminal 1-2-3 2 ✈	d				00 07							05 29		05 57				06 27				06 57
Hayes & Harlington	d	23p43	23p56		00 13		00 54		01 43	04 43	05 11	05 35	05 51	06 03	06 10		06 26	06 33	06 40		06 56	07 03
Southall	d	23p47	23p59		00 16		00 57			04 46	05 13	05 38	05 54	06 06	06 13			06 36	06 43			07 06
Hanwell	d											05 41		06 09				06 39				07 09
Greenford ⊖	d															06 16				06 46		
South Greenford	d															06 19				06 49		
Castle Bar Park	d															06 22				06 52		
Drayton Green	d															06 24				06 54		
West Ealing	d											05 43		06 11		06 26		06 41		06 56		07 11
Ealing Broadway ⊖	d	23p52	00 06		00 21		01 03		01 50	04 52	05 19	05 46	06 00	06 14	06 19	06 29	06 33	06 44	06 49	06 59	07 03	07 14
Acton Main Line	d										05 23		06 03			06 33				07 03		
London Paddington 15 ⊖	a	00 02	00 17	00 29	00 30	00 33	01 14	01 17	02 02	05 01	05 31	05 56	06 11	06 24	06 31	06 42	06 46	06 54	07 01	07 12	07 16	07 24

A The Night Riviera

Table 117

Saturdays

7 January to 24 March

Reading and Greenford - London

Network Diagram - see first Page of Table 116

		GW 1	GW ◇1 ☕	GW 1	GW 1	GW 1		GW ◇1	HC	GW 1	GW ◇1 ☕	GW 1	GW 1	GW ◇1	GW ◇1 ☕	GW 1		GW 1	HC	GW 1	GW ◇1 ☕	GW 1	GW ◇1 ☕	GW ◇1 ☕	GW 1
Oxford	d	05 49						06 31		06 07				07 01						06 42			07 31		
Reading 7	d	06 33	06 45		06 48	06 52		07 00		07 03	07 15	07 18	07 21	07 27	07 32					07 33	07 46	07 48	07 54	08 02	
Twyford 3	d	06 39			06 54					07 09		07 24								07 39		07 54			
Maidenhead 3	d	06 47			07 02					07 17		07 32								07 47		08 02			
Taplow	d				07 06							07 36										08 06			
Burnham	d				07 09							07 39						←				08 09			
Slough 3	a	06 54			07 14			07 16		07 24		07 44		07 42				07 44		07 54		08 14	08 09		
	d	06 54			07 14			07 17		07 24		07 44		07 42				07 44		07 54		08 14	08 09		
Langley	d	06 58								07 28		↪								07 58		↪			
Iver	d	07 01								07 31										08 01					
West Drayton	d	07 05			07 21					07 35								07 51		08 05					
Heathrow Terminal 4 ✈	d																								
Heathrow Terminal 1-2-3 2 ✈	d								07 27										07 57						
Hayes & Harlington	d	07 10			07 26				07 33	07 40								07 56	08 03	08 10					
Southall	d	07 13							07 36	07 43									08 06	08 13					
Hanwell	d								07 39										08 09						
Greenford ⊖	d			07 16												07 46									08 16
South Greenford	d			07 19												07 49									08 19
Castle Bar Park	d			07 22												07 52									08 22
Drayton Green	d			07 24												07 54									08 24
West Ealing	d			07 26					07 41							07 56			08 11						08 26
Ealing Broadway ⊖	d	07 19		07 29	07 33				07 44	07 49						07 59		08 03	08 14	08 19					08 29
Acton Main Line	d			07 33												08 03									08 33
London Paddington 15 ⊖	a	07 31	07 14	07 42	07 46	07 22		07 37	07 54	08 01	07 44		07 54	08 01	08 07	08 12		08 16	08 24	08 31	08 14		08 29	08 32	08 42

		GW 1		HC	GW 1		GW ◇1 ☕	GW 1	GW 1	GW ◇1	GW ◇1 ☕	GW 1		GW 1	HC	GW 1		GW ◇1 ☕	GW 1	GW ◇1 ☕	GW ◇1 ☕	GW ◇1 ☕		GW 1	GW 1
Oxford	d				07 07					08 01						07 37					08 31				
Reading 7	d				08 03		08 16	08 18	08 20	08 26	08 32					08 33		08 46	08 48	08 52	08 55	09 02			
Twyford 3	d				08 09			08 24								08 39			08 54						
Maidenhead 3	d				08 17			08 32								08 47			09 02						
Taplow	d							08 36											09 06						
Burnham	d	←						08 39						←					09 09						←
Slough 3	a	08 14			08 24			08 44		08 40				08 44		08 54			09 14		09 09				09 14
	d	08 14			08 24			08 44		08 41				08 44		08 54			09 14		09 11				09 14
Langley	d				08 28			↪								08 58			↪						
Iver	d				08 31											09 01									
West Drayton	d	08 21			08 35									08 51		09 05									09 21
Heathrow Terminal 4 ✈	d																								
Heathrow Terminal 1-2-3 2 ✈	d			08 27											08 57										
Hayes & Harlington	d	08 26		08 33	08 40									08 56	09 03	09 10									09 26
Southall	d			08 36	08 43										09 06	09 13									
Hanwell	d			08 39											09 09										
Greenford ⊖	d											08 46												09 16	
South Greenford	d											08 49												09 19	
Castle Bar Park	d											08 52												09 22	
Drayton Green	d											08 54												09 24	
West Ealing	d			08 41								08 56			09 11									09 26	
Ealing Broadway ⊖	d	08 33		08 44	08 49							08 59		09 03	09 14	09 19								09 29	09 33
Acton Main Line	d											09 03												09 33	
London Paddington 15 ⊖	a	08 46		08 54	09 01		08 44		08 52	08 59	09 02	09 12		09 16	09 24	09 31		09 14		09 21	09 29	09 32		09 42	09 46

		HC	GW 1		GW ◇1 ☕	GW ◇1 ☕	GW 1	GW 1		GW ◇1 ⊥o	GW ◇1 ☕	GW 1	GW 1	HC	GW 1	GW ◇1 ☕	GW ◇1 ☕	GW 1		GW ◇1 A ☕⊘	GW ◇1 ☕	GW 1	GW 1	HC	GW 1
Oxford	d		08 07							09 01					08 37					09 31					09 07
Reading 7	d		09 03		09 09	09 16	09 18	09 20		09 24	09 33				09 33	09 42	09 46	09 48		09 55	10 02				10 03
Twyford 3	d		09 09				09 24								09 39			09 54							10 09
Maidenhead 3	d		09 17				09 32								09 47			10 02							10 17
Taplow	d						09 36											10 06							
Burnham	d						09 39						←					10 09					←		
Slough 3	a		09 24				09 44			09 40			09 44		09 54			10 14		10 09			10 14		10 24
	d		09 24				09 44			09 40			09 44		09 54			10 14		10 10			10 14		10 24
Langley	d		09 28				↪								09 58			↪							10 28
Iver	d		09 31												10 01										10 31
West Drayton	d		09 35										09 51		10 05								10 21		10 35
Heathrow Terminal 4 ✈	d																								
Heathrow Terminal 1-2-3 2 ✈	d	09 27												09 57										10 27	
Hayes & Harlington	d	09 33	09 40										09 56	10 03	10 10								10 26	10 33	10 40
Southall	d	09 36	09 43											10 06	10 13									10 36	10 43
Hanwell	d	09 39												10 09										10 39	
Greenford ⊖	d											09 46										10 16			
South Greenford	d											09 49										10 19			
Castle Bar Park	d											09 52										10 22			
Drayton Green	d											09 54										10 24			
West Ealing	d	09 41										09 56		10 11								10 26		10 41	
Ealing Broadway ⊖	d	09 44	09 49									09 59	10 03	10 14	10 19							10 29	10 33	10 44	10 49
Acton Main Line	d											10 03										10 33			
London Paddington 15 ⊖	a	09 54	10 01		09 37	09 44		09 52		09 59	10 02	10 12	10 16	10 24	10 31	10 11	10 14			10 29	10 32	10 42	10 46	10 54	11 01

A ☕ from Reading ⊘ to Reading

Table 117

7 January to 24 March

Reading and Greenford - London

Network Diagram - see first Page of Table 116

		GW	GW	GW	GW	GW	GW	GW	HC	GW	GW	GW	GW	GW	GW	GW	GW	GW	HC	GW
		◇1 ☕	1	1	◇1 🍴	◇1 ☕	1	1		1	◇1 ☕	◇1 ☕	1	◇1 ☕	◇1 ☕	◇1 ☕	1	1		1
Oxford	d				10 01					09 37					10 31					10 07
Reading 7	d	10 13	10 18	10 18	10 25	10 33				10 33	10 39	10 46	10 48	10 53	10 55	11 02				11 03
Twyford 3	d			10 24						10 39			10 54							11 09
Maidenhead 3	d			10 32						10 47			11 02							11 17
Taplow	d			10 36									11 06							
Burnham	d			10 39				←					11 09					←		
Slough 3	a			10 44	10 40			10 44		10 54			11 14		11 09			11 14		11 24
	d			10 44	10 40			10 44		10 54			11 14		11 10			11 14		11 24
Langley	d			→						10 58			→							11 28
Iver	d									11 01										11 31
West Drayton	d							10 51		11 05								11 21		11 35
Heathrow Terminal 4 ✈	d																			
Heathrow Terminal 1-2-3 2 ✈	d								10 57										11 27	
Hayes & Harlington	d							10 56	11 03	11 10								11 26	11 33	11 40
Southall	d								11 06	11 13									11 36	11 43
Hanwell	d								11 09										11 39	
Greenford ⊖	d						10 46										11 16			
South Greenford	d						10 49										11 19			
Castle Bar Park	d						10 52										11 22			
Drayton Green	d						10 54										11 24			
West Ealing	d						10 56		11 11								11 26		11 41	
Ealing Broadway ⊖	d						10 59	11 03	11 14	11 19							11 29	11 33	11 44	11 49
Acton Main Line	d						11 03										11 33			
London Paddington 15 ⊖	a	10 39	10 52		10 59	11 02	11 12	11 16	11 24	11 31	11 08	11 14		11 24	11 29	11 33	11 42	11 46	11 54	12 01

		GW	GW	GW	GW	GW	GW	HC	GW	GW	GW	GW	GW	GW	GW	GW	HC	GW	GW	GW	GW
		◇1 ☕	1	1	◇1	1	1		1	◇1 ☕	1	1 ☕	◇1 🍴	◇1 ☕	1	1		1	◇1 ☕	1	1
Oxford	d				11 01				10 37				11 31					11 07			
Reading 7	d	11 14	11 18	11 21	11 25				11 33	11 45	11 48	11 53	11 55	12 02				12 03	12 13	12 18	12 18
Twyford 3	d		11 24						11 39		11 54							12 09			12 24
Maidenhead 3	d		11 32						11 47		12 02							12 17			12 32
Taplow	d		11 36								12 06										12 36
Burnham	d		11 39				←				12 09					←					12 39
Slough 3	a		11 44		11 39		11 44		11 54		12 14		12 09			12 14		12 24			12 44
	d		11 44		11 40		11 44		11 54		12 14		12 11			12 14		12 24			12 44
Langley	d		→						11 58		→							12 28			→
Iver	d								12 01									12 31			
West Drayton	d						11 51		12 05							12 21		12 35			
Heathrow Terminal 4 ✈	d																				
Heathrow Terminal 1-2-3 2 ✈	d							11 57									12 27				
Hayes & Harlington	d						11 56	12 03	12 10							12 26	12 33	12 40			
Southall	d							12 06	12 13								12 36	12 43			
Hanwell	d							12 09									12 39				
Greenford ⊖	d					11 46									12 16						
South Greenford	d					11 49									12 19						
Castle Bar Park	d					11 52									12 22						
Drayton Green	d					11 54									12 24						
West Ealing	d					11 56		12 11							12 26		12 41				
Ealing Broadway ⊖	d					11 59	12 03	12 14	12 19						12 29	12 33	12 44	12 49			
Acton Main Line	d					12 03									12 33						
London Paddington 15 ⊖	a	11 40		11 52	11 59	12 12	12 16	12 24	12 31	12 14		12 23	12 29	12 32	12 42	12 46	12 54	13 01	12 39	12 52	

		GW	GW	GW	HC	GW	GW	GW	GW	GW	GW	GW	GW	GW	HC	GW	GW	GW	GW	GW	GW
		◇1 🍴	1	1		1	◇1 ☕	◇1 ☕	1	◇1 ☕	◇1 🍴	◇1 ☕	1	1		1	◇1 ☕	1	◇1 ☕	◇1 🍴	1
Oxford	d	12 01				11 37					12 31					12 07				13 01	
Reading 7	d	12 25				12 33	12 39	12 45	12 48	12 54	12 55	13 02				13 03	13 12	13 18	13 20	13 25	
Twyford 3	d					12 39			12 54							13 09		13 24			
Maidenhead 3	d					12 47			13 02							13 17		13 32			
Taplow	d								13 06									13 36			
Burnham	d			←					13 09					←				13 39			
Slough 3	a	12 40		12 44		12 54			13 14		13 09			13 14		13 24		13 44		13 40	
	d	12 40		12 44		12 54			13 14		13 11			13 14		13 24		13 44		13 40	
Langley	d					12 58			→							13 28		→			
Iver	d					13 01										13 31					
West Drayton	d			12 51		13 05								13 21		13 35					
Heathrow Terminal 4 ✈	d																				
Heathrow Terminal 1-2-3 2 ✈	d				12 57										13 27						
Hayes & Harlington	d			12 56	13 03	13 10								13 26	13 33	13 40					
Southall	d				13 06	13 13									13 36	13 43					
Hanwell	d				13 09										13 39						
Greenford ⊖	d		12 46										13 16								13 46
South Greenford	d		12 49										13 19								13 49
Castle Bar Park	d		12 52										13 22								13 52
Drayton Green	d		12 54										13 24								13 54
West Ealing	d		12 56		13 11								13 26		13 41						13 56
Ealing Broadway ⊖	d		12 59	13 03	13 14	13 19							13 29	13 33	13 44	13 49					13 59
Acton Main Line	d		13 03										13 33								14 03
London Paddington 15 ⊖	a	12 59	13 12	13 16	13 24	13 31	13 07	13 12		13 21	13 30	13 33	13 42	13 46	13 54	14 01	13 41		13 46	13 59	14 12

Table 117

Saturdays

7 January to 24 March

Reading and Greenford - London

Network Diagram - see first Page of Table 116

		GW 1		HC	GW 1	GW ◇1 ☕	GW 1	GW 1	GW ◇1	GW ◇1 ☕	GW 1	GW 1		HC	GW 1		GW ◇1 ☕	GW 1	GW ◇1 ☕	GW ◇1 trolley	GW 1	GW 1		HC	GW 1
Oxford	d				12 37				13 31						13 07					14 01					13 37
Reading 7	d				13 33	13 45	13 48	13 51	13 55	14 02					14 03		14 13	14 18	14 19	14 25					14 33
Twyford 3	d				13 39		13 54								14 09			14 24							14 39
Maidenhead 3	d				13 47		14 02								14 17			14 32							14 47
Taplow	d						14 06											14 36							
Burnham	d	←					14 09					←						14 39				←			
Slough 3	a	13 44			13 54		14 14		14 09			14 14			14 24			14 44		14 40		14 44			14 54
	d	13 44			13 54		14 14		14 10			14 14			14 24			14 44		14 40		14 44			14 54
Langley	d				13 58		→								14 28			→							14 58
Iver	d				14 01										14 31										15 01
West Drayton	d	13 51			14 05							14 21			14 35							14 51			15 05
Heathrow Terminal 4 ✈	d																								
Heathrow Terminal 1-2-3 2 ✈	d			13 57										14 27										14 57	
Hayes & Harlington	d	13 56		14 03	14 10							14 26		14 33	14 40							14 56		15 03	15 10
Southall	d			14 06	14 13									14 36	14 43									15 06	15 13
Hanwell	d			14 09										14 39										15 09	
Greenford ⊖	d										14 16										14 46				
South Greenford	d										14 19										14 49				
Castle Bar Park	d										14 22										14 52				
Drayton Green	d										14 24										14 54				
West Ealing	d			14 11							14 26			14 41							14 56			15 11	
Ealing Broadway ⊖	d	14 03		14 14	14 19						14 29	14 33		14 44	14 49						14 59	15 03		15 14	15 19
Acton Main Line	d										14 33										15 03				
London Paddington 15 ⊖	a	14 16		14 24	14 31	14 14		14 23	14 29	14 32	14 42	14 46		14 54	15 01		14 39		14 45	14 59	15 12	15 16		15 24	15 31

			GW ◇1 ☕	GW ◇1 ☕	GW 1	GW ◇1 ☕	GW ◇1 A ☕	GW ◇1 A ☕		GW 1	GW 1	HC	GW 1		GW ◇1 B ☕	GW 1	GW 1	GW ◇1		GW 1	GW 1	HC	GW 1	GW ◇1 ☕	GW 1
Oxford	d						14 31						14 07					15 01					14 37		
Reading 7	d		14 39	14 45	14 48	14 53	14 55	15 02					15 03		15 12	15 18	15 19	15 25					15 33	15 45	15 48
Twyford 3	d				14 54								15 09			15 24							15 39		15 54
Maidenhead 3	d				15 02								15 17			15 32							15 47		16 02
Taplow	d				15 06											15 36									16 06
Burnham	d				15 09						←					15 39					←				16 09
Slough 3	a				15 14		15 10				15 14		15 24			15 44		15 40			15 44		15 54		16 14
	d				15 14		15 11				15 14		15 24			15 44		15 40			15 44		15 54		16 14
Langley	d				→								15 28			→							15 58		→
Iver	d												15 31										16 01		
West Drayton	d										15 21		15 35								15 51		16 05		
Heathrow Terminal 4 ✈	d																								
Heathrow Terminal 1-2-3 2 ✈	d											15 27										15 57			
Hayes & Harlington	d										15 26	15 33	15 40								15 56	16 03	16 10		
Southall	d											15 36	15 43									16 06	16 13		
Hanwell	d											15 39										16 09			
Greenford ⊖	d									15 16										15 46					
South Greenford	d									15 19										15 49					
Castle Bar Park	d									15 22										15 52					
Drayton Green	d									15 24										15 54					
West Ealing	d									15 26		15 41								15 56		16 11			
Ealing Broadway ⊖	d									15 29	15 33	15 44	15 49							15 59	16 03	16 14	16 19		
Acton Main Line	d									15 33										16 03					
London Paddington 15 ⊖	a		15 09	15 14		15 22	15 29	15 32		15 42	15 46	15 54	16 01		15 39		15 54	15 59		16 12	16 16	16 24	16 31	16 14	

		GW ◇1 ☕	GW ◇1 trolley	GW ◇1 ☕		GW 1	GW 1	HC	GW 1		GW ◇1 ☕	GW 1	GW 1	GW ◇1		GW 1	GW 1	HC	GW 1		GW ◇1 ☕	GW ◇1 ☕	GW 1	GW ◇1 ☕	
Oxford	d		15 31						15 07					16 01					15 37						
Reading 7	d	15 53	15 55	16 01					16 03		16 13	16 18	16 18	16 26					16 33		16 39	16 45	16 48	16 51	
Twyford 3	d								16 09				16 24						16 39				16 54		
Maidenhead 3	d								16 17				16 32						16 47				17 02		
Taplow	d												16 36										17 06		
Burnham	d						←						16 39				←						17 09		
Slough 3	a		16 10				16 14		16 24				16 44	16 40			16 44		16 54				17 14		
	d		16 11				16 14		16 24				16 44	16 41			16 44		16 54				17 14		
Langley	d								16 28				→						16 58				→		
Iver	d								16 31										17 01						
West Drayton	d						16 21		16 35								16 51		17 05						
Heathrow Terminal 4 ✈	d																								
Heathrow Terminal 1-2-3 2 ✈	d							16 27										16 57							
Hayes & Harlington	d						16 26	16 33	16 40								16 56	17 03	17 10						
Southall	d							16 36	16 43									17 06	17 13						
Hanwell	d							16 39										17 09							
Greenford ⊖	d					16 16										16 46									
South Greenford	d					16 19										16 49									
Castle Bar Park	d					16 22										16 52									
Drayton Green	d					16 24										16 54									
West Ealing	d					16 26		16 41								16 56		17 11							
Ealing Broadway ⊖	d					16 29	16 33	16 44	16 49							16 59	17 03	17 14	17 19						
Acton Main Line	d					16 33										17 03									
London Paddington 15 ⊖	a	16 23	16 29	16 32		16 42	16 46	16 54	17 01		16 39	16 52		16 59		17 12	17 16	17 24	17 31		17 07	17 14		17 21	

A from 7 January until 11 February

B from 7 January until 4 February, 24 March

Table 117

Reading and Greenford - London

Saturdays

7 January to 24 March

Network Diagram - see first Page of Table 116

		GW	GW	GW	GW	HC	GW	GW	GW	GW	GW	GW	GW	HC	GW	GW	GW	GW	GW	GW	GW	GW
		◇1	◇1	1	1		1	◇1	◇1	1	◇1	1	1		1	◇1	1	◇1	◇1	◇1	1	1
																		A		A		
		🍴	☕					☕	☕							☕		☕	☕	☕		
Oxford	d	16 31					16 07				17 01				16 37				17 31			
Reading 7	d	16 55	17 02				17 03	17 12	17 18	17 18	17 27				17 33	17 45	17 48	17 54	17 57	18 02		
Twyford 3	d						17 09			17 24					17 39		17 54					
Maidenhead 3	d						17 17			17 32					17 47		18 02					
Taplow	d									17 36							18 06					
Burnham	d				←					17 39			←				18 09					←
Slough 3	a	17 10			17 14		17 24			17 44	17 41		17 44		17 54		18 14		18 10			18 14
	d	17 11			17 14		17 24			17 44	17 42		17 44		17 54		18 14		18 11			18 14
Langley	d						17 28			→					17 58		→					
Iver	d						17 31								18 01							
West Drayton	d				17 21		17 35						17 51		18 05							18 21
Heathrow Terminal 4 ✈	d																					
Heathrow Terminal 1-2-3 2 ✈	d					17 27								17 57								
Hayes & Harlington	d				17 26	17 33	17 40						17 56	18 03	18 10							18 26
Southall	d					17 36	17 43							18 06	18 13							
Hanwell	d					17 39								18 09								
Greenford ⊖	d			17 16								17 46									18 16	
South Greenford	d			17 19								17 49									18 19	
Castle Bar Park	d			17 22								17 52									18 22	
Drayton Green	d			17 24								17 54									18 24	
West Ealing	d			17 26		17 41						17 56		18 11							18 26	
Ealing Broadway ⊖	d			17 29	17 33	17 44	17 49					17 59	18 03	18 14	18 19						18 29	18 33
Acton Main Line	d			17 33								18 03									18 33	
London Paddington 15 ⊖	a	17 29	17 32	17 42	17 46	17 54	18 01	17 38	17 51		18 00	18 12	18 16	18 24	18 31	18 14		18 21	18 29	18 32	18 42	18 46

		HC	GW	GW	GW	GW	GW	GW	GW	HC	GW	GW	GW	GW	GW	GW	GW	GW	GW	HC	GW
			1	◇1	1	1	◇1	1	1		1	◇1	◇1	1	◇1	◇1	◇1	1	1		1
				A											A	A					
				☕								☕	☕		☕	🍴	☕				
Oxford	d		17 07				18 01				17 37					18 31					18 07
Reading 7	d		18 03	18 13	18 18	18 19	18 25				18 33	18 39	18 45	18 48	18 50	18 56	19 02				19 03
Twyford 3	d		18 09		18 24						18 39			18 54							19 09
Maidenhead 3	d		18 17		18 32						18 47			19 02							19 17
Taplow	d				18 36									19 06							
Burnham	d				18 39				←					19 09					←		
Slough 3	a		18 24		18 44		18 40		18 44		18 54			19 14		19 10			19 14		19 24
	d		18 24		18 44		18 40		18 44		18 54			19 14		19 11			19 14		19 24
Langley	d		18 28		→						18 58			→							19 28
Iver	d		18 31								19 01										19 31
West Drayton	d		18 35						18 51		19 05								19 21		19 35
Heathrow Terminal 4 ✈	d																				
Heathrow Terminal 1-2-3 2 ✈	d	18 27								18 57										19 27	
Hayes & Harlington	d	18 33	18 40						18 56	19 03	19 10								19 26	19 33	19 40
Southall	d	18 36	18 43							19 06	19 13									19 36	19 43
Hanwell	d	18 39								19 09										19 39	
Greenford ⊖	d							18 46										19 16			
South Greenford	d							18 49										19 19			
Castle Bar Park	d							18 52										19 22			
Drayton Green	d							18 54										19 24			
West Ealing	d	18 41						18 56		19 11								19 26		19 41	
Ealing Broadway ⊖	d	18 44	18 49					18 59	19 03	19 14	19 19							19 29	19 33	19 44	19 49
Acton Main Line	d							19 03										19 33			
London Paddington 15 ⊖	a	18 54	19 01	18 39		18 52	18 59	19 12	19 16	19 24	19 31	19 08	19 14		19 22	19 29	19 32	19 42	19 46	19 54	20 01

		GW	GW	GW	GW	GW	GW	HC	GW	GW	GW	GW	GW	GW	GW	HC	GW	GW	GW	GW
		◇1	1	1	◇1	1	1		1	◇1	1	◇1	◇1	1	1		1	◇1	1	◇1
				A						A										
		☕								☕		🍴	☕					☕		
Oxford	d				19 01				18 37			19 31					19 07			20 01
Reading 7	d	19 12	19 18	19 20	19 25				19 33	19 45	19 48	19 55	20 03				20 03	20 09	20 18	20 25
Twyford 3	d		19 24						19 39		19 54						20 09		20 24	
Maidenhead 3	d		19 32						19 47		20 02						20 17		20 32	
Taplow	d		19 36								20 06								20 36	
Burnham	d		19 39				←				20 09				←				20 39	
Slough 3	a		19 44		19 40		19 44		19 54		20 14	20 10			20 14		20 24		20 44	20 40
	d		19 44		19 40		19 44		19 54		20 14	20 10			20 14		20 24		20 44	20 40
Langley	d		→						19 58		→						20 28		→	
Iver	d								20 01								20 31			
West Drayton	d						19 51		20 05						20 21		20 35			
Heathrow Terminal 4 ✈	d																			
Heathrow Terminal 1-2-3 2 ✈	d							19 57								20 27				
Hayes & Harlington	d						19 56	20 03	20 10						20 26	20 33	20 40			
Southall	d							20 06	20 13							20 36	20 43			
Hanwell	d							20 09								20 39				
Greenford ⊖	d					19 46								20 16						
South Greenford	d					19 49								20 19						
Castle Bar Park	d					19 52								20 22						
Drayton Green	d					19 54								20 24						
West Ealing	d					19 56		20 11						20 26		20 41				
Ealing Broadway ⊖	d					19 59	20 03	20 14	20 19					20 29	20 33	20 44	20 49			
Acton Main Line	d					20 03								20 33						
London Paddington 15 ⊖	a	19 39		19 52	19 59	20 12	20 16	20 24	20 31	20 14		20 29	20 32	20 42	20 46	20 54	21 01	20 37		20 59

A from 7 January until 11 February

Table 117

Saturdays

7 January to 24 March

Reading and Greenford - London

Network Diagram - see first Page of Table 116

		GW	GW	HC	GW	GW	GW	GW	GW	GW	GW	HC	GW	GW	GW	GW	GW	GW	GW	HC	GW
		1	1		1	◇1 ☕	◇1 ☕	1	◇1	1	1		1	◇1 ☕	◇1 ☕	1	◇1	1	1		1
Oxford	d				19 37				20 31				20 07				20 59				20 53
Reading 7	d				20 33	20 39	20 45	20 48	20 54				20 59	21 01	21 08	21 18	21 25				21 37
Twyford 3	d				20 39			20 54					21 05			21 24					21 43
Maidenhead 3	d				20 47			21 02					21 13			21 32					21 51
Taplow	d							21 06								21 36					
Burnham	d		←					21 09			←					21 39			←		
Slough 3	a		20 44		20 54			21 14	21 09		21 14		21 20			21 44	21 40		21 44		21 58
	d		20 44		20 54			21 14	21 09		21 14		21 24			21 44	21 40		21 44		21 58
Langley	d				20 58			↦					21 28			↦					22 02
Iver	d				21 01								21 31								22 05
West Drayton	d		20 51		21 05						21 21		21 35						21 51		22 09
Heathrow Terminal 4 ✈	d																				
Heathrow Terminal 1-2-3 2 ✈	d			20 57								21 27								21 57	
Hayes & Harlington	d		20 56	21 03	21 10						21 26	21 33	21 40						21 56	22 03	22 14
Southall	d			21 06	21 13							21 36	21 43							22 06	22 17
Hanwell	d			21 09								21 39								22 09	
Greenford ⊖	d	20 46								21 16								21 46			
South Greenford	d	20 49								21 19								21 49			
Castle Bar Park	d	20 52								21 22								21 52			
Drayton Green	d	20 54								21 24								21 54			
West Ealing	d	20 56		21 11						21 26		21 41						21 56		22 11	
Ealing Broadway ⊖	d	20 59	21 03	21 14	21 19					21 29	21 33	21 44	21 49					21 59	22 03	22 14	22 23
Acton Main Line	d	21 03								21 33								22 03			
London Paddington 15 ⊖	a	21 12	21 16	21 24	21 31	21 07	21 14		21 29	21 42	21 46	21 54	22 02	21 32	21 36		21 59	22 12	22 16	22 24	22 32

		GW	GW	GW	GW	HC	GW	GW	GW	HC	GW	GW	GW	GW	HC	GW	GW	GW	GW
		1	◇1 ☕	◇1	◇1 ☕		1	1	◇1		1	1	◇1 ☕	◇1		1	◇1	◇1 ☕	1
Oxford	d			21 31				21 50	22 10					22 35			23 01		23 13
Reading 7	d	21 48	21 54	22 00	22 03		22 18	22 33	22 38			22 48	23 05	23 09		23 18	23 29	23 51	00 06
Twyford 3	d	21 54					22 24	22 40				22 54				23 24			00 13
Maidenhead 3	d	22 02					22 32	22 47				23 02				23 32			00 21
Taplow	d	22 06					22 36					23 06				23 36			00 25
Burnham	d	22 09					22 39				←	23 09				23 39			00 28
Slough 3	a	22 14		22 13			22 44	22 54	22 52		22 54	23 14		23 26		23 44	23 44		00 32
	d	22 14		22 14			22 44	22 54	22 53		22 54	23 14		23 27		23 44	23 44		00 33
Langley	d							↦			22 58								00 37
Iver	d										23 01								00 40
West Drayton	d	22 21					22 51				23 05	23 21				23 51			00 43
Heathrow Terminal 4 ✈	d																		
Heathrow Terminal 1-2-3 2 ✈	d					22 27				22 57					23 27				
Hayes & Harlington	d	22 26				22 33	22 56			23 03	23 10	23 26			23 33	23 56			00 50
Southall	d					22 36				23 06	23 13				23 36				00 53
Hanwell	d					22 39				23 09					23 39				
Greenford ⊖	d																		
South Greenford	d																		
Castle Bar Park	d																		
Drayton Green	d																		
West Ealing	d					22 41				23 11					23 41				
Ealing Broadway ⊖	d	22 33				22 44	23 03			23 14	23 19	23 33			23 44	00 03			00 59
Acton Main Line	d																		
London Paddington 15 ⊖	a	22 46	22 22	22 31	22 38	22 54	23 16		23 11	23 24	23 29	23 46	23 36	23 46	23 54	00 16	00 10	00 34	01 08

Saturdays

from 31 March

		GW	GW	GW	HC	GW	GW	GW	GW	GW	GW	HC	GW	HC	GW	GW	GW	HC	GW	GW	GW	HC
		1	1	◇1		◇1 ☕	1	◇1	1	1	1		1		1	1	1		1	1	1	
Oxford	d			23p09				00 07	00 27		03 59								05 14			
Reading 7	d	22p48	23p15	23p45		23p55	00 15	00 38	01 12	04 10	04 40		05 10		05 33		05 48		06 03		06 18	
Twyford 3	d	22p54	23p22				00 21		01 18	04 16	04 46		05 16		05 39		05 54		06 09		06 24	
Maidenhead 3	d	23p02	23p29	23p58			00 29		01 26	04 24	04 54		05 24		05 47		06 02		06 17		06 32	
Taplow	d	23p05	23p33				00 32						05 28				06 06				06 36	
Burnham	d	23p08	23p36				00 35						05 31				06 09				06 39	
Slough 3	a	23p13	23p41	00 05			00 40	00 55	01 34	04 31	05 01		05 35		05 54		06 14		06 24		06 44	
	d	23p27	23p41	00 05			00 40	00 56	01 34	04 32	05 02		05 36		05 54		06 14		06 24		06 44	
Langley	d	23p31	23p45				00 44						05 40		05 58				06 28			
Iver	d	23p34	23p48										05 43		06 01				06 31			
West Drayton	d	23p38	23p51				00 49			04 38			05 45		06 05		06 21		06 35		06 51	
Heathrow Terminal 4 ✈	d				00 01							05 23		05 51								
Heathrow Terminal 1-2-3 2 ✈	d				00 07							05 29		05 57				06 27				06 57
Hayes & Harlington	d	23p43	23p56		00 13		00 54		01 43	04 43	05 11	05 35	05 51	06 03	06 10		06 26	06 33	06 40		06 56	07 03
Southall	d	23p47	23p59		00 16		00 57			04 46	05 13	05 38	05 54	06 06	06 13			06 36	06 43			07 06
Hanwell	d											05 41		06 09				06 39				07 09
Greenford ⊖	d															06 16				06 46		
South Greenford	d															06 19				06 49		
Castle Bar Park	d															06 22				06 52		
Drayton Green	d															06 24				06 54		
West Ealing	d											05 43		06 11		06 26		06 41		06 56		07 11
Ealing Broadway ⊖	d	23p52	00 06		00 21		01 03		01 50	04 52	05 19	05 46	06 00	06 14	06 19	06 29	06 33	06 44	06 49	06 59	07 03	07 14
Acton Main Line	d										05 23		06 03			06 33				07 03		
London Paddington 15 ⊖	a	00 02	00 17	00 29	00 30	00 33	01 14	01 17	02 02	05 01	05 31	05 56	06 11	06 24	06 31	06 42	06 46	06 54	07 01	07 12	07 16	07 24

A The Night Riviera

Table 117

Saturdays
from 31 March

Reading and Greenford - London

Network Diagram - see first Page of Table 116

		GW	GW	GW	GW	GW		GW	HC	GW	GW	GW	GW	GW	GW	GW		GW	HC	GW	GW	GW	GW	GW	GW
		1	◇1	1	1	1		◇1		1	◇1	1	1	◇1	◇1	1		1		1	◇1	1	◇1	◇1	1
			☕								☕				☕						☕		☕	☕	
Oxford	d	05 49						06 31		06 07				07 01						06 42			07 31		
Reading 7	d	06 33	06 45		06 48	06 52		07 00		07 03	07 15	07 18	07 21	07 27	07 32					07 33	07 46	07 48	07 54	08 02	
Twyford 3	d	06 39			06 54					07 09		07 24								07 39		07 54			
Maidenhead 3	d	06 47			07 02					07 17		07 32								07 47		08 02			
Taplow	d				07 06							07 36										08 06			
Burnham	d				07 09							07 39						←				08 09			
Slough 3	a	06 54			07 14			07 16		07 24		07 44		07 42				07 44		07 54		08 14	08 09		
	d	06 54			07 14			07 17		07 24		07 44		07 42				07 44		07 54		08 14	08 09		
Langley	d	06 58								07 28		→								07 58		→			
Iver	d	07 01								07 31										08 01					
West Drayton	d	07 05			07 21					07 35								07 51		08 05					
Heathrow Terminal 4 ✈	d																								
Heathrow Terminal 1-2-3 2 ✈	d								07 27										07 57						
Hayes & Harlington	d	07 10			07 26				07 33	07 40								07 56	08 03	08 10					
Southall	d	07 13							07 36	07 43									08 06	08 13					
Hanwell	d								07 39										08 09						
Greenford ⊖	d			07 16												07 46									08 16
South Greenford	d			07 19												07 49									08 19
Castle Bar Park	d			07 22												07 52									08 22
Drayton Green	d			07 24												07 54									08 24
West Ealing	d			07 26					07 41							07 56			08 11						08 26
Ealing Broadway ⊖	d	07 19		07 29	07 33				07 44	07 49						07 59		08 03	08 14	08 19					08 29
Acton Main Line	d			07 33												08 03									08 33
London Paddington 15 ⊖	a	07 31	07 14	07 42	07 46	07 22		07 37	07 54	08 01	07 44		07 54	08 01	08 07	08 12		08 16	08 24	08 31	08 14		08 29	08 32	08 42

		GW		HC	GW		GW	GW	GW	GW	GW	GW		GW	HC	GW		GW	GW	GW	GW	GW		GW	GW
		1			1		◇1	1	1	◇1	◇1	1		1		1		◇1	1	◇1	◇1	◇1		1	1
							☕				☕							☕		☕	☕	☕			
Oxford	d				07 07					08 01						07 37					08 31				
Reading 7	d				08 03		08 16	08 18	08 20	08 26	08 32					08 33		08 46	08 48	08 52	08 55	09 02			
Twyford 3	d				08 09			08 24								08 39			08 54						
Maidenhead 3	d				08 17			08 32								08 47			09 02						
Taplow	d							08 36											09 06						
Burnham	d	←						08 39						←					09 09						←
Slough 3	a	08 14			08 24			08 44		08 40				08 44		08 54			09 14		09 09				09 14
	d	08 14			08 24			08 44		08 41				08 44		08 54			09 14		09 11				09 14
Langley	d				08 28			→								08 58			→						
Iver	d				08 31											09 01									
West Drayton	d	08 21			08 35									08 51		09 05									09 21
Heathrow Terminal 4 ✈	d																								
Heathrow Terminal 1-2-3 2 ✈	d			08 27											08 57										
Hayes & Harlington	d	08 26		08 33	08 40									08 56	09 03	09 10									09 26
Southall	d			08 36	08 43										09 06	09 13									
Hanwell	d			08 39											09 09										
Greenford ⊖	d											08 46												09 16	
South Greenford	d											08 49												09 19	
Castle Bar Park	d											08 52												09 22	
Drayton Green	d											08 54												09 24	
West Ealing	d			08 41								08 56			09 11									09 26	
Ealing Broadway ⊖	d	08 33		08 44	08 49							08 59		09 03	09 14	09 19								09 29	09 33
Acton Main Line	d											09 03												09 33	
London Paddington 15 ⊖	a	08 46		08 54	09 01		08 44		08 52	08 59	09 02	09 12		09 16	09 24	09 31		09 14		09 21	09 29	09 32		09 42	09 46

		HC	GW		GW	GW	GW	GW		GW	GW	GW	GW	HC	GW	GW	GW	GW		GW	GW	GW	GW	HC	GW
			1		◇1	◇1	1	1		◇1	◇1	1	1		1	◇1	◇1	1		◇1	◇1	1	1		1
																				A					
					☕	☕				🍴	☕					☕	☕			☕⊘	☕				
Oxford	d		08 07							09 01					08 37					09 31					09 07
Reading 7	d		09 03		09 09	09 16	09 18	09 20		09 24	09 33				09 33	09 42	09 46	09 48		09 55	10 02				10 03
Twyford 3	d		09 09				09 24								09 39			09 54							10 09
Maidenhead 3	d		09 17				09 32								09 47			10 02							10 17
Taplow	d						09 36											10 06							
Burnham	d						09 39						←					10 09					←		
Slough 3	a		09 24				09 44			09 40			09 44		09 54			10 14		10 09			10 14		10 24
	d		09 24				09 44			09 40			09 44		09 54			10 14		10 10			10 14		10 24
Langley	d		09 28				→								09 58			→							10 28
Iver	d		09 31												10 01										10 31
West Drayton	d		09 35										09 51		10 05								10 21		10 35
Heathrow Terminal 4 ✈	d																								
Heathrow Terminal 1-2-3 2 ✈	d	09 27												09 57										10 27	
Hayes & Harlington	d	09 33	09 40										09 56	10 03	10 10								10 26	10 33	10 40
Southall	d	09 36	09 43											10 06	10 13									10 36	10 43
Hanwell	d	09 39												10 09										10 39	
Greenford ⊖	d											09 46										10 16			
South Greenford	d											09 49										10 19			
Castle Bar Park	d											09 52										10 22			
Drayton Green	d											09 54										10 24			
West Ealing	d	09 41										09 56		10 11								10 26		10 41	
Ealing Broadway ⊖	d	09 44	09 49									09 59	10 03	10 14	10 19							10 29	10 33	10 44	10 49
Acton Main Line	d											10 03										10 33			
London Paddington 15 ⊖	a	09 54	10 01		09 37	09 44		09 52		09 59	10 02	10 12	10 16	10 24	10 31	10 11	10 14			10 29	10 32	10 42	10 46	10 54	11 01

A ☕ from Reading ⊘ to Reading

Table 117

Saturdays

from 31 March

Reading and Greenford - London

Network Diagram - see first Page of Table 116

	GW	GW	GW	GW	GW	GW	GW	HC	GW	GW	GW	GW	GW	GW	GW	GW	GW	HC	GW
	◇1 ☕	1	1	◇1 🍴	◇1 ☕	1	1		1	◇1 ☕	◇1 ☕	1	◇1 ☕	◇1 ☕	◇1 ☕	1	1		1
Oxford d				10 01					09 37					10 31					10 07
Reading 7 d	10 13	10 18	10 18	10 25	10 33				10 33	10 39	10 46	10 48	10 53	10 55	11 02				11 03
Twyford 3 d			10 24						10 39			10 54							11 09
Maidenhead 3 d			10 32						10 47			11 02							11 17
Taplow d			10 36									11 06							
Burnham d			10 39				←					11 09					←		
Slough 3 a			10 44	10 40			10 44		10 54			11 14		11 09			11 14		11 24
d			10 44	10 40			10 44		10 54			11 14		11 10			11 14		11 24
Langley d			↳						10 58			↳							11 28
Iver d									11 01										11 31
West Drayton d							10 51		11 05								11 21		11 35
Heathrow Terminal 4 ✈ d																			
Heathrow Terminal 1-2-3 2 ✈ d								10 57										11 27	
Hayes & Harlington d							10 56	11 03	11 10								11 26	11 33	11 40
Southall d								11 06	11 13									11 36	11 43
Hanwell d								11 09										11 39	
Greenford ⊖ d						10 46										11 16			
South Greenford d						10 49										11 19			
Castle Bar Park d						10 52										11 22			
Drayton Green d						10 54										11 24			
West Ealing d						10 56		11 11								11 26		11 41	
Ealing Broadway ⊖ d						10 59	11 03	11 14	11 19							11 29	11 33	11 44	11 49
Acton Main Line d						11 03										11 33			
London Paddington 15 ⊖ a	10 39	10 52		10 59	11 02	11 12	11 16	11 24	11 31	11 08	11 14		11 24	11 29	11 33	11 42	11 46	11 54	12 01

	GW	GW	GW	GW	GW	GW	HC	GW	GW	GW	GW	GW	GW	GW	GW	HC	GW	GW	GW	GW
	◇1 ☕	1	1	◇1	1	1		1	◇1 ☕	1	R 1 ☕	◇1 🍴	◇1 ☕	1	1		1	◇1 ☕	1	1
Oxford d				11 01				10 37				11 31					11 07			
Reading 7 d	11 14	11 18	11 21	11 25				11 33	11 45	11 48	11 53	11 55	12 02				12 03	12 13	12 18	12 18
Twyford 3 d		11 24						11 39		11 54							12 09			12 24
Maidenhead 3 d		11 32						11 47		12 02							12 17			12 32
Taplow d		11 36								12 06										12 36
Burnham d		11 39				←				12 09					←					12 39
Slough 3 a		11 44		11 39		11 44		11 54		12 14		12 09			12 14		12 24			12 44
d		11 44		11 40		11 44		11 54		12 14		12 11			12 14		12 24			12 44
Langley d		↳						11 58		↳							12 28			↳
Iver d								12 01									12 31			
West Drayton d						11 51		12 05							12 21		12 35			
Heathrow Terminal 4 ✈ d																				
Heathrow Terminal 1-2-3 2 ✈ d							11 57									12 27				
Hayes & Harlington d						11 56	12 03	12 10							12 26	12 33	12 40			
Southall d							12 06	12 13								12 36	12 43			
Hanwell d							12 09									12 39				
Greenford ⊖ d					11 46									12 16						
South Greenford d					11 49									12 19						
Castle Bar Park d					11 52									12 22						
Drayton Green d					11 54									12 24						
West Ealing d					11 56		12 11							12 26		12 41				
Ealing Broadway ⊖ d					11 59	12 03	12 14	12 19						12 29	12 33	12 44	12 49			
Acton Main Line d					12 03									12 33						
London Paddington 15 ⊖ a	11 40		11 52	11 59	12 12	12 16	12 24	12 31	12 14		12 23	12 29	12 32	12 42	12 46	12 54	13 01	12 39	12 52	

	GW	GW	GW	HC	GW	GW	GW	GW	GW	GW	GW	GW	GW	HC	GW	GW	GW	GW	GW	GW
	◇1 🍴	1	1		1	◇1 ☕	◇1 ☕	1	◇1 ☕	◇1 🍴	◇1 ☕	1	1		1	◇1 ☕	1	◇1 ☕	◇1 🍴	1
Oxford d	12 01				11 37					12 31					12 07				13 01	
Reading 7 d	12 25				12 33	12 39	12 45	12 48	12 54	12 55	13 02				13 03	13 12	13 18	13 20	13 25	
Twyford 3 d					12 39			12 54							13 09		13 24			
Maidenhead 3 d					12 47			13 02							13 17		13 32			
Taplow d								13 06									13 36			
Burnham d			←					13 09					←				13 39			
Slough 3 a	12 40		12 44		12 54			13 14		13 09			13 14		13 24		13 44		13 40	
d	12 40		12 44		12 54			13 14		13 11			13 14		13 24		13 44		13 40	
Langley d					12 58			↳							13 28		↳			
Iver d					13 01										13 31					
West Drayton d			12 51		13 05								13 21		13 35					
Heathrow Terminal 4 ✈ d																				
Heathrow Terminal 1-2-3 2 ✈ d				12 57										13 27						
Hayes & Harlington d			12 56	13 03	13 10								13 26	13 33	13 40					
Southall d				13 06	13 13									13 36	13 43					
Hanwell d				13 09										13 39						
Greenford ⊖ d		12 46										13 16								13 46
South Greenford d		12 49										13 19								13 49
Castle Bar Park d		12 52										13 22								13 52
Drayton Green d		12 54										13 24								13 54
West Ealing d		12 56		13 11								13 26		13 41						13 56
Ealing Broadway ⊖ d		12 59	13 03	13 14	13 19							13 29	13 33	13 44	13 49					13 59
Acton Main Line d		13 03										13 33								14 03
London Paddington 15 ⊖ a	12 59	13 12	13 16	13 24	13 31	13 07	13 12		13 21	13 30	13 33	13 42	13 46	13 54	14 01	13 41		13 46	13 59	14 12

Table 117

Saturdays

from 31 March

Reading and Greenford - London

Network Diagram - see first Page of Table 116

		GW		HC	GW	GW	GW	GW	GW	GW	GW	GW		HC	GW		GW	GW	GW	GW	GW	GW		HC	GW
		1			1	◇1 🍴	1	1	◇1	◇1 🍴	1	1			1		◇1 🍴	1	◇1 🍴	◇1 🛒	1	1			1
Oxford	d				12 37				13 31						13 07					14 01					13 37
Reading 7	d				13 33	13 45	13 48	13 51	13 55	14 02					14 03		14 13	14 18	14 19	14 25					14 33
Twyford 3	d				13 39		13 54								14 09			14 24							14 39
Maidenhead 3	d				13 47		14 02								14 17			14 32							14 47
Taplow	d						14 06											14 36							
Burnham	d	←					14 09					←						14 39				←			
Slough 3	a	13 44			13 54		14 14		14 09			14 14			14 24			14 44		14 40		14 44			14 54
	d	13 44			13 54		14 14		14 10			14 14			14 24			14 44		14 40		14 44			14 54
Langley	d				13 58		→								14 28			→							14 58
Iver	d				14 01										14 31										15 01
West Drayton	d	13 51			14 05							14 21			14 35							14 51			15 05
Heathrow Terminal 4 ✈	d																								
Heathrow Terminal 1-2-3 2 ✈	d			13 57										14 27										14 57	
Hayes & Harlington	d	13 56		14 03	14 10							14 26		14 33	14 40							14 56		15 03	15 10
Southall	d			14 06	14 13									14 36	14 43									15 06	15 13
Hanwell	d			14 09										14 39										15 09	
Greenford ⊖	d										14 16										14 46				
South Greenford	d										14 19										14 49				
Castle Bar Park	d										14 22										14 52				
Drayton Green	d										14 24										14 54				
West Ealing	d			14 11							14 26			14 41							14 56			15 11	
Ealing Broadway ⊖	d	14 03		14 14	14 19						14 29	14 33		14 44	14 49						14 59	15 03		15 14	15 19
Acton Main Line	d										14 33										15 03				
London Paddington 15 ⊖	a	14 16		14 24	14 31	14 14		14 23	14 29	14 32	14 42	14 46		14 54	15 01		14 39		14 45	14 59	15 12	15 16		15 24	15 31

			GW	GW	GW	GW	GW	GW		GW	GW	HC	GW		GW	GW	GW	GW		GW	GW	HC	GW	GW	GW
			◇1 🍴	◇1 🍴	1	◇1 🍴	◇1 🍴	◇1 🍴		1	1		1		◇1 🍴	1	1	◇1		1	1		1	◇1 🍴	1
Oxford	d						14 31						14 07					15 01					14 37		
Reading 7	d		14 39	14 45	14 48	14 53	14 55	15 02					15 03		15 12	15 18	15 19	15 25					15 33	15 45	15 48
Twyford 3	d				14 54								15 09			15 24							15 39		15 54
Maidenhead 3	d				15 02								15 17			15 32							15 47		16 02
Taplow	d				15 06											15 36									16 06
Burnham	d				15 09						←					15 39					←				16 09
Slough 3	a				15 14		15 10				15 14		15 24			15 44		15 40			15 44		15 54		16 14
	d				15 14		15 11				15 14		15 24			15 44		15 40			15 44		15 54		16 14
Langley	d				→								15 28			→							15 58		→
Iver	d												15 31										16 01		
West Drayton	d										15 21		15 35								15 51		16 05		
Heathrow Terminal 4 ✈	d																								
Heathrow Terminal 1-2-3 2 ✈	d											15 27										15 57			
Hayes & Harlington	d										15 26	15 33	15 40								15 56	16 03	16 10		
Southall	d											15 36	15 43									16 06	16 13		
Hanwell	d											15 39										16 09			
Greenford ⊖	d									15 16										15 46					
South Greenford	d									15 19										15 49					
Castle Bar Park	d									15 22										15 52					
Drayton Green	d									15 24										15 54					
West Ealing	d									15 26		15 41								15 56		16 11			
Ealing Broadway ⊖	d									15 29	15 33	15 44	15 49							15 59	16 03	16 14	16 19		
Acton Main Line	d									15 33										16 03					
London Paddington 15 ⊖	a		15 09	15 14		15 22	15 29	15 32		15 42	15 46	15 54	16 01		15 39		15 54	15 59		16 12	16 16	16 24	16 31	16 14	

		GW	GW	GW		GW	GW	HC	GW		GW	GW	GW	GW		GW	GW	HC	GW		GW	GW	GW	GW	
		◇1 🍴	◇1 🛒	◇1 🍴		1	1		1		◇1 🍴	1	1	◇1		1	1		1		◇1 🍴	◇1 🍴	1	◇1 🍴	
Oxford	d		15 31						15 07					16 01					15 37						
Reading 7	d	15 53	15 55	16 01					16 03		16 13	16 18	16 18	16 26					16 33		16 39	16 45	16 48	16 51	
Twyford 3	d								16 09				16 24						16 39				16 54		
Maidenhead 3	d								16 17				16 32						16 47				17 02		
Taplow	d												16 36										17 06		
Burnham	d						←						16 39				←						17 09		
Slough 3	a		16 10				16 14		16 24				16 44	16 40			16 44		16 54				17 14		
	d		16 11				16 14		16 24				16 44	16 41			16 44		16 54				17 14		
Langley	d								16 28				→						16 58				→		
Iver	d								16 31										17 01						
West Drayton	d						16 21		16 35								16 51		17 05						
Heathrow Terminal 4 ✈	d																								
Heathrow Terminal 1-2-3 2 ✈	d							16 27										16 57							
Hayes & Harlington	d						16 26	16 33	16 40								16 56	17 03	17 10						
Southall	d							16 36	16 43									17 06	17 13						
Hanwell	d							16 39										17 09							
Greenford ⊖	d					16 16										16 46									
South Greenford	d					16 19										16 49									
Castle Bar Park	d					16 22										16 52									
Drayton Green	d					16 24										16 54									
West Ealing	d					16 26		16 41								16 56		17 11							
Ealing Broadway ⊖	d					16 29	16 33	16 44	16 49							16 59	17 03	17 14	17 19						
Acton Main Line	d					16 33										17 03									
London Paddington 15 ⊖	a	16 23	16 29	16 32		16 42	16 46	16 54	17 01		16 39	16 52		16 59		17 12	17 16	17 24	17 31		17 07	17 14		17 21	

Table 117

Saturdays
from 31 March

Reading and Greenford - London

Network Diagram - see first Page of Table 116

	GW ◇1 🛒	GW ◇1 ☕	GW 1	GW 1	HC	GW 1		GW ◇1 ☕	GW ◇1 ☕		GW 1	GW ◇1	GW 1	GW 1	HC	GW 1	GW ◇1 ☕	GW 1	GW ◇1 ☕		GW ◇1 ☕	GW ◇1 ☕	GW 1	GW 1
Oxford d	16 31					16 07						17 01				16 37					17 31			
Reading 7 d	16 55	17 02				17 03		17 12	17 18		17 18	17 27				17 33	17 45	17 48	17 54		17 57	18 02		
Twyford 3 d						17 09					17 24					17 39		17 54						
Maidenhead 3 d						17 17					17 32					17 47		18 02						
Taplow d											17 36							18 06						
Burnham d				←							17 39			←				18 09						←
Slough 3 a	17 10			17 14		17 24					17 44	17 41		17 44		17 54		18 14			18 10			18 14
d	17 11			17 14		17 24					17 44	17 42		17 44		17 54		18 14			18 11			18 14
Langley d						17 28					→					17 58		→						
Iver d						17 31										18 01								
West Drayton d				17 21		17 35								17 51		18 05								18 21
Heathrow Terminal 4 ✈ d																								
Heathrow Terminal 1-2-3 2 ✈ d					17 27										17 57									
Hayes & Harlington d				17 26	17 33	17 40								17 56	18 03	18 10								18 26
Southall d					17 36	17 43									18 06	18 13								
Hanwell d					17 39										18 09									
Greenford ⊖ d			17 16										17 46										18 16	
South Greenford d			17 19										17 49										18 19	
Castle Bar Park d			17 22										17 52										18 22	
Drayton Green d			17 24										17 54										18 24	
West Ealing d			17 26		17 41								17 56		18 11								18 26	
Ealing Broadway ⊖ d			17 29	17 33	17 44	17 49							17 59	18 03	18 14	18 19							18 29	18 33
Acton Main Line d			17 33										18 03										18 33	
London Paddington 15 ⊖ a	17 29	17 32	17 42	17 46	17 54	18 01		17 38	17 51			18 00	18 12	18 16	18 24	18 31	18 14		18 21		18 29	18 32	18 42	18 46

	HC	GW 1		GW ◇1 ☕	GW 1		GW 1	GW ◇1	GW 1	GW 1	HC	GW 1		GW ◇1 ☕	GW ◇1 ☕		GW 1	GW ◇1 ☕	GW ◇1 🛒	GW ◇1 ☕	GW 1	GW 1	HC	GW 1
Oxford d		17 07						18 01				17 37							18 31					18 07
Reading 7 d		18 03		18 13	18 18		18 19	18 25				18 33		18 39	18 45		18 48	18 50	18 56	19 02				19 03
Twyford 3 d		18 09			18 24							18 39					18 54							19 09
Maidenhead 3 d		18 17			18 32							18 47					19 02							19 17
Taplow d					18 36												19 06							
Burnham d					18 39					←							19 09					←		
Slough 3 a		18 24			18 44			18 40		18 44		18 54					19 14		19 10			19 14		19 24
d		18 24			18 44			18 40		18 44		18 54					19 14		19 11			19 14		19 24
Langley d		18 28			→							18 58					→							19 28
Iver d		18 31										19 01												19 31
West Drayton d		18 35								18 51		19 05										19 21		19 35
Heathrow Terminal 4 ✈ d																								
Heathrow Terminal 1-2-3 2 ✈ d	18 27										18 57												19 27	
Hayes & Harlington d	18 33	18 40								18 56	19 03	19 10										19 26	19 33	19 40
Southall d	18 36	18 43									19 06	19 13											19 36	19 43
Hanwell d	18 39										19 09												19 39	
Greenford ⊖ d									18 46												19 16			
South Greenford d									18 49												19 19			
Castle Bar Park d									18 52												19 22			
Drayton Green d									18 54												19 24			
West Ealing d	18 41								18 56		19 11										19 26		19 41	
Ealing Broadway ⊖ d	18 44	18 49							18 59	19 03	19 14	19 19									19 29	19 33	19 44	19 49
Acton Main Line d									19 03												19 33			
London Paddington 15 ⊖ a	18 54	19 01		18 39			18 52	18 59	19 12	19 16	19 24	19 31		19 08	19 14			19 22	19 29	19 32	19 42	19 46	19 54	20 01

			GW ◇1 ☕	GW 1	GW 1	GW ◇1	GW 1	GW 1	HC	GW 1	GW ◇1 ☕		GW 1	GW ◇1 🛒	GW ◇1 ☕	GW 1	GW 1	HC	GW 1		GW ◇1 ☕		GW 1	GW ◇1
Oxford d						19 01				18 37				19 31					19 07					20 01
Reading 7 d			19 12	19 18	19 20	19 25				19 33	19 45		19 48	19 55	20 03				20 03		20 09		20 18	20 25
Twyford 3 d				19 24						19 39			19 54						20 09				20 24	
Maidenhead 3 d				19 32						19 47			20 02						20 17				20 32	
Taplow d				19 36									20 06										20 36	
Burnham d				19 39				←					20 09				←						20 39	
Slough 3 a				19 44		19 40		19 44		19 54			20 14	20 10			20 14		20 24				20 44	20 40
d				19 44		19 40		19 44		19 54			20 14	20 10			20 14		20 24				20 44	20 40
Langley d				→						19 58			→						20 28				→	
Iver d										20 01									20 31					
West Drayton d								19 51		20 05							20 21		20 35					
Heathrow Terminal 4 ✈ d																								
Heathrow Terminal 1-2-3 2 ✈ d									19 57									20 27						
Hayes & Harlington d								19 56	20 03	20 10							20 26	20 33	20 40					
Southall d									20 06	20 13								20 36	20 43					
Hanwell d									20 09									20 39						
Greenford ⊖ d							19 46									20 16								
South Greenford d							19 49									20 19								
Castle Bar Park d							19 52									20 22								
Drayton Green d							19 54									20 24								
West Ealing d							19 56		20 11							20 26		20 41						
Ealing Broadway ⊖ d							19 59	20 03	20 14	20 19						20 29	20 33	20 44	20 49					
Acton Main Line d							20 03									20 33								
London Paddington 15 ⊖ a			19 39		19 52	19 59	20 12	20 16	20 24	20 31	20 14			20 29	20 32	20 42	20 46	20 54	21 01		20 37			20 59

Table 117

Saturdays
from 31 March

Reading and Greenford - London

Network Diagram - see first Page of Table 116

		GW 1	GW 1	HC	GW 1	GW ◇1 ☕	GW ◇1 ☕	GW 1		GW ◇1	GW ◇1 ☕	GW 1	GW 1	HC	GW 1		GW ◇1 ☕	GW 1		GW ◇1	GW 1	GW 1	HC	GW 1
Oxford	d				19 37					20 31					20 07					21 01				20 37
Reading 7	d				20 33	20 39	20 45	20 48		20 54	21 01				21 03		21 08	21 18		21 25				21 33
Twyford 3	d				20 39			20 54							21 09			21 24						21 39
Maidenhead 3	d				20 47			21 02							21 17			21 32						21 47
Taplow	d							21 06										21 36						
Burnham	d		←					21 09					←					21 39				←		
Slough 3	a		20 44		20 54			21 14		21 09			21 14		21 24			21 44		21 40		21 44		21 54
	d		20 44		20 54			21 14		21 09			21 14		21 24			21 44		21 40		21 44		21 54
Langley	d				20 58			→							21 28			→						21 58
Iver	d				21 01										21 31									22 01
West Drayton	d		20 51		21 05								21 21		21 35							21 51		22 05
Heathrow Terminal 4 ✈	d																							
Heathrow Terminal 1-2-3 2 ✈	d			20 57										21 27									21 57	
Hayes & Harlington	d		20 56	21 03	21 10								21 26	21 33	21 40							21 56	22 03	22 10
Southall	d			21 06	21 13									21 36	21 43								22 06	22 13
Hanwell	d			21 09										21 39									22 09	
Greenford ⊖	d	20 46										21 16									21 46			
South Greenford	d	20 49										21 19									21 49			
Castle Bar Park	d	20 52										21 22									21 52			
Drayton Green	d	20 54										21 24									21 54			
West Ealing	d	20 56		21 11								21 26		21 41							21 56		22 11	
Ealing Broadway ⊖	d	20 59	21 03	21 14	21 19							21 29	21 33	21 44	21 49						21 59	22 03	22 14	22 19
Acton Main Line	d	21 03										21 33									22 03			
London Paddington 15 ⊖	a	21 12	21 16	21 24	21 31	21 07	21 14			21 29	21 32	21 42	21 46	21 54	22 02		21 36			21 59	22 12	22 16	22 24	22 31

		GW 1	GW ◇1 ☕	GW ◇1		GW ◇1 ☕	HC	GW 1	GW ◇1	HC	GW 1		GW 1	GW ◇1 ☕		GW ◇1	HC	GW 1	GW ◇1	GW ◇1 ☕	GW 1
Oxford	d			21 31					22 01		21 50					22 35			23 01		23 07
Reading 7	d	21 48	21 50	22 01		22 03		22 18	22 29		22 33		22 48	23 05		23 09		23 18	23 29	23 51	00 03
Twyford 3	d	21 54						22 24			22 39		22 54					23 24			00 10
Maidenhead 3	d	22 02						22 32			22 47		23 02					23 32			00 18
Taplow	d	22 06						22 36					23 06					23 36			00 22
Burnham	d	22 09						22 39					23 09					23 39			00 25
Slough 3	a	22 14		22 14				22 44	22 43		22 54		23 14			23 26		23 44	23 44		00 29
	d	22 14		22 15				22 44	22 44		22 54		23 14			23 27		23 44	23 44		00 30
Langley	d										22 58										00 34
Iver	d										23 01										00 37
West Drayton	d	22 21						22 51			23 05		23 21					23 51			00 40
Heathrow Terminal 4 ✈	d																				
Heathrow Terminal 1-2-3 2 ✈	d						22 27			22 57							23 27				
Hayes & Harlington	d	22 26					22 33	22 56		23 03	23 10		23 26				23 33	23 56			00 45
Southall	d						22 36			23 06	23 13						23 36				00 48
Hanwell	d						22 39			23 09							23 39				
Greenford ⊖	d																				
South Greenford	d																				
Castle Bar Park	d																				
Drayton Green	d																				
West Ealing	d						22 41			23 11							23 41				
Ealing Broadway ⊖	d	22 33					22 44	23 03		23 14	23 19		23 33				23 44	00 03			00 54
Acton Main Line	d																				
London Paddington 15 ⊖	a	22 46	22 16	22 32		22 37	22 54	23 16	23 02	23 24	23 28		23 46	23 36		23 46	23 54	00 16	00 10	00 33	01 03

Sundays
until 1 January

		GW 1 A	GW ◇1 A	HC	GW ◇1 A ☕	GW 1 A	HC	GW 1	HC	GW 1		HC	GW 1	GW 1	HC	GW 1	GW ◇1 ☕	GW 1	GW ◇1	GW 1		GW ◇1 ☕	HC	GW 1	GW ◇1 ☕
Oxford	d		23p01			23p07													08 50					09 01	
Reading 7	d	23p18	23p29		23p51	00 03		06 22		07 22			08 03	08 18		08 52	09 03	09 19	09 23			09 45		09 52	10 00
Twyford 3	d	23p24				00 09		06 28		07 28				08 24		08 58		09 25						09 58	
Maidenhead 3	d	23p32				00 17		06 36		07 36				08 36		09 06		09 33						10 06	
Taplow	d	23p36				00 21																			
Burnham	d	23p39				00 24		06 40		07 40				08 40				09 38		←					
Slough 3	a	23p44	23p44			00 28		06 45		07 45			08 20	08 45		09 14		09 45	09 38	09 45				10 14	
	d	23p44	23p44			00 29		06 46		07 46			08 20	08 46		09 18		09 48	09 38	09 48				10 19	
Langley	d					00 33		06 50		07 50				08 50		09 23		→		09 50				10 23	
Iver	d					00 36																			
West Drayton	d	23p51				00 39		06 55		07 55				08 55		09 30				09 56				10 30	
Heathrow Terminal 4 ✈	d			00 01			06 07		07 07			08 07			09 07								10 07		
Heathrow Terminal 1-2-3 2 ✈	d			00 07			06 13		07 13			08 13			09 13								10 13		
Hayes & Harlington	d	23p56		00 13		00 44	06 19	07 02	07 19	08 02		08 19		09 02	09 19	09 34				10 01			10 19	10 34	
Southall	d			00 16		00 47	06 22	07 05	07 22	08 05		08 22		09 05	09 22	09 37							10 23	10 37	
Hanwell	d																								
Greenford ⊖	d																								
South Greenford	d																								
Castle Bar Park	d																								
Drayton Green	d																								
West Ealing	d																								
Ealing Broadway ⊖	d	00 03		00 21		00 53	06 27	07 11	07 27	08 11		08 27		09 11	09 27	09 42				10 08			10 28	10 42	
Acton Main Line	d																								
London Paddington 15 ⊖	a	00 16	00 10	00 30	00 34	01 02	06 36	07 20	07 36	08 20		08 36	08 44	09 20	09 36	09 51	09 44		10 00	10 18		10 22	10 36	10 51	10 44

A not 11 December

Table 117

Sundays

until 1 January

Reading and Greenford - London

Network Diagram - see first Page of Table 116

		GW	GW	GW	GW	GW		HC	GW		GW	GW	GW	GW	GW	GW		GW	HC	GW		GW	GW	GW	GW
		1	◇1	1	◇1 ☕	◇1 ☕			1		◇1 ☕	◇1	1	◇1	1	◇1 ☕		◇1 ☕		1		◇1 ☕	1	◇1	1
Oxford	d		09 50						10 05			10 44		10 55						11 05				11 50	
Reading 7	d	10 18	10 20		10 44	10 49			10 52		11 02	11 14	11 18	11 23		11 44		11 51		11 52		12 02	12 18	12 23	
Twyford 3	d	10 24							10 58			11 21	11 24							11 58			12 24		
Maidenhead 3	d	10 36							11 06			11 29	11 36							12 06			12 36		
Taplow	d																								
Burnham	d	10 40		←									11 41		←								12 40		←
Slough 3	a	10 45	10 35	10 45					11 14			11 35	11 45	11 42	11 45					12 14			12 45	12 38	12 45
	d	10 48	10 35	10 48					11 18			11 36	11 48	11 42	11 48					12 18			12 48	12 39	12 48
Langley	d	→		10 50					11 23				→		11 50					12 23			→		12 50
Iver	d																								
West Drayton	d			10 56					11 30						11 56					12 30					12 56
Heathrow Terminal 4 ✈	d							11 07											12 07						
Heathrow Terminal 1-2-3 2 ✈	d							11 13											12 13						
Hayes & Harlington	d			11 01				11 19	11 34						12 01				12 19	12 34					13 01
Southall	d							11 22	11 37										12 22	12 37					
Hanwell	d																								
Greenford ⊖	d																								
South Greenford	d																								
Castle Bar Park	d																								
Drayton Green	d																								
West Ealing	d																								
Ealing Broadway ⊖	d			11 08				11 27	11 42						12 08				12 27	12 42					13 08
Acton Main Line	d																								
London Paddington 15 ⊖	a		10 59	11 18	11 22	11 29		11 36	11 50		11 44	11 58		12 06	12 18	12 21		12 29	12 36	12 50		12 44		13 03	13 18

		GW		HC	GW		GW	GW	GW	GW	GW	GW		GW	HC	GW		GW	GW	GW	GW	GW		GW	HC
		◇1 ☕			1		◇1 ☕	◇1 ☕	1	◇1	1	◇1 ☕		◇1 ☕		1		◇1 ☕	1	◇1	1	◇1 ☕		◇1 ☕	
Oxford	d				12 05					12 50						13 05				13 50					
Reading 7	d	12 44			12 52		13 02	13 15	13 18	13 20		13 49		13 51		13 52		14 02	14 18	14 21		14 44		14 52	
Twyford 3	d				12 58				13 24							13 58			14 24						
Maidenhead 3	d				13 06				13 36							14 06			14 36						
Taplow	d																								
Burnham	d								13 40		←								14 40		←				
Slough 3	a				13 14				13 45	13 36	13 45					14 14			14 45	14 37	14 45				
	d				13 18				13 48	13 37	13 48					14 18			14 48	14 37	14 48				
Langley	d				13 23				→		13 50					14 23			→		14 50				
Iver	d																								
West Drayton	d				13 30						13 56					14 30					14 56				
Heathrow Terminal 4 ✈	d			13 07											14 07										15 07
Heathrow Terminal 1-2-3 2 ✈	d			13 13											14 13										15 13
Hayes & Harlington	d			13 19	13 34						14 01				14 19	14 34					15 01				15 19
Southall	d			13 22	13 37										14 22	14 37									15 22
Hanwell	d																								
Greenford ⊖	d																								
South Greenford	d																								
Castle Bar Park	d																								
Drayton Green	d																								
West Ealing	d																								
Ealing Broadway ⊖	d			13 27	13 42						14 08				14 27	14 42					15 08				15 27
Acton Main Line	d																								
London Paddington 15 ⊖	a	13 22		13 36	13 51		13 44	13 59		14 02	14 19	14 22		14 29	14 36	14 50		14 44		14 59	15 18	15 21		15 29	15 36

		GW		GW	GW	GW	GW	GW		GW	HC	GW		GW	GW	GW	GW	GW		GW	HC	GW		GW	GW
		1		◇1 ☕	1	◇1	1	◇1 ☕		◇1 ☕		1		◇1 ☕	1	◇1 ☕	1	◇1 ☕		◇1 ☕		1		◇1 ☕	◇1
Oxford	d	14 05				14 50						15 05				15 50						16 05			16 37
Reading 7	d	14 52		15 02	15 18	15 22		15 44		15 52		15 52		16 02	16 18	16 20		16 47		16 51		16 52		17 02	17 12
Twyford 3	d	14 58			15 24							15 58			16 24							16 58			17 20
Maidenhead 3	d	15 06			15 36							16 06			16 36							17 06			17 28
Taplow	d																								
Burnham	d				15 40		←					16 11			16 40		←					17 11			
Slough 3	a	15 14			15 45	15 36	15 45					16 14			16 45	16 33	16 45					17 14			17 35
	d	15 18			15 48	15 37	15 48					16 18			16 48	16 33	16 48					17 18			17 35
Langley	d	15 23			→		15 50					16 23			→		16 50					17 23			
Iver	d																								
West Drayton	d	15 30					15 56					16 30					16 56					17 30			
Heathrow Terminal 4 ✈	d										16 07										17 07				
Heathrow Terminal 1-2-3 2 ✈	d										16 13										17 13				
Hayes & Harlington	d	15 34					16 01				16 19	16 34					17 01				17 19	17 34			
Southall	d	15 37									16 22	16 37									17 22	17 37			
Hanwell	d																								
Greenford ⊖	d																								
South Greenford	d																								
Castle Bar Park	d																								
Drayton Green	d																								
West Ealing	d																								
Ealing Broadway ⊖	d	15 42					16 08				16 27	16 42					17 08				17 27	17 42			
Acton Main Line	d																								
London Paddington 15 ⊖	a	15 50		15 44		15 59	16 18	16 22		16 29	16 36	16 51		16 44		16 59	17 19	17 22		17 30	17 36	17 51		17 43	18 03

Table 117

Sundays

until 1 January

Reading and Greenford - London

Network Diagram - see first Page of Table 116

		GW	GW	GW		GW	GW	GW	GW	HC	GW		GW	GW		GW	GW	GW	GW	HC	GW		GW	GW	
		◇1 ⊡	1	◇1 ⊡		◇1 ⊡	1	◇1 ⊡	◇1 ⊡		1		◇1 ⊡	◇1 ⊡		1	◇1 ⊡	1	◇1 ⊡		1		◇1 ⊡	◇1 ⊡	
Oxford	d					16 50					17 05						17 50				18 05				
Reading 7	d	17 15	17 17	17 21		17 21		17 44	17 48		17 52		18 03	18 16		18 18	18 21		18 49		18 52		18 53	19 02	
Twyford 3	d		17 23								17 58					18 24					18 58				
Maidenhead 3	d		17 36								18 06					18 36					19 06				
Taplow	d																								
Burnham	d		17 40				←				18 11					18 40		←			19 11				
Slough 3	a		17 45			17 40	17 45				18 14					18 45	18 36	18 45			19 15				
	d		17 48			17 40	17 48				18 18					18 48	18 36	18 48			19 18				
Langley	d		→				17 54				18 23					→		18 50			19 23				
Iver	d																								
West Drayton	d						17 56				18 30							18 56			19 30				
Heathrow Terminal 4 ✈	d									18 07										19 07					
Heathrow Terminal 1-2-3 2 ✈	d									18 13										19 13					
Hayes & Harlington	d						18 01			18 19	18 34							19 01		19 19	19 34				
Southall	d									18 22	18 37									19 22	19 37				
Hanwell	d																								
Greenford ⊖	d																								
South Greenford	d																								
Castle Bar Park	d																								
Drayton Green	d																								
West Ealing	d																								
Ealing Broadway ⊖	d						18 08			18 27	18 42							19 08		19 27	19 42				
Acton Main Line	d																								
London Paddington 15 ⊖	a	17 58		18 00		18 06	18 18	18 22	18 29	18 36	18 51		18 44	18 59			19 02	19 18	19 22	19 36	19 51		19 29	19 44	

		GW	GW	GW	GW	GW	GW	GW	HC	GW			GW	GW	GW	GW	GW	GW	GW	HC		GW		GW	GW
		◇1 ⊡	1	◇1 ⊡	◇1 ⊡	◇1 ⊡	1	◇1 ⊡		1			◇1 ⊡	1	◇1 ⊡	◇1	◇1 ⊡	1	◇1 ⊡			1		◇1 ⊡	◇1 ⊡
Oxford	d				18 50					19 05						19 50						20 05			
Reading 7	d	19 14	19 18	19 25	19 28	19 34		19 47		19 52			20 03	20 18	20 23	20 23	20 32		20 47			20 52		21 15	21 18
Twyford 3	d		19 23							19 58				20 24								20 58			
Maidenhead 3	d		19 36							20 06				20 36								21 06			
Taplow	d																								
Burnham	d		19 40				←			20 11				20 40				←				21 11			
Slough 3	a		19 45		19 42		19 45			20 14				20 45		20 42		20 45				21 14			
	d		19 48		19 43		19 48			20 18				20 48		20 42		20 48				21 18			
Langley	d		→				19 50			20 23				→				20 54				21 24			
Iver	d																								
West Drayton	d						19 59			20 30								20 59				21 30			
Heathrow Terminal 4 ✈	d								20 07											21 07					
Heathrow Terminal 1-2-3 2 ✈	d								20 13											21 13					
Hayes & Harlington	d						20 03		20 19	20 34								21 03		21 19		21 34			
Southall	d								20 22	20 37								21 08		21 22		21 37			
Hanwell	d																								
Greenford ⊖	d																								
South Greenford	d																								
Castle Bar Park	d																								
Drayton Green	d																								
West Ealing	d																								
Ealing Broadway ⊖	d						20 09		20 27	20 42								21 12		21 27		21 42			
Acton Main Line	d																								
London Paddington 15 ⊖	a	19 59		20 02	20 06	20 14	20 18	20 22	20 36	20 51			20 44		20 59	21 03	21 13	21 21	21 29	21 36		21 51		21 59	22 02

		GW		GW	GW	GW		HC	GW		GW	GW	GW	GW	HC	GW		GW	GW	GW	GW				
		◇1		1	◇1 ⊡	◇1 ⊡			1		◇1 ⊡	◇1	◇1 ⊡	◇1 ⊡		1		1	◇1	◇1 ⊡	1				
Oxford	d	20 50							21 21			21 50						22 21	22 46						
Reading 7	d	21 22		21 24	21 32	21 47			22 10		22 18	22 22	22 37	22 38		22 40		23 00	23 22	23 30	23 35				
Twyford 3	d			21 30					22 16							22 49		23 07			23 41				
Maidenhead 3	d	21 35		21 38					22 24							22 57		23 15			23 49				
Taplow	d																								
Burnham	d			21 43					22 29							23 01					23 54				
Slough 3	a	21 42		21 48					22 33			22 43				23 06		23 22	23 40		23 58				
	d	21 42		21 48					22 34			22 44				23 06		23 22	23 41		23 59				
Langley	d			21 55					22 38							23 10		23 26			00 03				
Iver	d																								
West Drayton	d			21 59					22 43							23 15		23 31			00 08				
Heathrow Terminal 4 ✈	d							22 07							23 07										
Heathrow Terminal 1-2-3 2 ✈	d							22 13							23 13										
Hayes & Harlington	d			22 04				22 19	22 47						23 19	23 23		23 36			00 16				
Southall	d			22 08				22 22	22 51						23 22			23 39			00 20				
Hanwell	d																								
Greenford ⊖	d																								
South Greenford	d																								
Castle Bar Park	d																								
Drayton Green	d																								
West Ealing	d																								
Ealing Broadway ⊖	d			22 13				22 27	22 56						23 27	23 31		23 45			00 25				
Acton Main Line	d																								
London Paddington 15 ⊖	a	22 04		22 21	22 14	22 29		22 36	23 05		23 07	23 13	23 16	23 19	23 36	23 40		23 53	00 02	00 13	00 34				

Table 117

Sundays

8 January to 12 February

Reading and Greenford - London

Network Diagram - see first Page of Table 116

		GW	GW	HC	GW	GW	GW	HC	GW	GW	HC	GW	HC	GW	GW	GW	HC	GW	GW	GW	GW	GW	HC
		1	◇1		◇1 🍴	1	🚌		1	🚌		1		1	1	1		1	◇1 🍴	1	◇1	1	
Oxford	d		23p01			23p13															08 50		
Reading 7	d	23p18	23p29		23p51	00 06	05 52			06 52				08 17	08 19			08 52	09 06	09 19	09 23		
Twyford 3	d	23p24				00 13	06a25		06 30	07a25		07 30		08 23				08 58		09 25			
Maidenhead 3	d	23p32				00 21			06 36			07 36		0836				09 06		09 33			
Taplow	d	23p36				00 25																	
Burnham	d	23p39				00 28			06 40			07 40		08 40		←				09 38		←	
Slough 3	a	23p44	23p44			00 32			06 45			07 45		08 45	08 35	08 45		09 14		09 45	09 38	09 45	
	d	23p44	23p44			00 33			06 46			07 46		08 46	08 36	08 46		09 21		09 48	09 38	09 48	
Langley	d					00 37			06 50			07 50		→		08 50		09 25		→		09 50	
Iver	d					00 40																	
West Drayton	d	23p51				00 43			06 55			07 55				08 55		09 30				09 56	
Heathrow Terminal 4 ✈	d			00 01				06 07			07 07		08 07				09 07						10 07
Heathrow Terminal 1-2-3 2 ✈	d			00 07				06 13			07 13		08 13				09 13						10 13
Hayes & Harlington	d	23p56		00 13		00 50		06 19	07 02		07 19	08 02	08 19			09 02	09 19	09 34				10 01	10 19
Southall	d			00 16		00 53		06 22	07 05		07 22	08 05	08 22			09 05	09 22	09 37					10 23
Hanwell	d																						
Greenford ⊖	d																						
South Greenford	d																						
Castle Bar Park	d																						
Drayton Green	d																						
West Ealing	d																						
Ealing Broadway ⊖	d	00 03		00 21		00 59		06 27	07 11		07 27	08 11	08 27			09 11	09 27	09 43				10 08	10 28
Acton Main Line	d																						
London Paddington 15 ⊖	a	00 16	00 10	00 30	00 34	01 08		06 36	07 20		07 36	08 20	08 36		08 59	09 20	09 36	09 52	09 44		10 00	10 18	10 36

		GW	GW	GW	GW	GW	GW	HC	GW	GW	GW	GW	GW	GW	GW	GW	HC	GW	GW	GW	GW
		1	◇1 🍴	◇1 🍴	1	◇1	1		1	◇1 🍴	◇1 🍴	◇1 🍴	◇1	1	◇1	1		1	◇1 🍴	◇1 🍴	◇1 🍴
Oxford	d	09 00				09 48			09 53				10 44		10 55			10 39			
Reading 7	d	09 43	09 47	10 04	10 19	10 22			10 36	10 44	10 49	11 02	11 14	11 19	11 23			11 42	11 47	11 51	12 02
Twyford 3	d	09 49			10 25				10 47				11 21	11 25				11 49			
Maidenhead 3	d	10 06			10 36				11 06				11 29	11 33				12 06			
Taplow	d																				
Burnham	d				10 40		←							11 38		←					
Slough 3	a	10 14			10 45	10 37	10 45		11 15				11 35	11 42	11 37	11 42		12 15			
	d	10 18			10 48	10 37	10 48		11 18				11 36	11 48	11 38	11 48		12 18			
Langley	d	10 24			→		10 50		11 23					→		11 50		12 23			
Iver	d																				
West Drayton	d	10 30					10 56		11 30							11 56		12 29			
Heathrow Terminal 4 ✈	d							11 07									12 07				
Heathrow Terminal 1-2-3 2 ✈	d							11 13									12 13				
Hayes & Harlington	d	10 34					11 01	11 19	11 34							12 01	12 19	12 33			
Southall	d	10 37						11 22	11 37								12 22	12 37			
Hanwell	d																				
Greenford ⊖	d																				
South Greenford	d																				
Castle Bar Park	d																				
Drayton Green	d																				
West Ealing	d																				
Ealing Broadway ⊖	d	10 42					11 08	11 27	11 42							12 08	12 27	12 42			
Acton Main Line	d																				
London Paddington 15 ⊖	a	10 51	10 22	10 44		10 59	11 18	11 36	11 51	11 22	11 29	11 44	11 56		12 01	12 18	12 36	12 51	12 22	12 29	12 44

		GW	GW	GW	HC	GW	GW	GW	GW	GW	GW	GW	HC	GW	GW	GW	GW	GW	GW	GW
		1	◇1	1		1	◇1 🍴	◇1 🍴	1	◇1 🍴	◇1	1		1	◇1 🍴	◇1 🍴	◇1 🍴	1	◇1	1
Oxford	d		11 50			11 56					12 50			12 56					13 50	
Reading 7	d	12 18	12 23			12 42	12 44	13 02	13 18	13 23	13 25			13 42	13 49	13 51	14 06	14 18	14 21	
Twyford 3	d	12 24				12 48			13 24					13 50				14 24		
Maidenhead 3	d	12 32				13 06			13 36					14 06				14 32		
Taplow	d																			
Burnham	d	12 37		←					13 40			←						14 37		←
Slough 3	a	12 43	12 38	12 43		13 15			13 45		13 41	13 45		14 15				14 41	14 37	14 41
	d	12 48	12 39	12 48		13 18			13 48		13 41	13 48		14 19				14 48	14 37	14 48
Langley	d	→		12 52		13 23			→			13 50		14 24				→		14 50
Iver	d																			
West Drayton	d			12 56		13 30						13 58		14 29						14 56
Heathrow Terminal 4 ✈	d				13 07								14 07							
Heathrow Terminal 1-2-3 2 ✈	d				13 13								14 13							
Hayes & Harlington	d			13 01	13 19	13 34						14 01	14 19	14 34						15 01
Southall	d				13 22	13 37							14 22	14 38						
Hanwell	d																			
Greenford ⊖	d																			
South Greenford	d																			
Castle Bar Park	d																			
Drayton Green	d																			
West Ealing	d																			
Ealing Broadway ⊖	d			13 08	13 27	13 42						14 08	14 27	14 42						15 08
Acton Main Line	d																			
London Paddington 15 ⊖	a		13 03	13 18	13 36	13 51	13 22	13 44		13 59	14 04	14 19	14 36	14 51	14 22	14 29	14 44		14 59	15 18

Table 117

Sundays

8 January to 12 February

Reading and Greenford - London

Network Diagram - see first Page of Table 116

		HC	GW		GW	GW	GW	GW		GW	GW	HC	GW		GW	GW	GW	GW		GW	GW	HC	GW		GW
			1		◇1 🛒	◇1 🛒	◇1 🛒	1		◇1	1		1		◇1 🛒	◇1 🛒	◇1 🛒	1		◇1 🛒	1		1		◇1 🛒
Oxford	d		13 56							14 50			14 58							15 50			15 56		
Reading 7	d		14 42		14 49	14 52	15 06	15 18		15 22			15 44		15 49	15 52	16 06	16 18		16 24			16 44		16 49
Twyford 3	d		14 48					15 24					15 50					16 26					16 50		
Maidenhead 3	d		15 06					15 32					16 06					16 36					17 06		
Taplow	d																								
Burnham	d							15 37			←		16 11					16 40			←		17 11		
Slough 3	a		15 15					15 41		15 36	15 41		16 14					16 45		16 37	16 45		17 16		
	d		15 18					15 48		15 37	15 48		16 21					16 48		16 37	16 48		17 16		
Langley	d		15 23					→			15 50		16 25					→			16 50		17 21		
Iver	d																								
West Drayton	d		15 30								15 56		16 29								16 56		17 30		
Heathrow Terminal 4 ✈	d	15 07										16 07										17 07			
Heathrow Terminal 1-2-3 2 ✈	d	15 13										16 13										17 13			
Hayes & Harlington	d	15 19	15 34								16 01	16 19	16 34								17 01	17 19	17 34		
Southall	d	15 22	15 37									16 22	16 37									17 22	17 37		
Hanwell	d																								
Greenford ⊖	d																								
South Greenford	d																								
Castle Bar Park	d																								
Drayton Green	d																								
West Ealing	d																								
Ealing Broadway ⊖	d	15 27	15 42								16 08	16 27	16 43								17 08	17 27	17 42		
Acton Main Line	d																								
London Paddington 15 ⊖	a	15 36	15 51		15 22	15 29	15 44			15 59	16 18	16 36	16 51		16 22	16 29	16 44			17 02	17 19	17 36	17 51		17 22

		GW	GW	GW		GW	GW	GW	GW	GW	HC	GW		GW		GW	GW	GW	GW	GW	GW	HC	GW		
		◇1 🛒	1	◇1 🛒		◇1	◇1 🛒	◇1 🛒	◇1 🛒	1		1		◇1 🛒		◇1 🛒	◇1 🛒	1	◇1 🛒	◇1 🛒	1		1		
Oxford	d					16 37			16 50			16 56								17 50			17 55		
Reading 7	d	16 51	17 01	17 06		17 12	17 17	17 23	17 27			17 42		17 49		17 50	18 06	18 18	18 19	18 21			18 44		
Twyford 3	d		17 07			17 19						17 48						18 24					18 50		
Maidenhead 3	d		17 29			17 27						18 06						18 33					19 06		
Taplow	d																								
Burnham	d		17 34							←		18 11						18 38			←		19 12		
Slough 3	a		17 39			17 34			17 43	17 39		18 15						18 42		18 36	18 42		19 16		
	d		17 51			17 35			17 43	17 51		18 18						18 48		18 36	18 48		19 18		
Langley	d		→							17 55		18 23						→			18 50		19 23		
Iver	d																								
West Drayton	d									17 59		18 30									18 56		19 30		
Heathrow Terminal 4 ✈	d										18 07											19 07			
Heathrow Terminal 1-2-3 2 ✈	d										18 13											19 13			
Hayes & Harlington	d									18 03	18 19	18 34									19 01	19 19	19 34		
Southall	d										18 22	18 37										19 22	19 37		
Hanwell	d																								
Greenford ⊖	d																								
South Greenford	d																								
Castle Bar Park	d																								
Drayton Green	d																								
West Ealing	d																								
Ealing Broadway ⊖	d									18 09	18 27	18 42									19 08	19 27	19 42		
Acton Main Line	d																								
London Paddington 15 ⊖	a	17 30		17 43		17 58	18 01	18 04	18 06	18 19	18 36	18 51		18 22		18 29	18 44		18 58	19 03	19 18	19 36	19 51		

		GW	GW	GW	GW	GW	GW	GW	GW	GW		HC	GW		GW	GW	GW	GW	GW	GW		GW	GW	HC	GW
		◇1 🛒	◇1 🛒	◇1 🛒	1	◇1 🛒	◇1 🛒	◇1 🛒	◇1 🛒	1			1		◇1 🛒	◇1 🛒	1	◇1 🛒	◇1	◇1 🛒		1	◇1 🛒		1
Oxford	d							18 50					18 56						19 50						20 05
Reading 7	d	18 50	18 53	19 05	19 18	19 19	19 25	19 28	19 35				19 44		19 49	20 03	20 18	20 23	20 25	20 32			20 51		20 55
Twyford 3	d				19 24								19 50				20 24								21 02
Maidenhead 3	d				19 36								20 06				20 36								21 11
Taplow	d																								
Burnham	d				19 41					←			20 11				20 40					←			21 15
Slough 3	a				19 45			19 44		19 45			20 14				20 46		20 44			20 46			21 19
	d				19 48			19 44		19 48			20 18				20 48		20 44			20 48			21 21
Langley	d				→					19 50			20 24				→					20 50			21 25
Iver	d																								
West Drayton	d									19 59			20 29									20 56			21 30
Heathrow Terminal 4 ✈	d											20 07												21 07	
Heathrow Terminal 1-2-3 2 ✈	d											20 13												21 13	
Hayes & Harlington	d									20 03		20 19	20 34									21 01		21 19	21 34
Southall	d											20 22	20 36											21 22	21 36
Hanwell	d																								
Greenford ⊖	d																								
South Greenford	d																								
Castle Bar Park	d																								
Drayton Green	d																								
West Ealing	d																								
Ealing Broadway ⊖	d									20 09		20 27	20 43									21 08		21 27	21 43
Acton Main Line	d																								
London Paddington 15 ⊖	a	19 22	19 29	19 43		19 59	20 02	20 07	20 13	20 18		20 36	20 51		20 22	20 44		20 59	21 04	21 13		21 18	21 29	21 36	21 51

Table 117

Sundays

8 January to 12 February

Reading and Greenford - London

Network Diagram - see first Page of Table 116

		GW 1	GW ◇1 ☕	GW ◇1 ☕	GW ◇1	GW ◇1 ☕	GW 1	GW ◇1 ☕	HC	GW 1	GW ◇1 ☕	GW ◇1	HC	GW 1	GW ◇1 ☕	GW ◇1 ☕	GW 1	GW ◇1	GW ◇1 ☕	GW 1
Oxford	d				20 50					21 05		21 50					22 21	22 50		
Reading 7	d	21 18	21 20	21 23	21 27	21 32		21 49		21 56	22 21	22 23		22 29	22 41	22 54	23 10	23 24	23 30	23 36
Twyford 3	d	21 24								22 03				22 38			23 16			23 42
Maidenhead 3	d	21 36			21 39					22 11				22 46			23 24			23 50
Taplow	d																			
Burnham	d	21 40					←			22 15				22 50						23 55
Slough 3	a	21 46			21 45		21 46			22 21		22 40		22 56			23 31	23 41		23 59
	d	21 51			21 45		21 51			22 21		22 41		23 08			23 32	23 42		00 01
Langley	d	↪					21 55			22 25				23 12			23 36			00 05
Iver	d																			
West Drayton	d						21 59			22 30				23 17			23 41			00 10
Heathrow Terminal 4 ✈	d								22 07				23 07							
Heathrow Terminal 1-2-3 2 ✈	d								22 13				23 13							
Hayes & Harlington	d						22 03		22 19	22 34			23 19	23 23			23 47			00 16
Southall	d						22 07		22 22	22 38			23 22				23 50			00 20
Hanwell	d																			
Greenford ⊖	d																			
South Greenford	d																			
Castle Bar Park	d																			
Drayton Green	d																			
West Ealing	d																			
Ealing Broadway ⊖	d						22 12		22 27	22 43			23 27	23 31			23 55			00 25
Acton Main Line	d																			
London Paddington 15 ⊖	a		21 58	22 01	22 07	22 13	22 21	22 27	22 36	22 51	22 58	23 01	23 36	23 40	23 18	23 31	00 04	00 04	00 13	00 34

Sundays

19 February to 25 March

		GW 1	GW ◇1	HC	GW ◇1 ☕	GW 1	GW 🚌	HC	GW 1	GW 🚌	HC	GW 1	HC	GW 1	GW 1	GW 1	HC	GW 1	GW ◇1 ☕	GW 1	GW ◇1	GW ◇1 ☕	GW 1
Oxford	d		23p01			23p13															08 50		
Reading 7	d	23p18	23p29		23p51	00 06	05 52			06 52				08 17	08 19			08 52	09 03	09 19	09 23	09 32	
Twyford 3	d	23p24				00 13	06a25		06 30	07a25		07 30		08 23				08 58		09 25			
Maidenhead 3	d	23p32				00 21			06 38			07 38		08 36				09 06		09 33			
Taplow	d	23p36				00 25																	
Burnham	d	23p39				00 28			06 41			07 41		08 40		←				09 38			←
Slough 3	a	23p44	23p44			00 32			06 47			07 47		08 45	08 35	08 45		09 14		09 43	09 38		09 43
	d	23p44	23p44			00 33			06 47			07 47		08 46	08 36	08 46		09 19		09 46	09 38		09 46
Langley	d					00 37			06 51			07 51		↪		08 50		09 24		↪			09 50
Iver	d					00 40																	
West Drayton	d	23p51				00 43			06 56			07 56				08 55		09 30					09 55
Heathrow Terminal 4 ✈	d			00 01				06 07			07 07		08 07				09 07						
Heathrow Terminal 1-2-3 2 ✈	d			00 07				06 13			07 13		08 13				09 13						
Hayes & Harlington	d	23p56		00 13		00 50		06 19	07 02		07 19	08 02	08 19			09 02	09 19	09 34					10 02
Southall	d			00 16		00 53		06 22	07 05		07 22	08 05	08 22			09 05	09 22	09 37					
Hanwell	d																						
Greenford ⊖	d																						
South Greenford	d																						
Castle Bar Park	d																						
Drayton Green	d																						
West Ealing	d																						
Ealing Broadway ⊖	d	00 03		00 21		00 59		06 27	07 11		07 27	08 11	08 27			09 11	09 27	09 43					10 08
Acton Main Line	d																						
London Paddington 15 ⊖	a	00 16	00 10	00 30	00 34	01 08		06 36	07 20		07 36	08 20	08 36		08 59	09 20	09 36	09 52	09 44		10 00	10 07	10 18

		HC	GW 1	GW ◇1 ☕	GW 1	GW ◇1	GW ◇1 ☕	GW 1	HC	GW 1	GW ◇1 ☕	GW ◇1 ☕	GW ◇1	GW 1	GW ◇1	GW ◇1 ☕	GW 1	HC	GW 1	GW ◇1 ☕	GW ◇1 ☕
Oxford	d		09 10			09 48				09 53			10 44		10 55				10 39		
Reading 7	d		09 54	10 00	10 19	10 22	10 27			10 36	10 49	11 02	11 14	11 19	11 23	11 28			11 42	11 47	11 53
Twyford 3	d		10 00		10 25					10 47			11 21	11 25					11 49		
Maidenhead 3	d		10 08		10 36					11 06			11 29	11 33					12 06		
Taplow	d																				
Burnham	d				10 40			←						11 38			←				
Slough 3	a		10 17		10 45	10 37		10 45		11 15			11 35	11 42	11 37		11 42		12 15		
	d		10 19		10 48	10 37		10 48		11 18			11 36	11 48	11 38		11 48		12 18		
Langley	d		10 23		↪			10 50		11 23				↪			11 50		12 23		
Iver	d																				
West Drayton	d		10 30					10 56		11 30							11 56		12 29		
Heathrow Terminal 4 ✈	d	10 07							11 07									12 07			
Heathrow Terminal 1-2-3 2 ✈	d	10 13							11 13									12 13			
Hayes & Harlington	d	10 19	10 34					11 01	11 19	11 34							12 01	12 19	12 33		
Southall	d	10 23	10 37						11 22	11 37								12 22	12 37		
Hanwell	d																				
Greenford ⊖	d																				
South Greenford	d																				
Castle Bar Park	d																				
Drayton Green	d																				
West Ealing	d																				
Ealing Broadway ⊖	d	10 28	10 43					11 08	11 27	11 42							12 08	12 27	12 42		
Acton Main Line	d																				
London Paddington 15 ⊖	a	10 36	10 51	10 44		10 58	11 06	11 18	11 36	11 51	11 29	11 44	11 56		12 01	12 06	12 18	12 36	12 51	12 22	12 29

Table 117

Sundays

19 February to 25 March

Reading and Greenford - London

Network Diagram - see first Page of Table 116

		GW 1	GW ◇1	GW ◇1 ☕	GW 1	HC	GW 1	GW ◇1 ☕	GW 1	GW ◇1 ☕	GW ◇1	GW 1	HC	GW 1	GW ◇1 ☕	GW ◇1 ☕	GW ◇1 ☕	GW 1	GW ◇1	GW 1
Oxford	d		11 50				11 56				12 50			12 56					13 50	
Reading 7	d	12 18	12 23	12 27			12 42	12 44	13 18	13 23	13 25			13 44	13 49	13 52	14 04	14 18	14 21	
Twyford 3	d	12 24					12 48		13 24					13 50				14 24		
Maidenhead 3	d	12 32					13 06		13 36					14 06				14 32		
Taplow	d																			
Burnham	d	12 37			←				13 40			←						14 37		←
Slough 3	a	12 46	12 38		12 46		13 15		13 45		13 41	13 45		14 15				14 41	14 37	14 41
	d	12 48	12 43		12 48		13 18		13 48		13 41	13 48		14 18				14 48	14 37	14 48
Langley	d	→			12 50		13 23		→			13 50		14 23				→		14 50
Iver	d																			
West Drayton	d				12 56		13 30					13 58		14 29						14 56
Heathrow Terminal 4 ✈	d					13 07							14 07							
Heathrow Terminal 1-2-3 2 ✈	d					13 13							14 13							
Hayes & Harlington	d				13 01	13 19	13 34					14 01	14 19	14 33						15 01
Southall	d					13 22	13 37						14 22	14 37						
Hanwell	d																			
Greenford ⊖	d																			
South Greenford	d																			
Castle Bar Park	d																			
Drayton Green	d																			
West Ealing	d																			
Ealing Broadway ⊖	d				13 08	13 27	13 42					14 08	14 27	14 43						15 08
Acton Main Line	d																			
London Paddington 15 ⊖	a		13 07	13 03	13 18	13 36	13 51	13 22		13 59	14 04	14 19	14 36	14 51	14 22	14 29	14 44		14 59	15 18

		HC	GW 1	GW ◇1 ☕	GW ◇1 ☕	GW ◇1 ☕	GW 1	GW ◇1	GW 1	HC	GW 1	GW ◇1 ☕	GW ◇1 ☕	GW ◇1 ☕	GW 1	GW ◇1 ☕	GW ◇1 ☕	GW 1	HC	GW 1
Oxford	d		13 56					14 49			14 58						15 50			15 56
Reading 7	d		14 39	14 49	14 52	15 05	15 18	15 22			15 44	15 49	15 53	16 05	16 18	16 22	16 28			16 44
Twyford 3	d		14 51				15 24				15 50				16 26					16 50
Maidenhead 3	d		15 06				15 32				16 06				16 36					17i06
Taplow	d																			
Burnham	d						15 37		←		16 11				16 40			←		17 11
Slough 3	a		15 15				15 41	15 37	15 41		16 14				16 45		16 41	16 45		17 16
	d		15 18				15 48	15 37	15 48		16 21				16 48		16 41	16 48		17 16
Langley	d		15 23				→		15 50		16 25				→			16 50		17 21
Iver	d																			
West Drayton	d		15 30						15 56		16 29							16 56		17 30
Heathrow Terminal 4 ✈	d	15 07								16 07									17 07	
Heathrow Terminal 1-2-3 2 ✈	d	15 13								16 13									17 13	
Hayes & Harlington	d	15 19	15 34						16 01	16 19	16 34							17 01	17 19	17 34
Southall	d	15 22	15 37							16 22	16 37								17 22	17 37
Hanwell	d																			
Greenford ⊖	d																			
South Greenford	d																			
Castle Bar Park	d																			
Drayton Green	d																			
West Ealing	d																			
Ealing Broadway ⊖	d	15 27	15 42						16 08	16 27	16 43							17 08	17 27	17 42
Acton Main Line	d																			
London Paddington 15 ⊖	a	15 36	15 51	15 22	15 29	15 44		15 59	16 18	16 36	16 51	16 22	16 29	16 44		16 58	17 06	17 19	17 36	17 51

		GW ◇1 ☕	GW ◇1 ☕	GW 1	GW ◇1 ☕	GW ◇1	GW ◇1 ☕	GW ◇1 ☕	GW 1	HC	GW 1	GW ◇1 ☕	GW ◇1 ☕	GW 1	GW ◇1 ☕	GW ◇1 ☕	GW 1	HC	GW 1	GW ◇1 ☕
Oxford	d					16 37		16 50			16 56					17 50			17 55	
Reading 7	d	16 49	16 51	17 01	17 05	17 12	17 17	17 24			17 42	17 49	17 52	17 58	18 04	18 23			18 44	18 50
Twyford 3	d			17 07		17 19					17 48			18 04					18 50	
Maidenhead 3	d			17 29		17 27					18 06			18 26					19 06	
Taplow	d																			
Burnham	d			17 34					←		18 11			18 30			←		19 12	
Slough 3	a			17 39		17 34		17 44	17 39		18 15			18 35		18 38	18 35		19 16	
	d			17 51		17 35		17 44	17 51		18 18			18 48		18 38	18 48		19 18	
Langley	d			→					17 55		18 23			→			18 50		19 23	
Iver	d																			
West Drayton	d								17 59		18 30						18 56		19 30	
Heathrow Terminal 4 ✈	d									18 07								19 07		
Heathrow Terminal 1-2-3 2 ✈	d									18 13								19 13		
Hayes & Harlington	d								18 03	18 19	18 34						19 01	19 19	19 34	
Southall	d									18 22	18 37							19 22	19 37	
Hanwell	d																			
Greenford ⊖	d																			
South Greenford	d																			
Castle Bar Park	d																			
Drayton Green	d																			
West Ealing	d																			
Ealing Broadway ⊖	d								18 09	18 27	18 42						19 08	19 27	19 42	
Acton Main Line	d																			
London Paddington 15 ⊖	a	17 22	17 30		17 43	17 56	18 01	18 07	18 19	18 36	18 51	18 22	18 29		18 45	19 03	19 18	19 36	19 51	19 22

Table 117

Reading and Greenford - London

Sundays

19 February to 25 March

Network Diagram - see first Page of Table 116

	GW ◇1 ⊡	GW ◇1 ⊡	GW 1	GW ◇1 ⊡	GW ◇1 ⊡	GW ◇1 ⊡	GW 1	HC	GW 1	GW ◇1 ⊡	GW ◇1 ⊡	GW ◇1 ⊡	GW 1	GW ◇1 ⊡	GW ◇1	GW ◇1 ⊡	GW 1	GW ◇1 ⊡	HC	GW 1
Oxford d						18 50			18 56						19 49					20 05
Reading 7 d	18 53	19 06	19 18	19 19	19 25	19 30			19 44	19 49	19 53	20 06	20 18	20 23	20 25	20 34		20 51		20 55
Twyford 3 d			19 24						19 50				20 24							21 02
Maidenhead 3 d			19 36						20 06				20 36							21 11
Taplow d																				
Burnham d			19 41				←		20 11				20 40				←			21 15
Slough 3 a			19 45			19 44	19 45		20 14				20 46		20 42		20 46			21 19
d			19 48			19 44	19 48		20 18				20 48		20 44		20 48			21 21
Langley d			→				19 50		20 24				→				20 50			21 25
Iver d																				
West Drayton d							19 59		20 29								20 56			21 30
Heathrow Terminal 4 ✈ d								20 07											21 07	
Heathrow Terminal 1-2-3 2 ✈ d								20 13											21 13	
Hayes & Harlington d							20 03	20 19	20 34								21 01		21 19	21 34
Southall d								20 22	20 36										21 22	21 36
Hanwell d																				
Greenford ⊖ d																				
South Greenford d																				
Castle Bar Park d																				
Drayton Green d																				
West Ealing d																				
Ealing Broadway ⊖ d							20 09	20 27	20 43								21 08		21 27	21 43
Acton Main Line d																				
London Paddington 15 ⊖ a	19 29	19 43		19 59	20 02	20 07	20 18	20 36	20 51	20 22	20 31	20 43		20 59	21 04	21 13	21 18	21 30	21 36	21 51

	GW 1	GW ◇1 ⊡	GW ◇1	GW ◇1 ⊡	GW 1	GW ◇1 ⊡	HC	GW 1	GW ◇1 ⊡	GW ◇1	HC	GW 1	GW ◇1 ⊡	GW ◇1 ⊡	GW 1	GW ◇1 ⊡	GW ◇1	GW ◇1 ⊡	GW 1
Oxford d			20 50					21 05		21 50					22 17		22 50		
Reading 7 d	21 18	21 23	21 27	21 35		21 51		21 56	22 18	22 23		22 29	22 34	22 39	22 58	23 21	23 24	23 30	23 36
Twyford 3 d	21 24							22 02				22 38			23 05				23 42
Maidenhead 3 d	21 36		21 39					22 10				22 46			23 13				23 50
Taplow d																			
Burnham d	21 40				←			22 15				22 50							23 55
Slough 3 a	21 46		21 45		21 46			22 19		22 40		22 56			23 20		23 41		23 59
d	21 51		21 45		21 51			22 20		22 41		23 08			23 20		23 42		00 01
Langley d	→				21 55			22 24				23 12			23 24				00 05
Iver d																			
West Drayton d					21 59			22 29				23 17			23 29				00 10
Heathrow Terminal 4 ✈ d							22 07				23 07								
Heathrow Terminal 1-2-3 2 ✈ d							22 13				23 13								
Hayes & Harlington d					22 03		22 19	22 33			23 19	23 23			23 35				00 16
Southall d					22 07		22 22	22 37			23 22				23 38				00 20
Hanwell d																			
Greenford ⊖ d																			
South Greenford d																			
Castle Bar Park d																			
Drayton Green d																			
West Ealing d																			
Ealing Broadway ⊖ d					22 12		22 27	22 42			23 27	23 31			23 43				00 25
Acton Main Line d																			
London Paddington 15 ⊖ a		22 00	22 07	22 14	22 21	22 28	22 36	22 51	22 58	23 01	23 36	23 40	23 13	23 16	23 52	00 01	00 04	00 12	00 34

Sundays

from 1 April

	GW 1	GW ◇1	HC	GW ◇1 ⊡	GW 1	HC	GW 1	HC	GW 1	HC	GW 1	GW 1	HC	GW 1	GW ◇1 ⊡	GW 1	GW ◇1	GW 1	HC	GW 1	GW ◇1 ⊡	GW 1
Oxford d		23p01			23p07									08 05			08 50			09 00		
Reading 7 d	23p18	23p29		23p51	00 03		06 22		07 22		08 03	08 18		08 52	09 03	09 19	09 23			09 43	09 47	09 59
Twyford 3 d	23p24				00 10		06 28		07 28			08 24		08 58		09 25				09 49		10 05
Maidenhead 3 d	23p32				00 18		06 36		07 36			08 36		09 06		09 33				10 06		10 27
Taplow d	23p36				00 22																	
Burnham d	23p39				00 25		06 40		07 40			08 40				09 38		←				10 31
Slough 3 a	23p44	23p44			00 29		06 45		07 45		08 22	08 45		09 14		09 43	09 38	09 43		10 14		10 36
d	23p44	23p44			00 30		06 46		07 46		08 23	08 46		09 19		09 46	09 38	09 46		10 19		10 49
Langley d					00 34		06 50		07 50			08 50		09 24		→		09 50		10 23		→
Iver d					00 37																	
West Drayton d	23p51				00 40		06 55		07 55			08 55		09 30				09 55		10 30		
Heathrow Terminal 4 ✈ d			00 01			06 07		07 07		08 07			09 07						10 07			
Heathrow Terminal 1-2-3 2 ✈ d			00 07			06 13		07 13		08 13			09 13						10 13			
Hayes & Harlington d	23p56		00 13		00 45	06 19	07 02	07 19	08 02	08 19		09 02	09 19	09 34				10 02	10 19	10 34		
Southall d			00 16		00 48	06 22	07 05	07 22	08 05	08 22		09 05	09 22	09 37					10 23	10 37		
Hanwell d																						
Greenford ⊖ d																						
South Greenford d																						
Castle Bar Park d																						
Drayton Green d																						
West Ealing d																						
Ealing Broadway ⊖ d	00 03		00 21		00 54	06 27	07 11	07 27	08 11	08 27		09 11	09 27	09 43				10 08	10 28	10 43		
Acton Main Line d																						
London Paddington 15 ⊖ a	00 16	00 10	00 30	00 33	01 03	06 36	07 20	07 36	08 20	08 36	08 44	09 20	09 36	09 52	09 44		10 00	10 18	10 36	10 51	10 22	

Table 117

Sundays

from 1 April

Reading and Greenford - London

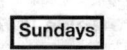

Network Diagram - see first Page of Table 116

		GW ◇1 ☕	GW ◇1	GW 1	HC	GW 1			GW ◇1 ☕	GW ◇1 ☕	GW 1	GW ◇1 ☕	GW ◇1	GW ◇1	GW ◇1	GW 1		HC	GW 1		GW ◇1 ☕	GW ◇1 ☕	GW 1	GW ◇1 ☕	GW ◇1
Oxford	d		09 48			09 54							10 44	10 55					10 39						11 50
Reading 7	d	10 00	10 22			10 39			10 44	10 52	10 58	11 02	11 14	11 23					11 42		11 47	11 52	12 00	12 05	12 23
Twyford 3	d					10 47					11 04		11 27						11 49				12 06		
Maidenhead 3	d					11 06					11 22		11 35						12 06				12 26		
Taplow	d																								
Burnham	d			←							11 29				←	←							12 30		
Slough 3	a		10 37	10 36		11 17					11 34		11 43	11 37	11 43	11 34			12 15				12 35		12 38
	d		10 37	10 49		11 19					11 48		11 44	11 38	11 44	11 48			12 18				12 48		12 39
Langley	d			10 51		11 24					→		→			11 50			12 23				→		
Iver	d																								
West Drayton	d			10 57		11 29										11 56			12 29						
Heathrow Terminal 4 ✈	d				11 07													12 07							
Heathrow Terminal 1-2-3 2 ✈	d				11 13													12 13							
Hayes & Harlington	d			11 02	11 19	11 33										12 01		12 19	12 33						
Southall	d				11 22	11 37												12 22	12 37						
Hanwell	d																								
Greenford ⊖	d																								
South Greenford	d																								
Castle Bar Park	d																								
Drayton Green	d																								
West Ealing	d																								
Ealing Broadway ⊖	d			11 09	11 27	11 42										12 08		12 27	12 42						
Acton Main Line	d																								
London Paddington 15 ⊖	a	10 44	10 58	11 19	11 36	11 51			11 22	11 29		11 44		12 01	12 03	12 18		12 36	12 51		12 22	12 29		12 42	13 03

		GW 1		HC	GW 1		GW ◇1 ☕	GW 1	GW ◇1 ☕	GW ◇1 ☕	GW ◇1	GW 1		HC	GW 1		GW ◇1 ☕	GW ◇1 ☕	GW 1	GW ◇1 ☕	GW ◇1	GW 1		HC	GW 1
Oxford	d				11 54						12 50				12 55						13 50				13 54
Reading 7	d				12 41		12 44	13 00	13 02	13 15	13 25				13 39		13 49	13 56	14 02	14 06	14 21				14 36
Twyford 3	d				12 49			13 06							13 48				14 08						14 44
Maidenhead 3	d				13 06			13 26							14 06				14 23						15 06
Taplow	d																								
Burnham	d	←						13 30				←							14 27			←			
Slough 3	a	12 35			13 15			13 35			13 40	13 35			14 15				14 32		14 37	14 32			15 15
	d	12 48			13 19			13 48			13 40	13 48			14 18				14 48		14 37	14 48			15 18
Langley	d	12 50			13 24			→				13 50			14 23				→			14 50			15 23
Iver	d																								
West Drayton	d	12 56			13 29							13 56			14 29							14 56			15 29
Heathrow Terminal 4 ✈	d			13 07										14 07										15 07	
Heathrow Terminal 1-2-3 2 ✈	d			13 13										14 13										15 13	
Hayes & Harlington	d	13 01		13 19	13 33							14 01		14 19	14 33							15 01		15 19	15 33
Southall	d			13 22	13 37									14 22	14 37									15 22	15 37
Hanwell	d																								
Greenford ⊖	d																								
South Greenford	d																								
Castle Bar Park	d																								
Drayton Green	d																								
West Ealing	d																								
Ealing Broadway ⊖	d	13 08		13 27	13 42							14 08		14 27	14 42							15 08		15 27	15 43
Acton Main Line	d																								
London Paddington 15 ⊖	a	13 18		13 36	13 51		13 22		13 42	13 59	14 05	14 19		14 36	14 51		14 22	14 33		14 43	14 59	15 18		15 36	15 51

			GW ◇1 ☕	GW ◇1 ☕	GW ◇1 ☕	GW 1	GW ◇1	GW 1		HC	GW 1		GW ◇1 ☕	GW 1	GW ◇1 ☕	GW ◇1 ☕	GW ◇1 ☕	GW 1		HC	GW 1		GW ◇1 ☕	GW ◇1 ☕	GW 1
Oxford	d						14 50				14 58						15 50				15 56				
Reading 7	d		14 47	14 53	15 07	15 18	15 26				15 44		15 49	15 58	16 02	16 21	16 26				16 43		16 49	16 55	17 01
Twyford 3	d					15 24					15 50			16 04							16 50				17 07
Maidenhead 3	d					15 36					16 06			16 31							17 06				17 29
Taplow	d																								
Burnham	d					15 40		←			16 11			16 35				←			17 11				17 34
Slough 3	a					15 45	15 41	15 45			16 14			16 45			16 40	16 45			17 16				17 39
	d					15 48	15 41	15 48			16 20			16 48			16 40	16 48			17 17				17 51
Langley	d					→		15 52			16 24			→				16 50			17 22				→
Iver	d																								
West Drayton	d							15 56			16 29							16 56			17 30				
Heathrow Terminal 4 ✈	d									16 07										17 07					
Heathrow Terminal 1-2-3 2 ✈	d									16 13										17 13					
Hayes & Harlington	d							16 01		16 19	16 34							17 01		17 19	17 34				
Southall	d									16 22	16 36									17 22	17 37				
Hanwell	d																								
Greenford ⊖	d																								
South Greenford	d																								
Castle Bar Park	d																								
Drayton Green	d																								
West Ealing	d																								
Ealing Broadway ⊖	d							16 08		16 27	16 43							17 08		17 27	17 42				
Acton Main Line	d																								
London Paddington 15 ⊖	a		15 23	15 29	15 43		16 03	16 18		16 36	16 51		16 22		16 42	16 59	17 05	17 19		17 36	17 51		17 22	17 32	

Table 117

Sundays
from 1 April

Reading and Greenford - London

Network Diagram - see first Page of Table 116

		GW ◇1 ☕	GW ◇1	GW ◇1 ☕		GW ◇1 ☕	GW ◇1 ☕	GW 1	HC	GW 1		GW ◇1 ☕	GW ◇1 ☕	GW 1		GW ◇1 ☕	GW ◇1 ☕	GW ◇1 ☕	GW 1	HC	GW 1		GW ◇1 ☕	GW ◇1 ☕	
Oxford	d		16 37				16 50			16 56								17 50			17 55				
Reading 7	d	17 06	17 10	17 18		17 23	17 27			17 44		17 49	17 54	17 58		18 02	18 21	18 26			18 43		18 50	18 56	
Twyford 3	d		17 17							17 51				18 04							18 50				
Maidenhead 3	d		17 25							18 06				18 26							19 06				
Taplow	d																								
Burnham	d							←		18 12				18 30					←		19 12				
Slough 3	a		17 33				17 47	17 39		18 15				18 35				18 41	18 35		19 16				
	d		17 33				17 47	17 51		18 20				18 48				18 41	18 48		19 20				
Langley	d							17 55		18 24				↪					18 50		19 24				
Iver	d																								
West Drayton	d							17 59		18 29									18 56		19 30				
Heathrow Terminal 4 ✈	d								18 07											19 07					
Heathrow Terminal 1-2-3 2 ✈	d								18 13											19 13					
Hayes & Harlington	d							18 03	18 19	18 34									19 00	19 19	19 33				
Southall	d								18 22	18 36										19 22	19 37				
Hanwell	d																								
Greenford ⊖	d																								
South Greenford	d																								
Castle Bar Park	d																								
Drayton Green	d																								
West Ealing	d																								
Ealing Broadway ⊖	d							18 09	18 27	18 43									19 08	19 27	19 42				
Acton Main Line	d																								
London Paddington 15 ⊖	a	17 44	17 57	18 03		18 06	18 13	18 19	18 36	18 51		18 22	18 29			18 43	18 59	19 06	19 18	19 36	19 51		19 22	19 32	

		GW ◇1 ☕	GW ◇1 ☕	GW 1	GW ◇1 ☕	GW ◇1 ☕	GW ◇1 ☕	GW 1	GW ◇1 ☕	HC		GW 1		GW 1	GW ◇1 ☕	GW ◇1 ☕	GW ◇1	GW 1	HC	GW 1			GW ◇1 ☕	GW ◇1 ☕	GW 1
Oxford	d					18 50						19 05					19 50			19 58					
Reading 7	d	19 05	19 14	19 20	19 25	19 30	19 38		19 50			19 56		20 03	20 18	20 23	20 24			20 38			20 43	20 50	21 18
Twyford 3	d			19 26								20 03		20 09						20 45					21 24
Maidenhead 3	d			19 40								20 12		20 26						21 11					21 36
Taplow	d																								
Burnham	d			19 44				←				20 16		20 30				←		21 16					21 41
Slough 3	a			19 50		19 44		19 50				20 19		20 36			20 42	20 36		21 19					21 45
	d			19 51		19 44		19 51				20 19		20 48			20 42	20 48		21 19					21 52
Langley	d			↪				19 55				20 24		↪				20 50		21 26					↪
Iver	d																								
West Drayton	d							19 59				20 29						20 56		21 30					
Heathrow Terminal 4 ✈	d									20 07									21 07						
Heathrow Terminal 1-2-3 2 ✈	d									20 13									21 13						
Hayes & Harlington	d							20 03		20 19		20 33						21 01	21 19	21 34					
Southall	d									20 22		20 37							21 22	21 37					
Hanwell	d																								
Greenford ⊖	d																								
South Greenford	d																								
Castle Bar Park	d																								
Drayton Green	d																								
West Ealing	d																								
Ealing Broadway ⊖	d							20 09		20 27		20 42						21 08	21 27	21 43					
Acton Main Line	d																								
London Paddington 15 ⊖	a	19 44	19 59		20 02	20 07	20 14	20 18	20 28	20 36		20 51			20 58	21 01	21 05	21 16	21 36	21 51			21 19	21 27	

		GW ◇1 ☕	GW ◇1 ☕	GW ◇1	GW ◇1 ☕	GW 1		GW ◇1 ☕	HC	GW 1			GW ◇1 ☕	GW ◇1	HC	GW 1		GW ◇1 ☕	GW ◇1 ☕	GW 1	GW ◇1	GW ◇1 ☕	GW 1		
Oxford	d			20 50						21 05				21 50						22 21	22 46				
Reading 7	d	21 20	21 23	21 28	21 32			21 49		21 56			22 18	22 23		22 29		22 39	22 45	23 00	23 22	23 30	23 36		
Twyford 3	d									22 03						22 38				23 06			23 42		
Maidenhead 3	d			21 40						22 11						22 46				23 14			23 50		
Taplow	d																								
Burnham	d					←				22 15						22 50							23 55		
Slough 3	a			21 46		21 45				22 21				22 40		22 56				23 21	23 42		23 59		
	d			21 46		21 52				22 21				22 41		23 08				23 22	23 43		00 01		
Langley	d					21 56				22 25						23 12				23 26			00 05		
Iver	d																								
West Drayton	d					22 00				22 30						23 17				23 31			00 10		
Heathrow Terminal 4 ✈	d								22 07						23 07										
Heathrow Terminal 1-2-3 2 ✈	d								22 13						23 13										
Hayes & Harlington	d					22 04			22 19	22 34					23 19	23 23				23 35			00 16		
Southall	d					22 08			22 22	22 38					23 22					23 39			00 20		
Hanwell	d																								
Greenford ⊖	d																								
South Greenford	d																								
Castle Bar Park	d																								
Drayton Green	d																								
West Ealing	d																								
Ealing Broadway ⊖	d					22 13			22 27	22 43					23 27	23 31				23 44			00 25		
Acton Main Line	d																								
London Paddington 15 ⊖	a	21 59	22 02	22 07	22 14	22 21		22 27	22 36	22 51			22 58	23 01	23 36	23 40		23 15	23 28	23 53	00 04	00 13	00 34		

London - Heathrow Airport

Network Diagram - see first Page of Table 116

Miles			HX	HX	HX 1	HX	HX 1	HX	HX 1	HX	HX 1		HX	HX 1	HX	HX 1	HX	HX 1	HX	HX 1	HX		HX 1	HX	HX 1
0	London Paddington 15 ⊖	d	04 42		05 10	05 13	05 25		05 40		05 55			06 10		06 25		06 40		06 55			07 10		07 25
14¾	Heathrow Terminals 1-2-3 2 ✈	a	05 04		05 26	05 35	05 40		05 55		06 10			06 25		06 40		06 55		07 10			07 25		07 40
—		d	05 05	05 16	05 29	05 36	05 41	05 44	05 56	06 03	06 11		06 18	06 26	06 33	06 41	06 48	06 56	07 03	07 11	07 18		07 26	07 33	07 41
—	Heathrow Terminal 4 ✈	a	05 10	05 20		05 41		05 48		06 07			06 22		06 37		06 52		07 07		07 22			07 37	
16¼	Heathrow Terminal 5 ✈	a			05 33		05 46		06 01		06 16			06 31		06 46		07 01		07 16			07 31		07 46

		HX	HX 1	HX	HX 1	HX	HX 1		HX	HX 1	HX	HX 1	HX	HX 1	HX	HX 1	HX		HX 1	HX	HX 1	HX	HX 1	HX	HX 1
London Paddington 15 ⊖	d		07 40		07 55		08 10			08 25		08 40		08 55		09 10			09 25		09 40		09 55		10 10
Heathrow Terminals 1-2-3 2 ✈	a		07 55		08 10		08 25			08 40		08 55		09 10		09 25			09 40		09 55		10 10		10 25
	d	07 48	07 56	08 03	08 11	08 18	08 26		08 33	08 41	08 48	08 56	09 03	09 11	09 18	09 26	09 33		09 41	09 48	09 56	10 03	10 11	10 18	10 26
Heathrow Terminal 4 ✈	a	07 52		08 07		08 22			08 37		08 52		09 07		09 22		09 37			09 52		10 07		10 22	
Heathrow Terminal 5 ✈	a		08 01		08 16		08 31			08 46		09 01		09 16		09 31			09 46		10 01		10 16		10 31

		HX	HX 1		HX	HX 1	HX	HX 1	HX	HX 1	HX	HX 1	HX		HX 1	HX	HX 1	HX	HX 1	HX	HX 1	HX	HX 1		HX
London Paddington 15 ⊖	d		10 25			10 40		10 55		11 10		11 25			11 40		11 55		12 10		12 25		12 40		
Heathrow Terminals 1-2-3 2 ✈	a		10 40			10 55		11 10		11 25		11 40			11 55		12 10		12 25		12 40		12 55		
	d	10 33	10 41		10 48	10 56	11 03	11 11	11 18	11 26	11 33	11 41	11 48		11 56	12 03	12 11	12 18	12 26	12 33	12 41	12 48	12 56		13 03
Heathrow Terminal 4 ✈	a	10 37			10 52		11 07		11 22		11 37		11 52			12 07		12 22		12 37		12 52			13 07
Heathrow Terminal 5 ✈	a		10 46			11 01		11 16		11 31		11 46			12 01		12 16		12 31		12 46		13 01		

		HX 1	HX	HX 1	HX	HX 1	HX	HX 1	HX		HX 1	HX	HX 1	HX	HX 1	HX	HX 1	HX	HX 1		HX	HX 1	HX	HX 1	HX
London Paddington 15 ⊖	d	12 55		13 10		13 25		13 40			13 55		14 10		14 25		14 40		14 55			15 10		15 25	
Heathrow Terminals 1-2-3 2 ✈	a	13 10		13 25		13 40		13 55			14 10		14 25		14 40		14 55		15 10			15 25		15 40	
	d	13 11	13 18	13 26	13 33	13 41	13 48	13 56	14 03		14 11	14 18	14 26	14 33	14 41	14 48	14 56	15 03	15 11		15 18	15 26	15 33	15 41	15 48
Heathrow Terminal 4 ✈	a		13 22		13 37		13 52		14 07			14 22		14 37		14 52		15 07			15 22		15 37		15 52
Heathrow Terminal 5 ✈	a	13 16		13 31		13 46		14 01			14 16		14 31		14 46		15 01		15 16			15 31		15 46	

		HX 1	HX	HX 1	HX		HX 1	HX	HX 1	HX	HX 1	HX	HX 1	HX	HX 1		HX	HX 1	HX	HX 1	HX	HX 1	HX	HX 1	HX
London Paddington 15 ⊖	d	15 40		15 55			16 10		16 25		16 40		16 55		17 10			17 25		17 40		17 55		18 10	
Heathrow Terminals 1-2-3 2 ✈	a	15 55		16 10			16 25		16 40		16 55		17 10		17 25			17 40		17 55		18 10		18 25	
	d	15 56	16 03	16 11	16 18		16 26	16 33	16 41	16 48	16 56	17 03	17 11	17 18	17 26		17 33	17 41	17 48	17 56	18 03	18 11	18 18	18 26	18 33
Heathrow Terminal 4 ✈	a		16 07		16 22			16 37		16 52		17 07		17 22			17 37		17 52		18 07		18 22		18 37
Heathrow Terminal 5 ✈	a	16 01		16 16			16 31		16 46		17 01		17 16		17 31			17 46		18 01		18 16		18 31	

			HX 1	HX	HX 1	HX	HX 1	HX	HX 1	HX	HX 1		HX	HX 1	HX	HX 1	HX	HX 1	HX	HX 1	HX		HX 1	HX	HX 1
London Paddington 15 ⊖	d		18 25		18 40		18 55		19 10		19 25			19 40		19 55		20 10		20 25			20 40		20 55
Heathrow Terminals 1-2-3 2 ✈	a		18 40		18 55		19 10		19 25		19 40			19 55		20 10		20 25		20 40			20 55		21 10
	d		18 41	18 48	18 56	19 03	19 11	19 18	19 26	19 33	19 41		19 48	19 56	20 03	20 11	20 18	20 26	20 33	20 41	20 48		20 56	21 03	21 11
Heathrow Terminal 4 ✈	a			18 52		19 07		19 22		19 37			19 52		20 07		20 22		20 37		20 52			21 07	
Heathrow Terminal 5 ✈	a		18 46		19 01		19 16		19 31		19 46			20 01		20 16		20 31		20 46			21 01		21 16

		HX	HX 1	HX	HX 1	HX	HX 1		HX	HX 1	HX	HX 1	HX	HX 1	HX	HX 1	HX		HX 1	HX	HX 1	HX	HX	HX 1	HX
London Paddington 15 ⊖	d		21 10		21 25		21 40			21 55		22 10		22 25		22 40			22 55		23 10		23 03	23 25	
Heathrow Terminals 1-2-3 2 ✈	a		21 25		21 40		21 55			22 10		22 25		22 40		22 55			23 10		23 25		23 35	23 40	
	d	21 18	21 26	21 33	21 41	21 48	21 56		22 03	22 11	22 18	22 26	22 33	22 41	22 48	22 56	23 03		23 11	23 18	23 26	23 33	23 37	23 41	23 48
Heathrow Terminal 4 ✈	a	21 22		21 37		21 52			22 07		22 22		22 37		22 52		23 07			23 22		23 37	23 41		23 52
Heathrow Terminal 5 ✈	a		21 31		21 46		22 01			22 16		22 31		22 46		23 01			23 16		23 31			23 46	

Saturdays

		HC	HX	HX 1	HX	HX 1	HX	HX 1	HX	HX 1		HX	HX 1	HX	HX 1	HX	HX 1	HX	HX 1	HX		HX 1	HX	HX 1	HX
London Paddington 15 ⊖	d	04 42		05 10	05 13	05 25		05 40		05 55			06 10		06 25		06 40		06 55			07 10		07 25	
Heathrow Terminals 1-2-3 2 ✈	a	05 04		05 26	05 35	05 40		05 55		06 10			06 25		06 40		06 55		07 10			07 25		07 40	
	d	05 05	05 16	05 29	05 36	05 41	05 44	05 56	06 03	06 11		06 18	06 26	06 33	06 41	06 48	06 56	07 03	07 11	07 18		07 26	07 33	07 41	07 48
Heathrow Terminal 4 ✈	a	05 10	05 20		05 41		05 48		06 07			06 22		06 37		06 52		07 07		07 22			07 37		07 52
Heathrow Terminal 5 ✈	a			05 33		05 46		06 01		06 16			06 31		06 46		07 01		07 16			07 31		07 46	

		HX 1	HX	HX 1	HX	HX 1		HX	HX 1	HX	HX 1	HX	HX 1	HX	HX 1	HX		HX 1	HX	HX 1	HX	HX 1	HX	HX 1	HX
London Paddington 15 ⊖	d	07 40		07 55		08 10			08 25		08 40		08 55		09 10			09 25		09 40		09 55		10 10	
Heathrow Terminals 1-2-3 2 ✈	a	07 55		08 10		08 25			08 40		08 55		09 10		09 25			09 40		09 55		10 10		10 25	
	d	07 56	08 03	08 11	08 18	08 26		08 33	08 41	08 48	08 56	09 03	09 11	09 18	09 26	09 33		09 41	09 48	09 56	10 03	10 11	10 18	10 26	10 33
Heathrow Terminal 4 ✈	a		08 07		08 22			08 37		08 52		09 07		09 22		09 37			09 52		10 07		10 22		10 37
Heathrow Terminal 5 ✈	a	08 01		08 16		08 31			08 46		09 01		09 16		09 31			09 46		10 01		10 16		10 31	

Table 118

Saturdays

London - Heathrow Airport

Network Diagram - see first Page of Table 116

	HX ■		HX	HX ■	HX	HX ■	HX	HX ■	HX	HX ■	HX		HX ■	HX	HX ■	HX	HX ■	HX	HX ■	HX	HX ■		HX	HX ■
London Paddington 15 ⊖ d	10 25			10 40		10 55		11 10		11 25			11 40		11 55		12 10		12 25		12 40			12 55
Heathrow Terminals 1-2-3 2 ✈ a	10 40			10 55		11 10		11 25		11 40			11 55		12 10		12 25		12 40		12 55			13 10
d	10 41		10 48	10 56	11 03	11 11	11 18	11 26	11 33	11 41	11 48		11 56	12 03	12 11	12 18	12 26	12 33	12 41	12 48	12 56		13 03	13 11
Heathrow Terminal 4 ✈ a			10 52		11 07		11 22		11 37		11 52			12 07		12 22		12 37		12 52			13 07	
Heathrow Terminal 5 ✈ a	10 46			11 01		11 16		11 31		11 46			12 01		12 16		12 31		12 46		13 01			13 16

	HX	HX ■	HX	HX ■	HX	HX ■	HX		HX ■	HX	HX ■	HX	HX ■	HX	HX ■	HX	HX ■		HX	HX ■	HX	HX ■	HX	HX ■
London Paddington 15 ⊖ d		13 10		13 25		13 40			13 55		14 10		14 25		14 40		14 55			15 10		15 25		15 40
Heathrow Terminals 1-2-3 2 ✈ a		13 25		13 40		13 55			14 10		14 25		14 40		14 55		15 10			15 25		15 40		15 55
d	13 18	13 26	13 33	13 41	13 48	13 56	14 03		14 11	14 18	14 26	14 33	14 41	14 48	14 56	15 03	15 11		15 18	15 26	15 33	15 41	15 48	15 56
Heathrow Terminal 4 ✈ a	13 22		13 37		13 52		14 07			14 22		14 37		14 52		15 07			15 22		15 37		15 52	
Heathrow Terminal 5 ✈ a		13 31		13 46		14 01			14 16		14 31		14 46		15 01		15 16			15 31		15 46		16 01

	HX	HX ■	HX		HX ■	HX	HX ■	HX	HX ■	HX	HX ■	HX	HX ■		HX	HX ■	HX	HX ■	HX	HX ■	HX	HX ■	HX	
London Paddington 15 ⊖ d		15 55			16 10		16 25		16 40		16 55		17 10			17 25		17 40		17 55		18 10		
Heathrow Terminals 1-2-3 2 ✈ a		16 10			16 25		16 40		16 55		17 10		17 25			17 40		17 55		18 10		18 25		
d	16 03	16 11	16 18		16 26	16 33	16 41	16 48	16 56	17 03	17 11	17 18	17 26		17 33	17 41	17 48	17 56	18 03	18 11	18 18	18 26	18 33	
Heathrow Terminal 4 ✈ a	16 07		16 22			16 37		16 52		17 07		17 22			17 37		17 52		18 07		18 22		18 37	
Heathrow Terminal 5 ✈ a		16 16			16 31		16 46		17 01		17 16		17 31			17 46		18 01		18 16		18 31		

	HX ■	HX	HX ■	HX	HX ■	HX	HX ■	HX	HX ■		HX	HX ■	HX	HX ■	HX	HX ■	HX	HX ■	HX		HX ■	HX	HX ■	HX
London Paddington 15 ⊖ d	18 25		18 40		18 55		19 10		19 25			19 40		19 55		20 10		20 25			20 40		20 55	
Heathrow Terminals 1-2-3 2 ✈ a	18 40		18 55		19 10		19 25		19 40			19 55		20 10		20 25		20 40			20 55		21 10	
d	18 41	18 48	18 56	19 03	19 11	19 18	19 26	19 33	19 41		19 48	19 56	20 03	20 11	20 18	20 26	20 33	20 41	20 48		20 56	21 03	21 11	21 18
Heathrow Terminal 4 ✈ a		18 52		19 07		19 22		19 37			19 52		20 07		20 22		20 37		20 52			21 07		21 22
Heathrow Terminal 5 ✈ a	18 46		19 01		19 16		19 31		19 46			20 01		20 16		20 31		20 46			21 01		21 16	

	HX ■	HX	HX ■	HX	HX ■		HX	HX ■	HX	HX ■	HX	HX ■	HX	HX ■	HX		HX ■	HX	HX ■	HX	HC	HX ■	HX	
London Paddington 15 ⊖ d	21 10		21 25		21 40			21 55		22 10		22 25		22 40			22 55		23 10		23 03	23 25		
Heathrow Terminals 1-2-3 2 ✈ a	21 25		21 40		21 55			22 10		22 25		22 40		22 55			23 10		23 25		23 35	23 40		
d	21 26	21 33	21 41	21 48	21 56		22 03	22 11	22 18	22 26	22 33	22 41	22 48	22 56	23 03		23 11	23 18	23 26	23 33	23 37	23 41	23 48	
Heathrow Terminal 4 ✈ a		21 37		21 52			22 07		22 22		22 37		22 52		23 07			23 22		23 37	23 41		23 52	
Heathrow Terminal 5 ✈ a	21 31		21 46		22 01			22 16		22 31		22 46		23 01			23 16		23 31			23 46		

Sundays

	HX ■	HX	HX ■	HC	HX ■	HX	HX ■	HX	HX		HX	HX	HX ■	HX	HX ■	HX	HX ■	HX	HX ■		HX	HX	HX ■	HX
London Paddington 15 ⊖ d	05 10		05 25	05 28	05 40		05 55		06 10			06 12	06 25		06 40		06 55		07 10			07 12	07 25	
Heathrow Terminals 1-2-3 2 ✈ a	05 26	05 34	05 41	05 45	05 56		06 11		06 26			06 34	06 41		06 56		07 11		07 26			07 34	07 41	
d	05 27	05 36	05 42	05 47	05 59	06 01	06 13	06 19	06 31		06 33	06 37	06 47	06 49	06 59	07 01	07 13	07 19	07 31		07 33	07 37	07 47	07 49
Heathrow Terminal 4 ✈ a		05 40		05 51		06 05		06 23			06 37	06 41		06 53		07 05		07 23			07 37	07 41		07 53
Heathrow Terminal 5 ✈ a	05 32		05 47		06 03		06 17		06 35				06 51		07 03		07 17		07 35				07 51	

	HX ■	HX	HX ■	HX	HX ■		HX	HX	HX ■	HX	HX ■	HX	HX ■	HX	HX ■		HX	HX	HX ■	HX	HX ■	HX	HX ■	HX
London Paddington 15 ⊖ d	07 40		07 55		08 10			08 12	08 25		08 40		08 55		09 10			09 12	09 25		09 40		09 55	
Heathrow Terminals 1-2-3 2 ✈ a	07 56		08 11		08 26			08 34	08 41		08 56		09 11		09 26			09 34	09 41		09 56		10 11	
d	07 59	08 01	08 13	08 19	08 31		08 33	08 37	08 47	08 49	08 59	09 01	09 13	09 19	09 31		09 33	09 37	09 47	09 49	09 59	10 01	10 13	10 19
Heathrow Terminal 4 ✈ a		08 05		08 23			08 37	08 41		08 53		09 05		09 23			09 37	09 41		09 53		10 05		10 23
Heathrow Terminal 5 ✈ a	08 03		08 17		08 35				08 51		09 03		09 17		09 35				09 51		10 03		10 17	

	HX ■		HX	HX	HX ■	HX	HX ■	HX	HX ■	HX	HX ■		HX	HX	HX ■	HX	HX ■	HX	HX ■	HX	HX		HX	HX
London Paddington 15 ⊖ d	10 10			10 12	10 25		10 40		10 55		11 10			11 12	11 25		11 40		11 55		12 10			12 12
Heathrow Terminals 1-2-3 2 ✈ a	10 26			10 34	10 41		10 56		11 11		11 26			11 34	11 41		11 56		12 11		12 26			12 34
d	10 31		10 33	10 37	10 47	10 49	10 59	11 01	11 13	11 19	11 31		11 33	11 37	11 47	11 49	11 59	12 01	12 13	12 19	12 31		12 33	12 37
Heathrow Terminal 4 ✈ a			10 37	10 41		10 53		11 05		11 23			11 37	11 41		11 53		12 05		12 23			12 37	12 41
Heathrow Terminal 5 ✈ a	10 35				10 51		11 03		11 17		11 35				11 51		12 03		12 17		12 35			

	HX	HX	HX ■	HX	HX ■	HX	HX ■		HX	HX	HX ■	HX	HX ■	HX	HX ■	HX	HX ■		HX	HX	HX ■	HX	HX ■	HX
London Paddington 15 ⊖ d	12 25		12 40		12 55		13 10			13 12	13 25		13 40		13 55		14 10			14 12	14 25		14 40	
Heathrow Terminals 1-2-3 2 ✈ a	12 41		12 56		13 11		13 26			13 34	13 41		13 56		14 11		14 26			14 34	14 41		14 56	
d	12 47	12 49	12 59	13 01	13 13	13 19	13 31		13 33	13 37	13 47	13 49	13 59	14 01	14 13	14 19	14 31		14 33	14 37	14 47	14 49	14 59	15 01
Heathrow Terminal 4 ✈ a		12 53		13 05		13 23			13 37	13 41		13 53		14 05		14 23			14 37	14 41		14 53		15 05
Heathrow Terminal 5 ✈ a	12 51		13 03		13 17		13 35				13 51		14 03		14 17		14 35				14 51		15 03	

Table 118

Sundays

London - Heathrow Airport

Network Diagram - see first Page of Table 116

		HX 1	HX	HX 1		HX	HX	HX 1	HX	HX 1	HX	HX 1	HX	HX 1		HX	HX	HX 1	HX	HX 1	HX	HX 1	HX	HX
London Paddington 15 ⊖	d	14 55		15 10			15 12	15 25		15 40		15 55		16 10			16 12	16 25		16 40		16 55		17 10
Heathrow Terminals 1-2-3 2 ✈	a	15 11		15 26			15 34	15 41		15 56		16 11		16 26			16 34	16 41		16 56		17 11		17 26
	d	15 13	15 19	15 31		15 33	15 37	15 47	15 49	15 59	16 01	16 13	16 19	16 31		16 33	16 37	16 47	16 49	16 59	17 01	17 13	17 19	17 31
Heathrow Terminal 4 ✈	a		15 23			15 37	15 41		15 53		16 05		16 23			16 37	16 41		16 53		17 05		17 23	
Heathrow Terminal 5 ✈	a	15 17		15 35				15 51		16 03		16 17		16 35				16 51		17 03		17 17		17 35

		HX	HC	HX	HX	HX	HX	HX	HX	HX		HX	HX	HX	HX	HX	HX	HX	HX	HX		HX	HX	HX	HX
London Paddington 15 ⊖	d		17 12	17 25		17 40		17 55		18 10			18 12	18 25		18 40		18 55		19 10			19 12	19 25	
Heathrow Terminals 1-2-3 2 ✈	a		17 34	17 41		17 56		18 11		18 26			18 34	18 41		18 56		19 11		19 26			19 34	19 41	
	d	17 33	17 37	17 47	17 49	17 59	18 01	18 13	18 19	18 31		18 33	18 37	18 47	18 49	18 59	19 01	19 13	19 19	19 31		19 33	19 37	19 47	19 49
Heathrow Terminal 4 ✈	a	17 37	17 41		17 53		18 05		18 23			18 37	18 41		18 53		19 05		19 23			19 37	19 41		19 53
Heathrow Terminal 5 ✈	a			17 51		18 03		18 17		18 35				18 51		19 03		19 17		19 35				19 51	

		HX	HX	HX	HX	HX		HX	HX	HX	HX	HX	HX	HX	HX	HX		HX	HX	HX	HX	HX	HX	HX	HX
London Paddington 15 ⊖	d	19 40		19 55		20 10			20 12	20 25		20 40		20 55		21 10			21 12	21 25		21 40		21 55	
Heathrow Terminals 1-2-3 2 ✈	a	19 56		20 11		20 26			20 34	20 41		20 56		21 11		21 26			21 34	21 41		21 56		22 11	
	d	19 59	20 01	20 13	20 19	20 31		20 33	20 37	20 47	20 49	20 59	21 01	21 13	21 19	21 31		21 33	21 37	21 47	21 49	21 59	22 01	22 13	22 19
Heathrow Terminal 4 ✈	a		20 05		20 23			20 37	20 41		20 53		21 05		21 23			21 37	21 41		21 53		22 05		22 23
Heathrow Terminal 5 ✈	a	20 03		20 17		20 35				20 51		21 03		21 17		21 35				21 51		22 03		22 17	

		HX		HX	HX	HX	HX	HX	HX	HX	HX	HX		HX	HX	HX	HX								
London Paddington 15 ⊖	d	22 10			22 12	22 25		22 40		22 55		23 10			23 12	23 25									
Heathrow Terminals 1-2-3 2 ✈	a	22 26			22 34	22 41		22 56		23 11		23 26			23 34	23 41									
	d	22 31		22 33	22 37	22 47	22 49	22 59	23 01	23 13	23 19	23 31		23 33	23 37	23 47	23 49								
Heathrow Terminal 4 ✈	a			22 37	22 41		22 53		23 05		23 23			23 37	23 41		23 53								
Heathrow Terminal 5 ✈	a	22 35				22 51		23 03		23 17		23 35				23 51									

Heathrow Airport - London

Network Diagram - see first Page of Table 116

Miles			HX MX 1	HX MO 1	HX MX	HX MO	HX	HX 1	HX	HX 1	HX		HX 1	HX	HX	HX 1	HX	HX 1	HX	HX 1	HX		HX 1	HX	HX 1
0	Heathrow Terminal 5	d	23p42	23p48	23p53	23p58		05 07		05 27			05 42			05 57		06 12		06 27			06 42		06 57
—	Heathrow Terminal 4	d					00 01		05 23		05 32			05 51	05 57		06 12		06 27		06 42			06 57	
1½	Heathrow Terminals 1-2-3 2	a	23p46	23p52	23p57	00 02	00 05	05 11	05 27	05 31	05 36		05 46	05 55	06 01	06 01	06 16	06 16	06 31	06 31	06 46		06 46	07 01	07 01
—		d	23p48	23p53	23p57	00 02	00 07	05 12	05 29	05 33			05 48	05 57		06 03		06 18		06 33			06 48		07 03
16¼	London Paddington 15	a	00 04	00 09			00 30	05 28	05 56	05 49			06 04	06 24		06 19		06 34		06 49			07 05		07 19

		HX	HX 1	HX	HX 1	HX	HX 1		HX	HX 1	HX	HX 1	HX	HX 1	HX	HX 1	HX		HX 1	HX	HX 1	HX	HX 1	HX	HX 1
Heathrow Terminal 5	d		07 12		07 27		07 42			07 57		08 12		08 27		08 42			08 57		09 12		09 27		09 42
Heathrow Terminal 4	d	07 12		07 27		07 42			07 57		08 12		08 27		08 42		08 57			09 12		09 27		09 42	
Heathrow Terminals 1-2-3 2	a	07 16	07 16	07 31	07 31	07 46	07 46		08 01	08 01	08 16	08 16	08 31	08 31	08 46	08 46	09 01		09 01	09 16	09 16	09 31	09 31	09 46	09 46
	d		07 18		07 33		07 48			08 03		08 18		08 33		08 48			09 03		09 18		09 33		09 48
London Paddington 15	a		07 35		07 49		08 04			08 19		08 35		08 49		09 04			09 19		09 35		09 49		10 05

		HX	HX 1		HX	HX 1	HX	HX 1	HX	HX 1	HX	HX 1	HX		HX 1	HX	HX 1	HX	HX 1	HX	HX 1	HX	HX 1		HX
Heathrow Terminal 5	d		09 57			10 12		10 27		10 42		10 57			11 12		11 27		11 42		11 57		12 12		
Heathrow Terminal 4	d	09 57			10 12		10 27		10 42		10 57		11 12			11 27		11 42		11 57		12 12			12 27
Heathrow Terminals 1-2-3 2	a	10 01	10 01		10 16	10 16	10 31	10 31	10 46	10 46	11 01	11 01	11 16		11 16	11 31	11 31	11 46	11 46	12 01	12 01	12 16	12 16		12 31
	d		10 03			10 18		10 33		10 48		11 03			11 18		11 33		11 48		12 03		12 18		
London Paddington 15	a		10 19			10 34		10 49		11 04		11 19			11 34		11 49		12 04		12 19		12 34		

		HX 1	HX	HX 1	HX	HX 1	HX	HX 1	HX		HX 1	HX	HX 1	HX	HX 1	HX	HX 1	HX	HX 1		HX	HX 1	HX	HX 1	HX
Heathrow Terminal 5	d	12 27		12 42		12 57		13 12			13 27		13 42		13 57		14 12		14 27			14 42		14 57	
Heathrow Terminal 4	d		12 42		12 57		13 12		13 27			13 42		13 57		14 12		14 27			14 42		14 57		15 12
Heathrow Terminals 1-2-3 2	a	12 31	12 46	12 46	13 01	13 01	13 16	13 16	13 31		13 31	13 46	13 46	14 01	14 01	14 16	14 16	14 31	14 31		14 46	14 46	15 01	15 01	15 16
	d	12 33		12 48		13 03		13 18			13 33		13 48		14 03		14 18		14 33			14 48		15 03	
London Paddington 15	a	12 49		13 04		13 19		13 35			13 49		14 04		14 19		14 34		14 49			15 04		15 19	

		HX 1	HX	HX 1	HX		HX 1	HX	HX 1	HX	HX 1	HX	HX 1	HX	HX 1		HX	HX 1	HX	HX 1	HX	HX 1	HX	HX 1	HX
Heathrow Terminal 5	d	15 12		15 27			15 42		15 57		16 12		16 27		16 42			16 57		17 12		17 27		17 42	
Heathrow Terminal 4	d		15 27		15 42			15 57		16 12		16 27		16 42			16 57		17 12		17 27		17 42		17 57
Heathrow Terminals 1-2-3 2	a	15 16	15 31	15 31	15 46		15 46	16 01	16 01	16 16	16 16	16 31	16 31	16 46	16 46		17 01	17 01	17 16	17 16	17 31	17 31	17 46	17 46	18 01
	d	15 18		15 33			15 48		16 03		16 18		16 33		16 48			17 03		17 18		17 33		17 48	
London Paddington 15	a	15 35		15 49			16 05		16 19		16 35		16 49		17 05			17 19		17 35		17 49		18 05	

			HX 1	HX	HX 1	HX	HX 1	HX	HX 1	HX	HX 1		HX	HX 1	HX	HX 1	HX	HX 1	HX	HX 1	HX		HX 1	HX	HX 1
Heathrow Terminal 5	d		17 57		18 12		18 27		18 42		18 57			19 12		19 27		19 42		19 57			20 12		20 27
Heathrow Terminal 4	d			18 12		18 27		18 42		18 57			19 12		19 27		19 42		19 57		20 12			20 27	
Heathrow Terminals 1-2-3 2	a		18 01	18 16	18 16	18 31	18 31	18 46	18 46	19 01	19 01		19 16	19 16	19 31	19 31	19 46	19 46	20 01	20 01	20 16		20 16	20 31	20 31
	d		18 03		18 18		18 33		18 48		19 03			19 18		19 33		19 48		20 03			20 18		20 33
London Paddington 15	a		18 19		18 35		18 49		19 05		19 19			19 35		19 49		20 04		20 19			20 34		20 49

		HX	HX 1	HX	HX 1	HX	HX 1		HX	HX 1	HX	HX 1	HX	HX 1	HX	HX 1	HX		HX 1	HX	HX 1	HX	HX 1	HX	HX 1
Heathrow Terminal 5	d		20 42		20 57		21 12			21 27		21 42		21 57		22 12			22 27		22 42		22 57		23 12
Heathrow Terminal 4	d	20 42		20 57		21 12			21 27		21 42		21 57		22 12		22 27			22 42		22 57		23 12	
Heathrow Terminals 1-2-3 2	a	20 46	20 46	21 01	21 01	21 16	21 16		21 31	21 31	21 46	21 46	22 01	22 01	22 16	22 16	22 31		22 31	22 46	22 46	23 01	23 01	23 16	23 16
	d		20 48		21 03		21 18			21 33		21 48		22 03		22 18			22 33		22 48		23 03		23 18
London Paddington 15	a		21 04		21 19		21 34			21 49		22 04		22 19		22 34			22 49		23 04		23 19		23 34

		HX	HX 1		HX 1	HX	HX
Heathrow Terminal 5	d		23 27		23 42		23 53
Heathrow Terminal 4	d	23 27				23 42	
Heathrow Terminals 1-2-3 2	a	23 31	23 31		23 46	23 46	23 57
	d		23 33		23 48		23 57
London Paddington 15	a		23 49		00 04		

Saturdays

		HX 1	HX	HX	HX 1	HX	HX 1	HX	HX 1	HX		HX	HX 1	HX	HX 1	HX	HX 1	HX	HX 1	HX		HX 1	HX	HX 1	HX
Heathrow Terminal 5	d	23p42	23p53		05 07		05 27		05 42				05 57		06 12		06 27		06 42			06 57		07 12	
Heathrow Terminal 4	d			00 01		05 23		05 32		05 51		05 57		06 12		06 27		06 42		06 57			07 12		07 27
Heathrow Terminals 1-2-3 2	a	23p46	23p57	00 05	05 11	05 27	05 31	05 36	05 46	05 55		06 01	06 01	06 16	06 16	06 31	06 31	06 46	06 46	07 01		07 01	07 16	07 16	07 31
	d	23p48	23p57	00 07	05 12	05 29	05 33		05 48	05 57			06 03		06 18		06 33		06 48			07 03		07 18	
London Paddington 15	a	00 04		00 30	05 28	05 56	05 49		06 04	06 24			06 19		06 34		06 49		07 04			07 19		07 34	

Table 118

Saturdays

Heathrow Airport - London

Network Diagram - see first Page of Table 116

		HX 1	HX	HX 1	HX	HX 1		HX	HX 1	HX	HX 1	HX	HX 1	HX	HX 1	HX		HX 1	HX	HX 1	HX	HX 1	HX	HX 1	HX
Heathrow Terminal 5 ✈	d	07 27		07 42		07 57			08 12		08 27		08 42		08 57			09 12		09 27		09 42		09 57	
Heathrow Terminal 4 ✈	d		07 42		07 57			08 12		08 27		08 42		08 57		09 12			09 27		09 42		09 57		10 12
Heathrow Terminals 1-2-3 2 ✈	a	07 31	07 46	07 46	08 01	08 01		08 16	08 16	08 31	08 31	08 46	08 46	09 01	09 01	09 16		09 16	09 31	09 31	09 46	09 46	10 01	10 01	10 16
	d	07 33		07 48		08 03			08 18		08 33		08 48		09 03			09 18		09 33		09 48		10 03	
London Paddington 15 ⊖	a	07 49		08 04		08 19			08 34		08 49		09 04		09 19			09 34		09 49		10 04		10 19	

		HX 1		HX	HX 1	HX	HX 1	HX	HX 1	HX	HX 1	HX		HX 1	HX	HX 1	HX	HX 1	HX	HX 1	HX	HX 1		HX	HX 1
Heathrow Terminal 5 ✈	d	10 12			10 27		10 42		10 57		11 12			11 27		11 42		11 57		12 12		12 27			12 42
Heathrow Terminal 4 ✈	d			10 27		10 42		10 57		11 12		11 27			11 42		11 57		12 12		12 27			12 42	
Heathrow Terminals 1-2-3 2 ✈	a	10 16		10 31	10 31	10 46	10 46	11 01	11 01	11 16	11 16	11 31		11 31	11 46	11 46	12 01	12 01	12 16	12 16	12 31	12 31		12 46	12 46
	d	10 18			10 33		10 48		11 03		11 18			11 33		11 48		12 03		12 18		12 33			12 48
London Paddington 15 ⊖	a	10 34			10 49		11 04		11 19		11 34			11 49		12 04		12 19		12 34		12 49			13 04

		HX	HX 1	HX	HX 1	HX	HX 1	HX		HX 1	HX	HX 1	HX	HX 1	HX	HX 1	HX	HX 1		HX	HX 1	HX	HX 1	HX	HX 1
Heathrow Terminal 5 ✈	d		12 57		13 12		13 27			13 42		13 57		14 12		14 27		14 42			14 57		15 12		15 27
Heathrow Terminal 4 ✈	d	12 57		13 12		13 27		13 42			13 57		14 12		14 27		14 42			14 57		15 12		15 27	
Heathrow Terminals 1-2-3 2 ✈	a	13 01	13 01	13 16	13 16	13 31	13 31	13 46		13 46	14 01	14 01	14 16	14 16	14 31	14 31	14 46	14 46		15 01	15 01	15 16	15 16	15 31	15 31
	d		13 03		13 18		13 33			13 48		14 03		14 18		14 33		14 48			15 03		15 18		15 33
London Paddington 15 ⊖	a		13 19		13 35		13 49			14 04		14 19		14 34		14 49		15 04			15 19		15 34		15 49

		HX	HX 1	HX		HX 1	HX	HX 1	HX	HX 1	HX	HX 1	HX	HX 1		HX	HX 1	HX	HX 1	HX	HX 1	HX	HX 1	HX	
Heathrow Terminal 5 ✈	d		15 42			15 57		16 12		16 27		16 42		16 57			17 12		17 27		17 42		17 57		
Heathrow Terminal 4 ✈	d	15 42		15 57			16 12		16 27		16 42		16 57			17 12		17 27		17 42		17 57		18 12	
Heathrow Terminals 1-2-3 2 ✈	a	15 46	15 46	16 01		16 01	16 16	16 16	16 31	16 31	16 46	16 46	17 01	17 01		17 16	17 16	17 31	17 31	17 46	17 46	18 01	18 01	18 16	
	d		15 48			16 03		16 18		16 33		16 48		17 03			17 18		17 33		17 48		18 03		
London Paddington 15 ⊖	a		16 04			16 19		16 34		16 49		17 04		17 19			17 34		17 49		18 04		18 19		

		HX 1	HX	HX 1	HX	HX 1	HX	HX 1	HX	HX 1		HX	HX 1	HX	HX 1	HX	HX 1	HX	HX 1	HX		HX 1	HX	HX 1	HX
Heathrow Terminal 5 ✈	d	18 12		18 27		18 42		18 57		19 12			19 27		19 42		19 57		20 12			20 27		20 42	
Heathrow Terminal 4 ✈	d		18 27		18 42		18 57		19 12			19 27		19 42		19 57		20 12		20 27			20 42		20 57
Heathrow Terminals 1-2-3 2 ✈	a	18 16	18 31	18 31	18 46	18 46	19 01	19 01	19 16	19 16		19 31	19 31	19 46	19 46	20 01	20 01	20 16	20 16	20 31		20 31	20 46	20 46	21 01
	d	18 18		18 33		18 48		19 03		19 18			19 33		19 48		20 03		20 18			20 33		20 48	
London Paddington 15 ⊖	a	18 34		18 49		19 04		19 19		19 34			19 49		20 04		20 19		20 34			20 49		21 04	

		HX 1	HX	HX 1	HX	HX 1		HX	HX 1	HX	HX 1	HX	HX 1	HX	HX 1	HX		HX 1	HX	HX 1	HX	HX 1	HX	HX 1	HX 1
Heathrow Terminal 5 ✈	d	20 57		21 12		21 27			21 42		21 57		22 12		22 27			22 42		22 57		23 12		23 27	23 42
Heathrow Terminal 4 ✈	d		21 12		21 27			21 42		21 57		22 12		22 27		22 42			22 57		23 12		23 27		
Heathrow Terminals 1-2-3 2 ✈	a	21 01	21 16	21 16	21 31	21 31		21 46	21 46	22 01	22 01	22 16	22 16	22 31	22 31	22 46		22 46	23 01	23 01	23 16	23 16	23 31	23 31	23 46
	d	21 03		21 18		21 33			21 48		22 03		22 18		22 33			22 48		23 03		23 18		23 33	23 48
London Paddington 15 ⊖	a	21 19		21 34		21 49			22 04		22 19		22 35		22 49			23 05		23 19		23 34		23 49	00 04

		HX		HX
Heathrow Terminal 5 ✈	d			23 53
Heathrow Terminal 4 ✈	d	23 42		
Heathrow Terminals 1-2-3 2 ✈	a	23 46		23 57
	d			23 57
London Paddington 15 ⊖	a			

Sundays

		HX 1	HX	HX	HX 1	HX 1	HX 1	HX 1	HX	HX 1		HX	HX	HX 1	HX	HX 1	HX	HX 1	HX	HX 1		HX	HX	HX 1	HX
Heathrow Terminal 5 ✈	d	23p42	23p53		05 03	05 18	05 33	05 48		06 03				06 18		06 33		06 48		07 03				07 18	
Heathrow Terminal 4 ✈	d			00 01					05 53			06 07	06 13		06 25		06 41		06 53			07 07	07 13		07 25
Heathrow Terminals 1-2-3 2 ✈	a	23p46	23p57	00 05	05 07	05 22	05 37	05 52	05 57	06 07		06 11	06 17	06 22	06 29	06 37	06 45	06 52	06 57	07 07		07 11	07 17	07 22	07 29
	d	23p48	23p57	00 07	05 08	05 23	05 38	05 53		06 08		06 13		06 23		06 38		06 53		07 08		07 13		07 23	
London Paddington 15 ⊖	a			00 30	05 24	05 39	05 54	06 09		06 24		06 36		06 39		06 54		07 09		07 24		07 36		07 39	

		HX 1	HX	HX 1	HX	HX 1		HX	HX	HX 1	HX	HX 1	HX	HX 1	HX	HX 1		HX	HX	HX 1	HX	HX 1	HX	HX 1	HX
Heathrow Terminal 5 ✈	d	07 33		07 48		08 03				08 18		08 33		08 48		09 03				09 18		09 33		09 48	
Heathrow Terminal 4 ✈	d		07 41		07 53			08 07	08 13		08 25		08 41		08 53			09 07	09 13		09 25		09 41		09 53
Heathrow Terminals 1-2-3 2 ✈	a	07 37	07 45	07 52	07 57	08 07		08 11	08 17	08 22	08 29	08 37	08 45	08 52	08 57	09 07		09 11	09 17	09 22	09 29	09 37	09 45	09 52	09 57
	d	07 38		07 53		08 08		08 13		08 23		08 38		08 53		09 08		09 13		09 23		09 38		09 53	
London Paddington 15 ⊖	a	07 54		08 09		08 24		08 36		08 39		08 54		09 09		09 24		09 36		09 39		09 54		10 09	

Table 118

Sundays

Heathrow Airport - London

Network Diagram - see first Page of Table 116

	HX 1		HX	HX	HX 1	HX	HX 1	HX	HX 1	HX	HX 1		HX	HX	HX 1	HX	HX 1	HX	HX 1	HX	HX 1		HX	HX
Heathrow Terminal 5 ✈ d	10 03				10 18		10 33		10 48		11 03				11 18		11 33		11 48		12 03			
Heathrow Terminal 4 ✈ d			10 07	10 13		10 25		10 41		10 53			11 07	11 13		11 25		11 41		11 53			12 07	12 13
Heathrow Terminals 1-2-3 2 ✈ a	10 07		10 11	10 17	10 22	10 29	10 37	10 45	10 52	10 57	11 07		11 11	11 17	11 22	11 29	11 37	11 45	11 52	11 57	12 07		12 11	12 17
d	10 08		10 13		10 23		10 38		10 53		11 08		11 13		11 23		11 38		11 53		12 08		12 13	
London Paddington 15 ⊖ a	10 24		10 36		10 39		10 54		11 09		11 24		11 36		11 39		11 54		12 09		12 24		12 36	

	HX 1	HX	HX 1	HX	HX 1	HX	HX 1		HX	HX	HX 1	HX	HX 1	HX	HX 1	HX	HX 1		HX	HX	HX 1	HX	HX 1	HX
Heathrow Terminal 5 ✈ d	12 18		12 33		12 48		13 03				13 18		13 33		13 48		14 03				14 18		14 33	
Heathrow Terminal 4 ✈ d		12 25		12 41		12 53			13 07	13 13		13 25		13 41		13 53			14 07	14 13		14 25		14 41
Heathrow Terminals 1-2-3 2 ✈ a	12 22	12 29	12 37	12 45	12 52	12 57	13 07		13 11	13 17	13 22	13 29	13 37	13 45	13 52	13 57	14 07		14 11	14 17	14 22	14 29	14 37	14 45
d	12 23		12 38		12 53		13 08		13 13		13 23		13 38		13 53		14 08		14 13		14 23		14 38	
London Paddington 15 ⊖ a	12 39		12 54		13 09		13 24		13 36		13 39		13 54		14 09		14 24		14 36		14 39		14 54	

	HX 1	HX	HX 1		HX	HX	HX 1	HX	HX 1	HX	HX 1	HX	HX 1		HX	HX	HX 1	HX	HX 1	HX	HX 1	HX	HX 1	
Heathrow Terminal 5 ✈ d	14 48		15 03				15 18		15 33		15 48		16 03				16 18		16 33		16 48		17 03	
Heathrow Terminal 4 ✈ d		14 53			15 07	15 13		15 25		15 41		15 53			16 07	16 13		16 25		16 41		16 53		
Heathrow Terminals 1-2-3 2 ✈ a	14 52	14 57	15 07		15 11	15 17	15 22	15 29	15 37	15 45	15 52	15 57	16 07		16 11	16 17	16 22	16 29	16 37	16 45	16 52	16 57	17 07	
d	14 53		15 08		15 13		15 23		15 38		15 53		16 08		16 13		16 23		16 38		16 53		17 08	
London Paddington 15 ⊖ a	15 09		15 24		15 36		15 39		15 54		16 09		16 24		16 36		16 39		16 54		17 09		17 24	

	HX	HX	HX 1	HX	HX 1	HX	HX 1	HX	HX 1		HX	HX	HX 1	HX	HX 1	HX	HX 1	HX	HX 1		HX	HX	HX 1	HX
Heathrow Terminal 5 ✈ d			17 18		17 33		17 48		18 03				18 18		18 33		18 48		19 03				19 18	
Heathrow Terminal 4 ✈ d	17 07	17 13		17 25		17 41		17 53			18 07	18 13		18 25		18 41		18 53			19 07	19 13		19 25
Heathrow Terminals 1-2-3 2 ✈ a	17 11	17 17	17 22	17 29	17 37	17 45	17 52	17 57	18 07		18 11	18 17	18 22	18 29	18 37	18 45	18 52	18 57	19 07		19 11	19 17	19 22	19 29
d	17 13		17 23		17 38		17 53		18 08		18 13		18 23		18 38		18 53		19 08		19 13		19 23	
London Paddington 15 ⊖ a	17 36		17 39		17 54		18 09		18 24		18 36		18 39		18 54		19 09		19 24		19 36		19 39	

	HX 1	HX	HX 1	HX	HX 1		HX	HX	HX 1	HX	HX 1	HX	HX 1	HX	HX 1		HX	HX	HX 1	HX	HX 1	HX	HX 1	HX
Heathrow Terminal 5 ✈ d	19 33		19 48		20 03				20 18		20 33		20 48		21 03				21 18		21 33		21 48	
Heathrow Terminal 4 ✈ d		19 41		19 53			20 07	20 13		20 25		20 41		20 53			21 07	21 13		21 25		21 41		21 53
Heathrow Terminals 1-2-3 2 ✈ a	19 37	19 45	19 52	19 57	20 07		20 11	20 17	20 22	20 29	20 37	20 45	20 52	20 57	21 07		21 11	21 17	21 22	21 29	21 37	21 45	21 52	21 57
d	19 38		19 53		20 08		20 13		20 23		20 38		20 53		21 08		21 13		21 23		21 38		21 53	
London Paddington 15 ⊖ a	19 54		20 09		20 24		20 36		20 39		20 54		21 09		21 24		21 36		21 39		21 54		22 09	

	HX 1		HX	HX	HX 1	HX	HX 1	HX	HX 1	HX	HX 1		HX	HX	HX 1	HX	HX 1	HX	HX 1	HX				
Heathrow Terminal 5 ✈ d	22 03				22 18		22 33		22 48		23 03				23 18		23 33		23 48	23 58				
Heathrow Terminal 4 ✈ d			22 07	22 13		22 25		22 41		22 53			23 07	23 13		23 25		23 41						
Heathrow Terminals 1-2-3 2 ✈ a	22 07		22 11	22 17	22 22	22 29	22 37	22 45	22 52	22 57	23 07		23 11	23 17	23 22	23 29	23 37	23 45	23 52	00 02				
d	22 08		22 13		22 23		22 38		22 53		23 08		23 13		23 23		23 38		23 53	00 02				
London Paddington 15 ⊖ a	22 24		22 36		22 39		22 54		23 09		23 24		23 36		23 43		23 56		00 09					

Table 119

Mondays to Fridays

Slough - Windsor & Eton

Network Diagram - see first Page of Table 116

Miles			GW [1]	GW [1]	GW [1]	GW [1]	GW [1]	GW [1]	GW [1]	GW [1]	GW [1]	GW [1]	GW [1]	GW [1]	GW [1]	GW [1]	GW [1]	GW [1]	GW [1]	GW [1]	GW [1]	GW [1]	GW [1]
0	Slough [3]	d	05 38	05 58	06 18	06 37	06 55	07 13	07 31	07 54	08 13	08 31	08 54	09 14	09 33	09 53	10 11	10 30	10 50	11 10	11 30	11 50	12 10
2¾	Windsor & Eton Central	a	05 44	06 04	06 24	06 43	07 01	07 19	07 37	08 00	08 19	08 37	09 00	09 20	09 39	09 59	10 17	10 36	10 56	11 16	11 36	11 56	12 16

		GW [1]	GW [1]	GW [1]	GW [1]	GW [1]	GW [1]	GW [1]	GW [1]	GW [1]	GW [1]	GW [1]	GW [1]	GW [1]	GW [1]	GW [1]	GW [1]	GW [1]	GW [1]	GW [1]	GW [1]	GW [1]	GW [1]
Slough [3]	d	12 30	12 50	13 10	13 30	13 50	14 10	14 30	14 50	15 10	15 30	15 50	16 21	16 43	17 01	17 21	17 40	17 58	18 16	18 40	18 58	19 16	19 40
Windsor & Eton Central	a	12 36	12 56	13 16	13 36	13 56	14 16	14 36	14 56	15 16	15 36	15 56	16 27	16 49	17 07	17 27	17 46	18 04	18 22	18 46	19 04	19 22	19 46

		GW [1]	GW [1]	GW [1]	GW [1]	GW [1]	GW [1]	GW [1]	GW [1]	GW [1]	GW [1]	GW [1]
Slough [3]	d	20 00	20 20	20 40	21 00	21 20	21 40	22 00	22 20	22 40	23 00	23 20
Windsor & Eton Central	a	20 06	20 26	20 46	21 06	21 26	21 46	22 06	22 26	22 46	23 06	23 26

Saturdays

		GW [1]	GW [1]	GW [1]	GW [1]	GW [1]	GW [1]	GW [1]	GW [1]	GW [1]	GW [1]	GW [1]	GW [1]	GW [1]	GW [1]	GW [1]	GW [1]	GW [1]	GW [1]	GW [1]	GW [1]	GW [1]	GW [1]
Slough [3]	d	06 17	06 47	07 17	07 47	08 17	08 47	09 17	09 47	10 17	10 37	10 57	11 17	11 37	11 57	12 17	12 37	12 57	13 17	13 37	13 57	14 17	14 37
Windsor & Eton Central	a	06 23	06 53	07 23	07 53	08 23	08 53	09 23	09 53	10 23	10 43	11 03	11 23	11 43	12 03	12 23	12 43	13 03	13 23	13 43	14 03	14 23	14 43

		GW [1]	GW [1]	GW [1]	GW [1]	GW [1]	GW [1]	GW [1]	GW [1]	GW [1]	GW [1]	GW [1]	GW [1]	GW [1]	GW [1]	GW [1]	GW [1]	GW [1]	GW [1]	GW [1]	GW [1]	GW [1]	GW [1]	GW [1]
Slough [3]	d	14 57	15 17	15 37	15 57	16 17	16 37	16 57	17 17	17 37	17 57	18 17	18 37	18 57	19 17	19 47	20 17	20 47	21 17	21 47	22 17	22 53	23 22	23 56
Windsor & Eton Central	a	15 03	15 23	15 43	16 03	16 23	16 43	17 03	17 23	17 43	18 03	18 23	18 43	19 03	19 23	19 53	20 23	20 53	21 23	21 53	22 23	22 59	23 28	00 02

Sundays

		GW [1] A	GW [1]	GW [1]	GW [1]	GW [1]	GW [1]	GW [1]	GW [1]	GW [1]	GW [1]	GW [1]	GW [1]	GW [1]	GW [1]	GW [1]	GW [1]	GW [1]	GW [1]	GW [1]	GW [1]	GW [1]	GW [1]
Slough [3]	d	23p56	08 22	08 52	09 22	09 52	10 12	10 32	10 52	11 12	11 32	11 52	12 12	12 32	12 52	13 12	13 32	13 52	14 12	14 32	14 52	15 12	15 32
Windsor & Eton Central	a	00 02	08 28	08 58	09 28	09 58	10 18	10 38	10 58	11 18	11 38	11 58	12 18	12 38	12 58	13 18	13 38	13 58	14 18	14 38	14 58	15 18	15 38

		GW [1]	GW [1]	GW [1]	GW [1]	GW [1]	GW [1]	GW [1]	GW [1]	GW [1]	GW [1]	GW [1]	GW [1]	GW [1]	GW [1]	GW [1]	GW [1]	GW [1]	GW [1]	GW [1]
Slough [3]	d	15 52	16 12	16 32	16 52	17 12	17 32	17 52	18 12	18 32	18 52	19 22	19 52	20 22	20 52	21 22	21 52	22 22	22 52	23 22
Windsor & Eton Central	a	15 58	16 18	16 38	16 58	17 18	17 38	17 58	18 18	18 38	18 58	19 28	19 58	20 28	20 58	21 28	21 58	22 28	22 58	23 28

A not 11 December

Table 119

Mondays to Fridays

Windsor & Eton - Slough

Network Diagram - see first Page of Table 116

Miles			GW [1]	GW [1]	GW [1]	GW [1]	GW [1]	GW [1]	GW [1]	GW [1]	GW [1]	GW [1]	GW [1]	GW [1]	GW [1]	GW [1]	GW [1]	GW [1]	GW [1]	GW [1]	GW [1]	GW [1]	GW [1]
0	Windsor & Eton Central	d	05 48	06 08	06 28	06 46	07 04	07 22	07 40	08 04	08 22	08 40	09 04	09 24	09 42	10 02	10 20	10 40	11 00	11 20	11 40	12 00	12 20
2¾	Slough [3]	a	05 54	06 14	06 34	06 52	07 10	07 28	07 46	08 10	08 28	08 46	09 10	09 30	09 48	10 08	10 26	10 46	11 06	11 26	11 46	12 06	12 26

		GW [1]	GW [1]	GW [1]	GW [1]	GW [1]	GW [1]	GW [1]	GW [1]	GW [1]	GW [1]	GW [1]	GW [1]	GW [1]	GW [1]	GW [1]	GW [1]	GW [1]	GW [1]	GW [1]	GW [1]	GW [1]	GW [1]
Windsor & Eton Central	d	12 40	13 00	13 20	13 40	14 00	14 20	14 40	15 00	15 20	15 40	16 00	16 30	16 52	17 10	17 30	17 49	18 07	18 28	18 49	19 07	19 27	19 50
Slough [3]	a	12 46	13 06	13 26	13 46	14 06	14 26	14 46	15 06	15 26	15 46	16 06	16 36	16 58	17 16	17 36	17 55	18 13	18 34	18 55	19 13	19 33	19 56

		GW [1]	GW [1]	GW [1]	GW [1]	GW [1]	GW [1]	GW [1]	GW [1]	GW [1]	GW [1]	GW [1]
Windsor & Eton Central	d	20 10	20 30	20 50	21 10	21 30	21 50	22 10	22 30	22 50	23 10	23 30
Slough [3]	a	20 16	20 36	20 56	21 16	21 36	21 56	22 16	22 36	22 56	23 16	23 36

Saturdays

		GW [1]	GW [1]	GW [1]	GW [1]	GW [1]	GW [1]	GW [1]	GW [1]	GW [1]	GW [1]	GW [1]	GW [1]	GW [1]	GW [1]	GW [1]	GW [1]	GW [1]	GW [1]	GW [1]	GW [1]	GW [1]	GW [1]
Windsor & Eton Central	d	06 27	06 57	07 27	07 57	08 27	08 57	09 27	09 57	10 27	10 47	11 07	11 27	11 47	12 07	12 27	12 47	13 07	13 27	13 47	14 07	14 27	14 47
Slough [3]	a	06 33	07 03	07 33	08 03	08 33	09 03	09 33	10 03	10 33	10 53	11 13	11 33	11 53	12 13	12 33	12 53	13 13	13 33	13 53	14 13	14 33	14 53

		GW [1]	GW [1]	GW [1]	GW [1]	GW [1]	GW [1]	GW [1]	GW [1]	GW [1]	GW [1]	GW [1]	GW [1]	GW [1]	GW [1]	GW [1]	GW [1]	GW [1]	GW [1]	GW [1]	GW [1]	GW [1]	GW [1]
Windsor & Eton Central	d	15 07	15 27	15 47	16 07	16 27	16 47	17 07	17 27	17 47	18 07	18 27	18 47	19 07	19 27	19 57	20 27	20 57	21 26	21 57	22 27	23 02	23 32
Slough [3]	a	15 13	15 33	15 53	16 13	16 33	16 53	17 13	17 33	17 53	18 13	18 33	18 53	19 13	19 33	20 03	20 33	21 03	21 32	22 03	22 33	23 08	23 38

Sundays

		GW [1]	GW [1]	GW [1]	GW [1]	GW [1]	GW [1]	GW [1]	GW [1]	GW [1]	GW [1]	GW [1]	GW [1]	GW [1]	GW [1]	GW [1]	GW [1]	GW [1]	GW [1]	GW [1]	GW [1]	GW [1]	GW [1]
Windsor & Eton Central	d	00 05	08 32	09 02	09 32	10 02	10 22	10 42	11 02	11 22	11 42	12 02	12 22	12 42	13 02	13 22	13 42	14 02	14 22	14 42	15 02	15 22	15 42
Slough [3]	a	00 11	08 38	09 08	09 38	10 08	10 28	10 48	11 08	11 28	11 48	12 08	12 28	12 48	13 08	13 28	13 48	14 08	14 28	14 48	15 08	15 28	15 48

		GW [1]	GW [1]	GW [1]	GW [1]	GW [1]	GW [1]	GW [1]	GW [1]	GW [1]	GW [1]	GW [1]	GW [1]	GW [1]	GW [1]	GW [1]	GW [1]	GW [1]	GW [1]	GW [1]
Windsor & Eton Central	d	16 02	16 22	16 42	17 02	17 22	17 42	18 02	18 22	18 42	19 02	19 32	20 02	20 32	21 02	21 32	22 02	22 32	23 02	23 32
Slough [3]	a	16 08	16 28	16 48	17 08	17 28	17 48	18 08	18 28	18 48	19 08	19 38	20 08	20 38	21 08	21 38	22 08	22 38	23 08	23 38

Table 120

Mondays to Fridays

Maidenhead - Marlow

Network Diagram - see first Page of Table 116

Miles			GW	GW	GW	GW	GW	GW	GW	GW	GW	GW	GW	GW	GW	GW	GW	GW	GW	GW	GW	GW	GW
			MX																				
			1	1	1	1	1	1	1	1	1	1	1	1	1	1	1	1	1	1	1	1	1
—	London Paddington 15 ⊖	d																					
0	**Maidenhead** 3	d	23p49	05 25	05 49		06 31		07 09		07 41		08 11		09 02	09 38	10 38	11 38	12 38	13 38	14 38	15 38	16 40
1¼	Furze Platt	d	23p53	05 29	05 53		06 35		07 13		07 45		08 15		09 06	09 42	10 42	11 42	12 42	13 42	14 42	15 42	16 44
3	Cookham	d	23p56	05 32	05 57		06 39		07 17		07 48		08 18		09 09	09 45	10 45	11 45	12 45	13 45	14 45	15 45	16 47
4½	Bourne End 3	a	23p59	05 36	06 01		06 43		07 21		07 52		08 22		09 13	09 49	10 49	11 49	12 49	13 49	14 49	15 49	16 51
—		d	00 04	05 40		06 18		06 49		07 28		07 57		08 25		09 53	10 53	11 53	12 53	13 53	14 53	15 53	16 55
7¼	**Marlow**	a	00 12	05 48		06 25		06 56		07 35		08 04		08 32		10 01	11 01	12 01	13 01	14 01	15 01	16 01	17 03

		GW	GW	GW	GW	GW	GW	GW	GW	GW	GW	GW	GW	GW
		1	1	1	1	1	1	1	1	1	1	1	1	1
London Paddington 15 ⊖	d		17 42				18 36							
Maidenhead 3	d	17 46	18 14		18 46		19 14		19 47		20 42	21 39	22 49	23 49
Furze Platt	d	17 50	18 18		18 49		19 18		19 51		20 46	21 43	22 53	23 53
Cookham	d	17 53	18 22		18 53		19 22		19 54		20 49	21 46	22 56	23 56
Bourne End 3	a	17 57	18 28		18 57		19 26		19 58		20 53	21 50	23 00	23 59
	d	18 01		18 31		19 02		19 31		20 01	20 57	21 54	23 04	00 04
Marlow	a	18 09		18 38		19 09		19 38		20 08	21 05	22 02	23 12	00 12

Saturdays

		GW	GW	GW	GW	GW	GW	GW	GW	GW	GW	GW	GW	GW	GW	GW	GW	GW	GW	GW
		1	1	1	1	1	1	1	1	1	1	1	1	1	1	1	1	1	1	1
London Paddington 15 ⊖	d																			
Maidenhead 3	d	23p49	06 38	07 38	08 38	09 38	10 38	11 38	12 38	13 38	14 38	15 38	16 38	17 38	18 38	19 38	20 38	21 38	22 38	23 38
Furze Platt	d	23p53	06 42	07 42	08 42	09 42	10 42	11 42	12 42	13 42	14 42	15 42	16 42	17 42	18 42	19 42	20 42	21 42	22 42	23 42
Cookham	d	23p56	06 45	07 45	08 45	09 45	10 45	11 45	12 45	13 45	14 45	15 45	16 45	17 45	18 45	19 45	20 45	21 45	22 45	23 45
Bourne End 3	a	23p59	06 49	07 49	08 49	09 49	10 49	11 49	12 49	13 49	14 49	15 49	16 49	17 49	18 49	19 49	20 49	21 49	22 49	23 49
	d	00 04	06 53	07 53	08 53	09 53	10 53	11 53	12 53	13 53	14 53	15 53	16 53	17 53	18 53	19 53	20 53	21 53	22 53	23 53
Marlow	a	00 12	07 01	08 01	09 01	10 01	11 01	12 01	13 01	14 01	15 01	16 01	17 01	18 01	19 01	20 01	21 01	22 01	23 01	00 01

Sundays

		GW	GW	GW	GW	GW	GW	GW	GW	GW	GW	GW	GW	GW	GW	GW
		1	1	1	1	1	1	1	1	1	1	1	1	1	1	1
		A														
London Paddington 15 ⊖	d															
Maidenhead 3	d	23p38	08 35	09 35	10 35	11 35	12 35	13 35	14 35	15 35	16 35	17 35	18 35	19 35	20 35	21 40
Furze Platt	d	23p42	08 39	09 39	10 39	11 39	12 39	13 39	14 39	15 39	16 39	17 39	18 39	19 39	20 39	21 44
Cookham	d	23p45	08 42	09 42	10 42	11 42	12 42	13 42	14 42	15 42	16 42	17 42	18 42	19 42	20 42	21 47
Bourne End 3	a	23p49	08 47	09 47	10 47	11 47	12 47	13 47	14 47	15 47	16 47	17 47	18 47	19 47	20 47	21 52
	d	23p53	08 51	09 51	10 51	11 51	12 51	13 51	14 51	15 51	16 51	17 51	18 51	19 51	20 51	21 56
Marlow	a	00 01	08 58	09 58	10 58	11 58	12 58	13 58	14 58	15 58	16 58	17 58	18 58	19 58	20 58	22 03

A not 11 December

Table 120

Mondays to Fridays

Marlow - Maidenhead

Network Diagram - see first Page of Table 116

Miles			GW	GW	GW	GW	GW	GW	GW	GW	GW	GW	GW	GW	GW	GW	GW	GW	GW	GW	GW	GW	GW
			MX																				
			1	1	1	1	1	1	1	1	1	1	1	1	1	1	1	1	1	1	1	1	1
0	**Marlow**	d	00 15	06 04		06 39		07 17		07 46		08 15		08 35		10 06	11 06	12 06	13 06	14 06	15 06	16 06	17 06
2¾	Bourne End 3	a	00 22	06 11		06 46		07 24		07 53		08 22		08 42		10 13	11 13	12 13	13 13	14 13	15 13	16 13	17 13
—		d	00 26		06 14		06 49		07 27		07 56		08 28	08 46	09 17	10 17	11 17	12 17	13 17	14 17	15 17	16 17	17 17
4¼	Cookham	d	00 30		06 17		06 52		07 30		07 59		08 31	08 50	09 20	10 21	11 21	12 21	13 21	14 21	15 21	16 21	17 21
6	Furze Platt	d	00 33		06 21		06 56		07 34		08 03		08 35	08 53	09 24	10 24	11 24	12 24	13 24	14 24	15 24	16 24	17 24
7¼	**Maidenhead** 3	a	00 38		06 25		07 00		07 38		08 07		08 39	08 58	09 28	10 29	11 29	12 29	13 29	14 29	15 29	16 29	17 29
—	London Paddington 15 ⊖	a							08 21				09 21										

		GW	GW	GW	GW	GW	GW	GW	GW	GW	GW	GW	GW
		1	1	1	1	1	1	1	1	1	1	1	1
Marlow	d	18 21		18 51		19 21		19 51		20 15	21 08	22 05	23 15
Bourne End 3	a	18 28		18 58		19 28		19 58		20 22	21 15	22 12	23 22
	d		18 31		19 01		19 32		20 05	20 26	21 19	22 16	23 26
Cookham	d		18 34		19 04		19 35		20 08	20 30	21 23	22 20	23 30
Furze Platt	d		18 37		19 07		19 38		20 12	20 33	21 26	22 23	23 33
Maidenhead 3	a		18 42		19 12		19 43		20 16	20 38	21 31	22 28	23 38
London Paddington 15 ⊖	a												

Saturdays

		GW	GW	GW	GW	GW	GW	GW	GW	GW	GW	GW	GW	GW	GW	GW	GW	GW	GW
		1	1	1	1	1	1	1	1	1	1	1	1	1	1	1	1	1	1
Marlow	d	00 15	07 06	08 06	09 06	10 06	11 06	12 06	13 06	14 06	15 06	16 06	17 06	18 06	19 06	20 06	21 06	22 06	23 06
Bourne End 3	a	00 22	07 13	08 13	09 13	10 13	11 13	12 13	13 13	14 13	15 13	16 13	17 13	18 13	19 13	20 13	21 13	22 13	23 13
	d	00 26	07 17	08 17	09 17	10 17	11 17	12 17	13 17	14 17	15 17	16 17	17 17	18 17	19 17	20 17	21 17	22 17	23 17
Cookham	d	00 30	07 21	08 21	09 21	10 21	11 21	12 21	13 21	14 21	15 21	16 21	17 21	18 21	19 21	20 21	21 21	22 21	23 21
Furze Platt	d	00 33	07 24	08 24	09 24	10 24	11 24	12 24	13 24	14 24	15 24	16 24	17 24	18 24	19 24	20 24	21 24	22 24	23 24
Maidenhead 3	a	00 38	07 29	08 29	09 29	10 29	11 29	12 29	13 29	14 29	15 29	16 29	17 29	18 29	19 29	20 29	21 29	22 29	23 29
London Paddington 15 ⊖	a																		

Sundays

		GW	GW	GW	GW	GW	GW	GW	GW	GW	GW	GW	GW	GW	GW	GW
		1	1	1	1	1	1	1	1	1	1	1	1	1	1	1
Marlow	d	00 06	09 01	10 01	11 01	12 01	13 01	14 01	15 01	16 01	17 01	18 01	19 01	20 01	21 01	22 06
Bourne End 3	a	00 13	09 08	10 08	11 08	12 08	13 08	14 08	15 08	16 08	17 08	18 08	19 08	20 08	21 08	22 13
	d	00 17	09 12	10 12	11 12	12 12	13 12	14 12	15 12	16 12	17 12	18 12	19 12	20 12	21 12	22 17
Cookham	d	00 21	09 16	10 16	11 16	12 16	13 16	14 16	15 16	16 16	17 16	18 16	19 16	20 16	21 16	22 20
Furze Platt	d	00 24	09 20	10 20	11 20	12 20	13 20	14 20	15 20	16 20	17 20	18 20	19 20	20 20	21 20	22 24
Maidenhead 3	a	00 29	09 24	10 24	11 24	12 24	13 24	14 24	15 24	16 24	17 24	18 24	19 24	20 24	21 24	22 28
London Paddington 15 ⊖	a															

Table 121

Mondays to Fridays

Twyford - Henley-on-Thames

Network Diagram - see first Page of Table 116

Miles			GW	GW	GW	GW	GW	GW	GW	GW	GW	GW	GW	GW	GW	GW	GW	GW	GW	GW	GW	GW	GW
			1	1	1	1	1	1	1	1	1	1	1	1	1	1	1	1	1	1	1	1	1
—	London Paddington 15 ⊖	d																			17 12		18 12
—	Reading 7	d					08 06																
0	**Twyford 3**	d	05 42	06 21	06 50	07 27	08 14	08 45	09 21	09 53	10 36	11 21	12 06	12 51	13 36	14 21	15 06	15 48	16 48	17 31	17 58	18 31	18 58
1¾	Wargrave	d	05 46	06 25	06 54	07 31	08 19	08 49	09 25	09 57	10 40	11 25	12 10	12 55	13 40	14 25	15 10	15 52	16 52	17 35	18 03	18 35	19 03
2¾	Shiplake	d	05 49	06 28	06 57	07 34	08 22	08 52	09 28	10 00	10 43	11 28	12 13	12 58	13 43	14 28	15 13	15 55	16 55	17 38	18 06	18 38	19 06
4½	**Henley-on-Thames**	a	05 54	06 33	07 02	07 39	08 26	08 57	09 33	10 05	10 48	11 33	12 18	13 03	13 48	14 33	15 18	16 00	17 00	17 43	18 13	18 43	19 13

		GW	GW	GW	GW	GW	GW
		1	1	1	1	1	1
London Paddington 15 ⊖	d	19 06					
Reading 7	d						
Twyford 3	d	19 38	20 09	20 47	21 50	23 00	23 37
Wargrave	d	19 42	20 13	20 51	21 54	23 04	23 41
Shiplake	d	19 45	20 16	20 54	21 57	23 07	23 44
Henley-on-Thames	a	19 52	20 21	20 59	22 02	23 12	23 49

Saturdays

		GW	GW	GW	GW	GW	GW	GW	GW	GW	GW	GW	GW	GW	GW	GW	GW	GW	GW
		1	1	1	1	1	1	1	1	1	1	1	1	1	1	1	1	1	1
London Paddington 15 ⊖	d																		
Reading 7	d																		
Twyford 3	d	06 57	07 50	08 50	09 50	10 50	11 50	12 50	13 50	14 50	15 50	16 50	17 50	18 50	19 50	20 50	21 50	22 50	23 50
Wargrave	d	07 01	07 54	08 54	09 54	10 54	11 54	12 54	13 54	14 54	15 54	16 54	17 54	18 54	19 54	20 54	21 54	22 54	23 54
Shiplake	d	07 04	07 57	08 57	09 57	10 57	11 57	12 57	13 57	14 57	15 57	16 57	17 57	18 57	19 57	20 57	21 57	22 57	23 57
Henley-on-Thames	a	07 09	08 02	09 02	10 02	11 02	12 02	13 02	14 02	15 02	16 02	17 02	18 02	19 02	20 02	21 02	22 02	23 02	00 02

Sundays

		GW	GW	GW	GW	GW	GW	GW	GW	GW	GW	GW	GW	GW	GW
		1	1	1	1	1	1	1	1	1	1	1	1	1	1
		A													
London Paddington 15 ⊖	d														
Reading 7	d														
Twyford 3	d	23p50	09 43	10 43	11 43	12 43	13 43	14 43	15 43	16 43	17 43	18 43	19 43	20 43	21 43
Wargrave	d	23p54	09 47	10 47	11 47	12 47	13 47	14 47	15 47	16 47	17 47	18 47	19 47	20 47	21 47
Shiplake	d	23p57	09 50	10 50	11 50	12 50	13 50	14 50	15 50	16 50	17 50	18 50	19 50	20 50	21 50
Henley-on-Thames	a	00§02	09 55	10 55	11 55	12 55	13 55	14 55	15 55	16 55	17 55	18 55	19 55	20 55	21 55

A not 11 December

Table 121

Mondays to Fridays

Henley-on-Thames - Twyford

Network Diagram - see first Page of Table 116

Miles			GW MX	GW	GW	GW	GW	GW	GW	GW	GW	GW	GW	GW	GW	GW	GW	GW	GW	GW	GW	GW	GW
			1	1	1	1	1	1	1	1	1	1	1	1	1	1	1	1	1	1	1	1	1
0	**Henley-on-Thames**	d	23p52	06 06	06 36	07 09	07 44	08 29	09 01	09 36	10 09	10 54	11 39	12 24	13 09	13 54	14 39	15 24	16 20	17 09	17 46	18 17	18 46
1¾	Shiplake	d	23p56	06 10	06 40	07 13	07 48	08 33	09 05	09 40	10 13	10 58	11 43	12 28	13 13	13 58	14 43	15 28	16 24	17 13	17 50	18 21	18 50
2¾	Wargrave	d	23p59	06 13	06 43	07 16	07 51	08 36	09 08	09 43	10 16	11 01	11 46	12 31	13 16	14 01	14 46	15 31	16 27	17 16	17 53	18 24	18 53
4½	**Twyford 3**	a	00 04	06 18	06 48	07 21	07 56	08 41	09 13	09 48	10 21	11 06	11 51	12 36	13 21	14 06	14 51	15 36	16 32	17 21	17 58	18 29	18 58
—	Reading 7	a	00 16																				
—	London Paddington 15 ⊖	a				07 57	08 28																

		GW	GW	GW	GW	GW	GW	GW
		1	1	1	1	1	1	1
Henley-on-Thames	d	19 16	19 55	20 24	21 02	22 06	23 15	23 52
Shiplake	d	19 20	19 59	20 28	21 06	22 10	23 19	23 56
Wargrave	d	19 23	20 02	20 31	21 09	22 13	23 22	23 59
Twyford 3	a	19 28	20 07	20 36	21 14	22 18	23 27	00 04
Reading 7	a							00 16
London Paddington 15 ⊖	a							

Saturdays

		GW	GW	GW	GW	GW	GW	GW	GW	GW	GW	GW	GW	GW	GW	GW	GW	GW	GW
		1	1	1	1	1	1	1	1	1	1	1	1	1	1	1	1	1	1
Henley-on-Thames	d	23p52	07 24	08 24	09 24	10 24	11 24	12 24	13 24	14 24	15 24	16 24	17 24	18 24	19 24	20 24	21 24	22 24	23 08
Shiplake	d	23p56	07 28	08 28	09 28	10 28	11 28	12 28	13 28	14 28	15 28	16 28	17 28	18 28	19 28	20 28	21 28	22 28	23 12
Wargrave	d	23p59	07 31	08 31	09 31	10 31	11 31	12 31	13 31	14 31	15 31	16 31	17 31	18 31	19 31	20 31	21 31	22 31	23 15
Twyford 3	a	00 04	07 36	08 36	09 36	10 36	11 36	12 36	13 36	14 36	15 36	16 36	17 36	18 36	19 36	20 36	21 36	22 36	23 20
Reading 7	a	00 16																	
London Paddington 15 ⊖	a																		

Sundays

		GW	GW	GW	GW	GW	GW	GW	GW	GW	GW	GW	GW	GW	GW
		1	1	1	1	1	1	1	1	1	1	1	1	1	1
Henley-on-Thames	d	00 08	10 03	11 03	12 03	13 03	14 03	15 03	16 03	17 03	18 03	19 03	20 03	21 03	22 01
Shiplake	d	00 12	10 07	11 07	12 07	13 07	14 07	15 07	16 07	17 07	18 07	19 07	20 07	21 07	22 05
Wargrave	d	00 15	10 10	11 10	12 10	13 10	14 10	15 10	16 10	17 10	18 10	19 10	20 10	21 10	22 08
Twyford 3	a	00 20	10 15	11 15	12 15	13 15	14 15	15 15	16 15	17 15	18 15	19 15	20 15	21 15	22 13
Reading 7	a														
London Paddington 15 ⊖	a														

Table 122

Mondays to Fridays

Reading - Basingstoke

Network Diagram - see first Page of Table 116

Miles			GW MO 1	GW 1	GW 1	GW 1	GW 1	GW 1	XC ◇1 🛒	GW 1	XC ◇1 🛒		GW 1	XC ◇1 🛒	GW 1	GW 1	XC ◇1 🛒	GW 1	XC ◇1 🛒	GW 1	XC ◇1 🛒		GW 1	GW 1	XC ◇1 🛒
0	**Reading 7**	d	23p37	05 39	06 07	06 39	07 07	07 39	07 46	08 07	08 15		08 39	08 46	09 08	09 39	09 46	10 07	10 15	10 39	10 46		11 07	11 39	11 46
1	Reading West	d	23p40	05 42	06 10	06 42	07 10	07 42		08 10			08 42		09 10	09 42		10 10		10 42			11 10	11 42	
7¼	Mortimer	d	23p48	05 50	06 18	06 50	07 18	07 50		08 18			08 50		09 18	09 50		10 18		10 50			11 18	11 50	
10½	Bramley (Hants)	d	23p53	05 55	06 23	06 55	07 23	07 55		08 23			08 55		09 23	09 55		10 23		10 55			11 23	11 55	
15½	**Basingstoke**	a	00 01	06 03	06 31	07 03	07 31	08 03	08 08	08 31	08 40		09 03	09 08	09 34	10 03	10 08	10 31	10 39	11 03	11 08		11 31	12 03	12 08

		GW 1	XC ◇1 🛒	GW 1	XC ◇1 🛒	GW 1	GW 1		XC ◇1 🛒	GW 1	XC ◇1 🛒	GW 1	XC ◇1 🛒	GW 1	GW 1	XC ◇1 🛒	GW 1		XC ◇1 🛒	GW 1	XC ◇1 🛒	GW 1	GW 1	XC ◇1 🛒	GW 1
Reading 7	d	12 07	12 15	12 39	12 46	13 07	13 39		13 46	14 07	14 15	14 39	14 46	15 07	15 39	15 46	16 07		16 15	16 39	16 46	17 07	17 41	17 46	18 07
Reading West	d	12 10		12 42		13 10	13 42			14 10		14 42		15 10	15 42		16 10			16 42		17 10	17 42		18 10
Mortimer	d	12 18		12 50		13 18	13 50			14 18		14 50		15 18	15 50		16 18			16 50		17 18	17 50		18 18
Bramley (Hants)	d	12 23		12 55		13 23	13 55			14 23		14 55		15 23	15 55		16 23			16 55		17 23	17 55		18 23
Basingstoke	a	12 32	12 39	13 03	13 08	13 31	14 03		14 08	14 31	14 39	15 03	15 08	15 31	16 03	16 08	16 31		16 39	17 03	17 08	17 31	18 05	18 08	18 31

		XC ◇1 🛒	GW 1		XC ◇1 🛒	GW 1	GW 1	XC ◇1 🛒	GW 1	GW 1	XC ◇1	GW 1	GW 1		XC ◇1	GW 1	XC ◇1	GW 1	GW 1
Reading 7	d	18 15	18 41		18 46	19 07	19 37	19 46	20 07	20 37	20 46	21 07	21 39		21 46	22 10	22 48	22 55	23 34
Reading West	d		18 42			19 10	19 40		20 10	20 40		21 10	21 42			22 13		22 58	23 37
Mortimer	d		18 50			19 18	19 48		20 18	20 48		21 18	21 50			22 21		23 06	23 45
Bramley (Hants)	d		18 55			19 23	19 53		20 23	20 53		21 23	21 55			22 26		23 11	23 50
Basingstoke	a	18 47	19 05		19 08	19 31	20 01	20 09	20 31	21 01	21 09	21 31	22 03		22 09	22 34	23 06	23 19	23 58

Saturdays

		GW 1	GW 1	GW 1	GW 1	XC ◇1 🛒	GW 1	XC ◇1 🛒	GW 1	XC ◇1 🛒		GW 1	GW 1	XC ◇1 🛒	GW 1	XC ◇1 🛒	GW 1	XC ◇1 🛒	GW 1	GW 1		XC ◇1 🛒	GW 1	XC ◇1 🛒	GW 1
Reading 7	d	06 07	06 39	07 07	07 39	07 46	08 07	08 23	08 39	08 46		09 07	09 39	09 46	10 07	10 15	10 39	10 46	11 07	11 39		11 46	12 07	12 15	12 39
Reading West	d	06 10	06 42	07 10	07 42		08 10		08 42			09 10	09 42		10 10		10 42		11 10	11 42			12 10		12 42
Mortimer	d	06 18	06 50	07 18	07 50		08 18		08 50			09 18	09 50		10 18		10 50		11 18	11 50			12 18		12 50
Bramley (Hants)	d	06 23	06 55	07 23	07 55		08 23		08 55			09 23	09 55		10 23		10 55		11 23	11 55			12 23		12 55
Basingstoke	a	06 32	07 03	07 32	08 03	08 08	08 31	08 40	09 03	09 08		09 31	10 03	10 08	10 31	10 39	11 03	11 08	11 31	12 03		12 08	12 31	12 40	13 03

		XC ◇1 🛒	GW 1	GW 1	XC ◇1 🛒	GW 1		XC ◇1 🛒	GW 1	XC ◇1 🛒	GW 1	GW 1	XC ◇1 🛒	GW 1	XC ◇1 🛒	GW 1		XC ◇1 🛒	GW 1	GW 1	XC ◇1 🛒	GW 1	XC ◇1 🛒	GW 1	XC ◇1 🛒
Reading 7	d	12 46	13 07	13 39	13 46	14 07		14 15	14 39	14 46	15 07	15 39	15 46	16 07	16 15	16 39		16 46	17 07	17 39	17 46	18 07	18 15	18 39	18 46
Reading West	d		13 10	13 42		14 10			14 42		15 10	15 42		16 10		16 42			17 10	17 42		18 10		18 42	
Mortimer	d		13 18	13 50		14 18			14 50		15 18	15 50		16 18		16 50			17 18	17 50		18 18		18 50	
Bramley (Hants)	d		13 23	13 55		14 23			14 55		15 23	15 55		16 23		16 55			17 23	17 55		18 23		18 55	
Basingstoke	a	13 08	13 31	14 03	14 08	14 31		14 40	15 03	15 08	15 31	16 03	16 08	16 31	16 40	17 03		17 08	17 31	18 03	18 08	18 31	18 40	19 03	19 08

		GW 1		GW 1	XC ◇1 🛒	GW 1	GW 1	XC ◇1	GW 1	GW 1	XC ◇1	GW 1		GW 1	XC ◇1	GW 1
Reading 7	d	19 07		19 39	19 46	20 07	20 39	20 46	21 07	21 39	21 47	22 07		22 39	22 49	23 07
Reading West	d	19 10		19 42		20 10	20 42		21 10	21 42		22 10		22 42		23 10
Mortimer	d	19 18		19 50		20 18	20 50		21 18	21 50		22 18		22 50		23 18
Bramley (Hants)	d	19 23		19 55		20 23	20 55		21 23	21 55		22 23		22 55		23 23
Basingstoke	a	19 31		20 03	20 08	20 31	21 03	21 08	21 31	22 03	22 09	22 31		23 03	23 06	23 31

Sundays

until 1 January

		GW 1	GW 1	GW 1	XC ◇1 🛒	GW 1	XC ◇1 🛒	GW 1	XC ◇1 ☕	GW 1		XC ◇1 ☕	GW 1	XC ◇1 ☕	GW 1	XC ◇1 ☕	GW 1	XC ◇1 ☕	GW 1	XC ◇1 ☕		GW 1	XC ◇1 ☕	GW 1	XC ◇1 ☕
Reading 7	d	07 37	08 37	09 37	09 53	10 37	10 53	11 37	11 53	12 37		12 53	13 37	13 53	14 37	14 53	15 37	15 53	16 37	16 53		17 37	17 53	18 37	18 53
Reading West	d	07 40	08 40	09 40		10 40		11 40		12 40			13 40		14 40		15 40		16 40			17 40		18 40	
Mortimer	d	07 48	08 48	09 48		10 48		11 48		12 48			13 48		14 48		15 48		16 48			17 48		18 48	
Bramley (Hants)	d	07 53	08 53	09 53		10 53		11 53		12 53			13 53		14 53		15 53		16 53			17 53		18 53	
Basingstoke	a	08 01	09 01	10 01	10 09	11 01	11 09	12 01	12 09	13 01		13 09	14 01	14 09	15 01	15 09	16 01	16 09	17 01	17 09		18 01	18 09	19 01	19 09

		GW 1	XC ◇1 ☕	GW 1	XC ◇1	GW 1		XC ◇1	GW 1	GW 1
Reading 7	d	19 37	19 53	20 37	20 53	21 37		21 53	22 37	23 37
Reading West	d	19 40		20 40		21 40			22 41	23 40
Mortimer	d	19 48		20 48		21 48			22 49	23 48
Bramley (Hants)	d	19 53		20 53		21 53			22 54	23 53
Basingstoke	a	20 01	20 09	21 01	21 09	22 01		22 09	23 02	00 01

Table 122

Sundays

8 January to 12 February

Reading - Basingstoke

Network Diagram - see first Page of Table 116

		GW	GW	GW	XC	GW	XC	GW	XC	GW		XC	GW	XC	GW	XC	GW	XC	GW	XC		GW	XC	GW	XC
		1	1	1	◇1	1	◇1	1	◇1	1		◇1	1	◇1	1	◇1	1	◇1	1	◇1		1	◇1	1	◇1
					🛒		🛒		☕			☕		☕		☕		☕		☕			☕		☕
Reading 7	d	07 37	08 37	09 37	09 53	10 37	10 53	11 37	11 53	12 37		12 53	13 37	13 53	14 37	14 53	15 37	15 53	16 37	16 53		17 37	17 53	18 37	18 53
Reading West	d	07 40	08 40	09 40		10 40		11 40		12 40			13 40		14 40		15 40		16 40			17 40		18 40	
Mortimer	d	07 48	08 48	09 48		10 48		11 48		12 48			13 48		14 48		15 48		16 48			17 48		18 48	
Bramley (Hants)	d	07 53	08 53	09 53		10 53		11 53		12 53			13 53		14 53		15 53		16 53			17 53		18 53	
Basingstoke	a	08 01	09 01	10 01	10 09	11 01	11 09	12 01	12 09	13 01		13 09	14 01	14 09	15 01	15 09	16 01	16 09	17 01	17 09		18 01	18 09	19 01	19 09

		GW	XC	GW	XC	GW		XC	GW	GW
		1	◇1	1	◇1	1		◇1	1	1
			☕							
Reading 7	d	19 37	19 53	20 37	20 53	21 37		21 53	22 37	23 37
Reading West	d	19 40		20 40		21 40			22 41	23 40
Mortimer	d	19 48		20 48		21 48			22 49	23 48
Bramley (Hants)	d	19 53		20 53		21 53			22 54	23 53
Basingstoke	a	20 01	20 09	21 01	21 09	22 01		22 09	23 02	00 01

Sundays

19 February to 25 March

		GW	GW	GW	XC	GW	XC	GW	XC	GW		XC	GW	XC	GW	XC	GW	XC	GW	XC		GW	XC	GW	XC
		1	1	1	◇1	1	◇1	1	◇1	1		◇1	1	◇1	1	◇1	1	◇1	1	◇1		1	◇1	1	◇1
					🛒		🛒		☕			☕		☕		☕		☕		☕			☕		☕
Reading 7	d	07 37	08 37	09 37	09 53	10 37	10 53	11 37	11 53	12 37		12 53	13 37	13 53	14 37	14 53	15 37	15 53	16 37	16 53		17 37	17 53	18 37	18 53
Reading West	d	07 40	08 40	09 40		10 40		11 40		12 40			13 40		14 40		15 40		16 40			17 40		18 40	
Mortimer	d	07 48	08 48	09 48		10 48		11 48		12 48			13 48		14 48		15 48		16 48			17 48		18 48	
Bramley (Hants)	d	07 53	08 53	09 53		10 53		11 53		12 53			13 53		14 53		15 53		16 53			17 53		18 53	
Basingstoke	a	08 01	09 01	10 01	10 09	11 01	11 09	12 01	12 09	13 01		13 09	14 01	14 09	15 01	15 09	16 01	16 09	17 01	17 09		18 01	18 09	19 01	19 09

		GW	XC	GW	XC	GW		XC	GW	GW
		1	◇1	1	◇1	1		◇1	1	1
			☕							
Reading 7	d	19 37	19 53	20 37	20 53	21 37		21 53	22 37	23 37
Reading West	d	19 40		20 40		21 40			22 41	23 40
Mortimer	d	19 48		20 48		21 48			22 49	23 48
Bramley (Hants)	d	19 53		20 53		21 53			22 54	23 53
Basingstoke	a	20 01	20 09	21 01	21 09	22 01		22 09	23 02	00 01

Sundays

from 1 April

		GW	GW	GW	XC	GW	XC	GW	XC	GW		XC	GW	XC	GW	XC	GW	XC	GW	XC		GW	XC	GW	XC
		1	1	1	◇1	1	◇1	1	◇1	1		◇1	1	◇1	1	◇1	1	◇1	1	◇1		1	◇1	1	◇1
					🛒		🛒		☕			☕		☕		☕		☕		☕			☕		☕
Reading 7	d	07 37	08 37	09 37	09 53	10 37	10 53	11 37	11 53	12 37		12 53	13 37	13 53	14 37	14 53	15 37	15 53	16 37	16 53		17 37	17 53	18 37	18 53
Reading West	d	07 40	08 40	09 40		10 40		11 40		12 40			13 40		14 40		15 40		16 40			17 40		18 40	
Mortimer	d	07 48	08 48	09 48		10 48		11 48		12 48			13 48		14 48		15 48		16 48			17 48		18 48	
Bramley (Hants)	d	07 53	08 53	09 53		10 53		11 53		12 53			13 53		14 53		15 53		16 53			17 53		18 53	
Basingstoke	a	08 01	09 01	10 01	10 09	11 01	11 09	12 01	12 09	13 01		13 09	14 01	14 09	15 01	15 09	16 01	16 09	17 01	17 09		18 01	18 09	19 01	19 09

		GW	XC	GW	XC	GW		XC	GW	GW
		1	◇1	1	◇1	1		◇1	1	1
			☕							
Reading 7	d	19 37	19 53	20 37	20 53	21 37		21 53	22 37	23 37
Reading West	d	19 40		20 40		21 40			22 41	23 40
Mortimer	d	19 48		20 48		21 48			22 49	23 48
Bramley (Hants)	d	19 53		20 53		21 53			22 54	23 53
Basingstoke	a	20 01	20 09	21 01	21 11	22 01		22 09	23 02	00 01

Basingstoke - Reading

Network Diagram - see first Page of Table 116

Mondays to Fridays

Miles			GW MX ■	GW MO ■	XC ◇■	GW ■	GW ■	XC ◇■	GW ■	GW ■	XC ◇■		GW ■	XC ◇■	GW ■	XC ◇■	GW ■	GW ■	XC ◇■	GW ■	XC ◇■		GW ■	XC ◇■	GW ■
0	**Basingstoke**	d	00 02	00 07	05 47	06 07	06 34	06 47	07 09	07 37	07 47		08 07	08 18	08 37	08 47	09 07	09 37	09 47	10 07	10 19		10 37	10 47	11 07
5	Bramley (Hants)	d	00 09	00 14		06 14	06 41		07 15	07 44			08 14		08 44		09 14	09 44		10 14			10 44		11 14
8¼	Mortimer	d	00 14	00 19		06 19	06 46		07 20	07 49			08 19		08 49		09 19	09 49		10 19			10 49		11 19
14½	Reading West	d	00 22	00 26		06 27	06 54		07 28	07 57			08 27		08 57		09 27	09 57		10 27			10 57		11 27
15½	**Reading 7**	a	00 26	00 30	06 04	06 32	06 57	07 04	07 32	08 00	08 04		08 30	08 36	09 00	09 04	09 30	10 00	10 04	10 30	10 36		11 00	11 04	11 30

		GW ■	XC ◇■	GW ■	XC ◇■	GW ■	XC ◇■		GW ■	GW ■	XC ◇■	GW ■	XC ◇■	GW ■	XC ◇■	GW ■	GW ■		XC ◇■	GW ■	XC ◇■	GW ■	XC ◇■	GW ■	GW ■
Basingstoke	d	11 37	11 47	12 07	12 18	12 37	12 47		13 07	13 37	13 47	14 07	14 19	14 37	14 47	15 07	15 37		15 47	16 07	16 18	16 37	16 47	17 07	17 37
Bramley (Hants)	d	11 44		12 14		12 44			13 14	13 44		14 14		14 44		15 14	15 44			16 14		16 44		17 14	17 44
Mortimer	d	11 49		12 19		12 49			13 19	13 49		14 19		14 49		15 19	15 49			16 19		16 49		17 19	17 49
Reading West	d	11 57		12 27		12 57			13 27	13 57		14 27		14 57		15 27	15 57			16 27		16 57		17 27	17 57
Reading 7	a	12 00	12 04	12 30	12 36	13 00	13 04		13 30	14 00	14 04	14 30	14 36	15 00	15 04	15 30	16 00		16 04	16 30	16 35	17 00	17 03	17 30	18 00

		XC ◇■	GW ■		XC ◇■	GW ■	XC ◇■	GW ■	GW ■	XC ◇■	GW ■	GW ■	XC ◇■		GW ■	GW ■	GW ■	GW ■	GW ■
Basingstoke	d	17 47	18 08		18 18	18 37	18 47	19 09	19 37	19 47	20 07	20 37	20 47		21 07	21 42	22 24	22 55	23 30
Bramley (Hants)	d		18 14			18 44		19 15	19 44		20 14	20 44			21 14	21 49	22 31	23 02	23 37
Mortimer	d		18 19			18 49		19 20	19 49		20 19	20 49			21 19	21 54	22 36	23 07	23 42
Reading West	d		18 27			18 57		19 28	19 57		20 27	20 57			21 27	22 02	22 44	23 15	23 50
Reading 7	a	18 04	18 31		18 36	19 00	19 04	19 32	20 01	20 04	20 30	21 01	21 04		21 30	22 05	22 47	23 18	23 53

Saturdays

		GW ■	XC ◇■	GW ■	XC ◇■	GW ■	XC ◇■	GW ■	XC ◇■	GW ■		XC ◇■	GW ■	XC ◇■	GW ■	GW ■	XC ◇■	GW ■	XC ◇■	GW ■		XC ◇■	GW ■	GW ■	XC ◇■
Basingstoke	d	00 02	05 41	06 37	06 47	07 07	07 25	07 37	07 47	08 07		08 19	08 37	08 47	09 07	09 37	09 47	10 07	10 19	10 37		10 47	11 07	11 37	11 47
Bramley (Hants)	d	00 09		06 44		07 14		07 44		08 14			08 44		09 14	09 44		10 14		10 44			11 14	11 44	
Mortimer	d	00 14		06 49		07 19		07 49		08 19			08 49		09 19	09 49		10 19		10 49			11 19	11 49	
Reading West	d	00 22		06 57		07 27		07 57		08 27			08 57		09 27	09 57		10 27		10 57			11 27	11 57	
Reading 7	a	00 26	05 59	07 00	07 04	07 31	07 42	08 00	08 04	08 31		08 35	09 00	09 04	09 31	10 00	10 04	10 31	10 34	11 00		11 04	11 31	12 00	12 04

		GW ■	XC ◇■	GW ■	XC ◇■	GW ■		GW ■	XC ◇■	GW ■	XC ◇■	GW ■	XC ◇■	GW ■	GW ■	XC ◇■		GW ■	XC ◇■	GW ■	XC ◇■	GW ■	GW ■	XC ◇■	GW ■
Basingstoke	d	12 07	12 19	12 37	12 47	13 07		13 37	13 47	14 07	14 19	14 37	14 47	15 07	15 37	15 47		16 07	16 19	16 37	16 47	17 07	17 37	17 47	18 07
Bramley (Hants)	d	12 14		12 44		13 14		13 44		14 14		14 44		15 14	15 44			16 14		16 44		17 14	17 44		18 14
Mortimer	d	12 19		12 49		13 19		13 49		14 19		14 49		15 19	15 49			16 19		16 49		17 19	17 49		18 19
Reading West	d	12 27		12 57		13 27		13 57		14 27		14 57		15 27	15 57			16 27		16 57		17 27	17 57		18 27
Reading 7	a	12 31	12 35	13 00	13 04	13 31		14 00	14 04	14 31	14 35	15 00	15 04	15 31	16 00	16 05		16 31	16 35	17 00	17 04	17 31	18 00	18 04	18 31

		XC ◇■		GW ■	XC ◇■	GW ■	GW ■	XC ◇■	GW ■	GW ■	XC ◇■	GW ■		GW ■	GW ■	GW ■	GW ■	GW ■
Basingstoke	d	18 19		18 37	18 47	19 07	19 37	19 47	20 08	20 37	20 47	21 07		21 39	22 07	22 37	23 07	23 37
Bramley (Hants)	d			18 44		19 14	19 44		20 14	20 44		21 14		21 44	22 14	22 44	23 14	23 44
Mortimer	d			18 49		19 19	19 49		20 19	20 49		21 19		21 49	22 19	22 49	23 19	23 49
Reading West	d			18 57		19 27	19 57		20 27	20 57		21 27		21 57	22 27	22 57	23 27	23 57
Reading 7	a	18 35		19 00	19 04	19 31	20 01	20 04	20 32	21 01	21 04	21 31		22 02	22 31	23 00	23 31	00 01

Sundays

until 1 January

		GW ■ A	GW ■	GW ■	XC ◇■	GW ■	XC ◇■	GW ■	XC ◇■	GW ■		XC ◇■	GW ■	XC ◇■	GW ■	XC ◇■	GW ■	XC ◇■	GW ■	XC ◇■		GW ■	XC ◇■	GW ■	XC ◇■
Basingstoke	d	23p37	08 07	09 07	09 47	10 07	10 47	11 07	11 47	12 07		12 47	13 07	13 47	14 07	14 47	15 07	15 47	16 07	16 47		17 07	17 47	18 07	18 47
Bramley (Hants)	d	23p44	08 14	09 14		10 14		11 14		12 14			13 14		14 14		15 14		16 14			17 14		18 14	
Mortimer	d	23p49	08 19	09 19		10 19		11 19		12 19			13 19		14 19		15 19		16 19			17 19		18 19	
Reading West	d	23p57	08 27	09 27		10 27		11 27		12 27			13 27		14 27		15 27		16 27			17 27		18 27	
Reading 7	a	00 01	08 30	09 30	10 04	10 30	11 03	11 30	12 03	12 30		13 02	13 30	14 03	14 30	15 04	15 30	16 03	16 30	17 03		17 30	18 04	18 30	19 03

		GW ■	XC ◇■	GW ■	XC ◇■	GW ■		GW ■	GW ■
Basingstoke	d	19 07	19 47	20 07	20 47	21 07		22 07	23 07
Bramley (Hants)	d	19 14		20 14		21 14		22 15	23 14
Mortimer	d	19 19		20 19		21 19		22 20	23 19
Reading West	d	19 28		20 27		21 27		22 30	23 27
Reading 7	a	19 31	20 03	20 30	21 03	21 30		22 33	23 30

A not 11 December

Table 122

Sundays

8 January to 12 February

Basingstoke - Reading

Network Diagram - see first Page of Table 116

		GW	GW	GW	XC	GW	XC	GW	XC	GW		XC	GW	XC	GW	XC	GW	XC	GW	XC		GW	XC	GW	XC
		1	1	1	◇1	1	◇1	1	◇1	1		◇1	1	◇1	1	◇1	1	◇1	1	◇1		1	◇1	1	◇1
					trolley		trolley		trolley			trolley		trolley		trolley		trolley		trolley			trolley		trolley
Basingstoke	d	23p37	08 07	09 07	09 47	10 07	10 47	11 07	11 47	12 07		12 47	13 07	13 47	14 07	14 47	15 07	15 47	16 07	16 47		17 07	17 47	18 07	18 47
Bramley (Hants)	d	23p44	08 14	09 14		10 14		11 14		12 14			13 14		14 14		15 14		16 14			17 14		18 14	
Mortimer	d	23p49	08 19	09 19		10 19		11 19		12 19			13 19		14 19		15 19		16 19			17 19		18 19	
Reading West	d	23p57	08 27	09 27		10 27		11 27		12 27			13 27		14 27		15 27		16 27			17 27		18 27	
Reading 7	a	00 01	08 30	09 30	10 04	10 30	11 03	11 30	12 03	12 30		13 03	13 30	14 03	14 30	15 04	15 30	16 03	16 30	17 03		17 30	18 03	18 30	19 03

		GW	XC	GW	XC	GW		GW	GW
		1	◇1	1	◇1	1		1	1
			trolley		trolley				
Basingstoke	d	19 07	19 47	20 07	20 47	21 07		22 07	23 07
Bramley (Hants)	d	19 14		20 14		21 14		22 15	23 14
Mortimer	d	19 19		20 19		21 19		22 20	23 19
Reading West	d	19 28		20 27		21 27		22 30	23 27
Reading 7	a	19 31	20 03	20 30	21 03	21 30		22 33	23 30

Sundays

19 February to 25 March

		GW	GW	GW	XC	GW	XC	GW	XC	GW		XC	GW	XC	GW	XC	GW	XC	GW	XC		GW	XC	GW	XC
		1	1	1	◇1	1	◇1	1	◇1	1		◇1	1	◇1	1	◇1	1	◇1	1	◇1		1	◇1	1	◇1
					trolley		trolley		trolley			trolley		trolley		trolley		trolley		trolley			trolley		trolley
Basingstoke	d	23p37	08 07	09 07	09 47	10 07	10 47	11 07	11 47	12 07		12 47	13 07	13 47	14 07	14 47	15 07	15 47	16 07	16 47		17 07	17 47	18 07	18 47
Bramley (Hants)	d	23p44	08 14	09 14		10 14		11 14		12 14			13 14		14 14		15 14		16 14			17 14		18 14	
Mortimer	d	23p49	08 19	09 19		10 19		11 19		12 19			13 19		14 19		15 19		16 19			17 19		18 19	
Reading West	d	23p57	08 27	09 27		10 27		11 27		12 27			13 27		14 27		15 27		16 27			17 27		18 27	
Reading 7	a	00 01	08 30	09 30	10 04	10 30	11 03	11 30	12 03	12 30		13 03	13 30	14 03	14 30	15 04	15 30	16 03	16 30	17 02		17 30	18 03	18 30	19 03

		GW	XC	GW	XC	GW		GW	GW
		1	◇1	1	◇1	1		1	1
			trolley		trolley				
Basingstoke	d	19 07	19 47	20 07	20 47	21 07		22 07	23 07
Bramley (Hants)	d	19 14		20 14		21 14		22 15	23 14
Mortimer	d	19 19		20 19		21 19		22 20	23 19
Reading West	d	19 28		20 27		21 27		22 30	23 27
Reading 7	a	19 31	20 03	20 30	21 03	21 30		22 33	23 30

Sundays

from 1 April

		GW	GW	GW	XC	GW	XC	GW	XC	GW		XC	GW	XC	GW	XC	GW	XC	GW	XC		GW	XC	GW	XC
		1	1	1	◇1	1	◇1	1	◇1	1		◇1	1	◇1	1	◇1	1	◇1	1	◇1		1	◇1	1	◇1
					trolley		trolley		trolley			trolley		trolley		trolley		trolley		trolley			trolley		trolley
Basingstoke	d	23p37	08 07	09 07	09 47	10 07	10 47	11 07	11 47	12 07		12 47	13 07	13 47	14 07	14 47	15 07	15 47	16 07	16 47		17 07	17 47	18 07	18 47
Bramley (Hants)	d	23p44	08 14	09 14		10 14		11 14		12 14			13 14		14 14		15 14		16 14			17 14		18 14	
Mortimer	d	23p49	08 19	09 19		10 19		11 19		12 19			13 19		14 19		15 19		16 19			17 19		18 19	
Reading West	d	23p57	08 27	09 27		10 27		11 27		12 27			13 27		14 27		15 27		16 27			17 27		18 27	
Reading 7	a	00 01	08 30	09 30	10 03	10 30	11 03	11 30	12 04	12 30		13 02	13 30	14 03	14 30	15 04	15 30	16 03	16 30	17 03		17 30	18 04	18 30	19 03

		GW	XC	GW	XC	GW		GW	GW
		1	◇1	1	◇1	1		1	1
			trolley		trolley				
Basingstoke	d	19 07	19 47	20 07	20 47	21 07		22 07	23 07
Bramley (Hants)	d	19 14		20 14		21 14		22 15	23 14
Mortimer	d	19 19		20 19		21 19		22 20	23 19
Reading West	d	19 28		20 27		21 27		22 30	23 27
Reading 7	a	19 31	20 03	20 30	21 03	21 30		22 33	23 30

Network Diagram for Table 123

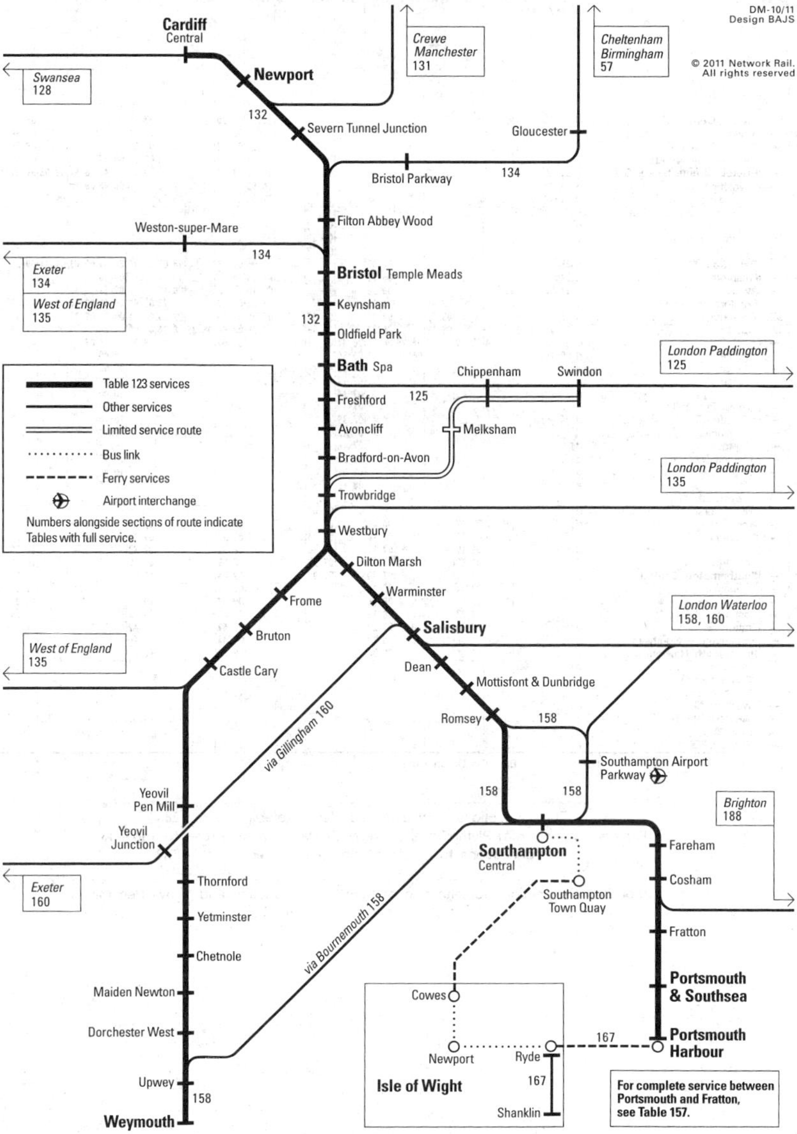

South Wales and Bristol - Weymouth and Portsmouth

Network Diagram - see first Page of Table 123

Miles	Miles	Miles			GW MX	GW MX ■ A 🛏 ☕	GW	GW	GW ◇1 ☕	GW	GW ◇	GW	GW		GW	GW ◇ 🛒	GW ◇1 B ☕	GW	GW ■ 🛒	GW ◇	SW ◇1	GW	GW ◇ 🛒		GW ◇1 ☕
0	0	—	**Cardiff Central** 7	d												06 28			07 30				08 30		
11¾	11¾	—	Newport (South Wales)	d												06 42			07 44				08 44		
21¾	21¾	—	Severn Tunnel Jn	d												06 53			07 55				08 55		
33¾	33¾	—	Filton Abbey Wood	d												07 09		07 28	08 09	08 23			09 09		
38¼	38¼	—	**Bristol Temple Meads** 10	d	23p20				05 20		05 44				06 48	07 22		07 49	08 22	08 41	08 51	09 05	09 22		
42¾	42¾	—	Keynsham	d	23p27						05 51				06 55			07 56		08 48	08 58				
48¾	48¾	—	Oldfield Park	d	23p34						05 58				07 02			08 03		08 55		09 17			
—	—	—	London Paddington 15 ⊖	d		23p45											07 06								09 06
—	—	0	Swindon	d									06 12												
—	—	16¾	Chippenham	d									06 28												
—	—	23	Melksham	d									06 37												
49¾	49¾	—	**Bath Spa** 7	d	23p38						06 02				07 06	07 35		08 07	08 35	08 59	09 07	09 21	09 35		
56¾	56¾	—	Freshford	d	23p47						06 12				07 15			08 16		09 08					
57¾	57¾	—	Avoncliff	d	23p50						06 14				07 18			08 19		09 11					
59	59	—	Bradford-on-Avon	d	23p54				05 44		06 18				07 22	07 47		08 23	08 47	09 15	09 20	09 33			
62¼	62¼	28½	Trowbridge	d	23p59				05 52		06 25		06 47		07 28	07 53		08 29	08 53	09 21	09 27	09 39	09 51		
66¼	66¼	32½	**Westbury**	a	00 07	01 35			05 59		06 32		06 55		07 35	08 00	08 25	08 36	09 00	09 28	09 33	09 49	09 58		
—	—	—		d	00 08		05 24	05 49		06 25	06 37	06 47	07 01			08 01			09 01	09 31	09 39		09 59		
—	72	—	Frome	d	00a19					06a35		06 56								09 40					
—	82½	—	Bruton	d								07 08								09 52					
—	86	—	Castle Cary	a								07 13								09 59					10 29
—	—	—		d								07 14								10 00					
—	97¾	—	Yeovil Pen Mill	d								07 35								10 14					
—	101	—	Thornford	d								07x39								10x18					
—	102	—	Yetminster	d								07x42								10x21					
—	104	—	Chetnole	d								07x46								10x25					
—	110½	—	Maiden Newton	d								07 58								10 37					
—	118¼	—	Dorchester West	d								08 09								10 48					
—	122¾	—	Upwey	a								08 16								10 55					
—	125¼	—	**Weymouth**	a								08 24								11 03					
67¾	—	—	Dilton Marsh	d									07x03												
71	—	—	Warminster	d			05 32	05 57			06 45		07 12			08 09			09 09		09 46		10 07		
90¾	—	—	**Salisbury**	a			05 55	06 18			07 10		07 36			08 32			09 32		10 09		10 29		
—	—	—		d				06 19			07 11		07 36			08 32			09 32				10 30		
107¼	—	—	Romsey	d				06 38			07 30		07 56			08 50			09 50				10 50		
115½	—	—	**Southampton Central**	a				06 49			07 40		08 09			09 04			10 04				11 04		
130	—	—	Fareham	a				07 14			08 05					09 27			10 27				11 27		
—	—	—		d				07 15			08 06					09 27			10 27				11 27		
135¾	—	—	Cosham	a				07 23			08 13					09 35			10 35				11 35		
139½	—	—	Fratton	a				07 34			08 20					09 42			10 42				11 42		
140½	—	—	Portsmouth & Southsea	a				07 38			08 24					09 46			10 46				11 46		
141¼	—	—	**Portsmouth Harbour**	a				07 45			08 30					09 55			10 54				11 54		
—	—	—	Havant	a																					
—	—	—	**Chichester** 4	a																					
—	—	—	Barnham	a																					
—	—	—	Worthing 4	a																					
—	—	—	Shoreham-by-Sea	a																					
—	—	—	Hove 2	a																					
—	—	—	Brighton 10	a																					

A The Night Riviera

B The Devon Express

For connections from Swansea please refer to Table 128.
For connections from Plymouth and Exeter St Davids please refer to Table 135.
For connections to Bournemouth please refer to Table 158

For Bus Connections for either to or from Yeovil Junction and Yeovil Pen Mill please see Table 123A

Table 123

Mondays to Fridays

South Wales and Bristol - Weymouth and Portsmouth

Network Diagram - see first Page of Table 123

		GW	GW	GW	GW	GW	GW	GW	GW	GW	GW	SW	GW	GW	GW	GW	GW	GW	GW	GW	GW	GW	SW
																		FO					
											R												
			◇	◇			◇	◇1	◇	◇		◇1	◇1	◇		◇		◇	◇	◇	◇1		◇1
								A			B												
				⌶			⌶	⌀		⌶	⌶	⌶	⊡	⌶		⌶				⌶	⌀		
Cardiff Central 7	d			09 30			10 30			11 30				12 30		13 30				14 30			
Newport (South Wales)	d			09 44			10 44			11 44				12 44		13 44				14 44			
Severn Tunnel Jn.	d			09 55																			
Filton Abbey Wood	d		09 23	10 09		10 25	11 09		11 23	12 09	12 25			13 09	13 23	14 09			14 25	15 09		15 23	
Bristol Temple Meads 10	d		09 49	10 22		10 49	11 22		11 49	12 22	12 39	12 51		13 22	13 49	14 22			14 48	15 22		15 44	15 51
Keynsham	d		09 56			10 56			11 56		12 46	12 58			13 56				14 55			15 51	15 58
Oldfield Park	d		10 03			11 03			12 03		12 53				14 03				15 02			15 58	
London Paddington 15 ⊖	d							11 06					12 18								15 06		
Swindon	d																						
Chippenham	d																						
Melksham	d																						
Bath Spa 7	d		10 07	10 35		11 07	11 35		12 07	12 35	12 57	13 07		13 35	14 07	14 35			15 06	15 35		16 02	16 07
Freshford	d		10 16			11 16			12 16		13 06				14 16				15 15			16 11	
Avoncliff	d		10 18			11 19			12 19		13 08				14 19				15 18			16 13	
Bradford-on-Avon	d		10 22	10 47		11 23	11 47		12 23	12 47	13 12	13 20		13 47	14 23	14 47			15 22	15 47		16 17	16 22
Trowbridge	d		10 29	10 53		11 29	11 53		12 29	12 53	13 19	13 27		13 53	14 29	14 53			15 28	15 53		16 24	16 28
Westbury	a		10 36	11 00		11 36	12 00	12 21	12 36	13 00	13 26	13 33	13 57	14 00	14 36	15 00			15 35	16 00	16 22	16 33	16 36
	d	10 08	10 37	11 01	11 11		12 01	12 22	12 37	13 01	13 27	13 39	13 59	14 01	14 37	15 01	15 11	15 20	15 38	16 01	16 23		16 39
Frome	d		10 46						12 49						14a50				15 47				
Bruton	d		10 58						13 01										15 58				
Castle Cary	a		11 03					12 39	13 06				14 16					15 46	16 04		16 41		
	d		11 03						13 06										16 09				
Yeovil Pen Mill	d		11 17						13 20										16 24				
Thornford	d		11x22						13x25										16x28				
Yetminster	d		11x25						13x28										16x31				
Chetnole	d		11x29						13x32										16x35				
Maiden Newton	d		11 41						13 44										16 47				
Dorchester West	d		11 54						13 54										16 58				
Upwey	a		12 02						14 02										17 05				
Weymouth	a		12 09						14 09										17 10				
Dilton Marsh	d	10x10			11x13						13x29						15x13						
Warminster	d	10a19		11 09	11 21		12 09			13 09	13 36	13 46		14 09		15 09	15a22			16 09			16 47
Salisbury	a			11 32	11 41		12 32			13 32	13 58	14 10		14 32		15 32				16 32			17 09
	d			11 32	11 42		12 32			13 32	13 59			14 32		15 32				16 32			
Romsey	d			11 50	12 10		12 50			13 50	14 19			14 50		15 50				16 50			
Southampton Central	a			12 04	12 22		13 04			14 04	14 32			15 04		16 04				17 04			
Fareham	a			12 27			13 27			14 27	14 55			15 27		16 27				17 27			
	d			12 27			13 27			14 27	14 56			15 27		16 27				17 27			
Cosham	a			12 35			13 35			14 35	15 04			15 35		16 35				17 35			
Fratton	a			12 42			13 42			14 42				15 42		16 42				17 42			
Portsmouth & Southsea	a			12 46			13 46			14 46				15 46		16 46				17 46			
Portsmouth Harbour	a			12 54			13 54			14 54				15 54		16 54				17 54			
Havant	a										15 10												
Chichester 4	a										15 21												
Barnham	a										15 29												
Worthing 4	a										15 45												
Shoreham-by-Sea	a										15 56												
Hove 2	a										16 07												
Brighton 10	a										16 14												

A The Mayflower

B ⌶ from Bristol Temple Mead

For connections from Swansea please refer to Table 128.
For connections from Plymouth and Exeter St Davids please refer to Table 135.
For connections to Bournemouth please refer to Table 158

For Bus Connections for either to or from Yeovil Junction and Yeovil Pen Mill please see Table 123A

South Wales and Bristol - Weymouth and Portsmouth

Network Diagram - see first Page of Table 123

		GW	GW	GW	GW		GW	GW	GW	GW	GW	GW	GW	GW	GW		GW	GW	GW	GW	GW	GW	GW	GW	GW
		◇ 🛒		◇				◇1 🍽	R 🛒	◇		◇1 🍽	R 🛒	◇			◇1 🍽	◇ 🛒	◇1 🍽		◇	◇1 🍽		◇1 🍽	◇
Cardiff Central 7	d	15 30							16 30				17 30					18 30			19 30				20 30
Newport (South Wales)	d	15 44							16 44				17 44					18 44			19 44				20 44
Severn Tunnel Jn	d								16 55				17 55					18 55							
Filton Abbey Wood	d	16 09		16 25	16 49		16 55		17 09	17 23	17 49		18 09		18 25			19 09		19 23	20 09				21 08
Bristol Temple Meads 10	d	16 22		16 49	17 07		17 14		17 22	17 49	18 07		18 22		18 49			19 22		19 49	20 22		20 49		21 23
Keynsham	d			16 56	17 14					17 56	18 14				18 56					19 56			20 56		
Oldfield Park	d			17 03	17 21		17 26			18 03	18 21				19 03					20 03			21 03		
London Paddington 15 ⊖	d							16 36				17 33					18 06		18 33			19 45		20 35	
Swindon	d													18 44											
Chippenham	d													19 01											
Melksham	d													19 11											
Bath Spa 7	d	16 35		17 07	17 25		17 31		17 37	18 07	18 25		18 35		19 07			19 35		20 07	20 35		21 07		21 36
Freshford	d			17 16			17 40			18 16	18 34				19 16					20 16			21 16		
Avoncliff	d			17 19						18 19	18 37				19 19					20 19			21 19		
Bradford-on-Avon	d	16 47		17 23	17 37		17 45		17 50	18 23	18 41		18 47		19 23			19 47		20 23	20 47		21 23		21 48
Trowbridge	d	16 53		17 30	17 44		17 51		17 57	18 29	18 47		18 53	19 20	19 29			19 53		20 29	20 53		21 29		21 55
Westbury	a	17 00		17 36	17 51		17 58	18 02	18 05	18 36	18 56	18 59	19 00	19 27	19 36		19 52	20 00	20 04	20 36	21 00	21 05	21 36	21 56	22 03
	d	17 01	17 11	17 39	17 54			18 04	18 05	18 40		19 01	19 02	19 41			19 53	20 01	20 05	20 37	21 01	21 05	21 38	21 57	22 03
Frome	d			17 48						18 49							20a04			20a48			21 49		
Bruton	d			18 00						19 01													22 01		
Castle Cary	a			18 05				18 20		19 06		19 17							20 23			21 23	22 06	22 14	
	d			18 06						19 06													22 06		
Yeovil Pen Mill	d			18 21						19 19													22 20		
Thornford	d			18x26						19x25													22x25		
Yetminster	d			18x29						19x28													22x28		
Chetnole	d			18x33						19x32													22x32		
Maiden Newton	d			18 45						19 44													22 44		
Dorchester West	d			18 58						19 54													22 54		
Upwey	a			19 06						20 02													23 02		
Weymouth	a			19 14						20 10													23 10		
Dilton Marsh	d		17x13		17x56									19x43											22x06
Warminster	d	17 09	17a22		18a05				18 13				19 09	19 51				20 09			21 09				22 11
Salisbury	a	17 32							18 35				19 32	20 13				20 32			21 32				22 32
	d	17 32							18 35				19 32	20 14				20 32			21 32				22 32
Romsey	d	17 50							18 54				19 50	20 35				20 50			21 50				22 53
Southampton Central	a	18 04							19 04				20 04	20 48				21 04			22 02				23 04
Fareham	a	18 27							19 27				20 27					21 27			22 42				23 27
	d	18 27							19 27				20 27					21 27			22 42				23 27
Cosham	a	18 35							19 34																
Fratton	a	18 48							19 42				20 42					21 41			22 56				23 44
Portsmouth & Southsea	a	18 52							19 46				20 46					21 45			22 59				23 48
Portsmouth Harbour	a	19 00							19 54				20 54					21 52			23 04				23 54
Havant	a																								
Chichester 4	a																								
Barnham	a																								
Worthing 4	a																								
Shoreham-by-Sea	a																								
Hove 2	a																								
Brighton 10	a																								

For connections from Swansea please refer to Table 128.
For connections from Plymouth and Exeter St Davids please refer to Table 135.
For connections to Bournemouth please refer to Table 158

For Bus Connections for either to or from Yeovil Junction and Yeovil Pen Mill please see Table 123A

South Wales and Bristol - Weymouth and Portsmouth

Network Diagram - see first Page of Table 123

		GW	SW	GW	GW
			1		R
					A
					🛏 ☕
Cardiff Central 7	d	21 00			
Newport (South Wales)	d	21 15			
Severn Tunnel Jn.	d	21 25			
Filton Abbey Wood	d	21 42			
Bristol Temple Meads 10	d	22 00	22 25	23 20	
Keynsham	d	22 07		23 27	
Oldfield Park	d	22 14		23 34	
London Paddington 15 ⊖	d				23 45
Swindon	d				
Chippenham	d				
Melksham	d				
Bath Spa 7	d	22 18	22 38	23 38	
Freshford	d	22 27		23 47	
Avoncliff	d	22 30		23 50	
Bradford-on-Avon	d	22 34	22 51	23 54	
Trowbridge	d	22 40	22 57	23 59	
Westbury	a	22 47	23 04	00 07	01 35
	d		23 08	00 08	
Frome	d			00a19	
Bruton	d				
Castle Cary	a				
	d				
Yeovil Pen Mill	d				
Thornford	d				
Yetminster	d				
Chetnole	d				
Maiden Newton	d				
Dorchester West	d				
Upwey	a				
Weymouth	a				
Dilton Marsh	d				
Warminster	d		23 15		
Salisbury	a		23 35		
	d				
Romsey	d				
Southampton Central	a				
Fareham	a				
	d				
Cosham	a				
Fratton	a				
Portsmouth & Southsea	a				
Portsmouth Harbour	a				
Havant	a				
Chichester 4	a				
Barnham	a				
Worthing 4	a				
Shoreham-by-Sea	a				
Hove 2	a				
Brighton 10	a				

A The Night Riviera

For connections from Swansea please refer to Table 128.
For connections from Plymouth and Exeter St Davids please refer to Table 135.
For connections to Bournemouth please refer to Table 158

For Bus Connections for either to or from Yeovil Junction and Yeovil Pen Mill please see Table 123A

Table 123

Saturdays

South Wales and Bristol - Weymouth and Portsmouth

Network Diagram - see first Page of Table 123

		GW	GW	GW	GW	GW	GW	GW	GW	GW	GW	GW	GW	SW	GW	GW	GW	GW	GW	GW	GW	GW	GW
			■			◇				◇		◇	◇	◇■	◇■	◇		◇	◇			◇	◇■
			A																B			B	
			🛏 ☕												☕				🍴			🍴	⌀
Cardiff Central ■	d									06 30		07 30				08 30			09 30			10 30	
Newport (South Wales)	d									06 44		07 44				08 44			09 44			10 44	
Severn Tunnel Jn	d									06 55		07 55				08 55			09 55				
Filton Abbey Wood	d									07 09		08 09	08 23			09 09		09 23	10 09		10 28	11 09	
Bristol Temple Meads ■	d	23p20				05 49			06 49	07 22	07 49	08 22	08 39	08 51		09 22		09 49	10 22		10 49	11 22	
Keynsham	d	23p27				05 56			06 56		07 56		08 46	08 58				09 56			10 56		
Oldfield Park	d	23p34				06 03			07 03		08 03		08 53					10 03			11 03		
London Paddington ■ ⊖	d		23p45												08 18								11 06
Swindon	d																						
Chippenham	d																						
Melksham	d																						
Bath Spa ■	d	23p38				06 07			07 07	07 35	08 07	08 35	08 57	09 07		09 35		10 07	10 35		11 07	11 35	
Freshford	d	23p47				06 16			07 16		08 16		09 06					10 16			11 16		
Avoncliff	d	23p50				06 18			07 18		08 19		09 08					10 18			11 18		
Bradford-on-Avon	d	23p54				06 22			07 22	07 47	08 23	08 47	09 13	09 20		09 47		10 22	10 47		11 22	11 47	
Trowbridge	d	23p59				06 28			07 29	07 53	08 29	08 53	09 19	09 27		09 53		10 29	10 53		11 29	11 53	
Westbury	a	00 07	01 35			06 36			07 36	08 01	08 36	09 01	09 27	09 34	09 59	10 01		10 36	11 01		11 36	12 01	12 22
	d	00 08		05 26	06 01	06 43	06 47	07 03		08 01		09 01	09 27	09 39	10 00	10 01	10 10	10 37	11 01	11 11		12 01	12 22
Frome	d	00a19					06 56						09 36					10 46					
Bruton	d						07 08						09 48					10 58					
Castle Cary	a						07 14						09 53		10 17			11 03					12 40
	d						07 15						09 53					11 03					
Yeovil Pen Mill	d						07 29						10 07					11 17					
Thornford	d						07x33						10x12					11x22					
Yetminster	d						07x36						10x15					11x25					
Chetnole	d						07x40						10x19					11x29					
Maiden Newton	d						07 52						10 31					11 41					
Dorchester West	d						08 03						10 38					11 54					
Upwey	a						08 10						10 49					12 02					
Weymouth	a						08 17						10 57					12 09					
Dilton Marsh	d							07x06									10x13			11x13			
Warminster	d			05 34	06 09	06 51		07 13		08 09		09 09		09 46		10 09	10a19		11 09	11 21		12 09	
Salisbury	a			05 58	06 31	07 12		07 34		08 32		09 31		10 09		10 31			11 32	11 42		12 32	
	d				06 32	07 24		07 36		08 32		09 32				10 32			11 32	11 43		12 32	
Romsey	d				06 50	07 44		07 55		08 50		09 50				10 50			11 50	12 04		12 50	
Southampton Central	a				07 02	08 02		08 07		09 03		10 03				11 03			12 03	12 20		13 03	
Fareham	a				07 27	08 27				09 27		10 27				11 27			12 27			13 27	
	d				07 27	08 27				09 27		10 27				11 27			12 27			13 27	
Cosham	a				07 35	08 35				09 35		10 35				11 35			12 35			13 35	
Fratton	a				07 42	08 42				09 42		10 42				11 42			12 42			13 42	
Portsmouth & Southsea	a				07 46	08 46				09 46		10 46				11 46			12 46			13 46	
Portsmouth Harbour	a				07 52	08 52				09 52		10 52				11 52			12 52			13 52	
Havant	a																						
Chichester ■	a																						
Barnham	a																						
Worthing ■	a																						
Shoreham-by-Sea	a																						
Hove ■	a																						
Brighton ■	a																						

A The Night Riviera

B 🍴 from Bristol Temple Meads

For connections from Swansea please refer to Table 128.
For connections from Plymouth and Exeter St Davids please refer to Table 135.
For connections to Bournemouth please refer to Table 158

For Bus Connections for either to or from Yeovil Junction and Yeovil Pen Mill please see Table 123A

Table 123

Saturdays

South Wales and Bristol - Weymouth and Portsmouth

Network Diagram - see first Page of Table 123

		GW	GW	GW	SW	GW	GW	GW	GW	GW	GW	GW	GW	GW	GW	SW	GW	GW	GW	GW	GW	GW	GW
				R																R			
		◇	◇	◇	◇1	◇1	◇		◇		◇	◇		◇1		◇1	◇		◇		◇1	◇	◇
			A																				
			trolley		trolley	buffet								buffet							buffet		
Cardiff Central 7	d		11 30				12 30		13 30			14 30					15 30			16 30			17 30
Newport (South Wales)	d		11 44				12 44		13 44			14 44					15 44			16 44			17 44
Severn Tunnel Jn.	d																			16 55			17 55
Filton Abbey Wood	d	11 23	12 09	12 28			13 09	13 23	14 09		14 25	15 09			15 22		16 09		16 28	17 09		17 23	18 09
Bristol Temple Meads 10	d	11 49	12 22	12 43	12 51		13 22	13 49	14 22		14 49	15 22			15 38	15 51	16 22		16 49	17 22		17 49	18 22
Keynsham	d	11 56		12 50	12 58			13 56			14 56				15 45	15 58			16 56			17 56	
Oldfield Park	d	12 03		12 57				14 03			15 03				15 52				17 03			18 03	
London Paddington 15 ⊖	d					12 18								15 06							17 06		
Swindon	d												15 22										
Chippenham	d												15 38										
Melksham	d												15 48										
Bath Spa 7	d	12 07	12 35	13 00	13 07		13 35	14 07	14 35		15 07	15 35			15 56	16 07	16 35		17 07	17 35		18 07	18 35
Freshford	d	12 16						14 16			15 16				16 05				17 16			18 16	
Avoncliff	d	12 18						14 18			15 18				16 08				17 19			18 19	
Bradford-on-Avon	d	12 22	12 47	13 13	13 20		13 47	14 22	14 47		15 22	15 47			16 12	16 24	16 47		17 23	17 47		18 23	18 47
Trowbridge	d	12 29	12 53	13 20	13 27		13 53	14 29	14 53		15 29	15 53	15 58		16 18	16 30	16 53		17 29	17 53		18 29	18 53
Westbury	a	12 36	13 01	13 27	13 33	13 57	14 01	14 36	15 01		15 36	16 01	16 05	16 22	16 25	16 37	17 01		17 36	18 01	18 22	18 36	19 01
	d	12 37	13 01	13 28	13 39	13 58	14 01	14 37	15 01	15 11	15 37	16 01		16 23		16 39	17 01	17 08	17 38	18 01	18 22	18 39	19 01
Frome	d	12 47						14a49			15 46								17 47			18 49	
Bruton	d	12 57									15 57								17 59			19 00	
Castle Cary	a	13 03				14 14					16 03			16 40					18 04		18 40	19 05	
	d	13 04									16 09								18 05			19 06	
Yeovil Pen Mill	d	13 17									16 24								18 21			19 19	
Thornford	d	13x22									16x28								18x26			19x24	
Yetminster	d	13x25									16x31								18x29			19x27	
Chetnole	d	13x29									16x35								18x33			19x31	
Maiden Newton	d	13 41									16 47								18 44			19 43	
Dorchester West	d	13 54									16 58								18 54			19 54	
Upwey	a	14 02									17 05								19 02			20 01	
Weymouth	a	14 08									17 10								19 10			20 09	
Dilton Marsh	d			13x31						15x14								17x10					
Warminster	d		13 09	13 37	13 46		14 09		15 09	15a23		16 09				16 47	17 09	17a19		18 09			19 09
Salisbury	a		13 32	13 59	14 10		14 32		15 32			16 32				17 09	17 32			18 32			19 32
	d		13 32	14 00			14 32		15 32			16 32					17 32			18 32			19 32
Romsey	d		13 50	14 20			14 50		15 50			16 50					17 50			18 50			19 50
Southampton Central	a		14 03	14 32			15 03		16 03			17 03					18 03			19 03			20 02
Fareham	a		14 27	14 54			15 27		16 27			17 27					18 27			19 27			20 27
	d		14 27	14 55			15 27		16 27			17 27					18 27			19 27			20 28
Cosham	a		14 35	15 03			15 35		16 35			17 35					18 35			19 35			
Fratton	a		14 42				15 42		16 42			17 42					18 42			19 42			20 42
Portsmouth & Southsea	a		14 46				15 46		16 46			17 46					18 46			19 46			20 46
Portsmouth Harbour	a		14 52				15 52		16 52			17 52					18 52			19 52			20 52
Havant	a			15 10																			
Chichester 4	a			15 21																			
Barnham	a			15 29																			
Worthing 4	a			15 44																			
Shoreham-by-Sea	a			15 55																			
Hove 2	a			16 07																			
Brighton 10	a			16 14																			

A trolley from Bristol Temple Meads

For connections from Swansea please refer to Table 128.
For connections from Plymouth and Exeter St Davids please refer to Table 135.
For connections to Bournemouth please refer to Table 158

For Bus Connections for either to or from Yeovil Junction and Yeovil Pen Mill please see Table 123A

Table 123

Saturdays

South Wales and Bristol - Weymouth and Portsmouth

Network Diagram - see first Page of Table 123

		GW	GW	GW	GW	GW	GW	GW	GW	GW	GW	GW	SW	GW	GW
				◇	◇1		◇	◇1			◇		1		
					A									B	C
					☕			☕							🚌
Cardiff Central 7	d			18 30			19 30				20 30				
Newport (South Wales)	d			18 44			19 44				20 44				
Severn Tunnel Jn.	d														
Filton Abbey Wood	d		18 28	19 09		19 24	20 09				21 08				
Bristol Temple Meads 10	d		18 49	19 22		19 49	20 22		20 49		21 22	22 00	22 23	23 11	
Keynsham	d		18 56			19 56			20 56			22 07		23 18	
Oldfield Park	d		19 03			20 03			21 03			22 14		23 25	
London Paddington 15 ⊖	d				19 06			20 06							
Swindon	d									21 08					
Chippenham	d									21 24					
Melksham	d									21 34					
Bath Spa 7	d		19 07	19 35		20 07	20 35		21 07		21 35	22 18	22 36	23 29	
Freshford	d		19 16			20 16			21 16			22 27		23 38	
Avoncliff	d		19 18			20 18			21 19			22 30		23 40	
Bradford-on-Avon	d		19 22	19 47		20 22	20 47		21 23		21 47	22 34	22 47	23 44	23 49
Trowbridge	d		19 29	19 53		20 29	20 53		21 29	21 43	21 53	22 40	22 53	23 50	00 02
Westbury	a		19 36	20 01	20 26	20 36	21 01	21 25	21 36	21 51	22 01	22 47	23 00	23 57	00 20
	d	19 09		20 01	20 27	20 37	21 01	21 26	21 39		22 01		23 04	23 58	00 21
Frome	d					20a48			21 49					00a08	00a38
Bruton	d								22 01						
Castle Cary	a				20 44			21 43	22 06						
	d								22 06						
Yeovil Pen Mill	d								22 20						
Thornford	d								22x25						
Yetminster	d								22x28						
Chetnole	d								22x32						
Maiden Newton	d								22 44						
Dorchester West	d								22 54						
Upwey	a								23 02						
Weymouth	a								23 10						
Dilton Marsh	d	19x12									22x05				
Warminster	d	19 19		20 09			21 09				22 10		23 11		
Salisbury	a	19 40		20 32			21 32				22 32		23 34		
	d	19 41		20 32			21 32				22 32				
Romsey	d	20 04		20 50			21 50				22 50				
Southampton Central	a	20 18		21 03			22 03				23 03				
Fareham	a			21 27			22 26				23 26				
	d			21 27			22 27				23 27				
Cosham	a														
Fratton	a			21 42			22 42				23 40				
Portsmouth & Southsea	a			21 46			22 46				23 44				
Portsmouth Harbour	a			21 52			22 52				23 52				
Havant	a														
Chichester 4	a														
Barnham	a														
Worthing 4	a														
Shoreham-by-Sea	a														
Hove 2	a														
Brighton 10	a														

A until 11 February, from 31 March

B until 24 March

C from 31 March

For connections from Swansea please refer to Table 128.
For connections from Plymouth and Exeter St Davids please refer to Table 135.
For connections to Bournemouth please refer to Table 158

For Bus Connections for either to or from Yeovil Junction and Yeovil Pen Mill please see Table 123A

Table 123

Sundays

until 1 January

South Wales and Bristol - Weymouth and Portsmouth

Network Diagram - see first Page of Table 123

		GW	GW	GW	GW	GW	GW	GW	GW	GW	GW	GW	GW	GW	SW	GW	GW	GW	GW	GW	GW	GW	GW
							R																
		◇	◇1	◇	◇1	◇	◇	◇1	◇	◇1		◇	◇1	◇	◇1	◇	◇1	◇	◇	◇	◇		◇1
							A																
			☕		☕		🛒	☕		☕			☕				☕						☕
Cardiff Central 7	d	08 05		09 15		10 08	11 08		12 08			13 08		14 08		15 08		16 08	16 35		17 08		
Newport (South Wales)	d	08 23		09 29		10 22	11 22		12 22			13 22		14 22		15 22		16 22	16 49		17 22		
Severn Tunnel Jn.	d	08 40		09 46		10 39	11 39		12 39			13 39		14 39		15 39		16 39			17 39		
Filton Abbey Wood	d	08 55		10 03		10 54	11 54		12 57			13 54		14 55		15 55		16 55	17 20		17 54		
Bristol Temple Meads 10	d	09 11		10 15		11 10	12 15		13 10		13 55	14 15		15 10	16 04	16 15		17 15	17 40	17 44	18 10		
Keynsham	d	09 18				11 17			13 17		14 02			15 17	16 11			17 22		17 51	18 17		
Oldfield Park	d	09 25				11 24			13 24		14 09			15 24				17 29		17 58	18 24		
London Paddington 15 ⊖	d		08 57		09 57			11 27		12 57			13 57				15 57						17 57
Swindon	d																					18 19	
Chippenham	d																					18 35	
Melksham	d																					18 45	
Bath Spa 7	d	09 28		10 29		11 27	12 27		13 27		14 13	14 27		15 27	16 20	16 27		17 33	17 52	18 01	18 27		
Freshford	d			10 40			12 38				14 23	14 37				16 38				18 11			
Avoncliff	d			10 42			12 40				14 25	14 39				16 40				18 13			
Bradford-on-Avon	d	09 41		10 46		11 40	12 44		13 40		14 29	14 43		15 40	16 31	16 44		17 46	18 05	18 17	18 40		
Trowbridge	d	09 47		10 53		11 47	12 51		13 47		14 36	14 49		15 46	16 37	16 51		17 52	18 12	18 24	18 46	18 54	
Westbury	a	09 57	10 23	11 00		11 54	13 00	13 05	13 54	14 18	14 43	14 56		15 57	16 44	16 58	17 23	17 59	18 19	18 31	18 53	19 06	19 28
	d	09 58		11 01		12 01	13 01	13 06	14 03		14 45	15 00		15 58	16 46	16 59	17 25	18 00	18 20	18 31	18 56		
Frome	d										14 54									18 39			
Bruton	d										15 06									18 52			
Castle Cary	a				11 34			13 24			15 10		15 35				17 41			18 57			
	d										15 11									18 58			
Yeovil Pen Mill	d										15 26									19 12			
Thornford	d										15x32									19x17			
Yetminster	d										15x35									19x20			
Chetnole	d										15x39									19x24			
Maiden Newton	d										15 50									19 36			
Dorchester West	d										16 01									19 47			
Upwey	a										16 10									19 55			
Weymouth	a										16 15									20 01			
Dilton Marsh	d	10x02				12x04			14x06					16x02		17x02			18x23				
Warminster	d	10 08		11 09		12 10	13 09		14 12			15 07		16 08	16 53	17 08		18 07	18 29		19 04		
Salisbury	a	10 32		11 32		12 32	13 32		14 34			15 32		16 32	17 16	17 32		18 32	18 52		19 32		
	d	10 33		11 33		12 33	13 33		14 48			15 32		16 33		17 33		18 32	18 56		19 32		
Romsey	d	10 51		11 51		12 52	13 51		15 10			15 50		16 51		17 51		18 50	19 14		19 50		
Southampton Central	a	11 03		12 03		13 05	14 03		15 21			16 02		17 03		18 03		19 02	19 25		20 02		
Fareham	a	11 27		12 28		13 33	14 26		15 50			16 26		17 27		18 27		19 27	19 48		20 26		
	d	11 27		12 28		13 34	14 27		15 51			16 26		17 27		18 27		19 27	19 49		20 26		
Cosham	a	11 34		12 35		13 42	14 34		16 01			16 34		17 34		18 34		19 35	19 57				
Fratton	a	11 41		12 42			14 41					16 41		17 41		18 41		19 42			20 41		
Portsmouth & Southsea	a	11 46		12 46			14 45					16 45		17 46		18 45		19 46			20 45		
Portsmouth Harbour	a	11 52		12 52			14 55					16 52		17 52		18 52		19 52			20 51		
Havant	a					14 03			16 11										20 09				
Chichester 4	a					14 19			16 22										20 20				
Barnham	a					14 27			16 30										20 28				
Worthing 4	a					14 45			16 45										20 50				
Shoreham-by-Sea	a					14 51			16 52										20 56				
Hove 2	a					15 00			16 58										21 03				
Brighton 10	a					15 06			17 06										21 09				

A 🛒 from Bristol Temple Meads

For connections from Swansea please refer to Table 128. For connections from Plymouth and Exeter St Davids please refer to Table 135.
For connections to Bournemouth please refer to Table 158

For Bus Connections for either to or from Yeovil Junction and Yeovil Pen Mill please see Table 123A

Table 123

Sundays
until 1 January

South Wales and Bristol - Weymouth and Portsmouth

Network Diagram - see first Page of Table 123

		GW	GW	GW	GW	GW	GW	GW	SW	GW	GW
		R	◇	◇ 1 ☕	◇	◇ 1 ☕		◇	1		🚲
Cardiff Central 7	d	17 40	18 08		19 08			20 18			22 00
Newport (South Wales)	d	17 54	18 22		19 22			20 31			22 19
Severn Tunnel Jn.	d		18 39		19 40			20 48			22 36
Filton Abbey Wood	d	18 23	18 56		19 55			21 05			22 53
Bristol Temple Meads 10	d	18 50	19 10		20 15		20 50	21 25	21 35	22 15	23 10
Keynsham	d		19 17				20 57			22 22	
Oldfield Park	d		19 24				21 04			22 29	
London Paddington 15 ⊖	d			18 57		19 57					
Swindon	d										
Chippenham	d										
Melksham	d										
Bath Spa 7	d	19 02	19 27		20 27		21 07	21 38	21 49	22 32	23 22
Freshford	d				20 38		21 17			22 42	
Avoncliff	d				20 40		21 20			22 45	
Bradford-on-Avon	d	19 15	19 40		20 44		21 24	21 50	22 00	22 49	23 35
Trowbridge	d	19 22	19 46		20 51		21 30	21 57	22 06	22 55	23 42
Westbury	a	19 29	19 53		20 58	21 28	21 37	22 04	22 13	23 02	23 49
	d	19 31	19 54		20 59	21 29	21 38	22 05	22 15		23 50
Frome	d						21 48				
Bruton	d						21 59				
Castle Cary	a			20 30		21 46	22 04				
	d						22 05				
Yeovil Pen Mill	d						22 19				
Thornford	d						22x23				
Yetminster	d						22x26				
Chetnole	d						22x30				
Maiden Newton	d						22 42				
Dorchester West	d						22 53				
Upwey	a						23 00				
Weymouth	a						23 06				
Dilton Marsh	d		19x58								23x53
Warminster	d	19 38	20 04		21 07			22 13	22 22		23a59
Salisbury	a	20 00	20 25		21 28			22 34	22 46		
	d	20 01	20 30		21 33			22 36			
Romsey	d	20 19	20 48		21 51			22 54			
Southampton Central	a	20 29	20 59		22 03			23 05			
Fareham	a	20 54	21 24		22 26			23 29			
	d	20 55	21 25		22 26			23 30			
Cosham	a										
Fratton	a	21 09	21 38		22 40			23 43			
Portsmouth & Southsea	a	21 15	21 41		22 44			23 46			
Portsmouth Harbour	a	21 26	21 48		22 50			23 54			
Havant	a										
Chichester 4	a										
Barnham	a										
Worthing 4	a										
Shoreham-by-Sea	a										
Hove 2	a										
Brighton 10	a										

For connections from Swansea please refer to Table 128.
For connections from Plymouth and Exeter St Davids please refer to Table 135.
For connections to Bournemouth please refer to Table 158

For Bus Connections for either to or from Yeovil Junction and Yeovil Pen Mill please see Table 123A

Table 123

Sundays

8 January to 12 February

South Wales and Bristol - Weymouth and Portsmouth

Network Diagram - see first Page of Table 123

		GW	GW	GW	GW	GW	GW	GW	GW	GW	GW	GW	GW	GW	SW	GW	GW	GW	GW	GW	GW	GW	GW
		◇	◇1 ☕	◇	◇1 ☕	◇	R ◇ A 🚲	◇1 ☕	◇	◇1 ☕		◇	◇1 ☕	◇	◇1	◇	◇1 ☕	◇	◇	◇	◇		◇1 ☕
Cardiff Central 7	d	08 05		09 15		10 08	11 08		12 08			13 08		14 08		15 08		16 08	16 35		17 08		
Newport (South Wales)	d	08 23		09 29		10 22	11 22		12 22			13 22		14 22		15 22		16 22	16 49		17 22		
Severn Tunnel Jn.	d	08 40		09 46		10 39	11 39		12 39			13 39		14 39		15 39		16 39			17 39		
Filton Abbey Wood	d	08 55		10 03		10 54	11 54		12 57			13 54		14 55		15 55		16 55	17 20		17 54		
Bristol Temple Meads 10	d	09 11		10 15		11 10	12 15		13 10		13 55	14 15		15 10	16 04	16 15		17 15	17 40	17 44	18 10		
Keynsham	d	09 18				11 17			13 17		14 02			15 17	16 11			17 22		17 51	18 17		
Oldfield Park	d	09 25				11 24			13 24		14 09			15 24				17 29		17 58	18 24		
London Paddington 15 ⊖	d		08 57		09 57			11 27		12 57			13 57				15 57						17 57
Swindon	d																					18 19	
Chippenham	d																					18 35	
Melksham	d																					18 45	
Bath Spa 7	d	09 28		10 29		11 27	12 27		13 27		14 13	14 27		15 27	16 20	16 27		17 33	17 52	18 01	18 27		
Freshford	d			10 40			12 38				14 23	14 37				16 38				18 11			
Avoncliff	d			10 42			12 40				14 25	14 39				16 40				18 13			
Bradford-on-Avon	d	09 41		10 46		11 40	12 44		13 40		14 29	14 43		15 40	16 31	16 44		17 46	18 05	18 17	18 40		
Trowbridge	d	09 47		10 53		11 47	12 51		13 47		14 36	14 49		15 46	16 37	16 51		17 52	18 12	18 24	18 46	18 54	
Westbury	a	09 57	10 23	11 00		11 54	13 00	13 05	13 54	14 18	14 43	14 56		15 57	16 44	16 58	17 23	17 59	18 19	18 31	18 53	19 06	19 28
	d	09 58		11 01		12 01	13 01	13 06	14 03		14 45	15 00		15 58	16 46	16 59	17 25	18 00	18 20	18 31	18 56		
Frome	d										14 54									18 39			
Bruton	d										15 06									18 52			
Castle Cary	a				11 34			13 24			15 10		15 35				17 41			18 57			
	d										15 11									18 58			
Yeovil Pen Mill	d										15 26									19 12			
Thornford	d										15x32									19x17			
Yetminster	d										15x35									19x20			
Chetnole	d										15x39									19x24			
Maiden Newton	d										15 50									19 36			
Dorchester West	d										16 01									19 47			
Upwey	a										16 10									19 55			
Weymouth	a										16 15									20 01			
Dilton Marsh	d	10x02				12x04			14x06					16x02		17x02			18x23				
Warminster	d	10 08		11 09		12 10	13 09		14 12			15 07		16 08	16 53	17 08		18 07	18 29		19 04		
Salisbury	a	10 32		11 32		12 32	13 32		14 34			15 32		16 32	17 16	17 32		18 32	18 52		19 32		
	d	10 33		11 33		12 33	13 33		14 48			15 32		16 33		17 33		18 32	18 56		19 32		
Romsey	d	10 51		11 51		12 52	13 51		15 10			15 50		16 51		17 51		18 50	19 14		19 50		
Southampton Central	a	11 03		12 03		13 05	14 03		15 21			16 02		17 03		18 03		19 02	19 25		20 02		
Fareham	a	11 27		12 28		13 33	14 26		15 50			16 26		17 27		18 27		19 27	19 48		20 26		
	d	11 27		12 28		13 34	14 27		15 51			16 26		17 27		18 27		19 27	19 49		20 26		
Cosham	a	11 34		12 35		13 42	14 34		16 01			16 34		17 34		18 34		19 35	19 57				
Fratton	a	11 41		12 42			14 41					16 41		17 41		18 41		19 42			20 41		
Portsmouth & Southsea	a	11 46		12 46			14 45					16 45		17 46		18 45		19 46			20 45		
Portsmouth Harbour	a	11 52		12 52			14 55					16 52		17 52		18 52		19 52			20 51		
Havant	a					14 03			16 11										20 09				
Chichester 4	a					14 19			16 22										20 20				
Barnham	a					14 27			16 30										20 28				
Worthing 4	a					14 45			16 45										20 50				
Shoreham-by-Sea	a					14 51			16 52										20 56				
Hove 2	a					15 00			16 58										21 03				
Brighton 10	a					15 06			17 06										21 09				

A 🚲 from Bristol Temple Meads

For connections from Swansea please refer to Table 128.
For connections from Plymouth and Exeter St Davids please refer to Table 135.
For connections to Bournemouth please refer to Table 158

For Bus Connections for either to or from Yeovil Junction and Yeovil Pen Mill please see Table 123A

Table 123

Sundays

8 January to 12 February

South Wales and Bristol - Weymouth and Portsmouth

Network Diagram - see first Page of Table 123

		GW	GW	GW	GW	GW		GW	GW	SW	GW	GW
		[R]	◇	◇ [1] [catering]	◇	◇ [1] [catering]			◇	[1]		[bicycle]
Cardiff Central [7]	d	17 40	18 08		19 08				20 18			22 00
Newport (South Wales)	d	17 54	18 22		19 22				20 31			22 19
Severn Tunnel Jn	d		18 39		19 40				20 48			22 36
Filton Abbey Wood	d	18 23	18 56		19 55				21 05			22 53
Bristol Temple Meads [10]	d	18 50	19 10		20 15			20 50	21 25	21 35	22 15	23 10
Keynsham	d		19 17					20 57			22 22	
Oldfield Park	d		19 24					21 04			22 29	
London Paddington [15] ⊖	d			18 57		19 57						
Swindon	d											
Chippenham	d											
Melksham	d											
Bath Spa [7]	d	19 02	19 27		20 27			21 07	21 38	21 49	22 32	23 22
Freshford	d				20 38			21 17			22 42	
Avoncliff	d				20 40			21 20			22 45	
Bradford-on-Avon	d	19 15	19 40		20 44			21 24	21 50	22 00	22 49	23 35
Trowbridge	d	19 22	19 46		20 51			21 30	21 57	22 06	22 55	23 42
Westbury	a	19 29	19 53		20 58	21 28		21 37	22 04	22 13	23 02	23 49
	d	19 31	19 54		20 59	21 29		21 38	22 05	22 15		23 50
Frome	d							21 48				
Bruton	d							21 59				
Castle Cary	a			20 30		21 46		22 04				
	d							22 05				
Yeovil Pen Mill	d							22 19				
Thornford	d							22x23				
Yetminster	d							22x26				
Chetnole	d							22x30				
Maiden Newton	d							22 42				
Dorchester West	d							22 53				
Upwey	a							23 00				
Weymouth	a							23 06				
Dilton Marsh	d		19x58									23x53
Warminster	d	19 38	20 04		21 07				22 13	22 22		23a59
Salisbury	a	20 00	20 25		21 28				22 34	22 46		
	d	20 01	20 30		21 33				22 36			
Romsey	d	20 19	20 48		21 51				22 54			
Southampton Central	a	20 29	20 59		22 03				23 05			
Fareham	a	20 54	21 24		22 26				23 29			
	d	20 55	21 25		22 26				23 30			
Cosham	a											
Fratton	a	21 09	21 38		22 40				23 43			
Portsmouth & Southsea	a	21 15	21 41		22 44				23 46			
Portsmouth Harbour	a	21 26	21 48		22 50				23 54			
Havant	a											
Chichester [4]	a											
Barnham	a											
Worthing [4]	a											
Shoreham-by-Sea	a											
Hove [2]	a											
Brighton [10]	a											

For connections from Swansea please refer to Table 128.
For connections from Plymouth and Exeter St Davids please refer to Table 135.
For connections to Bournemouth please refer to Table 158

For Bus Connections for either to or from Yeovil Junction and Yeovil Pen Mill please see Table 123A

Table 123

Sundays

19 February to 25 March

South Wales and Bristol - Weymouth and Portsmouth

Network Diagram - see first Page of Table 123

		GW	GW	GW	GW	GW	GW	GW	GW	GW	GW	GW	GW	GW	SW	GW	GW	GW	GW	GW	GW	GW	GW
		◇	◇1 ⊡	◇1 ⊡	◇	◇	R ◇ A	◇1 ⊡	◇	◇1 ⊡		◇	◇1 ⊡	◇	◇1	◇	◇1 ⊡	◇	◇	◇	◇		◇1 ⊡
Cardiff Central 7	d																						
Newport (South Wales)	d																						
Severn Tunnel Jn.	d																						
Filton Abbey Wood	d	08 54			10 03	10 54	11 54		12 57			13 54		14 55		15 55		16 55	17 20		17 55		
Bristol Temple Meads 10	d	09 10			10 15	11 10	12 15		13 10		13 55	14 15		15 10	16 04	16 15		17 15	17 40	17 44	18 10		
Keynsham	d	09 17				11 17			13 17		14 02			15 17	16 11			17 22		17 51	18 17		
Oldfield Park	d	09 24				11 24			13 24		14 09			15 24				17 29		17 58	18 24		
London Paddington 15 ⊖	d		08 57	09 57				11 27		12 57			13 57				15 57						17 55
Swindon	d																					18 19	
Chippenham	d																					18 35	
Melksham	d																					18 45	
Bath Spa 7	d	09 27			10 29	11 27	12 27		13 27		14 13	14 27		15 27	16 20	16 27		17 33	17 52	18 01	18 27		
Freshford	d				10 40		12 38				14 23	14 38				16 38				18 11			
Avoncliff	d				10 42		12 40				14 25	14 40				16 40				18 13			
Bradford-on-Avon	d	09 40			10 46	11 40	12 44		13 40		14 29	14 44		15 40	16 31	16 44		17 47	18 05	18 17	18 40		
Trowbridge	d	09 46			10 53	11 47	12 51		13 47		14 36	14 51		15 46	16 37	16 51		17 53	18 12	18 24	18 46	18 54	
Westbury	a	09 53	10 24		11 00	11 54	13 00	13 05	13 54	14 18	14 43	14 58		15 57	16 44	16 58	17 23	18 00	18 19	18 31	18 53	19 06	19 28
	d	09 59			11 01	12 01	13 01	13 06	14 03		14 45	15 00		15 58	16 46	16 59	17 25	18 01	18 20	18 31	18 56		
Frome	d										14 54									18 39			
Bruton	d										15 06									18 52			
Castle Cary	a			11 34				13 24			15 10		15 35				17 41			18 57			
	d										15 11									18 58			
Yeovil Pen Mill	d										15 26									19 12			
Thornford	d										15 32									19x17			
Yetminster	d										15 35									19x20			
Chetnole	d										15 39									19x24			
Maiden Newton	d										15 50									19 36			
Dorchester West	d										16 01									19 47			
Upwey	a										16 10									19 55			
Weymouth	a										16 15									20 01			
Dilton Marsh	d	10x02				12x04			14x06					16x02		17x02			18x23				
Warminster	d	10 08			11 09	12 10	13 09		14 12			15 08		16 08	16 53	17 08		18 09	18 29		19 04		
Salisbury	a	10 32			11 32	12 32	13 32		14 34			15 32		16 32	17 16	17 33		18 33	18 52		19 32		
	d	10 32			11 33	12 33	13 33		14 48			15 33		16 33		17 33		18 33	18 56		19 32		
Romsey	d	10 50			11 51	12 52	13 51		15 10			15 51		16 51		17 51		18 51	19 14		19 50		
Southampton Central	a	11 02			12 03	13 05	14 03		15 21			16 03		17 03		18 03		19 03	19 25		20 02		
Fareham	a	11 26			12 28	13 33	14 26		15 50			16 27		17 27		18 27		19 28	19 48		20 27		
	d	11 26			12 28	13 34	14 27		15 51			16 27		17 27		18 27		19 28	19 49		20 27		
Cosham	a	11 33			12 35	13 42	14 34		16 01			16 35		17 34		18 34		19 35	19 57				
Fratton	a	11 40			12 42		14 41					16 42		17 41		18 41		19 42			20 42		
Portsmouth & Southsea	a	11 45			12 46		14 45					16 46		17 46		18 45		19 46			20 45		
Portsmouth Harbour	a	11 52			12 52		14 55					16 52		17 51		18 52		19 51			20 49		
Havant	a					14 03			16 11										20 09				
Chichester 4	a					14 19			16 22										20 20				
Barnham	a					14 27			16 30										20 28				
Worthing 4	a					14 45			16 45										20 50				
Shoreham-by-Sea	a					14 51			16 52										20 56				
Hove 2	a					15 00			16 58										21 03				
Brighton 10	a					15 06			17 06										21 09				

A ⊼ from Bristol Temple Meads

For connections from Swansea please refer to Table 128.
For connections from Plymouth and Exeter St Davids please refer to Table 135.
For connections to Bournemouth please refer to Table 158

For Bus Connections for either to or from Yeovil Junction and Yeovil Pen Mill please see Table 123A

Table 123

Sundays

19 February to 25 March

South Wales and Bristol - Weymouth and Portsmouth

Network Diagram - see first Page of Table 123

		GW	GW	GW	GW	GW		GW	GW	SW	GW	GW
		B	◇	◇1 ᴅᴘ	◇	◇1 ᴅᴘ			◇	1		trolley
Cardiff Central 7	d											
Newport (South Wales)	d											
Severn Tunnel Jn.	d											
Filton Abbey Wood	d	18 25	18 55		19 55				21 06			22 52
Bristol Temple Meads 10	d	18 50	19 10		20 15			20 50	21 25	21 35	22 15	23 10
Keynsham	d		19 17					20 57			22 22	
Oldfield Park	d		19 24					21 04			22 29	
London Paddington 15 ⊖	d			18 57		19 57						
Swindon	d											
Chippenham	d											
Melksham	d											
Bath Spa 7	d	19 02	19 27		20 27			21 07	21 38	21 49	22 32	23 22
Freshford	d				20 38			21 18			22 42	
Avoncliff	d				20 40			21 20			22 45	
Bradford-on-Avon	d	19 15	19 40		20 44			21 24	21 50	22 00	22 49	23 35
Trowbridge	d	19 22	19 46		20 51			21 31	21 57	22 06	22 55	23 42
Westbury	a	19 29	19 53		20 58	21 28		21 38	22 04	22 13	23 02	23 49
	d	19 31	19 54		20 59	21 29		21 39	22 05	22 15		23 50
Frome	d							21 48				
Bruton	d							22 00				
Castle Cary	a			20 30		21 46		22 05				
	d							22 05				
Yeovil Pen Mill	d							22 19				
Thornford	d							22x24				
Yetminster	d							22x27				
Chetnole	d							22x31				
Maiden Newton	d							22 43				
Dorchester West	d							22 53				
Upwey	a							23 01				
Weymouth	a							23 06				
Dilton Marsh	d		19x53									23x53
Warminster	d	19 38	19 59		21 07				22 13	22 22		23a59
Salisbury	a	20 00	20 22		21 28				22 34	22 46		
	d	20 01	20 30		21 33				22 36			
Romsey	d	20 19	20 48		21 51				22 54			
Southampton Central	a	20 29	20 59		22 03				23 05			
Fareham	a	20 54	21 24		22 26				23 29			
	d	20 55	21 25		22 26				23 30			
Cosham	a											
Fratton	a	21 09	21 38		22 40				23 43			
Portsmouth & Southsea	a	21 15	21 41		22 44				23 46			
Portsmouth Harbour	a	21 24	21 46		22 50				23 50			
Havant	a											
Chichester 4	a											
Barnham	a											
Worthing 4	a											
Shoreham-by-Sea	a											
Hove 2	a											
Brighton 10	a											

For connections from Swansea please refer to Table 128.
For connections from Plymouth and Exeter St Davids please refer to Table 135.
For connections to Bournemouth please refer to Table 158

For Bus Connections for either to or from Yeovil Junction and Yeovil Pen Mill please see Table 123A

Table 123

Sundays

from 1 April

South Wales and Bristol - Weymouth and Portsmouth

Network Diagram - see first Page of Table 123

		GW	GW	GW	GW	GW	GW	GW	GW	GW	GW	GW	GW	GW	SW	GW	GW	GW	GW	GW	GW	GW	GW
							R																R
			◇	◇	◇1	◇	◇	◇1	◇	◇1		◇	◇1	◇	◇1	◇	◇1	◇	◇	◇	◇		
							A																
		bus			cup		trolley	cup		cup			cup				cup						
Cardiff Central 7	d		08 05	09 15		10 08	11 08		12 08			13 08		14 08		15 08		16 08	16 35		17 08		17 40
Newport (South Wales)	d		08 23	09 29		10 22	11 22		12 22			13 22		14 22		15 22		16 22	16 49		17 22		17 54
Severn Tunnel Jn.	d		08 40	09 46		10 39	11 39		12 39			13 39		14 39		15 39		16 39			17 39		
Filton Abbey Wood	d		08 55	10 03		10 54	11 54		12 57			13 54		14 55		15 55		16 55	17 20		17 54		18 23
Bristol Temple Meads 10	d		09 10	10 15		11 10	12 15		13 10		13 55	14 15		15 10	16 04	16 15		17 15	17 40	17 44	18 10		18 50
Keynsham	d		09 17			11 17			13 17		14 02			15 17	16 11			17 22		17 51	18 17		
Oldfield Park	d		09 24			11 24			13 24		14 09			15 24				17 29		17 58	18 24		
London Paddington 15 ⊖	d				09 30			11 30		12 30			13 30				15 30						
Swindon	d				10 34			12 34		13 34												18 19	
Chippenham	d																					18 35	
Melksham	d																					18 45	
Bath Spa 7	d		09 27	10 29		11 27	12 27		13 27		14 13	14 27		15 27	16 20	16 27		17 33	17 52	18 01	18 27		19 02
Freshford	d			10 40			12 38				14 23	14 37				16 38				18 11			
Avoncliff	d			10 42			12 40				14 25	14 39				16 40				18 13			
Bradford-on-Avon	d	23p49	09 40	10 46		11 40	12 44		13 40		14 29	14 43		15 40	16 31	16 44		17 46	18 05	18 17	18 40		19 15
Trowbridge	d	00 02	09 46	10 53		11 47	12 51		13 47		14 36	14 49		15 46	16 37	16 51		17 52	18 12	18 24	18 46	18 54	19 22
Westbury	a	00 20	09 53	11 00	11 05	11 54	13 00	13 08	13 54	14 06	14 43	14 56		15 57	16 44	16 58	17 03	17 59	18 19	18 31	18 53	19 06	19 29
	d	00 21	09 59	11 01	11 18	12 01	13 01		14 03		14 45	15 00		15 58	16 46	16 59	17 04	18 00	18 20	18 31	18 56		19 31
Frome	d	00a38									14 54									18 39			
Bruton	d										15 06									18 52			
Castle Cary	a				11 35						15 10		15 21				17 21			18 57			
	d										15 11									18 58			
Yeovil Pen Mill	d										15 26									19 12			
Thornford	d										15x32									19x17			
Yetminster	d										15x35									19x20			
Chetnole	d										15x39									19x24			
Maiden Newton	d										15 50									19 36			
Dorchester West	d										16 01									19 47			
Upwey	a										16 10									19 55			
Weymouth	a										16 15									20 01			
Dilton Marsh	d		10x02			12x04			14x06					16x02		17x02			18x23				
Warminster	d		10 08	11 09		12 10	13 09		14 12			15 07		16 08	16 53	17 08		18 07	18 29		19 04		19 38
Salisbury	a		10 32	11 32		12 32	13 32		14 34			15 32		16 32	17 16	17 32		18 32	18 52		19 32		20 00
	d		10 32	11 33		12 33	13 33		14 48			15 32		16 33		17 33		18 32	18 56		19 32		20 01
Romsey	d		10 50	11 51		12 52	13 51		15 10			15 50		16 51		17 51		18 50	19 14		19 50		20 19
Southampton Central	a		11 02	12 03		13 05	14 03		15 21			16 02		17 03		18 03		19 02	19 25		20 02		20 29
Fareham	a		11 26	12 28		13 33	14 26		15 50			16 26		17 27		18 27		19 27	19 48		20 26		20 54
	d		11 26	12 28		13 34	14 27		15 51			16 26		17 27		18 27		19 27	19 49		20 26		20 55
Cosham	a		11 33	12 35		13 42	14 34		16 01			16 34		17 34		18 34		19 35	19 57				
Fratton	a		11 40	12 42			14 41					16 41		17 41		18 41		19 42			20 41		21 09
Portsmouth & Southsea	a		11 45	12 46			14 45					16 45		17 46		18 45		19 46			20 45		21 15
Portsmouth Harbour	a		11 52	12 52			14 55					16 52		17 52		18 52		19 52			20 51		21 26
Havant	a					14 03			16 11										20 09				
Chichester 4	a					14 19			16 22										20 20				
Barnham	a					14 27			16 30										20 28				
Worthing 4	a					14 45			16 45										20 50				
Shoreham-by-Sea	a					14 51			16 52										20 56				
Hove 2	a					15 00			16 58										21 03				
Brighton 10	a					15 06			17 06										21 09				

A trolley from Bristol Temple Meads

For connections from Swansea please refer to Table 128.
For connections from Plymouth and Exeter St Davids please refer to Table 135.
For connections to Bournemouth please refer to Table 158

For Bus Connections for either to or from Yeovil Junction and Yeovil Pen Mill please see Table 123A

Table 123

Sundays

from 1 April

South Wales and Bristol - Weymouth and Portsmouth

Network Diagram - see first Page of Table 123

		GW	GW	GW	GW	GW		GW	GW	SW	GW	GW
		◇1	◇	◇1	◇	◇1			◇	1		
		⊏P		⊏P		⊏P						⊥o
Cardiff Central 7	d		18 08		19 08				20 18			22 00
Newport (South Wales)	d		18 22		19 22				20 31			22 19
Severn Tunnel Jn.	d		18 39		19 40				20 48			22 36
Filton Abbey Wood	d		18 56		19 55				21 05			22 53
Bristol Temple Meads 10	d		19 10		20 15			20 50	21 25	21 35	22 15	23 10
Keynsham	d		19 17					20 57			22 22	
Oldfield Park	d		19 24					21 04			22 29	
London Paddington 15 ⊖	d	17 57		18 57		19 57						
Swindon	d	19 01				21 01						
Chippenham	d											
Melksham	d											
Bath Spa 7	d		19 27		20 27			21 07	21 38	21 49	22 32	23 22
Freshford	d				20 38			21 17			22 42	
Avoncliff	d				20 40			21 20			22 45	
Bradford-on-Avon	d		19 40		20 44			21 24	21 50	22 00	22 49	23 35
Trowbridge	d		19 46		20 51			21 30	21 57	22 06	22 55	23 42
Westbury	a	19 32	19 53		20 58	21 35		21 37	22 04	22 13	23 02	23 49
	d		19 54		20 59	21 36		21 38	22 05	22 15		23 50
Frome	d							21 48				
Bruton	d							21 59				
Castle Cary	a			20 44		21 53		22 04				
	d							22 05				
Yeovil Pen Mill	d							22 19				
Thornford	d							22x23				
Yetminster	d							22x26				
Chetnole	d							22x30				
Maiden Newton	d							22 42				
Dorchester West	d							22 53				
Upwey	a							23 00				
Weymouth	a							23 06				
Dilton Marsh	d		19x58									23x53
Warminster	d		20 04		21 07				22 13	22 22		23a59
Salisbury	a		20 25		21 28				22 34	22 46		
	d		20 30		21 33				22 36			
Romsey	d		20 48		21 51				22 54			
Southampton Central	a		20 59		22 03				23 05			
Fareham	a		21 24		22 26				23 29			
	d		21 25		22 26				23 30			
Cosham	a											
Fratton	a		21 38		22 40				23 43			
Portsmouth & Southsea	a		21 41		22 44				23 46			
Portsmouth Harbour	a		21 48		22 50				23 54			
Havant	a											
Chichester 4	a											
Barnham	a											
Worthing 4	a											
Shoreham-by-Sea	a											
Hove 2	a											
Brighton 10	a											

For connections from Swansea please refer to Table 128.
For connections from Plymouth and Exeter St Davids please refer to Table 135.
For connections to Bournemouth please refer to Table 158

For Bus Connections for either to or from Yeovil Junction and Yeovil Pen Mill please see Table 123A

Table 123

Mondays to Fridays

Portsmouth and Weymouth - Bristol and South Wales

Network Diagram - see first Page of Table 123

Miles	Miles	Miles			GW	GW	GW	GW	GW	GW	GW	GW	SW		GW	GW	GW	GW	GW	GW	GW	GW	GW		GW
																		■							
						◇1	◇1			◇	◇1		1		◇		◇1		◇		◇	◇	◇1		◇
											A												A		
						🍽	🍽				⊘						🍽	⊼			⊼		⊘		⊼
—	—	—	Brighton 10	d																					
—	—	—	Hove 2	d																					
—	—	—	Shoreham-by-Sea	d																					
—	—	—	Worthing 4	d																					
—	—	—	Barnham	d																					
—	—	—	**Chichester** 4	d																					
—	—	—	Havant	d																					
0	—	—	**Portsmouth Harbour** ⛴	d														06 00			07 05				08 23
0¾	—	—	Portsmouth & Southsea	d														06 04			07 09				08 27
1¾	—	—	Fratton	d														06 08			07 13				08 31
5½	—	—	Cosham	d														06 15			07 21				08 39
11¼	—	—	Fareham	a														06 23			07 28				08 46
—	—	—		d														06 24			07 29				08 47
25¾	—	—	**Southampton Central** ⛴	d														06 46			07 52	08 23			09 10
34	—	—	Romsey	d														07 00			08 11	08 35			09 21
50½	—	—	**Salisbury**	a														07 18			08 29	09 00			09 39
—	—	—		d				06 02					06 40					07 19			08 30	09 03			09 40
70¼	—	—	Warminster	d				06 24					07 00			07 23		07 39			08 52	09 25			10 01
73½	—	—	Dilton Marsh	d				06x28								07x27		07x43				09x29			
—	0	—	**Weymouth**	d											05 33				06 40						
—	2½	—	Upwey	d											05 37				06 45						
—	7	—	Dorchester West	d											05 45				06 53						
—	14¾	—	Maiden Newton	d											05 57				07 05						
—	21¼	—	Chetnole	d											06x06				07x13						
—	23¼	—	Yetminster	d											06x08				07x16						
—	24¼	—	Thornford	d											06x10				07x18						
—	27½	—	Yeovil Pen Mill	d											06 20				07 30						
—	39¼	—	Castle Cary	a											06 33				07 43						
—	—	—		d							06 38				06 45		07 27		07 44				09 42		
—	42¾	—	Bruton	d											06 51				07 49						
—	53¼	—	Frome	d			06 07			06 45					07 04				08 02						
75	59	—	**Westbury**	a			06 17	06 33		06 54	06 59		07 08		07 12	07 32	07 45	07 47	08 09		09 01	09 35	10 00		10 09
—	—	—		d	05 58	06 06	06 18		06 38	06 55	07 01	07 04	07 09		07 18	07 38	07 51	07 53	08 17	08 45	09 10	09 38	10 01		10 10
79	63	4	Trowbridge	d	06 04				06 44	07 02		07 10	07 15		07 24	07 44		08 00	08 23	08 51	09 16	09 44			10 16
82¼	66¼	—	Bradford-on-Avon	d	06 10				06 50	07 08			07 21		07 30	07 50		08 06	08 29	08 57	09 22	09 50			10 22
83½	67½	—	Avoncliff	d	06 13				06 53	07 11					07 33	07 53			08 32	09 00		09 53			
84½	68½	—	Freshford	d	06 16				06 56	07 13					07 36	07 56		08 10	08 35	09 03		09 56			
91½	75½	—	Bath Spa 7	a	06 26				07 06	07 24			07 33		07 46	08 06		08 21	08 45	09 13	09 35	10 06			10 34
—	—	9½	Melksham	d								07 20													
—	—	15¾	Chippenham	a								07 30													
—	—	32½	Swindon	a								07 48													
—	—	—	London Paddington 15 ⊖	a		07 53	08 09				08 38						09 21						11 24		
92½	76½	—	Oldfield Park	a	06 30				07 10	07 28			07 37		07 50	08 10		08 25	08 49	09 17		10 10			
98½	82½	—	Keynsham	a	06 37				07 18	07 35			07 44		07 58	08 18		08 32	08 56	09 25	09 44	10 18			
103	87	—	**Bristol Temple Meads** 10	a	06 46				07 27	07 46			07 52		08 06	08 29		08 41	09 05	09 35	09 52	10 28			10 48
107½	91½	—	Filton Abbey Wood	a	07 01				07 42	08 01					08 21	08 48		09 01	09 21	09 48	10 03	10 48			11 01
119½	119½	—	Severn Tunnel Jn	a	07 14																				
129½	113½	—	Newport (South Wales)	a	07 25					08 27								09 25			10 26				11 26
141¼	125¼	—	**Cardiff Central** 7	a	07 44					08 46								09 43			10 41				11 43

A ⊘ to Westbury

For connections to Swansea please refer to Table 128.
For connections to Exeter St Davids and Plymouth please refer to Table 135.
For connections from Bournemouth please refer to Table 158

For Bus Connections for either to or from Yeovil Junction and Yeovil Pen Mill please see Table 123A

Portsmouth and Weymouth - Bristol and South Wales

Network Diagram - see first Page of Table 123

		GW	GW	GW	GW	SW	GW	GW	GW		GW	GW	GW	GW	SW	GW	GW	GW	GW		GW	GW	GW	GW	GW
		◇		◇1	◇	◇1	◇ A	◇			◇1	◇	◇	◇	◇1		◇	◇1			◇		◇1 C	◇1	B
					🛒		🛒	🛒			🍽	🛒		🛒				🍽			🛒		🍽	🍽	🛒
Brighton 10	d						08 59																		
Hove 2	d						09 03																		
Shoreham-by-Sea	d						09 13																		
Worthing 4	d						09 22																		
Barnham	d						09 38																		
Chichester 4	d						09 47																		
Havant	d						09 59																		
Portsmouth Harbour ⛴	d				09 23			10 23				11 23		12 23							13 23				14 23
Portsmouth & Southsea	d				09 27			10 27				11 27		12 27							13 27				14 27
Fratton	d				09 31			10 31				11 31		12 31							13 31				14 31
Cosham	d				09 39		10 05	10 39				11 39		12 39							13 39				14 39
Fareham	a				09 46		10 14	10 46				11 46		12 46							13 46				14 46
	d				09 47		10 15	10 47				11 47		12 47							13 47				14 47
Southampton Central ⛴	d				10 10		10 42	11 10				12 10	12 27	13 10							14 10				15 10
Romsey	d				10 21		10 54	11 21				12 21	12 39	13 21							14 21				15 21
Salisbury	a				10 39		11 13	11 39				12 39	13 02	13 39							14 39				15 39
	d				10 40	10 52	11 13	11 40				12 40	13 06	13 40	13 52						14 40				15 40
Warminster	d		10 25		11 01	11 12	11 34	12 01				13 01	13 34	14 01	14 12						15 01	15 28			16 01
Dilton Marsh	d		10x29										13x38									15x32			
Weymouth	d	08 53							11 10								13 10								
Upwey	d	08 58							11 15								13 15								
Dorchester West	d	09 06							11 23								13 23								
Maiden Newton	d	09 18							11 43								13 46								
Chetnole	d	09x26							11x50								13x53								
Yetminster	d	09x29							11x53								13x56								
Thornford	d	09x31							11x55								13x59								
Yeovil Pen Mill	d	09 41							12 05								14 08								
Castle Cary	a	09 54							12 19								14 22								
	d	09 55							12 23		12 45						14 22	14 44					15 51		
Bruton	d	10 01							12 29								14 28								
Frome	d	10 15							12 42								14 41		14 59					15 55	
Westbury	a	10 24	10 33		11 09	11 20	11 42	12 09	12 48		13 04	13 09	13 42	14 09	14 20		14 48	15 02	15 08		15 09	15 36		16 06	16 09
	d	10 38		11 05	11 10	11 21	11 43	12 10	12 52		13 05	13 10	13 44	14 10	14 21	14 38	14 51	15 03			15 10	15 38		16 08	16 10
Trowbridge	d	10 44			11 16	11 27	11 49	12 16	12 58			13 16	13 50	14 16	14 27	14 44	14 57				15 16	15 44			16 16
Bradford-on-Avon	d	10 50			11 22	11 33	11 55	12 22	13 04			13 22	13 56	14 22	14 33	14 50	15 03				15 22	15 50			16 22
Avoncliff	d	10 53					11 58		13 07				13 59			14 53	15 06					15 53			
Freshford	d	10 56					12 01		13 10				14 02			14 56	15 09					15 56			
Bath Spa 7	a	11 06			11 34	11 46	12 11	12 34	13 20			13 34	14 12	14 34	14 46	15 06	15 19				15 34	16 06			16 34
Melksham	d																								
Chippenham	a																								
Swindon	a																								
London Paddington 15 ⊖	a			12 23							14 44							16 22					17 24	17 54	
Oldfield Park	a	11 10					12 15		13 24				14 16			15 10						16 10			
Keynsham	a	11 18				11 54	12 22		13 32				14 24		14 54	15 18						16 18			
Bristol Temple Meads 10	a	11 28			11 48	12 05	12 31	12 48	13 41			13 48	14 35	14 48	15 05	15 28	15 34				15 48	16 29			16 48
Filton Abbey Wood	a	11 48			12 01		12 48	13 01				14 01	14 47	15 01			15 48				16 01	16 48			17 01
Severn Tunnel Jn.	a																								17 13
Newport (South Wales)	a				12 25			13 26				14 26		15 25							16 25				17 25
Cardiff Central 7	a				12 43			13 43				14 43		15 43							16 43				17 43

A 🛒 to Southampton Central

C The Torbay Express

For connections to Swansea please refer to Table 128.
For connections to Exeter St Davids and Plymouth please refer to Table 135.
For connections from Bournemouth please refer to Table 158

For Bus Connections for either to or from Yeovil Junction and Yeovil Pen Mill please see Table 123A

Table 123

Mondays to Fridays

Portsmouth and Weymouth - Bristol and South Wales

Network Diagram - see first Page of Table 123

		GW	GW	GW	GW	GW	GW	GW	GW	GW	GW	GW	GW	GW	GW	GW	GW	GW	GW	GW	SW	GW	GW
																		FO	FX				
		◇	R 🛒		R 🛒			◇ 🛒	◇	◇1 🍴	◇	◇	◇ 🛒	◇ 🛒	1		◇1 🍴	◇	◇		◇1		◇
Brighton 10	d												16 59										
Hove 2	d												17 03										
Shoreham-by-Sea	d												17 13										
Worthing 4	d												17 22										
Barnham	d												17 39										
Chichester 4	d												17 47										
Havant	d												17 58										
Portsmouth Harbour ⛴	d		15 23		16 23			17 23						18 23				19 23	19 23				20 23
Portsmouth & Southsea	d		15 27		16 27			17 27						18 27				19 27	19 27				20 27
Fratton	d		15 31		16 31			17 31						18 31				19 31	19 31				20 31
Cosham	d		15 39		16 39			17 39					18 05	18 39				19 39	19 39				
Fareham	a		15 46		16 46			17 46					18 12	18 46				19 46	19 46				20 46
	d		15 47		16 47			17 47					18 13	18 47				19 47	19 47				20 47
Southampton Central ⛴	d		16 10		17 10			18 10					18 42	19 10				20 10	20 10				21 10
Romsey	d		16 21		17 21			18 21					18 54	19 21				20 21	20 21				21 21
Salisbury	a		16 39		17 39			18 39					19 12	19 39				20 39	20 39				21 39
	d		16 40		17 40			18 40					19 13	19 40				20 40	20 40		20 57		21 40
Warminster	d		17 01	17 28	18 01	18 18		19 01					19 32	20 01				21 01	21 01		21 17		22 01
Dilton Marsh	d			17x32		18x22							19x37										
Weymouth	d	15 08							17 30													20 21	
Upwey	d	15 13							17 35													20 26	
Dorchester West	d	15 21							17 43													20 34	
Maiden Newton	d	15 33							17 54													20 45	
Chetnole	d	15x42							18x03													20x54	
Yetminster	d	15x45							18x06													20x57	
Thornford	d	15x47							18x08													20x59	
Yeovil Pen Mill	d	15 56							18 23													21 09	
Castle Cary	a	16 09							18 36													21 22	
	d	16 10							18 37	18 54							20 46					21 23	
Bruton	d	16 16							18 43													21 29	
Frome	d	16 29							19 06		←				20 15					21 02		21 42	
Westbury	a	16 38	17 09	17 36	18 09	18 28		19 09	19 17	19 12	19 17		19 40	20 09	20 26		21 04	21 08	21 08	21 12	21 25	21 51	22 09
	d	16 38	17 10	17 38	18 10		18 38	19 10	19 19	19 12	19 19	19 32	19 41	20 10		20 38	21 05	21 10	21 10		21 25	21 55	22 10
Trowbridge	d	16 44	17 16	17 44	18 16		18 44	19 16	→		19 25	19 38	19 48	20 16		20 44		21 16	21 16		21 31	22 02	22 16
Bradford-on-Avon	d	16 50	17 22	17 50	18 22		18 50	19 22			19 31		19 54	20 22		20 50		21 22	21 22		21 37	22 08	22 22
Avoncliff	d	16 53		17 53			18 54				19 34		19 56			20 53						22 11	
Freshford	d	16 56		17 56			18 56				19 37		19 58			20 56						22 13	
Bath Spa 7	a	17 06	17 34	18 06	18 34		19 06	19 34			19 47		20 12	20 34		21 06		21 34	21 34		21 50	22 24	22 34
Melksham	d											19 48											
Chippenham	a											20 01											
Swindon	a											20 21											
London Paddington 15 ⊖	a									20 39							22 30						
Oldfield Park	a	17 10		18 10			19 10				19 51		20 14			21 10						22 28	
Keynsham	a	17 18		18 17			19 18				19 59		20 21			21 18					21 58	22 35	
Bristol Temple Meads 10	a	17 29	17 48	18 28	18 48		19 29	19 48			20 08		20 30	20 48		21 28		21 48	21 48		22 06	22 44	22 48
Filton Abbey Wood	a	17 48	18 01	18 48	19 01		19 48	20 01						21 01				22 01	22 01				23 01
Severn Tunnel Jn.	a		18 13		19 13			20 16						21 13				22 17	22 17				23 16
Newport (South Wales)	a		18 25		19 26			20 27						21 26				22 29	22 36				23 34
Cardiff Central 7	a		18 43		19 46			20 43						21 44				22 52	23 00				23 56

For connections to Swansea please refer to Table 128.
For connections to Exeter St Davids and Plymouth please refer to Table 135.
For connections from Bournemouth please refer to Table 158

For Bus Connections for either to or from Yeovil Junction and Yeovil Pen Mill please see Table 123A

Portsmouth and Weymouth - Bristol and South Wales

Network Diagram - see first Page of Table 123

Station		GW	GW	GW
Brighton 10	d			
Hove 2	d			
Shoreham-by-Sea	d			
Worthing 4	d			
Barnham	d			
Chichester 4	d			
Havant	d			
Portsmouth Harbour ⛴	d			21 23
Portsmouth & Southsea	d			21 27
Fratton	d			21 31
Cosham	d			
Fareham	a			21 47
	d			21 48
Southampton Central ⛴	d	21 20		22 22
Romsey	d	21 31		22 34
Salisbury	a	21 51		22 58
	d	21 53		23 00
Warminster	d	22 15		23 20
Dilton Marsh	d	22x19		23x24
Weymouth	d			
Upwey	d			
Dorchester West	d			
Maiden Newton	d			
Chetnole	d			
Yetminster	d			
Thornford	d			
Yeovil Pen Mill	d			
Castle Cary	a			
	d			
Bruton	d			
Frome	d			
Westbury	a	22 26		23 31
	d		22 32	
Trowbridge	d		22 38	
Bradford-on-Avon	d		22 44	
Avoncliff	d		22 46	
Freshford	d		22 50	
Bath Spa 7	a		23 00	
Melksham	d			
Chippenham	a			
Swindon	a			
London Paddington 15 ⊖	a			
Oldfield Park	a		23 04	
Keynsham	a		23 12	
Bristol Temple Meads 10	a		23 23	
Filton Abbey Wood	a			
Severn Tunnel Jn.	a			
Newport (South Wales)	a			
Cardiff Central 7	a			

For connections to Swansea please refer to Table 128.
For connections to Exeter St Davids and Plymouth please refer to Table 135.
For connections from Bournemouth please refer to Table 158

For Bus Connections for either to or from Yeovil Junction and Yeovil Pen Mill please see Table 123A

Table 123

Saturdays

Portsmouth and Weymouth - Bristol and South Wales

Network Diagram - see first Page of Table 123

		GW	GW	GW	SW	GW	GW	GW	GW	GW		GW	GW	GW	GW	GW	GW	GW	GW	GW		SW	GW	GW	GW
					[1]		◇[1] ⊡	◇	◇				◇ A 🛒	◇	◇[1] ⊡	◇ A 🛒	◇		R [1] ⊡	◇ A 🛒		◇[1]	◇	◇	◇
Brighton [10]	d																						09 00		
Hove [2]	d																						09 04		
Shoreham-by-Sea	d																						09 13		
Worthing [4]	d																						09 22		
Barnham	d																						09 41		
Chichester [4]	d																						09 49		
Havant	d																						10 00		
Portsmouth Harbour ⛴	d							06 00					07 23			08 23				09 23				10 23	
Portsmouth & Southsea	d							06 04					07 27			08 27				09 27				10 27	
Fratton	d							06 08					07 31			08 31				09 31				10 31	
Cosham	d							06 19					07 39			08 39				09 39			10 06	10 39	
Fareham	a							06 27					07 46			08 46				09 46			10 15	10 46	
	d							06 28					07 47			08 47				09 47			10 16	10 47	
Southampton Central ⛴	d							06 53					08 10	08 27		09 10				10 10			10 42	11 10	
Romsey	d							07 11					08 21	08 38		09 21				10 21			10 53	11 21	
Salisbury	a							07 29					08 40	09 02		09 39				10 39			11 12	11 39	
	d	06 03			06 40			07 30					08 40	09 03		09 40				10 40		10 52	11 13	11 40	
Warminster	d	06 25			07 00	07 23		07 50					09 01	09 25		10 01		10 25		11 01		11 12	11 35	12 01	
Dilton Marsh	d	06x29				07x27		07x54						09x29				10x29							
Weymouth	d								06 38								08 46								11 10
Upwey	d								06 43								08 51								11 15
Dorchester West	d								06 51								08 59								11 26
Maiden Newton	d								07 03								09 11								11 43
Chetnole	d								07x11								09x19								11x50
Yetminster	d								07x14								09x22								11x53
Thornford	d								07x16								09x24								11x56
Yeovil Pen Mill	d								07 30								09 34								12 05
Castle Cary	a								07 43								09 47								12 19
	d						07 33		07 44						09 40		09 48								12 22
Bruton	d								07 49								09 54								12 27
Frome	d			06 49					08 02								10 07								12 39
Westbury	a	06 33		06 58	07 08	07 31	07 51	07 59	08 11				09 09	09 35	09 58	10 09	10 16	10 33		11 09		11 20	11 43	12 09	12 48
	d		06 38		07 09	07 38	07 56	08 02	08 17	08 38		09 05	09 10	09 38	09 59	10 10	10 38		11 02	11 10		11 21	11 47	12 10	12 49
Trowbridge	d		06 45		07 15	07 44		08 08	08 23	08 44		09 11	09 16	09 44		10 16	10 44			11 16		11 27	11 53	12 16	12 56
Bradford-on-Avon	d		06 51		07 21	07 50		08 14	08 29	08 50			09 22	09 50		10 22	10 50			11 22		11 33	11 59	12 22	13 02
Avoncliff	d		06 53			07 53			08 32	08 53				09 53			10 53						12 02		13 05
Freshford	d		06 56			07 56			08 35	08 56				09 56			10 56						12 05		13 07
Bath Spa [7]	a		07 06		07 33	08 06		08 30	08 45	09 06			09 34	10 06		10 34	11 06			11 34		11 46	12 15	12 34	13 18
Melksham	d											09 20													
Chippenham	a											09 30													
Swindon	a											09 49													
London Paddington [15] ⊖	a						09 21								11 24				12 23						
Oldfield Park	a		07 11		07 37	08 11			08 49	09 11				10 11			11 10						12 19		13 22
Keynsham	a		07 18		07 44	08 18			08 56	09 18				10 18			11 18					11 54	12 26		13 28
Bristol Temple Meads [10]	a		07 29		07 53	08 29		08 44	09 05	09 27			09 48	10 29		10 48	11 29			11 48		12 05	12 35	12 48	13 37
Filton Abbey Wood	a		07 48			08 48		09 01		09 48			10 01	10 48		11 01	11 48			12 01			12 48	13 01	13 48
Severn Tunnel Jn.	a																								
Newport (South Wales)	a							09 25					10 24			11 24				12 24				13 25	
Cardiff Central [7]	a							09 43					10 43			11 43				12 43				13 43	

A 🛒 to Bristol Temple Meads

For connections to Swansea please refer to Table 128.
For connections to Exeter St Davids and Plymouth please refer to Table 135.
For connections from Bournemouth please refer to Table 158

For Bus Connections for either to or from Yeovil Junction and Yeovil Pen Mill please see Table 123A

Table 123

Portsmouth and Weymouth - Bristol and South Wales

Network Diagram - see first Page of Table 123

		GW	GW	GW	GW	SW		GW	GW	GW	GW	GW	GW	GW	GW	GW		GW	GW	GW	GW	GW	GW	GW	GW
		◇1 ☕	◇	◇	◇	◇1		◇	◇1 A ⊘			◇		◇1	◇1 ☕	◇		◇	◇		■		◇	◇	◇1 ☕
Brighton 10	d																								
Hove 2	d																								
Shoreham-by-Sea	d																								
Worthing 4	d																								
Barnham	d																								
Chichester 4	d																								
Havant	d																								
Portsmouth Harbour ⛴	d		11 23		12 23							13 23				14 23			15 23		16 23		17 23		
Portsmouth & Southsea	d		11 27		12 27							13 27				14 27			15 27		16 27		17 27		
Fratton	d		11 31		12 31							13 31				14 31			15 31		16 31		17 31		
Cosham	d		11 39		12 39							13 39				14 39			15 39		16 39		17 39		
Fareham	a		11 46		12 46							13 46				14 46			15 46		16 46		17 46		
	d		11 47		12 47							13 47				14 47			15 47		16 47		17 47		
Southampton Central ⛴	d		12 10	12 27	13 10							14 10				15 10			16 10		17 10		18 10		
Romsey	d		12 21	12 38	13 21							14 21				15 21			16 21		17 21		18 21		
Salisbury	a		12 39	13 02	13 39							14 39				15 39			16 39		17 39		18 39		
	d		12 40	13 04	13 40	13 52						14 40				15 40			16 40		17 40		18 40		
Warminster	d		13 01	13 26	14 01	14 12						15 01	15 28			16 01			17 01	17 28	18 01		19 01		
Dilton Marsh	d			13x30									15x33							17 32					
Weymouth	d							13 10										15 08						17 28	
Upwey	d							13 15										15 13						17 33	
Dorchester West	d							13 23										15 21						17 41	
Maiden Newton	d							13 43										15 33						17 52	
Chetnole	d							13x51										15x42						18x01	
Yetminster	d							13x54										15x45						18x04	
Thornford	d							13x56										15x47						18x06	
Yeovil Pen Mill	d							14 06										15 56						18 18	
Castle Cary	a							14 19										16 09						18 31	
	d	12 45						14 20	14 44					15 49				16 10						18 32	18 53
Bruton	d							14 26										16 16						18 38	
Frome	d							14 39			14 59				15 55			16 29						19 05	
Westbury	a	13 03	13 09	13 34	14 09	14 20		14 48	15 02		15 08	15 09	15 36		16 05	16 09		16 38	17 09	17 36	18 09		19 09	19 13	19 11
	d	13 05	13 10	13 38	14 10	14 21		14 48	15 03	15 06		15 10	15 38		16 07	16 10		16 38	17 10	17 38	18 10	18 38	19 10	19 17	19 12
Trowbridge	d		13 16	13 44	14 16	14 27		14 55		15 12		15 16	15 44			16 16		16 44	17 16	17 44	18 16	18 44	19 16	→	
Bradford-on-Avon	d		13 22	13 50	14 22	14 33		15 01				15 22	15 50			16 22		16 50	17 22	17 50	18 22	18 50	19 22		
Avoncliff	d			13 53				15 04					15 53					16 53		17 53		18 53			
Freshford	d			13 56				15 06					15 56					16 56		17 56		18 56			
Bath Spa 7	a		13 34	14 06	14 34	14 46		15 17				15 35	16 06			16 34		17 06	17 34	18 06	18 34	19 07	19 34		
Melksham	d									15 21															
Chippenham	a									15 29															
Swindon	a									15 50															
London Paddington 15 ⊖	a	14 45							16 23					17 21	17 51										20 37
Oldfield Park	a			14 11				15 21					16 11					17 11		18 10		19 11			
Keynsham	a			14 18		14 54		15 28					16 18					17 18		18 18		19 18			
Bristol Temple Meads 10	a		13 48	14 28	14 48	15 05		15 36				15 49	16 29			16 48		17 29	17 48	18 29	18 48	19 29	19 48		
Filton Abbey Wood	a		14 01	14 48	15 01			15 48				16 01	16 48			17 01		17 48	18 01	18 48	19 01	19 48	20 01		
Severn Tunnel Jn.	a															17 14			18 13						
Newport (South Wales)	a		14 24		15 25							16 24				17 26			18 25		19 26		20 25		
Cardiff Central 7	a		14 43		15 43							16 43				17 43			18 43		19 43		20 43		

A ⊘ to Westbury

For connections to Swansea please refer to Table 128.
For connections to Exeter St Davids and Plymouth please refer to Table 135.
For connections from Bournemouth please refer to Table 158

For Bus Connections for either to or from Yeovil Junction and Yeovil Pen Mill please see Table 123A

Table 123

Saturdays

Portsmouth and Weymouth - Bristol and South Wales

Network Diagram - see first Page of Table 123

		GW		GW	GW	GW	GW	GW	GW	SW	GW	GW		GW
		◇		◇	◇1 ☕	◇			◇	◇1		◇		
Brighton 10	d			17 00										
Hove 2	d			17 04										
Shoreham-by-Sea	d			17 13										
Worthing 4	d			17 22										
Barnham	d			17 38										
Chichester 4	d			17 46										
Havant	d			18 00										
Portsmouth Harbour ⛴	d					18 23			19 23			20 23		
Portsmouth & Southsea	d					18 27			19 27			20 27		
Fratton	d					18 31			19 31			20 31		
Cosham	d			18 06		18 39			19 39					
Fareham	a			18 14		18 46			19 46			20 45		
	d			18 15		18 47			19 47			20 47		
Southampton Central ⛴	d			18 45		19 10			20 10			21 10		21 27
Romsey	d			18 56		19 21			20 21			21 21		21 38
Salisbury	a			19 14		19 39			20 39			21 40		22 02
	d			19 15		19 40			20 40	20 57		21 40		22 04
Warminster	d			19 36		20 01			21 01	21 17		22 01		22 26
Dilton Marsh	d			19x41										22x30
Weymouth	d										20 21			
Upwey	d										20 26			
Dorchester West	d										20 34			
Maiden Newton	d										20 45			
Chetnole	d										20x54			
Yetminster	d										20x57			
Thornford	d										20x59			
Yeovil Pen Mill	d										21 09			
Castle Cary	a										21 22			
	d				19 47						21 23			
Bruton	d										21 29			
Frome	d	←						20 53			21 42			
Westbury	a	19 13		19 45	20 05	20 09		21 02	21 09	21 25	21 51	22 10		22 34
	d	19 17		19 46	20 06	20 10	20 38		21 10	21 25	21 55	22 10		22 38
Trowbridge	d	19 23		19 52		20 16	20 44		21 16	21 31	22 02	22 16		22 44
Bradford-on-Avon	d	19 29		19 58		20 22	20 50		21 22	21 37	22 08	22 22		22 50
Avoncliff	d	19 32		20 01			20 53				22 11			22 53
Freshford	d	19 35		20 04			20 56				22 13			22 56
Bath Spa 7	a	19 45		20 14		20 34	21 07		21 37	21 50	22 24	22 34		23 07
Melksham	d													
Chippenham	a													
Swindon	a													
London Paddington 15 ⊖	a				21 32									
Oldfield Park	a	19 49		20 18			21 11				22 28			23 11
Keynsham	a	19 57		20 25			21 18			21 58	22 35			23 18
Bristol Temple Meads 10	a	20 05		20 33		20 48	21 29		21 51	22 06	22 44	22 50		23 31
Filton Abbey Wood	a					21 01			22 01			23 01		
Severn Tunnel Jn.	a								22 17			23 17		
Newport (South Wales)	a					21 25			22 38			23 35		
Cardiff Central 7	a					21 43			22 58			23 55		

For connections to Swansea please refer to Table 128.
For connections to Exeter St Davids and Plymouth please refer to Table 135.
For connections from Bournemouth please refer to Table 158

For Bus Connections for either to or from Yeovil Junction and Yeovil Pen Mill please see Table 123A

Table 123

Sundays
until 1 January

Portsmouth and Weymouth - Bristol and South Wales

Network Diagram - see first Page of Table 123

		GW	GW	GW	GW	GW	GW	GW	GW	GW		SW	GW	GW	GW	GW	GW	GW	GW	GW		GW	GW	GW	GW
		◇1 🍴		◇1 🍴	R		◇1 🍴	◇	◇	◇1 🍴		◇1	◇	◇	◇1 🍴	◇	R		◇1 🍴	◇		◇	◇	◇1 🍴	◇
Brighton 10	d								11 10													15 46			
Hove 2	d								11 14													15 50			
Shoreham-by-Sea	d								11 20													15 56			
Worthing 4	d								11 29													16 08			
Barnham	d								11 46													16 25			
Chichester 4	d								11 54													16 34			
Havant	d								12 10													16 48			
Portsmouth Harbour ⛴	d				09 08			11 08					13 08			14 08	15 08			16 08			17 08		
Portsmouth & Southsea	d				09 12			11 12					13 12			14 12	15 12			16 12			17 12		
Fratton	d				09 16			11 16					13 16			14 16	15 16			16 16			17 16		
Cosham	d				09 23			11 23	12 23				13 23			14 23	15 23			16 23		16 55	17 23		
Fareham	a				09 31			11 31	12 31				13 31			14 31	15 31			16 31		17 02	17 31		
	d				09 32			11 32	12 32				13 32			14 32	15 32			16 32		17 03	17 32		
Southampton Central ⛴	d				09 54			11 54	12 54				13 54			14 54	15 54			16 54		17 26	17 54		
Romsey	d				10 06			12 06	13 06				14 06			15 06	16 06			17 06		17 39	18 06		
Salisbury	a				10 24			12 24	13 24				14 24			15 24	16 24			17 24		18 00	18 24		
	d				10 29			12 27	13 26			13 55	14 27			15 28	16 27			17 27		18 01	18 27		
Warminster	d				10 50			12 48	13 46			14 15	14 48			15 48	16 48			17 48		18 21	18 48		
Dilton Marsh	d				10x55								14x53			15x53	16x53					18x26			
Weymouth	d													14 00											17 56
Upwey	d													14 05											18 01
Dorchester West	d													14 13											18 09
Maiden Newton	d													14 25											18 21
Chetnole	d													14x33											18x29
Yetminster	d													14x36											18x32
Thornford	d													14x38											18x34
Yeovil Pen Mill	d													14 48											18 44
Castle Cary	a													15 00											18 56
	d	09 34					12 33							15 03	15 34				17 37						18 59
Bruton	d													15 08											19 05
Frome	d		09 39											15 21											19 18
Westbury	a	09 51	09 48		10 58		12 52	12 54	13 55			14 23	14 56	15 30	15 51	15 56	16 56		17 54	17 57		18 30	18 55		19 27
	d	09 54	09 58	10 51	11 00	11 50	12 53	12 56	13 56	13 59		14 24	15 02	15 31	15 52	15 59	17 00	17 10	17 56	18 02		18 32	19 01	19 12	19 30
Trowbridge	d		10 04		11 06	11 56		13 02	14 02			14 30	15 08	15 37		16 05	17 06	17 16		18 08		18 38	19 07		19 36
Bradford-on-Avon	d		10 10		11 12	12 02		13 08	14 08			14 36	15 14	15 43		16 11	17 12			18 14		18 44	19 13		19 42
Avoncliff	d		10 13			12 05			14 11					15 46		16 14						18 47			19 45
Freshford	d		10 15			12 07			14 14					15 49		16 17						18 50			19 48
Bath Spa 7	a		10 26		11 25	12 19		13 22	14 24			14 49	15 27	16 00		16 28	17 25			18 27		19 00	19 26		19 59
Melksham	d																	17 25							
Chippenham	a																	17 35							
Swindon	a																	17 53							
London Paddington 15 ⊖	a	11 29		12 29			14 29			15 29					17 30				19 29					20 44	
Oldfield Park	a		10 30		11 28	12 23		13 25	14 27					16 03			17 28					19 04			20 02
Keynsham	a		10 37		11 35	12 30		13 32	14 35			14 57		16 11			17 35					19 11			20 10
Bristol Temple Meads 10	a		10 45		11 44	12 38		13 41	14 44			15 05	15 40	16 23		16 41	17 44			18 40		19 20	19 39		20 18
Filton Abbey Wood	a				11 55			13 55	14 55				15 55			16 55	17 55			18 55			19 55		
Severn Tunnel Jn.	a				12 10			14 07	15 07				16 07			17 10	18 07			19 07			20 10		
Newport (South Wales)	a				12 29			14 27	15 26				16 26			17 29	18 26			19 26			20 28		
Cardiff Central 7	a				12 44			14 51	15 41				16 44			17 46	18 44			19 42			20 46		

For connections to Swansea please refer to Table 128.
For connections to Exeter St Davids and Plymouth please refer to Table 135.
For connections from Bournemouth please refer to Table 158

For Bus Connections for either to or from Yeovil Junction and Yeovil Pen Mill please see Table 123A

Table 123

Sundays

until 1 January

Portsmouth and Weymouth - Bristol and South Wales

Network Diagram - see first Page of Table 123

		GW	GW	SW	GW	GW	GW	GW	GW	GW	GW	GW
			◇	◇1	◇1	◇	◇		◇1		◇	
					☕				☕			
Brighton 10	d					17 46						
Hove 2	d					17 50						
Shoreham-by-Sea	d					17 56						
Worthing 4	d					18 08						
Barnham	d					18 25						
Chichester 4	d					18 34						
Havant	d					18 48						
Portsmouth Harbour ⛴	d		18 08				19 08				20 08	22 03
Portsmouth & Southsea	d		18 12				19 12				20 12	22 12
Fratton	d		18 16				19 16				20 16	22 16
Cosham	d		18 23			18 55	19 23					
Fareham	a		18 31			19 02	19 31				20 31	22 31
	d		18 32			19 03	19 32				20 32	22 32
Southampton Central ⛴	d		18 54			19 30	19 54				20 54	22 57
Romsey	d		19 06			19 42	20 06				21 06	23 09
Salisbury	a		19 24			20 00	20 24				21 24	23 27
	d		19 25	19 55		20 03	20 27				21 27	23 28
Warminster	d		19 48	20 15		20 23	20 48				21 48	23 48
Dilton Marsh	d					20x28					21x53	23x53
Weymouth	d							20 09				
Upwey	d							20 14				
Dorchester West	d							20 22				
Maiden Newton	d							20 34				
Chetnole	d							20x42				
Yetminster	d							20x45				
Thornford	d							20x47				
Yeovil Pen Mill	d							20 57				
Castle Cary	a							21 09				
	d				20 07			21 10	21 19			
Bruton	d							21 16				
Frome	d							21 34		←		
Westbury	a		19 55	20 23	20 26	20 32	20 56	21 43	21 39	21 43	21 56	23 57
	d	19 35	20 01	20 23	20 27	20 36	21 02	21 45	21 40	21 45	22 00	
Trowbridge	d	19 42	20 07	20 29		20 42	21 08	→		21 51	22 06	
Bradford-on-Avon	d		20 13	20 35		20 48	21 14			21 57	22 12	
Avoncliff	d					20 51				22 00		
Freshford	d					20 54				22 03		
Bath Spa 7	a		20 26	20 48		21 09	21 27			22 14	22 25	
Melksham	d	19 53										
Chippenham	a	20 03										
Swindon	a	20 21										
London Paddington 15 ⊖	a				21 59				23 16			
Oldfield Park	a					21 12				22 17		
Keynsham	a			20 56		21 20				22 25		
Bristol Temple Meads 10	a		20 39	21 04		21 29	21 40			22 33	22 38	
Filton Abbey Wood	a		20 55				21 55				22 55	
Severn Tunnel Jn.	a		21 07				22 14				23 08	
Newport (South Wales)	a		21 26				22 31				23 26	
Cardiff Central 7	a		21 42				22 53				23 47	

For connections to Swansea please refer to Table 128.
For connections to Exeter St Davids and Plymouth please refer to Table 135.
For connections from Bournemouth please refer to Table 158

For Bus Connections for either to or from Yeovil Junction and Yeovil Pen Mill please see Table 123A

Table 123

Sundays

8 January to 12 February

Portsmouth and Weymouth - Bristol and South Wales

Network Diagram - see first Page of Table 123

		GW	GW	GW	GW	GW	GW	GW	GW	GW		SW	GW	GW	GW	GW	GW	GW	GW	GW		GW	GW	GW	GW
					R												R								
		◇1		◇1			◇1	◇	◇	◇1		◇1	◇	◇	◇1	◇			◇1	◇		◇	◇	◇1	◇
		⊡		⊡			⊡			⊡					⊡				⊡					⊡	
Brighton 10	d								11 10													15 46			
Hove 2	d								11 14													15 50			
Shoreham-by-Sea	d								11 20													15 56			
Worthing 4	d								11 29													16 08			
Barnham	d								11 46													16 25			
Chichester 4	d								11 54													16 34			
Havant	d								12 10													16 48			
Portsmouth Harbour ⛴	d				09 08			11 08					13 08			14 08	15 08			16 08			17 08		
Portsmouth & Southsea	d				09 12			11 12					13 12			14 12	15 12			16 12			17 12		
Fratton	d				09 16			11 16					13 16			14 16	15 16			16 16			17 16		
Cosham	d				09 23			11 23	12 23				13 23			14 23	15 23			16 23		16 55	17 23		
Fareham	a				09 31			11 31	12 31				13 31			14 31	15 31			16 31		17 02	17 31		
	d				09 32			11 32	12 32				13 32			14 32	15 32			16 32		17 03	17 32		
Southampton Central ⛴	d				09 54			11 54	12 54				13 54			14 54	15 54			16 54		17 26	17 54		
Romsey	d				10 06			12 06	13 06				14 06			15 06	16 06			17 06		17 39	18 06		
Salisbury	a				10 24			12 24	13 24				14 24			15 24	16 24			17 24		18 00	18 24		
	d				10 29			12 27	13 26			13 55	14 27			15 28	16 27			17 27		18 01	18 27		
Warminster	d				10 50			12 48	13 47			14 15	14 48			15 48	16 48			17 48		18 21	18 48		
Dilton Marsh	d				10x55								14x53			15x53	16x53					18x26			
Weymouth	d													14 00											17 56
Upwey	d													14 05											18 01
Dorchester West	d													14 13											18 09
Maiden Newton	d													14 25											18 21
Chetnole	d													14x33											18x29
Yetminster	d													14x36											18x32
Thornford	d													14x38											18x34
Yeovil Pen Mill	d													14 48											18 44
Castle Cary	a													15 00											18 56
	d	09 34					12 33							15 03	15 34				17 37						18 59
Bruton	d													15 08											19 05
Frome	d		09 39											15 21											19 18
Westbury	a	09 51	09 48		10 58		12 52	12 54	13 55			14 23	14 56	15 30	15 51	15 56	16 56		17 54	17 57		18 30	18 55		19 27
	d	09 54	09 58	10 51	11 00	11 50	12 53	12 56	13 56	13 59		14 24	15 02	15 31	15 52	15 59	17 00	17 10	17 56	18 02		18 32	19 01	19 12	19 30
Trowbridge	d		10 04		11 06	11 56		13 02	14 02			14 30	15 08	15 37		16 05	17 06	17 16		18 08		18 38	19 07		19 36
Bradford-on-Avon	d		10 10		11 12	12 02		13 08	14 08			14 36	15 14	15 43		16 11	17 12			18 14		18 44	19 13		19 42
Avoncliff	d		10 13			12 05			14 11					15 46		16 14						18 47			19 45
Freshford	d		10 15			12 07			14 14					15 49		16 17						18 50			19 48
Bath Spa 7	a		10 26		11 25	12 19		13 22	14 24			14 49	15 27	16 00		16 28	17 25			18 27		19 00	19 26		19 59
Melksham	d																	17 25							
Chippenham	a																	17 35							
Swindon	a																	17 53							
London Paddington 15 ⊖	a	11 29		12 29			14 29			15 29					17 30				19 29					20 44	
Oldfield Park	a		10 30		11 28	12 23		13 25	14 27					16 03			17 28					19 04			20 02
Keynsham	a		10 37		11 35	12 30		13 32	14 35			14 57		16 11			17 35					19 11			20 10
Bristol Temple Meads 10	a		10 45		11 44	12 38		13 41	14 44			15 05	15 40	16 23		16 41	17 44			18 40		19 20	19 39		20 18
Filton Abbey Wood	a				11 55			13 55	14 55				15 55			16 55	17 55			18 55			19 55		
Severn Tunnel Jn.	a				12 10			14 07	15 07				16 07			17 10	18 07			19 07			20 10		
Newport (South Wales)	a				12 29			14 27	15 26				16 26			17 29	18 26			19 26			20 28		
Cardiff Central 7	a				12 44			14 51	15 41				16 44			17 46	18 44			19 42			20 46		

For connections to Swansea please refer to Table 128.
For connections to Exeter St Davids and Plymouth please refer to Table 135.
For connections from Bournemouth please refer to Table 158

For Bus Connections for either to or from Yeovil Junction and Yeovil Pen Mill please see Table 123A

Table 123

Sundays

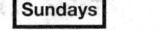

8 January to 12 February

Portsmouth and Weymouth - Bristol and South Wales

Network Diagram - see first Page of Table 123

		GW	GW	SW	GW	GW	GW	GW	GW	GW	GW	GW
			◇	◇1	◇1 ☕	◇	◇		◇1 ☕		◇	
Brighton 10	d					17 46						
Hove 2	d					17 50						
Shoreham-by-Sea	d					17 56						
Worthing 4	d					18 08						
Barnham	d					18 25						
Chichester 4	d					18 34						
Havant	d					18 48						
Portsmouth Harbour ⛴	d		18 08				19 08				20 08	22 03
Portsmouth & Southsea	d		18 12				19 12				20 12	22 12
Fratton	d		18 16				19 16				20 16	22 16
Cosham	d		18 23			18 55	19 23					
Fareham	a		18 31			19 02	19 31				20 31	22 31
	d		18 32			19 03	19 32				20 32	22 32
Southampton Central ⛴	d		18 54			19 30	19 54				20 54	22 57
Romsey	d		19 06			19 42	20 06				21 06	23 09
Salisbury	a		19 24			20 00	20 24				21 24	23 27
	d		19 25	19 55		20 03	20 27				21 27	23 28
Warminster	d		19 48	20 15		20 23	20 48				21 48	23 48
Dilton Marsh	d					20x28					21x53	23x53
Weymouth	d							20 09				
Upwey	d							20 14				
Dorchester West	d							20 22				
Maiden Newton	d							20 34				
Chetnole	d							20x42				
Yetminster	d							20x45				
Thornford	d							20x47				
Yeovil Pen Mill	d							20 57				
Castle Cary	a							21 09				
	d				20 07			21 10	21 19			
Bruton	d							21 16				
Frome	d							21 34		←		
Westbury	a		19 55	20 23	20 26	20 32	20 56	21 43	21 39	21 43	21 56	23 57
	d	19 35	20 01	20 23	20 27	20 36	21 02	21 45	21 40	21 45	22 00	
Trowbridge	d	19 42	20 07	20 29		20 42	21 08	→		21 51	22 06	
Bradford-on-Avon	d		20 13	20 35		20 48	21 14			21 57	22 12	
Avoncliff	d					20 51				22 00		
Freshford	d					20 54				22 03		
Bath Spa 7	a		20 26	20 48		21 09	21 27			22 14	22 25	
Melksham	d	19 53										
Chippenham	a	20 03										
Swindon	a	20 21										
London Paddington 15 ⊖	a				21 58				23 18			
Oldfield Park	a					21 12				22 17		
Keynsham	a			20 56		21 20				22 25		
Bristol Temple Meads 10	a		20 39	21 04		21 29	21 40			22 33	22 38	
Filton Abbey Wood	a		20 55				21 55				22 55	
Severn Tunnel Jn.	a		21 07				22 14				23 08	
Newport (South Wales)	a		21 26				22 31				23 26	
Cardiff Central 7	a		21 42				22 53				23 47	

For connections to Swansea please refer to Table 128.
For connections to Exeter St Davids and Plymouth please refer to Table 135.
For connections from Bournemouth please refer to Table 158

For Bus Connections for either to or from Yeovil Junction and Yeovil Pen Mill please see Table 123A

Table 123

Sundays

19 February to 25 March

Portsmouth and Weymouth - Bristol and South Wales

Network Diagram - see first Page of Table 123

		GW	GW	GW	GW	GW	GW	GW	GW	GW		SW	GW	GW	GW	GW	GW	GW	GW	GW		GW	GW	GW	GW
					R												R								
		◇1		◇1			◇1	◇	◇	◇1		◇1	◇	◇	◇1	◇			◇1	◇		◇	◇	◇1	◇
		☕		☕			☕			☕					☕				☕					☕	
Brighton 10	d								11 10													15 46			
Hove 2	d								11 14													15 50			
Shoreham-by-Sea	d								11 20													15 56			
Worthing 4	d								11 29													16 08			
Barnham	d								11 46													16 25			
Chichester 4	d								11 54													16 34			
Havant	d								12 10													16 48			
Portsmouth Harbour ⛴	d				09 08			11 08					13 08			14 08	15 08			16 08			17 08		
Portsmouth & Southsea	d				09 12			11 12					13 12			14 12	15 12			16 12			17 12		
Fratton	d				09 16			11 16					13 16			14 16	15 16			16 16			17 16		
Cosham	d				09 23			11 23	12 23				13 23			14 23	15 23			16 23		16 55	17 23		
Fareham	a				09 31			11 31	12 31				13 31			14 31	15 31			16 31		17 02	17 31		
	d				09 32			11 32	12 32				13 32			14 32	15 32			16 32		17 03	17 32		
Southampton Central ⛴	d				09 54			11 54	12 54				13 54			14 54	15 54			16 54		17 26	17 54		
Romsey	d				10 05			12 06	13 06				14 06			15 06	16 06			17 06		17 39	18 06		
Salisbury	a				10 23			12 24	13 24				14 24			15 24	16 24			17 24		18 00	18 24		
	d				10 29			12 27	13 26			13 55	14 27			15 27	16 27			17 27		18 01	18 27		
Warminster	d				10 50			12 48	13 46			14 15	14 48			15 48	16 48			17 48		18 21	18 48		
Dilton Marsh	d				10x55								14x53			15x53	16x53					18x26			
Weymouth	d													14 00											17 56
Upwey	d													14 05											18 01
Dorchester West	d													14 13											18 09
Maiden Newton	d													14 25											18 21
Chetnole	d													14x33											18x29
Yetminster	d													14x36											18x32
Thornford	d													14x38											18x34
Yeovil Pen Mill	d													14 48											18 44
Castle Cary	a													15 00											18 56
	d	09 26					12 33							15 03	15 34				17 37						18 59
Bruton	d													15 08											19 05
Frome	d	09 40												15 21											19 18
Westbury	a	09 49			10 58		12 52	12 54	13 55			14 23	14 56	15 30	15 51	15 56	16 56		17 54	17 57		18 30	18 55		19 27
	d	09 54	09 58	10 51	11 00	11 50	12 53	12 56	13 56	13 59		14 24	15 02	15 31	15 52	15 59	16 59	17 10	17 56	18 02		18 32	19 01	19 13	19 30
Trowbridge	d		10 04		11 06	11 56		13 02	14 02			14 30	15 08	15 37		16 05	17 05	17 16		18 08		18 38	19 07		19 36
Bradford-on-Avon	d		10 10		11 12	12 02		13 08	14 08			14 36	15 14	15 43		16 11	17 11			18 14		18 44	19 13		19 42
Avoncliff	d		10 13			12 05			14 11					15 46		16 14						18 47			19 45
Freshford	d		10 15			12 07			14 14					15 49		16 17						18 50			19 48
Bath Spa 7	a		10 26		11 25	12 19		13 22	14 24			14 49	15 27	16 00		16 29	17 24			18 27		19 00	19 26		19 59
Melksham	d																	17 25							
Chippenham	a																	17 35							
Swindon	a																	17 53							
London Paddington 15 ⊖	a	11 29		12 29			14 29			15 29					17 30				19 29					20 43	
Oldfield Park	a		10 30		11 28	12 23		13 25	14 27					16 03			17 27					19 04			20 02
Keynsham	a		10 37		11 35	12 30		13 32	14 35			14 57		16 11			17 34					19 11			20 10
Bristol Temple Meads 10	a		10 45		11 44	12 38		13 41	14 44			15 05	15 40	16 23		16 42	17 43			18 40		19 20	19 39		20 18
Filton Abbey Wood	a				11 55			13 55	14 55				15 55			16 55	17 55			18 55			19 55		
Severn Tunnel Jn.	a																								
Newport (South Wales)	a																								
Cardiff Central 7	a																								

For connections to Swansea please refer to Table 128.
For connections to Exeter St Davids and Plymouth please refer to Table 135.
For connections from Bournemouth please refer to Table 158

For Bus Connections for either to or from Yeovil Junction and Yeovil Pen Mill please see Table 123A

Table 123

Sundays

19 February to 25 March

Portsmouth and Weymouth - Bristol and South Wales

Network Diagram - see first Page of Table 123

		GW	GW	GW	SW	GW		GW	GW	GW	GW	GW	GW	GW
			◇	◇1	◇1	◇		◇	◇1		◇1		◇	
				🍴					🍴		🍴			
Brighton 10	d					17 46								
Hove 2	d					17 50								
Shoreham-by-Sea	d					17 56								
Worthing 4	d					18 08								
Barnham	d					18 25								
Chichester 4	d					18 34								
Havant	d					18 48								
Portsmouth Harbour ⛴	d		18 08					19 08					20 08	22 03
Portsmouth & Southsea	d		18 12					19 12					20 12	22 12
Fratton	d		18 16					19 16					20 16	22 16
Cosham	d		18 23			18 55		19 23						
Fareham	a		18 31			19 02		19 31					20 31	22 31
	d		18 32			19 03		19 32					20 32	22 32
Southampton Central ⛴	d		18 54			19 30		19 54					20 54	22 57
Romsey	d		19 06			19 42		20 06					21 06	23 09
Salisbury	a		19 24			20 00		20 24					21 24	23 27
	d		19 25		19 55	20 03		20 27					21 27	23 28
Warminster	d		19 48		20 15	20 23		20 48					21 48	23 48
Dilton Marsh	d					20x28							21x53	23x53
Weymouth	d									20 09				
Upwey	d									20 14				
Dorchester West	d									20 22				
Maiden Newton	d									20 34				
Chetnole	d									20x42				
Yetminster	d									20x45				
Thornford	d									20x47				
Yeovil Pen Mill	d									20 57				
Castle Cary	a									21 09				
	d								20 48	21 10	21 19			
Bruton	d									21 16				
Frome	d									21 34		←		
Westbury	a		19 55		20 23	20 32		20 56		21 43	21 39	21 43	21 56	23 57
	d	19 35	20 01	19 55	20 23	20 36		21 02		21 45	21 40	21 45	22 00	
Trowbridge	d	19 42	20 07		20 29	20 42		21 08		→		21 51	22 06	
Bradford-on-Avon	d		20 13		20 35	20 48		21 14				21 57	22 12	
Avoncliff	d					20 51						22 00		
Freshford	d					20 54						22 03		
Bath Spa 7	a		20 26		20 48	21 09		21 27				22 14	22 25	
Melksham	d	19 53												
Chippenham	a	20 03												
Swindon	a	20 21												
London Paddington 15 ⊖	a			21 30					22 28		23 16			
Oldfield Park	a					21 12						22 17		
Keynsham	a				20 56	21 20						22 25		
Bristol Temple Meads 10	a		20 39		21 04	21 29		21 40				22 33	22 41	
Filton Abbey Wood	a		20 55					21 55					22 55	
Severn Tunnel Jn.	a													
Newport (South Wales)	a													
Cardiff Central 7	a													

For connections to Swansea please refer to Table 128.
For connections to Exeter St Davids and Plymouth please refer to Table 135.
For connections from Bournemouth please refer to Table 158

For Bus Connections for either to or from Yeovil Junction and Yeovil Pen Mill please see Table 123A

Table 123

Sundays

from 1 April

Portsmouth and Weymouth - Bristol and South Wales

Network Diagram - see first Page of Table 123

		GW	GW	GW	GW	GW	GW	GW	GW	SW	GW	GW	GW	GW	GW	GW	GW	GW	GW	GW	GW	GW	GW
					R										R								
		◇1		◇1			◇1	◇1	◇	◇1	◇	◇	◇1	◇			◇1	◇	◇	◇		◇	◇1
		☕		☕			☕	☕					☕				☕						☕
Brighton 10	d								11 10										15 46				
Hove 2	d								11 14										15 50				
Shoreham-by-Sea	d								11 20										15 56				
Worthing 4	d								11 29										16 08				
Barnham	d								11 46										16 25				
Chichester 4	d								11 54										16 34				
Havant	d								12 10										16 48				
Portsmouth Harbour ⛴	d				09 08						13 08			14 08	15 08			16 08		17 08			
Portsmouth & Southsea	d				09 12						13 12			14 12	15 12			16 12		17 12			
Fratton	d				09 16						13 16			14 16	15 16			16 16		17 16			
Cosham	d				09 23				12 23		13 23			14 23	15 23			16 23	16 55	17 23			
Fareham	a				09 31				12 31		13 31			14 31	15 31			16 31	17 02	17 31			
	d				09 32				12 32		13 32			14 32	15 32			16 32	17 03	17 32			
Southampton Central ⛴	d				09 54				12 54		13 54			14 54	15 54			16 54	17 26	17 54			
Romsey	d				10 06				13 06		14 06			15 06	16 06			17 06	17 39	18 06			
Salisbury	a				10 24				13 24		14 24			15 24	16 24			17 24	18 00	18 24			
	d				10 29				13 26	13 55	14 27			15 28	16 27			17 27	18 01	18 27			
Warminster	d				10 50				13 46	14 15	14 48			15 48	16 48			17 48	18 21	18 48			
Dilton Marsh	d				10x55						14x53			15x53	16x53				18x26				
Weymouth	d											14 00										17 56	
Upwey	d											14 05										18 01	
Dorchester West	d											14 13										18 09	
Maiden Newton	d											14 25										18 21	
Chetnole	d											14x33										18x29	
Yetminster	d											14x36										18x32	
Thornford	d											14x38										18x34	
Yeovil Pen Mill	d											14 48										18 44	
Castle Cary	a											15 00										18 56	
	d	09 21					12 34					15 03	15 34				17 31					18 59	19 26
Bruton	d											15 08										19 05	
Frome	d		09 25									15 21										19 18	
Westbury	a	09 38	09 33		10 58		12 52		13 55	14 23	14 56	15 30	15 51	15 56	16 56		17 48	17 57	18 30	18 55		19 27	19 43
	d	09 41	09 45	10 51	11 00	11 50	12 53	13 54	13 58	14 24	15 02	15 31	15 52	15 59	17 00	17 10	17 51	18 02	18 32	19 01	19 22	19 30	19 45
Trowbridge	d		09 51		11 06	11 56			14 04	14 30	15 08	15 37		16 05	17 06	17 16		18 08	18 38	19 07	19 28	19 36	
Bradford-on-Avon	d		09 57		11 12	12 02			14 10	14 36	15 14	15 43		16 11	17 12			18 14	18 44	19 13		19 42	
Avoncliff	d		10 00			12 05			14 13			15 46		16 14					18 47			19 45	
Freshford	d		10 02			12 07			14 16			15 49		16 17					18 50			19 48	
Bath Spa 7	a		10 15		11 25	12 19			14 26	14 49	15 27	16 00		16 28	17 25			18 27	19 00	19 26		19 59	
Melksham	d															17 25					19 38		
Chippenham	a															17 35					19 48		
Swindon	a	10 18														17 53	18 26				20 06		20 19
London Paddington 15 ⊖	a	11 29		12 29			14 33	15 29					17 32				19 32						21 27
Oldfield Park	a		10 19		11 28	12 23			14 29			16 03			17 28				19 04			20 02	
Keynsham	a		10 26		11 35	12 30			14 37	14 57		16 11			17 35				19 11			20 10	
Bristol Temple Meads 10	a		10 33		11 44	12 38			14 46	15 05	15 40	16 23		16 41	17 44			18 40	19 20	19 39		20 18	
Filton Abbey Wood	a				11 55				14 57		15 55			16 55	17 55			18 55		19 55			
Severn Tunnel Jn.	a				12 10				15 09		16 07			17 10	18 07			19 07		20 10			
Newport (South Wales)	a				12 29				15 28		16 26			17 29	18 26			19 26		20 28			
Cardiff Central 7	a				12 44				15 43		16 44			17 46	18 44			19 42		20 46			

For connections to Swansea please refer to Table 128.
For connections to Exeter St Davids and Plymouth please refer to Table 135.
For connections from Bournemouth please refer to Table 158

For Bus Connections for either to or from Yeovil Junction and Yeovil Pen Mill please see Table 123A

Table 123

Sundays
from 1 April

Portsmouth and Weymouth - Bristol and South Wales

Network Diagram - see first Page of Table 123

		GW	SW	GW	GW	GW		GW	GW	GW	GW
		◇	◇1	◇	◇			◇1		◇	
								☕			
Brighton 10	d			17 46							
Hove 2	d			17 50							
Shoreham-by-Sea	d			17 56							
Worthing 4	d			18 08							
Barnham	d			18 25							
Chichester 4	d			18 34							
Havant	d			18 48							
Portsmouth Harbour ⛴	d	18 08			19 08					20 08	22 03
Portsmouth & Southsea	d	18 12			19 12					20 12	22 12
Fratton	d	18 16			19 16					20 16	22 16
Cosham	d	18 23		18 55	19 23						
Fareham	a	18 31		19 02	19 31					20 31	22 31
	d	18 32		19 03	19 32					20 32	22 32
Southampton Central ⛴	d	18 54		19 30	19 54					20 54	22 57
Romsey	d	19 06		19 42	20 06					21 06	23 09
Salisbury	a	19 24		20 00	20 24					21 24	23 27
	d	19 25	19 55	20 03	20 27					21 27	23 28
Warminster	d	19 48	20 15	20 23	20 48					21 48	23 48
Dilton Marsh	d			20x28						21x53	23x53
Weymouth	d					20 09					
Upwey	d					20 14					
Dorchester West	d					20 22					
Maiden Newton	d					20 34					
Chetnole	d					20x42					
Yetminster	d					20x45					
Thornford	d					20x47					
Yeovil Pen Mill	d					20 57					
Castle Cary	a					21 09					
	d					21 10		21 19			
Bruton	d					21 16					
Frome	d					21 34			←		
Westbury	a	19 55	20 23	20 32	20 56	21 43		21 39	21 43	21 56	23 57
	d	20 01	20 23	20 36	21 02	21 45		21 40	21 45	22 00	
Trowbridge	d	20 07	20 29	20 42	21 08	→			21 51	22 06	
Bradford-on-Avon	d	20 13	20 35	20 48	21 14				21 57	22 12	
Avoncliff	d			20 51					22 00		
Freshford	d			20 54					22 03		
Bath Spa 7	a	20 26	20 48	21 09	21 27				22 14	22 25	
Melksham	d										
Chippenham	a										
Swindon	a							22 15			
London Paddington 15 ⊖	a							23 28			
Oldfield Park	a			21 12					22 17		
Keynsham	a		20 56	21 20					22 25		
Bristol Temple Meads 10	a	20 39	21 04	21 29	21 40				22 33	22 38	
Filton Abbey Wood	a	20 55			21 55					22 55	
Severn Tunnel Jn.	a	21 07			22 14					23 08	
Newport (South Wales)	a	21 26			22 31					23 26	
Cardiff Central 7	a	21 42			22 53					23 47	

For connections to Swansea please refer to Table 128.
For connections to Exeter St Davids and Plymouth please refer to Table 135.
For connections from Bournemouth please refer to Table 158

For Bus Connections for either to or from Yeovil Junction and Yeovil Pen Mill please see Table 123A

Table 123A

Mondays to Fridays

Yeovil Pen Mill - Yeovil Junction

		GW BHX 🚌	GW BHX 🚌	GW BHX 🚌	GW BHX 🚌	GW BHX 🚌	GW BHX 🚌	GW BHX 🚌	GW BHX 🚌	GW BHX 🚌	GW BHX 🚌	GW BHX 🚌	GW BHX 🚌	GW BHX 🚌	GW BHX 🚌	GW BHX 🚌	GW BHX 🚌	GW BHX 🚌	GW BHX 🚌	GW BHX 🚌	GW BHX 🚌	GW BHX 🚌	GW BHX 🚌
Yeovil Pen Mill	d	07 20	07 50	08 20	08 50	09 20	09 50	10 20	10 50	11 20	11 50	12 20	12 50	13 20	13 50	14 20	14 50	15 20	15 50	16 20	16 50	17 20	17 50
Yeovil Bus Station	d	07 30	08 00	08 30	09 00	09 30	10 00	10 30	11 00	11 30	12 00	12 30	13 00	13 30	14 00	14 30	15 00	15 30	16 00	16 30	17 00	17 30	18 00
Yeovil Junction	a	07 35	08 05	08 35	09 05	09 35	10 05	10 35	11 05	11 35	12 05	12 35	13 05	13 35	14 05	14 35	15 05	15 35	16 05	16 35	17 05	17 35	18 05

		GW BHX 🚌	GW BHX 🚌	GW BHX 🚌	GW BHX 🚌
Yeovil Pen Mill	d	18 20	18 50	19 20	19 50
Yeovil Bus Station	d	18 30	19 00	19a30	20a00
Yeovil Junction	a	18 35	19 05		

Saturdays

		GW 🚌	GW 🚌	GW 🚌	GW 🚌	GW 🚌	GW 🚌	GW 🚌	GW 🚌	GW 🚌	GW 🚌	GW 🚌	GW 🚌	GW 🚌	GW 🚌	GW 🚌	GW 🚌	GW 🚌	GW 🚌	GW 🚌	GW 🚌	GW 🚌	GW 🚌
Yeovil Pen Mill	d	07 20	07 50	08 20	08 50	09 20	09 50	10 20	10 50	11 20	11 50	12 20	12 50	13 20	13 50	14 20	14 50	15 20	15 50	16 20	16 50	17 20	17 50
Yeovil Bus Station	d	07 30	08 00	08 30	09 00	09 30	10 00	10 30	11 00	11 30	12 00	12 30	13 00	13 30	14 00	14 30	15 00	15 30	16 00	16 30	17 00	17 30	18 00
Yeovil Junction	a	07 35	08 05	08 35	09 05	09 35	10 05	10 35	11 05	11 35	12 05	12 35	13 05	13 35	14 05	14 35	15 05	15 35	16 05	16 35	17 05	17 35	18 05

		GW 🚌	GW 🚌	GW 🚌	GW 🚌
Yeovil Pen Mill	d	18 20	18 50	19 20	19 50
Yeovil Bus Station	d	18 30	19 00	19a30	20a00
Yeovil Junction	a	18 35	19 05		

No Sunday Service

Table 123A

Mondays to Fridays

Yeovil Junction - Yeovil Pen Mill

		GW BHX 🚌	GW BHX 🚌	GW BHX 🚌	GW BHX 🚌	GW BHX 🚌	GW BHX 🚌	GW BHX 🚌	GW BHX 🚌	GW BHX 🚌	GW BHX 🚌	GW BHX 🚌	GW BHX 🚌	GW BHX 🚌	GW BHX 🚌	GW BHX 🚌	GW BHX 🚌	GW BHX 🚌	GW BHX 🚌	GW BHX 🚌	GW BHX 🚌	GW BHX 🚌	GW BHX 🚌
Yeovil Junction	d	06 50	07 20	07 50	08 20	08 50	09 20	09 50	10 20	10 50	11 20	11 50	12 20	12 50	13 20	13 50	14 20	14 50	15 20	15 50	16 20	16 50	17 20
Yeovil Bus Station	d	06 57	07 27	07 57	08 27	08 57	09 27	09 57	10 27	10 57	11 27	11 57	12 27	12 57	13 27	13 57	14 27	14 57	15 27	15 57	16 27	16 57	17 27
Yeovil Pen Mill	a	07 02	07 32	08 02	08 32	09 02	09 32	10 02	10 32	11 02	11 32	12 02	12 32	13 02	13 32	14 02	14 32	15 02	15 32	16 02	16 32	17 02	17 32

		GW BHX 🚌	GW BHX 🚌	GW BHX 🚌	GW BHX 🚌
Yeovil Junction	d	17 50	18 20	18 50	19 20
Yeovil Bus Station	d	17 57	18 27	18 57	19 27
Yeovil Pen Mill	a	18 02	18 32	19 02	19 32

Saturdays

		GW 🚌	GW 🚌	GW 🚌	GW 🚌	GW 🚌	GW 🚌	GW 🚌	GW 🚌	GW 🚌	GW 🚌	GW 🚌	GW 🚌	GW 🚌	GW 🚌	GW 🚌	GW 🚌	GW 🚌	GW 🚌	GW 🚌	GW 🚌	GW 🚌	GW 🚌
Yeovil Junction	d	06 50	07 20	07 50	08 20	08 50	09 20	09 50	10 20	10 50	11 20	11 50	12 20	12 50	13 20	13 50	14 20	14 50	15 20	15 50	16 20	16 50	17 20
Yeovil Bus Station	d	06 57	07 27	07 57	08 27	08 57	09 27	09 57	10 27	10 57	11 27	11 57	12 27	12 57	13 27	13 57	14 27	14 57	15 27	15 57	16 27	16 57	17 27
Yeovil Pen Mill	a	07 02	07 32	08 02	08 32	09 02	09 32	10 02	10 32	11 02	11 32	12 02	12 32	13 02	13 32	14 02	14 32	15 02	15 32	16 02	16 32	17 02	17 32

		GW 🚌	GW 🚌	GW 🚌	GW 🚌
Yeovil Junction	d	17 50	18 20	18 50	19 20
Yeovil Bus Station	d	17 57	18 27	18 57	19 27
Yeovil Pen Mill	a	18 02	18 32	19 02	19 32

No Sunday Service

Route Diagram for Table 125

DM-11/11
Design BAJS

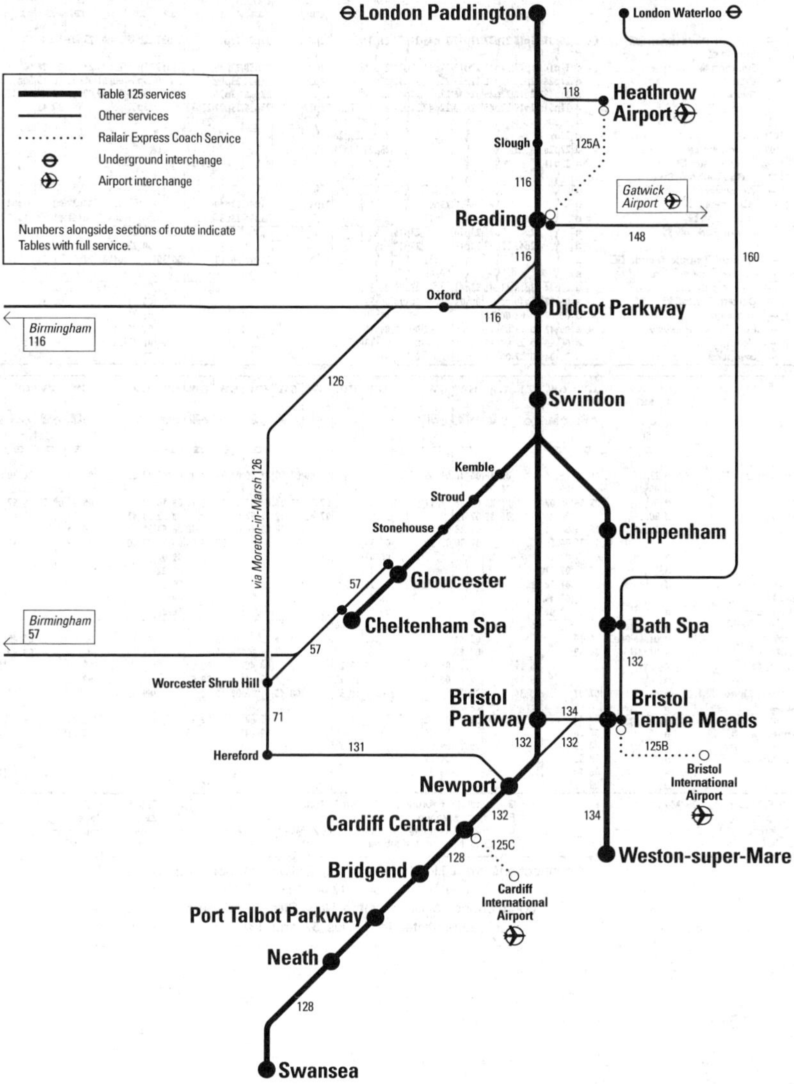

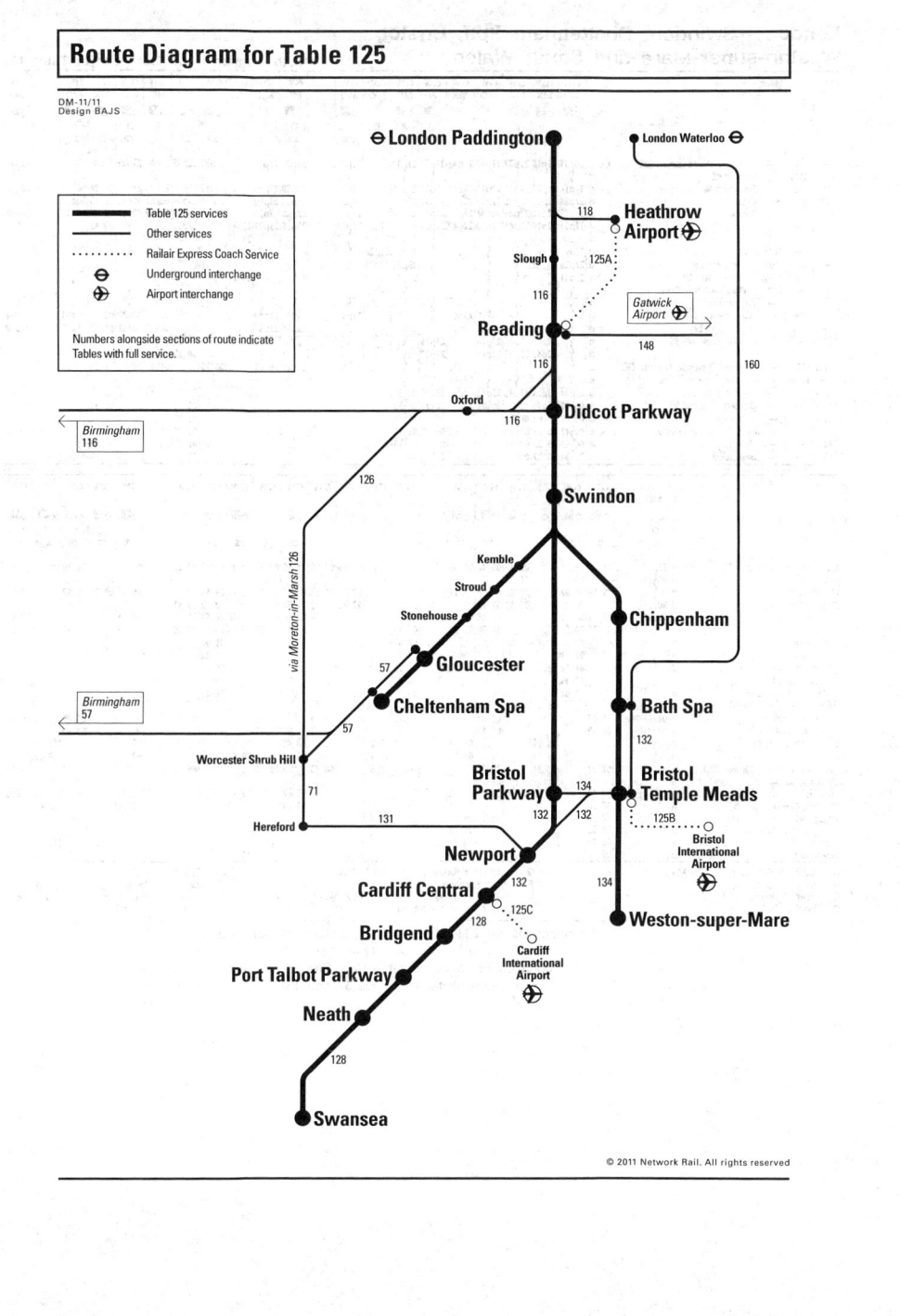

London - Swindon, Cheltenham Spa, Bristol, Weston-super-Mare and South Wales

Route Diagram - see first Page of Table 125

Miles	Miles	Miles			GW MO ◇1 A ☕	GW MX ◇1 ☕	GW MO ◇1 B ☕	GW MO ◇1 C ☕	GW MX ◇1 ☕	GW MO ◇1 D ☕	GW MO ◇1 A ☕	GW MO E	GW MO ◇1 F ☕	GW MO ◇1 D ☕	GW MX ◇1 ☕	GW MX	GW MO ◇1 ☕	GW MX ◇1 ☕	GW MO ◇1 F ☕	GW MO ◇1 D ☕	GW MX ◇1 ☕	GW MO ◇1 A ☕	GW MO ◇1 G ☕
—	—	—	**London Paddington 15** ⊖	d	20p37	21p15	21p37	21p37	21p45	21p37	21p37		22p03	22p03	22p15		22p37	22p45	23p03	23p03	23p30	23p37	23p37
18½	18½	18½	Slough 3	d																		00 01	00 02
36	36	36	**Reading 7**	d	21p14	21p41	22p12	22p12	22p11	22p14	22p15		22p45	22p50	22p49		23p15	23p19	23p47	23p46	00 08	00 15	00 15
53¼	53¼	53¼	Didcot Parkway	d	21p28	22p00	22p28	22p29	22p31	22p30	22p29		22p59	23p05	23p09		23b30	23p39	00s01	00s02	00 25	00s30	00s31
77¼	77¼	77¼	**Swindon**	a	21p48	22p18	22p45	22p46	22p48	22p49	22p54		23p17	23p25	23p26		23b48	23p55	00s19	00s21	00 44	00s47	00s49
—	—	—		d	21p51	22p19	22p46	22p50	22p49	22p51	22p56	22p57	23p17	23p25	23p27	23p33		23p57			00 45		
—	—	91	Kemble	d	22p06						23p09	23p11				23p47							
—	—	102¼	Stroud	d	22p21						23p24	23p26				00 02							
—	—	105	Stonehouse	d	22p26						23p29	23p31				00 07							
—	—	113¾	Gloucester 7	a	22p41						23p42	23p48				00 24							
—	—	120¼	**Cheltenham Spa**	a								00 05											
—	—	—	Worcester Shrub Hill	d																			
—	94	—	Chippenham	d					23p03				23p33	23p41	23p40				00s34	00s37	00 59	01s03	01s04
—	107	—	Bath Spa 7	a					23p17				23p46	23p54	23p54				00s49	00s51	01 13	01s17	01s19
111¾	—	—	Bristol Parkway 7	a		22p45	23p11	23p14		23p15							00s16	00 21					
—	—	—		d		22p45	23p12	23p16		23p17								00 23					
117¾	118½	—	**Bristol Temple Meads 10**	a					23p32				00 01	00 09	00 10		00 30		01 03	01 05	01 29	01 31	01 33
—	137½	—	Weston-super-Mare	a					00s05														
133½	—	—	Newport (South Wales)	a	23p44	23p19	23p41	23p41		23p42	00 31							00 51			02s10		
145¼	—	—	**Cardiff Central 7**	a	00 07	23p40	00 01	00 03		00 04	00 53							01 11			02 31		
165½	—	—	Bridgend	a	00 29	00 02	00 23			00 27	01 18							01 36					
177¾	—	—	Port Talbot Parkway	a	00 42	00 15	00 36			00 40	01 31							01 49					
183¼	—	—	Neath	a	00 50	00 22	00 44			00 48	01 38							01 57					
192¾	—	—	**Swansea**	a	01 04	00 37	00 57			01 01	01 52							02 10					

		GW MO ◇1 D ☕	GW	GW ◇1 ☕	GW ◇1 ☕	GW ◇	GW ◇1	GW ◇1 ☕	GW ◇1 ☕	GW	GW	GW 1	GW ◇1 ☕	GW ◇1 ☕	GW ◇1 H Ø	GW ◇1 I ☕	GW ◇1 ☕	GW ◇1 ☕	GW ◇1 ☕	GW ◇1 ☕	GW ◇1 ☕	GW ◇1 J ☕Ø	GW ◇1 ☕
London Paddington 15 ⊖	d	23p37		05 27	05 36		05 48	06 30	06 45			06 48	07 00	07 15	07 30	07 45	07 48	08 00	08 15	08 22	08 30	08 45	09 00
Slough 3	d	00 02			05 52		06 05					07 04								08 36			
Reading 7	d	00 15		05 56	06 07		06 22	06 56	07 11			07 22	07 26	07 42	07 57	08 11	08 16	08 27	08 42	08 52	08 57	09 11	09 27
Didcot Parkway	d	00s31			06 21		06 39	07 12				07 49	07 42	07 57			08 33	08 41	08 57		09 12		
Swindon	a	00s51		06 23	06 41			07 28	07 38				07 58	08 14	08 27	08 38	08 53	08 59	09 14		09 30	09 38	09 54
	d		06 12	06 25	06 50			07 30	07 38	07 54			08 00	08 15	08 27	08 38	08 54	09 00	09 15		09 31	09 38	09 55
Kemble	d				07 07					08 07							09 07						
Stroud	d				07 22					08 22							09 22						
Stonehouse	d				07 28					08 28							09 28						
Gloucester 7	a				07 45					08 50							09 44						
Cheltenham Spa	a				08 01					09 05							10 03						
Worcester Shrub Hill	d					06 49	08a10				09 06	09a15								10a44			
Chippenham	d	01s06	06a28	06 39				07 44					08 14		08 42			09 14			09 45		10 09
Bath Spa 7	a	01s21		06 52				07 57					08 27		08 55			09 29			09 59		10 23
Bristol Parkway 7	a					08 19			08 04		10 22			08 40		09 04			09 40			10 04	
	d					08 19			08 07		10 22			08 41		09 07			09 41			10 07	
Bristol Temple Meads 10	a	01 35		07 07		08 36		08 17			10 37		08 45		09 10			09 45			10 15		10 38
Weston-super-Mare	a																						
Newport (South Wales)	a			07 44					08 32					09 07		09 31			10 04			10 31	
Cardiff Central 7	a			08 00					08 46					09 24		09 48			10 21			10 46	
Bridgend	a			08 23					09 09							10 09						11 09	
Port Talbot Parkway	a			08 36					09 22							10 22						11 22	
Neath	a			08 44					09 30							10 30						11 30	
Swansea	a			08 57					09 45							10 44						11 43	

A from 20 February until 26 March
B from 2 April
C from 9 January until 13 February
D until 2 January
E until 13 February, MO from 2 April
F from 9 January
G from 9 January until 13 February, MO from 2 April
H The Merchant Venturer
I The St. David
J ☕ from Bridgend Ø to Bridgend
b Previous night, stops to set down only

For connections from Heathrow Airport, Gatwick Airport and Oxford please refer to Tables 125A, 148 and 116.
For connections to Birmingham New Street and Hereford please refer to Tables 57 and 131

London - Swindon, Cheltenham Spa, Bristol, Weston-super-Mare and South Wales

Route Diagram - see first Page of Table 125

		GW	GW	GW	GW		GW	GW	GW	GW	GW	GW	GW	GW	GW		GW	GW	GW	GW	GW	GW	GW	GW	GW
			◇1	R	◇1		◇1	◇1	◇1	◇1	◇1	◇1	◇1	◇1			◇1	◇1	◇	◇1	◇1	◇1	◇1	◇1	◇1
								A		B				A								A	C		
			☕		🛒		☕	☕⊘	☕	☕	☕	☕	☕	☕⊘			☕	☕		🛒	☕	☕⊘	☕	☕	☕
London Paddington 15 ⊖	d		09 15		09 21		09 30	09 45	09 48	10 00	10 15	10 22	10 30	10 45			11 00	11 15		11 20	11 30	11 45	11 48	12 00	12 15
Slough 3	d				09 36							10 36								11 36					
Reading 7	d		09 42		09 52		09 57	10 11	10 16	10 27	10 42	10 52	10 57	11 11			11 27	11 42		11 52	11 57	12 11	12 16	12 27	12 42
Didcot Parkway	d		09 57				10 12		10 33		10 57		11 12					11 57			12 12		12 33		12 57
Swindon	a		10 14				10 30	10 38	10 53	10 55	11 14		11 30	11 38			11 55	12 14			12 30	12 38	12 53	12 55	13 14
	d	09 54	10 15				10 31	10 38	10 54	10 55	11 15		11 30	11 38	11 54		11 55	12 15			12 30	12 38	12 54	12 55	13 15
Kemble	d	10 07							11 07						12 07								13 07		
Stroud	d	10 22							11 22						12 22								13 22		
Stonehouse	d	10 28							11 28						12 28								13 28		
Gloucester 7	a	10 50							11 44						12 50								13 44		
Cheltenham Spa	a	11 05							12 03						13 05								14 03		
Worcester Shrub Hill	d			11 06	11a34							12a44							13 06	13a31					
Chippenham	d						10 44			11 09			11 44				12 09				12 44			13 09	
Bath Spa 7	a						10 59			11 24			11 59				12 23				12 59			13 24	
Bristol Parkway 7	a		10 40	12 22				11 04			11 40			12 04				12 40	14 22			13 04			13 40
	d		10 41	12 22				11 07			11 41			12 07				12 41	14 22			13 07			13 41
Bristol Temple Meads 10	a			12 34			11 15			11 40			12 15				12 39		14 38		13 15			13 44	
Weston-super-Mare	a									12 06															
Newport (South Wales)	a		11 06					11 31			12 04			12 31				13 06				13 31			14 04
Cardiff Central 7	a		11 23					11 46			12 21			12 46				13 22				13 46			14 22
Bridgend	a							12 09						13 09								14 09			
Port Talbot Parkway	a							12 22						13 22								14 22			
Neath	a							12 30						13 30								14 30			
Swansea	a							12 43						13 44								14 43			

			GW	GW	GW	GW	GW	GW	GW	GW	GW		GW	GW	GW	GW	GW	GW	GW	GW	GW		GW	GW	GW
			◇1	◇1	◇1	◇1		◇1	◇1	◇1	◇1		◇1	◇1	◇	◇1	◇1	◇1		◇1	◇1		◇1	◇1	◇1
					A											D									
			🛒	☕	☕⊘	☕		☕	☕	☕	☕		☕	☕		🛒	☕	☕		☕	☕		☕	☕	☕
London Paddington 15 ⊖	d		12 21	12 30	12 45	13 00		13 15	13 30	13 45	13 48		14 00	14 15		14 21	14 30	14 45		15 00	15 15		15 30	15 45	15 48
Slough 3	d		12 36													14 36									
Reading 7	d		12 52	12 57	13 11	13 27		13 42	13 57	14 11	14 16		14 27	14 42		14 52	14 57	15 11		15 27	15 42		15 57	16 11	16 16
Didcot Parkway	d			13 12				13 57	14 12		14 33			14 57			15 12				15 57		16 12		16 33
Swindon	a			13 30	13 38	13 54		14 14	14 30	14 38	14 54		14 55	15 14			15 30	15 38		15 55	16 14		16 30	16 38	16 53
	d			13 32	13 38	13 55	13 54	14 15	14 30	14 38	14 54		14 55	15 15			15 30	15 38	15 54	15 55	16 15		16 30	16 38	16 54
Kemble	d						14 07				15 07								16 07						17 07
Stroud	d						14 22				15 22								16 22						17 22
Stonehouse	d						14 28				15 28								16 28						17 28
Gloucester 7	a						14 50				15 44								16 50						17 46
Cheltenham Spa	a						15 05				16 03								17 05						18 03
Worcester Shrub Hill	d		14a46												15 06	16a39									
Chippenham	d			13 44		14 09			14 44				15 09				15 44			16 10			16 45		
Bath Spa 7	a			13 59		14 23			14 59				15 24				15 59			16 24			16 59		
Bristol Parkway 7	a				14 04			14 40		15 04				15 40	16 22			16 05			16 40			17 04	
	d				14 07			14 41		15 07				15 41	16 22			16 07			16 41			17 07	
Bristol Temple Meads 10	a			14 15		14 39			15 15				15 40		16 37		16 15			16 39			17 15		
Weston-super-Mare	a																16 52						17 52		
Newport (South Wales)	a				14 30			15 06		15 31				16 05				16 30			17 06			17 31	
Cardiff Central 7	a				14 46			15 22		15 46				16 22				16 46			17 22			17 46	
Bridgend	a				15 09					16 09								17 09						18 09	
Port Talbot Parkway	a				15 22					16 22								17 22						18 22	
Neath	a				15 30					16 30								17 30						18 30	
Swansea	a				15 43					16 43								17 43						18 48	

		GW	GW	GW	GW	GW	GW		GW	GW	GW	GW	GW	GW	GW	GW	GW		GW	GW	GW	GW	GW	GW	GW
			◇1	◇1	◇1	◇1	◇1		◇	◇1	◇1		◇1	◇1	◇1	◇	◇1		◇1	◇1	◇1	◇1	◇1	◇1	◇1
							E				F									G		H			
			☕	☕	☕	☕	☕			☕	☕		☕	☕	☕		☕		☕	☕	☕	☕	☕	☕	☕
London Paddington 15 ⊖	d		15 51	16 00	16 15	16 30	16 45			17 00	17 15		17 22	17 30	17 45		17 48		17 50	18 00	18 15	18 22	18 30	18 45	18 47
Slough 3	d		16 06																						
Reading 7	d		16 22	16 27	16 41	16 57	17 11			17 26	17 41		17 50	17 56	18 11		18 16		18 22	18 27	18 41	18 50	18 56	19 11	19 18
Didcot Parkway	d				16 56	17 12				17 42	17 57			18 11			18 33			18 42	18 57		19 12		19 33
Swindon	a			16 55	17 13	17 30	17 38			17 58	18 14			18 28	18 38		18 53			18 59	19 14		19 28	19 38	19 52
	d			16 55	17 15	17 30	17 38		17 54	18 00	18 15			18 30	18 38	18 44	18 54			19 00	19 15		19 30	19 38	19 54
Kemble	d								18 07								19 07								20 07
Stroud	d								18 22								19 22								20 22
Stonehouse	d								18 28								19 28								20 28
Gloucester 7	a								18 49								19 45								20 45
Cheltenham Spa	a								19 05								20 03								21 02
Worcester Shrub Hill	d	17 06	18a08									19 07	19a34						20a03			20a41			
Chippenham	d			17 13		17 45				18 14				18 44		19a01				19 14			19 44		
Bath Spa 7	a			17 26		17 59				18 27				18 57						19 28			19 57		
Bristol Parkway 7	a	18 22			17 40		18 04				18 40	20 22			19 04						19 42			20 04	
	d	18 22			17 41		18 07				18 41	20 22			19 07						19 44			20 07	
Bristol Temple Meads 10	a	18 38		17 41		18 14				18 44		20 38		19 12						19 43			20 13		
Weston-super-Mare	a					18 51								19 48									20 53		
Newport (South Wales)	a				18 04		18 30				19 11				19 31						20 07			20 31	
Cardiff Central 7	a				18 19		18 48				19 26				19 48						20 22			20 48	
Bridgend	a				18 44		19 09				19 49				20 10						20 45			21 15	
Port Talbot Parkway	a				18 57		19 22				20 02				20 26						20 58			21 28	
Neath	a				19 04		19 30				20 10				20 33						21 05			21 36	
Swansea	a				19 18		19 46				20 23				20 47						21 19			21 49	

A ☕ from Bridgend ⊘ to Bridgend
B The Torbay Express
C The Cheltenham Spa Express
D 🛒 to Reading
E The Capitals United
F The Red Dragon
G The Bristolian
H The Cathedrals Express

For connections from Heathrow Airport, Gatwick Airport and Oxford please refer to Tables 125A, 148 and 116.
For connections to Birmingham New Street and Hereford please refer to Tables 57 and 131

London - Swindon, Cheltenham Spa, Bristol, Weston-super-Mare and South Wales

Route Diagram - see first Page of Table 125

		GW	GW		GW	GW	GW	GW	GW	GW	GW	GW	GW		GW	GW	GW	GW	GW	GW	GW	GW	GW		GW
			FX		FO														FO	FX	FO	FX			FO
		◇1	◇1		◇1	◇		◇1	◇1	◇1	◇1	◇1	◇1		◇1		◇1	◇1	◇1	◇1	◇1	◇1			◇1
													A						A						
		☕	☕		☕			☕	☕	☕	☕	☕	🛒		☕		☕	☕	🛒	☕	☕	☕			☕
London Paddington 15 ⊖	d	19 00	19 15		19 15			19 22	19 30	19 48	20 00	20 15	20 20		20 45		21 15	21 45	21 48	21 48	22 15	22 15			22 45
Slough 3	d							19 36					20 36						22 03	22 03					
Reading 7	d	19 27	19 41		19 41			19 52	19 57	20 18	20 27	20 41	20 52		21 11		21 41	22 11	22 22	22 22	22 41	22 49			23 11
Didcot Parkway	d	19 42	19 57		19 58				20 12	20 33	20 42	20 57			21 26		22 00	22 31			23 01	23 09			23 30
Swindon	a	20 00	20 13		20 13				20 30	20 52	21 00	21 14			21 43		22 18	22 48			23 19	23 26			23 48
	d	20 00	20 15		20 15	20 25			20 30	20 54	21 00	21 15			21 44	21 54	22 19	22 49			23 21	23 27	23 33		23 49
Kemble	d					20 38				21 11						22 07							23 47		
Stroud	d					20 53				21 26						22 22							00 02		
Stonehouse	d					20 59				21 31						22 28							00 07		
Gloucester 7	a					21 14				21 46						22 45							00 24		
Cheltenham Spa	a					21 29				22 02						23 05									
Worcester Shrub Hill	d						21 32	21a46		22a24			22a34						00a12	00a12					
Chippenham	d	20 15							20 44		21 16				21 58			23 03			23 33	23 40			
Bath Spa 7	a	20 29							20 59		21 29				22 11			23 17			23 47	23 54			
Bristol Parkway 7	a		20 40		20 40		23 04					21 40					22 45								00 14
	d		20 42		20 42		23 05					21 41					22 45								00 16
Bristol Temple Meads 10	a	20 44					23 19		21 15		21 44				22 30			23 32			00 03	00 10			
Weston-super-Mare	a								21 50									00s05							
Newport (South Wales)	a		21 04		21 04							22 03					23 19								00 38
Cardiff Central 7	a		21 19		21 23							22 23					23 40								00 53
Bridgend	a		21 45		21 51							22 46					00 02								01 19
Port Talbot Parkway	a		21 58		22 04							22 59					00 15								01 32
Neath	a		22 06		22 12							23 07					00 22								01 39
Swansea	a		22 19		22 25							23 20					00 37								01 53

		GW	GW	GW
		FX	FO	FX
		◇1	◇1	◇1
		☕	☕	☕
London Paddington 15 ⊖	d	22 45	23 30	23 30
Slough 3	d			
Reading 7	d	23 19	00 08	00 08
Didcot Parkway	d	23 39	00 25	00 25
Swindon	a	23 55	00 44	00 44
	d	23 57	00 45	00 45
Kemble	d			
Stroud	d			
Stonehouse	d			
Gloucester 7	a			
Cheltenham Spa	a			
Worcester Shrub Hill	d			
Chippenham	d		00 59	00 59
Bath Spa 7	a		01 13	01 13
Bristol Parkway 7	a	00 21		
	d	00 23		
Bristol Temple Meads 10	a		01 29	01 29
Weston-super-Mare	a			
Newport (South Wales)	a	00 51	02s02	02s10
Cardiff Central 7	a	01 11	02 19	02 31
Bridgend	a	01 36		
Port Talbot Parkway	a	01 49		
Neath	a	01 57		
Swansea	a	02 10		

Saturdays
until 31 December

		GW	GW	GW	GW	GW	GW	GW	GW	GW		GW	GW	GW	GW	GW	GW	GW	GW	GW		GW	GW	GW	GW
		◇1	◇1	◇1		◇1	◇1	◇	◇1	◇1			◇1	◇1		◇1	R 1	◇1	◇1	◇1		◇1	◇1	◇1	◇1
		☕	☕	☕		☕	☕						☕	☕			☕	☕	☕	☕		☕	☕	☕	☕
London Paddington 15 ⊖	d	21p15	21p45	22p15		22p45	23p30		05 21	06 21			06 30	07 00		07 21	07 30	07 45	08 00	08 15		08 21	08 30	08 45	09 00
Slough 3	d								05 38	06 38						07 38						08 39			
Reading 7	d	21p41	22p11	22p41		23p11	00 08		05 54	06 54			06 59	07 27		07 53	07 57	08 11	08 27	08 42		08 54	08 57	09 11	09 27
Didcot Parkway	d	22p00	22p31	23p01		23p30	00 25		06 08				07 12				08 12			08 56			09 12		
Swindon	a	22p18	22p48	23p19		23p48	00 44						07 30	07 54			08 30	08 38	08 55	09 15			09 30	09 38	09 54
	d	22p19	22p49	23p21	23p33	23p49	00 45					07 16	07 30	07 55			08 30	08 38	08 55	09 15			09 30	09 38	09 55
Kemble	d				23p47							07 30								09 31					
Stroud	d				00 02							07 45								09 46					
Stonehouse	d				00 07							07 50								09 51					
Gloucester 7	a				00 24							08 06								10 06					
Cheltenham Spa	a											08 24								10 22					
Worcester Shrub Hill	d							06 47	07a44	08a40					09 08	09a40						10a44			
Chippenham	d		23p03	23p33			00 59						07 44	08 09			08 44		09 09				09 44		10 09
Bath Spa 7	a		23p17	23p47			01 13						08 00	08 24			09 00		09 24				10 00		10 24
Bristol Parkway 7	a	22p45				00 14		08 19							10 24			09 04						10 04	
	d	22p45				00 16		08 19							10 25			09 07						10 07	
Bristol Temple Meads 10	a		23p32	00 03			01 29	08 34					08 15	08 39	10 39		09 15		09 39				10 15		10 39
Weston-super-Mare	a		00s05																						
Newport (South Wales)	a	23p19				00 38	02s02											09 30						10 31	
Cardiff Central 7	a	23p40				00 53	02 19											09 47						10 46	
Bridgend	a	00 02				01 19												10 09						11 09	
Port Talbot Parkway	a	00 15				01 32												10 22						11 22	
Neath	a	00 22				01 39												10 30						11 30	
Swansea	a	00 37				01 53												10 43						11 43	

A 🛒 to Reading

For connections from Heathrow Airport, Gatwick Airport and Oxford please refer to Tables 125A, 148 and 116.
For connections to Birmingham New Street and Hereford please refer to Tables 57 and 131

Table 125

Saturdays

until 31 December

London - Swindon, Cheltenham Spa, Bristol, Weston-super-Mare and South Wales

Route Diagram - see first Page of Table 125

		GW	GW	GW	GW	GW		GW	GW	GW	GW	GW	GW	GW	GW	GW		GW	GW	GW	GW	GW	GW	GW	GW
			◇1	◇1	◇1	◇1		🚌	◇1	◇1	◇1	◇1		◇	◇1	◇1		◇1	◇1	◇1	◇1	◇1	◇1		◇
											A					B		A							
			🍴	🍴	🍴	🍴			🍴	🍴	🍴⊘	🍴			🛒	🍴⊘		🍴⊘	🍴	🍴	🍴	🍴	🍴		
London Paddington 15 ⊖	d		09 30	09 45	10 00	10 15			10 21	10 30	10 45	11 00			11 21	11 30		11 45	12 00	12 15	12 30	12 45	13 00		
Slough 3	d								10 39						11 39										
Reading 7	d		09 57	10 11	10 27	10 42			10 54	10 57	11 11	11 27			11 54	11 58		12 11	12 27	12 42	12 57	13 11	13 27		
Didcot Parkway	d		10 12			10 56				11 12						12 12				12 56	13 12				
Swindon	a		10 30	10 38	10 54	11 15				11 30	11 38	11 54				12 30		12 38	12 54	13 15	13 30	13 38	13 55		
	d	10 14	10 30	10 38	10 55	11 15				11 30	11 38	11 55	12 14			12 30		12 38	12 55	13 15	13 30	13 38	13 55	14 14	
Kemble	d	10 28				11 31							12 28							13 31				14 28	
Stroud	d	10 43				11 46							12 43							13 46				14 43	
Stonehouse	d	10 48				11 51							12 48							13 51				14 48	
Gloucester 7	a	11 07				12 07							13 03							14 06				15 03	
Cheltenham Spa	a	11 23				12 22							13 24							14 22				15 25	
Worcester Shrub Hill	d							11 06	12a39					12 54	13a40										15 06
Chippenham	d		10 44		11 09					11 44		12 09				12 44			13 09		13 44		14 09		
Bath Spa 7	a		11 00		11 24					12 00		12 24				12 59			13 24		14 00		14 24		
Bristol Parkway 7	a			11 04				12 24			12 04			14 20				13 04				14 04			16 24
	d			11 07				12 25			12 07			14 20				13 07				14 07			16 25
Bristol Temple Meads 10	a		11 15		11 39			12 39		12 15		12 39		14 36		13 14			13 42		14 15		14 39		16 39
Weston-super-Mare	a																								
Newport (South Wales)	a			11 31							12 31							13 31				14 31			
Cardiff Central 7	a			11 46							12 46							13 47				14 46			
Bridgend	a			12 09							13 09							14 09				15 09			
Port Talbot Parkway	a			12 22							13 22							14 22				15 22			
Neath	a			12 30							13 30							14 30				15 30			
Swansea	a			12 43							13 43							14 43				15 43			

		GW		GW	GW	GW	GW	GW	GW	GW	GW	GW		GW	GW	GW	GW	GW	GW	GW	GW	GW		GW	GW
		◇1		◇1	◇1	◇1	◇1	◇1		◇1	◇1	◇1				◇1	◇1	◇1	◇1	◇1	◇1	◇1		◇1	◇1
																C									
		🛒		🍴	🍴	🍴	🍴	🛒		🍴	🍴	🍴				🛒	🍴	🍴	🍴	🍴	🍴	🍴		🍴	🍴
London Paddington 15 ⊖	d	13 21		13 30	13 45	14 00	14 15	14 21		14 30	14 45	15 00				15 21	15 30	15 45	16 00	16 15	16 21	16 30		16 45	17 00
Slough 3	d	13 39						14 39								15 39					16 39				
Reading 7	d	13 54		13 59	14 11	14 27	14 42	14 54		14 57	15 11	15 27				15 54	15 59	16 11	16 27	16 42	16 54	16 57		17 11	17 27
Didcot Parkway	d			14 12			14 56			15 12							16 12			16 56		17 12			
Swindon	a			14 30	14 38	14 54	15 15			15 30	15 38	15 54					16 30	16 38	16 54	17 15		17 30		17 38	17 54
	d			14 30	14 38	14 55	15 15		15 22	15 30	15 38	15 55		16 14			16 30	16 38	16 55	17 15		17 30		17 38	17 55
Kemble	d						15 31							16 28						17 31					
Stroud	d						15 46							16 43						17 46					
Stonehouse	d						15 51							16 48						17 51					
Gloucester 7	a						16 06							17 03						18 06					
Cheltenham Spa	a						16 22							17 25						18 22					
Worcester Shrub Hill	d	15a40						16a40							17 08	17a40					18a43				
Chippenham	d			14 44		15 09			15a38	15 44		16 09					16 44		17 09			17 44			18 09
Bath Spa 7	a			15 00		15 24				16 00		16 24					17 00		17 24			18 00			18 24
Bristol Parkway 7	a				15 04						16 04				18 24			17 04						18 04	
	d				15 07						16 07				18 25			17 07						18 07	
Bristol Temple Meads 10	a			15 15		15 41				16 15		16 39			18 39		17 15		17 39			18 15			18 39
Weston-super-Mare	a																					18 36			
Newport (South Wales)	a				15 31						16 31							17 29						18 30	
Cardiff Central 7	a				15 46						16 47							17 46						18 46	
Bridgend	a				16 09						17 09							18 09						19 09	
Port Talbot Parkway	a				16 22						17 22							18 22						19 22	
Neath	a				16 30						17 30							18 30						19 30	
Swansea	a				16 43						17 43							18 46						19 43	

		GW	GW	GW	GW	GW	GW	GW		GW	GW	GW	GW	GW	GW	GW	GW	GW		GW	GW	GW	GW	GW	GW
				◇1	◇1	◇1	◇1	◇1		◇1	◇1	◇1	◇1		◇1	◇1	◇1	◇1		◇1		◇1	◇1	◇1	◇1
																		C							
				🍴	🍴	🍴	🍴	🍴		🍴	🍴	🍴	🍴		🍴	🍴	🍴	🛒		🍴		🍴	🍴	🍴	🍴
London Paddington 15 ⊖	d			17 21	17 30	17 45	18 00	18 15		18 21	18 30	18 45	19 00		19 15	19 30	19 45	19 50		20 00		20 15	20 30	20 45	21 30
Slough 3	d			17 39						18 39								20 06							
Reading 7	d			17 54	17 57	18 11	18 27	18 42		18 54	18 57	19 11	19 27		19 42	19 57	20 11	20 22		20 27		20 42	20 57	21 13	21 57
Didcot Parkway	d				18 12			18 56			19 12				19 56	20 12				20 42		20 56	21 12		22 12
Swindon	a				18 30	18 38	18 54	19 15			19 29	19 38	19 54		20 14	20 30	20 38			21 00		21 15	21 30	21 40	22 30
	d	18 14			18 30	18 38	18 55	19 15			19 30	19 38	19 55	20 00	20 14	20 30	20 38			21 00	21 08	21 15	21 30	21 41	22 30
Kemble	d	18 28						19 31						20 15								21 31			
Stroud	d	18 43						19 46						20 30								21 46			
Stonehouse	d	18 48						19 51						20 35								21 51			
Gloucester 7	a	19 03						20 06						20 50								22 05			
Cheltenham Spa	a	19 25						20 22						21 03								22 20			
Worcester Shrub Hill	d		19 07	19a40						20a42								22a02							
Chippenham	d				18 44		19 09				19 44		20 09			20 45				21 14	21a24		21 45		22 44
Bath Spa 7	a				19 00		19 24				19 59		20 24			21 00				21 29			21 58		23 00
Bristol Parkway 7	a		20 24			19 05						20 05			20 40		21 04							22 06	
	d		20 25			19 07						20 07			20 40		21 07							22 11	
Bristol Temple Meads 10	a		20 39		19 15		19 38				20 15		20 40			21 16				21 45			22 14		23 15
Weston-super-Mare	a				19 50						20 36		21 26										22s47		
Newport (South Wales)	a					19 30						20 30			21 05		21 30							22 46	
Cardiff Central 7	a					19 46						20 44			21 23		21 47							23 06	
Bridgend	a					20 09						21 09			21 46		22 09							23 28	
Port Talbot Parkway	a					20 22						21 22			21 59		22 22							23 41	
Neath	a					20 30						21 30			22 07		22 30							23 49	
Swansea	a					20 43						21 43			22 19		22 43							00 02	

A 🍴 from Bridgend ⊘ to Bridgend

B 🍴 from Chippenham ⊘ to Chippenham

C 🛒 to Reading

For connections from Heathrow Airport, Gatwick Airport and Oxford please refer to Tables 125A, 148 and 116.
For connections to Birmingham New Street and Hereford please refer to Tables 57 and 131

Table 125

Saturdays

until 31 December

London - Swindon, Cheltenham Spa, Bristol, Weston-super-Mare and South Wales

Route Diagram - see first Page of Table 125

		GW	GW	GW	GW	GW
		◇1		◇1	◇1	◇1
				☕	☕	☕
London Paddington 15 ⊖	d	21 50		22 00	22 35	23 30
Slough 3	d	22 06				
Reading 7	d	22 23		22 27	23 02	23 59
Didcot Parkway	d	22 38		22 41	23 23	00 18
Swindon	a			22 59	23 40	00 37
	d		22 35	22 59	23 41	00 38
Kemble	d		22 49			
Stroud	d		23 04			
Stonehouse	d		23 09			
Gloucester 7	a		23 25			
Cheltenham Spa	a					
Worcester Shrub Hill	d	00a07				
Chippenham	d				23 55	00 53
Bath Spa 7	a				00 11	01 07
Bristol Parkway 7	a			23 27		
	d			23 28		
Bristol Temple Meads 10	a				00 25	01 21
Weston-super-Mare	a					
Newport (South Wales)	a			23 57		
Cardiff Central 7	a			00 18		
Bridgend	a					
Port Talbot Parkway	a					
Neath	a					
Swansea	a					

Saturdays

7 January to 24 March

		GW	GW	GW	GW	GW	GW	GW	GW	GW	GW	GW	GW	GW	GW	GW	GW	GW	GW	GW	GW	GW	GW
																R							
		◇1	◇1	◇1		◇1	◇1	◇	◇1	◇1		◇1	◇1		◇1	1	◇1	◇1	◇1	◇1	◇1	◇1	◇1
		☕	☕	☕		☕	☕					☕	☕			☕	☕	☕	☕	☕	☕	☕	☕
London Paddington 15 ⊖	d	21p15	21p45	22p15		22p45	23p30		05 21	06 21		06 30	07 00		07 21	07 30	07 45	08 00	08 15	08 21	08 30	08 45	09 00
Slough 3	d								05 38	06 38					07 38					08 39			
Reading 7	d	21p41	22p11	22p41		23p11	00 08		05 54	06 54		06 59	07 27		07 53	07 57	08 11	08 27	08 42	08 54	08 57	09 11	09 27
Didcot Parkway	d	22p00	22p31	23p01		23p30	00 25		06 08			07 12				08 12			08 56		09 12		
Swindon	a	22p18	22p48	23p19		23p48	00 44					07 30	07 54			08 30	08 38	08 55	09 15		09 30	09 38	09 54
	d	22p19	22p49	23p21	23p33	23p49	00 45				07 16	07 30	07 55			08 30	08 38	08 55	09 15		09 30	09 38	09 55
Kemble	d				23p47						07 30								09 31				
Stroud	d				00 02						07 45								09 46				
Stonehouse	d				00 07						07 50								09 51				
Gloucester 7	a				00 24						08 06								10 06				
Cheltenham Spa	a										08 24								10 22				
Worcester Shrub Hill	d							06 47	07a44	08a40				09 08	09a40					10a44			
Chippenham	d		23p03	23p33			00 59					07 44	08 09			08 44		09 09			09 44		10 09
Bath Spa 7	a		23p17	23p47			01 13					08 00	08 24			09 00		09 24			10 00		10 24
Bristol Parkway 7	a	22p45				00 14		08 19						10 24			09 04					10 04	
	d	22p45				00 16		08 19						10 25			09 07					10 07	
Bristol Temple Meads 10	a		23p32	00 03			01 29	08 34				08 15	08 39	10 39		09 15		09 39			10 15		10 39
Weston-super-Mare	a		00s05																				
Newport (South Wales)	a	23p19				00 38	02s02										09 30					10 31	
Cardiff Central 7	a	23p40				00 53	02 19										09 47					10 46	
Bridgend	a	00 02				01 19											10 09					11 09	
Port Talbot Parkway	a	00 15				01 32											10 22					11 22	
Neath	a	00 22				01 39											10 30					11 30	
Swansea	a	00 37				01 53											10 43					11 43	

		GW	GW	GW	GW	GW	GW	GW	GW	GW	GW	GW	GW	GW	GW	GW	GW	GW	GW	GW	GW	GW	GW
							R																
			◇1	◇1	◇1	◇1		◇1	◇1	◇1	◇1		◇	◇1	◇1	◇1	◇1	◇1	◇1	◇1	◇1		◇
										A					B	A							
			☕	☕	☕	☕		☕	☕	☕⊘	☕			🛒	☕⊘	☕⊘	☕	☕	☕	☕	☕		
London Paddington 15 ⊖	d		09 30	09 45	10 00	10 15		10 21	10 30	10 45	11 00			11 21	11 30	11 45	12 00	12 15	12 30	12 45	13 00		
Slough 3	d							10 39						11 39									
Reading 7	d		09 57	10 11	10 27	10 42		10 54	10 57	11 11	11 27			11 54	11 58	12 11	12 27	12 42	12 57	13 11	13 27		
Didcot Parkway	d		10 12			10 56			11 12						12 12			12 56	13 12				
Swindon	a		10 30	10 38	10 54	11 15			11 30	11 38	11 54				12 30	12 38	12 54	13 15	13 30	13 38	13 55		
	d	10 14	10 30	10 38	10 55	11 15			11 30	11 38	11 55	12 14			12 30	12 38	12 55	13 15	13 30	13 38	13 55	14 14	
Kemble	d	10 28				11 31						12 28						13 31				14 28	
Stroud	d	10 43				11 46						12 43						13 46				14 43	
Stonehouse	d	10 48				11 51						12 48						13 51				14 48	
Gloucester 7	a	11 07				12 07						13 03						14 06				15 03	
Cheltenham Spa	a	11 23				12 22						13 24						14 22				15 25	
Worcester Shrub Hill	d						11 06	12a39					12 54	13a40									15 06
Chippenham	d		10 44		11 09				11 44		12 09				12 44		13 09		13 44		14 09		
Bath Spa 7	a		11 00		11 24				12 00		12 24				12 59		13 24		14 00		14 24		
Bristol Parkway 7	a			11 04			12 24			12 04			14 20			13 04				14 04			16 24
	d			11 07			12 25			12 07			14 20			13 07				14 07			16 25
Bristol Temple Meads 10	a		11 15		11 39		12 39		12 15		12 39		14 36		13 14		13 42		14 15		14 39		16 39
Weston-super-Mare	a																						
Newport (South Wales)	a			11 31						12 31						13 31				14 31			
Cardiff Central 7	a			11 46						12 46						13 47				14 46			
Bridgend	a			12 09						13 09						14 09				15 09			
Port Talbot Parkway	a			12 22						13 22						14 22				15 22			
Neath	a			12 30						13 30						14 30				15 30			
Swansea	a			12 43						13 43						14 43				15 43			

A ☕ from Bridgend ⊘ to Bridgend

B ☕ from Chippenham ⊘ to Chippenham

For connections from Heathrow Airport, Gatwick Airport and Oxford please refer to Tables 125A, 148 and 116.
For connections to Birmingham New Street and Hereford please refer to Tables 57 and 131

Table 125

Saturdays

7 January to 24 March

London - Swindon, Cheltenham Spa, Bristol, Weston-super-Mare and South Wales

Route Diagram - see first Page of Table 125

		GW		GW	GW	GW	GW	GW	GW	GW	GW	GW		GW	GW	GW	GW	GW	GW	GW	GW	GW		GW	GW
		◇1		◇1	◇1	◇1	◇1	◇1		◇1	◇1	◇1				◇1	◇1	◇1	◇1	◇1	◇1	◇1		◇1	◇1
																A				B					
		🛒		☕	☕	☕	☕	🛒		☕	☕	☕				🛒	☕	☕	☕	☕	☕	☕		☕	☕
London Paddington 15 ⊖	d	13 21		13 30	13 45	14 00	14 15	14 21		14 30	14 45	15 00				15 21	15 30	15 45	16 00	16 15	16 21	16 30		16 45	17 00
Slough 3	d	13 39						14 39								15 39					16 39				
Reading 7	d	13 54		13 59	14 11	14 27	14 42	14 54		14 57	15 11	15 27				15 54	15 59	16 11	16 27	16 42	16 54	16 57		17 11	17 27
Didcot Parkway	d			14 12			14 56			15 12							16 12			16 56		17 12			
Swindon	a			14 30	14 38	14 54	15 15			15 30	15 38	15 54					16 30	16 38	16 54	17 15		17 30		17 38	17 54
	d			14 30	14 38	14 55	15 15		15 22	15 30	15 38	15 55		16 14			16 30	16 38	16 55	17 15		17 30		17 38	17 55
Kemble	d						15 31							16 28						17 31					
Stroud	d						15 46							16 43						17 46					
Stonehouse	d						15 51							16 48						17 51					
Gloucester 7	a						16 06							17 03						18 06					
Cheltenham Spa	a						16 22							17 25						18 22					
Worcester Shrub Hill	d	15a40						16a40							17 08	17a40					18a43				
Chippenham	d			14 44		15 09			15a38	15 44		16 09					16 44		17 09			17 44			18 09
Bath Spa 7	a			15 00		15 24				16 00		16 24					17 00		17 24			18 00			18 24
Bristol Parkway 7	a				15 04						16 04				18 24			17 04						18 04	
	d				15 07						16 07				18 25			17 07						18 07	
Bristol Temple Meads 10	a			15 15		15 41				16 15		16 39			18 39		17 15		17 39			18 15			18 39
Weston-super-Mare	a																					18 36			
Newport (South Wales)	a				15 31						16 31							17 29						18 30	
Cardiff Central 7	a				15 46						16 47							17 46						18 46	
Bridgend	a				16 09						17 09							18 09						19 09	
Port Talbot Parkway	a				16 22						17 22							18 22						19 22	
Neath	a				16 30						17 30							18 30						19 30	
Swansea	a				16 43						17 43							18 46						19 43	

		GW	GW	GW	GW	GW	GW	GW		GW	GW	GW	GW	GW	GW	GW	GW	GW		GW	GW	GW	GW	GW	GW
				◇1	◇1	◇1	◇1	◇1		◇1	◇1	◇1	◇1		◇1	◇1	◇1	◇1		◇1		◇1	◇1	◇1	◇1
																B		C						B	
				☕	☕	☕	☕	☕		☕	☕	☕	☕		☕	☕	☕	🛒		☕		☕	☕	☕	☕
London Paddington 15 ⊖	d			17 21	17 30	17 45	18 00	18 15		18 21	18 30	18 45	19 00		19 15	19 30	19 45	19 50		20 00		20 15	20 30	20 45	21 30
Slough 3	d			17 39						18 39								20 06							
Reading 7	d			17 54	17 57	18 11	18 27	18 42		18 54	18 57	19 11	19 27		19 42	19 57	20 11	20 22		20 27		20 42	20 59	21 13	21 57
Didcot Parkway	d				18 12			18 56			19 12				19 56	20 12				20 42		20 56	21 23		22 12
Swindon	a				18 30	18 38	18 54	19 15			19 29	19 38	19 54		20 14	20 30	20 38			21 00		21 15	21 40	21 42	22 30
	d	18 14			18 30	18 38	18 55	19 15			19 30	19 38	19 55	20 00	20 14	20 30	20 38			21 00	21 08	21 15	21 41	21 44	22 30
Kemble	d	18 28						19 31						20 15								21 31			
Stroud	d	18 43						19 46						20 30								21 46			
Stonehouse	d	18 48						19 51						20 35								21 51			
Gloucester 7	a	19 03						20 06						20 50								22 05			
Cheltenham Spa	a	19 25						20 22						21 03								22 20			
Worcester Shrub Hill	d		19 07	19a40						20a42								22a02							
Chippenham	d				18 44		19 09				19 44		20 09			20 45				21 14	21a24		21 55		22 44
Bath Spa 7	a				19 00		19 24				19 59		20 24			21 00				21 29			22 08		23 00
Bristol Parkway 7	a		20 24			19 05						20 05			20 40		21 04							22 08	
	d		20 25			19 07						20 07			20 40		21 07							22 11	
Bristol Temple Meads 10	a		20 39		19 15		19 38				20 15		20 40			21 16				21 45			22 25		23 15
Weston-super-Mare	a				19 50						20 36		21 26										22s57		
Newport (South Wales)	a					19 30						20 30			21 05		21 30							22 46	
Cardiff Central 7	a					19 46						20 44			21 23		21 47							23 06	
Bridgend	a					20 09						21 09			21 46		22 09							23 28	
Port Talbot Parkway	a					20 22						21 22			21 59		22 22							23 41	
Neath	a					20 30						21 30			22 07		22 30							23 49	
Swansea	a					20 43						21 43			22 19		22 43							00 02	

		GW	GW	GW		GW	GW
		◇1		◇1		◇1	◇1
				☕		☕	☕
London Paddington 15 ⊖	d	21 50		22 00		22 35	23 30
Slough 3	d	22 06					
Reading 7	d	22 23		22 27		23 02	23 59
Didcot Parkway	d	22 38		22 41		23 23	00 18
Swindon	a			22 59		23 41	00 37
	d		22 35	22 59		23 41	00 38
Kemble	d		22 49				
Stroud	d		23 04				
Stonehouse	d		23 09				
Gloucester 7	a		23 25				
Cheltenham Spa	a						
Worcester Shrub Hill	d	00a07					
Chippenham	d					23 55	00 53
Bath Spa 7	a					00 13	01 07
Bristol Parkway 7	a			23 27			
	d			23 28			
Bristol Temple Meads 10	a					00 27	01 21
Weston-super-Mare	a						
Newport (South Wales)	a			23 57			
Cardiff Central 7	a			00 18			
Bridgend	a						
Port Talbot Parkway	a						
Neath	a						
Swansea	a						

A 🛒 to Reading

B from 7 January until 11 February

C from 7 January until 11 February. 🛒 to Reading

For connections from Heathrow Airport, Gatwick Airport and Oxford please refer to Tables 125A, 148 and 116.
For connections to Birmingham New Street and Hereford please refer to Tables 57 and 131

Table 125

Saturdays
from 31 March

London - Swindon, Cheltenham Spa, Bristol, Weston-super-Mare and South Wales

Route Diagram - see first Page of Table 125

		GW	GW	GW	GW	GW	GW	GW	GW	GW		GW	GW	GW	GW	GW	GW	GW	GW	GW		GW	GW	GW	GW
																	R								
		◇1	◇1	◇1		◇1	◇1	◇	◇1	◇1			◇1	◇1		◇1	1	◇1	◇1	◇1		◇1	◇1	◇1	◇1
		🛒	🛒	🛒		🛒	🛒						🛒	🛒			🛒	🛒	🛒	🛒		🛒	🛒	🛒	🛒
London Paddington 15 ⊖	d	21p15	21p45	22p15		22p45	23p30		05 21	06 21			06 30	07 00		07 21	07 30	07 45	08 00	08 15		08 21	08 30	08 45	09 00
Slough 3	d								05 38	06 38						07 38						08 39			
Reading 7	d	21p41	22p11	22p41		23p11	00 08		05 54	06 54			06 59	07 27		07 53	07 57	08 11	08 27	08 42		08 54	08 57	09 11	09 27
Didcot Parkway	d	22p00	22p31	23p01		23p30	00 25		06 08				07 12				08 12			08 56			09 12		
Swindon	a	22p18	22p48	23p19		23p48	00 44						07 30	07 54			08 30	08 38	08 55	09 15			09 30	09 38	09 54
	d	22p19	22p49	23p21	23p33	23p49	00 45					07 16	07 30	07 55			08 30	08 38	08 55	09 15			09 30	09 38	09 55
Kemble	d				23p47							07 30								09 31					
Stroud	d				00 02							07 45								09 46					
Stonehouse	d				00 07							07 50								09 51					
Gloucester 7	a				00 24							08 06								10 06					
Cheltenham Spa	a											08 24								10 22					
Worcester Shrub Hill	d							06 47	07a44	08a40					09 08	09a40						10a44			
Chippenham	d		23p03	23p33			00 59						07 44	08 09			08 44		09 09				09 44		10 09
Bath Spa 7	a		23p17	23p47			01 13						08 00	08 24			09 00		09 24				10 00		10 24
Bristol Parkway 7	a	22p45				00 14		08 19							10 24			09 04						10 04	
	d	22p45				00 16		08 19							10 25			09 07						10 07	
Bristol Temple Meads 10	a		23p32	00 03			01 29	08 34					08 15	08 39	10 39		09 15		09 39				10 15		10 39
Weston-super-Mare	a		00s05																						
Newport (South Wales)	a	23p19				00 38	02s02											09 30						10 31	
Cardiff Central 7	a	23p40				00 53	02 19											09 47						10 46	
Bridgend	a	00 02				01 19												10 09						11 09	
Port Talbot Parkway	a	00 15				01 32												10 22						11 22	
Neath	a	00 22				01 39												10 30						11 30	
Swansea	a	00 37				01 53												10 43						11 43	

		GW	GW	GW	GW	GW		GW	GW	GW	GW	GW	GW	GW	GW	GW		GW	GW	GW	GW	GW	GW	GW	GW
								R																	
			◇1	◇1	◇1	◇1			◇1	◇1	◇1	◇1		◇	◇1	◇1		◇1	◇1	◇1	◇1	◇1	◇1		◇
											A					B		A							
			🛒	🛒	🛒	🛒			🛒	🛒	🛒⌀	🛒			🍽	🛒⌀		🛒⌀	🛒	🛒	🛒	🛒	🛒		
London Paddington 15 ⊖	d		09 30	09 45	10 00	10 15			10 21	10 30	10 45	11 00			11 21	11 30		11 45	12 00	12 15	12 30	12 45	13 00		
Slough 3	d								10 39						11 39										
Reading 7	d		09 57	10 11	10 27	10 42			10 54	10 57	11 11	11 27			11 54	11 58		12 11	12 27	12 42	12 57	13 11	13 27		
Didcot Parkway	d		10 12			10 56				11 12						12 12				12 56	13 12				
Swindon	a		10 30	10 38	10 54	11 15				11 30	11 38	11 54				12 30		12 38	12 54	13 15	13 30	13 38	13 55		
	d	10 14	10 30	10 38	10 55	11 15				11 30	11 38	11 55	12 14			12 30		12 38	12 55	13 15	13 30	13 38	13 55	14 14	
Kemble	d	10 28				11 31							12 28							13 31				14 28	
Stroud	d	10 43				11 46							12 43							13 46				14 43	
Stonehouse	d	10 48				11 51							12 48							13 51				14 48	
Gloucester 7	a	11 07				12 07							13 03							14 06				15 03	
Cheltenham Spa	a	11 23				12 22							13 24							14 22				15 25	
Worcester Shrub Hill	d							11 06	12a39					12 54	13a40										15 06
Chippenham	d		10 44		11 09					11 44		12 09				12 44			13 09		13 44		14 09		
Bath Spa 7	a		11 00		11 24					12 00		12 24				12 59			13 24		14 00		14 24		
Bristol Parkway 7	a			11 04				12 24			12 04			14 20				13 04				14 04			16 24
	d			11 07				12 25			12 07			14 20				13 07				14 07			16 25
Bristol Temple Meads 10	a		11 15		11 39			12 39		12 15		12 39		14 36		13 14			13 42		14 15		14 39		16 39
Weston-super-Mare	a																								
Newport (South Wales)	a			11 31							12 31							13 31				14 31			
Cardiff Central 7	a			11 46							12 46							13 47				14 46			
Bridgend	a			12 09							13 09							14 09				15 09			
Port Talbot Parkway	a			12 22							13 22							14 22				15 22			
Neath	a			12 30							13 30							14 30				15 30			
Swansea	a			12 43							13 43							14 43				15 43			

		GW		GW	GW	GW	GW	GW	GW	GW	GW	GW		GW	GW	GW	GW	GW	GW	GW	GW	GW		GW	GW
		◇1		◇1	◇1	◇1	◇1	◇1		◇1	◇1	◇1				◇1	◇1	◇1	◇1	◇1	◇1	◇1		◇1	◇1
																C									
		🍽		🛒	🛒	🛒	🛒	🍽		🛒	🛒	🛒				🍽	🛒	🛒	🛒	🛒	🛒	🛒		🛒	🛒
London Paddington 15 ⊖	d	13 21		13 30	13 45	14 00	14 15	14 21		14 30	14 45	15 00				15 21	15 30	15 45	16 00	16 15	16 21	16 30		16 45	17 00
Slough 3	d	13 39						14 39								15 39					16 39				
Reading 7	d	13 54		13 59	14 11	14 27	14 42	14 54		14 57	15 11	15 27				15 54	15 59	16 11	16 27	16 42	16 54	16 57		17 11	17 27
Didcot Parkway	d			14 12			14 56			15 12							16 12			16 56		17 12			
Swindon	a			14 30	14 38	14 54	15 15			15 30	15 38	15 54					16 30	16 38	16 54	17 15		17 30		17 38	17 54
	d			14 30	14 38	14 55	15 15		15 22	15 30	15 38	15 55		16 14			16 30	16 38	16 55	17 15		17 30		17 38	17 55
Kemble	d						15 31							16 28						17 31					
Stroud	d						15 46							16 43						17 46					
Stonehouse	d						15 51							16 48						17 51					
Gloucester 7	a						16 06							17 03						18 06					
Cheltenham Spa	a						16 22							17 25						18 22					
Worcester Shrub Hill	d	15a40						16a40							17 08	17a40					18a43				
Chippenham	d			14 44		15 09			15a38	15 44		16 09					16 44		17 09			17 44			18 09
Bath Spa 7	a			15 00		15 24				16 00		16 24					17 00		17 24			18 00			18 24
Bristol Parkway 7	a				15 04						16 04				18 24			17 04						18 04	
	d				15 07						16 07				18 25			17 07						18 07	
Bristol Temple Meads 10	a			15 15		15 41				16 15		16 39			18 39		17 15		17 39			18 15			18 39
Weston-super-Mare	a																					18 36			
Newport (South Wales)	a				15 31						16 31							17 29						18 30	
Cardiff Central 7	a				15 46						16 47							17 46						18 46	
Bridgend	a				16 09						17 09							18 09						19 09	
Port Talbot Parkway	a				16 22						17 22							18 22						19 22	
Neath	a				16 30						17 30							18 30						19 30	
Swansea	a				16 43						17 43							18 46						19 43	

A 🛒 from Bridgend ⌀ to Bridgend **B** 🛒 from Chippenham ⌀ to Chippenham **C** 🍽 to Reading

For connections from Heathrow Airport, Gatwick Airport and Oxford please refer to Tables 125A, 148 and 116.
For connections to Birmingham New Street and Hereford please refer to Tables 57 and 131

Table 125

Saturdays
from 31 March

London - Swindon, Cheltenham Spa, Bristol, Weston-super-Mare and South Wales

Route Diagram - see first Page of Table 125

	GW	GW	GW	GW	GW	GW	GW	GW	GW	GW	GW	GW	GW	GW	GW	GW	GW	GW	GW	GW	GW	GW
			◇1	◇1	◇1	◇1	◇1	◇1	◇1	◇1	◇1		◇1	◇1	◇1	◇1	◇1		◇1	◇1	◇1	◇1
																A						
			☕	☕	☕	☕	☕	☕	☕	☕	☕		☕	☕	☕	🛒	☕		☕	☕	☕	☕
London Paddington [15] ⊖ d			17 21	17 30	17 45	18 00	18 15	18 21	18 30	18 45	19 00		19 15	19 30	19 45	19 50	20 00		20 15	20 30	20 45	21 30
Slough [3] d			17 39					18 39								20 06						
Reading [7] d			17 54	17 57	18 11	18 27	18 42	18 54	18 57	19 11	19 27		19 42	19 57	20 11	20 22	20 27		20 42	20 57	21 13	21 57
Didcot Parkway d				18 12			18 56		19 12				19 56	20 12			20 42		20 56	21 12		22 12
Swindon a				18 30	18 38	18 54	19 15		19 29	19 38	19 54		20 14	20 30	20 38		21 00		21 15	21 30	21 40	22 30
d	18 14			18 30	18 38	18 55	19 15		19 30	19 38	19 55	20 00	20 14	20 30	20 38		21 00	21 08	21 15	21 30	21 41	22 30
Kemble d	18 28						19 31					20 15							21 31			
Stroud d	18 43						19 46					20 30							21 46			
Stonehouse d	18 48						19 51					20 35							21 51			
Gloucester [7] a	19 03						20 06					20 50							22 05			
Cheltenham Spa a	19 25						20 22					21 03							22 20			
Worcester Shrub Hill d		19 07	19a40					20a42								22a02						
Chippenham d				18 44		19 09			19 44		20 09			20 45			21 14	21a24		21 45		22 44
Bath Spa [7] a				19 00		19 24			19 59		20 24			21 00			21 29			21 58		23 00
Bristol Parkway [7] a		20 24			19 05					20 05			20 40		21 04						22 06	
d		20 25			19 07					20 07			20 40		21 07						22 11	
Bristol Temple Meads [10] a		20 39		19 15		19 38			20 15		20 40			21 16			21 45			22 14		23 15
Weston-super-Mare a				19 50					20 36		21 26									22s47		
Newport (South Wales) a					19 30					20 30			21 05		21 30						22 46	
Cardiff Central [7] a					19 46					20 44			21 23		21 47						23 06	
Bridgend a					20 09					21 09			21 46		22 09						23 28	
Port Talbot Parkway a					20 22					21 22			21 59		22 22						23 41	
Neath a					20 30					21 30			22 07		22 30						23 49	
Swansea a					20 43					21 43			22 19		22 43						00 02	

	GW	GW	GW	GW	GW
	◇1		◇1	◇1	◇1
			☕	☕	☕
London Paddington [15] ⊖ d	21 50		22 00	22 35	23 30
Slough [3] d	22 06				
Reading [7] d	22 23		22 27	23 02	23 59
Didcot Parkway d	22 38		22 41	23 23	00 18
Swindon a			22 59	23 40	00 38
d		22 35	22 59	23 41	00 38
Kemble d		22 49			
Stroud d		23 04			
Stonehouse d		23 09			
Gloucester [7] a		23 25			
Cheltenham Spa a					
Worcester Shrub Hill d	00a07				
Chippenham d				23 55	00 53
Bath Spa [7] a				00 11	01 08
Bristol Parkway [7] a			23 27		
d			23 28		
Bristol Temple Meads [10] a				00 25	01 23
Weston-super-Mare a					
Newport (South Wales) a			23 57		
Cardiff Central [7] a			00 18		
Bridgend a					
Port Talbot Parkway a					
Neath a					
Swansea a					

Sundays
until 1 January

	GW	GW	GW	GW	GW	GW	GW	GW	GW	GW	GW	GW	GW	GW	GW	GW	GW	GW	GW	GW	GW	GW
	◇1	◇1	◇1	◇1	◇1	◇1	◇1	◇1	◇1	◇1	◇1		◇1	◇1	◇1		◇1	◇1	◇1		◇1	
	B	B	B	B																		
	☕	☕	☕	☕	☕		☕	☕	☕	☕	☕		☕	☕	☕		☕	☕	☕		☕	
London Paddington [15] ⊖ d	20p45	22p00	22p35	23p30	08 00	08 03	08 30		09 03	09 30	09 35		10 03	10 37	10 42		11 03	11 37	12 03		12 37	
Slough [3] d	∫	∫	∫	∫		08 26					09 58				11 05							
Reading [7] d	21p13	22p27	23p02	23p59	08 34	08 45	09 06		09 38	10 06	10 11		10 38	11 12	11 21		11 38	12 12	12 38		13 12	
Didcot Parkway d	∫	22p41	23p23	00∫18	08 49	09 02	09 23		09 52	10 20	10 28		10 52	11 26	11 37		11 52	12 26	12 52		13 26	
Swindon a	21p40	22p59	23p40	00∫37	09 09		09 41		10 10	10 38			11 10	11 44			12 10	12 44	13 10		13 44	
d	21p41	22p59	23p41	00∫38	09 09		09 42	09 50	10 11	10 39		10 47	11 11	11 45		11 49	12 11	12 45	13 11	13 25	13 45	
Kemble d	∫	∫	∫	∫				10 03				11 01				12 04				13 39		
Stroud d	∫	∫	∫	∫				10 18				11 16				12 19				13 54		
Stonehouse d	∫	∫	∫	∫				10 23				11 21				12 24				13 59		
Gloucester [7] a	∫	∫	∫	∫				10 40				11 36				12 39				14 18		
Cheltenham Spa a	∫	∫	∫	∫				10 55				11 49				12 51				14 31		
Worcester Shrub Hill d	∫	∫	∫	∫		10a32					12a05				13a09							14 36
Chippenham d	∫	∫	23p55	00∫53	09 26				10 26				11 26				12 26		13 26			
Bath Spa [7] a	∫	∫	00∫11	01∫07	09 38				10 39				11 39				12 39		13 39			
Bristol Parkway [7] a	22p06	23p27	∫	∫			10 07			11 04				12 10				13 10			14 10	15 49
d	22p11	23p28	∫	∫			10 08			11 05				12 11				13 11			14 11	15 55
Bristol Temple Meads [10] a	∫	∫	00∫25	01∫21	09 53				10 57				11 54				12 54		13 54			16 09
Weston-super-Mare a	∫	∫											12 31						14 26			16 56
Newport (South Wales) a	22p46	23p57					10 33			11 32				12 37				13 37			14 37	
Cardiff Central [7] a	23p06	00∫18					10 51			11 50				12 56				13 56			14 57	
Bridgend a	23p28						11 14			12 13				13 18				14 18			15 18	
Port Talbot Parkway a	23p41						11 27			12 26				13 31				14 31			15 31	
Neath a	23p49						11 35			12 33				13 38				14 38			15 38	
Swansea a	00∫02						11 49			12 47				13 52				14 52			15 52	

A 🛒 to Reading

B not 11 December

For connections from Heathrow Airport, Gatwick Airport and Oxford please refer to Tables 125A, 148 and 116.
For connections to Birmingham New Street and Hereford please refer to Tables 57 and 131

Table 125

Sundays
until 1 January

London - Swindon, Cheltenham Spa, Bristol, Weston-super-Mare and South Wales

Route Diagram - see first Page of Table 125

		GW	GW	GW	GW	GW		GW	GW	GW	GW	GW	GW	GW	GW	GW		GW	GW	GW	GW	GW	GW	GW	GW
		◇1	◇1		◇1	◇1		◇1	◇1			◇1	◇1	◇1	◇1	◇1		◇1	◇1		◇1	◇1			◇1
		☕	☕		☕	☕		☕	☕				☕	☕		☕		☕	☕			☕			☕
London Paddington [15] ⊖	d	12 42	13 03		13 37	13 42		14 03	14 37			14 42	15 03	15 37	15 42	16 03		16 30	16 37		16 42	17 03			17 30
Slough [3]	d	13 07				14 06						15 05			16 05						17 04				
Reading [7]	d	13 23	13 38		14 12	14 21		14 38	15 12			15 21	15 38	16 12	16 21	16 38		17 05	17 12		17 24	17 38			18 06
Didcot Parkway	d	13 38	13 52		14 26	14 37		14 52	15 26			15 36	15 52	16 26	16 37	16 52			17 26		17 39	17 52			
Swindon	a		14 10		14 44			15 09	15 44				16 10	16 44		17 10		17 36	17 44			18 10			18 34
	d		14 11	14 21	14 45			15 11	15 45	16 01			16 11	16 45		17 11		17 36	17 45			18 11	18 19	18 22	18 34
Kemble	d			14 36						16 16								17 50						18 36	
Stroud	d			14 51						16 31								18 05						18 50	
Stonehouse	d			14 56						16 36								18 10						18 55	
Gloucester [7]	a			15 19						16 50								18 25						19 15	
Cheltenham Spa	a			15 33						17 04								18 46							
Worcester Shrub Hill	d	15a09				16a08					16 40	17a09			18a08					18 40	19a10				
Chippenham	d		14 26					15 25					16 26			17 26						18 26	18a35		18 49
Bath Spa [7]	a		14 39					15 38					16 39			17 39						18 39			19 06
Bristol Parkway [7]	a				15 10				16 10		17 57			17 10					18 10	19 57					
	d				15 11				16 11		17 58			17 11					18 11	19 58					
Bristol Temple Meads [10]	a		14 54					15 53			18 10		16 54			17 54				20 11		18 54			19 25
Weston-super-Mare	a												17 26												19 58
Newport (South Wales)	a				15 37				16 37					17 40					18 37						
Cardiff Central [7]	a				15 56				16 56					17 58					18 56						
Bridgend	a				16 18				17 18					18 21					19 18						
Port Talbot Parkway	a				16 31				17 31					18 35					19 31						
Neath	a				16 38				17 38					18 43					19 38						
Swansea	a				16 52				17 53					18 58					19 52						

		GW		GW	GW	GW	GW	GW	GW	GW	GW	GW		GW	GW	GW	GW	GW	GW	GW	GW	GW		GW	GW
		◇1		◇1	◇1	◇1	◇1		◇1	◇1		◇1		◇1	◇1	◇1	◇1	◇1	◇1	◇1	◇1			◇1	◇1
		☕		☕	☕	☕	☕			☕		☕		☕	☕	☕	☕	☕	☕	☕				☕	☕
London Paddington [15] ⊖	d	17 37		17 42	18 03	18 30	18 37		18 42	19 03		19 30		19 37	19 42	20 03	20 30	20 37	21 03	21 37	21 42			22 03	22 37
Slough [3]	d			18 04					19 07						20 06						22 06				
Reading [7]	d	18 12		18 25	18 38	19 06	19 12		19 27	19 38		20 06		20 13	20 21	20 38	21 06	21 12	21 38	22 14	22 22			22 50	23 15
Didcot Parkway	d	18 27		18 39	18 52		19 26		19 43	19 52				20 27	20 37	20 52		21 26	21 52	22 30	22 38			23 05	23s30
Swindon	a	18 43			19 10	19 35	19 43			20 10		20 34		20 44		21 10	21 34	21 43	22 10	22 49				23 25	23s48
	d	18 45			19 11	19 36	19 45			20 11	20 28	20 34		20 45		21 11	21 36	21 45	22 11	22 51		22 57		23 25	
Kemble	d					19 50					20 42						21 50					23 11			
Stroud	d					20 05					20 57						22 05					23 26			
Stonehouse	d					20 09					21 02						22 10					23 31			
Gloucester [7]	a					20 32					21 17						22 25					23 48			
Cheltenham Spa	a					20 49					21 33						22 41					00 05			
Worcester Shrub Hill	d			20a12				20 37	21a13						22a10						00a12				
Chippenham	d				19 26					20 26		20 49				21 26			22 26					23 41	
Bath Spa [7]	a				19 39					20 39		21 03				21 39			22 43					23 54	
Bristol Parkway [7]	a	19 14					20 10	21 53						21 10				22 10		23 15					00s16
	d	19 15					20 11	21 55						21 11				22 11		23 17					
Bristol Temple Meads [10]	a				19 54			22 07		20 54		21 18				21 54			22 58					00 09	00 30
Weston-super-Mare	a									21 26						22 27									
Newport (South Wales)	a	19 41					20 37							21 37				22 37		23 42					
Cardiff Central [7]	a	19 59					20 56							21 59				23 00		00 04					
Bridgend	a	20 22					21 18							22 22				23 21		00 27					
Port Talbot Parkway	a	20 35					21 31							22 35				23 35		00 40					
Neath	a	20 43					21 38							22 43				23 43		00 48					
Swansea	a	20 56					21 53							22 56				23 56		01 01					

		GW	GW
		◇1	◇1
		☕	☕
London Paddington [15] ⊖	d	23 03	23 37
Slough [3]	d		00 02
Reading [7]	d	23 46	00 15
Didcot Parkway	d	00s02	00s31
Swindon	a	00s21	00s51
	d		
Kemble	d		
Stroud	d		
Stonehouse	d		
Gloucester [7]	a		
Cheltenham Spa	a		
Worcester Shrub Hill	d		
Chippenham	d	00s37	01s06
Bath Spa [7]	a	00s51	01s21
Bristol Parkway [7]	a		
	d		
Bristol Temple Meads [10]	a	01 05	01 35
Weston-super-Mare	a		
Newport (South Wales)	a		
Cardiff Central [7]	a		
Bridgend	a		
Port Talbot Parkway	a		
Neath	a		
Swansea	a		

For connections from Heathrow Airport, Gatwick Airport and Oxford please refer to Tables 125A, 148 and 116.
For connections to Birmingham New Street and Hereford please refer to Tables 57 and 131

Table 125

Sundays

8 January to 12 February

London - Swindon, Cheltenham Spa, Bristol, Weston-super-Mare and South Wales

Route Diagram - see first Page of Table 125

		GW	GW	GW	GW	GW	GW	GW	GW	GW		GW	GW	GW	GW	GW	GW	GW	GW	GW		GW	GW	GW	GW
		◇1	◇1	◇1	◇1	◇1	◇1	◇1	◇1	◇1		◇1	◇1		◇1	◇1	◇1		◇1	◇1		◇1		◇1	
		☕	☕	☕	☕	☕		☕	☕	☕		☕	☕		☕	☕	☕		☕	☕		☕		☕	
London Paddington 15 ⊖	d	20p45	22p00	22p35	23p30	08 00	08 03	08 30		09 03		09 30	09 35		10 03	10 37	10 42		11 03	11 37		12 03		12 37	
Slough 3	d						08 26						09 58				11 05								
Reading 7	d	21p13	22p27	23p02	23p59	08 38	08 44	09 06		09 38		10 06	10 11		10 38	11 12	11 21		11 38	12 12		12 38		13 12	
Didcot Parkway	d		22p41	23p23	00 18	08 52	09 02	09 19		09 52		10 20	10 28		10 52	11 26	11 37		11 52	12 26		12 52		13 26	
Swindon	a	21p42	22p59	23p41	00 37	09 10		09 38		10 10		10 38			11 10	11 44			12 10	12 44		13 10		13 44	
	d	21p44	22p59	23p41	00 38	09 11		09 39	09 50	10 11		10 39		10 47	11 11	11 45		11 49	12 11	12 45		13 11	13 25	13 45	
Kemble	d								10 03					11 01				12 04					13 39		
Stroud	d								10 18					11 16				12 19					13 54		
Stonehouse	d								10 23					11 21				12 24					13 59		
Gloucester 7	a								10 40					11 36				12 39					14 18		
Cheltenham Spa	a								10 55					11 49				12 51					14 31		
Worcester Shrub Hill	d						10a32						12a05				13a09								14 36
Chippenham	d			23p55	00 53	09 26				10 26					11 26				12 26			13 26			
Bath Spa 7	a			00 13	01 07	09 39				10 39					11 40				12 39			13 39			
Bristol Parkway 7	a	22p08	23p27					10 04				11 04				12 10				13 10				14 10	15 49
	d	22p11	23p28					10 05				11 05				12 11				13 11				14 11	15 55
Bristol Temple Meads 10	a			00 27	01 21	09 54				10 54					11 55				12 54			13 54			16 09
Weston-super-Mare	a														12 31							14 26			16 56
Newport (South Wales)	a	22p46	23p57					10 30				11 32				12 38				13 37				14 37	
Cardiff Central 7	a	23p06	00 18					10 49				11 51				12 57				13 56				14 57	
Bridgend	a	23p28																							
Port Talbot Parkway	a	23p41																							
Neath	a	23p49																							
Swansea	a	00 02																							

		GW	GW	GW	GW	GW		GW	GW	GW	GW	GW	GW	GW	GW	GW		GW	GW	GW	GW	GW	GW	GW	GW
		◇1	◇1		◇1	◇1		◇1	◇1			◇1	◇1	◇1	◇1	◇1		◇1	◇1		◇1	◇1			◇1
		☕	☕		☕	☕		☕	☕				☕	☕		☕		☕	☕			☕			☕
London Paddington 15 ⊖	d	12 42	13 03		13 37	13 42		14 03	14 37			14 42	15 03	15 37	15 42	16 03		16 30	16 37		16 42	17 03			17 30
Slough 3	d	13 07				14 06						15 03			16 04						17 03				
Reading 7	d	13 23	13 38		14 12	14 21		14 38	15 12			15 21	15 38	16 12	16 21	16 38		17 05	17 12		17 26	17 38			18 06
Didcot Parkway	d	13 38	13 52		14 26	14 39		14 52	15 26			15 36	15 52	16 26	16 37	16 53			17 26		17 41	17 52			
Swindon	a		14 10		14 44			15 10	15 44				16 10	16 44		17 10		17 36	17 44			18 10			18 34
	d		14 11	14 21	14 45			15 11	15 45	16 01			16 12	16 45		17 12		17 36	17 45			18 11	18 19	18 22	18 34
Kemble	d			14 36						16 16								17 50						18 36	
Stroud	d			14 51						16 31								18 05						18 50	
Stonehouse	d			14 56						16 36								18 10						18 55	
Gloucester 7	a			15 19						16 50								18 25						19 15	
Cheltenham Spa	a			15 33						17 04								18 46							
Worcester Shrub Hill	d	15a09				16a08					16 40	17a09			18a08					18 40	19a10				
Chippenham	d		14 26					15 26					16 26			17 26						18 26	18a35		18 49
Bath Spa 7	a		14 39					15 38					16 39			17 39						18 39			19 06
Bristol Parkway 7	a				15 10				16 10		17 57			17 10					18 10	19 57					
	d				15 11				16 11		17 58			17 11					18 11	19 58					
Bristol Temple Meads 10	a		14 54					15 54			18 10		16 53			17 54				20 11		18 54			19 25
Weston-super-Mare	a												17 26												19 58
Newport (South Wales)	a				15 37				16 37					17 40					18 37						
Cardiff Central 7	a				15 56				16 57					18 00					18 57						
Bridgend	a																								
Port Talbot Parkway	a																								
Neath	a																								
Swansea	a																								

		GW		GW	GW	GW	GW	GW	GW	GW	GW	GW		GW	GW	GW	GW	GW	GW	GW	GW	GW		GW	GW
		◇1		◇1	◇1	◇1	◇1		◇1	◇1		◇1		◇1	◇1	◇1	◇1	◇1	◇1	◇1	◇1			◇1	◇1
		☕		☕	☕	☕	☕			☕		☕		☕	☕	☕	☕	☕	☕	☕				☕	☕
London Paddington 15 ⊖	d	17 37		17 42	18 03	18 30	18 37		18 42	19 03		19 30		19 37	19 42	20 03	20 30	20 37	21 03	21 37	21 42			22 03	22 37
Slough 3	d			18 04					19 08						20 06						22 06				
Reading 7	d	18 12		18 24	18 37	19 06	19 13		19 27	19 38		20 06		20 13	20 21	20 37	21 06	21 13	21 38	22 12	22 22			22 45	23 15
Didcot Parkway	d	18 26		18 39	18 52		19 26		19 43	19 52				20 27	20 37	20 52		21 26	21 52	22 29	22 38			22 59	23s30
Swindon	a	18 44			19 10	19 35	19 44			20 10		20 32		20 44		21 10	21 34	21 45	22 10	22 46				23 17	23s48
	d	18 45			19 11	19 36	19 45			20 11	20 28	20 34		20 45		21 11	21 36	21 45	22 11	22 50		22 57		23 17	
Kemble	d					19 50					20 42						21 50					23 11			
Stroud	d					20 05					20 57						22 05					23 26			
Stonehouse	d					20 09					21 02						22 10					23 31			
Gloucester 7	a					20 32					21 17						22 25					23 48			
Cheltenham Spa	a					20 49					21 33						22 41					00 05			
Worcester Shrub Hill	d			20a12				20 37	21a13						22a10						00a12				
Chippenham	d				19 26					20 26		20 49				21 26			22 26					23 33	
Bath Spa 7	a				19 39					20 39		21 03				21 39			22 43					23 46	
Bristol Parkway 7	a	19 10					20 10	21 53						21 10				22 10		23 14					00s16
	d	19 12					20 12	21 55						21 12				22 12		23 16					
Bristol Temple Meads 10	a				19 54			22 07		20 54		21 18				21 54			22 58					00 01	00 30
Weston-super-Mare	a									21 26						22 27									
Newport (South Wales)	a	19 37					20 37							21 37				22 37		23 41					
Cardiff Central 7	a	19 55					20 56							22 00				23 00		00 03					
Bridgend	a																								
Port Talbot Parkway	a																								
Neath	a																								
Swansea	a																								

For connections from Heathrow Airport, Gatwick Airport and Oxford please refer to Tables 125A, 148 and 116.
For connections to Birmingham New Street and Hereford please refer to Tables 57 and 131

Sundays

8 January to 12 February

London - Swindon, Cheltenham Spa, Bristol, Weston-super-Mare and South Wales

Route Diagram - see first Page of Table 125

		GW	GW
		◇1	◇1
		ꟾP	ꟾP
London Paddington 15 ⊖	d	23 03	23 37
Slough 3	d		00 02
Reading 7	d	23 47	00 15
Didcot Parkway	d	00s01	00s31
Swindon	a	00s19	00s49
	d		
Kemble	d		
Stroud	d		
Stonehouse	d		
Gloucester 7	a		
Cheltenham Spa	a		
Worcester Shrub Hill	d		
Chippenham	d	00s34	01s04
Bath Spa 7	a	00s49	01s19
Bristol Parkway 7	a		
	d		
Bristol Temple Meads 10	a	01 03	01 33
Weston-super-Mare	a		
Newport (South Wales)	a		
Cardiff Central 7	a		
Bridgend	a		
Port Talbot Parkway	a		
Neath	a		
Swansea	a		

Sundays

19 February to 25 March

		GW	GW	GW	GW	GW	GW	GW	GW	GW		GW	GW	GW	GW	GW	GW	GW	GW	GW		GW	GW	GW	GW
		◇1	◇1	◇1	◇1	◇1	◇1	◇1	◇1	◇1		◇1	◇1	◇1	◇1	◇1	◇1	◇1		◇1		◇1	◇1	◇1	◇1
		ꟾP	ꟾP	ꟾP	ꟾP	ꟾP		ꟾP	ꟾP	ꟾP		ꟾP	ꟾP	ꟾP	ꟾP	ꟾP	ꟾP	ꟾP		ꟾP		ꟾP	ꟾP	ꟾP	ꟾP
London Paddington 15 ⊖	d	22p00	22p35	23p30	07 57	08 00	08 03	09 03	09 30	09 35		10 03	10 30	10 42	11 03	11 30	12 03	12 30		12 42		13 03	13 30	13 42	14 03
Slough 3	d						08 26			09 58				11 05						13 07				14 06	
Reading 7	d	22p27	23p02	23p59	08 32	08 38	08 44	09 38	10 06	10 11		10 39	11 06	11 21	11 38	12 06	12 38	13 06		13 23		13 38	14 04	14 21	14 38
Didcot Parkway	d	22p41	23p23	00 18	08 47	08 52	09 02	09 52	10 19	10 28		10 52	11 19	11 37	11 53	12 19	12 52	13 19		13 38		13 51	14 19	14 37	14 52
Swindon	a	22p59	23p41	00 37	09 05	09 10		10 10	10 39			11 10	11 39		12 10	12 39	13 10	13 39				14 09	14 39		15 09
	d	22p59	23p41	00 38	09 08	09 11		10 11	10 40			11 11	11 40		12 12	12 40	13 11	13 40				14 09	14 40		15 11
Kemble	d				09 24				11 01							12 54		13 54					14 54		
Stroud	d				09 40				11 16							13 09		14 09					15 09		
Stonehouse	d				09 45				11 21							13 14		14 14					15 14		
Gloucester 7	a				09 59				11 36				12 28			13 28		14 28					15 28		
Cheltenham Spa	a																								
Worcester Shrub Hill	d						10a32			12a05				13a09					14 36	15a09				16a08	
Chippenham	d		23p55	00 53		09 26		10 26				11 26			12 26		13 26					14 25			15 25
Bath Spa 7	a		00 13	01 07		09 39		10 39				11 40			12 39		13 39					14 38			15 38
Bristol Parkway 7	a	23p27																	15 49						
	d	23p28																	15 55						
Bristol Temple Meads 10	a		00 27	01 21		09 54		10 54				11 55			12 54		13 54		16 09			14 52			15 53
Weston-super-Mare	a											12 31					14 26		16 56						
Newport (South Wales)	a	23p57			10 52				12 25				13 19			14 19		15 19					16 19		
Cardiff Central 7	a	00 18			11 06				12 44				13 37			14 37		15 39					16 39		
Bridgend	a				11 29				13 07				14 01			15 01		16 03					17 00		
Port Talbot Parkway	a				11 42				13 20				14 13			15 13		16 15					17 12		
Neath	a				11 51				13 28				14 21			15 21		16 23					17 19		
Swansea	a				12 04				13 41				14 36			15 34		16 36					17 33		

		GW	GW	GW	GW	GW		GW	GW	GW	GW	GW	GW	GW	GW	GW		GW	GW	GW	GW	GW	GW	GW	GW
		◇1		◇1	◇1	◇1		◇1	◇1	◇1	◇1		◇1	◇1		◇1		◇1	◇1	◇1	◇1	◇1		◇1	◇1
		ꟾP			ꟾP	ꟾP			ꟾP	ꟾP	ꟾP			ꟾP		ꟾP		ꟾP	ꟾP	ꟾP	ꟾP	ꟾP			ꟾP
London Paddington 15 ⊖	d	14 30		14 42	15 03	15 30		15 42	16 03	16 30	16 37		16 42	17 03		17 30		17 37	17 42	18 03	18 30	18 37		18 42	19 03
Slough 3	d			15 03				16 04					17 03						18 05					19 08	
Reading 7	d	15 05		15 21	15 37	16 06		16 21	16 38	17 06	17 13		17 26	17 38		18 06		18 12	18 25	18 37	19 05	19 12		19 27	19 38
Didcot Parkway	d	15 18		15 36	15 50	16 18		16 37	16 52	17 19			17 41	17 52		18 20			18 40	18 50	19 18			19 43	19 52
Swindon	a	15 38			16 09	16 39			17 10	17 37	17 43			18 10		18 39		18 43		19 09	19 39	19 44			20 10
	d	15 40			16 10	16 40			17 10	17 39	17 50			18 11	18 19	18 40		18 44		19 09	19 40	19 53			20 11
Kemble	d	15 54				16 54					18 03					19 00						20 06			
Stroud	d	16 09				17 09					18 18					19 15						20 21			
Stonehouse	d	16 14				17 14					18 23					19 20						20 26			
Gloucester 7	a	16 28				17 29				18 25	18 43					19 44					20 19	20 44			
Cheltenham Spa	a										19 02											21 03			
Worcester Shrub Hill	d		16 40	17a09				18a08				18 40	19a09						20a12				20 37	21a13	
Chippenham	d				16 25				17 26					18 26	18a35			18 57		19 25					20 26
Bath Spa 7	a				16 38				17 39					18 39				19 12		19 38					20 39
Bristol Parkway 7	a		17 57									19 57											21 53		
	d		17 58									19 58											21 55		
Bristol Temple Meads 10	a		18 10		16 53				17 54			20 11		18 54				19 26		19 53			22 07		20 54
Weston-super-Mare	a				17 26													20 00							21 26
Newport (South Wales)	a	17 19				18 19				19 16						20 37					21 11				
Cardiff Central 7	a	17 39				18 37				19 37						20 52					21 26				
Bridgend	a	18 00				19 00				20 01						21 15					21 51				
Port Talbot Parkway	a	18 13				19 13				20 13						21 28					22 04				
Neath	a	18 20				19 20				20 21						21 36					22 12				
Swansea	a	18 35				19 34				20 34						21 49					22 25				

For connections from Heathrow Airport, Gatwick Airport and Oxford please refer to Tables 125A, 148 and 116.
For connections to Birmingham New Street and Hereford please refer to Tables 57 and 131

Table 125

Sundays
19 February to 25 March

London - Swindon, Cheltenham Spa, Bristol, Weston-super-Mare and South Wales

Route Diagram - see first Page of Table 125

		GW		GW	GW	GW	GW	GW	GW	GW	GW	GW		GW	GW
		◇1		◇1	◇1	◇1	◇1	◇1	◇1	◇1	◇1	◇1		◇1	◇1
		🍴		🍴	🍴	🍴	🍴	🍴	🍴		🍴	🍴		🍴	🍴
London Paddington 15 ⊖	d	19 30		19 37	19 42	20 03	20 37	21 03	21 37	21 42	22 03	22 37		23 03	23 37
Slough 3	d				20 06					22 06					00 01
Reading 7	d	20 05		20 13	20 21	20 37	21 14	21 37	22 15	22 22	22 45	23 15		23 47	00 15
Didcot Parkway	d			20 28	20 37	20 51	21 28	21 50	22 29	22 38	22 59	23s30		00s01	00s30
Swindon	a	20 33		20 47		21 09	21 48	22 09	22 54		23 17	23s48		00s19	00s47
	d	20 33		20 50		21 10	21 51	22 10	22 56		23 17				
Kemble	d			21 05			22 06		23 09						
Stroud	d			21 20			22 21		23 24						
Stonehouse	d			21 25			22 26		23 29						
Gloucester 7	a			21 40			22 41		23 42						
Cheltenham Spa	a														
Worcester Shrub Hill	d				22a10					00a12					
Chippenham	d	20 48				21 25		22 25			23 33			00s34	01s03
Bath Spa 7	a	21 01				21 38		22 42			23 46			00s49	01s17
Bristol Parkway 7	a											00s16			
	d														
Bristol Temple Meads 10	a	21 16				21 53		22 57			00 01	00 30		01 03	01 31
Weston-super-Mare	a					22 27									
Newport (South Wales)	a			22 37			23 44		00 31						
Cardiff Central 7	a			22 57			00 07		00 53						
Bridgend	a			23 20			00 29		01 18						
Port Talbot Parkway	a			23 33			00 42		01 31						
Neath	a			23 41			00 50		01 38						
Swansea	a			23 54			01 04		01 52						

Sundays
from 1 April

		GW	GW	GW	GW	GW	GW	GW	GW	GW		GW	GW	GW	GW	GW	GW	GW	GW	GW		GW	GW	GW	GW
		◇1	◇1	◇1	◇1	◇1	◇1	◇1	◇1	◇1		◇1	◇1	◇1		◇1	◇1	◇1	◇1			◇1	◇1	◇1	◇1
		🍴	🍴	🍴	🍴	🍴		🍴	🍴	🍴		🍴	🍴	🍴		🍴	🍴	🍴	🍴			🍴	🍴	🍴	🍴
London Paddington 15 ⊖	d	20p45	22p00	22p35	23p30	08 00	08 03	08 30	08 37			09 03	09 30	09 35		09 42	10 03	10 37	10 42			11 03	11 30	11 37	12 03
Slough 3	d						08 26							09 58					11 05						
Reading 7	d	21p13	22p27	23p02	23p59	08 35	08 44	09 06	09 15			09 38	10 05	10 11		10 18	10 39	11 12	11 21			11 38	12 05	12 12	12 38
Didcot Parkway	d		22p41	23p23	00 18	08 49	09 02	09 21				09 52		10 28		10 32	10 52	11 26	11 37			11 52		12 26	12 52
Swindon	a	21p40	22p59	23p40	00 38	09 06		09 41	09 47			10 10	10 33			10 50	11 10	11 43				12 10	12 33	12 45	13 10
	d	21p41	22p59	23p41	00 38	09 08		09 43		09 50		10 11			10 47	10 51	11 11	11 45		11 49		12 11		12 45	13 10
Kemble	d									10 03					11 01					12 04					
Stroud	d									10 18					11 16					12 19					
Stonehouse	d									10 23					11 21					12 24					
Gloucester 7	a									10 40					11 36					12 39					
Cheltenham Spa	a									10 55					11 49					12 51					
Worcester Shrub Hill	d						10a32							12a05					13a09						
Chippenham	d			23p55	00 53	09 23						10 26					11 26					12 26			13 26
Bath Spa 7	a			00 11	01 08	09 37						10 39					11 40					12 39			13 39
Bristol Parkway 7	a	22p06	23p27					10 07								11 16		12 10						13 11	
	d	22p11	23p28					10 09								11 17		12 11						13 11	
Bristol Temple Meads 10	a			00 25	01 23	09 52						10 54					11 55					12 54			13 54
Weston-super-Mare	a																12 31					13 15			14 26
Newport (South Wales)	a	22p46	23p57					10 33								11 42		12 37						13 37	
Cardiff Central 7	a	23p06	00 18					10 51								12 01		12 56						13 56	
Bridgend	a	23p28						11 14								12 23		13 18						14 18	
Port Talbot Parkway	a	23p41						11 27								12 36		13 31						14 31	
Neath	a	23p49						11 36								12 44		13 38						14 38	
Swansea	a	00 02						11 49								12 58		13 52						14 52	

		GW	GW	GW	GW	GW		GW	GW	GW	GW	GW	GW	GW	GW	GW		GW	GW	GW	GW	GW	GW	GW	GW
			◇1	◇1		◇1		◇1		◇1	◇1	◇1	◇1			◇1		◇1	◇1	◇1	◇1	◇1	◇1		
			🍴	🍴		🍴		🍴		🍴	🍴	🍴	🍴					🍴	🍴		🍴	🍴	🍴		
London Paddington 15 ⊖	d		12 30	12 37		12 42		13 03		13 37	13 42	14 03	14 37			14 42		15 03	15 37	15 42	16 03	16 30	16 37		
Slough 3	d					13 07					14 06					15 03				16 04					
Reading 7	d		13 05	13 13		13 23		13 38		14 13	14 21	14 38	15 13			15 21		15 38	16 13	16 21	16 38	17 05	17 13		
Didcot Parkway	d			13 26		13 38		13 52		14 27	14 39	14 53	15 27			15 36		15 52	16 27	16 37	16 52		17 27		
Swindon	a		13 33	13 43				14 10		14 44		15 09	15 44					16 10	16 44		17 10	17 33	17 44		
	d	13 25		13 45				14 11	14 21	14 46		15 11	15 46	16 01				16 11	16 46		17 11		17 46	17 49	
Kemble	d	13 39							14 36					16 16										18 03	
Stroud	d	13 54							14 51					16 31										18 17	
Stonehouse	d	13 59							14 56					16 36										18 22	
Gloucester 7	a	14 18							15 13					16 50										18 43	
Cheltenham Spa	a	14 31							15 25					17 04											
Worcester Shrub Hill	d				14 36	15a09					16a08				16 40	17a09				18a08					18 40
Chippenham	d							14 27				15 25						16 26			17 26				
Bath Spa 7	a							14 40				15 38						16 39			17 39				
Bristol Parkway 7	a			14 10	15 49					15 11			16 11		17 57				17 11				18 11		19 57
	d			14 11	15 55					15 12			16 12		17 58				17 11				18 12		19 58
Bristol Temple Meads 10	a				16 09			14 54				15 53			18 10			16 54			17 54				20 11
Weston-super-Mare	a				16 56													17 26							
Newport (South Wales)	a			14 37						15 38			16 38						17 40				18 38		
Cardiff Central 7	a			14 56						15 57			16 57						17 58				18 57		
Bridgend	a			15 18						16 19			17 19						18 21				19 19		
Port Talbot Parkway	a			15 31						16 32			17 32						18 35				19 32		
Neath	a			15 38						16 38			17 39						18 43				19 39		
Swansea	a			15 52						16 53			17 54						18 58				19 53		

For connections from Heathrow Airport, Gatwick Airport and Oxford
please refer to Tables 125A, 148 and 116.
For connections to Birmingham New Street and Hereford
please refer to Tables 57 and 131

Table 125

Sundays
from 1 April

London - Swindon, Cheltenham Spa, Bristol, Weston-super-Mare and South Wales

Route Diagram - see first Page of Table 125

		GW		GW	GW	GW	GW	GW	GW	GW	GW	GW		GW	GW	GW	GW	GW	GW	GW	GW	GW		GW	GW
		◇1		◇1	◇1		◇1	◇1	◇1	◇1	◇1	◇1		◇1		◇1	◇1		◇1	◇1	◇1	◇1		◇1	◇1
				☕	☕		☕	☕	☕	☕	☕	☕		☕			☕		☕	☕	☕	☕		☕	☕
London Paddington 15 ⊖	d	16 42		16 57	17 03		17 30	17 37	17 42	17 57	18 03	18 30		18 37		18 42	19 03		19 30	19 37	19 42	19 57		20 03	20 30
Slough 3	d	17 04							18 05							19 07					20 06				
Reading 7	d	17 24		17 32	17 38		18 06	18 13	18 26	18 32	18 37	19 04		19 12		19 27	19 38		20 05	20 14	20 21	20 31		20 37	21 06
Didcot Parkway	d	17 39		17 46	17 52			18 27	18 40		18 51			19 26		19 43	19 52			20 28	20 37			20 51	
Swindon	a			18 08	18 10		18 34	18 43		19 00	19 09	19 35		19 43			20 10		20 33	20 47		20 59		21 08	21 35
	d			18 10	18 11	18 19	18 34	18 45			19 10	19 36		19 45			20 11	20 28	20 33	20 47				21 09	21 36
Kemble	d			18 23								19 50						20 42							21 50
Stroud	d			18 38								20 05						20 57							22 05
Stonehouse	d			18 43								20 09						21 02							22 10
Gloucester 7	a			18 57								20 32						21 17							22 25
Cheltenham Spa	a			19 18								20 49						21 33							22 41
Worcester Shrub Hill	d	19a10							20a12						20 37	21a13					22a10				
Chippenham	d				18 26	18a35	18 49				19 25						20 26		20 48					21 24	
Bath Spa 7	a				18 39		19 06				19 38						20 39		21 01					21 37	
Bristol Parkway 7	a							19 14						20 10	21 53					21 12					
	d							19 15						20 11	21 55					21 13					
Bristol Temple Meads 10	a				18 54		19 25				19 53				22 07		20 54		21 16					21 53	
Weston-super-Mare	a						19 58										21 26							22 27	
Newport (South Wales)	a							19 41						20 37						21 39					
Cardiff Central 7	a							19 59						20 56						22 01					
Bridgend	a							20 22						21 18						22 24					
Port Talbot Parkway	a							20 35						21 31						22 37					
Neath	a							20 43						21 38						22 45					
Swansea	a							20 56						21 53						22 58					

		GW	GW	GW	GW	GW	GW	GW		GW	GW
		◇1	◇1	◇1	◇1		◇1	◇1		◇1	◇1
		☕	☕	☕			☕	☕		☕	☕
London Paddington 15 ⊖	d	20 37	21 03	21 37	21 42		22 03	22 37		23 03	23 37
Slough 3	d				22 06						00 02
Reading 7	d	21 13	21 37	22 12	22 22		22 45	23 15		23 47	00 15
Didcot Parkway	d	21 27	21 51	22 28	22 38		22 59	23s30		00s01	00s31
Swindon	a	21 44	22 09	22 45			23 17	23s48		00s19	00s49
	d	21 46	22 10	22 46		22 57	23 17				
Kemble	d					23 11					
Stroud	d					23 26					
Stonehouse	d					23 31					
Gloucester 7	a					23 48					
Cheltenham Spa	a					00 05					
Worcester Shrub Hill	d				00a12						
Chippenham	d		22 25				23 33			00s34	01s04
Bath Spa 7	a		22 42				23 46			00s49	01s19
Bristol Parkway 7	a	22 11		23 11				00s16			
	d	22 12		23 12							
Bristol Temple Meads 10	a		22 57				00 01	00 30		01 03	01 33
Weston-super-Mare	a										
Newport (South Wales)	a	22 38		23 41							
Cardiff Central 7	a	23 01		00 01							
Bridgend	a	23 23		00 23							
Port Talbot Parkway	a	23 36		00 36							
Neath	a	23 43		00 44							
Swansea	a	23 57		00 57							

For connections from Heathrow Airport, Gatwick Airport and Oxford please refer to Tables 125A, 148 and 116.
For connections to Birmingham New Street and Hereford please refer to Tables 57 and 131

South Wales, Weston-super-Mare, Bristol, Cheltenham Spa and Swindon - London

Route Diagram - see first Page of Table 125

Miles	Miles	Miles			GW MO ◇1 A ☕	GW MO ◇1 B	GW MO ◇1 C	GW MO ◇1 D	GW MO ◇1 A ☕	GW MO ◇1 E ☕	GW MX ◇1 ☕	GW MX ◇1	GW MX R F 🛏 ☕	GW MO R E 🛏 ☕	GW ◇1 ☕	GW	GW ◇1 ☕	GW ◇1 ☕	GW ◇1 ☕	AW	GW ◇1 ☕	GW ◇1 ☕	GW ◇1 ☕
0	—	—	**Swansea**	d	19p59														03 57			04 58	
9½	—	—	Neath	d	20p11														04 09			05 10	
15	—	—	Port Talbot Parkway	d	20p18														04 17			05 18	
27¼	—	—	Bridgend	d	20p31														04 30			05 30	
47½	—	—	**Cardiff Central** 7	d	20p55														05 14			05 55	
59¼	—	—	Newport (South Wales)	d	21p10														05 32			06 09	
—	0	—	Weston-super-Mare	d							22p01												
—	19	—	**Bristol Temple Meads** 10	d					22p10	22p10	22p35		02 35	02 39	04 47		05 30				06 00		
81	—	—	Bristol Parkway 7	a															05 59			06 29	
—	—	—		d											04u57				06 01			06 31	
—	30½	—	Bath Spa 7	d					22p23	22p23	22p47						05 43				06 13		
—	43½	—	Chippenham	d					22p35	22p35	23p00						05 55				06 25		
—	—	—	Worcester Shrub Hill	d		21p34	21p34	21p34				22p43						05 11					05 21
—	—	0	**Cheltenham Spa**	d																05 37			05 54
—	—	6½	Gloucester 7	d	22p00											05 18				05a48			06 09
—	—	15½	Stonehouse	d	22p13											05 31							06 23
—	—	18	Stroud	d	22p19											05 36							06 29
—	—	29¼	Kemble	d	22p34											05 51							06 43
115½	60¼	43	**Swindon**	a	22p48				22p50	22p50	23p14		03 15	03 21	05 22	06 06	06 10		06 27		06 40	06 57	06 58
—	—	—		d	22p48				22p53	22p53	23p16		03 17	03 22	05 23		06 11		06 28		06 41	06 58	07 01
139½	84¼	67	Didcot Parkway	a		22p58	22p58	23p01	23p09	23p09	23p33	00 20			05 41		06 29	06 39	06 46		06 58		07 19
156¾	101½	84½	**Reading** 7	a	23p19	23p15	23p15	23p17	23p28	23p28	23p53	00 38	04s00	04s02	05 56		06 43	06 54	07 00		07 14	07 31	07 34
174¼	119	101¾	Slough 3	a		23p40	23p42	23p41				00 55					06 58						
192¾	137½	120¼	**London Paddington** 15 ⊖	a	00 01	00 02	00 04	00 04	00 12	00 13	00 33	01 17	05 25	05 05	06 24		07 16	07 30	07 32		07 44	08 02	08 07

		GW ◇1 ☕	XC ◇1	GW	AW	GW ◇1 ☕	GW ◇1 ☕	GW ◇1 ☕	GW ◇1 ☕	GW ◇1 ☕	GW ◇1 G ☕⊘	XC ◇1	GW ◇	XC ◇1	GW	GW ◇1 H ⊘	GW ◇1 I ☕	AW	GW ◇1 G ☕⊘	GW ◇1 ☕	GW ◇1 ☕	GW ◇1 J ☕⊘	AW
Swansea	d							05 27								05 58			06 28				
Neath	d							05 39								06 10			06 40				
Port Talbot Parkway	d							05 47								06 18			06 48				
Bridgend	d							05 59								06 30			07 00				
Cardiff Central 7	d				06 12			06 24						06 40		06 55		07 12	07 25				
Newport (South Wales)	d				06 28			06 38						06 55		07 09		07 27	07 39				
Weston-super-Mare	d									06 20							06 49				07 25		
Bristol Temple Meads 10	d					06 30	06 40			07 00							07 30				08 00		
Bristol Parkway 7	a							06 58								07 29			07 59				
	d							07 01								07 31			08 01				
Bath Spa 7	d					06 43	06 52			07 13							07 43				08 13		
Chippenham	d					06 55	07 05			07 25					07 31		07 55				08 25		
Worcester Shrub Hill	d	05 37									06 33		06 49							07 09		07 34	
Cheltenham Spa	d		06 03	06 24					06 31			06 43	07 16							07 30			07 45
Gloucester 7	d		06a16	06a34	07a20				06 46			06a53	07a26	07a44				08a20		07 45			07a57
Stonehouse	d								06 59											07 59			
Stroud	d								07 05											08 05			
Kemble	d								07 19											08 19			
Swindon	a					07 10	07 19	07 27	07 35	07 40					07 48	07 57	08 10		08 27	08 33	08 40		
	d					07 11	07 20	07 28	07 35	07 41						07 58	08 11		08 28	08 35	08 41		
Didcot Parkway	a	07 07				07 28		07 45	07 53	08 00							08 28		08 46	08 52	08 58		
Reading 7	a	07 25				07 43		08 00	08 12	08 16	08 21						08 44		09 01	09 07	09 14	09 14	
Slough 3	a																						
London Paddington 15 ⊖	a	07 59				08 14	08 16	08 33	08 40	08 44	08 51					08 54	09 14		09 29	09 39	09 44	09 47	

- **A** from 20 February until 26 March
- **B** until 2 January
- **C** from 2 Apri
- **D** from 9 January until 26 March
- **E** until 13 February, MO from 2 April
- **F** The Night Riviera
- **G** ☕ from Reading ⊘ to Reading
- **H** The Capitals United
- **I** The Bristolian
- **J** The Cathedrals Express. ☕ from Reading ⊘ to Reading

For connections from Hereford and Birmingham New Street please refer to Tables 131 and 57.
For connections to Oxford, Gatwick Airport and Heathrow Airport please refer to Tables 116, 148 and 125A

South Wales, Weston-super-Mare, Bristol, Cheltenham Spa and Swindon - London

Route Diagram - see first Page of Table 125

		XC	XC	GW	GW		GW	GW	GW	GW	AW	GW	GW	XC	GW		XC	AW	GW	GW	GW	GW	GW	XC	XC
		◇1	◇1	◇1			◇1		◇1	◇1		◇1	◇1	◇1			◇1		◇1	◇1	◇1	◇1		◇1	◇1
			A	B					B								A				C				A
		🛒	🛒	🍴⊘			🍴		🍴⊘	🍴		🍴	🛒	🛒			🛒		🍴	🍴	🍴	🍴		🛒	🛒
Swansea	d			06 58					07 28										07 58		08 28				
Neath	d			07 10					07 40										08 10		08 40				
Port Talbot Parkway	d			07 18					07 48										08 18		08 48				
Bridgend	d			07 30					08 00									08 21	08 30		09 00				
Cardiff Central 7	d		07 45	07 55					08 25								08 45	09 12	08 55		09 25				09 45
Newport (South Wales)	d		08 02	08 09					08 39								09 02	09 27	09 09		09 39				10 00
Weston-super-Mare	d						07 49															09 29			
Bristol Temple Meads 10	d				08 12		08 30	08 41				09 00								09 30		10 00			
Bristol Parkway 7	a			08 30				08 52	08 59										09 30		09 59				
	d			08 31				08 52	09 01										09 31		10 01				
Bath Spa 7	d				08 30		08 43					09 13								09 43		10 13			
Chippenham	d				08 44		08 55					09 25								09 55		10 25			
Worcester Shrub Hill	d												08 39		09 06										
Cheltenham Spa	d	08 16								08 31	08 45			09 12	09 34								09 40	10 11	
Gloucester 7	d	08a27	08a44					09a33		08 46	08a58			09a22	09a42		09a44	10a20					09 54	10a22	10a44
Stonehouse	d									08 59													10 06		
Stroud	d									09 05													10 11		
Kemble	d									09 19													10 27		
Swindon	a			08 57	09 03		09 10		09 27	09 33		09 40							09 57	10 10	10 27	10 40	10 44		
	d			08 59			09 11		09 29	09 35		09 41							09 59	10 11	10 29	10 41			
Didcot Parkway	a						09 28			09 52									10 16	10 28	10 46				
Reading 7	a			09 25			09 44		09 59	10 06		10 10	10 25						10 31	10 44	11 00	11 09			
Slough 3	a												10 39												
London Paddington 15 ⊖	a			09 59			10 15		10 32	10 37		10 39	11 00						11 07	11 14	11 32	11 38			

			GW	AW	GW	GW	GW	GW	GW	AW	GW		XC	GW	XC	GW	GW	GW	GW	GW	AW		XC	XC	GW
														R											
			◇1		◇1	◇1	◇	◇1	◇1		◇1		◇1		◇1	◇1	◇1	◇1	◇1				◇1	◇1	◇1
															A									A	
			🍴		🍴	🛒		🍴	🍴		🍴		🛒		🛒	🍴	🍴	🍴	🍴				🛒	🛒	🍴
Swansea	d							09 28										10 28							
Neath	d							09 40										10 40							
Port Talbot Parkway	d							09 48										10 48							
Bridgend	d			09 38				10 00										11 00							
Cardiff Central 7	d		09 55	10 12				10 25							10 45	10 55		11 25						11 45	11 55
Newport (South Wales)	d		10 09	10 27				10 39							11 00	11 09		11 39						12 02	12 09
Weston-super-Mare	d																								
Bristol Temple Meads 10	d				10 30		10 41				11 00						11 30		12 00						
Bristol Parkway 7	a		10 30				10 52	10 59								11 30		11 59							12 30
	d		10 31				10 52	11 01								11 31		12 01							12 31
Bath Spa 7	d				10 43						11 13						11 43		12 13						
Chippenham	d				10 55						11 25						11 55		12 25						
Worcester Shrub Hill	d					10 08								11 06											
Cheltenham Spa	d								10 31	10 45			11 11	11 32						11 40	11 45		12 11		
Gloucester 7	d			11a20			11a34		10 46	10a57			11a22	11a42	11a44					11 54	11a57		12a22	12a44	
Stonehouse	d								10 59											12 06					
Stroud	d								11 05											12 11					
Kemble	d								11 19											12 27					
Swindon	a		10 57		11 10			11 27	11 33		11 40					11 57	12 10	12 27	12 40	12 44					12 57
	d		10 59		11 11			11 29	11 35		11 41					11 59	12 11	12 29	12 41						12 59
Didcot Parkway	a		11 16		11 28				11 52							12 16	12 28	12 46							13 16
Reading 7	a		11 30		11 43	11 54		11 59	12 06		12 10					12 30	12 44	13 00	13 09						13 31
Slough 3	a					12 09																			
London Paddington 15 ⊖	a		12 02		12 14	12 29		12 32	12 37		12 40					13 00	13 14	13 32	13 38						14 06

		AW	GW	GW	GW	GW	GW		GW	XC	GW	XC	GW	AW	GW	GW	GW		GW	AW	XC	XC	GW	GW	GW
			◇1	◇1	◇	◇1	◇1		◇1	◇1	◇	◇1	◇1		◇1	◇1	◇1				◇1	◇1	◇1	◇1	◇1
						D						A				B						A			
			🍴	🛒		🍴	🍴		🍴	🛒		🛒	🍴	🛒	🍴	🍴⊘	🍴				🛒	🛒	🍴	🍴	🍴
Swansea	d					11 28										12 28									
Neath	d					11 40										12 40									
Port Talbot Parkway	d					11 48										12 48									
Bridgend	d	11 38				12 00								12 38		13 00									
Cardiff Central 7	d	12 12				12 25						12 45	12 55	13 12		13 25						13 45	13 55		
Newport (South Wales)	d	12 28				12 39						13 01	13 09	13 28		13 39						14 00	14 09		
Weston-super-Mare	d																								
Bristol Temple Meads 10	d		12 30		12 41				13 00						13 30		14 00							14 30	
Bristol Parkway 7	a				12 52	12 59							13 30			13 59							14 30		
	d				12 52	13 01							13 31			14 01							14 31		
Bath Spa 7	d		12 43						13 13						13 43		14 13							14 43	
Chippenham	d		12 55						13 25						13 55		14 25							14 55	
Worcester Shrub Hill	d			12 08							13 06														14 09
Cheltenham Spa	d						12 31			13 11	13 34								13 40	13 45	14 11				
Gloucester 7	d	13a20			13a31		12 46			13a22	13a42	13a44		14a20					13 54	13a57	14a22	14a44			
Stonehouse	d						12 59												14 06						
Stroud	d						13 05												14 11						
Kemble	d						13 19												14 27						
Swindon	a		13 10			13 27	13 33		13 40				13 57		14 10	14 27	14 40		14 44				14 57	15 10	
	d		13 11			13 29	13 35		13 41				13 59		14 11	14 29	14 41						14 59	15 11	
Didcot Parkway	a		13 28				13 52						14 15		14 28	14 46							15 15	15 28	
Reading 7	a		13 43	13 54		13 59	14 06		14 10				14 31		14 43	15 00	15 09						15 31	15 43	15 54
Slough 3	a			14 09																					16 09
London Paddington 15 ⊖	a		14 14	14 29		14 32	14 37		14 40				15 08		15 14	15 32	15 38						16 09	16 14	16 27

A 🛒 from Newport (South Wales

B 🍴 from Reading ⊘ to Reading

C The Red Dragon

D The St. David

For connections from Hereford and Birmingham New Street please refer to Tables 131 and 57.
For connections to Oxford, Gatwick Airport and Heathrow Airport please refer to Tables 116, 148 and 125A

South Wales, Weston-super-Mare, Bristol, Cheltenham Spa and Swindon - London

Route Diagram - see first Page of Table 125

		GW	GW		GW	AW	GW	GW	XC	GW	XC	GW	AW		GW	GW	GW	GW	GW	XC	XC	GW	AW		GW
																							R		
		◇	◇1		◇1		◇1	◇1	◇1	◇	◇1	◇1			◇1	◇1	1	◇1		◇1	◇1	◇1			◇1
					A						B							C							
			☕		☕	🛒	☕	🛒	🛒		🛒	☕			☕	☕		☕		🛒		☕	🛒		☕
Swansea	d		13 28													14 28									
Neath	d		13 40													14 40									
Port Talbot Parkway	d		13 48													14 48									
Bridgend	d		14 00										14 38			15 00									
Cardiff Central 7	d		14 25								14 45	14 55	15 12			15 25					15 45	15 55	16 05		
Newport (South Wales)	d		14 39								15 01	15 09	15 28			15 39					16 00	16 09	16 21		
Weston-super-Mare	d																								
Bristol Temple Meads 10	d	14 41					15 00								15 30			16 00							16 30
Bristol Parkway 7	a	14 51	15 00									15 30				15 59						16 30			
	d	14 52	15 01									15 31				16 01						16 31			
Bath Spa 7	d						15 13								15 43			16 13							16 43
Chippenham	d						15 25								15 55			16 25							16 55
Worcester Shrub Hill	d							14 41		15 06							15 42								
Cheltenham Spa	d				14 31	14 45			15 11	15 34									15 40	16 11					
Gloucester 7	d	15a32			14 46	14a56			15a22	15a42	15a44		16a21						15 54	16a22	16a44		17a14		
Stonehouse	d				14 59														16 06						
Stroud	d				15 05														16 11						
Kemble	d				15 19														16 27						
Swindon	a		15 27		15 33		15 40					15 57			16 10	16 27		16 40	16 44			16 57			17 10
	d		15 29		15 35		15 41					15 59			16 11	16 29		16 41				16 59			17 11
Didcot Parkway	a				15 52							16 16			16 28	16 46	17 04					17 16			17 28
Reading 7	a		16 00		16 06		16 13	16 24				16 31			16 43	17 00		17 09				17 31			17 44
Slough 3	a							16 39																	
London Paddington 15 ⊖	a		16 30		16 39		16 44	17 00				17 09			17 14	17 30		17 39				18 02			18 14

		GW	GW	GW	GW	AW	GW	XC	GW		XC	GW	AW	GW	GW	GW	AW	GW	XC		XC	GW	GW	AW	GW
		◇1		◇1	◇1		◇1	◇1			◇1	◇1		◇1	◇1	◇		◇1	◇1		◇1	◇1	◇1		◇1
																					B				
		☕		☕	☕		☕					☕		☕	☕			☕			🛒	☕	🛒		☕
Swansea	d			15 28											16 28										
Neath	d			15 40											16 40										
Port Talbot Parkway	d			15 48											16 48										
Bridgend	d			16 00									16 38		17 00									17 38	
Cardiff Central 7	d			16 25							16 45	16 55	17 12		17 25						17 45	17 55		18 12	
Newport (South Wales)	d			16 39							17 00	17 09	17 28		17 39						18 00	18 09		18 27	
Weston-super-Mare	d													17 10											18 08
Bristol Temple Meads 10	d		16 41				17 00							17 30				18 00							18 30
Bristol Parkway 7	a		16 52	16 59								17 30			17 59							18 30			
	d		16 52	17 01								17 31			18 01							18 31			
Bath Spa 7	d						17 13							17 43				18 13							18 43
Chippenham	d						17 25							17 55				18 25							18 55
Worcester Shrub Hill	d	16 03							17 06														17 31		
Cheltenham Spa	d				16 31	16 45		17 15	17 33							17 40	17 45		18 18						
Gloucester 7	d		17a33		16 46	16a56		17a26	17a42		17a44		18a21			17 54	17a57		18a29		18a44			19a20	
Stonehouse	d				16 59											18 06									
Stroud	d				17 05											18 11									
Kemble	d				17 19											18 25									
Swindon	a			17 27	17 33		17 40					17 57		18 10	18 27	18 41		18 40				18 57			19 10
	d			17 29	17 35		17 41					17 59		18 11	18 29			18 41				18 59			19 11
Didcot Parkway	a				17 52							18 16		18 28	18 46										19 28
Reading 7	a	17 54		18 00	18 06		18 12					18 31		18 46	19 01			19 09				19 25	19 32		19 44
Slough 3	a	18 10																					19 47		
London Paddington 15 ⊖	a	18 28		18 30	18 39		18 44					19 02		19 14	19 32			19 38				19 54	20 06		20 14

		GW	GW	GW	AW		XC	GW	GW	GW	XC	AW	GW	GW	GW		GW	XC	XC	XC	GW	GW	GW	GW	GW
																								FX	FO
			◇1	◇1			◇1	◇1	◇1		◇1			◇	◇1			◇1	◇1	◇1	◇1	◇1		◇1	◇1
			☕	☕				☕	☕						☕						☕			☕	☕
Swansea	d		17 28												18 28									19 29	19 29
Neath	d		17 40												18 40									19 40	19 40
Port Talbot Parkway	d		17 48												18 48									19 48	19 48
Bridgend	d		18 00												19 00									20 00	20 00
Cardiff Central 7	d		18 25								18 45				19 25					19 50				20 25	20 25
Newport (South Wales)	d		18 39								19 01				19 39					20 05				20 39	20 39
Weston-super-Mare	d																								
Bristol Temple Meads 10	d	18 41						19 30					19 41						20 00		20 30		20 41		
Bristol Parkway 7	a	18 52	18 59										19 52		19 59				20 08				20 52	21 01	21 01
	d	18 52	19 01										19 52		20 01				20 10				20 52	21 01	21 01
Bath Spa 7	d							19 43													20 43				
Chippenham	d							19 55						20 02							20 55				
Worcester Shrub Hill	d								18 55	19 07												20 03			
Cheltenham Spa	d			18 34	18 45		19 15			19 34		19 45					20 01	20 11							
Gloucester 7	d	19a30		18 51	18a56		19a27			19a42	19a45	19a56	20a32				20 13	20a22	20a38	20a53			21a31		
Stonehouse	d			19 04													20 25								
Stroud	d			19 09													20 30								
Kemble	d			19 23													20 44								
Swindon	a		19 27	19 38				20 10						20 21	20 27		21 03				21 10			21 29	21 29
	d		19 29	19 41				20 11							20 29						21 11			21 33	21 33
Didcot Parkway	a		19 46	19 58				20 28							20 46						21 28			21 52	21 52
Reading 7	a		20 00	20 14				20 44	20 54						21 00						21 43	21 55		22 11	22 11
Slough 3	a								21 09													22 13			
London Paddington 15 ⊖	a		20 32	20 46				21 14	21 29						21 32						22 14	22 39		22 44	22 45

A The Cheltenham Spa Express

B 🛒 from Newport (South Wales)

C The Merchant Venturer

For connections from Hereford and Birmingham New Street please refer to Tables 131 and 57.
For connections to Oxford, Gatwick Airport and Heathrow Airport please refer to Tables 116, 148 and 125A

South Wales, Weston-super-Mare, Bristol, Cheltenham Spa and Swindon - London

Route Diagram - see first Page of Table 125

Mondays to Fridays

		GW	GW	GW	GW	XC	XC	XC	AW	GW	GW	GW	GW	XC	GW	AW	GW	GW	LM	AW	AW
				FO	FX														FO	FO	FX
		1		◇1	◇1	◇1	◇1	◇1		◇1	◇1			◇1	◇1			◇1	A		
Swansea	d									20 28											
Neath	d									20 40											
Port Talbot Parkway	d									20 48											
Bridgend	d								20 38	21 00										22 38	22 38
Cardiff Central 7	d							21 05	21 12	21 25				21 50						23 20	23 19
Newport (South Wales)	d							21 21	21 27	21 39				22 05						23 40	23 40
Weston-super-Mare	d														22 01						
Bristol Temple Meads 10	d										21 50				22 35						
Bristol Parkway 7	a									21 59											
	d									22 01											
Bath Spa 7	d										22 02				22 47						
Chippenham	d										22 15				23 00						
Worcester Shrub Hill	d			21 03	21 03								21 32				22 28	22 43	23 46		
Cheltenham Spa	d	20 48	21 00			21 11	21 52					22 01	22 07			23 00	23 05		00 09		
Gloucester 7	d	21 04	21a11			21a22	22a01	22a02	22a21			22 14	22a21	22a46		23a12	23a17		00a20	00a39	00a39
Stonehouse	d	21 17										22 26									
Stroud	d	21 23										22 31									
Kemble	d	21 37										22 46									
Swindon	a	21 51								22 27	22 33	23 05			23 14						
	d									22 28	22 34				23 16						
Didcot Parkway	a										22 50				23 33			00 20			
Reading 7	a			22 58	22 58					23 02	23 06				23 53			00 38			
Slough 3	a			23 12	23 15													00 55			
London Paddington 15 ⊖	a			23 36	23 36					23 38	23 41				00 33			01 17			

Saturdays

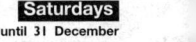

until 31 December

		GW	GW	LM	GW	GW	GW	GW	XC	XC	GW	GW	GW	XC	GW	AW	GW	GW	GW	XC	GW	AW	GW
		◇1	◇1		B	◇1		◇1	◇1	◇1	◇1	◇1	◇1	◇1			◇1	◇1	◇	◇1	◇1		◇1
Swansea	d							03 58			04 58						05 28				05 58		
Neath	d							04 10			05 10						05 40				06 10		
Port Talbot Parkway	d							04 18			05 18						05 48				06 18		
Bridgend	d							04 30			05 30						06 00				06 30		
Cardiff Central 7	d							04 55			05 55					06 12	06 25			06 40	06 55	07 12	
Newport (South Wales)	d							05 09			06 09					06 28	06 39			06 55	07 09	07 27	
Weston-super-Mare	d	22p01																06 24					
Bristol Temple Meads 10	d	22p35			02 35	05 30		06 00		06 15		06 30						07 00					07 30
Bristol Parkway 7	a									06 23	06 29						06 59				07 29		
	d									06 25	06 31						07 01				07 31		
Bath Spa 7	d	22p47				05 43		06 13				06 43						07 13					07 43
Chippenham	d	23p00				05 55		06 25				06 55						07 25					07 55
Worcester Shrub Hill	d		22p43	23p46									06 12						06 47				
Cheltenham Spa	d			00 09			05 30		06 04					06 43	06 48				07 13				
Gloucester 7	d			00a20			05 44		06a13	06a54				06a54	06a58	07a20			07a24	07a44		08a21	
Stonehouse	d						05 56																
Stroud	d						06 01																
Kemble	d						06 16																
Swindon	a	23p14			03 15	06 09	06 32	06 39			06 57	07 09					07 27	07 40			07 57		08 09
	d	23p16			03 17	06 11		06 41			06 59	07 11					07 29	07 41			07 59		08 11
Didcot Parkway	a	23p33	00 20			06 28		06 58			07 16	07 28					07 46	07 59			08 16		08 28
Reading 7	a	23p53	00 38		04s00	06 43		07 14			07 31	07 44	07 54				08 00	08 14			08 31		08 44
Slough 3	a		00 55										08 09										
London Paddington 15 ⊖	a	00 33	01 17		05 13	07 14		07 44			08 07	08 14	08 29				08 32	08 44			09 02		09 14

A until 23 March

B The Night Riviera

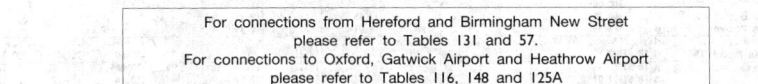

For connections from Hereford and Birmingham New Street please refer to Tables 131 and 57.
For connections to Oxford, Gatwick Airport and Heathrow Airport please refer to Tables 116, 148 and 125A

Table 125

Saturdays
until 31 December

South Wales, Weston-super-Mare, Bristol, Cheltenham Spa and Swindon - London

Route Diagram - see first Page of Table 125

		GW	GW	GW	GW	AW		XC	XC	GW	GW	GW	AW	GW	GW	GW		XC	AW	GW	GW	GW	XC	GW	GW
		◇1	◇1	◇1	◇1			◇1	◇1	◇1	◇1	◇1			◇1	◇1		◇1			◇1	◇1	◇1	◇1	◇1
									A	B		B			B			A							
		🍽	🍽	🍽	🍽			🛒	🛒	🍽Ø	🍽	🍽Ø			🍽Ø	🍽		🛒			🍽	🍽	🛒	🍽	🍽
Swansea	d		06 28							06 58					07 28						07 58				
Neath	d		06 40							07 10					07 40						08 10				
Port Talbot Parkway	d		06 48							07 18					07 48						08 18				
Bridgend	d		07 00							07 30					08 00				08 23		08 30				
Cardiff Central 7	d		07 25						07 45	07 55					08 25			08 45	09 12		08 55				
Newport (South Wales)	d		07 39						08 00	08 09					08 39			09 00	09 26		09 09				
Weston-super-Mare	d				07 24											08 30									
Bristol Temple Meads 10	d				08 00						08 30			08 41		09 00								09 30	
Bristol Parkway 7	a		07 59							08 30				08 52	08 59						09 30				
	d		08 01							08 31				08 52	09 01						09 31				
Bath Spa 7	d				08 13						08 43					09 13								09 43	
Chippenham	d				08 25						08 55					09 25				09 31				09 55	
Worcester Shrub Hill	d	07 08										08 04													09 02
Cheltenham Spa	d			07 30		07 45		08 11					08 45									08 59	09 11		
Gloucester 7	d			07 46		07a57		08a22	08a45				08a57	09a33				09a44	10a19			09 16	09a22		
Stonehouse	d			07 58																		09 29			
Stroud	d			08 03																		09 34			
Kemble	d			08 17																		09 48			
Swindon	a		08 27	08 33	08 39					08 58	09 09				09 27	09 40				09 49	09 57	10 02		10 10	
	d		08 29	08 35	08 41					08 59	09 11				09 29	09 41					09 59	10 04		10 11	
Didcot Parkway	a		08 46	08 51	08 58					09 16	09 28				09 46						10 16	10 21		10 28	
Reading 7	a	08 54	09 00	09 07	09 14					09 32	09 45	09 54			10 00	10 11					10 32	10 36		10 45	10 54
Slough 3	a	09 09										10 09													11 09
London Paddington 15 ⊖	a	09 29	09 32	09 37	09 44					10 02	10 14	10 29			10 32	10 39					11 02	11 08		11 14	11 29

		GW		GW	GW	GW	XC	XC	GW	GW	AW	AW		GW	GW	GW	GW	XC	XC	GW	GW	GW		GW	AW
																				R					
		◇1			◇1		◇1	◇1	◇1	◇1				◇	◇1	◇1	◇1	◇1	◇1		◇1	◇1		◇1	
								A											A						
		🍽			🍽		🛒	🛒	🍽	🛒					🍽	🍽	🍽	🛒	🛒		🍽	🛒		🍽	
Swansea	d	08 28													09 28									10 28	
Neath	d	08 40													09 40									10 40	
Port Talbot Parkway	d	08 48													09 48									10 48	
Bridgend	d	09 00										09 40			10 00									11 00	
Cardiff Central 7	d	09 25						09 45				10 12			10 25				10 45					11 25	
Newport (South Wales)	d	09 39						10 00				10 27			10 39				11 00					11 39	
Weston-super-Mare	d																								
Bristol Temple Meads 10	d				10 00				10 30					10 41		11 00					11 30				
Bristol Parkway 7	a	09 59												10 52	10 59									11 59	
	d	10 01												10 52	11 01									12 01	
Bath Spa 7	d				10 13				10 43							11 13					11 43				
Chippenham	d				10 25				10 55							11 25					11 55				
Worcester Shrub Hill	d			09 08						10 08										11 06		11 15			
Cheltenham Spa	d			09 35		10 01	10 11				10 45						11 00	11 11		11 34					11 45
Gloucester 7	d			09a44		10 15	10a22	10a44			10a56	11a21		11a32			11 16	11a22	11a44	11a44					11a57
Stonehouse	d					10 27											11 29								
Stroud	d					10 32											11 34								
Kemble	d					10 47											11 48								
Swindon	a	10 28			10 39	11 04			11 09						11 27	11 39	12 02				12 09			12 27	
	d	10 29			10 41				11 11						11 29	11 41	12 04				12 11			12 29	
Didcot Parkway	a	10 47							11 28						11 46		12 21				12 28			12 46	
Reading 7	a	11 01			11 12				11 44	11 54					12 00	12 11	12 37				12 44	12 53		13 00	
Slough 3	a									12 09												13 09			
London Paddington 15 ⊖	a	11 33			11 40				12 14	12 29					12 32	12 39	13 07				13 12	13 30		13 33	

		GW	GW	XC	XC	AW	GW	GW		GW	GW	GW	XC	GW	XC	GW	GW	AW		AW	GW	GW	GW	XC	XC
		◇1		◇1	◇1		◇1	◇		◇1	◇1	◇1	◇1	◇	◇1	◇1	◇1				◇1	◇1		◇1	◇1
					A										A										A
		🍽		🛒	🛒		🍽			🍽	🍽	🍽	🛒		🛒	🍽	🍽			🛒	🍽	🍽		🛒	🛒
Swansea	d									11 28											12 28				
Neath	d									11 40											12 40				
Port Talbot Parkway	d									11 48											12 48				
Bridgend	d					11 38				12 00										12 40	13 00				
Cardiff Central 7	d				11 45	12 12				12 25					12 45					13 12	13 25				13 45
Newport (South Wales)	d				12 00	12 27				12 39					13 00					13 27	13 39				14 00
Weston-super-Mare	d																								
Bristol Temple Meads 10	d	12 00					12 30	12 41			13 00					13 30						14 00			
Bristol Parkway 7	a							12 52		12 59											13 59				
	d							12 52		13 01											14 01				
Bath Spa 7	d	12 13					12 43				13 13					13 43						14 13			
Chippenham	d	12 25					12 55				13 25					13 55						14 25			
Worcester Shrub Hill	d													12 54			13 04								
Cheltenham Spa	d		12 01	12 11								13 00	13 11	13 20				13 45					14 01	14 11	
Gloucester 7	d		12 15	12a22	12a44	13a21		13a34				13 16	13a22	13a32	13a44			13a57		14a21			14 15	14a22	14a44
Stonehouse	d		12 27									13 29											14 27		
Stroud	d		12 32									13 34											14 32		
Kemble	d		12 47									13 48											14 47		
Swindon	a	12 40	13 04				13 09			13 27	13 39	14 02				14 09					14 27	14 39	15 04		
	d	12 41					13 11			13 29	13 41	14 04				14 11					14 29	14 41			
Didcot Parkway	a						13 28			13 46		14 21				14 28					14 46				
Reading 7	a	13 10					13 44			14 00	14 11	14 38				14 44	14 53				15 00	15 10			
Slough 3	a																15 10								
London Paddington 15 ⊖	a	13 41					14 14			14 32	14 39	15 09				15 14	15 29				15 32	15 39			

A 🛒 from Newport (South Wales)

B 🍽 from Reading Ø to Reading

For connections from Hereford and Birmingham New Street
please refer to Tables 131 and 57.
For connections to Oxford, Gatwick Airport and Heathrow Airport
please refer to Tables 116, 148 and 125A

Saturdays

until 31 December

South Wales, Weston-super-Mare, Bristol, Cheltenham Spa and Swindon - London

Route Diagram - see first Page of Table 125

		GW	AW	GW		GW	GW	GW	GW	XC	GW	GW	GW	XC		AW	GW	GW	GW	XC	XC	GW	GW	AW	
		◇1		◇		◇1	◇1		◇1	◇1	◇1	◇1	◇	◇1			◇1	◇1		◇1	◇1	◇1	◇1		
														A											
		⊡	⊥			⊡	⊡		⊡	⊥	⊡	⊥		⊥			⊡	⊡		⊥		⊡	⊡		
Swansea	d					13 28											14 28								
Neath	d					13 40											14 40								
Port Talbot Parkway	d					13 48											14 48								
Bridgend	d					14 00										14 38	15 00								
Cardiff Central 7	d					14 25								14 45		15 12	15 25				15 45				
Newport (South Wales)	d					14 39								15 00		15 27	15 39				16 00				
Weston-super-Mare	d																								
Bristol Temple Meads 10	d	14 30		14 41			15 00				15 30							16 00				16 30			
Bristol Parkway 7	a			14 52		14 59											15 59								
	d			14 52		15 01											16 01								
Bath Spa 7	d	14 43					15 13				15 43							16 13				16 43			
Chippenham	d	14 55					15 25	15 30			15 55							16 25				16 55			
Worcester Shrub Hill	d											15 01	15 06										16 04		
Cheltenham Spa	d		14 45						15 00	15 11			15 34						16 01	16 11				16 45	
Gloucester 7	d		14a56	15a32					15 16	15a22			15a42	15a44		16a19			16 15	16a22	16a44			16a56	
Stonehouse	d								15 29										16 27						
Stroud	d								15 34										16 32						
Kemble	d								15 48										16 47						
Swindon	a	15 09				15 27	15 39	15 50	16 02		16 09						16 27	16 39	17 04			17 09			
	d	15 11				15 29	15 41		16 04		16 11						16 29	16 41				17 11			
Didcot Parkway	a	15 28				15 46			16 21		16 28						16 46					17 28			
Reading 7	a	15 44				16 00	16 11		16 38		16 44	16 55					17 00	17 10				17 44	17 55		
Slough 3	a											17 10											18 10		
London Paddington 15 ⊖	a	16 14				16 32	16 39		17 07		17 14	17 29					17 32	17 38				18 14	18 29		

		AW	GW	GW	GW	GW	XC	XC	GW	GW		GW	AW	AW	GW	GW	GW	XC	XC	GW		GW	AW	AW	GW
				◇1	◇1	◇1	◇1	◇1	◇1	◇1					◇1	◇1		◇1	◇1	◇1		◇1			
																			A						
				⊡	⊡	⊡	⊥		⊡	⊥					⊡	⊡			⊥	⊡		⊥			
Swansea	d			15 28											16 28										
Neath	d			15 40											16 40										
Port Talbot Parkway	d			15 48											16 48										
Bridgend	d	15 40		16 00										16 38	17 00									17 38	
Cardiff Central 7	d	16 12		16 25				16 45						17 12	17 25				17 45					18 12	
Newport (South Wales)	d	16 26		16 39				17 00						17 27	17 39				18 00					18 27	
Weston-super-Mare	d																								
Bristol Temple Meads 10	d		16 41		17 00				17 30							18 00				18 30					18 41
Bristol Parkway 7	a		16 52	16 59											17 59										18 52
	d		16 52	17 01											18 01										18 52
Bath Spa 7	d				17 13				17 43							18 13				18 43					
Chippenham	d				17 25				17 55							18 25				18 55					
Worcester Shrub Hill	d									17 02		17 08										18 06			
Cheltenham Spa	d					17 00	17 11					17 34	17 45				18 01	18 18					18 45		
Gloucester 7	d	17a19	17a33			17 16	17a22	17a44				17a44	17a56	18a20			18 15	18a29	18a44				18a56	19a20	19a33
Stonehouse	d					17 29											18 27								
Stroud	d					17 34											18 32								
Kemble	d					17 48											18 47								
Swindon	a			17 27	17 39	18 02			18 09						18 27	18 39	19 04			19 09					
	d			17 29	17 41	18 04			18 11						18 29	18 41				19 11					
Didcot Parkway	a			17 46		18 21			18 28						18 46					19 28					
Reading 7	a			18 00	18 11	18 38			18 44	18 55					19 00	19 10				19 44		19 55			
Slough 3	a									19 10												20 10			
London Paddington 15 ⊖	a			18 32	18 39	19 08			19 14	19 29					19 32	19 39				20 14		20 29			

		GW	GW	XC	GW	GW		GW	XC	AW	GW	GW	GW	GW	GW	XC		XC	GW	XC	GW	GW	GW	GW	XC
		◇1	◇1	◇1	◇1	◇1			◇1			◇1		◇1	◇1	◇1		◇1		◇1		◇1	◇1		◇1
		⊡	⊡		⊡							⊡		⊡								⊡			
Swansea	d	17 28										18 28										19 28			
Neath	d	17 40										18 40										19 40			
Port Talbot Parkway	d	17 48										18 48										19 48			
Bridgend	d	18 00										19 00										20 00			
Cardiff Central 7	d	18 25							18 45			19 25						20 00				20 25			20 50
Newport (South Wales)	d	18 39							19 00			19 39						20 15				20 39			21 05
Weston-super-Mare	d													20 10											
Bristol Temple Meads 10	d				19 30						19 41			20 33							20 43				
Bristol Parkway 7	a	18 59									19 52	19 59									20 52	21 01			
	d	19 01									19 52	20 01									20 52	21 01			
Bath Spa 7	d				19 43									20 46											
Chippenham	d				19 55									20 58											
Worcester Shrub Hill	d					19 02		19 07							20 06								21 15		
Cheltenham Spa	d		19 00	19 11				19 34		19 45			20 01			20 11			21 02	21 11				21 19	
Gloucester 7	d		19 16	19a22				19a42	19a44	19a56	20a33		20 15			20a22		21a04	21a12	21a22	21a34			21 35	21a48
Stonehouse	d		19 29										20 27											21 47	
Stroud	d		19 34										20 32											21 52	
Kemble	d		19 48										20 47											22 07	
Swindon	a	19 27	20 03		20 09							20 27	21 03	21 13								21 29		22 24	
	d	19 29	20 05		20 11							20 29		21 14								21 29			
Didcot Parkway	a	19 46	20 22		20 28							20 46		21 31	21 43							21 47	22 47		
Reading 7	a	20 00	20 38		20 44	20 54						21 06		21 48	21 59							21 59	23 04		
Slough 3	a					21 09									22 14								23 23		
London Paddington 15 ⊖	a	20 32	21 07		21 14	21 29						21 36		22 16	22 32							22 37	23 43		

A ⊥ from Newport (South Wales)

For connections from Hereford and Birmingham New Street please refer to Tables 131 and 57.
For connections to Oxford, Gatwick Airport and Heathrow Airport please refer to Tables 116, 148 and 125A

Table 125

Saturdays
until 31 December

South Wales, Weston-super-Mare, Bristol, Cheltenham Spa and Swindon - London

Route Diagram - see first Page of Table 125

		GW		XC	GW	GW
		◇1		◇1		◇1
		☕				☕
Swansea	d					
Neath	d					
Port Talbot Parkway	d					
Bridgend	d					
Cardiff Central 7	d					
Newport (South Wales)	d					
Weston-super-Mare	d					21 53
Bristol Temple Meads 10	d	21 47				22 30
Bristol Parkway 7	a					
	d					
Bath Spa 7	d	22 02				22 43
Chippenham	d	22 15				22 55
Worcester Shrub Hill	d				21 31	
Cheltenham Spa	d			21 50	22 01	
Gloucester 7	d			21a59	22a10	
Stonehouse	d					
Stroud	d					
Kemble	d					
Swindon	a	22 29				23 10
	d	22 31				23 11
Didcot Parkway	a	22 48				23 28
Reading 7	a	23 04				23 51
Slough 3	a					
London Paddington 15 ⊖	a	23 36				00 34

Saturdays
7 January to 24 March

		GW	GW	LM	GW	GW	GW	GW	XC	XC		GW	GW	GW	XC	GW	AW	GW	GW	GW		XC	GW	AW	GW
					R																				
		◇1	◇1			◇1		◇1	◇1	◇1		◇1	◇1	◇1	◇1			◇1	◇1	◇		◇1	◇1		◇1
					A 🛏																				
		☕			☕	☕		☕		🛒		☕	☕	☕				☕	☕				☕		☕
Swansea	d							03 58				04 58						05 28					05 58		
Neath	d							04 10				05 10						05 40					06 10		
Port Talbot Parkway	d							04 18				05 18						05 48					06 18		
Bridgend	d							04 30				05 30						06 00					06 30		
Cardiff Central 7	d							04 55				05 55					06 12	06 25				06 40	06 55	07 12	
Newport (South Wales)	d							05 09				06 09					06 28	06 39				06 55	07 09	07 27	
Weston-super-Mare	d	22p01																	06 24						
Bristol Temple Meads 10	d	22p35			02 35	05 30		06 00		06 15			06 30						07 00						07 30
Bristol Parkway 7	a									06 23		06 29						06 59					07 29		
	d									06 25		06 31						07 01					07 31		
Bath Spa 7	d	22p47				05 43		06 13					06 43						07 13						07 43
Chippenham	d	23p00				05 55		06 25					06 55						07 25						07 55
Worcester Shrub Hill	d		22p43	23p46										06 12						06 47					
Cheltenham Spa	d			00 09			05 30		06 04						06 43	06 48				07 13					
Gloucester 7	d			00a20			05 44		06a13	06a54					06a54	06a58	07a20			07a24		07a44		08a21	
Stonehouse	d						05 56																		
Stroud	d						06 01																		
Kemble	d						06 16																		
Swindon	a	23p14			03 15	06 09	06 32	06 39				06 57	07 09					07 27	07 40				07 57		08 09
	d	23p16			03 17	06 11		06 41				06 59	07 11					07 29	07 41				07 59		08 11
Didcot Parkway	a	23p33	00 20			06 28		06 58				07 16	07 28					07 46	07 59				08 16		08 28
Reading 7	a	23p53	00 38		04s00	06 43		07 14				07 31	07 44	07 54				08 00	08 14				08 31		08 44
Slough 3	a		00 55											08 09											
London Paddington 15 ⊖	a	00 33	01 17		05 13	07 14		07 44				08 07	08 14	08 29				08 32	08 44				09 02		09 14

A The Night Riviera

For connections from Hereford and Birmingham New Street please refer to Tables 131 and 57.
For connections to Oxford, Gatwick Airport and Heathrow Airport please refer to Tables 116, 148 and 125A

Table 125

Saturdays

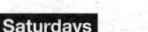

7 January to 24 March

South Wales, Weston-super-Mare, Bristol, Cheltenham Spa and Swindon - London

Route Diagram - see first Page of Table 125

		GW	GW	GW	GW	AW		XC	XC	GW	GW	GW	AW	GW	GW	GW		XC	AW	GW	GW	GW	XC	GW	GW
		◇1	◇1	◇1	◇1			◇1	◇1	◇1	◇1	◇1			◇1	◇1		◇1			◇1	◇1	◇1	◇1	◇1
									A	B		B			B			A							
		🍽	🍽	🍽	🍽			🛒	🛒	🍽Ø	🍽	🍽Ø			🍽Ø	🍽		🛒			🍽	🍽	🛒	🍽	🍽
Swansea	d		06 28							06 58					07 28						07 58				
Neath	d		06 40							07 10					07 40						08 10				
Port Talbot Parkway	d		06 48							07 18					07 48						08 18				
Bridgend	d		07 00							07 30					08 00				08 23		08 30				
Cardiff Central 7	d		07 25						07 45	07 55					08 25			08 45	09 12		08 55				
Newport (South Wales)	d		07 39						08 00	08 09					08 39			09 00	09 26		09 09				
Weston-super-Mare	d				07 24											08 30									
Bristol Temple Meads 10	d				08 00						08 30			08 41		09 00								09 30	
Bristol Parkway 7	a		07 59							08 30				08 52	08 59						09 30				
	d		08 01							08 31				08 52	09 01						09 31				
Bath Spa 7	d				08 13						08 43					09 13								09 43	
Chippenham	d				08 25						08 55					09 25				09 31				09 55	
Worcester Shrub Hill	d	07 08										08 04													09 02
Cheltenham Spa	d			07 30		07 45		08 11					08 45									08 59	09 11		
Gloucester 7	d			07 46		07a57		08a22	08a45				08a57	09a33				09a44	10a19			09e16	09a22		
Stonehouse	d			07 58																		09 29			
Stroud	d			08 03																		09 34			
Kemble	d			08 17																		09 48			
Swindon	a		08 27	08 33	08 39					08 58	09 09				09 27	09 40				09 49	09 57	10 02		10 10	
	d		08 29	08 35	08 41					08 59	09 11				09 29	09 41					09 59	10 04		10 11	
Didcot Parkway	a		08 46	08 51	08 58					09 16	09 28				09 46						10 16	10 21		10 28	
Reading 7	a	08 54	09 00	09 07	09 14					09 32	09 45	09 54			10 00	10 11					10 32	10 36		10 45	10 54
Slough 3	a	09 09										10 09													11 09
London Paddington 15 ⊖	a	09 29	09 32	09 37	09 44					10 02	10 14	10 29			10 32	10 39					11 02	11 08		11 14	11 29

		GW		GW	GW	GW	XC	XC	GW	GW	AW	AW		GW	GW	GW	GW	XC	XC	GW	GW	GW		GW	AW
																				▪					
		◇1			◇1		◇1	◇1	◇1	◇1				◇	◇1	◇1	◇1	◇1	◇1		◇1	◇1		◇1	
								A											A						
		🍽			🍽		🛒	🛒	🍽	🛒					🍽	🍽	🍽	🛒	🛒		🍽	🛒		🍽	
Swansea	d	08 28													09 28									10 28	
Neath	d	08 40													09 40									10 40	
Port Talbot Parkway	d	08 48													09 48									10 48	
Bridgend	d	09 00										09 40			10 00									11 00	
Cardiff Central 7	d	09 25						09 45				10 12			10 25				10 45					11 25	
Newport (South Wales)	d	09 39						10 00				10 27			10 39				11 00					11 39	
Weston-super-Mare	d																								
Bristol Temple Meads 10	d				10 00				10 30					10 41		11 00					11 30				
Bristol Parkway 7	a	09 59												10 52	10 59									11 59	
	d	10 01												10 52	11 01									12 01	
Bath Spa 7	d				10 13				10 43							11 13					11 43				
Chippenham	d				10 25				10 55							11 25					11 55				
Worcester Shrub Hill	d			09 08						10 08										11 06		11 15			
Cheltenham Spa	d			09 35		10 01	10 11				10 45						11 00	11 11		11 34					11 45
Gloucester 7	d			09a44		10 15	10a22	10a44			10a56	11a21		11a32			11 16	11a22	11a44	11a44					11a57
Stonehouse	d					10 27											11 29								
Stroud	d					10 32											11 34								
Kemble	d					10 47											11 48								
Swindon	a	10 28			10 39	11 04			11 09						11 27	11 39	12 02				12 09			12 27	
	d	10 29			10 41				11 11						11 29	11 41	12 04				12 11			12 29	
Didcot Parkway	a	10 47							11 28						11 46		12 21				12 28			12 46	
Reading 7	a	11 01			11 12				11 44	11 54					12 00	12 11	12 37				12 44	12 53		13 00	
Slough 3	a									12 09												13 09			
London Paddington 15 ⊖	a	11 33			11 40				12 14	12 29					12 32	12 39	13 07				13 12	13 30		13 33	

		GW	GW	XC	XC	AW	GW	GW		GW	GW	GW	XC	GW	XC	GW	GW	AW		AW	GW	GW	GW	XC	XC
		◇1		◇1	◇1		◇1	◇		◇1	◇1	◇1	◇1	◇	◇1	◇1	◇1				◇1	◇1		◇1	◇1
					A										A		C				C	D			A
		🍽		🛒	🛒		🍽			🍽	🍽	🍽	🛒		🛒	🍽	🍽			🛒	🍽	🍽		🛒	🛒
Swansea	d									11 28											12 28				
Neath	d									11 40											12 40				
Port Talbot Parkway	d									11 48											12 48				
Bridgend	d					11 38				12 00										12 40	13 00				
Cardiff Central 7	d				11 45	12 12				12 25					12 45					13 12	13 25				13 45
Newport (South Wales)	d				12 00	12 27				12 39					13 00					13 27	13 39				14 00
Weston-super-Mare	d																								
Bristol Temple Meads 10	d	12 00					12 30	12 41			13 00					13 30						14 00			
Bristol Parkway 7	a							12 52		12 59											13 59				
	d							12 52		13 01											14 01				
Bath Spa 7	d	12 13					12 43				13 13					13 43						14 13			
Chippenham	d	12 25					12 55				13 25					13 55						14 25			
Worcester Shrub Hill	d													12 54			13 04								
Cheltenham Spa	d		12 01	12 11								13 00	13 11	13 20				13 45					14 01	14 11	
Gloucester 7	d		12 15	12a22	12a44	13a21		13a34				13 16	13a22	13a32	13a44			13a57		14a21			14 15	14a22	14a44
Stonehouse	d		12 27									13 29											14 27		
Stroud	d		12 32									13 34											14 32		
Kemble	d		12 47									13 48											14 47		
Swindon	a	12 40	13 04				13 09			13 27	13 39	14 02				14 09					14 27	14 39	15 04		
	d	12 41					13 11			13 29	13 41	14 04				14 11					14 29	14 41			
Didcot Parkway	a						13 28			13 46		14 21				14 28					14 46				
Reading 7	a	13 10					13 44			14 00	14 11	14 38				14 44	14 53				15 00	15 10			
Slough 3	a																15 10								
London Paddington 15 ⊖	a	13 41					14 14			14 32	14 39	15 09				15 14	15 29				15 32	15 39			

A 🛒 from Newport (South Wales)

B 🍽 from Reading Ø to Reading

C from 7 January until 11 February

D from 7 January until 4 February, 24 March

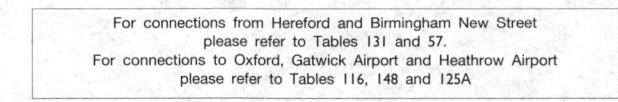

For connections from Hereford and Birmingham New Street please refer to Tables 131 and 57.
For connections to Oxford, Gatwick Airport and Heathrow Airport please refer to Tables 116, 148 and 125A

Table 125

Saturdays

7 January to 24 March

South Wales, Weston-super-Mare, Bristol, Cheltenham Spa and Swindon - London

Route Diagram - see first Page of Table 125

		GW	AW	GW		GW	GW	GW	GW	XC	GW	GW	GW	XC		AW	GW	GW	GW	XC	XC	GW	GW	AW	
		◇1		◇		◇1	◇1		◇1	◇1	◇1	◇1	◇	◇1			◇1	◇1		◇1	◇1	◇1	◇1		
														A											
		🍽	🛒			🍽	🍽		🍽	🛒	🍽	🛒		🛒			🍽	🍽		🛒		🍽	🍽		
Swansea	d					13 28											14 28								
Neath	d					13 40											14 40								
Port Talbot Parkway	d					13 48											14 48								
Bridgend	d					14 00										14 38	15 00								
Cardiff Central 7	d					14 25								14 45		15 12	15 25				15 45				
Newport (South Wales)	d					14 39								15 00		15 27	15 39				16 00				
Weston-super-Mare	d																								
Bristol Temple Meads 10	d	14 30		14 41			15 00				15 30							16 00				16 30			
Bristol Parkway 7	a			14 52		14 59											15 59								
	d			14 52		15 01											16 01								
Bath Spa 7	d	14 43					15 13				15 43							16 13				16 43			
Chippenham	d	14 55					15 25	15 30			15 55							16 25				16 55			
Worcester Shrub Hill	d											15 01	15 06										16 04		
Cheltenham Spa	d		14 45						15 00	15 11			15 34						16 01	16 11				16 45	
Gloucester 7	d		14a56	15a32					15 16	15a22			15a42	15a44		16a19			16 15	16a22	16a44			16a56	
Stonehouse	d								15 29										16 27						
Stroud	d								15 34										16 32						
Kemble	d								15 48										16 47						
Swindon	a	15 09				15 27	15 39	15 50	16 02		16 09						16 27	16 39	17 04			17 09			
	d	15 11				15 29	15 41		16 04		16 11						16 29	16 41				17 11			
Didcot Parkway	a	15 28				15 46			16 21		16 28						16 46					17 28			
Reading 7	a	15 44				16 00	16 11		16 38		16 44	16 55					17 00	17 10				17 44	17 55		
Slough 3	a											17 10											18 10		
London Paddington 15 ⊖	a	16 14				16 32	16 39		17 07		17 14	17 29					17 32	17 38				18 14	18 29		

		AW	GW	GW	GW	GW	XC	XC	GW	GW		GW	AW	AW	GW	GW	GW	XC	XC	GW		GW	AW	AW	GW
				◇1	◇1	◇1	◇1	◇1	◇1	◇1					◇1	◇1		◇1	◇1	◇1		◇1			
				B	B					B									A	B					
				🍽	🍽	🍽	🛒		🍽	🛒					🍽	🍽			🛒	🍽		🛒			
Swansea	d			15 28											16 28										
Neath	d			15 40											16 40										
Port Talbot Parkway	d			15 48											16 48										
Bridgend	d	15 40		16 00										16 38	17 00									17 38	
Cardiff Central 7	d	16 12		16 25				16 45						17 12	17 25				17 45					18 12	
Newport (South Wales)	d	16 26		16 39				17 00						17 27	17 39				18 00					18 27	
Weston-super-Mare	d																								
Bristol Temple Meads 10	d		16 41		17 00				17 30							18 00				18 30					18 41
Bristol Parkway 7	a		16 52	16 59											17 59										18 52
	d		16 52	17 01											18 01										18 52
Bath Spa 7	d				17 13				17 43							18 13				18 43					
Chippenham	d				17 25				17 55							18 25				18 55					
Worcester Shrub Hill	d									17 02		17 08										18 06			
Cheltenham Spa	d					17 00	17 11					17 34	17 45				18 01	18 18					18 45		
Gloucester 7	d	17a19	17a33			17 16	17a22	17a44				17a44	17a56	18a20			18 15	18a29	18a44				18a56	19a20	19a33
Stonehouse	d					17 29											18 27								
Stroud	d					17 34											18 32								
Kemble	d					17 48											18 47								
Swindon	a			17 27	17 39	18 02			18 09						18 27	18 39	19 04			19 09					
	d			17 29	17 41	18 04			18 11						18 29	18 41				19 11					
Didcot Parkway	a			17 46		18 21			18 28						18 46					19 28					
Reading 7	a			18 00	18 11	18 38			18 44	18 55					19 00	19 10				19 44		19 55			
Slough 3	a									19 10												20 10			
London Paddington 15 ⊖	a			18 32	18 39	19 08			19 14	19 29					19 32	19 39				20 14		20 29			

		GW	GW	XC	GW	GW		GW	XC	AW	GW	GW	GW	GW	GW	XC		XC	GW	XC	GW	GW	GW	XC	GW
		◇1	◇1	◇1	◇1	◇1			◇1			◇1		◇1	◇1	◇1		◇1		◇1		◇1		◇1	◇1
		🍽	🍽		🍽							🍽		🍽								🍽			🍽
Swansea	d	17 28										18 28										19 28			
Neath	d	17 40										18 40										19 40			
Port Talbot Parkway	d	17 48										18 48										19 48			
Bridgend	d	18 00										19 00										20 00			
Cardiff Central 7	d	18 25							18 45			19 25						20 00				20 25		20 50	
Newport (South Wales)	d	18 39							19 00			19 39						20 15				20 39		21 05	
Weston-super-Mare	d													20 10											
Bristol Temple Meads 10	d				19 30						19 41			20 33							20 43				21 47
Bristol Parkway 7	a	18 59									19 52	19 59									20 52	21 01			
	d	19 01									19 52	20 01									20 52	21 01			
Bath Spa 7	d				19 43									20 46											22 02
Chippenham	d				19 55									20 58											22 15
Worcester Shrub Hill	d					19 02		19 07							20 06										
Cheltenham Spa	d		19 00	19 11				19 34		19 45			20 01			20 11			21 02	21 11			21 19		
Gloucester 7	d		19 16	19a22				19a42	19a44	19a56	20a33		20 15			20a22		21a04	21a12	21a22	21a34		21 35	21a48	
Stonehouse	d		19 29										20 27										21 47		
Stroud	d		19 34										20 32										21 52		
Kemble	d		19 48										20 47										22 07		
Swindon	a	19 27	20 03		20 09							20 27	21 03	21 13								21 29	22 24		22 29
	d	19 29	20 05		20 11							20 29		21 14								21 29			22 31
Didcot Parkway	a	19 46	20 22		20 28							20 46		21 31	21 43							21 47			22 48
Reading 7	a	20 00	20 38		20 44	20 54						21 06		21 52	21 58							21 59			23 04
Slough 3	a					21 09									22 13										
London Paddington 15 ⊖	a	20 32	21 07		21 14	21 29						21 36		22 22	22 31							22 38			23 36

A 🛒 from Newport (South Wales)

B from 7 January until 11 February

For connections from Hereford and Birmingham New Street please refer to Tables 131 and 57.
For connections to Oxford, Gatwick Airport and Heathrow Airport please refer to Tables 116, 148 and 125A

Table 125

Saturdays
7 January to 24 March

South Wales, Weston-super-Mare, Bristol, Cheltenham Spa and Swindon - London

Route Diagram - see first Page of Table 125

		GW		XC	GW	GW
		◇1		◇1		◇1
						☕
Swansea	d					
Neath	d					
Port Talbot Parkway	d					
Bridgend	d					
Cardiff Central 7	d					
Newport (South Wales)	d					
Weston-super-Mare	d					21 53
Bristol Temple Meads 10	d					22 30
Bristol Parkway 7	a					
	d					
Bath Spa 7	d					22 43
Chippenham	d					22 55
Worcester Shrub Hill	d	21 15			21 31	
Cheltenham Spa	d			21 50	22 01	
Gloucester 7	d			21a59	22a10	
Stonehouse	d					
Stroud	d					
Kemble	d					
Swindon	a					23 10
	d					23 11
Didcot Parkway	a	22 47				23 28
Reading 7	a	23 08				23 51
Slough 3	a	23 26				
London Paddington 15 ⊖	a	23 46				00 34

Saturdays
from 31 March

		GW	GW	LM	GW	GW	GW	GW	XC	XC		GW	GW	GW	XC	GW	AW	GW	GW	GW		XC	GW	AW	GW
					R																				
		◇1	◇1			◇1		◇1	◇1	◇1		◇1	◇1	◇1	◇1			◇1	◇1	◇		◇1	◇1		◇1
					A 🛏																				
		☕			☕	☕		☕		🛒		☕	☕	☕				☕	☕				☕		☕
Swansea	d							03 58				04 58						05 28					05 58		
Neath	d							04 10				05 10						05 40					06 10		
Port Talbot Parkway	d							04 18				05 18						05 48					06 18		
Bridgend	d							04 30				05 30						06 00					06 30		
Cardiff Central 7	d							04 55				05 55					06 12	06 25				06 40	06 55	07 12	
Newport (South Wales)	d							05 09				06 09					06 28	06 39				06 55	07 09	07 27	
Weston-super-Mare	d	22p01																	06 24						
Bristol Temple Meads 10	d	22p35			02 35	05 30		06 00		06 15			06 30						07 00						07 30
Bristol Parkway 7	a									06 23		06 29						06 59					07 29		
	d									06 25		06 31						07 01					07 31		
Bath Spa 7	d	22p47				05 43		06 13					06 43						07 13						07 43
Chippenham	d	23p00				05 55		06 25					06 55						07 25						07 55
Worcester Shrub Hill	d		22p43	00 10										06 12						06 47					
Cheltenham Spa	d			00 33			05 30		06 04						06 43	06 48				07 13					
Gloucester 7	d			00a43			05 44		06a13	06a54					06a54	06a58	07a20			07a24		07a44		08a21	
Stonehouse	d						05 56																		
Stroud	d						06 01																		
Kemble	d						06 16																		
Swindon	a	23p14			03 15	06 09	06 32	06 39				06 57	07 09					07 27	07 40				07 57		08 09
	d	23p16			03 17	06 11		06 41				06 59	07 11					07 29	07 41				07 59		08 11
Didcot Parkway	a	23p33	00 20			06 28		06 58				07 16	07 28					07 46	07 59				08 16		08 28
Reading 7	a	23p53	00 38		04s00	06 43		07 14				07 31	07 44	07 54				08 00	08 14				08 31		08 44
Slough 3	a		00 55											08 09											
London Paddington 15 ⊖	a	00 33	01 17		05 13	07 14		07 44				08 07	08 14	08 29				08 32	08 44				09 02		09 14

A The Night Riviera

For connections from Hereford and Birmingham New Street please refer to Tables 131 and 57.
For connections to Oxford, Gatwick Airport and Heathrow Airport please refer to Tables 116, 148 and 125A

Table 125

Saturdays
from 31 March

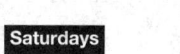

South Wales, Weston-super-Mare, Bristol, Cheltenham Spa and Swindon - London

Route Diagram - see first Page of Table 125

		GW	GW	GW	GW	AW		XC	XC	GW	GW	GW	AW	GW	GW	GW		XC	AW	GW	GW	GW	XC	GW	GW
		◇1 ☕	◇1 ☕	◇1 ☕	◇1 ☕			◇1 🛒	◇1 A 🛒	◇1 B ☕⊘	◇1 ☕	◇1 B ☕⊘			◇1 B ☕⊘	◇1 ☕		◇1 A 🛒			◇1 ☕	◇1 ☕	◇1 🛒	◇1 ☕	◇1 ☕
Swansea	d		06 28							06 58					07 28						07 58				
Neath	d		06 40							07 10					07 40						08 10				
Port Talbot Parkway	d		06 48							07 18					07 48						08 18				
Bridgend	d		07 00							07 30					08 00				08 23		08 30				
Cardiff Central 7	d		07 25						07 45	07 55					08 25			08 45	09 12		08 55				
Newport (South Wales)	d		07 39						08 00	08 09					08 39			09 00	09 26		09 09				
Weston-super-Mare	d				07 24											08 30									
Bristol Temple Meads 10	d				08 00						08 30			08 41		09 00								09 30	
Bristol Parkway 7	a		07 59							08 30				08 52	08 59						09 30				
	d		08 01							08 31				08 52	09 01						09 31				
Bath Spa 7	d				08 13						08 43					09 13								09 43	
Chippenham	d				08 25						08 55					09 25				09 31				09 55	
Worcester Shrub Hill	d	07 08										08 04													09 02
Cheltenham Spa	d			07 30		07 45		08 11					08 45									08 59	09 11		
Gloucester 7	d			07 46		07a57		08a22	08a45				08a57	09a33				09a44	10a19			09e16	09a22		
Stonehouse	d			07 58																		09 29			
Stroud	d			08 03																		09 34			
Kemble	d			08 17																		09 48			
Swindon	a		08 27	08 33	08 39					08 58	09 09				09 27	09 40				09 49	09 57	10 02		10 10	
	d		08 29	08 35	08 41					08 59	09 11				09 29	09 41					09 59	10 04		10 11	
Didcot Parkway	a		08 46	08 51	08 58					09 16	09 28				09 46						10 16	10 21		10 28	
Reading 7	a	08 54	09 00	09 07	09 14					09 32	09 45	09 54			10 00	10 11					10 32	10 36		10 45	10 54
Slough 3	a	09 09										10 09													11 09
London Paddington 15 ⊖	a	09 29	09 32	09 37	09 44					10 02	10 14	10 29			10 32	10 39					11 02	11 08		11 14	11 29

		GW		GW	GW	GW	XC	XC	GW	GW	AW	AW		GW	GW	GW	GW	XC	XC	GW	GW	GW		GW	AW
		◇1 ☕			◇1 ☕		◇1 🛒	◇1 A 🛒	◇1 ☕	◇1 🛒				◇	◇1 ☕	◇1 ☕	◇1 ☕	◇1 🛒	◇1 A 🛒	R	◇1 ☕	◇1 🛒		◇1 ☕	
Swansea	d	08 28													09 28									10 28	
Neath	d	08 40													09 40									10 40	
Port Talbot Parkway	d	08 48													09 48									10 48	
Bridgend	d	09 00										09 40			10 00									11 00	
Cardiff Central 7	d	09 25						09 45				10 12			10 25				10 45					11 25	
Newport (South Wales)	d	09 39						10 00				10 27			10 39				11 00					11 39	
Weston-super-Mare	d																								
Bristol Temple Meads 10	d				10 00				10 30					10 41		11 00					11 30				
Bristol Parkway 7	a	09 59												10 52	10 59									11 59	
	d	10 01												10 52	11 01									12 01	
Bath Spa 7	d				10 13				10 43							11 13					11 43				
Chippenham	d				10 25				10 55							11 25					11 55				
Worcester Shrub Hill	d			09 08						10 08										11 06		11 15			
Cheltenham Spa	d			09 35		10 01	10 11				10 45						11 00	11 11		11 34					11 45
Gloucester 7	d			09a44		10 15	10a22	10a44			10a56	11a21		11a32			11 16	11a22	11a44	11a44					11a57
Stonehouse	d					10 27											11 29								
Stroud	d					10 32											11 34								
Kemble	d					10 47											11 48								
Swindon	a	10 28			10 39	11 04			11 09						11 27	11 39	12 02				12 09			12 27	
	d	10 29			10 41				11 11						11 29	11 41	12 04				12 11			12 29	
Didcot Parkway	a	10 47							11 28						11 46		12 21				12 28			12 46	
Reading 7	a	11 01			11 12				11 44	11 54					12 00	12 11	12 37				12 44	12 53		13 00	
Slough 3	a									12 09												13 09			
London Paddington 15 ⊖	a	11 33			11 40				12 14	12 29					12 32	12 39	13 07				13 12	13 30		13 33	

		GW	GW	XC	XC	AW	GW	GW		GW	GW	GW	XC	GW	XC	GW	GW	AW		AW	GW	GW	GW	XC	XC
		◇1 ☕		◇1 🛒	◇1 A 🛒		◇1 ☕	◇		◇1 ☕	◇1 ☕	◇1 ☕	◇1 🛒	◇	◇1 A 🛒	◇1 ☕	◇1 ☕			🛒	◇1 ☕	◇1 ☕		◇1 🛒	◇1 A 🛒
Swansea	d									11 28											12 28				
Neath	d									11 40											12 40				
Port Talbot Parkway	d									11 48											12 48				
Bridgend	d					11 38				12 00										12 40	13 00				
Cardiff Central 7	d				11 45	12 12				12 25					12 45					13 12	13 25				13 45
Newport (South Wales)	d				12 00	12 27				12 39					13 00					13 27	13 39				14 00
Weston-super-Mare	d																								
Bristol Temple Meads 10	d	12 00					12 30	12 41			13 00					13 30						14 00			
Bristol Parkway 7	a							12 52		12 59											13 59				
	d							12 52		13 01											14 01				
Bath Spa 7	d	12 13					12 43				13 13					13 43						14 13			
Chippenham	d	12 25					12 55				13 25					13 55						14 25			
Worcester Shrub Hill	d													12 54			13 04								
Cheltenham Spa	d		12 01	12 11								13 00	13 11	13 20				13 45					14 01	14 11	
Gloucester 7	d		12 15	12a22	12a44	13a21		13a34				13 16	13a22	13a32	13a44			13a57		14a21			14 15	14a22	14a44
Stonehouse	d		12 27									13 29											14 27		
Stroud	d		12 32									13 34											14 32		
Kemble	d		12 47									13 48											14 47		
Swindon	a	12 40	13 04				13 09			13 27	13 39	14 02				14 09					14 27	14 39	15 04		
	d	12 41					13 11			13 29	13 41	14 04				14 11					14 29	14 41			
Didcot Parkway	a						13 28			13 46		14 21				14 28					14 46				
Reading 7	a	13 10					13 44			14 00	14 11	14 38				14 44	14 53				15 00	15 10			
Slough 3	a																15 10								
London Paddington 15 ⊖	a	13 41					14 14			14 32	14 39	15 09				15 14	15 29				15 32	15 39			

A 🛒 from Newport (South Wales)

B ☕ from Reading ⊘ to Reading

For connections from Hereford and Birmingham New Street please refer to Tables 131 and 57.
For connections to Oxford, Gatwick Airport and Heathrow Airport please refer to Tables 116, 148 and 125A

Table 125

Saturdays
from 31 March

South Wales, Weston-super-Mare, Bristol, Cheltenham Spa and Swindon - London

Route Diagram - see first Page of Table 125

		GW	AW	GW		GW	GW	GW	GW	XC	GW	GW	GW	XC		AW	GW	GW	GW	XC	XC	GW	GW	AW	
		◇1		◇		◇1	◇1		◇1	◇1	◇1	◇1	◇	◇1			◇1	◇1		◇1	◇1	◇1	◇1		
														A											
		🍴	🛒			🍴	🍴		🍴	🛒	🍴	🛒		🛒			🍴	🍴		🛒		🍴	🍴		
Swansea	d					13 28											14 28								
Neath	d					13 40											14 40								
Port Talbot Parkway	d					13 48											14 48								
Bridgend	d					14 00										14 38	15 00								
Cardiff Central 7	d					14 25								14 45		15 12	15 25				15 45				
Newport (South Wales)	d					14 39								15 00		15 27	15 39				16 00				
Weston-super-Mare	d																								
Bristol Temple Meads 10	d	14 30		14 41			15 00				15 30							16 00				16 30			
Bristol Parkway 7	a			14 52		14 59											15 59								
	d			14 52		15 01											16 01								
Bath Spa 7	d	14 43					15 13				15 43							16 13				16 43			
Chippenham	d	14 55					15 25	15 30			15 55							16 25				16 55			
Worcester Shrub Hill	d											15 01	15 06										16 04		
Cheltenham Spa	d		14 45						15 00	15 11			15 34						16 01	16 11				16 45	
Gloucester 7	d		14a56	15a32					15 16	15a22			15a42	15a44		16a19			16 15	16a22	16a44			16a56	
Stonehouse	d								15 29										16 27						
Stroud	d								15 34										16 32						
Kemble	d								15 48										16 47						
Swindon	a	15 09				15 27	15 39	15 50	16 02		16 09						16 27	16 39	17 04			17 09			
	d	15 11				15 29	15 41		16 04		16 11						16 29	16 41				17 11			
Didcot Parkway	a	15 28				15 46			16 21		16 28						16 46					17 28			
Reading 7	a	15 44				16 00	16 11		16 38		16 44	16 55					17 00	17 10				17 44	17 55		
Slough 3	a											17 10											18 10		
London Paddington 15 ⊖	a	16 14				16 32	16 39		17 07		17 14	17 29					17 32	17 38				18 14	18 29		

		AW	GW	GW	GW	GW	XC	XC	GW	GW		GW	AW	AW	GW	GW	GW	XC	XC	GW		GW	AW	AW	GW
				◇1	◇1	◇1	◇1	◇1	◇1	◇1					◇1	◇1		◇1	◇1	◇1		◇1			
																			A						
				🍴	🍴	🍴	🛒		🍴	🛒					🍴	🍴			🛒	🍴		🛒			
Swansea	d			15 28											16 28										
Neath	d			15 40											16 40										
Port Talbot Parkway	d			15 48											16 48										
Bridgend	d	15 40		16 00										16 38	17 00									17 38	
Cardiff Central 7	d	16 12		16 25				16 45						17 12	17 25				17 45					18 12	
Newport (South Wales)	d	16 26		16 39				17 00						17 27	17 39				18 00					18 27	
Weston-super-Mare	d																								
Bristol Temple Meads 10	d		16 41		17 00				17 30							18 00				18 30					18 41
Bristol Parkway 7	a		16 52	16 59											17 59										18 52
	d		16 52	17 01											18 01										18 52
Bath Spa 7	d				17 13				17 43							18 13				18 43					
Chippenham	d				17 25				17 55							18 25				18 55					
Worcester Shrub Hill	d									17 02		17 08										18 06			
Cheltenham Spa	d					17 00	17 11					17 34	17 45				18 01	18 18					18 45		
Gloucester 7	d	17a19	17a33			17 16	17a22	17a44				17a44	17a56	18a20			18 15	18a29	18a44				18a56	19a20	19a33
Stonehouse	d					17 29											18 27								
Stroud	d					17 34											18 32								
Kemble	d					17 48											18 47								
Swindon	a			17 27	17 39	18 02			18 09						18 27	18 39	19 04			19 09					
	d			17 29	17 41	18 04			18 11						18 29	18 41				19 11					
Didcot Parkway	a			17 46		18 21			18 28						18 46					19 28					
Reading 7	a			18 00	18 11	18 38			18 44	18 55					19 00	19 10				19 44		19 55			
Slough 3	a									19 10												20 10			
London Paddington 15 ⊖	a			18 32	18 39	19 08			19 14	19 29					19 32	19 39				20 14		20 29			

		GW	GW	XC	GW	GW		GW	XC	AW	GW	GW	GW	GW	GW	XC		XC	GW	XC	GW	GW	GW	GW	XC
		◇1	◇1	◇1	◇1	◇1			◇1			◇1		◇1	◇1	◇1		◇1		◇1		◇1	◇1		◇1
		🍴	🍴		🍴							🍴		🍴								🍴			
Swansea	d	17 28										18 28										19 28			
Neath	d	17 40										18 40										19 40			
Port Talbot Parkway	d	17 48										18 48										19 48			
Bridgend	d	18 00										19 00										20 00			
Cardiff Central 7	d	18 25							18 45			19 25						20 00				20 25			20 50
Newport (South Wales)	d	18 39							19 00			19 39						20 15				20 39			21 05
Weston-super-Mare	d													20 10											
Bristol Temple Meads 10	d				19 30						19 41			20 33							20 43				
Bristol Parkway 7	a	18 59									19 52	19 59									20 52	21 01			
	d	19 01									19 52	20 01									20 52	21 01			
Bath Spa 7	d				19 43									20 46											
Chippenham	d				19 55									20 58											
Worcester Shrub Hill	d					19 02		19 07							20 06								21 15		
Cheltenham Spa	d		19 00	19 11				19 34		19 45			20 01			20 11			21 02	21 11				21 19	
Gloucester 7	d		19 16	19a22				19a42	19a44	19a56	20a33		20 15			20a22		21a04	21a12	21a22	21a34			21 35	21a48
Stonehouse	d		19 29										20 27											21 47	
Stroud	d		19 34										20 32											21 52	
Kemble	d		19 48										20 47											22 07	
Swindon	a	19 27	20 03		20 09							20 27	21 03	21 13								21 29		22 24	
	d	19 29	20 05		20 11							20 29		21 14								21 29			
Didcot Parkway	a	19 46	20 22		20 28							20 46		21 31	21 43							21 47	22 47		
Reading 7	a	20 00	20 38		20 44	20 54						21 06		21 48	21 59							21 59	23 08		
Slough 3	a					21 09									22 14								23 26		
London Paddington 15 ⊖	a	20 32	21 07		21 14	21 29						21 36		22 16	22 32							22 37	23 46		

A 🛒 from Newport (South Wales)

For connections from Hereford and Birmingham New Street please refer to Tables 131 and 57.
For connections to Oxford, Gatwick Airport and Heathrow Airport please refer to Tables 116, 148 and 125A

Table 125

Saturdays
from 31 March

South Wales, Weston-super-Mare, Bristol, Cheltenham Spa and Swindon - London

Route Diagram - see first Page of Table 125

		GW		XC	GW	GW
		◇1		◇1		◇1
		☕				☕
Swansea	d					
Neath	d					
Port Talbot Parkway	d					
Bridgend	d					
Cardiff Central [7]	d					
Newport (South Wales)	d					
Weston-super-Mare	d					21 53
Bristol Temple Meads [10]	d	21 47				22 30
Bristol Parkway [7]	a					
	d					
Bath Spa [7]	d	22 02				22 43
Chippenham	d	22 15				22 55
Worcester Shrub Hill	d				21 31	
Cheltenham Spa	d			21 50	22 01	
Gloucester [7]	d			21a59	22a10	
Stonehouse	d					
Stroud	d					
Kemble	d					
Swindon	a	22 29				23 10
	d	22 31				23 11
Didcot Parkway	a	22 48				23 28
Reading [7]	a	23 04				23 49
Slough [3]	a					
London Paddington [15] ⊖	a	23 36				00 33

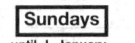

Sundays
until 1 January

		GW	GW	GW	GW	GW	XC	GW	GW	GW		GW	GW	GW	GW	GW	GW	XC	GW	GW	AW		XC	GW	XC
		◇1	◇1	1	◇1	◇1	◇1	◇1					◇1	◇1	◇1		◇1	◇1	◇1				◇1	◇1	◇1
		A																					B		
		☕	☕	☕	☕	☕	🛒	☕					☕		☕		☕	🛒	☕				🛒	☕	🛒
Swansea	d							08 07									09 21							10 21	
Neath	d							08 19									09 33							10 33	
Port Talbot Parkway	d							08 26									09 40							10 40	
Bridgend	d							08 38									09 52							10 52	
Cardiff Central [7]	d				07 55			09 05									10 15				10 23		10 45	11 15	
Newport (South Wales)	d				08 13			09 19									10 32				10 38		10 59	11 32	
Weston-super-Mare	d	21p53				08 11									09 56										
Bristol Temple Meads [10]	d	22c30	07 45	08 20		08 45	09 15					09 41	09 48		10 30				11 30						
Bristol Parkway [7]	a				08 42		09 23	09 46				09 53					10 59							11 59	
	d				08 43		09 25	09 48				09 53					11 01							12 01	
Bath Spa [7]	d	22p43	07 58	08 33		08 58							10 00		10 43				11 43						
Chippenham	d	22p55	08 10	08 45		09 10							10 12		10 55				11 55						
Worcester Shrub Hill	d													09 35											
Cheltenham Spa	d								09 24	10 05						10 24		10 53		11 24					11 53
Gloucester [7]	d						09a54		09 38	10a15		10a32				10 38		11a03		11 38	11a42		11a49		12a03
Stonehouse	d								09 50							10 50				11 50					
Stroud	d								09 55							10 55				11 55					
Kemble	d								10 09							11 09				12 09					
Swindon	a	23p10	08 25	09 00	09 08	09 24		10 13	10 24				10 27		11 10	11 24	11 26		12 10	12 24				12 27	
	d	23p11	08 26		09 09	09 29		10 14					10 29		11 11		11 29		12 11					12 29	
Didcot Parkway	a	23p28	08 43			09 45							10 45	11 07	11 28		11 46		12 29					12 46	
Reading [7]	a	23p51	09 01		09 43	09 59		10 42					11 00	11 23	11 42		12 01		12 42					13 00	
Slough [3]	a													11 42											
London Paddington [15] ⊖	a	00 34	09 44		10 22	10 44		11 22					11 44	12 06	12 21		12 44		13 22					13 44	

		GW	GW	GW	AW	XC		GW	GW	GW	GW	GW	XC	AW	XC	GW		GW	XC	AW	XC	GW	GW	GW	GW
		◇1	◇1			◇1		◇1		◇1		◇1	◇1		◇1	◇1		◇1	◇1		◇1	◇1		◇1	◇1
						B									B						B				
		☕				🛒		☕		☕		☕	🛒		🛒	☕			🛒		🛒	☕		☕	☕
Swansea	d									11 21						12 21								13 21	
Neath	d									11 33						12 33								13 33	
Port Talbot Parkway	d									11 40						12 40								13 40	
Bridgend	d									11 52						12 52								13 52	
Cardiff Central [7]	d					11 45				12 15				12 23	12 45	13 15					13 45			14 15	
Newport (South Wales)	d					11 59				12 32				12 38	12 59	13 32					13 59			14 32	
Weston-super-Mare	d											12 51													
Bristol Temple Meads [10]	d	12 00						12 30	12 41			13 30										14 30	14 41		
Bristol Parkway [7]	a								12 52	12 59						13 59							14 52	14 59	
	d								12 52	13 01						14 01							14 53	15 01	
Bath Spa [7]	d	12 13						12 43				13 43										14 43			
Chippenham	d	12 25						12 55				13 55										14 55			
Worcester Shrub Hill	d		11 30															13 30							14 30
Cheltenham Spa	d			12 00	12 18						13 01		13 11						14 12	14 18					
Gloucester [7]	d			12a11	12a28	12a46			13a31		13 15		13a21	13a34	13a47				14a22	14a29	14a46		15a35		
Stonehouse	d										13 27														
Stroud	d										13 32														
Kemble	d										13 46														
Swindon	a	12 40						13 10		13 27	14 01	14 10				14 26						15 10		15 26	
	d	12 41						13 11		13 29		14 11				14 29						15 11		15 29	
Didcot Parkway	a	12 58	13 01					13 28		13 46		14 28				14 46		15 03				15 28		15 46	16 02
Reading [7]	a	13 14	13 20					13 47		14 00		14 42				15 00		15 21				15 42		16 00	16 20
Slough [3]	a		13 36															15 36							16 33
London Paddington [15] ⊖	a	13 59	14 02					14 22		14 44		15 21				15 44		15 59				16 22		16 44	16 59

A not 11 December
B 🛒 from Newport (South Wales)
c Previous night, arr. 2212

For connections from Hereford and Birmingham New Street please refer to Tables 131 and 57.
For connections to Oxford, Gatwick Airport and Heathrow Airport please refer to Tables 116, 148 and 125A

Table 125

Sundays
until 1 January

South Wales, Weston-super-Mare, Bristol, Cheltenham Spa and Swindon - London

Route Diagram - see first Page of Table 125

		GW		GW	GW	XC	AW	XC	GW	GW	GW	GW		XC	AW	XC	GW	GW	GW	GW	GW	GW		GW	XC
					◇1	◇1		◇1	◇1	◇1	◇1	◇1		◇1		◇1	◇1		◇1		◇1	◇1			◇1
								A																	
					☕	🛒		🛒	☕	☕	☕	☕		🛒			☕		☕		☕	☕			🛒
Swansea	d								14 21										15 21						
Neath	d								14 33										15 33						
Port Talbot Parkway	d								14 40										15 40						
Bridgend	d								14 52										15 52						
Cardiff Central 7	d						14 23	14 45	15 15							15 45			16 15						
Newport (South Wales)	d						14 38	14 59	15 32							15 59			16 32						
Weston-super-Mare	d				14 51																				
Bristol Temple Meads 10	d				15 30					16 00							16 30	16 41			17 00				
Bristol Parkway 7	a								15 59									16 52	16 59						
	d								16 01									16 52	17 01						
Bath Spa 7	d				15 43					16 13							16 43				17 13				
Chippenham	d				15 55					16 25							16 55				17 25				
Worcester Shrub Hill	d			14 36								15 27										16 27		16 40	
Cheltenham Spa	d	14 46		15 01		15 11					15 46			16 11	16 18					16 33				17 08	17 11
Gloucester 7	d	15 03		15a10		15a21	15a37	15a46			16 02			16a21	16a29	16a46		17a32		16 47				17a16	17a21
Stonehouse	d	15 17									16 15									16 59					
Stroud	d	15 22									16 20									17 04					
Kemble	d	15 36									16 35									17 19					
Swindon	a	15 51			16 10				16 26	16 40	16 50						17 10		17 26	17 34	17 40				
	d				16 11				16 29	16 41	16 51						17 11		17 29		17 41				
Didcot Parkway	a				16 31				16 46	16 58		17 02					17 28		17 46		17 58	18 02			
Reading 7	a				16 46				17 00	17 13	17 18	17 21					17 42		18 01		18 14	18 21			
Slough 3	a											17 40										18 36			
London Paddington 15 ⊖	a				17 22				17 43	17 58	18 00	18 06					18 22		18 44		18 59	19 02			

		AW	XC	GW	GW	GW	GW	GW		GW	XC	XC	GW	GW	GW	AW	GW	XC		GW	AW	XC	GW	GW	GW
			◇1		◇1	◇1	◇1	◇1		◇1	◇1	◇1	◇1	◇1	◇1			◇1				◇1	◇1	◇1	
					☕	☕	☕	☕		☕	🛒		☕	☕				🛒					☕	☕	
Swansea	d					16 21							16 51											17 51	
Neath	d					16 33							17 03											18 03	
Port Talbot Parkway	d					16 40							17 10											18 10	
Bridgend	d					16 52							17 22											18 22	
Cardiff Central 7	d	16 23	16 45			17 15						17 45	17 50								18 23	18 45		18 50	
Newport (South Wales)	d	16 38	16 59			17 32						17 59	18 04								18 38	18 59		19 04	
Weston-super-Mare	d				17 02		17 29																		
Bristol Temple Meads 10	d				17 30		18 00							18 30						18 41			19 00		
Bristol Parkway 7	a					17 59							18 31							18 52				19 31	
	d					17 59							18 33							18 52				19 33	
Bath Spa 7	d				17 43		18 13							18 43									19 13		
Chippenham	d			17 35	17 55		18 25							18 55									19 25		20 05
Worcester Shrub Hill	d									17 27					18 27		18 40								
Cheltenham Spa	d							17 46			18 11					18 35	19 06	19 13							
Gloucester 7	d	17a37	17a46					18 02			18a22	18a46				18a46	19a17	19a26		19a33	19a38	19a47			
Stonehouse	d							18 15																	
Stroud	d							18 20																	
Kemble	d							18 34																	
Swindon	a			17 53	18 10	18 26	18 40	18 48					18 59	19 11									19 40	19 58	20 21
	d				18 11	18 29	18 41	18 49					18 59	19 11									19 41	19 59	
Didcot Parkway	a					18 46	18 59			19 02			19 16		20 04								19 58	20 16	
Reading 7	a				18 46	19 00	19 12	19 22		19 28			19 32	19 46	20 23								20 21	20 32	
Slough 3	a									19 42					20 42										
London Paddington 15 ⊖	a				19 22	19 44	19 59	20 02		20 06			20 14	20 22	21 03								20 59	21 13	

		GW	GW	GW		XC	GW	GW	XC	AW	GW	GW	GW	GW		XC	GW	GW	GW	XC	GW				
			◇1	◇1		◇1	◇1	◇1	◇1		◇1			◇1		◇1	◇1	◇1		◇1	◇1				
			☕				☕	☕						☕			☕				☕				
Swansea	d						18 51										19 59								
Neath	d						19 03										20 11								
Port Talbot Parkway	d						19 10										20 18								
Bridgend	d						19 22										20 30								
Cardiff Central 7	d					19 45	19 50									20 45	20 55								
Newport (South Wales)	d					20 00	20 04									20 59	21 09								
Weston-super-Mare	d		19 27											20 26											
Bristol Temple Meads 10	d		20 00										20 41	21 00							22 10				
Bristol Parkway 7	a						20 31						20 52				21 36								
	d						20 33						20 52				21 38								
Bath Spa 7	d		20 13											21 13							22 23				
Chippenham	d		20 25											21 24							22 35				
Worcester Shrub Hill	d			19 27							20 30	20 37						21 34							
Cheltenham Spa	d							20 05	20 11	20 18		21 03							21 46	21 52					
Gloucester 7	d	19 34				20a49		20 23	20a21	20a29		21a13	21a33			21a47			21 59	22a02					
Stonehouse	d	19 48						20 36											22 12						
Stroud	d	19 53						20 42											22 17						
Kemble	d	20 07						20 57											22 32						
Swindon	a	20 23	20 40				20 59	21 11						21 40			22 04		22 47		22 50				
	d		20 41				20 59	21 11						21 41			22 05				22 53				
Didcot Parkway	a		20 58	21 00			21 16	21 30			22 00			22 00				22 58			23 09				
Reading 7	a		21 16	21 21			21 32	21 45			22 19			22 17			22 36	23 15			23 28				
Slough 3	a			21 42							22 43							23 40							
London Paddington 15 ⊖	a		22 02	22 04			22 14	22 29			23 13			23 07			23 19	00 02			00 13				

A 🛒 from Newport (South Wales)

For connections from Hereford and Birmingham New Street please refer to Tables 131 and 57.
For connections to Oxford, Gatwick Airport and Heathrow Airport please refer to Tables 116, 148 and 125A

Table 125

Sundays

8 January to 12 February

South Wales, Weston-super-Mare, Bristol, Cheltenham Spa and Swindon - London

Route Diagram - see first Page of Table 125

		GW	GW	GW	GW	GW	XC	GW	GW	GW		GW	GW	GW	GW	GW	GW	XC	GW	GW		AW	XC	GW	XC
		◇1	◇1	1	◇1	◇1	◇1	◇1					◇1	◇1	◇1		◇1	◇1	◇1				◇1	◇1	◇1
																							A		
		☕	☕	☕	☕	☕	🛒	☕					☕		☕		☕	🛒	☕				🛒	☕	🛒
Swansea	d																								
Neath	d																								
Port Talbot Parkway	d																								
Bridgend	d																								
Cardiff Central 7	d				07 55			09 05									10 15					10 23	10 45	11 15	
Newport (South Wales)	d				08 13			09 19									10 32					10 38	10 59	11 32	
Weston-super-Mare	d	21p53				08 11									09 56										
Bristol Temple Meads 10	d	22b30	07 45	08 20		08 45	09 15					09 41	09 48		10 30				11 30						
Bristol Parkway 7	a				08 42		09 23	09 46				09 53					10 59							11 59	
	d				08 43		09 25	09 48				09 53					11 01							12 01	
Bath Spa 7	d	22p43	07 58	08 33		08 58							10 00		10 43				11 43						
Chippenham	d	22p55	08 10	08 45		09 10							10 12		10 55				11 55						
Worcester Shrub Hill	d													09 35											
Cheltenham Spa	d								09 24	10 05						10 24		10 53		11 24					11 53
Gloucester 7	d						09a54		09 38	10a15		10a32				10 38		11a03		11 38		11a42	11a49		12a03
Stonehouse	d								09 50							10 50				11 50					
Stroud	d								09 55							10 55				11 55					
Kemble	d								10 09							11 09				12 09					
Swindon	a	23p10	08 25	09 00	09 08	09 24		10 13	10 24				10 27		11 10	11 24	11 26		12 10	12 24				12 26	
	d	23p11	08 26		09 09	09 29		10 14					10 29		11 11		11 29		12 11					12 29	
Didcot Parkway	a	23p28	08 42			09 45							10 45	11 07	11 28		11 46		12 29					12 46	
Reading 7	a	23p51	09 01		09 45	09 59		10 42					11 00	11 23	11 45		12 01		12 44					13 00	
Slough 3	a													11 37											
London Paddington 15 ⊖	a	00 34	09 44		10 22	10 44		11 22					11 44	12 01	12 22		12 44		13 22					13 44	

			GW	GW	AW	XC		GW	GW	GW	GW	GW	XC	AW	XC	GW		GW	XC	AW	XC	GW	GW	GW	GW
			◇1			◇1		◇1		◇1		◇1	◇1		◇1	◇1		◇1	◇1		◇1	◇1		◇1	◇1
						A									A						A				
						🛒		☕		☕		☕	🛒		🛒	☕			🛒		🛒	☕		☕	☕
Swansea	d																								
Neath	d																								
Port Talbot Parkway	d																								
Bridgend	d																								
Cardiff Central 7	d					11 45				12 15				12 23	12 45	13 15					13 45			14 15	
Newport (South Wales)	d					11 59				12 32				12 38	12 59	13 32					13 59			14 32	
Weston-super-Mare	d											12 51													
Bristol Temple Meads 10	d							12 30	12 41			13 30										14 30	14 41		
Bristol Parkway 7	a								12 52	13 01						13 59							14 52	14 59	
	d								12 52	13 01						14 01							14 53	15 01	
Bath Spa 7	d							12 43				13 43										14 43			
Chippenham	d							12 55				13 55										14 55			
Worcester Shrub Hill	d		11 30															13 30							14 30
Cheltenham Spa	d			12 00	12 18						13 01		13 11						14 12	14 18					
Gloucester 7	d			12a11	12a28	12a46			13a31		13 15		13a21	13a34	13a47				14a22	14a29	14a46		15a35		
Stonehouse	d										13 27														
Stroud	d										13 32														
Kemble	d										13 46														
Swindon	a							13 10		13 26	14 01	14 10				14 26						15 10		15 26	
	d							13 11		13 29		14 11				14 29						15 11		15 29	
Didcot Parkway	a		13 02					13 28		13 46		14 31				14 46		15 03				15 31		15 46	16 02
Reading 7	a		13 25					13 47		14 00		14 47				15 00		15 21				15 47		16 00	16 23
Slough 3	a		13 41															15 36							16 37
London Paddington 15 ⊖	a		14 04					14 22		14 44		15 22				15 44		15 59				16 22		16 44	17 02

		GW		GW	GW	XC	AW	XC	GW	GW	GW	GW		XC	AW	XC	GW	GW	GW	GW	GW	GW		GW	XC
					◇1	◇1		◇1	◇1	◇1	◇1	◇1		◇1		◇1	◇1		◇1		◇1	◇1			◇1
								A																	
					☕	🛒		🛒	☕	☕	☕	☕		🛒			☕		☕		☕	☕			🛒
Swansea	d																								
Neath	d																								
Port Talbot Parkway	d																								
Bridgend	d																								
Cardiff Central 7	d						14 23	14 45	15 15							15 45			16 15						
Newport (South Wales)	d						14 38	14 59	15 32							15 59			16 32						
Weston-super-Mare	d				14 51																				
Bristol Temple Meads 10	d				15 30					16 00							16 30	16 41			17 00				
Bristol Parkway 7	a								15 59									16 52	16 59						
	d								16 01									16 52	17 01						
Bath Spa 7	d				15 43					16 13							16 43				17 13				
Chippenham	d				15 55					16 25							16 55				17 25				
Worcester Shrub Hill	d			14 36								15 27										16 27		16 40	
Cheltenham Spa	d	14 46		15 01		15 11					15 46			16 11	16 18					16 33				17 08	17 11
Gloucester 7	d	15 03		15a10		15a21	15a37	15a46			16 02			16a21	16a29	16a46		17a32		16 47				17a16	17a21
Stonehouse	d	15 17									16 15									16 59					
Stroud	d	15 22									16 20									17 04					
Kemble	d	15 36									16 35									17 19					
Swindon	a	15 51			16 10				16 26	16 40	16 50						17 10		17 26	17 34	17 40				
	d				16 11				16 29	16 41	16 51						17 11		17 29		17 41				
Didcot Parkway	a				16 31				16 46	16 58		17 02					17 28		17 46		17 58	18 02			
Reading 7	a				16 47				17 04	17 15	17 20	17 25					17 46		18 00		18 17	18 21			
Slough 3	a											17 43										18 36			
London Paddington 15 ⊖	a				17 22				17 43	18 01	18 04	18 06					18 22		18 44		18 58	19 03			

A 🛒 from Newport (South Wales)

b Previous night, arr. 2212

For connections from Hereford and Birmingham New Street please refer to Tables 131 and 57.
For connections to Oxford, Gatwick Airport and Heathrow Airport please refer to Tables 116, 148 and 125A

Table 125

Sundays

8 January to 12 February

South Wales, Weston-super-Mare, Bristol, Cheltenham Spa and Swindon - London

Route Diagram - see first Page of Table 125

		AW	XC	GW	GW	GW	GW	GW		GW	XC	XC	GW	GW	GW	AW	GW	XC		GW	AW	XC	GW	GW	GW
			◇1		◇1	◇1	◇1	◇1		◇1	◇1	◇1	◇1	◇1	◇1			◇1				◇1	◇1	◇1	
					🍴	🍴	🍴	🍴		🍴	🛒		🍴	🍴				🛒					🍴	🍴	
Swansea	d																								
Neath	d																								
Port Talbot Parkway	d																								
Bridgend	d																								
Cardiff Central 7	d	16 23	16 45			17 10						17 45	17 50								18 23	18 45		18 50	
Newport (South Wales)	d	16 38	16 59			17 27						17 59	18 04								18 38	18 59		19 04	
Weston-super-Mare	d				17 02		17 29																		
Bristol Temple Meads 10	d				17 30		18 00							18 30						18 41			19 00		
Bristol Parkway 7	a					18 00							18 31							18 52				19 31	
	d					18 01							18 33							18 52				19 33	
Bath Spa 7	d				17 43		18 13							18 43									19 13		
Chippenham	d			17 35	17 55		18 25							18 55									19 25		20 05
Worcester Shrub Hill	d									17 27					18 27		18 40								
Cheltenham Spa	d							17 46			18 11					18 35	19 06	19 13							
Gloucester 7	d	17a37	17a46					18 02			18a22	18a46				18a46	19a17	19a26		19a33	19a38	19a47			
Stonehouse	d							18 15																	
Stroud	d							18 20																	
Kemble	d							18 34																	
Swindon	a			17 53	18 10	18 26	18 40	18 48					18 59	19 11									19 40	19 58	20 21
	d				18 11	18 29	18 41	18 49					18 59	19 11									19 41	19 59	
Didcot Parkway	a					18 46	18 59			19 02			19 16		20 02								19 58	20 16	
Reading 7	a				18 46	19 00	19 17	19 22		19 28			19 33	19 47	20 25								20 21	20 31	
Slough 3	a									19 44					20 44										
London Paddington 15 ⊖	a				19 22	19 43	19 59	20 02		20 07			20 13	20 22	21 04								20 59	21 13	

		GW	GW	GW		XC	GW	GW	XC	AW	GW	GW	GW	GW		XC	GW	GW	GW	XC	GW				
			◇1	◇1		◇1	◇1	◇1	◇1		◇1			◇1		◇1	◇1	◇1		◇1	◇1				
			🍴				🍴	🍴						🍴			🍴				🍴				
Swansea	d																								
Neath	d																								
Port Talbot Parkway	d																								
Bridgend	d																								
Cardiff Central 7	d					19 45	19 50									20 45	21 15								
Newport (South Wales)	d					20 00	20 04									20 59	21 29								
Weston-super-Mare	d		19 27											20 26											
Bristol Temple Meads 10	d		20 00										20 41	21 00							22 10				
Bristol Parkway 7	a						20 31						20 52				21 56								
	d						20 33						20 52				21 58								
Bath Spa 7	d		20 13											21 13							22 23				
Chippenham	d		20 25											21 24							22 35				
Worcester Shrub Hill	d			19 27							20 30	20 37						21 34							
Cheltenham Spa	d							20 05	20 11	20 18		21 03							21 46	21 52					
Gloucester 7	d	19 34				20a49		20 23	20a21	20a29		21a13	21a33			21a47			21 59	22a02					
Stonehouse	d	19 48						20 36											22 12						
Stroud	d	19 53						20 42											22 17						
Kemble	d	20 07						20 57											22 32						
Swindon	a	20 23	20 40				20 59	21 11						21 40			22 24		22 47		22 50				
	d		20 41				20 59	21 11						21 40			22 25				22 53				
Didcot Parkway	a		20 58	21 00			21 16	21 28			22 00			21 59				23 01			23 09				
Reading 7	a		21 21	21 26			21 32	21 47			22 23			22 16			22 52	23 17			23 28				
Slough 3	a			21 45							22 40							23 41							
London Paddington 15 ⊖	a		22 01	22 07			22 13	22 27			23 01			22 58			23 31	00 04			00 13				

Sundays

19 February to 25 March

		GW	GW	GW	GW	GW	XC	GW	GW	GW		GW	GW	GW	GW	XC	AW	XC	GW	XC		GW	GW	GW	AW
		◇1	◇1	◇1	◇1	◇1	◇1		◇1	◇1		◇1	◇1	◇1		◇1		◇1	◇1	◇1		◇1	◇1		
																		A							
		🍴	🍴	🍴	🍴	🍴	🛒		🍴			🍴	🍴	🍴		🛒		🛒	🍴	🛒		🍴			
Swansea	d											07 55		09 05											
Neath	d											08 07		09 17											
Port Talbot Parkway	d											08 15		09 24											
Bridgend	d											08 27		09 36											
Cardiff Central 7	d					07 55						08 52		10 00			10 23	10 45							
Newport (South Wales)	d					08 13						09 06		10 16			10 38	10 59							
Weston-super-Mare	d	21p53			08 11								09 56												
Bristol Temple Meads 10	d	22g30	07 45	08 25	08 45		09 15	09 41	09 48				10 30						11 30			12 00			
Bristol Parkway 7	a			08 34			09 23	09 53																	
	d			08 35			09 25	09 53																	
Bath Spa 7	d	22p43	07 58		08 58				10 00				10 43						11 43			12 13			
Chippenham	d	22p55	08 10		09 10				10 12				10 55						11 55			12 25			
Worcester Shrub Hill	d									09 35													11 30		
Cheltenham Spa	d														10 05	10 53				11 53				12 00	12 18
Gloucester 7	d					09 11	09a54	10a32				10 01			10a15	11a03	11a42	11a49		12a03				12a11	12a32
Stonehouse	d											10 16													
Stroud	d											10 22													
Kemble	d											10 36													
Swindon	a	23p10	08 25	08 59	09 24	09 47			10 27			10 50	11 10	11 45					12 10			12 40			
	d	23p11	08 26	09 01	09 29	09 49			10 29			10 52	11 11	11 51					12 11			12 41			
Didcot Parkway	a	23p28	08 43		09 45	10 07			10 45	11 07			11 28	12 08					12 29			12 58	13 02		
Reading 7	a	23p51	09 01	09 30	09 58	10 25			11 00	11 23		11 25	11 45	12 26					12 44			13 21	13 25		
Slough 3	a									11 37													13 41		
London Paddington 15 ⊖	a	00 34	09 44	10 07	10 44	11 06			11 44	12 01		12 06	12 22	13 03					13 22			13 59	14 04		

A 🛒 from Newport (South Wales)

g Previous night, arr. 2212

For connections from Hereford and Birmingham New Street please refer to Tables 131 and 57.
For connections to Oxford, Gatwick Airport and Heathrow Airport please refer to Tables 116, 148 and 125A

Table 125

Sundays

19 February to 25 March

South Wales, Weston-super-Mare, Bristol, Cheltenham Spa and Swindon - London

Route Diagram - see first Page of Table 125

		GW	GW	XC	XC	GW		GW	GW	AW	XC	GW	XC	AW	GW	GW		XC	GW	GW	XC	GW		GW	GW
		◇1	◇1	◇1	◇1			◇1	◇1		◇1	◇1	◇1		◇1	◇1		◇1	◇1		◇1			◇1	◇1
				A							A							A							
		🍽	🍽	🛒	🛒			🍽	🍽		🛒		🛒		🍽	🍽		🛒	🍽		🛒			🍽	🍽
Swansea	d		10 25						11 25							12 30									13 25
Neath	d		10 38						11 37							12 42									13 37
Port Talbot Parkway	d		10 45						11 44							12 49									13 44
Bridgend	d		10 57						11 56							13 01									13 56
Cardiff Central 7	d		11 25	11 45					12 20	12 23	12 45					13 25		13 45							14 20
Newport (South Wales)	d		11 40	11 59					12 35	12 39	12 59					13 40		13 59							14 35
Weston-super-Mare	d							12 51																14 51	
Bristol Temple Meads 10	d	12 30				12 41		13 30							14 30							14 41		15 30	
Bristol Parkway 7	a					12 52																14 52			
	d					12 52																14 53			
Bath Spa 7	d	12 43						13 43							14 43									15 43	
Chippenham	d	12 55						13 55							14 55									15 55	
Worcester Shrub Hill	d											13 30							14 30	14 36					
Cheltenham Spa	d				13 11								14 12	14 18						15 01	15 11				
Gloucester 7	d		12 38	12a46	13a21	13a31			13 32	13a36	13a47		14a22	14a33		14 38		14a46		15a10	15a21	15a35			15 32
Stonehouse	d		12 52						13 46							14 52									15 48
Stroud	d		12 58						13 52							14 58									15 54
Kemble	d		13 12						14 06							15 12									16 08
Swindon	a	13 10	13 25					14 10	14 19						15 10	15 26								16 10	16 22
	d	13 11	13 29					14 11	14 29						15 11	15 29								16 11	16 29
Didcot Parkway	a	13 28	13 45					14 31	14 46			15 03			15 31	15 46			16 02					16 31	16 46
Reading 7	a	13 47	13 59					14 47	15 00			15 21			15 47	16 00			16 27					16 47	17 03
Slough 3	a											15 37							16 41						
London Paddington 15 ⊖	a	14 22	14 44					15 22	15 44			15 59			16 22	16 44			17 06					17 22	17 43

		AW		XC	GW	GW	XC	AW	GW	GW	XC	GW		GW	XC	GW	AW	XC	GW	GW	GW	GW		GW	GW
				◇1	◇1	◇1	◇1		◇1	◇1	◇1	◇1			◇1			◇1		◇1	◇1	◇1		◇1	◇1
				A																					
				🛒	🍽	🍽	🛒		🍽	🍽		🍽			🛒					🍽	🍽	🍽		🍽	🍽
Swansea	d									14 30											15 50				
Neath	d									14 42											16 02				
Port Talbot Parkway	d									14 49											16 09				
Bridgend	d									15 01											16 21				
Cardiff Central 7	d	14 23		14 45						15 26	15 45						16 23	16 45			16 50				
Newport (South Wales)	d	14 38		14 59						15 42	15 59						16 38	16 59			17 04				
Weston-super-Mare	d																			17 02		17 29			
Bristol Temple Meads 10	d				16 00				16 30							16 41				17 30		18 00			
Bristol Parkway 7	a															16 52									
	d															16 52									
Bath Spa 7	d				16 13				16 43											17 43		18 13			
Chippenham	d				16 25				16 55										17 35	17 55		18 25			
Worcester Shrub Hill	d					15 27						16 27		16 40											17 27
Cheltenham Spa	d						16 11	16 18						17 08	17 11									17 46	
Gloucester 7	d	15a37		15a46			16a21	16a29		16 38	16a46			17a16	17a21	17a32	17a37	17a46						18 02	
Stonehouse	d									16 52														18 15	
Stroud	d									16 58														18 20	
Kemble	d									17 12														18 34	
Swindon	a				16 40				17 10	17 26									17 53	18 10	18 28	18 40		18 48	
	d				16 41				17 11	17 29										18 11	18 29	18 41		18 49	
Didcot Parkway	a				16 58	17 02			17 28	17 45		18 02										18 59			19 02
Reading 7	a				17 15	17 24			17 46	17 59		18 23								18 46	19 00	19 17		19 22	19 29
Slough 3	a					17 44						18 38													19 44
London Paddington 15 ⊖	a				18 01	18 07			18 22	18 45		19 03								19 22	19 43	19 59		20 02	20 07

		XC	GW	GW	XC	GW	AW	GW		XC	GW	GW	GW	AW	XC	GW	GW	GW		GW	XC	AW	XC	GW	GW
		◇1	◇1	◇1	◇1	◇1				◇1		◇1	◇1		◇1		◇1	◇1		◇1	◇1		◇1		◇1
		🛒	🍽	🍽						🛒		🍽	🍽				🍽			🍽					🍽
Swansea	d			16 25									17 05							18 00					
Neath	d			16 40									17 17							18 14					
Port Talbot Parkway	d			16 47									17 24							18 21					
Bridgend	d			16 59									17 36							18 33					
Cardiff Central 7	d			17 25	17 45								18 00	18 23	18 45					18 56			19 45		
Newport (South Wales)	d			17 39	17 59								18 16	18 38	18 59					19 13			20 00		
Weston-super-Mare	d																								20 26
Bristol Temple Meads 10	d		18 30								18 41	19 00					20 00							20 41	21 00
Bristol Parkway 7	a										18 52													20 52	
	d										18 52													20 52	
Bath Spa 7	d		18 43									19 13					20 13								21 13
Chippenham	d		18 55									19 25				20 05	20 25								21 24
Worcester Shrub Hill	d					18 27		18 40										19 27							
Cheltenham Spa	d	18 11					18 35	19 06		19 13											20 11	20 18			
Gloucester 7	d	18a22		18 33	18a46		18a46	19a17		19a26	19a33			19a38	19a47					20 07	20a23	20a29	20a49	21a33	
Stonehouse	d			18 47																20 20					
Stroud	d			18 53																20 25					
Kemble	d			19 07																20 39					
Swindon	a		19 11	19 22								19 39	19 41			20 21	20 39			20 52					21 40
	d		19 11	19 23								19 41	20 01				20 41			20 59					21 40
Didcot Parkway	a					20 02						19 58	20 18				20 58	21 00		21 15					21 59
Reading 7	a		19 47	19 52		20 23						20 21	20 32				21 21	21 26		21 31					22 16
Slough 3	a					20 42												21 45							
London Paddington 15 ⊖	a		20 22	20 31		21 04						20 59	21 13				22 00	22 07		22 14					22 58

A 🛒 from Newport (South Wales)

For connections from Hereford and Birmingham New Street please refer to Tables 131 and 57.
For connections to Oxford, Gatwick Airport and Heathrow Airport please refer to Tables 116, 148 and 125A

Table 125

Sundays

19 February to 25 March

South Wales, Weston-super-Mare, Bristol, Cheltenham Spa and Swindon - London

Route Diagram - see first Page of Table 125

		GW	GW	GW		XC	GW	GW	XC	GW
		◇1	◇1			◇1	◇1	◇1	◇1	◇1
			⊡				⊡			⊡
Swansea	d		18 55				19 59			
Neath	d		19 09				20 11			
Port Talbot Parkway	d		19 16				20 18			
Bridgend	d		19 28				20 31			
Cardiff Central [7]	d		19 55			20 45	20 55			
Newport (South Wales)	d		20 13			20 59	21 10			
Weston-super-Mare	d									
Bristol Temple Meads [10]	d									22 10
Bristol Parkway [7]	a									
	d									
Bath Spa [7]	d									22 23
Chippenham	d									22 35
Worcester Shrub Hill	d	20 30		20 37				21 34		
Cheltenham Spa	d			21 03					21 52	
Gloucester [7]	d		21 07	21a13		21a47	22 00		22a02	
Stonehouse	d		21 21				22 13			
Stroud	d		21 27				22 19			
Kemble	d		21 41				22 34			
Swindon	a		21 55				22 48			22 50
	d		21 57				22 48			22 53
Didcot Parkway	a	22 00	22 13					23 01		23 09
Reading [7]	a	22 21	22 31				23 19	23 17		23 28
Slough [3]	a	22 40						23 41		
London Paddington [15] ⊖	a	23 01	23 13				00 01	00 04		00 12

Sundays

from 1 April

		GW	GW	GW	GW	GW	XC	GW	GW	GW		GW	GW	GW	GW	GW	GW	GW	XC	GW		GW	AW	XC	GW
		◇1	◇1	1	◇1	◇1	◇1	◇1	◇1					◇1	◇1	◇1		◇1	◇1	◇1				◇1	◇1
																								A	
		⊡	⊡	⊡	⊡	⊡	🍴	⊡	⊡					⊡		⊡		⊡	🍴	⊡				🍴	⊡
Swansea	d																								10 21
Neath	d																								10 33
Port Talbot Parkway	d																								10 40
Bridgend	d																								10 52
Cardiff Central [7]	d				07 55			09 05										10 15					10 23	10 45	11 15
Newport (South Wales)	d				08 13			09 19										10 32					10 38	10 59	11 32
Weston-super-Mare	d	21p53				08 11										09 56									
Bristol Temple Meads [10]	d	22b30	07 45	08 20		08 45	09 15						09 41	09 48		10 30				11 30					
Bristol Parkway [7]	a				08 42		09 23	09 46					09 53					10 59							11 59
	d				08 43		09 25	09 48					09 53					11 00							12 01
Bath Spa [7]	d	22p43	07 58	08 33		08 58								10 00		10 43				11 43					
Chippenham	d	22p55	08 10	08 45		09 10								10 12		10 55				11 55					
Worcester Shrub Hill	d														09 35										
Cheltenham Spa	d									09 24		10 05					10 24		10 53			11 24			
Gloucester [7]	d						09a54			09 38		10a15	10a32				10 38		11a03			11 38	11a42	11a49	
Stonehouse	d									09 50							10 50					11 50			
Stroud	d									09 55							10 55					11 55			
Kemble	d									10 09							11 09					12 09			
Swindon	a	23p10	08 25	09 00	09 08	09 24		10 13		10 24				10 27		11 10	11 24	11 29		12 10		12 24			12 27
	d	23p11	08 26		09 09	09 29		10 14	10 20					10 29		11 11		11 29		12 11					12 29
Didcot Parkway	a	23p28	08 43			09 45								10 45	11 07	11 28		11 49		12 29					12 46
Reading [7]	a	23p49	09 01		09 45	09 58		10 42	10 47					11 00	11 23	11 45		12 04		12 44					13 00
Slough [3]	a														11 37										
London Paddington [15] ⊖	a	00 33	09 44		10 22	10 44		11 22	11 29					11 44	12 01	12 22		12 42		13 22					13 42

		XC		GW	GW	AW		XC	GW	GW	GW	GW	GW	XC	AW	XC		GW	GW	XC	AW	XC	GW	GW	GW
		◇1		◇1				◇1	◇1		◇1		◇1	◇1		◇1		◇1	◇1	◇1		◇1	◇1		◇1
								A								A						A			
		🍴						🍴	⊡		⊡		⊡	🍴		🍴		⊡		🍴		🍴	⊡		⊡
Swansea	d										11 21							12 21							13 21
Neath	d										11 33							12 33							13 33
Port Talbot Parkway	d										11 40							12 40							13 40
Bridgend	d										11 52							12 52							13 52
Cardiff Central [7]	d							11 45			12 15				12 23	12 45		13 15				13 45			14 15
Newport (South Wales)	d							11 59			12 32				12 38	12 59		13 32				13 59			14 32
Weston-super-Mare	d												12 51												
Bristol Temple Meads [10]	d								12 30	12 41			13 30										14 30	14 41	
Bristol Parkway [7]	a									12 52	12 59							13 59						14 52	14 59
	d									12 52	13 02							14 01						14 53	15 01
Bath Spa [7]	d								12 43				13 43										14 43		
Chippenham	d								12 55				13 55										14 55		
Worcester Shrub Hill	d			11 30															13 30						
Cheltenham Spa	d	11 53			12 00	12 18						13 01		13 11						14 12	14 18				
Gloucester [7]	d	12a03			12a11	12a28		12a46		13a31		13 15		13a21	13a34	13a47				14a22	14a29	14a46		15a35	
Stonehouse	d											13 27													
Stroud	d											13 32													
Kemble	d											13 46													
Swindon	a								13 10		13 29	14 01	14 10					14 29					15 10		15 29
	d								13 11		13 29		14 11					14 29					15 11		15 29
Didcot Parkway	a			13 02					13 28		13 50		14 33					14 51	15 04				15 31		15 46
Reading [7]	a			13 25					13 47		14 05		14 45					15 05	15 25				15 47		16 00
Slough [3]	a			13 40															15 41						
London Paddington [15] ⊖	a			14 05					14 22		14 43		15 23					15 43	16 03				16 22		16 42

A 🍴 from Newport (South Wales)

b Previous night, arr. 2212

For connections from Hereford and Birmingham New Street please refer to Tables 131 and 57.
For connections to Oxford, Gatwick Airport and Heathrow Airport please refer to Tables 116, 148 and 125A

Table 125

Sundays

from 1 April

South Wales, Weston-super-Mare, Bristol, Cheltenham Spa and Swindon - London

Route Diagram - see first Page of Table 125

		GW		GW	GW	GW	XC	AW	XC	GW	GW	GW		GW	XC	AW	XC	GW	GW	GW	GW	GW		GW	GW
		◇1				◇1	◇1		◇1	◇1	◇1	◇1		◇1	◇1		◇1	◇1		◇1		◇1		◇1	
									A																
		☕				☕	🛒		🛒	☕	☕	☕		☕	🛒			☕		☕		☕		☕	
Swansea	d									14 21										15 21					
Neath	d									14 33										15 33					
Port Talbot Parkway	d									14 40										15 40					
Bridgend	d									14 52										15 52					
Cardiff Central [7]	d							14 23	14 45	15 15							15 45			16 15					
Newport (South Wales)	d							14 38	14 59	15 32							15 59			16 32					
Weston-super-Mare	d					14 51																			
Bristol Temple Meads [10]	d					15 30					16 00							16 30	16 41			17 00			
Bristol Parkway [7]	a									15 59									16 52	16 59					
	d									16 01									16 52	17 01					
Bath Spa [7]	d					15 43					16 13							16 43				17 13			
Chippenham	d					15 55					16 25							16 55				17 25			
Worcester Shrub Hill	d	14 30			14 36									15 27										16 27	16 40
Cheltenham Spa	d			14 46	15 01		15 11					15 46			16 11	16 18					16 33				17 08
Gloucester [7]	d			15 03	15a10		15a21	15a37	15a46			16 02			16a21	16a29	16a46		17a32		16 47				17a16
Stonehouse	d			15 17								16 15									16 59				
Stroud	d			15 22								16 20									17 04				
Kemble	d			15 36								16 35									17 19				
Swindon	a			15 51		16 10				16 27	16 40	16 50						17 10		17 27	17 34	17 41			
	d					16 11				16 33	16 41	16 51						17 11		17 29		17 41			
Didcot Parkway	a	16 02				16 31				16 50	17 00			17 02				17 28		17 46		17 58		18 02	
Reading [7]	a	16 25				16 47				17 04	17 16	17 20		17 26				17 46		18 00		18 19		18 25	
Slough [3]	a	16 40												17 47										18 41	
London Paddington [15] ⊖	a	17 05				17 22				17 44	18 03	18 06		18 13				18 22		18 43		18 59		19 06	

		XC	AW	XC	GW	GW	GW	GW		GW	GW	GW	XC	XC	GW	GW	GW	AW		GW	XC	GW	AW	XC	GW
		◇1		◇1		◇1	◇1	◇1		◇1	◇1	◇1	◇1	◇1	◇1	◇1	◇1				◇1			◇1	◇1
		🛒				☕	☕	☕		☕	☕	☕	🛒		☕	☕					🛒				☕
Swansea	d							16 21							16 51										
Neath	d							16 33							17 03										
Port Talbot Parkway	d							16 40							17 10										
Bridgend	d							16 52							17 22										
Cardiff Central [7]	d		16 23	16 45				17 13						17 45	17 50								18 23	18 45	
Newport (South Wales)	d		16 38	16 59				17 32						17 59	18 04								18 38	18 59	
Weston-super-Mare	d					17 02				17 29															
Bristol Temple Meads [10]	d					17 30				18 00						18 30						18 41			19 00
Bristol Parkway [7]	a							17 59							18 31							18 52			
	d							18 01							18 33							18 52			
Bath Spa [7]	d					17 43				18 13						18 43									19 13
Chippenham	d				17 35	17 55				18 25						18 55									19 25
Worcester Shrub Hill	d											17 27					18 27			18 40					
Cheltenham Spa	d	17 11									17 46		18 11					18 35		19 06	19 13				
Gloucester [7]	d	17a21	17a37	17a46							18 02		18a22	18a46				18a46		19a17	19a26	19a33	19a38	19a47	
Stonehouse	d										18 15														
Stroud	d										18 20														
Kemble	d										18 35														
Swindon	a				17 53	18 10		18 30		18 39	18 49				18 59	19 11									19 39
	d					18 11	18 27	18 31		18 41	18 50				19 01	19 11									19 41
Didcot Parkway	a							18 48		18 59		19 02			19 18		20 04								19 58
Reading [7]	a					18 46	18 55	19 02		19 12	19 22	19 30			19 36	19 48	20 24								20 16
Slough [3]	a											19 44					20 42								
London Paddington [15] ⊖	a					19 22	19 32	19 44		19 59	20 02	20 07			20 14	20 28	21 05								20 58

		GW	GW	GW		GW	GW	GW	XC	GW	GW	XC	AW	GW		GW	GW	GW	XC	GW	GW	GW	GW	XC	
		◇1		◇1			◇1	◇1	◇1	◇1	◇1	◇1		◇1				◇1	◇1	◇1	◇1	◇1		◇1	
		☕		☕			☕			☕	☕							☕		☕	☕				
Swansea	d	17 51								18 51										19 59					
Neath	d	18 03								19 03										20 11					
Port Talbot Parkway	d	18 10								19 10										20 18					
Bridgend	d	18 22								19 22										20 30					
Cardiff Central [7]	d	18 50							19 45	19 50									20 45	20 55					
Newport (South Wales)	d	19 04							20 00	20 04									20 59	21 09					
Weston-super-Mare	d						19 27											20 26							
Bristol Temple Meads [10]	d						20 00										20 41	21 00							
Bristol Parkway [7]	a	19 31								20 31							20 52			21 36					
	d	19 33								20 33							20 52			21 38					
Bath Spa [7]	d						20 13											21 13							
Chippenham	d		19 49				20 25											21 24							
Worcester Shrub Hill	d							19 27						20 30		20 37						21 34			
Cheltenham Spa	d										20 05	20 11	20 18			21 03							21 46	21 52	
Gloucester [7]	d					19 34			20a49		20 23	20a21	20a29			21a13	21a33		21a47				21 59	22a02	
Stonehouse	d					19 48					20 36												22 12		
Stroud	d					19 53					20 42												22 17		
Kemble	d					20 07					20 57												22 32		
Swindon	a	19 58	20 06			20 23	20 39			20 59	21 11							21 40		22 04			22 47		
	d	19 59		20 21			20 41			20 59	21 11							21 40		22 05	22 17				
Didcot Parkway	a	20 16					20 58	21 00		21 16	21 28			22 00				21 59				22 58			
Reading [7]	a	20 42		20 48			21 18	21 26		21 32	21 47			22 20				22 16		22 37	22 44	23 15			
Slough [3]	a							21 46						22 40								23 42			
London Paddington [15] ⊖	a	21 19		21 27			21 59	22 07		22 14	22 27			23 01				22 58		23 15	23 28	00 04			

A 🛒 from Newport (South Wales)

For connections from Hereford and Birmingham New Street please refer to Tables 131 and 57.
For connections to Oxford, Gatwick Airport and Heathrow Airport please refer to Tables 116, 148 and 125A

Table 125

Sundays
from 1 April

South Wales, Weston-super-Mare, Bristol, Cheltenham Spa and Swindon - London

Route Diagram - see first Page of Table 125

		GW
		◇1
		☕
Swansea	d	
Neath	d	
Port Talbot Parkway	d	
Bridgend	d	
Cardiff Central 7	d	
Newport (South Wales)	d	
Weston-super-Mare	d	
Bristol Temple Meads 10	d	22 10
Bristol Parkway 7	a	
	d	
Bath Spa 7	d	22 23
Chippenham	d	22 35
Worcester Shrub Hill	d	
Cheltenham Spa	d	
Gloucester 7	d	
Stonehouse	d	
Stroud	d	
Kemble	d	
Swindon	a	22 50
	d	22 53
Didcot Parkway	a	23 09
Reading 7	a	23 28
Slough 3	a	
London Paddington 15 ⊖	a	00 13

For connections from Hereford and Birmingham New Street please refer to Tables 131 and 57.
For connections to Oxford, Gatwick Airport and Heathrow Airport please refer to Tables 116, 148 and 125A

Table 125A

Mondays to Fridays

Reading - Heathrow Railair Link

Express Coach Service

		GW	GW	GW	GW	GW	GW	GW	GW	GW		GW	GW	GW	GW	GW	GW	GW	GW	GW		GW	GW	GW	GW
Reading 7	d	04 00	05 00	05 30	05 55	06 08	06 20	06 40	07 00	07 20		07 40	08 00	08 20	08 40	09 05	09 25	09 45	10 05	10 25		10 45	11 05	11 25	11 45
Heathrow Terminal 5 Bus	a	04 38	05 38	06 08	06 33	06 48	07 15	07 35	07 55	08 15		08 35	08 55	09 15	09 35	09 45	10 05	10 25	10 45	11 05		11 25	11 45	12 05	12 25
Heathrow Terminal 1 Bus	a	04 46	05 46	06 16	06 41	06 58	07 25	07 45	08 05	08 25		08 45	09 05	09 25	09 45	09 55	10 15	10 35	10 55	11 15		11 35	11 55	12 15	12 35
Heathrow Terminal 2 Bus	a																								
Heathrow Terminal 3 Bus	a	04 51	05 51	06 21	06 46	07 04	07 31	07 51	08 11	08 31		08 51	09 11	09 31	09 51	10 01	10 21	10 41	11 01	11 21		11 41	12 01	12 21	12 41

		GW	GW	GW	GW	GW		GW	GW	GW	GW	GW	GW	GW	GW	GW		GW	GW	GW	GW	GW	GW	GW	GW
Reading 7	d	12 05	12 25	12 45	13 05	13 25		13 45	14 05	14 25	14 45	15 05	15 25	15 45	16 05	16 25		16 45	17 05	17 25	17 45	18 05	18 35	19 05	19 35
Heathrow Terminal 5 Bus	a	12 45	13 05	13 25	13 45	14 05		14 25	14 45	15 05	15 25	15 45	16 05	16 25	16 45	17 05		17 25	17 45	18 05	18 25	18 45	19 15	19 45	20 15
Heathrow Terminal 1 Bus	a	12 55	13 15	13 35	13 55	14 15		14 35	14 55	15 15	15 35	15 55	16 15	16 35	16 55	17 15		17 35	17 55	18 15	18 35	18 55	19 25	19 55	20 25
Heathrow Terminal 2 Bus	a																								
Heathrow Terminal 3 Bus	a	13 01	13 21	13 41	14 01	14 21		14 41	15 01	15 21	15 41	16 01	16 21	16 41	17 01	17 21		17 41	18 01	18 21	18 41	19 01	19 31	20 01	20 31

		GW		GW	GW	GW	GW																		
Reading 7	d	20 05		20 35	21 05	22 05	23 05																		
Heathrow Terminal 5 Bus	a	20 43		21 13	21 43	22 43	23 43																		
Heathrow Terminal 1 Bus	a	20 51		21 21	21 51	22 51	23 51																		
Heathrow Terminal 2 Bus	a																								
Heathrow Terminal 3 Bus	a	20 56		21 26	21 56	22 56	23 56																		

Saturdays

		GW	GW	GW	GW	GW	GW	GW	GW	GW		GW	GW	GW	GW	GW	GW	GW	GW	GW		GW	GW	GW	GW
Reading 7	d	04 00	05 00	05 45	06 15	06 45	07 15	07 45	08 15	08 45		09 15	09 45	10 15	10 45	11 15	11 45	12 15	12 45	13 15		13 45	14 15	14 45	15 15
Heathrow Terminal 5 Bus	a	04 38	05 38	06 25	06 55	07 25	07 55	08 25	08 55	09 25		09 55	10 25	10 55	11 25	11 55	12 25	12 55	13 25	13 55		14 25	14 55	15 25	15 55
Heathrow Terminal 1 Bus	a	04 46	05 46	06 35	07 05	07 35	08 05	08 35	09 05	09 35		10 05	10 35	11 05	11 35	12 05	12 35	13 05	13 35	14 05		14 35	15 05	15 35	16 05
Heathrow Terminal 2 Bus	a																								
Heathrow Terminal 3 Bus	a	04 51	05 51	06 41	07 11	07 41	08 11	08 41	09 11	09 41		10 11	10 41	11 11	11 41	12 11	12 41	13 11	13 41	14 11		14 41	15 11	15 41	16 11

		GW	GW	GW	GW	GW		GW	GW	GW	GW	GW	GW	GW	GW										
Reading 7	d	15 45	16 15	16 45	17 15	17 45		18 15	18 45	19 15	19 45	20 25	20 55	22 05	23 05										
Heathrow Terminal 5 Bus	a	16 25	16 55	17 25	17 55	18 25		18 55	19 25	19 55	20 25	21 05	21 35	22 43	23 43										
Heathrow Terminal 1 Bus	a	16 35	17 05	17 35	18 05	18 35		19 05	19 35	20 05	20 35	21 15	21 45	22 51	23 51										
Heathrow Terminal 2 Bus	a																								
Heathrow Terminal 3 Bus	a	16 41	17 11	17 41	18 11	18 41		19 11	19 41	20 11	20 41	21 21	21 51	22 56	23 56										

Sundays

		GW	GW	GW	GW	GW	GW	GW	GW	GW		GW	GW	GW	GW	GW	GW	GW	GW	GW		GW	GW	GW	GW
Reading 7	d	04 00	05 00	05 45	06 15	06 45	07 15	07 45	08 15	08 45		09 15	09 45	10 15	10 45	11 15	11 45	12 15	12 45	13 15		13 45	14 15	14 45	15 15
Heathrow Terminal 5 Bus	a	04 38	05 38	06 25	06 55	07 25	07 55	08 25	08 55	09 25		09 55	10 25	10 55	11 25	11 55	12 25	12 55	13 25	13 55		14 25	14 55	15 25	15 55
Heathrow Terminal 1 Bus	a	04 46	05 46	06 35	07 05	07 35	08 05	08 35	09 05	09 35		10 05	10 35	11 05	11 35	12 05	12 35	13 05	13 35	14 05		14 35	15 05	15 35	16 05
Heathrow Terminal 2 Bus	a																								
Heathrow Terminal 3 Bus	a	04 51	05 51	06 41	07 11	07 41	08 11	08 41	09 11	09 41		10 11	10 41	11 11	11 41	12 11	12 41	13 11	13 41	14 11		14 41	15 11	15 41	16 11

		GW	GW	GW	GW	GW		GW	GW	GW	GW	GW	GW	GW	GW										
Reading 7	d	15 45	16 15	16 45	17 15	17 45		18 15	18 45	19 15	19 45	20 25	20 55	22 05	23 05										
Heathrow Terminal 5 Bus	a	16 25	16 55	17 25	17 55	18 25		18 55	19 25	19 55	20 25	21 05	21 35	22 43	23 43										
Heathrow Terminal 1 Bus	a	16 35	17 05	17 35	18 05	18 35		19 05	19 35	20 05	20 35	21 15	21 45	22 51	23 51										
Heathrow Terminal 2 Bus	a																								
Heathrow Terminal 3 Bus	a	16 41	17 11	17 41	18 11	18 41		19 11	19 41	20 11	20 41	21 21	21 51	22 56	23 56										

Table 125A

Mondays to Fridays

Heathrow - Reading Railair Link

Express Coach Service

	GW	GW	GW	GW	GW	GW	GW	GW	GW		GW	GW	GW	GW	GW	GW	GW	GW	GW		GW	GW	GW	GW
	🚌	🚌	🚌	🚌	🚌	🚌	🚌	🚌	🚌		🚌	🚌	🚌	🚌	🚌	🚌	🚌	🚌	🚌		🚌	🚌	🚌	🚌
Heathrow Central Bus Stn ✈ d	00 05	05 00	06 00	06 30	06 57	07 20	07 40	08 00	08 20		08 40	09 00	09 20	09 40	10 00	10 15	10 35	10 55	11 15		11 35	11 55	12 15	12 35
Heathrow Terminal 5 Bus ✈ d	00 13	05 08	06 08	06 38	07 05	07 28	07 50	08 10	08 30		08 50	09 10	09 30	09 50	10 10	10 25	10 45	11 05	11 25		11 45	12 05	12 25	12 45
Reading ■ a	00 51	05 46	06 46	07 21	07 48	08 21	08 46	09 06	09 26		09 39	09 59	10 13	10 33	10 53	11 08	11 28	11 48	12 08		12 28	12 48	13 08	13 28

	GW	GW	GW	GW	GW		GW	GW	GW	GW	GW	GW	GW	GW	GW		GW	GW	GW	GW	GW	GW	GW	GW
	🚌	🚌	🚌	🚌	🚌		🚌	🚌	🚌	🚌	🚌	🚌	🚌	🚌	🚌		🚌	🚌	🚌	🚌	🚌	🚌	🚌	🚌
Heathrow Central Bus Stn ✈ d	12 55	13 15	13 35	13 55	14 15		14 35	14 55	15 15	15 35	15 55	16 15	16 35	16 55	17 15		17 35	17 55	18 15	18 35	18 55	19 15	19 40	20 10
Heathrow Terminal 5 Bus ✈ d	13 05	13 25	13 45	14 05	14 25		14 45	15 05	15 25	15 45	16 05	16 25	16 45	17 05	17 25		17 45	18 05	18 25	18 45	19 05	19 25	19 50	20 20
Reading ■ a	13 48	14 08	14 28	14 48	15 08		15 28	15 48	16 08	16 28	16 48	17 14	17 34	17 54	18 14		18 34	18 54	19 14	19 34	19 54	20 14	20 31	21 01

	GW		GW	GW	GW	GW
	🚌		🚌	🚌	🚌	🚌
Heathrow Central Bus Stn ✈ d	20 40		21 10	21 40	22 15	23 05
Heathrow Terminal 5 Bus ✈ d	20 50		21 20	21 50	22 23	23 13
Reading ■ a	21 31		22 01	22 31	23 01	23 51

Saturdays

	GW	GW	GW	GW	GW	GW	GW	GW	GW		GW	GW	GW	GW	GW	GW	GW	GW	GW		GW	GW	GW	GW
	🚌	🚌	🚌	🚌	🚌	🚌	🚌	🚌	🚌		🚌	🚌	🚌	🚌	🚌	🚌	🚌	🚌	🚌		🚌	🚌	🚌	🚌
Heathrow Central Bus Stn ✈ d	00 05	05 00	06 00	07 00	07 30	08 00	08 30	09 00	09 30		10 00	10 30	11 00	11 30	12 00	12 30	13 00	13 30	14 00		14 30	15 00	15 30	16 00
Heathrow Terminal 5 Bus ✈ d	00 13	05 08	06 08	07 10	07 40	08 10	08 40	09 10	09 40		10 10	10 40	11 10	11 40	12 10	12 40	13 10	13 40	14 10		14 40	15 10	15 40	16 10
Reading ■ a	00 51	05 46	06 46	07 53	08 23	08 53	09 23	09 53	10 23		10 53	11 23	11 53	12 23	12 53	13 23	13 53	14 23	14 53		15 23	15 53	16 23	16 53

	GW	GW	GW	GW	GW		GW	GW	GW	GW	GW	GW	GW	GW
	🚌	🚌	🚌	🚌	🚌		🚌	🚌	🚌	🚌	🚌	🚌	🚌	🚌
Heathrow Central Bus Stn ✈ d	16 30	17 00	17 30	18 00	18 30		19 00	19 20	19 50	20 20	20 50	21 30	22 00	23 05
Heathrow Terminal 5 Bus ✈ d	16 40	17 10	17 40	18 10	18 40		19 10	19 30	20 00	20 30	21 00	21 38	22 08	23 13
Reading ■ a	17 23	17 53	18 23	18 53	19 23		19 53	20 13	20 43	21 13	21 43	22 19	22 49	23 51

Sundays

	GW	GW	GW	GW	GW	GW	GW	GW	GW		GW	GW	GW	GW	GW	GW	GW	GW	GW		GW	GW	GW	GW
	🚌	🚌	🚌	🚌	🚌	🚌	🚌	🚌	🚌		🚌	🚌	🚌	🚌	🚌	🚌	🚌	🚌	🚌		🚌	🚌	🚌	🚌
Heathrow Central Bus Stn ✈ d	00 05	05 00	06 00	07 00	07 30	08 00	08 30	09 00	09 30		10 00	10 30	11 00	11 30	12 00	12 30	13 00	13 30	14 00		14 30	15 00	15 30	16 00
Heathrow Terminal 5 Bus ✈ d	00 13	05 08	06 08	07 10	07 40	08 10	08 40	09 10	09 40		10 10	10 40	11 10	11 40	12 10	12 40	13 10	13 40	14 10		14 40	15 10	15 40	16 10
Reading ■ a	00 51	05 46	06 46	07 53	08 23	08 53	09 23	09 53	10 23		10 53	11 23	11 53	12 23	12 53	13 23	13 53	14 23	14 53		15 23	15 53	16 23	16 53

	GW	GW	GW	GW	GW		GW	GW	GW	GW	GW	GW	GW	GW
	🚌	🚌	🚌	🚌	🚌		🚌	🚌	🚌	🚌	🚌	🚌	🚌	🚌
Heathrow Central Bus Stn ✈ d	16 30	17 00	17 30	18 00	18 30		19 00	19 20	19 50	20 20	20 50	21 30	22 00	23 05
Heathrow Terminal 5 Bus ✈ d	16 40	17 10	17 40	18 10	18 40		19 10	19 30	20 00	20 30	21 00	21 38	22 08	23 13
Reading ■ a	17 23	17 53	18 23	18 53	19 23		19 53	20 13	20 43	21 13	21 43	22 19	22 49	23 51

Table 125B

Mondays to Fridays

Bristol - Bristol International Airport

Bus Service

		GW	GW	GW	GW	GW	GW	GW	GW	GW		GW	GW	GW	GW	GW	GW	GW	GW	GW		GW	GW	GW	GW
Bristol Temple Meads 10	d	23p53	00 13	02 42	03 57	04 52	05 12	05 32	05 52	06 12		06 22	06 32	06 42	06 52	07 02	07 12	07 22	07 32	07 46		07 56	08 06	08 16	08 26
Bristol Internatl Airport ✈	a	00 13	00 33	03 01	04 16	05 11	05 31	05 51	06 11	06 31		06 41	06 51	07 01	07 11	07 21	07 31	07 44	07 57	08 11		08 21	08 31	08 41	08 51

		GW	GW	GW	GW	GW		GW	GW	GW	GW	GW	GW	GW	GW	GW		GW	GW	GW	GW	GW	GW	GW	GW
Bristol Temple Meads 10	d	08 36	08 46	08 56	09 06	09 16		09 26	09 36	09 45	09 55	10 05	10 15	10 25	10 35	10 45		10 55	11 05	11 15	11 25	11 35	11 45	11 55	12 05
Bristol Internatl Airport ✈	a	09 01	09 11	09 21	09 31	09 41		09 49	09 58	10 07	10 17	10 27	10 37	10 47	10 57	11 07		11 17	11 27	11 37	11 47	11 57	12 07	12 17	12 27

		GW		GW	GW	GW	GW	GW	GW	GW	GW	GW		GW	GW	GW	GW	GW	GW	GW	GW	GW		GW	GW
Bristol Temple Meads 10	d	12 15		12 25	12 35	12 45	12 55	13 05	13 15	13 25	13 35	13 45		13 55	14 05	14 15	14 25	14 35	14 45	14 55	15 05	15 15		15 25	15 35
Bristol Internatl Airport ✈	a	12 37		12 47	12 57	13 07	13 17	13 27	13 37	13 47	13 57	14 07		14 17	14 27	14 37	14 47	14 57	15 07	15 17	15 27	15 37		15 50	16 02

		GW	GW	GW	GW	GW	GW	GW		GW	GW	GW	GW	GW	GW	GW	GW	GW		GW	GW	GW	GW	GW	GW
Bristol Temple Meads 10	d	15 48	15 58	16 08	16 18	16 28	16 38	16 48		16 58	17 08	17 18	17 28	17 38	17 48	17 58	18 08	18 15		18 25	18 35	18 45	18 55	19 05	19 15
Bristol Internatl Airport ✈	a	16 15	16 25	16 35	16 45	16 55	17 05	17 15		17 25	17 35	17 45	17 55	18 05	18 12	18 22	18 30	18 37		18 47	18 57	19 07	19 17	19 27	19 37

		GW	GW	GW		GW	GW	GW	GW	GW	GW	GW	GW	GW		GW	GW								
Bristol Temple Meads 10	d	19 35	19 55	20 13		20 33	20 53	21 13	21 33	21 53	22 13	22 33	22 53	23 13		23 33	23 53								
Bristol Internatl Airport ✈	a	19 57	20 17	20 33		20 53	21 13	21 33	21 53	22 13	22 33	22 53	23 13	23 33		23 53	00 13								

Saturdays

		GW	GW	GW	GW	GW	GW	GW	GW	GW		GW	GW	GW	GW	GW	GW	GW	GW	GW		GW	GW	GW	GW
Bristol Temple Meads 10	d	23p53	00 13	02 42	03 57	04 52	05 12	05 32	05 52	06 12		06 22	06 32	06 42	06 52	07 02	07 12	07 22	07 32	07 44		07 54	08 04	08 14	08 24
Bristol Internatl Airport ✈	a	00 13	00 33	03 01	04 16	05 11	05 31	05 51	06 11	06 31		06 41	06 51	07 01	07 11	07 21	07 31	07 42	07 52	08 04		08 14	08 24	08 34	08 44

		GW	GW	GW	GW	GW		GW	GW	GW	GW	GW	GW	GW	GW	GW		GW	GW	GW	GW	GW	GW	GW	GW
Bristol Temple Meads 10	d	08 34	08 44	08 54	09 04	09 14		09 24	09 34	09 45	09 55	10 05	10 15	10 25	10 35	10 45		10 55	11 05	11 15	11 25	11 35	11 45	11 55	12 05
Bristol Internatl Airport ✈	a	08 54	09 04	09 14	09 24	09 34		09 44	09 57	10 08	10 18	10 28	10 38	10 48	10 58	11 08		11 18	11 28	11 38	11 48	11 58	12 08	12 18	12 28

		GW		GW	GW	GW	GW	GW	GW	GW	GW	GW		GW	GW	GW	GW	GW	GW	GW	GW	GW		GW	GW
Bristol Temple Meads 10	d	12 15		12 25	12 35	12 45	12 55	13 05	13 15	13 25	13 35	13 45		13 55	14 05	14 15	14 25	14 35	14 45	14 55	15 05	15 15		15 25	15 35
Bristol Internatl Airport ✈	a	12 38		12 48	12 58	13 08	13 18	13 28	13 38	13 48	13 58	14 08		14 18	14 28	14 38	14 48	14 58	15 08	15 18	15 28	15 38		15 48	15 57

		GW	GW	GW	GW	GW	GW	GW		GW	GW	GW	GW	GW	GW	GW	GW	GW		GW	GW	GW	GW	GW	GW
Bristol Temple Meads 10	d	15 46	15 56	16 16	16 36	16 56	17 16	17 36		17 56	18 15	18 35	18 55	19 15	19 35	19 55	20 13	20 33		20 53	21 13	21 33	21 53	22 13	22 33
Bristol Internatl Airport ✈	a	16 08	16 18	16 38	16 58	17 18	17 38	17 58		18 18	18 38	18 58	19 18	19 38	19 58	20 18	20 33	20 53		21 13	21 33	21 53	22 13	22 33	22 53

		GW	GW	GW		GW																			
Bristol Temple Meads 10	d	22 53	23 13	23 33		23 53																			
Bristol Internatl Airport ✈	a	23 13	23 33	23 53		00 13																			

Sundays

		GW A	GW	GW	GW	GW	GW	GW	GW	GW		GW	GW	GW	GW	GW	GW	GW	GW	GW		GW	GW	GW	GW
Bristol Temple Meads 10	d	23p53	00 13	02 42	03 57	04 52	05 12	05 32	05 52	06 12		06 32	06 52	07 12	07 32	07 54	08 14	08 34	08 54	09 14		09 34	09 55	10 15	10 35
Bristol Internatl Airport ✈	a	00 13	00 33	03 01	04 16	05 11	05 31	05 51	06 11	06 31		06 51	07 11	07 31	07 51	08 13	08 33	08 53	09 13	09 33		09 56	10 17	10 37	10 57

		GW	GW	GW	GW	GW		GW	GW	GW	GW	GW	GW	GW	GW	GW		GW	GW	GW	GW	GW	GW	GW	GW
Bristol Temple Meads 10	d	10 55	11 15	11 25	11 35	11 45		11 55	12 05	12 15	12 25	12 35	12 45	12 55	13 05	13 15		13 25	13 35	13 45	13 55	14 05	14 15	14 25	14 35
Bristol Internatl Airport ✈	a	11 17	11 37	11 47	11 57	12 07		12 17	12 27	12 37	12 47	12 57	13 07	13 17	13 27	13 37		13 47	13 57	14 07	14 17	14 27	14 37	14 47	14 57

		GW		GW	GW	GW	GW	GW	GW	GW	GW	GW		GW	GW	GW	GW	GW	GW	GW	GW	GW		GW	GW
Bristol Temple Meads 10	d	14 45		14 55	15 05	15 15	15 25	15 35	15 45	15 55	16 15	16 35		16 55	17 15	17 35	17 55	18 15	18 35	18 55	19 15	19 35		19 55	20 13
Bristol Internatl Airport ✈	a	15 07		15 17	15 27	15 37	15 47	15 58	16 08	16 18	16 38	16 58		17 18	17 38	17 58	18 18	18 37	18 57	19 17	19 37	19 57		20 17	20 33

		GW	GW	GW	GW	GW	GW	GW		GW	GW	GW	GW												
Bristol Temple Meads 10	d	20 33	20 53	21 13	21 33	21 53	22 13	22 33		22 53	23 13	23 33	23 53												
Bristol Internatl Airport ✈	a	20 53	21 13	21 33	21 53	22 13	22 33	22 53		23 13	23 33	23 53	00 13												

A not 11 December

Bristol International Airport - Bristol

Bus Service

		GW	GW	GW	GW	GW	GW	GW	GW	GW		GW	GW	GW	GW	GW	GW	GW	GW	GW		GW	GW	GW	GW
Bristol Internatl Airport	d	23p50	00 50	03 05	04 20	05 20	06 00	06 20	06 40	06 50		07 00	07 10	07 20	07 30	07 40	07 50	08 00	08 10	08 20		08 30	08 40	08 50	09 00
Bristol Temple Meads 10	a	00 16	01 16	03 29	04 44	05 44	06 24	06 44	07 04	07 14		07 24	07 34	07 48	08 02	08 12	08 22	08 32	08 42	08 52		09 02	09 12	09 22	09 32

		GW	GW	GW	GW	GW		GW	GW	GW	GW	GW	GW	GW	GW	GW		GW	GW	GW	GW	GW	GW	GW	GW
Bristol Internatl Airport	d	09 10	09 20	09 30	09 40	09 50		10 00	10 10	10 20	10 30	10 40	10 50	11 00	11 10	11 20		11 30	11 40	11 50	12 00	12 10	12 20	12 30	12 40
Bristol Temple Meads 10	a	09 42	09 52	10 00	10 10	10 20		10 30	10 40	10 50	11 00	11 10	11 20	11 30	11 40	11 50		12 00	12 10	12 20	12 30	12 40	12 50	13 00	13 10

		GW		GW	GW	GW	GW	GW	GW	GW	GW	GW		GW	GW	GW	GW	GW	GW	GW	GW	GW		GW	GW
Bristol Internatl Airport	d	12 50		13 00	13 10	13 20	13 30	13 40	13 50	14 00	14 10	14 20		14 30	14 40	14 50	15 00	15 10	15 20	15 30	15 40	15 50		16 00	16 10
Bristol Temple Meads 10	a	13 20		13 30	13 40	13 50	14 00	14 10	14 20	14 30	14 40	14 50		15 00	15 10	15 20	15 30	15 40	15 52	16 03	16 13	16 23		16 33	16 43

		GW	GW	GW	GW	GW	GW	GW		GW	GW	GW	GW	GW	GW	GW	GW	GW		GW	GW	GW	GW	GW	GW
Bristol Internatl Airport	d	16 20	16 30	16 40	16 50	17 00	17 10	17 20		17 30	17 40	17 50	18 00	18 10	18 20	18 30	18 40	18 50		19 00	19 10	19 20	19 30	19 50	20 10
Bristol Temple Meads 10	a	16 53	17 03	17 13	17 23	17 33	17 43	17 53		18 03	18 13	18 21	18 30	18 40	18 50	19 00	19 10	19 20		19 30	19 40	19 50	20 00	20 17	20 36

		GW	GW	GW		GW	GW	GW	GW	GW	GW	GW	GW												
Bristol Internatl Airport	d	20 30	20 50	21 10		21 30	21 50	22 10	22 30	22 50	23 10	23 30	23 50												
Bristol Temple Meads 10	a	20 56	21 16	21 36		21 56	22 16	22 36	22 56	23 16	23 36	23 56	00 16												

Saturdays

		GW	GW	GW	GW	GW	GW	GW	GW	GW		GW	GW	GW	GW	GW	GW	GW	GW	GW		GW	GW	GW	GW
Bristol Internatl Airport	d	23p50	00 50	03 05	04 20	05 20	05 40	06 00	06 20	06 40		06 50	07 00	07 10	07 20	07 30	07 40	07 50	08 00	08 10		08 20	08 30	08 40	08 50
Bristol Temple Meads 10	a	00 16	01 16	03 29	04 44	05 44	06 04	06 24	06 44	07 04		07 14	07 24	07 34	07 45	07 56	08 06	08 16	08 26	08 36		08 46	08 56	09 06	09 16

		GW	GW	GW	GW	GW		GW	GW	GW	GW	GW	GW	GW	GW	GW		GW	GW	GW	GW	GW	GW	GW	GW
Bristol Internatl Airport	d	09 00	09 10	09 20	09 30	09 40		09 50	10 00	10 10	10 20	10 30	10 40	10 50	11 00	11 10		11 20	11 30	11 40	11 50	12 00	12 10	12 20	12 30
Bristol Temple Meads 10	a	09 26	09 36	09 48	09 59	10 09		10 19	10 29	10 39	10 49	10 59	11 09	11 19	11 29	11 39		11 49	11 59	12 09	12 19	12 29	12 39	12 49	12 59

		GW		GW	GW	GW	GW	GW	GW	GW	GW	GW		GW	GW	GW	GW	GW	GW	GW	GW	GW		GW	GW
Bristol Internatl Airport	d	12 40		12 50	13 00	13 10	13 20	13 30	13 40	13 50	14 00	14 10		14 20	14 30	14 40	14 50	15 00	15 10	15 20	15 30	15 40		15 50	16 00
Bristol Temple Meads 10	a	13 09		13 19	13 29	13 39	13 49	13 59	14 09	14 19	14 29	14 39		14 49	14 59	15 09	15 19	15 29	15 39	15 50	16 00	16 10		16 20	16 30

		GW	GW	GW	GW	GW	GW	GW		GW	GW	GW	GW	GW	GW	GW	GW	GW		GW	GW	GW	GW	GW	GW
Bristol Internatl Airport	d	16 10	16 20	16 30	16 50	17 10	17 30	17 50		18 10	18 30	18 50	19 10	19 30	19 50	20 10	20 30	20 50		21 10	21 30	21 50	22 10	22 30	22 50
Bristol Temple Meads 10	a	16 40	16 50	17 00	17 20	17 40	18 00	18 19		18 39	18 59	19 19	19 39	19 59	20 17	20 36	20 56	21 16		21 36	21 56	22 16	22 36	22 56	23 16

		GW	GW	GW																					
Bristol Internatl Airport	d	23 10	23 30	23 50																					
Bristol Temple Meads 10	a	23 36	23 56	00 16																					

Sundays

		GW A	GW	GW	GW	GW	GW	GW	GW	GW		GW	GW	GW	GW	GW	GW	GW	GW	GW		GW	GW	GW	GW
Bristol Internatl Airport	d	23p50	00 50	03 05	04 20	05 20	05 50	06 10	06 30	06 50		07 10	07 30	07 50	08 10	08 30	08 50	09 10	09 30	09 50		10 10	10 30	10 50	11 10
Bristol Temple Meads 10	a	00 16	01 16	03 29	04 44	05 44	06 14	06 34	06 54	07 14		07 34	07 55	08 15	08 35	08 55	09 15	09 35	09 57	10 17		10 37	10 57	11 17	11 37

		GW	GW	GW	GW	GW		GW	GW	GW	GW	GW	GW	GW	GW	GW		GW	GW	GW	GW	GW	GW	GW	GW
Bristol Internatl Airport	d	11 20	11 30	11 40	11 50	12 00		12 10	12 20	12 30	12 40	12 50	13 00	13 10	13 20	13 30		13 40	13 50	14 00	14 10	14 20	14 30	14 40	14 50
Bristol Temple Meads 10	a	11 47	11 57	12 07	12 17	12 27		12 37	12 47	12 57	13 07	13 17	13 27	13 37	13 47	13 57		14 07	14 17	14 27	14 37	14 47	14 57	15 07	15 17

		GW		GW	GW	GW	GW	GW	GW	GW	GW	GW		GW	GW	GW	GW	GW	GW	GW	GW	GW		GW	GW
Bristol Internatl Airport	d	15 00		15 10	15 20	15 30	15 40	15 50	16 00	16 10	16 20	16 30		16 50	17 10	17 30	17 50	18 10	18 30	18 50	19 10	19 30		19 50	20 10
Bristol Temple Meads 10	a	15 27		15 37	15 49	16 00	16 10	16 20	16 30	16 40	16 50	17 00		17 20	17 40	18 00	18 18	18 37	18 57	19 17	19 37	19 57		20 16	20 36

		GW	GW	GW	GW	GW	GW	GW		GW	GW	GW	GW												
Bristol Internatl Airport	d	20 30	20 50	21 10	21 30	21 50	22 10	22 30		22 50	23 10	23 30	23 50												
Bristol Temple Meads 10	a	20 56	21 16	21 36	21 56	22 16	22 36	22 56		23 16	23 36	23 56	00 16												

A not 11 December

London and Oxford - Worcester and Hereford

Network Diagram - see first Page of Table 116

Miles	Station		GW MX ◇1 ☕	GW MO ◇1 A	GW MO ◇1 B	GW 1	GW ◇1 C 🛒	GW 1 C 🛒	GW 1	GW ◇1 ☕	GW ◇1 🛒	GW ◇1	GW ◇1 ☕	GW ◇1 🛒	GW ◇1 🛒	GW ◇1 🛒	GW ◇1 D 🛒	GW ◇1 ☕	GW 1	GW ◇1 ☕	GW ◇1 ☕	GW ◇1 E ☕	GW ◇1 ☕
0	**London Paddington 15** ⊖	d	21p48	21p42	21p42		05 48	06 48		08 22	09 21	09 50	10 22	11 20	12 21	13 21	14 21	15 51		17 22	17 50	18 22	19 22
18½	Slough 3	d	22p03	22p06	22p06		06 05	07 04		08 36	09 36	10 06	10 36	11 36	12 36	13 36	14 36	16 06					19 36
36	Reading 7	d	22p22	22p22	22p22		06 22	07 22		08 52	09 52	10 22	10 52	11 52	12 52	13 52	14 52	16 22		17 50	18 22	18 50	19 52
53¼	Didcot Parkway	d		22p38	22p38		06 39	07 49															
63½	**Oxford**	d	22p52	22p51	22p51		06 56	08 04	08 58	09 21	10 25	10 48	11 19	12 19	13 21	14 19	15 19	16 49	17 32	18 17	18 49	19 22	20 19
70½	Hanborough	d	23p03	23p04	23p04		07 06	08 14	09 07	09 32	10 35	10 57	11 30	12 29	13 31	14 29	15 29	16 59	17 41	18 27		19 33	20 30
71½	Combe	d																	17 43				
75	Finstock	d																	17 48				
76¾	Charlbury	a	23p10	23p11	23p11		07 13	08 21	09 14	09 39	10 42	11 04	11 37	12 36	13 38	14 36	15 36	17 07	17 52	18 34	19 02	19 40	20 37
—		d	23p11	23p12	23p12		07 13	08 21	09 14	09 40	10 42	11 04	11 38	12 36	13 38	14 36	15 36	17 08	17 52	18 35	19 03	19 41	20 38
80½	Ascott-under-Wychwood	d																	17 57				
81¾	Shipton	d	23p18																18 00		19 11		
84¾	Kingham	d	23p24	23p21	23p21		07 22	08 30	09 23	09 49	10 51	11 13	11 47	12 45	13 47	14 45	15 45	17 18	18 05	18 45	19 18	19 51	20 47
91¾	Moreton-in-Marsh	a	23p31	23p29	23p29		07 30	08 38	09 35	09 57	10 59	11 22	11 55	12 53	13 55	14 54	15 53	17 26	18 13	18 53	19 26	19 59	20 55
—		d	23p32	23p32	23p32	05 46	07 30	08 38		09 58	10 59		11 56	12 53	13 55		15 53	17 27	18 13	18 54	19 27	20 00	20 56
101¾	Honeybourne	d	23p44	23p43	23p43		07 41	08 49		10 09			12 07	13 04	14 06		16 04	17 39	18 24	19 06		20 12	21 07
106¾	Evesham	a	23p50	23p50	23p50	06 00	07 48	08 56		10 17	11 14		12 15	13 11	14 12		16 11	17 46	18 31	19 13	19 43	20 19	21 15
—		d	23p52	23p52	23p53	06 00	07 51	08 56		10 24	11 14		12 24	13 11	14 26		16 20	17 47	18 40	19 14	19 44	20 20	21 19
112¾	Pershore	d	23p59	00 01	00 01	06 08	07 58	09 03		10 32	11 21		12 32	13 18	14 33		16 27	17 56	18 48	19 22	19 52	20 28	21 27
120½	**Worcester Shrub Hill 7**	a	00 12	00 12	00 12	06 19	08 10	09 15		10 44	11 34		12 44	13 31	14 46		16 39	18 08	18 59	19 34	20 03	20 41	21 46
121¼	**Worcester Foregate Street 7**	a				06 39	08 17	09 18		10 48	11 40		12 48	13 35	14 51		16 43		19 11	19 38		20 45	21 50
128	Malvern Link	a						09 27		11 02			12 58	13 50	15 05				19 20	19 48		20 54	22 02
128¾	Great Malvern	a						09 32		11 06			13 02	13 56	15 09				19 24	19 52		20 58	22 06
131¾	Colwall	a								11 14			13 16							19 58		21 04	22 25
136	Ledbury	a								11 22			13 24							20 06		21 12	22 33
149¾	**Hereford 7**	a								11 42			13 48							20 27		21 33	22 54

Station		GW ◇1 D 🛒	GW FO ◇1 D 🛒	GW FX ◇1 ☕
London Paddington 15 ⊖	d	20 20	21 48	21 48
Slough 3	d	20 36	22 03	22 03
Reading 7	d	20 52	22 22	22 22
Didcot Parkway	d			
Oxford	d	21 18	22 52	22 52
Hanborough	d	21 28	23 03	23 03
Combe	d			
Finstock	d			
Charlbury	a	21 35	23 10	23 10
	d	21 36	23 11	23 11
Ascott-under-Wychwood	d			
Shipton	d		23 18	23 18
Kingham	d	21 45	23 24	23 24
Moreton-in-Marsh	a	21 53	23 31	23 31
	d	21 54	23 32	23 32
Honeybourne	d	22 05	23 44	23 44
Evesham	a	22 13	23 50	23 50
	d	22 13	23 52	23 52
Pershore	d	22 21	23 59	23 59
Worcester Shrub Hill 7	a	22 34	00 12	00 12
Worcester Foregate Street 7	a	22 43		
Malvern Link	a	22 52		
Great Malvern	a	22 58		
Colwall	a			
Ledbury	a			
Hereford 7	a			

A until 13 February, MO from 2 April
B from 20 February until 26 March
C 🛒 from Oxford
D 🛒 to Oxford
E The Cathedrals Express

Saturdays

until 31 December

London and Oxford - Worcester and Hereford

Network Diagram - see first Page of Table 116

		GW	GW	GW	GW	GW	GW	GW	GW	GW	GW	GW	GW	GW	GW	GW
		◇1	◇1	◇1	◇1	◇1	◇1	◇1	◇1	◇1	◇1	◇1	◇1	◇1	◇1	◇1
		A		B	B						A				A	
		🛒		🛒	🛒	🍴	🍴	🛒	🛒	🛒	🛒	🍴	🍴	🍴	🛒	
London Paddington 15 ⊖	d	21p48	05 21	06 21	07 21	08 21	10 21	11 21	13 21	14 21	15 21	16 21	17 21	18 21	19 50	21 50
Slough 3	d	22p03	05 38	06 38	07 38	08 39	10 39	11 39	13 39	14 39	15 39	16 39	17 39	18 39	20 06	22 06
Reading 7	d	22p22	05 54	06 54	07 53	08 54	10 54	11 54	13 54	14 54	15 54	16 54	17 54	18 54	20 22	22 23
Didcot Parkway	d		06 08													22 38
Oxford	d	22p52	06 23	07 23	08 23	09 23	11 23	12 23	14 23	15 23	16 23	17 23	18 23	19 23	20 49	22 50
Hanborough	d	23p03	06 34	07 32	08 32	09 34	11 33	12 33	14 32	15 32	16 32	17 33	18 33	19 33	20 58	23 00
Combe	d															
Finstock	d															
Charlbury	a	23p10	06 41	07 39	08 39	09 41	11 40	12 40	14 39	15 39	16 39	17 40	18 40	19 40	21 05	23 07
	d	23p11	06 42	07 39	08 39	09 42	11 41	12 40	14 39	15 39	16 39	17 41	18 41	19 41	21 05	23 07
Ascott-under-Wychwood	d															
Shipton	d	23p18							14 46			17 48			21 12	23 14
Kingham	d	23p24	06 51	07 48	08 48	09 51	11 50	12 49	14 51	15 48	16 48	17 54	18 50	19 50	21 17	23 19
Moreton-in-Marsh	a	23p31	07 00	07 56	08 56	10 00	11 59	12 58	14 59	15 57	16 57	18 03	18 59	19 59	21 25	23 27
	d	23p32	07 00	07 56	08 56	10 00	11 59	12 58	14 59	15 57	16 57	18 03	18 59	19 59	21 25	23 27
Honeybourne	d	23p44	07 12	08 07	09 07	10 12	12 11	13 09	15 10	16 08	17 08	18 15	19 11	20 11	21 36	23 38
Evesham	a	23p50	07 20	08 15	09 15	10 20	12 19	13 17	15 18	16 16	17 16	18 23	19 19	20 19	21 43	23 45
	d	23p52	07 25	08 21	09 21	10 25	12 20	13 21	15 21	16 21	17 21	18 24	19 21	20 23	21 43	23 45
Pershore	d	23p59	07 32	08 28	09 28	10 32	12 27	13 28	15 28	16 28	17 28	18 31	19 28	20 30	21 50	23 53
Worcester Shrub Hill 7	a	00 12	07 44	08 40	09 40	10 44	12 39	13 40	15 40	16 40	17 40	18 43	19 40	20 42	22 02	00 07
Worcester Foregate Street 7	a		07 48	08 44	09 44	10 48	12 47	13 44	15 44	16 44	17 44	18 55	19 44	20 48	22 06	
Malvern Link	a		07 58	08 54	09 54	10 58	12 57	13 54	15 54	16 54	17 54	19 05		20 58	22 16	
Great Malvern	a		08 03	09 00	10 00	11 05	13 02	14 00	16 00	17 00	18 00	19 09		21 02	22 22	
Colwall	a					11 12	13 13					19 15		21 08		
Ledbury	a					11 20	13 21					19 23		21 16		
Hereford 7	a					11 41	13 40					19 45		21 34		

Saturdays

7 January to 24 March

		GW	GW	GW	GW	GW	GW	GW	GW	GW	GW	GW	GW	GW	GW	GW
		◇1	◇1	◇1	◇1	◇1	◇1	◇1	◇1	◇1	◇1	◇1	◇1	◇1	◇1	◇1
		A		B	B						A				C	
		🛒		🛒	🛒	🍴	🍴	🛒	🛒	🛒	🛒	🍴	🍴	🍴	🛒	
London Paddington 15 ⊖	d	21p48	05 21	06 21	07 21	08 21	10 21	11 21	13 21	14 21	15 21	16 21	17 21	18 21	19 50	21 50
Slough 3	d	22p03	05 38	06 38	07 38	08 39	10 39	11 39	13 39	14 39	15 39	16 39	17 39	18 39	20 06	22 06
Reading 7	d	22p22	05 54	06 54	07 53	08 54	10 54	11 54	13 54	14 54	15 54	16 54	17 54	18 54	20 22	22 23
Didcot Parkway	d		06 08													22 38
Oxford	d	22p52	06 23	07 23	08 23	09 23	11 23	12 23	14 23	15 23	16 23	17 23	18 23	19 23	20 49	22 50
Hanborough	d	23p03	06 34	07 32	08 32	09 34	11 33	12 33	14 32	15 32	16 32	17 33	18 33	19 33	20 58	23 00
Combe	d															
Finstock	d															
Charlbury	a	23p10	06 41	07 39	08 39	09 41	11 40	12 40	14 39	15 39	16 39	17 40	18 40	19 40	21 05	23 07
	d	23p11	06 42	07 39	08 39	09 42	11 41	12 40	14 39	15 39	16 39	17 41	18 41	19 41	21 05	23 07
Ascott-under-Wychwood	d															
Shipton	d	23p18							14 46			17 48			21 12	23 14
Kingham	d	23p24	06 51	07 48	08 48	09 51	11 50	12 49	14 51	15 48	16 48	17 54	18 50	19 50	21 17	23 19
Moreton-in-Marsh	a	23p31	07 00	07 56	08 56	10 00	11 59	12 58	14 59	15 57	16 57	18 03	18 59	19 59	21 25	23 27
	d	23p32	07 00	07 56	08 56	10 00	11 59	12 58	14 59	15 57	16 57	18 03	18 59	19 59	21 25	23 27
Honeybourne	d	23p44	07 12	08 07	09 07	10 12	12 11	13 09	15 10	16 08	17 08	18 15	19 11	20 11	21 36	23 38
Evesham	a	23p50	07 20	08 15	09 15	10 20	12 19	13 17	15 18	16 16	17 16	18 23	19 19	20 19	21 43	23 45
	d	23p52	07 25	08 21	09 21	10 25	12 20	13 21	15 21	16 21	17 21	18 24	19 21	20 23	21 43	23 45
Pershore	d	23p59	07 32	08 28	09 28	10 32	12 27	13 28	15 28	16 28	17 28	18 31	19 28	20 30	21 50	23 53
Worcester Shrub Hill 7	a	00 12	07 44	08 40	09 40	10 44	12 39	13 40	15 40	16 40	17 40	18 43	19 40	20 42	22 02	00 07
Worcester Foregate Street 7	a		07 48	08 44	09 44	10 48	12 47	13 44	15 44	16 44	17 44	18 55	19 44	20 48	22 06	
Malvern Link	a		07 58	08 54	09 54	10 58	12 57	13 54	15 54	16 54	17 54	19 05		20 58	22 16	
Great Malvern	a		08 03	09 00	10 00	11 05	13 02	14 00	16 00	17 00	18 00	19 09		21 02	22 22	
Colwall	a					11 12	13 13					19 15		21 08		
Ledbury	a					11 20	13 21					19 23		21 16		
Hereford 7	a					11 41	13 40					19 45		21 34		

A 🛒 to Oxford

B 🛒 from Oxford

C from 7 January until 11 February. 🛒 to Oxford

Table 126

Saturdays
from 31 March

London and Oxford - Worcester and Hereford

Network Diagram - see first Page of Table 116

		GW	GW	GW	GW	GW	GW	GW	GW	GW	GW	GW	GW	GW	GW	GW
		◇1	◇1	◇1	◇1	◇1	◇1	◇1	◇1	◇1	◇1	◇1	◇1	◇1	◇1	◇1
		A		B	B						A				A	
		[trolley]		[trolley]	[trolley]	[buffet]	[buffet]	[trolley]	[trolley]	[trolley]	[trolley]	[buffet]	[buffet]	[buffet]	[trolley]	
London Paddington 15 ⊖	d	21p48	05 21	06 21	07 21	08 21	10 21	11 21	13 21	14 21	15 21	16 21	17 21	18 21	19 50	21 50
Slough 3	d	22p03	05 38	06 38	07 38	08 39	10 39	11 39	13 39	14 39	15 39	16 39	17 39	18 39	20 06	22 06
Reading 7	d	22p22	05 54	06 54	07 53	08 54	10 54	11 54	13 54	14 54	15 54	16 54	17 54	18 54	20 22	22 23
Didcot Parkway	d		06 08													22 38
Oxford	d	22p52	06 23	07 23	08 23	09 23	11 23	12 23	14 23	15 23	16 23	17 23	18 23	19 23	20 49	22 50
Hanborough	d	23p03	06 34	07 32	08 32	09 34	11 33	12 33	14 32	15 32	16 32	17 33	18 33	19 33	20 58	23 00
Combe	d															
Finstock	d															
Charlbury	a	23p10	06 41	07 39	08 39	09 41	11 40	12 40	14 39	15 39	16 39	17 40	18 40	19 40	21 05	23 07
	d	23p11	06 42	07 39	08 39	09 42	11 41	12 40	14 39	15 39	16 39	17 41	18 41	19 41	21 05	23 07
Ascott-under-Wychwood	d															
Shipton	d	23p18							14 46			17 48			21 12	23 14
Kingham	d	23p24	06 51	07 48	08 48	09 51	11 50	12 49	14 51	15 48	16 48	17 54	18 50	19 50	21 17	23 19
Moreton-in-Marsh	a	23p31	07 00	07 56	08 56	10 00	11 59	12 58	14 59	15 57	16 57	18 03	18 59	19 59	21 25	23 27
	d	23p32	07 00	07 56	08 56	10 00	11 59	12 58	14 59	15 57	16 57	18 03	18 59	19 59	21 25	23 27
Honeybourne	d	23p44	07 12	08 07	09 07	10 12	12 11	13 09	15 10	16 08	17 08	18 15	19 11	20 11	21 36	23 38
Evesham	a	23p50	07 20	08 15	09 15	10 20	12 19	13 17	15 18	16 16	17 16	18 23	19 19	20 19	21 43	23 45
	d	23p52	07 25	08 21	09 21	10 25	12 20	13 21	15 21	16 21	17 21	18 24	19 21	20 23	21 43	23 45
Pershore	d	23p59	07 32	08 28	09 28	10 32	12 27	13 28	15 28	16 28	17 28	18 31	19 28	20 30	21 50	23 53
Worcester Shrub Hill 7	a	00 12	07 44	08 40	09 40	10 44	12 39	13 40	15 40	16 40	17 40	18 43	19 40	20 42	22 02	00 07
Worcester Foregate Street 7	a		07 48	08 44	09 44	10 48	12 47	13 44	15 44	16 44	17 44	18 55	19 44	20 48	22 06	
Malvern Link	a		07 58	08 54	09 54	10 58	12 57	13 54	15 54	16 54	17 54	19 05		20 58	22 16	
Great Malvern	a		08 03	09 00	10 00	11 05	13 02	14 00	16 00	17 00	18 00	19 09		21 02	22 22	
Colwall	a					11 12	13 13					19 15		21 08		
Ledbury	a					11 20	13 21					19 23		21 16		
Hereford 7	a					11 41	13 40					19 45		21 34		

Sundays
until 1 January

		GW	GW	GW	GW	GW	GW	GW	GW	GW	GW	GW	GW	GW
		◇1	◇1	◇1	◇1	◇1	◇1	◇1	◇1	◇1	◇1	◇1	◇1	◇1
		C												
				[buffet]	[buffet]	[buffet]	[buffet]				[buffet]		[buffet]	
London Paddington 15 ⊖	d	21p50	08 03	09 35	10 42	12 42	13 42	14 42	15 42	16 42	17 42	18 42	19 42	21 42
Slough 3	d	22p06	08 26	09 58	11 05	13 07	14 06	15 05	16 05	17 04	18 04	19 07	20 06	22 06
Reading 7	d	22p23	08 45	10 11	11 21	13 23	14 21	15 21	16 21	17 24	18 25	19 27	20 21	22 22
Didcot Parkway	d	22p38	09 02	10 28	11 37	13 38	14 37	15 36	16 37	17 39	18 39	19 43	20 37	22 38
Oxford	d	22p50	09 18	10 45	11 51	13 50	14 50	15 54	16 54	17 56	18 53	19 58	20 51	22 51
Hanborough	d	23p00	09 28	10 58	12 02	14 02		16 00		18 06	19 05	20 09	21 02	23 04
Combe	d													
Finstock	d													
Charlbury	a	23p07	09 35	11 05	12 09	14 09	15 04	16 08	17 04	18 13	19 12	20 16	21 09	23 11
	d	23p07	09 35	11 06	12 10	14 10	15 05	16 09	17 05	18 13	19 13	20 16	21 10	23 12
Ascott-under-Wychwood	d													
Shipton	d	23p14												
Kingham	d	23p19	09 44	11 16	12 19	14 20	15 15	16 19	17 14	18 22	19 21	20 25	21 18	23 21
Moreton-in-Marsh	a	23p27	09 52	11 24	12 27	14 27	15 25	16 27	17 23	18 30	19 28	20 33	21 26	23 29
	d	23p27	09 53	11 25	12 28	14 28	15 25	16 28	17 23	18 31	19 29	20 34	21 29	23 32
Honeybourne	d	23p38	10 04	11 36	12 39		15 38	16 40		18 42	19 41	20 45	21 40	23 43
Evesham	a	23p45	10 10	11 44	12 47	14 48	15 47	16 48	17 41	18 48	19 48	20 52	21 48	23 50
	d	23p45	10 13	11 46	12 48	14 49	15 47	16 48	17 48	18 51	19 51	20 52	21 48	23 52
Pershore	d	23p53	10 20	11 54	12 56	14 56	15 56	16 57	17 56	18 58	19 59	21 02	21 57	00 01
Worcester Shrub Hill 7	a	00 07	10 32	12 05	13 09	15 09	16 08	17 09	18 08	19 10	20 12	21 13	22 10	00 12
Worcester Foregate Street 7	a		10 35	12 09	13 12	15 12		17 12	18 10	19 13	20 16		22 13	
Malvern Link	a		10 47	12 19	13 22	15 22		17 22		19 23	20 24		22 23	
Great Malvern	a		10 50	12 22	13 26	15 26		17 26		19 26	20 29		22 27	
Colwall	a			12 28	13 32	15 32		17 32			20 37			
Ledbury	a			12 36	13 41	15 41		17 41			20 45			
Hereford 7	a			12 54	14 06	16 05		17 58			21 03			

A [trolley] to Oxford

B [trolley] from Oxford

C not 11 December

Table 126

London and Oxford - Worcester and Hereford

Network Diagram - see first Page of Table 116

Sundays

8 January to 12 February

		GW ◇1	GW ◇1	GW ◇1 ☕	GW ◇1 ☕	GW ◇1 ☕	GW ◇1 ☕	GW ◇1	GW ◇1	GW ◇1	GW ◇1 ☕	GW ◇1	GW ◇1 ☕	GW ◇1
London Paddington ■15 ⊖	d	21p50	08 03	09 35	10 42	12 42	13 42	14 42	15 42	16 42	17 42	18 42	19 42	21 42
Slough ■3	d	22p06	08 26	09 58	11 05	13 07	14 06	15 03	16 04	17 03	18 04	19 08	20 06	22 06
Reading ■7	d	22p23	08 44	10 11	11 21	13 23	14 21	15 21	16 21	17 26	18 24	19 27	20 21	22 22
Didcot Parkway	d	22p38	09 02	10 28	11 37	13 38	14 39	15 36	16 37	17 41	18 39	19 43	20 37	22 38
Oxford	d	22p50	09 18	10 45	11 51	13 50	14 50	15 54	16 54	17 58	18 53	19 58	20 51	22 51
Hanborough	d	23p00	09 28	10 58	12 02	14 02		16 02		18 07	19 04	20 09	21 02	23 04
Combe	d													
Finstock	d													
Charlbury	a	23p07	09 35	11 05	12 09	14 09	15 04	16 10	17 04	18 14	19 11	20 16	21 09	23 11
	d	23p07	09 35	11 06	12 10	14 10	15 05	16 11	17 05	18 15	19 12	20 16	21 10	23 12
Ascott-under-Wychwood	d													
Shipton	d	23p14												
Kingham	d	23p19	09 44	11 16	12 19	14 20	15 15	16 20	17 13	18 24	19 21	20 25	21 18	23 21
Moreton-in-Marsh	a	23p27	09 52	11 24	12 27	14 27	15 25	16 27	17 23	18 32	19 28	20 33	21 26	23 29
	d	23p27	09 53	11 25	12 28	14 28	15 25	16 28	17 24	18 32	19 29	20 34	21 29	23 32
Honeybourne	d	23p38	10 04	11 36	12 39		15 38	16 40		18 43	19 41	20 45	21 40	23 43
Evesham	a	23p45	10 10	11 44	12 47	14 48	15 47	16 48	17 41	18 50	19 48	20 52	21 48	23 50
	d	23p45	10 13	11 46	12 48	14 49	15 47	16 48	17 48	18 51	19 51	20 52	21 48	23 52
Pershore	d	23p53	10 20	11 54	12 56	14 56	15 56	16 57	17 56	18 58	19 59	21 02	21 57	00 01
Worcester Shrub Hill ■7	a	00 07	10 32	12 05	13 09	15 09	16 08	17 09	18 08	19 10	20 12	21 13	22 10	00 12
Worcester Foregate Street ■7	a		10 35	12 09	13 12	15 12		17 12	18 10	19 13	20 16		22 13	
Malvern Link	a		10 47	12 19	13 23	15 22		17 22		19 23	20 24		22 23	
Great Malvern	a		10 50	12 22	13 27	15 26		17 26		19 26	20 29		22 27	
Colwall	a			12 28	13 32	15 32		17 32			20 37			
Ledbury	a			12 36	13 41	15 41		17 41			20 45			
Hereford ■7	a			12 54	14 06	16 05		17 58			21 03			

Sundays

19 February to 25 March

		GW ◇1	GW ◇1	GW ◇1 ☕	GW ◇1 ☕	GW ◇1 ☕	GW ◇1 ☕	GW ◇1	GW ◇1	GW ◇1	GW ◇1 ☕	GW ◇1	GW ◇1 ☕	GW ◇1
London Paddington ■15 ⊖	d	21p50	08 03	09 35	10 42	12 42	13 42	14 42	15 42	16 42	17 42	18 42	19 42	21 42
Slough ■3	d	22p06	08 26	09 58	11 05	13 07	14 06	15 03	16 04	17 03	18 05	19 08	20 06	22 06
Reading ■7	d	22p23	08 44	10 11	11 21	13 23	14 21	15 21	16 21	17 26	18 25	19 27	20 21	22 22
Didcot Parkway	d	22p38	09 02	10 28	11 37	13 38	14 37	15 36	16 37	17 41	18 40	19 43	20 37	22 38
Oxford	d	22p50	09 18	10 45	11 51	13 50	14 50	15 51	16 51	17 58	18 53	19 58	20 51	22 51
Hanborough	d	23p00	09 28	10 58	12 02	14 02		16 00		18 07	19 05	20 09	21 02	23 04
Combe	d													
Finstock	d													
Charlbury	a	23p07	09 35	11 05	12 09	14 09	15 04	16 08	17 04	18 14	19 12	20 16	21 09	23 11
	d	23p07	09 35	11 06	12 10	14 10	15 05	16 09	17 05	18 15	19 13	20 16	21 10	23 12
Ascott-under-Wychwood	d													
Shipton	d	23p14												
Kingham	d	23p19	09 44	11 16	12 19	14 20	15 15	16 19	17 13	18 24	19 21	20 25	21 18	23 21
Moreton-in-Marsh	a	23p27	09 52	11 24	12 27	14 27	15 23	16 26	17 23	18 32	19 28	20 33	21 26	23 29
	d	23p27	09 53	11 25	12 28	14 28	15 23	16 28	17 24	18 32	19 29	20 34	21 29	23 32
Honeybourne	d	23p38	10 04	11 36	12 39		15 38	16 40		18 43	19 41	20 45	21 40	23 43
Evesham	a	23p45	10 10	11 44	12 47	14 48	15 47	16 48	17 41	18 50	19 48	20 52	21 48	23 50
	d	23p45	10 13	11 46	12 48	14 49	15 47	16 48	17 48	18 52	19 51	20 52	21 48	23 53
Pershore	d	23p53	10 20	11 54	12 56	14 56	15 56	16 57	17 56	19 00	19 59	21 02	21 57	00 01
Worcester Shrub Hill ■7	a	00 07	10 32	12 05	13 09	15 09	16 08	17 09	18 08	19 09	20 12	21 13	22 10	00 12
Worcester Foregate Street ■7	a		10 35	12 09	13 12	15 12		17 12	18 10	19 12	20 16		22 13	
Malvern Link	a		10 47	12 19	13 22	15 22		17 22		19 22	20 24		22 23	
Great Malvern	a		10 50	12 22	13 26	15 26		17 26		19 28	20 29		22 27	
Colwall	a			12 28	13 32	15 33		17 32			20 37			
Ledbury	a			12 36	13 41	15 41		17 41			20 45			
Hereford ■7	a			12 54	14 06	16 05		17 58			21 03			

Table 126

Sundays
from 1 April

London and Oxford - Worcester and Hereford

Network Diagram - see first Page of Table 116

		GW	GW	GW	GW	GW	GW	GW	GW	GW		GW	GW	GW	GW
		◇1	◇1	◇1	◇1	◇1	◇1	◇1	◇1	◇1		◇1	◇1	◇1	◇1
				☕	☕	☕	☕					☕		☕	
London Paddington 15 ⊖	d	21p50	08 03	09 35	10 42	12 42	13 42	14 42	15 42	16 42		17 42	18 42	19 42	21 42
Slough 3	d	22p06	08 26	09 58	11 05	13 07	14 06	15 03	16 04	17 04		18 05	19 07	20 06	22 06
Reading 7	d	22p23	08 44	10 11	11 21	13 23	14 21	15 21	16 21	17 24		18 26	19 27	20 21	22 22
Didcot Parkway	d	22p38	09 02	10 28	11 37	13 38	14 39	15 36	16 37	17 39		18 40	19 43	20 37	22 38
Oxford	d	22p50	09 18	10 45	11 51	13 50	14 50	15 51	16 51	17 56		18 54	19 58	20 51	22 51
Hanborough	d	23p00	09 28	10 58	12 02	14 02		16 00		18 06		19 05	20 09	21 02	23 04
Combe	d														
Finstock	d														
Charlbury	a	23p07	09 35	11 05	12 09	14 09	15 04	16 08	17 04	18 13		19 12	20 16	21 09	23 11
	d	23p07	09 35	11 06	12 10	14 10	15 05	16 09	17 05	18 13		19 13	20 16	21 10	23 12
Ascott-under-Wychwood	d														
Shipton	d	23p14													
Kingham	d	23p19	09 44	11 16	12 19	14 20	15 15	16 19	17 13	18 22		19 22	20 25	21 18	23 21
Moreton-in-Marsh	a	23p27	09 52	11 24	12 27	14 27	15 25	16 26	17 23	18 30		19 29	20 33	21 26	23 29
	d	23p27	09 53	11 25	12 28	14 28	15 25	16 28	17 24	18 31		19 30	20 34	21 29	23 32
Honeybourne	d	23p38	10 04	11 36	12 39		15 38	16 40		18 42		19 41	20 45	21 40	23 43
Evesham	a	23p45	10 10	11 44	12 47	14 48	15 47	16 48	17 41	18 48		19 49	20 52	21 48	23 50
	d	23p45	10 13	11 46	12 48	14 49	15 47	16 48	17 48	18 51		19 52	20 52	21 48	23 52
Pershore	d	23p53	10 20	11 54	12 56	14 56	15 56	16 57	17 56	18 58		20 00	21 02	21 57	00 01
Worcester Shrub Hill 7	a	00 07	10 32	12 05	13 09	15 09	16 08	17 09	18 08	19 10		20 12	21 13	22 10	00 12
Worcester Foregate Street 7	a		10 35	12 09	13 12	15 12		17 12	18 10	19 13		20 16		22 13	
Malvern Link	a		10 47	12 19	13 22	15 22		17 22		19 23		20 25		22 23	
Great Malvern	a		10 50	12 22	13 26	15 26		17 26		19 26		20 29		22 27	
Colwall	a			12 28	13 32	15 32		17 32				20 37			
Ledbury	a			12 36	13 41	15 41		17 41				20 45			
Hereford 7	a			12 54	14 06	16 05		17 58				21 03			

Hereford and Worcester - Oxford and London

Network Diagram - see first Page of Table 116

Miles			GW	GW	GW	GW	GW	GW	GW	GW	GW
			MO	MO	MO	MX					
			◇1	◇1	◇1	◇1	◇1	◇1	◇1	◇1	1
			A	B	C					D	
							🍴	🍴	🛒	🍴⊘	
0	**Hereford 7**	d				21p51				05 35	
13¾	Ledbury	d				22p09				05 52	
18	Colwall	d				22p17				05 59	
20¾	Great Malvern	d				22p22		05 18		06 04	
21¾	Malvern Link	d						05 21		06 08	
28½	**Worcester Foregate Street 7**	d				22p34		05 32		06 19	06 53
29¼	**Worcester Shrub Hill 7**	d	21p34	21p34	21p34	22p43	05 11	05 37		06 33	06 56
37	Pershore	d	21p44	21p44	21p44	22p52		05 46		06 41	07 05
43	Evesham	a	21p48	21p48	21p48	23p00	05 24	05 54		06 49	07 13
—		d	21p49	21p49	21p49	23p01	05 29	05 54		06 51	07 13
48	Honeybourne	d	21p57	21p57	21p57	23p08	05 36			06 58	
58	Moreton-in-Marsh	a	22p09	22p09	22p09	23p19	05 47	06 09		07 09	07 28
—		d	22p10	22p10	22p10	23p27	05 48	06 10		07 10	07 28
65	Kingham	d	22p19	22p19	22p19	23p36	05 56	06 18		07 19	07 36
68	Shipton	d									07 41
69¼	Ascott-under-Wychwood	d									07 43
73	Charlbury	a	22p29	22p29	22p29	23p45	06 05	06 27		07 28	07 49
—		d	22p29	22p29	22p29	23p45	06 06	06 30	07 15	07 30	07 49
74¾	Finstock	d									07 53
78¼	Combe	d									07 58
79¼	Hanborough	d	22p37	22p37	22p37		06 14	06 38	07 23	07 39	08 01
86¼	**Oxford**	a	22p46	22p46	22p46	23p58	06 24	06 52	07 31	07 49	08 12
96½	Didcot Parkway	a	22p58	22p58	23p01	00 20	06 39	07 07			
113¾	Reading 7	a	23p15	23p15	23p17	00 38	06 54	07 25	07 57	08 21	
131¼	Slough 3	a	23p40	23p42	23p41	00 55					
149¾	**London Paddington 15** ⊖	a	00 02	00 04	00 04	01 17	07 30	07 59	08 31	08 51	

Miles			GW	GW	GW	GW	GW	GW	GW	GW	GW	GW	GW	GW
			◇1	◇1	◇1	◇1	◇1	◇1	◇1	◇1	◇1	1	◇1	◇1
			E											
			🍴⊘	🛒		🛒	🛒	🛒	🍴	🛒			🍴	🛒
0	**Hereford 7**	d	06 44						13 14				15 14	
13¾	Ledbury	d	07 01						13 31				15 31	
18	Colwall	d	07 08						13 39				15 38	
20¾	Great Malvern	d	07 14			09 54			13 44	14 26		15 22	15 44	
21¾	Malvern Link	d	07 18			09 56			13 48	14 28			15 48	
28½	**Worcester Foregate Street 7**	d	07 29	08 26		10 05		12 06	13 59	14 38		15 34	15 59	17 28
29¼	**Worcester Shrub Hill 7**	d	07 34	08 39		10 08		12 08	14 09	14 41		15 42	16 03	17 31
37	Pershore	d	07 43	08 48		10 17		12 17	14 18	14 50		15 51	16 13	17 40
43	Evesham	a	07 51	08 56		10 25		12 25	14 26	14 58		15 59	16 21	17 48
—		d	07 52	09 04		10 31		12 31	14 30	15 06		15 59	16 21	17 48
48	Honeybourne	d	07 59	09 11		10 37		12 38	14 37	15 12			16 28	17 54
58	Moreton-in-Marsh	a	08 11	09 23		10 49		12 50	14 48	15 24		16 14	16 40	18 06
—		d	08 12	09 23	09 51	10 49	11 51	12 50	14 49	15 24	15 53	16 14	16 40	18 06
65	Kingham	d	08 21	09 31	09 58	10 57	11 58	12 58	14 57	15 32	16 00	16 22	16 49	18 14
68	Shipton	d											16 55	
69¼	Ascott-under-Wychwood	d												
73	Charlbury	a	08 30	09 40	10 07	11 06	12 07	13 06	15 06	15 41	16 08	16 31	17 01	18 23
—		d	08 31	09 40	10 07	11 06	12 07	13 06	15 07	15 41	16 09	16 31	17 11	18 37
74¾	Finstock	d												
78¼	Combe	d												
79¼	Hanborough	d	08 39	09 47	10 15	11 14	12 15	13 14	15 15	15 49	16 17		17 19	18 44
86¼	**Oxford**	a	08 49	09 58	10 25	11 28	12 29	13 25	15 25	15 59	16 27	16 46	17 29	19 02
96½	Didcot Parkway	a										17 04		
113¾	Reading 7	a	09 14	10 25	10 54	11 54	12 54	13 54	15 54	16 24	16 54		17 54	19 32
131¼	Slough 3	a		10 39	11 09	12 09	13 09	14 09	16 09	16 39	17 09		18 10	19 47
149¾	**London Paddington 15** ⊖	a	09 47	11 00	11 29	12 29	13 29	14 29	16 27	17 00	17 34		18 28	20 06

		GW	GW	GW	GW	GW
				FO	FX	
		◇1	◇1	◇1	◇1	◇1
		🍴				
Hereford 7	d					21 51
Ledbury	d					22 09
Colwall	d					22 17
Great Malvern	d		19 44			22 22
Malvern Link	d		19 46			
Worcester Foregate Street 7	d	18 49	19 54	20 59	20 59	22 34
Worcester Shrub Hill 7	d	18 55	20 03	21 03	21 03	22 43
Pershore	d	19 04	20 12	21 12	21 12	22 52
Evesham	a	19 12	20 20	21 20	21 20	23 00
	d	19 12	20 20	21 21	21 21	23 01
Honeybourne	d	19 20	20 27	21 28	21 28	23 08
Moreton-in-Marsh	a	19 31	20 39	21 39	21 39	23 19
	d	19 48	20 48	21 40	21 40	23 27
Kingham	d	19 56	20 56	21 48	21 48	23 36
Shipton	d					
Ascott-under-Wychwood	d					
Charlbury	a	20 05	21 05	21 57	21 57	23 45
	d	20 06	21 05	22 07	22 07	23 45
Finstock	d					
Combe	d					
Hanborough	d	20 14	21 12	22 15	22 15	
Oxford	a	20 24	21 27	22 27	22 27	23 58
Didcot Parkway	a					00 20
Reading 7	a	20 54	21 55	22 58	22 58	00 38
Slough 3	a	21 09	22 13	23 12	23 15	00 55
London Paddington 15 ⊖	a	21 29	22 39	23 36	23 36	01 17

A until 2 January
B from 2 April
C from 9 January until 26 March
D 🍴 from Reading ⊘ to Reading
E The Cathedrals Express. 🍴 from Reading ⊘ to Reading

Table 126

Saturdays

until 31 December

Hereford and Worcester - Oxford and London

Network Diagram - see first Page of Table 116

		GW	GW	GW	GW	GW	GW	GW	GW	GW		GW	GW	GW	GW	GW	GW	GW
		◇[1]	◇[1]	◇[1]	◇[1]	◇[1]	◇[1]	◇[1]	◇[1]	◇[1]		◇[1]	◇[1]	◇[1]	◇[1]	◇[1]	◇[1]	[1]
					A													
			☕	☕	☕⊘	☕	🛒	🛒	☕	🛒		☕	🛒	🛒				
Hereford [7]	d	21p51		06 17	07 10				12 13			15 13					20 20	
Ledbury	d	22p09		06 34	07 30				12 31			15 31					20 40	
Colwall	d	22p17		06 41	07 37				12 38			15 38					20 47	
Great Malvern	d	22p22	05 56	06 49	07 43	08 43	09 51	10 58	12 44	14 34		15 44	16 34	17 49	18 35		20 53	22 41
Malvern Link	d		05 59	06 53	07 46	08 47	09 54	11 01	12 48	14 37		15 48	16 37	17 52	18 38		20 57	22 44
Worcester Foregate Street [7]	d	22p34	06 09	07 04	07 59	08 58	10 04	11 11	12 59	14 57		15 59	16 54	18 02	18 48	20 02	21 11	22 53
Worcester Shrub Hill [7]	d	22p43	06 12	07 08	08 04	09 02	10 08	11 15	13 04	15 01		16 04	17 02	18 06	19 02	20 06	21 15	22 57
Pershore	d	22p52	06 21	07 17	08 13	09 11	10 16	11 23	13 13	15 09		16 12	17 10	18 15	19 10	20 15	21 24	23 06
Evesham	a	23p00	06 29	07 25	08 21	09 19	10 25	11 32	13 21	15 18		16 21	17 19	18 23	19 19	20 23	21 32	23 15
	d	23p01	06 30	07 26	08 26	09 32	10 32	11 32	13 30	15 26		16 22	17 26	18 27	19 27	20 24	21 33	
Honeybourne	d	23p08	06 36	07 33	08 33	09 39	10 38	11 38	13 37	15 32		16 28	17 32	18 33	19 33	20 31	21 39	
Moreton-in-Marsh	a	23p19	06 48	07 45	08 45	09 51	10 50	11 51	13 49	15 45		16 40	17 45	18 46	19 46	20 43	21 51	
	d	23p27	06 48	07 45	08 45	09 51	10 50	11 51	13 49	15 45		16 41	17 45	18 46	19 46	20 43	21 51	
Kingham	d	23p36	06 56	07 54	08 54	10 00	10 58	11 59	13 58	15 53		16 49	17 53	18 54	19 54	20 52	22 00	
Shipton	d			07 59	08 59							16 55					22 05	
Ascott-under-Wychwood	d																	
Charlbury	a	23p45	07 06	08 06	09 06	10 09	11 08	12 08	14 07	16 02		17 02	18 02	19 03	20 03	21 01	22 12	
	d	23p45	07 06	08 07	09 07	10 10	11 08	12 08	14 08	16 02		17 02	18 02	19 03	20 03	21 06	22 12	
Finstock	d																	
Combe	d																	
Hanborough	d		07 13	08 15	09 15	10 18	11 15	12 16	14 16	16 10		17 10	18 10	19 11	20 11	21 14	22 20	
Oxford	a	23p58	07 24	08 26	09 25	10 29	11 26	12 28	14 26	16 21		17 21	18 21	19 21	20 21	21 25	22 34	
Didcot Parkway	a	00 20														21 43	22 47	
Reading [7]	a	00 38	07 54	08 54	09 54	10 54	11 54	12 53	14 53	16 55		17 55	18 55	19 55	20 54	21 59	23 04	
Slough [3]	a	00 55	08 09	09 09	10 09	11 09	12 09	13 09	15 10	17 10		18 10	19 10	20 10	21 09	22 14	23 23	
London Paddington [15] ⊖	a	01 17	08 29	09 29	10 29	11 29	12 29	13 30	15 29	17 29		18 29	19 29	20 29	21 29	22 32	23 43	

Saturdays

7 January to 24 March

		GW	GW	GW	GW	GW	GW	GW	GW	GW		GW	GW	GW	GW	GW	GW	GW
		◇[1]	◇[1]	◇[1]	◇[1]	◇[1]	◇[1]	◇[1]	◇[1]	◇[1]		◇[1]	◇[1]	◇[1]	◇[1]	◇[1]	◇[1]	[1]
					A				B				B					
			☕	☕	☕⊘	☕	🛒	🛒	☕	🛒		☕	🛒	🛒				
Hereford [7]	d	21p51		06 17	07 10				12 13			15 13					20 20	
Ledbury	d	22p09		06 34	07 30				12 31			15 31					20 40	
Colwall	d	22p17		06 41	07 37				12 38			15 38					20 47	
Great Malvern	d	22p22	05 56	06 49	07 43	08 43	09 51	10 58	12 44	14 34		15 44	16 34	17 49	18 35		20 53	22 41
Malvern Link	d		05 59	06 53	07 46	08 47	09 54	11 01	12 48	14 37		15 48	16 37	17 52	18 38		20 57	22 44
Worcester Foregate Street [7]	d	22p34	06 09	07 04	07 59	08 58	10 04	11 11	12 59	14 57		15 59	16 54	18 02	18 48	20 02	21 11	22 53
Worcester Shrub Hill [7]	d	22p43	06 12	07 08	08 04	09 02	10 08	11 15	13 04	15 01		16 04	17b02	18 06	19c02	20 06	21 15	22 57
Pershore	d	22p52	06 21	07 17	08 13	09 11	10 16	11 23	13 13	15 09		16 12	17 10	18 15	19 10	20 15	21 24	23 06
Evesham	a	23p00	06 29	07 25	08 21	09 19	10 25	11 32	13 21	15 18		16 21	17 19	18 23	19 19	20 23	21 32	23 15
	d	23p01	06 30	07 26	08 26	09 32	10 32	11 32	13 30	15 26		16 22	17 26	18 27	19 27	20 24	21 33	
Honeybourne	d	23p08	06 36	07 33	08 33	09 39	10 38	11 38	13 37	15 32		16 28	17 32	18 33	19 33	20 31	21 39	
Moreton-in-Marsh	a	23p19	06 48	07 45	08 45	09 51	10 50	11 51	13 49	15 45		16 40	17 45	18 46	19 46	20 43	21 51	
	d	23p27	06 48	07 45	08 45	09 51	10 50	11 51	13 49	15 45		16 41	17 45	18 46	19 46	20 43	21 51	
Kingham	d	23p36	06 56	07 54	08 54	10 00	10 58	11 59	13 58	15 53		16 49	17 53	18 54	19 54	20 52	22 00	
Shipton	d			07 59	08 59							16 55					22 05	
Ascott-under-Wychwood	d																	
Charlbury	a	23p45	07 06	08 06	09 06	10 09	11 08	12 08	14 07	16 02		17 02	18 02	19 03	20 03	21 01	22 12	
	d	23p45	07 06	08 07	09 07	10 10	11 08	12 08	14 08	16 02		17 02	18 02	19 03	20 03	21 06	22 12	
Finstock	d																	
Combe	d																	
Hanborough	d		07 13	08 15	09 15	10 18	11 15	12 16	14 16	16 10		17 10	18 10	19 11	20 11	21 14	22 20	
Oxford	a	23p58	07 24	08 26	09 25	10 29	11 26	12 28	14 26	16 21		17 21	18 21	19 21	20 21	21 25	22 34	
Didcot Parkway	a	00 20														21 43	22 47	
Reading [7]	a	00 38	07 54	08 54	09 54	10 54	11 54	12 53	14 53	16 55		17 55	18 55	19 55	20 54	21 58	23 08	
Slough [3]	a	00 55	08 09	09 09	10 09	11 09	12 09	13 09	15 10	17 10		18 10	19 10	20 10	21 09	22 13	23 26	
London Paddington [15] ⊖	a	01 17	08 29	09 29	10 29	11 29	12 29	13 30	15 29	17 29		18 29	19 29	20 29	21 29	22 31	23 46	

A ☕ from Reading ⊘ to Reading

B from 7 January until 11 February

Table 126

Saturdays
from 31 March

Hereford and Worcester - Oxford and London

Network Diagram - see first Page of Table 116

		GW	GW	GW	GW	GW	GW	GW	GW	GW	GW	GW	GW	GW	GW	GW	GW
		◇1	◇1	◇1	◇1	◇1	◇1	◇1	◇1	◇1	◇1	◇1	◇1	◇1	◇1	◇1	1
					A												
			☕	☕	☕⊘	☕	🛒	🛒	☕	🛒	☕	🛒	🛒				
Hereford 7	d	21p51		06 17	07 10				12 13		15 13					20 20	
Ledbury	d	22p09		06 34	07 30				12 31		15 31					20 40	
Colwall	d	22p17		06 41	07 37				12 38		15 38					20 47	
Great Malvern	d	22p22	05 56	06 49	07 43	08 43	09 51	10 58	12 44	14 34	15 44	16 34	17 49	18 35		20 53	22 41
Malvern Link	d		05 59	06 53	07 46	08 47	09 54	11 01	12 48	14 37	15 48	16 37	17 52	18 38		20 57	22 44
Worcester Foregate Street 7	d	22p34	06 09	07 04	07 59	08 58	10 04	11 11	12 59	14 57	15 59	16 54	18 02	18 48	20 02	21 11	22 53
Worcester Shrub Hill 7	d	22p43	06 12	07 08	08 04	09 02	10 08	11 15	13 04	15 01	16 04	17 02	18 06	19 02	20 06	21 15	22 57
Pershore	d	22p52	06 21	07 17	08 13	09 11	10 16	11 23	13 13	15 09	16 12	17 10	18 15	19 10	20 15	21 24	23 06
Evesham	a	23p00	06 29	07 25	08 21	09 19	10 25	11 32	13 21	15 18	16 21	17 19	18 23	19 19	20 23	21 32	23 15
	d	23p01	06 30	07 26	08 26	09 32	10 32	11 32	13 30	15 26	16 22	17 26	18 27	19 27	20 24	21 33	
Honeybourne	d	23p08	06 36	07 33	08 33	09 39	10 38	11 38	13 37	15 32	16 28	17 32	18 33	19 33	20 31	21 39	
Moreton-in-Marsh	a	23p19	06 48	07 45	08 45	09 51	10 50	11 51	13 49	15 45	16 40	17 45	18 46	19 46	20 43	21 51	
	d	23p27	06 48	07 45	08 45	09 51	10 50	11 51	13 49	15 45	16 41	17 45	18 46	19 46	20 43	21 51	
Kingham	d	23p36	06 56	07 54	08 54	10 00	10 58	11 59	13 58	15 53	16 49	17 53	18 54	19 54	20 52	22 00	
Shipton	d			07 59	08 59						16 55					22 05	
Ascott-under-Wychwood	d																
Charlbury	a	23p45	07 06	08 06	09 06	10 09	11 08	12 08	14 07	16 02	17 02	18 02	19 03	20 03	21 01	22 12	
	d	23p45	07 06	08 07	09 07	10 10	11 08	12 08	14 08	16 02	17 02	18 02	19 03	20 03	21 06	22 12	
Finstock	d																
Combe	d																
Hanborough	d		07 13	08 15	09 15	10 18	11 15	12 16	14 16	16 10	17 10	18 10	19 11	20 11	21 14	22 20	
Oxford	a	23p58	07 24	08 26	09 25	10 29	11 26	12 28	14 26	16 21	17 21	18 21	19 21	20 21	21 25	22 34	
Didcot Parkway	a	00 20													21 43	22 47	
Reading 7	a	00 38	07 54	08 54	09 54	10 54	11 54	12 53	14 53	16 55	17 55	18 55	19 55	20 54	21 59	23 08	
Slough 3	a	00 55	08 09	09 09	10 09	11 09	12 09	13 09	15 10	17 10	18 10	19 10	20 10	21 09	22 14	23 26	
London Paddington 15 ⊖	a	01 17	08 29	09 29	10 29	11 29	12 29	13 30	15 29	17 29	18 29	19 29	20 29	21 29	22 32	23 46	

Sundays
until 1 January

		GW	GW	GW	GW	GW	GW	GW	GW	GW	GW	GW
		◇1	◇1	◇1	◇1	◇1	◇1	◇1	◇1	◇1	◇1	◇1
					☕	☕	☕	☕				
Hereford 7	d				13 32	14 32		16 35		18 30		
Ledbury	d				13 50	14 55		16 52		18 48		
Colwall	d				13 57	15 02		17 00		18 55		
Great Malvern	d	09 20	11 15	13 15	14 11	15 08		17 05		19 11	20 15	
Malvern Link	d	09 23	11 18	13 18	14 15	15 12		17 09		19 14	20 18	
Worcester Foregate Street 7	d	09 31	11 27	13 26	14 26	15 23		17 22	18 25	19 25	20 26	
Worcester Shrub Hill 7	d	09 35	11 30	13 30	14 30	15 27	16 27	17 27	18 27	19 27	20 30	21 34
Pershore	d	09 44	11 39	13 39	14 40	15 36	16 36	17 36	18 36	19 36	20 39	21 44
Evesham	a	09 52	11 48	13 47	14 48	15 45	16 45	17 45	18 45	19 45	20 48	21 48
	d	09 52	11 49	13 49	14 49	15 49	16 49	17 49	18 49	19 49	20 49	21 49
Honeybourne	d	09 58	11 56	13 54		15 57	16 55	17 57	18 57	19 57	20 55	21 57
Moreton-in-Marsh	a	10 10	12 06	14 08	15 06	16 09	17 09	18 09	19 09	20 09	21 09	22 09
	d	10 10	12 08	14 08	15 08	16 10	17 10	18 10	19 10	20 10	21 10	22 10
Kingham	d	10 18	12 16	14 16	15 16	16 19	17 19	18 19	19 19	20 19	21 19	22 19
Shipton	d											
Ascott-under-Wychwood	d											
Charlbury	a	10 28	12 25	14 24	15 26	16 29	17 29	18 29	19 28	20 29	21 27	22 29
	d	10 29	12 25	14 24	15 26	16 29	17 29	18 29	19 28	20 29	21 27	22 29
Finstock	d											
Combe	d											
Hanborough	d	10 36	12 33	14 32	15 34	16 37	17 37		19 37	20 36	21 36	22 37
Oxford	a	10 51	12 47	14 47	15 49	16 49	17 47	18 49	19 48	20 48	21 48	22 46
Didcot Parkway	a	11 07	13 01	15 03	16 02	17 02	18 02	19 02	20 04	21 00	22 00	22 58
Reading 7	a	11 23	13 20	15 21	16 20	17 21	18 21	19 28	20 23	21 21	22 19	23 15
Slough 3	a	11 42	13 36	15 36	16 33	17 40	18 36	19 42	20 42	21 42	22 43	23 40
London Paddington 15 ⊖	a	12 06	14 02	15 59	16 59	18 06	19 02	20 06	21 03	22 04	23 13	00 02

A ☕ from Reading ⊘ to Reading

Table 126

Sundays

8 January to 12 February

Hereford and Worcester - Oxford and London

Network Diagram - see first Page of Table 116

		GW	GW	GW	GW	GW	GW	GW	GW	GW	GW	GW
		◇1	◇1	◇1	◇1	◇1	◇1	◇1	◇1	◇1	◇1	◇1
					☕	☕	☕	☕				
Hereford 7	d				13 32	14 32		16 35		18 30		
Ledbury	d				13 50	14 55		16 52		18 48		
Colwall	d				13 57	15 02		17 00		18 55		
Great Malvern	d	09 20	11 15	13 15	14 11	15 08		17 05		19 11	20 15	
Malvern Link	d	09 23	11 18	13 18	14 15	15 12		17 09		19 14	20 18	
Worcester Foregate Street 7	d	09 31	11 27	13 26	14 26	15 23		17 22	18 25	19 25	20 26	
Worcester Shrub Hill 7	d	09 35	11 30	13 30	14 30	15 27	16 27	17 27	18 27	19 27	20 30	21 34
Pershore	d	09 44	11 39	13 39	14 40	15 36	16 36	17 36	18 36	19 36	20 39	21 44
Evesham	a	09 52	11 48	13 47	14 48	15 45	16 45	17 45	18 45	19 45	20 48	21 48
	d	09 52	11 49	13 49	14 49	15 49	16 49	17 49	18 49	19 49	20 49	21 49
Honeybourne	d	09 58	11 56	13 54		15 57	16 55	17 57	18 57	19 57	20 55	21 57
Moreton-in-Marsh	a	10 10	12 06	14 08	15 06	16 09	17 09	18 09	19 09	20 09	21 09	22 09
	d	10 10	12 08	14 08	15 08	16 10	17 10	18 10	19 10	20 10	21 10	22 10
Kingham	d	10 18	12 16	14 16	15 16	16 19	17 19	18 19	19 18	20 19	21 19	22 19
Shipton	d											
Ascott-under-Wychwood	d											
Charlbury	a	10 28	12 25	14 24	15 26	16 29	17 29	18 29	19 27	20 29	21 27	22 29
	d	10 29	12 25	14 24	15 26	16 29	17 29	18 29	19 27	20 29	21 27	22 29
Finstock	d											
Combe	d											
Hanborough	d	10 36	12 33	14 32	15 34	16 37	17 37		19 36	20 36	21 36	22 37
Oxford	a	10 51	12 47	14 47	15 49	16 49	17 47	18 49	19 48	20 48	21 48	22 46
Didcot Parkway	a	11 07	13 02	15 03	16 02	17 02	18 02	19 02	20 02	21 00	22 00	23 01
Reading 7	a	11 23	13 25	15 21	16 23	17 25	18 21	19 28	20 25	21 26	22 23	23 17
Slough 3	a	11 37	13 41	15 36	16 37	17 43	18 36	19 44	20 44	21 45	22 40	23 41
London Paddington 15 ⊖	a	12 01	14 04	15 59	17 02	18 06	19 03	20 07	21 04	22 07	23 01	00 04

Sundays

19 February to 25 March

		GW	GW	GW	GW	GW	GW	GW	GW	GW	GW	GW
		◇1	◇1	◇1	◇1	◇1	◇1	◇1	◇1	◇1	◇1	◇1
					☕	☕	☕	☕				
Hereford 7	d				13 32	14 32		16 35		18 30		
Ledbury	d				13 50	14 55		16 52		18 48		
Colwall	d				13 57	15 02		17 00		18 55		
Great Malvern	d	09 20	11 15	13 15	14 11	15 08		17 05		19 11	20 15	
Malvern Link	d	09 23	11 18	13 18	14 15	15 12		17 09		19 14	20 18	
Worcester Foregate Street 7	d	09 31	11 27	13 26	14 26	15 23		17 22	18 25	19 25	20 26	
Worcester Shrub Hill 7	d	09 35	11 30	13 30	14 30	15 27	16 27	17 27	18 27	19 27	20 30	21 34
Pershore	d	09 44	11 39	13 39	14 40	15 36	16 36	17 36	18 36	19 36	20 39	21 44
Evesham	a	09 52	11 48	13 47	14 48	15 45	16 45	17 45	18 45	19 45	20 48	21 48
	d	09 52	11 49	13 49	14 49	15 49	16 49	17 49	18 49	19 49	20 49	21 49
Honeybourne	d	09 58	11 56	13 54		15 57	16 55	17 57	18 57	19 57	20 55	21 57
Moreton-in-Marsh	a	10 10	12 06	14 08	15 06	16 09	17 09	18 09	19 09	20 09	21 09	22 09
	d	10 10	12 08	14 08	15 08	16 10	17 10	18 10	19 10	20 10	21 10	22 10
Kingham	d	10 18	12 16	14 16	15 16	16 19	17 19	18 19	19 18	20 19	21 19	22 19
Shipton	d											
Ascott-under-Wychwood	d											
Charlbury	a	10 28	12 25	14 24	15 26	16 29	17 29	18 29	19 27	20 29	21 27	22 29
	d	10 29	12 25	14 24	15 26	16 29	17 29	18 29	19 27	20 29	21 27	22 29
Finstock	d											
Combe	d											
Hanborough	d	10 36	12 33	14 32	15 34	16 37	17 37		19 36	20 36	21 36	22 37
Oxford	a	10 51	12 47	14 47	15 49	16 49	17 47	18 49	19 46	20 48	21 48	22 46
Didcot Parkway	a	11 07	13 02	15 03	16 02	17 02	18 02	19 02	20 02	21 00	22 00	23 01
Reading 7	a	11 23	13 25	15 21	16 27	17 24	18 23	19 29	20 23	21 26	22 21	23 17
Slough 3	a	11 37	13 41	15 37	16 41	17 44	18 38	19 44	20 42	21 45	22 40	23 41
London Paddington 15 ⊖	a	12 01	14 04	15 59	17 06	18 07	19 03	20 07	21 04	22 07	23 01	00 04

Table 126

Sundays

from 1 April

Hereford and Worcester - Oxford and London

Network Diagram - see first Page of Table 116

		GW	GW	GW	GW	GW	GW	GW	GW	GW		GW	GW
		◇1	◇1	◇1	◇1	◇1	◇1	◇1	◇1	◇1		◇1	◇1
					☕	☕	☕	☕					
Hereford 7	d				13 32	14 32		16 35		18 30			
Ledbury	d				13 50	14 55		16 52		18 48			
Colwall	d				13 57	15 02		17 00		18 55			
Great Malvern	d	09 20	11 15	13 15	14 11	15 08		17 05		19 11		20 15	
Malvern Link	d	09 23	11 18	13 18	14 15	15 12		17 09		19 14		20 18	
Worcester Foregate Street 7	d	09 31	11 27	13 26	14 26	15 23		17 22	18 25	19 25		20 26	
Worcester Shrub Hill 7	d	09 35	11 30	13 30	14 30	15 27	16 27	17 27	18 27	19 27		20 30	21 34
Pershore	d	09 44	11 39	13 39	14 40	15 36	16 36	17 36	18 36	19 36		20 39	21 44
Evesham	a	09 52	11 48	13 47	14 48	15 45	16 45	17 45	18 45	19 45		20 48	21 48
	d	09 52	11 49	13 49	14 49	15 49	16 49	17 49	18 49	19 49		20 49	21 49
Honeybourne	d	09 58	11 56	13 54		15 57	16 53	17 57	18 57	19 57		20 55	21 57
Moreton-in-Marsh	a	10 10	12 06	14 08	15 06	16 09	17 09	18 09	19 09	20 09		21 09	22 09
	d	10 10	12 08	14 08	15 08	16 10	17 10	18 10	19 10	20 10		21 10	22 10
Kingham	d	10 18	12 16	14 16	15 16	16 19	17 19	18 19	19 19	20 19		21 19	22 19
Shipton	d												
Ascott-under-Wychwood	d												
Charlbury	a	10 28	12 25	14 24	15 26	16 29	17 29	18 29	19 28	20 29		21 27	22 29
	d	10 29	12 25	14 24	15 26	16 29	17 29	18 29	19 28	20 29		21 27	22 29
Finstock	d												
Combe	d												
Hanborough	d	10 36	12 33	14 32	15 34	16 37	17 37		19 37	20 36		21 36	22 37
Oxford	a	10 51	12 47	14 48	15 49	16 49	17 45	18 49	19 48	20 48		21 48	22 46
Didcot Parkway	a	11 07	13 02	15 04	16 02	17 02	18 02	19 02	20 04	21 00		22 00	22 58
Reading 7	a	11 23	13 25	15 25	16 25	17 26	18 25	19 30	20 24	21 26		22 20	23 15
Slough 3	a	11 37	13 40	15 41	16 40	17 47	18 41	19 44	20 42	21 46		22 40	23 42
London Paddington 15 ⊖	a	12 01	14 05	16 03	17 05	18 13	19 06	20 07	21 05	22 07		23 01	00 04

Table 126A

Mondays to Fridays

Kingham - Chipping Norton

Bus Service

		GW BHX 🚌	GW BHX 🚌	GW BHX 🚌	GW BHX 🚌	GW BHX 🚌	GW BHX 🚌	GW BHX 🚌	GW BHX 🚌	GW BHX 🚌	GW BHX 🚌	GW BHX 🚌	GW BHX 🚌	GW BHX 🚌	GW BHX 🚌	GW BHX 🚌	GW BHX 🚌	GW BHX 🚌
Kingham	d	06 30	07 00	07 30	08 30	09 55	10 55	11 55	12 55	13 55	14 55	15 50	16 40	17 20	18 10	18 50	19 25	19 50
Chipping Norton West St	a	06 43	07 13	07 43	08 43	10 08	11 08	12 08	13 08	14 08	15 08	16 03	16 53	17 33	18 23	19 03	19 38	20 03

Saturdays

		GW 🚌	GW 🚌	GW 🚌	GW 🚌	GW 🚌	GW 🚌	GW 🚌	GW 🚌	GW 🚌	GW 🚌	GW 🚌	GW 🚌	GW 🚌
Kingham	d	08 15	08 55	09 55	10 55	11 55	12 55	13 55	14 55	15 50	16 50	17 55	18 50	19 50
Chipping Norton West St	a	08 28	09 08	10 08	11 08	12 08	13 08	14 08	15 08	16 03	17 03	18 08	19 03	20 03

Sundays

		GW 🚌	GW 🚌	GW 🚌
Kingham	d	13 17	17 17	18 22
Chipping Norton West St	a	13 29	17 29	18 34

Table 126A

Mondays to Fridays

Chipping Norton - Kingham

Bus Service

		GW BHX 🚌	GW BHX 🚌	GW BHX 🚌	GW BHX 🚌	GW BHX 🚌	GW BHX 🚌	GW BHX 🚌	GW BHX 🚌	GW BHX 🚌	GW BHX 🚌	GW BHX 🚌	GW BHX 🚌	GW BHX 🚌	GW BHX 🚌	GW BHX 🚌	GW BHX 🚌
Chipping Norton West St	d	06 07	06 45	07 15	08 00	09 30	10 35	11 35	12 35	13 35	14 35	15 30	16 20	16 55	17 45	18 25	19 10
Kingham	a	06 19	06 58	07 28	08 14	09 44	10 50	11 50	12 50	13 50	14 50	15 45	16 35	17 10	18 00	18 40	19 25

Saturdays

		GW 🚌	GW 🚌	GW 🚌	GW 🚌	GW 🚌	GW 🚌	GW 🚌	GW 🚌	GW 🚌	GW 🚌	GW 🚌	GW 🚌	GW 🚌
Chipping Norton West St	d	08 00	08 30	09 30	10 35	11 35	12 35	13 35	14 35	15 30	16 35	17 30	18 25	19 10
Kingham	a	08 14	08 44	09 44	10 50	11 50	12 50	13 50	14 50	15 45	16 50	17 45	18 40	19 25

Sundays

		GW 🚌	GW 🚌	GW 🚌
Chipping Norton West St	d	09 25	13 33	17 59
Kingham	a	09 39	13 47	18 13

Route Diagram for Tables 127, 128

DM-9/07(2)
Design BAJS

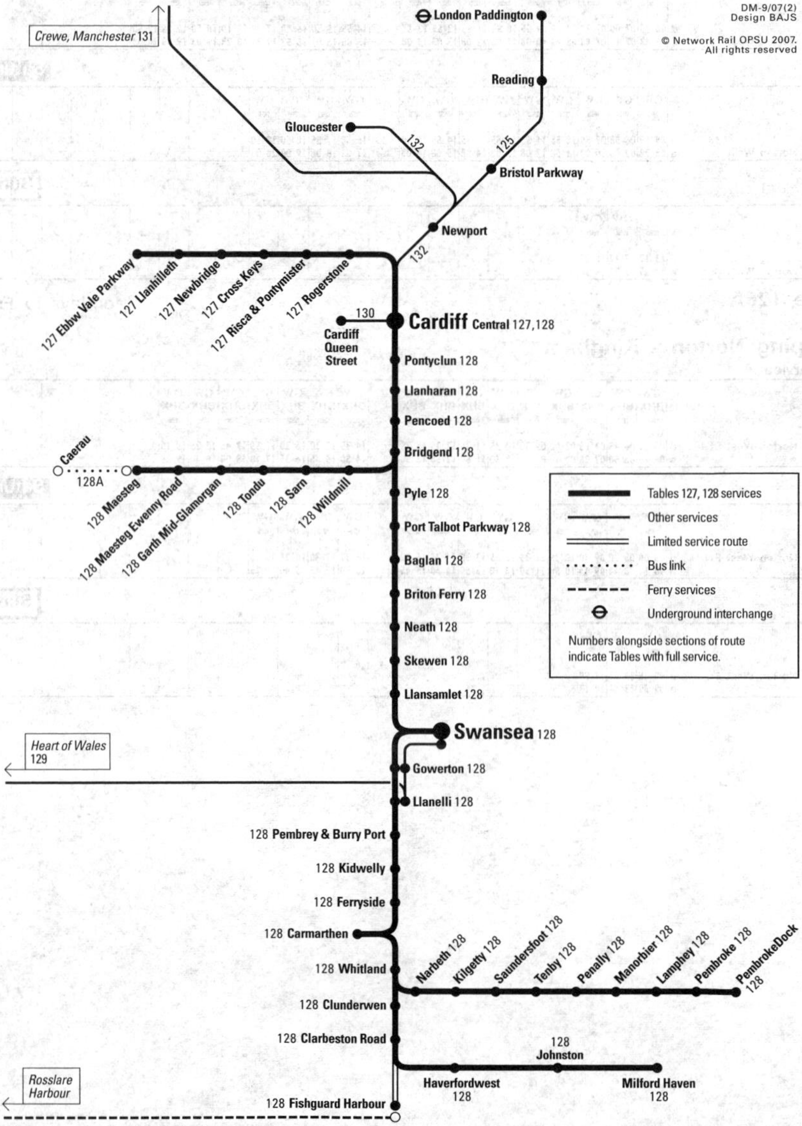

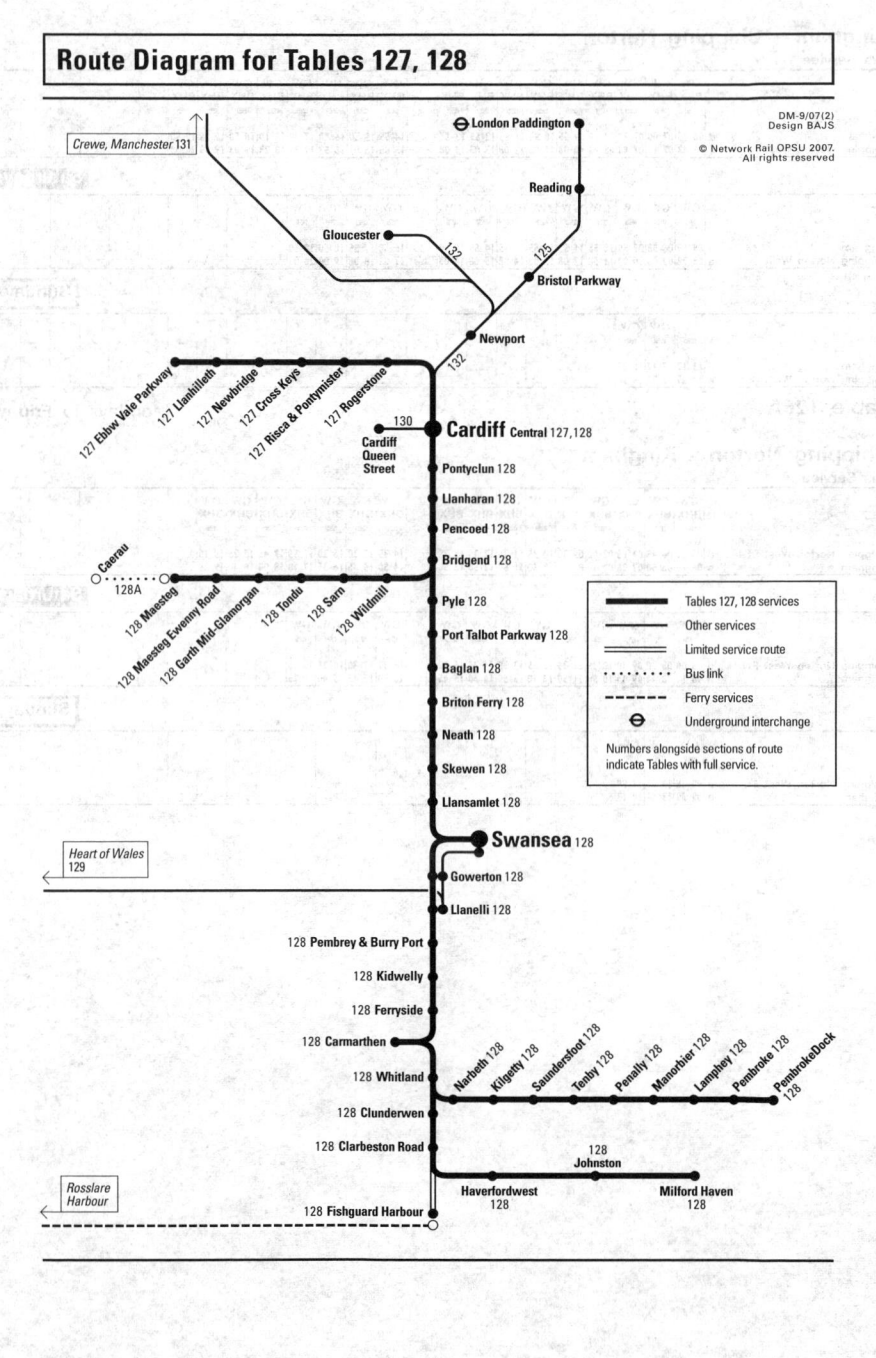

Table 127

Mondays to Fridays

Cardiff Central - Ebbw Vale Parkway

Route Diagram - see first Page of Table 127

Miles			AW MX	AW	AW	AW	AW	AW	AW	AW	AW	AW	AW	AW	AW	AW	AW	AW	AW	AW FX	AW FO
0	**Cardiff Central** 7	d	23p05	06 35	07 39	08 35	09 35	10 35	11 35	12 35	13 35	14 35	15 35	16 35	17 35	18 35	19 35	20 35	21 35	23 05	23 05
14	Rogerstone	d	23p27	06 57	08 00	08 57	09 57	10 57	11 57	12 57	13 57	14 57	15 57	16 57	17 57	18 57	19 57	20 57	21 57	23 27	23 29
15¼	Risca & Pontymister	d	23p30	07 00	08 04	09 00	10 00	11 00	12 00	13 00	14 00	15 00	16 00	17 00	18 00	19 00	20 00	21 00	22 00	23 30	23 32
17¼	Cross Keys	d	23p36	07 06	08 09	09 06	10 06	11 06	12 06	13 06	14 06	15 06	16 06	17 06	18 06	19 06	20 06	21 06	22 06	23 36	23 38
20¾	Newbridge (Ebbw Vale)	d	23p44	07 14	08 17	09 14	10 14	11 14	12 14	13 14	14 14	15 14	16 14	17 14	18 14	19 14	20 14	21 14	22 14	23 44	23 46
23½	Llanhilleth	d	23p50	07 20	08 23	09 20	10 20	11 20	12 20	13 20	14 20	15 20	16 20	17 20	18 20	19 20	20 20	21 20	22 20	23 50	23 52
28¾	**Ebbw Vale Parkway**	a	00 02	07 31	08 35	09 31	10 31	11 31	12 31	13 31	14 31	15 31	16 31	17 31	18 31	19 31	20 34	21 31	22 31	00 02	00 05

Saturdays

		AW	AW	AW	AW	AW	AW	AW	AW	AW	AW	AW	AW	AW	AW	AW	AW	AW	AW
Cardiff Central 7	d	23p05	06 35	07 39	08 35	09 35	10 35	11 35	12 35	13 35	14 35	15 35	16 35	17 35	18 35	19 35	20 35	21 35	23 05
Rogerstone	d	23p29	06 57	08 00	08 57	09 57	10 57	11 57	12 57	13 57	14 57	15 57	16 57	17 57	18 57	19 57	20 57	21 57	23 27
Risca & Pontymister	d	23p32	07 00	08 04	09 00	10 00	11 00	12 00	13 00	14 00	15 00	16 00	17 00	18 00	19 00	20 00	21 00	22 00	23 30
Cross Keys	d	23p38	07 06	08 09	09 06	10 06	11 06	12 06	13 06	14 06	15 06	16 06	17 06	18 06	19 06	20 06	21 06	22 06	23 36
Newbridge (Ebbw Vale)	d	23p46	07 14	08 17	09 14	10 14	11 14	12 14	13 14	14 14	15 14	16 14	17 14	18 14	19 14	20 14	21 14	22 14	23 44
Llanhilleth	d	23p52	07 20	08 23	09 20	10 20	11 20	12 20	13 20	14 20	15 20	16 20	17 20	18 20	19 20	20 20	21 20	22 20	23 50
Ebbw Vale Parkway	a	00 05	07 31	08 35	09 31	10 31	11 31	12 31	13 31	14 31	15 31	16 31	17 31	18 31	19 31	20 34	21 31	22 31	00 02

Sundays

		AW A	AW	AW	AW	AW	AW	AW	AW
Cardiff Central 7	d	23p05	07 40	09 24	11 30	13 30	15 32	17 30	19 30
Rogerstone	d	23p27	08 03	09 45	11 51	13 51	15 53	17 51	19 51
Risca & Pontymister	d	23p30	08 07	09 49	11 55	13 55	15 57	17 55	19 55
Cross Keys	d	23p36	08 13	09 55	12 01	14 01	16 03	18 01	20 01
Newbridge (Ebbw Vale)	d	23p44	08 21	10 03	12 09	14 09	16 11	18 09	20 09
Llanhilleth	d	23p50	08 28	10 10	12 16	14 16	16 18	18 16	20 16
Ebbw Vale Parkway	a	00 02	08 39	10 21	12 27	14 27	16 29	18 27	20 27

A not 11 December

Table 127

Mondays to Fridays

Ebbw Vale Parkway - Cardiff Central

Route Diagram - see first Page of Table 127

Miles			AW	AW	AW	AW	AW	AW	AW	AW	AW	AW	AW	AW	AW	AW	AW	AW FX	AW FO	AW
0	**Ebbw Vale Parkway**	d	06 40	07 40	08 40	09 40	10 40	11 40	12 40	13 40	14 40	15 40	16 40	17 40	18 40	19 40	20 40	21 40	21 40	22 40
5¼	Llanhilleth	d	06 48	07 48	08 48	09 48	10 48	11 48	12 48	13 48	14 48	15 48	16 48	17 48	18 48	19 48	20 48	21 48	21 48	22 48
8	Newbridge (Ebbw Vale)	d	06 54	07 54	08 54	09 54	10 54	11 54	12 54	13 54	14 54	15 54	16 54	17 54	18 54	19 54	20 54	21 54	21 54	22 54
11½	Cross Keys	d	07 02	08 02	09 02	10 02	11 02	12 02	13 02	14 02	15 02	16 02	17 02	18 02	19 02	20 02	21 02	22 02	22 02	23 02
13½	Risca & Pontymister	d	07 07	08 07	09 07	10 07	11 07	12 07	13 07	14 07	15 07	16 07	17 07	18 07	19 07	20 07	21 07	22 07	22 07	23 07
14¾	Rogerstone	d	07 11	08 11	09 11	10 11	11 11	12 11	13 11	14 11	15 11	16 11	17 11	18 11	19 11	20 11	21 11	22 11	22 11	23 11
28¾	**Cardiff Central** 7	a	07 37	08 37	09 37	10 37	11 37	12 37	13 37	14 37	15 37	16 37	17 37	18 37	19 39	20 39	21 38	22 40	22 41	23 37

Saturdays

		AW	AW	AW	AW	AW	AW	AW	AW	AW	AW	AW	AW	AW	AW	AW	AW	AW
Ebbw Vale Parkway	d	06 40	07 40	08 40	09 40	10 40	11 40	12 40	13 40	14 40	15 40	16 40	17 40	18 40	19 40	20 40	21 40	22 40
Llanhilleth	d	06 48	07 48	08 48	09 48	10 48	11 48	12 48	13 48	14 48	15 48	16 48	17 48	18 48	19 48	20 48	21 48	22 48
Newbridge (Ebbw Vale)	d	06 54	07 54	08 54	09 54	10 54	11 54	12 54	13 54	14 54	15 54	16 54	17 54	18 54	19 54	20 54	21 54	22 54
Cross Keys	d	07 02	08 02	09 02	10 02	11 02	12 02	13 02	14 02	15 02	16 02	17 02	18 02	19 02	20 02	21 02	22 02	23 02
Risca & Pontymister	d	07 07	08 07	09 07	10 07	11 07	12 07	13 07	14 07	15 07	16 07	17 07	18 07	19 07	20 07	21 07	22 07	23 07
Rogerstone	d	07 11	08 11	09 11	10 11	11 11	12 11	13 11	14 11	15 11	16 11	17 11	18 11	19 11	20 11	21 11	22 11	23 11
Cardiff Central 7	a	07 37	08 37	09 37	10 37	11 37	12 37	13 37	14 37	15 37	16 37	17 36	18 37	19 37	20 37	21 37	22 41	23 37

Sundays

		AW	AW	AW	AW	AW	AW A	AW B	AW A	AW B
Ebbw Vale Parkway	d	08 40	10 27	12 27	14 30	16 30	18 30	18 30	20 40	20 40
Llanhilleth	d	08 48	10 35	12 35	14 38	16 38	18 38	18 38	20 48	20 48
Newbridge (Ebbw Vale)	d	08 54	10 41	12 41	14 44	16 44	18 44	18 44	20 54	20 54
Cross Keys	d	09 02	10 49	12 49	14 52	16 52	18 52	18 52	21 02	21 02
Risca & Pontymister	d	09 07	10 54	12 54	14 57	16 57	18 57	18 57	21 07	21 07
Rogerstone	d	09 11	10 58	12 58	15 01	17 01	19 01	19 01	21 11	21 11
Cardiff Central 7	a	09 37	11 24	13 24	15 23	17 25	19 23	19 25	21 37	21 42

A until 12 February, from 1 April

B from 19 February until 25 March

Cardiff - Maesteg, Swansea and West Wales

Route Diagram - see first Page of Table 127

Miles	Miles			AW MX	AW MO	AW MO	AW MX	AW MO	AW MO	AW MO	AW MO	GW MO	AW	AW MX	GW MO	GW MX	GW MO	GW MO	GW MO	GW MO	GW MO	GW MO	GW MX
					◇		◇	◇		◇			[R]			◇1	◇1	◇1	◇1			◇1	◇1
					A	B		A	B	C	B	B			B		D	E	C	B	B	C	
											bus	bus			bus	catering	catering	catering	catering	bus	bus	catering	catering
—	—	London Paddington 15 ⊖	d													21p15	21p37	21p37	20p37			21p37	22p45
—	—	Reading 7	d													21p41	22p12	22p14	21p14			22p15	23p19
—	—	Manchester Piccadilly 10	d																				
—	—	Gloucester 7	d																22p42			23p43	
—	—	Bristol Parkway 7	d													22p45	23p12	23p17					00 23
—	—	Newport (South Wales)	d													23p19	23p42	23p43	23p44			00 32	00 52
0	—	**Cardiff Central 7**	d	21p04	22p30					22p30	22p29	23p15		23p15	23p13	23p43	00 04	00 08	00 10	00 15	00 13	00 54	01 13
11	—	Pontyclun	d											23p29									
14	—	Llanharan	d											23p34									
16¼	—	Pencoed	d											23p39									
20¼	0	Bridgend	d	21p27	22p51					22p51	23p04			23p45	23p48	00 02	00 24	00 28	00 29		00 48	01 19	01 36
—	1	Wildmill	d																				
—	2¼	Sarn	d																				
—	3	Tondu	d																				
—	7	Garth (Mid Glamorgan)	d																				
—	7¾	Maesteg (Ewenny Road)	d																				
—	8¼	Maesteg	a																				
26¼	—	Pyle	d	21p34										23p53									
32½	—	Port Talbot Parkway	d	21p45	23p05					23p05	23p24			00 01	00 13	00 15	00 37	00 41	00 43		01 13	01 32	01 49
34½	—	Baglan	d											00 05									
36¼	—	Briton Ferry	d											00 09									
38	—	Neath	d	21p52	23p13					23p13	23p44			00 13	00 28	00 22	00 45	00 49	00 51		01 28	01 39	01 57
41¾	—	Skewen	d											00 16									
43½	—	Llansamlet	d											00 20									
47½	—	**Swansea**	a	22p04	23p25					23p25	00 09	00 15		00 28	00 50	00 37	00 57	01 01	01 04	01 15	01 50	01 52	02 10
—	—		d	22p27	23p38	23p38	23p45			23p55				00 45									
53	—	Gowerton	d	22b41	23b49	23b49	23b56			00x06				00c55									
58¾	—	Llanelli	a	22p47	23p56	23p56	00 01			00 13				01s02									
—	—		d	22p49	23p58	23p58	00 03			00 15													
62¾	—	Pembrey & Burry Port	d	22p54	00 04	00 04	00 08			00 21				01s09									
68	—	Kidwelly	d	23b00	00x11	00x11				00x28				01c15									
72¼	—	Ferryside	d	23b06	00x17	00x17		←	←	00x34				01c21									
79¼	—	**Carmarthen**	a	23p18	00 30	00 30	00 28	00 30	00 30	00 47				01 40									
—	—		d	23p21	00 34	00 34	00 31	00 34	00 34	00 51													
93¼	—	Whitland	a	23p35	↪	↪	00 46	00 50	00 50	01 07													
—	—		d	23p36			00 46	00 50	00 50	01 07													
—	5¼	Narberth	d																				
—	10¾	Kilgetty	d																				
—	11½	Saundersfoot	d																				
—	15¾	**Tenby**	a																				
—	—		d																				
—	17	Penally	d																				
—	20¼	Manorbier	d																				
—	23¾	Lamphey	d																				
—	25¾	Pembroke	d																				
—	27¼	**Pembroke Dock**	a																				
98¾	—	Clunderwen	d	23b42																			
105¼	0	Clarbeston Road	d	23b51			01x00	01x03	01x03	01x20													
—	5¼	Haverfordwest	d	23p59																			
—	10	Johnston	d	00x07																			
—	14	**Milford Haven**	a	00 22																			
121	—	**Fishguard Harbour** ⛴	a				01 27	01 30	01 30	01 47													
—	—		d										02 45										
—	—	Rosslare Harbour ⛴	a										06 15										

A until 2 January, MO from 2 April
B from 9 January until 13 February
C from 20 February until 26 March
D from 2 April
E until 2 January
b Previous night, stops on request
c Stops to set down only, stops on request

When events are being held at the Millenium Stadium,
services are subject to alteration.
Please check times before travelling.

Cardiff - Maesteg, Swansea and West Wales

Route Diagram - see first Page of Table 127

		AW	AW	AW	AW	AW	AW	AW		AW	AW	AW	AW	AW	AW	GW	AW	AW		GW	AW	AW	AW	GW	AW
		◇								◇		◇			◇	◇1	◇	◇		◇1	◇			◇1	
																								A	
						bike				bike					bike	café	bike			café	bike			café	
London Paddington 15 ⊖	d															05 27				06 45				07 45	
Reading 7	d															05 56				07 11				08 11	
Manchester Piccadilly 10	d																								
Gloucester 7	d												05 50										07 58		
Bristol Parkway 7	d																			08 07				09 07	
Newport (South Wales)	d											06 17	06 44		07 35	07 44		08 01		08 32	08 38		08 52	09 32	
Cardiff Central 7	d									05 39	05 51	06 42	07 03		07 58	08 02	08 09	08 20		08 48	09 04	09 14	09 18	09 48	
Pontyclun	d									05 51	06 03		07 15					08 32					09 30		
Llanharan	d									05 56	06 08		07 20					08 37					09 35		
Pencoed	d									06 01	06 12		07 24					08 41					09 39		
Bridgend	d									06 07	06 20	07 02	07 32		08 17	08 23	08 29	08 49		09 09	09 23	09 34	09 46	10 09	
Wildmill	d										06 22		07 34					08 51					09 49		
Sarn	d										06 25		07 37					08 54					09 52		
Tondu	d										06 29		07 41					08 58					09 55		
Garth (Mid Glamorgan)	d										06 38		07 50					09 07					10 05		
Maesteg (Ewenny Road)	d										06 41		07 53					09 10					10 07		
Maesteg	a										06 45		07 57					09 15					10 12		
Pyle	d									06 15		07 10					08 37					09 43			
Port Talbot Parkway	d									06 23		07 18			08 30	08 36	08 45			09 22	09 36	09 52		10 22	
Baglan	d									06 27		07 22					08 49					09 55			
Briton Ferry	d									06 30		07 25					08 52					09 59			
Neath	d									06 34		07 29			08 37	08 44	08 56			09 30	09 43	10 03		10 30	
Skewen	d									06 38		07 33					09 00					10 06			
Llansamlet	d									06 42		07 37					09 04					10 10			
Swansea	a									06 51		07 45			08 50	08 57	09 12			09 45	09 55	10 21		10 44	
	d	04 36					05 50			06 53		07 50			09 01		09 16				10 00				
Gowerton	d						06x00			07x03		08x00			09x17						10x11				
Llanelli	a	04 52					06 07			07 10		08 07			09 24		09 32				10 17				
	d						06 09			07 11		08 08			09 25						10 19				
Pembrey & Burry Port	d						06 15			07 17		08 14			09 31						10 25				
Kidwelly	d						06x22			07x23		08x20			09x37						10x31				
Ferryside	d						06x28			07x29		08x26			09x43						10x36				
Carmarthen	a						06 42			07 43		08 40			09 55						10 51				
	d		04 53	05 38	05 50	05 58	06 43			07 46		08 45			09 57										10 58
Whitland	a		05 06	05 54	06 05	06 13	07 00			08 00		08 59			10 13										11 12
	d		05 06	05 54	06 05	06 13	07 00			08 00		09 02		09 07	10 14										11 13
Narberth	d			06x03			07x09					09x11													11x22
Kilgetty	d			06x13			07x19					09x21													11x32
Saundersfoot	d			06x15			07x21					09x23													11x34
Tenby	a			06 22			07 28					09 30													11 41
	d			06 25			07 42					09 43													11 49
Penally	d			06x28			07x45					09x46													11x52
Manorbier	d			06 35			07 52					09 53													11 58
Lamphey	d			06x42			07x59					10x00													12x06
Pembroke	d			06 45			08 02					10 03													12 09
Pembroke Dock	a			07 00			08 17					10 18													12 23
Clunderwen	d		05x13		06x12	06x19				08 07				09x14	10x20										
Clarbeston Road	d		05x21		06x20	06x27		07 34		08x14				09x22	10x28										
Haverfordwest	d		05 32			06 35				08 23					10 36										
Johnston	d		05x40			06x43				08x31					10x44										
Milford Haven	a		05 55			06 58				08 48					10 57										
Fishguard Harbour ⛴	a				06 44			07 58						09 46											
	d																								
Rosslare Harbour ⛴	a																								

A The St. David

When events are being held at the Millenium Stadium,
services are subject to alteration.
Please check times before travelling.

Table 128

Mondays to Fridays

Cardiff - Maesteg, Swansea and West Wales

Route Diagram - see first Page of Table 127

		AW	AW	AW		GW	AW	AW	AW	AW	AW	AW	GW	AW	AW		AW	GW	AW	AW	AW	AW	GW	AW	AW
		◇		◇		◇1	◇			R		◇	◇1		◇		◇	◇1				◇	◇1		◇
						A							A					A					A		
		trolley		trolley		bus Ø	trolley					trolley	bus Ø				trolley	bus Ø				trolley	bus Ø		trolley
London Paddington 15 ⊖	d					08 45							09 45					10 45					11 45		
Reading 7	d					09 11							10 11					11 11					12 11		
Manchester Piccadilly 10	d	06 30		07 30								08 30					09 30					10 30			11 30
Gloucester 7	d		08 58											10 58							11 58				
Bristol Parkway 7	d					10 07							11 07					12 07					13 07		
Newport (South Wales)	d	09 37	09 52	10 22		10 31						11 22	11 31	11 51			12 23	12 32			12 52	13 23	13 31		14 22
Cardiff Central 7	d	10 04	10 18	10 40		10 48	10 57		11 14		11 18	11 39	11 48	12 18			12 39	12 48		13 14	13 18	13 40	13 48	14 21	14 39
Pontyclun	d		10 30								11 30			12 30							13 30			14 33	
Llanharan	d		10 35								11 35			12 35							13 35			14 38	
Pencoed	d		10 39								11 39			12 39							13 39			14 42	
Bridgend	d	10 23	10 46	10 59		11 09			11 34		11 46	12 00	12 09	12 46			12 58	13 09		13 34	13 46	14 04	14 09	14 49	14 58
Wildmill	d		10 49								11 49			12 49							13 49			14 52	
Sarn	d		10 52								11 52			12 52							13 52			14 55	
Tondu	d		10 55								11 55			12 55							13 55			14 58	
Garth (Mid Glamorgan)	d		11 05								12 05			13 05							14 05			15 08	
Maesteg (Ewenny Road)	d		11 07								12 07			13 07							14 07			15 10	
Maesteg	a		11 12								12 14			13 12							14 12			15 15	
Pyle	d								11 42											13 42					
Port Talbot Parkway	d	10 36		11 12		11 22			11 50			12 12	12 22				13 11	13 22		13 50		14 18	14 22		15 11
Baglan	d								11 54											13 54					
Briton Ferry	d								11 57											13 57					
Neath	d	10 43		11 19		11 30			12 01			12 19	12 30				13 18	13 30		14 01		14 25	14 30		15 18
Skewen	d								12 05											14 05					
Llansamlet	d								12 09											14 09					
Swansea	a	10 55		11 34		11 43			12 20			12 33	12 43				13 33	13 44		14 20		14 34	14 43		15 34
	d	11 00		11 38				12 00				12 37			13 14		13 37		14 00			14 37			15 37
Gowerton	d							12x11											14x10						
Llanelli	a	11 18		11 52			12 01	12 18				13 01			13 31		13 52		14 17			14 53			15 52
	d	11 18		11 54			12 03	12 20				13 03					13 54		14 19			14 54			15 54
Pembrey & Burry Port	d	11 24		12 00				12 26				13 09					14 00		14 25			15 00			16 00
Kidwelly	d			12x06													14x06								16x06
Ferryside	d			12x11													14x11								16x11
Carmarthen	a	11 44		12 26				12 49				13 26					14 28		14 48			15 20			16 28
	d	11 48						12 51				13 30							14 51			15 28			
Whitland	a	12 01					12 45	13 06				13 45							15 05			15 43			
	d	12 01					12 45	13 06				13 45							15 06			15 43			
Narberth	d							13x15											15x15						
Kilgetty	d							13x25											15x25						
Saundersfoot	d							13x27											15x27						
Tenby	a							13 34											15 34						
	d							13 45											15 45						
Penally	d							13x48											15x48						
Manorbier	d							13 54											15 54						
Lamphey	d							14x02											16x02						
Pembroke	d							14 05											16 05						
Pembroke Dock	a							14 19											16 19						
Clunderwen	d	12x07										13x52										15x50			
Clarbeston Road	d	12x15										13x59										15x57			
Haverfordwest	d	12 23										14 08										16 06			
Johnston	d	12x31										14x16										16x14			
Milford Haven	a	12 48										14 31										16 29			
Fishguard Harbour ⛴	a						13 26																		
	d									14 30															
Rosslare Harbour ⛴	a									18 00															

A bus from Bridgend Ø to Bridgend

When events are being held at the Millenium Stadium,
services are subject to alteration.
Please check times before travelling.

Cardiff - Maesteg, Swansea and West Wales

Route Diagram - see first Page of Table 127

		GW		AW	AW	AW	GW	AW	AW	AW		GW	AW	AW	AW	AW	GW	AW	GW	AW		AW	GW	AW	AW
								▣					▣			▣								▣	
		◇1					◇1					◇1		◇	◇		◇1		◇1				◇1		
		A																					B		
		☕⊘					☕	🛒	🛒			☕	🛒	🛒		🛒	☕		☕				☕	🛒	
London Paddington 15 ⊖	d	12 45					13 45					14 45					15 45		16 15				16 45		
Reading 7	d	13 11					14 11					15 11					16 11		16 41				17 11		
Manchester Piccadilly 10	d							12 30					13 30			14 30								15 30	
Gloucester 7	d					13 58			14 58											16 58					17 59
Bristol Parkway 7	d	14 07					15 07					16 07					17 07		17 41				18 07		
Newport (South Wales)	d	14 31				14 52	15 32	15 37	15 52			16 31	16 40	17 01		17 22	17 31		18 04	17 52			18 31	18 41	18 53
Cardiff Central 7	d	14 48			15 14	15 18	15 48	16 04	16 18			16 48	17 04	17 18		17 39	17 48	18 04	18 22	18 12			18 50	19 04	19 12
Pontyclun	d					15 30			16 30					17 32						18 24					19 28
Llanharan	d					15 35			16 35					17 36						18 29					19 33
Pencoed	d					15 39			16 39					17 40						18 33					19 37
Bridgend	d	15 09			15 34	15 46	16 09	16 25	16 46			17 09	17 25	17 46		17 59	18 09	18 24	18 44	18 49			19 09	19 23	19 45
Wildmill	d					15 49			16 49					17 48						18 52					19 48
Sarn	d					15 52			16 52					17 51						18 55					19 51
Tondu	d					15 55			16 55					17 55						18 58					19 54
Garth (Mid Glamorgan)	d					16 05			17 05					18 04						19 08					20 04
Maesteg (Ewenny Road)	d					16 07			17 07					18 07						19 10					20 06
Maesteg	a					16 12			17 12					18 15						19 15					20 11
Pyle	d				15 42			16 33					17 32			18 07		18 33						19 30	
Port Talbot Parkway	d	15 22			15 50		16 22	16 41				17 22	17 40			18 17	18 22	18 41	18 57				19 22	19 38	
Baglan	d				15 54								17 42					18 45						19 41	
Briton Ferry	d				15 57								17 46					18 48						19 44	
Neath	d	15 30			16 01		16 30	16 48				17 30	17 50			18 25	18 30	18 52	19 04				19 30	19 48	
Skewen	d				16 05								17 54					18 56						19 53	
Llansamlet	d				16 09								17 58					19 00						19 57	
Swansea	a	15 43			16 20		16 43	17 01				17 43	18 05			18 37	18 48	19 11	19 18				19 46	20 04	
	d			16 00	16 40			17 05		17 35			18 09		18 21	18 41						19 35		20 08	
Gowerton	d			16x10	16 51			17x16		17x45			18 20			18x52								20x19	
Llanelli	a			16 17	16 58			17 22		17 52			18 26		18 35	18 59						19 51		20 25	
	d			16 19	16 59			17 24		17 54			18 28			19 00						19 52		20 27	
Pembrey & Burry Port	d			16 25	17 05			17 30		18 00			18 33			19 06						19 59		20 32	
Kidwelly	d				17x12			17x36		18x08			18 39									20x06			
Ferryside	d				17x18			17x41		18x14			18 45									20x12			
Carmarthen	a			16 48	17 30			17 53		18 30			18 57			19 27						20 28		20 55	
	d			16 51	17 35			17 56					19 02			19 30								21 00	
Whitland	a			17 05	17 50			18 13					19 18			19 45								21 15	
	d			17 06	17 50			18 14					19 18			19 46								21 15	
Narberth	d			17x15									19 28											21x24	
Kilgetty	d			17x25									19 38											21x33	
Saundersfoot	d			17x27									19 40											21x35	
Tenby	a			17 34									19 52											21 42	
	d			17 45																				21 43	
Penally	d			17x48																				21x46	
Manorbier	d			17 54																				21 52	
Lamphey	d			18x02																				22x00	
Pembroke	d			18 05																				22 03	
Pembroke Dock	a			18 19																				22 18	
Clunderwen	d				17x57			18x20								19x53									
Clarbeston Road	d				18x05			18x28								20x00									
Haverfordwest	d							18 36								20 09									
Johnston	d							18x44								20x17									
Milford Haven	a							18 59								20 32									
Fishguard Harbour ⛴	a				18 29																				
	d																								
Rosslare Harbour ⛴	a																								

A ☕ from Bridgend ⊘ to Bridgend

B The Capitals United

When events are being held at the Millenium Stadium,
services are subject to alteration.
Please check times before travelling.

Cardiff - Maesteg, Swansea and West Wales

Route Diagram - see first Page of Table 127

		GW	AW	AW	GW	AW		GW	GW	AW	AW	AW	GW		GW	AW		AW	GW	AW	AW	AW	GW	GW	GW
										FO	FX		FX		FO	FX		FO						FO	FX
				■																					
		◇**1**			◇**1**			◇**1**	◇**1**				◇**1**		◇**1**	◇		◇	◇**1**		◇		◇**1**	◇**1**	◇**1**
		A																							
		⊐		⊥	⊐			⊐	⊐				⊐		⊐	⊥		⊥	⊐				⊐	⊐	⊐
London Paddington **15** ⊖	d	17 15			17 45			18 15	18 45				19 15		19 15				20 15				21 15	22 45	22 45
Reading **7**	d	17 41			18 11			18 41	19 11				19 41		19 48				20 41				21 41	23 11	23 19
Manchester Piccadilly **10**	d			16 30												18 30		18 30							
Gloucester **7**	d					18 58						19 58													
Bristol Parkway **7**	d	18 41			19 07			19 44	20 07				20 42		20 43				21 41				22 45	00 16	00 23
Newport (South Wales)	d	19 11		19 22	19 31	19 52		20 08	20 33			20 52	21 04		21 07	21 52		21 52	22 05				23 19	00 38	00 52
Cardiff Central 7	d	19 28		19 46	19 51	20 13		20 24	20 54	21 04	21 04	21 10	21 22		21 22	22 09		22 09	22 26	22 35		23 15	23 43	00 55	01 13
Pontyclun	d					20 25						21 22				22 21		22 21				23 29			
Llanharan	d					20 30						21 27				22 25		22 25				23 34			
Pencoed	d					20 34						21 32				22 29		22 29				23 39			
Bridgend	d	19 49		20 05	20 10	20 41		20 45	21 15	21 27	21 27	21 41	21 45		21 45	22 35		22 35	22 46	22 59		23 45	00 02	01 19	01 36
Wildmill	d					20 44						21 43								23 01					
Sarn	d					20 47						21 46								23 04					
Tondu	d					20 50						21 50								23 08					
Garth (Mid Glamorgan)	d					21 00						21 59								23 17					
Maesteg (Ewenny Road)	d					21 02						22 02								23 20					
Maesteg	a					21 07						22 06								23 24					
Pyle	d									21 34	21 34											23 53			
Port Talbot Parkway	d	20 02		20 21	20 26			20 58	21 28	21 45	21 45		21 58		21 58	22 47		22 47	22 59			00 01	00 15	01 32	01 49
Baglan	d																					00 05			
Briton Ferry	d																					00 09			
Neath	d	20 10		20 28	20 33			21 05	21 36	21 52	21 52		22 06		22 06			22 54	23 07			00 13	00 22	01 39	01 57
Skewen	d																					00 16			
Llansamlet	d																					00 20			
Swansea	a	20 23		20 42	20 47			21 19	21 49	22 04	22 04		22 19		22 19			23 07	23 20			00 28	00 37	01 53	02 10
	d	20 32		20 52						22 30	22 27							23 11			23 45	00 45			
Gowerton	d									22x41	22x41							23x22			23x56	00c55			
Llanelli	a	20 48		21 07						22 47	22 47					23 16		23 29			00 01	01s02			
	d	20 49		21 09						22 49	22 49					23 18		23 30			00 03				
Pembrey & Burry Port	d	20 56		21 14						22 54	22 54					23 23		23 36			00 08	01s09			
Kidwelly	d									23x00	23x00					23x29		23x42				01c15			
Ferryside	d									23x06	23x06					23x35		23x47				01c21			
Carmarthen	a	21 20		21 35						23 18	23 18					23 56		00 04			00 28	01 40			
	d			21 38						23 21	23 21										00 31				
Whitland	a			21 52						23 35	23 35										00 46				
	d			21 53						23 36	23 36										00 46				
Narberth	d																								
Kilgetty	d																								
Saundersfoot	d																								
Tenby	a																								
	d																								
Penally	d																								
Manorbier	d																								
Lamphey	d																								
Pembroke	d																								
Pembroke Dock	a																								
Clunderwen	d			21x59						23x42	23x42														
Clarbeston Road	d		20 05	22x07						23x51	23x51										01x00				
Haverfordwest	d			22 20						23 59	23 59														
Johnston	d			22x28						00x07	00x07														
Milford Haven	a			22 43						00 22	00 22														
Fishguard Harbour ⛴	a		20 30																		01 27				
	d																								
Rosslare Harbour ⛴	a																								

A The Red Dragon

c Stops to set down only, stops on request

When events are being held at the Millenium Stadium, services are subject to alteration. Please check times before travelling.

Cardiff - Maesteg, Swansea and West Wales

Route Diagram - see first Page of Table 127

		AW	AW	AW	AW	AW	AW	GW	GW	AW		AW	AW	AW	AW	AW	AW	AW	AW	AW		AW	GW	GW	AW
			◇	◇		R		◇1	◇1	◇								◇		◇			1	◇1	
London Paddington 15 ⊖	d							21p15	22p45																
Reading 7	d							21p41	23p11																
Manchester Piccadilly 10	d		18p30																						
Gloucester 7	d																					05 50			
Bristol Parkway 7	d							22p45	00 16															07 11	
Newport (South Wales)	d		21p52					23p19	00 38													06 44		07 31	
Cardiff Central 7	d	21p04	22p09				23p15	23p43	00 55									05 39	05 51	06 42		07 04		07 48	
Pontyclun	d		22p21				23p29											05 51	06 03			07 16			
Llanharan	d		22p25				23p34											05 56	06 08			07 21			
Pencoed	d		22p29				23p39											06 01	06 12			07 25			
Bridgend	d	21p27	22p35				23p45	00 02	01 19									06 07	06 20	07 02		07 32		08 09	
Wildmill	d																		06 22			07 35			
Sarn	d																		06 25			07 38			
Tondu	d																		06 29			07 41			
Garth (Mid Glamorgan)	d																		06 38			07 51			
Maesteg (Ewenny Road)	d																		06 41			07 53			
Maesteg	a																		06 45			07 58			
Pyle	d	21p34					23p53											06 15		07 10					
Port Talbot Parkway	d	21p45	22p47				00 01	00 15	01 32									06 23		07 18				08 22	
Baglan	d						00 05											06 27		07 22					
Briton Ferry	d						00 09											06 30		07 25					
Neath	d	21p52	22p54				00 13	00 22	01 39									06 34		07 29				08 30	
Skewen	d						00 16											06 38		07 33					
Llansamlet	d						00 20											06 42		07 37					
Swansea	a	22p04	23p07				00 28	00 37	01 53									06 51		07 45				08 44	
	d	22p30	23p11	23p45	00 05		00 45			04 36						05 50		06 53		07 50			08 15		
Gowerton	d	22b41	23b22	23b56	00x16		00c55									06x00		07x03		08x00					
Llanelli	a	22p47	23p29	00 01	00 23		01s02			04 52						06 07		07 10		08 07			08 31		
	d	22p49	23p30	00 03	00 25											06 09		07 11		08 08			08 36		
Pembrey & Burry Port	d	22p54	23p36	00 08	00 31		01s09									06 15		07 17		08 14			08 43		
Kidwelly	d	23b00	23b42		00x38		01c15									06x22		07x23		08x20					
Ferryside	d	23b06	23b47		00x44		01c21									06x28		07x29		08x26					
Carmarthen	a	23p18	00 04	00 28	01 00		01 40									06 42		07 43		08 40			09 08		
	d	23p21		00 31								04 53	05 38	05 50	05 58	06 43		07 46		08 43					
Whitland	a	23p35		00 46								05 06	05 54	06 05	06 13	07 00		08 00		08 59					
	d	23p36		00 46								05 06	05 54	06 05	06 13	07 00		08 00		09 02					09 07
Narberth	d												06x03			07x09				09x11					
Kilgetty	d												06x13			07x19				09x21					
Saundersfoot	d												06x15			07x21				09x23					
Tenby	a												06 22			07 28				09 30					
	d												06 25			07 42				09 43					
Penally	d												06x28			07x45				09x46					
Manorbier	d												06 35			07 52				09 53					
Lamphey	d												06x42			07x59				10x00					
Pembroke	d												06 45			08 02				10 03					
Pembroke Dock	a												07 00			08 17				10 17					
Clunderwen	d	23b42										05x13		06x12	06x19			08 07							09x14
Clarbeston Road	d	23b51		01x00								05x21		06x20	06x27		07 34	08x14							09x22
Haverfordwest	d	23p59										05 32			06 35			08 23							
Johnston	d	00x07										05x40			06x43			08x31							
Milford Haven	a	00 22										05 55			06 58			08 48							
Fishguard Harbour ⛴	a			01 27										06 44			07 58								09 46
	d					02 45																			
Rosslare Harbour ⛴	a					06 15																			

b Previous night, stops on request

c Stops to set down only, stops on request

When events are being held at the Millenium Stadium,
services are subject to alteration.
Please check times before travelling.

Table 128

Saturdays

Cardiff - Maesteg, Swansea and West Wales

Route Diagram - see first Page of Table 127

		AW	AW	AW	AW	AW	AW	GW	AW	AW	AW	GW	AW	AW	AW	AW	AW	AW	GW	AW	AW	AW	GW	AW
		◇	◇		◇			◇■1		◇		◇■1	◇		◇	R			◇■1	◇		◇	◇■1	
																							A	
		🛒	🛒		🛒			🍽		🛒		🍽	🛒		🛒				🍽	🛒			🍽∅	
London Paddington ■15 ⊖	d							07 45				08 45							09 45				10 45	
Reading ■7	d							08 11				09 11							10 11				11 11	
Manchester Piccadilly ■10	d									06 30					07 30					08 30				
Gloucester ■7	d						07 58				08 58										10 58			
Bristol Parkway ■7	d							09 07				10 07							11 07				12 07	
Newport (South Wales)	d	07 38		08 01	08 33		08 52	09 31		09 38	09 52	10 31			10 36				11 31	11 37	11 52		12 31	
Cardiff Central ■7	d	07 58	08 09	08 22	09 04	09 14	09 18	09 48		10 04	10 18	10 48	10 54		11 04		11 14	11 21	11 48	12 04	12 18		12 48	
Pontyclun	d			08 34			09 30				10 30							11 33			12 30			
Llanharan	d			08 39			09 35				10 35							11 38			12 35			
Pencoed	d			08 43			09 39				10 39							11 42			12 39			
Bridgend	d	08 17	08 29	08 51	09 23	09 34	09 46	10 09		10 23	10 46	11 09			11 23		11 34	11 49	12 09	12 23	12 46		13 09	
Wildmill	d			08 53			09 49				10 49							11 52			12 49			
Sarn	d			08 56			09 52				10 52							11 55			12 52			
Tondu	d			09 00			09 55				10 55							11 58			12 55			
Garth (Mid Glamorgan)	d			09 09			10 05				11 05							12 08			13 05			
Maesteg (Ewenny Road)	d			09 12			10 07				11 07							12 10			13 07			
Maesteg	a			09 16			10 12				11 12							12 15			13 12			
Pyle	d		08 37			09 43											11 42							
Port Talbot Parkway	d	08 30	08 45		09 38	09 52		10 22		10 35		11 22			11 36		11 50		12 22	12 36			13 22	
Baglan	d		08 49			09 55											11 54							
Briton Ferry	d		08 52			09 59											11 57							
Neath	d	08 37	08 56		09 45	10 03		10 30		10 42		11 30			11 43		12 01		12 30	12 43			13 30	
Skewen	d		09 00			10 06											12 05							
Llansamlet	d		09 04			10 10											12 09							
Swansea	a	08 51	09 13		09 57	10 21		10 43		10 55		11 43			11 56		12 20		12 43	12 55			13 43	
	d	09 02	09 16		10 04					11 00				11 50	12 05					13 03		13 16		13 50
Gowerton	d	09x18			10x15									12x01										14x00
Llanelli	a	09 25	09 32		10 22					11 15			11 58	12 08	12 21					13 19		13 32		14 07
	d	09 26			10 22					11 17			11 58	12 10	12 22					13 20				14 09
Pembrey & Burry Port	d	09 32			10 28					11 23				12 16	12 28					13 26				14 15
Kidwelly	d	09x38			10x34										12x34									
Ferryside	d	09x44			10x40										12x40									
Carmarthen	a	09 56			10 53					11 42				12 39	12 51					13 46				14 39
	d	09 58							10 56	11 47				12 56						13 49				14 56
Whitland	a	10 14							11 10	12 01			12 34	13 11						14 03				15 10
	d	10 15							11 11	12 02			12 34	13 11						14 04				15 10
Narberth	d								11x20					13x20										15x19
Kilgetty	d								11x30					13x30										15x29
Saundersfoot	d								11x32					13x32										15x31
Tenby	a								11 39					13 39										15 38
	d								11 45					13 45										15 45
Penally	d								11x48					13x48										15x48
Manorbier	d								11 54					13 54										15 54
Lamphey	d								12x02					14x02										16x02
Pembroke	d								12 05					14 05										16 05
Pembroke Dock	a								12 20					14 19										16 19
Clunderwen	d	10x21								12x08										14x10				
Clarbeston Road	d	10x29								12x16										14x18				
Haverfordwest	d	10 37								12 24										14 26				
Johnston	d	10x45								12x32										14x34				
Milford Haven	a	10 59								12 47										14 49				
Fishguard Harbour ⛴	a												13 15											
	d															14 30								
Rosslare Harbour ⛴	a															18 00								

A 🍽 from Bridgend ∅ to Bridgend

When events are being held at the Millenium Stadium,
services are subject to alteration.
Please check times before travelling.

Table 128

Saturdays

Cardiff - Maesteg, Swansea and West Wales

Route Diagram - see first Page of Table 127

		AW		AW	AW	GW	AW	AW	GW	AW		AW		AW	AW	GW	AW	AW	GW	AW	AW	AW		AW	AW
																	R				R				
		◇				◇1	◇		◇1	◇						◇1			◇1			◇		◇	
						A																			
		trolley				buffet ⊘	trolley		buffet	trolley						buffet	trolley	trolley	buffet		trolley	trolley			
London Paddington 15 ⊖	d					11 45			12 45							13 45			14 45						
Reading 7	d					12 11			13 11							14 11			15 11						
Manchester Piccadilly 10	d	09 30					10 30			11 30							12 30				13 30				
Gloucester 7	d				11 58										13 58			14 58							
Bristol Parkway 7	d					13 07			14 07							15 07			16 07						
Newport (South Wales)	d	12 37			12 52	13 31	13 37		14 31	14 37					14 52	15 31	15 37	15 52	16 31		16 37	16 56			
Cardiff Central 7	d	13 04		13 14	13 18	13 48	14 04	14 21	14 48	15 04				15 14	15 18	15 48	16 04	16 18	16 48		17 04	17 18			17 38
Pontyclun	d				13 30			14 33							15 30			16 30				17 30			
Llanharan	d				13 35			14 38							15 35			16 35				17 35			
Pencoed	d				13 39			14 42							15 39			16 39				17 39			
Bridgend	d	13 23		13 34	13 46	14 09	14 23	14 49	15 09	15 23				15 34	15 46	16 09	16 23	16 46	17 09		17 25	17 46			17 58
Wildmill	d				13 49			14 52							15 49			16 49				17 48			
Sarn	d				13 52			14 55							15 52			16 52				17 51			
Tondu	d				13 55			14 58							15 55			16 55				17 55			
Garth (Mid Glamorgan)	d				14 05			15 08							16 05			17 05				18 04			
Maesteg (Ewenny Road)	d				14 07			15 10							16 07			17 07				18 07			
Maesteg	a				14 12			15 15							16 12			17 12				18 15			
Pyle	d			13 42										15 42			16 31				17 32				18 06
Port Talbot Parkway	d	13 36		13 50		14 22	14 36		15 22	15 36				15 50		16 22	16 39		17 22		17 40				18 14
Baglan	d			13 54										15 54							17 42				18 18
Briton Ferry	d			13 57										15 57							17 46				18 21
Neath	d	13 43		14 01		14 30	14 43		15 30	15 43				16 01		16 30	16 46		17 30		17 50				18 25
Skewen	d			14 05										16 05							17 54				18 29
Llansamlet	d			14 09										16 09							17 58				18 33
Swansea	a	13 55		14 20		14 43	14 55		15 43	15 55				16 20		16 43	16 58		17 43		18 05				18 44
	d	14 05					15 00			16 00		16 05		16 40			17 05			17 51	18 09			18 21	
Gowerton	d											16x16		16 51			17x16			18x01	18x20				
Llanelli	a	14 20					15 20			16 15		16 23		16 58			17 22			18 08	18 26			18 37	
	d	14 22					15 22			16 17		16 25		16 59			17 24			18 10	18 28				
Pembrey & Burry Port	d	14 28					15 28			16 23		16 31		17 05			17 30			18 16	18 33				
Kidwelly	d	14x34								16x29				17x12			17x36			18x24	18x39				
Ferryside	d	14x39								16x34				17x18			17x41			18x30	18x45				
Carmarthen	a	14 51					15 46			16 51		16 54		17 30			17 53			18 46	18 57				
	d						15 49					16 54		17 35			17 56				19 02				
Whitland	a						16 03					17 10		17 50			18 10				19 18				
	d						16 04					17 11		17 50			18 11				19 18				
Narberth	d											17x20									19x28				
Kilgetty	d											17x29									19x38				
Saundersfoot	d											17x31									19x40				
Tenby	a											17 38									19 50				
	d											17 43									19 50				
Penally	d											17x46									19x53				
Manorbier	d											17 53									20 00				
Lamphey	d											18x00									20x07				
Pembroke	d											18 03									20 10				
Pembroke Dock	a											18 18									20 20				
Clunderwen	d						16x10							17x57			18x17								
Clarbeston Road	d						16x18							18x05			18x25								
Haverfordwest	d						16 26										18 33								
Johnston	d						16x34										18x41								
Milford Haven	a						16 49										18 55								
Fishguard Harbour ⛴	a													18 29											
	d																								
Rosslare Harbour ⛴	a																								

A buffet from Bridgend ⊘ to Bridgend

When events are being held at the Millenium Stadium,
services are subject to alteration.
Please check times before travelling.

Table 128

Cardiff - Maesteg, Swansea and West Wales

Route Diagram - see first Page of Table 127

		GW	AW	AW	AW	GW	AW	AW		AW	GW	AW	GW	AW	GW	AW	AW	GW		GW	AW	AW	AW	GW	
			R				R					R													
		◇1				◇1					◇1		◇1		◇1			◇1		◇1	◇			◇1	
																								A	
		☕	🛒			☕	🛒				☕	🛒	☕		☕			☕		☕	🛒			☕	
London Paddington 15 ⊖	d	15 45				16 45					17 45				18 45			19 15		19 45				20 45	
Reading 7	d	16 11				17 11					18 11				19 11			19 42		20 11				21 13	
Manchester Piccadilly 10	d		14 30				15 30					16 30									18 30				
Gloucester 7	d			16 58				17 58						18 58			19 58								
Bristol Parkway 7	d	17 07				18 07					19 07				20 07			20 40		21 07				22 11	
Newport (South Wales)	d	17 31	17 37	17 52		18 31	18 37	18 52			19 31	19 41		19 52	20 31		20 52	21 07		21 31	21 45			22 46	
Cardiff Central 7	d	17 48	18 04	18 18		18 48	19 04	19 16			19 48	20 04		20 13	20 48	21 04	21 10	21 23		21 48	22 07		22 43	23 07	
Pontyclun	d			18 30				19 28						20 25			21 22				22 19		22 57		
Llanharan	d			18 35				19 33						20 30			21 27				22 23		23 02		
Pencoed	d			18 39				19 37						20 34			21 30				22 27		23 07		
Bridgend	d	18 09	18 25	18 46		19 09	19 23	19 45			20 09	20 23		20 41	21 09	21 23	21 41	21 46		22 09	22 33		23 13	23 28	
Wildmill	d			18 49				19 48						20 44			21 43								
Sarn	d			18 52				19 51						20 47			21 46								
Tondu	d			18 55				19 54						20 50			21 50								
Garth (Mid Glamorgan)	d			19 05				20 04						21 00			21 59								
Maesteg (Ewenny Road)	d			19 07				20 06						21 02			22 02								
Maesteg	a			19 13				20 11						21 07			22 06								
Pyle	d		18 33				19 30									21 31							23 21		
Port Talbot Parkway	d	18 22	18 41			19 22	19 38				20 22	20 36			21 22	21 39		21 59		22 22	22 45		23 30	23 41	
Baglan	d						19 41																23 34		
Briton Ferry	d						19 44																23 37		
Neath	d	18 30	18 49			19 30	19 48				20 30				21 30	21 46		22 07		22 30	22 52		23 41	23 49	
Skewen	d						19 53																23 45		
Llansamlet	d						19 57																23 49		
Swansea	a	18 46	19 02			19 43	20 04				20 43				21 43	21 57		22 19		22 43	23 05		23 57	00 02	
	d		19 05		19 35		20 08				21 00					22 25					23 10	23 45	00 09		
Gowerton	d		19x16				20x19						←			22x36					23x22		00s20		
Llanelli	a		19 23		19 51		20 25				21 16	21 05	21 16			22 42					23 29	00 01	00s28		
	d		19 24		19 52		20 27				21 16	21 06	21 16			22 44					23 30	00 02			
Pembrey & Burry Port	d		19 30		19 59		20 32				→	21 12	21 23			22 50					23 36	00 07	00s34		
Kidwelly	d				20x06											22x56					23x42		00s40		
Ferryside	d				20x12											23x01					23x47		00s46		
Carmarthen	a		19 51		20 28		20 55					21 31	21 48			23 18					00 04	00 28	01 04		
	d		19 55				21 00					22 05										00 31			
Whitland	a		20 10				21 15					22 19										00 46			
	d		20 10				21 15					22 20										00 46			
Narberth	d						21x24																		
Kilgetty	d						21x33																		
Saundersfoot	d						21x35																		
Tenby	a						21 42																		
	d						21 43																		
Penally	d						21x46																		
Manorbier	d						21 52																		
Lamphey	d						22x00																		
Pembroke	d						22 03																		
Pembroke Dock	a						22 18																		
Clunderwen	d		20x17									22x26													
Clarbeston Road	d		20x25							20 30		22x34										01x00			
Haverfordwest	d		20 33									22 42													
Johnston	d		20x41									22x50													
Milford Haven	a		20 56									23 05													
Fishguard Harbour ⛴	a									20 55												01 27			
	d																								
Rosslare Harbour ⛴	a																								

A until 11 February, from 31 March

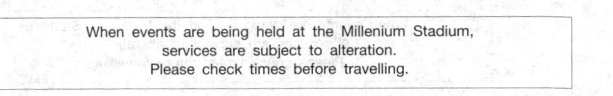

When events are being held at the Millenium Stadium,
services are subject to alteration.
Please check times before travelling.

Table 128

Sundays

until 1 January

Cardiff - Maesteg, Swansea and West Wales

Route Diagram - see first Page of Table 127

		AW	AW	AW	AW	GW	AW	AW	AW	AW		GW	AW	AW	GW	AW	GW	AW	GW	AW		AW	GW	AW	GW
					R									R						R					
		◇				◇1			◇	◇		◇1	◇		◇1		◇1		◇1			◇	◇1		◇1
		A	A	A		A																			
		🛒				☕			🛒			☕			☕	🛒	☕		☕	🛒			☕		☕
London Paddington 15 ⊖	d					20p45						08 30			09 30		10 37		11 37				12 37		13 37
Reading 7	d					21p13						09 06			10 06		11 12		12 12				13 12		14 12
Manchester Piccadilly 10	d	18p30																		10 30					
Gloucester 7	d																								
Bristol Parkway 7	d					22p11						10 08			11 05		12 11		13 11				14 11		15 11
Newport (South Wales)	d	21p45				22p46			09 27			10 33	11 00		11 32		12 37		13 37	13 29			14 37		15 37
Cardiff Central 7	d	22p07		22p43		23p07			09 50			10 54	11 18		11 53	12 05	12 57		13 57	14 03			14 57		15 57
Pontyclun	d	22p19		22p57					10 03											14 16					
Llanharan	d	22p23		23p02					10 08											14 21					
Pencoed	d	22p27		23p07					10 13											14 26					
Bridgend	d	22p33		23p13		23p28			10 20			11 15	11 38		12 14	12 26	13 19		14 19	14 33			15 19		16 19
Wildmill	d																								
Sarn	d																								
Tondu	d																								
Garth (Mid Glamorgan)	d																								
Maesteg (Ewenny Road)	d																								
Maesteg	a																								
Pyle	d			23p21					10 28							12 34				14 41					
Port Talbot Parkway	d	22p45		23p30		23p41			10 37			11 28	11 52		12 27	12 43	13 32		14 32	14 49			15 32		16 32
Baglan	d			23p34																					
Briton Ferry	d			23p37																					
Neath	d	22p52		23p41		23p49			10 45			11 36	12 00		12 34		13 39		14 39	14 57			15 39		16 39
Skewen	d			23p45																					
Llansamlet	d			23p49																					
Swansea	a	23p05		23p57		00 02			10 58			11 49	12 13		12 47		13 52		14 52	15 10			15 52		16 52
	d	23p10	23p45	00 09					11 01	11 06			12 15		12 58			14 11	14 58	15 13		15 26		16 26	17 05
Gowerton	d	23b22		00s20						11x16			12x26					14x22				15x36		16x37	
Llanelli	a	23p29	00 01	00s28					11 17	11 23			12 32		13 15	13 23		14 29	15 14	15 29		15 48		16 44	17 21
	d	23p30	00 02						11 19				12 34		13 16	13 23		14 31	15 15	15 30				16 46	17 22
Pembrey & Burry Port	d	23p36	00 07	00s34					11 25				12 39		13 23	13 29		14 37	15 22	15 36				16 52	17 29
Kidwelly	d	23b42		00s40					11x32				12x46					14x43						16x59	
Ferryside	d	23b47		00s46					11x38				12x52					14x49						17x05	
Carmarthen	a	00 04	00 28	01 04					11 51				13 05		13 44	13 56		15 04	15 43	15 59				17 19	17 50
	d		00 31				09 55	10 19	11 55				13 08			14 04		15 07		16 03				17 32	
Whitland	a		00 46				10 11	10 34	12 11				13 23			14 20		15 21		16 19				17 48	
	d		00 46				10 11	10 34	12 11				13 23			14 20		15 22		16 20				17 48	
Narberth	d							10x43										15x31						17x57	
Kilgetty	d							10x52										15x41						18x07	
Saundersfoot	d							10x54										15x43						18x09	
Tenby	a							11 01										15 50						18 16	
	d							11 11										15 54						18 19	
Penally	d							11x14										15x57						18x22	
Manorbier	d							11 20										16 03						18 29	
Lamphey	d							11x28										16x11						18x36	
Pembroke	d							11 31										16 14						18 40	
Pembroke Dock	a							11 44										16 29						18 55	
Clunderwen	d						10x19		12x19							14x28				16x28					
Clarbeston Road	d		01x00				10x27		12x27							14x36				16x36					
Haverfordwest	d						10 35		12 35							14 44				16 44					
Johnston	d						10x44		12x44							14x53				16x53					
Milford Haven	a						10 55		12 55							15 08				17 08					
Fishguard Harbour ⛴	a		01 27										13 59												
	d				02 45									14 30											
Rosslare Harbour ⛴	a				06 15									18 00											

A not 11 December

b Previous night, stops on request

When events are being held at the Millenium Stadium,
services are subject to alteration.
Please check times before travelling.

Table 128

Sundays
until 1 January

Cardiff - Maesteg, Swansea and West Wales

Route Diagram - see first Page of Table 127

		AW	GW	AW	GW	AW		GW	AW	AW	GW	AW	GW	GW	AW	GW		GW
		R				R												
			◇1		◇1			◇1			◇1	◇	◇1	◇1	◇	◇1		◇1
		🛒	☕		☕	🛒		☕			☕	🛒	☕	☕		☕		☕
London Paddington 15 ⊖	d		14 37		15 37			16 37			17 37		18 37	19 37		20 37		21 37
Reading 7	d		15 12		16 12			17 12			18 12		19 12	20 13		21 12		22 14
Manchester Piccadilly 10	d	12 30				14 30												
Gloucester 7	d																	
Bristol Parkway 7	d		16 11		17 11			18 11			19 15		20 11	21 11		22 11		23 17
Newport (South Wales)	d	15 46	16 37		17 41	17 34		18 37			19 41		20 37	21 37		22 38		23 43
Cardiff Central 7	d	16 16	16 57		18 01	18 06		18 57			20 01	20 15	20 57	22 01	22 30	23 01		00 08
Pontyclun	d					18 21												
Llanharan	d					18 26												
Pencoed	d					18 30												
Bridgend	d	16 37	17 19		18 22	18 38		19 19			20 22	20 37	21 19	22 22	22 51	23 22		00 28
Wildmill	d																	
Sarn	d																	
Tondu	d																	
Garth (Mid Glamorgan)	d																	
Maesteg (Ewenny Road)	d																	
Maesteg	a																	
Pyle	d	16 45				18 46						20 45						
Port Talbot Parkway	d	16 54	17 32		18 35	18 54		19 32			20 35	20 54	21 32	22 35	23 05	23 36		00 41
Baglan	d																	
Briton Ferry	d																	
Neath	d	17 02	17 39		18 43	19 02		19 39			20 43	21 02	21 39	22 43	23 13	23 44		00 49
Skewen	d																	
Llansamlet	d																	
Swansea	a	17 14	17 53		18 58	19 15		19 52			20 56	21 14	21 53	22 56	23 25	23 56		01 01
	d	17 25		18 11		19 20				20 35		21 18			23 38			
Gowerton	d			18x22						20x46					23x49			
Llanelli	a	17 41		18 29		19 36				20 54		21 34			23 56			
	d	17 41		18 31		19 36				20 55		21 34			23 58			
Pembrey & Burry Port	d	17 48		18 37		19 43				21 01		21 41			00 04			
Kidwelly	d			18x44						21x08					00x11			
Ferryside	d			18x50						21x14					00x17			
Carmarthen	a	18 14		19 03		20 05				21 32		22 04			00 30			
	d	18 20		19 06		20 07						22 05			00 34			
Whitland	a	18 36		19 22		20 23						22 21			00 50			
	d	18 37		19 22		20 30			20 30			22 22			00 50			
Narberth	d								20x37									
Kilgetty	d								20x46									
Saundersfoot	d								20x48									
Tenby	a								20 55									
	d								20 59									
Penally	d								21x02									
Manorbier	d								21 08									
Lamphey	d								21x16									
Pembroke	d								21 19									
Pembroke Dock	a								21 34									
Clunderwen	d	18x45		19x30		20x37						22x29						
Clarbeston Road	d	18x53		19x38		20x45						22x37			01x03			
Haverfordwest	d	19 01		19a46		20 54						22 46						
Johnston	d	19x10				21x02						22x54						
Milford Haven	a	19 25				21 19						23 10						
Fishguard Harbour ⛴	a														01 30			
	d																	
Rosslare Harbour ⛴	a																	

When events are being held at the Millenium Stadium,
services are subject to alteration.
Please check times before travelling.

Table 128

Sundays

8 January to 12 February

Cardiff - Maesteg, Swansea and West Wales

Route Diagram - see first Page of Table 127

		AW	AW	AW	AW	GW	AW	AW	AW	AW		AW	AW	GW	AW	GW	AW	GW	GW	AW	AW	AW	GW	GW	AW
					R												R								
		◇				◇1						◇						1							
							🚌						🚌	🚌		🚌			🚌	🚌		🚌	🚌	🚌	
		🛒				🍴												🍴							
London Paddington 15 ⊖	d					20p45																			
Reading 7	d					21p13																			
Manchester Piccadilly 10	d	18p30																							
Gloucester 7	d																								
Bristol Parkway 7	d					22p11																			
Newport (South Wales)	d	21p45				22p46																			
Cardiff Central 7	d	22p07		22p43		23p07	08 36						09 45	11 10		11 08			12 05	11 29		12 00	12 08	13 10	
Pontyclun	d	22p19		22p57									10 10												
Llanharan	d	22p23		23p02									10 18												
Pencoed	d	22p27		23p07									10 25												
Bridgend	d	22p33		23p13		23p28							10 40			11 43				12 04		12 35	12 43		
Wildmill	d																								
Sarn	d																								
Tondu	d																								
Garth (Mid Glamorgan)	d																								
Maesteg (Ewenny Road)	d																								
Maesteg	a																								
Pyle	d			23p21									10 55									12 50			
Port Talbot Parkway	d	22p45		23p30		23p41							11 15			12 08				12 24		13 10	13 08		
Baglan	d			23p34																					
Briton Ferry	d			23p37																					
Neath	d	22p52		23p41		23p49							11 35			12 23				12 44		13 30	13 23		
Skewen	d			23p45																					
Llansamlet	d			23p49																					
Swansea	a	23p05		23p57		00 02	10 51						12 00	12 10		12 45			13 05	13 09		13 55	13 45	14 10	
	d	23p10	23p45	00 09						11 01		11 06			12 15			13 00			13 22				14 11
Gowerton	d	23b22		00s20								11x15			12x26										14x22
Llanelli	a	23p29	00 01	00s28						11 17		11 22			12 32			13 16			13 38				14 29
	d	23p30	00 02							11 19					12 34			13 17			13 39				14 31
Pembrey & Burry Port	d	23p36	00 07	00s34						11 25					12 39			13 24			13 46				14 37
Kidwelly	d	23b42		00s40						11x32					12x46										14x43
Ferryside	d	23b47		00s46						11x38					12x52										14x49
Carmarthen	a	00 04	00 28	01 04						11 51					13 05			13 45			14 08				15 04
	d		00 31					09 55	10 19	11 55					13 08						14 10				15 07
Whitland	a		00 46					10 11	10 34	12 11					13 23						14 26				15 21
	d		00 46					10 11	10 34	12 11					13 23						14 27				15 22
Narberth	d								10x43																15x31
Kilgetty	d								10x52																15x41
Saundersfoot	d								10x54																15x43
Tenby	a								11 01																15 50
	d								11 11																15 54
Penally	d								11x14																15x57
Manorbier	d								11 20																16 03
Lamphey	d								11x28																16x11
Pembroke	d								11 31																16 14
Pembroke Dock	a								11 44																16 29
Clunderwen	d							10x19		12x19											14x34				
Clarbeston Road	d		01x00					10x27		12x27											14x42				
Haverfordwest	d							10 35		12 35											14 51				
Johnston	d							10x44		12x44											14x59				
Milford Haven	a							10 55		12 55											15 14				
Fishguard Harbour ⛴	a		01 27												13 59										
	d				02 45												14 30								
Rosslare Harbour ⛴	a				06 15												18 00								

b Previous night, stops on request

When events are being held at the Millenium Stadium, services are subject to alteration. Please check times before travelling.

Table 128

Sundays

8 January to 12 February

Cardiff - Maesteg, Swansea and West Wales

Route Diagram - see first Page of Table 127

		GW	GW		AW	AW		GW	GW	GW	AW	AW	GW	GW	AW	AW		GW	GW	GW	AW	GW	AW	GW	AW
						◇			1											1					
		🚌	🚌					🚌		🚌	🚌		🚌	🚌		🚌		🚌	🚌			🚌	🚌	🚌	
									☕											☕					
London Paddington 15 ⊖	d																								
Reading 7	d																								
Manchester Piccadilly 10	d																								
Gloucester 7	d																								
Bristol Parkway 7	d																								
Newport (South Wales)	d																								
Cardiff Central 7	d	13 08	14 10					14 08		15 10	14 00		15 08	16 10		16 06		16 08	17 10			17 08	17 29	18 15	
Pontyclun	d										14 25														
Llanharan	d										14 33														
Pencoed	d										14 40														
Bridgend	d	13 43						14 43			14 55		15 43			16 41		16 43				17 43			
Wildmill	d																								
Sarn	d																								
Tondu	d																								
Garth (Mid Glamorgan)	d																								
Maesteg (Ewenny Road)	d																								
Maesteg	a																								
Pyle	d										15 10					16 56									
Port Talbot Parkway	d	14 08						15 08			15 30		16 08			17 16		17 08				18 08			
Baglan	d																								
Briton Ferry	d																								
Neath	d	14 23						15 23			15 50		16 23			17 36		17 23				18 23			
Skewen	d																								
Llansamlet	d																								
Swansea	a	14 45	15 10					15 45		16 10	16 15		16 45	17 10		18 01		17 45	18 10			18 45	19 09	19 15	
	d				15 12	15 26			15 55			16 26			17 25					18 11	18 22				19 19
Gowerton	d					15x36						16x37									18x33				
Llanelli	a				15 28	15 48			16 14			16 44			17 41					18 27	18 40				19 35
	d				15 29				16 15			16 46			17 41					18 28	18 42				19 36
Pembrey & Burry Port	d				15 35				16 22			16 52			17 48					18 35	18 48				19 43
Kidwelly	d											16x59									18x55				
Ferryside	d											17x05									19x01				
Carmarthen	a				15 58				16 43			17 19			18 14					18 56	19 16				20 05
	d				16 03							17 32			18 20						19 18				20 07
Whitland	a				16 19							17 48			18 36						19 34				20 23
	d				16 20							17 48			18 37						19 35				20 30
Narberth	d											17x57													
Kilgetty	d											18x07													
Saundersfoot	d											18x09													
Tenby	a											18 16													
	d											18 19													
Penally	d											18x22													
Manorbier	d											18 29													
Lamphey	d											18x36													
Pembroke	d											18 40													
Pembroke Dock	a											18 55													
Clunderwen	d				16x28										18x45						19x42				20x37
Clarbeston Road	d				16x36										18x53						19x50				20x45
Haverfordwest	d				16 44										19 01						19a58				20 54
Johnston	d				16x53										19x10										21x02
Milford Haven	a				17 08										19 25										21 19
Fishguard Harbour ⛴	a																								
	d																								
Rosslare Harbour ⛴	a																								

When events are being held at the Millenium Stadium,
services are subject to alteration.
Please check times before travelling.

Table 128

Sundays

8 January to 12 February

Cardiff - Maesteg, Swansea and West Wales

Route Diagram - see first Page of Table 127

	GW		GW	AW	AW	AW	GW	AW	GW	AW	GW		GW	AW	GW	GW	AW	AW	GW	AW	GW		GW	
London Paddington 15 ⊖ d																								
Reading 7 d																								
Manchester Piccadilly 10 d																								
Gloucester 7 d																								
Bristol Parkway 7 d																								
Newport (South Wales) d																								
Cardiff Central 7 d	18 13		19 15	18 05			19 13	19 13	20 15		20 13		21 15	20 25	21 13	22 15	21 46		22 13	22 29	23 15		23 13	
Pontyclun d				18 30																				
Llanharan d				18 38																				
Pencoed d				18 45																				
Bridgend d	18 48			19 00			19 48				20 48			21 00	21 48		22 21		22 48	23 04			23 48	
Wildmill d																								
Sarn d																								
Tondu d																								
Garth (Mid Glamorgan) d																								
Maesteg (Ewenny Road) d																								
Maesteg a																								
Pyle d				19 15										21 15										
Port Talbot Parkway d	19 13			19 35			20 13				21 13			21 35	22 13		22 41		23 13	23 24			00 13	
Baglan d																								
Briton Ferry d																								
Neath d	19 28			19 55			20 28				21 28			21 55	22 28		23 01		23 28	23 44			00 28	
Skewen d																								
Llansamlet d																								
Swansea a	19 50		20 15	20 20			20 50	21 08	21 15		21 50		22 15	22 20	22 50	23 15	23 26		23 50	00 09	00 15		00 50	
d						20 35				21 18								23 38						
Gowerton d						20x46												23x49						
Llanelli a						20 54				21 34								23 56						
d						20 55				21 34								23 58						
Pembrey & Burry Port d						21 01				21 41								00 04						
Kidwelly d						21x08												00x11						
Ferryside d						21x14												00x17						
Carmarthen a						21 32				22 04								00 30						
d										22 05								00 34						
Whitland a										22 21								00 50						
d					20 30					22 22								00 50						
Narberth d					20x37																			
Kilgetty d					20x46																			
Saundersfoot d					20x48																			
Tenby a					20 55																			
d					20 59																			
Penally d					21x02																			
Manorbier d					21 08																			
Lamphey d					21x16																			
Pembroke d					21 19																			
Pembroke Dock a					21 34																			
Clunderwen d										22x29														
Clarbeston Road d										22x37								01x03						
Haverfordwest d										22 46														
Johnston d										22x54														
Milford Haven a										23 10														
Fishguard Harbour ⛴ a																		01 30						
d																								
Rosslare Harbour ⛴ a																								

When events are being held at the Millenium Stadium,
services are subject to alteration.
Please check times before travelling.

Table 128

Sundays

19 February to 25 March

Cardiff - Maesteg, Swansea and West Wales

Route Diagram - see first Page of Table 127

		AW	AW	AW	AW	AW	AW	AW	AW	GW		AW	AW	AW	GW	AW	GW	AW	AW	GW		GW	AW	AW	GW
		◇ 🛒			R			◇ 🛒	◇	◇1 ☕		◇	🛒	R	◇1 ☕		◇1 ☕	R 🛒	◇	◇1 ☕		◇1 ☕		R 🛒	◇1 ☕
London Paddington 15 ⊖	d									07 57					09 30		10 30			11 30		12 30			13 30
Reading 7	d									08 32					10 06		11 06			12 06		13 06			14 04
Manchester Piccadilly 10	d	18p30																10 30						12 30	
Gloucester 7	d									10 01					11 37		12 30			13 30		14 30			15 30
Bristol Parkway 7	d																								
Newport (South Wales)	d	21p45						09 27		10 53		11 00			12 26		13 19	13 29		14 19		15 19		15 46	16 19
Cardiff Central 7	d	22p07		22p43				09 50		11 10		11 18	12 05		12 48		13 40	14 02		14 40		15 40		16 16	16 40
Pontyclun	d	22p19		22p57				10 03										14 15							
Llanharan	d	22p23		23p02				10 08										14 20							
Pencoed	d	22p27		23p07				10 13										14 25							
Bridgend	d	22p33		23p13				10 20		11 30		11 38	12 26		13 08		14 01	14 32		15 01		16 03		16 37	17 00
Wildmill	d																								
Sarn	d																								
Tondu	d																								
Garth (Mid Glamorgan)	d																								
Maesteg (Ewenny Road)	d																								
Maesteg	a																								
Pyle	d			23p21				10 28					12 34					14 40						16 45	
Port Talbot Parkway	d	22p45		23p30				10 37		11 43		11 52	12 43		13 21		14 14	14 48		15 14		16 16		16 54	17 13
Baglan	d			23p34																					
Briton Ferry	d			23p37																					
Neath	d	22p52		23p41				10 45		11 52		12 00			13 29		14 21	14 56		15 21		16 23		17 02	17 19
Skewen	d			23p45																					
Llansamlet	d			23p49																					
Swansea	a	23p05		23p57				10 58		12 04		12 13			13 41		14 36	15 09		15 34		16 36		17 14	17 33
	d	23p10	23p45	00 09				11 01	11 06			12 15			13 54	14 11		15 12	15 26	15 45			16 41	17 25	17 46
Gowerton	d	23b22		00s20					11x16			12x26				14x22			15x36				16x52		
Llanelli	a	23p29	00 01	00s28				11 17	11 23			12 32	13 12		14 10	14 29		15 28	15 48	16 09			16 59	17 41	18 02
	d	23p30	00 02					11 19				12 34	13 12		14 11	14 31		15 29		16 11			17 01	17 41	18 03
Pembrey & Burry Port	d	23p36	00 07	00s34				11 25				12 39	13 18		14 18	14 37		15 35		16 17			17 07	17 48	18 10
Kidwelly	d	23b42		00s40				11x32				12x46				14x43							17x14		
Ferryside	d	23b47		00s46				11x38				12x52				14x49							17x20		
Carmarthen	a	00 04	00 28	01 04				11 51				13 05	13 42		14 39	15 04		15 58		16 39			17 33	18 14	18 31
	d		00 31			09 55	10 19	11 55				13 08	14 04			15 07		16 03					17 36	18 20	
Whitland	a		00 46			10 11	10 34	12 11				13 23	14 20			15 21		16 19					17 51	18 36	
	d		00 46			10 11	10 34	12 11				13 23	14 20			15 22		16 20					17 51	18 37	
Narberth	d						10x43									15x31							18x00		
Kilgetty	d						10x52									15x41							18x10		
Saundersfoot	d						10x54									15x43							18x12		
Tenby	a						11 01									15 50							18 19		
	d						11 11									15 54							18 22		
Penally	d						11x14									15x57							18x25		
Manorbier	d						11 20									16 03							18 32		
Lamphey	d						11x28									16x11							18x39		
Pembroke	d						11 31									16 14							18 43		
Pembroke Dock	a						11 44									16 29							18 58		
Clunderwen	d					10x19		12x19					14x28					16x28						18x45	
Clarbeston Road	d		01x00			10x27		12x27					14x36					16x36						18x53	
Haverfordwest	d					10 35		12 35					14 44					16 44						19 01	
Johnston	d					10x44		12x44					14x53					16x53						19x10	
Milford Haven	a					10 55		12 55					15 08					17 08						19 25	
Fishguard Harbour ⛴	a		01 27									13 59													
	d				02 45									14 30											
Rosslare Harbour ⛴	a				06 15									18 00											

b Previous night, stops on request

When events are being held at the Millenium Stadium,
services are subject to alteration.
Please check times before travelling.

Table 128

Sundays

19 February to 25 March

Cardiff - Maesteg, Swansea and West Wales

Route Diagram - see first Page of Table 127

		AW	GW	AW	GW	GW		AW	AW	AW	GW	GW	AW	GW	GW	GW
				R												
			◇1		◇1	◇1				◇	◇1	◇1	◇	◇1	◇1	◇1
			☕	🛒	☕	☕				🛒	☕	☕		☕	☕	☕
London Paddington 15 ⊖	d		14 30		15 30	16 30					17 30	18 30		19 37	20 37	21 37
Reading 7	d		15 05		16 06	17 06					18 06	19 05		20 13	21 14	22 15
Manchester Piccadilly 10	d			14 30												
Gloucester 7	d		16 30		17 30	18 27					19 46	20 20		21 42	22 42	23 43
Bristol Parkway 7	d															
Newport (South Wales)	d		17 19	17 34	18 19	19 16					20 38	21 13		22 38	23 44	00 32
Cardiff Central 7	d		17 40	18 06	18 40	19 40				20 15	20 53	21 29	22 30	22 59	00 10	00 54
Pontyclun	d			18 21												
Llanharan	d			18 26												
Pencoed	d			18 30												
Bridgend	d		18 01	18 38	19 01	20 01				20 37	21 15	21 51	22 51	23 21	00 29	01 19
Wildmill	d															
Sarn	d															
Tondu	d															
Garth (Mid Glamorgan)	d															
Maesteg (Ewenny Road)	d															
Maesteg	a															
Pyle	d			18 46						20 45						
Port Talbot Parkway	d		18 14	18 54	19 14	20 14				20 54	21 28	22 05	23 05	23 33	00 43	01 32
Baglan	d															
Briton Ferry	d															
Neath	d		18 20	19 02	19 20	20 21				21 02	21 36	22 12	23 13	23 42	00 51	01 39
Skewen	d															
Llansamlet	d															
Swansea	a		18 35	19 15	19 34	20 34				21 14	21 49	22 25	23 25	23 54	01 04	01 52
	d	18 11		19 40				20 55		21 18			23 55			
Gowerton	d	18x22						21x08					00x06			
Llanelli	a	18 29		20 00				21 15		21 34			00 13			
	d	18 31		20 01				21 17		21 34			00 15			
Pembrey & Burry Port	d	18 37		20 08				21 23		21 41			00 21			
Kidwelly	d	18x44						21x30					00x28			
Ferryside	d	18x50						21x36					00x34			
Carmarthen	a	19 03		20 30				21 54		22 04			00 47			
	d	19 06		20 35						22 05			00 51			
Whitland	a	19 22		20 51						22 21			01 07			
	d	19 22		20 57					20 56	22 22			01 07			
Narberth	d								21x03							
Kilgetty	d								21x12							
Saundersfoot	d								21x14							
Tenby	a								21 21							
	d								21 25							
Penally	d								21x28							
Manorbier	d								21 34							
Lamphey	d								21x42							
Pembroke	d								21 45							
Pembroke Dock	a								22 00							
Clunderwen	d	19x30		21x05						22x29						
Clarbeston Road	d	19x38		21x13						22x37			01x20			
Haverfordwest	d	19a46		21 21						22 46						
Johnston	d			21x30						22x54						
Milford Haven	a			21 47						23 10						
Fishguard Harbour ⛴	a												01 47			
	d															
Rosslare Harbour ⛴	a															

When events are being held at the Millenium Stadium,
services are subject to alteration.
Please check times before travelling.

Table 128

Sundays
from 1 April

Cardiff - Maesteg, Swansea and West Wales

Route Diagram - see first Page of Table 127

		AW	AW	AW	AW	GW	AW	AW	AW	AW		GW	AW	AW	GW	AW	GW	GW	AW	GW		AW	AW	GW	AW
				R										R								R			
		◇				◇1			◇	◇		◇1	◇		◇1		◇1	◇1		◇1			◇	◇1	
		🛒				☕			🛒			☕			☕	🛒	☕	☕		☕		🛒		☕	
London Paddington 15 ⊖	d					20p45						08 30			09 42			10 37		11 37				12 37	
Reading 7	d					21p13						09 06			10 18			11 12		12 12				13 13	
Manchester Piccadilly 10	d	18p30																				10 30			
Gloucester 7	d																								
Bristol Parkway 7	d					22p11						10 09			11 17			12 11		13 11				14 11	
Newport (South Wales)	d	21p45				22p46			09 27			10 33	11 00		11 43			12 37		13 37		13 29		14 37	
Cardiff Central 7	d	22p07			22p43	23p07			09 50			10 55	11 18		12 04	12 10		12 57		13 57		14 02		14 57	
Pontyclun	d	22p19			22p57				10 03													14 15			
Llanharan	d	22p23			23p02				10 08													14 20			
Pencoed	d	22p27			23p07				10 13													14 25			
Bridgend	d	22p33			23p13	23p28			10 20			11 15	11 38		12 24	12 31		13 19		14 19		14 32		15 19	
Wildmill	d																								
Sarn	d																								
Tondu	d																								
Garth (Mid Glamorgan)	d																								
Maesteg (Ewenny Road)	d																								
Maesteg	a																								
Pyle	d				23p21				10 28							12 39						14 40			
Port Talbot Parkway	d	22p45			23p30	23p41			10 37			11 28	11 52		12 37	12 48		13 32		14 32		14 48		15 32	
Baglan	d				23p34																				
Briton Ferry	d				23p37																				
Neath	d	22p52			23p41	23p49			10 45			11 37	12 00		12 45			13 39		14 39		14 56		15 39	
Skewen	d				23p45																				
Llansamlet	d				23p49																				
Swansea	a	23p05			23p57	00 02			10 58			11 49	12 13		12 58			13 52		14 52		15 09		15 52	
	d	23p10	23p45		00 09				11 01	11 06			12 15		13 08				14 11	14 58		15 12	15 26		16 26
Gowerton	d	23b22			00s20					11x16			12x26				←		14x22				15x36		16x37
Llanelli	a	23p29	00 01		00s28				11 17	11 23			12 32		13 24	13 17	13 24		14 29	15 14		15 28	15 48		16 44
	d	23p30	00 02						11 19				12 34		13 30	13 17	13 30		14 31	15 15		15 29			16 46
Pembrey & Burry Port	d	23p36	00 07		00s34				11 25				12 39		→	13 23	13 36		14 37	15 22		15 35			16 52
Kidwelly	d	23b42			00s40				11x32				12x46						14x43						16x59
Ferryside	d	23b47			00s46				11x38				12x52						14x49						17x05
Carmarthen	a	00 04	00 28		01 04				11 51				13 05			13 47	13 58		15 04	15 43		15 58			17 19
	d		00 31				09 55	10 19	11 55				13 08			14 04			15 07			16 03			17 32
Whitland	a		00 46				10 11	10 34	12 11				13 23			14 20			15 21			16 19			17 48
	d		00 46				10 11	10 34	12 11				13 23			14 20			15 22			16 20			17 48
Narberth	d							10x43											15x31						17x57
Kilgetty	d							10x52											15x41						18x07
Saundersfoot	d							10x54											15x43						18x09
Tenby	a							11 01											15 50						18 16
	d							11 11											15 54						18 19
Penally	d							11x14											15x57						18x22
Manorbier	d							11 20											16 03						18 29
Lamphey	d							11x28											16x11						18x36
Pembroke	d							11 31											16 14						18 40
Pembroke Dock	a							11 44											16 29						18 55
Clunderwen	d						10x19		12x19							14x28						16x28			
Clarbeston Road	d		01x00				10x27		12x27							14x36						16x36			
Haverfordwest	d						10 35		12 35							14 44						16 44			
Johnston	d						10x44		12x44							14x53						16x53			
Milford Haven	a						10 55		12 55							15 08						17 08			
Fishguard Harbour ⛴	a		01 27										13 59												
	d			02 45										14 30											
Rosslare Harbour ⛴	a			06 15										18 00											

b Previous night, stops on request

When events are being held at the Millenium Stadium, services are subject to alteration. Please check times before travelling.

Table 128

Sundays

from 1 April

Cardiff - Maesteg, Swansea and West Wales

Route Diagram - see first Page of Table 127

		GW	AW	GW	AW	GW		AW	GW	AW	AW	GW	AW	GW	GW	AW		GW	GW
			R					R											
		◇1		◇1		◇1			◇1			◇1	◇	◇1	◇1	◇		◇1	◇1
		☕	🛒	☕		☕		🛒	☕			☕	🛒	☕	☕			☕	☕
London Paddington 15 ⊖	d	13 37		14 37		15 37			16 37			17 37		18 37	19 37			20 37	21 37
Reading 7	d	14 13		15 13		16 13			17 13			18 13		19 12	20 14			21 13	22 12
Manchester Piccadilly 10	d		12 30					14 30											
Gloucester 7	d																		
Bristol Parkway 7	d	15 12		16 12		17 11			18 12			19 15		20 11	21 13			22 12	23 12
Newport (South Wales)	d	15 38	15 46	16 38		17 41		17 34	18 38			19 41		20 37	21 39			22 38	23 42
Cardiff Central 7	d	15 57	16 16	16 58		18 01		18 06	18 58			20 00	20 15	20 57	22 03	22 30		23 02	00 04
Pontyclun	d							18 21											
Llanharan	d							18 26											
Pencoed	d							18 30											
Bridgend	d	16 20	16 37	17 20		18 22		18 38	19 20			20 22	20 37	21 18	22 25	22 51		23 23	00 24
Wildmill	d																		
Sarn	d																		
Tondu	d																		
Garth (Mid Glamorgan)	d																		
Maesteg (Ewenny Road)	d																		
Maesteg	a																		
Pyle	d		16 45					18 46					20 45						
Port Talbot Parkway	d	16 33	16 54	17 33		18 35		18 54	19 33			20 35	20 54	21 32	22 37	23 05		23 37	00 37
Baglan	d																		
Briton Ferry	d																		
Neath	d	16 39	17 02	17 40		18 43		19 02	19 40			20 43	21 02	21 39	22 46	23 13		23 44	00 45
Skewen	d																		
Llansamlet	d																		
Swansea	a	16 53	17 14	17 54		18 58		19 15	19 53			20 56	21 14	21 53	22 58	23 25		23 57	00 57
	d	17 05	17 25		18 11			19 20			20 35		21 18			23 38			
Gowerton	d				18x22						20x46					23x49			
Llanelli	a	17 21	17 41		18 29			19 36			20 54		21 34			23 56			
	d	17 22	17 41		18 31			19 36			20 55		21 34			23 58			
Pembrey & Burry Port	d	17 29	17 48		18 37			19 43			21 01		21 41			00 04			
Kidwelly	d				18x44						21x08					00x11			
Ferryside	d				18x50						21x14					00x17			
Carmarthen	a	17 50	18 14		19 03			20 05			21 32		22 04			00 30			
	d		18 20		19 06			20 07					22 05			00 34			
Whitland	a		18 36		19 22			20 23					22 21			00 50			
	d		18 37		19 22			20 30		20 30			22 22			00 50			
Narberth	d									20x37									
Kilgetty	d									20x46									
Saundersfoot	d									20x48									
Tenby	a									20 55									
	d									20 59									
Penally	d									21x02									
Manorbier	d									21 08									
Lamphey	d									21x16									
Pembroke	d									21 19									
Pembroke Dock	a									21 34									
Clunderwen	d		18x45		19x30			20x37					22x29						
Clarbeston Road	d		18x53		19x38			20x45					22x37			01x03			
Haverfordwest	d		19 01		19a46			20 54					22 46						
Johnston	d		19x10					21x02					22x54						
Milford Haven	a		19 25					21 19					23 10						
Fishguard Harbour ⛴	a															01 30			
	d																		
Rosslare Harbour ⛴	a																		

When events are being held at the Millenium Stadium, services are subject to alteration. Please check times before travelling.

West Wales, Swansea and Maesteg - Cardiff

Route Diagram - see first Page of Table 127

Miles	Miles			GW	AW	AW	AW	AW	AW	AW	AW	AW	AW	AW	AW	GW	GW	GW	GW	AW	GW	GW	AW
				MO		MX	MO	MO	MO	MO	MO	MX	MX		MO		MO						
					🅁																		
				◇1				◇		◇				◇	◇	◇1	◇1	◇1	◇1	◇	◇1	◇1	
				A			B	C	B	A				D	A	E	B				F	G	
							🚌		🚌														
				🍴												🍴	🍴	🍴	🍴	☕	⊘	🍴⊘	
—	—	Rosslare Harbour ⛴	d		21p00																		
0	—	**Fishguard Harbour** ⛴	a		00 30																		
—	—		d											01 50	01 55								
—	0	**Milford Haven**	d					21p33		21p50	23p15	23p18	00 18										
—	4	Johnston	d					21b41		21b58	23b23	23b26	00x26										
—	8¾	Haverfordwest	d					21p49		22p06	23p30	23p33	00 33										
15¾	14	Clarbeston Road	d					21b57		22b14	23b39	23b41	00x41	02x10	02x15								
22¼	—	Clunderwen	d					22b05		22b22	23b46	23b48	00x48										
—	0	**Pembroke Dock**	d																				
—	2	Pembroke	d																				
—	3½	Lamphey	d																				
—	7	Manorbier	d																				
—	10¼	Penally	d																				
—	11½	**Tenby**	a																				
—	—		d																				
—	15¾	Saundersfoot	d																				
—	16½	Kilgetty	d																				
—	22	Narberth	d																				
27¾	27¼	Whitland	a					22p11		22p28	23p53	23p54	00 54	02 22	02 27								
—	—		d					22p14		22p31	23p53	23p54	00 54	02 22	02 27								
41¾	—	**Carmarthen**	a					22p31		22p48	00 14	00 16	01 16	02 39	02 44								
—	—		d	19p09				22p34		22p51				02 44	02 49					05 03			
48¾	—	Ferryside	d					22b44		23b01													
53	—	Kidwelly	d					22b50		23b07													
58¼	—	Pembrey & Burry Port	d	19p29				22p58		23p15										05 21			
62¼	—	Llanelli	a	19p35				23p04		23p21				03 06	03 11					05 26			
—	—		d	19p36				23p04		23p21				03 06	03 11					05 28			
68	—	Gowerton	d					23b12		23b29													
73½	—	**Swansea**	a	19p53				23p27		23p44				03 29	03 34								
—	—		d	19p59			22p06	23p30	23p40	23p47						03 57	03 57	04 58	05 27		05 58	06 28	
77½	—	Llansamlet	d																				
79¼	—	Skewen	d																				
83	—	Neath	d	20p11			22p31	23p42	00 05	23p59						04 09	04 09	05 10	05 39		06 10	06 40	
84¾	—	Briton Ferry	d																				
86½	—	Baglan	d																				
88½	—	Port Talbot Parkway	d	20p18			22p51	23p49	00 25	00 06						04 17	04 17	05 18	05 47	06 01	06 18	06 48	
94¾	—	Pyle	d				23p11	23p56	00 45	00 13										06 08			
—	0	Maesteg	d			22p15																	06 46
—	0½	Maesteg (Ewenny Road)	d			22p17																	06 48
—	1¼	Garth (Mid Glamorgan)	d			22p20																	06 51
—	5¼	Tondu	d			22p29																	07 00
—	6	Sarn	d			22p32																	07 03
—	7¼	Wildmill	d			22p34																	07 05
100¾	8¼	Bridgend	d	20p31		22p38	23p26	00 04	01 00	00 21						04 30	04 30	05 30	05 59	06 15	06 30	07 00	07 09
104¾	—	Pencoed	d			22p44														06 21			07 15
107	—	Llanharan	d			22p48														06 25			
110	—	Pontyclun	d			22p52														06 30			07 22
121	—	**Cardiff Central** 7	a	20p54		23p08	00 01	00 29	01 35	00 46						05 02	05 14	05 52	06 21	06 43	06 52	07 22	07 36
—	—	Newport (South Wales)	a	21p08		23p39										05 30	05 30	06 09	06 37	07 02	07 09	07 39	
—	—	Bristol Parkway 7	a													05 59	05 59	06 29	06 58		07 29	07 59	
—	—	Gloucester 7	a	21p58		00 39																	
—	—	Manchester Piccadilly 10	a																	10 15			
—	—	Reading 7	a	23p19												07 00	07 00	07 31	08 00			09 01	
—	—	London Paddington 15 ⊖	a	00 01												07 32	07 32	08 02	08 33		08 54	09 29	

A from 20 February until 26 March
B from 9 January until 13 February
C until 2 January, from 2 April
D until 17 February, MX from 21 February until 23 March, from 27 March
E until 6 January, MX from 10 January until 10 February, from 14 February
F The Capitals United
G 🍴 from Reading ⊘ to Reading
b Previous night, stops on request

When events are being held at the Millenium Stadium,
services are subject to alteration.
Please check times before travelling.

Table 128

Mondays to Fridays

West Wales, Swansea and Maesteg - Cardiff

Route Diagram - see first Page of Table 127

		AW	GW	AW	GW	AW	AW	AW		AW	GW	GW	AW	AW	AW	AW	GW	AW		AW	GW	AW	AW	AW	AW
			◇1	◇	◇1		◇				◇1	◇1	◇		◇		◇1	◇			◇1	◇			
			A		A							B													
		🛒	🍽⊘	🛒	🍽⊘		🛒				🍽	🍽	🛒				🍽	🛒			🍽	🛒			
Rosslare Harbour ⛴	d																								
Fishguard Harbour ⛴	a																								
	d							06 53										08 04							
Milford Haven	d						06 00						07 05									09 08			
Johnston	d						06x08						07x13									09x16			
Haverfordwest	d						06 15						07 20									09 23			
Clarbeston Road	d						06x23	07a16					07x28					08x25				09x31			
Clunderwen	d						06x30						07x35					08x33				09x38			
Pembroke Dock	d															07 09									09 09
Pembroke	d															07 17									09 17
Lamphey	d															07x20									09x20
Manorbier	d															07 28									09 29
Penally	d															07x34									09x34
Tenby	a															07 35									09 37
	d															07 38									09 38
Saundersfoot	d															07x44									09x46
Kilgetty	d															07x46									09x48
Narberth	d															07x56									09x58
Whitland	a						06 36						07 41			08 04		08 37				09 44			10 06
	d						06 36						07 41			08 05		08 38				09 44			10 07
Carmarthen	a						06 52						07 55			08 25		08 55				10 02			10 24
	d	05 50		06 15			06 57					07 30	08 01			08 30		09 00				10 04			10 31
Ferryside	d	06x00		06x25								07 42	08x11			08x40		09x10							
Kidwelly	d	06x05		06x30								07 49	08x16			08x46		09x15							
Pembrey & Burry Port	d	06 12		06 37			07 15					07 56	08 23			08 53		09 18				10 24			10 50
Llanelli	a	06 17		06 42			07 20					08 02	08 28			08 59		09 24				10 29			10 56
	d	06 18		06 44			07 22					08 04	08 30		08 45	09 00		09 25				10 31			10 57
Gowerton	d	06x24		06x50			07x28						08x36		08x53	09x08									11x04
Swansea	a	06 38		07 04			07 41					08 21	08 49		09 08	09 23		09 48				10 48			11 22
	d	06 42	06 58	07 06	07 28		07 45				07 58	08 28	08 55		09 11		09 28	09 55			10 28	10 55		11 10	
Llansamlet	d	06 46													09 18									11 17	
Skewen	d	06 50													09 22									11 21	
Neath	d	06 54	07 10	07 17	07 40		07 56				08 10	08 40	09 06		09 26		09 40	10 06			10 40	11 06		11 25	
Briton Ferry	d	06 58													09 30									11 28	
Baglan	d	07 01													09 33									11 32	
Port Talbot Parkway	d	07 05	07 18	07 24	07 48		08 03				08 18	08 48	09 13		09 37		09 48	10 13			10 48	11 13		11 36	
Pyle	d	07 12		07 31			08 09								09 44									11 43	
Maesteg	d									07 58				09 15						10 15			11 15		
Maesteg (Ewenny Road)	d									08 00				09 17						10 17			11 17		
Garth (Mid Glamorgan)	d									08 03				09 20						10 20			11 20		
Tondu	d									08 12				09 29						10 29			11 29		
Sarn	d									08 15				09 32						10 32			11 32		
Wildmill	d									08 17				09 34						10 34			11 34		
Bridgend	d	07 20	07 30	07 39	08 00	08 07	08 17			08 21	08 30	09 00	09 25	09 38	09 53		10 00	10 25		10 38	11 00	11 25	11 38	11 55	
Pencoed	d	07 26				08 13				08 27				09 44						10 44			11 44		
Llanharan	d			07 46			08 24							09 48						10 48			11 48		
Pontyclun	d	07 33				08 21				08 34				09 52						10 52			11 52		
Cardiff Central 7	a	07 47	07 52	08 02	08 22	08 34	08 43			08 48	08 52	09 22	09 46	10 07	10 17		10 22	10 48		11 09	11 22	11 48	12 08	12 18	
Newport (South Wales)	a		08 09	08 17	08 39		09 02			09 25	09 09	09 39	10 17	10 25			10 39	11 02			11 39	12 17	12 25		
Bristol Parkway 7	a		08 30		08 59						09 30	09 59					10 59				11 59				
Gloucester 7	a									10 20				11 20									13 20		
Manchester Piccadilly 10	a			11 15			12 15						13 15					14 15				15 15			
Reading 7	a		09 25		09 59						10 31	11 00					11 59				13 00				
London Paddington 15 ⊖	a		09 59		10 32						11 07	11 32					12 32				13 32				

A 🍽 from Reading ⊘ to Reading

B The Red Dragon

When events are being held at the Millenium Stadium,
services are subject to alteration.
Please check times before travelling.

Table 128

West Wales, Swansea and Maesteg - Cardiff

Route Diagram - see first Page of Table 127

		AW	GW		AW	AW	GW	AW	AW	AW	AW	AW	AW	GW		AW	AW	GW	AW	AW	AW	AW	AW	GW
													R						R	R				
			◇1		◇		◇1	◇	◇		◇			◇1		◇		◇1						◇1
			A				B																	
			🍴		🛒	🛒	🍴Ø	🛒	🛒		🛒			🍴		🛒		🍴	🛒	🛒			🛒	🍴
Rosslare Harbour ⛴	d												09 00											
Fishguard Harbour ⛴	a												12 30											
	d	09 56																		13 30				
Milford Haven	d							11 08											13 08					
Johnston	d							11x16											13x16					
Haverfordwest	d							11 23											13 23					
Clarbeston Road	d	10x17						11x31											13x31					
Clunderwen	d	10x25						11x38											13x38					
Pembroke Dock	d											11 09											13 09	
Pembroke	d											11 17											13 17	
Lamphey	d											11x20											13x20	
Manorbier	d											11 29											13 29	
Penally	d											11x34											13x34	
Tenby	a											11 37											13 37	
	d											11 43											13 41	
Saundersfoot	d											11x51											13x49	
Kilgetty	d											11x53											13x51	
Narberth	d											12x03											14x01	
Whitland	a	10 31						11 44				12 11							13 44	14 02			14 09	
	d	10 32						11 44				12 11							13 44	14 02			14 09	
Carmarthen	a	10 49						12 00				12 29							14 00	14 19			14 29	
	d				11 04			12 05				12 33				13 02			14 05	14 25			14 34	
Ferryside	d				11x14											13x12								
Kidwelly	d				11x19											13x17								
Pembrey & Burry Port	d				11 25			12 23				12 52				13 23			14 23				14 53	
Llanelli	a				11 31			12 28				12 58				13 29			14 28	14 47			14 59	
	d				11 32			12 30	12 42			12 59				13 30			14 30	14 47			14 59	
Gowerton	d				11x39							13x06							14x36					
Swansea	a				11 51			12 47	13 04			13 22				13 51			14 49				15 22	
	d		11 28		11 55		12 28	12 54			13 10			13 28		13 55		14 28	14 55			15 10		15 28
Llansamlet	d										13 17											15 17		
Skewen	d										13 21											15 21		
Neath	d		11 40		12 06		12 40	13 05			13 25			13 40		14 06		14 40	15 06			15 25		15 40
Briton Ferry	d										13 28											15 28		
Baglan	d										13 32											15 32		
Port Talbot Parkway	d		11 48		12 13		12 48	13 12			13 36			13 48		14 13		14 48	15 13			15 36		15 48
Pyle	d										13 43											15 43		
Maesteg	d					12 15				13 15							14 15				15 17			
Maesteg (Ewenny Road)	d					12 17				13 17							14 17				15 19			
Garth (Mid Glamorgan)	d					12 20				13 20							14 20				15 22			
Tondu	d					12 29				13 29							14 29				15 31			
Sarn	d					12 32				13 32							14 32				15 34			
Wildmill	d					12 34				13 34							14 34				15 36			
Bridgend	d		12 00		12 25	12 38	13 00	13 24		13 38	13 52			14 00		14 25	14 38	15 00	15 25		15 40	15 52		16 00
Pencoed	d					12 44				13 44							14 44				15 46			
Llanharan	d					12 48				13 48							14 48				15 50			
Pontyclun	d					12 52				13 52							14 52				15 54			
Cardiff Central 7	a		12 22		12 47	13 07	13 22	13 47		14 07	14 15			14 22		14 47	15 07	15 22	15 47	16 04	16 09	16 15		16 22
Newport (South Wales)	a		12 39		13 02	13 25	13 39	14 17						14 39		15 02	15 26	15 39	16 02	16 18				16 39
Bristol Parkway 7	a		12 59				13 59							15 00				15 59						16 59
Gloucester 7	a					14 20											16 21			17 14				
Manchester Piccadilly 10	a				16 15			17 14								18 13			19 15					
Reading 7	a		13 59				15 00							16 00				17 00						18 00
London Paddington 15 ⊖	a		14 32				15 32							16 30				17 30						18 30

A The St. David

B 🍴 from Reading Ø to Reading

When events are being held at the Millenium Stadium,
services are subject to alteration.
Please check times before travelling.

West Wales, Swansea and Maesteg - Cardiff

Route Diagram - see first Page of Table 127

		AW	AW	GW	AW	AW	AW	AW	GW	AW		AW	AW	GW	AW	AW	AW	AW	AW	GW FX		GW FO	AW	AW	GW
		■ 🛒		◇1 ☕	■ 🛒				◇1 ☕	◇ 🛒		◇		◇1 ☕						◇1 ☕		◇1 ☕			◇1 ☕
Rosslare Harbour ⛴	d																								
Fishguard Harbour ⛴	a																								
	d															19 00									
Milford Haven	d				15 08										17 08										
Johnston	d				15x16										17x16										
Haverfordwest	d				15 23										17 23										
Clarbeston Road	d				15x31										17x31	19a21									
Clunderwen	d				15x38										17x38										
Pembroke Dock	d							15 09											17 09						
Pembroke	d							15 17											17 17						
Lamphey	d							15x20											17x20						
Manorbier	d							15 29											17 29						
Penally	d							15x34											17x34						
Tenby	a							15 37											17 37						
	d							15 41											17 38						
Saundersfoot	d							15x49											17x46						
Kilgetty	d							15x51											17x48						
Narberth	d							16x01											17x58						
Whitland	a				15 44			16 09							17 44				18 06						
	d				15 44			16 09							17 45				18 07						
Carmarthen	a				16 00			16 27							18 02				18 24						
	d	15 05			16 05			16 31		17 04					18 07				18 31				18 59		
Ferryside	d	15x15								17x14					18x17								19x09		
Kidwelly	d	15x20								17x19					18x23								19x15		
Pembrey & Burry Port	d	15 27			16 23			16 50		17 25					18 30				18 50				19 23		
Llanelli	a	15 32			16 28			16 56		17 31					18 35				18 56				19 29		
	d	15 34			16 30			16 57		17 32		17 48			18 36				18 57				19 30		
Gowerton	d				16x36			17x04				17x57							19x04						
Swansea	a	15 51			16 49			17 22		17 49		18 18			18 54				19 22				19 49		
	d	15 55		16 28	16 55		17 10		17 28	17 55				18 28	19 00			19 10		19 29		19 29	19 52		20 28
Llansamlet	d						17 17											19 17							
Skewen	d						17 21											19 21							
Neath	d	16 06		16 40	17 06		17 25		17 40	18 06				18 40	19 11			19 25		19 40		19 40	20 03		20 40
Briton Ferry	d						17 28											19 28							
Baglan	d						17 32											19 32							
Port Talbot Parkway	d	16 13		16 48	17 13		17 36		17 48	18 13				18 48	19 19			19 36		19 48		19 48	20 10		20 48
Pyle	d						17 43											19 43							
Maesteg	d		16 15			17 15							18 20				19 17							20 15	
Maesteg (Ewenny Road)	d		16 17			17 17							18 22				19 19							20 17	
Garth (Mid Glamorgan)	d		16 20			17 20							18 25				19 22							20 20	
Tondu	d		16 29			17 29							18 34				19 31							20 29	
Sarn	d		16 32			17 32							18 37				19 34							20 32	
Wildmill	d		16 34			17 34							18 39				19 36							20 34	
Bridgend	d	16 25	16 38	17 00	17 25	17 38	17 54		18 00	18 25			18 43	19 00	19 32		19 40	19 51		20 00		20 00	20 24	20 38	21 00
Pencoed	d		16 44			17 44							18 49				19 46							20 44	
Llanharan	d		16 48			17 48							18 53				19 49							20 48	
Pontyclun	d		16 52			17 52							18 57				19 54							20 52	
Cardiff Central 7	a	16 46	17 07	17 22	17 47	18 07	18 20		18 22	18 46			19 13	19 22	19 57		20 10	20 17		20 22		20 22	20 46	21 08	21 22
Newport (South Wales)	a	17 02	17 25	17 39	18 02	18 25			18 39	19 03				19 39						20 38		20 38		21 25	21 38
Bristol Parkway 7	a			17 59					18 59					19 59						21 01		21 01			21 59
Gloucester 7	a		18 21			19 20																		22 21	
Manchester Piccadilly 10	a	20 15			21 05					22 13															
Reading 7	a			19 01					20 00					21 00						22 11		22 11			23 02
London Paddington 15 ⊖	a			19 32					20 32					21 32						22 44		22 45			23 38

When events are being held at the Millenium Stadium,
services are subject to alteration.
Please check times before travelling.

Table 128

Mondays to Fridays

West Wales, Swansea and Maesteg - Cardiff

Route Diagram - see first Page of Table 127

		AW	AW	AW	AW	AW	AW	AW	AW	AW	AW	AW	AW	AW	AW	AW
								FO	FX	FX	FX	FO				
							◇									R
Rosslare Harbour	d															21 00
Fishguard Harbour	a															00 30
	d					20 50										
Milford Haven	d	19 08			20 36										23 18	
Johnston	d	19x16			20x44										23x26	
Haverfordwest	d	19 23			20 51										23 33	
Clarbeston Road	d	19x31			20x59	21x12									23x41	
Clunderwen	d	19x38			21x06	21x19									23x48	
Pembroke Dock	d												21 09	22 23		
Pembroke	d												21 17	22 31		
Lamphey	d												21x20	22x34		
Manorbier	d												21 29	22 42		
Penally	d												21x34	22x48		
Tenby	a												21 37	22 50		
	d			19 57									21 42	22 50		
Saundersfoot	d			20x05									21x50	22x58		
Kilgetty	d			20x07									21x52	23x00		
Narberth	d			20x17									22x02	23x09		
Whitland	a	19 44		20 25	21 12	21 26							22 10	23 17	23 54	
	d	19 44		20 27	21 12	21 26							22 10	23 20	23 54	
Carmarthen	a	20 00		20 45	21 34	21 47							22 28	23 39	00 16	
	d	20 05		20 47									22 35			
Ferryside	d			20x58									22x45			
Kidwelly	d			21x04									22x51			
Pembrey & Burry Port	d	20 23		21 11									22 58			
Llanelli	a	20 28		21 17									23 04			
	d	20 29		21 17			21 43						23 05			
Gowerton	d						21x50						23x12			
Swansea	a	20 47		21 39			22 08						23 32			
	d	20 57		21 45							22 32	22 35				
Llansamlet	d			21 52							22 39	22 42				
Skewen	d			21 56							22 43	22 46				
Neath	d	21 08		22 00							22 47	22 50				
Briton Ferry	d			22 03							22 50	22 53				
Baglan	d			22 07							22 54	22 57				
Port Talbot Parkway	d	21 15		22 11							22 58	23 01				
Pyle	d			22 18							23 05	23 08				
Maesteg	d		21 15					22 15	22 15							
Maesteg (Ewenny Road)	d		21 17					22 17	22 17							
Garth (Mid Glamorgan)	d		21 20					22 20	22 20							
Tondu	d		21 29					22 29	22 29							
Sarn	d		21 32					22 32	22 32							
Wildmill	d		21 34					22 34	22 34							
Bridgend	d	21 27	21 38	22 26				22 38	22 38	22 52	23 13	23 16				
Pencoed	d		21 44					22 44	22 44							
Llanharan	d		21 48					22 48	22 48							
Pontyclun	d		21 52					22 52	22 52							
Cardiff Central 7	a	21 50	22 10	22 49				23 08	23 08	23 18	23 38	23 38				
Newport (South Wales)	a							23 38	23 39							
Bristol Parkway 7	a															
Gloucester 7	a							00 39	00 39							
Manchester Piccadilly 10	a															
Reading 7	a															
London Paddington 15 ⊖	a															

When events are being held at the Millenium Stadium, services are subject to alteration. Please check times before travelling.

Table 128

Saturdays

West Wales, Swansea and Maesteg - Cardiff

Route Diagram - see first Page of Table 127

Station		AW	AW	AW	AW	AW	GW	GW	GW	AW	GW	GW	AW	AW	GW	AW	GW	AW	AW	AW	GW	GW	AW
					R	◇	◇1	◇1	◇1	◇	◇1	◇1		◇	◇1		◇1	◇			◇1	◇1	◇
															A		A						
							⊐P	⊐P	⊐P	⊤	⊐P	⊐P		⊤	⊐P∅	⊤	⊐P∅	⊤			⊐P	⊐P	⊤
Rosslare Harbour ⛴	d				21p00																		
Fishguard Harbour ⛴	a				00 30																		
	d					01 50													06 53				
Milford Haven	d		23p18	00 18														06 00					07 05
Johnston	d		23b26	00x26														06x08					07x13
Haverfordwest	d		23p33	00 33														06 15					07 20
Clarbeston Road	d		23b41	00x41		02x10												06x23	07a16				07x28
Clunderwen	d		23b48	00x48														06x30					07x35
Pembroke Dock	d																						
Pembroke	d																						
Lamphey	d																						
Manorbier	d																						
Penally	d																						
Tenby	a																						
	d																						
Saundersfoot	d																						
Kilgetty	d																						
Narberth	d																						
Whitland	a		23p54	00 54		02 22												06 36					07 41
	d		23p54	00 54		02 22												06 36					07 41
Carmarthen	a		00 16	01 16		02 39												06 52					07 55
	d					02 44				05 04				05 55		06 20		06 57					08 01
Ferryside	d													06x05		06x30							08x11
Kidwelly	d													06x10		06x35							08x16
Pembrey & Burry Port	d									05 22				06 17		06 42		07 15					08 23
Llanelli	a					03 06				05 27				06 22		06 47		07 20					08 28
	d					03 06				05 29				06 24		06 48		07 22					08 30
Gowerton	d													06x30		06x55		07x28					08x36
Swansea	a					03 29								06 43		07 10		07 41					08 49
	d						03 58	04 58	05 28		05 58	06 28		06 47	06 58	07 13	07 28	07 45			07 58	08 28	08 55
Llansamlet	d															07 20							
Skewen	d															07 24							
Neath	d						04 10	05 10	05 40		06 10	06 40		06 58	07 10	07 28	07 40	07 56			08 10	08 40	09 06
Briton Ferry	d															07 31							
Baglan	d															07 35							
Port Talbot Parkway	d						04 18	05 18	05 48	06 02	06 18	06 48		07 05	07 18	07 39	07 48	08 03			08 18	08 48	09 13
Pyle	d									06 08				07 11		07 46		08 09					09 20
Maesteg	d	22p15											06 46							08 00			
Maesteg (Ewenny Road)	d	22p17											06 48							08 02			
Garth (Mid Glamorgan)	d	22p20											06 51							08 05			
Tondu	d	22p29											07 00							08 14			
Sarn	d	22p32											07 03							08 17			
Wildmill	d	22p34											07 05							08 19			
Bridgend	d	22p38					04 30	05 30	06 00	06 16	06 30	07 00	07 09	07 19	07 30	07 54	08 00	08 17		08 23	08 30	09 00	09 27
Pencoed	d	22p44								06 22			07 15			08 07		08 23					
Llanharan	d	22p48								06 25				07 26		08 11				08 31			
Pontyclun	d	22p52								06 30			07 22			08 15		08 30					
Cardiff Central 7	a	23p08					04 52	05 52	06 22	06 43	06 52	07 22	07 36	07 42	07 52	08 34	08 22	08 44		08 47	08 52	09 22	09 46
Newport (South Wales)	a	23p38					05 09	06 09	06 38	07 02	07 08	07 39		08 02	08 08		08 38	09 02		09 24	09 08	09 39	10 07
Bristol Parkway 7	a						05 36	06 29	06 59		07 29	07 59			08 30		08 59				09 30	09 59	
Gloucester 7	a	00 39																		10 19			
Manchester Piccadilly 10	a									10 14				11 15				12 15					13 15
Reading 7	a						07 14	07 31	08 00		08 31	09 00			09 32		10 00				10 32	11 01	
London Paddington 15 ⊖	a						07 44	08 07	08 32		09 02	09 32			10 02		10 32				11 02	11 33	

A ⊐P from Reading ∅ to Reading

b Previous night, stops on request

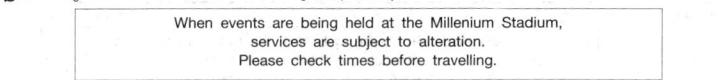

When events are being held at the Millenium Stadium,
services are subject to alteration.
Please check times before travelling.

West Wales, Swansea and Maesteg - Cardiff

Route Diagram - see first Page of Table 127

		AW	AW	AW	GW	AW	AW	GW	AW	AW	AW	AW	AW	GW	AW	AW	GW	AW	AW	AW	AW	AW	GW
			◇		◇1	◇		◇1	◇					◇1	◇		◇1	◇		◇	◇		◇1
																	A						
					🍴	🛒		🍴	🛒					🍴	🛒	🛒	🍴	🛒		🛒	🛒		🍴
Rosslare Harbour ⛴	d																						
Fishguard Harbour ⛴	a																						
	d					08 04							09 53										
Milford Haven	d								09 08									11 08					
Johnston	d								09x16									11x16					
Haverfordwest	d								09 23									11 23					
Clarbeston Road	d					08x25			09x31				10x14					11x31					
Clunderwen	d					08x33			09x38				10x22					11x38					
Pembroke Dock	d			07 09								09 09										11 09	
Pembroke	d			07 17								09 17										11 17	
Lamphey	d			07x20								09x20										11x20	
Manorbier	d			07 28								09 29										11 29	
Penally	d			07x34								09x34										11x34	
Tenby	a			07 35								09 37										11 37	
	d			07 38								09 37										11 41	
Saundersfoot	d			07x44								09x45										11x49	
Kilgetty	d			07x46								09x47										11x51	
Narberth	d			07x56								09x57										12x01	
Whitland	a			08 04		08 37			09 44			10 05	10 28					11 44				12 09	
	d			08 05		08 38			09 44			10 05	10 29					11 44				12 09	
Carmarthen	a			08 25		08 55			10 02			10 23	10 46					12 00				12 27	
	d			08 30		09 00		09 35	10 04			10 28			11 09			12 05				12 31	
Ferryside	d			08x40		09x10									11x19								
Kidwelly	d			08x46		09x15									11x24								
Pembrey & Burry Port	d			08 53		09 21		09 56	10 24			10 47			11 30			12 23				12 50	
Llanelli	a			08 59		09 27		10 01	10 29			10 53			11 36			12 28				12 56	
	d		08 45	09 00		09 28		10 03	10 31			10 53			11 37			12 30		12 37		12 57	
Gowerton	d		08x53	09x08								11x01			11x44							13x04	
Swansea	a		09 08	09 23		09 45		10 21	10 48			11 21			11 56			12 47		13 01		13 23	
	d		09 11		09 28	09 55		10 28	10 55		11 10			11 28	12 00		12 28	12 55		13 10	13 10		13 28
Llansamlet	d		09 19								11 17									13 17	13 17		
Skewen	d		09 23								11 21									13 21	13 21		
Neath	d		09 27		09 40	10 06		10 40	11 06		11 25			11 40	12 11		12 40	13 06		13 25	13 25		13 40
Briton Ferry	d		09 31								11 28									13 28	13 28		
Baglan	d		09 34								11 32									13 32	13 32		
Port Talbot Parkway	d		09 38		09 48	10 13		10 48	11 13		11 36			11 48	12 18		12 48	13 13		13 36	13 36		13 48
Pyle	d		09 46			10 19			11 20		11 43							13 20		13 43	13 43		
Maesteg	d	09 17					10 15			11 15						12 17			13 15				
Maesteg (Ewenny Road)	d	09 19					10 17			11 17						12 19			13 17				
Garth (Mid Glamorgan)	d	09 22					10 20			11 20						12 22			13 20				
Tondu	d	09 31					10 29			11 29						12 31			13 29				
Sarn	d	09 34					10 32			11 32						12 34			13 32				
Wildmill	d	09 36					10 34			11 34						12 36			13 34				
Bridgend	d	09 40	09 54		10 00	10 27	10 38	11 00	11 27	11 38	11 55			12 00	12 30	12 40	13 00	13 27	13 38	13 52	13 52		14 00
Pencoed	d	09 46					10 44			11 44						12 46			13 44				
Llanharan	d	09 50					10 48			11 48						12 50			13 48				
Pontyclun	d	09 54					10 52			11 52						12 54			13 52				
Cardiff Central 7	a	10 09	10 20		10 22	10 48	11 13	11 22	11 48	12 07	12 18			12 22	12 52	13 09	13 22	13 48	14 09	14 15	14 15		14 22
Newport (South Wales)	a	10 25			10 39	11 07		11 39	12 07	12 25				12 39	13 07	13 25	13 38	14 07					14 39
Bristol Parkway 7	a				10 59			11 59						12 59			13 59						14 59
Gloucester 7	a	11 21								13 21						14 21							
Manchester Piccadilly 10	a					14 15			15 15						16 15			17 15					
Reading 7	a				12 00			13 00						14 00			15 00						16 00
London Paddington 15 ⊖	a				12 32			13 33						14 32			15 32						16 32

A until 11 February, from 31 March

When events are being held at the Millenium Stadium,
services are subject to alteration.
Please check times before travelling.

Table 128

Saturdays

West Wales, Swansea and Maesteg - Cardiff

Route Diagram - see first Page of Table 127

		AW	AW	AW	GW	AW	AW	AW	AW	AW	GW		AW	AW	GW	AW	AW	AW	AW	GW	AW		AW	AW
			R			R	R						R			R								
		◇			◇1						◇1				◇1					◇1	◇		◇	
											A													
		(trolley)			(buffet)	(trolley)	(trolley)			(trolley)	(buffet)		(trolley)		(buffet)	(trolley)				(buffet)	(trolley)			
Rosslare Harbour (ship)	d		09 00																					
Fishguard Harbour (ship)	a		12 30																					
	d						13 30																	
Milford Haven	d					13 08										15 08								
Johnston	d					13x16										15x16								
Haverfordwest	d					13 23										15 23								
Clarbeston Road	d					13x31										15x31								
Clunderwen	d					13x38										15x38								
Pembroke Dock	d									13 09									15 09					
Pembroke	d									13 17									15 17					
Lamphey	d									13x20									15x20					
Manorbier	d									13 29									15 29					
Penally	d									13x34									15x34					
Tenby	a									13 37									15 37					
	d									13 42									15 40					
Saundersfoot	d									13x50									15x48					
Kilgetty	d									13x52									15x50					
Narberth	d									14x02									16x00					
Whitland	a					13 44	14 02			14 10						15 44			16 08					
	d					13 44	14 02			14 11						15 44			16 09					
Carmarthen	a					14 00	14 19			14 28						16 00			16 26					
	d	13 02				14 05	14 22			14 33			15 05			16 05			16 31		17 04			
Ferryside	d	13x12											15x15								17x14			
Kidwelly	d	13x17											15x20								17x19			
Pembrey & Burry Port	d	13 23				14 23				14 52			15 27			16 23			16 50		17 25			
Llanelli	a	13 29				14 28	14 44			14 58			15 32			16 28			16 56		17 31			
	d	13 30				14 30	14 45			14 58			15 34			16 30			16 57		17 32		17 41	
Gowerton	d					14x36										16x36			17x04				17x51	
Swansea	a	13 48				14 49				15 22			15 51			16 49			17 22		17 49		18 10	
	d	14 00			14 28	14 55			15 10		15 28		15 55		16 28	16 55		17 10		17 28	17 55			
Llansamlet	d								15 17									17 17						
Skewen	d								15 21									17 21						
Neath	d	14 11			14 40	15 06			15 25		15 40		16 06		16 40	17 06		17 25		17 40	18 06			
Briton Ferry	d								15 28									17 28						
Baglan	d								15 32									17 32						
Port Talbot Parkway	d	14 18			14 48	15 13			15 36		15 48		16 13		16 48	17 13		17 36		17 48	18 13			
Pyle	d								15 43				16 20			17 20		17 43						
Maesteg	d			14 15				15 17						16 15			17 15							18 20
Maesteg (Ewenny Road)	d			14 17				15 19						16 17			17 17							18 22
Garth (Mid Glamorgan)	d			14 20				15 22						16 20			17 20							18 25
Tondu	d			14 29				15 31						16 29			17 29							18 34
Sarn	d			14 32				15 34						16 32			17 32							18 37
Wildmill	d			14 34				15 36						16 34			17 34							18 39
Bridgend	d	14 30		14 38	15 00	15 25		15 40	15 52		16 00		16 27	16 38	17 00	17 27	17 38	17 54		18 00	18 25			18 43
Pencoed	d			14 44				15 46						16 44			17 44							18 49
Llanharan	d			14 48				15 50						16 48			17 48							18 53
Pontyclun	d			14 52				15 54						16 52			17 52							18 57
Cardiff Central 7	a	14 52		15 07	15 22	15 47	15 54	16 09	16 15		16 22		16 48	17 07	17 22	17 48	18 07	18 20		18 22	18 46			19 13
Newport (South Wales)	a	15 07		15 25	15 39	16 07		16 23	16 32		16 39		17 07	17 27	17 39	18 07	18 25			18 39	19 03			
Bristol Parkway 7	a				15 59						16 59				17 59					18 59				
Gloucester 7	a			16 19				17 19						18 20			19 20							
Manchester Piccadilly 10	a	18 15				19 15							20 15			21 15					22 15			
Reading 7	a				17 00						18 00				19 00					20 00				
London Paddington 15 ⊖	a				17 32						18 32				19 32					20 32				

A until 11 February, from 31 March

When events are being held at the Millenium Stadium, services are subject to alteration. Please check times before travelling.

Table 128

Saturdays

West Wales, Swansea and Maesteg - Cardiff

Route Diagram - see first Page of Table 127

		GW	AW	AW	AW	AW	AW	GW		GW	AW	AW	AW	AW	AW	AW	AW			AW	AW	AW	AW	AW	AW
		◇1			◇			◇1		◇1											◇				
								A		B												C	D		
		☕						☕		☕															
Rosslare Harbour ⛴	d																								
Fishguard Harbour ⛴	a																								
	d			19 00													21 00								
Milford Haven	d		17 08										19 08	19 08						21 16					
Johnston	d		17x16										19x16	19x16						21x24					
Haverfordwest	d		17 23										19 23	19 23						21 31					
Clarbeston Road	d		17x31	19a21									19x31	19x31			21x22			21x39					
Clunderwen	d		17x38										19x38	19x38			21x29			21x46					
Pembroke Dock	d						17 09									19 09									21 09
Pembroke	d						17 17									19 17									21 17
Lamphey	d						17x20									19 21									21x20
Manorbier	d						17 29									19 29									21 29
Penally	d						17x34									19 34									21x34
Tenby	a						17 37									19 37									21 37
	d						17 41									19 49									21 42
Saundersfoot	d						17x49									19x57									21x50
Kilgetty	d						17x51									19x59									21x52
Narberth	d						18x01									20x09									22x02
Whitland	a		17 44				18 11						19 44	19 44		20 17	21 36			21 52					22 10
	d		17 45				18 11						19 44	19 44		20 19	21 36			21 52					22 11
Carmarthen	a		18 03				18 29						20 02	20 02		20 37	21 57			22 14					22 28
	d		18 07				18 33				19 06		20 07	20 07		20 47									22 35
Ferryside	d		18x17													20x58									22x45
Kidwelly	d		18x23													21x04									22x51
Pembrey & Burry Port	d		18 30				18 52				19 25		20 25	20 25		21 11									22 58
Llanelli	a		18 35				18 58				19 31		20 30	20 30		21 17									23 04
	d		18 36				18 59				19 33		20 31	20 31		21 17					21 40				23 05
Gowerton	d						19x06														21x47				23x12
Swansea	a		18 54				19 23				19 51		20 50	20 50		21 39					22 10				23 30
	d	18 28	19 00			19 10		19 28		19 28	19 54		20 55	20 55		21 43								22 20	
Llansamlet	d					19 17										21 50								22 27	
Skewen	d					19 21										21 54								22 31	
Neath	d	18 40	19 11			19 25		19 40		19 40	20 05		21 06	21 06		21 58								22 35	
Briton Ferry	d					19 28										22 02								22 38	
Baglan	d					19 32										22 05								22 42	
Port Talbot Parkway	d	18 48	19 19			19 36		19 48		19 48	20 12		21 13	21 13		22 09								22 46	
Pyle	d					19 43										22 16								22 53	
Maesteg	d				19 15							20 15			21 15							22 15	22 15		
Maesteg (Ewenny Road)	d				19 17							20 17			21 17							22 17	22 17		
Garth (Mid Glamorgan)	d				19 20							20 20			21 20							22 20	22 20		
Tondu	d				19 29							20 29			21 29							22 29	22 29		
Sarn	d				19 32							20 32			21 32							22 32	22 32		
Wildmill	d				19 34							20 34			21 34							22 34	22 34		
Bridgend	d	19 00	19 32		19 38	19 51		20 00		20 00	20 25	20 38	21 25	21 25	21 38	22 25						22 38	22 38	23 01	
Pencoed	d				19 44							20 44			21 44							22 44	22 44		
Llanharan	d				19 47							20 48			21 48							22 48	22 48		
Pontyclun	d				19 52							20 52			21 52							22 52	22 52		
Cardiff Central 7	a	19 22	19 57		20 05	20 17		20 23		20 23	20 48	21 07	21 48	21 46	22 09	22 47						23 08	23 08	23 26	
Newport (South Wales)	a	19 39			20 24			20 39		20 39		21 25	22 05	22 05								23 36	23 37		
Bristol Parkway 7	a	19 59						21 01		21 01															
Gloucester 7	a											22 22										00 40			
Manchester Piccadilly 10	a				23 50																				
Reading 7	a	21 06						21 59		21 59															
London Paddington 15 ⊖	a	21 36						22 37		22 38															

A 17 December, 24 December, 31 December, from 31 March

B from 7 January until 24 March

C 17 December, 24 December, 31 December, from 18 February until 24 March

D from 7 January until 11 February, from 31 March

When events are being held at the Millenium Stadium, services are subject to alteration. Please check times before travelling.

Table 128

Saturdays

West Wales, Swansea and Maesteg - Cardiff

Route Diagram - see first Page of Table 127

		AW	AW	AW
				🅱
Rosslare Harbour ⛴	d			21 00
Fishguard Harbour ⛴	a			00 30
	d			
Milford Haven	d		23 18	
Johnston	d		23x26	
Haverfordwest	d		23 33	
Clarbeston Road	d		23x41	
Clunderwen	d		23x48	
Pembroke Dock	d	22 23		
Pembroke	d	22 31		
Lamphey	d	22x34		
Manorbier	d	22 42		
Penally	d	22x48		
Tenby	a	22 50		
	d	22 50		
Saundersfoot	d	22x58		
Kilgetty	d	23x00		
Narberth	d	23x09		
Whitland	a	23 17	23 54	
	d	23 20	23 54	
Carmarthen	a	23 39	00 16	
	d			
Ferryside	d			
Kidwelly	d			
Pembrey & Burry Port	d			
Llanelli	a			
	d			
Gowerton	d			
Swansea	a			
	d			
Llansamlet	d			
Skewen	d			
Neath	d			
Briton Ferry	d			
Baglan	d			
Port Talbot Parkway	d			
Pyle	d			
Maesteg	d			
Maesteg (Ewenny Road)	d			
Garth (Mid Glamorgan)	d			
Tondu	d			
Sarn	d			
Wildmill	d			
Bridgend	d			
Pencoed	d			
Llanharan	d			
Pontyclun	d			
Cardiff Central 7	a			
Newport (South Wales)	a			
Bristol Parkway 7	a			
Gloucester 7	a			
Manchester Piccadilly 10	a			
Reading 7	a			
London Paddington 15 ⊖	a			

When events are being held at the Millenium Stadium, services are subject to alteration. Please check times before travelling.

Table 128

Sundays

until 1 January

West Wales, Swansea and Maesteg - Cardiff

Route Diagram - see first Page of Table 127

		AW	AW	AW	AW	GW	GW	GW	AW	GW	AW	AW	GW	GW	AW	AW	GW	GW	AW	AW	AW	AW	GW
				R											R				R	R			
					◇	◇1	◇1	◇1		◇1	◇		◇1	◇1			◇1	◇1			◇		◇1
		A	A	A																			
						⊡	⊡	⊡		⊡	⊼		⊡	⊡	⊼		⊡	⊡		⊼		⊼	⊡
Rosslare Harbour	d			21p00															09 00				
Fishguard Harbour	a			00 30															12 30				
	d				01 50																	14 23	
Milford Haven	d		23p18												11 28					13 23			
Johnston	d		23b26												11x36					13x29			
Haverfordwest	d		23p33												11 43					13 36			
Clarbeston Road	d		23b41												11x52					13x45			
Clunderwen	d		23b48												11x59					13x52			
Pembroke Dock	d															11 55							
Pembroke	d															12 03							
Lamphey	d															12x06							
Manorbier	d															12 15							
Penally	d															12x20							
Tenby	a															12 23							
	d															12 23							
Saundersfoot	d															12x31							
Kilgetty	d															12x33							
Narberth	d															12x43							
Whitland	a		23p54		02s22										12 06	12 51				13 59		14 55	
	d		23p54												12 08	12 54				14 02		14 55	
Carmarthen	a		00 16		02s40										12 26	13 14				14 20		15 13	
	d								09 40		10 30	11 18			12 29	13 17				14 23		15 16	15 30
Ferryside	d								09x50			11x28				13x27						15x26	
Kidwelly	d								09x56			11x34				13x33						15x32	
Pembrey & Burry Port	d								10 03		10 49	11 42			12 49	13 40				14 42		15 39	15 50
Llanelli	a				03s06				10 09		10 54	11 48			12 55	13 46				14 48		15 47	15 56
	d								10 10		10 56	11 48			12 55	13 47				14 49	15 41	15 47	15 58
Gowerton	d								10x17			11x56				13x54						15x55	
Swansea	a				03s26				10 35		11 15	12 12			13 15	14 12				15 08	16 04	16 14	16 14
	d					08 07	09 21	10 21		11 21	11 32		12 21	13 21	13 43		14 21	15 21		15 33			16 21
Llansamlet	d																						
Skewen	d																						
Neath	d				03s45	08 19	09 33	10 33		11 33	11 43		12 33	13 33	13 54		14 33	15 33		15 44			16 33
Briton Ferry	d																						
Baglan	d																						
Port Talbot Parkway	d				03s52	08 26	09 40	10 40		11 40	11 50		12 40	13 40	14 01		14 40	15 40		15 51			16 40
Pyle	d										11 57				14 09					15 58			
Maesteg	d	22p15																					
Maesteg (Ewenny Road)	d	22p17																					
Garth (Mid Glamorgan)	d	22p20																					
Tondu	d	22p29																					
Sarn	d	22p32																					
Wildmill	d	22p34																					
Bridgend	d	22p38			04s06	08 38	09 52	10 52		11 52	12 05		12 52	13 52	14 17		14 52	15 52		16 06			16 52
Pencoed	d	22p44									12 11									16 12			
Llanharan	d	22p48									12 15									16 16			
Pontyclun	d	22p52									12 20									16 21			
Cardiff Central 7	a	23p08			04 35	09 01	10 14	11 14		12 14	12 35		13 14	14 14	14 40		15 14	16 14		16 36			17 12
Newport (South Wales)	a	23p36				09 18	10 31	11 31		12 31	12 52		13 31	14 31	15 12		15 31	16 31		16 52			17 31
Bristol Parkway 7	a					09 46	10 59	11 59		12 59			13 59	14 59			15 59	16 59					17 59
Gloucester 7	a	00 40																					
Manchester Piccadilly 10	a										16 15				18 17					20 17			
Reading 7	a					10 42	12 01	13 00		14 00			15 00	16 00			17 00	18 01					19 00
London Paddington 15 ⊖	a					11 22	12 44	13 44		14 44			15 44	16 44			17 43	18 44					19 44

A not 11 December

b Previous night, stops on request

When events are being held at the Millenium Stadium, services are subject to alteration. Please check times before travelling.

Table 128

Sundays
until 1 January

West Wales, Swansea and Maesteg - Cardiff

Route Diagram - see first Page of Table 127

		GW	AW	GW	GW	AW		AW	GW	AW	AW	AW	AW	AW	AW		AW	AW
			R															R
		◇1		◇1	◇1				◇1	◇			◇	◇				
		☕	🛒	☕	☕				☕									
Rosslare Harbour ⛴	d																	21 00
Fishguard Harbour ⛴	a																	00 30
	d																	
Milford Haven	d		15 28					17 30				19 38		21 33			23 15	
Johnston	d		15x36					17x38				19x46		21x41			23x23	
Haverfordwest	d		15 43					17 45				19 53		21 49			23 30	
Clarbeston Road	d		15x52					17x53				20x01		21x57			23x39	
Clunderwen	d		15x59					18x00				20x08		22x05			23x46	
Pembroke Dock	d					16 45					19 00				21 45			
Pembroke	d					16 53					19 08				21 53			
Lamphey	d					16x56					19x11				21x56			
Manorbier	d					17 05					19 20				22 05			
Penally	d					17x10					19x25				22x10			
Tenby	a					17 13					19 28				22 13			
	d					17 13					19 28				22 13			
Saundersfoot	d					17x21					19x36				22x21			
Kilgetty	d					17x23					19x38				22x23			
Narberth	d					17x33					19x48				22x33			
Whitland	a		16 06			17 41		18 06			19 56	20 14		22 11	22 41		23 53	
	d		16 09			17 44		18 08			19 59	20 17		22 14	22 44		23 53	
Carmarthen	a		16 26			18 04		18 29			20 16	20 36		22 31	23 05		00 14	
	d		16 31	16 55		18 07			19 09		20 19		21 05	22 34				
Ferryside	d		16x41			18x17					20x30			22x44				
Kidwelly	d		16x47			18x23					20x36			22x50				
Pembrey & Burry Port	d		16 55	17 15		18 31			19 29		20 43		21 24	22 58				
Llanelli	a		17 01	17 21		18 37			19 35		20 49		21 30	23 04				
	d		17 01	17 22		18 38			19 36	19 55	20 51		21 31	23 04				
Gowerton	d					18x46				20x02	20x58			23x12				
Swansea	a		17 20	17 39		19 06			19 53	20 16	21 17		21 48	23 27				
	d	16 51	17 30	17 51	18 51				19 59	20 40			21 52	23 30				
Llansamlet	d																	
Skewen	d																	
Neath	d	17 03	17 41	18 03	19 03				20 11	20 51			22 03	23 42				
Briton Ferry	d																	
Baglan	d																	
Port Talbot Parkway	d	17 10	17 48	18 10	19 10				20 18	20 58			22 10	23 49				
Pyle	d		17 55										22 17	23 56				
Maesteg	d																	
Maesteg (Ewenny Road)	d																	
Garth (Mid Glamorgan)	d																	
Tondu	d																	
Sarn	d																	
Wildmill	d																	
Bridgend	d	17 22	18 03	18 22	19 22				20 30	21 11			22 25	00 04				
Pencoed	d		18 09															
Llanharan	d		18 13															
Pontyclun	d		18 18															
Cardiff Central 7	a	17 45	18 34	18 45	19 45				20 53	21 36			22 49	00 29				
Newport (South Wales)	a	18 03	18 52	19 03	20 03				21 08				23 18					
Bristol Parkway 7	a	18 31		19 31	20 31				21 36									
Gloucester 7	a																	
Manchester Piccadilly 10	a		22 19															
Reading 7	a	19 32		20 32	21 32				22 36									
London Paddington 15 ⊖	a	20 14		21 13	22 14				23 19									

When events are being held at the Millenium Stadium,
services are subject to alteration.
Please check times before travelling.

Table 128

Sundays

8 January to 12 February

West Wales, Swansea and Maesteg - Cardiff

Route Diagram - see first Page of Table 127

		AW	AW	AW	AW	GW	GW	GW	GW	GW	GW	GW	AW	GW	AW	GW	AW	GW	AW	GW	GW	AW	GW
			R	◇	🚌	🚌	🚌	🚌	🚌	🚌	🚌	🚌		🚌		🚌	🚌	🚌		🚌	🚌		🚌
Rosslare Harbour ⛴	d		21p00																				
Fishguard Harbour ⛴	a		00 30																				
	d			01 50																			
Milford Haven	d	23p18																				11 20	
Johnston	d	23b26																				11x28	
Haverfordwest	d	23p33																				11 35	
Clarbeston Road	d	23b41																				11x44	
Clunderwen	d	23b48																				11x51	
Pembroke Dock	d																						
Pembroke	d																						
Lamphey	d																						
Manorbier	d																						
Penally	d																						
Tenby	a																						
	d																						
Saundersfoot	d																						
Kilgetty	d																						
Narberth	d																						
Whitland	a	23p54		02s22																		11 58	
	d	23p54																				12 00	
Carmarthen	a	00 16		02 42																		12 18	
	d				02 50								09 40		10 30				11 07			12 21	
Ferryside	d												09x50						11x17				
Kidwelly	d												09x56						11x23				
Pembrey & Burry Port	d												10 03		10 49				11 31			12 41	
Llanelli	a				03s30								10 09		10 54				11 37			12 47	
	d												10 10		10 56				11 37			12 47	
Gowerton	d												10x17						11x45				
Swansea	a				04s00								10 35		11 18				12 02			13 10	
	d					07 15	07 55	08 20	09 00	09 20	10 00	10 20		11 00		11 20	11 30	12 00		12 20	13 00		13 20
Llansamlet	d																						
Skewen	d																						
Neath	d				04s25	07 37		08 42		09 42		10 42				11 42	11 55			12 42			13 42
Briton Ferry	d																						
Baglan	d																						
Port Talbot Parkway	d				04s45	07 52		08 57		09 57		10 57				11 57	12 15			12 57			13 57
Pyle	d																12 35						
Maesteg	d																						
Maesteg (Ewenny Road)	d																						
Garth (Mid Glamorgan)	d																						
Tondu	d																						
Sarn	d																						
Wildmill	d																						
Bridgend	d				05s05	08 17		09 22		10 22		11 22				12 22	12 50			13 22			14 22
Pencoed	d																13 05						
Llanharan	d																13 12						
Pontyclun	d																13 20						
Cardiff Central 7	a				05 40	08 52	08 55	09 57	10 00	10 57	11 00	11 57		12 00		12 57	13 45	13 00		13 57	14 00		14 57
Newport (South Wales)	a																						
Bristol Parkway 7	a																						
Gloucester 7	a																						
Manchester Piccadilly 10	a																						
Reading 7	a																						
London Paddington 15 ⊖	a																						

b Previous night, stops on request

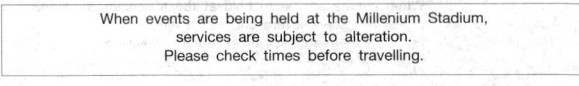

When events are being held at the Millenium Stadium,
services are subject to alteration.
Please check times before travelling.

Table 128

Sundays

8 January to 12 February

West Wales, Swansea and Maesteg - Cardiff

Route Diagram - see first Page of Table 127

		AW	GW	AW	GW		GW	GW	AW	AW	GW	AW	GW	GW	AW	AW		GW	GW	AW	AW	GW	GW	GW	GW
							1		R						◇								1		
		🚌	🚌		🚌			🚌			🚌	🚌	🚌	🚌				🚌	🚌		🚌	🚌		🚌	🚌
							☕									🛒							☕		
Rosslare Harbour ⛴	d								09 00																
Fishguard Harbour ⛴	a								12 30																
	d															14 23									
Milford Haven	d									13 23										15 28					
Johnston	d									13x29										15x36					
Haverfordwest	d									13 36										15 43					
Clarbeston Road	d									13x45										15x52					
Clunderwen	d									13x52										15x59					
Pembroke Dock	d			11 55																					
Pembroke	d			12 03																					
Lamphey	d			12x06																					
Manorbier	d			12 15																					
Penally	d			12x20																					
Tenby	a			12 23																					
	d			12 23																					
Saundersfoot	d			12x31																					
Kilgetty	d			12x33																					
Narberth	d			12x43																					
Whitland	a			12 51						13 59						14 55				16 06					
	d			12 54						14 02						14 55				16 09					
Carmarthen	a			13 14						14 20						15 13				16 26					
	d			13 17			14 00			14 23						15 16				16 31			16 55		
Ferryside	d			13x27												15x26				16x41					
Kidwelly	d			13x33												15x32				16x47					
Pembrey & Burry Port	d			13 40			14 20			14 42						15 39				16 55			17 15		
Llanelli	a			13 46			14 26			14 48						15 50				17 01			17 21		
	d			13 47			14 28			14 49					15 41	15 50				17 01			17 23		
Gowerton	d			13x54												15x58									
Swansea	a			14 12			14 44			15 10					16 08	16 17				17 22			17 39		
	d	13 25	14 00		14 20			15 00			15 20	15 25	15 55	16 00				16 35	16 55		17 32	17 35		17 55	18 35
Llansamlet	d																								
Skewen	d																								
Neath	d	13 50			14 42						15 42	15 50	16 17						17 17		17 57			18 17	
Briton Ferry	d																								
Baglan	d																								
Port Talbot Parkway	d	14 10			14 57						15 57	16 10	16 32						17 32		18 17			18 32	
Pyle	d	14 30										16 30									18 37				
Maesteg	d																								
Maesteg (Ewenny Road)	d																								
Garth (Mid Glamorgan)	d																								
Tondu	d																								
Sarn	d																								
Wildmill	d																								
Bridgend	d	14 45			15 22						16 22	16 45	16 57						17 57		18 52			18 57	
Pencoed	d											17 00									19 07				
Llanharan	d											17 07									19 14				
Pontyclun	d											17 15									19 22				
Cardiff Central 7	a	15 20	15 00		15 57			16 00			16 57	17 40	17 32	17 00				17 35	18 32		19 47	18 35		19 32	19 35
Newport (South Wales)	a																								
Bristol Parkway 7	a																								
Gloucester 7	a																								
Manchester Piccadilly 10	a																								
Reading 7	a																								
London Paddington 15 ⊖	a																								

When events are being held at the Millenium Stadium, services are subject to alteration. Please check times before travelling.

Table 128

Sundays

8 January to 12 February

West Wales, Swansea and Maesteg - Cardiff

Route Diagram - see first Page of Table 127

Station		AW		AW	GW	GW	GW	GW	AW	AW	AW	AW		AW	AW	AW	AW	AW	AW	AW
					🚌	1 ☕	🚌	🚌	◇	🚌					🚌				🚌	R
Rosslare Harbour ⛴	d																			21 00
Fishguard Harbour ⛴	a																			00 30
	d																			
Milford Haven	d			17 30								19 42				21 33		23 15		
Johnston	d			17x38								19x50				21x41		23x23		
Haverfordwest	d			17 45								19 59				21 49		23 30		
Clarbeston Road	d			17x53								20x07				21x57		23x39		
Clunderwen	d			18x00								20x14				22x05		23x46		
Pembroke Dock	d	16 45									19 00						21 45			
Pembroke	d	16 53									19 08						21 53			
Lamphey	d	16x56									19x11						21x56			
Manorbier	d	17 05									19 20						22 05			
Penally	d	17x10									19x25						22x10			
Tenby	a	17 13									19 28						22 13			
	d	17 13									19 28						22 13			
Saundersfoot	d	17x21									19x36						22x21			
Kilgetty	d	17x23									19x38						22x23			
Narberth	d	17x33									19x48						22x33			
Whitland	a	17 41		18 06							19 56	20 20				22 11	22 41	23 53		
	d	17 44		18 08							19 59	20 23				22 14	22 44	23 53		
Carmarthen	a	18 04		18 29							20 16	20 42				22 31	23 05	00 14		
	d	18 07				19 09					20 19			21 05		22 34				
Ferryside	d	18x17									20x30					22x44				
Kidwelly	d	18x23									20x36					22x50				
Pembrey & Burry Port	d	18 31				19 29					20 43			21 24		22 58				
Llanelli	a	18 37				19 35					20 49			21 30		23 04				
	d	18 38				19 37			19 55		20 51			21 31		23 04				
Gowerton	d	18x46							20x02		20x58					23x12				
Swansea	a	19 06				19 53			20 19		21 17			21 51		23 30				
	d				19 25		20 05	20 05		20 35					22 06				23 40	
Llansamlet	d																			
Skewen	d																			
Neath	d				19 47			20 27		21 00					22 31				00 05	
Briton Ferry	d																			
Baglan	d																			
Port Talbot Parkway	d				20 02			20 42		21 20					22 51				00 25	
Pyle	d														23 11				00 45	
Maesteg	d																			
Maesteg (Ewenny Road)	d																			
Garth (Mid Glamorgan)	d																			
Tondu	d																			
Sarn	d																			
Wildmill	d																			
Bridgend	d				20 27			21 07		21 40					23 26				01 00	
Pencoed	d																			
Llanharan	d																			
Pontyclun	d																			
Cardiff Central 7	a				21 02		21 05	21 42		22 15					00 01				01 35	
Newport (South Wales)	a																			
Bristol Parkway 7	a																			
Gloucester 7	a																			
Manchester Piccadilly 10	a																			
Reading 7	a																			
London Paddington 15 ⊖	a																			

When events are being held at the Millenium Stadium,
services are subject to alteration.
Please check times before travelling.

Table 128

Sundays

19 February to 25 March

West Wales, Swansea and Maesteg - Cardiff

Route Diagram - see first Page of Table 127

		AW	AW	AW	AW	GW	GW	GW	AW		GW	AW	AW	GW	GW	AW	AW	GW	AW	AW		GW	AW	AW	GW
				R												R			R	R					
					◇	◇1	◇1	◇1			◇1	◇		◇1	◇1			◇1				◇1	◇		◇1
						🍴	🍴	🍴			🍴	☕		🍴	🍴	☕		🍴		☕		🍴		☕	🍴
Rosslare Harbour ⛴	d			21p00															09 00						
Fishguard Harbour ⛴	a			00 30															12 30						
	d				01 50																			14 23	
Milford Haven	d		23p18													11 28				13 23					
Johnston	d		23b26													11x36				13x29					
Haverfordwest	d		23p33													11 43				13 36					
Clarbeston Road	d		23b41													11x52				13x45					
Clunderwen	d		23b48													11x59				13x52					
Pembroke Dock	d																11 55								
Pembroke	d																12 03								
Lamphey	d																12x06								
Manorbier	d																12 15								
Penally	d																12x20								
Tenby	a																12 23								
	d																12 23								
Saundersfoot	d																12x31								
Kilgetty	d																12x33								
Narberth	d																12x43								
Whitland	a		23p54		02s22											12 06	12 51			13 59				14 55	
	d		23p54													12 08	12 54			14 02				14 55	
Carmarthen	a		00 16		02s40											12 26	13 14			14 20				15 13	
	d								09 40			10 30	11 18			12 29	13 17			14 23				15 16	15 35
Ferryside	d								09x50				11x28				13x27							15x26	
Kidwelly	d								09x56				11x34				13x33							15x32	
Pembrey & Burry Port	d								10 03			10 49	11 42			12 49	13 40			14 42				15 39	15 57
Llanelli	a				03s06				10 09			10 54	11 48			12 55	13 46			14 48				15 47	16 03
	d								10 10			10 56	11 48			12 55	13 47			14 49			15 41	15 47	16 05
Gowerton	d								10x17				11x56				13x54							15x55	
Swansea	a				03s26				10 35			11 15	12 12			13 15	14 12			15 08			16 04	16 14	16 21
	d					07 55	09 05	10 25			11 25	11 32		12 30	13 25	13 43		14 30		15 33		15 50			16 25
Llansamlet	d																								
Skewen	d																								
Neath	d				03s45	08 07	09 17	10 38			11 37	11 43		12 42	13 37	13 54		14 42		15 44		16 02			16 40
Briton Ferry	d																								
Baglan	d																								
Port Talbot Parkway	d				03s52	08 15	09 24	10 45			11 44	11 50		12 49	13 44	14 01		14 49		15 51		16 09			16 47
Pyle	d											11 57				14 09				15 58					
Maesteg	d	22p15																							
Maesteg (Ewenny Road)	d	22p17																							
Garth (Mid Glamorgan)	d	22p20																							
Tondu	d	22p29																							
Sarn	d	22p32																							
Wildmill	d	22p34																							
Bridgend	d	22p38			04s06	08 27	09 36	10 57			11 56	12 05		13 01	13 56	14 17		15 01		16 06		16 21			16 59
Pencoed	d	22p44										12 11								16 12					
Llanharan	d	22p48										12 15								16 16					
Pontyclun	d	22p52										12 20								16 21					
Cardiff Central 7	a	23p08			04 35	08 52	09 58	11 20			12 19	12 35		13 24	14 19	14 40		15 24		16 36		16 44			17 21
Newport (South Wales)	a	23p36				09 05	10 15	11 39			12 34	12 52		13 39	14 34	15 12		15 39		16 52		17 03			17 38
Bristol Parkway 7	a																								
Gloucester 7	a	00 40				09 59		12 33			13 29			14 33	15 30			16 34							18 32
Manchester Piccadilly 10	a											16 15				18 17				20 17					
Reading 7	a					11 25	12 26	13 59			15 00			16 00	17 03			17 59				19 00			19 52
London Paddington 15 ⊖	a					12 06	13 03	14 44			15 44			16 44	17 43			18 45				19 43			20 31

b Previous night, stops on request

When events are being held at the Millenium Stadium,
services are subject to alteration.
Please check times before travelling.

Table 128

Sundays

19 February to 25 March

West Wales, Swansea and Maesteg - Cardiff

Route Diagram - see first Page of Table 127

		GW	AW	GW	GW	AW		AW	GW	AW	AW	AW	AW	AW	AW		AW	AW
			R															R
		◇1		◇1	◇1				◇1	◇			◇	◇				
		☕	🛒	☕	☕				☕									
Rosslare Harbour ⛴	d																	21 00
Fishguard Harbour ⛴	a																	00 30
	d																	
Milford Haven	d		15 28					17 30				19 38		21 50			23 15	
Johnston	d		15x36					17x38				19x46		21x58			23x23	
Haverfordwest	d		15 43					17 45				19 53		22 06			23 30	
Clarbeston Road	d		15x52					17x53				20x01		22x14			23x39	
Clunderwen	d		15x59					18x00				20x08		22x22			23x46	
Pembroke Dock	d					16 45					19 00				22 00			
Pembroke	d					16 53					19 08				22 08			
Lamphey	d					16x56					19x11				22x11			
Manorbier	d					17 05					19 20				22 20			
Penally	d					17x10					19x25				22x25			
Tenby	a					17 13					19 28				22 28			
	d					17 13					19 28				22 28			
Saundersfoot	d					17x21					19x36				22x36			
Kilgetty	d					17x23					19x38				22x38			
Narberth	d					17x33					19x48				22x48			
Whitland	a		16 06			17 41		18 06			19 56	20 14		22 28	22 56		23 53	
	d		16 09			17 44		18 08			19 59	20 17		22 31	22 59		23 53	
Carmarthen	a		16 26			18 04		18 29			20 16	20 36		22 48	23 20		00 14	
	d		16 31	17 10		18 07			19 09		20 19		21 05	22 51				
Ferryside	d		16x41			18x17					20x30			23x01				
Kidwelly	d		16x47			18x23					20x36			23x07				
Pembrey & Burry Port	d		16 55	17 30		18 31			19 29		20 43		21 24	23 15				
Llanelli	a		17 01	17 36		18 37			19 35		20 49		21 30	23 21				
	d		17 01	17 37		18 38			19 36	19 55	20 51		21 31	23 21				
Gowerton	d					18x46				20x02	20x58			23x29				
Swansea	a		17 20	17 55		19 09			19 53	20 16	21 17		21 48	23 44				
	d	17 05	17 30	18 00	18 55				19 59	20 40			21 52	23 47				
Llansamlet	d																	
Skewen	d																	
Neath	d	17 17	17 41	18 14	19 09				20 11	20 51			22 03	23 59				
Briton Ferry	d																	
Baglan	d																	
Port Talbot Parkway	d	17 24	17 48	18 21	19 16				20 18	20 58			22 10	00 06				
Pyle	d		17 55										22 17	00 13				
Maesteg	d																	
Maesteg (Ewenny Road)	d																	
Garth (Mid Glamorgan)	d																	
Tondu	d																	
Sarn	d																	
Wildmill	d																	
Bridgend	d	17 36	18 03	18 33	19 28				20 31	21 11			22 25	00 21				
Pencoed	d		18 09															
Llanharan	d		18 13															
Pontyclun	d		18 18															
Cardiff Central 7	a	17 59	18 34	18 56	19 51				20 54	21 36			22 49	00 46				
Newport (South Wales)	a	18 15	18 52	19 12	20 12				21 08				23 18					
Bristol Parkway 7	a																	
Gloucester 7	a			20 05	21 06				21 58									
Manchester Piccadilly 10	a		22 19															
Reading 7	a	20 32		21 31	22 31				23 19									
London Paddington 15 ⊖	a	21 13		22 14	23 13				00 01									

When events are being held at the Millenium Stadium,
services are subject to alteration.
Please check times before travelling.

Table 128

Sundays

from 1 April

West Wales, Swansea and Maesteg - Cardiff

Route Diagram - see first Page of Table 127

		AW	AW	AW	GW	GW	GW	GW	GW	AW	GW	AW	AW	GW	GW	AW	AW	GW	AW	GW	AW	AW	AW
			R	◇	🚌	🚌	🚌	🚌	◇1 ☕		◇1 ☕	◇ 🛒		◇1 ☕	◇1 ☕	R 🛒		◇1 ☕	R	◇1 ☕	R 🛒	◇	🛒
Rosslare Harbour ⛴	d		21p00																09 00				
Fishguard Harbour ⛴	a		00 30																12 30				
	d			01 50																			14 23
Milford Haven	d	23p18														11 28					13 23		
Johnston	d	23b26														11x36					13x29		
Haverfordwest	d	23p33														11 43					13 36		
Clarbeston Road	d	23b41														11x52					13x45		
Clunderwen	d	23b48														11x59					13x52		
Pembroke Dock	d																11 55						
Pembroke	d																12 03						
Lamphey	d																12x06						
Manorbier	d																12 15						
Penally	d																12x20						
Tenby	a																12 23						
	d																12 23						
Saundersfoot	d																12x31						
Kilgetty	d																12x33						
Narberth	d																12x43						
Whitland	a	23p54		02s22												12 06	12 51				13 59		14 55
	d	23p54														12 08	12 54				14 02		14 55
Carmarthen	a	00 16		02s40												12 26	13 14				14 20		15 13
	d									09 40		10 30	11 18			12 29	13 17				14 23		15 16
Ferryside	d									09x50			11x28				13x27						15x26
Kidwelly	d									09x56			11x34				13x33						15x32
Pembrey & Burry Port	d									10 03		10 49	11 42			12 49	13 40				14 42		15 39
Llanelli	a			03s06						10 09		10 54	11 48			12 55	13 46				14 48		15 45
	d									10 10		10 56	11 48			12 55	13 47				14 49	15 41	15 45
Gowerton	d									10x17			11x56				13x54						15x54
Swansea	a			03s26						10 35		11 15	12 12			13 15	14 12				15 08	16 04	16 13
	d				07 15	07 55	08 20	09 00	10 21		11 21	11 32		12 21	13 21	13 43		14 21		15 21	15 33		
Llansamlet	d																						
Skewen	d																						
Neath	d			03s45	07 37		08 42		10 33		11 33	11 43		12 33	13 33	13 54		14 33		15 33	15 44		
Briton Ferry	d																						
Baglan	d																						
Port Talbot Parkway	d			03s52	07 52		08 57		10 40		11 40	11 50		12 40	13 40	14 01		14 40		15 40	15 51		
Pyle	d											11 57				14 09					15 58		
Maesteg	d																						
Maesteg (Ewenny Road)	d																						
Garth (Mid Glamorgan)	d																						
Tondu	d																						
Sarn	d																						
Wildmill	d																						
Bridgend	d			04s06	08 17		09 22		10 52		11 52	12 05		12 52	13 52	14 17		14 52		15 52	16 06		
Pencoed	d											12 11									16 12		
Llanharan	d											12 15									16 16		
Pontyclun	d											12 20									16 21		
Cardiff Central 7	a			04 35	08 52	08 55	09 57	10 00	11 14		12 14	12 35		13 14	14 14	14 40		15 14		16 14	16 36		
Newport (South Wales)	a								11 31		12 31	12 52		13 31	14 31	15 12		15 31		16 31	16 52		
Bristol Parkway 7	a								11 59		12 59			13 59	14 59			15 59		16 59			
Gloucester 7	a																						
Manchester Piccadilly 10	a											16 15				18 17					20 17		
Reading 7	a								13 00		14 05			15 05	16 00			17 04		18 00			
London Paddington 15 ⊖	a								13 42		14 43			15 43	16 42			17 44		18 43			

b Previous night, stops on request

When events are being held at the Millenium Stadium,
services are subject to alteration.
Please check times before travelling.

Table 128

Sundays

from 1 April

West Wales, Swansea and Maesteg - Cardiff

Route Diagram - see first Page of Table 127

		GW	GW	AW	GW	GW		AW	AW	GW	AW	AW	AW	AW	AW		AW	AW	AW
				R															R
		◇1	◇1		◇1	◇1				◇1	◇			◇	◇				
		☕	☕	🍴	☕	☕				☕									
Rosslare Harbour ⛴	d																		21 00
Fishguard Harbour ⛴	a																		00 30
	d																		
Milford Haven	d			15 28					17 30				19 38		21 33			23 15	
Johnston	d			15x36					17x38				19x46		21x41			23x23	
Haverfordwest	d			15 43					17 45				19 53		21 49			23 30	
Clarbeston Road	d			15x52					17x53				20x01		21x57			23x39	
Clunderwen	d			15x59					18x00				20x08		22x05			23x46	
Pembroke Dock	d							16 45				19 00					21 45		
Pembroke	d							16 53				19 08					21 53		
Lamphey	d							16x56				19x11					21x56		
Manorbier	d							17 05				19 20					22 05		
Penally	d							17x10				19x25					22x10		
Tenby	a							17 13				19 28					22 13		
	d							17 13				19 28					22 13		
Saundersfoot	d							17x21				19x36					22x21		
Kilgetty	d							17x23				19x38					22x23		
Narberth	d							17x33				19x48					22x33		
Whitland	a			16 06				17 41	18 06			19 56	20 14		22 11		22 41	23 53	
	d			16 09				17 44	18 08			19 59	20 17		22 14		22 44	23 53	
Carmarthen	a			16 26				18 04	18 29			20 16	20 36		22 31		23 05	00 14	
	d	15 30		16 31	16 55			18 07		19 09		20 19		21 05	22 34				
Ferryside	d			16x41				18x17				20x30			22x44				
Kidwelly	d			16x47				18x23				20x36			22x50				
Pembrey & Burry Port	d	15 50		16 55	17 15			18 31		19 29		20 43		21 24	22 58				
Llanelli	a	15 56		17 01	17 21			18 37		19 35		20 49		21 30	23 04				
	d	15 58		17 01	17 22			18 38		19 36	19 55	20 51		21 31	23 04				
Gowerton	d							18x46			20x02	20x58			23x12				
Swansea	a	16 14		17 20	17 39			19 09		19 53	20 16	21 17		21 48	23 27				
	d	16 21	16 51	17 30	17 51	18 51				19 59	20 40			21 52	23 30				
Llansamlet	d																		
Skewen	d																		
Neath	d	16 33	17 03	17 41	18 03	19 03				20 11	20 51			22 03	23 42				
Briton Ferry	d																		
Baglan	d																		
Port Talbot Parkway	d	16 40	17 10	17 48	18 10	19 10				20 18	20 58			22 10	23 49				
Pyle	d			17 55										22 17	23 56				
Maesteg	d																		
Maesteg (Ewenny Road)	d																		
Garth (Mid Glamorgan)	d																		
Tondu	d																		
Sarn	d																		
Wildmill	d																		
Bridgend	d	16 52	17 22	18 03	18 22	19 22				20 30	21 11			22 25	00 04				
Pencoed	d			18 09															
Llanharan	d			18 13															
Pontyclun	d			18 18															
Cardiff Central 7	a	17 12	17 45	18 34	18 45	19 45				20 53	21 36			22 49	00 29				
Newport (South Wales)	a	17 29	18 03	18 52	19 03	20 03				21 08				23 18					
Bristol Parkway 7	a	17 59	18 31		19 31	20 31				21 36									
Gloucester 7	a																		
Manchester Piccadilly 10	a			22 19															
Reading 7	a	19 02	19 36		20 42	21 32				22 37									
London Paddington 15 ⊖	a	19 44	20 14		21 19	22 14				23 15									

When events are being held at the Millenium Stadium,
services are subject to alteration.
Please check times before travelling.

Network Diagram for Tables 129, 131

DM-12/11
Design BAJS

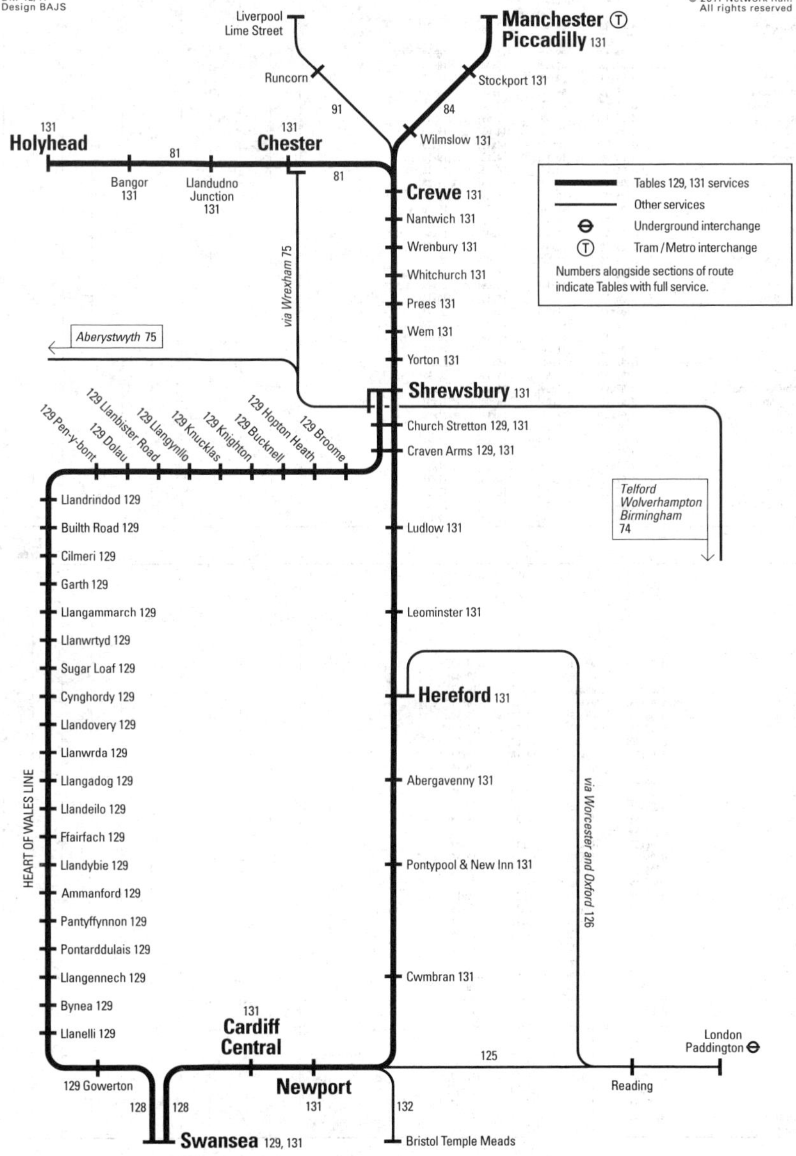

Swansea - Shrewsbury

HEART OF WALES LINE

Route Diagram - see first Page of Table 129

Miles			AW	AW	AW	AW
			◇	◇ 🛒	◇	◇
0	**Swansea**	d	04 36	09 16	13 14	18 21
5½	Gowerton	d				
11¼	Llanelli	d	04 53	09 34	13 35	18 39
14	Bynea	d	04x58	09x39	13x40	18x44
16	Llangennech	d	05x01	09x43	13x44	18x47
18¼	Pontarddulais	d	05x05	09x47	13x48	18x51
23	Pantyffynnon	d	05 13	09 55	13 56	18 59
24¼	Ammanford	d	05 16	09 58	13 59	19 02
26	Llandybie	d	05 20	10 02	14 03	19 06
30	Ffairfach	d	05x27	10x10	14x11	19x13
30¾	Llandeilo	a	05 30	10 12	14 13	19 16
—		d	05 32	10 15	14 16	19 18
36½	Llangadog	d	05 42	10 24	14 25	19 28
38¼	Llanwrda	d	05 45	10 28	14 29	19 31
42	Llandovery	a	05 52	10 34	14 35	19 38
—		d	05 54	10 37	14 38	19 40
46¾	Cynghordy	d	06x02	10x45	14x46	19x48
49½	Sugar Loaf	d	06x10	10x54	14x55	19x56
53½	Llanwrtyd	a	06 16	11 00	15 01	20 02
—		d	06 19	11 05	15 03	20 07
56¾	Llangammarch	d	06x24	11x11	15x09	20x12
58½	Garth (Powys)	d	06x28	11x17	15x13	20x16
62	Cilmeri	d	06x33	11x21	15x19	20x21
64	Builth Road	d	06x36	11x24	15x22	20x24
69¾	Llandrindod	a	06 47	11 36	15 34	20 36
—		d	06 55	11 40	15 40	20 40
73¼	Pen-y-bont	d	07x02	11x48	15x48	20x47
76¼	Dolau	d	07 07	11 53	15 53	20 52
79¾	Llanbister Road	d	07x13	11x59	15x59	20x58
82¾	Llangynllo	d	07x18	12x05	16x04	21x03
86¾	Knucklas	d	07x24	12x11	16x11	21x09
89¼	Knighton	a	07 30	12 16	16 16	21 14
—		d	07 32	12 18	16 19	21 17
93½	Bucknell	d	07 38	12 24	16 25	21 23
96½	Hopton Heath	d	07x42	12x28	16x29	21x27
99	Broome	d	07x46	12x32	16x34	21x31
101½	Craven Arms	a	07 53	12 39	16 40	21 38
108¾	Church Stretton	a	08 06	12 52	16 53	21 51
121½	**Shrewsbury**	a	08 22	13 08	17 09	22 08

Saturdays

		AW	AW	AW	AW
		◇	◇ 🛒	◇	◇
Swansea	d	04 36	09 16	13 16	18 21
Gowerton	d				
Llanelli	d	04 53	09 34	13 35	18 39
Bynea	d	04x58	09x39	13x39	18x44
Llangennech	d	05x01	09x43	13x43	18x47
Pontarddulais	d	05x05	09x47	13x48	18x51
Pantyffynnon	d	05 13	09 55	13 55	18 59
Ammanford	d	05 16	09 58	13 58	19 02
Llandybie	d	05 20	10 02	14 03	19 06
Ffairfach	d	05x27	10x10	14x10	19x13
Llandeilo	a	05 30	10 12	14 12	19 16
	d	05 32	10 15	14 15	19 18
Llangadog	d	05 42	10 24	14 24	19 28
Llanwrda	d	05 45	10 28	14 28	19 31
Llandovery	a	05 52	10 34	14 34	19 38
	d	05 54	10 37	14 37	19 40
Cynghordy	d	06x02	10x45	14x45	19x48
Sugar Loaf	d	06x10	10x54	14x53	19x56
Llanwrtyd	a	06 16	11 00	14 59	20 02
	d	06 19	11 05	15 01	20 07
Llangammarch	d	06x24	11x11	15x07	20x13
Garth (Powys)	d	06x28	11x15	15x11	20x16
Cilmeri	d	06x33	11x20	15x16	20x21
Builth Road	d	06x36	11x23	15x19	20x24
Llandrindod	a	06 47	11 35	15 31	20 36
	d	06 55	11 39	15 40	20 40
Pen-y-bont	d	07x02	11x46	15x47	20x47
Dolau	d	07x07	11 51	15 52	20 52
Llanbister Road	d	07x12	11x57	15x57	20x58
Llangynllo	d	07x17	12x02	16x02	21x03
Knucklas	d	07x23	12x08	16x08	21x09
Knighton	a	07 29	12 13	16 14	21 14
	d	07 32	12 16	16 16	21 17
Bucknell	d	07 38	12 22	16 22	21 23
Hopton Heath	d	07x42	12x26	16x26	21x27
Broome	d	07x46	12x30	16x30	21x31
Craven Arms	a	07 53	12 37	16 37	21 38
Church Stretton	a	08 06	12 51	16 51	21 51
Shrewsbury	a	08 22	13 09	17 11	22 08

When events are being held at the Millenium Stadium,
services are subject to alteration. Please check times before travelling.

Sundays
until 1 January

Swansea - Shrewsbury

HEART OF WALES LINE

Route Diagram - see first Page of Table 129

		AW ◇	AW ◇
Swansea	d	11 06	15 26
Gowerton	d	11x16	15x36
Llanelli	d	11 29	15 51
Bynea	d	11x34	15x56
Llangennech	d	11x38	16x00
Pontarddulais	d	11x42	16x04
Pantyffynnon	d	11 50	16 11
Ammanford	d	11 53	16 14
Llandybie	d	11 57	16 19
Ffairfach	d	12x05	16x26
Llandeilo	a	12 07	16 29
	d	12 10	16 31
Llangadog	d	12 19	16 41
Llanwrda	d	12 23	16 44
Llandovery	a	12 29	16 51
	d	12 32	16 53
Cynghordy	d	12x40	17x02
Sugar Loaf	d	12x49	17x10
Llanwrtyd	a	12 55	17 16
	d	12 57	17 19
Llangammarch	d	13x03	17x25
Garth (Powys)	d	13x07	17x29
Cilmeri	d	13x13	17x34
Builth Road	d	13x16	17x38
Llandrindod	a	13 28	17 49
	d	13 43	18 00
Pen-y-bont	d	13x51	18x08
Dolau	d	13 56	18 13
Llanbister Road	d	14x02	18x19
Llangynllo	d	14x07	18x24
Knucklas	d	14x14	18x31
Knighton	a	14 19	18 36
	d	14 22	18 39
Bucknell	d	14 28	18 45
Hopton Heath	d	14x32	18x49
Broome	d	14x37	18x54
Craven Arms	a	14 44	19 01
Church Stretton	a	14 57	19 15
Shrewsbury	a	15 15	19 31

Sundays
8 January to 25 March

		AW ◇ A	AW ◇ B	AW ◇
Swansea	d	11 06	11 06	15 26
Gowerton	d	11x15	11x16	15x36
Llanelli	d	11 29	11b29	15 55
Bynea	d	11x34	11x34	16x00
Llangennech	d	11x38	11x38	16x04
Pontarddulais	d	11x42	11x42	16x08
Pantyffynnon	d	11 50	11 50	16 15
Ammanford	d	11 53	11 53	16 18
Llandybie	d	11 57	11 57	16 23
Ffairfach	d	12x05	12x05	16x30
Llandeilo	a	12 07	12 07	16 33
	d	12 10	12 10	16 35
Llangadog	d	12 19	12 19	16 45
Llanwrda	d	12 23	12 23	16 48
Llandovery	a	12 29	12 29	16 55
	d	12 32	12 32	16 57
Cynghordy	d	12x40	12x40	17x06
Sugar Loaf	d	12x49	12x49	17x14
Llanwrtyd	a	12 55	12 55	17 20
	d	12 57	12 57	17 23
Llangammarch	d	13x03	13x03	17x29
Garth (Powys)	d	13x07	13x07	17x33
Cilmeri	d	13x13	13x13	17x38
Builth Road	d	13x16	13x16	17x42
Llandrindod	a	13 28	13 28	17 53
	d	13 43	13 43	18 00
Pen-y-bont	d	13x51	13x51	18x08
Dolau	d	13 56	13 56	18 13
Llanbister Road	d	14x02	14x02	18x19
Llangynllo	d	14x07	14x07	18x24
Knucklas	d	14x14	14x14	18x31
Knighton	a	14 19	14 19	18 36
	d	14 22	14 22	18 39
Bucknell	d	14 28	14 28	18 45
Hopton Heath	d	14x32	14x32	18x49
Broome	d	14x37	14x37	18x54
Craven Arms	a	14 44	14 44	19 01
Church Stretton	a	14 57	14 57	19 15
Shrewsbury	a	15 15	15 15	19 31

A from 8 January until 12 February

B from 19 February until 25 March

When events are being held at the Millenium Stadium,
services are subject to alteration. Please check times before travelling.

Table 129

Sundays

from 1 April

Swansea - Shrewsbury

HEART OF WALES LINE

Route Diagram - see first Page of Table 129

		AW ◇	AW ◇
Swansea	d	11 06	15 26
Gowerton	d	11x16	15x36
Llanelli	d	11 29	15 51
Bynea	d	11x34	15x56
Llangennech	d	11x38	16x00
Pontarddulais	d	11x42	16x04
Pantyffynnon	d	11 50	16 11
Ammanford	d	11 53	16 14
Llandybie	d	11 57	16 19
Ffairfach	d	12x05	16x26
Llandeilo	a	12 07	16 29
	d	12 10	16 31
Llangadog	d	12 19	16 41
Llanwrda	d	12 23	16 44
Llandovery	a	12 29	16 51
	d	12 32	16 53
Cynghordy	d	12x40	17x02
Sugar Loaf	d	12x49	17x10
Llanwrtyd	a	12 55	17 16
	d	12 57	17 19
Llangammarch	d	13x03	17x25
Garth (Powys)	d	13x07	17x29
Cilmeri	d	13x13	17x34
Builth Road	d	13x16	17x38
Llandrindod	a	13 28	17 49
	d	13 43	18 00
Pen-y-bont	d	13x51	18x08
Dolau	d	13 56	18 13
Llanbister Road	d	14x02	18x19
Llangynllo	d	14x07	18x24
Knucklas	d	14x14	18x31
Knighton	a	14 19	18 36
	d	14 22	18 39
Bucknell	d	14 28	18 45
Hopton Heath	d	14x32	18x49
Broome	d	14x37	18x54
Craven Arms	a	14 44	19 01
Church Stretton	a	14 57	19 15
Shrewsbury	a	15 15	19 31

When events are being held at the Millenium Stadium, services are subject to alteration. Please check times before travelling.

Shrewsbury - Swansea

HEART OF WALES LINE | **Route Diagram - see first Page of Table 129**

Miles			AW ◇	AW ◇	AW ◇	AW ◇
0	**Shrewsbury**	d	05 19	09 00	14 04	18 05
12¾	Church Stretton	d	05 36	09 18	14 22	18 22
20	Craven Arms	d	05 50	09 28	14 33	18 35
22½	Broome	d	05x55	09x34	14x39	18x40
25	Hopton Heath	d	05x59	09x38	14x43	18x44
28	Bucknell	d	06x03	09x43	14x48	18x48
32¼	Knighton	a	06 10	09 50	14 55	18 55
—		d	06 12	09 52	14 57	18 57
34¾	Knucklas	d	06x17	09x58	15x03	19x02
38¾	Llangynllo	d	06x25	10x06	15x11	19x10
41¾	Llanbister Road	d	06x30	10x11	15x16	19x15
45¼	Dolau	d	06x35	10x17	15x22	19x20
48½	Pen-y-bont	d	06x39	10x21	15x26	19x24
51¾	Llandrindod	a	06 46	10 28	15 35	19 31
—		d	06 52	10 31	15 40	19 34
57½	Builth Road	d	07x01	10x40	15x50	19x43
59½	Cilmeri	d	07x04	10x44	15x53	19x46
63	Garth (Powys)	d	07x09	10x49	15x59	19x52
64¾	Llangammarch	d	07x12	10x53	16x03	19x55
68	Llanwrtyd	a	07 18	10 59	16 09	20 01
—		d	07 21	11 07	16 11	20 10
70¾	Sugar Loaf	d	07x27	11x13	16x18	20x16
74¾	Cynghordy	d	07x33	11x20	16x25	20x23
79½	Llandovery	a	07 43	11 30	16 34	20 33
—		d	07 45	11 32	16 37	20 35
83¼	Llanwrda	d	07x51	11x38	16x43	20x41
85	Llangadog	d	07x54	11x42	16x47	20x45
90¾	Llandeilo	a	08 03	11 51	16 56	20 54
—		d	08 06	11 54	16 58	20 57
91½	Ffairfach	d	08 08	11 56	17 01	20 59
95½	Llandybie	d	08x15	12x04	17x08	21x07
97¼	Ammanford	d	08x20	12x08	17x13	21x11
98½	Pantyffynnon	d	08 23	12 11	17 16	21 14
103¼	Pontarddulais	d	08x30	12x18	17x23	21x21
105½	Llangennech	d	08x34	12x23	17x27	21x26
107½	Bynea	d	08x37	12x26	17x31	21x29
110¼	Llanelli	a	08 42	12 35	17 38	21 34
116	Gowerton	a	08x53		17x57	21x50
121½	**Swansea**	a	09 08	13 04	18 18	22 08

Saturdays

		AW ◇	AW ◇	AW ◇	AW ◇
Shrewsbury	d	05 19	09 00	14 05	18 05
Church Stretton	d	05 36	09 17	14 23	18 23
Craven Arms	d	05 47	09 30	14 36	18 36
Broome	d	05x52	09x35	14x42	18x42
Hopton Heath	d	05x56	09x39	14x45	18x45
Bucknell	d	06x00	09x43	14x50	18x50
Knighton	a	06 09	09 50	14 56	18 56
	d	06 11	09 52	14 59	18 59
Knucklas	d	06x15	09x57	15x04	19x04
Llangynllo	d	06x22	10x05	15x11	19x11
Llanbister Road	d	06x27	10x10	15x16	19x16
Dolau	d	06x33	10x15	15x21	19x22
Pen-y-bont	d	06x37	10x20	15x25	19x26
Llandrindod	a	06 48	10 29	15 34	19 35
	d	06 52	10 29	15 37	19 35
Builth Road	d	07x01	10x39	15x46	19x45
Cilmeri	d	07x04	10x42	15x50	19x48
Garth (Powys)	d	07x09	10x47	15x55	19x53
Llangammarch	d	07x12	10x51	15x59	19x57
Llanwrtyd	a	07 18	10 57	16 05	20 03
	d	07 21	11 06	16 08	20 10
Sugar Loaf	d	07x27	11x13	16x14	20x16
Cynghordy	d	07x33	11x20	16x21	20x23
Llandovery	a	07 43	11 29	16 31	20 33
	d	07 45	11 32	16 33	20 35
Llanwrda	d	07x51	11x37	16x39	20x41
Llangadog	d	07x54	11x41	16x43	20x45
Llandeilo	a	08 03	11 50	16 52	20 54
	d	08 06	11 53	16 55	20 57
Ffairfach	d	08 08	11 55	16 57	20 59
Llandybie	d	08x15	12x02	17x05	21x07
Ammanford	d	08x20	12x07	17x09	21x11
Pantyffynnon	d	08 23	12 10	17 12	21 14
Pontarddulais	d	08x30	12x17	17x19	21x21
Llangennech	d	08x34	12x21	17x24	21x26
Bynea	d	08x37	12x24	17x27	21x29
Llanelli	a	08 42	12 29	17 32	21 34
Gowerton	a	08x53		17x51	21x47
Swansea	a	09 08	13 01	18 10	22 10

When events are being held at the Millenium Stadium,
services are subject to alteration. Please check times before travelling.

Table 129

Sundays
until 1 January

Shrewsbury - Swansea

HEART OF WALES LINE

Route Diagram - see first Page of Table 129

		AW ◇	AW ◇
Shrewsbury	d	12 07	16 18
Church Stretton	d	12 25	16 36
Craven Arms	d	12 36	16 47
Broome	d	12x42	16x53
Hopton Heath	d	12x46	16x57
Bucknell	d	12x51	17x02
Knighton	a	12 58	17 08
	d	13 00	17 11
Knucklas	d	13x06	17x16
Llangynllo	d	13x14	17x24
Llanbister Road	d	13x19	17x29
Dolau	d	13x25	17x35
Pen-y-bont	d	13x29	17x40
Llandrindod	a	13 38	17 49
	d	13 41	17 54
Builth Road	d	13x50	18x04
Cilmeri	d	13x54	18x07
Garth (Powys)	d	13x59	18x13
Llangammarch	d	14x03	18x17
Llanwrtyd	a	14 09	18 23
	d	14 12	18 25
Sugar Loaf	d	14x18	18x32
Cynghordy	d	14x25	18x39
Llandovery	a	14 35	18 48
	d	14 37	18 51
Llanwrda	d	14x43	18x57
Llangadog	d	14x47	19x01
Llandeilo	a	14 56	19 10
	d	14 59	19 12
Ffairfach	d	15 01	19 15
Llandybie	d	15x09	19x22
Ammanford	d	15x13	19x27
Pantyffynnon	d	15 16	19 30
Pontarddulais	d	15x23	19x37
Llangennech	d	15x28	19x41
Bynea	d	15x31	19x45
Llanelli	a	15 36	19 50
Gowerton	a		20x02
Swansea	a	16 04	20 16

Sundays
8 January to 25 March

		AW ◇ A	AW ◇ B	AW ◇ A	AW ◇ B
Shrewsbury	d	12 07	12 07	16 18	16 18
Church Stretton	d	12 25	12 25	16 36	16 36
Craven Arms	d	12 36	12 36	16 47	16 47
Broome	d	12x42	12x42	16x53	16x53
Hopton Heath	d	12x46	12x46	16x57	16x57
Bucknell	d	12x51	12x51	17x02	17x02
Knighton	a	12 58	12 58	17 08	17 08
	d	13 00	13 00	17 11	17 11
Knucklas	d	13x06	13x06	17x16	17x16
Llangynllo	d	13x14	13x14	17x24	17x24
Llanbister Road	d	13x19	13x19	17x29	17x29
Dolau	d	13x25	13x25	17x35	17x35
Pen-y-bont	d	13x29	13x29	17x40	17x40
Llandrindod	a	13 38	13 38	17 49	17 49
	d	13 41	13 41	17 54	17 54
Builth Road	d	13x50	13x50	18x04	18x04
Cilmeri	d	13x54	13x54	18x07	18x07
Garth (Powys)	d	13x59	13x59	18x13	18x13
Llangammarch	d	14x03	14x03	18x17	18x17
Llanwrtyd	a	14 09	14 09	18 23	18 23
	d	14 12	14 12	18 25	18 25
Sugar Loaf	d	14x18	14x18	18x32	18x32
Cynghordy	d	14x25	14x25	18x39	18x39
Llandovery	a	14 35	14 35	18 48	18 48
	d	14 37	14 37	18 51	18 51
Llanwrda	d	14x43	14x43	18x57	18x57
Llangadog	d	14x47	14x47	19x01	19x01
Llandeilo	a	14 56	14 56	19 10	19 10
	d	14 59	14 59	19 12	19 12
Ffairfach	d	15 01	15 01	19 15	19 15
Llandybie	d	15x09	15x09	19x22	19x22
Ammanford	d	15x13	15x13	19x27	19x27
Pantyffynnon	d	15 16	15 16	19 30	19 30
Pontarddulais	d	15x23	15x23	19x37	19x37
Llangennech	d	15x28	15x28	19x41	19x41
Bynea	d	15x31	15x31	19x45	19x45
Llanelli	a	15 36	15 36	19 50	19 50
Gowerton	a			20x02	20x02
Swansea	a	16 04	16 08	20 16	20 19

A from 19 February until 25 March **B** from 8 January until 12 February

When events are being held at the Millenium Stadium,
services are subject to alteration. Please check times before travelling.

Table 129

Sundays
from 1 April

Shrewsbury - Swansea

HEART OF WALES LINE

Route Diagram - see first Page of Table 129

		AW ◇	AW ◇
Shrewsbury	d	12 07	16 18
Church Stretton	d	12 25	16 36
Craven Arms	d	12 36	16 47
Broome	d	12x42	16x53
Hopton Heath	d	12x46	16x57
Bucknell	d	12x51	17x02
Knighton	a	12 58	17 08
	d	13 00	17 11
Knucklas	d	13x06	17x16
Llangynllo	d	13x14	17x24
Llanbister Road	d	13x19	17x29
Dolau	d	13x25	17x35
Pen-y-bont	d	13x29	17x40
Llandrindod	a	13 38	17 49
	d	13 41	17 54
Builth Road	d	13x50	18x04
Cilmeri	d	13x54	18x07
Garth (Powys)	d	13x59	18x13
Llangammarch	d	14x03	18x17
Llanwrtyd	a	14 09	18 23
	d	14 12	18 25
Sugar Loaf	d	14x18	18x32
Cynghordy	d	14x25	18x39
Llandovery	a	14 35	18 48
	d	14 37	18 51
Llanwrda	d	14x43	18x57
Llangadog	d	14x47	19x01
Llandeilo	a	14 56	19 10
	d	14 59	19 12
Ffairfach	d	15 01	19 15
Llandybie	d	15x09	19x22
Ammanford	d	15x13	19x27
Pantyffynnon	d	15 16	19 30
Pontarddulais	d	15x23	19x37
Llangennech	d	15x28	19x41
Bynea	d	15x31	19x45
Llanelli	a	15 36	19 50
Gowerton	a		20x02
Swansea	a	16 04	20 16

When events are being held at the Millenium Stadium,
services are subject to alteration. Please check times before travelling.

Network Diagram for Table 130

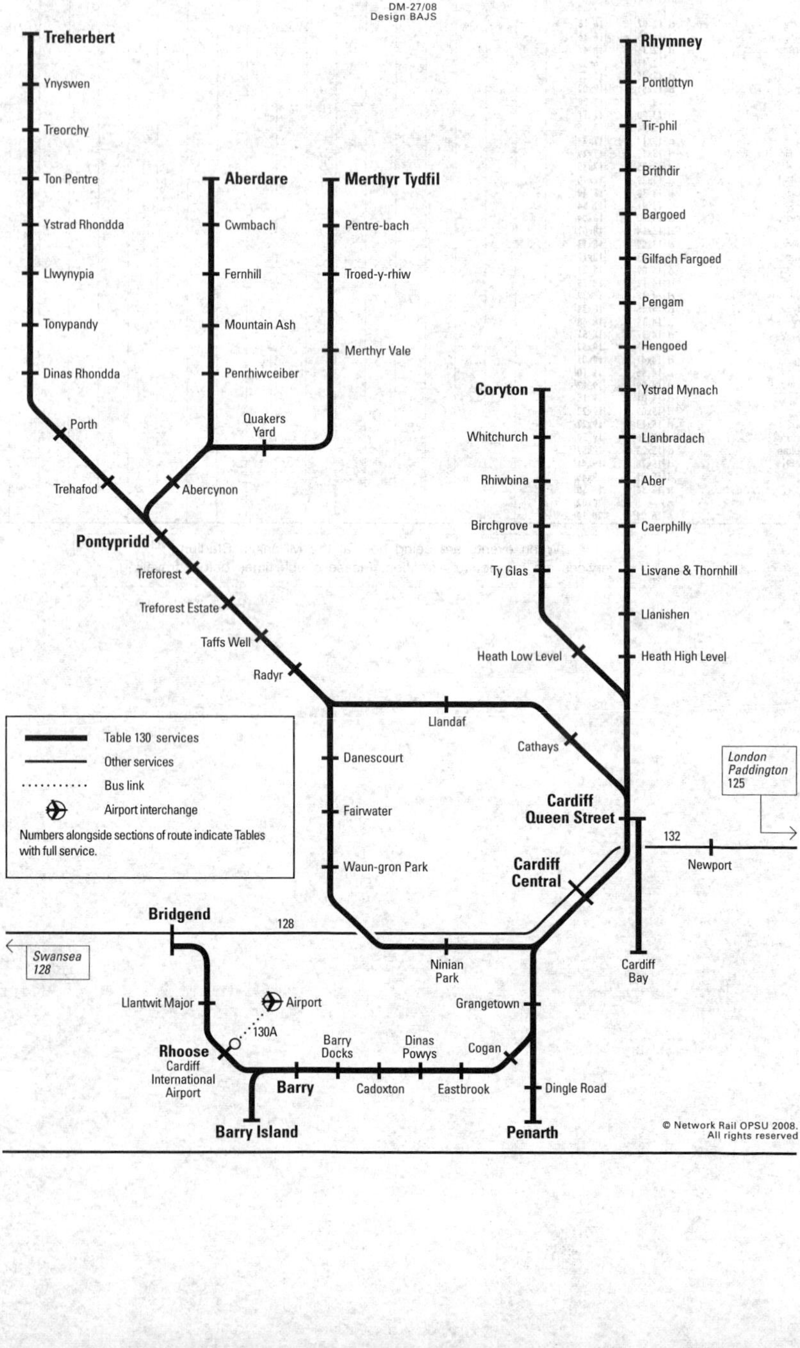

Treherbert, Aberdare, Merthyr, Pontypridd, Rhymney and Coryton - Cardiff, Penarth, Barry, Barry Island and Bridgend

Network Diagram - see first Page of Table 130

Miles	Miles	Miles	Miles	Miles			AW MX 🚌	AW MX	AW	AW	AW	AW	AW	AW	AW		AW	AW	AW	AW	AW	AW	AW	AW	AW
0	—	—	—	—	**Treherbert**	d													05 47						
0½	—	—	—	—	Ynyswen	d													05 49						
1¼	—	—	—	—	Treorchy	d													05 51						
2¾	—	—	—	—	Ton Pentre	d													05 53						
3¼	—	—	—	—	Ystrad Rhondda	a													05 56						
—	—	—	—	—		d													05 58						
4½	—	—	—	—	Llwynypia	d													06 00						
5½	—	—	—	—	Tonypandy	d													06 03						
6	—	—	—	—	Dinas Rhondda	d													06 05						
7½	—	—	—	—	Porth	a													06 08						
—	—	—	—	—		d													06 09						
8¾	—	—	—	—	Trehafod	d													06 12						
—	—	0	—	—	**Merthyr Tydfil**	d																			
—	—	1½	—	—	Pentre-bach	d																			
—	—	2¾	—	—	Troed Y Rhiw	d																			
—	—	4½	—	—	Merthyr Vale	a																			
—	—	—	—	—		d																			
—	—	6¾	—	—	Quakers Yard	d																			
—	—	—	—	0	**Aberdare** 3	d																			
—	—	—	—	1½	Cwmbach	d																			
—	—	—	—	2¾	Fernhill	d																			
—	—	—	—	3¾	Mountain Ash	a																			
—	—	—	—	—		d																			
—	—	—	—	5	Penrhiwceiber	d																			
—	—	8¼	—	7¾	Abercynon	d																			
10¾	—	11½	—	11	**Pontypridd** 3	a													06 17						
—	—	—	—	—		d						05 24							06 18						
11½	—	—	—	—	Trefforest	d						05 27							06 21						
14	—	—	—	—	Trefforest Estate	d						05 31													
16¼	—	—	—	—	Taffs Well 3	d						05 34							06 28						
18¼	—	—	0	—	Radyr 3	a						05 37							06 31						
—	—	—	—	—		d		23p10				05 37							06 31						
—	—	—	1½	—	Danescourt	d																			
—	—	—	2	—	Fairwater	d																			
—	—	—	2¼	—	Waun-gron Park	d																			
—	—	—	3¾	—	Ninian Park	d																			
19¼	—	—	—	—	Llandaf	d		23p12				05 40							06 34						
21¾	—	—	—	—	Cathays	d		23p16				05 45							06 39						
—	0	—	—	—	**Rhymney** 3	d																			06 10
—	1	—	—	—	Pontlottyn	d																			06 13
—	3½	—	—	—	Tir-phil	d																			06 17
—	4½	—	—	—	Brithdir	d																			06 20
—	6	—	—	—	Bargoed	a																			06 23
—	—	—	—	—		d																			06 27
—	6½	—	—	—	Gilfach Fargoed	d																			06 29
—	7½	—	—	—	Pengam	d																			06 32
—	9¼	—	—	—	Hengoed	d																			06 35
—	10½	—	—	—	Ystrad Mynach 3	d																			06 38
—	13	—	—	—	Llanbradach	d																			06 43
—	15	—	—	—	Aber	d																			06 47
—	15¾	—	—	—	Caerphilly 3	d											06 10								06 50
—	18¼	—	—	—	Lisvane & Thornhill	d											06 14								06 54
—	19¼	—	—	—	Llanishen	d											06 16								06 56
—	20¼	—	—	—	Heath High Level	d											06 19								06 59
—	—	0	—	—	**Coryton**	d																		06 45	
—	—	0½	—	—	Whitchurch (Cardiff)	d																		06 46	
—	—	0¾	—	—	Rhiwbina	d																		06 48	
—	—	1¼	—	—	Birchgrove	d																		06 50	
—	—	1½	—	—	Ty Glas	d																		06 51	
—	—	2¼	—	—	Heath Low Level	d																		06 54	
22½	22¾	4¾	—	—	**Cardiff Queen Street** 3	a		23p20				05 49					06 25		06 42					06 59	07 04
—	—	—	—	—		d		23p20				05 51					06 26	06 36	06 43	06 48		07 00		07 01	07 06
—	—	5¾	—	—	**Cardiff Bay**	a												06 40		06 52		07 04			
23	23¼	—	4¾	—	**Cardiff Central** 7	a		23p25				05 54					06 29		06 48					07 04	07 09
—	—	—	—	—		d		23p30	05 20	05 41	05 46	05 55	06 16	06 25	06 36		06 41				06 55		07 01		07 10
24	24¼	—	—	—	Grangetown	d		23p34	05 24	05 45	05 50	05 59	06 20	06 29	06 40		06 45				06 59		07 05		07 14
—	26¾	—	—	—	Dingle Road	d					05 54		06 24		06 44								07 11		
—	27	—	—	—	**Penarth**	a					05 59		06 29		06 49								07 16		
25¾	—	—	—	—	Cogan	d		23p37	05 28	05 48		06 03		06 33			06 48				07 03				07 18
26½	—	—	—	—	Eastbrook	d		23p40	05 30	05 51		06 05		06 35			06 51				07 05				07 20
27½	—	—	—	—	Dinas Powys	d		23p42	05 32	05 53		06 07		06 37			06 53				07 07				07 22
29½	—	—	—	—	Cadoxton	d		23p46	05 37	05 57		06 12		06 42			06 57				07 12				07 27
30¼	—	—	—	—	Barry Docks	d		23p49	05 40	06 00		06 15		06 45			07 00				07 15				07 30
31½	—	0	—	—	**Barry** 3	d	23p15	23p54	05 44	06 05		06 19		06 49			07 05				07 19				07 34
32¼	—	—	—	—	**Barry Island**	a		00 01	05 50			06 25		06 55							07 25				07 40
—	—	3¼	—	—	Rhoose Cardiff Int Airport ✈	d	23p30			06 12							07 12								
—	—	9¾	—	—	Llantwit Major	d	23p45			06 22							07 22								
—	—	19	—	—	**Bridgend**	a	00 10			06 39							07 39								

When events are being held at the Millenium Stadium,
services are subject to alteration. Please check times before travelling.

Treherbert, Aberdare, Merthyr, Pontypridd, Rhymney and Coryton - Cardiff, Penarth, Barry, Barry Island and Bridgend

Network Diagram - see first Page of Table 130

		AW	AW	AW	AW	AW	AW	AW	AW	AW	AW	AW	AW	AW	AW	AW	AW	AW	AW	AW	AW	AW
Treherbert	d	06 17										06 47										07 17
Ynyswen	d	06 19										06 49										07 19
Treorchy	d	06 21										06 51										07 21
Ton Pentre	d	06 23										06 53										07 23
Ystrad Rhondda	a	06 26										06 56										07 26
	d	06 28										06 58										07 28
Llwynypia	d	06 30										07 00										07 30
Tonypandy	d	06 33										07 03										07 33
Dinas Rhondda	d	06 35										07 05										07 35
Porth	a	06 38										07 08										07 38
	d	06 39										07 09										07 39
Trehafod	d	06 42										07 12										07 42
Merthyr Tydfil	d								06 38										07 08			
Pentre-bach	d								06 42										07 12			
Troed Y Rhiw	d								06 45										07 15			
Merthyr Vale	a								06 48										07 18			
	d								06 50										07 20			
Quakers Yard	d								06 55										07 25			
Aberdare ■	d				06 22										06 52							
Cwmbach	d				06 25										06 55							
Fernhill	d				06 28										06 58							
Mountain Ash	a				06 31										07 01							
	d				06 34										07 04							
Penrhiwceiber	d				06 37										07 07							
Abercynon	d				06 43				06 59						07 13				07 29			
Pontypridd ■	a	06 47			06 52				07 07			07 17			07 22				07 37			07 47
	d	06 48			06 54				07 09			07 18			07 24				07 39			07 48
Trefforest	d	06 51			06 57				07 12			07 21			07 27				07 42			07 51
Trefforest Estate	d								07 16										07 46			
Taffs Well ■	d	06 58	06 53		07 04				07 20			07 28			07 34				07 50			07 58
Radyr ■	a	07 01	06 56		07 07				07 23			07 31			07 37				07 53			08 01
	d	07 01	07 04		07 07				07 23			07 31	07 34		07 37				07 53			08 01
Danescourt	d		07 08										07 38									
Fairwater	d		07 10										07 40									
Waun-gron Park	d		07 12										07 42									
Ninian Park	d		07 15										07 45									
Llandaf	d	07 04			07 10				07 26			07 34			07 40				07 56			08 04
Cathays	d	07 09			07 15				07 31			07 39			07 45				08 01			08 09
Rhymney ■	d					06 34										07 02						
Pontlottyn	d					06 37										07 05						
Tir-phil	d					06 41										07 09						
Brithdir	d					06 44										07 12						
Bargoed	a					06 47										07 15						
	d					06 48					07 02					07 17				07 32		
Gilfach Fargoed	d										07 04					07 19						
Pengam	d					06 52					07 07					07 22				07 37		
Hengoed	d					06 56					07 10					07 25				07 40		
Ystrad Mynach ■	d					06 58					07 13					07 28				07 43		
Llanbradach	d					07 03					07 18					07 33				07 48		
Aber	d					07 07					07 22					07 37				07 52		
Caerphilly ■	d					07 10					07 25					07 40				07 55		
Lisvane & Thornhill	d					07 14					07 29					07 44				07 59		
Llanishen	d					07 16					07 31					07 46				08 01		
Heath High Level	d					07 19					07 34					07 49				08 04		
Coryton	d							07 15									07 45					
Whitchurch (Cardiff)	d							07 16									07 46					
Rhiwbina	d							07 18									07 48					
Birchgrove	d							07 20									07 50					
Ty Glas	d							07 21									07 51					
Heath Low Level	d							07 24									07 54					
Cardiff Queen Street ■	a	07 12			07 19	07 24		07 29	07 34		07 39	07 44			07 49	07 54	07 59		08 04	08 09		08 14
	d	07 13		07 12	07 21	07 26	07 24	07 31	07 36	07 36	07 41	07 46		07 48	07 51	07 56	08 01	08 00	08 06	08 11	08 12	08 16
Cardiff Bay	a			07 16			07 28			07 40				07 52				08 04			08 16	
Cardiff Central ■	a	07 16	07 20		07 24	07 29		07 34	07 39		07 44	07 52	07 50		07 54	07 59	08 04		08 09	08 14		08 22
	d	07 16			07 25	07 31			07 41		07 46				07 55	08 01			08 10	08 16		
Grangetown	d	07 20			07 29	07 35			07 45		07 50				07 59	08 05			08 14	08 20		
Dingle Road	d	07 26				07 41					07 56					08 11				08 26		
Penarth	a	07 31				07 46					08 01					08 16				08 31		
Cogan	d				07 33				07 48						08 03				08 18			
Eastbrook	d				07 35				07 51						08 05				08 20			
Dinas Powys	d				07 37				07 53						08 07				08 22			
Cadoxton	d				07 42				07 57						08 12				08 27			
Barry Docks	d				07 45				08 00						08 15				08 30			
Barry ■	d				07 49				08 05						08 19				08 34			
Barry Island	a				07 55										08 25				08 40			
Rhoose Cardiff Int Airport ✈	d								08 12													
Llantwit Major	d								08 22													
Bridgend	a								08 39													

When events are being held at the Millenium Stadium, services are subject to alteration. Please check times before travelling.

Treherbert, Aberdare, Merthyr, Pontypridd, Rhymney and Coryton - Cardiff, Penarth, Barry, Barry Island and Bridgend

Network Diagram - see first Page of Table 130

		AW	AW	AW	AW	AW	AW	AW	AW	AW	AW	AW	AW	AW	AW	AW	AW	AW	AW	AW	AW	AW	AW
Treherbert	d									07 45										08 17			
Ynyswen	d									07 47										08 19			
Treorchy	d									07 49										08 21			
Ton Pentre	d									07 51										08 23			
Ystrad Rhondda	a									07 54										08 26			
	d									07 58										08 28			
Llwynypia	d									08 00										08 30			
Tonypandy	d									08 03										08 33			
Dinas Rhondda	d									08 05										08 35			
Porth	a									08 08										08 38			
	d									08 09										08 39			
Trehafod	d									08 12										08 42			
Merthyr Tydfil	d						07 38										08 08						
Pentre-bach	d						07 42										08 12						
Troed Y Rhiw	d						07 45										08 15						
Merthyr Vale	a						07 48										08 18						
	d						07 50										08 20						
Quakers Yard	d						07 55										08 25						
Aberdare 3	d		07 22										07 52									08 22	
Cwmbach	d		07 25										07 55									08 25	
Fernhill	d		07 28										07 58									08 28	
Mountain Ash	a		07 31										08 01									08 31	
	d		07 34										08 04									08 34	
Penrhiwceiber	d		07 37										08 07									08 37	
Abercynon	d		07 43				07 59						08 13				08 29					08 43	
Pontypridd 3	a		07 52				08 07			08 17			08 22				08 37			08 47		08 52	
	d		07 54				08 09			08 18			08 24				08 39			08 48		08 54	
Trefforest	d		07 57				08 12			08 21			08 27				08 42			08 51		08 57	
Trefforest Estate	d						08 16										08 46						
Taffs Well 3	d		08 04				08 20			08 28			08 34				08 50			08 58		09 04	
Radyr 3	a		08 07				08 23			08 31			08 37				08 53			09 01		09 07	
	d	08 04	08 07				08 23			08 31	08 34		08 37				08 53			09 01	09 04	09 07	
Danescourt	d	08 08									08 38										09 08		
Fairwater	d	08 10									08 40										09 10		
Waun-gron Park	d	08 12									08 42										09 12		
Ninian Park	d	08 15									08 45										09 15		
Llandaf	d		08 10				08 26			08 34			08 40				08 56			09 04		09 10	
Cathays	d		08 15				08 31			08 39			08 45				09 01			09 09		09 15	
Rhymney 3	d			07 24					07 44														08 30
Pontlottyn	d			07 27					07 47														08 33
Tir-phil	d			07 31					07 51														08 37
Brithdir	d			07 34					07 54														08 40
Bargoed	a			07 37					08 00														08 44
	d			07 45					08 02					08 17				08 32					08 47
Gilfach Fargoed	d			07 47										08 19									
Pengam	d			07 50					08 07					08 22				08 37					08 52
Hengoed	d			07 54					08 10					08 25				08 40					08 55
Ystrad Mynach 3	d			07 57					08 13					08 28				08 43					08 58
Llanbradach	d			08 02					08 18					08 33				08 48					09 03
Aber	d			08 07					08 22					08 37				08 52					09 07
Caerphilly 3	d			08 10					08 25					08 40				08 55					09 10
Lisvane & Thornhill	d			08 14					08 29					08 44				08 59					09 14
Llanishen	d			08 16					08 31					08 46				09 01					09 16
Heath High Level	d			08 19					08 34					08 49				09 04					09 19
Coryton	d					08 15									08 45								
Whitchurch (Cardiff)	d					08 16									08 46								
Rhiwbina	d					08 18									08 48								
Birchgrove	d					08 20									08 50								
Ty Glas	d					08 21									08 51								
Heath Low Level	d					08 24									08 54								
Cardiff Queen Street 3	a		08 19	08 24		08 29	08 34		08 39	08 44			08 49	08 54	08 59		09 04	09 09		09 14		09 19	09 24
	d		08 21	08 26	08 24	08 31	08 36	08 36	08 41	08 46		08 48	08 51	08 56	09 01	09 00	09 06	09 11	09 12	09 16		09 21	09 26
Cardiff Bay	a				08 28			08 40				08 52				09 04			09 16				
Cardiff Central 7	a	08 20	08 24	08 29		08 34	08 39		08 47	08 52	08 50		08 54	08 59	09 04		09 09	09 14		09 22	09 20	09 24	09 29
	d		08 25	08 31			08 41						08 55	09 01			09 10	09 16				09 25	09 31
Grangetown	d		08 29	08 35			08 45						08 59	09 05			09 14	09 20				09 29	09 35
Dingle Road	d			08 41										09 11				09 26					09 41
Penarth	a			08 46										09 16				09 31					09 46
Cogan	d		08 33				08 48						09 03				09 18					09 33	
Eastbrook	d		08 35				08 51						09 05				09 20					09 35	
Dinas Powys	d		08 37				08 53						09 07				09 22					09 37	
Cadoxton	d		08 42				08 57						09 12				09 27					09 42	
Barry Docks	d		08 45				08 59						09 15				09 30					09 45	
Barry 3	d		08 49				09 03						09 19				09 34					09 49	
Barry Island	a		08 55										09 25				09 40					09 55	
Rhoose Cardiff Int Airport ✈	d						09 10																
Llantwit Major	d						09 19																
Bridgend	a						09 36																

When events are being held at the Millenium Stadium, services are subject to alteration. Please check times before travelling.

Table 130

Mondays to Fridays

Treherbert, Aberdare, Merthyr, Pontypridd, Rhymney and Coryton - Cardiff, Penarth, Barry, Barry Island and Bridgend

Network Diagram - see first Page of Table 130

Station		AW	AW	AW	AW	AW	AW	AW	AW	AW	AW	AW	AW	AW	AW	AW	AW	AW	AW	AW	AW	AW
Treherbert	d						08 47										09 17					
Ynyswen	d						08 49										09 19					
Treorchy	d						08 51										09 21					
Ton Pentre	d						08 53										09 23					
Ystrad Rhondda	a						08 56										09 26					
	d						08 58										09 28					
Llwynypia	d						09 00										09 30					
Tonypandy	d						09 03										09 33					
Dinas Rhondda	d						09 05										09 35					
Porth	a						09 08										09 38					
	d						09 09										09 39					
Trehafod	d						09 12										09 42					
Merthyr Tydfil	d			08 38									09 08									
Pentre-bach	d			08 42									09 12									
Troed Y Rhiw	d			08 45									09 15									
Merthyr Vale	a			08 48									09 18									
	d			08 50									09 20									
Quakers Yard	d			08 55									09 25									
Aberdare [3]	d									08 52									09 22			
Cwmbach	d									08 55									09 25			
Fernhill	d									08 58									09 28			
Mountain Ash	a									09 01									09 31			
	d									09 04									09 34			
Penrhiwceiber	d									09 07									09 37			
Abercynon	d			08 59						09 13			09 29						09 43			
Pontypridd [3]	a			09 07			09 17			09 22			09 37				09 47		09 52			
	d			09 09			09 18			09 24			09 39				09 48		09 54			
Trefforest	d			09 12			09 21			09 27			09 42				09 51		09 57			
Trefforest Estate	d			09 16									09 46									
Taffs Well [3]	d			09 20			09 28			09 34			09 50				09 58		10 04			
Radyr [3]	a			09 23			09 31			09 37			09 53				10 01		10 07			
	d			09 23			09 31	09 34		09 37			09 53				10 01	10 04	10 07			
Danescourt	d							09 38										10 08				
Fairwater	d							09 40										10 10				
Waun-gron Park	d							09 42										10 12				
Ninian Park	d							09 45										10 15				
Llandaf	d			09 26			09 34			09 40			09 56				10 04		10 10			
Cathays	d			09 31			09 39			09 45			10 01				10 09		10 15			
Rhymney [3]	d																			09 29		
Pontlottyn	d																			09 32		
Tir-phil	d																			09 36		
Brithdir	d																			09 39		
Bargoed	a																			09 42		
	d					09 02					09 17				09 32					09 47		
Gilfach Fargoed	d										09 19											
Pengam	d					09 07					09 22				09 37					09 52		
Hengoed	d					09 10					09 25				09 40					09 55		
Ystrad Mynach [3]	d					09 13					09 28				09 43					09 58		
Llanbradach	d					09 18					09 33				09 48					10 03		
Aber	d					09 22					09 37				09 52					10 07		
Caerphilly [3]	d					09 25					09 40				09 55					10 10		
Lisvane & Thornhill	d					09 29					09 44				09 59					10 14		
Llanishen	d					09 31					09 46				10 01					10 16		
Heath High Level	d					09 34					09 49				10 04					10 19		
Coryton	d		09 15									09 45										10 15
Whitchurch (Cardiff)	d		09 16									09 46										10 16
Rhiwbina	d		09 18									09 48										10 18
Birchgrove	d		09 20									09 50										10 20
Ty Glas	d		09 21									09 51										10 21
Heath Low Level	d		09 24									09 54										10 24
Cardiff Queen Street [3]	a		09 29	09 34		09 39	09 44			09 49	09 54	09 59		10 04	10 09		10 14		10 19	10 24		10 29
	d	09 24	09 31	09 36	09 36	09 41	09 46		09 48	09 51	09 56	10 01	10 00	10 06	10 11	10 12	10 16		10 21	10 26	10 24	10 31
Cardiff Bay	a	09 28			09 40				09 52				10 04			10 16					10 28	
Cardiff Central [7]	a		09 34	09 39		09 44	09 52	09 50		09 54	09 59	10 04		10 09	10 14		10 22	10 20	10 24	10 29		10 34
	d			09 41		09 46				09 55	10 01			10 10	10 16				10 25	10 31		
Grangetown	d			09 45		09 50				09 59	10 05			10 14	10 20				10 29	10 35		
Dingle Road	d					09 56					10 11				10 26					10 41		
Penarth	a					10 02					10 16				10 31					10 46		
Cogan	d			09 48						10 03				10 18					10 33			
Eastbrook	d			09 51						10 05				10 20					10 35			
Dinas Powys	d			09 53						10 07				10 22					10 37			
Cadoxton	d			09 57						10 12				10 27					10 42			
Barry Docks	d			09 59						10 15				10 30					10 45			
Barry [3]	d			10 03						10 19				10 34					10 49			
Barry Island	a									10 25				10 40					10 55			
Rhoose Cardiff Int Airport ✈	d			10 10																		
Llantwit Major	d			10 19																		
Bridgend	a			10 36																		

When events are being held at the Millenium Stadium, services are subject to alteration. Please check times before travelling.

Treherbert, Aberdare, Merthyr, Pontypridd, Rhymney and Coryton - Cardiff, Penarth, Barry, Barry Island and Bridgend

Network Diagram - see first Page of Table 130

		AW	AW	AW	AW	AW	AW	AW	AW		AW	AW	AW	AW	AW	AW	AW	AW	AW		AW	AW	AW	AW	AW
Treherbert	d				09 47																10 17				
Ynyswen	d				09 49																10 19				
Treorchy	d				09 51																10 21				
Ton Pentre	d				09 53																10 23				
Ystrad Rhondda	a				09 56																10 26				
	d				09 58																10 28				
Llwynypia	d				10 00																10 30				
Tonypandy	d				10 03																10 33				
Dinas Rhondda	d				10 05																10 35				
Porth	a				10 08																10 38				
	d				10 09																10 52				
Trehafod	d				10 12																10 55				
Merthyr Tydfil	d	09 38							10 04															10 38	
Pentre-bach	d	09 42							10 08															10 42	
Troed Y Rhiw	d	09 45							10 11															10 45	
Merthyr Vale	a	09 48							10 14															10 48	
	d	09 50							10 16															10 50	
Quakers Yard	d	09 55							10 22															10 55	
Aberdare 3	d							09 52										10 22							
Cwmbach	d							09 55										10 25							
Fernhill	d							09 58										10 28							
Mountain Ash	a							10 01										10 31							
	d							10 04										10 34							
Penrhiwceiber	d							10 07										10 37							
Abercynon	d	09 59						10 13	10 26									10 43						10 59	
Pontypridd 3	a	10 07			10 17			10 22	10 32									10 52			11 00			11 07	
	d	10 09			10 18			10 24						10 39				10 54			11 04			11 09	
Trefforest	d	10 12			10 21			10 27						10 42				10 57			11 07			11 12	
Trefforest Estate	d	10 16																						11 16	
Taffs Well 3	d	10 20			10 28			10 34						10 50				11 04			11 13			11 20	
Radyr 3	a	10 23			10 31			10 37						10 53				11 07			11 17			11 23	
	d	10 23			10 31	10 34		10 37						10 53		11 04		11 07			11 17			11 23	
Danescourt	d					10 38										11 08									
Fairwater	d					10 40										11 10									
Waun-gron Park	d					10 42										11 12									
Ninian Park	d					10 45										11 15									
Llandaf	d	10 26			10 34			10 40						10 56				11 10						11 26	
Cathays	d	10 31			10 39			10 45						11 01				11 15						11 31	
Rhymney 3	d																		10 29						
Pontlottyn	d																		10 32						
Tir-phil	d																		10 36						
Brithdir	d																		10 39						
Bargoed	a																		10 42						
	d			10 02							10 17				10 32				10 47						
Gilfach Fargoed	d										10 19														
Pengam	d			10 07							10 22				10 37				10 52						
Hengoed	d			10 10							10 25				10 40				10 55						
Ystrad Mynach 3	d			10 13							10 28				10 43				10 58						
Llanbradach	d			10 18							10 33				10 48				11 03						
Aber	d			10 22							10 37				10 52				11 07						
Caerphilly 3	d			10 25							10 40				10 55				11 10						
Lisvane & Thornhill	d			10 29							10 44				10 59				11 14						
Llanishen	d			10 31							10 46				11 01				11 16						
Heath High Level	d			10 34							10 49				11 04				11 19						
Coryton	d											10 45											11 15		
Whitchurch (Cardiff)	d											10 46											11 16		
Rhiwbina	d											10 48											11 18		
Birchgrove	d											10 50											11 20		
Ty Glas	d											10 51											11 21		
Heath Low Level	d											10 54											11 24		
Cardiff Queen Street 3	a	10 34		10 39	10 44			10 49			10 54	10 59		11 04	11 09			11 19	11 24				11 29	11 34	
	d	10 36	10 36	10 41	10 46		10 48	10 51			10 56	11 01	11 00	11 06	11 11		11 12	11 21	11 26			11 24	11 31	11 36	11 36
Cardiff Bay	a		10 40				10 52						11 04				11 16					11 28			11 40
Cardiff Central 7	a	10 39		10 44	10 52	10 50		10 54			10 59	11 04		11 09	11 14	11 20		11 24	11 29		11 34		11 34	11 39	
	d	10 41		10 46				10 55			11 01			11 10	11 16			11 25	11 31					11 41	
Grangetown	d	10 45		10 50				10 59			11 05			11 14	11 20			11 29	11 35					11 45	
Dingle Road	d			10 56							11 11				11 26				11 41						
Penarth	a			11 01							11 16				11 31				11 46						
Cogan	d	10 48						11 03						11 18				11 33						11 48	
Eastbrook	d	10 51						11 05						11 20				11 35						11 51	
Dinas Powys	d	10 53						11 07						11 22				11 37						11 53	
Cadoxton	d	10 57						11 12						11 27				11 42						11 57	
Barry Docks	d	11 00						11 15						11 30				11 45						12 00	
Barry 3	d	11 05						11 19						11 34				11 49						12 05	
Barry Island	a							11 25						11 40				11 55							
Rhoose Cardiff Int Airport ✈	d	11 12																						12 12	
Llantwit Major	d	11 22																						12 22	
Bridgend	a	11 39																						12 39	

When events are being held at the Millenium Stadium, services are subject to alteration. Please check times before travelling.

Table 130

Mondays to Fridays

Treherbert, Aberdare, Merthyr, Pontypridd, Rhymney and Coryton - Cardiff, Penarth, Barry, Barry Island and Bridgend

Network Diagram - see first Page of Table 130

		AW	AW	AW	AW		AW	AW	AW	AW	AW	AW	AW	AW	AW		AW	AW	AW	AW	AW	AW	AW	AW	AW
Treherbert	d		10 47											11 17										11 47	
Ynyswen	d		10 49											11 19										11 49	
Treorchy	d		10 51											11 21										11 51	
Ton Pentre	d		10 53											11 23										11 53	
Ystrad Rhondda	a		10 56											11 26										11 56	
	d		10 58											11 28										11 58	
Llwynypia	d		11 00											11 30										12 00	
Tonypandy	d		11 03											11 33										12 03	
Dinas Rhondda	d		11 05											11 35										12 05	
Porth	a		11 08											11 38										12 08	
	d		11 09											11 39										12 09	
Trehafod	d		11 12											11 42										12 12	
Merthyr Tydfil	d										11 08										11 38				
Pentre-bach	d										11 12										11 42				
Troed Y Rhiw	d										11 15										11 45				
Merthyr Vale	a										11 18										11 48				
	d										11 20										11 50				
Quakers Yard	d										11 25										11 55				
Aberdare 3	d						10 52										11 22								
Cwmbach	d						10 55										11 25								
Fernhill	d						10 58										11 28								
Mountain Ash	a						11 01										11 31								
	d						11 04										11 34								
Penrhiwceiber	d						11 07										11 37								
Abercynon	d						11 13				11 29						11 43				11 59				
Pontypridd 3	a		11 17				11 22				11 37			11 47			11 52				12 07			12 17	
	d		11 18				11 24				11 39			11 48			11 54				12 09			12 18	
Trefforest	d		11 21				11 27				11 42			11 51			11 57				12 12			12 21	
Trefforest Estate	d										11 46										12 16				
Taffs Well 3	d		11 28				11 34				11 50			11 58			12 04				12 20			12 28	
Radyr 3	a		11 31				11 37				11 53			12 01			12 07				12 23			12 31	
	d		11 31	11 34			11 37				11 53			12 01	12 04		12 07				12 23			12 31	12 34
Danescourt	d			11 38											12 08										12 38
Fairwater	d			11 40											12 10										12 40
Waun-gron Park	d			11 42											12 12										12 42
Ninian Park	d			11 45											12 15										12 45
Llandaf	d		11 34				11 40				11 56			12 04			12 10				12 26			12 34	
Cathays	d		11 39				11 45				12 01			12 09			12 15				12 31			12 39	
Rhymney 3	d																	11 29							
Pontlottyn	d																	11 32							
Tir-phil	d																	11 36							
Brithdir	d																	11 39							
Bargoed	a																	11 42							
	d	11 02						11 17				11 32						11 47					12 02		
Gilfach Fargoed	d							11 19																	
Pengam	d	11 07						11 22				11 37						11 52					12 07		
Hengoed	d	11 10						11 25				11 40						11 55					12 10		
Ystrad Mynach 3	d	11 13						11 28				11 43						11 58					12 13		
Llanbradach	d	11 18						11 33				11 48						12 03					12 18		
Aber	d	11 22						11 37				11 52						12 07					12 22		
Caerphilly 3	d	11 25						11 40				11 55						12 10					12 25		
Lisvane & Thornhill	d	11 29						11 44				11 59						12 14					12 29		
Llanishen	d	11 31						11 46				12 01						12 16					12 31		
Heath High Level	d	11 34						11 49				12 04						12 19					12 34		
Coryton	d								11 45											12 15					
Whitchurch (Cardiff)	d								11 46											12 16					
Rhiwbina	d								11 48											12 18					
Birchgrove	d								11 50											12 20					
Ty Glas	d								11 51											12 21					
Heath Low Level	d								11 54											12 24					
Cardiff Queen Street 3	a	11 39	11 44				11 49	11 54	11 59		12 04	12 09		12 14			12 19	12 24		12 29	12 34		12 39	12 44	
	d	11 41	11 46		11 48		11 51	11 56	12 01	12 00	12 06	12 11	12 12	12 16			12 21	12 26	12 24	12 31	12 36	12 36	12 41	12 46	
Cardiff Bay	a				11 52					12 04			12 16						12 28			12 40			
Cardiff Central 7	a	11 44	11 52	11 50			11 54	11 59	12 04		12 09	12 14		12 22	12 20		12 24	12 29		12 34	12 39		12 44	12 52	12 50
	d	11 46					11 55	12 01			12 10	12 16					12 25	12 31			12 41		12 46		
Grangetown	d	11 50					11 59	12 05			12 14	12 20					12 29	12 35			12 45		12 50		
Dingle Road	d	11 56						12 11				12 26						12 41					12 56		
Penarth	a	12 01						12 16				12 31						12 46					13 01		
Cogan	d						12 03				12 18						12 33				12 48				
Eastbrook	d						12 05				12 20						12 35				12 51				
Dinas Powys	d						12 07				12 22						12 37				12 53				
Cadoxton	d						12 12				12 27						12 42				12 57				
Barry Docks	d						12 15				12 30						12 45				13 00				
Barry 3	d						12 19				12 34						12 49				13 05				
Barry Island	a						12 25				12 40						12 55								
Rhoose Cardiff Int Airport ✈	d																				13 12				
Llantwit Major	d																				13 22				
Bridgend	a																				13 39				

When events are being held at the Millenium Stadium, services are subject to alteration. Please check times before travelling.

Treherbert, Aberdare, Merthyr, Pontypridd, Rhymney and Coryton - Cardiff, Penarth, Barry, Barry Island and Bridgend

Network Diagram - see first Page of Table 130

		AW	AW	AW	AW	AW	AW	AW	AW	AW	AW	AW	AW	AW	AW	AW	AW	AW	AW	AW	AW	AW
Treherbert	d									12 17									12 47			
Ynyswen	d									12 19									12 49			
Treorchy	d									12 21									12 51			
Ton Pentre	d									12 23									12 53			
Ystrad Rhondda	a									12 26									12 56			
	d									12 28									12 58			
Llwynypia	d									12 30									13 00			
Tonypandy	d									12 33									13 03			
Dinas Rhondda	d									12 35									13 05			
Porth	a									12 38									13 08			
	d									12 39									13 09			
Trehafod	d									12 42									13 12			
Merthyr Tydfil	d						12 08									12 38						
Pentre-bach	d						12 12									12 42						
Troed Y Rhiw	d						12 15									12 45						
Merthyr Vale	a						12 18									12 48						
	d						12 20									12 50						
Quakers Yard	d						12 25									12 55						
Aberdare [3]	d											12 22										12 52
Cwmbach	d											12 25										12 55
Fernhill	d											12 28										12 58
Mountain Ash	a											12 31										13 01
	d											12 34										13 04
Penrhiwceiber	d											12 37										13 07
Abercynon	d						12 29					12 43				12 59						13 13
Pontypridd [3]	a						12 37			12 48		12 52				13 07			13 17			13 22
	d						12 39			12 48		12 54				13 09			13 18			13 24
Trefforest	d						12 42			12 51		12 57				13 12			13 21			13 27
Trefforest Estate	d						12 46									13 16						
Taffs Well [3]	d						12 50			12 58		13 04				13 20			13 28			13 34
Radyr [3]	a						12 53			13 01		13 07				13 23			13 31			13 37
	d						12 53			13 01	13 04	13 07				13 23			13 31	13 34		13 37
Danescourt	d										13 08									13 38		
Fairwater	d										13 10									13 40		
Waun-gron Park	d										13 12									13 42		
Ninian Park	d										13 15									13 45		
Llandaf	d						12 56			13 04		13 10				13 26			13 34			13 40
Cathays	d						13 01			13 09		13 15				13 31			13 39			13 45
Rhymney [3]	d												12 29									
Pontlottyn	d												12 32									
Tir-phil	d												12 36									
Brithdir	d												12 39									
Bargoed	a												12 42									
	d			12 17				12 32					12 47					13 02				
Gilfach Fargoed	d			12 19																		
Pengam	d			12 22				12 37					12 52					13 07				
Hengoed	d			12 25				12 40					12 55					13 10				
Ystrad Mynach [3]	d			12 28				12 43					12 58					13 13				
Llanbradach	d			12 33				12 48					13 03					13 18				
Aber	d			12 37				12 52					13 07					13 22				
Caerphilly [3]	d			12 40				12 55					13 10					13 25				
Lisvane & Thornhill	d			12 44				12 59					13 14					13 29				
Llanishen	d			12 46				13 01					13 16					13 31				
Heath High Level	d			12 49				13 04					13 19					13 34				
Coryton	d				12 45										13 15							
Whitchurch (Cardiff)	d				12 46										13 16							
Rhiwbina	d				12 48										13 18							
Birchgrove	d				12 50										13 20							
Ty Glas	d				12 51										13 21							
Heath Low Level	d				12 54										13 24							
Cardiff Queen Street [3]	a			12 54	12 59		13 04	13 09		13 14		13 19	13 24		13 29	13 34		13 39	13 44			13 49
	d	12 48		12 56	13 01	13 00	13 06	13 11	13 12	13 16		13 21	13 26	13 24	13 31	13 36	13 36	13 41	13 46		13 48	13 51
Cardiff Bay	a	12 52				13 04			13 16					13 28			13 40				13 52	
Cardiff Central [7]	a			12 59	13 04		13 09	13 14		13 22	13 20	13 24	13 29		13 34	13 39		13 44	13 52	13 50		13 54
	d		12 55	13 01			13 10	13 16				13 25	13 31			13 41		13 46				13 55
Grangetown	d		12 59	13 05			13 14	13 20				13 29	13 35			13 45		13 50				13 59
Dingle Road	d			13 11				13 26					13 41					13 56				
Penarth	a			13 16				13 31					13 46					14 01				
Cogan	d		13 03				13 18					13 33				13 48						14 03
Eastbrook	d		13 05				13 20					13 35				13 51						14 05
Dinas Powys	d		13 07				13 22					13 37				13 53						14 07
Cadoxton	d		13 12				13 27					13 42				13 57						14 12
Barry Docks	d		13 15				13 30					13 45				14 00						14 15
Barry [3]	d		13 19				13 34					13 49				14 05						14 19
Barry Island	a		13 25				13 40					13 55										14 25
Rhoose Cardiff Int Airport ✈	d															14 12						
Llantwit Major	d															14 22						
Bridgend	a															14 39						

When events are being held at the Millenium Stadium, services are subject to alteration. Please check times before travelling.

Treherbert, Aberdare, Merthyr, Pontypridd, Rhymney and Coryton - Cardiff, Penarth, Barry, Barry Island and Bridgend

Network Diagram - see first Page of Table 130

		AW	AW	AW	AW	AW	AW		AW	AW	AW	AW	AW	AW	AW	AW	AW		AW	AW	AW	AW	AW	AW	AW
Treherbert	d								13 17										13 47						
Ynyswen	d								13 19										13 49						
Treorchy	d								13 21										13 51						
Ton Pentre	d								13 23										13 53						
Ystrad Rhondda	a								13 26										13 56						
	d								13 28										13 58						
Llwynypia	d								13 30										14 00						
Tonypandy	d								13 33										14 03						
Dinas Rhondda	d								13 35										14 05						
Porth	a								13 38										14 08						
	d								13 39										14 09						
Trehafod	d								13 42										14 12						
Merthyr Tydfil	d				13 08										13 38										
Pentre-bach	d				13 12										13 42										
Troed Y Rhiw	d				13 15										13 45										
Merthyr Vale	a				13 18										13 48										
	d				13 20										13 50										
Quakers Yard	d				13 25										13 55										
Aberdare 3	d																					13 52			
Cwmbach	d																					13 55			
Fernhill	d																					13 58			
Mountain Ash	a																					14 01			
	d																					14 04			
Penrhiwceiber	d																					14 07			
Abercynon	d				13 29						13 45				13 59							14 13			
Pontypridd 3	a				13 37				13 47		13 52				14 07				14 17			14 22			
	d				13 39				13 48		13 54				14 09				14 18			14 24			
Trefforest	d				13 42				13 51		13 57				14 12				14 21			14 27			
Trefforest Estate	d				13 46										14 16										
Taffs Well 3	d				13 50				13 58		14 04				14 20				14 28			14 34			
Radyr 3	a				13 53				14 01		14 07				14 23				14 31			14 37			
	d				13 53				14 01	14 04	14 07				14 23				14 31	14 34		14 37			
Danescourt	d									14 08										14 38					
Fairwater	d									14 10										14 40					
Waun-gron Park	d									14 12										14 42					
Ninian Park	d									14 15										14 45					
Llandaf	d				13 56				14 04		14 10				14 26				14 34			14 40			
Cathays	d				14 01				14 09		14 15				14 31				14 39			14 45			
Rhymney 3	d											13 29													
Pontlottyn	d											13 32													
Tir-phil	d											13 36													
Brithdir	d											13 39													
Bargoed	a											13 42													
	d	13 17				13 32						13 47					14 02						14 17		
Gilfach Fargoed	d	13 19																					14 19		
Pengam	d	13 22				13 37						13 52					14 07						14 22		
Hengoed	d	13 25				13 40						13 55					14 10						14 25		
Ystrad Mynach 3	d	13 28				13 43						13 58					14 13						14 28		
Llanbradach	d	13 33				13 48						14 03					14 18						14 33		
Aber	d	13 37				13 52						14 07					14 22						14 37		
Caerphilly 3	d	13 40				13 55						14 10					14 25						14 40		
Lisvane & Thornhill	d	13 44				13 59						14 14					14 29						14 44		
Llanishen	d	13 46				14 01						14 16					14 31						14 46		
Heath High Level	d	13 49				14 04						14 19					14 34						14 49		
Coryton	d		13 45											14 15										14 45	
Whitchurch (Cardiff)	d		13 46											14 16										14 46	
Rhiwbina	d		13 48											14 18										14 48	
Birchgrove	d		13 50											14 20										14 50	
Ty Glas	d		13 51											14 21										14 51	
Heath Low Level	d		13 54											14 24										14 54	
Cardiff Queen Street 3	a	13 54	13 59		14 04	14 09			14 14		14 19	14 24		14 29	14 34		14 39		14 44			14 49	14 54	14 59	
	d	13 56	14 01	14 00	14 06	14 11	14 12		14 16		14 21	14 26	14 24	14 31	14 36	14 36	14 41		14 46		14 48	14 51	14 56	15 01	15 00
Cardiff Bay	a			14 04			14 16						14 28			14 40					14 52				15 04
Cardiff Central 7	a	13 59	14 04		14 09	14 14			14 22	14 20	14 24	14 29		14 34	14 39		14 44		14 52	14 50		14 54	14 59	15 04	
	d	14 01			14 10	14 16					14 25	14 31			14 41		14 46					14 55	15 01		
Grangetown	d	14 05			14 14	14 20					14 29	14 35			14 45		14 50					14 59	15 05		
Dingle Road	d	14 11				14 26						14 41					14 56						15 11		
Penarth	a	14 16				14 31						14 46					15 01						15 16		
Cogan	d				14 18						14 33				14 48							15 03			
Eastbrook	d				14 20						14 35				14 51							15 05			
Dinas Powys	d				14 22						14 37				14 53							15 07			
Cadoxton	d				14 27						14 42				14 57							15 12			
Barry Docks	d				14 30						14 45				15 00							15 15			
Barry 3	d				14 34						14 49				15 05							15 19			
Barry Island	a				14 40						14 55											15 25			
Rhoose Cardiff Int Airport ✈	d														15 12										
Llantwit Major	d														15 22										
Bridgend	a														15 39										

When events are being held at the Millenium Stadium, services are subject to alteration. Please check times before travelling.

Treherbert, Aberdare, Merthyr, Pontypridd, Rhymney and Coryton - Cardiff, Penarth, Barry, Barry Island and Bridgend

Network Diagram - see first Page of Table 130

		AW	AW		AW	AW	AW	AW	AW	AW	AW	AW	AW		AW	AW	AW	AW	AW	AW	AW	AW	AW		AW
Treherbert	d								14 17							14 47									
Ynyswen	d								14 19							14 49									
Treorchy	d								14 21							14 51									
Ton Pentre	d								14 23							14 53									
Ystrad Rhondda	a								14 26							14 56									
	d								14 28							14 58									
Llwynypia	d								14 30							15 00									
Tonypandy	d								14 33							15 03									
Dinas Rhondda	d								14 35							15 05									
Porth	a								14 38							15 08									
	d								14 52							15 09									
Trehafod	d								14 55							15 12									
Merthyr Tydfil	d	14 08										14 38											15 08		
Pentre-bach	d	14 12										14 42											15 12		
Troed Y Rhiw	d	14 15										14 45											15 15		
Merthyr Vale	a	14 18										14 48											15 18		
	d	14 20										14 50											15 20		
Quakers Yard	d	14 25										14 55											15 25		
Aberdare 3	d						14 22												14 52						
Cwmbach	d						14 25												14 55						
Fernhill	d						14 28												14 58						
Mountain Ash	a						14 31												15 01						
	d						14 34												15 04						
Penrhiwceiber	d						14 37												15 07						
Abercynon	d	14 29					14 43					14 59							15 13				15 29		
Pontypridd 3	a	14 37					14 52		15 00			15 07				15 17			15 22				15 37		
	d	14 39					14 54		15 04			15 09				15 18			15 24				15 39		
Trefforest	d	14 42					14 57		15 07			15 12				15 21			15 27				15 42		
Trefforest Estate	d	14 46										15 16											15 46		
Taffs Well 3	d	14 50					15 04		15 13			15 20				15 28			15 34				15 50		
Radyr 3	a	14 53					15 07		15 17			15 23				15 31			15 37				15 53		
	d	14 53			15 04		15 07		15 17			15 23				15 31	15 34		15 37				15 53		
Danescourt	d				15 08												15 38								
Fairwater	d				15 10												15 40								
Waun-gron Park	d				15 12												15 42								
Ninian Park	d				15 15												15 45								
Llandaf	d	14 56					15 10					15 26				15 34			15 40				15 56		
Cathays	d	15 01					15 15					15 31				15 39			15 45				16 01		
Rhymney 3	d							14 29																	
Pontlottyn	d							14 32																	
Tir-phil	d							14 36																	
Brithdir	d							14 39																	
Bargoed	a							14 42																	
	d		14 32					14 47							15 02					15 17					15 32
Gilfach Fargoed	d																			15 19					
Pengam	d		14 37					14 52							15 07					15 22					15 37
Hengoed	d		14 40					14 55							15 10					15 25					15 40
Ystrad Mynach 3	d		14 43					14 58							15 13					15 28					15 43
Llanbradach	d		14 48					15 03							15 18					15 33					15 48
Aber	d		14 52					15 07							15 22					15 37					15 52
Caerphilly 3	d		14 55					15 10							15 25					15 40					15 55
Lisvane & Thornhill	d		14 59					15 14							15 29					15 44					15 59
Llanishen	d		15 01					15 16							15 31					15 46					16 01
Heath High Level	d		15 04					15 19							15 34					15 49					16 04
Coryton	d										15 15										15 45				
Whitchurch (Cardiff)	d										15 16										15 46				
Rhiwbina	d										15 18										15 48				
Birchgrove	d										15 20										15 50				
Ty Glas	d										15 21										15 51				
Heath Low Level	d										15 24										15 54				
Cardiff Queen Street 3	a	15 04	15 09				15 19	15 24			15 29	15 34			15 39	15 44			15 49	15 54	15 59		16 04		16 09
	d	15 06	15 11			15 12	15 21	15 26		15 24	15 31	15 36	15 36		15 41	15 46		15 48	15 51	15 56	16 01	16 00	16 06		16 11
Cardiff Bay	a					15 16				15 28			15 40					15 52				16 04			
Cardiff Central 7	a	15 09	15 14		15 20		15 24	15 29	15 34		15 34	15 39			15 44	15 52	15 50		15 54	15 59	16 04		16 09		16 14
	d	15 10	15 16				15 25	15 31				15 41			15 46				15 55	16 01			16 10		16 16
Grangetown	d	15 14	15 20				15 29	15 35				15 45			15 50				15 59	16 05			16 14		16 20
Dingle Road	d		15 26					15 41							15 56					16 11					16 26
Penarth	a		15 31					15 46							16 01					16 16					16 31
Cogan	d	15 18					15 33					15 48							16 03				16 18		
Eastbrook	d	15 20					15 35					15 51							16 05				16 20		
Dinas Powys	d	15 22					15 37					15 53							16 07				16 22		
Cadoxton	d	15 27					15 42					15 57							16 12				16 27		
Barry Docks	d	15 30					15 45					16 00							16 15				16 30		
Barry 3	d	15 34					15 49					16 05							16 19				16 34		
Barry Island	a	15 40					15 55												16 25				16 40		
Rhoose Cardiff Int Airport ✈	d											16 12													
Llantwit Major	d											16 22													
Bridgend	a											16 39													

When events are being held at the Millenium Stadium, services are subject to alteration. Please check times before travelling.

Treherbert, Aberdare, Merthyr, Pontypridd, Rhymney and Coryton - Cardiff, Penarth, Barry, Barry Island and Bridgend

Network Diagram - see first Page of Table 130

		AW	AW	AW	AW	AW	AW	AW	AW	AW	AW	AW	AW	AW	AW	AW	AW	AW	AW	AW	AW	AW	AW
Treherbert	d		15 13									15 47									16 17	
Ynyswen	d		15 15									15 49									16 19	
Treorchy	d		15 21									15 51									16 21	
Ton Pentre	d		15 23									15 53									16 23	
Ystrad Rhondda	a		15 26									15 56									16 26	
	d		15 28									15 58									16 28	
Llwynypia	d		15 30									16 00									16 30	
Tonypandy	d		15 33									16 03									16 33	
Dinas Rhondda	d		15 35									16 05									16 35	
Porth	a		15 38									16 08									16 38	
	d		15 39									16 09									16 39	
Trehafod	d		15 42									16 12									16 42	
Merthyr Tydfil	d								15 38										16 08				
Pentre-bach	d								15 42										16 12				
Troed Y Rhiw	d								15 45										16 15				
Merthyr Vale	a								15 48										16 18				
	d								15 50										16 20				
Quakers Yard	d								15 55										16 25				
Aberdare [3]	d				15 22										15 52								
Cwmbach	d				15 25										15 55								
Fernhill	d				15 28										15 58								
Mountain Ash	a				15 31										16 01								
	d				15 34										16 04								
Penrhiwceiber	d				15 37										16 07								
Abercynon	d				15 43				15 59						16 13				16 29				
Pontypridd [3]	a		15 47		15 52				16 07			16 17			16 22				16 37			16 47	
	d		15 48		15 54				16 09			16 18			16 24				16 39			16 48	
Trefforest	d		15 51		15 57				16 12			16 21			16 27				16 42			16 51	
Trefforest Estate	d								16 16										16 46				
Taffs Well [3]	d		15 58		16 04				16 20			16 28			16 34				16 50			16 58	
Radyr [3]	a		16 01		16 07				16 23			16 31			16 37				16 53			17 01	
	d		16 01	16 04	16 07				16 23			16 31	16 34		16 37				16 53			17 01	17 04
Danescourt	d			16 08									16 38										17 08
Fairwater	d			16 10									16 40										17 10
Waun-gron Park	d			16 12									16 42										17 12
Ninian Park	d			16 15									16 45										17 15
Llandaf	d		16 04		16 10				16 26			16 34			16 40				16 56			17 04	
Cathays	d		16 09		16 15				16 31			16 39			16 45				17 01			17 09	
Rhymney [3]	d					15 29																	
Pontlottyn	d					15 32																	
Tir-phil	d					15 36																	
Brithdir	d					15 39																	
Bargoed	a					15 42																	
	d					15 47					16 02					16 17				16 32			
Gilfach Fargoed	d															16 19							
Pengam	d					15 52					16 07					16 22				16 37			
Hengoed	d					15 55					16 10					16 25				16 40			
Ystrad Mynach [3]	d					15 58					16 13					16 28				16 43			
Llanbradach	d					16 03					16 18					16 33				16 48			
Aber	d					16 07					16 22					16 37				16 52			
Caerphilly [3]	d					16 10					16 25					16 40				16 55			
Lisvane & Thornhill	d					16 14					16 29					16 44				16 59			
Llanishen	d					16 16					16 31					16 46				17 01			
Heath High Level	d					16 19					16 34					16 49				17 04			
Coryton	d							16 15									16 45						
Whitchurch (Cardiff)	d							16 16									16 46						
Rhiwbina	d							16 18									16 48						
Birchgrove	d							16 20									16 50						
Ty Glas	d							16 21									16 51						
Heath Low Level	d							16 24									16 54						
Cardiff Queen Street [3]	a		16 14		16 19	16 24		16 29	16 34		16 39	16 44			16 49	16 54	16 59		17 04	17 09		17 14	
	d	16 12	16 16		16 21	16 26	16 24	16 31	16 36	16 36	16 41	16 46		16 48	16 51	16 56	17 01	17 00	17 06	17 11	17 12	17 16	
Cardiff Bay	a	16 16					16 28			16 40				16 52				17 04			17 16		
Cardiff Central [7]	a		16 22	16 20	16 24	16 32		16 34	16 39		16 44	16 52	16 50		16 54	16 59	17 04		17 09	17 14		17 22	17 20
	d				16 25				16 41		16 46				16 55	17 01			17 10	17 16			
Grangetown	d				16 29				16 45		16 50				16 59	17 05			17 14	17 20			
Dingle Road	d										16 56					17 11				17 26			
Penarth	a										17 01					17 16				17 31			
Cogan	d				16 33				16 48						17 03				17 18				
Eastbrook	d				16 35				16 51						17 05				17 20				
Dinas Powys	d				16 37				16 53						17 07				17 22				
Cadoxton	d				16 42				16 57						17 12				17 27				
Barry Docks	d				16 45				17 00						17 15				17 30				
Barry [3]	d				16 49				17 05						17 19				17 34				
Barry Island	a				16 55										17 25				17 40				
Rhoose Cardiff Int Airport ✈	d								17 12														
Llantwit Major	d								17 22														
Bridgend	a								17 39														

When events are being held at the Millenium Stadium, services are subject to alteration. Please check times before travelling.

Treherbert, Aberdare, Merthyr, Pontypridd, Rhymney and Coryton - Cardiff, Penarth, Barry, Barry Island and Bridgend

Network Diagram - see first Page of Table 130

		AW	AW	AW	AW	AW	AW	AW	AW	AW	AW	AW	AW	AW	AW	AW	AW	AW	AW	AW	AW	AW	AW
Treherbert	d								16 47										17 17				
Ynyswen	d								16 49										17 19				
Treorchy	d								16 51										17 21				
Ton Pentre	d								16 53										17 23				
Ystrad Rhondda	a								16 56										17 26				
	d								16 58										17 28				
Llwynypia	d								17 00										17 30				
Tonypandy	d								17 03										17 33				
Dinas Rhondda	d								17 05										17 35				
Porth	a								17 08										17 38				
	d								17 09										17 39				
Trehafod	d								17 12										17 42				
Merthyr Tydfil	d					16 38										17 08							
Pentre-bach	d					16 42										17 12							
Troed Y Rhiw	d					16 45										17 15							
Merthyr Vale	a					16 48										17 18							
	d					16 50										17 20							
Quakers Yard	d					16 55										17 25							
Aberdare 3	d	16 22										16 52									17 22		
Cwmbach	d	16 25										16 55									17 25		
Fernhill	d	16 28										16 58									17 28		
Mountain Ash	a	16 31										17 01									17 31		
	d	16 34										17 04									17 34		
Penrhiwceiber	d	16 37										17 07									17 37		
Abercynon	d	16 43				16 59						17 13				17 29					17 43		
Pontypridd 3	a	16 52				17 07			17 17			17 22				17 37			17 47		17 52		
	d	16 54				17 09			17 18			17 24				17 39			17 48		17 54		
Trefforest	d	16 57				17 12			17 21			17 27				17 42			17 51		17 57		
Trefforest Estate	d					17 16										17 46							
Taffs Well 3	d	17 04				17 20			17 28			17 34				17 50			17 58		18 04		
Radyr 3	a	17 07				17 23			17 31			17 37				17 53			18 01		18 07		
	d	17 07				17 23			17 31	17 34		17 37				17 53			18 01	18 04	18 07		
Danescourt	d									17 38										18 08			
Fairwater	d									17 40										18 10			
Waun-gron Park	d									17 42										18 12			
Ninian Park	d									17 45										18 15			
Llandaf	d	17 10				17 26			17 34			17 40				17 56			18 04		18 10		
Cathays	d	17 15				17 31			17 39			17 45				18 01			18 09		18 15		
Rhymney 3	d		16 29																			17 29	
Pontlottyn	d		16 32																			17 32	
Tir-phil	d		16 36																			17 36	
Brithdir	d		16 39																			17 39	
Bargoed	a		16 42																			17 42	
	d		16 47					17 02					17 17				17 32					17 47	
Gilfach Fargoed	d												17 19										
Pengam	d		16 52					17 07					17 22				17 37					17 52	
Hengoed	d		16 55					17 10					17 25				17 40					17 55	
Ystrad Mynach 3	d		16 58					17 13					17 28				17 43					17 58	
Llanbradach	d		17 03					17 18					17 33				17 48					18 03	
Aber	d		17 07					17 22					17 37				17 52					18 07	
Caerphilly 3	d		17 10					17 25					17 40				17 55					18 10	
Lisvane & Thornhill	d		17 14					17 29					17 44				17 59					18 14	
Llanishen	d		17 16					17 31					17 46				18 01					18 16	
Heath High Level	d		17 19					17 34					17 49				18 04					18 19	
Coryton	d				17 15									17 45									
Whitchurch (Cardiff)	d				17 16									17 46									
Rhiwbina	d				17 18									17 48									
Birchgrove	d				17 20									17 50									
Ty Glas	d				17 21									17 51									
Heath Low Level	d				17 24									17 54									
Cardiff Queen Street 3	a	17 19	17 24		17 29	17 34		17 39	17 44			17 49	17 54	17 59		18 04	18 09		18 14		18 19	18 24	
	d	17 21	17 26	17 24	17 31	17 36	17 36	17 41	17 46		17 48	17 51	17 56	18 01	18 00	18 06	18 11	18 12	18 16		18 21	18 26	18 24
Cardiff Bay	a			17 28			17 40				17 52				18 04			18 16					18 28
Cardiff Central 7	a	17 24	17 29		17 34	17 39		17 44	17 52	17 50		17 54	17 59	18 04		18 09	18 14		18 22	18 20	18 24	18 29	
	d	17 25	17 31			17 41		17 46				17 55	18 01			18 10	18 16				18 25	18 31	
Grangetown	d	17 29	17 35			17 45		17 50				17 59	18 05			18 14	18 20				18 29	18 35	
Dingle Road	d		17 41					17 56					18 11				18 26					18 41	
Penarth	a		17 46					18 01					18 16				18 31					18 46	
Cogan	d	17 33				17 48						18 03				18 18					18 33		
Eastbrook	d	17 35				17 51						18 05				18 20					18 35		
Dinas Powys	d	17 37				17 53						18 07				18 22					18 37		
Cadoxton	d	17 42				17 57						18 12				18 27					18 42		
Barry Docks	d	17 45				18 00						18 15				18 30					18 45		
Barry 3	d	17 49				18 05						18 19				18 34					18 49		
Barry Island	a	17 55										18 25				18 40					18 55		
Rhoose Cardiff Int Airport ✈	d					18 12																	
Llantwit Major	d					18 22																	
Bridgend	a					18 39																	

When events are being held at the Millenium Stadium, services are subject to alteration. Please check times before travelling.

Treherbert, Aberdare, Merthyr, Pontypridd, Rhymney and Coryton - Cardiff, Penarth, Barry, Barry Island and Bridgend

Network Diagram - see first Page of Table 130

		AW	AW	AW	AW	AW	AW	AW	AW	AW	AW	AW	AW	AW	AW	AW	AW	AW	AW	AW	AW	AW
Treherbert	d				17 47									18 17								18 47
Ynyswen	d				17 49									18 19								18 49
Treorchy	d				17 51									18 21								18 51
Ton Pentre	d				17 53									18 23								18 53
Ystrad Rhondda	a				17 56									18 26								18 56
	d				17 58									18 28								18 58
Llwynypia	d				18 00									18 30								19 00
Tonypandy	d				18 03									18 33								19 03
Dinas Rhondda	d				18 05									18 35								19 05
Porth	a				18 08									18 38								19 08
	d				18 09									18 39								19 09
Trehafod	d				18 12									18 42								19 12
Merthyr Tydfil	d		17 38									18 08								18 38		
Pentre-bach	d		17 42									18 12								18 42		
Troed Y Rhiw	d		17 45									18 15								18 45		
Merthyr Vale	a		17 48									18 18								18 48		
	d		17 50									18 20								18 50		
Quakers Yard	d		17 55									18 25								18 55		
Aberdare 3	d							17 52								18 22						
Cwmbach	d							17 55								18 25						
Fernhill	d							17 58								18 28						
Mountain Ash	a							18 01								18 31						
	d							18 04								18 34						
Penrhiwceiber	d							18 07								18 37						
Abercynon	d		17 59					18 13				18 29				18 43				18 59		
Pontypridd 3	a		18 07		18 17			18 22				18 37		18 47		18 52				19 07		19 17
	d		18 09		18 18			18 24				18 39		18 48		18 54				19 09		19 18
Trefforest	d		18 12		18 21			18 27				18 42		18 51		18 57				19 12		19 21
Trefforest Estate	d		18 16									18 46								19 16		
Taffs Well 3	d		18 20		18 28			18 34				18 50		18 58		19 04				19 20		19 28
Radyr 3	a		18 23		18 31			18 37				18 53		19 01		19 07				19 23		19 31
	d		18 23		18 31	18 34		18 37				18 53		19 01	19 04	19 07				19 23		19 31
Danescourt	d					18 38									19 08							
Fairwater	d					18 40									19 10							
Waun-gron Park	d					18 42									19 12							
Ninian Park	d					18 45									19 15							
Llandaf	d		18 26		18 34			18 40				18 56		19 04		19 10				19 26		19 34
Cathays	d		18 31		18 39			18 45				19 01		19 09		19 15				19 31		19 39
Rhymney 3	d																					
Pontlottyn	d																					
Tir-phil	d																					
Brithdir	d																					
Bargoed	a																					
	d								18 17								18 48					
Gilfach Fargoed	d								18 19								18 50					
Pengam	d								18 22								18 53					
Hengoed	d								18 25								18 56					
Ystrad Mynach 3	d								18 28								18 59					
Llanbradach	d								18 33								19 04					
Aber	d								18 37								19 08					
Caerphilly 3	d								18 40								19 11					
Lisvane & Thornhill	d								18 44								19 15					
Llanishen	d								18 46								19 17					
Heath High Level	d								18 49								19 20					
Coryton	d	18 15								18 45									19 15			
Whitchurch (Cardiff)	d	18 16								18 46									19 16			
Rhiwbina	d	18 18								18 48									19 18			
Birchgrove	d	18 20								18 50									19 20			
Ty Glas	d	18 21								18 51									19 21			
Heath Low Level	d	18 24								18 54									19 24			
Cardiff Queen Street 3	a	18 29	18 34		18 44			18 49	18 54	18 59		19 04		19 14		19 19	19 24		19 29	19 34		19 44
	d	18 31	18 36	18 36	18 46		18 48	18 51	18 56	19 01	19 00	19 06	19 12	19 16		19 21	19 26	19 24	19 31	19 36	19 36	19 46
Cardiff Bay	a			18 40			18 52				19 04		19 16					19 28			19 40	
Cardiff Central 7	a	18 34	18 39		18 52	18 50		18 54	18 59	19 06		19 10		19 22	19 22	19 24	19 29		19 34	19 39		19 52
	d		18 41					18 55	19 01							19 25	19 31			19 41		
Grangetown	d		18 45					18 59	19 05							19 29	19 35			19 45		
Dingle Road	d								19 11								19 41					
Penarth	a								19 16								19 46					
Cogan	d		18 48					19 03								19 33				19 48		
Eastbrook	d		18 51					19 05								19 35				19 51		
Dinas Powys	d		18 53					19 07								19 37				19 53		
Cadoxton	d		18 57					19 12								19 42				19 57		
Barry Docks	d		19 00					19 15								19 45				20 00		
Barry 3	d		19 05					19 19								19 49				20 05		
Barry Island	a							19 25								19 55						
Rhoose Cardiff Int Airport ✈	d		19 12																	20 12		
Llantwit Major	d		19 22																	20 22		
Bridgend	a		19 39																	20 39		

When events are being held at the Millenium Stadium, services are subject to alteration. Please check times before travelling.

Table 130

Mondays to Fridays

Treherbert, Aberdare, Merthyr, Pontypridd, Rhymney and Coryton - Cardiff, Penarth, Barry, Barry Island and Bridgend

Network Diagram - see first Page of Table 130

		AW	AW	AW	AW	AW	AW	AW	AW	AW	AW	AW	AW	AW	AW	AW	AW	AW	AW	AW	AW	AW	AW
Treherbert	d							19 17								19 47						20 17	
Ynyswen	d							19 19								19 49						20 19	
Treorchy	d							19 21								19 51						20 21	
Ton Pentre	d							19 23								19 53						20 23	
Ystrad Rhondda	a							19 26								19 56						20 26	
	d							19 28								19 58						20 28	
Llwynypia	d							19 30								20 00						20 30	
Tonypandy	d							19 33								20 03						20 33	
Dinas Rhondda	d							19 35								20 05						20 35	
Porth	a							19 38								20 08						20 38	
	d							19 39								20 09						20 39	
Trehafod	d							19 42								20 12						20 42	
Merthyr Tydfil	d					19 08							19 38										
Pentre-bach	d					19 12							19 42										
Troed Y Rhiw	d					19 15							19 45										
Merthyr Vale	a					19 18							19 48										
	d					19 20							19 50										
Quakers Yard	d					19 25							19 55										
Aberdare 3	d		18 52															19 52					
Cwmbach	d		18 55															19 55					
Fernhill	d		18 58															19 58					
Mountain Ash	a		19 01															20 01					
	d		19 04															20 04					
Penrhiwceiber	d		19 07															20 07					
Abercynon	d		19 13			19 29				19 43			19 59					20 13					
Pontypridd 3	a		19 22			19 37		19 47		19 52			20 07			20 18		20 22				20 47	
	d		19 24			19 39		19 48		19 54			20 09			20 18		20 24				20 48	
Trefforest	d		19 27			19 42		19 51		19 57			20 12			20 21		20 27				20 51	
Trefforest Estate	d					19 46							20 16										
Taffs Well 3	d		19 34			19 50		19 58		20 04			20 20			20 28		20 34				20 58	
Radyr 3	a		19 37			19 53		20 01		20 07			20 23			20 31		20 37				21 01	
	d		19 37			19 53		20 01	20 04	20 07			20 23			20 31		20 37				21 01	21 04
Danescourt	d								20 08														21 08
Fairwater	d								20 10														21 10
Waun-gron Park	d								20 12														21 12
Ninian Park	d								20 15														21 15
Llandaf	d		19 40			19 56		20 04		20 10			20 26			20 34		20 40				21 04	
Cathays	d		19 45			20 01		20 09		20 15			20 31			20 39		20 45				21 09	
Rhymney 3	d														19 45								
Pontlottyn	d														19 48								
Tir-phil	d														19 52								
Brithdir	d														19 55								
Bargoed	a														19 58								
	d														19 59								
Gilfach Fargoed	d														20 01								
Pengam	d														20 04								
Hengoed	d														20 07								
Ystrad Mynach 3	d														20 10								
Llanbradach	d														20 15								
Aber	d														20 19								
Caerphilly 3	d			19 40											20 22				20 40				
Lisvane & Thornhill	d			19 44											20 26				20 44				
Llanishen	d			19 46											20 28				20 46				
Heath High Level	d			19 49											20 31				20 49				
Coryton	d											20 15											
Whitchurch (Cardiff)	d											20 16											
Rhiwbina	d											20 18											
Birchgrove	d											20 20											
Ty Glas	d											20 21											
Heath Low Level	d											20 24											
Cardiff Queen Street 3	a		19 49	19 54		20 04		20 14		20 19		20 29	20 34		20 39	20 44		20 49	20 54			21 14	
	d	19 48	19 51	19 56	20 00	20 06	20 12	20 16		20 21	20 24	20 31	20 36	20 36	20 41	20 46	20 48	20 51	20 56	21 00	21 12	21 16	
Cardiff Bay	a	19 52			20 04		20 16				20 28			20 40			20 52			21 04	21 16		
Cardiff Central 7	a		19 57	19 59		20 09		20 22	20 24	20 24		20 34	20 39		20 47	20 52		20 57	20 59			21 22	21 25
	d			20 06		20 10				20 31			20 41					21 06	21 10				
Grangetown	d			20 10		20 14				20 35			20 45					21 10	21 14				
Dingle Road	d			20 14						20 41								21 14					
Penarth	a			20 19						20 46								21 19					
Cogan	d					20 18							20 48						21 18				
Eastbrook	d					20 20							20 51						21 20				
Dinas Powys	d					20 22							20 53						21 22				
Cadoxton	d					20 27							20 57						21 27				
Barry Docks	d					20 30							21 00						21 30				
Barry 3	d					20 34							21 05						21 34				
Barry Island	a					20 40													21 40				
Rhoose Cardiff Int Airport ✈	d												21 12										
Llantwit Major	d												21 22										
Bridgend	a												21 39										

When events are being held at the Millenium Stadium,
services are subject to alteration. Please check times before travelling.

Treherbert, Aberdare, Merthyr, Pontypridd, Rhymney and Coryton - Cardiff, Penarth, Barry, Barry Island and Bridgend

Network Diagram - see first Page of Table 130

		AW	AW		AW	AW	AW FO	AW FX	AW	AW	AW	AW	AW		AW	AW	AW	AW	AW	AW	AW FX	AW FO	AW		AW
Treherbert	d																21 17								
Ynyswen	d																21 19								
Treorchy	d																21 21								
Ton Pentre	d																21 23								
Ystrad Rhondda	a																21 26								
	d																21 28								
Llwynypia	d																21 30								
Tonypandy	d																21 33								
Dinas Rhondda	d																21 35								
Porth	a																21 38								
	d																21 39								
Trehafod	d																21 42								
Merthyr Tydfil	d						20 38	20 38													21 38	21 38			
Pentre-bach	d						20 42	20 42													21 42	21 42			
Troed Y Rhiw	d						20 45	20 45													21 45	21 45			
Merthyr Vale	a						20 48	20 48													21 48	21 48			
	d						20 50	20 50													21 50	21 50			
Quakers Yard	d						20 55	20 55													21 55	21 55			
Aberdare 3	d	20 22										20 54													
Cwmbach	d	20 25										20 57													
Fernhill	d	20 28										21 00													
Mountain Ash	a	20 31										21 03													
	d	20 34										21 04													
Penrhiwceiber	d	20 37										21 07													
Abercynon	d	20 43					20 59	20 59				21 13									21 59	21 59			
Pontypridd 3	a	20 52					21 07	21 07				21 22					21 47				22 07	22 07			
	d	20 54					21 09	21 09				21 24					21 48				22 09	22 09			
Trefforest	d	20 57					21 12	21 12				21 27					21 51				22 12	22 12			
Trefforest Estate	d						21 16	21 16													22 16	22 16			
Taffs Well 3	d	21 04					21 20	21 20				21 34					21 58				22 20	22 20			
Radyr 3	a	21 07					21 23	21 23				21 37					22 01				22 23	22 23			
	d	21 07					21 23	21 23				21 37					22 01	22 04			22 23	22 23			
Danescourt	d																	22 08							
Fairwater	d																	22 10							
Waun-gron Park	d																	22 12							
Ninian Park	d																	22 15							
Llandaf	d	21 10					21 26	21 26				21 40					22 04				22 26	22 26			
Cathays	d	21 15					21 31	21 31				21 45					22 09				22 31	22 31			
Rhymney 3	d									20 48									21 33						
Pontlottyn	d									20 51									21 36						
Tir-phil	d									20 55									21 40						
Brithdir	d									20 58									21 43						
Bargoed	a									21 01									21 46						
	d									21 02									21 47						
Gilfach Fargoed	d									21 04									21 49						
Pengam	d									21 07									21 52						
Hengoed	d									21 10									21 55						
Ystrad Mynach 3	d									21 13					21 39				21 58						
Llanbradach	d									21 18					21 44				22 03						
Aber	d									21 22					21 48				22 07						
Caerphilly 3	d									21 25					21 51				22 10						22 28
Lisvane & Thornhill	d									21 29					21 55				22 14						
Llanishen	d									21 31					21 57				22 16						
Heath High Level	d									21 34					22 00				22 19						
Coryton	d					21 15																			
Whitchurch (Cardiff)	d					21 16																			
Rhiwbina	d					21 18																			
Birchgrove	d					21 20																			
Ty Glas	d					21 21																			
Heath Low Level	d					21 24																			
Cardiff Queen Street 3	a	21 19				21 29	21 34	21 34		21 42		21 49			22 05		22 14		22 24		22 34	22 34			22 39
	d	21 21	21 24			21 31	21 36	21 36	21 36	21 44	21 48	21 51	22 00		22 06	22 12	22 16		22 26	22 24	22 36	22 36	22 36		22 39
Cardiff Bay	a		21 28						21 40		21 52		22 04			22 16				22 28			22 40		
Cardiff Central 7	a	21 27				21 34	21 39	21 39		21 47		21 54			22 09		22 22	22 20	22 29		22 39	22 39			22 43
	d				21 31		21 41	21 41				21 56			22 10				22 31		22 41	22 41			
Grangetown	d				21 35		21 45	21 45				22 00			22 14				22 35		22 45	22 45			
Dingle Road	d				21 41							22 04							22 41						
Penarth	a				21 46							22 09							22 46						
Cogan	d						21 48	21 48							22 18						22 48	22 48			
Eastbrook	d						21 51	21 51							22 20						22 51	22 51			
Dinas Powys	d						21 53	21 53							22 22						22 53	22 53			
Cadoxton	d						21 57	21 57							22 27						22 57	22 57			
Barry Docks	d						22 00	22 00							22 30						23 00	23 00			
Barry 3	d						22 05	22 05							22 34						23a05	23 05			
Barry Island	a														22 40										
Rhoose Cardiff Int Airport ✈	d						22 12	22 12														23 12			
Llantwit Major	d						22 22	22 22														23 22			
Bridgend	a						22 39	22 40														23 39			

When events are being held at the Millenium Stadium, services are subject to alteration. Please check times before travelling.

Table 130

Mondays to Fridays

Treherbert, Aberdare, Merthyr, Pontypridd, Rhymney and Coryton - Cardiff, Penarth, Barry, Barry Island and Bridgend

Network Diagram - see first Page of Table 130

		AW	AW	AW	AW	AW	AW FX	AW	AW		AW	AW	AW	AW
Treherbert	d													
Ynyswen	d													
Treorchy	d													
Ton Pentre	d													
Ystrad Rhondda	a													
	d													
Llwynypia	d													
Tonypandy	d													
Dinas Rhondda	d													
Porth	a													
	d													
Trehafod	d													
Merthyr Tydfil	d										22 38			
Pentre-bach	d										22 42			
Troed Y Rhiw	d										22 45			
Merthyr Vale	a										22 48			
	d										22 50			
Quakers Yard	d										22 55			
Aberdare 3	d		21 54									22 54		
Cwmbach	d		21 57									22 57		
Fernhill	d		22 00									23 00		
Mountain Ash	a		22 03									23 03		
	d		22 04									23 04		
Penrhiwceiber	d		22 07									23 07		
Abercynon	d		22 13								22 59	23 13		
Pontypridd 3	a		22 22								23 07	23 22		
	d		22 24								23 09			
Trefforest	d		22 27								23 12			
Trefforest Estate	d										23 16			
Taffs Well 3	d		22 34								23 20			
Radyr 3	a		22 37								23 23			
	d		22 37					23 10			23 23			
Danescourt	d													
Fairwater	d													
Waun-gron Park	d													
Ninian Park	d													
Llandaf	d		22 40					23 12			23 26			
Cathays	d		22 45					23 16			23 31			
Rhymney 3	d													
Pontlottyn	d													
Tir-phil	d													
Brithdir	d													
Bargoed	a													
	d													
Gilfach Fargoed	d													
Pengam	d													
Hengoed	d													
Ystrad Mynach 3	d													
Llanbradach	d													
Aber	d													
Caerphilly 3	d													
Lisvane & Thornhill	d													
Llanishen	d													
Heath High Level	d													
Coryton	d			22 45										
Whitchurch (Cardiff)	d			22 46										
Rhiwbina	d			22 48										
Birchgrove	d			22 50										
Ty Glas	d			22 51										
Heath Low Level	d			22 54										
Cardiff Queen Street 3	a		22 49	22 59				23 20			23 34			
	d	22 48	22 54	23 01	23 00	23 12		23 20	23 24		23 36		23 36	23 48
Cardiff Bay	a	22 52			23 04	23 16			23 28				23 40	23 52
Cardiff Central 7	a		23 00	23 06				23 25			23 42			
	d		23 12					23 30						
Grangetown	d		23 16					23 34						
Dingle Road	d		23 20											
Penarth	a		23 25											
Cogan	d							23 37						
Eastbrook	d							23 40						
Dinas Powys	d							23 42						
Cadoxton	d							23 46						
Barry Docks	d							23 49						
Barry 3	d						23 15	23 54						
Barry Island	a							00 01						
Rhoose Cardiff Int Airport ✈	d						23 30							
Llantwit Major	d						23 45							
Bridgend	a						00 10							

When events are being held at the Millenium Stadium, services are subject to alteration. Please check times before travelling.

Table 130

Saturdays

Treherbert, Aberdare, Merthyr, Pontypridd, Rhymney and Coryton - Cardiff, Penarth, Barry, Barry Island and Bridgend

Network Diagram - see first Page of Table 130

		AW	AW	AW	AW	AW	AW	AW	AW	AW	AW	AW	AW	AW	AW	AW	AW	AW	AW	AW	AW	AW	AW
Treherbert	d											05 47							06 17				
Ynyswen	d											05 49							06 19				
Treorchy	d											05 51							06 21				
Ton Pentre	d											05 53							06 23				
Ystrad Rhondda	a											05 56							06 26				
	d											05 58							06 28				
Llwynypia	d											06 00							06 30				
Tonypandy	d											06 03							06 33				
Dinas Rhondda	d											06 05							06 35				
Porth	a											06 08							06 38				
	d											06 09							06 39				
Trehafod	d											06 12							06 42				
Merthyr Tydfil	d																						
Pentre-bach	d																						
Troed Y Rhiw	d																						
Merthyr Vale	a																						
	d																						
Quakers Yard	d																						
Aberdare 3	d																					06 22	
Cwmbach	d																					06 25	
Fernhill	d																					06 28	
Mountain Ash	a																					06 31	
	d																					06 34	
Penrhiwceiber	d																					06 37	
Abercynon	d																					06 43	
Pontypridd 3	a											06 17							06 47			06 52	
	d					05 24						06 18							06 48			06 54	
Trefforest	d					05 27						06 21							06 51			06 57	
Trefforest Estate	d					05 31																	
Taffs Well 3	d					05 34						06 28							06 58	06 53		07 04	
Radyr 3	a					05 37						06 31							07 01	06 56		07 07	
	d	23p10				05 37						06 31							07 01	07 04		07 07	
Danescourt	d																			07 08			
Fairwater	d																			07 10			
Waun-gron Park	d																			07 12			
Ninian Park	d																			07 15			
Llandaf	d	23p12				05 40						06 34							07 04			07 10	
Cathays	d	23p16				05 45						06 39							07 09			07 15	
Rhymney 3	d																	06 10					06 34
Pontlottyn	d																	06 13					06 37
Tir-phil	d																	06 17					06 41
Brithdir	d																	06 20					06 44
Bargoed	a																	06 23					06 47
	d																	06 27					06 48
Gilfach Fargoed	d																	06 29					
Pengam	d																	06 32					06 52
Hengoed	d																	06 35					06 56
Ystrad Mynach 3	d																	06 38					06 58
Llanbradach	d																	06 43					07 03
Aber	d																	06 47					07 07
Caerphilly 3	d									06 10								06 50					07 10
Lisvane & Thornhill	d									06 14								06 54					07 14
Llanishen	d									06 16								06 56					07 16
Heath High Level	d									06 19								06 59					07 19
Coryton	d																06 45						
Whitchurch (Cardiff)	d																06 46						
Rhiwbina	d																06 48						
Birchgrove	d																06 50						
Ty Glas	d																06 51						
Heath Low Level	d																06 54						
Cardiff Queen Street 3	a	23p20				05 49				06 25		06 42					06 59	07 04	07 12			07 19	07 24
	d	23p20				05 51				06 26	06 36	06 43	06 48		07 00		07 01	07 06	07 13		07 12	07 21	07 26
Cardiff Bay	a										06 40		06 52		07 04						07 16		
Cardiff Central 7	a	23p25				05 54				06 29		06 48					07 04	07 09	07 16	07 20		07 24	07 29
	d	23p30	05 20	05 41	05 46	05 55	06 16	06 25	06 36	06 41				06 55		07 01		07 10	07 16			07 25	07 31
Grangetown	d	23p34	05 24	05 45	05 50	05 59	06 20	06 29	06 40	06 45				06 59		07 05		07 14	07 20			07 29	07 35
Dingle Road	d				05 54		06 24		06 44							07 11			07 26				07 41
Penarth	a				05 59		06 29		06 49							07 16			07 31				07 46
Cogan	d	23p37	05 28	05 48		06 03		06 33		06 48				07 03				07 18				07 33	
Eastbrook	d	23p40	05 30	05 51		06 05		06 35		06 51				07 05				07 20				07 35	
Dinas Powys	d	23p42	05 32	05 53		06 07		06 37		06 53				07 07				07 22				07 37	
Cadoxton	d	23p46	05 37	05 57		06 12		06 42		06 57				07 12				07 27				07 42	
Barry Docks	d	23p49	05 40	06 00		06 15		06 45		07 00				07 15				07 30				07 45	
Barry 3	d	23p54	05 44	06 05		06 19		06 49		07 05				07 19				07 34				07 49	
Barry Island	a	00 01	05 50			06 25		06 55						07 25				07 40				07 55	
Rhoose Cardiff Int Airport ✈	d			06 12						07 12													
Llantwit Major	d			06 22						07 22													
Bridgend	a			06 39						07 39													

When events are being held at the Millenium Stadium, services are subject to alteration. Please check times before travelling.

Table 130

Saturdays

Treherbert, Aberdare, Merthyr, Pontypridd, Rhymney and Coryton - Cardiff, Penarth, Barry, Barry Island and Bridgend

Network Diagram - see first Page of Table 130

		AW	AW	AW	AW	AW	AW	AW	AW	AW	AW	AW	AW	AW	AW	AW	AW	AW	AW	AW	AW	AW	AW
Treherbert	d						06 47										07 17						
Ynyswen	d						06 49										07 19						
Treorchy	d						06 51										07 21						
Ton Pentre	d						06 53										07 23						
Ystrad Rhondda	a						06 56										07 26						
	d						06 58										07 28						
Llwynypia	d						07 00										07 30						
Tonypandy	d						07 03										07 33						
Dinas Rhondda	d						07 05										07 35						
Porth	a						07 08										07 38						
	d						07 09										07 39						
Trehafod	d						07 12										07 42						
Merthyr Tydfil	d			06 38										07 08									07 38
Pentre-bach	d			06 42										07 12									07 42
Troed Y Rhiw	d			06 45										07 15									07 45
Merthyr Vale	a			06 48										07 18									07 48
	d			06 50										07 20									07 50
Quakers Yard	d			06 55										07 25									07 55
Aberdare 3	d									06 52									07 22				
Cwmbach	d									06 55									07 25				
Fernhill	d									06 58									07 28				
Mountain Ash	a									07 01									07 31				
	d									07 04									07 34				
Penrhiwceiber	d									07 07									07 37				
Abercynon	d			06 59						07 13				07 29					07 43				07 59
Pontypridd 3	a			07 07			07 17			07 22				07 37			07 47		07 52				08 07
	d			07 09			07 18			07 24				07 39			07 48		07 54				08 09
Trefforest	d			07 12			07 21			07 27				07 42			07 51		07 57				08 12
Trefforest Estate	d			07 16										07 46									08 16
Taffs Well 3	d			07 20			07 28			07 34				07 50			07 58		08 04				08 20
Radyr 3	a			07 23			07 31			07 37				07 53			08 01		08 07				08 23
	d			07 23			07 31	07 34		07 37				07 53			08 01	08 04	08 07				08 23
Danescourt	d							07 38										08 08					
Fairwater	d							07 40										08 10					
Waun-gron Park	d							07 42										08 12					
Ninian Park	d							07 45										08 15					
Llandaf	d			07 26			07 34			07 40				07 56			08 04		08 10				08 26
Cathays	d			07 31			07 39			07 45				08 01			08 09		08 15				08 31
Rhymney 3	d										07 02									07 24			
Pontlottyn	d										07 05									07 27			
Tir-phil	d										07 09									07 31			
Brithdir	d										07 12									07 34			
Bargoed	a										07 15									07 37			
	d					07 02					07 17				07 32					07 45			
Gilfach Fargoed	d					07 04					07 19									07 47			
Pengam	d					07 07					07 22				07 37					07 50			
Hengoed	d					07 10					07 25				07 40					07 54			
Ystrad Mynach 3	d					07 13					07 28				07 43					07 57			
Llanbradach	d					07 18					07 33				07 48					08 02			
Aber	d					07 22					07 37				07 52					08 07			
Caerphilly 3	d					07 25					07 40				07 55					08 10			
Lisvane & Thornhill	d					07 29					07 44				07 59					08 14			
Llanishen	d					07 31					07 46				08 01					08 16			
Heath High Level	d					07 34					07 49				08 04					08 19			
Coryton	d		07 15									07 45										08 15	
Whitchurch (Cardiff)	d		07 16									07 46										08 16	
Rhiwbina	d		07 18									07 48										08 18	
Birchgrove	d		07 20									07 50										08 20	
Ty Glas	d		07 21									07 51										08 21	
Heath Low Level	d		07 24									07 54										08 24	
Cardiff Queen Street 3	a		07 29	07 34		07 39	07 44			07 49	07 54	07 59		08 04	08 09		08 14		08 19	08 24		08 29	08 34
	d	07 24	07 31	07 36	07 36	07 41	07 46		07 48	07 51	07 56	08 01	08 00	08 06	08 11	08 12	08 16		08 21	08 26	08 24	08 31	08 36
Cardiff Bay	a	07 28			07 40				07 52				08 04			08 16					08 28		
Cardiff Central 7	a		07 34	07 39		07 44	07 52	07 50		07 54	07 59	08 04		08 09	08 14		08 22	08 20	08 24	08 29		08 34	08 39
	d			07 41		07 46				07 55	08 01			08 10	08 16				08 25	08 31			08 41
Grangetown	d			07 45		07 50				07 59	08 05			08 14	08 20				08 29	08 35			08 45
Dingle Road	d					07 56					08 11				08 26					08 41			
Penarth	a					08 01					08 16				08 31					08 46			
Cogan	d			07 48						08 03				08 18					08 33				08 48
Eastbrook	d			07 51						08 05				08 20					08 35				08 51
Dinas Powys	d			07 53						08 07				08 22					08 37				08 53
Cadoxton	d			07 57						08 12				08 27					08 42				08 57
Barry Docks	d			08 00						08 15				08 30					08 45				09 00
Barry 3	d			08 05						08 19				08 34					08 49				09 05
Barry Island	a									08 25				08 40					08 55				
Rhoose Cardiff Int Airport ✈	d			08 12																			09 12
Llantwit Major	d			08 22																			09 22
Bridgend	a			08 39																			09 39

When events are being held at the Millenium Stadium, services are subject to alteration. Please check times before travelling.

Table 130

Saturdays

Treherbert, Aberdare, Merthyr, Pontypridd, Rhymney and Coryton - Cardiff, Penarth, Barry, Barry Island and Bridgend

Network Diagram - see first Page of Table 130

		AW	AW	AW	AW	AW	AW	AW	AW	AW	AW	AW	AW	AW	AW	AW	AW	AW	AW	AW	AW	AW
Treherbert	d			07 45										08 17								
Ynyswen	d			07 47										08 19								
Treorchy	d			07 49										08 21								
Ton Pentre	d			07 51										08 23								
Ystrad Rhondda	a			07 54										08 26								
	d			07 58										08 28								
Llwynypia	d			08 00										08 30								
Tonypandy	d			08 03										08 33								
Dinas Rhondda	d			08 05										08 35								
Porth	a			08 08										08 38								
	d			08 09										08 39								
Trehafod	d			08 12										08 42								
Merthyr Tydfil	d										08 08									08 38		
Pentre-bach	d										08 12									08 42		
Troed Y Rhiw	d										08 15									08 45		
Merthyr Vale	a										08 18									08 48		
	d										08 20									08 50		
Quakers Yard	d										08 25									08 55		
Aberdare 3	d						07 52									08 22						
Cwmbach	d						07 55									08 25						
Fernhill	d						07 58									08 28						
Mountain Ash	a						08 01									08 31						
	d						08 04									08 34						
Penrhiwceiber	d						08 07									08 37						
Abercynon	d						08 13				08 29					08 43				08 59		
Pontypridd 3	a			08 17			08 22				08 37			08 47		08 52				09 07		
	d			08 18			08 24				08 39			08 48		08 54				09 09		
Trefforest	d			08 21			08 27				08 42			08 51		08 57				09 12		
Trefforest Estate	d										08 46									09 16		
Taffs Well 3	d			08 28			08 34				08 50			08 58		09 04				09 20		
Radyr 3	a			08 31			08 37				08 53			09 01		09 07				09 23		
	d			08 31	08 34		08 37				08 53			09 01	09 04	09 07				09 23		
Danescourt	d				08 38										09 08							
Fairwater	d				08 40										09 10							
Waun-gron Park	d				08 42										09 12							
Ninian Park	d				08 45										09 15							
Llandaf	d			08 34			08 40				08 56			09 04		09 10				09 26		
Cathays	d			08 39			08 45				09 01			09 09		09 15				09 31		
Rhymney 3	d		07 44														08 30					
Pontlottyn	d		07 47														08 33					
Tir-phil	d		07 51														08 37					
Brithdir	d		07 54														08 40					
Bargoed	a		08 00														08 44					
	d		08 02					08 17				08 32					08 47					09 02
Gilfach Fargoed	d							08 19														
Pengam	d		08 07					08 22				08 37					08 52					09 07
Hengoed	d		08 10					08 25				08 40					08 55					09 10
Ystrad Mynach 3	d		08 13					08 28				08 43					08 58					09 13
Llanbradach	d		08 18					08 33				08 48					09 03					09 18
Aber	d		08 22					08 37				08 52					09 07					09 22
Caerphilly 3	d		08 25					08 40				08 55					09 10					09 25
Lisvane & Thornhill	d		08 29					08 44				08 59					09 14					09 29
Llanishen	d		08 31					08 46				09 01					09 16					09 31
Heath High Level	d		08 34					08 49				09 04					09 19					09 34
Coryton	d								08 45										09 15			
Whitchurch (Cardiff)	d								08 46										09 16			
Rhiwbina	d								08 48										09 18			
Birchgrove	d								08 50										09 20			
Ty Glas	d								08 51										09 21			
Heath Low Level	d								08 54										09 24			
Cardiff Queen Street 3	a		08 39	08 44			08 49	08 54	08 59		09 04	09 09		09 14		09 19	09 24		09 29	09 34		09 39
	d	08 36	08 41	08 46		08 48	08 51	08 56	09 01	09 00	09 06	09 11	09 12	09 16		09 21	09 26	09 24	09 31	09 36	09 36	09 41
Cardiff Bay	a	08 40				08 52				09 04			09 16					09 28			09 40	
Cardiff Central 7	a		08 47	08 52	08 50		08 54	08 59	09 04		09 09	09 14		09 22	09 20	09 24	09 29		09 34	09 39		09 44
	d						08 55	09 01			09 10	09 16				09 25	09 31			09 41		09 46
Grangetown	d						08 59	09 05			09 14	09 20				09 29	09 35			09 45		09 50
Dingle Road	d							09 11				09 26					09 41					09 56
Penarth	a							09 16				09 31					09 46					10 02
Cogan	d						09 03				09 18					09 33				09 48		
Eastbrook	d						09 05				09 20					09 35				09 51		
Dinas Powys	d						09 07				09 22					09 37				09 53		
Cadoxton	d						09 12				09 27					09 42				09 57		
Barry Docks	d						09 15				09 30					09 45				10 00		
Barry 3	d						09 19				09 34					09 49				10 05		
Barry Island	a						09 25				09 40					09 55						
Rhoose Cardiff Int Airport ✈	d																			10 12		
Llantwit Major	d																			10 22		
Bridgend	a																			10 39		

When events are being held at the Millenium Stadium, services are subject to alteration. Please check times before travelling.

Treherbert, Aberdare, Merthyr, Pontypridd, Rhymney and Coryton - Cardiff, Penarth, Barry, Barry Island and Bridgend

Network Diagram - see first Page of Table 130

		AW	AW	AW	AW	AW	AW	AW	AW	AW	AW	AW	AW	AW	AW	AW	AW	AW	AW	AW	AW	AW	AW
Treherbert	d	08 47										09 17									09 47		
Ynyswen	d	08 49										09 19									09 49		
Treorchy	d	08 51										09 21									09 51		
Ton Pentre	d	08 53										09 23									09 53		
Ystrad Rhondda	a	08 56										09 26									09 56		
	d	08 58										09 28									09 58		
Llwynypia	d	09 00										09 30									10 00		
Tonypandy	d	09 03										09 33									10 03		
Dinas Rhondda	d	09 05										09 35									10 05		
Porth	a	09 08										09 38									10 08		
	d	09 09										09 39									10 09		
Trehafod	d	09 12										09 42									10 12		
Merthyr Tydfil	d								09 08									09 38					
Pentre-bach	d								09 12									09 42					
Troed Y Rhiw	d								09 15									09 45					
Merthyr Vale	a								09 18									09 48					
	d								09 20									09 50					
Quakers Yard	d								09 25									09 55					
Aberdare 3	d				08 52									09 22									
Cwmbach	d				08 55									09 25									
Fernhill	d				08 58									09 28									
Mountain Ash	a				09 01									09 31									
	d				09 04									09 34									
Penrhiwceiber	d				09 07									09 37									
Abercynon	d				09 13				09 29					09 43				09 59					
Pontypridd 3	a	09 17			09 22				09 37			09 47		09 52				10 07			10 17		
	d	09 18			09 24				09 39			09 48		09 54				10 09			10 18		
Trefforest	d	09 21			09 27				09 42			09 51		09 57				10 12			10 21		
Trefforest Estate	d								09 46									10 16					
Taffs Well 3	d	09 28			09 34				09 50			09 58		10 04				10 20			10 28		
Radyr 3	a	09 31			09 37				09 53			10 01		10 07				10 23			10 31		
	d	09 31	09 34		09 37				09 53			10 01	10 04	10 07				10 23			10 31	10 34	
Danescourt	d		09 38										10 08									10 38	
Fairwater	d		09 40										10 10									10 40	
Waun-gron Park	d		09 42										10 12									10 42	
Ninian Park	d		09 45										10 15									10 45	
Llandaf	d	09 34			09 40				09 56			10 04		10 10				10 26			10 34		
Cathays	d	09 39			09 45				10 01			10 09		10 15				10 31			10 39		
Rhymney 3	d														09 29								
Pontlottyn	d														09 32								
Tir-phil	d														09 36								
Brithdir	d														09 39								
Bargoed	a														09 42								
	d					09 17				09 32					09 47					10 02			
Gilfach Fargoed	d					09 19																	
Pengam	d					09 22				09 37					09 52					10 07			
Hengoed	d					09 25				09 40					09 55					10 10			
Ystrad Mynach 3	d					09 28				09 43					09 58					10 13			
Llanbradach	d					09 33				09 48					10 03					10 18			
Aber	d					09 37				09 52					10 07					10 22			
Caerphilly 3	d					09 40				09 55					10 10					10 25			
Lisvane & Thornhill	d					09 44				09 59					10 14					10 29			
Llanishen	d					09 46				10 01					10 16					10 31			
Heath High Level	d					09 49				10 04					10 19					10 34			
Coryton	d						09 45										10 15						
Whitchurch (Cardiff)	d						09 46										10 16						
Rhiwbina	d						09 48										10 18						
Birchgrove	d						09 50										10 20						
Ty Glas	d						09 51										10 21						
Heath Low Level	d						09 54										10 24						
Cardiff Queen Street 3	a	09 44			09 49	09 54	09 59		10 04	10 09		10 14		10 19	10 24		10 29	10 34		10 39	10 44		
	d	09 46		09 48	09 51	09 56	10 01	10 00	10 06	10 11	10 12	10 16		10 21	10 26	10 24	10 31	10 36	10 36	10 41	10 46		10 48
Cardiff Bay	a			09 52				10 04			10 16					10 28			10 40				10 52
Cardiff Central 7	a	09 52	09 50		09 54	09 59	10 04		10 09	10 14		10 22	10 20	10 24	10 29		10 34	10 39		10 44	10 52	10 50	
	d				09 55	10 01			10 10	10 16				10 25	10 31			10 41		10 46			
Grangetown	d				09 59	10 05			10 14	10 20				10 29	10 35			10 45		10 50			
Dingle Road	d					10 11				10 26					10 41					10 56			
Penarth	a					10 16				10 31					10 46					11 01			
Cogan	d				10 03				10 18					10 33				10 48					
Eastbrook	d				10 05				10 20					10 35				10 51					
Dinas Powys	d				10 07				10 22					10 37				10 53					
Cadoxton	d				10 12				10 27					10 42				10 57					
Barry Docks	d				10 15				10 30					10 45				11 00					
Barry 3	d				10 19				10 34					10 49				11 05					
Barry Island	a				10 25				10 40					10 55									
Rhoose Cardiff Int Airport ✈	d																	11 12					
Llantwit Major	d																	11 22					
Bridgend	a																	11 39					

When events are being held at the Millenium Stadium, services are subject to alteration. Please check times before travelling.

Table 130

Saturdays

Treherbert, Aberdare, Merthyr, Pontypridd, Rhymney and Coryton - Cardiff, Penarth, Barry, Barry Island and Bridgend

Network Diagram - see first Page of Table 130

		AW	AW	AW	AW	AW	AW	AW	AW	AW	AW	AW	AW	AW	AW	AW	AW	AW	AW	AW	AW	AW
Treherbert	d												10 17						10 47			
Ynyswen	d												10 19						10 49			
Treorchy	d												10 21						10 51			
Ton Pentre	d												10 23						10 53			
Ystrad Rhondda	a												10 26						10 56			
	d												10 28						10 58			
Llwynypia	d												10 30						11 00			
Tonypandy	d												10 33						11 03			
Dinas Rhondda	d												10 35						11 05			
Porth	a												10 38						11 08			
	d												10 52						11 09			
Trehafod	d												10 55						11 12			
Merthyr Tydfil	d		10 04													10 38						
Pentre-bach	d		10 08													10 42						
Troed Y Rhiw	d		10 11													10 45						
Merthyr Vale	a		10 14													10 48						
	d		10 16													10 50						
Quakers Yard	d		10 22													10 55						
Aberdare [3]	d	09 52									10 22											10 52
Cwmbach	d	09 55									10 25											10 55
Fernhill	d	09 58									10 28											10 58
Mountain Ash	a	10 01									10 31											11 01
	d	10 04									10 34											11 04
Penrhiwceiber	d	10 07									10 37											11 07
Abercynon	d	10 13	10 26								10 43					10 59						11 13
Pontypridd [3]	a	10 22	10 32								10 52		11 00			11 07			11 17			11 22
	d	10 24					10 39				10 54		11 04			11 09			11 18			11 24
Trefforest	d	10 27					10 42				10 57		11 07			11 12			11 21			11 27
Trefforest Estate	d															11 16						
Taffs Well [3]	d	10 34					10 50				11 04		11 13			11 20			11 28			11 34
Radyr [3]	a	10 37					10 53				11 07		11 17			11 23			11 31			11 37
	d	10 37					10 53		11 04		11 07		11 17			11 23			11 31	11 34		11 37
Danescourt	d								11 08											11 38		
Fairwater	d								11 10											11 40		
Waun-gron Park	d								11 12											11 42		
Ninian Park	d								11 15											11 45		
Llandaf	d	10 40					10 56				11 10					11 26			11 34			11 40
Cathays	d	10 45					11 01				11 15					11 31			11 39			11 45
Rhymney [3]	d											10 29										
Pontlottyn	d											10 32										
Tir-phil	d											10 36										
Brithdir	d											10 39										
Bargoed	a											10 42										
	d			10 17				10 32				10 47						11 02				
Gilfach Fargoed	d			10 19																		
Pengam	d			10 22				10 37				10 52						11 07				
Hengoed	d			10 25				10 40				10 55						11 10				
Ystrad Mynach [3]	d			10 28				10 43				10 58						11 13				
Llanbradach	d			10 33				10 48				11 03						11 18				
Aber	d			10 37				10 52				11 07						11 22				
Caerphilly [3]	d			10 40				10 55				11 10						11 25				
Lisvane & Thornhill	d			10 44				10 59				11 14						11 29				
Llanishen	d			10 46				11 01				11 16						11 31				
Heath High Level	d			10 49				11 04				11 19						11 34				
Coryton	d				10 45										11 15							
Whitchurch (Cardiff)	d				10 46										11 16							
Rhiwbina	d				10 48										11 18							
Birchgrove	d				10 50										11 20							
Ty Glas	d				10 51										11 21							
Heath Low Level	d				10 54										11 24							
Cardiff Queen Street [3]	a	10 49		10 54	10 59		11 04	11 09			11 19	11 24			11 29	11 34		11 39	11 44			11 49
	d	10 51		10 56	11 01	11 00	11 06	11 11		11 12	11 21	11 26		11 24	11 31	11 36	11 36	11 41	11 46		11 48	11 51
Cardiff Bay	a					11 04				11 16				11 28			11 40				11 52	
Cardiff Central [7]	a	10 54		10 59	11 04		11 09	11 14	11 20		11 24	11 29	11 34		11 34	11 39		11 44	11 52	11 50		11 54
	d	10 55		11 01			11 10	11 16			11 25	11 31				11 41		11 46				11 55
Grangetown	d	10 59		11 05			11 14	11 20			11 29	11 35				11 45		11 50				11 59
Dingle Road	d			11 11				11 26				11 41						11 56				
Penarth	a			11 16				11 31				11 46						12 01				
Cogan	d	11 03					11 18				11 33					11 48						12 03
Eastbrook	d	11 05					11 20				11 35					11 51						12 05
Dinas Powys	d	11 07					11 22				11 37					11 53						12 07
Cadoxton	d	11 12					11 27				11 42					11 57						12 12
Barry Docks	d	11 15					11 30				11 45					12 00						12 15
Barry [3]	d	11 19					11 34				11 49					12 05						12 19
Barry Island	a	11 25					11 40				11 55											12 25
Rhoose Cardiff Int Airport ✈	d															12 12						
Llantwit Major	d															12 22						
Bridgend	a															12 39						

When events are being held at the Millenium Stadium, services are subject to alteration. Please check times before travelling.

Table 130

Saturdays

Treherbert, Aberdare, Merthyr, Pontypridd, Rhymney and Coryton - Cardiff, Penarth, Barry, Barry Island and Bridgend

Network Diagram - see first Page of Table 130

		AW	AW	AW	AW	AW	AW	AW	AW	AW		AW	AW	AW	AW	AW	AW	AW	AW	AW		AW	AW	AW	AW
Treherbert	d							11 17										11 47							
Ynyswen	d							11 19										11 49							
Treorchy	d							11 21										11 51							
Ton Pentre	d							11 23										11 53							
Ystrad Rhondda	a							11 26										11 56							
	d							11 28										11 58							
Llwynypia	d							11 30										12 00							
Tonypandy	d							11 33										12 03							
Dinas Rhondda	d							11 35										12 05							
Porth	a							11 38										12 08							
	d							11 39										12 09							
Trehafod	d							11 42										12 12							
Merthyr Tydfil	d				11 08										11 38										12 08
Pentre-bach	d				11 12										11 42										12 12
Troed Y Rhiw	d				11 15										11 45										12 15
Merthyr Vale	a				11 18										11 48										12 18
	d				11 20										11 50										12 20
Quakers Yard	d				11 25										11 55										12 25
Aberdare 3	d									11 22															
Cwmbach	d									11 25															
Fernhill	d									11 28															
Mountain Ash	a									11 31															
	d									11 34															
Penrhiwceiber	d									11 37															
Abercynon	d				11 29					11 43					11 59										12 29
Pontypridd 3	a				11 37			11 47		11 52					12 07			12 17							12 37
	d				11 39			11 48		11 54					12 09			12 18							12 39
Trefforest	d				11 42			11 51		11 57					12 12			12 21							12 42
Trefforest Estate	d				11 46										12 16										12 46
Taffs Well 3	d				11 50			11 58		12 04					12 20			12 28							12 50
Radyr 3	a				11 53			12 01		12 07					12 23			12 31							12 53
	d				11 53			12 01	12 04	12 07					12 23			12 31	12 34						12 53
Danescourt	d								12 08										12 38						
Fairwater	d								12 10										12 40						
Waun-gron Park	d								12 12										12 42						
Ninian Park	d								12 15										12 45						
Llandaf	d				11 56			12 04		12 10					12 26			12 34							12 56
Cathays	d				12 01			12 09		12 15					12 31			12 39							13 01
Rhymney 3	d											11 29													
Pontlottyn	d											11 32													
Tir-phil	d											11 36													
Brithdir	d											11 39													
Bargoed	a											11 42													
	d	11 17				11 32						11 47					12 02					12 17			
Gilfach Fargoed	d	11 19																				12 19			
Pengam	d	11 22				11 37						11 52					12 07					12 22			
Hengoed	d	11 25				11 40						11 55					12 10					12 25			
Ystrad Mynach 3	d	11 28				11 43						11 58					12 13					12 28			
Llanbradach	d	11 33				11 48						12 03					12 18					12 33			
Aber	d	11 37				11 52						12 07					12 22					12 37			
Caerphilly 3	d	11 40				11 55						12 10					12 25					12 40			
Lisvane & Thornhill	d	11 44				11 59						12 14					12 29					12 44			
Llanishen	d	11 46				12 01						12 16					12 31					12 46			
Heath High Level	d	11 49				12 04						12 19					12 34					12 49			
Coryton	d		11 45											12 15									12 45		
Whitchurch (Cardiff)	d		11 46											12 16									12 46		
Rhiwbina	d		11 48											12 18									12 48		
Birchgrove	d		11 50											12 20									12 50		
Ty Glas	d		11 51											12 21									12 51		
Heath Low Level	d		11 54											12 24									12 54		
Cardiff Queen Street 3	a	11 54	11 59		12 04	12 09		12 14		12 19		12 24		12 29	12 34		12 39	12 44				12 54	12 59		13 04
	d	11 56	12 01	12 00	12 06	12 11	12 12	12 16		12 21		12 26	12 24	12 31	12 36	12 36	12 41	12 46		12 48		12 56	13 01	13 00	13 06
Cardiff Bay	a			12 04			12 16						12 28			12 40				12 52				13 04	
Cardiff Central 7	a	11 59	12 04		12 09	12 14		12 22	12 20	12 24		12 29		12 34	12 39		12 44	12 52	12 50			12 59	13 04		13 09
	d	12 01			12 10	12 16				12 25		12 31			12 41		12 46	12 55				13 01			13 10
Grangetown	d	12 05			12 14	12 20				12 29		12 35			12 45		12 50	12 59				13 05			13 14
Dingle Road	d	12 11				12 26						12 41					12 56					13 11			
Penarth	a	12 16				12 31						12 46					13 01					13 16			
Cogan	d				12 18					12 33					12 48			13 03							13 18
Eastbrook	d				12 20					12 35					12 51			13 05							13 20
Dinas Powys	d				12 22					12 37					12 53			13 07							13 22
Cadoxton	d				12 27					12 42					12 57			13 12							13 27
Barry Docks	d				12 30					12 45					13 00			13 15							13 30
Barry 3	d				12 34					12 49					13 05			13 19							13 34
Barry Island	a				12 40					12 55								13 25							13 40
Rhoose Cardiff Int Airport ✈	d														13 12										
Llantwit Major	d														13 22										
Bridgend	a														13 39										

When events are being held at the Millenium Stadium,
services are subject to alteration. Please check times before travelling.

Table 130

Saturdays

Treherbert, Aberdare, Merthyr, Pontypridd, Rhymney and Coryton - Cardiff, Penarth, Barry, Barry Island and Bridgend

Network Diagram - see first Page of Table 130

		AW	AW	AW	AW	AW		AW	AW	AW	AW	AW	AW	AW	AW	AW		AW	AW	AW	AW	AW	AW	AW	AW
Treherbert	d			12 17										12 47											13 17
Ynyswen	d			12 19										12 49											13 19
Treorchy	d			12 21										12 51											13 21
Ton Pentre	d			12 23										12 53											13 23
Ystrad Rhondda	a			12 26										12 56											13 26
	d			12 28										12 58											13 28
Llwynypia	d			12 30										13 00											13 30
Tonypandy	d			12 33										13 03											13 33
Dinas Rhondda	d			12 35										13 05											13 35
Porth	a			12 38										13 08											13 38
	d			12 39										13 09											13 39
Trehafod	d			12 42										13 12											13 42
Merthyr Tydfil	d										12 38											13 08			
Pentre-bach	d										12 42											13 12			
Troed Y Rhiw	d										12 45											13 15			
Merthyr Vale	a										12 48											13 18			
	d										12 50											13 20			
Quakers Yard	d										12 55											13 25			
Aberdare 3	d					12 22												12 52							
Cwmbach	d					12 25												12 55							
Fernhill	d					12 28												12 58							
Mountain Ash	a					12 31												13 01							
	d					12 34												13 04							
Penrhiwceiber	d					12 37												13 07							
Abercynon	d					12 43					12 59							13 13				13 29			
Pontypridd 3	a			12 48		12 52					13 07			13 17				13 22				13 37			13 47
	d			12 48		12 54					13 09			13 18				13 24				13 39			13 48
Trefforest	d			12 51		12 57					13 12			13 21				13 27				13 42			13 51
Trefforest Estate	d										13 16											13 46			
Taffs Well 3	d			12 58		13 04					13 20			13 28				13 34				13 50			13 58
Radyr 3	a			13 01		13 07					13 23			13 31				13 37				13 53			14 01
	d			13 01	13 04	13 07					13 23			13 31	13 34			13 37				13 53			14 01
Danescourt	d				13 08										13 38										
Fairwater	d				13 10										13 40										
Waun-gron Park	d				13 12										13 42										
Ninian Park	d				13 15										13 45										
Llandaf	d			13 04		13 10					13 26			13 34				13 40				13 56			14 04
Cathays	d			13 09		13 15					13 31			13 39				13 45				14 01			14 09
Rhymney 3	d							12 29																	
Pontlottyn	d							12 32																	
Tir-phil	d							12 36																	
Brithdir	d							12 39																	
Bargoed	a							12 42																	
	d	12 32						12 47					13 02						13 17				13 32		
Gilfach Fargoed	d																		13 19						
Pengam	d	12 37						12 52					13 07						13 22				13 37		
Hengoed	d	12 40						12 55					13 10						13 25				13 40		
Ystrad Mynach 3	d	12 43						12 58					13 13						13 28				13 43		
Llanbradach	d	12 48						13 03					13 18						13 33				13 48		
Aber	d	12 52						13 07					13 22						13 37				13 52		
Caerphilly 3	d	12 55						13 10					13 25						13 40				13 55		
Lisvane & Thornhill	d	12 59						13 14					13 29						13 44				13 59		
Llanishen	d	13 01						13 16					13 31						13 46				14 01		
Heath High Level	d	13 04						13 19					13 34						13 49				14 04		
Coryton	d									13 15										13 45					
Whitchurch (Cardiff)	d									13 16										13 46					
Rhiwbina	d									13 18										13 48					
Birchgrove	d									13 20										13 50					
Ty Glas	d									13 21										13 51					
Heath Low Level	d									13 24										13 54					
Cardiff Queen Street 3	a	13 09		13 14		13 19		13 24		13 29	13 34		13 39	13 44				13 49	13 54	13 59		14 04	14 09		14 14
	d	13 11	13 12	13 16		13 21		13 26	13 24	13 31	13 36	13 36	13 41	13 46		13 48		13 51	13 56	14 01	14 00	14 06	14 11	14 12	14 16
Cardiff Bay	a		13 16						13 28			13 40				13 52					14 04			14 16	
Cardiff Central 7	a	13 14		13 22	13 20	13 24		13 29		13 34	13 39		13 44	13 52	13 50			13 54	13 59	14 04		14 09	14 14		14 22
	d	13 16				13 25		13 31			13 41		13 46					13 55	14 01			14 10	14 16		
Grangetown	d	13 20				13 29		13 35			13 45		13 50					13 59	14 05			14 14	14 20		
Dingle Road	d	13 26						13 41					13 56						14 11				14 26		
Penarth	a	13 31						13 46					14 01						14 16				14 31		
Cogan	d					13 33					13 48							14 03				14 18			
Eastbrook	d					13 35					13 51							14 05				14 20			
Dinas Powys	d					13 37					13 53							14 07				14 22			
Cadoxton	d					13 42					13 57							14 12				14 27			
Barry Docks	d					13 45					14 00							14 15				14 30			
Barry 3	d					13 49					14 05							14 19				14 34			
Barry Island	a					13 55												14 25				14 40			
Rhoose Cardiff Int Airport ✈	d										14 12														
Llantwit Major	d										14 22														
Bridgend	a										14 39														

When events are being held at the Millenium Stadium, services are subject to alteration. Please check times before travelling.

Table 130

Saturdays

Treherbert, Aberdare, Merthyr, Pontypridd, Rhymney and Coryton - Cardiff, Penarth, Barry, Barry Island and Bridgend

Network Diagram - see first Page of Table 130

Station		AW		AW	AW	AW	AW	AW	AW	AW	AW	AW		AW	AW	AW	AW	AW	AW	AW	AW	AW		AW	AW
Treherbert	d										13 47														
Ynyswen	d										13 49														
Treorchy	d										13 51														
Ton Pentre	d										13 53														
Ystrad Rhondda	a										13 56														
	d										13 58														
Llwynypia	d										14 00														
Tonypandy	d										14 03														
Dinas Rhondda	d										14 05														
Porth	a										14 08														
	d										14 09														
Trehafod	d										14 12														
Merthyr Tydfil	d						13 38												14 08						
Pentre-bach	d						13 42												14 12						
Troed Y Rhiw	d						13 45												14 15						
Merthyr Vale	a						13 48												14 18						
	d						13 50												14 20						
Quakers Yard	d						13 55												14 25						
Aberdare 3	d														13 52									14 22	
Cwmbach	d														13 55									14 25	
Fernhill	d														13 58									14 28	
Mountain Ash	a														14 01									14 31	
	d														14 04									14 34	
Penrhiwceiber	d														14 07									14 37	
Abercynon	d			13 45				13 59							14 13				14 29					14 43	
Pontypridd 3	a			13 52				14 07			14 17				14 22				14 37					14 52	
	d			13 54				14 09			14 18				14 24				14 39					14 54	
Trefforest	d			13 57				14 12			14 21				14 27				14 42					14 57	
Trefforest Estate	d							14 16											14 46						
Taffs Well 3	d			14 04				14 20			14 28				14 34				14 50					15 04	
Radyr 3	a			14 07				14 23			14 31				14 37				14 53					15 07	
	d	14 04		14 07				14 23			14 31	14 34			14 37				14 53		15 04			15 07	
Danescourt	d	14 08										14 38									15 08				
Fairwater	d	14 10										14 40									15 10				
Waun-gron Park	d	14 12										14 42									15 12				
Ninian Park	d	14 15										14 45									15 15				
Llandaf	d			14 10				14 26			14 34				14 40				14 56					15 10	
Cathays	d			14 15				14 31			14 39				14 45				15 01					15 15	
Rhymney 3	d				13 29																				14 29
Pontlottyn	d				13 32																				14 32
Tir-phil	d				13 36																				14 36
Brithdir	d				13 39																				14 39
Bargoed	a				13 42																				14 42
	d				13 47					14 02						14 17				14 32					14 47
Gilfach Fargoed	d															14 19									
Pengam	d				13 52					14 07						14 22				14 37					14 52
Hengoed	d				13 55					14 10						14 25				14 40					14 55
Ystrad Mynach 3	d				13 58					14 13						14 28				14 43					14 58
Llanbradach	d				14 03					14 18						14 33				14 48					15 03
Aber	d				14 07					14 22						14 37				14 52					15 07
Caerphilly 3	d				14 10					14 25						14 40				14 55					15 10
Lisvane & Thornhill	d				14 14					14 29						14 44				14 59					15 14
Llanishen	d				14 16					14 31						14 46				15 01					15 16
Heath High Level	d				14 19					14 34						14 49				15 04					15 19
Coryton	d						14 15										14 45								
Whitchurch (Cardiff)	d						14 16										14 46								
Rhiwbina	d						14 18										14 48								
Birchgrove	d						14 20										14 50								
Ty Glas	d						14 21										14 51								
Heath Low Level	d						14 24										14 54								
Cardiff Queen Street 3	a			14 19	14 24		14 29	14 34		14 39	14 44				14 49	14 54	14 59		15 04	15 09				15 19	15 24
	d			14 21	14 26	14 24	14 31	14 36	14 36	14 41	14 46			14 48	14 51	14 56	15 01	15 00	15 06	15 11		15 12		15 21	15 26
Cardiff Bay	a					14 28			14 40					14 52				15 04				15 16			
Cardiff Central 7	a	14 20		14 24	14 29		14 34	14 39		14 44	14 52	14 50			14 54	14 59	15 04		15 09	15 14	15 20			15 24	15 29
	d			14 25	14 31			14 41		14 46					14 55	15 01			15 10	15 16				15 25	15 31
Grangetown	d			14 29	14 35			14 45		14 50					14 59	15 05			15 14	15 20				15 29	15 35
Dingle Road	d				14 41					14 56						15 11				15 26					15 41
Penarth	a				14 46					15 01						15 16				15 31					15 46
Cogan	d			14 33				14 48							15 03				15 18					15 33	
Eastbrook	d			14 35				14 51							15 05				15 20					15 35	
Dinas Powys	d			14 37				14 53							15 07				15 22					15 37	
Cadoxton	d			14 42				14 57							15 12				15 27					15 42	
Barry Docks	d			14 45				15 00							15 15				15 30					15 45	
Barry 3	d			14 49				15 05							15 19				15 34					15 49	
Barry Island	a			14 55											15 25				15 40					15 55	
Rhoose Cardiff Int Airport ✈	d							15 12																	
Llantwit Major	d							15 22																	
Bridgend	a							15 39																	

When events are being held at the Millenium Stadium, services are subject to alteration. Please check times before travelling.

Table 130

Saturdays

Treherbert, Aberdare, Merthyr, Pontypridd, Rhymney and Coryton - Cardiff, Penarth, Barry, Barry Island and Bridgend

Network Diagram - see first Page of Table 130

		AW	AW	AW	AW	AW	AW	AW	AW	AW	AW	AW	AW	AW	AW	AW	AW	AW	AW	AW	AW	AW	AW
Treherbert	d	14 17						14 47										15 13					
Ynyswen	d	14 19						14 49										15 15					
Treorchy	d	14 21						14 51										15 21					
Ton Pentre	d	14 23						14 53										15 23					
Ystrad Rhondda	a	14 26						14 56										15 26					
	d	14 28						14 58										15 28					
Llwynypia	d	14 30						15 00										15 30					
Tonypandy	d	14 33						15 03										15 33					
Dinas Rhondda	d	14 35						15 05										15 35					
Porth	a	14 38						15 08										15 38					
	d	14 52						15 09										15 39					
Trehafod	d	14 55						15 12										15 42					
Merthyr Tydfil	d				14 38										15 08								
Pentre-bach	d				14 42										15 12								
Troed Y Rhiw	d				14 45										15 15								
Merthyr Vale	a				14 48										15 18								
	d				14 50										15 20								
Quakers Yard	d				14 55										15 25								
Aberdare 3	d										14 52									15 22			
Cwmbach	d										14 55									15 25			
Fernhill	d										14 58									15 28			
Mountain Ash	a										15 01									15 31			
	d										15 04									15 34			
Penrhiwceiber	d										15 07									15 37			
Abercynon	d				14 59						15 13				15 29					15 43			
Pontypridd 3	a	15 00			15 07			15 17			15 22				15 37			15 47		15 52			
	d	15 04			15 09			15 18			15 24				15 39			15 48		15 54			
Trefforest	d	15 07			15 12			15 21			15 27				15 42			15 51		15 57			
Trefforest Estate	d				15 16										15 46								
Taffs Well 3	d	15 13			15 20			15 28			15 34				15 50			15 58		16 04			
Radyr 3	a	15 17			15 23			15 31			15 37				15 53			16 01		16 07			
	d	15 17			15 23			15 31	15 34		15 37				15 53			16 01	16 04	16 07			
Danescourt	d								15 38										16 08				
Fairwater	d								15 40										16 10				
Waun-gron Park	d								15 42										16 12				
Ninian Park	d								15 45										16 15				
Llandaf	d				15 26			15 34			15 40				15 56			16 04		16 10			
Cathays	d				15 31			15 39			15 45				16 01			16 09		16 15			
Rhymney 3	d																				15 29		
Pontlottyn	d																				15 32		
Tir-phil	d																				15 36		
Brithdir	d																				15 39		
Bargoed	a																				15 42		
	d						15 02					15 17				15 32					15 47		
Gilfach Fargoed	d											15 19											
Pengam	d						15 07					15 22				15 37					15 52		
Hengoed	d						15 10					15 25				15 40					15 55		
Ystrad Mynach 3	d						15 13					15 28				15 43					15 58		
Llanbradach	d						15 18					15 33				15 48					16 03		
Aber	d						15 22					15 37				15 52					16 07		
Caerphilly 3	d						15 25					15 40				15 55					16 10		
Lisvane & Thornhill	d						15 29					15 44				15 59					16 14		
Llanishen	d						15 31					15 46				16 01					16 16		
Heath High Level	d						15 34					15 49				16 04					16 19		
Coryton	d			15 15									15 45										16 15
Whitchurch (Cardiff)	d			15 16									15 46										16 16
Rhiwbina	d			15 18									15 48										16 18
Birchgrove	d			15 20									15 50										16 20
Ty Glas	d			15 21									15 51										16 21
Heath Low Level	d			15 24									15 54										16 24
Cardiff Queen Street 3	a			15 29	15 34		15 39	15 44			15 49	15 54	15 59		16 04	16 09		16 14		16 19	16 24		16 29
	d		15 24	15 31	15 36	15 36	15 41	15 46		15 48	15 51	15 56	16 01	16 00	16 06	16 11	16 12	16 16		16 21	16 26	16 24	16 31
Cardiff Bay	a		15 28			15 40				15 52				16 04			16 16					16 28	
Cardiff Central 7	a	15 34		15 34	15 39		15 44	15 52	15 50		15 54	15 59	16 04		16 09	16 14		16 22	16 20	16 24	16 32		16 34
	d				15 41		15 46				15 55	16 01			16 10	16 16				16 25			
Grangetown	d				15 45		15 50				15 59	16 05			16 14	16 20				16 29			
Dingle Road	d						15 56					16 11				16 26							
Penarth	a						16 01					16 16				16 31							
Cogan	d				15 48						16 03				16 18					16 33			
Eastbrook	d				15 51						16 05				16 20					16 35			
Dinas Powys	d				15 53						16 07				16 22					16 37			
Cadoxton	d				15 57						16 12				16 27					16 42			
Barry Docks	d				16 00						16 15				16 30					16 45			
Barry 3	d				16 05						16 19				16 34					16 49			
Barry Island	a										16 25				16 40					16 55			
Rhoose Cardiff Int Airport ✈	d				16 12																		
Llantwit Major	d				16 22																		
Bridgend	a				16 39																		

When events are being held at the Millenium Stadium, services are subject to alteration. Please check times before travelling.

Table 130

Saturdays

Treherbert, Aberdare, Merthyr, Pontypridd, Rhymney and Coryton - Cardiff, Penarth, Barry, Barry Island and Bridgend

Network Diagram - see first Page of Table 130

		AW	AW	AW	AW	AW	AW	AW	AW	AW	AW	AW	AW	AW	AW	AW	AW	AW	AW	AW	AW	AW
Treherbert	d				15 47										16 17							
Ynyswen	d				15 49										16 19							
Treorchy	d				15 51										16 21							
Ton Pentre	d				15 53										16 23							
Ystrad Rhondda	a				15 56										16 26							
	d				15 58										16 28							
Llwynypia	d				16 00										16 30							
Tonypandy	d				16 03										16 33							
Dinas Rhondda	d				16 05										16 35							
Porth	a				16 08										16 38							
	d				16 09										16 39							
Trehafod	d				16 12										16 42							
Merthyr Tydfil	d	15 38										16 08									16 38	
Pentre-bach	d	15 42										16 12									16 42	
Troed Y Rhiw	d	15 45										16 15									16 45	
Merthyr Vale	a	15 48										16 18									16 48	
	d	15 50										16 20									16 50	
Quakers Yard	d	15 55										16 25									16 55	
Aberdare 3	d							15 52									16 22					
Cwmbach	d							15 55									16 25					
Fernhill	d							15 58									16 28					
Mountain Ash	a							16 01									16 31					
	d							16 04									16 34					
Penrhiwceiber	d							16 07									16 37					
Abercynon	d	15 59						16 13				16 29					16 43				16 59	
Pontypridd 3	a	16 07			16 17			16 22				16 37			16 47		16 52				17 07	
	d	16 09			16 18			16 24				16 39			16 48		16 54				17 09	
Trefforest	d	16 12			16 21			16 27				16 42			16 51		16 57				17 12	
Trefforest Estate	d	16 16										16 46									17 16	
Taffs Well 3	d	16 20			16 28			16 34				16 50			16 58		17 04				17 20	
Radyr 3	a	16 23			16 31			16 37				16 53			17 01		17 07				17 23	
	d	16 23			16 32	16 34		16 37				16 53			17 01	17 04	17 07				17 23	
Danescourt	d					16 38										17 08						
Fairwater	d					16 40										17 10						
Waun-gron Park	d					16 42										17 12						
Ninian Park	d					16 45										17 15						
Llandaf	d	16 26			16 34			16 40				16 56			17 04		17 10				17 26	
Cathays	d	16 31			16 39			16 45				17 01			17 09		17 15				17 31	
Rhymney 3	d																	16 29				
Pontlottyn	d																	16 32				
Tir-phil	d																	16 36				
Brithdir	d																	16 39				
Bargoed	a																	16 42				
	d			16 02					16 17				16 32					16 47				
Gilfach Fargoed	d								16 19													
Pengam	d			16 07					16 22				16 37					16 52				
Hengoed	d			16 10					16 25				16 40					16 55				
Ystrad Mynach 3	d			16 13					16 28				16 43					16 58				
Llanbradach	d			16 18					16 33				16 48					17 03				
Aber	d			16 22					16 37				16 52					17 07				
Caerphilly 3	d			16 25					16 40				16 55					17 10				
Lisvane & Thornhill	d			16 29					16 44				16 59					17 14				
Llanishen	d			16 31					16 46				17 01					17 16				
Heath High Level	d			16 34					16 49				17 04					17 19				
Coryton	d									16 45										17 15		
Whitchurch (Cardiff)	d									16 46										17 16		
Rhiwbina	d									16 48										17 18		
Birchgrove	d									16 50										17 20		
Ty Glas	d									16 51										17 21		
Heath Low Level	d									16 54										17 24		
Cardiff Queen Street 3	a	16 34		16 39	16 44			16 49	16 54	16 59		17 04	17 09		17 14		17 19	17 24		17 29	17 34	
	d	16 36	16 36	16 41	16 46		16 48	16 51	16 56	17 01	17 00	17 06	17 11	17 12	17 16		17 21	17 26	17 24	17 31	17 36	17 36
Cardiff Bay	a		16 40				16 52				17 04			17 16					17 28			17 40
Cardiff Central 7	a	16 39		16 44	16 53	16 50		16 54	16 59	17 04		17 09	17 14		17 22	17 20	17 24	17 29		17 34	17 39	
	d	16 41		16 46				16 55	17 01			17 10	17 16				17 25	17 31			17 41	
Grangetown	d	16 45		16 50				16 59	17 05			17 14	17 20				17 29	17 35			17 45	
Dingle Road	d			16 56					17 11				17 26					17 41				
Penarth	a			17 01					17 16				17 31					17 46				
Cogan	d	16 48						17 03				17 18					17 33				17 48	
Eastbrook	d	16 51						17 05				17 20					17 35				17 51	
Dinas Powys	d	16 53						17 07				17 22					17 37				17 53	
Cadoxton	d	16 57						17 12				17 27					17 42				17 57	
Barry Docks	d	17 00						17 15				17 30					17 45				18 00	
Barry 3	d	17 05						17 19				17 34					17 49				18 05	
Barry Island	a							17 25				17 40					17 55					
Rhoose Cardiff Int Airport ✈	d	17 12																			18 12	
Llantwit Major	d	17 22																			18 22	
Bridgend	a	17 39																			18 39	

When events are being held at the Millenium Stadium, services are subject to alteration. Please check times before travelling.

Table 130

Saturdays

Treherbert, Aberdare, Merthyr, Pontypridd, Rhymney and Coryton - Cardiff, Penarth, Barry, Barry Island and Bridgend

Network Diagram - see first Page of Table 130

		AW	AW	AW	AW	AW	AW	AW	AW	AW	AW	AW	AW	AW	AW	AW	AW	AW	AW	AW	AW	AW	AW
Treherbert	d		16 47										17 17								17 47		
Ynyswen	d		16 49										17 19								17 49		
Treorchy	d		16 51										17 21								17 51		
Ton Pentre	d		16 53										17 23								17 53		
Ystrad Rhondda	a		16 56										17 26								17 56		
	d		16 58										17 28								17 58		
Llwynypia	d		17 00										17 30								18 00		
Tonypandy	d		17 03										17 33								18 03		
Dinas Rhondda	d		17 05										17 35								18 05		
Porth	a		17 08										17 38								18 08		
	d		17 09										17 39								18 09		
Trehafod	d		17 12										17 42								18 12		
Merthyr Tydfil	d									17 08									17 38				
Pentre-bach	d									17 12									17 42				
Troed Y Rhiw	d									17 15									17 45				
Merthyr Vale	a									17 18									17 48				
	d									17 20									17 50				
Quakers Yard	d									17 25									17 55				
Aberdare 3	d					16 52									17 22								
Cwmbach	d					16 55									17 25								
Fernhill	d					16 58									17 28								
Mountain Ash	a					17 01									17 31								
	d					17 04									17 34								
Penrhiwceiber	d					17 07									17 37								
Abercynon	d					17 13				17 29					17 43				17 59				
Pontypridd 3	a		17 17			17 22				17 37			17 47		17 52				18 07		18 17		
	d		17 18			17 24				17 39			17 48		17 54				18 09		18 18		
Trefforest	d		17 21			17 27				17 42			17 51		17 57				18 12		18 21		
Trefforest Estate	d									17 46									18 16				
Taffs Well 3	d		17 28			17 34				17 50			17 58		18 04				18 20		18 28		
Radyr 3	a		17 31			17 37				17 53			18 01		18 07				18 23		18 31		
	d		17 31	17 34		17 37				17 53			18 01	18 04	18 07				18 23		18 31	18 34	
Danescourt	d			17 38										18 08								18 38	
Fairwater	d			17 40										18 10								18 40	
Waun-gron Park	d			17 42										18 12								18 42	
Ninian Park	d			17 45										18 15								18 45	
Llandaf	d		17 34			17 40				17 56			18 04		18 10				18 26		18 34		
Cathays	d		17 39			17 45				18 01			18 09		18 15				18 31		18 39		
Rhymney 3	d															17 29							
Pontlottyn	d															17 32							
Tir-phil	d															17 36							
Brithdir	d															17 39							
Bargoed	a															17 42							
	d	17 02					17 17				17 32					17 47							
Gilfach Fargoed	d						17 19																
Pengam	d	17 07					17 22				17 37					17 52							
Hengoed	d	17 10					17 25				17 40					17 55							
Ystrad Mynach 3	d	17 13					17 28				17 43					17 58							
Llanbradach	d	17 18					17 33				17 48					18 03							
Aber	d	17 22					17 37				17 52					18 07							
Caerphilly 3	d	17 25					17 40				17 55					18 10							
Lisvane & Thornhill	d	17 29					17 44				17 59					18 14							
Llanishen	d	17 31					17 46				18 01					18 16							
Heath High Level	d	17 34					17 49				18 04					18 19							
Coryton	d							17 45										18 15					
Whitchurch (Cardiff)	d							17 46										18 16					
Rhiwbina	d							17 48										18 18					
Birchgrove	d							17 50										18 20					
Ty Glas	d							17 51										18 21					
Heath Low Level	d							17 54										18 24					
Cardiff Queen Street 3	a	17 39	17 44			17 49	17 54	17 59		18 04	18 09		18 14		18 19	18 24		18 29	18 34		18 44		
	d	17 41	17 46		17 48	17 51	17 56	18 01	18 00	18 06	18 11	18 12	18 16		18 21	18 26	18 24	18 31	18 36	18 36	18 46		18 48
Cardiff Bay	a				17 52				18 04			18 16					18 28			18 40			18 52
Cardiff Central 7	a	17 44	17 52	17 50		17 54	17 59	18 04		18 09	18 14		18 22	18 20	18 24	18 29		18 34	18 39		18 52	18 50	
	d	17 46				17 55	18 01			18 10	18 16				18 25	18 31			18 41				
Grangetown	d	17 50				17 59	18 05			18 14	18 20				18 29	18 35			18 45				
Dingle Road	d	17 56					18 11				18 26					18 41							
Penarth	a	18 01					18 16				18 31					18 46							
Cogan	d					18 03				18 18					18 33				18 48				
Eastbrook	d					18 05				18 20					18 35				18 51				
Dinas Powys	d					18 07				18 22					18 37				18 53				
Cadoxton	d					18 12				18 27					18 42				18 57				
Barry Docks	d					18 15				18 30					18 45				19 00				
Barry 3	d					18 19				18 34					18 49				19 05				
Barry Island	a					18 25				18 40					18 55								
Rhoose Cardiff Int Airport ✈	d																		19 12				
Llantwit Major	d																		19 22				
Bridgend	a																		19 39				

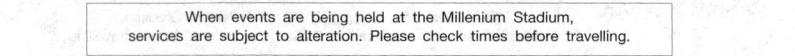

When events are being held at the Millenium Stadium, services are subject to alteration. Please check times before travelling.

Table 130

Saturdays

Treherbert, Aberdare, Merthyr, Pontypridd, Rhymney and Coryton - Cardiff, Penarth, Barry, Barry Island and Bridgend

Network Diagram - see first Page of Table 130

		AW	AW	AW	AW	AW		AW	AW	AW	AW	AW	AW	AW	AW	AW		AW	AW	AW	AW	AW	AW	AW	AW
Treherbert	d								18 17									18 47							19 17
Ynyswen	d								18 19									18 49							19 19
Treorchy	d								18 21									18 51							19 21
Ton Pentre	d								18 23									18 53							19 23
Ystrad Rhondda	a								18 26									18 56							19 26
	d								18 28									18 58							19 28
Llwynypia	d								18 30									19 00							19 30
Tonypandy	d								18 33									19 03							19 33
Dinas Rhondda	d								18 35									19 05							19 35
Porth	a								18 38									19 08							19 38
	d								18 39									19 09							19 39
Trehafod	d								18 42									19 12							19 42
Merthyr Tydfil	d					18 08									18 38								19 08		
Pentre-bach	d					18 12									18 42								19 12		
Troed Y Rhiw	d					18 15									18 45								19 15		
Merthyr Vale	a					18 18									18 48								19 18		
	d					18 20									18 50								19 20		
Quakers Yard	d					18 25									18 55								19 25		
Aberdare [3]	d	17 52									18 22									18 52					
Cwmbach	d	17 55									18 25									18 55					
Fernhill	d	17 58									18 28									18 58					
Mountain Ash	a	18 01									18 31									19 01					
	d	18 04									18 34									19 04					
Penrhiwceiber	d	18 07									18 37									19 07					
Abercynon	d	18 13				18 29					18 43				18 59					19 13			19 29		
Pontypridd [3]	a	18 22				18 37			18 47		18 52				19 07			19 17		19 22			19 37		19 47
	d	18 24				18 39			18 48		18 54				19 09			19 18		19 24			19 39		19 48
Trefforest	d	18 27				18 42			18 51		18 57				19 12			19 21		19 27			19 42		19 51
Trefforest Estate	d					18 46									19 16								19 46		
Taffs Well [3]	d	18 34				18 50			18 58		19 04				19 20			19 28		19 34			19 50		19 58
Radyr [3]	a	18 37				18 53			19 01		19 07				19 23			19 31		19 37			19 53		20 01
	d	18 37				18 53			19 01	19 04	19 07				19 23			19 31		19 37			19 53		20 01
Danescourt	d									19 08															
Fairwater	d									19 10															
Waun-gron Park	d									19 12															
Ninian Park	d									19 15															
Llandaf	d	18 40				18 56			19 04		19 10				19 26			19 34		19 40			19 56		20 04
Cathays	d	18 45				19 01			19 09		19 15				19 31			19 39		19 45			20 01		20 09
Rhymney [3]	d																								
Pontlottyn	d																								
Tir-phil	d																								
Brithdir	d																								
Bargoed	a																								
	d		18 17									18 48													
Gilfach Fargoed	d		18 19									18 50													
Pengam	d		18 22									18 53													
Hengoed	d		18 25									18 56													
Ystrad Mynach [3]	d		18 28									18 59													
Llanbradach	d		18 33									19 04													
Aber	d		18 37									19 08													
Caerphilly [3]	d		18 40									19 11									19 40				
Lisvane & Thornhill	d		18 44									19 15									19 44				
Llanishen	d		18 46									19 17									19 46				
Heath High Level	d		18 49									19 20									19 49				
Coryton	d			18 45										19 15											
Whitchurch (Cardiff)	d			18 46										19 16											
Rhiwbina	d			18 48										19 18											
Birchgrove	d			18 50										19 20											
Ty Glas	d			18 51										19 21											
Heath Low Level	d			18 54										19 24											
Cardiff Queen Street [3]	a	18 49	18 54	18 59		19 04			19 14		19 19	19 24		19 29	19 34			19 44		19 49	19 54		20 04		20 14
	d	18 51	18 56	19 01	19 00	19 06		19 12	19 16		19 21	19 26	19 24	19 31	19 36	19 36		19 46	19 48	19 51	19 56	20 00	20 06	20 12	20 16
Cardiff Bay	a				19 04			19 16					19 28			19 40			19 52			20 04		20 16	
Cardiff Central [7]	a	18 54	18 59	19 06		19 10			19 22	19 22	19 24	19 29		19 34	19 39			19 52		19 57	19 59		20 09		20 22
	d	18 55	19 01								19 25	19 31			19 41						20 06		20 10		
Grangetown	d	18 59	19 05								19 29	19 35			19 45						20 10		20 14		
Dingle Road	d		19 11									19 41									20 14				
Penarth	a		19 16									19 46									20 19				
Cogan	d	19 03									19 33				19 48								20 18		
Eastbrook	d	19 05									19 35				19 51								20 20		
Dinas Powys	d	19 07									19 37				19 53								20 22		
Cadoxton	d	19 12									19 42				19 57								20 27		
Barry Docks	d	19 15									19 45				20 00								20 30		
Barry [3]	d	19 19									19 49				20 05								20 34		
Barry Island	a	19 25									19 55												20 40		
Rhoose Cardiff Int Airport ✈	d														20 12										
Llantwit Major	d														20 22										
Bridgend	a														20 39										

When events are being held at the Millenium Stadium,
services are subject to alteration. Please check times before travelling.

Table 130

Saturdays

Treherbert, Aberdare, Merthyr, Pontypridd, Rhymney and Coryton - Cardiff, Penarth, Barry, Barry Island and Bridgend

Network Diagram - see first Page of Table 130

		AW	AW	AW	AW	AW	AW	AW	AW	AW	AW	AW	AW	AW	AW	AW	AW	AW	AW	AW	AW	AW
Treherbert	d								19 47						20 17							
Ynyswen	d								19 49						20 19							
Treorchy	d								19 51						20 21							
Ton Pentre	d								19 53						20 23							
Ystrad Rhondda	a								19 56						20 26							
	d								19 58						20 28							
Llwynypia	d								20 00						20 30							
Tonypandy	d								20 03						20 33							
Dinas Rhondda	d								20 05						20 35							
Porth	a								20 08						20 38							
	d								20 09						20 39							
Trehafod	d								20 12						20 42							
Merthyr Tydfil	d					19 38															20 38	
Pentre-bach	d					19 42															20 42	
Troed Y Rhiw	d					19 45															20 45	
Merthyr Vale	a					19 48															20 48	
	d					19 50															20 50	
Quakers Yard	d					19 55															20 55	
Aberdare [3]	d										19 52						20 22					
Cwmbach	d										19 55						20 25					
Fernhill	d										19 58						20 28					
Mountain Ash	a										20 01						20 31					
	d										20 04						20 34					
Penrhiwceiber	d										20 07						20 37					
Abercynon	d		19 43			19 59					20 13						20 43				20 59	
Pontypridd [3]	a		19 52			20 07			20 18		20 22				20 47		20 52				21 07	
	d		19 54			20 09			20 18		20 24				20 48		20 54				21 09	
Trefforest	d		19 57			20 12			20 21		20 27				20 51		20 57				21 12	
Trefforest Estate	d					20 16															21 16	
Taffs Well [3]	d		20 04			20 20			20 28		20 34				20 58		21 04				21 20	
Radyr [3]	a		20 07			20 23			20 31		20 37				21 01		21 07				21 23	
	d	20 04	20 07			20 23			20 31		20 37				21 01	21 04	21 07				21 23	
Danescourt	d	20 08														21 08						
Fairwater	d	20 10														21 10						
Waun-gron Park	d	20 12														21 12						
Ninian Park	d	20 15														21 15						
Llandaf	d		20 10			20 26			20 34		20 40				21 04		21 10				21 26	
Cathays	d		20 15			20 31			20 39		20 45				21 09		21 15				21 31	
Rhymney [3]	d							19 45														
Pontlottyn	d							19 48														
Tir-phil	d							19 52														
Brithdir	d							19 55														
Bargoed	a							19 58														
	d							19 59														
Gilfach Fargoed	d							20 01														
Pengam	d							20 04														
Hengoed	d							20 07														
Ystrad Mynach [3]	d							20 10														
Llanbradach	d							20 15														
Aber	d							20 19														
Caerphilly [3]	d							20 22				20 40										
Lisvane & Thornhill	d							20 26				20 44										
Llanishen	d							20 28				20 46										
Heath High Level	d							20 31				20 49										
Coryton	d				20 15															21 15		
Whitchurch (Cardiff)	d				20 16															21 16		
Rhiwbina	d				20 18															21 18		
Birchgrove	d				20 20															21 20		
Ty Glas	d				20 21															21 21		
Heath Low Level	d				20 24															21 24		
Cardiff Queen Street [3]	a		20 19		20 29	20 34		20 39	20 44		20 49	20 54			21 14		21 19			21 29	21 34	
	d		20 21	20 24	20 31	20 36	20 36	20 41	20 46	20 48	20 51	20 56	21 00	21 12	21 16		21 21	21 24		21 31	21 36	21 36
Cardiff Bay	a			20 28			20 40			20 52			21 04	21 16				21 28				21 40
Cardiff Central [7]	a	20 24	20 24		20 34	20 39		20 47	20 52		20 57	20 59			21 22	21 25	21 27			21 34	21 39	
	d		20 31			20 41					21 06	21 10							21 31		21 41	
Grangetown	d		20 35			20 45					21 10	21 14							21 35		21 45	
Dingle Road	d		20 41								21 14								21 41			
Penarth	a		20 46								21 19								21 46			
Cogan	d					20 48						21 18									21 48	
Eastbrook	d					20 51						21 20									21 51	
Dinas Powys	d					20 53						21 22									21 53	
Cadoxton	d					20 57						21 27									21 57	
Barry Docks	d					21 00						21 30									22 00	
Barry [3]	d					21 05						21 34									22 05	
Barry Island	a											21 40										
Rhoose Cardiff Int Airport ✈	d					21 12															22 12	
Llantwit Major	d					21 22															22 22	
Bridgend	a					21 39															22 39	

When events are being held at the Millenium Stadium, services are subject to alteration. Please check times before travelling.

Table 130

Saturdays

Treherbert, Aberdare, Merthyr, Pontypridd, Rhymney and Coryton - Cardiff, Penarth, Barry, Barry Island and Bridgend

Network Diagram - see first Page of Table 130

		AW	AW	AW	AW	AW	AW	AW		AW	AW	AW	AW	AW	AW	AW	AW	AW		AW	AW	AW	AW	AW	AW
Treherbert	d							21 17																	
Ynyswen	d							21 19																	
Treorchy	d							21 21																	
Ton Pentre	d							21 23																	
Ystrad Rhondda	a							21 26																	
	d							21 28																	
Llwynypia	d							21 30																	
Tonypandy	d							21 33																	
Dinas Rhondda	d							21 35																	
Porth	a							21 38																	
	d							21 39																	
Trehafod	d							21 42																	
Merthyr Tydfil	d												21 38											22 38	
Pentre-bach	d												21 42											22 42	
Troed Y Rhiw	d												21 45											22 45	
Merthyr Vale	a												21 48											22 48	
	d												21 50											22 50	
Quakers Yard	d												21 55											22 55	
Aberdare 3	d			20 54													21 54								22 54
Cwmbach	d			20 57													21 57								22 57
Fernhill	d			21 00													22 00								23 00
Mountain Ash	a			21 03													22 03								23 03
	d			21 04													22 04								23 04
Penrhiwceiber	d			21 07													22 07								23 07
Abercynon	d			21 13									21 59				22 13							22 59	23 13
Pontypridd 3	a			21 22				21 47					22 07				22 22							23 07	23 22
	d			21 24				21 48					22 09				22 24							23 09	
Trefforest	d			21 27				21 51					22 12				22 27							23 12	
Trefforest Estate	d												22 16											23 16	
Taffs Well 3	d			21 34				21 58					22 20				22 34							23 20	
Radyr 3	a			21 37				22 01					22 23				22 37							23 23	
	d			21 37				22 01		22 04			22 23				22 37					23 14		23 23	
Danescourt	d									22 08															
Fairwater	d									22 10															
Waun-gron Park	d									22 12															
Ninian Park	d									22 15															
Llandaf	d			21 40				22 04					22 26				22 40					23 16		23 26	
Cathays	d			21 45				22 09					22 31				22 45					23 20		23 31	
Rhymney 3	d	20 48									21 33														
Pontlottyn	d	20 51									21 36														
Tir-phil	d	20 55									21 40														
Brithdir	d	20 58									21 43														
Bargoed	a	21 01									21 46														
	d	21 02									21 47														
Gilfach Fargoed	d	21 04									21 49														
Pengam	d	21 07									21 52														
Hengoed	d	21 10									21 55														
Ystrad Mynach 3	d	21 13				21 39					21 58														
Llanbradach	d	21 18				21 44					22 03														
Aber	d	21 22				21 48					22 07														
Caerphilly 3	d	21 25				21 51					22 10				22 28										
Lisvane & Thornhill	d	21 29				21 55					22 14														
Llanishen	d	21 31				21 57					22 16														
Heath High Level	d	21 34				22 00					22 19														
Coryton	d																	22 45							
Whitchurch (Cardiff)	d																	22 46							
Rhiwbina	d																	22 48							
Birchgrove	d																	22 50							
Ty Glas	d																	22 51							
Heath Low Level	d																	22 54							
Cardiff Queen Street 3	a	21 42		21 49		22 05		22 14			22 24		22 34		22 39		22 49	22 59				23 24		23 34	
	d	21 44	21 48	21 51	22 00	22 06	22 12	22 16			22 26	22 24	22 36	22 36	22 39	22 48	22 54	23 01		23 00	23 12	23 25	23 24	23 36	
Cardiff Bay	a		21 52		22 04		22 16					22 28		22 40		22 52				23 04	23 16		23 28		
Cardiff Central 7	a	21 47		21 54		22 09		22 22		22 20	22 29		22 41		22 43		23 00	23 06				23 28		23 42	
	d			22 06		22 10					22 31						23 12					23 30			
Grangetown	d			22 10		22 14					22 35						23 16					23 34			
Dingle Road	d			22 14							22 41						23 20								
Penarth	a			22 19							22 46						23 25								
Cogan	d					22 18																23 37			
Eastbrook	d					22 20																23 40			
Dinas Powys	d					22 22																23 42			
Cadoxton	d					22 27																23 46			
Barry Docks	d					22 30																23 49			
Barry 3	d					22 34																23 54			
Barry Island	a					22 40																00 01			
Rhoose Cardiff Int Airport ✈	d																								
Llantwit Major	d																								
Bridgend	a																								

When events are being held at the Millenium Stadium, services are subject to alteration. Please check times before travelling.

Table 130

Saturdays

Treherbert, Aberdare, Merthyr, Pontypridd, Rhymney and Coryton - Cardiff, Penarth, Barry, Barry Island and Bridgend

Network Diagram - see first Page of Table 130

		AW	AW
Treherbert	d		
Ynyswen	d		
Treorchy	d		
Ton Pentre	d		
Ystrad Rhondda	a		
	d		
Llwynypia	d		
Tonypandy	d		
Dinas Rhondda	d		
Porth	a		
	d		
Trehafod	d		
Merthyr Tydfil	d		
Pentre-bach	d		
Troed Y Rhiw	d		
Merthyr Vale	a		
	d		
Quakers Yard	d		
Aberdare [3]	d		
Cwmbach	d		
Fernhill	d		
Mountain Ash	a		
	d		
Penrhiwceiber	d		
Abercynon	d		
Pontypridd [3]	a		
	d		
Trefforest	d		
Trefforest Estate	d		
Taffs Well [3]	d		
Radyr [3]	a		
	d		
Danescourt	d		
Fairwater	d		
Waun-gron Park	d		
Ninian Park	d		
Llandaf	d		
Cathays	d		
Rhymney [3]	d		
Pontlottyn	d		
Tir-phil	d		
Brithdir	d		
Bargoed	a		
	d		
Gilfach Fargoed	d		
Pengam	d		
Hengoed	d		
Ystrad Mynach [3]	d		
Llanbradach	d		
Aber	d		
Caerphilly [3]	d		
Lisvane & Thornhill	d		
Llanishen	d		
Heath High Level	d		
Coryton	d		
Whitchurch (Cardiff)	d		
Rhiwbina	d		
Birchgrove	d		
Ty Glas	d		
Heath Low Level	d		
Cardiff Queen Street [3]	a		
	d	23 36	23 48
Cardiff Bay	a	23 40	23 52
Cardiff Central [7]	a		
	d		
Grangetown	d		
Dingle Road	d		
Penarth	a		
Cogan	d		
Eastbrook	d		
Dinas Powys	d		
Cadoxton	d		
Barry Docks	d		
Barry [3]	d		
Barry Island	a		
Rhoose Cardiff Int Airport ✈	d		
Llantwit Major	d		
Bridgend	a		

When events are being held at the Millenium Stadium, services are subject to alteration. Please check times before travelling.

Table 130

Sundays
until 1 January

Treherbert, Aberdare, Merthyr, Pontypridd, Rhymney and Coryton - Cardiff, Penarth, Barry, Barry Island and Bridgend

Network Diagram - see first Page of Table 130

		AW	AW	AW	AW	AW	AW	AW	AW	AW		AW	AW	AW	AW	AW	AW	AW	AW	AW		AW	AW	AW	AW
		A																							
Treherbert	d						08 17																10 07		
Ynyswen	d						08 19																10 09		
Treorchy	d						08 21																10 11		
Ton Pentre	d						08 23																10 13		
Ystrad Rhondda	a						08 26																10 16		
	d						08 28																10 18		
Llwynypia	d						08 30																10 20		
Tonypandy	d						08 33																10 23		
Dinas Rhondda	d						08 35																10 25		
Porth	a						08 38																10 28		
	d						08 39																10 29		
Trehafod	d						08 42																10 32		
Merthyr Tydfil	d																09 38								
Pentre-bach	d																09 42								
Troed Y Rhiw	d																09 45								
Merthyr Vale	a																09 48								
	d																09 50								
Quakers Yard	d																09 55								
Aberdare 3	d																			09 54					
Cwmbach	d																			09 57					
Fernhill	d																			10 00					
Mountain Ash	a																			10 03					
	d																			10 04					
Penrhiwceiber	d																			10 07					
Abercynon	d																09 59			10 13					
Pontypridd 3	a						08 47										10 07			10 22			10 37		
	d						08 48										10 09			10 24			10 38		
Trefforest	d						08 51										10 12			10 27			10 41		
Trefforest Estate	d																								
Taffs Well 3	d						08 58										10 20			10 34			10 48		
Radyr 3	a						09 01										10 23			10 37			10 51		
	d	23p14					09 01										10 23			10 37			10 51		
Danescourt	d																								
Fairwater	d																								
Waun-gron Park	d																								
Ninian Park	d																								
Llandaf	d	23p16					09 04										10 26			10 40			10 54		
Cathays	d	23p20					09 09										10 31			10 45			10 59		
Rhymney 3	d												09 10												
Pontlottyn	d												09 13												
Tir-phil	d												09 17												
Brithdir	d												09 20												
Bargoed	a												09 23												
	d												09 25												
Gilfach Fargoed	d												09 27												
Pengam	d												09 30												
Hengoed	d												09 33												
Ystrad Mynach 3	d												09 36												
Llanbradach	d												09 41												
Aber	d												09 45												
Caerphilly 3	d												09 48												
Lisvane & Thornhill	d												09 52												
Llanishen	d												09 54												
Heath High Level	d												09 57												
Coryton	d																								
Whitchurch (Cardiff)	d																								
Rhiwbina	d																								
Birchgrove	d																								
Ty Glas	d																								
Heath Low Level	d																								
Cardiff Queen Street 3	a	23p24					09 14						10 02				10 34			10 49			11 02		
	d	23p25			09 00	09 12	09 16	09 24	09 36	09 48		10 00	10 04	10 12	10 24		10 36	10 36	10 48	10 51		11 00	11 04	11 12	11 24
Cardiff Bay	a				09 04	09 16		09 28	09 40	09 52		10 04		10 16	10 28			10 40	10 52			11 04		11 16	11 28
Cardiff Central 7	a	23p28					09 19						10 07				10 39			10 54			11 07		
	d	23p30	08 25	08 41			09 25						10 25			10 31	10 41			10 55			11 25		
Grangetown	d	23p34	08 29	08 45			09 29						10 29			10 35	10 45			10 59			11 29		
Dingle Road	d															10 41									
Penarth	a															10 46									
Cogan	d	23p37	08 33	08 48			09 33						10 33				10 48			11 03			11 33		
Eastbrook	d	23p40	08 35	08 51			09 35						10 35				10 51			11 05			11 35		
Dinas Powys	d	23p42	08 37	08 53			09 37						10 37				10 53			11 07			11 37		
Cadoxton	d	23p46	08 42	08 57			09 42						10 42				10 57			11 12			11 42		
Barry Docks	d	23p49	08 45	09 00			09 45						10 45				11 00			11 15			11 45		
Barry 3	d	23p54	08 49	09 05			09 49						10 49				11 05			11 19			11 49		
Barry Island	a	00 01	08 55				09 55						10 55							11 25			11 55		
Rhoose Cardiff Int Airport ✈	d			09 12													11 12								
Llantwit Major	d			09 22													11 22								
Bridgend	a			09 39													11 39								

A not 11 December

When events are being held at the Millenium Stadium, services are subject to alteration. Please check times before travelling.

Table 130

Sundays
until 1 January

Treherbert, Aberdare, Merthyr, Pontypridd, Rhymney and Coryton - Cardiff, Penarth, Barry, Barry Island and Bridgend

Network Diagram - see first Page of Table 130

		AW	AW	AW	AW	AW		AW	AW	AW	AW	AW	AW	AW	AW	AW		AW	AW	AW	AW	AW	AW	AW	AW
Treherbert	d															12 07									
Ynyswen	d															12 09									
Treorchy	d															12 11									
Ton Pentre	d															12 13									
Ystrad Rhondda	a															12 16									
	d															12 18									
Llwynypia	d															12 20									
Tonypandy	d															12 23									
Dinas Rhondda	d															12 25									
Porth	a															12 28									
	d															12 29									
Trehafod	d															12 32									
Merthyr Tydfil	d										11 38														
Pentre-bach	d										11 42														
Troed Y Rhiw	d										11 45														
Merthyr Vale	a										11 48														
	d										11 50														
Quakers Yard	d										11 55														
Aberdare 3	d			10 54																		12 54			
Cwmbach	d			10 57																		12 57			
Fernhill	d			11 00																		13 00			
Mountain Ash	a			11 03																		13 03			
	d			11 04																		13 04			
Penrhiwceiber	d			11 07																		13 07			
Abercynon	d			11 13							11 59											13 13			
Pontypridd 3	a			11 22							12 07					12 37						13 22			
	d			11 24							12 09					12 38						13 24			
Trefforest	d			11 27							12 12					12 41						13 27			
Trefforest Estate	d																								
Taffs Well 3	d			11 34							12 20					12 48						13 34			
Radyr 3	a			11 37							12 23					12 51						13 37			
	d			11 37							12 23					12 51						13 37			
Danescourt	d																								
Fairwater	d																								
Waun-gron Park	d																								
Ninian Park	d																								
Llandaf	d			11 40							12 26					12 54						13 40			
Cathays	d			11 45							12 31					12 59						13 45			
Rhymney 3	d					11 10																		13 10	
Pontlottyn	d					11 13																		13 13	
Tir-phil	d					11 17																		13 17	
Brithdir	d					11 20																		13 20	
Bargoed	a					11 23																		13 23	
	d					11 25																		13 25	
Gilfach Fargoed	d					11 27																		13 27	
Pengam	d					11 30																		13 30	
Hengoed	d					11 33																		13 33	
Ystrad Mynach 3	d					11 36																		13 36	
Llanbradach	d					11 41																		13 41	
Aber	d					11 45																		13 45	
Caerphilly 3	d					11 48																		13 48	
Lisvane & Thornhill	d					11 52																		13 52	
Llanishen	d					11 54																		13 54	
Heath High Level	d					11 57																		13 57	
Coryton	d																								
Whitchurch (Cardiff)	d																								
Rhiwbina	d																								
Birchgrove	d																								
Ty Glas	d																								
Heath Low Level	d																								
Cardiff Queen Street 3	a			11 49		12 02					12 34					13 02						13 49		14 02	
	d	11 36	11 48	11 51	12 00	12 04		12 12	12 24		12 36	12 36	12 48		13 00	13 04		13 12	13 24	13 36	13 48	13 51	14 00	14 04	14 12
Cardiff Bay	a	11 40	11 52		12 04			12 16	12 28			12 40	12 52		13 04			13 16	13 28	13 40	13 52		14 04		14 16
Cardiff Central 7	a			11 57		12 07					12 39					13 06						13 57		14 07	
	d					12 25				12 31	12 41			12 55		13 25								14 25	
Grangetown	d					12 29				12 35	12 45			12 59		13 29								14 29	
Dingle Road	d									12 41															
Penarth	a									12 46															
Cogan	d					12 33					12 48			13 03		13 33								14 33	
Eastbrook	d					12 35					12 51			13 05		13 35								14 35	
Dinas Powys	d					12 37					12 53			13 07		13 37								14 37	
Cadoxton	d					12 42					12 57			13 12		13 42								14 42	
Barry Docks	d					12 45					13 00			13 15		13 45								14 45	
Barry 3	d					12 49					13 05			13 19		13 49								14 49	
Barry Island	a					12 55								13 25		13 55								14 55	
Rhoose Cardiff Int Airport ✈	d										13 12														
Llantwit Major	d										13 22														
Bridgend	a										13 39														

When events are being held at the Millenium Stadium, services are subject to alteration. Please check times before travelling.

Table 130

Sundays
until 1 January

Treherbert, Aberdare, Merthyr, Pontypridd, Rhymney and Coryton - Cardiff, Penarth, Barry, Barry Island and Bridgend

Network Diagram - see first Page of Table 130

		AW		AW	AW	AW	AW	AW	AW	AW	AW	AW		AW	AW	AW	AW	AW	AW	AW	AW	AW		AW	AW
Treherbert	d										14 17														
Ynyswen	d										14 19														
Treorchy	d										14 21														
Ton Pentre	d										14 23														
Ystrad Rhondda	a										14 26														
	d										14 28														
Llwynypia	d										14 30														
Tonypandy	d										14 33														
Dinas Rhondda	d										14 35														
Porth	a										14 38														
	d										14 39														
Trehafod	d										14 42														
Merthyr Tydfil	d				13 38																		15 38			
Pentre-bach	d				13 42																		15 42			
Troed Y Rhiw	d				13 45																		15 45			
Merthyr Vale	a				13 48																		15 48			
	d				13 50																		15 50			
Quakers Yard	d				13 55																		15 55			
Aberdare 3	d															14 54									
Cwmbach	d															14 57									
Fernhill	d															15 00									
Mountain Ash	a															15 03									
	d															15 04									
Penrhiwceiber	d															15 07									
Abercynon	d				13 59											15 13						15 59			
Pontypridd 3	a				14 07						14 47					15 22						16 07			
	d				14 09						14 48					15 24						16 09			
Trefforest	d				14 12						14 51					15 27						16 12			
Trefforest Estate	d																								
Taffs Well 3	d				14 20						14 58					15 34						16 20			
Radyr 3	a				14 23						15 01					15 37						16 23			
	d				14 23						15 01					15 37						16 23			
Danescourt	d																								
Fairwater	d																								
Waun-gron Park	d																								
Ninian Park	d																								
Llandaf	d				14 26						15 04					15 40						16 26			
Cathays	d				14 31						15 09					15 45						16 31			
Rhymney 3	d																		15 22						
Pontlottyn	d																		15 25						
Tir-phil	d																		15 29						
Brithdir	d																		15 32						
Bargoed	a																		15 35						
	d																		15 37						
Gilfach Fargoed	d																		15 39						
Pengam	d																		15 42						
Hengoed	d																		15 45						
Ystrad Mynach 3	d																		15 48						
Llanbradach	d																		15 53						
Aber	d																		15 57						
Caerphilly 3	d																		16 00						
Lisvane & Thornhill	d																		16 04						
Llanishen	d																		16 06						
Heath High Level	d																		16 09						
Coryton	d																								
Whitchurch (Cardiff)	d																								
Rhiwbina	d																								
Birchgrove	d																								
Ty Glas	d																								
Heath Low Level	d																								
Cardiff Queen Street 3	a				14 34						15 14					15 49			16 14			16 34			
	d	14 24			14 36	14 36	14 48		15 00	15 12	15 16	15 24		15 36	15 48	15 51	16 00	16 12	16 16	16 24		16 36		16 36	16 48
Cardiff Bay	a	14 28				14 40	14 52		15 04	15 16		15 28		15 40	15 52		16 04	16 16		16 28				16 40	16 52
Cardiff Central 7	a				14 39						15 18					15 57			16 18			16 39			
	d			14 31	14 41			14 55			15 25								16 25		16 31	16 41			
Grangetown	d			14 35	14 45			14 59			15 29								16 29		16 35	16 45			
Dingle Road	d			14 41																	16 41				
Penarth	a			14 46																	16 46				
Cogan	d				14 48			15 03			15 33								16 33			16 48			
Eastbrook	d				14 51			15 05			15 35								16 35			16 51			
Dinas Powys	d				14 53			15 07			15 37								16 37			16 53			
Cadoxton	d				14 57			15 12			15 42								16 42			16 57			
Barry Docks	d				15 00			15 15			15 45								16 45			17 00			
Barry 3	d				15 05			15 19			15 49								16 49			17 05			
Barry Island	a							15 25			15 55								16 55						
Rhoose Cardiff Int Airport ✈	d				15 12																	17 12			
Llantwit Major	d				15 22																	17 22			
Bridgend	a				15 39																	17 39			

When events are being held at the Millenium Stadium,
services are subject to alteration. Please check times before travelling.

Table 130

Sundays
until 1 January

Treherbert, Aberdare, Merthyr, Pontypridd, Rhymney and Coryton - Cardiff, Penarth, Barry, Barry Island and Bridgend

Network Diagram - see first Page of Table 130

		AW	AW	AW	AW	AW	AW	AW	AW	AW	AW	AW	AW	AW	AW	AW	AW	AW	AW	AW	AW	AW	AW
Treherbert	d				16 17														18 17				
Ynyswen	d				16 19														18 19				
Treorchy	d				16 21														18 21				
Ton Pentre	d				16 23														18 23				
Ystrad Rhondda	a				16 26														18 26				
	d				16 28														18 28				
Llwynypia	d				16 30														18 30				
Tonypandy	d				16 33														18 33				
Dinas Rhondda	d				16 35														18 35				
Porth	a				16 38														18 38				
	d				16 39														18 39				
Trehafod	d				16 42														18 42				
Merthyr Tydfil	d														17 38								19 38
Pentre-bach	d														17 42								19 42
Troed Y Rhiw	d														17 45								19 45
Merthyr Vale	a														17 48								19 48
	d														17 50								19 50
Quakers Yard	d														17 55								19 55
Aberdare 3	d								16 54											18 54			
Cwmbach	d								16 57											18 57			
Fernhill	d								17 00											19 00			
Mountain Ash	a								17 03											19 03			
	d								17 04											19 04			
Penrhiwceiber	d								17 07											19 07			
Abercynon	d								17 13						17 59					19 13			19 59
Pontypridd 3	a				16 47				17 22						18 07				18 47	19 22			20 07
	d				16 48				17 24						18 09				18 48	19 24			20 09
Trefforest	d				16 51				17 27						18 12				18 51	19 27			20 12
Trefforest Estate	d																						
Taffs Well 3	d				16 58				17 34						18 20				18 58	19 34			20 20
Radyr 3	a				17 01				17 37						18 23				19 01	19 37			20 23
	d				17 01				17 37						18 23				19 01	19 37			20 23
Danescourt	d																						
Fairwater	d																						
Waun-gron Park	d																						
Ninian Park	d																						
Llandaf	d				17 04				17 40						18 26				19 04	19 40			20 26
Cathays	d				17 09				17 45						18 31				19 09	19 45			20 31
Rhymney 3	d											17 22									19 22		
Pontlottyn	d											17 25									19 25		
Tir-phil	d											17 29									19 29		
Brithdir	d											17 32									19 32		
Bargoed	a											17 35									19 35		
	d											17 37									19 37		
Gilfach Fargoed	d											17 39									19 39		
Pengam	d											17 42									19 42		
Hengoed	d											17 45									19 45		
Ystrad Mynach 3	d											17 48									19 48		
Llanbradach	d											17 53									19 53		
Aber	d											17 57									19 57		
Caerphilly 3	d											18 00									20 00		
Lisvane & Thornhill	d											18 04									20 04		
Llanishen	d											18 06									20 06		
Heath High Level	d											18 09									20 09		
Coryton	d																						
Whitchurch (Cardiff)	d																						
Rhiwbina	d																						
Birchgrove	d																						
Ty Glas	d																						
Heath Low Level	d																						
Cardiff Queen Street 3	a				17 14				17 49			18 14			18 34				19 14	19 48	20 14		20 34
	d		17 00	17 12	17 16	17 24	17 36	17 48	17 51	18 00	18 12	18 16	18 24		18 36	18 36	18 48		19 16	19 51	20 16		20 36
Cardiff Bay	a		17 04	17 16		17 28	17 40	17 52		18 04	18 16		18 28			18 40	18 52						
Cardiff Central 7	a				17 18				17 57			18 18			18 39				19 18	19 55	20 18		20 39
	d	16 55			17 25							18 25		18 31	18 41			18 55	19 25	19 55	20 25	20 31	20 41
Grangetown	d	16 59			17 29							18 29		18 35	18 45			18 59	19 29	19 59	20 29	20 35	20 45
Dingle Road	d													18 41								20 41	
Penarth	a													18 46								20 46	
Cogan	d	17 03			17 33							18 33			18 48			19 03	19 33	20 03	20 33		20 48
Eastbrook	d	17 05			17 35							18 35			18 51			19 05	19 35	20 05	20 35		20 51
Dinas Powys	d	17 07			17 37							18 37			18 53			19 07	19 37	20 07	20 37		20 53
Cadoxton	d	17 12			17 42							18 42			18 57			19 12	19 42	20 12	20 42		20 57
Barry Docks	d	17 15			17 45							18 45			19 00			19 15	19 45	20 15	20 45		21 00
Barry 3	d	17 19			17 49							18 49			19 05			19 19	19 49	20 19	20 49		21 05
Barry Island	a	17 25			17 55							18 55						19 25	19 55	20 25	20 55		
Rhoose Cardiff Int Airport ✈	d														19 12								21 12
Llantwit Major	d														19 22								21 22
Bridgend	a														19 39								21 39

When events are being held at the Millenium Stadium, services are subject to alteration. Please check times before travelling.

Table 130

Sundays
until 1 January

Treherbert, Aberdare, Merthyr, Pontypridd, Rhymney and Coryton - Cardiff, Penarth, Barry, Barry Island and Bridgend

Network Diagram - see first Page of Table 130

Station		AW	AW	AW		AW	AW
Treherbert	d		20 17				
Ynyswen	d		20 19				
Treorchy	d		20 21				
Ton Pentre	d		20 23				
Ystrad Rhondda	a		20 26				
	d		20 28				
Llwynypia	d		20 30				
Tonypandy	d		20 33				
Dinas Rhondda	d		20 35				
Porth	a		20 38				
	d		20 39				
Trehafod	d		20 42				
Merthyr Tydfil	d						21 38
Pentre-bach	d						21 42
Troed Y Rhiw	d						21 45
Merthyr Vale	a						21 48
	d						21 50
Quakers Yard	d						21 55
Aberdare ■	d			20 54			
Cwmbach	d			20 57			
Fernhill	d			21 00			
Mountain Ash	a			21 03			
	d			21 04			
Penrhiwceiber	d			21 07			
Abercynon	d			21 13			21 59
Pontypridd ■	a		20 47	21 22			22 07
	d		20 48	21 24			22 09
Trefforest	d		20 51	21 27			22 12
Trefforest Estate	d						
Taffs Well ■	d		20 58	21 34			22 20
Radyr ■	a		21 01	21 37			22 23
	d		21 01	21 37			22 23
Danescourt	d						
Fairwater	d						
Waun-gron Park	d						
Ninian Park	d						
Llandaf	d		21 04	21 40			22 26
Cathays	d		21 09	21 45			22 31
Rhymney ■	d						
Pontlottyn	d						
Tir-phil	d						
Brithdir	d						
Bargoed	a						
	d						
Gilfach Fargoed	d						
Pengam	d						
Hengoed	d						
Ystrad Mynach ■	d						
Llanbradach	d						
Aber	d						
Caerphilly ■	d						
Lisvane & Thornhill	d						
Llanishen	d						
Heath High Level	d						
Coryton	d						
Whitchurch (Cardiff)	d						
Rhiwbina	d						
Birchgrove	d						
Ty Glas	d						
Heath Low Level	d						
Cardiff Queen Street ■	a		21 14	21 49			22 34
	d		21 16	21 51			22 36
Cardiff Bay	a						
Cardiff Central ■	a		21 18	21 56			22 42
	d	20 55	21 25			22 25	
Grangetown	d	20 59	21 29			22 29	
Dingle Road	d						
Penarth	a						
Cogan	d	21 03	21 33			22 33	
Eastbrook	d	21 05	21 35			22 35	
Dinas Powys	d	21 07	21 37			22 37	
Cadoxton	d	21 12	21 42			22 42	
Barry Docks	d	21 15	21 45			22 45	
Barry ■	d	21 19	21 49			22 49	
Barry Island	a	21 25	21 55			22 55	
Rhoose Cardiff Int Airport ✈	d						
Llantwit Major	d						
Bridgend	a						

When events are being held at the Millenium Stadium, services are subject to alteration. Please check times before travelling.

Table 130

Sundays

8 January to 25 March

Treherbert, Aberdare, Merthyr, Pontypridd, Rhymney and Coryton - Cardiff, Penarth, Barry, Barry Island and Bridgend

Network Diagram - see first Page of Table 130

		AW	AW	AW	AW	AW	AW	AW	AW	AW		AW	AW	AW	AW	AW	AW	AW	AW	AW		AW	AW	AW	AW
			🚌	🚌					🚌								🚌	🚌					🚌		
Treherbert	d						08 17																		
Ynyswen	d						08 19																		
Treorchy	d						08 21																		
Ton Pentre	d						08 23																		
Ystrad Rhondda	a						08 26																		
	d						08 28																		
Llwynypia	d						08 30																		
Tonypandy	d						08 33																		
Dinas Rhondda	d						08 35																		
Porth	a						08 38																		
	d						08 39																		
Trehafod	d						08 42																		
Merthyr Tydfil	d																		09 38						
Pentre-bach	d																		09 42						
Troed Y Rhiw	d																		09 45						
Merthyr Vale	a																		09 48						
	d																		09 50						
Quakers Yard	d																		09 55						
Aberdare 3	d																							09 54	
Cwmbach	d																							09 57	
Fernhill	d																							10 00	
Mountain Ash	a																							10 03	
	d																							10 04	
Penrhiwceiber	d																							10 07	
Abercynon	d																		09 59					10 13	
Pontypridd 3	a						08 47												10 07					10 22	
	d						08 48												10 09					10 24	
Trefforest	d						08 51												10 12					10 27	
Trefforest Estate	d																								
Taffs Well 3	d						08 58												10 20					10 34	
Radyr 3	a						09 01												10 23					10 37	
	d	23p14					09 01												10 23					10 37	
Danescourt	d																								
Fairwater	d																								
Waun-gron Park	d																								
Ninian Park	d																								
Llandaf	d	23p16					09 04												10 26					10 40	
Cathays	d	23p20					09 09												10 31					10 45	
Rhymney 3	d													09 10											
Pontlottyn	d													09 13											
Tir-phil	d													09 17											
Brithdir	d													09 20											
Bargoed	a													09 23											
	d													09 25											
Gilfach Fargoed	d													09 27											
Pengam	d													09 30											
Hengoed	d													09 33											
Ystrad Mynach 3	d													09 36											
Llanbradach	d													09 41											
Aber	d													09 45											
Caerphilly 3	d													09 48											
Lisvane & Thornhill	d													09 52											
Llanishen	d													09 54											
Heath High Level	d													09 57											
Coryton	d																								
Whitchurch (Cardiff)	d																								
Rhiwbina	d																								
Birchgrove	d																								
Ty Glas	d																								
Heath Low Level	d																								
Cardiff Queen Street 3	a	23p24					09 14							10 02					10 34					10 49	
	d	23p25			09 00	09 12	09 16	09 24		09 36		09 48	10 00	10 04	10 12	10 24			10 36	10 36		10 48		10 51	11 00
Cardiff Bay	a				09 04	09 16		09 28		09 40		09 52	10 04		10 16	10 28				10 40		10 52			11 04
Cardiff Central 7	a	23p28					09 22							10 08					10 42					10 57	
	d	23p30	08 35	08 50					09 35								10 31	10 35					10 50		
Grangetown	d	23p34	08 40	08 55					09 40								10 36	10 40					10 55		
Dingle Road	d																10 46								
Penarth	a																10 51								
Cogan	d	23p37	08 45	09 00					09 45									10 45					11 00		
Eastbrook	d	23p40	08 50	09 05					09 50									10 50					11 05		
Dinas Powys	d	23p42	08 55	09 10					09 55									10 55					11 10		
Cadoxton	d	23p46	09 05	09 20					10 05									11 05					11 20		
Barry Docks	d	23p49	09 10	09 25					10 10									11 10					11 25		
Barry 3	d	23p54	09 15	09 30					10 15									11 15					11 30		
Barry Island	a	00 01	09 20						10 20									11 20							
Rhoose Cardiff Int Airport ✈	d			09 45																			11 45		
Llantwit Major	d			10 00																			12 00		
Bridgend	a			10 25																			12 25		

When events are being held at the Millenium Stadium, services are subject to alteration. Please check times before travelling.

Table 130

Sundays

8 January to 25 March

Treherbert, Aberdare, Merthyr, Pontypridd, Rhymney and Coryton - Cardiff, Penarth, Barry, Barry Island and Bridgend

Network Diagram - see first Page of Table 130

		AW	AW	AW	AW (bus)	AW		AW	AW	AW	AW	AW	AW	AW	AW	AW		AW	AW	AW	AW	AW	AW	AW	AW
Treherbert	d	10 07																			12 07				
Ynyswen	d	10 09																			12 09				
Treorchy	d	10 11																			12 11				
Ton Pentre	d	10 13																			12 13				
Ystrad Rhondda	a	10 16																			12 16				
	d	10 18																			12 18				
Llwynypia	d	10 20																			12 20				
Tonypandy	d	10 23																			12 23				
Dinas Rhondda	d	10 25																			12 25				
Porth	a	10 28																			12 28				
	d	10 29																			12 29				
Trehafod	d	10 32																			12 32				
Merthyr Tydfil	d														11 38										
Pentre-bach	d														11 42										
Troed Y Rhiw	d														11 45										
Merthyr Vale	a														11 48										
	d														11 50										
Quakers Yard	d														11 55										
Aberdare [3]	d								10 54																
Cwmbach	d								10 57																
Fernhill	d								11 00																
Mountain Ash	a								11 03																
	d								11 04																
Penrhiwceiber	d								11 07																
Abercynon	d								11 13						11 59										
Pontypridd [3]	a	10 37							11 22						12 07						12 37				
	d	10 38							11 24						12 09						12 38				
Trefforest	d	10 41							11 27						12 12						12 41				
Trefforest Estate	d																								
Taffs Well [3]	d	10 48							11 34						12 20						12 48				
Radyr [3]	a	10 51							11 37						12 23						12 51				
	d	10 51							11 37						12 23						12 51				
Danescourt	d																								
Fairwater	d																								
Waun-gron Park	d																								
Ninian Park	d																								
Llandaf	d	10 54							11 40						12 26						12 54				
Cathays	d	10 59							11 45						12 31						12 59				
Rhymney [3]	d											11 10													
Pontlottyn	d											11 13													
Tir-phil	d											11 17													
Brithdir	d											11 20													
Bargoed	a											11 23													
	d											11 25													
Gilfach Fargoed	d											11 27													
Pengam	d											11 30													
Hengoed	d											11 33													
Ystrad Mynach [3]	d											11 36													
Llanbradach	d											11 41													
Aber	d											11 45													
Caerphilly [3]	d											11 48													
Lisvane & Thornhill	d											11 52													
Llanishen	d											11 54													
Heath High Level	d											11 57													
Coryton	d																								
Whitchurch (Cardiff)	d																								
Rhiwbina	d																								
Birchgrove	d																								
Ty Glas	d																								
Heath Low Level	d																								
Cardiff Queen Street [3]	a	11 02							11 49			12 02			12 34						13 02				
	d	11 04	11 12	11 24		11 36		11 48	11 51	12 00		12 04	12 12	12 24	12 36	12 36		12 48		13 00	13 04	13 12	13 24	13 36	13 48
Cardiff Bay	a		11 16	11 28		11 40		11 52		12 04			12 16	12 28		12 40		12 52		13 04		13 16	13 28	13 40	13 52
Cardiff Central [7]	a	11 08							11 57			12 07			12 39						13 06				
	d				11 35						12 31	12 34			12 41				12 55		13 25				
Grangetown	d				11 40						12 35	12 38			12 45				12 59		13 29				
Dingle Road	d										12 41														
Penarth	a										12 46														
Cogan	d				11 45							12 42			12 48				13 03		13 33				
Eastbrook	d				11 50							12 44			12 51				13 05		13 35				
Dinas Powys	d				11 55							12 46			12 53				13 07		13 37				
Cadoxton	d				12 05							12 51			12 57				13 12		13 42				
Barry Docks	d				12 10							12 54			13 00				13 15		13 45				
Barry [3]	d				12 15							12 58			13 05				13 19		13 49				
Barry Island	a				12 20							13 04							13 25		13 55				
Rhoose Cardiff Int Airport ✈	d														13 12										
Llantwit Major	d														13 26										
Bridgend	a														13 49										

When events are being held at the Millenium Stadium, services are subject to alteration. Please check times before travelling.

Table 130

Sundays

8 January to 25 March

Treherbert, Aberdare, Merthyr, Pontypridd, Rhymney and Coryton - Cardiff, Penarth, Barry, Barry Island and Bridgend

Network Diagram - see first Page of Table 130

		AW		AW	AW	AW	AW	AW	AW	AW	AW	AW		AW	AW	AW	AW	AW	AW	AW	AW	AW		AW	AW
Treherbert	d															14 17									
Ynyswen	d															14 19									
Treorchy	d															14 21									
Ton Pentre	d															14 23									
Ystrad Rhondda	a															14 26									
	d															14 28									
Llwynypia	d															14 30									
Tonypandy	d															14 33									
Dinas Rhondda	d															14 35									
Porth	a															14 38									
	d															14 39									
Trehafod	d															14 42									
Merthyr Tydfil	d								13 38																
Pentre-bach	d								13 42																
Troed Y Rhiw	d								13 45																
Merthyr Vale	a								13 48																
	d								13 50																
Quakers Yard	d								13 55																
Aberdare [3]	d	12 54																		14 54					
Cwmbach	d	12 57																		14 57					
Fernhill	d	13 00																		15 00					
Mountain Ash	a	13 03																		15 03					
	d	13 04																		15 04					
Penrhiwceiber	d	13 07																		15 07					
Abercynon	d	13 13							13 59											15 13					
Pontypridd [3]	a	13 22							14 07							14 47				15 22					
	d	13 24							14 09							14 48				15 24					
Trefforest	d	13 27							14 12							14 51				15 27					
Trefforest Estate	d																								
Taffs Well [3]	d	13 34							14 20							14 58				15 34					
Radyr [3]	a	13 37							14 23							15 01				15 37					
	d	13 37							14 23							15 01				15 37					
Danescourt	d																								
Fairwater	d																								
Waun-gron Park	d																								
Ninian Park	d																								
Llandaf	d	13 40							14 26							15 04				15 40					
Cathays	d	13 45							14 31							15 09				15 45					
Rhymney [3]	d				13 10																			15 22	
Pontlottyn	d				13 13																			15 25	
Tir-phil	d				13 17																			15 29	
Brithdir	d				13 20																			15 32	
Bargoed	a				13 23																			15 35	
	d				13 25																			15 37	
Gilfach Fargoed	d				13 27																			15 39	
Pengam	d				13 30																			15 42	
Hengoed	d				13 33																			15 45	
Ystrad Mynach [3]	d				13 36																			15 48	
Llanbradach	d				13 41																			15 53	
Aber	d				13 45																			15 57	
Caerphilly [3]	d				13 48																			16 00	
Lisvane & Thornhill	d				13 52																			16 04	
Llanishen	d				13 54																			16 06	
Heath High Level	d				13 57																			16 09	
Coryton	d																								
Whitchurch (Cardiff)	d																								
Rhiwbina	d																								
Birchgrove	d																								
Ty Glas	d																								
Heath Low Level	d																								
Cardiff Queen Street [3]	a	13 49			14 02				14 34							15 14				15 49				16 14	
	d	13 51		14 00	14 04	14 12	14 24		14 36	14 36	14 48			15 00	15 12	15 16	15 24	15 36	15 48	15 51	16 00	16 12		16 16	16 24
Cardiff Bay	a			14 04		14 16	14 28			14 40	14 52			15 04	15 16		15 28	15 40	15 52		16 04	16 16			16 28
Cardiff Central [7]	a	13 57			14 07				14 39							15 18				15 57				16 18	
	d				14 25			14 31	14 41			14 55				15 25								16 25	
Grangetown	d				14 29			14 35	14 45			14 59				15 29								16 29	
Dingle Road	d							14 41																	
Penarth	a							14 46																	
Cogan	d				14 33				14 48			15 03				15 33								16 33	
Eastbrook	d				14 35				14 51			15 05				15 35								16 35	
Dinas Powys	d				14 37				14 53			15 07				15 37								16 37	
Cadoxton	d				14 42				14 57			15 12				15 42								16 42	
Barry Docks	d				14 45				15 00			15 15				15 45								16 45	
Barry [3]	d				14 49				15 05			15 19				15 49								16 49	
Barry Island	a				14 55							15 25				15 55								16 55	
Rhoose Cardiff Int Airport ✈	d								15 12																
Llantwit Major	d								15 22																
Bridgend	a								15 39																

When events are being held at the Millenium Stadium, services are subject to alteration. Please check times before travelling.

Table 130

Sundays

8 January to 25 March

Treherbert, Aberdare, Merthyr, Pontypridd, Rhymney and Coryton - Cardiff, Penarth, Barry, Barry Island and Bridgend

Network Diagram - see first Page of Table 130

Station		AW	AW	AW	AW	AW	AW	AW	AW	AW	AW	AW	AW	AW	AW	AW	AW	AW	AW	AW	AW	AW	AW
Treherbert	d								16 17														18 17
Ynyswen	d								16 19														18 19
Treorchy	d								16 21														18 21
Ton Pentre	d								16 23														18 23
Ystrad Rhondda	a								16 26														18 26
	d								16 28														18 28
Llwynypia	d								16 30														18 30
Tonypandy	d								16 33														18 33
Dinas Rhondda	d								16 35														18 35
Porth	a								16 38														18 38
	d								16 39														18 39
Trehafod	d								16 42														18 42
Merthyr Tydfil	d		15 38																17 38				
Pentre-bach	d		15 42																17 42				
Troed Y Rhiw	d		15 45																17 45				
Merthyr Vale	a		15 48																17 48				
	d		15 50																17 50				
Quakers Yard	d		15 55																17 55				
Aberdare 3	d												16 54										
Cwmbach	d												16 57										
Fernhill	d												17 00										
Mountain Ash	a												17 03										
	d												17 04										
Penrhiwceiber	d												17 07										
Abercynon	d		15 59										17 13						17 59				
Pontypridd 3	a		16 07						16 47				17 22						18 07				18 47
	d		16 09						16 48				17 24						18 09				18 48
Trefforest	d		16 12						16 51				17 27						18 12				18 51
Trefforest Estate	d																						
Taffs Well 3	d		16 20						16 58				17 34						18 20				18 58
Radyr 3	a		16 23						17 01				17 37						18 23				19 01
	d		16 23						17 01				17 37						18 23				19 01
Danescourt	d																						
Fairwater	d																						
Waun-gron Park	d																						
Ninian Park	d																						
Llandaf	d		16 26						17 04				17 40						18 26				19 04
Cathays	d		16 31						17 09				17 45						18 31				19 09
Rhymney 3	d															17 22							
Pontlottyn	d															17 25							
Tir-phil	d															17 29							
Brithdir	d															17 32							
Bargoed	a															17 35							
	d															17 37							
Gilfach Fargoed	d															17 39							
Pengam	d															17 42							
Hengoed	d															17 45							
Ystrad Mynach 3	d															17 48							
Llanbradach	d															17 53							
Aber	d															17 57							
Caerphilly 3	d															18 00							
Lisvane & Thornhill	d															18 04							
Llanishen	d															18 06							
Heath High Level	d															18 09							
Coryton	d																						
Whitchurch (Cardiff)	d																						
Rhiwbina	d																						
Birchgrove	d																						
Ty Glas	d																						
Heath Low Level	d																						
Cardiff Queen Street 3	a		16 34						17 14				17 49			18 14			18 34				19 14
	d		16 36	16 36	16 48		17 00	17 12	17 16	17 24	17 36	17 48	17 51	18 00	18 12	18 16	18 24		18 36	18 36	18 48		19 16
Cardiff Bay	a			16 40	16 52		17 04	17 16		17 28	17 40	17 52		18 04	18 16		18 28			18 40	18 52		
Cardiff Central 7	a		16 39						17 18				17 57			18 18			18 39				19 18
	d	16 31	16 41			16 55			17 25							18 25		18 31	18 41			18 55	19 25
Grangetown	d	16 35	16 45			16 59			17 29							18 29		18 35	18 45			18 59	19 29
Dingle Road	d	16 41																18 41					
Penarth	a	16 46																18 46					
Cogan	d		16 48			17 03			17 33							18 33			18 48			19 03	19 33
Eastbrook	d		16 51			17 05			17 35							18 35			18 51			19 05	19 35
Dinas Powys	d		16 53			17 07			17 37							18 37			18 53			19 07	19 37
Cadoxton	d		16 57			17 12			17 42							18 42			18 57			19 12	19 42
Barry Docks	d		17 00			17 15			17 45							18 45			19 00			19 15	19 45
Barry 3	d		17 05			17 19			17 49							18 49			19 05			19 19	19 49
Barry Island	a					17 25			17 55							18 55						19 25	19 55
Rhoose Cardiff Int Airport ✈	d		17 12																19 12				
Llantwit Major	d		17 22																19 22				
Bridgend	a		17 39																19 39				

When events are being held at the Millenium Stadium, services are subject to alteration. Please check times before travelling.

Table 130

Sundays

8 January to 25 March

Treherbert, Aberdare, Merthyr, Pontypridd, Rhymney and Coryton - Cardiff, Penarth, Barry, Barry Island and Bridgend

Network Diagram - see first Page of Table 130

		AW	AW	AW		AW	AW	AW	AW	AW	AW
Treherbert	d							20 17			
Ynyswen	d							20 19			
Treorchy	d							20 21			
Ton Pentre	d							20 23			
Ystrad Rhondda	a							20 26			
	d							20 28			
Llwynypia	d							20 30			
Tonypandy	d							20 33			
Dinas Rhondda	d							20 35			
Porth	a							20 38			
	d							20 39			
Trehafod	d							20 42			
Merthyr Tydfil	d					19 38					21 38
Pentre-bach	d					19 42					21 42
Troed Y Rhiw	d					19 45					21 45
Merthyr Vale	a					19 48					21 48
	d					19 50					21 50
Quakers Yard	d					19 55					21 55
Aberdare 3	d	18 54							20 54		
Cwmbach	d	18 57							20 57		
Fernhill	d	19 00							21 00		
Mountain Ash	a	19 03							21 03		
	d	19 04							21 04		
Penrhiwceiber	d	19 07							21 07		
Abercynon	d	19 13				19 59			21 13		21 59
Pontypridd 3	a	19 22				20 07		20 47	21 22		22 07
	d	19 24				20 09		20 48	21 24		22 09
Trefforest	d	19 27				20 12		20 51	21 27		22 12
Trefforest Estate	d										
Taffs Well 3	d	19 34				20 20		20 58	21 34		22 20
Radyr 3	a	19 37				20 23		21 01	21 37		22 23
	d	19 37				20 23		21 01	21 37		22 23
Danescourt	d										
Fairwater	d										
Waun-gron Park	d										
Ninian Park	d										
Llandaf	d	19 40				20 26		21 04	21 40		22 26
Cathays	d	19 45				20 31		21 09	21 45		22 31
Rhymney 3	d		19 22								
Pontlottyn	d		19 25								
Tir-phil	d		19 29								
Brithdir	d		19 32								
Bargoed	a		19 35								
	d		19 37								
Gilfach Fargoed	d		19 39								
Pengam	d		19 42								
Hengoed	d		19 45								
Ystrad Mynach 3	d		19 48								
Llanbradach	d		19 53								
Aber	d		19 57								
Caerphilly 3	d		20 00								
Lisvane & Thornhill	d		20 04								
Llanishen	d		20 06								
Heath High Level	d		20 09								
Coryton	d										
Whitchurch (Cardiff)	d										
Rhiwbina	d										
Birchgrove	d										
Ty Glas	d										
Heath Low Level	d										
Cardiff Queen Street 3	a	19 48	20 14			20 34		21 14	21 49		22 34
	d	19 51	20 16			20 36		21 16	21 51		22 36
Cardiff Bay	a										
Cardiff Central 7	a	19 55	20 18			20 39		21 18	21 56		22 42
	d	19 55	20 25	20 31		20 41	20 55	21 25		22 25	
Grangetown	d	19 59	20 29	20 35		20 45	20 59	21 29		22 29	
Dingle Road	d			20 41							
Penarth	a			20 46							
Cogan	d	20 03	20 33			20 48	21 03	21 33		22 33	
Eastbrook	d	20 05	20 35			20 51	21 05	21 35		22 35	
Dinas Powys	d	20 07	20 37			20 53	21 07	21 37		22 37	
Cadoxton	d	20 12	20 42			20 57	21 12	21 42		22 42	
Barry Docks	d	20 15	20 45			21 00	21 15	21 45		22 45	
Barry 3	d	20 19	20 49			21 05	21 19	21 49		22 49	
Barry Island	a	20 25	20 55				21 25	21 55		22 55	
Rhoose Cardiff Int Airport ✈	d					21 12					
Llantwit Major	d					21 22					
Bridgend	a					21 39					

When events are being held at the Millenium Stadium, services are subject to alteration. Please check times before travelling.

Table 130

Sundays
from 1 April

Treherbert, Aberdare, Merthyr, Pontypridd, Rhymney and Coryton - Cardiff, Penarth, Barry, Barry Island and Bridgend

Network Diagram - see first Page of Table 130

		AW	AW 🚌	AW 🚌	AW	AW 🚌	AW	AW	AW	AW 🚌		AW 🚌	AW	AW	AW 🚌	AW	AW 🚌	AW	AW 🚌	AW		AW	AW	AW	AW
Treherbert	d				08 17											10 07									
Ynyswen	d				08 19											10 09									
Treorchy	d				08 21											10 11									
Ton Pentre	d				08 23											10 13									
Ystrad Rhondda	a				08 26											10 16									
	d				08 28											10 18									
Llwynypia	d				08 30											10 20									
Tonypandy	d				08 33											10 23									
Dinas Rhondda	d				08 35											10 25									
Porth	a				08 38											10 28									
	d				08 39											10 29									
Trehafod	d				08 42											10 32									
Merthyr Tydfil	d								09 38															11 38	
Pentre-bach	d								09 42															11 42	
Troed Y Rhiw	d								09 45															11 45	
Merthyr Vale	a								09 48															11 48	
	d								09 50															11 50	
Quakers Yard	d								09 55															11 55	
Aberdare 3	d												09 54					10 54							
Cwmbach	d												09 57					10 57							
Fernhill	d												10 00					11 00							
Mountain Ash	a												10 03					11 03							
	d												10 04					11 04							
Penrhiwceiber	d												10 07					11 07							
Abercynon	d								09 59				10 13					11 13						11 59	
Pontypridd 3	a				08 47				10 07				10 22			10 37		11 22						12 07	
	d				08 48				10 09				10 24			10 38		11 24						12 09	
Trefforest	d				08 51				10 12				10 27			10 41		11 27						12 12	
Trefforest Estate	d																								
Taffs Well 3	d				08 58				10 20				10 34			10 48		11 34						12 20	
Radyr 3	a				09 01				10 23				10 37			10 51		11 37						12 23	
	d	23p14			09 01	09 11			10 23			10 33	10 37		10 47	10 57	11 01	11 37	11 47					12 23	
Danescourt	d																								
Fairwater	d																								
Waun-gron Park	d																								
Ninian Park	d																								
Llandaf	d	23p16				09 21						10 43			10 57		11 11		11 57					12 26	
Cathays	d	23p20				09 36						10 58			11 12		11 26		12 12					12 31	
Rhymney 3	d									09 10															
Pontlottyn	d									09 18															
Tir-phil	d									09 23															
Brithdir	d									09 28															
Bargoed	a									09 33															
	d									09 33															
Gilfach Fargoed	d									09 38															
Pengam	d									09 43															
Hengoed	d									09 53															
Ystrad Mynach 3	d									09 58															
Llanbradach	d									10 08															
Aber	d									10 18															
Caerphilly 3	d									10 23															
Lisvane & Thornhill	d									10 33															
Llanishen	d									10 38															
Heath High Level	d									10 43															
Coryton	d																								
Whitchurch (Cardiff)	d																								
Rhiwbina	d																								
Birchgrove	d																								
Ty Glas	d																								
Heath Low Level	d																								
Cardiff Queen Street 3	a	23p24				09 41				10 58		11 03			11 17		11 31		12 17					12 34	
	d	23p25				09 41				10 58		11 03			11 17		11 31		12 17	12 24				12 36	12 36
Cardiff Bay	a																			12 28					12 40
Cardiff Central 7	a	23p28			09 12	09 49			10 41	11 06		11 11	10 51		11 25	11 08	11 39	11 54	12 25					12 39	
	d	23p30	08 35	08 50	09 31		10 25	10 31						10 55		11 25						12 25	12 31	12 41	
Grangetown	d	23p34	08 40	08 55	09 35		10 29	10 35						10 59		11 29						12 29	12 35	12 45	
Dingle Road	d							10 41															12 41		
Penarth	a							10 46															12 46		
Cogan	d	23p37	08 45	09 00	09 39		10 33							11 03		11 33						12 33		12 48	
Eastbrook	d	23p40	08 50	09 05	09 41		10 35							11 05		11 35						12 35		12 51	
Dinas Powys	d	23p42	08 55	09 10	09 43		10 37							11 07		11 37						12 37		12 53	
Cadoxton	d	23p46	09 05	09 20	09 48		10 42							11 12		11 42						12 42		12 57	
Barry Docks	d	23p49	09 10	09 25	09 51		10 45							11 15		11 45						12 45		13 00	
Barry 3	d	23p54	09 15	09 30	09 55		10 49							11 19		11 49						12 49		13 05	
Barry Island	a	00 01	09 20		10 01		10 55							11 25		11 55						12 55			
Rhoose Cardiff Int Airport ✈	d			09 45																				13 12	
Llantwit Major	d			10 00																				13 26	
Bridgend	a			10 25																				13 49	

When events are being held at the Millenium Stadium, services are subject to alteration. Please check times before travelling.

Table 130

Sundays
from 1 April

Treherbert, Aberdare, Merthyr, Pontypridd, Rhymney and Coryton - Cardiff, Penarth, Barry, Barry Island and Bridgend

Network Diagram - see first Page of Table 130

		AW	AW	AW 🚌	AW	AW	AW	AW	AW	AW	AW	AW	AW	AW	AW	AW	AW	AW	AW	AW	AW	AW	AW
Treherbert	d					12 07																	
Ynyswen	d					12 09																	
Treorchy	d					12 11																	
Ton Pentre	d					12 13																	
Ystrad Rhondda	a					12 16																	
	d					12 18																	
Llwynypia	d					12 20																	
Tonypandy	d					12 23																	
Dinas Rhondda	d					12 25																	
Porth	a					12 28																	
	d					12 29																	
Trehafod	d					12 32																	
Merthyr Tydfil	d																13 38						
Pentre-bach	d																13 42						
Troed Y Rhiw	d																13 45						
Merthyr Vale	a																13 48						
	d																13 50						
Quakers Yard	d																13 55						
Aberdare 3	d										12 54												
Cwmbach	d										12 57												
Fernhill	d										13 00												
Mountain Ash	a										13 03												
	d										13 04												
Penrhiwceiber	d										13 07												
Abercynon	d										13 13						13 59						
Pontypridd 3	a					12 37					13 22						14 07						
	d					12 38					13 24						14 09						
Trefforest	d					12 41					13 27						14 12						
Trefforest Estate	d																						
Taffs Well 3	d					12 48					13 34						14 20						
Radyr 3	a					12 51					13 37						14 23						
	d					12 51					13 37						14 23						
Danescourt	d																						
Fairwater	d																						
Waun-gron Park	d																						
Ninian Park	d																						
Llandaf	d					12 54					13 40						14 26						
Cathays	d					12 59					13 45						14 31						
Rhymney 3	d			11 10															13 32				
Pontlottyn	d			11 18															13 35				
Tir-phil	d			11 23															13 39				
Brithdir	d			11 28															13 42				
Bargoed	a			11 33															13 45				
	d			11 33															13 47				
Gilfach Fargoed	d			11 38															13 51				
Pengam	d			11 43															13 56				
Hengoed	d			11 53															14 01				
Ystrad Mynach 3	d			11 58															14 06				
Llanbradach	d			12 08															14 13				
Aber	d			12 18															14 19				
Caerphilly 3	d			12 23															14 24				
Lisvane & Thornhill	d			12 33															14 29				
Llanishen	d			12 38															14 31				
Heath High Level	d			12 43															14 34				
Coryton	d																						
Whitchurch (Cardiff)	d																						
Rhiwbina	d																						
Birchgrove	d																						
Ty Glas	d																						
Heath Low Level	d																						
Cardiff Queen Street 3	a			12 58		13 02					13 49						14 34		14 39				
	d	12 48		12 58	13 00	13 04	13 12	13 24	13 36	13 48	13 51	14 00	14 12	14 24			14 36	14 36	14 41	14 48		15 00	15 12
Cardiff Bay	a	12 52			13 04		13 16	13 28	13 40	13 52		14 04	14 16	14 28				14 40		14 52		15 04	15 16
Cardiff Central 7	a			13 06		13 06					13 57						14 39		14 44				
	d		12 55			13 25									14 25	14 31	14 41				14 55		
Grangetown	d		12 59			13 29									14 29	14 35	14 45				14 59		
Dingle Road	d															14 41							
Penarth	a															14 46							
Cogan	d		13 03			13 33									14 33		14 48				15 03		
Eastbrook	d		13 05			13 35									14 35		14 51				15 05		
Dinas Powys	d		13 07			13 37									14 37		14 53				15 07		
Cadoxton	d		13 12			13 42									14 42		14 57				15 12		
Barry Docks	d		13 15			13 45									14 45		15 00				15 15		
Barry 3	d		13 19			13 49									14 49		15 05				15 19		
Barry Island	a		13 25			13 55									14 55						15 25		
Rhoose Cardiff Int Airport ✈	d																15 12						
Llantwit Major	d																15 22						
Bridgend	a																15 39						

When events are being held at the Millenium Stadium, services are subject to alteration. Please check times before travelling.

Table 130

Sundays
from 1 April

Treherbert, Aberdare, Merthyr, Pontypridd, Rhymney and Coryton - Cardiff, Penarth, Barry, Barry Island and Bridgend

Network Diagram - see first Page of Table 130

		AW		AW	AW	AW	AW	AW	AW	AW	AW	AW		AW	AW	AW	AW	AW	AW	AW	AW	AW		AW	AW
Treherbert	d	14 17																		16 17					
Ynyswen	d	14 19																		16 19					
Treorchy	d	14 21																		16 21					
Ton Pentre	d	14 23																		16 23					
Ystrad Rhondda	a	14 26																		16 26					
	d	14 28																		16 28					
Llwynypia	d	14 30																		16 30					
Tonypandy	d	14 33																		16 33					
Dinas Rhondda	d	14 35																		16 35					
Porth	a	14 38																		16 38					
	d	14 39																		16 39					
Trehafod	d	14 42																		16 42					
Merthyr Tydfil	d													15 38											
Pentre-bach	d													15 42											
Troed Y Rhiw	d													15 45											
Merthyr Vale	a													15 48											
	d													15 50											
Quakers Yard	d													15 55											
Aberdare 3	d						14 54																		16 54
Cwmbach	d						14 57																		16 57
Fernhill	d						15 00																		17 00
Mountain Ash	a						15 03																		17 03
	d						15 04																		17 04
Penrhiwceiber	d						15 07																		17 07
Abercynon	d						15 13							15 59											17 13
Pontypridd 3	a	14 47					15 22							16 07						16 47					17 22
	d	14 48					15 24							16 09						16 48					17 24
Trefforest	d	14 51					15 27							16 12						16 51					17 27
Trefforest Estate	d																								
Taffs Well 3	d	14 58					15 34							16 20						16 58					17 34
Radyr 3	a	15 01					15 37							16 23						17 01					17 37
	d	15 01					15 37							16 23						17 01					17 37
Danescourt	d																								
Fairwater	d																								
Waun-gron Park	d																								
Ninian Park	d																								
Llandaf	d	15 04					15 40							16 26						17 04					17 40
Cathays	d	15 09					15 45							16 31						17 09					17 45
Rhymney 3	d									15 22															
Pontlottyn	d									15 25															
Tir-phil	d									15 29															
Brithdir	d									15 32															
Bargoed	a									15 35															
	d									15 37															
Gilfach Fargoed	d									15 39															
Pengam	d									15 42															
Hengoed	d									15 45															
Ystrad Mynach 3	d									15 48															
Llanbradach	d									15 53															
Aber	d									15 57															
Caerphilly 3	d									16 00															
Lisvane & Thornhill	d									16 04															
Llanishen	d									16 06															
Heath High Level	d									16 09															
Coryton	d																								
Whitchurch (Cardiff)	d																								
Rhiwbina	d																								
Birchgrove	d																								
Ty Glas	d																								
Heath Low Level	d																								
Cardiff Queen Street 3	a	15 14					15 49			16 14				16 34						17 14					17 49
	d	15 16		15 24	15 36	15 48	15 51	16 00	16 12	16 16	16 24			16 36	16 36	16 48		17 00	17 12	17 16	17 24	17 36		17 48	17 51
Cardiff Bay	a			15 28	15 40	15 52		16 04	16 16		16 28				16 40	16 52		17 04	17 16		17 28	17 40		17 52	
Cardiff Central 7	a	15 18					15 57			16 18				16 39						17 18					17 57
	d	15 25								16 25		16 31		16 41			16 55			17 25					
Grangetown	d	15 29								16 29		16 35		16 45			16 59			17 29					
Dingle Road	d											16 41													
Penarth	a											16 46													
Cogan	d	15 33								16 33				16 48			17 03			17 33					
Eastbrook	d	15 35								16 35				16 51			17 05			17 35					
Dinas Powys	d	15 37								16 37				16 53			17 07			17 37					
Cadoxton	d	15 42								16 42				16 57			17 12			17 42					
Barry Docks	d	15 45								16 45				17 00			17 15			17 45					
Barry 3	d	15 49								16 49				17 05			17 19			17 49					
Barry Island	a	15 55								16 55							17 25			17 55					
Rhoose Cardiff Int Airport ✈	d													17 12											
Llantwit Major	d													17 22											
Bridgend	a													17 39											

When events are being held at the Millenium Stadium, services are subject to alteration. Please check times before travelling.

Table 130

Sundays
from 1 April

Treherbert, Aberdare, Merthyr, Pontypridd, Rhymney and Coryton - Cardiff, Penarth, Barry, Barry Island and Bridgend

Network Diagram - see first Page of Table 130

		AW	AW	AW	AW	AW	AW	AW		AW	AW	AW	AW	AW	AW	AW	AW	AW		AW	AW	AW			
Treherbert	d										18 17						20 17								
Ynyswen	d										18 19						20 19								
Treorchy	d										18 21						20 21								
Ton Pentre	d										18 23						20 23								
Ystrad Rhondda	a										18 26						20 26								
	d										18 28						20 28								
Llwynypia	d										18 30						20 30								
Tonypandy	d										18 33						20 33								
Dinas Rhondda	d										18 35						20 35								
Porth	a										18 38						20 38								
	d										18 39						20 39								
Trehafod	d										18 42						20 42								
Merthyr Tydfil	d						17 38									19 38						21 38			
Pentre-bach	d						17 42									19 42						21 42			
Troed Y Rhiw	d						17 45									19 45						21 45			
Merthyr Vale	a						17 48									19 48						21 48			
	d						17 50									19 50						21 50			
Quakers Yard	d						17 55									19 55						21 55			
Aberdare 3	d											18 54							20 54						
Cwmbach	d											18 57							20 57						
Fernhill	d											19 00							21 00						
Mountain Ash	a											19 03							21 03						
	d											19 04							21 04						
Penrhiwceiber	d											19 07							21 07						
Abercynon	d						17 59					19 13			19 59				21 13		21 59				
Pontypridd 3	a						18 07				18 47	19 22			20 07		20 47		21 22		22 07				
	d						18 09				18 48	19 24			20 09		20 48		21 24		22 09				
Trefforest	d						18 12				18 51	19 27			20 12		20 51		21 27		22 12				
Trefforest Estate	d																								
Taffs Well 3	d						18 20				18 58	19 34			20 20		20 58		21 34		22 20				
Radyr 3	a						18 23				19 01	19 37			20 23		21 01		21 37		22 23				
	d						18 23				19 01	19 37			20 23		21 01		21 37		22 23				
Danescourt	d																								
Fairwater	d																								
Waun-gron Park	d																								
Ninian Park	d																								
Llandaf	d						18 26				19 04	19 40			20 26		21 04		21 40		22 26				
Cathays	d						18 31				19 09	19 45			20 31		21 09		21 45		22 31				
Rhymney 3	d			17 22									19 22												
Pontlottyn	d			17 25									19 25												
Tir-phil	d			17 29									19 29												
Brithdir	d			17 32									19 32												
Bargoed	a			17 35									19 35												
	d			17 37									19 37												
Gilfach Fargoed	d			17 39									19 39												
Pengam	d			17 42									19 42												
Hengoed	d			17 45									19 45												
Ystrad Mynach 3	d			17 48									19 48												
Llanbradach	d			17 53									19 53												
Aber	d			17 57									19 57												
Caerphilly 3	d			18 00									20 00												
Lisvane & Thornhill	d			18 04									20 04												
Llanishen	d			18 06									20 06												
Heath High Level	d			18 09									20 09												
Coryton	d																								
Whitchurch (Cardiff)	d																								
Rhiwbina	d																								
Birchgrove	d																								
Ty Glas	d																								
Heath Low Level	d																								
Cardiff Queen Street 3	a			18 14			18 34					19 14	19 48	20 14		20 34		21 14		21 49		22 34			
	d	18 00	18 12	18 16	18 24		18 36	18 36		18 48		19 16	19 51	20 16		20 36		21 16		21 51		22 36			
Cardiff Bay	a	18 04	18 16		18 28			18 40		18 52															
Cardiff Central 7	a			18 18			18 39					19 18	19 55	20 18		20 39		21 18		21 56		22 42			
	d			18 25		18 31	18 41				18 55	19 25	19 55	20 25	20 31	20 41	20 55	21 25			22 25				
Grangetown	d			18 29		18 35	18 45				18 59	19 29	19 59	20 29	20 35	20 45	20 59	21 29			22 29				
Dingle Road	d					18 41									20 41										
Penarth	a					18 46									20 46										
Cogan	d			18 33			18 48				19 03	19 33	20 03	20 33		20 48	21 03	21 33			22 33				
Eastbrook	d			18 35			18 51				19 05	19 35	20 05	20 35		20 51	21 05	21 35			22 35				
Dinas Powys	d			18 37			18 53				19 07	19 37	20 07	20 37		20 53	21 07	21 37			22 37				
Cadoxton	d			18 42			18 57				19 12	19 42	20 12	20 42		20 57	21 12	21 42			22 42				
Barry Docks	d			18 45			19 00				19 15	19 45	20 15	20 45		21 00	21 15	21 45			22 45				
Barry 3	d			18 49			19 05				19 19	19 49	20 19	20 49		21 05	21 19	21 49			22 49				
Barry Island	a			18 55							19 25	19 55	20 25	20 55			21 25	21 55			22 55				
Rhoose Cardiff Int Airport ✈	d						19 12									21 12									
Llantwit Major	d						19 22									21 22									
Bridgend	a						19 39									21 39									

When events are being held at the Millenium Stadium, services are subject to alteration. Please check times before travelling.

Bridgend, Barry Island, Barry, Penarth and Cardiff - Coryton, Rhymney, Pontypridd, Merthyr, Aberdare and Treherbert

Network Diagram - see first Page of Table 130

Miles	Miles	Miles	Miles	Miles			AW	AW	AW	AW	AW	AW	AW	AW	AW	AW	AW	AW	AW	AW	AW	AW	AW	AW
—	—	0	—	—	**Bridgend**	d										05 42								
—	—	9¼	—	—	Llantwit Major	d										05 56								
—	—	15¾	—	—	Rhoose Cardiff Int Airport ✈	d										06 06								
0	—	—	—	—	**Barry Island**	d		05 15					05 51								06 25			
0¾	—	19	—	—	**Barry** 3	d		05 20					05 55			06 15					06 30			
2	—	—	—	—	Barry Docks	d		05 24					05 59			06 19					06 34			
2¾	—	—	—	—	Cadoxton	d		05 27					06 02			06 22					06 37			
4¾	—	—	—	—	Dinas Powys	d		05 31					06 06			06 26					06 41			
5¾	—	—	—	—	Eastbrook	d		05 33					06 08			06 28					06 43			
6½	—	—	—	—	Cogan	d		05 35					06 10			06 30					06 45			
—	0	—	—	—	**Penarth**	d						06 02						06 32						
—	0¼	—	—	—	Dingle Road	d						06 04						06 34						
8¼	2¾	—	—	—	Grangetown	d		05 39				06 08	06 14			06 34		06 38			06 49			
9¼	3¾	—	0	—	**Cardiff Central** 7	a		05 44				06 13	06 19			06 39		06 44			06 54			
—	—	—	—	—		d	05 26	05 46		05 56	06 11	06 15	06 21	06 26	06 36	06 41		06 46	06 51		06 56		07 06	07 06
—	—	0	—	—	**Cardiff Bay**	d											06 42			06 54		07 06		
9¾	4¼	1	—	—	**Cardiff Queen Street** 3	a	05 29	05 49		05 59	06 14	06 19	06 24	06 29	06 39	06 44	06 46	06 49	06 54	06 58	06 59	07 10	07 09	
—	—	—	—	—		d	05 30	05 50		06 00	06 15	06 20	06 25	06 30	06 40	06 45		06 50	06 55		07 00		07 10	
—	—	3½	—	—	Heath Low Level	d							06 30						07 00					
—	4½	—	—	—	Ty Glas	d							06 33						07 03					
—	—	4¾	—	—	Birchgrove	d							06 34						07 04					
—	—	5¼	—	—	Rhiwbina	d							06 36						07 06					
—	—	5½	—	—	Whitchurch (Cardiff)	d							06 38						07 08					
—	—	6	—	—	**Coryton**	a							06 43						07 13					
—	6¾	—	—	—	Heath High Level	d		05 55				06 25						06 55						
—	7¾	—	—	—	Llanishen	d		05 58				06 28						06 58						
—	8¾	—	—	—	Lisvane & Thornhill	d		06 00				06 30						07 00						
—	11¼	—	—	—	Caerphilly 3	d		06a08				06 36						07 06						
—	12	—	—	—	Aber	d						06 38						07 08						
—	14	—	—	—	Llanbradach	d						06 42						07 12						
—	16¾	—	—	—	Ystrad Mynach 3	d						06 47						07 17						
—	17¾	—	—	—	Hengoed	d						06 50						07 20						
—	19½	—	—	—	Pengam	d						06 53						07 23						
—	20½	—	—	—	Gilfach Fargoed	d																		
—	21	—	—	—	Bargoed	a						07 01						07 31						
—	—	—	—	—		d																		
—	22½	—	—	—	Brithdir	d																		
—	23½	—	—	—	Tir-phil	d																		
—	26	—	—	—	Pontlottyn	d																		
—	27	—	—	—	**Rhymney** 3	a																		
10½	—	—	—	—	Cathays	d	05 33			06 03	06 18			06 33	06 43	06 48					07 03		07 13	
13	—	—	—	—	Llandaf	d	05 37			06 07	06 22			06 37	06 47	06 52					07 07		07 17	
—	—	—	1	—	Ninian Park	d																		07 10
—	—	—	2½	—	Waun-gron Park	d																		07 13
—	—	—	3	—	Fairwater	d																		07 15
—	—	—	3½	—	Danescourt	d																		07 17
14	—	—	4¾	—	Radyr 3	a	05 40			06 10	06 24			06 40	06 50	06 54					07 10		07 20	07 24
—	—	—	—	—		d	05 40			06 10	06 24			06 40	06 50	06 55					07 10		07 20	
16	—	—	—	—	Taffs Well 3	d	05 44			06 14	06 28			06 44	06 54	06 59					07 14		07 24	
18¼	—	—	—	—	Trefforest Estate	d	05 48			06 18				06 48							07 18			
20¾	—	—	—	—	Trefforest	d	05 52			06 22	06 35			06 52	07 01	07 06					07 22		07 31	
21¾	—	0	—	0	**Pontypridd** 3	a	05 55			06 25	06 38			06 55	07 04	07 09					07 25		07 34	
—	—	—	—	—		d	05 57		06 11	06 27	06 41			06 57	07 06	07 11					07 27		07 36	
—	—	3¼	—	3¼	Abercynon	d	06 04		06 19	06 34	06 49			07 04		07 19					07 34			
—	—	—	—	6	Penrhiwceiber	d			06 24		06 54					07 24								
—	—	—	—	7¼	Mountain Ash	a			06 28		06 58					07 28								
—	—	—	—	—		d			06 33		07 03					07 33								
—	—	—	—	8¼	Fernhill	d			06 35		07 05					07 35								
—	—	—	—	9½	Cwmbach	d			06 39		07 09					07 39								
—	—	—	—	11	**Aberdare** 3	a			06 46		07 16					07 46								
—	—	4¾	—	—	Quakers Yard	d	06 09			06 39				07 09							07 39			
—	—	7	—	—	Merthyr Vale	a	06 14			06 44				07 14							07 44			
—	—	—	—	—		d	06 17			06 47				07 17							07 47			
—	—	8¾	—	—	Troed Y Rhiw	d	06 20			06 50				07 20							07 50			
—	—	10	—	—	Pentre-bach	d	06 23			06 53				07 23							07 53			
—	—	11½	—	—	**Merthyr Tydfil**	a	06 31			07 01				07 31							08 01			
23½	—	—	—	—	Trehafod	d									07 11								07 41	
24¾	—	—	—	—	Porth	a									07 14								07 44	
—	—	—	—	—		d									07 15								07 45	
26¼	—	—	—	—	Dinas Rhondda	d									07 19								07 49	
26¾	—	—	—	—	Tonypandy	d									07 21								07 51	
27¾	—	—	—	—	Llwynypia	d									07 23								07 53	
29	—	—	—	—	Ystrad Rhondda	a									07 26								07 56	
—	—	—	—	—		d									07 29								07 59	
29½	—	—	—	—	Ton Pentre	d									07 31								08 01	
30¾	—	—	—	—	Treorchy	d									07 34								08 04	
31¾	—	—	—	—	Ynyswen	d									07 37								08 07	
32¼	—	—	—	—	**Treherbert**	a									07 43								08 13	

When events are being held at the Millenium Stadium,
services are subject to alteration. Please check times before travelling.

Table 130

Mondays to Fridays

Bridgend, Barry Island, Barry, Penarth and Cardiff - Coryton, Rhymney, Pontypridd, Merthyr, Aberdare and Treherbert

Network Diagram - see first Page of Table 130

		AW	AW	AW	AW	AW	AW	AW	AW	AW	AW	AW	AW	AW	AW	AW	AW	AW	AW	AW	AW	AW
Bridgend	d										06 42											
Llantwit Major	d										06 56											
Rhoose Cardiff Int Airport ✈	d										07 06											
Barry Island	d					06 55										07 25					07 40	
Barry [3]	d					07 00					07 15					07 30					07 45	
Barry Docks	d					07 04					07 19					07 34					07 49	
Cadoxton	d					07 07					07 22					07 37					07 52	
Dinas Powys	d					07 11					07 26					07 41					07 56	
Eastbrook	d					07 13					07 28					07 43					07 58	
Cogan	d					07 15					07 30					07 45					08 00	
Penarth	d		07 02				07 17						07 32				07 47					08 02
Dingle Road	d		07 04				07 19						07 34				07 49					08 04
Grangetown	d		07 08			07 19	07 23				07 34		07 38			07 49	07 53				08 04	08 08
Cardiff Central [7]	a		07 14			07 24	07 29				07 39		07 44			07 54	07 59				08 09	08 14
	d	07 11	07 16		07 21	07 26	07 31		07 36	07 36	07 41		07 46	07 51		07 56	08 01		08 06	08 06	08 11	08 16
Cardiff Bay	d			07 18				07 30				07 42			07 54			08 06				
Cardiff Queen Street [3]	a	07 14	07 19	07 22	07 24	07 29	07 34	07 34	07 39		07 44	07 46	07 49	07 54	07 58	07 59	08 04	08 10	08 09		08 14	08 19
	d	07 15	07 20		07 25	07 30	07 35		07 40		07 45		07 50	07 55		08 00	08 05		08 10		08 15	08 20
Heath Low Level	d				07 30									08 00								
Ty Glas	d				07 33									08 03								
Birchgrove	d				07 34									08 04								
Rhiwbina	d				07 36									08 06								
Whitchurch (Cardiff)	d				07 38									08 08								
Coryton	a				07 43									08 13								
Heath High Level	d		07 25				07 40						07 55				08 10					08 25
Llanishen	d		07 28				07 43						07 58				08 13					08 28
Lisvane & Thornhill	d		07 30				07 45						08 00				08 15					08 30
Caerphilly [3]	d		07 36				07 51						08 06				08 21					08 36
Aber	d		07 38				07 53						08 08				08 23					08 38
Llanbradach	d		07 42				07 57						08 12				08 27					08 42
Ystrad Mynach [3]	d		07 47				08 02						08 17				08 32					08 47
Hengoed	d		07 50				08 05						08 20				08 35					08 50
Pengam	d		07 53				08 08						08 23				08 38					08 53
Gilfach Fargoed	d																08 41					
Bargoed	a		08 02				08 13						08 31				08 48					08 58
	d						08 14															08 59
Brithdir	d						08 18															09 03
Tir-phil	d						08 21															09 06
Pontlottyn	d						08 25															09 10
Rhymney [3]	a						08 31															09 16
Cathays	d	07 18				07 33			07 43		07 48					08 03			08 13		08 18	
Llandaf	d	07 22				07 37			07 47		07 52					08 07			08 17		08 22	
Ninian Park	d									07 40										08 10		
Waun-gron Park	d									07 43										08 13		
Fairwater	d									07 45										08 15		
Danescourt	d									07 47										08 17		
Radyr [3]	a	07 25				07 40			07 50	07 54	07 55					08 10			08 20	08 24	08 25	
	d	07 25				07 40			07 50		07 55					08 10			08 20		08 25	
Taffs Well [3]	d	07 29				07 44			07 54		07 59					08 14			08 24		08 29	
Trefforest Estate	d					07 48										08 18						
Trefforest	d	07 36				07 52			08 01		08 06					08 22			08 31		08 36	
Pontypridd [3]	a	07 39				07 55			08 04		08 09					08 25			08 34		08 39	
	d	07 41				07 57			08 06		08 11					08 27			08 36		08 41	
Abercynon	d	07 49				08 04					08 19					08 34					08 49	
Penrhiwceiber	d	07 54									08 24										08 54	
Mountain Ash	a	07 58									08 28										08 58	
	d	08 03									08 33										09 03	
Fernhill	d	08 05									08 35										09 05	
Cwmbach	d	08 09									08 39										09 09	
Aberdare [3]	a	08 16									08 46										09 16	
Quakers Yard	d					08 09										08 39						
Merthyr Vale	a					08 14										08 44						
	d					08 17										08 47						
Troed Y Rhiw	d					08 20										08 50						
Pentre-bach	d					08 23										08 53						
Merthyr Tydfil	a					08 31										09 01						
Trehafod	d								08 11										08 41			
Porth	a								08 14										08 44			
	d								08 15										08 45			
Dinas Rhondda	d								08 19										08 49			
Tonypandy	d								08 21										08 51			
Llwynypia	d								08 23										08 53			
Ystrad Rhondda	a								08 26										08 56			
	d								08 29										08 59			
Ton Pentre	d								08 31										09 01			
Treorchy	d								08 34										09 04			
Ynyswen	d								08 37										09 07			
Treherbert	a								08 43										09 13			

When events are being held at the Millenium Stadium,
services are subject to alteration. Please check times before travelling.

Table 130

Mondays to Fridays

Bridgend, Barry Island, Barry, Penarth and Cardiff - Coryton, Rhymney, Pontypridd, Merthyr, Aberdare and Treherbert

Network Diagram - see first Page of Table 130

Station		AW	AW	AW	AW	AW	AW	AW	AW	AW	AW	AW	AW	AW	AW	AW	AW	AW	AW	AW	AW	AW	AW
Bridgend	d								07 42														
Llantwit Major	d								07 56														
Rhoose Cardiff Int Airport ✈	d								08 06														
Barry Island	d			07 55										08 25					08 40				08 55
Barry 3	d			08 00					08 15					08 30					08 45				09 00
Barry Docks	d			08 04					08 19					08 34					08 49				09 04
Cadoxton	d			08 07					08 22					08 37					08 52				09 07
Dinas Powys	d			08 11					08 26					08 41					08 56				09 11
Eastbrook	d			08 13					08 28					08 43					08 58				09 13
Cogan	d			08 15					08 30					08 45					09 00				09 15
Penarth	d				08 17						08 32				08 47								
Dingle Road	d				08 19						08 34				08 49								
Grangetown	d			08 19	08 23				08 34		08 38			08 49	08 53				09 04				09 19
Cardiff Central 7	a			08 24	08 29				08 39		08 44			08 54	08 59				09 09				09 24
	d		08 21	08 26	08 31		08 36	08 36	08 41		08 46	08 51		08 56	09 01		09 06	09 06	09 11	09 16		09 21	09 26
Cardiff Bay	d	08 18				08 30				08 42			08 54			09 06					09 18		
Cardiff Queen Street 3	a	08 22	08 24	08 29	08 34	08 34	08 39		08 44	08 46	08 49	08 54	08 58	08 59	09 04	09 10	09 09		09 14	09 19	09 22	09 24	09 29
	d		08 25	08 30	08 35		08 40		08 45		08 50	08 55		09 00	09 05		09 10		09 15	09 20		09 25	09 30
Heath Low Level	d		08 30									09 00										09 30	
Ty Glas	d		08 33									09 03										09 33	
Birchgrove	d		08 34									09 04										09 34	
Rhiwbina	d		08 36									09 06										09 36	
Whitchurch (Cardiff)	d		08 38									09 08										09 38	
Coryton	a		08 43									09 13										09 43	
Heath High Level	d				08 40						08 55				09 10					09 25			
Llanishen	d				08 43						08 58				09 13					09 28			
Lisvane & Thornhill	d				08 45						09 00				09 15					09 30			
Caerphilly 3	d				08 51						09 06				09 21					09 36			
Aber	d				08 53						09 08				09 23					09 38			
Llanbradach	d				08 57						09 12				09 27					09 42			
Ystrad Mynach 3	d				09 02						09 17				09 32					09 47			
Hengoed	d				09 05						09 20				09 35					09 50			
Pengam	d				09 08						09 23				09 38					09 53			
Gilfach Fargoed	d														09 41								
Bargoed	a				09 16						09 31				09 48					09 58			
	d																			09 59			
Brithdir	d																			10 03			
Tir-phil	d																			10 06			
Pontlottyn	d																			10 10			
Rhymney 3	a																			10 16			
Cathays	d			08 33			08 43		08 48					09 03			09 13		09 18				09 33
Llandaf	d			08 37			08 47		08 52					09 07			09 17		09 22				09 37
Ninian Park	d							08 40										09 10					
Waun-gron Park	d							08 43										09 13					
Fairwater	d							08 45										09 15					
Danescourt	d							08 47										09 17					
Radyr 3	a			08 40			08 50	08 54	08 55					09 10			09 20	09 24	09 25				09 40
	d			08 40			08 50		08 55					09 10			09 20		09 25				09 40
Taffs Well 3	d			08 44			08 54		08 59					09 14			09 24		09 29				09 44
Trefforest Estate	d			08 48										09 18									09 48
Trefforest	d			08 52			09 01		09 06					09 22			09 31		09 36				09 52
Pontypridd 3	a			08 55			09 04		09 09					09 25			09 34		09 39				09 55
	d			08 57			09 06		09 11					09 27			09 36		09 41				09 57
Abercynon	d			09 04					09 19					09 34					09 49				10 04
Penrhiwceiber	d								09 24										09 54				
Mountain Ash	a								09 28										09 58				
	d								09 33										10 03				
Fernhill	d								09 35										10 05				
Cwmbach	d								09 39										10 09				
Aberdare 3	a								09 46										10 16				
Quakers Yard	d			09 09										09 39									10 09
Merthyr Vale	a			09 14										09 44									10 14
	d			09 17										09 47									10 17
Troed Y Rhiw	d			09 20										09 50									10 20
Pentre-bach	d			09 23										09 53									10 23
Merthyr Tydfil	a			09 31										10 01									10 31
Trehafod	d						09 11										09 41						
Porth	a						09 14										09 44						
	d						09 15										09 45						
Dinas Rhondda	d						09 19										09 49						
Tonypandy	d						09 21										09 51						
Llwynypia	d						09 23										09 53						
Ystrad Rhondda	a						09 26										09 56						
	d						09 29										09 59						
Ton Pentre	d						09 31										10 01						
Treorchy	d						09 34										10 04						
Ynyswen	d						09 37										10 07						
Treherbert	a						09 43										10 13						

When events are being held at the Millenium Stadium,
services are subject to alteration. Please check times before travelling.

Bridgend, Barry Island, Barry, Penarth and Cardiff - Coryton, Rhymney, Pontypridd, Merthyr, Aberdare and Treherbert

Network Diagram - see first Page of Table 130

		AW	AW		AW	AW	AW	AW	AW	AW	AW	AW	AW		AW	AW	AW	AW	AW	AW	AW	AW	AW		AW
Bridgend	d						08 42																		
Llantwit Major	d						08 56																		
Rhoose Cardiff Int Airport ✈	d						09 06																		
Barry Island	d											09 25							09 40				09 55		
Barry 3	d						09 15					09 30							09 45				10 00		
Barry Docks	d						09 19					09 34							09 49				10 04		
Cadoxton	d						09 22					09 37							09 52				10 07		
Dinas Powys	d						09 26					09 41							09 56				10 11		
Eastbrook	d						09 28					09 43							09 58				10 13		
Cogan	d						09 30					09 45							10 00				10 15		
Penarth	d	09 17							09 32				09 47							10 02					10 17
Dingle Road	d	09 19							09 34				09 49							10 04					10 19
Grangetown	d	09 23					09 34		09 38			09 49	09 53						10 04	10 08			10 19		10 23
Cardiff Central 7	a	09 29					09 39		09 44			09 54	09 59						10 09	10 14			10 24		10 29
	d	09 31			09 36	09 36	09 41		09 46	09 51		09 56	10 01			10 06	10 06		10 11	10 16		10 21	10 26		10 31
Cardiff Bay	d		09 30					09 42			09 54				10 06						10 18				
Cardiff Queen Street 3	a	09 34	09 34		09 39		09 44	09 46	09 49	09 54	09 58	09 59	10 04		10 10	10 09			10 14	10 19	10 22	10 24	10 29		10 34
	d	09 35			09 40		09 45		09 50	09 55		10 00	10 05			10 10			10 15	10 20		10 25	10 30		10 35
Heath Low Level	d									10 00												10 30			
Ty Glas	d									10 03												10 33			
Birchgrove	d									10 04												10 34			
Rhiwbina	d									10 06												10 36			
Whitchurch (Cardiff)	d									10 08												10 38			
Coryton	a									10 13												10 43			
Heath High Level	d	09 40							09 55				10 10							10 25					10 40
Llanishen	d	09 43							09 58				10 13							10 28					10 43
Lisvane & Thornhill	d	09 45							10 00				10 15							10 30					10 45
Caerphilly 3	d	09 51							10 06				10 21							10 36					10 51
Aber	d	09 53							10 08				10 23							10 38					10 53
Llanbradach	d	09 57							10 12				10 27							10 42					10 57
Ystrad Mynach 3	d	10 02							10 17				10 32							10 47					11 02
Hengoed	d	10 05							10 20				10 35							10 50					11 05
Pengam	d	10 08							10 23				10 38							10 53					11 08
Gilfach Fargoed	d												10 41												
Bargoed	a	10 16							10 31				10 48							10 58					11 16
	d																			10 59					
Brithdir	d																			11 03					
Tir-phil	d																			11 06					
Pontlottyn	d																			11 10					
Rhymney 3	a																			11 16					
Cathays	d				09 43		09 48					10 03				10 13			10 18				10 33		
Llandaf	d				09 47		09 52					10 07				10 17			10 22				10 37		
Ninian Park	d					09 40											10 10								
Waun-gron Park	d					09 43											10 13								
Fairwater	d					09 45											10 15								
Danescourt	d					09 47											10 17								
Radyr 3	a				09 50	09 54	09 55					10 10				10 20	10 24		10 25				10 40		
	d				09 50		09 55					10 10				10 20			10 25				10 40		
Taffs Well 3	d				09 54		09 59					10 14				10 24			10 29				10 44		
Trefforest Estate	d																						10 48		
Trefforest	d				10 01		10 06					10 22				10 31			10 36				10 52		
Pontypridd 3	a				10 04		10 09					10 30				10 34			10 39				10 55		
	d				10 06		10 11									10 36		10 35	10 41				10 57		
Abercynon	d						10 19											10 41	10 49				11 04		
Penrhiwceiber	d						10 24												10 54						
Mountain Ash	a						10 28												10 58						
	d						10 33												11 03						
Fernhill	d						10 35												11 05						
Cwmbach	d						10 39												11 09						
Aberdare 3	a						10 46												11 16						
Quakers Yard	d																	10 45					11 09		
Merthyr Vale	a																	10 50					11 14		
	d																	10 52					11 17		
Troed Y Rhiw	d																	10 55					11 20		
Pentre-bach	d																	10 58					11 23		
Merthyr Tydfil	a																	11 06					11 31		
Trehafod	d				10 11											10 41									
Porth	a				10 14											10 44									
	d				10 15											10 45									
Dinas Rhondda	d				10 19											10 49									
Tonypandy	d				10 21											10 51									
Llwynypia	d				10 23											10 53									
Ystrad Rhondda	a				10 26											10 56									
	d				10 29											10 59									
Ton Pentre	d				10 31											11 01									
Treorchy	d				10 34											11 04									
Ynyswen	d				10 37											11 07									
Treherbert	a				10 43											11 13									

When events are being held at the Millenium Stadium,
services are subject to alteration. Please check times before travelling.

Bridgend, Barry Island, Barry, Penarth and Cardiff - Coryton, Rhymney, Pontypridd, Merthyr, Aberdare and Treherbert

Network Diagram - see first Page of Table 130

		AW	AW	AW	AW	AW	AW	AW	AW		AW	AW	AW	AW	AW	AW	AW	AW	AW		AW	AW	AW	AW	AW
Bridgend	d				09 45																				
Llantwit Major	d				09 58																				
Rhoose Cardiff Int Airport ✈	d				10 08																				
Barry Island	d										10 25					10 40					10 55				
Barry 3	d				10 16						10 30					10 45					11 00				
Barry Docks	d				10 19						10 34					10 49					11 04				
Cadoxton	d				10 22						10 37					10 52					11 07				
Dinas Powys	d				10 26						10 41					10 56					11 11				
Eastbrook	d				10 28						10 43					10 58					11 13				
Cogan	d				10 30						10 45					11 00					11 15				
Penarth	d						10 32						10 47				11 02					11 17			
Dingle Road	d						10 34						10 49				11 04					11 19			
Grangetown	d				10 34		10 38				10 49		10 53			11 04	11 08				11 19	11 23			
Cardiff Central 7	a				10 42		10 44				10 54		10 59			11 09	11 14				11 24	11 29			
	d		10 36	10 36			10 46	10 51			10 56	10 54	11 01	11 06		11 11	11 16		11 21		11 26	11 31		11 36	11 36
Cardiff Bay	d	10 30				10 42			10 54						11 06			11 18					11 30		
Cardiff Queen Street 3	a	10 34	10 39			10 46	10 49	10 54	10 58		10 59		11 04		11 10	11 14	11 19	11 22	11 24		11 29	11 34	11 34	11 39	
	d		10 40				10 50	10 55			11 00		11 05			11 15	11 20		11 25		11 30	11 35		11 40	
Heath Low Level	d							11 00											11 30						
Ty Glas	d							11 03											11 33						
Birchgrove	d							11 04											11 34						
Rhiwbina	d							11 06											11 36						
Whitchurch (Cardiff)	d							11 08											11 38						
Coryton	a							11 13											11 43						
Heath High Level	d						10 55						11 10				11 25					11 40			
Llanishen	d						10 58						11 13				11 28					11 43			
Lisvane & Thornhill	d						11 00						11 15				11 30					11 45			
Caerphilly 3	d						11 06						11 21				11 36					11 51			
Aber	d						11 08						11 23				11 38					11 53			
Llanbradach	d						11 12						11 27				11 42					11 57			
Ystrad Mynach 3	d						11 17						11 32				11 47					12 02			
Hengoed	d						11 20						11 35				11 50					12 05			
Pengam	d						11 23						11 38				11 53					12 08			
Gilfach Fargoed	d												11 41												
Bargoed	a						11 31						11 48				11 58					12 16			
	d																11 59								
Brithdir	d																12 03								
Tir-phil	d																12 06								
Pontlottyn	d																12 10								
Rhymney 3	a																12 16								
Cathays	d		10 43								11 03					11 18					11 33			11 43	
Llandaf	d		10 47								11 07					11 22					11 37			11 47	
Ninian Park	d			10 40										11 10											11 40
Waun-gron Park	d			10 43										11 13											11 43
Fairwater	d			10 45										11 15											11 45
Danescourt	d			10 47										11 17											11 47
Radyr 3	a		10 50	10 54							11 10	11 02		11 24		11 25					11 40			11 50	11 54
	d		10 50								11 10	11 20				11 25					11 40			11 50	
Taffs Well 3	d		10 54								11 14	11 24				11 29					11 44			11 54	
Trefforest Estate	d										11 18										11 48				
Trefforest	d		11 01								11 22	11 31				11 36					11 52			12 01	
Pontypridd 3	a		11 04								11 25	11 34				11 39					11 55			12 04	
	d		11 06								11 27	11 36				11 41					11 57			12 06	
Abercynon	d										11 34					11 49					12 04				
Penrhiwceiber	d															11 54									
Mountain Ash	a															11 58									
	d															12 03									
Fernhill	d															12 05									
Cwmbach	d															12 09									
Aberdare 3	a															12 16									
Quakers Yard	d										11 39										12 09				
Merthyr Vale	a										11 44										12 14				
	d										11 47										12 17				
Troed Y Rhiw	d										11 50										12 20				
Pentre-bach	d										11 53										12 23				
Merthyr Tydfil	a										12 01										12 31				
Trehafod	d		11 11									11 41												12 11	
Porth	a		11 14									11 44												12 14	
	d		11 15									11 45												12 15	
Dinas Rhondda	d		11 19									11 49												12 19	
Tonypandy	d		11 21									11 51												12 21	
Llwynypia	d		11 23									11 53												12 23	
Ystrad Rhondda	a		11 26									11 56												12 26	
	d		11 29									11 59												12 29	
Ton Pentre	d		11 31									12 01												12 31	
Treorchy	d		11 34									12 04												12 34	
Ynyswen	d		11 37									12 07												12 37	
Treherbert	a		11 43									12 13												12 43	

When events are being held at the Millenium Stadium,
services are subject to alteration. Please check times before travelling.

Bridgend, Barry Island, Barry, Penarth and Cardiff - Coryton, Rhymney, Pontypridd, Merthyr, Aberdare and Treherbert

Network Diagram - see first Page of Table 130

		AW	AW	AW	AW	AW	AW	AW	AW	AW	AW	AW	AW	AW	AW	AW	AW	AW	AW	AW	AW	AW	AW
Bridgend	d	10 45																				11 42	
Llantwit Major	d	10 58																				11 56	
Rhoose Cardiff Int Airport ✈	d	11 08																				12 06	
Barry Island	d						11 25					11 40				11 55							
Barry 3	d	11 16					11 30					11 45				12 00						12 15	
Barry Docks	d	11 19					11 34					11 49				12 04						12 19	
Cadoxton	d	11 22					11 37					11 52				12 07						12 22	
Dinas Powys	d	11 26					11 41					11 56				12 11						12 26	
Eastbrook	d	11 28					11 43					11 58				12 13						12 28	
Cogan	d	11 30					11 45					12 00				12 15						12 30	
Penarth	d			11 32				11 47					12 02				12 17						
Dingle Road	d			11 34				11 49					12 04				12 19						
Grangetown	d	11 34		11 38			11 49	11 53				12 04	12 08			12 19	12 23					12 34	
Cardiff Central 7	a	11 39		11 44			11 54	11 59				12 09	12 14			12 24	12 29					12 44	
	d	11 41		11 46	11 51		11 56	12 01		12 06	12 06	12 11	12 16		12 21	12 26	12 31		12 36	12 36	12 41		
Cardiff Bay	d		11 42			11 54			12 06					12 18				12 30					12 42
Cardiff Queen Street 3	a	11 44	11 46	11 49	11 54	11 58	11 59	12 04	12 10	12 09		12 14	12 19	12 22	12 24	12 29	12 34	12 34	12 39		12 44		12 46
	d	11 45		11 50	11 55		12 00	12 05		12 10		12 15	12 20		12 25	12 30	12 35		12 40		12 45		
Heath Low Level	d				12 00										12 30								
Ty Glas	d				12 03										12 33								
Birchgrove	d				12 04										12 34								
Rhiwbina	d				12 06										12 36								
Whitchurch (Cardiff)	d				12 08										12 38								
Coryton	a				12 13										12 43								
Heath High Level	d			11 55				12 10					12 25				12 40						
Llanishen	d			11 58				12 13					12 28				12 43						
Lisvane & Thornhill	d			12 00				12 15					12 30				12 45						
Caerphilly 3	d			12 06				12 21					12 36				12 51						
Aber	d			12 08				12 23					12 38				12 53						
Llanbradach	d			12 12				12 27					12 42				12 57						
Ystrad Mynach 3	d			12 17				12 32					12 47				13 02						
Hengoed	d			12 20				12 35					12 50				13 05						
Pengam	d			12 23				12 38					12 53				13 08						
Gilfach Fargoed	d							12 41															
Bargoed	a			12 31				12 48					12 58				13 16						
	d												12 59										
Brithdir	d												13 03										
Tir-phil	d												13 06										
Pontlottyn	d												13 10										
Rhymney 3	a												13 16										
Cathays	d	11 48					12 03			12 13		12 18				12 33			12 43		12 48		
Llandaf	d	11 52					12 07			12 17		12 22				12 37			12 47		12 52		
Ninian Park	d										12 10									12 40			
Waun-gron Park	d										12 13									12 43			
Fairwater	d										12 15									12 45			
Danescourt	d										12 17									12 47			
Radyr 3	a	11 55					12 10			12 20	12 24	12 25				12 40			12 50	12 54	12 55		
	d	11 55					12 10			12 20		12 25				12 40			12 50		12 55		
Taffs Well 3	d	11 59					12 14			12 24		12 29				12 44			12 54		12 59		
Trefforest Estate	d						12 18									12 48							
Trefforest	d	12 06					12 22			12 31		12 36				12 52			13 01		13 06		
Pontypridd 3	a	12 09					12 25			12 34		12 42				12 55			13 04		13 09		
	d	12 11					12 27			12 36						12 57			13 06		13 11		
Abercynon	d	12 19					12 34									13 04					13 19		
Penrhiwceiber	d	12 24																			13 24		
Mountain Ash	a	12 28																			13 28		
	d	12 33																			13 33		
Fernhill	d	12 35																			13 35		
Cwmbach	d	12 39																			13 39		
Aberdare 3	a	12 46																			13 46		
Quakers Yard	d						12 39									13 09							
Merthyr Vale	a						12 44									13 14							
	d						12 47									13 17							
Troed Y Rhiw	d						12 50									13 20							
Pentre-bach	d						12 53									13 23							
Merthyr Tydfil	a						13 01									13 31							
Trehafod	d									12 41									13 11				
Porth	a									12 44									13 14				
	d									12 45									13 15				
Dinas Rhondda	d									12 49									13 19				
Tonypandy	d									12 51									13 21				
Llwynypia	d									12 53									13 23				
Ystrad Rhondda	a									12 56									13 26				
	d									12 59									13 29				
Ton Pentre	d									13 01									13 31				
Treorchy	d									13 04									13 34				
Ynyswen	d									13 07									13 37				
Treherbert	a									13 13									13 43				

When events are being held at the Millenium Stadium, services are subject to alteration. Please check times before travelling.

Table 130

Mondays to Fridays

Bridgend, Barry Island, Barry, Penarth and Cardiff - Coryton, Rhymney, Pontypridd, Merthyr, Aberdare and Treherbert

Network Diagram - see first Page of Table 130

		AW	AW	AW	AW	AW	AW	AW	AW	AW	AW	AW	AW	AW	AW	AW	AW	AW	AW	AW	AW	AW
Bridgend	d																		12 42			
Llantwit Major	d																		12 56			
Rhoose Cardiff Int Airport ✈	d																		13 06			
Barry Island	d				12 25					12 40				12 55								
Barry [3]	d				12 30					12 45				13 00					13 15			
Barry Docks	d				12 34					12 49				13 04					13 19			
Cadoxton	d				12 37					12 52				13 07					13 22			
Dinas Powys	d				12 41					12 56				13 11					13 26			
Eastbrook	d				12 43					12 58				13 13					13 28			
Cogan	d				12 45					13 00				13 15					13 30			
Penarth	d	12 32				12 47					13 02				13 17						13 32	
Dingle Road	d	12 34				12 49					13 04				13 19						13 34	
Grangetown	d	12 38			12 49	12 53				13 04	13 08			13 19	13 23				13 34		13 38	
Cardiff Central [7]	a	12 44			12 54	12 59				13 09	13 14			13 24	13 29				13 39		13 44	
	d	12 46	12 51		12 56	13 01		13 06	13 06	13 11	13 16		13 21	13 26	13 31		13 36	13 36	13 41		13 46	13 51
Cardiff Bay	d			12 54			13 06					13 18				13 30				13 42		
Cardiff Queen Street [3]	a	12 49	12 54	12 58	12 59	13 04	13 10	13 09		13 14	13 19	13 22	13 24	13 29	13 34	13 34	13 39		13 44	13 46	13 49	13 54
	d	12 50	12 55		13 00	13 05		13 10		13 15	13 20		13 25	13 30	13 35		13 40		13 45		13 50	13 55
Heath Low Level	d		13 00										13 30									14 00
Ty Glas	d		13 03										13 33									14 03
Birchgrove	d		13 04										13 34									14 04
Rhiwbina	d		13 06										13 36									14 06
Whitchurch (Cardiff)	d		13 08										13 38									14 08
Coryton	a		13 13										13 43									14 13
Heath High Level	d	12 55				13 10					13 25				13 40						13 55	
Llanishen	d	12 58				13 13					13 28				13 43						13 58	
Lisvane & Thornhill	d	13 00				13 15					13 30				13 45						14 00	
Caerphilly [3]	d	13 06				13 21					13 36				13 51						14 06	
Aber	d	13 08				13 23					13 38				13 53						14 08	
Llanbradach	d	13 12				13 27					13 42				13 57						14 12	
Ystrad Mynach [3]	d	13 17				13 32					13 47				14 02						14 17	
Hengoed	d	13 20				13 35					13 50				14 05						14 20	
Pengam	d	13 23				13 38					13 53				14 08						14 23	
Gilfach Fargoed	d					13 41																
Bargoed	a	13 31				13 48					13 58				14 16						14 31	
	d										13 59											
Brithdir	d										14 03											
Tir-phil	d										14 06											
Pontlottyn	d										14 10											
Rhymney [3]	a										14 16											
Cathays	d				13 03			13 13		13 18				13 33			13 43		13 48			
Llandaf	d				13 07			13 17		13 22				13 37			13 47		13 52			
Ninian Park	d								13 10									13 40				
Waun-gron Park	d								13 13									13 43				
Fairwater	d								13 15									13 45				
Danescourt	d								13 17									13 47				
Radyr [3]	a				13 10			13 20	13 24	13 25				13 40			13 50	13 54	13 55			
	d				13 10			13 20		13 25				13 40			13 50		13 55			
Taffs Well [3]	d				13 14			13 24		13 29				13 44			13 54		13 59			
Trefforest Estate	d				13 18									13 48								
Trefforest	d				13 22			13 31		13 36				13 52			14 01		14 06			
Pontypridd [3]	a				13 25			13 34		13 39				13 55			14 04		14 09			
	d				13 27			13 36		13 41				13 57			14 06		14 11			
Abercynon	d				13 34					13 49				14 04					14 19			
Penrhiwceiber	d									13 54									14 24			
Mountain Ash	a									13 58									14 28			
	d									14 03									14 33			
Fernhill	d									14 05									14 35			
Cwmbach	d									14 09									14 39			
Aberdare [3]	a									14 16									14 46			
Quakers Yard	d				13 39									14 09								
Merthyr Vale	a				13 44									14 14								
	d				13 47									14 17								
Troed Y Rhiw	d				13 50									14 20								
Pentre-bach	d				13 53									14 23								
Merthyr Tydfil	a				14 01									14 31								
Trehafod	d							13 41									14 11					
Porth	a							13 44									14 14					
	d							13 45									14 15					
Dinas Rhondda	d							13 49									14 19					
Tonypandy	d							13 51									14 21					
Llwynypia	d							13 53									14 23					
Ystrad Rhondda	a							13 56									14 26					
	d							13 59									14 29					
Ton Pentre	d							14 01									14 31					
Treorchy	d							14 04									14 34					
Ynyswen	d							14 07									14 37					
Treherbert	a							14 13									14 43					

When events are being held at the Millenium Stadium, services are subject to alteration. Please check times before travelling.

Bridgend, Barry Island, Barry, Penarth and Cardiff - Coryton, Rhymney, Pontypridd, Merthyr, Aberdare and Treherbert

Network Diagram - see first Page of Table 130

		AW	AW	AW	AW	AW	AW		AW	AW	AW	AW	AW	AW	AW	AW	AW		AW	AW	AW	AW	AW	AW	AW
Bridgend	d																		13 42						
Llantwit Major	d																		13 56						
Rhoose Cardiff Int Airport ✈	d																		14 06						
Barry Island	d		13 25						13 40				13 55												14 25
Barry 3	d		13 30						13 45				14 00						14 15						14 30
Barry Docks	d		13 34						13 49				14 04						14 19						14 34
Cadoxton	d		13 37						13 52				14 07						14 22						14 37
Dinas Powys	d		13 41						13 56				14 11						14 26						14 41
Eastbrook	d		13 43						13 58				14 13						14 28						14 43
Cogan	d		13 45						14 00				14 15						14 30						14 45
Penarth	d			13 47						14 02				14 17							14 32				
Dingle Road	d			13 49						14 04				14 19							14 34				
Grangetown	d		13 49	13 53					14 04	14 08			14 19	14 23					14 34		14 38				14 49
Cardiff Central 7	a		13 54	13 59					14 09	14 14			14 24	14 29					14 39		14 44				14 54
	d		13 56	14 01		14 06	14 06		14 11	14 16		14 21	14 26	14 31		14 36	14 36		14 41		14 46	14 51		14 51	14 56
Cardiff Bay	d	13 54			14 06						14 18				14 30					14 42			14 54		
Cardiff Queen Street 3	a	13 58	13 59	14 04	14 10	14 09			14 14	14 19	14 22	14 24	14 29	14 34	14 34	14 39			14 44	14 46	14 49	14 54	14 58		14 59
	d		14 00	14 05		14 10			14 15	14 20		14 25	14 30	14 35		14 40			14 45		14 50	14 55			15 00
Heath Low Level	d											14 30										15 00			
Ty Glas	d											14 33										15 03			
Birchgrove	d											14 34										15 04			
Rhiwbina	d											14 36										15 06			
Whitchurch (Cardiff)	d											14 38										15 08			
Coryton	a											14 43										15 13			
Heath High Level	d			14 10						14 25				14 40							14 55				
Llanishen	d			14 13						14 28				14 43							14 58				
Lisvane & Thornhill	d			14 15						14 30				14 45							15 00				
Caerphilly 3	d			14 21						14 36				14 51							15 06				
Aber	d			14 23						14 38				14 53							15 08				
Llanbradach	d			14 27						14 42				14 57							15 12				
Ystrad Mynach 3	d			14 32						14 47				15 02							15 17				
Hengoed	d			14 35						14 50				15 05							15 20				
Pengam	d			14 38						14 53				15 08							15 23				
Gilfach Fargoed	d			14 41																					
Bargoed	a			14 48						14 58				15 16							15 31				
	d									14 59															
Brithdir	d									15 03															
Tir-phil	d									15 06															
Pontlottyn	d									15 10															
Rhymney 3	a									15 16															
Cathays	d		14 03			14 13			14 18				14 33			14 43			14 48						15 03
Llandaf	d		14 07			14 17			14 22				14 37			14 47			14 52						15 07
Ninian Park	d						14 10										14 40								
Waun-gron Park	d						14 13										14 43								
Fairwater	d						14 15										14 45								
Danescourt	d						14 17										14 47								
Radyr 3	a		14 10			14 20	14 24		14 25				14 40			14 50	14 54		14 55					15 08	15 10
	d		14 10			14 20			14 25				14 40			14 50			14 55					15 20	15 10
Taffs Well 3	d		14 14			14 24			14 29				14 44			14 54			14 59					↦	15 14
Trefforest Estate	d		14 18										14 48												15 18
Trefforest	d		14 22			14 31			14 36				14 52			15 01			15 06						15 22
Pontypridd 3	a		14 25			14 34			14 39				14 55			15 04			15 09						15 25
	d		14 27			14 36			14 41				14 57			15 06			15 11						15 27
Abercynon	d		14 34						14 49				15 04						15 19						15 34
Penrhiwceiber	d								14 54										15 24						
Mountain Ash	a								14 58										15 28						
	d								15 03										15 33						
Fernhill	d								15 05										15 35						
Cwmbach	d								15 09										15 39						
Aberdare 3	a								15 16										15 46						
Quakers Yard	d		14 39										15 09												15 39
Merthyr Vale	a		14 44										15 14												15 44
	d		14 47										15 17												15 47
Troed Y Rhiw	d		14 50										15 20												15 50
Pentre-bach	d		14 53										15 23												15 53
Merthyr Tydfil	a		15 01										15 31												16 01
Trehafod	d					14 41										15 11									
Porth	a					14 44										15 14									
	d					14 45										15 15									
Dinas Rhondda	d					14 49										15 19									
Tonypandy	d					14 51										15 21									
Llwynypia	d					14 53										15 23									
Ystrad Rhondda	a					14 56										15 26									
	d					14 59										15 29									
Ton Pentre	d					15 01										15 31									
Treorchy	d					15 04										15 34									
Ynyswen	d					15 07										15 37									
Treherbert	a					15 13										15 43									

When events are being held at the Millenium Stadium,
services are subject to alteration. Please check times before travelling.

Table 130

Mondays to Fridays

Bridgend, Barry Island, Barry, Penarth and Cardiff - Coryton, Rhymney, Pontypridd, Merthyr, Aberdare and Treherbert

Network Diagram - see first Page of Table 130

		AW	AW	AW	AW	AW	AW	AW	AW	AW	AW	AW	AW	AW	AW	AW	AW	AW	AW	AW	AW	AW
Bridgend	d														14 42							
Llantwit Major	d														14 56							
Rhoose Cardiff Int Airport ✈	d														15 06							
Barry Island	d					14 40				14 55										15 25		
Barry 3	d					14 45				15 00					15 15					15 30		
Barry Docks	d					14 49				15 04					15 19					15 34		
Cadoxton	d					14 52				15 07					15 22					15 37		
Dinas Powys	d					14 56				15 11					15 26					15 41		
Eastbrook	d					14 58				15 13					15 28					15 43		
Cogan	d					15 00				15 15					15 30					15 45		
Penarth	d		14 47				15 02				15 17						15 32				15 47	
Dingle Road	d		14 49				15 04				15 19						15 34				15 49	
Grangetown	d		14 53			15 04	15 08			15 19	15 23				15 34		15 38			15 49	15 53	
Cardiff Central 7	a		14 59			15 09	15 14			15 24	15 29				15 39		15 44			15 54	15 59	
	d		15 01	15 06		15 11	15 16		15 21	15 26	15 31		15 36	15 36	15 41		15 46	15 51		15 56	16 01	
Cardiff Bay	d				15 06			15 18				15 30				15 42			15 54			16 06
Cardiff Queen Street 3	a		15 04		15 10	15 14	15 19	15 22	15 24	15 29	15 34	15 34	15 39		15 44	15 46	15 49	15 54	15 58	15 59	16 04	16 10
	d		15 05			15 15	15 20		15 25	15 30	15 35		15 40		15 45		15 50	15 55		16 00	16 05	
Heath Low Level	d								15 30									16 00				
Ty Glas	d								15 33									16 03				
Birchgrove	d								15 34									16 04				
Rhiwbina	d								15 36									16 06				
Whitchurch (Cardiff)	d								15 38									16 08				
Coryton	a								15 43									16 13				
Heath High Level	d		15 10				15 25				15 40						15 55				16 10	
Llanishen	d		15 13				15 28				15 43						15 58				16 13	
Lisvane & Thornhill	d		15 15				15 30				15 45						16 00				16 15	
Caerphilly 3	d		15 21				15 36				15 51						16 06				16 21	
Aber	d		15 23				15 38				15 53						16 08				16 23	
Llanbradach	d		15 27				15 42				15 57						16 12				16 27	
Ystrad Mynach 3	d		15 32				15 47				16 02						16 17				16 32	
Hengoed	d		15 35				15 50				16 05						16 20				16 35	
Pengam	d		15 38				15 53				16 08						16 23				16 38	
Gilfach Fargoed	d		15 41																		16 41	
Bargoed	a		15 48				15 58				16 16						16 31				16 48	
	d						15 59															
Brithdir	d						16 03															
Tir-phil	d						16 06															
Pontlottyn	d						16 10															
Rhymney 3	a						16 16															
Cathays	d					15 18				15 33			15 43		15 48					16 03		
Llandaf	d					15 22				15 37			15 47		15 52					16 07		
Ninian Park	d			15 10										15 40								
Waun-gron Park	d			15 13										15 43								
Fairwater	d			15 15										15 45								
Danescourt	d	←		15 17										15 47								
Radyr 3	a	15 08		15 24		15 25				15 40			15 50	15 54	15 55					16 10		
	d	15 20				15 25				15 40			15 50		15 55					16 10		
Taffs Well 3	d	15 24				15 29				15 44			15 54		15 59					16 14		
Trefforest Estate	d									15 48										16 18		
Trefforest	d	15 31				15 36				15 52			16 01		16 06					16 22		
Pontypridd 3	a	15 34				15 39				15 55			16 04		16 09					16 25		
	d	15 36				15 41				15 57			16 06		16 11					16 27		
Abercynon	d					15 49				16 04					16 19					16 34		
Penrhiwceiber	d					15 54									16 24							
Mountain Ash	a					15 58									16 28							
	d					16 03									16 33							
Fernhill	d					16 05									16 35							
Cwmbach	d					16 09									16 39							
Aberdare 3	a					16 16									16 46							
Quakers Yard	d									16 09										16 39		
Merthyr Vale	a									16 14										16 44		
	d									16 17										16 47		
Troed Y Rhiw	d									16 20										16 50		
Pentre-bach	d									16 23										16 53		
Merthyr Tydfil	a									16 31										17 01		
Trehafod	d	15 41											16 11									
Porth	a	15 44											16 14									
	d	15 45											16 15									
Dinas Rhondda	d	15 49											16 19									
Tonypandy	d	15 51											16 21									
Llwynypia	d	15 53											16 23									
Ystrad Rhondda	a	15 56											16 26									
	d	15 59											16 29									
Ton Pentre	d	16 01											16 31									
Treorchy	d	16 04											16 34									
Ynyswen	d	16 07											16 37									
Treherbert	a	16 13											16 43									

When events are being held at the Millenium Stadium, services are subject to alteration. Please check times before travelling.

Bridgend, Barry Island, Barry, Penarth and Cardiff - Coryton, Rhymney, Pontypridd, Merthyr, Aberdare and Treherbert

Network Diagram - see first Page of Table 130

		AW	AW	AW	AW	AW	AW	AW	AW	AW	AW	AW	AW	AW	AW	AW	AW	AW	AW	AW	AW	AW	AW
Bridgend	d												15 42										
Llantwit Major	d												15 56										
Rhoose Cardiff Int Airport ✈	d												16 06										
Barry Island	d			15 40				15 55										16 25					16 40
Barry 3	d			15 45				16 00					16 15					16 30					16 45
Barry Docks	d			15 49				16 04					16 19					16 34					16 49
Cadoxton	d			15 52				16 07					16 22					16 37					16 52
Dinas Powys	d			15 56				16 11					16 26					16 41					16 56
Eastbrook	d			15 58				16 13					16 28					16 43					16 58
Cogan	d			16 00				16 15					16 30					16 45					17 00
Penarth	d				16 02				16 17						16 32								
Dingle Road	d				16 04				16 19						16 34								
Grangetown	d			16 04	16 08			16 19	16 23				16 34		16 38			16 49					17 04
Cardiff Central 7	a			16 09	16 14			16 24	16 29				16 39		16 44			16 54					17 09
	d	16 06	16 06	16 11	16 16		16 21	16 26	16 31		16 36	16 36	16 41		16 46	16 51		16 56	17 01		17 06	17 06	17 11
Cardiff Bay	d					16 18				16 30				16 42			16 54			17 06			
Cardiff Queen Street 3	a	16 09		16 14	16 19	16 22	16 24	16 29	16 34	16 34	16 39		16 44	16 46	16 49	16 54	16 58	16 59	17 04	17 10	17 09		17 14
	d	16 10		16 15	16 20		16 25	16 30	16 35		16 40		16 45		16 50	16 55		17 00	17 05		17 10		17 15
Heath Low Level	d						16 30									17 00							
Ty Glas	d						16 33									17 03							
Birchgrove	d						16 34									17 04							
Rhiwbina	d						16 36									17 06							
Whitchurch (Cardiff)	d						16 38									17 08							
Coryton	a						16 43									17 13							
Heath High Level	d				16 25				16 40						16 55				17 10				
Llanishen	d				16 28				16 43						16 58				17 13				
Lisvane & Thornhill	d				16 30				16 45						17 00				17 15				
Caerphilly 3	d				16 36				16 51						17 06				17 21				
Aber	d				16 38				16 53						17 08				17 23				
Llanbradach	d				16 42				16 57						17 12				17 27				
Ystrad Mynach 3	d				16 47				17 02						17 17				17 33				
Hengoed	d				16 50				17 05						17 20				17 35				
Pengam	d				16 53				17 08						17 23				17 39				
Gilfach Fargoed	d																		17 42				
Bargoed	a				16 58				17 16						17 31				17 45				
	d				16 59														17 47				
Brithdir	d				17 03														17 50				
Tir-phil	d				17 06														17 53				
Pontlottyn	d				17 10														17 58				
Rhymney 3	a				17 16														18 04				
Cathays	d	16 13		16 18				16 33			16 43		16 48					17 03			17 13		17 18
Llandaf	d	16 17		16 22				16 37			16 47		16 52					17 07			17 17		17 22
Ninian Park	d		16 10									16 40										17 10	
Waun-gron Park	d		16 13									16 43										17 13	
Fairwater	d		16 15									16 45										17 15	
Danescourt	d		16 17									16 47										17 17	
Radyr 3	a	16 20	16 24	16 25				16 40			16 50	16 54	16 55					17 10			17 20	17 24	17 25
	d	16 20		16 25				16 40			16 50		16 55					17 10			17 20		17 25
Taffs Well 3	d	16 24		16 29				16 44			16 54		16 59					17 14			17 24		17 29
Trefforest Estate	d							16 48										17 18					
Trefforest	d	16 31		16 36				16 52			17 01		17 06					17 22			17 31		17 36
Pontypridd 3	a	16 34		16 39				16 55			17 04		17 09					17 25			17 34		17 39
	d	16 36		16 41				16 57			17 06		17 11					17 27			17 36		17 41
Abercynon	d			16 49				17 04					17 19					17 34					17 49
Penrhiwceiber	d			16 54									17 24										17 54
Mountain Ash	a			16 58									17 28										17 58
	d			17 03									17 33										18 03
Fernhill	d			17 05									17 35										18 05
Cwmbach	d			17 09									17 39										18 09
Aberdare 3	a			17 16									17 46										18 16
Quakers Yard	d							17 09										17 39					
Merthyr Vale	a							17 14										17 44					
	d							17 17										17 47					
Troed Y Rhiw	d							17 20										17 50					
Pentre-bach	d							17 23										17 53					
Merthyr Tydfil	a							17 31										18 01					
Trehafod	d	16 41									17 11										17 41		
Porth	a	16 44									17 14										17 44		
	d	16 45									17 15										17 45		
Dinas Rhondda	d	16 49									17 19										17 49		
Tonypandy	d	16 51									17 21										17 51		
Llwynypia	d	16 53									17 23										17 53		
Ystrad Rhondda	a	16 56									17 26										17 56		
	d	16 59									17 29										17 59		
Ton Pentre	d	17 01									17 31										18 01		
Treorchy	d	17 04									17 34										18 04		
Ynyswen	d	17 07									17 37										18 07		
Treherbert	a	17 13									17 43										18 13		

When events are being held at the Millenium Stadium, services are subject to alteration. Please check times before travelling.

Bridgend, Barry Island, Barry, Penarth and Cardiff - Coryton, Rhymney, Pontypridd, Merthyr, Aberdare and Treherbert

Network Diagram - see first Page of Table 130

		AW	AW	AW	AW	AW	AW	AW	AW	AW	AW	AW	AW	AW	AW	AW	AW	AW	AW	AW	AW	AW	AW
Bridgend	d									16 42													
Llantwit Major	d									16 56													
Rhoose Cardiff Int Airport ✈	d									17 06													
Barry Island	d				16 55										17 25					17 40			
Barry 3	d				17 00					17 15					17 30					17 45			
Barry Docks	d				17 04					17 19					17 34					17 49			
Cadoxton	d				17 07					17 22					17 37					17 52			
Dinas Powys	d				17 11					17 26					17 41					17 56			
Eastbrook	d				17 13					17 28					17 43					17 58			
Cogan	d				17 15					17 30					17 45					18 00			
Penarth	d	17 02				17 17						17 32				17 47					18 02		
Dingle Road	d	17 04				17 19						17 34				17 49					18 04		
Grangetown	d	17 08			17 19	17 23				17 34		17 38			17 49	17 53				18 04	18 08		
Cardiff Central 7	a	17 14			17 24	17 29				17 39		17 44			17 54	17 59				18 09	18 14		
	d	17 16		17 21	17 26	17 31		17 36	17 36	17 41		17 46	17 51		17 56	18 01		18 06	18 06	18 11	18 16		18 21
Cardiff Bay	d		17 18				17 30				17 42			17 54			18 06					18 18	
Cardiff Queen Street 3	a	17 19	17 22	17 24	17 29	17 34	17 34	17 39		17 44	17 46	17 49	17 54	17 58	17 59	18 04	18 10	18 09		18 14	18 19	18 22	18 24
	d	17 20		17 25	17 30	17 35		17 40		17 45		17 50	17 55		18 00	18 05		18 10		18 15	18 20		18 25
Heath Low Level	d			17 30									18 00										18 30
Ty Glas	d			17 33									18 03										18 33
Birchgrove	d			17 34									18 04										18 34
Rhiwbina	d			17 36									18 06										18 36
Whitchurch (Cardiff)	d			17 38									18 08										18 38
Coryton	a			17 43									18 13										18 43
Heath High Level	d	17 25				17 40						17 55				18 10					18 25		
Llanishen	d	17 28				17 43						17 59				18 13					18 28		
Lisvane & Thornhill	d	17 30				17 45						18 02				18 15					18 30		
Caerphilly 3	d	17 36				17 51						18 07				18 21					18 36		
Aber	d	17 38				17 53						18 10				18 23					18 38		
Llanbradach	d	17 42				17 57						18 14				18 27					18 42		
Ystrad Mynach 3	d	17 47				18 02						18 20				18 32					18a51		
Hengoed	d	17 50				18 05						18 23				18 35							
Pengam	d	17 53				18 08						18 27				18 38							
Gilfach Fargoed	d					18 11						18 30				18 41							
Bargoed	a	18 01				18 14						18 34				18 48							
	d					18 16						18 44											
Brithdir	d					18 20						18 48											
Tir-phil	d					18 23						18 51											
Pontlottyn	d					18 27						18 55											
Rhymney 3	a					18 33						19 01											
Cathays	d				17 33			17 43		17 48					18 03			18 13		18 18			
Llandaf	d				17 37			17 47		17 52					18 07			18 17		18 22			
Ninian Park	d								17 40										18 10				
Waun-gron Park	d								17 43										18 13				
Fairwater	d								17 45										18 15				
Danescourt	d								17 47										18 17				
Radyr 3	a				17 40			17 50	17 54	17 55					18 10			18 20	18 24	18 25			
	d				17 40			17 50		17 55					18 10			18 20		18 25			
Taffs Well 3	d				17 44			17 54		17 59					18 14			18 24		18 29			
Trefforest Estate	d				17 48										18 18								
Trefforest	d				17 52			18 01		18 06					18 22			18 31		18 36			
Pontypridd 3	a				17 55			18 04		18 09					18 25			18 34		18 42			
	d				17 57			18 06		18 11					18 27			18 36					
Abercynon	d				18 04					18 19					18 34								
Penrhiwceiber	d									18 24													
Mountain Ash	a									18 28													
	d									18 33													
Fernhill	d									18 35													
Cwmbach	d									18 39													
Aberdare 3	a									18 46													
Quakers Yard	d				18 09										18 39								
Merthyr Vale	a				18 14										18 44								
	d				18 17										18 47								
Troed Y Rhiw	d				18 20										18 50								
Pentre-bach	d				18 23										18 53								
Merthyr Tydfil	a				18 31										19 01								
Trehafod	d							18 11										18 41					
Porth	a							18 14										18 44					
	d							18 15										18 45					
Dinas Rhondda	d							18 19										18 49					
Tonypandy	d							18 21										18 51					
Llwynypia	d							18 23										18 53					
Ystrad Rhondda	a							18 26										18 56					
	d							18 29										18 59					
Ton Pentre	d							18 31										19 01					
Treorchy	d							18 34										19 04					
Ynyswen	d							18 37										19 07					
Treherbert	a							18 43										19 13					

When events are being held at the Millenium Stadium,
services are subject to alteration. Please check times before travelling.

Bridgend, Barry Island, Barry, Penarth and Cardiff - Coryton, Rhymney, Pontypridd, Merthyr, Aberdare and Treherbert

Network Diagram - see first Page of Table 130

		AW	AW	AW	AW	AW	AW	AW	AW	AW	AW	AW	AW	AW	AW	AW	AW	AW	AW	AW	AW	AW
Bridgend	d						17 42															18 42
Llantwit Major	d						17 56															18 56
Rhoose Cardiff Int Airport ✈	d						18 06															19 06
Barry Island	d	17 55									18 25					18 40		18 55				
Barry 3	d	18 00					18 15				18 30					18 45		19 00				19 15
Barry Docks	d	18 04					18 19				18 34					18 49		19 04				19 19
Cadoxton	d	18 07					18 22				18 37					18 52		19 07				19 22
Dinas Powys	d	18 11					18 26				18 41					18 56		19 11				19 26
Eastbrook	d	18 13					18 28				18 43					18 58		19 13				19 28
Cogan	d	18 15					18 30				18 45					19 00		19 15				19 30
Penarth	d		18 17					18 32					18 47						19 17			
Dingle Road	d		18 19					18 34					18 49						19 19			
Grangetown	d	18 19	18 23				18 34	18 38			18 49		18 53			19 04		19 19	19 23			19 34
Cardiff Central 7	a	18 24	18 29				18 39	18 47			18 55		18 59			19 09		19 24	19 29			19 39
	d	18 26	18 31		18 36	18 36	18 41			18 51			19 01		19 06	19 11		19 26	19 31		19 36	19 41
Cardiff Bay	d			18 30					18 42			18 54		19 06			19 18			19 30		
Cardiff Queen Street 3	a	18 29	18 34	18 34	18 38		18 44		18 46	18 54		18 58	19 04	19 10	19 09	19 14	19 22	19 29	19 34	19 34		19 44
	d	18 30	18 35		18 40		18 50			18 55			19 05		19 10	19 15		19 30	19 35			19 45
Heath Low Level	d									19 00												
Ty Glas	d									19 03												
Birchgrove	d									19 04												
Rhiwbina	d									19 06												
Whitchurch (Cardiff)	d									19 08												
Coryton	a									19 13												
Heath High Level	d		18 40										19 10						19 40			
Llanishen	d		18 43										19 13						19 43			
Lisvane & Thornhill	d		18 45										19 15						19 45			
Caerphilly 3	d		18 51										19a23						19 51			
Aber	d		18 53																19 53			
Llanbradach	d		18 57																19 57			
Ystrad Mynach 3	d		19 02																20 02			
Hengoed	d		19 05																20 05			
Pengam	d		19 08																20 08			
Gilfach Fargoed	d		19 11																20 11			
Bargoed	a		19 14																20 15			
	d		19 16																20 16			
Brithdir	d		19 20																20 20			
Tir-phil	d		19 23																20 23			
Pontlottyn	d		19 27																20 27			
Rhymney 3	a		19 34																20 33			
Cathays	d	18 33			18 43		18 52								19 13	19 18		19 33				19 48
Llandaf	d	18 37			18 47		18 56								19 17	19 22		19 37				19 52
Ninian Park	d					18 40															19 40	
Waun-gron Park	d					18 43															19 43	
Fairwater	d					18 45															19 45	
Danescourt	d					18 47															19 47	
Radyr 3	a	18 40			18 50	18 54	18 58								19 20	19 25		19 40			19 54	19 55
	d	18 40			18 50		18 58								19 20	19 25		19 40				19 55
Taffs Well 3	d	18 44			18 54		19 03								19 24	19 29		19 44				19 59
Trefforest Estate	d	18 48																19 48				
Trefforest	d	18 52			19 01		19 10								19 31	19 36		19 52				20 06
Pontypridd 3	a	18 55			19 04		19 13								19 34	19 39		19 55				20 09
	d	18 57			19 06		19 14								19 36	19 41		19 57				20 11
Abercynon	d	19 04					19 21									19 49		20 04				20 21
Penrhiwceiber	d						19 26									19 54						20 26
Mountain Ash	a						19 30									19 56						20 30
	d						19 33									20 03						20 33
Fernhill	d						19 35									20 05						20 35
Cwmbach	d						19 39									20 09						20 39
Aberdare 3	a						19 46									20 16						20 46
Quakers Yard	d	19 09																20 08				
Merthyr Vale	a	19 14																20 13				
	d	19 17																20 15				
Troed Y Rhiw	d	19 20																20 19				
Pentre-bach	d	19 23																20 22				
Merthyr Tydfil	a	19 31																20 30				
Trehafod	d				19 11										19 41							
Porth	a				19 14										19 44							
	d				19 15										19 45							
Dinas Rhondda	d				19 19										19 49							
Tonypandy	d				19 21										19 51							
Llwynypia	d				19 23										19 53							
Ystrad Rhondda	a				19 26										19 56							
	d				19 29										19 59							
Ton Pentre	d				19 31										20 01							
Treorchy	d				19 34										20 04							
Ynyswen	d				19 37										20 07							
Treherbert	a				19 43										20 13							

When events are being held at the Millenium Stadium, services are subject to alteration. Please check times before travelling.

Bridgend, Barry Island, Barry, Penarth and Cardiff - Coryton, Rhymney, Pontypridd, Merthyr, Aberdare and Treherbert

Network Diagram - see first Page of Table 130

Station		AW	AW	AW	AW	AW	AW	AW	AW	AW	AW	AW	AW	AW	AW	AW	AW	AW	AW	AW	AW	AW	AW
Bridgend	d												19 42										
Llantwit Major	d												19 56										
Rhoose Cardiff Int Airport ✈	d												20 06										
Barry Island	d				19 25				19 55												20 55		
Barry 3	d				19 30				20 00				20 15								21 00		
Barry Docks	d				19 34				20 04				20 19								21 04		
Cadoxton	d				19 37				20 07				20 22								21 07		
Dinas Powys	d				19 41				20 11				20 26								21 11		
Eastbrook	d				19 43				20 13				20 28								21 13		
Cogan	d				19 45				20 15				20 30								21 15		
Penarth	d					19 47				20 20							20 47						
Dingle Road	d					19 49				20 22							20 49						
Grangetown	d				19 49	19 53			20 19	20 26			20 34				20 53				21 19		
Cardiff Central 7	a				19 56	19 59			20 24	20 31			20 39				20 59				21 24		
	d		19 51		20 01	20 06			20 26	20 31		20 36	20 41		20 51		21 01		21 06		21 26		21 31
Cardiff Bay	d	19 42		19 54			20 06	20 18			20 30			20 42		20 54		21 06		21 18		21 30	
Cardiff Queen Street 3	a	19 46	19 54	19 58	20 04	20 09	20 10	20 22	20 29	20 34	20 34		20 44	20 46	20 54	20 58	21 04	21 10	21 09	21 22	21 29	21 34	21 34
	d		19 55		20 05	20 10			20 30	20 35			20 45		20 55		21 05		21 10		21 30		21 35
Heath Low Level	d		20 00												21 00								
Ty Glas	d		20 03												21 03								
Birchgrove	d		20 04												21 04								
Rhiwbina	d		20 06												21 06								
Whitchurch (Cardiff)	d		20 08												21 08								
Coryton	a		20 13												21 13								
Heath High Level	d				20 10					20 40							21 10						21 40
Llanishen	d				20 13					20 43							21 13						21 43
Lisvane & Thornhill	d				20 15					20 45							21 15						21 45
Caerphilly 3	d				20a27					20 51							21 21						21 51
Aber	d									20 53							21 23						21 53
Llanbradach	d									20 57							21 27						21 57
Ystrad Mynach 3	d									21 02							21a36						22 02
Hengoed	d									21 05													22 05
Pengam	d									21 08													22 08
Gilfach Fargoed	d									21 11													22 11
Bargoed	a									21 15													22 15
	d									21 16													22 16
Brithdir	d									21 20													22 20
Tir-phil	d									21 23													22 23
Pontlottyn	d									21 27													22 27
Rhymney 3	a									21 34													22 34
Cathays	d					20 13			20 33				20 48						21 13		21 33		
Llandaf	d					20 17			20 37				20 52						21 17		21 37		
Ninian Park	d											20 40											
Waun-gron Park	d											20 43											
Fairwater	d											20 45											
Danescourt	d											20 47											
Radyr 3	a					20 20			20 40			20 54	20 55						21 20		21 40		
	d					20 20			20 40				20 55						21 20		21 40		
Taffs Well 3	d					20 24			20 44				20 59						21 24		21 44		
Trefforest Estate	d								20 48												21 48		
Trefforest	d					20 31			20 52				21 06						21 31		21 52		
Pontypridd 3	a					20 34			20 55				21 09						21 34		21 55		
	d					20 36			20 57				21 11						21 36		21 57		
Abercynon	d								21 04				21 19								22 04		
Penrhiwceiber	d												21 24										
Mountain Ash	a												21 28										
	d												21 29										
Fernhill	d												21 31										
Cwmbach	d												21 35										
Aberdare 3	a												21 42										
Quakers Yard	d								21 08												22 08		
Merthyr Vale	a								21 13												22 13		
	d								21 15												22 15		
Troed Y Rhiw	d								21 19												22 19		
Pentre-bach	d								21 22												22 22		
Merthyr Tydfil	a								21 30												22 30		
Trehafod	d					20 41													21 41				
Porth	a					20 44													21 44				
	d					20 45													21 45				
Dinas Rhondda	d					20 49													21 49				
Tonypandy	d					20 51													21 51				
Llwynypia	d					20 53													21 53				
Ystrad Rhondda	a					20 56													21 56				
	d					20 59													21 59				
Ton Pentre	d					21 01													22 01				
Treorchy	d					21 04													22 04				
Ynyswen	d					21 07													22 07				
Treherbert	a					21 13													22 13				

When events are being held at the Millenium Stadium, services are subject to alteration. Please check times before travelling.

Bridgend, Barry Island, Barry, Penarth and Cardiff - Coryton, Rhymney, Pontypridd, Merthyr, Aberdare and Treherbert

Network Diagram - see first Page of Table 130

		AW	AW	AW	AW	AW	AW	AW	AW	AW	AW	AW	AW	AW	AW	AW	AW	AW	AW	AW	AW	AW
Bridgend	d			20 42											21 42							
Llantwit Major	d			20 56											21 56							
Rhoose Cardiff Int Airport ✈	d			21 06											22 06							
Barry Island	d											21 55										
Barry [3]	d			21 15								22 00			22 15							
Barry Docks	d			21 19								22 04			22 19							
Cadoxton	d			21 22								22 07			22 22							
Dinas Powys	d			21 26								22 11			22 26							
Eastbrook	d			21 28								22 13			22 28							
Cogan	d			21 30								22 15			22 30							
Penarth	d		21 20				21 47							22 20							22 47	
Dingle Road	d		21 22				21 49							22 22							22 49	
Grangetown	d		21 26	21 34			21 53					22 19		22 26	22 34						22 53	
Cardiff Central [7]	a		21 37	21 39			21 59					22 24		22 33	22 39						23 00	
	d	21 36		21 41			22 01		22 06		22 21	22 26		22 35	22 41		22 46		22 55		23 15	
Cardiff Bay	d				21 42	21 54		22 06		22 18			22 30			22 42		22 54		23 06		23 18
Cardiff Queen Street [3]	a			21 44	21 46	21 58	22 04	22 10	22 09	22 22	22 24	22 29	22 34	22 38	22 44	22 46	22 49	22 58		23 10	23 18	23 22
	d			21 45			22 05		22 10		22 25	22 30		22 39	22 45		22 50				23 19	
Heath Low Level	d										22 30											
Ty Glas	d										22 33											
Birchgrove	d										22 34											
Rhiwbina	d										22 36											
Whitchurch (Cardiff)	d										22 38											
Coryton	a										22 43											
Heath High Level	d						22 10							22 44							23 24	
Llanishen	d						22 13							22 47							23 27	
Lisvane & Thornhill	d						22 15							22 49							23 29	
Caerphilly [3]	d						22a23							22 55							23 35	
Aber	d													22 57							23 37	
Llanbradach	d													23 01							23 41	
Ystrad Mynach [3]	d													23 06							23a50	
Hengoed	d													23 09								
Pengam	d													23 12								
Gilfach Fargoed	d													23 15								
Bargoed	a													23 19								
	d													23 20								
Brithdir	d													23 24								
Tir-phil	d													23 27								
Pontlottyn	d													23 31								
Rhymney [3]	a													23 37								
Cathays	d			21 48					22 13			22 33			22 48		22 53					
Llandaf	d			21 52					22 17			22 37			22 52		22 57					
Ninian Park	d	21 40																	22 59			
Waun-gron Park	d	21 43																	23 02			
Fairwater	d	21 45																	23 04			
Danescourt	d	21 47																	23 06			
Radyr [3]	a	21 54		21 55					22 20			22 40			22 55		22 59		23 14			
	d			21 55					22 20			22 40			22 55		22 59					
Taffs Well [3]	d			21 59					22 24			22 44			22 59		23 03					
Trefforest Estate	d											22 48										
Trefforest	d			22 06					22 31			22 52			23 06		23 10					
Pontypridd [3]	a			22 09					22 34			22 55			23 09		23 14					
	d			22 11					22 36			22 57			23 11		23 15					
Abercynon	d			22 19								23 04			23 19							
Penrhiwceiber	d			22 24											23 24							
Mountain Ash	a			22 28											23 28							
	d			22 29											23 29							
Fernhill	d			22 31											23 31							
Cwmbach	d			22 35											23 35							
Aberdare [3]	a			22 42											23 42							
Quakers Yard	d											23 08										
Merthyr Vale	a											23 13										
	d											23 15										
Troed Y Rhiw	d											23 19										
Pentre-bach	d											23 22										
Merthyr Tydfil	a											23 30										
Trehafod	d								22 41								23 20					
Porth	a								22 44								23 23					
	d								22 45								23 24					
Dinas Rhondda	d								22 49								23 28					
Tonypandy	d								22 51								23 30					
Llwynypia	d								22 53								23 32					
Ystrad Rhondda	a								22 56								23 35					
	d								22 59								23 38					
Ton Pentre	d								23 01								23 40					
Treorchy	d								23 04								23 43					
Ynyswen	d								23 07								23 46					
Treherbert	a								23 13								23 52					

When events are being held at the Millenium Stadium, services are subject to alteration. Please check times before travelling.

Bridgend, Barry Island, Barry, Penarth and Cardiff - Coryton, Rhymney, Pontypridd, Merthyr, Aberdare and Treherbert

Network Diagram - see first Page of Table 130

		AW	AW FX 🚌	AW	AW FO	AW FX	AW	AW	AW
Bridgend	d		22 15		22 42				
Llantwit Major	d		22 40		22 56				
Rhoose Cardiff Int Airport ✈	d		22 55		23 06				
Barry Island	d	22 44							
Barry 3	d	22 49	23a10		23 15	23 15			
Barry Docks	d	22 53			23 19	23 19			
Cadoxton	d	22 56			23 22	23 22			
Dinas Powys	d	23 00			23 26	23 26			
Eastbrook	d	23 02			23 28	23 28			
Cogan	d	23 04			23 30	23 30			
Penarth	d			23 26					
Dingle Road	d			23 28					
Grangetown	d	23 08		23 32	23 34	23 34			
Cardiff Central 7	a	23 13		23 40	23 42	23 42			
	d	23 26							
Cardiff Bay	d						23 30	23 42	23 54
Cardiff Queen Street 3	a	23 29					23 34	23 46	23 58
	d	23 30							
Heath Low Level	d								
Ty Glas	d								
Birchgrove	d								
Rhiwbina	d								
Whitchurch (Cardiff)	d								
Coryton	a								
Heath High Level	d								
Llanishen	d								
Lisvane & Thornhill	d								
Caerphilly 3	d								
Aber	d								
Llanbradach	d								
Ystrad Mynach 3	d								
Hengoed	d								
Pengam	d								
Gilfach Fargoed	d								
Bargoed	a								
	d								
Brithdir	d								
Tir-phil	d								
Pontlottyn	d								
Rhymney 3	a								
Cathays	d	23 33							
Llandaf	d	23 37							
Ninian Park	d								
Waun-gron Park	d								
Fairwater	d								
Danescourt	d								
Radyr 3	a	23 40							
	d	23 40							
Taffs Well 3	d	23 44							
Trefforest Estate	d								
Trefforest	d	23 52							
Pontypridd 3	a	23 58							
	d								
Abercynon	d								
Penrhiwceiber	d								
Mountain Ash	a								
	d								
Fernhill	d								
Cwmbach	d								
Aberdare 3	a								
Quakers Yard	d								
Merthyr Vale	a								
	d								
Troed Y Rhiw	d								
Pentre-bach	d								
Merthyr Tydfil	a								
Trehafod	d								
Porth	a								
	d								
Dinas Rhondda	d								
Tonypandy	d								
Llwynypia	d								
Ystrad Rhondda	a								
	d								
Ton Pentre	d								
Treorchy	d								
Ynyswen	d								
Treherbert	a								

When events are being held at the Millenium Stadium, services are subject to alteration. Please check times before travelling.

Table 130

Saturdays

Bridgend, Barry Island, Barry, Penarth and Cardiff - Coryton, Rhymney, Pontypridd, Merthyr, Aberdare and Treherbert

Network Diagram - see first Page of Table 130

		AW	AW	AW	AW	AW	AW	AW	AW	AW	AW	AW	AW	AW	AW	AW	AW	AW	AW	AW	AW	AW	AW
Bridgend	d										05 42												
Llantwit Major	d										05 56												
Rhoose Cardiff Int Airport ✈	d										06 06												
Barry Island	d		05 15					05 51								06 25							
Barry 3	d		05 20					05 55			06 15					06 30							
Barry Docks	d		05 24					05 59			06 19					06 34							
Cadoxton	d		05 27					06 02			06 22					06 37							
Dinas Powys	d		05 31					06 06			06 26					06 41							
Eastbrook	d		05 33					06 08			06 28					06 43							
Cogan	d		05 35					06 10			06 30					06 45							
Penarth	d						06 02						06 32								07 02		
Dingle Road	d						06 04						06 34								07 04		
Grangetown	d		05 39				06 08	06 14			06 34		06 38			06 49					07 08		
Cardiff Central 7	a		05 44				06 13	06 19			06 39		06 44			06 54					07 14		
	d	05 26	05 46		05 56	06 11	06 15	06 21	06 26	06 36	06 41		06 46	06 51		06 56		07 06	07 06	07 11	07 16		07 21
Cardiff Bay	d											06 42			06 54		07 06					07 18	
Cardiff Queen Street 3	a	05 29	05 49		05 59	06 14	06 19	06 24	06 29	06 39	06 44	06 46	06 49	06 54	06 58	06 59	07 10	07 09		07 14	07 19	07 22	07 24
	d	05 30	05 50		06 00	06 15	06 20	06 25	06 30	06 40	06 45		06 50	06 55		07 00		07 10		07 15	07 20		07 25
Heath Low Level	d							06 30						07 00									07 30
Ty Glas	d							06 33						07 03									07 33
Birchgrove	d							06 34						07 04									07 34
Rhiwbina	d							06 36						07 06									07 36
Whitchurch (Cardiff)	d							06 38						07 08									07 38
Coryton	a							06 43						07 13									07 43
Heath High Level	d		05 55				06 25						06 55								07 25		
Llanishen	d		05 58				06 28						06 58								07 28		
Lisvane & Thornhill	d		06 00				06 30						07 00								07 30		
Caerphilly 3	d		06a08				06 36						07 06								07 36		
Aber	d						06 38						07 08								07 38		
Llanbradach	d						06 42						07 12								07 42		
Ystrad Mynach 3	d						06 47						07 17								07 47		
Hengoed	d						06 50						07 20								07 50		
Pengam	d						06 53						07 23								07 53		
Gilfach Fargoed	d																						
Bargoed	a						07 01						07 31								08 02		
	d																						
Brithdir	d																						
Tir-phil	d																						
Pontlottyn	d																						
Rhymney 3	a																						
Cathays	d	05 33			06 03	06 18			06 33	06 43	06 48					07 03		07 13		07 18			
Llandaf	d	05 37			06 07	06 22			06 37	06 47	06 52					07 07		07 17		07 22			
Ninian Park	d																		07 10				
Waun-gron Park	d																		07 13				
Fairwater	d																		07 15				
Danescourt	d																		07 17				
Radyr 3	a	05 40			06 10	06 24			06 40	06 50	06 54					07 10		07 20	07 24	07 25			
	d	05 40			06 10	06 24			06 40	06 50	06 55					07 10		07 20		07 25			
Taffs Well 3	d	05 44			06 14	06 28			06 44	06 54	06 59					07 14		07 24		07 29			
Trefforest Estate	d	05 48			06 18				06 48							07 18							
Trefforest	d	05 52			06 22	06 35			06 52	07 01	07 06					07 22		07 31		07 36			
Pontypridd 3	a	05 55			06 25	06 38			06 55	07 04	07 09					07 25		07 34		07 39			
	d	05 57		06 11	06 27	06 41			06 57	07 06	07 11					07 27		07 36		07 41			
Abercynon	d	06 04		06 19	06 34	06 49			07 04		07 19					07 34				07 49			
Penrhiwceiber	d			06 24		06 54					07 24									07 54			
Mountain Ash	a			06 28		06 58					07 28									07 58			
	d			06 33		07 03					07 33									08 03			
Fernhill	d			06 35		07 05					07 35									08 05			
Cwmbach	d			06 39		07 09					07 39									08 09			
Aberdare 3	a			06 46		07 16					07 46									08 16			
Quakers Yard	d	06 09			06 39				07 09							07 39							
Merthyr Vale	a	06 14			06 44				07 14							07 44							
	d	06 17			06 47				07 17							07 47							
Troed Y Rhiw	d	06 20			06 50				07 20							07 50							
Pentre-bach	d	06 23			06 53				07 23							07 53							
Merthyr Tydfil	a	06 31			07 01				07 31							08 01							
Trehafod	d									07 11								07 41					
Porth	a									07 14								07 44					
	d									07 15								07 45					
Dinas Rhondda	d									07 19								07 49					
Tonypandy	d									07 21								07 51					
Llwynypia	d									07 23								07 53					
Ystrad Rhondda	a									07 26								07 56					
	d									07 29								07 59					
Ton Pentre	d									07 31								08 01					
Treorchy	d									07 34								08 04					
Ynyswen	d									07 37								08 07					
Treherbert	a									07 43								08 13					

When events are being held at the Millenium Stadium, services are subject to alteration. Please check times before travelling.

Table 130

Saturdays

Bridgend, Barry Island, Barry, Penarth and Cardiff - Coryton, Rhymney, Pontypridd, Merthyr, Aberdare and Treherbert

Network Diagram - see first Page of Table 130

		AW	AW	AW	AW	AW	AW	AW	AW	AW	AW	AW	AW	AW	AW	AW	AW	AW	AW	AW	AW	AW	AW
Bridgend	d						06 42																
Llantwit Major	d						06 56																
Rhoose Cardiff Int Airport ✈	d						07 06																
Barry Island	d	06 55										07 25					07 40				07 55		
Barry 3	d	07 00					07 15					07 30					07 45				08 00		
Barry Docks	d	07 04					07 19					07 34					07 49				08 04		
Cadoxton	d	07 07					07 22					07 37					07 52				08 07		
Dinas Powys	d	07 11					07 26					07 41					07 56				08 11		
Eastbrook	d	07 13					07 28					07 43					07 58				08 13		
Cogan	d	07 15					07 30					07 45					08 00				08 15		
Penarth	d		07 17						07 32				07 47					08 02				08 17	
Dingle Road	d		07 19						07 34				07 49					08 04				08 19	
Grangetown	d	07 19	07 23				07 34		07 38			07 49	07 53				08 04	08 08			08 19	08 23	
Cardiff Central 7	a	07 24	07 29				07 39		07 44			07 54	07 59				08 09	08 14			08 24	08 29	
	d	07 26	07 31		07 36	07 36	07 41		07 46	07 51		07 56	08 01		08 06	08 06	08 11	08 16		08 21	08 26	08 31	
Cardiff Bay	d			07 30				07 42			07 54			08 06					08 18				08 30
Cardiff Queen Street 3	a	07 29	07 34	07 34	07 39		07 44	07 46	07 49	07 54	07 58	07 59	08 04	08 10	08 09		08 14	08 19	08 22	08 24	08 29	08 34	08 34
	d	07 30	07 35		07 40		07 45		07 50	07 55		08 00	08 05		08 10		08 15	08 20		08 25	08 30	08 35	
Heath Low Level	d									08 00										08 30			
Ty Glas	d									08 03										08 33			
Birchgrove	d									08 04										08 34			
Rhiwbina	d									08 06										08 36			
Whitchurch (Cardiff)	d									08 08										08 38			
Coryton	a									08 13										08 43			
Heath High Level	d		07 40						07 55				08 10					08 25				08 40	
Llanishen	d		07 43						07 58				08 13					08 28				08 43	
Lisvane & Thornhill	d		07 45						08 00				08 15					08 30				08 45	
Caerphilly 3	d		07 51						08 06				08 21					08 36				08 51	
Aber	d		07 53						08 08				08 23					08 38				08 53	
Llanbradach	d		07 57						08 12				08 27					08 42				08 57	
Ystrad Mynach 3	d		08 02						08 17				08 32					08 47				09 02	
Hengoed	d		08 05						08 20				08 35					08 50				09 05	
Pengam	d		08 08						08 23				08 38					08 53				09 08	
Gilfach Fargoed	d												08 41										
Bargoed	a		08 13						08 31				08 48					08 58				09 16	
	d		08 14															08 59					
Brithdir	d		08 18															09 03					
Tir-phil	d		08 21															09 06					
Pontlottyn	d		08 25															09 10					
Rhymney 3	a		08 31															09 16					
Cathays	d	07 33			07 43		07 48					08 03			08 13		08 18				08 33		
Llandaf	d	07 37			07 47		07 52					08 07			08 17		08 22				08 37		
Ninian Park	d					07 40										08 10							
Waun-gron Park	d					07 43										08 13							
Fairwater	d					07 45										08 15							
Danescourt	d					07 47										08 17							
Radyr 3	a	07 40			07 50	07 54	07 55					08 10			08 20	08 24	08 25				08 40		
	d	07 40			07 50		07 55					08 10			08 20		08 25				08 40		
Taffs Well 3	d	07 44			07 54		07 59					08 14			08 24		08 29				08 44		
Trefforest Estate	d	07 48										08 18									08 48		
Trefforest	d	07 52			08 01		08 06					08 22			08 31		08 36				08 52		
Pontypridd 3	a	07 55			08 04		08 09					08 25			08 34		08 39				08 55		
	d	07 57			08 06		08 11					08 27			08 36		08 41				08 57		
Abercynon	d	08 04					08 19					08 34					08 49				09 04		
Penrhiwceiber	d						08 24										08 54						
Mountain Ash	a						08 28										08 58						
	d						08 33										09 03						
Fernhill	d						08 35										09 05						
Cwmbach	d						08 39										09 09						
Aberdare 3	a						08 46										09 16						
Quakers Yard	d	08 09										08 39									09 09		
Merthyr Vale	a	08 14										08 44									09 14		
	d	08 17										08 47									09 17		
Troed Y Rhiw	d	08 20										08 50									09 20		
Pentre-bach	d	08 23										08 53									09 23		
Merthyr Tydfil	a	08 31										09 01									09 31		
Trehafod	d				08 11										08 41								
Porth	a				08 14										08 44								
	d				08 15										08 45								
Dinas Rhondda	d				08 19										08 49								
Tonypandy	d				08 21										08 51								
Llwynypia	d				08 23										08 53								
Ystrad Rhondda	a				08 26										08 56								
	d				08 29										08 59								
Ton Pentre	d				08 31										09 01								
Treorchy	d				08 34										09 04								
Ynyswen	d				08 37										09 07								
Treherbert	a				08 43										09 13								

When events are being held at the Millenium Stadium, services are subject to alteration. Please check times before travelling.

Table 130

Saturdays

Bridgend, Barry Island, Barry, Penarth and Cardiff - Coryton, Rhymney, Pontypridd, Merthyr, Aberdare and Treherbert

Network Diagram - see first Page of Table 130

		AW		AW	AW	AW	AW	AW	AW	AW	AW	AW		AW	AW	AW	AW	AW	AW	AW	AW	AW		AW	AW
Bridgend	d				07 42																				
Llantwit Major	d				07 56																				
Rhoose Cardiff Int Airport ✈	d				08 06																				
Barry Island	d									08 25						08 40				08 55					
Barry 3	d				08 15					08 30						08 45				09 00					
Barry Docks	d				08 19					08 34						08 49				09 04					
Cadoxton	d				08 22					08 37						08 52				09 07					
Dinas Powys	d				08 26					08 41						08 56				09 11					
Eastbrook	d				08 28					08 43						08 58				09 13					
Cogan	d				08 30					08 45						09 00				09 15					
Penarth	d						08 32				08 47										09 17				
Dingle Road	d						08 34				08 49										09 19				
Grangetown	d				08 34		08 38			08 49	08 53					09 04				09 19	09 23				
Cardiff Central 7	a				08 39		08 44			08 54	08 59					09 09				09 24	09 29				
	d	08 36		08 36	08 41		08 46	08 51		08 56	09 01			09 06	09 06	09 11	09 16		09 21	09 26	09 31			09 36	09 36
Cardiff Bay	d					08 42			08 54			09 06						09 18				09 30			
Cardiff Queen Street 3	a	08 39			08 44	08 46	08 49	08 54	08 58	08 59	09 04	09 10		09 09		09 14	09 19	09 22	09 24	09 29	09 34	09 34		09 39	
	d	08 40			08 45		08 50	08 55		09 00	09 05			09 10		09 15	09 20		09 25	09 30	09 35			09 40	
Heath Low Level	d							09 00											09 30						
Ty Glas	d							09 03											09 33						
Birchgrove	d							09 04											09 34						
Rhiwbina	d							09 06											09 36						
Whitchurch (Cardiff)	d							09 08											09 38						
Coryton	a							09 13											09 43						
Heath High Level	d						08 55				09 10						09 25				09 40				
Llanishen	d						08 58				09 13						09 28				09 43				
Lisvane & Thornhill	d						09 00				09 15						09 30				09 45				
Caerphilly 3	d						09 06				09 21						09 36				09 51				
Aber	d						09 08				09 23						09 38				09 53				
Llanbradach	d						09 12				09 27						09 42				09 57				
Ystrad Mynach 3	d						09 17				09 32						09 47				10 02				
Hengoed	d						09 20				09 35						09 50				10 05				
Pengam	d						09 23				09 38						09 53				10 08				
Gilfach Fargoed	d										09 41														
Bargoed	a						09 31				09 48						09 58				10 16				
	d																09 59								
Brithdir	d																10 03								
Tir-phil	d																10 06								
Pontlottyn	d																10 10								
Rhymney 3	a																10 16								
Cathays	d	08 43			08 48					09 03				09 13		09 18				09 33				09 43	
Llandaf	d	08 47			08 52					09 07				09 17		09 22				09 37				09 47	
Ninian Park	d			08 40											09 10										09 40
Waun-gron Park	d			08 43											09 13										09 43
Fairwater	d			08 45											09 15										09 45
Danescourt	d			08 47											09 17										09 47
Radyr 3	a	08 50		08 54	08 55					09 10				09 20	09 24	09 25				09 40				09 50	09 54
	d	08 50			08 55					09 10				09 20		09 25				09 40				09 50	
Taffs Well 3	d	08 54			08 59					09 14				09 24		09 29				09 44				09 54	
Trefforest Estate	d									09 18										09 48					
Trefforest	d	09 01			09 06					09 22				09 31		09 36				09 52				10 01	
Pontypridd 3	a	09 04			09 09					09 25				09 34		09 39				09 55				10 04	
	d	09 06			09 11					09 27				09 36		09 41				09 57				10 06	
Abercynon	d				09 19					09 34						09 49				10 04					
Penrhiwceiber	d				09 24											09 54									
Mountain Ash	a				09 28											09 58									
	d				09 33											10 03									
Fernhill	d				09 35											10 05									
Cwmbach	d				09 39											10 09									
Aberdare 3	a				09 46											10 16									
Quakers Yard	d									09 39										10 09					
Merthyr Vale	a									09 44										10 14					
	d									09 47										10 17					
Troed Y Rhiw	d									09 50										10 20					
Pentre-bach	d									09 53										10 23					
Merthyr Tydfil	a									10 01										10 31					
Trehafod	d	09 11												09 41										10 11	
Porth	a	09 14												09 44										10 14	
	d	09 15												09 45										10 15	
Dinas Rhondda	d	09 19												09 49										10 19	
Tonypandy	d	09 21												09 51										10 21	
Llwynypia	d	09 23												09 53										10 23	
Ystrad Rhondda	a	09 26												09 56										10 26	
	d	09 29												09 59										10 29	
Ton Pentre	d	09 31												10 01										10 31	
Treorchy	d	09 34												10 04										10 34	
Ynyswen	d	09 37												10 07										10 37	
Treherbert	a	09 43												10 13										10 43	

When events are being held at the Millenium Stadium, services are subject to alteration. Please check times before travelling.

Table 130

Saturdays

Bridgend, Barry Island, Barry, Penarth and Cardiff - Coryton, Rhymney, Pontypridd, Merthyr, Aberdare and Treherbert

Network Diagram - see first Page of Table 130

		AW	AW	AW	AW	AW	AW	AW	AW	AW	AW	AW	AW	AW	AW	AW	AW	AW	AW	AW	AW	AW	AW
Bridgend	d	08 42																				09 42	
Llantwit Major	d	08 56																				09 56	
Rhoose Cardiff Int Airport ✈	d	09 06																				10 06	
Barry Island	d						09 25						09 40				09 55						
Barry 3	d	09 15					09 30						09 45				10 00					10 15	
Barry Docks	d	09 19					09 34						09 49				10 04					10 19	
Cadoxton	d	09 22					09 37						09 52				10 07					10 22	
Dinas Powys	d	09 26					09 41						09 56				10 11					10 26	
Eastbrook	d	09 28					09 43						09 58				10 13					10 28	
Cogan	d	09 30					09 45						10 00				10 15					10 30	
Penarth	d			09 32				09 47						10 02				10 17					
Dingle Road	d			09 34				09 49						10 04				10 19					
Grangetown	d	09 34		09 38			09 49	09 53					10 04	10 08			10 19	10 23				10 34	
Cardiff Central 7	a	09 39		09 44			09 54	09 59					10 09	10 14			10 24	10 29				10 42	
	d	09 41		09 46	09 51		09 56	10 01		10 06	10 06		10 11	10 16		10 21	10 26	10 31		10 36	10 36		
Cardiff Bay	d		09 42			09 54			10 06						10 18				10 30				10 42
Cardiff Queen Street 3	a	09 44	09 46	09 49	09 54	09 58	09 59	10 04	10 10	10 09			10 14	10 19	10 22	10 24	10 29	10 34	10 34	10 39			10 46
	d	09 45		09 50	09 55		10 00	10 05		10 10			10 15	10 20		10 25	10 30	10 35		10 40			
Heath Low Level	d				10 00											10 30							
Ty Glas	d				10 03											10 33							
Birchgrove	d				10 04											10 34							
Rhiwbina	d				10 06											10 36							
Whitchurch (Cardiff)	d				10 08											10 38							
Coryton	a				10 13											10 43							
Heath High Level	d			09 55				10 10						10 25				10 40					
Llanishen	d			09 58				10 13						10 28				10 43					
Lisvane & Thornhill	d			10 00				10 15						10 30				10 45					
Caerphilly 3	d			10 06				10 21						10 36				10 51					
Aber	d			10 08				10 23						10 38				10 53					
Llanbradach	d			10 12				10 27						10 42				10 57					
Ystrad Mynach 3	d			10 17				10 32						10 47				11 02					
Hengoed	d			10 20				10 35						10 50				11 05					
Pengam	d			10 23				10 38						10 53				11 08					
Gilfach Fargoed	d							10 41															
Bargoed	a			10 31				10 48						10 58				11 16					
	d													10 59									
Brithdir	d													11 03									
Tir-phil	d													11 06									
Pontlottyn	d													11 10									
Rhymney 3	a													11 16									
Cathays	d	09 48					10 03			10 13			10 18				10 33			10 43			
Llandaf	d	09 52					10 07			10 17			10 22				10 37			10 47			
Ninian Park	d										10 10										10 40		
Waun-gron Park	d										10 13										10 43		
Fairwater	d										10 15										10 45		
Danescourt	d										10 17										10 47		
Radyr 3	a	09 55					10 10			10 20	10 24		10 25				10 40			10 50	10 54		
	d	09 55					10 10			10 20			10 25				10 40			10 50			
Taffs Well 3	d	09 59					10 14			10 24			10 29				10 44			10 54			
Trefforest Estate	d																10 48						
Trefforest	d	10 06					10 22			10 31			10 36				10 52			11 01			
Pontypridd 3	a	10 09					10 30			10 34			10 39				10 55			11 04			
	d	10 11								10 36		10 35	10 41				10 57			11 06			
Abercynon	d	10 19										10 41	10 49				11 04						
Penrhiwceiber	d	10 24											10 54										
Mountain Ash	a	10 28											10 58										
	d	10 33											11 03										
Fernhill	d	10 35											11 05										
Cwmbach	d	10 39											11 09										
Aberdare 3	a	10 46											11 16										
Quakers Yard	d											10 45					11 09						
Merthyr Vale	a											10 50					11 14						
	d											10 52					11 17						
Troed Y Rhiw	d											10 55					11 20						
Pentre-bach	d											10 58					11 23						
Merthyr Tydfil	a											11 06					11 31						
Trehafod	d									10 41										11 11			
Porth	a									10 44										11 14			
	d									10 45										11 15			
Dinas Rhondda	d									10 49										11 19			
Tonypandy	d									10 51										11 21			
Llwynypia	d									10 53										11 23			
Ystrad Rhondda	a									10 56										11 26			
	d									10 59										11 29			
Ton Pentre	d									11 01										11 31			
Treorchy	d									11 04										11 34			
Ynyswen	d									11 07										11 37			
Treherbert	a									11 13										11 43			

When events are being held at the Millenium Stadium,
services are subject to alteration. Please check times before travelling.

Table 130

Saturdays

Bridgend, Barry Island, Barry, Penarth and Cardiff - Coryton, Rhymney, Pontypridd, Merthyr, Aberdare and Treherbert

Network Diagram - see first Page of Table 130

		AW	AW	AW	AW	AW	AW	AW	AW	AW	AW	AW	AW	AW	AW	AW	AW	AW	AW	AW	AW	AW
Bridgend	d																			10 42		
Llantwit Major	d																			10 56		
Rhoose Cardiff Int Airport ✈	d																			11 06		
Barry Island	d					10 25					10 40				10 55							
Barry 3	d					10 30					10 45				11 00					11 15		
Barry Docks	d					10 34					10 49				11 04					11 19		
Cadoxton	d					10 37					10 52				11 07					11 22		
Dinas Powys	d					10 41					10 56				11 11					11 26		
Eastbrook	d					10 43					10 58				11 13					11 28		
Cogan	d					10 45					11 00				11 15					11 30		
Penarth	d	10 32						10 47				11 02				11 17						11 32
Dingle Road	d	10 34						10 49				11 04				11 19						11 34
Grangetown	d	10 38				10 49		10 53			11 04	11 08			11 19	11 23				11 34		11 38
Cardiff Central 7	a	10 44				10 54		10 59			11 09	11 14			11 24	11 29				11 39		11 44
	d	10 46	10 51		10 51	10 56		11 01	11 06		11 11	11 16		11 21	11 26	11 31		11 36	11 36	11 41		11 46
Cardiff Bay	d			10 54						11 06			11 18				11 30				11 42	
Cardiff Queen Street 3	a	10 49	10 54	10 58		10 59		11 04		11 10	11 14	11 19	11 22	11 24	11 29	11 34	11 34	11 39		11 44	11 46	11 49
	d	10 50	10 55			11 00		11 05			11 15	11 20		11 25	11 30	11 35		11 40		11 45		11 50
Heath Low Level	d		11 00											11 30								
Ty Glas	d		11 03											11 33								
Birchgrove	d		11 04											11 34								
Rhiwbina	d		11 06											11 36								
Whitchurch (Cardiff)	d		11 08											11 38								
Coryton	a		11 13											11 43								
Heath High Level	d	10 55						11 10				11 25				11 40						11 55
Llanishen	d	10 58						11 13				11 28				11 43						11 58
Lisvane & Thornhill	d	11 00						11 15				11 30				11 45						12 00
Caerphilly 3	d	11 06						11 21				11 36				11 51						12 06
Aber	d	11 08						11 23				11 38				11 53						12 08
Llanbradach	d	11 12						11 27				11 42				11 57						12 12
Ystrad Mynach 3	d	11 17						11 32				11 47				12 02						12 17
Hengoed	d	11 20						11 35				11 50				12 05						12 20
Pengam	d	11 23						11 38				11 53				12 08						12 23
Gilfach Fargoed	d							11 41														
Bargoed	a	11 31						11 48				11 58				12 16						12 31
	d											11 59										
Brithdir	d											12 03										
Tir-phil	d											12 06										
Pontlottyn	d											12 10										
Rhymney 3	a											12 16										
Cathays	d					11 03					11 18				11 33			11 43		11 48		
Llandaf	d					11 07					11 22				11 37			11 47		11 52		
Ninian Park	d								11 10										11 40			
Waun-gron Park	d								11 13										11 43			
Fairwater	d								11 15										11 45			
Danescourt	d						←		11 17										11 47			
Radyr 3	a				11 02	11 10	11 02		11 24		11 25				11 40			11 50	11 54	11 55		
	d				11 20	11 10	11 20				11 25				11 40			11 50		11 55		
Taffs Well 3	d				↪	11 14	11 24				11 29				11 44			11 54		11 59		
Trefforest Estate	d					11 18									11 48							
Trefforest	d					11 22	11 31				11 36				11 52			12 01		12 06		
Pontypridd 3	a					11 25	11 34				11 39				11 55			12 04		12 09		
	d					11 27	11 36				11 41				11 57			12 06		12 11		
Abercynon	d					11 34					11 49				12 04					12 19		
Penrhiwceiber	d										11 54									12 24		
Mountain Ash	a										11 58									12 28		
	d										12 03									12 33		
Fernhill	d										12 05									12 35		
Cwmbach	d										12 09									12 39		
Aberdare 3	a										12 16									12 46		
Quakers Yard	d					11 39									12 09							
Merthyr Vale	a					11 44									12 14							
	d					11 47									12 17							
Troed Y Rhiw	d					11 50									12 20							
Pentre-bach	d					11 53									12 23							
Merthyr Tydfil	a					12 01									12 31							
Trehafod	d						11 41											12 11				
Porth	a						11 44											12 14				
	d						11 45											12 15				
Dinas Rhondda	d						11 49											12 19				
Tonypandy	d						11 51											12 21				
Llwynypia	d						11 53											12 23				
Ystrad Rhondda	a						11 56											12 26				
	d						11 59											12 29				
Ton Pentre	d						12 01											12 31				
Treorchy	d						12 04											12 34				
Ynyswen	d						12 07											12 37				
Treherbert	a						12 13											12 43				

When events are being held at the Millenium Stadium, services are subject to alteration. Please check times before travelling.

Table 130

Saturdays

Bridgend, Barry Island, Barry, Penarth and Cardiff - Coryton, Rhymney, Pontypridd, Merthyr, Aberdare and Treherbert

Network Diagram - see first Page of Table 130

		AW	AW	AW	AW	AW	AW	AW	AW	AW	AW	AW	AW	AW	AW	AW	AW	AW	AW	AW	AW	AW	AW
Bridgend	d																	11 42					
Llantwit Major	d																	11 56					
Rhoose Cardiff Int Airport ✈	d																	12 06					
Barry Island	d			11 25					11 40				11 55										12 25
Barry 3	d			11 30					11 45				12 00					12 15					12 30
Barry Docks	d			11 34					11 49				12 04					12 19					12 34
Cadoxton	d			11 37					11 52				12 07					12 22					12 37
Dinas Powys	d			11 41					11 56				12 11					12 26					12 41
Eastbrook	d			11 43					11 58				12 13					12 28					12 43
Cogan	d			11 45					12 00				12 15					12 30					12 45
Penarth	d				11 47					12 02				12 17						12 32			
Dingle Road	d				11 49					12 04				12 19						12 34			
Grangetown	d			11 49	11 53				12 04	12 08			12 19	12 23				12 34		12 38			12 49
Cardiff Central 7	a			11 54	11 59				12 09	12 14			12 24	12 29				12 39		12 44			12 54
	d	11 51		11 56	12 01		12 06	12 06	12 11	12 16		12 21	12 26	12 31		12 36	12 36	12 41		12 46	12 51		12 56
Cardiff Bay	d		11 54			12 06					12 18				12 30				12 42			12 54	
Cardiff Queen Street 3	a	11 54	11 58	11 59	12 04	12 10	12 09		12 14	12 19	12 22	12 24	12 29	12 34	12 34	12 39		12 44	12 46	12 49	12 54	12 58	12 59
	d	11 55		12 00	12 05		12 10		12 15	12 20		12 25	12 30	12 35		12 40		12 45		12 50	12 55		13 00
Heath Low Level	d	12 00										12 30									13 00		
Ty Glas	d	12 03										12 33									13 03		
Birchgrove	d	12 04										12 34									13 04		
Rhiwbina	d	12 06										12 36									13 06		
Whitchurch (Cardiff)	d	12 08										12 38									13 08		
Coryton	a	12 13										12 43									13 13		
Heath High Level	d				12 10					12 25				12 40						12 55			
Llanishen	d				12 13					12 28				12 43						12 58			
Lisvane & Thornhill	d				12 15					12 30				12 45						13 00			
Caerphilly 3	d				12 21					12 36				12 51						13 06			
Aber	d				12 23					12 38				12 53						13 08			
Llanbradach	d				12 27					12 42				12 57						13 12			
Ystrad Mynach 3	d				12 32					12 47				13 02						13 17			
Hengoed	d				12 35					12 50				13 05						13 20			
Pengam	d				12 38					12 53				13 08						13 23			
Gilfach Fargoed	d				12 41																		
Bargoed	a				12 48					12 58				13 16						13 31			
	d									12 59													
Brithdir	d									13 03													
Tir-phil	d									13 06													
Pontlottyn	d									13 10													
Rhymney 3	a									13 16													
Cathays	d			12 03			12 13		12 18				12 33			12 43		12 48					13 03
Llandaf	d			12 07			12 17		12 22				12 37			12 47		12 52					13 07
Ninian Park	d							12 10									12 40						
Waun-gron Park	d							12 13									12 43						
Fairwater	d							12 15									12 45						
Danescourt	d							12 17									12 47						
Radyr 3	a			12 10			12 20	12 24	12 25				12 40			12 50	12 54	12 55					13 10
	d			12 10			12 20		12 25				12 40			12 50		12 55					13 10
Taffs Well 3	d			12 14			12 24		12 29				12 44			12 54		12 59					13 14
Trefforest Estate	d			12 18									12 48										13 18
Trefforest	d			12 22			12 31		12 36				12 52			13 01		13 06					13 22
Pontypridd 3	a			12 25			12 34		12 42				12 55			13 04		13 09					13 25
	d			12 27			12 36						12 57			13 06		13 11					13 27
Abercynon	d			12 34									13 04					13 19					13 34
Penrhiwceiber	d																	13 24					
Mountain Ash	a																	13 28					
	d																	13 33					
Fernhill	d																	13 35					
Cwmbach	d																	13 39					
Aberdare 3	a																	13 46					
Quakers Yard	d			12 39									13 09										13 39
Merthyr Vale	a			12 44									13 14										13 44
	d			12 47									13 17										13 47
Troed Y Rhiw	d			12 50									13 20										13 50
Pentre-bach	d			12 53									13 23										13 53
Merthyr Tydfil	a			13 01									13 31										14 01
Trehafod	d						12 41									13 11							
Porth	a						12 44									13 14							
	d						12 45									13 15							
Dinas Rhondda	d						12 49									13 19							
Tonypandy	d						12 51									13 21							
Llwynypia	d						12 53									13 23							
Ystrad Rhondda	a						12 56									13 26							
	d						12 59									13 29							
Ton Pentre	d						13 01									13 31							
Treorchy	d						13 04									13 34							
Ynyswen	d						13 07									13 37							
Treherbert	a						13 13									13 43							

When events are being held at the Millenium Stadium, services are subject to alteration. Please check times before travelling.

Table 130

Saturdays

Bridgend, Barry Island, Barry, Penarth and Cardiff - Coryton, Rhymney, Pontypridd, Merthyr, Aberdare and Treherbert

Network Diagram - see first Page of Table 130

		AW	AW	AW	AW	AW	AW	AW	AW	AW	AW	AW	AW	AW	AW	AW	AW	AW	AW	AW	AW	AW	AW
Bridgend	d														12 42								
Llantwit Major	d														12 56								
Rhoose Cardiff Int Airport ✈	d														13 06								
Barry Island	d					12 40				12 55										13 25			
Barry ■	d					12 45				13 00					13 15					13 30			
Barry Docks	d					12 49				13 04					13 19					13 34			
Cadoxton	d					12 52				13 07					13 22					13 37			
Dinas Powys	d					12 56				13 11					13 26					13 41			
Eastbrook	d					12 58				13 13					13 28					13 43			
Cogan	d					13 00				13 15					13 30					13 45			
Penarth	d	12 47					13 02				13 17						13 32				13 47		
Dingle Road	d	12 49					13 04				13 19						13 34				13 49		
Grangetown	d	12 53				13 04	13 08			13 19	13 23				13 34		13 38			13 49	13 53		
Cardiff Central ■	a	12 59				13 09	13 14			13 24	13 29				13 39		13 44			13 54	13 59		
	d	13 01		13 06	13 06	13 11	13 16		13 21	13 26	13 31		13 36	13 36	13 41		13 46	13 51		13 56	14 01		14 06
Cardiff Bay	d		13 06					13 18				13 30				13 42			13 54			14 06	
Cardiff Queen Street ■	a	13 04	13 10	13 09		13 14	13 19	13 22	13 24	13 29	13 34	13 34	13 39		13 44	13 46	13 49	13 54	13 58	13 59	14 04	14 10	14 09
	d	13 05		13 10		13 15	13 20		13 25	13 30	13 35		13 40		13 45		13 50	13 55		14 00	14 05		14 10
Heath Low Level	d								13 30									14 00					
Ty Glas	d								13 33									14 03					
Birchgrove	d								13 34									14 04					
Rhiwbina	d								13 36									14 06					
Whitchurch (Cardiff)	d								13 38									14 08					
Coryton	a								13 43									14 13					
Heath High Level	d	13 10					13 25				13 40						13 55				14 10		
Llanishen	d	13 13					13 28				13 43						13 58				14 13		
Lisvane & Thornhill	d	13 15					13 30				13 45						14 00				14 15		
Caerphilly ■	d	13 21					13 36				13 51						14 06				14 21		
Aber	d	13 23					13 38				13 53						14 08				14 23		
Llanbradach	d	13 27					13 42				13 57						14 12				14 27		
Ystrad Mynach ■	d	13 32					13 47				14 02						14 17				14 32		
Hengoed	d	13 35					13 50				14 05						14 20				14 35		
Pengam	d	13 38					13 53				14 08						14 23				14 38		
Gilfach Fargoed	d	13 41																			14 41		
Bargoed	a	13 48					13 58				14 16						14 31				14 48		
	d						13 59																
Brithdir	d						14 03																
Tir-phil	d						14 06																
Pontlottyn	d						14 10																
Rhymney ■	a						14 16																
Cathays	d			13 13		13 18				13 33			13 43		13 48					14 03			14 13
Llandaf	d			13 17		13 22				13 37			13 47		13 52					14 07			14 17
Ninian Park	d				13 10									13 40									
Waun-gron Park	d				13 13									13 43									
Fairwater	d				13 15									13 45									
Danescourt	d				13 17									13 47									
Radyr ■	a			13 20	13 24	13 25				13 40			13 50	13 54	13 55					14 10			14 20
	d			13 20		13 25				13 40			13 50		13 55					14 10			14 20
Taffs Well ■	d			13 24		13 29				13 44			13 54		13 59					14 14			14 24
Trefforest Estate	d									13 48										14 18			
Trefforest	d			13 31		13 36				13 52			14 01		14 06					14 22			14 31
Pontypridd ■	a			13 34		13 39				13 55			14 04		14 09					14 25			14 34
	d			13 36		13 41				13 57			14 06		14 11					14 27			14 36
Abercynon	d					13 49				14 04					14 19					14 34			
Penrhiwceiber	d					13 54									14 24								
Mountain Ash	a					13 58									14 28								
	d					14 03									14 33								
Fernhill	d					14 05									14 35								
Cwmbach	d					14 09									14 39								
Aberdare ■	a					14 16									14 46								
Quakers Yard	d									14 09										14 39			
Merthyr Vale	a									14 14										14 44			
	d									14 17										14 47			
Troed Y Rhiw	d									14 20										14 50			
Pentre-bach	d									14 23										14 53			
Merthyr Tydfil	a									14 31										15 01			
Trehafod	d			13 41									14 11										14 41
Porth	a			13 44									14 14										14 44
	d			13 45									14 15										14 45
Dinas Rhondda	d			13 49									14 19										14 49
Tonypandy	d			13 51									14 21										14 51
Llwynypia	d			13 53									14 23										14 53
Ystrad Rhondda	a			13 56									14 26										14 56
	d			13 59									14 29										14 59
Ton Pentre	d			14 01									14 31										15 01
Treorchy	d			14 04									14 34										15 04
Ynyswen	d			14 07									14 37										15 07
Treherbert	a			14 13									14 43										15 13

When events are being held at the Millenium Stadium, services are subject to alteration. Please check times before travelling.

Table 130

Saturdays

Bridgend, Barry Island, Barry, Penarth and Cardiff - Coryton, Rhymney, Pontypridd, Merthyr, Aberdare and Treherbert

Network Diagram - see first Page of Table 130

		AW	AW	AW	AW	AW	AW	AW	AW	AW	AW	AW	AW	AW	AW	AW	AW	AW	AW	AW	AW	AW
Bridgend	d											13 42										
Llantwit Major	d											13 56										
Rhoose Cardiff Int Airport ✈	d											14 06										
Barry Island	d		13 40				13 55											14 25				
Barry 3	d		13 45				14 00					14 15						14 30				
Barry Docks	d		13 49				14 04					14 19						14 34				
Cadoxton	d		13 52				14 07					14 22						14 37				
Dinas Powys	d		13 56				14 11					14 26						14 41				
Eastbrook	d		13 58				14 13					14 28						14 43				
Cogan	d		14 00				14 15					14 30						14 45				
Penarth	d			14 02				14 17						14 32						14 47		
Dingle Road	d			14 04				14 19						14 34						14 49		
Grangetown	d		14 04	14 08			14 19	14 23				14 34		14 38				14 49		14 53		
Cardiff Central 7	a		14 09	14 14			14 24	14 29				14 39		14 44				14 54		14 59		
	d	14 06	14 11	14 16		14 21	14 26	14 31		14 36	14 36	14 41		14 46	14 51		14 51	14 56		15 01	15 06	
Cardiff Bay	d				14 18				14 30				14 42			14 54						15 06
Cardiff Queen Street 3	a		14 14	14 19	14 22	14 24	14 29	14 34	14 34	14 39		14 44	14 46	14 49	14 54	14 58		14 59		15 04		15 10
	d		14 15	14 20		14 25	14 30	14 35		14 40		14 45		14 50	14 55			15 00		15 05		
Heath Low Level	d					14 30									15 00							
Ty Glas	d					14 33									15 03							
Birchgrove	d					14 34									15 04							
Rhiwbina	d					14 36									15 06							
Whitchurch (Cardiff)	d					14 38									15 08							
Coryton	a					14 43									15 13							
Heath High Level	d			14 25				14 40						14 55						15 10		
Llanishen	d			14 28				14 43						14 58						15 13		
Lisvane & Thornhill	d			14 30				14 45						15 00						15 15		
Caerphilly 3	d			14 36				14 51						15 06						15 21		
Aber	d			14 38				14 53						15 08						15 23		
Llanbradach	d			14 42				14 57						15 12						15 27		
Ystrad Mynach 3	d			14 47				15 02						15 17						15 32		
Hengoed	d			14 50				15 05						15 20						15 35		
Pengam	d			14 53				15 08						15 23						15 38		
Gilfach Fargoed	d																			15 41		
Bargoed	a			14 58				15 16						15 31						15 48		
	d			14 59																		
Brithdir	d			15 03																		
Tir-phil	d			15 06																		
Pontlottyn	d			15 10																		
Rhymney 3	a			15 16																		
Cathays	d		14 18				14 33			14 43		14 48						15 03				
Llandaf	d		14 22				14 37			14 47		14 52						15 07				
Ninian Park	d	14 10									14 40										15 10	
Waun-gron Park	d	14 13									14 43										15 13	
Fairwater	d	14 15									14 45										15 15	
Danescourt	d	14 17									14 47								←		15 17	
Radyr 3	a	14 24	14 25				14 40			14 50	14 54	14 55					15 08	15 10	15 08		15 24	
	d		14 25				14 40			14 50		14 55					15 20	15 10	15 20			
Taffs Well 3	d		14 29				14 44			14 54		14 59					→	15 14	15 24			
Trefforest Estate	d						14 48											15 18				
Trefforest	d		14 36				14 52			15 01		15 06						15 22	15 31			
Pontypridd 3	a		14 39				14 55			15 04		15 09						15 25	15 34			
	d		14 41				14 57			15 06		15 11						15 27	15 36			
Abercynon	d		14 49				15 04					15 19						15 34				
Penrhiwceiber	d		14 54									15 24										
Mountain Ash	a		14 58									15 28										
	d		15 03									15 33										
Fernhill	d		15 05									15 35										
Cwmbach	d		15 09									15 39										
Aberdare 3	a		15 16									15 46										
Quakers Yard	d						15 09											15 39				
Merthyr Vale	a						15 14											15 44				
	d						15 17											15 47				
Troed Y Rhiw	d						15 20											15 50				
Pentre-bach	d						15 23											15 53				
Merthyr Tydfil	a						15 31											16 01				
Trehafod	d									15 11									15 41			
Porth	a									15 14									15 44			
	d									15 15									15 45			
Dinas Rhondda	d									15 19									15 49			
Tonypandy	d									15 21									15 51			
Llwynypia	d									15 23									15 53			
Ystrad Rhondda	a									15 26									15 56			
	d									15 29									15 59			
Ton Pentre	d									15 31									16 01			
Treorchy	d									15 34									16 04			
Ynyswen	d									15 37									16 07			
Treherbert	a									15 43									16 13			

When events are being held at the Millenium Stadium,
services are subject to alteration. Please check times before travelling.

Table 130

Saturdays

Bridgend, Barry Island, Barry, Penarth and Cardiff - Coryton, Rhymney, Pontypridd, Merthyr, Aberdare and Treherbert

Network Diagram - see first Page of Table 130

		AW	AW	AW	AW	AW	AW	AW	AW	AW	AW	AW	AW	AW	AW	AW	AW	AW	AW	AW	AW	AW	AW
Bridgend	d										14 42												
Llantwit Major	d										14 56												
Rhoose Cardiff Int Airport ✈	d										15 06												
Barry Island	d	14 40				14 55										15 25					15 40		
Barry 3	d	14 45				15 00					15 15					15 30					15 45		
Barry Docks	d	14 49				15 04					15 19					15 34					15 49		
Cadoxton	d	14 52				15 07					15 22					15 37					15 52		
Dinas Powys	d	14 56				15 11					15 26					15 41					15 56		
Eastbrook	d	14 58				15 13					15 28					15 43					15 58		
Cogan	d	15 00				15 15					15 30					15 45					16 00		
Penarth	d		15 02				15 17						15 32				15 47					16 02	
Dingle Road	d		15 04				15 19						15 34				15 49					16 04	
Grangetown	d	15 04	15 08			15 19	15 23				15 34		15 38			15 49	15 53				16 04	16 08	
Cardiff Central 7	a	15 09	15 14			15 24	15 29				15 39		15 44			15 54	15 59				16 09	16 14	
	d	15 11	15 16		15 21	15 26	15 31		15 36	15 36	15 41		15 46	15 51		15 56	16 01		16 06	16 06	16 11	16 16	
Cardiff Bay	d			15 18				15 30				15 42			15 54			16 06					16 18
Cardiff Queen Street 3	a	15 14	15 19	15 22	15 24	15 29	15 34	15 34	15 39		15 44	15 46	15 49	15 54	15 58	15 59	16 04	16 10	16 09		16 14	16 19	16 22
	d	15 15	15 20		15 25	15 30	15 35		15 40		15 45		15 50	15 55		16 00	16 05		16 10		16 15	16 20	
Heath Low Level	d				15 30									16 00									
Ty Glas	d				15 33									16 03									
Birchgrove	d				15 34									16 04									
Rhiwbina	d				15 36									16 06									
Whitchurch (Cardiff)	d				15 38									16 08									
Coryton	a				15 43									16 13									
Heath High Level	d		15 25				15 40						15 55				16 10					16 25	
Llanishen	d		15 28				15 43						15 58				16 13					16 28	
Lisvane & Thornhill	d		15 30				15 45						16 00				16 15					16 30	
Caerphilly 3	d		15 36				15 51						16 06				16 21					16 36	
Aber	d		15 38				15 53						16 08				16 23					16 38	
Llanbradach	d		15 42				15 57						16 12				16 27					16 42	
Ystrad Mynach 3	d		15 47				16 02						16 17				16 32					16 47	
Hengoed	d		15 50				16 05						16 20				16 35					16 50	
Pengam	d		15 53				16 08						16 23				16 38					16 53	
Gilfach Fargoed	d																16 41						
Bargoed	a		15 58				16 16						16 31				16 48					16 58	
	d		15 59																			16 59	
Brithdir	d		16 03																			17 03	
Tir-phil	d		16 06																			17 06	
Pontlottyn	d		16 10																			17 10	
Rhymney 3	a		16 16																			17 16	
Cathays	d	15 18				15 33			15 43		15 48					16 03			16 13		16 18		
Llandaf	d	15 22				15 37			15 47		15 52					16 07			16 17		16 22		
Ninian Park	d									15 40										16 10			
Waun-gron Park	d									15 43										16 13			
Fairwater	d									15 45										16 15			
Danescourt	d									15 47										16 17			
Radyr 3	a	15 25				15 40			15 50	15 54	15 55					16 10			16 20	16 24	16 25		
	d	15 25				15 40			15 50		15 55					16 10			16 20		16 25		
Taffs Well 3	d	15 29				15 44			15 54		15 59					16 14			16 24		16 29		
Trefforest Estate	d					15 48										16 18							
Trefforest	d	15 36				15 52			16 01		16 06					16 22			16 31		16 36		
Pontypridd 3	a	15 39				15 55			16 04		16 09					16 25			16 34		16 39		
	d	15 41				15 57			16 06		16 11					16 27			16 36		16 41		
Abercynon	d	15 49				16 04					16 19					16 34					16 49		
Penrhiwceiber	d	15 54									16 24										16 54		
Mountain Ash	a	15 58									16 28										16 58		
	d	16 03									16 33										17 03		
Fernhill	d	16 05									16 35										17 05		
Cwmbach	d	16 09									16 39										17 09		
Aberdare 3	a	16 16									16 46										17 16		
Quakers Yard	d					16 09										16 39							
Merthyr Vale	a					16 14										16 44							
	d					16 17										16 47							
Troed Y Rhiw	d					16 20										16 50							
Pentre-bach	d					16 23										16 53							
Merthyr Tydfil	a					16 31										17 01							
Trehafod	d								16 11										16 41				
Porth	a								16 14										16 44				
	d								16 15										16 45				
Dinas Rhondda	d								16 19										16 49				
Tonypandy	d								16 21										16 51				
Llwynypia	d								16 23										16 53				
Ystrad Rhondda	a								16 26										16 56				
	d								16 29										16 59				
Ton Pentre	d								16 31										17 01				
Treorchy	d								16 34										17 04				
Ynyswen	d								16 37										17 07				
Treherbert	a								16 43										17 13				

When events are being held at the Millenium Stadium, services are subject to alteration. Please check times before travelling.

Table 130

Saturdays

Bridgend, Barry Island, Barry, Penarth and Cardiff - Coryton, Rhymney, Pontypridd, Merthyr, Aberdare and Treherbert

Network Diagram - see first Page of Table 130

		AW	AW	AW	AW	AW	AW	AW	AW	AW	AW	AW	AW	AW	AW	AW	AW	AW	AW	AW	AW	AW
Bridgend	d							15 42														
Llantwit Major	d							15 56														
Rhoose Cardiff Int Airport ✈	d							16 06														
Barry Island	d		15 55										16 25					16 40				16 55
Barry 3	d		16 00					16 15					16 30					16 45				17 00
Barry Docks	d		16 04					16 19					16 34					16 49				17 04
Cadoxton	d		16 07					16 22					16 37					16 52				17 07
Dinas Powys	d		16 11					16 26					16 41					16 56				17 11
Eastbrook	d		16 13					16 28					16 43					16 58				17 13
Cogan	d		16 15					16 30					16 45					17 00				17 15
Penarth	d			16 17						16 32									17 02			
Dingle Road	d			16 19						16 34									17 04			
Grangetown	d		16 19	16 23				16 34		16 38			16 49					17 04	17 08			17 19
Cardiff Central 7	a		16 24	16 29				16 39		16 44			16 54					17 09	17 14			17 24
	d	16 21	16 26	16 31		16 36	16 36	16 41		16 46	16 51		16 56	17 01		17 06	17 06	17 11	17 16		17 21	17 26
Cardiff Bay	d				16 30				16 42			16 54			17 06					17 18		
Cardiff Queen Street 3	a	16 24	16 29	16 34	16 34	16 39		16 44	16 46	16 49	16 54	16 58	16 59	17 04	17 10	17 09		17 14	17 19	17 22	17 24	17 29
	d	16 25	16 30	16 35		16 40		16 45		16 50	16 55		17 00	17 05		17 10		17 15	17 20		17 25	17 30
Heath Low Level	d	16 30									17 00										17 30	
Ty Glas	d	16 33									17 03										17 33	
Birchgrove	d	16 34									17 04										17 34	
Rhiwbina	d	16 36									17 06										17 36	
Whitchurch (Cardiff)	d	16 38									17 08										17 38	
Coryton	a	16 43									17 13										17 43	
Heath High Level	d			16 40						16 55				17 10					17 25			
Llanishen	d			16 43						16 58				17 13					17 28			
Lisvane & Thornhill	d			16 45						17 00				17 15					17 30			
Caerphilly 3	d			16 51						17 06				17 21					17 36			
Aber	d			16 53						17 08				17 23					17 38			
Llanbradach	d			16 57						17 12				17 27					17 42			
Ystrad Mynach 3	d			17 02						17 17				17 33					17 47			
Hengoed	d			17 05						17 20				17 35					17 50			
Pengam	d			17 08						17 23				17 39					17 53			
Gilfach Fargoed	d													17 42								
Bargoed	a			17 16						17 31				17 45					18 01			
	d													17 47								
Brithdir	d													17 50								
Tir-phil	d													17 53								
Pontlottyn	d													17 58								
Rhymney 3	a													18 04								
Cathays	d		16 33			16 43		16 48					17 03			17 13		17 18				17 33
Llandaf	d		16 37			16 47		16 52					17 07			17 17		17 22				17 37
Ninian Park	d						16 40										17 10					
Waun-gron Park	d						16 43										17 13					
Fairwater	d						16 45										17 15					
Danescourt	d						16 47										17 17					
Radyr 3	a		16 40			16 50	16 54	16 55					17 10			17 20	17 24	17 25				17 40
	d		16 40			16 50		16 55					17 10			17 20		17 25				17 40
Taffs Well 3	d		16 44			16 54		16 59					17 14			17 24		17 29				17 44
Trefforest Estate	d		16 48										17 18									17 48
Trefforest	d		16 52			17 01		17 06					17 22			17 31		17 36				17 52
Pontypridd 3	a		16 55			17 04		17 09					17 25			17 34		17 39				17 55
	d		16 57			17 06		17 11					17 27			17 36		17 41				17 57
Abercynon	d		17 04					17 19					17 34					17 49				18 04
Penrhiwceiber	d							17 24										17 54				
Mountain Ash	a							17 28										17 58				
	d							17 33										18 03				
Fernhill	d							17 35										18 05				
Cwmbach	d							17 39										18 09				
Aberdare 3	a							17 46										18 16				
Quakers Yard	d		17 09										17 39									18 09
Merthyr Vale	a		17 14										17 44									18 14
	d		17 17										17 47									18 17
Troed Y Rhiw	d		17 20										17 50									18 20
Pentre-bach	d		17 23										17 53									18 23
Merthyr Tydfil	a		17 31										18 01									18 31
Trehafod	d					17 11										17 41						
Porth	a					17 14										17 44						
	d					17 15										17 45						
Dinas Rhondda	d					17 19										17 49						
Tonypandy	d					17 21										17 51						
Llwynypia	d					17 23										17 53						
Ystrad Rhondda	a					17 26										17 56						
	d					17 29										17 59						
Ton Pentre	d					17 31										18 01						
Treorchy	d					17 34										18 04						
Ynyswen	d					17 37										18 07						
Treherbert	a					17 43										18 13						

When events are being held at the Millenium Stadium,
services are subject to alteration. Please check times before travelling.

Table 130

Saturdays

Bridgend, Barry Island, Barry, Penarth and Cardiff - Coryton, Rhymney, Pontypridd, Merthyr, Aberdare and Treherbert

Network Diagram - see first Page of Table 130

		AW	AW	AW	AW	AW	AW	AW	AW	AW	AW	AW	AW	AW	AW	AW	AW	AW	AW	AW	AW	AW	AW
Bridgend	d					16 42																	
Llantwit Major	d					16 56																	
Rhoose Cardiff Int Airport ✈	d					17 06																	
Barry Island	d										17 25					17 40				17 55			
Barry [3]	d					17 15					17 30					17 45				18 00			
Barry Docks	d					17 19					17 34					17 49				18 04			
Cadoxton	d					17 22					17 37					17 52				18 07			
Dinas Powys	d					17 26					17 41					17 56				18 11			
Eastbrook	d					17 28					17 43					17 58				18 13			
Cogan	d					17 30					17 45					18 00				18 15			
Penarth	d	17 17						17 32				17 47					18 02				18 17		
Dingle Road	d	17 19						17 34				17 49					18 04				18 19		
Grangetown	d	17 23				17 34		17 38			17 49	17 53				18 04	18 08			18 19	18 23		
Cardiff Central [7]	a	17 29				17 39		17 44			17 54	17 59				18 09	18 14			18 24	18 29		
	d	17 31		17 36	17 36	17 41		17 46	17 51		17 56	18 01		18 06	18 06	18 11	18 16		18 21	18 26	18 31		18 36
Cardiff Bay	d		17 30				17 42			17 54			18 06					18 18				18 30	
Cardiff Queen Street [3]	a	17 34	17 34	17 39		17 44	17 46	17 49	17 54	17 58	17 59	18 04	18 10	18 09		18 14	18 19	18 22	18 24	18 29	18 34	18 34	18 38
	d	17 35		17 40		17 45		17 50	17 55		18 00	18 05		18 10		18 15	18 20		18 25	18 30	18 35		18 40
Heath Low Level	d								18 00										18 30				
Ty Glas	d								18 03										18 33				
Birchgrove	d								18 04										18 34				
Rhiwbina	d								18 06										18 36				
Whitchurch (Cardiff)	d								18 08										18 38				
Coryton	a								18 13										18 43				
Heath High Level	d	17 40						17 55				18 10					18 25				18 40		
Llanishen	d	17 43						17 59				18 13					18 28				18 43		
Lisvane & Thornhill	d	17 45						18 02				18 15					18 30				18 45		
Caerphilly [3]	d	17 51						18 07				18 21					18 36				18 51		
Aber	d	17 53						18 10				18 23					18 38				18 53		
Llanbradach	d	17 57						18 14				18 27					18 42				18 57		
Ystrad Mynach [3]	d	18 02						18 20				18 32					18a51				19 02		
Hengoed	d	18 05						18 23				18 35									19 05		
Pengam	d	18 08						18 27				18 38									19 08		
Gilfach Fargoed	d	18 11						18 30				18 41									19 11		
Bargoed	a	18 14						18 34				18 48									19 14		
	d	18 16						18 44													19 16		
Brithdir	d	18 20						18 48													19 20		
Tir-phil	d	18 23						18 51													19 23		
Pontlottyn	d	18 27						18 55													19 27		
Rhymney [3]	a	18 33						19 01													19 34		
Cathays	d			17 43		17 48					18 03			18 13		18 18				18 33			18 43
Llandaf	d			17 47		17 52					18 07			18 17		18 22				18 37			18 47
Ninian Park	d				17 40										18 10								
Waun-gron Park	d				17 43										18 13								
Fairwater	d				17 45										18 15								
Danescourt	d				17 47										18 17								
Radyr [3]	a			17 50	17 54	17 55					18 10			18 20	18 24	18 25				18 40			18 50
	d			17 50		17 55					18 10			18 20		18 25				18 40			18 50
Taffs Well [3]	d			17 54		17 59					18 14			18 24		18 29				18 44			18 54
Trefforest Estate	d										18 18									18 48			
Trefforest	d			18 01		18 06					18 22			18 31		18 36				18 52			19 01
Pontypridd [3]	a			18 04		18 09					18 25			18 34		18 42				18 55			19 04
	d			18 06		18 11					18 27			18 36						18 57			19 06
Abercynon	d					18 19					18 34									19 04			
Penrhiwceiber	d					18 24																	
Mountain Ash	a					18 28																	
	d					18 33																	
Fernhill	d					18 35																	
Cwmbach	d					18 39																	
Aberdare [3]	a					18 46																	
Quakers Yard	d										18 39									19 09			
Merthyr Vale	a										18 44									19 14			
	d										18 47									19 17			
Troed Y Rhiw	d										18 50									19 20			
Pentre-bach	d										18 53									19 23			
Merthyr Tydfil	a										19 01									19 31			
Trehafod	d			18 11										18 41									19 11
Porth	a			18 14										18 44									19 14
	d			18 15										18 45									19 15
Dinas Rhondda	d			18 19										18 49									19 19
Tonypandy	d			18 21										18 51									19 21
Llwynypia	d			18 23										18 53									19 23
Ystrad Rhondda	a			18 26										18 56									19 26
	d			18 29										18 59									19 29
Ton Pentre	d			18 31										19 01									19 31
Treorchy	d			18 34										19 04									19 34
Ynyswen	d			18 37										19 07									19 37
Treherbert	a			18 43										19 13									19 43

When events are being held at the Millenium Stadium, services are subject to alteration. Please check times before travelling.

Table 130

Saturdays

Bridgend, Barry Island, Barry, Penarth and Cardiff - Coryton, Rhymney, Pontypridd, Merthyr, Aberdare and Treherbert

Network Diagram - see first Page of Table 130

		AW	AW	AW	AW	AW		AW	AW	AW	AW	AW	AW	AW	AW	AW		AW	AW	AW	AW	AW	AW	AW	AW
Bridgend	d		17 42																	18 42					
Llantwit Major	d		17 56																	18 56					
Rhoose Cardiff Int Airport ✈	d		18 06																	19 06					
Barry Island	d							18 25					18 40		18 55									19 25	
Barry 3	d		18 15					18 30					18 45		19 00					19 15				19 30	
Barry Docks	d		18 19					18 34					18 49		19 04					19 19				19 34	
Cadoxton	d		18 22					18 37					18 52		19 07					19 22				19 37	
Dinas Powys	d		18 26					18 41					18 56		19 11					19 26				19 41	
Eastbrook	d		18 28					18 43					18 58		19 13					19 28				19 43	
Cogan	d		18 30					18 45					19 00		19 15					19 30				19 45	
Penarth	d			18 32						18 47						19 17									19 47
Dingle Road	d			18 34						18 49						19 19									19 49
Grangetown	d		18 34	18 38				18 49		18 53			19 04		19 19	19 23				19 34				19 49	19 53
Cardiff Central 7	a		18 39	18 47				18 55		18 59			19 09		19 24	19 29				19 39				19 54	19 59
	d	18 36	18 41			18 51				19 01		19 06	19 11		19 26	19 31			19 36	19 41		19 51		20 01	20 06
Cardiff Bay	d				18 42				18 54		19 06			19 18				19 30			19 42		19 54		
Cardiff Queen Street 3	a		18 44		18 46	18 54			18 58	19 04	19 10	19 09	19 14	19 22	19 29	19 34		19 34		19 44	19 46	19 54	19 58	20 04	20 09
	d		18 50			18 55				19 05		19 10	19 15		19 30	19 35				19 45		19 55		20 05	20 10
Heath Low Level	d					19 00																20 00			
Ty Glas	d					19 03																20 03			
Birchgrove	d					19 04																20 04			
Rhiwbina	d					19 06																20 06			
Whitchurch (Cardiff)	d					19 08																20 08			
Coryton	a					19 13																20 13			
Heath High Level	d									19 10						19 40								20 10	
Llanishen	d									19 13						19 43								20 13	
Lisvane & Thornhill	d									19 15						19 45								20 15	
Caerphilly 3	d									19a23						19 51								20a27	
Aber	d															19 53									
Llanbradach	d															19 57									
Ystrad Mynach 3	d															20 02									
Hengoed	d															20 05									
Pengam	d															20 08									
Gilfach Fargoed	d															20 11									
Bargoed	a															20 15									
	d															20 16									
Brithdir	d															20 20									
Tir-phil	d															20 23									
Pontlottyn	d															20 27									
Rhymney 3	a															20 33									
Cathays	d		18 52									19 13	19 18		19 33					19 48					20 13
Llandaf	d		18 56									19 17	19 22		19 37					19 52					20 17
Ninian Park	d	18 40																	19 40						
Waun-gron Park	d	18 43																	19 43						
Fairwater	d	18 45																	19 45						
Danescourt	d	18 47																	19 47						
Radyr 3	a	18 54	18 58									19 20	19 25		19 40				19 54	19 55					20 20
	d		18 58									19 20	19 25		19 40					19 55					20 20
Taffs Well 3	d		19 03									19 24	19 29		19 44					19 59					20 24
Trefforest Estate	d														19 48										
Trefforest	d		19 10									19 31	19 36		19 52					20 06					20 31
Pontypridd 3	a		19 13									19 34	19 39		19 55					20 09					20 34
	d		19 14									19 36	19 41		19 57					20 11					20 36
Abercynon	d		19 21										19 49		20 04					20 21					
Penrhiwceiber	d		19 26										19 54							20 26					
Mountain Ash	a		19 30										19 56							20 30					
	d		19 33										20 03							20 33					
Fernhill	d		19 35										20 05							20 35					
Cwmbach	d		19 39										20 09							20 39					
Aberdare 3	a		19 46										20 16							20 46					
Quakers Yard	d														20 08										
Merthyr Vale	a														20 13										
	d														20 15										
Troed Y Rhiw	d														20 19										
Pentre-bach	d														20 22										
Merthyr Tydfil	a														20 30										
Trehafod	d											19 41													20 41
Porth	a											19 44													20 44
	d											19 45													20 45
Dinas Rhondda	d											19 49													20 49
Tonypandy	d											19 51													20 51
Llwynypia	d											19 53													20 53
Ystrad Rhondda	a											19 56													20 56
	d											19 59													20 59
Ton Pentre	d											20 01													21 01
Treorchy	d											20 04													21 04
Ynyswen	d											20 07													21 07
Treherbert	a											20 13													21 13

When events are being held at the Millenium Stadium, services are subject to alteration. Please check times before travelling.

Table 130

Saturdays

Bridgend, Barry Island, Barry, Penarth and Cardiff - Coryton, Rhymney, Pontypridd, Merthyr, Aberdare and Treherbert

Network Diagram - see first Page of Table 130

		AW	AW	AW	AW	AW	AW	AW	AW	AW	AW	AW	AW	AW	AW	AW	AW	AW	AW	AW	AW	AW
Bridgend	d							19 42													20 42	
Llantwit Major	d							19 56													20 56	
Rhoose Cardiff Int Airport ✈	d							20 06													21 06	
Barry Island	d			19 55												20 55						
Barry 3	d			20 00				20 15								21 00					21 15	
Barry Docks	d			20 04				20 19								21 04					21 19	
Cadoxton	d			20 07				20 22								21 07					21 22	
Dinas Powys	d			20 11				20 26								21 11					21 26	
Eastbrook	d			20 13				20 28								21 13					21 28	
Cogan	d			20 15				20 30								21 15					21 30	
Penarth	d				20 20							20 47								21 20		
Dingle Road	d				20 22							20 49								21 22		
Grangetown	d			20 19	20 26			20 34				20 53				21 19				21 26	21 34	
Cardiff Central 7	a			20 24	20 31			20 39				20 59				21 24				21 37	21 39	
	d			20 26	20 31		20 36	20 41		20 51		21 01		21 06		21 26		21 31	21 36		21 41	
Cardiff Bay	d	20 06	20 18			20 30			20 42		20 54		21 06		21 18		21 30					21 42
Cardiff Queen Street 3	a	20 10	20 22	20 29	20 34	20 34		20 44	20 46	20 54	20 58	21 04	21 10	21 09	21 22	21 29	21 34	21 34			21 44	21 46
	d			20 30	20 35			20 45		20 55		21 05		21 10		21 30		21 35			21 45	
Heath Low Level	d									21 00												
Ty Glas	d									21 03												
Birchgrove	d									21 04												
Rhiwbina	d									21 06												
Whitchurch (Cardiff)	d									21 08												
Coryton	a									21 13												
Heath High Level	d				20 40							21 10						21 40				
Llanishen	d				20 43							21 13						21 43				
Lisvane & Thornhill	d				20 45							21 15						21 45				
Caerphilly 3	d				20 51							21 20						21 51				
Aber	d				20 53							21 22						21 53				
Llanbradach	d				20 57							21 26						21 57				
Ystrad Mynach 3	d				21 02							21a36						22 02				
Hengoed	d				21 05													22 05				
Pengam	d				21 08													22 08				
Gilfach Fargoed	d				21 11													22 11				
Bargoed	a				21 15													22 15				
	d				21 16													22 16				
Brithdir	d				21 20													22 20				
Tir-phil	d				21 23													22 23				
Pontlottyn	d				21 27													22 27				
Rhymney 3	a				21 34													22 34				
Cathays	d			20 33				20 48						21 13		21 33					21 48	
Llandaf	d			20 37				20 52						21 17		21 37					21 52	
Ninian Park	d						20 40												21 40			
Waun-gron Park	d						20 43												21 43			
Fairwater	d						20 45												21 45			
Danescourt	d						20 47												21 47			
Radyr 3	a			20 40			20 54	20 55						21 20		21 40			21 54		21 55	
	d			20 40				20 55						21 20		21 40					21 55	
Taffs Well 3	d			20 44				20 59						21 24		21 44					21 59	
Trefforest Estate	d			20 48												21 48						
Trefforest	d			20 52				21 06						21 31		21 52					22 06	
Pontypridd 3	a			20 55				21 09						21 34		21 55					22 09	
	d			20 57				21 11						21 36		21 57					22 11	
Abercynon	d			21 04				21 19								22 04					22 19	
Penrhiwceiber	d							21 24													22 24	
Mountain Ash	a							21 28													22 28	
	d							21 29													22 29	
Fernhill	d							21 31													22 31	
Cwmbach	d							21 35													22 35	
Aberdare 3	a							21 42													22 42	
Quakers Yard	d			21 08												22 08						
Merthyr Vale	a			21 13												22 13						
	d			21 15												22 15						
Troed Y Rhiw	d			21 19												22 19						
Pentre-bach	d			21 22												22 22						
Merthyr Tydfil	a			21 30												22 30						
Trehafod	d													21 41								
Porth	a													21 44								
	d													21 45								
Dinas Rhondda	d													21 49								
Tonypandy	d													21 51								
Llwynypia	d													21 53								
Ystrad Rhondda	a													21 56								
	d													21 59								
Ton Pentre	d													22 01								
Treorchy	d													22 04								
Ynyswen	d													22 07								
Treherbert	a													22 13								

When events are being held at the Millenium Stadium, services are subject to alteration. Please check times before travelling.

Table 130

Saturdays

Bridgend, Barry Island, Barry, Penarth and Cardiff - Coryton, Rhymney, Pontypridd, Merthyr, Aberdare and Treherbert

Network Diagram - see first Page of Table 130

		AW	AW	AW	AW	AW	AW	AW	AW	AW	AW	AW	AW	AW	AW	AW	AW	AW	AW	AW	AW	AW	AW
Bridgend	d										21 42										22 42		
Llantwit Major	d										21 56										22 56		
Rhoose Cardiff Int Airport ✈	d										22 06										23 06		
Barry Island	d							21 55											22 44				
Barry 3	d							22 00			22 15								22 49		23 15		
Barry Docks	d							22 04			22 19								22 53		23 19		
Cadoxton	d							22 07			22 22								22 56		23 22		
Dinas Powys	d							22 11			22 26								23 00		23 26		
Eastbrook	d							22 13			22 28								23 02		23 28		
Cogan	d							22 15			22 30								23 04		23 30		
Penarth	d		21 47							22 20							22 47			23 26			
Dingle Road	d		21 49							22 22							22 49			23 28			
Grangetown	d		21 53					22 19		22 26	22 34						22 53		23 08	23 32	23 34		
Cardiff Central 7	a		21 59					22 24		22 33	22 39						23 00		23 13	23 40	23 42		
	d		22 01		22 06		22 21	22 26		22 35	22 41		22 46		22 55		23 15		23 26				
Cardiff Bay	d	21 54		22 06		22 18			22 30			22 42		22 54		23 06		23 18				23 30	23 42
Cardiff Queen Street 3	a	21 58	22 04	22 10	22 09	22 22	22 24	22 29	22 34	22 38	22 44	22 46	22 49	22 58		23 10	23 18	23 22	23 29			23 34	23 46
	d		22 05		22 10		22 25	22 30		22 39	22 45		22 50				23 19		23 30				
Heath Low Level	d						22 30																
Ty Glas	d						22 33																
Birchgrove	d						22 34																
Rhiwbina	d						22 36																
Whitchurch (Cardiff)	d						22 38																
Coryton	a						22 43																
Heath High Level	d		22 10							22 44							23 24						
Llanishen	d		22 13							22 47							23 27						
Lisvane & Thornhill	d		22 15							22 49							23 29						
Caerphilly 3	d		22a23							22 55							23 35						
Aber	d									22 57							23 37						
Llanbradach	d									23 01							23 41						
Ystrad Mynach 3	d									23 06							23a50						
Hengoed	d									23 09													
Pengam	d									23 12													
Gilfach Fargoed	d									23 15													
Bargoed	a									23 19													
	d									23 20													
Brithdir	d									23 24													
Tir-phil	d									23 27													
Pontlottyn	d									23 31													
Rhymney 3	a									23 37													
Cathays	d				22 13			22 33			22 48		22 53						23 33				
Llandaf	d				22 17			22 37			22 52		22 57						23 37				
Ninian Park	d														22 59								
Waun-gron Park	d														23 02								
Fairwater	d														23 04								
Danescourt	d														23 06								
Radyr 3	a				22 20			22 40			22 55		22 59		23 14				23 40				
	d				22 20			22 40			22 55		22 59						23 40				
Taffs Well 3	d				22 24			22 44			22 59		23 03						23 44				
Trefforest Estate	d							22 48															
Trefforest	d				22 31			22 52			23 06		23 10						23 52				
Pontypridd 3	a				22 34			22 55			23 09		23 14						23 58				
	d				22 36			22 57			23 11		23 15										
Abercynon	d							23 04			23 19												
Penrhiwceiber	d										23 24												
Mountain Ash	a										23 28												
	d										23 29												
Fernhill	d										23 31												
Cwmbach	d										23 35												
Aberdare 3	a										23 42												
Quakers Yard	d							23 08															
Merthyr Vale	a							23 13															
	d							23 15															
Troed Y Rhiw	d							23 19															
Pentre-bach	d							23 22															
Merthyr Tydfil	a							23 30															
Trehafod	d				22 41								23 20										
Porth	a				22 44								23 23										
	d				22 45								23 24										
Dinas Rhondda	d				22 49								23 28										
Tonypandy	d				22 51								23 30										
Llwynypia	d				22 53								23 32										
Ystrad Rhondda	a				22 56								23 35										
	d				22 59								23 38										
Ton Pentre	d				23 01								23 40										
Treorchy	d				23 04								23 43										
Ynyswen	d				23 07								23 46										
Treherbert	a				23 13								23 52										

When events are being held at the Millenium Stadium, services are subject to alteration. Please check times before travelling.

Table 130

Saturdays

Bridgend, Barry Island, Barry, Penarth and Cardiff - Coryton, Rhymney, Pontypridd, Merthyr, Aberdare and Treherbert

Network Diagram - see first Page of Table 130

		AW
Bridgend	d	
Llantwit Major	d	
Rhoose Cardiff Int Airport ✈	d	
Barry Island	d	
Barry [3]	d	
Barry Docks	d	
Cadoxton	d	
Dinas Powys	d	
Eastbrook	d	
Cogan	d	
Penarth	d	
Dingle Road	d	
Grangetown	d	
Cardiff Central [7]	a	
	d	
Cardiff Bay	d	23 54
Cardiff Queen Street [3]	a	23 58
	d	
Heath Low Level	d	
Ty Glas	d	
Birchgrove	d	
Rhiwbina	d	
Whitchurch (Cardiff)	d	
Coryton	a	
Heath High Level	d	
Llanishen	d	
Lisvane & Thornhill	d	
Caerphilly [3]	d	
Aber	d	
Llanbradach	d	
Ystrad Mynach [3]	d	
Hengoed	d	
Pengam	d	
Gilfach Fargoed	d	
Bargoed	a	
	d	
Brithdir	d	
Tir-phil	d	
Pontlottyn	d	
Rhymney [3]	a	
Cathays	d	
Llandaf	d	
Ninian Park	d	
Waun-gron Park	d	
Fairwater	d	
Danescourt	d	
Radyr [3]	a	
	d	
Taffs Well [3]	d	
Trefforest Estate	d	
Trefforest	d	
Pontypridd [3]	a	
	d	
Abercynon	d	
Penrhiwceiber	d	
Mountain Ash	a	
	d	
Fernhill	d	
Cwmbach	d	
Aberdare [3]	a	
Quakers Yard	d	
Merthyr Vale	a	
	d	
Troed Y Rhiw	d	
Pentre-bach	d	
Merthyr Tydfil	a	
Trehafod	d	
Porth	a	
	d	
Dinas Rhondda	d	
Tonypandy	d	
Llwynypia	d	
Ystrad Rhondda	a	
	d	
Ton Pentre	d	
Treorchy	d	
Ynyswen	d	
Treherbert	a	

When events are being held at the Millenium Stadium, services are subject to alteration. Please check times before travelling.

Table 130

Sundays
until 1 January

Bridgend, Barry Island, Barry, Penarth and Cardiff - Coryton, Rhymney, Pontypridd, Merthyr, Aberdare and Treherbert

Network Diagram - see first Page of Table 130

		AW	AW	AW	AW	AW	AW	AW	AW	AW	AW	AW	AW	AW	AW	AW	AW	AW	AW	AW	AW	AW	AW
Bridgend	d															09 42							
Llantwit Major	d															09 56							
Rhoose Cardiff Int Airport ✈	d															10 06							
Barry Island	d								08 55						09 55								
Barry 3	d								09 00						10 00	10 15							
Barry Docks	d								09 04						10 04	10 19							
Cadoxton	d								09 07						10 07	10 22							
Dinas Powys	d								09 11						10 11	10 26							
Eastbrook	d								09 13						10 13	10 28							
Cogan	d								09 15						10 15	10 30							
Penarth	d																		10 47				
Dingle Road	d																		10 49				
Grangetown	d								09 19						10 19	10 34			10 53				
Cardiff Central 7	a								09 24						10 24	10 42			10 59				
	d	08 26	08 41	08 54	09 00				09 41				10 06		10 26						11 00		
Cardiff Bay	d					09 06	09 18	09 30		09 42	09 54	10 06		10 18			10 30	10 42		10 54		11 06	11 18
Cardiff Queen Street 3	a	08 29	08 44	08 57	09 03	09 10	09 22	09 34	09 44	09 46	09 58	10 10	10 09	10 22	10 29		10 34	10 46		10 58	11 03	11 10	11 22
	d	08 30	08 45		09 04				09 45				10 10		10 30						11 04		
Heath Low Level	d																						
Ty Glas	d																						
Birchgrove	d																						
Rhiwbina	d																						
Whitchurch (Cardiff)	d																						
Coryton	a																						
Heath High Level	d												10 15										
Llanishen	d												10 18										
Lisvane & Thornhill	d												10 20										
Caerphilly 3	d												10 26										
Aber	d												10 28										
Llanbradach	d												10 32										
Ystrad Mynach 3	d												10 37										
Hengoed	d												10 40										
Pengam	d												10 43										
Gilfach Fargoed	d												10 46										
Bargoed	a												10 49										
	d												10 49										
Brithdir	d												10 53										
Tir-phil	d												10 56										
Pontlottyn	d												11 00										
Rhymney 3	a												11 07										
Cathays	d	08 33	08 48		09 07				09 48						10 33						11 07		
Llandaf	d	08 37	08 52		09 11				09 52						10 37						11 11		
Ninian Park	d																						
Waun-gron Park	d																						
Fairwater	d																						
Danescourt	d																						
Radyr 3	a	08 40	08 55		09 14				09 55						10 40						11 14		
	d	08 40	08 55		09 14				09 55						10 40						11 14		
Taffs Well 3	d	08 44	08 59		09 18				09 59						10 44						11 18		
Trefforest Estate	d																						
Trefforest	d	08 52	09 06		09 25				10 06						10 52						11 25		
Pontypridd 3	a	08 55	09 09		09 28				10 09						10 55						11 28		
	d	08 57	09 11		09 30				10 11						10 57						11 30		
Abercynon	d	09 05	09 19						10 19						11 05								
Penrhiwceiber	d		09 24						10 24														
Mountain Ash	a		09 28						10 28														
	d		09 29						10 29														
Fernhill	d		09 31						10 31														
Cwmbach	d		09 35						10 35														
Aberdare 3	a		09 42						10 42														
Quakers Yard	d	09 09													11 09								
Merthyr Vale	a	09 14													11 14								
	d	09 16													11 16								
Troed Y Rhiw	d	09 20													11 20								
Pentre-bach	d	09 23													11 23								
Merthyr Tydfil	a	09 31													11 31								
Trehafod	d				09 35																11 35		
Porth	a				09 38																11 38		
	d				09 39																11 39		
Dinas Rhondda	d				09 43																11 43		
Tonypandy	d				09 45																11 45		
Llwynypia	d				09 47																11 47		
Ystrad Rhondda	a				09 50																11 50		
	d				09 53																11 53		
Ton Pentre	d				09 55																11 55		
Treorchy	d				09 58																11 58		
Ynyswen	d				10 01																12 01		
Treherbert	a				10 07																12 07		

When events are being held at the Millenium Stadium,
services are subject to alteration. Please check times before travelling.

Table 130

Sundays
until 1 January

Bridgend, Barry Island, Barry, Penarth and Cardiff - Coryton, Rhymney, Pontypridd, Merthyr, Aberdare and Treherbert

Network Diagram - see first Page of Table 130

		AW	AW	AW	AW	AW	AW	AW	AW	AW	AW	AW	AW	AW	AW	AW	AW	AW	AW	AW	AW	AW	AW
Bridgend	d									11 42													
Llantwit Major	d									11 56													
Rhoose Cardiff Int Airport ✈	d									12 06													
Barry Island	d		10 55			11 25			11 55										12 55			13 25	
Barry 3	d		11 00			11 30			12 00	12 15									13 00			13 30	
Barry Docks	d		11 04			11 34			12 04	12 19									13 04			13 34	
Cadoxton	d		11 07			11 37			12 07	12 22									13 07			13 37	
Dinas Powys	d		11 11			11 41			12 11	12 26									13 11			13 41	
Eastbrook	d		11 13			11 43			12 13	12 28									13 13			13 43	
Cogan	d		11 15			11 45			12 15	12 30									13 15			13 45	
Penarth	d												12 47										
Dingle Road	d												12 49										
Grangetown	d		11 19			11 49			12 19	12 34			12 53						13 19			13 49	
Cardiff Central 7	a		11 24			11 54			12 24	12 42			12 59						13 24			13 54	
	d		11 41			12 06			12 26							13 06			13 41			14 06	
Cardiff Bay	d	11 30		11 42	11 54		12 06	12 18			12 30	12 42		12 54	13 06		13 18	13 30		13 42	13 54		14 06
Cardiff Queen Street 3	a	11 34	11 44	11 46	11 58	12 09	12 10	12 22	12 29		12 34	12 46		12 58	13 10	13 09	13 22	13 34	13 44	13 46	13 58	14 09	14 10
	d		11 45			12 10			12 30							13 10			13 45			14 10	
Heath Low Level	d																						
Ty Glas	d																						
Birchgrove	d																						
Rhiwbina	d																						
Whitchurch (Cardiff)	d																						
Coryton	a																						
Heath High Level	d					12 15																14 15	
Llanishen	d					12 18																14 18	
Lisvane & Thornhill	d					12 20																14 20	
Caerphilly 3	d					12 26																14 26	
Aber	d					12 28																14 28	
Llanbradach	d					12 32																14 32	
Ystrad Mynach 3	d					12 37																14 37	
Hengoed	d					12 40																14 40	
Pengam	d					12 43																14 43	
Gilfach Fargoed	d					12 46																14 46	
Bargoed	a					12 49																14 49	
	d					12 49																14 49	
Brithdir	d					12 53																14 53	
Tir-phil	d					12 56																14 56	
Pontlottyn	d					13 00																15 00	
Rhymney 3	a					13 07																15 07	
Cathays	d		11 48						12 33							13 13			13 48				
Llandaf	d		11 52						12 37							13 17			13 52				
Ninian Park	d																						
Waun-gron Park	d																						
Fairwater	d																						
Danescourt	d																						
Radyr 3	a		11 55						12 40							13 20			13 55				
	d		11 55						12 40							13 20			13 55				
Taffs Well 3	d		11 59						12 44							13 24			13 59				
Trefforest Estate	d																						
Trefforest	d		12 06						12 52							13 31			14 06				
Pontypridd 3	a		12 09						12 55							13 34			14 09				
	d		12 11						12 57							13 36			14 11				
Abercynon	d		12 19						13 05										14 19				
Penrhiwceiber	d		12 24																14 24				
Mountain Ash	a		12 28																14 28				
	d		12 29																14 29				
Fernhill	d		12 31																14 31				
Cwmbach	d		12 35																14 35				
Aberdare 3	a		12 42																14 42				
Quakers Yard	d								13 09														
Merthyr Vale	a								13 14														
	d								13 16														
Troed Y Rhiw	d								13 20														
Pentre-bach	d								13 23														
Merthyr Tydfil	a								13 31														
Trehafod	d															13 41							
Porth	a															13 44							
	d															13 45							
Dinas Rhondda	d															13 49							
Tonypandy	d															13 51							
Llwynypia	d															13 53							
Ystrad Rhondda	a															13 56							
	d															13 59							
Ton Pentre	d															14 01							
Treorchy	d															14 04							
Ynyswen	d															14 07							
Treherbert	a															14 13							

When events are being held at the Millenium Stadium, services are subject to alteration. Please check times before travelling.

Table 130

Sundays

until 1 January

Bridgend, Barry Island, Barry, Penarth and Cardiff - Coryton, Rhymney, Pontypridd, Merthyr, Aberdare and Treherbert

Network Diagram - see first Page of Table 130

		AW		AW	AW	AW	AW	AW	AW	AW	AW	AW		AW	AW	AW	AW	AW	AW	AW	AW	AW		AW	AW
Bridgend	d				13 42																	15 42			
Llantwit Major	d				13 56																	15 56			
Rhoose Cardiff Int Airport ✈	d				14 06																	16 06			
Barry Island	d			13 55											14 55			15 25			15 55				
Barry 3	d			14 00	14 15										15 00			15 30			16 00	16 15			
Barry Docks	d			14 04	14 19										15 04			15 34			16 04	16 19			
Cadoxton	d			14 07	14 22										15 07			15 37			16 07	16 22			
Dinas Powys	d			14 11	14 26										15 11			15 41			16 11	16 26			
Eastbrook	d			14 13	14 28										15 13			15 43			16 13	16 28			
Cogan	d			14 15	14 30										15 15			15 45			16 15	16 30			
Penarth	d							14 47																	
Dingle Road	d							14 49																	
Grangetown	d			14 19	14 34			14 53							15 19			15 49			16 19	16 34			
Cardiff Central 7	a			14 24	14 42			14 59							15 24			15 54			16 24	16 42			
	d			14 26							15 06				15 41			16 06			16 26				
Cardiff Bay	d	14 18				14 30	14 42		14 54	15 06		15 18		15 30		15 42	15 54		16 06	16 18				16 30	16 42
Cardiff Queen Street 3	a	14 22		14 29		14 34	14 46		14 58	15 10	15 09	15 22		15 34	15 44	15 46	15 58	16 09	16 10	16 22	16 29			16 34	16 46
	d			14 30							15 10				15 45			16 10			16 30				
Heath Low Level	d																								
Ty Glas	d																								
Birchgrove	d																								
Rhiwbina	d																								
Whitchurch (Cardiff)	d																								
Coryton	a																								
Heath High Level	d																	16 15							
Llanishen	d																	16 18							
Lisvane & Thornhill	d																	16 20							
Caerphilly 3	d																	16 26							
Aber	d																	16 28							
Llanbradach	d																	16 32							
Ystrad Mynach 3	d																	16 37							
Hengoed	d																	16 40							
Pengam	d																	16 43							
Gilfach Fargoed	d																	16 46							
Bargoed	a																	16 49							
	d																	16 49							
Brithdir	d																	16 53							
Tir-phil	d																	16 56							
Pontlottyn	d																	17 00							
Rhymney 3	a																	17 07							
Cathays	d			14 33							15 13				15 48						16 33				
Llandaf	d			14 37							15 17				15 52						16 37				
Ninian Park	d																								
Waun-gron Park	d																								
Fairwater	d																								
Danescourt	d																								
Radyr 3	a			14 40							15 20				15 55						16 40				
	d			14 40							15 20				15 55						16 40				
Taffs Well 3	d			14 44							15 24				15 59						16 44				
Trefforest Estate	d																								
Trefforest	d			14 52							15 31				16 06						16 52				
Pontypridd 3	a			14 55							15 34				16 09						16 55				
	d			14 57							15 36				16 11						16 57				
Abercynon	d			15 05											16 19						17 05				
Penrhiwceiber	d														16 24										
Mountain Ash	a														16 28										
	d														16 29										
Fernhill	d														16 31										
Cwmbach	d														16 35										
Aberdare 3	a														16 42										
Quakers Yard	d			15 09																	17 09				
Merthyr Vale	a			15 14																	17 14				
	d			15 16																	17 16				
Troed Y Rhiw	d			15 20																	17 20				
Pentre-bach	d			15 23																	17 23				
Merthyr Tydfil	a			15 31																	17 31				
Trehafod	d										15 41														
Porth	a										15 44														
	d										15 45														
Dinas Rhondda	d										15 49														
Tonypandy	d										15 51														
Llwynypia	d										15 53														
Ystrad Rhondda	a										15 56														
	d										15 59														
Ton Pentre	d										16 01														
Treorchy	d										16 04														
Ynyswen	d										16 07														
Treherbert	a										16 13														

When events are being held at the Millenium Stadium, services are subject to alteration. Please check times before travelling.

Table 130

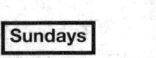

Sundays
until 1 January

Bridgend, Barry Island, Barry, Penarth and Cardiff - Coryton, Rhymney, Pontypridd, Merthyr, Aberdare and Treherbert

Network Diagram - see first Page of Table 130

		AW	AW	AW	AW	AW	AW	AW	AW	AW	AW	AW	AW	AW	AW	AW	AW	AW	AW	AW	AW	AW	AW
Bridgend	d														17 42								
Llantwit Major	d														17 56								
Rhoose Cardiff Int Airport ✈	d														18 06								
Barry Island	d							16 55			17 25			17 55							18 55	19 25	19 55
Barry 3	d							17 00			17 30			18 00	18 15						19 00	19 30	20 00
Barry Docks	d							17 04			17 34			18 04	18 19						19 04	19 34	20 04
Cadoxton	d							17 07			17 37			18 07	18 22						19 07	19 37	20 07
Dinas Powys	d							17 11			17 41			18 11	18 26						19 11	19 41	20 11
Eastbrook	d							17 13			17 43			18 13	18 28						19 13	19 43	20 13
Cogan	d							17 15			17 45			18 15	18 30						19 15	19 45	20 15
Penarth	d	16 47																18 47					
Dingle Road	d	16 49																18 49					
Grangetown	d	16 53						17 19			17 49			18 19	18 34			18 53			19 19	19 49	20 19
Cardiff Central 7	a	16 59						17 24			17 54			18 24	18 42			19 00			19 24	19 54	20 24
	d				17 06			17 41			18 06			18 26						19 06	19 41	20 06	20 26
Cardiff Bay	d		16 54	17 06		17 18	17 30		17 42	17 54		18 06	18 18			18 30	18 42		18 54				
Cardiff Queen Street 3	a		16 58	17 10	17 09	17 22	17 34	17 44	17 46	17 58	18 09	18 10	18 22	18 29		18 34	18 46		18 57	19 09	19 44	20 09	20 29
	d				17 10			17 45			18 10			18 30						19 10	19 45	20 10	20 30
Heath Low Level	d																						
Ty Glas	d																						
Birchgrove	d																						
Rhiwbina	d																						
Whitchurch (Cardiff)	d																						
Coryton	a																						
Heath High Level	d										18 15											20 15	
Llanishen	d										18 18											20 18	
Lisvane & Thornhill	d										18 20											20 20	
Caerphilly 3	d										18 26											20 26	
Aber	d										18 28											20 28	
Llanbradach	d										18 32											20 32	
Ystrad Mynach 3	d										18 37											20 37	
Hengoed	d										18 40											20 40	
Pengam	d										18 43											20 43	
Gilfach Fargoed	d										18 46											20 46	
Bargoed	a										18 49											20 49	
	d										18 49											20 49	
Brithdir	d										18 53											20 53	
Tir-phil	d										18 56											20 56	
Pontlottyn	d										19 00											21 00	
Rhymney 3	a										19 07											21 07	
Cathays	d				17 13			17 48						18 33						19 13	19 48		20 33
Llandaf	d				17 17			17 52						18 37						19 17	19 52		20 37
Ninian Park	d																						
Waun-gron Park	d																						
Fairwater	d																						
Danescourt	d																						
Radyr 3	a				17 20			17 55						18 40						19 20	19 55		20 40
	d				17 20			17 55						18 40						19 20	19 55		20 40
Taffs Well 3	d				17 24			17 59						18 44						19 24	19 59		20 44
Trefforest Estate	d																						
Trefforest	d				17 31			18 06						18 52						19 31	20 06		20 52
Pontypridd 3	a				17 34			18 09						18 55						19 34	20 09		20 55
	d				17 36			18 11						18 57						19 36	20 11		20 57
Abercynon	d							18 19						19 05							20 19		21 05
Penrhiwceiber	d							18 24													20 24		
Mountain Ash	a							18 28													20 28		
	d							18 29													20 29		
Fernhill	d							18 31													20 31		
Cwmbach	d							18 35													20 35		
Aberdare 3	a							18 42													20 42		
Quakers Yard	d													19 09									21 09
Merthyr Vale	a													19 14									21 14
	d													19 16									21 16
Troed Y Rhiw	d													19 20									21 20
Pentre-bach	d													19 23									21 23
Merthyr Tydfil	a													19 31									21 31
Trehafod	d				17 41															19 41			
Porth	a				17 44															19 44			
	d				17 45															19 45			
Dinas Rhondda	d				17 49															19 49			
Tonypandy	d				17 51															19 51			
Llwynypia	d				17 53															19 53			
Ystrad Rhondda	a				17 56															19 56			
	d				17 59															19 59			
Ton Pentre	d				18 01															20 01			
Treorchy	d				18 04															20 04			
Ynyswen	d				18 07															20 07			
Treherbert	a				18 13															20 13			

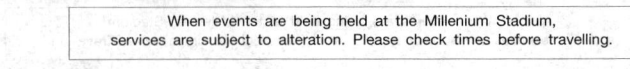

When events are being held at the Millenium Stadium,
services are subject to alteration. Please check times before travelling.

Table 130

Sundays
until 1 January

Bridgend, Barry Island, Barry, Penarth and Cardiff - Coryton, Rhymney, Pontypridd, Merthyr, Aberdare and Treherbert

Network Diagram - see first Page of Table 130

		AW	AW	AW		AW	AW	AW	AW	AW	AW
Bridgend	d	19 42								21 42	
Llantwit Major	d	19 56								21 56	
Rhoose Cardiff Int Airport ✈	d	20 06								22 06	
Barry Island	d		20 25				20 55	21 25	21 55		22 55
Barry 3	d	20 15	20 30				21 00	21 30	22 00	22 15	23 00
Barry Docks	d	20 19	20 34				21 04	21 34	22 04	22 19	23 04
Cadoxton	d	20 22	20 37				21 07	21 37	22 07	22 22	23 07
Dinas Powys	d	20 26	20 41				21 11	21 41	22 11	22 26	23 11
Eastbrook	d	20 28	20 43				21 13	21 43	22 13	22 28	23 13
Cogan	d	20 30	20 45				21 15	21 45	22 15	22 30	23 15
Penarth	d			20 47							
Dingle Road	d			20 49							
Grangetown	d	20 34	20 49	20 53			21 19	21 49	22 19	22 34	23 19
Cardiff Central 7	a	20 42	20 54	21 00			21 26	21 54	22 26	22 42	23 26
	d		21 06			21 16		22 06			
Cardiff Bay	d										
Cardiff Queen Street 3	a		21 09			21 19		22 09			
	d		21 10			21 20		22 10			
Heath Low Level	d										
Ty Glas	d										
Birchgrove	d										
Rhiwbina	d										
Whitchurch (Cardiff)	d										
Coryton	a										
Heath High Level	d					21 25					
Llanishen	d					21 28					
Lisvane & Thornhill	d					21 30					
Caerphilly 3	d					21 36					
Aber	d					21 38					
Llanbradach	d					21 42					
Ystrad Mynach 3	d					21 47					
Hengoed	d					21 50					
Pengam	d					21 53					
Gilfach Fargoed	d					21 56					
Bargoed	a					21 59					
	d					21 59					
Brithdir	d					22 03					
Tir-phil	d					22 06					
Pontlottyn	d					22 10					
Rhymney 3	a					22 17					
Cathays	d		21 13					22 13			
Llandaf	d		21 17					22 17			
Ninian Park	d										
Waun-gron Park	d										
Fairwater	d										
Danescourt	d										
Radyr 3	a		21 20					22 20			
	d		21 20					22 20			
Taffs Well 3	d		21 24					22 24			
Trefforest Estate	d										
Treforest	d		21 31					22 31			
Pontypridd 3	a		21 34					22 34			
	d		21 36					22 36			
Abercynon	d										
Penrhiwceiber	d										
Mountain Ash	a										
	d										
Fernhill	d										
Cwmbach	d										
Aberdare 3	a										
Quakers Yard	d										
Merthyr Vale	a										
	d										
Troed Y Rhiw	d										
Pentre-bach	d										
Merthyr Tydfil	a										
Trehafod	d		21 41					22 41			
Porth	a		21 44					22 44			
	d		21 45					22 45			
Dinas Rhondda	d		21 49					22 49			
Tonypandy	d		21 51					22 51			
Llwynypia	d		21 53					22 53			
Ystrad Rhondda	a		21 56					22 56			
	d		21 59					22 59			
Ton Pentre	d		22 01					23 01			
Treorchy	d		22 04					23 04			
Ynyswen	d		22 07					23 07			
Treherbert	a		22 13					23 13			

When events are being held at the Millenium Stadium, services are subject to alteration. Please check times before travelling.

Table 130

Sundays

8 January to 25 March

Bridgend, Barry Island, Barry, Penarth and Cardiff - Coryton, Rhymney, Pontypridd, Merthyr, Aberdare and Treherbert

Network Diagram - see first Page of Table 130

		AW	AW	AW	AW	AW (bus)	AW	AW	AW	AW	AW	AW	AW	AW	AW (bus)	AW	AW	AW	AW	AW	AW	AW (bus)	AW (bus)
Bridgend	d																					09 30	
Llantwit Major	d																					09 55	
Rhoose Cardiff Int Airport ✈	d																					10 10	
Barry Island	d					08 30									09 30								10 30
Barry 3	d					08 35									09 35							10 25	10 35
Barry Docks	d					08 40									09 40							10 30	10 40
Cadoxton	d					08 45									09 45							10 35	10 45
Dinas Powys	d					08 55									09 55							10 45	10 55
Eastbrook	d					09 00									10 00							10 50	11 00
Cogan	d					09 05									10 05							10 55	11 05
Penarth	d																						
Dingle Road	d																						
Grangetown	d					09 10									10 10							11 00	11 10
Cardiff Central 7	a					09 15									10 15							11 05	11 15
	d	08 26	08 41	08 54	09 00					09 41				10 06			10 26				11 00		
Cardiff Bay	d						09 06	09 18	09 30		09 42	09 54	10 06			10 18		10 30	10 42	10 54			
Cardiff Queen Street 3	a	08 29	08 44	08 57	09 03		09 10	09 22	09 34	09 44	09 46	09 58	10 10	10 09		10 22	10 29	10 34	10 46	10 58	11 03		
	d	08 30	08 45		09 04					09 45				10 10			10 30				11 04		
Heath Low Level	d																						
Ty Glas	d																						
Birchgrove	d																						
Rhiwbina	d																						
Whitchurch (Cardiff)	d																						
Coryton	a																						
Heath High Level	d													10 15									
Llanishen	d													10 18									
Lisvane & Thornhill	d													10 20									
Caerphilly 3	d													10 26									
Aber	d													10 28									
Llanbradach	d													10 32									
Ystrad Mynach 3	d													10 37									
Hengoed	d													10 40									
Pengam	d													10 43									
Gilfach Fargoed	d													10 46									
Bargoed	a													10 49									
	d													10 49									
Brithdir	d													10 53									
Tir-phil	d													10 56									
Pontlottyn	d													11 00									
Rhymney 3	a													11 07									
Cathays	d	08 33	08 48		09 07					09 48							10 33				11 07		
Llandaf	d	08 37	08 52		09 11					09 52							10 37				11 11		
Ninian Park	d																						
Waun-gron Park	d																						
Fairwater	d																						
Danescourt	d																						
Radyr 3	a	08 40	08 55		09 14					09 55							10 40				11 14		
	d	08 40	08 55		09 14					09 55							10 40				11 14		
Taffs Well 3	d	08 44	08 59		09 18					09 59							10 44				11 18		
Treforest Estate	d																						
Treforest	d	08 52	09 06		09 25					10 06							10 52				11 25		
Pontypridd 3	a	08 55	09 09		09 28					10 09							10 55				11 28		
	d	08 57	09 11		09 30					10 11							10 57				11 30		
Abercynon	d	09 05	09 19							10 19							11 05						
Penrhiwceiber	d		09 24							10 24													
Mountain Ash	a		09 28							10 28													
	d		09 29							10 29													
Fernhill	d		09 31							10 31													
Cwmbach	d		09 35							10 35													
Aberdare 3	a		09 42							10 42													
Quakers Yard	d	09 09															11 09						
Merthyr Vale	a	09 14															11 14						
	d	09 16															11 16						
Troed Y Rhiw	d	09 20															11 20						
Pentre-bach	d	09 23															11 23						
Merthyr Tydfil	a	09 31															11 31						
Trehafod	d				09 35																11 35		
Porth	a				09 38																11 38		
	d				09 39																11 39		
Dinas Rhondda	d				09 43																11 43		
Tonypandy	d				09 45																11 45		
Llwynypia	d				09 47																11 47		
Ystrad Rhondda	a				09 50																11 50		
	d				09 53																11 53		
Ton Pentre	d				09 55																11 55		
Treorchy	d				09 58																11 58		
Ynyswen	d				10 01																12 01		
Treherbert	a				10 07																12 07		

When events are being held at the Millenium Stadium, services are subject to alteration. Please check times before travelling.

Table 130

Sundays

8 January to 25 March

Bridgend, Barry Island, Barry, Penarth and Cardiff - Coryton, Rhymney, Pontypridd, Merthyr, Aberdare and Treherbert

Network Diagram - see first Page of Table 130

		AW 🚌	AW	AW	AW	AW		AW 🚌	AW	AW	AW	AW	AW 🚌	AW	AW	AW		AW	AW	AW	AW	AW	AW 🚌	AW	AW
Bridgend	d							10 30																	
Llantwit Major	d							10 55																	
Rhoose Cardiff Int Airport ✈	d							11 10																	
Barry Island	d												11 30										12 30		
Barry ■	d							11 25					11 35										12 35		
Barry Docks	d							11 30					11 40										12 40		
Cadoxton	d							11 35					11 45										12 45		
Dinas Powys	d							11 45					11 55										12 55		
Eastbrook	d							11 50					12 00										13 00		
Cogan	d							11 55					12 05										13 05		
Penarth	d	11 00																	12 47						
Dingle Road	d	11 05																	12 49						
Grangetown	d	11 15						12 00					12 10						12 53				13 10		
Cardiff Central ■	a	11 20						12 05					12 15						12 59				13 15		
	d					11 41						12 06			12 26							13 06			
Cardiff Bay	d		11 06	11 18	11 30				11 42	11 54	12 06			12 18		12 30		12 42		12 54	13 06			13 18	13 30
Cardiff Queen Street ■	a		11 10	11 22	11 34	11 44			11 46	11 58	12 10	12 09		12 22	12 29	12 34		12 46		12 58	13 10	13 09		13 22	13 34
	d					11 45						12 10			12 30							13 10			
Heath Low Level	d																								
Ty Glas	d																								
Birchgrove	d																								
Rhiwbina	d																								
Whitchurch (Cardiff)	d																								
Coryton	a																								
Heath High Level	d											12 15													
Llanishen	d											12 18													
Lisvane & Thornhill	d											12 20													
Caerphilly ■	d											12 26													
Aber	d											12 28													
Llanbradach	d											12 32													
Ystrad Mynach ■	d											12 37													
Hengoed	d											12 40													
Pengam	d											12 43													
Gilfach Fargoed	d											12 46													
Bargoed	a											12 49													
	d											12 49													
Brithdir	d											12 53													
Tir-phil	d											12 56													
Pontlottyn	d											13 00													
Rhymney ■	a											13 07													
Cathays	d					11 48									12 33							13 13			
Llandaf	d					11 52									12 37							13 17			
Ninian Park	d																								
Waun-gron Park	d																								
Fairwater	d																								
Danescourt	d																								
Radyr ■	a					11 55									12 40							13 20			
	d					11 55									12 40							13 20			
Taffs Well ■	d					11 59									12 44							13 24			
Trefforest Estate	d																								
Treforest	d					12 06									12 52							13 31			
Pontypridd ■	a					12 09									12 55							13 34			
	d					12 11									12 57							13 36			
Abercynon	d					12 19									13 05										
Penrhiwceiber	d					12 24																			
Mountain Ash	a					12 28																			
	d					12 29																			
Fernhill	d					12 31																			
Cwmbach	d					12 35																			
Aberdare ■	a					12 42																			
Quakers Yard	d														13 09										
Merthyr Vale	a														13 14										
	d														13 16										
Troed Y Rhiw	d														13 20										
Pentre-bach	d														13 23										
Merthyr Tydfil	a														13 31										
Trehafod	d																					13 41			
Porth	a																					13 44			
	d																					13 45			
Dinas Rhondda	d																					13 49			
Tonypandy	d																					13 51			
Llwynypia	d																					13 53			
Ystrad Rhondda	a																					13 56			
	d																					13 59			
Ton Pentre	d																					14 01			
Treorchy	d																					14 04			
Ynyswen	d																					14 07			
Treherbert	a																					14 13			

When events are being held at the Millenium Stadium, services are subject to alteration. Please check times before travelling.

Table 130

Sundays

8 January to 25 March

Bridgend, Barry Island, Barry, Penarth and Cardiff - Coryton, Rhymney, Pontypridd, Merthyr, Aberdare and Treherbert

Network Diagram - see first Page of Table 130

		AW		AW 🚌	AW	AW	AW	AW	AW	AW	AW	AW		AW	AW	AW	AW	AW	AW	AW	AW	AW		AW	AW
Bridgend	d			12 30							13 50														
Llantwit Major	d			12 55							14 10														
Rhoose Cardiff Int Airport ✈	d			13 10							14 24														
Barry Island	d	13 04					13 25			13 55											14 55				15 25
Barry 3	d	13 09		13 25			13 30			14 00	14 33										15 00				15 30
Barry Docks	d	13 13		13 30			13 34			14 04	14 37										15 04				15 34
Cadoxton	d	13 16		13 35			13 37			14 07	14 40										15 07				15 37
Dinas Powys	d	13 20		13 45			13 41			14 11	14 44										15 11				15 41
Eastbrook	d	13 22		13 50			13 43			14 13	14 46										15 13				15 43
Cogan	d	13 24		13 55			13 45			14 15	14 48										15 15				15 45
Penarth	d														14 50										
Dingle Road	d														14 52										
Grangetown	d	13 28		14 00			13 49			14 19	14 52				14 56						15 19				15 49
Cardiff Central 7	a	13 33		14 05			13 54			14 24	15 00				15 03						15 24				15 54
	d	13 41					14 06			14 26								15 06			15 41				16 06
Cardiff Bay	d				13 42	13 54		14 06	14 18			14 30		14 42		14 54	15 06		15 18	15 30		15 42		15 54	
Cardiff Queen Street 3	a	13 44			13 46	13 58	14 09	14 10	14 22	14 29		14 34		14 46		14 58	15 10	15 09	15 22	15 34	15 44	15 46		15 58	16 09
	d	13 45					14 10			14 30								15 10			15 45				16 10
Heath Low Level	d																								
Ty Glas	d																								
Birchgrove	d																								
Rhiwbina	d																								
Whitchurch (Cardiff)	d																								
Coryton	a																								
Heath High Level	d						14 15																		16 15
Llanishen	d						14 18																		16 18
Lisvane & Thornhill	d						14 20																		16 20
Caerphilly 3	d						14 26																		16 26
Aber	d						14 28																		16 28
Llanbradach	d						14 32																		16 32
Ystrad Mynach 3	d						14 37																		16 37
Hengoed	d						14 40																		16 40
Pengam	d						14 43																		16 43
Gilfach Fargoed	d						14 46																		16 46
Bargoed	a						14 49																		16 49
	d						14 49																		16 49
Brithdir	d						14 53																		16 53
Tir-phil	d						14 56																		16 56
Pontlottyn	d						15 00																		17 00
Rhymney 3	a						15 07																		17 07
Cathays	d	13 48								14 33								15 13			15 48				
Llandaf	d	13 52								14 37								15 17			15 52				
Ninian Park	d																								
Waun-gron Park	d																								
Fairwater	d																								
Danescourt	d																								
Radyr 3	a	13 55								14 40								15 20			15 55				
	d	13 55								14 40								15 20			15 55				
Taffs Well 3	d	13 59								14 44								15 24			15 59				
Trefforest Estate	d																								
Trefforest	d	14 06								14 52								15 31			16 06				
Pontypridd 3	a	14 09								14 55								15 34			16 09				
	d	14 11								14 57								15 36			16 11				
Abercynon	d	14 19								15 05											16 19				
Penrhiwceiber	d	14 24																			16 24				
Mountain Ash	a	14 28																			16 28				
	d	14 29																			16 29				
Fernhill	d	14 31																			16 31				
Cwmbach	d	14 35																			16 35				
Aberdare 3	a	14 42																			16 42				
Quakers Yard	d									15 09															
Merthyr Vale	a									15 14															
	d									15 16															
Troed Y Rhiw	d									15 20															
Pentre-bach	d									15 23															
Merthyr Tydfil	a									15 31															
Trehafod	d																	15 41							
Porth	a																	15 44							
	d																	15 45							
Dinas Rhondda	d																	15 49							
Tonypandy	d																	15 51							
Llwynypia	d																	15 53							
Ystrad Rhondda	a																	15 56							
	d																	15 59							
Ton Pentre	d																	16 01							
Treorchy	d																	16 04							
Ynyswen	d																	16 07							
Treherbert	a																	16 13							

When events are being held at the Millenium Stadium, services are subject to alteration. Please check times before travelling.

Table 130 **Sundays**

8 January to 25 March

Bridgend, Barry Island, Barry, Penarth and Cardiff - Coryton, Rhymney, Pontypridd, Merthyr, Aberdare and Treherbert

Network Diagram - see first Page of Table 130

		AW	AW	AW	AW	AW	AW	AW	AW	AW	AW	AW	AW	AW	AW	AW	AW	AW	AW	AW	AW	AW	AW
Bridgend	d				15 42																17 42		
Llantwit Major	d				15 56																17 56		
Rhoose Cardiff Int Airport ✈	d				16 06																18 06		
Barry Island	d			15 55										16 55			17 25			17 55			
Barry 3	d			16 00	16 15									17 00			17 30			18 00	18 15		
Barry Docks	d			16 04	16 19									17 04			17 34			18 04	18 19		
Cadoxton	d			16 07	16 22									17 07			17 37			18 07	18 22		
Dinas Powys	d			16 11	16 26									17 11			17 41			18 11	18 26		
Eastbrook	d			16 13	16 28									17 13			17 43			18 13	18 28		
Cogan	d			16 15	16 30									17 15			17 45			18 15	18 30		
Penarth	d							16 47															
Dingle Road	d							16 49															
Grangetown	d			16 19	16 34			16 53						17 19			17 49			18 19	18 34		
Cardiff Central 7	a			16 24	16 42			16 59						17 24			17 54			18 24	18 42		
	d			16 26							17 06			17 41			18 06			18 26			
Cardiff Bay	d	16 06	16 18			16 30	16 42		16 54	17 06		17 18	17 30		17 42	17 54		18 06	18 18			18 30	18 42
Cardiff Queen Street 3	a	16 10	16 22	16 29		16 34	16 46		16 58	17 10	17 09	17 22	17 34	17 44	17 46	17 58	18 09	18 10	18 22	18 29		18 34	18 46
	d			16 30							17 10			17 45			18 10			18 30			
Heath Low Level	d																						
Ty Glas	d																						
Birchgrove	d																						
Rhiwbina	d																						
Whitchurch (Cardiff)	d																						
Coryton	a																						
Heath High Level	d																18 15						
Llanishen	d																18 18						
Lisvane & Thornhill	d																18 20						
Caerphilly 3	d																18 26						
Aber	d																18 28						
Llanbradach	d																18 32						
Ystrad Mynach 3	d																18 37						
Hengoed	d																18 40						
Pengam	d																18 43						
Gilfach Fargoed	d																18 46						
Bargoed	a																18 49						
	d																18 49						
Brithdir	d																18 53						
Tir-phil	d																18 56						
Pontlottyn	d																19 00						
Rhymney 3	a																19 07						
Cathays	d			16 33							17 13			17 48						18 33			
Llandaf	d			16 37							17 17			17 52						18 37			
Ninian Park	d																						
Waun-gron Park	d																						
Fairwater	d																						
Danescourt	d																						
Radyr 3	a			16 40							17 20			17 55						18 40			
	d			16 40							17 20			17 55						18 40			
Taffs Well 3	d			16 44							17 24			17 59						18 44			
Trefforest Estate	d																						
Trefforest	d			16 52							17 31			18 06						18 52			
Pontypridd 3	a			16 55							17 34			18 09						18 55			
	d			16 57							17 36			18 11						18 57			
Abercynon	d			17 05										18 19						19 05			
Penrhiwceiber	d													18 24									
Mountain Ash	a													18 28									
	d													18 29									
Fernhill	d													18 31									
Cwmbach	d													18 35									
Aberdare 3	a													18 42									
Quakers Yard	d			17 09																19 09			
Merthyr Vale	a			17 14																19 14			
	d			17 16																19 16			
Troed Y Rhiw	d			17 20																19 20			
Pentre-bach	d			17 23																19 23			
Merthyr Tydfil	a			17 31																19 31			
Trehafod	d										17 41												
Porth	a										17 44												
	d										17 45												
Dinas Rhondda	d										17 49												
Tonypandy	d										17 51												
Llwynypia	d										17 53												
Ystrad Rhondda	a										17 56												
	d										17 59												
Ton Pentre	d										18 01												
Treorchy	d										18 04												
Ynyswen	d										18 07												
Treherbert	a										18 13												

When events are being held at the Millenium Stadium,
services are subject to alteration. Please check times before travelling.

Table 130

Sundays

8 January to 25 March

Bridgend, Barry Island, Barry, Penarth and Cardiff - Coryton, Rhymney, Pontypridd, Merthyr, Aberdare and Treherbert

Network Diagram - see first Page of Table 130

Station		AW	AW	AW	AW	AW	AW	AW	AW	AW	AW	AW	AW	AW	AW	AW
Bridgend	d							19 42							21 42	
Llantwit Major	d							19 56							21 56	
Rhoose Cardiff Int Airport ✈	d							20 06							22 06	
Barry Island	d				18 55	19 25	19 55		20 25			20 55	21 25	21 55		22 55
Barry [3]	d				19 00	19 30	20 00	20 15	20 30			21 00	21 30	22 00	22 15	23 00
Barry Docks	d				19 04	19 34	20 04	20 19	20 34			21 04	21 34	22 04	22 19	23 04
Cadoxton	d				19 07	19 37	20 07	20 22	20 37			21 07	21 37	22 07	22 22	23 07
Dinas Powys	d				19 11	19 41	20 11	20 26	20 41			21 11	21 41	22 11	22 26	23 11
Eastbrook	d				19 13	19 43	20 13	20 28	20 43			21 13	21 43	22 13	22 28	23 13
Cogan	d				19 15	19 45	20 15	20 30	20 45			21 15	21 45	22 15	22 30	23 15
Penarth	d	18 47								20 47						
Dingle Road	d	18 49								20 49						
Grangetown	d	18 53			19 19	19 49	20 19	20 34	20 49	20 53		21 19	21 49	22 19	22 34	23 19
Cardiff Central [7]	a	19 00			19 24	19 54	20 24	20 42	20 54	21 00		21 26	21 54	22 26	22 42	23 26
	d			19 06	19 41	20 06	20 26		21 06		21 16		22 06			
Cardiff Bay	d		18 54													
Cardiff Queen Street [3]	a		18 57	19 09	19 44	20 09	20 29		21 09		21 19		22 09			
	d			19 10	19 45	20 10	20 30		21 10		21 20		22 10			
Heath Low Level	d															
Ty Glas	d															
Birchgrove	d															
Rhiwbina	d															
Whitchurch (Cardiff)	d															
Coryton	a															
Heath High Level	d					20 15					21 25					
Llanishen	d					20 18					21 28					
Lisvane & Thornhill	d					20 20					21 30					
Caerphilly [3]	d					20 26					21 36					
Aber	d					20 28					21 38					
Llanbradach	d					20 32					21 42					
Ystrad Mynach [3]	d					20 37					21 47					
Hengoed	d					20 40					21 50					
Pengam	d					20 43					21 53					
Gilfach Fargoed	d					20 46					21 56					
Bargoed	a					20 49					21 59					
	d					20 49					21 59					
Brithdir	d					20 53					22 03					
Tir-phil	d					20 56					22 06					
Pontlottyn	d					21 00					22 10					
Rhymney [3]	a					21 07					22 17					
Cathays	d			19 13	19 48		20 33		21 13				22 13			
Llandaf	d			19 17	19 52		20 37		21 17				22 17			
Ninian Park	d															
Waun-gron Park	d															
Fairwater	d															
Danescourt	d															
Radyr [3]	a			19 20	19 55		20 40		21 20				22 20			
	d			19 20	19 55		20 40		21 20				22 20			
Taffs Well [3]	d			19 24	19 59		20 44		21 24				22 24			
Trefforest Estate	d															
Treforest	d			19 31	20 06		20 52		21 31				22 31			
Pontypridd [3]	a			19 34	20 09		20 55		21 34				22 34			
	d			19 36	20 11		20 57		21 36				22 36			
Abercynon	d				20 19		21 05									
Penrhiwceiber	d				20 24											
Mountain Ash	a				20 28											
	d				20 29											
Fernhill	d				20 31											
Cwmbach	d				20 35											
Aberdare [3]	a				20 42											
Quakers Yard	d						21 09									
Merthyr Vale	a						21 14									
	d						21 16									
Troed Y Rhiw	d						21 20									
Pentre-bach	d						21 23									
Merthyr Tydfil	a						21 31									
Trehafod	d			19 41					21 41				22 41			
Porth	a			19 44					21 44				22 44			
	d			19 45					21 45				22 45			
Dinas Rhondda	d			19 49					21 49				22 49			
Tonypandy	d			19 51					21 51				22 51			
Llwynypia	d			19 53					21 53				22 53			
Ystrad Rhondda	a			19 56					21 56				22 56			
	d			19 59					21 59				22 59			
Ton Pentre	d			20 01					22 01				23 01			
Treorchy	d			20 04					22 04				23 04			
Ynyswen	d			20 07					22 07				23 07			
Treherbert	a			20 13					22 13				23 13			

When events are being held at the Millenium Stadium, services are subject to alteration. Please check times before travelling.

Table 130

Sundays
from 1 April

Bridgend, Barry Island, Barry, Penarth and Cardiff - Coryton, Rhymney, Pontypridd, Merthyr, Aberdare and Treherbert

Network Diagram - see first Page of Table 130

		AW 🚌	AW 🚌	AW	AW 🚌	AW	AW	AW 🚌	AW 🚌	AW	AW 🚌	AW 🚌	AW 🚌	AW 🚌	AW	AW	AW	AW 🚌	AW 🚌	AW	AW 🚌	AW	AW
Bridgend	d																	09 30			10 30		
Llantwit Major	d																	09 55			10 55		
Rhoose Cardiff Int Airport ✈	d																	10 10			11 10		
Barry Island	d								08 30				09 30		10 06					10 55		11 25	
Barry [3]	d								08 35				09 35		10 11			10 25		11 00	11 25	11 30	
Barry Docks	d								08 40				09 40		10 15			10 30		11 04	11 30	11 34	
Cadoxton	d								08 45				09 45		10 18			10 35		11 07	11 35	11 37	
Dinas Powys	d								08 55				09 55		10 22			10 45		11 11	11 45	11 41	
Eastbrook	d								09 00				10 00		10 24			10 50		11 13	11 50	11 43	
Cogan	d								09 05				10 05		10 26			10 55		11 15	11 55	11 45	
Penarth	d																10 47						
Dingle Road	d																10 49						
Grangetown	d								09 10				10 10		10 30		10 53	11 00		11 19	12 00	11 49	
Cardiff Central [7]	a								09 15				10 15		10 37		11 01	11 05		11 29	12 05	11 56	
	d	07 52	08 07	08 26	08 26	08 45	09 00	09 07		09 41	09 52	10 06		10 26		11 00			11 07	11 41			12 10
Cardiff Bay	d																						
Cardiff Queen Street [3]	a	08 00	08 15		08 34			09 15			10 00	10 14		10 34					11 15				12 13
	d	08 00	08 15		08 34			09 15			10 00	10 14		10 34					11 15				12 14
Heath Low Level	d																						
Ty Glas	d																						
Birchgrove	d																						
Rhiwbina	d																						
Whitchurch (Cardiff)	d																						
Coryton	a																						
Heath High Level	d											10 29											12 19
Llanishen	d											10 34											12 22
Lisvane & Thornhill	d											10 39											12 24
Caerphilly [3]	d											10 49											12 30
Aber	d											10 54											12 32
Llanbradach	d											11 04											12 41
Ystrad Mynach [3]	d											11 14											12 51
Hengoed	d											11 19											12 59
Pengam	d											11 29											13 02
Gilfach Fargoed	d											11 34											13 05
Bargoed	a											11 39											13 08
	d											11 39											13 08
Brithdir	d											11 44											13 12
Tir-phil	d											11 49											13 15
Pontlottyn	d											11 54											13 19
Rhymney [3]	a											12 02											13 26
Cathays	d	08 05	08 20		08 39			09 20			10 05			10 39					11 20				
Llandaf	d	08 20	08 35		08 54			09 35			10 20			10 54					11 35				
Ninian Park	d																						
Waun-gron Park	d																						
Fairwater	d																						
Danescourt	d																						
Radyr [3]	a	08 30	08 45	08 40	09 04	08 55	09 11	09 45		09 52	10 30			11 04		11 11			11 45	11 52			
	d			08 40		08 55	09 14			09 55						11 14				11 55			
Taffs Well [3]	d			08 44		08 59	09 18			09 59						11 18				11 59			
Trefforest Estate	d																						
Trefforest	d			08 52		09 06	09 25			10 06						11 25				12 06			
Pontypridd [3]	a			08 55		09 09	09 28			10 09						11 28				12 09			
	d			08 57		09 11	09 30			10 11						11 30				12 11			
Abercynon	d			09 05		09 19				10 19										12 19			
Penrhiwceiber	d					09 24				10 24										12 24			
Mountain Ash	a					09 28				10 28										12 28			
	d					09 29				10 29										12 29			
Fernhill	d					09 31				10 31										12 31			
Cwmbach	d					09 35				10 35										12 35			
Aberdare [3]	a					09 42				10 42										12 42			
Quakers Yard	d			09 09																			
Merthyr Vale	a			09 14																			
	d			09 16																			
Troed Y Rhiw	d			09 20																			
Pentre-bach	d			09 23																			
Merthyr Tydfil	a			09 31																			
Trehafod	d						09 35									11 35							
Porth	a						09 38									11 38							
	d						09 39									11 39							
Dinas Rhondda	d						09 43									11 43							
Tonypandy	d						09 45									11 45							
Llwynypia	d						09 47									11 47							
Ystrad Rhondda	a						09 50									11 50							
	d						09 53									11 53							
Ton Pentre	d						09 55									11 55							
Treorchy	d						09 58									11 58							
Ynyswen	d						10 01									12 01							
Treherbert	a						10 07									12 07							

When events are being held at the Millenium Stadium, services are subject to alteration. Please check times before travelling.

Table 130

Sundays
from 1 April

Bridgend, Barry Island, Barry, Penarth and Cardiff - Coryton, Rhymney, Pontypridd, Merthyr, Aberdare and Treherbert

Network Diagram - see first Page of Table 130

Station		AW	AW	AW	AW	AW		AW	AW	AW	AW	AW	AW	AW	AW	AW		AW	AW	AW	AW	AW	AW	AW	AW
Bridgend	d																				13 50				
Llantwit Major	d																				14 10				
Rhoose Cardiff Int Airport ✈	d																				14 24				
Barry Island	d		11 55										12 55			13 25				13 55					
Barry 3	d		12 00										13 00			13 30				14 00	14 33				
Barry Docks	d		12 04										13 04			13 34				14 04	14 37				
Cadoxton	d		12 07										13 07			13 37				14 07	14 40				
Dinas Powys	d		12 11										13 11			13 41				14 11	14 44				
Eastbrook	d		12 13										13 13			13 43				14 13	14 46				
Cogan	d		12 15										13 15			13 45				14 15	14 48				
Penarth	d					12 47																		14 50	
Dingle Road	d					12 49																		14 52	
Grangetown	d		12 19			12 53							13 19			13 49				14 19	14 52			14 56	
Cardiff Central 7	a		12 24			12 59							13 24			13 54				14 24	15 00			15 03	
	d	12 18	12 26							13 06			13 41			14 06				14 26					
Cardiff Bay	d			12 30	12 42			12 54	13 06		13 18	13 30		13 42	13 54			14 06	14 18			14 30	14 42		14 54
Cardiff Queen Street 3	a	12 21	12 29	12 34	12 46			12 58	13 10	13 09	13 22	13 34	13 44	13 46	13 58	14 09		14 10	14 22	14 29		14 34	14 46		14 58
	d		12 30							13 10			13 45			14 10				14 30					
Heath Low Level	d																								
Ty Glas	d																								
Birchgrove	d																								
Rhiwbina	d																								
Whitchurch (Cardiff)	d																								
Coryton	a																								
Heath High Level	d															14 15									
Llanishen	d															14 18									
Lisvane & Thornhill	d															14 20									
Caerphilly 3	d															14 26									
Aber	d															14 28									
Llanbradach	d															14 32									
Ystrad Mynach 3	d															14 37									
Hengoed	d															14 40									
Pengam	d															14 43									
Gilfach Fargoed	d															14 46									
Bargoed	a															14 49									
	d															14 49									
Brithdir	d															14 53									
Tir-phil	d															14 56									
Pontlottyn	d															15 00									
Rhymney 3	a															15 07									
Cathays	d		12 33							13 13			13 48							14 33					
Llandaf	d		12 37							13 17			13 52							14 37					
Ninian Park	d																								
Waun-gron Park	d																								
Fairwater	d																								
Danescourt	d																								
Radyr 3	a		12 40							13 20			13 55							14 40					
	d		12 40							13 20			13 55							14 40					
Taffs Well 3	d		12 44							13 24			13 59							14 44					
Trefforest Estate	d																								
Trefforest	d		12 52							13 31			14 06							14 52					
Pontypridd 3	a		12 55							13 34			14 09							14 55					
	d		12 57							13 36			14 11							14 57					
Abercynon	d		13 05										14 19							15 05					
Penrhiwceiber	d												14 24												
Mountain Ash	a												14 28												
	d												14 29												
Fernhill	d												14 31												
Cwmbach	d												14 35												
Aberdare 3	a												14 42												
Quakers Yard	d		13 09																	15 09					
Merthyr Vale	a		13 14																	15 14					
	d		13 16																	15 16					
Troed Y Rhiw	d		13 20																	15 20					
Pentre-bach	d		13 23																	15 23					
Merthyr Tydfil	a		13 31																	15 31					
Trehafod	d									13 41															
Porth	a									13 44															
	d									13 45															
Dinas Rhondda	d									13 49															
Tonypandy	d									13 51															
Llwynypia	d									13 53															
Ystrad Rhondda	a									13 56															
	d									13 59															
Ton Pentre	d									14 01															
Treorchy	d									14 04															
Ynyswen	d									14 07															
Treherbert	a									14 13															

When events are being held at the Millenium Stadium, services are subject to alteration. Please check times before travelling.

Table 130

Sundays
from 1 April

Bridgend, Barry Island, Barry, Penarth and Cardiff - Coryton, Rhymney, Pontypridd, Merthyr, Aberdare and Treherbert

Network Diagram - see first Page of Table 130

		AW	AW	AW	AW	AW	AW	AW	AW	AW	AW	AW	AW	AW	AW	AW	AW	AW	AW	AW	AW	AW
Bridgend	d												15 42									
Llantwit Major	d												15 56									
Rhoose Cardiff Int Airport ✈	d												16 06									
Barry Island	d					14 55			15 25			15 55										16 55
Barry 3	d					15 00			15 30			16 00	16 15									17 00
Barry Docks	d					15 04			15 34			16 04	16 19									17 04
Cadoxton	d					15 07			15 37			16 07	16 22									17 07
Dinas Powys	d					15 11			15 41			16 11	16 26									17 11
Eastbrook	d					15 13			15 43			16 13	16 28									17 13
Cogan	d					15 15			15 45			16 15	16 30									17 15
Penarth	d															16 47						
Dingle Road	d															16 49						
Grangetown	d					15 19			15 49			16 19	16 34			16 53						17 19
Cardiff Central 7	a					15 24			15 54			16 24	16 42			16 59						17 24
	d		15 06			15 41			16 06			16 26							17 06			17 41
Cardiff Bay	d	15 06		15 18	15 30		15 42	15 54		16 06	16 18			16 30	16 42		16 54	17 06		17 18	17 30	
Cardiff Queen Street 3	a	15 10	15 09	15 22	15 34	15 44	15 46	15 58	16 09	16 10	16 22	16 29		16 34	16 46		16 58	17 10	17 09	17 22	17 34	17 44
	d		15 10			15 45			16 10			16 30							17 10			17 45
Heath Low Level	d																					
Ty Glas	d																					
Birchgrove	d																					
Rhiwbina	d																					
Whitchurch (Cardiff)	d																					
Coryton	a																					
Heath High Level	d								16 15													
Llanishen	d								16 18													
Lisvane & Thornhill	d								16 20													
Caerphilly 3	d								16 26													
Aber	d								16 28													
Llanbradach	d								16 32													
Ystrad Mynach 3	d								16 37													
Hengoed	d								16 40													
Pengam	d								16 43													
Gilfach Fargoed	d								16 46													
Bargoed	a								16 49													
	d								16 49													
Brithdir	d								16 53													
Tir-phil	d								16 56													
Pontlottyn	d								17 00													
Rhymney 3	a								17 07													
Cathays	d		15 13			15 48						16 33							17 13			17 48
Llandaf	d		15 17			15 52						16 37							17 17			17 52
Ninian Park	d																					
Waun-gron Park	d																					
Fairwater	d																					
Danescourt	d																					
Radyr 3	a		15 20			15 55						16 40							17 20			17 55
	d		15 20			15 55						16 40							17 20			17 55
Taffs Well 3	d		15 24			15 59						16 44							17 24			17 59
Trefforest Estate	d																					
Trefforest	d		15 31			16 06						16 52							17 31			18 06
Pontypridd 3	a		15 34			16 09						16 55							17 34			18 09
	d		15 36			16 11						16 57							17 36			18 11
Abercynon	d					16 19						17 05										18 19
Penrhiwceiber	d					16 24																18 24
Mountain Ash	a					16 28																18 28
	d					16 29																18 29
Fernhill	d					16 31																18 31
Cwmbach	d					16 35																18 35
Aberdare 3	a					16 42																18 42
Quakers Yard	d											17 09										
Merthyr Vale	a											17 14										
	d											17 16										
Troed Y Rhiw	d											17 20										
Pentre-bach	d											17 23										
Merthyr Tydfil	a											17 31										
Trehafod	d		15 41																17 41			
Porth	a		15 44																17 44			
	d		15 45																17 45			
Dinas Rhondda	d		15 49																17 49			
Tonypandy	d		15 51																17 51			
Llwynypia	d		15 53																17 53			
Ystrad Rhondda	a		15 56																17 56			
	d		15 59																17 59			
Ton Pentre	d		16 01																18 01			
Treorchy	d		16 04																18 04			
Ynyswen	d		16 07																18 07			
Treherbert	a		16 13																18 13			

When events are being held at the Millenium Stadium,
services are subject to alteration. Please check times before travelling.

Table 130

Sundays
from 1 April

Bridgend, Barry Island, Barry, Penarth and Cardiff - Coryton, Rhymney, Pontypridd, Merthyr, Aberdare and Treherbert

Network Diagram - see first Page of Table 130

		AW	AW	AW	AW	AW	AW	AW		AW	AW	AW	AW	AW	AW	AW	AW	AW		AW	AW	AW	AW	AW	AW
Bridgend	d							17 42										19 42							
Llantwit Major	d							17 56										19 56							
Rhoose Cardiff Int Airport ✈	d							18 06										20 06							
Barry Island	d			17 25			17 55								18 55	19 25	19 55			20 25			20 55	21 25	21 55
Barry 3	d			17 30			18 00	18 15							19 00	19 30	20 00	20 15		20 30			21 00	21 30	22 00
Barry Docks	d			17 34			18 04	18 19							19 04	19 34	20 04	20 19		20 34			21 04	21 34	22 04
Cadoxton	d			17 37			18 07	18 22							19 07	19 37	20 07	20 22		20 37			21 07	21 37	22 07
Dinas Powys	d			17 41			18 11	18 26							19 11	19 41	20 11	20 26		20 41			21 11	21 41	22 11
Eastbrook	d			17 43			18 13	18 28							19 13	19 43	20 13	20 28		20 43			21 13	21 43	22 13
Cogan	d			17 45			18 15	18 30							19 15	19 45	20 15	20 30		20 45			21 15	21 45	22 15
Penarth	d											18 47									20 47				
Dingle Road	d											18 49									20 49				
Grangetown	d			17 49			18 19	18 34				18 53			19 19	19 49	20 19	20 34		20 49	20 53		21 19	21 49	22 19
Cardiff Central 7	a			17 54			18 24	18 42				19 00			19 24	19 54	20 24	20 42		20 54	21 00		21 26	21 54	22 26
	d			18 06			18 26							19 06	19 41	20 06	20 26			21 06		21 16		22 06	
Cardiff Bay	d	17 42	17 54		18 06	18 18				18 30	18 42		18 54												
Cardiff Queen Street 3	a	17 46	17 58	18 09	18 10	18 22	18 29			18 34	18 46		18 57	19 09	19 44	20 09	20 29			21 09		21 19		22 09	
	d			18 10			18 30							19 10	19 45	20 10	20 30			21 10		21 20		22 10	
Heath Low Level	d																								
Ty Glas	d																								
Birchgrove	d																								
Rhiwbina	d																								
Whitchurch (Cardiff)	d																								
Coryton	a																								
Heath High Level	d			18 15												20 15						21 25			
Llanishen	d			18 18												20 18						21 28			
Lisvane & Thornhill	d			18 20												20 20						21 30			
Caerphilly 3	d			18 26												20 26						21 36			
Aber	d			18 28												20 28						21 38			
Llanbradach	d			18 32												20 32						21 42			
Ystrad Mynach 3	d			18 37												20 37						21 47			
Hengoed	d			18 40												20 40						21 50			
Pengam	d			18 43												20 43						21 53			
Gilfach Fargoed	d			18 46												20 46						21 56			
Bargoed	a			18 49												20 49						21 59			
	d			18 49												20 49						21 59			
Brithdir	d			18 53												20 53						22 03			
Tir-phil	d			18 56												20 56						22 06			
Pontlottyn	d			19 00												21 00						22 10			
Rhymney 3	a			19 07												21 07						22 17			
Cathays	d						18 33							19 13	19 48		20 33			21 13				22 13	
Llandaf	d						18 37							19 17	19 52		20 37			21 17				22 17	
Ninian Park	d																								
Waun-gron Park	d																								
Fairwater	d																								
Danescourt	d																								
Radyr 3	a						18 40							19 20	19 55		20 40			21 20				22 20	
	d						18 40							19 20	19 55		20 40			21 20				22 20	
Taffs Well 3	d						18 44							19 24	19 59		20 44			21 24				22 24	
Trefforest Estate	d																								
Trefforest	d						18 52							19 31	20 06		20 52			21 31				22 31	
Pontypridd 3	a						18 55							19 34	20 09		20 55			21 34				22 34	
	d						18 57							19 36	20 11		20 57			21 36				22 36	
Abercynon	d						19 05								20 19		21 05								
Penrhiwceiber	d														20 24										
Mountain Ash	a														20 28										
	d														20 29										
Fernhill	d														20 31										
Cwmbach	d														20 35										
Aberdare 3	a														20 42										
Quakers Yard	d						19 09										21 09								
Merthyr Vale	a						19 14										21 14								
	d						19 16										21 16								
Troed Y Rhiw	d						19 20										21 20								
Pentre-bach	d						19 23										21 23								
Merthyr Tydfil	a						19 31										21 31								
Trehafod	d													19 41						21 41				22 41	
Porth	a													19 44						21 44				22 44	
	d													19 45						21 45				22 45	
Dinas Rhondda	d													19 49						21 49				22 49	
Tonypandy	d													19 51						21 51				22 51	
Llwynypia	d													19 53						21 53				22 53	
Ystrad Rhondda	a													19 56						21 56				22 56	
	d													19 59						21 59				22 59	
Ton Pentre	d													20 01						22 01				23 01	
Treorchy	d													20 04						22 04				23 04	
Ynyswen	d													20 07						22 07				23 07	
Treherbert	a													20 13						22 13				23 13	

When events are being held at the Millenium Stadium,
services are subject to alteration. Please check times before travelling.

Table 130

Sundays
from 1 April

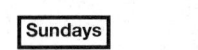

Bridgend, Barry Island, Barry, Penarth and Cardiff - Coryton, Rhymney, Pontypridd, Merthyr, Aberdare and Treherbert

Network Diagram - see first Page of Table 130

		AW	AW
Bridgend	d	21 42	
Llantwit Major	d	21 56	
Rhoose Cardiff Int Airport ✈	d	22 06	
Barry Island	d		22 55
Barry 3	d	22 15	23 00
Barry Docks	d	22 19	23 04
Cadoxton	d	22 22	23 07
Dinas Powys	d	22 26	23 11
Eastbrook	d	22 28	23 13
Cogan	d	22 30	23 15
Penarth	d		
Dingle Road	d		
Grangetown	d	22 34	23 19
Cardiff Central 7	a	22 42	23 26
	d		
Cardiff Bay	d		
Cardiff Queen Street 3	a		
	d		
Heath Low Level	d		
Ty Glas	d		
Birchgrove	d		
Rhiwbina	d		
Whitchurch (Cardiff)	d		
Coryton	a		
Heath High Level	d		
Llanishen	d		
Lisvane & Thornhill	d		
Caerphilly 3	d		
Aber	d		
Llanbradach	d		
Ystrad Mynach 3	d		
Hengoed	d		
Pengam	d		
Gilfach Fargoed	d		
Bargoed	a		
	d		
Brithdir	d		
Tir-phil	d		
Pontlottyn	d		
Rhymney 3	a		
Cathays	d		
Llandaf	d		
Ninian Park	d		
Waun-gron Park	d		
Fairwater	d		
Danescourt	d		
Radyr 3	a		
	d		
Taffs Well 3	d		
Trefforest Estate	d		
Trefforest	d		
Pontypridd 3	a		
	d		
Abercynon	d		
Penrhiwceiber	d		
Mountain Ash	a		
	d		
Fernhill	d		
Cwmbach	d		
Aberdare 3	a		
Quakers Yard	d		
Merthyr Vale	a		
	d		
Troed Y Rhiw	d		
Pentre-bach	d		
Merthyr Tydfil	a		
Trehafod	d		
Porth	a		
	d		
Dinas Rhondda	d		
Tonypandy	d		
Llwynypia	d		
Ystrad Rhondda	a		
	d		
Ton Pentre	d		
Treorchy	d		
Ynyswen	d		
Treherbert	a		

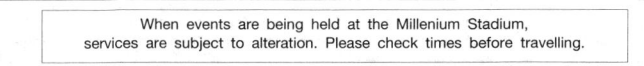

When events are being held at the Millenium Stadium, services are subject to alteration. Please check times before travelling.

Table 131

Cardiff - Crewe, Liverpool and Manchester

Route Diagram - see first Page of Table 129

Miles	Miles			AW	AW	AW	AW	AW	AW	AW	AW	AW		AW	AW	AW	AW	AW	AW	AW	AW	AW		AW	AW
				MX	MX	MO	MX	MO	MO	MX															
				◇	◇	◇	◇	◇	◇			◇		◇	◇		◇	◇	◇	◇		◇		◇	◇
								A	B																
														T	T			T	T	T		T		T	T
—	—	Swansea	d					21p52									04 36			07 06		07 45			08 55
0	0	**Cardiff Central [7]**	d	19p34	20p53	21p04	21p55	23c00	23p00	00 30		04 35		05 10	05 40			06 50	07 21	08 05		08 50		09 21	10 05
—	—	London Paddington [15] ⊖	d																						
—	—	Reading [7]	d																						
11¾	11¾	**Newport (South Wales)**	d	19p48	21p10	21p19	22p11	23p20	23p20	00 59		04 52		05 28	05 57			07 04	07 36	08 19		09 04		09 36	10 19
18¾	18¾	Cwmbran	d	19p58	21p20	21p30	22p23	23p29	23p29	01 10		05 03		05 38	06 08			07 14	07 46	08 29		09 14		09 46	10 29
21¾	21¾	Pontypool and New Inn	d	20p03		21p36	22p29	23p35	23p35	01 16		05 09		05 44	06 13				07 52					09 52	
31¼	31¼	Abergavenny	d	20p12	21p33	21p46	22p39	23p45	23p45	01 27		05 18		05 53	06 23			07 27	08 01	08 42		09 27		10 01	10 42
55¼	55¼	**Hereford [7]**	a	20p38	21p57	22p12	23p05	00 17	00 17	01 57		05 46		06 17	06 47			07 51	08 25	09 07		09 51		10 25	11 06
—	—		d	20p39	21p59	22p14	23p07					05 47		06 25	06 49			07 53	08 27	09 08		09 53		10 27	11 08
67¾	67¾	Leominster	d	20p52	22p12	22p27	23p20					06 00		06 38	07 02			08 06		09 21		10 06			11 21
78¾	78¾	Ludlow	d	21p03	22p23	22p38	23p31					06 11		06 49	07 13			08 17	08 48	09 32		10 17		10 48	11 32
86	86	Craven Arms	d	21p12	22p31	22p48	23p41					06 20		06 57	07 21		07 54	08 25	08 56			10 25		10 56	
93¼	93¼	Church Stretton	d	21p21	22p40	22p57	23p50					06 29		07 06	07 30		08 07	08 34	09 05			10 39		11 05	
106	106	**Shrewsbury**	a	21p37	22p54	23p14	00 05					06 43		07 20	07 44		08 22	08 48	09 19	09 58		10 52		11 19	11 58
—	—		d	21p39	23p06	23p19	00 10				05 44	06 44		07 24	07 46	07 57		08 50	09 24	10 00	10 18	10 53		11 24	11 59
113¼	113¼	Yorton	d		23b15	23b28	00x19				05x52					08x06					10x28				
116¾	116¾	Wem	d		23p20	23p34	00 24				05 58	06 56			07 57	08 12					10 34				
120	120	Prees	d		23b25	23b39	00x29				06x03					08x17					10x39				
125	125	Whitchurch (Shrops)	d		23p32	23p46	00 36				06 10	07 04			08 06	08 25		09 06			10 46	11 11			
129¾	129¾	Wrenbury	d		23b38	23b52	00x42				06x17					08x31					10x53				
134¼	134¼	Nantwich	d		23p44	23p59	00 49				06 23	07 13			08 15	08 38		09 16			10 59	11 19			
138¾	138¾	**Crewe [10]**	a		23p53	00 09	01 04				06 35	07 24			08 24	08 47		09 25		10 29	11 09	11 29			12 29
—	—	Chester	a	22p34	00 27	00 33								08 19					10 19					12 19	
—	—	Llandudno Junction	a	23p49										09 11					11 14					13 11	
—	—	Bangor (Gwynedd)	a	00 13										09 33					11 38					13 28	
—	—	Holyhead	a	00 58										10 14					12 14					14 13	
157¾	—	Wilmslow	a									07 44			08 45			09 48		10 49		11 48			12 48
163¾	—	Stockport	a									07 54			08 58			09 58		10 58		11 58			12 58
169¾	—	**Manchester Piccadilly [10]** ⛴	a									08 10			09 15			10 15		11 15		12 15			13 15

		GW	AW	AW	AW	AW	AW	GW		AW	AW	AW	AW	AW	AW	AW	AW	AW		AW		AW	AW	AW	AW
																				BHX					
																	R	R		R			R	R	R
		◇[1]		◇	◇	◇	◇	◇[1]			◇	◇	◇		◇	◇									
		⊡		T	T	T	T	⊡			T	T	T		T		T	T		⊠			T	T	T
Swansea	d			09 55	09 16		10 55				11 55		12 54		13 55	13 14		14 55					15 55		16 55
Cardiff Central [7]	d			10 50		11 21	12 05				12 50	13 21	14 05		14 50		15 21	15 50		16 15			16 50	17 21	17 50
London Paddington [15] ⊖	d	08 22						10 22																	
Reading [7]	d	08 52						10 52																	
Newport (South Wales)	d			11 04		11 36	12 19				13 04	13 36	14 19		15 04		15 36	16 04		16 29			17 04	17 36	18 04
Cwmbran	d			11 14		11 46	12 29				13 14	13 46	14 29		15 14		15 46	16 14		16 40			17 14	17 46	18 14
Pontypool and New Inn	d					11 52						13 52					15 52	16 19						17 52	18 19
Abergavenny	d			11 27		12 01	12 42				13 26	14 01	14 43		15 27		16 01	16 29		16 54			17 27	18 01	18 29
Hereford [7]	a	11 42		11 51		12 25	13 06	13 48			13 53	14 25	15 06		15 51		16 25	16 53					17 51	18 25	18 53
	d			11 53		12 27	13 08				13 55	14 27	15 08		15 53		16 27	16 54					17 53	18 27	18 54
Leominster	d			12 06			13 21				14 08		15 21		16 06		16 40	17 07					18 06		19 07
Ludlow	d			12 17		12 48	13 32				14 19	14 48	15 32		16 17		16 51	17 18					18 17	18 48	19 18
Craven Arms	d			12 25	12 39	12 56					14 27	14 56			16 25	16 40		17 27					18 25		19 27
Church Stretton	d			12 38	12 52	13 05					14 36	15 05				16 53	17 05	17 36					18 34		19 36
Shrewsbury	a			12 52	13 08	13 19	13 58				14 50	15 19	15 58		16 48	17 09	17 19	17 50		18 05			18 48	19 14	19 50
	d		12 24	12 54		13 24	13 59			14 24	14 52	15 24	15 59	16 24	16 50		17 24	17 51		18 06		18 25	18 50	19 24	19 51
Yorton	d		12x34							14x34				16x34								18 35			
Wem	d		12 40							14 40				16 40	17 01							18 41			
Prees	d		12x45							14x45				16x45								18 46			
Whitchurch (Shrops)	d		12 52	13 10						14 52	15 08			16 52	17 10			18 09				18 53	19 06		
Wrenbury	d		12x59							14x59				16x59								19 00			
Nantwich	d		13 05	13 20						15 05	15 18			17 05	17 19			18 19				19 06	19 16		
Crewe [10]	a		13 15	13 29			14 29			15 15	15 27		16 29	17 15	17 28			18 28		18 42		19 16	19 25		20 22
Chester	a					14 19						16 20					18 20			19 06				20 20	
Llandudno Junction	a					15 11						17 13					19 12			19 52				21 24	
Bangor (Gwynedd)	a					15 28						17 34					19 33			20 09				21 41	
Holyhead	a					16 15						18 19					20 18			20 49				22 25	
Wilmslow	a			13 48			14 48				15 47		16 48		17 47			18 48					19 48		20 40
Stockport	a			13 58			14 58				15 58		16 58		17 57			18 58					19 58		20 50
Manchester Piccadilly [10] ⛴	a			14 15			15 15				16 15		17 14		18 13			19 15					20 15		21 05

A until 2 January, from 20 February
B from 9 January until 13 February
b Previous night, stops on request
c Previous night, arr. 2249

For connections from Bristol Temple Meads please refer to Table 132.
For connections to Runcorn and Liverpool Lime Street please refer to Table 91

When events are being held at the Millenium Stadium,
services are subject to alteration. Please check times before travelling.

Table 131

Mondays to Fridays

Cardiff - Crewe, Liverpool and Manchester

Route Diagram - see first Page of Table 129

		AW BHX [R]	AW	AW ◇		GW ◇[1]	AW ◇	AW ◇	AW ◇	GW ◇[1] A	AW ◇	GW ◇[1]	AW ◇
Swansea	d			17 55				18 21					
Cardiff Central [7]	d	18 18		18 50			19 34		20 17		20 53		21 55
London Paddington [15]	d					17 22				18 22		19 22	
Reading [7]	d					17 50				18 50		19 52	
Newport (South Wales)	d	18 32		19 05			19 48		20 31		21 10		22 11
Cwmbran	d			19 15			19 58		20 41		21 20		22 23
Pontypool and New Inn	d			19 20			20 03		20 47				22 29
Abergavenny	d	18 53		19 30			20 12		20 56		21 33		22 39
Hereford [7]	a	19 17		19 54		20 27	20 38		21 21	21 33	21 57	22 54	23 05
	d	19 18		19 55			20 39		21 22		21 59		23 07
Leominster	d			20 08			20 52		21 35		22 12		23 20
Ludlow	d			20 19			21 03		21 46		22 23		23 31
Craven Arms	d			20 28			21 12	21 38	21 54		22 31		23 41
Church Stretton	d			20 37			21 21	21 51	22 03		22 40		23 50
Shrewsbury	a	20 03		20 51			21 37	22 08	22 17		22 54		00 05
	d	20 05	20 32	20 52			21 39		22 19		23 06		00 10
Yorton	d		20x39						22x27		23x15		00x19
Wem	d		20 44						22 31		23 20		00 24
Prees	d		20x49						22x35		23x25		00x29
Whitchurch (Shrops)	d		20 56	21 10					22 42		23 32		00 36
Wrenbury	d		21x02						22x48		23x38		00x42
Nantwich	d		21 08	21 20					22 53		23 44		00 49
Crewe [10]	a		21 19	21 29					23 03		23 53		01 04
Chester	a	20 56					22 34				00 27		
Llandudno Junction	a	21 44					23 49						
Bangor (Gwynedd)	a	22 02					00 13						
Holyhead	a	22 35					00 58						
Wilmslow	a			21 48					23 22				
Stockport	a			21 58					23 30				
Manchester Piccadilly [10]	a			22 13					23 48				

Saturdays

		AW ◇	AW ◇	AW ◇	AW	AW	AW ◇	AW ◇	AW ◇	AW		AW ◇	AW ◇	AW ◇	AW ◇	AW	AW ◇	AW ◇	AW ◇	GW ◇[1]		AW	AW ◇	AW ◇	AW ◇
Swansea	d											04 36			06 47		07 45		08 55				09 55	09 16	
Cardiff Central [7]	d	19p34	20p53	21p55	00 30		04 35	05 20	05 40				06 50	07 21	07 50		08 50	09 21	09 55				10 55		11 21
London Paddington [15]	d																			08 21					
Reading [7]	d																			08 54					
Newport (South Wales)	d	19p48	21p10	22p11	00 46		04 52	05 35	05 57				07 04	07 36	08 04		09 04	09 36	10 09				11 09		11 36
Cwmbran	d	19p58	21p20	22p23	00 56		05 03	05 45	06 08				07 14	07 46	08 14		09 14	09 46	10 19				11 19		11 46
Pontypool and New Inn	d	20p03		22p29	01 02		05 09	05 51	06 13					07 51				09 51							11 50
Abergavenny	d	20p12	21p33	22p39	01 13		05 18	06 00	06 23				07 27	08 01	08 27		09 27	10 01	10 32				11 32		12 00
Hereford [7]	a	20p38	21p57	23p05	01 43		05 46	06 24	06 46				07 51	08 26	08 51		09 51	10 26	10 56	11 41			11 56		12 26
	d	20p39	21p59	23p07			05 47	06 26	06 49				07 53	08 27	08 53		09 53	10 28	10 58				11 58		12 28
Leominster	d	20p52	22p12	23p20			06 00	06 40	07 02				08 06		09 06		10 06		11 11				12 11		
Ludlow	d	21p03	22p23	23p31			06 11	06 51	07 13				08 17	08 48	09 17		10 17	10 49	11 22				12 22		12 49
Craven Arms	d	21p12	22p31	23p41			06 20	06 59	07 21			07 54	08 25	08 56			10 25	10 57					12 30	12 37	12 57
Church Stretton	d	21p21	22p40	23p50			06 29	07 08	07 30			08 07	08 34	09 05			10 34	11 06					12 39	12 51	13 06
Shrewsbury	a	21p37	22p54	00 05			06 43	07 22	07 44			08 22	08 51	09 19	09 43		10 48	11 20	11 48				12 53	13 09	13 20
	d	21p39	23p06	00 10		05 44	06 44	07 24	07 46	07 57			08 52	09 24	09 44	10 18	10 50	11 24	11 49			12 24	12 55		13 24
Yorton	d		23b15	00x19		05x52				08x06						10x28						12x34			
Wem	d		23p20	00 24		05 58	06 56		07 57	08 12						10 34						12 40			
Prees	d		23b25	00x29		06x03				08x17						10x39						12x45			
Whitchurch (Shrops)	d		23p32	00 36		06 10	07 04		08 06	08 25			09 09		10 01	10 46	11 06		12 06			12 52			
Wrenbury	d		23b38	00x42		06x17				08x31						10x53						12x59			
Nantwich	d		23p44	00 49		06 23	07 13		08 15	08 38			09 18		10 10	10 59	11 16		12 15			13 05			
Crewe [10]	a		23p53	01 04		06 35	07 22		08 24	08 47			09 27		10 20	11 09	11 25		12 24			13 15	13 26		
Chester	a	22p34	00 27					08 18						10 19				12 19							14 19
Llandudno Junction	a	23p49						09 11						11 11				13 11							15 11
Bangor (Gwynedd)	a	00 13						09 33						11 33				13 28							15 28
Holyhead	a	00 58						10 14						12 09				14 13							16 13
Wilmslow	a						07 44		08 45				09 47		10 48		11 48		12 48				13 48		
Stockport	a						08 01		08 58				09 57		10 58		11 58		12 58				13 58		
Manchester Piccadilly [10]	a						08 20		09 15				10 14		11 15		12 15		13 15				14 15		

A The Cathedrals Express

b Previous night, stops on request

For connections from Bristol Temple Meads please refer to Table 132.
For connections to Runcorn and Liverpool Lime Street please refer to Table 91

When events are being held at the Millenium Stadium,
services are subject to alteration. Please check times before travelling.

Table 131

Saturdays

Cardiff - Crewe, Liverpool and Manchester

Route Diagram - see first Page of Table 129

		AW	GW	AW	AW	AW		AW	AW	AW	AW	AW	AW	AW	AW	AW		AW	AW	GW	AW	AW	AW	AW	AW
												R	R			R		R	R						
		◇	◇1		◇	◇		◇		◇	◇									◇1		◇	◇	◇	◇
																		A							
		trolley	restaurant		trolley	trolley		trolley		trolley		trolley	trolley			trolley		trolley	trolley	restaurant		trolley			
Swansea	d	10 55			12 00			12 55		14 00	13 16		14 55	15 10		15 55			16 55			17 55		18 21	
Cardiff Central 7	d	11 55			12 55	13 21		13 55		14 55		15 21	15 55	16 19		16 55		17 21	17 55			18 50	19 34		20 10
London Paddington 15 ⊖	d		10 21																	16 21					
Reading 7	d		10 54																	16 54					
Newport (South Wales)	d	12 09			13 09	13 36		14 09		15 09		15 36	16 09	16 34		17 09		17 35	18 09			19 04	19 48		20 26
Cwmbran	d	12 19			13 19	13 46		14 19		15 19		15 46	16 19	16 44		17 19		17 46	18 19			19 15	19 58		20 37
Pontypool and New Inn	d					13 50						15 52	16 24	16 50				17 52	18 24			19 20	20 03		20 42
Abergavenny	d	12 32			13 32	14 01		14 32		15 32		16 01	16 34	17a02		17 32		18 01	18 34			19 29	20 12		20 52
Hereford 7	a	12 56	13 40		13 56	14 26		14 56		15 56		16 25	16 58			17 56		18 25	18 58	19 45		19 53	20 38		21 17
	d	12 58			13 58	14 26		14 58		15 58		16 27	16 59			17 58		18 27	18 59			19 55	20 39		21 20
Leominster	d	13 11			14 11			15 11		16 11		16 40	17 12			18 11			19 12			20 08	20 52		21 33
Ludlow	d	13 22			14 22	14 47		15 22		16 22		16 51	17 23			18 22		18 48	19 23			20 19	21 03		21 44
Craven Arms	d				14 30	14 55				16 30	16 38					18 30		18 56				20 27	21 12	21 38	21 53
Church Stretton	d				14 39	15 04				16 39	16 51	17 05				18 39		19 05				20 36	21 21	21 51	22 03
Shrewsbury	a	13 48			14 53	15 18		15 48		16 53	17 11	17 19	17 49			18 53		19 19	19 49			20 53	21 35	22 08	22 17
	d	13 49		14 24	14 55	15 24		15 49	16 24	16 55		17 24	17 51		18 25	18 55		19 24	19 51		20 32	20 57	21 37		22 19
Yorton	d			14x34					16x34						18x35						20x39				22x27
Wem	d			14 40					16 40						18 41						20 44				22 32
Prees	d			14x45					16x45						18x46						20x49				22x36
Whitchurch (Shrops)	d	14 06		14 52				16 06	16 52				18 07		18 53				20 07		20 56				22 44
Wrenbury	d			14x59					16x59						19x00						21x02				22x49
Nantwich	d	14 15		15 05				16 15	17 05				18 17		19 06				20 17		21 08				22 55
Crewe 10	a	14 24		15 15	15 25			16 24	17 15	17 26			18 28		19 16	19 26			20 26		21 19	21 28			23 04
Chester	a					16 22						18 19						20 19					22 31		
Llandudno Junction	a					17 14						19 14						21 24					23 38		
Bangor (Gwynedd)	a					17 35						19 32						21 41							
Holyhead	a					18 20						20 18						22 25							
Wilmslow	a	14 48			15 45			16 48		17 45			18 48			19 48			20 45			21 50			23 24
Stockport	a	14 58			15 58			16 58		17 58			18 58			19 58			20 58			22 00			23 32
Manchester Piccadilly 10 ⇌	a	15 15			16 15			17 15		18 15			19 15			20 15			21 15			22 15			23 50

		GW		AW	AW	AW
		◇1		◇		
		restaurant				
Swansea	d				20 55	
Cardiff Central 7	d			20 55	21 49	
London Paddington 15 ⊖	d	18 21				
Reading 7	d	18 54				
Newport (South Wales)	d			21 10	22 07	
Cwmbran	d			21 21	22 19	
Pontypool and New Inn	d				22 24	
Abergavenny	d			21 34	22 34	
Hereford 7	a	21 34		21 58	22 58	
	d			22 00		
Leominster	d			22 14		
Ludlow	d			22 25		
Craven Arms	d			22 33		
Church Stretton	d			22 42		
Shrewsbury	a			22 57		
	d			23 06		23 50
Yorton	d			23x14		23x58
Wem	d			23 20		00 04
Prees	d			23x24		00x07
Whitchurch (Shrops)	d			23 31		00 15
Wrenbury	d			23x36		00x20
Nantwich	d			23 42		00 26
Crewe 10	a			23 53		00 38
Chester	a			00 24		
Llandudno Junction	a					
Bangor (Gwynedd)	a					
Holyhead	a					
Wilmslow	a					
Stockport	a					
Manchester Piccadilly 10 ⇌	a					

A trolley from Shrewsbury

For connections from Bristol Temple Meads please refer to Table 132.
For connections to Runcorn and Liverpool Lime Street please refer to Table 91

When events are being held at the Millenium Stadium, services are subject to alteration. Please check times before travelling.

Table 131

Sundays
until 1 January

Cardiff - Crewe, Liverpool and Manchester

Route Diagram - see first Page of Table 129

		AW	AW	AW	AW	AW	AW	GW	AW	AW	GW	AW	AW	AW	AW	GW	AW	AW	AW	GW	AW	AW	AW
													R	R	R		R	R	R			R	R
		◇		◇	◇	◇	◇	◇1	◇	◇	◇1	◇				◇1	◇			◇1	◇		
		A	A														B						
					🛒	🛒	🛒	☕	🛒	🛒	☕			🛒	🛒	☕	🛒	🛒	🛒				🛒
Swansea	d									11 32		11 06			13 43				15 33		15 26		17 30
Cardiff Central 7	d	20p55			08 30	09 30	10 35		11 35	12 40			13 22	13 40	14 56		15 22	15 56	16 40			17 35	18 40
London Paddington 15 ⊖	d	∫						09 35			10 42					12 42				14 42			
Reading 7	d	∫						10 11			11 21					13 23				15 21			
Newport (South Wales)	d	21p10			08 49	09 50	10 51		11 50	12 54			13 36	13 54	15 14		15 36	16 14	16 54			17 49	18 54
Cwmbran	d	21p21			09 00	10 00	11 02		12 04	13 09			13 47	14 09	15 24		15 47	16 24	17 09			18 04	19 09
Pontypool and New Inn	d	∫			09 06	10 06	11 08		12 10	13 15							15 52		17 15			18 10	
Abergavenny	d	21p34			09 15	10 16	11 18		12 20	13 25			14 00	14 22	15 38		16 02	16 37	17 25			18 20	19 22
Hereford 7	a	21p58			09 40	10 40	11 44	12 54	12 44	13 49	14 06		14 26	14 47	16 02	16 05	16 27	17 02	17 49	17 58		18 44	19 47
	d	22p00			09 41	10 43	11 50		12 57	13 55			14 26	14 48	16 04		16 28	17 04	17 53			18 49	19 49
Leominster	d	22p14			09 55	10 56	12 03		13 10	14 08				15 01			16 41		18 07			19 03	20 03
Ludlow	d	22p25			10 06	11 07	12 14		13 21	14 19			14 48	15 12	16 25		16 52	17 26	18 18			19 14	20 14
Craven Arms	d	22p33			10 14		12 24			14 28		14 44					17 00		18 26		19 03		20 22
Church Stretton	d	22p42			10 23		12 33			14 37		14 57					17 09		18 35		19 16		20 31
Shrewsbury	a	22p57			10 37	11 36	12 48		13 47	14 51		15 15	15 21	15 38	16 51		17 23	17 52	18 49		19 31	19 40	20 45
	d	23p06	23p50	09 55	10 39	11 37	12 51		13 50	14 53			15 22	15 40	16 53		17 30	17 54	18 54			19 41	20 48
Yorton	d	23b14	23b58			11x45								15x48								19x49	
Wem	d	23p20	00∫04		10 51	11 51								15 54								19 55	
Prees	d	23b24	00x07			11x55								15x58								19x59	
Whitchurch (Shrops)	d	23p31	00∫15		11 00	12 03								16 06								20 06	
Wrenbury	d	23b36	00x20			12x08								16x11								20x11	
Nantwich	d	23p42	00∫26		11 09	12 15								16 18								20 18	
Crewe 10	a	23p53	00∫38	10 25	11 22	12 25	13 26		14 22	15 25				16 27	17 25			18 25	19 24			20 27	21 21
Chester	a	00∫24											16 18				18 25						
Llandudno Junction	a												17 29				19 22						
Bangor (Gwynedd)	a												17 52				19 45						
Holyhead	a												18 37				20 18						
Wilmslow	a			10 46	11 41	12 46	13 49		14 46	15 46				16 46	17 45			18 46	19 46			20 45	21 45
Stockport	a			10 58		12 58	14 00		14 58	15 58				16 58	17 58			18 58	19 58			20 57	21 58
Manchester Piccadilly 10 ⛴	a			11 12	12 02	13 15	14 19		15 15	16 15				17 15	18 17			19 15	20 17			21 14	22 19

		AW	GW	AW	AW	AW
		◇	◇1	◇	◇	◇
			☕			
Swansea	d					21 52
Cardiff Central 7	d	19 40			21 04	23 00
London Paddington 15 ⊖	d		17 42			
Reading 7	d		18 25			
Newport (South Wales)	d	19 55			21 19	23 20
Cwmbran	d	20 10			21 30	23 29
Pontypool and New Inn	d	20 16			21 36	23 35
Abergavenny	d	20 26			21 46	23 45
Hereford 7	a	20 52	21 03		22 12	00 17
	d	20 54			22 14	
Leominster	d	21 08			22 27	
Ludlow	d	21 19			22 38	
Craven Arms	d	21 29			22 48	
Church Stretton	d	21 38			22 57	
Shrewsbury	a	21 55			23 14	
	d			22 32	23 19	
Yorton	d				23x28	
Wem	d				23 34	
Prees	d				23x39	
Whitchurch (Shrops)	d				23 46	
Wrenbury	d				23x52	
Nantwich	d				23 59	
Crewe 10	a			23 03	00 09	
Chester	a			23 31	00 33	
Llandudno Junction	a					
Bangor (Gwynedd)	a					
Holyhead	a					
Wilmslow	a					
Stockport	a					
Manchester Piccadilly 10 ⛴	a					

A not 11 December

B ◇ from Shrewsbury R to Shrewsbury

b Previous night, stops on request

For connections from Bristol Temple Meads please refer to Table 132.
For connections to Runcorn and Liverpool Lime Street please refer to Table 91

When events are being held at the Millenium Stadium,
services are subject to alteration. Please check times before travelling.

Table 131

Sundays

8 January to 12 February

Cardiff - Crewe, Liverpool and Manchester

Route Diagram - see first Page of Table 129

		AW	AW	AW	AW	AW	AW	GW	AW	AW	GW	AW	AW	AW	AW	GW	AW	AW	AW	GW	AW	AW	AW
													R	R	R		R	R	R			R	R
		◇		◇	◇	◇	◇	◇1	◇	◇	◇1	◇				◇1	◇			◇1	◇		
																	A						
					(trolley)	(trolley)	(trolley)	(buffet)	(trolley)	(trolley)	(buffet)			(trolley)	(trolley)	(buffet)	(trolley)	(trolley)	(trolley)				(trolley)
Swansea	d											11 06									15 26		
Cardiff Central 7	d	20p55			08 30	09 30	10 35		11 35	12 40			13 22	13 40	14 56		15 22	15 56	16 40			17 35	18 40
London Paddington 15 ⊖	d							09 35			10 42					12 42				14 42			
Reading 7	d							10 11			11 21					13 23				15 21			
Newport (South Wales)	d	21p10			08 49	09 50	10 51		11 51	12 54			13 36	13 54	15 14		15 36	16 15	16 54			17 49	18 54
Cwmbran	d	21p21			09 00	10 00	11 02		12 05	13 09			13 47	14 09	15 24		15 47	16 25	17 09			18 04	19 09
Pontypool and New Inn	d				09 06	10 06	11 08		12 11	13 15							15 52		17 15			18 10	
Abergavenny	d	21p34			09 15	10 16	11 18		12 22	13 25			14 00	14 22	15 38		16 02	16 39	17 25			18 20	19 22
Hereford 7	a	21p58			09 40	10 40	11 44	12 54	12 48	13 49	14 06		14 26	14 47	16 02	16 05	16 27	17 05	17 49	17 58		18 44	19 47
	d	22p00			09 41	10 43	11 50		12 55	13 55			14 26	14 48	16 04		16 28	17 07	17 53			18 49	19 49
Leominster	d	22p14			09 55	10 56	12 03		13 08	14 08				15 01			16 41		18 07			19 03	20 03
Ludlow	d	22p25			10 06	11 07	12 14		13 19	14 19			14 48	15 12	16 25		16 52	17 28	18 18			19 14	20 14
Craven Arms	d	22p33			10 14		12 24			14 28		14 44					17 00		18 26		19 03		20 22
Church Stretton	d	22p42			10 23		12 33			14 37		14 57					17 09		18 35		19 16		20 31
Shrewsbury	a	22p57			10 37	11 36	12 48		13 48	14 51		15 15	15 21	15 38	16 51		17 23	17 56	18 49		19 31	19 40	20 45
	d	23p06	23p50	09 55	10 39	11 37	12 51		13 50	14 53			15 22	15 40	16 53		17 30	17 58	18 54			19 41	20 48
Yorton	d	23b14	23b58			11x45								15x48								19x49	
Wem	d	23p20	00 04		10 51	11 51								15 54								19 55	
Prees	d	23b24	00x07			11x55								15x58								19x59	
Whitchurch (Shrops)	d	23p31	00 15		11 00	12 03								16 06								20 06	
Wrenbury	d	23b36	00x20			12x08								16x11								20x11	
Nantwich	d	23p42	00 26		11 09	12 15								16 18								20 18	
Crewe 10	a	23p53	00 38	10 25	11 22	12 25	13 26		14 28	15 25				16 27	17 25			18 33	19 24			20 27	21 21
Chester	a	00 24											16 18				18 25						
Llandudno Junction	a												17 29				19 22						
Bangor (Gwynedd)	a												17 52				19 45						
Holyhead	a												18 37				20 18						
Wilmslow	a			10 46	11 41	12 46	13 49		14 49	15 46				16 46	17 45			18 54	19 46			20 45	21 45
Stockport	a			10 58		12 58	14 00		14 58	15 58				16 58	17 58			19 02	19 58			20 57	21 58
Manchester Piccadilly 10	a			11 12	12 02	13 15	14 19		15 15	16 15				17 15	18 17			19 16	20 17			21 14	22 19

		AW	GW	AW	AW	AW
		◇	◇1	◇	◇	◇
			(buffet)			
Swansea	d					
Cardiff Central 7	d	19 40			21 04	23 00
London Paddington 15 ⊖	d		17 42			
Reading 7	d		18 24			
Newport (South Wales)	d	19 55			21 19	23 20
Cwmbran	d	20 10			21 30	23 29
Pontypool and New Inn	d	20 16			21 36	23 35
Abergavenny	d	20 26			21 46	23 45
Hereford 7	a	20 52	21 03		22 12	00 17
	d	20 54			22 14	
Leominster	d	21 08			22 27	
Ludlow	d	21 19			22 38	
Craven Arms	d	21 29			22 48	
Church Stretton	d	21 38			22 57	
Shrewsbury	a	21 55			23 14	
	d			22 32	23 19	
Yorton	d				23x28	
Wem	d				23 34	
Prees	d				23x39	
Whitchurch (Shrops)	d				23 46	
Wrenbury	d				23x52	
Nantwich	d				23 59	
Crewe 10	a			23 03	00 09	
Chester	a			23 31	00 33	
Llandudno Junction	a					
Bangor (Gwynedd)	a					
Holyhead	a					
Wilmslow	a					
Stockport	a					
Manchester Piccadilly 10	a					

A ◇ from Shrewsbury R to Shrewsbury

b Previous night, stops on request

For connections from Bristol Temple Meads please refer to Table 132.
For connections to Runcorn and Liverpool Lime Street please refer to Table 91

When events are being held at the Millenium Stadium,
services are subject to alteration. Please check times before travelling.

Table 131

Sundays

19 February to 25 March

Cardiff - Crewe, Liverpool and Manchester

Route Diagram - see first Page of Table 129

		AW	AW	AW	AW	AW	AW	GW	AW	AW	GW	AW	AW	AW	AW	GW	AW	AW	AW	GW	AW	AW	AW
													R	R	R		R	R	R			R	R
		◇		◇	◇	◇	◇	◇1	◇	◇	◇1	◇				◇1	◇			◇1	◇		
																	A						
					trolley	trolley	trolley	buffet	trolley	trolley	buffet			trolley	trolley	buffet	trolley	trolley	trolley				trolley
Swansea	d									11 32		11 06			13 43				15 33		15 26		17 30
Cardiff Central 7	d	20p55			08 30	09 30	10 35		11 35	12 40			13 22	13 40	14 56		15 22	15 56	16 40			17 35	18 40
London Paddington 15 ⊖	d							09 35			10 42					12 42				14 42			
Reading 7	d							10 11			11 21					13 23				15 21			
Newport (South Wales)	d	21p10			08 49	09 50	10 51		11 50	12 54			13 36	13 54	15 14		15 36	16 14	16 54			17 49	18 54
Cwmbran	d	21p21			09 00	10 00	11 02		12 04	13 09			13 47	14 09	15 24		15 47	16 24	17 09			18 04	19 09
Pontypool and New Inn	d				09 06	10 06	11 08		12 10	13 15							15 52		17 15			18 10	
Abergavenny	d	21p34			09 15	10 16	11 18		12 20	13 25			14 00	14 22	15 38		16 02	16 37	17 25			18 20	19 22
Hereford 7	a	21p58			09 40	10 40	11 44	12 54	12 44	13 49	14 06		14 26	14 47	16 02	16 05	16 27	17 02	17 49	17 58		18 44	19 47
	d	22p00			09 41	10 43	11 50		12 57	13 55			14 26	14 48	16 04		16 28	17 04	17 53			18 49	19 49
Leominster	d	22p14			09 55	10 56	12 03		13 10	14 08				15 01			16 41		18 07			19 03	20 03
Ludlow	d	22p25			10 06	11 07	12 14		13 21	14 19			14 48	15 12	16 25		16 52	17 26	18 18			19 14	20 14
Craven Arms	d	22p33			10 14		12 24			14 28		14 44					17 00		18 26		19 03		20 22
Church Stretton	d	22p42			10 23		12 33			14 37		14 57					17 09		18 35		19 16		20 31
Shrewsbury	a	22p57			10 37	11 36	12 48		13 47	14 51		15 15	15 21	15 38	16 51		17 23	17 52	18 49		19 31	19 40	20 45
	d	23p06	23p50	09 55	10 39	11 37	12 51		13 50	14 53			15 22	15 40	16 53		17 30	17 54	18 54			19 41	20 48
Yorton	d	23b14	23b58			11x45								15x48								19x49	
Wem	d	23p20	00 04		10 51	11 51								15 54								19 55	
Prees	d	23b24	00x07			11x55								15x58								19x59	
Whitchurch (Shrops)	d	23p31	00 15		11 00	12 03								16 06								20 06	
Wrenbury	d	23b36	00x20			12x08								16x11								20x11	
Nantwich	d	23p42	00 26		11 09	12 15								16 18								20 18	
Crewe 10	a	23p53	00 38	10 25	11 22	12 25	13 26		14 22	15 25				16 27	17 25			18 25	19 24			20 27	21 21
Chester	a	00 24											16 18				18 25						
Llandudno Junction	a												17 29				19 22						
Bangor (Gwynedd)	a												17 52				19 45						
Holyhead	a												18 37				20 18						
Wilmslow	a			10 46	11 41	12 46	13 49		14 46	15 46				16 46	17 45			18 46	19 46			20 45	21 45
Stockport	a			10 58		12 58	14 00		14 58	15 58				16 58	17 58			18 58	19 58			20 57	21 58
Manchester Piccadilly 10	a			11 12	12 02	13 15	14 19		15 15	16 15				17 15	18 17			19 15	20 17			21 14	22 19

		AW	GW	AW	AW	AW
		◇	◇1	◇	◇	◇
			buffet			
Swansea	d					21 52
Cardiff Central 7	d	19 40			21 04	23 00
London Paddington 15 ⊖	d		17 42			
Reading 7	d		18 25			
Newport (South Wales)	d	19 55			21 19	23 20
Cwmbran	d	20 10			21 30	23 29
Pontypool and New Inn	d	20 16			21 36	23 35
Abergavenny	d	20 26			21 46	23 45
Hereford 7	a	20 52	21 03		22 12	00 17
	d	20 54			22 14	
Leominster	d	21 08			22 27	
Ludlow	d	21 19			22 38	
Craven Arms	d	21 29			22 48	
Church Stretton	d	21 38			22 57	
Shrewsbury	a	21 55			23 14	
	d			22 32	23 19	
Yorton	d				23x28	
Wem	d				23 34	
Prees	d				23x39	
Whitchurch (Shrops)	d				23 46	
Wrenbury	d				23x52	
Nantwich	d				23 59	
Crewe 10	a			23 03	00 09	
Chester	a			23 31	00 33	
Llandudno Junction	a					
Bangor (Gwynedd)	a					
Holyhead	a					
Wilmslow	a					
Stockport	a					
Manchester Piccadilly 10	a					

A ◇ from Shrewsbury R to Shrewsbury

b Previous night, stops on request

For connections from Bristol Temple Meads please refer to Table 132.
For connections to Runcorn and Liverpool Lime Street please refer to Table 91

When events are being held at the Millenium Stadium,
services are subject to alteration. Please check times before travelling.

Table 131

Sundays
from 1 April

Cardiff - Crewe, Liverpool and Manchester

Route Diagram - see first Page of Table 129

		AW	AW	AW	AW	AW	AW	GW	AW	AW	GW	AW	AW	AW	AW	GW	AW	AW	AW	GW	AW	AW	AW
													R	R	R		R	R	R			R	R
		◇		◇	◇	◇	◇	◇**1**	◇	◇	◇**1**	◇				◇**1**	◇ A			◇**1**	◇		
					🛒	🛒	🛒	☕	🛒	🛒	☕			🛒	🛒	☕	🛒	🛒	🛒				🛒
Swansea	d									11 32		11 06			13 43				15 33		15 26		17 30
Cardiff Central 7	d	20p55			08 30	09 30	10 35		11 35	12 40			13 22	13 40	14 56		15 22	15 56	16 40			17 35	18 40
London Paddington 15 ⊖	d							09 35			10 42					12 42				14 42			
Reading 7	d							10 11			11 21					13 23				15 21			
Newport (South Wales)	d	21p10			08 49	09 50	10 51		11 50	12 54			13 36	13 54	15 14		15 36	16 14	16 54			17 49	18 54
Cwmbran	d	21p21			09 00	10 00	11 02		12 04	13 09			13 47	14 09	15 24		15 47	16 24	17 09			18 04	19 09
Pontypool and New Inn	d				09 06	10 06	11 08		12 10	13 15							15 52		17 15			18 10	
Abergavenny	d	21p34			09 15	10 16	11 18		12 20	13 25			14 00	14 22	15 38		16 02	16 37	17 25			18 20	19 22
Hereford 7	a	21p58			09 40	10 40	11 44	12 54	12 44	13 49	14 06		14 26	14 47	16 02	16 05	16 27	17 02	17 49	17 58		18 44	19 47
	d	22p00			09 41	10 43	11 50		12 57	13 55			14 26	14 48	16 04		16 28	17 04	17 53			18 49	19 49
Leominster	d	22p14			09 55	10 56	12 03		13 10	14 08				15 01			16 41		18 07			19 03	20 03
Ludlow	d	22p25			10 06	11 07	12 14		13 21	14 19			14 48	15 12	16 25		16 52	17 26	18 18			19 14	20 14
Craven Arms	d	22p33			10 14		12 24			14 28		14 44					17 00		18 26		19 03		20 22
Church Stretton	d	22p42			10 23		12 33			14 37		14 57					17 09		18 35		19 16		20 31
Shrewsbury	a	22p57			10 37	11 36	12 48		13 47	14 51		15 15	15 21	15 38	16 51		17 23	17 52	18 49		19 31	19 40	20 45
	d	23p06	23p50	09 55	10 39	11 37	12 51		13 50	14 53			15 22	15 40	16 53		17 30	17 54	18 54			19 41	20 48
Yorton	d	23b14	23b58			11x45								15x48								19x49	
Wem	d	23p20	00 04		10 51	11 51								15 54								19 55	
Prees	d	23b24	00x07			11x55								15x58								19x59	
Whitchurch (Shrops)	d	23p31	00 15		11 00	12 03								16 06								20 06	
Wrenbury	d	23b36	00x20			12x08								16x11								20x11	
Nantwich	d	23p42	00 26		11 09	12 15								16 18								20 18	
Crewe 10	a	23p53	00 38	10 25	11 22	12 25	13 26		14 22	15 25				16 27	17 25			18 25	19 24			20 27	21 21
Chester	a	00 24											16 18				18 25						
Llandudno Junction	a												17 29				19 22						
Bangor (Gwynedd)	a												17 52				19 45						
Holyhead	a												18 37				20 18						
Wilmslow	a			10 46	11 41	12 46	13 49		14 46	15 46				16 46	17 45			18 46	19 46			20 45	21 45
Stockport	a			10 58		12 58	14 00		14 58	15 58				16 58	17 58			18 58	19 58			20 57	21 58
Manchester Piccadilly 10 ⛴	a			11 12	12 02	13 15	14 19		15 15	16 15				17 15	18 17			19 15	20 17			21 14	22 19

		AW	GW	AW	AW	AW
		◇	◇**1**	◇	◇	◇
			☕			
Swansea	d					21 52
Cardiff Central 7	d	19 40			21 04	23 00
London Paddington 15 ⊖	d		17 42			
Reading 7	d		18 26			
Newport (South Wales)	d	19 55			21 19	23 20
Cwmbran	d	20 10			21 30	23 29
Pontypool and New Inn	d	20 16			21 36	23 35
Abergavenny	d	20 26			21 46	23 45
Hereford 7	a	20 52	21 03		22 12	00 17
	d	20 54			22 14	
Leominster	d	21 08			22 27	
Ludlow	d	21 19			22 38	
Craven Arms	d	21 29			22 48	
Church Stretton	d	21 38			22 57	
Shrewsbury	a	21 55			23 14	
	d			22 32	23 19	
Yorton	d				23x28	
Wem	d				23 34	
Prees	d				23x39	
Whitchurch (Shrops)	d				23 46	
Wrenbury	d				23x52	
Nantwich	d				23 59	
Crewe 10	a			23 03	00 09	
Chester	a			23 31	00 33	
Llandudno Junction	a					
Bangor (Gwynedd)	a					
Holyhead	a					
Wilmslow	a					
Stockport	a					
Manchester Piccadilly 10 ⛴	a					

A ◇ from Shrewsbury R to Shrewsbury

b Previous night, stops on request

For connections from Bristol Temple Meads please refer to Table 132.
For connections to Runcorn and Liverpool Lime Street please refer to Table 91

When events are being held at the Millenium Stadium,
services are subject to alteration. Please check times before travelling.

Table 131

Mondays to Fridays

Manchester, Liverpool and Crewe - Cardiff

Route Diagram - see first Page of Table 129

Miles	Miles			GW MX	AW MX	AW MO	AW MX	AW MX	AW MO	AW	AW	AW		AW	GW	AW			GW	AW	AW	AW		AW	AW BHX
				◇1	◇	◇	◇	◇		A	B	◇		◇	◇1 C ⊡∅	◇ ⍑			◇1 D ⊡∅	◇	◇ ⍑	◇ ⍑		◇ ⍑	◇ E ⊠⍑
0	—	**Manchester Piccadilly** 10 ✈	d		20p30	20p30		22p35		00§50														06 30	
6	—	Stockport	d		20p39	20p39		22p44		§														06 39	
12	—	Wilmslow	d		20p46	20p47		22p52		§														06 46	
—	—	Holyhead	d							§												04 25			05 32
—	—	Bangor (Gwynedd)	d							§												04 57			06 02
—	—	Llandudno Junction	d							§												05 15			06 21
—	—	Chester	d						23p00	§	04§22									05 15		06 18			07 08
31	35½	**Crewe** 10	d		21p08	21c13		23p14	23p23	01a31	04a44					04 54					05 55			07 08	07 33
35½	40	Nantwich	d		21p17	21p21		23p22	23p31							05 02					06 03			07 17	
40	44½	Wrenbury	d		21b23	21b26		23b27	23b37												06x09				
44¾	49¼	Whitchurch (Shrops)	d		21p30	21p35		23p34	23p45							05 13					06 16				
49¾	54¼	Prees	d		21b36	21b40		23b40	23b51												06x22				
53	57½	Wem	d		21p41	21p47		23p45	23p57							05 22					06 27				
56½	61	Yorton	d		21b46	21b51		23b50	00x02												06x32				
63¾	68¼	**Shrewsbury**	a		21p55	22p03		00 04	00 14							05 33				06 10	06 42	07 17		07 42	08 09
—	—		d		21p57	22p04	23p08							05 19		05 40				06 13	06 44	07 19		07 44	08 10
76½	81	Church Stretton	d		22p12	22p20	23p24							05 36		05 55				06 29	06 59			07 59	
83¾	88¼	Craven Arms	d		22p20	22p29	23p32							05 50		06 03				06 37	07 07			08 07	
91	95½	Ludlow	d		22p27	22p37	23p41									06 10				06 45	07 14	07 46		08 15	
102	106½	Leominster	d		22p38	22p49	23p52									06 21				06 56	07 25	07 56		08 26	
114½	119	**Hereford** 7	a		22p56	23p03	00 07									06 36				07 10	07 43	08 12		08 40	
—	—		d	21p51	22p58	23p05	00 09					05 25			05 35	06 42			06 44	07 13	07 45	08 13		08 42	
138½	143	Abergavenny	d		23p21	23p29	00 33					05 49				07 05				07 36	08 08	08 36		09 05	
148	152½	Pontypool and New Inn	d		23p30	23p39						05 59				07 15				07 46	08 17	08 46			
151	155½	Cwmbran	d		23p35	23p44	00 46					06 04				07 20				07 51	08 22	08 51		09 17	
158	162½	**Newport (South Wales)**	a		23p46	23p54	00 57					06 16				07 33				08 01	08 37	09 02		09 34	09 40
—	—	Reading 7	a	00 38											08 21				09 14						
—	—	London Paddington 15 ⊖	a	01 17											08 51				09 47						
169¾	174½	**Cardiff Central** 7	a		00 02	00 20	01 18					06 33				07 51				08 17	08 53	09 23		09 57	09 58
—	—	Swansea	a									07 45		09 08		08 50					09 55			10 55	

		AW	AW	AW	AW	AW	AW FO	AW FX		AW	AW	AW	AW	AW	AW	GW	AW	AW	AW		AW	AW	GW	AW	AW
			◇ ⍑	◇ ⍑	◇ ⍑	◇ ⍑				◇ ⍑	◇ ⍑	◇ ⍑	◇ ⍑	◇ ⍑		◇1 ⊡	◇ ⍑	R ⍑	R ⍑		◇		◇1 ⊡	R ⍑	◇ ⍑
Manchester Piccadilly 10 ✈	d		07 30			08 30						09 30		10 30			11 30		12 30					13 30	
Stockport	d		07 39			08 39						09 39		10 39			11 39		12 39					13 39	
Wilmslow	d		07 46			08 46						09 46		10 46			11 46		12 46					13 46	
Holyhead	d				06 28					07 15	07 51		08 05					10 33							12 39
Bangor (Gwynedd)	d				07 06					08 02	08 21		09 02					11 05							13 07
Llandudno Junction	d				07 24					08 25	08 39		09 25					11 25							13 25
Chester	d				08 19					09 19	19 27		10 20					12 19							14 19
Crewe 10	d	07 40	08 08			09 08	09 20	09 20		09 49		10 08		11 08	11 20		12 08		13 08			13 20		14 08	
Nantwich	d	07 47					09 28	09 28		09 56					11 28							13 28		14 17	
Wrenbury	d	07x53					09x34	09x34							11x35							13x35			
Whitchurch (Shrops)	d	08 00					09 42	09 42		10 07					11 43							13 43		14 28	
Prees	d	08x06					09x48	09x48							11x49							13x49			
Wem	d	08 12					09 54	09 54		10 16					11 55							13 55			
Yorton	d	08x17					10x00	10x00							12x01							14x01			
Shrewsbury	a	08 28	08 37		09 13	09 37	10 11	10 12		10 27	10 22	10 37	11 14	11 37	12 11		12 37	13 14	13 37			14 11		14 45	15 13
	d		08 40	09 00	09 14	09 40					10 24	10 39	11 16	11 39			12 40	13 15	13 40		14 04			14 50	15 15
Church Stretton	d			09 18	09 30							10 54		11 54				13 30			14 22			15 05	15 30
Craven Arms	d			09 28	09 38								11 37					13 38			14 33			15 13	15 38
Ludlow	d		09 06		09 45	10 06						11 08	11 44	12 08			13 06	13 45	14 06					15 20	15 46
Leominster	d		09 16			10 16						11 18		12 18			13 16		14 16					15 31	
Hereford 7	a		09 32		10 09	10 32						11 34	12 06	12 34			13 32	14 09	14 32					15 49	16 09
	d		09 33		10 10	10 33						11 35	12 08	12 35		13 14	13 33	14 11	14 33				15 14	15 51	16 11
Abergavenny	d		09 56		10 33	10 56						11 58	12 31	12 58			13 56	14 33	14 56					16 14	16 34
Pontypool and New Inn	d				10 43								12 42					14 44						16 23	16 44
Cwmbran	d		10 09		10 48	11 09						12 11	12 47	13 11			14 09	14 49	15 09					16 28	16 49
Newport (South Wales)	a		10 20		11 01	11 20					11 51	12 22	13 00	13 22			14 20	14 58	15 22					16 39	16 59
Reading 7	a															15 54							17 54		
London Paddington 15 ⊖	a															16 27							18 28		
Cardiff Central 7	a		10 37		11 15	11 37					12 08	12 38	13 22	13 39			14 37	15 19	15 53					16 55	17 15
Swansea	a		11 34	13 04		12 33						13 33		14 34			15 34		17 01		18 18			18 05	

A from 3 January until 6 January
B until 26 March, MO from 2 April
C ⊡ from Reading ∅ to Reading
D The Cathedrals Express. ⊡ from Reading ∅ to Reading
E ⊠ to Crewe ⍑ from Crewe
b Previous night, stops on request
c Previous night, arr. 2107

For connections from Liverpool Lime Street
and Runcorn please refer to Table 91.
For connections to Bristol Temple Meads please refer to Table 132

When events are being held at the Millenium Stadium,
services are subject to alteration. Please check times before travelling.

Table 131

Mondays to Fridays

Manchester, Liverpool and Crewe - Cardiff

Route Diagram - see first Page of Table 129

		AW	AW	AW	AW		AW	AW	AW		AW	AW	AW	AW	AW		AW		GW	AW	AW	AW	AW		
													FX	FO	FO		FX								
		■		■			■				■														
					◇			◇				◇	◇	◇	◇		◇		◇1	◇		◇	◇		
		⊥		⊥	⊥		⊥				⊥	⊥	⊥	⊥											
Manchester Piccadilly 10	d	14 30		15 30			16 30				17 30		18 30	18 30	19 30		19 30			20 30	21 35		22 35		
Stockport	d	14 39		15 39			16 39				17 39		18 39	18 39	19 39		19 39			20 39	21 44		22 44		
Wilmslow	d	14 46		15 46			16 46				17 46		18 46	18 46	19 46		19 46			20 46	21 51		22 52		
Holyhead	d				14 34							16 38													
Bangor (Gwynedd)	d				15 04							17 06													
Llandudno Junction	d				15 27							17 25													
Chester	d				16 19							18 18													
Crewe 10	d	15 08	15 20	16 08			17 08		17 20		18 08		19 08	19 08	20 08		20 08			21 08	22 12		23 14		
Nantwich	d		15 28	16 17					17 28		18 17		19 17	19 17	20 17		20 17			21 17	22 20		23 22		
Wrenbury	d		15x35						17x35				19x23	19x23						21x23	22x26		23x27		
Whitchurch (Shrops)	d		15 43	16 28					17 43		18 28		19 29	19 29	20 28		20 28			21 30	22 33		23 34		
Prees	d		15x49						17x49				19x35	19x35						21x36	22x39		23x40		
Wem	d		15 55	16 36					17 55		18 36		19 40	19 40	20 36		20 36			21 41	22 44		23 45		
Yorton	d		16x01						18x01				19x45	19x45						21x46	22x49		23x50		
Shrewsbury	a	15 37	16 11	16 47	17 14		17 37		18 11		18 47	19 15	19 55	19 55	20 47		20 47			21 55	23 01		00 04		
	d	15 40		16 50	17 16		17 40	18 05			18 50	19 17	19 56	19 56	20 50		20 50			21 57		23 08			
Church Stretton	d			17 06	17 31			18 22			19 05		20 11	20 11	21 05		21 05			22 12		23 24			
Craven Arms	d			17 14	17 39			18 35			19 13		20 19	20 19	21 13		21 13			22 20		23 32			
Ludlow	d	16 06		17 21	17 46		18 06				19 20	19 44	20 27	20 27	21 20		21 20			22 27		23 41			
Leominster	d	16 16		17 32	17 57		18 16				19 31		20 37	20 37	21 31		21 31			22 38		23 52			
Hereford 7	a	16 32		17 49	18 12		18 32				19 46	20 08	20 53	20 53	21 46		21 46			22 56		00 07			
	d	16 33		17 51	18 14		18 33				19 48	20 09	20 54	20 54	21 50		21 50		21 51	22 58		00 09			
Abergavenny	d	16 56		18 14	18 37		18 56				20 11	20 32	21 22	21 22	22 16		22 16			23 21		00 33			
Pontypool and New Inn	d			18 24							20 21		21 32	21 32						23 30					
Cwmbran	d	17 09		18 29	18 49		19 09				20 26	20 45	21 37	21 37	22 28		22 28			23 35		00 46			
Newport (South Wales)	a	17 21		18 39	19 00		19 22				20 37	20 58	21 50	21 50	22 39		22 41			23 46		00 57			
Reading 7	a																		00 38						
London Paddington 15 ⊖	a																		01 17						
Cardiff Central 7	a	17 37		18 55	19 21		19 43				20 58	21 19	22 06	22 06	22 55		23 04			00 02		01 18			
Swansea	a	18 37		20 04			20 42	22 08						23 07											

Saturdays

		GW	AW	AW	AW	AW	AW	AW	GW	AW			AW	GW	AW	AW	AW	AW	AW	AW		AW	AW	AW	AW
		◇1	◇	◇	◇		◇		◇1	◇				◇1	◇	◇	◇		◇	◇		◇	◇		◇
														A											
									🍽	⊥				🍽⊘	⊥	⊥	⊥		⊥	⊥		⊥	⊥		⊥
Manchester Piccadilly 10	d		20p30		22p35												06 30		07 30				08 30		09 30
Stockport	d		20p39		22p44												06 39		07 39				08 39		09 39
Wilmslow	d		20p46		22p52												06 46		07 46				08 46		09 46
Holyhead	d															04 25						06 35			
Bangor (Gwynedd)	d															04 57						07 07			
Llandudno Junction	d															05 15						07 25			
Chester	d					04 22										06 12						08 19			
Crewe 10	d		21p08		23p14	04a44				04 54					05 55		07 08	07 20	08 08				09 08	09 20	10 08
Nantwich	d		21p17		23p22					05 02					06 03		07 17	07 27	08 17					09 28	
Wrenbury	d		21c23		23c27										06x09			07x34						09x34	
Whitchurch (Shrops)	d		21p30		23p34					05 13					06 16		07 28	07 41	08 27					09 42	
Prees	d		21c36		23c40										06x22			07x47						09x48	
Wem	d		21p41		23p45					05 22					06 27		07 36	07 53						09 54	
Yorton	d		21c46		23c50										06x32			07x58						10x00	
Shrewsbury	a		21p55		00 04					05 33					06 42	07 17	07 47	08 08	08 45			09 13	09 37	10 12	10 36
	d		21p57	23p08			05 19			05 40			06 13		06 44	07 19	07 50		08 46	09 00		09 15	09 40		10 38
Church Stretton	d		22p12	23p24			05 36			05 55			06 28		06 59		08 05		09 01	09 17			09 55		10 54
Craven Arms	d		22p20	23p32			05 47			06 03			06 36		07 07		08 13		09 09	09 30			10 03		11 02
Ludlow	d		22p27	23p41						06 10			06 44		07 14	07 45	08 20		09 17			09 42	10 10		11 09
Leominster	d		22p38	23p52						06 21			06 55		07 25	07 55	08 31		09 27				10 21		11 20
Hereford 7	a		22p56	00 07						06 37			07 09		07 40	08 11	08 49		09 43			10 05	10 36		11 44
	d	21p51	22p58	00 09				05 42	06 17	06 42			07 11	07 10	07 44	08 12	08 51		09 44			10 07	10 38		11 46
Abergavenny	d		23p21	00 33				06 07		07 05			07 34		08 07	08 35	09 14		10 07			10 30	11 01		12 09
Pontypool and New Inn	d		23p30					06 18		07 15			07 44		08 16	08 45						10 40			
Cwmbran	d		23p35	00 46				06 23		07 20			07 49		08 21	08 50	09 26		10 20			10 45	11 13		12 21
Newport (South Wales)	a		23p46	00 57				06 34		07 37			08 00		08 31	09 01	09 37		10 35			10 55	11 27		12 35
Reading 7	a	00 38							08 54					09 54											
London Paddington 15 ⊖	a	01 17							09 29					10 29											
Cardiff Central 7	a		00 02	01 18				06 54		07 53			08 19		08 50	09 22	09 58		10 53			11 15	11 53		12 53
Swansea	a						09 08			08 51					09 57		10 55		11 56	13 01			12 55		13 55

A 🍽 from Reading ⊘ to Reading

c Previous night, stops on request

For connections from Liverpool Lime Street and Runcorn please refer to Table 91.
For connections to Bristol Temple Meads please refer to Table 132

When events are being held at the Millenium Stadium, services are subject to alteration. Please check times before travelling.

Table 131

Saturdays

Manchester, Liverpool and Crewe - Cardiff

Route Diagram - see first Page of Table 129

		AW	GW	AW	AW	AW	AW	AW	AW	AW	GW	AW	AW	AW	AW	AW	AW	AW	AW	AW	AW	AW
							R	R				R		R		R		R			R	
		◇	◇1	◇		◇			◇		◇1		◇				◇		◇			◇
			A																			
		✠	🍽	✠		✠	✠	✠			🍽	✠	✠	✠		✠	✠	✠			✠	✠
Manchester Piccadilly 10	d			10 30		11 30		12 30				13 30		14 30		15 30		16 30			17 30	
Stockport	d			10 39		11 39		12 39				13 39		14 39		15 39		16 39			17 39	
Wilmslow	d			10 46		11 46		12 46				13 46		14 46		15 46		16 46			17 46	
Holyhead	d	08 20					10 33						12 38				14 23					16 38
Bangor (Gwynedd)	d	09 02					11 05						13 07				14 53					17 07
Llandudno Junction	d	09 25					11 25						13 25				15 16					17 25
Chester	d	10 19					12 19						14 19				16 19					18 20
Crewe 10	d			11 08	11 20	12 08		13 08		13 20		14 08		15 08	15 20	16 08		17 08		17 20	18 08	
Nantwich	d				11 31	12 17				13 28		14 17			15 28	16 17		17 17		17 28	18 17	
Wrenbury	d				11x42					13x35					15x35					17x35		
Whitchurch (Shrops)	d				11 49	12 27				13 43		14 27			15 43	16 27		17 27		17 43	18 28	
Prees	d				11x56					13x49					15x49					17x49		
Wem	d				12 02					13 55					15 55					17 55		
Yorton	d				12x08					14x01					16x01					18x01		
Shrewsbury	a	11 14		11 37	12 18	12 45	13 13	13 37		14 11		14 43	15 13	15 37	16 11	16 43	17 14	17 43		18 11	18 45	19 15
	d	11 15		11 40		12 46	13 15	13 40	14 05			14 45	15 15	15 40		16 45	17 16	17 45	18 05		18 47	19 16
Church Stretton	d			11 55		13 01		13 55	14 23			15 00		15 55		17 00		18 00	18 23		19 02	
Craven Arms	d			12 03		13 09		14 03	14 36			15 08		16 03		17 08		18 08	18 36		19 10	
Ludlow	d	11 41		12 10		13 17	13 40	14 10				15 15	15 41	16 10		17 15	17 42	18 15			19 17	19 41
Leominster	d			12 21		13 27		14 21				15 26		16 21		17 26		18 26			19 28	
Hereford 7	a	12 04		12 36		13 44	14 04	14 36				15 41	16 03	16 36		17 41	18 05	18 41			19 49	20 09
	d	12 06	12 13	12 38		13 46	14 06	14 38			15 13	15 46	16 06	16 38		17 46	18 07	18 43			19 51	20 11
Abergavenny	d	12 29		13 01		14 09	14 28	15 01				16 09	16 29	17 01		18 09	18 30	19 06			20 14	20 34
Pontypool and New Inn	d	12 39					14 39						16 39				18 40				20 23	
Cwmbran	d	12 44		13 13		14 21	14 44	15 13				16 21	16 44	17 13		18 21	18 45	19 18			20 28	20 46
Newport (South Wales)	a	12 54		13 28		14 33	15 05	15 35				16 33	16 54	17 33		18 33	18 55	19 34			20 39	21 00
Reading 7	a		14 53								17 55											
London Paddington 15 ⊖	a		15 29								18 29											
Cardiff Central 7	a	13 15		13 53		14 53	15 26	15 53				16 53	17 08	17 53		18 53	19 16	19 58			21 00	21 21
Swansea	a			14 55		15 55		16 58	18 10			18 05		19 02		20 04			22 10			

		GW	AW	AW	AW	AW	AW	AW
		◇1	◇					
			✠					
Manchester Piccadilly 10	d		18 30	19 30	20 30	21 35	22 35	
Stockport	d		18 39	19 39	20 39	21 44	22 44	
Wilmslow	d		18 46	19 46	20 46	21 51	22 52	
Holyhead	d							
Bangor (Gwynedd)	d							
Llandudno Junction	d							
Chester	d							
Crewe 10	d		19 10	20 08	21 08	22 12	23 14	
Nantwich	d		19 18	20 17	21 17	22 20	23 22	
Wrenbury	d		19x24		21x23	22x26	23x27	
Whitchurch (Shrops)	d		19 31	20 27	21 29	22 33	23 34	
Prees	d		19x37		21x35	22x39	23x40	
Wem	d		19 42	20 36	21 40	22 44	23 45	
Yorton	d		19x47		21x45	22x49	23x50	
Shrewsbury	a		19 56	20 47	21 53	23 01	00 04	
	d		19 58	20 48	21 55			
Church Stretton	d		20 13	21 03	22 10			
Craven Arms	d		20 21	21 11	22 18			
Ludlow	d		20 28	21 19	22 26			
Leominster	d		20 39	21 29	22 37			
Hereford 7	a		20 54	21 45	22 51			
	d	20 20	20 56	21 46	22 53			23 15
Abergavenny	d		21 19	22 09	23 16			23 38
Pontypool and New Inn	d		21 28		23 25			
Cwmbran	d		21 33	22 22	23 30			23 50
Newport (South Wales)	a		21 44	22 33	23 45			00 02
Reading 7	a	23 08						
London Paddington 15 ⊖	a	23 46						
Cardiff Central 7	a		22 04	22 53	00 05			00 26
Swansea	a		23 05					

A until 11 February, from 31 March

For connections from Liverpool Lime Street
and Runcorn please refer to Table 91.
For connections to Bristol Temple Meads please refer to Table 132

When events are being held at the Millenium Stadium,
services are subject to alteration. Please check times before travelling.

Table 131

Sundays

until 1 January

Manchester, Liverpool and Crewe - Cardiff

Route Diagram - see first Page of Table 129

		AW	AW	AW	AW		AW	AW	AW	AW		GW	AW	AW	GW	AW	AW	GW	AW	AW		AW	GW	AW	AW
									R				R			R	R		R			R		R	R
							◇	◇		◇		◇1		◇	◇1			◇1		◇			◇1		
		A	A	A	bus																				
								⊥	⊥			bistro	⊥	⊥	bistro	⊥	⊥	bistro	⊥			⊥		⊥	⊥
Manchester Piccadilly 10	d	20p30	22p35					09 30	10 30				11 24			12 30	13 30		14 30			15 30		16 30	17 30
Stockport	d	20p39	22p44					09 39	10 39				11 40			12 40	13 40		14 39			15 39		16 39	17 39
Wilmslow	d	20p46	22p52					09 47	10 48				11 47			12 48	13 47		14 47			15 47		16 47	17 47
Holyhead	d													10 20											
Bangor (Gwynedd)	d													10 59											
Llandudno Junction	d													11 22											
Chester	d													12 21											
Crewe 10	d	21p08	23p14					10 13	11 11				12 13			13 13	14 13		15 10			16 13		17 13	18 13
Nantwich	d	21p17	23p22					10 22								13 21								17 21	
Wrenbury	d	21b23	23b27					10x27								13x26								17x26	
Whitchurch (Shrops)	d	21p29	23p34					10 35								13 34								17 34	
Prees	d	21b35	23b40					10x40								13x39								17x39	
Wem	d	21p40	23p45					10 46								13 45								17 45	
Yorton	d	21b45	23b50					10x50								13x49								17x49	
Shrewsbury	a	21p53	00 04					11 01	11 41				12 43	13 18		13 59	14 43		15 44			16 43		18 00	18 43
	d	21p55			07 50			11 03	11 45	12 07			12 44	13 19		14 01	14 44		15 47	16 18		16 44		18 01	18 44
Church Stretton	d	22p10						11 19		12 25				13 35			15 00			16 36		17 00			
Craven Arms	d	22p18						11 27		12 36				13 43			15 08			16 47		17 08			
Ludlow	d	22p26						11 36	12 13				13 12	13 51		14 28	15 16		16 17			17 16		18 29	19 12
Leominster	d	22p37						11 47	12 23				13 22	14 02		14 39	15 26		16 28			17 26		18 39	
Hereford 7	a	22p51			09 50			12 02	12 38				13 37	14 17		14 53	15 41		16 43			17 41		18 54	19 34
	d	22p53		23p15			10 09	12 03	12 39			13 32	13 39	14 19	14 32	14 56	15 43	16 35	16 44			17 43	18 30	18 57	19 36
Abergavenny	d	23p16		23p38			10 33	12 27	13 02				14 02	14 42		15 19	16 06		17 08			18 06		19 20	19 59
Pontypool and New Inn	d	23p25					10 43		13 12					14 52			16 16					18 16			
Cwmbran	d	23p30		23p50			10 48	12 40	13 17				14 14	14 57		15 31	16 21		17 21			18 21		19 33	20 11
Newport (South Wales)	a	23p45		00 02			10 59	12 51	13 28				14 28	15 07		15 45	16 31		17 33			18 31		19 49	20 22
Reading 7	a											16 20			17 21			19 28					21 21		
London Paddington 15 ⊖	a											16 59			18 06			20 06					22 04		
Cardiff Central 7	a	00 05		00 26			11 16	13 13	13 44				14 49	15 31		16 02	16 52		17 50			18 50		20 06	20 43
Swansea	a						12 13		15 10	16 04						17 14			19 15	20 16					

		AW	AW	AW	AW	AW		AW
		R		R				
			◇		◇	◇		
		⊥	⊥	⊥				
Manchester Piccadilly 10	d			18 30	19 30	20 30		
Stockport	d			18 39	19 39	20 39		
Wilmslow	d			18 47	19 47	20 47		
Holyhead	d	16 25	18 25					
Bangor (Gwynedd)	d	17 04	19 04					
Llandudno Junction	d	17 25	19 24					
Chester	d	18 24	20 27					23 00
Crewe 10	d		20a48	19 13	20 13	21 13		23 23
Nantwich	d			19 21		21 21		23 31
Wrenbury	d			19x26		21x26		23x37
Whitchurch (Shrops)	d			19 34		21 35		23 45
Prees	d			19x39		21x40		23x51
Wem	d			19 45		21 47		23 57
Yorton	d			19x49		21x51		00x02
Shrewsbury	a	19 20		20 00	20 42	22 03		00 14
	d	19 21		20 01	20 43	22 04		
Church Stretton	d	19 37			20 59	22 20		
Craven Arms	d	19 45			21 07	22 29		
Ludlow	d	19 53		20 29	21 15	22 37		
Leominster	d	20 04		20 39	21 25	22 49		
Hereford 7	a	20 18		20 54	21 40	23 03		
	d	20 21		20 55	21 42	23 05		
Abergavenny	d	20 46		21 18	22 05	23 29		
Pontypool and New Inn	d	20 56			22 15	23 39		
Cwmbran	d	21 01		21 31	22 20	23 44		
Newport (South Wales)	a	21 14		21 44	22 32	23 54		
Reading 7	a							
London Paddington 15 ⊖	a							
Cardiff Central 7	a	21 36		22 05	22 59	00 20		
Swansea	a							

A not 11 December

b Previous night, stops on request

For connections from Liverpool Lime Street and Runcorn please refer to Table 91.
For connections to Bristol Temple Meads please refer to Table 132

When events are being held at the Millenium Stadium, services are subject to alteration. Please check times before travelling.

Table 131

Sundays

8 January to 12 February

Manchester, Liverpool and Crewe - Cardiff

Route Diagram - see first Page of Table 129

		AW	AW	AW	AW	XC	AW	AW	AW	AW	GW	AW	AW	GW	AW	AW	GW	AW	AW	AW	GW	AW
									R			R			R	R		R		R		R
						◇1	◇	◇		◇	◇1		◇	◇1			◇1		◇		◇1	
Manchester Piccadilly 10	d	20p30	22p35			09 27		09 30	10 30			11 24			12 30	13 30		14 30		15 30		16 30
Stockport	d	20p39	22p44			09 36		09 39	10 39			11 40			12 40	13 40		14 39		15 39		16 39
Wilmslow	d	20p46	22p52			09 43		09 47	10 48			11 47			12 48	13 47		14 47		15 47		16 47
Holyhead	d												10 20									
Bangor (Gwynedd)	d												10 59									
Llandudno Junction	d												11 22									
Chester	d												12 21									
Crewe 10	d	21p08	23p14			10a01		10 13	11 11			12 13			13 13	14 13		15 10		16 13		17 13
Nantwich	d	21p17	23p22					10 22							13 21							17 21
Wrenbury	d	21b23	23b27					10x27							13x26							17x26
Whitchurch (Shrops)	d	21p29	23p34					10 35							13 34							17 34
Prees	d	21b35	23b40					10x40							13x39							17x39
Wem	d	21p40	23p45					10 46							13 45							17 45
Yorton	d	21b45	23b50					10x50							13x49							17x49
Shrewsbury	a	21p53	00 04					11 01	11 41			12 43	13 18		13 59	14 43		15 44		16 47		18 00
	d	21p55			07 50			11 03	11 45	12 07		12 44	13 19		14 01	14 44		15 47	16 18	16 48		18 01
Church Stretton	d	22p10						11 19		12 25			13 35			15 00			16 36	17 04		
Craven Arms	d	22p18						11 27		12 36			13 43			15 08			16 47	17 13		
Ludlow	d	22p26						11 36	12 13			13 12	13 52		14 28	15 16		16 17		17 21		18 29
Leominster	d	22p37						11 47	12 23			13 22	14 04		14 39	15 26		16 28		17 33		18 39
Hereford 7	a	22p51			09 50			12 02	12 38			13 37	14 19		14 53	15 41		16 43		17 47		18 54
	d	22p53		23p15			10 09	12 03	12 39		13 32	13 39	14 21	14 32	14 56	15 43	16 35	16 45		17 49	18 30	18 57
Abergavenny	d	23p16		23p38			10 33	12 27	13 02			14 02	14 45		15 19	16 06		17 09		18 13		19 20
Pontypool and New Inn	d	23p25					10 43		13 12				14 56			16 16				18 23		
Cwmbran	d	23p30		23p50			10 48	12 40	13 17			14 14	15 01		15 31	16 21		17 22		18 28		19 33
Newport (South Wales)	a	23p45		00 02			10 59	12 51	13 28			14 28	15 15		15 45	16 31		17 34		18 45		19 49
Reading 7	a										16 23			17 25			19 28				21 26	
London Paddington 15 ⊖	a										17 02			18 06			20 07				22 07	
Cardiff Central 7	a	00 05		00 26			11 19	13 13	13 49			14 49	15 35		16 07	16 52		17 57		19 03		20 06
Swansea	a									16 08									20 19			

		AW	AW	AW	AW	AW	AW	AW
		R	R		R			
				◇		◇	◇	
Manchester Piccadilly 10	d	17 30			18 30	19 30	20 30	
Stockport	d	17 39			18 39	19 39	20 39	
Wilmslow	d	17 47			18 47	19 47	20 47	
Holyhead	d		16 25	18 25				
Bangor (Gwynedd)	d		17 04	19 04				
Llandudno Junction	d		17 25	19 24				
Chester	d		18 24	20 27				23 00
Crewe 10	d	18 13		20a48	19 13	20 10	21 13	23 23
Nantwich	d				19 21		21 21	23 31
Wrenbury	d				19x26		21x26	23x37
Whitchurch (Shrops)	d				19 34		21 35	23 45
Prees	d				19x39		21x40	23x51
Wem	d				19 45		21 47	23 57
Yorton	d				19x49		21x51	00x02
Shrewsbury	a	18 43	19 20		20 00	20 44	22 03	00 14
	d	18 44	19 21		20 01	20 45	22 04	
Church Stretton	d		19 37			21 01	22 20	
Craven Arms	d		19 45			21 10	22 29	
Ludlow	d	19 12	19 53		20 29	21 18	22 37	
Leominster	d		20 04		20 39	21 30	22 49	
Hereford 7	a	19 34	20 18		20 54	21 44	23 03	
	d	19 36	20 21		20 55	21 46	23 05	
Abergavenny	d	19 59	20 46		21 18	22 10	23 29	
Pontypool and New Inn	d		20 56			22 21	23 39	
Cwmbran	d	20 11	21 01		21 31	22 26	23 44	
Newport (South Wales)	a	20 22	21 14		21 44	22 43	23 54	
Reading 7	a							
London Paddington 15 ⊖	a							
Cardiff Central 7	a	20 43	21 36		22 05	23 05	00 20	
Swansea	a							

b Previous night, stops on request

For connections from Liverpool Lime Street
and Runcorn please refer to Table 91.
For connections to Bristol Temple Meads please refer to Table 132

When events are being held at the Millenium Stadium,
services are subject to alteration. Please check times before travelling.

Table 131

Sundays

19 February to 25 March

Manchester, Liverpool and Crewe - Cardiff

Route Diagram - see first Page of Table 129

		AW	AW	AW	AW		XC	AW	AW	AW		AW	GW	AW	AW	GW	AW	AW	GW	AW		AW	AW	GW	AW
										R				R			R	R		R			R		R
							◇1	◇	◇			◇	◇1		◇	◇1			◇1			◇		◇1	
					🚌																				
							🍴		🍴	🍴			🍽	🍴	🍴	🍽	🍴	🍴	🍽	🍴			🍴		🍴
Manchester Piccadilly 10	d	20p30	22p35				09 27		09 30	10 30				11 24			12 30	13 30		14 30			15 30		16 30
Stockport	d	20p39	22p44				09 36		09 39	10 39				11 40			12 40	13 40		14 39			15 39		16 39
Wilmslow	d	20p46	22p52				09 43		09 47	10 48				11 47			12 48	13 47		14 47			15 47		16 47
Holyhead	d														10 20										
Bangor (Gwynedd)	d														10 59										
Llandudno Junction	d														11 22										
Chester	d														12 21										
Crewe 10	d	21p08	23p14				10a01		10 13	11 11				12 13			13 13	14 13		15 10			16 13		17 13
Nantwich	d	21p17	23p22						10 22								13 21								17 21
Wrenbury	d	21b23	23b27						10x27								13x26								17x26
Whitchurch (Shrops)	d	21p29	23p34						10 35								13 34								17 34
Prees	d	21b35	23b40						10x40								13x39								17x39
Wem	d	21p40	23p45						10 46								13 45								17 45
Yorton	d	21b45	23b50						10x50								13x49								17x49
Shrewsbury	a	21p53	00 04						11 01	11 41				12 43	13 18		13 59	14 43		15 44			16 43		18 00
	d	21p55			07 50				11 03	11 45		12 07		12 44	13 19		14 01	14 44		15 47		16 18	16 44		18 01
Church Stretton	d	22p10							11 19			12 25			13 35			15 00				16 36	17 00		
Craven Arms	d	22p18							11 27			12 36			13 43			15 08				16 47	17 08		
Ludlow	d	22p26							11 36	12 13				13 12	13 51		14 28	15 16		16 17			17 16		18 29
Leominster	d	22p37							11 47	12 23				13 22	14 02		14 39	15 26		16 28			17 26		18 39
Hereford 7	a	22p51			09 50				12 02	12 38				13 37	14 17		14 53	15 41		16 43			17 41		18 54
	d	22p53		23p15				10 09	12 03	12 39			13 32	13 39	14 19	14 32	14 56	15 43	16 35	16 44			17 43	18 30	18 57
Abergavenny	d	23p16		23p38				10 33	12 27	13 02				14 02	14 42		15 19	16 06		17 08			18 06		19 20
Pontypool and New Inn	d	23p25						10 43		13 12					14 52			16 16					18 16		
Cwmbran	d	23p30		23p50				10 48	12 40	13 17				14 14	14 57		15 31	16 21		17 21			18 21		19 33
Newport (South Wales)	a	23p45		00 02				10 59	12 51	13 28				14 28	15 07		15 45	16 31		17 33			18 31		19 49
Reading 7	a												16 27			17 24			19 29					21 26	
London Paddington 15 ⊖	a												17 06			18 07			20 07					22 07	
Cardiff Central 7	a	00 05		00 26				11 16	13 13	13 44				14 49	15 31		16 02	16 52		17 50			18 50		20 06
Swansea	a							12 13		15 09		16 04					17 14			19 15		20 16			

		AW	AW	AW	AW	AW		AW	AW
		R	R		R				
				◇		◇		◇	
		🍴	🍴	🍴	🍴				
Manchester Piccadilly 10	d	17 30			18 30	19 30		20 30	
Stockport	d	17 39			18 39	19 39		20 39	
Wilmslow	d	17 47			18 47	19 47		20 47	
Holyhead	d		16 25	18 25					
Bangor (Gwynedd)	d		17 04	19 04					
Llandudno Junction	d		17 25	19 24					
Chester	d		18 24	20 27					23 00
Crewe 10	d	18 13		20a48	19 13	20 13		21 13	23 23
Nantwich	d				19 21			21 21	23 31
Wrenbury	d				19x26			21x26	23x37
Whitchurch (Shrops)	d				19 34			21 35	23 45
Prees	d				19x39			21x40	23x51
Wem	d				19 45			21 47	23 57
Yorton	d				19x49			21x51	00x02
Shrewsbury	a	18 43	19 20		20 00	20 43		22 03	00 14
	d	18 44	19 21		20 01	20 44		22 04	
Church Stretton	d		19 37			21 00		22 20	
Craven Arms	d		19 45			21 08		22 29	
Ludlow	d	19 12	19 53		20 29	21 16		22 37	
Leominster	d		20 04		20 39	21 26		22 49	
Hereford 7	a	19 34	20 18		20 54	21 41		23 03	
	d	19 36	20 21		20 55	21 43		23 05	
Abergavenny	d	19 59	20 46		21 18	22 06		23 29	
Pontypool and New Inn	d		20 56			22 16		23 39	
Cwmbran	d	20 11	21 01		21 31	22 21		23 44	
Newport (South Wales)	a	20 22	21 20		21 44	22 31		23 54	
Reading 7	a								
London Paddington 15 ⊖	a								
Cardiff Central 7	a	20 43	21 45		22 05	22 57		00 20	
Swansea	a								

b Previous night, stops on request

For connections from Liverpool Lime Street and Runcorn please refer to Table 91. For connections to Bristol Temple Meads please refer to Table 132

When events are being held at the Millenium Stadium, services are subject to alteration. Please check times before travelling.

Table 131

Sundays

from 1 April

Manchester, Liverpool and Crewe - Cardiff

Route Diagram - see first Page of Table 129

		AW	AW	AW	AW	AW	AW	AW	AW	GW	AW	AW	GW	AW	AW	GW	AW	AW	AW	GW	AW	AW
								[R]			[R]			[R]	[R]		[R]		[R]		[R]	[R]
						◇	◇		◇	◇[1]		◇	◇[1]			◇[1]		◇		◇[1]		
					[bus]		[trolley]	[trolley]		[buffet]	[trolley]	[trolley]	[buffet]	[trolley]	[trolley]	[buffet]	[trolley]		[trolley]		[trolley]	[trolley]
Manchester Piccadilly [10] ⇌	d	20p30	22p35				09 30	10 30			11 24			12 30	13 30		14 30		15 30		16 30	17 30
Stockport	d	20p39	22p44				09 39	10 39			11 40			12 40	13 40		14 39		15 39		16 39	17 39
Wilmslow	d	20p46	22p52				09 47	10 48			11 47			12 48	13 47		14 47		15 47		16 47	17 47
Holyhead	d											10 20										
Bangor (Gwynedd)	d											10 59										
Llandudno Junction	d											11 22										
Chester	d											12 21										
Crewe [10]	d	21p08	23p14				10 13	11 11			12 13			13 13	14 13		15 10		16 13		17 13	18 13
Nantwich	d	21p17	23p22				10 22							13 21							17 21	
Wrenbury	d	21b23	23b27				10x27							13x26							17x26	
Whitchurch (Shrops)	d	21p29	23p34				10 35							13 34							17 34	
Prees	d	21b35	23b40				10x40							13x39							17x39	
Wem	d	21p40	23p45				10 46							13 45							17 45	
Yorton	d	21b45	23b50				10x50							13x49							17x49	
Shrewsbury	a	21p53	00 04				11 01	11 41			12 43	13 18		13 59	14 43		15 44		16 43		18 00	18 43
	d	21p55			07 50		11 03	11 45	12 07		12 44	13 19		14 01	14 44		15 47	16 18	16 44		18 01	18 44
Church Stretton	d	22p10					11 19		12 25			13 35			15 00			16 36	17 00			
Craven Arms	d	22p18					11 27		12 36			13 43			15 08			16 47	17 08			
Ludlow	d	22p26					11 36	12 13			13 12	13 51		14 28	15 16		16 17		17 16		18 29	19 12
Leominster	d	22p37					11 47	12 23			13 22	14 02		14 39	15 26		16 28		17 26		18 39	
Hereford [7]	a	22p51			09 50		12 02	12 38			13 37	14 17		14 53	15 41		16 43		17 41		18 54	19 34
	d	22p53		23p15		10 09	12 03	12 39		13 32	13 39	14 19	14 32	14 56	15 43	16 35	16 44		17 43	18 30	18 57	19 36
Abergavenny	d	23p16		23p38		10 33	12 27	13 02			14 02	14 42		15 19	16 06		17 08		18 06		19 20	19 59
Pontypool and New Inn	d	23p25				10 43		13 12				14 52			16 16				18 16			
Cwmbran	d	23p30		23p50		10 48	12 40	13 17			14 14	14 57		15 31	16 21		17 21		18 21		19 33	20 11
Newport (South Wales)	a	23p45		00 02		10 59	12 51	13 28			14 28	15 07		15 45	16 31		17 33		18 31		19 49	20 22
Reading [7]	a									16 25			17 26			19 30				21 26		
London Paddington [15] ⊖	a									17 05			18 13			20 07				22 07		
Cardiff Central [7]	a	00 05		00 26		11 16	13 13	13 44			14 49	15 31		16 02	16 52		17 50		18 50		20 06	20 43
Swansea	a					12 13		15 09	16 04					17 14			19 15	20 16				

		AW	AW	AW	AW	AW	AW
		[R]		[R]			
			◇		◇	◇	
		[trolley]	[trolley]	[trolley]			
Manchester Piccadilly [10] ⇌	d			18 30	19 30	20 30	
Stockport	d			18 39	19 39	20 39	
Wilmslow	d			18 47	19 47	20 47	
Holyhead	d	16 25	18 25				
Bangor (Gwynedd)	d	17 04	19 04				
Llandudno Junction	d	17 25	19 24				
Chester	d	18 24	20 27				23 00
Crewe [10]	d		20a48	19 13	20 13	21 13	23 23
Nantwich	d			19 21		21 21	23 31
Wrenbury	d			19x26		21x26	23x37
Whitchurch (Shrops)	d			19 34		21 35	23 45
Prees	d			19x39		21x40	23x51
Wem	d			19 45		21 47	23 57
Yorton	d			19x49		21x51	00x02
Shrewsbury	a	19 20		20 00	20 42	22 03	00 14
	d	19 21		20 01	20 43	22 04	
Church Stretton	d	19 37			20 59	22 20	
Craven Arms	d	19 45			21 07	22 29	
Ludlow	d	19 53		20 29	21 15	22 37	
Leominster	d	20 04		20 39	21 25	22 49	
Hereford [7]	a	20 18		20 54	21 40	23 03	
	d	20 21		20 55	21 42	23 05	
Abergavenny	d	20 46		21 18	22 05	23 29	
Pontypool and New Inn	d	20 56			22 15	23 39	
Cwmbran	d	21 01		21 31	22 20	23 44	
Newport (South Wales)	a	21 14		21 46	22 32	23 54	
Reading [7]	a						
London Paddington [15] ⊖	a						
Cardiff Central [7]	a	21 36		22 07	22 59	00 20	
Swansea	a						

b Previous night, stops on request

For connections from Liverpool Lime Street
and Runcorn please refer to Table 91.
For connections to Bristol Temple Meads please refer to Table 132

When events are being held at the Millenium Stadium,
services are subject to alteration. Please check times before travelling.

Network Diagram for Tables 132, 133 ,134

DM-26/05
Design BAJS

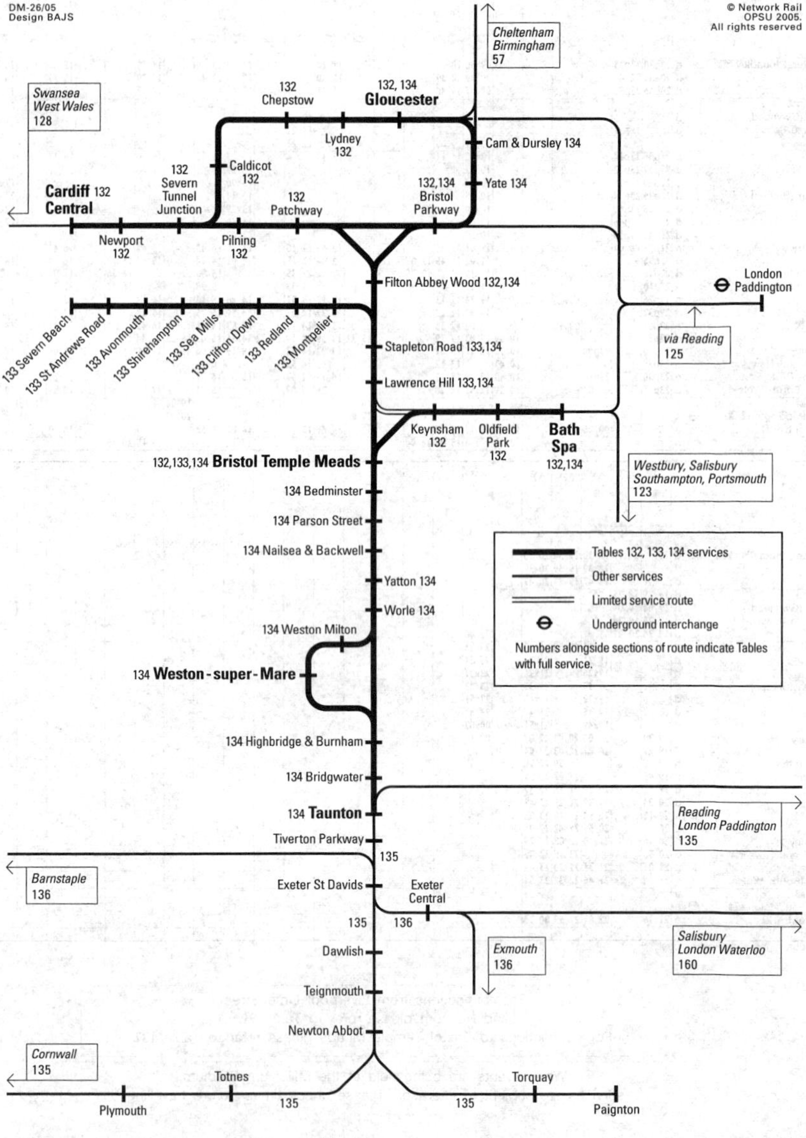

Cardiff - Gloucester, Bristol and Bath Spa

Network Diagram - see first Page of Table 132

Miles	Miles	Miles			AW MX	GW MX	AW MX	AW	AW	GW	GW	AW	GW		GW	GW	AW	GW	GW	GW	GW	GW	GW		XC
								◇	◇ 🛒	◇1 ☕	◇1 ☕	◇ 🛒	◇		◇1 ☕	◇1 ☕		◇1 ☕	◇1 ☕	◇1 ☕		◇1 ☕	◇ 🛒		◇1
0	0	0	**Cardiff Central 7**	d	23p19	23p27	00 30	04 35	05 10	05 14		05 40			05 55		06 12	06 24					06 28		06 40
11¾	11¾	11¾	Newport (South Wales)	a	23p39	23p44	00 48	04 50	05 25	05 30		05 55			06 09		06 26	06 37					06 41		06 53
—	—	—		d	23p40	23p45				05 32					06 09		06 28	06 38					06 42		06 55
21¾	21¾	21¾	Severn Tunnel Jn	d	23p58	00 03											06 38						06 53		07 05
—	—	22½	Caldicot	d	00 01												06 40								07 08
—	—	29¼	Chepstow	d	00 10												06 49								07 16
—	—	37	Lydney	d	00 19												06 58								07 25
—	—	56½	**Gloucester 7**	a	00 39												07 20								07 44
28¾	28¾	—	Pilning	d																					
32¼	32¼	—	Patchway	d		00 16																	07 06		
—	33½	—	**Bristol Parkway 7**	a						05 59					06 29			06 58							
—	—	—		d																					
33¾	—	—	Filton Abbey Wood	d		00 20																	07 09		
38¼	—	—	**Bristol Temple Meads 10**	a		00 33																	07 17		
—	—	—		d							05 30		05 44			06 00			06 30	06 40	06 48	07 00	07 22		
42¾	—	—	Keynsham	d									05 51								06 55				
48¾	—	—	Oldfield Park	d									05 58								07 02				
49¾	—	—	**Bath Spa 7**	a							05 41		06 01			06 11			06 41	06 51	07 05	07 11	07 34		

		AW	GW	GW	GW	XC	AW	AW	GW		GW	GW	GW	XC	GW	GW	GW	GW	AW		GW	SW	GW	GW	GW
		◇ 🛒	◇1 A ☕		◇1 B Ø	◇1		◇ 🛒	◇1 ☕			◇1 Ø	R 🛒	◇1 C 🛒	◇1 ☕	◇	◇1 Ø	◇	◇ 🛒		◇1 Ø	◇1	◇1 ☕		◇ 🛒
Cardiff Central 7	d	06 50			06 55	07 00	07 12	07 21				07 25	07 30	07 45			07 55	08 00	08 05		08 25				08 30
Newport (South Wales)	a	07 02			07 09	07 13	07 26	07 34				07 39	07 44	07 59			08 09	08 13	08 17		08 39				08 42
	d				07 09	07 15	07 27					07 39	07 44	08 02			08 09	08 15			08 39				08 44
Severn Tunnel Jn	d					07 25	07 38						07 55					08 26							08 55
Caldicot	d						07 40																		
Chepstow	d						07 49																		
Lydney	d						07 58							08 25											
Gloucester 7	a						08 20							08 44											
Pilning	d																								
Patchway	d					07 37												08 39							
Bristol Parkway 7	a				07 29							07 59					08 30				08 59				
	d			07 25							07 49					08 19									
Filton Abbey Wood	d			07 28		07 41					07 53		08 09			08 23		08 42							09 09
Bristol Temple Meads 10	a			07 39		07 51					08 01		08 17			08 36		08 50							09 17
	d		07 30	07 49					08 00		08 12		08 22		08 30	08 41						08 51	09 00	09 05	09 22
Keynsham	d			07 56							08 19					08 48						08 58			
Oldfield Park	d			08 03							08 26					08 55								09 17	
Bath Spa 7	a		07 41	08 05					08 11		08 28		08 34		08 41	08 58						09 05	09 11	09 19	09 34

		XC	AW	GW	GW		GW	GW	AW	AW	GW	GW	GW	XC	GW		GW	GW	GW	AW	AW	GW	GW	GW	XC
		◇1 C 🛒	◇ 🛒	◇1 ☕	◇		◇1 ☕	◇		◇ 🛒	◇1 D ☕	◇1 ☕	◇ 🛒	◇1 C 🛒	◇1 ☕			◇1 ☕		◇ 🛒		◇1 ☕	◇1 ☕	◇ 🛒	◇1 C 🛒
Cardiff Central 7	d	08 45	08 50				08 55	09 00	09 12	09 21	09 25		09 30	09 45				09 55	10 00	10 05	10 12	10 25		10 30	10 45
Newport (South Wales)	a	08 59	09 02				09 09	09 13	09 25	09 34	09 39		09 42	09 58				10 08	10 13	10 17	10 25	10 39		10 42	10 58
	d	09 02					09 09	09 15	09 27		09 39		09 44	10 00				10 09	10 15		10 27	10 39		10 44	11 00
Severn Tunnel Jn	d							09 26	09 37				09 55						10 26		10 38				
Caldicot	d								09 39												10 40				
Chepstow	d								09 48					10 18							10 49				
Lydney	d								09 57												10 58				11 25
Gloucester 7	a	09 44							10 20					10 44							11 20				11 44
Pilning	d																								
Patchway	d							09 39											10 39						
Bristol Parkway 7	a						09 30				09 59							10 30				10 59			
	d				09 20												10 22								
Filton Abbey Wood	d				09 23			09 42					10 09				10 25		10 42					11 09	
Bristol Temple Meads 10	a				09 34			09 53					10 18				10 37		10 51					11 18	
	d			09 30	09 49							10 00	10 22		10 30		10 49						11 00	11 22	
Keynsham	d				09 56												10 56								
Oldfield Park	d				10 03												11 03								
Bath Spa 7	a			09 41	10 05							10 11	10 34		10 41		11 06						11 11	11 34	

A The Bristolian
B The Capitals United
C 🛒 from Newport (South Wales)
D The Red Dragon

When events are being held at the Millenium Stadium,
services are subject to alteration. Please check times before travelling.

Cardiff - Gloucester, Bristol and Bath Spa

Network Diagram - see first Page of Table 132

			AW	GW	GW	GW	GW	AW	GW	GW	GW		XC	GW	GW	GW	GW	AW	AW	GW	SW		GW	GW	XC
			◇ 🛒	◇1 ☕	◇	◇1 ☕		◇ 🛒	◇1 ☕	◇1 ☕	◇ 🛒		◇1 A 🛒	◇1 ☕	[R] B 🛒	◇1 ☕		◇ 🛒		◇1 C ☕	◇1 🛒		◇1 ☕	◇ 🛒	◇1 A 🛒
Cardiff Central [7]	d		10 50			10 55	11 00	11 21	11 25		11 30		11 45			11 55	12 00	12 05	12 12	12 25				12 30	12 45
Newport (South Wales)	a		11 02			11 08	11 13	11 34	11 39		11 42		11 59			12 08	12 13	12 17	12 25	12 39				12 42	12 59
	d					11 09	11 15		11 39		11 44		12 02			12 09	12 15		12 28	12 39				12 44	13 01
Severn Tunnel Jn	d						11 26										12 26		12 39						
Caldicot	d																		12 42						
Chepstow	d												12 18						12 51						13 18
Lydney	d																		13 00						
Gloucester [7]	a												12 44						13 20						13 44
Pilning	d																								
Patchway	d						11 39										12 39								
Bristol Parkway [7]	a					11 30			11 59							12 30				12 59					
	d				11 20										12 22										
Filton Abbey Wood	d				11 23		11 42				12 09				12 25		12 42							13 09	
Bristol Temple Meads [10]	a				11 34		11 51				12 18				12 34		12 51							13 18	
	d			11 30	11 49					12 00	12 22			12 30	12 39						12 51		13 00	13 22	
Keynsham	d				11 56										12 46						12 58				
Oldfield Park	d				12 03										12 53										
Bath Spa [7]	a			11 41	12 06					12 12	12 34			12 41	12 55						13 05		13 11	13 34	

		AW	GW	GW	GW	GW	AW		AW	GW	GW	GW	XC	GW	GW	GW	GW		AW	GW	GW	GW	XC	AW	GW
		◇ 🛒	◇1 ☕		◇1 ☕	◇	🛒		◇ 🛒	◇1 Ø	◇1 ☕	◇ 🛒	◇1 A 🛒	◇1 ☕	◇	◇1 ☕			◇ 🛒	◇1 ☕	◇1 ☕	◇ 🛒	◇1 A 🛒	◇ 🛒	◇1 ☕
Cardiff Central [7]	d	12 50			12 55	13 00	13 12		13 21	13 25		13 30	13 45			13 55	14 00		14 05	14 25		14 30	14 45	14 50	
Newport (South Wales)	a	13 02			13 08	13 13	13 25		13 34	13 39		13 42	13 58			14 08	14 13		14 17	14 39		14 42	14 59	15 02	
	d				13 09	13 15	13 28			13 39		13 44	14 00			14 09	14 15			14 39		14 44	15 01		
Severn Tunnel Jn	d					13 26	13 39										14 26								
Caldicot	d						13 41																		
Chepstow	d						13 50																15 18		
Lydney	d						13 59						14 25												
Gloucester [7]	a						14 20						14 44										15 44		
Pilning	d																								
Patchway	d					13 39											14 39								
Bristol Parkway [7]	a				13 30					13 59						14 30				15 00					
	d			13 20											14 22										
Filton Abbey Wood	d			13 23		13 42						14 09			14 25		14 42					15 09			
Bristol Temple Meads [10]	a			13 35		13 51						14 17			14 38		14 51					15 17			
	d		13 30	13 49							14 00	14 22		14 30	14 48						15 00	15 22			15 30
Keynsham	d			13 56											14 55										
Oldfield Park	d			14 03											15 02										
Bath Spa [7]	a		13 41	14 06							14 11	14 34		14 41	15 05						15 11	15 34			15 41

		GW	GW		GW	AW	AW	SW	GW	GW	GW	GW	XC		AW	GW	GW	GW	GW	AW			GW		GW
			◇1 ☕				[R] 🛒	◇1	◇1 D ☕		◇1 ☕	◇ 🛒	◇1		[R] 🛒	◇1 ☕	◇	◇1 ☕		[R] 🛒			◇1 ☕		
Cardiff Central [7]	d		14 55		15 00	15 12	15 21				15 25	15 30	15 45		15 50			15 55	16 00	16 05					
Newport (South Wales)	a		15 08		15 13	15 26	15 34				15 39	15 43	15 58		16 02			16 08	16 13	16 18					
	d		15 09		15 15	15 28					15 39	15 44	16 00					16 09	16 15	16 21					
Severn Tunnel Jn	d				15 26	15 37													16 26	16 32					
Caldicot	d					15 40														16 34					
Chepstow	d					15 49							16 18							16 43					
Lydney	d					15 58														16 52					
Gloucester [7]	a					16 21							16 44							17 14					
Pilning	d																								
Patchway	d				15 39														16 39						
Bristol Parkway [7]	a		15 30								15 59							16 30							
	d	15 20								15 53							16 22								16 46
Filton Abbey Wood	d	15 23			15 42					15 56		16 09					16 25		16 42						16 49
Bristol Temple Meads [10]	a	15 36			15 51							16 18					16 37		16 51						17 02
	d	15 44						15 51	16 00			16 22				16 30	16 49						17 00		17 07
Keynsham	d	15 51						15 58		16 11							16 56								17 14
Oldfield Park	d	15 58								16 18							17 03								17 21
Bath Spa [7]	a	16 00						16 05	16 11	16 21		16 34				16 41	17 06						17 11		17 24

A 🛒 from Newport (South Wales)

B 🛒 from Bristol Temple Meads

C The St. David

D The Merchant Venturer

When events are being held at the Millenium Stadium, services are subject to alteration. Please check times before travelling.

Cardiff - Gloucester, Bristol and Bath Spa

Network Diagram - see first Page of Table 132

		GW	GW	GW	XC	AW	GW	GW	GW		GW	AW	AW	GW	GW	GW	GW	XC	AW		GW	GW	GW	GW	AW
				R		R							R				R		R						
		◇1			◇1		◇1	◇	◇1					◇1		◇1		◇1			◇1		◇1		
																		A							
		☕		🛒		🛒	☕		☕				🛒	☕		☕	🛒	🛒	🛒		☕		☕		
Cardiff Central [7]	d	16 25		16 30	16 45	16 50			16 55		17 00	17 12	17 21			17 25	17 30	17 45	17 50				17 55	18 00	18 12
Newport (South Wales)	a	16 39		16 42	16 58	17 02			17 08		17 13	17 25	17 34			17 39	17 42	17 58	18 02				18 08	18 13	18 25
	d	16 39		16 44	17 00				17 09		17 15	17 28				17 39	17 44	18 00					18 09	18 15	18 27
Severn Tunnel Jn	d			16 55							17 26	17 39					17 55							18 26	18 38
Caldicot	d											17 41													18 40
Chepstow	d											17 50						18 18							18 49
Lydney	d				17 25							17 59													18 58
Gloucester [7]	a				17 44							18 21						18 44							19 20
Pilning	d																								
Patchway	d										17 39													18 39	
Bristol Parkway [7]	a	16 59							17 30							17 59							18 30		
	d							17 20							17 46							18 22			
Filton Abbey Wood	d		16 55	17 09				17 23			17 43				17 49		18 09					18 25		18 42	
Bristol Temple Meads [10]	a		17 03	17 18				17 36			17 53				18 01		18 17					18 38		18 53	
	d		17 14	17 22			17 30	17 49						18 00	18 07		18 22				18 30	18 49			
Keynsham	d							17 56							18 14							18 56			
Oldfield Park	d		17 26					18 03							18 21							19 03			
Bath Spa [7]	a		17 30	17 35			17 41	18 06						18 11	18 24		18 34				18 41	19 06			

		AW BHX	GW	GW	XC		AW	GW	GW	GW	GW	GW	AW	XC	GW		GW	GW	AW	GW	GW	AW	GW	GW	XC
		R																							
			◇1	◇	◇1		◇	◇1			◇1	◇	◇	◇1	◇1				◇	◇1	◇	◇	◇1		◇1
		🛒	☕	🛒			🛒	☕			☕				☕					☕			☕		
Cardiff Central [7]	d	18 18	18 25	18 30	18 45		18 50			19 00	19 25	19 30	19 34	19 50				20 00	20 17	20 25	20 30	20 53		21 00	21 05
Newport (South Wales)	a	18 30	18 39	18 42	18 59		19 03			19 13	19 39	19 42	19 46	20 03				20 13	20 29	20 38	20 44	21 07		21 13	21 18
	d		18 39	18 44	19 01					19 15	19 39	19 44		20 05				20 15		20 39	20 44			21 15	21 21
Severn Tunnel Jn	d			18 55						19 26				20 15				20 26						21 25	
Caldicot	d													20 18											
Chepstow	d				19 18									20 26											
Lydney	d													20 35											
Gloucester [7]	a				19 45									20 53											22 02
Pilning	d																								
Patchway	d									19 39								20 39						21 39	
Bristol Parkway [7]	a		18 59								19 59									21 01					
	d								19 20																
Filton Abbey Wood	d			19 09					19 23	19 42		20 09						20 42			21 08			21 42	
Bristol Temple Meads [10]	a			19 17					19 35	19 51		20 17						20 53			21 19			21 51	
	d			19 22				19 30	19 49			20 22			20 30		20 49				21 23		21 50	22 00	
Keynsham	d								19 56								20 56							22 07	
Oldfield Park	d								20 03								21 03							22 14	
Bath Spa [7]	a			19 34				19 41	20 06			20 34			20 41		21 06				21 36		22 01	22 17	

			AW	GW	GW	SW	XC	XC	AW	GW	GW		GW	GW	AW FX	AW FO	GW
				◇1		1		◇1	◇	◇1							
				☕						☕							
Cardiff Central [7]	d		21 12	21 25	21 30		21 40	21 50	21 55		22 04			22 49	23 19	23 20	23 27
Newport (South Wales)	a		21 25	21 38	21 43		21 55	22 03	22 08		22 16			23 06	23 39	23 38	23 44
	d		21 27	21 39	21 44		21 56	22 05			22 18			23 06	23 40	23 40	23 45
Severn Tunnel Jn	d		21 38		21 55						22 35			23 24	23 58	23 58	00 03
Caldicot	d		21 40												00 01	00 01	
Chepstow	d		21 49												00 10	00 09	
Lydney	d		21 58												00 19	00 18	
Gloucester [7]	a		22 21					22 46							00 39	00 39	
Pilning	d																
Patchway	d										22 48						00 16
Bristol Parkway [7]	a			21 59													
	d																
Filton Abbey Wood	d				22 09						22 52			23 40			00 20
Bristol Temple Meads [10]	a				22 22		22 29				23 05			23 49			00 33
	d					22 25				22 35			23 20				
Keynsham	d												23 27				
Oldfield Park	d												23 34				
Bath Spa [7]	a					22 37				22 46			23 37				

A 🛒 from Newport (South Wales)

When events are being held at the Millenium Stadium, services are subject to alteration. Please check times before travelling.

Table 132

Saturdays

Cardiff - Gloucester, Bristol and Bath Spa

Network Diagram - see first Page of Table 132

		AW	GW	AW	AW	GW	GW	GW	AW	AW		GW	AW	GW	GW	GW	GW	GW	XC	AW		GW	GW	GW	XC
					◇	◇[1]	◇	◇[1]	◇	◇		◇[1]		◇[1]	◇[1]		◇[1]	◇	◇[1]	◇		◇[1]	◇[1]		◇[1]
						buffet		buffet	trolley	trolley		buffet		buffet	buffet		buffet			trolley		buffet	buffet		trolley
Cardiff Central [7]	d	23p20	23p27	00 30	04 35			04 55	05 20	05 40		05 55	06 12	06 25				06 30	06 40	06 50		06 55			07 00
Newport (South Wales)	a	23p38	23p44	00 43	04 50			05 09	05 33	05 55		06 09	06 25	06 38				06 43	06 53	07 02		07 08			07 13
	d	23p40	23p45					05 09				06 09	06 28	06 39				06 44	06 55			07 09			07 15
Severn Tunnel Jn	d	23p58	00 03										06 39					06 55	07 05						07 25
Caldicot	d	00 01											06 41						07 08						
Chepstow	d	00 09											06 50						07 16						
Lydney	d	00 18											06 59						07 25						
Gloucester [7]	a	00 39											07 20						07 44						
Pilning	d																								
Patchway	d		00 16																						07 37
Bristol Parkway [7]	a							05 36				06 29		06 59								07 29			
	d							05 42																	
Filton Abbey Wood	d		00 20															07 09							07 41
Bristol Temple Meads [10]	a		00 33					05 53										07 18							07 51
	d					05 30	05 49	06 00							06 30	06 49	07 00	07 22					07 30	07 49	
Keynsham	d						05 56									06 56								07 56	
Oldfield Park	d						06 03									07 03								08 03	
Bath Spa [7]	a					05 41	06 05	06 11							06 41	07 05	07 11	07 34					07 41	08 05	

		AW	AW	GW	GW	GW		XC	AW	GW	GW	GW	SW	GW	GW	GW		GW	XC	AW	GW	GW	GW	GW	AW
			◇	◇[1]	◇[1]	◇		◇[1]	◇	◇[1]	◇	◇[1]	◇[1]		◇[1]	◇[1]		◇	◇[1]	◇	◇[1]	◇	◇[1]		
								A											A						
			trolley	buffet	buffet			trolley	trolley	buffet		Ø			Ø	buffet			trolley	trolley	buffet		buffet		
Cardiff Central [7]	d	07 12	07 21	07 25		07 30		07 45	07 50			07 55		08 00	08 25			08 30	08 45	08 50			08 55	09 00	09 12
Newport (South Wales)	a	07 25	07 34	07 39		07 42		07 59	08 02			08 08		08 13	08 38			08 42	08 58	09 02			09 08	09 13	09 24
	d	07 27		07 39		07 44		08 00				08 09		08 15	08 39			08 44	09 00				09 09	09 15	09 26
Severn Tunnel Jn	d	07 38				07 55								08 26				08 55						09 26	09 36
Caldicot	d	07 40																							09 38
Chepstow	d	07 49																							09 48
Lydney	d	07 58						08 26																	09 56
Gloucester [7]	a	08 21						08 45											09 44						10 19
Pilning	d													08 32											
Patchway	d													08 39										09 39	
Bristol Parkway [7]	a			07 59								08 30			08 59								09 30		
	d										08 19											09 20			
Filton Abbey Wood	d					08 09					08 23			08 42				09 09				09 23		09 42	
Bristol Temple Meads [10]	a					08 18					08 34			08 52				09 18				09 34		09 51	
	d				08 00	08 22				08 30	08 39		08 51			09 00		09 22			09 30	09 49			
Keynsham	d										08 46		08 58									09 56			
Oldfield Park	d										08 53											10 03			
Bath Spa [7]	a				08 11	08 34				08 41	08 55		09 05			09 11		09 34			09 41	10 05			

		AW		GW	GW	GW	XC	AW	GW	GW	GW	AW		GW	GW	GW	XC	AW	GW	GW	GW	AW		GW	GW
		◇		◇[1]	◇[1]	◇	◇[1]	◇	◇[1]					◇[1]	◇[1]	◇	◇[1]	◇	◇[1]	◇		◇		◇[1]	◇[1]
						B	A									B	A								
		trolley		buffet	buffet	trolley	trolley	trolley	buffet					buffet	buffet	trolley	trolley	trolley	buffet			trolley		buffet	buffet
Cardiff Central [7]	d	09 21		09 25		09 30	09 45	09 55			10 00	10 12		10 25		10 30	10 45	10 55			11 00	11 21		11 25	
Newport (South Wales)	a	09 34		09 39		09 42	09 58	10 07			10 13	10 25		10 39		10 42	10 58	11 07			11 13	11 34		11 39	
	d			09 39		09 44	10 00				10 15	10 27		10 39		10 44	11 00				11 15			11 39	
Severn Tunnel Jn	d					09 55					10 26	10 38									11 26				
Caldicot	d											10 40													
Chepstow	d						10 18					10 49													
Lydney	d											10 58					11 25								
Gloucester [7]	a						10 44					11 21					11 44								
Pilning	d																								
Patchway	d										10 39										11 39				
Bristol Parkway [7]	a			09 59										10 59										11 59	
	d									10 25										11 20					
Filton Abbey Wood	d					10 09				10 28	10 42					11 09				11 23	11 42				
Bristol Temple Meads [10]	a					10 18				10 39	10 51					11 18				11 33	11 51				
	d				10 00	10 22			10 30	10 49					11 00	11 22			11 30	11 49					12 00
Keynsham	d									10 56										11 56					
Oldfield Park	d									11 03										12 03					
Bath Spa [7]	a				10 11	10 34			10 41	11 05					11 11	11 34			11 41	12 05					12 11

A trolley from Newport (South Wales)

B trolley from Bristol Temple Meads

When events are being held at the Millenium Stadium,
services are subject to alteration. Please check times before travelling.

Table 132

Saturdays

Cardiff - Gloucester, Bristol and Bath Spa

Network Diagram - see first Page of Table 132

		GW	XC	AW	GW	GW	GW	AW		GW	SW	GW	GW	XC	AW	GW	GW	GW		AW	AW	GW	GW	GW	XC
		◇ A trolley	◇1 B trolley	◇ trolley	◇1 buffet	R ◇				◇1 buffet	◇1 trolley	◇1 buffet	◇	◇1 B trolley	◇ trolley	◇1 buffet				trolley	◇ trolley	◇1 D buffet	◇1 E buffet	◇	◇1 B trolley
Cardiff Central 7	d	11 30	11 45	11 55			12 00	12 12		12 25			12 30	12 45	12 55			13 00		13 12	13 21	13 25		13 30	13 45
Newport (South Wales)	a	11 42	11 58	12 07			12 13	12 25		12 39			12 42	12 59	13 07			13 13		13 25	13 34	13 38		13 42	13 58
	d	11 44	12 00				12 15	12 27		12 39			12 44	13 00				13 15		13 27		13 39		13 44	14 00
Severn Tunnel Jn	d						12 26	12 38										13 26		13 39					
Caldicot	d							12 40												13 40					
Chepstow	d		12 18					12 49						13 18						13 49					
Lydney	d							12 58												13 58					14 25
Gloucester 7	a		12 44					13 21						13 44						14 21					14 44
Pilning	d																								
Patchway	d						12 39											13 39							
Bristol Parkway 7	a									12 59												13 59			
	d					12 25											13 20								
Filton Abbey Wood	d	12 09				12 28	12 42						13 09				13 23	13 42						14 09	
Bristol Temple Meads 10	a	12 18				12 39	12 51						13 18				13 34	13 53						14 18	
	d	12 22			12 30	12 43					12 51	13 00	13 22			13 30	13 49						14 00	14 22	
Keynsham	d					12 50					12 58						13 56								
Oldfield Park	d					12 57											14 03								
Bath Spa 7	a	12 34			12 41	13 00					13 05	13 11	13 34			13 41	14 05						14 11	14 34	

		AW	GW	GW		GW	GW	GW	GW	XC	AW	GW	GW	GW		AW	AW	GW	SW	GW	GW	XC	AW	GW	
		◇ trolley	◇1 buffet	◇			◇1 buffet	◇1 buffet	◇	◇1 B trolley	◇ trolley	◇1 buffet					R trolley	◇1 buffet	◇1	◇1 buffet	◇	◇1	R trolley	◇1 buffet	
Cardiff Central 7	d	13 55				14 00	14 25		14 30	14 45	14 55			15 00		15 12	15 21	15 25			15 30	15 45	15 55		
Newport (South Wales)	a	14 07				14 13	14 39		14 42	14 59	15 07			15 13		15 25	15 34	15 39			15 42	15 58	16 07		
	d					14 15	14 39		14 44	15 00				15 15		15 27		15 39			15 44	16 00			
Severn Tunnel Jn	d					14 26								15 26		15 37									
Caldicot	d															15 38									
Chepstow	d									15 18						15 47						16 18			
Lydney	d															15 56									
Gloucester 7	a									15 44						16 19						16 44			
Pilning	d																								
Patchway	d					14 39								15 39											
Bristol Parkway 7	a						14 59											15 59							
	d			14 20									15 19												
Filton Abbey Wood	d			14 25		14 42			15 09				15 22	15 42							16 09				
Bristol Temple Meads 10	a			14 36		14 51			15 18				15 33	15 51							16 18				
	d		14 30	14 49				15 00	15 22			15 30	15 38						15 51	16 00	16 22			16 30	
Keynsham	d			14 56									15 45						15 58						
Oldfield Park	d			15 03									15 52												
Bath Spa 7	a		14 41	15 05				15 11	15 34			15 41	15 54						16 05	16 11	16 34			16 41	

		GW	GW	AW	AW	GW	GW	GW	XC	AW		GW	GW	GW	AW	AW	GW	GW	GW	XC		AW	GW	GW	GW
		◇				◇1 D buffet	◇1 D buffet	R	◇1	R trolley		◇1 buffet	◇			R	◇1 buffet	◇1 buffet	◇	◇1 B trolley		R trolley	◇1 D buffet		
Cardiff Central 7	d		16 00	16 12	16 19	16 25		16 30	16 45	16 55				17 00	17 12	17 21	17 25		17 30	17 45		17 55			18 00
Newport (South Wales)	a		16 13	16 23	16 32	16 39		16 42	16 58	17 07				17 13	17 27	17 33	17 39		17 42	17 58		18 07			18 13
	d		16 15	16 26		16 39		16 44	17 00					17 15	17 27		17 39		17 44	18 00					18 15
Severn Tunnel Jn	d		16 26	16 38				16 55						17 26	17 38				17 55						18 26
Caldicot	d			16 40											17 40										
Chepstow	d			16 49											17 49					18 18					
Lydney	d			16 58					17 25						17 58										
Gloucester 7	a			17 19					17 44						18 20					18 44					
Pilning	d																								
Patchway	d		16 39											17 39											18 39
Bristol Parkway 7	a					16 59											17 59								
	d	16 25											17 20											18 25	
Filton Abbey Wood	d	16 28	16 42					17 09					17 23	17 42					18 09					18 28	18 42
Bristol Temple Meads 10	a	16 39	16 51					17 18					17 34	17 51					18 18					18 39	18 51
	d	16 49					17 00	17 22				17 30	17 49					18 00	18 22				18 30	18 49	
Keynsham	d	16 56											17 56											18 56	
Oldfield Park	d	17 03											18 03											19 03	
Bath Spa 7	a	17 06					17 11	17 34				17 41	18 06					18 11	18 34				18 41	19 05	

A trolley from Bristol Temple Meads

B trolley from Newport (South Wales)

D until 11 February, from 31 March

E until 4 February, from 24 March

When events are being held at the Millenium Stadium,
services are subject to alteration. Please check times before travelling.

Cardiff - Gloucester, Bristol and Bath Spa

Network Diagram - see first Page of Table 132

		AW	GW	GW	XC	AW		GW	GW	GW	GW	GW	AW	GW	GW	XC		AW	GW	GW	GW	XC	AW	GW	GW
			◇1 🍴	◇	◇1	◇ 🛒		◇1 🍴			◇1 🍴	◇	◇	◇1 🍴		◇1		◇	◇1 🍴		◇	◇1	◇	◇1 🍴	
Cardiff Central 7	d	18 12	18 25	18 30	18 45	18 50				19 00	19 25	19 30	19 34		19 55	20 00		20 10	20 25		20 30	20 50	20 55		21 00
Newport (South Wales)	a	18 25	18 39	18 42	18 59	19 03				19 13	19 39	19 42	19 46		20 08	20 13		20 24	20 39		20 43	21 03	21 08		21 13
	d	18 27	18 39	18 44	19 00					19 15	19 39	19 44			20 10	20 15			20 39		20 44	21 05			21 15
Severn Tunnel Jn	d	18 38								19 26					20 21	20 25									21 26
Caldicot	d	18 40														20 28									
Chepstow	d	18 49			19 18											20 36									
Lydney	d	18 58														20 45									
Gloucester 7	a	19 20			19 44											21 04						21 48			
Pilning	d																								
Patchway	d									19 39					20 34										21 38
Bristol Parkway 7	a		18 59								19 59								21 01						
	d								19 21																
Filton Abbey Wood	d			19 09					19 24	19 42		20 09			20 40						21 08				21 42
Bristol Temple Meads 10	a			19 18					19 36	19 51		20 18			20 48						21 18				21 49
	d			19 22				19 30	19 49			20 22		20 33						20 49	21 22			21 47	
Keynsham	d								19 56											20 56					
Oldfield Park	d								20 03											21 03					
Bath Spa 7	a			19 34				19 41	20 05			20 34		20 44						21 06	21 34			22 01	

		AW		GW	SW	XC	AW	GW	GW	GW	AW	AW		AW
											SO	SO		
					1			◇1 🍴			A	B		B 🚌
Cardiff Central 7	d	21 12				21 30	21 49		22 00		23 20	23 20		
Newport (South Wales)	a	21 25				21 42	22 05		22 13		23 36	23 37		
	d	21 27				21 44			22 16		23 38			23 50
Severn Tunnel Jn	d	21 38							22 35		23 55			00 15
Caldicot	d	21 40									23 58			00 25
Chepstow	d	21 49									00 07			00 40
Lydney	d	21 58									00 16			01 00
Gloucester 7	a	22 22									00 40			01 40
Pilning	d													
Patchway	d								22 48					
Bristol Parkway 7	a													
	d													
Filton Abbey Wood	d								22 52					
Bristol Temple Meads 10	a					22 24			23 00					
	d			22 00	22 23			22 30		23 11				
Keynsham	d			22 07						23 18				
Oldfield Park	d			22 14						23 25				
Bath Spa 7	a			22 17	22 34			22 41		23 27				

Sundays
until 1 January

		AW	GW	GW	GW	GW	GW	AW	GW	GW		GW	AW	GW	GW	GW	AW	AW	XC	GW		GW	GW	GW	AW
		C	◇1 🍴	◇1 🍴	1 🍴	◇1 🍴	◇	◇ 🛒	◇1 🍴	◇1 🍴		◇	◇ 🛒	◇1 🍴	◇	◇1 🍴		◇ 🛒	◇1 D 🛒	◇1 🍴		◇1 🍴	1 ◇ E 🛒	◇1 🍴	◇ 🛒
Cardiff Central 7	d	23p20		07 55			08 05	08 30	09 05			09 15	09 30		10 08	10 15	10 23	10 35	10 45				11 08	11 15	11 35
Newport (South Wales)	a	23p36		08 11			08 21	08 47	09 18			09 27	09 48		10 20	10 31	10 36	10 48	10 57				11 20	11 31	11 49
	d	23p38		08 13			08 23		09 19			09 29			10 22	10 32	10 38		10 59				11 22	11 32	
Severn Tunnel Jn	d	23p55					08 40					09 46			10 39		10 56						11 39		
Caldicot	d	23p58															10 58								
Chepstow	d	00 07															11 07								
Lydney	d	00 16															11 16								
Gloucester 7	a	00 40															11 42		11 49						
Pilning	d																								
Patchway	d											09 59													
Bristol Parkway 7	a			08 42					09 46							10 59								11 59	
	d																								
Filton Abbey Wood	d						08 55					10 03			10 54								11 54		
Bristol Temple Meads 10	a						09 05					10 13			11 03								12 04		
	d		07 45		08 20	08 45	09 11			09 48		10 15		10 30	11 10					11 30		12 00	12 15		
Keynsham	d						09 18								11 17										
Oldfield Park	d						09 25								11 24										
Bath Spa 7	a		07 57		08 31	08 57	09 27			09 58		10 29		10 41	11 26					11 41		12 11	12 27		

A from 17 December to 31 December, from 18 February until 24 March

B from 7 January until 11 February, from 31 March

C not 11 December

D 🛒 from Newport (South Wales)

E 🛒 from Bristol Temple Meads

When events are being held at the Millenium Stadium, services are subject to alteration. Please check times before travelling.

Table 132

Sundays

until 1 January

Cardiff - Gloucester, Bristol and Bath Spa

Network Diagram - see first Page of Table 132

		XC	GW	GW	GW	AW		AW	XC	GW	GW	GW	GW	AW	AW	XC		GW	GW	GW	AW	XC	AW	GW	GW
														R	R								R		
		◇1	◇1	◇	◇1			◇	◇1	◇1		◇	◇1			◇1		◇1	◇	◇1		◇1		◇1	◇1
		A							A							A						A			
		🛒	☕		☕			🛒	🛒	☕			☕		🛒	🛒		☕		☕		🛒	🛒	☕	☕
Cardiff Central [7]	d	11 45		12 08	12 15	12 23		12 40	12 45			13 08	13 15	13 22	13 40	13 45			14 08	14 15	14 23	14 45	14 56		
Newport (South Wales)	a	11 57		12 20	12 31	12 36		12 52	12 57			13 20	13 31	13 35	13 52	13 57			14 20	14 31	14 36	14 57	15 12		
	d	11 59		12 22	12 32	12 38			12 59			13 22	13 32			13 59			14 22	14 32	14 38	14 59			
Severn Tunnel Jn	d			12 39		12 56						13 39							14 39		14 56				
Caldicot	d					12 58															14 58				
Chepstow	d					13 07															15 07				
Lydney	d					13 16															15 16				
Gloucester [7]	a	12 46				13 34			13 47							14 46					15 37	15 46			
Pilning	d																								
Patchway	d			12 52																					
Bristol Parkway [7]	a				12 59								13 59							14 59					
	d																								
Filton Abbey Wood	d			12 57								13 54							14 55						
Bristol Temple Meads [10]	a			13 05								14 04							15 04						
	d		12 30	13 10						13 30	13 55	14 15						14 30	15 10					15 30	16 00
Keynsham	d			13 17							14 02								15 17						
Oldfield Park	d			13 24							14 09								15 24						
Bath Spa [7]	a		12 41	13 26						13 41	14 12	14 26						14 41	15 26					15 41	16 11

		SW		GW	GW	AW	XC	AW	GW	GW	GW	GW		AW	GW	GW	AW	XC	GW	GW	GW	GW		AW	GW
						R		R									R							R	
		◇1		◇	◇1		◇1		◇1	◇1	◇	◇1			◇1	◇		◇1	◇	◇1	◇	◇1			◇1
					☕	🛒		🛒	☕	☕		☕			☕		🛒			☕		☕			☕
Cardiff Central [7]	d			15 08	15 15	15 22	15 45	15 56			16 08	16 15		16 23		16 35	16 40	16 45			17 08	17 15		17 35	
Newport (South Wales)	a			15 20	15 31	15 35	15 57	16 12			16 20	16 31		16 36		16 47	16 52	16 57			17 20	17 31		17 48	
	d			15 22	15 32		15 59				16 22	16 32		16 38		16 49		16 59			17 22	17 32			
Severn Tunnel Jn	d			15 39							16 39			16 56							17 39				
Caldicot	d													16 58											
Chepstow	d													17 07											
Lydney	d													17 16											
Gloucester [7]	a						16 46							17 37				17 46							
Pilning	d																								
Patchway	d			15 52																					
Bristol Parkway [7]	a				15 59							16 59										17 59			
	d																								
Filton Abbey Wood	d			15 55							16 55					17 20					17 54				
Bristol Temple Meads [10]	a			16 04							17 06					17 29					18 04				
	d	16 04		16 15					16 30	17 00	17 15				17 30	17 40			17 44	18 00	18 10				18 30
Keynsham	d	16 11									17 22								17 51		18 17				
Oldfield Park	d										17 29								17 58		18 24				
Bath Spa [7]	a	16 18		16 27					16 41	17 11	17 30				17 41	17 52			18 00	18 12	18 26				18 41

		GW	XC	GW	GW	GW	AW	AW		XC	GW	GW	GW	AW	XC	GW	GW	GW		GW	AW	XC	GW	AW	SW
		R						R																	
			◇1	◇1	◇1	◇				◇1	◇1	◇1	◇	◇	◇1	◇1		◇1		◇		◇1	◇1	◇	1
				☕	☕			🛒			☕	☕				☕		☕					☕		
Cardiff Central [7]	d	17 40	17 45	17 50		18 08	18 23	18 40		18 45	18 50		19 08	19 40	19 45	19 50				20 18	20 23	20 45	20 55	21 04	
Newport (South Wales)	a	17 52	17 57	18 03		18 20	18 36	18 52		18 57	19 03		19 20	19 53	19 58	20 03				20 30	20 36	20 57	21 08	21 17	
	d	17 54	17 59	18 04		18 22	18 38			18 59	19 04		19 22		20 00	20 04				20 31	20 38	20 59	21 09		
Severn Tunnel Jn	d					18 39	18 56						19 40							20 48	20 56				
Caldicot	d						18 58														20 58				
Chepstow	d						19 07														21 07				
Lydney	d						19 16														21 16				
Gloucester [7]	a		18 46				19 38			19 47					20 49						21 41	21 47			
Pilning	d																								
Patchway	d					18 52																			
Bristol Parkway [7]	a			18 31							19 31					20 31							21 36		
	d																								
Filton Abbey Wood	d	18 23				18 56							19 55							21 05					
Bristol Temple Meads [10]	a	18 33				19 06							20 05							21 13					
	d	18 50			19 00	19 10						20 00	20 15				20 50	21 00		21 25					21 35
Keynsham	d					19 17											20 57								
Oldfield Park	d					19 24											21 04								
Bath Spa [7]	a	19 02			19 11	19 26						20 11	20 27				21 06	21 12		21 37					21 47

		GW	GW	GW		AW	AW
		◇1					◇
		☕		🛒			
Cardiff Central [7]	d			22 00		22 30	23 00
Newport (South Wales)	a			22 17		22 47	23 18
	d			22 19		22 49	
Severn Tunnel Jn	d			22 36		23 06	
Caldicot	d					23 09	
Chepstow	d					23 18	
Lydney	d					23 27	
Gloucester [7]	a					23 51	
Pilning	d						
Patchway	d			22 49			
Bristol Parkway [7]	a						
	d						
Filton Abbey Wood	d			22 53			
Bristol Temple Meads [10]	a			22 59			
	d	22 10	22 15	23 10			
Keynsham	d		22 22				
Oldfield Park	d		22 29				
Bath Spa [7]	a	22 22	22 31	23 22			

A 🛒 from Newport (South Wales)

When events are being held at the Millenium Stadium, services are subject to alteration. Please check times before travelling.

Table 132

Sundays

8 January to 12 February

Cardiff - Gloucester, Bristol and Bath Spa

Network Diagram - see first Page of Table 132

		AW	GW	GW	GW	GW	GW	AW	GW	GW		GW	AW	GW	GW	GW	AW	AW	XC	GW		GW	GW	GW	AW
																							[R]		
			◇[1]	◇[1]	[1]	◇[1]	◇	◇	◇[1]	◇[1]		◇	◇	◇[1]	◇	◇[1]		◇	◇[1]	◇[1]		◇[1]	◇	◇[1]	◇
																			A				B		
		🚌	☕	☕	☕	☕		🛒	☕	☕			🛒	☕		☕		🛒	🛒	☕		☕	🛒	☕	🛒
Cardiff Central [7]	d			07 55			08 05	08 30	09 05			09 15	09 30		10 08	10 15	10 23	10 35	10 45				11 08	11 15	11 35
Newport (South Wales)	a			08 11			08 21	08 47	09 18			09 27	09 48		10 20	10 31	10 36	10 48	10 57				11 20	11 31	11 50
	d	23p50		08 13			08 23		09 19			09 29			10 22	10 32	10 38		10 59				11 22	11 32	
Severn Tunnel Jn	d	00 15					08 40					09 46			10 39		10 56						11 39		
Caldicot	d	00 25															10 58								
Chepstow	d	00 40															11 07								
Lydney	d	01 00															11 16								
Gloucester [7]	a	01 40															11 42		11 49						
Pilning	d																								
Patchway	d											09 59													
Bristol Parkway [7]	a			08 42					09 46							10 59								11 59	
	d																								
Filton Abbey Wood	d						08 55					10 03			10 54								11 54		
Bristol Temple Meads [10]	a						09 05					10 13			11 03								12 04		
	d		07 45		08 20	08 45	09 11			09 48		10 15		10 30	11 10					11 30		12 00	12 15		
Keynsham	d						09 18								11 17										
Oldfield Park	d						09 25								11 24										
Bath Spa [7]	a		07 57		08 31	08 57	09 27			09 58		10 29		10 41	11 26					11 41		12 11	12 27		

		XC	GW	GW	GW	AW		AW	XC	GW	GW	GW	GW	AW	AW	XC		GW	GW	GW	AW	XC	AW	GW	GW
														[R]	[R]								[R]		
		◇[1]	◇[1]	◇	◇[1]			◇	◇[1]	◇[1]		◇	◇[1]			◇[1]		◇[1]	◇	◇[1]		◇[1]		◇[1]	◇[1]
		A							A							A						A			
		🛒	☕		☕			🛒	🛒	☕			☕		🛒	🛒		☕		☕		🛒	🛒	☕	☕
Cardiff Central [7]	d	11 45		12 08	12 15	12 23		12 40	12 45			13 08	13 15	13 22	13 40	13 45			14 08	14 15	14 23	14 45	14 56		
Newport (South Wales)	a	11 57		12 20	12 31	12 36		12 52	12 57			13 20	13 31	13 35	13 52	13 57			14 20	14 31	14 36	14 57	15 12		
	d	11 59		12 22	12 32	12 38			12 59			13 22	13 32			13 59			14 22	14 32	14 38	14 59			
Severn Tunnel Jn	d			12 39		12 56						13 39							14 39		14 56				
Caldicot	d					12 58															14 58				
Chepstow	d					13 07															15 07				
Lydney	d					13 16															15 16				
Gloucester [7]	a	12 46				13 34			13 47							14 46					15 37	15 46			
Pilning	d																								
Patchway	d			12 52																					
Bristol Parkway [7]	a				13 01								13 59							14 59					
	d																								
Filton Abbey Wood	d			12 57								13 54							14 55						
Bristol Temple Meads [10]	a			13 05								14 04							15 04						
	d		12 30	13 10						13 30	13 55	14 15						14 30	15 10					15 30	16 00
Keynsham	d			13 17							14 02								15 17						
Oldfield Park	d			13 24							14 09								15 24						
Bath Spa [7]	a		12 41	13 26						13 41	14 12	14 26						14 41	15 26					15 41	16 11

		SW		GW	GW	AW	XC	AW	GW	GW	GW	GW		AW	GW	GW	AW	XC	GW	GW	GW	GW		AW	GW
						[R]		[R]									[R]							[R]	
		◇[1]		◇	◇[1]		◇[1]		◇[1]	◇[1]	◇	◇[1]			◇[1]	◇		◇[1]	◇	◇[1]	◇	◇[1]			◇[1]
					☕	🛒		🛒	☕	☕		☕			☕		🛒			☕		☕			☕
Cardiff Central [7]	d			15 08	15 15	15 22	15 45	15 56			16 08	16 15		16 23		16 35	16 40	16 45			17 08	17 10		17 35	
Newport (South Wales)	a			15 20	15 31	15 35	15 57	16 13			16 20	16 31		16 36		16 47	16 52	16 57			17 20	17 25		17 48	
	d			15 22	15 32		15 59				16 22	16 32		16 38		16 49		16 59			17 22	17 27			
Severn Tunnel Jn	d			15 39							16 39			16 56							17 39				
Caldicot	d													16 58											
Chepstow	d													17 07											
Lydney	d													17 16											
Gloucester [7]	a						16 46							17 37				17 46							
Pilning	d																								
Patchway	d			15 52																					
Bristol Parkway [7]	a				15 59							16 59										18 00			
	d																								
Filton Abbey Wood	d			15 55							16 55					17 20					17 54				
Bristol Temple Meads [10]	a			16 04							17 06					17 29					18 04				
	d	16 04		16 15					16 30	17 00	17 15				17 30	17 40			17 44	18 00	18 10				18 30
Keynsham	d	16 11									17 22								17 51		18 17				
Oldfield Park	d										17 29								17 58		18 24				
Bath Spa [7]	a	16 18		16 27					16 41	17 11	17 30				17 41	17 52			18 00	18 12	18 26				18 41

A 🛒 from Newport (South Wales)

B 🛒 from Bristol Temple Meads

When events are being held at the Millenium Stadium, services are subject to alteration. Please check times before travelling.

Table 132

Sundays

8 January to 12 February

Cardiff - Gloucester, Bristol and Bath Spa

Network Diagram - see first Page of Table 132

		GW	XC	GW	GW	GW	AW	AW		XC	GW	GW	GW	AW	XC	GW	GW	GW		GW	AW	XC	AW	GW	SW
		R	◇1	◇1 ☕	◇1 ☕	◇		R 🛒		◇1	◇1 ☕	◇1 ☕	◇	◇	◇1	◇1 ☕		◇1 ☕		◇		◇1	◇	◇1 ☕	1
Cardiff Central 7	d	17 40	17 45	17 50		18 08	18 23	18 40		18 45	18 50		19 08	19 40	19 45	19 50				20 18	20 23	20 45	21 04	21 15	
Newport (South Wales)	a	17 52	17 57	18 03		18 20	18 36	18 52		18 57	19 03		19 20	19 53	19 58	20 03				20 30	20 36	20 57	21 17	21 28	
	d	17 54	17 59	18 04		18 22	18 38			18 59	19 04		19 22		20 00	20 04				20 31	20 38	20 59		21 29	
Severn Tunnel Jn	d					18 39	18 56						19 40							20 48	20 56				
Caldicot	d						18 58														20 58				
Chepstow	d						19 07														21 07				
Lydney	d						19 16														21 16				
Gloucester 7	a		18 46				19 38			19 47					20 49						21 41	21 47			
Pilning	d																								
Patchway	d					18 52																			
Bristol Parkway 7	a			18 31							19 31					20 31								21 56	
	d																								
Filton Abbey Wood	d	18 23				18 56							19 55							21 05					
Bristol Temple Meads 10	a	18 33				19 06							20 05							21 13					
	d	18 50			19 00	19 10						20 00	20 15				20 50	21 00		21 25					21 35
Keynsham	d					19 17											20 57								
Oldfield Park	d					19 24											21 04								
Bath Spa 7	a	19 02			19 11	19 26						20 11	20 27				21 06	21 12		21 37					21 47

		GW	GW	GW		AW	AW
		◇1 ☕		🛒			◇
Cardiff Central 7	d			22 00		22 30	23 00
Newport (South Wales)	a			22 17		22 47	23 18
	d			22 19		22 49	
Severn Tunnel Jn	d			22 36		23 06	
Caldicot	d					23 09	
Chepstow	d					23 18	
Lydney	d					23 27	
Gloucester 7	a					23 51	
Pilning	d						
Patchway	d			22 49			
Bristol Parkway 7	a						
	d						
Filton Abbey Wood	d			22 53			
Bristol Temple Meads 10	a			22 59			
	d	22 10	22 15	23 10			
Keynsham	d		22 22				
Oldfield Park	d		22 29				
Bath Spa 7	a	22 22	22 31	23 22			

Sundays

19 February to 25 March

		AW	GW	GW	GW	GW	GW	AW	GW	GW		GW	GW	AW	GW	GW	GW	GW	GW	GW		GW	AW	AW	XC
			◇1 ☕	◇1 ☕	◇1 ☕	◇	🚌	◇ 🛒	🚌	🚌		◇1 ☕	🚌	◇ 🛒	◇1 ☕	◇	🚌	◇1 ☕	◇1 ☕	◇		🚌		◇ 🛒	◇1 A 🛒
Cardiff Central 7	d	23p20		07 55				08 30				08 52		09 30				10 00					10 23	10 35	10 45
Newport (South Wales)	a	23p36		08 11				08 47				09 05		09 48				10 15					10 36	10 48	10 57
	d	23p38		08 13			08 25			09 00		09 06	09 15				10 00	10 16				10 25	10 38		10 59
Severn Tunnel Jn	d	23p55		08 35					09 00			09 25						10a33					10 56		
Caldicot	d	23p58																					10 58		
Chepstow	d	00 07																					11 07		
Lydney	d	00 16																					11 16		
Gloucester 7	a	00 40		09 09								09 59											11 42		11 49
Pilning	d																								
Patchway	d								09 35																
Bristol Parkway 7	a						09 05		09 40	09 40			09 55				10 40					11 05			
	d					08 51	09 05									10 01				10 51					
Filton Abbey Wood	d					08 54										10 03				10 54					
Bristol Temple Meads 10	a					09 05	09 25									10 13				11 02					
	d		07 45		08 45	09 10									09 48	10 15			10 30	11 10					
Keynsham	d					09 17														11 17					
Oldfield Park	d					09 24														11 24					
Bath Spa 7	a		07 57		08 57	09 26									09 58	10 29			10 41	11 26					

A 🛒 from Newport (South Wales)

When events are being held at the Millenium Stadium, services are subject to alteration. Please check times before travelling.

Table 132

Sundays

19 February to 25 March

Cardiff - Gloucester, Bristol and Bath Spa

Network Diagram - see first Page of Table 132

		GW	GW	GW	GW	AW		GW	GW	GW	XC	GW	GW	AW	GW	GW		GW	AW	XC	GW	GW	AW	GW	GW
				◇1	◇1	◇		◇1	R ◇ A		◇1 B		◇1		◇1	◇			◇	◇1 B			R	◇1	◇1
		🚌	🚌	☕	☕	🛒		☕	🛒	🚌	🛒	🚌	☕		☕			🚌	🛒	🛒	🚌	🚌		☕	☕
Cardiff Central 7	d			11 25		11 35					11 45		12 20	12 23					12 40	12 45			13 22	13 25	
Newport (South Wales)	a			11 39		11 49					11 57		12 34	12 37					12 52	12 57			13 35	13 39	
	d		11 00	11 40						11 50	11 59	12 00	12 35	12 39				12 44		12 59		13 00		13 40	
Severn Tunnel Jn	d	11 00		11 59									12 54	12 56							13 00			13 59	
Caldicot	d													12 57											
Chepstow	d													13 06											
Lydney	d													13 15											
Gloucester 7	a			12 33							12 46		13 29	13 36						13 47				14 33	
Pilning	d																								
Patchway	d	11 35																			13 35				
Bristol Parkway 7	a	11 40	11 40							12 30		12 40						13 24			13 40	13 40			
	d								11 51							12 54									
Filton Abbey Wood	d								11 54							12 57									
Bristol Temple Meads 10	a								12 03							13 05									
	d				11 30			12 00	12 15						12 30	13 10									13 30
Keynsham	d															13 17									
Oldfield Park	d															13 24									
Bath Spa 7	a				11 41			12 11	12 27						12 41	13 26									13 41

		GW		GW	GW	AW	XC	GW	GW	AW	GW	GW		GW	GW	XC	GW	GW	AW	AW	GW	GW		GW	SW
				◇		R	◇1 B		◇1		◇1	◇1		◇		◇1 B			R	R	◇1	◇1		◇1	◇1
					🚌	🛒	🛒	🚌	☕		☕	☕			🚌	🛒	🚌	🚌	🛒	🛒	☕	☕		☕	
Cardiff Central 7	d					13 40	13 45		14 20	14 23						14 45			14 56	15 22	15 26				
Newport (South Wales)	a					13 52	13 57		14 34	14 38						14 57			15 12	15 35	15 39				
	d				13 50		13 59	14 00	14 35	14 38					14 45	14 59		15 00			15 42				
Severn Tunnel Jn	d								14 54	14 56							15 00				16 00				
Caldicot	d									14 58															
Chepstow	d									15 07															
Lydney	d									15 16															
Gloucester 7	a						14 46		15 30	15 37						15 46					16 34				
Pilning	d																								
Patchway	d																15 35								
Bristol Parkway 7	a				14 30			14 40							15 25		15 40	15 40							
	d			13 51										14 51											
Filton Abbey Wood	d			13 54										14 55											
Bristol Temple Meads 10	a			14 03										15 04											
	d	13 55		14 15							14 30	15 00		15 10								15 30		16 00	16 04
Keynsham	d	14 02												15 17											16 11
Oldfield Park	d	14 09												15 24											
Bath Spa 7	a	14 12		14 27							14 41	15 11		15 26								15 41		16 11	16 18

		GW	GW	XC	GW	AW	GW	GW	GW		GW	AW	AW	XC	GW	GW	GW	GW	GW		GW	GW	GW	GW	GW
		◇		◇1		R	◇1	C ◇1	◇				R	◇1	◇1	◇		◇1			◇	◇1	◇		
			🚌		🚌	🛒	☕	☕			🚌		🛒		☕		🚌	☕	🚌			☕		🚌	🚌
Cardiff Central 7	d			15 45		15 56						16 23	16 40	16 45				16 50							
Newport (South Wales)	a			15 57		16 12						16 36	16 52	16 57				17 03							
	d		15 50	15 59	16 00						16 27	16 38		16 59			17 00							17 13	17 30
Severn Tunnel Jn	d											16 56							17 00						
Caldicot	d											16 58													
Chepstow	d											17 07													
Lydney	d											17 16													
Gloucester 7	a			16 46								17 37		17 46											
Pilning	d																								
Patchway	d																		17 35						
Bristol Parkway 7	a		16 30		16 40						17 07						17 40		17 40					17 53	18 10
	d	15 51							16 51							17 17							17 51		
Filton Abbey Wood	d	15 55							16 55							17 20							17 55		
Bristol Temple Meads 10	a	16 04							17 06							17 29							18 04		
	d	16 15					16 30	17 00	17 15						17 30	17 40					17 44	18 00	18 10		
Keynsham	d								17 22												17 51		18 17		
Oldfield Park	d								17 29												17 58		18 24		
Bath Spa 7	a	16 27					16 41	17 11	17 30						17 41	17 52					18 00	18 12	18 26		

A 🛒 from Bristol Temple Meads

B 🛒 from Newport (South Wales)

C from 4 March to 25 March

When events are being held at the Millenium Stadium,
services are subject to alteration. Please check times before travelling.

Table 132

Sundays

19 February to 25 March

Cardiff - Gloucester, Bristol and Bath Spa

Network Diagram - see first Page of Table 132

		GW	AW	GW	GW		GW	XC	GW	GW	GW	GW	GW	AW	AW		XC	GW	GW	GW	GW	GW	GW	AW	XC
			R		R										R										
		◇1		◇1				◇1	◇1	◇1	◇						◇1			◇1	◇1	◇		◇	◇1
							🚌					🚌	🚌					🚌	🚌				🚌		
		☕		☕					☕	☕					🛒					☕	☕				
Cardiff Central 7	d	17 25	17 35					17 45	18 00					18 23	18 40		18 45			18 56				19 40	19 45
Newport (South Wales)	a	17 38	17 48					17 57	18 15					18 36	18 52		18 57			19 12				19 53	19 58
	d	17 39					17 48	17 59				18 25	18 30	18 38			18 59		19 00	19 13			19 22		20 00
Severn Tunnel Jn	d	17 58												18 56				19 00		19 31					
Caldicot	d													18 58											
Chepstow	d													19 07											
Lydney	d													19 16											
Gloucester 7	a	18 32						18 46						19 38			19 47			20 05					20 49
Pilning	d																								
Patchway	d																	19 35							
Bristol Parkway 7	a						18 28					19 05	19 10					19 40	19 40				20 02		
	d				18 20						18 51											19 51			
Filton Abbey Wood	d				18 25						18 55											19 55			
Bristol Temple Meads 10	a				18 33						19 06											20 05			
	d			18 30	18 50					19 00	19 10										20 00	20 15			
Keynsham	d										19 17														
Oldfield Park	d										19 24														
Bath Spa 7	a			18 41	19 02					19 11	19 26										20 11	20 27			

		GW	GW	GW	AW	XC	GW	GW	GW	GW		GW	AW	GW	GW	SW	GW	GW	GW	GW		AW	AW		
			◇1			◇1		◇1	◇1	◇			◇			1	◇1						◇		
		🚌		🚌								🚌		🚌	🚌					🚌					
			☕					☕	☕								☕		🛒						
Cardiff Central 7	d		19 55		20 23	20 45		20 55					21 04		21 30					22 00		22 30	23 00		
Newport (South Wales)	a		20 12		20 36	20 57		21 08					21 17		22 00							22 47	23 18		
	d	20 00	20 13	20 22	20 38	20 59		21 10						21 25	22 00					22u30		22 49			
Severn Tunnel Jn	d		20 32		20 56							21 00		21 50						22 55		23 06			
Caldicot	d				20 58																	23 09			
Chepstow	d				21 07																	23 18			
Lydney	d				21 16																	23 27			
Gloucester 7	a		21 06		21 41	21 47		21 58														23 51			
Pilning	d																								
Patchway	d											21 35		22 25											
Bristol Parkway 7	a	20 40		21 02								21 40		22 30	22 40					23 30					
	d									21 02									22 49	23 30					
Filton Abbey Wood	d									21 06									22 52						
Bristol Temple Meads 10	a									21 13									23 00	23 50					
	d						20 50		21 00	21 25						21 35	22 10	22 15	23 10						
Keynsham	d						20 57											22 22							
Oldfield Park	d						21 04											22 29							
Bath Spa 7	a						21 07		21 12	21 37						21 47	22 22	22 31	23 22						

Sundays

from 1 April

		AW	GW	GW	GW	GW	GW	AW	GW	GW		GW	AW	GW	GW	GW	AW	AW	XC	GW		GW	GW	GW	AW
																							R		
			◇1	◇1	1	◇1	◇	◇	◇1	◇1		◇	◇	◇1	◇	◇1		◇	◇1	◇1		◇1	◇	◇1	◇
																			B				C		
		🚌																							
			☕	☕	☕	☕		🛒	☕	☕			🛒	☕		☕		🛒	🛒	☕		☕	🛒	☕	🛒
Cardiff Central 7	d			07 55			08 05	08 30	09 05			09 15	09 30		10 08	10 15	10 23	10 35	10 45				11 08	11 15	11 35
Newport (South Wales)	a			08 11			08 21	08 47	09 18			09 27	09 48		10 20	10 30	10 36	10 48	10 57				11 20	11 31	11 49
	d	23p50		08 13			08 23		09 19			09 29			10 22	10 32	10 38		10 59				11 22	11 32	
Severn Tunnel Jn	d	00 15					08 40					09 46			10 39		10 56						11 39		
Caldicot	d	00 25															10 58								
Chepstow	d	00 40															11 07								
Lydney	d	01 00															11 16								
Gloucester 7	a	01 40															11 42		11 49						
Pilning	d																								
Patchway	d											09 59													
Bristol Parkway 7	a			08 42					09 46							10 59								11 59	
	d																								
Filton Abbey Wood	d						08 55					10 03			10 54								11 54		
Bristol Temple Meads 10	a						09 05					10 13			11 03								12 04		
	d		07 45		08 20	08 45	09 10			09 48		10 15		10 30	11 10					11 30		12 00	12 15		
Keynsham	d						09 17								11 17										
Oldfield Park	d						09 24								11 24										
Bath Spa 7	a		07 57		08 31	08 57	09 26			09 58		10 29		10 41	11 26					11 41		12 11	12 27		

B 🛒 from Newport (South Wales)

C 🛒 from Bristol Temple Meads

When events are being held at the Millenium Stadium, services are subject to alteration. Please check times before travelling.

Table 132

Sundays from 1 April

Cardiff - Gloucester, Bristol and Bath Spa

Network Diagram - see first Page of Table 132

		XC	GW	GW	GW	AW		AW	XC	GW	GW	GW	GW	AW	AW	XC		GW	GW	GW	AW	XC	AW	GW	GW
		◇1 A (trolley)	◇1 (buffet)	◇	◇1 (buffet)			◇ (trolley)	◇1 A (trolley)	◇1 (buffet)		◇	◇1 (buffet)	R	R (trolley)	◇1 A (trolley)		◇1 (buffet)	◇	◇1 (buffet)		◇1 A (trolley)	R (trolley)	◇1 (buffet)	◇1 (buffet)
Cardiff Central 7	d	11 45		12 08	12 15	12 23		12 40	12 45			13 08	13 15	13 22	13 40	13 45			14 08	14 15	14 23	14 45	14 56		
Newport (South Wales)	a	11 57		12 20	12 31	12 36		12 52	12 57			13 20	13 31	13 35	13 52	13 57			14 20	14 31	14 36	14 57	15 12		
	d	11 59		12 22	12 32	12 38			12 59			13 22	13 32			13 59			14 22	14 32	14 38	14 59			
Severn Tunnel Jn	d			12 39		12 56						13 39							14 39		14 56				
Caldicot	d					12 58															14 58				
Chepstow	d					13 07															15 07				
Lydney	d					13 16															15 16				
Gloucester 7	a	12 46				13 34			13 47							14 46					15 37	15 46			
Pilning	d																								
Patchway	d			12 52																					
Bristol Parkway 7	a				12 59								13 59							14 59					
	d																								
Filton Abbey Wood	d			12 57								13 54							14 55						
Bristol Temple Meads 10	a			13 05								14 04							15 04						
	d		12 30	13 10						13 30	13 55	14 15						14 30	15 10					15 30	16 00
Keynsham	d			13 17							14 02								15 17						
Oldfield Park	d			13 24							14 09								15 24						
Bath Spa 7	a		12 41	13 26						13 41	14 12	14 26						14 41	15 26					15 41	16 11

		SW		GW	GW	AW	XC	AW	GW	GW	GW	GW		AW	GW	GW	AW	XC	GW	GW	GW	GW		AW	GW
		◇1		◇	◇1 (buffet)	R (trolley)	◇1	R (trolley)	◇1 (buffet)	◇1 (buffet)	◇	◇1 (buffet)			◇1 (buffet)	◇	R (trolley)	◇1	◇	◇1 (buffet)	◇	◇1 (buffet)		R	◇1 (buffet)
Cardiff Central 7	d			15 08	15 15	15 22	15 45	15 56			16 08	16 15		16 23		16 35	16 40	16 45			17 08	17 13		17 35	
Newport (South Wales)	a			15 20	15 31	15 35	15 57	16 12			16 20	16 31		16 36		16 47	16 52	16 57			17 20	17 29		17 48	
	d			15 22	15 32		15 59				16 22	16 32		16 38		16 49		16 59			17 22	17 32			
Severn Tunnel Jn	d			15 39							16 39			16 56							17 39				
Caldicot	d													16 58											
Chepstow	d													17 07											
Lydney	d													17 16											
Gloucester 7	a						16 46							17 37				17 46							
Pilning	d																								
Patchway	d			15 52																					
Bristol Parkway 7	a				15 59							16 59										17 59			
	d																								
Filton Abbey Wood	d			15 55							16 55					17 20					17 54				
Bristol Temple Meads 10	a			16 04							17 06					17 29					18 04				
	d	16 04		16 15					16 30	17 00	17 15				17 30	17 40			17 44	18 00	18 10				18 30
Keynsham	d	16 11									17 22								17 51		18 17				
Oldfield Park	d										17 29								17 58		18 24				
Bath Spa 7	a	16 18		16 27					16 41	17 11	17 30				17 41	17 52			18 00	18 12	18 26				18 41

		GW	XC	GW	GW	GW	AW	AW		XC	GW	GW	GW	AW	XC	GW	GW	GW		GW	AW	XC	GW	AW	SW
		R	◇1	◇1 (buffet)	◇1 (buffet)	◇		R (trolley)		◇1	◇1 (buffet)	◇1 (buffet)	◇	◇	◇1	◇1 (buffet)		◇1 (buffet)		◇		◇1	◇1 (buffet)	◇	1
Cardiff Central 7	d	17 40	17 45	17 50		18 08	18 23	18 40		18 45	18 50		19 08	19 40	19 45	19 50				20 18	20 23	20 45	20 55	21 04	
Newport (South Wales)	a	17 52	17 57	18 03		18 20	18 36	18 52		18 57	19 03		19 20	19 53	19 58	20 03				20 30	20 36	20 57	21 08	21 17	
	d	17 54	17 59	18 04		18 22	18 38			18 59	19 04		19 22		20 00	20 04				20 31	20 38	20 59	21 09		
Severn Tunnel Jn	d					18 39	18 56						19 40							20 48	20 56				
Caldicot	d						18 58														20 58				
Chepstow	d						19 07														21 07				
Lydney	d						19 16														21 16				
Gloucester 7	a		18 46				19 38			19 47					20 49						21 41	21 47			
Pilning	d																								
Patchway	d					18 52																			
Bristol Parkway 7	a			18 31							19 31					20 31							21 36		
	d																								
Filton Abbey Wood	d	18 23				18 56							19 55							21 05					
Bristol Temple Meads 10	a	18 33				19 06							20 05							21 13					
	d	18 50			19 00	19 10						20 00	20 15				20 50	21 00		21 25					21 35
Keynsham	d					19 17											20 57								
Oldfield Park	d					19 24											21 04								
Bath Spa 7	a	19 02			19 11	19 26						20 11	20 27				21 06	21 12		21 37					21 47

		GW	GW	GW		AW	AW
		◇1 (buffet)		(trolley)			◇
Cardiff Central 7	d			22 00		22 30	23 00
Newport (South Wales)	a			22 17		22 47	23 18
	d			22 19		22 49	
Severn Tunnel Jn	d			22 36		23 06	
Caldicot	d					23 09	
Chepstow	d					23 18	
Lydney	d					23 27	
Gloucester 7	a					23 51	
Pilning	d						
Patchway	d			22 49			
Bristol Parkway 7	a						
	d						
Filton Abbey Wood	d			22 53			
Bristol Temple Meads 10	a			22 59			
	d	22 10	22 15	23 10			
Keynsham	d		22 22				
Oldfield Park	d		22 29				
Bath Spa 7	a	22 22	22 31	23 22			

A (trolley) from Newport (South Wales)

When events are being held at the Millenium Stadium, services are subject to alteration. Please check times before travelling.

Bath Spa, Bristol and Gloucester - Cardiff

Network Diagram - see first Page of Table 132

Miles	Miles	Miles	Station		GW	GW	GW	GW	GW	AW	GW	AW	AW		GW	GW	GW	GW	GW	AW	GW	GW	GW		GW
					MO	MO	MO	MO	MO	MX		MO	MX		MO	MO	MO	MX	MX	MX	MO	MO	MX		MO
						◇1	◇1	◇1	◇1	◇	◇1	◇				◇1	◇1	◇1	◇1	◇	◇1	◇1	◇1		◇1
					A	B	C	D	A		E				A	A	D				E	D			A
					🚌	☕	☕	☕	☕		☕				🚌	☕	☕	☕	☕		☕	☕	☕		☕
0	—	—	**Bath Spa 7**	d							23p47						23p55	23p56					01 15		
1	—	—	Oldfield Park	d																					
7	—	—	Keynsham	d																					
11½	—	—	**Bristol Temple Meads 10**	a							00 01						00 09	00 10			01 03	01 05	01 29		01 31
—	—	—		d																			01 36		
16	—	—	Filton Abbey Wood	d																					
—	0	—	**Bristol Parkway 7**	a																					
—	—	—		d	23p10	23p12	23p16	23p17							23p40				00 23						
17½	—	—	Patchway	d																					
21	4¾	—	Pilning	d																					
—	—	0	**Gloucester 7**	d					22p42				23p13			23p43									
—	—	19½	Lydney	d									23p33												
—	—	27¼	Chepstow	d									23p42												
—	—	34	Caldicot	d									23p51												
28	11¾	34¾	Severn Tunnel Jn	d	23p40				23p21				23p54			00 16									
38	21¾	44¾	Newport (South Wales)	a	00s06	23p41	23p41	23p42	23p44				00 06		00 20	00 31			00 51				02s10		
—	—	—		d		23p42	23p42	23p43	23p44	23p47		23p55	00 07			00 32			00 52	00 59					
49¾	33½	56½	**Cardiff Central 7**	a	00 35	00 01	00 03	00 04	00 07	00 02		00 20	00 35			00 53			01 11	01 18			02 31		

Station		GW	GW	XC	XC	AW	GW	AW	GW		XC	XC	GW	AW	GW	XC	AW	GW	GW		GW	SW	GW	GW	GW
		MO	MO	MX	MO																				
		◇1	◇1	1	1	◇					◇1	◇1		◇	◇1	◇1	◇				◇	1	◇1	◇	◇1
		F	D																						
		☕	☕								🍴			🍴	☕								☕		☕
Bath Spa 7	d										06 09		06 28		06 54				07 08		07 25	07 35		07 48	07 59
Oldfield Park	d												06 31						07 11		07 28	07 38		07 51	
Keynsham	d												06 38						07 18		07 35	07 45		07 58	08 08
Bristol Temple Meads 10	a	01 33	01 35								06 20		06 46		07 07				07 27		07 46	07 52		08 06	08 17
	d			05 19	05 19		05 54		06 19		06 27		06 50		07 14			07 19	07 34		07 54			08 10	
Filton Abbey Wood	d						06 01		06 31				07 02		07 22			07 30	07 43		08 01			08 22	
Bristol Parkway 7	a			05 28	05 28						06 37							07 33	07 47					08 29	
	d			05 38	05 38													07 40	07 48				08 07		
Patchway	d						06 06		06 35									07 44			08 06				
Pilning	d																								
Gloucester 7	d							05 50				06 18				07 01			08a29						
Lydney	d							06 09				06 37				07 20									
Chepstow	d							06 19				06 46				07 29									
Caldicot	d							06 26				06 55				07 38									
Severn Tunnel Jn.	d						06 17	06 29	06 47			06 58	07 14			07 41		07 56							
Newport (South Wales)	a			05 58	06 08		06 28	06 41	06 58			07 09	07 25		07 44	07 52		08 07			08 27		08 32		
	d			06 00	06 10	06 17	06 29	06 44	07 00			07 10	07 27	07 35	07 44	07 53	08 01	08 09			08 27		08 32		
Cardiff Central 7	a			06 18	06 24	06 33	06 48	07 00	07 20			07 26	07 44	07 51	08 00	08 08	08 17	08 24			08 46		08 46		

Station		AW	AW	AW	GW		GW	XC	GW	GW	GW	GW	GW	GW	AW		AW	AW	GW	GW	XC	GW	GW	AW	GW
										R							BHX								
		◇		◇			◇1	◇1			◇1	◇1	◇	◇1	◇		◇			◇1	◇1		◇1	◇	◇
								G				H		I							G				
		🍴		🍴			☕	🍴		🍴	☕	☕		Ø	🍴		🍴			☕	🍴		☕	🍴	🍴
Bath Spa 7	d								08 08	08 22	08 29		08 47	08 57								09 15	09 30		09 36
Oldfield Park	d								08 11	08 25			08 49									09 18			
Keynsham	d								08 18	08 34			08 57									09 25			09 44
Bristol Temple Meads 10	a								08 29	08 41	08 45		09 05	09 10								09 35	09 45		09 52
	d				08 21				08 41	08 54			09 10						09 21			09 41			09 56
Filton Abbey Wood	d				08 33				08 48	09 01			09 22						09 30			09 48			10 03
Bristol Parkway 7	a								08 52				09 28									09 52			
	d						08 41		08 52			09 07								09 41		09 52			
Patchway	d				08 37														09 35						
Pilning	d																								
Gloucester 7	d		07 58					08 28	09a33									08 58			09 24	10a33			
Lydney	d		08 17															09 17							
Chepstow	d		08 27					08 54										09 27			09 50				
Caldicot	d		08 35															09 36							
Severn Tunnel Jn.	d		08 38		08 49													09 38	09 46						
Newport (South Wales)	a		08 50		09 02		09 07	09 12		09 25		09 31						09 51	09 58	10 04	10 09				10 26
	d	08 38	08 52	09 03	09 03		09 08	09 14		09 25		09 32			09 37		09 41	09 52	10 00	10 05	10 11			10 22	10 26
Cardiff Central 7	a	08 53	09 07	09 23	09 24		09 24	09 30		09 43		09 48			09 57		09 58	10 07	10 18	10 21	10 25			10 37	10 41

A from 20 February until 26 March
B from 2 April
C from 9 January until 13 February
D until 2 January
E from 9 January
F from 9 January until 13 February, from 2 April
G 🍴 to Newport (South Wales)
H The St. David
I The Merchant Venturer

When events are being held at the Millenium Stadium, services are subject to alteration. Please check times before travelling.

Bath Spa, Bristol and Gloucester - Cardiff

Network Diagram - see first Page of Table 132

			GW ◇1 ☕	GW ◇1 ⌀	AW ◇ 🛒	GW	GW ◇1 ☕	XC ◇1 A 🛒	GW ◇	GW ◇1 ☕	AW ◇ 🛒		GW ◇ 🛒	GW ◇1 ☕	GW ◇1 ⌀	AW	AW BHX R 🛒	GW ◇	GW ◇1 ☕	XC ◇1 A 🛒	GW ◇		GW ◇1 B ☕	AW ◇ 🛒	GW ◇ 🛒
Bath Spa 7	d		10 00						10 08	10 24			10 36	11 00							11 08		11 24		11 36
Oldfield Park	d								10 11												11 11				
Keynsham	d								10 18												11 18				
Bristol Temple Meads 10	a		10 15						10 28	10 38			10 48	11 15							11 28		11 40		11 48
	d					10 21			10 41				10 54					11 21			11 41				11 54
Filton Abbey Wood	d					10 30			10 48				11 01					11 30			11 48				12 01
Bristol Parkway 7	a								10 52												11 52				
	d			10 07			10 41		10 52						11 07				11 41		11 52				
Patchway	d					10 35												11 35							
Pilning	d																								
Gloucester 7	d							10 24	11a34							10 58				11 24	12a33				
Lydney	d							10 43								11 17									
Chepstow	d															11 27				11 50					
Caldicot	d															11 35									
Severn Tunnel Jn.	d					10 46										11 38		11 46							
Newport (South Wales)	a			10 31		11 02	11 06	11 11					11 26		11 31	11 50		11 58	12 04	12 10					12 25
	d			10 31	11 01	11 02	11 06	11 12			11 22		11 27		11 31	11 51	11 53	12 00	12 04	12 11				12 23	12 26
Cardiff Central 7	a			10 46	11 15	11 23	11 23	11 27			11 37		11 43		11 46	12 12	12 08	12 18	12 21	12 28				12 38	12 43

		SW ◇1	GW ◇1 ☕	GW ◇1 ⌀	AW	GW	AW ◇ 🛒		GW ◇1 ☕	XC ◇1 A 🛒	GW ◇	GW ◇1 ☕	AW ◇ 🛒	GW ◇ 🛒	GW ◇1 ☕	GW ◇1 ⌀	GW		GW	GW ◇1 ☕	GW ◇1 ☕	XC ◇1 A 🛒	AW ◇ 🛒	GW ◇ 🛒	GW ◇1 ☕
Bath Spa 7	d	11 47	12 00								12 13	12 24		12 36	13 00				13 22	13 24				13 36	14 00
Oldfield Park	d										12 15								13 25						
Keynsham	d	11 55									12 23								13 32						
Bristol Temple Meads 10	a	12 05	12 15								12 31	12 39		12 48	13 15				13 41	13 44				13 48	14 15
	d					12 21					12 41			12 54			13 21							13 54	
Filton Abbey Wood	d					12 30					12 48			13 01			13 30							14 01	
Bristol Parkway 7	a										12 52														
	d			12 07					12 41		12 52					13 07					13 41				
Patchway	d					12 35											13 35								
Pilning	d																								
Gloucester 7	d				11 58					12 24	13a31											13 24			
Lydney	d				12 17																	13 43			
Chepstow	d				12 27					12 50															
Caldicot	d				12 35																				
Severn Tunnel Jn.	d				12 38	12 46											13 46								
Newport (South Wales)	a			12 31	12 50	13 00			13 06	13 11				13 26		13 31	13 58				14 04	14 09		14 26	
	d			12 32	12 52	13 01	13 00		13 06	13 12			13 23	13 26		13 31	14 00				14 05	14 11	14 22	14 27	
Cardiff Central 7	a			12 46	13 07	13 22	13 22		13 22	13 29			13 39	13 43		13 46	14 18				14 22	14 29	14 37	14 43	

		GW ◇1 ⌀	AW		AW R 🛒	GW	GW ◇1 ☕	XC ◇1 A 🛒	GW ◇	GW ◇1 ☕	GW ◇ 🛒	SW ◇1	GW ◇1 ☕		GW ◇1 ☕	AW R 🛒	AW 🛒	GW ◇	GW ◇1 ☕	GW	XC ◇1 A 🛒	GW ◇	GW ◇1 ☕		GW ◇ 🛒
Bath Spa 7	d								14 14	14 24	14 36	14 47	15 00							15 08		15 21	15 24		15 36
Oldfield Park	d								14 17											15 11					
Keynsham	d								14 24			14 55								15 18					
Bristol Temple Meads 10	a								14 35	14 39	14 48	15 05	15 15							15 28		15 34	15 40		15 48
	d					14 21			14 41		14 54							15 21		15 34		15 41			15 54
Filton Abbey Wood	d					14 30			14 48		15 01							15 30				15 48			16 01
Bristol Parkway 7	a								14 51											15 48		15 52			
	d	14 07					14 41		14 52						15 07				15 41			15 52			
Patchway	d					14 35												15 35							
Pilning	d																								
Gloucester 7	d		13 58					14 24	15a32								14 58				15 24	16a33			
Lydney	d		14 17														15 17								
Chepstow	d		14 27					14 50									15 27				15 50				
Caldicot	d		14 35														15 35								
Severn Tunnel Jn.	d		14 38			14 46											15 38	15 46							
Newport (South Wales)	a	14 30	14 50			15 02	15 06	15 11			15 25				15 31		15 50	15 58	16 05		16 10				16 25
	d	14 31	14 52		15 00	15 03	15 06	15 12			15 26				15 32	15 37	15 52	16 00	16 06		16 12				16 25
Cardiff Central 7	a	14 46	15 07		15 19	15 24	15 22	15 29			15 43				15 46	15 53	16 10	16 18	16 22		16 29				16 43

A 🛒 to Newport (South Wales)

B The Torbay Express

When events are being held at the Millenium Stadium, services are subject to alteration. Please check times before travelling.

Bath Spa, Bristol and Gloucester - Cardiff

Network Diagram - see first Page of Table 132

		GW	GW	AW	AW	GW	GW	XC	GW		GW	AW	GW	GW	GW	AW	GW	GW	GW		XC	GW	GW	GW	GW
		◇1 ☕	◇1 ☕	R 🛒	◇ 🛒		◇1 ☕	◇1 A 🛒			◇1 ☕	R 🛒	R 🛒	◇1 ☕			◇1 ☕		◇1 ☕		◇1	◇	◇1 ☕	R 🛒	◇1 ☕
Bath Spa 7	d	16 00							16 08		16 24		16 36		16 43		17 00					17 08	17 27	17 36	18 00
Oldfield Park	d								16 11													17 11			
Keynsham	d								16 18						16 51							17 18			
Bristol Temple Meads 10	a	16 15							16 29		16 39		16 48		16 59		17 15					17 29	17 41	17 48	18 14
	d					16 24			16 41				16 54		17 10			17 21				17 41		17 54	
Filton Abbey Wood	d					16 30			16 48				17 01		17 22			17 30				17 48		18 01	
Bristol Parkway 7	a								16 52						17 27							17 52			
	d		16 07				16 41		16 52					17 07					17 41			17 52			
Patchway	d					16 35												17 35							
Pilning	d																								
Gloucester 7	d							16 24	17a33							16 58					17 27	18a33			
Lydney	d							16 43								17 17									
Chepstow	d							16 52								17 27									
Caldicot	d															17 35									
Severn Tunnel Jn.	d					16 46							17 14			17 38		17 46						18 14	
Newport (South Wales)	a		16 30			17 00	17 06	17 11					17 25	17 31		17 50		17 58	18 04		18 10			18 25	
	d		16 31	16 40	17 01	17 01	17 06	17 12				17 22	17 27	17 31		17 52		18 00	18 04		18 11			18 26	
Cardiff Central 7	a		16 46	16 55	17 15	17 25	17 22	17 28				17 37	17 43	17 46		18 10		18 17	18 19		18 27			18 43	

		GW	AW	AW	AW		GW	GW	XC	GW	GW	AW	GW	GW	GW		AW	GW	GW	XC	GW	GW	GW	GW	GW
		◇1 B ☕	R 🛒		◇ 🛒			◇1 C ☕	◇1		◇1 ☕	R 🛒	R 🛒	◇1 ☕	◇1 ☕				◇1 ☕	◇1		◇1 ☕	◇1 D ☕	◇ 🛒	◇
Bath Spa 7	d									18 08	18 29		18 36	18 59							19 08	19 24	19 30	19 36	19 49
Oldfield Park	d									18 11											19 11				19 52
Keynsham	d									18 18											19 18				19 59
Bristol Temple Meads 10	a									18 28	18 44		18 48	19 12							19 29	19 41	19 43	19 48	20 08
	d						18 21			18 41			18 54					19 21			19 41			19 54	
Filton Abbey Wood	d						18 30			18 48			19 01					19 30			19 48			20 01	
Bristol Parkway 7	a									18 52											19 52				
	d	18 07						18 41		18 52					19 07				19 44		19 52				
Patchway	d						18 35											19 35							
Pilning	d																								
Gloucester 7	d			17 59					18 31	19a30							18 58			19 28	20a32				
Lydney	d			18 18													19 17								
Chepstow	d			18 28													19 27								
Caldicot	d			18 36													19 34								
Severn Tunnel Jn.	d			18 39			18 50						19 14				19 37	19 46						20 16	
Newport (South Wales)	a	18 30		18 51			19 06	19 11	19 16				19 26		19 31		19 50	20 01	20 07	20 11				20 27	
	d	18 31	18 41	18 53	19 01		19 06	19 11	19 17			19 22	19 26		19 31		19 52	20 02	20 08	20 13				20 28	
Cardiff Central 7	a	18 48	18 55	19 09	19 21		19 24	19 26	19 33			19 43	19 46		19 48		20 09	20 20	20 22	20 27				20 43	

			GW	GW	AW	XC	AW	GW	GW	GW FO	AW		GW FX	GW FO	XC	GW	GW	AW	GW	GW	GW		GW	XC FO	XC FX
			◇1 ☕	◇1 ☕	R 🛒	◇1		◇ 🛒	◇1 ☕	◇1 ☕	◇ 🛒		◇1 ☕	◇1 ☕	◇1	◇ 🛒	◇1 ☕	◇ 🛒			◇1 ☕		◇1 ☕	◇1	◇1
Bath Spa 7	d		19 59					20 12	20 30							20 36	21 00			21 08	21 30				
Oldfield Park	d							20 14												21 11					
Keynsham	d							20 21												21 18					
Bristol Temple Meads 10	a		20 13					20 30	20 44							20 48	21 15			21 28	21 44				
	d					20 15										20 54			21 19						
Filton Abbey Wood	d					20 22										21 01			21 30						
Bristol Parkway 7	a																								
	d			20 07						20 34			20 42	20 42									21 41		
Patchway	d					20 25													21 34						
Pilning	d																								
Gloucester 7	d						19 58								20 24									21 24	21 24
Lydney	d						20 17																	21 43	21 43
Chepstow	d						20 27																	21 52	21 52
Caldicot	d						20 36																	22 01	22 01
Severn Tunnel Jn.	d					20 37	20 39									21 14			21 46					22 04	22 04
Newport (South Wales)	a			20 31		20 47	20 51			20 58			21 04	21 04	21 11	21 26			21 58				22 03	22 15	22 15
	d			20 33	20 39	20 49	20 52			21 00	21 00		21 04	21 04	21 13	21 26		21 52	21 59				22 05	22 16	22 16
Cardiff Central 7	a			20 48	20 58	21 02	21 10			21 17	21 19		21 19	21 23	21 27	21 44		22 06	22 18				22 23	22 31	22 35

A 🛒 to Newport (South Wales)
B The Capitals United
C The Red Dragon
D The Bristolian

When events are being held at the Millenium Stadium, services are subject to alteration. Please check times before travelling.

Table 132

Bath Spa, Bristol and Gloucester - Cardiff

Network Diagram - see first Page of Table 132

		GW FO	GW FX	SW	GW	GW	AW FO		AW FX	GW	GW	GW	GW	AW	AW FO	AW FX	GW FO		GW FX						
		◇	◇	◇**1**	◇**1** ☕		◇		◇	◇**1** ☕	◇		◇**1** ☕	◇			◇**1** ☕		◇**1** ☕						
Bath Spa 7	d	21 36	21 36	21 51	22 13	22 25					22 36	23 02	23 19				23 49		23 56						
Oldfield Park	d					22 28						23 05													
Keynsham	d			21 59		22 36						23 12													
Bristol Temple Meads 10	a	21 48	21 48	22 06	22 30	22 44					22 48	23 23	23 32				00 03		00 10						
	d	21 54	21 54								22 54														
Filton Abbey Wood	d	22 01	22 01								23 01														
Bristol Parkway 7	a																								
	d									22 45															
Patchway	d	22 06	22 06								23 06														
Pilning	d																								
Gloucester 7	d														23 13	23 13									
Lydney	d														23 33	23 33									
Chepstow	d														23 42	23 42									
Caldicot	d														23 51	23 51									
Severn Tunnel Jn.	d	22 18	22 18								23 17				23 54	23 54									
Newport (South Wales)	a	22 29	22 36							23 19	23 34				00 06	00 06									
	d	22 30	22 37				22 40		22 42	23 19	23 35			23 47	00 07	00 07									
Cardiff Central 7	a	22 52	23 00				22 55		23 04	23 40	23 56			00 02	00 33	00 35									

Saturdays

		AW	AW	GW	GW	AW	GW	AW	AW	XC		GW	GW	AW	XC	GW	GW	SW	AW	GW		GW	AW	AW	GW
		◇		◇**1** ☕	◇**1** ☕	◇	◇**1** ☕			◇**1**		◇**1**		◇ 🛒	◇**1**			**1**				◇**1** ☕	◇ 🛒		
Bath Spa 7	d			23p49			01 15										07 08	07 35				08 00			
Oldfield Park	d																07 11	07 38							
Keynsham	d																07 18	07 45							
Bristol Temple Meads 10	a			00 03			01 29										07 29	07 53				08 15			
	d						01 36					06 46	06 50			07 21	07 41			07 54					08 20
Filton Abbey Wood	d											06 54	07 02			07 30	07 48			08 01					08 30
Bristol Parkway 7	a											06 58					07 52								
	d				00 16							07 11					07 52								
Patchway	d															07 34									08 35
Pilning	d																								
Gloucester 7	d		23p13						05 50	06 15					07 00		08a32							07 58	
Lydney	d		23p33						06 09	06 34					07 20									08 17	
Chepstow	d		23p42						06 19	06 43					07 29									08 27	
Caldicot	d		23p51						06 27	06 52					07 38									08 35	
Severn Tunnel Jn.	d		23p54						06 30	06 55			07 14		07 41	07 46								08 38	08 46
Newport (South Wales)	a		00 06		00 38		02s02		06 42	07 06		07 31	07 25		07 52	07 58				08 26				08 50	09 01
	d	23p47	00 07		00 38	00 59		06 38	06 44	07 07		07 31	07 26	07 38	07 53	07 58			08 01	08 27			08 33	08 52	09 01
Cardiff Central 7	a	00 02	00 33		00 53	01 18	02 19	06 54	07 00	07 22		07 47	07 44	07 53	08 08	08 18			08 19	08 43			08 50	09 10	09 21

		AW	XC	GW	GW	GW		GW	GW	GW	AW	AW	GW	XC	GW	GW		GW	GW	GW	AW	AW	GW	XC	GW
		◇ 🛒	◇**1** A 🛒		◇**1** ☕	◇		◇	**1** ☕	◇**1** ☕	◇ 🛒			◇**1** A 🛒		◇**1** ☕		◇ B 🛒	◇**1** ☕	◇**1** ☕	◇ 🛒	◇ 🛒		◇**1** A 🛒	◇
Bath Spa 7	d			08 08	08 24	08 30		08 47	09 00						09 08	09 24		09 36	10 00						10 08
Oldfield Park	d			08 11				08 49							09 11										10 11
Keynsham	d			08 18				08 57							09 18										10 18
Bristol Temple Meads 10	a			08 29	08 39	08 44		09 05	09 15						09 27	09 39		09 48	10 15						10 29
	d			08 41		08 54							09 21		09 41			09 54					10 21		10 41
Filton Abbey Wood	d			08 48		09 01							09 30		09 48			10 01					10 30		10 48
Bristol Parkway 7	a			08 52											09 52										10 52
	d			08 52						09 07					09 52					10 07					10 52
Patchway	d												09 35										10 35		
Pilning	d																								
Gloucester 7	d		08 24	09a33								08 58		09 24	10a33									10 24	11a32
Lydney	d											09 17												10 43	
Chepstow	d		08 50									09 27		09 50											
Caldicot	d											09 35													
Severn Tunnel Jn.	d											09 38	09 46										10 46		
Newport (South Wales)	a		09 07			09 25				09 30		09 50	09 58	10 07				10 24		10 31			11 00	11 08	
	d	09 02	09 09			09 25				09 31	09 38	09 52	09 59	10 09				10 24		10 31	10 36	10 57	11 01	11 09	
Cardiff Central 7	a	09 22	09 23			09 43				09 47	09 58	10 07	10 18	10 23				10 43		10 46	10 53	11 15	11 22	11 24	

A 🛒 to Newport (South Wales)

B 🛒 to Bristol Temple Meads

When events are being held at the Millenium Stadium, services are subject to alteration. Please check times before travelling.

Table 132

Saturdays

Bath Spa, Bristol and Gloucester - Cardiff

Network Diagram - see first Page of Table 132

		GW		GW	GW	GW	AW	AW	GW	XC	GW	GW		GW	SW	GW	GW	AW	AW	AW	GW	XC		GW	GW
		◇1		◇	◇1	◇1	◇			◇1	◇	◇1		◇	◇1	◇1	◇1	◇		◇		◇1		◇	◇1
				A						B				A								B			
		⊡		⊼	⊡	⊡	⊼			⊼		⊡		⊼		⊡	Ø	⊼		⊼		⊼			⊡
Bath Spa 7	d	10 24		10 36	11 00						11 08	11 24		11 36	11 47	12 00								12 17	12 24
Oldfield Park	d										11 11													12 19	
Keynsham	d										11 18				11 55									12 27	
Bristol Temple Meads 10	a	10 39		10 48	11 15						11 29	11 39		11 48	12 05	12 15								12 35	12 39
	d			10 54					11 21		11 41			11 54							12 21			12 41	
Filton Abbey Wood	d			11 01					11 30		11 48			12 01							12 30			12 48	
Bristol Parkway 7	a										11 52													12 52	
	d					11 07					11 52						12 07							12 52	
Patchway	d								11 35												12 35				
Pilning	d																								
Gloucester 7	d							10 58		11 24	12a33								11 58			12 24		13a34	
Lydney	d							11 17											12 17						
Chepstow	d							11 27		11 50									12 27			12 50			
Caldicot	d							11 35											12 35						
Severn Tunnel Jn.	d							11 38	11 46										12 38		12 46				
Newport (South Wales)	a			11 24		11 31		11 50	11 58	12 07				12 24			12 31		12 50		13 00	13 11			
	d			11 24		11 31	11 37	11 52	11 59	12 09				12 24			12 31	12 37	12 52	12 56	13 01	13 12			
Cardiff Central 7	a			11 43		11 46	11 53	12 07	12 18	12 23				12 43			12 46	12 53	13 07	13 15	13 18	13 27			

		GW	GW	GW	AW	GW	XC	GW		GW	GW	GW	GW	AW	AW	GW	AW	XC		GW	GW	GW	SW	GW	GW
																	R								
		◇	◇1	◇1	◇		◇1	◇		◇1	◇	◇1	◇1	◇				◇1		◇	◇1	◇	◇1	◇1	◇1
							B											B							
			⊡	Ø	⊼		⊼			⊡		⊡	⊡	⊼			⊼	⊼			⊡			⊡	⊡
Bath Spa 7	d	12 36	13 00					13 19		13 24	13 36	14 00								14 08	14 24	14 36	14 47	15 00	
Oldfield Park	d							13 22												14 11					
Keynsham	d							13 29												14 18			14 55		
Bristol Temple Meads 10	a	12 48	13 14					13 37		13 42	13 48	14 15								14 28	14 39	14 48	15 05	15 15	
	d	12 54				13 21		13 41			13 54					14 21				14 41		14 54			
Filton Abbey Wood	d	13 01				13 30		13 48			14 01					14 30				14 48		15 01			
Bristol Parkway 7	a							13 52												14 52					
	d			13 07				13 52					14 07							14 52					15 07
Patchway	d					13 35										14 35									
Pilning	d																								
Gloucester 7	d						13 24	14a33							13 58			14 24		15a32					
Lydney	d						13 43								14 17										
Chepstow	d														14 27			14 50							
Caldicot	d														14 35										
Severn Tunnel Jn.	d					13 46									14 38	14 46									
Newport (South Wales)	a	13 25		13 31		13 58	14 08				14 24		14 31		14 50	14 59		15 11				15 25			15 31
	d	13 25		13 31	13 37	13 59	14 09				14 24		14 31	14 37	14 52	15 00	15 06	15 12				15 25			15 31
Cardiff Central 7	a	13 43		13 47	13 53	14 18	14 24				14 43		14 46	14 53	15 09	15 18	15 26	15 27				15 43			15 46

		AW	AW	GW		XC	GW	GW	GW	GW	GW	AW	AW	GW		XC	GW	GW	GW	GW	GW	AW	AW	GW	
		R										R										R			
						◇1	◇	◇1	◇	◇1	◇1		◇			◇1		◇1	◇	◇1	◇1				
						B										B									
		⊼	⊼			⊼		⊡		⊡	⊡	⊼	⊼			⊼		⊡		⊡	⊡	⊼			
Bath Spa 7	d						15 18	15 24	15 36	16 00							16 08	16 24	16 36	17 00					
Oldfield Park	d						15 21										16 11								
Keynsham	d						15 28										16 18								
Bristol Temple Meads 10	a						15 36	15 41	15 49	16 15							16 29	16 39	16 48	17 15					
	d			15 21			15 41		15 54					16 21			16 41		16 54					17 21	
Filton Abbey Wood	d			15 30			15 48		16 01					16 30			16 48		17 01					17 30	
Bristol Parkway 7	a						15 52										16 52								
	d						15 52				16 07						16 52				17 07				
Patchway	d			15 35										16 35										17 35	
Pilning	d			15 41																					
Gloucester 7	d		14 58			15 24	16a33									16 24	17a33						16 58		
Lydney	d		15 17													16 43							17 17		
Chepstow	d		15 27			15 50										16 52							17 27		
Caldicot	d		15 35																				17 35		
Severn Tunnel Jn.	d		15 38	15 46										16 46					17 14				17 38	17 46	
Newport (South Wales)	a		15 50	16 01		16 08			16 24		16 31			17 00		17 10			17 26		17 29		17 50	17 58	
	d	15 37	15 52	16 01		16 10			16 24		16 31	16 37	16 56	17 01		17 11			17 26		17 31	17 37	17 52	18 00	
Cardiff Central 7	a	15 53	16 07	16 18		16 25			16 43		16 47	16 53	17 08	17 18		17 26			17 43		17 46	17 53	18 10	18 18	

A ⊼ to Bristol Temple Meads

B ⊼ to Newport (South Wales)

When events are being held at the Millenium Stadium, services are subject to alteration. Please check times before travelling.

Table 132

Saturdays

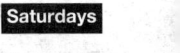

Bath Spa, Bristol and Gloucester - Cardiff

Network Diagram - see first Page of Table 132

		XC	GW	GW	GW	GW	GW	AW	AW	AW		GW	XC	GW	GW	GW	GW	GW	AW	AW		GW	XC	GW	GW
		◇1 🛒	◇	◇1 ☕	◇	◇1 ☕	◇1 ☕	R 🛒		◇ 🛒			◇1		◇1 ☕	R	◇1 ☕	◇1 ☕	R 🛒				◇1		◇1 ☕
Bath Spa 7	d		17 08	17 24	17 36	18 00								18 08	18 24	18 36	19 00							19 08	19 24
Oldfield Park	d		17 11											18 11										19 11	
Keynsham	d		17 18											18 18										19 18	
Bristol Temple Meads 10	a		17 29	17 39	17 48	18 15								18 29	18 39	18 48	19 15							19 29	19 38
	d		17 41		17 54							18 21		18 41		18 54						19 21		19 41	
Filton Abbey Wood	d		17 48		18 01							18 30		18 48		19 01						19 28		19 48	
Bristol Parkway 7	a		17 52											18 52										19 52	
	d		17 52				18 07							18 52				19 07						19 52	
Patchway	d											18 35										19 33			
Pilning	d																								
Gloucester 7	d	17 24	18a33						17 58				18 31	19a33						18 58			19 24	20a33	
Lydney	d								18 17											19 17					
Chepstow	d								18 27											19 27					
Caldicot	d								18 35											19 34					
Severn Tunnel Jn.	d				18 14				18 38			18 47								19 37		19 46			
Newport (South Wales)	a	18 05			18 25		18 30		18 50			19 05	19 12			19 26		19 30		19 50		19 58	20 05		
	d	18 07			18 25		18 31	18 37	18 52	18 57		19 05	19 14			19 26		19 31	19 41	19 52		19 58	20 07		
Cardiff Central 7	a	18 21			18 43		18 46	18 53	19 10	19 16		19 23	19 29			19 43		19 46	19 58	20 11		20 18	20 21		

		GW	GW	GW	GW	AW		AW	XC	GW	GW	AW	GW	XC	GW	GW		GW	GW	AW	GW	XC	GW	AW	GW
		◇	◇	◇1 ☕	◇1 ☕	R 🛒			◇1 🛒	◇	◇1 ☕	◇ 🛒	◇1 ☕	◇1	◇	◇1 A ☕		◇1 ☕		◇ 🛒		◇1	◇1 ☕		◇
Bath Spa 7	d	19 36	19 47	20 00						20 16	20 24				20 36	21 00			21 08				21 30		21 39
Oldfield Park	d		19 50							20 18									21 11						
Keynsham	d		19 57							20 25									21 18						
Bristol Temple Meads 10	a	19 48	20 05	20 15						20 33	20 40				20 48	21 16			21 29				21 45		21 51
	d	19 54							20 21						20 54						21 29				21 54
Filton Abbey Wood	d	20 01							20 28						21 01						21 36				22 01
Bristol Parkway 7	a																								
	d				20 07								20 40					21 07							
Patchway	d								20 32												21 41				22 06
Pilning	d																								
Gloucester 7	d							19 58						20 24								21 24			
Lydney	d							20 17														21 43			
Chepstow	d							20 27														21 52			
Caldicot	d							20 35														22 01			
Severn Tunnel Jn.	d							20 38	20 42												21 52	22 04			22 18
Newport (South Wales)	a	20 25			20 30			20 50	20 55				21 05	21 11	21 25			21 30			22 09	22 21			22 38
	d	20 25			20 31	20 40		20 52	20 57			21 02	21 07	21 13	21 25			21 31		21 45	22 11	22 21		22 34	22 38
Cardiff Central 7	a	20 43			20 44	21 00		21 09	21 11			21 21	21 23	21 29	21 43			21 47		22 04	22 30	22 43		22 53	22 58

		SW		GW SO	GW	GW	GW	GW	GW	GW	AW	GW		AW SO	AW
		◇1		◇1 B ☕	◇1 C ☕	◇1 A ☕		◇	◇1 ☕			◇1 ☕		D	E 🚌
Bath Spa 7	d	21 51		22 00	22 11		22 25	22 36	23 00	23 08					
Oldfield Park	d						22 28			23 11					
Keynsham	d	21 59					22 36			23 18					
Bristol Temple Meads 10	a	22 06		22 14	22 25		22 44	22 50	23 15	23 31					
	d							22 54							
Filton Abbey Wood	d							23 01							
Bristol Parkway 7	a														
	d					22 11						23 28			
Patchway	d							23 06							
Pilning	d														
Gloucester 7	d													23 09	23 09
Lydney	d													23 28	23 49
Chepstow	d													23 38	00 09
Caldicot	d													23 46	00 24
Severn Tunnel Jn.	d							23 18						23 49	00 34
Newport (South Wales)	a					22 46		23 35				23 57		00 07	00 59
	d					22 46		23 36			23 46	23 58		00 09	00 59
Cardiff Central 7	a					23 06		23 55			00 05	00 18		00 35	01 29

A until 11 February, from 31 March

B from 17 December to 31 December, from 31 March

C from 7 January until 24 March

D from 17 December to 31 December, from 18 February until 24 March

E from 7 January until 11 February, from 31 March

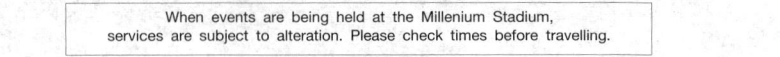

When events are being held at the Millenium Stadium, services are subject to alteration. Please check times before travelling.

Table 132

Sundays

until 1 January

Bath Spa, Bristol and Gloucester - Cardiff

Network Diagram - see first Page of Table 132

		AW	GW	AW	AW	GW	GW	AW	GW	GW		GW	GW	GW	AW	GW	AW	XC	GW	GW		GW	XC	GW	GW
		A	◇1 A ☕	A	A	◇1 A ☕	◇1 A ☕	◇ 🛒	◇	◇1 ☕		◇1 ☕		◇1 ☕	◇	◇1 ☕		◇1 🛒	R	◇1 ☕		◇1 ☕	◇1 🛒		◇1 ☕
Bath Spa 7	d					00 13	01 08			09 39			10 27	10 40					11 26	11 40				12 20	12 40
Oldfield Park	d												10 30						11 29					12 23	
Keynsham	d												10 37						11 36					12 30	
Bristol Temple Meads 10	a					00 25	01 21			09 53			10 45	10 57					11 44	11 54				12 38	12 54
	d								09 48										11 48						
Filton Abbey Wood	d								09 55										11 55						
Bristol Parkway 7	a																								
	d		23p28									10 08				11 05						12 11			
Patchway	d																		12 00						
Pilning	d																								
Gloucester 7	d				23p09												10 48	11 05					12 05		
Lydney	d				23p28												11 07								
Chepstow	d				23p38												11 17								
Caldicot	d				23p46												11 25								
Severn Tunnel Jn.	d				23p49				10 08								11 28		12 11						
Newport (South Wales)	a		23p57		00 07				10 25			10 33				11 32	11 46	11 48	12 29			12 37	12 52		
	d	23p46	23p58	00 04	00 09			09 27	10 26			10 33			11 00	11 32	11 48	11 50	12 29			12 37	12 53		
Cardiff Central 7	a	00 05	00 18	00 26	00 35			09 42	10 41			10 51			11 16	11 50	12 06	12 08	12 44			12 56	13 12		

		AW	AW	AW	GW	XC		GW	GW	AW	GW	AW	XC	GW	AW	GW		SW	GW	AW	XC	GW	GW	GW	AW
		◇ 🛒	R 🛒		◇1 ☕	◇1 B 🛒		◇	◇1 ☕	R 🛒	◇1 ☕	◇ 🛒	◇1 B 🛒	◇		◇1 ☕		◇1	◇1 ☕	R 🛒	◇1 B 🛒	◇	◇1 ☕	◇	R 🛒
Bath Spa 7	d							13 23	13 40					14 26		14 40		14 50				15 28	15 40	16 01	
Oldfield Park	d							13 26						14 28										16 03	
Keynsham	d							13 33						14 36				14 58						16 11	
Bristol Temple Meads 10	a							13 41	13 54					14 44		14 54		15 05				15 40	15 53	16 23	
	d							13 48						14 48								15 48			
Filton Abbey Wood	d							13 55						14 55								15 55			
Bristol Parkway 7	a																								
	d				13 11						14 11								15 11						
Patchway	d																								
Pilning	d																								
Gloucester 7	d			12 30		13 23							14 24		14 33						15 23				
Lydney	d			12 49											14 52										
Chepstow	d			12 59											15 02										
Caldicot	d			13 07											15 10										
Severn Tunnel Jn.	d			13 10				14 08						15 08	15 16							16 08			
Newport (South Wales)	a			13 33	13 37	14 06		14 27			14 37		15 08	15 26	15 34				15 37		16 06	16 26			
	d	12 52	13 29	13 34	13 37	14 08		14 28		14 30	14 37	15 07	15 09	15 26	15 36				15 37	15 46	16 08	16 26			16 31
Cardiff Central 7	a	13 13	13 44	13 52	13 56	14 26		14 51		14 49	14 57	15 31	15 31	15 41	15 53				15 56	16 02	16 26	16 44			16 52

		GW		XC	GW	GW	AW	AW	GW	XC	GW	GW		AW	GW	XC	GW	GW	GW	GW	GW	AW		AW	XC
		◇1 ☕		◇1 B 🛒	◇	◇1 ☕	R 🛒		◇1 ☕	◇1 🛒	R	◇1 ☕		R 🛒	◇1 ☕	◇1 B 🛒	◇	◇1 ☕	◇	◇1 ☕	◇1 ☕	R 🛒			◇1 B 🛒
Bath Spa 7	d				16 28	16 40					17 26	17 40					18 28	18 40	19 02	19 07					
Oldfield Park	d										17 29								19 04						
Keynsham	d										17 36								19 12						
Bristol Temple Meads 10	a				16 41	16 54					17 44	17 54					18 40	18 54	19 20	19 25					
	d				16 48						17 48						18 48								
Filton Abbey Wood	d				16 55						17 55						18 55								
Bristol Parkway 7	a																								
	d	16 11							17 11						18 11						19 15				
Patchway	d				17 00																				
Pilning	d																								
Gloucester 7	d			16 23				16 37		17 23						18 23								18 48	19 28
Lydney	d							16 56																19 07	
Chepstow	d							17 07																19 17	
Caldicot	d							17 13																19 25	
Severn Tunnel Jn.	d				17 11			17 16			18 08						19 08							19 32	
Newport (South Wales)	a	16 37		17 06	17 29			17 37	17 40	18 07	18 26				18 37	19 07	19 26				19 41			19 54	20 11
	d	16 37		17 08	17 29		17 34	17 38	17 41	18 09	18 26			18 33	18 37	19 08	19 26				19 41	19 51		19 56	20 13
Cardiff Central 7	a	16 56		17 27	17 46		17 50	17 57	17 58	18 29	18 44			18 50	18 56	19 27	19 42				19 59	20 06		20 12	20 31

A not 11 December

B 🛒 to Newport (South Wales)

When events are being held at the Millenium Stadium, services are subject to alteration. Please check times before travelling.

Table 132

Sundays
until 1 January

Bath Spa, Bristol and Gloucester - Cardiff

Network Diagram - see first Page of Table 132

		AW	GW	GW	GW	GW	XC	AW		GW	AW	GW	SW	GW	GW	GW	AW	GW		GW	GW	AW	GW	GW	AW
		R						R									R								
			◇	◇1	◇	◇1	◇1			◇		◇1	◇1	◇1	◇	◇1		◇		◇1		◇	◇1	◇	
		🛒		☕		☕		🛒				☕		☕		☕	🛒			☕			☕		
Bath Spa 7	d		19 27	19 40	20 00					20 27		20 40	20 49	21 03	21 11			21 28		21 40	22 15			22 26	
Oldfield Park	d				20 02										21 13						22 17				
Keynsham	d				20 10								20 57		21 21						22 25				
Bristol Temple Meads 10	a		19 39	19 54	20 18					20 39		20 54	21 04	21 18	21 29			21 40		21 54	22 33			22 38	
	d		19 48							20 48								21 48						22 48	
Filton Abbey Wood	d		19 55							20 55								21 55						22 55	
Bristol Parkway 7	a																								
	d					20 11										21 11							22 11		
Patchway	d		20 00															22 02							
Pilning	d																								
Gloucester 7	d						20 23				20 31														22 33
Lydney	d										20 50														22 52
Chepstow	d										21 00														23 02
Caldicot	d										21 10														23 10
Severn Tunnel Jn.	d		20 11							21 08	21 13							22 15						23 09	23 14
Newport (South Wales)	a		20 28			20 37	21 06			21 26	21 31					21 37		22 31					22 37	23 26	23 33
	d	20 23	20 29			20 37	21 08	21 14		21 26	21 33					21 37	21 46	22 31				22 33	22 38	23 27	23 34
Cardiff Central 7	a	20 43	20 46			20 56	21 26	21 36		21 42	21 49					21 59	22 05	22 53				22 59	23 00	23 47	23 54

		GW	GW	AW		GW
		◇1	◇1	◇		◇1
		☕	☕			☕
Bath Spa 7	d	22 44				23 55
Oldfield Park	d					
Keynsham	d					
Bristol Temple Meads 10	a	22 58				00 09
	d					
Filton Abbey Wood	d					
Bristol Parkway 7	a					
	d		23 17			
Patchway	d					
Pilning	d					
Gloucester 7	d					
Lydney	d					
Chepstow	d					
Caldicot	d					
Severn Tunnel Jn.	d					
Newport (South Wales)	a		23 42			
	d		23 43	23 55		
Cardiff Central 7	a		00 04	00 20		

Sundays
8 January to 12 February

		AW	GW	AW	AW	GW	GW	AW	GW	GW		GW	GW	GW	AW	GW	AW	XC	GW	GW		GW	XC	GW	GW
																			R						
			◇1			◇1	◇1		◇	◇1		◇1		◇1	◇	◇1		◇1		◇1		◇1	◇1		◇1
					🚌																				
			☕			☕	☕			☕		☕		☕		☕		🛒		☕		☕	🛒		☕
Bath Spa 7	d					00 13	01 08			09 40			10 27	10 40					11 26	11 40				12 20	12 40
Oldfield Park	d												10 30						11 29					12 23	
Keynsham	d												10 37						11 36					12 30	
Bristol Temple Meads 10	a					00 27	01 21			09 54			10 45	10 54					11 44	11 55				12 38	12 54
	d								09 48										11 48						
Filton Abbey Wood	d								09 55										11 55						
Bristol Parkway 7	a																								
	d		23p28									10 05				11 05						12 11			
Patchway	d																		12 00						
Pilning	d																								
Gloucester 7	d				23p09												10 48	11 05					12 05		
Lydney	d				23p49												11 07								
Chepstow	d				00 09												11 17								
Caldicot	d				00 24												11 25								
Severn Tunnel Jn.	d				00 34				10 08								11 28		12 11						
Newport (South Wales)	a		23p57		00 59				10 25			10 30				11 32	11 46	11 48	12 29			12 38	12 52		
	d	23p46	23p58	00 04	00 59			09 22	10 26			10 30			11 00	11 32	11 48	11 50	12 29			12 38	12 53		
Cardiff Central 7	a	00 05	00 18	00 26	01 29			09 37	10 41			10 49			11 19	11 51	12 06	12 08	12 44			12 57	13 12		

When events are being held at the Millenium Stadium,
services are subject to alteration. Please check times before travelling.

Table 132

Sundays

8 January to 12 February

Bath Spa, Bristol and Gloucester - Cardiff

Network Diagram - see first Page of Table 132

		AW	AW	AW	GW	XC		GW	GW	AW	GW	XC	AW	GW	AW	GW		SW	GW	AW	XC	GW	GW	GW	AW
			R							R										R					R
		◇			◇1	◇1		◇	◇1		◇1	◇1	◇	◇		◇1		◇1	◇1		◇1	◇	◇1	◇	
						A						A									A				
		🛒	🛒		☕	🛒			☕	🛒	☕	🛒	🛒			☕			☕	🛒	🛒		☕		🛒
Bath Spa 7	d							13 23	13 40					14 26		14 40		14 50				15 28	15 40	16 01	
Oldfield Park	d							13 26						14 28										16 03	
Keynsham	d							13 33						14 36				14 58						16 11	
Bristol Temple Meads 10	a							13 41	13 54					14 44		14 52		15 05				15 40	15 54	16 23	
	d							13 48						14 48								15 48			
Filton Abbey Wood	d							13 55						14 55								15 55			
Bristol Parkway 7	a																								
	d				13 11						14 11								15 11						
Patchway	d																								
Pilning	d																								
Gloucester 7	d			12 30		13 23						14 24			14 33						15 23				
Lydney	d			12 49											14 52										
Chepstow	d			12 59											15 02										
Caldicot	d			13 07											15 10										
Severn Tunnel Jn.	d			13 10				14 08						15 08	15 16							16 08			
Newport (South Wales)	a			13 33	13 37	14 06		14 27			14 37	15 08		15 26	15 34				15 37		16 06	16 26			
	d	12 52	13 29	13 34	13 37	14 08		14 28		14 30	14 37	15 09	15 16	15 26	15 36				15 37	15 46	16 08	16 26			16 31
Cardiff Central 7	a	13 13	13 49	13 52	13 56	14 26		14 51		14 49	14 57	15 31	15 35	15 41	15 53				15 56	16 07	16 26	16 44			16 52

		GW		XC	GW	GW	AW	AW	GW	XC	GW	GW		GW	AW	XC	GW	GW	GW	GW	GW	AW		AW	XC
							R				R				R							R			
		◇1		◇1	◇	◇1			◇1	◇1		◇1		◇1		◇1	◇	◇1	◇	◇1	◇1				◇1
				A												A									A
		☕		🛒		☕	🛒		☕	🛒		☕		☕	🛒	🛒		☕		☕	☕	🛒			🛒
Bath Spa 7	d				16 28	16 41					17 26	17 40					18 28	18 40	19 02	19 07					
Oldfield Park	d										17 29								19 04						
Keynsham	d										17 36								19 12						
Bristol Temple Meads 10	a				16 41	16 53					17 44	17 54					18 40	18 54	19 20	19 25					
	d				16 48						17 48						18 48								
Filton Abbey Wood	d				16 55						17 55						18 55								
Bristol Parkway 7	a																								
	d	16 11							17 11					18 11							19 12				
Patchway	d				17 00																				
Pilning	d																								
Gloucester 7	d			16 23				16 37		17 23						18 23								18 48	19 28
Lydney	d							16 56																19 07	
Chepstow	d							17 07																19 17	
Caldicot	d							17 13																19 25	
Severn Tunnel Jn.	d				17 11			17 16			18 08						19 08							19 32	
Newport (South Wales)	a	16 37		17 06	17 29			17 37	17 40	18 07	18 26			18 37		19 07	19 26				19 37			19 54	20 11
	d	16 37		17 08	17 29		17 35	17 38	17 41	18 09	18 26			18 37	18 46	19 08	19 26				19 37	19 51		19 56	20 13
Cardiff Central 7	a	16 57		17 27	17 46		17 57	17 57	18 00	18 29	18 44			18 57	19 03	19 27	19 42				19 55	20 06		20 12	20 31

		AW	GW	GW	GW	GW	XC	AW		GW	AW	GW	SW	GW	GW	GW	AW	GW		GW	GW	GW	AW	GW	AW
		R						R									R								
			◇	◇1	◇	◇1	◇1			◇		◇1	◇1	◇1	◇	◇1		◇		◇1	◇1		◇	◇	
		🛒		☕		☕		🛒				☕		☕		☕	🛒			☕	☕				
Bath Spa 7	d		19 27	19 40	20 00					20 27		20 40	20 49	21 03	21 11			21 28		21 40		22 15		22 26	
Oldfield Park	d				20 02										21 13							22 17			
Keynsham	d				20 10								20 57		21 21							22 25			
Bristol Temple Meads 10	a		19 39	19 54	20 18					20 39		20 54	21 04	21 18	21 29			21 40		21 54		22 33		22 38	
	d		19 48							20 48								21 48						22 48	
Filton Abbey Wood	d		19 55							20 55								21 55						22 55	
Bristol Parkway 7	a																								
	d					20 12										21 12					22 12				
Patchway	d		20 00															22 02							
Pilning	d																								
Gloucester 7	d						20 23				20 31														22 33
Lydney	d										20 50														22 52
Chepstow	d										21 00														23 02
Caldicot	d										21 10														23 10
Severn Tunnel Jn.	d		20 11							21 08	21 13							22 15						23 09	23 14
Newport (South Wales)	a		20 28			20 37	21 06			21 26	21 31					21 37		22 31			22 37			23 26	23 33
	d	20 23	20 29			20 37	21 08	21 14		21 26	21 33					21 37	21 46	22 31			22 37		22 44	23 27	23 34
Cardiff Central 7	a	20 43	20 46			20 56	21 26	21 36		21 42	21 49					22 00	22 05	22 53			23 00		23 05	23 47	23 54

A 🛒 to Newport (South Wales)

When events are being held at the Millenium Stadium,
services are subject to alteration. Please check times before travelling.

Table 132

Sundays

8 January to 12 February

Bath Spa, Bristol and Gloucester - Cardiff

Network Diagram - see first Page of Table 132

		GW	GW	GW	AW
		◇1 🍴	◇1 🍴	◇1 🍴	◇
Bath Spa 7	d	22 44		23 47	
Oldfield Park	d				
Keynsham	d				
Bristol Temple Meads 10	a	22 58		00 01	
	d				
Filton Abbey Wood	d				
Bristol Parkway 7	a				
	d		23 16		
Patchway	d				
Pilning	d				
Gloucester 7	d				
Lydney	d				
Chepstow	d				
Caldicot	d				
Severn Tunnel Jn.	d				
Newport (South Wales)	a		23 41		
	d		23 42		23 55
Cardiff Central 7	a		00 03		00 20

Sundays

19 February to 25 March

		AW	GW	AW	AW	GW	GW	AW	GW	GW		GW	GW	GW	GW	GW	AW	AW	XC	GW		GW	GW	GW	GW
			◇1 🍴			◇1 🍴	◇1 🍴	◇ 🛒	◇1 🍴	🚌		◇1 🍴	🚌	🚌		◇1 🍴	◇		◇1 🛒	🚌		R	◇1 🍴	◇1 🍴	🚌
Bath Spa 7	d					00 13	01 08		09 40						10 27	10 40						11 26		11 40	
Oldfield Park	d														10 30							11 29			
Keynsham	d														10 37							11 36			
Bristol Temple Meads 10	a					00 27	01 21		09 54						10 45	10 54						11 44		11 55	
	d																					11 48			
Filton Abbey Wood	d																					11 55			
Bristol Parkway 7	a																					11 59			
	d		23p28							10 00			10 15	10 15						11 35					12 10
Patchway	d												10 20												
Pilning	d																								
Gloucester 7	d				23p09							10 01						10 48	11 05				11 37		
Lydney	d				23p28													11 07							
Chepstow	d				23p38													11 17							
Caldicot	d				23p46													11 25							
Severn Tunnel Jn.	d				23p49							10 34	10a45					11 28					12 11		
Newport (South Wales)	a		23p57		00 07					10 40		10 52		10 55				11 46	11 48	12 15			12 25		12 50
	d	23p46	23p58	00 04	00 09			09 27				10 53					11 00	11 48	11 50				12 26		
Cardiff Central 7	a	00 05	00 18	00 26	00 35			09 42				11 06					11 16	12 06	12 08				12 44		

		XC	GW	GW	GW	AW		GW	GW	AW	AW	GW	GW	XC	GW	GW		AW	GW	GW	GW	GW	GW	SW	AW
		◇1 🛒	🚌		◇1 🍴	◇ 🛒		🚌	◇1 🍴	R 🛒		🚌	◇	◇1 A 🛒	◇1 🍴	◇1 🍴		R 🛒	🚌	🚌	🚌	◇	◇1 🍴	◇1	◇ 🛒
Bath Spa 7	d			12 20	12 41								13 23			13 40						14 26	14 39	14 50	
Oldfield Park	d			12 23									13 26									14 28			
Keynsham	d			12 30									13 33									14 36		14 58	
Bristol Temple Meads 10	a			12 38	12 54								13 41			13 54						14 44	14 52	15 05	
	d												13 48									14 48			
Filton Abbey Wood	d												13 55									14 55			
Bristol Parkway 7	a												13 59									14 59			
	d		12 15					12 25				13 25							14 10	14 15	14 25				
Patchway	d		12 20																	14 20					
Pilning	d																								
Gloucester 7	d	12 05							12 30		12 34			13 23	13 30										
Lydney	d										12 53														
Chepstow	d										13 03														
Caldicot	d										13 11														
Severn Tunnel Jn.	d		12a45						13 03		13 14				14 03					14a45					
Newport (South Wales)	a	12 52						13 05	13 19		13 33	14 05		14 06	14 19				14 50		15 05				
	d	12 53				12 52			13 19	13 29	13 34			14 08	14 19			14 30							15 07
Cardiff Central 7	a	13 12				13 13			13 37	13 44	13 52			14 26	14 37			14 49							15 31

A 🛒 to Newport (South Wales)

When events are being held at the Millenium Stadium,
services are subject to alteration. Please check times before travelling.

Table 132

Sundays

19 February to 25 March

Bath Spa, Bristol and Gloucester - Cardiff

Network Diagram - see first Page of Table 132

		XC		GW	AW	AW	GW	GW	XC	GW	GW	GW		GW	AW	GW	GW	GW	XC	GW	GW	GW		AW	AW
						R									R									R	
		◇1		◇1					◇1	◇	◇1	◇1		◇					◇1	◇	◇1	◇1			
		A							A										A						
							🚌	🚌								🚌	🚌	🚌							
		🛒		☕		🛒			🛒		☕	☕			🛒				🛒		☕	☕		🛒	
Bath Spa 7	d									15 28		15 40		16 01						16 29		16 39			
Oldfield Park	d													16 03											
Keynsham	d													16 11											
Bristol Temple Meads 10	a									15 40		15 53		16 23						16 42		16 53			
	d									15 48										16 48					
Filton Abbey Wood	d									15 55										16 55					
Bristol Parkway 7	a									15 59										16 59					
	d						15 10	15 25								16 10	16 15	16 25							
Patchway	d																16 20								
Pilning	d																								
Gloucester 7	d	14 24		14 30	14 35				15 23		15 30								16 23		16 30				16 37
Lydney	d				14 54																				16 56
Chepstow	d				15 04																				17 07
Caldicot	d				15 12																				17 13
Severn Tunnel Jn.	d			15 03	15 15						16 03						16a45				17 03				17 16
Newport (South Wales)	a	15 08		15 19	15 33		15 50	16 05	16 06		16 19					16 50		17 05	17 06		17 19				17 37
	d	15 09		15 19	15 35	15 46			16 08		16 19				16 31				17 08		17 19			17 34	17 38
Cardiff Central 7	a	15 31		15 39	15 53	16 02			16 26		16 39				16 52				17 27		17 39			17 50	17 57

		GW	GW	XC	GW	GW	GW	AW		GW	GW	GW	XC	GW	GW	GW	GW	GW		GW	AW	AW	XC	GW	GW
					R			R													R				
				◇1		◇1	◇1						◇1	◇1	◇	◇1	◇			◇1			◇1		◇
													A										A		
		🚌	🚌							🚌	🚌	🚌						🚌						🚌	
				🛒		☕	☕	🛒					🛒	☕		☕				☕	🛒		🛒		
Bath Spa 7	d				17 25		17 40								18 28	18 40	19 02			19 13					19 27
Oldfield Park	d				17 28												19 04								
Keynsham	d				17 35												19 12								
Bristol Temple Meads 10	a				17 43		17 54								18 40	18 54	19 20			19 26					19 39
	d				17 48										18 48										19 48
Filton Abbey Wood	d				17 55										18 55										19 55
Bristol Parkway 7	a				17 59										18 59										19 59
	d	17 10	17 25							18 10	18 15	18 25						19 10						19 35	
Patchway	d										18 20														
Pilning	d																								
Gloucester 7	d			17 23		17 30							18 23	18 27								18 48	19 28		
Lydney	d																					19 07			
Chepstow	d																					19 17			
Caldicot	d																					19 25			
Severn Tunnel Jn.	d					18 03					18a45			19 00								19 32			
Newport (South Wales)	a	17 50	18 05	18 07		18 19				18 50		19 05	19 07	19 16				19 50				19 54	20 11	20 15	
	d			18 09		18 19		18 33					19 08	19 16							19 51	19 56	20 13		
Cardiff Central 7	a			18 29		18 37		18 50					19 29	19 37							20 06	20 12	20 31		

		GW	GW	AW		GW	GW	GW	GW	GW	XC	GW	GW	SW		GW	GW	AW	AW	AW	GW	GW	GW	GW	
				R														R		R					
		◇1	◇			◇1				◇1	◇1	◇	◇1	◇1		◇1	◇						◇	◇1	
							🚌	🚌	🚌												🚌	🚌			
		☕		🛒		☕				☕			☕			☕		🛒		🛒				☕	
Bath Spa 7	d	19 38	20 00									20 27	20 40	20 49		21 03	21 11						21 28	21 39	
Oldfield Park	d		20 02														21 13								
Keynsham	d		20 10											20 57			21 21								
Bristol Temple Meads 10	a	19 53	20 18									20 39	20 54	21 04		21 16	21 29						21 40	21 53	
	d											20 48											21 48		
Filton Abbey Wood	d											20 55											21 55		
Bristol Parkway 7	a											20 59											22 01		
	d						20 10	20 15	20 25												21 10	21 35			
Patchway	d							20 20																	
Pilning	d																								
Gloucester 7	d					19 46				20 20	20 25								20 31						
Lydney	d																		20 50						
Chepstow	d																		21 00						
Caldicot	d																		21 10						
Severn Tunnel Jn.	d					20 19		20a45		20 54									21 13		21 40				
Newport (South Wales)	a					20 37	20 50		21 05	21 11	21 12								21 31		22s00	22 15			
	d			20 23		20 38				21 13	21 14							21 21	21 33	21 46					
Cardiff Central 7	a			20 43		20 52				21 26	21 32							21 45	21 49	22 05	22 35				

A 🛒 to Newport (South Wales)

When events are being held at the Millenium Stadium, services are subject to alteration. Please check times before travelling.

Table 132

Sundays

19 February to 25 March

Bath Spa, Bristol and Gloucester - Cardiff

Network Diagram - see first Page of Table 132

		GW	AW	GW	GW	GW	GW	GW	AW	GW		GW	GW	AW	GW	GW	GW								
			◇	◇1 ☕	🚌	🚌	🚌	◇		◇1 ☕		◇1 ☕	◇1 ☕	◇	🚌	🚌	◇1 ☕								
Bath Spa 7	d	22 15						22 26				22 44	23 47												
Oldfield Park	d	22 17																							
Keynsham	d	22 25																							
Bristol Temple Meads 10	a	22 33						22 41				22 57	00 01												
	d							22 48																	
Filton Abbey Wood	d							22 55																	
Bristol Parkway 7	a							22 59																	
	d				22 10	22 15	22 40								23 10	23 40									
Patchway	d					22 20																			
Pilning	d																								
Gloucester 7	d			21 42					22 33	22 42							23 43								
Lydney	d								22 52																
Chepstow	d								23 02																
Caldicot	d								23 10																
Severn Tunnel Jn.	d			22 15	22 40	22a45			23 14	23 21					23 40		00 16								
Newport (South Wales)	a			22 37	23s00		23 20		23 33	23 44					00s06	00 20	00 31								
	d		22 31	22 38					23 34	23 44				23 55			00 32								
Cardiff Central 7	a		22 57	22 57	23 35				23 54	00 07				00 20	00 35		00 53								

Sundays

from 1 April

		AW	GW	AW	AW	GW	GW	AW	GW	GW		GW	GW	GW	AW	GW	AW	XC	GW	GW		GW	XC	GW	GW
			◇1 ☕		🚌	◇1 ☕	◇1 ☕	◇ 🛒	◇	◇1 ☕		◇1 ☕		◇1 ☕	◇	◇1 ☕		◇1 🛒	R	◇1 ☕		◇1 ☕	◇1 🛒		◇1 ☕
Bath Spa 7	d					00 13	01 08			09 38			10 16	10 40					11 26	11 40				12 20	12 40
Oldfield Park	d												10 19						11 29					12 23	
Keynsham	d												10 26						11 36					12 30	
Bristol Temple Meads 10	a					00 25	01 23			09 52			10 33	10 54					11 44	11 55				12 38	12 54
	d								09 48										11 48						
Filton Abbey Wood	d								09 55										11 55						
Bristol Parkway 7	a																								
	d		23p28									10 09				11 17						12 11			
Patchway	d																		12 00						
Pilning	d																								
Gloucester 7	d				23p09												10 48	11 05					12 05		
Lydney	d				23p49												11 07								
Chepstow	d				00 09												11 17								
Caldicot	d				00 24												11 25								
Severn Tunnel Jn.	d				00 34				10 08								11 28		12 11						
Newport (South Wales)	a		23p57		00 59				10 25			10 33				11 42	11 46	11 48	12 29			12 37	12 52		
	d	23p46	23p58	00 04	00 59			09 27	10 26			10 33			11 00	11 43	11 48	11 50	12 29			12 37	12 53		
Cardiff Central 7	a	00 05	00 18	00 26	01 29			09 42	10 41			10 51			11 16	12 01	12 06	12 08	12 44			12 56	13 12		

		AW	AW	AW	GW	XC		GW	GW	AW	GW	AW	XC	GW	AW	GW	SW		GW	AW	XC	GW	GW	GW	AW
		◇ 🛒	R 🛒		◇1 ☕	◇1 A 🛒		◇	◇1 ☕	R 🛒	◇1 ☕	◇ 🛒	◇1 A 🛒	◇		◇1 ☕	◇1		◇1 ☕	R 🛒	◇1 A 🛒	◇	◇1 ☕	◇	R 🛒
Bath Spa 7	d							13 24	13 40					14 28		14 42	14 50					15 28	15 40	16 01	
Oldfield Park	d							13 27						14 30										16 03	
Keynsham	d							13 34						14 38			14 58							16 11	
Bristol Temple Meads 10	a							13 41	13 54					14 46		14 54	15 05					15 40	15 53	16 23	
	d							13 48						14 50								15 48			
Filton Abbey Wood	d							13 55						14 57								15 55			
Bristol Parkway 7	a																								
	d				13 11						14 11								15 12						
Patchway	d																								
Pilning	d																								
Gloucester 7	d			12 30		13 23							14 24		14 33						15 23				
Lydney	d			12 49											14 52										
Chepstow	d			12 59											15 02										
Caldicot	d			13 07											15 10										
Severn Tunnel Jn.	d			13 10				14 08						15 10	15 16							16 08			
Newport (South Wales)	a			13 33	13 37	14 06		14 27			14 37		15 08	15 28	15 34				15 38		16 06	16 26			
	d	12 52	13 29	13 34	13 37	14 08		14 28		14 30	14 37	15 07	15 09	15 28	15 36				15 38	15 46	16 08	16 26			16 31
Cardiff Central 7	a	13 13	13 44	13 52	13 56	14 26		14 47		14 49	14 56	15 31	15 31	15 43	15 53				15 57	16 02	16 26	16 44			16 52

A 🛒 to Newport (South Wales)

When events are being held at the Millenium Stadium,
services are subject to alteration. Please check times before travelling.

Table 132

Sundays
from 1 April

Bath Spa, Bristol and Gloucester - Cardiff

Network Diagram - see first Page of Table 132

		GW	XC		GW	GW	AW	AW	GW	XC	GW	GW	AW		GW	XC	GW	GW	GW	GW	GW	AW	AW		XC
							R				R		R									R			
		◇1	◇1		◇	◇1			◇1	◇1		◇1			◇1	◇1	◇	◇1	◇	◇1	◇1				◇1
			A													A									A
		☕	🛒			☕	🛒		☕	🛒		☕	🛒		☕	🛒		☕		☕	☕	🛒			🛒
Bath Spa 7	d				16 28	16 40					17 26	17 40					18 28	18 40	19 02	19 07					
Oldfield Park	d										17 29								19 04						
Keynsham	d										17 36								19 12						
Bristol Temple Meads 10	a				16 41	16 54					17 44	17 54					18 40	18 54	19 20	19 25					
	d				16 48						17 48						18 48								
Filton Abbey Wood	d				16 55						17 55						18 55								
Bristol Parkway 7	a																								
	d	16 12							17 11						18 12						19 15				
Patchway	d				17 00																				
Pilning	d																								
Gloucester 7	d		16 23					16 37		17 23						18 23							18 48		19 28
Lydney	d							16 56															19 07		
Chepstow	d							17 07															19 17		
Caldicot	d							17 13															19 25		
Severn Tunnel Jn.	d				17 11			17 16			18 08						19 08						19 32		
Newport (South Wales)	a	16 38	17 06		17 29			17 37	17 40	18 07	18 26				18 38	19 07	19 26				19 41		19 54		20 11
	d	16 38	17 08		17 29		17 34	17 38	17 41	18 09	18 26		18 33		18 38	19 08	19 26				19 41	19 51	19 56		20 13
Cardiff Central 7	a	16 57	17 27		17 46		17 50	17 57	17 58	18 29	18 44		18 50		18 57	19 27	19 42				19 59	20 06	20 12		20 31

		AW	GW	GW	GW	GW	XC	AW	GW		AW	GW	SW	GW	GW	GW	AW	GW	GW		GW	AW	GW	GW	AW
		R						R									R								
			◇	◇1	◇	◇1	◇1		◇			◇1	◇1	◇1	◇	◇1		◇	◇1			◇	◇1	◇	
		🛒		☕		☕		🛒				☕		☕		☕	🛒		☕				☕		
Bath Spa 7	d		19 27	19 39	20 00				20 27			20 40	20 49	21 03	21 11			21 28	21 38		22 15			22 26	
Oldfield Park	d				20 02										21 13						22 17				
Keynsham	d				20 10								20 57		21 21						22 25				
Bristol Temple Meads 10	a		19 39	19 53	20 18				20 39			20 54	21 04	21 16	21 29			21 40	21 53		22 33			22 38	
	d		19 48						20 48									21 48						22 48	
Filton Abbey Wood	d		19 55						20 55									21 55						22 55	
Bristol Parkway 7	a																								
	d					20 11										21 13							22 12		
Patchway	d		20 00															22 02							
Pilning	d																								
Gloucester 7	d						20 23				20 31														22 33
Lydney	d										20 50														22 52
Chepstow	d										21 00														23 02
Caldicot	d										21 10														23 10
Severn Tunnel Jn.	d		20 11						21 08		21 13							22 15						23 09	23 14
Newport (South Wales)	a		20 28			20 37	21 06		21 26		21 31					21 39		22 31					22 38	23 26	23 33
	d	20 23	20 29			20 37	21 08	21 14	21 26		21 33					21 39	21 48	22 31				22 33	22 38	23 27	23 34
Cardiff Central 7	a	20 43	20 46			20 56	21 26	21 36	21 42		21 49					22 01	22 07	22 53				22 59	23 01	23 47	23 54

		GW	GW	GW	AW
		◇1	◇1	◇1	◇
		☕	☕	☕	
Bath Spa 7	d	22 44		23 47	
Oldfield Park	d				
Keynsham	d				
Bristol Temple Meads 10	a	22 57		00 01	
	d				
Filton Abbey Wood	d				
Bristol Parkway 7	a				
	d		23 12		
Patchway	d				
Pilning	d				
Gloucester 7	d				
Lydney	d				
Chepstow	d				
Caldicot	d				
Severn Tunnel Jn.	d				
Newport (South Wales)	a		23 41		
	d		23 42		23 55
Cardiff Central 7	a		00 01		00 20

A 🛒 to Newport (South Wales)

When events are being held at the Millenium Stadium, services are subject to alteration. Please check times before travelling.

Bristol - Avonmouth and Severn Beach

Network Diagram - see first Page of Table 132

Miles			GW	GW	GW	GW	GW	GW	GW	GW	GW	GW ◇	GW	GW	GW ◇	GW	GW	GW	GW	GW	GW	GW	GW
0	**Bristol Temple Meads 10**	d	05 24	05 48	06 19	06 30	06 50	07 04	07 19	07 47	08 03	08 10	08 36	08 44	09 10	09 16	09 47	10 03	10 34	10 45	11 16	11 44	12 03
1	Lawrence Hill	d	05 27		06 22	06 33	06 53	07 07	07 22	07 50	08 06	08 13	08 39	08 47	09 13	09 19	09 49		10 37	10 49	11 19	11 47	
1½	Stapleton Road	d	05 29	05 51	06a24	06 35	06a55	07 09	07a24	07a52	08 08	08a15	08 41	08a49	09a15	09 21	09a50	10 07	10 39	10a51	11 21	11a49	12 07
2¾	Montpelier	d	05 32	05 55		06 39		07 12			08 11		08 45			09 24		10 10	10 42		11 24		12 10
3¼	Redland	d	05 34	05 57		06 41		07 14			08 13		08 47			09 26		10 12	10 44		11 26		12 12
4	Clifton Down	d	05 37	06 00		06 44		07 17			08 17		08 52			09 29		10 17	10 48		11 29		12 17
6	Sea Mills	d	05 41	06 04		06 48		07 21			08 21		08 56			09 33		10 21	10 52		11 33		12 21
7¼	Shirehampton	d	05 45	06 07		06 52		07 24			08 25		08 59			09 37		10 25	10 56		11 37		12 25
9	Avonmouth 2	d	05 49	06a14		06 56		07 30			08a31		09a06			09 40		10a31	11a02		11 40		12a31
10	St Andrews Road	d	05x52			06x59		07x33								09x44					11x44		
13½	**Severn Beach**	a	06 01			07 07		07 41								09 53					11 53		

		GW	GW	GW	GW	GW	GW	GW	GW	GW	GW	GW	GW	GW	GW	GW	GW	GW	GW	GW	GW	GW	GW
Bristol Temple Meads 10	d	12 34	12 44	13 16	13 46	14 03	14 34	14 45	15 16	15 45	16 03	16 15	16 35	16 44	17 10	17 16	17 46	18 03	18 21	18 48	19 21	19 33	19 45
Lawrence Hill	d	12 37	12 47	13 19	13 47		14 37	14 47	15 19	15 47	16 06	16 18	16 37	16 47	17 13	17 19	17 47	18 06	18 24	18 51	19 24	19 36	19 47
Stapleton Road	d	12 39	12a49	13 21	13a50	14 07	14 39	14a49	15 21	15a50	16 07	16a20	16 39	16a49	17a15	17 21	17a49	18 07	18a26	18 53	19a26	19 38	19a50
Montpelier	d	12 42		13 24		14 10	14 42		15 24		16 10		16 42			17 24		18 10		18 57		19 41	
Redland	d	12 44		13 26		14 12	14 44		15 26		16 12		16 44			17 26		18 12		18 59		19 43	
Clifton Down	d	12 48		13 29		14 17	14 48		15 29		16 17		16 48			17 29		18 17		19 08		19 46	
Sea Mills	d	12 52		13 33		14 21	14 52		15 33		16 21		16 52			17 33		18 21		19 12		19 50	
Shirehampton	d	12 56		13 37		14 25	14 56		15 37		16 25		16 56			17 37		18 25		19 16		19 54	
Avonmouth 2	d	13a02		13 40		14a31	15a02		15 40		16a31		17a02			17 40		18 29		19a22		20a00	
St Andrews Road	d			13x44					15x44							17x44		18x32					
Severn Beach	a			13 53					15 53							17 53		18 40					

		GW	GW	GW
Bristol Temple Meads 10	d	20 34	21 19	22 16
Lawrence Hill	d	20 37	21 22	22 19
Stapleton Road	d	20 39	21a24	22 21
Montpelier	d	20 42		22 24
Redland	d	20 44		22 26
Clifton Down	d	20 48		22 29
Sea Mills	d	20 52		22 33
Shirehampton	d	20 56		22 37
Avonmouth 2	d	20 59		22 40
St Andrews Road	d	21x02		22x44
Severn Beach	a	21 11		22 53

Saturdays

		GW	GW	GW	GW	GW	GW	GW	GW (bus)	GW	GW	GW	GW	GW	GW	GW	GW (bus)	GW	GW	GW	GW	GW	GW
Bristol Temple Meads 10	d	06 03	06 34	06 50	07 16	07 47	08 03	08 20		08 34	08 45	09 16	09 21	09 45	10 03	10 21		10 34	10 45	11 16	11 21	11 45	12 03
Lawrence Hill	d		06 37	06 53	07 19	07 50	08 06	08 23		08 37	08 48	09 19		09 48				10 37	10 48	11 19		11 48	
Stapleton Road	d	06 07	06 39	06a55	07 21	07a52	08 07	08a25		08 39	08a50	09 21	09a24	09a50	10 07	10a24		10 39	10a50	11 21	11a24	11a50	12 07
Montpelier	d	06 10	06 42		07 24		08 10			08 42		09 24			10 10			10 42		11 24			12 10
Redland	d	06 12	06 44		07 26		08 12			08 44		09 26			10 12			10 44		11 26			12 12
Clifton Down	d	06 17	06 48		07 29		08 17			08 48		09 29			10 17			10 48		11 29			12 17
Sea Mills	d	06 21	06 52		07 33		08 21			08 52		09 33			10 21			10 52		11 33			12 21
Shirehampton	d	06 25	06 56		07 37		08 25			08 56		09 37			10 25			10 56		11 37			12 25
Avonmouth 2	d	06a31	07a02		07 40		08a31		08 33	09a02		09 40			10a31		10 33	11a02		11 40			12a31
St Andrews Road	d				07x44				08x36			09x44					10x36			11x44			
Severn Beach	a				07 53				08 48			09 53					10 48			11 53			

		GW	GW (bus)	GW	GW	GW	GW	GW	GW	GW	GW (bus)	GW	GW	GW	GW	GW	GW	GW	GW (bus)	GW	GW	GW	GW
Bristol Temple Meads 10	d	12 21		12 34	12 45	13 16	13 21	13 45	14 03	14 21		14 34	14 45	15 16	15 21	15 45	16 03	16 21		16 34	16 45	17 16	17 21
Lawrence Hill	d			12 37	12 48	13 19		13 48				14 37	14 48	15 19		15 48	16 06			16 37	16 48	17 19	
Stapleton Road	d	12a25		12 39	12a50	13 21	13a24	13a50	14 07	14a25		14 39	14a50	15 21	15a24	15a50	16 07	16a25		16 39	16a50	17 21	17a24
Montpelier	d			12 42		13 24			14 10			14 42		15 24			16 10			16 42		17 24	
Redland	d			12 44		13 26			14 12			14 44		15 26			16 12			16 44		17 26	
Clifton Down	d			12 48		13 29			14 17			14 48		15 29			16 17			16 48		17 29	
Sea Mills	d			12 52		13 33			14 21			14 52		15 33			16 21			16 52		17 33	
Shirehampton	d			12 56		13 37			14 25			14 56		15 37			16 25			16 56		17 37	
Avonmouth 2	d		12 33	13a02		13 40			14a31		14 33	15a02		15 40			16a31		16 33	17a02		17 40	
St Andrews Road	d		12x36			13x44					14x36			15x44					16x36			17x44	
Severn Beach	a		12 48			13 53					14 48			15 53					16 48			17 53	

		GW	GW	GW	GW	GW	GW	GW	GW
Bristol Temple Meads 10	d	17 45	18 03	18 21	18 45	19 03	19 45	20 34	22 16
Lawrence Hill	d	17 48	18 06		18 48	19 06	19 48	20 37	22 19
Stapleton Road	d	17a50	18 07	18a24	18a50	19 07	19a50	20 39	22 21
Montpelier	d		18 10			19 10		20 42	22 24
Redland	d		18 12			19 12		20 44	22 26
Clifton Down	d		18 17			19 17		20 48	22 29
Sea Mills	d		18 21			19 21		20 52	22 33
Shirehampton	d		18 25			19 25		20 56	22 37
Avonmouth 2	d		18 29			19 29		20 59	22 40
St Andrews Road	d		18x32			19x32		21x02	22x44
Severn Beach	a		18 40			19 40		21 11	22 53

Sundays

		GW	GW	GW ◇	GW	GW	GW	GW	GW	GW	GW
Bristol Temple Meads 10	d	09 08	10 23	11 23	12 23	13 23	14 23	15 23	16 23	16 53	17 53
Lawrence Hill	d	09 11	10 26	11 26	12 26	13 26	14 26	15 26	16 26	16 56	17 56
Stapleton Road	d	09 13	10 28	11 28	12 28	13 28	14 28	15 28	16 28	16 58	17 58
Montpelier	d	09 16	10 31	11 31	12 31	13 31	14 31	15 31	16 31	17 02	18 01
Redland	d	09 18	10 33	11 33	12 33	13 33	14 33	15 33	16 33	17 04	18 03
Clifton Down	d	09 21	10 36	11 36	12 36	13 36	14 36	15 36	16 36	17 06	18 06
Sea Mills	d	09 25	10 40	11 40	12 40	13 40	14 40	15 40	16 40	17 10	18 10
Shirehampton	d	09 29	10 44	11 43	12 44	13 44	14 44	15 44	16 44	17 14	18 14
Avonmouth 2	d	09 33	10a49	11a47	12a49	13a49	14a49	15a49	16a47	17 18	18a17
St Andrews Road	d	09x36								17x21	
Severn Beach	a	09 43								17 28	

Table 133

Mondays to Fridays

Severn Beach and Avonmouth - Bristol

Network Diagram - see first Page of Table 132

Miles			GW MX	GW	GW	GW	GW	GW	GW	GW	GW		GW	GW	GW	GW	GW	GW	GW	GW	GW		GW	GW	GW
													◇						◇						
0	**Severn Beach**	d		06 03				07 18	07 54							09 54					11 54				
3½	St Andrews Road	d		06x09				07x24	08x00							10x00					12x00				
4½	Avonmouth 2	d		06 13	06 31			07 28	08 04		08 38			09 15		10 04		10 35		11 15	12 04		12 35		13 15
6	Shirehampton	d		06 17	06 34			07 32	08 07		08 41			09 18		10 07		10 38		11 18	12 07		12 38		13 18
7½	Sea Mills	d		06 21	06 38			07 36	08 11		08 45			09 22		10 11		10 42		11 22	12 11		12 42		13 22
9½	Clifton Down	d		06 26	06 44			07 40	08 16		08 52			09 30		10 16		10 48		11 31	12 16		12 48		13 31
10¼	Redland	d		06 28	06 46			07 44	08 19		08 54			09 32		10 19		10 51		11 34	12 19		12 51		13 34
10¾	Montpelier	d		06 30	06 48			07 46	08 21		08 56			09 34		10 21		10 53		11 36	12 21		12 53		13 36
12	Stapleton Road	d	00 25	06 36	06 53	07 07	07 33	07 52	08 27	08 53	09 01		09 29	09 39	09 43	10 25	10 30	10 59	11 29	11 40	12 25		12 59	13 29	13 40
12½	Lawrence Hill	d	00 27	06 38	06 56	07 09	07 35	07 55	08 29	08 55	09 03		09 31	09 41			10 32	11 01	11 31	11 42			13 01	13 31	13 42
13½	**Bristol Temple Meads 10**	a	00 33	06 41	07 02	07 12	07 39	07 58	08 32	09 01	09 10		09 34	09 48	09 50	10 32	10 37	11 10	11 34	11 49	12 32		13 10	13 35	13 50

		GW	GW	GW	GW	GW	GW		GW	GW	GW	GW	GW	GW	GW	GW	GW		GW	GW	GW	GW	GW	GW	GW
			◇						◇			◇													
Severn Beach	d	13 54					15 54									17 54			18 44					21 29	
St Andrews Road	d	14x00					16x00									18x00			18x50					21x35	
Avonmouth 2	d	14 04		14 35		15 15	16 04				16 35		17 15			18 04			18 54		19 32	20 01		21 39	
Shirehampton	d	14 07		14 38		15 18	16 07				16 38		17 18			18 07			18 58		19 35	20 04		21 43	
Sea Mills	d	14 11		14 42		15 22	16 11				16 42		17 22			18 11			19 02		19 39	20 08		21 47	
Clifton Down	d	14 16		14 48		15 31	16 16				16 48		17 31			18 16			19 13		19 46	20 13		21 52	
Redland	d	14 19		14 51		15 34	16 19				16 51		17 34			18 19			19 15		19 49	20 16		21 54	
Montpelier	d	14 21		14 53		15 36	16 21				16 53		17 36			18 21			19 17		19 51	20 18		21 56	
Stapleton Road	d	14 25	14 31	14 59	15 29	15 40	16 24		16 31	16 54	17 00	17 29	17 40	17 54	18 19	18 25	18 31		19 22	19 29	19 56	20 22	20 31	22 02	22 58
Lawrence Hill	d		14 33	15 01	15 31	15 42			16 33	16 56	17 02	17 31	17 42	17 56		18 27	18 32		19 24	19 31	19 58	20 24	20 33	22 04	23 00
Bristol Temple Meads 10	a	14 32	14 38	15 10	15 36	15 50	16 32		16 37	17 02	17 10	17 36	17 50	18 01	18 24	18 34	18 38		19 28	19 35	20 04	20 32	20 38	22 07	23 05

		GW
Severn Beach	d	22 54
St Andrews Road	d	23x00
Avonmouth 2	d	23 04
Shirehampton	d	23 07
Sea Mills	d	23 11
Clifton Down	d	23 16
Redland	d	23 19
Montpelier	d	23 21
Stapleton Road	d	23 25
Lawrence Hill	d	23 27
Bristol Temple Meads 10	a	23 32

Saturdays

		GW	GW	GW	GW	GW	GW	GW	GW	GW		GW	GW	GW	GW	GW	GW	GW	GW	GW		GW	GW	GW	GW
																		R							
								◇							◇										◇
							🚌							🚌						🚌					
Severn Beach	d				07 54		08 55			09 54				10 55			11 54			12 55				13 54	
St Andrews Road	d				08x00		09x07			10x00				11x07			12x00			13x07				14x00	
Avonmouth 2	d		06 35	07 15	08 04	08 35	09a10		09 15	10 04			10 35	11a10		11 15	12 04		12 35	13a10			13 15	14 04	
Shirehampton	d		06 38	07 18	08 07	08 38			09 18	10 07			10 38			11 18	12 07		12 38				13 18	14 07	
Sea Mills	d		06 42	07 22	08 11	08 42			09 22	10 11			10 42			11 22	12 11		12 42				13 22	14 11	
Clifton Down	d		06 48	07 31	08 16	08 47			09 30	10 16			10 48			11 31	12 16		12 47				13 31	14 16	
Redland	d		06 50	07 34	08 19	08 50			09 33	10 19			10 51			11 34	12 19		12 50				13 34	14 19	
Montpelier	d		06 52	07 36	08 21	08 52			09 35	10 21			10 53			11 36	12 21		12 52				13 36	14 21	
Stapleton Road	d	00 25	06 55	07 40	08 24	08 54		09 29	09 39	10 24		10 32	10 59		11 28	11 39	12 24	12 32	12 54			13 27	13 40	14 24	14 31
Lawrence Hill	d	00 27	06 57	07 42	08 26	08 56		09 31	09 41			10 34	11 01		11 30	11 41		12 34	12 56			13 29	13 41		14 33
Bristol Temple Meads 10	a	00 33	07 04	07 49	08 32	09 05		09 34	09 47	10 32		10 39	11 09		11 33	11 48	12 32	12 39	13 07			13 34	13 48	14 32	14 36

		GW	GW	GW	GW	GW		GW	GW	GW	GW	GW	GW	GW	GW	GW		GW	GW	GW	GW
								◇			◇										
			🚌							🚌											
Severn Beach	d		14 55			15 54				16 55			17 54			18 54		19 47		21 31	22 54
St Andrews Road	d		15x07			16x00				17x07			18x00			19x00		19x53		21x35	23x00
Avonmouth 2	d	14 35	15a10		15 15	16 04			16 35	17a10		17 15	18 04			19 04		19 57		21 39	23 04
Shirehampton	d	14 38			15 18	16 07			16 38			17 18	18 07			19 07		20 00		21 43	23 07
Sea Mills	d	14 42			15 22	16 11			16 42			17 22	18 11			19 11		20 04		21 47	23 11
Clifton Down	d	14 48			15 31	16 16			16 47			17 31	18 16			19 29		20 09		21 52	23 16
Redland	d	14 51			15 34	16 19			16 50			17 34	18 19			19 31		20 12		21 54	23 19
Montpelier	d	14 53			15 36	16 21			16 52			17 36	18 21			19 33		20 14		21 56	23 21
Stapleton Road	d	14 59		15 27	15 39	16 24		16 34	16 54		17 29	17 39	18 24	18 34	19 29	19 40		20 17	20 34	22 02	23 24
Lawrence Hill	d	15 01		15 29	15 41			16 36	16 56		17 31	17 41	18 26	18 36	19 31	19 42		20 19	20 36	22 04	23 26
Bristol Temple Meads 10	a	15 09		15 33	15 48	16 32		16 39	17 07		17 34	17 48	18 31	18 39	19 36	19 46		20 25	20 39	22 09	23 32

Sundays

		GW	GW	GW	GW	GW	GW	GW	GW	GW		GW
Severn Beach	d	09 46								17 42		
St Andrews Road	d	09x52								17x48		
Avonmouth 2	d	09 56	10 52	11 52	12 52	13 52	14 52	15 52	16 52	17 52		18 22
Shirehampton	d	09 59	10 55	11 55	12 55	13 55	14 55	15 55	16 55	17 56		18 25
Sea Mills	d	10 03	10 59	11 59	12 59	13 59	14 59	15 59	16 59	18 00		18 29
Clifton Down	d	10 08	11 04	12 04	13 04	14 04	15 04	16 04	17 07	18 06		18 34
Redland	d	10 11	11 07	12 07	13 07	14 07	15 07	16 07	17 10	18 09		18 37
Montpelier	d	10 13	11 09	12 09	13 09	14 09	15 09	16 09	17 12	18 11		18 39
Stapleton Road	d	10 16	11 13	12 14	13 13	14 13	15 13	16 13	17 16	18 15		18 43
Lawrence Hill	d	10 18	11 15	12 16	13 15	14 15	15 15	16 15	17 18	18 17		18 45
Bristol Temple Meads 10	a	10 21	11 20	12 20	13 20	14 20	15 20	16 20	17 22	18 23		18 47

Gloucester - Taunton

Network Diagram - see first Page of Table 132

Miles			GW MX	GW MX	XC MX	GW MO	GW MX	GW	GW	XC	GW		GW	GW	GW	GW	XC	GW	GW	XC	GW		GW	GW	XC
				◇1 🛏	◇1 A	◇1 🛏		◇	1	◇1	◇				◇ 🚲		◇1			◇1 🚲	R 🚲			◇	◇1 🚲
0	Gloucester 7	d												06 16		06 42			07 10					07 40	
13	Cam & Dursley	d												06 32		06 58			07 25					07 54	
28	Yate	d												06 45		07 12			07 40					08 09	
34	Bristol Parkway 7	a												06 54		07 23			07 48					08 19	
—		d			00 03						06 24			06 58		07 25			07 49	07 58			08 12	08 19	08 26
35¼	Filton Abbey Wood	d					00 20				06 27			07 01	07 09	07 28	07 41		07 53		08 09		08 15	08 23	
38¼	Stapleton Road	d					00 25							07 07		07 33									
38¾	Lawrence Hill	d					00 27							07 09		07 35									
39¾	Bristol Temple Meads 10	a			00 13	00 30	00 33				06 35			07 12	07 17	07 39	07 51		08 01	08 08	08 17		08 23	08 36	08 40
—		d	23p06	23p35				05 24	06 03	06 34	06 42		06 48	07 18				07 51		08 10			08 25		08 44
40¾	Bedminster	d	23p10										06 50					07 53					08 27		
41½	Parson Street	d	23p12										06 53					07 55					08 29		
47¾	Nailsea & Backwell	d	23p20	23b45					06 14				07 02	07 28				08 04					08 38		
51¾	Yatton	d	23p26	23b52					06 21				07 07	07 33				08 09					08 44		
55¾	Worle	d	23p32	23b58					06 27				07 12	07 39				08 15					08 50		
58½	Weston Milton	d	23p37										07 18					08 20					08 55		
59¾	Weston-super-Mare	a	23p40	00s05				05 43	06 36		07 02		07 23	07 47				08 26					08 58		
—		d	23p42					05 45			07 06			07 49									09 00		
67¼	Highbridge & Burnham	d	23p54	00s16				05 55			07 17			08 00									09 10		
73½	Bridgwater	d	00 02	00s24				06 03			07 25			08 08									09 18		
85¼	Taunton	a	00s14	00s36				06 16		07 06	07 38			08 24						08 41			09 33		09 15

		GW	GW	GW	XC	GW	GW		GW	XC	GW	GW	XC	GW	GW	GW	XC		GW	XC	GW	GW	GW	XC	GW
		◇		◇1 B ⌀	◇1 🚲	◇ 🚲			◇	◇1 🚲		◇	◇1 🚲	◇ 🚲			◇1 🚲			◇1 🚲	◇ 🚲		◇	◇1 🚲	◇1 C 🛏
Gloucester 7	d								08 41							09 45							10 41		
Cam & Dursley	d								08 56							09 59							10 56		
Yate	d								09 10							10 13							11 10		
Bristol Parkway 7	a								09 19							10 22							11 19		
	d		08 45		08 55		09 12		09 20	09 26	09 34		09 56		10 12	10 22	10 27			10 55		11 12	11 20	11 28	
Filton Abbey Wood	d	08 42	08 48			09 09	09 15		09 23		09 37	09 42		10 09	10 15	10 25			10 42		11 09	11 15	11 23		
Stapleton Road	d		08 53						09 29		09 43					10 30							11 29		
Lawrence Hill	d		08 55						09 31							10 32							11 31		
Bristol Temple Meads 10	a	08 50	09 01		09 14	09 17	09 23		09 34	09 38	09 50	09 53	10 08	10 18	10 23	10 37	10 41		10 51	11 12	11 18	11 23	11 34	11 37	
	d	08 55		09 13			09 26			09 44		09 55			10 25		10 44		10 53	11 15		11 25		11 44	11 47
Bedminster	d						09 28								10 27							11 27			
Parson Street	d						09 31								10 29							11 29			
Nailsea & Backwell	d	09 03					09 40					10 03			10 38				11 03			11 38			
Yatton	d	09 08					09 45					10 08			10 44				11 08			11 44			
Worle	d	09 14					09 51					10 14			10 50				11 14			11 50			
Weston Milton	d						09 56								10 55							11 55			
Weston-super-Mare	a	09 22					10 01					10 22			11 00				11 21	11 32		12 00			12 06
	d	09 29										10 23							11 23	11 37					12 07
Highbridge & Burnham	d	09 40										10 34							11 34						
Bridgwater	d	09 48										10 42							11 42						
Taunton	a	10 01		09 45						10 16		10 58					11 16		11 57	12 00				12 15	12 29

		GW	XC		GW	GW	GW	XC	GW	XC	GW	GW	GW		XC	GW	XC	GW	GW	GW	XC	GW	XC		GW
			◇1 🚲		◇ 🚲		R	◇1 🚲		◇1 🚲	◇ 🚲				◇1 🚲	◇	◇1 🚲	◇ 🚲		◇	◇1 🚲		◇1 🚲		◇ 🚲
Gloucester 7	d						11 45						12 41							13 45					
Cam & Dursley	d						11 59						12 56							13 59					
Yate	d						12 13						13 10							14 13					
Bristol Parkway 7	a						12 22						13 19							14 22					
	d		11 56			12 12	12 22	12 30		12 56		13 12	13 20		13 27		13 59		14 12	14 22	14 29		14 59		
Filton Abbey Wood	d	11 42			12 09	12 15	12 25		12 42		13 09	13 15	13 23			13 42		14 09	14 15	14 25		14 42			15 09
Stapleton Road	d												13 29							14 31					
Lawrence Hill	d												13 31							14 33					
Bristol Temple Meads 10	a	11 51	12 08		12 18	12 23	12 34	12 40	12 51	13 10	13 18	13 23	13 35		13 38	13 51	14 09	14 17	14 23	14 38	14 41	14 51	15 10		15 17
	d	11 53				12 25		12 44	12 53			13 25			13 44	13 53			14 25		14 44	14 53	15 13		
Bedminster	d					12 27						13 27							14 27						
Parson Street	d					12 29						13 29							14 29						
Nailsea & Backwell	d	12 03				12 38			13 03			13 38				14 03			14 38			15 03			
Yatton	d	12 08				12 44			13 08			13 44				14 08			14 44			15 08			
Worle	d	12 14				12 50			13 14			13 50				14 14			14 50			15 14			
Weston Milton	d					12 55						13 55							14 55						
Weston-super-Mare	a	12 20				13 00			13 21			14 00				14 21			15 00			15 22			
	d	12 22							13 23							14 23						15 28			
Highbridge & Burnham	d	12 33							13 34							14 34						15 38			
Bridgwater	d	12 41							13 42							14 42						15 46			
Taunton	a	12 57						13 16	13 59						14 15	14 55					15 16	16 01	15 44		

A from 27 March
B The Merchant Venturer
C The Torbay Express
b Previous night, stops to set down only

For connections from London Paddington please refer to Table 125

Gloucester - Taunton

Network Diagram - see first Page of Table 132

		GW	GW	XC	GW	GW	XC	GW	GW		GW	GW	XC	GW	GW	GW	XC	GW	GW		GW	GW	XC	GW	GW
																		■							
				◇1			◇1	◇	◇1			◇	◇1				◇1		◇1			◇	◇1		
				🛒			🛒	🛒	☕				🛒				🛒	🛒	☕				🛒		
Gloucester 7	d		14 41									15 45										16 41			
Cam & Dursley	d		14 56									15 59										16 56			
Yate	d		15 10									16 13										17 10			
Bristol Parkway 7	a		15 20									16 22										17 20			
	d	15 12	15 20	15 26		15 53	15 57				16 12	16 22	16 29		16 46		16 58				17 12	17 20	17 27		17 46
Filton Abbey Wood	d	15 15	15 23		15 42	15a56		16 09			16 15	16 25		16 42	16 49	16 55		17 09			17 15	17 23		17 43	17 49
Stapleton Road	d		15 29									16 31			16 54							17 29			17 54
Lawrence Hill	d		15 31									16 33			16 56							17 31			17 56
Bristol Temple Meads 10	a	15 23	15 36	15 39	15 51		16 08	16 18			16 23	16 37	16 40	16 51	17 02	17 03	17 10	17 18			17 23	17 36	17 39	17 53	18 01
	d	15 25		15 44	15 53				16 18		16 25		16 44	16 53			17 13		17 18		17 25		17 44	17 55	
Bedminster	d	15 27			15 55						16 27			16 55							17 27			17 58	
Parson Street	d	15 29			15 57						16 29			16 57							17 29			18 01	
Nailsea & Backwell	d	15 38			16 03				16 29		16 38			17 03					17 28		17 38			18 09	
Yatton	d	15 44			16 08				16 36		16 44			17 08					17 34		17 44			18 15	
Worle	d	15 50			16 14				16 43		16 50			17 14					17 41		17 50			18 21	
Weston Milton	d	15 55			16 21						16 55			17 22							17 55			18 25	
Weston-super-Mare	a	16 00			16 24				16 52		17 00			17 27					17 52		18 00			18 29	
	d				16 24									17 28										18 30	
Highbridge & Burnham	d				16 37									17 38										18 41	
Bridgwater	d				16 45									17 46										18 49	
Taunton	a			16 15	17 00								17 15	18 01			17 44						18 15	19 03	

		XC	GW	GW	GW		GW	XC	GW	XC	GW	GW	GW	XC	GW		XC	GW	GW	GW	GW	XC	GW	XC	GW
			■																						
		◇1		◇1				◇1		◇1	◇1	◇		◇1			◇1	◇	◇1			◇1		◇1	◇1
																						A		A	
		🛒	🛒	☕				🛒		🛒	☕	🛒		🛒			🛒		☕			🛒		🛒	☕
Gloucester 7	d						17 45						18 41								19 45				
Cam & Dursley	d						17 58						18 56								19 59				
Yate	d						18 12						19 10								20 13				
Bristol Parkway 7	a						18 22						19 20								20 22				
	d	18 00			18 12		18 22	18 29		18 57			19 20	19 29			19 58			20 11	20 22	20 29		20 56	
Filton Abbey Wood	d		18 09		18 15		18 25		18 42			19 09	19 23		19 42			20 09		20 14	20 25		20 42		
Stapleton Road	d				18 19		18 31						19 29								20 31				
Lawrence Hill	d						18 32						19 31								20 33				
Bristol Temple Meads 10	a	18 10	18 17		18 24		18 38	18 41	18 53	19 06		19 17	19 35	19 38	19 51		20 09	20 17		20 24	20 38	20 40	20 53	21 07	
	d			18 20	18 26			18 44	18 56		19 15			19 44	19 55				20 18			20 44	20 55	21 12	21 18
Bedminster	d				18 27				18 57						19 57								20 57		
Parson Street	d				18 29				18 59						19 59								20 59		
Nailsea & Backwell	d			18 31	18 38				19 08		19 25				20 08				20 29				21 08		21 27
Yatton	d			18 38	18 44				19 13		19 32				20 13				20 36				21 13		21 34
Worle	d			18 45	18 50				19 19		19 38				20 19				20 44				21 19		21 40
Weston Milton	d				18 54				19 23		19 43				20 23				20 49				21 23		
Weston-super-Mare	a			18 51	19 00				19 28		19 48				20 27				20 53				21 27		21 50
	d			18 55					19 29		19 57				20 29								21 33		
Highbridge & Burnham	d			19 08					19 40						20 39								21 44		
Bridgwater	d			19 15					19 48						20 47								21 52		
Taunton	a			19 28				19 15	20 03		20 23			20 16	21 02							21 16	22 07	21 43	

			GW	XC	GW	GW	GW	XC	GW	XC	GW		GW	GW	GW	XC	GW
			◇	◇1		◇		◇1		◇1					◇1	◇1	
				A												B	
				🛒											☕		
Gloucester 7	d						21 14			22 05				22 28			
Cam & Dursley	d						21 29										
Yate	d						21 43										
Bristol Parkway 7	a						21 52			22 32				23 04			
	d			21 27			21 52	22 02		22 34				23 05		23 23	
Filton Abbey Wood	d		21 08		21 42		21 56		22 09		22 52						23 40
Stapleton Road	d										22 58						
Lawrence Hill	d										23 00						
Bristol Temple Meads 10	a		21 19	21 36	21 51		22 10	22 13	22 22	22 44	23 05			23 19		23 40	23 49
	d			21 44		21 56							23 06		23 35		
Bedminster	d					21 58							23 10				
Parson Street	d					22 00							23 12				
Nailsea & Backwell	d					22 09							23 20		23s45		
Yatton	d					22 13							23 26		23s52		
Worle	d					22 19							23 32		23s58		
Weston Milton	d					22 23							23 37				
Weston-super-Mare	a					22 28							23 40		00s05		
	d					22 29							23 42				
Highbridge & Burnham	d					22 40							23 54		00s16		
Bridgwater	d					22 48							00 02		00s24		
Taunton	a			22 15		23 01							00s14		00s36		

A 🛒 to Bristol Temple Meads

B until 23 March

For connections from London Paddington please refer to Table 125

Table 134

Gloucester - Taunton

Network Diagram - see first Page of Table 132

		GW	GW	XC	GW	GW	GW	XC	GW	GW		GW	GW	GW	XC	GW	XC	GW	GW	GW		XC	GW	XC	GW
			◇1 ⊥P	◇1 A		◇	◇1 ⊥P	◇1		◇				◇	◇1 ⊥o		◇1 ⊥o	◇		◇		◇1 ⊥o		◇1 ⊥o	R 1 ⊥P
Gloucester 7	d												06 19			07 02				07 40					
Cam & Dursley	d												06 35			07 15				07 54					
Yate	d												06 48			07 30				08 09					
Bristol Parkway 7	a												06 58			07 39				08 19					
	d			00 03			05 42						06 58			07 40	07 56		08 12	08 19		08 26		08 56	
Filton Abbey Wood	d				00 20								07 02	07 09	07 41	07 46		08 09	08 15	08 23			08 42		
Stapleton Road	d				00 25																				
Lawrence Hill	d				00 27																				
Bristol Temple Meads 10	a			00 13	00 33		05 53						07 11	07 18	07 51	07 54	08 05	08 18	08 23	08 34		08 38	08 52	09 08	
	d	23p06	23p35			05 24		06 08	06 18	06 36		06 48	07 18			07 56	08 11		08 25			08 44	08 56		09 17
Bedminster	d	23p10										06 50	07 21						08 27						
Parson Street	d	23p12										06 53	07 23						08 29						
Nailsea & Backwell	d	23p20	23b45						06 28			07 01	07 28			08 03			08 38				09 03		
Yatton	d	23p26	23b52						06 34			07 06	07 34			08 08			08 44				09 07		
Worle	d	23p32	23b58						06 40			07 12	07 40			08 14			08 50				09 13		
Weston Milton	d	23p37										07 17	07 46						08 55						
Weston-super-Mare	a	23p40	00s05			05 43			06 45	06 55		07 22	07 47			08 24			09 00				09 23		
	d	23p42				05 45			06 47	06 56			07 50										09 32		
Highbridge & Burnham	d	23p54	00s16			05 55			06 58				08 01										09 44		
Bridgwater	d	00 02	00s24			06 03			07 06				08 09										09 52		
Taunton	a	00s14	00s36			06 16		07 14	07 20	07 24			08 24				08 42					09 14	10 06		09 50

		GW	GW	GW	XC	GW		XC	GW	GW	GW	XC	GW	XC	GW	GW		GW	XC	GW	XC	GW	GW	GW	XC
		◇		◇	◇1 ⊥o			◇1 ⊥o	◇			◇1 ⊥o		◇1 ⊥o	◇			◇	◇1 ⊥o		◇1 ⊥o	◇		R	◇1 ⊥o
Gloucester 7	d			08 42							09 46							10 42						11 46	
Cam & Dursley	d			08 56							10 02							10 56						12 01	
Yate	d			09 11							10 16							11 10						12 16	
Bristol Parkway 7	a			09 19							10 24							11 19						12 24	
	d		09 12	09 20	09 26			09 57		10 12	10 25	10 31		10 59		11 12		11 20	11 26		11 56		12 12	12 25	12 31
Filton Abbey Wood	d	09 09	09 15	09 23		09 42			10 09	10 15	10 28		10 42		11 09	11 15		11 23		11 42		12 09	12 15	12 28	
Stapleton Road	d			09 29							10 32							11 28						12 32	
Lawrence Hill	d			09 31							10 34							11 30						12 34	
Bristol Temple Meads 10	a	09 18	09 23	09 34	09 38	09 51		10 06	10 18	10 23	10 39	10 42	10 51	11 09	11 18	11 23		11 33	11 37	11 51	12 08	12 18	12 23	12 39	12 42
	d		09 25		09 44	09 55				10 25		10 44	10 53	11 12		11 25			11 44	11 53			12 25		12 44
Bedminster	d		09 27							10 27						11 27							12 27		
Parson Street	d		09 29							10 29						11 29							12 29		
Nailsea & Backwell	d		09 38			10 03				10 38			11 03			11 38				12 03			12 38		
Yatton	d		09 44			10 08				10 44			11 08			11 44				12 08			12 44		
Worle	d		09 50			10 14				10 50			11 14			11 50				12 14			12 50		
Weston Milton	d		09 55							10 55						11 55							12 55		
Weston-super-Mare	a		10 00			10 22				11 00			11 21	11 29		12 00				12 22			13 00		
	d					10 23							11 23	11 39						12 23					
Highbridge & Burnham	d					10 34							11 34							12 34					
Bridgwater	d					10 42							11 42							12 42					
Taunton	a				10 17	10 59						11 15	11 56	11 59					12 15	12 57					13 15

		GW		XC	GW	GW	GW	XC	GW	XC	GW	GW		GW	XC	GW	XC	GW	GW	GW	XC	GW		XC	GW
				◇1 ⊥o	◇			◇1 ⊥o		◇1 ⊥o	◇			◇	◇1 ⊥o		◇1 ⊥o	◇			◇1 ⊥o			◇1 ⊥o	◇
Gloucester 7	d						12 42							13 42						14 42					
Cam & Dursley	d						12 56							13 57						14 56					
Yate	d						13 11							14 11						15 10					
Bristol Parkway 7	a						13 19							14 20						15 18					
	d			12 57		13 12	13 20	13 26		13 58		14 12		14 20	14 28		14 59		15 12	15 19	15 25			15 57	
Filton Abbey Wood	d	12 42			13 09	13 15	13 23		13 42		14 09	14 15		14 25		14 42		15 09	15 15	15 22		15 42			16 09
Stapleton Road	d						13 27							14 31						15 27					
Lawrence Hill	d						13 29							14 33						15 29					
Bristol Temple Meads 10	a	12 51		13 07	13 18	13 23	13 34	13 38	13 53	14 08	14 18	14 23		14 36	14 41	14 51	15 09	15 18	15 23	15 33	15 37	15 51		16 08	16 18
	d	12 53				13 25		13 44	13 55			14 25			14 44	14 53	15 12		15 25		15 44	15 53			
Bedminster	d					13 27						14 27							15 27						
Parson Street	d					13 29			13 59			14 29							15 29						
Nailsea & Backwell	d	13 03				13 38			14 07			14 38				15 03			15 38			16 03			
Yatton	d	13 08				13 44			14 12			14 44				15 08			15 44			16 08			
Worle	d	13 14				13 50			14 18			14 50				15 14			15 50			16 14			
Weston Milton	d					13 55						14 55							15 55						
Weston-super-Mare	a	13 22				14 00			14 23			15 00				15 22			16 00			16 22			
	d	13 23							14 23							15 23						16 23			
Highbridge & Burnham	d	13 34							14 34							15 34						16 34			
Bridgwater	d	13 42							14 42							15 42						16 42			
Taunton	a	13 59						14 15	15 01						15 16	15 59	15 43				16 15	16 57			

A from 31 March

b Previous night, stops to set down only

For connections from London Paddington please refer to Table 125

Table 134

Saturdays

Gloucester - Taunton

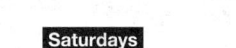

Network Diagram - see first Page of Table 132

		GW	GW	XC	GW	XC	GW	GW		GW	XC	GW	XC	GW	GW	GW	GW	XC		GW	XC	GW	GW	GW	GW
							R																		
			◇	◇1		◇1				◇	◇1		◇1	◇	◇1			◇1			◇1	◇	◇1		
				[trolley]		[trolley]					[trolley]		[trolley]		[buffet]			[trolley]			[trolley]		[buffet]		
Gloucester 7	d		15 45							16 42							17 46								18 42
Cam & Dursley	d		15 59							16 56							18 01								18 56
Yate	d		16 13							17 10							18 16								19 11
Bristol Parkway 7	a		16 24							17 18							18 24								19 20
	d	16 12	16 25	16 31		16 56		17 12		17 20	17 26		17 56			18 12	18 25	18 31			18 56			19 12	19 21
Filton Abbey Wood	d	16 15	16 28		16 42		17 09	17 15		17 23		17 42		18 09		18 15	18 28			18 42		19 09		19 15	19 24
Stapleton Road	d		16 34							17 29							18 34								19 29
Lawrence Hill	d		16 36							17 31							18 36								19 31
Bristol Temple Meads 10	a	16 23	16 39	16 42	16 51	17 07	17 18	17 23		17 34	17 38	17 51	18 07	18 18		18 23	18 39	18 42		18 51	19 05	19 18		19 24	19 36
	d	16 25		16 44	16 53	17 10		17 25			17 44	17 53			18 18	18 25		18 44		18 53			19 18		
Bedminster	d	16 27						17 27								18 27									
Parson Street	d	16 29						17 29								18 29									
Nailsea & Backwell	d	16 38			17 03			17 38				18 03				18 38				19 03			19 30		
Yatton	d	16 44			17 08			17 44				18 08				18 44				19 08			19 37		
Worle	d	16 50			17 14			17 50				18 14				18 50				19 14			19 43		
Weston Milton	d	16 55						17 55								18 55				19 20					
Weston-super-Mare	a	17 00			17 22			18 00				18 22			18 36	19 00				19 23			19 50		
	d				17 23							18 23			18 40					19 23					
Highbridge & Burnham	d				17 34							18 34								19 34					
Bridgwater	d				17 42							18 42								19 42					
Taunton	a			17 17	17 59	17 41					18 15	18 56			19 06			19 15		19 59					

		XC	GW	XC		GW	GW	GW	GW	XC	GW	GW	XC	XC		GW	XC	GW	GW	GW	XC	GW	GW	XC	
		◇1		◇1		◇1	◇			◇1		◇1	◇1	◇1		◇	◇1		◇		◇1	◇1	◇1	◇1	
										A			B	C			A					D	E		
		[trolley]		[trolley]		[buffet]				[trolley]		[buffet]	[trolley]	[trolley]			[trolley]				[trolley]	[buffet]	[buffet]		
Gloucester 7	d								19 45											21 16				22 04	
Cam & Dursley	d								19 59											21 30					
Yate	d								20 13											21 44					
Bristol Parkway 7	a								20 24											21 53				22 30	
	d	19 27		19 57				20 17	20 25	20 31			20 56	20 56			21 24			21 53	21 59			22 31	
Filton Abbey Wood	d		19 42				20 09	20 20	20 28		20 40					21 08		21 42		21 57					
Stapleton Road	d								20 34																
Lawrence Hill	d								20 36																
Bristol Temple Meads 10	a	19 39	19 51	20 06			20 18	20 29	20 39	20 42	20 48		21 06	21 05		21 18	21 35	21 49		22 05	22 12			22 41	
	d	19 44	19 53			20 15				20 44		20 55		21 11			21 44		21 59			22 17	22 27		
Bedminster	d																		22 01						
Parson Street	d																		22 03						
Nailsea & Backwell	d		20 03									21 04							22 12			22s27	22s38		
Yatton	d		20 08									21 11							22 18			22s34	22s44		
Worle	d		20 14									21 17							22 24			22s40	22s51		
Weston Milton	d		20 20									21 22													
Weston-super-Mare	a		20 23			20 36						21 26							22 29			22s47	22s57		
	d		20 24			20 38						21 26							22 31						
Highbridge & Burnham	d		20 34									21 39							22 42			22s58	23s08		
Bridgwater	d		20 42									21 46							22 50			23s05	23s16		
Taunton	a	20 15	20 59			21 03				21 15		21 58		21 42			22 15		23 03			23 17	23 28		

		GW
Gloucester 7	d	
Cam & Dursley	d	
Yate	d	
Bristol Parkway 7	a	
	d	
Filton Abbey Wood	d	22 52
Stapleton Road	d	
Lawrence Hill	d	
Bristol Temple Meads 10	a	23 00
	d	
Bedminster	d	
Parson Street	d	
Nailsea & Backwell	d	
Yatton	d	
Worle	d	
Weston Milton	d	
Weston-super-Mare	a	
	d	
Highbridge & Burnham	d	
Bridgwater	d	
Taunton	a	

A [trolley] to Bristol Temple Meads

B from 18 February until 24 March

C until 11 February, from 31 March. [trolley] to Bristol Temple Meads

D until 31 December and then from 31 March

E from 7 January until 24 March

For connections from London Paddington please refer to Table 125

Table 134

Sundays

until 1 January

Gloucester - Taunton

Network Diagram - see first Page of Table 132

		GW	GW	XC	GW	GW	XC	GW	GW	GW		XC	GW	GW	XC	GW	GW	XC	GW	GW		GW	XC	GW	GW
		◇	◇	◇1 trolley	◇		◇1 trolley	◇1 cup	◇			◇1 trolley	◇		◇1 trolley	◇1 cup	■	◇1 trolley	◇				◇1 trolley	◇1 cup	◇
Gloucester 7	d													10 18								12 17			
Cam & Dursley	d													10 32								12 31			
Yate	d													10 46								12 46			
Bristol Parkway 7	a													10 52								12 54			
	d											10 23		10 55	11 41			12 41				12 58	13 23		
Filton Abbey Wood	d				08 55				10 03				10 54	10 58			11 54		12 57			13 01			13 54
Stapleton Road	d									10 16															
Lawrence Hill	d									10 18															
Bristol Temple Meads 10	a				09 05				10 13	10 21		10 32	11 03	11 07	11 52		12 04	12 51	13 05			13 10	13 32		14 04
	d	07 30	08 28	08 44		09 05	09 48	09 55		10 23		10 44		11 10	11 54	11 55		12 54		13 05			13 44	13 55	
Bedminster	d																								
Parson Street	d																								
Nailsea & Backwell	d		08 38			09 13				10 33				11 20		12 07				13 15				14 06	
Yatton	d	07 43	08 43			09 20				10 38				11 25		12 12				13 20				14 12	
Worle	d		08 49			09 26				10 44				11 31		12 19				13 26				14 19	
Weston Milton	d																								
Weston-super-Mare	a	07 52	08 55			09 35				10 50				11 37		12 31				13 31				14 26	
	d	07 53	08 59							10 55				11 38						13 33					
Highbridge & Burnham	d		09 10							11 09				11 48						13 44					
Bridgwater	d	08 09	09 18							11 17				11 56						13 52					
Taunton	a	08 22	09 31	09 15			10 19	10 27		11 31		11 15		12 10	12 26			13 26		14 06			14 15		

		XC	GW	GW	XC	GW		XC	GW	GW	GW	XC	GW	XC	GW	GW		XC	GW	GW	XC	GW	GW	GW	XC
		◇1 trolley	◇1 cup	◇	◇1 trolley			◇1 trolley		◇		◇1 trolley		◇1 trolley	◇1 cup	◇		◇1 trolley		◇	◇1 trolley	◇	◇		◇1 trolley
Gloucester 7	d										15 13													17 20	
Cam & Dursley	d										15 27													17 34	
Yate	d										15 41													17 49	
Bristol Parkway 7	a										15 49													17 57	
	d	14 23			14 56			15 26			15 55	16 00		16 23				16 57			17 22			17 58	18 02
Filton Abbey Wood	d			14 55						15 55	15 57					16 55				17 20		17 54		18 01	
Stapleton Road	d																								
Lawrence Hill	d												←												
Bristol Temple Meads 10	a	14 32		15 04	15 07			15 36		16 04	16 09	16 11	16 09	16 35		17 06		17 08		17 29	17 35	18 04		18 10	18 13
	d	14 44	14 55			15 10		15 44	15 55		16 25	16 14	16 25	16 44	16 55				17 25		17 44		18 07		
Bedminster	d					15 13			15 58		↪								17 28						
Parson Street	d								16 00																
Nailsea & Backwell	d					15 22			16 08				16 35		17 06				17 37				18 17		
Yatton	d					15 28			16 14				16 40		17 12				17 43				18 23		
Worle	d					15 34			16 20				16 46		17 18				17 49				18 29		
Weston Milton	d					15 39							16 52						17 58						
Weston-super-Mare	a					15 42			16 25				16 56		17 26				18 01				18 35		
	d								16 28						17 30								18 36		
Highbridge & Burnham	d								16 40														18 47		
Bridgwater	d								16 48														18 55		
Taunton	a	15 15	15 29					16 14	17 03			16 45		17 15	17 53						18 18		19 09		

		GW		XC	GW	GW	XC	GW	XC	GW	GW	XC		GW	XC	GW	XC	GW	XC	GW	GW	XC		XC	GW
		■		◇1 trolley		◇	◇1 trolley	◇1 cup	◇1 trolley	◇		◇1 trolley			◇1 A trolley	◇1 cup	◇1 trolley	◇	◇1 A trolley	◇1 cup		◇1		◇1	trolley
Gloucester 7	d										19 20										21 15			22 07	
Cam & Dursley	d										19 35										21 31				
Yate	d										19 49										21 45				
Bristol Parkway 7	a										19 57										21 53			22 34	
	d			18 24			18 58		19 23		19 58	20 03			20 23		20 58		21 23		21 55	22 00		22 34	
Filton Abbey Wood	d	18 23				18 56				19 55	20 01							21 05			21 58				22 53
Stapleton Road	d				18 43																				
Lawrence Hill	d				18 45																				
Bristol Temple Meads 10	a	18 33		18 40	18 47	19 06	19 08		19 35	20 05	20 11	20 14			20 35		21 08	21 13	21 32		22 07	22 10		22 45	22 59
	d			18 44	19 05			19 27	19 44			20 19		20 25	20 44	20 55			21 44	21 55					
Bedminster	d				19 08									20 28											
Parson Street	d				19 10																				
Nailsea & Backwell	d				19 18			19 38						20 36		21 06				22 06					
Yatton	d				19 24			19 44						20 42		21 12				22 12					
Worle	d				19 30			19 51						20 48		21 19				22 19					
Weston Milton	d				19 34																				
Weston-super-Mare	a				19 38			19 58				20 36		20 53		21 26				22 27					
	d				19 40							20 37		20 58		21 27									
Highbridge & Burnham	d				19 51									21 09											
Bridgwater	d				19 59									21 17											
Taunton	a			19 15	20 13				20 18			20 58		21 33	21 15	21 50			22 15						

A trolley to Bristol Temple Meads

For connections from London Paddington please refer to Table 125

Table 134

Gloucester - Taunton

Sundays
until 1 January

Network Diagram - see first Page of Table 132

		XC	GW	XC
		◇1		◇1
Gloucester 7	d			
Cam & Dursley	d			
Yate	d			
Bristol Parkway 7	a			
	d	22 54		23 23
Filton Abbey Wood	d			
Stapleton Road	d			
Lawrence Hill	d			
Bristol Temple Meads 10	a	23 07		23 33
	d		23 10	
Bedminster	d		23 13	
Parson Street	d		23 15	
Nailsea & Backwell	d		23 23	
Yatton	d		23 29	
Worle	d		23 35	
Weston Milton	d		23 40	
Weston-super-Mare	a		23 43	
	d			
Highbridge & Burnham	d			
Bridgwater	d			
Taunton	a			

Sundays
8 January to 12 February

		GW	GW	XC	GW	GW	XC	GW	GW	GW		XC	GW	GW	XC	GW	GW	XC	GW	GW		GW	XC	GW	GW
																	B								
		◇	◇	◇1	◇		◇1	◇1	◇			◇1	◇		◇1	◇1		◇1	◇				◇1	◇1	◇
				🛒			🛒	☕				🛒			🛒	☕		🛒					🛒	☕	
Gloucester 7	d													10 18								12 17			
Cam & Dursley	d													10 32								12 31			
Yate	d													10 46								12 46			
Bristol Parkway 7	a													10 52								12 54			
	d											10 23		10 55	11 41			12 41				12 58	13 23		
Filton Abbey Wood	d				08 55				10 03				10 54	10 58			11 54		12 57			13 01			13 54
Stapleton Road	d									10 16															
Lawrence Hill	d									10 18															
Bristol Temple Meads 10	a				09 05				10 13	10 21		10 32	11 03	11 07	11 52		12 04	12 51	13 05			13 10	13 32		14 04
	d	07 30	08 28	08 44		09 05	09 48	09 55		10 23		10 44		11 10	11 54	11 55		12 54		13 05			13 44	13 55	
Bedminster	d																								
Parson Street	d																								
Nailsea & Backwell	d		08 38			09 13				10 33				11 20		12 07				13 15				14 06	
Yatton	d	07 43	08 43			09 20				10 38				11 25		12 12				13 20				14 12	
Worle	d		08 49			09 26				10 44				11 31		12 20				13 26				14 19	
Weston Milton	d																								
Weston-super-Mare	a	07 52	08 55			09 35				10 50				11 37		12 31				13 31				14 26	
	d	07 53	08 59							10 55				11 38						13 33					
Highbridge & Burnham	d		09 10							11 09				11 48						13 44					
Bridgwater	d	08 09	09 18							11 17				11 56						13 52					
Taunton	a	08 22	09 31	09 15			10 19	10 29		11 31		11 15		12 10	12 26			13 26		14 06			14 15		

		XC	GW	GW	XC	GW		XC	GW	GW	GW	XC	GW	XC	GW	GW		XC	GW	GW	XC	GW	GW	GW	XC
		◇1	◇1	◇	◇1			◇1		◇		◇1		◇1	◇1	◇		◇1		◇	◇1	◇	◇		◇1
		🛒	☕		🛒			🛒				🛒		🛒	☕			🛒			🛒				🛒
Gloucester 7	d										15 13													17 20	
Cam & Dursley	d										15 27													17 34	
Yate	d										15 41													17 49	
Bristol Parkway 7	a										15 49													17 57	
	d	14 23			14 56			15 26			15 55	16 00		16 23				16 57			17 22			17 58	18 02
Filton Abbey Wood	d			14 55						15 55	15 57					16 55				17 20		17 54		18 01	
Stapleton Road	d																								
Lawrence Hill	d												←												
Bristol Temple Meads 10	a	14 32		15 04	15 07			15 36		16 04	16 09	16 11	16 09	16 35		17 06		17 08		17 29	17 35	18 04		18 10	18 13
	d	14 44	14 55			15 10		15 44	15 55		16 25	16 14	16 25	16 44	16 55				17 25		17 44		18 07		
Bedminster	d					15 13			15 58		↦								17 28						
Parson Street	d								16 00																
Nailsea & Backwell	d					15 22			16 08				16 35		17 06				17 37				18 17		
Yatton	d					15 28			16 14				16 40		17 12				17 43				18 23		
Worle	d					15 34			16 20				16 46		17 19				17 49				18 29		
Weston Milton	d					15 39							16 52						17 58						
Weston-super-Mare	a					15 42			16 25				16 56		17 26				18 01				18 35		
	d								16 28						17 31								18 36		
Highbridge & Burnham	d								16 40														18 47		
Bridgwater	d								16 48														18 55		
Taunton	a	15 15	15 31					16 14	17 03			16 45		17 15	17 53						18 18		19 09		

For connections from London Paddington please refer to Table 125

Table 134

Gloucester - Taunton

Sundays

8 January to 12 February

Network Diagram - see first Page of Table 132

		GW		XC	GW	GW	XC	GW	XC	GW	GW	XC		GW	XC	GW	XC	GW	XC	GW	GW	XC		XC	GW
		R		◇1 [trolley]		◇	◇1 [trolley]	◇1 [buffet]	◇1 [trolley]	◇		◇1 [trolley]			◇1 A [trolley]	◇1 [buffet]	◇1 [trolley]	◇	◇1 A [trolley]	◇1 [buffet]		◇1		◇1	[trolley]
Gloucester 7	d										19 20										21 15			22 07	
Cam & Dursley	d										19 35										21 31				
Yate	d										19 49										21 45				
Bristol Parkway 7	a										19 57										21 53			22 34	
	d			18 24			18 58		19 23		19 58	20 03			20 23		20 58		21 23		21 55	22 00		22 34	
Filton Abbey Wood	d	18 23				18 56				19 55	20 01							21 05			21 58				22 53
Stapleton Road	d				18 43																				
Lawrence Hill	d				18 45																				
Bristol Temple Meads 10	a	18 33		18 40	18 47	19 06	19 08		19 35	20 05	20 11	20 14			20 35		21 08	21 13	21 32		22 07	22 10		22 45	22 59
	d			18 44	19 05			19 25	19 44			20 19		20 25	20 44	20 55			21 44	21 55					
Bedminster	d				19 08									20 28											
Parson Street	d				19 10																				
Nailsea & Backwell	d				19 18			19 36						20 36		21 06				22 06					
Yatton	d				19 24			19 42						20 42		21 12				22 12					
Worle	d				19 30			19 49						20 48		21 19				22 19					
Weston Milton	d				19 34																				
Weston-super-Mare	a				19 38			19 58				20 36		20 53		21 26				22 27					
	d				19 40							20 37		20 58		21 27									
Highbridge & Burnham	d				19 51									21 09											
Bridgwater	d				19 59									21 17											
Taunton	a			19 15	20 13				20 18			20 58		21 33	21 15	21 50			22 15						

		XC	GW	XC
		◇1		◇1
Gloucester 7	d			
Cam & Dursley	d			
Yate	d			
Bristol Parkway 7	a			
	d	22 54		23 23
Filton Abbey Wood	d			
Stapleton Road	d			
Lawrence Hill	d			
Bristol Temple Meads 10	a	23 07		23 33
	d		23 10	
Bedminster	d		23 13	
Parson Street	d		23 15	
Nailsea & Backwell	d		23 23	
Yatton	d		23 29	
Worle	d		23 35	
Weston Milton	d		23 40	
Weston-super-Mare	a		23 43	
	d			
Highbridge & Burnham	d			
Bridgwater	d			
Taunton	a			

Sundays

19 February to 25 March

		GW	GW	XC	GW	GW	GW	XC	GW	GW		GW	XC	GW	GW	XC	GW	GW	XC	GW		GW	GW	XC	GW
		◇	◇	◇1 [trolley]	◇		[bus]	◇1 [trolley]	◇1 [buffet]	◇			◇1 [trolley]	◇		◇1 [trolley]	◇1 [buffet]	R	◇1 [trolley]	◇				◇1 [trolley]	◇1 [buffet]
Gloucester 7	d														10 18								12 17		
Cam & Dursley	d														10 32								12 31		
Yate	d														10 46								12 46		
Bristol Parkway 7	a														10 52								12 54		
	d				08 51		09 05			10 01			10 23	10 51	10 55	11 41		11 51	12 41	12 54			12 58	13 23	
Filton Abbey Wood	d				08 54					10 03				10 54	10 58			11 54		12 57			13 01		
Stapleton Road	d											10 16													
Lawrence Hill	d											10 18													
Bristol Temple Meads 10	a				09 05		09 25			10 13		10 21	10 32	11 02	11 07	11 52		12 03	12 51	13 05			13 10	13 35	
	d	07 45	08 28	08 44		09 05		09 48	09 55			10 23	10 44		11 10	11 54	11 55		12 54			13 05		13 44	13 55
Bedminster	d																								
Parson Street	d																								
Nailsea & Backwell	d		08 38			09 13						10 33			11 20		12 07					13 15			14 06
Yatton	d	07 57	08 45			09 20						10 38			11 25		12 12					13 20			14 12
Worle	d		08 51			09 26						10 44			11 31		12 20					13 26			14 19
Weston Milton	d																								
Weston-super-Mare	a	08 06	08 57			09 35						10 50			11 37		12 31					13 31			14 26
	d	08 07	09 06									10 55			11 38							13 33			
Highbridge & Burnham	d		09 15									11 09			11 48							13 44			
Bridgwater	d	08 21	09 23									11 17			11 56							13 52			
Taunton	a	08 32	09 34	09 15				10 19	10 29			11 31	11 15		12 10	12 26			13 26			14 06		14 15	

A [trolley] to Bristol Temple Meads

For connections from London Paddington please refer to Table 125

Table 134

Sundays

19 February to 25 March

Gloucester - Taunton

Network Diagram - see first Page of Table 132

		GW	XC	GW	GW	XC		GW	XC	GW	GW	GW	XC
		◇	◇1	◇1	◇	◇1			◇1		◇		◇1
			trolley	buffet		trolley			trolley				trolley
Gloucester 7	d											15 13	
Cam & Dursley	d											15 27	
Yate	d											15 41	
Bristol Parkway 7	a											15 49	
	d	13 51	14 23		14 51	14 56			15 26		15 51	15 55	16 00
Filton Abbey Wood	d	13 54			14 55						15 55	15 57	
Stapleton Road	d												
Lawrence Hill	d												
Bristol Temple Meads 10	a	14 03	14 32		15 04	15 07			15 36		16 04	16 09	16 13
	d		14 44	14 55				15 10	15 44	15 55		16 25	
Bedminster	d							15 13		15 58			
Parson Street	d									16 00			
Nailsea & Backwell	d							15 22		16 08		16 35	
Yatton	d							15 28		16 14		16 40	
Worle	d							15 34		16 20		16 46	
Weston Milton	d							15 39				16 52	
Weston-super-Mare	a							15 42		16 25		16 56	
	d									16 28			
Highbridge & Burnham	d									16 40			
Bridgwater	d									16 48			
Taunton	a		15 15	15 30					16 14	17 03			

		XC	GW	GW		XC	GW	GW	XC	GW	GW	GW	XC
		◇1	◇1	◇		◇1		◇	◇1	◇	◇		◇1
		trolley	buffet			trolley			trolley				trolley
Gloucester 7	d											17 20	
Cam & Dursley	d											17 34	
Yate	d											17 49	
Bristol Parkway 7	a											17 57	
	d	16 23		16 51		16 57		17 17	17 22	17 51		17 58	18 02
Filton Abbey Wood	d			16 55				17 20		17 55		18 01	
Stapleton Road	d												
Lawrence Hill	d												
Bristol Temple Meads 10	a	16 35		17 06		17 08		17 29	17 35	18 04		18 10	18 13
	d	16 44	16 55				17 25		17 44		18 07		
Bedminster	d						17 28						
Parson Street	d												
Nailsea & Backwell	d		17 06				17 37				18 17		
Yatton	d		17 12				17 43				18 23		
Worle	d		17 19				17 49				18 29		
Weston Milton	d						17 58						
Weston-super-Mare	a		17 26				18 01				18 35		
	d		17 31								18 36		
Highbridge & Burnham	d										18 47		
Bridgwater	d										18 55		
Taunton	a	17 15	17 53						18 18		19 09		

		GW		XC	GW	GW	XC	GW	XC	GW	GW	XC	
		R		◇1		◇	◇1	◇1	◇1	◇		◇1	
				trolley			trolley	buffet	trolley			trolley	
Gloucester 7	d										19 20		
Cam & Dursley	d										19 35		
Yate	d										19 49		
Bristol Parkway 7	a										19 57		
	d	18 20		18 28		18 51	18 58		19 23	19 51	19 58	20 03	
Filton Abbey Wood	d	18 25				18 55				19 55	20 01		
Stapleton Road	d				18 43								
Lawrence Hill	d				18 45								
Bristol Temple Meads 10	a	18 33		18 40	18 47	19 06	19 08		19 35	20 05	20 11	20 14	
	d			18 44	19 05			19 29	19 44				
Bedminster	d				19 08								
Parson Street	d				19 10								
Nailsea & Backwell	d				19 18			19 39					
Yatton	d				19 24			19 46					
Worle	d				19 30			19 52					
Weston Milton	d				19 34								
Weston-super-Mare	a				19 38			20 00					
	d				19 40								
Highbridge & Burnham	d				19 51								
Bridgwater	d				19 59								
Taunton	a			19 15	20 13				20 18				

		GW	XC	GW	XC	GW	XC	GW	GW	XC		XC	GW
			◇1 A	◇1	◇1	◇	◇1 A	◇1		◇1		◇1	
			trolley	buffet	trolley		trolley	buffet					trolley
Gloucester 7	d								21 15			22 07	
Cam & Dursley	d								21 31				
Yate	d								21 45				
Bristol Parkway 7	a								21 53			22 34	
	d		20 23		20 58	21 02	21 23		21 55	22 00		22 34	22 49
Filton Abbey Wood	d					21 06			21 58				22 52
Stapleton Road	d												
Lawrence Hill	d												
Bristol Temple Meads 10	a		20 35		21 08	21 13	21 32		22 07	22 10		22 45	23 00
	d	20 25	20 44	20 55			21 44	21 55					
Bedminster	d	20 28											
Parson Street	d												
Nailsea & Backwell	d	20 36		21 06				22 06					
Yatton	d	20 42		21 12				22 12					
Worle	d	20 48		21 19				22 19					
Weston Milton	d												
Weston-super-Mare	a	20 53		21 26				22 27					
	d	20 58		21 27									
Highbridge & Burnham	d	21 09											
Bridgwater	d	21 17											
Taunton	a	21 33	21 15	21 50			22 15						

		GW	XC	GW
			◇1	
				bus
Gloucester 7	d			
Cam & Dursley	d			
Yate	d			
Bristol Parkway 7	a			
	d		23 23	23 30
Filton Abbey Wood	d			
Stapleton Road	d			
Lawrence Hill	d			
Bristol Temple Meads 10	a		23 33	23 50
	d	23 10		
Bedminster	d	23 13		
Parson Street	d	23 15		
Nailsea & Backwell	d	23 23		
Yatton	d	23 29		
Worle	d	23 35		
Weston Milton	d	23 40		
Weston-super-Mare	a	23 43		
	d			
Highbridge & Burnham	d			
Bridgwater	d			
Taunton	a			

A trolley to Bristol Temple Meads

For connections from London Paddington please refer to Table 125

Table 134

Sundays

from 1 April

Gloucester - Taunton

Network Diagram - see first Page of Table 132

		GW	GW	XC	GW	GW	XC	GW	GW	GW		XC	GW	GW	XC	GW	GW	XC	GW	GW		GW	GW	XC	GW
																	R								
		◇	◇	◇1	◇		◇1	◇1	◇			◇1	◇		◇1	◇1		◇1	◇1	◇				◇1	◇1
				🛒			🛒	☕				🛒			🛒	☕		🛒	☕					🛒	☕
Gloucester 7	d													10 18									12 17		
Cam & Dursley	d													10 32									12 31		
Yate	d													10 46									12 46		
Bristol Parkway 7	a													10 52									12 54		
	d											10 23		10 55	11 41			12 41					12 58	13 23	
Filton Abbey Wood	d				08 55				10 03				10 54	10 58			11 54			12 57			13 01		
Stapleton Road	d									10 16															
Lawrence Hill	d									10 18															
Bristol Temple Meads 10	a				09 05				10 13	10 21		10 32	11 03	11 07	11 52		12 04	12 51		13 05			13 10	13 32	
	d	07 30	08 28	08 44		09 05	09 48	09 54		10 23		10 44		11 10	11 54	11 55		12 54	12 55			13 05		13 44	13 55
Bedminster	d																								
Parson Street	d																								
Nailsea & Backwell	d		08 38			09 13				10 33				11 20		12 07						13 15			14 06
Yatton	d	07 43	08 43			09 20				10 38				11 25		12 12						13 20			14 12
Worle	d		08 49			09 26				10 44				11 31		12 20						13 26			14 19
Weston Milton	d																								
Weston-super-Mare	a	07 52	08 55			09 35				10 50				11 37		12 31			13 15			13 31			14 26
	d	07 53	08 59							10 55				11 38					13 17			13 33			
Highbridge & Burnham	d		09 10							11 09				11 48								13 44			
Bridgwater	d	08 09	09 18							11 17				11 56								13 52			
Taunton	a	08 22	09 31	09 15			10 19	10 28		11 31		11 15		12 10	12 26			13 26	13 38			14 06		14 15	

		GW	XC	GW	GW	XC		GW	XC	GW	GW	GW	XC	GW	XC	GW		GW	XC	GW	GW	XC	GW	GW	XC
		◇	◇1	◇1	◇	◇1			◇1		◇		◇1		◇1	◇1		◇	◇1		◇	◇1	◇		◇1
			🛒	☕		🛒			🛒				🛒		🛒	☕			🛒			🛒			🛒
Gloucester 7	d											15 13												17 20	
Cam & Dursley	d											15 27												17 34	
Yate	d											15 41												17 49	
Bristol Parkway 7	a											15 49												17 57	
	d		14 23			14 56			15 26			15 55	16 00		16 23				16 57			17 22		17 58	18 02
Filton Abbey Wood	d	13 54			14 55						15 55	15 57						16 55			17 20		17 54	18 01	
Stapleton Road	d																								
Lawrence Hill	d													←											
Bristol Temple Meads 10	a	14 04	14 32		15 04	15 07			15 36		16 04	16 09	16 11	16 09	16 35			17 06	17 08		17 29	17 35	18 04	18 10	18 13
	d		14 44	14 55				15 10	15 44	15 55		16 25	16 14	16 25	16 44	16 55				17 25		17 44			
Bedminster	d							15 13		15 58		→								17 28					
Parson Street	d									16 00															
Nailsea & Backwell	d							15 22		16 08				16 35		17 06				17 37					
Yatton	d							15 28		16 14				16 40		17 12				17 43					
Worle	d							15 34		16 20				16 46		17 19				17 49					
Weston Milton	d							15 39						16 52						17 58					
Weston-super-Mare	a							15 42		16 25				16 56		17 26				18 01					
	d									16 28						17 31									
Highbridge & Burnham	d									16 40															
Bridgwater	d									16 48															
Taunton	a		15 15	15 31					16 14	17 03			16 45		17 15	17 53						18 18			

		GW		GW	XC	GW	GW	XC	GW	XC	GW	GW		XC	GW	XC	GW	XC	GW	XC	GW	GW		XC	XC
				R																					
		◇			◇1		◇	◇1	◇1	◇1	◇			◇1		◇1	◇1	◇1	◇	◇1	◇1			◇1	◇1
																A				A					
					🛒			🛒	☕	🛒				🛒		🛒	☕	🛒		🛒	☕				
Gloucester 7	d											19 20										21 15			22 07
Cam & Dursley	d											19 35										21 31			
Yate	d											19 49										21 45			
Bristol Parkway 7	a											19 57										21 53			22 34
	d				18 24			18 58		19 23		19 58		20 03		20 23		20 58		21 23		21 55		22 00	22 34
Filton Abbey Wood	d			18 23			18 56				19 55	20 01							21 05			21 58			
Stapleton Road	d					18 43																			
Lawrence Hill	d					18 45																			
Bristol Temple Meads 10	a			18 33	18 40	18 47	19 06	19 08		19 35	20 05	20 11		20 14		20 35		21 08	21 13	21 32		22 07		22 10	22 45
	d	18 25			18 44	19 05			19 27	19 44				20 19	20 25	20 44	20 55			21 44	21 55				
Bedminster	d					19 08									20 28										
Parson Street	d					19 10																			
Nailsea & Backwell	d	18 35				19 18			19 38						20 36		21 06				22 06				
Yatton	d	18 41				19 24			19 44						20 42		21 12				22 12				
Worle	d	18 47				19 30			19 51						20 48		21 19				22 19				
Weston Milton	d					19 34																			
Weston-super-Mare	a	18 53				19 38			19 58					20 36	20 53		21 26				22 27				
	d	18 58				19 40								20 37	20 58		21 27								
Highbridge & Burnham	d	19 09				19 51									21 09										
Bridgwater	d	19 17				19 59									21 17										
Taunton	a	19 32			19 15	20 13				20 18				20 58	21 33	21 15	21 50			22 15					

A 🛒 to Bristol Temple Meads

For connections from London Paddington please refer to Table 125

Table 134

Sundays

from 1 April

Gloucester - Taunton

Network Diagram - see first Page of Table 132

		GW	XC	GW	XC
			◇1		◇1
		ꝏ			
Gloucester 7	d				
Cam & Dursley	d				
Yate	d				
Bristol Parkway 7	a				
	d		22 54		23 23
Filton Abbey Wood	d	22 53			
Stapleton Road	d				
Lawrence Hill	d				
Bristol Temple Meads 10	a	22 59	23 07		23 33
	d			23 10	
Bedminster	d			23 13	
Parson Street	d			23 15	
Nailsea & Backwell	d			23 23	
Yatton	d			23 29	
Worle	d			23 35	
Weston Milton	d			23 40	
Weston-super-Mare	a			23 43	
	d				
Highbridge & Burnham	d				
Bridgwater	d				
Taunton	a				

For connections from London Paddington please refer to Table 125

Table 134

Mondays to Fridays

Taunton - Gloucester

Network Diagram - see first Page of Table 132

Miles			GW MO	GW MX	XC	GW	GW	XC	GW	GW	GW	XC	GW	GW	GW	GW	XC	GW	GW	GW	GW	XC
				R A 🛏 ☕	1			◇1 🛒			◇1 ☕	◇1 🛒	◇1 ☕		◇1 B ☕		◇1 🛒			◇	◇1 ☕	◇1 🛒
0	**Taunton**	d		01 36					05 27					06 02		06 34	06 50				06 55	
11¾	Bridgwater	d							05 39					06 14		06 46					07 05	
18	Highbridge & Burnham	d							05 47					06 21		06 54					07 13	
25¾	**Weston-super-Mare**	a							05 58					06 32		07 04					07 24	
—		d	23p47						06 00		06 20			06 36	06 49	07 08					07 25	
27	Weston Milton	d	23p50								06 25			06 39	06 53	07 11						
29½	Worle	d	23p54						06 05		06 30			06 43	06 59	07 15					07 32	
33½	Yatton	d	23p59						06 12		06 37			06 49	07 06	07 21					07 39	
37½	Nailsea & Backwell	d	00 06						06 18		06 44			06 55	07 13	07 27					07 46	
43¾	Parson Street	d												07 02		07 34						
44½	Bedminster	d	00 15											07 05		07 36			←			
45½	**Bristol Temple Meads 10**	a	00 19	02 34					06 30		06 54			07 09	07 23	07 41	07 24		07 41		07 57	
—		d			05 19	05 54	06 19	06 27		06 50		07 00	07 14	07 19		07 47	07 30	07 34	07 47	07 54		08 00
46½	Lawrence Hill	d					06 22			06 53				07 22		→			07 50			
47	Stapleton Road	d					06 25			06 56				07 24					07 52			
50	Filton Abbey Wood	d				06a01	06a30			07a01			07a21	07 30				07 43	07 59	08a01		
51¼	**Bristol Parkway 7**	a			05 28			06 37				07 08		07 33			07 38	07 47	08 05			08 08
—		d																07 48				
57½	Yate	d																07 57				
72¼	Cam & Dursley	d																08 10				
85¼	**Gloucester 7**	a																08 29				

		GW	GW	GW	GW	XC	GW	GW	XC	GW	GW	GW	GW	XC	GW	GW	GW	GW	XC	GW	GW	XC	GW
		◇		◇1 ☕		◇1 🛒			◇1 🛒	R 🛒	◇			◇1 🛒			◇1 ☕	◇ 🛒	◇1 🛒			◇1 🛒	◇
Taunton	d			07 12	07 36	07 51			08 13				08 36	08 51			09 05				09 37	09 51	
Bridgwater	d			07 23	07 48								08 48								09 49		
Highbridge & Burnham	d			07 31	07 56								08 56								09 56		
Weston-super-Mare	a			07 41	08 06				08 32				09 08				09 27				10 07		
	d		07 37	07 49	08 08				08 34			08 41	09 10				09 29			09 45	10 10		
Weston Milton	d		07 40	07 53	08 11							08 44	09 13								10 13		
Worle	d		07 44	07 59	08 15							08 48	09 17							09 50	10 17		
Yatton	d		07 49	08 06	08 21							08 54	09 23				09 40			09 56	10 23		
Nailsea & Backwell	d		07 55	08 13	08 27							09 00	09 29				09 46			10 02	10 29		
Parson Street	d		08 02		08 34							09 07	09 36								10 36		
Bedminster	d		08 04		08 36			←				09 10	09 38			←					10 39		
Bristol Temple Meads 10	a		08 09	08 24	08 41	08 26		08 41	08 53			09 14	09 42	09 26		09 42	09 56			10 13	10 42	10 25	
	d	08 10	08 21		08 44	08 30	08 41	08 44	09 00	08 54	09 10	09 21	09 47	09 30	09 41	09 47		09 56	10 00	10 21	10 45	10 30	10 41
Lawrence Hill	d	08 13			→			08 47			09 13		→			09 49					→		
Stapleton Road	d	08 16						08 49			09 15					09 50							
Filton Abbey Wood	d	08 22	08a32				08 48	08 55		09a01	09 22	09a30			09 48	09 55		10a03		10a30			10 48
Bristol Parkway 7	a	08 29				08 38	08 52	09 03	09 08		09 28			09 38	09 52	10 03			10 08			10 38	10 52
	d						08 52								09 52								10 52
Yate	d						09 01								10 01								11 01
Cam & Dursley	d						09 14								10 14								11 14
Gloucester 7	a						09 33								10 33								11 34

		GW	GW	XC	GW	XC	GW	GW	GW	GW	XC	GW	GW	XC	GW	GW	GW	XC	GW	XC	GW	GW
			◇ 🛒	◇1 🛒	◇	◇1 🛒	◇		◇ 🛒		◇1 🛒	◇1 ☕		◇1 🛒	◇		◇ 🛒	◇1 🛒		◇1 🛒		
Taunton	d				10 07	10 51				11 04	11 18	11 26		11 51					12 07	12 51		
Bridgwater	d				10 19					11 16									12 19			
Highbridge & Burnham	d				10 27					11 24									12 27			
Weston-super-Mare	a				10 38					11 34									12 38			
	d				10 39			11 10		11 45						12 10			12 39			13 10
Weston Milton	d							11 13								12 13						13 13
Worle	d				10 45			11 17		11 50						12 17			12 45			13 17
Yatton	d				10 51			11 23		11 56						12 23			12 51			13 23
Nailsea & Backwell	d				10 57			11 29		12 02						12 29			12 57			13 29
Parson Street	d							11 36								12 36						13 36
Bedminster	d	←						11 39					←			12 39						13 39
Bristol Temple Meads 10	a	10 42			11 11	11 23		11 43		12 11	11 52	11 58	12 11	12 23		12 43			13 09	13 24		13 42
	d	10 45	10 54	11 00	11 21	11 30	11 41	11 44	11 54	12 21	12 00		12 21	12 30	12 41	12 44	12 54	13 00	13 21	13 30	13 41	13 46
Lawrence Hill	d	10 49						11 47		→						12 47						13 47
Stapleton Road	d	10 52						11 50								12 50						13 50
Filton Abbey Wood	d	10 57	11a01		11a30		11 48	11 55	12a01				12a30		12 48	12 55	13a01		13a30		13 48	13 55
Bristol Parkway 7	a	11 03		11 08		11 38	11 52	12 03			12 08			12 38	12 52	13 03		13 08		13 38	13 52	14 03
	d						11 52								12 52						13 52	
Yate	d						12 01								13 01						14 01	
Cam & Dursley	d						12 14								13 14						14 14	
Gloucester 7	a						12 33								13 31						14 33	

A The Night Riviera

B The Bristolian

For connections to London Paddington please refer to Table 125

Taunton - Gloucester

Network Diagram - see first Page of Table 132

		GW	GW	XC	GW	XC	GW	GW	GW		XC	GW	XC	GW	GW	GW	GW	XC	GW		GW	XC	GW	GW	GW
		◇ 🚲		◇1 🚲		◇1 🚲	◇		◇ 🚲		◇1 🚲	◇	◇1 🚲		◇		◇ 🚲	◇1 🚲				◇1 🚲			R 🚲
Taunton	d		13 07	13 16		13 54						14 07	14 54					15 12			15 15	15 51			
Bridgwater	d		13 19									14 19									15 27				
Highbridge & Burnham	d		13 27									14 27									15 34				
Weston-super-Mare	a		13 38									14 37						15 37			15 45				
	d		13 39					14 10				14 39				15 10		15 38			15 45			16 10	
Weston Milton	d							14 13								15 13								16 13	
Worle	d		13 45					14 17				14 45				15 17					15 50			16 17	
Yatton	d		13 51					14 23				14 51				15 23					15 56			16 23	
Nailsea & Backwell	d		13 57					14 29				14 57				15 29					16 02			16 29	
Parson Street	d							14 36								15 36								16 36	
Bedminster	d				↤			14 39								15 39								16 39	
Bristol Temple Meads 10	a		14 11	13 55	14 11	14 26		14 43				15 08	15 26			15 43		15 55			16 15	16 26		16 43	
	d	13 54	14 21	14 00	14 21	14 30	14 41	14 45	14 54		15 00	15 21	15 30	15 34	15 41	15 45	15 54	16 00	16 15		16 24	16 30	16 41	16 44	16 54
Lawrence Hill	d		↦					14 47								15 47			16 18					16 47	
Stapleton Road	d							14 50								15 50			16 20					16 50	
Filton Abbey Wood	d	14a01			14a30		14 48	14 55	15a01			15a30			15 48	15 55	16a01		16 26		16a30		16 48	16 55	17a01
Bristol Parkway 7	a			14 08		14 38	14 51	15 03			15 08		15 38	15 48	15 52	16 03		16 08	16 34			16 38	16 52	17 03	
	d						14 52								15 52								16 52		
Yate	d						15 01								16 01								17 01		
Cam & Dursley	d						15 14								16 14								17 14		
Gloucester 7	a						15 32								16 33								17 33		

		XC	GW	GW	XC		GW	GW	GW	GW	GW	XC	GW	XC	GW		GW	GW	GW	XC	GW	XC	GW	GW	GW
		◇1 🚲			◇1 🚲		◇1 ☕	◇		R 🚲		◇1 🚲		◇1 🚲	◇1 ☕				R 🚲	◇1 🚲		◇1 🚲			◇ 🚲
Taunton	d			16 07	16 54						17 06	17 22		17 51							18 08	18 54			
Bridgwater	d			16 19							17 17										18 19				
Highbridge & Burnham	d			16 27							17 25										18 27				
Weston-super-Mare	a			16 37							17 37										18 38				
	d			16 39			17 10		17 15		17 38				18 08			18 15			18 39			19 10	
Weston Milton	d			16 42							17 41										18 43			19 13	
Worle	d			16 45					17 21		17 45							18 21			18 45			19 17	
Yatton	d			16 51					17 26		17 51							18 27			18 51			19 23	
Nailsea & Backwell	d			16 57					17 32		17 57							18 33			18 57			19 29	
Parson Street	d										18 04										19 07			19 36	
Bedminster	d			17 07							18 06		↤								19 09			19 39	
Bristol Temple Meads 10	a			17 11	17 26		17 30		17 44		18 14	17 53	18 14	18 24	18 28			18 44			19 13	19 26		19 43	
	d	17 00	17 10	17 21	17 30			17 41	17 46	17 54	18 21	18 00	18 21	18 30			18 41	18 48	18 54	19 00	19 21	19 30	19 41	19 45	19 54
Lawrence Hill	d		17 13						17 47		↦		18 24					18 51			19 24			19 47	
Stapleton Road	d		17 16						17 49				18 26					18a53			19 26			19 50	
Filton Abbey Wood	d		17 22	17a30				17 48	17 55	18a01			18a30				18 48		19a01		19a30		19 48	19 55	20a01
Bristol Parkway 7	a	17 08	17 27		17 38			17 52	18 03			18 08		18 38			18 52			19 08		19 38	19 52	20 03	
	d							17 52									18 52						19 52		
Yate	d							18 01									19 01						20 01		
Cam & Dursley	d							18 14									19 14						20 14		
Gloucester 7	a							18 33									19 30						20 32		

			XC	XC	GW	XC	GW	GW	GW	GW	GW		XC MTWO	XC ThFO	GW	GW	GW	GW	GW	GW	GW		GW		
			◇1	◇1		◇1 A 🚲		◇ 🚲			◇1 ☕		◇1	◇1	◇	1		◇1 ☕	◇	◇ D	◇ E				
Taunton	d				19 10	19 51				20 30	21 15		21 19	21 19				21 29		22⌇02	22⌇23		22 45		
Bridgwater	d				19 22					20 42								21 39		⌇	⌇		22 57		
Highbridge & Burnham	d				19 31					20 50								21 47		⌇	⌇		23 05		
Weston-super-Mare	a				19 42					21 00								21 57		22⌇26	22⌇47		23 15		
	d				19 49					21 02						21 34		22 01		22⌇30	22⌇49		23 17		
Weston Milton	d									21 05						21 38				⌇	⌇		23 20		
Worle	d				19 55					21 09						21 43		22 08		⌇	⌇		23 24		
Yatton	d				20 01					21 14						21 50		22 15		⌇	⌇		23 30		
Nailsea & Backwell	d				20 07					21 20						21 56		22 21		⌇	⌇		23 36		
Parson Street	d									21 27										⌇	⌇		23 42		
Bedminster	d									21 29										⌇	⌇		23 45		
Bristol Temple Meads 10	a				20 19	20 24				21 35	21 47		21 52	21 51		22 06		22 31		22⌇56	23⌇15		23 51		
	d		20 00	20 15		20 30	20 41	20 54	21 19				22 00	22 00	21 54		22 11		22 54						
Lawrence Hill	d								21 22																
Stapleton Road	d								21 24																
Filton Abbey Wood	d			20a21			20 48	21a01	21a30						22a01		22 18		23a01						
Bristol Parkway 7	a		20 08			20 38	20 52						22 08	22 08			22 22								
	d		20 10				20 52										22 22								
Yate	d						21 01										22 31								
Cam & Dursley	d						21 14										22 44								
Gloucester 7	a		20 38				21 31										23 03								

A 🚲 to Bristol Temple Meads
D until 30 December
E from 2 January

For connections to London Paddington please refer to Table 125

Table 134

Taunton - Gloucester

Network Diagram - see first Page of Table 132

		GW	XC	GW	GW	GW	GW	XC	GW	GW		XC	GW	GW	GW	GW	XC	GW	GW	XC		GW	GW	GW	GW
		R A 🛏 🍴	◇1 🛒		◇1		◇1 🍴	◇1 🛒				◇1 🛒				◇1 🍴	◇1 🛒			◇1 🛒				◇	◇1 🍴
Taunton	d	01 36		05 28						06 35		06 51				06 54			07 35	07 51					07 59
Bridgwater	d			05 40						06 48						07 05			07 47						08 10
Highbridge & Burnham	d			05 48						06 55						07 12			07 55						08 17
Weston-super-Mare	a			05 59						07 06						07 24			08 06						08 27
	d			06 01			06 24			07 08						07 24		07 37	08 06						08 30
Weston Milton	d			06 04						07 11								07 40	08 09						
Worle	d			06 07			06 32			07 16						07 32		07 44	08 15						
Yatton	d			06 12			06 39			07 22						07 39		07 49	08 21						08 41
Nailsea & Backwell	d			06 18			06 45			07 28						07 46		07 55	08 27						08 47
Parson Street	d			06 29						07 35								08 02	08 36						
Bedminster	d			06 31						07 38				←				08 04	08 38				←		
Bristol Temple Meads 10	a	02 34		06 34			06 56			07 42		07 24		07 42		07 58		08 10	08 41	08 23			08 41		08 57
	d		06 15		06 46	06 50		07 00	07 21	07 47		07 30	07 41	07 47	07 54		08 00	08 20	08 45	08 30		08 41	08 45	08 54	
Lawrence Hill	d					06 53				→				07 50				08 23	→				08 48		
Stapleton Road	d					06 56								07 52				08 25					08 50		
Filton Abbey Wood	d				06 54	07a01			07a29				07 48	07 59	08a00			08a30				08 48	08 56	09a01	
Bristol Parkway 7	a		06 23		06 58			07 08				07 38	07 52	08 05			08 08			08 38		08 52	09 03		
	d		06 25										07 52									08 52			
Yate	d												08 01									09 01			
Cam & Dursley	d												08 14									09 14			
Gloucester 7	a		06 54										08 32									09 33			

		XC	GW	XC	GW	GW		GW	XC	GW	XC	GW	GW	GW	XC	GW		GW	XC	GW	GW	GW	GW	XC	GW
		◇1 🛒		◇1 🛒				◇	◇1 🛒		◇1 🛒	◇		◇	◇1 🛒			◇1 🍴	◇1 🛒	◇		◇		◇1 🛒	
Taunton	d	08 13		08 51						09 10	09 51					10 12		10 45	10 51				11 07	11 18	
Bridgwater	d									09 22						10 24							11 19		
Highbridge & Burnham	d									09 30						10 32							11 27		
Weston-super-Mare	a									09 42						10 40							11 37		
	d		08 39			09 10				09 44			10 10			10 40					11 10		11 39		
Weston Milton	d					09 13							10 13								11 13				
Worle	d		08 45			09 18				09 49			10 18			10 46					11 18		11 45		
Yatton	d		08 51			09 23				09 55			10 23			10 52					11 23		11 51		
Nailsea & Backwell	d		08 57			09 29				10 01			10 29			10 58					11 29		11 57		
Parson Street	d					09 36							10 36								11 36				
Bedminster	d					09 38							10 38								11 38				←
Bristol Temple Meads 10	a	08 48	09 08	09 25		09 43				10 13	10 25		10 43			11 13		11 24	11 25		11 43		12 10	11 54	12 10
	d	09 00	09 21	09 30	09 41	09 45		09 54	10 00	10 21	10 30	10 41	10 45	10 54	11 00	11 21			11 30	11 41	11 45	11 54	12 21	12 00	12 21
Lawrence Hill	d					09 48							10 48								11 48		→		
Stapleton Road	d		09 25			09 50				10 25			10 50			11 25					11 50				12 25
Filton Abbey Wood	d		09a30		09 48	09 56		10a01		10a30		10 48	10 56	11a01		11a30				11 48	11 56	12a01			12a29
Bristol Parkway 7	a	09 08		09 38	09 52	10 03			10 08		10 38	10 52	11 03		11 08				11 38	11 52	12 03			12 08	
	d				09 52							10 52								11 52					
Yate	d				10 01							11 01								12 01					
Cam & Dursley	d				10 14							11 14								12 14					
Gloucester 7	a				10 33							11 32								12 33					

		XC		GW	GW	GW	XC	GW	XC	GW	GW	GW		GW	XC	GW	XC	GW	GW	GW	XC	GW		XC	GW
		◇1 🛒		◇		◇	◇1 🛒		◇1 🛒	◇		◇			◇1 🛒		◇1 🛒	◇		◇	◇1 🛒			◇1 🛒	◇
Taunton	d	11 51						12 07	12 51					13 07	13 16		13 54					14 07		14 52	
Bridgwater	d							12 19						13 19								14 19			
Highbridge & Burnham	d							12 27						13 27								14 27			
Weston-super-Mare	a							12 37						13 37								14 37			
	d				12 10			12 39			13 10			13 39					14 10			14 39			
Weston Milton	d				12 13						13 13								14 13						
Worle	d				12 18			12 45			13 18			13 45					14 18			14 45			
Yatton	d				12 23			12 51			13 23			13 51					14 23			14 51			
Nailsea & Backwell	d				12 29			12 57			13 29			13 57					14 29			14 57			
Parson Street	d				12 36						13 36								14 36						
Bedminster	d				12 38						13 38					←			14 38						
Bristol Temple Meads 10	a	12 24			12 43			13 09	13 23		13 43			14 11	13 55	14 11	14 26		14 43			15 10		15 24	
	d	12 30		12 41	12 45	12 54	13 00	13 21	13 30	13 41	13 45	13 54		14 21	14 00	14 21	14 30	14 41	14 45	14 54	15 00	15 21		15 30	15 41
Lawrence Hill	d				12 48						13 48			→					14 48						
Stapleton Road	d				12 50			13 25			13 50					14 25			14 50			15 25			
Filton Abbey Wood	d			12 48	12 56	13a01		13a30		13 48	13 56	14a01				14a30		14 48	14 56	15a01		15a30			15 48
Bristol Parkway 7	a	12 38		12 52	13 03		13 08		13 38	13 52	14 03				14 08		14 38	14 52	15 03		15 08			15 38	15 52
	d			12 52						13 52								14 52							15 52
Yate	d			13 01						14 01								15 01							16 01
Cam & Dursley	d			13 14						14 14								15 14							16 14
Gloucester 7	a			13 34						14 33								15 32							16 33

A The Night Riviera

For connections to London Paddington please refer to Table 125

Taunton - Gloucester

Network Diagram - see first Page of Table 132

		GW	XC	GW	GW	XC	GW	GW		GW	XC	GW	XC	GW	GW	GW	GW	XC		GW	XC	GW	GW	GW	XC
																								R	
			◇1	◇		◇1				◇	◇1		◇1	◇		◇		◇1			◇1				◇1
			trolley			trolley					trolley		trolley					trolley			trolley				trolley
Taunton	d		15 04		15 07	15 51						16 07	16 51				17 07	17 21			17 51				
Bridgwater	d				15 19							16 19					17 17								
Highbridge & Burnham	d				15 27							16 27					17 25								
Weston-super-Mare	a		15 23		15 37							16 37					17 37								
	d	15 10	15 30		15 39			16 10				16 39			17 10		17 40						18 10		
Weston Milton	d	15 13						16 13							17 13								18 13		
Worle	d	15 18			15 45			16 18				16 45			17 18		17 45						18 18		
Yatton	d	15 23			15 51			16 23				16 51			17 23		17 51						18 23		
Nailsea & Backwell	d	15 29			15 57			16 29				16 57			17 29		17 57						18 29		
Parson Street	d	15 36						16 36				17 04			17 36								18 36		
Bedminster	d	15 38						16 38							17 38					←			18 38		
Bristol Temple Meads 10	a	15 43	15 49		16 09	16 24		16 43				17 11	17 24		17 43		18 11	17 53		18 11	18 24		18 43		
	d	15 45	16 00	15 54	16 21	16 30	16 41	16 45		16 54	17 00	17 21	17 30	17 41	17 45	17 54	18 21	18 00		18 21	18 30	18 41	18 45	18 54	19 00
Lawrence Hill	d	15 48						16 48							17 48		→						18 48		
Stapleton Road	d	15 50			16 25			16 50				17 25			17 50					18 25			18 50		
Filton Abbey Wood	d	15 56		16a01	16a30		16 48	16 56		17a01		17a30		17 48	17 56	18a01				18a30		18 48	18 56	19a01	
Bristol Parkway 7	a	16 03	16 08			16 38	16 52	17 03			17 08		17 38	17 52	18 03			18 08			18 38	18 52	19 03		19 08
	d						16 52							17 52								18 52			
Yate	d						17 01							18 01								19 01			
Cam & Dursley	d						17 14							18 14								19 14			
Gloucester 7	a						17 33							18 33								19 33			

		GW	XC	GW		GW	GW	XC	GW	XC	XC	GW	GW	GW		GW	GW	GW	GW	GW	GW	GW			
			◇1				◇	◇1		◇1	◇1	◇1		◇			◇1	◇		◇1		◇			
			trolley							trolley	trolley	cup					cup			cup					
Taunton	d	18 07	18 54						19 07		19 51					20 17	21 14			21 30	21 35				
Bridgwater	d	18 19							19 19							20 29					21 47				
Highbridge & Burnham	d	18 27							19 27							20 37					21 55				
Weston-super-Mare	a	18 37							19 37							20 48				21 51	22 05				
	d	18 39				19 10			19 39			20 10				20 50				21 53	22 07				
Weston Milton	d					19 13										20 53					22 10				
Worle	d	18 45				19 18			19 45							20 57					22 14				
Yatton	d	18 51				19 23			19 51							21 03					22 20				
Nailsea & Backwell	d	18 57				19 29			19 57							21 09					22 26				
Parson Street	d					19 36										21 17					22 33				
Bedminster	d					19 38										21 19					22 36				
Bristol Temple Meads 10	a	19 09	19 26			19 43			20 09		20 24	20 30				21 24	21 47			22 12	22 42				
	d	19 21	19 30	19 41		19 45	19 54	20 00		20 21	20 30		20 43	20 54		21 29		21 54	22 06			22 54			
Lawrence Hill	d					19 48																			
Stapleton Road	d					19 50																			
Filton Abbey Wood	d	19a28		19 48		19 56	20a01			20a27			20 48	21a01		21a36		22a01	22 14			23a01			
Bristol Parkway 7	a		19 38	19 52		20 03		20 08			20 38		20 52						22 17						
	d			19 52									20 52						22 18						
Yate	d			20 01									21 04						22 28						
Cam & Dursley	d			20 14									21 18						22 43						
Gloucester 7	a			20 33									21 34						23 01						

Sundays

until 1 January

		GW	XC	GW	GW	GW	XC	GW	XC	GW		GW	GW	XC	GW	XC	GW	XC	GW	GW		XC	XC	GW	GW
										R															
		◇1	◇1		◇	◇1	◇1	◇	◇1				◇1	◇1		◇1	◇1	◇1	◇			◇1	◇1		◇
		cup	trolley			cup	trolley		trolley				cup	trolley		trolley	cup	trolley				trolley	trolley		
Taunton	d				08 35			10 19	10 51			11 36	11 48	11 53		12 00		12 51		13 11		13 25	13 51		
Bridgwater	d				08 47			10 31				11 48								13 23					
Highbridge & Burnham	d				08 55			10 39				11 55								13 30					
Weston-super-Mare	a				09 06			10 49				12 05				12 20				13 41					
	d	08 11			09 08	09 56		10 51				12 07				12 21	12 51			13 43					
Weston Milton	d				09 11							12 10								13 46					
Worle	d	08 18			09 15	10 03		10 57				12 18					12 58			13 50					
Yatton	d	08 25			09 21	10 10		11 03				12 23					13 05			13 56					
Nailsea & Backwell	d	08 31			09 27	10 16		11 09				12 29					13 12			14 02					
Parson Street	d																								
Bedminster	d											12 40													
Bristol Temple Meads 10	a	08 42			09 38	10 27		11 20	11 27			12 43	12 23	12 27		12 45	13 20	13 26		14 14		13 57	14 26		
	d		09 15	09 41	09 48		10 30	11 23	11 30	11 48				12 30	12 41	13 00		13 30	13 48			14 00	14 30	14 41	14 48
Lawrence Hill	d							11 26																	
Stapleton Road	d							11a28																	
Filton Abbey Wood	d			09 48	09a55					11a55					12 48				13a55					14 48	14a55
Bristol Parkway 7	a		09 23	09 53			10 38		11 38					12 38	12 52	13 08		13 38				14 08	14 38	14 52	
	d		09 25	09 53											12 52									14 53	
Yate	d			10 03											13 02									15 03	
Cam & Dursley	d			10 17											13 16									15 17	
Gloucester 7	a		09 54	10 32											13 31									15 35	

For connections to London Paddington please refer to Table 125

Table 134

Sundays

until 1 January

Taunton - Gloucester

Network Diagram - see first Page of Table 132

		XC	GW	XC	GW	XC		GW	XC	GW	GW	GW	XC	GW	XC	GW		GW	GW	XC	GW	GW	XC	GW	GW
																		R							
		◇1	◇1	◇1	◇	◇1			◇1		◇		◇1	◇1	◇1	◇			◇1	◇1		◇1	◇1		◇
		🛒	☕			🛒			🛒				🛒	☕	🛒				☕	🛒		☕	🛒		
Taunton	d			14 54				15 18	15 54				16 01	16 40	16 53				16 59		17 19	17 48	17 51		
Bridgwater	d							15 30											17 10		17 30				
Highbridge & Burnham	d							15 37											17 18		17 37				
Weston-super-Mare	a							15 47					16 20	17 01					17 28		17 48				
	d		14 51					15 49				16 14	16 30	17 02		17 07			17 29		17 50				
Weston Milton	d							15 52				16 17				17 10									
Worle	d		14 58					15 56				16 22				17 17					17 56				
Yatton	d		15 05					16 02				16 28				17 23			17 40		18 02				
Nailsea & Backwell	d		15 11					16 08				16 34				17 29			17 46		18 08				
Parson Street	d											16 41													
Bedminster	d											16 44				17 39									
Bristol Temple Meads 10	a		15 20	15 27				16 20	16 27			16 49	16 52	17 22	17 26	17 42			17 58		18 20	18 25	18 27		
	d	15 00		15 30	15 48	16 00			16 30	16 41	16 48	16 53	17 00		17 30			17 48		18 00			18 30	18 41	18 48
Lawrence Hill	d											16 56													
Stapleton Road	d											16a58													
Filton Abbey Wood	d				15a55					16 48	16a55							17a55						18 48	18a55
Bristol Parkway 7	a	15 08		15 38		16 08			16 38	16 52			17 08		17 38					18 08			18 38	18 52	
	d									16 52														18 52	
Yate	d									17 02														19 02	
Cam & Dursley	d									17 16														19 16	
Gloucester 7	a									17 32														19 33	

		GW		XC	GW	XC	GW	GW	XC	XC	GW	GW		GW	GW	GW	GW	XC	GW	GW	GW				
				◇1	◇	◇1	◇	◇1	◇1	◇1		◇		◇1		◇	◇1	◇1		◇					
				🛒		🛒		☕	🛒	🛒				☕			☕								
Taunton	d				18 22	18 52		18 57	19 25	19 54					20 20		21 23		21 35						
Bridgwater	d				18 34			19 07							20 32				21 48						
Highbridge & Burnham	d				18 41			19 14							20 40				21 55						
Weston-super-Mare	a				18 52			19 25							20 51				22 05						
	d	18 16			18 53			19 27						20 26	20 55				22 07		23 47				
Weston Milton	d	18 19													20 58				22 10		23 50				
Worle	d	18 24			18 59									20 33	21 03						23 54				
Yatton	d	18 30			19 04			19 36						20 39	21 09				22 18		23 59				
Nailsea & Backwell	d	18 36			19 10			19 42						20 46	21 15				22 24		00 06				
Parson Street	d	18 43																							
Bedminster	d	18 46													21 26				22 34		00 15				
Bristol Temple Meads 10	a	18 50			19 23	19 26		19 54	19 57	20 27				20 57	21 31		22 00		22 38		00 19				
	d			19 00		19 30	19 48		20 00	20 30	20 41	20 48				21 48		22 10		22 48					
Lawrence Hill	d																								
Stapleton Road	d																								
Filton Abbey Wood	d						19a55				20 48	20a55				21a55				22a55					
Bristol Parkway 7	a			19 08		19 38			20 08	20 38	20 52							22 18							
	d										20 52														
Yate	d										21 02														
Cam & Dursley	d										21 16														
Gloucester 7	a										21 33														

Sundays

8 January to 12 February

		GW	XC	GW	GW	GW	XC	GW	XC	GW		GW	GW	XC	GW	XC	GW	XC	GW	GW		XC	XC	GW	GW
										R															
		◇1	◇1		◇	◇1	◇1	◇	◇1				◇1	◇1		◇1	◇1	◇1	◇			◇1	◇1		◇
		☕	🛒			☕	🛒		🛒				☕	🛒		🛒	☕	🛒				🛒	🛒		
Taunton	d				08 35			10 19	10 51			11 36	11 48	11 53		12 00		12 51		13 11		13 25	13 51		
Bridgwater	d				08 47			10 31				11 48								13 23					
Highbridge & Burnham	d				08 55			10 39				11 55								13 30					
Weston-super-Mare	a				09 06			10 49				12 05				12 20				13 41					
	d	08 11			09 08	09 56		10 51				12 07				12 21	12 51			13 43					
Weston Milton	d				09 11							12 10								13 46					
Worle	d	08 18			09 15	10 03		10 57				12 18					12 58			13 50					
Yatton	d	08 25			09 21	10 10		11 03				12 23					13 05			13 56					
Nailsea & Backwell	d	08 31			09 27	10 16		11 09				12 29					13 12			14 02					
Parson Street	d																								
Bedminster	d											12 40													
Bristol Temple Meads 10	a	08 42			09 38	10 27		11 20	11 27			12 43	12 23	12 27		12 45	13 20	13 26		14 14		13 57	14 26		
	d		09 15	09 41	09 48		10 30	11 23	11 30	11 48				12 30	12 41	13 00		13 30	13 48			14 00	14 30	14 41	14 48
Lawrence Hill	d							11 26																	
Stapleton Road	d							11a28																	
Filton Abbey Wood	d			09 48	09a55					11a55					12 48				13a55					14 48	14a55
Bristol Parkway 7	a		09 23	09 53			10 38		11 38					12 38	12 52	13 08		13 38				14 08	14 38	14 52	
	d		09 25	09 53											12 52									14 53	
Yate	d			10 03											13 02									15 03	
Cam & Dursley	d			10 17											13 16									15 17	
Gloucester 7	a		09 54	10 32											13 31									15 35	

For connections to London Paddington please refer to Table 125

Table 134

Taunton - Gloucester

Sundays

8 January to 12 February

Network Diagram - see first Page of Table 132

		XC	GW	XC	GW	XC		GW	XC	GW	GW	GW	XC	GW	XC	GW		GW	GW	XC	GW	GW	XC	GW	GW
		◇1	◇1	◇1	◇	◇1			◇1		◇		◇1	◇1	◇1	◇		R	◇1	◇1		◇1	◇1		◇
		🛒	☕			🛒			🛒				🛒	☕	🛒				☕	🛒		☕	🛒		
Taunton	d			14 54				15 18	15 54				16 01	16 40	16 53				16 59		17 19	17 48	17 51		
Bridgwater	d							15 30											17 10		17 30				
Highbridge & Burnham	d							15 37											17 18		17 37				
Weston-super-Mare	a							15 47					16 20	17 01					17 28		17 48				
	d		14 51					15 49				16 14	16 30	17 02		17 07			17 29		17 50				
Weston Milton	d							15 52				16 17				17 10									
Worle	d		14 58					15 56				16 22				17 17					17 56				
Yatton	d		15 05					16 02				16 28				17 23			17 40		18 02				
Nailsea & Backwell	d		15 11					16 08				16 34				17 29			17 46		18 08				
Parson Street	d											16 41													
Bedminster	d											16 44				17 39									
Bristol Temple Meads 10	a		15 20	15 27				16 20	16 27			16 49	16 52	17 22	17 26	17 42			17 58		18 20	18 25	18 27		
	d	15 00		15 30	15 48	16 00			16 30	16 41	16 48	16 53	17 00		17 30			17 48		18 00			18 30	18 41	18 48
Lawrence Hill	d											16 56													
Stapleton Road	d											16a58													
Filton Abbey Wood	d				15a55					16 48	16a55							17a55						18 48	18a55
Bristol Parkway 7	a	15 08		15 38		16 08			16 38	16 52			17 08		17 38					18 08			18 38	18 52	
	d									16 52														18 52	
Yate	d									17 02														19 02	
Cam & Dursley	d									17 16														19 16	
Gloucester 7	a									17 32														19 33	

		GW		XC	GW	XC	GW	GW	XC	XC	GW	GW		GW	GW	GW	GW	XC	GW	GW	GW				
				◇1	◇	◇1	◇	◇1	◇1	◇1		◇		◇1		◇	◇1	◇1		◇					
				🛒		🛒		☕	🛒	🛒				☕			☕								
Taunton	d				18 22	18 52		18 57	19 25	19 54					20 20		21 23		21 35						
Bridgwater	d				18 34			19 07							20 32				21 48						
Highbridge & Burnham	d				18 41			19 14							20 40				21 55						
Weston-super-Mare	a				18 52			19 25							20 51				22 05						
	d	18 16			18 53			19 27						20 26	20 55				22 07		23 47				
Weston Milton	d	18 19													20 58				22 10		23 50				
Worle	d	18 24			18 59									20 33	21 03						23 54				
Yatton	d	18 30			19 04			19 36						20 39	21 09				22 18		23 59				
Nailsea & Backwell	d	18 36			19 10			19 42						20 46	21 15				22 24		00 06				
Parson Street	d	18 43																							
Bedminster	d	18 46													21 26				22 34		00 15				
Bristol Temple Meads 10	a	18 50			19 23	19 26		19 54	19 57	20 27				20 57	21 31		22 00		22 38		00 19				
	d			19 00		19 30	19 48		20 00	20 30	20 41	20 48				21 48		22 10		22 48					
Lawrence Hill	d																								
Stapleton Road	d																								
Filton Abbey Wood	d						19a55				20 48	20a55				21a55				22a55					
Bristol Parkway 7	a			19 08		19 38			20 08	20 38	20 52							22 18							
	d										20 52														
Yate	d										21 02														
Cam & Dursley	d										21 16														
Gloucester 7	a										21 33														

Sundays

19 February to 25 March

		GW	GW	XC	GW	GW	GW	GW	XC	GW		XC	GW	GW	GW	XC	GW	XC	GW	XC		GW	XC	GW	XC
		◇1	◇1	◇1	◇			◇1	◇1	◇		◇1	R		◇1	◇1		◇1	◇1	◇1		◇	◇1		◇1
		☕	☕	🛒				☕	🛒			🛒			☕	🛒		🛒	☕	🛒			🛒		🛒
Taunton	d				08 35					10 19				11 36	11 50			12 00		12 51				13 11	13 51
Bridgwater	d				08 47					10 31				11 48										13 23	
Highbridge & Burnham	d				08 55					10 39				11 55										13 30	
Weston-super-Mare	a				09 06					10 49				12 05				12 20						13 41	
	d		08 11		09 08			09 56		10 51				12 07				12 21	12 51					13 43	
Weston Milton	d				09 11									12 10										13 46	
Worle	d		08 18		09 15			10 03		10 57				12 18					12 58					13 50	
Yatton	d		08 25		09 21			10 10		11 03				12 23					13 05					13 56	
Nailsea & Backwell	d		08 31		09 27			10 16		11 09				12 29					13 12					14 02	
Parson Street	d																								
Bedminster	d													12 40											
Bristol Temple Meads 10	a		08 42		09 39			10 27		11 20				12 43	12 24			12 45	13 20	13 26				14 14	14 26
	d	08 25		09 15		09 41	09 49		10 30	11 23		11 30	11 48			12 30	12 41	13 00		13 30		13 48	14 00		14 30
Lawrence Hill	d									11 26															
Stapleton Road	d									11a28															
Filton Abbey Wood	d					09 48	09 56						11 55				12 48					13 55			
Bristol Parkway 7	a	08 34		09 23		09 53	10 05		10 38			11 38	11 59			12 38	12 52	13 08		13 38		13 59	14 08		14 38
	d			09 25		09 53											12 52								
Yate	d					10 03											13 02								
Cam & Dursley	d					10 17											13 16								
Gloucester 7	a			09 54		10 32											13 31								

For connections to London Paddington please refer to Table 125

Table 134

Sundays

19 February to 25 March

Taunton - Gloucester

Network Diagram - see first Page of Table 132

		GW	GW	XC	GW	XC		GW	XC	GW	XC	GW	GW	GW	XC	GW		XC	GW	GW	GW	XC	GW	GW	XC
																				B					
			◇	◇1	◇1	◇1		◇	◇1		◇1		◇		◇1	◇1		◇1	◇		◇1	◇1		◇1	◇1
				🛒	☕	🛒			🛒		🛒				🛒	☕		🛒			☕	🛒		☕	🛒
Taunton	d					14 54				15 18	15 54					16 40		16 54			16 59		17 19	17 48	17 51
Bridgwater	d									15 30											17 10		17 30		
Highbridge & Burnham	d									15 37											17 18		17 37		
Weston-super-Mare	a									15 47						17 01					17 28		17 48		
	d				14 51					15 49				16 14		17 02			17 07		17 29		17 50		
Weston Milton	d									15 52				16 17					17 10						
Worle	d				14 58					15 56				16 22					17 17				17 56		
Yatton	d				15 05					16 02				16 28					17 22		17 40		18 02		
Nailsea & Backwell	d				15 11					16 08				16 34					17 28		17 46		18 08		
Parson Street	d													16 41											
Bedminster	d													16 44					17 39						
Bristol Temple Meads 10	a				15 20	15 27				16 20	16 27			16 49		17 20		17 27	17 42		17 58		18 20	18 22	18 27
	d	14 41	14 48	15 00		15 30		15 48	16 00		16 30	16 41	16 48	16 53	17 00			17 30		17 48		18 00			18 30
Lawrence Hill	d													16 56											
Stapleton Road	d													16a58											
Filton Abbey Wood	d	14 48	14 55					15 55				16 48	16 55							17 55					
Bristol Parkway 7	a	14 52	14 59	15 08		15 38		15 59	16 08		16 38	16 52	16 59		17 08			17 38		17 59		18 08			18 38
	d	14 53										16 52													
Yate	d	15 03										17 02													
Cam & Dursley	d	15 17										17 16													
Gloucester 7	a	15 35										17 32													

		GW		GW	GW	XC	GW	XC	GW	XC	XC	GW		GW	GW	GW	XC	GW	XC	GW	GW	GW	GW		
				◇		◇1	◇	◇1	◇	◇1	◇1			◇	◇1	◇	◇1	◇	◇1	◇1		◇			
						🛒		🛒		🛒	🛒				☕					☕					
Taunton	d						18 40	18 52			19 54					20 20	20 40		21 13	21 26	21 35				
Bridgwater	d						18 52									20 32					21 48				
Highbridge & Burnham	d						19 00									20 40					21 55				
Weston-super-Mare	a						19 10									20 51					22 05				
	d				18 16		19 15								20 26	20 55					22 07		23 47		
Weston Milton	d				18 19											20 58					22 10		23 50		
Worle	d				18 24		19 20								20 33	21 05							23 54		
Yatton	d				18 30		19 26								20 39	21 11					22 18		23 59		
Nailsea & Backwell	d				18 36		19 32								20 46	21 17					22 24		00 06		
Parson Street	d				18 43																				
Bedminster	d				18 46											21 28					22 34		00 15		
Bristol Temple Meads 10	a				18 50		19 44	19 27			20 27				20 57	21 31	21 13		21 50	22 00	22 38		00 19		
	d	18 41		18 48		19 00		19 30	19 48	20 00	20 30	20 41		20 48			21 20	21 48	22 10			22 48			
Lawrence Hill	d																								
Stapleton Road	d																								
Filton Abbey Wood	d	18 48		18 55					19 55			20 48		20 55				21 55				22 55			
Bristol Parkway 7	a	18 52		18 59		19 08		19 38	19 59	20 08	20 38	20 52		20 59			21 28	22 01	22 18			22 59			
	d	18 52										20 52													
Yate	d	19 02										21 02													
Cam & Dursley	d	19 16										21 16													
Gloucester 7	a	19 33										21 33													

Sundays

from 1 April

		GW	XC	GW	GW	GW	XC	GW	XC	GW		GW	GW	XC	GW	XC	GW	XC	GW	XC		XC	GW	GW	XC
										B															
		◇1	◇1		◇	◇1	◇1	◇	◇1				◇1	◇1		◇1	◇1	◇1		◇1		◇1		◇	◇1
		☕	🛒			☕	🛒		🛒				☕	🛒		🛒	☕	🛒		🛒		🛒			🛒
Taunton	d				08 35			10 19	10 51			11 36	11 48	11 53		12 00		12 51	13 11	13 25		13 51			
Bridgwater	d				08 47			10 31				11 48							13 23						
Highbridge & Burnham	d				08 55			10 39				11 55							13 30						
Weston-super-Mare	a				09 06			10 49				12 05				12 20			13 41						
	d	08 11			09 08	09 56		10 51				12 07				12 21	12 51		13 43						
Weston Milton	d				09 11							12 10							13 46						
Worle	d	08 18			09 15	10 03		10 57				12 18					12 58		13 50						
Yatton	d	08 25			09 21	10 10		11 03				12 23					13 05		13 56						
Nailsea & Backwell	d	08 31			09 27	10 16		11 09				12 29					13 12		14 02						
Parson Street	d																								
Bedminster	d											12 40													
Bristol Temple Meads 10	a	08 42			09 38	10 27		11 20	11 27			12 43	12 23	12 27		12 45	13 22	13 26	14 14	13 57		14 26			
	d		09 15	09 41	09 48		10 30	11 23	11 30	11 48				12 30	12 41	13 00		13 30		14 00		14 30	14 41	14 50	15 00
Lawrence Hill	d							11 26																	
Stapleton Road	d							11a28																	
Filton Abbey Wood	d			09 48	09a55					11a55					12 48								14 48	14a57	
Bristol Parkway 7	a		09 23	09 53			10 38		11 38					12 38	12 52	13 08		13 38		14 08		14 38	14 52		15 08
	d		09 25	09 53											12 52								14 53		
Yate	d			10 03											13 02								15 03		
Cam & Dursley	d			10 17											13 16								15 17		
Gloucester 7	a		09 54	10 32											13 31								15 35		

For connections to London Paddington please refer to Table 125

Table 134

Sundays
from 1 April

Taunton - Gloucester

Network Diagram - see first Page of Table 132

		GW	XC	GW	XC	GW		XC	GW	GW	GW	XC	GW	XC	GW	GW		GW	XC	GW	GW	XC	GW	GW	GW
																R									
		◇1	◇1	◇	◇1			◇1		◇		◇1	◇1	◇1	◇			◇1	◇1		◇1	◇1		◇	
		☕			🛒			🛒				🛒	☕	🛒				☕	🛒		☕	🛒			
Taunton	d		14 54			15 18		15 54				16 01	16 40	16 53				16 59		17 19	17 48	17 51			
Bridgwater	d					15 30												17 10		17 30					
Highbridge & Burnham	d					15 37												17 18		17 37					
Weston-super-Mare	a					15 47						16 20	17 01					17 28		17 48					
	d	14 51				15 49					16 14	16 30	17 02		17 07			17 29		17 50					18 16
Weston Milton	d					15 52					16 17				17 10										18 19
Worle	d	14 58				15 56					16 22				17 17					17 56					18 24
Yatton	d	15 05				16 02					16 28				17 23			17 40		18 02					18 30
Nailsea & Backwell	d	15 11				16 08					16 34				17 29			17 46		18 08					18 36
Parson Street	d										16 41														18 43
Bedminster	d										16 44				17 39										18 46
Bristol Temple Meads 10	a	15 20	15 27			16 20		16 27			16 49	16 54	17 20	17 26	17 42			17 58		18 20	18 25	18 27			18 50
	d		15 30	15 48	16 00			16 30	16 41	16 48	16 53	17 00		17 30		17 48			18 00			18 30	18 41	18 48	
Lawrence Hill	d										16 56														
Stapleton Road	d										16a58														
Filton Abbey Wood	d			15a55					16 48	16a55						17a55							18 48	18a55	
Bristol Parkway 7	a		15 38		16 08			16 38	16 52			17 08		17 38					18 08			18 38	18 52		
	d								16 52														18 52		
Yate	d								17 02														19 02		
Cam & Dursley	d								17 16														19 16		
Gloucester 7	a								17 32														19 33		

		XC		GW	XC	GW	GW	XC	XC	GW	GW	GW		GW	GW	GW	XC	GW	GW	GW					
		◇1		◇	◇1	◇	◇1	◇1	◇1		◇	◇1			◇	◇1	◇1		◇						
		🛒			🛒		☕	🛒	🛒			☕				☕									
Taunton	d			18 22	18 52		18 57	19 25	19 54					20 20		21 23		21 35							
Bridgwater	d			18 34			19 07							20 32				21 48							
Highbridge & Burnham	d			18 41			19 14							20 40				21 55							
Weston-super-Mare	a			18 52			19 25							20 51				22 05							
	d			19 12			19 27					20 26		20 55				22 07		23 47					
Weston Milton	d													20 58				22 10		23 50					
Worle	d			19 18								20 33		21 03						23 54					
Yatton	d			19 23			19 36					20 39		21 09				22 18		23 59					
Nailsea & Backwell	d			19 29			19 42					20 46		21 15				22 24		00 06					
Parson Street	d																								
Bedminster	d													21 26				22 34		00 15					
Bristol Temple Meads 10	a			19 42	19 26		19 54	19 57	20 27			20 57		21 31		22 00		22 38		00 19					
	d	19 00			19 30	19 48		20 00	20 30	20 41	20 48				21 48		22 10		22 48						
Lawrence Hill	d																								
Stapleton Road	d																								
Filton Abbey Wood	d					19a55				20 48	20a55				21a55				22a55						
Bristol Parkway 7	a	19 08			19 38			20 08	20 38	20 52							22 18								
	d									20 52															
Yate	d									21 02															
Cam & Dursley	d									21 16															
Gloucester 7	a									21 33															

For connections to London Paddington please refer to Table 125

Route Diagram for Tables 135, 136, 139, 140, 142, 143, 144

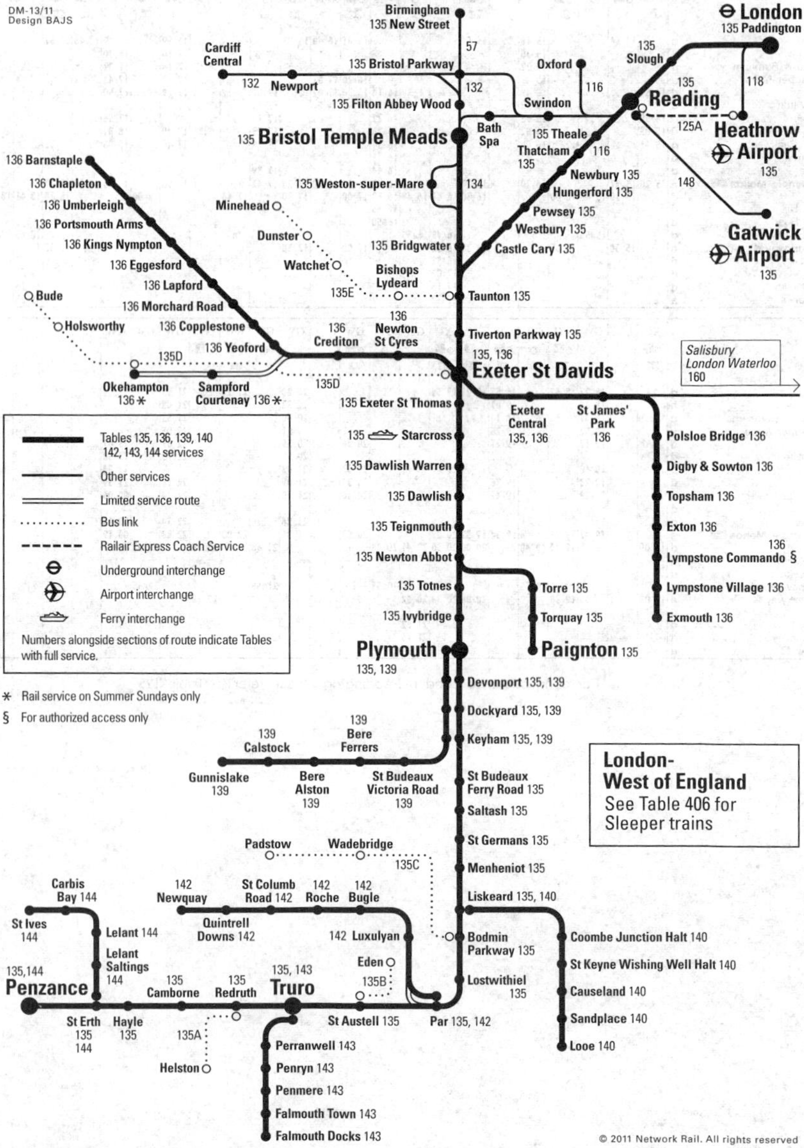

London and Birmingham - Devon and Cornwall

Route Diagram - see first Page of Table 135

Miles	Miles			GW	GW	GW	XC	GW	GW	GW	GW	XC		XC	GW	GW	GW	GW	GW	GW	GW	GW		GW	GW
				MX	MO	MO	MO	MX	MX	MX	MX	MO		MX		MO									
						◇1		◇1		◇1	R	◇1		◇1		R				1		1		◇	
					A	B	A				C														
0	—	**London Paddington** 15 ⊖	d			19p57		20p35		21p45	23p45					23p50									
18½	—	Slough 3	d																						
36	—	**Reading** 7	d			20p31		21p02		22p11	00u37					00u37									
41¼	—	Theale	d																						
49½	—	Thatcham	d																						
53	—	Newbury	d					21p18																	
61½	—	Hungerford	d																						
75¼	—	Pewsey	d					21p38																	
95½	—	Westbury	d			21p36		21p57			01 45														
115¼	—	Castle Cary	d			21p54		22p15																	
—	0	**Birmingham New Street** 12	d																						
—	—	Cardiff Central 7	d																						
—	—	Newport (South Wales)	d																						
—	—	Swindon	d							22p49															
—	87	Bristol Parkway 7	d																						
—	88¼	Filton Abbey Wood	d																						
—	—	Bath Spa 7	d							23p19															
—	92¾	**Bristol Temple Meads** 10	d						23p06	23p35						02 55								05 24	
—	112¾	Weston-super-Mare	d						23p42	00s05														05 45	
—	126½	Bridgwater	d						00 02	00s24														06 03	
143	138¼	Taunton	d			22p19		22p37	00s14	00s36	02 35													06 18	
157¼	—	Tiverton Parkway	d			22p33		22p50	00s31	00s49														06 33	
173¾	—	**Exeter St Davids** 6	a			22p52		23p06	00 50	01 07	03 06					04 04								06 51	
—	—	Exmouth	d																						06 45
—	—	Exeter Central	d																						07 12
—	—	**Exeter St Davids** 6	d			22p52	22p55	23p08			03 11					04 35		05 34	06 11		06 28			06 55	07 18
174¾	—	Exeter St Thomas	d															05 38	06 14					06 58	07 21
182¼	—	Starcross	d															05 46	06 22					07 07	07 29
184¼	—	Dawlish Warren	d															05 51	06 27					07 12	07 34
185¾	—	Dawlish	d			23p06												05 55	06 31		06 42			07 16	07 38
188¾	—	Teignmouth	d			23p12												06 00	06 36		06 47			07 21	07 43
193¾	—	Newton Abbot	a			23p19	23b25	23p28			03 31					04 55		06 07	06 44		06 55			07 28	07 50
—	—		d		23p10	23p19		23p28			03 33					04 56	05 42	06 09	06 45		06 55	07 06		07 28	07 52
—	5¼	Torre	d														05 50	06 17	06 53			07 15			08 00
—	6	Torquay	d														05 53	06 20	06 56			07 20			08 03
—	8¼	Paignton	a														06 00	06 28	07 06			07 29			08 12
202½	—	Totnes	d		23p35	23p32	23b50	23p42													07 09			07 42	
214	—	Ivybridge	d																		07 26			07 58	
225¾	—	**Plymouth**	a		00 20	00 01	00 35	00 11			04 12					05 35					07 40			08 11	
—	—		d	22p31							05 43	05 43		06 28		06 28				07 02	07 53			08 14	
227	—	Devonport	d																	07 07				08 17	
227½	—	Dockyard	d																						
228	—	Keyham	d																						
228¾	—	St Budeaux Ferry Road	d																						
230	—	Saltash	d	22p40																07 15	08 02			08 24	
235	—	St Germans	d	22p47																07 23	08 09			08 31	
240¼	—	Menheniot	d																						
243½	—	Liskeard 6	d	22p59							06 08	06 08		06 51		07 09				07 36	08 21			08 43	
252½	—	Bodmin Parkway	d	23p11							06 22	06 22		07 03		07 23				07 49	08 33			08 55	
256	—	Lostwithiel	d	23p16							06 28	06 28		07 09		07 29				07 55	08 40			09 00	
260½	—	Par	d	23p24							06 37	06 37		07 15		07 38				08 04	08a54			09 08	
—	—	Newquay	a																						
265	—	St Austell	d	23p31							06 46	06 46		07 22		07 46				08 11				09 16	
279½	—	Truro	d	23p50							07 06	07 06		07 39		08 06				08 30				09 34	
288½	—	Redruth	d	00 03							07 18	07 18		07 50		08 20				08 42				09 47	
292	—	Camborne	d	00 09							07 26	07 26		07 57		08 27				08 48				09 53	
298	—	Hayle	d	00 16							07 35	07 35		08 05		08 38				08 57				10 00	
299½	—	St Erth	d	00 20							07 41	07 41		08 11	08 28	08 45				09 02				10 08	
305¼	—	**Penzance**	a	00 40							07 53	07 53		08 19	08 40	08 59				09 12				10 16	

A from 20 February until 26 March
B from 2 April
C The Night Riviera
b Previous night, stops to set down only

For connections from Heathrow Airport, Gatwick Airport and Oxford please refer to Tables 125A, 148 and 116

London and Birmingham - Devon and Cornwall

Route Diagram - see first Page of Table 135

		XC	GW	GW	GW	GW	XC	GW	GW	XC	GW	GW	GW	XC	GW	GW	GW	GW	GW	XC	GW	GW	XC
		◇1			◇		◇1	◇1	◇	◇1		◇1	◇	◇1		◇1	◇	◇	◇	◇1		◇1	◇1
								A				B										C	
							[trolley]	[restaurant]		[trolley]		[restaurant] ⊘		[trolley]		[restaurant]				[trolley]		[restaurant] ⊘	[trolley]
London Paddington 15 ⊖	d							07 06				07 30				09 06						10 06	
Slough 3	d																						
Reading 7	d							07 33				07 57				09 33						10u33	
Theale	d																						
Thatcham	d																						
Newbury	d							07 48															
Hungerford	d																						
Pewsey	d							08 07															
Westbury	d							08 25															
Castle Cary	d															10 29							
Birmingham New Street 12	d						06 42			07 12				08 12						09 12			09 42
Cardiff Central 7	d												08 00						09 00				
Newport (South Wales)	d												08 15						09 15				
Swindon	d											08 27											
Bristol Parkway 7	d				06 24		07 58			08 26				09 26						10 27			10 55
Filton Abbey Wood	d				06 27								08 42						09 42				
Bath Spa 7	d											08 57											
Bristol Temple Meads 10	d	06 34			06 42		08 10			08 44		09 13	08 55	09 44					09 55	10 44			11 15
Weston-super-Mare	d				07 06								09 29						10 23				11 37
Bridgwater	d				07 25								09 48						10 42				
Taunton	d	07 08			07 39		08 43	09 02		09 17		09 46	10 02	10 17		10 51			10 58	11 18			12 02
Tiverton Parkway	d	07 20			07 54		08 55	09 15		09 29				10 30		11 04			11 14	11 30			12 14
Exeter St Davids 6	a	07 34			08 12		09 08	09 30		09 42		10 11	10 33	10 45		11 20			11 32	11 45		12 08	12 30
Exmouth	d		07 14			08 23					09 23				10 23						11 23		
Exeter Central	d		07 43			08 50					09 50				10 50						11 50		
Exeter St Davids 6	d	07 36	07 50		08 14	08 58	09 10	09 32	09 35	09 44	09 56	10 13	10 34	10 46	10 56	11 22			11 35	11 47	11 56	12 08	12 32
Exeter St Thomas	d		07 53			09 01					09 59				10 59						11 59		
Starcross	d		08 01			09 09					10 07				11 07						12 07		
Dawlish Warren	d		08 06			09 21					10 12		10 46		11 12						12 22		
Dawlish	d		08 10			09 25					10 16		10 50		11 16						12 27		12 44
Teignmouth	d		08 15			09 30					10 21		10 55		11 21						12 32		12 49
Newton Abbot	a	07 54	08 22		08 35	09 37	09 29	09 52	09 56	10 02	10 30	10 34	11 02	11 06	11 29	11 41			11 55	12 06	12 39	12 29	12 55
	d	07 55	08 24		08 35	09 39	09 30	09 56	09 57	10 03	10 39	10 36	11 03	11 07	11 30	11 42			11 56	12 07	12 40	12 29	12 56
Torre	d		08 33			09 47		10 05			10 47		11 12		11 38						12 49		
Torquay	d		08 36			09 50	09 42	10 09			10 50		11 15		11 41						12 52		13 08
Paignton	a		08 44			09 57	09 47	10 19			10 59		11 24		11 51						13 00		13 14
Totnes	d	08 07			08 49				10 10	10 17		10 49		11 21		11 55			12 09	12 21			
Ivybridge	d				09 05				10 27										12 26				
Plymouth	a	08 34			09 19				10 41	10 46		11 17		11 48		12 25			12 42	12 49		13 06	
	d				09 21				10 42			11 20						12 39				13 11	
Devonport	d				09 24																		
Dockyard	d																						
Keyham	d																						
St Budeaux Ferry Road	d								10 48														
Saltash	d				09 31				10 53									12 48					
St Germans	d				09 38				11 00									12 55					
Menheniot	d																						
Liskeard 6	d				09 50				11 12			11 44						13 07				13 35	
Bodmin Parkway	d				10 02				11 24			11 57						13 19				13 48	
Lostwithiel	d				10 07				11 29									13 24					
Par	d			09 17	10 15				11 37			12 09					12 13	13 32				14 00	
Newquay	a			10 09													13 01						
St Austell	d				10 22				11 44			12 16						13 39				14 07	
Truro	d				10 40				12 02			12 34						13 57				14 25	
Redruth	d				10 53				12 15			12 46						14 10				14 37	
Camborne	d				10 59				12 21			12 53						14 16				14 45	
Hayle	d				11 06				12 28									14 23				14 54	
St Erth	d				11 10				12 32			13 05						14 28				14 59	
Penzance	a				11 23				12 42			13 17						14 39				15 11	

A The Devon Express

B The Merchant Venturer. [restaurant] from Taunton ⊘ to Taunton

C The Cornish Riveira. [restaurant] from Newton Abbot ⊘ to Newton Abbot

For connections from Heathrow Airport, Gatwick Airport and Oxford please refer to Tables 125A, 148 and 116

Table 135

Mondays to Fridays

London and Birmingham - Devon and Cornwall

Route Diagram - see first Page of Table 135

		XC	GW	GW	GW	GW	GW	XC	GW	GW	GW	XC	GW	GW	GW	GW	GW	GW	GW	XC	XC	GW
		◇1	◇1		◇		◇1	◇1		◇1		◇1	◇1		◇		◇1	◇		◇1	◇1	
			A				B			C							D					
		🛒	🍴				🍴⊘	🛒		🍴⊘		🛒	🍴				🍴⊘			🛒	🛒	
London Paddington 15 ⊖	d		10 00				11 06			12 06			12 18				13 06					
Slough 3	d																					
Reading 7	d		10 27				11 33			12 33			12 48				13 33					
Theale	d												12 56									
Thatcham	d												13 04									
Newbury	d												13 12									
Hungerford	d												13 21									
Pewsey	d						12 03						13 40									
Westbury	d						12 22						13 59									
Castle Cary	d						12 39						14 16									
Birmingham New Street 12	d	10 12						11 12				12 12								13 12	13 42	
Cardiff Central 7	d																	13 00				
Newport (South Wales)	d																	13 15				
Swindon	d		10 55																			
Bristol Parkway 7	d	11 28						12 30				13 27								14 29	14 59	
Filton Abbey Wood	d																	13 42				
Bath Spa 7	d		11 24																			
Bristol Temple Meads 10	d	11 44	11 47					12 44				13 44						13 53		14 44	15 13	
Weston-super-Mare	d		12 07															14 23				
Bridgwater	d																	14 42				
Taunton	d	12 17	12 29				13 02	13 18				14 17	14a41				14 48	14 56		15 18	15 46	
Tiverton Parkway	d	12 29					13 15	13 30				14 29					15 01	15 11		15 30	15 58	
Exeter St Davids 6	a	12 42	12 55				13 31	13 45		14 08		14 42					15 17	15 31		15 46	16 13	
Exmouth	d			12 23					13 23					14 23								15 23
Exeter Central	d			12 50					13 50					14 50								15 50
Exeter St Davids 6	d	12 44	12 56	13 03			13 33	13 47	13 56	14 08		14 44		14 56			15 18			15 48		15 56
Exeter St Thomas	d			13 06					13 59					14 59								15 59
Starcross	d			13 15					14 07					15 07								16 07
Dawlish Warren	d			13 20					14 23					15 12								16 12
Dawlish	d		13 08	13 24					14 27					15 16								16 16
Teignmouth	d		13 14	13 29					14 32					15 21								16 21
Newton Abbot	a	13 02	13 22	13 36			13 52	14 06	14 40	14 28		15 02		15 29			15 39			16 07		16 30
	d	13 03	13 22	13 38			13 53	14 07	14 41	14 29	14 50	15 03		15 30			15 39		15 58	16 08		16 30
Torre	d			13 46					14 49					15 38								16 38
Torquay	d		13 34	13 49					14 52					15 41								16 41
Paignton	a		13 43	13 58					15 00					15 51								16 51
Totnes	d	13 16					14 06	14 21			15 02	15 16					15 53		16 11	16 22		
Ivybridge	d										15 19								16 28			
Plymouth	a	13 41					14 36	14 48		15 06	15 37	15 41					16 22		16 42	16 49		
	d					13 53				15 12						15 57			17 04			
Devonport	d															16 00			17 07			
Dockyard	d															16x01			17x08			
Keyham	d															16 03			17 10			
St Budeaux Ferry Road	d															16 06			17 13			
Saltash	d					14 02										16 11			17 17			
St Germans	d					14 09										16 18			17 24			
Menheniot	d															16x25			17x32			
Liskeard 6	d					14 21				15 36						16 32			17a40			
Bodmin Parkway	d					14 33				15 49						16 44						
Lostwithiel	d					14 38										16 49						
Par	d				14 08	14 46				16 01					16 10	16 57						
Newquay	a				14 56										17 02							
St Austell	d					14 53				16 08						17 06						
Truro	d					15 11				16 26						17 23						
Redruth	d					15 24				16 38						17 36						
Camborne	d					15 30				16 46						17 42						
Hayle	d					15 37				16 55						17 50						
St Erth	d					15 42				17 00						17 54						
Penzance	a					15 53				17 12						18 07						

A The Torbay Express

B The Mayflower. 🍴 from Taunton ⊘ to Taunton

C The Royal Duchy. 🍴 from Newton Abbot ⊘ to Newton Abbot

D 🍴 from Newton Abbot ⊘ to Newton Abbot

For connections from Heathrow Airport, Gatwick Airport and Oxford please refer to Tables 125A, 148 and 116

London and Birmingham - Devon and Cornwall

Route Diagram - see first Page of Table 135

		GW	GW	GW	XC	GW	GW	GW	GW	GW	GW	GW	GW	XC	GW	XC	GW	GW	GW	XC	GW	GW	GW
						FO															FX	FO	
			◇1		◇1	◇			◇				◇1	◇1		◇1	◇1			◇1	◇1	◇1	◇1
			A										A	B						B			
			⊐⊘		🛒								⊐⊘	🛒		🛒	⊐			🛒	⊐	⊐	⊐
London Paddington 15 ⊖	d		14 06										15 06				16 06				16 36	16 36	17 03
Slough 3	d																						
Reading 7	d		14 33										15 33				16 33				17 04	17 04	17 32
Theale	d																						
Thatcham	d																						
Newbury	d																				17 19	17 19	17 48
Hungerford	d																				17 29	17 29	
Pewsey	d												16 03								17 44	17 44	
Westbury	d					15 20							16 23								18 04	18 04	
Castle Cary	d					15 49							16 41								18 21	18 21	
Birmingham New Street 12	d				14 12									15 12		15 42				16 12			
Cardiff Central 7	d																						
Newport (South Wales)	d																						
Swindon	d																						
Bristol Parkway 7	d				15 26									16 29		16 58				17 27			
Filton Abbey Wood	d																						
Bath Spa 7	d																						
Bristol Temple Meads 10	d				15 44									16 44		17 13				17 44			
Weston-super-Mare	d																						
Bridgwater	d																						
Taunton	d		15 49		16 17	16 24							17 05	17 17		17 45	17 50			18 17	18 43	18 43	18 52
Tiverton Parkway	d		16 02		16 29	16 41							17 18	17 29		17 57	18 03			18 29	18 56	18 56	19 05
Exeter St Davids 6	a		16 18		16 42	17 02							17 34	17 42		18 11	18 19			18 42	19 14	19 14	19 21
Exmouth	d			15 53				16 55										17 58					
Exeter Central	d			16 20			16 46	17 21							17 45			18 25					
Exeter St Davids 6	d	16 05	16 20	16 26	16 44		16 56	17 26					17 35	17 45	17 50	18 12	18 22	18 30		18 46		19 14	19 22
Exeter St Thomas	d			16 29			16 59	17 29							17 54			18 33					
Starcross	d			16 37			17 07	17 37							18 02			18 42					
Dawlish Warren	d	16 18		16 42			17 12	17 49							18 07			18 47					
Dawlish	d	16 22		16 46			17 16	17 53							18 11	18 24		18 51					
Teignmouth	d	16 27		16 51			17 21	17 58							18 16	18 29		18 56					
Newton Abbot	a	16 35	16 39	16 58	17 02		17 29	18 05					17 56	18 10	18 23	18 35	18 42	19 03		19 07		19 34	19 42
	d	16 48	16 40	17 00	17 04		17 30	18 09					17 57	18 12	18 25	18 37	18 43	19 10		19 08		19 35	19 42
Torre	d			17 08			17 38	18 17							18 33			19 18					
Torquay	d			17 11			17 41	18 20							18 36	18 48		19 21					
Paignton	a			17 20			17 51	18 30							18 45	18 55		19 30					
Totnes	d	17 02	16 53		17 16								18 10	18 24			18 56			19 21			19 56
Ivybridge	d	17 19															19 12						
Plymouth	a	17 34	17 21		17 42								18 38	18 50			19 26			19 46		20 15	20 24
	d		17 23							17 55	18 17	18 23	18 41	19 01			19 31			19 49			20 26
Devonport	d										18 20	18 26											
Dockyard	d										18x21	18x27											
Keyham	d										18 23	18a29											
St Budeaux Ferry Road	d										18 25												
Saltash	d		17 34							18 03	18 31						19 40						20 37
St Germans	d		17 41								18 38												20 44
Menheniot	d										18x45												
Liskeard 6	d		17 54							18 20	18a53		19 07	19 24			19 57			20 12			20 56
Bodmin Parkway	d		18 07							18 32			19 19	19 36			20 10			20 25			21 09
Lostwithiel	d		18 13							18 37													
Par	d		18 22						18 29	18 45			19 31	19 47			20 22		20 28	20 36			21 21
Newquay	a								19 21										21 20				
St Austell	d		18 29							18 52			19 39	19 54			20 29			20 43			21 28
Truro	d		18 47							19 10			20 00	20 11			20 47			21 02			21 46
Redruth	d		18 59							19 23			20 10	20 26			20 59			21 16			21 58
Camborne	d		19 07							19 29			20 18	20 32			21 07			21 23			
Hayle	d		19 16							19 36													22 11
St Erth	d		19 21							19 42			20 28	20 44			21 20			21 34			22 16
Penzance	a		19 33							19 54			20 40	20 52			21 31			21 42			22 30

A ⊐ from Newton Abbot ⊘ to Newton Abbot

B 🛒 to Plymouth

For connections from Heathrow Airport, Gatwick Airport and Oxford please refer to Tables 125A, 148 and 116

London and Birmingham - Devon and Cornwall

Route Diagram - see first Page of Table 135

Station		GW	XC	GW	GW	GW		GW	GW	XC	GW FX	GW FO	GW FO	GW FX	GW	GW FX		XC	XC	GW	GW	XC	GW	GW	GW
			◇1	◇1	◇1			◇1	◇1	◇1	◇1	◇1	R 1	R 1				◇1	◇1	◇1		◇1	◇1	◇	
			A					B										D	D			D			
			[trolley]	[buffet]	[buffet]			[restaurant] [buffet]	[buffet]	[trolley]	[buffet]	[buffet]	[restaurant] [buffet]	[restaurant] [buffet]				[trolley]	[trolley]	[buffet]		[trolley]	[buffet]		
London Paddington 15 ⊖	d			17 06	17 33			18 03	18 06		18 33	18 33	19 03	19 03						19 45			20 35		
Slough 3	d																								
Reading 7	d			17 36	18 04			18 33	18 37		19 02	19 02	19u33	19 33						20 12			21 02		
Theale	d			17 45					18 45																
Thatcham	d			17 55					18 55																
Newbury	d			18 02	18 19				19 02		19 17	19 17	19 50	19 50						20 27			21 18		
Hungerford	d			18 16					19 16		19 27	19 27													
Pewsey	d			18 34	18 41				19 34		19 46	19 46								20 47			21 38		
Westbury	d				19 01				19a52		20 05	20 05								21 05			21 57		
Castle Cary	d				19 19						20 23	20 23								21 26			22 15		
Birmingham New Street 12	d		17 12							18 12								19 12	19 42			20 12			
Cardiff Central 7	d																								
Newport (South Wales)	d																								
Swindon	d																								
Bristol Parkway 7	d		18 29							19 29								20 29	20 56			21 27			
Filton Abbey Wood	d																								
Bath Spa 7	d			19 24																					
Bristol Temple Meads 10	d		18 44	19a41						19 44								20 44	21 12			21 44		21 56	23 06
Weston-super-Mare	d																							22 29	23 42
Bridgwater	d																							22 48	00 02
Taunton	d		19 17		19 41			19 48		20 18	20 46	20 46	20 54	20 54				21 17	21 45	21 48		22 17	22 37	23 03	00s14
Tiverton Parkway	d		19 29		19 54					20 30	20 59	20 59	21 07	21 07				21 30	21 57	22 02		22 29	22 50	23 18	00s31
Exeter St Davids 6	a		19 42		20 09			20 13		20 44	21 15	21 15	21 23	21 23				21 43	22 11	22 18		22 43	23 06	23 36	00 50
Exmouth	d	18 55																			22 05				
Exeter Central	d	19 21													21 21						22 31				
Exeter St Davids 6	d	19 28	19 44		20 19			20 15		20 46		21 16	21 25	21 25	21 29			21 45	22 12	22 19	22 37	22 44	23 08		
Exeter St Thomas	d	19 31			20 24										21 32						22 40				
Starcross	d	19 39			20 33										21 40						22 48				
Dawlish Warren	d	19 44			20 38										21 45						22 59				
Dawlish	d	19 48			20 43										21 49						23 03				
Teignmouth	d	19 53			20 50										21 54						23 08				
Newton Abbot	a	20 00	20 04		20 57			20 34		21 03		21 36	21 44	21 44	22 01			22 04	22 30	22 39	23 15	23 05	23 28		
	d	20 09	20 06		20 58			20 35		21 05		21 36	21 45	21 45	22 03			22 06	22 32	22 40	23 16	23 07	23 28		
Torre	d	20 17			21 08										22 11						23 24				
Torquay	d	20 20			21 12										22 14						23 27				
Paignton	a	20 29			21 22										22 23						23 37				
Totnes	d		20 18					20 48		21 18			21 58	21 58				22 17	22 44	22 53		23 19	23 42		
Ivybridge	d																			23 10					
Plymouth	a		20 44					21 16		21 48		22 14	22 26	22 26				22 43	23 14	23 25		23 45	00 11		
	d		20 51					21 19					22 29			22 31									
Devonport	d																								
Dockyard	d																								
Keyham	d																								
St Budeaux Ferry Road	d																								
Saltash	d												22 40			22 40									
St Germans	d												22 47			22 47									
Menheniot	d																								
Liskeard 6	d		21 14					21 44					22 59			22 59									
Bodmin Parkway	d		21 27					21 58					23 11			23 11									
Lostwithiel	d		21 32										23 16			23 16									
Par	d		21 40					22 10					23 24			23 24									
Newquay	a																								
St Austell	d		21 47					22 18					23 31			23 31									
Truro	d		22 04					22 36					23 50			23 50									
Redruth	d		22 15					22 48					00 03			00 03									
Camborne	d		22 22										00 09			00 09									
Hayle	d		22 30										00 16			00 16									
St Erth	d		22 35			22 45							00 20			00 20									
Penzance	a		22 43			22 57		23 13					00 40			00 40									

A [trolley] to Plymouth
B The Golden Hind.
D [trolley] to Bristol Temple Meads

For connections from Heathrow Airport, Gatwick Airport and Oxford please refer to Tables 125A, 148 and 116

London and Birmingham - Devon and Cornwall

Route Diagram - see first Page of Table 135

Station		GW	GW FO	GW FX
			R	R
		◇1		
			A	A
			🛏	🛏
		☕	☕	☕
London Paddington 15 ⊖	d	21 45	23 45	23 45
Slough 3	d			
Reading 7	d	22 11	00u37	00u37
Theale	d			
Thatcham	d			
Newbury	d			
Hungerford	d			
Pewsey	d			
Westbury	d		01 37	01 45
Castle Cary	d			
Birmingham New Street 12	d			
Cardiff Central 7	d			
Newport (South Wales)	d			
Swindon	d	22 49		
Bristol Parkway 7	d			
Filton Abbey Wood	d			
Bath Spa 7	d	23 19		
Bristol Temple Meads 10	d	23 35		
Weston-super-Mare	d	00s05		
Bridgwater	d	00s24		
Taunton	d	00s36	02 35	02 35
Tiverton Parkway	d	00s49		
Exeter St Davids 6	a	01 07	03 06	03 06
Exmouth	d			
Exeter Central	d			
Exeter St Davids 6	d		03 11	03 11
Exeter St Thomas	d			
Starcross	d			
Dawlish Warren	d			
Dawlish	d			
Teignmouth	d			
Newton Abbot	a		03 31	03 31
	d		03 33	03 33
Torre	d			
Torquay	d			
Paignton	a			
Totnes	d			
Ivybridge	d			
Plymouth	a		04 14	04 12
	d		05 43	05 43
Devonport	d			
Dockyard	d			
Keyham	d			
St Budeaux Ferry Road	d			
Saltash	d			
St Germans	d			
Menheniot	d			
Liskeard 6	d		06 08	06 08
Bodmin Parkway	d		06 22	06 22
Lostwithiel	d		06 28	06 28
Par	d		06 37	06 37
Newquay	a			
St Austell	d		06 46	06 46
Truro	d		07 06	07 06
Redruth	d		07 18	07 18
Camborne	d		07 26	07 26
Hayle	d		07 35	07 35
St Erth	d		07 41	07 41
Penzance	a		07 53	07 53

A The Night Riviera

For connections from Heathrow Airport, Gatwick Airport and Oxford please refer to Tables 125A, 148 and 116

Table 135

Saturdays

London and Birmingham - Devon and Cornwall

Route Diagram - see first Page of Table 135

		GW	GW	GW	GW	GW	GW	GW	GW	GW		GW	XC	GW	GW	GW	XC	GW	GW	GW		GW	GW	XC	GW
		R 1 ✕ ☕	◇1 ☕		◇1 ☕		R B 🛏 ☕						◇1		◇		◇1			◇				◇1 trolley	
London Paddington 15 ⊖	d	19p03	20p35		21p45		23p45																		
Slough 3	d																								
Reading 7	d	19b33	21p02		22p11		00u37																		
Theale	d																								
Thatcham	d																								
Newbury	d	19p50	21p18																						
Hungerford	d																								
Pewsey	d		21p38																						
Westbury	d		21p57				01 37																		
Castle Cary	d		22p15																						
Birmingham New Street 12	d																							06 42	
Cardiff Central 7	d																								
Newport (South Wales)	d																								
Swindon	d				22p49																				
Bristol Parkway 7	d																							07 56	
Filton Abbey Wood	d																								
Bath Spa 7	d				23p19																				
Bristol Temple Meads 10	d			23p06	23p35										05 24		06 08			06 36				08 11	
Weston-super-Mare	d			23p42	00s05										05 45					06 56					
Bridgwater	d			00 02	00s24										06 03										
Taunton	d	20p54	22p37	00s14	00s36		02 35								06 18		07 17			07 25				08 43	
Tiverton Parkway	d	21p07	22p50	00s31	00s49										06 33		07 29			07 41				08 55	
Exeter St Davids 6	a	21p23	23p06	00 50	01 07		03 06								06 52		07 42			07 59				09 09	
Exmouth	d																	07 15					08 23		
Exeter Central	d																	07 43					08 50		
Exeter St Davids 6	d	21p25	23p08				03 11	05 18	05 36	06 11					06 56		07 44	07 50		08 00		08 37	08 56	09 10	
Exeter St Thomas	d							05 22	05 40	06 14					06 59			07 53		08 04			08 59		
Starcross	d							05 30	05 48	06 22					07 05			08 01					09 07		
Dawlish Warren	d							05 35	05 53	06 27					07 10			08 06					09 24		
Dawlish	d							05 39	05 57	06 31					07 14			08 10		08 17		08 51	09 28		
Teignmouth	d							05 44	06 02	06 36					07 19			08 15		08 22		08 56	09 33		
Newton Abbot	a	21p44	23p28				03 31	05 51	06 09	06 45					07 26		08 02	08 22		08 29		09 03	09 40	09 28	
	d	21p45	23p28				03 33	05 52	06 11	06 45					07 26	07 40	08 03	08 24		08 31		09 06	09 41	09 30	
Torre	d							06 00	06 19	06 53						07 48		08 32					09 50		
Torquay	d							06 03	06 22	06 56						07 51		08 35				09 16	09 53	09 41	
Paignton	a							06 11	06 30	07 06						07 59		08 44				09 25	10 01	09 47	
Totnes	d	21p58	23p42												07 40		08 16			08 45					
Ivybridge	d														07 56					09 02					
Plymouth	a	22p26	00 11				04 14								08 13		08 41			09 16					
	d	22p29					05 43						06 28		08 18					09 19					09 51
Devonport	d														08 21										09 54
Dockyard	d																								
Keyham	d																								
St Budeaux Ferry Road	d																								
Saltash	d	22p40													08 28					09 28					10 01
St Germans	d	22p47													08 35					09 36					10 08
Menheniot	d																								10x15
Liskeard 6	d	22p59					06 08						06 51		08 47					09 49					10 22
Bodmin Parkway	d	23p11					06 22						07 03		08 59					10 02					10 34
Lostwithiel	d	23p16					06 28						07 08		09 04										10 39
Par	d	23p24				06 09	06 37					06 52	07 15		09 12				09 18	10 14					10 46
Newquay	a											07 44							10 10						
St Austell	d	23p31				06 16	06 46						07 21		09 20					10 22					10 54
Truro	d	23p50				06 35	07 06						07 38		09 37					10 40					11 10
Redruth	d	00 03				06 48	07 18						07 50		09 50					10 55					11 24
Camborne	d	00 09				06 54	07 26						07 56		09 56					11 02					11 30
Hayle	d	00 16				07 01	07 35						08 04		10 03					11 10					11 38
St Erth	d	00 20				07 04	07 41						08 10	08 28	10 08					11 18					11 42
Penzance	a	00 40				07 16	07 53						08 19	08 40	10 18					11 26					11 55

B The Night Riviera

b Previous night, stops to pick up only

For connections from Heathrow Airport, Gatwick Airport and Oxford please refer to Tables 125A, 148 and 116

Table 135

Saturdays

London and Birmingham - Devon and Cornwall

Route Diagram - see first Page of Table 135

		GW	XC	GW	GW	GW		GW	XC	GW	GW	GW	XC	GW	GW	GW		GW	XC	XC	GW	GW	GW	GW	GW
					R																				
			◇1		◇1				◇1	◇1		◇1	◇1		◇	◇		◇1	◇1	◇1			◇		◇1
					A							B						B							B
			🛒		🍴				🛒	🍴		🍴⊘	🛒					🍴⊘	🛒	🛒					🍴⊘
London Paddington 15 ⊖	d				07 30					08 18		09 06						10 06							11 06
Slough 3	d																								
Reading 7	d				07 57					08 48		09 32						10 33							11 32
Theale	d									08 58															
Thatcham	d									09 07															
Newbury	d									09 14															
Hungerford	d									09 23															
Pewsey	d									09 41															12 03
Westbury	d									10 00															12 22
Castle Cary	d									10 18															12 40
Birmingham New Street 12	d		07 12						08 12				09 12						09 42	10 12					
Cardiff Central 7	d																								
Newport (South Wales)	d																								
Swindon	d				08 30																				
Bristol Parkway 7	d		08 26						09 26				10 31						10 59	11 26					
Filton Abbey Wood	d																								
Bath Spa 7	d				09 00																				
Bristol Temple Meads 10	d		08 44		09 17				09 44				10 44						11 12	11 44					
Weston-super-Mare	d																		11 39						
Bridgwater	d																								
Taunton	d		09 17		09 51				10 18	10 40		10 48	11 17						12 01	12 17					13 02
Tiverton Parkway	d		09 29						10 30	10 53		11 01	11 29						12 13	12 29					13 15
Exeter St Davids 6	a		09 41		10 16				10 46	11 09		11 17	11 42					12 09	12 26	12 42					13 31
Exmouth	d			09 23							10 23			11 23								12 23			
Exeter Central	d			09 52				10 30			10 50			11 50								12 50			
Exeter St Davids 6	d	09 28	09 44	09 58	10 19	10 25		10 35	10 48		10 56	11 19	11 45	11 56				12 11	12 29	12 45	12 52	12 56			13 33
Exeter St Thomas	d			09 59							10 59			11 59								12 59			
Starcross	d			10 07							11 07			12 07								13 07			
Dawlish Warren	d			10 12				10 47			11 12			12 12							13 04	13 12			
Dawlish	d			10 16				10 51			11 16			12 16					12 41		13 08	13 16			
Teignmouth	d			10 21				10 56			11 21			12 21					12 46		13 13	13 21			
Newton Abbot	a	09 48	10 02	10 30	10 38	10 46		11 03	11 09		11 29	11 38	12 03	12 29				12 31	12 52	13 03	13 20	13 29			13 51
	d	09 49	10 03	10 31	10 39	10 48		11 04	11 10		11 30	11 38	12 05	12 36				12 32	12 53	13 05	13 21	13 30			13 53
Torre	d			10 39		10 56					11 38			12 43								13 38			
Torquay	d			10 42		10 59		11 14			11 41			12 46					13 05			13 41			
Paignton	a			10 50		11 07		11 23			11 51			12 54					13 11			13 49			
Totnes	d	10 02	10 16		10 52				11 24			11 52	12 17							13 17	13 34				14 05
Ivybridge	d	10 19										12 07									13 50				
Plymouth	a	10 32	10 41		11 20				11 51			12 24	12 43					13 13		13 43	14 05				14 34
	d	10 33			11 23											12 44		13 15						14 15	
Devonport	d																								
Dockyard	d																								
Keyham	d																								
St Budeaux Ferry Road	d	10 39																							
Saltash	d	10 44														12 53								14 24	
St Germans	d	10 51														13 00								14 32	
Menheniot	d																								
Liskeard 6	d	11 03			11 47											13 12		13 40						14 45	
Bodmin Parkway	d	11 15			12 00											13 24		13 54						14 58	
Lostwithiel	d	11 20														13 29								15 04	
Par	d	11 28			12 11										12 15	13 37		14 06					14 08	15 12	
Newquay	a														13 07								14 55		
St Austell	d	11 37			12 19											13 45		14 14						15 21	
Truro	d	11 55			12 37											14 02		14 30						15 39	
Redruth	d	12 08			12 49											14 15		14 44						15 53	
Camborne	d	12 14			12 56											14 21		14 50						16 00	
Hayle	d	12 21														14 28		15 00							
St Erth	d	12 25			13 08											14 33		15 05						16 12	
Penzance	a	12 36			13 20											14 42		15 17						16 21	

A ◇ from Exeter St Davids R to Exeter St Davids

B 🍴 from Newton Abbot ⊘ to Newton Abbot

For connections from Heathrow Airport, Gatwick Airport and Oxford please refer to Tables 125A, 148 and 116

Table 135

Saturdays

London and Birmingham - Devon and Cornwall

Route Diagram - see first Page of Table 135

		XC		GW	GW	GW	XC	GW	GW	GW	GW	GW		XC	XC	GW	GW	GW	GW	XC	GW	GW		GW	GW
												R													
		◇1			◇1		◇1	◇1		◇		1		◇1	◇1				◇1	◇1				◇	
					A																				
		🛒			🍽⊘		🛒	🍽				🍽		🛒	🛒				🍽	🛒					
London Paddington 15 ⊖	d				12 06			12 18				13 06							14 06						
Slough 3	d																								
Reading 7	d				12 32			12 48				13 32							14 32						
Theale	d							12 57																	
Thatcham	d							13 05																	
Newbury	d							13 13																	
Hungerford	d							13 21																	
Pewsey	d							13 39																	
Westbury	d							13 58																	
Castle Cary	d							14 14																	
Birmingham New Street 12	d	11 12					12 12							13 12	13 42					14 12					
Cardiff Central 7	d																								
Newport (South Wales)	d																								
Swindon	d																								
Bristol Parkway 7	d	12 31					13 26							14 28	14 59					15 25					
Filton Abbey Wood	d																								
Bath Spa 7	d																								
Bristol Temple Meads 10	d	12 44					13 44							14 44	15 12					15 44					
Weston-super-Mare	d																								
Bridgwater	d																								
Taunton	d	13 17					14 17	14a37				14 48		15 18	15 44				15 48	16 17					
Tiverton Parkway	d	13 29					14 29					15 01		15 30	15 56				16 01	16 29					
Exeter St Davids 6	a	13 42			14 09		14 42					15 17		15 45	16 10				16 17	16 42					
Exmouth	d			13 23					14 23								15 23					16 55			
Exeter Central	d			13 50					14 50								15 50				16 48	17 21			
Exeter St Davids 6	d	13 44		13 57	14 11	14 30	14 44		14 56			15 18		15 47			15 57		16 18	16 44	16 56	17 27			
Exeter St Thomas	d			13 59					14 59								15 59				16 59	17 30			
Starcross	d			14 07					15 07								16 07				17 07	17 35			
Dawlish Warren	d			14 24		14 42			15 12								16 12				17 12	17 49			
Dawlish	d			14 28		14 46			15 16								16 16				17 16	17 53			
Teignmouth	d			14 33		14 51			15 21								16 21				17 21	17 58			
Newton Abbot	a	14 02		14 41	14 30	14 58	15 02		15 29			15 39		16 06			16 29		16 38	17 02	17 29	18 05			
	d	14 04		14 42	14 32	15 00	15 04		15 30			15 39		16 07		16 18	16 30		16 39	17 04	17 30	18 09			
Torre	d			14 50		15 08			15 38								16 38				17 38	18 17			
Torquay	d			14 53		15 11			15 41								16 41				17 41	18 20			
Paignton	a			15 01		15 19			15 51								16 51				17 51	18 27			
Totnes	d	14 16					15 16					15 53		16 21		16 31			16 52	17 16					
Ivybridge	d															16 47			17 08						
Plymouth	a	14 42			15 09		15 42					16 20		16 48		17 05			17 23	17 42					
	d				15 11						16 03	16 26							17 26						17 52
Devonport	d																								17 55
Dockyard	d																								17x57
Keyham	d																								17 59
St Budeaux Ferry Road	d																								18 01
Saltash	d										16 12														18 06
St Germans	d										16 19														18 12
Menheniot	d										16x27														18x19
Liskeard 6	d				15 36						16 33	16 50							17 51						18 26
Bodmin Parkway	d				15 49						16 45	17 03							18 03						18 38
Lostwithiel	d										16 50														18 44
Par	d				16 01					16 15	16 57								18 16					18 21	18 52
Newquay	a									17 07														19 13	
St Austell	d				16 08						17 05	17 20							18 23						18 59
Truro	d				16 26						17 23	17 37							18 41						19 17
Redruth	d				16 38						17 36	17 50							18 53						19 30
Camborne	d				16 46						17 42	17 57							19 01						19 36
Hayle	d										17 49	18 06													19 43
St Erth	d				16 57						17 54	18 12						18 32	19 12						19 48
Penzance	a				17 09						18 03	18 24						18 44	19 24						19 57

A 🍽 from Newton Abbot ⊘ to Newton Abbot

For connections from Heathrow Airport, Gatwick Airport and Oxford please refer to Tables 125A, 148 and 116

Table 135

Saturdays

London and Birmingham - Devon and Cornwall

Route Diagram - see first Page of Table 135

		GW	XC	GW	XC	GW	GW	GW	XC	GW	GW	GW	GW	GW	XC	XC	GW	GW	XC	GW	GW	XC	XC
		◇1	◇1	1	◇1	◇1			◇1				◇1	◇1	◇1	◇1		◇1	◇1		◇1	◇1	◇1
			A			C			A						D	E					C	F	G
		[restaurant]	[trolley]		[trolley]	[restaurant]			[trolley]				[restaurant]	[restaurant]	[trolley]	[trolley]		[restaurant]	[trolley]		[restaurant]	[trolley]	[trolley]
London Paddington 15 ⊖	d	15 06				16 06							17 06	16 30				18 06			19 06		
Slough 3	d																						
Reading 7	d	15 32				16 32							17 32	16 57				18 32			19 32		
Theale	d																						
Thatcham	d																						
Newbury	d																				19 49		
Hungerford	d																						
Pewsey	d	16 04											18 03								20 09		
Westbury	d	16 23											18 22								20 27		
Castle Cary	d	16 40											18 41								20 44		
Birmingham New Street 12	d		15 12		15 42				16 12						17 12	17 12			18 12			19 12	19 42
Cardiff Central 7	d																						
Newport (South Wales)	d																						
Swindon	d													17 30									
Bristol Parkway 7	d		16 31		16 56				17 26						18 31	18 31			19 27			20 31	20 56
Filton Abbey Wood	d																						
Bath Spa 7	d													18 00									
Bristol Temple Meads 10	d		16 44		17 10				17 44					18 18	18 44	18 44			19 44			20 44	21 11
Weston-super-Mare	d													18 40									
Bridgwater	d																						
Taunton	d	17 03	17 18		17 42	17 49			18 17				19 02	19 06	19 17	19 17		19 47	20 17		21 07	21 17	21 44
Tiverton Parkway	d	17 16	17 31		17 54	18 02			18 29				19 15	19 21	19 29	19 29			20 29		21 20	21 29	21 56
Exeter St Davids 6	a	17 31	17 46		18 08	18 18			18 42				19 31	19 36	19 43	19 43		20 13	20 42		21 36	21 42	22 09
Exmouth	d						17 55										19 38			20 08			
Exeter Central	d						18 21										20 01			20 35			
Exeter St Davids 6	d	17 34	17 48	17 53	18 10	18 20	18 27		18 46	18 56	19 16		19 34	19 39	19 45	19 45	20 07	20 16	20 45	20 56	21 38	21 45	22 11
Exeter St Thomas	d						18 29				19 19						20 10			20 59			
Starcross	d						18 37				19 27						20 18			21 07			
Dawlish Warren	d			18 05			18 42				19 32						20 32			21 12			
Dawlish	d			18 09	18 22		18 46			19 09	19 36						20 36			21 16			
Teignmouth	d			18 14	18 27		18 51			19 14	19 41						20 41			21 21			
Newton Abbot	a	17 53	18 10	18 21	18 33	18 40	18 59		19 04	19 21	19 48		19 53	19 58	20 03	20 03	20 48	20 37	21 03	21 28	21 58	22 04	22 29
	d	17 55	18 12	18 22	18 35	18 41	19 01		19 05	19 22	19 50		19 54	19 59	20 05	20 05	20 49	20 37	21 05	21 30	21 58	22 08	22 30
Torre	d						19 09				19 58			20 09			20 57			21 38			
Torquay	d				18 46		19 12			19 32	20 01			20 12			21 00			21 41			
Paignton	a				18 53		19 21			19 40	20 09			20 21			21 07			21 48			
Totnes	d	18 08	18 25	18 35		18 54			19 18				20 07		20 17	20 17		20 51	21 17		22 12	22 21	22 43
Ivybridge	d			18 51		19 11																	
Plymouth	a	18 36	18 52	19 05		19 26			19 43				20 35		20 43	20 43		21 19	21 43		22 40	22 47	23 08
	d	18 41	18 56	19 08					19 48				20 38		20 58	20 58		21 20					
Devonport	d																						
Dockyard	d																						
Keyham	d																						
St Budeaux Ferry Road	d																						
Saltash	d			19 17									20 49										
St Germans	d			19 24									20 56										
Menheniot	d																						
Liskeard 6	d	19 06	19 19	19 36					20 11				21 08		21 25	21 25		21 45					
Bodmin Parkway	d	19 19	19 34	19 48					20 23				21 21		21 38	21 38		21 59					
Lostwithiel	d			19 53					20 29														
Par	d	19 31	19 45	20 01				20 15	20 36				21 33		21 49	21 49		22 11					
Newquay	a							21 07															
St Austell	d	19 39	19 53	20 08					20 43				21 43		21 56	21 56		22 18					
Truro	d	20 00	20 12	20 26					21 02				22 03		22 13	22 13		22 36					
Redruth	d	20 10	20 27	20 43					21 13				22 13		22 28	22 28		22 48					
Camborne	d	20 18	20 35	20 49					21 19						22 35	22 35		22 56					
Hayle	d								21 27									23 03					
St Erth	d	20 29	20 46	20 58					21 32			22 20	22 30		22 46	22 46		23 09					
Penzance	a	20 40	20 56	21 08					21 43			22 32	22 42		22 54	22 54		23 22					

A [trolley] to Plymouth
C until 11 February, from 31 March
D from 18 February
E until 11 February. [trolley] to Plymouth
F [trolley] to Bristol Temple Meads
G until 11 February, from 31 March. [trolley] to Bristol Temple Meads

For connections from Heathrow Airport, Gatwick Airport and Oxford please refer to Tables 125A, 148 and 116

Table 135

Saturdays

London and Birmingham - Devon and Cornwall

Route Diagram - see first Page of Table 135

		GW	GW	XC	GW	XC	GW	GW	GW	GW
		◇1	◇1	◇1		◇1	◇	◇1	◇1	
		A	B	C	B	D		E	F	B
					(bus)					(bus)
		(catering)	(catering)	(trolley)		(trolley)		(catering)	(catering)	
London Paddington 15 ⊖	d	20 06	20 06					20 30	20 30	
Slough 3	d									
Reading 7	d	20 33	20 33					20 57	20 59	
Theale	d									
Thatcham	d									
Newbury	d	20 47	20 47							
Hungerford	d									
Pewsey	d	21 07	21 07							
Westbury	d	21 26	21 26							
Castle Cary	d	21 43	21 43							
Birmingham New Street 12	d			20 12		20 12				
Cardiff Central 7	d									
Newport (South Wales)	d									
Swindon	d							21 30	21 41	
Bristol Parkway 7	d			21 24		21 24				
Filton Abbey Wood	d									
Bath Spa 7	d							22 00	22 11	
Bristol Temple Meads 10	d			21b44		21 44	21 59	22 17	22 27	
Weston-super-Mare	d						22 31	22s47	22s57	
Bridgwater	d						22 50	23s05	23s16	
Taunton	d	22 06	22 06	22 17		22 17	23 03	23 18	23 28	
Tiverton Parkway	d	22 19	22 19	22 29	22 29	22 29	23 18	23 31	23 41	
Exeter St Davids 6	a	22 35	22 35	22 43		22 43	23 36	23 47	23 57	
Exmouth	d									
Exeter Central	d									
Exeter St Davids 6	d	22 38	22 38			22 46				
Exeter St Thomas	d									
Starcross	d									
Dawlish Warren	d									
Dawlish	d	22 48	22 48							
Teignmouth	d	22 54	22 54							
Newton Abbot	a	23 02	23 04			23 10				
	d	23 02				23 11				23 13
Torre	d									
Torquay	d									
Paignton	a									
Totnes	d	23 16				23 27				23 39
Ivybridge	d									
Plymouth	a	23 46			23 49	23 53				00 24
	d									
Devonport	d									
Dockyard	d									
Keyham	d									
St Budeaux Ferry Road	d									
Saltash	d									
St Germans	d									
Menheniot	d									
Liskeard 6	d									
Bodmin Parkway	d									
Lostwithiel	d									
Par	d									
Newquay	a									
St Austell	d									
Truro	d									
Redruth	d									
Camborne	d									
Hayle	d									
St Erth	d									
Penzance	a									

A until 11 February, from 31 March
B from 18 February until 24 March
C from 18 February until 24 March. (trolley) to Bristol Temple Meads
D until 11 February, from 31 March. (trolley) to Bristol Temple Meads
E unitl 31 December, and then from 31 March
F from 7 January until 24 March

For connections from Heathrow Airport, Gatwick Airport and Oxford please refer to Tables 125A, 148 and 116

Table 135

Sundays

until 1 January

London and Birmingham - Devon and Cornwall

Route Diagram - see first Page of Table 135

		GW	GW	GW	GW	XC	GW	GW	XC	GW	GW	GW	GW	XC	GW	GW	GW	XC	GW	GW	GW	XC	GW
					◇	◇1		◇	◇1		◇1	◇1		◇1			◇1	◇1		◇1		◇1	
														A									
			🛒			🛒			🛒		🍽	🍽		🛒			🍽	🛒		🍽		🛒	
London Paddington 15 ⊖	d										08 00	08 57					09 57			10 57			
Slough 3	d																						
Reading 7	d										08 34	09 33					10 33			11 33			
Theale	d																						
Thatcham	d																						
Newbury	d											09 49											
Hungerford	d																						
Pewsey	d																11 05						
Westbury	d											10 24											
Castle Cary	d																11 35						
Birmingham New Street 12	d													09 12				10 30				11 30	
Cardiff Central 7	d																						
Newport (South Wales)	d																						
Swindon	d										09 09												
Bristol Parkway 7	d													10 23				11 41				12 41	
Filton Abbey Wood	d																						
Bath Spa 7	d										09 39												
Bristol Temple Meads 10	d				07 30	08 44		08 28	09 48		09 55			10 44				11 54				12 54	
Weston-super-Mare	d				07 53			08 59															
Bridgwater	d				08 09			09 18															
Taunton	d				08 24	09 16		09 32	10 21		10 28	11 00		11 16			11 57	12 27		12 47		13 26	
Tiverton Parkway	d				08 39	09 28		09 48	10 33		10 42	11 13		11 29				12 39				13 39	
Exeter St Davids 6	a				08 56	09 42		10 05	10 46		10 58	11 29		11 42			12 21	12 56		13 14		13 55	
Exmouth	d						09 10			10 21					11 24				12 29				13 24
Exeter Central	d						09 36			10 48					11 52				12 55		13 20		13 50
Exeter St Davids 6	d	08 52			09 05	09 44	09 54	10 06	10 48	10 53	11 00	11 29		11 44	11 57	12 15	12 24	12 58	13 01	13 15	13 25	13 57	14 00
Exeter St Thomas	d	08 55					09 57			10 56					12 00								14 03
Starcross	d	09 03					10 05			11 04					12 08								14 11
Dawlish Warren	d	09 08					10 10			11 09					12 13				13 12				14 16
Dawlish	d	09 12			09 18		10 14	10 21		11 13	11 19				12 17				13 16		13 38		14 20
Teignmouth	d	09 17			09 23		10 19	10 26		11 18	11 25				12 22				13 21		13 43		14 25
Newton Abbot	a	09 24			09 30	10 03	10 26	10 31	11 07	11 25	11 31	11 49		12 02	12 29	12 35	12 43	13 17	13 28	13 35	13 50	14 16	14 32
	d	09 26			09 30	10 04	10 37	10 33	11 09	11 27	11 32	11 50		12 03	12 31	12 36	12 45	13 18	13 29	13 37	13 52	14 17	14 34
Torre	d	09 34					10 45			11 35					12 39				13 37		14 00		14 42
Torquay	d	09 37					10 48			11 38					12 42				13 40		14 03		14 45
Paignton	a	09 44					10 54			11 45					12 49				13 47		14 10		14 52
Totnes	d				09 43	10 17		10 46	11 21		11 45	12 04		12 16		12 48	12 57	13 32				14 31	
Ivybridge	d				10 00											13 04							
Plymouth	a				10 14	10 43		11 15	11 48		12 13	12 33		12 42		13 17	13 26	13 59		14 14		14 57	
	d		09 15		10 15			11 15				12 35		12 55						14 20			
Devonport	d				10 19																		
Dockyard	d																						
Keyham	d																						
St Budeaux Ferry Road	d		09 21																				
Saltash	d		09 25		10 26			11 26															
St Germans	d		09 31		10 33			11 33															
Menheniot	d				10x41																		
Liskeard 6	d		09 43		10 47			11 45				12 59		13 18						14 44			
Bodmin Parkway	d		09 55		10 59			11 57				13 13		13 30						14 58			
Lostwithiel	d		10 01		11 04			12 02															
Par	d		10 09	10 18	11 12			12 10				13 24	13 31	13 41									
Newquay	a			11 10									14 23										
St Austell	d		10 16		11 21			12 18				13 31		13 48						15 14			
Truro	d		10 35		11 40			12 35				13 50		14 05						15 32			
Redruth	d		10 48		11 53			12 48				14 02		14 19						15 43			
Camborne	d		10 54		11 59			12 54				14 10		14 25						15 51			
Hayle	d		11 01		12 06			13 01															
St Erth	d		11 06		12 10			13 06				14 23		14 37						16 03			
Penzance	a		11 18		12 21			13 16				14 33		14 49						16 21			

A 🛒 to Plymouth

For connections from Heathrow Airport, Gatwick Airport and Oxford please refer to Tables 125A, 148 and 116

Table 135

Sundays
until 1 January

London and Birmingham - Devon and Cornwall

Route Diagram - see first Page of Table 135

		GW	GW	GW	XC	GW		GW	GW	GW	XC	GW	GW	GW	GW	XC		GW	XC	GW	GW	XC	GW	GW	GW
		◇1		◇1	◇1			◇	◇1		◇1	◇1		◇	◇1	◇1			◇1		◇1	◇1		◇1	
																						A			
		🍴	🛒	🍴	🛒				🍴		🛒	🍴			🍴	🛒			🛒		🍴	🛒		🍴	
London Paddington 15 ⊖	d	11 27		11 57					12 57			13 03			13 57						14 57			15 57	
Slough 3	d																								
Reading 7	d	12 03		12 33					13 33			13 38			14 33						15 33			16 33	
Theale	d																								
Thatcham	d																								
Newbury	d			12 49											14 49									16 48	
Hungerford	d																								
Pewsey	d	12 41																							
Westbury	d	13 06							14 20															17 25	
Castle Cary	d	13 24													15 36									17 42	
Birmingham New Street 12	d				12 12						13 12					14 12			14 42			15 12			
Cardiff Central 7	d																								
Newport (South Wales)	d																								
Swindon	d											14 11													
Bristol Parkway 7	d				13 23						14 23					15 26			16 00			16 23			
Filton Abbey Wood	d																								
Bath Spa 7	d											14 40													
Bristol Temple Meads 10	d				13 44						14 44	14 55				15 44			16 14			16 44			
Weston-super-Mare	d																								
Bridgwater	d																								
Taunton	d	13 45		13 54	14 17				14 56		15 17	15 30			15 56	16 15			16 46		16 52	17 17		18 05	
Tiverton Parkway	d	13 58			14 29				15 09		15 29					16 27			16 58		17 05	17 29		18 18	
Exeter St Davids 6	a	14 14		14 20	14 44				15 24		15 43	15 54			16 22	16 44			17 12		17 20	17 43		18 36	
Exmouth	d					14 31							15 24					16 24					17 24		
Exeter Central	d					14 57				15 20			15 50					16 50					17 50		
Exeter St Davids 6	d	14 15		14 22	14 46	15 03			15 25	15 31	15 44	15 56	16 00	16 10	16 23	16 45		16 56	17 14		17 22	17 44	17 56	18 37	
Exeter St Thomas	d												16 03	16 12									17 59		
Starcross	d												16 11										18 07		
Dawlish Warren	d												16 16										18 12		
Dawlish	d	14 29				15 15				15 43			16 20	16 25				17 09	17 26				18 16		
Teignmouth	d	14 35				15 20				15 48			16 25	16 30				17 14	17 31				18 21		
Newton Abbot	a	14 42		14 45	15 04	15 27			15 46	15 55	16 02	16 16	16 32	16 36	16 42	17 04		17 21	17 37		17 40	18 02	18 28	18 57	
	d	14 42		14 47	15 04	15 28			15 46	15 56	16 03	16 17	16 33	16 36	16 43	17 06		17 22	17 38		17 41	18 03	18 29	18 59	
Torre	d					15 37				16 04			16 41					17 31					18 37		
Torquay	d	14 54				15 40				16 07			16 44					17 34	17 50				18 40		
Paignton	a	15 03				15 50				16 15			16 51					17 41	17 56				18 47		
Totnes	d			14 59	15 18				16 00		16 16			16 52	17 01	17 19					17 56	18 16			
Ivybridge	d													17 08											
Plymouth	a			15 28	15 43				16 29		16 42	16 55		17 22	17 30	17 46					18 22	18 42		19 36	
	d		14 58	15 35					16 35					17 35							18 25	18 55			19 43
Devonport	d																								
Dockyard	d																								
Keyham	d																								
St Budeaux Ferry Road	d																								
Saltash	d		15 07											17 44											19 52
St Germans	d		15 14											17 51											19 59
Menheniot	d													17x59											
Liskeard 6	d		15 26	15 57					16 59					18 05							18 51	19 18			20 11
Bodmin Parkway	d		15 39	16 12					17 12					18 17							19 05	19 30			20 23
Lostwithiel	d		15 45											18 22											20 28
Par	d		15 53	16 24				16 30	17 23					18 30							19 16	19 41			20 36
Newquay	a							17 22																	
St Austell	d		16 00	16 32					17 31					18 37							19 24	19 52			20 43
Truro	d		16 19	16 50					17 49					18 55							19 41	20 09			21 00
Redruth	d		16 32	17 02					18 02					19 08							19 54	20 20			21 14
Camborne	d		16 38	17 10					18 10					19 14							20 05	20 28			21 20
Hayle	d		16 45											19 21											21 27
St Erth	d		16 50	17 22					18 22					19 25						20 05	20 16	20 39			21 32
Penzance	a		17 00	17 35					18 33					19 37						20 14	20 27	20 47			21 42

A 🛒 to Plymouth

For connections from Heathrow Airport, Gatwick Airport and Oxford please refer to Tables 125A, 148 and 116

Sundays

until 1 January

London and Birmingham - Devon and Cornwall

Route Diagram - see first Page of Table 135

		XC	GW	GW	GW	XC	GW	GW	XC	GW	GW	XC	XC	GW	GW	GW	XC	GW	GW
		◇1		◇1	◇	◇1 A		◇1	◇1		◇1	◇1	◇1 B	◇1		◇1	◇1 B	◇1	
London Paddington 15 ⊖	d			16 57				17 57			18 57			19 03		19 57		20 57	23 50
Slough 3	d																		
Reading 7	d			17 33				18 33			19 33			19 38		20 33		21 33	00u37
Theale	d																		
Thatcham	d																		
Newbury	d							18 50								20 50			
Hungerford	d																		
Pewsey	d							19 10								21 10			
Westbury	d							19 29								21 29			
Castle Cary	d										20 30					21 47			
Birmingham New Street 12	d	16 12				17 12			18 12			18 42	19 12				20 12		
Cardiff Central 7	d																		
Newport (South Wales)	d																		
Swindon	d													20 11					
Bristol Parkway 7	d	17 22				18 24			19 23			20 03	20 23				21 23		
Filton Abbey Wood	d																		
Bath Spa 7	d													20 40					
Bristol Temple Meads 10	d	17 44			18 07	18 44			19 44			20 19	20 44	20 55			21 44		02 55
Weston-super-Mare	d				18 36							20 37		21 27					
Bridgwater	d				18 55														
Taunton	d	18 20		18 50	19 10	19 17		20 03	20 20		20 52	20 59	21 17	21 51		22 07	22 17	22s49	
Tiverton Parkway	d	18 32		19 03	19 25	19 29		20 17	20 32		21 05	21 12	21 29	22 04		22 20	22 29	23s03	
Exeter St Davids 6	a	18 46		19 18	19 43	19 47		20 32	20 46		21 21	21 27	21 43	22 19		22 36	22 46	23 19	04 04
Exmouth	d		18 24				19 24			20 24					21 24				
Exeter Central	d		18 49				19 50			20 50					21 50				
Exeter St Davids 6	d	18 47	18 56	19 20		19 49	19 56	20 32	20 47	20 56	21 22	21 30	21 44		21 56	22 37	22 47		04 35
Exeter St Thomas	d		18 59				19 59								21 59				
Starcross	d		19 07				20 07								22 07				
Dawlish Warren	d		19 12				20 12								22 12				
Dawlish	d		19 16				20 16			21 09	21 36	21 42			22 16				
Teignmouth	d		19 21				20 21			21 14	21 42	21 47			22 21				
Newton Abbot	a	19 05	19 28	19 39		20 07	20 28	20 54	21 05	21 21	21 48	21 54	22 02		22 28	22 57	23 05		04 55
	d	19 07	19 30	19 39		20 08	20 30	20 54	21 07	21 22	21 49	21 56	22 04		22 30	22 58	23 07		04 56
Torre	d		19 38				20 38			21 31					22 38				
Torquay	d		19 41				20 41			21 34					22 41				
Paignton	a		19 48				20 48			21 41					22 49				
Totnes	d	19 19		19 55		20 21		21 08	21 19		22 03		22 20			23 11	23 21		
Ivybridge	d																		
Plymouth	a	19 45		20 21		20 46		21 35	21 45		22 30	22 37	22 45			23 40	23 47		05 35
	d			20 25		20 50		21 40											06 28
Devonport	d																		
Dockyard	d																		
Keyham	d																		
St Budeaux Ferry Road	d																		
Saltash	d																		
St Germans	d																		
Menheniot	d																		
Liskeard 6	d			20 49		21 13		22 04											07 09
Bodmin Parkway	d			21 02		21 25		22 17											07 23
Lostwithiel	d																		07 29
Par	d			21 13		21 36		22 30											07 38
Newquay	a																		
St Austell	d			21 20		21 43		22 38											07 46
Truro	d			21 37		22 01		22 53											08 06
Redruth	d			21 51		22 12		23 08											08 20
Camborne	d			21 57		22 19		23 15											08 27
Hayle	d																		08 38
St Erth	d			22 10		22 30		23 27											08 45
Penzance	a			22 22		22 38		23 38											08 59

A to Plymouth

B to Bristol Temple Meads

For connections from Heathrow Airport, Gatwick Airport and Oxford please refer to Tables 125A, 148 and 116

Table 135

Sundays

8 January to 12 February

London and Birmingham - Devon and Cornwall

Route Diagram - see first Page of Table 135

		GW	GW	GW	GW	XC	GW	GW	XC	GW		GW	GW	GW	XC	GW	GW	GW	XC	GW		GW	GW	XC	GW
					◇	◇1		◇	◇1			◇1	◇1		◇1			◇1	◇1			◇1		◇1	
															A										
			⊥			⊥			⊥			⊏P	⊏P		⊥			⊏P	⊥			⊏P		⊥	
London Paddington 15 ⊖	d											08 00	08 57					09 57				10 57			
Slough 3	d																								
Reading 7	d											08 38	09 33					10 33				11 33			
Theale	d																								
Thatcham	d																								
Newbury	d												09 49												
Hungerford	d																								
Pewsey	d																	11 05							
Westbury	d												10 24												
Castle Cary	d																	11 35							
Birmingham New Street 12	d														09 12				10 30					11 30	
Cardiff Central 7	d																								
Newport (South Wales)	d																								
Swindon	d											09 11													
Bristol Parkway 7	d														10 23				11 41					12 41	
Filton Abbey Wood	d																								
Bath Spa 7	d											09 40													
Bristol Temple Meads 10	d				07 30	08 44		08 28	09 48			09 55			10 44				11 54					12 54	
Weston-super-Mare	d				07 53			08 59																	
Bridgwater	d				08 09			09 18																	
Taunton	d				08 24	09 16		09 32	10 21			10 29	11 00		11 16			11 57	12 27			12 47		13 26	
Tiverton Parkway	d				08 39	09 28		09 48	10 33			10 43	11 13		11 29				12 39					13 39	
Exeter St Davids 6	a				08 56	09 42		10 05	10 46			10 59	11 29		11 42			12 21	12 56			13 14		13 55	
Exmouth	d						09 10			10 21						11 24				12 29					13 24
Exeter Central	d						09 36			10 48						11 52				12 55			13 20		13 50
Exeter St Davids 6	d	08 52			09 05	09 44	09 54	10 06	10 48	10 53		11 02	11 29		11 44	11 57	12 15	12 24	12 58	13 01		13 15	13 25	13 57	14 00
Exeter St Thomas	d	08 55					09 57			10 56						12 00									14 03
Starcross	d	09 03					10 05			11 04						12 08									14 11
Dawlish Warren	d	09 08					10 10			11 09						12 13				13 12					14 16
Dawlish	d	09 12			09 18		10 14	10 21		11 13		11 19				12 17				13 16			13 38		14 20
Teignmouth	d	09 17			09 23		10 19	10 26		11 18		11 25				12 22				13 21			13 43		14 25
Newton Abbot	a	09 24			09 30	10 03	10 26	10 31	11 07	11 25		11 31	11 49		12 02	12 29	12 35	12 43	13 17	13 28		13 36	13 50	14 16	14 32
	d	09 26			09 30	10 04	10 37	10 33	11 09	11 27		11 32	11 50		12 03	12 31	12 36	12 45	13 18	13 29		13 38	13 52	14 17	14 34
Torre	d	09 34					10 45			11 35						12 39				13 37			14 00		14 42
Torquay	d	09 37					10 48			11 38						12 42				13 40			14 03		14 45
Paignton	a	09 44					10 54			11 45						12 49				13 47			14 10		14 52
Totnes	d				09 43	10 17		10 46	11 21			11 45	12 04		12 16		12 48	12 57	13 32					14 31	
Ivybridge	d				10 00												13 04								
Plymouth	a				10 14	10 43		11 15	11 48			12 13	12 33		12 42		13 17	13 26	13 59			14 14		14 57	
	d		09 15		10 15			11 15					12 35		12 55							14 20			
Devonport	d				10 19																				
Dockyard	d																								
Keyham	d																								
St Budeaux Ferry Road	d		09 21																						
Saltash	d		09 25		10 26			11 26																	
St Germans	d		09 31		10 33			11 33																	
Menheniot	d				10x41																				
Liskeard 6	d		09 43		10 47			11 45					12 59		13 18							14 44			
Bodmin Parkway	d		09 55		10 59			11 57					13 13		13 30							14 58			
Lostwithiel	d		10 01		11 04			12 02																	
Par	d		10 09	10 18	11 12			12 10					13 24	13 31	13 41										
Newquay	a			11 10										14 23											
St Austell	d		10 16		11 21			12 18					13 31		13 48							15 14			
Truro	d		10 35		11 40			12 35					13 50		14 05							15 32			
Redruth	d		10 48		11 53			12 48					14 02		14 19							15 43			
Camborne	d		10 54		11 59			12 54					14 10		14 25							15 51			
Hayle	d		11 01		12 06			13 01																	
St Erth	d		11 06		12 10			13 06					14 23		14 37							16 03			
Penzance	a		11 18		12 21			13 16					14 33		14 49							16 21			

A ⊥ to Plymouth

For connections from Heathrow Airport, Gatwick Airport and Oxford please refer to Tables 125A, 148 and 116

Table 135

Sundays

8 January to 12 February

London and Birmingham - Devon and Cornwall

Route Diagram - see first Page of Table 135

		GW	GW	GW	XC	GW		GW	GW	GW	XC	GW	GW	GW	GW	XC		GW	XC	GW	GW	XC	GW	GW	GW
		◇1		◇1	◇1			◇	◇1		◇1	◇1		◇	◇1	◇1			◇1		◇1	◇1		◇1	
																						A			
		☕	🛒	☕	🛒				☕		🛒	☕			☕	🛒			🛒		☕	🛒		☕	
London Paddington 15 ⊖	d	11 27		11 57					12 57			13 03			13 57						14 57			15 57	
Slough 3	d																								
Reading 7	d	12 03		12 33					13 33			13 38			14 33						15 33			16 33	
Theale	d																								
Thatcham	d																								
Newbury	d			12 49											14 49									16 48	
Hungerford	d																								
Pewsey	d	12 41																							
Westbury	d	13 06							14 20															17 25	
Castle Cary	d	13 24													15 36									17 42	
Birmingham New Street 12	d				12 12						13 12					14 12			14 42			15 12			
Cardiff Central 7	d																								
Newport (South Wales)	d																								
Swindon	d											14 11													
Bristol Parkway 7	d				13 23						14 23					15 26			16 00			16 23			
Filton Abbey Wood	d																								
Bath Spa 7	d											14 41													
Bristol Temple Meads 10	d				13 44						14 44	14 55				15 44			16 14			16 44			
Weston-super-Mare	d																								
Bridgwater	d																								
Taunton	d	13 45		13 54	14 17				14 56		15 17	15 31			15 56	16 15			16 46		16 52	17 17		18 05	
Tiverton Parkway	d	13 58			14 29				15 09		15 29					16 27			16 58		17 05	17 29		18 18	
Exeter St Davids 6	a	14 14		14 20	14 44				15 24		15 43	15 56			16 22	16 44			17 12		17 20	17 43		18 36	
Exmouth	d					14 31							15 24					16 24					17 24		
Exeter Central	d					14 57				15 20			15 50					16 50					17 50		
Exeter St Davids 6	d	14 15		14 22	14 46	15 03			15 25	15 31	15 44	15 57	16 00	16 10	16 23	16 45		16 56	17 14		17 22	17 44	17 56	18 37	
Exeter St Thomas	d												16 03	16 12									17 59		
Starcross	d												16 11										18 07		
Dawlish Warren	d												16 16										18 12		
Dawlish	d	14 29				15 15				15 43			16 20	16 25				17 09	17 26				18 16		
Teignmouth	d	14 35				15 20				15 48			16 25	16 30				17 14	17 31				18 21		
Newton Abbot	a	14 42		14 45	15 04	15 27			15 46	15 55	16 02	16 18	16 32	16 36	16 42	17 04		17 21	17 37		17 40	18 02	18 28	18 57	
	d	14 42		14 47	15 04	15 28			15 46	15 56	16 03	16 18	16 33	16 36	16 43	17 06		17 22	17 38		17 41	18 03	18 29	18 59	
Torre	d					15 37				16 04			16 41					17 31					18 37		
Torquay	d	14 54				15 40				16 07			16 44					17 34	17 50				18 40		
Paignton	a	15 02				15 50				16 15			16 51					17 41	17 56				18 47		
Totnes	d			14 59	15 18				16 00		16 16			16 52	17 01	17 19					17 56	18 16			
Ivybridge	d													17 08											
Plymouth	a			15 28	15 43				16 29		16 42	16 56		17 22	17 30	17 46					18 22	18 42		19 36	
	d		14 58	15 35					16 35					17 35							18 25	18 55			19 43
Devonport	d																								
Dockyard	d																								
Keyham	d																								
St Budeaux Ferry Road	d																								
Saltash	d		15 07											17 44											19 52
St Germans	d		15 14											17 51											19 59
Menheniot	d													17x59											
Liskeard 6	d		15 26	15 57					16 59					18 05							18 51	19 18			20 11
Bodmin Parkway	d		15 39	16 12					17 12					18 17							19 05	19 30			20 23
Lostwithiel	d		15 45											18 22											20 28
Par	d		15 53	16 24				16 30	17 23					18 30							19 16	19 41			20 36
Newquay	a							17 22																	
St Austell	d		16 00	16 32					17 31					18 37							19 24	19 52			20 43
Truro	d		16 19	16 50					17 49					18 55							19 41	20 09			21 00
Redruth	d		16 32	17 02					18 02					19 08							19 54	20 20			21 14
Camborne	d		16 38	17 10					18 10					19 14							20 05	20 28			21 20
Hayle	d		16 45											19 21											21 27
St Erth	d		16 50	17 22					18 22					19 25						20 05	20 16	20 39			21 32
Penzance	a		17 00	17 35					18 33					19 37						20 14	20 27	20 47			21 42

A 🛒 to Plymouth

For connections from Heathrow Airport, Gatwick Airport and Oxford please refer to Tables 125A, 148 and 116

Table 135

Sundays

8 January to 12 February

London and Birmingham - Devon and Cornwall

Route Diagram - see first Page of Table 135

		XC		GW	GW	GW	XC	GW	GW	XC	GW	GW		XC	XC	GW	GW	GW	XC	GW	GW
		◇ 1			◇ 1	◇	◇ 1 A		◇ 1	◇ 1		◇ 1		◇ 1	◇ 1 B	◇ 1		◇ 1	◇ 1 B	◇ 1	R
		trolley			buffet		trolley		buffet	trolley		buffet		trolley	trolley	buffet		buffet	trolley	buffet	sleeper, buffet
London Paddington 15 ⊖	d				16 57				17 57			18 57				19 03		19 57		20 57	23 50
Slough 3	d																				
Reading 7	d				17 33				18 33			19 33				19 38		20 33		21 33	00u37
Theale	d																				
Thatcham	d																				
Newbury	d								18 50									20 50			
Hungerford	d																				
Pewsey	d								19 10									21 10			
Westbury	d								19 29									21 29			
Castle Cary	d											20 30						21 47			
Birmingham New Street 12	d	16 12					17 12			18 12				18 42	19 12				20 12		
Cardiff Central 7	d																				
Newport (South Wales)	d																				
Swindon	d															20 11					
Bristol Parkway 7	d	17 22					18 24			19 23				20 03	20 23				21 23		
Filton Abbey Wood	d																				
Bath Spa 7	d															20 40					
Bristol Temple Meads 10	d	17 44				18 07	18 44			19 44				20 19	20 44	20 55			21 44		02 55
Weston-super-Mare	d					18 36								20 37		21 27					
Bridgwater	d					18 55															
Taunton	d	18 20			18 50	19 10	19 17		20 03	20 20		20 52		20 59	21 17	21 51		22 07	22 17	22s49	
Tiverton Parkway	d	18 32			19 03	19 25	19 29		20 17	20 32		21 05		21 12	21 29	22 04		22 20	22 29	23s03	
Exeter St Davids 6	a	18 46			19 18	19 43	19 47		20 32	20 46		21 21		21 27	21 43	22 19		22 36	22 46	23 19	04 04
Exmouth	d			18 24				19 24			20 24						21 24				
Exeter Central	d			18 49				19 50			20 50						21 50				
Exeter St Davids 6	d	18 47		18 56	19 20		19 49	19 56	20 32	20 47	20 56	21 22		21 30	21 44		21 56	22 37	22 47		04 35
Exeter St Thomas	d			18 59				19 59									21 59				
Starcross	d			19 07				20 07									22 07				
Dawlish Warren	d			19 12				20 12									22 12				
Dawlish	d			19 16				20 16			21 09	21 36		21 42			22 16				
Teignmouth	d			19 21				20 21			21 14	21 42		21 47			22 21				
Newton Abbot	a	19 05		19 28	19 39		20 07	20 28	20 54	21 05	21 21	21 48		21 54	22 02		22 28	22 57	23 05		04 55
	d	19 07		19 30	19 39		20 08	20 30	20 54	21 07	21 22	21 49		21 56	22 04		22 30	22 58	23 07		04 56
Torre	d			19 38				20 38			21 31						22 38				
Torquay	d			19 41				20 41			21 34						22 41				
Paignton	a			19 48				20 48			21 41						22 49				
Totnes	d	19 19			19 55		20 21		21 08	21 19		22 03			22 20			23 11	23 21		
Ivybridge	d																				
Plymouth	a	19 45			20 21		20 46		21 35	21 45		22 30		22 37	22 45			23 40	23 47		05 35
	d				20 25		20 50		21 40												06 28
Devonport	d																				
Dockyard	d																				
Keyham	d																				
St Budeaux Ferry Road	d																				
Saltash	d																				
St Germans	d																				
Menheniot	d																				
Liskeard 6	d				20 49		21 13		22 04												07 09
Bodmin Parkway	d				21 02		21 25		22 17												07 23
Lostwithiel	d																				07 29
Par	d				21 13		21 36		22 30												07 38
Newquay	a																				
St Austell	d				21 20		21 43		22 38												07 46
Truro	d				21 37		22 01		22 53												08 06
Redruth	d				21 51		22 12		23 08												08 20
Camborne	d				21 57		22 19		23 15												08 27
Hayle	d																				08 38
St Erth	d				22 10		22 30		23 27												08 45
Penzance	a				22 22		22 38		23 38												08 59

A trolley to Plymouth

B trolley to Bristol Temple Meads

For connections from Heathrow Airport, Gatwick Airport and Oxford please refer to Tables 125A, 148 and 116

Table 135

Sundays

19 February to 25 March

London and Birmingham - Devon and Cornwall

Route Diagram - see first Page of Table 135

		GW	GW	GW	GW	GW	GW	GW	GW	XC		GW	XC	GW	GW	XC	GW	GW	GW	XC		GW	XC	GW	XC
						◇							◇1					◇		◇1					
		🚌		🚌			🚌			🚌		🚌		🚌		🚌			🚌				🚌	🚌	🚌
			🛒										🛒		☕					🛒					
London Paddington 15 ⊖	d																								
Slough 3	d																								
Reading 7	d																								
Theale	d																								
Thatcham	d																								
Newbury	d																								
Hungerford	d																								
Pewsey	d																								
Westbury	d																								
Castle Cary	d																								
Birmingham New Street 12	d																								
Cardiff Central 7	d																								
Newport (South Wales)	d																								
Swindon	d																								
Bristol Parkway 7	d																								
Filton Abbey Wood	d																								
Bath Spa 7	d																								
Bristol Temple Meads 10	d					07 45							08 44					08 28		09 48					
Weston-super-Mare	d					08 07												09 06							
Bridgwater	d					08 21												09 23							
Taunton	d					08 36							09 16					09 35		10 21					
Tiverton Parkway	d					08 48	09 00			09 40			09 28	10 00				09 48		10 33			10 45	10 55	
Exeter St Davids 6	a					09 04							09 42					10 03		10 46					
Exmouth	d																09 10					10 21			
Exeter Central	d																09 36					10 48			
Exeter St Davids 6	d				08 52	09 06							09 44				09 54	10 04		10 48		10 53			
Exeter St Thomas	d				08 55												09 57					10 56			
Starcross	d				09 03												10 05					11 04			
Dawlish Warren	d				09 08												10 10					11 09			
Dawlish	d				09 12	09 19											10 14	10 18				11 13			
Teignmouth	d				09 17	09 25											10 19	10 24				11 18			
Newton Abbot	a				09 24	09 31							10 03				10 26	10 30		11 07		11 25			
	d	23p13		08 55	09 26							09 46				10 25	10 37		10 40			11 27			11 30
Torre	d				09 34												10 45					11 35			
Torquay	d				09 37												10 48					11 38			
Paignton	a				09 44												10 54					11 45			
Totnes	d	23p39		09 20								10 11				10 50			11 05						11 55
Ivybridge	d			09 50								10 41													
Plymouth	a	00 24		10 20			10 20			11 00		11 11		11 20		11 35			11 50				12 05	12 15	12 40
	d		09 15						10 30						11 30										
Devonport	d								10 35																
Dockyard	d																								
Keyham	d																								
St Budeaux Ferry Road	d		09 21																						
Saltash	d		09 25						10 43						11 42										
St Germans	d		09 31						10 51						11 50										
Menheniot	d								10x59						11x58										
Liskeard 6	d		09 43						11 06						12 05										
Bodmin Parkway	d		09 55						11 19						12 18										
Lostwithiel	d		10 01						11 25						12 24										
Par	d		10 09					10 18	11 34						12 32										
Newquay	a							11 10																	
St Austell	d		10 16						11 41						12 39										
Truro	d		10 35						12 00						12 58										
Redruth	d		10 48						12 12						13 10										
Camborne	d		10 54						12 19						13 16										
Hayle	d		11 01						12 28						13 25										
St Erth	d		11 06						12 34						13 31										
Penzance	a		11 18						12 45						13 42										

For connections from Heathrow Airport, Gatwick Airport and Oxford please refer to Tables 125A, 148 and 116

Table 135

Sundays

19 February to 25 March

London and Birmingham - Devon and Cornwall

Route Diagram - see first Page of Table 135

		GW	GW	GW	GW	XC		XC	XC	GW	XC	GW	GW	GW	GW	GW		XC	GW	XC	GW	GW	GW	XC	GW
		◇1			◇1	◇1		◇1							◇1			◇1					◇1		◇1
			🚌	🚌					🚌	🚌	🚌		🚌	🚌		🚌				🚌	🚌			🚌	
		🍴			🍴	🛒									🍴			🛒					🍴		🍴
London Paddington 15 ⊖	d	08 00			08 57										09 57										10 55
Slough 3	d																								
Reading 7	d	08 38			09 33										10 33										11 33
Theale	d																								
Thatcham	d																								
Newbury	d				09 50																				
Hungerford	d																								
Pewsey	d														11 05										
Westbury	d				10 24																				
Castle Cary	d														11 34										
Birmingham New Street 12	d					09 12												10 28							
Cardiff Central 7	d																								
Newport (South Wales)	d																								
Swindon	d	09 11																							
Bristol Parkway 7	d					10 23												11 41							
Filton Abbey Wood	d																								
Bath Spa 7	d	09 40																							
Bristol Temple Meads 10	d	09 55				10 44												11 54							
Weston-super-Mare	d																								
Bridgwater	d																								
Taunton	d	10 29			11 01	11 16									11 57			12 27							12 47
Tiverton Parkway	d	10 43	11 25		11 16	11 29			11 40				12 20		12 13			12 39		12 50	13 15				13 05
Exeter St Davids 6	a	10 59			11 32	11 42									12 27			12 56							13 14
Exmouth	d											11 24							12 29						
Exeter Central	d											11 52							12 55						
Exeter St Davids 6	d	11 02			11 33	11 44						11 57			12 30			12 58	13 01						13 15
Exeter St Thomas	d											12 00													
Starcross	d											12 08													
Dawlish Warren	d											12 13							13 12						
Dawlish	d	11 19										12 17							13 16						
Teignmouth	d	11 25										12 22							13 21						
Newton Abbot	a	11 31			11 54	12 03						12 29			12 49			13 17	13 28						13 41
	d			11 36						12 05	12 25	12 31		12 38		13 00			13 29					13 40	
Torre	d											12 39							13 37						
Torquay	d											12 42							13 40						
Paignton	a											12 49							13 47						
Totnes	d			12 01						12 30	12 50			13 03		13 25								14 05	
Ivybridge	d													13 33											
Plymouth	a		12 45	12 46					13 00	13 15	13 35		13 40	14 03		14 10				14 10	14 35			14 50	
	d							12 55															14 45		
Devonport	d																								
Dockyard	d																								
Keyham	d																								
St Budeaux Ferry Road	d																								
Saltash	d																								
St Germans	d																								
Menheniot	d																								
Liskeard 6	d							13 18															15 09		
Bodmin Parkway	d							13 30															15 23		
Lostwithiel	d																								
Par	d							13 41														13 45	15 34		
Newquay	a																					14 37			
St Austell	d							13 48															15 42		
Truro	d							14 08															16 01		
Redruth	d							14 19															16 12		
Camborne	d							14 26															16 20		
Hayle	d																								
St Erth	d							14 37															16 31		
Penzance	a							14 46															16 48		

For connections from Heathrow Airport, Gatwick Airport and Oxford please refer to Tables 125A, 148 and 116

Table 135

Sundays

19 February to 25 March

London and Birmingham - Devon and Cornwall

Route Diagram - see first Page of Table 135

		GW		XC	GW	XC	GW	GW	GW	GW	XC	GW		GW	XC	GW	XC	GW	XC	GW	GW	GW		GW	XC
						◇1			◇			◇1		◇1			◇1				◇1			◇1	
				bus	bus			bus			bus				bus	bus			bus			bus			bus
						trolley				trolley		restaurant		restaurant			trolley				restaurant			restaurant	
London Paddington 15 ⊖	d											11 27		11 57							12 57				
Slough 3	d																								
Reading 7	d											12 03		12 33							13 32				
Theale	d																								
Thatcham	d																								
Newbury	d													12 49											
Hungerford	d																								
Pewsey	d											12 41													
Westbury	d											13 06									14 20				
Castle Cary	d											13 24													
Birmingham New Street 12	d					11 30											12 12								
Cardiff Central 7	d																								
Newport (South Wales)	d																								
Swindon	d																								
Bristol Parkway 7	d					12 41											13 23								
Filton Abbey Wood	d																								
Bath Spa 7	d																								
Bristol Temple Meads 10	d					12 54											13 44								
Weston-super-Mare	d																								
Bridgwater	d																								
Taunton	d					13 26						13 45		13 54			14 17				14 56				
Tiverton Parkway	d			13 50		13 39		14 15				13 58		14 09	14 40		14 29				15 11	15 20			15 40
Exeter St Davids 6	a					13 55						14 14		14 25			14 44				15 27				
Exmouth	d						13 24											14 31							
Exeter Central	d	13 20					13 50											14 57		15 20					
Exeter St Davids 6	d	13 25				13 57	14 00					14 15		14 26			14 46	15 03		15 25	15 29				
Exeter St Thomas	d						14 03																		
Starcross	d						14 11																		
Dawlish Warren	d						14 16													15 42					
Dawlish	d	13 38					14 20					14 29						15 15		15 46					
Teignmouth	d	13 43					14 25					14 35						15 20		15 51					
Newton Abbot	a	13 50				14 16	14 32					14 42		14 47			15 05	15 27		15 58	15 51				
	d	13 52			13 55		14 34				14 40	14 42				14 55		15 28	15 30	15 59					
Torre	d	14 00					14 42											15 37		16 07					
Torquay	d	14 03					14 45					14 54						15 40		16 10					
Paignton	a	14 10					14 52					15 02						15 50		16 18					
Totnes	d				14 30						15 05					15 20			15 55						
Ivybridge	d																								
Plymouth	a			15 10	15 20			15 35			15 50				16 00	16 05			16 40			16 40			17 00
	d									15 45														16 50	
Devonport	d																								
Dockyard	d																								
Keyham	d																								
St Budeaux Ferry Road	d																								
Saltash	d									15 54															
St Germans	d									16 01															
Menheniot	d																								
Liskeard 6	d									16 13														17 13	
Bodmin Parkway	d									16 26														17 26	
Lostwithiel	d									16 32															
Par	d								15 45	16 40														17 39	
Newquay	a								16 37																
St Austell	d									16 47														17 45	
Truro	d									17 06														18 10	
Redruth	d									17 19														18 23	
Camborne	d									17 25														18 31	
Hayle	d									17 32															
St Erth	d									17 37														18 44	
Penzance	a									17 47														18 54	

For connections from Heathrow Airport, Gatwick Airport and Oxford please refer to Tables 125A, 148 and 116

Table 135

Sundays

19 February to 25 March

London and Birmingham - Devon and Cornwall

Route Diagram - see first Page of Table 135

		GW	XC	GW	XC	GW	GW	GW		GW	XC	GW	GW	GW	XC	GW	GW	XC		GW	GW	XC	XC	GW	XC
			◇1				◇1			◇1			◇1		◇1					◇1		◇1			◇1
		🚌		🚌	🚌			🚌			🚌	🚌		🚌			🚌	🚌					🚌	🚌	
			🛒				☕			☕			☕		🛒					☕					🛒
London Paddington 15 ⊖	d						13 03						13 57							14 57					
Slough 3	d																								
Reading 7	d						13 38						14 33							15 32					
Theale	d																								
Thatcham	d																								
Newbury	d												14 49												
Hungerford	d																								
Pewsey	d																								
Westbury	d																								
Castle Cary	d												15 36												
Birmingham New Street 12	d		13 12												14 12										15 12
Cardiff Central 7	d																								
Newport (South Wales)	d																								
Swindon	d						14 09																		
Bristol Parkway 7	d		14 23												15 26										16 23
Filton Abbey Wood	d																								
Bath Spa 7	d						14 39																		
Bristol Temple Meads 10	d		14 44				14 55								15 44										16 44
Weston-super-Mare	d																								
Bridgwater	d																								
Taunton	d		15 17				15 31						15 56		16 15					16 52					17 17
Tiverton Parkway	d		15 29	15 51			15 47	16 20			16 40		16 13		16 27		17 15			17 07			17 40		17 29
Exeter St Davids 6	a		15 43				16 01						16 32		16 44					17 22					17 43
Exmouth	d					15 24										16 24									
Exeter Central	d					15 50										16 50									
Exeter St Davids 6	d		15 44			15 56	16 03						16 34		16 45	16 56				17 24					17 44
Exeter St Thomas	d					15 59																			
Starcross	d					16 07																			
Dawlish Warren	d					16 19																			
Dawlish	d					16 23	16 20									17 09									
Teignmouth	d					16 28	16 26									17 14									
Newton Abbot	a		16 05			16 35	16 32						16 53		17 06	17 21				17 44					18 13
	d	16 00			16 30	16 36						16 40		17 00		17 22		17 30						17 55	
Torre	d					16 44										17 31									
Torquay	d					16 47										17 34									
Paignton	a					16 54										17 41									
Totnes	d	16 25			16 55							17 05		17 25				17 55						18 20	
Ivybridge	d											17 35													
Plymouth	a	17 10		17 11	17 40			17 40			18 00	18 05		18 10			18 35	18 40					19 00	19 05	
	d									17 50												18 55			
Devonport	d																								
Dockyard	d																								
Keyham	d																								
St Budeaux Ferry Road	d																								
Saltash	d									18 00															
St Germans	d									18 08															
Menheniot	d									18x16															
Liskeard 6	d									18 21												19 18			
Bodmin Parkway	d									18 34												19 30			
Lostwithiel	d									18 42															
Par	d									18 51												19 41			
Newquay	a																								
St Austell	d									18 56												19 52			
Truro	d									19 15												20 09			
Redruth	d									19 27												20 20			
Camborne	d									19 35												20 28			
Hayle	d									19 46															
St Erth	d									19 52											20 05	20 39			
Penzance	a									20 02											20 14	20 47			

For connections from Heathrow Airport, Gatwick Airport and Oxford please refer to Tables 125A, 148 and 116

Table 135

Sundays

19 February to 25 March

London and Birmingham - Devon and Cornwall

Route Diagram - see first Page of Table 135

Station		GW	XC	GW	GW	XC	GW	XC	GW	GW	GW	XC	GW	GW	XC	XC	GW	GW	XC	GW	GW	GW
				◇1		◇1	◇1						◇1	◇	◇1	◇1				◇1		
			bus	restaurant	bus	trolley	restaurant	bus	bus		bus	bus	restaurant		trolley		bus		bus	restaurant	bus	trolley
London Paddington 15 ⊖	d			15 57									16 57							17 55		
Slough 3	d																					
Reading 7	d			16 33									17 32							18 32		
Theale	d																					
Thatcham	d																					
Newbury	d			16 48																18 50		
Hungerford	d																					
Pewsey	d																			19 10		
Westbury	d			17 25																19 29		
Castle Cary	d			17 42																		
Birmingham New Street 12	d					16 12									17 12							
Cardiff Central 7	d																					
Newport (South Wales)	d																					
Swindon	d																					
Bristol Parkway 7	d					17 22									18 28							
Filton Abbey Wood	d																					
Bath Spa 7	d																					
Bristol Temple Meads 10	d					17 44								18 07	18 44							
Weston-super-Mare	d													18 36								
Bridgwater	d													18 55								
Taunton	d			18 05		18 20							18 50	19 10	19 17					20 03		
Tiverton Parkway	d			18 20	18 25	18 32		18 45			19 10		19 06	19 25	19 29					20 19	20 25	
Exeter St Davids 6	a			18 36		18 46							19 21	19 43	19 47					20 35		
Exmouth	d	17 24								18 24								19 24				
Exeter Central	d	17 50								18 49								19 50				
Exeter St Davids 6	d	17 58		18 37		18 47				18 56			19 23					19 56		20 36		
Exeter St Thomas	d	18 01								18 59								19 59				
Starcross	d	18 09								19 07								20 07				
Dawlish Warren	d	18 14								19 12								20 12				
Dawlish	d	18 18								19 16								20 16				
Teignmouth	d	18 23								19 21								20 21				
Newton Abbot	a	18 30		18 57		19 06				19 28			19 42					20 28		20 56		
	d	18 31	18 30						19 10	19 30		19 30					19 55	20 30	20 30			
Torre	d	18 39								19 38								20 38				
Torquay	d	18 42								19 41								20 41				
Paignton	a	18 49								19 48								20 48				
Totnes	d		18 55						19 35			19 55					20 20		20 55			
Ivybridge	d																					
Plymouth	a		19 40		19 45			20 05	20 20		20 30	20 40					21 05		21 40		21 45	
	d						19 55									20 50						21 55
Devonport	d																					
Dockyard	d																					
Keyham	d																					
St Budeaux Ferry Road	d																					
Saltash	d						20 05															
St Germans	d						20 13															
Menheniot	d																					
Liskeard 6	d						20 23									21 13						22 19
Bodmin Parkway	d						20 37									21 25						22 32
Lostwithiel	d						20 44															
Par	d						20 52									21 36						22 44
Newquay	a																					
St Austell	d						20 59									21 43						22 51
Truro	d						21 17									22 01						23 10
Redruth	d						21 29									22 12						23 23
Camborne	d						21 38									22 19						23 29
Hayle	d						21 47															
St Erth	d						21 51									22 30						23 39
Penzance	a						22 03									22 38						23 50

For connections from Heathrow Airport, Gatwick Airport and Oxford please refer to Tables 125A, 148 and 116

Table 135

Sundays

19 February to 25 March

London and Birmingham - Devon and Cornwall

Route Diagram - see first Page of Table 135

		XC	GW	GW	GW	XC	XC	GW	XC	XC		GW	GW	GW	GW	XC	GW	XC	GW	GW		XC	GW		
																							■		
							◇1	◇1	◇1			◇1			◇1	◇1			◇1						
									A							A									
		bus	bus		bus	bus				bus			bus				bus	bus		bus		bus	sleeper		
							trolley	restaurant	trolley			restaurant			restaurant	trolley			restaurant				restaurant		
London Paddington 15 ⊖	d							18 57				19 03			19 57				20 57				23 50		
Slough 3	d																								
Reading 7	d							19 32				19 38			20 32				21 32				00u37		
Theale	d																								
Thatcham	d																								
Newbury	d														20 50										
Hungerford	d																								
Pewsey	d														21 10										
Westbury	d														21 29										
Castle Cary	d							20 30							21 47										
Birmingham New Street 12	d						18 12		19 12							20 12									
Cardiff Central 7	d																								
Newport (South Wales)	d																								
Swindon	d											20 11													
Bristol Parkway 7	d						19 23		20 23							21 23									
Filton Abbey Wood	d																								
Bath Spa 7	d											20 40													
Bristol Temple Meads 10	d						19 44		20 44			20 55				21 44							02 55		
Weston-super-Mare	d											21 27													
Bridgwater	d																								
Taunton	d						20 20	20 52	21 17			21 51			22 07	22 17			22s49						
Tiverton Parkway	d	20 45			21 15	19 40	20 32	21 06	21 29	21 40		22 04			22 23	22 29	22 30	22 40	23s03						
Exeter St Davids 6	a						20 45	21 22	21 42			22 19			22 39	22 45			23 19				04 04		
Exmouth	d			20 24										21 24											
Exeter Central	d			20 50										21 50											
Exeter St Davids 6	d			20 56				21 23						21 56	22 39							22 55	04 35		
Exeter St Thomas	d													21 59											
Starcross	d													22 07											
Dawlish Warren	d													22 12											
Dawlish	d			21 09				21 37						22 16											
Teignmouth	d			21 14				21 43						22 21											
Newton Abbot	a			21 21				21 50						22 28	23 01							23s25	04 55		
	d		21 06	21 22									22 00	22 30						23 10			04 56		
Torre	d			21 31										22 38											
Torquay	d			21 34										22 41											
Paignton	a			21 41										22 49											
Totnes	d		21 31										22 25							23 35		23s50			
Ivybridge	d																								
Plymouth	a	22 05	22 16		22 35	23 00				23 00			23 10				23 50	23 59		00 20		00 35	05 35		
	d																						06 28		
Devonport	d																								
Dockyard	d																								
Keyham	d																								
St Budeaux Ferry Road	d																								
Saltash	d																								
St Germans	d																								
Menheniot	d																								
Liskeard 6	d																						07 09		
Bodmin Parkway	d																						07 23		
Lostwithiel	d																						07 29		
Par	d																						07 38		
Newquay	a																								
St Austell	d																						07 46		
Truro	d																						08 06		
Redruth	d																						08 20		
Camborne	d																						08 27		
Hayle	d																						08 38		
St Erth	d																						08 45		
Penzance	a																						08 59		

A trolley to Bristol Temple Meads

For connections from Heathrow Airport, Gatwick Airport and Oxford please refer to Tables 125A, 148 and 116

Table 135

Sundays

from 1 April

London and Birmingham - Devon and Cornwall

Route Diagram - see first Page of Table 135

		GW	GW	GW	GW	XC	GW	GW	XC	GW	GW	GW	GW	GW	XC	GW	GW	GW	XC	GW	GW	GW	XC
					◇	◇1		◇	◇1		◇1	◇1			◇1 A			◇1	◇1		◇1		◇1
			[trolley]			[trolley]			[trolley]		[restaurant]	[restaurant]	[bus]		[trolley]			[restaurant]	[trolley]		[restaurant]		[trolley]
London Paddington 15 ⊖	d										08 00	08 37						09 30			10 30		
Slough 3	d																						
Reading 7	d										08 35	09 15						10 05			11 05		
Theale	d																						
Thatcham	d																						
Newbury	d																						
Hungerford	d																						
Pewsey	d												09 30										
Westbury	d																	11 18					
Castle Cary	d																	11 36					
Birmingham New Street 12	d														09 12				10 30				11 30
Cardiff Central 7	d																						
Newport (South Wales)	d																						
Swindon	d										09 08	09 48	10a15										
Bristol Parkway 7	d														10 23				11 41				12 41
Filton Abbey Wood	d																						
Bath Spa 7	d										09 38												
Bristol Temple Meads 10	d				07 30	08 44		08 28	09 48		09 54				10 44				11 54				12 54
Weston-super-Mare	d				07 53			08 59															
Bridgwater	d				08 09			09 18															
Taunton	d				08 24	09 16		09 32	10 21		10 28	11 00			11 16			11 57	12 27		12 45		13 26
Tiverton Parkway	d				08 39	09 28		09 48	10 33		10 42	11 13			11 29				12 39		12 58		13 39
Exeter St Davids 6	a				08 56	09 42		10 05	10 46		10 58	11 29			11 42			12 22	12 56		13 13		13 55
Exmouth	d						09 10			10 21						11 24				12 29			
Exeter Central	d						09 36			10 48						11 52				12 55		13 20	
Exeter St Davids 6	d	08 52			09 05	09 44	09 54	10 06	10 48	10 53	11 01	11 29			11 44	11 57	12 15	12 24	12 58	13 01	13 16	13 25	13 57
Exeter St Thomas	d	08 55					09 57			10 56						12 00							
Starcross	d	09 03					10 05			11 04						12 08							
Dawlish Warren	d	09 08					10 10			11 09						12 13				13 12			
Dawlish	d	09 12			09 18		10 14	10 21		11 13	11 19					12 17				13 16		13 38	
Teignmouth	d	09 17			09 23		10 19	10 26		11 18	11 25					12 22				13 21		13 43	
Newton Abbot	a	09 24			09 30	10 03	10 26	10 31	11 07	11 25	11 31	11 49			12 02	12 29	12 35	12 44	13 17	13 28	13 36	13 50	14 16
	d	09 26			09 30	10 04	10 37	10 33	11 09	11 27	11 32	11 50			12 03	12 31	12 36	12 45	13 18	13 29	13 38	13 52	14 17
Torre	d	09 34					10 45			11 35						12 39				13 37		14 00	
Torquay	d	09 37					10 48			11 38						12 42				13 40		14 03	
Paignton	a	09 44					10 54			11 45						12 49				13 47		14 10	
Totnes	d				09 43	10 17		10 46	11 21		11 45	12 04			12 16		12 48	12 58	13 32				14 31
Ivybridge	d				10 00												13 04						
Plymouth	a				10 14	10 43		11 15	11 48		12 13	12 31			12 42		13 17	13 26	13 59		14 15		14 57
	d		09 15		10 15			11 15				12 35			12 55						14 20		
Devonport	d				10 19																		
Dockyard	d																						
Keyham	d																						
St Budeaux Ferry Road	d		09 21																				
Saltash	d		09 25		10 26			11 26															
St Germans	d		09 31		10 33			11 33															
Menheniot	d				10x41																		
Liskeard 6	d		09 43		10 47			11 45				12 59			13 18						14 44		
Bodmin Parkway	d		09 55		10 59			11 57				13 14			13 30						14 58		
Lostwithiel	d		10 01		11 04			12 02															
Par	d		10 09	10 18	11 12			12 10				13 25		13 31	13 41								
Newquay	a			11 10										14 23									
St Austell	d		10 16		11 21			12 18				13 31			13 48						15 14		
Truro	d		10 35		11 40			12 35				13 51			14 05						15 32		
Redruth	d		10 48		11 53			12 48				14 02			14 19						15 43		
Camborne	d		10 54		11 59			12 54				14 10			14 25						15 51		
Hayle	d		11 01		12 06			13 01															
St Erth	d		11 06		12 10			13 06				14 23			14 37						16 03		
Penzance	a		11 18		12 21			13 16				14 33			14 49						16 21		

A [trolley] to Plymouth

For connections from Heathrow Airport, Gatwick Airport and Oxford please refer to Tables 125A, 148 and 116

Table 135

Sundays

from 1 April

London and Birmingham - Devon and Cornwall

Route Diagram - see first Page of Table 135

		GW	GW	GW	GW	GW		XC	GW	GW	GW	GW	XC	GW	GW	GW		GW	GW	GW	XC	GW	GW	GW	XC
			◇1			◇1		◇1		◇	◇1		◇1	◇1					◇	◇1	◇1			◇1	◇1
				[bus]											[bus]			[bus]							
			[restaurant]		[trolley]	[restaurant]		[trolley]			[restaurant]		[trolley]	[restaurant]						[restaurant]	[trolley]			[restaurant]	[trolley]
London Paddington 15 ⊖	d		11 03			11 30					12 30			13 03						13 30				14 30	
Slough 3	d																								
Reading 7	d		11 38			12 05					13 05			13 38						14 05				15 05	
Theale	d																								
Thatcham	d																								
Newbury	d																								
Hungerford	d																								
Pewsey	d			11 34											14 34			15 30							
Westbury	d																								
Castle Cary	d																			15 26					
Birmingham New Street 12	d							12 12					13 12								14 12				14 42
Cardiff Central 7	d																								
Newport (South Wales)	d																								
Swindon	d		12 11	12a19		12 34					13 34			14 11	15a19			16a15							
Bristol Parkway 7	d							13 23					14 23								15 26				16 00
Filton Abbey Wood	d																								
Bath Spa 7	d		12 40											14 42											
Bristol Temple Meads 10	d		12 55					13 44					14 44	14 55							15 44				16 14
Weston-super-Mare	d		13 17																						
Bridgwater	d																								
Taunton	d		13 40			13 54		14 17			14 56		15 17	15 31						15 46	16 15			16 37	16 46
Tiverton Parkway	d							14 29			15 09		15 29								16 27			16 50	16 58
Exeter St Davids 6	a		14 04			14 18		14 44			15 24		15 43	15 56						16 12	16 44			17 05	17 12
Exmouth	d	13 24							14 31							15 24						16 24			
Exeter Central	d	13 50							14 57			15 20				15 50						16 50			
Exeter St Davids 6	d	14 00	14 06			14 18		14 46	15 03		15 25	15 31	15 44	15 57		16 00			16 10	16 25	16 45	16 56		17 07	17 14
Exeter St Thomas	d	14 03														16 03			16 12						
Starcross	d	14 11														16 11									
Dawlish Warren	d	14 16														16 16									
Dawlish	d	14 20	14 26						15 15			15 43				16 20			16 25			17 09			17 26
Teignmouth	d	14 25	14 32						15 20			15 48				16 25			16 30			17 14			17 31
Newton Abbot	a	14 32	14 38			14 43		15 04	15 27		15 46	15 55	16 02	16 18		16 32			16 36	16 43	17 04	17 21		17 26	17 37
	d	14 34	14 41			14 44		15 04	15 28		15 46	15 56	16 03	16 18		16 33			16 36	16 44	17 06	17 22		17 26	17 38
Torre	d	14 42							15 37			16 04				16 41						17 31			
Torquay	d	14 45	14 53						15 40			16 07				16 44						17 34			17 50
Paignton	a	14 52	15 00						15 50			16 15				16 51						17 41			17 56
Totnes	d					14 57		15 18			16 00		16 16						16 52	16 59	17 19			17 42	
Ivybridge	d																		17 08						
Plymouth	a					15 25		15 43			16 29		16 42	16 56					17 22	17 31	17 46			18 09	
	d				14 58	15 35					16 35								17 35					18 25	
Devonport	d																								
Dockyard	d																								
Keyham	d																								
St Budeaux Ferry Road	d																								
Saltash	d				15 07														17 44						
St Germans	d				15 14														17 51						
Menheniot	d																		17x59						
Liskeard 6	d				15 26	15 57					16 58								18 05					18 51	
Bodmin Parkway	d				15 39	16 12					17 11								18 17					19 05	
Lostwithiel	d				15 45														18 22						
Par	d				15 53	16 24				16 30	17 23								18 30					19 16	
Newquay	a									17 22															
St Austell	d				16 00	16 32					17 29								18 37					19 24	
Truro	d				16 19	16 50					17 48								18 55					19 41	
Redruth	d				16 32	17 02					18 00								19 08					19 54	
Camborne	d				16 38	17 10					18 08								19 14					20 05	
Hayle	d				16 45														19 21						
St Erth	d				16 50	17 22					18 22								19 25				20 05	20 16	
Penzance	a				17 00	17 35					18 32								19 37				20 14	20 27	

For connections from Heathrow Airport, Gatwick Airport and Oxford please refer to Tables 125A, 148 and 116

Table 135

Sundays
from 1 April

London and Birmingham - Devon and Cornwall

Route Diagram - see first Page of Table 135

		XC		GW	GW	GW	XC	GW	GW	XC	GW	GW		GW	GW	XC	GW	XC	GW	XC	GW	GW		GW	XC
		◇1			◇1		◇1		◇1	◇1		◇			◇1	◇1		◇1	◇1	◇1	◇1				◇1
		A								A										B					B
											bus											bus			
		trolley			buffet		trolley		buffet	trolley					buffet	trolley		trolley	buffet	trolley	buffet				trolley
London Paddington 15 ⊖	d				15 30				16 30						17 57				18 57		19 03				
Slough 3	d																								
Reading 7	d				16 05				17 05						18 32				19 32		19 38				
Theale	d																								
Thatcham	d																								
Newbury	d																								
Hungerford	d																								
Pewsey	d										17 55											20 05			
Westbury	d				17 04																				
Castle Cary	d				17 22														20 45						
Birmingham New Street 12	d	15 12					16 12			17 12						18 12		18 42		19 12					20 12
Cardiff Central 7	d																								
Newport (South Wales)	d																								
Swindon	d								17 34		18a40				19 01						20 11	20a50			
Bristol Parkway 7	d	16 23					17 22			18 24						19 23		20 03		20 23					21 23
Filton Abbey Wood	d																								
Bath Spa 7	d																				20 40				
Bristol Temple Meads 10	d	16 44					17 44			18 44		18 25				19 44		20 19		20 44	20 55				21 44
Weston-super-Mare	d											18 58						20 37			21 27				
Bridgwater	d											19 17													
Taunton	d	17 17			17 44		18 20		18 50	19 17		19 32			20 07	20 20		20 59	21 07	21 17	21 51				22 17
Tiverton Parkway	d	17 29			17 57		18 32		19 02	19 29		19 48			20 21	20 32		21 12	21 20	21 29	22 04				22 29
Exeter St Davids 6	a	17 43			18 12		18 46		19 18	19 47		20 06			20 36	20 46		21 25	21 37	21 43	22 19				22 46
Exmouth	d			17 24				18 24						19 24			20 24							21 24	
Exeter Central	d			17 50				18 49						19 50			20 50							21 50	
Exeter St Davids 6	d	17 44		17 56	18 13		18 47	18 56	19 20	19 49				19 56	20 36	20 47	20 56	21 28	21 37	21 46				21 56	22 47
Exeter St Thomas	d			17 59				18 59						19 59										21 59	
Starcross	d			18 07				19 07						20 07										22 07	
Dawlish Warren	d			18 12				19 12						20 12										22 12	
Dawlish	d			18 16				19 16						20 16			21 09	21 40						22 16	
Teignmouth	d			18 21				19 21						20 21			21 14	21 45						22 21	
Newton Abbot	a	18 02		18 28	18 33		19 05	19 28	19 40	20 07				20 28	20 58	21 05	21 21	21 51	21 58	22 07				22 28	23 05
	d	18 03		18 29	18 35		19 07	19 30	19 40	20 08				20 30	21 12	21 07	21 22	21 52	21 58	22 09				22 30	23 07
Torre	d			18 37				19 38						20 38			21 31							22 38	
Torquay	d			18 40				19 41						20 41			21 34							22 41	
Paignton	a			18 47				19 48						20 48			21 41							22 49	
Totnes	d	18 16					19 19		19 54	20 21					21 28	21 19			22 13	22 25					23 21
Ivybridge	d																								
Plymouth	a	18 42			19 12		19 45		20 22	20 46					21 55	21 45		22 32	22 40	22 50					23 47
	d	18 55				19 43			20 25	20 50					21 56										
Devonport	d																								
Dockyard	d																								
Keyham	d																								
St Budeaux Ferry Road	d																								
Saltash	d					19 52																			
St Germans	d					19 59																			
Menheniot	d																								
Liskeard 6	d	19 18				20 11			20 49	21 13					22 21										
Bodmin Parkway	d	19 30				20 23			21 02	21 25					22 35										
Lostwithiel	d					20 28																			
Par	d	19 41				20 36			21 13	21 36					22 48										
Newquay	a																								
St Austell	d	19 52				20 43			21 20	21 43					22 56										
Truro	d	20 09				21 00			21 37	22 01					23 13										
Redruth	d	20 20				21 14			21 51	22 12					23 26										
Camborne	d	20 28				21 20			21 57	22 19					23 33										
Hayle	d					21 27																			
St Erth	d	20 39				21 32			22 10	22 30					23 45										
Penzance	a	20 47				21 42			22 22	22 38					23 56										

A trolley to Plymouth

B trolley to Bristol Temple Meads

For connections from Heathrow Airport, Gatwick Airport and Oxford please refer to Tables 125A, 148 and 116

Table 135

Sundays

from 1 April

London and Birmingham - Devon and Cornwall

Route Diagram - see first Page of Table 135

		GW	GW	GW	GW
					R
		◇1	◇1		
				🚌	🛏
		☕	☕		☕
London Paddington 15 ⊖	d	19 57	20 57		23 50
Slough 3	d				
Reading 7	d	20 31	21 31		00u37
Theale	d				
Thatcham	d				
Newbury	d				
Hungerford	d				
Pewsey	d			22 00	
Westbury	d	21 36			
Castle Cary	d	21 54			
Birmingham New Street 12	d				
Cardiff Central 7	d				
Newport (South Wales)	d				
Swindon	d			22a45	
Bristol Parkway 7	d				
Filton Abbey Wood	d				
Bath Spa 7	d				
Bristol Temple Meads 10	d				02 55
Weston-super-Mare	d				
Bridgwater	d				
Taunton	d	22 19	22s59		
Tiverton Parkway	d	22 33	23s13		
Exeter St Davids 6	a	22 52	23 29		04 04
Exmouth	d				
Exeter Central	d				
Exeter St Davids 6	d	22 52			04 35
Exeter St Thomas	d				
Starcross	d				
Dawlish Warren	d				
Dawlish	d	23 06			
Teignmouth	d	23 12			
Newton Abbot	a	23 19			04 55
	d	23 19			04 56
Torre	d				
Torquay	d				
Paignton	a				
Totnes	d	23 32			
Ivybridge	d				
Plymouth	a	00 01			05 35
	d				06 28
Devonport	d				
Dockyard	d				
Keyham	d				
St Budeaux Ferry Road	d				
Saltash	d				
St Germans	d				
Menheniot	d				
Liskeard 6	d				07 09
Bodmin Parkway	d				07 23
Lostwithiel	d				07 29
Par	d				07 38
Newquay	a				
St Austell	d				07 46
Truro	d				08 06
Redruth	d				08 20
Camborne	d				08 27
Hayle	d				08 38
St Erth	d				08 45
Penzance	a				08 59

For connections from Heathrow Airport, Gatwick Airport and Oxford please refer to Tables 125A, 148 and 116

Cornwall and Devon - Birmingham and London

Route Diagram - see first Page of Table 135

Miles	Miles			GW	GW	GW	GW	GW	GW	XC	GW	GW		GW	GW	GW	XC	GW	GW	GW	GW	XC		XC	GW
				MO	MO	MX	MO	MO	MX	MX															
							R	R	R																
				◇1	◇1					◇1	◇1	◇1		◇1		◇1	◇1	◇1	◇1			◇1		◇1	◇1
				A	B		A	B	C					D					D						E
							🛏	🛏	🛏																
				🍴	🍴		🍴	🍴	🍴		🍴	🍴		🍴⊘		🍴	🛒	🍴	🍴⊘			🛒		🛒	🍴⊘
0	—	**Penzance**	d				21p15	21p15	21p45	22p08															05 05
5¾	—	St Erth	d				21p25	21p25	21p55	22p16															
7¼	—	Hayle	d							22p20															
13¾	—	Camborne	d				21p38	21p38	22p07	22p30															
16¾	—	Redruth	d				21p45	21p45	22p14	22p36															05 25
25¾	—	Truro	d				22p00	22p00	22p27	22p48															05 38
40¼	—	St Austell	d				22p18	22p18	22p45	23p04															05 55
—	—	Newquay	d																						
44¾	—	Par	d						22p54	23p12															
49¼	—	Lostwithiel	d							23p19															
52¾	—	Bodmin Parkway	d				22p35	22p35	23p06	23p26															06 11
61¾	—	Liskeard 6	d				22p50	22p50	23p21	23p39															06 26
65	—	Menheniot	d																						
70¼	—	St Germans	d																						
75¼	—	Saltash	d																						
76½	—	St Budeaux Ferry Road	d																						
77¼	—	Keyham	d																						
77¾	—	Dockyard	d																						
78¼	—	Devonport	d																						
79½	—	**Plymouth**	a				23p15	23p15	23p45	00 04															06 51
—	—		d	19p55			23p20	01 50	23p51							05 09	05 20	05 30	05 53			06 25			06 55
90¼	—	Ivybridge	d																						
102¾	—	Totnes	d				23p48	02 18	00 20								05 45	05 58				06 50			
—	0	Paignton	d			23p41														06 10	06 34			07 02	
—	2¼	Torquay	d			23p46														06 15	06 39			07 08	
—	3	Torre	d			23p49														06 18	06 42				
111½	8¼	Newton Abbot	a	20p31		23p57	23p59	02 29	00 32							05 45	05 56	06 09	06 28	06 26	06 50	07 01		07 18	07 30
—	—		d	20p32	20p32	23p59	00 01	02 31	00 33							05 47	06 02	06 11	06 31	06 34	06 52	07 03		07 19	07 32
116½	—	Teignmouth	d			00 06										05 54				06 41	06 59			07 26	
119¼	—	Dawlish	d			00 11												06 21		06 46	07 04			07 31	
121	—	Dawlish Warren	d			00 16														06 51	07 15				
123	—	Starcross	d			00 20														06 55	07 19				
130½	—	Exeter St Thomas	d			00 29														07 04	07 28				
131½	—	**Exeter St Davids** 6	a	20p53	20p53	00 34	00 40	02 57	00 55							06 10	06 19	06 33	06 51	07 09	07 33	07 21		07 43	07 52
—	—	Exeter Central	a																	07 14	07 39				
—	—	Exmouth	a																	07 43	08 18				
—	—	**Exeter St Davids** 6	d	20p55	20p55		01 06	02 59	01 06					05 46	06 00	06 12	06 22	06 35	06 52			07 23		07 45	07 53
148	—	Tiverton Parkway	d	21p10	21p12									06 02	06 17	06 27	06 36	06 51				07 37		07 58	
162¼	—	Taunton	d	21p23	21p26				01 36					06 17	06 34	06 55	06 50	07 06	07 18			07 51		08 13	08 19
—	11¾	Bridgwater	a												06 46	07 05									
—	25¾	Weston-super-Mare	a												07 04	07 24								08 32	
—	45½	**Bristol Temple Meads** 10	a	22p00	22p00		02 14		02 34						07 41	07 57	07 24					08 26		08 53	
—	—	Bath Spa 7	a	22p22	22p22											08 11									
—	—	Filton Abbey Wood	a												07 58										
—	51¼	Bristol Parkway 7	a												08 05		07 38					08 38		09 08	
—	—	Swindon	a	22p50	22p50		03 21		03 15							08 40									
—	—	Newport (South Wales)	a																						
—	—	Cardiff Central 7	a																						
—	138¼	**Birmingham New Street** 12	a														08 56					09 56		10 26	
190	—	Castle Cary	d											06 38				07 27							
209¾	—	Westbury	d								06 06	06 18		07 01				07 51							
230	—	Pewsey	d								06 24	06 36		07 19				08 09							
243¾	—	Hungerford	a								06 36	06 54		07 32											
252¼	—	Newbury	a								06 49	07 08		07 46				08 29							
255¾	—	Thatcham	a								06 56	07 15													
264½	—	Theale	a								07 06	07 25													
269¼	—	**Reading** 7	a	23p28	23p28		04s02	05s11	04s00		07 19	07 37		08 06		09 14		08 50	08 32						09 32
286¾	—	Slough 3	a																						
305¼	—	**London Paddington** 15 ⊖	a	00 13	00 12		05 05	06 09	05 25		07 53	08 09		08 38		09 44		09 21	09 00						10 02

A until 13 February, from 2 April
B from 20 February until 26 March
C The Night Riviera
D 🍴 from Reading ⊘ to Reading
E The Golden Hind. 🍴 to Plymouth 🍴 from Reading ⊘ from Plymouth to Reading

For connections to Oxford, Gatwick Airport and Heathrow Airport please refer to Tables 116, 148 and 125A

Cornwall and Devon - Birmingham and London

Route Diagram - see first Page of Table 135

		GW	GW	XC	GW	GW	GW	GW		XC	GW	GW	GW	XC	XC	GW	GW	XC		GW	GW	GW	GW	XC	XC
																				R					
				◇1	◇1	◇1		◇		◇1	◇1			◇1	◇1	◇1		◇1		1		◇1		◇1	◇1
						A				B	A							B		C					B
				🛒	🍽	🍽Ø				🛒	🍽Ø			🛒	🛒	🍽		🛒		🍽Ø		🍽		🛒	🛒
Penzance	d	05 21				05 41		06 00		06 28	06 45	06 55				07 41		08 28		08 44	08 57				09 40
St Erth	d							06 09		06 36	06 55	07a03				07 51		08 36		08 54	09a05				09 48
Hayle	d	05 31						06 12								07 55									09 52
Camborne	d	05 40				05 58		06 21		06 46	07 06					08 05		08 46		09 06					10 01
Redruth	d					06 05		06 27		06 52	07 13					08 12		08 52		09 13					10 08
Truro	d	05a55				06 18		06 39		07 04	07 26					08 25		09 04		09 26					10 19
St Austell	d					06 35		06 56		07 20	07 44					08 43		09 20		09 43					10 35
Newquay	d																								
Par	d					06 43		07 03		07 28	07 52					08 51		09 28		09 51					10 43
Lostwithiel	d					06 51		07 10			08 00														10 50
Bodmin Parkway	d					06 57		07 16		07 39	08 06					09 03		09 39		10 03					10 57
Liskeard 6	d					07 11		07 29		07 53	08 20					09 16		09 51		10 16					11 09
Menheniot	d							07x33																	
St Germans	d					07 22		07 41			08 31					09 27									
Saltash	d					07 30		07 48			08 39					09 35									
St Budeaux Ferry Road	d							07 52																	
Keyham	d							07 54																	
Dockyard	d							07x56																	
Devonport	d							07 58																	
Plymouth	a					07 41		08 04		08 20	08 49					09 46		10 18		10 41					11 39
	d			07 25		07 48		08 06		08 25	08 53			09 25		09 48		10 25		10 44				11 25	11 50
Ivybridge	d							08 21			09 08					10 03									
Totnes	d			07 50		08 16		08 36		08 50	09 23			09 50		10 19		10 50						11 50	12 15
Paignton	d		07 12		07 40		08 23						09 13		10 07		10 15					11 06	11 23		
Torquay	d		07 17		07 46		08 28						09 18		10 13		10 23					11 12	11 28		
Torre	d		07 20		07 50		08 31						09 21				10 26					11 16	11 31		
Newton Abbot	a		07 27	08 01	07 58	08 27	08 39	08 48		09 01	09 34		09 29	10 01	10 23	10 31	10 35	11 01				11 24	11 39	12 01	12 26
	d		07 37	08 03	08 06	08 29	08 41	08 49		09 03	09 36		09 39	10 03	10 24	10 32	10 36	11 03				11 26	11 41	12 03	12 28
Teignmouth	d		07 45		08 13		08 48	08 56					09 46		10 31		10 44					11 33	11 48		
Dawlish	d		07 50		08 19		08 53	09 01					09 51		10 36		10 49					11 39	11 53		
Dawlish Warren	d		07 55				08 58						09 55				10 53						11 58		
Starcross	d		07 59		08 25		09 02						09 59				10 57						12 02		
Exeter St Thomas	d		08 09		08 34		09 11						10 09				11 07						12 11		
Exeter St Davids 6	a		08 14	08 21	08 39	08 49	09 15	09 18		09 22	09 56		10 16	10 21	10 48	10 54	11 10	11 21		11 38		11 52	12 16	12 21	12 46
Exeter Central	a		08 19				09 21						10 21				11 21						12 21		
Exmouth	a		08 48				09 50						10 50				11 50						12 50		
Exeter St Davids 6	d			08 23	08 41	08 51		09 33		09 23	09 58			10 23	10 50	10 56		11 23		11 40		11 55		12 23	12 48
Tiverton Parkway	d			08 37		09 06		09 50		09 37	10 13			10 37	11 03	11 11		11 37				12 09		12 37	13 02
Taunton	d			08 51	09 05	09 21		10 07		09 51	10 28			10 51	11 18	11 26		11 51				12 24		12 51	13 16
Bridgwater	a							10 19																	
Weston-super-Mare	a				09 27			10 38																	
Bristol Temple Meads 10	a			09 26	09 56			11 11		10 25				11 23	11 52	11 58		12 23						13 24	13 55
Bath Spa 7	a				10 11											12 12									
Filton Abbey Wood	a							11 30																	
Bristol Parkway 7	a			09 38						10 38				11 38	12 08			12 38						13 38	14 08
Swindon	a				10 40											12 40									
Newport (South Wales)	a							11 58																	
Cardiff Central 7	a							12 18																	
Birmingham New Street 12	a			10 56						11 58				12 56	13 26			13 56						14 56	15 26
Castle Cary	d					09 42																12 45			
Westbury	d					10 01					11 05											13 05			
Pewsey	d					10 18																13 21			
Hungerford	a																					13 39			
Newbury	a																					13 48			
Thatcham	a																					13 55			
Theale	a																					14 04			
Reading 7	a				11 09	10 50					11 50					13 09				13 15		14 15			
Slough 3	a																								
London Paddington 15 ⊖	a				11 38	11 24					12 23					13 38				13 44		14 44			

A 🍽 to Plymouth 🍽 from Reading Ø from Plymouth to Reading

B 🛒 from Plymouth

C The Cornish Riviera. 🍽 to Plymouth 🍽 from Reading Ø from Plymouth to Reading

For connections to Oxford, Gatwick Airport and Heathrow Airport please refer to Tables 116, 148 and 125A

Cornwall and Devon - Birmingham and London

Route Diagram - see first Page of Table 135

		GW	GW	GW	XC	GW	GW	GW	GW	XC	XC	GW	GW	GW	GW	GW	XC	GW	GW	GW	XC	GW
		◇		■ 1	◇1	◇	◇	◇1		◇1	◇1	◇	◇	◇1	◇1 C		◇1		◇1 D	◇	◇1	
				✕ ▭	⊥			✕ ▭		⊥	⊥			▭	▭		⊥		▭		⊥	
Penzance	d			10 00		10 46						11 41								12 51		
St Erth	d			10 10		10 55						11 50								13 03		
Hayle	d					10 58						11 53								13 06		
Camborne	d			10 21		11 07						12 02								13 15		
Redruth	d			10 28		11 13						12 08								13 21		
Truro	d			10 41		11 25						12 19								13 32		
St Austell	d			10 58		11 42						12 36								13 49		
Newquay	d	10 13											13 03									
Par	d	11a02		11 07		11 50						12 44	13a52							13 57		
Lostwithiel	d					11 56						12 50								14 04		
Bodmin Parkway	d			11 19		12 02						12 56								14 10		
Liskeard 6	d			11 33		12 16						13 09								14 23		
Menheniot	d											13x13										
St Germans	d					12 27						13 22								14 34		
Saltash	d					12 34						13 29								14 42		
St Budeaux Ferry Road	d																					
Keyham	d																					
Dockyard	d																					
Devonport	d																					
Plymouth	a			11 58		12 45						13 39								14 51		
	d			12 01	12 23			12 55		13 23		13 41					14 25		15 00	15 08	15 23	
Ivybridge	d											13 56								15 23		
Totnes	d			12 29	12 49			13 23		13 49		14 11					14 50		15 28	15 38	15 49	
Paignton	d		12 13				12 48		13 13		14 01				14 15	14 23		15 13				16 12
Torquay	d		12 18				12 53		13 18		14 07				14 21	14 28		15 18				16 17
Torre	d		12 21				12 56		13 21							14 31		15 21				16 21
Newton Abbot	a		12 30	12 41	13 01		13 04	13 34	13 30	14 01	14 17	14 24			14 31	14 39	15 01	15 29	15 39	15 52	16 01	16 29
	d		12 31	12 42	13 03		13 06	13 36	13 41	14 03	14 18				14 33	14 41	15 03	15 31	15 41		16 03	16 31
Teignmouth	d		12 38				13 13		13 48		14 25				14 40	14 48		15 38				16 38
Dawlish	d		12 43				13 18		13 53		14 30				14 46	14 53		15 43				16 43
Dawlish Warren	d		12 54						13 58							14 58		15 54				16 54
Starcross	d		12 58						14 02							15 02		15 58				16 58
Exeter St Thomas	d		13 07						14 11							15 11		16 07				17 07
Exeter St Davids 6	a		13 13	13 02	13 23		13 31	13 56	14 16	14 23	14 42				14 59	15 16	15 21	16 13	16 01		16 23	17 13
Exeter Central	a		13 21						14 21							15 21		16 21				17 21
Exmouth	a		13 50						14 50							15 50		16 50				17 51
Exeter St Davids 6	d			13 04	13 25		13 33	13 58		14 25	14 44				15 01		15 23		16 03		16 25	
Tiverton Parkway	d			13 19	13 39		13 50			14 39	14 57				15 15		15 37		16 17		16 39	
Taunton	d			13 34	13 54		14 07	14 23		14 54	15 12			15 23	15 30		15 51		16 31		16 54	
Bridgwater	a						14 18															
Weston-super-Mare	a						14 37				15 37											
Bristol Temple Meads 10	a				14 26		15 08			15 26	15 55						16 26				17 26	
Bath Spa 7	a																					
Filton Abbey Wood	a						15 30															
Bristol Parkway 7	a				14 38					15 38	16 08						16 38				17 38	
Swindon	a																					
Newport (South Wales)	a						15 58															
Cardiff Central 7	a						16 18															
Birmingham New Street 12	a				15 56					16 58	17 26						17 56				18 55	
Castle Cary	d							14 44							15 51							
Westbury	d							15 03						16 08								
Pewsey	d													16 25								
Hungerford	a													16 39								
Newbury	a													16 48								
Thatcham	a													16 55								
Theale	a													17 04								
Reading 7	a			14 50				15 50						17 15	16 49				17 49			
Slough 3	a																					
London Paddington 15 ⊖	a			15 24				16 22						17 54	17 24				18 21			

C The Torbay Express

D The Mayflower

For connections to Oxford, Gatwick Airport and Heathrow Airport please refer to Tables 116, 148 and 125A

Cornwall and Devon - Birmingham and London

Route Diagram - see first Page of Table 135

		XC	GW	GW	XC	GW	GW	GW	GW	XC		GW	GW	GW	GW	GW	XC	GW	GW	GW		GW	GW	GW	GW
																			FX	FO				FX	FO
		◇1	◇1	◇	◇1	◇		◇1		◇1				◇1			◇1		◇	◇		◇		◇1	◇1
			A											B			C								
		🛒	☕		🛒			☕		🛒				☕⊘			🛒							☕	☕
Penzance	d		14 00			14 49								16 00					16 44	16 44					
St Erth	d		14 10			14 58								16 10					16 53	16 53					
Hayle	d					15 01													16 56	16 56					
Camborne	d		14 21			15 10								16 20					17 05	17 05					
Redruth	d		14 28			15 16								16 28					17 11	17 11					
Truro	d		14 41			15 27								16 41					17 24	17 24					
St Austell	d		14 58			15 44								16 58					17 41	17 41					
Newquay	d			14 58																		17 22			
Par	d		15 06	15a47		15 52								17 07					17 48	17 48		18a13			
Lostwithiel	d					15 58								17 14					17 55	17 55					
Bodmin Parkway	d		15 18			16 04								17 21					18 01	18 01					
Liskeard 6	d		15 31			16 17								17 34	17 49				18 14	18 14					
Menheniot	d					16x21																			
St Germans	d					16 30									18 00				18 25	18 25					
Saltash	d					16 37									18 07				18 32	18 32					
St Budeaux Ferry Road	d					16 41									18 12										
Keyham	d					16 43																			
Dockyard	d					16x45																			
Devonport	d					16 47																			
Plymouth	a		15 56			16 52								18 00	18 19				18 42	18 42					
	d		16 00		16 25			16 57		17 23			17 45	18 03			18 25		18 44	18 44					
Ivybridge	d							17 12					18 02						18 59	18 59					
Totnes	d		16 28		16 50			17 28		17 49			18 17	18 31			18 50		19 14	19 14					
Paignton	d						16 55		17 26			17 52				18 35		18 52					19 32		
Torquay	d						17 00		17 31			17 57				18 40		18 57					19 37		
Torre	d						17 03		17 34			18 00				18 43							19 40		
Newton Abbot	a		16 39		17 01		17 11	17 38	17 42	18 01		18 08	18 29	18 43		18 50	19 01	19 07	19 26	19 26			19 48		
	d		16 41		17 03		17 13	17 41	17 44	18 03		18 10	18 30	18 44		18 53	19 03	19 09	19 27	19 27			19 50		
Teignmouth	d						17 20		17 51			18 17	18 37			19 00		19 16					19 57		
Dawlish	d						17 25		17 56			18 22	18 43			19 05		19 21					20 02		
Dawlish Warren	d						17 30		18 01			18 27	18 47			19 16		19 26					20 07		
Starcross	d						17 34		18 05			18 31				19 20							20 11		
Exeter St Thomas	d						17 43		18 14			18 40				19 29							20 20		
Exeter St Davids 6	a		17 01		17 21		17 50	18 01	18 18	18 23		18 46	18 59	19 03		19 33	19 21	19 40	19 49	19 49			20 26		
Exeter Central	a						17 55		18 23			18 53											20 33		
Exmouth	a						18 25		18 52			19 23											21 01		
Exeter St Davids 6	d	16 54	17 03		17 23			18 03		18 25				19 06			19 23			19 49				19 55	
Tiverton Parkway	d	17 08	17 18		17 37			18 17		18 39				19 21			19 37			20 06				20 10	
Taunton	d	17 22	17 32		17 51			18 31		18 54				19 36			19 51			20a22				20 25	20 27
Bridgwater	a																								
Weston-super-Mare	a																								
Bristol Temple Meads 10	a	17 53			18 24					19 26							20 24								
Bath Spa 7	a																								
Filton Abbey Wood	a																								
Bristol Parkway 7	a	18 08			18 38					19 38							20 38								
Swindon	a																								
Newport (South Wales)	a																								
Cardiff Central 7	a																								
Birmingham New Street 12	a	19 26			19 56					20 52							22 06								
Castle Cary	d							18 54																20 46	20 46
Westbury	d							19 12																21 05	21 05
Pewsey	d							19 29																21 22	21 22
Hungerford	a																								
Newbury	a							19 49																21 42	21 42
Thatcham	a																								
Theale	a																								
Reading 7	a		18 49					20 06						20 50										21 59	21 59
Slough 3	a																								
London Paddington 15 ⊖	a		19 24					20 39						21 21										22 30	22 30

A The Royal Duchy

B ☕ to Plymouth ☕ from Reading ⊘ from Plymouth to Reading

C 🛒 to Bristol Temple Meads

For connections to Oxford, Gatwick Airport and Heathrow Airport please refer to Tables 116, 148 and 125A

Cornwall and Devon - Birmingham and London

Route Diagram - see first Page of Table 135

		GW	GW	GW	XC ThFO	XC MTWO	GW	GW	GW	GW	GW FX	GW FO	GW	GW	GW	GW	GW FO	GW FX	XC
		◇1 ⊡			◇1	◇1		◇ C	1			1		◇ D			R E ⊡	R E ⊡	◇1
Penzance	d	17 39		19 16							20 18	20 18					21 45	21 45	22 08
St Erth	d	17 49		19 25							20 27	20 27					21 55	21 55	22 16
Hayle	d	17 53		19 28							20 32	20 32							22 20
Camborne	d	18 03		19 37							20 41	20 41					22 07	22 07	22 30
Redruth	d	18 11		19 43							20 49	20 49					22 14	22 14	22 36
Truro	d	18 23		19 55							21 02	21 02					22 27	22 27	22 48
St Austell	d	18 40		20 12							21 19	21 19					22 45	22 45	23 04
Newquay	d		19 25										21 26						
Par	d	18 49	20a13	20 19							21 27	21 27	22a16				22 54	22 54	23 12
Lostwithiel	d			20 26							21 34	21 34							23 19
Bodmin Parkway	d	19 01		20 32							21 40	21 40					23 06	23 06	23 26
Liskeard 6	d	19 14		20 45							21 53	21 53					23 21	23 21	23 39
Menheniot	d			20x49															
St Germans	d			20 58							22 04	22 04							
Saltash	d			21 05							22 12	22 12							
St Budeaux Ferry Road	d			21 09															
Keyham	d			21 11															
Dockyard	d			21x13															
Devonport	d			21 15															
Plymouth	a	19 39		21 20							22 25	22 25					23 45	23 45	00 04
	d	19 42								21 25							23 51	23 51	
Ivybridge	d									21 40									
Totnes	d	20 10								21 55							00 20	00 20	
Paignton	d				20 14	20 14	20 34		21 31						22 30	23 41			
Torquay	d				20 20	20 20	20 39		21 37						22 35	23 46			
Torre	d						20 42		21 41						22 38	23 49			
Newton Abbot	a	20 21			20 30	20 30	20 50		21 52	22 01					22 46	23 57	00 32	00 32	
	d	20 23			20 31	20 31	20 52			22 02					22 48	23 59	00 33	00 33	
Teignmouth	d						20 59			22 14					22 55	00 06			
Dawlish	d						21 04			22 19					23 00	00 11			
Dawlish Warren	d						21 09			22 23					23 05	00 16			
Starcross	d						21 13			22 27					23 09	00 20			
Exeter St Thomas	d						21 22			22 36					23 18	00 29			
Exeter St Davids 6	a	20 43			20 50	20 50	21 28			22 40					23 22	00 34	00 55	00 55	
Exeter Central	a						21 35												
Exmouth	a						22 02												
Exeter St Davids 6	d	20 45			20 52	20 52		21 28						21 49			01 06	01 06	
Tiverton Parkway	d	21 00			21 04	21 04		21 45						22 06					
Taunton	d	21 15			21 19	21 19		22 02						22 23			01 36	01 36	
Bridgwater	a																		
Weston-super-Mare	a							22 26						22 47					
Bristol Temple Meads 10	a	21 47			21 51	21 52		22 56						23 15			02 34	02 34	
Bath Spa 7	a	22 01																	
Filton Abbey Wood	a																		
Bristol Parkway 7	a				22 08	22 08													
Swindon	a	22 33															03 15	03 15	
Newport (South Wales)	a																		
Cardiff Central 7	a																		
Birmingham New Street 12	a				23 44	23 44													
Castle Cary	d																		
Westbury	d																		
Pewsey	d																		
Hungerford	a																		
Newbury	a																		
Thatcham	a																		
Theale	a																		
Reading 7	a	23 06															04s00	04s00	
Slough 3	a																		
London Paddington 15 ⊖	a	23 41															05 13	05 25	

C until 30 December

D from 2 January

E The Night Riviera

For connections to Oxford, Gatwick Airport and Heathrow Airport please refer to Tables 116, 148 and 125A

Table 135

Saturdays

Cornwall and Devon - Birmingham and London

Route Diagram - see first Page of Table 135

		GW	GW	XC	GW	GW	XC	GW	GW	GW		XC	GW	XC	GW	GW	XC	GW	GW	GW		GW	XC	GW	GW
			R																						R
				◇1			◇1	◇1				◇1	◇1	◇1		◇1	◇1		◇1				◇1		1
			A													B			C				D		
			[sleeper]																						
			[buffet]				[trolley]	[buffet]				[trolley]	[buffet]	[trolley]		[buffet] ⊘	[trolley]		[buffet] ⊘				[trolley]		[buffet]
Penzance	d		21p45	22p08	05 20													05 37					06 30	06 41	06 50
St Erth	d		21p55	22p16														05 45					06 38	06a49	07 00
Hayle	d			22p20														05 48					06 41		
Camborne	d		22p07	22p30	05 37													05 58					06 51		07 11
Redruth	d		22p14	22p36	05 43													06 04					06 57		07 18
Truro	d		22p27	22p48	05a55													06 15					07 09		07 31
St Austell	d		22p45	23p04														06 32					07 25		07 48
Newquay	d																								
Par	d		22p54	23p12														06 39					07 32		07 56
Lostwithiel	d			23p19														06 46					07 39		08 04
Bodmin Parkway	d		23p06	23p26														06 52					07 46		08 10
Liskeard 6	d		23p21	23p39														07 07					07 58		08 23
Menheniot	d																	07x11							
St Germans	d																	07 19							
Saltash	d																	07 26							
St Budeaux Ferry Road	d																	07 30							
Keyham	d																	07 32							
Dockyard	d																	07x34							
Devonport	d																	07 36							
Plymouth	a		23p45	00 04														07 42					08 22		08 49
	d		23p51				05 25	05 40				06 25				06 55	07 25		07 47			08 06	08 25		08 52
Ivybridge	d																					08 21			
Totnes	d		00 20				05 50	06 07				06 50					07 50		08 14			08 35	08 50		09 19
Paignton	d	23p41							06 13	06 34				07 02	07 11					08 06					
Torquay	d	23p46							06 18	06 39				07 08	07 16					08 11					
Torre	d	23p49							06 21	06 42					07 19					08 14					
Newton Abbot	a	23p57	00 32				06 01	06 18	06 29	06 50		07 01		07 18	07 27	07 30	08 01		08 26	08 22		08 47	09 01		09 30
	d	23p59	00 33				06 03	06 20	06 31	06 52		07 03		07 19		07 32	08 03		08 27	08 34		08 48	09 03		09 32
Teignmouth	d	00 06							06 38	06 59				07 26						08 41		08 55			
Dawlish	d	00 11							06 43	07 04				07 31						08 46		09 00			
Dawlish Warren	d	00 16							06 48	07 15										08 51					
Starcross	d	00 20							06 52	07 19										08 55					
Exeter St Thomas	d	00 29							07 01	07 28										09 04					
Exeter St Davids 6	a	00 34	00 55				06 21	06 40	07 06	07 33		07 21		07 43		07 52	08 21		08 47	09 09		09 16	09 21		09 52
Exeter Central	a								07 14	07 39										09 21					
Exmouth	a								07 43	08 18										09 50					
Exeter St Davids 6	d		01 06			06 00	06 23	06 41				07 23	07 29	07 45		07 54	08 23		08 49				09 23		09 54
Tiverton Parkway	d					06 18	06 37	06 56				07 37	07 44	07 58		08 09	08 37		09 04				09 37		10 09
Taunton	d		01 36			06 35	06 51	07 11				07 51	07 59	08 13		08 24	08 51		09 19				09 51		10 24
Bridgwater	a					06 47							08 09												
Weston-super-Mare	a					07 06							08 27												
Bristol Temple Meads 10	a		02 34			07 42	07 24					08 23	08 57	08 48			09 25						10 25		
Bath Spa 7	a												09 11												
Filton Abbey Wood	a					07 58																			
Bristol Parkway 7	a					08 05	07 38					08 38		09 08			09 38						10 38		
Swindon	a		03 15										09 40												
Newport (South Wales)	a																								
Cardiff Central 7	a																								
Birmingham New Street 12	a						08 56					09 56		10 26			10 56						11 56		
Castle Cary	d							07 33											09 40						
Westbury	d							07 56											09 59						11 02
Pewsey	d							08 13											10 16						
Hungerford	a																								
Newbury	a							08 33																	
Thatcham	a																								
Theale	a																								
Reading 7	a		04s00					08 52					10 11			09 39			10 51						11 51
Slough 3	a																								
London Paddington 15 ⊖	a		05 13					09 21					10 39			10 11			11 24						12 23

A The Night Riviera

B [buffet] from Reading ⊘ to Reading

C [buffet] from Castle Cary ⊘ to Castle Cary

D [trolley] from Plymouth

For connections to Oxford, Gatwick Airport and Heathrow Airport please refer to Tables 116, 148 and 125A

Table 135

Saturdays

Cornwall and Devon - Birmingham and London

Route Diagram - see first Page of Table 135

		GW	GW	GW	GW	XC		GW	XC	GW	GW	XC	GW	GW	GW	GW		GW	XC	XC	GW	GW	GW	XC	GW
		◇		◇1		◇1			◇1	◇1		◇1	◇1					◇1	◇1	◇1	◇		◇1	◇1	
												A													
				🍴		🛒			🛒	🍴		🛒	🍴					🍴	🛒	🛒			🍴	🛒	
Penzance	d							07 35		07 59		08 28	08 45	08 54						09 43			10 00		10 36
St Erth	d							07 48		08 09		08 36	08 55	09a02						09 51			10 10		10 45
Hayle	d							07 52		08 13															10 48
Camborne	d							08 02		08 23		08 46	09 06							10 01			10 21		10 58
Redruth	d							08 09		08 30		08 52	09 13							10 07			10 28		11 04
Truro	d							08 20		08 43		09 04	09 26							10 19			10 41		11 15
St Austell	d							08 36		09 01		09 20	09 43							10 35			10 58		11 32
Newquay	d	07 48																			10 12				
Par	d	08a39						08 44		09 09		09 28	09 51							10 42	11a01		11 07		11 39
Lostwithiel	d							08 51												10 49					11 46
Bodmin Parkway	d							08 57		09 20		09 39	10 03							10 56			11 18		11 52
Liskeard 6	d							09 10		09 33		09 51	10 16							11 09			11 31		12 06
Menheniot	d																								12x10
St Germans	d							09 22																	12 17
Saltash	d							09 29																	12 23
St Budeaux Ferry Road	d																								
Keyham	d																								
Dockyard	d																								
Devonport	d																								
Plymouth	a							09 40		09 59		10 18	10 40							11 33			11 59		12 36
	d					09 25				10 02		10 25	10 44						11 25	11 48			12 00	12 23	
Ivybridge	d									10 17													12 15		
Totnes	d					09 50				10 31		10 50							11 50	12 13			12 29	12 49	
Paignton	d		09 04	09 18	09 30				10 07		10 23				10 56	11 13						12 13			
Torquay	d		09 09	09 25	09 35				10 13		10 28				11 01	11 18						12 18			
Torre	d		09 12	09 29	09 38						10 31				11 04	11 21						12 21			
Newton Abbot	a		09 20	09 38	09 47	10 01			10 23	10 43	10 38	11 01			11 12	11 29			12 01	12 24		12 30	12 41	13 01	
	d		09 35	09 39	09 48	10 03			10 24	10 44	10 47	11 03			11 23	11 41			12 03	12 25		12 32	12 42	13 03	
Teignmouth	d		09 42	09 49	09 56				10 31		10 55				11 30	11 48						12 39			
Dawlish	d		09 47	09 57	10 02				10 36		11 00				11 35	11 53						12 44			
Dawlish Warren	d		09 52	10 02	10 07						11 04				11 40	11 58						12 55			
Starcross	d		09 56												11 44	12 02						12 59			
Exeter St Thomas	d		10 05												11 53	12 11						13 08			
Exeter St Davids 6	a		10 10	10 13	10 18	10 21			10 48	11 04	11 16	11 21	11 38		11 58	12 16			12 21	12 44		13 13	13 02	13 23	
Exeter Central	a		10 21								11 21					12 21						13 21			
Exmouth	a		10 50								11 50					12 50						13 50			
Exeter St Davids 6	d			10 15		10 23			10 50	11 06		11 23	11 40					11 54	12 23	12 48			13 04	13 25	
Tiverton Parkway	d			10 30		10 37			11 03	11 21		11 37						12 09	12 37	13 02			13 19	13 39	
Taunton	d			10 45		10 51			11 18	11 36		11 51						12 24	12 51	13 16			13 34	13 54	
Bridgwater	a																								
Weston-super-Mare	a																								
Bristol Temple Meads 10	a			11 24		11 25			11 54			12 24							13 23	13 55				14 26	
Bath Spa 7	a			11 41																					
Filton Abbey Wood	a																								
Bristol Parkway 7	a					11 38			12 08			12 38							13 38	14 08				14 38	
Swindon	a			12 09																					
Newport (South Wales)	a																								
Cardiff Central 7	a																								
Birmingham New Street 12	a					12 56			13 26			13 56							14 56	15 26				15 55	
Castle Cary	d																	12 45							
Westbury	d																	13 05							
Pewsey	d																	13 22							
Hungerford	a																	13 39							
Newbury	a																	13 49							
Thatcham	a																	13 56							
Theale	a																	14 05							
Reading 7	a			12 44						12 52			13 17					14 19					14 51		
Slough 3	a																								
London Paddington 15 ⊖	a			13 12						13 21			13 46					14 45					15 22		

A 🛒 from Plymouth

For connections to Oxford, Gatwick Airport and Heathrow Airport please refer to Tables 116, 148 and 125A

Table 135

Saturdays

Cornwall and Devon - Birmingham and London

Route Diagram - see first Page of Table 135

		GW		GW	GW	XC	GW	GW	XC	GW	GW	GW		XC	GW	GW	GW	XC	GW	GW	GW	XC		GW	GW
				◇1		◇1	◇	◇	◇1	◇1	◇1			◇1	◇		◇1	◇1				◇1		◇1	◇
				A							B						C							C	
				⊡⊘		ᴛ			ᴛ	⊡	⊡⊘			ᴛ			⊡	ᴛ				ᴛ		⊡	
Penzance	d			10 58			11 46								13 00									14 01	
St Erth	d			11 08			11 56								13 09									14 11	
Hayle	d						12 00								13 12										
Camborne	d			11 19			12 10								13 21									14 22	
Redruth	d			11 26			12 16								13 27									14 29	
Truro	d			11 39			12 29								13 38									14 42	
St Austell	d			11 56			12 47								13 55									14 59	
Newquay	d							13 09																	14 59
Par	d						12 55	13a59							14 03									15 07	15a48
Lostwithiel	d						13 02								14 09										
Bodmin Parkway	d			12 13			13 09								14 15									15 19	
Liskeard 6	d			12 26			13 23								14 28									15 33	
Menheniot	d						13x28																		
St Germans	d						13 36								14 39										
Saltash	d						13 45								14 47										
St Budeaux Ferry Road	d																								
Keyham	d																								
Dockyard	d																								
Devonport	d														14 52										
Plymouth	a			12 52			13 55								14 58									15 58	
	d			12 54		13 25					14 00			14 25			15 04	15 25		15 32				16 01	
Ivybridge	d																			15 47					
Totnes	d			13 21		13 50								14 50			15 31	15 50		16 01				16 28	
Paignton	d	12 43			13 13				13 53			14 13				15 13			15 43		16 13				
Torquay	d	12 48			13 18				13 59			14 18				15 18			15 48		16 18				
Torre	d				13 21							14 21				15 21					16 21				
Newton Abbot	a	12 58		13 34	13 29	14 01			14 09		14 35	14 29		15 01		15 29	15 42	16 01	15 58	16 13	16 29			16 41	
	d	13 06		13 35	13 41	14 03			14 10		14 36	14 40		15 03		15 34	15 44	16 03	16 09		16 31			16 41	
Teignmouth	d	13 13			13 48				14 17			14 48				15 42			16 16		16 38				
Dawlish	d	13 18			13 53				14 22			14 53				15 47			16 21		16 43				
Dawlish Warren	d	13 23			13 58							14 57				15 58					16 55				
Starcross	d				14 02							15 01				16 02					16 59				
Exeter St Thomas	d				14 11							15 11				16 12					17 08				
Exeter St Davids 6	a	13 35		13 55	14 16	14 21			14 34		14 56	15 15		15 21		16 15	16 04	16 21	16 34		17 15			17 01	
Exeter Central	a				14 21							15 21				16 21			16 44		17 21				
Exmouth	a				14 50							15 50				16 50					17 50				
Exeter St Davids 6	d			13 57		14 23			14 36		14 58			15 23			16 06	16 23				16 53		17 03	
Tiverton Parkway	d					14 37			14 49		15 13			15 37			16 21	16 37				17 07		17 17	
Taunton	d			14 23		14 52			15 04	15 19	15 28			15 51			16 36	16 51				17 21		17 32	
Bridgwater	a																								
Weston-super-Mare	a								15 23																
Bristol Temple Meads 10	a					15 24			15 49					16 24				17 24				17 53			
Bath Spa 7	a																								
Filton Abbey Wood	a																								
Bristol Parkway 7	a					15 38			16 08					16 38				17 38				18 08			
Swindon	a																								
Newport (South Wales)	a																								
Cardiff Central 7	a																								
Birmingham New Street 12	a					16 56			17 26					17 56				18 56				19 26			
Castle Cary	d			14 44							15 49														
Westbury	d			15 03						16 07															
Pewsey	d									16 25															
Hungerford	a									16 41															
Newbury	a									16 52															
Thatcham	a									16 58															
Theale	a									17 07															
Reading 7	a			15 51						17 17	16 50						17 53							18 49	
Slough 3	a																								
London Paddington 15 ⊖	a			16 23						17 51	17 21						18 21							19 22	

A ⊡ to Plymouth ⊡ from Reading ⊘ from Plymouth to Reading

B ⊡ from Reading ⊘ to Reading

C until 11 February, from 31 March

For connections to Oxford, Gatwick Airport and Heathrow Airport please refer to Tables 116, 148 and 125A

Cornwall and Devon - Birmingham and London

Route Diagram - see first Page of Table 135

		XC	GW	GW	GW	XC	GW	GW	GW	XC	GW	GW	GW	GW	GW	GW	GW	GW	GW	GW	GW	GW	GW
		◇1	◇	◇1		◇1			◇1	◇1			◇			◇1				1			
Penzance	d		14 52						15 52			16 41				17 40	18 50					19 06	
St Erth	d		15 01						16 02			16 51				17 50	18a58					19 15	
Hayle	d		15 04									16 55				17 54						19 18	
Camborne	d		15 14						16 13			17 05				18 04						19 27	
Redruth	d		15 20						16 20			17 12				18 11						19 33	
Truro	d		15 31						16 33			17 25				18 24						19 44	
St Austell	d		15 48						16 51			17 43				18 41						20 01	
Newquay	d												17 21					19 17					21 18
Par	d		15 55						16 59			17 51	18a10			18 49		20a03				20 09	22 09
Lostwithiel	d		16 02						17 06			17 58										20 15	22 18
Bodmin Parkway	d		16 08						17 13			18 05				19 01						20 21	22 24
Liskeard 6	d		16 21						17 26			18 19				19 14						20 34	22 37
Menheniot	d		16x25																			20x39	22x41
St Germans	d		16 33									18 31										20 47	22 49
Saltash	d		16 39									18 38										20 54	22 55
St Budeaux Ferry Road	d																					20 58	22 59
Keyham	d																					21 00	23 01
Dockyard	d																					21x02	23x03
Devonport	d																					21 04	23 05
Plymouth	a		16 51						17 51			18 49				19 39						21 10	23 12
	d	16 25		16 57		17 23		17 38	17 54	18 25		18 51				19 42						21 15	
Ivybridge	d			17 12				17 53				19 07										21 30	
Totnes	d	16 50		17 27		17 49		18 07	18 21	18 50		19 22				20 09						21 44	
Paignton	d				17 13		17 52				18 53			19 21	19 50				20 13	20 46	21 13		
Torquay	d				17 18		17 57				18 58			19 26	19 55				20 18	20 52	21 18		
Torre	d				17 21		18 00				19 01			19 29					20 21		21 21		
Newton Abbot	a	17 01		17 38	17 29	18 01	18 08	18 19	18 32	19 01	19 10	19 34		19 38	20 05	20 20			20 29	21 02	21 29	21 56	
	d	17 03		17 40	17 43	18 03	18 10	18 19	18 34	19 03	19 12	19 35		19 40	20 07	20 22			20 31	21 04	21 31	21 56	
Teignmouth	d				17 50		18 17	18 26			19 19	19 43		19 47	20 14				20 38		21 38	22 03	
Dawlish	d				17 55		18 22	18 31			19 24	19 48		19 52	20 19				20 43		21 43	22 08	
Dawlish Warren	d				18 00		18 27	18 47			19 29			20 06	20 24				20 48		21 48		
Starcross	d				18 04		18 31				19 33			20 10					20 52		21 52		
Exeter St Thomas	d				18 13		18 40				19 42			20 20					21 01		22 01		
Exeter St Davids 6	a	17 21		18 00	18 18	18 23	18 46	18 59	18 54	19 21	19 45	20 01		20 25	20 36	20 42			21 05	21 24	22 05	22 22	
Exeter Central	a				18 23		18 53							20 33									
Exmouth	a				18 52		19 22							21 01									
Exeter St Davids 6	d	17 23		18 02		18 25			18 56	19 23						20 44							
Tiverton Parkway	d	17 37		18 17		18 39			19 11	19 37						20 59							
Taunton	d	17 51		18 32		18 54			19 26	19 51						21 14							
Bridgwater	a																						
Weston-super-Mare	a																						
Bristol Temple Meads 10	a	18 24				19 26				20 24						21 47							
Bath Spa 7	a															22 01							
Filton Abbey Wood	a																						
Bristol Parkway 7	a	18 38				19 38				20 38													
Swindon	a															22 29							
Newport (South Wales)	a																						
Cardiff Central 7	a																						
Birmingham New Street 12	a	19 58				20 53				21 53													
Castle Cary	d			18 53					19 47														
Westbury	d			19 12					20 06														
Pewsey	d								20 23														
Hungerford	a																						
Newbury	a			19 45																			
Thatcham	a																						
Theale	a																						
Reading 7	a			20 07					20 58							23 04							
Slough 3	a																						
London Paddington 15 ⊖	a			20 37					21 32							23 36							

For connections to Oxford, Gatwick Airport and Heathrow Airport please refer to Tables 116, 148 and 125A

Table 135

Saturdays

Cornwall and Devon - Birmingham and London

Route Diagram - see first Page of Table 135

		XC	GW
		◇1	
Penzance	d	21 32	
St Erth	d	21 42	
Hayle	d		
Camborne	d	21 53	
Redruth	d	22 00	
Truro	d	22 13	
St Austell	d	22 30	
Newquay	d		
Par	d	22 38	
Lostwithiel	d		
Bodmin Parkway	d	22 49	
Liskeard 6	d	23 02	
Menheniot	d		
St Germans	d		
Saltash	d		
St Budeaux Ferry Road	d		
Keyham	d		
Dockyard	d		
Devonport	d		
Plymouth	a	23 27	
	d		
Ivybridge	d		
Totnes	d		
Paignton	d		21 53
Torquay	d		21 58
Torre	d		22 01
Newton Abbot	a		22 09
	d		22 11
Teignmouth	d		22 18
Dawlish	d		22 23
Dawlish Warren	d		22 28
Starcross	d		22 32
Exeter St Thomas	d		22 41
Exeter St Davids 6	a		22 45
Exeter Central	a		
Exmouth	a		
Exeter St Davids 6	d		
Tiverton Parkway	d		
Taunton	d		
Bridgwater	a		
Weston-super-Mare	a		
Bristol Temple Meads 10	a		
Bath Spa 7	a		
Filton Abbey Wood	a		
Bristol Parkway 7	a		
Swindon	a		
Newport (South Wales)	a		
Cardiff Central 7	a		
Birmingham New Street 12	a		
Castle Cary	d		
Westbury	d		
Pewsey	d		
Hungerford	a		
Newbury	a		
Thatcham	a		
Theale	a		
Reading 7	a		
Slough 3	a		
London Paddington 15 ⊖	a		

For connections to Oxford, Gatwick Airport and Heathrow Airport please refer to Tables 116, 148 and 125A

Table 135

Sundays

until 1 January

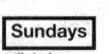

Cornwall and Devon - Birmingham and London

Route Diagram - see first Page of Table 135

		GW	GW	GW	GW	XC	GW	GW	XC	XC		GW	GW	XC	GW	GW	GW	XC	XC	GW		XC	GW	GW	XC
		◇	◇1	◇	◇1	◇1		◇1	◇1	◇1		◇1		◇1		◇1	◇	◇1	◇1			◇1	◇1		◇1
														A											
			R		R	T		R	T	T		R		T		R		T	T			T	R		
Penzance	d											08 35		09 30		09 47							11 00	11 45	
St Erth	d											08 44		09 38		09 57							11 10	11a53	
Hayle	d											08 49													
Camborne	d											09 00		09 48		10 08							11 23		
Redruth	d											09 06		09 54		10 14							11 29		
Truro	d											09 20		10 06		10 27							11 42		
St Austell	d											09 36		10 22		10 44							11 59		
Newquay	d																11 12								
Par	d											09 45		10 30		10 53	12a01						12 07		
Lostwithiel	d																								
Bodmin Parkway	d											09 57		10 41		11 06							12 19		
Liskeard 6	d											10 10		10 53		11 19							12 33		
Menheniot	d																								
St Germans	d															11 30									
Saltash	d											10 28													
St Budeaux Ferry Road	d																								
Keyham	d																								
Dockyard	d																								
Devonport	d																								
Plymouth	a											10 35		11 17		11 44							12 58		
	d				08 40	09 25		10 10	10 25			10 40		11 25		11 45		12 00	12 25			12 52	13 00		13 23
Ivybridge	d																								
Totnes	d				09 07	09 50		10 40	10 50			11 07		11 50		12 15			12 50				13 28		13 49
Paignton	d						09 49			10 50			11 00		11 49					12 57					
Torquay	d						09 54			10 56			11 05		11 54					13 02					
Torre	d						09 57						11 08		11 57					13 05					
Newton Abbot	a				09 19	10 01	10 05	10 52	11 01	11 06		11 19	11 16	12 01	12 05	12 28		12 34	13 01	13 13		13 26	13 40		14 01
	d				09 21	10 03	10 07	10 54	11 03	11 08		11 21	11 25	12 03	12 07	12 29		12 36	13 03	13 15		13 27	13 41		14 03
Teignmouth	d				09 28		10 14			11 15			11 32		12 14					13 22					
Dawlish	d				09 34		10 19			11 20			11 37		12 19					13 27					
Dawlish Warren	d						10 24								12 24										
Starcross	d						10 28								12 28										
Exeter St Thomas	d						10 37								12 37										
Exeter St Davids 6	a				09 47	10 21	10 41	11 14	11 21	11 30		11 41	11 52	12 21	12 42	12 49		12 55	13 21	13 41		13 46	14 01		14 23
Exeter Central	a						10 49						11 58		12 51					13 51					
Exmouth	a						11 18						12 25		13 20					14 18					
Exeter St Davids 6	d	08 01	08 43	09 35	09 49	10 23		11 18	11 23	11 32		11 43		12 23		12 50		12 57	13 23			13 48	14 03		14 25
Tiverton Parkway	d	08 18	08 58	09 53		10 37		11 33	11 37	11 46		11 58		12 37				13 10	13 37				14 17		14 39
Taunton	d	08 35	09 12	10 19	10 14	10 51		11 48	11 53	12 00		12 12		12 51		13 16		13 25	13 51				14 32		14 54
Bridgwater	a	08 46		10 31																					
Weston-super-Mare	a	09 06		10 49						12 20															
Bristol Temple Meads 10	a	09 38		11 20		11 27		12 23	12 27	12 45				13 26				13 57	14 26			14 40			15 27
Bath Spa 7	a							12 41																	
Filton Abbey Wood	a	09 55																							
Bristol Parkway 7	a					11 38			12 38	13 08				13 38				14 08	14 38			15 08			15 38
Swindon	a							13 10																	
Newport (South Wales)	a	10 25																							
Cardiff Central 7	a	10 41																							
Birmingham New Street 12	a					12 50			13 50	14 26				14 50				15 27	15 50			16 26			16 50
Castle Cary	d		09 34									12 33													
Westbury	d		09 54		10 51							12 53				13 59									
Pewsey	d		10 11									13 10													
Hungerford	a																								
Newbury	a		10 31		11 26							13 30													
Thatcham	a																								
Theale	a																								
Reading 7	a		10 48		11 49			13 47				13 51				14 48							15 50		
Slough 3	a																								
London Paddington 15 ⊖	a		11 29		12 29			14 22				14 29				15 29							16 29		

A T from Plymouth

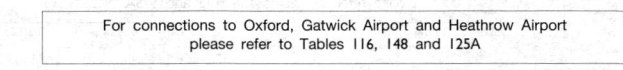

For connections to Oxford, Gatwick Airport and Heathrow Airport please refer to Tables 116, 148 and 125A

Table 135

Sundays
until 1 January

Cornwall and Devon - Birmingham and London

Route Diagram - see first Page of Table 135

		GW	GW	GW	GW	XC	XC	GW	GW	GW	XC	GW	GW	GW	GW	GW	GW	XC	GW	GW	GW	GW	XC
			◇1			◇1	◇1		◇1	◇1	◇1	◇1		◇1	◇		◇1	◇1		◇	◇	◇1	◇1
							A																A
			🍴			🛒	🛒		🍴	🍴	🛒	🍴		🍴			🍴	🛒				🍴	🛒
Penzance	d				12 05		12 30		12 56						13 41					14 40		15 00	15 30
St Erth	d				12 14		12 40		13 06						13 51					14 49		15 10	15 38
Hayle	d						12 44								13 54					14 52			
Camborne	d				12 25		12 56		13 19						14 04					15 01		15 22	15 51
Redruth	d				12 31		13 02		13 25						14 10					15 07		15 29	15 57
Truro	d				12 43		13 14		13 38						14 21					15 18		15 41	16 09
St Austell	d				12 59		13 30		13 56						14 38					15 35		15 59	16 25
Newquay	d																				15 10		
Par	d				13 06		13 38		14 03						14 45					15 43	15a59	16 07	16 33
Lostwithiel	d				13 13		13 45								14 52					15 49			
Bodmin Parkway	d				13 19		13 52		14 16						14 58					15 55		16 18	16 44
Liskeard 6	d				13 33		14 04		14 29						15 11					16 09		16 31	16 56
Menheniot	d				13 38																		
St Germans	d				13 46										15 21					16 19			
Saltash	d				13 54										15 29					16 27			
St Budeaux Ferry Road	d																						
Keyham	d																						
Dockyard	d																						
Devonport	d																						
Plymouth	a				14 03		14 28		14 54						15 39					16 37		16 57	17 20
	d		13 44		14 06	14 23	14 35		14 58	15 05	15 23			15 43	15 49		16 10	16 25		16 38		17 00	17 26
Ivybridge	d				14 21										16 07					16 53			
Totnes	d		14 11		14 35	14 49	15 00		15 25	15 35	15 49			16 11	16 21		16 42	16 50		17 07		17 28	17 52
Paignton	d	13 51		14 19				14 57				15 45	15 54			16 21			16 55				
Torquay	d	13 56		14 24				15 02				15 51	15 59			16 26			17 00				
Torre	d	13 59		14 27				15 05				15 56	16 02			16 29			17 03				
Newton Abbot	a	14 07	14 23	14 35	14 47	15 01	15 11	15 13	15 37	15 47	16 01	16 04	16 10	16 22	16 33	16 37	16 53	17 01	17 11	17 19		17 39	18 02
	d	14 08	14 25	14 37	14 48	15 03	15 12	15 15	15 38	15 48	16 03	16 05	16 11	16 24	16 34	16 38	16 55	17 03	17 12	17 20		17 40	18 04
Teignmouth	d	14 15		14 44	14 55			15 22				16 13	16 18			16 45			17 19	17 27			
Dawlish	d	14 20		14 49	15 00			15 27				16 18	16 23			16 50			17 24	17 32			
Dawlish Warren	d	14 25		14 54									16 28			16 55			17 29				
Starcross	d	14 29		14 58												16 59							
Exeter St Thomas	d	14 38		15 07												17 08							
Exeter St Davids 6	a	14 43	14 46	15 12	15 16	15 23	15 31	15 41	15 58	16 08	16 23	16 32	16 40	16 44	16 55	17 13	17 17	17 21	17 41	17 46		18 01	18 21
Exeter Central	a	14 51		15 17				15 51					16 51			17 18			17 51				
Exmouth	a	15 18						16 18					17 18						18 18				
Exeter St Davids 6	d		14 47			15 25	15 33		16 01	16 10	16 24	16 34		16 45			17 19	17 23		17 51		18 02	18 23
Tiverton Parkway	d					15 38	15 46		16 16	16 25	16 37			17 01			17 34	17 37				18 18	18 38
Taunton	d		15 12			15 54	16 01		16 31	16 40	16 53	16 59		17 15			17 48	17 51		18 22		18 33	18 52
Bridgwater	a											17 09								18 33			
Weston-super-Mare	a						16 20			17 01		17 28								18 52			
Bristol Temple Meads 10	a					16 27	16 52			17 22	17 26	17 58					18 25	18 27		19 23			19 26
Bath Spa 7	a									17 41		18 12					18 41						
Filton Abbey Wood	a																						
Bristol Parkway 7	a					16 38	17 08				17 38							18 38					19 38
Swindon	a									18 10		18 40					19 11						
Newport (South Wales)	a																						
Cardiff Central 7	a																						
Birmingham New Street 12	a					17 49	18 27				18 51							19 50					20 50
Castle Cary	d		15 34											17 37									
Westbury	d		15 52											17 56								19 12	
Pewsey	d		16 10											18 13									
Hungerford	a																						
Newbury	a		16 31											18 33									
Thatcham	a																						
Theale	a																						
Reading 7	a		16 48						17 47	18 46		19 12		18 51			19 46					19 58	
Slough 3	a																						
London Paddington 15 ⊖	a		17 30						18 29	19 22		19 59		19 29			20 22					20 44	

A 🛒 from Plymouth

For connections to Oxford, Gatwick Airport and Heathrow Airport please refer to Tables 116, 148 and 125A

Table 135

Sundays

until 1 January

Cornwall and Devon - Birmingham and London

Route Diagram - see first Page of Table 135

		GW	GW	XC	GW	GW	XC	GW	GW	GW	GW	GW	GW	GW	GW	GW	GW
																	■
			◇1	◇1	◇1		◇1		◇1		◇1						
																	[sleeper]
			[restaurant]	[trolley]	[restaurant]		[trolley]		[restaurant]		[restaurant]			[trolley]			[restaurant]
Penzance	d				16 10				17 25				19 00	20 05			21 15
St Erth	d				16 21				17 34				19 09	20 14			21 25
Hayle	d													20 17			
Camborne	d				16 33				17 46				19 20	20 26			21 38
Redruth	d				16 40				17 53				19 26	20 32			21 45
Truro	d				16 53				18 05				19 38	20 44			22 00
St Austell	d				17 10				18 24				19 55	21 01			22 18
Newquay	d					17 30											
Par	d				17 17	18a19			18 32				20 03	21 09			
Lostwithiel	d												20 09				
Bodmin Parkway	d				17 29				18 44				20 15	21 21			22 35
Liskeard 6	d				17 42				18 57				20 28	21 35			22 50
Menheniot	d												20x33				
St Germans	d												20 41				
Saltash	d				18 00								20 48				
St Budeaux Ferry Road	d																
Keyham	d																
Dockyard	d																
Devonport	d												20 56				
Plymouth	a				18 10				19 21				21 00	22 00			23 15
	d		17 45		18 10		18 23		19 25		19 55		21 15				23 20
Ivybridge	d																
Totnes	d		18 13		18 40		18 49		19 52				21 42				23 48
Paignton	d	17 49		18 20				18 55		19 55		20 55			21 52	23 00	
Torquay	d	17 54		18 26				19 00		20 00		21 00			21 57	23 05	
Torre	d	17 57						19 03		20 03		21 03			22 00	23 08	
Newton Abbot	a	18 05	18 25	18 36	18 52		19 01	19 11	20 04	20 11	20 31	21 11	21 54		22 08	23 16	23 59
	d	18 07	18 26	18 37	18 52		19 03	19 13	20 05	20 13	20 32	21 13	21 55		22 10	23 18	00 01
Teignmouth	d	18 14						19 20		20 20		21 20	22 02		22 17	23 25	
Dawlish	d	18 19						19 25		20 25		21 25	22 07		22 22	23 30	
Dawlish Warren	d	18 24						19 30		20 30					22 27	23 35	
Starcross	d	18 28						19 34		20 34					22 31	23 39	
Exeter St Thomas	d	18 37						19 43		20 43					22 40	23 48	
Exeter St Davids 6	a	18 40	18 47	18 56	19 14		19 23	19 48	20 25	20 48	20 53	21 40	22 21		22 43	23 52	00 40
Exeter Central	a	18 51						19 54		20 54		21 51			22 51		
Exmouth	a	19 18						20 21		21 21		22 18			23 18		
Exeter St Davids 6	d		18 49	18 58	19 16		19 25		20 26		20 55						01 06
Tiverton Parkway	d			19 11	19 31		19 38		20 42		21 10						
Taunton	d		19 12	19 25	19 45		19 54		20 55		21 23						
Bridgwater	a																
Weston-super-Mare	a																
Bristol Temple Meads 10	a			19 57			20 27				22 00						02 14
Bath Spa 7	a										22 22						
Filton Abbey Wood	a																
Bristol Parkway 7	a			20 08			20 38										
Swindon	a										22 50						03 21
Newport (South Wales)	a																
Cardiff Central 7	a																
Birmingham New Street 12	a			21 20			21 51										
Castle Cary	d				20 07				21 19								
Westbury	d				20 27				21 40								
Pewsey	d								21 58								
Hungerford	a																
Newbury	a		20 18						22 18								
Thatcham	a																
Theale	a																
Reading 7	a		20 45		21 13				22 36		23 28						04s02
Slough 3	a																
London Paddington 15 ⊖	a		21 29		21 59				23 16		00 13						05 05

For connections to Oxford, Gatwick Airport and Heathrow Airport please refer to Tables 116, 148 and 125A

Table 135

Sundays

8 January to 12 February

Cornwall and Devon - Birmingham and London

Route Diagram - see first Page of Table 135

		GW	GW	GW	GW	XC	GW	GW	XC	XC		GW	GW	XC	GW	GW	GW	XC	XC	GW		XC	GW	GW	XC
		◇	◇1	◇	◇1	◇1		◇1	◇1	◇1		◇1		◇1		◇1	◇	◇1	◇1			◇1	◇1		◇1
														A											
			⊏		⊏	⊥		⊏	⊥	⊥		⊏		⊥		⊏		⊥	⊥			⊥	⊏		
Penzance	d											08 35		09 30		09 47							11 00	11 45	
St Erth	d											08 44		09 38		09 57							11 10	11a53	
Hayle	d											08 49													
Camborne	d											09 00		09 48		10 08							11 23		
Redruth	d											09 06		09 54		10 14							11 29		
Truro	d											09 20		10 06		10 27							11 42		
St Austell	d											09 36		10 22		10 44							11 59		
Newquay	d																11 12								
Par	d											09 45		10 30		10 53	12a01						12 07		
Lostwithiel	d																								
Bodmin Parkway	d											09 57		10 41		11 06							12 19		
Liskeard 6	d											10 10		10 53		11 19							12 33		
Menheniot	d																								
St Germans	d															11 30									
Saltash	d											10 28													
St Budeaux Ferry Road	d																								
Keyham	d																								
Dockyard	d																								
Devonport	d																								
Plymouth	a											10 35		11 17		11 44							12 58		
	d				08 40	09 25		10 10	10 25			10 40		11 25		11 45		12 00	12 25			12 52	13 00		13 23
Ivybridge	d																								
Totnes	d				09 07	09 50		10 40	10 50			11 07		11 50		12 15			12 50				13 28		13 49
Paignton	d						09 49			10 50			11 00		11 49					12 57					
Torquay	d						09 54			10 56			11 05		11 54					13 02					
Torre	d						09 57						11 08		11 57					13 05					
Newton Abbot	a				09 19	10 01	10 05	10 52	11 01	11 06		11 19	11 16	12 01	12 05	12 28		12 34	13 01	13 13		13 26	13 40		14 01
	d				09 21	10 03	10 07	10 54	11 03	11 08		11 21	11 25	12 03	12 07	12 29		12 36	13 03	13 15		13 27	13 41		14 03
Teignmouth	d				09 28		10 14			11 15			11 32		12 14					13 22					
Dawlish	d				09 34		10 19			11 20			11 37		12 19					13 27					
Dawlish Warren	d						10 24								12 24										
Starcross	d						10 28								12 28										
Exeter St Thomas	d						10 37								12 37										
Exeter St Davids 6	a				09 47	10 21	10 41	11 14	11 21	11 30		11 41	11 52	12 21	12 42	12 49		12 55	13 21	13 41		13 46	14 01		14 23
Exeter Central	a						10 49						11 58		12 51					13 51					
Exmouth	a						11 18						12 25		13 20					14 18					
Exeter St Davids 6	d	08 01	08 43	09 35	09 49	10 23		11 18	11 23	11 32		11 43		12 23		12 50		12 57	13 23			13 48	14 03		14 25
Tiverton Parkway	d	08 18	08 58	09 53		10 37		11 33	11 37	11 46		11 58		12 37				13 10	13 37				14 17		14 39
Taunton	d	08 35	09 12	10 19	10 14	10 51		11 48	11 53	12 00		12 12		12 51		13 16		13 25	13 51				14 32		14 54
Bridgwater	a	08 46		10 31																					
Weston-super-Mare	a	09 06		10 49						12 20															
Bristol Temple Meads 10	a	09 38		11 20		11 27		12 23	12 27	12 45				13 26				13 57	14 26			14 40			15 27
Bath Spa 7	a							12 41																	
Filton Abbey Wood	a	09 55																							
Bristol Parkway 7	a					11 38			12 38	13 08				13 38				14 08	14 38			15 08			15 38
Swindon	a							13 10																	
Newport (South Wales)	a	10 25																							
Cardiff Central 7	a	10 41																							
Birmingham New Street 12	a					12 50			13 50	14 26				14 50				15 27	15 50			16 26			16 50
Castle Cary	d		09 34									12 33													
Westbury	d		09 54		10 51							12 53				13 59									
Pewsey	d		10 11									13 10													
Hungerford	a																								
Newbury	a		10 31		11 26							13 30													
Thatcham	a																								
Theale	a																								
Reading 7	a		10 48		11 49			13 47				13 51				14 48							15 50		
Slough 3	a																								
London Paddington 15 ⊖	a		11 29		12 29			14 22				14 29				15 29							16 29		

A ⊥ from Plymouth

For connections to Oxford, Gatwick Airport and Heathrow Airport please refer to Tables 116, 148 and 125A

Table 135

Sundays

8 January to 12 February

Cornwall and Devon - Birmingham and London

Route Diagram - see first Page of Table 135

		GW	GW	GW	GW	XC		XC	GW	GW	GW	XC	GW	GW	GW	GW		GW	GW	XC	GW	GW	GW	GW	XC
			◇1			◇1		◇1		◇1	◇1	◇1	◇1		◇1	◇			◇1	◇1		◇	◇	◇1	◇1
								A																	A
			🍽			🛒		🛒		🍽	🍽	🛒	🍽		🍽				🍽	🛒				🍽	🛒
Penzance	d				12 05			12 30		12 56						13 41						14 40		15 00	15 30
St Erth	d				12 14			12 40		13 06						13 51						14 49		15 10	15 38
Hayle	d							12 44								13 54						14 52			
Camborne	d				12 25			12 56		13 19						14 04						15 01		15 22	15 51
Redruth	d				12 31			13 02		13 25						14 10						15 07		15 29	15 57
Truro	d				12 43			13 14		13 38						14 21						15 18		15 41	16 09
St Austell	d				12 59			13 30		13 56						14 38						15 35		15 59	16 25
Newquay	d																						15 10		
Par	d				13 06			13 38		14 03						14 45						15 43	15a59	16 07	16 33
Lostwithiel	d				13 13			13 45								14 52						15 49			
Bodmin Parkway	d				13 19			13 52		14 16						14 58						15 55		16 18	16 44
Liskeard 6	d				13 33			14 04		14 29						15 11						16 09		16 31	16 56
Menheniot	d				13 38																				
St Germans	d				13 46											15 21						16 19			
Saltash	d				13 54											15 29						16 27			
St Budeaux Ferry Road	d																								
Keyham	d																								
Dockyard	d																								
Devonport	d																								
Plymouth	a				14 03			14 28		14 54						15 39						16 37		16 57	17 20
	d		13 44		14 06	14 23		14 35		14 58	15 05	15 23			15 43	15 49			16 10	16 25		16 38		17 00	17 26
Ivybridge	d				14 21											16 07						16 53			
Totnes	d		14 11		14 35	14 49		15 00		15 25	15 35	15 49			16 11	16 21			16 42	16 50		17 07		17 28	17 52
Paignton	d	13 51		14 19					14 57				15 45	15 54				16 21			16 55				
Torquay	d	13 56		14 24					15 02				15 51	15 59				16 26			17 00				
Torre	d	13 59		14 27					15 05				15 56	16 02				16 29			17 03				
Newton Abbot	a	14 07	14 23	14 35	14 47	15 01		15 11	15 13	15 37	15 47	16 01	16 04	16 10	16 22	16 33		16 37	16 53	17 01	17 11	17 19		17 39	18 02
	d	14 08	14 25	14 37	14 48	15 03		15 12	15 15	15 38	15 48	16 03	16 05	16 11	16 24	16 34		16 38	16 55	17 03	17 12	17 20		17 40	18 04
Teignmouth	d	14 15		14 44	14 55				15 22				16 13	16 18				16 45			17 19	17 27			
Dawlish	d	14 20		14 49	15 00				15 27				16 18	16 23				16 50			17 24	17 32			
Dawlish Warren	d	14 25		14 54										16 28				16 55			17 29				
Starcross	d	14 29		14 58														16 59							
Exeter St Thomas	d	14 38		15 07														17 08							
Exeter St Davids 6	a	14 43	14 46	15 12	15 16	15 23		15 31	15 41	15 58	16 08	16 23	16 32	16 40	16 44	16 55		17 13	17 17	17 21	17 41	17 46		18 01	18 21
Exeter Central	a	14 51		15 17					15 51					16 51				17 18			17 51				
Exmouth	a	15 18							16 18					17 18							18 18				
Exeter St Davids 6	d		14 47			15 25		15 33		16 01	16 10	16 24	16 34		16 45				17 19	17 23		17 51		18 02	18 23
Tiverton Parkway	d					15 38		15 46		16 16	16 25	16 37			17 01				17 34	17 37				18 18	18 38
Taunton	d		15 12			15 54		16 01		16 31	16 40	16 53	16 59		17 15				17 48	17 51		18 22		18 33	18 52
Bridgwater	a												17 09									18 33			
Weston-super-Mare	a							16 20			17 01		17 28									18 52			
Bristol Temple Meads 10	a					16 27		16 52			17 22	17 26	17 58						18 25	18 27		19 23			19 26
Bath Spa 7	a										17 41		18 12						18 41						
Filton Abbey Wood	a																								
Bristol Parkway 7	a					16 38		17 08				17 38								18 38					19 38
Swindon	a										18 10		18 40						19 11						
Newport (South Wales)	a																								
Cardiff Central 7	a																								
Birmingham New Street 12	a					17 49		18 27				18 51								19 50					20 50
Castle Cary	d		15 34												17 37										
Westbury	d		15 52												17 56									19 12	
Pewsey	d		16 10												18 13										
Hungerford	a																								
Newbury	a		16 31												18 33										
Thatcham	a																								
Theale	a																								
Reading 7	a		16 48							17 50	18 46		19 17		18 51				19 47					19 59	
Slough 3	a																								
London Paddington 15 ⊖	a		17 30							18 29	19 22		19 59		19 29				20 22					20 44	

A 🛒 from Plymouth

For connections to Oxford, Gatwick Airport and Heathrow Airport please refer to Tables 116, 148 and 125A

Table 135

Sundays

8 January to 12 February

Cornwall and Devon - Birmingham and London

Route Diagram - see first Page of Table 135

		GW		GW	XC	GW	GW	XC	GW	GW	GW	GW		GW	GW	GW	GW	GW	GW
																			R
				◇1	◇1	◇1		◇1		◇1		◇1							
				☕	🛒	☕		🛒		☕		☕				🛒			🛏 ☕
Penzance	d					16 10				17 25					19 00	20 05			21 15
St Erth	d					16 21				17 34					19 09	20 14			21 25
Hayle	d															20 17			
Camborne	d					16 33				17 46					19 20	20 26			21 38
Redruth	d					16 40				17 53					19 26	20 32			21 45
Truro	d					16 53				18 05					19 38	20 44			22 00
St Austell	d					17 10				18 24					19 55	21 01			22 18
Newquay	d						17 30												
Par	d					17 17	18a19			18 32					20 03	21 09			
Lostwithiel	d														20 09				
Bodmin Parkway	d					17 29				18 44					20 15	21 21			22 35
Liskeard 6	d					17 42				18 57					20 28	21 35			22 50
Menheniot	d														20x33				
St Germans	d														20 41				
Saltash	d					18 00									20 48				
St Budeaux Ferry Road	d																		
Keyham	d																		
Dockyard	d																		
Devonport	d														20 56				
Plymouth	a					18 10				19 21					21 00	22 00			23 15
	d			17 45		18 10		18 23		19 25		19 55			21 15				23 20
Ivybridge	d																		
Totnes	d			18 13		18 40		18 49		19 52					21 42				23 48
Paignton	d	17 49			18 20				18 55		19 55			20 55			21 52	23 00	
Torquay	d	17 54			18 26				19 00		20 00			21 00			21 57	23 05	
Torre	d	17 57							19 03		20 03			21 03			22 00	23 08	
Newton Abbot	a	18 05		18 25	18 36	18 52		19 01	19 11	20 04	20 11	20 31		21 11	21 54		22 08	23 16	23 59
	d	18 07		18 26	18 37	18 52		19 03	19 13	20 05	20 13	20 32		21 13	21 55		22 10	23 18	00 01
Teignmouth	d	18 14							19 20		20 20			21 20	22 02		22 17	23 25	
Dawlish	d	18 19							19 25		20 25			21 25	22 07		22 22	23 30	
Dawlish Warren	d	18 24							19 30		20 30						22 27	23 35	
Starcross	d	18 28							19 34		20 34						22 31	23 39	
Exeter St Thomas	d	18 37							19 43		20 43						22 40	23 48	
Exeter St Davids 6	a	18 40		18 47	18 56	19 14		19 23	19 48	20 25	20 48	20 53		21 40	22 21		22 43	23 52	00 40
Exeter Central	a	18 51							19 54		20 54			21 51			22 51		
Exmouth	a	19 18							20 21		21 21			22 18			23 18		
Exeter St Davids 6	d			18 49	18 58	19 16		19 25		20 26		20 55							01 06
Tiverton Parkway	d				19 11	19 31		19 38		20 42		21 10							
Taunton	d			19 12	19 25	19 45		19 54		20 55		21 23							
Bridgwater	a																		
Weston-super-Mare	a																		
Bristol Temple Meads 10	a				19 57			20 27				22 00							02 14
Bath Spa 7	a											22 22							
Filton Abbey Wood	a																		
Bristol Parkway 7	a				20 08			20 38											
Swindon	a											22 50							03 21
Newport (South Wales)	a																		
Cardiff Central 7	a																		
Birmingham New Street 12	a				21 20			21 51											
Castle Cary	d					20 07				21 19									
Westbury	d					20 27				21 40									
Pewsey	d									21 58									
Hungerford	a																		
Newbury	a			20 18						22 18									
Thatcham	a																		
Theale	a																		
Reading 7	a			20 50		21 18				22 40		23 28							04s02
Slough 3	a																		
London Paddington 15 ⊖	a			21 29		21 58				23 18		00 13							05 05

For connections to Oxford, Gatwick Airport and Heathrow Airport please refer to Tables 116, 148 and 125A

Table 135

Sundays

19 February to 25 March

Cornwall and Devon - Birmingham and London

Route Diagram - see first Page of Table 135

		GW	GW	GW	GW	GW	GW	GW	XC	GW	GW	XC	GW	GW	GW	XC	XC	GW	GW	GW	GW	XC	XC
			◇	◇1	◇	◇1				◇1	◇1	◇1		◇1			◇1			◇1	◇1		◇1
		🚌						🚌	🚌				🚌			🚌			🚌			🚌	
				☕		☕				☕	☕	🍴		☕			🍴			☕	☕		🍴
Penzance	d									08 15										09 15			
St Erth	d									08 23										09 25			
Hayle	d									08 29													
Camborne	d									08 39										09 36			
Redruth	d									08 45										09 42			
Truro	d									08 59										09 55			
St Austell	d									09 15										10 13			
Newquay	d																						
Par	d									09 24										10 21			
Lostwithiel	d																						
Bodmin Parkway	d									09 36										10 33			
Liskeard 6	d									09 49										10 46			
Menheniot	d																						
St Germans	d																			10 58			
Saltash	d									10 06													
St Budeaux Ferry Road	d																						
Keyham	d																						
Dockyard	d																						
Devonport	d																						
Plymouth	a									10 15										11 14			
	d	07 55						09 35	09 40							10 30			11 05			11 30	
Ivybridge	d																						
Totnes	d	08 40						10 20	10 25				10 45			11 25			11 50			12 15	
Paignton	d						09 49					10 50			11 00			11 49					
Torquay	d						09 54					10 56			11 05			11 54					
Torre	d						09 57								11 08			11 57					
Newton Abbot	a	09 05					10 05	10 45	10 50			11 06	11 10		11 16	11 40		12 05	12 15			12 40	
	d					09 15	10 07				10 55	11 08		11 18	11 25		12 00	12 07			12 25		13 03
Teignmouth	d					09 22	10 14					11 15			11 32			12 14					
Dawlish	d					09 28	10 19					11 20			11 37			12 19					
Dawlish Warren	d						10 24											12 24					
Starcross	d						10 28											12 28					
Exeter St Thomas	d						10 37											12 37					
Exeter St Davids 6	a					09 41	10 41				11 15	11 30		11 38	11 52		12 18	12 42			12 45		13 21
Exeter Central	a						10 49								11 58			12 51					
Exmouth	a						11 18								12 25			13 20					
Exeter St Davids 6	d		08 01	08 35	09 35	09 43					11 18	11 32		11 40			12 23				12 46		13 23
Tiverton Parkway	d		08 18	08 50	09 53	10 01					11 35	11 46		11 57			12 37				13 03		13 37
Taunton	d		08 35	09 04	10 19	10 14					11 50	12 00		12 12			12 51				13 16		13 51
Bridgwater	a		08 46		10 31																		
Weston-super-Mare	a		09 06		10 49							12 20											
Bristol Temple Meads 10	a		09 39		11 20						12 24	12 45					13 26						14 26
Bath Spa 7	a										12 41												
Filton Abbey Wood	a																						
Bristol Parkway 7	a											13 08					13 38						14 38
Swindon	a										13 10												
Newport (South Wales)	a																						
Cardiff Central 7	a																						
Birmingham New Street 12	a											14 26					14 50						15 50
Castle Cary	d			09 26										12 33									
Westbury	d			09 54		10 51								12 53							13 59		
Pewsey	d			10 11										13 10									
Hungerford	a																						
Newbury	a			10 31		11 26								13 30									
Thatcham	a																						
Theale	a																						
Reading 7	a			10 48		11 49					13 47			13 51							14 48		
Slough 3	a																						
London Paddington 15 ⊖	a			11 29		12 29					14 22			14 29							15 29		

For connections to Oxford, Gatwick Airport and Heathrow Airport please refer to Tables 116, 148 and 125A

Table 135

Sundays

19 February to 25 March

Cornwall and Devon - Birmingham and London

Route Diagram - see first Page of Table 135

		GW	GW	XC	GW	XC		GW	XC	GW	GW	GW	GW	GW	GW	XC		GW	XC	GW	GW	GW	XC	GW	XC
				◇1	◇			◇1	◇1		◇1			◇1					◇1				◇1	◇1	
			(bus)			(bus)				(bus)						(bus)					(bus)	(bus)			(bus)
								(catering)	(trolley)		(catering)			(catering)					(trolley)					(catering)	
Penzance	d			10 35							11 17	11 45						12 05					12 30		
St Erth	d			10 43							11 26	11a53						12 13					12 40		
Hayle	d																						12 44		
Camborne	d			10 53							11 38							12 25					12 56		
Redruth	d			10 59							11 44							12 31					13 02		
Truro	d			11 11							11 58							12 42					13 14		
St Austell	d			11 27							12 15							12 59					13 30		
Newquay	d				11 12																				
Par	d			11 35	12a01						12 23							13 06					13 38		
Lostwithiel	d																	13 13					13 45		
Bodmin Parkway	d			11 46							12 35							13 19					13 52		
Liskeard 6	d			11 58							12 48							13 32					14 04		
Menheniot	d																	13 37							
St Germans	d																	13 45							
Saltash	d																	13 53							
St Budeaux Ferry Road	d																								
Keyham	d																								
Dockyard	d																								
Devonport	d																								
Plymouth	a			12 22							13 15							14 02					14 28		
	d		12 20			12 30				12 55						13 30					14 15	14 11			14 30
Ivybridge	d																								
Totnes	d		13 05			13 15				13 40						14 15					15 00	15 11			15 15
Paignton	d	12 57											13 51		14 19					14 57					
Torquay	d	13 02											13 56		14 24					15 02					
Torre	d	13 05											13 59		14 27					15 05					
Newton Abbot	a	13 13	13 30			13 40				14 05			14 07		14 35	14 40				15 13	15 25	15 36			15 40
	d	13 15						13 42	14 03				14 08	14 20	14 37				15 01	15 15				15 38	
Teignmouth	d	13 22											14 15		14 44					15 22					
Dawlish	d	13 27											14 20		14 49					15 27					
Dawlish Warren	d												14 33		14 54										
Starcross	d														14 58										
Exeter St Thomas	d														15 07										
Exeter St Davids 6	a	13 41						14 02	14 23				14 45	14 40	15 12				15 21	15 41				15 58	
Exeter Central	a	13 51											14 51		15 17					15 51					
Exmouth	a	14 18											15 18							16 18					
Exeter St Davids 6	d							14 04	14 25					14 41					15 25					16 00	
Tiverton Parkway	d							14 20	14 39					14 58					15 38					16 18	
Taunton	d							14 32	14 54					15 12					15 54					16 31	
Bridgwater	a																								
Weston-super-Mare	a																								
Bristol Temple Meads 10	a								15 27										16 27						
Bath Spa 7	a																								
Filton Abbey Wood	a																								
Bristol Parkway 7	a								15 38										16 38						
Swindon	a																								
Newport (South Wales)	a																								
Cardiff Central 7	a																								
Birmingham New Street 12	a								16 50										17 49						
Castle Cary	d													15 34											
Westbury	d													15 52											
Pewsey	d													16 10											
Hungerford	a																								
Newbury	a													16 31											
Thatcham	a																								
Theale	a																								
Reading 7	a							15 51						16 48										17 48	
Slough 3	a																								
London Paddington 15 ⊖	a							16 29						17 30										18 29	

For connections to Oxford, Gatwick Airport and Heathrow Airport
please refer to Tables 116, 148 and 125A

Table 135

Sundays

19 February to 25 March

Cornwall and Devon - Birmingham and London

Route Diagram - see first Page of Table 135

		GW	XC	GW	GW	GW	GW	GW	GW	XC	GW	GW	GW	GW	XC	GW	GW	XC	GW	GW	GW	XC
		◇1	◇1	◇1				◇1			◇1	◇		◇1	◇1				◇1	◇1	◇	◇1
					🚌				🚌	🚌							🚌	🚌				
		⊡	⊼	⊡				⊡			⊡			⊡	⊼				⊡	⊡		⊼
Penzance	d					13 20					13 55								14 30			
St Erth	d					13 29					14 03								14 40			
Hayle	d					13 32													14 44			
Camborne	d					13 42					14 16								14 55			
Redruth	d					13 48					14 22								15 02			
Truro	d					13 59					14 35								15 15			
St Austell	d					14 16					14 52								15 33			
Newquay	d											14 45										
Par	d					14 23					15 01	15a34							15 41			
Lostwithiel	d					14 30													15 48			
Bodmin Parkway	d					14 36					15 12								15 55			
Liskeard 6	d					14 49					15 27								16 08			
Menheniot	d																					
St Germans	d					14 59													16 19			
Saltash	d					15 07					15 44								16 28			
St Budeaux Ferry Road	d																					
Keyham	d																					
Dockyard	d																					
Devonport	d																					
Plymouth	a					15 17					15 53								16 38			
	d				15 00				15 28	15 30							16 02	16 30				
Ivybridge	d																16 27					
Totnes	d				15 45				16 13	16 15							17 02	17 15				
Paignton	d			15 45			15 54						16 22			16 58						
Torquay	d			15 51			15 59						16 27			17 03						
Torre	d			15 56			16 02						16 30			17 06						
Newton Abbot	a			16 04	16 10		16 10		16 28	16 40			16 41			17 14	17 27	17 40				
	d	15 46	16 01	16 05			16 11	16 21					16 41	16 55	17 03	17 15				17 40		18 04
Teignmouth	d			16 13			16 18						16 49			17 22						
Dawlish	d			16 18			16 23						16 54			17 27						
Dawlish Warren	d						16 34						16 58			17 32						
Starcross	d															17 36						
Exeter St Thomas	d															17 45						
Exeter St Davids 6	a	16 06	16 21	16 32			16 46	16 41					17 11	17 15	17 21	17 49				18 00		18 21
Exeter Central	a						16 52						17 18			17 55						
Exmouth	a						17 19									18 21						
Exeter St Davids 6	d	16 08	16 25	16 34				16 42						17 17	17 23					18 02	18 09	18 23
Tiverton Parkway	d	16 25	16 38					17 01						17 34	17 37					18 19		18 38
Taunton	d	16 40	16 54	16 59				17 15						17 48	17 51					18 34	18 40	18 52
Bridgwater	a			17 09																	18 51	
Weston-super-Mare	a	17 01		17 28																	19 10	
Bristol Temple Meads 10	a	17 20	17 27	17 58										18 22	18 27						19 44	19 27
Bath Spa 7	a	17 41		18 12										18 41								
Filton Abbey Wood	a																					
Bristol Parkway 7	a		17 38												18 38							19 38
Swindon	a	18 10		18 40										19 11								
Newport (South Wales)	a																					
Cardiff Central 7	a																					
Birmingham New Street 12	a		18 51												19 50							20 50
Castle Cary	d							17 37														
Westbury	d							17 56												19 13		
Pewsey	d							18 13														
Hungerford	a																					
Newbury	a							18 33														
Thatcham	a																					
Theale	a																					
Reading 7	a	18 46		19 17				18 51						19 47						19 58		
Slough 3	a																					
London Paddington 15 ⊖	a	19 22		19 59				19 29						20 22						20 43		

For connections to Oxford, Gatwick Airport and Heathrow Airport please refer to Tables 116, 148 and 125A

Table 135

Sundays

19 February to 25 March

Cornwall and Devon - Birmingham and London

Route Diagram - see first Page of Table 135

		GW	GW	GW	XC	GW	GW	XC		XC	GW	GW	XC	GW	GW	GW	XC	GW		GW	GW	GW	GW	XC	GW
					◇1		◇1			◇1				◇1		◇1	◇1	◇1						◇1	◇1
			🚌	🚌				🚌				🚌	🚌		🚌						🚌				
							☕			🛒				☕		☕		☕					🛒		☕
Penzance	d				15 30											16 59						19 00	20 05		
St Erth	d				15 38											17 09						19 09	20 14		
Hayle	d																						20 17		
Camborne	d				15 51											17 22						19 20	20 26		
Redruth	d				15 57											17 29						19 26	20 32		
Truro	d				16 09											17 41						19 38	20 44		
St Austell	d				16 25											18 00						19 55	21 01		
Newquay	d					17 14																			
Par	d				16 33	18a03										18 08						20 03	21 09		
Lostwithiel	d																					20 09			
Bodmin Parkway	d				16 44											18 19						20 15	21 21		
Liskeard 6	d				16 56											18 32						20 28	21 35		
Menheniot	d																					20x33			
St Germans	d																					20 41			
Saltash	d															18 49						20 48			
St Budeaux Ferry Road	d																								
Keyham	d																								
Dockyard	d																								
Devonport	d																					20 56			
Plymouth	a				17 19											18 59						20 59	22 00		
	d		16 55	16 50				17 30				18 10	18 20		18 35						19 10				
Ivybridge	d			17 15																					
Totnes	d		17 45	17 50				18 15				18 55	19 05		19 25						19 20				
Paignton	d	17 49									18 55									19 55					
Torquay	d	17 54									19 00									20 00					
Torre	d	17 57									19 03									20 03					
Newton Abbot	a	18 05	18 10	18 15				18 40			19 11	19 20	19 30		19 50					20 11	20 20				
	d	18 07					18 24			19 03	19 13			19 32			19 50	20 01		20 13					20 32
Teignmouth	d	18 14									19 20									20 20					
Dawlish	d	18 19									19 25									20 25					
Dawlish Warren	d	18 24									19 30									20 30					
Starcross	d	18 28									19 34									20 34					
Exeter St Thomas	d	18 37									19 43									20 43					
Exeter St Davids 6	a	18 40					18 44			19 23	19 48			19 52			20 07	20 21		20 48					20 53
Exeter Central	a	18 51									19 54									20 54					
Exmouth	a	19 18									20 21									21 21					
Exeter St Davids 6	d						18 46			19 25				19 54			20 10	20 22						20 45	20 55
Tiverton Parkway	d						19 04			19 38				20 12			20 24	20 42						20 58	21 12
Taunton	d						19 15			19 54				20 26			20 40	20 55						21 13	21 26
Bridgwater	a																								
Weston-super-Mare	a																								
Bristol Temple Meads 10	a									20 27							21 13							21 50	22 00
Bath Spa 7	a																								22 22
Filton Abbey Wood	a																								
Bristol Parkway 7	a									20 38							21 28							22 18	
Swindon	a																								22 50
Newport (South Wales)	a																								
Cardiff Central 7	a																								
Birmingham New Street 12	a									21 51							22 46							23 39	
Castle Cary	d													20 48				21 19							
Westbury	d						19 55											21 40							
Pewsey	d																	21 58							
Hungerford	a																								
Newbury	a						20 27											22 18							
Thatcham	a																								
Theale	a																								
Reading 7	a						20 50							21 49				22 38							23 28
Slough 3	a																								
London Paddington 15 ⊖	a						21 30							22 28				23 16							00 12

For connections to Oxford, Gatwick Airport and Heathrow Airport please refer to Tables 116, 148 and 125A

Table 135

Sundays

19 February to 25 March

Cornwall and Devon - Birmingham and London

Route Diagram - see first Page of Table 135

		GW	GW	GW		GW
Penzance	d					21 15
St Erth	d					21 25
Hayle	d					
Camborne	d					21 38
Redruth	d					21 45
Truro	d					22 00
St Austell	d					22 18
Newquay	d					
Par	d					
Lostwithiel	d					
Bodmin Parkway	d					22 35
Liskeard 6	d					22 50
Menheniot	d					
St Germans	d					
Saltash	d					
St Budeaux Ferry Road	d					
Keyham	d					
Dockyard	d					
Devonport	d					
Plymouth	a					23 15
	d					01 50
Ivybridge	d					
Totnes	d					02 18
Paignton	d	20 55	21 52	23 00		
Torquay	d	21 00	21 57	23 05		
Torre	d	21 03	22 00	23 08		
Newton Abbot	a	21 11	22 08	23 16		02 29
	d	21 13	22 10	23 18		02 31
Teignmouth	d	21 20	22 17	23 25		
Dawlish	d	21 25	22 22	23 30		
Dawlish Warren	d		22 27	23 35		
Starcross	d		22 31	23 39		
Exeter St Thomas	d		22 40	23 48		
Exeter St Davids 6	a	21 40	22 43	23 52		02 57
Exeter Central	a	21 51	22 51			
Exmouth	a	22 18	23 18			
Exeter St Davids 6	d					02 59
Tiverton Parkway	d					
Taunton	d					
Bridgwater	a					
Weston-super-Mare	a					
Bristol Temple Meads 10	a					
Bath Spa 7	a					
Filton Abbey Wood	a					
Bristol Parkway 7	a					
Swindon	a					
Newport (South Wales)	a					
Cardiff Central 7	a					
Birmingham New Street 12	a					
Castle Cary	d					
Westbury	d					
Pewsey	d					
Hungerford	a					
Newbury	a					
Thatcham	a					
Theale	a					
Reading 7	a					05s11
Slough 3	a					
London Paddington 15 ⊖	a					06 09

For connections to Oxford, Gatwick Airport and Heathrow Airport please refer to Tables 116, 148 and 125A

Table 135

Sundays
from 1 April

Cornwall and Devon - Birmingham and London

Route Diagram - see first Page of Table 135

		GW	GW	GW	GW	XC	GW	GW	XC	XC		GW	GW	XC	GW	GW	GW	XC	XC	GW		XC	GW	GW	XC
		◇	◇1	◇	◇1	◇1		◇1	◇1	◇1		◇1		◇1		◇1	◇	◇1	◇1			◇1	◇1		◇1
														A											
			☕		☕	🛒		☕	🛒	🛒		☕		🛒		☕		🛒	🛒			🛒	☕		
Penzance	d											08 35		09 30		09 47							11 04	11 45	
St Erth	d											08 44		09 38		09 57							11 14	11a53	
Hayle	d											08 49													
Camborne	d											09 00		09 48		10 08							11 27		
Redruth	d											09 06		09 54		10 14							11 33		
Truro	d											09 20		10 06		10 27							11 47		
St Austell	d											09 36		10 22		10 44							12 03		
Newquay	d																11 12								
Par	d											09 45		10 30		10 53	12a01						12 11		
Lostwithiel	d																								
Bodmin Parkway	d											09 57		10 41		11 06							12 24		
Liskeard 6	d											10 10		10 53		11 19							12 37		
Menheniot	d																								
St Germans	d															11 30									
Saltash	d											10 28													
St Budeaux Ferry Road	d																								
Keyham	d																								
Dockyard	d																								
Devonport	d																								
Plymouth	a											10 35		11 17		11 44							13 02		
	d				08 40	09 25		10 10	10 25			10 40		11 25		11 45		12 00	12 25			12 52	13 07		13 23
Ivybridge	d																								
Totnes	d				09 07	09 50		10 40	10 50			11 07		11 50		12 15			12 50				13 34		13 49
Paignton	d						09 49			10 50			11 00		11 49					12 57					
Torquay	d						09 54			10 56			11 05		11 54					13 02					
Torre	d						09 57						11 08		11 57					13 05					
Newton Abbot	a				09 19	10 01	10 05	10 52	11 01	11 06		11 19	11 16	12 01	12 05	12 28		12 34	13 01	13 13		13 26	13 46		14 01
	d				09 20	10 03	10 07	10 54	11 03	11 08		11 21	11 25	12 03	12 07	12 29		12 36	13 03	13 15		13 27	13 47		14 03
Teignmouth	d				09 27		10 14			11 15			11 32		12 14					13 22					
Dawlish	d				09 33		10 19			11 20			11 37		12 19					13 27					
Dawlish Warren	d						10 24								12 24										
Starcross	d						10 28								12 28										
Exeter St Thomas	d						10 37								12 37										
Exeter St Davids 6	a				09 47	10 21	10 41	11 14	11 21	11 30		11 41	11 52	12 21	12 42	12 49		12 55	13 21	13 41		13 46	14 07		14 23
Exeter Central	a						10 49						11 58		12 51					13 51					
Exmouth	a						11 18						12 25		13 20					14 18					
Exeter St Davids 6	d	08 01	08 30	09 35	09 48	10 23		11 18	11 23	11 32		11 43		12 23		12 50		12 57	13 23			13 48	14 09		14 25
Tiverton Parkway	d	08 18	08 45	09 53		10 37		11 33	11 37	11 46		11 58		12 37				13 10	13 37				14 23		14 39
Taunton	d	08 35	08 59	10 19	10 14	10 51		11 48	11 53	12 00		12 13		12 51		13 16		13 25	13 51				14 38		14 54
Bridgwater	a	08 46		10 31																					
Weston-super-Mare	a	09 06		10 49						12 20															
Bristol Temple Meads 10	a	09 38		11 20		11 27		12 23	12 27	12 45				13 26				13 57	14 26			14 40			15 27
Bath Spa 7	a							12 41																	
Filton Abbey Wood	a	09 55																							
Bristol Parkway 7	a					11 38			12 38	13 08				13 38				14 08	14 38			15 08			15 38
Swindon	a							13 10																	
Newport (South Wales)	a	10 25																							
Cardiff Central 7	a	10 41																							
Birmingham New Street 12	a					12 50			13 50	14 26				14 50				15 27	15 50			16 26			16 50
Castle Cary	d		09 21									12 34													
Westbury	d		09 41		10 51							12 53				13 54									
Pewsey	d																								
Hungerford	a																								
Newbury	a																								
Thatcham	a																								
Theale	a																								
Reading 7	a		10 47		11 50			13 47				13 56				14 52							16 18		
Slough 3	a																								
London Paddington 15 ⊖	a		11 29		12 29			14 22				14 33				15 29							16 59		

A 🛒 from Plymouth

For connections to Oxford, Gatwick Airport and Heathrow Airport please refer to Tables 116, 148 and 125A

Table 135

Sundays
from 1 April

Cornwall and Devon - Birmingham and London

Route Diagram - see first Page of Table 135

		GW	GW	GW	GW	XC		XC	GW	GW	GW	XC	GW	GW	GW	GW		GW	GW	XC	GW	GW	GW	GW	XC
			◇[1]			◇[1]		◇[1]		◇[1]	◇[1]	◇[1]	◇[1]	◇[1]		◇			◇[1]	◇[1]		◇	◇	◇[1]	◇[1]
								A																	A
			☕			🛒		🛒		☕	☕	🛒	☕	☕					☕	🛒				☕	🛒
Penzance	d				12 05			12 25		12 43						13 41						14 40		15 10	15 30
St Erth	d				12 14			12 33		12 52						13 51						14 49		15 20	15 38
Hayle	d							12 37								13 54						14 52			
Camborne	d				12 25			12 46		13 06						14 04						15 01		15 32	15 51
Redruth	d				12 31			12 53		13 12						14 10						15 07		15 39	15 57
Truro	d				12 43			13 04		13 25						14 21						15 18		15 51	16 09
St Austell	d				12 59			13 21		13 43						14 38						15 35		16 09	16 25
Newquay	d																						15 10		
Par	d				13 06			13 28		13 50						14 45						15 43	15a59	16 17	16 33
Lostwithiel	d				13 13			13 35								14 52						15 49			
Bodmin Parkway	d				13 19			13 42		14 03						14 58						15 55		16 28	16 44
Liskeard [6]	d				13 33			13 55		14 16						15 11						16 09		16 41	16 56
Menheniot	d				13 38																				
St Germans	d				13 46											15 21						16 19			
Saltash	d				13 54											15 29						16 27			
St Budeaux Ferry Road	d																								
Keyham	d																								
Dockyard	d																								
Devonport	d																								
Plymouth	a				14 03			14 19		14 42						15 39						16 37		17 07	17 20
	d		13 44		14 06	14 23		14 35		14 45	15 05	15 23		15 33		15 49			16 10	16 25		16 38		17 10	17 26
Ivybridge	d				14 21											16 07						16 53			
Totnes	d		14 11		14 35	14 49		15 00		15 12	15 35	15 49		16 01		16 21			16 42	16 50		17 07		17 38	17 52
Paignton	d	13 51		14 19					14 57				15 45		16 00			16 21			16 55				
Torquay	d	13 56		14 24					15 02				15 51		16 05			16 26			17 00				
Torre	d	13 59		14 27					15 05				15 56		16 08			16 29			17 03				
Newton Abbot	a	14 07	14 23	14 35	14 47	15 01		15 11	15 13	15 24	15 47	16 01	16 04	16 12	16 16	16 33		16 37	16 53	17 01	17 11	17 19		17 49	18 02
	d	14 08	14 25	14 37	14 48	15 03		15 12	15 15	15 25	15 48	16 03	16 05	16 14	16 17	16 34		16 38	16 55	17 03	17 12	17 20		17 51	18 04
Teignmouth	d	14 15		14 44	14 55				15 22				16 13		16 24			16 45			17 19	17 27			
Dawlish	d	14 20		14 49	15 00				15 27				16 18		16 29			16 50			17 24	17 32			
Dawlish Warren	d	14 25		14 54											16 34			16 55			17 29				
Starcross	d	14 29		14 58														16 59							
Exeter St Thomas	d	14 38		15 07														17 08							
Exeter St Davids [6]	a	14 43	14 46	15 12	15 16	15 23		15 31	15 41	15 45	16 08	16 23	16 32	16 38	16 46	16 55		17 13	17 17	17 21	17 41	17 46		18 11	18 21
Exeter Central	a	14 51		15 17					15 51						16 52			17 18			17 51				
Exmouth	a	15 18							16 18						17 19						18 18				
Exeter St Davids [6]	d		14 47			15 25		15 33		15 47	16 10	16 24	16 34	16 39					17 19	17 23		17 51		18 13	18 23
Tiverton Parkway	d					15 38		15 46		16 02	16 25	16 37		16 55					17 34	17 37				18 28	18 38
Taunton	d		15 12			15 54		16 01		16 17	16 40	16 53	16 59	17 09					17 48	17 51		18 22		18 43	18 52
Bridgwater	a												17 09									18 33			
Weston-super-Mare	a							16 20			17 01		17 28									18 52			
Bristol Temple Meads [10]	a					16 27		16 54			17 20	17 26	17 58						18 25	18 27		19 42			19 26
Bath Spa [7]	a										17 41		18 12						18 41						
Filton Abbey Wood	a																								
Bristol Parkway [7]	a					16 38		17 08				17 38								18 38					19 38
Swindon	a										18 10		18 39						19 11						
Newport (South Wales)	a																								
Cardiff Central [7]	a																								
Birmingham New Street [12]	a					17 49		18 27				18 51								19 50					20 50
Castle Cary	d		15 34											17 31											
Westbury	d		15 52											17 51											
Pewsey	d																								
Hungerford	a																								
Newbury	a																								
Thatcham	a																								
Theale	a																								
Reading [7]	a		16 53							17 52	18 46		19 12	18 55					19 48					20 21	
Slough [3]	a																								
London Paddington [15] ⊖	a		17 32							18 29	19 22		19 59	19 32					20 28					21 01	

A 🛒 from Plymouth

For connections to Oxford, Gatwick Airport and Heathrow Airport please refer to Tables 116, 148 and 125A

Table 135

Sundays
from 1 April

Cornwall and Devon - Birmingham and London

Route Diagram - see first Page of Table 135

		GW		GW	XC	GW	GW	XC	GW	GW	GW	GW		GW	GW	GW	GW	GW	GW
				◇1 🍴	◇1 🛒	◇1 🍴		◇1 🛒		◇1 🍴		◇1 🍴				🛒			R 🛏 🍴
Penzance	d					16 10				17 25					19 00	20 05			21 15
St Erth	d					16 21				17 34					19 09	20 14			21 25
Hayle	d															20 17			
Camborne	d					16 33				17 47					19 20	20 26			21 38
Redruth	d					16 40				17 54					19 26	20 32			21 45
Truro	d					16 53				18 06					19 38	20 44			22 00
St Austell	d					17 10				18 24					19 55	21 01			22 18
Newquay	d						17 30												
Par	d					17 17	18a19			18 32					20 03	21 09			
Lostwithiel	d														20 09				
Bodmin Parkway	d					17 29				18 44					20 15	21 21			22 35
Liskeard 6	d					17 42				18 57					20 28	21 35			22 50
Menheniot	d														20x33				
St Germans	d														20 41				
Saltash	d					18 00									20 48				
St Budeaux Ferry Road	d																		
Keyham	d																		
Dockyard	d																		
Devonport	d														20 56				
Plymouth	a					18 10				19 21					21 00	22 00			23 15
	d			17 35		18 10		18 23		19 25		19 55			21 15				23 20
Ivybridge	d																		
Totnes	d			18 03		18 40		18 49		19 52					21 42				23 48
Paignton	d	17 49			18 20				18 55		19 55			20 55			21 52	23 00	
Torquay	d	17 54			18 26				19 00		20 00			21 00			21 57	23 05	
Torre	d	17 57							19 03		20 03			21 03			22 00	23 08	
Newton Abbot	a	18 05		18 15	18 36	18 52		19 01	19 11	20 04	20 11	20 31		21 11	21 54		22 08	23 16	23 59
	d	18 07		18 16	18 37	18 52		19 03	19 13	20 05	20 13	20 32		21 13	21 55		22 10	23 18	00 01
Teignmouth	d	18 14							19 20		20 20			21 20	22 02		22 17	23 25	
Dawlish	d	18 19							19 25		20 25			21 25	22 07		22 22	23 30	
Dawlish Warren	d	18 30							19 30		20 30						22 27	23 35	
Starcross	d	18 34							19 34		20 34						22 31	23 39	
Exeter St Thomas	d	18 43							19 43		20 43						22 40	23 48	
Exeter St Davids 6	a	18 46		18 37	18 56	19 13		19 23	19 48	20 25	20 48	20 53		21 40	22 21		22 43	23 52	00 40
Exeter Central	a	18 53							19 54		20 54			21 51			22 51		
Exmouth	a	19 20							20 21		21 21			22 18			23 18		
Exeter St Davids 6	d			18 39	18 58	19 15		19 25		20 26		20 55							01 06
Tiverton Parkway	d				19 11	19 30		19 38		20 42		21 10							
Taunton	d			19 05	19 25	19 44		19 54		20 57		21 23							
Bridgwater	a																		
Weston-super-Mare	a																		
Bristol Temple Meads 10	a				19 57			20 27				22 00							02 14
Bath Spa 7	a											22 22							
Filton Abbey Wood	a																		
Bristol Parkway 7	a				20 08			20 38											
Swindon	a											22 50							03 21
Newport (South Wales)	a																		
Cardiff Central 7	a																		
Birmingham New Street 12	a				21 20			21 51											
Castle Cary	d			19 26						21 19									
Westbury	d			19 45						21 40									
Pewsey	d																		
Hungerford	a																		
Newbury	a																		
Thatcham	a																		
Theale	a																		
Reading 7	a			20 48		21 21				22 44		23 28							04s02
Slough 3	a																		
London Paddington 15 ⊖	a			21 27		22 02				23 28		00 13							05 05

For connections to Oxford, Gatwick Airport and Heathrow Airport please refer to Tables 116, 148 and 125A

Table 135A

Mondays to Fridays

Redruth - Helston

Bus Service

	GW	GW	GW	GW	GW	GW	GW	GW	GW	GW	GW	GW	GW	GW
	BHX	BHX	BHX	BHX	BHX	BHX	BHX	BHX	BHX	BHX	BHX	BHX	BHX	BHX
	A													
Redruth d	08 00	09 05	10 15	11 05	12 05	13 05	14 05	15 05	16 05	17 00	18 15	19 15	21 15	23 25
Helston Coinagehall St a	08 38	09 37	10 47	11 37	12 37	13 37	14 37	15 37	16 37	17 42	18 47	19 47	21 47	23 51

Saturdays

	GW	GW	GW	GW	GW	GW	GW	GW	GW	GW	GW	GW	GW	GW
	A	A												
Redruth d	08 00	09 05	10 15	11 05	12 05	13 05	14 05	15 05	16 05	17 10	18 15	19 15	21 15	23 25
Helston Coinagehall St a	08 29	09 37	10 47	11 37	12 37	13 37	14 37	15 37	16 37	17 42	18 47	19 47	21 47	23 51

Sundays

	GW	GW	GW	GW	GW
Redruth d	09 50	11 50	13 50	15 50	17 50
Helston Coinagehall St a	10 19	12 19	14 19	16 19	18 19

A Operates on School Holidays only

Table 135A

Mondays to Fridays

Helston - Redruth

Bus Service

	GW	GW	GW	GW	GW	GW	GW	GW	GW	GW	GW	GW	GW	GW
	BHX	BHX	BHX	BHX	BHX	BHX	BHX	BHX	BHX	BHX	BHX	BHX	BHX	BHX
								A		B				
Helston Coinagehall St d	07 05	08 06	09 35	10 27	11 27	12 27	13 27	14 27	15 15	16 30	17 30	18 30	19 50	21 50
Redruth a	07 39	08 55	10 09	11 01	12 01	13 01	14 01	15 01	16 01	17 04	18 04	19 02	20 22	22 22

Saturdays

	GW	GW	GW	GW	GW	GW	GW	GW	GW	GW	GW	GW	GW	GW
Helston Coinagehall St d	07 05	08 13	09 35	10 27	11 27	12 27	13 27	14 27	15 27	16 30	17 30	18 30	19 50	21 50
Redruth a	07 39	08 47	10 09	11 01	12 01	13 01	14 01	15 01	16 01	17 04	18 04	19 02	20 22	22 22

Sundays

	GW	GW	GW	GW	GW
Helston Coinagehall St d	08 50	10 50	12 50	14 50	16 50
Redruth a	09 21	11 21	13 21	15 21	17 21

A Operates during School Holidays only

B Runs during school holidays only.

Table 135B

Mondays to Fridays

St. Austell - Eden Project

Bus Service

		GW	GW	GW	GW	GW	GW	GW	GW	GW	GW	GW	GW	GW	GW	GW	GW	GW	GW	GW
			BHX	BHX			BHX		BHX	BHX			BHX		BHX		BHX		BHX	
St Austell	d	08 35	08 50	09 30	09 35	10 35	10 40	11 35	11 50	12 30	12 35	13 35	13 55	14 35	15 02	15 35	16 10	16 35	17 05	17 35
Eden Project	a	08 57	09 09	09 49	09 57	10 57	10 59	11 57	12 09	12 49	12 57	13 57	14 14	14 57	15 21	15 57	16 29	16 57	17 24	17 57

Saturdays

		GW	GW	GW	GW	GW	GW	GW	GW	GW	GW	GW	GW	GW	GW	GW	GW	GW	GW
St Austell	d	08 35	08 50	09 30	09 35	10 35	10 40	11 35	12 05	12 35	13 35	13 55	14 35	15 02	15 35	15 50	16 35	17 00	17 35
Eden Project	a	08 57	09 09	09 49	09 57	10 57	10 59	11 57	12 24	12 57	13 57	14 14	14 57	15 21	15 57	16 09	16 57	17 19	17 57

Sundays

		GW	GW	GW	GW	GW	GW	GW	GW	GW	GW	GW	GW
St Austell	d	08 50	10 35	11 35	11 40	12 30	12 35	13 35	14 35	14 45	15 35	16 25	17 10
Eden Project	a	09 09	10 57	11 57	11 59	12 49	12 57	13 54	14 57	15 04	15 57	16 44	17 29

Table 135B

Mondays to Fridays

Eden Project - St. Austell

Bus Service

		GW	GW	GW	GW	GW	GW	GW	GW	GW	GW	GW	GW	GW	GW	GW	GW	GW
			BHX	BHX			BHX		BHX			BHX		BHX		BHX		
Eden Project	d	09 00	09 10	09 55	10 00	11 00	11 15	12 00	12 10	13 00	14 00	14 25	15 00	15 22	16 00	16 30	17 00	18 00
St Austell	a	09 24	09 29	10 14	10 24	11 24	11 34	12 24	12 29	13 24	14 24	14 44	15 24	15 41	16 24	16 49	17 24	18 24

Saturdays

		GW	GW	GW	GW	GW	GW	GW	GW	GW	GW	GW	GW	GW	GW	GW	GW	GW	GW
Eden Project	d	09 00	09 10	09 55	10 00	11 00	11 15	12 00	13 00	13 15	14 00	14 25	15 00	15 22	16 00	16 25	17 00	17 55	18 00
St Austell	a	09 24	09 29	10 14	10 24	11 24	11 34	12 24	13 24	13 34	14 24	14 44	15 24	15 41	16 24	16 44	17 24	18 14	18 24

Sundays

		GW	GW	GW	GW	GW	GW	GW	GW	GW	GW	GW	GW
Eden Project	d	09 50	11 00	12 00	13 05	14 00	14 25	15 00	15 15	16 00	16 05	16 50	18 00
St Austell	a	10 09	11 20	12 20	13 24	14 20	14 44	15 20	15 34	16 24	16 24	17 09	18 19

Table 135C

Mondays to Saturdays

Bodmin - Wadebridge and Padstow

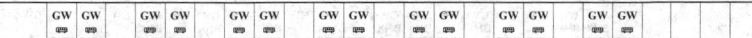

Bus Service

		GW	GW	GW	GW	GW	GW	GW	GW	GW	GW	GW	GW	GW	GW
		🚌	🚌	🚌	🚌	🚌	🚌	🚌	🚌	🚌	🚌	🚌	🚌	🚌	🚌
		BHX	BHX	BHX	BHX	BHX	BHX	BHX	BHX	BHX	BHX	BHX	BHX	BHX	BHX
Bodmin Parkway	d	07 25	08 30	09 30	10 30	11 30	12 30	13 30	14 30	15 30	16 30	17 30	18 30	19 30	22 00
Bodmin Mount Folly	a	07 35	08 40	09 40	10 40	11 40	12 40	13 40	14 40	15 40	16 40	17 40	18 40	19 40	22 10
Wadebridge Bus Station	a	07 55	09 00	10 00	11 00	12 00	13 00	14 00	15 00	16 00	17 00	18 00	19 00	20 00	22 30
Padstow Old Rly Station	a	08 27	09 27	10 27	11 27	12 27	13 27	14 27	15 27	16 27	17 27	18 27	19 27	20 27	22 57

Sundays

		GW	GW	GW	GW	GW	GW
		🚌	🚌	🚌	🚌	🚌	🚌
Bodmin Parkway	d	09 30	11 30	13 30	15 30	17 30	19 30
Bodmin Mount Folly	a	09 40	11 40	13 40	15 40	17 40	19 40
Wadebridge Bus Station	a	10 00	12 00	14 00	16 00	18 00	20 00
Padstow Old Rly Station	a	10 27	12 27	14 27	16 27	18 27	20 27

Table 135C

Mondays to Saturdays

Padstow and Wadebridge - Bodmin

Bus Service

		GW	GW	GW	GW	GW	GW	GW	GW	GW	GW	GW	GW	GW	GW
		BHX	BHX	BHX	BHX	BHX		BHX	BHX	BHX	BHX	BHX	BHX		BHX
		🚌	🚌	🚌	🚌	🚌	🚌	🚌	🚌	🚌	🚌	🚌	🚌	🚌	🚌
Padstow Old Rly Station	d	06 30	07 30	08 30	09 30	10 30	11 30	12 30	13 30	14 30	15 30	16 30	17 30	18 30	20 30
Wadebridge Bus Station	d	06 55	07 55	08 55	09 55	10 55	11 55	12 55	13 55	14 55	15 55	16 55	17 55	18 55	20 55
Bodmin Mount Folly	d	07 15	08 15	09 15	10 15	11 15	12 15	13 15	14 15	15 15	16 15	17 15	18 15	19 15	21 15
Bodmin Parkway	a	07 25	08 25	09 25	10 25	11 25	12 25	13 25	14 25	15 25	16 25	17 25	18 25	19 25	21 25

Sundays

		GW	GW	GW	GW	GW	GW
		🚌	🚌	🚌	🚌	🚌	🚌
Padstow Old Rly Station	d	08 30	10 30	12 30	14 30	16 30	18 30
Wadebridge Bus Station	d	08 55	10 55	12 55	14 55	16 55	18 55
Bodmin Mount Folly	d	09 15	11 15	13 15	15 15	17 15	19 15
Bodmin Parkway	a	09 25	11 25	13 25	15 25	17 25	19 25

Table 135D

Mondays to Saturdays

Exeter - Okehampton, Holsworthy and Bude

Bus Service

		GW	GW	GW	GW	GW	GW	GW	GW	GW	GW	GW	GW	GW	GW	GW	GW	GW
		🚌	🚌	🚌	🚌	🚌	🚌	🚌	🚌	🚌	🚌	🚌	🚌	🚌	🚌	🚌	🚌	🚌
Exeter St Davids	d	08 00	08 50	09 45	10 20	10 45	11 20	11 45	12 20	13 20	13 20	13 45	14 20	15 20	15 45	16 20	17 55	18 35
Okehampton West Street	a	08 45	09 40	10 25	11 05	11 25	12 10	12 25	13 05	14 00	14 05	14 25	15 10	16 10	16 25	17 00	18 35	19 20
Holsworthy Library	a			11 03				13 03		14 40		15 03			17 03		19 13	19 55
Holsworthy Cattle Market	a																	
Bude Strand	a			11 25				13 25		15 00		15 25			17 25		19 35	20 15

Sundays

		GW	GW	GW	GW	GW	GW
		🚌	🚌	🚌	🚌	🚌	🚌
Exeter St Davids	d	10 20	11 50	13 20	15 20	16 50	17 50
Okehampton West Street	a	11 05	12 40	14 05	16 05	17 30	18 40
Holsworthy Library	a		13 15				19 15
Holsworthy Cattle Market	a						
Bude Strand	a		13 35				19 35

Table 135D

Mondays to Saturdays

Bude, Holsworthy and Okehampton - Exeter

Bus Service

		GW	GW	GW	GW	GW	GW	GW	GW	GW	GW	GW	GW	GW	GW	GW	GW
																	SX
		BHX	BHX	BHX	BHX	BHX	BHX	BHX	BHX	BHX	BHX	BHX	BHX	BHX	BHX	BHX	BHX
		🚌	🚌	🚌	🚌	🚌	🚌	🚌	🚌	🚌	🚌	🚌	🚌	🚌	🚌	🚌	🚌
Bude Strand	d	06 40				08 40		09 00			11 30			13 30			15 27
Holsworthy Church	d	07 02				09 05		09 22			11 52			13 52			15 57
Holsworthy Cattle Market	d																
Okehampton West Street	d	07 45	09 10	09 25	09 35	09 45	09 55	10 05	11 10	11 40	12 35	13 10	14 10	14 35	15 10	15 40	16 40
Exeter St Davids	a	08 25	09 55	10 00	10 15	10 20	10 40	10 45	11 45	12 25	13 15	13 55	14 50	15 15	15 45	16 25	17 25

		GW	GW
			SO
		BHX	
		🚌	🚌
Bude Strand	d	15 30	15 30
Holsworthy Church	d	15 55	15 57
Holsworthy Cattle Market	d		
Okehampton West Street	d	16 40	16 40
Exeter St Davids	a	17x25	17 25

Sundays

		GW	GW	GW	GW	GW
		🚌	🚌	🚌	🚌	🚌
Bude Strand	d	09 45				15 45
Holsworthy Church	d	10 05				16 05
Holsworthy Cattle Market	d					
Okehampton West Street	d	10 40	11 45	14 15	14 45	16 40
Exeter St Davids	a	11 30	12 30	15 00	15 30	17 30

Taunton - Watchet, Dunster and Minehead

Bus Service

		GW SX BHX	GW	GW	GW	GW	GW A	GW B	GW C	GW D	GW E	GW F	GW G	GW H	GW I	GW J	GW K	GW L	GW M	GW N	GW O
Taunton	d	05 41	06 21	07 17	07 47	08 17	08 47	09 17	09 47	10 17	10 47	11 17	11 47	12 17	12 47	13 17	13 47	14 17	14 47	15 17	15 47
Bishops Lydeard Hithermead	a	05 56	06 36	07 32	08 02	08 32	09 02	09 32	10 02	10 32	11 02	11 32	12 02	12 32	13 02	13 32	14 02	14 32	15 02	15 32	16 02
Watchet (West Somerset Ry)	a	06 25	07 05	08 01	08 31	09 01	09 35	10 05	10 35	11 05	11 35	12 05	12 35	13 05	13 35	14 05	14 35	15 05	15 35	16 05	16 35
Dunster Steep	a	06 39	07 19	08 19	08 49	09 19	09 53	10 23	10 53	11 23	11 53	12 23	12 53	13 23	13 53	14 23	14 53	15 23	15 53	16 23	16 53
Minehead Parade	a	06 47	07 27	08 27	08 57	09 27	10 01	10 31	11 01	11 31	12 01	12 31	13 01	13 31	14 01	14 31	15 01	15 31	16 01	16 31	17 01
Minehead Butlins	a	06 52	07 32	08 32	09 02	09 32	10 06	10 36	11 06	11 36	12 06	12 36	13 06	13 36	14 06	14 36	15 06	15 36	16 06	16 36	17 06

		GW SX BHX P	GW	GW SX BHX	GW SO	GW BHX	GW	GW BHX	GW	GW
Taunton	d	16 17	16 47	17 12	17 12	17 37	18 07	18 37	20 16	22 16
Bishops Lydeard Hithermead	a	16 32	17 02	.	17 27	17 52	18 22	18 52	20 31	22 31
Watchet (West Somerset Ry)	a	17 05	17 31	17 54	17 56	18 21	18 51	19 21	21 00	23 00
Dunster Steep	a	17 23	17 49	18 12	18 14	18 39	19 09	19 39	21 14	23 14
Minehead Parade	a	17 31	17 57	18 20	18 22	18 47	19 17	19 47	21 22	23 22
Minehead Butlins	a	17 36	18 02	18 25	18 27	18 52	19 22	19 52	21 27	23 27

Sundays

		GW BHX	GW Q	GW R	GW	GW S	GW	GW T	GW	GW	GW
Taunton	d	08 22	09 22	11 28	12 38	13 38	14 38	15 38	16 38	17 38	19 38
Bishops Lydeard Hithermead	a	08 37	09 37	11 43	12 53	13 53	14 53	15 53	16 53	17 53	19 53
Watchet (West Somerset Ry)	a	09 10	10 10	12 13	13 22	14 23	15 22	16 23	17 22	18 22	20 22
Dunster Steep	a	09 28	10 28	12 30	13 39	14 40	15 39	16 40	17 39	18 39	20 39
Minehead Parade	a	09 36	10 36	12 38	13 47	14 48	15 47	16 48	17 47	18 47	20 47
Minehead Butlins	a	09 41	10 41	12 43	13 52	14 53	15 52	16 53	17 52	18 52	20 52

Also stops at West Somerset Railway (WSR) Station at

A 0906 on railway operating days
B 0936 on railway operating days
C 1006 on railway operating days
D 1036 on railway operating days
E 1106 on railway operating days
F 1136 on railway operating days
G 1206 on railway operating days
H 1236 on railway operating days
I 1306 on railway operating days
J 1336 on railway operating days
K 1406 on railway operating days
L 1436 on railway operating days
M 1506 on railway operating days
N 1536 on railway operating days
O 1606 on railway operating days
P 1636 on railway operating days
Q 0941 on railway operating days
R 1146 on railway operating days
S 1356 on railway operating days
T 1556 on railway operating days

Minehead, Dunster and Watchet - Taunton

Bus Service

		GW BHX	GW BHX	GW SX BHX	GW SX BHX	GW SO	GW BHX	GW	GW BHX	GW BHX	GW SX BHX	GW SO	GW BHX	GW A BHX	GW B BHX	GW C BHX	GW D BHX	GW E BHX	GW F BHX	GW G BHX	GW H BHX
Minehead Butlins	d	05 45	06 30	06 50	07 00	07 00	07 50	08 20	08 50	09 20	09 50	09 50	10 20	10 50	11 20	11 50	12 20	12 50	13 20	13 50	14 20
Minehead Bancks Street	d	05 50	06 35	06 58	07 08	07 10	08 00	08 30	09 00	09 30	10 00	10 00	10 30	11 00	11 30	12 00	12 30	13 00	13 30	14 00	14 30
Dunster Steep	d	05 58	06 43	07 06	07 16	07 18	08 08	08 38	09 08	09 38	10 08	10 08	10 38	11 08	11 38	12 08	12 38	13 08	13 38	14 08	14 38
Watchet (West Somerset Ry)	d	06 13	06 58	07 25	07 35	07 37	08 27	08 57	09 27	09 57	10 27	10 27	10 57	11 27	11 57	12 27	12 57	13 27	13 57	14 27	14 57
Bishops Lydeard Hithermead	d	06 41	07 26	07 54	.....	08 06	08 56	09 26	09 56	10 26	10 56	10 57	11 26	12 00	12 30	13 00	13 30	14 00	14 30	15 00	15 30
Taunton	a	06 55	07 40	08 14	08 23	08 20	09 10	09 40	10 10	10 40	11 10	11 10	11 40	12 14	12 44	13 14	13 44	14 14	14 44	15 14	15 44

		GW BHX I	GW BHX J	GW BHX K	GW BHX L	GW BHX M	GW N	GW BHX O	GW BHX	GW BHX
Minehead Butlins	d	14 50	15 20	15 50	16 20	16 50	17 20	17 50	19 40	21 30
Minehead Bancks Street	d	15 00	15 30	16 00	16 30	17 00	17 30	18 00	19 45	21 35
Dunster Steep	d	15 08	15 38	16 08	16 38	17 08	17 38	18 08	19 53	21 43
Watchet (West Somerset Ry)	d	15 27	15 57	16 27	16 57	17 27	17 57	18 27	20 08	21 58
Bishops Lydeard Hithermead	d	16 00	16 30	17 00	17 30	18 00	18 30	19 00	20 36	22 26
Taunton	a	16 14	16 44	17 14	17 44	18 14	18 44	19 14	20 50	22 40

Sundays

		GW	GW	GW A	GW P	GW	GW Q	GW	GW R	GW	GW
Minehead Butlins	d	08 50	09 50	10 50	12 58	13 58	14 58	15 58	16 58	17 58	18 58
Minehead Bancks Street	d	09 00	10 00	11 00	13 06	14 06	15 06	16 06	17 06	18 06	19 06
Dunster Steep	d	09 08	10 08	11 08	13 14	14 14	15 14	16 14	17 14	18 14	19 14
Watchet (West Somerset Ry)	d	09 27	10 27	11 27	13 32	14 32	15 32	16 32	17 32	18 32	19 32
Bishops Lydeard Hithermead	d	09 56	10 56	12 00	14 03	15 00	16 03	17 00	18 03	19 00	20 00
Taunton	a	10 10	11 10	12 14	14 16	15 13	16 16	17 13	18 16	19 13	20 13

Also stops at West Somerset Railway (WSR) Station at

A 1156 on railway operating days
B 1226 on railway operating days
C 1256 on railway operating days
D 1326 on railway operating days
E 1356 on railway operating days
F 1426 on railway operating days
G 1456 on railway operating days
H 1526 on railway operating days
I 1556 on railway operating days
J 1626 on railway operating days
K 1656 on railway operating days
L 1726 on railway operating days
M 1756 on railway operating days
N 1826 on railway operating days
O 1856 on railway operating days
P 1359 on railway operating days
Q 1559 on railway operating days
R 1759 on railway operating days

Table 136

Mondays to Fridays

Exmouth - Exeter - Barnstaple

Route Diagram - see first Page of Table 135

Miles	Miles			SW MX ◇1 🛒	GW MO	GW MX	GW	SW 1	GW	GW	SW 1	GW		SW 1	GW	GW	GW	GW	GW	SW ◇1	GW	GW		SW ◇1 🛒	GW
0	—	**Exmouth**	d		23p59	00 02			06 12	06 45		07 14			07 53		08 23		08 53		09 23	09 53			10 23
2	—	Lympstone Village	d		00 03	00 06			06 16	06 49		07 18			07 57		08 27		08 57		09 27	09 57			10 27
3	—	Lympstone Commando	d		00x04	00x07			06x17	06x52		07x20			07x58		08x29		08x58		09x28				10x28
3½	—	Exton	d		00x06	00x09			06x19	06x53		07x21			08x00		08x30		09x00		09x30				10x30
5	—	Topsham	d		00 11	00 14			06 24	06 58		07 29			08 05		08 35		09 05		09 35	10 05			10 35
7	—	Digby & Sowton	d		00 16	00 19			06 29	07 03		07 33			08 10		08 40		09 10		09 40	10 10			10 40
9	—	Polsloe Bridge	d		00 19	00 22			06 32	07 06		07 37			08 14		08 44		09 14		09 44				10 44
10	—	St James' Park	d		00 22	00 25			06 35	07 09		07 40			08 17	08 34	08 47		09 17		09 47				10 47
10½	—	**Exeter Central**	a		00 24	00s27			06 37	07 11		07 42			08 20	08 36	08 49		09 19		09 50	10 16			10 49
—	—		d	23p57	00 25			06 32	06 38	07 12	07 39	07 43		08 15	08 24	08 37	08 50	09 06	09 20	09 39	09 50	10 17		10 39	10 50
11¼	—	**Exeter St Davids** 6	a	00 01	00 28	00 31		06 35	06 41	07 15	07 42	07 46		08 18	08 26	08 42	08 54	09 11	09 24	09 42	09 54	10 21		10 42	10 54
—	—		d				05 54		06 48						08 31				09 27			10 27			
15½	—	Newton St Cyres	d																						
18¼	0	Crediton	d				06 05		06 59						08 42				09 38			10 38			
21¾	3½	Yeoford	d				06x11		07x05						08x48				09x44			10x44			
—	14¼	Sampford Courtenay	d																						
—	18	Okehampton	a																						
24½	—	Copplestone	d				06x16		07x10						08x53				09x49			10x49			
26¼	—	Morchard Road	d						07x13						08x56				09x52			10x52			
28¾	—	Lapford	d						07x17																
32½	—	Eggesford	d				06 31		07 33						09 11				10 08			11 08			
36½	—	Kings Nympton	d						07x38						09x17										
39¼	—	Portsmouth Arms	d						07x43																
43½	—	Umberleigh	d				06x45		07x49						09x27				10x23			11x23			
45¾	—	Chapelton	d						07x53																
50¼	—	**Barnstaple**	a				06 59		08 01						09 39				10 35			11 35			

		GW	SW ◇1 🛒	GW	GW	SW ◇1 🛒	GW	GW		SW ◇1 🛒	GW	GW	SW ◇1 🛒	GW	GW	SW ◇1 🛒	GW	GW		SW ◇1 🛒	GW	GW	GW	SW ◇1 🛒	GW
Exmouth	d	10 53		11 23	11 53		12 23	12 53			13 23	13 53		14 23	14 53		15 23	15 53				16 25	16 55		
Lympstone Village	d	10 57		11 27	11 57		12 27	12 57			13 27	13 57		14 27	14 57		15 27	15 57				16 29	16 59		
Lympstone Commando	d			11x28			12x28				13x28			14x28			15x28	15x58				16x30	17x00		
Exton	d			11x30			12x30				13x30			14x30			15x30	16x00				16x32	17x02		
Topsham	d	11 05		11 35	12 05		12 35	13 05			13 35	14 05		14 35	15 05		15 35	16 05				16 37	17 07		
Digby & Sowton	d	11 10		11 40	12 10		12 40	13 10			13 40	14 10		14 40	15 10		15 40	16 10				16 42	17 12		
Polsloe Bridge	d			11 44			12 44				13 44			14 44			15 44	16 14				16 46	17 15		
St James' Park	d			11 47			12 47				13 47			14 47			15 47	16 17			16 43	16 48	17 18		17 40
Exeter Central	a	11 16		11 49	12 16		12 49	13 16			13 49	14 16		14 49	15 16		15 49	16 19			16 45	16 51	17 20		17 42
	d	11 17	11 39	11 50	12 17	12 39	12 50	13 17		13 39	13 50	14 17	14 39	14 50	15 17	15 39	15 50	16 20		16 37	16 46	16 53	17 21	17 36	17 45
Exeter St Davids 6	a	11 21	11 42	11 54	12 21	12 42	12 54	13 21		13 42	13 54	14 21	14 42	14 54	15 21	15 42	15 54	16 25		16 42	16 49	16 56	17 24	17 42	17 48
	d	11 27			12 27			13 27				14 27			15 27							16 57			
Newton St Cyres	d																								
Crediton	d	11 38			12 38			13 38				14 38			15 38							17 08			
Yeoford	d	11x44			12x44			13x44				14x44			15x44							17x15			
Sampford Courtenay	d																								
Okehampton	a																								
Copplestone	d	11x49			12x49			13x49				14x49			15x49							17x19			
Morchard Road	d	11x52			12x52			13x52				14x52			15x52							17x22			
Lapford	d																					17x27			
Eggesford	d	12 08			13 08			14 08				15 08			16 08							17 37			
Kings Nympton	d							14x15														17x44			
Portsmouth Arms	d																								
Umberleigh	d	12x23			13x23			14x23				15x23			16x23							17x54			
Chapelton	d																								
Barnstaple	a	12 35			13 37			14 37				15 35			16 35							18 07			

		GW	GW	SW ◇1 🛒		GW	GW	GW	SW ◇1 🛒	GW	GW	SW ◇1 🛒	GW	GW		GW	SW ◇1 🛒	GW	GW	SW ◇1 🛒	GW FO	GW	SW ◇1 🛒		
Exmouth	d	17 25	17 58			18 27		18 55		19 35	20 08					21 04			22 05			23 10			
Lympstone Village	d	17 29	18 02			18 31		18 59		19 42	20 12					21 08			22 09			23 14			
Lympstone Commando	d	17x30	18x04					19x00			20x13					21x09			22x10			23x15			
Exton	d	17x32	18x06					19x02			20x15					21x11			22x12			23x17			
Topsham	d	17 37	18 11			18 37		19 07		19 49	20 20					21 16			22 17			23 22			
Digby & Sowton	d	17 42	18 15			18 42		19 12		19 54	20 25					21 21			22 22			23 27			
Polsloe Bridge	d	17 45	18 19					19 15			20 28					21 24			22 25			23 30			
St James' Park	d	17 48	18 21					19 18			20 31					21 27			22 28			23 33			
Exeter Central	a	17 50	18 24			18 49		19 20		20 00	20 34					21 29			22 30			23 36			
	d	17 51	18 25	18 39		18 49	18 58	19 21	19 40	20 01	20 35	20 40	20 55	21 21		21 30	21 39	21 55	22 31	22 42	22 48	23 37	23 57		
Exeter St Davids 6	a	17 55	18 28	18 42		18 53	19 02	19 25	19 45	20 05	20 38	20 44	20 58	21 25		21 34	21 44	22 00	22 34	22 45	22 51	23 41	00 01		
	d	17 57				18 57							21 00								22 52				
Newton St Cyres	d	18x04				19x04							21x07												
Crediton	d	18 11				19 11							21 14								23 05				
Yeoford	d	18x17				19x17							21x20								23x11				
Sampford Courtenay	d																								
Okehampton	a																								
Copplestone	d	18x22				19x22							21x26								23x16				
Morchard Road	d	18x25				19x25							21x29								23x19				
Lapford	d	18x29											21x33								23x23				
Eggesford	d	18 41				19 42							21 43								23 33				
Kings Nympton	d	18x48											21x48								23x39				
Portsmouth Arms	d	18x52											21x53												
Umberleigh	d	18x59				19x56							21x59								23x49				
Chapelton	d	19x03											22x03												
Barnstaple	a	19 13				20 08							22 13								23 59				

For connections at Exeter St Davids please refer to Table 135

Table 136

Saturdays

Exmouth - Exeter - Barnstaple

Route Diagram - see first Page of Table 135

		SW	GW	GW	SW	GW	SW	GW	SW	GW		GW	GW	SW	GW	GW	GW	SW	GW	GW		SW	GW	GW	SW
		◇1 ⊤			1		1		1					◇1				◇1 ⊤				◇1 ⊤			◇1 ⊤
Exmouth	d		00 02			06 12		07 15		07 53		08 23	08 53		09 23	09 53			10 23	10 53			11 23	11 53	
Lympstone Village	d		00 06			06 16		07 19		07 57		08 27	08 57		09 27	09 57			10 27	10 57			11 27	11 57	
Lympstone Commando	d		00x07			06x17		07x21		07x58		08x29	08x58		09x28	09x58			10x28	10x58			11x28	11x58	
Exton	d		00x09			06x19		07x22		08x00		08x30	09x00		09x30				10x30				11x30		
Topsham	d		00 14			06 24		07 29		08 05		08 35	09 05		09 35	10 05			10 35	11 05			11 35	12 05	
Digby & Sowton	d		00 19			06 29		07 33		08 10		08 40	09 10		09 40	10 10			10 40	11 10			11 40	12 10	
Polsloe Bridge	d		00 22			06 32		07 37		08 14		08 44	09 14		09 44				10 44				11 44		
St James' Park	d		00 25			06 35		07 40		08 17		08 47	09 17		09 47				10 47				11 47		
Exeter Central	a		00s27			06 37		07 42		08 20		08 49	09 19		09 50	10 16			10 49	11 16			11 49	12 16	
	d	23p57			06 32	06 38	07 39	07 43	08 15	08 24		08 50	09 20	09 39	09 52	10 17	10 30	10 39	10 50	11 17		11 39	11 50	12 17	12 39
Exeter St Davids 6	a	00 01	00 31		06 35	06 41	07 42	07 46	08 18	08 26		08 54	09 24	09 42	09 54	10 21	10 33	10 42	10 54	11 21		11 42	11 54	12 21	12 42
	d			05 54		06 55				08 31			09 27			10 27				11 27				12 27	
Newton St Cyres	d																								
Crediton	d			06 05		07 06				08 42			09 38			10 38				11 38				12 38	
Yeoford	d			06x11		07x12				08x48			09x44			10x44				11x44				12x44	
Sampford Courtenay	d																								
Okehampton	a																								
Copplestone	d			06x16		07x18				08x53			09x49			10x49				11x49				12x49	
Morchard Road	d					07x21				08x56			09x52			10x52				11x52				12x52	
Lapford	d					07x25																			
Eggesford	d			06 31		07 38				09 11			10 08			11 08				12 08				13 08	
Kings Nympton	d					07x43				09x17															
Portsmouth Arms	d					07x48																			
Umberleigh	d			06x45		07x54				09x27			10x23			11x23				12x23				13x23	
Chapelton	d					07x58																			
Barnstaple	a			06 59		08 07				09 39			10 35			11 35				12 35				13 37	

		GW	GW	SW	GW	GW	SW	GW	GW	SW	GW	GW	SW	GW	GW	GW		GW	SW	GW	GW	SW	GW	GW	SW
				◇1 ⊤			◇1 ⊤			◇1 ⊤			◇1 ⊤						◇1 ⊤			◇1 ⊤			◇1 ⊤
Exmouth	d	12 23	12 53		13 23	13 53		14 23	14 53		15 23	15 53			16 25			16 55		17 25	17 55		18 27	18 55	
Lympstone Village	d	12 27	12 57		13 27	13 57		14 27	14 57		15 27	15 57			16 29			16 59		17 29	17 59		18 31	18 59	
Lympstone Commando	d	12x28	12x58		13x28	13x58		14x28	14x58		15x28	15x58			16x30			17x00		17x30	18x01			19x00	
Exton	d	12x30			13x30			14x30			15x30	16x00			16x32			17x02		17x32	18x03			19x02	
Topsham	d	12 35	13 05		13 35	14 05		14 35	15 05		15 35	16 05			16 37			17 07		17 37	18 07		18 37	19 07	
Digby & Sowton	d	12 40	13 10		13 40	14 10		14 40	15 10		15 40	16 10			16 42			17 12		17 42	18 12		18 42	19 12	
Polsloe Bridge	d	12 44			13 44			14 44			15 44	16 14			16 46			17 15		17 45	18 15			19 15	
St James' Park	d	12 47			13 47			14 47			15 47	16 17			16 48	17 05		17 18		17 48	18 18			19 18	
Exeter Central	a	12 49	13 16		13 49	14 16		14 49	15 16		15 49	16 19			16 51	17 07		17 20		17 50	18 20		18 49	19 20	
	d	12 50	13 17	13 39	13 50	14 17	14 39	14 50	15 17	15 39	15 50	16 20	16 37	16 48	16 53	17 08		17 21	17 39	17 51	18 21	18 37	18 49	19 21	19 39
Exeter St Davids 6	a	12 54	13 21	13 42	13 54	14 22	14 42	14 54	15 21	15 42	15 54	16 25	16 42	16 51	16 56	17 11		17 24	17 42	17 55	18 26	18 42	18 53	19 25	19 42
	d		13 27			14 27			15 27						16 57					17 57			18 57		
Newton St Cyres	d																			18x04			19x04		
Crediton	d		13 38			14 38			15 38						17 08					18 11			19 11		
Yeoford	d		13x44			14x44			15x44						17x15					18x17			19x18		
Sampford Courtenay	d																								
Okehampton	a																								
Copplestone	d		13x49			14x49			15x49						17x19					18x22			19x22		
Morchard Road	d		13x52			14x52			15x52						17x22					18x25			19x25		
Lapford	d														17x27					18x29					
Eggesford	d		14 08			15 08			16 08						17 37					18 41			19 42		
Kings Nympton	d		14x15												17x44					18x48					
Portsmouth Arms	d																			18x52					
Umberleigh	d		14x23			15x23			16x23						17x54					18x59			19x56		
Chapelton	d																			19x03					
Barnstaple	a		14 37			15 35			16 35						18 07					19 13			20 08		

		GW		GW	SW	GW	GW	SW	GW	SW	GW	GW
					◇1 ⊤			◇1 ⊤		◇1 ⊤		
Exmouth	d	19 38		20 08			21 04		22 11		23 10	23 43
Lympstone Village	d	19 42		20 12			21 08		22 15		23 14	23 47
Lympstone Commando	d			20x13			21x09		22x16		23x15	23x48
Exton	d			20x15			21x11		22x18		23x17	23x50
Topsham	d	19 49		20 20			21 16		22 23		23 22	23 55
Digby & Sowton	d	19 54		20 25			21 21		22 28		23 27	23 59
Polsloe Bridge	d			20 28			21 24		22 31		23 30	00 03
St James' Park	d			20 31			21 27		22 34		23 33	00 06
Exeter Central	a	20 00		20 34			21 29		22 36		23 36	00 08
	d	20 01		20 35	20 40	20 52	21 30	21 39	22 37	22 42	23 37	00 09
Exeter St Davids 6	a	20 05		20 38	20 43	20 55	21 34	21 42	22 40	22 45	23 41	00 14
	d					21 00						
Newton St Cyres	d					21x07						
Crediton	d					21 14						
Yeoford	d					21x20						
Sampford Courtenay	d											
Okehampton	a											
Copplestone	d					21x26						
Morchard Road	d					21x29						
Lapford	d					21x33						
Eggesford	d					21 43						
Kings Nympton	d					21x48						
Portsmouth Arms	d					21x53						
Umberleigh	d					21x59						
Chapelton	d					22x03						
Barnstaple	a					22 13						

For connections at Exeter St Davids please refer to Table 135

Table 136

Sundays

Exmouth - Exeter - Barnstaple

Route Diagram - see first Page of Table 135

		GW	GW	SW	GW	GW	SW	GW	SW	GW		GW	SW	GW	GW	SW	GW	GW	SW	GW		GW	SW	GW	GW
		A		1			◇1		◇1 🚲				◇1 🚲			◇1 🚲			◇1 🚲				◇1 🚲		
Exmouth	d	23p43			09 10			10 21		11 24				12 29			13 24			14 31				15 24	
Lympstone Village	d	23p47			09 14			10 25		11 28				12 33			13 28			14 35				15 28	
Lympstone Commando	d	23b48			09x15			10x26		11x29				12x34			13x29			14x36				15x29	
Exton	d	23b50			09x17			10x28		11x31				12x36			13x31			14x38				15x31	
Topsham	d	23p55			09 22			10 33		11 36				12 41			13 36			14 43				15 36	
Digby & Sowton	d	23p59			09 27			10 38		11 41				12 46			13 41			14 48				15 41	
Polsloe Bridge	d	00 03			09 30			10 41		11 44				12 49			13 44			14 51				15 44	
St James' Park	d	00 06			09 33			10 44		11 47				12 52			13 47			14 54				15 47	
Exeter Central	a	00 08			09 36			10 46		11 49				12 54			13 49			14 56				15 49	
	d	00 09		08 58	09 36		10 42	10 48	11 42	11 53		11 59	12 42	12 55	13 20	13 42	13 50	13 55	14 42	14 57		15 20	15 42	15 50	15 59
Exeter St Davids 6	a	00 14		09 01	09 40		10 45	10 51	11 45	11 56		12 02	12 45	12 58	13 23	13 45	13 53	13 58	14 45	15 01		15 23	15 45	15 53	16 02
	d		08 39			09 53						12 03						13 59							16 04
Newton St Cyres	d		08x47									12x11													16x12
Crediton	d		08 53			10 04						12 17						14 20							16 19
Yeoford	d		09x00			10x11						12x24						14x27							16x26
Sampford Courtenay	d																								
Okehampton	a																								
Copplestone	d		09x05			10x16						12x30						14x33							16x31
Morchard Road	d		09x08			10x19						12x33						14x36							16x34
Lapford	d		09x12									12 37													16x38
Eggesford	d		09 22			10 31						12 46						14 48							16 45
Kings Nympton	d		09x29									12x52						14x54							16x53
Portsmouth Arms	d		09x33									12x57						14x59							16x56
Umberleigh	d		09x40			10x46						13x03						15x05							17x04
Chapelton	d		09x44									13x07													17x08
Barnstaple	a		09 52			10 57						13 14						15 15							17 17

		SW	GW	SW	GW	GW		GW	GW	SW	GW	SW	GW	GW	SW	GW		SW	GW	SW	GW	GW	GW		
		◇1 🚲		◇1 🚲	B	C		B	C	◇1 🚲		◇1 🚲			◇1 🚲			◇1 🚲		◇1 🚲					
Exmouth	d		16 24		17 24	17 24					18 24		19 24			20 24			21 24		22 29	23 29	23 59		
Lympstone Village	d		16 28		17 28	17 28					18 28		19 28			20 28			21 28		22 33	23 33	00 03		
Lympstone Commando	d		16x29		17x29	17x29					18x29		19x29			20x29			21x29		22x34	23x34	00x04		
Exton	d		16x31		17x31	17x31					18x31		19x31			20x31			21x31		22x36	23x36	00x06		
Topsham	d		16 36		17 36	17 36					18 35		19 36			20 36			21 36		22 42	23 42	00 11		
Digby & Sowton	d		16 41		17 41	17 41					18 40		19 41			20 41			21 41		22 46	23 47	00 16		
Polsloe Bridge	d		16 44		17 44	17 44					18 43		19 44			20 44			21 44		22 50	23 50	00 19		
St James' Park	d		16 47		17 47	17 47					18 46		19 47			20 47			21 47		22 53	23 53	00 22		
Exeter Central	a		16 49		17 49	17 49					18 48		19 49			20 49			21 49		22 55	23 55	00 24		
	d	16 42	16 50	17 42	17 50	17 50		17 56	17 56	18 42	18 49	19 42	19 50	19 56	20 42	20 50		21 42	21 50	22 42	22 56	23 56	00 25		
Exeter St Davids 6	a	16 45	16 53	17 45	17 53	17 55		17 59	18 00	18 45	18 53	19 45	19 53	19 59	20 45	20 53		21 45	21 53	22 45	22 59	23 59	00 28		
	d							17 59	18 04					20 01											
Newton St Cyres	d													20x08											
Crediton	d							18 16	18 18					20 18											
Yeoford	d							18x23	18x25					20x24											
Sampford Courtenay	d																								
Okehampton	a																								
Copplestone	d							18x28	18x30					20x30											
Morchard Road	d							18x31	18x33					20x33											
Lapford	d													20x37											
Eggesford	d							18 44	18 46					20x47											
Kings Nympton	d													20x52											
Portsmouth Arms	d													20x57											
Umberleigh	d							18x58	19x00					21x03											
Chapelton	d													21x07											
Barnstaple	a							19 08	19 10					21 15											

A not 11 December
B until 12 February, from 1 April
C from 19 February until 25 March
b Previous night, stops on request

For connections at Exeter St Davids please refer to Table 135

Barnstaple - Exeter - Exmouth

Route Diagram - see first Page of Table 135

Miles	Miles			SW ◇1 🚲	GW	GW	GW	SW ◇1 🚲	GW	SW ◇1 🚲	GW	GW		GW	SW ◇1 🚲	GW	GW	GW	SW ◇1 🚲	GW	GW	SW ◇1 🚲		GW	GW
0	—	**Barnstaple**	d									07 00								08 43				09 43	
4¼	—	Chapelton	d									07x05													
6¾	—	Umberleigh	d									07x09								08x51				09x51	
10¾	—	Portsmouth Arms	d									07x16													
13¾	—	Kings Nympton	d									07x21								09x03					
17½	—	Eggesford	d									07 30								09 07				10 07	
21½	—	Lapford	d									07x35								09x14					
23¾	—	Morchard Road	d									07x40								09x17				10x16	
25½	—	Copplestone	d									07x43								09x22				10x20	
—	0	Okehampton	d																						
—	3¾	Sampford Courtenay	d																						
28½	14½	Yeoford	d									07x48								09x25				10x24	
32	18	Crediton	d									07 55								09 37				10 37	
34¾	—	Newton St Cyres	d									07x58													
39	—	**Exeter St Davids** 6	a									08 07								09 48				10 48	
—	—		d	05 10	05 44	06 06	06 29	06 41	07 11	07 26	07 36	08 09		08 16	08 26	08 48	08 59	09 18	09 26	09 50	10 18	10 26		10 50	11 18
39¾	—	**Exeter Central**	a	05 13	05 47	06 09	06 32	06 44	07 14	07 29	07 39	08 12		08 19	08 29	08 51	09 04	09 21	09 29	09 53	10 21	10 29		10 53	11 21
—	—		d		05 48	06 10	06 39		07 15		07 52	08 13		08 20		08 52		09 22		09 54	10 22			10 54	11 22
40¼	—	St James' Park	d			06 12	06 41		07 17		07 54	08a17		08 22		08 54		09 24			10 24				11 24
41¼	—	Polsloe Bridge	d			06 15	06 44		07 20		07 57			08 25		08 57		09 27			10 27				11 27
43¼	—	Digby & Sowton	d		05 54	06 19	06 48		07 24		08 01			08 29		09 01		09 31		10 01	10 31			11 01	11 31
45¼	—	Topsham	d		05 58	06 25	06 57		07 28		08 05			08 35		09 05		09 35		10 05	10 35			11 05	11 35
46¾	—	Exton	d			06x27	07x00		07x31		08x08			08x38		09x08		09x38			10x38				11x38
47¼	—	Lympstone Commando	d			06x29	07x02		07x33		08x10			08x40		09x10		09x40			10x40				11x40
48¼	—	Lympstone Village	d		06 03	06 31	07 05		07 36		08 13			08 43		09 13		09 43		10 11	10 43			11 11	11 43
50¼	—	**Exmouth**	a		06 10	06 38	07 10		07 43		08 18			08 48		09 20		09 50		10 19	10 50			11 19	11 50

		SW ◇1 🚲	GW	GW	SW ◇1 🚲	GW	GW	SW ◇1 🚲		GW	GW	SW ◇1 🚲	GW	GW	SW ◇1 🚲	GW	GW	GW		SW ◇1 🚲	GW	GW	GW	SW ◇1 🚲	SW 1
Barnstaple	d		10 43			11 43				12 43			13 43			14 43					15 43				
Chapelton	d																								
Umberleigh	d		10x51			11x51				12x51			13x51			14x51					15x51				
Portsmouth Arms	d																								
Kings Nympton	d									13x02															
Eggesford	d		11 07			12 07				13 07			14 07			15 07					16 07				
Lapford	d																								
Morchard Road	d		11x16			12x16				13x16			14x16			15x16					16x16				
Copplestone	d		11x20			12x20				13x20			14x20			15x20					16x20				
Okehampton	d																								
Sampford Courtenay	d																								
Yeoford	d		11x24			12x24				13x24			14x24			15x24					16x24				
Crediton	d		11 37			12 37				13 37			14 37			15 37					16 37				
Newton St Cyres	d																								
Exeter St Davids 6	a		11 48			12 48				13 48			14 48			15 48					16 48				
	d	11 26	11 50	12 18	12 26	12 50	13 18	13 26		13 50	14 18	14 26	14 51	15 18	15 26	15 50	16 08	16 18		16 26	16 50	17 10	17 18	17 26	17 46
Exeter Central	a	11 29	11 53	12 21	12 29	12 53	13 21	13 29		13 53	14 21	14 29	14 54	15 21	15 29	15 53	16 11	16 21		16 29	16 53	17 13	17 21	17 29	17 49
	d		11 54	12 22		12 54	13 22			13 54	14 22		14 55	15 22		15 54	16 12	16 22			16 54	17 14	17 22		
St James' Park	d			12 24			13 24				14 24			15 24			16a16	16 24			16 56	17a18	17 24		
Polsloe Bridge	d			12 27			13 27				14 27			15 27				16 27			16 59		17 27		
Digby & Sowton	d		12 01	12 31		13 01	13 31			14 01	14 31		15 01	15 31		16 01		16 31			17 03		17 31		
Topsham	d		12 05	12 35		13 05	13 35			14 05	14 35		15 05	15 35		16 05		16 37			17 07		17 37		
Exton	d			12x38			13x38				14x38			15x38				16x38			17x10		17x38		
Lympstone Commando	d			12x40			13x40				14x40			15x40				16x40			17x12		17x40		
Lympstone Village	d		12 11	12 43		13 11	13 43			14 11	14 43		15 11	15 43		16 11		16 43			17 15		17 43		
Exmouth	a		12 19	12 50		13 19	13 50			14 19	14 50		15 19	15 50		16 19		16 50			17 22		17 51		

		GW	GW	SW ◇1 🚲		GW	GW	SW ◇1	GW	GW	SW ◇1 🚲	GW	GW	SW 1		GW	GW	GW	SW 1	GW					
Barnstaple	d					17 08			18 13	19 16							20 24			22 16					
Chapelton	d					17x14																			
Umberleigh	d					17x18			18x21	19x24							20x32			22x24					
Portsmouth Arms	d								18x28																
Kings Nympton	d					17 29			18x33																
Eggesford	d					17 37			18 40	19 40							20 49			22 40					
Lapford	d					17 43			18x47																
Morchard Road	d					17x46			18x51	19x49							20x58			22x48					
Copplestone	d					17x50			18x55	19x53							21x01			22x52					
Okehampton	d																								
Sampford Courtenay	d																								
Yeoford	d					17x54			18x59	19x57							21x05			22x56					
Crediton	d					18 12			19 12	20 06							21 16			23 05					
Newton St Cyres	d					18x15				20x09							21x19			23x08					
Exeter St Davids 6	a					18 29			19 25	20 17							21 34			23 16					
	d	17 52	18 20	18 26		18 33	18 50	19 26	19 32	20 19	20 26	20 30	21 14	21 23		21 32	21 38	22 36	22 57	23 28					
Exeter Central	a	17 55	18 23	18 29		18 38	18 53	19 29	19 35	20 24	20 29	20 33	21 19	21 26		21 35	21 41	22 39	23 00	23 31					
	d	17 56	18 24				18 54		19 36			20 34				21 35		22 40		23 32					
St James' Park	d	17 58	18 26				18 56		19 38			20 36				21 37		22 42		23 34					
Polsloe Bridge	d	18 01	18 29				18 59		19 41			20 39				21 40		22 45		23 37					
Digby & Sowton	d	18 05	18 33				19 03		19 45			20 43				21 44		22 49		23 41					
Topsham	d	18 09	18 37				19 07		19 49			20 47				21 49		22 53		23 45					
Exton	d	18x12	18x38				19x10		19x52			20x49				21x51		22x56		23x47					
Lympstone Commando	d	18x14	18x40				19x12		19x54			20x51				21x53		22x58		23x49					
Lympstone Village	d	18 17	18 43				19 15		19 57			20 54				21 56		23 01		23 52					
Exmouth	a	18 25	18 52				19 23		20 03			21 01				22 02		23 08		23 59					

For connections at Exeter St Davids please refer to Table 135

Table 136

Saturdays

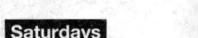

Barnstaple - Exeter - Exmouth

Route Diagram - see first Page of Table 135

		GW	SW	GW	GW	SW	GW	SW	GW	GW		SW	GW	GW	SW	GW	GW	SW	GW	GW		SW	GW	GW	SW
			◇1			◇1		◇1				◇1			◇1			◇1				◇1			◇1
			🍴			🍴		🍴				🍴			🍴			🍴				🍴			🍴
Barnstaple	d	00 05								07 08						08 43			09 43				10 43		
Chapelton	d									07x13															
Umberleigh	d									07x17						08x51			09x51				10x51		
Portsmouth Arms	d									07x24															
Kings Nympton	d									07x29						09x02									
Eggesford	d	00 29								07 38						09 07			10 07				11 07		
Lapford	d									07x43						09x14									
Morchard Road	d									07x48						09x17			10x16				11x16		
Copplestone	d									07x51						09x22			10x20				11x20		
Okehampton	d																								
Sampford Courtenay	d																								
Yeoford	d									07x57						09x25			10x24				11x24		
Crediton	d	00 47								08 04						09 37			10 37				11 37		
Newton St Cyres	d									08x07															
Exeter St Davids 6	a	01 00								08 16						09 48			10 48				11 48		
	d		05 10	05 44	06 29	06 41	07 11	07 26	07 36	08 16		08 26	08 48	09 18	09 26	09 50	10 18	10 26	10 50	11 18		11 26	11 50	12 18	12 26
Exeter Central	a		05 13	05 47	06 32	06 44	07 14	07 29	07 39	08 19		08 29	08 51	09 21	09 29	09 51	10 21	10 29	10 51	11 21		11 29	11 51	12 21	12 29
	d			05 48	06 39		07 15		07 52	08 20			08 52	09 22		09 52	10 22		10 52	11 22			11 52	12 22	
St James' Park	d				06 41		07 17		07 54	08 23			08 54	09 24		09 54	10 24			11 24				12 24	
Polsloe Bridge	d				06 44		07 20		07 57	08 27			08 57	09 27		09 57	10 27			11 27				12 27	
Digby & Sowton	d			05 54	06 48		07 24		08 01	08 31			09 01	09 31		10 01	10 31		11 01	11 31			12 01	12 31	
Topsham	d			05 58	06 52		07 28		08 05	08 35			09 05	09 35		10 05	10 35		11 05	11 35			12 05	12 35	
Exton	d				06x54		07x31		08x08	08x38			09x08	09x38		10x08	10x38			11x38				12x38	
Lympstone Commando	d				06x56		07x33		08x10	08x40			09x10	09x40		10x10	10x40		11x09	11x40			12x09	12x40	
Lympstone Village	d			06 03	06 59		07 36		08 13	08 43			09 13	09 43		10 11	10 43		11 11	11 43			12 11	12 43	
Exmouth	a			06 10	07 04		07 43		08 18	08 48			09 20	09 50		10 19	10 50		11 19	11 50			12 19	12 50	

		GW	GW	SW	GW	GW		SW	GW	GW	SW	GW	GW	SW	GW	GW		GW	GW	SW	GW	GW	SW	GW	SW
				◇1				◇1			◇1			◇1						◇1			◇1		◇1
				🍴				🍴			🍴			🍴						🍴			🍴		
Barnstaple	d	11 43			12 43				13 43			14 43				15 43		17 08							
Chapelton	d																	17x14							
Umberleigh	d	11x51			12x51				13x51			14x51				15x51		17x18							
Portsmouth Arms	d																								
Kings Nympton	d				13x02													17x29							
Eggesford	d	12 07			13 07				14 07			15 07				16 07		17 37							
Lapford	d																	17x43							
Morchard Road	d	12x16			13x16				14x16			15x16				16x16		17x46							
Copplestone	d	12x20			13x20				14x20			15x20				16x20		17x50							
Okehampton	d																								
Sampford Courtenay	d																								
Yeoford	d	12x24			13x24				14x24			15x24				16x24		17x54							
Crediton	d	12 37			13 37				14 37			15 37				16 37		18 10							
Newton St Cyres	d																	18x13							
Exeter St Davids 6	a	12 48			13 48				14 48			15 48				16 48		18 22							
	d	12 50	13 18	13 26	13 50	14 18		14 26	14 50	15 18	15 26	15 50	16 18	16 26	16 41	16 50			17 18	17 26	17 50	18 20	18 26	18 50	19 26
Exeter Central	a	12 51	13 21	13 29	13 51	14 21		14 29	14 51	15 21	15 29	15 51	16 21	16 29	16 44	16 53			17 21	17 29	17 53	18 23	18 29	18 53	19 29
	d	12 52	13 22		13 52	14 22			14 52	15 22		15 52	16 22			16 54			17 22		17 54	18 24		18 54	
St James' Park	d		13 24		13 54	14 24				15 24		15 57	16 24			16 56			17 24		17 56	18 26		18 56	
Polsloe Bridge	d		13 27			14 27				15 27			16 27			16 59			17 27		17 59	18 29		18 59	
Digby & Sowton	d	13 01	13 31		14 01	14 31			15 01	15 31		16 01	16 31			17 03			17 31		18 03	18 33		19 03	
Topsham	d	13 05	13 35		14 05	14 35			15 05	15 35		16 05	16 37			17 07			17 37		18 07	18 37		19 07	
Exton	d		13x38			14x38				15x38			16x38			17x10			17x38		18x10	18x38		19x10	
Lympstone Commando	d	13x09	13x40		14x09	14x40			15x09	15x40		16x09	16x40			17x12			17x40		18x12	18x40		19x12	
Lympstone Village	d	13 11	13 43		14 11	14 43			15 11	15 43		16 11	16 43			17 15			17 43		18 15	18 43		19 15	
Exmouth	a	13 19	13 50		14 19	14 50			15 19	15 50		16 19	16 50			17 22			17 50		18 22	18 52		19 22	

		GW		GW	SW	GW	SW	GW	GW	GW	GW	SW		GW
					◇1		1					1		
					🍴									
Barnstaple	d	18 13		19 16				20 24		22 18				
Chapelton	d									22x23				
Umberleigh	d	18x21		19x24				20x32		22x27				
Portsmouth Arms	d	18x28								22x34				
Kings Nympton	d	18x33								22x39				
Eggesford	d	18 40		19 40				20 49		22 47				
Lapford	d	18x47								22x52				
Morchard Road	d	18x51		19x49				20x58		22x57				
Copplestone	d	18x55		19x53				21x01		23x00				
Okehampton	d													
Sampford Courtenay	d													
Yeoford	d	18x59		19x58				21x06		23x05				
Crediton	d	19 11		20 06				21 16		23 13				
Newton St Cyres	d			20x09				21x19		23x16				
Exeter St Davids 6	a	19 24		20 18				21 30		23 26				
	d	19 32		20 20	20 26	20 30	21 26	21 32	21 38		22 36	22 57		23 06
Exeter Central	a	19 35		20 25	20 29	20 33	21 29	21 37	21 41		22 39	23 00		23 09
	d	19 36				20 34			21 42		22 40			23 10
St James' Park	d	19 38				20 36			21 44		22 42			23 12
Polsloe Bridge	d	19 41				20 39			21 47		22 45			23 15
Digby & Sowton	d	19 45				20 43			21 51		22 49			23 19
Topsham	d	19 49				20 47			21 55		22 53			23 23
Exton	d	19x52				20x49			21x57		22x56			23x25
Lympstone Commando	d	19x54				20x51			21x59		22x58			23x27
Lympstone Village	d	19 57				20 54			22 03		23 01			23 31
Exmouth	a	20 03				21 01			22 09		23 08			23 36

For connections at Exeter St Davids please refer to Table 135

Table 136

Sundays

Barnstaple - Exeter - Exmouth

Route Diagram - see first Page of Table 135

		GW	SW	GW	SW	GW	GW	SW	GW	SW		GW	GW	SW	GW	SW	GW	GW	GW	SW		GW	SW	GW	GW
			◇1		◇1			◇1		◇1				◇1		◇1				◇1			◇1		
																									A
			🚲		🚲			🚲		🚲				🚲		🚲				🚲			🚲		
Barnstaple	d						10 00					11 26					13 24							15 23	
Chapelton	d						10x06										13x30								
Umberleigh	d						10x10					11x34					13x33							15x31	
Portsmouth Arms	d						10x17										13x41							15x38	
Kings Nympton	d						10x22										13x46							15x43	
Eggesford	d						10 32					11 52					13 54							15 52	
Lapford	d						10x37										14x00								
Morchard Road	d						10x41					12x00					14x04							16x00	
Copplestone	d						10x45					12x04					14x07							16x03	
Okehampton	d																								
Sampford Courtenay	d																								
Yeoford	d						10x50					12x09					14x13							16x09	
Crediton	d						10 58					12 18					14 21							16 17	
Newton St Cyres	d						11x01					12x21					14x25							16x21	
Exeter St Davids 6	a						11 11					12 32					14 33							16 28	
	d	08 30	09 26	09 45	10 26	10 46	11 13	11 26	11 55	12 26		12 33	12 48	13 26	13 48	14 26	14 35	14 48	15 14	15 26		15 48	16 26	16 30	16⟆48
Exeter Central	a	08 33	09 29	09 48	10 29	10 49	11 16	11 29	11 58	12 29		12 36	12 51	13 29	13 51	14 29	14 38	14 51	15 17	15 29		15 51	16 29	16 33	16⟆51
	d	08 34		09 49		10 52			11 59				12 53		13 52			14 52				15 51			16⟆51
St James' Park	d	08 36		09 51		10 54			12 01				12 55		13 54			14 54				15 53			16⟆53
Polsloe Bridge	d	08 39		09 54		10 57			12 04				12 58		13 57			14 57				15 56			16⟆56
Digby & Sowton	d	08 43		09 58		11 01			12 08				13 02		14 01			15 01				16 00			17⟆00
Topsham	d	08 47		10 03		11 05			12 12				13 07		14 06			15 06				16 05			17⟆05
Exton	d	08x49		10x05		11x07			12x14				13x09		14x08			15x08				16x07			17x07
Lympstone Commando	d	08x51		10x07		11x09			12x16				13x11		14x10			15x10				16x09			17x09
Lympstone Village	d	08 55		10 10		11 13			12 20				13 14		14 13			15 13				16 13			17⟆13
Exmouth	a	09 00		10 15		11 18			12 25				13 20		14 18			15 18				16 18			17⟆18

		GW	GW	SW	GW	GW		SW	GW	GW	GW	GW	SW	GW	SW	GW		SW	GW	GW	GW	SW	GW		
				◇1				◇1					◇1		◇1			1				1			
		B			C	D				E	F														
				🚲				🚲																	
Barnstaple	d								17 20			19 20							21 30						
Chapelton	d								17x25										21x36						
Umberleigh	d								17x29			19x28							21x39						
Portsmouth Arms	d								17x36										21x47						
Kings Nympton	d								17x41										21x52						
Eggesford	d								17 50			19 45							22 00						
Lapford	d								17x55										22x06						
Morchard Road	d								18x00			19x53							22x10						
Copplestone	d								18x03			19x57							22x13						
Okehampton	d																								
Sampford Courtenay	d																								
Yeoford	d								18x09			20x02							22x19						
Crediton	d								18 18			20 15							22 28						
Newton St Cyres	d								18x22			20x18							22x31						
Exeter St Davids 6	a								18 32			20 27							22 42						
	d	16⟆49	17 15	17 26	17⟆48	17⟆52		18 26	18 33	18⟆48	18⟆50		19 26	19 51	20 26	20 51		21 26		21 48	22 48	23 15	23 25		
Exeter Central	a	16⟆52	17 18	17 29	17⟆51	17⟆55		18 29	18 36	18⟆51	18⟆53		19 29	19 54	20 29	20 54		21 29		21 51	22 51	23 18	23 28		
	d	16⟆52			17⟆51	17⟆55				18⟆52	18⟆54			19 55		20 55				21 51	22 52		23 29		
St James' Park	d	16⟆54			17⟆53	17⟆57				18⟆54	18⟆56			19 57		20 57				21 53	22 54		23 31		
Polsloe Bridge	d	16⟆57			17⟆56	18⟆00				18⟆57	18⟆59			20 00		21 00				21 56	22 57		23 34		
Digby & Sowton	d	17⟆01			18⟆00	18⟆04				19⟆01	19⟆03			20 04		21 04				22 00	23 01		23 38		
Topsham	d	17⟆06			18⟆05	18⟆08				19⟆06	19⟆08			20 08		21 08				22 05	23 06		23 42		
Exton	d	17x08			18x07	18x10				19x08	19x10			20x10		21x10				22x07	23x08		23x44		
Lympstone Commando	d	17x10			18x09	18x12				19x11	19x13			20x12		21x12				22x09	23x11		23x46		
Lympstone Village	d	17⟆14			18⟆13	18⟆16				19⟆13	19⟆15			20 16		21 16				22 13	23 13		23 50		
Exmouth	a	17⟆19			18⟆18	18⟆21				19⟆18	19⟆20			20 21		21 21				22 18	23 18		23 54		

A until 12 February
B from 19 February
C until 12 February, from 1 April
D from 19 February until 25 March
E until 25 March
F from 1 April

For connections at Exeter St Davids please refer to Table 135

Plymouth - Gunnislake

Route Diagram - see first Page of Table 135

Miles			GW	GW	GW	GW	GW	GW	GW	GW	GW		GW	GW	GW	GW	GW	GW	GW
					1 ☕	◇		◇	◇										
0	**Plymouth**	d	05 06	06 41	07 02	08 14	08 40	09 21	10 42	10 54	12 54		14 54	15 57	16 38	17 04	18 17	18 23	21 31
1¼	Devonport	d		06 44	07a06	08a17	08 43	09a24		10 57	12 57		14 57	16 00	16 41	17 07	18 20	18 26	21 34
1¾	Dockyard	d		06x45			08x44			10x58	12x58		14x58	16x01	16x42	17x08	18x21	18x27	21x35
2¼	Keyham	d		06 47			08 46			11 00	13 00		15 00	16 03	16 44	17 10	18 23	18 29	21 37
—	St Budeaux Ferry Road	a							10 48					16 06		17 13	18 25		
3¼	St Budeaux Victoria Road	d	05 12	06 51			08 50			11 04	13 04		15 04		16 48			18 33	21 41
7½	Bere Ferrers	d		06 58			08 57			11 11	13 11		15 11		16 55			18 40	21 48
10¼	Bere Alston	a	05 25	07 05			09 04			11 18	13 19		15 18		17 02			18 47	21 55
—		d	05 27	07 07			09 06			11 20	13 20		15 20		17 04			18 49	21 57
12	Calstock	d	05 34	07 14			09 13			11 27	13 27		15 27		17 11			18 56	22 04
15	**Gunnislake**	a	05 50	07 27			09 26			11 40	13 41		15 40		17 24			19 09	22 17

Saturdays

		GW	GW	GW	GW	GW	GW	GW	GW	GW		GW	GW	GW
			◇											
Plymouth	d	06 40	08 18	08 40	09 51	10 33	10 54	12 54	14 47	16 38		17 52	18 23	21 31
Devonport	d	06 43	08a21	08 43	09a54		10 57	12 57	14 50	16 41		17 55	18 26	21 34
Dockyard	d	06x44		08x44			10x58	12x58	14x51	16x42		17x57	18x27	21x35
Keyham	d	06 46		08 46			11 00	13 00	14 53	16 44		17 59	18 29	21 37
St Budeaux Ferry Road	a					10 39						18 00		
St Budeaux Victoria Road	d	06 50		08 50			11 04	13 04	14 57	16 48			18 33	21 41
Bere Ferrers	d	06 57		08 57			11 11	13 11	15 04	16 55			18 40	21 48
Bere Alston	a	07 04		09 04			11 18	13 18	15 11	17 02			18 47	21 55
	d	07 06		09 06			11 20	13 20	15 13	17 04			18 49	21 57
Calstock	d	07 13		09 13			11 27	13 27	15 20	17 11			18 56	22 04
Gunnislake	a	07 26		09 26			11 40	13 40	15 33	17 25			19 09	22 17

Sundays

		GW	GW	GW	GW	GW	GW	GW	GW	GW		GW
				◇								
				A	B			B	A	B		A
		trolley										
Plymouth	d	09 15	09 30	10 15	10 30	11 40	13 45	15 36	15 40	17 43		17 45
Devonport	d		09 33	10a19	10a34	11 43	13 48	15 39	15 43	17 46		17 48
Dockyard	d		09x34			11x44	13x49	15x40	15x44	17x47		17x49
Keyham	d		09 36			11 46	13 51	15 42	15 46	17 49		17 51
St Budeaux Ferry Road	a	09 21										
St Budeaux Victoria Road	d		09 40			11 50	13 55	15 46	15 50	17 53		17 55
Bere Ferrers	d		09 47			11 57	14 02	15 53	15 57	18 00		18 02
Bere Alston	a		09 54			12 04	14 09	16 00	16 04	18 07		18 09
	d		09 56			12 06	14 11	16 02	16 06	18 09		18 11
Calstock	d		10 03			12 13	14 18	16 09	16 13	18 16		18 18
Gunnislake	a		10 16			12 26	14 31	16 22	16 26	18 29		18 31

A until 12 February, from 1 April

B from 19 February until 25 March

Table 139

Mondays to Fridays

Gunnislake - Plymouth

Route Diagram - see first Page of Table 135

Miles			GW	GW ◇	GW	GW	GW	GW	GW	GW ◇	GW		GW	GW	GW	GW
0	**Gunnislake**	d	05 50		07 31	09 29	11 45	13 45	15 45		17 29			19 13		22 21
3	Calstock	d	06 01		07 42	09 40	11 56	13 56	15 56		17 40			19 24		22 32
4¾	Bere Alston	a	06 08		07 49	09 47	12 03	14 03	16 03		17 47			19 31		22 39
—		d	06 10		07 51	09 49	12 05	14 05	16 05		17 49			19 33		22 41
7½	Bere Ferrers	d	06 15		07 56	09 54	12 10	14 10	16 10		17 54			19 38		22 46
11¾	St Budeaux Victoria Road	d	06 24		08 05	10 03	12 19	14 19	16 19		18 03			19 47		22 55
—	St Budeaux Ferry Road	d		07 52						16 41			18 12		21 09	
12¾	Keyham	d	06 26	07 54	08 07	10 05	12 21	14 21	16 21	16 43	18 05			19 49	21 11	22 57
13¼	Dockyard	d	06x28	07x56	08x09	10x07	12x23	14x23	16x23	16x45	18x07			19x51	21x13	22x59
13¾	Devonport	d	06 31	07 58	08 11	10 09	12 25	14 25	16 25	16 47	18 09			19 53	21 15	23 01
15	**Plymouth**	a	06 36	08 04	08 17	10 14	12 30	14 30	16 30	16 52	18 14		18 19	19 58	21 20	23 06

Saturdays

		GW	GW	GW	GW	GW	GW ◇	GW	GW	GW		GW	GW	GW
Gunnislake	d		07 31	09 29	11 45	13 45		15 45	17 29	19 17			22 21	
Calstock	d		07 42	09 40	11 56	13 56		15 56	17 40	19 28			22 32	
Bere Alston	a		07 49	09 47	12 03	14 03		16 03	17 47	19 35			22 39	
	d		07 51	09 49	12 05	14 05		16 05	17 49	19 37			22 41	
Bere Ferrers	d		07 56	09 54	12 10	14 10		16 10	17 54	19 42			22 46	
St Budeaux Victoria Road	d		08 05	10 03	12 19	14 19		16 19	18 03	19 51			22 55	
St Budeaux Ferry Road	d	07 30										20 58		22 59
Keyham	d	07 32	08 07	10 05	12 21	14 21		16 21	18 05	19 53		21 00	22 57	23 01
Dockyard	d	07x34	08x09	10x07	12x23	14x23		16x23	18x07	19x55		21x02	22x59	23x03
Devonport	d	07 36	08 11	10 09	12 25	14 25	14 52	16 25	18 09	19 57		21 04	23 01	23 05
Plymouth	a	07 42	08 17	10 14	12 30	14 30	14 58	16 30	18 14	20 02		21 10	23 06	23 12

Sundays

		GW	GW	GW	GW	GW	GW A	GW B
Gunnislake	d	10 25	12 45	14 45	16 54	18 44		
Calstock	d	10 36	12 56	14 56	17 05	18 55		
Bere Alston	a	10 43	13 03	15 03	17 12	19 02		
	d	10 45	13 05	15 05	17 14	19 04		
Bere Ferrers	d	10 50	13 10	15 10	17 19	19 09		
St Budeaux Victoria Road	d	10 59	13 19	15 19	17 28	19 18		
St Budeaux Ferry Road	d							
Keyham	d	11 01	13 21	15 21	17 30	19 20		
Dockyard	d	11x03	13x23	15x23	17x32	19x22		
Devonport	d	11 05	13 25	15 25	17 34	19 24	20 56	20 56
Plymouth	a	11 10	13 30	15 30	17 39	19 29	20 59	21 00

A from 19 February until 25 March

B until 12 February, from 1 April

Table 140

Mondays to Fridays

Liskeard - Looe

Route Diagram - see first Page of Table 135

Miles			GW	GW	GW	GW	GW	GW	GW	GW	GW		GW	GW	GW
0	**Liskeard** 6	d	06 05	07 14	08 33	09 58	11 18	12 15	13 19	14 28	15 41		16 41	18 01	19 18
2	Coombe Junction Halt	a			08 39	10 04									
—		d			08 42	10 07									
3¾	St Keyne Wishing Well Halt	d	06x17	07x26	08x48	10x13		12x27	13x31		15x53		16x53	18x13	19x31
5	Causeland	d	06x21	07x30	08x52	10x17		12x31	13x35		15x57		16x57	18x17	19x33
6½	Sandplace	d	06x24	07x33	08x56	10x20		12x34	13x38		16x00		17x00	18x20	19x38
8¾	**Looe**	a	06 36	07 45	09 04	10 29	11 46	12 46	13 50	14 56	16 12		17 12	18 32	19 49

Saturdays

		GW	GW	GW	GW	GW	GW	GW	GW	GW		GW	GW	GW
Liskeard 6	d	06 01	07 12	08 35	09 58	11 08	12 12	13 24	14 28	15 42		16 56	18 01	19 28
Coombe Junction Halt	a			08 41	10 04									
	d			08 44	10 06									
St Keyne Wishing Well Halt	d	06x13	07x24	08x50	10x13		12x24	13x37		15x54		17x09	18x13	19x41
Causeland	d	06x17	07x28	08x54	10x17		12x28	13x40		15x58		17x12	18x17	19x43
Sandplace	d	06x20	07x31	08x58	10x20		12x31	13x44		16x01		17x16	18x20	19x48
Looe	a	06 32	07 43	09 06	10 29	11 36	12 43	13 55	14 56	16 13		17 27	18 32	19 59

Sundays

Liskeard 6	d
Coombe Junction Halt	a
	d
St Keyne Wishing Well Halt	d
Causeland	d
Sandplace	d
Looe	a

For connections at Liskeard please refer to Table 135

Table 140

Mondays to Fridays

Looe - Liskeard

Route Diagram - see first Page of Table 135

Miles			GW	GW	GW	GW	GW	GW	GW	GW	GW		GW	GW	GW
0	**Looe**	d	06 37	07 46	09 09	10 32	11 47	12 47	13 51	14 57	16 13		17 15	18 33	19 52
2¼	Sandplace	d	06x42	07x51	09x14	10x37		12x52		15x02			17x20	18x38	19x57
3¾	Causeland	d	06x46	07x55	09x18	10x41		12x56		15x06			17x24	18x42	20x01
5	St Keyne Wishing Well Halt	d	06x49	07x58	09x21	10x44		12x59		15x09			17x27	18x45	20x04
6¾	Coombe Junction Halt	a			09 27	10 50									
—		d			09 29	10 52									
8¾	**Liskeard** 6	a	07 05	08 14	09 40	11 03	12 11	13 17	14 15	15 25	16 39		17 43	19 01	20 22

Saturdays

		GW	GW	GW	GW	GW	GW	GW	GW	GW		GW	GW	GW
Looe	d	06 33	07 47	09 09	10 32	11 37	12 44	13 56	14 56	16 14		17 28	18 33	20 00
Sandplace	d	06x38	07x52	09x14	10x37		12x49		15x01	16x19		17x33	18x38	20x05
Causeland	d	06x42	07x56	09x18	10x41		12x53		15x05	16x23		17x37	18x42	20x09
St Keyne Wishing Well Halt	d	06x45	07x59	09x21	10x45		12x56		15x08	16x27		17x41	18x45	20x13
Coombe Junction Halt	a			09 27	10 50									
	d			09 29	10 52									
Liskeard 6	a	07 01	08 15	09 40	11 03	12 01	13 12	14 20	15 25	16 44		17 58	19 01	20 28

Sundays

Looe	d
Sandplace	d
Causeland	d
St Keyne Wishing Well Halt	d
Coombe Junction Halt	a
	d
Liskeard 6	a

For connections at Liskeard please refer to Table 135

Table 142

Mondays to Fridays

Par - Newquay

Route Diagram - see first Page of Table 135

Miles			GW	GW ◇	GW ◇	GW ◇	GW ◇	GW
0	**Par**	d	09 17	12 13	14 08	16 10	18 29	20 28
4¼	Luxulyan	d	09x28			16x21	18x40	20x39
6¼	Bugle	d	09x34	12x30	14x25	16x26	18x46	20x45
8¾	Roche	d	09x38			16x32	18x50	20x49
14½	St Columb Road	d	09x50			16x43	19x02	21x01
18¼	Quintrell Downs	d	09 58			16 51	19 10	21 09
20¾	**Newquay**	a	10 09	13 01	14 56	17 02	19 21	21 20

Saturdays

		GW	GW	GW ◇	GW ◇	GW ◇	GW ◇	GW
Par	d	06 52	09 18	12 15	14 08	16 15	18 21	20 15
Luxulyan	d	07x03	09x29	12x26		16x26	18x32	20x26
Bugle	d	07x09	09x35	12x32	14x25	16x32	18x38	20x32
Roche	d	07x14	09x39	12x37		16x37	18x43	20x37
St Columb Road	d	07x25	09x51	12x48		16x48	18x54	20x48
Quintrell Downs	d	07 33	09 59	12 56		16 56	19 02	20 56
Newquay	a	07 44	10 10	13 07	14 55	17 07	19 13	21 07

Sundays
until 12 February

		GW	GW	GW ◇
Par	d	10 18	13 31	16 30
Luxulyan	d	10x29	13x42	16x41
Bugle	d	10x35	13x48	16x47
Roche	d	10x40	13x53	16x52
St Columb Road	d	10x51	14x04	17x03
Quintrell Downs	d	10 59	14 12	17 11
Newquay	a	11 10	14 23	17 22

Sundays
19 February to 25 March

		GW	GW	GW ◇
Par	d	10 18	13 45	15 45
Luxulyan	d	10x29	13x56	15x56
Bugle	d	10x35	14x02	16x02
Roche	d	10x40	14x07	16x07
St Columb Road	d	10x51	14x18	16x18
Quintrell Downs	d	10 59	14 26	16 26
Newquay	a	11 10	14 37	16 37

Sundays
from 1 April

		GW	GW	GW ◇
Par	d	10 18	13 31	16 30
Luxulyan	d	10x29	13x42	16x41
Bugle	d	10x35	13x48	16x47
Roche	d	10x40	13x53	16x52
St Columb Road	d	10x51	14x04	17x03
Quintrell Downs	d	10 59	14 12	17 11
Newquay	a	11 10	14 23	17 22

For connections at Par please refer to Table 135

Table 142

Mondays to Fridays

Newquay - Par

Route Diagram - see first Page of Table 135

Miles			GW ◇	GW ◇	GW ◇	GW ◇	GW	GW
0	**Newquay**	d	10 13	13 03	14 58	17 22	19 25	21 26
2½	Quintrell Downs	d	10 19	13 09	15 04	17 28	19 31	21 32
6½	St Columb Road	d	10x26	13x16	15x11	17x35		21x39
12	Roche	d	10x38	13x28	15x23	17x47		21x51
14½	Bugle	d	10x42	13x32	15x27	17x51	19x54	21x55
16½	Luxulyan	d	10x48	13x38	15x33	17x57		22x01
20¾	**Par**	a	11 02	13 52	15 47	18 13	20 13	22 16

Saturdays

		GW ◇	GW ◇	GW ◇	GW ◇	GW ◇	GW	GW
Newquay	d	07 48	10 12	13 09	14 59	17 21	19 17	21 18
Quintrell Downs	d	07 54	10 18	13 15	15 05	17 27	19 23	21 24
St Columb Road	d	08x02	10x26	13x23	15x13	17x35		21x32
Roche	d	08x13	10x37	13x34	15x24	17x46		21x43
Bugle	d	08x18	10x42	13x39	15x29	17x51	19x46	21x48
Luxulyan	d	08x23	10x47	13x44	15x34	17x56		21x53
Par	a	08 39	11 01	13 59	15 48	18 10	20 03	22 07

Sundays

until 12 February

		GW ◇	GW ◇	GW
Newquay	d	11 12	15 10	17 30
Quintrell Downs	d	11 18	15 16	17 36
St Columb Road	d	11x26	15x24	17x44
Roche	d	11x37	15x35	17x55
Bugle	d	11x42	15x40	18x00
Luxulyan	d	11x47	15x45	18x05
Par	a	12 01	15 59	18 19

Sundays

19 February to 25 March

		GW ◇	GW ◇	GW
Newquay	d	11 12	14 45	17 14
Quintrell Downs	d	11 18	14 51	17 20
St Columb Road	d	11x26	14x59	17x28
Roche	d	11x37	15x10	17x39
Bugle	d	11x42	15x15	17x44
Luxulyan	d	11x47	15x20	17x49
Par	a	12 01	15 34	18 03

Sundays

from 1 April

		GW ◇	GW ◇	GW
Newquay	d	11 12	15 10	17 30
Quintrell Downs	d	11 18	15 16	17 36
St Columb Road	d	11x26	15x24	17x44
Roche	d	11x37	15x35	17x55
Bugle	d	11x42	15x40	18x00
Luxulyan	d	11x47	15x45	18x05
Par	a	12 01	15 59	18 19

For connections at Par please refer to Table 135

Table 143

Mondays to Fridays

Truro - Falmouth

Route Diagram - see first Page of Table 135

Miles			GW	GW	GW	GW	GW	GW	GW	GW	GW		GW	GW	GW	GW	GW	GW	GW	GW	GW		GW	GW	GW
0	**Truro**	d	06 04	06 31	07 14	07 47	08 20	08 50	09 20	09 50	10 20		10 50	11 20	11 50	12 20	12 50	13 20	13 50	14 20	14 50		15 20	15 50	16 20
4¼	Perranwell	d	06x10	06x37	07x20	07x53	08x26		09x26		10x26			11x26		12x26		13x26		14x26			15x26		16x26
8¼	Penryn	d	06 18	06 45	07 28	08 01	08 34	09 04	09 34	10 04	10 34		11 04	11 34	12 04	12 34	13 04	13 34	14 04	14 34	15 04		15 34	16 04	16 34
10¼	Penmere	d	06 23	06 50	07 33	08 06	08 39	09 09	09 39	10 09	10 39		11 09	11 39	12 09	12 39	13 09	13 39	14 09	14 39	15 09		15 39	16 09	16 39
11¾	Falmouth Town	d	06 26	06 53	07 36	08 09	08 42	09 12	09 42	10 12	10 42		11 12	11 42	12 12	12 42	13 12	13 42	14 12	14 42	15 12		15 42	16 12	16 42
12¼	**Falmouth Docks**	a	06 28	06 55	07 38	08 11	08 44	09 14	09 44	10 14	10 44		11 14	11 44	12 14	12 44	13 14	13 44	14 14	14 44	15 14		15 44	16 14	16 44

		GW	GW	GW	GW	GW	GW		GW	GW
Truro	d	16 51	17 27	17 59	18 31	19 02	20 04		21 05	22 08
Perranwell	d	16x57	17x33	18x05	18x37	19x08	20x10		21x11	22x14
Penryn	d	17 05	17 41	18 13	18 45	19 16	20 18		21 19	22 22
Penmere	d	17 10	17 46	18 18	18 50	19 21	20 23		21 24	22 27
Falmouth Town	d	17 13	17 49	18 21	18 53	19 24	20 26		21 27	22 30
Falmouth Docks	a	17 15	17 51	18 23	18 55	19 26	20 28		21 29	22 32

Saturdays

		GW	GW	GW	GW	GW	GW	GW	GW	GW		GW	GW	GW	GW	GW	GW	GW	GW	GW		GW	GW	GW	GW
Truro	d	06 04	06 31	07 14	07 47	08 20	08 50	09 20	09 50	10 20		10 50	11 20	11 50	12 20	12 50	13 20	13 50	14 20	14 50		15 20	15 50	16 20	16 51
Perranwell	d	06x10	06x37	07x19	07x53	08x26		09x26		10x26			11x26		12x26		13x26		14x26			15x26		16x26	16x57
Penryn	d	06 18	06 45	07 27	08 01	08 34	09 04	09 34	10 04	10 34		11 04	11 34	12 04	12 34	13 04	13 34	14 04	14 34	15 04		15 34	16 04	16 34	17 05
Penmere	d	06 23	06 50	07 32	08 06	08 39	09 09	09 39	10 09	10 39		11 09	11 39	12 09	12 39	13 09	13 39	14 09	14 39	15 09		15 39	16 09	16 39	17 10
Falmouth Town	d	06 26	06 53	07 35	08 09	08 42	09 12	09 42	10 12	10 42		11 12	11 42	12 12	12 42	13 12	13 42	14 12	14 42	15 12		15 42	16 12	16 42	17 13
Falmouth Docks	a	06 28	06 55	07 38	08 11	08 44	09 14	09 44	10 14	10 44		11 14	11 44	12 14	12 44	13 14	13 44	14 14	14 44	15 14		15 44	16 14	16 44	17 15

		GW	GW	GW	GW	GW		GW	GW
Truro	d	17 27	17 59	18 31	19 02	20 04		21 05	22 06
Perranwell	d	17x33	18x05	18x37	19x08	20x10		21x11	22x12
Penryn	d	17 41	18 13	18 45	19 16	20 18		21 19	22 20
Penmere	d	17 46	18 18	18 50	19 21	20 23		21 24	22 25
Falmouth Town	d	17 49	18 21	18 53	19 24	20 26		21 27	22 28
Falmouth Docks	a	17 51	18 23	18 55	19 26	20 28		21 29	22 30

Sundays

until 12 February

		GW	GW	GW	GW	GW	GW	GW	GW	GW		GW
Truro	d	10 38	12 09	13 07	14 10	15 35	17 00	18 10	19 46	21 03		22 04
Perranwell	d	10x45	12x16	13x14	14x17	15x42	17x07	18x17	19x53	21x10		22x11
Penryn	d	10 52	12 23	13 21	14 24	15 49	17 14	18 24	20 00	21 17		22 18
Penmere	d	10 57	12 28	13 26	14 29	15 53	17 19	18 29	20 05	21 22		22 23
Falmouth Town	d	11 00	12 31	13 29	14 32	15 56	17 22	18 32	20 08	21 25		22 26
Falmouth Docks	a	11 02	12 33	13 31	14 34	16 00	17 24	18 34	20 10	21 27		22 28

Sundays

19 February to 25 March

		GW	GW	GW	GW	GW	GW	GW	GW	GW		GW
Truro	d	10 38	12 09	13 10	14 12	15 35	16 43	18 15	19 46	21 03		22 04
Perranwell	d	10x45	12x16	13x17	14x19	15x42	16x50	18x22	19x53	21x10		22x11
Penryn	d	10 52	12 23	13 24	14 26	15 49	16 57	18 29	20 00	21 17		22 18
Penmere	d	10 57	12 28	13 29	14 31	15 53	17 02	18 34	20 05	21 22		22 23
Falmouth Town	d	11 00	12 31	13 32	14 34	15 56	17 05	18 37	20 08	21 25		22 26
Falmouth Docks	a	11 02	12 33	13 34	14 36	16 00	17 07	18 39	20 10	21 27		22 28

Sundays

from 1 April

		GW	GW	GW	GW	GW	GW	GW	GW	GW		GW
Truro	d	10 38	12 09	13 07	14 10	15 35	17 00	18 10	19 46	21 03		22 04
Perranwell	d	10x45	12x16	13x14	14x17	15x42	17x07	18x17	19x53	21x10		22x11
Penryn	d	10 52	12 23	13 21	14 24	15 49	17 14	18 24	20 00	21 17		22 18
Penmere	d	10 57	12 28	13 26	14 29	15 53	17 19	18 29	20 05	21 22		22 23
Falmouth Town	d	11 00	12 31	13 29	14 32	15 56	17 22	18 32	20 08	21 25		22 26
Falmouth Docks	a	11 02	12 33	13 31	14 34	16 00	17 24	18 34	20 10	21 27		22 28

For connections at Truro please refer to Table 135

Table 143

Mondays to Fridays

Falmouth - Truro

Route Diagram - see first Page of Table 135

Miles			GW	GW	GW	GW	GW	GW	GW	GW	GW		GW	GW	GW	GW	GW	GW	GW	GW	GW		GW	GW	GW
0	**Falmouth Docks**	d	06 31	07 15	07 47	08 20	08 50	09 20	09 50	10 20	10 50		11 20	11 50	12 20	12 50	13 20	13 50	14 20	14 50	15 20		15 50	16 20	16 50
0½	Falmouth Town	d	06 34	07 18	07 50	08 23	08 53	09 23	09 53	10 23	10 53		11 23	11 53	12 23	12 53	13 23	13 53	14 23	14 53	15 23		15 53	16 23	16 53
2	Penmere	d	06 37	07 21	07 53	08 26	08 56	09 26	09 56	10 26	10 56		11 26	11 56	12 26	12 56	13 26	13 56	14 26	14 56	15 26		15 56	16 26	16 56
4	Penryn	d	06 45	07 29	08 01	08 34	09 04	09 34	10 04	10 34	11 04		11 34	12 04	12 34	13 04	13 34	14 04	14 34	15 04	15 34		16 04	16 34	17 04
8	Perranwell	d	06x51	07x35	08x07	08x40		09x40		10x40			11x40		12x40		13x40		14x40		15x40			16x40	17x11
12¼	**Truro**	a	06 59	07 43	08 15	08 48	09 18	09 48	10 18	10 48	11 18		11 48	12 17	12 48	13 18	13 48	14 18	14 48	15 18	15 48		16 18	16 48	17 19

		GW	GW	GW	GW	GW	GW		GW	GW
Falmouth Docks	d	17 27	17 59	18 31	19 02	19 29	20 31		21 32	22 35
Falmouth Town	d	17 30	18 02	18 34	19 05	19 32	20 34		21 35	22 38
Penmere	d	17 33	18 05	18 37	19 08	19 35	20 37		21 38	22 41
Penryn	d	17 40	18 13	18 45	19 16	19 40	20 42		21 43	22 46
Perranwell	d	17x48	18x19	18x51	19x22	19x46	20x48		21x49	22x52
Truro	a	17 55	18 27	18 59	19 30	19 55	20 57		21 59	23 02

Saturdays

		GW	GW	GW	GW	GW	GW	GW	GW	GW		GW	GW	GW	GW	GW	GW	GW	GW	GW		GW	GW	GW	GW
Falmouth Docks	d	06 31	07 15	07 47	08 20	08 50	09 20	09 50	10 20	10 50		11 20	11 50	12 20	12 50	13 20	13 50	14 20	14 50	15 20		15 50	16 20	16 51	17 27
Falmouth Town	d	06 34	07 18	07 50	08 23	08 53	09 23	09 53	10 23	10 53		11 23	11 53	12 23	12 53	13 23	13 53	14 23	14 53	15 23		15 53	16 23	16 53	17 30
Penmere	d	06 37	07 21	07 53	08 26	08 56	09 26	09 56	10 26	10 56		11 26	11 56	12 26	12 56	13 26	13 56	14 26	14 56	15 26		15 56	16 26	16 56	17 33
Penryn	d	06 45	07 29	08 01	08 34	09 04	09 34	10 04	10 34	11 04		11 34	12 04	12 34	13 04	13 34	14 04	14 34	15 04	15 34		16 04	16 34	17 04	17 40
Perranwell	d	06x51	07x35	08x07	08x40		09x40		10x40			11x40		12x40		13x40		14x40		15x40			16x40	17x11	17x48
Truro	a	06 59	07 43	08 15	08 48	09 18	09 48	10 18	10 48	11 18		11 48	12 18	12 48	13 18	13 48	14 18	14 48	15 18	15 48		16 18	16 48	17 19	17 55

		GW	GW	GW	GW	GW		GW	GW
Falmouth Docks	d	17 59	18 31	19 02	19 29	20 31		21 32	22 33
Falmouth Town	d	18 02	18 34	19 05	19 32	20 34		21 35	22 36
Penmere	d	18 05	18 37	19 08	19 35	20 37		21 38	22 39
Penryn	d	18 13	18 45	19 16	19 40	20 42		21 43	22 44
Perranwell	d	18x19	18x51	19x22	19x46	20x48		21x49	22x50
Truro	a	18 27	18 59	19 30	19 55	20 57		21 58	23 00

Sundays

until 12 February

		GW	GW	GW	GW	GW	GW	GW	GW	GW		GW
Falmouth Docks	d	11 09	12 35	13 34	14 44	16 14	17 30	18 37	20 13	21 30		22 32
Falmouth Town	d	11 12	12 39	13 37	14 47	16 17	17 33	18 40	20 16	21 33		22 35
Penmere	d	11 15	12 42	13 40	14 50	16 20	17 36	18 43	20 19	21 36		22 38
Penryn	d	11 20	12 47	13 45	14 55	16 25	17 41	18 48	20 24	21 40		22 43
Perranwell	d	11x27	12x54	13x52	15x02	16x32	17x48	18x55	20x31	21x47		22x50
Truro	a	11 35	13 02	14 00	15 10	16 39	17 56	19 03	20 39	21 55		23 01

Sundays

19 February to 25 March

		GW	GW	GW	GW	GW	GW	GW	GW	GW		GW
Falmouth Docks	d	11 09	12 35	13 37	14 44	16 14	17 10	18 42	20 13	21 30		22 32
Falmouth Town	d	11 12	12 39	13 40	14 47	16 17	17 13	18 45	20 16	21 33		22 35
Penmere	d	11 15	12 42	13 43	14 50	16 20	17 16	18 48	20 19	21 36		22 38
Penryn	d	11 20	12 47	13 48	14 55	16 25	17 21	18 53	20 24	21 40		22 43
Perranwell	d	11x27	12x54	13x55	15x02	16x32	17x28	19x00	20x31	21x47		22x50
Truro	a	11 35	13 05	14 03	15 10	16 39	17 36	19 08	20 39	21 55		23 01

Sundays

from 1 April

		GW	GW	GW	GW	GW	GW	GW	GW	GW		GW
Falmouth Docks	d	11 09	12 35	13 34	14 44	16 14	17 30	18 37	20 13	21 30		22 32
Falmouth Town	d	11 12	12 39	13 37	14 47	16 17	17 33	18 40	20 16	21 33		22 35
Penmere	d	11 15	12 42	13 40	14 50	16 20	17 36	18 43	20 19	21 36		22 38
Penryn	d	11 20	12 47	13 45	14 55	16 25	17 41	18 48	20 24	21 40		22 43
Perranwell	d	11x27	12x54	13x52	15x02	16x32	17x48	18x55	20x31	21x47		22x50
Truro	a	11 35	13 02	14 00	15 10	16 39	17 56	19 03	20 39	21 55		23 01

For connections at Truro please refer to Table 135

 Mondays to Fridays

St Erth - St Ives

Route Diagram - see first Page of Table 135

Miles			GW	GW	GW	GW	GW	GW	GW	GW	GW		GW	GW	GW	GW	GW	GW	GW	GW	GW		GW	GW	GW
—	Penzance	d	06 55		08 57																				
0	**St Erth**	d	07 03	08 01	09 05	09 38	10 18	10 48	11 18	11 48	12 18		12 48	13 18	13 48	14 18	14 48	15 18	15 48	16 18	16 48		17 17	17 48	18 18
0¾	Lelant Saltings	d			09 09	09 41	10 21	10 51	11 21	11 51	12 21		12 51	13 21	13 51	14 21	14 51	15 21	15 51	16 21			17 20		18 21
1	Lelant	d	07x07	08x03	09x10																16x50			17x50	18x22
3	Carbis Bay	d	07 12	08 09	09 16	09 47		10 57		11 57			12 57		13 57		14 57		15 57		16 56			17 56	18 27
4¼	**St Ives**	a	07 15	08 14	09 19	09 52	10 31	11 02	11 31	12 02	12 31		13 02	13 31	14 02	14 31	15 02	15 31	16 02	16 31	17 01		17 30	18 01	18 33

		GW	GW	GW	GW	GW	GW		GW
Penzance	d								
St Erth	d	18 48	19 18	19 48	20 18	20 48	21 23		21 58
Lelant Saltings	d		19 21		20 21				22 01
Lelant	d	18x51		19x51		20x51	21x25		22x02
Carbis Bay	d	18 56		19 56		20 56	21 31		22 08
St Ives	a	19 03	19 31	20 01	20 31	21 02	21 36		22 13

Saturdays

		GW	GW	GW	GW	GW	GW	GW	GW	GW		GW	GW	GW	GW	GW	GW	GW	GW	GW		GW	GW	GW	GW
Penzance	d	06 41		08 54																				18 50	
St Erth	d	06 50	08 00	09 03	09 35	10 13	10 48	11 20	11 48	12 18		12 48	13 18	13 48	14 18	14 48	15 18	15 48	16 18	16 48		17 17	17 59	18 59	19 53
Lelant Saltings	d			09 06	09 38	10 16	10 51	11 23	11 51	12 21		12 51	13 21	13 51	14 21	14 51	15 21	15 51	16 21			17 20	18 02	19 02	19 56
Lelant	d	06x53	08x03	09x08																16x51			18x04	19x04	19x58
Carbis Bay	d	06 58	08 08	09 13	09 44		10 57		11 57			12 57		13 57		14 57		15 57		16 56		17 26	18 09	19 09	20 03
St Ives	a	07 03	08 13	09 18	09 49	10 26	11 02	11 33	12 02	12 31		13 02	13 31	14 02	14 31	15 02	15 31	16 02	16 31	17 01		17 31	18 13	19 14	20 07

		GW	GW	GW
Penzance	d			
St Erth	d	20 33	21 06	21 47
Lelant Saltings	d	20 36	21 07	21 48
Lelant	d	20x38	21x09	21x50
Carbis Bay	d	20 43	21 14	21 55
St Ives	a	20 47	21 19	22 01

Sundays

		GW	GW	GW	GW	GW	GW	GW	GW	GW		GW	GW	GW	GW	GW
Penzance	d	11 45														
St Erth	d	11 56	12 30	13 18	13 48	14 18	14 48	15 18	15 48	16 18		16 48	17 18	17 48	18 30	19 30
Lelant Saltings	d	11 59	12 33	13 21	13 51	14 21	14 51	15 21	15 51	16 21		16 51	17 21	17 51	18 33	19 33
Lelant	d	12x01												17x53	18x35	19x35
Carbis Bay	d	12 06	12 39		13 57		14 57		15 57			16 57		17 58	18 40	19 40
St Ives	a	12 12	12 44	13 31	14 02	14 31	15 02	15 31	16 02	16 31		17 02	17 31	18 02	18 45	19 45

For connections at St Erth please refer to Table 135

Table 144

Mondays to Fridays

St Ives - St Erth

Route Diagram - see first Page of Table 135

Miles			GW	GW	GW	GW	GW	GW	GW	GW	GW		GW	GW	GW	GW	GW	GW	GW	GW	GW		GW	GW	GW
0	**St Ives**	d	07 25	08 15	09 22	09 53	10 33	11 03	11 33	12 03	12 33		13 03	13 33	14 03	14 33	15 03	15 33	16 03	16 33	17 03		17 31	18 03	18 33
1¼	Carbis Bay	d	07 28	08 18	09 25		10 36		11 36		12 36			13 36		14 36		15 36		16 36			17 34		18 36
3¼	Lelant	d	07x33	08x23	09x30																		17x39		18x41
3½	Lelant Saltings	d			09 33		10 43		11 43		12 43			13 43	14 13	14 43	15 13	15 43	16 13	16 43	17 12		17 42	18 13	18 44
4¼	**St Erth**	a	07 37	08 28	09 37	10 05	10 47	11 16	11 47	12 16	12 47		13 16	13 47	14 17	14 47	15 17	15 47	16 17	16 47	17 16		17 45	18 17	18 48
—	Penzance	a		08 40																					

		GW	GW	GW	GW	GW	GW		GW
St Ives	d	19 03	19 32	20 03	20 33	21 03	21 37		22 31
Carbis Bay	d		19 35		20 36	21 06	21 40		22 34
Lelant	d		19x40		20x41	21x11	21x45		22x39
Lelant Saltings	d		19 43	20 12	20 44	21 14			22 41
St Erth	a	19 16	19 47	20 16	20 47	21 18	21 51		22 45
Penzance	a								22 57

Saturdays

		GW	GW	GW	GW	GW	GW	GW	GW	GW		GW	GW	GW	GW	GW	GW	GW	GW	GW		GW	GW	GW	GW
St Ives	d	07 12	08 15	09 20	09 50	10 27	11 03	11 33	12 03	12 33		13 03	13 33	14 03	14 33	15 03	15 33	16 03	16 33	17 03		17 32	18 17	19 26	20 10
Carbis Bay	d	07 15	08 18	09 23		10 30		11 36		12 36			13 36		14 36		15 36		16 36			17 35	18 20	19 29	20 13
Lelant	d	07x20	08x23			10x35																17x40	18x25	19x34	20x18
Lelant Saltings	d			09 30		10 38		11 43		12 43			13 43	14 12	14 43	15 12	15 43	16 12	16 43	17 12		17 43	18 28	19 37	20 21
St Erth	a	07 24	08 27	09 33	10 00	10 40	11 13	11 47	12 15	12 47		13 15	13 47	14 14	14 47	15 16	15 47	16 16	16 46	17 16		17 45	18 31	19 41	20 23
Penzance	a		08 40																				18 44		

		GW	GW	GW
St Ives	d	20 49	21 24	22 05
Carbis Bay	d	20 52	21 27	22 08
Lelant	d	20x57	21x32	22x13
Lelant Saltings	d	21 00	21 35	22 16
St Erth	a	21 02	21 37	22 19
Penzance	a			22 32

Sundays

		GW	GW	GW	GW	GW	GW	GW	GW	GW		GW	GW	GW	GW	GW
St Ives	d	12 13	12 48	13 33	14 03	14 33	15 03	15 33	16 03	16 33		17 03	17 33	18 03	18 50	19 50
Carbis Bay	d	12 16	12 51	13 36		14 36		15 36		16 36			17 36		18 51	19 53
Lelant	d	12x21												18x10	18x58	19x58
Lelant Saltings	d	12 24	12 58	13 43	14 12	14 43	15 12	15 43	16 12	16 43		17 12	17 43	18 13	19 01	20 01
St Erth	a	12 26	13 00	13 45	14 16	14 45	15 14	15 45	16 16	16 47		17 16	17 47	18 17	19 03	20 04
Penzance	a															20 14

For connections at St Erth please refer to Table 135

Network Diagram for Tables 148, 149

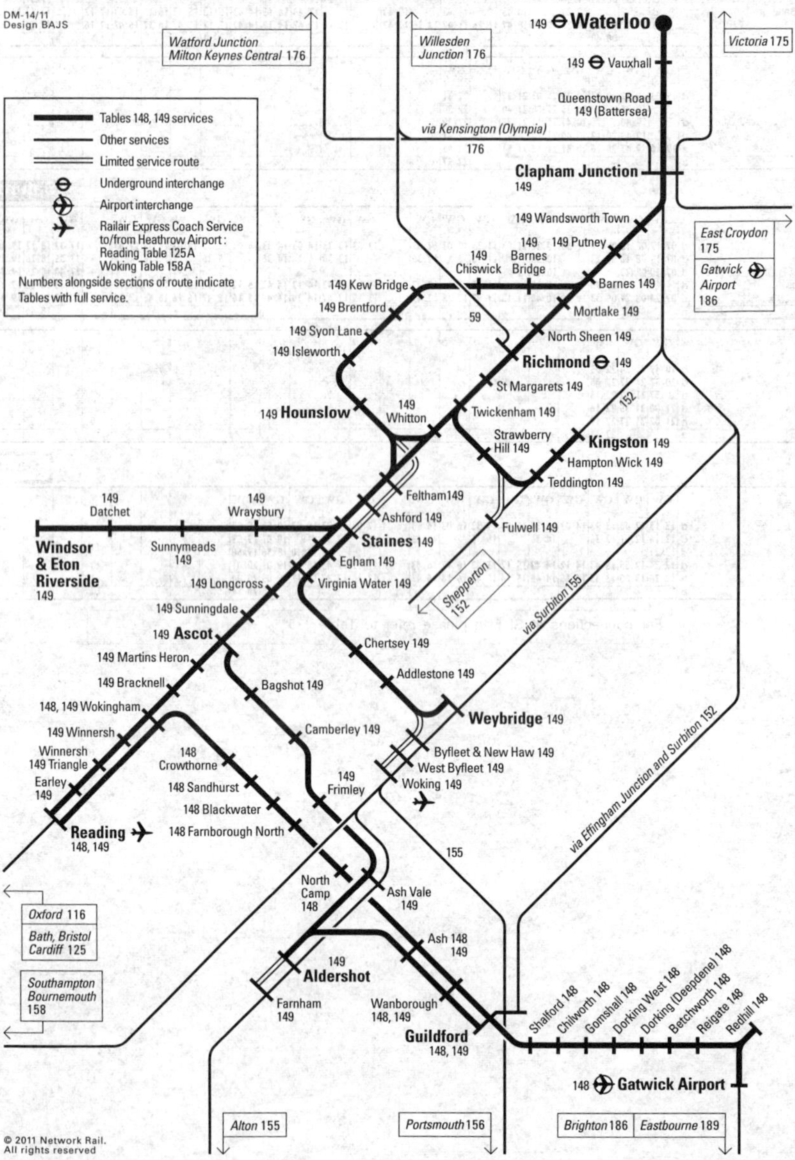

Reading - Guildford, Redhill and Gatwick Airport

Network Diagram - see first Page of Table 148

Miles			GW	GW	GW	GW	GW	GW	GW		GW		GW	GW	GW	GW	GW	GW	GW	GW	GW		GW	GW	GW
			MX	MO	MX																				
			1	1	1	1	1	1	1		1		1	1	1	1	1	1	1	1	1		1	1	1
0	**Reading** 7	149 d	22p34	23p15	23p34	04 34	05 24	05 54	06 06		06 34		07 04	07 34	08 04	08 20	08 34	09 04	09 34	10 04	10 34		11 04	11 34	12 04
6¾	Wokingham	149 d	22p43	23p24	23p43	04 43	05 33	06 03	06 16		06 43		07 13	07 43	08 13	08 29	08 43	09 13	09 43	10 13	10 43		11 13	11 43	12 13
10	Crowthorne	d	22p48	23p29	23p48			06 08	06 21				07 18	07 48	08 18	08 34		09 18		10 18			11 18		12 18
11½	Sandhurst	d	22p52	23p33	23p52			06 12	06 25				07 22	07 52	08 22	08 38		09 22		10 22			11 22		12 22
13½	Blackwater	d	22p55	23p36	23p55	04 51	05 41	06 15	06 28		06 51		07 25	07 55	08 25	08 41	08 51	09 25	09 51	10 25	10 51		11 25	11 51	12 25
15½	Farnborough North	d	23p00	23p41	23p59			06 20	06 33				07 30	08 00	08 30	08 46		09 30		10 30			11 30		12 30
17½	North Camp	d	23p04	23p45	00 04	04 57	05 48	06 24	06 37		06 57		07 34	08 04	08 34	08 50	09 01	09 34	09 57	10 34	10 57		11 34	11 57	12 34
19½	Ash 5	149 d	23p08	23p49	00 08			06 28	06 41				07 38	08 08	08 38	08 54		09 38		10 38			11 38		12 38
21½	Wanborough	149 d			00 12			06 32																	
25¾	**Guildford**	149 a	23p17	23p58	00 19	05 09	05 59	06 39	06 50		07 08		07 47	08 17	08 47	09 03	09 13	09 47	10 09	10 47	11 08		11 47	12 08	12 47
—		d	23p18	23p59	00 21	05 10	06 00	06 43	06 58		07 10		07 48	08 18	08 48	09 04	09 13	09 48	10 10	10 48	11 10		11 48	12 10	12 48
27¾	Shalford	d	23p23					06 48	07a04				07 53		08 53	09a11		09 53		10 53			11 53		12 53
29¾	Chilworth	d	23p27					06 52					07 57		08 57			09 57					11 57		
33½	Gomshall	d	23p34					06 58					08 04		09 04			10 04					12 04		
38¼	Dorking West	d	23p41					07 06					08 11		09 11					11 06					13 06
39	Dorking Deepdene	d	23p44	00 19	00 37	05 26	06 17	07 08			07 26		08 14	08 35	09 14		09 30	10 11	10 26	11 08	11 26		12 11	12 26	13 08
41¾	Betchworth	d	23p49					07 13					08 19		09 19					11 13					13 13
44½	Reigate	186 d	23p54	00 26	00 45	05 34	06 24	07 18			07 34		08 24	08 42	09 24		09 37	10 19	10 34	11 19	11 34		12 19	12 34	13 19
46½	**Redhill**	186 a	23p58	00 30	00 49	05 39	06 29	07 24			07 38		08 30	08 46	09 30		09 42	10 25	10 38	11 25	11 38		12 25	12 38	13 25
52¼	**Gatwick Airport** 10	186 a	00 11	00 41	01 03	05 54	06 40				07 50			08 59			09 59		10 50		11 50			12 50	

		GW	GW	GW	GW	GW	GW		GW	GW	GW	GW	GW	GW	GW	GW	GW	GW	GW	GW	GW	XC	GW	GW	GW
																								FX	FO
		1	1	1	1	1	1		1	1	1	1	1	1	1	1	1	1	1	1	1	◇1	1	1	1
Reading 7	149 d	12 34	13 04	13 34	14 04	14 34	15 04		15 28	16 04	16 34	16 51	17 04	17 34	18 04	18 34	19 04	19 34	20 04	20 34	21 34	22 23	22 34	23 34	23 34
Wokingham	149 d	12 43	13 13	13 43	14 13	14 43	15 13		15 39	16 13	16 43	17 00	17 13	17 43	18 13	18 43	19 13	19 43	20 13	20 43	21 43		22 43	23 43	
Crowthorne	d		13 18		14 18		15 18		15 44	16 18		17 06	17 18	17 48	18 18		19 18		20 18		21 48		22 48	23 48	23 48
Sandhurst	d		13 22		14 22		15 22		15 48	16 22		17 10	17 22	17 52	18 22		19 22		20 22		21 52		22 52	23 52	23 52
Blackwater	d	12 51	13 25	13 51	14 25	14 51	15 25		15 51	16 25	16 51	17 13	17 25	17 55	18 25	18 51	19 25	19 51	20 25	20 51	21 55		22 55	23 55	23 55
Farnborough North	d		13 30		14 30		15 30			16 30		17 18	17 30	18 00	18 30		19 30		20 30		22 00		23 00	23 59	23 59
North Camp	d	12 57	13 34	13 57	14 34	14 57	15 34		15 57	16 34	16 57	17 22	17 34	18 04	18 34	18 57	19 34	19 57	20 34	20 57	22 04		23 04	00 04	00 04
Ash 5	149 d		13 38		14 38		15 38			16 38		17 26	17 38	18 08	18 38		19 38		20 38		22 08		23 08	00 08	00 08
Wanborough	149 d									16 42			17 42		18 42									00 12	00 12
Guildford	149 a	13 08	13 47	14 08	14 47	15 08	15 47		16 08	16 49	17 08	17 35	17 49	18 17	18 50	19 08	19 47	20 08	20 47	21 08	22 17	22 59	23 17	00 19	00 19
	d	13 10	13 48	14 10	14 48	15 10	15 48		16 10	16 50	17 10	17 40	17 50	18 18	18 54	19 10	19 48	20 10	20 48	21 10	22 18		23 18	00 21	00 21
Shalford	d		13 53		14 53		15 53		16 15	16 55		17a48	17 55		18 59		19a55		20 53	21 15	22 23		23 23		
Chilworth	d		13 57				15 57			16 59			17 59		19 03				20 58	21 19			23 27		
Gomshall	d		14 04				16 04			17 06			18 06		19 10				21 04	21 25			23 34		
Dorking West	d				15 06				16 28	17 13			18 13		19 17				21 12	21 33			23 41		
Dorking Deepdene	d	13 26	14 11	14 26	15 08	15 26	16 11		16 30	17 16	17 26		18 16	18 35	19 20	19 27		20 26	21 14	21 35	22 37		23 44	00 37	00 37
Betchworth	d				15 13		16 16			17 21			18 21		19 25				21 19	21 40			23 49		
Reigate	186 d	13 34	14 19	14 34	15 19	15 34	16 21		16 38	17 26	17 34		18 26	18 42	19 30	19 36		20 34	21 24	21 45	22 44		23 54	00 45	00 45
Redhill	186 a	13 38	14 25	14 38	15 25	15 38	16 27		16 42	17 32	17 38		18 32	18 47	19 35	19 40		20 38	21 30	21 49	22 48		23 58	00 49	00 49
Gatwick Airport 10	186 a	13 50		14 50		15 50			16 59		17 54			19 00		19 55		20 50		22 06	23 06		00 11	01 03	01 03

Saturdays

Reading - Guildford, Redhill and Gatwick Airport

Network Diagram - see first Page of Table 148

			GW 1	GW 1	GW 1	GW 1	GW 1	GW 1	GW 1	GW 1	GW 1	GW 1	GW 1	GW 1	GW 1	GW 1	GW 1	GW 1	GW 1	GW 1	GW 1	GW 1	GW 1	GW 1
Reading 7	149	d	22p34	23p34	04 34	05 34	06 04	06 34	07 04	07 34	08 04	08 34	09 04	09 34	10 04	10 34	11 04	11 34	12 04	12 34	13 04	13 34	14 04	14 34
Wokingham	149	d	22p43		04 43	05 43	06 13	06 43	07 13	07 43	08 13	08 43	09 13	09 43	10 13	10 43	11 13	11 43	12 13	12 43	13 13	13 43	14 13	14 43
Crowthorne		d	22p48	23p48			06 18		07 18		08 18		09 18		10 18		11 18		12 18		13 18		14 18	
Sandhurst		d	22p52	23p52			06 22		07 22		08 22		09 22		10 22		11 22		12 22		13 22		14 22	
Blackwater		d	22p55	23p55	04 51	05 51	06 25	06 51	07 25	07 51	08 25	08 51	09 25	09 51	10 25	10 51	11 25	11 51	12 25	12 51	13 25	13 51	14 25	14 51
Farnborough North		d	23p00	23p59			06 30		07 30		08 30		09 30		10 30		11 30		12 30		13 30		14 30	
North Camp		d	23p04	00 04	04 57	05 57	06 34	06 57	07 34	07 57	08 34	08 57	09 34	09 57	10 34	10 57	11 34	11 57	12 34	12 57	13 34	13 57	14 34	14 57
Ash 5	149	d	23p08	00 08			06 38		07 38		08 38		09 38		10 38		11 38		12 38		13 38		14 38	
Wanborough	149	d		00 12																				
Guildford	149	a	23p17	00 19	05 08	06 08	06 47	07 09	07 47	08 08	08 47	09 08	09 47	10 08	10 47	11 08	11 47	12 08	12 47	13 08	13 47	14 08	14 47	15 08
		d	23p18	00 21	05 10	06 10	06 48	07 10	07 48	08 10	08 48	09 10	09 48	10 10	10 48	11 10	11 48	12 10	12 48	13 10	13 48	14 10	14 48	15 10
Shalford		d	23p23				06 53		07 53		08 53		09 53		10 53		11 53		12 53		13 53		14 53	
Chilworth		d	23p27						07 57				09 57				11 57				13 57			
Gomshall		d	23p34						08 04				10 04				12 04				14 04			
Dorking West		d	23p41				07 06				09 06				11 06				13 06				15 06	
Dorking Deepdene		d	23p44	00 37	05 26	06 26	07 08	07 26	08 11	08 26	09 08	09 26	10 11	10 26	11 08	11 26	12 11	12 26	13 08	13 26	14 11	14 26	15 08	15 26
Betchworth		d	23p49				07 13				09 13				11 13				13 13				15 13	
Reigate	186	d	23p54	00 45	05 34	06 34	07 18	07 34	08 19	08 34	09 18	09 34	10 19	10 34	11 18	11 34	12 19	12 34	13 18	13 34	14 19	14 34	15 18	15 34
Redhill	186	a	23p58	00 49	05 39	06 39	07 25	07 39	08 25	08 38	09 25	09 38	10 25	10 38	11 25	11 38	12 25	12 38	13 25	13 38	14 25	14 38	15 25	15 38
Gatwick Airport 10	186	a	00 11	01 03	05 58	06 50		07 50		08 50		09 50		10 50		11 50		12 50		13 50		14 50		15 50

			GW 1	GW 1	GW 1	GW 1	GW 1	GW 1	GW 1	GW 1	GW 1	GW 1	GW 1	GW 1	GW 1	GW 1	GW 1
Reading 7	149	d	15 04	15 34	16 04	16 34	17 04	17 34	18 04	18 34	19 04	19 34	20 04	20 34	21 34	22 34	23 34
Wokingham	149	d	15 13	15 43	16 13	16 43	17 13	17 43	18 13	18 43	19 13	19 43	20 13	20 43	21 43	22 43	
Crowthorne		d	15 18		16 18		17 18		18 18		19 18		20 18		21 48	22 48	23 48
Sandhurst		d	15 22		16 22		17 22		18 22		19 22		20 22		21 52	22 52	23 52
Blackwater		d	15 25	15 51	16 25	16 51	17 25	17 51	18 25	18 51	19 25	19 51	20 25	20 51	21 55	22 55	23 55
Farnborough North		d	15 30		16 30		17 30		18 30		19 30		20 30		22 00	23 00	23 59
North Camp		d	15 34	15 57	16 34	16 57	17 34	17 57	18 34	18 57	19 34	19 57	20 34	20 57	22 04	23 04	00 04
Ash 5	149	d	15 38		16 38		17 38		18 38		19 38		20 38		22 08	23 08	00 08
Wanborough	149	d															00 12
Guildford	149	a	15 47	16 08	16 47	17 08	17 47	18 08	18 47	19 08	19 47	20 08	20 47	21 08	22 17	23 17	00 19
		d	15 48	16 10	16 48	17 10	17 48	18 10	18 48	19 10	19 48	20 10	20 48	21 10	22 18	23 18	00 21
Shalford		d	15 53		16 53		17 53		18 53		19 53		20 53	21 15	22 23	23 23	
Chilworth		d	15 57				17 57				19 57			21 19		23 27	
Gomshall		d	16 04				18 04				20 04			21 25		23 34	
Dorking West		d			17 06				19 06				21 06		22 36	23 41	
Dorking Deepdene		d	16 11	16 26	17 08	17 26	18 11	18 26	19 08	19 26	20 11	20 26	21 08	21 33	22 38	23 44	00 37
Betchworth		d			17 13				19 13				21 13		22 43	23 49	
Reigate	186	d	16 19	16 34	17 18	17 34	18 19	18 34	19 18	19 34	20 19	20 34	21 18	21 40	22 48	23 54	00 45
Redhill	186	a	16 25	16 38	17 25	17 38	18 25	18 38	19 25	19 38	20 25	20 38	21 25	21 44	22 52	23 58	00 49
Gatwick Airport 10	186	a		16 50		17 50		18 50		19 50		20 50		21 59	23 05	00 10	01 02

Sundays

until 1 January

			GW 1	GW 1	GW 1	GW 1	GW 1	GW 1	GW 1	GW 1	GW 1	GW 1	GW 1	GW 1	GW 1	GW 1	GW 1	GW 1	GW 1	GW 1	GW 1	XC ◇1	GW 1
			A	A																			
Reading 7	149	d	22p34	23p34	06 03	07 03	08 03	09 03	10 03	11 03	12 03	13 03	14 03	15 03	16 03	17 03	18 03	19 03	20 03	21 03	22 03	22 14	23 15
Wokingham	149	d	22p43		06 11	07 11	08 11	09 11	10 11	11 11	12 11	13 11	14 11	15 11	16 11	17 11	18 11	19 11	20 11	21 11	22 11		23 24
Crowthorne		d	22p48	23p48		07 17		09 17		11 17		13 17		15 17		17 17		19 17		21 17			23 29
Sandhurst		d	22p52	23p52		07 21		09 21		11 21		13 21		15 21		17 21		19 21		21 21			23 33
Blackwater		d	22p55	23p55	06 20	07 24	08 19	09 24	10 19	11 24	12 19	13 24	14 19	15 24	16 19	17 24	18 19	19 24	20 19	21 24	22 19		23 36
Farnborough North		d	23p00	23p59		07 29		09 29		11 29		13 29		15 29		17 29		19 29		21 29			23 41
North Camp		d	23p04	00 04	06 27	07 33	08 26	09 33	10 26	11 33	12 26	13 33	14 26	15 33	16 26	17 33	18 26	19 33	20 26	21 33	22 26		23 45
Ash 5	149	d	23p08	00 08		07 37		09 37		11 37		13 37		15 37		17 37		19 37		21 37			23 49
Wanborough	149	d		00 12																			
Guildford	149	a	23p17	00 19	06 38	07 46	08 37	09 46	10 37	11 46	12 37	13 46	14 37	15 46	16 37	17 46	18 37	19 46	20 37	21 46	22 37	22 42	23 58
		d	23p18	00 21	06 40	07 47	08 39	09 47	10 39	11 47	12 39	13 47	14 39	15 47	16 39	17 47	18 39	19 47	20 39	21 47	22 39		23 59
Shalford		d	23p23				08 44		10 44		12 44		14 44		16 44		18 44		20 44		22 44		
Chilworth		d	23p27				08 48		10 48		12 48		14 48		16 48		18 48		20 48		22 48		
Gomshall		d	23p34				08 54		10 54		12 54		14 54		16 54		18 54		20 54		22 54		
Dorking West		d	23p41				09 02		11 02		13 02		15 02		17 02		19 02		21 02		23 02		
Dorking Deepdene		d	23p44	00 37	06 57	08 04	09 04	10 04	11 04	12 04	13 04	14 04	15 04	16 04	17 04	18 04	19 04	20 04	21 04	22 04	23 04		00 19
Betchworth		d	23p49				09 09		11 09		13 09		15 09		17 09		19 09		21 09		23 09		
Reigate	186	d	23p54	00 45	07 05	08 13	09 13	10 13	11 13	12 13	13 13	14 13	15 13	16 13	17 13	18 13	19 13	20 13	21 13	22 13	23 13		00 26
Redhill	186	a	23p58	00 49	07 09	08 18	09 18	10 18	11 18	12 18	13 18	14 18	15 18	16 18	17 18	18 18	19 18	20 18	21 18	22 18	23 18		00 30
Gatwick Airport 10	186	a	00 10	01 02	07 27	08 31	09 31	10 30	11 30	12 30	13 30	14 30	15 30	16 30	17 30	18 30	19 30	20 30	21 30	22 30	23 31		00 41

A not 11 December

Table 148

Sundays

8 January to 25 March

Reading - Guildford, Redhill and Gatwick Airport

Network Diagram - see first Page of Table 148

			GW 1	GW 1	GW 1	GW 1	GW 1	GW 1	GW 1	GW 1	GW 1	GW 1	GW 1	GW 1	GW 1	GW 1	GW 1	GW 1	GW 1	GW 1	GW 1	XC ◇1	GW 1
Reading 7	149	d	22p34	23p34	06 03	07 03	08 03	09 03	10 03	11 03	12 03	13 03	14 03	15 03	16 03	17 03	18 03	19 03	20 03	21 03	22 03	22 14	23 15
Wokingham	149	d	22p43		06 11	07 11	08 11	09 11	10 11	11 11	12 11	13 11	14 11	15 11	16 11	17 11	18 11	19 11	20 11	21 11	22 11		23 24
Crowthorne		d	22p48	23p48		07 17		09 17		11 17		13 17		15 17		17 17		19 17		21 17			23 29
Sandhurst		d	22p52	23p52		07 21		09 21		11 21		13 21		15 21		17 21		19 21		21 21			23 33
Blackwater		d	22p55	23p55	06 20	07 24	08 19	09 24	10 19	11 24	12 19	13 24	14 19	15 24	16 19	17 24	18 19	19 24	20 19	21 24	22 19		23 36
Farnborough North		d	23p00	23p59		07 29		09 29		11 29		13 29		15 29		17 29		19 29		21 29			23 41
North Camp		d	23p04	00 04	06 27	07 33	08 26	09 33	10 26	11 33	12 26	13 33	14 26	15 33	16 26	17 33	18 26	19 33	20 26	21 33	22 26		23 45
Ash 5	149	d	23p08	00 08		07 37		09 37		11 37		13 37		15 37		17 37		19 37		21 37			23 49
Wanborough	149	d		00 12																			
Guildford	149	a	23p17	00 19	06 38	07 46	08 37	09 46	10 37	11 46	12 37	13 46	14 37	15 46	16 37	17 46	18 37	19 46	20 37	21 46	22 37	22 42	23 58
		d	23p18	00 21	06 40	07 47	08 39	09 47	10 39	11 47	12 39	13 47	14 39	15 47	16 39	17 47	18 39	19 47	20 39	21 47	22 39		23 59
Shalford		d	23p23				08 44		10 44		12 44		14 44		16 44		18 44		20 44		22 44		
Chilworth		d	23p27				08 48		10 48		12 48		14 48		16 48		18 48		20 48		22 48		
Gomshall		d	23p34				08 54		10 54		12 54		14 54		16 54		18 54		20 54		22 54		
Dorking West		d	23p41				09 02		11 02		13 02		15 02		17 02		19 02		21 02		23 02		
Dorking Deepdene		d	23p44	00 37	06 57	08 04	09 04	10 04	11 04	12 04	13 04	14 04	15 04	16 04	17 04	18 04	19 04	20 04	21 04	22 04	23 04		00 19
Betchworth		d	23p49				09 09		11 09		13 09		15 09		17 09		19 09		21 09		23 09		
Reigate	186	d	23p54	00 45	07 05	08 13	09 13	10 13	11 13	12 13	13 13	14 13	15 13	16 13	17 13	18 13	19 13	20 13	21 13	22 13	23 13		00 26
Redhill	186	a	23p58	00 49	07 09	08 18	09 18	10 18	11 18	12 18	13 18	14 18	15 18	16 18	17 18	18 18	19 18	20 18	21 18	22 18	23 18		00 30
Gatwick Airport 10	186	a	00 10	01 02	07 27	08 31	09 31	10 30	11 30	12 30	13 30	14 30	15 30	16 30	17 30	18 30	19 30	20 30	21 30	22 30	23 31		00 41

Sundays

from 1 April

			GW 1	GW 1	GW 1	GW 1	GW 1	GW 1	GW 1	GW 1	GW 1	GW 1	GW 1	GW 1	GW 1	GW 1	GW 1	GW 1	GW 1	GW 1	GW 1	XC ◇1	GW 1
Reading 7	149	d	22p34	23p34	06 03	07 03	08 03	09 03	10 03	11 03	12 03	13 03	14 03	15 03	16 03	17 03	18 03	19 03	20 03	21 03	22 03	22 14	23 15
Wokingham	149	d	22p43		06 11	07 11	08 11	09 11	10 11	11 11	12 11	13 11	14 11	15 11	16 11	17 11	18 11	19 11	20 11	21 11	22 11		23 24
Crowthorne		d	22p48	23p48		07 17		09 17		11 17		13 17		15 17		17 17		19 17		21 17			23 29
Sandhurst		d	22p52	23p52		07 21		09 21		11 21		13 21		15 21		17 21		19 21		21 21			23 33
Blackwater		d	22p55	23p55	06 20	07 24	08 19	09 24	10 19	11 24	12 19	13 24	14 19	15 24	16 19	17 24	18 19	19 24	20 19	21 24	22 19		23 36
Farnborough North		d	23p00	23p59		07 29		09 29		11 29		13 29		15 29		17 29		19 29		21 29			23 41
North Camp		d	23p04	00 04	06 27	07 33	08 26	09 33	10 26	11 33	12 26	13 33	14 26	15 33	16 26	17 33	18 26	19 33	20 26	21 33	22 26		23 45
Ash 5	149	d	23p08	00 08		07 37		09 37		11 37		13 37		15 37		17 37		19 37		21 37			23 49
Wanborough	149	d		00 12																			
Guildford	149	a	23p17	00 19	06 38	07 46	08 37	09 46	10 37	11 46	12 37	13 46	14 37	15 46	16 37	17 46	18 37	19 46	20 37	21 46	22 37	22 42	23 58
		d	23p18	00 21	06 40	07 47	08 39	09 47	10 39	11 47	12 39	13 47	14 39	15 47	16 39	17 47	18 39	19 47	20 39	21 47	22 39		23 59
Shalford		d	23p23				08 44		10 44		12 44		14 44		16 44		18 44		20 44		22 44		
Chilworth		d	23p27				08 48		10 48		12 48		14 48		16 48		18 48		20 48		22 48		
Gomshall		d	23p34				08 54		10 54		12 54		14 54		16 54		18 54		20 54		22 54		
Dorking West		d	23p41				09 02		11 02		13 02		15 02		17 02		19 02		21 02		23 02		
Dorking Deepdene		d	23p44	00 37	06 57	08 04	09 04	10 04	11 04	12 04	13 04	14 04	15 04	16 04	17 04	18 04	19 04	20 04	21 04	22 04	23 04		00 19
Betchworth		d	23p49				09 09		11 09		13 09		15 09		17 09		19 09		21 09		23 09		
Reigate	186	d	23p54	00 45	07 05	08 13	09 13	10 13	11 13	12 13	13 13	14 13	15 13	16 13	17 13	18 13	19 13	20 13	21 13	22 13	23 13		00 26
Redhill	186	a	23p58	00 49	07 09	08 18	09 18	10 18	11 18	12 18	13 18	14 18	15 18	16 18	17 18	18 18	19 18	20 18	21 18	22 18	23 18		00 30
Gatwick Airport 10	186	a	00 10	01 02	07 27	08 31	09 31	10 30	11 30	12 30	13 30	14 30	15 30	16 30	17 30	18 30	19 30	20 30	21 30	22 30	23 31		00 41

Gatwick Airport, Redhill and Guildford - Reading

Network Diagram - see first Page of Table 148

Miles	Station			GW MX [1]	GW MO [1]	GW MX [1]	XC ◇[1]	GW [1]	GW [1]	GW [1]	GW [1]	GW [1]	GW [1]	GW [1]	GW [1]	GW [1]	GW [1]	GW [1]	GW [1]	GW [1]	GW [1]	GW [1]	GW [1]	GW [1]
0	**Gatwick Airport** [10]	186	d	22p22	23p08	23p18		05 31	05 56			06 58		07 58			09 07		10 03		11 03		12 03	
5¾	**Redhill**	186	d	22p33	23p20	23p28		05 43	06 13	06 24		07 10	07 28	08 08	08 33		09 23	09 34	10 13	10 34	11 13	11 34	12 13	12 34
—	Reigate	186	d	22p38	23p24	23p33		05 49	06 18	06 28		07 15	07 32	08 13	08 37		09 28	09 38	10 18	10 38	11 18	11 38	12 18	12 38
10½	Betchworth		d	22p43						06 33			07 37		08 42			09 43		10 43				12 43
13¼	Dorking Deepdene		d	22p47	23p32	23p40		05 56	06 25	06 37		07 22	07 41	08 20	08 46		09 35	09 47	10 25	10 47	11 25	11 45	12 25	12 47
14	Dorking West		d	22p50						06 40			07 44		08 49			09 50		10 50				12 50
18¾	Gomshall		d	22p58						06 48		07 30	07 52		08 57			09 58				11 53		
22½	Chilworth		d	23p04						06 54			07 58		09 03			10 04				11 59		
24½	Shalford		d	23p08						06 58	07 21		08 02		09 07	09 31		10 08		11 03		12 03		13 03
26½	**Guildford**		a	23p12	23p49	00 01		06 12	06 41	07 03	07 25	07 41	08 06	08 36	09 11	09 36	09 53	10 12	10 42	11 08	11 42	12 08	12 42	13 08
—			d	23p14	23p52	00 02	06 02	06 13	06 43	07 04	07 27	07 43	08 13	08 38	09 13	09 38	09 54	10 14	10 44	11 09	11 44	12 09	12 44	13 09
30¾	Wanborough	149	d	23p21				06 20		07 12			08 20		09 20									
32¾	Ash [5]	149	d	23p26	00 01			06 25	06 52	07 16	07 36	07 52	08 25		09 25	09 47		10 23		11 19		12 19		13 19
34¾	North Camp		d	23p30	00 05	00 14		06 29	06 56	07 20	07 41	07 56	08 29	08 50	09 29	09 51		10 27	10 56	11 23	11 56	12 23	12 56	13 23
36¾	Farnborough North		d	23p34	00 09			06 33	07 00	07 24	07 45	08 00	08 33		09 33			10 31		11 27		12 27		13 27
38¾	Blackwater		d	23p38	00 14	00 20		06 37	07 05	07 29	07 49	08 05	08 37	08 56	09 37	09 58		10 36	11 02	11 31	12 02	12 31	13 02	13 31
40¾	Sandhurst		d	23p42	00 16			06 41	07 08	07 32	07 53	08 08	08 41		09 41			10 39		11 35		12 35		13 35
42¼	Crowthorne		d	23p46	00 20			06 45	07 12	07 36	07 57	08 12	08 45		09 45			10 43		11 39		12 39		13 39
45½	Wokingham	149	d	23p51	00 25	00 29		06 50	07 17	07 41	08 02	08 17	08 50	09 04	09 51	10 06		10 48	11 10	11 44	12 10	12 44	13 10	13 44
52¼	**Reading** [7]	149	a	00 01	00 37	00 39	06 31	06 58	07 29	07 52	08 17	08 28	09 00	09 17	10 01	10 17	10 23	10 59	11 19	11 54	12 19	12 54	13 19	13 54

Station			GW [1]	GW [1]	GW [1]	GW [1]	GW [1]	GW [1]	GW [1]	GW [1]	GW [1]	GW [1]	GW [1]	GW [1]	GW [1]	GW [1]	GW [1]	GW [1]	GW [1]	GW [1]	GW [1]	GW [1]	GW [1]
Gatwick Airport [10]	186	d	13 03		14 03		15 03		16 03		17 03			18 03		19 16		20 03		21 03		22 22	23 18
Redhill	186	d	13 13	13 34	14 13	14 34	15 13	15 29	16 13	16 32	17 13		17 43	18 13	18 43	19 26		20 13	20 34	21 13	21 35	22 33	23 28
Reigate	186	d	13 18	13 38	14 18	14 38	15 18	15 34	16 18	16 36	17 18		17 48	18 18	18 47	19 30		20 18	20 40	21 18	21 39	22 38	23 33
Betchworth		d				14 43		15 38		16 41			17 52		18 52				20 45		21 44	22 43	
Dorking Deepdene		d	13 25	13 45	14 25	14 47	15 25	15 43	16 25	16 45	17 25		17 57	18 25	18 56	19 37		20 25	20 49	21 25	21 48	22 47	23 40
Dorking West		d				14 50		15 45					17 59		18 59				20 52		21 51	22 50	
Gomshall		d		13 53				15 53		16 53			18 07		19 07				21 00		21 59	22 58	
Chilworth		d		13 59				15 59		16 59			18 13		19 13				21 06		22 05	23 04	
Shalford		d		14 03		15 03		16 03		17 03		17 58	18 17		19 17		20 02		21 10		22 09	23 08	
Guildford		a	13 42	14 08	14 42	15 08	15 42	16 08	16 42	17 08	17 43	18 02	18 22	18 41	19 22	19 54	20 06	20 42	21 14	21 42	22 13	23 12	00 01
		d	13 44	14 09	14 44	15 09	15 44	16 14	16 44	17 09	17 44	18 04	18 26	18 47	19 36	19 55	20 10	20 44	21 16	21 44	22 15	23 14	00 02
Wanborough	149	d																				23 21	
Ash [5]	149	d		14 19		15 19		16 24		17 19	17 54	18 14	18 35		19 46		20 19		21 25		22 23	23 26	
North Camp		d	13 56	14 23	14 56	15 23	15 56	16 28	16 56	17 23	17 58	18 18	18 39	19 01	19 50	20 07	20 23	20 56	21 29	21 56	22 27	23 30	00 14
Farnborough North		d		14 27		15 27		16 32		17 27	18 02	18 22	18 42		19 54		20 27		21 33		22 31	23 34	
Blackwater		d	14 02	14 31	15 02	15 31	16 02	16 36	17 02	17 31	18 07	18 27	18 47	19 07	19 58	20 14	20 31	21 02	21 38	22 02	22 36	23 38	00 20
Sandhurst		d		14 35		15 35		16 40		17 35		18 30	18 51		20 02		20 35		21 41		22 39	23 42	
Crowthorne		d		14 39		15 39		16 44		17 39		18 34	18 59		20 06		20 39		21 45		22 43	23 46	
Wokingham	149	d	14 10	14 44	15 10	15 43	16 10	16 48	17 10	17 44	18 15	18 39	19 04	19 15	20 11	20 22	20 43	21 10	21 50	22 10	22 48	23 51	00 29
Reading [7]	149	a	14 19	14 54	15 19	15 54	16 24	17 00	17 19	17 54	18 24	18 50	19 17	19 25	20 21	20 32	20 55	21 19	22 01	22 19	23 01	00 01	00 39

Saturdays

Station			GW [1]	GW [1]	XC ◇[1]	GW [1]	GW [1]	GW [1]	GW [1]	GW [1]	GW [1]	GW [1]	GW [1]	GW [1]	GW [1]	GW [1]	GW [1]	GW [1]	GW [1]	GW [1]	GW [1]	GW [1]	GW [1]	GW [1]
Gatwick Airport [10]	186	d	22p22	23p18		05 31	06 03		07 03		08 03		09 03		10 03		11 03		12 03		13 03		14 03	
Redhill	186	d	22p33	23p28		05 41	06 13	06 34	07 13	07 34	08 13	08 34	09 13	09 34	10 13	10 34	11 13	11 34	12 13	12 34	13 13	13 34	14 13	14 34
Reigate	186	d	22p38	23p33		05 47	06 18	06 38	07 18	07 38	08 18	08 38	09 18	09 38	10 18	10 38	11 18	11 38	12 18	12 38	13 18	13 38	14 18	14 38
Betchworth		d	22p43					06 43				08 43				10 43				12 43				14 43
Dorking Deepdene		d	22p47	23p40		05 54	06 25	06 47	07 25	07 45	08 25	08 47	09 25	09 45	10 25	10 47	11 25	11 45	12 25	12 47	13 25	13 45	14 25	14 47
Dorking West		d	22p50					06 50				08 50				10 50				12 50				14 50
Gomshall		d	22p58							07 53				09 53				11 53				13 53		
Chilworth		d	23p04							07 59				09 59				11 59				13 59		
Shalford		d	23p08					07 03		08 03		09 03		10 03		11 03		12 03		13 03		14 03		15 03
Guildford		a	23p12	00 01		06 12	06 43	07 08	07 41	08 08	08 42	09 08	09 42	10 08	10 42	11 08	11 42	12 08	12 42	13 08	13 42	14 08	14 42	15 08
		d	23p14	00 02	06 09	06 12	06 44	07 09	07 44	08 09	08 44	09 09	09 44	10 09	10 44	11 09	11 44	12 09	12 44	13 09	13 44	14 09	14 44	15 09
Wanborough	149	d	23p21			06 21																		
Ash [5]	149	d	23p26			06 24		07 19		08 19		09 19		10 19		11 19		12 19		13 19		14 19		15 19
North Camp		d	23p30	00 14		06 28	06 56	07 23	07 56	08 23	08 56	09 23	09 56	10 23	10 56	11 23	11 56	12 23	12 56	13 23	13 56	14 23	14 56	15 23
Farnborough North		d	23p34			06 32		07 27		08 27		09 27		10 27		11 27		12 27		13 27		14 27		15 27
Blackwater		d	23p38	00 20		06 38	07 02	07 31	08 02	08 31	09 02	09 31	10 02	10 31	11 02	11 31	12 02	12 31	13 02	13 31	14 02	14 31	15 02	15 31
Sandhurst		d	23p42			06 40		07 35		08 35		09 35		10 35		11 35		12 35		13 35		14 35		15 35
Crowthorne		d	23p46			06 44		07 39		08 39		09 39		10 39		11 39		12 39		13 39		14 39		15 39
Wokingham	149	d	23p51	00 29		06 49	07 10	07 44	08 10	08 44	09 10	09 44	10 10	10 44	11 10	11 44	12 10	12 44	13 10	13 44	14 10	14 44	15 10	15 44
Reading [7]	149	a	00 01	00 39	06 44	07 03	07 19	07 54	08 19	08 54	09 19	09 54	10 19	10 54	11 19	11 54	12 19	12 54	13 19	13 54	14 19	14 54	15 19	15 54

Table 148

Saturdays

Gatwick Airport, Redhill and Guildford - Reading

Network Diagram - see first Page of Table 148

			GW	GW	GW	GW	GW	GW	GW	GW	GW	GW	GW	GW	GW	GW	GW	GW	GW
			1	1	1	1	1	1	1	1	1	1	1	1	1	1	1	1	1
																		A	B
Gatwick Airport 10	186	d	15 03		16 03		17 03		18 03		19 03		20 03		21 03		22 22	23 18	23 18
Redhill	186	d	15 13	15 34	16 13	16 34	17 13	17 34	18 13	18 34	19 13	19 34	20 13	20 34	21 13	21 36	22 33	23 28	23 28
Reigate	186	d	15 18	15 38	16 18	16 38	17 18	17 38	18 18	18 38	19 18	19 38	20 18	20 38	21 18	21 40	22 38	23 33	23 33
Betchworth		d				16 43				18 43				20 43			22 43		
Dorking Deepdene		d	15 25	15 45	16 25	16 47	17 25	17 45	18 25	18 47	19 25	19 45	20 25	20 47	21 25	21 47	22 47	23 40	23 40
Dorking West		d				16 50				18 50				20 50			22 50		
Gomshall		d		15 53				17 53				19 53				21 55	22 58		
Chilworth		d		15 59				17 59				19 59				22 01	23 04		
Shalford		d		16 03		17 03		18 03		19 03		20 03		21 03		22 05	23 08		
Guildford		a	15 42	16 08	16 42	17 08	17 42	18 08	18 42	19 08	19 42	20 08	20 42	21 08	21 42	22 13	23 13	00 01	00 01
		d	15 44	16 09	16 44	17 09	17 44	18 09	18 44	19 09	19 44	20 09	20 44	21 09	21 44	22 14	23 14	00 02	00 02
Wanborough	149	d															23 22		
Ash 5	149	d		16 19		17 19		18 19		19 19		20 19		21 19		22 24	23 26		
North Camp		d	15 56	16 23	16 56	17 23	17 56	18 23	18 56	19 23	19 56	20 23	20 56	21 23	21 56	22 28	23 30	00 14	00 14
Farnborough North		d		16 27		17 27		18 27		19 27		20 27		21 27		22 32	23 34		
Blackwater		d	16 02	16 31	17 02	17 31	18 02	18 31	19 02	19 31	20 02	20 31	21 02	21 31	22 02	22 36	23 39	00 20	00 20
Sandhurst		d		16 35		17 35		18 35		19 35		20 35		21 35		22 40	23 42		
Crowthorne		d		16 39		17 39		18 39		19 39		20 39		21 39		22 44	23 46		
Wokingham	149	d	16 10	16 44	17 10	17 44	18 10	18 44	19 10	19 44	20 10	20 44	21 10	21 44	22 10	22 49	23 51	00 29	00 29
Reading 7	149	a	16 19	16 54	17 19	17 54	18 19	18 54	19 19	19 54	20 19	20 54	21 19	21 54	22 19	22 57	00 01	00 37	00 38

Sundays

until 1 January

			GW	GW	GW	GW	GW	GW	GW	GW	XC	GW	GW	GW	GW	GW	GW	GW	GW	GW	GW	GW	GW
			1	1	1	1	1	1	1	1	◇1	1	1	1	1	1	1	1	1	1	1	1	1
			C	C																			
Gatwick Airport 10	186	d	22p22	23p18	06 08	07 08	08 08	09 08	10 08	11 08		12 08	13 08	14 08	15 08	16 08	17 08	18 08	19 08	20 08	21 08	22 08	23 08
Redhill	186	d	22p33	23p28	06 20	07 20	08 19	09 20	10 19	11 20		12 19	13 20	14 19	15 20	16 19	17 20	18 19	19 20	20 19	21 20	22 19	23 20
Reigate	186	d	22p38	23p33	06 24	07 24	08 23	09 24	10 23	11 24		12 23	13 24	14 23	15 24	16 23	17 24	18 23	19 24	20 23	21 24	22 23	23 24
Betchworth		d	22p43				08 28		10 28			12 28		14 28		16 28		18 28		20 28		22 28	
Dorking Deepdene		d	22p47	23p40	06 32	07 32	08 32	09 32	10 32	11 32		12 32	13 32	14 31	15 32	16 31	17 32	18 31	19 32	20 31	21 32	22 31	23 32
Dorking West		d	22p50				08 35		10 35			12 35		14 35		16 35		18 35		20 35		22 35	
Gomshall		d	22p58				08 43		10 43			12 43		14 43		16 43		18 43		20 43		22 43	
Chilworth		d	23p04				08 49		10 49			12 49		14 49		16 49		18 49		20 49		22 49	
Shalford		d	23p08				08 53		10 53			12 53		14 53		16 53		18 53		20 53		22 53	
Guildford		a	23p13	00 01	06 49	07 50	08 57	09 50	10 57	11 52		12 57	13 50	14 57	15 50	16 57	17 50	18 57	19 50	20 57	21 50	22 57	23 49
		d	23p14	00 02	06 50	07 52	08 59	09 52	10 59	11 52	12 14	12 59	13 52	14 59	15 52	16 59	17 52	18 59	19 52	20 58	21 52	22 59	23 52
Wanborough	149	d	23p22																				
Ash 5	149	d	23p26			08 02		10 02		12 02			14 02		16 02		18 02		20 02		22 02		00 01
North Camp		d	23p30	00 14	07 02	08 06	09 11	10 06	11 11	12 06		13 11	14 06	15 11	16 06	17 11	18 06	19 11	20 06	21 10	22 06	23 11	00 05
Farnborough North		d	23p34			08 10		10 10		12 10			14 10		16 10		18 10		20 10		22 10		00 09
Blackwater		d	23p39	00 20	07 09	08 14	09 17	10 14	11 17	12 14		13 17	14 14	15 17	16 14	17 17	18 14	19 17	20 14	21 17	22 14	23 17	00 14
Sandhurst		d	23p42			08 18		10 18		12 18			14 18		16 18		18 18		20 18		22 18		00 16
Crowthorne		d	23p46			08 22		10 22		12 22			14 22		16 22		18 22		20 22		22 22		00 20
Wokingham	149	d	23p51	00 29	07 17	08 26	09 26	10 26	11 26	12 26		13 26	14 26	15 26	16 26	17 26	18 26	19 26	20 26	21 26	22 26	23 26	00 25
Reading 7	149	a	00 01	00 38	07 25	08 35	09 35	10 35	11 35	12 35	12 50	13 35	14 35	15 35	16 35	17 35	18 35	19 35	20 35	21 35	22 38	23 37	00 37

Sundays

8 January to 25 March

			GW	GW	GW	GW	GW	GW	GW	GW	GW	GW	GW	GW	GW	GW	GW	GW	GW	GW	GW	GW
			1	1	1	1	1	1	1	1	1	1	1	1	1	1	1	1	1	1	1	1
Gatwick Airport 10	186	d	22p22	23p18	06 08	07 08	08 08	09 08	10 08	11 08	12 08	13 08	14 08	15 08	16 08	17 08	18 08	19 08	20 08	21 08	22 08	23 08
Redhill	186	d	22p33	23p28	06 20	07 20	08 19	09 20	10 19	11 20	12 19	13 20	14 19	15 20	16 19	17 20	18 19	19 20	20 19	21 20	22 19	23 20
Reigate	186	d	22p38	23p33	06 24	07 24	08 23	09 24	10 23	11 24	12 23	13 24	14 23	15 24	16 23	17 24	18 23	19 24	20 23	21 24	22 23	23 24
Betchworth		d	22p43				08 28		10 28		12 28		14 28		16 28		18 28		20 28		22 28	
Dorking Deepdene		d	22p47	23p40	06 32	07 32	08 32	09 32	10 32	11 32	12 32	13 32	14 31	15 32	16 31	17 32	18 31	19 32	20 31	21 32	22 31	23 32
Dorking West		d	22p50				08 35		10 35		12 35		14 35		16 35		18 35		20 35		22 35	
Gomshall		d	22p58				08 43		10 43		12 43		14 43		16 43		18 43		20 43		22 43	
Chilworth		d	23p04				08 49		10 49		12 49		14 49		16 49		18 49		20 49		22 49	
Shalford		d	23p08				08 53		10 53		12 53		14 53		16 53		18 53		20 53		22 53	
Guildford		a	23p13	00 01	06 49	07 50	08 57	09 50	10 57	11 52	12 57	13 50	14 57	15 50	16 57	17 50	18 57	19 50	20 57	21 50	22 57	23 49
		d	23p14	00 02	06 50	07 52	08 59	09 52	10 59	11 52	12 59	13 52	14 59	15 52	16 59	17 52	18 59	19 52	20 58	21 52	22 59	23 52
Wanborough	149	d	23p22																			
Ash 5	149	d	23p26			08 02		10 02		12 02		14 02		16 02		18 02		20 02		22 02		00 01
North Camp		d	23p30	00 14	07 02	08 06	09 11	10 06	11 11	12 06	13 11	14 06	15 11	16 06	17 11	18 06	19 11	20 06	21 10	22 06	23 11	00 05
Farnborough North		d	23p34			08 10		10 10		12 10		14 10		16 10		18 10		20 10		22 10		00 09
Blackwater		d	23p39	00 20	07 09	08 14	09 17	10 14	11 17	12 14	13 17	14 14	15 17	16 14	17 17	18 14	19 17	20 14	21 17	22 14	23 17	00 14
Sandhurst		d	23p42			08 18		10 18		12 18		14 18		16 18		18 18		20 18		22 18		00 16
Crowthorne		d	23p46			08 22		10 22		12 22		14 22		16 22		18 22		20 22		22 22		00 20
Wokingham	149	d	23p51	00 29	07 17	08 26	09 26	10 26	11 26	12 26	13 26	14 26	15 26	16 26	17 26	18 26	19 26	20 26	21 26	22 26	23 26	00 25
Reading 7	149	a	00 01	00 37	07 25	08 35	09 35	10 35	11 35	12 35	13 35	14 35	15 35	16 35	17 35	18 35	19 35	20 35	21 35	22 38	23 37	00 37

A from 7 January until 24 March

B until 31 December and then from 31 March

C not 11 December

Table 148

Sundays
from 1 April

Gatwick Airport, Redhill and Guildford - Reading

Network Diagram - see first Page of Table 148

			GW 1	GW 1	GW 1	GW 1	GW 1	GW 1	GW 1	GW 1	XC ◇1
Gatwick Airport 10	186	d	22p22	23p18	06 08	07 08	08 08	09 08	10 08	11 08	.
Redhill	186	d	22p33	23p28	06 20	07 20	08 19	09 20	10 19	11 20	.
Reigate	186	d	22p38	23p33	06 24	07 24	08 23	09 24	10 23	11 24	.
Betchworth		d	22p43	.	.	.	08 28	.	10 28	.	.
Dorking Deepdene		d	22p47	23p40	06 32	07 32	08 32	09 32	10 32	11 32	.
Dorking West		d	22p50	.	.	.	08 35	.	10 35	.	.
Gomshall		d	22p58	.	.	.	08 43	.	10 43	.	.
Chilworth		d	23p04	.	.	.	08 49	.	10 49	.	.
Shalford		d	23p08	.	.	.	08 53	.	10 53	.	.
Guildford		a	23p13	00 01	06 49	07 50	08 57	09 50	10 57	11 52	.
		d	23p14	00 02	06 50	07 52	08 59	09 52	10 59	11 52	12 14
Wanborough	149	d	23p22	.	.	.	.	.	.	.	.
Ash 5	149	d	23p26	.	.	08 02	.	10 02	.	12 02	.
North Camp		d	23p30	00 14	07 02	08 06	09 11	10 06	11 11	12 06	.
Farnborough North		d	23p34	.	.	08 10	.	10 10	.	12 10	.
Blackwater		d	23p39	00 20	07 09	08 14	09 17	10 14	11 17	12 14	.
Sandhurst		d	23p42	.	.	08 18	.	10 18	.	12 18	.
Crowthorne		d	23p46	.	.	08 22	.	10 22	.	12 22	.
Wokingham	149	d	23p51	00 29	07 17	08 26	09 26	10 26	11 26	12 26	.
Reading 7	149	a	00 01	00 38	07 25	08 35	09 35	10 35	11 35	12 35	12 50

			GW 1	GW 1	GW 1	GW 1	GW 1	GW 1	GW 1	GW 1	GW 1	GW 1	GW 1	GW 1
Gatwick Airport 10	186	d	12 08	13 08	14 08	15 08	16 08	17 08	18 08	19 08	20 08	21 08	22 08	23 08
Redhill	186	d	12 19	13 20	14 19	15 20	16 19	17 20	18 19	19 20	20 19	21 20	22 19	23 20
Reigate	186	d	12 23	13 24	14 23	15 24	16 23	17 24	18 23	19 24	20 23	21 24	22 23	23 24
Betchworth		d	12 28	.	14 28	.	16 28	.	18 28	.	20 28	.	22 28	.
Dorking Deepdene		d	12 32	13 32	14 31	15 32	16 31	17 32	18 31	19 32	20 31	21 32	22 31	23 32
Dorking West		d	12 35	.	14 35	.	16 35	.	18 35	.	20 35	.	22 35	.
Gomshall		d	12 43	.	14 43	.	16 43	.	18 43	.	20 43	.	22 43	.
Chilworth		d	12 49	.	14 49	.	16 49	.	18 49	.	20 49	.	22 49	.
Shalford		d	12 53	.	14 53	.	16 53	.	18 53	.	20 53	.	22 53	.
Guildford		a	12 57	13 50	14 57	15 50	16 57	17 50	18 57	19 50	20 57	21 50	22 57	23 49
		d	12 59	13 52	14 59	15 52	16 59	17 52	18 59	19 52	20 58	21 52	22 59	23 52
Wanborough	149	d	.	.	.	.	.	.	.	.	.	.	.	.
Ash 5	149	d	.	14 02	.	16 02	.	18 02	.	20 02	.	22 02	.	00 01
North Camp		d	13 11	14 06	15 11	16 06	17 11	18 06	19 11	20 06	21 10	22 06	23 11	00 05
Farnborough North		d	.	14 10	.	16 10	.	18 10	.	20 10	.	22 10	.	00 09
Blackwater		d	13 17	14 14	15 17	16 14	17 17	18 14	19 17	20 14	21 17	22 14	23 17	00 14
Sandhurst		d	.	14 18	.	16 18	.	18 18	.	20 18	.	22 18	.	00 16
Crowthorne		d	.	14 22	.	16 22	.	18 22	.	20 22	.	22 22	.	00 20
Wokingham	149	d	13 26	14 26	15 26	16 26	17 26	18 26	19 26	20 26	21 26	22 26	23 26	00 25
Reading 7	149	a	13 35	14 35	15 35	16 35	17 35	18 35	19 35	20 35	21 35	22 38	23 37	00 37

London - Hounslow, Richmond, Kingston, Windsor, Weybridge, Ascot, Guildford and Reading

Network Diagram - see first Page of Table 148

Miles	Miles	Miles			SW MO 1	SW MX 1	SW MO	SW MX	SW MO 1	SW MX	SW MX 1	SW MX	SW MX		SW MX	SW MX	SW MX 1	SW MO 1	SW MX	SW MO	SW MO	SW 1	SW 1		SW MX
0	—	0	**London Waterloo** [15] ⊖	d	22p39	22p50	22p50	22p52	23p09	23p13	23p20	23p22	23p33		23p38			23p39			23p44				23p52
1¼	—	1¼	Vauxhall ⊖	d	22p43		22p54	22p56	23p13	23p17		23p26	23p37					23p43			23p48				23p56
2¾	—	2¾	Queenstown Rd.(Battersea)	d			22p57	22p59				23p29	23p40								23p51				23p59
4	—	4	**Clapham Junction** [10]	d	22p49	22p58	23p00	23p02	23p19	23p23	23p28	23p32	23p43		23p46			23p49			23p54				00 02
4¾	—	4¾	Wandsworth Town	d			23p03	23p05				23p35	23p46								23p57				00 05
5¾	—	5¾	Putney	d	22p53		23p06	23p08	23p23	23p27		23p38	23p49					23p53			23p59				00 08
7	0	7	Barnes	d			23p09	23p12				23p42	23p52								00 03				00 12
—	0½	—	Barnes Bridge	d			23p11	23p14				23p44													00 14
—	1½	—	Chiswick	d			23p13	23p17				23p47													00 17
—	2½	—	Kew Bridge	d			23p16	23p20				23p50													00 20
—	3½	—	Brentford	d			23p19	23p23				23p53													00 23
—	4¼	—	Syon Lane	d			23p21	23p25				23p55													00 25
—	5	—	Isleworth	d			23p23	23p27				23p57													00 27
—	6½	—	**Hounslow**	d			23p26	23p31				00 01													00 31
8¼	—	8¼	Mortlake	d									23p54								00 05				
9	—	9	North Sheen	d									23p56						←		00 07				
9¾	—	9¾	**Richmond** ⊖	d	22p59	23p06			23p29	23p33	23p37		23p59		23p54			23p59	23p59		00 10				
10¾	—	10¾	St Margarets	d									↦						00 01		00 12				
11¼	—	11¼	Twickenham	a	23p02	23p10			23p32	23p36	23p41				23p58			00 02	00 03		00 14				
—	—	—		d	23p03	23p10			23p33	23p37	23p41				23p58			00 03	00 04		00 15				
12¼	—	—	Strawberry Hill	d															00 07						
12½	—	—	Fulwell	a																					
13½	—	—	Teddington	a															00 11						
14¾	—	—	Hampton Wick	a															00 14						
15¼	—	—	**Kingston**	a															00 16						
—	—	12½	Whitton	d						23p40						←					00 18				
—	—	14¾	Feltham	d	23p09	23p16	23p32	23p36	23p39	23p44	23p48	00 06			00 04	00 06		00 09			00 22				00 37
—	—	17½	Ashford (Surrey)	d			23p36	23p40		23p48		↦				00 10					00 26				↦
0	—	19	**Staines**	d	23p15	23p23	23p40	23p44	23p45	23p52	23p56				00 11	00 14		00 15		00 21	00a30				
2½	—	—	Wraysbury	d						23p56															
3¾	—	—	Sunnymeads	d						23p59															
4¾	—	—	Datchet	d						00 02															
6¾	—	—	**Windsor & Eton Riverside**	a						00 06															
—	—	21	Egham	d	23p20	23p27	23p45	23p49	23p50		00 01				00 15	00 19		00 20		00s25					
0	—	23¾	Virginia Water	a	23p24	23p31	23p49	23p53	23p54		00 05				00 19	00 23		00 24		00s30					
—	—	—		d	23p24	23p31	23p49	23p53	23p54		00 05				00 19	00 23		00 24							
2½	—	—	Chertsey	d			23p55	23p59								00 29				00s35					
4	—	—	Addlestone	d			23p58	00 02								00a32				00s38					
5	—	—	**Weybridge**	a																					
7¼	—	—	Byfleet & New Haw	d			00 02	00 06												00s42					
8½	—	—	West Byfleet	d			00 05	00 09												00s45					
11	—	—	Woking	a			00 11	00 15												00 51					
—	—	25¼	Longcross	d																					
—	—	27	Sunningdale	d	23p29	23p37			23p59		00 11				00 25			00 29							
—	0	29	**Ascot** [3]	d	23p34	23p43			00 04		00 15				00 30		00 32	00 34							
—	3¼	—	Bagshot	d													00 38								
—	6½	—	Camberley	a													00 44								
—	8¾	—	Frimley	d													00 48								
—	12	—	Ash Vale	d													00 57								
—	14½	—	**Aldershot**	a													01s02								
—	—	—		d																		06 08	06 38		
—	17¼	—	Ash [5]	d																		06 15	06 45		
—	19¼	—	Wanborough	d																		06 18	06 48		
—	23½	—	**Guildford**	a																		06 25	06 55		
—	—	31¼	Martins Heron	d	23p38	23p47			00 08		00 19				00 34			00 38							
—	—	32¼	Bracknell	d	23p41	23p50			00 11		00 23				00 37			00 41							
—	—	36¾	**Wokingham**	d	23p48	23p57			00 18		00 32				00 44			00 48							
—	—	38¾	Winnersh	d	23p51	23p59			00 21		00 36							00 51							
—	—	39¼	Winnersh Triangle	d	23p53	00 02			00 23		00 38							00 53							
—	—	40½	Earley	d	23p56	00 05			00 26		00 40							00 56							
—	—	43½	**Reading** [7]	a	00 01	00 10			00 31		00 45				00 52			01 01							

Table 149

Mondays to Fridays

London - Hounslow, Richmond, Kingston, Windsor, Weybridge, Ascot, Guildford and Reading

Network Diagram - see first Page of Table 148

		SW MX	SW MX	SW	SW	SW 1	SW	SW 1	SW	SW	SW	SW 1	SW 1	SW	SW	SW	SW	SW 1	SW	SW 1	SW	SW 1	SW
London Waterloo 15 ⊖	d	23p58		00 18				05 05		05 33			05 50		05 58	06 03			06 15	06 20			06 22
Vauxhall ⊖	d	00 02		00 22				05 09		05 37					06 02	06 07			06 19				06 26
Queenstown Rd.(Battersea)	d			00 25				05 12		05 40						06 10			06 22				06 29
Clapham Junction 10	d	00 08		00 29				05 15		05 43			05 58		06 08	06 13			06 25	06 28			06 32
Wandsworth Town	d			00 32				05 18		05 46						06 16			06 28				06 35
Putney	d	00 12		00 35				05 21		05 49					06 12	06 19			06 31				06 38
Barnes	d			00 38				05 24		05 52						06 22			06 35				06 42
Barnes Bridge	d																						06 44
Chiswick	d																						06 47
Kew Bridge	d																						06 50
Brentford	d																						06 53
Syon Lane	d																						06 55
Isleworth	d																						06 57
Hounslow	d																						07 01
Mortlake	d			00 40				05 26		05 54						06 24			06 37				
North Sheen	d			00 42				05 28		05 56						06 26			06 39		←		
Richmond ⊖	d	00 18		00 45				05 31		05 59			06 06		06 18	06 29			06 42	06 36	06 42		
St Margarets	d			00 47				05 33		06 01						06 31			→		06 44		
Twickenham	a	00 21		00 49				05 35		06 03			06 10		06 21	06 33				06 40	06 46		
	d	00 22		00 50	04 52			05 36	05 53	06 05			06 10	06 17	06 22	06 34				06 40	06 47		
Strawberry Hill	d			00s53	04 55					06 08						06 37							
Fulwell	a																						
Teddington	a			00s56	04 58					06 11						06 40							
Hampton Wick	a			00s59	05 01					06 14						06 44							
Kingston	a			01 01	05 03					06 16						06 46							
Whitton	d	00 25	←					05 39	05 56					06a20	06 25						06a50		
Feltham	d	00 29	00 37					05 43	06 00				06 16		06 29					06 46			07 06
Ashford (Surrey)	d	00 33	00 41					05 47	06 04						06 33								→
Staines	d	00a37	00a46			05 23	05 44	05 53	06 08		06 14		06 23		06 37		06 44			06 53			
Wraysbury	d								06 12						06 41								
Sunnymeads	d								06 15						06 44								
Datchet	d								06 18						06 47								
Windsor & Eton Riverside	a								06 22						06 51								
Egham	d					05 27	05 49	05 57			06 19		06 27				06 49			06 57			
Virginia Water	a					05 31	05 53	06 01			06 23		06 31				06 53			07 01			
	d					05 31	05 53	06 01			06 23		06 31				06 53			07 01			
Chertsey	d						05 59				06 29						06 59						
Addlestone	d						06 02				06 32						07 02						
Weybridge	a						06 07				06 37						07 07						
Byfleet & New Haw	d																						
West Byfleet	d																						
Woking	a																						
Longcross	d												06 35							07 05			
Sunningdale	d					05 37		06 07					06 37							07 07			
Ascot 3	d					05 43		06 13				06 23	06 43					06 53		07 13		07 23	
Bagshot	d											06 29						06 59				07 29	
Camberley	a											06 35						07 05				07 35	
Frimley	d											06 43						07 13				07 43	
Ash Vale	d											06 49						07 19				07 49	
Aldershot	a											06 56						07 26				07 54	
	d											07 08						07 38				08 08	
Ash 5	d											07 15						07 45				08 15	
Wanborough	d											07 18						07 48				08 18	
Guildford	a											07 25						07 55				08 25	
Martins Heron	d					05 47		06 17					06 47							07 17			
Bracknell	d					05 50		06 20					06 50							07 20			
Wokingham	d					05 57		06 27					06 57							07 27			
Winnersh	d					06 00		06 30					07 00							07 30			
Winnersh Triangle	d					06 02		06 32					07 02							07 32			
Earley	d					06 05		06 35					07 05							07 35			
Reading 7	a					06 10		06 40					07 10							07 40			

London - Hounslow, Richmond, Kingston, Windsor, Weybridge, Ascot, Guildford and Reading

Network Diagram - see first Page of Table 148

Station		SW	SW	SW	SW	SW	SW 1	SW	SW 1	SW	SW	SW	SW	SW	SW	SW 1	SW	SW	SW	SW 1	SW	SW	SW
London Waterloo 15 ⊖	d	06 28		06 33		06 45	06 50			06 52	06 58		07 03		07 15	07 20		07 22	07 28			07 33	07 37
Vauxhall ⊖	d	06 32		06 37		06 49				06 56	07 02		07 07		07 19			07 26	07 32			07 37	07 41
Queenstown Rd.(Battersea)	d			06 40		06 52				06 59			07 10		07 22			07 29				07 40	07 44
Clapham Junction 10	d	06 38		06 43		06 55	06 58			07 02	07 08		07 13		07 25	07 28		07 32	07 38			07 43	07 47
Wandsworth Town	d			06 46		06 58				07 05			07 16		07 28			07 35				07 46	07 50
Putney	d	06 42		06 49		07 01				07 08	07 12		07 19		07 31			07 38	07 42			07 49	07 53
Barnes	d			06 52		07 05				07 12			07 22		07 35			07 42				07 52	07 57
Barnes Bridge	d									07 14								07 44					07 59
Chiswick	d									07 17								07 47					08 02
Kew Bridge	d									07 20								07 50					08 05
Brentford	d									07 23								07 53					08 08
Syon Lane	d									07 25								07 55					08 10
Isleworth	d									07 27								07 57					08 12
Hounslow	d				06 48					07 31								08 01					08a18
Mortlake	d			06 54		07 07							07 24		07 37							07 54	
North Sheen	d			06 56		07 09		←					07 26		07 39		←					07 56	
Richmond ⊖	d	06 48		06 59		07 12	07 06	07 12			07 18		07 29		07 42	07 36	07 42		07 48	07 54		07 59	
St Margarets	d			07 01		→		07 14					07 31		→		07 44					08 01	
Twickenham	a	06 51		07 03	06 56		07 10	07 16			07 21		07 33			07 40	07 46		07 51	07 57		08 03	
	d	06 52		07 04			07 10	07 17			07 22		07 34	07 37		07 40	07 47		07 52	07 58		08 04	
Strawberry Hill	d			07 07									07 37	07 47								08 07	
Fulwell	a																						
Teddington	a			07 10									07 40	07 50								08 10	
Hampton Wick	a			07 14									07 44	07 52								08 14	
Kingston	a			07 16									07 46	07 54								08 16	
Whitton	d	06 55	←					07a20			07 25	←					07a50		07 55		←		
Feltham	d	06 59	07 06				07 16			07 36	07 29	07 36				07 46		08 06	07 59	08 04	08 06		
Ashford (Surrey)	d	07 03	07 10							→	07 33	07 40						→	08 03	08 08	08 10		
Staines	d	07 07	07 14				07 23				07 37	07 44				07 53			08 07	08 12	08 14		
Wraysbury	d	07 11									07 41								08 11				
Sunnymeads	d	07 14									07 44								08 14				
Datchet	d	07 17									07 47								08 17				
Windsor & Eton Riverside	a	07 21									07 51								08 21				
Egham	d		07 19				07 27					07 49				07 57				08 16	08 19		
Virginia Water	a		07 23				07 31					07 53				08 01					08 23		
	d		07 23				07 31					07 53				08 01					08 23		
Chertsey	d		07 29									07 59									08 29		
Addlestone	d		07 32									08 02									08 32		
Weybridge	a		07 37									08 07									08 38		
Byfleet & New Haw	d																						
West Byfleet	d																						
Woking	a																						
Longcross	d						07 35									08 05							
Sunningdale	d						07 37									08 07							
Ascot 3	d						07 43		07 53							08 13				08 26			
Bagshot	d								07 59											08 32			
Camberley	a								08 05											08 38			
Frimley	d								08 13											08 43			
Ash Vale	d								08 19											08 49			
Aldershot	a								08 24											08 54			
	d								08 38											09 08			
Ash 5	d								08 45											09 15			
Wanborough	d								08 48											09 18			
Guildford	a								08 55											09 25			
Martins Heron	d						07 47									08 17							
Bracknell	d						07 50									08 20							
Wokingham	d						07 57									08 27							
Winnersh	d						08 00									08 30							
Winnersh Triangle	d						08 02									08 32							
Earley	d						08 05									08 35							
Reading 7	a						08 10									08 40							

London - Hounslow, Richmond, Kingston, Windsor, Weybridge, Ascot, Guildford and Reading

Network Diagram - see first Page of Table 148

			SW	SW	SW 1	SW	SW 1	SW	SW	SW	SW 1		SW	SW	SW	SW	SW 1	SW	SW 1	SW	SW		SW	SW 1	SW
London Waterloo 15 ⊖	d			07 45	07 50			07 52	07 58	08 03	08 07				08 10	08 15	08 20			08 22	08 28		08 33	08 37	
Vauxhall ⊖	d			07 49				07 56	08 02	08 07					08 14	08 19				08 26	08 32		08 37		
Queenstown Rd.(Battersea)	d			07 52				07 59		08 10					08 17	08 22				08 29			08 40		
Clapham Junction 10	d			07 55	07 58			08 02	08 08	08 13	08 16				08 20	08 25	08 28			08 32	08 38		08 43	08 45	
Wandsworth Town	d			07 58				08 05		08 16					08 23	08 28				08 35			08 46		
Putney	d			08 01				08 08	08 12	08 19					08 26	08 31				08 38	08 42		08 49		
Barnes	d			08 05				08 12		08 23					08 29	08 35				08 42			08 52		
Barnes Bridge	d							08 14							08 31					08 44					
Chiswick	d							08 17							08 34					08 47					
Kew Bridge	d							08 20							08 36					08 50					
Brentford	d							08 23							08 39					08 53					
Syon Lane	d							08 25							08 41					08 55					
Isleworth	d							08 27							08 43					08 57					
Hounslow	d							08 31							08 48					09 01					
Mortlake	d			08 07						08 25						08 37							08 54		
North Sheen	d			08 09		←				08 27				←		08 39		←					08 56		
Richmond ⊖	d			08 12	08 06	08 12			08 18	08 30	08 24			08 30		08 42	08 36	08 42			08 48		08 59	08 54	
St Margarets	d			↪		08 14				↪				08 32		↪		08 44					↪		
Twickenham	a				08 10	08 16			08 21		08 28			08 34			08 40	08 46			08 51			08 57	
	d		08 07		08 10	08 17			08 22		08 28			08 35			08 40	08 47			08 52			08 58	
Strawberry Hill	d		08 17											08 38											
Fulwell	a																								
Teddington	a		08 20											08 41											
Hampton Wick	a		08 22											08 44											
Kingston	a		08 24											08 46											
Whitton	d					08a20			08 25				←		08a53			08a50			08 55				←
Feltham	d				08 16			08 36	08 29		08 34		08 36				08 46			09 06	08 59			09 04	09 06
Ashford (Surrey)	d							↪	08 33		08 38		08 40							↪	09 03			09 08	09 10
Staines	d				08 23				08 37		08 42		08 44				08 53				09 07			09 12	09 14
Wraysbury	d								08 41												09 11				
Sunnymeads	d								08 44												09 14				
Datchet	d								08 47												09 17				
Windsor & Eton Riverside	a								08 51												09 21				
Egham	d				08 27						08 47		08 49				08 57							09 16	09 19
Virginia Water	a				08 31						08 51		08 53				09 01							09 20	09 23
	d				08 31						08 51		08 53				09 01							09 20	09 23
Chertsey	d												08 59												09 29
Addlestone	d												09 02												09 32
Weybridge	a												09 08												09 37
Byfleet & New Haw	d																								
West Byfleet	d																								
Woking	a																								
Longcross	d				08 35						08 54														
Sunningdale	d				08 37						08 58						09 07							09 26	
Ascot 3	d				08 43		08 53				09 02						09 13		09 23					09 30	
Bagshot	d						08 59												09 29						
Camberley	a						09 05												09 35						
Frimley	d						09 13												09 43						
Ash Vale	d						09 19												09 49						
Aldershot	a						09 25												09 54						
	d						09 38												10 08						
Ash 5	d						09 45												10 15						
Wanborough	d						09 48												10 18						
Guildford	a						09 55												10 25						
Martins Heron	d				08 47						09 06						09 17							09 34	
Bracknell	d				08 50						09 10						09 20							09 38	
Wokingham	d				08 57						09 17						09 27							09 47	
Winnersh	d				09 00						09 20						09 30								
Winnersh Triangle	d				09 02						09 22						09 32								
Earley	d				09 05						09 25						09 35								
Reading 7	a				09 10						09 30						09 40							09 55	

Table 149

Mondays to Fridays

London - Hounslow, Richmond, Kingston, Windsor, Weybridge, Ascot, Guildford and Reading

Network Diagram - see first Page of Table 148

		SW	SW	SW	SW	SW	SW	SW	SW	SW	SW	SW	SW	SW	SW	SW	SW	SW	SW	SW	SW	SW	SW
					1		1							1		1							1
London Waterloo 15 ⊖	d		08 40	08 43	08 50			08 52	08 58		09 03	09 07	09 15	09 20			09 22	09 28		09 33	09 37	09 45	09 50
Vauxhall ⊖	d		08 44	08 47				08 56	09 02		09 07	09 11	09 19				09 26	09 32		09 37	09 41	09 49	
Queenstown Rd.(Battersea)	d		08 47	08 50				08 59			09 10	09 14	09 22				09 29			09 40	09 44	09 52	
Clapham Junction 10	d		08 50	08 55	08 58			09 02	09 08		09 13	09 17	09 25	09 28			09 32	09 38		09 43	09 47	09 55	09 58
Wandsworth Town	d		08 53	08 58				09 05			09 16	09 20	09 28				09 35			09 46	09 50	09 58	
Putney	d		08 56	09 01				09 08	09 12		09 19	09 23	09 31				09 38	09 42		09 49	09 53	10 01	
Barnes	d		08 59	09 05				09 12			09 22	09 27	09 35				09 42			09 52	09 57	10 05	
Barnes Bridge	d		09 01					09 14				09 29					09 44				09 59		
Chiswick	d		09 03					09 17				09 32					09 47				10 02		
Kew Bridge	d		09 06					09 20				09 35					09 50				10 05		
Brentford	d		09 09					09 23				09 38					09 53				10 08		
Syon Lane	d		09 11					09 25				09 40					09 55				10 10		
Isleworth	d		09 13					09 27				09 42					09 57				10 12		
Hounslow	d		09 18					09 31				09 48					10 01				10 18		
Mortlake	d			09 07							09 24		09 37							09 54		10 07	
North Sheen	d	←		09 09		←					09 26		09 39		←					09 56		10 09	
Richmond ⊖	d	08 59		09 12	09 06	09 12			09 18		09 29		09 42	09 36	09 42			09 48		09 59		10 12	10 06
St Margarets	d	09 01		→		09 14					09 31		→		09 44					10 01		→	
Twickenham	a	09 03			09 10	09 16			09 21		09 33			09 40	09 46			09 51		10 03			10 10
	d	09 04			09 10	09 17			09 22		09 34			09 40	09 47			09 52		10 04			10 10
Strawberry Hill	d	09 07									09 37									10 07			
Fulwell	a																						
Teddington	a	09 10									09 40									10 10			
Hampton Wick	a	09 14									09 44									10 14			
Kingston	a	09 16									09 46									10 16			
Whitton	d		09a23			09a20			09 25	←		09a53			09a50			09 55	←		10a26		
Feltham	d				09 16			09 36	09 29	09 36				09 46			10 06	09 59	10 06				10 16
Ashford (Surrey)	d							→	09 33	09 40							→	10 03	10 10				
Staines	d				09 23				09 37	09 44				09 53				10 07	10 14				10 23
Wraysbury	d								09 41									10 11					
Sunnymeads	d								09 44									10 14					
Datchet	d								09 47									10 17					
Windsor & Eton Riverside	a								09 51									10 21					
Egham	d				09 27					09 49				09 57					10 19				10 27
Virginia Water	a				09 31					09 53				10 01					10 23				10 31
	d				09 31					09 53				10 01					10 23				10 31
Chertsey	d									09 59									10 29				
Addlestone	d									10 02									10 32				
Weybridge	a									10 07									10 37				
Byfleet & New Haw	d																						
West Byfleet	d																						
Woking	a																						
Longcross	d																						
Sunningdale	d				09 37									10 07									10 37
Ascot 3	d				09 43		09 53							10 13		10 23							10 43
Bagshot	d						09 59									10 29							
Camberley	a						10 05									10 35							
Frimley	d						10 13									10 43							
Ash Vale	d						10 19									10 49							
Aldershot	a						10 24									10 54							
	d						10 38									11 08							
Ash 5	d						10 45									11 15							
Wanborough	d						10 48									11 18							
Guildford	a						10 55									11 25							
Martins Heron	d				09 47									10 17									10 47
Bracknell	d				09 50									10 20									10 50
Wokingham	d				09 57									10 27									10 57
Winnersh	d				10 00									10 30									11 00
Winnersh Triangle	d				10 02									10 32									11 02
Earley	d				10 05									10 35									11 05
Reading 7	a				10 10									10 40									11 10

London - Hounslow, Richmond, Kingston, Windsor, Weybridge, Ascot, Guildford and Reading

Network Diagram - see first Page of Table 148

Station		SW	SW 1	SW	SW	SW	SW	SW	SW	SW 1	SW	SW 1	SW	SW	SW	SW	SW	SW	SW 1	SW	SW 1	SW
London Waterloo 15 ⊖	d			09 52	09 58		10 03	10 07	10 15	10 20			10 22	10 28		10 33	10 37	10 45	10 50			10 52
Vauxhall ⊖	d			09 56	10 02		10 07	10 11	10 19				10 26	10 32		10 37	10 41	10 49				10 56
Queenstown Rd.(Battersea)	d			09 59			10 10	10 14	10 22				10 29			10 40	10 44	10 52				10 59
Clapham Junction 10	d			10 02	10 08		10 13	10 17	10 25	10 28			10 32	10 38		10 43	10 47	10 55	10 58			11 02
Wandsworth Town	d			10 05			10 16	10 20	10 28				10 35			10 46	10 50	10 58				11 05
Putney	d			10 08	10 12		10 19	10 23	10 31				10 38	10 42		10 49	10 53	11 01				11 08
Barnes	d			10 12			10 22	10 27	10 35				10 42			10 52	10 57	11 05				11 12
Barnes Bridge	d			10 14				10 29					10 44				10 59					11 14
Chiswick	d			10 17				10 32					10 47				11 02					11 17
Kew Bridge	d			10 20				10 35					10 50				11 05					11 20
Brentford	d			10 23				10 38					10 53				11 08					11 23
Syon Lane	d			10 25				10 40					10 55				11 10					11 25
Isleworth	d			10 27				10 42					10 57				11 12					11 27
Hounslow	d			10 31				10 48					11 01				11 18					11 31
Mortlake	d						10 24		10 37							10 54		11 07				
North Sheen	d	←					10 26		10 39		←					10 56		11 09		←		
Richmond ⊖	d	10 12			10 18		10 29		10 42	10 36	10 42			10 48		10 59		11 12	11 06	11 12		
St Margarets	d	10 14					10 31		↦		10 44					11 01		↦		11 14		
Twickenham	a	10 16			10 21		10 33			10 40	10 46			10 51		11 03			11 10	11 16		
	d	10 17			10 22		10 34			10 40	10 47			10 52		11 04			11 10	11 17		
Strawberry Hill	d						10 37									11 07						
Fulwell	a																					
Teddington	a						10 40									11 10						
Hampton Wick	a						10 44									11 14						
Kingston	a						10 46									11 16						
Whitton	d	10a20			10 25	←		10a56			10a50			10 55	←		11a23			11a20		
Feltham	d			10 36	10 29	10 36				10 46			11 06	10 59	11 06				11 16			11 36
Ashford (Surrey)	d			↦	10 33	10 40							↦	11 03	11 10							↦
Staines	d				10 37	10 44				10 53				11 07	11 14				11 23			
Wraysbury	d				10 41									11 11								
Sunnymeads	d				10 44									11 14								
Datchet	d				10 47									11 17								
Windsor & Eton Riverside	a				10 51									11 21								
Egham	d					10 49				10 57					11 19				11 27			
Virginia Water	a					10 53				11 01					11 23				11 31			
	d					10 53				11 01					11 23				11 31			
Chertsey	d					10 59									11 29							
Addlestone	d					11 02									11 32							
Weybridge	a					11 07									11 37							
Byfleet & New Haw	d																					
West Byfleet	d																					
Woking	a																					
Longcross	d																					
Sunningdale	d									11 07									11 37			
Ascot 3	d		10 53							11 13		11 23							11 43		11 53	
Bagshot	d		10 59									11 29									11 59	
Camberley	a		11 05									11 35									12 05	
Frimley	d		11 13									11 43									12 13	
Ash Vale	d		11 19									11 49									12 19	
Aldershot	a		11 24									11 54									12 24	
	d		11 38									12 08									12 38	
Ash 5	d		11 45									12 15									12 45	
Wanborough	d		11 48									12 18									12 48	
Guildford	a		11 55									12 25									12 55	
Martins Heron	d									11 17									11 47			
Bracknell	d									11 20									11 50			
Wokingham	d									11 27									11 57			
Winnersh	d									11 30									12 00			
Winnersh Triangle	d									11 32									12 02			
Earley	d									11 35									12 05			
Reading 7	a									11 40									12 10			

London - Hounslow, Richmond, Kingston, Windsor, Weybridge, Ascot, Guildford and Reading

Network Diagram - see first Page of Table 148

		SW	SW	SW	SW	SW	SW 1	SW	SW 1	SW	SW	SW	SW	SW	SW	SW 1	SW	SW 1	SW	SW	SW	SW	SW
London Waterloo 15 ⊖	d	10 58		11 03	11 07	11 15	11 20			11 22	11 28		11 33	11 37	11 45	11 50			11 52	11 58		12 03	12 07
Vauxhall ⊖	d	11 02		11 07	11 11	11 19				11 26	11 32		11 37	11 41	11 49				11 56	12 02		12 07	12 11
Queenstown Rd.(Battersea)	d			11 10	11 14	11 22				11 29			11 40	11 44	11 52				11 59			12 10	12 14
Clapham Junction 10	d	11 08		11 13	11 17	11 25	11 28			11 32	11 38		11 43	11 47	11 55	11 58			12 02	12 08		12 13	12 17
Wandsworth Town	d			11 16	11 20	11 28				11 35			11 46	11 50	11 58				12 05			12 16	12 20
Putney	d	11 12		11 19	11 23	11 31				11 38	11 42		11 49	11 53	12 01				12 08	12 12		12 19	12 23
Barnes	d			11 22	11 27	11 35				11 42			11 52	11 57	12 05				12 12			12 22	12 27
Barnes Bridge	d				11 29					11 44				11 59					12 14				12 29
Chiswick	d				11 32					11 47				12 02					12 17				12 32
Kew Bridge	d				11 35					11 50				12 05					12 20				12 35
Brentford	d				11 38					11 53				12 08					12 23				12 38
Syon Lane	d				11 40					11 55				12 10					12 25				12 40
Isleworth	d				11 42					11 57				12 12					12 27				12 42
Hounslow	d				11 48					12 01				12 18					12 31				12 48
Mortlake	d			11 24		11 37							11 54		12 07							12 24	
North Sheen	d			11 26		11 39		←					11 56		12 09		←					12 26	
Richmond ⊖	d	11 18		11 29		11 42	11 36	11 42			11 48		11 59		12 12	12 06	12 12			12 18		12 29	
St Margarets	d			11 31		→		11 44					12 01		→		12 14					12 31	
Twickenham	a	11 21		11 33			11 40	11 46			11 51		12 03			12 10	12 16			12 21		12 33	
	d	11 22		11 34			11 40	11 47			11 52		12 04			12 10	12 17			12 22		12 34	
Strawberry Hill	d			11 37									12 07									12 37	
Fulwell	a																						
Teddington	a			11 40									12 10									12 40	
Hampton Wick	a			11 44									12 14									12 44	
Kingston	a			11 46									12 16									12 46	
Whitton	d	11 25	←		11a53			11a50			11 55	←		12a23			12a20			12 25	←		12a53
Feltham	d	11 29	11 36				11 46			12 06	11 59	12 06				12 16			12 36	12 29	12 36		
Ashford (Surrey)	d	11 33	11 40							→	12 03	12 10							→	12 33	12 40		
Staines	d	11 37	11 44				11 53				12 07	12 14				12 23				12 37	12 44		
Wraysbury	d	11 41									12 11									12 41			
Sunnymeads	d	11 44									12 14									12 44			
Datchet	d	11 47									12 17									12 47			
Windsor & Eton Riverside	a	11 51									12 21									12 51			
Egham	d		11 49				11 57					12 19				12 27					12 49		
Virginia Water	a		11 53				12 01					12 23				12 31					12 53		
	d		11 53				12 01					12 23				12 31					12 53		
Chertsey	d		11 59									12 29									12 59		
Addlestone	d		12 02									12 32									13 02		
Weybridge	a		12 07									12 37									13 07		
Byfleet & New Haw	d																						
West Byfleet	d																						
Woking	a																						
Longcross	d																						
Sunningdale	d						12 07									12 37							
Ascot 3	d						12 13		12 23							12 43		12 53					
Bagshot	d								12 29									12 59					
Camberley	a								12 35									13 05					
Frimley	d								12 43									13 13					
Ash Vale	d								12 49									13 19					
Aldershot	a								12 54									13 24					
	d								13 08									13 38					
Ash 5	d								13 15									13 45					
Wanborough	d								13 18									13 48					
Guildford	a								13 25									13 55					
Martins Heron	d						12 17									12 47							
Bracknell	d						12 20									12 50							
Wokingham	d						12 27									12 57							
Winnersh	d						12 30									13 00							
Winnersh Triangle	d						12 32									13 02							
Earley	d						12 35									13 05							
Reading 7	a						12 40									13 10							

London - Hounslow, Richmond, Kingston, Windsor, Weybridge, Ascot, Guildford and Reading

Network Diagram - see first Page of Table 148

		SW	SW ■1	SW	SW ■1	SW	SW	SW	SW	SW	SW	SW ■1	SW	SW ■1	SW	SW	SW	SW	SW	SW	SW ■1	SW	SW ■1
London Waterloo ■15 ⊖	d	12 15	12 20			12 22	12 28		12 33	12 37	12 45	12 50			12 52	12 58		13 03	13 07	13 15	13 20		
Vauxhall ⊖	d	12 19				12 26	12 32		12 37	12 41	12 49				12 56	13 02		13 07	13 11	13 19			
Queenstown Rd.(Battersea)	d	12 22				12 29			12 40	12 44	12 52				12 59			13 10	13 14	13 22			
Clapham Junction ■10	d	12 25	12 28			12 32	12 38		12 43	12 47	12 55	12 58			13 02	13 08		13 13	13 17	13 25	13 28		
Wandsworth Town	d	12 28				12 35			12 46	12 50	12 58				13 05			13 16	13 20	13 28			
Putney	d	12 31				12 38	12 42		12 49	12 53	13 01				13 08	13 12		13 19	13 23	13 31			
Barnes	d	12 35				12 42			12 52	12 57	13 05				13 12			13 22	13 27	13 35			
Barnes Bridge	d					12 44				12 59					13 14				13 29				
Chiswick	d					12 47				13 02					13 17				13 32				
Kew Bridge	d					12 50				13 05					13 20				13 35				
Brentford	d					12 53				13 08					13 23				13 38				
Syon Lane	d					12 55				13 10					13 25				13 40				
Isleworth	d					12 57				13 12					13 27				13 42				
Hounslow	d					13 01				13 18					13 31				13 48				
Mortlake	d	12 37							12 54		13 07							13 24		13 37			
North Sheen	d	12 39		←					12 56		13 09		←					13 26		13 39		←	
Richmond ⊖	d	12 42	12 36	12 42			12 48		12 59		13 12	13 06	13 12			13 18		13 29		13 42	13 36	13 42	
St Margarets	d	↦		12 44					13 01		↦		13 14					13 31		↦		13 44	
Twickenham	a		12 40	12 46			12 51		13 03			13 10	13 16			13 21		13 33			13 40	13 46	
	d		12 40	12 47			12 52		13 04			13 10	13 17			13 22		13 34			13 40	13 47	
Strawberry Hill	d								13 07									13 37					
Fulwell	a																						
Teddington	a								13 10									13 40					
Hampton Wick	a								13 14									13 44					
Kingston	a								13 16									13 46					
Whitton	d			12a50			12 55	←		13a23			13a20			13 25	←		13a53			13a50	
Feltham	d		12 46			13 06	12 59	13 06				13 16			13 36	13 29	13 36				13 46		
Ashford (Surrey)	d					↦	13 03	13 10							↦	13 33	13 40						
Staines	d		12 53				13 07	13 14				13 23				13 37	13 44				13 53		
Wraysbury	d						13 11									13 41							
Sunnymeads	d						13 14									13 44							
Datchet	d						13 17									13 47							
Windsor & Eton Riverside	a						13 21									13 51							
Egham	d		12 57					13 19				13 27					13 49				13 57		
Virginia Water	a		13 01					13 23				13 31					13 53				14 01		
	d		13 01					13 23				13 31					13 53				14 01		
Chertsey	d							13 29									13 59						
Addlestone	d							13 32									14 02						
Weybridge	a							13 37									14 07						
Byfleet & New Haw	d																						
West Byfleet	d																						
Woking	a																						
Longcross	d											13 35											
Sunningdale	d		13 07									13 37									14 07		
Ascot ■3	d		13 13		13 23							13 43		13 53							14 13		14 23
Bagshot	d				13 29									13 59									14 29
Camberley	a				13 35									14 05									14 35
Frimley	d				13 43									14 13									14 43
Ash Vale	d				13 49									14 19									14 49
Aldershot	a				13 54									14 24									14 54
	d				14 08									14 38									15 08
Ash ■5	d				14 15									14 45									15 15
Wanborough	d				14 18									14 48									15 18
Guildford	a				14 25									14 55									15 25
Martins Heron	d		13 17									13 47									14 17		
Bracknell	d		13 20									13 50									14 20		
Wokingham	d		13 27									13 57									14 27		
Winnersh	d		13 30									14 00									14 30		
Winnersh Triangle	d		13 32									14 02									14 32		
Earley	d		13 35									14 05									14 35		
Reading ■7	a		13 40									14 10									14 40		

London - Hounslow, Richmond, Kingston, Windsor, Weybridge, Ascot, Guildford and Reading

Network Diagram - see first Page of Table 148

			SW	SW	SW	SW	SW	SW	SW 1	SW	SW 1		SW	SW	SW	SW	SW	SW	SW 1	SW	SW 1		SW	SW	SW
London Waterloo 15 ⊖	d		13 22	13 28		13 33	13 37	13 45	13 50				13 52	13 58		14 03	14 07	14 15	14 20				14 22	14 28	
Vauxhall ⊖	d		13 26	13 32		13 37	13 41	13 49					13 56	14 02		14 07	14 11	14 19					14 26	14 32	
Queenstown Rd.(Battersea)	d		13 29			13 40	13 44	13 52					13 59			14 10	14 14	14 22					14 29		
Clapham Junction 10	d		13 32	13 38		13 43	13 47	13 55	13 58				14 02	14 08		14 13	14 17	14 25	14 28				14 32	14 38	
Wandsworth Town	d		13 35			13 46	13 50	13 58					14 05			14 16	14 20	14 28					14 35		
Putney	d		13 38	13 42		13 49	13 53	14 01					14 08	14 12		14 19	14 23	14 31					14 38	14 42	
Barnes	d		13 42			13 52	13 57	14 05					14 12			14 22	14 27	14 35					14 42		
Barnes Bridge	d		13 44				13 59						14 14				14 29						14 44		
Chiswick	d		13 47				14 02						14 17				14 32						14 47		
Kew Bridge	d		13 50				14 05						14 20				14 35						14 50		
Brentford	d		13 53				14 08						14 23				14 38						14 53		
Syon Lane	d		13 55				14 10						14 25				14 40						14 55		
Isleworth	d		13 57				14 12						14 27				14 42						14 57		
Hounslow	d		14 01				14 18						14 31				14 48						15 01		
Mortlake	d					13 54		14 07								14 24		14 37							
North Sheen	d					13 56		14 09		←						14 26		14 39		←					
Richmond ⊖	d			13 48		13 59		14 12	14 06	14 12				14 18		14 29		14 42	14 36	14 42				14 48	
St Margarets	d					14 01		↪		14 14						14 31		↪		14 44					
Twickenham	a			13 51		14 03			14 10	14 16				14 21		14 33			14 40	14 46				14 51	
	d			13 52		14 04			14 10	14 17				14 22		14 34			14 40	14 47				14 52	
Strawberry Hill	d					14 07										14 37									
Fulwell	a																								
Teddington	a					14 10										14 40									
Hampton Wick	a					14 14										14 44									
Kingston	a					14 16										14 46									
Whitton	d			13 55	←		14a23			14a20				14 25	←		14a53			14a50				14 55	←
Feltham	d		14 06	13 59	14 06				14 16				14 36	14 29	14 36				14 46				15 06	14 59	15 06
Ashford (Surrey)	d		↪	14 03	14 10								↪	14 33	14 40								↪	15 03	15 10
Staines	d			14 07	14 14				14 23					14 37	14 44				14 53					15 07	15 14
Wraysbury	d			14 11										14 41										15 11	
Sunnymeads	d			14 14										14 44										15 14	
Datchet	d			14 17										14 47										15 17	
Windsor & Eton Riverside	a			14 21										14 51										15 21	
Egham	d				14 19				14 27						14 49				14 57						15 19
Virginia Water	a				14 23				14 31						14 53				15 01						15 23
	d				14 23				14 31						14 53				15 01						15 23
Chertsey	d				14 29										14 59										15 29
Addlestone	d				14 32										15 02										15 32
Weybridge	a				14 37										15 07										15 37
Byfleet & New Haw	d																								
West Byfleet	d																								
Woking	a																								
Longcross	d																								
Sunningdale	d								14 37										15 07						
Ascot 3	d								14 43		14 53								15 13		15 23				
Bagshot	d										14 59										15 29				
Camberley	a										15 05										15 35				
Frimley	d										15 13										15 43				
Ash Vale	d										15 19										15 49				
Aldershot	a										15 24										15 54				
	d										15 38										16 08				
Ash 5	d										15 45										16 15				
Wanborough	d										15 48										16 18				
Guildford	a										15 55										16 25				
Martins Heron	d								14 47										15 17						
Bracknell	d								14 50										15 20						
Wokingham	d								14 57										15 27						
Winnersh	d								15 00										15 30						
Winnersh Triangle	d								15 02										15 32						
Earley	d								15 05										15 35						
Reading 7	a								15 10										15 40						

London - Hounslow, Richmond, Kingston, Windsor, Weybridge, Ascot, Guildford and Reading

Network Diagram - see first Page of Table 148

		SW	SW	SW	SW	SW	SW		SW	SW	SW	SW	SW	SW	SW	SW	SW		SW	SW	SW	SW	SW	SW	SW
					1		1								1		1								1
London Waterloo [15] ⊖	d	14 33	14 37	14 45	14 50				14 52	14 58		15 03	15 07	15 15	15 20				15 22	15 28		15 33	15 37	15 45	15 50
Vauxhall ⊖	d	14 37	14 41	14 49					14 56	15 02		15 07	15 11	15 19					15 26	15 32		15 37	15 41	15 49	
Queenstown Rd.(Battersea)	d	14 40	14 44	14 52					14 59			15 10	15 14	15 22					15 29			15 40	15 44	15 52	
Clapham Junction [10]	d	14 43	14 47	14 55	14 58				15 02	15 08		15 13	15 17	15 25	15 28				15 32	15 38		15 43	15 47	15 55	15 58
Wandsworth Town	d	14 46	14 50	14 58					15 05			15 16	15 20	15 28					15 35			15 46	15 50	15 58	
Putney	d	14 49	14 53	15 01					15 08	15 12		15 19	15 23	15 31					15 38	15 42		15 49	15 53	16 01	
Barnes	d	14 52	14 57	15 05					15 12			15 22	15 27	15 35					15 42			15 52	15 57	16 05	
Barnes Bridge	d		14 59						15 14				15 29						15 44				15 59		
Chiswick	d		15 02						15 17				15 32						15 47				16 02		
Kew Bridge	d		15 05						15 20				15 35						15 50				16 05		
Brentford	d		15 08						15 23				15 38						15 53				16 08		
Syon Lane	d		15 10						15 25				15 40						15 55				16 10		
Isleworth	d		15 12						15 27				15 42						15 57				16 12		
Hounslow	d		15 18						15 31				15 48						16 01				16 18		
Mortlake	d	14 54		15 07								15 24		15 37								15 54		16 07	
North Sheen	d	14 56		15 09		←						15 26		15 39		←						15 56		16 09	
Richmond ⊖	d	14 59		15 12	15 06	15 12				15 18		15 29		15 42	15 36	15 42				15 48		15 59		16 12	16 06
St Margarets	d	15 01		↪		15 14						15 31		↪		15 44						16 01		↪	
Twickenham	a	15 03			15 10	15 16				15 21		15 33			15 40	15 46				15 51		16 03			16 10
	d	15 04			15 10	15 17				15 22		15 34			15 40	15 47				15 52		16 04			16 10
Strawberry Hill	d	15 07										15 37										16 07			
Fulwell	a																								
Teddington	a	15 10										15 40										16 10			
Hampton Wick	a	15 14										15 44										16 14			
Kingston	a	15 16										15 46										16 16			
Whitton	d		15a23			15a20				15 25	←		15a53			15a50				15 55	←		16a23		
Feltham	d				15 16				15 36	15 29	15 36				15 46				16 06	15 59	16 06				16 16
Ashford (Surrey)	d								↪	15 33	15 40								↪	16 03	16 10				
Staines	d				15 23					15 37	15 44				15 53					16 07	16 14				16 23
Wraysbury	d									15 41										16 11					
Sunnymeads	d									15 44										16 14					
Datchet	d									15 47										16 17					
Windsor & Eton Riverside	a									15 51										16 21					
Egham	d				15 27						15 49				15 57						16 19				16 27
Virginia Water	a				15 31						15 53				16 01						16 23				16 31
	d				15 31						15 53				16 01						16 23				16 31
Chertsey	d										15 59										16 29				
Addlestone	d										16 02										16 32				
Weybridge	a										16 07										16 37				
Byfleet & New Haw	d																								
West Byfleet	d																								
Woking	a																								
Longcross	d																								
Sunningdale	d				15 37										16 07										16 37
Ascot [3]	d				15 43		15 53								16 13		16 23								16 43
Bagshot	d						15 59										16 29								
Camberley	a						16 05										16 35								
Frimley	d						16 13										16 43								
Ash Vale	d						16 19										16 49								
Aldershot	a						16 24										16 54								
	d						16 38										17 08								
Ash [5]	d						16 45										17 15								
Wanborough	d						16 48										17 18								
Guildford	a						16 55										17 25								
Martins Heron	d				15 47										16 17										16 47
Bracknell	d				15 50										16 20										16 50
Wokingham	d				15 57										16 27										16 57
Winnersh	d				16 00										16 30										17 00
Winnersh Triangle	d				16 02										16 32										17 02
Earley	d				16 05										16 35										17 05
Reading [7]	a				16 10										16 40										17 10

London - Hounslow, Richmond, Kingston, Windsor, Weybridge, Ascot, Guildford and Reading

Network Diagram - see first Page of Table 148

		SW	SW		SW	SW	SW	SW	SW	SW	SW	SW	SW		SW	SW	SW	SW	SW	SW	SW	SW	SW		SW
			1					◇1					◇1			1	◇	◇		◇1	◇				
London Waterloo 15 ⊖	d				15 52	15 58	16 01	16 05			16 07	16 15	16 20				16 22	16 28	16 31	16 35			16 37		16 45
Vauxhall ⊖	d				15 56	16 02	16 05	16 09			16 11	16 19					16 26	16 32	16 35	16 39			16 41		16 49
Queenstown Rd.(Battersea)	d				15 59		16 08				16 14	16 22					16 29		16 38				16 44		16 52
Clapham Junction 10	d				16 02	16 08	16 11	16 15			16 17	16 25	16 28				16 32	16 38	16 41	16 45			16 47		16 55
Wandsworth Town	d				16 05		16 14				16 20	16 28					16 35		16 44				16 50		16 58
Putney	d				16 08	16 12	16 17				16 23	16 31					16 38	16 42	16 47				16 53		17 01
Barnes	d				16 12		16 22				16 27	16 35					16 42		16 52				16 57		17 05
Barnes Bridge	d				16 14						16 29						16 44						16 59		
Chiswick	d				16 17						16 32						16 47						17 02		
Kew Bridge	d				16 20						16 35						16 50						17 05		
Brentford	d				16 23						16 38						16 53						17 08		
Syon Lane	d				16 25						16 40						16 55						17 10		
Isleworth	d				16 27						16 42						16 57						17 12		
Hounslow	d				16 31						16 48						17 01						17 18		
Mortlake	d						16 24					16 37							16 54						17 07
North Sheen	d	←					16 26			←		16 39			←				16 56			←			17 09
Richmond ⊖	d	16 12				16 18	16 29	16 23		16 29		16 42	16 36		16 42			16 48	16 59	16 53		16 59			17 12
St Margarets	d	16 14					→			16 31		→			16 44				→			17 01			→
Twickenham	a	16 16				16 21		16 27		16 33			16 40		16 46			16 51		16 57		17 03			
	d	16 17				16 22		16 27		16 34			16 40		16 47			16 52		16 57		17 04			
Strawberry Hill	d									16 37												17 07			
Fulwell	a																								
Teddington	a									16 42												17 12			
Hampton Wick	a									16 46												17 16			
Kingston	a									16 48												17 18			
Whitton	d	16a20				16 25			←		16a53				16a50			16 55			←		17a23		
Feltham	d				16 36	16 29		16 33	16 36				16 46				17 06	16 59		17 03	17 06				
Ashford (Surrey)	d				→	16 33		16 37	16 40								→	17 03		17 07	17 10				
Staines	d					16 37		16 41	16 44				16 53					17 07		17 11	17 14				
Wraysbury	d					16 41												17 11							
Sunnymeads	d					16 44												17 14							
Datchet	d					16 47												17 17							
Windsor & Eton Riverside	a					16 51												17 23							
Egham	d							16 46	16 49				16 57							17 16	17 19				
Virginia Water	a							16 50	16 53				17 01							17 20	17 23				
	d							16 50	16 53				17 01							17 20	17 23				
Chertsey	d								16 59												17 29				
Addlestone	d								17 02												17 32				
Weybridge	a								17 07												17 40				
Byfleet & New Haw	d																								
West Byfleet	d																								
Woking	a																								
Longcross	d																			17 23					
Sunningdale	d							16 55					17 07							17 27					
Ascot 3	d		16 53					17 00					17 13			17 23				17 31					
Bagshot	d		16 59													17 29									
Camberley	a		17 05													17 35									
Frimley	d		17 13													17 43									
Ash Vale	d		17 19													17 49									
Aldershot	a		17 24													17 54									
	d		17 38													18 08									
Ash 5	d		17 45													18 15									
Wanborough	d		17 48													18 18									
Guildford	a		17 55													18 25									
Martins Heron	d							17 04					17 17							17 35					
Bracknell	d							17 07					17 20							17 39					
Wokingham	d							17 17					17 27							17 47					
Winnersh	d												17 30												
Winnersh Triangle	d												17 32												
Earley	d												17 35												
Reading 7	a							17 27					17 42							17 58					

London - Hounslow, Richmond, Kingston, Windsor, Weybridge, Ascot, Guildford and Reading

Network Diagram - see first Page of Table 148

		SW	SW	SW	SW	SW	SW	SW	SW		SW	SW	SW	SW	SW	SW	SW	SW	SW		SW	SW	SW	SW	SW
		◇1		◇	◇		◇1	◇						◇1		◇	1	◇	1		1		◇1	◇	
London Waterloo 15 ⊖	d	16 50		16 52	16 58	17 01	17 05				17 07	17 13	17 15	17 20		17 22	17 25	17 28				17 31	17 35		
Vauxhall ⊖	d			16 56	17 02	17 05	17 09				17 11	17 17	17 19			17 26		17 32				17 35	17 39		
Queenstown Rd.(Battersea)	d			16 59		17 08					17 14		17 22			17 29						17 38			
Clapham Junction 10	d	16 58		17 02	17 08	17 11	17 15				17 17	17 23	17 25	17 28		17 32		17 38				17 41	17 45		
Wandsworth Town	d			17 05		17 14					17 20		17 28			17 35						17 44			
Putney	d			17 08	17 12	17 17					17 23	17 27	17 31			17 38		17 42				17 47			
Barnes	d			17 12		17 22					17 27		17 35			17 42						17 52			
Barnes Bridge	d			17 14							17 29					17 44									
Chiswick	d			17 17							17 32					17 47									
Kew Bridge	d			17 20							17 35					17 50									
Brentford	d			17 23							17 38					17 53									
Syon Lane	d			17 25							17 40					17 55									
Isleworth	d			17 27							17 42					17 57									
Hounslow	d			17 31							17 48					18 01									
Mortlake	d					17 24							17 37									17 54			
North Sheen	d		←			17 26			←				17 39		←							17 56			←
Richmond ⊖	d	17 06	17 12		17 18	17 29	17 23		17 29			17 33	17 42	17 36	17 42			17 48				17 59	17 53		17 59
St Margarets	d		17 14			↪			17 31				↪		17 44							↪			18 01
Twickenham	a	17 10	17 16		17 21		17 27		17 33			17 37		17 40	17 46			17 51					17 57		18 03
	d	17 10	17 17		17 22		17 27		17 34			17 37		17 40	17 47			17 52					17 57		18 04
Strawberry Hill	d								17 37			17 41													18 07
Fulwell	a																								
Teddington	a								17 42			17 46													18 12
Hampton Wick	a								17 46			17 54													18 16
Kingston	a								17 48			17 56													18 18
Whitton	d		17a20		17 25			←			17a53				17a50			17 55						←	
Feltham	d	17 16		17 36	17 29		17 33	17 36						17 46		18 06		17 59					18 03	18 06	
Ashford (Surrey)	d			↪	17 33		17 37	17 40								↪		18 03					18 07	18 10	
Staines	d	17 23			17 37		17 41	17 44						17 53				18 07					18 11	18 14	
Wraysbury	d				17 41													18 11							
Sunnymeads	d				17 44													18 14							
Datchet	d				17 47													18 17							
Windsor & Eton Riverside	a				17 53													18 23							
Egham	d	17 27					17 46	17 49						17 57									18 16	18 19	
Virginia Water	a	17 31					17 50	17 53						18 01									18 20	18 23	
	d	17 31					17 50	17 53						18 01									18 20	18 23	
Chertsey	d							17 59																18 29	
Addlestone	d							18 02																18 32	
Weybridge	a							18 10																18 40	
Byfleet & New Haw	d																								
West Byfleet	d																								
Woking	a																17 50								
Longcross	d																								
Sunningdale	d	17 37					17 55							18 07									18 25		
Ascot 3	d	17 43					18 00							18 13							18 23		18 30		
Bagshot	d						18 06														18 29				
Camberley	a						18 12														18 35				
Frimley	d						18 17														18 43				
Ash Vale	d						18 24										18 03				18 49				
Aldershot	a						18 31										18 08				18 54				
	d																		18 38		19 08				
Ash 5	d																		18 45		19 15				
Wanborough	d																		18 48		19 18				
Guildford	a																		18 55		19 25				
Martins Heron	d	17 47												18 17									18 34		
Bracknell	d	17 50												18 20									18 37		
Wokingham	d	17 57												18 27									18 47		
Winnersh	d	18 00												18 30											
Winnersh Triangle	d	18 02												18 32											
Earley	d	18 05												18 35											
Reading 7	a	18 12												18 42									18 57		

London - Hounslow, Richmond, Kingston, Windsor, Weybridge, Ascot, Guildford and Reading

Network Diagram - see first Page of Table 148

		SW	SW	SW	SW	SW	SW	SW	SW	SW	SW	SW	SW	SW	SW	SW	SW	SW	SW	SW	SW	SW	SW
					◇ 1		◇	◇		◇ 1	◇					◇ 1		◇	1	◇	1	1	
London Waterloo 15 ⊖	d	17 37	17 43	17 45	17 50		17 52	17 58	18 01	18 05			18 07	18 13	18 15	18 20		18 22	18 25	18 28			18 31
Vauxhall ⊖	d	17 41	17 47	17 49			17 56	18 02	18 05	18 09			18 11	18 17	18 19			18 26		18 32			18 35
Queenstown Rd.(Battersea)	d	17 44		17 52			17 59		18 08				18 14		18 22			18 29					18 38
Clapham Junction 10	d	17 47	17 53	17 55	17 58		18 02	18 08	18 11	18 15			18 17	18 23	18 25	18 28		18 32		18 38			18 41
Wandsworth Town	d	17 50		17 58			18 05		18 14				18 20		18 28			18 35					18 44
Putney	d	17 53	17 57	18 01			18 08	18 12	18 17				18 23	18 27	18 31			18 38		18 42			18 47
Barnes	d	17 57		18 05			18 12		18 22				18 27		18 35			18 42					18 52
Barnes Bridge	d	17 59					18 14						18 29					18 44					
Chiswick	d	18 02					18 17						18 32					18 47					
Kew Bridge	d	18 05					18 20						18 35					18 50					
Brentford	d	18 08					18 23						18 38					18 53					
Syon Lane	d	18 10					18 25						18 40					18 55					
Isleworth	d	18 12					18 27						18 42					18 57					
Hounslow	d	18 18					18 31						18 48					19 01					
Mortlake	d			18 07					18 24						18 37								18 54
North Sheen	d			18 09		←			18 26			←			18 39		←						18 56
Richmond ⊖	d		18 03	18 12	18 06	18 12		18 18	18 29	18 23		18 29		18 33	18 42	18 36	18 42			18 48			18 59
St Margarets	d			↪		18 14			↪			18 31			↪		18 44						↪
Twickenham	a		18 07		18 10	18 16		18 21		18 27		18 33		18 37		18 40	18 46			18 51			
	d		18 07		18 10	18 17		18 22		18 27		18 34		18 37		18 40	18 47			18 52			
Strawberry Hill	d		18 11									18 37		18 41									
Fulwell	a		18 13											18 43									
Teddington	a											18 42											
Hampton Wick	a											18 46											
Kingston	a											18 48											
Whitton	d	18a23				18a20		18 25			←		18a53				18a50			18 55			
Feltham	d				18 16		18 36	18 29		18 33	18 36					18 46		19 06		18 59			
Ashford (Surrey)	d						↪	18 33		18 37	18 40							↪		19 03			
Staines	d				18 23			18 37		18 41	18 44					18 53				19 07			
Wraysbury	d							18 41												19 11			
Sunnymeads	d							18 44												19 14			
Datchet	d							18 47												19 17			
Windsor & Eton Riverside	a							18 53												19 23			
Egham	d				18 27					18 46	18 49					18 57							
Virginia Water	a				18 31					18 50	18 53					19 01							
	d				18 31					18 50	18 53					19 01							
Chertsey	d										18 59												
Addlestone	d										19 02												
Weybridge	a										19 10												
Byfleet & New Haw	d																						
West Byfleet	d																						
Woking	a																		18 52				
Longcross	d				18 35																		
Sunningdale	d				18 37					18 55						19 07							
Ascot 3	d				18 43					19 02						19 13						19 23	
Bagshot	d									19 08												19 29	
Camberley	a									19 14												19 35	
Frimley	d									19 19												19 43	
Ash Vale	d									19 26									19 05			19 49	
Aldershot	a									19 34									19 10			19 54	
	d																				19 38	20 08	
Ash 5	d																				19 45	20 15	
Wanborough	d																				19 48	20 18	
Guildford	a																				19 55	20 25	
Martins Heron	d				18 47											19 17							
Bracknell	d				18 50											19 20							
Wokingham	d				18 57											19 27							
Winnersh	d				19 00											19 30							
Winnersh Triangle	d				19 02											19 32							
Earley	d				19 05											19 35							
Reading 7	a				19 12											19 42							

London - Hounslow, Richmond, Kingston, Windsor, Weybridge, Ascot, Guildford and Reading

Network Diagram - see first Page of Table 148

		SW ◇1	SW ◇	SW	SW	SW	SW	SW ◇1	SW	SW 1	SW ◇	SW ◇	SW	SW 1	SW ◇	SW	SW	SW	SW 1	SW	SW 1	SW
London Waterloo 15 ⊖	d	18 35			18 37	18 43	18 45	18 50			18 52	18 58	19 01	19 05			19 07	19 15	19 20			19 22
Vauxhall ⊖	d	18 39			18 41	18 47	18 49				18 56	19 02	19 05	19 09			19 11	19 19				19 26
Queenstown Rd.(Battersea)	d				18 44		18 52				18 59		19 08				19 14	19 22				19 29
Clapham Junction 10	d	18 45			18 47	18 53	18 55	18 58			19 02	19 08	19 11	19 15			19 17	19 25	19 28			19 32
Wandsworth Town	d				18 50		18 58				19 05		19 14				19 20	19 28				19 35
Putney	d				18 53	18 57	19 01				19 08	19 12	19 17				19 23	19 31				19 38
Barnes	d				18 57		19 05				19 12		19 22				19 27	19 35				19 42
Barnes Bridge	d				18 59						19 14						19 29					19 44
Chiswick	d				19 02						19 17						19 32					19 47
Kew Bridge	d				19 05						19 20						19 35					19 50
Brentford	d				19 08						19 23						19 38					19 53
Syon Lane	d				19 10						19 25						19 40					19 55
Isleworth	d				19 12						19 27						19 42					19 57
Hounslow	d				19 18						19 31						19 48					20 01
Mortlake	d						19 07						19 24					19 37				
North Sheen	d			←			19 09		←				19 26			←		19 39		←		
Richmond ⊖	d	18 53		18 59		19 03	19 12	19 06	19 12			19 18	19 29	19 23		19 29		19 42	19 36	19 42		
St Margarets	d			19 01			→		19 14				→			19 31		→		19 44		
Twickenham	a	18 57		19 03		19 07		19 10	19 16			19 21		19 27		19 33			19 40	19 46		
	d	18 57		19 04		19 07		19 10	19 17			19 22		19 27		19 34			19 40	19 47		
Strawberry Hill	d			19 07		19 11										19 37						
Fulwell	a					19 13																
Teddington	a			19 12												19 42						
Hampton Wick	a			19 16												19 46						
Kingston	a			19 18												19 48						
Whitton	d		←		19a23				19a20			19 25			←		19a53			19a50		
Feltham	d	19 03	19 06					19 16			19 36	19 29		19 33	19 36				19 46			20 06
Ashford (Surrey)	d	19 07	19 10								→	19 33		19 37	19 40							→
Staines	d	19 11	19 14					19 23				19 37		19 41	19 44				19 53			
Wraysbury	d											19 41										
Sunnymeads	d											19 44										
Datchet	d											19 47										
Windsor & Eton Riverside	a											19 53										
Egham	d	19 16	19 19					19 27						19 46	19 49				19 57			
Virginia Water	a	19 20	19 23					19 31						19 50	19 53				20 01			
	d	19 20	19 23					19 31						19 50	19 53				20 01			
Chertsey	d		19 29												19 59							
Addlestone	d		19 32												20 02							
Weybridge	a		19 40												20 10							
Byfleet & New Haw	d																					
West Byfleet	d																					
Woking	a																					
Longcross	d																					
Sunningdale	d	19 25						19 37						19 55					20 07			
Ascot 3	d	19 30						19 43		19 53				20 00					20 13		20 23	
Bagshot	d									19 59											20 29	
Camberley	a									20 05											20 35	
Frimley	d									20 13											20 43	
Ash Vale	d									20 19											20 49	
Aldershot	a									20 24											20 54	
	d									20 38											21 08	
Ash 5	d									20 45											21 15	
Wanborough	d									20 48											21 18	
Guildford	a									20 55											21 25	
Martins Heron	d	19 34						19 47						20 04					20 17			
Bracknell	d	19 37						19 50						20 07					20 20			
Wokingham	d	19 47						19 57						20 17					20 27			
Winnersh	d							20 00											20 30			
Winnersh Triangle	d							20 02											20 32			
Earley	d							20 05											20 35			
Reading 7	a	19 57						20 12						20 25					20 40			

London - Hounslow, Richmond, Kingston, Windsor, Weybridge, Ascot, Guildford and Reading

Network Diagram - see first Page of Table 148

		SW	SW	SW	SW	SW	SW 1		SW	SW 1	SW	SW	SW	SW	SW	SW	SW 1		SW	SW 1	SW 1	SW	SW	SW	SW
London Waterloo 15 ⊖	d	19 28		19 33	19 37	19 45	19 50				19 52	19 58		20 03	20 07	20 15	20 20					20 22	20 28		20 33
Vauxhall ⊖	d	19 32		19 37	19 41	19 49					19 56	20 02		20 07	20 11	20 19						20 26	20 32		20 37
Queenstown Rd.(Battersea)	d			19 40	19 44	19 52					19 59			20 10	20 14	20 22						20 29			20 40
Clapham Junction 10	d	19 38		19 43	19 47	19 55	19 58				20 02	20 08		20 13	20 17	20 25	20 28					20 32	20 38		20 43
Wandsworth Town	d			19 46	19 50	19 58					20 05			20 16	20 20	20 28						20 35			20 46
Putney	d	19 42		19 49	19 53	20 01					20 08	20 12		20 19	20 23	20 31						20 38	20 42		20 49
Barnes	d			19 52	19 57	20 05					20 12			20 22	20 27	20 35						20 42			20 52
Barnes Bridge	d				19 59						20 14				20 29							20 44			
Chiswick	d				20 02						20 17				20 32							20 47			
Kew Bridge	d				20 05						20 20				20 35							20 50			
Brentford	d				20 08						20 23				20 38							20 53			
Syon Lane	d				20 10						20 25				20 40							20 55			
Isleworth	d				20 12						20 27				20 42							20 57			
Hounslow	d				20 18						20 31				20 48							21 01			
Mortlake	d			19 54		20 07								20 24		20 37									20 54
North Sheen	d			19 56		20 09			←					20 26		20 39			←						20 56
Richmond ⊖	d	19 48		19 59		20 12	20 06		20 12			20 18		20 29		20 42	20 36		20 42				20 48		20 59
St Margarets	d			20 01		↪			20 14					20 31		↪			20 44						21 01
Twickenham	a	19 51		20 03			20 10		20 16			20 21		20 33			20 40		20 46				20 51		21 03
	d	19 52		20 04			20 10		20 17			20 22		20 34			20 40		20 47				20 52		21 04
Strawberry Hill	d			20 07										20 37											21 07
Fulwell	a																								
Teddington	a			20 10										20 40											21 10
Hampton Wick	a			20 14										20 44											21 14
Kingston	a			20 16										20 46											21 16
Whitton	d	19 55	←		20a23				20a20			20 25	←		20a53				20a50				20 55	←	
Feltham	d	19 59	20 06				20 16				20 36	20 29	20 36				20 46					21 06	20 59	21 06	
Ashford (Surrey)	d	20 03	20 10								↪	20 33	20 40									↪	21 03	21 10	
Staines	d	20 07	20 14				20 23					20 37	20 44				20 53						21 07	21 14	
Wraysbury	d	20 11										20 41											21 11		
Sunnymeads	d	20 14										20 44											21 14		
Datchet	d	20 17										20 47											21 17		
Windsor & Eton Riverside	a	20 21										20 51											21 21		
Egham	d		20 19				20 27						20 49				20 57							21 19	
Virginia Water	a		20 23				20 31						20 53				21 01							21 23	
	d		20 23				20 31						20 53				21 01							21 23	
Chertsey	d		20 29										20 59											21 29	
Addlestone	d		20 32										21 02											21 32	
Weybridge	a		20 37										21 07											21 37	
Byfleet & New Haw	d																								
West Byfleet	d																								
Woking	a																								
Longcross	d																								
Sunningdale	d						20 37										21 07								
Ascot 3	d						20 43			20 53							21 13			21 23					
Bagshot	d									20 59										21 29					
Camberley	a									21 05										21 35					
Frimley	d									21 13										21 43					
Ash Vale	d									21 19										21 49					
Aldershot	a									21 24										21 54					
	d									21 38										22 08	22 38				
Ash 5	d									21 45										22 15	22 45				
Wanborough	d									21 48										22 18	22 48				
Guildford	a									21 55										22 25	22 55				
Martins Heron	d						20 47										21 17								
Bracknell	d						20 50										21 20								
Wokingham	d						20 57										21 27								
Winnersh	d						21 00										21 30								
Winnersh Triangle	d						21 02										21 32								
Earley	d						21 05										21 35								
Reading 7	a						21 10										21 40								

London - Hounslow, Richmond, Kingston, Windsor, Weybridge, Ascot, Guildford and Reading

Network Diagram - see first Page of Table 148

Station		SW	SW		SW 1	SW	SW	SW	SW	SW	SW	SW	SW 1		SW	SW 1	SW	SW	SW	SW	SW	SW	SW 1		SW
London Waterloo 15 ⊖	d	20 37	20 45		20 50		20 52	20 58		21 03	21 07	21 15	21 20				21 22	21 28		21 33	21 37	21 45	21 50		
Vauxhall ⊖	d	20 41	20 49				20 56	21 02		21 07	21 11	21 19					21 26	21 32		21 37	21 41	21 49			
Queenstown Rd.(Battersea)	d	20 44	20 52				20 59			21 10	21 14	21 22					21 29			21 40	21 44	21 52			
Clapham Junction 10	d	20 47	20 55		20 58		21 02	21 08		21 13	21 17	21 25	21 28				21 32	21 38		21 43	21 47	21 55	21 58		
Wandsworth Town	d	20 50	20 58				21 05			21 16	21 20	21 28					21 35			21 46	21 50	21 58			
Putney	d	20 53	21 01				21 08	21 12		21 19	21 23	21 31					21 38	21 42		21 49	21 53	22 01			
Barnes	d	20 57	21 05				21 12			21 22	21 27	21 35					21 42			21 52	21 57	22 05			
Barnes Bridge	d	20 59					21 14				21 29						21 44				21 59				
Chiswick	d	21 02					21 17				21 32						21 47				22 02				
Kew Bridge	d	21 05					21 20				21 35						21 50				22 05				
Brentford	d	21 08					21 23				21 38						21 53				22 08				
Syon Lane	d	21 10					21 25				21 40						21 55				22 10				
Isleworth	d	21 12					21 27				21 42						21 57				22 12				
Hounslow	d	21 18					21 31				21 48						22 01				22 18				
Mortlake	d		21 07							21 24		21 37								21 54		22 07			
North Sheen	d		21 09			←				21 26		21 39			←					21 56		22 09			←
Richmond ⊖	d		21 12		21 06	21 12		21 18		21 29		21 42	21 36		21 42			21 48		21 59		22 12	22 06		22 12
St Margarets	d		↪			21 14				21 31		↪			21 44					22 01		↪			22 14
Twickenham	a				21 10	21 16		21 21		21 33			21 40		21 46			21 51		22 03			22 10		22 16
	d				21 10	21 17		21 22		21 34			21 40		21 47			21 52		22 04			22 10		
Strawberry Hill	d									21 37										22 07					
Fulwell	a																								
Teddington	a									21 40										22 10					
Hampton Wick	a									21 44										22 14					
Kingston	a									21 46										22 16					
Whitton	d	21a23				21a20		21 25	←		21a53				21a50			21 55	←		22a23				
Feltham	d				21 16		21 36	21 29	21 36				21 46				22 06	21 59	22 06				22 16		
Ashford (Surrey)	d						↪	21 33	21 40								↪	22 03	22 10						
Staines	d				21 23			21 37	21 44				21 53					22 07	22 14				22 23		
Wraysbury	d							21 41										22 11							
Sunnymeads	d							21 44										22 14							
Datchet	d							21 47										22 17							
Windsor & Eton Riverside	a							21 51										22 21							
Egham	d				21 27				21 49				21 57						22 19				22 27		
Virginia Water	a				21 31				21 53				22 01						22 23				22 31		
	d				21 31				21 53				22 01						22 23				22 31		
Chertsey	d								21 59										22 29						
Addlestone	d								22 02										22 32						
Weybridge	a								22 07										22 37						
Byfleet & New Haw	d																								
West Byfleet	d																								
Woking	a																								
Longcross	d																								
Sunningdale	d				21 37								22 07										22 37		
Ascot 3	d				21 43								22 13			22 23							22 43		
Bagshot	d															22 29									
Camberley	a															22 35									
Frimley	d															22 43									
Ash Vale	d															22 49									
Aldershot	a															22 54									
	d															23 08									
Ash 5	d															23 15									
Wanborough	d															23 18									
Guildford	a															23 25									
Martins Heron	d				21 47								22 17										22 47		
Bracknell	d				21 50								22 20										22 50		
Wokingham	d				21 57								22 27										22 57		
Winnersh	d				22 00								22 30										23 00		
Winnersh Triangle	d				22 02								22 32										23 02		
Earley	d				22 05								22 35										23 05		
Reading 7	a				22 10								22 40										23 10		

London - Hounslow, Richmond, Kingston, Windsor, Weybridge, Ascot, Guildford and Reading

Network Diagram - see first Page of Table 148

		SW	SW	SW	SW	SW	SW	SW	SW		SW	SW	SW	SW	SW	SW	SW	SW	SW		SW	SW	SW	SW	SW
						1	1						1						1						
London Waterloo 15 ⊖	d	21 52	21 58		22 03	22 20		22 22	22 28			22 33	22 50	22 52	22 58		23 03	23 13	23 20		23 22	23 33	23 38		
Vauxhall ⊖	d	21 56	22 02		22 07			22 26	22 32			22 37		22 56	23 02		23 07	23 17			23 26	23 37			
Queenstown Rd.(Battersea)	d	21 59			22 10			22 29				22 40		22 59			23 10				23 29	23 40			
Clapham Junction 10	d	22 02	22 08		22 13	22 28		22 32	22 38			22 43	22 58	23 02	23 08		23 13	23 23	23 28		23 32	23 43	23 46		
Wandsworth Town	d	22 05			22 16			22 35				22 46		23 05			23 16				23 35	23 46			
Putney	d	22 08	22 12		22 19			22 38	22 42			22 49		23 08	23 12		23 19	23 27			23 38	23 49			
Barnes	d	22 12			22 22			22 42				22 52		23 12			23 22				23 42	23 52			
Barnes Bridge	d	22 14						22 44						23 14							23 44				
Chiswick	d	22 17						22 47						23 17							23 47				
Kew Bridge	d	22 20						22 50						23 20							23 50				
Brentford	d	22 23						22 53						23 23							23 53				
Syon Lane	d	22 25						22 55						23 25							23 55				
Isleworth	d	22 27						22 57						23 27							23 57				
Hounslow	d	22 31						23 01						23 31							00 01				
Mortlake	d				22 24							22 54					23 24					23 54			
North Sheen	d				22 26							22 56					23 26					23 56			←
Richmond ⊖	d		22 18		22 29	22 36			22 48			22 59	23 06		23 18		23 29	23 33	23 37			23 59	23 54		23 59
St Margarets	d				22 31							23 01					23 31					→			00 01
Twickenham	a		22 21		22 33	22 40			22 51			23 03	23 10		23 21		23 33	23 36	23 41				23 58		00 03
	d		22 22		22 34	22 40			22 52			23 04	23 10		23 22		23 34	23 37	23 41				23 58		00 04
Strawberry Hill	d				22 37							23 07					23 37								00 07
Fulwell	a																								
Teddington	a				22 40							23 10					23 40								00 11
Hampton Wick	a				22 44							23 14					23 44								00 14
Kingston	a				22 46							23 16					23 46								00 16
Whitton	d		22 25	←					22 55		←				23 25	←		23 40						←	
Feltham	d	22 36	22 29	22 36		22 46		23 06	22 59		23 06		23 16	23 36	23 29	23 36		23 44	23 48		00 06		00 04	00 06	
Ashford (Surrey)	d	→	22 33	22 40				→	23 03		23 10			→	23 33	23 40		23 48			→			00 10	
Staines	d		22 37	22 44		22 53			23 07		23 14		23 23		23 37	23 44		23 52	23 56				00 11	00 14	
Wraysbury	d		22 41						23 11						23 41			23 56							
Sunnymeads	d		22 44						23 14						23 44			23 59							
Datchet	d		22 47						23 17						23 47			00 02							
Windsor & Eton Riverside	a		22 51						23 21						23 51			00 06							
Egham	d			22 49		22 57					23 19		23 27			23 49			00 01				00 15	00 19	
Virginia Water	a			22 53		23 01					23 23		23 31			23 53			00 05				00 19	00 23	
	d			22 53		23 01					23 23		23 31			23 53			00 05				00 19	00 23	
Chertsey	d			22 59							23 29					23 59								00 29	
Addlestone	d			23 02							23a32					00 02								00a32	
Weybridge	a			23 07							23 37														
Byfleet & New Haw	d															00 06									
West Byfleet	d															00 09									
Woking	a															00 15									
Longcross	d																								
Sunningdale	d					23 07							23 37						00 11				00 25		
Ascot 3	d					23 13	23 23						23 43						00 15				00 30		
Bagshot	d						23 29																		
Camberley	a						23 35																		
Frimley	d						23 43																		
Ash Vale	d						23 49																		
Aldershot	a						23 54																		
	d																								
Ash 5	d																								
Wanborough	d																								
Guildford	a																								
Martins Heron	d					23 17							23 47						00 19				00 34		
Bracknell	d					23 20							23 50						00 23				00 37		
Wokingham	d					23 27							23 57						00 32				00 44		
Winnersh	d					23 30							23 59						00 36						
Winnersh Triangle	d					23 32							00 02						00 38						
Earley	d					23 35							00 05						00 40						
Reading 7	a					23 40							00 10						00 45				00 52		

London - Hounslow, Richmond, Kingston, Windsor, Weybridge, Ascot, Guildford and Reading

Network Diagram - see first Page of Table 148

			SW	SW	SW
London Waterloo 15	⊖	d	23 52	23 58	
Vauxhall	⊖	d	23 56	00 02	
Queenstown Rd.(Battersea)		d	23 59		
Clapham Junction 10		d	00 02	00 08	
Wandsworth Town		d	00 05		
Putney		d	00 08	00 12	
Barnes		d	00 12		
Barnes Bridge		d	00 14		
Chiswick		d	00 17		
Kew Bridge		d	00 20		
Brentford		d	00 23		
Syon Lane		d	00 25		
Isleworth		d	00 27		
Hounslow		d	00 31		
Mortlake		d			
North Sheen		d			
Richmond	⊖	d		00 18	
St Margarets		d			
Twickenham		a		00 21	
		d		00 22	
Strawberry Hill		d			
Fulwell		a			
Teddington		a			
Hampton Wick		a			
Kingston		a			
Whitton		d		00 25	←
Feltham		d	00 37	00 29	00 37
Ashford (Surrey)		d	→	00 33	00 41
Staines		d		00a37	00a46
Wraysbury		d			
Sunnymeads		d			
Datchet		d			
Windsor & Eton Riverside		a			
Egham		d			
Virginia Water		a			
		d			
Chertsey		d			
Addlestone		d			
Weybridge		a			
Byfleet & New Haw		d			
West Byfleet		d			
Woking		a			
Longcross		d			
Sunningdale		d			
Ascot 3		d			
Bagshot		d			
Camberley		a			
Frimley		d			
Ash Vale		d			
Aldershot		a			
		d			
Ash 5		d			
Wanborough		d			
Guildford		a			
Martins Heron		d			
Bracknell		d			
Wokingham		d			
Winnersh		d			
Winnersh Triangle		d			
Earley		d			
Reading 7		a			

Table 149

Saturdays

London - Hounslow, Richmond, Kingston, Windsor, Weybridge, Ascot, Guildford and Reading

Network Diagram - see first Page of Table 148

		SW 1	SW	SW	SW 1	SW	SW	SW	SW	SW		SW 1	SW 1	SW 1	SW 1	SW	SW	SW	SW	SW		SW 1	SW	SW 1	SW
London Waterloo 15 ⊖	d	22p50	22p52	23p13	23p20	23p22	23p33	23p38								23p52	23p58		00 18					05 05	
Vauxhall ⊖	d		22p56	23p17		23p26	23p37									23p56	00 02		00 22					05 09	
Queenstown Rd.(Battersea)	d		22p59			23p29	23p40									23p59			00 25					05 12	
Clapham Junction 10	d	22p58	23p02	23p23	23p28	23p32	23p43	23p46								00 02	00 08		00 29					05 15	
Wandsworth Town	d		23p05			23p35	23p46									00 05			00 32					05 18	
Putney	d		23p08	23p27		23p38	23p49									00 08	00 12		00 35					05 21	
Barnes	d		23p12			23p42	23p52									00 12			00 38					05 24	
Barnes Bridge	d		23p14			23p44										00 14									
Chiswick	d		23p17			23p47										00 17									
Kew Bridge	d		23p20			23p50										00 20									
Brentford	d		23p23			23p53										00 23									
Syon Lane	d		23p25			23p55										00 25									
Isleworth	d		23p27			23p57										00 27									
Hounslow	d		23p31			00 01										00 31									
Mortlake	d						23p54												00 40					05 26	
North Sheen	d						23p56			←									00 42					05 28	
Richmond ⊖	d	23p06		23p33	23p37		23p59	23p54		23p59							00 18		00 45					05 31	
St Margarets	d						→			00 01									00 47					05 33	
Twickenham	a	23p10		23p36	23p41			23p58		00 03							00 21		00 49					05 35	
	d	23p10		23p37	23p41			23p58		00 04							00 22		00 50	04 52				05 36	05 38
Strawberry Hill	d									00 07									00s53	04 55					
Fulwell	a																								
Teddington	a									00 11									00s56	04 58					
Hampton Wick	a									00 14									00s59	05 01					
Kingston	a									00 16									01 01	05 03					
Whitton	d			23p40					←								00 25	←						05 39	05a41
Feltham	d	23p16	23p36	23p44	23p48	00 06		00 04	00 06							00 37	00 29	00 37						05 43	
Ashford (Surrey)	d		23p40	23p48		→			00 10							→	00 33	00 41						05 47	
Staines	d	23p23	23p44	23p52	23p56			00 11	00 14								00a37	00a46				05 23	05 44	05 53	
Wraysbury	d			23p56																					
Sunnymeads	d			23p59																					
Datchet	d			00 02																					
Windsor & Eton Riverside	a			00 06																					
Egham	d	23p27	23p49		00 01			00 15	00 19													05 27	05 49	05 57	
Virginia Water	a	23p31	23p53		00 05			00 19	00 23													05 31	05 53	06 01	
	d	23p31	23p53		00 05			00 19	00 23													05 31	05 53	06 01	
Chertsey	d		23p59						00 29														05 59		
Addlestone	d		00 02						00a32														06 02		
Weybridge	a																						06 07		
Byfleet & New Haw	d		00 06																						
West Byfleet	d		00 09																						
Woking	a		00 15																						
Longcross	d																								
Sunningdale	d	23p37			00 11			00 25														05 37		06 07	
Ascot 3	d	23p43			00 15			00 30				00 32										05 43		06 13	
Bagshot	d											00 38													
Camberley	a											00 44													
Frimley	d											00 48													
Ash Vale	d											00 57													
Aldershot	a											01s02													
	d												06 08	06 38	07 08										
Ash 5	d												06 15	06 45	07 15										
Wanborough	d												06 18	06 48	07 18										
Guildford	a												06 25	06 55	07 25										
Martins Heron	d	23p47			00 19			00 34														05 47		06 17	
Bracknell	d	23p50			00 23			00 37														05 50		06 20	
Wokingham	d	23p57			00 32			00 44														05 57		06 27	
Winnersh	d	23p59			00 36																	06 00		06 30	
Winnersh Triangle	d	00 02			00 38																	06 02		06 32	
Earley	d	00 05			00 40																	06 05		06 35	
Reading 7	a	00 10			00 45			00 52														06 10		06 40	

London - Hounslow, Richmond, Kingston, Windsor, Weybridge, Ascot, Guildford and Reading

Network Diagram - see first Page of Table 148

		SW	SW	SW	SW 1	SW		SW	SW	SW 1	SW 1	SW 1	SW	SW	SW	SW		SW 1	SW 1	SW	SW	SW	SW	SW	SW 1
London Waterloo 15 ⊖	d		05 33		05 50	05 58		06 03			06 20		06 22	06 28		06 33		06 50		06 52	06 58		07 03	07 15	07 20
Vauxhall ⊖	d		05 37			06 02		06 07					06 26	06 32		06 37				06 56	07 02		07 07	07 19	
Queenstown Rd.(Battersea)	d		05 40					06 10					06 29			06 40				06 59			07 10	07 22	
Clapham Junction 10	d		05 43		05 58	06 08		06 13			06 28		06 32	06 38		06 43		06 58		07 02	07 08		07 13	07 25	07 28
Wandsworth Town	d		05 46					06 16					06 35			06 46				07 05			07 16	07 28	
Putney	d		05 49			06 12		06 19					06 38	06 42		06 49				07 08	07 12		07 19	07 31	
Barnes	d		05 52					06 22					06 42			06 52				07 12			07 22	07 35	
Barnes Bridge	d												06 44							07 14					
Chiswick	d												06 47							07 17					
Kew Bridge	d												06 50							07 20					
Brentford	d												06 53							07 23					
Syon Lane	d												06 55							07 25					
Isleworth	d												06 57							07 27					
Hounslow	d												07 01							07 31					
Mortlake	d		05 54					06 24								06 54							07 24	07 37	
North Sheen	d		05 56					06 26								06 56							07 26	07 39	
Richmond ⊖	d		05 59		06 06	06 18		06 29			06 36			06 48		06 59		07 06			07 18		07 29	07 42	07 36
St Margarets	d		06 01					06 31								07 01							07 31	↪	
Twickenham	a		06 03		06 10	06 21		06 33			06 40			06 51		07 03		07 10			07 21		07 33		07 40
	d	05 53	06 04		06 10	06 22		06 34			06 40			06 52		07 04		07 10			07 22		07 34		07 40
Strawberry Hill	d		06 07					06 37								07 07							07 37		
Fulwell	a																								
Teddington	a		06 10					06 40								07 10							07 40		
Hampton Wick	a		06 14					06 44								07 14							07 44		
Kingston	a		06 16					06 46								07 16							07 46		
Whitton	d	05 56				06 25								06 55	↩						07 25	↩			
Feltham	d	06 00			06 16	06 29					06 46		07 06	06 59	07 06			07 16		07 36	07 29	07 36			07 46
Ashford (Surrey)	d	06 04				06 33							↪	07 03	07 10					↪	07 33	07 40			
Staines	d	06 08		06 16	06 23	06 37			06 44		06 53			07 07	07 14			07 23			07 37	07 44			07 53
Wraysbury	d	06 12				06 41								07 11							07 41				
Sunnymeads	d	06 15				06 44								07 14							07 44				
Datchet	d	06 18				06 47								07 17							07 47				
Windsor & Eton Riverside	a	06 22				06 51								07 21							07 51				
Egham	d			06 20	06 27				06 49		06 57				07 19			07 27				07 49			07 57
Virginia Water	a			06 25	06 31				06 53		07 01				07 23			07 31				07 53			08 01
	d			06 25	06 31				06 53		07 01				07 23			07 31				07 53			08 01
Chertsey	d			06 30					06 59						07 29							07 59			
Addlestone	d			06 33					07 02						07 32							08 02			
Weybridge	a			06 38					07 07						07 37							08 07			
Byfleet & New Haw	d																								
West Byfleet	d																								
Woking	a																								
Longcross	d																								
Sunningdale	d				06 37						07 07							07 37							08 07
Ascot 3	d				06 43					06 53	07 13							07 43	07 53						08 13
Bagshot	d									06 59									07 59						
Camberley	a									07 05									08 05						
Frimley	d									07 13									08 13						
Ash Vale	d									07 19									08 19						
Aldershot	a									07 24									08 24						
	d									07 38		08 08							08 38						
Ash 5	d									07 45		08 15							08 45						
Wanborough	d									07 48		08 18							08 48						
Guildford	a									07 55		08 25							08 55						
Martins Heron	d				06 47						07 17							07 47							08 17
Bracknell	d				06 50						07 20							07 50							08 20
Wokingham	d				06 57						07 27							07 57							08 27
Winnersh	d				07 00						07 30							08 00							08 30
Winnersh Triangle	d				07 02						07 32							08 02							08 32
Earley	d				07 05						07 35							08 05							08 35
Reading 7	a				07 10						07 40							08 10							08 40

Table 149

Saturdays

London - Hounslow, Richmond, Kingston, Windsor, Weybridge, Ascot, Guildford and Reading

Network Diagram - see first Page of Table 148

		SW		SW 1	SW	SW	SW	SW	SW	SW	SW 1	SW		SW 1	SW	SW	SW	SW	SW	SW	SW 1	SW		SW 1	SW
London Waterloo 15 ⊖	d				07 22	07 28		07 33	07 37	07 45	07 50				07 52	07 58		08 03	08 07	08 15	08 20				08 22
Vauxhall ⊖	d				07 26	07 32		07 37	07 41	07 49					07 56	08 02		08 07	08 11	08 19					08 26
Queenstown Rd.(Battersea)	d				07 29			07 40	07 44	07 52					07 59			08 10	08 14	08 22					08 29
Clapham Junction 10	d				07 32	07 38		07 43	07 47	07 55	07 58				08 02	08 08		08 13	08 17	08 25	08 28				08 32
Wandsworth Town	d				07 35			07 46	07 50	07 58					08 05			08 16	08 20	08 28					08 35
Putney	d				07 38	07 42		07 49	07 53	08 01					08 08	08 12		08 19	08 23	08 31					08 38
Barnes	d				07 42			07 52	07 57	08 05					08 12			08 22	08 27	08 35					08 42
Barnes Bridge	d				07 44				07 59						08 14				08 29						08 44
Chiswick	d				07 47				08 02						08 17				08 32						08 47
Kew Bridge	d				07 50				08 05						08 20				08 35						08 50
Brentford	d				07 53				08 08						08 23				08 38						08 53
Syon Lane	d				07 55				08 10						08 25				08 40						08 55
Isleworth	d				07 57				08 12						08 27				08 42						08 57
Hounslow	d				08 01				08 18						08 31				08 48						09 01
Mortlake	d							07 54		08 07								08 24		08 37					
North Sheen	d	←						07 56		08 09		←						08 26		08 39		←			
Richmond ⊖	d	07 42				07 48		07 59		08 12	08 06	08 12				08 18		08 29		08 42	08 36	08 42			
St Margarets	d	07 44						08 01		→		08 14						08 31		→		08 44			
Twickenham	a	07 46				07 51		08 03			08 10	08 16				08 21		08 33			08 40	08 46			
	d	07 47				07 52		08 04			08 10	08 17				08 22		08 34			08 40	08 47			
Strawberry Hill	d							08 07										08 37							
Fulwell	a																								
Teddington	a							08 10										08 40							
Hampton Wick	a							08 14										08 44							
Kingston	a							08 16										08 46							
Whitton	d	07a50				07 55	←		08a23			08a20				08 25	←		08a53			08a50			
Feltham	d				08 06	07 59	08 06				08 16				08 36	08 29	08 36				08 46				09 06
Ashford (Surrey)	d				→	08 03	08 10								→	08 33	08 40								→
Staines	d					08 07	08 14				08 23					08 37	08 44				08 53				
Wraysbury	d					08 11										08 41									
Sunnymeads	d					08 14										08 44									
Datchet	d					08 17										08 47									
Windsor & Eton Riverside	a					08 21										08 51									
Egham	d						08 19				08 27						08 49				08 57				
Virginia Water	a						08 23				08 31						08 53				09 01				
	d						08 23				08 31						08 53				09 01				
Chertsey	d						08 29										08 59								
Addlestone	d						08 32										09 02								
Weybridge	a						08 37										09 07								
Byfleet & New Haw	d																								
West Byfleet	d																								
Woking	a																								
Longcross	d																								
Sunningdale	d										08 37										09 07				
Ascot 3	d			08 23							08 43			08 53							09 13			09 23	
Bagshot	d			08 29										08 59										09 29	
Camberley	a			08 35										09 05										09 35	
Frimley	d			08 43										09 13										09 43	
Ash Vale	d			08 49										09 19										09 49	
Aldershot	a			08 54										09 24										09 54	
	d			09 08										09 38										10 08	
Ash 5	d			09 15										09 45										10 15	
Wanborough	d			09 18										09 48										10 18	
Guildford	a			09 25										09 55										10 25	
Martins Heron	d										08 47										09 17				
Bracknell	d										08 50										09 20				
Wokingham	d										08 57										09 27				
Winnersh	d										09 00										09 30				
Winnersh Triangle	d										09 02										09 32				
Earley	d										09 05										09 35				
Reading 7	a										09 10										09 40				

London - Hounslow, Richmond, Kingston, Windsor, Weybridge, Ascot, Guildford and Reading

Network Diagram - see first Page of Table 148

		SW	SW	SW	SW	SW	SW [1]	SW		SW [1]	SW	SW	SW	SW	SW	SW	SW [1]	SW		SW [1]	SW	SW	SW	SW	SW
London Waterloo [15] ⊖	d	08 28		08 33	08 37	08 45	08 50				08 52	08 58		09 03	09 07	09 15	09 20				09 22	09 28		09 33	09 37
Vauxhall ⊖	d	08 32		08 37	08 41	08 49					08 56	09 02		09 07	09 11	09 19					09 26	09 32		09 37	09 41
Queenstown Rd.(Battersea)	d			08 40	08 44	08 52					08 59			09 10	09 14	09 22					09 29			09 40	09 44
Clapham Junction [10]	d	08 38		08 43	08 47	08 55	08 58				09 02	09 08		09 13	09 17	09 25	09 28				09 32	09 38		09 43	09 47
Wandsworth Town	d			08 46	08 50	08 58					09 05			09 16	09 20	09 28					09 35			09 46	09 50
Putney	d	08 42		08 49	08 53	09 01					09 08	09 12		09 19	09 23	09 31					09 38	09 42		09 49	09 53
Barnes	d			08 52	08 57	09 05					09 12			09 22	09 27	09 35					09 42			09 52	09 57
Barnes Bridge	d				08 59						09 14				09 29						09 44				09 59
Chiswick	d				09 02						09 17				09 32						09 47				10 02
Kew Bridge	d				09 05						09 20				09 35						09 50				10 05
Brentford	d				09 08						09 23				09 38						09 53				10 08
Syon Lane	d				09 10						09 25				09 40						09 55				10 10
Isleworth	d				09 12						09 27				09 42						09 57				10 12
Hounslow	d				09 18						09 31				09 48						10 01				10 18
Mortlake	d			08 54		09 07								09 24		09 37								09 54	
North Sheen	d			08 56		09 09		←						09 26		09 39		←						09 56	
Richmond ⊖	d	08 48		08 59		09 12	09 06	09 12				09 18		09 29		09 42	09 36	09 42				09 48		09 59	
St Margarets	d			09 01		→		09 14						09 31		→		09 44						10 01	
Twickenham	a	08 51		09 03			09 10	09 16				09 21		09 33			09 40	09 46				09 51		10 03	
	d	08 52		09 04			09 10	09 17				09 22		09 34			09 40	09 47				09 52		10 04	
Strawberry Hill	d			09 07										09 37										10 07	
Fulwell	a																								
Teddington	a			09 10										09 40										10 10	
Hampton Wick	a			09 14										09 44										10 14	
Kingston	a			09 16										09 46										10 16	
Whitton	d	08 55	←		09a23			09a20				09 25	←		09a53			09a50				09 55	←		10a23
Feltham	d	08 59	09 06				09 16				09 36	09 29	09 36				09 46				10 06	09 59	10 06		
Ashford (Surrey)	d	09 03	09 10								→	09 33	09 40								→	10 03	10 10		
Staines	d	09 07	09 14				09 23					09 37	09 44				09 53					10 07	10 14		
Wraysbury	d	09 11										09 41										10 11			
Sunnymeads	d	09 14										09 44										10 14			
Datchet	d	09 17										09 47										10 17			
Windsor & Eton Riverside	a	09 21										09 51										10 21			
Egham	d		09 19				09 27						09 49				09 57						10 19		
Virginia Water	a		09 23				09 31						09 53				10 01						10 23		
	d		09 23				09 31						09 53				10 01						10 23		
Chertsey	d		09 29										09 59										10 29		
Addlestone	d		09 32										10 02										10 32		
Weybridge	a		09 37										10 07										10 37		
Byfleet & New Haw	d																								
West Byfleet	d																								
Woking	a																								
Longcross	d																								
Sunningdale	d						09 37										10 07								
Ascot [3]	d						09 43			09 53							10 13			10 23					
Bagshot	d									09 59										10 29					
Camberley	a									10 05										10 35					
Frimley	d									10 13										10 43					
Ash Vale	d									10 19										10 49					
Aldershot	a									10 24										10 54					
	d									10 38										11 08					
Ash [5]	d									10 45										11 15					
Wanborough	d									10 48										11 18					
Guildford	a									10 55										11 25					
Martins Heron	d						09 47										10 17								
Bracknell	d						09 50										10 20								
Wokingham	d						09 57										10 27								
Winnersh	d						10 00										10 30								
Winnersh Triangle	d						10 02										10 32								
Earley	d						10 05										10 35								
Reading [7]	a						10 10										10 40								

London - Hounslow, Richmond, Kingston, Windsor, Weybridge, Ascot, Guildford and Reading

Network Diagram - see first Page of Table 148

		SW	SW 1	SW		SW 1	SW	SW	SW	SW	SW	SW	SW 1	SW		SW 1	SW	SW	SW	SW	SW	SW	SW 1	SW	
London Waterloo 15 ⊖	d	09 45	09 50				09 52	09 58		10 03	10 07	10 15	10 20				10 22	10 28		10 33	10 37	10 45	10 50		
Vauxhall ⊖	d	09 49					09 56	10 02		10 07	10 11	10 19					10 26	10 32		10 37	10 41	10 49			
Queenstown Rd.(Battersea)	d	09 52					09 59			10 10	10 14	10 22					10 29			10 40	10 44	10 52			
Clapham Junction 10	d	09 55	09 58				10 02	10 08		10 13	10 17	10 25	10 28				10 32	10 38		10 43	10 47	10 55	10 58		
Wandsworth Town	d	09 58					10 05			10 16	10 20	10 28					10 35			10 46	10 50	10 58			
Putney	d	10 01					10 08	10 12		10 19	10 23	10 31					10 38	10 42		10 49	10 53	11 01			
Barnes	d	10 05					10 12			10 22	10 27	10 35					10 42			10 52	10 57	11 05			
Barnes Bridge	d						10 14				10 29						10 44				10 59				
Chiswick	d						10 17				10 32						10 47				11 02				
Kew Bridge	d						10 20				10 35						10 50				11 05				
Brentford	d						10 23				10 38						10 53				11 08				
Syon Lane	d						10 25				10 40						10 55				11 10				
Isleworth	d						10 27				10 42						10 57				11 12				
Hounslow	d						10 31				10 48						11 01				11 18				
Mortlake	d	10 07								10 24		10 37								10 54		11 07			
North Sheen	d	10 09		←						10 26		10 39		←						10 56		11 09		←	
Richmond ⊖	d	10 12	10 06	10 12				10 18		10 29		10 42	10 36	10 42				10 48		10 59		11 12	11 06	11 12	
St Margarets	d	↪		10 14						10 31		↪		10 44						11 01		↪		11 14	
Twickenham	a		10 10	10 16				10 21		10 33			10 40	10 46				10 51		11 03			11 10	11 16	
	d		10 10	10 17				10 22		10 34			10 40	10 47				10 52		11 04			11 10	11 17	
Strawberry Hill	d									10 37										11 07					
Fulwell	a																								
Teddington	a									10 40										11 10					
Hampton Wick	a									10 44										11 14					
Kingston	a									10 46										11 16					
Whitton	d			10a20				10 25	←		10a53			10a50				10 55	←		11a23			11a20	
Feltham	d		10 16				10 36	10 29	10 36				10 46				11 06	10 59	11 06				11 16		
Ashford (Surrey)	d						↪	10 33	10 40								↪	11 03	11 10						
Staines	d		10 23					10 37	10 44				10 53					11 07	11 14				11 23		
Wraysbury	d							10 41										11 11							
Sunnymeads	d							10 44										11 14							
Datchet	d							10 47										11 17							
Windsor & Eton Riverside	a							10 51										11 21							
Egham	d		10 27						10 49				10 57						11 19				11 27		
Virginia Water	a		10 31						10 53				11 01						11 23				11 31		
	d		10 31						10 53				11 01						11 23				11 31		
Chertsey	d								10 59										11 29						
Addlestone	d								11 02										11 32						
Weybridge	a								11 07										11 37						
Byfleet & New Haw	d																								
West Byfleet	d																								
Woking	a																								
Longcross	d																								
Sunningdale	d		10 37										11 07										11 37		
Ascot 3	d		10 43			10 53							11 13			11 23							11 43		
Bagshot	d					10 59										11 29									
Camberley	a					11 05										11 35									
Frimley	d					11 13										11 43									
Ash Vale	d					11 19										11 49									
Aldershot	a					11 24										11 54									
	d					11 38										12 08									
Ash 5	d					11 45										12 15									
Wanborough	d					11 48										12 18									
Guildford	a					11 55										12 25									
Martins Heron	d		10 47										11 17										11 47		
Bracknell	d		10 50										11 20										11 50		
Wokingham	d		10 57										11 27										11 57		
Winnersh	d		11 00										11 30										12 00		
Winnersh Triangle	d		11 02										11 32										12 02		
Earley	d		11 05										11 35										12 05		
Reading 7	a		11 10										11 40										12 10		

Table 149

Saturdays

London - Hounslow, Richmond, Kingston, Windsor, Weybridge, Ascot, Guildford and Reading

Network Diagram - see first Page of Table 148

		SW 1	SW	SW	SW	SW	SW	SW	SW 1	SW		SW 1	SW	SW	SW	SW	SW	SW	SW 1	SW		SW 1	SW	SW	SW
London Waterloo 15 ⊖	d		10 52	10 58		11 03	11 07	11 15	11 20				11 22	11 28		11 33	11 37	11 45	11 50				11 52	11 58	
Vauxhall ⊖	d		10 56	11 02		11 07	11 11	11 19					11 26	11 32		11 37	11 41	11 49					11 56	12 02	
Queenstown Rd.(Battersea)	d		10 59			11 10	11 14	11 22					11 29			11 40	11 44	11 52					11 59		
Clapham Junction 10	d		11 02	11 08		11 13	11 17	11 25	11 28				11 32	11 38		11 43	11 47	11 55	11 58				12 02	12 08	
Wandsworth Town	d		11 05			11 16	11 20	11 28					11 35			11 46	11 50	11 58					12 05		
Putney	d		11 08	11 12		11 19	11 23	11 31					11 38	11 42		11 49	11 53	12 01					12 08	12 12	
Barnes	d		11 12			11 22	11 27	11 35					11 42			11 52	11 57	12 05					12 12		
Barnes Bridge	d		11 14				11 29						11 44				11 59						12 14		
Chiswick	d		11 17				11 32						11 47				12 02						12 17		
Kew Bridge	d		11 20				11 35						11 50				12 05						12 20		
Brentford	d		11 23				11 38						11 53				12 08						12 23		
Syon Lane	d		11 25				11 40						11 55				12 10						12 25		
Isleworth	d		11 27				11 42						11 57				12 12						12 27		
Hounslow	d		11 31				11 48						12 01				12 18						12 31		
Mortlake	d					11 24		11 37								11 54		12 07							
North Sheen	d					11 26		11 39		←						11 56		12 09		←					
Richmond ⊖	d			11 18		11 29		11 42	11 36	11 42				11 48		11 59		12 12	12 06	12 12				12 18	
St Margarets	d					11 31		→		11 44						12 01		→		12 14					
Twickenham	a			11 21		11 33			11 40	11 46				11 51		12 03			12 10	12 16				12 21	
	d			11 22		11 34			11 40	11 47				11 52		12 04			12 10	12 17				12 22	
Strawberry Hill	d					11 37										12 07									
Fulwell	a																								
Teddington	a					11 40										12 10									
Hampton Wick	a					11 44										12 14									
Kingston	a					11 46										12 16									
Whitton	d			11 25	←		11a53			11a50				11 55	←		12a23			12a20				12 25	←
Feltham	d		11 36	11 29	11 36				11 46				12 06	11 59	12 06				12 16				12 36	12 29	12 36
Ashford (Surrey)	d		→	11 33	11 40								→	12 03	12 10								→	12 33	12 40
Staines	d			11 37	11 44				11 53					12 07	12 14				12 23					12 37	12 44
Wraysbury	d			11 41										12 11										12 41	
Sunnymeads	d			11 44										12 14										12 44	
Datchet	d			11 47										12 17										12 47	
Windsor & Eton Riverside	a			11 51										12 21										12 51	
Egham	d				11 49				11 57						12 19				12 27						12 49
Virginia Water	a				11 53				12 01						12 23				12 31						12 53
	d				11 53				12 01						12 23				12 31						12 53
Chertsey	d				11 59										12 29										12 59
Addlestone	d				12 02										12 32										13 02
Weybridge	a				12 07										12 37										13 07
Byfleet & New Haw	d																								
West Byfleet	d																								
Woking	a																								
Longcross	d																								
Sunningdale	d								12 07										12 37						
Ascot 3	d	11 53							12 13			12 23							12 43			12 53			
Bagshot	d	11 59										12 29										12 59			
Camberley	a	12 05										12 35										13 05			
Frimley	d	12 13										12 43										13 13			
Ash Vale	d	12 19										12 49										13 19			
Aldershot	a	12 24										12 54										13 24			
	d	12 38										13 08										13 38			
Ash 5	d	12 45										13 15										13 45			
Wanborough	d	12 48										13 18										13 48			
Guildford	a	12 55										13 25										13 55			
Martins Heron	d								12 17										12 47						
Bracknell	d								12 20										12 50						
Wokingham	d								12 27										12 57						
Winnersh	d								12 30										13 00						
Winnersh Triangle	d								12 32										13 02						
Earley	d								12 35										13 05						
Reading 7	a								12 40										13 10						

Table 149

Saturdays

London - Hounslow, Richmond, Kingston, Windsor, Weybridge, Ascot, Guildford and Reading

Network Diagram - see first Page of Table 148

		SW	SW	SW	SW	SW		SW	SW	SW	SW	SW	SW	SW	SW	SW		SW	SW	SW	SW	SW	SW	SW	SW
					1			1							1			1							1
London Waterloo 15 ⊖	d	12 03	12 07	12 15	12 20				12 22	12 28		12 33	12 37	12 45	12 50				12 52	12 58		13 03	13 07	13 15	13 20
Vauxhall ⊖	d	12 07	12 11	12 19					12 26	12 32		12 37	12 41	12 49					12 56	13 02		13 07	13 11	13 19	
Queenstown Rd.(Battersea)	d	12 10	12 14	12 22					12 29			12 40	12 44	12 52					12 59			13 10	13 14	13 22	
Clapham Junction 10	d	12 13	12 17	12 25	12 28				12 32	12 38		12 43	12 47	12 55	12 58				13 02	13 08		13 13	13 17	13 25	13 28
Wandsworth Town	d	12 16	12 20	12 28					12 35			12 46	12 50	12 58					13 05			13 16	13 20	13 28	
Putney	d	12 19	12 23	12 31					12 38	12 42		12 49	12 53	13 01					13 08	13 12		13 19	13 23	13 31	
Barnes	d	12 22	12 27	12 35					12 42			12 52	12 57	13 05					13 12			13 22	13 27	13 35	
Barnes Bridge	d		12 29						12 44				12 59						13 14				13 29		
Chiswick	d		12 32						12 47				13 02						13 17				13 32		
Kew Bridge	d		12 35						12 50				13 05						13 20				13 35		
Brentford	d		12 38						12 53				13 08						13 23				13 38		
Syon Lane	d		12 40						12 55				13 10						13 25				13 40		
Isleworth	d		12 42						12 57				13 12						13 27				13 42		
Hounslow	d		12 48						13 01				13 18						13 31				13 48		
Mortlake	d	12 24		12 37								12 54		13 07								13 24		13 37	
North Sheen	d	12 26		12 39		←						12 56		13 09		←						13 26		13 39	
Richmond ⊖	d	12 29		12 42	12 36	12 42				12 48		12 59		13 12	13 06	13 12				13 18		13 29		13 42	13 36
St Margarets	d	12 31		→		12 44						13 01		→		13 14						13 31		→	
Twickenham	a	12 33			12 40	12 46				12 51		13 03			13 10	13 16				13 21		13 33			13 40
	d	12 34			12 40	12 47				12 52		13 04			13 10	13 17				13 22		13 34			13 40
Strawberry Hill	d	12 37										13 07										13 37			
Fulwell	a																								
Teddington	a	12 40										13 10										13 40			
Hampton Wick	a	12 44										13 14										13 44			
Kingston	a	12 46										13 16										13 46			
Whitton	d		12a53			12a50				12 55	←		13a23			13a20				13 25	←		13a53		
Feltham	d				12 46				13 06	12 59	13 06				13 16				13 36	13 29	13 36				13 46
Ashford (Surrey)	d								→	13 03	13 10								→	13 33	13 40				
Staines	d				12 53					13 07	13 14				13 23					13 37	13 44				13 53
Wraysbury	d									13 11										13 41					
Sunnymeads	d									13 14										13 44					
Datchet	d									13 17										13 47					
Windsor & Eton Riverside	a									13 21										13 51					
Egham	d				12 57						13 19				13 27						13 49				13 57
Virginia Water	a				13 01						13 23				13 31						13 53				14 01
	d				13 01						13 23				13 31						13 53				14 01
Chertsey	d										13 29										13 59				
Addlestone	d										13 32										14 02				
Weybridge	a										13 37										14 07				
Byfleet & New Haw	d																								
West Byfleet	d																								
Woking	a																								
Longcross	d																								
Sunningdale	d				13 07										13 37										14 07
Ascot 3	d				13 13			13 23							13 43			13 53							14 13
Bagshot	d							13 29										13 59							
Camberley	a							13 35										14 05							
Frimley	d							13 43										14 13							
Ash Vale	d							13 49										14 19							
Aldershot	a							13 54										14 24							
	d							14 08										14 38							
Ash 5	d							14 15										14 45							
Wanborough	d							14 18										14 48							
Guildford	a							14 25										14 55							
Martins Heron	d				13 17										13 47										14 17
Bracknell	d				13 20										13 50										14 20
Wokingham	d				13 27										13 57										14 27
Winnersh	d				13 30										14 00										14 30
Winnersh Triangle	d				13 32										14 02										14 32
Earley	d				13 35										14 05										14 35
Reading 7	a				13 40										14 10										14 40

Table 149

Saturdays

London - Hounslow, Richmond, Kingston, Windsor, Weybridge, Ascot, Guildford and Reading

Network Diagram - see first Page of Table 148

		SW		SW 1	SW	SW	SW	SW	SW	SW	SW 1	SW		SW 1	SW	SW	SW	SW	SW	SW	SW 1	SW		SW 1	SW
London Waterloo 15 ⊖	d				13 22	13 28		13 33	13 37	13 45	13 50				13 52	13 58		14 03	14 07	14 15	14 20				14 22
Vauxhall ⊖	d				13 26	13 32		13 37	13 41	13 49					13 56	14 02		14 07	14 11	14 19					14 26
Queenstown Rd.(Battersea)	d				13 29			13 40	13 44	13 52					13 59			14 10	14 14	14 22					14 29
Clapham Junction 10	d				13 32	13 38		13 43	13 47	13 55	13 58				14 02	14 08		14 13	14 17	14 25	14 28				14 32
Wandsworth Town	d				13 35			13 46	13 50	13 58					14 05			14 16	14 20	14 28					14 35
Putney	d				13 38	13 42		13 49	13 53	14 01					14 08	14 12		14 19	14 23	14 31					14 38
Barnes	d				13 42			13 52	13 57	14 05					14 12			14 22	14 27	14 35					14 42
Barnes Bridge	d				13 44				13 59						14 14				14 29						14 44
Chiswick	d				13 47				14 02						14 17				14 32						14 47
Kew Bridge	d				13 50				14 05						14 20				14 35						14 50
Brentford	d				13 53				14 08						14 23				14 38						14 53
Syon Lane	d				13 55				14 10						14 25				14 40						14 55
Isleworth	d				13 57				14 12						14 27				14 42						14 57
Hounslow	d				14 01				14 18						14 31				14 48						15 01
Mortlake	d							13 54		14 07								14 24		14 37					
North Sheen	d	←						13 56		14 09		←						14 26		14 39		←			
Richmond ⊖	d	13 42				13 48		13 59		14 12	14 06	14 12				14 18		14 29		14 42	14 36	14 42			
St Margarets	d	13 44						14 01		→		14 14						14 31		→		14 44			
Twickenham	a	13 46				13 51		14 03			14 10	14 16				14 21		14 33			14 40	14 46			
	d	13 47				13 52		14 04			14 10	14 17				14 22		14 34			14 40	14 47			
Strawberry Hill	d							14 07										14 37							
Fulwell	a																								
Teddington	a							14 10										14 40							
Hampton Wick	a							14 14										14 44							
Kingston	a							14 16										14 46							
Whitton	d	13a50				13 55	←		14a23			14a20				14 25	←		14a53			14a50			
Feltham	d				14 06	13 59	14 06				14 16				14 36	14 29	14 36				14 46				15 06
Ashford (Surrey)	d				→	14 03	14 10								→	14 33	14 40								→
Staines	d					14 07	14 14				14 23					14 37	14 44				14 53				
Wraysbury	d					14 11										14 41									
Sunnymeads	d					14 14										14 44									
Datchet	d					14 17										14 47									
Windsor & Eton Riverside	a					14 21										14 51									
Egham	d						14 19				14 27						14 49				14 57				
Virginia Water	a						14 23				14 31						14 53				15 01				
	d						14 23				14 31						14 53				15 01				
Chertsey	d						14 29										14 59								
Addlestone	d						14 32										15 02								
Weybridge	a						14 37										15 07								
Byfleet & New Haw	d																								
West Byfleet	d																								
Woking	a																								
Longcross	d																								
Sunningdale	d										14 37										15 07				
Ascot 3	d			14 23							14 43			14 53							15 13			15 23	
Bagshot	d			14 29										14 59										15 29	
Camberley	a			14 35										15 05										15 35	
Frimley	d			14 43										15 13										15 43	
Ash Vale	d			14 49										15 19										15 49	
Aldershot	a			14 54										15 24										15 54	
	d			15 08										15 38										16 08	
Ash 5	d			15 15										15 45										16 15	
Wanborough	d			15 18										15 48										16 18	
Guildford	a			15 25										15 55										16 25	
Martins Heron	d										14 47										15 17				
Bracknell	d										14 50										15 20				
Wokingham	d										14 57										15 27				
Winnersh	d										15 00										15 30				
Winnersh Triangle	d										15 02										15 32				
Earley	d										15 05										15 35				
Reading 7	a										15 10										15 40				

Table 149

Saturdays

London - Hounslow, Richmond, Kingston, Windsor, Weybridge, Ascot, Guildford and Reading

Network Diagram - see first Page of Table 148

		SW	SW	SW	SW	SW	SW 1	SW		SW 1	SW	SW	SW	SW	SW	SW	SW 1	SW		SW 1	SW	SW	SW	SW	SW
London Waterloo 15 ⊖	d	14 28		14 33	14 37	14 45	14 50				14 52	14 58		15 03	15 07	15 15	15 20				15 22	15 28		15 33	15 37
Vauxhall ⊖	d	14 32		14 37	14 41	14 49					14 56	15 02		15 07	15 11	15 19					15 26	15 32		15 37	15 41
Queenstown Rd.(Battersea)	d			14 40	14 44	14 52					14 59			15 10	15 14	15 22					15 29			15 40	15 44
Clapham Junction 10	d	14 38		14 43	14 47	14 55	14 58				15 02	15 08		15 13	15 17	15 25	15 28				15 32	15 38		15 43	15 47
Wandsworth Town	d			14 46	14 50	14 58					15 05			15 16	15 20	15 28					15 35			15 46	15 50
Putney	d	14 42		14 49	14 53	15 01					15 08	15 12		15 19	15 23	15 31					15 38	15 42		15 49	15 53
Barnes	d			14 52	14 57	15 05					15 12			15 22	15 27	15 35					15 42			15 52	15 57
Barnes Bridge	d				14 59						15 14				15 29						15 44				15 59
Chiswick	d				15 02						15 17				15 32						15 47				16 02
Kew Bridge	d				15 05						15 20				15 35						15 50				16 05
Brentford	d				15 08						15 23				15 38						15 53				16 08
Syon Lane	d				15 10						15 25				15 40						15 55				16 10
Isleworth	d				15 12						15 27				15 42						15 57				16 12
Hounslow	d				15 18						15 31				15 48						16 01				16 18
Mortlake	d			14 54		15 07								15 24		15 37								15 54	
North Sheen	d			14 56		15 09		←						15 26		15 39		←						15 56	
Richmond ⊖	d	14 48		14 59		15 12	15 06	15 12				15 18		15 29		15 42	15 36	15 42				15 48		15 59	
St Margarets	d			15 01		→		15 14						15 31		→		15 44						16 01	
Twickenham	a	14 51		15 03			15 10	15 16				15 21		15 33			15 40	15 46				15 51		16 03	
	d	14 52		15 04			15 10	15 17				15 22		15 34			15 40	15 47				15 52		16 04	
Strawberry Hill	d			15 07										15 37										16 07	
Fulwell	a																								
Teddington	a			15 10										15 40										16 10	
Hampton Wick	a			15 14										15 44										16 14	
Kingston	a			15 16										15 46										16 16	
Whitton	d	14 55	←		15a23			15a20				15 25	←		15a53			15a50				15 55	←		16a23
Feltham	d	14 59	15 06				15 16				15 36	15 29	15 36				15 46				16 06	15 59	16 06		
Ashford (Surrey)	d	15 03	15 10								→	15 33	15 40								→	16 03	16 10		
Staines	d	15 07	15 14				15 23					15 37	15 44				15 53					16 07	16 14		
Wraysbury	d	15 11										15 41										16 11			
Sunnymeads	d	15 14										15 44										16 14			
Datchet	d	15 17										15 47										16 17			
Windsor & Eton Riverside	a	15 22										15 51										16 21			
Egham	d		15 19				15 27						15 49				15 57						16 19		
Virginia Water	a		15 23				15 31						15 53				16 01						16 23		
	d		15 23				15 31						15 53				16 01						16 23		
Chertsey	d		15 29										15 59										16 29		
Addlestone	d		15 32										16 02										16 32		
Weybridge	a		15 37										16 07										16 42		
Byfleet & New Haw	d																								
West Byfleet	d																								
Woking	a																								
Longcross	d																								
Sunningdale	d						15 37										16 07								
Ascot 3	d						15 43			15 53							16 13			16 23					
Bagshot	d									15 59										16 29					
Camberley	a									16 05										16 35					
Frimley	d									16 13										16 43					
Ash Vale	d									16 19										16 49					
Aldershot	a									16 24										16 54					
	d									16 38										17 08					
Ash 5	d									16 45										17 15					
Wanborough	d									16 48										17 18					
Guildford	a									16 55										17 25					
Martins Heron	d						15 47										16 17								
Bracknell	d						15 50										16 20								
Wokingham	d						15 57										16 27								
Winnersh	d						16 00										16 30								
Winnersh Triangle	d						16 02										16 32								
Earley	d						16 05										16 35								
Reading 7	a						16 10										16 40								

Table 149

Saturdays

London - Hounslow, Richmond, Kingston, Windsor, Weybridge, Ascot, Guildford and Reading

Network Diagram - see first Page of Table 148

		SW	SW 1	SW		SW 1	SW	SW	SW	SW	SW	SW	SW 1	SW		SW 1	SW	SW	SW	SW	SW	SW	SW 1	SW
London Waterloo 15 ⊖	d	15 45	15 50				15 52	15 58		16 03	16 07	16 15	16 20				16 22	16 28		16 33	16 37	16 45	16 50	
Vauxhall ⊖	d	15 49					15 56	16 02		16 07	16 11	16 19					16 26	16 32		16 37	16 41	16 49		
Queenstown Rd.(Battersea)	d	15 52					15 59			16 10	16 14	16 22					16 29			16 40	16 44	16 52		
Clapham Junction 10	d	15 55	15 58				16 02	16 08		16 13	16 17	16 25	16 28				16 32	16 38		16 43	16 47	16 55	16 58	
Wandsworth Town	d	15 58					16 05			16 16	16 20	16 28					16 35			16 46	16 50	16 58		
Putney	d	16 01					16 08	16 12		16 19	16 23	16 31					16 38	16 42		16 49	16 53	17 01		
Barnes	d	16 05					16 12			16 22	16 27	16 35					16 42			16 52	16 57	17 05		
Barnes Bridge	d						16 14				16 29						16 44				16 59			
Chiswick	d						16 17				16 32						16 47				17 02			
Kew Bridge	d						16 20				16 35						16 50				17 05			
Brentford	d						16 23				16 38						16 53				17 08			
Syon Lane	d						16 25				16 40						16 55				17 10			
Isleworth	d						16 27				16 42						16 57				17 12			
Hounslow	d						16 31				16 48						17 01				17 18			
Mortlake	d	16 07								16 24		16 37								16 54		17 07		
North Sheen	d	16 09		←						16 26		16 39		←						16 56		17 09		←
Richmond ⊖	d	16 12	16 06	16 12				16 18		16 29		16 42	16 36	16 42				16 48		16 59		17 12	17 06	17 12
St Margarets	d	→		16 14						16 31		→		16 44						17 01		→		17 14
Twickenham	a		16 10	16 16				16 21		16 33			16 40	16 46				16 51		17 03			17 10	17 16
	d		16 10	16 17				16 22		16 34			16 40	16 47				16 52		17 04			17 10	17 17
Strawberry Hill	d									16 37										17 07				
Fulwell	a																							
Teddington	a									16 40										17 10				
Hampton Wick	a									16 44										17 14				
Kingston	a									16 46										17 16				
Whitton	d			16a20				16 25	←		16a53			16a50				16 55	←		17a23			17a20
Feltham	d		16 16				16 36	16 29	16 36				16 46				17 06	16 59	17 06				17 16	
Ashford (Surrey)	d						→	16 33	16 40								→	17 03	17 10					
Staines	d		16 23					16 37	16 44				16 53					17 07	17 14				17 23	
Wraysbury	d							16 41										17 11						
Sunnymeads	d							16 44										17 14						
Datchet	d							16 47										17 17						
Windsor & Eton Riverside	a							16 51										17 21						
Egham	d		16 27						16 49				16 57						17 19				17 27	
Virginia Water	a		16 31						16 53				17 01						17 23				17 31	
	d		16 31						16 53				17 01						17 23				17 31	
Chertsey	d								16 59										17 29					
Addlestone	d								17 02										17 32					
Weybridge	a								17 07										17 37					
Byfleet & New Haw	d																							
West Byfleet	d																							
Woking	a																							
Longcross	d																							
Sunningdale	d		16 37										17 07										17 37	
Ascot 3	d		16 43			16 53							17 13			17 23							17 43	
Bagshot	d					16 59										17 29								
Camberley	a					17 05										17 35								
Frimley	d					17 13										17 43								
Ash Vale	d					17 19										17 49								
Aldershot	a					17 24										17 54								
	d					17 38										18 08								
Ash 5	d					17 45										18 15								
Wanborough	d					17 48										18 18								
Guildford	a					17 55										18 25								
Martins Heron	d		16 47										17 17										17 47	
Bracknell	d		16 50										17 20										17 50	
Wokingham	d		16 57										17 27										17 57	
Winnersh	d		17 00										17 30										18 00	
Winnersh Triangle	d		17 02										17 32										18 02	
Earley	d		17 05										17 35										18 05	
Reading 7	a		17 10										17 40										18 10	

Table 149

Saturdays

London - Hounslow, Richmond, Kingston, Windsor, Weybridge, Ascot, Guildford and Reading

Network Diagram - see first Page of Table 148

		SW 1	SW	SW	SW	SW	SW	SW	SW 1	SW		SW 1	SW	SW	SW	SW	SW	SW	SW 1	SW		SW 1	SW	SW	SW
London Waterloo 15 ⊖	d		16 52	16 58		17 03	17 07	17 15	17 20				17 22	17 28		17 33	17 37	17 45	17 50				17 52	17 58	
Vauxhall ⊖	d		16 56	17 02		17 07	17 11	17 19					17 26	17 32		17 37	17 41	17 49					17 56	18 02	
Queenstown Rd.(Battersea)	d		16 59			17 10	17 14	17 22					17 29			17 40	17 44	17 52					17 59		
Clapham Junction 10	d		17 02	17 08		17 13	17 17	17 25	17 28				17 32	17 38		17 43	17 47	17 55	17 58				18 02	18 08	
Wandsworth Town	d		17 05			17 16	17 20	17 28					17 35			17 46	17 50	17 58					18 05		
Putney	d		17 08	17 12		17 19	17 23	17 31					17 38	17 42		17 49	17 53	18 01					18 08	18 12	
Barnes	d		17 12			17 22	17 27	17 35					17 42			17 52	17 57	18 05					18 12		
Barnes Bridge	d		17 14				17 29						17 44				17 59						18 14		
Chiswick	d		17 17				17 32						17 47				18 02						18 17		
Kew Bridge	d		17 20				17 35						17 50				18 05						18 20		
Brentford	d		17 23				17 38						17 53				18 08						18 23		
Syon Lane	d		17 25				17 40						17 55				18 10						18 25		
Isleworth	d		17 27				17 42						17 57				18 12						18 27		
Hounslow	d		17 31				17 48						18 01				18 18						18 31		
Mortlake	d					17 24		17 37								17 54		18 07							
North Sheen	d					17 26		17 39		←						17 56		18 09		←					
Richmond ⊖	d			17 18		17 29		17 42	17 36	17 42				17 48		17 59		18 12	18 06	18 12				18 18	
St Margarets	d					17 31		↦		17 44						18 01		↦		18 14					
Twickenham	a			17 21		17 33			17 40	17 46				17 51		18 03			18 10	18 16				18 21	
	d			17 22		17 34			17 40	17 47				17 52		18 04			18 10	18 17				18 22	
Strawberry Hill	d					17 37										18 07									
Fulwell	a																								
Teddington	a					17 40										18 10									
Hampton Wick	a					17 44										18 14									
Kingston	a					17 46										18 16									
Whitton	d			17 25	←		17a53			17a50				17 55	←		18a23			18a20				18 25	←
Feltham	d		17 36	17 29	17 36				17 46				18 06	17 59	18 06				18 16				18 36	18 29	18 36
Ashford (Surrey)	d		↦	17 33	17 40								↦	18 03	18 10								↦	18 33	18 40
Staines	d			17 37	17 44				17 53					18 07	18 14				18 23					18 37	18 44
Wraysbury	d			17 41										18 11										18 41	
Sunnymeads	d			17 44										18 14										18 44	
Datchet	d			17 47										18 17										18 47	
Windsor & Eton Riverside	a			17 51										18 21										18 51	
Egham	d				17 49				17 57						18 19				18 27						18 49
Virginia Water	a				17 53				18 01						18 23				18 31						18 53
	d				17 53				18 01						18 23				18 31						18 53
Chertsey	d				17 59										18 29										18 59
Addlestone	d				18 02										18 32										19 02
Weybridge	a				18 07										18 37										19 07
Byfleet & New Haw	d																								
West Byfleet	d																								
Woking	a																								
Longcross	d																								
Sunningdale	d								18 07										18 37						
Ascot 3	d	17 53							18 13			18 23							18 43			18 53			
Bagshot	d	17 59										18 29										18 59			
Camberley	a	18 05										18 35										19 05			
Frimley	d	18 13										18 43										19 13			
Ash Vale	d	18 19										18 49										19 19			
Aldershot	a	18 24										18 54										19 24			
	d	18 38										19 08										19 38			
Ash 5	d	18 45										19 15										19 45			
Wanborough	d	18 48										19 18										19 48			
Guildford	a	18 55										19 25										19 55			
Martins Heron	d								18 17										18 47						
Bracknell	d								18 20										18 50						
Wokingham	d								18 27										18 57						
Winnersh	d								18 30										19 00						
Winnersh Triangle	d								18 32										19 02						
Earley	d								18 35										19 05						
Reading 7	a								18 40										19 10						

Table 149

Saturdays

London - Hounslow, Richmond, Kingston, Windsor, Weybridge, Ascot, Guildford and Reading

Network Diagram - see first Page of Table 148

		SW	SW	SW	SW [1]	SW		SW [1]	SW	SW	SW	SW	SW	SW	SW [1]	SW		SW [1]	SW	SW	SW	SW	SW	SW	SW [1]
London Waterloo [15] ⊖	d	18 03	18 07	18 15	18 20				18 22	18 28		18 33	18 37	18 45	18 50				18 52	18 58		19 03	19 07	19 15	19 20
Vauxhall ⊖	d	18 07	18 11	18 19					18 26	18 32		18 37	18 41	18 49					18 56	19 02		19 07	19 11	19 19	
Queenstown Rd.(Battersea)	d	18 10	18 14	18 22					18 29			18 40	18 44	18 52					18 59			19 10	19 14	19 22	
Clapham Junction [10]	d	18 13	18 17	18 25	18 28				18 32	18 38		18 43	18 47	18 55	18 58				19 02	19 08		19 13	19 17	19 25	19 28
Wandsworth Town	d	18 16	18 20	18 28					18 35			18 46	18 50	18 58					19 05			19 16	19 20	19 28	
Putney	d	18 19	18 23	18 31					18 38	18 42		18 49	18 53	19 01					19 08	19 12		19 19	19 23	19 31	
Barnes	d	18 22	18 27	18 35					18 42			18 52	18 57	19 05					19 12			19 22	19 27	19 35	
Barnes Bridge	d		18 29						18 44				18 59						19 14				19 29		
Chiswick	d		18 32						18 47				19 02						19 17				19 32		
Kew Bridge	d		18 35						18 50				19 05						19 20				19 35		
Brentford	d		18 38						18 53				19 08						19 23				19 38		
Syon Lane	d		18 40						18 55				19 10						19 25				19 40		
Isleworth	d		18 42						18 57				19 12						19 27				19 42		
Hounslow	d		18 48						19 01				19 18						19 31				19 48		
Mortlake	d	18 24		18 37								18 54		19 07								19 24		19 37	
North Sheen	d	18 26		18 39		←						18 56		19 09		←						19 26		19 39	
Richmond ⊖	d	18 29		18 42	18 36	18 42				18 48		18 59		19 12	19 06	19 12				19 18		19 29		19 42	19 36
St Margarets	d	18 31		→		18 44						19 01		→		19 14						19 31		→	
Twickenham	a	18 33			18 40	18 46				18 51		19 03			19 10	19 16				19 21		19 33			19 40
	d	18 34			18 40	18 47				18 52		19 04			19 10	19 17				19 22		19 34			19 40
Strawberry Hill	d	18 37										19 07										19 37			
Fulwell	a																								
Teddington	a	18 40										19 10										19 40			
Hampton Wick	a	18 44										19 14										19 44			
Kingston	a	18 46										19 16										19 46			
Whitton	d		18a53			18a50				18 55	←		19a23			19a20				19 25	←		19a53		
Feltham	d				18 46				19 06	18 59	19 06				19 16				19 36	19 29	19 36				19 46
Ashford (Surrey)	d								→	19 03	19 10								→	19 33	19 40				
Staines	d				18 53					19 07	19 14				19 23					19 37	19 44				19 53
Wraysbury	d									19 11										19 41					
Sunnymeads	d									19 14										19 44					
Datchet	d									19 17										19 47					
Windsor & Eton Riverside	a									19 21										19 51					
Egham	d				18 57						19 19				19 27						19 49				19 57
Virginia Water	a				19 01						19 23				19 31						19 53				20 01
	d				19 01						19 23				19 31						19 53				20 01
Chertsey	d										19 29										19 59				
Addlestone	d										19 32										20 02				
Weybridge	a										19 37										20 07				
Byfleet & New Haw	d																								
West Byfleet	d																								
Woking	a																								
Longcross	d																								
Sunningdale	d				19 07										19 37										20 07
Ascot [3]	d				19 13			19 23							19 43			19 53							20 13
Bagshot	d							19 29										19 59							
Camberley	a							19 35										20 05							
Frimley	d							19 43										20 13							
Ash Vale	d							19 49										20 19							
Aldershot	a							19 54										20 24							
	d							20 08										20 38							
Ash [5]	d							20 15										20 45							
Wanborough	d							20 18										20 48							
Guildford	a							20 25										20 55							
Martins Heron	d				19 17										19 47										20 17
Bracknell	d				19 20										19 50										20 20
Wokingham	d				19 27										19 57										20 27
Winnersh	d				19 30										20 00										20 30
Winnersh Triangle	d				19 32										20 02										20 32
Earley	d				19 35										20 05										20 35
Reading [7]	a				19 40										20 10										20 40

London - Hounslow, Richmond, Kingston, Windsor, Weybridge, Ascot, Guildford and Reading

Network Diagram - see first Page of Table 148

		SW		SW ■1	SW	SW	SW	SW	SW	SW	SW ■1	SW		SW ■1	SW	SW	SW	SW	SW	SW	SW ■1	SW		SW ■1	SW ■1
London Waterloo ■15 ⊖	d				19 22	19 28		19 33	19 37	19 45	19 50				19 52	19 58		20 03	20 07	20 15	20 20				
Vauxhall ⊖	d				19 26	19 32		19 37	19 41	19 49					19 56	20 02		20 07	20 11	20 19					
Queenstown Rd.(Battersea)	d				19 29			19 40	19 44	19 52					19 59			20 10	20 14	20 22					
Clapham Junction ■10	d				19 32	19 38		19 43	19 47	19 55	19 58				20 02	20 08		20 13	20 17	20 25	20 28				
Wandsworth Town	d				19 35			19 46	19 50	19 58					20 05			20 16	20 20	20 28					
Putney	d				19 38	19 42		19 49	19 53	20 01					20 08	20 12		20 19	20 23	20 31					
Barnes	d				19 42			19 52	19 57	20 05					20 12			20 22	20 27	20 35					
Barnes Bridge	d				19 44				19 59						20 14				20 29						
Chiswick	d				19 47				20 02						20 17				20 32						
Kew Bridge	d				19 50				20 05						20 20				20 35						
Brentford	d				19 53				20 08						20 23				20 38						
Syon Lane	d				19 55				20 10						20 25				20 40						
Isleworth	d				19 57				20 12						20 27				20 42						
Hounslow	d				20 01				20 18						20 31				20 48						
Mortlake	d							19 54		20 07								20 24		20 37					
North Sheen	d	←						19 56		20 09		←						20 26		20 39		←			
Richmond ⊖	d	19 42				19 48		19 59		20 12	20 06	20 12				20 18		20 29		20 42	20 36	20 42			
St Margarets	d	19 44						20 01		→		20 14						20 31		→		20 44			
Twickenham	a	19 46				19 51		20 03			20 10	20 16				20 21		20 33			20 40	20 46			
	d	19 47				19 52		20 04			20 10	20 17				20 22		20 34			20 40	20 47			
Strawberry Hill	d							20 07										20 37							
Fulwell	a																								
Teddington	a							20 10										20 40							
Hampton Wick	a							20 14										20 44							
Kingston	a							20 16										20 46							
Whitton	d	19a50				19 55	←		20a23			20a20				20 25	←		20a53			20a50			
Feltham	d				20 06	19 59	20 06				20 16				20 36	20 29	20 36				20 46				
Ashford (Surrey)	d				→	20 03	20 10								→	20 33	20 40								
Staines	d					20 07	20 14				20 23					20 37	20 44				20 53				
Wraysbury	d					20 11										20 41									
Sunnymeads	d					20 14										20 44									
Datchet	d					20 17										20 47									
Windsor & Eton Riverside	a					20 21										20 51									
Egham	d						20 19				20 27						20 49				20 57				
Virginia Water	a						20 23				20 31						20 53				21 01				
	d						20 23				20 31						20 53				21 01				
Chertsey	d						20 29										20 59								
Addlestone	d						20 32										21 02								
Weybridge	a						20 37										21 07								
Byfleet & New Haw	d																								
West Byfleet	d																								
Woking	a																								
Longcross	d																								
Sunningdale	d										20 37										21 07				
Ascot ■3	d			20 23							20 43			20 53							21 13			21 23	
Bagshot	d			20 29										20 59										21 29	
Camberley	a			20 35										21 05										21 35	
Frimley	d			20 43										21 13										21 43	
Ash Vale	d			20 49										21 19										21 49	
Aldershot	a			20 54										21 24										21 54	
	d			21 08										21 38										22 08	22 38
Ash ■5	d			21 15										21 45										22 15	22 45
Wanborough	d			21 18										21 48										22 18	22 48
Guildford	a			21 25										21 55										22 25	22 55
Martins Heron	d										20 47										21 17				
Bracknell	d										20 50										21 20				
Wokingham	d										20 57										21 27				
Winnersh	d										21 00										21 30				
Winnersh Triangle	d										21 02										21 32				
Earley	d										21 05										21 35				
Reading ■7	a										21 10										21 40				

London - Hounslow, Richmond, Kingston, Windsor, Weybridge, Ascot, Guildford and Reading

Network Diagram - see first Page of Table 148

		SW	SW	SW	SW	SW	SW	SW 1		SW	SW	SW	SW	SW	SW	SW	SW 1	SW		SW 1	SW	SW	SW	SW	SW
London Waterloo 15 ⊖	d	20 22	20 28		20 33	20 37	20 45	20 50			20 52	20 58		21 03	21 07	21 15	21 20				21 22	21 28		21 33	21 37
Vauxhall ⊖	d	20 26	20 32		20 37	20 41	20 49				20 56	21 02		21 07	21 11	21 19					21 26	21 32		21 37	21 41
Queenstown Rd.(Battersea)	d	20 29			20 40	20 44	20 52				20 59			21 10	21 14	21 22					21 29			21 40	21 44
Clapham Junction 10	d	20 32	20 38		20 43	20 47	20 55	20 58			21 02	21 08		21 13	21 17	21 25	21 28				21 32	21 38		21 43	21 47
Wandsworth Town	d	20 35			20 46	20 50	20 58				21 05			21 16	21 20	21 28					21 35			21 46	21 50
Putney	d	20 38	20 42		20 49	20 53	21 01				21 08	21 12		21 19	21 23	21 31					21 38	21 42		21 49	21 53
Barnes	d	20 42			20 52	20 57	21 05				21 12			21 22	21 27	21 35					21 42			21 52	21 57
Barnes Bridge	d	20 44				20 59					21 14				21 29						21 44				21 59
Chiswick	d	20 47				21 02					21 17				21 32						21 47				22 02
Kew Bridge	d	20 50				21 05					21 20				21 35						21 50				22 05
Brentford	d	20 53				21 08					21 23				21 38						21 53				22 08
Syon Lane	d	20 55				21 10					21 25				21 40						21 55				22 10
Isleworth	d	20 57				21 12					21 27				21 42						21 57				22 12
Hounslow	d	21 01				21 18					21 31				21 48						22 01				22 18
Mortlake	d				20 54		21 07							21 24		21 37								21 54	
North Sheen	d				20 56		21 09			←				21 26		21 39		←						21 56	
Richmond ⊖	d		20 48		20 59		21 12	21 06		21 12		21 18		21 29		21 42	21 36	21 42				21 48		21 59	
St Margarets	d				21 01		→			21 14				21 31		→		21 44						22 01	
Twickenham	a		20 51		21 03			21 10		21 16		21 21		21 33			21 40	21 46				21 51		22 03	
	d		20 52		21 04			21 10		21 17		21 22		21 34			21 40	21 47				21 52		22 04	
Strawberry Hill	d				21 07									21 37										22 07	
Fulwell	a																								
Teddington	a				21 10									21 40										22 10	
Hampton Wick	a				21 14									21 44										22 14	
Kingston	a				21 16									21 46										22 16	
Whitton	d		20 55	←		21a23				21a20		21 25	←		21a53			21a50				21 55	←		22a23
Feltham	d	21 06	20 59	21 06				21 16			21 36	21 29	21 36				21 46				22 06	21 59	22 06		
Ashford (Surrey)	d	→	21 03	21 10							→	21 33	21 40								→	22 03	22 10		
Staines	d		21 07	21 14				21 23				21 37	21 44				21 53					22 07	22 14		
Wraysbury	d		21 11									21 41										22 11			
Sunnymeads	d		21 14									21 44										22 14			
Datchet	d		21 17									21 47										22 17			
Windsor & Eton Riverside	a		21 21									21 51										22 21			
Egham	d			21 19				21 27					21 49				21 57						22 19		
Virginia Water	a			21 23				21 31					21 53				22 01						22 23		
	d			21 23				21 31					21 53				22 01						22 23		
Chertsey	d			21 29									21 59										22 29		
Addlestone	d			21 32									22 02										22 32		
Weybridge	a			21 37									22 07										22 37		
Byfleet & New Haw	d																								
West Byfleet	d																								
Woking	a																								
Longcross	d																								
Sunningdale	d							21 37									22 07								
Ascot 3	d							21 43									22 13			22 23					
Bagshot	d																			22 29					
Camberley	a																			22 35					
Frimley	d																			22 43					
Ash Vale	d																			22 49					
Aldershot	a																			22 54					
	d																			23 08					
Ash 5	d																			23 15					
Wanborough	d																			23 18					
Guildford	a																			23 25					
Martins Heron	d							21 47									22 17								
Bracknell	d							21 50									22 20								
Wokingham	d							21 57									22 27								
Winnersh	d							22 00									22 30								
Winnersh Triangle	d							22 02									22 32								
Earley	d							22 05									22 35								
Reading 7	a							22 10									22 40								

Table 149

Saturdays

London - Hounslow, Richmond, Kingston, Windsor, Weybridge, Ascot, Guildford and Reading

Network Diagram - see first Page of Table 148

		SW	SW 1	SW		SW	SW	SW	SW	SW 1	SW 1	SW	SW	SW		SW	SW 1	SW	SW	SW	SW	SW	SW 1	SW	
London Waterloo 15 ⊖	d	21 45	21 50			21 52	21 58		22 03	22 20		22 22	22 28			22 33	22 50	22 52	22 58		23 03	23 13	23 20	23 22	
Vauxhall ⊖	d	21 49				21 56	22 02		22 07			22 26	22 32			22 37		22 56	23 02		23 07	23 17		23 26	
Queenstown Rd.(Battersea)	d	21 52				21 59			22 10			22 29				22 40		22 59			23 10			23 29	
Clapham Junction 10	d	21 55	21 58			22 02	22 08		22 13	22 28		22 32	22 38			22 43	22 58	23 02	23 08		23 13	23 23	23 28	23 32	
Wandsworth Town	d	21 58				22 05			22 16			22 35				22 46		23 05			23 16			23 35	
Putney	d	22 01				22 08	22 12		22 19			22 38	22 42			22 49		23 08	23 12		23 19	23 27		23 38	
Barnes	d	22 05				22 12			22 22			22 42				22 52		23 12			23 22			23 42	
Barnes Bridge	d					22 14						22 44						23 14						23 44	
Chiswick	d					22 17						22 47						23 17						23 47	
Kew Bridge	d					22 20						22 50						23 20						23 50	
Brentford	d					22 23						22 53						23 23						23 53	
Syon Lane	d					22 25						22 55						23 25						23 55	
Isleworth	d					22 27						22 57						23 27						23 57	
Hounslow	d					22 31						23 01						23 31						00 01	
Mortlake	d	22 07							22 24							22 54					23 24				
North Sheen	d	22 09		←					22 26							22 56					23 26				
Richmond ⊖	d	22 12	22 06	22 12			22 18		22 29	22 36			22 48			22 59	23 06		23 18		23 29	23 33	23 37		
St Margarets	d	→		22 14					22 31							23 01					23 31				
Twickenham	a		22 10	22 16			22 21		22 33	22 40			22 51			23 03	23 10		23 21		23 33	23 37	23 41		
	d		22 10				22 22		22 34	22 40			22 52			23 04	23 10		23 22		23 34	23 37	23 41		
Strawberry Hill	d								22 37							23 07					23 37				
Fulwell	a																								
Teddington	a								22 40							23 10					23 40				
Hampton Wick	a								22 44							23 14					23 44				
Kingston	a								22 46							23 16					23 46				
Whitton	d						22 25	←					22 55	←					23 25	←		23 40			
Feltham	d		22 16			22 36	22 29	22 36		22 46		23 06	22 59	23 06			23 16	23 36	23 29	23 36		23 44	23 48	00 06	
Ashford (Surrey)	d					→	22 33	22 40				→	23 03	23 10				→	23 33	23 40		23 48		→	
Staines	d		22 23				22 37	22 44		22 53			23 07	23 14			23 23		23 37	23 44		23 52	23 56		
Wraysbury	d						22 41						23 11						23 41			23 56			
Sunnymeads	d						22 44						23 14						23 44			23 59			
Datchet	d						22 47						23 17						23 47			00 02			
Windsor & Eton Riverside	a						22 51						23 21						23 51			00 06			
Egham	d		22 27					22 49		22 57				23 19			23 27			23 49			00 01		
Virginia Water	a		22 31					22 53		23 01				23 23			23 31			23 53			00 05		
	d		22 31					22 53		23 01				23 23			23 31			23 53			00 05		
Chertsey	d							22 59						23 29						23 59					
Addlestone	d							23 02						23a32						00 02					
Weybridge	a							23 07						00 38											
Byfleet & New Haw	d																			00 06					
West Byfleet	d																			00 09					
Woking	a																			00 15					
Longcross	d																								
Sunningdale	d		22 37							23 07							23 37						00 11		
Ascot 3	d		22 43							23 13	23 23						23 43						00 15		
Bagshot	d										23 29														
Camberley	a										23 35														
Frimley	d										23 43														
Ash Vale	d										23 49														
Aldershot	a										23 54														
	d																								
Ash 5	d																								
Wanborough	d																								
Guildford	a																								
Martins Heron	d		22 47							23 17							23 47						00 19		
Bracknell	d		22 50							23 20							23 50						00 23		
Wokingham	d		22 57							23 27							23 57						00 32		
Winnersh	d		23 00							23 30							23 59						00 36		
Winnersh Triangle	d		23 02							23 32							00 02						00 38		
Earley	d		23 05							23 35							00 05						00 40		
Reading 7	a		23 10							23 40							00 10						00 45		

Table 149

Saturdays

London - Hounslow, Richmond, Kingston, Windsor, Weybridge, Ascot, Guildford and Reading

Network Diagram - see first Page of Table 148

		SW	SW	SW	SW	SW	SW	SW
London Waterloo 15 ⊖	d	23 33	23 38			23 52	23 58	
Vauxhall ⊖	d	23 37				23 56	00 02	
Queenstown Rd.(Battersea)	d	23 40				23 59		
Clapham Junction 10	d	23 43	23 46			00 02	00 08	
Wandsworth Town	d	23 46				00 05		
Putney	d	23 49				00 08	00 12	
Barnes	d	23 52				00 12		
Barnes Bridge	d					00 14		
Chiswick	d					00 17		
Kew Bridge	d					00 20		
Brentford	d					00 23		
Syon Lane	d					00 25		
Isleworth	d					00 27		
Hounslow	d					00 31		
Mortlake	d	23 54						
North Sheen	d	23 56			←			
Richmond ⊖	d	23 59	23 54		23 59		00 18	
St Margarets	d	↦			00 01			
Twickenham	a		23 58		00 04		00 21	
	d		23 58		00 04		00 22	
Strawberry Hill	d				00 07			
Fulwell	a							
Teddington	a				00 11			
Hampton Wick	a				00 14			
Kingston	a				00 16			
Whitton	d			←			00 25	←
Feltham	d		00 04	00 06		00 36	00 29	00 36
Ashford (Surrey)	d			00 10		↦	00 33	00 40
Staines	d		00 11	00 14			00a37	00a46
Wraysbury	d							
Sunnymeads	d							
Datchet	d							
Windsor & Eton Riverside	a							
Egham	d		00 15	00 19				
Virginia Water	a		00 19	00 23				
	d		00 19	00 23				
Chertsey	d			00 29				
Addlestone	d			00a32				
Weybridge	a			00 38				
Byfleet & New Haw	d							
West Byfleet	d							
Woking	a							
Longcross	d							
Sunningdale	d		00 25					
Ascot 3	d		00 30					
Bagshot	d							
Camberley	a							
Frimley	d							
Ash Vale	d							
Aldershot	a							
	d							
Ash 5	d							
Wanborough	d							
Guildford	a							
Martins Heron	d		00 34					
Bracknell	d		00 37					
Wokingham	d		00 44					
Winnersh	d							
Winnersh Triangle	d							
Earley	d							
Reading 7	a		00 52					

Table 149

Sundays

London - Hounslow, Richmond, Kingston, Windsor, Weybridge, Ascot, Guildford and Reading

Network Diagram - see first Page of Table 148

		SW	SW	SW	SW	SW	SW	SW	SW	SW		SW	SW	SW	SW	SW	SW		SW			SW	SW	SW	SW
		1			1							1	1												1
		A	A	A	A	A	A	A	A	A				A	A	A									
London Waterloo 15 ⊖	d	22p50	22p52	23p13	23p20	23p22	23p33	23p38						23p52	23p58		00 18		06 14				06 44		07 09
Vauxhall ⊖	d		22p56	23p17		23p26	23p37							23p56	00 02		00 22		06 18				06 48		07 13
Queenstown Rd.(Battersea)	d		22p59			23p29	23p40							23p59			00 26		06 21				06 51		
Clapham Junction 10	d	22p58	23p02	23p23	23p28	23p32	23p43	23p46						00 02	00 08		00 29		06 24				06 54		07 19
Wandsworth Town	d		23p05			23p35	23p46							00 05			00 32		06 27				06 57		
Putney	d		23p08	23p27		23p38	23p49							00 08	00 12		00 35		06 30				07 00		07 23
Barnes	d		23p12			23p42	23p52							00 12			00 38		06 33				07 03		
Barnes Bridge	d		23p14			23p44								00 14											
Chiswick	d		23p17			23p47								00 17											
Kew Bridge	d		23p20			23p50								00 20											
Brentford	d		23p23			23p53								00 23											
Syon Lane	d		23p25			23p55								00 25											
Isleworth	d		23p27			23p57								00 27											
Hounslow	d		23p31			00 01								00 31											
Mortlake	d						23p54										00 40		06 35				07 05		
North Sheen	d						23p56			←							00 42		06 37				07 07		
Richmond ⊖	d	23p06		23p33	23p37		23p59	23p54		23p59					00 18		00 45		06 40				07 10		07 29
St Margarets	d						→			00 01							00 47		06 42				07 12		
Twickenham	a	23p10		23p37	23p41			23p58		00 04					00 21		00 49		06 44				07 14		07 32
	d	23p10		23p37	23p41			23p58		00 04					00 22		00 50		06 45				07 15		07 33
Strawberry Hill	d									00 07							00s53		06 49						
Fulwell	a																								
Teddington	a									00 11							00s56		06 52						
Hampton Wick	a									00 14							00s59		06 57						
Kingston	a									00 16							01 01		06 59						
Whitton	d			23p40					←						00 25	←							07 18		
Feltham	d	23p16	23p36	23p44	23p48	00 06		00 04	00 06					00 36	00 29	00 36							07 22		07 39
Ashford (Surrey)	d		23p40	23p48		→			00 10					→	00 33	00 40							07 26		
Staines	d	23p23	23p44	23p52	23p56			00 11	00 14						00a37	00a46						06 32	07 30	07 40	07 45
Wraysbury	d			23p56																			07 34		
Sunnymeads	d			23p59																			07 37		
Datchet	d			00 02																			07 40		
Windsor & Eton Riverside	a			00 06																			07 44		
Egham	d	23p27	23p49		00 01			00 15	00 19													06 36		07 45	07 50
Virginia Water	a	23p31	23p53		00 05			00 19	00 23													06 41		07 49	07 54
	d	23p31	23p53		00 05			00 19	00 23													06 41		07 49	07 54
Chertsey	d		23p59						00 29													06 46		07 55	
Addlestone	d		00 02						00a32													06 49		07 58	
Weybridge	a																					06 53			
Byfleet & New Haw	d		00 06																					08 02	
West Byfleet	d		00 09																					08 05	
Woking	a		00 15																					08 11	
Longcross	d																								
Sunningdale	d	23p37			00 11			00 25																	07 59
Ascot 3	d	23p43			00 15			00 30				00 32													08 04
Bagshot	d											00 38													
Camberley	a											00 44													
Frimley	d											00 48													
Ash Vale	d											00 57													
Aldershot	a											01s02													
	d												07 48												
Ash 5	d												07 55												
Wanborough	d												07 58												
Guildford	a												08 05												
Martins Heron	d	23p47			00 19			00 34																	08 08
Bracknell	d	23p50			00 23			00 37																	08 11
Wokingham	d	23p57			00 32			00 44																	08 18
Winnersh	d	23p59			00 36																				08 21
Winnersh Triangle	d	00 02			00 38																				08 23
Earley	d	00 05			00 40																				08 26
Reading 7	a	00 10			00 45			00 52																	08 31

A not 11 December

Table 149

Sundays

London - Hounslow, Richmond, Kingston, Windsor, Weybridge, Ascot, Guildford and Reading

Network Diagram - see first Page of Table 148

		SW	SW ■1	SW ■1	SW	SW		SW ■1	SW	SW ■1	SW ■1	SW	SW	SW ■1	SW	SW		SW ■1	SW ■1	SW	SW	SW ■1	SW	SW	SW ■1
London Waterloo 15 ⊖	d	07 14			07 44	07 50		08 09	08 14		08 39	08 44	08 50	09 09	09 14	09 25			09 39	09 44	09 50	10 09	10 14	10 25	
Vauxhall ⊖	d	07 18			07 48	07 54		08 13	08 18		08 43	08 48	08 54	09 13	09 18	09 29			09 43	09 48	09 54	10 13	10 18	10 29	
Queenstown Rd.(Battersea)	d	07 21			07 51	07 57			08 21			08 51	08 57		09 21					09 51	09 57		10 21		
Clapham Junction 10	d	07 24			07 54	08 00		08 19	08 24		08 49	08 54	09 00	09 19	09 24	09 35			09 49	09 54	10 00	10 19	10 24	10 35	
Wandsworth Town	d	07 27			07 57	08 03			08 27			08 57	09 03		09 27					09 57	10 03		10 27		
Putney	d	07 30			08 00	08 06		08 23	08 30		08 53	09 00	09 06	09 23	09 30	09 39			09 53	10 00	10 06	10 23	10 30	10 39	
Barnes	d	07 33			08 03	08 09			08 33			09 03	09 09		09 33					10 03	10 09		10 33		
Barnes Bridge	d					08 11							09 11								10 11				
Chiswick	d					08 13							09 13								10 13				
Kew Bridge	d					08 16							09 16								10 16				
Brentford	d					08 19							09 19								10 19				
Syon Lane	d					08 21							09 21								10 21				
Isleworth	d					08 23							09 23								10 23				
Hounslow	d					08 26							09 26								10 26				
Mortlake	d	07 35			08 05				08 35			09 05			09 35					10 05			10 35		
North Sheen	d	07 37			08 07				08 37			09 07			09 37					10 07			10 37		
Richmond ⊖	d	07 40			08 10			08 29	08 40		08 59	09 10		09 29	09 40	09 45			09 59	10 10		10 29	10 40	10 45	
St Margarets	d	07 42			08 12				08 42			09 12			09 42					10 12			10 42		
Twickenham	a	07 44			08 14			08 32	08 44		09 02	09 14		09 32	09 44	09 48			10 02	10 14		10 32	10 44	10 48	
	d	07 45			08 15			08 33	08 45		09 03	09 15		09 33	09 45	09 49			10 03	10 15		10 33	10 45	10 49	
Strawberry Hill	d	07 49							08 49						09 49								10 49		
Fulwell	a																								
Teddington	a	07 52							08 52						09 52								10 52		
Hampton Wick	a	07 57							08 57						09 57								10 57		
Kingston	a	07 59							08 59						09 59								10 59		
Whitton	d				08 18							09 18				09 52				10 18				10 52	
Feltham	d				08 22	08 32		08 39			09 09	09 22	09 32	09 39		09 56			10 09	10 22	10 32	10 39		10 56	
Ashford (Surrey)	d				08 26	08 36						09 26	09 36			10 00				10 26	10 36			11 00	
Staines	d			08 15	08 30	08 40		08 45			09 15	09 30	09 40	09 45		10 04			10 15	10 30	10 40	10 45		11 04	
Wraysbury	d				08 34							09 34								10 34					
Sunnymeads	d				08 37							09 37								10 37					
Datchet	d				08 40							09 40				10 12				10 40				11 12	
Windsor & Eton Riverside	a				08 44							09 44				10 16				10 44				11 16	
Egham	d			08 20		08 45		08 50			09 20		09 45	09 50					10 20		10 45	10 50			
Virginia Water	a			08 24		08 49		08 54			09 24		09 49	09 54					10 24		10 49	10 54			
	d			08 24		08 49		08 54			09 24		09 49	09 54					10 24		10 49	10 54			
Chertsey	d					08 55							09 55								10 55				
Addlestone	d					08 58							09 58								10 58				
Weybridge	a																								
Byfleet & New Haw	d					09 02							10 02								11 02				
West Byfleet	d					09 05							10 05								11 05				
Woking	a					09 11							10 11								11 11				
Longcross	d																								
Sunningdale	d			08 29				08 59			09 29			09 59					10 29			10 59			
Ascot 3	d		08 13	08 34				09 04		09 13	09 34			10 04				10 13	10 34			11 04			11 13
Bagshot	d		08 19							09 19								10 19							11 19
Camberley	a		08 25							09 25								10 25							11 25
Frimley	d		08 29							09 29								10 29							11 29
Ash Vale	d		08 36							09 36								10 36							11 36
Aldershot	a		08 41							09 41								10 41							11 41
	d		08 48							09 48								10 48							11 48
Ash 5	d		08 55							09 55								10 55							11 55
Wanborough	d		08 58							09 58								10 58							11 58
Guildford	a		09 05							10 05								11 05							12 05
Martins Heron	d			08 38				09 08			09 38			10 08					10 38			11 08			
Bracknell	d			08 41				09 11			09 41			10 11					10 41			11 11			
Wokingham	d			08 48				09 18			09 48			10 18					10 48			11 18			
Winnersh	d			08 51				09 21			09 51			10 21					10 51			11 21			
Winnersh Triangle	d			08 53				09 23			09 53			10 23					10 53			11 23			
Earley	d			08 56				09 26			09 56			10 26					10 56			11 26			
Reading 7	a			09 01				09 31			10 01			10 31					11 01			11 31			

Table 149

Sundays

London - Hounslow, Richmond, Kingston, Windsor, Weybridge, Ascot, Guildford and Reading

Network Diagram - see first Page of Table 148

		SW ■		SW	SW	SW ■	SW	SW	SW ■	SW ■	SW	SW		SW ■	SW	SW	SW ■	SW ■	SW	SW	SW ■	SW		SW	SW ■
London Waterloo 15 ⊖	d	10 39		10 44	10 50	11 09	11 14	11 25		11 39	11 44	11 50		12 09	12 14	12 25		12 39	12 44	12 50	13 09	13 14		13 25	
Vauxhall ⊖	d	10 43		10 48	10 54	11 13	11 19	11 29		11 43	11 48	11 54		12 13	12 19	12 29		12 43	12 48	12 54	13 13	13 18		13 29	
Queenstown Rd.(Battersea)	d			10 51	10 57		11 22				11 51	11 57			12 22				12 51	12 57		13 21			
Clapham Junction 10	d	10 49		10 54	11 00	11 19	11 25	11 35		11 49	11 54	12 00		12 19	12 25	12 35		12 49	12 54	13 00	13 19	13 24		13 35	
Wandsworth Town	d			10 57	11 03		11 28				11 57	12 03			12 28				12 57	13 03		13 27			
Putney	d	10 53		11 00	11 06	11 23	11 31	11 39		11 53	12 00	12 06		12 23	12 31	12 39		12 53	13 00	13 06	13 23	13 30		13 39	
Barnes	d			11 03	11 09		11 34				12 03	12 09			12 34				13 03	13 09		13 33			
Barnes Bridge	d				11 11							12 11								13 11					
Chiswick	d				11 13							12 13								13 13					
Kew Bridge	d				11 16							12 16								13 16					
Brentford	d				11 19							12 19								13 19					
Syon Lane	d				11 21							12 21								13 21					
Isleworth	d				11 23							12 23								13 23					
Hounslow	d				11 26							12 26								13 26					
Mortlake	d			11 05			11 36				12 05				12 36				13 05			13 35			
North Sheen	d			11 07			11 38				12 07				12 38				13 07			13 37			
Richmond ⊖	d	10 59		11 10		11 29	11 41	11 45		11 59	12 10			12 29	12 41	12 45		12 59	13 10		13 29	13 40		13 45	
St Margarets	d			11 12			11 43				12 12				12 43				13 12			13 42			
Twickenham	a	11 02		11 14		11 32	11 45	11 48		12 02	12 14			12 32	12 45	12 48		13 02	13 14		13 32	13 44		13 48	
	d	11 03		11 15		11 33	11 46	11 49		12 03	12 15			12 33	12 46	12 49		13 03	13 15		13 33	13 45		13 49	
Strawberry Hill	d						11 50								12 50							13 49			
Fulwell	a																								
Teddington	a						11 53								12 53							13 52			
Hampton Wick	a						11 57								12 57							13 57			
Kingston	a						11 59								12 59							13 59			
Whitton	d			11 18				11 52			12 18					12 52			13 18					13 52	
Feltham	d	11 09		11 22	11 32	11 39		11 56		12 09	12 22	12 32		12 39		12 56		13 09	13 22	13 32	13 39			13 56	
Ashford (Surrey)	d			11 26	11 36			12 00			12 26	12 36				13 00			13 26	13 36				14 00	
Staines	d	11 15		11 30	11 40	11 45		12 04		12 15	12 30	12 40		12 45		13 04		13 15	13 30	13 40	13 45			14 04	
Wraysbury	d			11 34							12 34								13 34						
Sunnymeads	d			11 37							12 37								13 37						
Datchet	d			11 40				12 12			12 40					13 12			13 40					14 12	
Windsor & Eton Riverside	a			11 44				12 16			12 44					13 16			13 44					14 16	
Egham	d	11 20			11 45	11 50				12 20		12 45		12 50				13 20		13 45	13 50				
Virginia Water	a	11 24			11 49	11 54				12 24		12 49		12 54				13 24		13 49	13 54				
	d	11 24			11 49	11 54				12 24		12 49		12 54				13 24		13 49	13 54				
Chertsey	d				11 55							12 55								13 55					
Addlestone	d				11 58							12 58								13 58					
Weybridge	a																								
Byfleet & New Haw	d				12 02							13 02								14 02					
West Byfleet	d				12 05							13 05								14 05					
Woking	a				12 11							13 11								14 11					
Longcross	d																								
Sunningdale	d	11 29				11 59				12 29				12 59				13 29			13 59				
Ascot 3	d	11 34				12 04			12 13	12 34				13 04			13 13	13 34			14 04				14 13
Bagshot	d								12 19								13 19								14 19
Camberley	a								12 25								13 25								14 25
Frimley	d								12 29								13 29								14 29
Ash Vale	d								12 36								13 36								14 36
Aldershot	a								12 41								13 41								14 41
	d								12 48								13 48								14 48
Ash 5	d								12 55								13 55								14 55
Wanborough	d								12 58								13 58								14 58
Guildford	a								13 05								14 05								15 05
Martins Heron	d	11 38				12 08				12 38				13 08				13 38			14 08				
Bracknell	d	11 41				12 11				12 41				13 11				13 41			14 11				
Wokingham	d	11 48				12 18				12 48				13 18				13 48			14 18				
Winnersh	d	11 51				12 21				12 51				13 21				13 51			14 21				
Winnersh Triangle	d	11 53				12 23				12 53				13 23				13 53			14 23				
Earley	d	11 56				12 26				12 56				13 26				13 56			14 26				
Reading 7	a	12 01				12 31				13 01				13 31				14 01			14 31				

Table 149

Sundays

London - Hounslow, Richmond, Kingston, Windsor, Weybridge, Ascot, Guildford and Reading

Network Diagram - see first Page of Table 148

Station		SW ■1	SW	SW	SW
London Waterloo ■15 ⊖	d	13 39	13 44	13 50	13 56
Vauxhall ⊖	d	13 43	13 48	13 54	14 00
Queenstown Rd.(Battersea)	d		13 51	13 57	14 03
Clapham Junction ■10	d	13 49	13 54	14 00	14 06
Wandsworth Town	d		13 57	14 03	14 09
Putney	d	13 53	14 00	14 06	14 12
Barnes	d		14 03	14 09	14 15
Barnes Bridge	d			14 11	
Chiswick	d			14 13	
Kew Bridge	d			14 16	
Brentford	d			14 19	
Syon Lane	d			14 21	
Isleworth	d			14 23	
Hounslow	d			14 26	
Mortlake	d		14 05		14 17
North Sheen	d		14 07		14 19
Richmond ⊖	d	13 59	14 10		14 22
St Margarets	d		14 12		14 24
Twickenham	a	14 02	14 14		14 26
	d	14 03	14 15		14 27
Strawberry Hill	d				14 30
Fulwell	a				
Teddington	a				14 33
Hampton Wick	a				14 36
Kingston	a				14 38
Whitton	d		14 18		
Feltham	d	14 09	14 22	14 32	
Ashford (Surrey)	d		14 26	14 36	
Staines	d	14 15	14 30	14 40	
Wraysbury	d		14 34		
Sunnymeads	d		14 37		
Datchet	d		14 40		
Windsor & Eton Riverside	a		14 44		
Egham	d	14 20		14 45	
Virginia Water	a	14 24		14 49	
	d	14 24		14 49	
Chertsey	d			14 55	
Addlestone	d			14 58	
Weybridge	a				
Byfleet & New Haw	d			15 02	
West Byfleet	d			15 05	
Woking	a			15 11	
Longcross	d				
Sunningdale	d	14 29			
Ascot ■3	d	14 34			
Bagshot	d				
Camberley	a				
Frimley	d				
Ash Vale	d				
Aldershot	a				
	d				
Ash ■5	d				
Wanborough	d				
Guildford	a				
Martins Heron	d	14 38			
Bracknell	d	14 41			
Wokingham	d	14 48			
Winnersh	d	14 51			
Winnersh Triangle	d	14 53			
Earley	d	14 56			
Reading ■7	a	15 01			

and at the same minutes past each hour until

Station		SW		SW ■1	SW	SW ■1	SW ■1	SW	SW	SW	SW ■1	SW		SW ■1	SW ■1	SW	SW	SW	SW ■1
London Waterloo ■15 ⊖	d	19 56		20 09	20 14		20 39	20 44	20 50	20 56	21 09	21 14			21 39	21 44	21 50	21 56	22 09
Vauxhall ⊖	d	20 00		20 13	20 18		20 43	20 48	20 54	21 00	21 13	21 18			21 43	21 48	21 54	22 00	22 13
Queenstown Rd.(Battersea)	d	20 03			20 21			20 51	20 57	21 03		21 21				21 51	21 57	22 03	
Clapham Junction ■10	d	20 06		20 19	20 24		20 49	20 54	21 00	21 06	21 19	21 24			21 49	21 54	22 00	22 06	22 19
Wandsworth Town	d	20 09			20 27			20 57	21 03	21 09		21 27				21 57	22 03	22 09	
Putney	d	20 12		20 23	20 30		20 53	21 00	21 06	21 12	21 23	21 30			21 53	22 00	22 06	22 12	22 23
Barnes	d	20 15			20 33			21 03	21 09	21 15		21 33				22 03	22 09	22 15	
Barnes Bridge	d								21 11								22 11		
Chiswick	d								21 13								22 13		
Kew Bridge	d								21 16								22 16		
Brentford	d								21 19								22 19		
Syon Lane	d								21 21								22 21		
Isleworth	d								21 23								22 23		
Hounslow	d								21 26								22 26		
Mortlake	d	20 17			20 35			21 05		21 17		21 35				22 05		22 17	
North Sheen	d	20 19			20 37			21 07		21 19		21 37				22 07		22 19	
Richmond ⊖	d	20 22		20 29	20 40		20 59	21 10		21 22	21 29	21 40			21 59	22 10		22 22	22 29
St Margarets	d	20 24			20 42			21 12		21 24		21 42				22 12		22 24	
Twickenham	a	20 26		20 32	20 44		21 02	21 14		21 26	21 32	21 44			22 02	22 14		22 26	22 32
	d	20 27		20 33	20 45		21 03	21 15		21 27	21 33	21 45			22 03	22 15		22 27	22 33
Strawberry Hill	d	20 30			20 49					21 30		21 49						22 30	
Fulwell	a																		
Teddington	a	20 33			20 52					21 33		21 52						22 33	
Hampton Wick	a	20 36			20 57					21 36		21 57						22 36	
Kingston	a	20 38			20 59					21 38		21 59						22 38	
Whitton	d							21 18								22 18			
Feltham	d			20 39			21 09	21 22	21 32		21 39				22 09	22 22	22 32		22 39
Ashford (Surrey)	d							21 26	21 36							22 26	22 36		
Staines	d			20 45			21 15	21 30	21 40		21 45				22 15	22 30	22 40		22 45
Wraysbury	d							21 34								22 34			
Sunnymeads	d							21 37								22 37			
Datchet	d							21 40								22 40			
Windsor & Eton Riverside	a							21 44								22 44			
Egham	d			20 50			21 20		21 45		21 50				22 20		22 45		22 50
Virginia Water	a			20 54			21 24		21 49		21 54				22 24		22 49		22 54
	d			20 54			21 24		21 49		21 54				22 24		22 49		22 54
Chertsey	d								21 55								22 55		
Addlestone	d								21 58								22 58		
Weybridge	a																		
Byfleet & New Haw	d								22 02								23 02		
West Byfleet	d								22 05								23 05		
Woking	a								22 11								23 11		
Longcross	d																		
Sunningdale	d			20 59			21 29				21 59				22 29				22 59
Ascot ■3	d			21 04		21 13	21 34				22 04			22 13	22 34				23 04
Bagshot	d					21 19								22 19					
Camberley	a					21 25								22 25					
Frimley	d					21 29								22 29					
Ash Vale	d					21 36								22 36					
Aldershot	a					21 41								22 41					
	d					21 48								22 48					
Ash ■5	d					21 55								22 55					
Wanborough	d					21 58								22 58					
Guildford	a					22 05								23 05					
Martins Heron	d			21 08			21 38				22 08				22 38				23 08
Bracknell	d			21 11			21 41				22 11				22 41				23 11
Wokingham	d			21 18			21 48				22 18				22 48				23 18
Winnersh	d			21 21			21 51				22 21				22 51				23 21
Winnersh Triangle	d			21 23			21 53				22 23				22 53				23 23
Earley	d			21 26			21 56				22 26				22 56				23 26
Reading ■7	a			21 31			22 01				22 31				23 01				23 31

Table 149

Sundays

London - Hounslow, Richmond, Kingston, Windsor, Weybridge, Ascot, Guildford and Reading

Network Diagram - see first Page of Table 148

		SW	SW 1	SW 1	SW	SW	SW	SW 1	SW	SW 1	SW
London Waterloo 15 ⊖	d	22 14		22 39	22 44	22 50	22 56	23 09	23 14	23 39	23 44
Vauxhall ⊖	d	22 18		22 43	22 48	22 54	23 00	23 13	23 18	23 43	23 48
Queenstown Rd.(Battersea)	d	22 21			22 51	22 57	23 03		23 21		23 51
Clapham Junction 10	d	22 24		22 49	22 54	23 00	23 06	23 19	23 24	23 49	23 54
Wandsworth Town	d	22 27			22 57	23 03	23 09		23 27		23 57
Putney	d	22 30		22 53	23 00	23 06	23 12	23 23	23 30	23 53	23 59
Barnes	d	22 33			23 03	23 09	23 15		23 33		00 03
Barnes Bridge	d					23 11					
Chiswick	d					23 13					
Kew Bridge	d					23 16					
Brentford	d					23 19					
Syon Lane	d					23 21					
Isleworth	d					23 23					
Hounslow	d					23 26					
Mortlake	d	22 35			23 05		23 17		23 35		00 05
North Sheen	d	22 37			23 07		23 19		23 37		00 07
Richmond ⊖	d	22 40		22 59	23 10		23 22	23 29	23 40	23 59	00 10
St Margarets	d	22 42			23 12		23 24		23 42		00 12
Twickenham	a	22 44		23 02	23 14		23 26	23 32	23 44	00 02	00 14
	d	22 45		23 03	23 15		23 27	23 33	23 45	00 03	00 15
Strawberry Hill	d	22 49					23 30		23 48		
Fulwell	a										
Teddington	a	22 52					23 33		23 51		
Hampton Wick	a	22 57					23 36		23 54		
Kingston	a	22 59					23 38		23 56		
Whitton	d				23 18						00 18
Feltham	d			23 09	23 22	23 32		23 39		00 09	00 22
Ashford (Surrey)	d				23 26	23 36					00 26
Staines	d			23 15	23 30	23 40		23 45		00 15	00a30
Wraysbury	d				23 34						
Sunnymeads	d				23 37						
Datchet	d				23 40						
Windsor & Eton Riverside	a				23 44						
Egham	d			23 20		23 45		23 50		00 20	
Virginia Water	a			23 24		23 49		23 54		00 24	
	d			23 24		23 49		23 54		00 24	
Chertsey	d					23 55					
Addlestone	d					23 58					
Weybridge	a										
Byfleet & New Haw	d					00 02					
West Byfleet	d					00 05					
Woking	a					00 11					
Longcross	d										
Sunningdale	d			23 29				23 59		00 29	
Ascot 3	d		23 13	23 34				00 04		00 34	
Bagshot	d		23 19								
Camberley	a		23 25								
Frimley	d		23 29								
Ash Vale	d		23 36								
Aldershot	a		23 41								
	d										
Ash 5	d										
Wanborough	d										
Guildford	a										
Martins Heron	d			23 38				00 08		00 38	
Bracknell	d			23 41				00 11		00 41	
Wokingham	d			23 48				00 18		00 48	
Winnersh	d			23 51				00 21		00 51	
Winnersh Triangle	d			23 53				00 23		00 53	
Earley	d			23 56				00 26		00 56	
Reading 7	a			00 01				00 31		01 01	

Reading, Guildford, Ascot, Weybridge, Windsor, Kingston, Richmond and Hounslow - London

Network Diagram - see first Page of Table 148

Miles	Miles	Miles	Miles			SW MO	SW MO	SW MX [1]	SW MX	SW MO [1]	SW MX	SW MX [1]	SW	SW	SW	SW	SW	SW	SW	SW ◇	SW ◇	SW ◇	SW ◇[1]	SW [1]
—	—	0	—	**Reading [7]**	d			22p42		22p54		23p12											05 42	
—	—	3	—	Earley	d			22p47		22p59		23p17											05 47	
—	—	4¼	—	Winnersh Triangle	d			22p49		23p01		23p19											05 49	
—	—	4¾	—	Winnersh	d			22p51		23p03		23p21											05 51	
—	—	6¾	—	**Wokingham**	d			22p56		23p08		23p26											05 56	
—	—	11¼	—	Bracknell	d			23p02		23p14		23p32											06 02	
—	—	12¼	—	Martins Heron	d			23p05		23p17		23p35											06 05	
—	0	—	—	**Guildford**	d																			
—	4¼	—	—	Wanborough	d																			
—	6¼	—	—	Ash [5]	d																			
—	9	—	—	**Aldershot**	a																			
—	—	—	—		d																			05 58
—	11½	—	—	Ash Vale	d																			06 02
—	14¾	—	—	Frimley	d																			06 10
—	17	—	—	Camberley	a																			06 14
—	—	—	—		d																			06 18
—	20¼	—	—	Bagshot	d																			06 23
—	23½	14½	—	**Ascot [3]**	d			23p10		23p22		23p40											06 10	06a30
—	—	16½	—	Sunningdale	d			23p13		23p25		23p43											06 13	
—	—	18¼	—	Longcross	d																			
0	—	—	—	Woking	d		22p52													05 27				
2½	—	—	—	West Byfleet	d		22p56													05 32				
3¾	—	—	—	Byfleet & New Haw	d		23p00													05 35				
5¼	—	—	—	**Weybridge**	d																			
7	—	—	—	Addlestone	d		23p04													05 39				
8½	—	—	—	Chertsey	d		23p07													05 42				
11	—	20¼	—	Virginia Water	a		23p12	23p19		23p30		23p49								05 47			06 19	
—	—	—	—		d		23p12	23p19		23p30		23p49								05 54			06 19	
—	—	22½	—	Egham	d		23p16	23p23		23p34		23p53								05 57			06 23	
—	—	—	0	**Windsor & Eton Riverside**	d	23p01															05 53			
—	—	—	2	Datchet	d	23p04															05 56			
—	—	—	3	Sunnymeads	d	23p07															05 59			
—	—	—	4¼	Wraysbury	d	23p10															06 02			
—	—	24½	6¾	**Staines**	d	23p16	23p21	23p29		23p39		23p59		04 58			05 37			06 03	06 08		06 29	
—	—	26	—	Ashford (Surrey)	d	23p19	23p24							05 01			05 40			06 06	06 11			
—	—	28¾	—	Feltham	d	23p24	23p29	23p35		23p46		00 05		05 06			05 45			06 11	06 16		06 35	
—	—	31	—	Whitton	d	23p28								05 10			05 49				06 20			
0	—	—	—	**Kingston**	d				23p29		23p55		01 17						05 59					
0½	—	—	—	Hampton Wick	d				23p31		23p57		01s22						06 01					
1¾	—	—	—	Teddington	d				23p35		23p59		01 25						06 05					
2¾	—	—	—	Fulwell	d											05 36								
3	—	—	—	Strawberry Hill	d				23p38		00 03		01 28			05 38			06 08					
4	—	32¼	—	Twickenham	a	23p31		23p40	23p42	23p51	00 07	00 10		05 13		05 42	05 52		06 12		06 23		06 40	
—	—	—	—		d	23p32		23p41	23p43	23p51		00 11		05 13		05 43	05 53		06 13		06 23		06 41	
4½	—	32¾	—	St Margarets	d	23p34			23p45					05 15		05 45			06 15					
5½	—	33¾	—	**Richmond** ⊖	d	23p37		23p45	23p49	23p56		00 15		05 19		05 49	05 58		06 19		06 28		06 45	
6¼	—	34½	—	North Sheen	d	23p39			23p51					05 21		05 51			06 21					
7	—	35¼	—	Mortlake	d	23p42			23p53					05 23		05 53			06 23					
—	0	—	—	**Hounslow**	d		23p35								05 31			06 01		06 16				
—	—	—	—	Isleworth	d		23p38								05 34			06 04		06 19				
—	2¼	—	—	Syon Lane	d		23p40								05 36			06 06		06 21				
—	3	—	—	Brentford	d		23p42								05 39			06 09		06 24				
—	4	—	—	Kew Bridge	d		23p45								05 41			06 11		06 26				
—	5	—	—	Chiswick	d		23p47								05 44			06 14		06 29				
—	6	—	—	Barnes Bridge	d		23p50								05 46			06 16		06 31				
8½	6½	36½	—	Barnes	d	23p45	23p53		23p56					05 26	05 49	05 56		06 19	06 26	06 34		←		
9½	—	37¾	—	Putney	d	23p48	23p56		23p59	00 02				05 29	05 52	05 59	06 04	06 22	06 29	06 37	06 34	06 37	06 52	
10½	—	38¾	—	Wandsworth Town	d	23p51	23p59		00 02					05 32	05 55	06 02		06 25	06 32	→		06 40		
11¼	—	39½	—	Clapham Junction [10]	d	23p54	00 02	23p54	00 05	00 07		00 24		05 35	05 58	06 05	06 09	06 28	06 35		06 39	06 43	06 56	
12½	—	41¾	—	Queenstown Rd.(Battersea)	d	23p57	00 05		00 08					05 38	06 01	06 08		06 31	06 38			06 46		
14	—	42¼	—	Vauxhall ⊖	d	23p59	00 08		00 12	00 12				05 42	06 05	06 12	06 15	06 35	06 42		06 45	06 50		
15¼	—	43½	—	**London Waterloo [15]** ⊖	a	00 05	00 13	00 04	00 16	00 17		00 37		05 46	06 09	06 16	06 19	06 39	06 46		06 49	06 56	07 07	

Reading, Guildford, Ascot, Weybridge, Windsor, Kingston, Richmond and Hounslow - London

Network Diagram - see first Page of Table 148

		SW	SW	SW	SW	SW	SW	SW	SW	SW		SW	SW	SW	SW	SW	SW	SW	SW	SW		SW	SW	SW	SW
					◇				◇ 1				◇	◇	◇			◇ 1	1	◇ 1			◇	◇	◇
Reading 7	d								06 12											06 42					
Earley	d								06 17											06 47					
Winnersh Triangle	d								06 19											06 49					
Winnersh	d								06 21											06 51					
Wokingham	d								06 26											06 56					
Bracknell	d								06 32											07 02					
Martins Heron	d								06 35											07 05					
Guildford	d																		06 30						
Wanborough	d																		06 36						
Ash 5	d																		06 40						
Aldershot	a																		06 47						
	d																	06 28							
Ash Vale	d																	06 32							
Frimley	d																	06 40							
Camberley	a																	06 44							
	d																	06 47							
Bagshot	d																	06 52							
Ascot 3	d								06 40									06 59		07 10					
Sunningdale	d								06 43									07 02		07 13					
Longcross	d																								
Woking	d																								
West Byfleet	d																								
Byfleet & New Haw	d																								
Weybridge	d												06 33										07 03		
Addlestone	d												06 37										07 07		
Chertsey	d												06 40										07 10		
Virginia Water	a								06 49				06 45					07 08		07 19			07 15		
	d								06 49				06 54					07 08		07 19			07 24		
Egham	d								06 53				06 57					07 12		07 23			07 27		
Windsor & Eton Riverside	d				06 23									06 53										07 23	
Datchet	d				06 26									06 56										07 26	
Sunnymeads	d				06 29									06 59										07 29	
Wraysbury	d				06 32									07 02										07 32	
Staines	d			06 33	06 38				06 59				07 03	07 08				07 18		07 29			07 33	07 38	
Ashford (Surrey)	d			06 36	06 41								07 06	07 11				07 21					07 36	07 41	
Feltham	d			06 41	06 46				07 05				07 11	07 16				07 26		07 35			07 41	07 46	
Whitton	d	06 20			06 50		06 50	06 53						07 20			07 20	07 30						07 50	
Kingston	d		06 29									06 59										07 29			
Hampton Wick	d		06 31									07 01										07 31			
Teddington	d		06 35									07 05										07 35			
Fulwell	d															07 12									
Strawberry Hill	d		06 38									07 08				07 14						07 38			
Twickenham	a		06 42		06 53			06 56	07 10			07 12		07 23		07 18		07 33		07 40		07 42		07 53	
	d		06 43		06 53			06 58	07 11			07 13		07 23		07 27		07 33		07 41		07 43		07 53	
St Margarets	d		06 45					07 00				07 15				07 29						07 45			
Richmond ⊖	d		06 49		06 58			07 04	07 15			07 19		07 28		07 32		07 38		07 45		07 49		07 58	
North Sheen	d		06 51					07 06				07 21				07 34						07 51			
Mortlake	d		06 53					07 08				07 23				07 37						07 53			
Hounslow	d	06 31		06 46			07 01						07 16				07 31						07 46		
Isleworth	d	06 34		06 49			07 04						07 19				07 34						07 49		
Syon Lane	d	06 36		06 51			07 06						07 21				07 36						07 51		
Brentford	d	06 39		06 54			07 09						07 24				07 39						07 54		
Kew Bridge	d	06 41		06 56			07 11						07 26				07 41						07 56		
Chiswick	d	06 44		06 59			07 14						07 29				07 44						07 59		
Barnes Bridge	d	06 46		07 01			07 16			←			07 31				07 46						08 01		
Barnes	d	06 49	06 56	07 04		←	07 19	07 11		07 19		07 26	07 34		←	07 40	07 49					07 56	08 04		←
Putney	d	06 52	06 59	07 07	07 04	07 07	→	07 14	07 22	07 22		07 29	07 37	07 34	07 37	07 43	07 52					07 59	08 07	08 04	08 07
Wandsworth Town	d	06 55	07 02	→		07 10		07 17		07 25		07 32	→		07 40	07 46	07 55					08 02	→		08 10
Clapham Junction 10	d	06 58	07 05		07 09	07 13		07 20	07 26	07 28		07 35		07 39	07 43	07 49	07 58	07 47		07 54		08 05		08 09	08 13
Queenstown Rd.(Battersea)	d	07 01	07 08			07 16		07 23		07 31		07 38			07 46	07 52	08 01					08 08			08 16
Vauxhall ⊖	d	07 05	07 12		07 15	07 20		07 27		07 35		07 42		07 45	07 50	07 56	08 05	07 53				08 12		08 15	08 20
London Waterloo 15 ⊖	a	07 11	07 18		07 21	07 28		07 34	07 37	07 43		07 48		07 51	07 58	08 04	08 11	07 59		08 06		08 18		08 21	08 28

Reading, Guildford, Ascot, Weybridge, Windsor, Kingston, Richmond and Hounslow - London

Network Diagram - see first Page of Table 148

		SW	SW	SW	SW	SW	SW	SW	SW	SW	SW	SW	SW	SW	SW	SW	SW	SW	SW	SW	SW	SW	SW
				◇1	1	◇1		◇	◇1	◇	◇			◇1	◇1	1		◇	◇	◇			◇1
Reading 7	d					07 12			07 24						07 42								08 12
Earley	d					07 17									07 47								08 17
Winnersh Triangle	d					07 19									07 49								08 19
Winnersh	d					07 21									07 51								08 21
Wokingham	d					07 26			07 33						07 56								08 26
Bracknell	d					07 32			07 39						08 02								08 32
Martins Heron	d					07 35			07 42						08 05								08 35
Guildford	d				07 00											07 30							
Wanborough	d				07 06											07 36							
Ash 5	d				07 10											07 40							
Aldershot	a				07 17											07 47							
	d			07 00										07 30		08 00							
Ash Vale	d			07 04										07 34		08 04							
Frimley	d			07 10										07 40		08 10							
Camberley	a			07 14										07 44		08 14							
	d			07 17										07 47		08 18							
Bagshot	d			07 22										07 52		08 23							
Ascot 3	d			07 29		07 40			07 47					07 59	08 10	08a30							08 40
Sunningdale	d			07 32		07 43			07 50					08 02	08 13								08 43
Longcross	d														08 16								08 46
Woking	d																						
West Byfleet	d																						
Byfleet & New Haw	d																						
Weybridge	d							07 33										08 03					
Addlestone	d							07 37										08 07					
Chertsey	d							07 40										08 10					
Virginia Water	a			07 38				07 45	07 55					08 08	08 19			08 15					08 49
	d			07 38				07 51	07 55					08 08	08 19			08 24					08 49
Egham	d			07 42		07 50		07 54	07 58					08 12	08 23			08 27					08 53
Windsor & Eton Riverside	d									07 53									08 23				
Datchet	d									07 56									08 26				
Sunnymeads	d									07 59									08 29				
Wraysbury	d									08 02									08 32				
Staines	d			07 48		07 56		08 00	08 04	08 08				08 18	08 29			08 33	08 38				08 59
Ashford (Surrey)	d			07 51				08 03		08 11				08 21				08 36	08 41				
Feltham	d			07 56		08 02		08 08	08 12	08 16				08 26	08 35			08 41	08 46				09 05
Whitton	d		07 50	08 00						08 20			08 20	08 30					08 50		08 50	08 53	
Kingston	d						07 59										08 29						
Hampton Wick	d						08 01										08 31						
Teddington	d						08 05										08 35						
Fulwell	d	07 42										08 12											
Strawberry Hill	d	07 44					08 08					08 14					08 38						
Twickenham	a	07 48		08 03		08 09	08 12		08 17	08 23		08 18		08 33	08 40		08 42		08 53			08 56	09 10
	d	07 57		08 03		08 09	08 13		08 18	08 23		08 27		08 33	08 41		08 43		08 53			08 58	09 11
St Margarets	d	07 59					08 15					08 29					08 45					09 00	
Richmond ⊖	d	08 02		08 08		08 14	08 19		08 24	08 28		08 32		08 38	08 45		08 49		08 58			09 04	09 15
North Sheen	d	08 04					08 21					08 34					08 51					09 06	
Mortlake	d	08 07					08 23					08 37					08 53					09 08	
Hounslow	d		08 01					08 16					08 31					08 46			09 01		
Isleworth	d		08 04					08 19					08 34					08 49			09 04		
Syon Lane	d		08 06					08 21					08 36					08 51			09 06		
Brentford	d		08 09					08 24					08 39					08 54			09 09		
Kew Bridge	d		08 11					08 26					08 41					08 56			09 11		
Chiswick	d		08 14					08 29					08 44					08 59			09 14		
Barnes Bridge	d		08 16					08 31					08 46					09 01			09 16		
Barnes	d	08 10	08 19				08 26	08 34			←	08 40	08 49				08 56	09 04		←	09 19	09 11	
Putney	d	08 13	08 22				08 29	08 37		08 34	08 37	08 43	08 52				08 59	09 07	09 04	09 07	→	09 14	
Wandsworth Town	d	08 16	08 25				08 32	→			08 40	08 46	08 55				09 02	→		09 10		09 17	
Clapham Junction 10	d	08 19	08 28	08 17		08 22	08 35		08 33	08 39	08 43	08 49	08 58	08 47	08 54		09 05		09 09	09 13		09 20	09 24
Queenstown Rd.(Battersea)	d	08 22	08 31				08 38				08 46	08 52	09 01				09 08			09 16		09 23	
Vauxhall ⊖	d	08 26	08 35	08 23			08 42		08 38	08 45	08 50	08 56	09 05	08 53			09 12		09 15	09 20		09 27	
London Waterloo 15 ⊖	a	08 34	08 43	08 29		08 38	08 49		08 46	08 51	08 58	09 04	09 13	09 00	09 06		09 18		09 21	09 28		09 34	09 34

Reading, Guildford, Ascot, Weybridge, Windsor, Kingston, Richmond and Hounslow - London

Network Diagram - see first Page of Table 148

		SW	SW 1	SW	SW ◇	SW ◇	SW ◇	SW	SW	SW 1	SW	SW 1	SW	SW	SW	SW	SW	SW	SW 1	SW	SW	SW
Reading 7	d									08 42									09 12			
Earley	d									08 47									09 17			
Winnersh Triangle	d									08 49									09 19			
Winnersh	d									08 51									09 21			
Wokingham	d									08 56									09 26			
Bracknell	d									09 02									09 32			
Martins Heron	d									09 05									09 35			
Guildford	d		08 00									08 30										
Wanborough	d		08 06									08 36										
Ash 5	d		08 10									08 40										
Aldershot	a		08 17									08 47										
	d		08 30									09 00										
Ash Vale	d		08 34									09 04										
Frimley	d		08 40									09 10										
Camberley	a		08 44									09 14										
	d		08 48									09 18										
Bagshot	d		08 53									09 23										
Ascot 3	d		09a00							09 10		09a30							09 40			
Sunningdale	d									09 13									09 43			
Longcross	d									09 16												
Woking	d																					
West Byfleet	d																					
Byfleet & New Haw	d																					
Weybridge	d				08 33									09 03								09 33
Addlestone	d				08 37									09 07								09 37
Chertsey	d				08 40									09 10								09 40
Virginia Water	a				08 45					09 19				09 15					09 49			09 45
	d				08 54					09 19				09 24					09 49			09 54
Egham	d				08 57					09 23				09 27					09 53			09 57
Windsor & Eton Riverside	d					08 53									09 23							
Datchet	d					08 56									09 26							
Sunnymeads	d					08 59									09 29							
Wraysbury	d					09 02									09 32							
Staines	d				09 03	09 08				09 29				09 33	09 38				09 59			10 03
Ashford (Surrey)	d				09 06	09 11								09 36	09 41							10 06
Feltham	d				09 11	09 16				09 35				09 41	09 46				10 05			10 11
Whitton	d					09 20		09 20	09 23						09 50		09 50	09 53				
Kingston	d			08 59									09 29								09 59	
Hampton Wick	d			09 01									09 31								10 01	
Teddington	d			09 05									09 35								10 05	
Fulwell	d																					
Strawberry Hill	d			09 08									09 38								10 08	
Twickenham	a			09 12		09 23			09 26	09 40			09 42		09 53			09 56	10 10		10 12	
	d			09 13		09 23			09 28	09 41			09 43		09 53			09 58	10 11		10 13	
St Margarets	d			09 15					09 30				09 45					10 00			10 15	
Richmond ⊖	d			09 19		09 28			09 34	09 45			09 49		09 58			10 04	10 15		10 19	
North Sheen	d			09 21					09 36				09 51					10 06			10 21	
Mortlake	d			09 23					09 38				09 53					10 08			10 23	
Hounslow	d				09 16			09 31						09 46			10 01					10 16
Isleworth	d				09 19			09 34						09 49			10 04					10 19
Syon Lane	d				09 21			09 36						09 51			10 06					10 21
Brentford	d				09 24			09 39						09 54			10 09					10 24
Kew Bridge	d				09 26			09 41						09 56			10 11					10 26
Chiswick	d				09 29			09 44						09 59			10 14					10 29
Barnes Bridge	d	←			09 31			09 46			←			10 01			10 16			←		10 31
Barnes	d	09 19		09 26	09 34		←	09 49	09 41		09 49		09 56	10 04		←	10 19	10 11		10 19	10 26	10 34
Putney	d	09 22		09 29	09 37	09 34	09 37	→	09 44		09 52		09 59	10 07	10 04	10 07	→	10 14		10 22	10 29	10 37
Wandsworth Town	d	09 25		09 32	→		09 40		09 47		09 55		10 02	→		10 10		10 17		10 25	10 32	→
Clapham Junction 10	d	09 28		09 35		09 39	09 43		09 50	09 54	09 58		10 05		10 09	10 13		10 20	10 24	10 28	10 35	
Queenstown Rd.(Battersea)	d	09 31		09 38			09 46		09 53		10 01		10 08			10 16		10 23		10 31	10 38	
Vauxhall ⊖	d	09 35		09 42		09 45	09 50		09 57		10 05		10 12		10 15	10 20		10 27		10 35	10 42	
London Waterloo 15 ⊖	a	09 43		09 48		09 51	09 58		10 02	10 04	10 11		10 16		10 19	10 26		10 32	10 34	10 41	10 46	

Reading, Guildford, Ascot, Weybridge, Windsor, Kingston, Richmond and Hounslow - London

Network Diagram - see first Page of Table 148

		SW	SW 1	SW	SW 1	SW	SW	SW 1	SW	SW	SW	SW	SW 1	SW	SW 1	SW	SW	SW 1	SW	SW 1	SW	SW	SW
Reading 7	d		09 25					09 42					09 56					10 12					
Earley	d		09 30					09 47					10 01					10 17					
Winnersh Triangle	d		09 32					09 49					10 03					10 19					
Winnersh	d		09 34					09 51					10 05					10 21					
Wokingham	d		09 39					09 56					10 10					10 26					
Bracknell	d		09 46					10 02					10 16					10 32					
Martins Heron	d		09 49					10 05					10 19					10 35					
Guildford	d				09 00										09 30					10 00			
Wanborough	d				09 06										09 36					10 06			
Ash 5	d				09 10										09 40					10 10			
Aldershot	a				09 17										09 47					10 17			
	d				09 30										10 00					10 30			
Ash Vale	d				09 34										10 04					10 34			
Frimley	d				09 40										10 10					10 40			
Camberley	a				09 44										10 14					10 44			
	d				09 48										10 18					10 48			
Bagshot	d				09 53										10 23					10 53			
Ascot 3	d		09 55		10a00			10 10					10 25		10a30			10 40		11a00			
Sunningdale	d		09 58					10 13					10 28					10 43					
Longcross	d																						
Woking	d																						
West Byfleet	d																						
Byfleet & New Haw	d																						
Weybridge	d										10 03											10 33	
Addlestone	d										10 07											10 37	
Chertsey	d										10 10											10 40	
Virginia Water	a		10 03					10 19			10 15		10 33					10 49				10 45	
	d		10 03					10 19			10 24		10 33					10 49				10 54	
Egham	d		10 06					10 23			10 27		10 36					10 53				10 57	
Windsor & Eton Riverside	d	09 53										10 23											10 53
Datchet	d	09 56										10 26											10 56
Sunnymeads	d	09 59										10 29											10 59
Wraysbury	d	10 02										10 32											11 02
Staines	d	10 08	10 14					10 29			10 33	10 38	10 44					10 59				11 03	11 08
Ashford (Surrey)	d	10 11									10 36	10 41										11 06	11 11
Feltham	d	10 16	10 20					10 35			10 41	10 46	10 50					11 05				11 11	11 16
Whitton	d	10 20				10 20	10 26					10 50				10 50	10 56						11 20
Kingston	d									10 29											10 59		
Hampton Wick	d									10 31											11 01		
Teddington	d									10 35											11 05		
Fulwell	d																						
Strawberry Hill	d									10 38											11 08		
Twickenham	a	10 23	10 27				10 28	10 40		10 42		10 53	10 57				10 58	11 10			11 12		11 23
	d	10 23	10 27				10 28	10 41		10 43		10 53	10 57				10 58	11 11			11 13		11 23
St Margarets	d						10 30			10 45							11 00				11 15		
Richmond	⊖ d	10 28	10 32				10 34	10 45		10 49		10 58	11 02				11 04	11 15			11 19		11 28
North Sheen	d						10 36			10 51							11 06				11 21		
Mortlake	d						10 38			10 53							11 08				11 23		
Hounslow	d					10 31					10 46					11 01						11 16	
Isleworth	d					10 34					10 49					11 04						11 19	
Syon Lane	d					10 36					10 51					11 06						11 21	
Brentford	d					10 39					10 54					11 09						11 24	
Kew Bridge	d					10 41					10 56					11 11						11 26	
Chiswick	d					10 44					10 59					11 14						11 29	
Barnes Bridge	d					10 46			←		11 01					11 16			←			11 31	
Barnes	d			←		10 49	10 41		10 49	10 56	11 04			←		11 19	11 11		11 19		11 26	11 34	
Putney	d	10 34		10 37		→	10 44		10 52	10 59	11 07	11 04		11 07		→	11 14		11 22		11 29	11 37	11 34
Wandsworth Town	d			10 40			10 47		10 55	11 02	→			11 10			11 17		11 25		11 32	→	
Clapham Junction 10	d	10 39	10 42	10 43			10 50	10 54	10 58	11 05		11 09	11 12	11 13			11 20	11 24	11 28		11 35		11 39
Queenstown Rd.(Battersea)	d			10 47			10 53		11 01	11 08				11 17			11 23		11 31		11 38		
Vauxhall	⊖ d	10 45		10 50			10 57		11 05	11 12		11 15		11 20			11 27		11 35		11 42		11 45
London Waterloo 15	⊖ a	10 49	10 53	10 56			11 02	11 04	11 11	11 16		11 19	11 25	11 27			11 32	11 34	11 41		11 46		11 49

Table 149

Mondays to Fridays

Reading, Guildford, Ascot, Weybridge, Windsor, Kingston, Richmond and Hounslow - London

Network Diagram - see first Page of Table 148

		SW	SW	SW	SW	SW	SW	SW	SW	SW	SW	SW	SW	SW	SW	SW	SW	SW	SW	SW	SW	SW
					■1		■1							■1		■1						
Reading ■7	d				10 42									11 12								
Earley	d				10 47									11 17								
Winnersh Triangle	d				10 49									11 19								
Winnersh	d				10 51									11 21								
Wokingham	d				10 56									11 26								
Bracknell	d				11 02									11 32								
Martins Heron	d				11 05									11 35								
Guildford	d						10 30									11 00						
Wanborough	d						10 36									11 06						
Ash ■5	d						10 40									11 10						
Aldershot	a						10 47									11 17						
	d						11 00									11 30						
Ash Vale	d						11 04									11 34						
Frimley	d						11 10									11 40						
Camberley	a						11 14									11 44						
	d						11 18									11 48						
Bagshot	d						11 23									11 53						
Ascot ■3	d				11 10		11a30							11 40		12a00						
Sunningdale	d				11 13									11 43								
Longcross	d																					
Woking	d																					
West Byfleet	d																					
Byfleet & New Haw	d																					
Weybridge	d								11 03									11 33				
Addlestone	d								11 07									11 37				
Chertsey	d								11 10									11 40				
Virginia Water	a				11 19				11 15					11 49				11 45				
	d				11 19				11 24					11 49				11 54				
Egham	d				11 23				11 27					11 53				11 57				
Windsor & Eton Riverside	d									11 23									11 53			
Datchet	d									11 26									11 56			
Sunnymeads	d									11 29									11 59			
Wraysbury	d									11 32									12 02			
Staines	d				11 29				11 33	11 38				11 59				12 03	12 08			
Ashford (Surrey)	d								11 36	11 41								12 06	12 11			
Feltham	d				11 35				11 41	11 46				12 05				12 11	12 16			
Whitton	d		11 20	11 23						11 50		11 50	11 53						12 20		12 20	12 23
Kingston	d							11 29									11 59					
Hampton Wick	d							11 31									12 01					
Teddington	d							11 35									12 05					
Fulwell	d																					
Strawberry Hill	d							11 38									12 08					
Twickenham	a			11 26	11 40			11 42		11 53			11 56	12 10			12 12		12 23			12 26
	d			11 28	11 41			11 43		11 53			11 58	12 11			12 13		12 23			12 28
St Margarets	d			11 30				11 45					12 00				12 15					12 30
Richmond ⊖	d			11 34	11 45			11 49		11 58			12 04	12 15			12 19		12 28			12 34
North Sheen	d			11 36				11 51					12 06				12 21					12 36
Mortlake	d			11 38				11 53					12 08				12 23					12 38
Hounslow	d		11 31						11 46			12 01						12 16			12 31	
Isleworth	d		11 34						11 49			12 04						12 19			12 34	
Syon Lane	d		11 36						11 51			12 06						12 21			12 36	
Brentford	d		11 39						11 54			12 09						12 24			12 39	
Kew Bridge	d		11 41						11 56			12 11						12 26			12 41	
Chiswick	d		11 44						11 59			12 14						12 29			12 44	
Barnes Bridge	d		11 46			←			12 01			12 16			←			12 31			12 46	
Barnes	d	←	11 49	11 41		11 49		11 56	12 04		←	12 19	12 11		12 19		12 26	12 34		←	12 49	12 41
Putney	d	11 37	→	11 44		11 52		11 59	12 07	12 04	12 07	→	12 14		12 22		12 29	12 37	12 34	12 37	→	12 44
Wandsworth Town	d	11 40		11 47		11 55		12 02	→		12 10		12 17		12 25		12 32	→		12 40		12 47
Clapham Junction ■10	d	11 43		11 50	11 54	11 58		12 05		12 09	12 13		12 20	12 25	12 28		12 35		12 39	12 43		12 50
Queenstown Rd.(Battersea)	d	11 46		11 53		12 01		12 08			12 16		12 23		12 31		12 38			12 46		12 53
Vauxhall ⊖	d	11 50		11 57		12 05		12 12		12 15	12 20		12 27		12 35		12 42		12 45	12 50		12 57
London Waterloo ■15 ⊖	a	11 56		12 02	12 04	12 11		12 16		12 19	12 26		12 32	12 34	12 41		12 46		12 49	12 56		13 02

Reading, Guildford, Ascot, Weybridge, Windsor, Kingston, Richmond and Hounslow - London

Network Diagram - see first Page of Table 148

		SW 1	SW	SW 1	SW	SW	SW	SW	SW	SW		SW 1	SW	SW 1	SW	SW	SW	SW	SW	SW		SW 1	SW	SW 1	SW
Reading 7	d	11 42										12 12										12 42			
Earley	d	11 47										12 17										12 47			
Winnersh Triangle	d	11 49										12 19										12 49			
Winnersh	d	11 51										12 21										12 51			
Wokingham	d	11 56										12 26										12 56			
Bracknell	d	12 02										12 32										13 02			
Martins Heron	d	12 05										12 35										13 05			
Guildford	d			11 30										12 00										12 30	
Wanborough	d			11 36										12 06										12 36	
Ash 5	d			11 40										12 10										12 40	
Aldershot	a			11 47										12 17										12 47	
	d			12 00										12 30										13 00	
Ash Vale	d			12 04										12 34										13 04	
Frimley	d			12 10										12 40										13 10	
Camberley	a			12 14										12 44										13 14	
	d			12 18										12 48										13 18	
Bagshot	d			12 23										12 53										13 23	
Ascot 3	d	12 10		12a30								12 40		13a00								13 10		13a30	
Sunningdale	d	12 13										12 43										13 13			
Longcross	d																					13 16			
Woking	d																								
West Byfleet	d																								
Byfleet & New Haw	d																								
Weybridge	d					12 03										12 33									
Addlestone	d					12 07										12 37									
Chertsey	d					12 10										12 40									
Virginia Water	a	12 19				12 15						12 49				12 45						13 19			
	d	12 19				12 24						12 49				12 54						13 19			
Egham	d	12 23				12 27						12 53				12 57						13 23			
Windsor & Eton Riverside	d						12 23										12 53								
Datchet	d						12 26										12 56								
Sunnymeads	d						12 29										12 59								
Wraysbury	d						12 32										13 02								
Staines	d	12 29				12 33	12 38					12 59				13 03	13 08					13 29			
Ashford (Surrey)	d					12 36	12 41									13 06	13 11								
Feltham	d	12 35				12 41	12 46					13 05				13 11	13 16					13 35			
Whitton	d						12 50		12 50	12 53							13 20		13 20	13 23					
Kingston	d				12 29										12 59										13 29
Hampton Wick	d				12 31										13 01										13 31
Teddington	d				12 35										13 05										13 35
Fulwell	d																								
Strawberry Hill	d				12 38										13 08										13 38
Twickenham	a	12 40			12 42		12 53			12 56		13 10			13 12		13 23			13 26		13 40			13 42
	d	12 41			12 43		12 53			12 58		13 11			13 13		13 23			13 28		13 41			13 43
St Margarets	d				12 45					13 00					13 15					13 30					13 45
Richmond ⊖	d	12 45			12 49		12 58			13 04		13 15			13 19		13 28			13 34		13 45			13 49
North Sheen	d				12 51					13 06					13 21					13 36					13 51
Mortlake	d				12 53					13 08					13 23					13 38					13 53
Hounslow	d					12 46			13 01							13 16			13 31						
Isleworth	d					12 49			13 04							13 19			13 34						
Syon Lane	d					12 51			13 06							13 21			13 36						
Brentford	d					12 54			13 09							13 24			13 39						
Kew Bridge	d					12 56			13 11							13 26			13 41						
Chiswick	d					12 59			13 14							13 29			13 44						
Barnes Bridge	d		←			13 01			13 16				←			13 31			13 46				←		
Barnes	d		12 49		12 56	13 04		←	13 19	13 11			13 19		13 26	13 34		←	13 49	13 41			13 49		13 56
Putney	d		12 52		12 59	13 07	13 04	13 07	→	13 14			13 22		13 29	13 37	13 34	13 37	→	13 44			13 52		13 59
Wandsworth Town	d		12 55		13 02	→		13 10		13 17			13 25		13 32	→		13 40		13 47			13 55		14 02
Clapham Junction 10	d	12 54	12 58		13 05		13 09	13 13		13 20		13 24	13 28		13 35		13 39	13 43		13 50		13 54	13 58		14 05
Queenstown Rd.(Battersea)	d		13 01		13 08			13 16		13 23			13 31		13 38			13 46		13 53			14 01		14 08
Vauxhall ⊖	d		13 05		13 12		13 15	13 20		13 27			13 35		13 42		13 45	13 50		13 57			14 05		14 12
London Waterloo 15 ⊖	a	13 04	13 11		13 16		13 19	13 26		13 32		13 34	13 41		13 46		13 49	13 56		14 02		14 04	14 11		14 16

Reading, Guildford, Ascot, Weybridge, Windsor, Kingston, Richmond and Hounslow - London

Network Diagram - see first Page of Table 148

		SW	SW	SW	SW	SW	SW 1	SW	SW 1	SW	SW	SW	SW	SW	SW	SW 1	SW	SW 1	SW	SW	SW	SW	SW
Reading 7	d						13 12									13 42							
Earley	d						13 17									13 47							
Winnersh Triangle	d						13 19									13 49							
Winnersh	d						13 21									13 51							
Wokingham	d						13 26									13 56							
Bracknell	d						13 32									14 02							
Martins Heron	d						13 35									14 05							
Guildford	d								13 00									13 30					
Wanborough	d								13 06									13 36					
Ash 5	d								13 10									13 40					
Aldershot	a								13 17									13 47					
	d								13 30									14 00					
Ash Vale	d								13 34									14 04					
Frimley	d								13 40									14 10					
Camberley	a								13 44									14 14					
	d								13 48									14 18					
Bagshot	d								13 53									14 23					
Ascot 3	d						13 40		14a00							14 10		14a30					
Sunningdale	d						13 43									14 13							
Longcross	d																						
Woking	d																						
West Byfleet	d																						
Byfleet & New Haw	d																						
Weybridge	d	13 03									13 33									14 03			
Addlestone	d	13 07									13 37									14 07			
Chertsey	d	13 10									13 40									14 10			
Virginia Water	a	13 15					13 49				13 45					14 19				14 15			
	d	13 24					13 49				13 54					14 19				14 24			
Egham	d	13 27					13 53				13 57					14 23				14 27			
Windsor & Eton Riverside	d		13 23									13 53									14 23		
Datchet	d		13 26									13 56									14 26		
Sunnymeads	d		13 29									13 59									14 29		
Wraysbury	d		13 32									14 02									14 32		
Staines	d	13 33	13 38				13 59				14 03	14 08				14 29				14 33	14 38		
Ashford (Surrey)	d	13 36	13 41								14 06	14 11								14 36	14 41		
Feltham	d	13 41	13 46				14 05				14 11	14 16				14 35				14 41	14 46		
Whitton	d		13 50		13 50	13 53						14 20		14 20	14 23						14 50		14 50
Kingston	d									13 59									14 29				
Hampton Wick	d									14 01									14 31				
Teddington	d									14 05									14 35				
Fulwell	d																						
Strawberry Hill	d									14 08									14 38				
Twickenham	a		13 53			13 56	14 10			14 12		14 23			14 26	14 40			14 42		14 53		
	d		13 53			13 58	14 11			14 13		14 23			14 28	14 41			14 43		14 53		
St Margarets	d					14 00				14 15					14 30				14 45				
Richmond ⊖	d		13 58			14 04	14 15			14 19		14 28			14 34	14 45			14 49		14 58		
North Sheen	d					14 06				14 21					14 36				14 51				
Mortlake	d					14 08				14 23					14 38				14 53				
Hounslow	d	13 46			14 01						14 16			14 31						14 46			15 01
Isleworth	d	13 49			14 04						14 19			14 34						14 49			15 04
Syon Lane	d	13 51			14 06						14 21			14 36						14 51			15 06
Brentford	d	13 54			14 09						14 24			14 39						14 54			15 09
Kew Bridge	d	13 56			14 11						14 26			14 41						14 56			15 11
Chiswick	d	13 59			14 14						14 29			14 44						14 59			15 14
Barnes Bridge	d	14 01			14 16			←			14 31			14 46			←			15 01			15 16
Barnes	d	14 04		←	14 19	14 11		14 19		14 26	14 34		←	14 49	14 41		14 49		14 56	15 04		←	15 19
Putney	d	14 07	14 04	14 07	↪	14 14		14 22		14 29	14 37	14 34	14 37	↪	14 44		14 52		14 59	15 07	15 04	15 07	↪
Wandsworth Town	d	↪		14 10		14 17		14 25		14 32	↪		14 40		14 47		14 55		15 02	↪		15 10	
Clapham Junction 10	d		14 09	14 13		14 20	14 24	14 28		14 35		14 39	14 43		14 50	14 54	14 58		15 05		15 09	15 13	
Queenstown Rd.(Battersea)	d			14 16		14 23		14 31		14 38			14 46		14 53		15 01		15 08			15 16	
Vauxhall ⊖	d		14 15	14 20		14 27		14 35		14 42		14 45	14 50		14 57		15 05		15 12		15 15	15 20	
London Waterloo 15 ⊖	a		14 19	14 26		14 32	14 34	14 41		14 46		14 49	14 56		15 02	15 04	15 11		15 16		15 19	15 26	

Reading, Guildford, Ascot, Weybridge, Windsor, Kingston, Richmond and Hounslow - London

Network Diagram - see first Page of Table 148

		SW		SW 1	SW	SW 1	SW	SW	SW	SW	SW	SW		SW 1	SW	SW 1	SW	SW	SW	SW	SW	SW		SW 1	SW
Reading 7	d			14 12										14 42										15 12	
Earley	d			14 17										14 47										15 17	
Winnersh Triangle	d			14 19										14 49										15 19	
Winnersh	d			14 21										14 51										15 21	
Wokingham	d			14 26										14 56										15 26	
Bracknell	d			14 32										15 02										15 32	
Martins Heron	d			14 35										15 05										15 35	
Guildford	d					14 00										14 30									
Wanborough	d					14 06										14 36									
Ash 5	d					14 10										14 40									
Aldershot	a					14 17										14 47									
	d					14 30										15 00									
Ash Vale	d					14 34										15 04									
Frimley	d					14 40										15 10									
Camberley	a					14 44										15 14									
	d					14 48										15 18									
Bagshot	d					14 53										15 23									
Ascot 3	d			14 40		15a00								15 10		15a30								15 40	
Sunningdale	d			14 43										15 13										15 43	
Longcross	d																								
Woking	d																								
West Byfleet	d																								
Byfleet & New Haw	d																								
Weybridge	d							14 33										15 03							
Addlestone	d							14 37										15 07							
Chertsey	d							14 40										15 10							
Virginia Water	a			14 49				14 45						15 19				15 15						15 49	
	d			14 49				14 54						15 19				15 24						15 49	
Egham	d			14 53				14 57						15 23				15 27						15 53	
Windsor & Eton Riverside	d								14 53										15 23						
Datchet	d								14 56										15 26						
Sunnymeads	d								14 59										15 29						
Wraysbury	d								15 02										15 32						
Staines	d			14 59				15 03	15 08					15 29				15 33	15 38					15 59	
Ashford (Surrey)	d							15 06	15 11									15 36	15 41						
Feltham	d			15 05				15 11	15 16					15 35				15 41	15 46					16 05	
Whitton	d	14 53							15 20		15 20	15 23							15 50		15 50	15 53			
Kingston	d						14 59										15 29								
Hampton Wick	d						15 01										15 31								
Teddington	d						15 05										15 35								
Fulwell	d																								
Strawberry Hill	d						15 08										15 38								
Twickenham	a	14 56		15 10			15 12		15 23			15 26		15 40			15 42		15 53			15 56		16 10	
	d	14 58		15 11			15 13		15 23			15 28		15 41			15 43		15 53			15 58		16 11	
St Margarets	d	15 00					15 15					15 30					15 45					16 00			
Richmond ⊖	d	15 04		15 15			15 19		15 28			15 34		15 45			15 49		15 58			16 04		16 15	
North Sheen	d	15 06					15 21					15 36					15 51					16 06			
Mortlake	d	15 08					15 23					15 38					15 53					16 08			
Hounslow	d							15 16			15 31							15 46			16 01				
Isleworth	d							15 19			15 34							15 49			16 04				
Syon Lane	d							15 21			15 36							15 51			16 06				
Brentford	d							15 24			15 39							15 54			16 09				
Kew Bridge	d							15 26			15 41							15 56			16 11				
Chiswick	d							15 29			15 44							15 59			16 14				
Barnes Bridge	d				←			15 31			15 46				←			16 01			16 16				←
Barnes	d	15 11			15 19		15 26	15 34		←	15 49	15 41			15 49		15 56	16 04		←	16 19	16 11			16 19
Putney	d	15 14			15 22		15 29	15 37	15 34	15 37	→	15 44			15 52		15 59	16 07	16 04	16 07	→	16 14			16 22
Wandsworth Town	d	15 17			15 25		15 32	→		15 40		15 47			15 55		16 02	→		16 10		16 17			16 25
Clapham Junction 10	d	15 20		15 24	15 28		15 35		15 39	15 43		15 50		15 54	15 58		16 05		16 09	16 13		16 20		16 24	16 28
Queenstown Rd.(Battersea)	d	15 23			15 31		15 38			15 46		15 53			16 01		16 08			16 16		16 23			16 31
Vauxhall ⊖	d	15 27			15 35		15 42		15 45	15 50		15 57			16 05		16 12		16 15	16 20		16 27			16 35
London Waterloo 15 ⊖	a	15 32		15 34	15 41		15 46		15 49	15 56		16 02		16 05	16 11		16 19		16 19	16 26		16 32		16 34	16 41

Reading, Guildford, Ascot, Weybridge, Windsor, Kingston, Richmond and Hounslow - London

Network Diagram - see first Page of Table 148

		SW 1	SW	SW	SW	SW	SW	SW	SW 1	SW	SW 1	SW	SW	SW	SW	SW	SW	SW 1	SW	SW 1	SW	SW	SW
Reading 7	d								15 42									16 12					
Earley	d								15 47									16 17					
Winnersh Triangle	d								15 49									16 19					
Winnersh	d								15 51									16 21					
Wokingham	d								15 56									16 26					
Bracknell	d								16 02									16 32					
Martins Heron	d								16 05									16 35					
Guildford	d	15 00									15 30									16 00			
Wanborough	d	15 06									15 36									16 06			
Ash 5	d	15 10									15 40									16 10			
Aldershot	a	15 17									15 47									16 17			
	d	15 30									16 00									16 30			
Ash Vale	d	15 34									16 04									16 34			
Frimley	d	15 40									16 10									16 40			
Camberley	a	15 44									16 14									16 44			
	d	15 48									16 18									16 48			
Bagshot	d	15 53									16 23									16 53			
Ascot 3	d	16a00							16 10		16a30							16 40		17a00			
Sunningdale	d								16 13									16 43					
Longcross	d																						
Woking	d																						
West Byfleet	d																						
Byfleet & New Haw	d																						
Weybridge	d			15 33									16 03									16 33	
Addlestone	d			15 37									16 07									16 37	
Chertsey	d			15 40									16 10									16 40	
Virginia Water	a			15 45					16 19				16 15					16 49				16 45	
	d			15 54					16 19				16 24					16 49				16 54	
Egham	d			15 57					16 23				16 27					16 53				16 57	
Windsor & Eton Riverside	d				15 53									16 23									16 53
Datchet	d				15 56									16 26									16 56
Sunnymeads	d				15 59									16 29									16 59
Wraysbury	d				16 02									16 32									17 02
Staines	d			16 03	16 08				16 29				16 33	16 38				16 59				17 03	17 08
Ashford (Surrey)	d			16 06	16 11								16 36	16 41								17 06	17 11
Feltham	d			16 11	16 16				16 35				16 41	16 46				17 05				17 11	17 16
Whitton	d				16 20		16 20	16 23						16 50		16 50	16 53						17 20
Kingston	d		15 59									16 29									16 59		
Hampton Wick	d		16 01									16 31									17 01		
Teddington	d		16 05									16 35									17 05		
Fulwell	d																						
Strawberry Hill	d		16 08									16 38									17 08		
Twickenham	a		16 12		16 23			16 26	16 40			16 42		16 53			16 56	17 10			17 12		17 23
	d		16 13		16 23			16 28	16 41			16 43		16 53			16 58	17 11			17 13		17 23
St Margarets	d		16 15					16 30				16 45					17 00				17 15		
Richmond ⊖	d		16 19		16 28			16 34	16 45			16 49		16 58			17 04	17 15			17 19		17 28
North Sheen	d		16 21					16 36				16 51					17 06				17 21		
Mortlake	d		16 23					16 38				16 53					17 08				17 23		
Hounslow	d			16 16			16 31						16 46			17 01						17 16	
Isleworth	d			16 19			16 34						16 49			17 04						17 19	
Syon Lane	d			16 21			16 36						16 51			17 06						17 21	
Brentford	d			16 24			16 39						16 54			17 09						17 24	
Kew Bridge	d			16 26			16 41						16 56			17 11						17 26	
Chiswick	d			16 29			16 44						16 59			17 14						17 29	
Barnes Bridge	d			16 31			16 46			←			17 01			17 16			←			17 31	
Barnes	d		16 26	16 34		←	16 49	16 41		16 49		16 56	17 04		←	17 19	17 11		17 19		17 26	17 34	
Putney	d		16 29	16 37	16 34	16 37	→	16 44		16 52		16 59	17 07	17 05	17 07	→	17 14		17 22		17 29	17 37	17 34
Wandsworth Town	d		16 32	→		16 40		16 47		16 55		17 02	→		17 10		17 17		17 25		17 32	→	
Clapham Junction 10	d		16 35		16 39	16 43		16 50	16 54	16 58		17 05		17 09	17 13		17 20	17 24	17 28		17 35		17 39
Queenstown Rd.(Battersea)	d		16 38			16 46		16 53		17 01		17 08			17 16		17 23		17 31		17 38		
Vauxhall ⊖	d		16 42		16 45	16 50		16 57		17 05		17 12		17 15	17 20		17 27		17 35		17 42		17 45
London Waterloo 15 ⊖	a		16 49		16 49	16 56		17 02	17 04	17 11		17 19		17 19	17 26		17 32	17 33	17 41		17 49		17 49

Reading, Guildford, Ascot, Weybridge, Windsor, Kingston, Richmond and Hounslow - London

Network Diagram - see first Page of Table 148

		SW	SW	SW	SW 1	SW	SW 1	SW	SW	SW	SW	SW	SW	SW 1	SW	SW	SW	SW	SW	SW 1	SW 1	SW
Reading 7	d				16 42									17 12						17 22		
Earley	d				16 47									17 17						17 27		
Winnersh Triangle	d				16 49									17 19						17 29		
Winnersh	d				16 51									17 21						17 31		
Wokingham	d				16 56									17 26						17 36		
Bracknell	d				17 02									17 32						17 42		
Martins Heron	d				17 05									17 35						17 45		
Guildford	d						16 30														17 00	
Wanborough	d						16 36														17 06	
Ash 5	d						16 40														17 10	
Aldershot	a						16 47														17 17	
	d						17 00														17 30	
Ash Vale	d						17 04														17 34	
Frimley	d						17 10														17 40	
Camberley	a						17 14														17 44	
	d						17 18														17 48	
Bagshot	d						17 23														17 53	
Ascot 3	d				17 10		17a30							17 40						17 55	18a00	
Sunningdale	d				17 13									17 43						17 58		
Longcross	d				17 16																	
Woking	d																					
West Byfleet	d																					
Byfleet & New Haw	d																					
Weybridge	d								17 03								17 37					
Addlestone	d								17 07								17 41					
Chertsey	d								17 10								17 44					
Virginia Water	a				17 19				17 15					17 49			17 49			18 03		
	d				17 19				17 24					17 49			17 54			18 03		
Egham	d				17 23				17 27					17 53			17 57			18 06		
Windsor & Eton Riverside	d									17 23								17 53				
Datchet	d									17 26								17 56				
Sunnymeads	d									17 29								17 59				
Wraysbury	d									17 32								18 02				
Staines	d				17 29				17 33	17 38				17 59			18 03	18 08		18 14		
Ashford (Surrey)	d								17 36	17 41							18 06	18 11				
Feltham	d				17 35				17 41	17 46				18 05			18 11	18 16		18 20		
Whitton	d		17 20	17 23						17 50		17 50	17 53					18 20				18 20
Kingston	d							17 29								17 59						
Hampton Wick	d							17 31								18 01						
Teddington	d							17 35								18 05						
Fulwell	d																					
Strawberry Hill	d							17 38								18 08						
Twickenham	a			17 26	17 40			17 42		17 53			17 56	18 10		18 12		18 23				
	d			17 28	17 41			17 43		17 53			17 58	18 11		18 13		18 23				
St Margarets	d			17 30				17 45					18 00			18 15						
Richmond ⊖	d			17 34	17 45			17 49		17 58			18 04	18 15		18 19		18 28				
North Sheen	d			17 36				17 51					18 06			18 21						
Mortlake	d			17 38				17 53					18 08			18 23						
Hounslow	d		17 31						17 46			18 01					18 16			18 26		18 31
Isleworth	d		17 34						17 49			18 04					18 19					18 34
Syon Lane	d		17 36						17 51			18 06					18 21					18 36
Brentford	d		17 39						17 54			18 09					18 24			18 31		18 39
Kew Bridge	d		17 41						17 56			18 11					18 26					18 41
Chiswick	d		17 44						17 59			18 14					18 29					18 44
Barnes Bridge	d		17 46			←			18 01			18 16			←		18 31					18 46
Barnes	d	←	17 49	17 41		17 49		17 56	18 04		←	18 19	18 11		18 19	18 26	18 34		←			18 49
Putney	d	17 37	→	17 44		17 52		17 59	18 07	18 04	18 07	→	18 14		18 22	18 29	18 37	18 34	18 37	18 39		→
Wandsworth Town	d	17 40		17 47		17 55		18 02	→		18 10		18 17		18 25	18 32	→		18 40			
Clapham Junction 10	d	17 43		17 50	17 54	17 58		18 05		18 09	18 13		18 20	18 24	18 28	18 35		18 39	18 43	18 44		
Queenstown Rd.(Battersea)	d	17 46		17 53		18 01		18 08			18 16		18 23		18 31	18 38			18 46			
Vauxhall ⊖	d	17 50		17 57		18 05		18 12		18 15	18 20		18 27		18 35	18 42		18 45	18 50			
London Waterloo 15 ⊖	a	17 56		18 02	18 04	18 11		18 19		18 19	18 26		18 32	18 34	18 41	18 49		18 49	18 56	18 56		

Reading, Guildford, Ascot, Weybridge, Windsor, Kingston, Richmond and Hounslow - London

Network Diagram - see first Page of Table 148

		SW	SW 1	SW	SW	SW	SW	SW	SW 1	SW 1	SW	SW	SW 1	SW	SW 1	SW	SW	SW	SW	SW	SW	SW 1	SW
Reading 7	d		17 42						17 53				18 12									18 42	
Earley	d		17 47						17 58				18 17									18 47	
Winnersh Triangle	d		17 49						18 00				18 19									18 49	
Winnersh	d		17 51						18 02				18 21									18 51	
Wokingham	d		17 56						18 07				18 26									18 56	
Bracknell	d		18 02						18 13				18 32									19 02	
Martins Heron	d		18 05						18 16				18 35									19 05	
Guildford	d									17 30					18 00								
Wanborough	d									17 36					18 06								
Ash 5	d									17 40					18 10								
Aldershot	a									17 47					18 17								
	d									18 00					18 30								
Ash Vale	d									18 04					18 34								
Frimley	d									18 10					18 40								
Camberley	a									18 14					18 44								
	d									18 18					18 48								
Bagshot	d									18 23					18 53								
Ascot 3	d		18 10						18 25	18a30			18 40		19a00							19 10	
Sunningdale	d		18 13						18 28				18 43									19 13	
Longcross	d		18 16										18 46									19 16	
Woking	d																						
West Byfleet	d																						
Byfleet & New Haw	d																						
Weybridge	d					18 07											18 37						
Addlestone	d					18 11											18 41						
Chertsey	d					18 14											18 44						
Virginia Water	a		18 19			18 19			18 33				18 49				18 49					19 19	
	d		18 19			18 24			18 33				18 49				18 54					19 19	
Egham	d		18 23			18 27			18 37				18 53				18 57					19 23	
Windsor & Eton Riverside	d						18 23											18 53					
Datchet	d						18 26											18 56					
Sunnymeads	d						18 29											18 59					
Wraysbury	d						18 32											19 02					
Staines	d		18 29			18 33	18 38		18 44				18 59				19 03	19 08				19 29	
Ashford (Surrey)	d					18 36	18 41										19 06	19 11					
Feltham	d		18 35			18 41	18 46		18 50				19 05				19 11	19 16				19 35	
Whitton	d	18 23					18 50				18 50	18 53						19 20		19 20	19 23		
Kingston	d				18 29											18 59							
Hampton Wick	d				18 31											19 01							
Teddington	d				18 35											19 05							
Fulwell	d																						
Strawberry Hill	d				18 38											19 08							
Twickenham	a	18 26	18 40		18 42		18 53					18 56	19 10			19 12		19 23			19 26	19 40	
	d	18 28	18 41		18 43		18 53					18 58	19 11			19 13		19 23			19 28	19 41	
St Margarets	d	18 30			18 45							19 00				19 15					19 30		
Richmond ⊖	d	18 34	18 45		18 49		18 58					19 04	19 15			19 19		19 28			19 34	19 45	
North Sheen	d	18 36			18 51							19 06				19 21					19 36		
Mortlake	d	18 38			18 53							19 08				19 23					19 38		
Hounslow	d					18 46			18 56		19 01						19 16			19 31			
Isleworth	d					18 49					19 04						19 19			19 34			
Syon Lane	d					18 51					19 06						19 21			19 36			
Brentford	d					18 54			19 01		19 09						19 24			19 39			
Kew Bridge	d					18 56					19 11						19 26			19 41			
Chiswick	d					18 59					19 14						19 29			19 44			
Barnes Bridge	d			←		19 01					19 16			←			19 31			19 46			←
Barnes	d	18 41		18 49	18 56	19 04		←			19 19	19 11		19 19		19 26	19 34		←	19 49	19 41		19 49
Putney	d	18 44		18 52	18 59	19 07	19 04	19 07	19 09		→	19 14		19 22		19 29	19 37	19 34	19 37	→	19 44		19 52
Wandsworth Town	d	18 47		18 55	19 02	→		19 10				19 17		19 25		19 32	→		19 40		19 47		19 55
Clapham Junction 10	d	18 50	18 54	18 58	19 05		19 09	19 13	19 14			19 20	19 24	19 28		19 35		19 39	19 43		19 50	19 54	19 58
Queenstown Rd.(Battersea)	d	18 53		19 01	19 08			19 16				19 23		19 31		19 38			19 46		19 53		20 01
Vauxhall ⊖	d	18 57		19 05	19 12		19 15	19 20				19 27		19 35		19 42		19 45	19 50		19 57		20 05
London Waterloo 15 ⊖	a	19 02	19 04	19 11	19 16		19 19	19 26	19 28			19 32	19 34	19 41		19 46		19 49	19 56		20 02	20 04	20 09

Reading, Guildford, Ascot, Weybridge, Windsor, Kingston, Richmond and Hounslow - London

Network Diagram - see first Page of Table 148

		SW	SW	SW	SW	SW		SW	SW	SW	SW	SW	SW	SW	SW	SW		SW	SW	SW	SW	SW	SW	SW	SW
		1	1								1		1								1		1		
Reading 7	d	18 52									19 12										19 42				
Earley	d	18 57									19 17										19 47				
Winnersh Triangle	d	18 59									19 19										19 49				
Winnersh	d	19 01									19 21										19 51				
Wokingham	d	19 06									19 26										19 56				
Bracknell	d	19 12									19 32										20 02				
Martins Heron	d	19 15									19 35										20 05				
Guildford	d		18 30										19 00										19 30		
Wanborough	d		18 36										19 06										19 36		
Ash 5	d		18 40										19 10										19 40		
Aldershot	a		18 47										19 17										19 47		
	d		19 00										19 30										20 00		
Ash Vale	d		19 04										19 34										20 04		
Frimley	d		19 10										19 40										20 10		
Camberley	a		19 14										19 44										20 14		
	d		19 18										19 48										20 18		
Bagshot	d		19 23										19 53										20 23		
Ascot 3	d	19a19	19a30								19 40		20a00								20 10		20a30		
Sunningdale	d										19 43										20 13				
Longcross	d										19 46										20 16				
Woking	d																								
West Byfleet	d																								
Byfleet & New Haw	d																								
Weybridge	d				19 07										19 37										20 03
Addlestone	d				19 11										19 41										20 07
Chertsey	d				19 14										19 44										20 10
Virginia Water	a				19 19						19 49				19 49						20 19				20 15
	d				19 24						19 49				19 54						20 19				20 24
Egham	d				19 27						19 53				19 57						20 23				20 27
Windsor & Eton Riverside	d					19 23										19 53									
Datchet	d					19 26										19 56									
Sunnymeads	d					19 29										19 59									
Wraysbury	d					19 32										20 02									
Staines	d				19 33	19 38					19 59				20 03	20 08					20 29				20 33
Ashford (Surrey)	d				19 36	19 41									20 06	20 11									20 36
Feltham	d				19 41	19 46					20 05				20 11	20 16					20 35				20 41
Whitton	d					19 50			19 50	19 53						20 20			20 20	20 23					
Kingston	d			19 29										19 59										20 29	
Hampton Wick	d			19 31										20 01										20 31	
Teddington	d			19 35										20 05										20 35	
Fulwell	d																								
Strawberry Hill	d			19 38										20 08										20 38	
Twickenham	a			19 42		19 53				19 56	20 10			20 12		20 23				20 26	20 40			20 42	
	d			19 43		19 53				19 58	20 11			20 13		20 23				20 28	20 41			20 43	
St Margarets	d			19 45						20 00				20 15						20 30				20 45	
Richmond ⊖	d			19 49		19 58				20 04	20 15			20 19		20 28				20 34	20 45			20 49	
North Sheen	d			19 51						20 06				20 21						20 36				20 51	
Mortlake	d			19 53						20 08				20 23						20 38				20 53	
Hounslow	d				19 46				20 01						20 16				20 31						20 46
Isleworth	d				19 49				20 04						20 19				20 34						20 49
Syon Lane	d				19 51				20 06						20 21				20 36						20 51
Brentford	d				19 54				20 09						20 24				20 39						20 54
Kew Bridge	d				19 56				20 11						20 26				20 41						20 56
Chiswick	d				19 59				20 14						20 29				20 44						20 59
Barnes Bridge	d				20 01				20 16			←			20 31				20 46			←			21 01
Barnes	d			19 56	20 04			←	20 19	20 11		20 19		20 26	20 34			←	20 49	20 41		20 49		20 56	21 04
Putney	d			19 59	20 07	20 04		20 07	→	20 14		20 22		20 29	20 37	20 34		20 37	→	20 44		20 52		20 59	21 07
Wandsworth Town	d			20 02	→			20 10		20 17		20 25		20 32	→			20 40		20 47		20 55		21 02	→
Clapham Junction 10	d			20 05		20 09		20 13		20 20	20 24	20 28		20 35		20 39		20 43		20 50	20 54	20 58		21 05	
Queenstown Rd.(Battersea)	d			20 08				20 16		20 23		20 31		20 38				20 46		20 53		21 01		21 08	
Vauxhall ⊖	d			20 12		20 15		20 20		20 27		20 35		20 42		20 45		20 50		20 57		21 05		21 12	
London Waterloo 15 ⊖	a			20 16		20 19		20 26		20 32	20 34	20 41		20 46		20 49		20 56		21 02	21 04	21 11		21 16	

Reading, Guildford, Ascot, Weybridge, Windsor, Kingston, Richmond and Hounslow - London

Network Diagram - see first Page of Table 148

		SW	SW	SW	SW	SW 1	SW	SW 1	SW 1	SW	SW	SW	SW	SW	SW	SW 1	SW	SW	SW	SW	SW	SW
Reading 7	d					20 12										20 42						
Earley	d					20 17										20 47						
Winnersh Triangle	d					20 19										20 49						
Winnersh	d					20 21										20 51						
Wokingham	d					20 26										20 56						
Bracknell	d					20 32										21 02						
Martins Heron	d					20 35										21 05						
Guildford	d							20 00	20 30													
Wanborough	d							20 06	20 36													
Ash 5	d							20 10	20 40													
Aldershot	a							20 17	20 47													
	d							20 30														
Ash Vale	d							20 34														
Frimley	d							20 40														
Camberley	a							20 44														
	d							20 48														
Bagshot	d							20 53														
Ascot 3	d					20 40		21a00								21 10						
Sunningdale	d					20 43										21 13						
Longcross	d					20 46																
Woking	d																					
West Byfleet	d																					
Byfleet & New Haw	d																					
Weybridge	d										20 33								21 03			
Addlestone	d										20 37								21 07			
Chertsey	d										20 40								21 10			
Virginia Water	a					20 49					20 45					21 19			21 15			
	d					20 49					20 54					21 19			21 24			
Egham	d					20 53					20 57					21 23			21 27			
Windsor & Eton Riverside	d	20 23										20 53								21 23		
Datchet	d	20 26										20 56								21 26		
Sunnymeads	d	20 29										20 59								21 29		
Wraysbury	d	20 32										21 02								21 32		
Staines	d	20 38				20 59					21 03	21 08				21 29			21 33	21 38		
Ashford (Surrey)	d	20 41									21 06	21 11							21 36	21 41		
Feltham	d	20 46				21 05					21 11	21 16				21 35			21 41	21 46		
Whitton	d	20 50		20 50	20 53							21 20		21 20	21 23					21 50		21 50
Kingston	d									20 59								21 29				
Hampton Wick	d									21 01								21 31				
Teddington	d									21 05								21 35				
Fulwell	d																					
Strawberry Hill	d									21 08								21 38				
Twickenham	a	20 53			20 56	21 10				21 12		21 23			21 26	21 40		21 42		21 53		
	d	20 53			20 58	21 11				21 13		21 23			21 28	21 41		21 43		21 53		
St Margarets	d				21 00					21 15					21 30			21 45				
Richmond ⊖	d	20 58			21 04	21 15				21 19		21 28			21 34	21 45		21 49		21 58		
North Sheen	d				21 06					21 21					21 36			21 51				
Mortlake	d				21 08					21 23					21 38			21 53				
Hounslow	d			21 01							21 16			21 31					21 46			22 01
Isleworth	d			21 04							21 19			21 34					21 49			22 04
Syon Lane	d			21 06							21 21			21 36					21 51			22 06
Brentford	d			21 09							21 24			21 39					21 54			22 09
Kew Bridge	d			21 11							21 26			21 41					21 56			22 11
Chiswick	d			21 14							21 29			21 44					21 59			22 14
Barnes Bridge	d			21 16			←				21 31			21 46			←		22 01			22 16
Barnes	d		←	21 19	21 11		21 19			21 26	21 34		←	21 49	21 41		21 49	21 56	22 04		←	22 19
Putney	d	21 04	21 07	→	21 14		21 22			21 29	21 37	21 34	21 37	→	21 44		21 52	21 59	22 07	22 04	22 07	→
Wandsworth Town	d		21 10		21 17		21 25			21 32	→		21 40		21 47		21 55	22 02	→		22 10	
Clapham Junction 10	d	21 09	21 13		21 20	21 24	21 28			21 35		21 39	21 43		21 50	21 54	21 58	22 05		22 09	22 13	
Queenstown Rd.(Battersea)	d		21 16		21 23		21 31			21 38			21 46		21 53		22 01	22 08			22 16	
Vauxhall ⊖	d	21 15	21 20		21 27		21 35			21 42		21 45	21 50		21 57		22 05	22 12		22 15	22 20	
London Waterloo 15 ⊖	a	21 19	21 26		21 32	21 34	21 41			21 46		21 49	21 56		22 02	22 04	22 11	22 16		22 19	22 26	

Reading, Guildford, Ascot, Weybridge, Windsor, Kingston, Richmond and Hounslow - London

Network Diagram - see first Page of Table 148

		SW	SW [1]	SW	SW [1]	SW [1]	SW	SW		SW	SW	SW	SW [1]	SW	SW	SW	SW	SW [1]		SW [1]	SW [1]	SW	SW	SW	SW
Reading [7]	d		21 12										21 42					22 12							
Earley	d		21 17										21 47					22 17							
Winnersh Triangle	d		21 19										21 49					22 19							
Winnersh	d		21 21										21 51					22 21							
Wokingham	d		21 26										21 56					22 26							
Bracknell	d		21 32										22 02					22 32							
Martins Heron	d		21 35										22 05					22 35							
Guildford	d				21 00	21 30														22 00	22 30				
Wanborough	d				21 06	21 36														22 06	22 36				
Ash [5]	d				21 10	21 40														22 10	22 40				
Aldershot	a				21 17	21 47														22 17	22 47				
	d				21 30															22 30					
Ash Vale	d				21 34															22 34					
Frimley	d				21 40															22 40					
Camberley	a				21 44															22 44					
	d				21 48															22 48					
Bagshot	d				21 53															22 53					
Ascot [3]	d		21 40		22a00								22 10					22 40		23a00					
Sunningdale	d		21 43										22 13					22 43							
Longcross	d																								
Woking	d																								
West Byfleet	d																								
Byfleet & New Haw	d																								
Weybridge	d							21 33							22 03								22 33		
Addlestone	d							21 37							22 07								22 37		
Chertsey	d							21 40							22 10								22 40		
Virginia Water	a		21 49					21 45					22 19		22 15			22 49					22 45		
	d		21 49					21 54					22 19		22 24			22 49					22 54		
Egham	d		21 53					21 57					22 23		22 27			22 53					22 57		
Windsor & Eton Riverside	d									21 53						22 23								22 53	
Datchet	d									21 56						22 26								22 56	
Sunnymeads	d									21 59						22 29								22 59	
Wraysbury	d									22 02						22 32								23 02	
Staines	d		21 59					22 03		22 08			22 29		22 33	22 38		22 59					23 03	23 08	
Ashford (Surrey)	d							22 06		22 11					22 36	22 41							23 06	23 11	
Feltham	d		22 05					22 11		22 16			22 35		22 41	22 46		23 05					23 11	23 16	
Whitton	d	21 53								22 20		22 23				22 50								23 20	
Kingston	d						21 59							22 29								22 59			
Hampton Wick	d						22 01							22 31								23 01			
Teddington	d						22 05							22 35								23 05			
Fulwell	d																								
Strawberry Hill	d						22 08							22 38								23 08			
Twickenham	a	21 56	22 10				22 12			22 23		22 26	22 40	22 42		22 53		23 10				23 12		23 23	
	d	21 58	22 11				22 13			22 23		22 28	22 41	22 43		22 53		23 11				23 13		23 23	
St Margarets	d	22 00					22 15					22 30		22 45								23 15			
Richmond ⊖	d	22 04	22 15				22 19			22 28		22 34	22 45	22 49		22 58		23 15				23 19		23 28	
North Sheen	d	22 06					22 21					22 36		22 51								23 21			
Mortlake	d	22 08					22 23					22 38		22 53								23 23			
Hounslow	d							22 16							22 46								23 16		
Isleworth	d							22 19							22 49								23 19		
Syon Lane	d							22 21							22 51								23 21		
Brentford	d							22 24							22 54								23 24		
Kew Bridge	d							22 26							22 56								23 26		
Chiswick	d							22 29							22 59								23 29		
Barnes Bridge	d			←				22 31							23 01								23 31		
Barnes	d	22 11		22 19			22 26	22 34			←	22 41		22 56	23 04		←					23 26	23 34		←
Putney	d	22 14		22 22			22 29	22 37		22 34	22 37	22 44		22 59	23 07	23 04	23 07					23 29	23 37	23 34	23 37
Wandsworth Town	d	22 17		22 25			22 32	→			22 40	22 47		23 02	→		23 10					23 32	→		23 40
Clapham Junction [10]	d	22 20	22 24	22 28			22 35			22 39	22 43	22 50	22 54	23 05		23 09	23 13	23 24				23 35		23 39	23 43
Queenstown Rd.(Battersea)	d	22 23		22 31			22 38				22 46	22 53		23 08			23 16					23 38			23 46
Vauxhall ⊖	d	22 27		22 35			22 42			22 45	22 50	22 57		23 12		23 15	23 20					23 42		23 45	23 50
London Waterloo [15] ⊖	a	22 32	22 34	22 41			22 46			22 49	22 56	23 02	23 04	23 16		23 19	23 26	23 34				23 46		23 49	23 56

Reading, Guildford, Ascot, Weybridge, Windsor, Kingston, Richmond and Hounslow - London

Network Diagram - see first Page of Table 148

		SW ■1	SW	SW	SW	SW	SW ■1	SW ■1	SW ■1	SW
Reading ■7	d	22 42					23 12			
Earley	d	22 47					23 17			
Winnersh Triangle	d	22 49					23 19			
Winnersh	d	22 51					23 21			
Wokingham	d	22 56					23 26			
Bracknell	d	23 02					23 32			
Martins Heron	d	23 05					23 35			
Guildford	d							23 00	23 30	
Wanborough	d							23 06	23 36	
Ash ■5	d							23 10	23 40	
Aldershot	a							23 17	23 47	
	d							23 30		
Ash Vale	d							23 34		
Frimley	d							23 40		
Camberley	a							23 44		
	d							23 48		
Bagshot	d							23 53		
Ascot ■8	d	23 10					23 40	00a01		
Sunningdale	d	23 13					23 43			
Longcross	d									
Woking	d									
West Byfleet	d									
Byfleet & New Haw	d									
Weybridge	d		23 03							23 33
Addlestone	d		23 07							23 37
Chertsey	d		23 10							23 40
Virginia Water	a	23 19	23 15				23 49			23 45
	d	23 19	23 24				23 49			23 54
Egham	d	23 23	23 27				23 53			23 57
Windsor & Eton Riverside	d			23 28						
Datchet	d			23 31						
Sunnymeads	d			23 34						
Wraysbury	d			23 37						
Staines	d	23 29	23a32	23a42			23 59			00a02
Ashford (Surrey)	d									
Feltham	d	23 35					00 05			
Whitton	d									
Kingston	d				23 29	23 55				
Hampton Wick	d				23 31	23 57				
Teddington	d				23 35	23 59				
Fulwell	d									
Strawberry Hill	d				23 38	00 03				
Twickenham	a	23 40			23 42	00 07	00 10			
	d	23 41			23 43		00 11			
St Margarets	d				23 45					
Richmond ⊖	d	23 45			23 49		00 15			
North Sheen	d				23 51					
Mortlake	d				23 53					
Hounslow	d									
Isleworth	d									
Syon Lane	d									
Brentford	d									
Kew Bridge	d									
Chiswick	d									
Barnes Bridge	d									
Barnes	d				23 56					
Putney	d				23 59					
Wandsworth Town	d				00 02					
Clapham Junction ■10	d	23 54			00 05		00 24			
Queenstown Rd.(Battersea)	d				00 08					
Vauxhall ⊖	d				00 12					
London Waterloo ■15 ⊖	a	00 04			00 16		00 37			

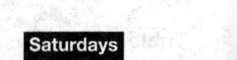

Reading, Guildford, Ascot, Weybridge, Windsor, Kingston, Richmond and Hounslow - London

Network Diagram - see first Page of Table 148

		SW [1]	SW	SW	SW [1]	SW	SW	SW	SW	SW	SW		SW	SW	SW	SW	SW [1]	SW [1]	SW	SW	SW		SW	SW [1]	SW	SW
Reading [7]	d	22p42			23p12												05 42							06 12		
Earley	d	22p47			23p17												05 47							06 17		
Winnersh Triangle	d	22p49			23p19												05 49							06 19		
Winnersh	d	22p51			23p21												05 51							06 21		
Wokingham	d	22p56			23p26												05 56							06 26		
Bracknell	d	23p02			23p32												06 02							06 32		
Martins Heron	d	23p05			23p35												06 05							06 35		
Guildford	d																									
Wanborough	d																									
Ash [5]	d																									
Aldershot	a																									
	d																	06 00								
Ash Vale	d																	06 04								
Frimley	d																	06 10								
Camberley	a																	06 14								
	d																	06 18								
Bagshot	d																	06 23								
Ascot [3]	d	23p10			23p40												06 10	06a30						06 40		
Sunningdale	d	23p13			23p43												06 13							06 43		
Longcross	d																									
Woking	d													05 27												
West Byfleet	d													05 32												
Byfleet & New Haw	d													05 35												
Weybridge	d																									06 33
Addlestone	d													05 39												06 37
Chertsey	d													05 42												06 40
Virginia Water	a	23p19			23p49									05 47			06 19							06 49		06 45
	d	23p19			23p49									05 54			06 19							06 49		06 54
Egham	d	23p23			23p53									05 57			06 23							06 53		06 57
Windsor & Eton Riverside	d														05 53						06 23					
Datchet	d														05 56						06 26					
Sunnymeads	d														05 59						06 29					
Wraysbury	d														06 02						06 32					
Staines	d	23p29			23p59		04 58			05 37				06 03	06 08		06 29			06 33	06 38			06 59		07 03
Ashford (Surrey)	d						05 01			05 40				06 06	06 11					06 36	06 41					07 06
Feltham	d	23p35			00 05		05 06			05 45				06 11	06 16		06 35			06 41	06 46			07 05		07 11
Whitton	d						05 10		05 41	05 49					06 20						06 50					
Kingston	d		23p29	23p55		01 17							05 59						06 29						06 59	
Hampton Wick	d		23p31	23p57		01s22							06 01						06 31						07 01	
Teddington	d		23p35	23p59		01 25							06 05						06 35						07 05	
Fulwell	d																									
Strawberry Hill	d		23p38	00 03		01 28		05 38					06 08						06 38						07 08	
Twickenham	a	23p40	23p42	00 07	00 10		05 13	05 41		05 52			06 12		06 23		06 40		06 42		06 53			07 10	07 12	
	d	23p41	23p43		00 11		05 13	05 43		05 53			06 13		06 23		06 41		06 43		06 53			07 11	07 13	
St Margarets	d		23p45				05 15	05 45					06 15						06 45						07 15	
Richmond ⊖	d	23p45	23p49		00 15		05 19	05 49		05 58			06 19		06 28		06 45		06 49		06 58			07 15	07 19	
North Sheen	d		23p51				05 21	05 51					06 21						06 51						07 21	
Mortlake	d		23p53				05 23	05 53					06 23						06 53						07 23	
Hounslow	d								05 46					06 16						06 46						07 16
Isleworth	d								05 49					06 19						06 49						07 19
Syon Lane	d								05 51					06 21						06 51						07 21
Brentford	d								05 54					06 24						06 54						07 24
Kew Bridge	d								05 56					06 26						06 56						07 26
Chiswick	d								05 59					06 29						06 59						07 29
Barnes Bridge	d								06 01					06 31						07 01						07 31
Barnes	d		23p56				05 26	05 56	06 04		←		06 26	06 34		←			06 56	07 04			←		07 26	07 34
Putney	d		23p59				05 29	05 59	06 07	06 04	06 07		06 29	06 37	06 34	06 37			06 59	07 07	07 04		07 07		07 29	07 37
Wandsworth Town	d		00 02				05 32	06 02	→		06 10		06 32	→		06 40			07 02	→			07 10		07 32	→
Clapham Junction [10]	d	23p54	00 05		00 24		05 35	06 05		06 09	06 13		06 35		06 39	06 43	06 54		07 05		07 09		07 13	07 24	07 35	
Queenstown Rd.(Battersea)	d		00 08				05 38	06 08			06 16		06 38			06 46			07 08				07 16		07 38	
Vauxhall ⊖	d		00 12				05 42	06 12		06 15	06 20		06 42		06 45	06 50			07 12		07 15		07 20		07 42	
London Waterloo [15] ⊖	a	00 04	00 16		00 37		05 46	06 16		06 19	06 26		06 46		06 49	06 56	07 04		07 16		07 19		07 26	07 34	07 46	

Table 149

Saturdays

Reading, Guildford, Ascot, Weybridge, Windsor, Kingston, Richmond and Hounslow - London

Network Diagram - see first Page of Table 148

		SW	SW	SW 1	SW 1	SW		SW	SW	SW	SW	SW	SW 1	SW 1	SW	SW		SW	SW	SW	SW	SW	SW 1	SW	SW 1
Reading 7	d			06 42									07 12										07 42		
Earley	d			06 47									07 17										07 47		
Winnersh Triangle	d			06 49									07 19										07 49		
Winnersh	d			06 51									07 21										07 51		
Wokingham	d			06 56									07 26										07 56		
Bracknell	d			07 02									07 32										08 02		
Martins Heron	d			07 05									07 35										08 05		
Guildford	d				06 30									07 00											07 30
Wanborough	d				06 36									07 06											07 36
Ash 5	d				06 40									07 10											07 40
Aldershot	a				06 47									07 17											07 47
	d				07 00									07 30											08 00
Ash Vale	d				07 04									07 34											08 04
Frimley	d				07 10									07 40											08 10
Camberley	a				07 14									07 44											08 14
	d				07 18									07 48											08 18
Bagshot	d				07 23									07 53											08 23
Ascot 3	d			07 10	07a30								07 40	08a00									08 10		08a30
Sunningdale	d			07 13									07 43										08 13		
Longcross	d																								
Woking	d																								
West Byfleet	d																								
Byfleet & New Haw	d																								
Weybridge	d								07 03									07 33							
Addlestone	d								07 07									07 37							
Chertsey	d								07 10									07 40							
Virginia Water	a			07 19					07 15				07 49					07 45					08 19		
	d			07 19					07 24				07 49					07 54					08 19		
Egham	d			07 23					07 27				07 53					07 57					08 23		
Windsor & Eton Riverside	d	06 53								07 23									07 53						
Datchet	d	06 56								07 26									07 56						
Sunnymeads	d	06 59								07 29									07 59						
Wraysbury	d	07 02								07 32									08 02						
Staines	d	07 08		07 29					07 33	07 38			07 59					08 03	08 08				08 29		
Ashford (Surrey)	d	07 11							07 36	07 41								08 06	08 11						
Feltham	d	07 16		07 35					07 41	07 46			08 05					08 11	08 16				08 35		
Whitton	d	07 20								07 50					07 50				08 20		08 20	08 23			
Kingston	d							07 29								07 59									
Hampton Wick	d							07 31								08 01									
Teddington	d							07 35								08 05									
Fulwell	d																								
Strawberry Hill	d							07 38								08 08									
Twickenham	a	07 23		07 40				07 42		07 53			08 10			08 12			08 23			08 26	08 40		
	d	07 23		07 41				07 43		07 53		07 58	08 11			08 13			08 23			08 28	08 41		
St Margarets	d							07 45				08 00				08 15						08 30			
Richmond ⊖	d	07 28		07 45				07 49		07 58		08 04	08 15			08 19			08 28			08 34	08 45		
North Sheen	d							07 51				08 06				08 21						08 36			
Mortlake	d							07 53				08 08				08 23						08 38			
Hounslow	d					07 31			07 46						08 01			08 16			08 31				
Isleworth	d					07 34			07 49						08 04			08 19			08 34				
Syon Lane	d					07 36			07 51						08 06			08 21			08 36				
Brentford	d					07 39			07 54						08 09			08 24			08 39				
Kew Bridge	d					07 41			07 56						08 11			08 26			08 41				
Chiswick	d					07 44			07 59						08 14			08 29			08 44				
Barnes Bridge	d					07 46			08 01						08 16			08 31			08 46			←	
Barnes	d		←			07 49		07 56	08 04		←	08 11			08 19	08 26		08 34		←	08 49	08 41		08 49	
Putney	d	07 34	07 37			07 52		07 59	08 07	08 04	08 07	08 14			08 22	08 29		08 37	08 34	08 37	↪	08 44		08 52	
Wandsworth Town	d		07 40			07 55		08 02	↪		08 10	08 17			08 25	08 32		↪		08 40		08 47		08 55	
Clapham Junction 10	d	07 39	07 43	07 54		07 58		08 05		08 09	08 13	08 20	08 24		08 28	08 35			08 39	08 43		08 50	08 54	08 58	
Queenstown Rd.(Battersea)	d		07 46			08 01		08 08			08 16	08 23			08 31	08 38				08 46		08 53		09 01	
Vauxhall ⊖	d	07 45	07 50			08 05		08 12		08 15	08 20	08 27			08 35	08 42			08 45	08 50		08 57		09 05	
London Waterloo 15 ⊖	a	07 49	07 56	08 04		08 11		08 16		08 19	08 26	08 32	08 34		08 41	08 46			08 49	08 56		09 02	09 04	09 11	

Reading, Guildford, Ascot, Weybridge, Windsor, Kingston, Richmond and Hounslow - London

Network Diagram - see first Page of Table 148

		SW	SW	SW	SW	SW	SW	SW [1]	SW	SW [1]	SW	SW	SW	SW	SW	SW	SW [1]	SW	SW [1]	SW	SW	SW
Reading [7]	d							08 12									08 42					
Earley	d							08 17									08 47					
Winnersh Triangle	d							08 19									08 49					
Winnersh	d							08 21									08 51					
Wokingham	d							08 26									08 56					
Bracknell	d							08 32									09 02					
Martins Heron	d							08 35									09 05					
Guildford	d									08 00									08 30			
Wanborough	d									08 06									08 36			
Ash [5]	d									08 10									08 40			
Aldershot	a									08 17									08 47			
	d									08 30									09 00			
Ash Vale	d									08 34									09 04			
Frimley	d									08 40									09 10			
Camberley	a									08 44									09 14			
	d									08 48									09 18			
Bagshot	d									08 53									09 23			
Ascot [3]	d							08 40		09a00							09 10		09a30			
Sunningdale	d							08 43									09 13					
Longcross	d																					
Woking	d																					
West Byfleet	d																					
Byfleet & New Haw	d																					
Weybridge	d		08 03									08 33									09 03	
Addlestone	d		08 07									08 37									09 07	
Chertsey	d		08 10									08 40									09 10	
Virginia Water	a		08 15					08 49				08 45					09 19				09 15	
	d		08 24					08 49				08 54					09 19				09 24	
Egham	d		08 27					08 53				08 57					09 23				09 27	
Windsor & Eton Riverside	d			08 23									08 53									09 23
Datchet	d			08 26									08 56									09 26
Sunnymeads	d			08 29									08 59									09 29
Wraysbury	d			08 32									09 02									09 32
Staines	d		08 33	08 38				08 59				09 03	09 08				09 29				09 33	09 38
Ashford (Surrey)	d		08 36	08 41								09 06	09 11								09 36	09 41
Feltham	d		08 41	08 46				09 05				09 11	09 16				09 35				09 41	09 46
Whitton	d			08 50		08 50	08 53						09 20		09 20	09 23						09 50
Kingston	d	08 29									08 59									09 29		
Hampton Wick	d	08 31									09 01									09 31		
Teddington	d	08 35									09 05									09 35		
Fulwell	d																					
Strawberry Hill	d	08 38									09 08									09 38		
Twickenham	a	08 42		08 53			08 56	09 10			09 12		09 23			09 26	09 40			09 42		09 53
	d	08 43		08 53			08 58	09 11			09 13		09 23			09 28	09 41			09 43		09 53
St Margarets	d	08 45					09 00				09 15					09 30				09 45		
Richmond ⊖	d	08 49		08 58			09 04	09 15			09 19		09 28			09 34	09 45			09 49		09 58
North Sheen	d	08 51					09 06				09 21					09 36				09 51		
Mortlake	d	08 53					09 08				09 23					09 38				09 53		
Hounslow	d		08 46			09 01						09 16			09 31						09 46	
Isleworth	d		08 49			09 04						09 19			09 34						09 49	
Syon Lane	d		08 51			09 06						09 21			09 36						09 51	
Brentford	d		08 54			09 09						09 24			09 39						09 54	
Kew Bridge	d		08 56			09 11						09 26			09 41						09 56	
Chiswick	d		08 59			09 14						09 29			09 44						09 59	
Barnes Bridge	d		09 01			09 16			←			09 31			09 46			←			10 01	
Barnes	d	08 56	09 04		←	09 19	09 11		09 19		09 26	09 34		←	09 49	09 41		09 49		09 56	10 04	
Putney	d	08 59	09 07	09 04	09 07	→	09 14		09 22		09 29	09 37	09 34	09 37	→	09 44		09 52		09 59	10 07	10 04
Wandsworth Town	d	09 02	→		09 10		09 17		09 25		09 32	→		09 40		09 47		09 55		10 02	→	
Clapham Junction [10]	d	09 05		09 09	09 13		09 20	09 24	09 28		09 35		09 39	09 43		09 50	09 54	09 58		10 05		10 09
Queenstown Rd.(Battersea)	d	09 08			09 16		09 23		09 31		09 38			09 46		09 53		10 01		10 08		
Vauxhall ⊖	d	09 12		09 15	09 20		09 27		09 35		09 42		09 45	09 50		09 57		10 05		10 12		10 15
London Waterloo [15] ⊖	a	09 16		09 19	09 26		09 32	09 34	09 41		09 46		09 49	09 56		10 02	10 04	10 11		10 16		10 19

Table 149

Saturdays

Reading, Guildford, Ascot, Weybridge, Windsor, Kingston, Richmond and Hounslow - London

Network Diagram - see first Page of Table 148

		SW	SW	SW	SW	SW	SW	SW	SW	SW	SW	SW	SW	SW	SW	SW	SW	SW	SW	SW	SW	SW	SW
					1		1							1		1							1
Reading 7	d				09 12									09 42									10 12
Earley	d				09 17									09 47									10 17
Winnersh Triangle	d				09 19									09 49									10 19
Winnersh	d				09 21									09 51									10 21
Wokingham	d				09 26									09 56									10 26
Bracknell	d				09 32									10 02									10 32
Martins Heron	d				09 35									10 05									10 35
Guildford	d						09 00									09 30							
Wanborough	d						09 06									09 36							
Ash 5	d						09 10									09 40							
Aldershot	a						09 17									09 47							
	d						09 30									10 00							
Ash Vale	d						09 34									10 04							
Frimley	d						09 40									10 10							
Camberley	a						09 44									10 14							
	d						09 48									10 18							
Bagshot	d						09 53									10 23							
Ascot 3	d				09 40		10a00							10 10		10a30							10 40
Sunningdale	d				09 43									10 13									10 43
Longcross	d																						
Woking	d																						
West Byfleet	d																						
Byfleet & New Haw	d																						
Weybridge	d								09 33									10 03					
Addlestone	d								09 37									10 07					
Chertsey	d								09 40									10 10					
Virginia Water	a				09 49				09 45					10 19				10 15					10 49
	d				09 49				09 54					10 19				10 24					10 49
Egham	d				09 53				09 57					10 23				10 27					10 53
Windsor & Eton Riverside	d									09 53									10 23				
Datchet	d									09 56									10 26				
Sunnymeads	d									09 59									10 29				
Wraysbury	d									10 02									10 32				
Staines	d				09 59				10 03	10 08				10 29				10 33	10 38				10 59
Ashford (Surrey)	d								10 06	10 11								10 36	10 41				
Feltham	d				10 05				10 11	10 16				10 35				10 41	10 46				11 05
Whitton	d		09 50	09 53						10 20		10 20	10 23						10 50		10 50	10 53	
Kingston	d							09 59									10 29						
Hampton Wick	d							10 01									10 31						
Teddington	d							10 05									10 35						
Fulwell	d																						
Strawberry Hill	d							10 08									10 38						
Twickenham	a			09 56	10 10			10 12		10 23			10 26	10 40			10 42		10 53			10 56	11 10
	d			09 58	10 11			10 13		10 23			10 28	10 41			10 43		10 53			10 58	11 11
St Margarets	d			10 00				10 15					10 30				10 45					11 00	
Richmond ⊖	d			10 04	10 15			10 19		10 28			10 34	10 45			10 49		10 58			11 04	11 15
North Sheen	d			10 06				10 21					10 36				10 51					11 06	
Mortlake	d			10 08				10 23					10 38				10 53					11 08	
Hounslow	d		10 01						10 16			10 31						10 46			11 01		
Isleworth	d		10 04						10 19			10 34						10 49			11 04		
Syon Lane	d		10 06						10 21			10 36						10 51			11 06		
Brentford	d		10 09						10 24			10 39						10 54			11 09		
Kew Bridge	d		10 11						10 26			10 41						10 56			11 11		
Chiswick	d		10 14						10 29			10 44						10 59			11 14		
Barnes Bridge	d		10 16			←			10 31			10 46			←			11 01			11 16		
Barnes	d	←	10 19	10 11		10 19		10 26	10 34		←	10 49	10 41		10 49		10 56	11 04		←	11 19	11 11	
Putney	d	10 07	↪	10 14		10 22		10 29	10 37	10 34	10 37	↪	10 44		10 52		10 59	11 07	11 04	11 07	↪	11 14	
Wandsworth Town	d	10 10		10 17		10 25		10 32	↪		10 40		10 47		10 55		11 02	↪		11 10		11 17	
Clapham Junction 10	d	10 13		10 20	10 24	10 28		10 35		10 39	10 43		10 50	10 54	10 58		11 05		11 09	11 13		11 20	11 24
Queenstown Rd.(Battersea)	d	10 16		10 23		10 31		10 38			10 46		10 53		11 01		11 08			11 16		11 23	
Vauxhall ⊖	d	10 20		10 27		10 35		10 42		10 45	10 50		10 57		11 05		11 12		11 15	11 20		11 27	
London Waterloo 15 ⊖	a	10 26		10 32	10 34	10 41		10 46		10 49	10 56		11 02	11 04	11 11		11 16		11 19	11 26		11 32	11 34

Saturdays

Reading, Guildford, Ascot, Weybridge, Windsor, Kingston, Richmond and Hounslow - London

Network Diagram - see first Page of Table 148

		SW	SW 1	SW		SW	SW	SW	SW	SW	SW 1	SW	SW 1	SW		SW	SW	SW	SW	SW	SW 1	SW	SW 1	SW	
Reading 7	d										10 42										11 12				
Earley	d										10 47										11 17				
Winnersh Triangle	d										10 49										11 19				
Winnersh	d										10 51										11 21				
Wokingham	d										10 56										11 26				
Bracknell	d										11 02										11 32				
Martins Heron	d										11 05										11 35				
Guildford	d		10 00										10 30										11 00		
Wanborough	d		10 06										10 36										11 06		
Ash 5	d		10 10										10 40										11 10		
Aldershot	a		10 17										10 47										11 17		
	d		10 30										11 00										11 30		
Ash Vale	d		10 34										11 04										11 34		
Frimley	d		10 40										11 10										11 40		
Camberley	a		10 44										11 14										11 44		
	d		10 48										11 18										11 48		
Bagshot	d		10 53										11 23										11 53		
Ascot 3	d		11a00								11 10		11a30								11 40		12a00		
Sunningdale	d										11 13										11 43				
Longcross	d																								
Woking	d																								
West Byfleet	d																								
Byfleet & New Haw	d																								
Weybridge	d					10 33										11 03									
Addlestone	d					10 37										11 07									
Chertsey	d					10 40										11 10									
Virginia Water	a					10 45					11 19					11 15					11 49				
	d					10 54					11 19					11 24					11 49				
Egham	d					10 57					11 23					11 27					11 53				
Windsor & Eton Riverside	d						10 53										11 23								
Datchet	d						10 56										11 26								
Sunnymeads	d						10 59										11 29								
Wraysbury	d						11 02										11 32								
Staines	d					11 03	11 08				11 29					11 33	11 38				11 59				
Ashford (Surrey)	d					11 06	11 11									11 36	11 41								
Feltham	d					11 11	11 16				11 35					11 41	11 46				12 05				
Whitton	d						11 20		11 20	11 23							11 50		11 50	11 53					
Kingston	d			10 59										11 29										11 59	
Hampton Wick	d			11 01										11 31										12 01	
Teddington	d			11 05										11 35										12 05	
Fulwell	d																								
Strawberry Hill	d			11 08										11 38										12 08	
Twickenham	a			11 12			11 23			11 26	11 40			11 42			11 53			11 56	12 10			12 12	
	d			11 13			11 23			11 28	11 41			11 43			11 53			11 58	12 11			12 13	
St Margarets	d			11 15						11 30				11 45						12 00				12 15	
Richmond ⊖	d			11 19			11 28			11 34	11 45			11 49			11 58			12 04	12 15			12 19	
North Sheen	d			11 21						11 36				11 51						12 06				12 21	
Mortlake	d			11 23						11 38				11 53						12 08				12 23	
Hounslow	d					11 16			11 31							11 46			12 01						
Isleworth	d					11 19			11 34							11 49			12 04						
Syon Lane	d					11 21			11 36							11 51			12 06						
Brentford	d					11 24			11 39							11 54			12 09						
Kew Bridge	d					11 26			11 41							11 56			12 11						
Chiswick	d					11 29			11 44							11 59			12 14						
Barnes Bridge	d	←				11 31			11 46			←				12 01			12 16			←			
Barnes	d	11 19		11 26		11 34		←	11 49	11 41		11 49		11 56		12 04		←	12 19	12 11		12 19		12 26	
Putney	d	11 22		11 29		11 37	11 34	11 37	→	11 44		11 52		11 59		12 07	12 04	12 07	→	12 14		12 22		12 29	
Wandsworth Town	d	11 25		11 32		→		11 40		11 47		11 55		12 02		→		12 10		12 17		12 25		12 32	
Clapham Junction 10	d	11 28		11 35			11 39	11 43		11 50	11 54	11 58		12 05			12 09	12 13		12 20	12 24	12 28		12 35	
Queenstown Rd.(Battersea)	d	11 31		11 38				11 46		11 53		12 01		12 08				12 16		12 23		12 31		12 38	
Vauxhall ⊖	d	11 35		11 42			11 45	11 50		11 57		12 05		12 12			12 15	12 20		12 27		12 35		12 42	
London Waterloo 15 ⊖	a	11 41		11 46			11 49	11 56		12 02	12 04	12 11		12 16			12 19	12 26		12 32	12 34	12 41		12 46	

Table 149

Saturdays

Reading, Guildford, Ascot, Weybridge, Windsor, Kingston, Richmond and Hounslow - London

Network Diagram - see first Page of Table 148

		SW	SW	SW	SW	SW	SW 1	SW	SW 1	SW	SW	SW	SW	SW	SW	SW 1	SW	SW 1	SW	SW	SW	SW	SW
Reading 7	d						11 42									12 12							
Earley	d						11 47									12 17							
Winnersh Triangle	d						11 49									12 19							
Winnersh	d						11 51									12 21							
Wokingham	d						11 56									12 26							
Bracknell	d						12 02									12 32							
Martins Heron	d						12 05									12 35							
Guildford	d								11 30									12 00					
Wanborough	d								11 36									12 06					
Ash 5	d								11 40									12 10					
Aldershot	a								11 47									12 17					
	d								12 00									12 30					
Ash Vale	d								12 04									12 34					
Frimley	d								12 10									12 40					
Camberley	a								12 14									12 44					
	d								12 18									12 48					
Bagshot	d								12 23									12 53					
Ascot 3	d						12 10		12a30							12 40		13a00					
Sunningdale	d						12 13									12 43							
Longcross	d																						
Woking	d																						
West Byfleet	d																						
Byfleet & New Haw	d																						
Weybridge	d	11 33									12 03									12 33			
Addlestone	d	11 37									12 07									12 37			
Chertsey	d	11 40									12 10									12 40			
Virginia Water	a	11 45					12 19				12 15					12 49				12 45			
	d	11 54					12 19				12 24					12 49				12 54			
Egham	d	11 57					12 23				12 27					12 53				12 57			
Windsor & Eton Riverside	d		11 53									12 23									12 53		
Datchet	d		11 56									12 26									12 56		
Sunnymeads	d		11 59									12 29									12 59		
Wraysbury	d		12 02									12 32									13 02		
Staines	d	12 03	12 08				12 29				12 33	12 38				12 59				13 03	13 08		
Ashford (Surrey)	d	12 06	12 11								12 36	12 41								13 06	13 11		
Feltham	d	12 11	12 16				12 35				12 41	12 46				13 05				13 11	13 16		
Whitton	d		12 20		12 20	12 23						12 50		12 50	12 53						13 20		13 20
Kingston	d									12 29									12 59				
Hampton Wick	d									12 31									13 01				
Teddington	d									12 35									13 05				
Fulwell	d																						
Strawberry Hill	d									12 38									13 08				
Twickenham	a		12 23			12 27	12 40			12 42		12 53			12 56	13 10			13 12		13 23		
	d		12 23			12 28	12 41			12 43		12 53			12 58	13 11			13 13		13 23		
St Margarets	d					12 30				12 45					13 00				13 15				
Richmond ⊖	d		12 28			12 34	12 45			12 49		12 58			13 04	13 15			13 19		13 28		
North Sheen	d					12 36				12 51					13 06				13 21				
Mortlake	d					12 38				12 53					13 08				13 23				
Hounslow	d	12 16			12 31						12 46			13 01						13 16			13 31
Isleworth	d	12 19			12 34						12 49			13 04						13 19			13 34
Syon Lane	d	12 21			12 36						12 51			13 06						13 21			13 36
Brentford	d	12 24			12 39						12 54			13 09						13 24			13 39
Kew Bridge	d	12 26			12 41						12 56			13 11						13 26			13 41
Chiswick	d	12 29			12 44						12 59			13 14						13 29			13 44
Barnes Bridge	d	12 31			12 46			←			13 01			13 16			←			13 31			13 46
Barnes	d	12 34		←	12 49	12 41		12 49		12 56	13 04		←	13 19	13 11		13 19		13 26	13 34		←	13 49
Putney	d	12 37	12 34	12 37	→	12 44		12 52		12 59	13 07	13 04	13 07	→	13 14		13 22		13 29	13 37	13 34	13 37	→
Wandsworth Town	d	→		12 40		12 47		12 55		13 02	→		13 10		13 17		13 25		13 32	→		13 40	
Clapham Junction 10	d		12 39	12 43		12 50	12 54	12 58		13 05		13 09	13 13		13 20	13 24	13 28		13 35		13 39	13 43	
Queenstown Rd.(Battersea)	d			12 46		12 53		13 01		13 08			13 16		13 23		13 31		13 38			13 46	
Vauxhall ⊖	d		12 45	12 50		12 57		13 05		13 12		13 15	13 20		13 27		13 35		13 42		13 45	13 50	
London Waterloo 15 ⊖	a		12 49	12 56		13 02	13 04	13 11		13 16		13 19	13 26		13 32	13 34	13 41		13 46		13 49	13 56	

Table 149

Saturdays

Reading, Guildford, Ascot, Weybridge, Windsor, Kingston, Richmond and Hounslow - London

Network Diagram - see first Page of Table 148

		SW	SW 1	SW	SW 1	SW	SW	SW	SW	SW	SW	SW 1	SW	SW 1	SW	SW	SW	SW	SW	SW	SW 1	SW	SW 1
Reading 7	d		12 42									13 12									13 42		
Earley	d		12 47									13 17									13 47		
Winnersh Triangle	d		12 49									13 19									13 49		
Winnersh	d		12 51									13 21									13 51		
Wokingham	d		12 56									13 26									13 56		
Bracknell	d		13 02									13 32									14 02		
Martins Heron	d		13 05									13 35									14 05		
Guildford	d				12 30									13 00									13 30
Wanborough	d				12 36									13 06									13 36
Ash 5	d				12 40									13 10									13 40
Aldershot	a				12 47									13 17									13 47
	d				13 00									13 30									14 00
Ash Vale	d				13 04									13 34									14 04
Frimley	d				13 10									13 40									14 10
Camberley	a				13 14									13 44									14 14
	d				13 18									13 48									14 18
Bagshot	d				13 23									13 53									14 23
Ascot 3	d		13 10		13a30							13 40		14a00							14 10		14a30
Sunningdale	d		13 13									13 43									14 13		
Longcross	d																						
Woking	d																						
West Byfleet	d																						
Byfleet & New Haw	d																						
Weybridge	d						13 03									13 33							
Addlestone	d						13 07									13 37							
Chertsey	d						13 10									13 40							
Virginia Water	a		13 19				13 15					13 49				13 45					14 19		
	d		13 19				13 24					13 49				13 54					14 19		
Egham	d		13 23				13 27					13 53				13 57					14 23		
Windsor & Eton Riverside	d							13 23									13 53						
Datchet	d							13 26									13 56						
Sunnymeads	d							13 29									13 59						
Wraysbury	d							13 32									14 02						
Staines	d		13 29				13 33	13 38				13 59				14 03	14 08				14 29		
Ashford (Surrey)	d						13 36	13 41								14 06	14 11						
Feltham	d		13 35				13 41	13 46				14 05				14 11	14 16				14 35		
Whitton	d	13 23						13 50		13 50	13 53						14 20		14 20	14 23			
Kingston	d					13 29									13 59								
Hampton Wick	d					13 31									14 01								
Teddington	d					13 35									14 05								
Fulwell	d																						
Strawberry Hill	d					13 38									14 08								
Twickenham	a	13 26	13 40			13 42		13 53			13 56	14 10			14 12		14 23			14 26	14 40		
	d	13 28	13 41			13 43		13 53			13 58	14 11			14 13		14 23			14 28	14 41		
St Margarets	d	13 30				13 45					14 00				14 15					14 30			
Richmond ⊖	d	13 34	13 45			13 49		13 58			14 04	14 15			14 19		14 28			14 34	14 45		
North Sheen	d	13 36				13 51					14 06				14 21					14 36			
Mortlake	d	13 38				13 53					14 08				14 23					14 38			
Hounslow	d						13 46			14 01						14 16			14 31				
Isleworth	d						13 49			14 04						14 19			14 34				
Syon Lane	d						13 51			14 06						14 21			14 36				
Brentford	d						13 54			14 09						14 24			14 39				
Kew Bridge	d						13 56			14 11						14 26			14 41				
Chiswick	d						13 59			14 14						14 29			14 44				
Barnes Bridge	d			←			14 01			14 16			←			14 31			14 46			←	
Barnes	d	13 41		13 49		13 56	14 04		←	14 19	14 11		14 19		14 26	14 34		←	14 49	14 41		14 49	
Putney	d	13 44		13 52		13 59	14 07	14 04	14 07	→	14 14		14 22		14 29	14 37	14 34	14 37	→	14 44		14 52	
Wandsworth Town	d	13 47		13 55		14 02	→		14 10		14 17		14 25		14 32	→		14 40		14 47		14 55	
Clapham Junction 10	d	13 50	13 54	13 58		14 05		14 09	14 13		14 20	14 24	14 28		14 35		14 39	14 43		14 50	14 54	14 58	
Queenstown Rd.(Battersea)	d	13 53		14 01		14 08			14 16		14 23		14 31		14 38			14 46		14 53		15 01	
Vauxhall ⊖	d	13 57		14 05		14 12		14 15	14 20		14 27		14 35		14 42		14 45	14 50		14 57		15 05	
London Waterloo 15 ⊖	a	14 02	14 04	14 11		14 16		14 19	14 26		14 32	14 34	14 41		14 46		14 49	14 56		15 02	15 04	15 11	

Table 149

Saturdays

Reading, Guildford, Ascot, Weybridge, Windsor, Kingston, Richmond and Hounslow - London

Network Diagram - see first Page of Table 148

		SW		SW	SW	SW	SW	SW	SW	SW	SW	SW		SW	SW	SW	SW	SW	SW	SW	SW	SW		SW	SW
									1		1								1		1				
Reading 7	d								14 12										14 42						
Earley	d								14 17										14 47						
Winnersh Triangle	d								14 19										14 49						
Winnersh	d								14 21										14 51						
Wokingham	d								14 26										14 56						
Bracknell	d								14 32										15 02						
Martins Heron	d								14 35										15 05						
Guildford	d										14 00										14 30				
Wanborough	d										14 06										14 36				
Ash 5	d										14 10										14 40				
Aldershot	a										14 17										14 47				
	d										14 30										15 00				
Ash Vale	d										14 34										15 04				
Frimley	d										14 40										15 10				
Camberley	a										14 44										15 14				
	d										14 48										15 18				
Bagshot	d										14 53										15 23				
Ascot 3	d								14 40		15a00								15 10		15a30				
Sunningdale	d								14 43										15 13						
Longcross	d																								
Woking	d																								
West Byfleet	d																								
Byfleet & New Haw	d																								
Weybridge	d			14 03										14 33										15 03	
Addlestone	d			14 07										14 37										15 07	
Chertsey	d			14 10										14 40										15 10	
Virginia Water	a			14 15					14 49					14 45					15 19					15 15	
	d			14 24					14 49					14 54					15 19					15 24	
Egham	d			14 27					14 53					14 57					15 23					15 27	
Windsor & Eton Riverside	d				14 23										14 53										15 23
Datchet	d				14 26										14 56										15 26
Sunnymeads	d				14 29										14 59										15 29
Wraysbury	d				14 32										15 02										15 32
Staines	d			14 33	14 38				14 59					15 03	15 08				15 29					15 33	15 38
Ashford (Surrey)	d			14 36	14 41									15 06	15 11									15 36	15 41
Feltham	d			14 41	14 46				15 05					15 11	15 16				15 35					15 41	15 46
Whitton	d				14 50		14 50	14 53							15 20		15 20	15 23							15 50
Kingston	d	14 29										14 59										15 29			
Hampton Wick	d	14 31										15 01										15 31			
Teddington	d	14 35										15 05										15 35			
Fulwell	d																								
Strawberry Hill	d	14 38										15 08										15 38			
Twickenham	a	14 42			14 53			14 56	15 10			15 12			15 23			15 26	15 40			15 42			15 53
	d	14 43			14 53			14 58	15 11			15 13			15 23			15 28	15 41			15 43			15 53
St Margarets	d	14 45						15 00				15 15						15 30				15 45			
Richmond ⊖	d	14 49			14 58			15 04	15 15			15 19			15 28			15 34	15 45			15 49			15 58
North Sheen	d	14 51						15 06				15 21						15 36				15 51			
Mortlake	d	14 53						15 08				15 23						15 38				15 53			
Hounslow	d			14 46			15 01							15 16			15 31							15 46	
Isleworth	d			14 49			15 04							15 19			15 34							15 49	
Syon Lane	d			14 51			15 06							15 21			15 36							15 51	
Brentford	d			14 54			15 09							15 24			15 39							15 54	
Kew Bridge	d			14 56			15 11							15 26			15 41							15 56	
Chiswick	d			14 59			15 14							15 29			15 44							15 59	
Barnes Bridge	d			15 01			15 16			←				15 31			15 46			←				16 01	
Barnes	d	14 56		15 04		←	15 19	15 11		15 19		15 26		15 34		←	15 49	15 41		15 49		15 56		16 04	
Putney	d	14 59		15 07	15 04	15 07	→	15 14		15 22		15 29		15 37	15 34	15 37	→	15 44		15 52		15 59		16 07	16 04
Wandsworth Town	d	15 02		→		15 10		15 17		15 25		15 32		→		15 40		15 47		15 55		16 02		→	
Clapham Junction 10	d	15 05			15 09	15 13		15 20	15 24	15 28		15 35			15 39	15 43		15 50	15 54	15 58		16 05			16 09
Queenstown Rd.(Battersea)	d	15 08				15 16		15 23		15 31		15 38				15 46		15 53		16 01		16 08			
Vauxhall ⊖	d	15 12			15 15	15 20		15 27		15 35		15 42			15 45	15 50		15 57		16 05		16 12			16 15
London Waterloo 15 ⊖	a	15 16			15 19	15 26		15 32	15 34	15 41		15 46			15 49	15 56		16 02	16 04	16 11		16 16			16 19

Table 149

Saturdays

Reading, Guildford, Ascot, Weybridge, Windsor, Kingston, Richmond and Hounslow - London

Network Diagram - see first Page of Table 148

		SW	SW	SW	SW [1]	SW	SW [1]	SW		SW	SW	SW	SW	SW	SW [1]	SW	SW [1]	SW		SW	SW	SW	SW	SW	SW [1]
Reading [7]	d				15 12										15 42										16 12
Earley	d				15 17										15 47										16 17
Winnersh Triangle	d				15 19										15 49										16 19
Winnersh	d				15 21										15 51										16 21
Wokingham	d				15 26										15 56										16 26
Bracknell	d				15 32										16 02										16 32
Martins Heron	d				15 35										16 05										16 35
Guildford	d						15 00										15 30								
Wanborough	d						15 06										15 36								
Ash [5]	d						15 10										15 40								
Aldershot	a						15 17										15 47								
	d						15 30										16 00								
Ash Vale	d						15 34										16 04								
Frimley	d						15 40										16 10								
Camberley	a						15 44										16 14								
	d						15 48										16 18								
Bagshot	d						15 53										16 23								
Ascot [3]	d				15 40		16a00								16 10		16a30								16 40
Sunningdale	d				15 43										16 13										16 43
Longcross	d																								
Woking	d																								
West Byfleet	d																								
Byfleet & New Haw	d																								
Weybridge	d									15 33										16 03					
Addlestone	d									15 37										16 07					
Chertsey	d									15 40										16 10					
Virginia Water	a				15 49					15 45					16 19					16 15					16 49
	d				15 49					15 54					16 19					16 24					16 49
Egham	d				15 53					15 57					16 23					16 27					16 53
Windsor & Eton Riverside	d										15 53										16 23				
Datchet	d										15 56										16 26				
Sunnymeads	d										15 59										16 29				
Wraysbury	d										16 02										16 32				
Staines	d				15 59					16 03	16 08				16 29					16 33	16 38				16 59
Ashford (Surrey)	d									16 06	16 11									16 36	16 41				
Feltham	d				16 05					16 11	16 16				16 35					16 41	16 46				17 05
Whitton	d		15 50	15 53							16 20		16 20	16 23							16 50		16 50	16 53	
Kingston	d							15 59										16 29							
Hampton Wick	d							16 01										16 31							
Teddington	d							16 05										16 35							
Fulwell	d																								
Strawberry Hill	d							16 08										16 38							
Twickenham	a			15 56	16 10			16 12			16 23			16 26	16 40			16 42			16 53			16 56	17 10
	d			15 58	16 11			16 13			16 23			16 28	16 41			16 43			16 53			16 58	17 11
St Margarets	d			16 00				16 15						16 30				16 45						17 00	
Richmond ⊖	d			16 04	16 15			16 19			16 28			16 34	16 45			16 49			16 58			17 04	17 15
North Sheen	d			16 06				16 21						16 36				16 51						17 06	
Mortlake	d			16 08				16 23						16 38				16 53						17 08	
Hounslow	d		16 01							16 16			16 31							16 46			17 01		
Isleworth	d		16 04							16 19			16 34							16 49			17 04		
Syon Lane	d		16 06							16 21			16 36							16 51			17 06		
Brentford	d		16 09							16 24			16 39							16 54			17 09		
Kew Bridge	d		16 11							16 26			16 41							16 56			17 11		
Chiswick	d		16 14							16 29			16 44							16 59			17 14		
Barnes Bridge	d		16 16			←				16 31			16 46			←				17 01			17 16		
Barnes	d	←	16 19	16 11		16 19		16 26		16 34		←	16 49	16 41		16 49		16 56		17 04		←	17 19	17 11	
Putney	d	16 07	→	16 14		16 22		16 29		16 37	16 34	16 37	→	16 44		16 52		16 59		17 07	17 04	17 07	→	17 14	
Wandsworth Town	d	16 10		16 17		16 25		16 32		→		16 40		16 47		16 55		17 02		→		17 10		17 17	
Clapham Junction [10]	d	16 13		16 20	16 24	16 28		16 35			16 39	16 43		16 50	16 54	16 58		17 05			17 09	17 13		17 20	17 24
Queenstown Rd.(Battersea)	d	16 16		16 23		16 31		16 38				16 46		16 53		17 01		17 08				17 16		17 23	
Vauxhall ⊖	d	16 20		16 27		16 35		16 42			16 45	16 50		16 57		17 05		17 12			17 15	17 20		17 27	
London Waterloo [15] ⊖	a	16 26		16 32	16 34	16 41		16 46			16 49	16 56		17 02	17 04	17 11		17 16			17 19	17 26		17 32	17 34

Table 149

Saturdays

Reading, Guildford, Ascot, Weybridge, Windsor, Kingston, Richmond and Hounslow - London

Network Diagram - see first Page of Table 148

		SW	SW [1]	SW	SW	SW	SW	SW	SW	SW [1]	SW	SW [1]	SW	SW	SW	SW	SW	SW	SW [1]	SW	SW [1]	SW
Reading [7]	d									16 42									17 12			
Earley	d									16 47									17 17			
Winnersh Triangle	d									16 49									17 19			
Winnersh	d									16 51									17 21			
Wokingham	d									16 56									17 26			
Bracknell	d									17 02									17 32			
Martins Heron	d									17 05									17 35			
Guildford	d		16 00									16 30									17 00	
Wanborough	d		16 06									16 36									17 06	
Ash [5]	d		16 10									16 40									17 10	
Aldershot	a		16 17									16 47									17 17	
	d		16 30									17 00									17 30	
Ash Vale	d		16 34									17 04									17 34	
Frimley	d		16 40									17 10									17 40	
Camberley	a		16 44									17 14									17 44	
	d		16 48									17 18									17 48	
Bagshot	d		16 53									17 23									17 53	
Ascot [3]	d		17a00							17 10		17a30							17 40		18a00	
Sunningdale	d									17 13									17 43			
Longcross	d																					
Woking	d																					
West Byfleet	d																					
Byfleet & New Haw	d																					
Weybridge	d				16 33									17 03								
Addlestone	d				16 37									17 07								
Chertsey	d				16 40									17 10								
Virginia Water	a				16 45					17 19				17 15					17 49			
	d				16 54					17 19				17 24					17 49			
Egham	d				16 57					17 23				17 27					17 53			
Windsor & Eton Riverside	d					16 53									17 23							
Datchet	d					16 56									17 26							
Sunnymeads	d					16 59									17 29							
Wraysbury	d					17 02									17 32							
Staines	d				17 03	17 08				17 29				17 33	17 38				17 59			
Ashford (Surrey)	d				17 06	17 11								17 36	17 41							
Feltham	d				17 11	17 16				17 35				17 41	17 46				18 05			
Whitton	d					17 20		17 20	17 23						17 50		17 50	17 53				
Kingston	d			16 59									17 29									17 59
Hampton Wick	d			17 01									17 31									18 01
Teddington	d			17 05									17 35									18 05
Fulwell	d																					
Strawberry Hill	d			17 08									17 38									18 08
Twickenham	a			17 12		17 23			17 26	17 40			17 42		17 53			17 56	18 10			18 12
	d			17 13		17 23			17 28	17 41			17 43		17 53			17 58	18 11			18 13
St Margarets	d			17 15					17 30				17 45					18 00				18 15
Richmond ⊖	d			17 19		17 28			17 34	17 45			17 49		17 58			18 04	18 15			18 19
North Sheen	d			17 21					17 36				17 51					18 06				18 21
Mortlake	d			17 23					17 38				17 53					18 08				18 23
Hounslow	d				17 16			17 31						17 46			18 01					
Isleworth	d				17 19			17 34						17 49			18 04					
Syon Lane	d				17 21			17 36						17 51			18 06					
Brentford	d				17 24			17 39						17 54			18 09					
Kew Bridge	d				17 26			17 41						17 56			18 11					
Chiswick	d				17 29			17 44						17 59			18 14					
Barnes Bridge	d	←			17 31			17 46			←			18 01			18 16			←		
Barnes	d	17 19		17 26	17 34		←	17 49	17 41		17 49		17 56	18 04		←	18 19	18 11		18 19		18 26
Putney	d	17 22		17 29	17 37	17 34	17 37	→	17 44		17 52		17 59	18 07	18 04	18 07	→	18 14		18 22		18 29
Wandsworth Town	d	17 25		17 32	→		17 40		17 47		17 55		18 02	→		18 10		18 17		18 25		18 32
Clapham Junction [10]	d	17 28		17 35		17 39	17 43		17 50	17 54	17 58		18 05		18 09	18 13		18 20	18 24	18 28		18 35
Queenstown Rd.(Battersea)	d	17 31		17 38			17 46		17 53		18 01		18 08			18 16		18 23		18 31		18 38
Vauxhall ⊖	d	17 35		17 42		17 45	17 50		17 57		18 05		18 12		18 15	18 20		18 27		18 35		18 42
London Waterloo [15] ⊖	a	17 41		17 46		17 49	17 56		18 02	18 04	18 11		18 16		18 19	18 26		18 32	18 34	18 41		18 46

Table 149

Saturdays

Reading, Guildford, Ascot, Weybridge, Windsor, Kingston, Richmond and Hounslow - London

Network Diagram - see first Page of Table 148

		SW	SW	SW	SW	SW	SW 1	SW	SW 1	SW		SW	SW	SW	SW	SW	SW 1	SW	SW 1	SW		SW	SW	SW	SW
Reading 7	d						17 42										18 12								
Earley	d						17 47										18 17								
Winnersh Triangle	d						17 49										18 19								
Winnersh	d						17 51										18 21								
Wokingham	d						17 56										18 26								
Bracknell	d						18 02										18 32								
Martins Heron	d						18 05										18 35								
Guildford	d								17 30										18 00						
Wanborough	d								17 36										18 06						
Ash 5	d								17 40										18 10						
Aldershot	a								17 47										18 17						
	d								18 00										18 30						
Ash Vale	d								18 04										18 34						
Frimley	d								18 10										18 40						
Camberley	a								18 14										18 44						
	d								18 18										18 48						
Bagshot	d								18 23										18 53						
Ascot 3	d						18 10		18a30								18 40		19a00						
Sunningdale	d						18 13										18 43								
Longcross	d																								
Woking	d																								
West Byfleet	d																								
Byfleet & New Haw	d																								
Weybridge	d	17 33										18 03										18 33			
Addlestone	d	17 37										18 07										18 37			
Chertsey	d	17 40										18 10										18 40			
Virginia Water	a	17 45					18 19					18 15					18 49					18 45			
	d	17 54					18 19					18 24					18 49					18 54			
Egham	d	17 57					18 23					18 27					18 53					18 57			
Windsor & Eton Riverside	d		17 53										18 23										18 53		
Datchet	d		17 56										18 26										18 56		
Sunnymeads	d		17 59										18 29										18 59		
Wraysbury	d		18 02										18 32										19 02		
Staines	d	18 03	18 08				18 29					18 33	18 38				18 59					19 03	19 08		
Ashford (Surrey)	d	18 06	18 11									18 36	18 41									19 06	19 11		
Feltham	d	18 11	18 16				18 35					18 41	18 46				19 05					19 11	19 16		
Whitton	d		18 20		18 20	18 23							18 50		18 50	18 53							19 20		19 20
Kingston	d									18 29										18 59					
Hampton Wick	d									18 31										19 01					
Teddington	d									18 35										19 05					
Fulwell	d																								
Strawberry Hill	d									18 38										19 08					
Twickenham	a		18 23			18 26	18 40			18 42			18 53			18 56	19 10			19 12			19 23		
	d		18 23			18 28	18 41			18 43			18 53			18 58	19 11			19 13			19 23		
St Margarets	d					18 30				18 45						19 00				19 15					
Richmond ⊖	d		18 28			18 34	18 45			18 49			18 58			19 04	19 15			19 19			19 28		
North Sheen	d					18 36				18 51						19 06				19 21					
Mortlake	d					18 38				18 53						19 08				19 23					
Hounslow	d	18 16			18 31							18 46			19 01							19 16			19 31
Isleworth	d	18 19			18 34							18 49			19 04							19 19			19 34
Syon Lane	d	18 21			18 36							18 51			19 06							19 21			19 36
Brentford	d	18 24			18 39							18 54			19 09							19 24			19 39
Kew Bridge	d	18 26			18 41							18 56			19 11							19 26			19 41
Chiswick	d	18 29			18 44							18 59			19 14							19 29			19 44
Barnes Bridge	d	18 31			18 46			←				19 01			19 16			←				19 31			19 46
Barnes	d	18 34		←	18 49	18 41		18 49		18 56		19 04		←	19 19	19 11		19 19		19 26		19 34		←	19 49
Putney	d	18 37	18 34	18 37	→	18 44		18 52		18 59		19 07	19 04	19 07	→	19 14		19 22		19 29		19 37	19 34	19 37	→
Wandsworth Town	d	→		18 40		18 47		18 55		19 02		→		19 10		19 17		19 25		19 32		→		19 40	
Clapham Junction 10	d		18 39	18 43		18 50	18 54	18 58		19 05			19 09	19 13		19 20	19 24	19 28		19 35			19 39	19 43	
Queenstown Rd.(Battersea)	d			18 46		18 53		19 01		19 08				19 16		19 23		19 31		19 38				19 46	
Vauxhall ⊖	d		18 45	18 50		18 57		19 05		19 12			19 15	19 20		19 27		19 35		19 42			19 45	19 50	
London Waterloo 15 ⊖	a		18 49	18 56		19 02	19 04	19 11		19 16			19 19	19 26		19 32	19 34	19 41		19 46			19 49	19 56	

Reading, Guildford, Ascot, Weybridge, Windsor, Kingston, Richmond and Hounslow - London

Network Diagram - see first Page of Table 148

		SW	SW 1	SW	SW 1	SW		SW	SW	SW	SW	SW	SW 1	SW	SW 1	SW		SW	SW	SW	SW	SW	SW 1	SW	SW 1
Reading 7	d		18 42										19 12										19 42		
Earley	d		18 47										19 17										19 47		
Winnersh Triangle	d		18 49										19 19										19 49		
Winnersh	d		18 51										19 21										19 51		
Wokingham	d		18 56										19 26										19 56		
Bracknell	d		19 02										19 32										20 02		
Martins Heron	d		19 05										19 35										20 05		
Guildford	d				18 30										19 00										19 30
Wanborough	d				18 36										19 06										19 36
Ash 5	d				18 40										19 10										19 40
Aldershot	a				18 47										19 17										19 47
	d				19 00										19 30										20 00
Ash Vale	d				19 04										19 34										20 04
Frimley	d				19 10										19 40										20 10
Camberley	a				19 14										19 44										20 14
	d				19 18										19 48										20 18
Bagshot	d				19 23										19 53										20 23
Ascot 3	d		19 10		19a30								19 40		20a00								20 10		20a30
Sunningdale	d		19 13										19 43										20 13		
Longcross	d																								
Woking	d																								
West Byfleet	d																								
Byfleet & New Haw	d																								
Weybridge	d							19 03										19 33							
Addlestone	d							19 07										19 37							
Chertsey	d							19 10										19 40							
Virginia Water	a		19 19					19 15					19 49					19 45					20 19		
	d		19 19					19 24					19 49					19 54					20 19		
Egham	d		19 23					19 27					19 53					19 57					20 23		
Windsor & Eton Riverside	d								19 23										19 53						
Datchet	d								19 26										19 56						
Sunnymeads	d								19 29										19 59						
Wraysbury	d								19 32										20 02						
Staines	d		19 29					19 33	19 38				19 59					20 03	20 08				20 29		
Ashford (Surrey)	d							19 36	19 41									20 06	20 11						
Feltham	d		19 35					19 41	19 46				20 05					20 11	20 16				20 35		
Whitton	d	19 23							19 50		19 50	19 53							20 20		20 20	20 23			
Kingston	d					19 29										19 59									
Hampton Wick	d					19 31										20 01									
Teddington	d					19 35										20 05									
Fulwell	d																								
Strawberry Hill	d					19 38										20 08									
Twickenham	a	19 26	19 40			19 42			19 53			19 56	20 10			20 12			20 23			20 26	20 40		
	d	19 28	19 41			19 43			19 53			19 58	20 11			20 13			20 23			20 28	20 41		
St Margarets	d	19 30				19 45						20 00				20 15						20 30			
Richmond ⊖	d	19 34	19 45			19 49			19 58			20 04	20 15			20 19			20 28			20 34	20 45		
North Sheen	d	19 36				19 51						20 06				20 21						20 36			
Mortlake	d	19 38				19 53						20 08				20 23						20 38			
Hounslow	d							19 46			20 01							20 16			20 31				
Isleworth	d							19 49			20 04							20 19			20 34				
Syon Lane	d							19 51			20 06							20 21			20 36				
Brentford	d							19 54			20 09							20 24			20 39				
Kew Bridge	d							19 56			20 11							20 26			20 41				
Chiswick	d							19 59			20 14							20 29			20 44				
Barnes Bridge	d			←				20 01			20 16			←				20 31			20 46			←	
Barnes	d	19 41		19 49		19 56		20 04		←	20 19	20 11		20 19		20 26		20 34		←	20 49	20 41		20 49	
Putney	d	19 44		19 52		19 59		20 07	20 04	20 07	→	20 14		20 22		20 29		20 37	20 34	20 37	→	20 44		20 52	
Wandsworth Town	d	19 47		19 55		20 02		→		20 10		20 17		20 25		20 32		→		20 40		20 47		20 55	
Clapham Junction 10	d	19 50	19 54	19 58		20 05			20 09	20 13		20 20	20 24	20 28		20 35			20 39	20 43		20 50	20 54	20 58	
Queenstown Rd.(Battersea)	d	19 53		20 01		20 08				20 16		20 23		20 31		20 38				20 46		20 53		21 01	
Vauxhall ⊖	d	19 57		20 05		20 12			20 15	20 20		20 27		20 35		20 42			20 45	20 50		20 57		21 05	
London Waterloo 15 ⊖	a	20 02	20 04	20 11		20 16			20 19	20 26		20 32	20 34	20 41		20 46			20 49	20 56		21 02	21 04	21 11	

Table 149

Saturdays

Reading, Guildford, Ascot, Weybridge, Windsor, Kingston, Richmond and Hounslow - London

Network Diagram - see first Page of Table 148

		SW		SW	SW	SW	SW	SW	SW ■1	SW	SW ■	SW ■1		SW	SW	SW	SW	SW	SW	SW ■1	SW	SW		SW	SW
Reading ■7	d								20 12											20 42					
Earley	d								20 17											20 47					
Winnersh Triangle	d								20 19											20 49					
Winnersh	d								20 21											20 51					
Wokingham	d								20 26											20 56					
Bracknell	d								20 32											21 02					
Martins Heron	d								20 35											21 05					
Guildford	d										20 00	20 30													
Wanborough	d										20 06	20 36													
Ash ■5	d										20 10	20 40													
Aldershot	a										20 17	20 47													
	d										20 30														
Ash Vale	d										20 34														
Frimley	d										20 40														
Camberley	a										20 44														
	d										20 48														
Bagshot	d										20 53														
Ascot ■3	d								20 40		21a00									21 10					
Sunningdale	d								20 43											21 13					
Longcross	d																								
Woking	d																								
West Byfleet	d																								
Byfleet & New Haw	d																								
Weybridge	d			20 03											20 33									21 03	
Addlestone	d			20 07											20 37									21 07	
Chertsey	d			20 10											20 40									21 10	
Virginia Water	a			20 15					20 49						20 45					21 19				21 15	
	d			20 24					20 49						20 54					21 19				21 24	
Egham	d			20 27					20 53						20 57					21 23				21 27	
Windsor & Eton Riverside	d				20 23											20 53									21 23
Datchet	d				20 26											20 56									21 26
Sunnymeads	d				20 29											20 59									21 29
Wraysbury	d				20 32											21 02									21 32
Staines	d			20 33	20 38				20 59						21 03	21 08				21 29				21 33	21 38
Ashford (Surrey)	d			20 36	20 41										21 06	21 11								21 36	21 41
Feltham	d			20 41	20 46				21 05						21 11	21 16				21 35				21 41	21 46
Whitton	d				20 50		20 50	20 53								21 20		21 20	21 23						21 50
Kingston	d	20 29												20 59								21 29			
Hampton Wick	d	20 31												21 01								21 31			
Teddington	d	20 35												21 05								21 35			
Fulwell	d																								
Strawberry Hill	d	20 38												21 08								21 38			
Twickenham	a	20 42			20 53			20 56	21 10					21 12		21 23			21 26	21 40		21 42			21 53
	d	20 43			20 53			20 58	21 11					21 13		21 23			21 28	21 41		21 43			21 53
St Margarets	d	20 45						21 00						21 15					21 30			21 45			
Richmond ⊖	d	20 49			20 58			21 04	21 15					21 19		21 28			21 34	21 45		21 49			21 58
North Sheen	d	20 51						21 06						21 21					21 36			21 51			
Mortlake	d	20 53						21 08						21 23					21 38			21 53			
Hounslow	d			20 46			21 01								21 16			21 31						21 46	
Isleworth	d			20 49			21 04								21 19			21 34						21 49	
Syon Lane	d			20 51			21 06								21 21			21 36						21 51	
Brentford	d			20 54			21 09								21 24			21 39						21 54	
Kew Bridge	d			20 56			21 11								21 26			21 41						21 56	
Chiswick	d			20 59			21 14								21 29			21 44						21 59	
Barnes Bridge	d			21 01			21 16			←					21 31			21 46			←			22 01	
Barnes	d	20 56		21 04		←	21 19	21 11		21 19				21 26	21 34		←	21 49	21 41		21 49	21 56		22 04	
Putney	d	20 59		21 07	21 04	21 07	→	21 14		21 22				21 29	21 37	21 34	21 37	→	21 44		21 52	21 59		22 07	22 04
Wandsworth Town	d	21 02		→		21 10		21 17		21 25				21 32	→		21 40		21 47		21 55	22 02		→	
Clapham Junction ■10	d	21 05			21 09	21 13		21 20	21 24	21 28				21 35		21 39	21 43		21 50	21 54	21 58	22 05			22 09
Queenstown Rd.(Battersea)	d	21 08				21 16		21 23		21 31				21 38			21 46		21 53		22 01	22 08			
Vauxhall ⊖	d	21 12			21 15	21 20		21 27		21 35				21 42		21 45	21 50		21 57		22 05	22 12			22 15
London Waterloo ■15 ⊖	a	21 16			21 19	21 26		21 32	21 34	21 41				21 46		21 49	21 56		22 02	22 04	22 11	22 16			22 19

Table 149

Saturdays

Reading, Guildford, Ascot, Weybridge, Windsor, Kingston, Richmond and Hounslow - London

Network Diagram - see first Page of Table 148

		SW	SW	SW	SW 1	SW	SW 1	SW 1		SW	SW	SW	SW	SW	SW 1	SW	SW	SW		SW	SW 1	SW 1	SW 1	SW	SW
Reading 7	d				21 12										21 42						22 12				
Earley	d				21 17										21 47						22 17				
Winnersh Triangle	d				21 19										21 49						22 19				
Winnersh	d				21 21										21 51						22 21				
Wokingham	d				21 26										21 56						22 26				
Bracknell	d				21 32										22 02						22 32				
Martins Heron	d				21 35										22 05						22 35				
Guildford	d						21 00	21 30														22 00	22 30		
Wanborough	d						21 06	21 36														22 06	22 36		
Ash 5	d						21 10	21 40														22 10	22 40		
Aldershot	a						21 17	21 47														22 17	22 47		
	d						21 30															22 30			
Ash Vale	d						21 34															22 34			
Frimley	d						21 40															22 40			
Camberley	a						21 44															22 44			
	d						21 48															22 48			
Bagshot	d						21 53															22 53			
Ascot 3	d				21 40		22a00								22 10						22 40	23a00			
Sunningdale	d				21 43										22 13						22 43				
Longcross	d																								
Woking	d																								
West Byfleet	d																								
Byfleet & New Haw	d																								
Weybridge	d										21 33						22 03								22 33
Addlestone	d										21 37						22 07								22 37
Chertsey	d										21 40						22 10								22 40
Virginia Water	a				21 49						21 45				22 19		22 15				22 49				22 45
	d				21 49						21 54				22 19		22 24				22 49				22 54
Egham	d				21 53						21 57				22 23		22 27				22 53				22 57
Windsor & Eton Riverside	d											21 53						22 23							
Datchet	d											21 56						22 26							
Sunnymeads	d											21 59						22 29							
Wraysbury	d											22 02						22 32							
Staines	d				21 59						22 03	22 08			22 29		22 33	22 38			22 59				23 03
Ashford (Surrey)	d										22 06	22 11					22 36	22 41							23 06
Feltham	d				22 05						22 11	22 16			22 35		22 41	22 46			23 05				23 11
Whitton	d		21 50	21 53								22 20		22 23				22 50							
Kingston	d									21 59						22 29								22 59	
Hampton Wick	d									22 01						22 31								23 01	
Teddington	d									22 05						22 35								23 05	
Fulwell	d																								
Strawberry Hill	d									22 08						22 38								23 08	
Twickenham	a			21 56	22 10					22 12		22 23		22 26	22 40	22 42		22 53			23 10			23 12	
	d			21 58	22 11					22 13		22 23		22 28	22 41	22 43		22 53			23 11			23 13	
St Margarets	d			22 00						22 15				22 30		22 45								23 15	
Richmond ⊖	d			22 04	22 15					22 19		22 28		22 34	22 45	22 49		22 58			23 15			23 19	
North Sheen	d			22 06						22 21				22 36		22 51								23 21	
Mortlake	d			22 08						22 23				22 38		22 53								23 23	
Hounslow	d		22 01								22 16						22 46								23 16
Isleworth	d		22 04								22 19						22 49								23 19
Syon Lane	d		22 06								22 21						22 51								23 21
Brentford	d		22 09								22 24						22 54								23 24
Kew Bridge	d		22 11								22 26						22 56								23 26
Chiswick	d		22 14								22 29						22 59								23 29
Barnes Bridge	d		22 16			←					22 31						23 01								23 31
Barnes	d	←	22 19	22 11		22 19				22 26	22 34		←	22 41		22 56	23 04			←				23 26	23 34
Putney	d	22 07	→	22 14		22 22				22 29	22 37	22 34	22 37	22 44		22 59	23 07	23 04		23 07				23 29	23 37
Wandsworth Town	d	22 10		22 17		22 25				22 32	→		22 40	22 47		23 02	→			23 10				23 32	→
Clapham Junction 10	d	22 13		22 20	22 24	22 28				22 35		22 39	22 43	22 50	22 54	23 05		23 09		23 13	23 24			23 35	
Queenstown Rd.(Battersea)	d	22 16		22 23		22 31				22 38			22 46	22 53		23 08				23 16				23 38	
Vauxhall ⊖	d	22 20		22 27		22 35				22 42		22 45	22 50	22 57		23 12		23 15		23 20				23 42	
London Waterloo 15 ⊖	a	22 26		22 32	22 34	22 41				22 46		22 49	22 56	23 02	23 04	23 17		23 19		23 26	23 34			23 46	

Table 149

Saturdays

Reading, Guildford, Ascot, Weybridge, Windsor, Kingston, Richmond and Hounslow - London

Network Diagram - see first Page of Table 148

		SW	SW	SW	SW	SW	SW	SW	SW	SW	SW	SW
				1					1	1	1	
Reading 7	d			22 42					23 12			
Earley	d			22 47					23 17			
Winnersh Triangle	d			22 49					23 19			
Winnersh	d			22 51					23 21			
Wokingham	d			22 56					23 26			
Bracknell	d			23 02					23 32			
Martins Heron	d			23 05					23 35			
Guildford	d									23 00	23 30	
Wanborough	d									23 06	23 36	
Ash 5	d									23 10	23 40	
Aldershot	a									23 17	23 47	
	d									23 30		
Ash Vale	d									23 34		
Frimley	d									23 40		
Camberley	a									23 44		
	d									23 48		
Bagshot	d									23 53		
Ascot 3	d			23 10					23 40	00a01		
Sunningdale	d			23 13					23 43			
Longcross	d											
Woking	d											
West Byfleet	d											
Byfleet & New Haw	d											
Weybridge	d				23 03							23 33
Addlestone	d				23 07							23 37
Chertsey	d				23 10							23 40
Virginia Water	a			23 19	23 15				23 49			23 45
	d			23 19	23 24				23 49			23 54
Egham	d			23 23	23 27				23 53			23 57
Windsor & Eton Riverside	d	22 53				23 28						
Datchet	d	22 56				23 31						
Sunnymeads	d	22 59				23 34						
Wraysbury	d	23 02				23 37						
Staines	d	23 08		23 29	23a32	23a42			23 59			00a02
Ashford (Surrey)	d	23 11										
Feltham	d	23 16		23 35					00 05			
Whitton	d	23 20										
Kingston	d						23 29	23 55				
Hampton Wick	d						23 31	23 57				
Teddington	d						23 35	23 59				
Fulwell	d											
Strawberry Hill	d						23 38	00 03				
Twickenham	a	23 23		23 40			23 42	00 07	00 10			
	d	23 23		23 41			23 43		00 11			
St Margarets	d						23 45					
Richmond ⊖	d	23 28		23 45			23 49		00 15			
North Sheen	d						23 51					
Mortlake	d						23 53					
Hounslow	d											
Isleworth	d											
Syon Lane	d											
Brentford	d											
Kew Bridge	d											
Chiswick	d											
Barnes Bridge	d											
Barnes	d		←				23 56					
Putney	d	23 34	23 37				23 59					
Wandsworth Town	d		23 40				00 02					
Clapham Junction 10	d	23 39	23 43	23 54			00 05		00 24			
Queenstown Rd.(Battersea)	d		23 46				00 08					
Vauxhall ⊖	d	23 45	23 50				00 12					
London Waterloo 15 ⊖	a	23 49	23 56	00 02			00 16		00 37			

Table 149

Sundays

Reading, Guildford, Ascot, Weybridge, Windsor, Kingston, Richmond and Hounslow - London

Network Diagram - see first Page of Table 148

		SW 1 A	SW A	SW A	SW 1 A	SW	SW	SW	SW	SW 1	SW	SW	SW	SW 1	SW	SW 1	SW 1	SW	SW	SW 1	SW	SW 1	SW 1
Reading 7	d	22p42			23p12									07 54		08 24				08 54		09 24	
Earley	d	22p47			23p17									07 59		08 29				08 59		09 29	
Winnersh Triangle	d	22p49			23p19									08 01		08 31				09 01		09 31	
Winnersh	d	22p51			23p21									08 03		08 33				09 03		09 33	
Wokingham	d	22p56			23p26									08 08		08 38				09 08		09 38	
Bracknell	d	23p02			23p32									08 14		08 44				09 14		09 44	
Martins Heron	d	23p05			23p35									08 17		08 47				09 17		09 47	
Guildford	d									07 17							08 17						09 17
Wanborough	d									07 23							08 23						09 23
Ash 5	d									07 27							08 27						09 27
Aldershot	a									07 34							08 34						09 34
	d									07 40							08 40						09 40
Ash Vale	d									07 45							08 45						09 45
Frimley	d									07 51							08 51						09 51
Camberley	a									07 55							08 55						09 55
	d									07 55							08 55						09 55
Bagshot	d									08 01							09 01						10 01
Ascot 3	d	23p10			23p40					08a07				08 22		08 52	09a07			09 22		09 52	10a07
Sunningdale	d	23p13			23p43									08 25		08 55				09 25		09 55	
Longcross	d																						
Woking	d												07 52						08 52				
West Byfleet	d												07 56						08 56				
Byfleet & New Haw	d												08 00						09 00				
Weybridge	d								07 00														
Addlestone	d								07 04				08 04						09 04				
Chertsey	d								07 07				08 07						09 07				
Virginia Water	a	23p19			23p49				07 12				08 12	08 30		09 00			09 12	09 30		10 00	
	d	23p19			23p49				07 12				08 12	08 30		09 00			09 12	09 30		10 00	
Egham	d	23p23			23p53				07 16				08 16	08 34		09 04			09 16	09 34		10 04	
Windsor & Eton Riverside	d							07 01				08 01						09 01					
Datchet	d							07 04				08 04						09 04					
Sunnymeads	d							07 07				08 07						09 07					
Wraysbury	d							07 10				08 10						09 10					
Staines	d	23p29			23p59			07 16	07 21			08 16	08 21	08 39		09 09		09 16	09 21	09 39		10 09	
Ashford (Surrey)	d							07 19	07 24			08 19	08 24					09 19	09 24				
Feltham	d	23p35			00 05			07 24	07 29			08 24	08 29	08 46		09 16		09 24	09 29	09 46		10 16	
Whitton	d							07 28				08 28						09 28					
Kingston	d		23p29	23p55		02 11	06 49				07 49				08 49						09 49		
Hampton Wick	d		23p31	23p57		02s13	06 51				07 51				08 51						09 51		
Teddington	d		23p35	23p59		02s15	06 56				07 56				08 56						09 56		
Fulwell	d																						
Strawberry Hill	d		23p38	00 03		02s18	06 59				07 59				08 59						09 59		
Twickenham	a	23p40	23p42	00 07	00 10	02 22	07 02	07 31			08 02	08 31		08 51	09 02	09 21		09 31		09 51	10 02	10 21	
	d	23p41	23p43		00 11		07 03	07 32			08 03	08 32		08 51	09 03	09 21		09 32		09 51	10 03	10 21	
St Margarets	d		23p45				07 05	07 34			08 05	08 34			09 05			09 34			10 05		
Richmond ⊖	d	23p45	23p49		00 15		07 09	07 37			08 09	08 37		08 56	09 09	09 26		09 37		09 56	10 09	10 26	
North Sheen	d		23p51				07 11	07 39			08 11	08 39			09 11			09 39			10 11		
Mortlake	d		23p53				07 13	07 42			08 13	08 42			09 13			09 42			10 13		
Hounslow	d								07 35				08 35						09 35				
Isleworth	d								07 38				08 38						09 38				
Syon Lane	d								07 40				08 40						09 40				
Brentford	d								07 42				08 42						09 42				
Kew Bridge	d								07 45				08 45						09 45				
Chiswick	d								07 47				08 47						09 47				
Barnes Bridge	d								07 50				08 50						09 50				
Barnes	d		23p56				07 16	07 45	07 53		08 16	08 45	08 53		09 16			09 45	09 53		10 16		
Putney	d		23p59				07 19	07 48	07 56		08 19	08 48	08 56	09 02	09 19	09 32		09 48	09 56	10 02	10 19	10 32	
Wandsworth Town	d		00 02				07 22	07 51	07 59		08 22	08 51	08 59		09 22			09 51	09 59		10 22		
Clapham Junction 10	d	23p54	00 05		00 24		07 25	07 54	08 02		08 25	08 54	09 02	09 07	09 25	09 37		09 54	10 02	10 07	10 25	10 37	
Queenstown Rd.(Battersea)	d		00 08				07 28	07 57	08 05		08 28	08 57	09 05		09 28			09 57	10 05		10 28		
Vauxhall ⊖	d		00 12				07 32	08 00	08 08		08 32	09 00	09 08	09 12	09 32	09 42		10 00	10 08	10 12	10 32	10 42	
London Waterloo 15 ⊖	a	00 02	00 16		00 37		07 41	08 10	08 13		08 41	09 10	09 13	09 23	09 41	09 53		10 10	10 13	10 23	10 41	10 53	

A not 11 December

Table 149

Sundays

Reading, Guildford, Ascot, Weybridge, Windsor, Kingston, Richmond and Hounslow - London

Network Diagram - see first Page of Table 148

		SW	SW	SW 1	SW	SW		SW 1	SW 1	SW	SW	SW 1	SW	SW	SW 1	SW 1		SW	SW	SW 1	SW	SW	SW 1	SW 1	SW
Reading 7	d			09 54				10 24				10 54			11 24					11 54			12 24		
Earley	d			09 59				10 29				10 59			11 29					11 59			12 29		
Winnersh Triangle	d			10 01				10 31				11 01			11 31					12 01			12 31		
Winnersh	d			10 03				10 33				11 03			11 33					12 03			12 33		
Wokingham	d			10 08				10 38				11 08			11 38					12 08			12 38		
Bracknell	d			10 14				10 44				11 14			11 44					12 14			12 44		
Martins Heron	d			10 17				10 47				11 17			11 47					12 17			12 47		
Guildford	d								10 17							11 17								12 17	
Wanborough	d								10 23							11 23								12 23	
Ash 5	d								10 27							11 27								12 27	
Aldershot	a								10 34							11 34								12 34	
	d								10 40							11 40								12 40	
Ash Vale	d								10 45							11 45								12 45	
Frimley	d								10 51							11 51								12 51	
Camberley	a								10 55							11 55								12 55	
	d								10 55							11 55								12 55	
Bagshot	d								11 01							12 01								13 01	
Ascot 3	d			10 22				10 52	11a07			11 22			11 52	12a07				12 22			12 52	13a07	
Sunningdale	d			10 25				10 55				11 25			11 55					12 25			12 55		
Longcross	d																								
Woking	d		09 52								10 52								11 52						
West Byfleet	d		09 56								10 56								11 56						
Byfleet & New Haw	d		10 00								11 00								12 00						
Weybridge	d																								
Addlestone	d		10 04								11 04								12 04						
Chertsey	d		10 07								11 07								12 07						
Virginia Water	a		10 12	10 30				11 00			11 12	11 30			12 00				12 12	12 30			13 00		
	d		10 12	10 30				11 00			11 12	11 30			12 00				12 12	12 30			13 00		
Egham	d		10 16	10 34				11 04			11 16	11 34			12 04				12 16	12 34			13 04		
Windsor & Eton Riverside	d	10 01			10 34					11 01			11 34					12 01			12 34				
Datchet	d	10 04			10 37					11 04			11 37					12 04			12 37				
Sunnymeads	d	10 07								11 07								12 07							
Wraysbury	d	10 10								11 10								12 10							
Staines	d	10 16	10 21	10 39	10 45			11 09		11 16	11 21	11 39	11 45		12 09			12 16	12 21	12 39	12 45		13 09		
Ashford (Surrey)	d	10 19	10 24		10 48					11 19	11 24		11 48					12 19	12 24		12 48				
Feltham	d	10 24	10 29	10 46	10 53			11 16		11 24	11 29	11 46	11 53		12 16			12 24	12 29	12 46	12 53		13 16		
Whitton	d	10 28			10 57					11 28			11 57					12 28			12 57				
Kingston	d					10 49								11 49								12 49			13 11
Hampton Wick	d					10 51								11 51								12 51			13 13
Teddington	d					10 56								11 56								12 56			13 16
Fulwell	d																								
Strawberry Hill	d					10 59								11 59								12 59			13 19
Twickenham	a	10 31		10 51	11 00	11 02		11 21		11 31		11 51	12 00	12 02	12 21			12 31		12 51	13 00	13 02	13 21		13 22
	d	10 32		10 51	11 01	11 03		11 21		11 32		11 51	12 01	12 03	12 21			12 32		12 51	13 01	13 03	13 21		13 23
St Margarets	d	10 34				11 05				11 34				12 05				12 34				13 05			13 25
Richmond ⊖	d	10 37		10 56	11 05	11 09		11 26		11 37		11 56	12 05	12 09	12 26			12 37		12 56	13 05	13 09	13 26		13 29
North Sheen	d	10 39				11 11				11 39				12 11				12 39				13 11			13 31
Mortlake	d	10 42				11 13				11 42				12 13				12 42				13 13			13 33
Hounslow	d		10 35								11 35								12 35						
Isleworth	d		10 38								11 38								12 38						
Syon Lane	d		10 40								11 40								12 40						
Brentford	d		10 42								11 42								12 42						
Kew Bridge	d		10 45								11 45								12 45						
Chiswick	d		10 47								11 47								12 47						
Barnes Bridge	d		10 50								11 50								12 50						
Barnes	d	10 45	10 53			11 16				11 45	11 53			12 16				12 45	12 53			13 16			13 36
Putney	d	10 48	10 56	11 02	11 14	11 19		11 32		11 48	11 56	12 02	12 14	12 19	12 32			12 48	12 56	13 02	13 14	13 19	13 32		13 39
Wandsworth Town	d	10 51	10 59			11 22				11 51	11 59			12 22				12 51	12 59			13 22			13 42
Clapham Junction 10	d	10 53	11 02	11 07	11 18	11 25		11 37		11 53	12 02	12 07	12 18	12 25	12 37			12 53	13 02	13 07	13 18	13 25	13 37		13 45
Queenstown Rd.(Battersea)	d	10 57	11 05			11 28				11 57	12 05			12 28				12 57	13 05			13 28			13 48
Vauxhall ⊖	d	11 00	11 08	11 12	11 24	11 32		11 42		12 00	12 08	12 12	12 24	12 32	12 42			13 00	13 08	13 12	13 24	13 32	13 42		13 52
London Waterloo 15 ⊖	a	11 10	11 13	11 23	11 34	11 41		11 53		12 10	12 13	12 23	12 34	12 41	12 53			13 10	13 13	13 23	13 34	13 41	13 53		14 00

Table 149

Sundays

Reading, Guildford, Ascot, Weybridge, Windsor, Kingston, Richmond and Hounslow - London

Network Diagram - see first Page of Table 148

		SW		SW	SW	SW	SW	SW	SW	SW	SW	SW		SW	SW	SW	SW		SW	SW	SW		SW	SW
					1			1	1					1			1		1	1				
Reading 7	d				12 54			13 24						13 54			14 24		20 24					
Earley	d				12 59			13 29						13 59			14 29		20 29					
Winnersh Triangle	d				13 01			13 31						14 01			14 31		20 31					
Winnersh	d				13 03			13 33						14 03			14 33		20 33					
Wokingham	d				13 08			13 38						14 08			14 38		20 38					
Bracknell	d				13 14			13 44						14 14			14 44		20 44					
Martins Heron	d				13 17			13 47						14 17			14 47		20 47					
Guildford	d								13 17											20 17				
Wanborough	d								13 23											20 23				
Ash 5	d								13 27											20 27				
Aldershot	a								13 34											20 34				
	d								13 40											20 40				
Ash Vale	d								13 45											20 45				
Frimley	d								13 51											20 51				
Camberley	a								13 55											20 55				
	d								13 55											20 55				
Bagshot	d								14 01											21 01				
Ascot 3	d				13 22			13 52	14a07					14 22			14 52		20 52	21a07				
Sunningdale	d				13 25			13 55						14 25			14 55		20 55					
Longcross	d																							
Woking	d			12 52								13 52												20 52
West Byfleet	d			12 56								13 56												20 56
Byfleet & New Haw	d			13 00								14 00												21 00
Weybridge	d																							
Addlestone	d			13 04								14 04												21 04
Chertsey	d			13 07								14 07												21 07
Virginia Water	a			13 12	13 30			14 00				14 12		14 30			15 00	and at the same minutes past each hour until	21 00					21 12
	d			13 12	13 30			14 00				14 12		14 30			15 00		21 00					21 12
Egham	d			13 16	13 34			14 04				14 16		14 34			15 04		21 04					21 16
Windsor & Eton Riverside	d	13 01				13 34					14 01				14 34								21 01	
Datchet	d	13 04				13 37					14 04				14 37								21 04	
Sunnymeads	d	13 07									14 07												21 07	
Wraysbury	d	13 10									14 10												21 10	
Staines	d	13 16		13 21	13 39	13 45		14 09			14 16	14 21		14 39	14 45		15 09		21 09				21 16	21 21
Ashford (Surrey)	d	13 19		13 24		13 48					14 19	14 24			14 48								21 19	21 24
Feltham	d	13 24		13 29	13 46	13 53		14 16			14 24	14 29		14 46	14 53		15 16		21 16				21 24	21 29
Whitton	d	13 28				13 57					14 28				14 57								21 28	
Kingston	d						13 49			14 11						14 49					21 11			
Hampton Wick	d						13 51			14 13						14 51					21 13			
Teddington	d						13 56			14 16						14 56					21 16			
Fulwell	d																							
Strawberry Hill	d						13 59			14 19						14 59					21 19			
Twickenham	a	13 31			13 51	14 00	14 02	14 21		14 22	14 31			14 51	15 00	15 02	15 21		21 21		21 22		21 31	
	d	13 32			13 51	14 01	14 03	14 21		14 23	14 32			14 51	15 01	15 03	15 21		21 21		21 23		21 32	
St Margarets	d	13 34					14 05			14 25	14 34					15 05					21 25		21 34	
Richmond ⊖	d	13 37			13 56	14 05	14 09	14 26		14 29	14 37			14 56	15 05	15 09	15 26		21 26		21 29		21 37	
North Sheen	d	13 39					14 11			14 31	14 39					15 11					21 31		21 39	
Mortlake	d	13 42					14 13			14 33	14 42					15 13					21 33		21 42	
Hounslow	d			13 35								14 35												21 35
Isleworth	d			13 38								14 38												21 38
Syon Lane	d			13 40								14 40												21 40
Brentford	d			13 42								14 42												21 42
Kew Bridge	d			13 45								14 45												21 45
Chiswick	d			13 47								14 47												21 47
Barnes Bridge	d			13 50								14 50												21 50
Barnes	d	13 45		13 53			14 16			14 36	14 45	14 53				15 16					21 36		21 45	21 53
Putney	d	13 48		13 56	14 02	14 14	14 19	14 32		14 39	14 48	14 56		15 02	15 14	15 19	15 32		21 32		21 39		21 48	21 56
Wandsworth Town	d	13 51		13 59			14 22			14 42	14 51	14 59				15 22					21 42		21 51	21 59
Clapham Junction 10	d	13 54		14 02	14 07	14 18	14 25	14 37		14 45	14 54	15 02		15 07	15 18	15 25	15 37		21 37		21 45		21 54	22 02
Queenstown Rd.(Battersea)	d	13 57		14 05			14 28			14 48	14 57	15 05				15 28					21 48		21 57	22 05
Vauxhall ⊖	d	14 00		14 08	14 12	14 24	14 32	14 42		14 52	15 00	15 08		15 12	15 24	15 32	15 42		21 42		21 52		22 00	22 08
London Waterloo 15 ⊖	a	14 10		14 13	14 23	14 34	14 41	14 53		15 00	15 05	15 13		15 18	15 29	15 36	15 48		21 48		22 00		22 05	22 13

Table 149

Sundays

Reading, Guildford, Ascot, Weybridge, Windsor, Kingston, Richmond and Hounslow - London

Network Diagram - see first Page of Table 148

		SW ■1	SW	SW ■1	SW ■1	SW	SW	SW		SW ■1	SW	SW ■1	SW ■1	SW	SW	SW	SW ■1	SW ■1	
Reading ■7	d	20 54		21 24						21 54		22 24					22 54		
Earley	d	20 59		21 29						21 59		22 29					22 59		
Winnersh Triangle	d	21 01		21 31						22 01		22 31					23 01		
Winnersh	d	21 03		21 33						22 03		22 33					23 03		
Wokingham	d	21 08		21 38						22 08		22 38					23 08		
Bracknell	d	21 14		21 44						22 14		22 44					23 14		
Martins Heron	d	21 17		21 47						22 17		22 47					23 17		
Guildford	d				21 17								22 17					23 17	
Wanborough	d				21 23								22 23					23 23	
Ash ■5	d				21 27								22 27					23 27	
Aldershot	a				21 34								22 34					23 34	
	d				21 40								22 40						
Ash Vale	d				21 45								22 45						
Frimley	d				21 51								22 51						
Camberley	a				21 55								22 55						
	d				21 55								22 55						
Bagshot	d				22 01								23 01						
Ascot ■3	d	21 22		21 52	22a07					22 22		22 52	23a07				23 22		
Sunningdale	d	21 25		21 55						22 25		22 55					23 25		
Longcross	d																		
Woking	d							21 52								22 52			
West Byfleet	d							21 56								22 56			
Byfleet & New Haw	d							22 00								23 00			
Weybridge	d																		
Addlestone	d							22 04								23 04			
Chertsey	d							22 07								23 07			
Virginia Water	a	21 30		22 00				22 12		22 30		23 00				23 12	23 30		
	d	21 30		22 00				22 12		22 30		23 00				23 12	23 30		
Egham	d	21 34		22 04				22 16		22 34		23 04				23 16	23 34		
Windsor & Eton Riverside	d						22 01								23 01				
Datchet	d						22 04								23 04				
Sunnymeads	d						22 07								23 07				
Wraysbury	d						22 10								23 10				
Staines	d	21 39		22 09			22 16	22 21		22 39		23 09			23 16	23 21	23 39		
Ashford (Surrey)	d						22 19	22 24							23 19	23 24			
Feltham	d	21 46		22 16			22 24	22 29		22 46		23 16			23 24	23 29	23 46		
Whitton	d						22 28								23 28				
Kingston	d		21 49			22 11					22 49			23 11					23 47
Hampton Wick	d		21 51			22 13					22 51			23 13					23 49
Teddington	d		21 56			22 16					22 56			23 16					23 51
Fulwell	d																		
Strawberry Hill	d		21 59			22 19					22 59			23 19					23 54
Twickenham	a	21 51	22 02	22 21		22 22	22 31			22 51	23 02	23 21		23 22	23 31		23 51		
	d	21 51	22 03	22 21		22 23	22 32			22 51	23 03	23 21		23 23	23 32		23 51		
St Margarets	d		22 05			22 25	22 34				23 05			23 25	23 34				
Richmond ⊖	d	21 56	22 09	22 26		22 29	22 37			22 56	23 09	23 26		23 29	23 37		23 56		
North Sheen	d		22 11			22 31	22 39				23 11			23 31	23 39				
Mortlake	d		22 13			22 33	22 42				23 13			23 33	23 42				
Hounslow	d							22 35								23 35			
Isleworth	d							22 38								23 38			
Syon Lane	d							22 40								23 40			
Brentford	d							22 42								23 42			
Kew Bridge	d							22 45								23 45			
Chiswick	d							22 47								23 47			
Barnes Bridge	d							22 50								23 50			
Barnes	d		22 16			22 36	22 45	22 53			23 16			23 36	23 45	23 53			
Putney	d	22 02	22 19	22 32		22 39	22 48	22 56		23 02	23 19	23 32		23 39	23 48	23 56	00 02		
Wandsworth Town	d		22 22			22 42	22 51	22 59			23 22			23 42	23 51	23 59			
Clapham Junction ■10	d	22 07	22 25	22 37		22 45	22 54	23 02		23 07	23 25	23 37		23 45	23 54	00 02	00 07		
Queenstown Rd.(Battersea)	d		22 28			22 48	22 57	23 05			23 28			23 48	23 57	00 05			
Vauxhall ⊖	d	22 12	22 32	22 42		22 52	23 00	23 08		23 12	23 32	23 42		23 52	23 59	00 08	00 12		
London Waterloo ■15 ⊖	a	22 18	22 36	22 48		23 00	23 05	23 13		23 18	23 36	23 48		23 59	00 05	00 13	00 17		

Network Diagram for Table 152

DM-15/11
Design BAJS

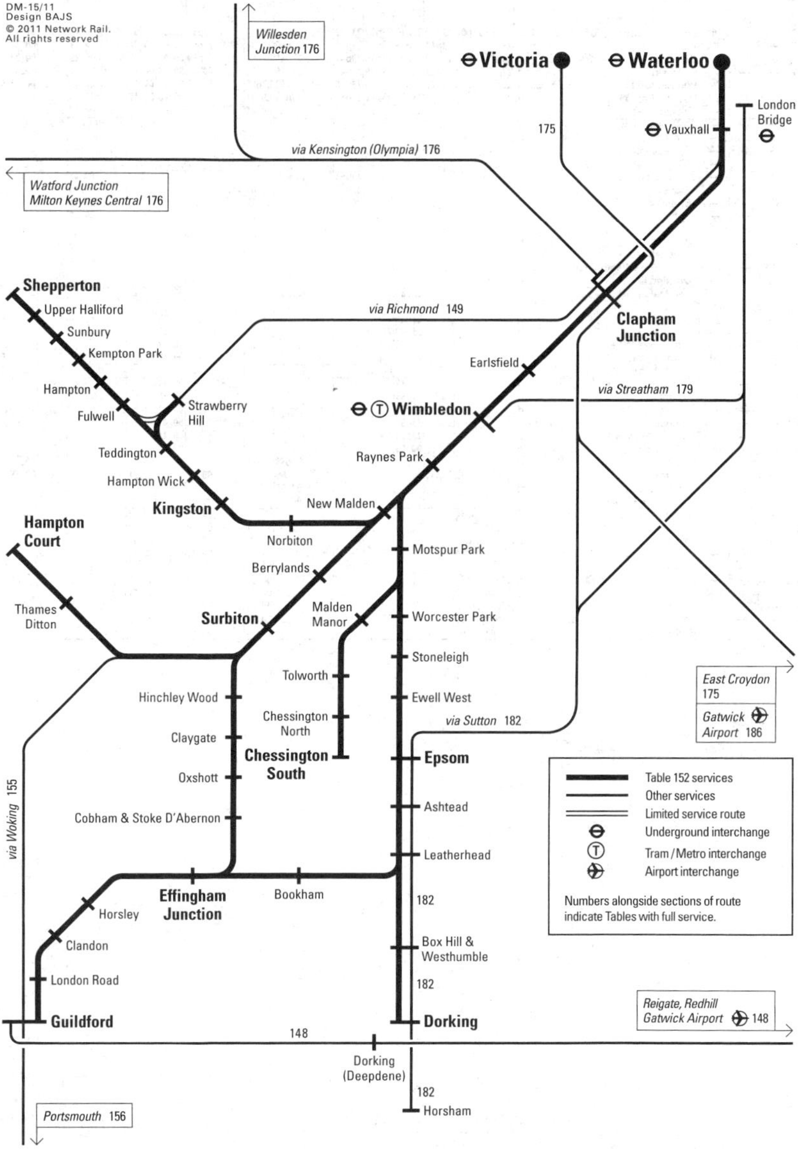

London - Chessington South, Dorking, Guildford, Shepperton and Hampton Court

Network Diagram - see first Page of Table 152

Miles	Miles	Miles	Miles	Miles			SW MX	SW MO	SW MO	SW MX	SW MX	SW MO	SW MX	SW MX	SW MX	SW MX	SW MO	SW MX	SW MX	SW MX	SW	SW 1
0	—	—	—	0	**London Waterloo** 15 ⊖	d	23p03	23p00	23p10	23p12	23p27	23p32	23p36	23p42	23p50	23p57	00 01	00 09	00 15	00 27	00 42	05 00
1¼	—	—	—	1¼	Vauxhall ⊖	d	23p07	23p04	23p14	23p16	23p31	23p36	23p40	23p46	23p54	00 01	00 04	00 13	00 19	00 31	00 46	05 04
4	—	—	—	4	**Clapham Junction** 10	d	23p12	23p09	23p19	23p21	23p36	23p41	23p45	23p51	23p59	00 06	00 09	00 20	00 25	00 37		05 11
5½	—	—	—	5½	Earlsfield	d	23p15	23p12	23p22	23p24	23p39	23p44	23p48	23p54	00 02	00 09	00 12	00 23	00 29	00s41		05 14
7¼	—	—	—	7¼	**Wimbledon** 6 ⊖	d	23p19	23p16	23p26	23p28	23p43	23p48	23p52	23p58	00 06	00 13	00 16	00 27	00 33	00 45	01 05	05 18
8¾	—	0	0	8¾	Raynes Park 6	d				23p31	23p46	23p52	23p55	00 01		00 16	00 19		00 36	00 48	01 08	
—	—	1	1	—	Motspur Park	d						23p55		00 04					00 38			
—	—	—	2½	—	Malden Manor	d																
—	—	—	3½	—	Tolworth	d																
—	—	—	4½	—	Chessington North	d																
—	—	—	5¼	—	**Chessington South**	a																
—	—	2	—	—	Worcester Park	d						23p57		00 06					00 41			
—	—	3¼	—	—	Stoneleigh	d						23p59		00 09					00 44			
—	—	4¼	—	—	Ewell West	d						00 03		00 12					00 46			
—	—	5½	—	—	**Epsom** 3	a						00 06		00 15					00 50			
—	—	—	—	—		d								00 19								
—	—	7½	—	—	Ashtead	d								00 23								
—	0	9¼	—	—	Leatherhead	d								00 26								
—	—	12½	—	—	Box Hill & Westhumble	d																
—	—	13¼	—	—	**Dorking** 4	a																
9¾	—	—	—	9¾	New Malden 6	d				23p34	23p49		23p58			00 19	00 22			00 50	01 11	
—	—	—	—	11¼	Norbiton	d				23p37	23p52					00 22					01 14	
—	—	—	—	12	Kingston	a				23p40	23p55					00 25					01 17	
—	—	—	—	—		d				23p40	23p55					00 25					01 17	
—	—	—	—	12½	Hampton Wick	d				23p42	23p57					00 27					01s22	
—	—	—	—	13¾	Teddington	d				23p45	23p59					00 30					01s25	
—	—	—	—	—	Strawberry Hill	a					00 03										01 28	
—	—	—	—	14¾	Fulwell	d				23p49						00 34						
—	—	—	—	16½	Hampton	d				23p53						00 38						
—	—	—	—	18¼	Kempton Park	d				23p56						00 41						
—	—	—	—	18¾	Sunbury	d				23p58						00 43						
—	—	—	—	19¼	Upper Halliford	d				23p59						00 45						
—	—	—	—	20¾	**Shepperton**	a				00 03						00 48						
11	—	—	—	—	Berrylands	d							23p59				00 25			00s53		
12	—	—	0	—	**Surbiton** 6	d	23p27	23p32	23p35				00 05		00 14		00 31	00 35		00a56		05 26
—	—	—	2	—	Thames Ditton	d							00 09									
—	—	—	3	—	**Hampton Court**	a							00 12									
14	—	—	—	—	Hinchley Wood	d	23p31	23p36							00 18		00 35					
15¼	—	—	—	—	Claygate	d	23p34	23p39							00 20		00 38					
17	—	—	—	—	Oxshott	d	23p37	23p42							00 24		00 41					
19	—	—	—	—	Cobham & Stoke D'abernon	d	23p41	23p46							00 27		00 45					
—	2½	—	—	—	Bookham	d								00 31								
21¼	4¼	—	—	—	Effingham Junction 6	d	23p45	23p50						00 36	00 32		00 49					
22¼	—	—	—	—	Horsley	d	23p48	23p53						00 39	00 34		00 52					
25½	—	—	—	—	Clandon	d	23p53	23p58						00 44	00 39		00 57					
28¾	—	—	—	—	London Road (Guildford)	d	23p58	00 03						00 49	00 44		01 02					
30	—	—	—	—	**Guildford**	a	00 02	00 07	00 13					00 53	00 48		01 06	01 07				06 00

London - Chessington South, Dorking, Guildford, Shepperton and Hampton Court

Network Diagram - see first Page of Table 152

			SW	SW 1	SW	SW		SW	SW	SW			SW	SW	SW	SW	SW	SW	SW	SW	SW			SW	SW
London Waterloo 15 ⊖	d		05 12	05 20				05 47	05 50					06 03	06 06	06 12	06 16	06 20	06 24	06 27	06 33			06 36	06 39
Vauxhall ⊖	d		05 16	05 24				05 51	05 54					06 07	06 10	06 16	06 20	06 24	06 28	06 31	06 37			06 40	06 43
Clapham Junction 10	d		05 21	05 29				05 56	05 59					06 12	06 15	06 21	06 25	06 29	06 33	06 36	06 42			06 45	06 48
Earlsfield	d		05 24	05 32				05 59	06 02					06 15	06 18	06 24	06 28	06 32	06 36	06 39	06 45			06 48	06 51
Wimbledon 6 ⊖	d		05 28	05 36	05 49			06 03	06 06	06 13			06 16	06 19	06 22	06 28	06 32	06 36	06 40	06 43	06 49			06 52	06 55
Raynes Park 6	d		05 31					06 06		06 16			06 19		06 25	06 31	06 35		06 43	06 46				06 55	06 58
Motspur Park	d							06 09					06 21				06 38		06 46						
Malden Manor	d												06 25				06 41								
Tolworth	d												06 27				06 44								
Chessington North	d												06 30				06 47								
Chessington South	a												06 32				06 49								
Worcester Park	d							06 11											06 48						07 02
Stoneleigh	d							06 14											06 51						07 05
Ewell West	d							06 17											06 54						07 08
Epsom 3	a							06 20											06 57						07 11
	d							06 21											06 58						07 12
Ashtead	d							06 25											07 02						07 16
Leatherhead	d							06 28											07 05						07 19
Box Hill & Westhumble	d																								
Dorking 4	a																		07 11						
New Malden 6	d		05 34							06 19					06 28	06 34				06 49				06 58	
Norbiton	d		05 37							06 22						06 37				06 52					
Kingston	a		05 40							06 25						06 40				06 55					
	d		05 40			05 59				06 29						06 40				06 59					
Hampton Wick	d		05 42			06 01				06 31						06 42				07 01					
Teddington	d		05 45			06 05				06 35						06 45				07 05					
Strawberry Hill	a					06 08				06 38										07 08					
Fulwell	d		05 49													06 49									
Hampton	d		05 53													06 53									
Kempton Park	d		05 56													06 56									
Sunbury	d		05 58													06 58									
Upper Halliford	d		06 00													07 00									
Shepperton	a		06 03													07 03									
Berrylands	d														06 30									07 00	
Surbiton 6	d			05 44	05 57				06a13					06 27	06 35			06 44			06 57			07 05	
Thames Ditton	d														06 39									07 09	
Hampton Court	a														06 42									07 12	
Hinchley Wood	d				06 01									06 31							07 01				
Claygate	d				06 04									06 34							07 04				
Oxshott	d				06 07									06 37							07 07				
Cobham & Stoke D'abernon	d				06 11									06 41							07 11				
Bookham	d							06 33																	07 24
Effingham Junction 6	d				06 15			06 37						06 45							07 15				07a28
Horsley	d				06 18									06 48							07 18				
Clandon	d				06 23									06 53							07 23				
London Road (Guildford)	d				06 28			06 46						06 58							07 28				
Guildford	a			06 21	06 32			06 50						07 02				07 20			07 32				

London - Chessington South, Dorking, Guildford, Shepperton and Hampton Court

Network Diagram - see first Page of Table 152

		SW	SW	SW	SW	SW	SW	SW	SW	SW	SW	SW	SW	SW	SW	SW	SW	SW	SW	SW	SW
London Waterloo 15 ⊖	d	06 42	06 46	06 50	06 54	06 57	07 03	07 06	07 09	07 12	07 16	07 20	07 24	07 27	07 33	07 36	07 39	07 42	07 46	07 50	07 54
Vauxhall ⊖	d	06 46	06 50	06 54	06 58	07 01	07 07	07 10	07 13	07 16	07 20	07 24	07 28	07 31	07 37	07 40	07 43	07 46	07 50	07 54	07 58
Clapham Junction 10	d	06 51	06 55	06 59	07 03	07 06	07 12	07 15	07 18	07 21	07 25	07 29	07 33	07 36	07 42	07 45	07 48	07 51	07 55	07 59	08 03
Earlsfield	d	06 54	06 58	07 02	07 06	07 09	07 15	07 18	07 21	07 24	07 28	07 32	07 36	07 39	07 45	07 48	07 51	07 54	07 58	08 02	08 06
Wimbledon 6 ⊖	d	06 58	07 02	07 06	07 10	07 13	07 19	07 22	07 25	07 28	07 32	07 36	07 40	07 43	07 49	07 52	07 55	07 58	08 02	08 06	08 10
Raynes Park 6	d	07 01	07 05		07 13	07 16		07 25	07 28	07 31	07 35		07 43	07 46		07 55	07 58	08 01	08 05		08 13
Motspur Park	d		07 08		07 16				07 31		07 38		07 46				08 01		08 08		08 16
Malden Manor	d		07 11								07 41								08 11		
Tolworth	d		07 14								07 44								08 14		
Chessington North	d		07 17								07 47								08 17		
Chessington South	a		07 19								07 49								08 19		
Worcester Park	d				07 18				07 33				07 48				08 03				08 18
Stoneleigh	d				07 21				07 36				07 51				08 06				08 21
Ewell West	d				07 24				07 39				07 54				08 09				08 24
Epsom 3	a				07 27				07 42				07 58				08 13				08 27
	d				07 28								07 58				08 17				08 28
Ashtead	d				07 32								08 02				08 21				08 32
Leatherhead	d				07 35								08 05				08 24				08 35
Box Hill & Westhumble	d																				
Dorking 4	a				07 41								08 12								08 41
New Malden 6	d	07 04				07 19		07 28		07 34				07 49		07 58		08 04			
Norbiton	d	07 07				07 22				07 37				07 52				08 07			
Kingston	a	07 10				07 25				07 40				07 55				08 10			
	d	07 10				07 29				07 40				07 59				08 10			
Hampton Wick	d	07 12				07 31				07 42				08 01				08 12			
Teddington	d	07 15				07 35				07 45				08 05				08 15			
Strawberry Hill	a					07 38								08 08							
Fulwell	d	07 19								07 49								08 19			
Hampton	d	07 23								07 53								08 23			
Kempton Park	d	07 26								07 56								08 26			
Sunbury	d	07 28								07 58								08 28			
Upper Halliford	d	07 30								08 00								08 30			
Shepperton	a	07 33								08 03								08 33			
Berrylands	d							07 30								08 00					
Surbiton 6	d			07 14			07 27	07 35				07a43			07 57	08 05				08 14	
Thames Ditton	d							07 39								08 09					
Hampton Court	a							07 42								08 12					
Hinchley Wood	d						07 31								08 01						
Claygate	d						07 34								08 04						
Oxshott	d						07 37								08 07						
Cobham & Stoke D'abernon	d						07 41								08 11						
Bookham	d																08 29				
Effingham Junction 6	d						07 45								08 15		08 33				
Horsley	d						07 48								08 18		08 36				
Clandon	d						07 53								08 23		08 41				
London Road (Guildford)	d						07 58								08 28		08 46				
Guildford	a			07 47			08 02								08 32		08 50			08 50	

		SW	SW	SW	SW	SW	SW	SW	SW	SW	SW	SW	SW	SW	SW	SW	SW	SW	SW
London Waterloo 15 ⊖	d	07 57	08 03	08 06	08 09	08 12	08 16	08 20	08 24	08 27	08 33	08 36	08 39	08 42	08 46	08 50	08 54	08 57	09 03
Vauxhall ⊖	d	08 01	08 07	08 10	08 13	08 16	08 20	08 24	08 28	08 31	08 37	08 40	08 43	08 46	08 50	08 54	08 58	09 01	09 07
Clapham Junction 10	d	08 06	08 12	08 15	08 18	08 21	08 25	08 29	08 33	08 36	08 42	08 45	08 48	08 51	08 55	08 59	09 03	09 06	09 12
Earlsfield	d	08 09	08 15	08 18	08 21	08 24	08 28	08 32	08 36	08 39	08 45	08 48	08 51	08 54	08 58	09 02	09 06	09 09	09 15
Wimbledon 6 ⊖	d	08 13	08 19	08 22	08 25	08 28	08 32	08 36	08 40	08 43	08 49	08 52	08 55	08 58	09 02	09 06	09 10	09 13	09 19
Raynes Park 6	d	08 16		08 25	08 28	08 31	08 35		08 43	08 46		08 55	08 58	09 01	09 05		09 13	09 16	
Motspur Park	d				08 31		08 38		08 46				09 01		09 08		09 16		
Malden Manor	d						08 41								09 11				
Tolworth	d						08 44								09 14				
Chessington North	d						08 47								09 17				
Chessington South	a						08 49								09 19				
Worcester Park	d				08 33				08 48				09 03				09 18		
Stoneleigh	d				08 36				08 51				09 06				09 21		
Ewell West	d				08 39				08 54				09 09				09 24		
Epsom 3	a				08 42				08 57				09 16				09 27		
	d				08 47				08 58				09 17				09 28		
Ashtead	d				08 51				09 02				09 21				09 32		
Leatherhead	d				08 54				09 05				09 24				09 35		
Box Hill & Westhumble	d																		
Dorking 4	a								09 11								09 41		
New Malden 6	d	08 19		08 28		08 34				08 49		08 58		09 04				09 19	
Norbiton	d	08 22				08 37				08 52				09 07				09 22	
Kingston	a	08 25				08 39				08 55				09 10				09 25	
	d	08 29				08 40				08 59				09 10				09 29	
Hampton Wick	d	08 31				08 42				09 01				09 12				09 31	
Teddington	d	08 35				08 45				09 05				09 15				09 35	
Strawberry Hill	a	08 38								09 08								09 38	
Fulwell	d					08 49								09 19					
Hampton	d					08 53								09 23					
Kempton Park	d					08 56								09 26					
Sunbury	d					08 58								09 28					
Upper Halliford	d					09 00								09 30					
Shepperton	a					09 04								09 33					
Berrylands	d			08 30								09 00							
Surbiton 6	d		08 27	08 35				08a43			08 57	09 05				09a13			09 27
Thames Ditton	d			08 39								09 09							
Hampton Court	a			08 42								09 12							
Hinchley Wood	d		08 31								09 01								09 31
Claygate	d		08 34								09 04								09 34
Oxshott	d		08 37								09 07								09 37
Cobham & Stoke D'abernon	d		08 41								09 11								09 41
Bookham	d				08 59								09 29						
Effingham Junction 6	d		08 45		09 03						09 15		09 33						09 45
Horsley	d		08 48		09 06						09 18		09 36						09 48
Clandon	d		08 53		09 11						09 23		09 41						09 53
London Road (Guildford)	d		08 58		09 16						09 28		09 46						09 58
Guildford	a		09 04		09 20						09 32		09 50						10 02

London - Chessington South, Dorking, Guildford, Shepperton and Hampton Court

Network Diagram - see first Page of Table 152

		SW	SW	SW	SW	SW	SW	SW	SW	SW	SW	SW	SW	SW	SW	SW	SW	SW	SW	SW	SW
London Waterloo 15 ⊖	d	09 06	09 09	09 12	09 16	09 20	09 24	09 27	09 33	09 36	09 39	09 42	09 46	09 50	09 54	09 57	10 03	10 06	10 09	10 12	10 16
Vauxhall ⊖	d	09 10	09 13	09 16	09 20	09 24	09 28	09 31	09 37	09 40	09 43	09 46	09 50	09 54	09 58	10 01	10 07	10 10	10 13	10 16	10 20
Clapham Junction 10	d	09 15	09 18	09 21	09 25	09 29	09 33	09 36	09 42	09 45	09 48	09 51	09 55	09 59	10 03	10 06	10 12	10 15	10 18	10 21	10 25
Earlsfield	d	09 18	09 21	09 24	09 28	09 32	09 36	09 39	09 45	09 48	09 51	09 54	09 58	10 02	10 06	10 09	10 15	10 18	10 21	10 24	10 28
Wimbledon 6 ⊖	d	09 22	09 25	09 28	09 32	09 36	09 40	09 43	09 49	09 52	09 55	09 58	10 02	10 06	10 10	10 13	10 19	10 22	10 25	10 28	10 32
Raynes Park 6	d	09 25	09 28	09 31	09 35		09 43	09 46		09 55	09 58	10 01	10 05		10 13	10 16		10 25	10 28	10 31	10 35
Motspur Park	d		09 31		09 38		09 46				10 01		10 08		10 16				10 31		10 38
Malden Manor	d				09 41								10 11								10 41
Tolworth	d				09 44								10 14								10 44
Chessington North	d				09 47								10 17								10 47
Chessington South	a				09 49								10 19								10 49
Worcester Park	d		09 33				09 48				10 03				10 18				10 33		
Stoneleigh	d		09 36				09 51				10 06				10 21				10 36		
Ewell West	d		09 39				09 54				10 09				10 24				10 39		
Epsom 3	a		09 42				09 57				10 16				10 27				10 46		
	d		09 47				09 58				10 17				10 28				10 47		
Ashtead	d		09 51				10 02				10 21				10 32				10 51		
Leatherhead	d		09 54				10 05				10 24				10 35				10 54		
Box Hill & Westhumble	d																				
Dorking 4	a						10 11								10 41						
New Malden 6	d	09 28		09 34				09 49		09 58		10 04				10 19		10 28		10 34	
Norbiton	d			09 37				09 52				10 07				10 22				10 37	
Kingston	a			09 40				09 55				10 10				10 25				10 40	
	d			09 40				09 59				10 10				10 29				10 40	
Hampton Wick	d			09 42				10 01				10 12				10 31				10 42	
Teddington	d			09 45				10 05				10 15				10 35				10 45	
Strawberry Hill	a							10 08								10 38					
Fulwell	d			09 49								10 19								10 49	
Hampton	d			09 53								10 23								10 53	
Kempton Park	d			09 56								10 26								10 56	
Sunbury	d			09 58								10 28								10 58	
Upper Halliford	d			10 00								10 30								11 00	
Shepperton	a			10 03								10 33								11 03	
Berrylands	d	09 30								10 00								10 30			
Surbiton 6	d	09 35				09a43			09 57	10 05				10a13			10 27	10 35			
Thames Ditton	d	09 39								10 09								10 39			
Hampton Court	a	09 42								10 12								10 42			
Hinchley Wood	d								10 01								10 31				
Claygate	d								10 04								10 34				
Oxshott	d								10 07								10 37				
Cobham & Stoke D'abernon	d								10 11								10 41				
Bookham	d		09 59								10 29								10 59		
Effingham Junction 6	d		10 03						10 15		10 33						10 45		11 03		
Horsley	d		10 06						10 18		10 36						10 48		11 06		
Clandon	d		10 11						10 23		10 41						10 53		11 11		
London Road (Guildford)	d		10 16						10 28		10 46						10 58		11 16		
Guildford	a		10 20						10 32		10 50						11 02		11 20		

London - Chessington South, Dorking, Guildford, Shepperton and Hampton Court

Network Diagram - see first Page of Table 152

		SW		SW	SW		SW		SW	SW	SW	SW	SW	SW	SW		SW		SW	SW	SW	SW	SW	SW	SW
London Waterloo 15 ⊖	d	10 20		10 24	10 27		10 33		10 36	10 39	10 42	10 46	10 50	10 54	10 57		11 03		11 06	11 09	11 12	11 16	11 20	11 24	11 27
Vauxhall ⊖	d	10 24		10 28	10 31		10 37		10 40	10 43	10 46	10 50	10 54	10 58	11 01		11 07		11 10	11 13	11 16	11 20	11 24	11 28	11 31
Clapham Junction 10	d	10 29		10 33	10 36		10 42		10 45	10 48	10 51	10 55	10 59	11 03	11 06		11 12		11 15	11 18	11 21	11 25	11 29	11 33	11 36
Earlsfield	d	10 32		10 36	10 39		10 45		10 48	10 51	10 54	10 58	11 02	11 06	11 09		11 15		11 18	11 21	11 24	11 28	11 32	11 36	11 39
Wimbledon 6 ⊖	d	10 36		10 40	10 43		10 49		10 52	10 55	10 58	11 02	11 06	11 10	11 13		11 19		11 22	11 25	11 28	11 32	11 36	11 40	11 43
Raynes Park 6	d			10 43	10 46				10 55	10 58	11 01	11 05		11 13	11 16				11 25	11 28	11 31	11 35		11 43	11 46
Motspur Park	d			10 46						11 01		11 08		11 16						11 31		11 38		11 46	
Malden Manor	d											11 11										11 41			
Tolworth	d											11 14										11 44			
Chessington North	d											11 17										11 47			
Chessington South	a											11 19										11 49			
Worcester Park	d			10 48						11 03				11 18						11 33				11 48	
Stoneleigh	d			10 51						11 06				11 21						11 36				11 51	
Ewell West	d			10 54						11 09				11 24						11 39				11 54	
Epsom 3	a			10 57						11 16				11 27						11 46				11 57	
	d			10 58						11 17				11 28						11 47				11 58	
Ashtead	d			11 02						11 21				11 32						11 51				12 02	
Leatherhead	d			11 05						11 24				11 35						11 54				12 05	
Box Hill & Westhumble	d																								
Dorking 4	a			11 11										11 41										12 11	
New Malden 6	d				10 49				10 58		11 04				11 19				11 28		11 34				11 49
Norbiton	d				10 52						11 07				11 22						11 37				11 52
Kingston	a				10 55						11 10				11 25						11 40				11 55
	d				10 59						11 10				11 29						11 40				11 59
Hampton Wick	d				11 01						11 12				11 31						11 42				12 01
Teddington	d				11 05						11 15				11 35						11 45				12 05
Strawberry Hill	a				11 08										11 38										12 08
Fulwell	d										11 19										11 49				
Hampton	d										11 23										11 53				
Kempton Park	d										11 26										11 56				
Sunbury	d										11 28										11 58				
Upper Halliford	d										11 30										12 00				
Shepperton	a										11 33										12 03				
Berrylands	d								11 00										11 30						
Surbiton 6	d	10a43					10 57		11 05				11a13				11 27		11 35				11a43		
Thames Ditton	d								11 09										11 39						
Hampton Court	a								11 12										11 42						
Hinchley Wood	d						11 01										11 31								
Claygate	d						11 04										11 34								
Oxshott	d						11 07										11 37								
Cobham & Stoke D'abernon	d						11 11										11 41								
Bookham	d									11 29										11 59					
Effingham Junction 6	d						11 15			11 33							11 45			12 03					
Horsley	d						11 18			11 36							11 48			12 06					
Clandon	d						11 23			11 41							11 53			12 11					
London Road (Guildford)	d						11 28			11 46							11 58			12 16					
Guildford	a						11 32			11 50							12 02			12 20					

London - Chessington South, Dorking, Guildford, Shepperton and Hampton Court

Network Diagram - see first Page of Table 152

			SW		SW	SW	SW	SW	SW	SW	SW		SW		SW	SW	SW	SW	SW	SW	SW		SW		SW
London Waterloo 15 ⊖	d		11 33		11 36	11 39	11 42	11 46	11 50	11 54	11 57		12 03		12 06	12 09	12 12	12 16	12 20	12 24	12 27		12 33		12 36
Vauxhall ⊖	d		11 37		11 40	11 43	11 46	11 50	11 54	11 58	12 01		12 07		12 10	12 13	12 16	12 20	12 24	12 28	12 31		12 37		12 40
Clapham Junction 10	d		11 42		11 45	11 48	11 51	11 55	11 59	12 03	12 06		12 12		12 15	12 18	12 21	12 25	12 29	12 33	12 36		12 42		12 45
Earlsfield	d		11 45		11 48	11 51	11 54	11 58	12 02	12 06	12 09		12 15		12 18	12 21	12 24	12 28	12 32	12 36	12 39		12 45		12 48
Wimbledon 6 ⊖	d		11 49		11 52	11 55	11 58	12 02	12 06	12 10	12 13		12 19		12 22	12 25	12 28	12 32	12 36	12 40	12 43		12 49		12 52
Raynes Park 6	d				11 55	11 58	12 01	12 05		12 13	12 16				12 25	12 28	12 31	12 35		12 43	12 46				12 55
Motspur Park	d					12 01		12 08		12 16						12 31		12 38		12 46					
Malden Manor	d							12 11										12 41							
Tolworth	d							12 14										12 44							
Chessington North	d							12 17										12 47							
Chessington South	a							12 19										12 49							
Worcester Park	d					12 03				12 18						12 33				12 48					
Stoneleigh	d					12 06				12 21						12 36				12 51					
Ewell West	d					12 09				12 24						12 39				12 54					
Epsom 3	a					12 16				12 27						12 46				12 57					
	d					12 17				12 28						12 47				12 58					
Ashtead	d					12 21				12 32						12 51				13 02					
Leatherhead	d					12 24				12 35						12 54				13 05					
Box Hill & Westhumble	d																								
Dorking 4	a									12 41										13 11					
New Malden 6	d				11 58		12 04				12 19				12 28		12 34				12 49				12 58
Norbiton	d						12 07				12 22						12 37				12 52				
Kingston	a						12 10				12 25						12 40				12 55				
	d						12 10				12 29						12 40				12 59				
Hampton Wick	d						12 12				12 31						12 42				13 01				
Teddington	d						12 15				12 35						12 45				13 05				
Strawberry Hill	a										12 38										13 08				
Fulwell	d						12 19										12 49								
Hampton	d						12 23										12 53								
Kempton Park	d						12 26										12 56								
Sunbury	d						12 28										12 58								
Upper Halliford	d						12 30										13 00								
Shepperton	a						12 33										13 03								
Berrylands	d				12 00										12 30										13 00
Surbiton 6	d		11 57		12 05				12a13				12 27		12 35				12a43				12 57		13 05
Thames Ditton	d				12 09										12 39										13 09
Hampton Court	a				12 12										12 42										13 12
Hinchley Wood	d		12 01										12 31										13 01		
Claygate	d		12 04										12 34										13 04		
Oxshott	d		12 07										12 37										13 07		
Cobham & Stoke D'abernon	d		12 11										12 41										13 11		
Bookham	d					12 29										12 59									
Effingham Junction 6	d		12 15			12 33							12 45			13 03							13 15		
Horsley	d		12 18			12 36							12 48			13 06							13 18		
Clandon	d		12 23			12 41							12 53			13 11							13 23		
London Road (Guildford)	d		12 28			12 46							12 58			13 16							13 28		
Guildford	a		12 32			12 50							13 02			13 20							13 32		

		SW	SW	SW	SW	SW	SW		SW		SW	SW	SW	SW	SW	SW	SW		SW		SW	SW	SW	SW	SW
London Waterloo 15 ⊖	d	12 39	12 42	12 46	12 50	12 54	12 57		13 03		13 06	13 09	13 12	13 16	13 20	13 24	13 27		13 33		13 36	13 39	13 42	13 46	13 50
Vauxhall ⊖	d	12 43	12 46	12 50	12 54	12 58	13 01		13 07		13 10	13 13	13 16	13 20	13 24	13 28	13 31		13 37		13 40	13 43	13 46	13 50	13 54
Clapham Junction 10	d	12 48	12 51	12 55	12 59	13 03	13 06		13 12		13 15	13 18	13 21	13 25	13 29	13 33	13 36		13 42		13 45	13 48	13 51	13 55	13 59
Earlsfield	d	12 51	12 54	12 58	13 02	13 06	13 09		13 15		13 18	13 21	13 24	13 28	13 32	13 36	13 39		13 45		13 48	13 51	13 54	13 58	14 02
Wimbledon 6 ⊖	d	12 55	12 58	13 02	13 06	13 10	13 13		13 19		13 22	13 25	13 28	13 32	13 36	13 40	13 43		13 49		13 52	13 55	13 58	14 02	14 06
Raynes Park 6	d	12 58	13 01	13 05		13 13	13 16				13 25	13 28	13 31	13 35		13 43	13 46				13 55	13 58	14 01	14 05	
Motspur Park	d	13 01		13 08		13 16						13 31		13 38		13 46						14 01		14 08	
Malden Manor	d			13 11										13 41										14 11	
Tolworth	d			13 14										13 44										14 14	
Chessington North	d			13 17										13 47										14 17	
Chessington South	a			13 19										13 49										14 19	
Worcester Park	d	13 03				13 18						13 33				13 48						14 03			
Stoneleigh	d	13 06				13 21						13 36				13 51						14 06			
Ewell West	d	13 09				13 24						13 39				13 54						14 09			
Epsom 3	a	13 16				13 27						13 46				13 57						14 16			
	d	13 17				13 28						13 47				13 58						14 17			
Ashtead	d	13 21				13 32						13 51				14 02						14 21			
Leatherhead	d	13 24				13 35						13 54				14 05						14 24			
Box Hill & Westhumble	d																								
Dorking 4	a					13 41										14 11									
New Malden 6	d		13 04				13 19				13 28		13 34				13 49				13 58		14 04		
Norbiton	d		13 07				13 22						13 37				13 52						14 07		
Kingston	a		13 10				13 25						13 40				13 55						14 10		
	d		13 10				13 29						13 40				13 59						14 10		
Hampton Wick	d		13 12				13 31						13 42				14 01						14 12		
Teddington	d		13 15				13 35						13 45				14 05						14 15		
Strawberry Hill	a						13 38										14 08								
Fulwell	d		13 19										13 49										14 19		
Hampton	d		13 23										13 53										14 23		
Kempton Park	d		13 26										13 56										14 26		
Sunbury	d		13 28										13 58										14 28		
Upper Halliford	d		13 30										14 00										14 30		
Shepperton	a		13 33										14 03										14 33		
Berrylands	d										13 30										14 00				
Surbiton 6	d				13a13				13 27		13 35				13a43				13 57		14 05				14a13
Thames Ditton	d										13 39										14 09				
Hampton Court	a										13 42										14 12				
Hinchley Wood	d								13 31										14 01						
Claygate	d								13 34										14 04						
Oxshott	d								13 37										14 07						
Cobham & Stoke D'abernon	d								13 41										14 11						
Bookham	d	13 29										13 59										14 29			
Effingham Junction 6	d	13 33							13 45			14 03							14 15			14 33			
Horsley	d	13 36							13 48			14 06							14 18			14 36			
Clandon	d	13 41							13 53			14 11							14 23			14 41			
London Road (Guildford)	d	13 46							13 58			14 16							14 28			14 46			
Guildford	a	13 50							14 02			14 20							14 32			14 50			

London - Chessington South, Dorking, Guildford, Shepperton and Hampton Court

Network Diagram - see first Page of Table 152

		SW	SW		SW		SW	SW	SW	SW	SW	SW	SW		SW		SW	SW	SW	SW	SW	SW	SW		SW
London Waterloo 15 ⊖	d	13 54	13 57		14 03		14 06	14 09	14 12	14 16	14 20	14 24	14 27		14 33		14 36	14 39	14 42	14 46	14 50	14 54	14 57		15 03
Vauxhall ⊖	d	13 58	14 01		14 07		14 10	14 13	14 16	14 20	14 24	14 28	14 31		14 37		14 40	14 43	14 46	14 50	14 54	14 58	15 01		15 07
Clapham Junction 10	d	14 03	14 06		14 12		14 15	14 18	14 21	14 25	14 29	14 33	14 36		14 42		14 45	14 48	14 51	14 55	14 59	15 03	15 06		15 12
Earlsfield	d	14 06	14 09		14 15		14 18	14 21	14 24	14 28	14 32	14 36	14 39		14 45		14 48	14 51	14 54	14 58	15 02	15 06	15 09		15 15
Wimbledon 6 ⊖	d	14 10	14 13		14 19		14 22	14 25	14 28	14 32	14 36	14 40	14 43		14 49		14 52	14 55	14 58	15 02	15 06	15 10	15 13		15 19
Raynes Park 6	d	14 13	14 16				14 25	14 28	14 31	14 35		14 43	14 46				14 55	14 58	15 01	15 05		15 13	15 16		
Motspur Park	d	14 16						14 31		14 38		14 46						15 01		15 08		15 16			
Malden Manor	d									14 41										15 11					
Tolworth	d									14 44										15 14					
Chessington North	d									14 47										15 17					
Chessington South	a									14 49										15 19					
Worcester Park	d	14 18						14 33				14 48						15 03				15 18			
Stoneleigh	d	14 21						14 36				14 51						15 06				15 21			
Ewell West	d	14 24						14 39				14 54						15 09				15 24			
Epsom 3	a	14 27						14 46				14 57						15 16				15 27			
	d	14 28						14 47				14 58						15 17				15 28			
Ashtead	d	14 32						14 51				15 02						15 21				15 32			
Leatherhead	d	14 35						14 54				15 05						15 24				15 35			
Box Hill & Westhumble	d																								
Dorking 4	a	14 41										15 11										15 41			
New Malden 6	d		14 19				14 28		14 34				14 49				14 58		15 04				15 19		
Norbiton	d		14 22						14 37				14 52						15 07				15 22		
Kingston	a		14 25						14 40				14 55						15 10				15 25		
	d		14 29						14 40				14 59						15 10				15 29		
Hampton Wick	d		14 31						14 42				15 01						15 12				15 31		
Teddington	d		14 35						14 45				15 05						15 15				15 35		
Strawberry Hill	a		14 38										15 08										15 38		
Fulwell	d								14 49										15 19						
Hampton	d								14 53										15 23						
Kempton Park	d								14 56										15 26						
Sunbury	d								14 58										15 28						
Upper Halliford	d								15 00										15 30						
Shepperton	a								15 03										15 33						
Berrylands	d						14 30										15 00								
Surbiton 6	d				14 27		14 35				14a43				14 57		15 05				15a13				15 27
Thames Ditton	d						14 39										15 09								
Hampton Court	a						14 42										15 12								
Hinchley Wood	d				14 31										15 01										15 31
Claygate	d				14 34										15 04										15 34
Oxshott	d				14 37										15 07										15 37
Cobham & Stoke D'abernon	d				14 41										15 11										15 41
Bookham	d							14 59										15 29							
Effingham Junction 6	d				14 45			15 03							15 15			15 33							15 45
Horsley	d				14 48			15 06							15 18			15 36							15 48
Clandon	d				14 53			15 11							15 23			15 41							15 53
London Road (Guildford)	d				14 58			15 16							15 28			15 46							15 58
Guildford	a				15 02			15 20							15 32			15 50							16 02

			SW	SW	SW	SW	SW	SW	SW		SW		SW	SW	SW	SW	SW	SW	SW			SW	SW	SW	SW
London Waterloo 15 ⊖	d		15 06	15 09	15 12	15 16	15 20	15 24	15 27		15 33		15 36	15 39	15 42	15 46	15 50	15 54	15 57			16 03	16 06	16 09	16 12
Vauxhall ⊖	d		15 10	15 13	15 16	15 20	15 24	15 28	15 31		15 37		15 40	15 43	15 46	15 50	15 54	15 58	16 01			16 07	16 10	16 13	16 16
Clapham Junction 10	d		15 15	15 18	15 21	15 25	15 29	15 33	15 36		15 42		15 45	15 48	15 51	15 55	15 59	16 03	16 06			16 12	16 15	16 18	16 21
Earlsfield	d		15 18	15 21	15 24	15 28	15 32	15 36	15 39		15 45		15 48	15 51	15 54	15 58	16 02	16 06	16 09			16 15	16 18	16 21	16 24
Wimbledon 6 ⊖	d		15 22	15 25	15 28	15 32	15 36	15 40	15 43		15 49		15 52	15 55	15 58	16 02	16 06	16 10	16 13			16 19	16 22	16 25	16 28
Raynes Park 6	d		15 25	15 28	15 31	15 35		15 43	15 46				15 55	15 58	16 01	16 05		16 13	16 16				16 25	16 28	16 31
Motspur Park	d			15 31		15 38		15 46						16 01		16 08		16 16						16 31	
Malden Manor	d					15 41										16 11									
Tolworth	d					15 44										16 14									
Chessington North	d					15 47										16 17									
Chessington South	a					15 49										16 19									
Worcester Park	d			15 33				15 48						16 03				16 18						16 33	
Stoneleigh	d			15 36				15 51						16 06				16 21						16 36	
Ewell West	d			15 39				15 54						16 09				16 24						16 39	
Epsom 3	a			15 46				15 57						16 15				16 27						16 46	
	d			15 47				15 58						16 17				16 28						16 47	
Ashtead	d			15 51				16 02						16 21				16 32						16 51	
Leatherhead	d			15 54				16 05						16 24				16 35						16 54	
Box Hill & Westhumble	d																								
Dorking 4	a							16 11										16 41							
New Malden 6	d		15 28		15 34				15 49				15 58		16 04				16 19				16 28		16 34
Norbiton	d				15 37				15 52						16 07				16 22						16 37
Kingston	a				15 40				15 55						16 10				16 25						16 40
	d				15 40				15 59						16 10				16 29						16 40
Hampton Wick	d				15 42				16 01						16 12				16 31						16 42
Teddington	d				15 45				16 05						16 15				16 35						16 45
Strawberry Hill	a								16 08										16 38						
Fulwell	d				15 49										16 19										16 49
Hampton	d				15 53										16 23										16 53
Kempton Park	d				15 56										16 26										16 56
Sunbury	d				15 58										16 28										16 58
Upper Halliford	d				16 00										16 30										17 00
Shepperton	a				16 03										16 33										17 05
Berrylands	d		15 30										16 00										16 30		
Surbiton 6	d		15 35				15a43				15 57		16 05				16a13					16 27	16 35		
Thames Ditton	d		15 39										16 09										16 39		
Hampton Court	a		15 42										16 12										16 44		
Hinchley Wood	d										16 01											16 31			
Claygate	d										16 04											16 34			
Oxshott	d										16 07											16 37			
Cobham & Stoke D'abernon	d										16 11											16 41			
Bookham	d			15 59										16 29										16 59	
Effingham Junction 6	d			16 03							16 15			16 33								16 45		17 03	
Horsley	d			16 06							16 18			16 36								16 48		17 06	
Clandon	d			16 11							16 23			16 41								16 53		17 11	
London Road (Guildford)	d			16 16							16 28			16 46								16 58		17 16	
Guildford	a			16 20							16 32			16 50								17 04		17 22	

London - Chessington South, Dorking, Guildford, Shepperton and Hampton Court

Network Diagram - see first Page of Table 152

		SW	SW	SW	SW	SW	SW	SW	SW	SW	SW	SW	SW	SW	SW	SW	SW	SW	SW	SW
														1						
London Waterloo 15 ⊖	d	16 16	16 20	16 24	16 27	16 33	16 36	16 39	16 42	16 46	16 50	16 54	16 57	17 02	17 02	17 06	17 09	17 12	17 16	17 20
Vauxhall ⊖	d	16 20	16 24	16 28	16 31	16 37	16 40	16 43	16 46	16 50	16 54	16 58	17 01		17 07	17 10	17 13	17 16	17 20	17 24
Clapham Junction 10	d	16 25	16 29	16 33	16 36	16 42	16 45	16 48	16 51	16 55	16 59	17 03	17 06		17 12	17 15	17 18	17 21	17 25	17 29
Earlsfield	d	16 28	16 32	16 36	16 39	16 45	16 48	16 51	16 54	16 58	17 02	17 06	17 09		17 15	17 18	17 21	17 24	17 28	17 32
Wimbledon 6 ⊖	d	16 32	16 36	16 40	16 43	16 49	16 52	16 55	16 58	17 02	17 06	17 10	17 13		17 19	17 22	17 25	17 28	17 32	17 36
Raynes Park 6	d	16 35		16 43	16 46		16 55	16 58	17 01	17 05		17 13	17 16			17 25	17 28	17 31	17 35	
Motspur Park	d	16 38		16 46				17 01		17 08		17 16					17 31		17 38	
Malden Manor	d	16 41								17 11									17 41	
Tolworth	d	16 44								17 14									17 44	
Chessington North	d	16 47								17 17									17 47	
Chessington South	a	16 51								17 21									17 51	
Worcester Park	d			16 48				17 03				17 18					17 33			
Stoneleigh	d			16 51				17 06				17 21					17 36			
Ewell West	d			16 54				17 09				17 24					17 39			
Epsom 3	a			16 57				17 12				17 27					17 42			
	d			16 58				17 17				17 28					17 47			
Ashtead	d			17 02				17 21				17 32					17 51			
Leatherhead	d			17 05				17 24				17 35					17 54			
Box Hill & Westhumble	d			17 10								17 40								
Dorking 4	a			17 14								17 44								
New Malden 6	d				16 49		16 58		17 04				17 19			17 28		17 34		
Norbiton	d				16 52				17 07				17 22					17 37		
Kingston	a				16 55				17 10				17 25					17 40		
	d				16 59				17 10				17 29					17 40		
Hampton Wick	d				17 01				17 12				17 31					17 42		
Teddington	d				17 05				17 15				17 35					17 45		
Strawberry Hill	a				17 08								17 38							
Fulwell	d								17 19									17 49		
Hampton	d								17 23									17 53		
Kempton Park	d								17 26									17 56		
Sunbury	d								17 28									17 58		
Upper Halliford	d								17 30									18 00		
Shepperton	a								17 35									18 06		
Berrylands	d						17 00									17 30				
Surbiton 6	d		16a43			16 57	17 05				17a13			17 18	17 27	17 35				17a43
Thames Ditton	d						17 09									17 39				
Hampton Court	a						17 14									17 44				
Hinchley Wood	d					17 01									17 31					
Claygate	d					17 04									17 34					
Oxshott	d					17 07									17 37					
Cobham & Stoke D'abernon	d					17 11									17 41					
Bookham	d							17 29									17 59			
Effingham Junction 6	d					17 15		17 33							17 45		18a05			
Horsley	d					17 18		17 36							17 48					
Clandon	d					17 23		17 41							17 53					
London Road (Guildford)	d					17 28		17 46							17 58					
Guildford	a					17 34		17 52						17 56	18 04					

London - Chessington South, Dorking, Guildford, Shepperton and Hampton Court

Network Diagram - see first Page of Table 152

Station			SW	SW	SW		SW	SW	SW	SW			SW	SW	SW	SW	SW	SW		SW	SW		SW	SW	SW
							1													1					
London Waterloo 15 ⊖	d		17 24	17 27	17 30		17 32	17 32	17 36	17 39			17 42	17 46	17 50	17 54	17 57	18 00		18 02	18 02		18 06	18 09	18 13
Vauxhall ⊖	d		17 28	17 31	17 34			17 37	17 40	17 43			17 46	17 50	17 54	17 58	18 01	18 04			18 07		18 10	18 13	18 17
Clapham Junction 10	d		17 33	17 36	17 39			17 42	17 45	17 48			17 51	17 55	17 59	18 03	18 06	18 09			18 12		18 15	18 18	
Earlsfield	d		17 36	17 39	17 42			17 45	17 48	17 51			17 54	17 58	18 02	18 06	18 09	18 12			18 15		18 18	18 21	
Wimbledon 6 ⊖	d		17 40	17 43	17 46			17 49	17 52	17 55			17 58	18 02	18 06	18 10	18 13	18 16			18 19		18 22	18 25	
Raynes Park 6	d		17 43	17 46	17 49				17 55	17 58			18 01	18 05		18 13	18 16	18 19					18 25	18 28	
Motspur Park	d				17 52					18 01				18 08				18 22						18 31	
Malden Manor	d													18 11											
Tolworth	d													18 14											
Chessington North	d													18 17											
Chessington South	a													18 21											
Worcester Park	d		17 47		17 54					18 03						18 17		18 24						18 33	
Stoneleigh	d				17 57					18 06								18 27						18 36	
Ewell West	d				18 00					18 09								18 30						18 39	
Epsom 3	a		17 54		18 07					18 15						18 24		18 35						18 46	
	d		17 54							18 17						18 24								18 47	
Ashtead	d		17 58							18 21						18 28								18 51	
Leatherhead	d		18 01							18 24						18 31								18 54	
Box Hill & Westhumble	d		18 06													18 36									
Dorking 4	a		18 11													18 41									
New Malden 6	d			17 49					17 58				18 04				18 19						18 28		
Norbiton	d			17 52									18 07				18 22								
Kingston	a			17 55									18 10				18 25								
	d			17 59									18 10				18 29								
Hampton Wick	d			18 01									18 12				18 31								
Teddington	d			18 05									18 15				18 35								
Strawberry Hill	a			18 08													18 38								18 41
Fulwell	d										18 13		18 19												18 43
Hampton	d										18 17		18 23												18 47
Kempton Park	d												18 26												
Sunbury	d										18 21		18 28												18 51
Upper Halliford	d										18 23		18 30												18 53
Shepperton	a										18 28		18 40												18 58
Berrylands	d								18 00														18 30		
Surbiton 6	d						17 48	17 57	18 05						18a13					18a17	18 27		18 35		
Thames Ditton	d								18 09														18 39		
Hampton Court	a								18 14														18 44		
Hinchley Wood	d							18 05													18 35				
Claygate	d							18 08													18 38				
Oxshott	d							18 11													18 41				
Cobham & Stoke D'abernon	d							18 15													18 45				
Bookham	d									18 29														18 59	
Effingham Junction 6	d							18 20		18a42											18 50			19 03	
Horsley	d							18 22													18 52			19 06	
Clandon	d							18 27													18 57			19 11	
London Road (Guildford)	d							18 32													19 02			19 16	
Guildford	a						18 29	18 38													19 09			19 22	

London - Chessington South, Dorking, Guildford, Shepperton and Hampton Court

Network Diagram - see first Page of Table 152

		SW	SW	SW	SW	SW	SW			SW	SW	SW	SW	SW	SW	SW	SW		SW	SW	SW		SW 1	SW	SW
London Waterloo 15 ⊖	d	18 12	18 16	18 20	18 24	18 27	18 30			18 32	18 36	18 39	18 43	18 42	18 46	18 48	18 50		18 54	18 57	19 00		19 02	19 02	19 06
Vauxhall ⊖	d	18 16	18 20	18 24	18 28	18 31	18 34			18 37	18 40	18 43	18 47	18 46	18 50		18 54		18 58	19 01	19 04			19 07	19 10
Clapham Junction 10	d	18 21	18 25	18 29	18 33	18 36	18 39			18 42	18 45	18 48		18 51	18 55		18 59		19 03	19 06	19 09			19 12	19 15
Earlsfield	d	18 24	18 28	18 32	18 36	18 39	18 42			18 45	18 48	18 51		18 54	18 58		19 02		19 06	19 09	19 12			19 15	19 18
Wimbledon 6 ⊖	d	18 28	18 32	18 36	18 40	18 43	18 46			18 49	18 52	18 55		18 58	19 02		19 06		19 10	19 13	19 16			19 19	19 22
Raynes Park 6	d	18 31	18 35		18 43	18 46	18 49				18 55	18 58		19 01	19 05				19 13	19 16	19 19				19 25
Motspur Park	d		18 38				18 52					19 01			19 08						19 22				
Malden Manor	d		18 41												19 11										
Tolworth	d		18 44												19 14										
Chessington North	d		18 47												19 17										
Chessington South	a		18 51												19 21										
Worcester Park	d				18 47		18 54					19 03							19 17		19 24				
Stoneleigh	d						18 57					19 06									19 27				
Ewell West	d						19 00					19 09									19 30				
Epsom 3	a				18 54		19 07					19 16							19 24		19 35				
	d				18 54							19 17							19 24						
Ashtead	d				18 58							19 21							19 28						
Leatherhead	d				19 01							19 24							19 31						
Box Hill & Westhumble	d				19 06														19 36						
Dorking 4	a				19 11														19 41						
New Malden 6	d	18 34				18 49					18 58			19 04						19 19					19 28
Norbiton	d	18 37				18 52								19 07						19 22					
Kingston	a	18 40				18 55								19 10						19 25					
	d	18 40				18 59								19 10						19 29					
Hampton Wick	d	18 42				19 01								19 12						19 31					
Teddington	d	18 45				19 05								19 15						19 35					
Strawberry Hill	a					19 08							19 11							19 38					
Fulwell	d	18 49											19 13	19 19											
Hampton	d	18 53											19 17	19 23											
Kempton Park	d	18 56												19 26											
Sunbury	d	18 58											19 21	19 28											
Upper Halliford	d	19 00											19 23	19 30											
Shepperton	a	19 10											19 28	19 36											
Berrylands	d										19 00														19 30
Surbiton 6	d			18a43						18 57	19 05					19 06	19a13						19a17	19 27	19 35
Thames Ditton	d										19 09														19 39
Hampton Court	a										19 14														19 42
Hinchley Wood	d									19 01						19 10								19 31	
Claygate	d									19 04						19 13								19 34	
Oxshott	d									19 07						19 16								19 37	
Cobham & Stoke D'abernon	d									19 11						19 20								19 41	
Bookham	d											19 29													
Effingham Junction 6	d									19 15		19 33				19 24								19 45	
Horsley	d									19 18		19 36				19 27								19 48	
Clandon	d									19 23		19 41				19 32								19 53	
London Road (Guildford)	d									19 28		19 46				19 37								19 58	
Guildford	a									19 34		19 52				19 43								20 02	

London - Chessington South, Dorking, Guildford, Shepperton and Hampton Court

Network Diagram - see first Page of Table 152

		SW	SW		SW	SW	SW	SW	SW	SW		SW	SW		SW	SW	SW	SW	SW	SW		SW	SW		SW
London Waterloo 15 ⊖	d	19 09	19 12		19 16	19 20	19 23	19 24	19 27	19 33		19 36	19 39		19 42	19 46	19 50	19 54	19 57	20 03		20 06	20 09		20 12
Vauxhall ⊖	d	19 13	19 16		19 20	19 24		19 28	19 31	19 37		19 40	19 43		19 46	19 50	19 54	19 58	20 01	20 07		20 10	20 13		20 16
Clapham Junction 10	d	19 18	19 21		19 25	19 29		19 33	19 36	19 42		19 45	19 48		19 51	19 55	19 59	20 03	20 06	20 12		20 15	20 18		20 21
Earlsfield	d	19 21	19 24		19 28	19 32		19 36	19 39	19 45		19 48	19 51		19 54	19 58	20 02	20 06	20 09	20 15		20 18	20 21		20 24
Wimbledon 6 ⊖	d	19 25	19 28		19 32	19 36		19 40	19 43	19 49		19 52	19 55		19 58	20 02	20 06	20 10	20 13	20 19		20 22	20 25		20 28
Raynes Park 6	d	19 28	19 31		19 35			19 43	19 46			19 55	19 58		20 01	20 05		20 13	20 16			20 25	20 28		20 31
Motspur Park	d	19 31			19 38			19 46					20 01			20 08		20 16					20 31		
Malden Manor	d				19 41											20 11									
Tolworth	d				19 44											20 14									
Chessington North	d				19 47											20 17									
Chessington South	a				19 49											20 19									
Worcester Park	d	19 33						19 48					20 03					20 18					20 33		
Stoneleigh	d	19 36						19 51					20 06					20 21					20 36		
Ewell West	d	19 39						19 54					20 09					20 24					20 39		
Epsom 3	a	19 44						19 57					20 16					20 27					20 42		
	d	19 47						19 58					20 17										20 43		
Ashtead	d	19 51						20 02					20 21										20 47		
Leatherhead	d	19 54						20 05					20 24										20 50		
Box Hill & Westhumble	d							20 10															20 55		
Dorking 4	a							20 14															20 57		
New Malden 6	d		19 34						19 49			19 58			20 04				20 19			20 28			20 34
Norbiton	d		19 37						19 52						20 07				20 22						20 37
Kingston	a		19 40						19 55						20 10				20 25						20 40
	d		19 40						19 59						20 10				20 29						20 40
Hampton Wick	d		19 42						20 01						20 12				20 31						20 42
Teddington	d		19 45						20 05						20 15				20 35						20 45
Strawberry Hill	a								20 08										20 38						
Fulwell	d		19 49												20 19										20 49
Hampton	d		19 53												20 23										20 53
Kempton Park	d		19 56												20 26										20 56
Sunbury	d		19 58												20 28										20 58
Upper Halliford	d		20 00												20 30										21 00
Shepperton	a		20 03												20 33										21 03
Berrylands	d											20 00										20 30			
Surbiton 6	d					19a43	19a39			19 57		20 05					20a13			20 27		20 35			
Thames Ditton	d											20 09										20 39			
Hampton Court	a											20 12										20 42			
Hinchley Wood	d									20 01										20 31					
Claygate	d									20 04										20 34					
Oxshott	d									20 07										20 37					
Cobham & Stoke D'abernon	d									20 11										20 41					
Bookham	d	19 59											20 29												
Effingham Junction 6	d	20 03								20 15			20 33							20 45					
Horsley	d	20 06								20 18			20 36							20 48					
Clandon	d	20 11								20 23			20 41							20 53					
London Road (Guildford)	d	20 16								20 28			20 46							20 58					
Guildford	a	20 20								20 32			20 50							21 02					

		SW	SW	SW	SW	SW		SW	SW		SW	SW	SW	SW	SW	SW		SW	SW		SW	SW	SW	SW	
London Waterloo 15 ⊖	d	20 16	20 20	20 24	20 27	20 33		20 36	20 39		20 42	20 46	20 50	20 54	20 57	21 03		21 09	21 12		21 20	21 24	21 27	21 33	
Vauxhall ⊖	d	20 20	20 24	20 28	20 31	20 37		20 40	20 43		20 46	20 50	20 54	20 58	21 01	21 07		21 13	21 16		21 24	21 28	21 31	21 37	
Clapham Junction 10	d	20 25	20 29	20 33	20 36	20 42		20 45	20 48		20 51	20 55	20 59	21 03	21 06	21 12		21 18	21 21		21 29	21 33	21 36	21 42	
Earlsfield	d	20 28	20 32	20 36	20 39	20 45		20 48	20 51		20 54	20 58	21 02	21 06	21 09	21 15		21 21	21 24		21 32	21 36	21 39	21 45	
Wimbledon 6 ⊖	d	20 32	20 36	20 40	20 43	20 49		20 52	20 55		20 58	21 02	21 06	21 10	21 13	21 19		21 25	21 28		21 36	21 40	21 43	21 49	
Raynes Park 6	d	20 35		20 43	20 46			20 55	20 58		21 01	21 05		21 13	21 16			21 28	21 31			21 43	21 46		
Motspur Park	d	20 38		20 46					21 01			21 08		21 16				21 31				21 46			
Malden Manor	d	20 41										21 11													
Tolworth	d	20 44										21 14													
Chessington North	d	20 47										21 17													
Chessington South	a	20 49										21 19													
Worcester Park	d			20 48					21 03					21 18				21 33				21 48			
Stoneleigh	d			20 51					21 06					21 21				21 36				21 51			
Ewell West	d			20 54					21 09					21 24				21 39				21 54			
Epsom 3	a			20 57					21 12					21 27				21 42				21 57			
	d								21 13									21 43							
Ashtead	d								21 17									21 47							
Leatherhead	d								21 20									21 50							
Box Hill & Westhumble	d																	21 55							
Dorking 4	a																	21 57							
New Malden 6	d				20 49			20 58			21 04				21 19				21 34				21 49		
Norbiton	d				20 52						21 07				21 22				21 37				21 52		
Kingston	a				20 55						21 10				21 25				21 40				21 55		
	d				20 59						21 10				21 29				21 40				21 59		
Hampton Wick	d				21 01						21 12				21 31				21 42				22 01		
Teddington	d				21 05						21 15				21 35				21 45				22 05		
Strawberry Hill	a				21 08										21 38								22 08		
Fulwell	d										21 19								21 49						
Hampton	d										21 23								21 53						
Kempton Park	d										21 26								21 56						
Sunbury	d										21 28								21 58						
Upper Halliford	d										21 30								22 00						
Shepperton	a										21 33								22 03						
Berrylands	d							21 00																	
Surbiton 6	d		20a43			20 57		21 05					21a13			21 27					21a43			21 57	
Thames Ditton	d							21 09																	
Hampton Court	a							21 12																	
Hinchley Wood	d					21 01										21 31								22 01	
Claygate	d					21 04										21 34								22 04	
Oxshott	d					21 07										21 37								22 07	
Cobham & Stoke D'abernon	d					21 11										21 41								22 11	
Bookham	d								21 25																
Effingham Junction 6	d					21 15			21 29							21 45								22 15	
Horsley	d					21 18			21 32							21 48								22 18	
Clandon	d					21 23			21 37							21 53								22 23	
London Road (Guildford)	d					21 28			21 42							21 58								22 28	
Guildford	a					21 32			21 46							22 02								22 32	

Table 152

Mondays to Fridays

London - Chessington South, Dorking, Guildford, Shepperton and Hampton Court

Network Diagram - see first Page of Table 152

		SW	SW	SW	SW		SW	SW	SW	SW		SW	SW	SW	SW		SW		SW	SW	SW	SW	SW	SW	SW
London Waterloo [15] ⊖	d	21 36	21 39	21 42	21 46		21 50	21 54	21 57	22 03		22 09	22 12	22 20	22 27		22 33		22 36	22 39	22 42	22 50	22 57	23 00	23 03
Vauxhall ⊖	d	21 40	21 43	21 46	21 50		21 54	21 58	22 01	22 07		22 13	22 16	22 24	22 31		22 37		22 40	22 43	22 46	22 54	23 01	23 04	23 07
Clapham Junction [10]	d	21 45	21 48	21 51	21 55		21 59	22 03	22 06	22 12		22 18	22 21	22 29	22 36		22 42		22 45	22 48	22 51	22 59	23 06	23 09	23 12
Earlsfield	d	21 48	21 51	21 54	21 58		22 02	22 06	22 09	22 15		22 21	22 24	22 32	22 39		22 45		22 48	22 51	22 54	23 02	23 09	23 12	23 15
Wimbledon [6] ⊖	d	21 52	21 55	21 58	22 02		22 06	22 10	22 13	22 19		22 25	22 28	22 36	22 43		22 49		22 52	22 55	22 58	23 06	23 13	23 16	23 19
Raynes Park [6]	d	21 55	21 58	22 01	22 05			22 13	22 16			22 28	22 31		22 46				22 55	22 58	23 01		23 16	23 19	
Motspur Park	d		22 01		22 08			22 16				22 31								23 01				23 22	
Malden Manor	d				22 11																			23 25	
Tolworth	d				22 14																			23 28	
Chessington North	d				22 17																			23 31	
Chessington South	a				22 19																			23 33	
Worcester Park	d		22 03					22 18				22 33								23 03					
Stoneleigh	d		22 06					22 21				22 36								23 06					
Ewell West	d		22 09					22 24				22 39								23 09					
Epsom [3]	a		22 12					22 27				22 42								23 12					
	d		22 13									22 43								23 13					
Ashtead	d		22 17									22 47								23 17					
Leatherhead	d		22 20									22 50								23 20					
Box Hill & Westhumble	d											22 55													
Dorking [4]	a											22 57													
New Malden [6]	d	21 58		22 04					22 19				22 34		22 49				22 58		23 04		23 19		
Norbiton	d			22 07					22 22				22 37		22 52						23 07		23 22		
Kingston	a			22 10					22 25				22 40		22 55						23 10		23 25		
	d			22 10					22 29				22 40		22 59						23 10		23 29		
Hampton Wick	d			22 12					22 31				22 42		23 01						23 12		23 31		
Teddington	d			22 15					22 35				22 45		23 05						23 15		23 35		
Strawberry Hill	a								22 38						23 08								23 38		
Fulwell	d			22 19									22 49								23 19				
Hampton	d			22 23									22 53								23 23				
Kempton Park	d			22 26									22 56								23 26				
Sunbury	d			22 28									22 58								23 28				
Upper Halliford	d			22 30									23 00								23 30				
Shepperton	a			22 33									23 03								23 33				
Berrylands	d	22 00																	23 00						
Surbiton [6]	d	22 05					22 14			22 27				22a43			22 57		23 05			23a13			23 27
Thames Ditton	d	22 09																	23 09						
Hampton Court	a	22 12																	23 12						
Hinchley Wood	d									22 31							23 01								23 31
Claygate	d									22 34							23 04								23 34
Oxshott	d									22 37							23 07								23 37
Cobham & Stoke D'abernon	d									22 41							23 11								23 41
Bookham	d		22 25																	23 25					
Effingham Junction [6]	d		22 29							22 45							23 15			23 29					23 45
Horsley	d		22 32							22 48							23 18			23 32					23 48
Clandon	d		22 37							22 53							23 23			23 37					23 53
London Road (Guildford)	d		22 42							22 58							23 28			23 42					23 58
Guildford	a		22 46				22 47			23 02							23 32			23 46					00 02

				SW	SW	SW	SW		SW	SW	SW		SW
London Waterloo [15] ⊖	d			23 09	23 12	23 20	23 27		23 36	23 42	23 50		23 57
Vauxhall ⊖	d			23 13	23 16	23 24	23 31		23 40	23 46	23 54		00 01
Clapham Junction [10]	d			23 18	23 21	23 29	23 36		23 45	23 51	23 59		00 06
Earlsfield	d			23 21	23 24	23 32	23 39		23 48	23 54	00 02		00 09
Wimbledon [6] ⊖	d			23 25	23 28	23 36	23 43		23 52	23 58	00 06		00 13
Raynes Park [6]	d			23 28	23 31		23 46		23 55	00 01			00 16
Motspur Park	d			23 31						00 04			
Malden Manor	d												
Tolworth	d												
Chessington North	d												
Chessington South	a												
Worcester Park	d			23 33						00 06			
Stoneleigh	d			23 36						00 09			
Ewell West	d			23 39						00 12			
Epsom [3]	a			23 42						00 15			
	d			23 43						00 19			
Ashtead	d			23 47						00 23			
Leatherhead	d			23 50						00 26			
Box Hill & Westhumble	d			23 55									
Dorking [4]	a			23 57									
New Malden [6]	d				23 34		23 49		23 58				00 19
Norbiton	d				23 37		23 52						00 22
Kingston	a				23 40		23 55						00 25
	d				23 40		23 55						00 25
Hampton Wick	d				23 42		23 57						00 27
Teddington	d				23 45		23 59						00 30
Strawberry Hill	a						00 03						
Fulwell	d				23 49								00 34
Hampton	d				23 53								00 38
Kempton Park	d				23 56								00 41
Sunbury	d				23 58								00 43
Upper Halliford	d				23 59								00 45
Shepperton	a				00 03								00 48
Berrylands	d								23 59				
Surbiton [6]	d					23a43			00 05		00 14		
Thames Ditton	d								00 09				
Hampton Court	a								00 12				
Hinchley Wood	d										00 18		
Claygate	d										00 20		
Oxshott	d										00 24		
Cobham & Stoke D'abernon	d										00 27		
Bookham	d									00 31			
Effingham Junction [6]	d									00 36	00 32		
Horsley	d									00 39	00 34		
Clandon	d									00 44	00 39		
London Road (Guildford)	d									00 49	00 44		
Guildford	a									00 53	00 48		

London - Chessington South, Dorking, Guildford, Shepperton and Hampton Court

Network Diagram - see first Page of Table 152

Station		SW	SW	SW		SW	SW	SW	SW	SW		SW		SW	SW	SW 1	SW	SW 1	SW			SW	SW		SW
London Waterloo 15 ⊖	d	23p03	23p12	23p27		23p36	23p42	23p50	23p57	00 09		00 15		00 27	00 42	05 00	05 12	05 20				05 50			06 06
Vauxhall ⊖	d	23p07	23p16	23p31		23p40	23p46	23p54	00 01	00 13		00 19		00 31	00 46	05 04	05 16	05 24				05 54			06 10
Clapham Junction 10	d	23p12	23p21	23p36		23p45	23p51	23p59	00 06	00 20		00 25		00 37	00 51	05 11	05 21	05 29				05 59			06 15
Earlsfield	d	23p15	23p24	23p39		23p48	23p54	00 02	00 09	00 23		00 29		00s41		05 14	05 24	05 32				06 02			06 18
Wimbledon 6 ⊖	d	23p19	23p28	23p43		23p52	23p58	00 06	00 13	00 27		00 33		00 45	01 05	05 18	05 28	05 36				06 06	06 13		06 22
Raynes Park 6	d		23p31	23p46		23p55	00 01		00 16			00 36		00 48	01 08		05 31						06 16		06 25
Motspur Park	d						00 04					00 38													
Malden Manor	d																								
Tolworth	d																								
Chessington North	d																								
Chessington South	a																								
Worcester Park	d						00 06					00 41													
Stoneleigh	d						00 09					00 44													
Ewell West	d						00 12					00 46													
Epsom 3	a						00 15					00 50													
	d						00 19																		
Ashtead	d						00 23																		
Leatherhead	d						00 26																		
Box Hill & Westhumble	d																								
Dorking 4	a																								
New Malden 6	d		23p34	23p49		23p58			00 19					00 50	01 11		05 34						06 19		06 28
Norbiton	d		23p37	23p52					00 22						01 14		05 37						06 22		
Kingston	a		23p40	23p55					00 25						01 17		05 40						06 25		
	d		23p40	23p55					00 25						01 17		05 40		05 59				06 29		
Hampton Wick	d		23p42	23p57					00 27						01s19		05 42		06 01				06 31		
Teddington	d		23p45	23p59					00 30						01s22		05 45		06 05				06 35		
Strawberry Hill	a			00 03											01 28				06 08				06 38		
Fulwell	d		23p49						00 34								05 49								
Hampton	d		23p53						00 38								05 53								
Kempton Park	d		23p56						00 41								05 56								
Sunbury	d		23p58						00 43								05 58								
Upper Halliford	d		23p59						00 45								06 00								
Shepperton	a		00 03						00 48								06 03								
Berrylands	d					23p59								00s53											06 30
Surbiton 6	d	23p27				00 05		00 14		00 35				00a56		05 26		05 44				06a13			06 35
Thames Ditton	d					00 09																			06 39
Hampton Court	a					00 12																			06 42
Hinchley Wood	d	23p31						00 18																	
Claygate	d	23p34						00 20																	
Oxshott	d	23p37						00 24																	
Cobham & Stoke D'abernon	d	23p41						00 27																	
Bookham	d						00 31																		
Effingham Junction 6	d	23p45					00 36	00 32																	
Horsley	d	23p48					00 39	00 34																	
Clandon	d	23p53					00 44	00 39																	
London Road (Guildford)	d	23p58					00 49	00 44																	
Guildford	a	00 02					00 53	00 48		01 07						06 00		06 23							

Table 152

Saturdays

London - Chessington South, Dorking, Guildford, Shepperton and Hampton Court

Network Diagram - see first Page of Table 152

		SW	SW	SW	SW	SW			SW	SW	SW	SW	SW	SW	SW			SW	SW	SW	SW	SW	SW	SW	SW
London Waterloo 15 ⊖	d	06 12	06 16	06 20	06 27	06 33			06 36	06 39	06 42	06 46	06 50	06 57	07 03			07 06	07 09	07 12	07 16	07 20	07 24	07 27	07 33
Vauxhall ⊖	d	06 16	06 20	06 24	06 31	06 37			06 40	06 43	06 46	06 50	06 54	07 01	07 07			07 10	07 13	07 16	07 20	07 24	07 28	07 31	07 37
Clapham Junction 10	d	06 21	06 25	06 29	06 36	06 42			06 45	06 48	06 51	06 55	06 59	07 06	07 12			07 15	07 18	07 21	07 25	07 29	07 33	07 36	07 42
Earlsfield	d	06 24	06 28	06 32	06 39	06 45			06 48	06 51	06 54	06 58	07 02	07 09	07 15			07 18	07 21	07 24	07 28	07 32	07 36	07 39	07 45
Wimbledon 6 ⊖	d	06 28	06 32	06 36	06 43	06 49			06 52	06 55	06 58	07 02	07 06	07 13	07 19			07 22	07 25	07 28	07 32	07 36	07 40	07 43	07 49
Raynes Park 6	d	06 31	06 35		06 46				06 55	06 58	07 01	07 05		07 16				07 25	07 28	07 31	07 35		07 43	07 46	
Motspur Park	d		06 38							07 01		07 08							07 31		07 38		07 46		
Malden Manor	d		06 41									07 11									07 41				
Tolworth	d		06 44									07 14									07 44				
Chessington North	d		06 47									07 17									07 47				
Chessington South	a		06 49									07 19									07 49				
Worcester Park	d									07 03									07 33				07 48		
Stoneleigh	d									07 06									07 36				07 51		
Ewell West	d									07 09									07 39				07 54		
Epsom 3	a									07 16									07 46				07 57		
	d									07 17									07 47				07 58		
Ashtead	d									07 21									07 51				08 02		
Leatherhead	d									07 24									07 54				08 05		
Box Hill & Westhumble	d																								
Dorking 4	a																						08 11		
New Malden 6	d	06 34			06 49				06 58		07 04			07 19				07 28		07 34				07 49	
Norbiton	d	06 37			06 52						07 07			07 22						07 37				07 52	
Kingston	a	06 40			06 55						07 10			07 25						07 40				07 55	
	d	06 40			06 59						07 10			07 29						07 40				07 59	
Hampton Wick	d	06 42			07 01						07 12			07 31						07 42				08 01	
Teddington	d	06 45			07 05						07 15			07 35						07 45				08 05	
Strawberry Hill	a				07 08									07 38										08 08	
Fulwell	d	06 49									07 19									07 49					
Hampton	d	06 53									07 23									07 53					
Kempton Park	d	06 56									07 26									07 56					
Sunbury	d	06 58									07 28									07 58					
Upper Halliford	d	07 00									07 30									08 00					
Shepperton	a	07 03									07 33									08 03					
Berrylands	d								07 00									07 30							
Surbiton 6	d			06a43		06 57			07 05				07a13		07 27			07 35				07a43			07 57
Thames Ditton	d								07 09									07 39							
Hampton Court	a								07 12									07 42							
Hinchley Wood	d					07 01									07 31										08 01
Claygate	d					07 04									07 34										08 04
Oxshott	d					07 07									07 37										08 07
Cobham & Stoke D'abernon	d					07 11									07 41										08 11
Bookham	d									07 29									07 59						
Effingham Junction 6	d					07 15				07 33					07 45				08 03						08 15
Horsley	d					07 18				07 36					07 48				08 06						08 18
Clandon	d					07 23				07 41					07 53				08 11						08 23
London Road (Guildford)	d					07 28				07 46					07 58				08 16						08 28
Guildford	a					07 32				07 50					08 02				08 20						08 32

				SW	SW	SW	SW	SW	SW	SW	SW			SW	SW	SW	SW	SW	SW	SW	SW			SW	SW
London Waterloo 15 ⊖	d			07 36	07 39	07 42	07 46	07 50	07 54	07 57	08 03			08 06	08 09	08 12	08 16	08 20	08 24	08 27	08 33			08 36	08 39
Vauxhall ⊖	d			07 40	07 43	07 46	07 50	07 54	07 58	08 01	08 07			08 10	08 13	08 16	08 20	08 24	08 28	08 31	08 37			08 40	08 43
Clapham Junction 10	d			07 45	07 48	07 51	07 55	07 59	08 03	08 06	08 12			08 15	08 18	08 21	08 25	08 29	08 33	08 36	08 42			08 45	08 48
Earlsfield	d			07 48	07 51	07 54	07 58	08 02	08 06	08 09	08 15			08 18	08 21	08 24	08 28	08 32	08 36	08 39	08 45			08 48	08 51
Wimbledon 6 ⊖	d			07 52	07 55	07 58	08 02	08 06	08 10	08 13	08 19			08 22	08 25	08 28	08 32	08 36	08 40	08 43	08 49			08 52	08 55
Raynes Park 6	d			07 55	07 58	08 01	08 05		08 13	08 16				08 25	08 28	08 31	08 35		08 43	08 46				08 55	08 58
Motspur Park	d				08 01		08 08		08 16						08 31		08 38		08 46						09 01
Malden Manor	d						08 11										08 41								
Tolworth	d						08 14										08 44								
Chessington North	d						08 17										08 47								
Chessington South	a						08 19										08 49								
Worcester Park	d				08 03				08 18						08 33				08 48						09 03
Stoneleigh	d				08 06				08 21						08 36				08 51						09 06
Ewell West	d				08 09				08 24						08 39				08 54						09 09
Epsom 3	a				08 16				08 27						08 46				08 57						09 16
	d				08 17				08 28						08 47				08 58						09 17
Ashtead	d				08 21				08 32						08 51				09 02						09 21
Leatherhead	d				08 24				08 35						08 54				09 05						09 24
Box Hill & Westhumble	d																								
Dorking 4	a								08 41										09 11						
New Malden 6	d			07 58		08 04				08 19				08 28		08 34				08 49				08 58	
Norbiton	d					08 07				08 22						08 37				08 52					
Kingston	a					08 10				08 25						08 40				08 55					
	d					08 10				08 29						08 40				08 59					
Hampton Wick	d					08 12				08 31						08 42				09 01					
Teddington	d					08 15				08 35						08 45				09 05					
Strawberry Hill	a									08 38										09 08					
Fulwell	d					08 19										08 49									
Hampton	d					08 23										08 53									
Kempton Park	d					08 26										08 56									
Sunbury	d					08 28										08 58									
Upper Halliford	d					08 30										09 00									
Shepperton	a					08 33										09 03									
Berrylands	d			08 00										08 30										09 00	
Surbiton 6	d			08 05				08a13			08 27			08 35				08a43			08 57			09 05	
Thames Ditton	d			08 09										08 39										09 09	
Hampton Court	a			08 12										08 42										09 12	
Hinchley Wood	d										08 31										09 01				
Claygate	d										08 34										09 04				
Oxshott	d										08 37										09 07				
Cobham & Stoke D'abernon	d										08 41										09 11				
Bookham	d				08 29										08 59										09 29
Effingham Junction 6	d				08 33						08 45				09 03						09 15				09 33
Horsley	d				08 36						08 48				09 06						09 18				09 36
Clandon	d				08 41						08 53				09 11						09 23				09 41
London Road (Guildford)	d				08 46						08 58				09 16						09 28				09 46
Guildford	a				08 50						09 02				09 20						09 32				09 50

London - Chessington South, Dorking, Guildford, Shepperton and Hampton Court

Network Diagram - see first Page of Table 152

		SW	SW	SW	SW	SW	SW			SW	SW	SW	SW	SW	SW	SW	SW			SW	SW	SW	SW	SW	SW
London Waterloo 15 ⊖	d	08 42	08 46	08 50	08 54	08 57	09 03			09 06	09 09	09 12	09 16	09 20	09 24	09 27	09 33			09 36	09 39	09 42	09 46	09 50	09 54
Vauxhall ⊖	d	08 46	08 50	08 54	08 58	09 01	09 07			09 10	09 13	09 16	09 20	09 24	09 28	09 31	09 37			09 40	09 43	09 46	09 50	09 54	09 58
Clapham Junction 10	d	08 51	08 55	08 59	09 03	09 06	09 12			09 15	09 18	09 21	09 25	09 29	09 33	09 36	09 42			09 45	09 48	09 51	09 55	09 59	10 03
Earlsfield	d	08 54	08 58	09 02	09 06	09 09	09 15			09 18	09 21	09 24	09 28	09 32	09 36	09 39	09 45			09 48	09 51	09 54	09 58	10 02	10 06
Wimbledon 6 ⊖	d	08 58	09 02	09 06	09 10	09 13	09 19			09 22	09 25	09 28	09 32	09 36	09 40	09 43	09 49			09 52	09 55	09 58	10 02	10 06	10 10
Raynes Park 6	d	09 01	09 05		09 13	09 16				09 25	09 28	09 31	09 35		09 43	09 46				09 55	09 58	10 01	10 05		10 13
Motspur Park	d		09 08		09 16						09 31		09 38		09 46						10 01		10 08		10 16
Malden Manor	d		09 11										09 41										10 11		
Tolworth	d		09 14										09 44										10 14		
Chessington North	d		09 17										09 47										10 17		
Chessington South	a		09 19										09 49										10 19		
Worcester Park	d				09 18						09 33				09 48						10 03				10 18
Stoneleigh	d				09 21						09 36				09 51						10 06				10 21
Ewell West	d				09 24						09 39				09 54						10 09				10 24
Epsom 3	a				09 27						09 46				09 57						10 16				10 27
	d				09 28						09 47				09 58						10 17				10 28
Ashtead	d				09 32						09 51				10 02						10 21				10 32
Leatherhead	d				09 35						09 54				10 05						10 24				10 35
Box Hill & Westhumble	d																								
Dorking 4	a				09 41										10 11										10 41
New Malden 6	d	09 04				09 19				09 28		09 34				09 49				09 58		10 04			
Norbiton	d	09 07				09 22						09 37				09 52						10 07			
Kingston	a	09 10				09 25						09 40				09 55						10 10			
	d	09 10				09 29						09 40				09 59						10 10			
Hampton Wick	d	09 12				09 31						09 42				10 01						10 12			
Teddington	d	09 15				09 35						09 45				10 05						10 15			
Strawberry Hill	a					09 38										10 08									
Fulwell	d	09 19										09 49										10 19			
Hampton	d	09 23										09 53										10 23			
Kempton Park	d	09 26										09 56										10 26			
Sunbury	d	09 28										09 58										10 28			
Upper Halliford	d	09 30										10 00										10 30			
Shepperton	a	09 33										10 03										10 33			
Berrylands	d									09 30										10 00					
Surbiton 6	d			09a13			09 27			09 35				09a43			09 57			10 05				10a13	
Thames Ditton	d									09 39										10 09					
Hampton Court	a									09 42										10 12					
Hinchley Wood	d						09 31										10 01								
Claygate	d						09 34										10 04								
Oxshott	d						09 37										10 07								
Cobham & Stoke D'abernon	d						09 41										10 11								
Bookham	d										09 59										10 29				
Effingham Junction 6	d						09 45				10 03						10 15				10 33				
Horsley	d						09 48				10 06						10 18				10 36				
Clandon	d						09 53				10 11						10 23				10 41				
London Road (Guildford)	d						09 58				10 16						10 28				10 46				
Guildford	a						10 02				10 20						10 32				10 50				

		SW	SW			SW	SW	SW	SW	SW	SW	SW	SW			SW	SW	SW	SW	SW	SW	SW	SW		
London Waterloo 15 ⊖	d	09 57	10 03			10 06	10 09	10 12	10 16	10 20	10 24	10 27	10 33			10 36	10 39	10 42	10 46	10 50	10 54	10 57	11 03		
Vauxhall ⊖	d	10 01	10 07			10 10	10 13	10 16	10 20	10 24	10 28	10 31	10 37			10 40	10 43	10 46	10 50	10 54	10 58	11 01	11 07		
Clapham Junction 10	d	10 06	10 12			10 15	10 18	10 21	10 25	10 29	10 33	10 36	10 42			10 45	10 48	10 51	10 55	10 59	11 03	11 06	11 12		
Earlsfield	d	10 09	10 15			10 18	10 21	10 24	10 28	10 32	10 36	10 39	10 45			10 48	10 51	10 54	10 58	11 02	11 06	11 09	11 15		
Wimbledon 6 ⊖	d	10 13	10 19			10 22	10 25	10 28	10 32	10 36	10 40	10 43	10 49			10 52	10 55	10 58	11 02	11 06	11 10	11 13	11 19		
Raynes Park 6	d	10 16				10 25	10 28	10 31	10 35		10 43	10 46				10 55	10 58	11 01	11 05		11 13	11 16			
Motspur Park	d						10 31		10 38		10 46						11 01		11 08		11 16				
Malden Manor	d								10 41										11 11						
Tolworth	d								10 44										11 14						
Chessington North	d								10 47										11 17						
Chessington South	a								10 49										11 19						
Worcester Park	d						10 33				10 48						11 03				11 18				
Stoneleigh	d						10 36				10 51						11 06				11 21				
Ewell West	d						10 39				10 54						11 09				11 24				
Epsom 3	a						10 46				10 57						11 16				11 27				
	d						10 47				10 58						11 17				11 28				
Ashtead	d						10 51				11 02						11 21				11 32				
Leatherhead	d						10 54				11 05						11 24				11 35				
Box Hill & Westhumble	d																								
Dorking 4	a										11 11										11 41				
New Malden 6	d	10 19				10 28		10 34				10 49				10 58		11 04				11 19			
Norbiton	d	10 22						10 37				10 52						11 07				11 22			
Kingston	a	10 25						10 40				10 55						11 10				11 25			
	d	10 29						10 40				10 59						11 10				11 29			
Hampton Wick	d	10 31						10 42				11 01						11 12				11 31			
Teddington	d	10 35						10 45				11 05						11 15				11 35			
Strawberry Hill	a	10 38										11 08										11 38			
Fulwell	d							10 49										11 19							
Hampton	d							10 53										11 23							
Kempton Park	d							10 56										11 26							
Sunbury	d							10 58										11 28							
Upper Halliford	d							11 00										11 30							
Shepperton	a							11 03										11 33							
Berrylands	d					10 30										11 00									
Surbiton 6	d		10 27			10 35				10a43			10 57			11 05				11a13			11 27		
Thames Ditton	d					10 39										11 09									
Hampton Court	a					10 42										11 12									
Hinchley Wood	d		10 31										11 01										11 31		
Claygate	d		10 34										11 04										11 34		
Oxshott	d		10 37										11 07										11 37		
Cobham & Stoke D'abernon	d		10 41										11 11										11 41		
Bookham	d						10 59										11 29								
Effingham Junction 6	d		10 45				11 03						11 15				11 33						11 45		
Horsley	d		10 48				11 06						11 18				11 36						11 48		
Clandon	d		10 53				11 11						11 23				11 41						11 53		
London Road (Guildford)	d		10 58				11 16						11 28				11 46						11 58		
Guildford	a		11 02				11 20						11 32				11 50						12 02		

Table 152

Saturdays

London - Chessington South, Dorking, Guildford, Shepperton and Hampton Court

Network Diagram - see first Page of Table 152

		SW	SW	SW	SW	SW	SW	SW	SW	SW	SW	SW	SW	SW	SW	SW	SW	SW	SW	SW	SW
London Waterloo [15] ⊖	d	11 06	11 09	11 12	11 16	11 20	11 24	11 27	11 33	11 36	11 39	11 42	11 46	11 50	11 54	11 57	12 03	12 06	12 09	12 12	12 16
Vauxhall ⊖	d	11 10	11 13	11 16	11 20	11 24	11 28	11 31	11 37	11 40	11 43	11 46	11 50	11 54	11 58	12 01	12 07	12 10	12 13	12 16	12 20
Clapham Junction [10]	d	11 15	11 18	11 21	11 25	11 29	11 33	11 36	11 42	11 45	11 48	11 51	11 55	11 59	12 03	12 06	12 12	12 15	12 18	12 21	12 25
Earlsfield	d	11 18	11 21	11 24	11 28	11 32	11 36	11 39	11 45	11 48	11 51	11 54	11 58	12 02	12 06	12 09	12 15	12 18	12 21	12 24	12 28
Wimbledon [6] ⊖	d	11 22	11 25	11 28	11 32	11 36	11 40	11 43	11 49	11 52	11 55	11 58	12 02	12 06	12 10	12 13	12 19	12 22	12 25	12 28	12 32
Raynes Park [6]	d	11 25	11 28	11 31	11 35		11 43	11 46		11 55	11 58	12 01	12 05		12 13	12 16		12 25	12 28	12 31	12 35
Motspur Park	d		11 31		11 38		11 46				12 01		12 08		12 16				12 31		12 38
Malden Manor	d				11 41								12 11								12 41
Tolworth	d				11 44								12 14								12 44
Chessington North	d				11 47								12 17								12 47
Chessington South	a				11 49								12 19								12 49
Worcester Park	d		11 33				11 48				12 03				12 18				12 33		
Stoneleigh	d		11 36				11 51				12 06				12 21				12 36		
Ewell West	d		11 39				11 54				12 09				12 24				12 39		
Epsom [3]	a		11 46				11 57				12 16				12 27				12 46		
	d		11 47				11 58				12 17				12 28				12 47		
Ashtead	d		11 51				12 02				12 21				12 32				12 51		
Leatherhead	d		11 54				12 05				12 24				12 35				12 54		
Box Hill & Westhumble	d																				
Dorking [4]	a						12 11								12 41						
New Malden [6]	d	11 28		11 34				11 49		11 58		12 04				12 19		12 28		12 34	
Norbiton	d			11 37				11 52				12 07				12 22				12 37	
Kingston	a			11 40				11 55				12 10				12 25				12 40	
	d			11 40				11 59				12 10				12 29				12 40	
Hampton Wick	d			11 42				12 01				12 12				12 31				12 42	
Teddington	d			11 45				12 05				12 15				12 35				12 45	
Strawberry Hill	a							12 08								12 38					
Fulwell	d			11 49								12 19								12 49	
Hampton	d			11 53								12 23								12 53	
Kempton Park	d			11 56								12 26								12 56	
Sunbury	d			11 58								12 28								12 58	
Upper Halliford	d			12 00								12 30								13 00	
Shepperton	a			12 03								12 33								13 03	
Berrylands	d	11 30								12 00								12 30			
Surbiton [6]	d	11 35				11a43			11 57	12 05				12a13			12 27	12 35			
Thames Ditton	d	11 39								12 09								12 39			
Hampton Court	a	11 42								12 12								12 42			
Hinchley Wood	d								12 01								12 31				
Claygate	d								12 04								12 34				
Oxshott	d								12 07								12 37				
Cobham & Stoke D'abernon	d								12 11								12 41				
Bookham	d		11 59								12 29								12 59		
Effingham Junction [6]	d		12 03						12 15		12 33						12 45		13 03		
Horsley	d		12 06						12 18		12 36						12 48		13 06		
Clandon	d		12 11						12 23		12 41						12 53		13 11		
London Road (Guildford)	d		12 16						12 28		12 46						12 58		13 16		
Guildford	a		12 20						12 32		12 50						13 02		13 20		

		SW	SW	SW	SW	SW	SW	SW	SW	SW	SW	SW	SW	SW	SW	SW	SW	SW	SW	SW	SW
London Waterloo [15] ⊖	d	12 20	12 24	12 27	12 33	12 36	12 39	12 42	12 46	12 50	12 54	12 57	13 03	13 06	13 09	13 12	13 16	13 20	13 24	13 27	13 33
Vauxhall ⊖	d	12 24	12 28	12 31	12 37	12 40	12 43	12 46	12 50	12 54	12 58	13 01	13 07	13 10	13 13	13 16	13 20	13 24	13 28	13 31	13 37
Clapham Junction [10]	d	12 29	12 33	12 36	12 42	12 45	12 48	12 51	12 55	12 59	13 03	13 06	13 12	13 15	13 18	13 21	13 25	13 29	13 33	13 36	13 42
Earlsfield	d	12 32	12 36	12 39	12 45	12 48	12 51	12 54	12 58	13 02	13 06	13 09	13 15	13 18	13 21	13 24	13 28	13 32	13 36	13 39	13 45
Wimbledon [6] ⊖	d	12 36	12 40	12 43	12 49	12 52	12 55	12 58	13 02	13 06	13 10	13 13	13 19	13 22	13 25	13 28	13 32	13 36	13 40	13 43	13 49
Raynes Park [6]	d		12 43	12 46		12 55	12 58	13 01	13 05		13 13	13 16		13 25	13 28	13 31	13 35		13 43	13 46	
Motspur Park	d		12 46				13 01		13 08		13 16				13 31		13 38		13 46		
Malden Manor	d								13 11								13 41				
Tolworth	d								13 14								13 44				
Chessington North	d								13 17								13 47				
Chessington South	a								13 19								13 49				
Worcester Park	d		12 48				13 03				13 18				13 33				13 48		
Stoneleigh	d		12 51				13 06				13 21				13 36				13 51		
Ewell West	d		12 54				13 09				13 24				13 39				13 54		
Epsom [3]	a		12 57				13 16				13 27				13 46				13 57		
	d		12 58				13 17				13 28				13 47				13 58		
Ashtead	d		13 02				13 21				13 32				13 51				14 02		
Leatherhead	d		13 05				13 24				13 35				13 54				14 05		
Box Hill & Westhumble	d																				
Dorking [4]	a		13 11								13 41								14 11		
New Malden [6]	d			12 49		12 58		13 04				13 19		13 28		13 34				13 49	
Norbiton	d			12 52				13 07				13 22				13 37				13 52	
Kingston	a			12 55				13 10				13 25				13 40				13 55	
	d			12 59				13 10				13 29				13 40				13 59	
Hampton Wick	d			13 01				13 12				13 31				13 42				14 01	
Teddington	d			13 05				13 15				13 35				13 45				14 05	
Strawberry Hill	a			13 08								13 38								14 08	
Fulwell	d							13 19								13 49					
Hampton	d							13 23								13 53					
Kempton Park	d							13 26								13 56					
Sunbury	d							13 28								13 58					
Upper Halliford	d							13 30								14 00					
Shepperton	a							13 33								14 03					
Berrylands	d					13 00								13 30							
Surbiton [6]	d	12a43			12 57	13 05				13a13			13 27	13 35				13a43			13 57
Thames Ditton	d					13 09								13 39							
Hampton Court	a					13 12								13 42							
Hinchley Wood	d				13 01								13 31								14 01
Claygate	d				13 04								13 34								14 04
Oxshott	d				13 07								13 37								14 07
Cobham & Stoke D'abernon	d				13 11								13 41								14 11
Bookham	d						13 29								13 59						
Effingham Junction [6]	d				13 15		13 33						13 45		14 03						14 15
Horsley	d				13 18		13 36						13 48		14 06						14 18
Clandon	d				13 23		13 41						13 53		14 11						14 23
London Road (Guildford)	d				13 28		13 46						13 58		14 16						14 28
Guildford	a				13 32		13 50						14 02		14 20						14 32

Table 152

Saturdays

London - Chessington South, Dorking, Guildford, Shepperton and Hampton Court

Network Diagram - see first Page of Table 152

				SW	SW	SW	SW	SW	SW	SW	SW			SW	SW	SW	SW	SW	SW	SW	SW			SW	SW
London Waterloo 15 ⊖	d			13 36	13 39	13 42	13 46	13 50	13 54	13 57	14 03			14 06	14 09	14 12	14 16	14 20	14 24	14 27	14 33			14 36	14 39
Vauxhall ⊖	d			13 40	13 43	13 46	13 50	13 54	13 58	14 01	14 07			14 10	14 13	14 16	14 20	14 24	14 28	14 31	14 37			14 40	14 43
Clapham Junction 10	d			13 45	13 48	13 51	13 55	13 59	14 03	14 06	14 12			14 15	14 18	14 21	14 25	14 29	14 33	14 36	14 42			14 45	14 48
Earlsfield	d			13 48	13 51	13 54	13 58	14 02	14 06	14 09	14 15			14 18	14 21	14 24	14 28	14 32	14 36	14 39	14 45			14 48	14 51
Wimbledon 6 ⊖	d			13 52	13 55	13 58	14 02	14 06	14 10	14 13	14 19			14 22	14 25	14 28	14 32	14 36	14 40	14 43	14 49			14 52	14 55
Raynes Park 6	d			13 55	13 58	14 01	14 05		14 13	14 16				14 25	14 28	14 31	14 35		14 43	14 46				14 55	14 58
Motspur Park	d				14 01		14 08		14 16						14 31		14 38		14 46						15 01
Malden Manor	d						14 11										14 41								
Tolworth	d						14 14										14 44								
Chessington North	d						14 17										14 47								
Chessington South	a						14 19										14 49								
Worcester Park	d				14 03				14 18						14 33				14 48						15 03
Stoneleigh	d				14 06				14 21						14 36				14 51						15 06
Ewell West	d				14 09				14 24						14 39				14 54						15 09
Epsom 3	a				14 16				14 27						14 46				14 57						15 16
	d				14 17				14 28						14 47				14 58						15 17
Ashtead	d				14 21				14 32						14 51				15 02						15 21
Leatherhead	d				14 24				14 35						14 54				15 05						15 24
Box Hill & Westhumble	d																								
Dorking 4	a								14 41										15 11						
New Malden 6	d			13 58		14 04				14 19				14 28		14 34				14 49				14 58	
Norbiton	d					14 07				14 22						14 37				14 52					
Kingston	a					14 10				14 25						14 40				14 55					
	d					14 10				14 29						14 40				14 59					
Hampton Wick	d					14 12				14 31						14 42				15 01					
Teddington	d					14 15				14 35						14 45				15 05					
Strawberry Hill	a									14 38										15 08					
Fulwell	d					14 19										14 49									
Hampton	d					14 23										14 53									
Kempton Park	d					14 26										14 56									
Sunbury	d					14 28										14 58									
Upper Halliford	d					14 30										15 00									
Shepperton	a					14 33										15 03									
Berrylands	d			14 00										14 30										15 00	
Surbiton 6	d			14 05				14a13			14 27			14 35				14a43			14 57			15 05	
Thames Ditton	d			14 09										14 39										15 09	
Hampton Court	a			14 12										14 42										15 12	
Hinchley Wood	d										14 31										15 01				
Claygate	d										14 34										15 04				
Oxshott	d										14 37										15 07				
Cobham & Stoke D'abernon	d										14 41										15 11				
Bookham	d				14 29										14 59										15 29
Effingham Junction 6	d				14 33						14 45				15 03						15 15				15 33
Horsley	d				14 36						14 48				15 06						15 18				15 36
Clandon	d				14 41						14 53				15 11						15 23				15 41
London Road (Guildford)	d				14 46						14 58				15 16						15 28				15 46
Guildford	a				14 50						15 02				15 20						15 32				15 50

		SW	SW	SW	SW	SW	SW			SW	SW	SW	SW	SW	SW	SW	SW			SW	SW	SW	SW	SW	SW
London Waterloo 15 ⊖	d	14 42	14 46	14 50	14 54	14 57	15 03			15 06	15 09	15 12	15 16	15 20	15 24	15 27	15 33			15 36	15 39	15 42	15 46	15 50	15 54
Vauxhall ⊖	d	14 46	14 50	14 54	14 58	15 01	15 07			15 10	15 13	15 16	15 20	15 24	15 28	15 31	15 37			15 40	15 43	15 46	15 50	15 54	15 58
Clapham Junction 10	d	14 51	14 55	14 59	15 03	15 06	15 12			15 15	15 18	15 21	15 25	15 29	15 33	15 36	15 42			15 45	15 48	15 51	15 55	15 59	16 03
Earlsfield	d	14 54	14 58	15 02	15 06	15 09	15 15			15 18	15 21	15 24	15 28	15 32	15 36	15 39	15 45			15 48	15 51	15 54	15 58	16 02	16 06
Wimbledon 6 ⊖	d	14 58	15 02	15 06	15 10	15 13	15 19			15 22	15 25	15 28	15 32	15 36	15 40	15 43	15 49			15 52	15 55	15 58	16 02	16 06	16 10
Raynes Park 6	d	15 01	15 05		15 13	15 16				15 25	15 28	15 31	15 35		15 43	15 46				15 55	15 58	16 01	16 05		16 13
Motspur Park	d		15 08		15 16						15 31		15 38		15 46						16 01		16 08		16 16
Malden Manor	d		15 11										15 41										16 11		
Tolworth	d		15 14										15 44										16 14		
Chessington North	d		15 17										15 47										16 17		
Chessington South	a		15 19										15 49										16 19		
Worcester Park	d				15 18						15 33				15 48						16 03				16 18
Stoneleigh	d				15 21						15 36				15 51						16 06				16 21
Ewell West	d				15 24						15 39				15 54						16 09				16 24
Epsom 3	a				15 27						15 46				15 57						16 16				16 27
	d				15 28						15 47				15 58						16 17				16 28
Ashtead	d				15 32						15 51				16 02						16 21				16 32
Leatherhead	d				15 35						15 54				16 05						16 24				16 35
Box Hill & Westhumble	d																								
Dorking 4	a				15 41										16 11										16 41
New Malden 6	d	15 04				15 19				15 28		15 34				15 49				15 58		16 04			
Norbiton	d	15 07				15 22						15 37				15 52						16 07			
Kingston	a	15 10				15 25						15 40				15 55						16 10			
	d	15 10				15 29						15 40				15 59						16 10			
Hampton Wick	d	15 12				15 31						15 42				16 01						16 12			
Teddington	d	15 15				15 35						15 45				16 05						16 15			
Strawberry Hill	a					15 38										16 08									
Fulwell	d	15 19										15 49										16 19			
Hampton	d	15 23										15 53										16 23			
Kempton Park	d	15 26										15 56										16 26			
Sunbury	d	15 28										15 58										16 28			
Upper Halliford	d	15 30										16 00										16 30			
Shepperton	a	15 33										16 03										16 33			
Berrylands	d									15 30										16 00					
Surbiton 6	d			15a13			15 27			15 35				15a43			15 57			16 05				16a13	
Thames Ditton	d									15 39										16 09					
Hampton Court	a									15 42										16 12					
Hinchley Wood	d						15 31										16 01								
Claygate	d						15 34										16 04								
Oxshott	d						15 37										16 07								
Cobham & Stoke D'abernon	d						15 41										16 11								
Bookham	d										15 59										16 29				
Effingham Junction 6	d						15 45				16 03						16 15				16 33				
Horsley	d						15 48				16 06						16 18				16 36				
Clandon	d						15 53				16 11						16 23				16 41				
London Road (Guildford)	d						15 58				16 16						16 28				16 46				
Guildford	a						16 02				16 20						16 32				16 50				

Table 152

Saturdays

London - Chessington South, Dorking, Guildford, Shepperton and Hampton Court

Network Diagram - see first Page of Table 152

		SW	SW	SW	SW	SW	SW	SW	SW	SW	SW	SW	SW	SW	SW	SW	SW	SW	SW
London Waterloo 15 ⊖	d	15 57	16 03	16 06	16 09	16 12	16 16	16 20	16 24	16 27	16 33	16 36	16 39	16 42	16 46	16 50	16 54	16 57	17 03
Vauxhall ⊖	d	16 01	16 07	16 10	16 13	16 16	16 20	16 24	16 28	16 31	16 37	16 40	16 43	16 46	16 50	16 54	16 58	17 01	17 07
Clapham Junction 10	d	16 06	16 12	16 15	16 18	16 21	16 25	16 29	16 33	16 36	16 42	16 45	16 48	16 51	16 55	16 59	17 03	17 06	17 12
Earlsfield	d	16 09	16 15	16 18	16 21	16 24	16 28	16 32	16 36	16 39	16 45	16 48	16 51	16 54	16 58	17 02	17 06	17 09	17 15
Wimbledon 6 ⊖	d	16 13	16 19	16 22	16 25	16 28	16 32	16 36	16 40	16 43	16 49	16 52	16 55	16 58	17 02	17 06	17 10	17 13	17 19
Raynes Park 6	d	16 16		16 25	16 28	16 31	16 35		16 43	16 46		16 55	16 58	17 01	17 05		17 13	17 16	
Motspur Park	d				16 31		16 38		16 46				17 01		17 08		17 16		
Malden Manor	d						16 41								17 11				
Tolworth	d						16 44								17 14				
Chessington North	d						16 47								17 17				
Chessington South	a						16 49								17 19				
Worcester Park	d				16 33				16 48				17 03				17 18		
Stoneleigh	d				16 36				16 51				17 06				17 21		
Ewell West	d				16 39				16 54				17 09				17 24		
Epsom 3	a				16 46				16 57				17 16				17 27		
	d				16 47				16 58				17 17				17 28		
Ashtead	d				16 51				17 02				17 21				17 32		
Leatherhead	d				16 54				17 05				17 24				17 35		
Box Hill & Westhumble	d																		
Dorking 4	a								17 11								17 41		
New Malden 6	d	16 19		16 28		16 34				16 49		16 58		17 04				17 19	
Norbiton	d	16 22				16 37				16 52				17 07				17 22	
Kingston	a	16 25				16 40				16 55				17 10				17 25	
	d	16 29				16 40				16 59				17 10				17 29	
Hampton Wick	d	16 31				16 42				17 01				17 12				17 31	
Teddington	d	16 35				16 45				17 05				17 15				17 35	
Strawberry Hill	a	16 38								17 08								17 38	
Fulwell	d					16 49								17 19					
Hampton	d					16 53								17 23					
Kempton Park	d					16 56								17 26					
Sunbury	d					16 58								17 28					
Upper Halliford	d					17 00								17 30					
Shepperton	a					17 03								17 33					
Berrylands	d			16 30								17 00							
Surbiton 6	d		16 27	16 35				16a43			16 57	17 05				17a13			17 27
Thames Ditton	d			16 39								17 09							
Hampton Court	a			16 42								17 12							
Hinchley Wood	d		16 31								17 01								17 31
Claygate	d		16 34								17 04								17 34
Oxshott	d		16 37								17 07								17 37
Cobham & Stoke D'abernon	d		16 41								17 11								17 41
Bookham	d				16 59								17 29						
Effingham Junction 6	d		16 45		17 03						17 15		17 33						17 45
Horsley	d		16 48		17 06						17 18		17 36						17 48
Clandon	d		16 53		17 11						17 23		17 41						17 53
London Road (Guildford)	d		16 58		17 16						17 28		17 46						17 58
Guildford	a		17 02		17 20						17 32		17 50						18 02

		SW	SW	SW	SW	SW	SW	SW	SW	SW	SW	SW	SW	SW	SW	SW	SW	SW	SW	SW	SW
London Waterloo 15 ⊖	d	17 06	17 09	17 12	17 16	17 20	17 24	17 27	17 33	17 36	17 39	17 42	17 46	17 50	17 54	17 57	18 03	18 06	18 09	18 12	18 16
Vauxhall ⊖	d	17 10	17 13	17 16	17 20	17 24	17 28	17 31	17 37	17 40	17 43	17 46	17 50	17 54	17 58	18 01	18 07	18 10	18 13	18 16	18 20
Clapham Junction 10	d	17 15	17 18	17 21	17 25	17 29	17 33	17 36	17 42	17 45	17 48	17 51	17 55	17 59	18 03	18 06	18 12	18 15	18 18	18 21	18 25
Earlsfield	d	17 18	17 21	17 24	17 28	17 32	17 36	17 39	17 45	17 48	17 51	17 54	17 58	18 02	18 06	18 09	18 15	18 18	18 21	18 24	18 28
Wimbledon 6 ⊖	d	17 22	17 25	17 28	17 32	17 36	17 40	17 43	17 49	17 52	17 55	17 58	18 02	18 06	18 10	18 13	18 19	18 22	18 25	18 28	18 32
Raynes Park 6	d	17 25	17 28	17 31	17 35		17 43	17 46		17 55	17 58	18 01	18 05		18 13	18 16		18 25	18 28	18 31	18 35
Motspur Park	d		17 31		17 38		17 46				18 01		18 08		18 16				18 31		18 38
Malden Manor	d				17 41								18 11								18 41
Tolworth	d				17 44								18 14								18 44
Chessington North	d				17 47								18 17								18 47
Chessington South	a				17 49								18 19								18 49
Worcester Park	d		17 33				17 48				18 03				18 18				18 33		
Stoneleigh	d		17 36				17 51				18 06				18 21				18 36		
Ewell West	d		17 39				17 54				18 09				18 24				18 39		
Epsom 3	a		17 46				17 57				18 16				18 27				18 46		
	d		17 47				17 58				18 17				18 28				18 47		
Ashtead	d		17 51				18 02				18 21				18 32				18 51		
Leatherhead	d		17 54				18 05				18 24				18 35				18 54		
Box Hill & Westhumble	d																				
Dorking 4	a						18 11								18 41						
New Malden 6	d	17 28		17 34				17 49		17 58		18 04				18 19		18 28		18 34	
Norbiton	d			17 37				17 52				18 07				18 22				18 37	
Kingston	a			17 40				17 55				18 10				18 25				18 40	
	d			17 40				17 59				18 10				18 29				18 40	
Hampton Wick	d			17 42				18 01				18 12				18 31				18 42	
Teddington	d			17 45				18 05				18 15				18 35				18 45	
Strawberry Hill	a							18 08								18 38					
Fulwell	d			17 49								18 19								18 49	
Hampton	d			17 53								18 23								18 53	
Kempton Park	d			17 56								18 26								18 56	
Sunbury	d			17 58								18 28								18 58	
Upper Halliford	d			18 00								18 30								19 00	
Shepperton	a			18 03								18 33								19 03	
Berrylands	d	17 30								18 00								18 30			
Surbiton 6	d	17 35				17a43			17 57	18 05				18a13			18 27	18 35			
Thames Ditton	d	17 39								18 09								18 39			
Hampton Court	a	17 42								18 12								18 42			
Hinchley Wood	d								18 01								18 31				
Claygate	d								18 04								18 34				
Oxshott	d								18 07								18 37				
Cobham & Stoke D'abernon	d								18 11								18 41				
Bookham	d		17 59								18 29								18 59		
Effingham Junction 6	d		18 03						18 15		18 33						18 45		19 03		
Horsley	d		18 06						18 18		18 36						18 48		19 06		
Clandon	d		18 11						18 23		18 41						18 53		19 11		
London Road (Guildford)	d		18 16						18 28		18 46						18 58		19 16		
Guildford	a		18 20						18 32		18 50						19 02		19 20		

Table 152

Saturdays

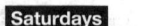

London - Chessington South, Dorking, Guildford, Shepperton and Hampton Court

Network Diagram - see first Page of Table 152

Station		SW	SW	SW	SW	SW	SW	SW	SW	SW	SW	SW	SW	SW	SW	SW	SW	SW	SW	SW	SW
London Waterloo [15] ⊖	d	18 20	18 24	18 27	18 33	18 36	18 39	18 42	18 46	18 50	18 54	18 57	19 03	19 06	19 09	19 12	19 16	19 20	19 24	19 27	19 33
Vauxhall ⊖	d	18 24	18 28	18 31	18 37	18 40	18 43	18 46	18 50	18 54	18 58	19 01	19 07	19 10	19 13	19 16	19 20	19 24	19 28	19 31	19 37
Clapham Junction [10]	d	18 29	18 33	18 36	18 42	18 45	18 48	18 51	18 55	18 59	19 03	19 06	19 12	19 15	19 18	19 21	19 25	19 29	19 33	19 36	19 42
Earlsfield	d	18 32	18 36	18 39	18 45	18 48	18 51	18 54	18 58	19 02	19 06	19 09	19 15	19 18	19 21	19 24	19 28	19 32	19 36	19 39	19 45
Wimbledon [6] ⊖	d	18 36	18 40	18 43	18 49	18 52	18 55	18 58	19 02	19 06	19 10	19 13	19 19	19 22	19 25	19 28	19 32	19 36	19 40	19 43	19 49
Raynes Park [6]	d		18 43	18 46		18 55	18 58	19 01	19 05		19 13	19 16		19 25	19 28	19 31	19 35		19 43	19 46	
Motspur Park	d		18 46				19 01		19 08		19 16				19 31		19 38		19 46		
Malden Manor	d								19 11								19 41				
Tolworth	d								19 14								19 44				
Chessington North	d								19 17								19 47				
Chessington South	a								19 19								19 49				
Worcester Park	d		18 48				19 03				19 18				19 33				19 48		
Stoneleigh	d		18 51				19 06				19 21				19 36				19 51		
Ewell West	d		18 54				19 09				19 24				19 39				19 54		
Epsom [3]	a		18 57				19 16				19 27				19 46				19 57		
	d		18 58				19 17				19 28				19 47				19 58		
Ashtead	d		19 02				19 21				19 32				19 51				20 02		
Leatherhead	d		19 05				19 24				19 35				19 54				20 05		
Box Hill & Westhumble	d																				
Dorking [4]	a		19 11								19 41								20 11		
New Malden [6]	d			18 49		18 58		19 04				19 19		19 28		19 34				19 49	
Norbiton	d			18 52				19 07				19 22				19 37				19 52	
Kingston	a			18 55				19 10				19 25				19 40				19 55	
	d			18 59				19 10				19 29				19 40				19 59	
Hampton Wick	d			19 01				19 12				19 31				19 42				20 01	
Teddington	d			19 05				19 15				19 35				19 45				20 05	
Strawberry Hill	a			19 08								19 38								20 08	
Fulwell	d							19 19								19 49					
Hampton	d							19 23								19 53					
Kempton Park	d							19 26								19 56					
Sunbury	d							19 28								19 58					
Upper Halliford	d							19 30								20 00					
Shepperton	a							19 33								20 03					
Berrylands	d					19 00								19 30							
Surbiton [6]	d	18a43			18 57	19 05				19a13			19 27	19 35				19a43			19 57
Thames Ditton	d					19 09								19 39							
Hampton Court	a					19 12								19 42							
Hinchley Wood	d				19 01								19 31								20 01
Claygate	d				19 04								19 34								20 04
Oxshott	d				19 07								19 37								20 07
Cobham & Stoke D'abernon	d				19 11								19 41								20 11
Bookham	d						19 29								19 59						
Effingham Junction [6]	d				19 15		19 33						19 45		20 03						20 15
Horsley	d				19 18		19 36						19 48		20 06						20 18
Clandon	d				19 23		19 41						19 53		20 11						20 23
London Road (Guildford)	d				19 28		19 46						19 58		20 16						20 28
Guildford	a				19 32		19 50						20 02		20 20						20 32

Station		SW	SW	SW	SW	SW	SW	SW	SW	SW	SW	SW	SW	SW	SW	SW	SW	SW	SW
London Waterloo [15] ⊖	d	19 36	19 39	19 42	19 46	19 50	19 54	19 57	20 03	20 06	20 09	20 12	20 16	20 20	20 24	20 27	20 33	20 36	20 39
Vauxhall ⊖	d	19 40	19 43	19 46	19 50	19 54	19 58	20 01	20 07	20 10	20 13	20 16	20 20	20 24	20 28	20 31	20 37	20 40	20 43
Clapham Junction [10]	d	19 45	19 48	19 51	19 55	19 59	20 03	20 06	20 12	20 15	20 18	20 21	20 25	20 29	20 33	20 36	20 42	20 45	20 48
Earlsfield	d	19 48	19 51	19 54	19 58	20 02	20 06	20 09	20 15	20 18	20 21	20 24	20 28	20 32	20 36	20 39	20 45	20 48	20 51
Wimbledon [6] ⊖	d	19 52	19 55	19 58	20 02	20 06	20 10	20 13	20 19	20 22	20 25	20 28	20 32	20 36	20 40	20 43	20 49	20 52	20 55
Raynes Park [6]	d	19 55	19 58	20 01	20 05		20 13	20 16		20 25	20 28	20 31	20 35		20 43	20 46		20 55	20 58
Motspur Park	d		20 01		20 08		20 16				20 31		20 38		20 46				21 01
Malden Manor	d				20 11								20 41						
Tolworth	d				20 14								20 44						
Chessington North	d				20 17								20 47						
Chessington South	a				20 19								20 49						
Worcester Park	d		20 03				20 18				20 33				20 48				21 03
Stoneleigh	d		20 06				20 21				20 36				20 51				21 06
Ewell West	d		20 09				20 24				20 39				20 54				21 09
Epsom [3]	a		20 16				20 27				20 46				20 57				21 16
	d		20 17								20 47								21 17
Ashtead	d		20 21								20 51								21 21
Leatherhead	d		20 24								20 54								21 24
Box Hill & Westhumble	d																		
Dorking [4]	a										21 00								
New Malden [6]	d	19 58		20 04				20 19		20 28		20 34				20 49		20 58	
Norbiton	d			20 07				20 22				20 37				20 52			
Kingston	a			20 10				20 25				20 40				20 55			
	d			20 10				20 29				20 40				20 59			
Hampton Wick	d			20 12				20 31				20 42				21 01			
Teddington	d			20 15				20 35				20 45				21 05			
Strawberry Hill	a							20 38								21 08			
Fulwell	d			20 19								20 49							
Hampton	d			20 23								20 53							
Kempton Park	d			20 26								20 56							
Sunbury	d			20 28								20 58							
Upper Halliford	d			20 30								21 00							
Shepperton	a			20 33								21 03							
Berrylands	d	20 00								20 30								21 00	
Surbiton [6]	d	20 05				20a13			20 27	20 35				20a43			20 57	21 05	
Thames Ditton	d	20 09								20 39								21 09	
Hampton Court	a	20 12								20 42								21 12	
Hinchley Wood	d								20 31								21 01		
Claygate	d								20 34								21 04		
Oxshott	d								20 37								21 07		
Cobham & Stoke D'abernon	d								20 41								21 11		
Bookham	d		20 29																21 29
Effingham Junction [6]	d		20 33						20 45								21 15		21 33
Horsley	d		20 36						20 48								21 18		21 36
Clandon	d		20 41						20 53								21 23		21 41
London Road (Guildford)	d		20 46						20 58								21 28		21 46
Guildford	a		20 50						21 02								21 32		21 50

London - Chessington South, Dorking, Guildford, Shepperton and Hampton Court

Network Diagram - see first Page of Table 152

		SW	SW	SW	SW	SW	SW	SW	SW	SW	SW	SW	SW	SW	SW	SW	SW	SW	SW	SW	SW
London Waterloo 15 ⊖	d	20 42	20 46	20 50	20 54	20 57	21 03	21 09	21 12	21 20	21 24	21 27	21 33	21 36	21 39	21 42	21 46	21 50	21 54	21 57	22 03
Vauxhall ⊖	d	20 46	20 50	20 54	20 58	21 01	21 07	21 13	21 16	21 24	21 28	21 31	21 37	21 40	21 43	21 46	21 50	21 54	21 58	22 01	22 07
Clapham Junction 10	d	20 51	20 55	20 59	21 03	21 06	21 12	21 18	21 21	21 29	21 33	21 36	21 42	21 45	21 48	21 51	21 55	21 59	22 03	22 06	22 12
Earlsfield	d	20 54	20 58	21 02	21 06	21 09	21 15	21 21	21 24	21 32	21 36	21 39	21 45	21 48	21 51	21 54	21 58	22 02	22 06	22 09	22 15
Wimbledon 6 ⊖	d	20 58	21 02	21 06	21 10	21 13	21 19	21 25	21 28	21 36	21 40	21 43	21 49	21 52	21 55	21 58	22 02	22 06	22 10	22 13	22 19
Raynes Park 6	d	21 01	21 05		21 13	21 16		21 28	21 31		21 43	21 46		21 55	21 58	22 01	22 05		22 13	22 16	
Motspur Park	d		21 08		21 16			21 31			21 46				22 01		22 08		22 16		
Malden Manor	d		21 11														22 11				
Tolworth	d		21 14														22 14				
Chessington North	d		21 17														22 17				
Chessington South	a		21 19														22 19				
Worcester Park	d				21 18			21 33			21 48				22 03				22 18		
Stoneleigh	d				21 21			21 36			21 51				22 06				22 21		
Ewell West	d				21 24			21 39			21 54				22 09				22 24		
Epsom 3	a				21 27			21 46			21 57				22 16				22 27		
	d							21 47							22 17						
Ashtead	d							21 51							22 21						
Leatherhead	d							21 54							22 24						
Box Hill & Westhumble	d																				
Dorking 4	a							22 00													
New Malden 6	d	21 04				21 19			21 34			21 49		21 58		22 04				22 19	
Norbiton	d	21 07				21 22			21 37			21 52				22 07				22 22	
Kingston	a	21 10				21 25			21 40			21 55				22 10				22 25	
	d	21 10				21 29			21 40			21 59				22 10				22 29	
Hampton Wick	d	21 12				21 31			21 42			22 01				22 12				22 31	
Teddington	d	21 15				21 35			21 45			22 05				22 15				22 35	
Strawberry Hill	a					21 38						22 08								22 38	
Fulwell	d	21 19							21 49							22 19					
Hampton	d	21 23							21 53							22 23					
Kempton Park	d	21 26							21 56							22 26					
Sunbury	d	21 28							21 58							22 28					
Upper Halliford	d	21 30							22 00							22 30					
Shepperton	a	21 33							22 03							22 33					
Berrylands	d													22 00							
Surbiton 6	d			21a13			21 27			21a43			21 57	22 05				22 14			22 27
Thames Ditton	d													22 09							
Hampton Court	a													22 12							
Hinchley Wood	d						21 31						22 01								22 31
Claygate	d						21 34						22 04								22 34
Oxshott	d						21 37						22 07								22 37
Cobham & Stoke D'abernon	d						21 41						22 11								22 41
Bookham	d														22 29						
Effingham Junction 6	d						21 45						22 15		22 33						22 45
Horsley	d						21 48						22 18		22 36						22 48
Clandon	d						21 53						22 23		22 41						22 53
London Road (Guildford)	d						21 58						22 28		22 46						22 58
Guildford	a						22 02						22 32		22 50			22 47			23 02

		SW	SW	SW	SW	SW	SW	SW	SW	SW	SW	SW	SW	SW	SW	SW	SW	SW
London Waterloo 15 ⊖	d	22 09	22 12	22 20	22 27	22 33	22 36	22 39	22 42	22 50	22 57	23 00	23 03	23 09	23 12	23 20	23 27	23 36
Vauxhall ⊖	d	22 13	22 16	22 24	22 31	22 37	22 40	22 43	22 46	22 54	23 01	23 04	23 07	23 13	23 16	23 24	23 31	23 40
Clapham Junction 10	d	22 18	22 21	22 29	22 36	22 42	22 45	22 48	22 51	22 59	23 06	23 09	23 12	23 18	23 21	23 29	23 36	23 45
Earlsfield	d	22 21	22 24	22 32	22 39	22 45	22 48	22 51	22 54	23 02	23 09	23 12	23 15	23 21	23 24	23 32	23 39	23 48
Wimbledon 6 ⊖	d	22 25	22 28	22 36	22 43	22 49	22 52	22 55	22 58	23 06	23 13	23 16	23 19	23 25	23 28	23 36	23 43	23 52
Raynes Park 6	d	22 28	22 31		22 46		22 55	22 58	23 01		23 16	23 19		23 28	23 31		23 46	23 55
Motspur Park	d	22 31						23 01				23 22		23 31				
Malden Manor	d											23 25						
Tolworth	d											23 28						
Chessington North	d											23 31						
Chessington South	a											23 33						
Worcester Park	d	22 33						23 03						23 33				
Stoneleigh	d	22 36						23 06						23 36				
Ewell West	d	22 39						23 09						23 39				
Epsom 3	a	22 46						23 12						23 42				
	d	22 47						23 17						23 47				
Ashtead	d	22 51						23 21						23 51				
Leatherhead	d	22 54						23 24						23 54				
Box Hill & Westhumble	d																	
Dorking 4	a	23 00												00 01				
New Malden 6	d		22 34		22 49		22 58		23 04		23 19				23 34		23 49	23 58
Norbiton	d		22 37		22 52				23 07		23 22				23 37		23 52	
Kingston	a		22 40		22 55				23 10		23 25				23 40		23 55	
	d		22 40		22 59				23 10		23 29				23 40		23 55	
Hampton Wick	d		22 42		23 01				23 12		23 31				23 42		23 57	
Teddington	d		22 45		23 05				23 15		23 35				23 45		23 59	
Strawberry Hill	a				23 08						23 38						00 03	
Fulwell	d		22 49						23 19						23 49			
Hampton	d		22 53						23 23						23 53			
Kempton Park	d		22 56						23 26						23 56			
Sunbury	d		22 58						23 28						23 58			
Upper Halliford	d		23 00						23 30						23 59			
Shepperton	a		23 03						23 33						00 03			
Berrylands	d						23 00											23 59
Surbiton 6	d			22a43		22 57	23 05			23a13			23 27			23a43		00 05
Thames Ditton	d						23 09											00 09
Hampton Court	a						23 12											00 12
Hinchley Wood	d					23 01							23 31					
Claygate	d					23 04							23 34					
Oxshott	d					23 07							23 37					
Cobham & Stoke D'abernon	d					23 11							23 41					
Bookham	d							23 29										
Effingham Junction 6	d					23 15		23 33					23 45					
Horsley	d					23 18		23 36					23 48					
Clandon	d					23 23		23 41					23 53					
London Road (Guildford)	d					23 28		23 46					23 58					
Guildford	a					23 32		23 50					00 02					

London - Chessington South, Dorking, Guildford, Shepperton and Hampton Court

Network Diagram - see first Page of Table 152

Station			SW	SW	SW
London Waterloo 15	⊖	d	23 42	23 50	23 57
Vauxhall	⊖	d	23 46	23 54	00 01
Clapham Junction 10		d	23 51	23 59	00 06
Earlsfield		d	23 54	00 02	00 09
Wimbledon 6	⊖	d	23 58	00 06	00 13
Raynes Park 6		d	00 01		00 16
Motspur Park		d	00 04		
Malden Manor		d			
Tolworth		d			
Chessington North		d			
Chessington South		a			
Worcester Park		d	00 06		
Stoneleigh		d	00 09		
Ewell West		d	00 12		
Epsom 3		a	00 15		
		d	00 19		
Ashtead		d	00 23		
Leatherhead		d	00 26		
Box Hill & Westhumble		d			
Dorking 4		a			
New Malden 6		d			00 19
Norbiton		d			00 22
Kingston		a			00 25
		d			00 25
Hampton Wick		d			00 27
Teddington		d			00 30
Strawberry Hill		a			
Fulwell		d			00 34
Hampton		d			00 38
Kempton Park		d			00 41
Sunbury		d			00 43
Upper Halliford		d			00 45
Shepperton		a			00 48
Berrylands		d			
Surbiton 6		d		00 14	
Thames Ditton		d			
Hampton Court		a			
Hinchley Wood		d		00 18	
Claygate		d		00 20	
Oxshott		d		00 24	
Cobham & Stoke D'abernon		d		00 27	
Bookham		d	00 31		
Effingham Junction 6		d	00 36	00 32	
Horsley		d	00 39	00 34	
Clandon		d	00 44	00 39	
London Road (Guildford)		d	00 49	00 44	
Guildford		a	00 53	00 48	

Table 152

Sundays

London - Chessington South, Dorking, Guildford, Shepperton and Hampton Court

Network Diagram - see first Page of Table 152

		SW	SW	SW	SW	SW	SW	SW	SW	SW	SW	SW	SW	SW	SW	SW	SW	SW	SW	SW	SW
		A	A	A	A	A	A	A	A	A											
London Waterloo 15 ⊖	d	23p03	23p09	23p12	23p27	23p33	23p36	23p42	23p50	23p57	00 09	00 15	00 27	00 42	01 42	06 18		06 57			07 10
Vauxhall ⊖	d	23p07	23p13	23p16	23p31	23p37	23p40	23p46	23p54	00 01	00 13	00 19	00 31	00 46	01 46	06 22		07 01			07 14
Clapham Junction 10	d	23p12	23p18	23p21	23p36		23p45	23p51	23p59	00 06	00 20	00 25	00 37		01 53	06 27		07 06			07 19
Earlsfield	d	23p15	23p21	23p24	23p39		23p48	23p54	00 02	00 09	00 23	00 29	00s41					07 09			07 22
Wimbledon 6 ⊖	d	23p19	23p25	23p28	23p43		23p52	23p58	00 06	00 13	00 27	00 33	00 45	01 05	01 59	06 34	06 48	07 13	07 16	07 20	07 26
Raynes Park 6	d		23p28	23p31	23p46		23p55	00 01		00 16		00 36	00 48	01 08	02 02	06 37	06 52	07 16		07 23	
Motspur Park	d		23p31					00 04				00 38					06 55			07 26	
Malden Manor	d																				
Tolworth	d																				
Chessington North	d																				
Chessington South	a																				
Worcester Park	d		23p33					00 06				00 41					06 57			07 28	
Stoneleigh	d		23p36					00 09				00 44					07 00			07 31	
Ewell West	d		23p39					00 12				00 46					07 03			07 34	
Epsom 3	a		23p42					00 15				00 50					07 06			07 37	
	d		23p47					00 19													
Ashtead	d		23p51					00 23													
Leatherhead	d		23p54					00 26													
Box Hill & Westhumble	d																				
Dorking 4	a		00 01																		
New Malden 6	d			23p34	23p49		23p58			00 19			00 50	01 11	02 04	06 40		07 19			
Norbiton	d			23p37	23p52					00 22				01 14	02 08	06 43					
Kingston	a			23p40	23p55	00 16				00 25				01 17	02 10	06 46					
	d			23p40	23p55					00 25				01 17	02 11	06 49					
Hampton Wick	d			23p42	23p57					00 27				01s22	02s13	06 51					
Teddington	d			23p45	23p59					00 30				01s25	02s15	06 56					
Strawberry Hill	a				00 03									01 28	02s18	06 59					
Fulwell	d			23p49						00 34											
Hampton	d			23p53						00 38											
Kempton Park	d			23p56						00 41											
Sunbury	d			23p58						00 43											
Upper Halliford	d			23p59						00 45											
Shepperton	a			00 03						00 48											
Berrylands	d						23p59						00s53					07 21			
Surbiton 6	d	23p27					00 05		00 14		00 35		00a56					07 25	07 32		07 35
Thames Ditton	d						00 09											07 30			
Hampton Court	a						00 12											07 33			
Hinchley Wood	d	23p31							00 18										07 36		
Claygate	d	23p34							00 20										07 39		
Oxshott	d	23p37							00 24										07 42		
Cobham & Stoke D'abernon	d	23p41							00 27										07 46		
Bookham	d							00 31													
Effingham Junction 6	d	23p45						00 36	00 32										07 50		
Horsley	d	23p48						00 39	00 34										07 53		
Clandon	d	23p53						00 44	00 39										07 58		
London Road (Guildford)	d	23p58						00 49	00 44										08 03		
Guildford	a	00 02						00 53	00 48		01 07								08 07		08 14

A not 11 December

Table 152

Sundays

London - Chessington South, Dorking, Guildford, Shepperton and Hampton Court

Network Diagram - see first Page of Table 152

			SW	SW	SW	SW		SW	SW	SW	SW	SW	SW	SW		SW		SW	SW	SW	SW	SW	SW	SW	SW
London Waterloo 15 ⊖	d		07 18		07 27			07 40	07 48		07 57		08 02	08 10		08 18		08 21	08 27	08 32	08 40	08 48	08 51	08 57	
Vauxhall ⊖	d		07 22		07 31			07 44	07 52		08 01		08 06	08 14		08 22		08 25	08 31	08 36	08 44	08 52	08 55	09 01	
Clapham Junction 10	d		07 27		07 36			07 49	07 57		08 06		08 11	08 19		08 27		08 30	08 36	08 41	08 49	08 57	09 00	09 06	
Earlsfield	d		07 30		07 39			07 52	08 00		08 09		08 14	08 22		08 30		08 33	08 39	08 44	08 52	09 00	09 03	09 09	
Wimbledon 6 ⊖ ⛴	d		07 34	07 37	07 43	07 48		07 56	08 04	08 07	08 13	08 17	08 18	08 26		08 34		08 37	08 43	08 48	08 56	09 04	09 07	09 13	09 17
Raynes Park 6	d		07 37	07 40	07 46	07 52			08 07	08 10	08 16		08 22			08 37		08 40	08 46	08 52		09 07	09 10	09 16	
Motspur Park	d			07 43		07 55				08 13			08 25					08 43		08 55			09 13		
Malden Manor	d			07 46						08 16								08 46					09 16		
Tolworth	d			07 49						08 19								08 49					09 19		
Chessington North	d			07 52						08 22								08 52					09 22		
Chessington South	a			07 54						08 24								08 54					09 24		
Worcester Park	d					07 57							08 27							08 57					
Stoneleigh	d					08 00							08 30							09 00					
Ewell West	d					08 03							08 33							09 03					
Epsom 3	a					08 06							08 36							09 06					
	d					08 08							08 38							09 08					
Ashtead	d					08 12							08 42							09 12					
Leatherhead	d					08 15							08 45							09 15					
Box Hill & Westhumble	d																								
Dorking 4	a												08 51												
New Malden 6	d		07 40		07 49				08 10		08 19					08 40			08 49			09 10		09 19	
Norbiton	d		07 43						08 13							08 43						09 13			
Kingston	a		07 46						08 16							08 46						09 16			
	d		07 49						08 16							08 49						09 16			
Hampton Wick	d		07 51						08 18							08 51						09 18			
Teddington	d		07 56						08 21							08 56						09 21			
Strawberry Hill	a		07 59													08 59									
Fulwell	d								08 25													09 25			
Hampton	d								08 29													09 29			
Kempton Park	d								08 32													09 32			
Sunbury	d								08 34													09 34			
Upper Halliford	d								08 36													09 36			
Shepperton	a								08 39													09 39			
Berrylands	d				07 51						08 21								08 51					09 21	
Surbiton 6	d				07 55			08 05			08 25	08 32		08 35					08 55		09 05			09 25	09 32
Thames Ditton	d				08 00						08 30								09 00					09 30	
Hampton Court	a				08 03						08 33								09 03					09 33	
Hinchley Wood	d											08 36													09 36
Claygate	d											08 39													09 39
Oxshott	d											08 42													09 42
Cobham & Stoke D'abernon	d											08 46													09 46
Bookham	d					08 21														09 21					
Effingham Junction 6	d					08 25						08 50								09 25					09 50
Horsley	d					08 27						08 53								09 27					09 53
Clandon	d					08 32						08 58								09 32					09 58
London Road (Guildford)	d					08 37						09 03								09 37					10 03
Guildford	a					08 41		08 40				09 07		09 10						09 41	09 40				10 07

		SW		SW		SW	SW	SW	SW	SW	SW	SW		SW	SW	SW	SW		SW	SW	SW	SW		SW	SW
London Waterloo 15 ⊖	d	09 02		09 10		09 18	09 21	09 27	09 32	09 40	09 48	09 51		09 57		10 02	10 10		10 18	10 21	10 27	10 32		10 40	10 48
Vauxhall ⊖	d	09 06		09 14		09 22	09 25	09 31	09 36	09 44	09 52	09 55		10 01		10 06	10 14		10 22	10 25	10 31	10 36		10 44	10 52
Clapham Junction 10	d	09 11		09 19		09 27	09 30	09 36	09 41	09 49	09 57	10 00		10 06		10 11	10 19		10 27	10 30	10 36	10 41		10 49	10 57
Earlsfield	d	09 14		09 22		09 30	09 33	09 39	09 44	09 52	10 00	10 03		10 09		10 14	10 22		10 30	10 33	10 39	10 44		10 52	11 00
Wimbledon 6 ⊖ ⛴	d	09 18		09 26		09 34	09 37	09 43	09 48	09 56	10 04	10 07		10 13	10 17	10 18	10 26		10 34	10 37	10 43	10 48		10 56	11 04
Raynes Park 6	d	09 22				09 37	09 40	09 46	09 52		10 07	10 10		10 16		10 22			10 37	10 40	10 46	10 52			11 07
Motspur Park	d	09 25					09 43		09 55			10 13				10 25				10 43		10 55			
Malden Manor	d						09 46					10 16								10 46					
Tolworth	d						09 49					10 19								10 49					
Chessington North	d						09 52					10 22								10 52					
Chessington South	a						09 54					10 24								10 54					
Worcester Park	d	09 27							09 57							10 27						10 57			
Stoneleigh	d	09 30							10 00							10 30						11 00			
Ewell West	d	09 33							10 03							10 33						11 03			
Epsom 3	a	09 36							10 06							10 36						11 06			
	d	09 38							10 08							10 38						11 08			
Ashtead	d	09 42							10 12							10 42						11 12			
Leatherhead	d	09 45							10 15							10 45						11 15			
Box Hill & Westhumble	d																								
Dorking 4	a	09 51														10 51									
New Malden 6	d					09 40		09 49			10 10			10 19					10 40		10 49				11 10
Norbiton	d					09 43					10 13								10 43						11 13
Kingston	a					09 46					10 16								10 46						11 16
	d					09 49					10 16								10 49						11 16
Hampton Wick	d					09 51					10 18								10 51						11 18
Teddington	d					09 56					10 21								10 56						11 21
Strawberry Hill	a					09 59													10 59						
Fulwell	d										10 25														11 25
Hampton	d										10 29														11 29
Kempton Park	d										10 32														11 32
Sunbury	d										10 34														11 34
Upper Halliford	d										10 36														11 36
Shepperton	a										10 39														11 39
Berrylands	d							09 51						10 21							10 51				
Surbiton 6	d			09 35				09 55		10 05				10 25	10 32		10 35				10 55			11 05	
Thames Ditton	d							10 00						10 30							11 00				
Hampton Court	a							10 03						10 33							11 03				
Hinchley Wood	d														10 36										
Claygate	d														10 39										
Oxshott	d														10 42										
Cobham & Stoke D'abernon	d														10 46										
Bookham	d								10 21													11 21			
Effingham Junction 6	d								10 25						10 50							11 25			
Horsley	d								10 27						10 53							11 27			
Clandon	d								10 32						10 58							11 32			
London Road (Guildford)	d								10 37						11 03							11 37			
Guildford	a			10 10					10 41	10 44					11 07		11 14					11 41		11 44	

Table 152

Sundays

London - Chessington South, Dorking, Guildford, Shepperton and Hampton Court

Network Diagram - see first Page of Table 152

		SW	SW	SW	SW	SW		SW		SW	SW	SW	SW	SW	SW	SW	SW	SW		SW		SW	SW	SW	SW
London Waterloo 15 ⊖	d	10 51	10 57		11 02	11 10		11 18		11 21	11 27	11 32	11 40	11 48	11 51	11 57		12 02		12 10		12 18	12 21	12 27	12 32
Vauxhall ⊖	d	10 55	11 01		11 06	11 14		11 22		11 25	11 31	11 36	11 44	11 52	11 55	12 01		12 06		12 14		12 22	12 25	12 31	12 36
Clapham Junction 10	d	11 00	11 06		11 11	11 19		11 27		11 30	11 36	11 41	11 49	11 57	12 00	12 06		12 11		12 19		12 27	12 30	12 36	12 41
Earlsfield	d	11 03	11 09		11 14	11 22		11 30		11 33	11 39	11 44	11 52	12 00	12 03	12 09		12 14		12 22		12 30	12 33	12 39	12 44
Wimbledon 6 ⊖	d	11 07	11 13	11 17	11 18	11 26		11 34		11 37	11 43	11 48	11 56	12 04	12 07	12 13	12 17	12 18		12 26		12 34	12 37	12 43	12 48
Raynes Park 6	d	11 10	11 16		11 22			11 37		11 40	11 46	11 52		12 07	12 10	12 16		12 22				12 37	12 40	12 46	12 52
Motspur Park	d	11 13			11 25					11 43		11 55			12 13			12 25					12 43		12 55
Malden Manor	d	11 16								11 46					12 16								12 46		
Tolworth	d	11 19								11 49					12 19								12 49		
Chessington North	d	11 22								11 52					12 22								12 52		
Chessington South	a	11 24								11 54					12 24								12 54		
Worcester Park	d				11 27							11 57						12 27							12 57
Stoneleigh	d				11 30							12 00						12 30							13 00
Ewell West	d				11 33							12 03						12 33							13 03
Epsom 3	a				11 36							12 06						12 36							13 06
	d				11 38							12 08						12 38							13 08
Ashtead	d				11 42							12 12						12 42							13 12
Leatherhead	d				11 45							12 15						12 45							13 15
Box Hill & Westhumble	d																								
Dorking 4	a				11 51													12 51							
New Malden 6	d		11 19					11 40			11 49			12 10		12 19						12 40		12 49	
Norbiton	d							11 43						12 13								12 43			
Kingston	a							11 46						12 16								12 46			
	d							11 49						12 16								12 49			
Hampton Wick	d							11 51						12 18								12 51			
Teddington	d							11 56						12 21								12 56			
Strawberry Hill	a							11 59														12 59			
Fulwell	d													12 25											
Hampton	d													12 29											
Kempton Park	d													12 32											
Sunbury	d													12 34											
Upper Halliford	d													12 36											
Shepperton	a													12 39											
Berrylands	d		11 21								11 51					12 21								12 51	
Surbiton 6	d		11 25	11 32		11 35					11 55		12 05			12 25	12 32			12 35				12 55	
Thames Ditton	d		11 30								12 00					12 30								13 00	
Hampton Court	a		11 33								12 03					12 33								13 03	
Hinchley Wood	d			11 36													12 36								
Claygate	d			11 39													12 39								
Oxshott	d			11 42													12 42								
Cobham & Stoke D'abernon	d			11 46													12 46								
Bookham	d											12 21													13 21
Effingham Junction 6	d			11 50								12 25					12 50								13 25
Horsley	d			11 53								12 27					12 53								13 27
Clandon	d			11 58								12 32					12 58								13 32
London Road (Guildford)	d			12 03								12 37					13 03								13 37
Guildford	a			12 07		12 14						12 41	12 44				13 07			13 14					13 41

		SW	SW	SW		SW	SW	SW	SW	SW		SW	SW	SW		SW	SW	SW	SW	SW		SW	SW	SW	
London Waterloo 15 ⊖	d	12 40		12 48		12 51	12 57	13 00	13 02	13 10		13 18	13 21	13 27		13 32	13 40		13 48	13 51		13 57	14 00	14 02	
Vauxhall ⊖	d	12 44		12 52		12 55	13 01	13 04	13 06	13 14		13 22	13 25	13 31		13 36	13 44		13 52	13 55		14 01	14 04	14 06	
Clapham Junction 10	d	12 49		12 57		13 00	13 06	13 09	13 11	13 19		13 27	13 30	13 36		13 41	13 49		13 57	14 00		14 06	14 09	14 11	
Earlsfield	d	12 52		13 00		13 03	13 09	13 12	13 14	13 22		13 30	13 33	13 39		13 44	13 52		14 00	14 03		14 09	14 12	14 14	
Wimbledon 6 ⊖	d	12 56		13 04		13 07	13 13	13 16	13 18	13 26		13 34	13 37	13 43		13 48	13 56		14 04	14 07		14 13	14 16	14 18	
Raynes Park 6	d			13 07		13 10	13 16		13 22			13 37	13 40	13 46		13 52			14 07	14 10		14 16		14 22	
Motspur Park	d					13 13			13 25				13 43			13 55				14 13				14 25	
Malden Manor	d					13 16							13 46							14 16					
Tolworth	d					13 19							13 49							14 19					
Chessington North	d					13 22							13 52							14 22					
Chessington South	a					13 24							13 54							14 24					
Worcester Park	d								13 27							13 57								14 27	
Stoneleigh	d								13 30							14 00								14 30	
Ewell West	d								13 33							14 03								14 33	
Epsom 3	a								13 36							14 06								14 36	
	d								13 38							14 08								14 38	
Ashtead	d								13 42							14 12								14 42	
Leatherhead	d								13 45							14 15								14 45	
Box Hill & Westhumble	d																								
Dorking 4	a								13 51															14 51	
New Malden 6	d			13 10			13 19					13 40		13 49					14 10			14 19			
Norbiton	d			13 13								13 43							14 13						
Kingston	a			13 16								13 46							14 16						
	d		13 11	13 16								13 49						14 11	14 16						
Hampton Wick	d		13 13	13 18								13 51						14 13	14 18						
Teddington	d		13 16	13 21								13 56						14 16	14 21						
Strawberry Hill	a		13 19									13 59						14 19							
Fulwell	d			13 25															14 25						
Hampton	d			13 29															14 29						
Kempton Park	d			13 32															14 32						
Sunbury	d			13 34															14 34						
Upper Halliford	d			13 36															14 36						
Shepperton	a			13 39															14 39						
Berrylands	d						13 21							13 51								14 21			
Surbiton 6	d	13 05					13 25	13 32		13 35				13 55			14 05					14 25	14 32		
Thames Ditton	d						13 30							14 00								14 30			
Hampton Court	a						13 33							14 03								14 33			
Hinchley Wood	d							13 36															14 36		
Claygate	d							13 39															14 39		
Oxshott	d							13 42															14 42		
Cobham & Stoke D'abernon	d							13 46															14 46		
Bookham	d															14 21									
Effingham Junction 6	d							13 50								14 25							14 50		
Horsley	d							13 53								14 27							14 53		
Clandon	d							13 58								14 32							14 58		
London Road (Guildford)	d							14 03								14 37							15 03		
Guildford	a	13 44						14 07		14 14						14 41	14 44						15 07		

Table 152

Sundays

London - Chessington South, Dorking, Guildford, Shepperton and Hampton Court

Network Diagram - see first Page of Table 152

		SW		SW	SW	SW	SW	SW	SW	SW		SW		SW	SW	SW	SW		SW	SW		SW	SW	SW	SW
London Waterloo 15 ⊖	d	14 10		14 18	14 21	14 27	14 32	14 40		14 48		14 51		14 57	15 00	15 02	15 10		15 18	15 21		15 27	15 32	15 40	
Vauxhall ⊖	d	14 14		14 22	14 25	14 31	14 36	14 44		14 52		14 55		15 01	15 04	15 06	15 14		15 22	15 25		15 31	15 36	15 44	
Clapham Junction 10	d	14 19		14 27	14 30	14 36	14 41	14 49		14 57		15 00		15 06	15 09	15 11	15 19		15 27	15 30		15 36	15 41	15 49	
Earlsfield	d	14 22		14 30	14 33	14 39	14 44	14 52		15 00		15 03		15 09	15 12	15 14	15 22		15 30	15 33		15 39	15 44	15 52	
Wimbledon 6 ⊖	d	14 26		14 34	14 37	14 43	14 48	14 56		15 04		15 07		15 13	15 16	15 18	15 26		15 34	15 37		15 43	15 48	15 56	
Raynes Park 6	d			14 37	14 40	14 46	14 52			15 07		15 10		15 16		15 22			15 37	15 40		15 46	15 52		
Motspur Park	d				14 43		14 55					15 13				15 25				15 43			15 55		
Malden Manor	d				14 46							15 16								15 46					
Tolworth	d				14 49							15 19								15 49					
Chessington North	d				14 52							15 22								15 52					
Chessington South	a				14 54							15 24								15 54					
Worcester Park	d						14 57									15 27							15 57		
Stoneleigh	d						15 00									15 30							16 00		
Ewell West	d						15 03									15 33							16 03		
Epsom 3	a						15 06									15 36							16 06		
	d						15 08									15 38							16 08		
Ashtead	d						15 12									15 42							16 12		
Leatherhead	d						15 15									15 45							16 15		
Box Hill & Westhumble	d																								
Dorking 4	a															15 51									
New Malden 6	d			14 40		14 49				15 10				15 19					15 40			15 49			
Norbiton	d			14 43						15 13									15 43						
Kingston	a			14 46						15 16									15 46						
	d			14 49					15 11	15 16									15 49						16 11
Hampton Wick	d			14 51					15 13	15 18									15 51						16 13
Teddington	d			14 56					15 16	15 21									15 56						16 16
Strawberry Hill	a			14 59					15 19										15 59						16 19
Fulwell	d									15 25															
Hampton	d									15 29															
Kempton Park	d									15 32															
Sunbury	d									15 34															
Upper Halliford	d									15 36															
Shepperton	a									15 39															
Berrylands	d					14 51								15 21								15 51			
Surbiton 6	d	14 35				14 55		15 05						15 25	15 32		15 35					15 55		16 05	
Thames Ditton	d					15 00								15 30								16 00			
Hampton Court	a					15 03								15 33								16 03			
Hinchley Wood	d														15 36										
Claygate	d														15 39										
Oxshott	d														15 42										
Cobham & Stoke D'abernon	d														15 46										
Bookham	d						15 21																16 21		
Effingham Junction 6	d						15 25								15 50								16 25		
Horsley	d						15 27								15 53								16 27		
Clandon	d						15 32								15 58								16 32		
London Road (Guildford)	d						15 37								16 03								16 37		
Guildford	a	15 14					15 41	15 44							16 07		16 14						16 41	16 44	

		SW	SW		SW	SW		SW	SW		SW	SW	SW	SW	SW	SW		SW	SW		SW	SW	SW	SW	
London Waterloo 15 ⊖	d	15 48	15 51		15 57	16 00		16 02	16 10		16 18	16 21	16 27	16 32	16 40			16 48	16 51		16 57	17 00	17 02	17 10	
Vauxhall ⊖	d	15 52	15 55		16 01	16 04		16 06	16 14		16 22	16 25	16 31	16 36	16 44			16 52	16 55		17 01	17 04	17 06	17 14	
Clapham Junction 10	d	15 57	16 00		16 06	16 09		16 11	16 19		16 27	16 30	16 36	16 41	16 49			16 57	17 00		17 06	17 09	17 11	17 19	
Earlsfield	d	16 00	16 03		16 09	16 12		16 14	16 22		16 30	16 33	16 39	16 44	16 52			17 00	17 03		17 09	17 12	17 14	17 22	
Wimbledon 6 ⊖	d	16 04	16 07		16 13	16 16		16 18	16 26		16 34	16 37	16 43	16 48	16 56			17 04	17 07		17 13	17 16	17 18	17 26	
Raynes Park 6	d	16 07	16 10		16 16			16 22			16 37	16 40	16 46	16 52				17 07	17 10		17 16		17 22		
Motspur Park	d		16 13					16 25				16 43		16 55					17 13				17 25		
Malden Manor	d		16 16									16 46							17 16						
Tolworth	d		16 19									16 49							17 19						
Chessington North	d		16 22									16 52							17 22						
Chessington South	a		16 24									16 54							17 24						
Worcester Park	d							16 27						16 57									17 27		
Stoneleigh	d							16 30						17 00									17 30		
Ewell West	d							16 33						17 03									17 33		
Epsom 3	a							16 36						17 06									17 36		
	d							16 38						17 08									17 38		
Ashtead	d							16 42						17 12									17 42		
Leatherhead	d							16 45						17 15									17 45		
Box Hill & Westhumble	d																								
Dorking 4	a							16 51															17 51		
New Malden 6	d	16 10			16 19						16 40		16 49					17 10			17 19				
Norbiton	d	16 13									16 43							17 13							
Kingston	a	16 16									16 46							17 16							
	d	16 16									16 49					17 11		17 16							
Hampton Wick	d	16 18									16 51					17 13		17 18							
Teddington	d	16 21									16 56					17 16		17 21							
Strawberry Hill	a										16 59					17 19									
Fulwell	d	16 25																17 25							
Hampton	d	16 29																17 29							
Kempton Park	d	16 32																17 32							
Sunbury	d	16 34																17 34							
Upper Halliford	d	16 36																17 36							
Shepperton	a	16 39																17 39							
Berrylands	d				16 21								16 51								17 21				
Surbiton 6	d				16 25	16 32			16 35				16 55		17 05						17 25	17 32		17 35	
Thames Ditton	d				16 30								17 00								17 30				
Hampton Court	a				16 33								17 03								17 33				
Hinchley Wood	d					16 36																17 36			
Claygate	d					16 39																17 39			
Oxshott	d					16 42																17 42			
Cobham & Stoke D'abernon	d					16 46																17 46			
Bookham	d													17 21											
Effingham Junction 6	d					16 50								17 25								17 50			
Horsley	d					16 53								17 27								17 53			
Clandon	d					16 58								17 32								17 58			
London Road (Guildford)	d					17 03								17 37								18 03			
Guildford	a					17 07			17 14					17 41	17 44							18 07		18 14	

Table 152

Sundays

London - Chessington South, Dorking, Guildford, Shepperton and Hampton Court

Network Diagram - see first Page of Table 152

		SW		SW	SW	SW	SW	SW	SW	SW		SW		SW	SW	SW		SW	SW	SW	SW	SW		SW	SW
London Waterloo 15 ⊖	d	17 18		17 21	17 27	17 32	17 40		17 48	17 51		17 57		18 00	18 02	18 10		18 18	18 21	18 27	18 32	18 40			18 48
Vauxhall ⊖	d	17 22		17 25	17 31	17 36	17 44		17 52	17 55		18 01		18 04	18 06	18 14		18 22	18 25	18 31	18 36	18 44			18 52
Clapham Junction 10	d	17 27		17 30	17 36	17 41	17 49		17 57	18 00		18 06		18 09	18 11	18 19		18 27	18 30	18 36	18 41	18 49			18 57
Earlsfield	d	17 30		17 33	17 39	17 44	17 52		18 00	18 03		18 09		18 12	18 14	18 22		18 30	18 33	18 39	18 44	18 52			19 00
Wimbledon 6 ⊖	d	17 34		17 37	17 43	17 48	17 56		18 04	18 07		18 13		18 16	18 18	18 26		18 34	18 37	18 43	18 48	18 56			19 04
Raynes Park 6	d	17 37		17 40	17 46	17 52			18 07	18 10		18 16			18 22			18 37	18 40	18 46	18 52				19 07
Motspur Park	d			17 43		17 55				18 13					18 25				18 43		18 55				
Malden Manor	d			17 46						18 16									18 46						
Tolworth	d			17 49						18 19									18 49						
Chessington North	d			17 52						18 22									18 52						
Chessington South	a			17 54						18 24									18 54						
Worcester Park	d					17 57									18 27						18 57				
Stoneleigh	d					18 00									18 30						19 00				
Ewell West	d					18 03									18 33						19 03				
Epsom 3	a					18 06									18 36						19 06				
	d					18 08									18 38						19 08				
Ashtead	d					18 12									18 42						19 12				
Leatherhead	d					18 15									18 45						19 15				
Box Hill & Westhumble	d																								
Dorking 4	a														18 51										
New Malden 6	d	17 40			17 49				18 10			18 19						18 40		18 49					19 10
Norbiton	d	17 43							18 13									18 43							19 13
Kingston	a	17 46							18 16									18 46							19 16
	d	17 49						18 11	18 16									18 49						19 11	19 16
Hampton Wick	d	17 51						18 13	18 18									18 51						19 13	19 18
Teddington	d	17 56						18 16	18 21									18 56						19 16	19 21
Strawberry Hill	a	17 59						18 19										18 59						19 19	
Fulwell	d								18 25																19 25
Hampton	d								18 29																19 29
Kempton Park	d								18 32																19 32
Sunbury	d								18 34																19 34
Upper Halliford	d								18 36																19 36
Shepperton	a								18 39																19 39
Berrylands	d				17 51							18 21								18 51					
Surbiton 6	d				17 55		18 05					18 25		18 32		18 35				18 55		19 05			
Thames Ditton	d				18 00							18 30								19 00					
Hampton Court	a				18 03							18 33								19 03					
Hinchley Wood	d													18 36											
Claygate	d													18 39											
Oxshott	d													18 42											
Cobham & Stoke D'abernon	d													18 46											
Bookham	d					18 21															19 21				
Effingham Junction 6	d					18 25								18 50							19 25				
Horsley	d					18 27								18 53							19 27				
Clandon	d					18 32								18 58							19 32				
London Road (Guildford)	d					18 37								19 03							19 37				
Guildford	a					18 41	18 44							19 07		19 14					19 41	19 44			

		SW		SW	SW	SW	SW			SW	SW	SW	SW	SW	SW	SW		SW		SW	SW	SW		SW	SW
London Waterloo 15 ⊖	d	18 51		18 57	19 00	19 02	19 10			19 18	19 21	19 27	19 32	19 40		19 48		19 57		20 00	20 02	20 10		20 18	20 21
Vauxhall ⊖	d	18 55		19 01	19 04	19 06	19 14			19 22	19 25	19 31	19 36	19 44		19 52		20 01		20 04	20 06	20 14		20 22	20 25
Clapham Junction 10	d	19 00		19 06	19 09	19 11	19 19			19 27	19 30	19 36	19 41	19 49		19 57		20 06		20 09	20 11	20 19		20 27	20 30
Earlsfield	d	19 03		19 09	19 12	19 14	19 22			19 30	19 33	19 39	19 44	19 52		20 00		20 09		20 12	20 14	20 22		20 30	20 33
Wimbledon 6 ⊖	d	19 07		19 13	19 16	19 18	19 26			19 34	19 37	19 43	19 48	19 56		20 04		20 13		20 16	20 18	20 26		20 34	20 37
Raynes Park 6	d	19 10		19 16		19 22				19 37	19 40	19 46	19 52			20 07		20 16			20 22			20 37	20 40
Motspur Park	d	19 13				19 25					19 43		19 55								20 25				20 43
Malden Manor	d	19 16									19 46														20 46
Tolworth	d	19 19									19 49														20 49
Chessington North	d	19 22									19 52														20 52
Chessington South	a	19 24									19 54														20 54
Worcester Park	d					19 27							19 57								20 27				
Stoneleigh	d					19 30							20 00								20 30				
Ewell West	d					19 33							20 03								20 33				
Epsom 3	a					19 36							20 06								20 36				
	d					19 38							20 08								20 38				
Ashtead	d					19 42							20 12								20 42				
Leatherhead	d					19 45							20 15								20 45				
Box Hill & Westhumble	d																								
Dorking 4	a					19 51															20 51				
New Malden 6	d			19 19						19 40		19 49				20 10		20 19						20 40	
Norbiton	d									19 43						20 13								20 43	
Kingston	a									19 46						20 16								20 46	
	d									19 49					20 11	20 16								20 49	
Hampton Wick	d									19 51					20 13	20 18								20 51	
Teddington	d									19 56					20 16	20 21								20 56	
Strawberry Hill	a									19 59					20 19									20 59	
Fulwell	d															20 25									
Hampton	d															20 29									
Kempton Park	d															20 32									
Sunbury	d															20 34									
Upper Halliford	d															20 36									
Shepperton	a															20 39									
Berrylands	d			19 21								19 51						20 21							
Surbiton 6	d			19 25	19 32		19 35					19 55		20 05				20 25		20 32		20 35			
Thames Ditton	d			19 30								20 00						20 30							
Hampton Court	a			19 33								20 03						20 33							
Hinchley Wood	d				19 36															20 36					
Claygate	d				19 39															20 39					
Oxshott	d				19 42															20 42					
Cobham & Stoke D'abernon	d				19 46															20 46					
Bookham	d												20 21												
Effingham Junction 6	d				19 50								20 25							20 50					
Horsley	d				19 53								20 27							20 53					
Clandon	d				19 58								20 32							20 58					
London Road (Guildford)	d				20 03								20 37							21 03					
Guildford	a				20 07		20 14						20 41	20 44						21 07		21 14			

Table 152

Sundays

London - Chessington South, Dorking, Guildford, Shepperton and Hampton Court

Network Diagram - see first Page of Table 152

		SW	SW	SW	SW	SW	SW	SW	SW	SW	SW	SW	SW	SW	SW	SW	SW	SW	SW
London Waterloo 15 ⊖	d	20 27	20 32	20 40		20 48	20 57	21 00	21 02	21 10	21 18	21 21	21 32	21 40		21 48	21 57	22 00	22 02
Vauxhall ⊖	d	20 31	20 36	20 44		20 52	21 01	21 04	21 06	21 14	21 22	21 25	21 36	21 44		21 52	22 01	22 04	22 06
Clapham Junction 10	d	20 36	20 41	20 49		20 57	21 06	21 09	21 11	21 19	21 27	21 30	21 41	21 49		21 57	22 06	22 09	22 11
Earlsfield	d	20 39	20 44	20 52		21 00	21 09	21 12	21 14	21 22	21 30	21 33	21 44	21 52		22 00	22 09	22 12	22 14
Wimbledon 6 ⊖	d	20 43	20 48	20 56		21 04	21 13	21 16	21 18	21 26	21 34	21 37	21 48	21 56		22 04	22 13	22 16	22 18
Raynes Park 6	d	20 46	20 52			21 07	21 16		21 22		21 37	21 40	21 52			22 07	22 16		22 22
Motspur Park	d		20 55						21 25			21 43	21 55						22 25
Malden Manor	d											21 46							
Tolworth	d											21 49							
Chessington North	d											21 52							
Chessington South	a											21 54							
Worcester Park	d		20 57						21 27				21 57						22 27
Stoneleigh	d		21 00						21 30				22 00						22 30
Ewell West	d		21 03						21 33				22 03						22 33
Epsom 3	a		21 06						21 36				22 06						22 36
	d		21 08						21 38				22 08						22 38
Ashtead	d		21 12						21 42				22 12						22 42
Leatherhead	d		21 15						21 45				22 15						22 45
Box Hill & Westhumble	d																		
Dorking 4	a								21 51										22 51
New Malden 6	d	20 49				21 10	21 19				21 40					22 10	22 19		
Norbiton	d					21 13					21 43					22 13			
Kingston	a					21 16					21 46					22 16			
	d				21 11	21 16					21 49				22 11	22 16			
Hampton Wick	d				21 13	21 18					21 51				22 13	22 18			
Teddington	d				21 16	21 21					21 56				22 16	22 21			
Strawberry Hill	a				21 19						21 59				22 19				
Fulwell	d					21 25										22 25			
Hampton	d					21 29										22 29			
Kempton Park	d					21 32										22 32			
Sunbury	d					21 34										22 34			
Upper Halliford	d					21 36										22 36			
Shepperton	a					21 39										22 39			
Berrylands	d	20 51					21 21										22 21		
Surbiton 6	d	20 55		21 05			21 25	21 32		21 35				22 05			22 25	22 32	
Thames Ditton	d	21 00					21 30										22 30		
Hampton Court	a	21 03					21 33										22 33		
Hinchley Wood	d							21 36										22 36	
Claygate	d							21 39										22 39	
Oxshott	d							21 42										22 42	
Cobham & Stoke D'abernon	d							21 46										22 46	
Bookham	d		21 21										22 21						
Effingham Junction 6	d		21 25					21 50					22 25					22 50	
Horsley	d		21 27					21 53					22 27					22 53	
Clandon	d		21 32					21 58					22 32					22 58	
London Road (Guildford)	d		21 37					22 03					22 37					23 03	
Guildford	a		21 41	21 44				22 07		22 14			22 41	22 44				23 07	

London - Chessington South, Dorking, Guildford, Shepperton and Hampton Court

Network Diagram - see first Page of Table 152

		SW		SW	SW	SW	SW	SW	SW	SW			SW	SW	SW	SW		SW	SW	SW 1
London Waterloo 15 ⊖	d	22 10		22 18	22 21	22 32	22 40		22 48	22 51			22 57	23 00	23 02	23 10		23 18	23 32	23 40
Vauxhall ⊖	d	22 14		22 22	22 25	22 36	22 44		22 52	22 55			23 01	23 04	23 06	23 14		23 22	23 36	23 44
Clapham Junction 10	d	22 19		22 27	22 30	22 41	22 49		22 57	23 00			23 06	23 09	23 11	23 19		23 27	23 41	23 49
Earlsfield	d	22 22		22 30	22 33	22 44	22 52		23 00	23 03			23 09	23 12	23 14	23 22		23 30	23 44	23 52
Wimbledon 6 ⊖	d	22 26		22 34	22 37	22 48	22 56		23 04	23 07			23 13	23 16	23 18	23 26		23 34	23 48	23 56
Raynes Park 6	d			22 37	22 40	22 52			23 07	23 10			23 16		23 22			23 37	23 52	
Motspur Park	d				22 43	22 55				23 13					23 25				23 55	
Malden Manor	d				22 46					23 16										
Tolworth	d				22 49					23 19										
Chessington North	d				22 52					23 22										
Chessington South	a				22 54					23 24										
Worcester Park	d					22 57									23 27				23 57	
Stoneleigh	d					23 00									23 30				23 59	
Ewell West	d					23 03									23 33				00 03	
Epsom 3	a					23 06									23 36				00 06	
	d					23 08														
Ashtead	d					23 12														
Leatherhead	d					23 15														
Box Hill & Westhumble	d																			
Dorking 4	a																			
New Malden 6	d			22 40					23 10				23 19					23 40		
Norbiton	d			22 43					23 13									23 43		
Kingston	a			22 46					23 16									23 46		
	d			22 49				23 11	23 16									23 47		
Hampton Wick	d			22 51				23 13	23 18									23 49		
Teddington	d			22 56				23 16	23 21									23 51		
Strawberry Hill	a			22 59				23 19										23 54		
Fulwell	d								23 25											
Hampton	d								23 29											
Kempton Park	d								23 32											
Sunbury	d								23 34											
Upper Halliford	d								23 36											
Shepperton	a								23 39											
Berrylands	d												23 21							
Surbiton 6	d	22 35					23 05						23 25	23 32		23 35				00a04
Thames Ditton	d												23 30							
Hampton Court	a												23 33							
Hinchley Wood	d													23 36						
Claygate	d													23 39						
Oxshott	d													23 42						
Cobham & Stoke D'abernon	d													23 46						
Bookham	d					23 21														
Effingham Junction 6	d					23 25								23 50						
Horsley	d					23 27								23 53						
Clandon	d					23 32								23 58						
London Road (Guildford)	d					23 37								00 03						
Guildford	a	23 13				23 41	23 45							00 07		00 13				

Hampton Court, Shepperton, Guildford, Dorking and Chessington South - London

Network Diagram - see first Page of Table 152

Miles	Miles	Miles	Miles	Miles			SW MO	SW MX	SW MX	SW MX		SW MO	SW MX	SW MO	SW MX		SW	SW	SW	SW	SW	SW	SW	SW	SW
0	—	—	—	—	**Guildford**	d			23p08								04 00		04 58			05 14			05 38
1¼	—	—	—	—	London Road (Guildford)	d			23p12										05 02						05 42
4½	—	—	—	—	Clandon	d			23p17										05 07						05 47
7¾	—	—	—	—	Horsley	d			23p21										05 11						05 51
8¾	0	—	—	—	Effingham Junction 6	d			23p24										05 16						05 54
—	1¾	—	—	—	Bookham	d													05 19						
11	—	—	—	—	Cobham & Stoke d'Abernon	d			23p28																05 58
13	—	—	—	—	Oxshott	d			23p31																06 01
14¾	—	—	—	—	Claygate	d			23p34																06 04
16	—	—	—	—	Hinchley Wood	d			23p37																06 07
—	—	—	0	—	**Hampton Court**	d						23p45												05 54	
—	—	—	1	—	Thames Ditton	d						23p47												05 56	
18	—	—	3	—	**Surbiton 6**	d			23p42			23p53					04 24					05 57	06 01	06 02	06 12
19	—	—	—	—	Berrylands	d						23p55												06 04	
—	—	—	—	0	**Shepperton**	d	23p11	23p11												05 23					
—	—	—	—	1½	Upper Halliford	d	23p14	23p14												05 26					
—	—	—	—	2	Sunbury	d	23p16	23p16												05 28					
—	—	—	—	2½	Kempton Park	d	23p18	23p18																	
—	—	—	—	4¼	Hampton	d	23p21	23p21												05 33					
—	—	—	—	6	Fulwell	d	23p24	23p24												05 36					
—	—	—	0	—	Strawberry Hill	d				23p37			00 07					04 55		05 38					
—	—	—	1¼	7	Teddington	d	23p29	23p29		23p41			00 11	00s56	00s56			04 59			05 44				
—	—	—	—	8¼	Hampton Wick	d	23p31	23p31		23p44			00 14	00s59	00s59			05 01			05 46				
—	—	—	—	8¾	Kingston	a	23p33	23p33		23p46			00 16	01 01	01 01			05 03			05 48				
—	—	—	—	—		d	23p34	23p34		23p49								05 04			05 49				
—	—	—	—	9½	Norbiton	d	23p36	23p36		23p51								05 06			05 51				
20	—	—	—	11	New Malden 6	d	23p40	23p41		23p55		23p58						05 10			05 55			06 07	
—	—	0	—	—	**Dorking 4**	d																			
—	—	0¾	—	—	Box Hill & Westhumble	d																			
—	4½	4	—	—	Leatherhead	d													05 24						
—	—	5¾	—	—	Ashtead	d													05 28						
—	—	7¾	—	—	**Epsom 3**	a													05 32						
—	—	—	—	—		d													05 34						
—	—	9	—	—	Ewell West	d													05 37						
—	—	10	—	—	Stoneleigh	d													05 40						
—	—	11¼	—	—	Worcester Park	d													05 42						
—	0	—	—	—	**Chessington South**	d																			
—	0¾	—	—	—	Chessington North	d																			
—	1¾	—	—	—	Tolworth	d																			
—	2¾	—	—	—	Malden Manor	d																			
—	3¾	12¼	—	—	Motspur Park	d													05 46						
21¼	5¼	13¼	—	12	Raynes Park 6	d	23p43	23p43		23p58		00 01						05 13	05 49		05 58			06 10	
22¾	6¾	14¾	—	13½	**Wimbledon 6** ⊖	d	23p47	23p50	23p53	00 02		00a04					04 32	05 17	05 53		06 02	06 05		06 14	06 20
24½	8½	16½	—	15¼	Earlsfield	d	23p50	23p53	23p56	00 05								05 21	05 57		06 05	06 08		06 17	06 24
26	10	18	—	16¾	**Clapham Junction 10**	d	23p54	23p57	23p59	00 09							04 44	05 25	06 01		06 09	06 12		06 21	06 28
28¾	12¾	20¾	—	19½	Vauxhall ⊖	d	23p59	00 02	00 05	00 14								05 30	06 06	06 12	06 14	06 17		06 26	06 33
30	14	22	—	20¾	**London Waterloo 15** ⊖	a	00 04	00 10	00 14	00 22							04 53	05 35	06 11	06 16	06 19	06 22	06 20	06 31	06 37

Hampton Court, Shepperton, Guildford, Dorking and Chessington South - London

Network Diagram - see first Page of Table 152

			SW		SW	SW	SW	SW	SW	SW	SW		SW	SW		SW	SW	SW	SW 1	SW	SW		SW	SW	SW
Guildford	d									05 58	06 07										06 28		06 37		
London Road (Guildford)	d									06 02	06 11										06 32		06 41		
Clandon	d									06 07	06 16										06 37		06 46		
Horsley	d									06 11	06 20										06 41		06 50		
Effingham Junction 6	d									06 16	06 24										06 48		06 54		
Bookham	d									06 19											06 51				
Cobham & Stoke d'Abernon	d										06 27												06 57		
Oxshott	d										06 31												07 01		
Claygate	d										06 34												07 04		
Hinchley Wood	d										06 37												07 07		
Hampton Court	d							06 24										06 54							
Thames Ditton	d							06 26										06 56							
Surbiton 6	d					06 28		06 32			06 42					06 57		07 02	07 08				07 12		
Berrylands	d							06 34										07 04							
Shepperton	d								06 11											06 41					
Upper Halliford	d								06 14											06 44					
Sunbury	d								06 16											06 46					
Kempton Park	d																								
Hampton	d								06 21											06 51					
Fulwell	d								06 24											06 54					
Strawberry Hill	d				06 08									06 37											07 07
Teddington	d				06 11				06 29					06 41						06 59					07 11
Hampton Wick	d				06 14				06 31					06 44						07 01					07 14
Kingston	a				06 16				06 33					06 46						07 03					07 16
	d				06 19				06 34					06 49						07 04					07 19
Norbiton	d				06 21				06 36					06 51						07 06					07 21
New Malden 6	d				06 25			06 37	06 40					06 55				07 07		07 10					07 25
Dorking 4	d		05 48														06 32								
Box Hill & Westhumble	d		05 50														06 34								
Leatherhead	d		05 56							06 24							06 39				06 56				
Ashtead	d		05 59							06 28							06 43				06 59				
Epsom 3	a		06 04							06 32							06 47				07 04				
	d		06 04				06 18			06 34							06 48				07 04				
Ewell West	d		06 07				06 21			06 37							06 51				07 07				
Stoneleigh	d		06 10				06 24			06 40							06 53				07 10				
Worcester Park	d		06 12				06 27			06 42							06 56				07 12				
Chessington South	d												06 40											07 10	
Chessington North	d												06 42											07 12	
Tolworth	d												06 44											07 14	
Malden Manor	d												06 47											07 17	
Motspur Park	d		06 16				06 30			06 46			06 50				07 00				07 16			07 20	
Raynes Park 6	d		06 19		06 28		06 34	06 40	06 43	06 49			06 54	06 58			07 04	07 10		07 13	07 19			07 24	07 28
Wimbledon 6 ⊖ ⛴	d		06 23		06 32	06 35	06 38	06 44	06 47	06 53	06 50		06 58	07 02		07 05	07 08	07 14		07 17	07 23		07 20	07 28	07 32
Earlsfield	d		06 27		06 35	06 39	06 42	06 47	06 50	06 57	06 54		07 01	07 05		07 08	07 11	07 17		07 20	07 27		07 24	07 31	07 35
Clapham Junction 10	d		06 31		06 39	06 43	06 46	06 51	06 54	07 01	06 58		07 05	07 09		07 12	07 15	07 21		07 24	07 31		07 28	07 35	07 39
Vauxhall ⊖	d		06 36		06 44	06 48	06 51	06 56	06 59	07 06	07 03		07 10	07 14		07 17	07 20	07 26		07 29	07 36		07 33	07 40	07 44
London Waterloo 15 ⊖	a		06 40		06 49	06 52	06 55	07 03	07 06	07 12	07 09		07 17	07 21		07 24	07 27	07 33	07 26	07 36	07 42		07 39	07 47	07 51

Hampton Court, Shepperton, Guildford, Dorking and Chessington South - London

Network Diagram - see first Page of Table 152

			SW 1	SW	SW	SW	SW		SW	SW 1	SW	SW	SW	SW	SW	SW			SW 1	SW	SW	SW	SW	SW	SW 1
Guildford	d											06 58	07 07	07 17											
London Road (Guildford)	d											07 02	07 11	07 21											
Clandon	d											07 07	07 16	07 26											
Horsley	d											07 11	07 20	07 30											
Effingham Junction 6	d											07 16	07 24	07 34											
Bookham	d											07 19													
Cobham & Stoke d'Abernon	d												07 27	07 37											
Oxshott	d												07 31	07 41											
Claygate	d												07 34	07 44											
Hinchley Wood	d												07 37	07 47											
Hampton Court	d								07 24															07 54	
Thames Ditton	d								07 26															07 56	
Surbiton 6	d		07 27						07 32	07 38			07 42	07 53					07 57					08 02	08 08
Berrylands	d								07 34															08 04	
Shepperton	d						07 00				07 11										07 30				
Upper Halliford	d						07 03				07 14										07 33				
Sunbury	d						07 05				07 16										07 35				
Kempton Park	d																								
Hampton	d						07 09				07 21										07 39				
Fulwell	d						07 12				07 24										07 42				
Strawberry Hill	d						07 14									07 37					07 44	07 47			
Teddington	d				07 20						07 29					07 41						07 50			
Hampton Wick	d				07 22						07 31					07 44						07 52			
Kingston	a				07 24						07 33					07 46						07 54			
	d				07 26						07 34					07 49						07 56			
Norbiton	d				07 28						07 36					07 51						07 58			
New Malden 6	d				07 32				07 37		07 40		07 46			07 55						08 02		08 07	
Dorking 4	d			07 02																07 32					
Box Hill & Westhumble	d			07 04																07 34					
Leatherhead	d			07 09								07 26								07 39					
Ashtead	d			07 13								07 29								07 43					
Epsom 3	a			07 17								07 34								07 47					
	d			07 18		07 22						07 34								07 48			07 52		
Ewell West	d					07 25						07 37											07 55		
Stoneleigh	d					07 27						07 40											07 57		
Worcester Park	d			07 25		07 30						07 43								07 55			08 00		
Chessington South	d														07 40										
Chessington North	d														07 42										
Tolworth	d														07 44										
Malden Manor	d														07 47										
Motspur Park	d					07 34						07 46			07 50								08 04		
Raynes Park 6	d			07 31	07 34	07 37			07 40		07 43	07 50			07 54	07 58				08 01		08 04	08 07	08 10	
Wimbledon 6 ⊖ ⛴	d			07 35	07 38	07 41			07 44		07 47	07 54	07 51		07 58	08 02				08 05		08 08	08 11	08 14	
Earlsfield	d			07 38	07 42	07 45			07 48		07 51	07 58	07 54		08 01	08 05				08 08		08 12	08 15	08 18	
Clapham Junction 10	d			07 42	07 46	07 49			07 52		07 55	08 02	07 58		08 05	08 09				08 12		08 16	08 19	08 22	
Vauxhall ⊖	d			07 47	07 51	07 54	07 56		07 57		08 00	08 07	08 03		08 10	08 14				08 17	08 26	08 21	08 24	08 27	
London Waterloo 15 ⊖	a		07 49	07 54	07 57	08 00	08 04		08 04	07 56	08 06	08 13	08 11	08 13	08 17	08 21			08 19	08 24	08 34	08 27	08 30	08 33	08 26

Hampton Court, Shepperton, Guildford, Dorking and Chessington South - London

Network Diagram - see first Page of Table 152

		SW	SW		SW	SW 1	SW 1	SW	SW		SW	SW	SW		SW	SW	SW 1	SW	SW	SW	SW	SW			SW
Guildford	d				07 37														07 58	08 07					
London Road (Guildford)	d				07 41														08 02	08 11					
Clandon	d				07 46														08 07	08 16					
Horsley	d				07 50														08 11	08 20					
Effingham Junction 6	d		07 46		07 54														08 16	08 24					
Bookham	d		07 49																08 19						
Cobham & Stoke d'Abernon	d				07 57															08 27					
Oxshott	d				08 01															08 31					
Claygate	d				08 04															08 34					
Hinchley Wood	d				08 07															08 37					
Hampton Court	d															08 24									
Thames Ditton	d															08 26									
Surbiton 6	d				08 12	08 19	08 25									08 32	08 38			08 42	08 48				
Berrylands	d															08 34									
Shepperton	d	07 41										08 00						08 11							
Upper Halliford	d	07 44										08 03						08 14							
Sunbury	d	07 46										08 05						08 16							
Kempton Park	d																								
Hampton	d	07 51										08 09						08 21							
Fulwell	d	07 54										08 12						08 24							
Strawberry Hill	d								08 07			08 14	08 17												08 38
Teddington	d	07 59							08 11				08 20					08 29							08 41
Hampton Wick	d	08 01							08 14				08 22					08 31							08 44
Kingston	a	08 03							08 16				08 24					08 33							08 46
	d	08 04							08 19				08 26					08 34							08 49
Norbiton	d	08 06							08 21				08 28					08 36							08 51
New Malden 6	d	08 10			08 16				08 25				08 32			08 37		08 40							08 55
Dorking 4	d										08 02														
Box Hill & Westhumble	d										08 04														
Leatherhead	d		07 56								08 09								08 25						
Ashtead	d		07 59								08 13								08 28						
Epsom 3	a		08 04								08 17								08 33						
	d		08 04								08 18				08 22				08 34						
Ewell West	d		08 07												08 25				08 37						
Stoneleigh	d		08 10												08 27				08 40						
Worcester Park	d		08 13								08 25				08 30				08 42						
Chessington South	d							08 10														08 40			
Chessington North	d							08 12														08 42			
Tolworth	d							08 14														08 44			
Malden Manor	d							08 17														08 47			
Motspur Park	d		08 16					08 20							08 34				08 46			08 50			
Raynes Park 6	d	08 13	08 20					08 24	08 28		08 31		08 34		08 37	08 40		08 43	08 49			08 54			08 58
Wimbledon 6 ⊖	d	08 17	08 24		08 21			08 28	08 32		08 35		08 38		08 41	08 44		08 47	08 53			08 58			09 02
Earlsfield	d	08 21	08 28		08 24			08 31	08 35		08 38		08 42		08 45	08 48		08 51	08 57			09 01			09 05
Clapham Junction 10	d	08 25	08 32		08 28			08 35	08 39		08 42		08 46		08 49	08 52		08 55	09 01			09 05			09 09
Vauxhall ⊖	d	08 30	08 37		08 33			08 40	08 44		08 47	08 56	08 51		08 54	08 57		09 00	09 06			09 10			09 14
London Waterloo 15 ⊖	a	08 36	08 43		08 40	08 36	08 46	08 47	08 51		08 54	09 04	08 57		09 00	09 03	08 59	09 06	09 12	09 01	09 06	09 17			09 21

Hampton Court, Shepperton, Guildford, Dorking and Chessington South - London

Network Diagram - see first Page of Table 152

		SW	SW	SW	SW	SW	SW	SW 1	SW		SW		SW	SW	SW	SW	SW	SW	SW		SW		SW	SW	SW
Guildford	d	08 20					08 37						08 46				08 58	09 08							
London Road (Guildford)	d						08 41										09 02	09 12							
Clandon	d						08 46										09 07	09 17							
Horsley	d						08 50										09 11	09 21							
Effingham Junction 6	d					08 48	08 54										09 16	09 24							
Bookham	d					08 51											09 19								
Cobham & Stoke d'Abernon	d						08 57											09 28							
Oxshott	d						09 01											09 31							
Claygate	d						09 04											09 34							
Hinchley Wood	d						09 07											09 37							
Hampton Court	d			08 54											09 24										09 54
Thames Ditton	d			08 56											09 26										09 56
Surbiton 6	d	08 57		09 02			09 12	09 19					09 27		09 32			09 42					09 57		10 02
Berrylands	d			09 04											09 34										10 04
Shepperton	d				08 41											09 11									
Upper Halliford	d				08 44											09 14									
Sunbury	d				08 46											09 16									
Kempton Park	d															09 18									
Hampton	d				08 51											09 21									
Fulwell	d				08 54											09 24									
Strawberry Hill	d										09 07										09 37				
Teddington	d				08 59						09 11					09 29					09 41				
Hampton Wick	d				09 01						09 14					09 31					09 44				
Kingston	a				09 03						09 16					09 33					09 46				
	d				09 04						09 19					09 34					09 49				
Norbiton	d				09 06						09 21					09 36					09 51				
New Malden 6	d			09 07	09 10						09 25				09 37	09 40					09 55				10 07
Dorking 4	d		08 31											09 02										09 35	
Box Hill & Westhumble	d		08 33											09 04											
Leatherhead	d		08 38			08 56								09 09			09 24							09 41	
Ashtead	d		08 42			08 59								09 13			09 28							09 45	
Epsom 3	a		08 46			09 04								09 17			09 32							09 49	
	d		08 48			09 04								09 18			09 35							09 50	
Ewell West	d		08 51			09 07								09 21			09 38							09 53	
Stoneleigh	d		08 54			09 10								09 24			09 40							09 55	
Worcester Park	d		08 57			09 12								09 27			09 43							09 58	
Chessington South	d								09 10										09 40						
Chessington North	d								09 12										09 42						
Tolworth	d								09 14										09 44						
Malden Manor	d								09 17										09 47						
Motspur Park	d		09 00			09 16			09 20					09 30			09 46		09 50					10 01	
Raynes Park 6	d		09 04	09 10	09 13	09 19			09 24		09 28			09 34	09 40	09 43	09 49		09 53		09 58			10 04	10 10
Wimbledon 6 ⊖ ⛴	d	09 05	09 08	09 14	09 17	09 23	09 20		09 28		09 32		09 35	09 38	09 44	09 47	09 53	09 50	09 57		10 02		10 05	10 08	10 14
Earlsfield	d	09 08	09 12	09 17	09 20	09 27	09 24		09 31		09 35		09 38	09 42	09 47	09 50	09 57	09 54	10 01		10 05		10 08	10 12	10 17
Clapham Junction 10	d	09 12	09 16	09 21	09 24	09 31	09 28		09 35		09 39		09 42	09 46	09 51	09 54	10 01	09 58	10 05		10 09		10 12	10 16	10 21
Vauxhall ⊖	d	09 17	09 21	09 26	09 29	09 36	09 33		09 40		09 44		09 47	09 51	09 56	09 59	10 06	10 03	10 10		10 14		10 17	10 21	10 26
London Waterloo 15 ⊖	a	09 24	09 27	09 33	09 36	09 42	09 39	09 40	09 47		09 51		09 54	09 57	10 01	10 04	10 10	10 07	10 15		10 19		10 22	10 25	10 31

Hampton Court, Shepperton, Guildford, Dorking and Chessington South - London

Network Diagram - see first Page of Table 152

		SW	SW	SW	SW		SW		SW	SW	SW	SW	SW	SW	SW		SW		SW	SW	SW	SW	SW	SW	SW
Guildford	d		09 28	09 38									09 58	10 08									10 28	10 38	
London Road (Guildford)	d		09 32	09 42									10 02	10 12									10 32	10 42	
Clandon	d		09 37	09 47									10 07	10 17									10 37	10 47	
Horsley	d		09 41	09 51									10 11	10 21									10 41	10 51	
Effingham Junction 6	d		09 46	09 54									10 16	10 24									10 46	10 54	
Bookham	d		09 49										10 19										10 49		
Cobham & Stoke d'Abernon	d			09 58										10 28										10 58	
Oxshott	d			10 01										10 31										11 01	
Claygate	d			10 04										10 34										11 04	
Hinchley Wood	d			10 07										10 37										11 07	
Hampton Court	d										10 24										10 54				
Thames Ditton	d										10 26										10 56				
Surbiton 6	d			10 12					10 27		10 32			10 42					10 57		11 02			11 12	
Berrylands	d										10 34										11 04				
Shepperton	d	09 41										10 11										10 41			
Upper Halliford	d	09 44										10 14										10 44			
Sunbury	d	09 46										10 16										10 46			
Kempton Park	d	09 48										10 18										10 48			
Hampton	d	09 51										10 21										10 51			
Fulwell	d	09 54										10 24										10 54			
Strawberry Hill	d						10 07										10 37								
Teddington	d	09 59					10 11					10 29					10 41					10 59			
Hampton Wick	d	10 01					10 14					10 31					10 44					11 01			
Kingston	a	10 03					10 16					10 33					10 46					11 03			
	d	10 04					10 19					10 34					10 49					11 04			
Norbiton	d	10 06					10 21					10 36					10 51					11 06			
New Malden 6	d	10 10					10 25				10 37	10 40					10 55				11 07	11 10			
Dorking 4	d									10 05										10 35					
Box Hill & Westhumble	d																								
Leatherhead	d		09 54							10 11			10 24							10 41			10 54		
Ashtead	d		09 58							10 14			10 28							10 44			10 58		
Epsom 3	a		10 02							10 19			10 32							10 49			11 02		
	d		10 05							10 20			10 35							10 50			11 05		
Ewell West	d		10 08							10 23			10 38							10 53			11 08		
Stoneleigh	d		10 10							10 25			10 40							10 55			11 10		
Worcester Park	d		10 13							10 28			10 43							10 58			11 13		
Chessington South	d				10 10										10 40										11 10
Chessington North	d				10 12										10 42										11 12
Tolworth	d				10 14										10 44										11 14
Malden Manor	d				10 17										10 47										11 17
Motspur Park	d		10 16		10 20					10 31			10 46		10 50					11 01			11 16		11 20
Raynes Park 6	d	10 13	10 19		10 23		10 28			10 34	10 40	10 43	10 49		10 53		10 58			11 04	11 10	11 13	11 19		11 23
Wimbledon 6 ⊖	d	10 17	10 23	10 20	10 27		10 32		10 35	10 38	10 44	10 47	10 53	10 50	10 57		11 02		11 05	11 08	11 14	11 17	11 23	11 20	11 27
Earlsfield	d	10 20	10 27	10 24	10 31		10 35		10 38	10 42	10 47	10 50	10 57	10 54	11 01		11 05		11 08	11 12	11 17	11 20	11 27	11 24	11 31
Clapham Junction 10	d	10 24	10 31	10 28	10 35		10 39		10 42	10 46	10 51	10 54	11 01	10 58	11 05		11 09		11 12	11 16	11 21	11 24	11 31	11 28	11 35
Vauxhall ⊖	d	10 29	10 36	10 33	10 40		10 44		10 47	10 51	10 56	10 59	11 06	11 03	11 10		11 14		11 17	11 21	11 26	11 29	11 36	11 33	11 40
London Waterloo 15 ⊖	a	10 34	10 40	10 37	10 45		10 49		10 52	10 55	11 01	11 04	11 10	11 07	11 15		11 19		11 22	11 25	11 31	11 34	11 40	11 37	11 45

			SW		SW	SW	SW	SW	SW	SW	SW		SW		SW	SW	SW	SW	SW	SW	SW		SW		SW
Guildford	d								10 58	11 08									11 28	11 38					
London Road (Guildford)	d								11 02	11 12									11 32	11 42					
Clandon	d								11 07	11 17									11 37	11 47					
Horsley	d								11 11	11 21									11 41	11 51					
Effingham Junction 6	d								11 16	11 24									11 46	11 54					
Bookham	d								11 19										11 49						
Cobham & Stoke d'Abernon	d									11 28										11 58					
Oxshott	d									11 31										12 01					
Claygate	d									11 34										12 04					
Hinchley Wood	d									11 37										12 07					
Hampton Court	d						11 24										11 54								
Thames Ditton	d						11 26										11 56								
Surbiton 6	d				11 27		11 32			11 42					11 57		12 02			12 12					12 27
Berrylands	d						11 34										12 04								
Shepperton	d							11 11										11 41							
Upper Halliford	d							11 14										11 44							
Sunbury	d							11 16										11 46							
Kempton Park	d							11 18										11 48							
Hampton	d							11 21										11 51							
Fulwell	d							11 24										11 54							
Strawberry Hill	d		11 07										11 37										12 07		
Teddington	d		11 11					11 29					11 41					11 59					12 11		
Hampton Wick	d		11 14					11 31					11 44					12 01					12 14		
Kingston	a		11 16					11 33					11 46					12 03					12 16		
	d		11 19					11 34					11 49					12 04					12 19		
Norbiton	d		11 21					11 36					11 51					12 06					12 21		
New Malden 6	d		11 25				11 37	11 40					11 55				12 07	12 10					12 25		
Dorking 4	d					11 05										11 35									
Box Hill & Westhumble	d																								
Leatherhead	d					11 11			11 24							11 41			11 54						
Ashtead	d					11 14			11 28							11 44			11 58						
Epsom 3	a					11 19			11 32							11 49			12 02						
	d					11 20			11 35							11 50			12 05						
Ewell West	d					11 23			11 38							11 53			12 08						
Stoneleigh	d					11 25			11 40							11 55			12 10						
Worcester Park	d					11 28			11 43							11 58			12 13						
Chessington South	d										11 40										12 10				
Chessington North	d										11 42										12 12				
Tolworth	d										11 44										12 14				
Malden Manor	d										11 47										12 17				
Motspur Park	d					11 31			11 46		11 50					12 01			12 16		12 20				
Raynes Park 6	d		11 28			11 34	11 40	11 43	11 49		11 53		11 58			12 04	12 10	12 13	12 19		12 23		12 28		
Wimbledon 6 ⊖	d		11 32		11 35	11 38	11 44	11 47	11 53	11 50	11 57		12 02		12 05	12 08	12 14	12 17	12 23	12 20	12 27		12 32		12 35
Earlsfield	d		11 35		11 38	11 42	11 47	11 50	11 57	11 54	12 01		12 05		12 08	12 12	12 17	12 20	12 27	12 24	12 31		12 35		12 38
Clapham Junction 10	d		11 39		11 42	11 46	11 51	11 54	12 01	11 58	12 05		12 09		12 12	12 16	12 21	12 24	12 31	12 28	12 35		12 39		12 42
Vauxhall ⊖	d		11 44		11 47	11 51	11 56	11 59	12 06	12 03	12 10		12 14		12 17	12 21	12 26	12 29	12 36	12 33	12 40		12 44		12 47
London Waterloo 15 ⊖	a		11 49		11 52	11 55	12 01	12 04	12 10	12 07	12 15		12 19		12 22	12 25	12 31	12 34	12 40	12 37	12 45		12 49		12 52

Hampton Court, Shepperton, Guildford, Dorking and Chessington South - London

Network Diagram - see first Page of Table 152

		SW	SW	SW	SW	SW	SW	SW	SW	SW	SW	SW 1	SW	SW	SW	SW	SW	SW	SW	SW	SW
Guildford	d				11 58	12 08								12 28	12 38						
London Road (Guildford)	d				12 02	12 12								12 32	12 42						
Clandon	d				12 07	12 17								12 37	12 47						
Horsley	d				12 11	12 21								12 41	12 51						
Effingham Junction 6	d				12 16	12 24								12 46	12 54						
Bookham	d				12 19									12 49							
Cobham & Stoke d'Abernon	d					12 28									12 58						
Oxshott	d					12 31									13 01						
Claygate	d					12 34									13 04						
Hinchley Wood	d					12 37									13 07						
Hampton Court	d		12 24								12 54									13 24	
Thames Ditton	d		12 26								12 56									13 26	
Surbiton 6	d		12 32			12 42			12 57		13 02	13 08			13 12			13 27		13 32	
Berrylands	d		12 34								13 04									13 34	
Shepperton	d			12 11									12 41								13 11
Upper Halliford	d			12 14									12 44								13 14
Sunbury	d			12 16									12 46								13 16
Kempton Park	d			12 18									12 48								13 18
Hampton	d			12 21									12 51								13 21
Fulwell	d			12 24									12 54								13 24
Strawberry Hill	d							12 37									13 07				
Teddington	d			12 29				12 41					12 59				13 11				13 29
Hampton Wick	d			12 31				12 44					13 01				13 14				13 31
Kingston	a			12 33				12 46					13 03				13 16				13 33
	d			12 34				12 49					13 04				13 19				13 34
Norbiton	d			12 36				12 51					13 06				13 21				13 36
New Malden 6	d		12 37	12 40				12 55			13 07		13 10				13 25			13 37	13 40
Dorking 4	d	12 05								12 35									13 05		
Box Hill & Westhumble	d																				
Leatherhead	d	12 11			12 24					12 41				12 54					13 11		
Ashtead	d	12 14			12 28					12 44				12 58					13 14		
Epsom 3	a	12 19			12 32					12 49				13 02					13 19		
	d	12 20			12 35					12 50				13 05					13 20		
Ewell West	d	12 23			12 38					12 53				13 08					13 23		
Stoneleigh	d	12 25			12 40					12 55				13 10					13 25		
Worcester Park	d	12 28			12 43					12 58				13 13					13 28		
Chessington South	d						12 40									13 10					
Chessington North	d						12 42									13 12					
Tolworth	d						12 44									13 14					
Malden Manor	d						12 47									13 17					
Motspur Park	d	12 31			12 46		12 50			13 01				13 16		13 20			13 31		
Raynes Park 6	d	12 34	12 40	12 43	12 49		12 53	12 58		13 04	13 10		13 13	13 19		13 23	13 28		13 34	13 40	13 43
Wimbledon 6 ⊖ 🚋	d	12 38	12 44	12 47	12 53	12 50	12 57	13 02	13 05	13 08	13 14		13 17	13 23	13 20	13 27	13 32	13 35	13 38	13 44	13 47
Earlsfield	d	12 42	12 47	12 50	12 57	12 54	13 01	13 05	13 08	13 12	13 17		13 20	13 27	13 24	13 31	13 35	13 38	13 42	13 47	13 50
Clapham Junction 10	d	12 46	12 51	12 54	13 01	12 58	13 05	13 09	13 12	13 16	13 21		13 24	13 31	13 28	13 35	13 39	13 42	13 46	13 51	13 54
Vauxhall ⊖	d	12 51	12 56	12 59	13 06	13 03	13 10	13 14	13 17	13 21	13 26		13 29	13 36	13 33	13 40	13 44	13 47	13 51	13 56	13 59
London Waterloo 15 ⊖	a	12 55	13 01	13 04	13 10	13 07	13 15	13 19	13 22	13 25	13 31	13 25	13 34	13 40	13 37	13 45	13 49	13 52	13 55	14 01	14 04

Hampton Court, Shepperton, Guildford, Dorking and Chessington South - London

Network Diagram - see first Page of Table 152

		SW	SW		SW	SW		SW	SW	SW	SW	SW	SW		SW	SW		SW	SW	SW	SW	SW	SW		SW
Guildford	d	12 58	13 08									13 28	13 38									13 58	14 08		
London Road (Guildford)	d	13 02	13 12									13 32	13 42									14 02	14 12		
Clandon	d	13 07	13 17									13 37	13 47									14 07	14 17		
Horsley	d	13 11	13 21									13 41	13 51									14 11	14 21		
Effingham Junction 6	d	13 16	13 24									13 46	13 54									14 16	14 24		
Bookham	d	13 19										13 49										14 19			
Cobham & Stoke d'Abernon	d		13 28										13 58										14 28		
Oxshott	d		13 31										14 01										14 31		
Claygate	d		13 34										14 04										14 34		
Hinchley Wood	d		13 37										14 07										14 37		
Hampton Court	d									13 54										14 24					
Thames Ditton	d									13 56										14 26					
Surbiton 6	d		13 42					13 57		14 02			14 12					14 27		14 32			14 42		
Berrylands	d									14 04										14 34					
Shepperton	d										13 41										14 11				
Upper Halliford	d										13 44										14 14				
Sunbury	d										13 46										14 16				
Kempton Park	d										13 48										14 18				
Hampton	d										13 51										14 21				
Fulwell	d										13 54										14 24				
Strawberry Hill	d					13 37										14 07									
Teddington	d					13 41					13 59					14 11					14 29				
Hampton Wick	d					13 44					14 01					14 14					14 31				
Kingston	a					13 46					14 03					14 16					14 33				
	d					13 49					14 04					14 19					14 34				
Norbiton	d					13 51					14 06					14 21					14 36				
New Malden 6	d					13 55				14 07	14 10					14 25				14 37	14 40				
Dorking 4	d								13 35										14 05						
Box Hill & Westhumble	d																								
Leatherhead	d	13 24							13 41			13 54							14 11			14 24			
Ashtead	d	13 28							13 44			13 58							14 14			14 28			
Epsom 3	a	13 32							13 49			14 02							14 19			14 32			
	d	13 35							13 50			14 05							14 20			14 35			
Ewell West	d	13 38							13 53			14 08							14 23			14 38			
Stoneleigh	d	13 40							13 55			14 10							14 25			14 40			
Worcester Park	d	13 43							13 58			14 13							14 28			14 43			
Chessington South	d				13 40										14 10										14 40
Chessington North	d				13 42										14 12										14 42
Tolworth	d				13 44										14 14										14 44
Malden Manor	d				13 47										14 17										14 47
Motspur Park	d	13 46			13 50				14 01			14 16			14 20				14 31			14 46			14 50
Raynes Park 6	d	13 49			13 53	13 58			14 04	14 10	14 13	14 19			14 23	14 28			14 34	14 40	14 43	14 49			14 53
Wimbledon 6 ⊖	d	13 53	13 50		13 57	14 02		14 05	14 08	14 14	14 17	14 23	14 20		14 27	14 32		14 35	14 38	14 44	14 47	14 53	14 50		14 57
Earlsfield	d	13 57	13 54		14 01	14 05		14 08	14 12	14 17	14 20	14 27	14 24		14 31	14 35		14 38	14 42	14 47	14 50	14 57	14 54		15 01
Clapham Junction 10	d	14 01	13 58		14 05	14 09		14 12	14 16	14 21	14 24	14 31	14 28		14 35	14 39		14 42	14 46	14 51	14 54	15 01	14 58		15 05
Vauxhall ⊖	d	14 06	14 03		14 10	14 14		14 17	14 21	14 26	14 29	14 36	14 33		14 40	14 44		14 47	14 51	14 56	14 59	15 06	15 03		15 10
London Waterloo 15 ⊖	a	14 10	14 07		14 15	14 19		14 22	14 25	14 31	14 34	14 40	14 37		14 45	14 49		14 52	14 55	15 01	15 04	15 10	15 07		15 15

		SW		SW	SW	SW	SW	SW	SW		SW	SW		SW	SW	SW	SW	SW	SW		SW	SW		SW	SW
Guildford	d							14 28	14 38									14 58	15 08						
London Road (Guildford)	d							14 32	14 42									15 02	15 12						
Clandon	d							14 37	14 47									15 07	15 17						
Horsley	d							14 41	14 51									15 11	15 21						
Effingham Junction 6	d							14 46	14 54									15 16	15 24						
Bookham	d							14 49										15 19							
Cobham & Stoke d'Abernon	d								14 58										15 28						
Oxshott	d								15 01										15 31						
Claygate	d								15 04										15 34						
Hinchley Wood	d								15 07										15 37						
Hampton Court	d					14 54										15 24									
Thames Ditton	d					14 56										15 26									
Surbiton 6	d			14 57		15 02			15 12					15 27		15 32			15 42					15 57	
Berrylands	d					15 04										15 34									
Shepperton	d						14 41										15 11								
Upper Halliford	d						14 44										15 14								
Sunbury	d						14 46										15 16								
Kempton Park	d						14 48										15 18								
Hampton	d						14 51										15 21								
Fulwell	d						14 54										15 24								
Strawberry Hill	d	14 37										15 07										15 37			
Teddington	d	14 41					14 59					15 11					15 29					15 41			
Hampton Wick	d	14 44					15 01					15 14					15 31					15 44			
Kingston	a	14 46					15 03					15 16					15 33					15 46			
	d	14 49					15 04					15 19					15 34					15 49			
Norbiton	d	14 51					15 06					15 21					15 36					15 51			
New Malden 6	d	14 55				15 07	15 10					15 25				15 37	15 40					15 55			
Dorking 4	d				14 35										15 05										15 35
Box Hill & Westhumble	d																								
Leatherhead	d				14 41			14 54							15 11			15 24							15 41
Ashtead	d				14 44			14 58							15 14			15 28							15 44
Epsom 3	a				14 49			15 02							15 19			15 32							15 49
	d				14 50			15 05							15 20			15 35							15 50
Ewell West	d				14 53			15 08							15 23			15 38							15 53
Stoneleigh	d				14 55			15 10							15 25			15 40							15 55
Worcester Park	d				14 58			15 13							15 28			15 43							15 58
Chessington South	d										15 10										15 40				
Chessington North	d										15 12										15 42				
Tolworth	d										15 14										15 44				
Malden Manor	d										15 17										15 47				
Motspur Park	d				15 01			15 16			15 20				15 31			15 46			15 50				16 01
Raynes Park 6	d	14 58			15 04	15 10	15 13	15 19			15 23	15 28			15 34	15 40	15 43	15 49			15 53	15 58			16 04
Wimbledon 6 ⊖	d	15 02		15 05	15 08	15 14	15 17	15 23	15 20		15 27	15 32		15 35	15 38	15 44	15 47	15 53	15 50		15 57	16 02		16 05	16 08
Earlsfield	d	15 05		15 08	15 12	15 17	15 20	15 27	15 24		15 31	15 35		15 38	15 42	15 47	15 50	15 57	15 54		16 01	16 05		16 08	16 12
Clapham Junction 10	d	15 09		15 12	15 16	15 21	15 24	15 31	15 28		15 35	15 39		15 42	15 46	15 51	15 54	16 01	15 58		16 05	16 09		16 12	16 16
Vauxhall ⊖	d	15 14		15 17	15 21	15 26	15 29	15 36	15 33		15 40	15 44		15 47	15 51	15 56	15 59	16 06	16 03		16 10	16 14		16 17	16 21
London Waterloo 15 ⊖	a	15 19		15 22	15 25	15 31	15 34	15 40	15 37		15 45	15 49		15 52	15 55	16 01	16 04	16 10	16 07		16 15	16 19		16 22	16 25

Hampton Court, Shepperton, Guildford, Dorking and Chessington South - London

Network Diagram - see first Page of Table 152

Station		SW	SW	SW	SW		SW	SW		SW	SW	SW	SW	SW	SW		SW	SW		SW	SW	SW	SW	SW	SW
Guildford	d			15 28	15 38									15 58	16 08									16 28	16 38
London Road (Guildford)	d			15 32	15 42									16 02	16 12									16 32	16 42
Clandon	d			15 37	15 47									16 07	16 17									16 37	16 47
Horsley	d			15 41	15 51									16 11	16 21									16 41	16 51
Effingham Junction 6	d			15 46	15 54									16 16	16 24									16 46	16 54
Bookham	d			15 49										16 19										16 49	
Cobham & Stoke d'Abernon	d				15 58										16 28										16 58
Oxshott	d				16 01										16 31										17 01
Claygate	d				16 04										16 34										17 04
Hinchley Wood	d				16 07										16 37										17 07
Hampton Court	d	15 54										16 24										16 54			
Thames Ditton	d	15 56										16 26										16 56			
Surbiton 6	d	16 02			16 12					16 27		16 32			16 42					16 57		17 02			17 12
Berrylands	d	16 04										16 34										17 04			
Shepperton	d		15 41										16 11										16 41		
Upper Halliford	d		15 44										16 14										16 44		
Sunbury	d		15 46										16 16										16 46		
Kempton Park	d		15 48										16 18										16 48		
Hampton	d		15 51										16 21										16 51		
Fulwell	d		15 54										16 24										16 54		
Strawberry Hill	d							16 07										16 37							
Teddington	d		15 59					16 11					16 29					16 43					16 59		
Hampton Wick	d		16 01					16 14					16 31					16 46					17 01		
Kingston	a		16 03					16 16					16 33					16 48					17 03		
	d		16 04					16 19					16 34					16 49					17 04		
Norbiton	d		16 06					16 21					16 36					16 51					17 06		
New Malden 6	d	16 07	16 10					16 25				16 37	16 40					16 55				17 07	17 10		
Dorking 4	d										16 05										16 35				
Box Hill & Westhumble	d																								
Leatherhead	d			15 54							16 11			16 24							16 41			16 54	
Ashtead	d			15 58							16 14			16 28							16 44			16 58	
Epsom 3	a			16 02							16 19			16 32							16 49			17 02	
	d			16 05							16 20			16 35							16 50			17 05	
Ewell West	d			16 08							16 23			16 38							16 53			17 08	
Stoneleigh	d			16 10							16 25			16 40							16 55			17 10	
Worcester Park	d			16 13							16 28			16 43							16 58			17 13	
Chessington South	d						16 10										16 40								
Chessington North	d						16 12										16 42								
Tolworth	d						16 14										16 44								
Malden Manor	d						16 17										16 47								
Motspur Park	d			16 16			16 20				16 31			16 46			16 50				17 01			17 16	
Raynes Park 6	d	16 10	16 13	16 19			16 23	16 28			16 34	16 40	16 43	16 49			16 53	16 58			17 04	17 10	17 13	17 19	
Wimbledon 6 ⊖ ⛴	d	16 14	16 17	16 23	16 20		16 27	16 32		16 35	16 38	16 44	16 47	16 53	16 50		16 57	17 02		17 05	17 08	17 14	17 17	17 23	17 20
Earlsfield	d	16 17	16 20	16 27	16 24		16 31	16 35		16 38	16 42	16 47	16 50	16 57	16 54		17 01	17 05		17 08	17 12	17 17	17 20	17 27	17 24
Clapham Junction 10	d	16 21	16 24	16 31	16 28		16 35	16 39		16 42	16 46	16 51	16 54	17 01	16 58		17 05	17 09		17 12	17 16	17 21	17 24	17 31	17 28
Vauxhall ⊖	d	16 26	16 29	16 36	16 33		16 40	16 44		16 47	16 51	16 56	16 59	17 06	17 03		17 10	17 14		17 17	17 21	17 26	17 29	17 36	17 33
London Waterloo 15 ⊖	a	16 31	16 34	16 40	16 37		16 45	16 49		16 52	16 55	17 01	17 05	17 10	17 07		17 16	17 19		17 22	17 25	17 31	17 35	17 40	17 37

Hampton Court, Shepperton, Guildford, Dorking and Chessington South - London

Network Diagram - see first Page of Table 152

			SW	SW		SW	SW	SW	SW	SW	SW		SW	SW		SW	SW	SW	SW	SW	SW		SW	SW	SW
Guildford	d									16 58	17 08										17 28		17 38		
London Road (Guildford)	d									17 02	17 12										17 32		17 42		
Clandon	d									17 07	17 17										17 37		17 47		
Horsley	d									17 11	17 21										17 41		17 51		
Effingham Junction 6	d									17 16	17 24										17 46		17 54		
Bookham	d									17 19											17 49				
Cobham & Stoke d'Abernon	d										17 28												17 58		
Oxshott	d										17 31												18 01		
Claygate	d										17 34												18 04		
Hinchley Wood	d										17 37												18 07		
Hampton Court	d							17 24											17 54						
Thames Ditton	d							17 26											17 56						
Surbiton 6	d					17 27		17 32			17 42					17 57			18 02				18 12		
Berrylands	d							17 34											18 04						
Shepperton	d								17 11											17 41					
Upper Halliford	d								17 14											17 44					
Sunbury	d								17 16											17 46					
Kempton Park	d								17 18											17 48					
Hampton	d								17 21											17 51					
Fulwell	d								17 24											17 54					
Strawberry Hill	d			17 07										17 37				17 41							18 07
Teddington	d			17 13					17 29					17 43				17 52		17 59					18 13
Hampton Wick	d			17 16					17 31					17 46				17 54		18 01					18 16
Kingston	a			17 18					17 33					17 48				17 56		18 03					18 18
	d			17 19					17 34					17 49				17 58		18 04					18 19
Norbiton	d			17 21					17 36					17 51				18 00		18 06					18 21
New Malden 6	d			17 25				17 37	17 40					17 55				18 04	18 07	18 10					18 25
Dorking 4	d						17 05										17 35								
Box Hill & Westhumble	d																								
Leatherhead	d						17 11			17 24							17 41				17 54				
Ashtead	d						17 14			17 28							17 45				17 58				
Epsom 3	a						17 19			17 32							17 49				18 02				
	d						17 20			17 35							17 50				18 05				
Ewell West	d						17 23			17 38							17 53				18 08				
Stoneleigh	d						17 25			17 40							17 55				18 10				
Worcester Park	d						17 28			17 43							17 58				18 13				
Chessington South	d		17 10										17 40											18 10	
Chessington North	d		17 12										17 42											18 12	
Tolworth	d		17 14										17 44											18 14	
Malden Manor	d		17 17										17 47											18 17	
Motspur Park	d		17 20				17 31			17 46			17 50				18 01				18 16			18 20	
Raynes Park 6	d		17 23	17 28			17 34	17 40	17 43	17 49			17 53	17 58			18 04	18 07	18 10	18 13	18 19			18 23	18 28
Wimbledon 6 ⊖ ⛴	d		17 27	17 32		17 35	17 38	17 44	17 47	17 53	17 50		17 57	18 02		18 05	18 08	18 11	18 14	18 17	18 23		18 20	18 27	18 32
Earlsfield	d		17 31	17 35		17 38	17 42	17 47	17 50	17 57	17 54		18 01	18 05		18 08	18 12	18 15	18 17	18 20	18 27		18 24	18 31	18 35
Clapham Junction 10	d		17 35	17 39		17 42	17 46	17 51	17 54	18 01	17 58		18 05	18 09		18 12	18 16	18 19	18 21	18 24	18 31		18 28	18 35	18 39
Vauxhall ⊖	d		17 40	17 44		17 47	17 51	17 56	17 59	18 06	18 03		18 10	18 14		18 17	18 21	18 24	18 26	18 29	18 36		18 33	18 40	18 44
London Waterloo 15 ⊖	a		17 45	17 49		17 52	17 55	18 01	18 05	18 10	18 07		18 15	18 19		18 23	18 25	18 29	18 31	18 35	18 40		18 37	18 47	18 49

Hampton Court, Shepperton, Guildford, Dorking and Chessington South - London

Network Diagram - see first Page of Table 152

		SW	SW	SW	SW	SW	SW	SW	SW	SW	SW	SW	SW	SW	SW	SW	SW	SW	SW	SW
Guildford	d					17 58	18 08							18 38						
London Road (Guildford)	d					18 02	18 12							18 42						
Clandon	d					18 07	18 17							18 47						
Horsley	d					18 11	18 21							18 51						
Effingham Junction 6	d					18 16	18 24							18 54					18 59	
Bookham	d					18 19													19 02	
Cobham & Stoke d'Abernon	d						18 28							18 58						
Oxshott	d						18 31							19 01						
Claygate	d						18 34							19 04						
Hinchley Wood	d						18 37							19 07						
Hampton Court	d			18 24								18 54								19 24
Thames Ditton	d			18 26								18 56								19 26
Surbiton 6	d	18 27		18 32			18 42			18 57		19 02		19 12				19 27		19 32
Berrylands	d			18 34								19 04								19 34
Shepperton	d				18 11								18 36							
Upper Halliford	d				18 14								18 39							
Sunbury	d				18 16								18 41							
Kempton Park	d				18 18								18 43							
Hampton	d				18 21								18 51							
Fulwell	d				18 24								18 54							
Strawberry Hill	d								18 37								19 07			
Teddington	d				18 29				18 43				18 59				19 13			
Hampton Wick	d				18 31				18 46				19 01				19 16			
Kingston	a				18 33				18 48				19 03				19 18			
	d				18 34				18 49				19 04				19 19			
Norbiton	d				18 36				18 51				19 06				19 21			
New Malden 6	d			18 37	18 40				18 55			19 07	19 10				19 25			19 37
Dorking 4	d		18 05								18 35				18 50					
Box Hill & Westhumble	d																			
Leatherhead	d		18 11			18 24					18 41				18 56				19 08	
Ashtead	d		18 14			18 28					18 45				18 59				19 12	
Epsom 3	a		18 19			18 32					18 49				19 04				19 16	
	d		18 20			18 35					18 50				19 05				19 20	
Ewell West	d		18 23			18 38					18 53				19 08				19 23	
Stoneleigh	d		18 25			18 40					18 55				19 10				19 25	
Worcester Park	d		18 28			18 43					18 58				19 13				19 28	
Chessington South	d							18 40								19 10				
Chessington North	d							18 42								19 12				
Tolworth	d							18 44								19 14				
Malden Manor	d							18 47								19 17				
Motspur Park	d		18 31			18 46		18 50			19 01				19 16	19 20			19 31	
Raynes Park 6	d		18 34	18 40	18 43	18 49		18 53	18 58		19 04	19 10	19 13		19 19	19 23	19 28		19 34	19 40
Wimbledon 6 ⊖ ⛴	d	18 35	18 38	18 44	18 47	18 53	18 50	18 57	19 02	19 05	19 08	19 14	19 17	19 20	19 23	19 27	19 32	19 35	19 38	19 44
Earlsfield	d	18 38	18 42	18 47	18 50	18 57	18 54	19 01	19 05	19 08	19 12	19 17	19 20	19 24	19 27	19 31	19 35	19 38	19 42	19 47
Clapham Junction 10	d	18 42	18 46	18 51	18 54	19 01	18 58	19 05	19 09	19 12	19 16	19 21	19 24	19 28	19 31	19 35	19 39	19 42	19 46	19 51
Vauxhall ⊖	d	18 47	18 51	18 56	18 59	19 06	19 03	19 10	19 14	19 17	19 21	19 26	19 29	19 33	19 36	19 40	19 44	19 47	19 51	19 56
London Waterloo 15 ⊖	a	18 52	18 55	19 01	19 05	19 10	19 07	19 14	19 19	19 23	19 27	19 31	19 34	19 37	19 41	19 45	19 49	19 52	19 55	20 01

Table 152

Mondays to Fridays

Hampton Court, Shepperton, Guildford, Dorking and Chessington South - London

Network Diagram - see first Page of Table 152

		SW	SW	SW	SW	SW	SW	SW	SW	SW	SW	SW	SW	SW	SW	SW	SW	SW	SW	SW
Guildford	d		19 08								19 28	19 38							19 58	20 08
London Road (Guildford)	d		19 12								19 32	19 42							20 02	20 12
Clandon	d		19 17								19 37	19 47							20 07	20 17
Horsley	d		19 21								19 41	19 51							20 11	20 21
Effingham Junction 6	d		19 25								19 46	19 54							20 16	20 24
Bookham	d										19 49								20 19	
Cobham & Stoke d'Abernon	d		19 28									19 58								20 28
Oxshott	d		19 32									20 01								20 31
Claygate	d		19 35									20 04								20 34
Hinchley Wood	d		19 37									20 07								20 37
Hampton Court	d								19 54								20 24			
Thames Ditton	d								19 56								20 26			
Surbiton 6	d		19 42				19 57		20 02			20 12			20 27		20 32			20 42
Berrylands	d								20 04								20 34			
Shepperton	d	19 06								19 41								20 11		
Upper Halliford	d	19 09								19 44								20 14		
Sunbury	d	19 11								19 46								20 16		
Kempton Park	d	19 13								19 48								20 18		
Hampton	d	19 21								19 51								20 21		
Fulwell	d	19 24								19 54								20 24		
Strawberry Hill	d					19 37								20 07						
Teddington	d	19 29				19 43				19 59				20 11				20 29		
Hampton Wick	d	19 31				19 46				20 01				20 14				20 31		
Kingston	a	19 33				19 48				20 04				20 16				20 33		
	d	19 34				19 49				20 04				20 19				20 34		
Norbiton	d	19 36				19 51				20 06				20 21				20 36		
New Malden 6	d	19 40				19 55			20 07	20 10				20 25			20 37	20 40		
Dorking 4	d							19 33								20 05				
Box Hill & Westhumble	d																			
Leatherhead	d							19 39			19 54					20 11			20 24	
Ashtead	d							19 42			19 58					20 14			20 28	
Epsom 3	a							19 47			20 02					20 19			20 32	
	d			19 35				19 50			20 05					20 20			20 35	
Ewell West	d			19 38				19 53			20 08					20 23			20 38	
Stoneleigh	d			19 40				19 55			20 10					20 25			20 40	
Worcester Park	d			19 43				19 58			20 13					20 28			20 43	
Chessington South	d				19 40								20 10							
Chessington North	d				19 42								20 12							
Tolworth	d				19 44								20 14							
Malden Manor	d				19 47								20 17							
Motspur Park	d			19 46	19 50			20 01			20 16		20 20			20 31			20 46	
Raynes Park 6	d	19 43		19 49	19 53	19 58		20 04	20 10	20 13	20 19		20 23	20 28		20 34	20 40	20 43	20 49	
Wimbledon 6 ⊖	d	19 47	19 50	19 53	19 57	20 02	20 05	20 08	20 14	20 17	20 23	20 20	20 27	20 32	20 35	20 38	20 44	20 47	20 53	20 50
Earlsfield	d	19 50	19 54	19 57	20 01	20 05	20 08	20 12	20 17	20 20	20 27	20 24	20 31	20 35	20 38	20 42	20 47	20 50	20 57	20 54
Clapham Junction 10	d	19 54	19 58	20 01	20 05	20 09	20 12	20 16	20 21	20 24	20 31	20 28	20 35	20 39	20 42	20 46	20 51	20 54	21 01	20 58
Vauxhall ⊖	d	19 59	20 03	20 06	20 10	20 14	20 17	20 21	20 26	20 29	20 36	20 33	20 40	20 44	20 47	20 51	20 56	20 59	21 06	21 03
London Waterloo 15 ⊖	a	20 04	20 07	20 10	20 15	20 19	20 22	20 25	20 31	20 35	20 41	20 38	20 46	20 49	20 52	20 55	21 01	21 04	21 10	21 07

Hampton Court, Shepperton, Guildford, Dorking and Chessington South - London

Network Diagram - see first Page of Table 152

		SW	SW		SW	SW	SW	SW	SW		SW	SW	SW		SW	SW	SW	SW	SW		SW	SW	SW		SW
Guildford	d								20 38							20 46			21 08						
London Road (Guildford)	d								20 42							20 50			21 12						
Clandon	d								20 47							20 55			21 17						
Horsley	d								20 51							20 59			21 21						
Effingham Junction [6]	d								20 54							21 03			21 24						
Bookham	d															21 06									
Cobham & Stoke d'Abernon	d								20 58										21 28						
Oxshott	d								21 01										21 31						
Claygate	d								21 04										21 34						
Hinchley Wood	d								21 07										21 37						
Hampton Court	d						20 54										21 24								
Thames Ditton	d						20 56										21 26								
Surbiton [6]	d				20 57		21 02		21 12						21 27		21 32		21 42						21 57
Berrylands	d						21 04										21 34								
Shepperton	d							20 41										21 11							
Upper Halliford	d							20 44										21 14							
Sunbury	d							20 46										21 16							
Kempton Park	d							20 48										21 18							
Hampton	d							20 51										21 21							
Fulwell	d							20 54										21 24							
Strawberry Hill	d		20 37										21 07										21 37		
Teddington	d		20 41					20 59					21 11					21 29					21 41		
Hampton Wick	d		20 44					21 01					21 14					21 31					21 44		
Kingston	a		20 46					21 03					21 16					21 33					21 46		
	d		20 49					21 04					21 19					21 34					21 49		
Norbiton	d		20 51					21 06					21 21					21 36					21 51		
New Malden [6]	d		20 55				21 07	21 10					21 25				21 37	21 40					21 55		
Dorking [4]	d					20 35																			
Box Hill & Westhumble	d																								
Leatherhead	d					20 41										21 11									
Ashtead	d					20 44										21 14									
Epsom [3]	a					20 49										21 19									
	d					20 50					21 05					21 20					21 35				
Ewell West	d					20 53					21 08					21 23					21 38				
Stoneleigh	d					20 55					21 10					21 25					21 40				
Worcester Park	d					20 58					21 13					21 28					21 43				
Chessington South	d	20 40										21 10										21 40			
Chessington North	d	20 42										21 12										21 42			
Tolworth	d	20 44										21 14										21 44			
Malden Manor	d	20 47										21 17										21 47			
Motspur Park	d	20 50				21 01					21 16	21 20				21 31					21 46	21 50			
Raynes Park [6]	d	20 53	20 58			21 04	21 10	21 13			21 19	21 23	21 28			21 34	21 40	21 43			21 49	21 53	21 58		
Wimbledon [6] ⊖	d	20 57	21 02		21 05	21 08	21 14	21 17	21 20		21 23	21 27	21 32		21 35	21 38	21 44	21 47	21 50		21 53	21 57	22 02		22 05
Earlsfield	d	21 01	21 05		21 08	21 12	21 17	21 20	21 24		21 27	21 31	21 35		21 38	21 42	21 47	21 50	21 54		21 57	22 01	22 05		22 08
Clapham Junction [10]	d	21 05	21 09		21 12	21 16	21 21	21 24	21 28		21 31	21 35	21 39		21 42	21 46	21 51	21 54	21 58		22 01	22 05	22 09		22 12
Vauxhall ⊖	d	21 10	21 14		21 17	21 21	21 26	21 29	21 33		21 36	21 40	21 44		21 47	21 51	21 56	21 59	22 03		22 06	22 10	22 14		22 17
London Waterloo [15] ⊖	a	21 15	21 19		21 22	21 25	21 31	21 34	21 37		21 40	21 45	21 49		21 52	21 55	22 01	22 04	22 07		22 10	22 16	22 19		22 22

		SW	SW	SW	SW			SW	SW	SW	SW	SW	SW	SW			SW	SW	SW	SW	SW		SW	SW	SW
Guildford	d			21 38					21 46			22 08					22 20			22 38			22 46	22 55	
London Road (Guildford)	d			21 42					21 50			22 12								22 42			22 50		
Clandon	d			21 47					21 55			22 17								22 47			22 55		
Horsley	d			21 51					21 59			22 21								22 51			22 59		
Effingham Junction [6]	d			21 54					22 03			22 24								22 54			23 03		
Bookham	d								22 06														23 06		
Cobham & Stoke d'Abernon	d			21 58								22 28								22 58					
Oxshott	d			22 01								22 31								23 01					
Claygate	d			22 04								22 34								23 04					
Hinchley Wood	d			22 07								22 37								23 07					
Hampton Court	d									22 24															23 24
Thames Ditton	d									22 26															23 26
Surbiton [6]	d			22 12				22 27		22 32		22 42					22 57			23 12				23 30	23 33
Berrylands	d									22 34															23 35
Shepperton	d		21 41								22 11								22 41						
Upper Halliford	d		21 44								22 14								22 44						
Sunbury	d		21 46								22 16								22 46						
Kempton Park	d		21 48								22 18								22 48						
Hampton	d		21 51								22 21								22 51						
Fulwell	d		21 54								22 24								22 54						
Strawberry Hill	d				22 07									22 37							23 07				
Teddington	d		21 59		22 11						22 29			22 41					22 59		23 11				
Hampton Wick	d		22 01		22 14						22 31			22 44					23 01		23 14				
Kingston	a		22 03		22 16						22 33			22 46					23 03		23 16				
	d		22 04		22 19						22 34			22 49					23 04		23 19				
Norbiton	d		22 06		22 21						22 36			22 51					23 06		23 21				
New Malden [6]	d		22 10		22 25					22 37	22 40			22 55					23 10		23 25				23 38
Dorking [4]	d	21 35																22 35							
Box Hill & Westhumble	d																								
Leatherhead	d	21 41							22 11									22 41					23 11		
Ashtead	d	21 44							22 14									22 44					23 14		
Epsom [3]	a	21 49							22 19									22 49					23 19		
	d	21 50							22 20									22 50					23 20		
Ewell West	d	21 53							22 23									22 53					23 23		
Stoneleigh	d	21 55							22 25									22 55					23 25		
Worcester Park	d	21 58							22 28									22 58					23 28		
Chessington South	d												22 40												
Chessington North	d												22 42												
Tolworth	d												22 44												
Malden Manor	d												22 47												
Motspur Park	d	22 01							22 31				22 50					23 01					23 31		
Raynes Park [6]	d	22 04	22 13		22 28				22 34	22 40	22 43		22 53	22 58				23 04	23 13		23 28		23 37		23 41
Wimbledon [6] ⊖	d	22 08	22 17	22 20	22 32			22 35	22 38	22 44	22 47	22 50	22 57	23 02			23 05	23 08	23 17	23 20	23 32		23 41	23 37	23a45
Earlsfield	d	22 12	22 20	22 24	22 35			22 38	22 42	22 47	22 50	22 54	23 01	23 05			23 08	23 12	23 20	23 24	23 36		23 44	23 41	
Clapham Junction [10]	d	22 16	22 24	22 28	22 39			22 42	22 46	22 51	22 54	22 58	23 05	23 09			23 12	23 16	23 24	23 28	23 40		23 48	23 45	
Vauxhall ⊖	d	22 21	22 29	22 33	22 44			22 47	22 51	22 56	22 59	23 03	23 10	23 14			23 17	23 21	23 29	23 33	23 45		23 53	23 50	
London Waterloo [15] ⊖	a	22 25	22 34	22 39	22 49			22 52	22 55	23 01	23 04	23 07	23 15	23 19			23 23	23 27	23 34	23 37	23 49		23 58	23 54	

Table 152

Mondays to Fridays

Hampton Court, Shepperton, Guildford, Dorking and Chessington South - London

Network Diagram - see first Page of Table 152

		SW	SW	SN	SW	SW
Guildford	d		23 08			
London Road (Guildford)	d		23 12			
Clandon	d		23 17			
Horsley	d		23 21			
Effingham Junction 6	d		23 24			
Bookham	d					
Cobham & Stoke d'Abernon	d		23 28			
Oxshott	d		23 31			
Claygate	d		23 34			
Hinchley Wood	d		23 37			
Hampton Court	d					
Thames Ditton	d					
Surbiton 6	d		23 42			
Berrylands	d					
Shepperton	d	23 11				
Upper Halliford	d	23 14				
Sunbury	d	23 16				
Kempton Park	d	23 18				
Hampton	d	23 21				
Fulwell	d	23 24				
Strawberry Hill	d					23 37
Teddington	d	23 29				23 41
Hampton Wick	d	23 31				23 44
Kingston	a	23 33				23 46
	d	23 34				23 49
Norbiton	d	23 36				23 51
New Malden 6	d	23 41				23 55
Dorking 4	d			23 30		
Box Hill & Westhumble	d					
Leatherhead	d			23 36		
Ashtead	d			23 39		
Epsom 3	a			23 45		
	d					
Ewell West	d					
Stoneleigh	d					
Worcester Park	d					
Chessington South	d				23 40	
Chessington North	d				23 42	
Tolworth	d				23 44	
Malden Manor	d				23 47	
Motspur Park	d				23 50	
Raynes Park 6	d	23 43			23 54	23 58
Wimbledon 6 ⊖ ⛴	d	23 50	23 53		23a57	00 02
Earlsfield	d	23 53	23 56			00 05
Clapham Junction 10	d	23 57	23 59			00 09
Vauxhall ⊖	d	00 02	00 05			00 14
London Waterloo 15 ⊖	a	00 10	00 14			00 22

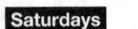

Hampton Court, Shepperton, Guildford, Dorking and Chessington South - London

Network Diagram - see first Page of Table 152

		SW	SW	SW		SW	SW	SW	SW	SW			SW	SW	SW	SW	SW		SW	SW		SW	SW	SW	SW
Guildford	d		23p08					04 00						05 14											
London Road (Guildford)	d		23p12																						
Clandon	d		23p17																						
Horsley	d		23p21																						
Effingham Junction 6	d		23p24																						
Bookham	d																								
Cobham & Stoke d'Abernon	d		23p28																						
Oxshott	d		23p31																						
Claygate	d		23p34																						
Hinchley Wood	d		23p37																						
Hampton Court	d														05 54					06 24					
Thames Ditton	d														05 56					06 26					
Surbiton 6	d		23p42					04 24						05 57	06 02				06 27	06 32					
Berrylands	d														06 04					06 34					
Shepperton	d	23p11																				06 11			
Upper Halliford	d	23p14																				06 14			
Sunbury	d	23p16																				06 16			
Kempton Park	d	23p18																				06 18			
Hampton	d	23p21																				06 21			
Fulwell	d	23p24																				06 24			
Strawberry Hill	d			23p37		00 07			04 55								06 07								06 37
Teddington	d	23p29		23p41		00 11	00s56		04 59				05 44				06 11					06 29			06 41
Hampton Wick	d	23p31		23p44		00 14	00s59		05 01				05 46				06 14					06 31			06 44
Kingston	a	23p33		23p46		00 16	01 01		05 03				05 48				06 16					06 33			06 46
	d	23p34		23p49					05 04				05 49				06 19					06 34			06 49
Norbiton	d	23p36		23p51					05 06				05 51				06 21					06 36			06 51
New Malden 6	d	23p41		23p55					05 10				05 55		06 07		06 25			06 37		06 40			06 55
Dorking 4	d																								
Box Hill & Westhumble	d																								
Leatherhead	d																								
Ashtead	d																								
Epsom 3	a																								
	d									05 35						06 05							06 35		
Ewell West	d									05 38						06 08							06 38		
Stoneleigh	d									05 40						06 10							06 40		
Worcester Park	d									05 43						06 13							06 43		
Chessington South	d																							06 40	
Chessington North	d																							06 42	
Tolworth	d																							06 44	
Malden Manor	d																							06 47	
Motspur Park	d									05 46						06 16							06 46	06 50	
Raynes Park 6	d	23p43		23p58					05 13	05 49			05 58		06 10	06 19	06 28			06 40		06 43	06 49	06 53	06 58
Wimbledon 6 ⊖	d	23p50	23p53	00 02				04 32	05 17	05 53			06 02	06 05	06 14	06 23	06 32		06 35	06 44		06 47	06 53	06 57	07 02
Earlsfield	d	23p53	23p56	00 05					05 21	05 57			06 05	06 08	06 17	06 27	06 35		06 38	06 47		06 50	06 57	07 01	07 05
Clapham Junction 10	d	23p57	23p59	00 09				04 44	05 25	06 01			06 09	06 12	06 21	06 31	06 39		06 42	06 51		06 54	07 01	07 05	07 09
Vauxhall ⊖	d	00 02	00 05	00 14					05 30	06 06			06 14	06 17	06 26	06 36	06 44		06 47	06 56		06 59	07 06	07 10	07 14
London Waterloo 15 ⊖	a	00 10	00 14	00 22				04 53	05 35	06 11			06 19	06 22	06 31	06 40	06 49		06 52	07 01		07 04	07 10	07 15	07 19

			SW	SW	SW	SW		SW	SW	SW		SW	SW	SW	SW	SW		SW	SW		SW	SW	SW	SW	SW
Guildford	d					06 28		06 38							06 58	07 08								07 28	07 38
London Road (Guildford)	d					06 32		06 42							07 02	07 12								07 32	07 42
Clandon	d					06 37		06 47							07 07	07 17								07 37	07 47
Horsley	d					06 41		06 51							07 11	07 21								07 41	07 51
Effingham Junction 6	d					06 46		06 54							07 16	07 24								07 46	07 54
Bookham	d					06 49									07 19									07 49	
Cobham & Stoke d'Abernon	d							06 58								07 28									07 58
Oxshott	d							07 01								07 31									08 01
Claygate	d							07 04								07 34									08 04
Hinchley Wood	d							07 07								07 37									08 07
Hampton Court	d			06 54									07 24									07 54			
Thames Ditton	d			06 56									07 26									07 56			
Surbiton 6	d		06 57	07 02				07 12				07 27	07 32			07 42					07 57	08 02			08 12
Berrylands	d			07 04									07 34									08 04			
Shepperton	d				06 41									07 11									07 41		
Upper Halliford	d				06 44									07 14									07 44		
Sunbury	d				06 46									07 16									07 46		
Kempton Park	d				06 48									07 18									07 48		
Hampton	d				06 51									07 21									07 51		
Fulwell	d				06 54									07 24									07 54		
Strawberry Hill	d									07 07									07 37						
Teddington	d				06 59					07 11				07 29					07 41				07 59		
Hampton Wick	d				07 01					07 14				07 31					07 44				08 01		
Kingston	a				07 03					07 16				07 33					07 46				08 03		
	d				07 04					07 19				07 34					07 49				08 04		
Norbiton	d				07 06					07 21				07 36					07 51				08 06		
New Malden 6	d			07 07	07 10					07 25			07 37	07 40					07 55			08 07	08 10		
Dorking 4	d																								
Box Hill & Westhumble	d																								
Leatherhead	d					06 54									07 24									07 54	
Ashtead	d					06 58									07 28									07 58	
Epsom 3	a					07 02									07 32									08 02	
	d					07 05									07 35									08 05	
Ewell West	d					07 08									07 38									08 08	
Stoneleigh	d					07 10									07 40									08 10	
Worcester Park	d					07 13									07 43									08 13	
Chessington South	d								07 10									07 40							
Chessington North	d								07 12									07 42							
Tolworth	d								07 14									07 44							
Malden Manor	d								07 17									07 47							
Motspur Park	d					07 16			07 20						07 46			07 50						08 16	
Raynes Park 6	d			07 10	07 13	07 19			07 23	07 28			07 40	07 43	07 49			07 53	07 58			08 10	08 13	08 19	
Wimbledon 6 ⊖	d		07 05	07 14	07 17	07 23		07 20	07 27	07 32		07 35	07 44	07 47	07 53	07 50		07 57	08 02		08 05	08 14	08 17	08 23	08 20
Earlsfield	d		07 08	07 17	07 20	07 27		07 24	07 31	07 35		07 38	07 47	07 50	07 57	07 54		08 01	08 05		08 08	08 17	08 20	08 27	08 24
Clapham Junction 10	d		07 12	07 21	07 24	07 31		07 28	07 35	07 39		07 42	07 51	07 54	08 01	07 58		08 05	08 09		08 12	08 21	08 24	08 31	08 28
Vauxhall ⊖	d		07 17	07 26	07 29	07 36		07 33	07 40	07 44		07 47	07 56	07 59	08 06	08 03		08 10	08 14		08 17	08 26	08 29	08 36	08 33
London Waterloo 15 ⊖	a		07 22	07 31	07 34	07 40		07 37	07 45	07 49		07 52	08 01	08 04	08 10	08 07		08 15	08 19		08 22	08 31	08 34	08 40	08 37

Table 152

Saturdays

Hampton Court, Shepperton, Guildford, Dorking and Chessington South - London

Network Diagram - see first Page of Table 152

		SW		SW		SW	SW	SW	SW	SW	SW	SW		SW		SW	SW	SW	SW	SW	SW	SW		SW	
Guildford	d									07 58	08 08									08 28	08 38				
London Road (Guildford)	d									08 02	08 12									08 32	08 42				
Clandon	d									08 07	08 17									08 37	08 47				
Horsley	d									08 11	08 21									08 41	08 51				
Effingham Junction 6	d									08 16	08 24									08 46	08 54				
Bookham	d									08 19										08 49					
Cobham & Stoke d'Abernon	d										08 28										08 58				
Oxshott	d										08 31										09 01				
Claygate	d										08 34										09 04				
Hinchley Wood	d										08 37										09 07				
Hampton Court	d							08 24										08 54							
Thames Ditton	d							08 26										08 56							
Surbiton 6	d					08 27		08 32			08 42					08 57		09 02			09 12				
Berrylands	d							08 34										09 04							
Shepperton	d								08 11										08 41						
Upper Halliford	d								08 14										08 44						
Sunbury	d								08 16										08 46						
Kempton Park	d								08 18										08 48						
Hampton	d								08 21										08 51						
Fulwell	d								08 24										08 54						
Strawberry Hill	d			08 07										08 37										09 07	
Teddington	d			08 11					08 29					08 41					08 59					09 11	
Hampton Wick	d			08 14					08 31					08 44					09 01					09 14	
Kingston	a			08 16					08 33					08 46					09 03					09 16	
	d			08 19					08 34					08 49					09 04					09 19	
Norbiton	d			08 21					08 36					08 51					09 06					09 21	
New Malden 6	d			08 25				08 37	08 40					08 55				09 07	09 10					09 25	
Dorking 4	d						08 05										08 35								
Box Hill & Westhumble	d																								
Leatherhead	d						08 11			08 24							08 41			08 54					
Ashtead	d						08 14			08 28							08 44			08 58					
Epsom 3	a						08 19			08 32							08 49			09 02					
	d						08 20			08 35							08 50			09 05					
Ewell West	d						08 23			08 38							08 53			09 08					
Stoneleigh	d						08 25			08 40							08 55			09 10					
Worcester Park	d						08 28			08 43							08 58			09 13					
Chessington South	d	08 10										08 40										09 10			
Chessington North	d	08 12										08 42										09 12			
Tolworth	d	08 14										08 44										09 14			
Malden Manor	d	08 17										08 47										09 17			
Motspur Park	d	08 20					08 31			08 46		08 50					09 01			09 16		09 20			
Raynes Park 6	d	08 23		08 28			08 34	08 40	08 43	08 49		08 53		08 58			09 04	09 10	09 13	09 19		09 23		09 28	
Wimbledon 6 ⊖	d	08 27		08 32		08 35	08 38	08 44	08 47	08 53	08 50	08 57		09 02		09 05	09 08	09 14	09 17	09 23	09 20	09 27		09 32	
Earlsfield	d	08 31		08 35		08 38	08 42	08 47	08 50	08 57	08 54	09 01		09 05		09 08	09 12	09 17	09 20	09 27	09 24	09 31		09 35	
Clapham Junction 10	d	08 35		08 39		08 42	08 46	08 51	08 54	09 01	08 58	09 05		09 09		09 12	09 16	09 21	09 24	09 31	09 28	09 35		09 39	
Vauxhall ⊖	d	08 40		08 44		08 47	08 51	08 56	08 59	09 06	09 03	09 10		09 14		09 17	09 21	09 26	09 29	09 36	09 33	09 40		09 44	
London Waterloo 15 ⊖	a	08 45		08 49		08 52	08 55	09 01	09 04	09 10	09 07	09 15		09 19		09 22	09 25	09 31	09 34	09 40	09 37	09 45		09 49	

		SW	SW	SW	SW	SW	SW	SW		SW		SW	SW	SW	SW	SW	SW	SW		SW		SW	SW	SW	SW
Guildford	d					08 58	09 08									09 28	09 38								
London Road (Guildford)	d					09 02	09 12									09 32	09 42								
Clandon	d					09 07	09 17									09 37	09 47								
Horsley	d					09 11	09 21									09 41	09 51								
Effingham Junction 6	d					09 16	09 24									09 46	09 54								
Bookham	d					09 19										09 49									
Cobham & Stoke d'Abernon	d						09 28										09 58								
Oxshott	d						09 31										10 01								
Claygate	d						09 34										10 04								
Hinchley Wood	d						09 37										10 07								
Hampton Court	d			09 24										09 54										10 24	
Thames Ditton	d			09 26										09 56										10 26	
Surbiton 6	d	09 27		09 32			09 42					09 57		10 02			10 12					10 27		10 32	
Berrylands	d			09 34										10 04										10 34	
Shepperton	d				09 11										09 41										10 11
Upper Halliford	d				09 14										09 44										10 14
Sunbury	d				09 16										09 46										10 16
Kempton Park	d				09 18										09 48										10 18
Hampton	d				09 21										09 51										10 21
Fulwell	d				09 24										09 54										10 24
Strawberry Hill	d									09 37										10 07					
Teddington	d				09 29					09 41					09 59					10 11					10 29
Hampton Wick	d				09 31					09 44					10 01					10 14					10 31
Kingston	a				09 33					09 46					10 03					10 16					10 33
	d				09 34					09 49					10 04					10 19					10 34
Norbiton	d				09 36					09 51					10 06					10 21					10 36
New Malden 6	d			09 37	09 40					09 55				10 07	10 10					10 25				10 37	10 40
Dorking 4	d		09 05										09 35										10 05		
Box Hill & Westhumble	d																								
Leatherhead	d		09 11			09 24							09 41			09 54							10 11		
Ashtead	d		09 14			09 28							09 44			09 58							10 14		
Epsom 3	a		09 19			09 32							09 49			10 02							10 19		
	d		09 20			09 35							09 50			10 05							10 20		
Ewell West	d		09 23			09 38							09 53			10 08							10 23		
Stoneleigh	d		09 25			09 40							09 55			10 10							10 25		
Worcester Park	d		09 28			09 43							09 58			10 13							10 28		
Chessington South	d							09 40										10 10							
Chessington North	d							09 42										10 12							
Tolworth	d							09 44										10 14							
Malden Manor	d							09 47										10 17							
Motspur Park	d		09 31			09 46		09 50					10 01			10 16		10 20					10 31		
Raynes Park 6	d		09 34	09 40	09 43	09 49		09 53		09 58			10 04	10 10	10 13	10 19		10 23		10 28			10 34	10 40	10 43
Wimbledon 6 ⊖	d	09 35	09 38	09 44	09 47	09 53	09 50	09 57		10 02		10 05	10 08	10 14	10 17	10 23	10 20	10 27		10 32		10 35	10 38	10 44	10 47
Earlsfield	d	09 38	09 42	09 47	09 50	09 57	09 54	10 01		10 05		10 08	10 12	10 17	10 20	10 27	10 24	10 31		10 35		10 38	10 42	10 47	10 50
Clapham Junction 10	d	09 42	09 46	09 51	09 54	10 01	09 58	10 05		10 09		10 12	10 16	10 21	10 24	10 31	10 28	10 35		10 39		10 42	10 46	10 51	10 54
Vauxhall ⊖	d	09 47	09 51	09 56	09 59	10 06	10 03	10 10		10 14		10 17	10 21	10 26	10 29	10 36	10 33	10 40		10 44		10 47	10 51	10 56	10 59
London Waterloo 15 ⊖	a	09 52	09 55	10 01	10 04	10 10	10 07	10 15		10 19		10 22	10 25	10 31	10 34	10 40	10 37	10 45		10 49		10 52	10 55	11 01	11 04

Hampton Court, Shepperton, Guildford, Dorking and Chessington South - London

Network Diagram - see first Page of Table 152

		SW	SW	SW		SW		SW	SW	SW	SW	SW	SW	SW		SW		SW	SW	SW	SW	SW	SW	SW	
Guildford	d	09 58	10 08									10 28	10 38									10 58	11 08		
London Road (Guildford)	d	10 02	10 12									10 32	10 42									11 02	11 12		
Clandon	d	10 07	10 17									10 37	10 47									11 07	11 17		
Horsley	d	10 11	10 21									10 41	10 51									11 11	11 21		
Effingham Junction 6	d	10 16	10 24									10 46	10 54									11 16	11 24		
Bookham	d	10 19										10 49										11 19			
Cobham & Stoke d'Abernon	d		10 28										10 58										11 28		
Oxshott	d		10 31										11 01										11 31		
Claygate	d		10 34										11 04										11 34		
Hinchley Wood	d		10 37										11 07										11 37		
Hampton Court	d									10 54										11 24					
Thames Ditton	d									10 56										11 26					
Surbiton 6	d		10 42					10 57		11 02			11 12					11 27		11 32			11 42		
Berrylands	d									11 04										11 34					
Shepperton	d										10 41										11 11				
Upper Halliford	d										10 44										11 14				
Sunbury	d										10 46										11 16				
Kempton Park	d										10 48										11 18				
Hampton	d										10 51										11 21				
Fulwell	d										10 54										11 24				
Strawberry Hill	d					10 37										11 07									
Teddington	d					10 41					10 59					11 11					11 29				
Hampton Wick	d					10 44					11 01					11 14					11 31				
Kingston	a					10 46					11 03					11 16					11 33				
	d					10 49					11 04					11 19					11 34				
Norbiton	d					10 51					11 06					11 21					11 36				
New Malden 6	d					10 55				11 07	11 10					11 25				11 37	11 40				
Dorking 4	d								10 35										11 05						
Box Hill & Westhumble	d																								
Leatherhead	d	10 24							10 41			10 54							11 11			11 24			
Ashtead	d	10 28							10 44			10 58							11 14			11 28			
Epsom 3	a	10 32							10 49			11 02							11 19			11 32			
	d	10 35							10 50			11 05							11 20			11 35			
Ewell West	d	10 38							10 53			11 08							11 23			11 38			
Stoneleigh	d	10 40							10 55			11 10							11 25			11 40			
Worcester Park	d	10 43							10 58			11 13							11 28			11 43			
Chessington South	d			10 40										11 10										11 40	
Chessington North	d			10 42										11 12										11 42	
Tolworth	d			10 44										11 14										11 44	
Malden Manor	d			10 47										11 17										11 47	
Motspur Park	d	10 46		10 50					11 01			11 16		11 20					11 31			11 46		11 50	
Raynes Park 6	d	10 49		10 53		10 58			11 04	11 10	11 13	11 19		11 23		11 28			11 34	11 40	11 43	11 49		11 53	
Wimbledon 6 ⊖	d	10 53	10 50	10 57		11 02		11 05	11 08	11 14	11 17	11 23	11 20	11 27		11 32		11 35	11 38	11 44	11 47	11 53	11 50	11 57	
Earlsfield	d	10 57	10 54	11 01		11 05		11 08	11 12	11 17	11 20	11 27	11 24	11 31		11 35		11 38	11 42	11 47	11 50	11 57	11 54	12 01	
Clapham Junction 10	d	11 01	10 58	11 05		11 09		11 12	11 16	11 21	11 24	11 31	11 28	11 35		11 39		11 42	11 46	11 51	11 54	12 01	11 58	12 05	
Vauxhall ⊖	d	11 06	11 03	11 10		11 14		11 17	11 21	11 26	11 29	11 36	11 33	11 40		11 44		11 47	11 51	11 56	11 59	12 06	12 03	12 10	
London Waterloo 15 ⊖	a	11 10	11 07	11 15		11 19		11 22	11 25	11 31	11 34	11 40	11 37	11 45		11 49		11 52	11 55	12 01	12 04	12 10	12 07	12 15	

		SW		SW	SW	SW	SW	SW	SW	SW		SW		SW	SW	SW	SW	SW	SW	SW		SW		SW	SW
Guildford	d							11 28	11 38									11 58	12 08						
London Road (Guildford)	d							11 32	11 42									12 02	12 12						
Clandon	d							11 37	11 47									12 07	12 17						
Horsley	d							11 41	11 51									12 11	12 21						
Effingham Junction 6	d							11 46	11 54									12 16	12 24						
Bookham	d							11 49										12 19							
Cobham & Stoke d'Abernon	d								11 58										12 28						
Oxshott	d								12 01										12 31						
Claygate	d								12 04										12 34						
Hinchley Wood	d								12 07										12 37						
Hampton Court	d					11 54										12 24									
Thames Ditton	d					11 56										12 26									
Surbiton 6	d			11 57		12 02			12 12					12 27		12 32			12 42					12 57	
Berrylands	d					12 04										12 34									
Shepperton	d						11 41										12 11								
Upper Halliford	d						11 44										12 14								
Sunbury	d						11 46										12 16								
Kempton Park	d						11 48										12 18								
Hampton	d						11 51										12 21								
Fulwell	d						11 54										12 24								
Strawberry Hill	d	11 37										12 07										12 37			
Teddington	d	11 41					11 59					12 11					12 29					12 41			
Hampton Wick	d	11 44					12 01					12 14					12 31					12 44			
Kingston	a	11 46					12 03					12 16					12 33					12 46			
	d	11 49					12 04					12 19					12 34					12 49			
Norbiton	d	11 51					12 06					12 21					12 36					12 51			
New Malden 6	d	11 55				12 07	12 10					12 25				12 37	12 40					12 55			
Dorking 4	d				11 35										12 05										12 35
Box Hill & Westhumble	d																								
Leatherhead	d				11 41			11 54							12 11			12 24							12 41
Ashtead	d				11 44			11 58							12 14			12 28							12 44
Epsom 3	a				11 49			12 02							12 19			12 32							12 49
	d				11 50			12 05							12 20			12 35							12 50
Ewell West	d				11 53			12 08							12 23			12 38							12 53
Stoneleigh	d				11 55			12 10							12 25			12 40							12 55
Worcester Park	d				11 58			12 13							12 28			12 43							12 58
Chessington South	d									12 10										12 40					
Chessington North	d									12 12										12 42					
Tolworth	d									12 14										12 44					
Malden Manor	d									12 17										12 47					
Motspur Park	d				12 01			12 16		12 20					12 31			12 46		12 50					13 01
Raynes Park 6	d	11 58			12 04	12 10	12 13	12 19		12 23		12 28			12 34	12 40	12 43	12 49		12 53		12 58			13 04
Wimbledon 6 ⊖	d	12 02		12 05	12 08	12 14	12 17	12 23	12 20	12 27		12 32		12 35	12 38	12 44	12 47	12 53	12 50	12 57		13 02		13 05	13 08
Earlsfield	d	12 05		12 08	12 12	12 17	12 20	12 27	12 24	12 31		12 35		12 38	12 42	12 47	12 50	12 57	12 54	13 01		13 05		13 08	13 12
Clapham Junction 10	d	12 09		12 12	12 16	12 21	12 24	12 31	12 28	12 35		12 39		12 42	12 46	12 51	12 54	13 01	12 58	13 05		13 09		13 12	13 16
Vauxhall ⊖	d	12 14		12 17	12 21	12 26	12 29	12 36	12 33	12 40		12 44		12 47	12 51	12 56	12 59	13 06	13 03	13 10		13 14		13 17	13 21
London Waterloo 15 ⊖	a	12 19		12 22	12 25	12 31	12 34	12 40	12 37	12 45		12 49		12 52	12 55	13 01	13 04	13 10	13 07	13 15		13 19		13 22	13 25

Hampton Court, Shepperton, Guildford, Dorking and Chessington South - London

Network Diagram - see first Page of Table 152

		SW	SW	SW	SW	SW		SW		SW	SW	SW	SW	SW	SW	SW		SW		SW	SW	SW	SW	SW	SW
Guildford	d			12 28	12 38									12 58	13 08									13 28	13 38
London Road (Guildford)	d			12 32	12 42									13 02	13 12									13 32	13 42
Clandon	d			12 37	12 47									13 07	13 17									13 37	13 47
Horsley	d			12 41	12 51									13 11	13 21									13 41	13 51
Effingham Junction 6	d			12 46	12 54									13 16	13 24									13 46	13 54
Bookham	d			12 49										13 19										13 49	
Cobham & Stoke d'Abernon	d				12 58										13 28										13 58
Oxshott	d				13 01										13 31										14 01
Claygate	d				13 04										13 34										14 04
Hinchley Wood	d				13 07										13 37										14 07
Hampton Court	d	12 54										13 24										13 54			
Thames Ditton	d	12 56										13 26										13 56			
Surbiton 6	d	13 02			13 12					13 27		13 32			13 42					13 57		14 02			14 12
Berrylands	d	13 04										13 34										14 04			
Shepperton	d		12 41										13 11										13 41		
Upper Halliford	d		12 44										13 14										13 44		
Sunbury	d		12 46										13 16										13 46		
Kempton Park	d		12 48										13 18										13 48		
Hampton	d		12 51										13 21										13 51		
Fulwell	d		12 54										13 24										13 54		
Strawberry Hill	d							13 07										13 37							
Teddington	d		12 59					13 11					13 29					13 41					13 59		
Hampton Wick	d		13 01					13 14					13 31					13 44					14 01		
Kingston	a		13 03					13 16					13 33					13 46					14 03		
	d		13 04					13 19					13 34					13 49					14 04		
Norbiton	d		13 06					13 21					13 36					13 51					14 06		
New Malden 6	d	13 07	13 10					13 25				13 37	13 40					13 55				14 07	14 10		
Dorking 4	d										13 05										13 35				
Box Hill & Westhumble	d																								
Leatherhead	d			12 54							13 11			13 24							13 41			13 54	
Ashtead	d			12 58							13 14			13 28							13 44			13 58	
Epsom 3	a			13 02							13 19			13 32							13 49			14 02	
	d			13 05							13 20			13 35							13 50			14 05	
Ewell West	d			13 08							13 23			13 38							13 53			14 08	
Stoneleigh	d			13 10							13 25			13 40							13 55			14 10	
Worcester Park	d			13 13							13 28			13 43							13 58			14 13	
Chessington South	d					13 10										13 40									
Chessington North	d					13 12										13 42									
Tolworth	d					13 14										13 44									
Malden Manor	d					13 17										13 47									
Motspur Park	d			13 16		13 20					13 31			13 46		13 50					14 01			14 16	
Raynes Park 6	d	13 10	13 13	13 19		13 23		13 28			13 34	13 40	13 43	13 49		13 53		13 58			14 04	14 10	14 13	14 19	
Wimbledon 6 ⊖	d	13 14	13 17	13 23	13 20	13 27		13 32		13 35	13 38	13 44	13 47	13 53	13 50	13 57		14 02		14 05	14 08	14 14	14 17	14 23	14 20
Earlsfield	d	13 17	13 20	13 27	13 24	13 31		13 35		13 38	13 42	13 47	13 50	13 57	13 54	14 01		14 05		14 08	14 12	14 17	14 20	14 27	14 24
Clapham Junction 10	d	13 21	13 24	13 31	13 28	13 35		13 39		13 42	13 46	13 51	13 54	14 01	13 58	14 05		14 09		14 12	14 16	14 21	14 24	14 31	14 28
Vauxhall ⊖	d	13 26	13 29	13 36	13 33	13 40		13 44		13 47	13 51	13 56	13 59	14 06	14 03	14 10		14 14		14 17	14 21	14 26	14 29	14 36	14 33
London Waterloo 15 ⊖	a	13 31	13 34	13 40	13 37	13 45		13 49		13 52	13 55	14 01	14 04	14 10	14 07	14 15		14 19		14 22	14 25	14 31	14 34	14 40	14 37

		SW		SW		SW	SW	SW	SW	SW	SW	SW		SW		SW	SW	SW	SW	SW	SW	SW		SW	
Guildford	d									13 58	14 08									14 28	14 38				
London Road (Guildford)	d									14 02	14 12									14 32	14 42				
Clandon	d									14 07	14 17									14 37	14 47				
Horsley	d									14 11	14 21									14 41	14 51				
Effingham Junction 6	d									14 16	14 24									14 46	14 54				
Bookham	d									14 19										14 49					
Cobham & Stoke d'Abernon	d										14 28										14 58				
Oxshott	d										14 31										15 01				
Claygate	d										14 34										15 04				
Hinchley Wood	d										14 37										15 07				
Hampton Court	d							14 24										14 54							
Thames Ditton	d							14 26										14 56							
Surbiton 6	d					14 27		14 32			14 42					14 57		15 02			15 12				
Berrylands	d							14 34										15 04							
Shepperton	d								14 11										14 41						
Upper Halliford	d								14 14										14 44						
Sunbury	d								14 16										14 46						
Kempton Park	d								14 18										14 48						
Hampton	d								14 21										14 51						
Fulwell	d								14 24										14 54						
Strawberry Hill	d			14 07										14 37										15 07	
Teddington	d			14 11					14 29					14 41					14 59					15 11	
Hampton Wick	d			14 14					14 31					14 44					15 01					15 14	
Kingston	a			14 16					14 33					14 46					15 03					15 16	
	d			14 19					14 34					14 49					15 04					15 19	
Norbiton	d			14 21					14 36					14 51					15 06					15 21	
New Malden 6	d			14 25				14 37	14 40					14 55				15 07	15 10					15 25	
Dorking 4	d						14 05										14 35								
Box Hill & Westhumble	d																								
Leatherhead	d						14 11			14 24							14 41			14 54					
Ashtead	d						14 14			14 28							14 44			14 58					
Epsom 3	a						14 19			14 32							14 49			15 02					
	d						14 20			14 35							14 50			15 05					
Ewell West	d						14 23			14 38							14 53			15 08					
Stoneleigh	d						14 25			14 40							14 55			15 10					
Worcester Park	d						14 28			14 43							14 58			15 13					
Chessington South	d	14 10										14 40										15 10			
Chessington North	d	14 12										14 42										15 12			
Tolworth	d	14 14										14 44										15 14			
Malden Manor	d	14 17										14 47										15 17			
Motspur Park	d	14 20					14 31			14 46		14 50					15 01			15 16		15 20			
Raynes Park 6	d	14 23		14 28			14 34	14 40	14 43	14 49		14 53		14 58			15 04	15 10	15 13	15 19		15 23		15 28	
Wimbledon 6 ⊖	d	14 27		14 32		14 35	14 38	14 44	14 47	14 53	14 50	14 57		15 02		15 05	15 08	15 14	15 17	15 23	15 20	15 27		15 32	
Earlsfield	d	14 31		14 35		14 38	14 42	14 47	14 50	14 57	14 54	15 01		15 05		15 08	15 12	15 17	15 20	15 27	15 24	15 31		15 35	
Clapham Junction 10	d	14 35		14 39		14 42	14 46	14 51	14 54	15 01	14 58	15 05		15 09		15 12	15 16	15 21	15 24	15 31	15 28	15 35		15 39	
Vauxhall ⊖	d	14 40		14 44		14 47	14 51	14 56	14 59	15 06	15 03	15 10		15 14		15 17	15 21	15 26	15 29	15 36	15 33	15 40		15 44	
London Waterloo 15 ⊖	a	14 45		14 49		14 52	14 55	15 01	15 04	15 10	15 07	15 15		15 19		15 22	15 25	15 31	15 34	15 40	15 37	15 45		15 49	

Table 152

Saturdays

Hampton Court, Shepperton, Guildford, Dorking and Chessington South - London

Network Diagram - see first Page of Table 152

		SW	SW	SW	SW	SW	SW	SW		SW		SW	SW	SW	SW	SW	SW	SW		SW		SW	SW	SW	SW
Guildford	d					14 58	15 08									15 28	15 38								
London Road (Guildford)	d					15 02	15 12									15 32	15 42								
Clandon	d					15 07	15 17									15 37	15 47								
Horsley	d					15 11	15 21									15 41	15 51								
Effingham Junction 6	d					15 16	15 24									15 46	15 54								
Bookham	d					15 19										15 49									
Cobham & Stoke d'Abernon	d						15 28										15 58								
Oxshott	d						15 31										16 01								
Claygate	d						15 34										16 04								
Hinchley Wood	d						15 37										16 07								
Hampton Court	d			15 24										15 54										16 24	
Thames Ditton	d			15 26										15 56										16 26	
Surbiton 6	d	15 27		15 32			15 42					15 57		16 02			16 12					16 27		16 32	
Berrylands	d			15 34										16 04										16 34	
Shepperton	d				15 11										15 41										16 11
Upper Halliford	d				15 14										15 44										16 14
Sunbury	d				15 16										15 46										16 16
Kempton Park	d				15 18										15 48										16 18
Hampton	d				15 21										15 51										16 21
Fulwell	d				15 24										15 54										16 24
Strawberry Hill	d									15 37										16 07					
Teddington	d				15 29					15 41					15 59					16 11					16 29
Hampton Wick	d				15 31					15 44					16 01					16 14					16 31
Kingston	a				15 33					15 46					16 03					16 16					16 33
	d				15 34					15 49					16 04					16 19					16 34
Norbiton	d				15 36					15 51					16 06					16 21					16 36
New Malden 6	d			15 37	15 40					15 55				16 07	16 10					16 25				16 37	16 40
Dorking 4	d		15 05										15 35										16 05		
Box Hill & Westhumble	d																								
Leatherhead	d		15 11			15 24							15 41			15 54							16 11		
Ashtead	d		15 14			15 28							15 44			15 58							16 14		
Epsom 3	a		15 19			15 32							15 49			16 02							16 19		
	d		15 20			15 35							15 50			16 05							16 20		
Ewell West	d		15 23			15 38							15 53			16 08							16 23		
Stoneleigh	d		15 25			15 40							15 55			16 10							16 25		
Worcester Park	d		15 28			15 43							15 58			16 13							16 28		
Chessington South	d							15 40										16 10							
Chessington North	d							15 42										16 12							
Tolworth	d							15 44										16 14							
Malden Manor	d							15 47										16 17							
Motspur Park	d		15 31			15 46		15 50					16 01			16 16		16 20					16 31		
Raynes Park 6	d		15 34	15 40	15 43	15 49		15 53		15 58			16 04	16 10	16 13	16 19		16 23		16 28			16 34	16 40	16 43
Wimbledon 6 ⊖	d	15 35	15 38	15 44	15 47	15 53	15 50	15 57		16 02		16 05	16 08	16 14	16 17	16 23	16 20	16 27		16 32		16 35	16 38	16 44	16 47
Earlsfield	d	15 38	15 42	15 47	15 50	15 57	15 54	16 01		16 05		16 08	16 12	16 17	16 20	16 27	16 24	16 31		16 35		16 38	16 42	16 47	16 50
Clapham Junction 10	d	15 42	15 46	15 51	15 54	16 01	15 58	16 05		16 09		16 12	16 16	16 21	16 24	16 31	16 28	16 35		16 39		16 42	16 46	16 51	16 54
Vauxhall ⊖	d	15 47	15 51	15 56	15 59	16 06	16 03	16 10		16 14		16 17	16 21	16 26	16 29	16 36	16 33	16 40		16 44		16 47	16 51	16 56	16 59
London Waterloo 15 ⊖	a	15 52	15 55	16 01	16 04	16 10	16 07	16 15		16 19		16 22	16 25	16 31	16 34	16 40	16 37	16 45		16 49		16 52	16 55	17 01	17 04

		SW	SW	SW		SW		SW	SW	SW	SW	SW	SW	SW		SW		SW	SW	SW	SW	SW	SW	SW	
Guildford	d	15 58	16 08									16 28	16 38									16 58	17 08		
London Road (Guildford)	d	16 02	16 12									16 32	16 42									17 02	17 12		
Clandon	d	16 07	16 17									16 37	16 47									17 07	17 17		
Horsley	d	16 11	16 21									16 41	16 51									17 11	17 21		
Effingham Junction 6	d	16 16	16 24									16 46	16 54									17 16	17 24		
Bookham	d	16 19										16 49										17 19			
Cobham & Stoke d'Abernon	d		16 28										16 58										17 28		
Oxshott	d		16 31										17 01										17 31		
Claygate	d		16 34										17 04										17 34		
Hinchley Wood	d		16 37										17 07										17 37		
Hampton Court	d									16 54										17 24					
Thames Ditton	d									16 56										17 26					
Surbiton 6	d		16 42					16 57		17 02			17 12					17 27		17 32			17 42		
Berrylands	d									17 04										17 34					
Shepperton	d										16 41										17 11				
Upper Halliford	d										16 44										17 14				
Sunbury	d										16 46										17 16				
Kempton Park	d										16 48										17 18				
Hampton	d										16 51										17 21				
Fulwell	d										16 54										17 24				
Strawberry Hill	d					16 37										17 07									
Teddington	d					16 41					16 59					17 11					17 29				
Hampton Wick	d					16 44					17 01					17 14					17 31				
Kingston	a					16 46					17 03					17 16					17 33				
	d					16 49					17 04					17 19					17 34				
Norbiton	d					16 51					17 06					17 21					17 36				
New Malden 6	d					16 55				17 07	17 10					17 25				17 37	17 40				
Dorking 4	d								16 35										17 05						
Box Hill & Westhumble	d																								
Leatherhead	d	16 24							16 41			16 54							17 11			17 24			
Ashtead	d	16 28							16 44			16 58							17 14			17 28			
Epsom 3	a	16 32							16 49			17 02							17 19			17 32			
	d	16 35							16 50			17 05							17 20			17 35			
Ewell West	d	16 38							16 53			17 08							17 23			17 38			
Stoneleigh	d	16 40							16 55			17 10							17 25			17 40			
Worcester Park	d	16 43							16 58			17 13							17 28			17 43			
Chessington South	d			16 40										17 10										17 40	
Chessington North	d			16 42										17 12										17 42	
Tolworth	d			16 44										17 14										17 44	
Malden Manor	d			16 47										17 17										17 47	
Motspur Park	d	16 46		16 50					17 01			17 16		17 20					17 31			17 46		17 50	
Raynes Park 6	d	16 49		16 53		16 58			17 04	17 10	17 13	17 19		17 23		17 28			17 34	17 40	17 43	17 49		17 53	
Wimbledon 6 ⊖	d	16 53	16 50	16 57		17 02		17 05	17 08	17 14	17 17	17 23	17 20	17 27		17 32		17 35	17 38	17 44	17 47	17 53	17 50	17 57	
Earlsfield	d	16 57	16 54	17 01		17 05		17 08	17 12	17 17	17 20	17 27	17 24	17 31		17 35		17 38	17 42	17 47	17 50	17 57	17 54	18 01	
Clapham Junction 10	d	17 01	16 58	17 05		17 09		17 12	17 16	17 21	17 24	17 31	17 28	17 35		17 39		17 42	17 46	17 51	17 54	18 01	17 58	18 05	
Vauxhall ⊖	d	17 06	17 03	17 10		17 14		17 17	17 21	17 26	17 29	17 36	17 33	17 40		17 44		17 47	17 51	17 56	17 59	18 06	18 03	18 10	
London Waterloo 15 ⊖	a	17 10	17 07	17 15		17 19		17 22	17 25	17 31	17 34	17 40	17 37	17 45		17 49		17 52	17 55	18 01	18 04	18 10	18 07	18 15	

Hampton Court, Shepperton, Guildford, Dorking and Chessington South - London

Network Diagram - see first Page of Table 152

		SW		SW	SW	SW	SW	SW	SW	SW		SW		SW	SW	SW	SW	SW	SW	SW		SW		SW	SW
Guildford	d							17 28	17 38									17 58	18 08						
London Road (Guildford)	d							17 32	17 42									18 02	18 12						
Clandon	d							17 37	17 47									18 07	18 17						
Horsley	d							17 41	17 51									18 11	18 21						
Effingham Junction 6	d							17 46	17 54									18 16	18 24						
Bookham	d							17 49										18 19							
Cobham & Stoke d'Abernon	d								17 58										18 28						
Oxshott	d								18 01										18 31						
Claygate	d								18 04										18 34						
Hinchley Wood	d								18 07										18 37						
Hampton Court	d					17 54										18 24									
Thames Ditton	d					17 56										18 26									
Surbiton 6	d			17 57		18 02			18 12					18 27		18 32			18 42					18 57	
Berrylands	d					18 04										18 34									
Shepperton	d						17 41										18 11								
Upper Halliford	d						17 44										18 14								
Sunbury	d						17 46										18 16								
Kempton Park	d						17 48										18 18								
Hampton	d						17 51										18 21								
Fulwell	d						17 54										18 24								
Strawberry Hill	d	17 37										18 07										18 37			
Teddington	d	17 41					17 59					18 11					18 29					18 41			
Hampton Wick	d	17 44					18 01					18 14					18 31					18 44			
Kingston	a	17 46					18 03					18 16					18 33					18 46			
	d	17 49					18 04					18 19					18 34					18 49			
Norbiton	d	17 51					18 06					18 21					18 36					18 51			
New Malden 6	d	17 55				18 07	18 10					18 25				18 37	18 40					18 55			
Dorking 4	d				17 35										18 05										18 35
Box Hill & Westhumble	d																								
Leatherhead	d				17 41			17 54							18 11			18 24							18 41
Ashtead	d				17 44			17 58							18 14			18 28							18 44
Epsom 3	a				17 49			18 02							18 19			18 32							18 49
	d				17 50			18 05							18 20			18 35							18 50
Ewell West	d				17 53			18 08							18 23			18 38							18 53
Stoneleigh	d				17 55			18 10							18 25			18 40							18 55
Worcester Park	d				17 58			18 13							18 28			18 43							18 58
Chessington South	d									18 10										18 40					
Chessington North	d									18 12										18 42					
Tolworth	d									18 14										18 44					
Malden Manor	d									18 17										18 47					
Motspur Park	d				18 01			18 16		18 20					18 31			18 46		18 50					19 01
Raynes Park 6	d	17 58			18 04	18 10	18 13	18 19		18 23		18 28			18 34	18 40	18 43	18 49		18 53		18 58			19 04
Wimbledon 6 ⊖	d	18 02		18 05	18 08	18 14	18 17	18 23	18 20	18 27		18 32		18 35	18 38	18 44	18 47	18 53	18 50	18 57		19 02		19 05	19 08
Earlsfield	d	18 05		18 08	18 12	18 17	18 20	18 27	18 24	18 31		18 35		18 38	18 42	18 47	18 50	18 57	18 54	19 01		19 05		19 08	19 12
Clapham Junction 10	d	18 09		18 12	18 16	18 21	18 24	18 31	18 28	18 35		18 39		18 42	18 46	18 51	18 54	19 01	18 58	19 05		19 09		19 12	19 16
Vauxhall ⊖	d	18 14		18 17	18 21	18 26	18 29	18 36	18 33	18 40		18 44		18 47	18 51	18 56	18 59	19 06	19 03	19 10		19 14		19 17	19 21
London Waterloo 15 ⊖	a	18 19		18 22	18 25	18 31	18 34	18 40	18 37	18 45		18 49		18 52	18 55	19 01	19 04	19 10	19 07	19 15		19 19		19 22	19 25

		SW	SW	SW	SW	SW		SW		SW	SW	SW	SW	SW	SW	SW		SW		SW	SW	SW	SW	SW	SW
Guildford	d			18 28	18 38									18 58	19 08									19 28	19 38
London Road (Guildford)	d			18 32	18 42									19 02	19 12									19 32	19 42
Clandon	d			18 37	18 47									19 07	19 17									19 37	19 47
Horsley	d			18 41	18 51									19 11	19 21									19 41	19 51
Effingham Junction 6	d			18 46	18 54									19 16	19 24									19 46	19 54
Bookham	d			18 49										19 19										19 49	
Cobham & Stoke d'Abernon	d				18 58										19 28										19 58
Oxshott	d				19 01										19 31										20 01
Claygate	d				19 04										19 34										20 04
Hinchley Wood	d				19 07										19 37										20 07
Hampton Court	d	18 54										19 24										19 54			
Thames Ditton	d	18 56										19 26										19 56			
Surbiton 6	d	19 02			19 12					19 27		19 32			19 42					19 57		20 02			20 12
Berrylands	d	19 04										19 34										20 04			
Shepperton	d		18 41										19 11										19 41		
Upper Halliford	d		18 44										19 14										19 44		
Sunbury	d		18 46										19 16										19 46		
Kempton Park	d		18 48										19 18										19 48		
Hampton	d		18 51										19 21										19 51		
Fulwell	d		18 54										19 24										19 54		
Strawberry Hill	d							19 07										19 37							
Teddington	d		18 59					19 11					19 29					19 41					19 59		
Hampton Wick	d		19 01					19 14					19 31					19 44					20 01		
Kingston	a		19 03					19 16					19 33					19 46					20 03		
	d		19 04					19 19					19 34					19 49					20 04		
Norbiton	d		19 06					19 21					19 36					19 51					20 06		
New Malden 6	d	19 07	19 10					19 25				19 37	19 40					19 55				20 07	20 10		
Dorking 4	d										19 05										19 35				
Box Hill & Westhumble	d																								
Leatherhead	d			18 54							19 11			19 24							19 41			19 54	
Ashtead	d			18 58							19 14			19 28							19 44			19 58	
Epsom 3	a			19 02							19 19			19 32							19 49			20 02	
	d			19 05							19 20			19 35							19 50			20 05	
Ewell West	d			19 08							19 23			19 38							19 53			20 08	
Stoneleigh	d			19 10							19 25			19 40							19 55			20 10	
Worcester Park	d			19 13							19 28			19 43							19 58			20 13	
Chessington South	d					19 10										19 40									
Chessington North	d					19 12										19 42									
Tolworth	d					19 14										19 44									
Malden Manor	d					19 17										19 47									
Motspur Park	d			19 16		19 20					19 31			19 46		19 50					20 01			20 16	
Raynes Park 6	d	19 10	19 13	19 19		19 23		19 28			19 34	19 40	19 43	19 49		19 53		19 58			20 04	20 10	20 13	20 19	
Wimbledon 6 ⊖	d	19 14	19 17	19 23	19 20	19 27		19 32		19 35	19 38	19 44	19 47	19 53	19 50	19 57		20 02		20 05	20 08	20 14	20 17	20 23	20 20
Earlsfield	d	19 17	19 20	19 27	19 24	19 31		19 35		19 38	19 42	19 47	19 50	19 57	19 54	20 01		20 05		20 08	20 12	20 17	20 20	20 27	20 24
Clapham Junction 10	d	19 21	19 24	19 31	19 28	19 35		19 39		19 42	19 46	19 51	19 54	20 01	19 58	20 05		20 09		20 12	20 16	20 21	20 24	20 31	20 28
Vauxhall ⊖	d	19 26	19 29	19 36	19 33	19 40		19 44		19 47	19 51	19 56	19 59	20 06	20 03	20 10		20 14		20 17	20 21	20 26	20 29	20 36	20 33
London Waterloo 15 ⊖	a	19 31	19 34	19 40	19 37	19 45		19 49		19 52	19 55	20 01	20 04	20 10	20 07	20 15		20 19		20 22	20 25	20 31	20 34	20 40	20 37

Hampton Court, Shepperton, Guildford, Dorking and Chessington South - London

Network Diagram - see first Page of Table 152

		SW		SW		SW	SW	SW	SW	SW	SW	SW		SW		SW	SW	SW	SW	SW	SW	SW		SW	
Guildford	d									19 58	20 08									20 38					
London Road (Guildford)	d									20 02	20 12									20 42					
Clandon	d									20 07	20 17									20 47					
Horsley	d									20 11	20 21									20 51					
Effingham Junction 6	d									20 16	20 24									20 54					
Bookham	d									20 19															
Cobham & Stoke d'Abernon	d										20 28									20 58					
Oxshott	d										20 31									21 01					
Claygate	d										20 34									21 04					
Hinchley Wood	d										20 37									21 07					
Hampton Court	d							20 24										20 54							
Thames Ditton	d							20 26										20 56							
Surbiton 6	d					20 27		20 32			20 42					20 57		21 02		21 12					
Berrylands	d							20 34										21 04							
Shepperton	d								20 11										20 41						
Upper Halliford	d								20 14										20 44						
Sunbury	d								20 16										20 46						
Kempton Park	d								20 18										20 48						
Hampton	d								20 21										20 51						
Fulwell	d								20 24										20 54						
Strawberry Hill	d			20 07										20 37										21 07	
Teddington	d			20 11					20 29					20 41					20 59					21 11	
Hampton Wick	d			20 14					20 31					20 44					21 01					21 14	
Kingston	a			20 16					20 33					20 46					21 03					21 16	
	d			20 19					20 34					20 49					21 04					21 19	
Norbiton	d			20 21					20 36					20 51					21 06					21 21	
New Malden 6	d			20 25				20 37	20 40					20 55				21 07	21 10					21 25	
Dorking 4	d						20 05										20 35								
Box Hill & Westhumble	d																								
Leatherhead	d						20 11			20 24							20 41								
Ashtead	d						20 14			20 28							20 44								
Epsom 3	a						20 19			20 32							20 49								
	d						20 20			20 35							20 50				21 05				
Ewell West	d						20 23			20 38							20 53				21 08				
Stoneleigh	d						20 25			20 40							20 55				21 10				
Worcester Park	d						20 28			20 43							20 58				21 13				
Chessington South	d	20 10										20 40										21 10			
Chessington North	d	20 12										20 42										21 12			
Tolworth	d	20 14										20 44										21 14			
Malden Manor	d	20 17										20 47										21 17			
Motspur Park	d	20 20					20 31			20 46		20 50					21 01				21 16	21 20			
Raynes Park 6	d	20 23		20 28			20 34	20 40	20 43	20 49		20 53		20 58			21 04	21 10	21 13		21 19	21 23		21 28	
Wimbledon 6 ⊖ ⇌	d	20 27		20 32		20 35	20 38	20 44	20 47	20 53	20 50	20 57		21 02		21 05	21 08	21 14	21 17	21 20	21 23	21 27		21 32	
Earlsfield	d	20 31		20 35		20 38	20 42	20 47	20 50	20 57	20 54	21 01		21 05		21 08	21 12	21 17	21 20	21 24	21 27	21 31		21 35	
Clapham Junction 10	d	20 35		20 39		20 42	20 46	20 51	20 54	21 01	20 58	21 05		21 09		21 12	21 16	21 21	21 24	21 28	21 31	21 35		21 39	
Vauxhall ⊖	d	20 40		20 44		20 47	20 51	20 56	20 59	21 06	21 03	21 10		21 14		21 17	21 21	21 26	21 29	21 33	21 36	21 40		21 44	
London Waterloo 15 ⊖	a	20 45		20 49		20 52	20 55	21 01	21 04	21 10	21 07	21 15		21 19		21 23	21 25	21 31	21 34	21 37	21 40	21 45		21 49	

		SW	SW	SW	SW	SW	SW	SW		SW		SW	SW	SW	SW	SW		SW		SW	SW	SW	SW	SW	SW
Guildford	d		20 46			21 08									21 38					21 46			22 08		
London Road (Guildford)	d		20 50			21 12									21 42					21 50			22 12		
Clandon	d		20 55			21 17									21 47					21 55			22 17		
Horsley	d		20 59			21 21									21 51					21 59			22 21		
Effingham Junction 6	d		21 03			21 24									21 54					22 03			22 24		
Bookham	d		21 06																	22 06					
Cobham & Stoke d'Abernon	d					21 28									21 58								22 28		
Oxshott	d					21 31									22 01								22 31		
Claygate	d					21 34									22 04								22 34		
Hinchley Wood	d					21 37									22 07								22 37		
Hampton Court	d			21 24																	22 24				
Thames Ditton	d			21 26																	22 26				
Surbiton 6	d	21 27		21 32		21 42						21 57			22 12			22 27			22 32		22 42		
Berrylands	d			21 34																	22 34				
Shepperton	d				21 11									21 41								22 11			
Upper Halliford	d				21 14									21 44								22 14			
Sunbury	d				21 16									21 46								22 16			
Kempton Park	d				21 18									21 48								22 18			
Hampton	d				21 21									21 51								22 21			
Fulwell	d				21 24									21 54								22 24			
Strawberry Hill	d									21 37						22 07									22 37
Teddington	d				21 29					21 41				21 59		22 11						22 29			22 41
Hampton Wick	d				21 31					21 44				22 01		22 14						22 31			22 44
Kingston	a				21 33					21 46				22 03		22 16						22 33			22 46
	d				21 34					21 49				22 04		22 19						22 34			22 49
Norbiton	d				21 36					21 51				22 06		22 21						22 36			22 51
New Malden 6	d			21 37	21 40					21 55				22 10		22 25					22 37	22 40			22 55
Dorking 4	d												21 35												
Box Hill & Westhumble	d																								
Leatherhead	d		21 11										21 41							22 11					
Ashtead	d		21 14										21 44							22 14					
Epsom 3	a		21 19										21 49							22 19					
	d		21 20				21 35						21 50							22 20					
Ewell West	d		21 23				21 38						21 53							22 23					
Stoneleigh	d		21 25				21 40						21 55							22 25					
Worcester Park	d		21 28				21 43						21 58							22 28					
Chessington South	d							21 40																22 40	
Chessington North	d							21 42																22 42	
Tolworth	d							21 44																22 44	
Malden Manor	d							21 47																22 47	
Motspur Park	d		21 31				21 46	21 50					22 01							22 31				22 50	
Raynes Park 6	d		21 34	21 40	21 43		21 49	21 53		21 58			22 04	22 13		22 28				22 34	22 40	22 43		22 53	22 58
Wimbledon 6 ⊖ ⇌	d	21 35	21 38	21 44	21 47	21 50	21 53	21 57		22 02		22 05	22 08	22 17	22 20	22 32		22 35		22 38	22 44	22 47	22 50	22 57	23 02
Earlsfield	d	21 38	21 42	21 47	21 50	21 54	21 57	22 01		22 05		22 08	22 12	22 20	22 24	22 35		22 38		22 42	22 47	22 50	22 54	23 01	23 05
Clapham Junction 10	d	21 42	21 46	21 51	21 54	21 58	22 01	22 05		22 09		22 12	22 16	22 24	22 28	22 39		22 42		22 46	22 51	22 54	22 58	23 05	23 09
Vauxhall ⊖	d	21 47	21 51	21 56	21 59	22 03	22 06	22 10		22 14		22 17	22 21	22 29	22 33	22 44		22 47		22 51	22 56	22 59	23 03	23 10	23 14
London Waterloo 15 ⊖	a	21 52	21 55	22 01	22 04	22 07	22 10	22 15		22 19		22 22	22 25	22 34	22 39	22 49		22 52		22 55	23 01	23 04	23 07	23 15	23 19

Table 152

Saturdays

Hampton Court, Shepperton, Guildford, Dorking and Chessington South - London

Network Diagram - see first Page of Table 152

			SW	SW		SW	SW	SW		SW	SW	SW	SW	SW		SN	SW	SW
Guildford	d		22 20				22 38			22 46	22 55			23 08				
London Road (Guildford)	d						22 42			22 50				23 12				
Clandon	d						22 47			22 55				23 17				
Horsley	d						22 51			22 59				23 21				
Effingham Junction 6	d						22 54			23 03				23 24				
Bookham	d									23 06								
Cobham & Stoke d'Abernon	d						22 58							23 28				
Oxshott	d						23 01							23 31				
Claygate	d						23 04							23 34				
Hinchley Wood	d						23 07							23 37				
Hampton Court	d											23 24						
Thames Ditton	d											23 26						
Surbiton 6	d		22 57				23 12				23 30	23 33		23 42				
Berrylands	d											23 35						
Shepperton	d					22 41							23 11					
Upper Halliford	d					22 44							23 14					
Sunbury	d					22 46							23 16					
Kempton Park	d					22 48							23 18					
Hampton	d					22 51							23 21					
Fulwell	d					22 54							23 24					
Strawberry Hill	d							23 07										23 37
Teddington	d					22 59		23 11					23 29					23 41
Hampton Wick	d					23 01		23 14					23 31					23 44
Kingston	a					23 03		23 16					23 33					23 46
	d					23 04		23 19					23 34					23 49
Norbiton	d					23 06		23 21					23 36					23 51
New Malden 6	d					23 10		23 25				23 38	23 41					23 55
Dorking 4	d			22 35												23 30		
Box Hill & Westhumble	d																	
Leatherhead	d			22 41						23 11						23 36		
Ashtead	d			22 44						23 14						23 39		
Epsom 3	a			22 49						23 19						23 45		
	d			22 50						23 20								
Ewell West	d			22 53						23 23								
Stoneleigh	d			22 55						23 25								
Worcester Park	d			22 58						23 28								
Chessington South	d																23 40	
Chessington North	d																23 42	
Tolworth	d																23 44	
Malden Manor	d																23 47	
Motspur Park	d			23 01						23 31							23 50	
Raynes Park 6	d			23 04		23 13		23 28		23 37		23 41	23 43				23 54	23 58
Wimbledon 6 ⊖	d		23 05	23 08		23 17	23 20	23 32		23 41	23 37	23 46	23 49	23 52			23a57	00 02
Earlsfield	d		23 08	23 12		23 20	23 24	23 35		23 44	23 41	23 50	23 53	23 56				00 05
Clapham Junction 10	d		23 12	23 16		23 24	23 28	23 39		23 48	23 45	23 53	23 56	23 58				00 09
Vauxhall ⊖	d		23 17	23 21		23 29	23 33	23 44		23 53	23 50	23 58	00 01	00 04				00 15
London Waterloo 15 ⊖	a		23 22	23 25		23 34	23 37	23 49		23 58	23 54	00 03	00 06	00 14				00 22

Table 152

Sundays

Hampton Court, Shepperton, Guildford, Dorking and Chessington South - London

Network Diagram - see first Page of Table 152

		SW	SW	SW	SW	SW	SW	SW	SW	SW	SW	SW	SW	SW		SW	SW	SW	SW	SW	SW	SW		SW ■1	SW
		A	A	A	A	A	A																		
Guildford	d			23p08												06 57				07 27					
London Road (Guildford)	d			23p12																					
Clandon	d			23p17																					
Horsley	d			23p21																					
Effingham Junction ■6	d			23p24																					
Bookham	d																								
Cobham & Stoke d'Abernon	d			23p28																					
Oxshott	d			23p31																					
Claygate	d			23p34																					
Hinchley Wood	d			23p37																					
Hampton Court	d	23p24																	07 35						08 05
Thames Ditton	d	23p26																	07 37						08 07
Surbiton ■6	d	23p33		23p42									07 00			07 30			07 43	08 00				08 10	08 13
Berrylands	d	23p35																	07 45						08 15
Shepperton	d		23p11															07 11							
Upper Halliford	d		23p14															07 14							
Sunbury	d		23p16															07 16							
Kempton Park	d		23p18															07 18							
Hampton	d		23p21															07 21							
Fulwell	d		23p24															07 24							
Strawberry Hill	d				23p37	23p38	00 07							06 49								07 49			
Teddington	d		23p29		23p41		00 11	00s56						06 55				07 29				07 55			
Hampton Wick	d		23p31		23p44		00 14	00s59						06 57				07 31				07 57			
Kingston	a		23p33		23p46		00 16	01 01						06 59				07 33				07 59			
	d		23p34		23p49									07 04				07 34				08 04			
Norbiton	d		23p36		23p51									07 06				07 36				08 06			
New Malden ■6	d	23p38	23p41		23p55									07 10				07 40	07 48			08 10			08 18
Dorking ■4	d																								
Box Hill & Westhumble	d																								
Leatherhead	d																								
Ashtead	d																								
Epsom ■3	a																								
	d																07 24				07 54				
Ewell West	d																07 27				07 57				
Stoneleigh	d																07 29				07 59				
Worcester Park	d																07 32				08 02				
Chessington South	d																								
Chessington North	d																								
Tolworth	d																								
Malden Manor	d																								
Motspur Park	d																07 35				08 05				
Raynes Park ■6	d	23p41	23p43		23p58									07 13			07 38	07 43	07 51		08 08	08 13			08 21
Wimbledon ■6 ⊖	d	23p46	23p49	23p52	00 02				05 31	06 12	06 42	07 31	07 08	07 19		07 38	07 42	07 47	07 55	08 08	08 12	08 17		08 20	08 25
Earlsfield	d	23p50	23p53	23p56	00 05						06 46	07 34	07 11	07 22		07 41	07 46	07 50	07 58	08 11	08 16	08 20			08 28
Clapham Junction ■10	d	23p53	23p56	23p58	00 09				05 38	06 20	06 50	07 38	07 15	07 26		07 45	07 50	07 54	08 02	08 15	08 20	08 24		08 28	08 34
Vauxhall ⊖	d	23p58	00 01	00 04	00 15	00 12			05 43	06 25	06 55	07 43	07 20	07 31		07 50	07 55	07 59	08 07	08 20	08 25	08 29			08 39
London Waterloo ■15 ⊖	a	00 03	00 06	00 14	00 22	00 16			05 54	06 34	07 04	07 53	07 30	07 41		08 00	08 04	08 07	08 17	08 30	08 34	08 39		08 41	08 47

A not 11 December

Table 152

Sundays

Hampton Court, Shepperton, Guildford, Dorking and Chessington South - London

Network Diagram - see first Page of Table 152

		SW	SW	SW	SW	SW	SW	SW	SW	SW	SW		SW	SW	SW	SW	SW	SW	SW	SW	SW	SW	SW		SW
Guildford	d			07 57					08 20	08 27					08 50	08 57					09 20	09 27			
London Road (Guildford)	d								08 24						08 54						09 24				
Clandon	d		07 50						08 29						08 59						09 29				
Horsley	d		07 54						08 33						09 03						09 33				
Effingham Junction 6	d		07 59						08 36						09 06						09 36				
Bookham	d		08 03						08 39												09 39				
Cobham & Stoke d'Abernon	d		08 06												09 10										
Oxshott	d														09 13										
Claygate	d		08 10												09 16										
Hinchley Wood	d		08 13												09 19										
Hampton Court	d		08 16				08 35						09 05						09 35						10 05
Thames Ditton	d		08 19				08 37						09 07						09 37						10 07
Surbiton 6	d			08 30			08 43			09 00			09 13		09 24	09 30			09 43			10 00			10 13
Berrylands	d						08 45						09 15						09 45						10 15
Shepperton	d		08 24			08 11												09 11							
Upper Halliford	d					08 14												09 14							
Sunbury	d					08 16												09 16							
Kempton Park	d					08 18												09 18							
Hampton	d					08 21												09 21							
Fulwell	d					08 24												09 24							
Strawberry Hill	d										08 49												09 49		
Teddington	d					08 29					08 55							09 29					09 55		
Hampton Wick	d					08 31					08 57							09 31					09 57		
Kingston	a					08 33					08 59							09 33					09 59		
	d					08 34					09 04							09 34					10 04		
Norbiton	d					08 36					09 06							09 36					10 06		
New Malden 6	d					08 40	08 48				09 10		09 18					09 40	09 48				10 10		10 18
Dorking 4	d																09 08								
Box Hill & Westhumble	d																								
Leatherhead	d								08 45								09 15				09 45				
Ashtead	d								08 48								09 18				09 48				
Epsom 3	a								08 53								09 23				09 53				
	d				08 24				08 54								09 24				09 54				
Ewell West	d				08 27				08 57								09 27				09 57				
Stoneleigh	d				08 29				08 59								09 29				09 59				
Worcester Park	d				08 32				09 02								09 32				10 02				
Chessington South	d							08 40						09 10						09 40					
Chessington North	d							08 42						09 12						09 42					
Tolworth	d	08 10						08 44						09 14						09 44					
Malden Manor	d	08 12						08 47						09 17						09 47					
Motspur Park	d	08 14			08 35			08 50	09 05					09 20			09 35			09 50	10 05				
Raynes Park 6	d	08 17			08 38	08 43	08 51	08 54	09 08		09 13		09 21	09 24			09 38	09 43	09 51	09 54	10 08		10 13		10 21
Wimbledon 6 ⊖	d	08 20		08 38	08 42	08 47	08 55	08 58	09 12	09 08	09 17		09 25	09 28	09a33	09 38	09 42	09 47	09 55	09 58	10 12	10 08	10 17		10 25
Earlsfield	d	08 24		08 41	08 46	08 50	08 58	09 01	09 16	09 11	09 20		09 28	09 31		09 41	09 46	09 50	09 58	10 01	10 16	10 11	10 20		10 28
Clapham Junction 10	d	08 28	08a33	08 45	08 50	08 54	09 02	09 09	09 20	09 15	09 24		09 33	09 36		09 45	09 50	09 54	10 06	10 09	10 20	10 15	10 24		10 32
Vauxhall ⊖	d	08 31		08 50	08 55	08 59	09 07	09 14	09 25	09 20	09 29		09 38	09 41		09 50	09 55	09 59	10 11	10 14	10 25	10 20	10 32		10 37
London Waterloo 15 ⊖	a	08 37		09 00	09 04	09 07	09 17	09 20	09 34	09 30	09 39		09 47	09 50		10 00	10 04	10 07	10 17	10 20	10 34	10 30	10 39		10 45

		SW		SW	SW	SW	SW	SW	SW	SW	SW	SW			SW	SW	SW	SW	SW	SW	SW	SW		SW	SW
Guildford	d			09 50	09 57					10 20	10 27						10 50	10 57						11 20	11 27
London Road (Guildford)	d			09 54						10 24							10 54							11 24	
Clandon	d			09 59						10 29							10 59							11 29	
Horsley	d			10 03						10 33							11 03							11 33	
Effingham Junction 6	d			10 06						10 36							11 06							11 36	
Bookham	d									10 39														11 39	
Cobham & Stoke d'Abernon	d			10 10													11 10								
Oxshott	d			10 13													11 13								
Claygate	d			10 16													11 16								
Hinchley Wood	d			10 19													11 19								
Hampton Court	d							10 35							11 05						11 35				
Thames Ditton	d							10 37							11 07						11 37				
Surbiton 6	d			10 24	10 30			10 43			11 00				11 13		11 24	11 30			11 43				12 00
Berrylands	d							10 45							11 15						11 45				
Shepperton	d						10 11													11 11					
Upper Halliford	d						10 14													11 14					
Sunbury	d						10 16													11 16					
Kempton Park	d						10 18													11 18					
Hampton	d						10 21													11 21					
Fulwell	d						10 24													11 24					
Strawberry Hill	d											10 49													
Teddington	d						10 29					10 55								11 29					
Hampton Wick	d						10 31					10 57								11 31					
Kingston	a						10 33					10 59								11 33					
	d						10 34					11 04								11 34					
Norbiton	d						10 36					11 06								11 36					
New Malden 6	d						10 40	10 48				11 10			11 18					11 40	11 48				
Dorking 4	d					10 08													11 08						
Box Hill & Westhumble	d																								
Leatherhead	d					10 15				10 45									11 15					11 45	
Ashtead	d					10 18				10 48									11 18					11 48	
Epsom 3	a					10 23				10 53									11 23					11 53	
	d					10 24				10 54									11 24					11 54	
Ewell West	d					10 27				10 57									11 27					11 57	
Stoneleigh	d					10 29				10 59									11 29					11 59	
Worcester Park	d					10 32				11 02									11 32					12 02	
Chessington South	d	10 10							10 40							11 10						11 40			
Chessington North	d	10 12							10 42							11 12						11 42			
Tolworth	d	10 14							10 44							11 14						11 44			
Malden Manor	d	10 17							10 47							11 17						11 47			
Motspur Park	d	10 20				10 35			10 50	11 05						11 20			11 35			11 50		12 05	
Raynes Park 6	d	10 24				10 38	10 43	10 51	10 54	11 08		11 13			11 21	11 24			11 38	11 43	11 51	11 54		12 08	
Wimbledon 6 ⊖	d	10 28		10a33	10 38	10 42	10 47	10 55	10 58	11 12	11 08	11 17			11 25	11 28	11a33	11 38	11 42	11 47	11 55	11 58		12 12	12 08
Earlsfield	d	10 31			10 41	10 46	10 50	10 58	11 01	11 16	11 11	11 20			11 28	11 31		11 41	11 46	11 50	11 58	12 01		12 16	12 11
Clapham Junction 10	d	10 36			10 45	10 50	10 54	11 02	11 05	11 20	11 15	11 24			11 32	11 35		11 45	11 50	11 54	12 02	12 05		12 20	12 15
Vauxhall ⊖	d	10 41			10 50	10 55	10 59	11 07	11 13	11 25	11 20	11 32			11 37	11 40		11 50	11 55	11 59	12 07	12 13		12 25	12 20
London Waterloo 15 ⊖	a	10 50			11 00	11 04	11 07	11 17	11 20	11 34	11 30	11 39			11 47	11 50		12 00	12 04	12 07	12 17	12 22		12 34	12 30

Table 152

Sundays

Hampton Court, Shepperton, Guildford, Dorking and Chessington South - London

Network Diagram - see first Page of Table 152

		SW		SW	SW	SW	SW	SW		SW	SW	SW	SW	SW	SW		SW	SW		SW	SW		SW	SW	SW
Guildford	d					11 50	11 57						12 20	12 27						12 50	12 57				
London Road (Guildford)	d					11 54							12 24							12 54					
Clandon	d					11 59							12 29							12 59					
Horsley	d					12 03							12 33							13 03					
Effingham Junction 6	d					12 06							12 36							13 06					
Bookham	d												12 39												
Cobham & Stoke d'Abernon	d					12 10														13 10					
Oxshott	d					12 13														13 13					
Claygate	d					12 16														13 16					
Hinchley Wood	d					12 19														13 19					
Hampton Court	d			12 05							12 35						13 05								13 35
Thames Ditton	d			12 07							12 37						13 07								13 37
Surbiton 6	d			12 13		12 24	12 30				12 43			13 00			13 13			13 24	13 30				13 43
Berrylands	d			12 15							12 45						13 15								13 45
Shepperton	d									12 11														13 11	
Upper Halliford	d									12 14														13 14	
Sunbury	d									12 16														13 16	
Kempton Park	d									12 18														13 18	
Hampton	d									12 21														13 21	
Fulwell	d									12 24														13 24	
Strawberry Hill	d	11 50													12 50										
Teddington	d	11 55								12 29					12 55									13 29	
Hampton Wick	d	11 57								12 31					12 57									13 31	
Kingston	a	11 59								12 33					12 59									13 33	
	d	12 04								12 34					13 04									13 34	
Norbiton	d	12 06								12 36					13 06									13 36	
New Malden 6	d	12 10		12 18						12 40	12 48				13 10		13 18							13 40	13 48
Dorking 4	d							12 08															13 08		
Box Hill & Westhumble	d																								
Leatherhead	d							12 15					12 45										13 15		
Ashtead	d							12 18					12 48										13 18		
Epsom 3	a							12 23					12 53										13 23		
	d							12 24					12 54										13 24		
Ewell West	d							12 27					12 57										13 27		
Stoneleigh	d							12 29					12 59										13 29		
Worcester Park	d							12 32					13 02										13 32		
Chessington South	d				12 10							12 40						13 10							
Chessington North	d				12 12							12 42						13 12							
Tolworth	d				12 14							12 44						13 14							
Malden Manor	d				12 17							12 47						13 17							
Motspur Park	d				12 20			12 35				12 50	13 05					13 20					13 35		
Raynes Park 6	d	12 13		12 21	12 24			12 38		12 43	12 51	12 54	13 08		13 13		13 21	13 24					13 38	13 43	13 51
Wimbledon 6 ⊖	d	12 17		12 25	12 28	12 31	12 38	12 42		12 47	12 55	12 58	13 12	13 08	13 17		13 25	13 28		13 31	13 38		13 42	13 47	13 55
Earlsfield	d	12 20		12 28	12 31	12 35	12 41	12 46		12 50	12 58	13 01	13 16	13 11	13 20		13 28	13 31		13 35	13 41		13 46	13 50	13 58
Clapham Junction 10	d	12 24		12 32	12 35	12 39	12 45	12 50		12 54	13 02	13 05	13 20	13 15	13 24		13 32	13 35		13 39	13 45		13 50	13 54	14 02
Vauxhall ⊖	d	12 29		12 37	12 40	12 44	12 50	12 55		12 59	13 07	13 10	13 25	13 20	13 29		13 37	13 40		13 44	13 50		13 55	13 59	14 07
London Waterloo 15 ⊖	a	12 39		12 47	12 50	12 53	13 00	13 04		13 07	13 17	13 20	13 34	13 30	13 39		13 47	13 50		13 53	14 00		14 04	14 07	14 17

		SW	SW	SW		SW		SW	SW	SW	SW		SW	SW		SW	SW	SW	SW	SW	SW		SW	SW	
Guildford	d		13 20	13 27						13 50	13 57								14 20	14 27					
London Road (Guildford)	d		13 24							13 54									14 24						
Clandon	d		13 29							13 59									14 29						
Horsley	d		13 33							14 03									14 33						
Effingham Junction 6	d		13 36							14 06									14 36						
Bookham	d		13 39																14 39						
Cobham & Stoke d'Abernon	d									14 10															
Oxshott	d									14 13															
Claygate	d									14 16															
Hinchley Wood	d									14 19															
Hampton Court	d							14 05									14 35						15 05		
Thames Ditton	d							14 07									14 37						15 07		
Surbiton 6	d			14 00				14 13		14 24	14 30						14 43			15 00			15 13		
Berrylands	d							14 15									14 45						15 15		
Shepperton	d													14 11											
Upper Halliford	d													14 14											
Sunbury	d													14 16											
Kempton Park	d													14 18											
Hampton	d													14 21											
Fulwell	d													14 24											
Strawberry Hill	d					13 49										14 30					14 49				
Teddington	d					13 55								14 29		14 33					14 55				
Hampton Wick	d					13 57								14 31		14 36					14 57				
Kingston	a					13 59								14 33		14 38					14 59				
	d					14 04								14 34							15 04				
Norbiton	d					14 06								14 36							15 06				
New Malden 6	d					14 10		14 18						14 40			14 48				15 10		15 18		
Dorking 4	d												14 08												
Box Hill & Westhumble	d																								
Leatherhead	d		13 45										14 15						14 45						
Ashtead	d		13 48										14 18						14 48						
Epsom 3	a		13 53										14 23						14 53						
	d		13 54										14 24						14 54						
Ewell West	d		13 57										14 27						14 57						
Stoneleigh	d		13 59										14 29						14 59						
Worcester Park	d		14 02										14 32						15 02						
Chessington South	d	13 40							14 10									14 40						15 10	
Chessington North	d	13 42							14 12									14 42						15 12	
Tolworth	d	13 44							14 14									14 44						15 14	
Malden Manor	d	13 47							14 17									14 47						15 17	
Motspur Park	d	13 50	14 05						14 20				14 35					14 50	15 05					15 20	
Raynes Park 6	d	13 54	14 08			14 13		14 21	14 24				14 38	14 43			14 51	14 54	15 08		15 13		15 21	15 24	
Wimbledon 6 ⊖	d	13 58	14 12	14 08		14 17		14 25	14 28	14 31	14 38		14 42	14 47			14 55	14 58	15 12	15 08	15 17		15 25	15 28	
Earlsfield	d	14 01	14 16	14 11		14 20		14 28	14 31	14 35	14 41		14 46	14 50			14 58	15 01	15 16	15 11	15 20		15 28	15 31	
Clapham Junction 10	d	14 05	14 20	14 15		14 24		14 32	14 35	14 39	14 45		14 50	14 54			15 02	15 05	15 20	15 15	15 24		15 32	15 35	
Vauxhall ⊖	d	14 10	14 25	14 20		14 29		14 37	14 40	14 44	14 50		14 55	14 59			15 07	15 10	15 25	15 20	15 29		15 37	15 40	
London Waterloo 15 ⊖	a	14 20	14 34	14 30		14 34		14 42	14 45	14 48	14 55		14 59	15 04			15 12	15 15	15 29	15 25	15 34		15 42	15 45	

Table 152

Sundays

Hampton Court, Shepperton, Guildford, Dorking and Chessington South - London

Network Diagram - see first Page of Table 152

		SW	SW		SW	SW	SW	SW	SW	SW		SW	SW		SW	SW	SW	SW		SW		SW	SW	SW	SW
Guildford	d	14 50	14 57							15 20		15 27					15 50	15 57							
London Road (Guildford)	d	14 54								15 24							15 54								
Clandon	d	14 59								15 29							15 59								
Horsley	d	15 03								15 33							16 03								
Effingham Junction 6	d	15 06								15 36							16 06								
Bookham	d									15 39															
Cobham & Stoke d'Abernon	d	15 10															16 10								
Oxshott	d	15 13															16 13								
Claygate	d	15 16															16 16								
Hinchley Wood	d	15 19															16 19								
Hampton Court	d							15 35							16 05									16 35	
Thames Ditton	d							15 37							16 07									16 37	
Surbiton 6	d	15 24	15 30					15 43				16 00			16 13		16 24	16 30						16 43	
Berrylands	d							15 45							16 15									16 45	
Shepperton	d					15 11																16 11			
Upper Halliford	d					15 14																16 14			
Sunbury	d					15 16																16 16			
Kempton Park	d					15 18																16 18			
Hampton	d					15 21																16 21			
Fulwell	d					15 24																16 24			
Strawberry Hill	d						15 30						15 49										16 30		
Teddington	d					15 29	15 33						15 55									16 29	16 33		
Hampton Wick	d					15 31	15 36						15 57									16 31	16 36		
Kingston	a					15 33	15 38						15 59									16 33	16 38		
	d					15 34							16 04									16 34			
Norbiton	d					15 36							16 06									16 36			
New Malden 6	d					15 40		15 48					16 10		16 18							16 40		16 48	
Dorking 4	d				15 08															16 08					
Box Hill & Westhumble	d																								
Leatherhead	d				15 15					15 45										16 15					
Ashtead	d				15 18					15 48										16 18					
Epsom 3	a				15 23					15 53										16 23					
	d				15 24					15 54										16 24					
Ewell West	d				15 27					15 57										16 27					
Stoneleigh	d				15 29					15 59										16 29					
Worcester Park	d				15 32					16 02										16 32					
Chessington South	d								15 40							16 10									16 40
Chessington North	d								15 42							16 12									16 42
Tolworth	d								15 44							16 14									16 44
Malden Manor	d								15 47							16 17									16 47
Motspur Park	d				15 35				15 50	16 05						16 20				16 35					16 50
Raynes Park 6	d				15 38	15 43		15 51	15 54	16 08			16 13		16 21	16 24				16 38		16 43		16 51	16 54
Wimbledon 6 ⊖	d	15 31	15 38		15 42	15 47		15 55	15 58	16 12		16 08	16 17		16 25	16 28	16 31	16 38		16 42		16 47		16 55	16 58
Earlsfield	d	15 35	15 41		15 46	15 50		15 58	16 01	16 16		16 11	16 20		16 28	16 31	16 35	16 41		16 46		16 50		16 58	17 01
Clapham Junction 10	d	15 39	15 45		15 50	15 54		16 02	16 05	16 20		16 15	16 24		16 32	16 35	16 39	16 45		16 50		16 54		17 02	17 05
Vauxhall ⊖	d	15 44	15 50		15 55	15 59		16 07	16 10	16 25		16 20	16 29		16 37	16 40	16 44	16 50		16 55		16 59		17 07	17 10
London Waterloo 15 ⊖	a	15 48	15 55		15 59	16 04		16 12	16 15	16 29		16 25	16 34		16 42	16 45	16 48	16 55		16 59		17 04		17 12	17 15

		SW	SW	SW		SW		SW	SW	SW		SW	SW	SW	SW	SW		SW	SW	SW		SW	SW	SW	SW
Guildford	d	16 20	16 27						16 50	16 57								17 20	17 27					17 50	17 57
London Road (Guildford)	d	16 24							16 54									17 24						17 54	
Clandon	d	16 29							16 59									17 29						17 59	
Horsley	d	16 33							17 03									17 33						18 03	
Effingham Junction 6	d	16 36							17 06									17 36						18 06	
Bookham	d	16 39																17 39							
Cobham & Stoke d'Abernon	d								17 10															18 10	
Oxshott	d								17 13															18 13	
Claygate	d								17 16															18 16	
Hinchley Wood	d								17 19															18 19	
Hampton Court	d					17 05									17 35							18 05			
Thames Ditton	d					17 07									17 37							18 07			
Surbiton 6	d		17 00			17 13			17 24	17 30					17 43				18 00			18 13		18 24	18 30
Berrylands	d					17 15									17 45							18 15			
Shepperton	d												17 11												
Upper Halliford	d												17 14												
Sunbury	d												17 16												
Kempton Park	d												17 18												
Hampton	d												17 21												
Fulwell	d												17 24												
Strawberry Hill	d			16 49										17 30						17 49					
Teddington	d			16 55									17 29	17 33						17 55					
Hampton Wick	d			16 57									17 31	17 36						17 57					
Kingston	a			16 59									17 33	17 38						17 59					
	d			17 04									17 34							18 04					
Norbiton	d			17 06									17 36							18 06					
New Malden 6	d			17 10		17 18							17 40		17 48					18 10		18 18			
Dorking 4	d											17 08													
Box Hill & Westhumble	d																								
Leatherhead	d	16 45										17 15						17 45							
Ashtead	d	16 48										17 18						17 48							
Epsom 3	a	16 53										17 23						17 53							
	d	16 54										17 24						17 54							
Ewell West	d	16 57										17 27						17 57							
Stoneleigh	d	16 59										17 29						17 59							
Worcester Park	d	17 02										17 32						18 02							
Chessington South	d							17 10								17 40							18 10		
Chessington North	d							17 12								17 42							18 12		
Tolworth	d							17 14								17 44							18 14		
Malden Manor	d							17 17								17 47							18 17		
Motspur Park	d	17 05						17 20				17 35				17 50		18 05					18 20		
Raynes Park 6	d	17 08		17 13		17 21		17 24				17 38	17 43		17 51	17 54		18 08		18 13		18 21	18 24		
Wimbledon 6 ⊖	d	17 12	17 08	17 17		17 25		17 28	17 31	17 38		17 42	17 47		17 55	17 58		18 12	18 08	18 17		18 25	18 28	18 31	18 38
Earlsfield	d	17 16	17 11	17 20		17 28		17 31	17 35	17 41		17 46	17 50		17 58	18 01		18 16	18 11	18 20		18 28	18 31	18 35	18 41
Clapham Junction 10	d	17 20	17 15	17 24		17 32		17 35	17 39	17 45		17 50	17 54		18 02	18 05		18 20	18 15	18 24		18 32	18 35	18 39	18 45
Vauxhall ⊖	d	17 25	17 20	17 29		17 37		17 40	17 44	17 50		17 55	17 59		18 07	18 10		18 25	18 20	18 29		18 37	18 40	18 44	18 50
London Waterloo 15 ⊖	a	17 29	17 25	17 34		17 42		17 45	17 48	17 55		17 59	18 04		18 12	18 15		18 29	18 25	18 34		18 42	18 45	18 48	18 55

Hampton Court, Shepperton, Guildford, Dorking and Chessington South - London

Network Diagram - see first Page of Table 152

				SW	SW	SW	SW	SW	SW	SW	SW			SW	SW	SW	SW		SW	SW	SW	SW		SW	SW
Guildford	d								18 20	18 27						18 50	18 57								19 20
London Road (Guildford)	d								18 24							18 54									19 24
Clandon	d								18 29							18 59									19 29
Horsley	d								18 33							19 03									19 33
Effingham Junction 6	d								18 36							19 06									19 36
Bookham	d								18 39																19 39
Cobham & Stoke d'Abernon	d															19 10									
Oxshott	d															19 13									
Claygate	d															19 16									
Hinchley Wood	d															19 19									
Hampton Court	d						18 35							19 05								19 35			
Thames Ditton	d						18 37							19 07								19 37			
Surbiton 6	d						18 43			19 00				19 13		19 24	19 30					19 43			
Berrylands	d						18 45							19 15								19 45			
Shepperton	d				18 11															19 11					
Upper Halliford	d				18 14															19 14					
Sunbury	d				18 16															19 16					
Kempton Park	d				18 18															19 18					
Hampton	d				18 21															19 21					
Fulwell	d				18 24															19 24					
Strawberry Hill	d					18 30					18 49										19 30				
Teddington	d				18 29	18 33					18 55									19 29	19 33				
Hampton Wick	d				18 31	18 36					18 57									19 31	19 36				
Kingston	a				18 33	18 38					18 59									19 33	19 38				
	d				18 34						19 04									19 34					
Norbiton	d				18 36						19 06									19 36					
New Malden 6	d				18 40		18 48				19 10			19 18						19 40		19 48			
Dorking 4	d			18 08															19 08						
Box Hill & Westhumble	d																								
Leatherhead	d			18 15					18 45										19 15						19 45
Ashtead	d			18 18					18 48										19 18						19 48
Epsom 3	a			18 23					18 53										19 23						19 53
	d			18 24					18 54										19 24						19 54
Ewell West	d			18 27					18 57										19 27						19 57
Stoneleigh	d			18 29					18 59										19 29						19 59
Worcester Park	d			18 32					19 02										19 32						20 02
Chessington South	d							18 40							19 10									19 40	
Chessington North	d							18 42							19 12									19 42	
Tolworth	d							18 44							19 14									19 44	
Malden Manor	d							18 47							19 17									19 47	
Motspur Park	d			18 35				18 50	19 05						19 20				19 35					19 50	20 05
Raynes Park 6	d			18 38	18 43		18 51	18 54	19 08		19 13			19 21	19 24				19 38	19 43		19 51		19 54	20 08
Wimbledon 6 ⊖	d			18 42	18 47		18 55	18 58	19 12	19 08	19 17			19 25	19 28	19 31	19 38		19 42	19 47		19 55		19 58	20 12
Earlsfield	d			18 46	18 50		18 58	19 01	19 16	19 11	19 20			19 28	19 31	19 35	19 41		19 46	19 50		19 58		20 01	20 16
Clapham Junction 10	d			18 50	18 54		19 02	19 05	19 20	19 15	19 24			19 32	19 35	19 39	19 45		19 50	19 54		20 02		20 05	20 20
Vauxhall ⊖	d			18 55	18 59		19 07	19 10	19 25	19 20	19 29			19 37	19 40	19 44	19 50		19 55	19 59		20 07		20 10	20 25
London Waterloo 15 ⊖	a			18 59	19 04		19 12	19 15	19 29	19 25	19 34			19 42	19 45	19 48	19 55		19 59	20 04		20 12		20 15	20 29

		SW	SW		SW	SW	SW	SW			SW	SW	SW	SW	SW	SW	SW			SW	SW	SW	SW		SW
Guildford	d	19 27					19 50	19 57							20 20	20 27						20 50	20 57		
London Road (Guildford)	d						19 54								20 24							20 54			
Clandon	d						19 59								20 29							20 59			
Horsley	d						20 03								20 33							21 03			
Effingham Junction 6	d						20 06								20 36							21 06			
Bookham	d														20 39										
Cobham & Stoke d'Abernon	d						20 10															21 10			
Oxshott	d						20 13															21 13			
Claygate	d						20 16															21 16			
Hinchley Wood	d						20 19															21 19			
Hampton Court	d				20 05									20 35						21 05					
Thames Ditton	d				20 07									20 37						21 07					
Surbiton 6	d	20 00			20 13		20 24	20 30						20 43		21 00				21 13		21 24	21 30		
Berrylands	d				20 15									20 45						21 15					
Shepperton	d											20 11													
Upper Halliford	d											20 14													
Sunbury	d											20 16													
Kempton Park	d											20 18													
Hampton	d											20 21													
Fulwell	d											20 24													
Strawberry Hill	d		19 49										20 30				20 49								
Teddington	d		19 55									20 29	20 33				20 55								
Hampton Wick	d		19 57									20 31	20 36				20 57								
Kingston	a		19 59									20 33	20 38				20 59								
	d		20 04									20 34					21 04								
Norbiton	d		20 06									20 36					21 06								
New Malden 6	d		20 10		20 18							20 40		20 48			21 10			21 18					
Dorking 4	d										20 08														21 08
Box Hill & Westhumble	d																								
Leatherhead	d										20 15				20 45										21 15
Ashtead	d										20 18				20 48										21 18
Epsom 3	a										20 23				20 53										21 23
	d										20 24				20 54										21 24
Ewell West	d										20 27				20 57										21 27
Stoneleigh	d										20 29				20 59										21 29
Worcester Park	d										20 32				21 02										21 32
Chessington South	d					20 10															21 10				
Chessington North	d					20 12															21 12				
Tolworth	d					20 14															21 14				
Malden Manor	d					20 17															21 17				
Motspur Park	d					20 20					20 35				21 05						21 20				21 35
Raynes Park 6	d		20 13		20 21	20 24					20 38	20 43		20 51	21 08		21 13			21 21	21 24				21 38
Wimbledon 6 ⊖	d	20 08	20 17		20 25	20 28	20 31	20 38			20 42	20 47		20 55	21 12	21 08	21 17			21 25	21 28	21 31	21 38		21 42
Earlsfield	d	20 11	20 20		20 28	20 31	20 35	20 41			20 46	20 50		20 58	21 16	21 11	21 20			21 28	21 31	21 35	21 41		21 46
Clapham Junction 10	d	20 15	20 24		20 32	20 35	20 39	20 45			20 50	20 54		21 02	21 20	21 15	21 24			21 32	21 35	21 39	21 45		21 50
Vauxhall ⊖	d	20 20	20 29		20 37	20 40	20 44	20 50			20 55	20 59		21 07	21 25	21 20	21 29			21 37	21 40	21 44	21 50		21 55
London Waterloo 15 ⊖	a	20 25	20 34		20 42	20 45	20 48	20 55			21 00	21 04		21 13	21 29	21 25	21 35			21 42	21 45	21 48	21 55		22 00

Table 152

Sundays

Hampton Court, Shepperton, Guildford, Dorking and Chessington South - London

Network Diagram - see first Page of Table 152

		SW	SW	SW	SW	SW	SW	SW	SW	SW	SW	SW	SW	SW	SW	SW	SW	SW	SW
Guildford	d				21 20	21 27				21 50	21 57			22 20	22 27				
London Road (Guildford)	d				21 24					21 54				22 24					
Clandon	d				21 29					21 59				22 29					
Horsley	d				21 33					22 03				22 33					
Effingham Junction 6	d				21 36					22 06				22 36					
Bookham	d				21 39									22 39					
Cobham & Stoke d'Abernon	d									22 10									
Oxshott	d									22 13									
Claygate	d									22 16									
Hinchley Wood	d									22 19									
Hampton Court	d			21 35				22 05										23 05	
Thames Ditton	d			21 37				22 07										23 07	
Surbiton 6	d			21 43		22 00		22 13		22 24	22 30				23 00			23 13	
Berrylands	d			21 45				22 15										23 15	
Shepperton	d	21 11											22 11						
Upper Halliford	d	21 14											22 14						
Sunbury	d	21 16											22 16						
Kempton Park	d	21 18											22 18						
Hampton	d	21 21											22 21						
Fulwell	d	21 24											22 24						
Strawberry Hill	d		21 30				21 49									22 30	22 49		
Teddington	d	21 29	21 33				21 55						22 29			22 33	22 55		
Hampton Wick	d	21 31	21 36				21 57						22 31			22 36	22 57		
Kingston	a	21 33	21 38				21 59						22 33			22 38	22 59		
	d	21 34					22 04						22 34				23 04		
Norbiton	d	21 36					22 06						22 36				23 06		
New Malden 6	d	21 40		21 48			22 10	22 18					22 40				23 10	23 18	
Dorking 4	d											22 08							
Box Hill & Westhumble	d																		
Leatherhead	d				21 45							22 15		22 45					
Ashtead	d				21 48							22 18		22 48					
Epsom 3	a				21 53							22 23		22 53					
	d				21 54							22 24		22 54					
Ewell West	d				21 57							22 27		22 57					
Stoneleigh	d				21 59							22 29		22 59					
Worcester Park	d				22 02							22 32		23 02					
Chessington South	d								22 10										23 10
Chessington North	d								22 12										23 12
Tolworth	d								22 14										23 14
Malden Manor	d								22 17										23 17
Motspur Park	d				22 05				22 20			22 35		23 05					23 20
Raynes Park 6	d	21 43		21 51	22 08		22 13	22 21	22 24			22 38	22 43	23 08			23 13	23 21	23 24
Wimbledon 6 ⊖ ⛴	d	21 47		21 55	22 12	22 08	22 17	22 25	22 28	22 31	22 38	22 42	22 47	23 12	23 08		23 17	23 25	23 28
Earlsfield	d	21 50		21 58	22 16	22 11	22 20	22 28	22 31	22 35	22 41	22 46	22 50	23 16	23 11		23 20	23 28	23 31
Clapham Junction 10	d	21 54		22 02	22 20	22 15	22 24	22 32	22 35	22 39	22 45	22 50	22 54	23 20	23 15		23 24	23 32	23 35
Vauxhall ⊖	d	21 59		22 07	22 25	22 20	22 29	22 37	22 40	22 44	22 50	22 55	22 59	23 25	23 20		23 29	23 37	23 40
London Waterloo 15 ⊖	a	22 04		22 12	22 29	22 25	22 35	22 42	22 45	22 48	22 55	23 00	23 04	23 29	23 25		23 35	23 42	23 45

		SW	SW	SW	SW	SW	SW	SW	SW
Guildford	d	22 50	22 57						
London Road (Guildford)	d	22 54							
Clandon	d	22 59							
Horsley	d	23 03							
Effingham Junction 6	d	23 06							
Bookham	d								
Cobham & Stoke d'Abernon	d	23 10							
Oxshott	d	23 13							
Claygate	d	23 16							
Hinchley Wood	d	23 19							
Hampton Court	d							23 45	
Thames Ditton	d							23 47	
Surbiton 6	d	23 24	23 30					23 53	
Berrylands	d							23 55	
Shepperton	d				23 11				
Upper Halliford	d				23 14				
Sunbury	d				23 16				
Kempton Park	d				23 18				
Hampton	d				23 21				
Fulwell	d				23 24				
Strawberry Hill	d					23 30			23 48
Teddington	d				23 29	23 33			23 51
Hampton Wick	d				23 31	23 36			23 54
Kingston	a				23 33	23 38			23 56
	d				23 34				
Norbiton	d				23 36				
New Malden 6	d				23 40			23 58	
Dorking 4	d			23 08					
Box Hill & Westhumble	d								
Leatherhead	d			23 15					
Ashtead	d			23 18					
Epsom 3	a			23 23					
	d			23 24					
Ewell West	d			23 27					
Stoneleigh	d			23 29					
Worcester Park	d			23 32					
Chessington South	d						23 40		
Chessington North	d						23 42		
Tolworth	d						23 44		
Malden Manor	d						23 47		
Motspur Park	d			23 35	23 43		23 50		
Raynes Park 6	d			23 38	23 43		23 54	00 01	
Wimbledon 6 ⊖ ⛴	d	23 31	23 38	23 42	23 47		23a59	00a04	
Earlsfield	d	23 35	23 41	23 46	23 50				
Clapham Junction 10	d	23 39	23 45	23 50	23 54				
Vauxhall ⊖	d	23 44	23 50	23 55	23 59				
London Waterloo 15 ⊖	a	23 48	23 55	23 59	00 04				

Network Diagram for Tables 155, 156, 157

DM-16/11
Design BAJS

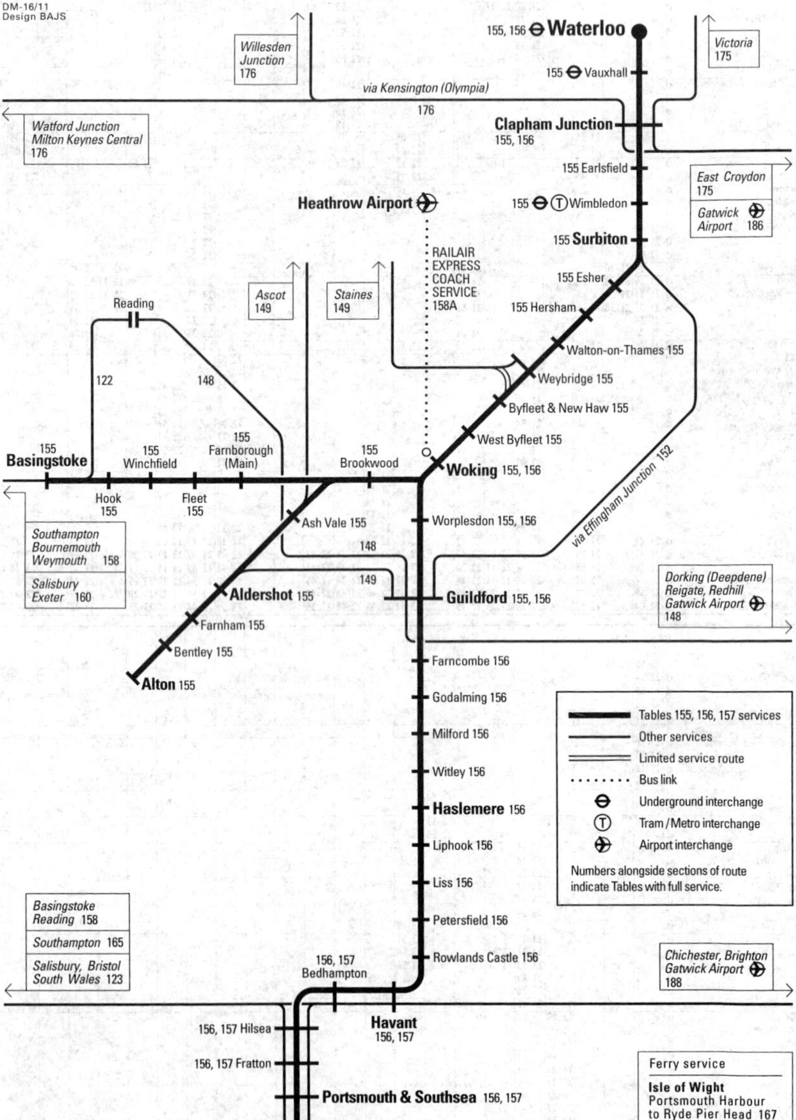

London - Woking, Guildford, Alton and Basingstoke

Network Diagram - see first Page of Table 155

Miles	Miles	Miles			SW	SW	SW	SW	SW		SW	SW	SW		SW	SW	SW	SW	SW	SW	SW	SW	SW		SW
					MO	MO	MX	MX	MO		MO	MX	MX		MX	MO	MX	MO	MX	MO	MX	MO	MX		MX
					1			1	1			1			1	1	1			1	1	1	1		1
0	—	—	**London Waterloo** 15 ⊖	d	22p37	22p50	22p52	22p53	23p07		23p10	23p12	23p20		23p23	23p30	23p35			23p35	23p40	23p40	23p45		23p48
1¼	—	—	Vauxhall ⊖	d		22p54	22p56				23p14		23p24									23p44			
4	—	—	Clapham Junction 10	d	22p46			23b00	23p15		23p19		23p29		23b30	23b39	23b42			23b44	23b47	23p49	23b52		23b55
—	—	—		d		23p00	23p02					23b19													
5½	—	—	Earlsfield	d							23p22		23p32									23p52			
7¼	—	—	Wimbledon 6 ⊖	d	22p53				23p22		23p26		23p36						←			23p56			
12	—	—	**Surbiton** 6	d	23p02			23p11	23p30		23p35	23p38	23p44		23p41				23p44			00 05			00 09
14½	—	—	Esher	d							23p39		→						23p48			00 09			
16	—	—	Hersham	d							23p42								23p51			00 12			
17	—	—	Walton-on-Thames	d	23p09						23p45	23p45							23p54			00 15			00 16
19	—	—	Weybridge	d	23p13						23p49	23p49							23p57			00 19			00 20
20½	—	—	Byfleet & New Haw	d		00 02	00 06				23p51								00 01			00 21			
21¾	—	—	West Byfleet	d		00 05	00 09	23p21			23p54				23p55			←	00 03			00 24			
24½	0	—	**Woking**	a	23p19	00 11	00 15	23p29	23p42		23p59	23p55			23p59	00 01	00 01	23p59	00 08	00 07	00 06	00 30	00 11		00 26
—	—	—																							
—	—	—		d	23p26			23p30	23p46	23p49	00 05	23p57			00 01	00 03	00 03	00 05		00 08	00 08	00 35	00 13		00 28
—	2½	—	Worplesdon	d							→											→	00 18		
—	6	—	**Guildford**	a												00 10		00 13					00 24		
28	—	0	Brookwood	d	23p32			23p36	23p51	23p55		00 03			00 07										00 34
—	—	4½	Ash Vale	d	23p40			23p44		00 03					00 15										
—	—	7	**Aldershot**	a	23p45			23p49		00 07					00 19										
—	—	—		d	23p48			23p50		00 08					00 20										
—	—	10	Farnham	a	23p54			23p55		00 13					00 25										
—	—	—		d	23p55			23p58		00 14					00 26										
—	—	14	Bentley	d				00 04		00 24					00 33										
—	—	18¾	**Alton**	a	00 07			00 11		00 31					00 40										
33¼	—	—	Farnborough (Main)	d					23p59			00 10					00 14			00 18					00 41
36½	—	—	Fleet	d					00 04			00 16					00 20			00 24					00 47
40	—	—	Winchfield	d					00 10			00 21													00s52
42¼	—	—	Hook	d					00 14			00 26													00s57
47¾	—	—	**Basingstoke**	a					00 21			00 33					00 33			00 39	00 27				01 06

		SW	SW	SW	SW	SW	SW	SW	SW		SW	SW	SW	SW	SW	SW	SW	SW	SW		SW	SW	SW	SW	SW
		MO	MX	MX	MO	MX	MO																		
		1	1	1			1	1	1		1	◇1	1	1	1	1		1	1		1		◇1	1	
London Waterloo 15 ⊖	d		00 05			00 09	00 50	01 05	05 00		05 20	05 30					05 50	06 12	06 15			06 20	06 30		
Vauxhall ⊖	d					00 13		01 09	05 04		05 24						05 54					06 24			
Clapham Junction 10	d		00u12			00 20	00 57		05 11		05 29	05u37					05 59	06u19	06u22			06 29	06u37		
	d							01 15																	
Earlsfield	d					00 23			05 14		05 32						06 02					06 32			
Wimbledon 6 ⊖	d		00u18			00 27		01s27	05 18		05 36	05 43					06 06					06 36			
Surbiton 6	d					00 35		01s35	05 26		05 44						06 14	06 30				06 44			
Esher	d					00s39			05 30		05 48						06 18					06 48			
Hersham	d					00s42			05 33		05 51						06 21					06 51			
Walton-on-Thames	d					00s44			05 37		05 54						06 24	06 37				06 54			
Weybridge	d					00s48			05 41		05 57						06 27	06 41				06 57			
Byfleet & New Haw	d					00s51			05 44		06 00						06 30					07 00			
West Byfleet	d	←			00s45	00s54			05 47		06 03			←			06 33				←	07 03			←
Woking	a	00 30	00 35		00 51	00 58	01 16	01 48	05 51		06 08	05 59		06 08			06 38	06 48	06 41		06 48	07 07	06 56		07 07
	d	00 35	00 37	00 40		01 00	01 18	01 49	05 53		06 11	06 01	06 02	06 11	06 19	06 30		06 50	06 43		06 50	07 10	06 57	06 58	07 10
Worplesdon	d										→			06 16				→	06 48			→			
Guildford	a					01 07	01s26		06 00					06 21					06 53						07 20
Brookwood	d	00 41		00 45									06 08		06 25	06 36					06 56			07 06	
Ash Vale	d	00 48		00 53									06 16			06 44								07 14	
Aldershot	a	00 53		00 58									06 21			06 49								07 19	
	d	00 54		00 59									06 21			06 50								07 20	
Farnham	a	00 59		01 04									06 27			06 55								07 25	
	d			01 05									06 27			06 56								07 26	
Bentley	d			01s11									06 34			07 02								07 32	
Alton	a			01 18									06 41			07 10								07 40	
Farnborough (Main)	d							01s58							06 33						07 04				
Fleet	d							02s04							06 38						07 09				
Winchfield	d														06 44						07 15				
Hook	d														06 48						07 19				
Basingstoke	a		00 55					02s16				06 20			06 58						07 28		07 16		

b Previous night, stops to pick up only

London - Woking, Guildford, Alton and Basingstoke

Network Diagram - see first Page of Table 155

		SW 1	SW 1	SW 1	SW		SW 1	SW ◇1 🛒	SW	SW 1	SW 1	SW 1	SW	SW 1	SW 1 🛒		SW 1	SW ◇1 🛒	SW	SW 1 🛒	SW 1	SW 1	SW ◇1 🛒	SW 1	SW
London Waterloo 15 ⊖	d	06 42	06 45		06 50		06 53	07 10		07 12	07 15		07 20	07 23	07 30			07 35		07 39	07 42	07 45	07 50		07 50
Vauxhall ⊖	d				06 54								07 24												07 54
Clapham Junction 10	d	06u49	06u52		06 59		07u00	07u17		07u20	07u23		07 29	07u30						07u46		07u52	07u57		07 59
	d																								
Earlsfield	d				07 02								07 32												08 02
Wimbledon 6 ⊖	d				07 06				←				07 36						←						08 06
Surbiton 6	d	07 00			07 14		07 11		07 14	07 31			07 44	07 41					07 44		08 00				08 14
Esher	d				→				07 18				→						07 48						→
Hersham	d								07 21										07 51						
Walton-on-Thames	d	07 07							07 24	07 38									07 54		08 07				
Weybridge	d	07 11							07 27	07 42									07 57		08 11				
Byfleet & New Haw	d								07 30										08 00						
West Byfleet	d			←			07 21		07 33			←		07 51			←		08 03					←	
Woking	a	07 18	07 11	07 18			07 26	07 35	07 37	07 48	07 42	07 48		07 59	07 54		07 59	07 58	08 08		08 18	08 12	08 15	08 18	
	d	07 19	07 13	07 19			07 30	07 36	07 39	07 50	07 44	07 50		08 00	07 55		08 00	08 00			08 19	08 14	08 16	08 19	
Worplesdon	d	→	07 18							→	07 49			→							→	08 19			
Guildford	a		07 23						07 47		07 54				08 03							08 24			
Brookwood	d			07 25			07 36					07 56					08 06							08 25	
Ash Vale	d						07 44										08 14								
Aldershot	a						07 49										08 19								
	d						07 50										08 20								
Farnham	a						07 55										08 25								
	d						07 56										08 26								
Bentley	d						08 02										08 32								
Alton	a						08 10										08 39								
Farnborough (Main)	d			07 33								08 03								08 13				08 33	
Fleet	d			07 38								08 09								08 19				08 38	
Winchfield	d			07 44								08 14												08 44	
Hook	d			07 48								08 19												08 48	
Basingstoke	a			07 56				07 55				08 26						08 19		08 32			08 37	08 58	

			SW 1	SW 1 🛒	SW 1	SW ◇1 🛒	SW 1	SW	SW 1	SW 1	SW ◇1 🛒		SW 1	SW	SW 1	SW 1 🛒	SW ◇1 🛒	SW 1	SW	SW 1	SW 1		SW 1	SW ◇1 🛒	SW 1
London Waterloo 15 ⊖	d		07 53	08 00		08 05	08 09		08 12	08 15	08 20			08 20	08 23	08 30	08 35			08 39	08 42		08 45	08 50	
Vauxhall ⊖	d													08 24											
Clapham Junction 10	d		08u00			08u12			08u19	08u22	08u27			08 29						08u46			08u52		
	d																								
Earlsfield	d													08 32											
Wimbledon 6 ⊖	d							←						08 36					←						
Surbiton 6	d		08 11					08 14	08 30					08 44	08 41				08 44		09 00				
Esher	d							08 18						→					08 48						
Hersham	d							08 21											08 51						
Walton-on-Thames	d							08 24	08 37										08 54		09 07				
Weybridge	d							08 27	08 41										08 57		09 11				
Byfleet & New Haw	d							08 30											09 00						
West Byfleet	d		08 21		←			08 33					←		08 51			←	09 03						←
Woking	a		08 29	08 24	08 29		08 33	08 37	08 49	08 42	08 46		08 49		09 00	08 55	08 58	09 00	09 08		09 18		09 11	09 15	09 18
	d		08 30	08 25	08 30		08 35	08 39	08 49	08 44	08 46		08 49		09 00	08 55		09 00			09 19		09 13	09 16	09 19
Worplesdon	d		→						→	08 49					→						→		09 18		
Guildford	a			08 35				08 50		08 54						09 05							09 23		
Brookwood	d				08 36								08 55					09 06							09 25
Ash Vale	d				08 44													09 14							
Aldershot	a				08 49													09 20							
	d				08 50													09 20							
Farnham	a				08 55													09 26							
	d				08 56													09 26							
Bentley	d				09 02																				
Alton	a				09 10													09 39							
Farnborough (Main)	d						08 45						09 03							09 13					09 33
Fleet	d												09 08							09 19					09 38
Winchfield	d												09 14												09 44
Hook	d												09 18												09 48
Basingstoke	a					08 47	08 58				09 05		09 28							09 31				09 36	09 58

London - Woking, Guildford, Alton and Basingstoke

Network Diagram - see first Page of Table 155

		SW	SW 1	SW 1 🚲	SW 1	SW ◇1 🚲	SW 1		SW	SW 1	SW 1	SW ◇1 🚲	SW 1	SW	SW 1	SW 1 🚲	SW ◇1 🚲		SW 1	SW	SW 1	SW 1	SW 1	SW ◇1 🚲	SW 1
London Waterloo 15 ⊖	d	08 50	08 53	09 00		09 05	09 09			09 12	09 15	09 20		09 20	09 23	09 30	09 35				09 39	09 42	09 45	09 50	
Vauxhall ⊖	d	08 54												09 24											
Clapham Junction 10	d	08 59	09u00			09u12				09u19	09u22	09u27		09 29							09u46		09u52		
	d																								
Earlsfield	d	09 02												09 32											
Wimbledon 6 ⊖	d	09 06							←					09 36						←					
Surbiton 6	d	09 14	09 11						09 14	09 30				09 44	09 41					09 44		10 00			
Esher	d	↪							09 18					↪						09 48					
Hersham	d								09 21											09 51					
Walton-on-Thames	d								09 24	09 37										09 54		10 07			
Weybridge	d								09 27	09 41										09 57		10 11			
Byfleet & New Haw	d								09 30											10 00					
West Byfleet	d		09 21		←				09 33				←		09 51				←	10 03					←
Woking	a		09 29	09 24	09 29		09 33		09 38	09 48	09 42	09 45	09 48		09 59	09 54	09 58		09 59	10 08		10 18	10 11	10 14	10 18
	d		09 30	09 25	09 30		09 35			09 49	09 43	09 46	09 49		10 00	09 55			10 00			10 19	10 13	10 16	10 19
Worplesdon	d		↪							↪					↪							↪	10 18		
Guildford	a			09 33							09 52					10 03							10 23		
Brookwood	d				09 36								09 55						10 06						10 25
Ash Vale	d				09 44														10 14						
Aldershot	a				09 49														10 19						
	d				09 50														10 20						
Farnham	a				09 55														10 25						
	d				09 56														10 26						
Bentley	d				10 02																				
Alton	a				10 10														10 37						
Farnborough (Main)	d						09 45						10 03								10 13				10 33
Fleet	d												10 08								10 19				10 38
Winchfield	d												10 14												10 44
Hook	d												10 18												10 48
Basingstoke	a					09 47	09 58					10 05	10 28								10 31			10 36	10 58

		SW	SW 1		SW 1 🚲	SW 1	SW ◇1 🚲	SW 1	SW	SW 1	SW 1	SW ◇1 🚲	SW 1		SW	SW 1	SW 1 🚲	SW ◇1 🚲	SW 1	SW	SW 1	SW 1	SW 1		SW ◇1 🚲
London Waterloo 15 ⊖	d	09 50	09 53		10 00		10 05	10 09		10 12	10 15	10 20			10 20	10 23	10 30	10 35			10 39	10 42	10 45		10 50
Vauxhall ⊖	d	09 54													10 24										
Clapham Junction 10	d	09 59	10u00				10u12			10u19	10u22	10u27			10 29						10u46		10u52		
	d																								
Earlsfield	d	10 02													10 32										
Wimbledon 6 ⊖	d	10 06							←						10 36					←					
Surbiton 6	d	10 14	10 11						10 14	10 30					10 44	10 41				10 44		11 00			
Esher	d	↪							10 18						↪					10 48					
Hersham	d								10 21											10 51					
Walton-on-Thames	d								10 24	10 37										10 54		11 07			
Weybridge	d								10 27	10 41										10 57		11 11			
Byfleet & New Haw	d								10 30											11 00					
West Byfleet	d		10 21			←			10 33				←			10 51			←	11 03					
Woking	a		10 29		10 24	10 29		10 33	10 38	10 48	10 41	10 45	10 48			10 59	10 54	10 58	10 59	11 08		11 18	11 11		11 14
	d		10 30		10 25	10 30		10 35		10 49	10 43	10 46	10 49			11 00	10 55		11 00			11 19	11 13		11 16
Worplesdon	d		↪							↪						↪						↪	11 18		
Guildford	a				10 33						10 50						11 03						11 23		
Brookwood	d					10 36							10 55						11 06						
Ash Vale	d					10 44													11 14						
Aldershot	a					10 49													11 19						
	d					10 50													11 20						
Farnham	a					10 55													11 25						
	d					10 56																			
Bentley	d					11 02																			
Alton	a					11 10																			
Farnborough (Main)	d							10 45					11 03								11 13				
Fleet	d												11 08								11 19				
Winchfield	d												11 14												
Hook	d												11 18												
Basingstoke	a						10 47	10 58				11 05	11 28								11 31				11 36

London - Woking, Guildford, Alton and Basingstoke

Network Diagram - see first Page of Table 155

		SW 1	SW	SW 1	SW 1 🚲	SW 1	SW ◇1 🚲	SW 1	SW		SW 1	SW 1	SW ◇1 🚲	SW 1	SW	SW 1	SW 1 🚲	SW ◇1 🚲	SW 1		SW	SW 1	SW 1	SW 1	SW ◇1 🚲
London Waterloo 15 ⊖	d		10 50	10 53	11 00		11 05	11 09			11 12	11 15	11 20		11 20	11 23	11 30	11 35				11 39	11 42	11 45	11 50
Vauxhall ⊖	d		10 54												11 24										
Clapham Junction 10	d		10 59	11u00			11u12				11u19	11u22	11u27		11 29							11u46		11u52	
	d																								
Earlsfield	d		11 02												11 32										
Wimbledon 6 ⊖	d		11 06						←						11 36						←				
Surbiton 6	d		11 14	11 11					11 14		11 30				11 44	11 41					11 44		12 00		
Esher	d		→						11 18						→						11 48				
Hersham	d								11 21												11 51				
Walton-on-Thames	d								11 24		11 37										11 54		12 07		
Weybridge	d								11 27		11 41										11 57		12 11		
Byfleet & New Haw	d								11 30												12 00				
West Byfleet	d	←		11 21		←			11 33					←		11 51			←		12 03				
Woking	a	11 18		11 29	11 24	11 29		11 33	11 38		11 48	11 41	11 45	11 48		11 59	11 54	11 58	11 59		12 08		12 18	12 11	12 14
	d	11 19		11 30	11 25	11 30		11 35			11 49	11 43	11 46	11 49		12 00	11 55		12 00				12 19	12 13	12 16
Worplesdon	d			→							→					→							→	12 18	
Guildford	a				11 33							11 50					12 03							12 23	
Brookwood	d	11 25				11 36								11 55					12 06						
Ash Vale	d					11 44													12 14						
Aldershot	a					11 49													12 19						
	d					11 50													12 20						
Farnham	a					11 55													12 25						
	d					11 56													12 26						
Bentley	d					12 02																			
Alton	a					12 10													12 37						
Farnborough (Main)	d	11 33						11 45						12 03								12 13			
Fleet	d	11 38												12 08								12 19			
Winchfield	d	11 44												12 14											
Hook	d	11 48												12 18											
Basingstoke	a	11 58					11 47	11 58					12 05	12 28								12 31			12 36

		SW 1	SW	SW 1	SW 1 🚲		SW 1	SW ◇1 🚲	SW 1	SW	SW 1	SW 1	SW ◇1 🚲	SW 1	SW		SW 1	SW 1 🚲	SW ◇1 🚲	SW 1	SW	SW 1	SW 1	SW 1	SW ◇1 🚲
London Waterloo 15 ⊖	d		11 50	11 53	12 00			12 05	12 09		12 12	12 15	12 20		12 20		12 23	12 30	12 35			12 39	12 42	12 45	12 50
Vauxhall ⊖	d		11 54												12 24										
Clapham Junction 10	d		11 59	12u00				12u12			12u19	12u22	12u27		12 29							12u46		12u52	
	d																								
Earlsfield	d		12 02												12 32										
Wimbledon 6 ⊖	d		12 06							←					12 36						←				
Surbiton 6	d		12 14	12 11						12 14	12 30				12 44		12 41				12 44		13 00		
Esher	d		→							12 18					→						12 48				
Hersham	d									12 21											12 51				
Walton-on-Thames	d									12 24	12 37										12 54		13 07		
Weybridge	d									12 27	12 41										12 57		13 11		
Byfleet & New Haw	d									12 30											13 00				
West Byfleet	d	←		12 21			←			12 33				←			12 51			←	13 03				
Woking	a	12 18		12 29	12 24		12 29		12 33	12 38	12 48	12 41	12 45	12 48			12 59	12 54	12 58	12 59	13 08		13 18	13 11	13 14
	d	12 19		12 30	12 25		12 30		12 35		12 49	12 43	12 46	12 49			13 00	12 55		13 00			13 19	13 13	13 16
Worplesdon	d			→							→						→						→	13 18	
Guildford	a				12 33							12 50						13 03						13 23	
Brookwood	d	12 25					12 36							12 55						13 06					
Ash Vale	d						12 44													13 14					
Aldershot	a						12 49													13 19					
	d						12 50													13 20					
Farnham	a						12 55													13 25					
	d						12 56													13 26					
Bentley	d						13 02																		
Alton	a						13 10													13 37					
Farnborough (Main)	d	12 33							12 45					13 03								13 13			
Fleet	d	12 38												13 08								13 19			
Winchfield	d	12 44												13 14											
Hook	d	12 48												13 18											
Basingstoke	a	12 58						12 47	12 58				13 05	13 28								13 31			13 36

London - Woking, Guildford, Alton and Basingstoke

Network Diagram - see first Page of Table 155

			SW	SW	SW	SW	SW	SW	SW	SW	SW		SW	SW	SW	SW	SW	SW	SW	SW	SW		SW	SW	SW
			1		1	1	1	◇1	1		1		1	◇1	1		1	1	◇1	1			1	1	1
						🚲		🚲						🚲				🚲	🚲						
London Waterloo 15 ⊖	d			12 50	12 53	13 00		13 05	13 09		13 12		13 15	13 20		13 20	13 23	13 30	13 35				13 39	13 42	13 45
Vauxhall ⊖	d			12 54												13 24									
Clapham Junction 10	d			12 59	13u00			13u12			13u19		13u22	13u27		13 29							13u46		13u52
	d																								
Earlsfield	d			13 02												13 32									
Wimbledon 6 ⊖	d			13 06						←						13 36					←				
Surbiton 6	d			13 14	13 11					13 14	13 30					13 44	13 41				13 44			14 00	
Esher	d			↪						13 18						↪					13 48				
Hersham	d									13 21											13 51				
Walton-on-Thames	d									13 24	13 37										13 54			14 07	
Weybridge	d									13 27	13 41										13 57			14 11	
Byfleet & New Haw	d									13 30											14 00				
West Byfleet	d		←		13 21		←			13 33					←		13 51			←	14 03				
Woking	a		13 18		13 29	13 24	13 29		13 33	13 38	13 48		13 41	13 45	13 48		13 59	13 54	13 58	13 59	14 08			14 18	14 11
	d		13 19		13 30	13 25	13 30		13 35		13 49		13 43	13 46	13 49		14 00	13 55		14 00				14 19	14 13
Worplesdon	d				↪						↪						↪							↪	14 18
Guildford	a					13 33							13 50					14 03							14 23
Brookwood	d		13 25				13 36								13 55					14 06					
Ash Vale	d						13 44													14 14					
Aldershot	a						13 49													14 19					
	d						13 50													14 20					
Farnham	a						13 55													14 25					
	d						13 56													14 26					
Bentley	d						14 02																		
Alton	a						14 11													14 37					
Farnborough (Main)	d		13 33						13 45						14 03								14 13		
Fleet	d		13 38												14 08								14 19		
Winchfield	d		13 44												14 14										
Hook	d		13 48												14 18										
Basingstoke	a		13 58					13 47	13 58					14 05	14 28								14 31		

		SW	SW	SW	SW	SW	SW		SW	SW	SW	SW	SW	SW	SW	SW	SW		SW	SW	SW	SW	SW	SW	SW
		◇1	1		1	1	1		◇1	1		1	1	◇1	1		1		1	◇1	1		1	1	1
		🚲				🚲			🚲					🚲					🚲	🚲					
London Waterloo 15 ⊖	d	13 50		13 50	13 53	14 00			14 05	14 09		14 12	14 15	14 20		14 20	14 23		14 30	14 35			14 39	14 42	14 45
Vauxhall ⊖	d			13 54												14 24									
Clapham Junction 10	d			13 59	14u00				14u12			14u19	14u22	14u27		14 29							14u46		14u52
	d																								
Earlsfield	d			14 02												14 32									
Wimbledon 6 ⊖	d			14 06							←					14 36						←			
Surbiton 6	d			14 14	14 11						14 14	14 30				14 44	14 41					14 44		15 00	
Esher	d			↪							14 18					↪						14 48			
Hersham	d										14 21											14 51			
Walton-on-Thames	d										14 24	14 37										14 54		15 07	
Weybridge	d										14 27	14 41										14 57		15 11	
Byfleet & New Haw	d										14 30											15 00			
West Byfleet	d		←		14 21		←				14 33				←		14 51				←	15 03			
Woking	a	14 14	14 18		14 29	14 24	14 29			14 33	14 38	14 48	14 41	14 45	14 48		14 59		14 54	14 58	14 59	15 08		15 18	15 11
	d	14 16	14 19		14 30	14 25	14 30			14 35		14 49	14 43	14 46	14 49		15 00		14 55		15 00			15 19	15 13
Worplesdon	d				↪							↪					↪							↪	15 18
Guildford	a					14 33							14 50						15 03						15 23
Brookwood	d		14 25				14 36								14 55						15 06				
Ash Vale	d						14 44														15 14				
Aldershot	a						14 49														15 19				
	d						14 50														15 20				
Farnham	a						14 55														15 25				
	d						14 56														15 26				
Bentley	d						15 02																		
Alton	a						15 10														15 37				
Farnborough (Main)	d		14 33							14 45					15 03								15 13		
Fleet	d		14 38												15 08								15 19		
Winchfield	d		14 44												15 14										
Hook	d		14 48												15 18										
Basingstoke	a	14 36	14 58						14 47	14 58				15 05	15 28								15 31		

London - Woking, Guildford, Alton and Basingstoke

Network Diagram - see first Page of Table 155

		SW ◇1 ⚲	SW 1		SW	SW 1	SW 1 ⚲	SW 1	SW ◇1 ⚲	SW 1	SW	SW 1	SW 1		SW ◇1 ⚲	SW 1	SW	SW 1	SW 1 ⚲	SW ◇1 ⚲	SW 1	SW	SW 1		SW 1
London Waterloo 15 ⊖	d	14 50			14 50	14 53	15 00		15 05	15 09		15 12	15 15		15 20		15 20	15 23	15 30	15 35			15 39		15 42
Vauxhall ⊖	d				14 54												15 24								
Clapham Junction 10	d				14 59	15u00			15u12			15u19	15u22		15u27		15 29						15u46		
	d																								
Earlsfield	d				15 02												15 32								
Wimbledon 6 ⊖	d				15 06						←						15 36					←			
Surbiton 6	d				15 14	15 11					15 14	15 30					15 44	15 41				15 44			16 00
Esher	d				↦						15 18						↦					15 48			
Hersham	d										15 21											15 51			
Walton-on-Thames	d										15 24	15 37										15 54			16 07
Weybridge	d										15 27	15 41										15 57			16 11
Byfleet & New Haw	d										15 30											16 00			
West Byfleet	d		←			15 21		←			15 33					←		15 51			←	16 03			
Woking	a	15 14	15 18			15 29	15 24	15 29		15 33	15 38	15 48	15 41		15 45	15 48		15 59	15 54	15 58	15 59	16 08			16 18
	d	15 16	15 19			15 30	15 25	15 30		15 35		15 49	15 43		15 46	15 49		16 00	15 55		16 00				16 19
Worplesdon	d					↦						↦	15 48					↦							↦
Guildford	a						15 33						15 53						16 03						
Brookwood	d		15 25					15 36								15 55					16 06				
Ash Vale	d							15 44													16 14				
Aldershot	a							15 49													16 19				
	d							15 50													16 20				
Farnham	a							15 55													16 25				
	d							15 56													16 26				
Bentley	d							16 02																	
Alton	a							16 10													16 37				
Farnborough (Main)	d		15 33							15 45						16 03							16 13		
Fleet	d		15 38													16 08							16 19		
Winchfield	d		15 44													16 14									
Hook	d		15 48													16 18									
Basingstoke	a	15 36	15 58						15 47	15 58					16 05	16 28							16 31		

		SW 1	SW ◇1 ⚲	SW 1	SW	SW 1	SW 1 ⚲	SW 1	SW ◇1 ⚲		SW 1	SW	SW 1	SW 1	SW ◇1 ⚲	SW 1	SW	SW 1	SW 1 ⚲		SW 1	SW	SW ◇1 ⚲	SW 1	SW 1
London Waterloo 15 ⊖	d	15 45	15 50		15 50	15 53	16 00		16 05		16 09		16 12	16 15	16 20		16 20	16 25	16 30				16 35	16 39	16 42
Vauxhall ⊖	d				15 54												16 24								
Clapham Junction 10	d	15u52	15u57		15 59	16u00			16u12				16u19	16u22	16u27		16 29							16u46	
	d																								
Earlsfield	d				16 02												16 32								
Wimbledon 6 ⊖	d				16 06							←					16 36					←			
Surbiton 6	d				16 14	16 11						16 14	16 30				16 44	16 41				16 44			17 00
Esher	d				↦							16 18					↦					16 48			
Hersham	d											16 21										16 51			
Walton-on-Thames	d											16 24	16 37									16 54			17 07
Weybridge	d											16 27	16 41									16 57			17 11
Byfleet & New Haw	d											16 30										17 00			
West Byfleet	d			←		16 21		←				16 33				←		16 51			←	17 03			
Woking	a	16 11	16 15	16 18		16 29	16 24	16 29			16 33	16 38	16 48	16 41	16 45	16 48		16 59	16 54		16 59	17 10			17 18
	d	16 13	16 16	16 19		16 30	16 25	16 30			16 35		16 49	16 43	16 46	16 49		17 00	16 55		17 00				17 19
Worplesdon	d					↦							↦	16 48				↦							↦
Guildford	a	16 20					16 33							16 53					17 03						
Brookwood	d			16 25				16 36								16 55					17 06				
Ash Vale	d							16 44													17 14				
Aldershot	a							16 49													17 19				
	d							16 50													17 20				
Farnham	a							16 55													17 25				
	d							16 56													17 26				
Bentley	d							17 02													17 32				
Alton	a							17 10													17 41				
Farnborough (Main)	d			16 33							16 45					17 03								17 13	
Fleet	d			16 38												17 08								17 19	
Winchfield	d			16 44												17 14									
Hook	d			16 48												17 18									
Basingstoke	a		16 36	16 58					16 47		16 58				17 05	17 30								17 31	

London - Woking, Guildford, Alton and Basingstoke

Network Diagram - see first Page of Table 155

		SW 1	SW ◇1 🚲	SW 1	SW		SW 1	SW 1 🚲	SW 1	SW 1	SW 1	SW 1	SW 1	SW 1	SW ◇1 🚲		SW	SW 1	SW 1	SW 1	SW 1 🚲	SW	SW 1	SW 1	SW 1
London Waterloo 15 ⊖	d	16 45	16 50		16 50		16 55	17 00		17 02	17 09	17 12	17 15		17 20		17 20	17 23	17 25		17 30		17 32	17 39	17 41
Vauxhall ⊖	d				16 54												17 24								
Clapham Junction 10	d	16u52	16u57		16 59		17u02										17 29								
	d																								
Earlsfield	d				17 02												17 32								
Wimbledon 6 ⊖	d				17 06												17 36					←			
Surbiton 6	d				17 14					17 18							17 44	17 39				17 44	17 48		
Esher	d				17 18					17 22							↪					17 48	17 52		
Hersham	d				17 21					17 25												17 51	17 55		
Walton-on-Thames	d				17 24					17 29												17 54	17 59		
Weybridge	d				17 27					17 33												17 57	18 03		
Byfleet & New Haw	d				17 30					17 36												18 00	18 06		
West Byfleet	d			←	17 33		17 21		←	17 39				←						←		18 03	18 09		
Woking	a	17 11		17 18	17 43		17 29	17 24	17 29	17 44	17 32	17 36	17 38	17 44				17 51	17 50	17 51	17 54	18 10	18 14	18 02	
	d	17 13	17u16	17 19			17 30	17 25	17 30	17 46	17 34	17 37	17 40	17 46	17u46			17 52	17 51	17 52	17 56		18 16	18 04	
Worplesdon	d						↪	17 30		↪			17 45					↪			18 00		↪		
Guildford	a	17 20						17 36					17 51	17 56							18 06				
Brookwood	d			17 25					17 36			17 43								18 00					18 11
Ash Vale	d								17 44										18 03						
Aldershot	a								17 49										18 08						
	d								17 50										18 09						
Farnham	a								17 55										18 14						
	d								17 56										18 15						
Bentley	d								18 02										18 24						
Alton	a								18 11										18 32						
Farnborough (Main)	d			17 33								17 51								18 08					18 19
Fleet	d			17 38								17 56								18 13					18 24
Winchfield	d			17 44								18 02								18 19					18 30
Hook	d			17 48								18 06								18 23					18 34
Basingstoke	a		17 36	18 00							17 52	18 16			18 05					18 32				18 22	18 45

			SW 1	SW 1	SW 1	SW ◇1 🚲	SW	SW 1	SW 1	SW 1	SW		SW 1 🚲	SW 1	SW 1	SW 1	SW 1	SW 1	SW ◇1 🚲	SW	SW 1		SW 1	SW 1 🚲	SW
London Waterloo 15 ⊖	d		17 45	17 48		17 50	17 50	17 53	17 55				18 00	18 02	18 09	18 12	18 15	18 18	18 20	18 20	18 23		18 25	18 30	
Vauxhall ⊖	d						17 54													18 24					
Clapham Junction 10	d						17 59												18u27	18 29			18u33		
	d																								
Earlsfield	d						18 02													18 32					
Wimbledon 6 ⊖	d						18 06				←									18 36					←
Surbiton 6	d						18 14	18 09			18 14			18 18						18 44	18 40				18 44
Esher	d						↪				18 18			18 22						↪					18 48
Hersham	d										18 21			18 25											18 51
Walton-on-Thames	d										18 24			18 29											18 54
Weybridge	d										18 27			18 33											18 57
Byfleet & New Haw	d										18 30			18 36											19 00
West Byfleet	d				←			18 19		←	18 33			18 39											19 03
Woking	a			18 11	18 14			18 23	18 20	18 23	18 41			18 48	18 33			18 42	18 45		18 52		18 52	18 57	19 12
	d			18 13	18 16			18 25	18 21	18 25					18 35			18 43	18 46		18 54		18 53	18 58	
Worplesdon	d				18 21			↪										18 48							
Guildford	a		18 21		18 29								18 32				18 50	18 54						19 06	
Brookwood	d								18 27							18 41					19 02				
Ash Vale	d								18 35														19 05		
Aldershot	a								18 40														19 10		
	d								18 41														19 11		
Farnham	a								18 46														19 16		
	d								18 48														19 18		
Bentley	d								18 54														19 24		
Alton	a								19 03														19 33		
Farnborough (Main)	d									18 39						18 48					19 10				
Fleet	d									18 44						18 54					19 15				
Winchfield	d									18 50						18 59					19 21				
Hook	d									18 54						19 04					19 25				
Basingstoke	a			18 31		18 37				19 03					18 53	19 16			19 05		19 34				

London - Woking, Guildford, Alton and Basingstoke

Network Diagram - see first Page of Table 155

		SW 1	SW 1	SW 1	SW 1	SW ◇1 🛒	SW 1		SW	SW 1	SW 1 🛒	SW 1	SW ◇1 🛒	SW 1	SW 1	SW 1	SW ◇1 🛒		SW	SW 1	SW 1 🛒	SW ◇1 🛒	SW 1	SW 1	SW 1
London Waterloo 15 ⊖	d	18 32	18 39	18 41	18 45	18 50			18 50	18 55	19 00	19 02	19 05	19 09	19 12	19 15	19 20		19 20	19 25	19 30	19 35		19 39	19 42
Vauxhall ⊖	d								18 54										19 24						
Clapham Junction 10	d		18u46						18 59	19u02			19u12		19u19	19u22	19u27		19 29	19u32				19u46	
	d																								
Earlsfield	d								19 02										19 32						
Wimbledon 6 ⊖	d								19 06										19 36						
Surbiton 6	d	18 48							19 14			19 18							19 44						20 00
Esher	d	18 52							19 18			19 22							19 48						
Hersham	d	18 55							19 21			19 25							19 51						
Walton-on-Thames	d	18 59							19 24			19 29							19 54						20 07
Weybridge	d	19 03							19 27			19 33							19 57						20 11
Byfleet & New Haw	d	19 06							19 30			19 36							20 00						
West Byfleet	d	19 09			19 08		←		19 33			19 39							20 03	19 51			←		
Woking	a	19 18	19 05		19 13	19 17	19 18		19 42	19 21	19 24	19 48		19 33	19 38	19 43	19 45		20 08	19 59	19 54	19 58	19 59		20 18
	d	19 20	19 06		19 14	19 18	19 20			19 23	19 25			19 35	19 39	19 45	19 46			20 00	19 55		20 00		20 19
Worplesdon	d	↪									19 30									↪					↪
Guildford	a				19 23						19 36					19 52					20 03				
Brookwood	d			19 13						19 30					19 45								20 06		
Ash Vale	d									19 37													20 14		
Aldershot	a									19 42													20 19		
	d									19 43													20 20		
Farnham	a									19 48													20 25		
	d									19 49													20 26		
Bentley	d									19 55													20 32		
Alton	a									20 04													20 39		
Farnborough (Main)	d			19 20			19 31							19 45	19 53									20 13	
Fleet	d			19 26			19 37								19 58									20 19	
Winchfield	d			19 31			19 42								20 04										
Hook	d			19 36			19 47								20 09										
Basingstoke	a		19 28	19 47		19 37	19 59						19 47	19 58	20 16		20 06							20 31	

		SW 1	SW ◇1 🛒		SW 1	SW	SW 1	SW 1 🛒	SW 1	SW ◇1 🛒	SW 1	SW	SW 1		SW 1	SW ◇1 🛒	SW 1	SW	SW 1	SW 1 🛒	SW ◇1 🛒	SW 1	SW		SW 1
London Waterloo 15 ⊖	d	19 45	19 50			19 50	19 53	20 00		20 05	20 09		20 12		20 15	20 20		20 20	20 23	20 30	20 35				20 39
Vauxhall ⊖	d					19 54												20 24							
Clapham Junction 10	d	19u52				19 59	20u00			20u12			20u19		20u22	20u27		20 29							20u46
	d																								
Earlsfield	d					20 02												20 32							
Wimbledon 6 ⊖	d					20 06						←						20 36					←		
Surbiton 6	d					20 14	20 11					20 14	20 30					20 44	20 41				20 44		
Esher	d					↪						20 18						↪					20 48		
Hersham	d											20 21											20 51		
Walton-on-Thames	d											20 24	20 37										20 54		
Weybridge	d											20 27	20 41										20 57		
Byfleet & New Haw	d											20 30											21 00		
West Byfleet	d				←		20 21		←			20 33					←		20 51			←	21 03		
Woking	a	20 11	20 14		20 18		20 29	20 24	20 29		20 33	20 38	20 48		20 41	20 45	20 48		20 59	20 54	20 58	20 59	21 08		
	d	20 13	20 16		20 19		20 30	20 25	20 30		20 35		20 49		20 43	20 46	20 49		21 00	20 55		21 00			
Worplesdon	d	20 18					↪						↪						↪						
Guildford	a	20 23						20 33							20 50					21 03					
Brookwood	d				20 25				20 36								20 55					21 06			
Ash Vale	d								20 44													21 14			
Aldershot	a								20 49													21 19			
	d								20 50													21 20			
Farnham	a								20 55													21 25			
	d								20 56													21 26			
Bentley	d								21 02													21 32			
Alton	a								21 10													21 39			
Farnborough (Main)	d				20 33						20 45						21 03								21 13
Fleet	d				20 38												21 08								21 19
Winchfield	d				20 44												21 14								
Hook	d				20 48												21 18								
Basingstoke	a		20 36		20 58					20 47	20 58					21 05	21 28								21 31

London - Woking, Guildford, Alton and Basingstoke

Network Diagram - see first Page of Table 155

		SW 1	SW 1	SW 1	SW	SW 1	SW 1 🚲	SW 1	SW ◇1 🚲		SW	SW 1	SW ◇1 🚲	SW	SW 1	SW 1 🚲	SW ◇1 🚲	SW 1	SW		SW 1	SW 1	SW 1	SW 1	SW
London Waterloo 15 ⊖	d	20 42	20 45		20 50	20 53	21 00		21 05			21 12	21 20	21 20	21 23	21 30	21 35				21 39	21 42	21 45		21 50
Vauxhall ⊖	d				20 54									21 24											21 54
Clapham Junction 10	d		20u52		20 59	21u00			21u12			21u19	21u27	21 29							21u46		21u52		21 59
	d																								
Earlsfield	d				21 02									21 32											22 02
Wimbledon 6 ⊖	d				21 06						←			21 36					←						22 06
Surbiton 6	d	21 00			21 14	21 11					21 14	21 30		21 44	21 41				21 44			22 00			22 14
Esher	d				↦						21 18			↦					21 48						↦
Hersham	d										21 21								21 51						
Walton-on-Thames	d	21 07									21 24	21 37							21 54			22 07			
Weybridge	d	21 11									21 27	21 41							21 57			22 11			
Byfleet & New Haw	d										21 30								22 00						
West Byfleet	d			←		21 21		←			21 33				21 51			←	22 03					←	
Woking	a	21 18	21 11	21 18		21 29	21 24	21 29	21 31		21 38	21 48	21 45		21 59	21 54	21 58	21 59	22 08			22 18	22 11	22 18	
	d	21 19	21 13	21 19		21 30	21 25	21 30	21 32			21 49	21 49		22 00	21 55		22 00				22 19	22 13	22 19	
Worplesdon	d	↦	21 18			↦									↦							↦	22 18		
Guildford	a		21 23				21 33									22 03							22 23		
Brookwood	d			21 25				21 36				21 55						22 06						22 25	
Ash Vale	d							21 44										22 14							
Aldershot	a							21 49										22 19							
	d							21 50										22 20							
Farnham	a							21 55										22 25							
	d							21 56										22 26							
Bentley	d							22 02										22 32							
Alton	a							22 10										22 39							
Farnborough (Main)	d			21 33								22 03									22 13			22 33	
Fleet	d			21 38								22 08									22 19			22 38	
Winchfield	d			21 44								22 14												22 44	
Hook	d			21 48								22 18												22 48	
Basingstoke	a			21 58					21 51			22 28	22 12								22 31			22 58	

		SW 1	SW 1	SW 1	SW ◇1 🚲		SW	SW 1	SW 1 🚲	SW	SW 1	SW 1	SW ◇1 🚲	SW 1	SW		SW 1	SW 1	SW 1	SW 1	SW	SW	SW 1	SW ◇1	SW
London Waterloo 15 ⊖	d	21 53	22 00		22 05			22 12	22 20	22 20	22 23	22 30	22 35				22 39	22 42	22 45		22 50	22 52	22 53	23 05	
Vauxhall ⊖	d									22 24											22 54	22 56			
Clapham Junction 10	d	22u00			22u12			22u19	22u27	22 29	22u30						22u46	22u49	22u52		22 59		23u00	23u12	
	d																					23 02			
Earlsfield	d									22 32											23 02				
Wimbledon 6 ⊖	d						←			22 36					←						23 06				←
Surbiton 6	d	22 11					22 14	22 30		22 44	22 41				22 44			23 00			23 14		23 11		23 14
Esher	d						22 18			↦					22 48						↦				23 18
Hersham	d						22 21								22 51										23 21
Walton-on-Thames	d						22 24	22 37							22 54			23 07							23 24
Weybridge	d						22 27	22 41							22 57			23 11							23 27
Byfleet & New Haw	d						22 30								23 00							00 06			23 30
West Byfleet	d	22 21		←			22 33				22 51			←	23 03					←		00 09	23 21		23 33
Woking	a	22 29	22 24	22 29	22 31		22 37	22 48	22 45		22 59	22 54	22 58	22 59	23 08			23 18	23 11	23 18		00 15	23 29	23 31	23 38
	d	22 30	22 25	22 30	22 32		22 39	22 49	22 49		23 00	22 55		23 00				23 19	23 13	23 19			23 30	23 32	
Worplesdon	d	↦									↦							↦	23 18						
Guildford	a		22 33				22 47					23 03							23 23						
Brookwood	d			22 36				22 55						23 06						23 25			23 36		
Ash Vale	d			22 44										23 14									23 44		
Aldershot	a			22 49										23 19									23 49		
	d			22 50										23 20									23 50		
Farnham	a			22 55										23 25									23 55		
	d			22 56										23 26									23 58		
Bentley	d			23 02										23 33									00 04		
Alton	a			23 10										23 40									00 11		
Farnborough (Main)	d							23 03									23 16			23 33					
Fleet	d							23 08									23 21			23 38					
Winchfield	d							23 14												23 44					
Hook	d							23 18												23 48					
Basingstoke	a				22 51			23 27	23 09								23 33			23 57				23 53	

London - Woking, Guildford, Alton and Basingstoke

Network Diagram - see first Page of Table 155

			SW 1	SW 1	SW 1	SW	SW 1	SW 1	SW	SW 1	SW 1		SW 1												
London Waterloo 15 ⊖	d		23 12	23 15		23 20	23 23	23 35		23 40	23 45		23 48												
Vauxhall ⊖	d					23 24																			
Clapham Junction 10	d			23u22		23 29	23u30	23u42		23u47	23u52		23u55												
	d		23u19																						
Earlsfield	d					23 32																			
Wimbledon 6 ⊖	d					23 36			←																
Surbiton 6	d		23 38			23 44	23 41		23 44				00 09												
Esher	d					↪			23 48																
Hersham	d								23 51																
Walton-on-Thames	d		23 45						23 54				00 16												
Weybridge	d		23 49						23 57				00 20												
Byfleet & New Haw	d								00 01																
West Byfleet	d				←		23 55		00 03																
Woking	a		23 55	23 41	23 55		23 59	00 01	00 08	00 06	00 11		00 26												
	d		23 57	23 43	23 57		00 01	00 03		00 08	00 13		00 28												
Worplesdon	d		↪								00 18														
Guildford	a			23 51							00 24														
Brookwood	d				00 03		00 07						00 34												
Ash Vale	d						00 15																		
Aldershot	a						00 19																		
	d						00 20																		
Farnham	a						00 25																		
	d						00 26																		
Bentley	d						00 33																		
Alton	a						00 40																		
Farnborough (Main)	d				00 10			00 14					00 41												
Fleet	d				00 16			00 20					00 47												
Winchfield	d				00 21								00s52												
Hook	d				00 26								00s57												
Basingstoke	a				00 33			00 33		00 27			01 06												

Saturdays

		SW	SW 1	SW 1	SW	SW 1	SW 1	SW	SW 1	SW 1		SW 1	SW 1	SW 1	SW	SW 1	SW 1	SW 1	SW ◇1	SW 1		SW 1	SW 1	SW 1	SW
London Waterloo 15 ⊖	d	22p52	22p53	23p12	23p20	23p23	23p35		23p40	23p45		23p48	00 05		00 09	01 05	05 00	05 20	05 30						05 50
Vauxhall ⊖	d	22p56			23p24										00 13	01 09	05 04	05 24							05 54
Clapham Junction 10	d		23b00		23p29	23b30	23b42		23b47	23b52		23b55	00u12		00 20	01 15	05 11	05 29	05u37						05 59
	d	23p02		23b19																					
Earlsfield	d				23p32										00 23		05 14	05 32							06 02
Wimbledon 6 ⊖	d				23p36			←					00u18		00 27	01s20	05 18	05 36	05 43						06 06
Surbiton 6	d		23p11	23p38	23p44	23p41		23p44				00 09			00 35	01s28	05 26	05 44							06 14
Esher	d				↪			23p48							00s39		05 30	05 48							06 18
Hersham	d							23p51							00s42		05 33	05 51							06 21
Walton-on-Thames	d			23p45				23p54				00 16			00s44		05 37	05 54							06 24
Weybridge	d			23p49				23p57				00 20			00s48		05 41	05 57							06 27
Byfleet & New Haw	d	00 06						00 01							00s51		05 44	06 00							06 30
West Byfleet	d	00 09	23p21			23p55		00 03							00s54		05 47	06 03				←			06 33
Woking	a	00 15	23p29	23p55		23p59	00 01	00 08	00 06	00 11		00 26	00 35		00 58	01 41	05 51	06 08	05 59			06 08			06 38
	d		23p30	23p57		00 01	00 03		00 08	00 13		00 28	00 37	00 40	01 00	01 42	05 53	06 13	06 01	06 02		06 13	06 19	06 30	
Worplesdon	d									00 18								↪				06 18			
Guildford	a									00 24					01 07		06 00					06 23			
Brookwood	d		23p36	00 03		00 07						00 34		00 45						06 08			06 25	06 36	
Ash Vale	d		23p44			00 15								00 53						06 16				06 44	
Aldershot	a		23p49			00 19								00 58						06 21				06 49	
	d		23p50			00 20								00 59						06 21				06 50	
Farnham	a		23p55			00 25								01 04						06 27				06 55	
	d		23p58			00 26								01 05						06 27				06 56	
Bentley	d		00 04			00 33								01s11						06 34				07 02	
Alton	a		00 11			00 40								01 18						06 41				07 10	
Farnborough (Main)	d			00 10			00 14					00 41				01s51							06 33		
Fleet	d			00 16			00 20					00 47				01s57							06 38		
Winchfield	d			00 21								00s52											06 43		
Hook	d			00 26								00s57											06 48		
Basingstoke	a			00 33			00 33		00 27			01 06	00 55			02s09			06 20				06 58		

b Previous night, stops to pick up only

Table 155

Saturdays

London - Woking, Guildford, Alton and Basingstoke

Network Diagram - see first Page of Table 155

		SW 1	SW 1	SW 1	SW	SW ◇1		SW 1	SW 1	SW 1	SW 1	SW	SW 1	SW ◇1 🛒	SW	SW 1		SW 1	SW 1	SW	SW 1	SW 1	SW 1	SW ◇1	SW
London Waterloo 15 ⊖	d	06 12	06 15		06 20	06 30			06 42	06 45		06 50	06 53	07 10		07 12		07 15		07 20	07 23	07 30		07 35	
Vauxhall ⊖	d				06 24							06 54								07 24					
Clapham Junction 10	d	06u19	06u22		06 29	06u37			06u49	06u52		06 59	07u00	07u17		07u20		07u23		07 29	07u30				
	d																								
Earlsfield	d				06 32							07 02								07 32					
Wimbledon 6 ⊖	d				06 36							07 06			←					07 36					←
Surbiton 6	d	06 30			06 44				07 00			07 14	07 11		07 14	07 31				07 44	07 41				07 44
Esher	d				06 48							→			07 18					→					07 48
Hersham	d				06 51										07 21										07 51
Walton-on-Thames	d	06 37			06 54				07 07						07 24	07 38									07 54
Weybridge	d	06 41			06 57				07 11						07 27	07 42									07 57
Byfleet & New Haw	d				07 00										07 30										08 00
West Byfleet	d			←	07 03						←		07 21		07 33				←		07 51		←		08 03
Woking	a	06 48	06 41	06 48	07 08	06 56			07 18	07 11	07 18		07 26	07 35	07 38	07 48		07 42	07 48		07 59	07 54	07 59	07 58	08 08
	d	06 49	06 43	06 49		06 57		07 00	07 19	07 13	07 19		07 30	07 36		07 50		07 44	07 50		08 00	07 55	08 00	08 00	
Worplesdon	d	→							→	07 18						→					→				
Guildford	a		06 51							07 23								07 51				08 03			
Brookwood	d			06 55				07 06			07 25		07 36						07 56				08 06		
Ash Vale	d							07 14					07 44										08 14		
Aldershot	a							07 19					07 49										08 19		
	d							07 20					07 50										08 20		
Farnham	a							07 25					07 55										08 25		
	d							07 26					07 56										08 26		
Bentley	d							07 32					08 02										08 32		
Alton	a							07 40					08 10										08 39		
Farnborough (Main)	d			07 03							07 33								08 03						
Fleet	d			07 08							07 38								08 09						
Winchfield	d			07 14							07 44								08 14						
Hook	d			07 18							07 48								08 19						
Basingstoke	a			07 28		07 16					07 58			07 57					08 28					08 20	

		SW 1		SW 1	SW 1	SW ◇1 🛒	SW 1	SW	SW 1	SW 1	SW 1	SW ◇1		SW 1	SW	SW 1	SW 1	SW ◇1 🛒	SW 1	SW	SW 1	SW 1		SW ◇1 🛒	SW 1
London Waterloo 15 ⊖	d	07 39		07 42	07 45	07 50		07 50	07 53	08 00		08 05		08 09		08 12	08 15	08 20		08 20	08 23	08 30		08 35	
Vauxhall ⊖	d							07 54												08 24					
Clapham Junction 10	d	07u46			07u52	07u57		07 59	08u00			08u12				08u19	08u22	08u27		08 29					
	d																								
Earlsfield	d							08 02												08 32					
Wimbledon 6 ⊖	d							08 06							←					08 36					
Surbiton 6	d			08 00				08 14	08 11						08 14	08 30				08 44	08 41				
Esher	d							→							08 18					→					
Hersham	d														08 21										
Walton-on-Thames	d			08 07											08 24	08 37									
Weybridge	d			08 11											08 27	08 41									
Byfleet & New Haw	d														08 30										
West Byfleet	d						←		08 21		←				08 33				←		08 51				←
Woking	a			08 18	08 11	08 15	08 18		08 29	08 24	08 29			08 33	08 38	08 48	08 41	08 45	08 48		08 59	08 54		08 58	08 59
	d			08 19	08 13	08 16	08 19		08 30	08 25	08 30			08 35		08 49	08 43	08 46	08 49		09 00	08 55			09 00
Worplesdon	d			→	08 18				→							→					→				
Guildford	a				08 23					08 33							08 50					09 03			
Brookwood	d						08 25				08 36								08 55						09 06
Ash Vale	d										08 44														09 14
Aldershot	a										08 49														09 19
	d										08 50														09 20
Farnham	a										08 55														09 25
	d										08 56														09 26
Bentley	d										09 02														
Alton	a										09 10														09 37
Farnborough (Main)	d	08 13					08 33							08 45					09 03						
Fleet	d	08 19					08 38												09 08						
Winchfield	d						08 44												09 14						
Hook	d						08 48												09 18						
Basingstoke	a	08 31				08 36	08 58					08 47		08 58				09 05	09 28						

Table 155

London - Woking, Guildford, Alton and Basingstoke

Network Diagram - see first Page of Table 155

Station		SW	SW 1	SW 1	SW 1	SW ◇1 🚲	SW 1	SW		SW 1	SW 1 🚲	SW 1	SW ◇1 🚲	SW 1	SW	SW 1	SW 1	SW ◇1 🚲		SW 1	SW	SW 1	SW 1 🚲	SW ◇1 🚲	SW 1
London Waterloo 15 ⊖	d		08 39	08 42	08 45	08 50		08 50		08 53	09 00		09 05	09 09		09 12	09 15	09 20			09 20	09 23	09 30	09 35	
Vauxhall ⊖	d							08 54													09 24				
Clapham Junction 10	d		08u46		08u52			08 59		09u00			09u12			09u19	09u22	09u27			09 29				
	d																								
Earlsfield	d							09 02													09 32				
Wimbledon 6 ⊖	d	←						09 06							←						09 36				
Surbiton 6	d	08 44		09 00				09 14		09 11					09 14	09 30					09 44	09 41			
Esher	d	08 48						→							09 18						→				
Hersham	d	08 51													09 21										
Walton-on-Thames	d	08 54		09 07											09 24	09 37									
Weybridge	d	08 57		09 11											09 27	09 41									
Byfleet & New Haw	d	09 00													09 30										
West Byfleet	d	09 03					←			09 21		←			09 33					←		09 51			←
Woking	a	09 08		09 18	09 11	09 14	09 18			09 29	09 24	09 29		09 33	09 38	09 48	09 41	09 45		09 48		09 59	09 54	09 58	09 59
	d			09 19	09 13	09 16	09 19			09 30	09 25	09 30		09 35		09 49	09 43	09 46		09 49		10 00	09 55		10 00
Worplesdon	d			→	09 18					→						→						→			
Guildford	a				09 23						09 33						09 50						10 03		
Brookwood	d						09 25					09 36								09 55					10 06
Ash Vale	d											09 44													10 14
Aldershot	a											09 49													10 19
	d											09 50													10 20
Farnham	a											09 55													10 25
	d											09 56													10 26
Bentley	d											10 02													
Alton	a											10 10													10 37
Farnborough (Main)	d		09 13				09 33							09 45						10 03					
Fleet	d		09 19				09 38													10 08					
Winchfield	d						09 44													10 14					
Hook	d						09 48													10 18					
Basingstoke	a		09 31			09 36	09 58						09 47	09 58				10 05		10 28					

Station		SW	SW 1	SW 1		SW 1	SW ◇1 🚲	SW 1	SW	SW 1	SW 1 🚲	SW 1	SW ◇1 🚲	SW 1		SW	SW 1	SW 1	SW ◇1 🚲	SW 1	SW	SW 1	SW 1 🚲	SW ◇1 🚲	
London Waterloo 15 ⊖	d		09 39	09 42		09 45	09 50		09 50	09 53	10 00		10 05	10 09			10 12	10 15	10 20		10 20	10 23	10 30	10 35	
Vauxhall ⊖	d								09 54												10 24				
Clapham Junction 10	d		09u46			09u52			09 59	10u00			10u12				10u19	10u22	10u27		10 29				
	d																								
Earlsfield	d								10 02												10 32				
Wimbledon 6 ⊖	d	←							10 06							←					10 36				
Surbiton 6	d	09 44		10 00					10 14	10 11						10 14	10 30				10 44	10 41			
Esher	d	09 48							→							10 18					→				
Hersham	d	09 51														10 21									
Walton-on-Thames	d	09 54		10 07												10 24	10 37								
Weybridge	d	09 57		10 11												10 27	10 41								
Byfleet & New Haw	d	10 00														10 30									
West Byfleet	d	10 03						←		10 21		←				10 33				←		10 51			
Woking	a	10 08		10 18		10 11	10 14	10 18		10 29	10 24	10 29		10 33		10 38	10 48	10 41	10 45	10 48		10 59	10 54	10 58	
	d			10 19		10 13	10 16	10 19		10 30	10 25	10 30		10 35			10 49	10 43	10 46	10 49		11 00	10 55		
Worplesdon	d			→		10 18				→							→					→			
Guildford	a					10 23					10 33							10 50					11 03		
Brookwood	d							10 25				10 36								10 55					
Ash Vale	d											10 44													
Aldershot	a											10 49													
	d											10 50													
Farnham	a											10 55													
	d											10 56													
Bentley	d											11 02													
Alton	a											11 10													
Farnborough (Main)	d		10 13					10 33						10 45						11 03					
Fleet	d		10 19					10 38												11 08					
Winchfield	d							10 44												11 14					
Hook	d							10 48												11 18					
Basingstoke	a		10 31				10 36	10 58					10 47	10 58					11 05	11 28					

Table 155

Saturdays

London - Woking, Guildford, Alton and Basingstoke

Network Diagram - see first Page of Table 155

		SW	SW	SW	SW	SW	SW	SW	SW	SW		SW	SW	SW	SW	SW	SW	SW	SW	SW		SW	SW	SW	SW
		1		1	1	1	◇1 🚲	1		1		1 🚲	1	◇1 🚲	1		1	1	◇1 🚲	1			1	1 🚲	◇1 🚲
London Waterloo 15 ⊖	d			10 39	10 42	10 45	10 50		10 50	10 53		11 00		11 05	11 09		11 12	11 15	11 20			11 20	11 23	11 30	11 35
Vauxhall ⊖	d								10 54													11 24			
Clapham Junction 10	d			10u46		10u52			10 59	11u00				11u12			11u19	11u22	11u27			11 29			
	d																								
Earlsfield	d								11 02													11 32			
Wimbledon 6 ⊖	d		←						11 06							←						11 36			
Surbiton 6	d		10 44		11 00				11 14	11 11						11 14	11 30					11 44	11 41		
Esher	d		10 48						↪							11 18						↪			
Hersham	d		10 51													11 21									
Walton-on-Thames	d		10 54		11 07											11 24	11 37								
Weybridge	d		10 57		11 11											11 27	11 41								
Byfleet & New Haw	d		11 00													11 30									
West Byfleet	d	←	11 03					←		11 21			←			11 33				←			11 51		
Woking	a	10 59	11 08		11 18	11 11	11 14	11 18		11 29		11 24	11 29		11 33	11 38	11 48	11 41	11 45	11 48			11 59	11 54	11 58
	d	11 00			11 19	11 13	11 16	11 19		11 30		11 25	11 30		11 35		11 49	11 43	11 46	11 49			12 00	11 55	
Worplesdon	d				↪	11 18				↪							↪						↪		
Guildford	a					11 23						11 33						11 50						12 03	
Brookwood	d	11 06						11 25					11 36							11 55					
Ash Vale	d	11 14											11 44												
Aldershot	a	11 19											11 49												
	d	11 20											11 50												
Farnham	a	11 25											11 55												
	d	11 26											11 56												
Bentley	d												12 02												
Alton	a	11 37											12 10												
Farnborough (Main)	d			11 13				11 33							11 45					12 03					
Fleet	d			11 19				11 38												12 08					
Winchfield	d							11 44												12 14					
Hook	d							11 48												12 18					
Basingstoke	a			11 31			11 36	11 58						11 47	11 58				12 05	12 28					

		SW	SW	SW	SW	SW		SW	SW	SW	SW	SW	SW	SW	SW	SW		SW	SW	SW	SW	SW	SW	SW	SW
		1		1	1	1		◇1 🚲	1		1	1 🚲	1	◇1 🚲	1			1	1	◇1 🚲	1		1	1 🚲	◇1 🚲
London Waterloo 15 ⊖	d			11 39	11 42	11 45		11 50		11 50	11 53	12 00		12 05	12 09			12 12	12 15	12 20		12 20	12 23	12 30	12 35
Vauxhall ⊖	d									11 54												12 24			
Clapham Junction 10	d			11u46		11u52				11 59	12u00			12u12				12u19	12u22	12u27		12 29			
	d																								
Earlsfield	d									12 02												12 32			
Wimbledon 6 ⊖	d		←							12 06						←						12 36			
Surbiton 6	d		11 44		12 00					12 14	12 11					12 14		12 30				12 44	12 41		
Esher	d		11 48							↪						12 18						↪			
Hersham	d		11 51													12 21									
Walton-on-Thames	d		11 54		12 07											12 24		12 37							
Weybridge	d		11 57		12 11											12 27		12 41							
Byfleet & New Haw	d		12 00													12 30									
West Byfleet	d	←	12 03						←		12 21		←			12 33					←		12 51		
Woking	a	11 59	12 08		12 18	12 11		12 14	12 18		12 29	12 24	12 29		12 33	12 38		12 48	12 41	12 45	12 48		12 59	12 54	12 58
	d	12 00			12 19	12 13		12 16	12 19		12 30	12 25	12 30		12 35			12 49	12 43	12 46	12 49		13 00	12 55	
Worplesdon	d				↪	12 18					↪							↪					↪		
Guildford	a					12 23						12 33							12 50					13 03	
Brookwood	d	12 06							12 25				12 36								12 55				
Ash Vale	d	12 14											12 44												
Aldershot	a	12 19											12 49												
	d	12 20											12 50												
Farnham	a	12 25											12 55												
	d	12 26											12 56												
Bentley	d												13 02												
Alton	a	12 37											13 10												
Farnborough (Main)	d			12 13					12 33						12 45						13 03				
Fleet	d			12 19					12 38												13 08				
Winchfield	d								12 44												13 14				
Hook	d								12 48												13 18				
Basingstoke	a			12 31				12 36	12 58					12 47	12 58					13 05	13 28				

London - Woking, Guildford, Alton and Basingstoke

Network Diagram - see first Page of Table 155

		SW 1		SW	SW 1	SW 1	SW 1	SW ◇1 ⚲	SW 1	SW	SW 1	SW 1 ⚲		SW 1	SW ◇1 ⚲	SW 1	SW	SW 1	SW 1	SW ◇1 ⚲	SW 1	SW		SW 1	SW 1 ⚲
London Waterloo 15 ⊖	d				12 39	12 42	12 45	12 50		12 50	12 53	13 00			13 05	13 09		13 12	13 15	13 20		13 20		13 23	13 30
Vauxhall ⊖	d									12 54												13 24			
Clapham Junction 10	d				12u46		12u52			12 59	13u00				13u12			13u19	13u22	13u27		13 29			
	d																								
Earlsfield	d									13 02												13 32			
Wimbledon 6 ⊖	d			←						13 06							←					13 36			
Surbiton 6	d			12 44		13 00				13 14	13 11						13 14	13 30				13 44		13 41	
Esher	d			12 48						↪							13 18					↪			
Hersham	d			12 51													13 21								
Walton-on-Thames	d			12 54		13 07											13 24	13 37							
Weybridge	d			12 57		13 11											13 27	13 41							
Byfleet & New Haw	d			13 00													13 30								
West Byfleet	d	←		13 03					←		13 21			←			13 33				←			13 51	
Woking	a	12 59		13 08		13 18	13 11	13 14	13 18		13 29	13 24		13 29		13 33	13 38	13 48	13 41	13 45	13 48			13 59	13 54
	d	13 00				13 19	13 13	13 16	13 19		13 30	13 25		13 30		13 35		13 49	13 43	13 46	13 49			14 00	13 55
Worplesdon	d					→	13 18				→							↪						↪	
Guildford	a						13 23					13 33							13 50						14 03
Brookwood	d	13 06							13 25					13 36							13 55				
Ash Vale	d	13 14												13 44											
Aldershot	a	13 19												13 49											
	d	13 20												13 50											
Farnham	a	13 25												13 55											
	d	13 26												13 56											
Bentley	d													14 02											
Alton	a	13 37												14 10											
Farnborough (Main)	d				13 13				13 33							13 45					14 03				
Fleet	d				13 19				13 38												14 08				
Winchfield	d								13 44												14 14				
Hook	d								13 48												14 18				
Basingstoke	a				13 31			13 36	13 58						13 47	13 58				14 05	14 28				

		SW ◇1 ⚲	SW 1	SW	SW 1	SW 1	SW 1	SW ◇1 ⚲		SW 1	SW	SW 1	SW 1 ⚲	SW 1	SW ◇1 ⚲	SW 1	SW	SW 1		SW 1	SW ◇1 ⚲	SW 1	SW	SW 1	SW 1 ⚲
London Waterloo 15 ⊖	d	13 35			13 39	13 42	13 45	13 50			13 50	13 53	14 00		14 05	14 09		14 12		14 15	14 20		14 20	14 23	14 30
Vauxhall ⊖	d										13 54												14 24		
Clapham Junction 10	d				13u46		13u52				13 59	14u00			14u12			14u19		14u22	14u27		14 29		
	d																								
Earlsfield	d										14 02												14 32		
Wimbledon 6 ⊖	d			←							14 06						←						14 36		
Surbiton 6	d			13 44		14 00					14 14	14 11					14 14	14 30					14 44	14 41	
Esher	d			13 48							↪						14 18						↪		
Hersham	d			13 51													14 21								
Walton-on-Thames	d			13 54		14 07											14 24	14 37							
Weybridge	d			13 57		14 11											14 27	14 41							
Byfleet & New Haw	d			14 00													14 30								
West Byfleet	d		←	14 03						←		14 21		←			14 33					←		14 51	
Woking	a	13 58	13 59	14 08		14 18	14 11	14 14		14 18		14 29	14 24	14 29		14 33	14 38	14 48		14 41	14 45	14 48		14 59	14 54
	d		14 00			14 19	14 13	14 16		14 19		14 30	14 25	14 30		14 35		14 49		14 43	14 46	14 49		15 00	14 55
Worplesdon	d					→	14 18					→						↪						↪	
Guildford	a						14 23						14 33							14 50					15 03
Brookwood	d		14 06							14 25				14 36								14 55			
Ash Vale	d		14 14											14 44											
Aldershot	a		14 19											14 49											
	d		14 20											14 50											
Farnham	a		14 25											14 55											
	d		14 26											14 56											
Bentley	d													15 02											
Alton	a		14 37											15 10											
Farnborough (Main)	d				14 13					14 33						14 45						15 03			
Fleet	d				14 19					14 38												15 08			
Winchfield	d									14 44												15 14			
Hook	d									14 48												15 18			
Basingstoke	a				14 31			14 36		14 58					14 47	14 58					15 05	15 28			

Table 155

Saturdays

London - Woking, Guildford, Alton and Basingstoke

Network Diagram - see first Page of Table 155

		SW ◇1 ⊥	SW 1	SW		SW 1	SW 1	SW 1	SW ◇1 ⊥	SW 1	SW	SW 1	SW 1 ⊥	SW 1		SW ◇1 ⊥	SW 1	SW	SW 1	SW 1	SW ◇1 ⊥	SW 1	SW	SW 1	
London Waterloo 15 ⊖	d	14 35				14 39	14 42	14 45	14 50		14 50	14 53	15 00			15 05	15 09		15 12	15 15	15 20		15 20	15 23	
Vauxhall ⊖	d										14 54												15 24		
Clapham Junction 10	d					14u46		14u52			14 59	15u00				15u12			15u19	15u22	15u27		15 29		
	d																								
Earlsfield	d										15 02												15 32		
Wimbledon 6 ⊖	d			←							15 06							←					15 36		
Surbiton 6	d			14 44			15 00				15 14	15 11						15 14	15 30				15 44	15 41	
Esher	d			14 48							↪							15 18					↪		
Hersham	d			14 51														15 21							
Walton-on-Thames	d			14 54			15 07											15 24	15 37						
Weybridge	d			14 57			15 11											15 27	15 41						
Byfleet & New Haw	d			15 00														15 30							
West Byfleet	d		←	15 03						←		15 21		←				15 33				←		15 51	
Woking	a	14 58	14 59	15 08			15 18	15 11	15 14	15 18		15 29	15 24	15 29			15 33	15 38	15 48	15 41	15 45	15 48		15 59	
	d		15 00				15 19	15 13	15 16	15 19		15 30	15 25	15 30			15 35		15 49	15 43	15 46	15 49		16 00	
Worplesdon	d						↪	15 18				↪							↪					↪	
Guildford	a							15 23					15 33							15 50					
Brookwood	d		15 06							15 25				15 36								15 55			
Ash Vale	d		15 14											15 44											
Aldershot	a		15 19											15 49											
	d		15 20											15 50											
Farnham	a		15 25											15 55											
	d		15 26											15 56											
Bentley	d													16 02											
Alton	a		15 37											16 10											
Farnborough (Main)	d					15 13				15 33							15 45					16 03			
Fleet	d					15 19				15 38												16 08			
Winchfield	d									15 44												16 14			
Hook	d									15 48												16 18			
Basingstoke	a					15 31			15 36	15 58						15 47	15 58				16 05	16 28			

		SW 1 ⊥	SW ◇1 ⊥	SW 1	SW	SW 1	SW 1	SW 1	SW ◇1 ⊥	SW 1		SW	SW 1	SW 1 ⊥	SW 1	SW ◇1 ⊥	SW 1	SW	SW 1	SW 1		SW ◇1 ⊥	SW 1	SW	SW 1
London Waterloo 15 ⊖	d	15 30	15 35			15 39	15 42	15 45	15 50			15 50	15 53	16 00		16 05	16 09		16 12	16 15		16 20		16 20	16 23
Vauxhall ⊖	d											15 54												16 24	
Clapham Junction 10	d					15u46		15u52				15 59	16u00			16u12			16u19	16u22		16u27		16 29	
	d																								
Earlsfield	d											16 02												16 32	
Wimbledon 6 ⊖	d				←							16 06						←						16 36	
Surbiton 6	d				15 44		16 00					16 14	16 11					16 14	16 30					16 44	16 41
Esher	d				15 48							↪						16 18						↪	
Hersham	d				15 51													16 21							
Walton-on-Thames	d				15 54		16 07											16 24	16 37						
Weybridge	d				15 57		16 11											16 27	16 41						
Byfleet & New Haw	d				16 00													16 30							
West Byfleet	d			←	16 03					←			16 21		←			16 33					←		16 51
Woking	a	15 54	15 58	15 59	16 08		16 18	16 11	16 14	16 18			16 29	16 24	16 29		16 33	16 38	16 48	16 41		16 45	16 48		16 59
	d	15 55		16 00			16 19	16 13	16 16	16 19			16 30	16 25	16 30		16 35		16 49	16 43		16 46	16 49		17 00
Worplesdon	d						↪	16 18					↪						↪						↪
Guildford	a	16 03						16 23						16 33						16 50					
Brookwood	d			16 06						16 25					16 36								16 55		
Ash Vale	d			16 14											16 44										
Aldershot	a			16 19											16 49										
	d			16 20											16 50										
Farnham	a			16 25											16 55										
	d			16 26											16 56										
Bentley	d														17 02										
Alton	a			16 37											17 10										
Farnborough (Main)	d					16 13				16 33							16 45						17 03		
Fleet	d					16 19				16 38													17 08		
Winchfield	d									16 44													17 14		
Hook	d									16 48													17 18		
Basingstoke	a					16 31			16 36	16 58						16 47	16 58					17 05	17 28		

London - Woking, Guildford, Alton and Basingstoke

Network Diagram - see first Page of Table 155

Station		SW [1] 🚲	SW ◇[1] 🚲	SW [1]	SW	SW [1]		SW [1]	SW [1]	SW ◇[1] 🚲	SW [1]	SW	SW [1]	SW [1] 🚲	SW [1]	SW ◇[1] 🛒		SW [1]	SW	SW [1]	SW [1]	SW ◇[1] 🚲	SW [1]	SW	SW [1]
London Waterloo [15] ⊖	d	16 30	16 35			16 39		16 42	16 45	16 50		16 50	16 53	17 00		17 05		17 09		17 12	17 15	17 20		17 20	17 23
Vauxhall ⊖	d											16 54												17 24	
Clapham Junction [10]	d					16u46			16u52			16 59	17u00			17u12				17u19	17u22	17u27		17 29	
	d																								
Earlsfield	d											17 02												17 32	
Wimbledon [6] ⊖	d				←							17 06							←					17 36	
Surbiton [6]	d				16 44			17 00				17 14	17 11						17 14	17 30				17 44	17 41
Esher	d				16 48							↦							17 18					↦	
Hersham	d				16 51														17 21						
Walton-on-Thames	d				16 54			17 07											17 24	17 37					
Weybridge	d				16 57			17 11											17 27	17 41					
Byfleet & New Haw	d				17 00														17 30						
West Byfleet	d			←	17 03						←		17 21		←				17 33				←		17 51
Woking	a	16 54	16 58	16 59	17 08			17 18	17 11	17 14	17 18		17 29	17 24	17 29			17 33	17 38	17 48	17 41	17 45	17 48		17 59
	d	16 55		17 00				17 19	17 13	17 16	17 19		17 30	17 25	17 30			17 35		17 49	17 43	17 46	17 49		18 00
Worplesdon	d							↦	17 18				↦							↦					↦
Guildford	a	17 03							17 23					17 33							17 50				
Brookwood	d			17 06							17 25				17 36								17 55		
Ash Vale	d			17 14											17 44										
Aldershot	a			17 19											17 49										
	d			17 20											17 50										
Farnham	a			17 25											17 55										
	d			17 26											17 56										
Bentley	d			17 32											18 02										
Alton	a			17 39											18 10										
Farnborough (Main)	d					17 13					17 33							17 45					18 03		
Fleet	d					17 19					17 38												18 08		
Winchfield	d										17 44												18 14		
Hook	d										17 48												18 18		
Basingstoke	a					17 31				17 36	17 58					17 47		17 58				18 05	18 28		

Station		SW [1] 🚲		SW ◇[1] 🚲	SW [1]	SW	SW [1]	SW [1]	SW [1]	SW ◇[1] 🚲	SW [1]	SW		SW [1]	SW [1] 🚲	SW [1]	SW ◇[1] 🚲	SW [1]	SW	SW [1]	SW [1]	SW ◇[1] 🚲		SW [1]	SW
London Waterloo [15] ⊖	d	17 30		17 35			17 39	17 42	17 45	17 50		17 50		17 53	18 00		18 05	18 09		18 12	18 15	18 20			18 20
Vauxhall ⊖	d											17 54													18 24
Clapham Junction [10]	d						17u46		17u52			17 59		18u00			18u12			18u19	18u22	18u27			18 29
	d																								
Earlsfield	d											18 02													18 32
Wimbledon [6] ⊖	d					←						18 06							←						18 36
Surbiton [6]	d					17 44		18 00				18 14		18 11					18 14	18 30					18 44
Esher	d					17 48						↦							18 18						↦
Hersham	d					17 51													18 21						
Walton-on-Thames	d					17 54		18 07											18 24	18 37					
Weybridge	d					17 57		18 11											18 27	18 41					
Byfleet & New Haw	d					18 00													18 30						
West Byfleet	d				←	18 03					←			18 21		←			18 33					←	
Woking	a	17 54		17 58	17 59	18 08		18 18	18 11	18 14	18 18			18 29	18 24	18 29		18 33	18 38	18 48	18 41	18 45		18 48	
	d	17 55			18 00			18 19	18 13	18 16	18 19			18 30	18 25	18 30		18 35		18 49	18 43	18 46		18 49	
Worplesdon	d							↦	18 18					↦						↦					
Guildford	a	18 03							18 23						18 33						18 50				
Brookwood	d				18 06						18 25					18 36								18 55	
Ash Vale	d				18 14											18 44									
Aldershot	a				18 19											18 49									
	d				18 20											18 50									
Farnham	a				18 25											18 55									
	d				18 26											18 56									
Bentley	d				18 32											19 02									
Alton	a				18 39											19 10									
Farnborough (Main)	d						18 13				18 33							18 45						19 03	
Fleet	d						18 19				18 38													19 08	
Winchfield	d										18 44													19 14	
Hook	d										18 48													19 18	
Basingstoke	a						18 31			18 36	18 58						18 47	18 58				19 05		19 28	

Table 155 **Saturdays**

London - Woking, Guildford, Alton and Basingstoke

Network Diagram - see first Page of Table 155

		SW 1	SW 1 ⚲	SW ◇1 ⚲	SW 1	SW	SW 1	SW 1		SW 1	SW ◇1 ⚲	SW 1	SW	SW 1	SW 1 ⚲	SW 1	SW ◇1 ⚲	SW 1		SW	SW 1	SW 1	SW ◇1 ⚲	SW 1	SW
London Waterloo 15 ⊖	d	18 23	18 30	18 35			18 39	18 42		18 45	18 50		18 50	18 53	19 00		19 05	19 09			19 12	19 15	19 20		19 20
Vauxhall ⊖	d												18 54												19 24
Clapham Junction 10	d						18u46			18u52			18 59	19u00			19u12				19u19	19u22	19u27		19 29
	d																								
Earlsfield	d												19 02												19 32
Wimbledon 6 ⊖	d					←							19 06							←					19 36
Surbiton 6	d	18 41				18 44		19 00					19 14	19 11						19 14	19 30				19 44
Esher	d					18 48							↪							19 18					↪
Hersham	d					18 51														19 21					
Walton-on-Thames	d					18 54		19 07												19 24	19 37				
Weybridge	d					18 57		19 11												19 27	19 41				
Byfleet & New Haw	d					19 00														19 30					
West Byfleet	d	18 51			←	19 03						←		19 21		←				19 33				←	
Woking	a	18 59	18 54	18 58	18 59	19 08		19 18		19 11	19 15	19 18		19 29	19 24	19 29		19 33		19 38	19 48	19 41	19 45	19 48	
	d	19 00	18 55		19 00			19 19		19 13	19 16	19 19		19 30	19 25	19 30		19 35			19 49	19 43	19 46	19 49	
Worplesdon	d	↪						↪		19 18				↪							↪				
Guildford	a		19 03							19 23					19 33							19 50			
Brookwood	d				19 06							19 25				19 36								19 55	
Ash Vale	d				19 14											19 44									
Aldershot	a				19 19											19 49									
	d				19 20											19 50									
Farnham	a				19 25											19 55									
	d				19 26											19 56									
Bentley	d				19 32											20 02									
Alton	a				19 39											20 10									
Farnborough (Main)	d						19 13					19 33						19 45						20 03	
Fleet	d						19 19					19 38												20 08	
Winchfield	d											19 44												20 14	
Hook	d											19 48												20 18	
Basingstoke	a						19 31				19 36	19 58					19 47	19 58					20 05	20 28	

		SW 1	SW 1 ⚲	SW ◇1 ⚲		SW 1	SW	SW 1	SW 1	SW 1	SW ◇1 ⚲	SW 1	SW	SW 1		SW 1	SW 1	SW ◇1 ⚲	SW 1	SW	SW 1	SW 1	SW ◇1 ⚲	SW 1	
London Waterloo 15 ⊖	d	19 23	19 30	19 35				19 39	19 42	19 45	19 50		19 50	19 53		20 00		20 05	20 09		20 12	20 15	20 20		
Vauxhall ⊖	d												19 54												
Clapham Junction 10	d							19u46		19u52			19 59	20u00				20u12			20u19	20u22	20u27		
	d																								
Earlsfield	d												20 02												
Wimbledon 6 ⊖	d						←						20 06							←					
Surbiton 6	d	19 41					19 44		20 00				20 14	20 11						20 14	20 30				
Esher	d						19 48						↪							20 18					
Hersham	d						19 51													20 21					
Walton-on-Thames	d						19 54		20 07											20 24	20 37				
Weybridge	d						19 57		20 11											20 27	20 41				
Byfleet & New Haw	d						20 00													20 30					
West Byfleet	d	19 51				←	20 03					←		20 21			←			20 33				←	
Woking	a	19 59	19 54	19 58		19 59	20 08		20 18	20 11	20 14	20 18		20 29		20 24	20 29		20 33	20 38	20 48	20 41	20 45	20 48	
	d	20 00	19 55			20 00			20 19	20 13	20 16	20 19		20 30		20 25	20 30		20 35		20 49	20 43	20 46	20 49	
Worplesdon	d	↪							↪	20 18				↪							↪				
Guildford	a		20 03							20 23						20 33						20 50			
Brookwood	d					20 06						20 25					20 36							20 55	
Ash Vale	d					20 14											20 44								
Aldershot	a					20 19											20 49								
	d					20 20											20 50								
Farnham	a					20 25											20 55								
	d					20 26											20 56								
Bentley	d					20 32											21 02								
Alton	a					20 39											21 10								
Farnborough (Main)	d							20 13				20 33							20 45					21 03	
Fleet	d							20 19				20 38												21 08	
Winchfield	d											20 44												21 14	
Hook	d											20 48												21 18	
Basingstoke	a							20 31			20 36	20 58						20 47	20 58				21 05	21 28	

Table 155

Saturdays

London - Woking, Guildford, Alton and Basingstoke

Network Diagram - see first Page of Table 155

		SW	SW 1	SW 1	SW ◇1 trolley	SW 1	SW	SW 1	SW 1	SW 1		SW 1	SW	SW 1	SW 1	SW 1	SW ◇1 trolley	SW	SW 1	SW ◇1 trolley		SW	SW 1	SW 1	SW ◇1 trolley
London Waterloo 15 ⊖	d	20 20	20 23	20 30	20 35			20 39	20 42	20 45			20 50	20 53	21 00		21 05		21 12	21 20		21 20	21 23	21 30	21 35
Vauxhall ⊖	d	20 24											20 54									21 24			
Clapham Junction 10	d	20 29						20u46		20u52			20 59	21u00			21u12		21u19	21u27		21 29			
	d																								
Earlsfield	d	20 32											21 02									21 32			
Wimbledon 6 ⊖	d	20 36					←						21 06					←				21 36			
Surbiton 6	d	20 44	20 41				20 44		21 00				21 14	21 11				21 14	21 30			21 44	21 41		
Esher	d	↪					20 48						↪					21 18				↪			
Hersham	d						20 51											21 21							
Walton-on-Thames	d						20 54		21 07									21 24	21 37						
Weybridge	d						20 57		21 11									21 27	21 41						
Byfleet & New Haw	d						21 00											21 30							
West Byfleet	d		20 51			←	21 03					←		21 21		←		21 33					21 51		
Woking	a		20 59	20 54	20 58	20 59	21 08		21 18	21 11		21 18		21 29	21 24	21 29	21 31	21 38	21 48	21 45			21 59	21 54	21 58
	d		21 00	20 55		21 00			21 19	21 13		21 19		21 30	21 25	21 30	21 32		21 49	21 49			22 00	21 55	
Worplesdon	d		↪						↪	21 18				↪									↪		
Guildford	a			21 03						21 23					21 33									22 03	
Brookwood	d					21 06						21 25				21 36			21 55						
Ash Vale	d					21 14										21 44									
Aldershot	a					21 19										21 49									
	d					21 20										21 50									
Farnham	a					21 25										21 55									
	d					21 26										21 56									
Bentley	d					21 32										22 02									
Alton	a					21 39										22 10									
Farnborough (Main)	d							21 13				21 33							22 03						
Fleet	d							21 19				21 38							22 08						
Winchfield	d											21 44							22 14						
Hook	d											21 48							22 18						
Basingstoke	a							21 31				21 58					21 51		22 25	22 12					

		SW 1	SW	SW 1	SW 1	SW 1		SW 1	SW	SW 1	SW 1	SW 1	SW ◇1 trolley	SW	SW 1	SW 1 trolley		SW	SW 1	SW 1	SW ◇1 trolley	SW 1	SW	SW 1	SW 1
London Waterloo 15 ⊖	d			21 39	21 42	21 45			21 50	21 53	22 00		22 05		22 12	22 20		22 20	22 23	22 30	22 35			22 39	22 42
Vauxhall ⊖	d								21 54									22 24							
Clapham Junction 10	d			21u46		21u52			21 59	22u00			22u12		22u19	22u27		22 29	22u30					22u46	22u49
	d																								
Earlsfield	d								22 02									22 32							
Wimbledon 6 ⊖	d		←						22 06					←				22 36					←		
Surbiton 6	d		21 44		22 00				22 14	22 11				22 14	22 30			22 44	22 41				22 44		23 00
Esher	d		21 48						↪					22 18				↪					22 48		
Hersham	d		21 51											22 21									22 51		
Walton-on-Thames	d		21 54		22 07									22 24	22 37								22 54		23 07
Weybridge	d		21 57		22 11									22 27	22 41								22 57		23 11
Byfleet & New Haw	d		22 00											22 30									23 00		
West Byfleet	d	←	22 03					←		22 21		←		22 33					22 51			←	23 03		
Woking	a	21 59	22 08		22 18	22 11		22 18		22 29	22 24	22 29	22 31	22 37	22 48	22 45			22 59	22 54	22 58	22 59	23 08		23 18
	d	22 00			22 19	22 13		22 19		22 30	22 25	22 30	22 32	22 39	22 49	22 49			23 00	22 55		23 00			23 19
Worplesdon	d				↪	22 18				↪									↪						↪
Guildford	a					22 23					22 33			22 47						23 03					
Brookwood	d	22 06						22 25				22 36			22 55							23 06			
Ash Vale	d	22 14										22 44										23 14			
Aldershot	a	22 19										22 49										23 19			
	d	22 20										22 50										23 20			
Farnham	a	22 25										22 55										23 25			
	d	22 26										22 56										23 26			
Bentley	d	22 32										23 02										23 33			
Alton	a	22 39										23 10										23 40			
Farnborough (Main)	d			22 13				22 33							23 03									23 16	
Fleet	d			22 19				22 38							23 08									23 21	
Winchfield	d							22 44							23 14										
Hook	d							22 48							23 18										
Basingstoke	a			22 31				22 58					22 51		23 25	23 10								23 34	

Table 155

Saturdays

London - Woking, Guildford, Alton and Basingstoke

Network Diagram - see first Page of Table 155

		SW 1		SW 1	SW	SW	SW 1	SW ◇1	SW	SW 1	SW 1	SW 1		SW	SW 1	SW 1	SW	SW 1	SW 1	SW 1
London Waterloo 15 ⊖	d	22 45			22 50	22 52	22 53	23 05		23 12	23 15			23 20	23 23	23 35		23 40	23 45	23 48
Vauxhall ⊖	d				22 54	22 56								23 24						
Clapham Junction 10	d	22u52			22 59		23u00	23u12			23u22			23 29	23u30	23u42		23u47	23u52	23u54
	d					23 02				23u19										
Earlsfield	d				23 02									23 32						
Wimbledon 6 ⊖	d				23 06				←					23 36			←			
Surbiton 6	d				23 14		23 11		23 14	23 38				23 44	23 41		23 44			00 09
Esher	d				→				23 18					→			23 48			
Hersham	d								23 21								23 51			
Walton-on-Thames	d								23 24	23 45							23 54			00 16
Weybridge	d								23 27	23 49							23 57			00 20
Byfleet & New Haw	d					00 06			23 30								23 59			
West Byfleet	d			←		00 09	23 21		23 33			←			23 55		00 03			
Woking	a	23 11		23 18		00 15	23 29	23 31	23 38	23 55	23 41	23 55			23 59	00 01	00 08	00 06	00 11	00 26
	d	23 13		23 19			23 30	23 32		23 57	23 43	23 57			00 01	00 03		00 08	00 13	00 28
Worplesdon	d	23 18								→									00 18	
Guildford	a	23 23									23 51								00 24	
Brookwood	d			23 25			23 36					00 03			00 07					00 34
Ash Vale	d						23 44								00 15					
Aldershot	a						23 49								00 19					
	d						23 50								00 20					
Farnham	a						23 55								00 25					
	d						23 58								00 26					
Bentley	d						00 04								00 33					
Alton	a						00 11								00 40					
Farnborough (Main)	d			23 33								00 10				00 14				00 41
Fleet	d			23 38								00 16				00 20				00 47
Winchfield	d			23 44								00 21								00s52
Hook	d			23 48								00 26								00s57
Basingstoke	a			23 55				23 51				00 33				00 33		00 27		01 06

Sundays

		SW A	SW 1 A	SW 1 A	SW A	SW 1 A	SW 1 A	SW A	SW 1 A	SW 1 A		SW 1 A	SW 1	SW 1	SW	SW 1	SW 1	SW 1	SW 1	SW		SW	SW	SW	SW ◇1
London Waterloo 15 ⊖	d	22p52	22p53	23p12	23p20	23p23	23p35		23p40	23p45		23p48	00 05		00 09	01 05				07 10			07 40	07 50	07 54
Vauxhall ⊖	d	22p56			23p24										00 13	01 09				07 14			07 44	07 54	
Clapham Junction 10	d		23b00		23p29	23b30	23b42		23b47	23b52		23b54	00u12		00 20					07 19			07 49		08u03
	d	23p02		23b19												01 15								08 00	
Earlsfield	d				23p32										00 23					07 22			07 52		
Wimbledon 6 ⊖	d				23p36			←					00u18		00 27	01s27				07 26			07 56		
Surbiton 6	d		23p11	23p38	23p44	23p41		23p44				00 09			00 35	01s35				07 35			08 05		
Esher	d				→			23p48							00s39					07 39			08 09		
Hersham	d							23p51							00s42					07 42			08 12		
Walton-on-Thames	d			23p45				23p54				00 16			00s44					07 45			08 15		
Weybridge	d			23p49				23p57				00 20			00s48					07 49			08 19		
Byfleet & New Haw	d	00 06						23p59							00s51					07 51		08 02	08 21	09 02	
West Byfleet	d	00 09	23p21			23p55		00 03							00s54					07 54		08 05	08 24	09 05	
Woking	a	00 15	23p29	23p55		23p59	00 01	00 08	00 06	00 11		00 26	00 35		00 58	01 48				07 59		08 11	08 29	09 11	08 27
	d		23p30	23p57		00 01	00 03		00 08	00 13		00 28	00 37	00 40	01 00	01 49	07 32	07 46	07 49	08 05			08 32		08 28
Worplesdon	d									00 18													→		
Guildford	a									00 24					01 07		07 39			08 14					
Brookwood	d		23p36	00 03		00 07						00 34		00 45				07 51	07 55						
Ash Vale	d		23p44			00 15								00 53					08 03						
Aldershot	a		23p49			00 19								00 58					08 07						
	d		23p50			00 20								00 59					08 08						
Farnham	a		23p55			00 25								01 04					08 13						
	d		23p58			00 26								01 05					08 14						
Bentley	d		00 04			00 33								01s11					08 24						
Alton	a		00 11			00 40								01 18					08 31						
Farnborough (Main)	d			00 10			00 14					00 41				01s58		07 59							
Fleet	d			00 16			00 20					00 47				02s04		08 04							
Winchfield	d			00 21								00s52						08 10							
Hook	d			00 26								00s57						08 14							
Basingstoke	a			00 33			00 33		00 27			01 06	00 55			02s16		08 21							08 46

A not 11 December

b Previous night, stops to pick up only

Sundays

London - Woking, Guildford, Alton and Basingstoke

Network Diagram - see first Page of Table 155

		SW	SW 1	SW 1		SW		SW ◇1 🚲	SW 1	SW	SW 1	SW ◇1	SW	SW	SW ◇1	SW		SW 1	SW 1		SW	SW ◇1 🚲	SW 1	SW	SW 1
London Waterloo 15 ⊖	d		08 00	08 07		08 10		08 15			08 30	08 35	08 40	08 50	08 54			09 00	09 07		09 10	09 15			09 30
Vauxhall ⊖	d					08 14							08 44	08 54							09 14				
Clapham Junction 10	d		08u09	08 15		08 19		08u22			08u39	08u45	08 49		09u03			09u09	09 15		09 19	09u22			09u39
	d													09 00											
Earlsfield	d					08 22							08 52								09 22				
Wimbledon 6 ⊖	d			08 22		08 26							08 56						09 22		09 26				
Surbiton 6	d			08 30		08 35							09 05						09 30		09 35				
Esher	d					08 39							09 09								09 39				
Hersham	d					08 42							09 12								09 42				
Walton-on-Thames	d					08 45							09 15								09 45				
Weybridge	d					08 49							09 19								09 49				
Byfleet & New Haw	d					08 51							09 21	10 02							09 51				
West Byfleet	d	←				08 54			←	←			09 24	10 05		←					09 54		←	←	
Woking	a	08 29	08 34	08 42		08 59		08 46	08 42	08 59	09 03	09 08	09 29	10 11	09 27	09 29		09 34	09 42		09 59	09 46	09 42	09 59	10 03
	d	08 32	08 35	08 46	08 49	09 02		08 47	08 49	09 02	09 04	09 09	09 32		09 28	09 32		09 35	09 46	09 49	10 02	09 47	09 49	10 02	10 04
Worplesdon	d				→	→							→							→	→				
Guildford	a	08 40	08 43							09 10	09 12					09 40		09 43						10 10	10 12
Brookwood	d			08 51					08 55										09 51				09 55		
Ash Vale	d								09 03														10 03		
Aldershot	a								09 07														10 07		
	d								09 08														10 08		
Farnham	a								09 13														10 13		
	d								09 14														10 14		
Bentley	d								09 24														10 24		
Alton	a								09 31														10 31		
Farnborough (Main)	d			08 59															09 59						
Fleet	d			09 04															10 04						
Winchfield	d			09 10															10 10						
Hook	d			09 14															10 14						
Basingstoke	a			09 21				09 06				09 28			09 46				10 21			10 06			

		SW ◇1		SW	SW	SW ◇1	SW 1	SW	SW 1		SW	SW ◇1 🚲		SW 1	SW 1	SW	SW ◇1 🚲	SW	SW	SW ◇1	SW 1	SW		SW 1	
London Waterloo 15 ⊖	d	09 35		09 40	09 50	09 54	10 00		10 07		10 10	10 15			10 30		10 35	10 40	10 50	10 54	11 00			11 07	
Vauxhall ⊖	d			09 44	09 54						10 14							10 44	10 54						
Clapham Junction 10	d	09u45		09 49		10u03	10u09		10 15		10 19	10u22			10u39		10u45	10 49		11u04	11u09			11 15	
	d				10 00														11 00						
Earlsfield	d			09 52							10 22							10 52							
Wimbledon 6 ⊖	d			09 56					10 22		10 26							10 56						11 22	
Surbiton 6	d			10 05					10 30		10 35							11 05						11 30	
Esher	d			10 09							10 39							11 09							
Hersham	d			10 12							10 42							11 12							
Walton-on-Thames	d			10 15							10 45							11 15							
Weybridge	d			10 19							10 49							11 19							
Byfleet & New Haw	d			10 21	11 02						10 51							11 21	12 02						
West Byfleet	d			10 24	11 05			←			10 54			←		←		11 24	12 05			←			
Woking	a	10 08		10 29	11 11	10 26	10 31	10 29	10 42		10 59	10 45		10 42	11 01	10 59	11 06	11 29	12 11	11 26	11 31	11 29		11 42	
	d	10 09		10 35		10 28	10 32	10 35	10 46	10 49	11 05	10 46		10 49	11 02	11 05	11 07	11 35		11 28	11 32	11 35		11 46	11 49
Worplesdon	d			→						→	→							→							→
Guildford	a						10 40	10 44							11 10	11 14					11 40	11 44			
Brookwood	d								10 51					10 55										11 51	
Ash Vale	d													11 03											
Aldershot	a													11 07											
	d													11 08											
Farnham	a													11 13											
	d													11 14											
Bentley	d													11 24											
Alton	a													11 31											
Farnborough (Main)	d								10 59															11 59	
Fleet	d								11 04															12 04	
Winchfield	d								11 10															12 10	
Hook	d								11 14															12 14	
Basingstoke	a	10 28				10 46			11 21			11 05					11 26			11 46				12 21	

Table 155

Sundays

London - Woking, Guildford, Alton and Basingstoke

Network Diagram - see first Page of Table 155

		SW	SW ◇1 ⚒	SW 1	SW 1 ⚒	SW	SW ◇1 ⚒	SW		SW	SW ◇1 ⚒	SW 1	SW	SW 1		SW	SW ◇1 ⚒	SW 1		SW 1 ⚒	SW	SW ◇1 ⚒	SW	SW	SW ◇1 ⚒
London Waterloo 15 ⊖	d	11 10	11 15		11 30		11 35	11 40		11 50	11 54	12 00		12 07		12 10	12 15			12 30		12 35	12 40	12 50	12 54
Vauxhall ⊖	d	11 14						11 44		11 54						12 14							12 44	12 54	
Clapham Junction 10	d	11 19	11u22		11u39		11u45	11 49			12u04	12u09		12 15		12 19	12u22			12u39		12u42	12 49		13u03
	d									12 00														13 00	
Earlsfield	d	11 22						11 52								12 22							12 52		
Wimbledon 6 ⊖	d	11 26						11 56						12 22		12 26							12 56		
Surbiton 6	d	11 35						12 05						12 30		12 35							13 05		
Esher	d	11 39						12 09								12 39							13 09		
Hersham	d	11 42						12 12								12 42							13 12		
Walton-on-Thames	d	11 45						12 15								12 45							13 15		
Weybridge	d	11 49						12 19								12 49							13 19		
Byfleet & New Haw	d	11 51						12 21		13 02						12 51							13 21	14 02	
West Byfleet	d	11 54		←		←		12 24		13 05			←			12 54		←			←		13 24	14 05	
Woking	a	11 59	11 45	11 42	12 01	11 59	12 06	12 29		13 11	12 26	12 31	12 29	12 42		12 59	12 45	12 42		13 01	12 59	13 06	13 29	14 11	13 26
	d	12 05	11 46	11 49	12 02	12 05	12 07	12 35			12 28	12 32	12 35	12 46	12 49	13 05	12 46	12 49		13 02	13 05	13 07	13 35		13 28
Worplesdon	d	↪						↪							↪	↪							↪		
Guildford	a				12 10	12 14						12 40	12 44							13 10	13 14				
Brookwood	d			11 55										12 51				12 55							
Ash Vale	d			12 03														13 03							
Aldershot	a			12 07														13 07							
	d			12 08														13 08							
Farnham	a			12 13														13 13							
	d			12 14														13 14							
Bentley	d			12 24														13 24							
Alton	a			12 31														13 31							
Farnborough (Main)	d													12 59											
Fleet	d													13 04											
Winchfield	d													13 10											
Hook	d													13 14											
Basingstoke	a		12 05				12 26				12 46			13 21			13 05					13 26			13 46

		SW 1	SW	SW 1			SW	SW ◇1 ⚒	SW 1	SW 1 ⚒	SW	SW ◇1 ⚒	SW	SW	SW ◇1 ⚒		SW 1	SW	SW 1		SW	SW ◇1 ⚒	SW 1	SW 1 ⚒	SW
London Waterloo 15 ⊖	d	13 00		13 07			13 10	13 15		13 30		13 35	13 40	13 50	13 54		14 00		14 07		14 10	14 15		14 30	
Vauxhall ⊖	d						13 14						13 44	13 54							14 14				
Clapham Junction 10	d	13u09		13 15			13 19	13u22		13u39		13u42	13 49		14u03		14u09		14 15		14 19	14u22		14u39	
	d													14 00											
Earlsfield	d						13 22						13 52								14 22				
Wimbledon 6 ⊖	d			13 22			13 26						13 56						14 22		14 26				
Surbiton 6	d			13 30			13 35						14 05						14 30		14 35				
Esher	d						13 39						14 09								14 39				
Hersham	d						13 42						14 12								14 42				
Walton-on-Thames	d						13 45						14 15								14 45				
Weybridge	d						13 49						14 19								14 49				
Byfleet & New Haw	d						13 51						14 21	15 02							14 51				
West Byfleet	d		←				13 54		←		←		14 24	15 05				←			14 54		←		←
Woking	a	13 31	13 29	13 42			13 59	13 45	13 42	14 01	13 59	14 06	14 29	15 11	14 26		14 31	14 29	14 42		14 59	14 45	14 42	15 01	14 59
	d	13 32	13 35	13 46	13 49		14 05	13 46	13 49	14 02	14 05	14 07	14 35		14 28		14 32	14 35	14 46	14 49	15 05	14 46	14 49	15 02	15 05
Worplesdon	d				↪		↪						↪							↪	↪				
Guildford	a	13 40	13 44							14 10	14 14						14 40	14 44						15 10	15 14
Brookwood	d			13 51					13 55										14 51				14 55		
Ash Vale	d								14 03														15 03		
Aldershot	a								14 07														15 07		
	d								14 08														15 08		
Farnham	a								14 13														15 13		
	d								14 14														15 14		
Bentley	d								14 24														15 24		
Alton	a								14 31														15 31		
Farnborough (Main)	d			13 59															14 59						
Fleet	d			14 04															15 04						
Winchfield	d			14 10															15 10						
Hook	d			14 14															15 14						
Basingstoke	a			14 21				14 05				14 26			14 46				15 21			15 05			

Table 155

Sundays

London - Woking, Guildford, Alton and Basingstoke

Network Diagram - see first Page of Table 155

			SW ◇1 🛒	SW	SW	SW ◇1 🛒	SW 1	SW	SW 1		SW		SW ◇1 🛒	SW 1	SW 1 🛒	SW	SW ◇1 🛒	SW 1		SW	SW		SW ◇1 🛒	SW 1	SW
London Waterloo 15 ⊖	d		14 35	14 40	14 50	14 54	15 00		15 07		15 10		15 15		15 30		15 35	15 37		15 40	15 50		15 54	16 00	
Vauxhall ⊖	d			14 44	14 54						15 14									15 44	15 54				
Clapham Junction 10	d		14u42	14 49		15u03	15u09		15 15		15 19		15u22		15u39		15u42	15 46		15 49			16u03	16u09	
	d				15 00																16 00				
Earlsfield	d			14 52							15 22									15 52					
Wimbledon 6 ⊖	d			14 56					15 22		15 26							15 53		15 56					
Surbiton 6	d			15 05					15 30		15 35							16 02		16 05					
Esher	d			15 09							15 39									16 09					
Hersham	d			15 12							15 42									16 12					
Walton-on-Thames	d			15 15							15 45							16 09		16 15					
Weybridge	d			15 19							15 49							16 13		16 19					
Byfleet & New Haw	d			15 21	16 02						15 51									16 21	17 02				
West Byfleet	d			15 24	16 05			←			15 54			←		←				16 24	17 05				←
Woking	a		15 06	15 29	16 11	15 26	15 31	15 29	15 42		15 59		15 45	15 42	16 01	15 59	16 06	16 19		16 29	17 11		16 26	16 31	16 29
	d		15 07	15 35		15 28	15 32	15 35	15 46	15 49	16 05		15 46	15 49	16 02	16 05	16 07	16 23	16 26	16 35			16 28	16 32	16 35
Worplesdon	d			→						→	→									→					
Guildford	a						15 40	15 44							16 10	16 14								16 40	16 44
Brookwood	d								15 51					15 55				16 28	16 32						
Ash Vale	d													16 03					16 40						
Aldershot	a													16 07					16 45						
	d													16 08					16 46						
Farnham	a													16 13					16 51						
	d													16 14					16 55						
Bentley	d													16 24											
Alton	a													16 31					17 07						
Farnborough (Main)	d								15 59									16 36							
Fleet	d								16 04									16 41							
Winchfield	d								16 10																
Hook	d								16 14																
Basingstoke	a		15 26			15 46			16 21				16 05				16 26	16 54					16 46		

		SW 1		SW	SW ◇1 🛒	SW 1	SW 1 🛒		SW	SW ◇1 🛒	SW 1		SW	SW	SW ◇1 🛒	SW 1	SW		SW 1		SW	SW ◇1 🛒	SW 1	SW 1 🛒	SW
London Waterloo 15 ⊖	d	16 07		16 10	16 15		16 30			16 35	16 37		16 40	16 50	16 54	17 00			17 07		17 10	17 15		17 30	
Vauxhall ⊖	d			16 14									16 44	16 54							17 14				
Clapham Junction 10	d	16 15		16 19	16u22		16u39			16u42	16 46		16 49		17u03	17u09			17 15		17 19	17u22		17u39	
	d													17 00											
Earlsfield	d			16 22									16 52								17 22				
Wimbledon 6 ⊖	d	16 22		16 26							16 53		16 56						17 22		17 26				
Surbiton 6	d	16 30		16 35							17 02		17 05						17 30		17 35				
Esher	d			16 39									17 09								17 39				
Hersham	d			16 42									17 12								17 42				
Walton-on-Thames	d			16 45							17 09		17 15								17 45				
Weybridge	d			16 49							17 13		17 19								17 49				
Byfleet & New Haw	d			16 51									17 21	18 02							17 51				
West Byfleet	d			16 54		←			←				17 24	18 05			←				17 54		←		←
Woking	a	16 42		16 59	16 45	16 42	17 01		16 59	17 06	17 19		17 29	18 11	17 26	17 31	17 29		17 42		17 59	17 45	17 42	18 01	17 59
	d	16 46	16 49	17 05	16 46	16 49	17 02		17 05	17 07	17 23	17 26	17 35		17 28	17 32	17 35		17 46	17 49	18 05	17 46	17 49	18 02	18 05
Worplesdon	d		→	→									→							→	→				
Guildford	a						17 10		17 14							17 40	17 44							18 10	18 14
Brookwood	d	16 51				16 55					17 28	17 32							17 51				17 55		
Ash Vale	d					17 03						17 40											18 03		
Aldershot	a					17 07						17 45											18 07		
	d					17 08						17 46											18 08		
Farnham	a					17 13						17 51											18 13		
	d					17 14						17 55											18 14		
Bentley	d					17 24																	18 24		
Alton	a					17 31						18 07											18 31		
Farnborough (Main)	d	16 59									17 36								17 59						
Fleet	d	17 04									17 41								18 04						
Winchfield	d	17 10																	18 10						
Hook	d	17 14																	18 14						
Basingstoke	a	17 21			17 05					17 26	17 54				17 46				18 21			18 05			

Table 155

Sundays

London - Woking, Guildford, Alton and Basingstoke

Network Diagram - see first Page of Table 155

		SW ◇1 🚲	SW 1			SW	SW	SW ◇1 🚲	SW 1	SW	SW 1		SW	SW ◇1 🚲		SW 1	SW 1 🚲	SW	SW ◇1 🚲	SW 1		SW	SW	SW ◇1 🚲	
London Waterloo 15 ⊖	d	17 35	17 37			17 40	17 50	17 54	18 00		18 07		18 10	18 15			18 30		18 35	18 37		18 40	18 50	18 54	
Vauxhall ⊖	d					17 44	17 54						18 14									18 44	18 54		
Clapham Junction 10	d	17u42	17 46			17 49		18u03	18u09		18 15		18 19	18u22			18u39		18u42	18 46		18 49		19u03	
	d						18 00																19 00		
Earlsfield	d					17 52							18 22									18 52			
Wimbledon 6 ⊖	d		17 53			17 56					18 22		18 26							18 53		18 56			
Surbiton 6	d		18 02			18 05					18 30		18 35							19 02		19 05			
Esher	d					18 09							18 39									19 09			
Hersham	d					18 12							18 42									19 12			
Walton-on-Thames	d		18 09			18 15							18 45							19 09		19 15			
Weybridge	d		18 13			18 19							18 49							19 13		19 19			
Byfleet & New Haw	d					18 21	19 02						18 51									19 21	20 02		
West Byfleet	d					18 24	19 05			←			18 54			←		←				19 24	20 05		
Woking	a	18 06	18 19			18 29	19 11	18 26	18 31	18 29	18 42		18 59	18 45		18 42	19 01	18 59	19 06	19 19		19 29	20 11	19 26	
	d	18 07	18 23	18 26		18 35		18 28	18 32	18 35	18 46	18 49	19 05	18 46		18 49	19 02	19 05	19 07	19 23	19 26	19 35		19 28	
Worplesdon	d					→						→	→									→			
Guildford	a								18 40	18 44							19 10	19 14							
Brookwood	d		18 28	18 32							18 51					18 55				19 28	19 32				
Ash Vale	d			18 40												19 03					19 40				
Aldershot	a			18 45												19 07					19 45				
	d			18 46												19 08					19 46				
Farnham	a			18 51												19 13					19 51				
	d			18 55												19 14					19 55				
Bentley	d															19 24									
Alton	a			19 07												19 31					20 07				
Farnborough (Main)	d		18 36								18 59									19 36					
Fleet	d		18 41								19 04									19 41					
Winchfield	d										19 10														
Hook	d										19 14														
Basingstoke	a	18 26	18 54					18 46			19 21			19 05					19 26	19 54				19 46	

		SW 1	SW	SW 1		SW	SW ◇1 🚲	SW 1	SW 1 🚲	SW		SW ◇1 🚲	SW 1		SW	SW	SW ◇1	SW 1	SW	SW 1			SW	SW ◇1 🚲	SW 1
London Waterloo 15 ⊖	d	19 00		19 07		19 10	19 15		19 30			19 35	19 37		19 40	19 50	19 54	20 00		20 07			20 10	20 15	
Vauxhall ⊖	d					19 14									19 44	19 54							20 14		
Clapham Junction 10	d	19u09		19 15		19 19	19u22		19u39			19u42	19 46		19 49		20u03	20u09		20 15			20 19	20u22	
	d															20 00									
Earlsfield	d					19 22									19 52								20 22		
Wimbledon 6 ⊖	d			19 22		19 26							19 53		19 56					20 22			20 26		
Surbiton 6	d			19 30		19 35							20 02		20 05					20 30			20 35		
Esher	d					19 39									20 09								20 39		
Hersham	d					19 42									20 12								20 42		
Walton-on-Thames	d					19 45							20 09		20 15								20 45		
Weybridge	d					19 49							20 13		20 19								20 49		
Byfleet & New Haw	d					19 51									20 21	21 02							20 51		
West Byfleet	d		←			19 54		←		←					20 24	21 05			←				20 54		←
Woking	a	19 31	19 29	19 42		19 59	19 45	19 42	20 01	19 59		20 06	20 19		20 29	21 11	20 26	20 31	20 29	20 42			20 59	20 45	20 42
	d	19 32	19 35	19 46	19 49	20 05	19 46	19 49	20 02	20 05		20 07	20 23	20 26	20 35		20 28	20 32	20 35	20 46	20 49		21 05	20 46	20 49
Worplesdon	d				→	→									→						→		→		
Guildford	a	19 40	19 44						20 10	20 14								20 40	20 44						
Brookwood	d			19 51				19 55					20 28	20 32						20 51					20 55
Ash Vale	d							20 03						20 40											21 03
Aldershot	a							20 07						20 45											21 07
	d							20 08						20 46											21 08
Farnham	a							20 13						20 51											21 13
	d							20 14						20 55											21 14
Bentley	d							20 24																	21 24
Alton	a							20 31						21 07											21 31
Farnborough (Main)	d			19 59									20 36							20 59					
Fleet	d			20 04									20 41							21 04					
Winchfield	d			20 10																21 10					
Hook	d			20 14																21 14					
Basingstoke	a			20 21			20 05					20 26	20 54				20 46			21 21				21 05	

London - Woking, Guildford, Alton and Basingstoke

Network Diagram - see first Page of Table 155

		SW	SW	SW	SW		SW		SW	SW	SW	SW	SW		SW	SW	SW		SW	SW	SW	SW		SW	SW
		1 🛒		◇1 🛒	1					◇1	1		1			◇1 🛒	1		1		◇1 🛒	1			
London Waterloo 15	⊖ d	20 30		20 35	20 37		20 40		20 50	20 54	21 00		21 07		21 10	21 15			21 30		21 35	21 37		21 40	21 50
Vauxhall	⊖ d						20 44		20 54						21 14									21 44	21 54
Clapham Junction 10	d	20u39		20u42	20 46		20 49			21u03	21u09		21 15		21 19	21u22			21u39		21u42	21 46		21 49	
	d								21 00																22 00
Earlsfield	d						20 52								21 22									21 52	
Wimbledon 6	⊖ d				20 53		20 56						21 22		21 26							21 53		21 56	
Surbiton 6	d				21 02		21 05						21 30		21 35							22 02		22 05	
Esher	d						21 09								21 39									22 09	
Hersham	d						21 12								21 42									22 12	
Walton-on-Thames	d				21 09		21 15								21 45							22 09		22 15	
Weybridge	d				21 13		21 19								21 49							22 13		22 19	
Byfleet & New Haw	d						21 21		22 02						21 51									22 21	23 02
West Byfleet	d		←				21 24		22 05			←			21 54		←			←				22 24	23 05
Woking	a	21 01	20 59	21 06	21 19		21 29		22 11	21 26	21 31	21 29	21 42		21 59	21 45	21 42		22 01	21 59	22 06	22 19		22 29	23 11
	d	21 02	21 05	21 07	21 23	21 26	21 35			21 28	21 32	21 35	21 46	21 49	22 05	21 46	21 49		22 02	22 05	22 07	22 23	22 26	22 35	
Worplesdon	d						→							→	→									→	
Guildford	a	21 10	21 14								21 40	21 44							22 10	22 14					
Brookwood	d				21 28	21 32							21 51				21 55					22 28	22 32		
Ash Vale	d					21 40											22 03						22 40		
Aldershot	a					21 45											22 07						22 45		
	d					21 46											22 08						22 46		
Farnham	a					21 51											22 13						22 51		
	d					21 55											22 14						22 55		
Bentley	d																22 24								
Alton	a					22 07											22 31						23 07		
Farnborough (Main)	d				21 36								21 59									22 36			
Fleet	d				21 41								22 04									22 41			
Winchfield	d												22 10												
Hook	d												22 14												
Basingstoke	a			21 26	21 54					21 46			22 21			22 05					22 26	22 54			

		SW	SW		SW	SW		SW	SW	SW	SW	SW	SW			SW	SW	SW	SW	SW	SW		SW	SW	
		◇1	1			1			1 🛒	1	1		1					◇1 🛒	1		1			1	
London Waterloo 15	⊖ d	21 54	22 00			22 07		22 10	22 15		22 30		22 37			22 40	22 50	22 54	23 00		23 07		23 10	23 30	
Vauxhall	⊖ d							22 14								22 44	22 54						23 14		
Clapham Junction 10	d	22u03	22u09			22 15		22 19	22u22		22u39		22 46			22 49		23u03	23u09		23 15		23 19	23u39	
	d																23 00								
Earlsfield	d							22 22								22 52							23 22		
Wimbledon 6	⊖ d					22 22		22 26					22 53			22 56					23 22		23 26		
Surbiton 6	d					22 30		22 35					23 02			23 05					23 30		23 35		
Esher	d							22 39								23 09							23 39		
Hersham	d							22 42								23 12							23 42		
Walton-on-Thames	d							22 45					23 09			23 15							23 45		
Weybridge	d							22 49					23 13			23 19							23 49		
Byfleet & New Haw	d							22 51								23 21	00 02						23 51		
West Byfleet	d				←			22 54		←		←				23 24	00 05			←			23 54		
Woking	a	22 26	22 31		22 29	22 42		22 59	22 45	22 42	23 01	22 59	23 19			23 29	00 11	23 26	23 31	23 29	23 42		23 59	00 01	
	d	22 28	22 32		22 35	22 46	22 49	23 05	22 46	22 49	23 02	23 05	23 23	23 26		23 35		23 28	23 32	23 35	23 46	23 49	00 05	00 03	
Worplesdon	d						→	→								→							→		
Guildford	a		22 40		22 44						23 10	23 13							23 40	23 45				00 10	
Brookwood	d					22 51				22 55			23 28	23 32							23 51	23 55			
Ash Vale	d									23 03				23 40								00 03			
Aldershot	a									23 07				23 45								00 07			
	d									23 08				23 48								00 08			
Farnham	a									23 13				23 54								00 13			
	d									23 14				23 55								00 14			
Bentley	d									23 24												00 24			
Alton	a									23 31				00 07								00 31			
Farnborough (Main)	d					22 59							23 36								23 59				
Fleet	d					23 04							23 41								00 04				
Winchfield	d					23 10															00 10				
Hook	d					23 14															00 14				
Basingstoke	a	22 46				23 21			23 05				23 54					23 46			00 21				

Table 155

Sundays

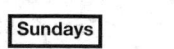

London - Woking, Guildford, Alton and Basingstoke

Network Diagram - see first Page of Table 155

			SW	SW 1	SW 1
London Waterloo 15	⊖	d		23 35	23 40
Vauxhall	⊖	d			23 44
Clapham Junction 10		d		23u44	23 49
		d			
Earlsfield		d			23 52
Wimbledon 6	⊖	d			23 56
Surbiton 6		d			00 05
Esher		d			00 09
Hersham		d			00 12
Walton-on-Thames		d			00 15
Weybridge		d			00 19
Byfleet & New Haw		d			00 21
West Byfleet		d	←		00 24
Woking		a	23 59	00 07	00 30
		d	00 05	00 08	00 35
Worplesdon		d			
Guildford		a	00 13		
Brookwood		d			00 41
Ash Vale		d			00 48
Aldershot		a			00 53
		d			00 54
Farnham		a			00 59
		d			
Bentley		d			
Alton		a			
Farnborough (Main)		d		00 18	
Fleet		d		00 24	
Winchfield		d			
Hook		d			
Basingstoke		a		00 39	

Basingstoke, Alton, Guildford and Woking - Waterloo

Network Diagram - see first Page of Table 155

Miles	Miles	Miles			SW MO	SW MX 1	SW MO 1	SW MX 1	SW MX 1	SW MO 1	SW MX 1	SW MO 1	SW MX 1		SW MO ◇1	SW MO 1	SW MX 1	SW	SW ◇	SW 1	SW	SW	SW 1		SW
0	—	—	**Basingstoke**	d				22p54	23p13						23p44		23p44			04 54					
5½	—	—	Hook	d				23p01									23p51			05 01					
7¾	—	—	Winchfield	d				23p05									23p55			05 05					
11¼	—	—	Fleet	d				23p10									00 01			05 10					
14½	—	—	Farnborough (Main)	d				23p16									00 06			05 16					
—	0	—	**Alton**	d		22p44	22p45																		
—	4¾	—	Bentley	d		22p51																			
—	8¾	—	Farnham	a		22p56	22p55																		
—	—	—		d		22p58	23p00																		
—	11¾	—	**Aldershot**	d		23p04	23p06																		
—	14¾	—	Ash Vale	d		23p09	23p11																		
19¾	18¾	—	Brookwood	d		23p16	23p18	23p23									00 13			05 23					
—	—	0	**Guildford**	d								23p35	23p39			00 05		04 00			05 14		05 50		
—	—	3½	Worplesdon	d							←		23p44								05 19		05 55		
23½	—	6	**Woking**	a		23p21	23p24	23p28	23p31		23p28	23p42	23p49		00 02	00 13	00 18	04 08		05 28	05 24		06 00		
—	—	—		d	22p52	23p22	23p28	23p33	23p32		23p33	23p45	23p56		00 04		00 20	04 10	05 27	05 29	05 33	05 43	06 01		06 04
26	—	—	West Byfleet	d	22p56	23p27		→			23p37						00 25		05 32		05 37	05 47			06 08
27¼	—	—	Byfleet & New Haw	d	23p00						23p40								05 35		05 40				06 11
28¾	—	—	Weybridge	d			23p34				23p43						00 29				05 43	05 51			06 14
30¾	—	—	Walton-on-Thames	d			23p38				23p47						00 33				05 47	05 55			06 18
31¾	—	—	Hersham	d							23p49										05 49				06 20
33¼	—	—	Esher	d							23p52										05 52				06 23
35¾	—	—	**Surbiton** [6]	a		23p37	23p45				23p57						00 39	04 24		05 40	05 56	06 01			06 27
40½	—	—	Wimbledon [6] ⊖	a			23p53				00 06						00 47	04 31		05 48	06 04				06 35
42¼	—	—	Earlsfield	a						←											06 08				06 39
43¾	—	—	Clapham Junction [10]	a		23p51	23p59		23p55	23p59		00 04	00 19		00 23		00 53	04 43			06 12		06 20		06 42
—	—	—		a	00 01		→				00 21								06 43	06 00					→
46½	—	—	Vauxhall ⊖	a	00 08						00 30								06 49	06 07	06 17				
47¾	—	—	**London Waterloo** [15] ⊖	a	00 13	00 02			00 09	00 10	00 35	00 14	00 33		00 33		01 04	04 53	06 56	06 12	06 22	06 20	06 29		

		SW 1	SW 1	SW ◇1 🚲	SW	SW 1	SW 1	SW 1	SW		SW 1	SW 1 🚲	SW 1	SW ◇1 🚲	SW 1	SW	SW ◇1 🚲	SW 1	SW 1		SW 1	SW 1	SW 1	SW ◇1 🚲	SW 1
Basingstoke	d	05 39	05 54	05 59				06 23						06 27			06 35						06 42	06 51	
Hook	d		06 01					06 31																	
Winchfield	d		06 05					06 35																	
Fleet	d	05 50	06 10					06 40															06 54		
Farnborough (Main)	d	05 56	06 16					06 46															07 00		
Alton	d					05 42									06 12										
Bentley	d					05 49									06 19										
Farnham	a					05 54									06 24										
	d					05 56									06 26										
Aldershot	d					06 02									06 32										
Ash Vale	d					06 07									06 37										
Brookwood	d		06 23			06 14		06 53							06 44										
Guildford	d										06 24	06 31									06 53				07 07
Worplesdon	d						←				06 30							←			06 59				
Woking	a	06 04	06 28	06 18		06 19	06 28	06 58			06 35	06 39		06 46	06 49		06 53	06 58			07 03		07 10		07 15
	d	06 06	06 29	06 19		06 20	06 29	06 59	06 32		06 37	06 41	06 41	06 47	06 50		06 55	06 59	07 02		07 05	07 07	07 11		07 17
West Byfleet	d		→			06 25		→	06 36				06 46						07 07			07 16			
Byfleet & New Haw	d								06 39				06 49									07 19			
Weybridge	d								06 43				06 52						07 11			07 22			
Walton-on-Thames	d								06 47				06 57						07 16			07 27			
Hersham	d								06 49				07 00						07 19			07 30			
Esher	d								06 52				07 03						07 22			07 33			
Surbiton [6]	a					06 35	06 40		06 56				07 07						07 26			07 37			
Wimbledon [6] ⊖	a						06 47		07 04																
Earlsfield	a				←				07 08							←									
Clapham Junction [10]	a	06 25		06 38	06 42	06 46	06 54		07 12		06 58	07 02			07 10	07 12	07 14	07 20			07 24			07 28	
	a								→																
Vauxhall ⊖	a				06 47											07 17									
London Waterloo [15] ⊖	a	06 34		06 49	06 52	06 54	07 04				07 08	07 12	07 26	07 14	07 20	07 24	07 24	07 31	07 49		07 36	07 56	07 41	07 39	07 45

Table 155

Mondays to Fridays

Basingstoke, Alton, Guildford and Woking - Waterloo

Network Diagram - see first Page of Table 155

		SW	SW	SW	SW		SW	SW	SW	SW	SW	SW	SW	SW	SW	SW	SW	SW	SW	SW	SW	SW	SW	SW	SW
		1	1 🚲	1	1		1	1	◇1	1	1	1	1		1	1	◇1 🚲	1 🚲	1	1	1	1	1	1	
Basingstoke	d			06 54	07 06		07 17									07 24	07 29				07 36	07 47			
Hook	d			07 01	07 13											07 31					07 43				
Winchfield	d			07 05	07 17											07 35					07 47				
Fleet	d			07 10	07 22											07 40					07 52				
Farnborough (Main)	d			07 16	07 28											07 46					07 58				
Alton	d	06 44											07 14												
Bentley	d	06 51											07 21												
Farnham	a	06 56											07 26												
	d	06 58											07 28							07 39					
Aldershot	d	07 04											07 34							07 46					
Ash Vale	d	07 09											07 39							07 50					
Brookwood	d	07 16		07 23									07 46			07 53				07 57					
Guildford	d		07 17							07 34					07 45			07 54						08 03	
Worplesdon	d									07 40					07 50								←		
Woking	a	07 21	07 25	07 28									07 51		07 54	07 58				08 03	08 08	08 05	08 08	08 11	
	d	07 22	07 26	07 29				07 32	07 40			07 47	07 52		07 56	07 59			08 02	08 05	08 09	08 06	08 09	08 12	08 17
West Byfleet	d							07 37			07 46	07 54							08 06	08 16	→				08 26
Byfleet & New Haw	d										07 49	07 57								08 19					08 29
Weybridge	d							07 41			07 52	08 01							08 11	08 22					08 32
Walton-on-Thames	d							07 46			07 57	08 06							08 15	08 27					08 36
Hersham	d							07 49			08 00	08 09							08 17	08 30					08 39
Esher	d							07 52			08 03	08 13							08 20	08 33					08 43
Surbiton 6	a							07 56			08 07	08 18							08 24	08 37					08 47
Wimbledon 6 ⊖	a																								
Earlsfield	a																								
Clapham Junction 10	a																								
	a																								
Vauxhall ⊖	a																								
London Waterloo 15 ⊖	a	07 51	07 54	07 59	08 06		08 01	08 19	08 08	08 11	08 26	08 36	08 22		08 24	08 29	08 14	08 32	08 46	08 59		08 34	08 39	08 41	09 06

			SW	SW	SW	SW	SW	SW	SW	SW	SW		SW	SW	SW	SW	SW	SW	SW	SW	SW		SW	SW	SW
			1	◇1 🚲	1	1 🚲	1	1		1	1		1	1	1	◇1 🚲	1		◇1 🚲	1	1 🚲		1	1	
Basingstoke	d		07 52	07 59				08 05		08 16				08 24		08 29			08 35				08 43		
Hook	d		07 59					08 12						08 31											
Winchfield	d		08 04					08 16						08 35											
Fleet	d		08 09					08 22						08 40									08 54		
Farnborough (Main)	d		08 16					08 28						08 46									09 00		
Alton	d				07 44												08 14								
Bentley	d				07 51												08 21								
Farnham	a				07 56												08 26								
	d				07 58												08 28								
Aldershot	d				08 04												08 34								
Ash Vale	d				08 09												08 39								
Brookwood	d		08 23		08 16									08 53			08 46								
Guildford	d					08 15			08 20				08 31								08 54				08 46
Worplesdon	d					08 20	←				←		08 37							←					08 51
Woking	a		08 28	08 18	08 21	08 26	08 28	08 38	08 30	08 34	08 38		08 41	08 58		08 48	08 51		08 53	08 58					08 59
	d		08 29	08 19	08 23	08 27	08 29	08 39	08 32	08 36	08 39		08 43	08 59	08 47	08 49	08 52		08 55	08 59					09 02
West Byfleet	d		→					→	08 36					→	08 54										09 06
Byfleet & New Haw	d								08 39						08 57										09 09
Weybridge	d								08 43						09 02										09 13
Walton-on-Thames	d								08 47						09 07										09 17
Hersham	d								08 49						09 10										09 19
Esher	d								08 52						09 13									←	09 22
Surbiton 6	a								08 56						09 18					09 10				09 18	09 26
Wimbledon 6 ⊖	a								09 04						→										09 34
Earlsfield	a								09 08									←							09 38
Clapham Junction 10	a								09 12				09 03					09 12	09 14				09 26		09 42
	a								→																→
Vauxhall ⊖	a																	09 17							
London Waterloo 15 ⊖	a			08 46	08 52	08 55	09 00			09 03	09 10		09 13			09 17	09 21	09 24	09 25	09 29	09 31		09 38	09 40	

Basingstoke, Alton, Guildford and Woking - Waterloo

Network Diagram - see first Page of Table 155

		SW	SW	SW	SW	SW	SW		SW	SW	SW	SW	SW	SW	SW	SW	SW		SW	SW	SW	SW	SW	SW	SW
		1	1	◇1		1	◇1		1	1	1		1	1	1	◇1			1	◇1	1	1	1	1	
				🍴			🍴		🍴							🍴				🍴	🍴	🍴			
Basingstoke	d		08 54	08 59									09 17		09 24	09 30				09 36		09 43		09 54	
Hook	d		09 01												09 31									10 01	
Winchfield	d		09 05												09 35									10 05	
Fleet	d		09 10												09 40							09 54		10 10	
Farnborough (Main)	d		09 16										09 30		09 46							10 00		10 16	
Alton	d					08 44													09 14						
Bentley	d					08 51													09 21						
Farnham	a					08 56													09 26						
	d					08 58													09 28						
Aldershot	d					09 04													09 34						
Ash Vale	d					09 09													09 39						
Brookwood	d		09 23			09 16									09 53				09 46					10 23	
Guildford	d	09 03							09 17					09 34							09 47				
Worplesdon	d										←			09 40									←		
Woking	a	09 11	09 28	09 18		09 21			09 27		09 28		09 39	09 44	09 58	09 49			09 51	09 54	09 59		09 58	10 28	
	d	09 13	09 29	09 19		09 22	09 24		09 28		09 29	09 33	09 41	09 46	09 59	09 50			09 52	09 56	09 59		09 59	10 29	10 03
West Byfleet	d		→			09 27						09 37			→				09 57					→	10 07
Byfleet & New Haw	d											09 40													10 10
Weybridge	d										09 36	09 43											10 06		10 13
Walton-on-Thames	d										09 40	09 47											10 10		10 17
Hersham	d											09 49													10 19
Esher	d											09 52													10 22
Surbiton 6	a					09 37					09 46	09 56							10 07				10 16		10 26
Wimbledon 6 ⊖	a											10 04													10 34
Earlsfield	a				←					←		10 08					←								10 38
Clapham Junction 10	a	09 32		09 38	09 42	09 50	09 43			09 50	09 57	10 12		10 05		10 09	10 12			10 15		10 25			10 42
	a					→						→													→
Vauxhall ⊖	a				09 47												10 17								
London Waterloo 15 ⊖	a	09 43		09 51	09 54		09 53		09 55	09 59	10 05		10 08	10 13		10 19	10 22		10 25	10 23	10 27	10 34	10 36		

		SW	SW		SW	SW	SW	SW	SW	SW	SW	SW	SW		SW	SW	SW	SW	SW	SW	SW	SW	SW		SW
		1	◇1		◇1		1	1	1		1	1	1		◇1	◇1		1	1	1	1	1			1
			🍴		🍴			🍴							🍴	🍴			🍴						
Basingstoke	d		09 57								10 17		10 24		10 30	10 35				10 43		10 54			
Hook	d												10 31									11 01			
Winchfield	d												10 35									11 05			
Fleet	d												10 40							10 54		11 10			
Farnborough (Main)	d										10 30		10 46							11 00		11 16			
Alton	d						09 44											10 14							
Bentley	d						09 51											10 21							
Farnham	a						09 56											10 26							
	d						09 58											10 28							
Aldershot	d						10 04											10 34							
Ash Vale	d						10 09											10 39							
Brookwood	d						10 16						10 53					10 46				11 23			
Guildford	d	10 02						10 17				10 34							10 47						11 02
Worplesdon	d								←			10 40									←				
Woking	a	10 11	10 15				10 21	10 25	10 28		10 39	10 44	10 58		10 49			10 51	10 57		10 58	11 28			11 11
	d	10 12	10 17		10 21		10 22	10 26	10 29	10 33	10 41	10 46	10 59		10 50			10 52	10 59		10 59	11 29	11 03		11 12
West Byfleet	d						10 27			10 37			→					10 57				→	11 07		
Byfleet & New Haw	d									10 40													11 10		
Weybridge	d								10 36	10 43											11 06		11 13		
Walton-on-Thames	d								10 40	10 47											11 10		11 17		
Hersham	d									10 49													11 19		
Esher	d									10 52													11 22		
Surbiton 6	a						10 37		10 46	10 56								11 07			11 16		11 26		
Wimbledon 6 ⊖	a									11 04													11 34		
Earlsfield	a					←				11 08							←						11 38		
Clapham Junction 10	a	10 31	10 36			10 42	10 48		10 57	11 12		11 05				11 12	11 12			11 25			11 42		11 31
	a									→													→		
Vauxhall ⊖	a					10 47											11 17								
London Waterloo 15 ⊖	a	10 40	10 49		10 49	10 52	10 57	10 51	11 05		11 08	11 13			11 19	11 20	11 22	11 27	11 24	11 34	11 36				11 40

Basingstoke, Alton, Guildford and Woking - Waterloo

Network Diagram - see first Page of Table 155

		SW ◇1 🛒	SW ◇1 🛒	SW	SW 1	SW 1 🛒	SW 1	SW	SW 1		SW 1	SW 1	SW ◇1 🛒	SW ◇1 🛒	SW	SW 1	SW 1 🛒	SW 1	SW 1		SW 1	SW	SW 1	SW ◇1 🛒	SW ◇1 🛒
Basingstoke	d	10 57							11 17			11 24	11 30	11 35				11 43			11 54			11 57	
Hook	d											11 31									12 01				
Winchfield	d											11 35									12 05				
Fleet	d											11 40						11 54			12 10				
Farnborough (Main)	d								11 30			11 46						12 00			12 16				
Alton	d				10 44											11 15									
Bentley	d				10 51																				
Farnham	a				10 56											11 25									
	d				10 58											11 28									
Aldershot	d				11 04											11 34									
Ash Vale	d				11 09											11 39									
Brookwood	d				11 16							11 53				11 46					12 23				
Guildford	d					11 17					11 34						11 47						12 02		
Worplesdon	d						←				11 40								←						
Woking	a	11 15			11 21	11 25	11 28		11 39		11 44	11 58	11 49			11 51	11 57		11 58		12 28		12 11	12 15	
	d	11 17	11 21		11 22	11 26	11 29	11 33	11 41		11 46	11 59	11 50			11 52	11 59		11 59		12 29	12 03	12 12	12 17	12 21
West Byfleet	d				11 27			11 37				→				11 57					→	12 07			
Byfleet & New Haw	d							11 40														12 10			
Weybridge	d						11 36	11 43											12 06			12 13			
Walton-on-Thames	d						11 40	11 47											12 10			12 17			
Hersham	d							11 49														12 19			
Esher	d							11 52														12 22			
Surbiton 6	a				11 37		11 46	11 56								12 07			12 16			12 26			
Wimbledon 6 ⊖	a							12 04														12 34			
Earlsfield	a			←				12 08							←							12 38			
Clapham Junction 10	a	11 36		11 42	11 48		11 57	12 12			12 05			12 12	12 12			12 25				12 42	12 31	12 36	
	a							→														→			
Vauxhall ⊖	a			11 47											12 17										
London Waterloo 15 ⊖	a	11 49	11 49	11 52	11 57	11 51	12 06		12 08		12 13		12 19	12 20	12 22	12 27	12 23	12 34	12 36				12 40	12 49	12 49

		SW	SW 1	SW 1 🛒	SW 1		SW	SW 1	SW 1	SW 1	SW ◇1 🛒	SW ◇1 🛒	SW	SW 1	SW 1 🛒		SW 1	SW 1	SW 1	SW	SW 1	SW ◇1 🛒	SW ◇1 🛒	SW	SW 1
Basingstoke	d							12 17		12 24	12 30	12 35					12 43		12 54			12 57			
Hook	d									12 31									13 01						
Winchfield	d									12 35									13 05						
Fleet	d									12 40							12 54		13 10						
Farnborough (Main)	d							12 30		12 46							13 00		13 16						
Alton	d		11 44																						12 44
Bentley	d		11 51																						12 51
Farnham	a		11 56																						12 56
	d		11 58											12 28											12 58
Aldershot	d		12 04											12 34											13 04
Ash Vale	d		12 09											12 39											13 09
Brookwood	d		12 16							12 53				12 46					13 23						13 16
Guildford	d			12 17					12 34						12 47						13 02				
Worplesdon	d				←				12 40									←							
Woking	a		12 21	12 25	12 28			12 39	12 44	12 58	12 49			12 51	12 57			12 58	13 28		13 11	13 15			13 21
	d		12 22	12 26	12 29		12 33	12 41	12 46	12 59	12 50			12 52	12 59			12 59	13 29	13 03	13 12	13 17	13 21		13 22
West Byfleet	d		12 27				12 37			→				12 57					→	13 07					13 27
Byfleet & New Haw	d						12 40													13 10					
Weybridge	d				12 36		12 43											13 06		13 13					
Walton-on-Thames	d				12 40		12 47											13 10		13 17					
Hersham	d						12 49													13 19					
Esher	d						12 52													13 22					
Surbiton 6	a		12 37		12 46		12 56							13 07				13 16		13 26					13 37
Wimbledon 6 ⊖	a						13 04													13 34					
Earlsfield	a	←					13 08						←							13 38				←	
Clapham Junction 10	a	12 42	12 48		12 57		13 12		13 05			13 12	13 12				13 25			13 42	13 31	13 36		13 42	13 48
	a						→													→					
Vauxhall ⊖	a	12 47											13 17											13 47	
London Waterloo 15 ⊖	a	12 52	12 57	12 51	13 05			13 07	13 13		13 19	13 20	13 22	13 25	13 23		13 34	13 36			13 40	13 49	13 49	13 52	13 57

Basingstoke, Alton, Guildford and Woking - Waterloo

Network Diagram - see first Page of Table 155

			SW [1] ⚲	SW [1]	SW	SW [1]	SW [1]	SW [1]	SW ◇[1] ⚲	SW ◇[1] ⚲	SW		SW [1]	SW [1] ⚲	SW [1]	SW [1]	SW [1]	SW	SW [1]	SW ◇[1] ⚲	SW ◇[1] ⚲		SW	SW [1]	SW [1] ⚲
Basingstoke	d					13 17		13 24	13 30	13 35					13 43		13 54			13 57					
Hook	d							13 31									14 01								
Winchfield	d							13 35									14 05								
Fleet	d							13 40							13 54		14 10								
Farnborough (Main)	d					13 30		13 46							14 00		14 16								
Alton	d												13 15											13 44	
Bentley	d																							13 51	
Farnham	a												13 25											13 56	
	d												13 28											13 58	
Aldershot	d												13 34											14 04	
Ash Vale	d												13 39											14 09	
Brookwood	d							13 53					13 46				14 23							14 16	
Guildford	d		13 17				13 34							13 47					14 02						14 17
Worplesdon	d			←			13 40									←									
Woking	a		13 25	13 28		13 39	13 44	13 58	13 49				13 51	13 57		13 58	14 28		14 11	14 15				14 21	14 25
	d		13 26	13 29	13 33	13 41	13 46	13 59	13 50				13 52	13 59		13 59	14 29	14 03	14 12	14 17	14 21			14 22	14 26
West Byfleet	d				13 37			→					13 57				→	14 07						14 27	
Byfleet & New Haw	d				13 40													14 10							
Weybridge	d			13 36	13 43											14 06		14 13							
Walton-on-Thames	d			13 40	13 47											14 10		14 17							
Hersham	d				13 49													14 19							
Esher	d				13 52													14 22							
Surbiton [6]	a			13 46	13 56								14 07			14 16		14 26						14 37	
Wimbledon [6] ⊖	a				14 04													14 34							
Earlsfield	a				14 08						←							14 38					←		
Clapham Junction [10]	a			13 57	14 12		14 05			14 12	14 12				14 25			14 42	14 31	14 36			14 42	14 48	
	a				→													→							
Vauxhall ⊖	a										14 17												14 47		
London Waterloo [15] ⊖	a		13 51	14 05		14 07	14 13		14 19	14 20	14 22		14 25	14 23	14 34	14 36			14 40	14 49	14 49		14 52	14 57	14 51

		SW [1]	SW	SW [1]	SW [1]	SW [1]	SW ◇[1] ⚲		SW ◇[1] ⚲	SW	SW [1]	SW [1] ⚲	SW [1]	SW [1]	SW [1]	SW	SW [1]		SW ◇[1] ⚲	SW ◇[1] ⚲	SW	SW [1]	SW [1] ⚲	SW [1]	SW
Basingstoke	d			14 17		14 24	14 30		14 35				14 43		14 54				14 57						
Hook	d					14 31									15 01										
Winchfield	d					14 35									15 05										
Fleet	d					14 40							14 54		15 10										
Farnborough (Main)	d			14 30		14 46							15 00		15 16										
Alton	d										14 15											14 44			
Bentley	d																					14 51			
Farnham	a										14 25											14 56			
	d										14 28											14 58			
Aldershot	d										14 34											15 04			
Ash Vale	d										14 39											15 09			
Brookwood	d					14 53					14 46				15 23							15 16			
Guildford	d				14 34							14 47					15 02						15 17		
Worplesdon	d	←			14 40									←										←	
Woking	a	14 28		14 39	14 44	14 58	14 49				14 51	14 57		14 58	15 28		15 11		15 15			15 21	15 25	15 28	
	d	14 29	14 33	14 41	14 46	14 59	14 50				14 52	14 59		14 59	15 29	15 03	15 12		15 17	15 21		15 22	15 26	15 29	15 33
West Byfleet	d		14 37			→					14 57				→	15 07						15 27			15 37
Byfleet & New Haw	d		14 40													15 10									15 40
Weybridge	d	14 36	14 43											15 06		15 13								15 36	15 43
Walton-on-Thames	d	14 40	14 47											15 10		15 17								15 40	15 47
Hersham	d		14 49													15 19									15 49
Esher	d		14 52													15 22									15 52
Surbiton [6]	a	14 46	14 56								15 07			15 16		15 26						15 37		15 46	15 56
Wimbledon [6] ⊖	a		15 04													15 34									16 04
Earlsfield	a		15 08							←						15 38					←				16 08
Clapham Junction [10]	a	14 57	15 12		15 05				15 12	15 12			15 25			15 42	15 31		15 36		15 42	15 48		15 57	16 12
	a		→													→									→
Vauxhall ⊖	a									15 17											15 47				
London Waterloo [15] ⊖	a	15 05		15 08	15 13		15 19		15 20	15 22	15 25	15 23	15 34	15 37			15 43		15 49	15 49	15 52	15 57	15 51	16 05	

Basingstoke, Alton, Guildford and Woking - Waterloo

Network Diagram - see first Page of Table 155

		SW 1	SW 1		SW 1	SW ◇1 🚲	SW ◇1 🚲	SW	SW 1	SW 1 🚲	SW 1	SW 1	SW 1		SW	SW 1	SW ◇1 🚲	SW ◇1 🚲	SW	SW 1	SW 1 🚲	SW 1	SW		SW 1
Basingstoke	d	15 17			15 24	15 30	15 35				15 43		15 54				15 57								16 17
Hook	d				15 31								16 01												
Winchfield	d				15 35								16 05												
Fleet	d				15 40						15 54		16 10												
Farnborough (Main)	d	15 30			15 46						16 00		16 16												16 30
Alton	d								15 15											15 44					
Bentley	d																			15 51					
Farnham	a								15 25											15 56					
	d								15 28											15 58					
Aldershot	d								15 34											16 04					
Ash Vale	d								15 39											16 09					
Brookwood	d				15 53				15 46				16 23							16 16					
Guildford	d		15 34							15 47						16 00					16 17				
Worplesdon	d		15 40									←				16 06						←			
Woking	a	15 39	15 44		15 58	15 49			15 51	15 57		15 58	16 28			16 11	16 15			16 21	16 25	16 28			16 39
	d	15 41	15 46		15 59	15 50			15 52	15 59		15 59	16 29		16 03	16 12	16 17	16 21		16 22	16 26	16 29	16 33		16 41
West Byfleet	d				→				15 57				→		16 07					16 27			16 37		
Byfleet & New Haw	d														16 10								16 40		
Weybridge	d											16 06			16 13							16 36	16 43		
Walton-on-Thames	d											16 10			16 17							16 40	16 47		
Hersham	d														16 19								16 49		
Esher	d														16 22								16 52		
Surbiton 6	a								16 07			16 16			16 26					16 37		16 46	16 56		
Wimbledon 6 ⊖	a														16 34								17 04		
Earlsfield	a							←							16 38				←				17 08		
Clapham Junction 10	a		16 05				16 12	16 12			16 25				16 42	16 31	16 36		16 42	16 48		16 57	17 12		
	a														→								→		
Vauxhall ⊖	a							16 17											16 47						
London Waterloo 15 ⊖	a	16 07	16 13			16 19	16 20	16 22	16 29	16 24	16 34	16 36				16 40	16 49	16 49	16 52	16 59	16 51	17 08			17 08

		SW 1	SW 1	SW ◇1 🚲	SW ◇1 🚲	SW	SW 1	SW 1	SW 1		SW 1	SW 1	SW	SW 1 🚲	SW ◇1 🚲	SW ◇1 🚲	SW	SW 1	SW 1 🚲		SW 1	SW	SW 1	SW 1	SW 1
Basingstoke	d		16 24	16 30	16 35						16 43	16 54			16 57								17 17		17 24
Hook	d		16 31									17 01													17 31
Winchfield	d		16 35									17 05													17 35
Fleet	d		16 40								16 54	17 10													17 40
Farnborough (Main)	d		16 46								17 00	17 16											17 30		17 46
Alton	d						16 15											16 44							
Bentley	d																	16 51							
Farnham	a						16 25											16 56							
	d						16 28											16 58							
Aldershot	d						16 34											17 04							
Ash Vale	d						16 39											17 09							
Brookwood	d		16 53				16 46					17 23						17 16							17 53
Guildford	d	16 34						16 47						17 00					17 17					17 34	
Worplesdon	d	16 40							←					17 06							←			17 40	
Woking	a	16 44	16 58	16 49			16 51	16 57	16 58			17 28		17 11	17 15			17 21	17 25		17 28		17 39	17 44	17 58
	d	16 46	16 59	16 50			16 52	16 59	16 59			17 29	17 03	17 12	17 17	17 21		17 22	17 26		17 29	17 33	17 41	17 46	17 59
West Byfleet	d		→				16 57					→	17 07					17 27				17 37			→
Byfleet & New Haw	d												17 10									17 40			
Weybridge	d								17 06				17 13								17 36	17 43			
Walton-on-Thames	d								17 10				17 17								17 40	17 47			
Hersham	d												17 19									17 49			
Esher	d												17 22									17 52			
Surbiton 6	a						17 07		17 16				17 26					17 37			17 46	17 56			
Wimbledon 6 ⊖	a												17 34									18 04			
Earlsfield	a					←							17 38				←					18 08			
Clapham Junction 10	a	17 05			17 12	17 12					17 25		17 42	17 31	17 36		17 42	17 48			17 57	18 12		18 05	
	a												→									→			
Vauxhall ⊖	a					17 17											17 47								
London Waterloo 15 ⊖	a	17 14		17 19	17 20	17 22	17 29	17 27	17 35		17 36			17 43	17 44	17 50	17 52	17 59	17 54		18 09		18 08	18 14	

Basingstoke, Alton, Guildford and Woking - Waterloo

Network Diagram - see first Page of Table 155

		SW	SW	SW	SW		SW	SW	SW	SW	SW	SW	SW	SW	SW		SW	SW	SW	SW	SW	SW	SW	SW	SW
		◇1		◇1	1		1	1	1	1		1	◇1	◇1			1	1	1		1	1	1	◇1	
		🚲		🚲								🚲	🚲	🚲				🚲						🚲	
Basingstoke	d	17 30		17 36				17 43		17 54			17 57								18 17		18 24	18 30	
Hook	d									18 01													18 31		
Winchfield	d									18 05													18 35		
Fleet	d							17 54		18 10													18 40		
Farnborough (Main)	d							18 00		18 16											18 30		18 46		
Alton	d				17 14												17 44								
Bentley	d				17 21												17 51								
Farnham	a				17 26												17 56								
	d				17 28												17 58								
Aldershot	d				17 34												18 04								
Ash Vale	d				17 39												18 09								
Brookwood	d				17 46					18 23							18 16						18 53		
Guildford	d						17 47					18 00						18 17				18 34			
Worplesdon	d								←			18 06							←			18 40			
Woking	a	17 49			17 51		17 58		17 58	18 28		18 11	18 15				18 21		18 28		18 39	18 44	18 58	18 49	
	d	17 51			17 52		17 59		17 59	18 29	18 03	18 12	18 17	18 21			18 22		18 29	18 33	18 41	18 46	18 59	18 50	
West Byfleet	d				17 57					→	18 07						18 27			18 37			→		
Byfleet & New Haw	d										18 10									18 40					
Weybridge	d								18 06		18 13								18 36	18 43					
Walton-on-Thames	d								18 10		18 17								18 40	18 47					
Hersham	d										18 19									18 49					
Esher	d										18 22									18 52					
Surbiton 6	a				18 07				18 16		18 26						18 37		18 47	18 56					
Wimbledon 6 ⊖	a										18 34									19 04					
Earlsfield	a		←								18 38				←					19 08					←
Clapham Junction 10	a		18 12	18 12				18 25			18 42	18 31	18 36		18 42		18 48		18 58	19 11		19 05			19 11
	a										→									→					
Vauxhall ⊖	a		18 17												18 47										19 16
London Waterloo 15 ⊖	a	18 21	18 23	18 23	18 29		18 27	18 34	18 38			18 43	18 45	18 47	18 52		18 57	18 59	19 06		19 08	19 13		19 19	19 23

			SW	SW	SW	SW	SW	SW	SW	SW	SW		SW	SW	SW	SW	SW	SW	SW	SW	SW		SW	SW	SW
			◇1	1	1	1	1		1	◇1	1		◇1	1	1		1	1	1	◇1			◇1	1	1
			🚲			🚲				🚲			🚲	🚲						🚲			🚲		🚲
Basingstoke	d		18 35				18 43		18 54	19 02							19 17		19 24	19 30			19 35		
Hook	d								19 01										19 31						
Winchfield	d								19 05										19 35						
Fleet	d						18 54		19 10										19 40						
Farnborough (Main)	d						19 00		19 16								19 30		19 46						
Alton	d			18 14							18 35													19 07	
Bentley	d			18 23							18 42														
Farnham	a			18 27							18 47													19 17	
	d			18 28							18 58													19 28	
Aldershot	d			18 34							19 04													19 34	
Ash Vale	d			18 39							19 09													19 39	
Brookwood	d			18 46					19 23		19 16								19 53					19 46	
Guildford	d					18 55								19 21				19 34							19 47
Worplesdon	d				←										←			19 40							
Woking	a			18 52	18 58	19 03			19 28	19 20	19 21			19 28	19 28		19 39	19 45	19 58	19 49				19 51	19 57
	d			18 52	18 59	19 05		19 03	19 29	19 22	19 22		19 25	19 30	19 29	19 33	19 41	19 46	19 59	19 50				19 52	19 59
West Byfleet	d			18 57				19 07	→		19 27					19 37			→					19 57	
Byfleet & New Haw	d							19 10								19 40									
Weybridge	d				19 06			19 13							19 36	19 43									
Walton-on-Thames	d				19 10			19 17							19 40	19 47									
Hersham	d							19 19								19 49									
Esher	d							19 22								19 52									
Surbiton 6	a			19 07	19 16			19 26			19 37				19 46	19 56								20 07	
Wimbledon 6 ⊖	a							19 34								20 04									
Earlsfield	a							19 38								20 08					←				
Clapham Junction 10	a		19 12				19 26	19 41		19 41	19 48				19 57	20 11		20 05			20 11		20 12		
	a															→									
Vauxhall ⊖	a							19 46													20 16				
London Waterloo 15 ⊖	a		19 20	19 25	19 39	19 29	19 34	19 52		19 49	19 57		19 51	19 59	20 05		20 08	20 14		20 19	20 22		20 20	20 26	20 24

Table 155

Mondays to Fridays

Basingstoke, Alton, Guildford and Woking - Waterloo

Network Diagram - see first Page of Table 155

		SW 1	SW 1	SW	SW 1	SW ◇1 (trolley)	SW		SW 1	SW 1	SW 1	SW ◇1 (trolley)	SW 1
Basingstoke	d	19 43									19 54	20 09	
Hook	d										20 01		
Winchfield	d										20 05		
Fleet	d	19 54									20 10		
Farnborough (Main)	d	20 00									20 16		
Alton	d								19 35				
Bentley	d								19 42				
Farnham	a								19 47				
	d								19 58				
Aldershot	d								20 04				
Ash Vale	d								20 09				
Brookwood	d								20 16		20 23		
Guildford	d				20 02					20 17			
Worplesdon	d		←										
Woking	a		19 58		20 11				20 21	20 25	20 28	20 29	
	d		19 59	20 03	20 12	20 21			20 22	20 26	20 29	20 30	
West Byfleet	d			20 07					20 27				
Byfleet & New Haw	d			20 10									
Weybridge	d		20 06	20 13							20 36		
Walton-on-Thames	d		20 10	20 17							20 40		
Hersham	d			20 19									
Esher	d			20 22									
Surbiton 6	a		20 16	20 26					20 37		20 46		
Wimbledon 6 ⊖	a			20 35									
Earlsfield	a			20 38			←						←
Clapham Junction 10	a	20 25		20 41	20 31		20 41		20 48		20 57	20 52	20 57
	a			↪							↪		
Vauxhall ⊖	a						20 46						
London Waterloo 15 ⊖	a	20 34	20 36		20 40	20 49	20 52		20 57	20 50		21 00	21 05

		SW	SW 1	SW 1	SW 1		SW 1	SW ◇1 (trolley)	SW 1	SW	SW 1	SW ◇1 (trolley)	SW
Basingstoke	d		20 17				20 24	20 36			20 43		
Hook	d						20 31						
Winchfield	d						20 35						
Fleet	d						20 40				20 54		
Farnborough (Main)	d		20 30				20 46				21 00		
Alton	d			20 15									
Bentley	d												
Farnham	a			20 25									
	d			20 28									
Aldershot	d			20 34									
Ash Vale	d			20 39									
Brookwood	d			20 46			20 53						
Guildford	d				20 39				20 47				
Worplesdon	d				20 44								
Woking	a		20 39	20 51	20 52		20 58		20 56		21 09		
	d	20 33	20 41	20 52	20 53		20 59		20 59	21 03	21 10	21 21	
West Byfleet	d	20 37		20 57						21 07			
Byfleet & New Haw	d	20 40								21 10			
Weybridge	d	20 43					21 06			21 13			
Walton-on-Thames	d	20 47					21 10			21 17			
Hersham	d	20 49								21 19			
Esher	d	20 52								21 22			
Surbiton 6	a	20 56		21 07			21 16			21 26			
Wimbledon 6 ⊖	a	21 05								21 34			
Earlsfield	a	21 08								21 38			←
Clapham Junction 10	a	21 11			21 12			21 16		21 42	21 29		21 42
	a									↪			
Vauxhall ⊖	a	21 16											21 47
London Waterloo 15 ⊖	a	21 22	21 07	21 29	21 21		21 34	21 24	21 27		21 38	21 49	21 52

		SW 1	SW 1		SW 1	SW ◇1 (trolley)	SW 1	SW	SW 1	SW	SW 1	SW 1	SW ◇1
Basingstoke	d				20 54	21 09						21 24	21 35
Hook	d				21 01							21 31	
Winchfield	d				21 05							21 35	
Fleet	d				21 10							21 40	
Farnborough (Main)	d				21 16							21 46	
Alton	d	20 44									21 15		
Bentley	d	20 51											
Farnham	a	20 56									21 25		
	d	20 58									21 28		
Aldershot	d	21 04									21 34		
Ash Vale	d	21 09									21 39		
Brookwood	d	21 16			21 23						21 46	21 53	
Guildford	d		21 17						21 39				
Worplesdon	d								21 44				
Woking	a	21 21	21 25		21 28	21 29			21 49		21 51	21 58	
	d	21 22	21 26		21 29	21 30		21 33	21 50		21 52	21 59	
West Byfleet	d	21 27						21 37			21 57		
Byfleet & New Haw	d							21 40					
Weybridge	d				21 36			21 43				22 06	
Walton-on-Thames	d				21 40			21 47				22 10	
Hersham	d							21 49					
Esher	d							21 52					
Surbiton 6	a	21 37			21 46			21 56			22 07	22 16	
Wimbledon 6 ⊖	a							22 04					
Earlsfield	a						←	22 08		←			
Clapham Junction 10	a	21 48			21 57	21 52	21 57	22 12	22 09	22 12			22 14
	a				↪			↪					
Vauxhall ⊖	a									22 17			
London Waterloo 15 ⊖	a	21 57	21 50			22 04	22 06		22 18	22 22	22 27	22 34	22 22

			SW 1	SW	SW 1	SW 1	SW	SW 1	SW 1	SW ◇1	SW 1		SW 1
Basingstoke	d				21 43				21 54	22 09			
Hook	d								22 01				
Winchfield	d								22 05				
Fleet	d				21 54				22 10				
Farnborough (Main)	d				22 00				22 16				
Alton	d							21 44					
Bentley	d							21 51					
Farnham	a							21 56					
	d							21 58					
Aldershot	d							22 04					
Ash Vale	d							22 09					
Brookwood	d							22 16	22 23				
Guildford	d		21 47										
Worplesdon	d												
Woking	a		21 57		22 09			22 21	22 28	22 28			
	d		21 59	22 03	22 10	22 21		22 22	22 29	22 29			
West Byfleet	d			22 07				22 27					
Byfleet & New Haw	d			22 10									
Weybridge	d			22 13					22 36				
Walton-on-Thames	d			22 17					22 40				
Hersham	d			22 19									
Esher	d			22 22									
Surbiton 6	a			22 26				22 37	22 46				
Wimbledon 6 ⊖	a			22 34									
Earlsfield	a			22 38			←				←		←
Clapham Junction 10	a			22 42	22 29		22 42	22 52	22 57	22 48	22 52		22 57
	a			↪				↪	↪				
Vauxhall ⊖	a						22 47						
London Waterloo 15 ⊖	a		22 27		22 38	22 49	22 52			22 58	23 01		23 08

Basingstoke, Alton, Guildford and Woking - Waterloo

Network Diagram - see first Page of Table 155

		SW	SW	SW	SW	SW	SW	SW	SW		SW	SW	SW	SW	SW	SW	SW	SW FO	SW FX		SW	SW			
			1		1	1	◇1	1			1		1	1	1	1	1	1	1		1	1			
Basingstoke	d					22 24	22 36				22 43			22 54	23 13						23 44				
Hook	d					22 31								23 01							23 51				
Winchfield	d					22 35								23 05							23 55				
Fleet	d					22 40					22 54			23 10							00 01				
Farnborough (Main)	d					22 46					23 00			23 16							00 06				
Alton	d				22 15								22 44				23 15					23 46			
Bentley	d												22 51									23 53			
Farnham	a				22 25								22 56				23 25					23 58			
	d				22 28								22 58				23 28								
Aldershot	d				22 34								23 04				23 34								
Ash Vale	d				22 39								23 09				23 39								
Brookwood	d				22 46	22 53							23 16	23 23			23 46				00 13				
Guildford	d	22 20	22 39						22 55									23 39	23 39						
Worplesdon	d		22 44					←								←		23 44	23 44						
Woking	a	22 32	22 49		22 51	22 58	22 54	22 58	23 05		23 09		23 21	23 28	23 31	23 28	23 51	23 49	23 49		00 18				
	d	22 33	22 50		22 52	22 59	22 55	22 59	23 06		23 10		23 22	23 33	23 32	23 33		23 56	23 56		00 20				
West Byfleet	d	22 37			22 57	→			23 10				23 27	→		23 37					00 25				
Byfleet & New Haw	d	22 40							23 13							23 40									
Weybridge	d	22 43						23 06	23 16							23 43					00 29				
Walton-on-Thames	d	22 47						23 10	23 20							23 47					00 33				
Hersham	d	22 49							23 22							23 49									
Esher	d	22 52							23 25							23 52									
Surbiton 6	a	22 56			23 07			23 16	23 29				23 37			23 57					00 39				
Wimbledon 6 ⊖	a	23 04							23 37							00 06					00 47				
Earlsfield	a	23 08		←					23 41			←													
Clapham Junction 10	a	23 12	23 09	23 12			23 14		23 44		23 29	23 44	23 51		23 55			00 19	00 19		00 53				
	a	→							→							00 21									
Vauxhall ⊖	a			23 17								23 49				00 30									
London Waterloo 15 ⊖	a		23 19	23 23	23 27		23 23	23 32			23 42	23 54	00 02		00 09	00 35		00 32	00 33		01 04				

Saturdays

		SW	SW	SW	SW	SW	SW	SW	SW	SW		SW	SW	SW	SW	SW	SW	SW	SW	SW		SW	SW	SW	SW
		1	1	1	1	1	1			1			1		1	◇1 trolley		1	1			1	◇1 trolley		1
Basingstoke	d		22p54	23p13			23p44			04 54			05 54			05 59			06 24				06 30		
Hook	d		23p01				23p51			05 01			06 01						06 31						
Winchfield	d		23p05				23p55			05 05			06 05						06 35						
Fleet	d		23p10				00 01			05 10			06 10						06 40						
Farnborough (Main)	d		23p16				00 06			05 16			06 16						06 46						
Alton	d	22p44																							06 14
Bentley	d	22p51																							06 21
Farnham	a	22p56																							06 26
	d	22p58																							06 28
Aldershot	d	23p04																							06 34
Ash Vale	d	23p09																							06 39
Brookwood	d	23p16	23p23				00 13			05 23			06 23						06 53						06 46
Guildford	d					23p39		04 00				05 14			06 02							06 34			
Worplesdon	d				←	23p44						05 19						←				06 40			
Woking	a	23p21	23p28	23p31	23p28	23p49	00 18	04 08		05 28		05 24	06 28		06 11	06 18		06 28	06 58			06 44	06 49		06 51
	d	23p22	23p33	23p32	23p33	23p56	00 20	04 10	05 27	05 29		05 33	06 29	06 03	06 13	06 19		06 29	06 59	06 33		06 46	06 50		06 52
West Byfleet	d	23p27	→		23p37		00 25		05 32			05 37	→	06 07					→	06 37					06 57
Byfleet & New Haw	d				23p40				05 35			05 40		06 10						06 40					
Weybridge	d				23p43		00 29					05 43		06 13				06 36		06 43					
Walton-on-Thames	d				23p47		00 33					05 47		06 17				06 40		06 47					
Hersham	d				23p49							05 49		06 19						06 49					
Esher	d				23p52							05 52		06 22						06 52					
Surbiton 6	a	23p37			23p57		00 39	04 24		05 40		05 56		06 26				06 46		06 56					07 07
Wimbledon 6 ⊖	a				00 06		00 47	04 31		05 48		06 04		06 34						07 04					
Earlsfield	a											06 08		06 38			←			07 08				←	
Clapham Junction 10	a	23p51		23p55		00 19	00 53	04 43				06 12		06 42	06 32	06 38	06 42	06 57		07 12		07 05		07 12	07 18
	a				00 21				06 43	06 00				→						→					
Vauxhall ⊖	a				00 30				06 49	06 07		06 17					06 47							07 17	
London Waterloo 15 ⊖	a	00 02		00 09	00 35	00 32	01 04	04 53	06 56	06 12		06 22			06 40	06 49	06 52	07 05				07 13	07 19	07 22	07 27

Table 155

Saturdays

Basingstoke, Alton, Guildford and Woking - Waterloo

Network Diagram - see first Page of Table 155

		SW 1	SW 1	SW 1	SW	SW 1		SW ◇1 trolley	SW	SW 1	SW ◇1 trolley	SW 1	SW 1	SW	SW 1	SW ◇1 trolley		SW	SW 1	SW 1 trolley	SW 1	SW	SW 1	SW 1	SW 1
Basingstoke	d	06 40		06 54				06 57			07 09		07 24			07 30							07 43		07 54
Hook	d			07 01									07 31												08 01
Winchfield	d			07 05									07 35												08 05
Fleet	d			07 10									07 40										07 54		08 10
Farnborough (Main)	d			07 16									07 46										08 00		08 16
Alton	d									06 44									07 14						
Bentley	d									06 51									07 21						
Farnham	a									06 56									07 26						
	d									06 58									07 28						
Aldershot	d									07 04									07 34						
Ash Vale	d									07 09									07 39						
Brookwood	d			07 23						07 16			07 53						07 46						08 23
Guildford	d					07 02									07 34					07 47				08 02	
Worplesdon	d		←									←			07 40						←				
Woking	a	06 58	06 58	07 28		07 11		07 15		07 21	07 27	07 28	07 58		07 44	07 49			07 51	07 57	07 58		08 09	08 10	08 28
	d	07 00	06 59	07 29	07 03	07 12		07 17		07 22	07 29	07 29	07 59	07 33	07 46	07 50			07 52	07 59	07 59	08 03	08 11	08 13	08 29
West Byfleet	d			↪	07 07					07 27			↪	07 37					07 57			08 07			↪
Byfleet & New Haw	d				07 10									07 40								08 10			
Weybridge	d		07 06		07 13							07 36		07 43							08 06	08 13			
Walton-on-Thames	d		07 10		07 17							07 40		07 47							08 10	08 17			
Hersham	d				07 19									07 49								08 19			
Esher	d				07 22									07 52								08 22			
Surbiton 6	a		07 16		07 26					07 37		07 46		07 56					08 07		08 16	08 26			
Wimbledon 6 ⊖	a				07 34									08 04								08 34			
Earlsfield	a				07 38				←					08 08				←				08 38			
Clapham Junction 10	a	07 23			07 42	07 31		07 36	07 42	07 50		07 57		08 12	08 05			08 12				08 42	08 30	08 33	
	a				↪									↪								↪			
Vauxhall ⊖	a								07 47									08 17							
London Waterloo 15 ⊖	a	07 31	07 33			07 40		07 49	07 52	07 58	07 53	08 05			08 13	08 19		08 22	08 25	08 23	08 34		08 39	08 42	

		SW ◇1 trolley		SW	SW 1	SW ◇1 trolley	SW 1 trolley	SW 1	SW	SW 1	SW 1	SW 1		SW ◇1 trolley	SW ◇1 trolley	SW	SW 1	SW 1 trolley	SW 1	SW 1	SW 1	SW		SW 1	SW ◇1 trolley
Basingstoke	d	07 57								08 17		08 24		08 30	08 35				08 43		08 54				08 57
Hook	d											08 31									09 01				
Winchfield	d											08 35									09 05				
Fleet	d											08 40							08 54		09 10				
Farnborough (Main)	d									08 30		08 46							09 00		09 16				
Alton	d				07 44												08 14								
Bentley	d				07 51												08 21								
Farnham	a				07 56												08 26								
	d				07 58												08 28								
Aldershot	d				08 04												08 34								
Ash Vale	d				08 09												08 39								
Brookwood	d				08 16							08 53					08 46				09 23				
Guildford	d						08 17				08 34							08 47						09 02	
Worplesdon	d							←			08 40									←					
Woking	a	08 17			08 21		08 26	08 28		08 39	08 44	08 58		08 49			08 51	08 57		08 58	09 28			09 11	09 15
	d	08 18			08 22	08 23	08 27	08 29	08 33	08 41	08 46	08 59		08 50			08 52	08 59		08 59	09 29	09 03		09 12	09 17
West Byfleet	d				08 27				08 37			↪					08 57				↪	09 07			
Byfleet & New Haw	d								08 40													09 10			
Weybridge	d							08 36	08 43											09 06		09 13			
Walton-on-Thames	d							08 40	08 47											09 10		09 17			
Hersham	d								08 49													09 19			
Esher	d								08 52													09 22			
Surbiton 6	a				08 37			08 46	08 56								09 07			09 16		09 26			
Wimbledon 6 ⊖	a								09 04													09 34			
Earlsfield	a			←					09 08							←						09 38			
Clapham Junction 10	a	08 37		08 42	08 49			08 57	09 12		09 05				09 12	09 12			09 25			09 42		09 31	09 36
	a								↪													↪			
Vauxhall ⊖	a			08 47												09 17									
London Waterloo 15 ⊖	a	08 49		08 52	08 58	08 49	08 51	09 05		09 08	09 13			09 19	09 20	09 22	09 25	09 23	09 34	09 36				09 40	09 49

Basingstoke, Alton, Guildford and Woking - Waterloo

Network Diagram - see first Page of Table 155

		SW ◇1 🛒	SW	SW 1	SW 1 🛒	SW 1	SW	SW 1		SW 1	SW 1	SW ◇1 🛒	SW ◇1 🛒	SW	SW 1	SW 1 🛒	SW 1	SW 1		SW 1	SW	SW 1	SW ◇1 🛒	SW ◇1 🛒	SW
Basingstoke	d							09 17			09 24	09 30	09 35				09 43			09 54			09 57		
Hook	d										09 31									10 01					
Winchfield	d										09 35									10 05					
Fleet	d										09 40						09 54			10 10					
Farnborough (Main)	d							09 30			09 46						10 00			10 16					
Alton	d			08 44											09 14										
Bentley	d			08 51											09 21										
Farnham	a			08 56											09 26										
	d			08 58											09 28										
Aldershot	d			09 04											09 34										
Ash Vale	d			09 09											09 39										
Brookwood	d			09 16							09 53				09 46					10 23					
Guildford	d				09 17					09 34						09 47						10 02			
Worplesdon	d					←				09 40								←							
Woking	a			09 21	09 25	09 28		09 39		09 44	09 58	09 49			09 51	09 57		09 58		10 28		10 11	10 15		
	d	09 21		09 22	09 26	09 29	09 33	09 41		09 46	09 59	09 50			09 52	09 59		09 59		10 29	10 03	10 12	10 17	10 21	
West Byfleet	d			09 27			09 37				→				09 57					→	10 07				
Byfleet & New Haw	d						09 40														10 10				
Weybridge	d					09 36	09 43											10 06			10 13				
Walton-on-Thames	d					09 40	09 47											10 10			10 17				
Hersham	d						09 49														10 19				
Esher	d						09 52														10 22				
Surbiton 6	a			09 37		09 46	09 56								10 07			10 16			10 26				
Wimbledon 6 ⊖	a						10 04														10 34				
Earlsfield	a		←				10 08							←							10 38				←
Clapham Junction 10	a		09 42	09 48		09 57	10 12			10 05			10 12	10 12			10 25				10 42	10 31	10 36		10 42
	a						→														→				
Vauxhall ⊖	a		09 47											10 17											10 47
London Waterloo 15 ⊖	a	09 49	09 52	09 57	09 51	10 05		10 07		10 13		10 19	10 20	10 22	10 25	10 23	10 34	10 36				10 40	10 49	10 49	10 52

		SW 1	SW 1 🛒	SW 1		SW	SW 1	SW 1	SW 1	SW ◇1 🛒	SW ◇1 🛒	SW	SW 1	SW 1 🛒		SW 1	SW 1	SW 1	SW	SW 1	SW ◇1 🛒	SW ◇1 🛒	SW	SW 1	
Basingstoke	d						10 17		10 24	10 30	10 35					10 43		10 54			10 57				
Hook	d								10 31									11 01							
Winchfield	d								10 35									11 05							
Fleet	d								10 40							10 54		11 10							
Farnborough (Main)	d						10 30		10 46							11 00		11 16							
Alton	d	09 44											10 14											10 44	
Bentley	d	09 51											10 21											10 51	
Farnham	a	09 56											10 26											10 56	
	d	09 58											10 28											10 58	
Aldershot	d	10 04											10 34											11 04	
Ash Vale	d	10 09											10 39											11 09	
Brookwood	d	10 16							10 53				10 46					11 23						11 16	
Guildford	d		10 17					10 34						10 47						11 02					
Worplesdon	d			←				10 40									←								
Woking	a	10 21	10 25	10 28			10 39	10 44	10 58	10 49			10 51	10 57			10 58	11 28		11 11	11 15			11 21	
	d	10 22	10 26	10 29		10 33	10 41	10 46	10 59	10 50			10 52	10 59			10 59	11 29	11 03	11 12	11 17	11 21		11 22	
West Byfleet	d	10 27				10 37			→				10 57					→	11 07					11 27	
Byfleet & New Haw	d					10 40													11 10						
Weybridge	d			10 36		10 43											11 06		11 13						
Walton-on-Thames	d			10 40		10 47											11 10		11 17						
Hersham	d					10 49													11 19						
Esher	d					10 52													11 22						
Surbiton 6	a	10 37		10 46		10 56							11 07				11 16		11 26					11 37	
Wimbledon 6 ⊖	a					11 04													11 34						
Earlsfield	a					11 08						←							11 38				←		
Clapham Junction 10	a	10 48		10 57		11 12		11 05			11 12	11 12				11 25			11 42	11 31	11 36		11 42	11 48	
	a					→													→						
Vauxhall ⊖	a											11 17											11 47		
London Waterloo 15 ⊖	a	10 57	10 51	11 05			11 07	11 13		11 19	11 20	11 22	11 25	11 23		11 34	11 36			11 40	11 49	11 49	11 52	11 57	

Basingstoke, Alton, Guildford and Woking - Waterloo

Network Diagram - see first Page of Table 155

		SW 1 🛒	SW 1	SW	SW 1	SW 1	SW 1	SW ◇1 🛒	SW ◇1 🛒	SW		SW 1	SW 1 🛒	SW 1	SW 1	SW 1	SW	SW 1	SW ◇1 🛒	SW ◇1 🛒		SW	SW 1	SW 1 🛒	SW 1
Basingstoke	d				11 17		11 24	11 30	11 35					11 43		11 54			11 57						
Hook	d						11 31									12 01									
Winchfield	d						11 35									12 05									
Fleet	d						11 40							11 54		12 10									
Farnborough (Main)	d				11 30		11 46							12 00		12 16									
Alton	d											11 15											11 44		
Bentley	d																						11 51		
Farnham	a											11 25											11 56		
	d											11 28											11 58		
Aldershot	d											11 34											12 04		
Ash Vale	d											11 39											12 09		
Brookwood	d						11 53					11 46				12 23							12 16		
Guildford	d	11 17				11 34							11 47					12 02						12 17	
Worplesdon	d		←			11 40									←										←
Woking	a	11 25	11 28		11 39	11 44	11 58	11 49				11 51	11 57		11 58	12 28		12 11	12 15				12 21	12 25	12 28
	d	11 26	11 29	11 33	11 41	11 46	11 59	11 50				11 52	11 59		11 59	12 29	12 03	12 12	12 17	12 21			12 22	12 26	12 29
West Byfleet	d			11 37			→					11 57				→	12 07						12 27		
Byfleet & New Haw	d			11 40													12 10								
Weybridge	d		11 36	11 43											12 06		12 13								12 36
Walton-on-Thames	d		11 40	11 47											12 10		12 17								12 40
Hersham	d			11 49													12 19								
Esher	d			11 52													12 22								
Surbiton 6	a		11 46	11 56								12 07			12 16		12 26						12 37		12 46
Wimbledon 6 ⊖	a			12 04													12 34								
Earlsfield	a			12 08						←							12 38					←			
Clapham Junction 10	a		11 57	12 12		12 05			12 12	12 12				12 25			12 42	12 31	12 36			12 42	12 48		12 57
	a			→													→								
Vauxhall ⊖	a									12 17												12 47			
London Waterloo 15 ⊖	a	11 51	12 05		12 07	12 13		12 19	12 21	12 22		12 29	12 27	12 34	12 36			12 43	12 49	12 51		12 52	12 59	12 57	13 05

		SW	SW 1	SW 1	SW 1	SW ◇1 🛒		SW ◇1 🛒	SW	SW 1	SW 1 🛒	SW 1	SW 1	SW 1	SW	SW 1		SW ◇1 🛒	SW ◇1 🛒	SW	SW 1	SW 1 🛒	SW 1	SW	SW 1
Basingstoke	d		12 17		12 24	12 30		12 35				12 43		12 54				12 57							13 17
Hook	d				12 31									13 01											
Winchfield	d				12 35									13 05											
Fleet	d				12 40							12 54		13 10											
Farnborough (Main)	d		12 30		12 46							13 00		13 16											13 30
Alton	d									12 15											12 44				
Bentley	d																				12 51				
Farnham	a									12 25											12 56				
	d									12 28											12 58				
Aldershot	d									12 34											13 04				
Ash Vale	d									12 39											13 09				
Brookwood	d				12 53					12 46				13 23							13 16				
Guildford	d			12 34							12 47					13 02						13 17			
Worplesdon	d			12 40									←										←		
Woking	a		12 39	12 44	12 58	12 49				12 51	12 57		12 58	13 28		13 11		13 15			13 21	13 25	13 28		13 39
	d	12 33	12 41	12 46	12 59	12 50				12 52	12 59		12 59	13 29	13 03	13 12		13 17	13 21		13 22	13 26	13 29	13 33	13 41
West Byfleet	d	12 37			→					12 57				→	13 07						13 27			13 37	
Byfleet & New Haw	d	12 40													13 10									13 40	
Weybridge	d	12 43											13 06		13 13								13 36	13 43	
Walton-on-Thames	d	12 47											13 10		13 17								13 40	13 47	
Hersham	d	12 49													13 19									13 49	
Esher	d	12 52													13 22									13 52	
Surbiton 6	a	12 56								13 07			13 16		13 26						13 37		13 46	13 56	
Wimbledon 6 ⊖	a	13 04													13 34									14 04	
Earlsfield	a	13 08							←						13 38					←				14 08	
Clapham Junction 10	a	13 12		13 05				13 12	13 12			13 25			13 42	13 31		13 36		13 42	13 48		13 57	14 12	
	a	→													→									→	
Vauxhall ⊖	a								13 17											13 47					
London Waterloo 15 ⊖	a		13 07	13 13		13 19		13 21	13 22	13 29	13 27	13 34	13 36			13 43		13 49	13 51	13 52	13 59	13 57	14 05		14 07

Table 155

Saturdays

Basingstoke, Alton, Guildford and Woking - Waterloo

Network Diagram - see first Page of Table 155

		SW 1		SW 1	SW ◇1 [trolley]	SW ◇1 [trolley]	SW	SW 1	SW 1 [trolley]	SW 1	SW 1	SW 1		SW	SW 1	SW ◇1 [trolley]	SW ◇1 [trolley]	SW	SW 1	SW 1 [trolley]	SW 1	SW		SW 1	SW 1
Basingstoke	d			13 24	13 30	13 35				13 43		13 54				13 57								14 17	
Hook	d			13 31								14 01													
Winchfield	d			13 35								14 05													
Fleet	d			13 40						13 54		14 10													
Farnborough (Main)	d			13 46						14 00		14 16												14 30	
Alton	d							13 15											13 44						
Bentley	d																		13 51						
Farnham	a							13 25											13 56						
	d							13 28											13 58						
Aldershot	d							13 34											14 04						
Ash Vale	d							13 39											14 09						
Brookwood	d			13 53				13 46				14 23							14 16						
Guildford	d	13 34							13 47						14 02					14 17					14 34
Worplesdon	d	13 40									←										←				14 40
Woking	a	13 44		13 58	13 49			13 51	13 57		13 58	14 28			14 11	14 15			14 21	14 25	14 28			14 39	14 44
	d	13 46		13 59	13 50			13 52	13 59		13 59	14 29		14 03	14 12	14 17	14 21		14 22	14 26	14 29	14 33		14 41	14 46
West Byfleet	d			↪				13 57				↪		14 07					14 27			14 37			
Byfleet & New Haw	d													14 10								14 40			
Weybridge	d										14 06			14 13							14 36	14 43			
Walton-on-Thames	d										14 10			14 17							14 40	14 47			
Hersham	d													14 19								14 49			
Esher	d													14 22								14 52			
Surbiton 6	a							14 07			14 16			14 26					14 37		14 46	14 56			
Wimbledon 6 ⊖	a													14 34								15 04			
Earlsfield	a						←							14 38				←				15 08			
Clapham Junction 10	a	14 05				14 12	14 12			14 25				14 42	14 31	14 36		14 42	14 48		14 57	15 12			15 05
	a													↪								↪			
Vauxhall ⊖	a						14 17											14 47							
London Waterloo 15 ⊖	a	14 14			14 19	14 21	14 22	14 29	14 27	14 34	14 36				14 41	14 49	14 51	14 52	14 59	14 57	15 05			15 07	15 14

		SW 1	SW ◇1 [trolley]	SW ◇1 [trolley]	SW	SW 1	SW 1 [trolley]	SW 1		SW 1	SW 1	SW	SW 1	SW ◇1 [trolley]	SW ◇1 [trolley]	SW	SW 1	SW 1 [trolley]		SW 1	SW	SW 1	SW 1	SW 1	SW ◇1 [trolley]
Basingstoke	d	14 24	14 30	14 35				14 43			14 54			14 57								15 17		15 24	15 30
Hook	d	14 31									15 01													15 31	
Winchfield	d	14 35									15 05													15 35	
Fleet	d	14 40						14 54			15 10													15 40	
Farnborough (Main)	d	14 46						15 00			15 16											15 30		15 46	
Alton	d					14 15											14 44								
Bentley	d																14 51								
Farnham	a					14 25											14 56								
	d					14 28											14 58								
Aldershot	d					14 34											15 04								
Ash Vale	d					14 39											15 09								
Brookwood	d	14 53				14 46					15 23						15 16							15 53	
Guildford	d						14 47						15 02					15 17					15 34		
Worplesdon	d									←										←			15 40		
Woking	a	14 58	14 49			14 51	14 57			14 58	15 28		15 11	15 15			15 21	15 25		15 28		15 39	15 44	15 58	15 49
	d	14 59	14 50			14 52	14 59			14 59	15 29	15 03	15 12	15 17	15 21		15 22	15 26		15 29	15 33	15 41	15 46	15 59	15 50
West Byfleet	d	↪				14 57					↪	15 07					15 27				15 37			↪	
Byfleet & New Haw	d											15 10									15 40				
Weybridge	d									15 06		15 13								15 36	15 43				
Walton-on-Thames	d									15 10		15 17								15 40	15 47				
Hersham	d											15 19									15 49				
Esher	d											15 22									15 52				
Surbiton 6	a					15 07				15 16		15 26					15 37			15 46	15 56				
Wimbledon 6 ⊖	a											15 34									16 04				
Earlsfield	a				←							15 38				←					16 08				
Clapham Junction 10	a			15 12	15 12			15 25				15 42	15 31	15 36		15 42	15 48			15 57	16 12		16 05		
	a											↪									↪				
Vauxhall ⊖	a				15 17											15 47									
London Waterloo 15 ⊖	a		15 19	15 21	15 22	15 29	15 27	15 34		15 36			15 41	15 49	15 51	15 52	15 59	15 57		16 05		16 07	16 13		16 19

Basingstoke, Alton, Guildford and Woking - Waterloo

Network Diagram - see first Page of Table 155

		SW ◇1 ⚲	SW	SW 1		SW 1 ⚲	SW 1	SW 1	SW 1	SW	SW 1	SW ◇1 ⚲	SW ◇1 ⚲	SW		SW 1	SW 1 ⚲	SW 1	SW	SW 1	SW 1	SW 1	SW ◇1 ⚲	SW ◇1 ⚲	
Basingstoke	d	15 35					15 43		15 54			15 57								16 17		16 24	16 30	16 35	
Hook	d								16 01													16 31			
Winchfield	d								16 05													16 35			
Fleet	d						15 54		16 10													16 40			
Farnborough (Main)	d						16 00		16 16											16 30		16 46			
Alton	d			15 15												15 44									
Bentley	d															15 51									
Farnham	a			15 25												15 56									
	d			15 28												15 58									
Aldershot	d			15 34												16 04									
Ash Vale	d			15 39												16 09									
Brookwood	d			15 46					16 23							16 16						16 53			
Guildford	d					15 47					16 02						16 17				16 34				
Worplesdon	d							←										←			16 40				
Woking	a			15 51		15 57		15 58	16 28		16 11	16 15				16 21	16 25	16 28		16 39	16 44	16 58	16 49		
	d			15 52		15 59		15 59	16 29	16 03	16 12	16 17	16 21			16 22	16 26	16 29	16 33	16 41	16 46	16 59	16 50		
West Byfleet	d			15 57					→	16 07						16 27			16 37			→			
Byfleet & New Haw	d									16 10									16 40						
Weybridge	d							16 06		16 13								16 36	16 43						
Walton-on-Thames	d							16 10		16 17								16 40	16 47						
Hersham	d									16 19									16 49						
Esher	d									16 22									16 52						
Surbiton 6	a			16 07				16 16		16 26						16 37		16 46	16 56						
Wimbledon 6 ⊖	a									16 34									17 04						
Earlsfield	a		←							16 38				←					17 08						
Clapham Junction 10	a	16 12	16 12				16 25			16 42	16 31	16 36		16 42		16 48		16 57	17 12		17 05			17 12	
	a									→									→						
Vauxhall ⊖	a		16 17											16 47											
London Waterloo 15 ⊖	a	16 20	16 22	16 25		16 23	16 34	16 36			16 40	16 49	16 49	16 52		16 57	16 51	17 05		17 07	17 13		17 19	17 20	

		SW	SW 1	SW 1 ⚲	SW 1	SW 1	SW 1	SW	SW 1	SW ◇1 ⚲		SW ◇1 ⚲	SW	SW 1	SW 1 ⚲	SW 1	SW	SW 1	SW 1	SW 1		SW ◇1 ⚲	SW ◇1 ⚲	SW	SW 1
Basingstoke	d				16 43		16 54			16 57								17 17		17 24		17 30	17 35		
Hook	d						17 01													17 31					
Winchfield	d						17 05													17 35					
Fleet	d				16 54		17 10													17 40					
Farnborough (Main)	d				17 00		17 16											17 30		17 46					
Alton	d		16 15											16 44											17 15
Bentley	d													16 51											
Farnham	a		16 25											16 56											17 25
	d		16 28											16 58											17 28
Aldershot	d		16 34											17 04											17 34
Ash Vale	d		16 39											17 09											17 39
Brookwood	d		16 46				17 23							17 16						17 53					17 46
Guildford	d			16 47					17 02						17 17				17 34						
Worplesdon	d					←										←			17 40						
Woking	a		16 51	16 57		16 58	17 28		17 11	17 15				17 21	17 25	17 28		17 39	17 44	17 58		17 49			17 51
	d		16 52	16 59		16 59	17 29	17 03	17 12	17 17		17 21		17 22	17 26	17 29	17 33	17 41	17 46	17 59		17 50			17 52
West Byfleet	d		16 57				→	17 07						17 27			17 37			→					17 57
Byfleet & New Haw	d							17 10									17 40								
Weybridge	d					17 06		17 13								17 36	17 43								
Walton-on-Thames	d					17 10		17 17								17 40	17 47								
Hersham	d							17 19									17 49								
Esher	d							17 22									17 52								
Surbiton 6	a		17 07			17 16		17 26						17 37		17 46	17 56								18 07
Wimbledon 6 ⊖	a							17 34									18 04								
Earlsfield	a	←						17 38					←				18 08							←	
Clapham Junction 10	a	17 12			17 25			17 42	17 31	17 36			17 42	17 48		17 57	18 12		18 05				18 12	18 12	
	a							→									→								
Vauxhall ⊖	a	17 17											17 47											18 17	
London Waterloo 15 ⊖	a	17 22	17 25	17 23	17 34	17 36			17 40	17 49		17 49	17 52	17 57	17 51	18 05		18 07	18 13			18 19	18 20	18 22	18 25

Table 155

Saturdays

Basingstoke, Alton, Guildford and Woking - Waterloo

Network Diagram - see first Page of Table 155

		SW 1 🚲	SW 1	SW 1	SW 1	SW		SW 1	SW ◇1 🚲	SW ◇1 🚲	SW	SW 1	SW 1	SW 1	SW	SW 1		SW 1	SW 1	SW ◇1 🚲	SW ◇1 🚲	SW	SW 1	SW 1 🚲	SW 1
Basingstoke	d		17 43		17 54				17 57							18 17			18 24	18 30	18 35				18 43
Hook	d				18 01														18 31						
Winchfield	d				18 05														18 35						
Fleet	d		17 54		18 10														18 40						18 54
Farnborough (Main)	d		18 00		18 16											18 30			18 46						19 00
Alton	d											17 44											18 15		
Bentley	d											17 51													
Farnham	a											17 56											18 25		
	d											17 58											18 28		
Aldershot	d											18 04											18 34		
Ash Vale	d											18 09											18 39		
Brookwood	d				18 23							18 16							18 53				18 46		
Guildford	d	17 47						18 02					18 17					18 34						18 47	
Worplesdon	d			←										←				18 40							
Woking	a	17 57		17 58	18 28			18 11	18 15			18 21	18 25	18 28		18 39		18 44	18 58	18 49			18 51	18 57	
	d	17 59		17 59	18 29	18 03		18 12	18 17	18 21		18 22	18 26	18 29	18 33	18 41		18 46	18 59	18 50			18 52	18 59	
West Byfleet	d				→	18 07						18 27			18 37				→				18 57		
Byfleet & New Haw	d					18 10									18 40										
Weybridge	d			18 06		18 13								18 36	18 43										
Walton-on-Thames	d			18 10		18 17								18 40	18 47										
Hersham	d					18 19									18 49										
Esher	d					18 22									18 52										
Surbiton 6	a			18 16		18 26						18 37		18 46	18 56								19 07		
Wimbledon 6 ⊖	a					18 34									19 04										
Earlsfield	a					18 38					←				19 08							←			
Clapham Junction 10	a		18 25			18 42		18 31	18 36		18 42	18 48		18 57	19 12			19 05			19 12	19 12			19 25
	a					→									→										
Vauxhall ⊖	a										18 47											19 17			
London Waterloo 15 ⊖	a	18 23	18 34	18 36				18 40	18 49	18 49	18 52	18 57	18 51	19 05		19 07		19 13		19 19	19 20	19 22	19 25	19 23	19 34

		SW 1		SW 1	SW	SW 1	SW ◇1 🚲	SW ◇1 🚲	SW	SW 1	SW 1	SW 1		SW	SW 1	SW 1	SW 1	SW ◇1 🚲	SW ◇1 🚲	SW	SW 1	SW 1		SW 1	SW 1
Basingstoke	d			18 54			18 57								19 17		19 24	19 30	19 35					19 43	
Hook	d			19 01													19 31								
Winchfield	d			19 05													19 35								
Fleet	d			19 10													19 40							19 54	
Farnborough (Main)	d			19 16											19 30		19 46							20 00	
Alton	d									18 44											19 15				
Bentley	d									18 51															
Farnham	a									18 56											19 25				
	d									18 58											19 28				
Aldershot	d									19 04											19 34				
Ash Vale	d									19 09											19 39				
Brookwood	d			19 23						19 16							19 53				19 46				
Guildford	d					19 02					19 17					19 34						19 47			
Worplesdon	d	←										←				19 40									←
Woking	a	18 58		19 28		19 11	19 15			19 21	19 25	19 28			19 39	19 44	19 58	19 49			19 51	19 57			19 58
	d	18 59		19 29	19 03	19 12	19 17	19 21		19 22	19 26	19 29		19 33	19 41	19 46	19 59	19 50			19 52	19 59			19 59
West Byfleet	d			→	19 07					19 27				19 37			→				19 57				
Byfleet & New Haw	d				19 10									19 40											
Weybridge	d	19 06			19 13							19 36		19 43											20 06
Walton-on-Thames	d	19 10			19 17							19 40		19 47											20 10
Hersham	d				19 19									19 49											
Esher	d				19 22									19 52											
Surbiton 6	a	19 16			19 26					19 37		19 46		19 56							20 07				20 16
Wimbledon 6 ⊖	a				19 34									20 04											
Earlsfield	a				19 38				←					20 08						←					
Clapham Junction 10	a				19 42	19 31	19 36		19 42	19 48		19 57		20 12		20 05			20 12	20 12				20 25	
	a				→									→											
Vauxhall ⊖	a								19 47											20 17					
London Waterloo 15 ⊖	a	19 36				19 40	19 49	19 49	19 52	19 57	19 51	20 05			20 07	20 13		20 19	20 20	20 22	20 25	20 23		20 34	20 36

Table 155

Saturdays

Basingstoke, Alton, Guildford and Woking - Waterloo

Network Diagram - see first Page of Table 155

		SW	SW 1	SW ◇1 🚲	SW	SW 1	SW 1	SW 1		SW ◇1 🚲	SW 1	SW	SW 1	SW 1	SW 1	SW 1	SW ◇1 🚲	SW 1		SW	SW 1	SW ◇1 🚲	SW	SW 1	SW 1
Basingstoke	d							19 54		20 09			20 17			20 24	20 35				20 43				
Hook	d							20 01								20 31									
Winchfield	d							20 05								20 35									
Fleet	d							20 10								20 40					20 54				
Farnborough (Main)	d							20 16					20 30			20 46					21 00				
Alton	d					19 44								20 15										20 44	
Bentley	d					19 51																		20 51	
Farnham	a					19 56								20 25										20 56	
	d					19 58								20 28										20 58	
Aldershot	d					20 04								20 34										21 04	
Ash Vale	d					20 09								20 39										21 09	
Brookwood	d					20 16		20 23						20 46		20 53								21 16	
Guildford	d		20 02				20 17								20 39			20 47							21 17
Worplesdon	d														20 44										
Woking	a		20 11			20 21	20 25	20 28		20 29			20 39	20 51	20 52	20 58		20 57			21 09			21 21	21 25
	d	20 03	20 12	20 21		20 22	20 26	20 29		20 30		20 33	20 41	20 52	20 53	20 59		20 59		21 03	21 10	21 21		21 22	21 26
West Byfleet	d	20 07				20 27						20 37		20 57						21 07				21 27	
Byfleet & New Haw	d	20 10										20 40								21 10					
Weybridge	d	20 13						20 36				20 43				21 06				21 13					
Walton-on-Thames	d	20 17						20 40				20 47				21 10				21 17					
Hersham	d	20 19										20 49								21 19					
Esher	d	20 22										20 52								21 22					
Surbiton 6	a	20 26				20 37		20 46				20 56		21 07		21 16				21 26				21 37	
Wimbledon 6 ⊖	a	20 34										21 04								21 34					
Earlsfield	a	20 38			←						←	21 08								21 38			←		
Clapham Junction 10	a	20 42	20 31		20 42	20 48		20 57		20 52	20 57	21 12			21 12		21 16			21 42	21 29		21 42	21 48	
	a	↪						↪												↪					
Vauxhall ⊖	a				20 47							21 17											21 47		
London Waterloo 15 ⊖	a		20 40	20 49	20 52	20 57	20 50			21 04	21 05	21 23	21 07	21 29	21 21	21 34	21 24	21 27			21 38	21 49	21 52	21 57	21 50

		SW 1	SW ◇1 🚲	SW 1		SW	SW 1	SW	SW 1	SW 1	SW ◇1	SW 1	SW	SW 1		SW 1	SW	SW 1	SW 1	SW ◇1	SW 1	SW 1	SW	SW 1	
Basingstoke	d	20 54	21 09							21 24	21 35			21 43					21 54	22 09					
Hook	d	21 01								21 31									22 01						
Winchfield	d	21 05								21 35									22 05						
Fleet	d	21 10								21 40				21 54					22 10						
Farnborough (Main)	d	21 16								21 46				22 00					22 16						
Alton	d								21 15									21 44							
Bentley	d																	21 51							
Farnham	a								21 25									21 56							
	d								21 28									21 58							
Aldershot	d								21 34									22 04							
Ash Vale	d								21 39									22 09							
Brookwood	d	21 23							21 46	21 53								22 16	22 23						
Guildford	d						21 39					21 49											22 20	22 39	
Worplesdon	d						21 44																	22 44	
Woking	a	21 28	21 29				21 49		21 51	21 58		21 57		22 09				22 21	22 28	22 28			22 32	22 49	
	d	21 29	21 30			21 33	21 50		21 52	21 59		21 59	22 03	22 10		22 21		22 22	22 29	22 29			22 33	22 50	
West Byfleet	d					21 37			21 57				22 07					22 27					22 37		
Byfleet & New Haw	d					21 40							22 10										22 40		
Weybridge	d	21 36				21 43				22 06			22 13						22 36				22 43		
Walton-on-Thames	d	21 40				21 47				22 10			22 17						22 40				22 47		
Hersham	d					21 49							22 19										22 49		
Esher	d					21 52							22 22										22 52		
Surbiton 6	a	21 46				21 56			22 07	22 16			22 26					22 37	22 46				22 56		
Wimbledon 6 ⊖	a					22 04							22 34										23 04		
Earlsfield	a			←		22 08		←					22 38				←				←	←	23 08		
Clapham Junction 10	a	21 57	21 52	21 57		22 12	22 09	22 12			22 14		22 42	22 29			22 42	22 52	22 57	22 48	22 52	22 57	23 12	23 09	
	a	↪				↪							↪					↪	↪				↪		
Vauxhall ⊖	a							22 17									22 47								
London Waterloo 15 ⊖	a		22 04	22 07			22 18	22 22	22 27	22 34	22 22	22 24		22 38		22 49	22 52			22 57	23 01	23 05		23 18	

Table 155

Saturdays

Basingstoke, Alton, Guildford and Woking - Waterloo

Network Diagram - see first Page of Table 155

		SW	SW	SW	SW	SW	SW	SW	SW	SW		SW	SW	SW	SW	SW	SW	SW							
			1	1	◇1	1		1		1		1	1	1	1	1	1	1							
Basingstoke	d			22 24	22 35			22 43				22 54	23 13				23 44								
Hook	d			22 31								23 01					23 51								
Winchfield	d			22 35								23 05					23 55								
Fleet	d			22 40				22 54				23 10					00 01								
Farnborough (Main)	d			22 46				23 00				23 16					00 06								
Alton	d		22 15							22 44					23 15			23 46							
Bentley	d									22 51								23 53							
Farnham	a		22 25							22 56					23 25			23 58							
	d		22 28							22 58					23 28										
Aldershot	d		22 34							23 04					23 34										
Ash Vale	d		22 39							23 09					23 39										
Brookwood	d		22 46	22 53						23 16		23 23			23 46		00 13								
Guildford	d						22 55									23 39									
Worplesdon	d					←								←		23 44									
Woking	a		22 51	22 58	22 53	22 58	23 05	23 09		23 21		23 28	23 31	23 28	23 51	23 49	00 18								
	d		22 52	22 59	22 55	22 59	23 06	23 10		23 22		23 33	23 32	23 33		23 56	00 20								
West Byfleet	d		22 57	→			23 10			23 27		→		23 37			00 25								
Byfleet & New Haw	d						23 13							23 40											
Weybridge	d					23 06	23 16							23 43			00 29								
Walton-on-Thames	d					23 10	23 20							23 47			00 33								
Hersham	d						23 22							23 49											
Esher	d						23 25							23 52											
Surbiton 6	a		23 07			23 16	23 29			23 37				23 57			00 39								
Wimbledon 6 ⊖	a						23 37							00 06			00 47								
Earlsfield	a	←					23 41		←																
Clapham Junction 10	a	23 12			23 14		23 44	23 29	23 44	23 48			23 52			00 18	00 53								
	a						→							00 21											
Vauxhall ⊖	a	23 17							23 49					00 30											
London Waterloo 15 ⊖	a	23 22	23 28		23 22	23 32		23 39	23 54	00 01			00 03	00 35		00 32	01 04								

Sundays

		SW	SW	SW	SW	SW	SW	SW	SW	SW	SW		SW	SW	SW	SW	SW	SW	SW	SW	SW		SW	SW	SW
		1	1	1	1	1	1			1	1			◇1		1		1		1			◇1		1
		A	A	A	A	A	A							🛒									🛒		
Basingstoke	d		22p54	23p13			23p44			07 16				07 20				07 44					08 10		
Hook	d		23p01	⌇			23p51			07 23															
Winchfield	d		23p05	⌇			23p55			07 27															
Fleet	d		23p10	⌇			00⌇01			07 32															
Farnborough (Main)	d		23p16	⌇			00⌇06			07 38															
Alton	d	22p44	⌇	⌇			⌇																		
Bentley	d	22p51	⌇	⌇			⌇																		
Farnham	a	22p56	⌇	⌇			⌇																		
	d	22p58	⌇	⌇			⌇				07 30														
Aldershot	d	23p04	⌇	⌇			⌇				07 36														
Ash Vale	d	23p09	⌇	⌇			⌇				07 41														
Brookwood	d	23p16	23p23	⌇			00⌇13			07 45	07 48														
Guildford	d	⌇	⌇	⌇		23p39	⌇		06 57				07 27						07 57	08 05				08 27	08 35
Worplesdon	d	⌇	⌇	⌇	←	23p44	⌇									←									
Woking	a	23p21	23p28	23p31	23p28	23p49	00⌇18		07 05	07 50	07 54		07 35	07 39		07 50		08 02	08 05	08 13			08 28	08 35	08 42
	d	23p22	23p33	23p32	23p33	23p56	00⌇20	06 36	07 06	07 58			07 36	07 40		07 58	07 52	08 04	08 06	08 15			08 30	08 36	08 45
West Byfleet	d	23p27	→	⌇	23p37	⌇	00⌇25	06 40	07 10	→			07 40				07 56		08 10					08 40	
Byfleet & New Haw	d	⌇		⌇	23p40	⌇	⌇	06 43	07 13				07 43				08 00		08 13					08 43	
Weybridge	d	⌇		⌇	23p43	⌇	00⌇29	06 46	07 16				07 46						08 16					08 46	
Walton-on-Thames	d	⌇		⌇	23p47	⌇	00⌇33	06 50	07 20				07 50						08 20					08 50	
Hersham	d	⌇		⌇	23p49	⌇	⌇	06 52	07 22				07 52						08 22					08 52	
Esher	d	⌇		⌇	23p52	⌇	⌇	06 55	07 25				07 55						08 25					08 55	
Surbiton 6	a	23p37		⌇	23p57	⌇	00⌇39	06 59	07 29				07 59			08 09			08 29					08 59	
Wimbledon 6 ⊖	a	⌇		⌇	00⌇06	⌇	00⌇47	07 07	07 37				08 07			08 19			08 37					09 07	
Earlsfield	a	⌇		⌇	⌇	⌇	⌇	07 11	07 41				08 11		←				08 41		←			09 11	
Clapham Junction 10	a	23p48		23p52	⌇	00⌇18	00⌇53	07 15	07 45				08 15	08 05	08 15	08 27		08 30	08 45	08 40	08 45		08 57	09 15	09 06
	a	⌇		⌇	00⌇21	⌇	⌇						→				09 01		→					→	
Vauxhall ⊖	a	⌇		⌇	00⌇30	⌇	⌇	07 20	07 50						08 20		09 08				08 50				
London Waterloo 15 ⊖	a	00⌇01		00⌇03	00⌇35	00⌇32	01⌇04	07 30	08 00					08 19	08 30	08 41	09 13	08 42		08 49	09 00		09 09		09 19

A not 11 December

Sundays

Basingstoke, Alton, Guildford and Woking - Waterloo

Network Diagram - see first Page of Table 155

		SW	SW	SW 1	SW 1	SW 1	SW		SW 1	SW	SW ◇1 🛒	SW	SW 1	SW	SW	SW 1	SW 1		SW 1	SW	SW 1	SW ◇1 🛒	SW	SW ◇1 🛒	SW
Basingstoke	d			08 16		08 44					09 10					09 16			09 44			10 00		10 10	
Hook	d			08 23												09 23									
Winchfield	d			08 27												09 27									
Fleet	d			08 32												09 32									
Farnborough (Main)	d			08 38												09 38									
Alton	d				08 15												09 15								
Bentley	d				08 23												09 23								
Farnham	a				08 28												09 28								
	d				08 30												09 30								
Aldershot	d				08 36												09 36								
Ash Vale	d				08 41												09 41								
Brookwood	d			08 45	08 48											09 45	09 48								
Guildford	d						08 57		09 05			09 27	09 35							09 57	10 05				10 27
Worplesdon	d																								
Woking	a			08 50	08 54	09 02	09 05		09 15		09 28	09 35	09 42			09 50	09 54		10 02	10 05	10 15	10 19		10 28	10 35
	d		08 52	08 58		09 04	09 06		09 15		09 30	09 36	09 45		09 52	09 58			10 04	10 06	10 15	10 20		10 30	10 36
West Byfleet	d		08 56				09 10					09 40			09 56					10 10					10 40
Byfleet & New Haw	d		09 00				09 13					09 43			10 00					10 13					10 43
Weybridge	d						09 16					09 46								10 16					10 46
Walton-on-Thames	d						09 20					09 50								10 20					10 50
Hersham	d						09 22					09 52								10 22					10 52
Esher	d						09 25					09 55								10 25					10 55
Surbiton 6	a			09 09			09 29					09 59				10 09				10 29					10 59
Wimbledon 6 ⊖	a			09 19			09 37					10 07				10 17				10 37					11 07
Earlsfield	a	←					09 41			←		10 11		←						10 41			←		11 11
Clapham Junction 10	a	09 15		09 26		09 30	09 45		09 38	09 45	09 57	10 15	10 04	10 15		10 23			10 27	10 45	10 35	10 40	10 45	10 49	11 15
	a		10 01				↪					↪			11 01					↪					↪
Vauxhall ⊖	a	09 20	10 08							09 50				10 20	11 08								10 50		
London Waterloo 15 ⊖	a	09 30	10 13	09 39		09 43			09 49	10 00	10 08		10 19	10 30	11 13	10 38			10 42		10 49	10 54	11 00	11 04	

		SW 1 🛒	SW		SW	SW 1	SW 1	SW 1 🛒	SW	SW 1	SW ◇1 🛒	SW	SW ◇1 🛒		SW	SW 1 🛒	SW	SW	SW 1	SW 1	SW 1 🛒	SW	SW 1		SW ◇1 🛒
Basingstoke	d					10 16		10 44			11 00		11 10						11 16		11 44				12 00
Hook	d					10 23													11 23						
Winchfield	d					10 27													11 27						
Fleet	d					10 32													11 32						
Farnborough (Main)	d					10 38													11 38						
Alton	d						10 15													11 15					
Bentley	d						10 23													11 23					
Farnham	a						10 28													11 28					
	d						10 30													11 30					
Aldershot	d						10 36													11 36					
Ash Vale	d						10 41													11 41					
Brookwood	d					10 45	10 48												11 45	11 48					
Guildford	d	10 35							10 57	11 06					11 27	11 35						11 57	12 06		
Worplesdon	d																								
Woking	a	10 42				10 50	10 54	11 02	11 05	11 13	11 18		11 28		11 35	11 42			11 50	11 54	12 02	12 05	12 13		12 18
	d	10 45			10 52	10 58		11 04	11 06	11 15	11 20		11 30		11 36	11 45		11 52	11 58		12 04	12 06	12 15		12 20
West Byfleet	d				10 56				11 10						11 40			11 56				12 10			
Byfleet & New Haw	d				11 00				11 13						11 43			12 00				12 13			
Weybridge	d								11 16						11 46							12 16			
Walton-on-Thames	d								11 20						11 50							12 20			
Hersham	d								11 22						11 52							12 22			
Esher	d								11 25						11 55							12 25			
Surbiton 6	a					11 09			11 29						11 59				12 09			12 29			
Wimbledon 6 ⊖	a					11 17			11 37						12 07				12 17			12 37			
Earlsfield	a		←						11 41			←			12 11		←					12 41			
Clapham Junction 10	a	11 04	11 15			11 23		11 27	11 45	11 34	11 39	11 45	11 49		12 15	12 04	12 15		12 23		12 27	12 45	12 34		12 39
	a				12 01				↪						↪			13 01				↪			
Vauxhall ⊖	a		11 20		12 08							11 50					12 20	13 08							
London Waterloo 15 ⊖	a	11 19	11 30		12 13	11 38		11 42		11 49	11 54	12 00	12 03			12 19	12 30	13 13	12 39		12 42		12 49		12 49

Table 155

Sundays

Basingstoke, Alton, Guildford and Woking - Waterloo

Network Diagram - see first Page of Table 155

		SW	SW	SW	SW	SW	SW	SW	SW		SW	SW	SW	SW	SW	SW	SW	SW	SW		SW	SW	SW	SW
			◇■1		■1			■1	■1		■1		■1	◇■1		◇■1		■1				■1	■1	■1
			⏉		⏉						⏉			⏉		⏉		⏉						⏉
Basingstoke	d		12 10					12 16			12 44			13 00		13 10						13 16		13 44
Hook	d							12 23														13 23		
Winchfield	d							12 27														13 27		
Fleet	d							12 32														13 32		
Farnborough (Main)	d							12 38														13 38		
Alton	d								12 15														13 15	
Bentley	d								12 23														13 23	
Farnham	a								12 28														13 28	
	d								12 30														13 30	
Aldershot	d								12 36														13 36	
Ash Vale	d								12 41														13 41	
Brookwood	d							12 45	12 48													13 45	13 48	
Guildford	d			12 27	12 35							12 57	13 05				13 27	13 35						
Worplesdon	d																							
Woking	a		12 28	12 35	12 42			12 50	12 54		13 02	13 05	13 13	13 18		13 28	13 35	13 42				13 50	13 54	14 02
	d		12 30	12 36	12 45		12 52	12 58			13 04	13 06	13 15	13 20		13 30	13 36	13 45			13 52	13 58		14 04
West Byfleet	d			12 40			12 56					13 10					13 40				13 56			
Byfleet & New Haw	d			12 43			13 00					13 13					13 43				14 00			
Weybridge	d			12 46								13 16					13 46							
Walton-on-Thames	d			12 50								13 20					13 50							
Hersham	d			12 52								13 22					13 52							
Esher	d			12 55								13 25					13 55							
Surbiton ■6	a			12 59				13 09				13 29					13 59					14 09		
Wimbledon ■6 ⊖	a			13 07				13 17				13 37					14 07					14 17		
Earlsfield	a	←		13 11		←						13 41			←		14 11		←					
Clapham Junction ■10	a	12 45	12 49	13 15	13 04	13 15		13 23			13 27	13 45	13 34	13 39	13 45	13 49	14 15	14 04	14 15			14 23		14 27
	a			→			14 01					→					→				15 01			
Vauxhall ⊖	a	12 50				13 20	14 08								13 50				14 20		15 08			
London Waterloo ■15 ⊖	a	13 00	13 04		13 14	13 30	14 13	13 39			13 37		13 44	13 49	14 00	13 59		14 14	14 30		15 13	14 34		14 37

		SW	SW	SW	SW	SW		SW	SW	SW	SW	SW	SW	SW	SW	SW		SW	SW	SW	SW	SW	SW	SW	SW
		■1	■1		■1	◇■1		■1		◇■1	■1	■1		■1				■1	■1	■1	■1	■1		■1	◇■1
						⏉				⏉				⏉						⏉					⏉
Basingstoke	d	13 50				14 00				14 10								14 16		14 44	14 50				15 00
Hook	d																	14 23							
Winchfield	d																	14 27							
Fleet	d	14 02																14 32			15 02				
Farnborough (Main)	d	14 08																14 38			15 08				
Alton	d		13 45																14 15			14 45			
Bentley	d																		14 23						
Farnham	a		13 55																14 28			14 55			
	d		14 00																14 30			15 00			
Aldershot	d		14 06																14 36			15 06			
Ash Vale	d		14 11																14 41			15 11			
Brookwood	d	14 15	14 18															14 45	14 48		15 15	15 18			
Guildford	d			13 57	14 05								14 27	14 35									14 57	15 05	
Worplesdon	d							←																	
Woking	a	14 20	14 24	14 05	14 13	14 18		14 20		14 28			14 35	14 42				14 50	14 54	15 02	15 20	15 24	15 05	15 13	15 18
	d	14 28		14 06	14 15	14 20		14 28		14 30			14 36	14 45		14 52		14 58		15 04	15 28		15 06	15 15	15 20
West Byfleet	d	→		14 10									14 40			14 56					→		15 10		
Byfleet & New Haw	d			14 13									14 43			15 00							15 13		
Weybridge	d			14 16				14 34					14 46										15 16		
Walton-on-Thames	d			14 20				14 38					14 50										15 20		
Hersham	d			14 22									14 52										15 22		
Esher	d			14 25									14 55										15 25		
Surbiton ■6	a			14 29				14 45					14 59					15 09					15 29		
Wimbledon ■6 ⊖	a			14 37				14 53					15 07					15 17					15 37		
Earlsfield	a			14 41					←		←	←	15 11		←								15 41		
Clapham Junction ■10	a			14 45	14 34	14 39		14 59	14 45	14 49	14 59	14 59	15 15	15 04	15 15			15 23		15 27			15 45	15 34	15 39
	a			→				→					→			16 01							→		
Vauxhall ⊖	a								14 50						15 20	16 08									
London Waterloo ■15 ⊖	a				14 44	14 49			14 55	14 59	15 10	15 10		15 14	15 25	16 13		15 34		15 37				15 44	15 49

Table 155

Sundays

Basingstoke, Alton, Guildford and Woking - Waterloo

Network Diagram - see first Page of Table 155

		SW		SW	SW	SW	SW	SW	SW	SW	SW	SW	SW		SW	SW	SW	SW	SW	SW	SW	SW	SW		SW
		1			◇1 ⚲	1	1		1 ⚲			1	1		1 ⚲	1	1		1	◇1 ⚲	1		◇1 ⚲		1
Basingstoke	d				15 10							15 16			15 44	15 50				16 00			16 10		
Hook	d											15 23													
Winchfield	d											15 27													
Fleet	d											15 32				16 02									
Farnborough (Main)	d											15 38				16 08									
Alton	d												15 15				15 45								
Bentley	d												15 23												
Farnham	a												15 28				15 55								
	d												15 30				16 00								
Aldershot	d												15 36				16 06								
Ash Vale	d												15 41				16 11								
Brookwood	d											15 45	15 48			16 15	16 18								
Guildford	d							15 27	15 35									15 57	16 05						
Worplesdon	d	←																			←				
Woking	a	15 20			15 28			15 35	15 42			15 50	15 54		16 02	16 20	16 24	16 05	16 13	16 18	16 20		16 28		
	d	15 28			15 30			15 36	15 45		15 52	15 58			16 04	16 28		16 06	16 15	16 20	16 28		16 30		
West Byfleet	d							15 40			15 56					↪		16 10							
Byfleet & New Haw	d							15 43			16 00							16 13							
Weybridge	d	15 34						15 46										16 16			16 34				
Walton-on-Thames	d	15 38						15 50										16 20			16 38				
Hersham	d							15 52										16 22							
Esher	d							15 55										16 25							
Surbiton 6	a	15 45						15 59				16 09						16 29			16 45				
Wimbledon 6 ⊖	a	15 53						16 07				16 17						16 37			16 53				
Earlsfield	a			←		←	←	16 11		←								16 41				←			←
Clapham Junction 10	a	15 59		15 45	15 49	15 59	15 59	16 15	16 04	16 15		16 23			16 27			16 45	16 34	16 39	16 59	16 45	16 49		16 59
	a	↪						↪			17 01							↪			↪				
Vauxhall ⊖	a			15 50						16 20	17 08											16 50			
London Waterloo 15 ⊖	a			15 55	15 59	16 10	16 10		16 14	16 25	17 13	16 34			16 37				16 44	16 49		16 55	16 59		17 10

		SW	SW	SW	SW	SW	SW	SW	SW		SW	SW	SW	SW	SW	SW	SW	SW	SW		SW	SW	SW	SW	SW
		1		1 ⚲			1	1	1 ⚲		1	1		1	◇1 ⚲	1		◇1 ⚲	1		1		1 ⚲		
Basingstoke	d						16 16		16 44		16 50				17 00			17 10							
Hook	d						16 23																		
Winchfield	d						16 27																		
Fleet	d						16 32				17 02														
Farnborough (Main)	d						16 38				17 08														
Alton	d							16 15				16 45													
Bentley	d							16 23																	
Farnham	a							16 28				16 55													
	d							16 30				17 00													
Aldershot	d							16 36				17 06													
Ash Vale	d							16 41				17 11													
Brookwood	d						16 45	16 48			17 15	17 18													
Guildford	d		16 27	16 35									16 57	17 05								17 27	17 35		
Worplesdon	d															←									
Woking	a		16 35	16 42			16 50	16 54	17 02		17 20	17 24	17 05	17 13	17 18	17 20		17 28				17 35	17 42		
	d		16 36	16 45		16 52	16 58		17 04		17 28		17 06	17 15	17 20	17 28		17 30				17 36	17 45		17 52
West Byfleet	d		16 40			16 56					↪		17 10									17 40			17 56
Byfleet & New Haw	d		16 43			17 00							17 13									17 43			18 00
Weybridge	d		16 46										17 16			17 34						17 46			
Walton-on-Thames	d		16 50										17 20			17 38						17 50			
Hersham	d		16 52										17 22									17 52			
Esher	d		16 55										17 25									17 55			
Surbiton 6	a		16 59				17 09						17 29			17 45						17 59			
Wimbledon 6 ⊖	a		17 07				17 17						17 37			17 53						18 07			
Earlsfield	a	←	17 11		←								17 41				←		←		←	18 11		←	
Clapham Junction 10	a	16 59	17 15	17 04	17 15		17 23		17 27				17 45	17 34	17 39	17 59	17 45	17 49	17 59		17 59	18 15	18 04	18 15	
	a		↪			18 01							↪			↪						↪			19 01
Vauxhall ⊖	a				17 20	18 08											17 50							18 20	19 08
London Waterloo 15 ⊖	a	17 10		17 14	17 25	18 13	17 34		17 37					17 44	17 49		17 55	17 59	18 10		18 10		18 14	18 25	19 13

Table 155

Sundays

Basingstoke, Alton, Guildford and Woking - Waterloo

Network Diagram - see first Page of Table 155

		SW 1	SW 1	SW 1 ⊥	SW 1	SW 1		SW	SW 1	SW ◇1 ⊥	SW 1	SW	SW ◇1 ⊥	SW 1	SW 1	SW		SW 1 ⊥	SW	SW	SW 1	SW 1	SW 1	SW 1	SW 1
Basingstoke	d	17 16		17 44	17 50					18 00			18 10								18 16		18 44	18 50	
Hook	d	17 23																			18 23				
Winchfield	d	17 27																			18 27				
Fleet	d	17 32			18 02																18 32			19 02	
Farnborough (Main)	d	17 38			18 08																18 38			19 08	
Alton	d		17 15			17 45																18 15			18 45
Bentley	d		17 23																			18 23			
Farnham	a		17 28			17 55																18 28			18 55
	d		17 30			18 00																18 30			19 00
Aldershot	d		17 36			18 06																18 36			19 06
Ash Vale	d		17 41			18 11																18 41			19 11
Brookwood	d	17 45	17 48		18 15	18 18															18 45	18 48		19 15	19 18
Guildford	d							17 57	18 05							18 27		18 35							
Worplesdon	d										←														
Woking	a	17 50	17 54	18 02	18 20	18 24		18 05	18 13	18 18	18 20		18 28			18 35		18 42			18 50	18 54	19 02	19 20	19 24
	d	17 58		18 04	18 28			18 06	18 15	18 20	18 28		18 30			18 36		18 45		18 52	18 58		19 04	19 28	
West Byfleet	d				→			18 10								18 40				18 56				→	
Byfleet & New Haw	d							18 13								18 43				19 00					
Weybridge	d							18 16			18 34					18 46									
Walton-on-Thames	d							18 20			18 38					18 50									
Hersham	d							18 22								18 52									
Esher	d							18 25								18 55									
Surbiton 6	a	18 09						18 29			18 45					18 59					19 09				
Wimbledon 6	⊖ a	18 17						18 37			18 53					19 07					19 17				
Earlsfield	a							18 41				←		←	←	19 11			←						
Clapham Junction 10	a	18 23		18 27				18 45	18 34	18 39	18 59	18 45	18 49	18 59	18 59	19 15		19 04	19 15		19 23		19 27		
	a							→			→					→				20 01					
Vauxhall	⊖ a											18 50							19 20	20 08					
London Waterloo 15	⊖ a	18 34		18 37					18 44	18 49		18 55	18 59	19 10	19 10			19 14	19 25	20 13	19 34		19 37		

		SW		SW 1	SW ◇1 ⊥	SW 1	SW	SW ◇1 ⊥	SW 1	SW 1	SW	SW 1 ⊥		SW	SW	SW 1	SW 1	SW 1	SW 1	SW 1	SW	SW 1		SW ◇1 ⊥	SW 1
Basingstoke	d				19 00			19 10								19 16		19 44	19 50					20 00	
Hook	d															19 23									
Winchfield	d															19 27									
Fleet	d															19 32			20 02						
Farnborough (Main)	d															19 38			20 08						
Alton	d																19 15			19 45					
Bentley	d																19 23								
Farnham	a																19 28			19 55					
	d																19 30			20 00					
Aldershot	d																19 36			20 06					
Ash Vale	d																19 41			20 11					
Brookwood	d															19 45	19 48		20 15	20 18					
Guildford	d	18 57		19 05							19 27	19 35									19 57	20 05			
Worplesdon	d					←																			←
Woking	a	19 05		19 13	19 18	19 20		19 28			19 35	19 42				19 50	19 54	20 02	20 20	20 24	20 05	20 13		20 18	20 20
	d	19 06		19 15	19 20	19 28		19 30			19 36	19 45			19 52	19 58		20 04	20 28		20 06	20 15		20 20	20 28
West Byfleet	d	19 10									19 40				19 56				→		20 10				
Byfleet & New Haw	d	19 13									19 43				20 00						20 13				
Weybridge	d	19 16				19 34					19 46										20 16				20 34
Walton-on-Thames	d	19 20				19 38					19 50										20 20				20 38
Hersham	d	19 22									19 52										20 22				
Esher	d	19 25									19 55										20 25				
Surbiton 6	a	19 29				19 45					19 59					20 09					20 29				20 45
Wimbledon 6	⊖ a	19 37				19 53					20 07					20 17					20 37				20 53
Earlsfield	a	19 41					←		←	←	20 11			←							20 41				
Clapham Junction 10	a	19 45		19 34	19 39	19 59	19 45	19 49	19 59	19 59	20 15	20 04		20 15		20 23		20 27			20 45	20 34		20 39	20 59
	a	→				→					→				21 01						→				→
Vauxhall	⊖ a						19 50							20 20	21 08										
London Waterloo 15	⊖ a			19 44	19 49		19 55	19 59	20 10	20 10		20 14		20 25	21 13	20 34		20 37				20 44		20 49	

Table 155

Sundays

Basingstoke, Alton, Guildford and Woking - Waterloo

Network Diagram - see first Page of Table 155

		SW	SW ◇1 🚲	SW 1	SW 1	SW	SW 1	SW		SW	SW 1	SW 1	SW 1	SW 1	SW 1	SW	SW 1	SW ◇1 🚲		SW 1	SW	SW ◇1 🚲	SW 1	SW 1	SW
Basingstoke	d		20 10								20 16		20 44	20 50				21 00				21 10			
Hook	d										20 23														
Winchfield	d										20 27														
Fleet	d										20 32			21 02											
Farnborough (Main)	d										20 38			21 08											
Alton	d											20 15			20 45										
Bentley	d											20 23													
Farnham	a											20 28			20 55										
	d											20 30			21 00										
Aldershot	d											20 36			21 06										
Ash Vale	d											20 41			21 11										
Brookwood	d										20 45	20 48		21 15	21 18										
Guildford	d					20 27	20 35									20 57	21 05								21 27
Worplesdon	d																			←					
Woking	a		20 28			20 35	20 42				20 50	20 54	21 02	21 20	21 24	21 05	21 13	21 18		21 20		21 28			21 35
	d		20 30			20 36	20 45			20 52	20 58		21 04	21 28		21 06	21 15	21 20		21 28		21 30			21 36
West Byfleet	d					20 40				20 56					↪	21 10									21 40
Byfleet & New Haw	d					20 43				21 00						21 13									21 43
Weybridge	d					20 46										21 16				21 34					21 46
Walton-on-Thames	d					20 50										21 20				21 38					21 50
Hersham	d					20 52										21 22									21 52
Esher	d					20 55										21 25									21 55
Surbiton 6	a					20 59					21 09					21 29				21 45					21 59
Wimbledon 6 ⊖	a					21 07					21 17					21 37				21 53					22 07
Earlsfield	a	←		←	←	21 11		←								21 41					←		←	←	22 11
Clapham Junction 10	a	20 45	20 49	20 59	20 59	21 15	21 04	21 15			21 23		21 27			21 45	21 34	21 39		21 59	21 45	21 49	21 59	21 59	22 15
	a					↪				22 01						↪				↪					↪
Vauxhall ⊖	a	20 50						21 20		22 08											21 50				
London Waterloo 15 ⊖	a	20 55	20 59	21 10	21 10		21 14	21 25		22 13	21 34		21 37				21 44	21 49			21 55	21 59	22 10	22 10	

		SW 1	SW	SW		SW 1	SW 1	SW 1	SW	SW 1	SW	SW 1	SW 1	SW ◇1		SW 1	SW 1	SW	SW 1	SW	SW	SW 1	SW 1	SW 1	
Basingstoke	d					21 16		21 44				21 50		22 10								22 16		22 44	
Hook	d					21 23																22 23			
Winchfield	d					21 27																22 27			
Fleet	d					21 32						22 02										22 32			
Farnborough (Main)	d					21 38						22 08										22 38			
Alton	d						21 15						21 45										22 15		
Bentley	d						21 23																22 23		
Farnham	a						21 28						21 55										22 28		
	d						21 30						22 00										22 30		
Aldershot	d						21 36						22 06										22 36		
Ash Vale	d						21 41						22 11										22 41		
Brookwood	d					21 45	21 48					22 15	22 18									22 45	22 48		
Guildford	d	21 35							21 57	22 05								22 27	22 35						
Worplesdon	d																								
Woking	a	21 42				21 50	21 54	22 02	22 05	22 13		22 21	22 24	22 28				22 35	22 42			22 50	22 54	23 02	
	d	21 45		21 52		21 58		22 04	22 06	22 15		22 28		22 30				22 36	22 45		22 52	22 58		23 04	
West Byfleet	d			21 56					22 10									22 40			22 56				
Byfleet & New Haw	d			22 00					22 13									22 43			23 00				
Weybridge	d								22 16			22 34						22 46							
Walton-on-Thames	d								22 20			22 38						22 50							
Hersham	d								22 22									22 52							
Esher	d								22 25									22 55							
Surbiton 6	a					22 09			22 29			22 45						22 59				23 09			
Wimbledon 6 ⊖	a					22 17			22 37			22 53						23 07				23 17			
Earlsfield	a		←						22 41		←					←	←	23 11		←					
Clapham Junction 10	a	22 04	22 15			22 23		22 27	22 45	22 34	22 45	22 59		22 49		22 59	22 59	23 15	23 04	23 15		23 23		23 27	
	a			23 01					↪			↪						↪			00 01				
Vauxhall ⊖	a		22 20	23 08							22 50									23 20	00 08				
London Waterloo 15 ⊖	a	22 14	22 25	23 13		22 34		22 37		22 44	22 55			22 59		23 10	23 10		23 14	23 25	00 13	23 34		23 37	

Table 155

Sundays

Basingstoke, Alton, Guildford and Woking - Waterloo

Network Diagram - see first Page of Table 155

		SW	SW 1	SW	SW 1	SW 1	SW 1	SW 1	SW ◇1
Basingstoke	d						23 16		23 44
Hook	d						23 23		
Winchfield	d						23 27		
Fleet	d						23 32		
Farnborough (Main)	d						23 38		
Alton	d				22 45			23 15	
Bentley	d							23 23	
Farnham	a				22 55			23 28	
	d				23 00			23 30	
Aldershot	d				23 06			23 36	
Ash Vale	d				23 11			23 41	
Brookwood	d				23 18		23 45	23 48	
Guildford	d	22 57	23 05			23 35			
Worplesdon	d								
Woking	a	23 05	23 13		23 24	23 42	23 50	23 54	00 02
	d	23 06	23 15		23 28	23 45			00 04
West Byfleet	d	23 10							
Byfleet & New Haw	d	23 13							
Weybridge	d	23 16			23 34				
Walton-on-Thames	d	23 20			23 38				
Hersham	d	23 22							
Esher	d	23 25							
Surbiton 6	a	23 29			23 45				
Wimbledon 6 ⊖	a	23 37			23 53				
Earlsfield	a	23 41		⟵					
Clapham Junction 10	a	23 45	23 34	23 45	23 59	00 04			00 23
	a	⟶							
Vauxhall ⊖	a			23 50					
London Waterloo 15 ⊖	a		23 44	23 55	00 10	00 14			00 33

Table 156

Mondays to Fridays

London - Guildford, Haslemere and Portsmouth

Network Diagram - see first Page of Table 155

Miles			SW MX ■1	SW MO ■1	SW MX ■1	SW MO ■1	SW MX ■1	SW MO ■1	SW MX ■1	SW MO ■1	SW ■1		SW ■1	SW ■1	SW ■1	SW ■1	SW ■1	SW ■1	SW ■1 🛒	SW ■1	SW ■1		SW ■1 🛒	SW ■1	SW ■1
0	**London Waterloo** ■15 ⊖	d	22p30	22p30	22p45	23p00	23p15	23p30	23p45	00 50				05 00	05 20	06 15	06 45	07 15	07 30		07 45		08 00		08 15
4	Clapham Junction ■10	d		22b39	22b52	23b09	23b22	23b39	23b52	00 57				05 11	05 29	06u22	06u52	07u23			07u52				08u22
24½	**Woking**	a	22p54	23p01	23p11	23p31	23p41	00 01	00 11	01 16				05 51	06 08	06 41	07 11	07 42	07 54		08 12		08 24		08 42
—		d	22p55	23p02	23p13	23p32	23p43	00 03	00 13	01 18				05 53	06 11	06 43	07 13	07 44	07 55		08 14		08 25		08 44
26¾	Worplesdon	d			23p18				00 18						06 16	06 48	07 18	07 49			08 19				08 49
30¼	**Guildford**	a	23p03	23p10	23p23	23p40	23p51	00 10	00 24	01s26				06 00	06 21	06 53	07 23	07 54	08 03		08 24		08 35		08 54
—		d	23p04	23p12	23p25	23p42	23p52	00 12	00 25				05 15	06 04	06 30	06 55	07 25	07 56	08 04		08 26		08 39		08 56
33½	Farncombe	d	23p10		23p31	23p48	23p58		00 31					06 10	06 36	07 01	07 31	08 02			08 32				09 02
34½	Godalming	d	23p13		23p34	23p51	00 02		00 34					06 13	06 39	07 04	07 34	08 05	08 11		08 35				09 05
36¼	Milford (Surrey)	d			23p38	23p55			00s38					06 17	06 43	07 08	07 38	08 09			08 39				09 09
38½	Witley	d			23p42	23p59			00s43					06 21	06 47	07 12	07 42	08 13		←	08 43			←	09 13
43	**Haslemere** ■4	a	23p24	23p26	23p49	00 06	00 12	00 26	00 49				05 29	06 28	06 54	07 19	07 49	08 20	08 24	08 20	08 50		08 54	08 50	09 20
—		d	23p25	23p27	23p50	00 07	00 13	00 27	00 50				05 30	06 28	06 55	07 20	07 53	08 30	08 25	08 30	08 58		08 55	08 58	
46¾	Liphook	d			23p55	00 12			00s55				05 35	06 33	07 00	07 25	07 59	→		08 35	→			09 03	
51½	Liss	d			00 01	00 18			01s01				05 41	06 39	07 06	07 31	08 05			08 41				09 09	
55	Petersfield	d	23p36	23p38	00 06	00 23	00 24	00 38	01 06				05 46	06 45	07 11	07 36	08 11		08 36	08 46			09 06	09 15	
63¼	Rowlands Castle	d			00 16	00 33			01s16				05 56	06 54	07 21	07 46	08 21			08 56				09 24	
66½	**Havant**	a	23p48	23p50	00 21	00 38	00 36	00 50	01 21	02s00			06 01	06 59	07 27	07 51	08 26		08 49	09 04			09 19	09 29	
—		d	23p49	23p51	00 22	00 39	00 37	00 51	01 21		04 40		06 02	07 00	07 28	07 52	08 27		08 50	09 05			09 20	09 30	
67¼	Bedhampton	a			00 24	00 41			01s24		04 42		06 04	07 02	07 30	07 54	08 29			09 07				09 32	
70½	Hilsea	a			00 30				01s29		04 48		06 10	07 08	07 37	08 00	08 35			09 13				09 38	
72¾	Fratton	a	23p58	23p59	00 34	00 49	00 46	01 00	01s33	02s10	04 52		06 14	07 12	07 41	08 04	08 39		08 58	09 17			09 28	09 42	
73¾	**Portsmouth & Southsea**	a	00 02	00 04	00 38	00 53	00 50	01 04	01 37	02s14	04 55		06 18	07 16	07 46	08 07	08 43		09 02	09 20			09 32	09 46	
74½	**Portsmouth Harbour** ⛴	a	00 07	00 09		00 58	00 55	01 09		02 19	04 59		06 22	07 20		08 12	08 48		09 07	09 26			09 37		

		SW ■1 🛒	SW ■1	SW ■1 🛒	SW ■1	SW ■1	SW ■1 🛒		SW ■1	SW ■1 🛒	SW ■1	SW ■1	SW ■1 🛒	SW ■1	SW ■1 🛒	SW ■1	SW ■1		SW ■1 🛒	SW ■1	SW ■1 🛒	SW ■1	SW ■1	SW ■1 🛒	SW ■1
London Waterloo ■15 ⊖	d	08 30	08 45	09 00		09 15	09 30		09 45	10 00		10 15	10 30	10 45	11 00		11 15		11 30	11 45	12 00		12 15	12 30	12 45
Clapham Junction ■10	d		08u52			09u22			09u52			10u22		10u52			11u22			11u52			12u22		12u52
Woking	a	08 55	09 11	09 24		09 42	09 54		10 11	10 24		10 41	10 54	11 11	11 24		11 41		11 54	12 11	12 24		12 41	12 54	13 11
	d	08 55	09 13	09 25		09 43	09 55		10 13	10 25		10 43	10 55	11 13	11 25		11 43		11 55	12 13	12 25		12 43	12 55	13 13
Worplesdon	d		09 18						10 18					11 18						12 18					13 18
Guildford	a	09 05	09 23	09 33		09 52	10 03		10 23	10 33		10 50	11 03	11 23	11 33		11 50		12 03	12 23	12 33		12 50	13 03	13 23
	d	09 07	09 25	09 34		09 54	10 04		10 25	10 34		10 52	11 04	11 25	11 34		11 52		12 04	12 25	12 34		12 52	13 04	13 25
Farncombe	d		09 31			10 00			10 31			10 58		11 31			11 58			12 31			12 58		13 31
Godalming	d		09 34			10 03			10 34			11 01		11 34			12 01			12 34			13 01		13 34
Milford (Surrey)	d					10 07						11 05					12 05						13 05		
Witley	d				←	10 11					←	11 09				←	12 09					←	13 09		
Haslemere ■4	a	09 24	09 45	09 49	09 45	10 19	10 22		10 45	10 49	10 45	11 16	11 20	11 45	11 49	11 45	12 16		12 20	12 45	12 49	12 45	13 16	13 20	13 45
	d	09 25	09 55	09 50	09 55		10 23		10 55	10 50	10 55		11 21	11 55	11 50	11 55			12 21	12 55	12 50	12 55		13 21	13 55
Liphook	d		→		10 00				→		11 00			→		12 00				→		13 00			→
Liss	d				10 06						11 06					12 06						13 06			
Petersfield	d	09 36		10 01	10 11		10 34			11 01	11 11		11 32		12 01	12 11			12 32		13 01	13 11		13 32	
Rowlands Castle	d				10 21						11 21					12 21						13 21			
Havant	a	09 49		10 15	10 26		10 49			11 15	11 26		11 49		12 15	12 26			12 49		13 15	13 26		13 49	
	d	09 50		10 16	10 27		10 50			11 16	11 27		11 50		12 16	12 27			12 50		13 16	13 27		13 50	
Bedhampton	a				10 29						11 29					12 29						13 29			
Hilsea	a				10 36						11 36					12 36						13 36			
Fratton	a	09 59		10 24	10 40		10 59			11 24	11 40		11 59		12 24	12 40			12 59		13 24	13 40		13 59	
Portsmouth & Southsea	a	10 02		10 28	10 44		11 02			11 28	11 44		12 02		12 28	12 44			13 02		13 28	13 44		14 02	
Portsmouth Harbour ⛴	a	10 07		10 33			11 07			11 33			12 07		12 33				13 07		13 33			14 07	

		SW ■1 🛒	SW ■1		SW ■1	SW ■1 🛒	SW ■1	SW ■1 🛒	SW ■1	SW ■1	SW ■1 🛒	SW ■1	SW ■1 🛒		SW ■1	SW ■1	SW ■1 🛒	SW ■1	SW ■1	SW ■1 🛒	SW ■1	SW ■1	SW ■1 🛒		SW ■1
London Waterloo ■15 ⊖	d	13 00			13 15	13 30	13 45	14 00		14 15	14 30	14 45	15 00			15 15	15 30		15 45	16 00		16 15	16 30		
Clapham Junction ■10	d				13u22		13u52			14u22		14u52				15u22			15u52			16u22			
Woking	a	13 24			13 41	13 54	14 11	14 24		14 41	14 54	15 11	15 24			15 41	15 54		16 11	16 24		16 41	16 54		
	d	13 25			13 43	13 55	14 13	14 25		14 43	14 55	15 13	15 25			15 43	15 55		16 13	16 25		16 43	16 55		
Worplesdon	d						14 18					15 18				15 48						16 48			
Guildford	a	13 33			13 50	14 03	14 23	14 33		14 50	15 03	15 23	15 33			15 53	16 03		16 20	16 33		16 53	17 03		
	d	13 34			13 52	14 04	14 25	14 34		14 52	15 04	15 25	15 34			15 55	16 04		16 22	16 34		16 55	17 04		
Farncombe	d				13 58		14 31			14 58		15 31				16 01			16 28			17 01			
Godalming	d				14 01		14 34			15 01		15 34				16 04			16 31			17 04			
Milford (Surrey)	d				14 05					15 05						16 08			16 35			17 08			
Witley	d		←		14 09				←	15 09					←	16 12		←	16 39		←	17 12			←
Haslemere ■4	a	13 49	13 45		14 16	14 20	14 45	14 49	14 45	15 16	15 20	15 45	15 49		15 45	16 19	16 23	16 19	16 46	16 50	16 46	17 19	17 23		17 19
	d	13 50	13 55			14 21	14 55	14 50	14 55		15 21	15 55	15 50		15 55	16 29	16 24	16 29	16 55	16 51	16 55	17 29	17 24		17 29
Liphook	d		14 00				→		15 00			→			16 00	→		16 34	→		17 00	→			17 34
Liss	d		14 06						15 06						16 06			16 40			17 06				17 40
Petersfield	d	14 01	14 11			14 32		15 01	15 11		15 32		16 01		16 11		16 35	16 45		17 02	17 11		17 35		17 45
Rowlands Castle	d		14 21						15 21						16 21			16 55			17 21				17 55
Havant	a	14 15	14 26			14 49		15 14	15 26		15 49		16 15		16 26		16 49	17 03		17 15	17 26		17 49		18 03
	d	14 16	14 27			14 50		15 16	15 27		15 50		16 16		16 27		16 50	17 04		17 16	17 27		17 50		18 04
Bedhampton	a		14 29						15 29						16 29			17 06			17 29				18 07
Hilsea	a		14 36						15 36						16 36			17 11			17 36				18 12
Fratton	a	14 24	14 40			14 58		15 24	15 40		15 59		16 24		16 40		16 59	17 15		17 24	17 40		17 59		18 16
Portsmouth & Southsea	a	14 28	14 44			15 02		15 28	15 44		16 02		16 28		16 44		17 02	17 20		17 28	17 44		18 02		18 20
Portsmouth Harbour ⛴	a	14 33				15 07		15 33			16 07		16 33		16 49		17 07	17 26		17 35			18 09		18 28

b Previous night, stops to pick up only

London - Guildford, Haslemere and Portsmouth

Network Diagram - see first Page of Table 155

		SW 1	SW 1 🚲	SW 1	SW 1	SW 1 🚲	SW 1	SW 1	SW 1 🚲		SW 1	SW 1	SW 1	SW 1 🚲	SW 1	SW 1 🚲	SW 1	SW 1	SW 1 🚲		SW 1	SW 1	SW 1 🚲	SW 1	SW 1
London Waterloo 15 ⊖	d	16 45	17 00		17 15	17 30		17 45	18 00			18 15	18 18	18 30	18 45	19 00		19 15	19 30			19 45	20 00		20 15
Clapham Junction 10	d	16u52																19u22				19u52			20u22
Woking	a	17 11	17 24		17 38	17 54							18 42	18 57	19 13	19 24		19 43	19 54			20 11	20 24		20 41
	d	17 13	17 25		17 40	17 56							18 43	18 58	19 14	19 25		19 45	19 55			20 13	20 25		20 43
Worplesdon	d		17 30		17 45	18 00							18 48			19 30						20 18			
Guildford	a	17 20	17 36		17 51	18 06		18 21	18 32			18 50	18 54	19 06	19 23	19 36		19 52	20 03			20 23	20 33		20 50
	d	17 22	17 37		17 54	18 08		18 23	18 33			18 51	18 57	19 08	19 24	19 37		19 54	20 04			20 25	20 34		20 52
Farncombe	d	17 28			18 00			18 29					19 03		19 30			20 00				20 31	20 40		20 58
Godalming	d	17 31			18 03	18 15		18 32	18 40				19 06	19 14	19 33			20 03	20 11			20 34	20 43		21 01
Milford (Surrey)	d	17 35			18 07			18 36					19 10		19 37			20 07				20 38			21 05
Witley	d	17 39		←	18 11		←	18 40			←		19 14		19 41		←	20 11			←	20 42		←	21 09
Haslemere 4	a	17 46	17 51	17 46	18 18	18 25	18 18	18 49	18 51		18 49	19 05	19 23	19 25	19 49	19 52	19 49	20 18	20 22		20 18	20 49	20 54	20 49	21 16
	d	17 56	17 52	17 56	18 31	18 26	18 31	18 56	18 52		18 56	19 06		19 26	19 57	19 53	19 57	20 27	20 22		20 27	20 59	20 55	20 59	
Liphook	d	→		18 01	→		18 36	→			19 01	19 11			→		20 02	→			20 32	→		21 04	
Liss	d			18 07			18 42				19 07	19 17					20 08				20 38			21 10	
Petersfield	d		18 03	18 12		18 37	18 47		19 03		19 12	19 23		19 37		20 04	20 13		20 33		20 43		21 06	21 16	
Rowlands Castle	d			18 22			18 57				19 22	19 32					20 23				20 53			21 25	
Havant	a		18 19	18 29		18 50	19 02		19 16		19 29	19 40		19 50		20 16	20 28		20 48		21 00		21 18	21 30	
	d		18 20	18 30		18 51	19 03		19 17			19 41		19 51		20 17	20 29		20 49				21 19	21 31	
Bedhampton	a			18 32			19 06					19 44					20 31							21 34	
Hilsea	a			18 39			19 11					19 49					20 37							21 41	
Fratton	a		18 28	18 43		18 59	19 15		19 25			19 55		19 59		20 25	20 41		20 57				21 28	21 45	
Portsmouth & Southsea	a		18 32	18 46		19 03			19 29					20 03		20 29	20 44		21 01				21 32	21 48	
Portsmouth Harbour ⛴	a		18 39			19 10			19 36					20 10		20 34	20 52		21 06				21 37		

		SW 1 🚲	SW 1	SW 1 🚲	SW 1		SW 1 🚲	SW 1	SW 1	SW 1	SW 1	SW 1	SW 1	SW 1
London Waterloo 15 ⊖	d	20 30	20 45	21 00			21 30	21 45	22 00		22 30	22 45	23 15	23 45
Clapham Junction 10	d		20u52					21u52				22u52	23u22	23u52
Woking	a	20 54	21 11	21 24			21 54	22 11	22 24		22 54	23 11	23 41	00 11
	d	20 55	21 13	21 25			21 55	22 13	22 25		22 55	23 13	23 43	00 13
Worplesdon	d		21 18					22 18				23 18		00 18
Guildford	a	21 03	21 23	21 33			22 03	22 23	22 33		23 03	23 23	23 51	00 24
	d	21 04	21 25	21 34			22 04	22 25	22 34		23 04	23 25	23 52	00 25
Farncombe	d		21 31	21 40			22 10	22 31	22 40		23 10	23 31	23 58	00 31
Godalming	d	21 11	21 34	21 43			22 13	22 34	22 43		23 13	23 34	00 02	00 34
Milford (Surrey)	d		21 38					22 38				23 38		00s38
Witley	d		21 42		←			22 42		←		23 42		00s43
Haslemere 4	a	21 21	21 49	21 54	21 49		22 24	22 49	22 54	22 49	23 24	23 49	00 12	00 49
	d	21 22	21 59	21 55	21 59		22 25	22 59	22 55	22 59	23 25	23 50	00 13	00 50
Liphook	d		→		22 04			→		23 04		23 55		00s55
Liss	d				22 10					23 10		00 01		01s01
Petersfield	d	21 33		22 06	22 16		22 36		23 06	23 15	23 36	00 06	00 24	01 06
Rowlands Castle	d				22 25					23 25		00 16		01s16
Havant	a	21 45		22 18	22 30		22 48		23 18	23 30	23 48	00 21	00 36	01 21
	d	21 46		22 19	22 31		22 49		23 19	23 31	23 49	00 22	00 37	01 21
Bedhampton	a				22 34					23 33		00 24		01s24
Hilsea	a				22 39					23 39		00 30		01s29
Fratton	a	21 54		22 28	22 43		22 59		23 28	23 43	23 58	00 34	00 46	01s33
Portsmouth & Southsea	a	21 58		22 32	22 47		23 04		23 32	23 47	00 02	00 38	00 50	01 37
Portsmouth Harbour ⛴	a	22 02		22 37			23 08		23 37		00 07		00 55	

Saturdays

		SW 1	SW 1	SW 1	SW 1	SW 1	SW 1	SW 1	SW 1	SW 1		SW 1	SW 1	SW 1	SW 1	SW 1	SW 1	SW 1	SW 1	SW 1		SW 1 🚲	SW 1	SW 1	SW 1 🚲
London Waterloo 15 ⊖	d	22p30	22p45	23p15	23p45			05 00	05 20	06 15		06 45	07 15	07 30	07 45	08 00		08 15	08 30	08 45		09 00		09 15	09 30
Clapham Junction 10	d		22b52	23b22	23b52			05 11	05 29	06u22		06u52	07u23		07u52			08u22		08u52				09u22	
Woking	a	22p54	23p11	23p41	00 11			05 51	06 08	06 41		07 11	07 42	07 54	08 11	08 24		08 41	08 54	09 11		09 24		09 41	09 54
	d	22p55	23p13	23p43	00 13			05 53	06 13	06 43		07 13	07 44	07 55	08 13	08 25		08 43	08 55	09 13		09 25		09 43	09 55
Worplesdon	d		23p18		00 18				06 18			07 18			08 18					09 18					
Guildford	a	23p03	23p23	23p51	00 24			06 00	06 23	06 51		07 23	07 51	08 03	08 23	08 33		08 50	09 03	09 23		09 33		09 50	10 03
	d	23p04	23p25	23p52	00 25		05 15	06 02	06 25	06 53		07 25	07 53	08 04	08 25	08 34		08 52	09 04	09 25		09 34		09 52	10 04
Farncombe	d	23p10	23p31	23p58	00 31			06 08	06 31	06 59		07 31	07 59		08 31			08 58		09 31				09 58	
Godalming	d	23p13	23p34	00 02	00 34			06 11	06 34	07 02		07 34	08 02		08 34			09 01		09 34				10 01	
Milford (Surrey)	d		23p38		00s38			06 15		07 06			08 06					09 05						10 05	
Witley	d		23p42		00s43			06 19		07 10			08 10				←	09 09					←	10 09	
Haslemere 4	a	23p24	23p49	00 12	00 49		05 29	06 26	06 44	07 17		07 44	08 17	08 20	08 45	08 49	08 45	09 16	09 20	09 45		09 49	09 45	10 16	10 20
	d	23p25	23p50	00 13	00 50		05 30		06 45			07 45		08 21	08 55	08 50	08 55		09 21	09 55		09 50	09 55		10 21
Liphook	d		23p55		00s55		05 35		06 50			07 50			→		09 00			→			10 00		
Liss	d		00 01		01s01		05 41		06 56			07 56					09 06						10 06		
Petersfield	d	23p36	00 06	00 24	01 06		05 46		07 01			08 01		08 32		09 01	09 11		09 32			10 01	10 11		10 32
Rowlands Castle	d		00 16		01s16		05 56		07 11			08 11					09 21						10 21		
Havant	a	23p48	00 21	00 36	01 21		06 01		07 19			08 16		08 49		09 15	09 26		09 49			10 15	10 26		10 49
	d	23p49	00 22	00 37	01 21	04 40	06 02		07 20			08 17		08 50		09 16	09 27		09 50			10 16	10 27		10 50
Bedhampton	a		00 24		01s24	04 42	06 04		07 22			08 19					09 29						10 29		
Hilsea	a		00 30		01s29	04 48	06 10		07 27			08 25					09 36						10 36		
Fratton	a	23p58	00 34	00 46	01s33	04 52	06 14		07 31			08 29		08 59		09 24	09 40		09 59			10 24	10 40		10 59
Portsmouth & Southsea	a	00 02	00 38	00 50	01 37	04 55	06 18		07 35			08 32		09 02		09 28	09 44		10 02			10 28	10 44		11 02
Portsmouth Harbour ⛴	a	00 07		00 55		05 00	06 22		07 40			08 37		09 07		09 33			10 07			10 33			11 07

b Previous night, stops to pick up only

Table 156

Saturdays

London - Guildford, Haslemere and Portsmouth

Network Diagram - see first Page of Table 155

Station		SW 1	SW 1 (trolley)	SW 1	SW 1	SW 1 (trolley)		SW 1	SW 1 (trolley)	SW 1	SW 1	SW 1 (trolley)	SW 1	SW 1 (trolley)	SW 1	SW 1		SW 1 (trolley)	SW 1	SW 1 (trolley)	SW 1	SW 1	SW 1 (trolley)	SW 1	SW 1 (trolley)
London Waterloo 15 ⊖	d	09 45	10 00		10 15	10 30		10 45	11 00		11 15	11 30	11 45	12 00		12 15		12 30	12 45	13 00		13 15	13 30	13 45	14 00
Clapham Junction 10	d	09u52			10u22			10u52			11u22		11u52			12u22			12u52			13u22		13u52	
Woking	a	10 11	10 24		10 41	10 54		11 11	11 24		11 41	11 54	12 11	12 24		12 41		12 54	13 11	13 24		13 41	13 54	14 11	14 24
	d	10 13	10 25		10 43	10 55		11 13	11 25		11 43	11 55	12 13	12 25		12 43		12 55	13 13	13 25		13 43	13 55	14 13	14 25
Worplesdon	d	10 18						11 18					12 18						13 18					14 18	
Guildford	a	10 23	10 33		10 50	11 03		11 23	11 33		11 50	12 03	12 23	12 33		12 50		13 03	13 23	13 33		13 50	14 03	14 23	14 33
	d	10 25	10 34		10 52	11 04		11 25	11 34		11 52	12 04	12 25	12 34		12 52		13 04	13 25	13 34		13 52	14 04	14 25	14 34
Farncombe	d	10 31			10 58			11 31			11 58		12 31			12 58			13 31			13 58		14 31	
Godalming	d	10 34			11 01			11 34			12 01		12 34			13 01			13 34			14 01		14 34	
Milford (Surrey)	d				11 05						12 05					13 05						14 05			
Witley	d			↩	11 09					↩	12 09				↩	13 09					↩	14 09			
Haslemere 4	a	10 45	10 49	10 45	11 16	11 20		11 45	11 49	11 45	12 16	12 20	12 45	12 49	12 45	13 16		13 20	13 45	13 49	13 45	14 16	14 20	14 45	14 49
	d	10 55	10 50	10 55		11 21		11 55	11 50	11 55		12 21	12 55	12 50	12 55			13 21	13 55	13 50	13 55		14 21	14 55	14 50
Liphook	d	↪		11 00				↪		12 00			↪		13 00				↪		14 00			↪	
Liss	d			11 06						12 06					13 06						14 06				
Petersfield	d		11 01	11 11		11 32			12 01	12 11		12 32		13 01	13 11			13 32		14 01	14 11		14 32		15 01
Rowlands Castle	d			11 21						12 21					13 21						14 21				
Havant	a		11 15	11 26		11 49			12 15	12 26		12 49		13 15	13 26			13 49		14 15	14 26		14 49		15 14
	d		11 16	11 27		11 50			12 16	12 27		12 50		13 16	13 27			13 50		14 16	14 27		14 50		15 16
Bedhampton	a			11 29						12 29					13 29						14 29				
Hilsea	a			11 36						12 36					13 36						14 36				
Fratton	a		11 24	11 40		11 59			12 24	12 40		12 59		13 24	13 40			13 59		14 24	14 40		14 59		15 24
Portsmouth & Southsea	a		11 28	11 44		12 02			12 28	12 44		13 02		13 28	13 44			14 02		14 28	14 44		15 02		15 28
Portsmouth Harbour ⛴	a		11 33			12 07			12 33			13 07		13 33				14 07		14 33			15 07		15 33

Station		SW 1		SW 1	SW 1 (trolley)	SW 1	SW 1 (trolley)	SW 1	SW 1	SW 1 (trolley)	SW 1	SW 1 (trolley)		SW 1	SW 1	SW 1 (trolley)	SW 1	SW 1 (trolley)	SW 1	SW 1	SW 1 (trolley)	SW 1		SW 1 (trolley)	SW 1
London Waterloo 15 ⊖	d			14 15	14 30	14 45	15 00		15 15	15 30	15 45	16 00			16 15	16 30	16 45	17 00		17 15	17 30	17 45		18 00	
Clapham Junction 10	d			14u22		14u52			15u22		15u52				16u22		16u52			17u22		17u52			
Woking	a			14 41	14 54	15 11	15 24		15 41	15 54	16 11	16 24			16 41	16 54	17 11	17 24		17 41	17 54	18 11		18 24	
	d			14 43	14 55	15 13	15 25		15 43	15 55	16 13	16 25			16 43	16 55	17 13	17 25		17 43	17 55	18 13		18 25	
Worplesdon	d					15 18					16 18						17 18					18 18			
Guildford	a			14 50	15 03	15 23	15 33		15 50	16 03	16 23	16 33			16 50	17 03	17 23	17 33		17 50	18 03	18 23		18 33	
	d			14 52	15 04	15 25	15 34		15 52	16 04	16 25	16 34			16 52	17 04	17 25	17 34		17 52	18 04	18 25		18 34	
Farncombe	d			14 58		15 31			15 58		16 31				16 58		17 31			17 58		18 31			
Godalming	d			15 01		15 34			16 01		16 34				17 01		17 34			18 01		18 34			
Milford (Surrey)	d			15 05					16 05						17 05					18 05					
Witley	d	↩		15 09				↩	16 09					↩	17 09				↩	18 09					↩
Haslemere 4	a	14 45		15 16	15 20	15 45	15 49	15 45	16 16	16 20	16 45	16 49		16 45	17 16	17 20	17 45	17 49	17 45	18 16	18 20	18 45		18 49	18 45
	d	14 55			15 21	15 55	15 50	15 55		16 21	16 55	16 50		16 55		17 21	17 55	17 50	17 55		18 21	18 55		18 50	18 55
Liphook	d	15 00				↪		16 00			↪			17 00			↪		18 00			↪			19 00
Liss	d	15 06						16 06						17 06					18 06						19 06
Petersfield	d	15 11			15 32		16 01	16 11		16 32		17 01		17 11		17 32		18 01	18 11		18 32			19 01	19 11
Rowlands Castle	d	15 21						16 21						17 21					18 21						19 21
Havant	a	15 26			15 49		16 15	16 26		16 49		17 15		17 26		17 49		18 15	18 26		18 49			19 15	19 26
	d	15 27			15 50		16 16	16 27		16 50		17 16		17 27		17 50		18 16	18 27		18 50			19 16	19 27
Bedhampton	a	15 29						16 29						17 29					18 29						19 29
Hilsea	a	15 36						16 36						17 36					18 36						19 36
Fratton	a	15 40			15 59		16 24	16 40		16 59		17 24		17 40		17 59		18 24	18 40		18 59			19 24	19 40
Portsmouth & Southsea	a	15 44			16 02		16 28	16 44		17 02		17 28		17 44		18 02		18 28	18 44		19 02			19 28	19 44
Portsmouth Harbour ⛴	a				16 07		16 33			17 07		17 33				18 07		18 33			19 07			19 33	

Station		SW 1	SW 1 (trolley)	SW 1	SW 1 (trolley)	SW 1	SW 1	SW 1 (trolley)		SW 1	SW 1	SW 1	SW 1	SW 1	SW 1	SW 1	SW 1	SW 1		SW 1	SW 1	SW 1	SW 1	SW 1	SW 1
London Waterloo 15 ⊖	d	18 15	18 30	18 45	19 00		19 15	19 30		19 45	20 00		20 15	20 30	20 45	21 00		21 30		21 45	22 00		22 30	22 45	23 15
Clapham Junction 10	d	18u22		18u52			19u22			19u52			20u22		20u52					21u52				22u52	23u22
Woking	a	18 41	18 54	19 11	19 24		19 41	19 54		20 11	20 24		20 41	20 54	21 11	21 24		21 54		22 11	22 24		22 54	23 11	23 41
	d	18 43	18 55	19 13	19 25		19 43	19 55		20 13	20 25		20 43	20 55	21 13	21 25		21 55		22 13	22 25		22 55	23 13	23 43
Worplesdon	d			19 18						20 18					21 18					22 18				23 18	
Guildford	a	18 50	19 03	19 23	19 33		19 50	20 03		20 23	20 33		20 50	21 03	21 23	21 33		22 03		22 23	22 33		23 03	23 23	23 51
	d	18 52	19 04	19 25	19 34		19 52	20 04		20 25	20 34		20 52	21 04	21 25	21 34		22 04		22 25	22 34		23 04	23 25	23 52
Farncombe	d	18 58		19 31			19 58			20 31			20 58		21 31	21 40		22 10		22 31	22 40		23 10	23 31	23 58
Godalming	d	19 01		19 34			20 01			20 34			21 01		21 34	21 43		22 13		22 34	22 43		23 13	23 34	00 02
Milford (Surrey)	d	19 05					20 05						21 05		21 38					22 38				23 38	
Witley	d	19 09				↩	20 09					↩	21 09		21 42		↩			22 42		↩		23 42	
Haslemere 4	a	19 16	19 20	19 45	19 49	19 45	20 16	20 20		20 45	20 49	20 45	21 16	21 20	21 49	21 54	21 49	22 24		22 49	22 54	22 49	23 24	23 49	00 12
	d		19 21	19 55	19 50	19 55		20 21		20 55	20 50	20 55		21 21	21 59	21 55	21 59	22 25		22 59	22 55	22 59	23 25	23 50	00 13
Liphook	d			↪		20 00				↪		21 00			↪		22 04			↪		23 04		23 55	
Liss	d					20 06						21 06					22 10					23 10		00 01	
Petersfield	d		19 32		20 01	20 11		20 32			21 01	21 11		21 32		22 06	22 15	22 36			23 06	23 15	23 36	00 06	00 24
Rowlands Castle	d					20 21						21 21					22 25					23 25		00 16	
Havant	a		19 49		20 15	20 29		20 49			21 15	21 26		21 45		22 18	22 30	22 48			23 18	23 30	23 48	00 21	00 36
	d		19 50		20 16	20 30		20 50			21 16	21 27		21 46		22 19	22 31	22 49			23 19	23 31	23 49	00 22	00 37
Bedhampton	a					20 32						21 29					22 33					23 33		00 24	
Hilsea	a					20 41						21 36					22 41					23 41		00 30	
Fratton	a		19 59		20 24	20 45		20 59			21 24	21 40		21 54		22 28	22 45	22 58			23 28	23 45	23 58	00 34	00 46
Portsmouth & Southsea	a		20 02		20 28	20 48		21 02			21 28	21 43		21 58		22 32	22 49	23 02			23 32	23 48	00 02	00 38	00 50
Portsmouth Harbour ⛴	a		20 07		20 33			21 07			21 33			22 03		22 36	22 53	23 08			23 37	23 53	00 07		00 55

London - Guildford, Haslemere and Portsmouth

Network Diagram - see first Page of Table 155

Saturdays

		SW 1
London Waterloo 15 ⊖	d	23 45
Clapham Junction 10	d	23u52
Woking	a	00 11
	d	00 13
Worplesdon	d	00 18
Guildford	a	00 24
	d	00 25
Farncombe	d	00 31
Godalming	d	00 34
Milford (Surrey)	d	00s38
Witley	d	00s43
Haslemere 4	a	00 49
	d	00 50
Liphook	d	00s55
Liss	d	01s01
Petersfield	d	01 06
Rowlands Castle	d	01s16
Havant	a	01 21
	d	01 21
Bedhampton	a	01s24
Hilsea	a	01s29
Fratton	a	01s33
Portsmouth & Southsea	a	01 37
Portsmouth Harbour ⛴	a	

Sundays

		SW 1	SW 1	SW 1	SW 1	SW 1	SW 1	SW 1	SW 1	SW 1	SW 1	SW 1	SW 1	SW 1	SW 1	SW 1	SW 1	SW 1	SW 1	SW 1	SW 1	SW 1	SW 1
		A	A	A	A									🛒		🛒		🛒		🛒		🛒	
London Waterloo 15 ⊖	d	22p30	22p45	23p15	23p45		08 00	08 30	09 00	09 30	10 00	10 30	11 00	11 30	12 00	12 30	13 00	13 30	14 00	14 30	15 00	15 30	16 00
Clapham Junction 10	d	ʃ	22b52	23b22	23b52		08u09	08u39	09u09	09u39	10u09	10u39	11u09	11u39	12u09	12u39	13u09	13u39	14u09	14u39	15u09	15u39	16u09
Woking	a	22p54	23p11	23p41	00ʃ11		08 34	09 03	09 34	10 03	10 31	11 01	11 31	12 01	12 31	13 01	13 31	14 01	14 31	15 01	15 31	16 01	16 31
	d	22p55	23p13	23p43	00ʃ13	07 32	08 35	09 04	09 35	10 04	10 32	11 02	11 32	12 02	12 32	13 02	13 32	14 02	14 32	15 02	15 32	16 02	16 32
Worplesdon	d	ʃ	23p18	ʃ	00ʃ18																		
Guildford	a	23p03	23p23	23p51	00ʃ24	07 39	08 43	09 12	09 43	10 12	10 40	11 10	11 40	12 10	12 40	13 10	13 40	14 10	14 40	15 10	15 40	16 10	16 40
	d	23p04	23p25	23p52	00ʃ25	07 41	08 45	09 14	09 45	10 14	10 42	11 12	11 42	12 12	12 42	13 12	13 42	14 12	14 42	15 12	15 42	16 12	16 42
Farncombe	d	23p10	23p31	23p58	00ʃ31	07 48	08 53		09 53		10 48		11 48		12 48		13 48		14 48		15 48		16 48
Godalming	d	23p13	23p34	00ʃ02	00ʃ34	07 51	08 56		09 56		10 51		11 51		12 51		13 51		14 51		15 51		16 51
Milford (Surrey)	d	ʃ	23p38	ʃ	00s38	07 55	09 00		10 00		10 55		11 55		12 55		13 55		14 55		15 55		16 55
Witley	d	ʃ	23p42	ʃ	00s43	07 59	09 04		10 04		10 59		11 59		12 59		13 59		14 59		15 59		16 59
Haslemere 4	a	23p24	23p49	00ʃ12	00ʃ49	08 06	09 11	09 28	10 11	10 28	11 06	11 26	12 06	12 26	13 06	13 26	14 06	14 26	15 06	15 26	16 06	16 26	17 06
	d	23p25	23p50	00ʃ13	00ʃ50	08 07	09 12	09 29	10 12	10 29	11 07	11 27	12 07	12 27	13 07	13 27	14 07	14 27	15 07	15 27	16 07	16 27	17 07
Liphook	d	ʃ	23p55	ʃ	00s55	08 12	09 17		10 17		11 12		12 12		13 12		14 12		15 12		16 12		17 12
Liss	d	ʃ	00ʃ01	ʃ	01s01	08 18	09 23		10 23		11 18		12 18		13 18		14 18		15 18		16 18		17 18
Petersfield	d	23p36	00ʃ06	00ʃ24	01ʃ06	08 23	09 28	09 40	10 28	10 40	11 23	11 38	12 23	12 38	13 23	13 38	14 23	14 38	15 23	15 38	16 23	16 38	17 23
Rowlands Castle	d	ʃ	00ʃ16	ʃ	01s16	08 33	09 38		10 38		11 33		12 33		13 33		14 33		15 33		16 33		17 33
Havant	a	23p48	00ʃ21	00ʃ36	01ʃ21	08 38	09 44	09 52	10 44	10 52	11 38	11 50	12 38	12 50	13 38	13 50	14 38	14 50	15 38	15 50	16 38	16 50	17 38
	d	23p49	00ʃ22	00ʃ37	01ʃ21	08 39	09 45	09 53	10 45	10 53	11 39	11 51	12 39	12 51	13 39	13 51	14 39	14 51	15 39	15 51	16 39	16 51	17 39
Bedhampton	a	ʃ	00ʃ24	ʃ	01s24	08 41	09 47		10 47		11 41		12 41		13 41		14 41		15 41		16 41		17 41
Hilsea	a	ʃ	00ʃ30	ʃ	01s29																		
Fratton	a	23p58	00ʃ34	00ʃ46	01s33	08 49	09 55	10 01	10 55	11 01	11 49	12 00	12 49	13 00	13 49	14 00	14 49	15 00	15 49	16 00	16 49	17 00	17 49
Portsmouth & Southsea	a	00ʃ02	00ʃ38	00ʃ50	01ʃ37	08 53	09 59	10 06	10 59	11 05	11 53	12 04	12 53	13 04	13 53	14 04	14 53	15 04	15 54	16 04	16 53	17 04	17 53
Portsmouth Harbour ⛴	a	00ʃ07		00ʃ55		08 57	10 04	10 11	11 04	11 11	11 58	12 09	12 58	13 11	13 58	14 11	14 58	15 11	15 58	16 11	16 58	17 11	17 58

		SW 1	SW 1	SW 1	SW 1	SW 1	SW 1	SW 1	SW 1	SW 1	SW 1	SW 1	SW 1	SW 1	SW 1	SW 1
		🛒		🛒		🛒		🛒		🛒						
London Waterloo 15 ⊖	d	16 30	17 00	17 30	18 00	18 30	19 00	19 30	20 00	20 30	21 00	21 30	22 00	22 30	23 00	23 30
Clapham Junction 10	d	16u39	17u09	17u39	18u09	18u39	19u09	19u39	20u09	20u39	21u09	21u39	22u09	22u39	23u09	23u39
Woking	a	17 01	17 31	18 01	18 31	19 01	19 31	20 01	20 31	21 01	21 31	22 01	22 31	23 01	23 31	00 01
	d	17 02	17 32	18 02	18 32	19 02	19 32	20 02	20 32	21 02	21 32	22 02	22 32	23 02	23 32	00 03
Worplesdon	d															
Guildford	a	17 10	17 40	18 10	18 40	19 10	19 40	20 10	20 40	21 10	21 40	22 10	22 40	23 10	23 40	00 10
	d	17 12	17 42	18 12	18 42	19 12	19 42	20 12	20 42	21 12	21 42	22 12	22 42	23 12	23 42	00 12
Farncombe	d		17 48		18 48		19 48		20 48		21 48		22 48		23 48	
Godalming	d		17 51		18 51		19 51		20 51		21 51		22 51		23 51	
Milford (Surrey)	d		17 55		18 55		19 55		20 55		21 55		22 55		23 55	
Witley	d		17 59		18 59		19 59		20 59		21 59		22 59		23 59	
Haslemere 4	a	17 26	18 06	18 26	19 06	19 26	20 06	20 26	21 06	21 26	22 06	22 26	23 06	23 26	00 06	00 26
	d	17 27	18 07	18 27	19 07	19 27	20 07	20 27	21 07	21 27	22 07	22 27	23 07	23 27	00 07	00 27
Liphook	d		18 12		19 12		20 12		21 12		22 12		23 12		00 12	
Liss	d		18 18		19 18		20 18		21 18		22 18		23 18		00 18	
Petersfield	d	17 38	18 23	18 38	19 23	19 38	20 23	20 38	21 23	21 38	22 23	22 38	23 23	23 38	00 23	00 38
Rowlands Castle	d		18 33		19 33		20 33		21 33		22 33		23 33		00 33	
Havant	a	17 50	18 38	18 50	19 38	19 50	20 38	20 50	21 38	21 50	22 38	22 50	23 38	23 50	00 38	00 50
	d	17 51	18 39	18 51	19 39	19 51	20 39	20 51	21 39	21 51	22 39	22 51	23 39	23 51	00 39	00 51
Bedhampton	a		18 41		19 41		20 41		21 41		22 41		23 41		00 41	
Hilsea	a															
Fratton	a	18 00	18 49	19 00	19 49	20 00	20 49	21 00	21 49	22 00	22 49	23 00	23 49	23 59	00 49	01 00
Portsmouth & Southsea	a	18 04	18 53	19 04	19 53	20 04	20 53	21 04	21 53	22 04	22 53	23 04	23 53	00 04	00 53	01 04
Portsmouth Harbour ⛴	a	18 11	18 58	19 11	19 58	20 11	20 58	21 09	21 58	22 11	22 58	23 09	23 58	00 09	00 58	01 09

A not 11 December

b Previous night, stops to pick up only

Table 156

Mondays to Fridays

Portsmouth, Haslemere and Guildford - London

Network Diagram - see first Page of Table 155

Miles	Station		SW MX 1	SW MO 1	SW MO 1	SW MX 1	SW 1	SW 1	SW 1 🚲	SW 1	SW 1
0	**Portsmouth Harbour** ⛴	d	22p18	22p32	22p48	23p19	04 30		05 19		05 50
0¾	**Portsmouth & Southsea**	d	22p24	22p37	22p53	23p24	04 35		05 24		05 55
1¾	Fratton	d	22p28	22p41	22p57	23p28	04 39		05 28		05 59
4	Hilsea	d	22p32			23p32	04 43		05 32		06 03
7¼	Bedhampton	d	22p37		23p04	23p37	04 48		05 37		06 08
8	**Havant**	a	22p39	22p49	23p07	23p39	04 50		05 40		06 10
—		d	22p40	22p50	23p07	23p40	04 51		05 41		06 11
11¼	Rowlands Castle	d	22p46		23p13	23p46	04 57		05 46		06 16
19½	Petersfield	d	22p57	23p04	23p24	23p57	05 08		05 57		06 29
23	Liss	d	23p02		23p29	00 02	05 13		06 02		06 34
27¾	Liphook	d	23p09		23p36	00 09	05 20		06 09		06 41
31½	**Haslemere** 4	a	23p15	23p16	23p41	00 15	05 25		06 15		06 46
—		d	23p15	23p17	23p42	00 15	05 26	06 00	06 16	06 30	06 47
36	Witley	d	23p21		23p48	00 21	05 32	06 06		06 36	
38¼	Milford (Surrey)	d	23p25		23p52	00 25	05 36	06 11		06 40	
40	Godalming	d	23p29		23p56	00 29	05 40	06 15		06 44	06 57
41	Farncombe	d	23p32		23p59	00 32	05 43	06 18		06 47	07 00
44¼	**Guildford**	a	23p37	23p31	00 04	00 37	05 48	06 23	06 29	06 52	07 06
—		d	23p39	23p35	00 05		05 50	06 24	06 31	06 53	07 07
47¾	Worplesdon	d	23p44				05 55	06 30		06 59	
50½	**Woking**	a	23p49	23p42	00 13		06 00	06 35	06 39	07 03	07 15
—		d	23p56	23p45			06 01	06 37	06 41	07 05	07 17
70½	Clapham Junction 10	a	00 19	00 04			06 20	06 58	07 02	07 24	
74½	**London Waterloo** 15 ⊖	a	00 33	00 14			06 29	07 08	07 12	07 36	07 45

Miles	Station		SW 1 🚲	SW 1	SW 1	SW 1 🚲	SW 1	SW 1	SW 1 🚲	SW 1	SW 1	SW 1 🚲	SW 1	SW 1 🚲
0	**Portsmouth Harbour** ⛴	d	06 15			06 42		06 55	07 13		07 29	07 45		08 15
0¾	**Portsmouth & Southsea**	d	06 20			06 47		07 00	07 18		07 33	07 50		08 20
1¾	Fratton	d	06 24			06 51		07 04	07 22		07 37	07 54		08 24
4	Hilsea	d			06 42			07 08			07 41			
7¼	Bedhampton	d			06 47			07 13			07 48			
8	**Havant**	a	06 33		06 49	06 59		07 15	07 30		07 50	08 03		08 32
—		d	06 34		06 50	07 00	07 11	07 16	07 32		07 52	08 04		08 34
11¼	Rowlands Castle	d			06 56			07 22			07 57			
19½	Petersfield	d	06 48		07 07	07 14	07 25	07 33	07 46		08 08	08 18		08 48
23	Liss	d			07 12	07 20		07 38			08 13			
27¾	Liphook	d			07 19	07 27		07 45		←	08 20		←	
31½	**Haslemere** 4	a	07 01		07 25	07 33	07 38	07 51	07 59	07 51	08 26	08 31	08 26	09 01
—		d	07 02	07 10	07 26	07 35	07 40	08 07	08 00	08 07	08 39	08 32	08 39	09 02
36	Witley	d		07 16			07 46	→		08 13	→		08 45	
38¼	Milford (Surrey)	d		07 21			07 50			08 17			08 49	
40	Godalming	d		07 25	07 35	07 45	07 54			08 21			08 53	
41	Farncombe	d		07 28	07 38		07 57			08 25			08 57	
44¼	**Guildford**	a	07 15	07 33	07 43	07 52	08 02		08 13	08 30		08 46	09 02	09 15
—		d	07 17	07 34	07 45	07 54	08 03		08 15	08 31		08 54	09 03	09 17
47¾	Worplesdon	d		07 40	07 50				08 20	08 37				
50½	**Woking**	a	07 25		07 54		08 11		08 26	08 41			09 11	09 27
—		d	07 26		07 56		08 12		08 27	08 43			09 13	09 28
70½	Clapham Junction 10	a								09 03			09 32	
74½	**London Waterloo** 15 ⊖	a	07 54	08 11	08 24	08 32	08 41		08 55	09 13		09 31	09 43	09 55

Station		SW 1	SW 1 🚲	SW 1	SW 1 🚲	SW 1	SW 1 🚲	SW 1	SW 1 🚲	SW 1	SW 1 🚲	SW 1
Portsmouth Harbour ⛴	d		08 45		09 15	09 18	09 45		10 15		10 45	
Portsmouth & Southsea	d	08 24	08 50		09 20	09 24	09 50		10 20	10 24	10 50	
Fratton	d	08 28	08 54		09 24	09 28	09 54		10 24	10 28	10 54	
Hilsea	d	08 32				09 32				10 32		
Bedhampton	d	08 37				09 37				10 37		
Havant	a	08 40	09 03		09 33	09 39	10 03		10 33	10 39	11 03	
	d	08 40	09 04		09 34	09 40	10 04		10 34	10 40	11 04	
Rowlands Castle	d	08 46				09 46				10 46		
Petersfield	d	08 57	09 18		09 48	09 57	10 18		10 48	10 57	11 18	
Liss	d	09 02				10 02				11 02		
Liphook	d	09 09				10 09				11 09		
Haslemere 4	a	09 15	09 31		10 01	10 15	10 31		11 01	11 15	11 31	
	d	09 15	09 32	09 39	10 02	10 15	10 32	10 39	11 02	11 15	11 32	11 39
Witley	d			09 45				10 45				11 45
Milford (Surrey)	d			09 49				10 49				11 49
Godalming	d	09 25		09 53		10 25		10 53		11 25		11 53
Farncombe	d	09 28		09 56		10 28		10 56		11 28		11 56
Guildford	a	09 33	09 45	10 01	10 15	10 33	10 46	11 01	11 15	11 33	11 45	12 01
	d	09 34	09 47	10 02	10 17	10 34	10 47	11 02	11 17	11 34	11 47	12 02
Worplesdon	d	09 40				10 40				11 40		
Woking	a	09 44	09 59	10 11	10 25	10 44	10 57	11 11	11 25	11 44	11 57	12 11
	d	09 46	09 59	10 12	10 26	10 46	10 59	11 12	11 26	11 46	11 59	12 12
Clapham Junction 10	a	10 05		10 31		11 05		11 31		12 05		12 31
London Waterloo 15 ⊖	a	10 13	10 27	10 40	10 51	11 13	11 24	11 40	11 51	12 13	12 23	12 40

Station		SW 1 🚲	SW 1	SW 1 🚲	SW 1	SW 1 🚲	SW 1	SW 1 🚲	SW 1	SW 1 🚲	SW 1	SW 1 🚲
Portsmouth Harbour ⛴	d	11 15		11 45		12 15		12 45		13 15		13 45
Portsmouth & Southsea	d	11 20	11 24	11 50		12 20	12 24	12 50		13 20	13 24	13 50
Fratton	d	11 24	11 28	11 54		12 24	12 28	12 54		13 24	13 28	13 54
Hilsea	d		11 32				12 32				13 32	
Bedhampton	d		11 37				12 37				13 37	
Havant	a	11 33	11 39	12 03		12 33	12 39	13 03		13 33	13 39	14 03
	d	11 34	11 40	12 04		12 34	12 40	13 04		13 34	13 40	14 04
Rowlands Castle	d		11 46				12 46				13 46	
Petersfield	d	11 48	11 57	12 18		12 48	12 57	13 18		13 48	13 57	14 18
Liss	d		12 02				13 02				14 02	
Liphook	d		12 09				13 09				14 09	
Haslemere 4	a	12 01	12 15	12 31		13 01	13 15	13 31		14 01	14 15	14 31
	d	12 02	12 15	12 32	12 39	13 02	13 15	13 32	13 39	14 02	14 15	14 32
Witley	d				12 45				13 45			
Milford (Surrey)	d				12 49				13 49			
Godalming	d		12 25		12 53		13 25		13 53		14 25	
Farncombe	d		12 28		12 56		13 28		13 56		14 28	
Guildford	a	12 15	12 33	12 45	13 01	13 15	13 33	13 45	14 01	14 15	14 33	14 45
	d	12 17	12 34	12 47	13 02	13 17	13 34	13 47	14 02	14 17	14 34	14 47
Worplesdon	d		12 40				13 40				14 40	
Woking	a	12 25	12 44	12 57	13 11	13 25	13 44	13 57	14 11	14 25	14 44	14 57
	d	12 26	12 46	12 59	13 12	13 26	13 46	13 59	14 12	14 26	14 46	14 59
Clapham Junction 10	a		13 05		13 31		14 05		14 31		15 05	
London Waterloo 15 ⊖	a	12 51	13 13	13 23	13 40	13 51	14 13	14 23	14 40	14 51	15 13	15 23

Station		SW 1	SW 1 🚲	SW 1	SW 1 🚲	SW 1	SW 1 🚲	SW 1	SW 1	SW 1 🚲	SW 1 🚲	SW 1
Portsmouth Harbour ⛴	d		14 15		14 45		15 15			15 45	16 15	
Portsmouth & Southsea	d		14 20	14 24	14 50		15 20	15 24		15 50	16 20	16 24
Fratton	d		14 24	14 28	14 54		15 24	15 28		15 54	16 24	16 28
Hilsea	d			14 32				15 32				16 32
Bedhampton	d			14 37				15 37				16 37
Havant	a		14 33	14 39	15 03		15 33	15 39		16 03	16 33	16 39
	d		14 34	14 40	15 04		15 34	15 40	15 54	16 04	16 34	16 40
Rowlands Castle	d			14 46				15 46				16 46
Petersfield	d		14 48	14 57	15 18		15 48	15 57	16 10	16 18	16 48	16 57
Liss	d			15 02				16 02		16 23		17 02
Liphook	d			15 09				16 09		16 30		17 09
Haslemere 4	a		15 01	15 15	15 31		16 01	16 15	16 23	16 36	17 01	17 15
	d	14 39	15 02	15 15	15 32	15 37	16 02	16 15	16 24	16 37	17 02	17 15
Witley	d	14 45				15 43			16 30	16 43		
Milford (Surrey)	d	14 49				15 47			16 34	16 47		
Godalming	d	14 53		15 25		15 51		16 25	16 38	16 51		17 25
Farncombe	d	14 56		15 28		15 54		16 28	16 41	16 54		17 28
Guildford	a	15 01	15 15	15 33	15 45	15 59	16 15	16 33	16 46	16 59	17 15	17 33
	d	15 02	15 17	15 34	15 47	16 00	16 17	16 34	16 47	17 00	17 17	17 34
Worplesdon	d			15 40		16 06		16 40		17 06		17 40
Woking	a	15 11	15 25	15 44	15 57	16 11	16 25	16 44	16 57	17 11	17 25	17 44
	d	15 12	15 26	15 46	15 59	16 12	16 26	16 46	16 59	17 12	17 26	17 46
Clapham Junction 10	a	15 31		16 05		16 31		17 05		17 31		18 05
London Waterloo 15 ⊖	a	15 43	15 51	16 13	16 24	16 40	16 51	17 14	17 27	17 43	17 54	18 14

Station		SW 1 🚲	SW 1 🚲	SW 1	SW 1 🚲	SW 1 🚲	SW 1	SW 1 🚲	SW 1	SW 1	SW 1
Portsmouth Harbour ⛴	d	16 45	17 15	17 18	17 45	18 15		18 45		19 15	
Portsmouth & Southsea	d	16 50	17 20	17 24	17 50	18 20	18 24	18 50		19 20	19 24
Fratton	d	16 54	17 24	17 28	17 54	18 24	18 28	18 54		19 24	19 28
Hilsea	d			17 32			18 32				19 32
Bedhampton	d			17 37			18 37				19 37
Havant	a	17 03	17 33	17 39	18 03	18 33	18 39	19 03		19 33	19 39
	d	17 04	17 34	17 40	18 04	18 34	18 40	19 04		19 34	19 40
Rowlands Castle	d			17 46			18 46				19 46
Petersfield	d	17 18	17 48	17 57	18 18	18 48	18 57	19 18		19 48	19 57
Liss	d	17 23		18 02			19 02				20 02
Liphook	d	17 30		18 09			19 09				20 09
Haslemere 4	a	17 36	18 01	18 15	18 31	19 01	19 15	19 31		20 01	20 15
	d	17 37	18 02	18 15	18 32	19 02	19 15	19 32	19 39	20 02	20 15
Witley	d	17 43			18 38				19 45		20 21
Milford (Surrey)	d	17 47			18 42				19 49		20 25
Godalming	d	17 51		18 25	18 46	19 11	19 25		19 53		20 29
Farncombe	d	17 54		18 28	18 49	19 14	19 28		19 56		20 32
Guildford	a	17 59	18 15	18 33	18 54	19 19	19 33	19 45	20 01	20 15	20 37
	d	18 00	18 17	18 34	18 55	19 21	19 34	19 47	20 02	20 17	20 39
Worplesdon	d	18 06		18 40			19 40				20 44
Woking	a	18 11		18 44	19 03	19 28	19 45	19 57	20 11	20 25	20 52
	d	18 12		18 46	19 05	19 30	19 46	19 59	20 12	20 26	20 53
Clapham Junction 10	a	18 31		19 05			20 05		20 31		21 12
London Waterloo 15 ⊖	a	18 43	18 59	19 13	19 29	19 59	20 14	20 24	20 40	20 50	21 21

Portsmouth, Haslemere and Guildford - London

Network Diagram - see first Page of Table 155

Station		SW **1**	SW **1**	SW **1**	SW **1**	SW **1**	SW **1**	SW FO **1**	SW FX **1**		SW **1**	SW **1**
Portsmouth Harbour ⛴	d	19 45	20 15	20 18	20 45	21 18	21 28	22 18	22 18		22 28	23 19
Portsmouth & Southsea	d	19 50	20 20	20 24	20 50	21 24	21 33	22 24	22 24		22 33	23 24
Fratton	d	19 54	20 24	20 28	20 54	21 28	21 37	22 28	22 28		22 37	23 28
Hilsea	d			20 32		21 32	21 41	22 32	22 32		22 41	23 32
Bedhampton	d			20 37		21 37	21 47	22 37	22 37		22 46	23 37
Havant	a	20 03	20 33	20 39	21 03	21 40	21 52	22 39	22 39		22 53	23 39
	d	20 04	20 34	20 40	21 04	21 40		22 40	22 40			23 40
Rowlands Castle	d			20 46		21 46		22 46	22 46			23 46
Petersfield	d	20 18	20 48	20 57	21 18	21 57		22 57	22 57			23 57
Liss	d			21 02		22 02		23 02	23 02			00 02
Liphook	d			21 09		22 09		23 09	23 09			00 09
Haslemere **4**	a	20 31	21 01	21 15	21 31	22 15		23 15	23 15			00 15
	d	20 32	21 02	21 15	21 32	22 15		23 15	23 15			00 15
Witley	d			21 21		22 21		23 21	23 21			00 21
Milford (Surrey)	d			21 25		22 25		23 25	23 25			00 25
Godalming	d			21 29		22 29		23 29	23 29			00 29
Farncombe	d			21 32		22 32		23 32	23 32			00 32
Guildford	a	20 45	21 16	21 37	21 45	22 37		23 37	23 37			00 37
	d	20 47	21 17	21 39	21 47	22 39		23 39	23 39			
Worplesdon	d			21 44		22 44		23 44	23 44			
Woking	a	20 56	21 25	21 49	21 57	22 49		23 49	23 49			
	d	20 59	21 26	21 50	21 59	22 50		23 56	23 56			
Clapham Junction **10**	a			22 09		23 09		00 19	00 19			
London Waterloo **15** ⊖	a	21 27	21 50	22 18	22 27	23 19		00 32	00 33			

Saturdays

Station		SW **1**	SW **1**	SW **1**	SW **1**	SW **1**	SW **1**	SW **1** 🛒	SW **1**	SW **1** 🛒		SW **1**	SW **1** 🛒	SW **1**	SW **1** 🛒	SW **1**	SW **1** 🛒	SW **1**	SW **1** 🛒	SW **1**		SW **1** 🛒	SW **1**	SW **1** 🛒	SW **1**
Portsmouth Harbour ⛴	d	22p18	23p19	04 43	05 19		06 19	06 45		07 15			07 45		08 15		08 45		09 15			09 45		10 15	
Portsmouth & Southsea	d	22p24	23p24	04 48	05 24		06 24	06 50		07 20		07 24	07 50		08 20	08 24	08 50		09 20	09 24		09 50		10 20	10 24
Fratton	d	22p28	23p28	04 52	05 28		06 28	06 54		07 24		07 28	07 54		08 24	08 28	08 54		09 24	09 28		09 54		10 24	10 28
Hilsea	d	22p32	23p32	04 56	05 32		06 32					07 32				08 32				09 32					10 32
Bedhampton	d	22p37	23p37	05 01	05 37		06 37					07 37				08 37				09 37					10 37
Havant	a	22p39	23p39	05 03	05 39		06 40	07 03		07 33		07 39	08 03		08 33	08 39	09 03		09 33	09 39		10 03		10 33	10 39
	d	22p40	23p40	05 04	05 40		06 41	07 04		07 34		07 40	08 04		08 34	08 40	09 04		09 34	09 40		10 04		10 34	10 40
Rowlands Castle	d	22p46	23p46	05 09	05 46		06 46					07 46				08 46				09 46					10 46
Petersfield	d	22p57	23p57	05 20	05 57		06 57	07 18		07 48		07 57	08 18		08 48	08 57	09 18		09 48	09 57		10 18		10 48	10 57
Liss	d	23p02	00 02	05 25	06 02		07 02					08 02				09 02				10 02					11 02
Liphook	d	23p09	00 09	05 32	06 09		07 09					08 09				09 09				10 09					11 09
Haslemere **4**	a	23p15	00 15	05 38	06 14		07 14	07 31		08 01		08 14	08 31		09 01	09 15	09 31		10 01	10 15		10 31		11 01	11 15
	d	23p15	00 15	05 39	06 15	06 39	07 15	07 32	07 39	08 02		08 15	08 32	08 39	09 02	09 15	09 32	09 39	10 02	10 15		10 32	10 39	11 02	11 15
Witley	d	23p21	00 21	05 45		06 45			07 45					08 45				09 45					10 45		
Milford (Surrey)	d	23p25	00 25	05 49		06 49			07 49					08 49				09 49					10 49		
Godalming	d	23p29	00 29	05 53	06 25	06 53	07 25		07 53			08 25		08 53		09 25		09 53		10 25			10 53		11 25
Farncombe	d	23p32	00 32	05 56	06 28	06 56	07 28		07 56			08 28		08 56		09 28		09 56		10 28			10 56		11 28
Guildford	a	23p37	00 37	06 01	06 33	07 01	07 33	07 45	08 01	08 15		08 33	08 45	09 01	09 15	09 33	09 45	10 01	10 15	10 33		10 45	11 01	11 15	11 33
	d	23p39		06 02	06 34	07 02	07 34	07 47	08 02	08 17		08 34	08 47	09 02	09 17	09 34	09 47	10 02	10 17	10 34		10 47	11 02	11 17	11 34
Worplesdon	d	23p44			06 40		07 40					08 40				09 40				10 40					11 40
Woking	a	23p49		06 11	06 44	07 11	07 44	07 57	08 10	08 26		08 44	08 57	09 11	09 25	09 44	09 57	10 11	10 25	10 44		10 57	11 11	11 25	11 44
	d	23p56		06 13	06 46	07 12	07 46	07 59	08 13	08 27		08 46	08 59	09 12	09 26	09 46	09 59	10 12	10 26	10 46		10 59	11 12	11 26	11 46
Clapham Junction **10**	a	00 19		06 32	07 05	07 31	08 05		08 33			09 05		09 31		10 05		10 31		11 05			11 31		12 05
London Waterloo **15** ⊖	a	00 32		06 40	07 13	07 40	08 13	08 23	08 42	08 51		09 13	09 23	09 40	09 51	10 13	10 23	10 40	10 51	11 13		11 23	11 40	11 51	12 13

Station		SW **1** 🛒	SW **1**	SW **1** 🛒	SW **1**	SW **1** 🛒		SW **1**	SW **1** 🛒	SW **1**	SW **1** 🛒	SW **1**	SW **1** 🛒	SW **1**	SW **1** 🛒	SW **1**		SW **1** 🛒	SW **1**	SW **1** 🛒	SW **1**	SW **1** 🛒	SW **1**	SW **1** 🛒	SW **1**
Portsmouth Harbour ⛴	d	10 45		11 15		11 45			12 15		12 45		13 15		13 45			14 15		14 45		15 15		15 45	
Portsmouth & Southsea	d	10 50		11 20	11 24	11 50			12 20	12 24	12 50		13 20	13 24	13 50			14 20	14 24	14 50		15 20	15 24	15 50	
Fratton	d	10 54		11 24	11 28	11 54			12 24	12 28	12 54		13 24	13 28	13 54			14 24	14 28	14 54		15 24	15 28	15 54	
Hilsea	d				11 32					12 32				13 32					14 32				15 32		
Bedhampton	d				11 37					12 37				13 37					14 37				15 37		
Havant	a	11 03		11 33	11 39	12 03			12 33	12 39	13 03		13 33	13 39	14 03			14 33	14 39	15 03		15 33	15 39	16 03	
	d	11 04		11 34	11 40	12 04			12 34	12 40	13 04		13 34	13 40	14 04			14 34	14 40	15 04		15 34	15 40	16 04	
Rowlands Castle	d				11 46					12 46				13 46					14 46				15 46		
Petersfield	d	11 18		11 48	11 57	12 18			12 48	12 57	13 18		13 48	13 57	14 18			14 48	14 57	15 18		15 48	15 57	16 18	
Liss	d				12 02					13 02				14 02					15 02				16 02		
Liphook	d				12 09					13 09				14 09					15 09				16 09		
Haslemere **4**	a	11 31		12 01	12 15	12 31			13 01	13 15	13 31		14 01	14 15	14 31			15 01	15 15	15 31		16 01	16 15	16 31	
	d	11 32	11 39	12 02	12 15	12 32		12 39	13 02	13 15	13 32	13 39	14 02	14 15	14 32	14 39		15 02	15 15	15 32	15 39	16 02	16 15	16 32	16 39
Witley	d		11 45					12 45				13 45				14 45					15 45				16 45
Milford (Surrey)	d		11 49					12 49				13 49				14 49					15 49				16 49
Godalming	d		11 53		12 25			12 53		13 25		13 53		14 25		14 53			15 25		15 53		16 25		16 53
Farncombe	d		11 56		12 28			12 56		13 28		13 56		14 28		14 56			15 28		15 56		16 28		16 56
Guildford	a	11 45	12 01	12 15	12 33	12 45		13 01	13 15	13 33	13 45	14 01	14 15	14 33	14 45	15 01		15 15	15 33	15 45	16 01	16 15	16 33	16 45	17 01
	d	11 47	12 02	12 17	12 34	12 47		13 02	13 17	13 34	13 47	14 02	14 17	14 34	14 47	15 02		15 17	15 34	15 47	16 02	16 17	16 34	16 47	17 02
Worplesdon	d				12 40					13 40				14 40					15 40				16 40		
Woking	a	11 57	12 11	12 25	12 44	12 57		13 11	13 25	13 44	13 57	14 11	14 25	14 44	14 57	15 11		15 25	15 44	15 57	16 11	16 25	16 44	16 57	17 11
	d	11 59	12 12	12 26	12 46	12 59		13 12	13 26	13 46	13 59	14 12	14 26	14 46	14 59	15 12		15 26	15 46	15 59	16 12	16 26	16 46	16 59	17 12
Clapham Junction **10**	a		12 31		13 05			13 31		14 05		14 31		15 05		15 31			16 05		16 31		17 05		17 31
London Waterloo **15** ⊖	a	12 27	12 43	12 57	13 13	13 27		13 43	13 57	14 14	14 27	14 41	14 57	15 14	15 27	15 41		15 57	16 13	16 23	16 40	16 51	17 13	17 23	17 40

Table 156

Saturdays

Portsmouth, Haslemere and Guildford - London

Network Diagram - see first Page of Table 155

		SW	SW	SW	SW	SW	SW	SW	SW	SW	SW
		1	1	1	1	1	1	1	1	1	1
		🚲		🚲				🚲			
Portsmouth Harbour ⛴	d	16 15		16 45			17 18	17 45		18 15	
Portsmouth & Southsea	d	16 20	16 24	16 50		17 10	17 24	17 50		18 20	18 24
Fratton	d	16 24	16 28	16 54		17 14	17 28	17 54		18 24	18 28
Hilsea	d		16 32			17 18	17 32				18 32
Bedhampton	d		16 37			17 23	17 37				18 37
Havant	a	16 33	16 39	17 03		17 25	17 39	18 03		18 33	18 39
	d	16 34	16 40	17 04		17 26	17 40	18 04		18 34	18 40
Rowlands Castle	d		16 46			17 32	17 46				18 46
Petersfield	d	16 48	16 57	17 18		17 43	17 57	18 18		18 48	18 57
Liss	d		17 02			17 48	18 02				19 02
Liphook	d		17 09			17 55	18 09				19 09
Haslemere 4	a	17 01	17 15	17 31		18 01	18 15	18 31		19 01	19 15
	d	17 02	17 15	17 32	17 39	18 02	18 15	18 32	18 39	19 02	19 15
Witley	d				17 45				18 45		
Milford (Surrey)	d				17 49				18 49		
Godalming	d		17 25		17 53		18 25		18 53		19 25
Farncombe	d		17 28		17 56		18 28		18 56		19 28
Guildford	a	17 15	17 33	17 45	18 01	18 15	18 33	18 45	19 01	19 15	19 33
	d	17 17	17 34	17 47	18 02	18 17	18 34	18 47	19 02	19 17	19 34
Worplesdon	d		17 40				18 40				19 40
Woking	a	17 25	17 44	17 57	18 11	18 25	18 44	18 57	19 11	19 25	19 44
	d	17 26	17 46	17 59	18 12	18 26	18 46	18 59	19 12	19 26	19 46
Clapham Junction 10	a		18 05		18 31		19 05		19 31		20 05
London Waterloo 15 ⊖	a	17 51	18 13	18 23	18 40	18 51	19 13	19 23	19 40	19 51	20 13

		SW	SW	SW	SW	SW	SW	SW	SW	SW	SW	SW
		1	1	1	1	1	1	1	1	1	1	1
Portsmouth Harbour ⛴	d	18 45		19 15		19 45	20 15		20 45	21 18	22 18	23 19
Portsmouth & Southsea	d	18 50		19 20	19 24	19 50	20 20	20 24	20 50	21 24	22 24	23 24
Fratton	d	18 54		19 24	19 28	19 54	20 24	20 28	20 54	21 28	22 28	23 28
Hilsea	d				19 32			20 32		21 32	22 32	23 32
Bedhampton	d				19 37			20 37		21 37	22 37	23 37
Havant	a	19 03		19 33	19 39	20 03	20 33	20 39	21 03	21 39	22 39	23 39
	d	19 04		19 34	19 40	20 04	20 34	20 40	21 04	21 40	22 40	23 40
Rowlands Castle	d				19 46			20 46		21 46	22 46	23 46
Petersfield	d	19 18		19 48	19 57	20 18	20 48	20 57	21 18	21 57	22 57	23 57
Liss	d				20 02			21 02		22 02	23 02	00 02
Liphook	d				20 09			21 09		22 09	23 09	00 09
Haslemere 4	a	19 31		20 01	20 15	20 31	21 01	21 15	21 31	22 15	23 15	00 15
	d	19 32	19 39	20 02	20 15	20 32	21 02	21 15	21 32	22 15	23 15	00 15
Witley	d		19 45		20 21			21 21		22 21	23 21	00 21
Milford (Surrey)	d		19 49		20 25			21 25		22 25	23 25	00 25
Godalming	d		19 53		20 29			21 29		22 29	23 29	00 29
Farncombe	d		19 56		20 32			21 32		22 32	23 32	00 32
Guildford	a	19 45	20 01	20 15	20 37	20 45	21 15	21 37	21 47	22 37	23 37	00 37
	d	19 47	20 02	20 17	20 39	20 47	21 17	21 39	21 49	22 39	23 39	
Worplesdon	d				20 44			21 44		22 44	23 44	
Woking	a	19 57	20 11	20 25	20 52	20 57	21 25	21 49	21 57	22 49	23 49	
	d	19 59	20 12	20 26	20 53	20 59	21 26	21 50	21 59	22 50	23 56	
Clapham Junction 10	a		20 31		21 12			22 09		23 09	00 18	
London Waterloo 15 ⊖	a	20 23	20 40	20 50	21 21	21 27	21 50	22 18	22 24	23 18	00 32	

Sundays

		SW	SW	SW	SW	SW	SW	SW	SW	SW
		1	1	1	1	1	1	1	1	1
		A	A							
									🚲	
Portsmouth Harbour ⛴	d	22p18	23p19	06 48	07 32	07 48	08 32	08 48	09 32	09 48
Portsmouth & Southsea	d	22p24	23p24	06 53	07 37	07 53	08 37	08 53	09 37	09 53
Fratton	d	22p28	23p28	06 57	07 41	07 57	08 41	08 57	09 41	09 57
Hilsea	d	22p32	23p32							
Bedhampton	d	22p37	23p37	07 04		08 04		09 04		10 04
Havant	a	22p39	23p39	07 07	07 49	08 07	08 49	09 07	09 49	10 07
	d	22p40	23p40	07 07	07 50	08 07	08 50	09 07	09 50	10 07
Rowlands Castle	d	22p46	23p46	07 13		08 13		09 13		10 13
Petersfield	d	22p57	23p57	07 24	08 04	08 24	09 04	09 24	10 04	10 24
Liss	d	23p02	00 02	07 29		08 29		09 29		10 29
Liphook	d	23p09	00 09	07 36		08 36		09 36		10 36
Haslemere 4	a	23p15	00 15	07 41	08 16	08 41	09 16	09 41	10 16	10 41
	d	23p15	00 15	07 42	08 17	08 42	09 17	09 42	10 17	10 42
Witley	d	23p21	00 21	07 48		08 48		09 48		10 48
Milford (Surrey)	d	23p25	00 25	07 52		08 52		09 52		10 52
Godalming	d	23p29	00 29	07 56		08 56		09 56		10 56
Farncombe	d	23p32	00 32	07 59		08 59		09 59		10 59
Guildford	a	23p37	00 37	08 04	08 31	09 04	09 31	10 04	10 31	11 04
	d	23p39		08 05	08 35	09 05	09 35	10 05	10 35	11 06
Worplesdon	d	23p44								
Woking	a	23p49		08 13	08 42	09 15	09 42	10 15	10 42	11 13
	d	23p56		08 15	08 45	09 15	09 45	10 15	10 45	11 15
Clapham Junction 10	a	00 18		08 40	09 06	09 38	10 04	10 35	11 04	11 34
London Waterloo 15 ⊖	a	00 32		08 49	09 19	09 49	10 19	10 49	11 19	11 49

		SW	SW	SW	SW	SW	SW	SW	SW	SW	SW	SW	SW	SW
		1	1	1	1	1	1	1	1	1	1	1	1	1
		🚲		🚲		🚲		🚲		🚲		🚲		🚲
Portsmouth Harbour ⛴	d	10 32	10 48	11 32	11 48	12 32	12 48	13 32	13 48	14 32	14 48	15 32	15 48	16 32
Portsmouth & Southsea	d	10 37	10 53	11 37	11 53	12 37	12 53	13 37	13 53	14 37	14 53	15 37	15 53	16 37
Fratton	d	10 41	10 57	11 41	11 57	12 41	12 57	13 41	13 57	14 41	14 57	15 41	15 57	16 41
Hilsea	d													
Bedhampton	d		11 04		12 04		13 04		14 04		15 04		16 04	
Havant	a	10 49	11 07	11 49	12 07	12 49	13 07	13 49	14 07	14 49	15 07	15 49	16 07	16 49
	d	10 50	11 07	11 50	12 07	12 50	13 07	13 50	14 07	14 50	15 07	15 50	16 07	16 50
Rowlands Castle	d		11 13		12 13		13 13		14 13		15 13		16 13	
Petersfield	d	11 04	11 24	12 04	12 24	13 04	13 24	14 04	14 24	15 04	15 24	16 04	16 24	17 04
Liss	d		11 29		12 29		13 29		14 29		15 29		16 29	
Liphook	d		11 36		12 36		13 36		14 36		15 36		16 36	
Haslemere 4	a	11 16	11 41	12 16	12 41	13 16	13 41	14 16	14 41	15 16	15 41	16 16	16 41	17 16
	d	11 17	11 42	12 17	12 42	13 17	13 42	14 17	14 42	15 17	15 42	16 17	16 42	17 17
Witley	d		11 48		12 48		13 48		14 48		15 48		16 48	
Milford (Surrey)	d		11 52		12 52		13 52		14 52		15 52		16 52	
Godalming	d		11 56		12 56		13 56		14 56		15 56		16 56	
Farncombe	d		11 59		12 59		13 59		14 59		15 59		16 59	
Guildford	a	11 31	12 04	12 31	13 04	13 31	14 04	14 31	15 04	15 31	16 04	16 31	17 04	17 31
	d	11 35	12 06	12 35	13 05	13 35	14 05	14 35	15 05	15 35	16 05	16 35	17 05	17 35
Worplesdon	d													
Woking	a	11 42	12 13	12 42	13 13	13 42	14 13	14 42	15 13	15 42	16 13	16 42	17 13	17 42
	d	11 45	12 15	12 45	13 15	13 45	14 15	14 45	15 15	15 45	16 15	16 45	17 15	17 45
Clapham Junction 10	a	12 04	12 34	13 04	13 34	14 04	14 34	15 04	15 34	16 04	16 34	17 04	17 34	18 04
London Waterloo 15 ⊖	a	12 19	12 49	13 14	13 44	14 14	14 44	15 14	15 44	16 14	16 44	17 14	17 44	18 14

		SW	SW	SW	SW	SW	SW	SW	SW	SW	SW	SW	SW	SW
		1	1	1	1	1	1	1	1	1	1	1	1	1
			🚲		🚲									
Portsmouth Harbour ⛴	d	16 48	17 32	17 48	18 32	18 48	19 32	19 48	20 32	20 48	21 32	21 48	22 32	22 48
Portsmouth & Southsea	d	16 53	17 37	17 53	18 37	18 53	19 37	19 53	20 37	20 53	21 37	21 53	22 37	22 53
Fratton	d	16 57	17 41	17 57	18 41	18 57	19 41	19 57	20 41	20 57	21 41	21 57	22 41	22 57
Hilsea	d													
Bedhampton	d	17 04		18 04		19 04		20 04		21 04		22 04		23 04
Havant	a	17 07	17 49	18 07	18 49	19 07	19 49	20 07	20 49	21 07	21 49	22 07	22 49	23 07
	d	17 07	17 50	18 07	18 50	19 07	19 50	20 07	20 50	21 07	21 50	22 07	22 50	23 07
Rowlands Castle	d	17 13		18 13		19 13		20 13		21 13		22 13		23 13
Petersfield	d	17 24	18 04	18 24	19 04	19 24	20 04	20 24	21 04	21 24	22 04	22 24	23 04	23 24
Liss	d	17 29		18 29		19 29		20 29		21 29		22 29		23 29
Liphook	d	17 36		18 36		19 36		20 36		21 36		22 36		23 36
Haslemere 4	a	17 41	18 16	18 41	19 16	19 41	20 16	20 41	21 16	21 41	22 16	22 41	23 16	23 41
	d	17 42	18 17	18 42	19 17	19 42	20 17	20 42	21 17	21 42	22 17	22 42	23 17	23 42
Witley	d	17 48		18 48		19 48		20 48		21 48		22 48		23 48
Milford (Surrey)	d	17 52		18 52		19 52		20 52		21 52		22 52		23 52
Godalming	d	17 56		18 56		19 56		20 56		21 56		22 56		23 56
Farncombe	d	17 59		18 59		19 59		20 59		21 59		22 59		23 59
Guildford	a	18 04	18 31	19 04	19 31	20 04	20 31	21 04	21 31	22 04	22 31	23 04	23 31	00 04
	d	18 05	18 35	19 05	19 35	20 05	20 35	21 05	21 35	22 05	22 35	23 05	23 35	00 05
Worplesdon	d													
Woking	a	18 13	18 42	19 13	19 42	20 13	20 42	21 13	21 42	22 13	22 42	23 13	23 42	00 13
	d	18 15	18 45	19 15	19 45	20 15	20 45	21 15	21 45	22 15	22 45	23 15	23 45	
Clapham Junction 10	a	18 34	19 04	19 34	20 04	20 34	21 04	21 34	22 04	22 34	23 04	23 34	00 04	
London Waterloo 15 ⊖	a	18 44	19 14	19 44	20 14	20 44	21 14	21 44	22 14	22 44	23 14	23 44	00 14	

A not 11 December

Havant - Portsmouth Harbour

(Complete service) **Network Diagram - see first Page of Table 155**

		SW	SW	SW	SW	SW	SW	SW	SW	SW		SW	SW	SW	SN	SN	SW	SN	SW	SN		SW	SW	SW	GW
		MX	MO	MO	MX	MX	MX	MO	MO			MX	MO												
		1	1	1	1	1	1	1	1	1		1	1	1			1	1	1			1	1	1	
Havant	d	23p49	23p51			00 22	00 37	00 39	00 51			01 21		04 40	05 21	05 40	06 02	06 13		06 53			07 00		
Bedhampton	d					00 25		00 41				01s24		04 43			06 05	06 15		06 56			07 03		
Hilsea	d			23p59	00 03	00 30						01s29		04 48			06 10	06 20	06 34	07 01		07 05	07 08	07 13	
Fratton	d	23p59	00 01	00 04	00 08	00 34	00 47	00 50	01 01			01s33	02s10	04 52	05 30	05 49	06 15	06 25	06 41	07 05		07 09	07 12	07 17	07 35
Portsmouth & Southsea	a	00 02	00 04	00 08	00 11	00 38	00 50	00 53	01 04	01s08		01 37	02s14	04 55	05 33	05 52	06 18	06 28	06 44	07 08		07 12	07 16	07 22	07 38
	d	00 03	00 05	00 09	00 13		00 51	00 54	01 05					04 56	05 33	05 52	06 19	06 28	06 45	07 09		07 13	07 17		07 39
Portsmouth Harbour ⛴	a	00 07	00 09	00 13	00 16		00 55	00 58	01 09	01 12			02 19	04 59	05 37	05 56	06 22	06 32	06 49	07 12		07 17	07 20		07 45

		SW	SW	SN	SN	SW		SW	SN	SW	GW	SN	SW	SW	SN	SW		SW	SN	SW	SW	SW	SW	GW	SN
		1	1		1	1		1		1	◇		1	1	1	1 ⊥		1		1	1 ⊥	1	1	◇ ⊥	
Havant	d		07 28	07 35	07 41	07 52			07 58			08 22	08 27		08 44	08 50			09 01	09 05	09 20		09 30		09 33
Bedhampton	d		07 31	07 37		07 55			08 00			08 25	08 30							09 08			09 33		09 36
Hilsea	d	07 35	07 37	07 42		08 00		08 03	08 05	08 09		08 30	08 35	08 45				09 05		09 13		09 33	09 38		09 42
Fratton	d	07 39	07 42	07 47	07 50	08 04		08 07	08 10	08 13	08 21	08 34	08 40	08 49	08 53	08 59		09 10	09 13	09 17	09 29	09 37	09 43	09 42	09 47
Portsmouth & Southsea	a	07 42	07 46	07 50	07 53	08 07		08 11	08 15	08 19	08 24	08 37	08 43	08 52	08 56	09 02		09 13	09 17	09 20	09 32	09 42	09 46	09 46	09 50
	d	07 43			07 53	08 09		08 13	08 17	08 21	08 24	08 38	08 45	08 54	08 57	09 04		09 14	09 18	09 22	09 34			09 46	
Portsmouth Harbour ⛴	a	07 48			07 58	08 12		08 16	08 20	08 24	08 30	08 41	08 48	08 57	09 02	09 07		09 18	09 21	09 26	09 37			09 55	

		SN		SW	SW	SN	SW	SW	SW	GW	SN	SN		SW	SW	SN	SW	SW	SW	GW	SN	SN		SW	SW
		◇1		1 ⊥	1		1 ⊥	1	1	▪ ⊥		◇1		1 ⊥	1		1 ⊥	1	1	◇ ⊥		◇1		1 ⊥	1
Havant	d	09 46		09 50		10 07	10 16		10 27		10 32	10 46		10 50		11 05	11 16		11 27		11 32	11 46		11 50	
Bedhampton	d								10 30		10 34								11 30		11 34				
Hilsea	d				10 03			10 33	10 36		10 42				11 03			11 33	11 36		11 42				12 03
Fratton	d	09 55		09 59	10 08	10 16	10 25	10 37	10 40	10 42	10 47	10 55		10 59	11 08	11 14	11 25	11 37	11 40	11 42	11 47	11 55		11 59	12 08
Portsmouth & Southsea	a	09 58		10 02	10 11	10 19	10 28	10 42	10 44	10 46	10 50	10 58		11 02	11 11	11 17	11 28	11 42	11 44	11 46	11 50	11 58		12 02	12 11
	d	09 58		10 04	10 12	10 20	10 29			10 46		10 58		11 04	11 12	11 17	11 29			11 46		11 58		12 04	12 12
Portsmouth Harbour ⛴	a	10 02		10 07	10 18	10 23	10 33			10 54		11 02		11 07	11 18	11 21	11 33			11 54		12 02		12 07	12 18

		SN	SW	SW	SW	GW	SN	SN		SW	SW	SN	SW	SW	SW	GW	SN	SN		SW	SW	SN	SW	SW	SW
			1 ⊥	1	1	◇ ⊥		◇1		1 ⊥	1		1 ⊥	1	1	◇ ⊥		◇1		1 ⊥	1		1 ⊥	1	1
Havant	d	12 05	12 16		12 27		12 32	12 46		12 50		13 05	13 16		13 27		13 32	13 46		13 50		14 05	14 16		14 27
Bedhampton	d				12 30		12 34								13 30		13 34								14 30
Hilsea	d			12 33	12 36		12 42				13 03			13 33	13 36		13 42				14 03			14 33	14 36
Fratton	d	12 14	12 25	12 37	12 40	12 42	12 47	12 55		12 59	13 08	13 14	13 25	13 37	13 40	13 42	13 47	13 55		13 59	14 08	14 14	14 25	14 37	14 40
Portsmouth & Southsea	a	12 17	12 28	12 42	12 44	12 46	12 50	12 58		13 02	13 11	13 17	13 28	13 42	13 44	13 46	13 50	13 58		14 02	14 11	14 17	14 28	14 42	14 44
	d	12 17	12 29			12 46		12 58		13 04	13 12	13 17	13 29			13 46		13 58		14 04	14 12	14 17	14 29		
Portsmouth Harbour ⛴	a	12 21	12 33			12 54		13 02		13 07	13 18	13 21	13 33			13 54		14 02		14 07	14 18	14 21	14 33		

		GW	SN	SN		SW	SW	SN	SW	SW	SW	GW	SN	SN		SW	SW	SN	SN	SW	SW	SW	GW	SN	
		◇ ⊥		◇1		1 ⊥	1		1 ⊥	1	1	◇ ⊥		◇1		1 ⊥	1			1 ⊥	1	1	◇ ⊥		
Havant	d		14 32	14 46		14 50		15 05	15 16		15 27		15 32	15 46		15 50		16 02	16 09	16 16		16 27		16 32	
Bedhampton	d		14 34								15 30		15 34					16 04				16 30		16 34	
Hilsea	d		14 42				15 03			15 33	15 36		15 42				16 03				16 33	16 36		16 42	
Fratton	d	14 42	14 47	14 55		14 59	15 08	15 14	15 25	15 37	15 40	15 42	15 47	15 55		15 59	16 08	16 12	16 18	16 25	16 37	16 40	16 42	16 47	
Portsmouth & Southsea	a	14 46	14 50	14 58		15 02	15 11	15 17	15 28	15 42	15 44	15 46	15 50	15 58		16 02	16 11	16 15	16 21	16 28	16 40	16 44	16 46	16 50	
	d	14 46		14 58		15 04	15 12	15 17	15 29			15 46		15 58		16 04	16 12	16 16	16 22	16 29	16 41	16 45	16 46		
Portsmouth Harbour ⛴	a	14 54		15 02		15 07	15 18	15 21	15 33			15 54		16 02		16 07	16 18	16 21	16 26	16 33	16 44	16 49	16 54		

		SN	SW	SW	SN	SW	SN	SW	SW	SW		SW	GW	SN	SW	SN	SW	SW	SN	SW		SW	SW	SW	SN
		◇1	1 ⊥	1		1		1 ⊥	1	1		1	◇ ⊥	1	1 ⊥	◇1	1	1		1 ⊥		1	1	1	
Havant	d	16 46	16 50		17 00	17 04	17 09	17 16				17 27		17 32	17 50	17 54		18 04	18 13	18 20				18 30	18 34
Bedhampton	d				17 02	17 06						17 30		17 34		17 56		18 07						18 33	18 36
Hilsea	d			17 03	17 07	17 11				17 33		17 36		17 42		18 01	18 04	18 12				18 33		18 39	18 42
Fratton	d	16 55	16 59	17 08	17 12	17 16	17 19	17 25	17 32	17 37		17 40	17 42	17 47	17 59	18 06	18 09	18 17	18 22	18 29		18 37	18 40	18 43	18 46
Portsmouth & Southsea	a	16 58	17 02	17 11	17 16	17 20	17 22	17 28	17 35	17 42		17 44	17 46	17 50	18 02	18 09	18 12	18 20	18 25	18 32		18 41	18 43	18 46	18 49
	d	16 58	17 04	17 12	17 16	17 21		17 30	17 36				17 46		18 04	18 09	18 14	18 22	18 26	18 33			18 45		
Portsmouth Harbour ⛴	a	17 02	17 07	17 18	17 20	17 26		17 35	17 40				17 54		18 09	18 15	18 20	18 28	18 31	18 39			18 51		

		GW	SW	SN	SW	SN		SW	SW	SW	GW	SN	SN	SW	SW	SN		SW	SW	SW	GW	SW	SN	SW	SN
		◇ ⊥	1 ⊥	◇1	1			1 ⊥	1	1	▪ ⊥		◇1	1 ⊥	1			1 ⊥	1	1	▪ ⊥	1 ⊥	◇1	1	1
Havant	d		18 51	18 54		19 08		19 17				19 33	19 46	19 51		20 07		20 17		20 29		20 49	20 52		21 10
Bedhampton	d			18 57								19 35								20 32					
Hilsea	d			19 02	19 05				19 28	19 33		19 43			20 02				20 33	20 37				21 03	
Fratton	d	18 48	19 00	19 06	19 09	19 18		19 26	19 33	19 37	19 42	19 47	19 56	20 00	20 08	20 16		20 26	20 37	20 41	20 42	20 58	21 02	21 08	21 19
Portsmouth & Southsea	a	18 52	19 03	19 09	19 12	19 21		19 29	19 36	19 42	19 46	19 50	20 00	20 03	20 11	20 19		20 29	20 42	20 44	20 46	21 01	21 06	21 11	21 23
	d	18 52	19 05		19 14	19 21		19 31	19 38		19 46		20 00	20 05	20 12			20 31		20 46	20 46	21 03		21 13	21 23
Portsmouth Harbour ⛴	a	19 00	19 10		19 20	19 26		19 36	19 43		19 54		20 06	20 10	20 20			20 34		20 52	20 54	21 06		21 16	21 27

Table 157

Mondays to Fridays

Havant - Portsmouth Harbour

(Complete service)

Network Diagram - see first Page of Table 155

		SW ■1 🚲		SW ■1	GW ◇ 🚲	SW ■1	SW ■1 🚲	SN ◇■1 🚲	SW ■1	SN	SW ■1 🚲	SW ■1		SW ■1	SN	GW ◇	SW ■1 🚲	SN	SW ■1	SW ■1	SW ■1	SW ■1		GW ◇	SN ■1
Havant	d	21 19				21 31	21 46	21 49		22 10	22 19			22 31	22 43		22 49	23 11	23 19			23 31			23 34
Bedhampton	d					21 34								22 34								23 34			
Hilsea	d			21 33		21 41			22 03			22 33		22 39						23 24	23 33	23 39			
Fratton	d	21 29		21 37	21 42	21 45	21 55	21 58	22 08	22 19	22 29	22 37		22 44	22 52	22 56	23 00	23 20	23 29	23 33	23 37	23 44		23 44	23 47
Portsmouth & Southsea	a	21 32		21 40	21 45	21 48	21 58	22 01	22 11	22 22	22 32	22 42		22 47	22 55	22 59	23 04	23 23	23 32	23 36	23 40	23 47		23 48	23 54
	d	21 33		21 41	21 46		21 58	22 02	22 13	22 22	22 33				22 56	22 59	23 05	23 24	23 33	23 36				23 48	
Portsmouth Harbour ⛴	a	21 37		21 45	21 52		22 02	22 05	22 16	22 26	22 37				22 59	23 04	23 08	23 27	23 37	23 40				23 54	

		SW ■1
Havant	d	23 49
Bedhampton	d	
Hilsea	d	
Fratton	d	23 59
Portsmouth & Southsea	a	00 02
	d	00 03
Portsmouth Harbour ⛴	a	00 07

Saturdays

		SW ■1	SW ■1	SW ■1	SW ■1	SW ■1	SW ■1	SW ■1	SN ◇	SN ■1		SN ■1	SW ■1	SW ■1	SN	SN	SW ■1	SN ■1	SW ■1	SW ■1		GW	SN	SN	SW ■1
Havant	d	23p49		00 22	00 37		01 21	04 40	05 34	05 49		05 57	06 02		06 32	06 46		07 04	07 20				07 32	07 46	
Bedhampton	d			00 25			01s24	04 43					06 05		06 34				07 22				07 34		
Hilsea	d		00 03	00 30			01s29	04 48					06 10	06 33	06 42		07 03		07 27	07 33			07 42		08 03
Fratton	d	23p59	00 08	00 34	00 47		01s33	04 52	05 43	05 58		06 06	06 15	06 37	06 47	06 55	07 08	07 13	07 32	07 37		07 42	07 47	07 55	08 08
Portsmouth & Southsea	a	00 02	00 11	00 38	00 50	01s08	01 37	04 55	05 46	06 01		06 09	06 18	06 42	06 50	06 58	07 11	07 16	07 35	07 42		07 46	07 50	07 58	08 11
	d	00 03	00 13		00 51			04 57		06 01		06 09	06 19			06 58	07 12	07 16	07 36			07 46		07 59	08 13
Portsmouth Harbour ⛴	a	00 07	00 16		00 55	01 12		05 00		06 05		06 16	06 22			07 02	07 16	07 20	07 40			07 52		08 02	08 18

		SN	SW ■1	SW ■1	GW ◇	SN		SN ■1	SW ■1	SW ■1	SN	SW ■1	SW ■1	SW ■1	GW ◇	SN		SN ◇■1	SW ■1	SW ■1	SN	SW ■1 🚲	SW ■1	SW ■1	GW ◇
Havant	d	08 04	08 17			08 32		08 46	08 50		09 04	09 16		09 27		09 32		09 46	09 50		10 07	10 16		10 27	
Bedhampton	d		08 20			08 34								09 30		09 34								10 30	
Hilsea	d		08 25	08 33		08 42				09 04			09 33	09 36		09 42				10 03			10 33	10 36	
Fratton	d	08 13	08 29	08 37	08 42	08 47		08 55	08 59	09 09	09 13	09 25	09 37	09 40	09 42	09 47		09 55	09 59	10 08	10 16	10 25	10 37	10 40	10 42
Portsmouth & Southsea	a	08 16	08 32	08 42	08 46	08 50		08 58	09 02	09 12	09 16	09 28	09 42	09 44	09 46	09 50		09 58	10 02	10 11	10 19	10 28	10 42	10 44	10 46
	d	08 16	08 34		08 46			08 59	09 04	09 13	09 16	09 29			09 46			09 58	10 04	10 12	10 20	10 29			10 46
Portsmouth Harbour ⛴	a	08 20	08 37		08 52			09 02	09 07	09 18	09 20	09 33			09 52			10 02	10 07	10 18	10 23	10 33			10 52

		SN		SN ◇■1	SW ■1 🚲	SW ■1	SN	SW ■1 🚲	SW ■1	SW ■1	GW ◇	SN		SN ◇■1	SW ■1 🚲	SW ■1	SN	SW ■1 🚲	SW ■1	SW ■1	GW ◇ 🚲	SN		SN ◇■1	SW ■1 🚲
Havant	d	10 32		10 46	10 50		11 05	11 16		11 27		11 32		11 46	11 50		12 05	12 16		12 27		12 32		12 46	12 50
Bedhampton	d	10 34								11 30		11 34								12 30		12 34			
Hilsea	d	10 43				11 03			11 33	11 36		11 42				12 03			12 33	12 36		12 42			
Fratton	d	10 47		10 55	10 59	11 08	11 14	11 25	11 37	11 40	11 42	11 47		11 55	11 59	12 08	12 14	12 25	12 37	12 40	12 42	12 47		12 55	12 59
Portsmouth & Southsea	a	10 50		10 58	11 02	11 11	11 17	11 28	11 42	11 44	11 46	11 50		11 58	12 02	12 11	12 17	12 28	12 42	12 44	12 46	12 50		12 58	13 02
	d			10 58	11 04	11 12	11 17	11 29			11 46			11 58	12 04	12 12	12 17	12 29			12 46			12 58	13 04
Portsmouth Harbour ⛴	a			11 02	11 07	11 18	11 21	11 33			11 52			12 02	12 07	12 18	12 21	12 33			12 52			13 02	13 07

		SW ■1	SN	SW ■1 🚲	SW ■1	SW ■1	GW ◇ 🚲	SN		SN ◇■1	SW ■1 🚲	SW ■1	SN	SW ■1 🚲	SW ■1	SW ■1	GW ◇ 🚲	SN		SN ◇■1	SW ■1 🚲	SW ■1	SN	SW ■1 🚲	SW ■1
Havant	d		13 05	13 16		13 27		13 32		13 46	13 50		14 05	14 16		14 27		14 32		14 46	14 50		15 05	15 16	
Bedhampton	d					13 30		13 34								14 30		14 34							
Hilsea	d	13 03			13 33	13 36		13 42				14 03			14 33	14 36		14 42				15 03			15 33
Fratton	d	13 08	13 14	13 25	13 37	13 40	13 42	13 47		13 55	13 59	14 08	14 14	14 25	14 37	14 40	14 42	14 47		14 55	14 59	15 08	15 14	15 25	15 37
Portsmouth & Southsea	a	13 11	13 17	13 28	13 42	13 44	13 46	13 50		13 58	14 02	14 11	14 17	14 28	14 42	14 44	14 46	14 50		14 58	15 02	15 11	15 17	15 28	15 42
	d	13 12	13 17	13 29			13 46			13 58	14 04	14 12	14 17	14 29			14 46			14 58	15 04	15 12	15 17	15 29	
Portsmouth Harbour ⛴	a	13 18	13 21	13 33			13 52			14 02	14 07	14 18	14 21	14 33			14 52			15 02	15 07	15 18	15 21	15 33	

		SW ■1	GW ◇	SN		SN ◇■1	SW ■1 🚲	SW ■1	SN	SW ■1 🚲	SW ■1	SW ■1	GW ◇	SN		SN ◇■1	SW ■1 🚲	SW ■1	SN	SW ■1 🚲	SW ■1	SW ■1	GW ◇	SN	
Havant	d	15 27		15 32		15 46	15 50		16 05	16 16		16 27		16 32		16 46	16 50		17 05	17 16		17 27		17 32	
Bedhampton	d	15 30		15 34								16 30		16 34								17 30		17 34	
Hilsea	d	15 36		15 42				16 03			16 33	16 36		16 42				17 03			17 33	17 36		17 42	
Fratton	d	15 40	15 42	15 47		15 55	15 59	16 08	16 14	16 25	16 37	16 40	16 42	16 47		16 55	16 59	17 08	17 14	17 25	17 37	17 40	17 42	17 47	
Portsmouth & Southsea	a	15 44	15 46	15 50		15 58	16 02	16 11	16 17	16 28	16 40	16 44	16 46	16 50		16 58	17 02	17 11	17 17	17 28	17 42	17 44	17 46	17 50	
	d		15 46			15 58	16 04	16 12	16 17	16 29	16 41		16 46			16 58	17 04	17 12	17 17	17 29			17 46		
Portsmouth Harbour ⛴	a		15 52			16 02	16 07	16 18	16 21	16 33	16 44		16 52			17 02	17 07	17 18	17 21	17 33			17 52		

Table 157

Saturdays

Havant - Portsmouth Harbour

(Complete service)

Network Diagram - see first Page of Table 155

		SN	SW	SW	SN	SW	SW	SW	GW	SN		SN	SW	SW	SN	SW	SW	SW	GW	SN		SN	SW	SW	SN
		◇1	1	1		1	1	1	◇			◇1	1	1		1	1	1	R			◇1	1	1	1
			🛒			🛒							🛒			🛒							🛒		
Havant	d	17 46	17 50		18 06	18 16		18 27		18 32		18 46	18 50		19 05	19 16		19 27		19 32		19 46	19 50		20 10
Bedhampton	d							18 30		18 34								19 30		19 34					
Hilsea	d			18 03			18 33	18 36		18 42				19 03			19 33	19 36		19 42				20 03	
Fratton	d	17 55	17 59	18 08	18 15	18 25	18 37	18 40	18 42	18 47		18 55	18 59	19 08	19 14	19 25	19 37	19 40	19 42	19 47		19 55	19 59	20 08	20 19
Portsmouth & Southsea	a	17 58	18 02	18 11	18 18	18 28	18 42	18 44	18 46	18 50		18 58	19 02	19 11	19 17	19 28	19 42	19 44	19 46	19 50		19 58	20 02	20 11	20 22
	d	17 58	18 04	18 12	18 19	18 29			18 46			18 58	19 04	19 12	19 17	19 29			19 46			19 58	20 04	20 12	20 22
Portsmouth Harbour ⛴	a	18 02	18 07	18 18	18 22	18 33			18 52			19 02	19 07	19 18	19 21	19 33			19 52			20 02	20 07	20 18	20 26

		SW	SW	GW	SW	SN		SW	SW	SN	SW	SW	SW	GW	SW	SN		SW	SN	SW	SW	GW	SW	SN	SW
		1	1	◇	1	◇1		1	1	1	1	1	1	◇	1	◇1		1		1	1	◇	1		1
		🛒						🛒																	
Havant	d	20 16			20 30	20 46		20 50		21 10	21 16		21 27		21 46	21 49			22 10	22 19			22 31	22 43	22 49
Bedhampton	d				20 33								21 30										22 34		
Hilsea	d		20 37		20 41				21 03			21 33	21 36					22 03			22 33		22 41		
Fratton	d	20 25	20 41	20 42	20 45	20 55		20 59	21 08	21 19	21 25	21 37	21 40	21 42	21 55	21 59		22 08	22 19	22 29	22 37	22 42	22 45	22 52	22 59
Portsmouth & Southsea	a	20 28	20 44	20 46	20 48	20 58		21 02	21 11	21 22	21 28	21 40	21 43	21 46	21 58	22 02		22 11	22 22	22 32	22 40	22 46	22 49	22 55	23 02
	d	20 29		20 46		20 58		21 04	21 12	21 22	21 29	21 41		21 46	22 00	22 03		22 12	22 22	22 33	22 41	22 46	22 50	22 56	23 03
Portsmouth Harbour ⛴	a	20 33		20 52		21 02		21 07	21 18	21 26	21 33	21 45		21 52	22 03	22 06		22 18	22 26	22 36	22 47	22 52	22 53	22 59	23 08

		SW		SN	SW	SW	GW	SW	SN	SW
		1			1	1	◇	1		1
Havant	d			23 10	23 19			23 31	23 36	23 49
Bedhampton	d							23 34		
Hilsea	d	23 03				23 33		23 41		
Fratton	d	23 08		23 19	23 29	23 37	23 41	23 45	23 48	23 59
Portsmouth & Southsea	a	23 11		23 22	23 32	23 40	23 44	23 48	23 51	00 02
	d	23 12		23 22	23 33		23 45	23 50		00 03
Portsmouth Harbour ⛴	a	23 18		23 26	23 37		23 52	23 53		00 07

Sundays

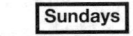

until 12 February

		SW	SW	SW	SW	SW	SW	SN	SW	SW		SN	SW	SW	SN	SW	SN	SW	SW	SN		SW	SW	SN	SW
		1	1	1	1	1	1	1	1	1		1	1	1	1	1	1	1	1	1		1	1	◇1	1
		A	A	A	A		A																		
Havant	d	23p49		00⌇22	00⌇37		01⌇21	07 10				08 11		08 39	08 49		09 11		09 45	09 49		09 53		10 17	
Bedhampton	d	⌇		00⌇25	⌇		01s24							08 41	08 51				09 47	09 51					
Hilsea	d	⌇	00⌇03	00⌇30	⌇		01s29		07 26	08 00			08 26			09 00		09 26					10 04		10 26
Fratton	d	23p59	00⌇07	00⌇34	00⌇47		01s33	07 19	07 30	08 04		08 20	08 30	08 50	08 59	09 04	09 20	09 30	09 56	09 59		10 02	10 08	10 26	10 30
Portsmouth & Southsea	a	00⌇02	00⌇11	00⌇38	00⌇50	01s08	01⌇37	07 22	07 33	08 08		08 23	08 33	08 53	09 03	09 08	09 23	09 33	09 59	10 03		10 06	10 11	10 29	10 33
	d	00⌇03	00⌇12		00⌇51			07 22		08 09		08 23		08 54	09 04	09 09	09 23		10 00	10 04		10 08	10 12	10 30	
Portsmouth Harbour ⛴	a	00⌇07	00⌇16		00⌇55	01 12		07 26		08 13		08 27		08 57	09 07	09 13	09 27		10 04	10 07		10 11	10 15	10 35	

		SN	SW	SW	SW	SN		SW	GW	SW	SN	SW	SW	SN	SW	GW		SW	SN	SW	SW	SN	SW	SW	SN
		1	1	1	1	◇1		1	◇	1	1	1	1	◇1	1	◇		1	1	1	1	◇1	1	1	1
																				🛒					
Havant	d	10 41	10 45	10 53		11 17				11 39	11 44	11 51		12 17				12 39	12 44	12 51		13 17		13 39	13 44
Bedhampton	d	10 43	10 47							11 41	11 46							12 41	12 46					13 41	13 46
Hilsea	d				11 04			11 26					12 00		12 26						13 00		13 26		
Fratton	d	10 51	10 56	11 02	11 08	11 26		11 30	11 42	11 50	11 54	12 01	12 04	12 26	12 30	12 43		12 50	12 54	13 01	13 04	13 26	13 30	13 50	13 54
Portsmouth & Southsea	a	10 54	10 59	11 05	11 11	11 29		11 33	11 46	11 53	11 57	12 04	12 08	12 29	12 33	12 46		12 53	12 57	13 04	13 08	13 29	13 33	13 53	13 57
	d	10 55	11 00	11 07	11 12	11 30			11 46	11 54	11 58	12 05	12 09	12 30		12 46		12 54	12 58	13 05	13 09	13 30		13 54	13 58
Portsmouth Harbour ⛴	a	10 58	11 04	11 11	11 15	11 35			11 52	11 58	12 01	12 09	12 13	12 35		12 52		12 58	13 01	13 11	13 13	13 35		13 58	14 01

		SW		SW	SN	SW	GW	SW	SN	SW	SW	SN		SW	SW	SN	SW	SW	SN	SW	GW	SW		SN	SW
		1		1	◇1	1	◇	1	1	1	1	◇1		1	1	1	1	1	◇1	1	◇	1		1	1
		🛒					🛒			🛒							🛒								🛒
Havant	d	13 51			14 17			14 39	14 44	14 51		15 17			15 39	15 44	15 51		16 17			16 39		16 44	16 51
Bedhampton	d							14 41	14 46						15 41	15 46						16 41		16 46	
Hilsea	d			14 00		14 26					15 00			15 26				16 00		16 26					
Fratton	d	14 01		14 04	14 26	14 30	14 42	14 50	14 54	15 01	15 04	15 26		15 30	15 50	15 54	16 01	16 04	16 26	16 30	16 41	16 50		16 54	17 01
Portsmouth & Southsea	a	14 04		14 08	14 29	14 33	14 45	14 53	14 57	15 04	15 08	15 29		15 33	15 54	15 57	16 04	16 08	16 29	16 33	16 45	16 53		16 57	17 04
	d	14 05		14 09	14 30		14 45	14 54	14 58	15 05	15 09	15 30			15 54	15 58	16 05	16 09	16 30		16 45	16 54		16 58	17 05
Portsmouth Harbour ⛴	a	14 11		14 13	14 35		14 55	14 58	15 01	15 11	15 13	15 35			15 58	16 01	16 11	16 13	16 35		16 52	16 58		17 01	17 11

		SW	SN	SW	GW	SW	SN	SW		SW	SN	SW	GW	SW	SN	SW	SW	SN		SW	GW	SW	SN	SW	SW
		1	◇1	1	◇	1	1	1		1	◇1	1	◇	1	1	1	1	◇1		1	◇	1	1	1	1
								🛒								🛒								🛒	
Havant	d		17 17			17 39	17 44	17 51			18 17			18 39	18 44	18 51		19 17				19 39	19 44	19 51	
Bedhampton	d					17 41	17 46							18 41	18 46							19 41	19 46		
Hilsea	d	17 00		17 26						18 00		18 26					19 00			19 26					20 00
Fratton	d	17 04	17 26	17 30	17 42	17 50	17 54	18 01		18 04	18 26	18 30	18 42	18 50	18 54	19 01	19 04	19 26		19 30	19 42	19 50	19 54	20 01	20 04
Portsmouth & Southsea	a	17 08	17 29	17 33	17 46	17 53	17 57	18 04		18 08	18 29	18 33	18 45	18 53	18 57	19 04	19 08	19 29		19 33	19 46	19 53	19 57	20 04	20 08
	d	17 09	17 30		17 46	17 54	17 58	18 05		18 09	18 30		18 45	18 54	18 58	19 05	19 09	19 30			19 46	19 54	19 58	20 05	20 09
Portsmouth Harbour ⛴	a	17 13	17 35		17 52	17 58	18 01	18 11		18 13	18 35		18 52	18 58	19 01	19 11	19 13	19 35			19 52	19 58	20 01	20 11	20 13

A not 11 December

Table 157

Sundays
until 12 February

Havant - Portsmouth Harbour

(Complete service)

Network Diagram - see first Page of Table 155

		SN	SW	GW		SW	SN	SW	SW	GW	SN	SW	GW	SW		SN	SW	SW	SN	SW	GW	SW	SN	GW
		◇1	1	◇		1	1	1 🛒	1	R	◇1	1	◇	1		1	1 🛒	1	◇1	1	◇	1	1	
Havant	d	20 17				20 39	20 44	20 51			21 17			21 39		21 44	21 51		22 17			22 39	22 44	22 47
Bedhampton	d					20 41	20 46							21 41		21 46						22 41	22 46	
Hilsea	d		20 26						21 00			21 26						22 00		22 26				
Fratton	d	20 26	20 30	20 41		20 50	20 54	21 01	21 04	21 10	21 26	21 30	21 38	21 50		21 54	22 01	22 04	22 26	22 30	22 41	22 50	22 54	22 57
Portsmouth & Southsea	a	20 29	20 33	20 45		20 53	20 57	21 04	21 08	21 15	21 29	21 33	21 41	21 53		21 57	22 04	22 08	22 29	22 33	22 44	22 53	22 57	23 00
	d	20 30		20 45		20 54	20 58	21 05	21 09	21 15	21 30		21 42	21 54		21 58	22 05	22 09	22 30		22 44	22 54	22 58	23 00
Portsmouth Harbour ⛴	a	20 35		20 51		20 58	21 01	21 09	21 13	21 26	21 35		21 48	21 58		22 01	22 11	22 13	22 35		22 50	22 58	23 01	23 04

		SW	SW	SW	SN	GW	SW	SW	SW
		1	1	1	◇1	◇	1	1	1
Havant	d	22 51			23 22		23 39	23 51	
Bedhampton	d						23 41		
Hilsea	d		23 00	23 24					23 59
Fratton	d	23 01	23 04	23 29	23 32	23 43	23 50	00 01	00 04
Portsmouth & Southsea	a	23 04	23 08	23 32	23 35	23 46	23 53	00 04	00 08
	d	23 05	23 09		23 36	23 47	23 54	00 05	00 09
Portsmouth Harbour ⛴	a	23 09	23 13		23 39	23 54	23 58	00 09	00 13

Sundays
19 February to 25 March

		SW	SW	SW	SW	SW	SW	SN	SW	SW		SN	SW	SW	SN	SW	SN	SW	SW	SN		SW	SW	SN	SW
		1	1	1	1	1	1	1	1	1		1	1	1	1	1	1	1	1	1		1	1	◇1	1
Havant	d	23p49		00 22	00 37		01 21	07 10				08 11		08 39	08 49		09 11		09 45	09 49		09 53		10 17	
Bedhampton	d			00 25			01s24							08 41	08 51				09 47	09 51					
Hilsea	d		00 03	00 30			01s29		07 26	08 00			08 26			09 00		09 26					10 04		10 26
Fratton	d	23p59	00 07	00 34	00 47		01s33	07 19	07 30	08 04		08 20	08 30	08 50	08 59	09 04	09 20	09 30	09 56	09 59		10 02	10 08	10 26	10 30
Portsmouth & Southsea	a	00 02	00 11	00 38	00 50	01s08	01 37	07 22	07 33	08 08		08 23	08 33	08 53	09 03	09 08	09 23	09 33	09 59	10 03		10 06	10 11	10 29	10 33
	d	00 03	00 12		00 51			07 22		08 09		08 23		08 54	09 04	09 09	09 23		10 00	10 04		10 08	10 12	10 30	
Portsmouth Harbour ⛴	a	00 07	00 16		00 55	01 12		07 26		08 13		08 27		08 57	09 07	09 13	09 27		10 04	10 07		10 11	10 15	10 35	

		SN	SW	SW	SW	SN		SW	GW	SW	SN	SW	SW	SN	SW	GW		SW	SN	SW	SW	SN	SW	SW	SN
		1	1	1	1	◇1		1	◇	1	1	1	1	◇1	1	◇		1	1	1 🛒	1	◇1	1	1	1
Havant	d	10 41	10 45	10 53		11 17				11 39	11 44	11 51		12 17				12 39	12 44	12 51		13 17		13 39	13 44
Bedhampton	d	10 43	10 47							11 41	11 46							12 41	12 46					13 41	13 46
Hilsea	d				11 04			11 26					12 00		12 26						13 00		13 26		
Fratton	d	10 51	10 56	11 02	11 08	11 26		11 30	11 41	11 50	11 54	12 01	12 04	12 26	12 30	12 43		12 50	12 54	13 01	13 04	13 26	13 30	13 50	13 54
Portsmouth & Southsea	a	10 54	10 59	11 05	11 11	11 29		11 33	11 45	11 53	11 57	12 04	12 08	12 29	12 33	12 46		12 53	12 57	13 04	13 08	13 29	13 33	13 53	13 57
	d	10 55	11 00	11 07	11 12	11 30			11 45	11 54	11 58	12 05	12 09	12 30		12 46		12 54	12 58	13 05	13 09	13 30		13 54	13 58
Portsmouth Harbour ⛴	a	10 58	11 04	11 11	11 15	11 35			11 52	11 58	12 01	12 09	12 13	12 35		12 52		12 58	13 01	13 11	13 13	13 35		13 58	14 01

		SW		SW	SN	SW	GW	SW	SN	SW	SW	SN		SW	SW	SN	SW	SW	SN	SW	GW	SW		SN	SW
		1 🛒		1	◇1	1	◇ 🛒	1	1	1 🛒	1	◇1		1	1	1	1 🛒	1	◇1	1	◇	1		1	1 🛒
Havant	d	13 51			14 17			14 39	14 44	14 51		15 17			15 39	15 44	15 51		16 17			16 39		16 44	16 51
Bedhampton	d							14 41	14 46						15 41	15 46						16 41		16 46	
Hilsea	d			14 00		14 26					15 00			15 26				16 00		16 26					
Fratton	d	14 01		14 04	14 26	14 30	14 42	14 50	14 54	15 01	15 04	15 26		15 30	15 50	15 54	16 01	16 04	16 26	16 30	16 42	16 50		16 54	17 01
Portsmouth & Southsea	a	14 04		14 08	14 29	14 33	14 45	14 53	14 57	15 04	15 08	15 29		15 33	15 54	15 57	16 04	16 08	16 29	16 33	16 46	16 53		16 57	17 04
	d	14 05		14 09	14 30		14 45	14 54	14 58	15 05	15 09	15 30			15 54	15 58	16 05	16 09	16 30		16 47	16 54		16 58	17 05
Portsmouth Harbour ⛴	a	14 11		14 13	14 35		14 55	14 58	15 01	15 11	15 13	15 35			15 58	16 01	16 11	16 13	16 35		16 52	16 58		17 01	17 11

		SW	SN	SW	GW	SW	SN	SW		SW	SN	SW	GW	SW	SN	SW	SW	SN		SW	GW	SW	SN	SW	SW
		1	◇1	1	◇	1	1	1 🛒		1	◇1	1	◇	1	1	1 🛒	1	◇1		1	◇	1	1	1 🛒	1
Havant	d		17 17			17 39	17 44	17 51			18 17			18 39	18 44	18 51		19 17				19 39	19 44	19 51	
Bedhampton	d					17 41	17 46							18 41	18 46							19 41	19 46		
Hilsea	d	17 00		17 26						18 00		18 26					19 00			19 26					20 00
Fratton	d	17 04	17 26	17 30	17 42	17 50	17 54	18 01		18 04	18 26	18 30	18 42	18 50	18 54	19 01	19 04	19 26		19 30	19 43	19 50	19 54	20 01	20 04
Portsmouth & Southsea	a	17 08	17 29	17 33	17 46	17 53	17 57	18 04		18 08	18 29	18 33	18 45	18 53	18 57	19 04	19 08	19 29		19 33	19 46	19 53	19 57	20 04	20 08
	d	17 09	17 30		17 46	17 54	17 58	18 05		18 09	18 30		18 45	18 54	18 58	19 05	19 09	19 30			19 46	19 54	19 58	20 05	20 09
Portsmouth Harbour ⛴	a	17 13	17 35		17 51	17 58	18 01	18 11		18 13	18 35		18 52	18 58	19 01	19 11	19 13	19 35			19 51	19 58	20 01	20 11	20 13

		SN	SW	GW		SW	SN	SW	SW	GW	SN	SW	GW	SW		SN	SW	SW	SN	SW	GW	SW	SN	GW
		◇1	1	◇		1	1	1 🛒	1	R	◇1	1	◇	1		1	1 🛒	1	◇1	1	◇	1	1	
Havant	d	20 17				20 39	20 44	20 51			21 17			21 39		21 44	21 51		22 17			22 39	22 44	22 47
Bedhampton	d					20 41	20 46							21 41		21 46						22 41	22 46	
Hilsea	d		20 26						21 00			21 26						22 00		22 26				
Fratton	d	20 26	20 30	20 42		20 50	20 54	21 01	21 04	21 10	21 26	21 30	21 38	21 50		21 54	22 01	22 04	22 26	22 30	22 41	22 50	22 54	22 57
Portsmouth & Southsea	a	20 29	20 33	20 45		20 53	20 57	21 04	21 08	21 15	21 29	21 33	21 41	21 53		21 57	22 04	22 08	22 29	22 33	22 44	22 53	22 57	23 00
	d	20 30		20 46		20 54	20 58	21 05	21 09	21 15	21 30		21 42	21 54		21 58	22 05	22 09	22 30		22 44	22 54	22 58	23 00
Portsmouth Harbour ⛴	a	20 35		20 49		20 58	21 01	21 09	21 13	21 24	21 35		21 46	21 58		22 01	22 11	22 13	22 35		22 50	22 58	23 01	23 04

Table 157

Sundays

19 February to 25 March

Havant - Portsmouth Harbour

(Complete service)

Network Diagram - see first Page of Table 155

		SW 1	SW 1	SW 1	SN ◇1	GW ◇	SW 1	SW 1	SW 1
Havant	d	22 51			23 22		23 39	23 51	
Bedhampton	d						23 41		
Hilsea	d		23 00	23 24					23 59
Fratton	d	23 01	23 04	23 29	23 32	23 43	23 50	00 01	00 04
Portsmouth & Southsea	a	23 04	23 08	23 32	23 35	23 46	23 53	00 04	00 08
	d	23 05	23 09		23 36	23 47	23 54	00 05	00 09
Portsmouth Harbour ⛴	a	23 09	23 13		23 39	23 50	23 58	00 09	00 13

Sundays

from 1 April

		SW 1	SW 1	SW 1	SW 1	SW 1	SW 1	SN 1	SW 1	SW 1		SN 1	SW 1	SW 1	SN 1	SW 1	SN 1	SW 1	SW 1	SN 1		SW 1	SW 1	SN ◇1	SW 1
Havant	d	23p49		00 22	00 37		01 21	07 10				08 11		08 39	08 49		09 11		09 45	09 49		09 53		10 17	
Bedhampton	d			00 25			01s24							08 41	08 51				09 47	09 51					
Hilsea	d		00 03	00 30			01s29		07 26	08 00			08 26			09 00		09 26					10 04		10 26
Fratton	d	23p59	00 07	00 34	00 47		01s33	07 19	07 30	08 04		08 20	08 30	08 50	08 59	09 04	09 20	09 30	09 56	09 59		10 02	10 08	10 26	10 30
Portsmouth & Southsea	a	00 02	00 11	00 38	00 50	01s08	01 37	07 22	07 33	08 08		08 23	08 33	08 53	09 03	09 08	09 23	09 33	09 59	10 03		10 06	10 11	10 29	10 33
	d	00 03	00 12		00 51			07 22		08 09		08 23		08 54	09 04	09 09	09 23		10 00	10 04		10 08	10 12	10 30	
Portsmouth Harbour ⛴	a	00 07	00 16		00 55	01 12		07 26		08 13		08 27		08 57	09 07	09 13	09 27		10 04	10 07		10 11	10 15	10 35	

		SN 1	SW 1	SW 1	SW 1	SN ◇1		SW 1	GW ◇	SW 1	SN 1	SW 1	SW 1	SN ◇1	SW 1	GW ◇		SW 1	SN 1	SW 1 (trolley)	SW 1	SN ◇1	SW 1	SW 1	SN 1
Havant	d	10 41	10 45	10 53		11 17				11 39	11 44	11 51		12 17				12 39	12 44	12 51		13 17		13 39	13 44
Bedhampton	d	10 43	10 47							11 41	11 46							12 41	12 46					13 41	13 46
Hilsea	d				11 04			11 26					12 00		12 26						13 00		13 26		
Fratton	d	10 51	10 56	11 02	11 08	11 26		11 30	11 41	11 50	11 54	12 01	12 04	12 26	12 30	12 43		12 50	12 54	13 01	13 04	13 26	13 30	13 50	13 54
Portsmouth & Southsea	a	10 54	10 59	11 05	11 11	11 29		11 33	11 45	11 53	11 57	12 04	12 08	12 29	12 33	12 46		12 53	12 57	13 04	13 08	13 29	13 33	13 53	13 57
	d	10 55	11 00	11 07	11 12	11 30			11 45	11 54	11 58	12 05	12 09	12 30		12 46		12 54	12 58	13 05	13 09	13 30		13 54	13 58
Portsmouth Harbour ⛴	a	10 58	11 04	11 11	11 15	11 35			11 52	11 58	12 01	12 09	12 13	12 35		12 52		12 58	13 01	13 11	13 13	13 35		13 58	14 01

		SW 1 (trolley)		SW 1	SN ◇1	SW 1	GW ◇ (trolley)	SW 1	SN 1	SW 1 (trolley)	SW 1	SN ◇1		SW 1	SW 1	SN 1	SW 1 (trolley)	SW 1	SN ◇1	SW 1	GW ◇	SW 1		SN 1	SW 1 (trolley)
Havant	d	13 51			14 17			14 39	14 44	14 51		15 17			15 39	15 44	15 51		16 17			16 39		16 44	16 51
Bedhampton	d							14 41	14 46						15 41	15 46						16 41		16 46	
Hilsea	d			14 00		14 26					15 00			15 26				16 00		16 26					
Fratton	d	14 01		14 04	14 26	14 30	14 42	14 50	14 54	15 01	15 04	15 26		15 30	15 50	15 54	16 01	16 04	16 26	16 30	16 41	16 50		16 54	17 01
Portsmouth & Southsea	a	14 04		14 08	14 29	14 33	14 45	14 53	14 57	15 04	15 08	15 29		15 33	15 54	15 57	16 04	16 08	16 29	16 33	16 45	16 53		16 57	17 04
	d	14 05		14 09	14 30		14 45	14 54	14 58	15 05	15 09	15 30			15 54	15 58	16 05	16 09	16 30		16 45	16 54		16 58	17 05
Portsmouth Harbour ⛴	a	14 11		14 13	14 35		14 55	14 58	15 01	15 11	15 13	15 35			15 58	16 01	16 11	16 13	16 35		16 52	16 58		17 01	17 11

		SW 1	SN ◇1	SW 1	GW ◇	SW 1	SN 1	SW 1 (trolley)		SW 1	SN ◇1	SW 1	GW ◇	SW 1	SN 1	SW 1 (trolley)	SW 1	SN ◇1		SW 1	GW ◇	SW 1	SN 1	SW 1 (trolley)	SW 1
Havant	d		17 17			17 39	17 44	17 51			18 17			18 39	18 44	18 51		19 17				19 39	19 44	19 51	
Bedhampton	d					17 41	17 46							18 41	18 46							19 41	19 46		
Hilsea	d	17 00		17 26						18 00		18 26					19 00			19 26					20 00
Fratton	d	17 04	17 26	17 30	17 42	17 50	17 54	18 01		18 04	18 26	18 30	18 42	18 50	18 54	19 01	19 04	19 26		19 30	19 42	19 50	19 54	20 01	20 04
Portsmouth & Southsea	a	17 08	17 29	17 33	17 46	17 53	17 57	18 04		18 08	18 29	18 33	18 45	18 53	18 57	19 04	19 08	19 29		19 33	19 46	19 53	19 57	20 04	20 08
	d	17 09	17 30		17 46	17 54	17 58	18 05		18 09	18 30		18 45	18 54	18 58	19 05	19 09	19 30			19 46	19 54	19 58	20 05	20 09
Portsmouth Harbour ⛴	a	17 13	17 35		17 52	17 58	18 01	18 11		18 13	18 35		18 52	18 58	19 01	19 11	19 13	19 35			19 52	19 58	20 01	20 11	20 13

		SN ◇1	SW 1	GW ◇		SW 1	SN 1	SW 1 (trolley)	SW 1	GW R	SN ◇1	SW 1	GW ◇	SW 1		SN 1	SW 1 (trolley)	SW 1	SN ◇1	SW 1	GW ◇	SW 1	SN 1	GW	
Havant	d	20 17				20 39	20 44	20 51			21 17			21 39		21 44	21 51		22 17			22 39	22 44	22 47	
Bedhampton	d					20 41	20 46							21 41		21 46						22 41	22 46		
Hilsea	d		20 26						21 00			21 26						22 00		22 26					
Fratton	d	20 26	20 30	20 41		20 50	20 54	21 01	21 04	21 10	21 26	21 30	21 38	21 50		21 54	22 01	22 04	22 26	22 30	22 41	22 50	22 54	22 57	
Portsmouth & Southsea	a	20 29	20 33	20 45		20 53	20 57	21 04	21 08	21 15	21 29	21 33	21 41	21 53		21 57	22 04	22 08	22 29	22 33	22 44	22 53	22 57	23 00	
	d	20 30		20 45		20 54	20 58	21 05	21 09	21 15	21 30		21 42	21 54		21 58	22 05	22 09	22 30		22 44	22 54	22 58	23 00	
Portsmouth Harbour ⛴	a	20 35		20 51		20 58	21 01	21 09	21 13	21 26	21 35		21 48	21 58		22 01	22 11	22 13	22 35		22 50	22 58	23 01	23 04	

		SW 1	SW 1	SW 1	SN ◇1	GW ◇	SW 1	SW 1	SW 1
Havant	d	22 51			23 22		23 39	23 51	
Bedhampton	d						23 41		
Hilsea	d		23 00	23 24					23 59
Fratton	d	23 01	23 04	23 29	23 32	23 43	23 50	00 01	00 04
Portsmouth & Southsea	a	23 04	23 08	23 32	23 35	23 46	23 53	00 04	00 08
	d	23 05	23 09		23 36	23 47	23 54	00 05	00 09
Portsmouth Harbour ⛴	a	23 09	23 13		23 39	23 54	23 58	00 09	00 13

Table 157

Mondays to Fridays

Portsmouth Harbour - Havant

(Complete service)

Network Diagram - see first Page of Table 155

		SW 1	SW 1	SW 1	SW 1 ⊼	SN 1	SW 1	SN ◇1	SW 1	GW ▪ ⊼		SN	SW 1 ⊼	SW 1	SW 1	SW 1 ⊼	SN ◇1	SW 1	SW 1	GW ⊼		GW ◇ ⊼	SW 1 ⊼	SN	SW 1
Portsmouth Harbour ⛴	d	04 30	05 00		05 19	05 33	05 43	05 47	05 50	06 00		06 04	06 15		06 23	06 42	06 46	06 50	06 55	07 01		07 05	07 13	07 20	07 24
Portsmouth & Southsea	a	04 33	05 03		05 22	05 36	05 46	05 50	05 53	06 03		06 07	06 18		06 26	06 45	06 49	06 53	06 58	07 04		07 08	07 16	07 23	07 27
	d	04 35	05 05	05 16	05 24	05 37	05 48	05 51	05 55	06 04		06 08	06 20	06 23	06 28	06 47	06 50	06 55	07 00	07 05		07 09	07 18	07 24	07 29
Fratton	d	04 39	05 09	05 20	05 28	05 41	05 52	05 55	05 59	06a07		06 12	06 24	06 27	06 32	06 51	06 54	06 59	07 04	07 10		07a13	07 22	07 28	07 33
Hilsea	d	04 43	05a13	05a24	05 32	05 45	05a56	05 59	06 03					06a31	06a36		06 58	07a03	07 08						07a37
Bedhampton	d	04 48			05 37	05 50		06 04	06 08								07 03		07 13						
Havant	a	04 50			05 40	05 52		06 06	06 10			06 20	06 33			06 59	07 05		07 15	07 19			07 30	07 36	

		SW 1	SW 1	SW 1 ⊼	SW 1	SN		SW 1	SN ◇1	SW 1 ⊼	SW 1	GW ◇ ⊼	SN	SW 1	SW 1 ⊼	SN		SW 1	SN ◇1	SW 1 ⊼	SW 1	GW ◇ ⊼	SN	SW 1	SW 1 ⊼
Portsmouth Harbour ⛴	d	07 29		07 45	07 55			08 05	08 10	08 15		08 23	08 29	08 33	08 45	08 51		08 59	09 12	09 15	09 18	09 23	09 29	09 33	09 45
Portsmouth & Southsea	a	07 32		07 48	07 58			08 08	08 13	08 18		08 26	08 32	08 36	08 48	08 54		09 02	09 15	09 18	09 22	09 26	09 32	09 36	09 48
	d	07 33	07 38	07 50	08 00	08 03		08 10	08 14	08 20	08 24	08 27	08 33	08 38	08 50	08 55		09 04	09 16	09 20	09 24	09 27	09 33	09 38	09 50
Fratton	d	07 37	07 42	07 54	08 04	08 07		08 13	08 18	08 24	08 28	08a31	08 37	08 42	08 54	08 59		09 08	09 20	09 24	09 28	09a31	09 37	09 42	09 54
Hilsea	d	07 41	07a46		08a08	08 11		08a17			08 32			08a46		09 04		09a12			09 32			09a46	
Bedhampton	d	07 48				08 16					08 37					09 13					09 37				
Havant	a	07 50		08 03		08 18			08 26	08 32	08 40		08 45		09 03	09 15			09 29	09 33	09 39		09 45		10 03

		SN		SW 1	SN ◇1	SW 1 ⊼	SW 1	GW ◇ ⊼	SN	SW 1	SW 1 ⊼	SN		SW 1	SN ◇1	SW 1 ⊼	SW 1	GW ◇ ⊼	SN	SW 1	SW 1 ⊼	SN		SW 1	SN ◇1
Portsmouth Harbour ⛴	d			09 59	10 12	10 15		10 23	10 29	10 33	10 45			10 59	11 12	11 15		11 23	11 29		11 45			11 59	12 12
Portsmouth & Southsea	a			10 02	10 15	10 18		10 26	10 32	10 36	10 48			11 02	11 15	11 18		11 26	11 32		11 48			12 02	12 15
	d	09 59		10 04	10 16	10 20	10 24	10 27	10 33	10 38	10 50	10 59		11 04	11 16	11 20	11 24	11 27	11 33	11 38	11 50	11 59		12 04	12 16
Fratton	d	10 04		10 08	10 20	10 24	10 28	10a31	10 37	10 42	10 54	11 04		11 08	11 20	11 24	11 28	11a31	11 37	11 42	11 54	12 04		12 08	12 20
Hilsea	d	10 08		10a12			10 32			10a46		11 08		11a12			11 32			11a46		12 08		12a12	
Bedhampton	d	10 13					10 37					11 13					11 37					12 13			
Havant	a	10 15			10 29	10 33	10 39		10 45		11 03	11 15			11 29	11 33	11 39		11 45		12 03	12 15			12 29

		SW 1 ⊼	SW 1	GW ◇ ⊼	SN	SW 1	SW 1 ⊼	SN		SW 1	SN ◇1	SW 1 ⊼	SW 1	GW ◇ ⊼	SN	SW 1	SW 1 ⊼	SN		SW 1	SN ◇1	SW 1 ⊼	SW 1	GW ▪ ⊼	SN
Portsmouth Harbour ⛴	d	12 15		12 23	12 29		12 45			12 59	13 12	13 15		13 23	13 29		13 45			13 59	14 12	14 15		14 23	14 29
Portsmouth & Southsea	a	12 18		12 26	12 32		12 48			13 02	13 15	13 18		13 26	13 32		13 48			14 02	14 15	14 18		14 26	14 32
	d	12 20	12 24	12 27	12 33	12 38	12 50	12 59		13 04	13 16	13 20	13 24	13 27	13 33	13 38	13 50	13 59		14 04	14 16	14 20	14 24	14 27	14 33
Fratton	d	12 24	12 28	12a31	12 37	12 42	12 54	13 04		13 08	13 20	13 24	13 28	13a31	13 37	13 42	13 54	14 04		14 08	14 20	14 24	14 28	14a31	14 37
Hilsea	d		12 32			12a46		13 08		13a12			13 32			13a46		14 08		14a12			14 32		
Bedhampton	d		12 37					13 13					13 37					14 13					14 37		
Havant	a	12 33	12 39		12 45		13 03	13 15			13 29	13 33	13 39		13 45		14 03	14 15			14 29	14 33	14 39		14 45

		SW 1	SW 1 ⊼	SN		SW 1	SN ◇1	SW 1 ⊼	SW 1	GW ▪ ⊼	SN	SW 1	SW 1 ⊼	SN		SW 1	SN ◇1	SW 1 ⊼	SW 1	GW ▪ ⊼	SN	SW 1	SN	SW 1 ⊼	
Portsmouth Harbour ⛴	d		14 45			14 59	15 12	15 15		15 23	15 29		15 45			15 59	16 12	16 15		16 23	16 29		16 40	16 45	
Portsmouth & Southsea	a		14 48			15 02	15 15	15 18		15 26	15 32		15 48			16 02	16 15	16 18		16 26	16 32		16 44	16 48	
	d	14 38	14 50	14 59		15 04	15 16	15 20	15 24	15 27	15 33	15 38	15 50	15 59		16 04	16 16	16 20	16 24	16 27	16 33	16 38	16 46	16 50	
Fratton	d	14 42	14 54	15 04		15 08	15 20	15 24	15 28	15a31	15 37	15 42	15 54	16 04		16 08	16 20	16 24	16 28	16a31	16 37	16 42	16 50	16 54	
Hilsea	d	14a46		15 08		15a12			15 32			15a46		16 08		16a12			16 32			16a46	16 54		
Bedhampton	d			15 14					15 37					16 13					16 37						
Havant	a		15 03	15 17			15 29	15 33	15 39		15 45		16 03	16 15			16 29	16 33	16 39		16 45		16 59	17 03	

		SW 1	SN	SW 1	SN ◇1	SW 1 ⊼	SW 1	GW ◇ ⊼	SN	SW 1		SN	SW 1 ⊼	SN 1	SW 1	SW 1 ⊼	SW 1	GW ◇ ⊼	SN 1	SW 1		SN	SW 1 ⊼	SN	SW 1
Portsmouth Harbour ⛴	d	16 49		16 59	17 12	17 15	17 18	17 23	17 29	17 33			17 45		17 59	18 15		18 23	18 28			18 37	18 45		18 59
Portsmouth & Southsea	a	16 53		17 02	17 15	17 18	17 22	17 26	17 32	17 36			17 48		18 02	18 18		18 26	18 31			18 40	18 48		19 02
	d	16 55	17 00	17 04	17 16	17 20	17 24	17 27	17 33	17 38		17 46	17 50	17 59	18 04	18 20	18 24	18 27	18 32	18 38		18 42	18 50	18 59	19 04
Fratton	d	16 59	17 04	17 08	17 20	17 24	17 28	17a31	17 37	17 42		17 50	17 54	18 04	18 08	18 24	18 28	18a31	18 36	18 42		18 46	18 54	19 04	19 08
Hilsea	d	17a03	17 08	17a12			17 32			17a46		17 54		18 08	18a12		18 32			18a46		18 50		19 08	19a12
Bedhampton	d		17 14				17 37							18 13			18 37							19 13	
Havant	a		17 17		17 29	17 33	17 39		17 45			17 59	18 03	18 15		18 33	18 39		18 44			18 56	19 03	19 15	

		SW 1	SW 1	GW ◇	SN 1	SW 1		SN 1	SW 1	SN	SW 1	SW 1	SW 1	GW ◇	SN	SW 1		SN 1	SW 1	SW 1	SN 1	SW 1	GW	SW 1	SW 1
Portsmouth Harbour ⛴	d	19 15		19 23				19 40	19 45		19 59	20 15	20 18	20 23				20 40	20 45	20 59		21 18	21 23	21 28	
Portsmouth & Southsea	a	19 18		19 26				19 43	19 48		20 02	20 18	20 22	20 26				20 43	20 48	21 02		21 21	21 26	21 31	
	d	19 20	19 24	19 27	19 32	19 38		19 44	19 50	19 59	20 04	20 20	20 24	20 27	20 32	20 38		20 44	20 50	21 04	21 15	21 24	21 27	21 33	21 38
Fratton	d	19 24	19 28	19a31	19 36	19 42		19 48	19 54	20 04	20 08	20 24	20 28	20a31	20 36	20 42		20 48	20 54	21 08	21 19	21 28	21a31	21 37	21 42
Hilsea	d		19 32			19a46				20 08	20a12		20 32			20a46				21a12	21 23	21 32		21 41	21a46
Bedhampton	d		19 37							20 14			20 37								21 28	21 37		21 47	
Havant	a	19 33	19 39		19 46			19 56	20 03	20 16		20 33	20 39		20 44			20 56	21 03		21 30	21 40		21 52	

Portsmouth Harbour - Havant

(Complete service)

Network Diagram - see first Page of Table 155

	SN [1]		SW [1]	SN	SW [1]	SW [1]	SW [1]	SN	SN	SW [1]	SW [1]
Portsmouth Harbour ⛴ d	21 40		21 54	22 15	22 18	22 28	22 33	22 44	23 15	23 19	23 24
Portsmouth & Southsea a	21 43		21 57	22 18	22 21	22 31	22 37	22 47	23 18	23 22	23 27
d	21 44		21 59	22 19	22 24	22 33	22 38	22 48	23 19	23 24	23 29
Fratton d	21 48		22 03	22 23	22 28	22 37	22 42	22 52	23 23	23 28	23 33
Hilsea d	21 52		22a07	22 27	22 32	22 41	22a46	22 56	23 27	23 32	23a37
Bedhampton d	21 57			22 32	22 37	22 46		23 01	23 33	23 37	
Havant a	21 59			22 34	22 39	22 53		23 05	23 36	23 39	

Saturdays

	SW [1]	SN ◇[1]	SW [1]	SW [1]	SW [1]	SN	GW ◇	SN ◇[1]	SW [1]		SN [1]	SW [1]	SW [1] 🚲	GW	SN	SW [1]	SN ◇[1]	SW [1] 🚲	SW [1]		GW ◇ 🚲	SN	SW [1]	SW [1] 🚲
Portsmouth Harbour ⛴ d	04 43			05 19	05 50		06 00	06 12	06 19		06 29		06 45	06 48		06 59	07 12	07 15			07 23	07 29		07 45
Portsmouth & Southsea a	04 46			05 22	05 53		06 03	06 15	06 22		06 32		06 48	06 53		07 02	07 15	07 18			07 26	07 32		07 48
d	04 48	04 56	05 16	05 24	05 55	05 59	06 04	06 16	06 24		06 33	06 38	06 50	06 54	06 56	07 04	07 16	07 20	07 24		07 27	07 33	07 38	07 50
Fratton d	04 52	05 00	05 20	05 28	05 59	06 04	06a07	06 20	06 28		06 37	06 42	06 54	06 58	07 01	07 08	07 20	07 24	07 28		07a30	07 37	07 42	07 54
Hilsea d	04 56		05a24	05 32	06a03	06 08			06 32			06a46			07 05	07a12			07 32				07a46	
Bedhampton d	05 01			05 37		06 13			06 37						07 13				07 37					
Havant a	05 03	05 08		05 39		06 15		06 29	06 40		06 45		07 03	07 08	07 15		07 29	07 33	07 39			07 45		08 03

	SN	SW [1]	SN ◇[1]	SW [1] 🚲	SW [1]		GW ◇ 🚲	SN	SW [1]	SW [1] 🚲	SN	SW [1]	SN ◇[1]	SW [1] 🚲	SW [1]		GW ◇ 🚲	SN	SW [1]	SW [1] 🚲	SN	SW [1]	SN ◇[1]	SW [1] 🚲
Portsmouth Harbour ⛴ d		07 59	08 12	08 15			08 23	08 29		08 45		08 59	09 12	09 15			09 23	09 29		09 45		09 59	10 12	10 15
Portsmouth & Southsea a		08 02	08 15	08 18			08 26	08 32		08 48		09 02	09 15	09 18			09 26	09 32		09 48		10 02	10 15	10 18
d	07 59	08 04	08 16	08 20	08 24		08 27	08 33	08 38	08 50	08 59	09 04	09 16	09 20	09 24		09 27	09 33	09 38	09 50	09 59	10 04	10 16	10 20
Fratton d	08 04	08 08	08 20	08 24	08 28		08a30	08 37	08 42	08 54	09 04	09 08	09 20	09 24	09 28		09a30	09 37	09 42	09 54	10 04	10 08	10 20	10 24
Hilsea d	08 08	08a12			08 32				08a46		09 08	09a12			09 32				09a46		10 08	10a12		
Bedhampton d	08 13				08 37						09 13				09 37						10 13			
Havant a	08 15		08 29	08 33	08 39			08 45		09 03	09 15		09 29	09 33	09 39			09 45		10 03	10 15		10 29	10 33

	SW [1]		GW ◇	SN	SW [1]	SW [1] 🚲	SN	SW [1]	SN ◇[1]	SW [1] 🚲	SW [1]		GW ◇	SN	SW [1]	SW [1] 🚲	SN	SW [1]	SN ◇[1]	SW [1] 🚲	SW [1]		GW ◇	SN
Portsmouth Harbour ⛴ d			10 23	10 29		10 45		10 59	11 12	11 15			11 23	11 29		11 45		11 59	12 12	12 15			12 23	12 29
Portsmouth & Southsea a			10 26	10 32		10 48		11 02	11 15	11 18			11 26	11 32		11 48		12 02	12 15	12 18			12 26	12 32
d	10 24		10 27	10 33	10 38	10 50	10 59	11 04	11 16	11 20	11 24		11 27	11 33	11 38	11 50	11 59	12 04	12 16	12 20	12 24		12 27	12 33
Fratton d	10 28		10a30	10 37	10 42	10 54	11 04	11 08	11 20	11 24	11 28		11a30	11 37	11 42	11 54	12 04	12 08	12 20	12 24	12 28		12a30	12 37
Hilsea d	10 32				10a46		11 08	11a12			11 32				11a46		12 08	12a12			12 32			
Bedhampton d	10 37						11 13				11 37						12 13				12 37			
Havant a	10 39			10 45		11 03	11 15		11 29	11 33	11 39			11 45		12 03	12 15		12 29	12 33	12 39			12 45

	SW [1]	SW [1] 🚲	SN	SW [1]	SN ◇[1]	SW [1] 🚲	SW [1]		GW ◇	SN	SW [1]	SW [1] 🚲	SN	SW [1]	SN ◇[1]	SW [1] 🚲	SW [1]		GW ◇	SN	SW [1]	SW [1] 🚲	SN	SW [1]
Portsmouth Harbour ⛴ d		12 45		12 59	13 12	13 15			13 23	13 29		13 45		13 59	14 12	14 15			14 23	14 29		14 45		14 59
Portsmouth & Southsea a		12 48		13 02	13 15	13 18			13 26	13 32		13 48		14 02	14 15	14 18			14 26	14 32		14 48		15 02
d	12 38	12 50	12 59	13 04	13 16	13 20	13 24		13 27	13 33	13 38	13 50	13 59	14 04	14 16	14 20	14 24		14 27	14 33	14 38	14 50	14 59	15 04
Fratton d	12 42	12 54	13 04	13 08	13 20	13 24	13 28		13a30	13 37	13 42	13 54	14 04	14 08	14 20	14 24	14 28		14a30	14 37	14 42	14 54	15 04	15 08
Hilsea d	12a46		13 08	13a12			13 32				13a46		14 08	14a12			14 32				14a46		15 08	15a12
Bedhampton d			13 13				13 37						14 13				14 37						15 14	
Havant a		13 03	13 15		13 29	13 33	13 39			13 45		14 03	14 15		14 29	14 33	14 39			14 45		15 03	15 17	

	SN ◇[1]	SW [1] 🚲	SW [1]		GW ◇	SN	SW [1]	SW [1] 🚲	SN	SW [1]	SN ◇[1]	SW [1] 🚲	SW [1]		GW [R]	SN	SW [1]	SW [1] 🚲	SN	SW [1]	SW [1]	SN ◇[1]	SW [1]	
Portsmouth Harbour ⛴ d	15 12	15 15			15 23	15 29		15 45		15 59	16 12	16 15			16 23	16 29		16 45		16 59		17 12	17 18	
Portsmouth & Southsea a	15 15	15 18			15 26	15 32		15 48		16 02	16 15	16 18			16 26	16 32		16 48		17 02		17 15	17 22	
d	15 16	15 20	15 24		15 27	15 33	15 38	15 50	15 59	16 04	16 16	16 20	16 24		16 27	16 33	16 38	16 50	16 59	17 04	17 10	17 16	17 24	
Fratton d	15 20	15 24	15 28		15a30	15 37	15 42	15 54	16 04	16 08	16 20	16 24	16 28		16a31	16 37	16 42	16 54	17 04	17 08	17 14	17 20	17 28	
Hilsea d			15 32				15a46		16 08	16a12			16 32				16a46		17 08	17a12	17 18		17 32	
Bedhampton d			15 37						16 13				16 37						17 13		17 23		17 37	
Havant a	15 29	15 33	15 39			15 45		16 03	16 15		16 29	16 33	16 39			16 45		17 03	17 15		17 25	17 29	17 39	

	GW ◇	SN	SW [1]	SW [1] 🚲	SN [1]	SW [1]	SN	SW [1]	SW [1]		GW ◇	SN	SW [1]	SW [1]	SN	SW [1]	SN [1]	SW [1]	SW [1]		GW ◇	SN	SW [1]	SW [1]
Portsmouth Harbour ⛴ d	17 23	17 29	17 33	17 45		17 59	18 12	18 15			18 23	18 29		18 45		18 59	19 12	19 15			19 23	19 29		19 45
Portsmouth & Southsea a	17 26	17 32	17 36	17 48		18 02	18 15	18 18			18 27	18 32		18 48		19 02	19 15	19 18			19 26	19 32		19 48
d	17 27	17 33	17 38	17 50	17 59	18 04	18 16	18 20	18 24		18 27	18 33	18 38	18 50	18 59	19 04	19 16	19 20	19 24		19 27	19 33	19 38	19 50
Fratton d	17a31	17 37	17 42	17 54	18 04	18 08	18 20	18 24	18 28		18a31	18 37	18 42	18 54	19 04	19 08	19 20	19 24	19 28		19a30	19 37	19 42	19 54
Hilsea d			17a46		18 08	18a12			18 32				18a46		19 08	19a12			19 32				19a46	
Bedhampton d					18 13				18 37						19 13				19 37					
Havant a		17 45		18 03	18 15		18 29	18 33	18 39			18 45		19 03	19 15		19 29	19 33	19 39			19 45		20 03

Table 157

Saturdays

Portsmouth Harbour - Havant

(Complete service)

Network Diagram - see first Page of Table 155

		SN	SW	SW	SW	GW		SN	SW	SN	SW	SW	SN	SW	SW	SN		SW	SN	SW	SW	SN	SN	SW	SW
			1	1	1	◇		1	1		1	1	1	1	1	1		1	1	1	1			1	1
Portsmouth Harbour ⛴	d		19 59	20 15		20 23		20 28		20 40	20 45	20 59	21 11	21 18		21 40		21 54	22 15	22 18	22 33	22 44	23 15	23 19	23 24
Portsmouth & Southsea	a		20 02	20 18		20 26		20 31		20 43	20 48	21 02	21 14	21 21		21 43		21 57	22 18	22 21	22 37	22 47	23 18	23 22	23 28
	d	19 59	20 04	20 20	20 24	20 27		20 32	20 38	20 44	20 50	21 04	21 15	21 24	21 38	21 44		21 59	22 19	22 24	22 38	22 48	23 19	23 24	23 29
Fratton	d	20 04	20 08	20 24	20 28	20a30		20 36	20 42	20 48	20 54	21 08	21 19	21 28	21 42	21 48		22 03	22 23	22 28	22 42	22 52	23 23	23 28	23 33
Hilsea	d	20 08	20a12		20 32				20a46	20 52		21a12	21 23	21 32	21a46	21 52		22a07	22 27	22 32	22a46	22 56	23 27	23 32	23a37
Bedhampton	d	20 13			20 37								21 28	21 37		21 57			22 32	22 37		23 01	23 33	23 37	
Havant	a	20 15		20 33	20 39			20 44		20 58	21 03		21 30	21 39		21 59			22 34	22 39		23 05	23 36	23 39	

Sundays

until 12 February

		SW	SW	SN	SW	SW	SW	SN	SW	SN		SW	SW	SW	SN	SW	GW	SN	SW	SW		SW	SN	SW	SN
		1	1	1	1	1	1	◇1	1	1		1	1	1	◇1	1	R	1	1 🛒	1 🛒		1	◇1	1	1
Portsmouth Harbour ⛴	d	06 37	06 48	07 14	07 17	07 32		07 43	07 48	08 14		08 17	08 32		08 43	08 48	09 08	09 14	09 17	09 32			09 43	09 48	10 14
Portsmouth & Southsea	a	06 40	06 51	07 17	07 20	07 35		07 46	07 51	08 17		08 20	08 35		08 46	08 51	09 11	09 17	09 20	09 35			09 46	09 51	10 17
	d	06 42	06 53	07 18	07 22	07 37	07 42	07 47	07 53	08 18		08 22	08 37	08 42	08 47	08 53	09 12	09 18	09 22	09 37		09 42	09 47	09 53	10 18
Fratton	d	06 46	06 57	07 22	07 26	07 41	07 46	07 51	07 57	08 22		08 26	08 41	08 46	08 51	08 57	09a15	09 22	09 26	09 41		09 46	09 51	09 57	10 22
Hilsea	d	06a50			07a30		07a50					08a30		08a50					09a30			09a50			
Bedhampton	d		07 04	07 30					08 04	08 30						09 04		09 30						10 04	10 30
Havant	a		07 07	07 32		07 49		07 59	08 07	08 32			08 49		08 59	09 07		09 32		09 49			09 59	10 07	10 32

		SW	SW	SW	SN	SW		GW	SN	SW	SW	SW	SN	SW	SN	SW		SW	SW	SN	SW	GW	SN	SW	SW
		1 🛒	1 🛒	1	◇1	1		◇	1	1 🛒	1 🛒	1	◇1	1	1	1 🛒		1 🛒	1	◇1	1	◇	1	1 🛒	1 🛒
Portsmouth Harbour ⛴	d	10 17	10 32		10 43	10 48		11 08	11 14	11 17	11 32		11 43	11 48	12 14	12 17		12 32		12 43	12 48	13 08	13 14	13 17	13 32
Portsmouth & Southsea	a	10 20	10 35		10 46	10 51		11 11	11 17	11 20	11 35		11 46	11 51	12 17	12 20		12 35		12 46	12 51	13 11	13 17	13 20	13 35
	d	10 22	10 37	10 42	10 47	10 53		11 12	11 18	11 22	11 37	11 42	11 47	11 53	12 18	12 22		12 37	12 42	12 47	12 53	13 12	13 18	13 22	13 37
Fratton	d	10 26	10 41	10 46	10 51	10 57		11a15	11 22	11 26	11 41	11 46	11 51	11 57	12 22	12 26		12 41	12 46	12 51	12 57	13a15	13 22	13 26	13 41
Hilsea	d	10a30		10a50						11a30		11a50				12a30			12a50					13a30	
Bedhampton	d					11 04			11 32					12 04	12 32						13 04		13 32		
Havant	a		10 49		10 59	11 07			11 34		11 49		11 59	12 07	12 34			12 49		12 59	13 07		13 34		13 49

		SW		SN	SW	GW	SN	SW	SW	SW	SN	SW		GW	SN	SW	SW	SW	SN	SW	GW	SN		SW	SW
		1		◇1	1	◇	1	1 🛒	1 🛒	1	◇1	1		R	1	1 🛒	1 🛒	1	◇1	1	◇	1		1 🛒	1 🛒
Portsmouth Harbour ⛴	d			13 43	13 48	14 08	14 14	14 17	14 32		14 43	14 48		15 08	15 14	15 17	15 32		15 43	15 48	16 08	16 14		16 17	16 32
Portsmouth & Southsea	a			13 46	13 51	14 11	14 17	14 20	14 35		14 46	14 51		15 11	15 17	15 20	15 35		15 46	15 51	16 11	16 17		16 20	16 35
	d	13 42		13 47	13 53	14 12	14 18	14 22	14 37	14 42	14 47	14 53		15 12	15 18	15 22	15 37	15 42	15 47	15 53	16 12	16 18		16 22	16 37
Fratton	d	13 46		13 51	13 57	14a15	14 22	14 26	14 41	14 46	14 51	14 57		15a15	15 22	15 26	15 41	15 46	15 51	15 57	16a15	16 22		16 26	16 41
Hilsea	d	13a50						14a30		14a50						15a30		15a50						16a30	
Bedhampton	d				14 04		14 30					15 04			15 30					16 04		16 30			
Havant	a			13 59	14 07		14 32		14 49		14 59	15 07			15 32		15 49		15 59	16 07		16 32			16 49

		SW	SN	SW	GW	SN	SW	SW		SW	SN	SW	GW	SN	SW	SW	SW	SN		SW	GW	SN	SW	SW	SW
		1	◇1	1	◇	1	1	1 🛒		1	◇1	1	◇	1	1	1 🛒	1	◇1		1	◇	1	1	1	1
Portsmouth Harbour ⛴	d		16 43	16 48	17 08	17 14	17 17	17 32			17 43	17 48	18 08	18 14	18 17	18 32		18 43		18 48	19 08	19 14	19 17	19 32	
Portsmouth & Southsea	a		16 46	16 51	17 11	17 17	17 20	17 35			17 46	17 51	18 11	18 17	18 20	18 35		18 46		18 51	19 11	19 17	19 20	19 35	
	d	16 42	16 47	16 53	17 12	17 18	17 22	17 37		17 42	17 47	17 53	18 12	18 18	18 22	18 37	18 42	18 47		18 53	19 12	19 18	19 22	19 37	19 42
Fratton	d	16 46	16 51	16 57	17a15	17 22	17 26	17 41		17 46	17 51	17 57	18a15	18 22	18 26	18 41	18 46	18 51		18 57	19a15	19 22	19 26	19 41	19 46
Hilsea	d	16a50					17a30			17a50					18a30		18a50						19a30		19a50
Bedhampton	d			17 04		17 30						18 04		18 30						19 04		19 30			
Havant	a		16 59	17 07		17 32		17 49			17 59	18 07		18 32		18 49		18 59		19 07		19 32		19 49	

		SN	SW	GW		SN	SW	SW	SW	SN	SW	SN	SW	SW		SW	SN	SW	GW	SN	SW	SW	SW	SN	
		◇1	1	◇		1	1	1	1	1	1	1	1	1		1	1	1		1	1	1	1	1	
Portsmouth Harbour ⛴	d	19 43	19 48	20 08		20 14	20 17	20 32		20 43	20 48	21 14	21 17	21 32			21 43	21 48	22 03	22 14	22 17	22 32		22 43	
Portsmouth & Southsea	a	19 46	19 51	20 11		20 17	20 20	20 35		20 46	20 51	21 17	21 20	21 35			21 46	21 51	22 11	22 17	22 20	22 35		22 46	
	d	19 47	19 53	20 12		20 18	20 22	20 37	20 42	20 47	20 53	21 18	21 22	21 37		21 42	21 47	21 53	22 12	22 18	22 22	22 37	22 42	22 47	
Fratton	d	19 51	19 57	20a15		20 22	20 26	20 41	20 46	20 51	20 57	21 22	21 26	21 41		21 46	21 51	21 57	22a15	22 22	22 26	22 41	22 46	22 51	
Hilsea	d						20a30		20a50				21a30			21a50					22a30		22a50		
Bedhampton	d		20 04			20 30					21 04	21 30						22 04		22 32					
Havant	a	19 59	20 07			20 32		20 49		20 59	21 07	21 32		21 49			21 59	22 07		22 35		22 49		22 59	

		SW	SW
		1	1
Portsmouth Harbour ⛴	d	22 48	23 17
Portsmouth & Southsea	a	22 51	23 20
	d	22 53	23 22
Fratton	d	22 57	23 26
Hilsea	d		23a30
Bedhampton	d	23 04	
Havant	a	23 07	

Table 157

Sundays

19 February to 25 March

Portsmouth Harbour - Havant

(Complete service)

Network Diagram - see first Page of Table 155

		SW	SW	SN	SW	SW	SW	SN	SW	SN		SW	SW	SW	SN	SW	GW	SN	SW	SW		SW	SN	SW	SN
		1	1	1	1	1	1	◇1	1	1		1	1	1	◇1	1	■	1	1 🛒	1 🛒		1	◇1	1	1
Portsmouth Harbour ⛴	d	06 37	06 48	07 14	07 17	07 32		07 43	07 48	08 14		08 17	08 32		08 43	08 48	09 08	09 14	09 17	09 32			09 43	09 48	10 14
Portsmouth & Southsea	a	06 40	06 51	07 17	07 20	07 35		07 46	07 51	08 17		08 20	08 35		08 46	08 51	09 11	09 17	09 20	09 35			09 46	09 51	10 17
	d	06 42	06 53	07 18	07 22	07 37	07 42	07 47	07 53	08 18		08 22	08 37	08 42	08 47	08 53	09 12	09 18	09 22	09 37		09 42	09 47	09 53	10 18
Fratton	d	06 46	06 57	07 22	07 26	07 41	07 46	07 51	07 57	08 22		08 26	08 41	08 46	08 51	08 57	09a15	09 22	09 26	09 41		09 46	09 51	09 57	10 22
Hilsea	d	06a50			07a30		07a50					08a30		08a50					09a30			09a50			
Bedhampton	d		07 04	07 30					08 04	08 30						09 04		09 30						10 04	10 30
Havant	a		07 07	07 32		07 49		07 59	08 07	08 32			08 49		08 59	09 07		09 32		09 49			09 59	10 07	10 32

		SW	SW	SW	SN	SW		GW	SN	SW	SW	SW	SN	SW	SN	SW		SW	SW	SN	SW	GW	SN	SW	SW
		1 🛒	1 🛒	1	◇1	1		◇	1	1 🛒	1 🛒	1	◇1	1	1	1 🛒		1 🛒	1	◇1	1	◇	1	1 🛒	1 🛒
Portsmouth Harbour ⛴	d	10 17	10 32		10 43	10 48		11 08	11 14	11 17	11 32		11 43	11 48	12 14	12 17		12 32		12 43	12 48	13 08	13 14	13 17	13 32
Portsmouth & Southsea	a	10 20	10 35		10 46	10 51		11 11	11 17	11 20	11 35		11 46	11 51	12 17	12 20		12 35		12 46	12 51	13 11	13 17	13 20	13 35
	d	10 22	10 37	10 42	10 47	10 53		11 12	11 18	11 22	11 37	11 42	11 47	11 53	12 18	12 22		12 37	12 42	12 47	12 53	13 12	13 18	13 22	13 37
Fratton	d	10 26	10 41	10 46	10 51	10 57		11a15	11 22	11 26	11 41	11 46	11 51	11 57	12 22	12 26		12 41	12 46	12 51	12 57	13a15	13 22	13 26	13 41
Hilsea	d	10a30		10a50						11a30		11a50				12a30			12a50					13a30	
Bedhampton	d					11 04			11 32					12 04	12 32						13 04		13 32		
Havant	a		10 49		10 59	11 07			11 34		11 49		11 59	12 07	12 34			12 49		12 59	13 07		13 34		13 49

		SW		SN	SW	GW	SN	SW	SW	SW	SN	SW		GW	SN	SW	SW	SW	SN	SW	GW	SN		SW	SW
		1		◇1	1	◇	1	1 🛒	1 🛒	1	◇1	1		■	1	1 🛒	1 🛒	1	◇1	1	◇	1		1 🛒	1 🛒
Portsmouth Harbour ⛴	d			13 43	13 48	14 08	14 14	14 17	14 32		14 43	14 48		15 08	15 14	15 17	15 32		15 43	15 48	16 08	16 14		16 17	16 32
Portsmouth & Southsea	a			13 46	13 51	14 11	14 17	14 20	14 35		14 46	14 51		15 11	15 17	15 20	15 35		15 46	15 51	16 11	16 17		16 20	16 35
	d	13 42		13 47	13 53	14 12	14 18	14 22	14 37	14 42	14 47	14 53		15 12	15 18	15 22	15 37	15 42	15 47	15 53	16 12	16 18		16 22	16 37
Fratton	d	13 46		13 51	13 57	14a15	14 22	14 26	14 41	14 46	14 51	14 57		15a15	15 22	15 26	15 41	15 46	15 51	15 57	16a15	16 22		16 26	16 41
Hilsea	d	13a50						14a30		14a50						15a30		15a50						16a30	
Bedhampton	d				14 04		14 30					15 04			15 30					16 04		16 30			
Havant	a			13 59	14 07		14 32		14 49		14 59	15 07			15 32		15 49		15 59	16 07		16 32			16 49

		SW	SN	SW	GW	SN	SW	SW		SW	SN	SW	GW	SN	SW	SW	SW	SN		SW	GW	SN	SW	SW	SW
		1	◇1	1	◇	1	1	1 🛒		1	◇1	1	◇	1	1	1 🛒	1	◇1		1	◇	1	1	1	1
Portsmouth Harbour ⛴	d		16 43	16 48	17 08	17 14	17 17	17 32			17 43	17 48	18 08	18 14	18 17	18 32		18 43		18 48	19 08	19 14	19 17	19 32	
Portsmouth & Southsea	a		16 46	16 51	17 11	17 17	17 20	17 35			17 46	17 51	18 11	18 17	18 20	18 35		18 46		18 51	19 11	19 17	19 20	19 35	
	d	16 42	16 47	16 53	17 12	17 18	17 22	17 37		17 42	17 47	17 53	18 12	18 18	18 22	18 37	18 42	18 47		18 53	19 12	19 18	19 22	19 37	19 42
Fratton	d	16 46	16 51	16 57	17a15	17 22	17 26	17 41		17 46	17 51	17 57	18a15	18 22	18 26	18 41	18 46	18 51		18 57	19a15	19 22	19 26	19 41	19 46
Hilsea	d	16a50					17a30			17a50					18a30		18a50						19a30		19a50
Bedhampton	d			17 04		17 30						18 04		18 30						19 04		19 30			
Havant	a		16 59	17 07		17 32		17 49			17 59	18 07		18 32		18 49		18 59		19 07		19 32		19 49	

		SN	SW	GW		SN	SW	SW	SW	SN	SW	SN	SW	SW		SW	SN	SW	GW	SN	SW	SW	SW	SN	
		◇1	1	◇		1	1	1	1	1	1	1	1	1		1	1	1		1	1	1	1	1	
Portsmouth Harbour ⛴	d	19 43	19 48	20 08		20 14	20 17	20 32		20 43	20 48	21 14	21 17	21 32			21 43	21 48	22 03	22 14	22 17	22 32		22 43	
Portsmouth & Southsea	a	19 46	19 51	20 11		20 17	20 20	20 35		20 46	20 51	21 17	21 20	21 35			21 46	21 51	22 11	22 17	22 20	22 35		22 46	
	d	19 47	19 53	20 12		20 18	20 22	20 37	20 42	20 47	20 53	21 18	21 22	21 37		21 42	21 47	21 53	22 12	22 18	22 22	22 37	22 42	22 47	
Fratton	d	19 51	19 57	20a15		20 22	20 26	20 41	20 46	20 51	20 57	21 22	21 26	21 41		21 46	21 51	21 57	22a15	22 22	22 26	22 41	22 46	22 51	
Hilsea	d						20a30		20a50				21a30			21a50					22a30		22a50		
Bedhampton	d		20 04			20 30					21 04	21 30						22 04		22 32					
Havant	a	19 59	20 07			20 32		20 49		20 59	21 07	21 32		21 49			21 59	22 07		22 35		22 49		22 59	

		SW	SW
		1	1
Portsmouth Harbour ⛴	d	22 48	23 17
Portsmouth & Southsea	a	22 51	23 20
	d	22 53	23 22
Fratton	d	22 57	23 26
Hilsea	d		23a30
Bedhampton	d	23 04	
Havant	a	23 07	

Sundays

from 1 April

		SW	SW	SN	SW	SW	SW	SN	SW	SN		SW	SW	SW	SN	SW	GW	SN	SW	SW		SW	SN	SW	SN
		1	1	1	1	1	1	◇1	1	1		1	1	1	◇1	1	■	1	1 🛒	1 🛒		1	◇1	1	1
Portsmouth Harbour ⛴	d	06 37	06 48	07 14	07 17	07 32		07 43	07 48	08 14		08 17	08 32		08 43	08 48	09 08	09 14	09 17	09 32			09 43	09 48	10 14
Portsmouth & Southsea	a	06 40	06 51	07 17	07 20	07 35		07 46	07 51	08 17		08 20	08 35		08 46	08 51	09 11	09 17	09 20	09 35			09 46	09 51	10 17
	d	06 42	06 53	07 18	07 22	07 37	07 42	07 47	07 53	08 18		08 22	08 37	08 42	08 47	08 53	09 12	09 18	09 22	09 37		09 42	09 47	09 53	10 18
Fratton	d	06 46	06 57	07 22	07 26	07 41	07 46	07 51	07 57	08 22		08 26	08 41	08 46	08 51	08 57	09a15	09 22	09 26	09 41		09 46	09 51	09 57	10 22
Hilsea	d	06a50			07a30		07a50					08a30		08a50					09a30			09a50			
Bedhampton	d		07 04	07 30					08 04	08 30						09 04		09 30						10 04	10 30
Havant	a		07 07	07 32		07 49		07 59	08 07	08 32			08 49		08 59	09 07		09 32		09 49			09 59	10 07	10 32

Table 157

Sundays
from 1 April

Portsmouth Harbour - Havant

(Complete service)

Network Diagram - see first Page of Table 155

		SW 1 🚲	SW 1 🚲	SW 1	SN ◇1	SW 1		SN 1	SW 1 🚲	SW 1 🚲	SW 1	SN ◇1	SW 1	SN 1	SW 1 🚲	SW 1 🚲		SW 1	SN ◇1	SW 1	GW ◇	SN 1	SW 1 🚲	SW 1 🚲	SW 1
Portsmouth Harbour ⛴	d	10 17	10 32		10 43	10 48		11 14	11 17	11 32		11 43	11 48	12 14	12 17	12 32			12 43	12 48	13 08	13 14	13 17	13 32	
Portsmouth & Southsea	a	10 20	10 35		10 46	10 51		11 17	11 20	11 35		11 46	11 51	12 17	12 20	12 35			12 46	12 51	13 11	13 17	13 20	13 35	
	d	10 22	10 37	10 42	10 47	10 53		11 18	11 22	11 37	11 42	11 47	11 53	12 18	12 22	12 37		12 42	12 47	12 53	13 12	13 18	13 22	13 37	13 42
Fratton	d	10 26	10 41	10 46	10 51	10 57		11 22	11 26	11 41	11 46	11 51	11 57	12 22	12 26	12 41		12 46	12 51	12 57	13a15	13 22	13 26	13 41	13 46
Hilsea	d	10a30		10a50					11a30		11a50				12a30			12a50					13a30		13a50
Bedhampton	d					11 04		11 32					12 04	12 32						13 04		13 32			
Havant	a		10 49		10 59	11 07		11 34		11 49		11 59	12 07	12 34		12 49			12 59	13 07		13 34		13 49	

		SN ◇1		SW 1	GW ◇	SN 1	SW 1 🚲	SW 1 🚲	SW 1	SN ◇1	SW 1	GW R		SN 1	SW 1 🚲	SW 1 🚲	SW 1	SN ◇1	SW 1	GW ◇	SN 1	SW 1 🚲		SW 1 🚲	SW 1
Portsmouth Harbour ⛴	d	13 43		13 48	14 08	14 14	14 17	14 32		14 43	14 48	15 08		15 14	15 17	15 32		15 43	15 48	16 08	16 14	16 17		16 32	
Portsmouth & Southsea	a	13 46		13 51	14 11	14 17	14 20	14 35		14 46	14 51	15 11		15 17	15 20	15 35		15 46	15 51	16 11	16 17	16 20		16 35	
	d	13 47		13 53	14 12	14 18	14 22	14 37	14 42	14 47	14 53	15 12		15 18	15 22	15 37	15 42	15 47	15 53	16 12	16 18	16 22		16 37	16 42
Fratton	d	13 51		13 57	14a15	14 22	14 26	14 41	14 46	14 51	14 57	15a15		15 22	15 26	15 41	15 46	15 51	15 57	16a15	16 22	16 26		16 41	16 46
Hilsea	d						14a30		14a50						15a30		15a50					16a30			16a50
Bedhampton	d			14 04		14 30					15 04			15 30					16 04		16 30				
Havant	a	13 59		14 07		14 32		14 49		14 59	15 07			15 32		15 49		15 59	16 07		16 32			16 49	

		SN ◇1	SW 1	GW ◇	SN 1	SW 1	SW 1 🚲	SW 1		SN ◇1	SW 1	GW ◇	SN 1	SW 1	SW 1 🚲	SW 1	SN ◇1	SW 1		GW ◇	SN 1	SW 1	SW 1	SW 1	SN ◇1
Portsmouth Harbour ⛴	d	16 43	16 48	17 08	17 14	17 17	17 32			17 43	17 48	18 08	18 14	18 17	18 32		18 43	18 48		19 08	19 14	19 17	19 32		19 43
Portsmouth & Southsea	a	16 46	16 51	17 11	17 17	17 20	17 35			17 46	17 51	18 11	18 17	18 20	18 35		18 46	18 51		19 11	19 17	19 20	19 35		19 46
	d	16 47	16 53	17 12	17 18	17 22	17 37	17 42		17 47	17 53	18 12	18 18	18 22	18 37	18 42	18 47	18 53		19 12	19 18	19 22	19 37	19 42	19 47
Fratton	d	16 51	16 57	17a15	17 22	17 26	17 41	17 46		17 51	17 57	18a15	18 22	18 26	18 41	18 46	18 51	18 57		19a15	19 22	19 26	19 41	19 46	19 51
Hilsea	d					17a30		17a50						18a30		18a50						19a30		19a50	
Bedhampton	d		17 04		17 30						18 04		18 30					19 04			19 30				
Havant	a	16 59	17 07		17 32		17 49			17 59	18 07		18 32		18 49		18 59	19 07			19 32		19 49		19 59

		SW 1	GW ◇	SN 1		SW 1	SW 1	SW 1	SN 1	SW 1	SN 1	SW 1	SW 1	SW 1		SN 1	SW 1	GW	SN 1	SW 1	SW 1	SW 1	SN 1	SW 1	
Portsmouth Harbour ⛴	d	19 48	20 08	20 14		20 17	20 32		20 43	20 48	21 14	21 17	21 32			21 43	21 48	22 03	22 14	22 17	22 32		22 43	22 48	
Portsmouth & Southsea	a	19 51	20 11	20 17		20 20	20 35		20 46	20 51	21 17	21 20	21 35			21 46	21 51	22 11	22 17	22 20	22 35		22 46	22 51	
	d	19 53	20 12	20 18		20 22	20 37	20 42	20 47	20 53	21 18	21 22	21 37	21 42		21 47	21 53	22 12	22 18	22 22	22 37	22 42	22 47	22 53	
Fratton	d	19 57	20a15	20 22		20 26	20 41	20 46	20 51	20 57	21 22	21 26	21 41	21 46		21 51	21 57	22a15	22 22	22 26	22 41	22 46	22 51	22 57	
Hilsea	d					20a30		20a50				21a30		21a50						22a30		22a50			
Bedhampton	d	20 04		20 30						21 04	21 30						22 04		22 32					23 04	
Havant	a	20 07		20 32			20 49		20 59	21 07	21 32		21 49			21 59	22 07		22 35		22 49		22 59	23 07	

		SW 1
Portsmouth Harbour ⛴	d	23 17
Portsmouth & Southsea	a	23 20
	d	23 22
Fratton	d	23 26
Hilsea	d	23a30
Bedhampton	d	
Havant	a	

Network Diagram for Table 158

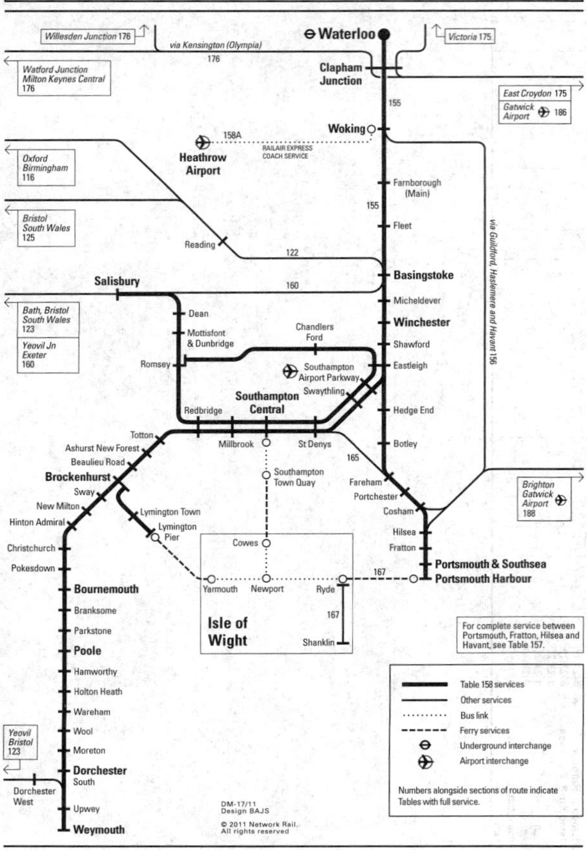

London - Basingstoke, Southampton, Romsey Lymington, Bournemouth and Weymouth

Network Diagram - see first Page of Table 158

Miles	Miles			SW	SW	SW		SW	SW	SW	SW	SW	SW	SW	SW	SW	SW	SW	SW	SW	SW	SW	SW	SW
				MX	MO	MO		MX	MO	MX	MX	MX	MO	MX		MX	MX	MO						
				◇1	◇1	◇1		◇1	◇1	1	◇1	1	◇1	◇1	1	1	1	1	1	1	1	1	1	1
				A	A																			
				⌶	⌶			⌶			⌶		⌶											
0	—	**London Waterloo** 15 ⊖	d	21p35	21p35	21p54		22p05			22p35	22p39	22p54	23p05		23p35	00 05	00 50	01 05					
4	—	**Clapham Junction** 10	d		21b42	22b03		22b12				22b46	23b03	23b12		23b42	00u12	00 57						
—	—		d																01 15					
24¼	—	**Woking**	d	22p00	22p07	22p28		22p32			23p00		23p28	23p32		00 03	00 37	01 18	01 49					
33¼	—	Farnborough (Main)	d									23p16				00 14			01s58					
36½	—	Fleet	d									23p21				00 20			02s04					
—	—	Reading 7	d																					
47¾	—	**Basingstoke**	a		22p26	22p46		22p51				23p33	23p46	23p53		00 33	00 55		02s16					
—	—		d		22p28	22p48		22p52				23p34	23p48	23p53		00 35	00 56							
58	—	Micheldever	d			22p58							23p58	00 03										
66½	—	**Winchester**	d	22p33	22p44	23p08		23p09			23p33	23p51	00 08	00 14		00 51	01 13		02s33					
69¾	—	Shawford	d									23p55												
—	0	**Romsey**	d							23p07														
—	5¼	Chandlers Ford	d							23p14														
73½	0	Eastleigh 8	a			23p17		23p17		23p22		00 01	00 18	00 22		00 59	01 21		02s42					
—	—																							
—	—		d			23p22	23p26	23p18		23p22		00 02	00 22	00 23	00 30	01 00	01 22				06 00			
—	4½	Hedge End	d				23p32								00s36						06 06			
—	5½	Botley	d				23p36								00s39						06 10			
—	11	Fareham	d				23p44								00s47						06 19			
—	14¼	Portchester	d				23p49								00s53						06 24			
—	16¾	Cosham	d				23p54								00s57						06 29			
—	18¼	Hilsea	a				23p59														06 33			
—	20½	Fratton	a				00 04								01s05			02s10			06 40			
—	21½	**Portsmouth & Southsea**	a				00 08								01s08			02s14			06 44			
—	22¼	**Portsmouth Harbour** ⛴	a				00 13								01 12			02 19			06 49			
75	—	**Southampton Airport Pkwy** ✈	d	22p42	22p53	23p27		23p22		23p26	23p42	00 06	00 27	00 28		01 05	01 26		02s46					
75¾	—	Swaythling	d							23p28														
77¼	—	St Denys	d						←	23p31			00s31	00s32					02s51					
79¼	—	**Southampton Central** ⛴	a	22p49	23p00	23p34		23p29	23p34	23p36	23p49	00 13	00 36	00 37		01 12	01 35		02 56					
—	—		d	22p51	23p03	23p35		23p31	23p35	23p38	23p51		00 37	00 38			01 37							
80¼	—	Millbrook (Hants)	d			→				23p40														
82	0	Redbridge	d							23p44														
—	6	**Romsey**	d							23p56														
—	9¾	Mottisfont & Dunbridge	d							00 01														
—	13½	Dean	d							00 07														
—	22½	**Salisbury**	a							00 19														
82½	—	Totton	d					23p36	23p41				00s42	00s43			01s42							
85½	—	Ashurst New Forest	d					23p41	23p45															
88	—	Beaulieu Road	d																					
92¾	0	**Brockenhurst** 3	a	23p04	23p16			23p49	23p53		00 04		00s53	00s54			01s53							
—	—		d	23p05	23p17			23p50	23p54		00 05									05 59			06 16	06 29
—	4¾	Lymington Town	d																	06 07				06 37
—	5¼	**Lymington Pier**	a																	06 10				06 40
95½	—	Sway	d					23p54	23p59														06 20	
98½	—	New Milton	d		23p24			23p59	00 04				01s01	01s02			02s00						06 25	
101	—	Hinton Admiral	d					00 03	00 08														06 29	
104¼	—	Christchurch	d					00 08	00 13				01s08	01s09			02s07						06 34	
106¼	—	Pokesdown	d					00 11	00 16				01s12	01s13			02s11						06 38	
108	—	**Bournemouth**	a	23p25	23p34			00 15	00 20		00 21		01 16	01 17			02 15						06 42	
—	—		d	23p29	23p39			00 17	00 22		00 22		01 17	01 18								06 11	06 44	
110¼	—	Branksome	d	23p35	23p44			00 22	00 27		00 27		01s22	01s23								06 16	06 49	
112	—	Parkstone (Dorset)	d	23p38	23p47			00 25	00 30		00 30		01s25	01s26								06 19	06 52	
113¾	—	**Poole** 4	a	23p41	23p50			00 29	00 34		00 35		01 29	01 30								06 23	06 55	
—	—		d	23p42	23p51																	06 24	06 57	
116	—	Hamworthy	d	23p47	23p56																	06 29	07 02	
118¾	—	Holton Heath	d																			06 33	07 06	
120¾	—	Wareham	d	23p54	00 03																	06 38	07 11	
125¾	—	Wool	d	00 01	00 10																	06 44	07 17	
130¼	—	Moreton (Dorset)	d	00 07	00 17																	06 50	07 23	
135¾	—	**Dorchester South**	d	00 15	00 25																	06 58	07 31	
—	—	Dorchester West	d																					
140½	—	Upwey	d	00 21	00 32																	07 05	07 38	
142¾	—	**Weymouth**	a	00 26	00 36																	07 09	07 42	

A ⌶ to Bournemouth

b Previous night, stops to pick up only

London - Basingstoke, Southampton, Romsey Lymington, Bournemouth and Weymouth

Network Diagram - see first Page of Table 158

		SW	SW	GW	SW	GW	SW	GW	SW	SW	SW	SW	SW	SW	SW	GW	SW	SW	SW	SW	GW	GW		SW	GW
		■	■	▪	■		■		◇■	■	■	■	■	■	■	◇	■	■	◇■	■	◇			◇■	◇
				🍴												🍴									
London Waterloo 15 ⊖	d								05 30										06 30					06 12	
Clapham Junction 10	d								05u37										06u37					06u19	
	d																								
Woking	d								06 01								06 19		06 57					06 50	
Farnborough (Main)	d																								
Fleet	d																								
Reading 7	d																								
Basingstoke	a								06 20								06 58		07 16					07 28	
	d	05 40							06 21						06 55		07 00		07 18					07 30	
Micheldever	d	05 50															07 10							07 41	
Winchester	d	05 59			06 18				06 38						07 11		07 19		07 34					07 50	
Shawford	d				06 23										07 16									07 55	
Romsey	d		05 58			06 38								07 07						07 13	07 30	07 56			
Chandlers Ford	d		06 06											07 14											
Eastleigh 3	a	06 07	06 11		06 28				06 47					07 20	07 22		07 27		07 43	07 49				08 00	
	d	06 08	06 13		06 29				06 48	06 50	07 02			07 21	07 24		07 28		07 44	07 50				08 02	
Hedge End	d				06 35						07 08						07 34								
Botley	d				06 39						07 12						07 38								
Fareham	d			06 24	06 50	07 15					07 20					07 29	07 48				08 06				
Portchester	d				06 55						07 25						07 53								
Cosham	d				07 00	07 23					07 29						07 58				08 14				
Hilsea	a				07 05						07 35						08 03								
Fratton	a				07 09	07 34					07 39						08 07				08 20				
Portsmouth & Southsea	a				07 12	07 38					07 42						08 13				08 24				
Portsmouth Harbour ⛴	a				07 17	07 45					07 48						08 16				08 30				
Southampton Airport Pkwy ✈	d	06 13	06 17						06 53					07 25	07 29				07 49					08 06	
Swaythling	d	06 15	06 20											07 27	07 31									08 09	
St Denys	d	06 18	06 24											07 30	07 34									08 12	
Southampton Central ⛴	a	06 23	06 29	06 45					07 00					07 35	07 39	07 50			07 57			08 09		08 17	
	d	06 25	06 30	06 46					07 01				07 19	07 37		07 52			08 00					08 19	08 23
Millbrook (Hants)	d		06 33										07 21	07 40										08 21	
Redbridge	d		06 36										07 25	07 43										08 25	
Romsey	d		06 44	07 00						07a03				07 51		08 11				08a03					08 35
Mottisfont & Dunbridge	d		06 49											07 56											
Dean	d		06 55											08 02											
Salisbury	a		07 07	07 18										08 15		08 29									09 00
Totton	d	06 30							07 07				07 28						08 05					08 28	
Ashurst New Forest	d	06 35											07 32											08 32	
Beaulieu Road	d												07 37											08 37	
Brockenhurst 3	a	06 43							07 17				07 43						08 16					08 43	
	d	06 44					06 59		07 18			07 29	07 44					07 59	08 17					08 44	
Lymington Town	d						07 07					07 37						08 07							
Lymington Pier	a						07 10					07 40						08 10							
Sway	d	06 48							07 23				07 48						08 21					08 48	
New Milton	d	06 53							07 28				07 53						08 26					08 53	
Hinton Admiral	d	06 57							07 32				07 57						08 30					08 57	
Christchurch	d	07 02							07 37				08 02						08 35					09 02	
Pokesdown	d	07 06							07 40				08 06						08 39					09 06	
Bournemouth	a	07 10							07 44				08 10						08 43					09 10	
	d	07 11							07 46				08 11						08 44					09 11	
Branksome	d	07 16							07 51				08 16						08 49					09 16	
Parkstone (Dorset)	d	07 19							07 54				08 19						08 52					09 19	
Poole 4	a	07 23							07 57				08 23						08 56					09 23	
	d	07 24							07 58				08 24						08 57					09 24	
Hamworthy	d	07 29							08 03				08 29						09 02					09 29	
Holton Heath	d	07 33							08 07				08 33											09 33	
Wareham	d	07 38							08 12				08 38						09 09					09 38	
Wool	d	07 44							08 19				08 44						09 15					09 44	
Moreton (Dorset)	d	07 50							08 25				08 50						09 21					09 50	
Dorchester South	d	07 58							08 33				08 58						09 29					09 58	
Dorchester West	d							08 09																	
Upwey	d	08 05						08 17	08 40				09 05						09 36					10 05	
Weymouth	a	08 09						08 24	08 44				09 09						09 40					10 09	

London - Basingstoke, Southampton, Romsey Lymington, Bournemouth and Weymouth

Network Diagram - see first Page of Table 158

		SW		SW	XC		SW	SW	SW	GW	GW	SW	GW	SW	XC		SW	SW	SW	SW	XC	SW	SW	SW	GW
		■		■	◇■		■	◇■	■	◇	◇	■	◇	■	◇■		◇■	■	■	■	◇■	◇■	■	■	◇
								A									A					A			
					🍴			🍴		🍴	🍴			🍴			🍴	🍴			🍴	🍴	🍴		🍴
London Waterloo 15 ⊖	d		06 42					07 35						07 39			08 05			08 09		08 35			
Clapham Junction 10	d		06u49											07u46			08u12								
	d																								
Woking	d		07 19					08 00												08 35		09 00			
Farnborough (Main)	d		07 33											08 13						08 45					
Fleet	d		07 38											08 19											
Reading 7	d				07 46										08 15						08 46				
Basingstoke	a		07 56		08 08			08 19						08 32	08 40		08 47			08 58	09 08				
	d		08 00		08 10			08 20						08 33	08 42		08 49			09 00	09 10				
Micheldever	d		08 10																	09 10					
Winchester	d		08 19		08 25			08 37						08 50	08 57		09 05			09 19	09 25	09 33			
Shawford	d		08 24											08 54											
Romsey	d	08 07							08 13		08 50								09 07					09 19	
Chandlers Ford	d	08 14																	09 14						
Eastleigh 3	a	08 20	08 30					08 47	08 49					09 00					09 20	09 27				09 50	
	d	08 21	08 31					08 48	08 50					09 01					09 21	09 28				09 51	
Hedge End	d		08 37																	09 34					
Botley	d		08 42																	09 38					
Fareham	d		08 51							08 47	09 27									09 48					09 47
Portchester	d		08 56																	09 53					
Cosham	d		09 01								09 35									09 58					
Hilsea	a		09 05																	10 03					
Fratton	a		09 10								09 42									10 07					
Portsmouth & Southsea	a		09 14								09 46									10 11					
Portsmouth Harbour ⛴	a		09 18								09 55									10 18					
Southampton Airport Pkwy ✈	d	08 25			08 33			08 52						09 05	09 09		09 14		09 25		09 33	09 42			
Swaythling	d	08 27																	09 27						
St Denys	d	08 30																←	09 30						
Southampton Central ⛴	a	08 35			08 44			08 59		09 08				09 15	09 17		09 22	09 15	09 35		09 41	09 49			10 08
	d	08 37			08 46			09 01		09 10				09 30			09 24	09 30	09 37		09 43	09 51			10 10
Millbrook (Hants)	d	08 40												→					09 40						
Redbridge	d	08 43																	09 43						
Romsey	d	08 51							09a03	09 21									09 51					10a03	10 21
Mottisfont & Dunbridge	d	08 56																	09 56						
Dean	d	09 02																	10 02						
Salisbury	a	09 15								09 39									10 15						10 39
Totton	d							09 06										09 35							
Ashurst New Forest	d																	09 40							
Beaulieu Road	d																						←		
Brockenhurst 3	a				08 59			09 17									09 37	09 49			09 56	10 04	09 49		
	d			08 29	09 00		08 59	09 18				09 29					09 38	10 16			09 57	10 05	10 16		
Lymington Town	d			08 37			09 07					09 37						→							
Lymington Pier	a			08 40			09 10					09 40													
Sway	d							09 22															10 20		
New Milton	d							09 27									09 45						10 25		
Hinton Admiral	d							09 31															10 29		
Christchurch	d							09 36									09 52						10 34		
Pokesdown	d							09 40									09 56						10 38		
Bournemouth	a				09 14			09 44									10 00				10 12	10 20	10 42		
	d							09 45									10 04					10 24	10 43		
Branksome	d							09 50														10 29	10 48		
Parkstone (Dorset)	d							09 53														10 32	10 51		
Poole 4	a							09 57									10 13					10 36	10 55		
	d							09 58									10 14					10 37			
Hamworthy	d							10 03									10 19					10 42			
Holton Heath	d																10 23								
Wareham	d							10 10									10 28					10 49			
Wool	d																10 35								
Moreton (Dorset)	d																10 41								
Dorchester South	d							10 26									10 54					11 05			
Dorchester West	d												10 48												
Upwey	d												10 55				11 01								
Weymouth	a							10 34					11 03				11 06					11 13			

A 🍴 to Bournemouth

London - Basingstoke, Southampton, Romsey Lymington, Bournemouth and Weymouth

Network Diagram - see first Page of Table 158

		SW	SW	SW	SW	GW	GW	SW	SW	SW	SW	XC	GW	SW	SW	GW	GW	SW	SW	XC	SW	SW	SW
		1	1	◇1 A ☕	1	◇ B ☕	■ ☕	1	1	1	1	◇1 ☕	◇	◇1 A ☕	1	◇ ☕	◇ ☕	1	1	◇1 ☕	◇1 A ☕	1	1
London Waterloo 15 ⊖	d		08 39	09 05					09 09					09 35					09 39		10 05		
Clapham Junction 10	d		08u46	09u12															09u46		10u12		
	d																						
Woking	d								09 35					10 00									
Farnborough (Main)	d		09 13						09 45										10 13				
Fleet	d		09 19																10 19				
Reading 7	d											09 46								10 15			
Basingstoke	a		09 31	09 47					09 58			10 08							10 31	10 39	10 47		
	d		09 33	09 49					10 00			10 10							10 33	10 40	10 49		
Micheldever	d								10 10														
Winchester	d		09 49	10 05					10 19			10 25		10 33					10 49	10 55	11 05		
Shawford	d		09 54																10 54				
Romsey	d						09 50	10 07		10 19							10 50						11 07
Chandlers Ford	d							10 14															11 14
Eastleigh 3	a		10 02					10 20	10 27	10 49									10 59				11 20
	d		10 03					10 21	10 28	10 50									11 00				11 21
Hedge End	d								10 34														
Botley	d								10 38														
Fareham	d					10 15	10 27		10 48							10 47	11 27						
Portchester	d								10 53														
Cosham	d						10 35		10 58								11 35						
Hilsea	a								11 03														
Fratton	a						10 42		11 07								11 42						
Portsmouth & Southsea	a						10 46		11 11								11 46						
Portsmouth Harbour ⛴	a						10 54		11 18								11 54						
Southampton Airport Pkwy ✈	d		10 08	10 14				10 25				10 33		10 42					11 05	11 09	11 14		11 25
Swaythling	d							10 27															11 27
St Denys	d				←			10 30														←	11 30
Southampton Central ⛴	a		10 18	10 22	10 18	10 40		10 35				10 43		10 49		11 08			11 12	11 16	11 22	11 12	11 35
	d		10 30	10 24	10 30	10 42		10 44				10 45		10 51		11 10			11 30		11 24	11 30	11 37
Millbrook (Hants)	d		→					10 48											→				11 40
Redbridge	d							10 51															11 43
Romsey	d					10 54		10 59		11a03						11 21							11 51
Mottisfont & Dunbridge	d							11 04															11 56
Dean	d							11 10															12 02
Salisbury	a					11 13		11 22								11 39							12 15
Totton	d				10 35																	11 35	
Ashurst New Forest	d				10 40																	11 40	
Beaulieu Road	d				10 44										←							11 44	
Brockenhurst 3	a			10 37	10 51							10 58		11 04	10 51						11 37	11 51	
	d	10 12		10 38	11 16						10 42	10 59		11 05	11 16			11 12			11 38	12 16	
Lymington Town	d	10 20			→						10 50							11 20				→	
Lymington Pier	a	10 23									10 53							11 23					
Sway	d														11 20								
New Milton	d			10 45											11 25						11 45		
Hinton Admiral	d														11 29								
Christchurch	d			10 52											11 34						11 52		
Pokesdown	d			10 56											11 38						11 56		
Bournemouth	a			11 00								11 12		11 20	11 42						12 00		
	d			11 04										11 24	11 43						12 04		
Branksome	d													11 29	11 48								
Parkstone (Dorset)	d													11 32	11 51								
Poole 4	a			11 13										11 36	11 55						12 13		
	d			11 14										11 37							12 14		
Hamworthy	d			11 19										11 42							12 19		
Holton Heath	d			11 23																	12 23		
Wareham	d			11 28										11 49							12 28		
Wool	d			11 35																	12 35		
Moreton (Dorset)	d			11 41																	12 41		
Dorchester South	d			11 49										12 05							12 49		
Dorchester West	d												11 54										
Upwey	d			11 55									12 02								12 55		
Weymouth	a			12 00									12 09	12 13							13 00		

A ☕ to Bournemouth

B ☕ to Southampton Central

London - Basingstoke, Southampton, Romsey Lymington, Bournemouth and Weymouth

Network Diagram - see first Page of Table 158

		SW	SW	SW	XC	SW	SW	GW	GW	GW	SW	SW	SW	SW	GW	SW	SW	SW	SW	XC	GW	SW	SW
		1	1	1	◇1 ☕	◇1 A ☕	1	◇ ☕	◇ ☕		1	1	◇1 A ☕	1	◇	1	1	1	1	◇1 ☕	◇	◇1 A ☕	1
London Waterloo 15 ⊖	d	10 09				10 35						10 39	11 05				11 09					11 35	
Clapham Junction 10	d											10u46	11u12										
	d																						
Woking	d	10 35				11 00											11 35					12 00	
Farnborough (Main)	d	10 45										11 13					11 45						
Fleet	d											11 19											
Reading 7	d				10 46															11 46			
Basingstoke	a	10 58			11 08							11 31	11 47				11 58			12 08			
	d	11 00			11 10							11 33	11 49				12 00			12 10			
Micheldever	d	11 10															12 10						
Winchester	d	11 19			11 25	11 33						11 49	12 05				12 19			12 25		12 33	
Shawford	d											11 54											
Romsey	d		11 20						11 50	12 10						12 07		12 19					
Chandlers Ford	d															12 14							
Eastleigh 3	a	11 27	11 49									11 59				12 20	12 27	12 49					
	d	11 28	11 50									12 00				12 21	12 28	12 50					
Hedge End	d	11 34															12 34						
Botley	d	11 38															12 38						
Fareham	d	11 48						11 47	12 27								12 48						
Portchester	d	11 53															12 53						
Cosham	d	11 58							12 35								12 58						
Hilsea	a	12 03															13 03						
Fratton	a	12 07							12 42								13 07						
Portsmouth & Southsea	a	12 11							12 46								13 11						
Portsmouth Harbour ⛴	a	12 18							12 54								13 18						
Southampton Airport Pkwy ✈	d				11 33	11 42						12 05	12 14			12 25				12 33		12 42	
Swaythling	d															12 27							
St Denys	d													←		12 30							
Southampton Central ⛴	a				11 43	11 49		12 08		12 22		12 15	12 22	12 15		12 35				12 41		12 49	
	d				11 45	11 51		12 10				12 30	12 24	12 30	12 27	12 37				12 43		12 51	
Millbrook (Hants)	d											→				12 40							
Redbridge	d															12 43							
Romsey	d		12a03					12 21							12 39	12 51		13a03					
Mottisfont & Dunbridge	d															12 56							
Dean	d															13 02							
Salisbury	a							12 39							13 02	13 15							
Totton	d													12 35									
Ashurst New Forest	d													12 40									
Beaulieu Road	d						←																←
Brockenhurst 3	a				11 58	12 04	11 51						12 37	12 51						12 56		13 04	12 51
	d			11 42	11 59	12 05	12 16				12 12		12 38	13 16					12 42	12 57		13 05	13 16
Lymington Town	d			11 50							12 20			→					12 50				
Lymington Pier	a			11 53							12 23								12 53				
Sway	d						12 20																13 20
New Milton	d						12 25						12 45										13 25
Hinton Admiral	d						12 29																13 29
Christchurch	d						12 34						12 52										13 34
Pokesdown	d						12 38						12 56										13 38
Bournemouth	a				12 12	12 20	12 42						13 00							13 10		13 20	13 42
	d					12 24	12 43						13 04									13 24	13 43
Branksome	d					12 29	12 48															13 29	13 48
Parkstone (Dorset)	d					12 32	12 51															13 32	13 51
Poole 4	a					12 36	12 55						13 13									13 36	13 55
	d					12 37							13 14									13 37	
Hamworthy	d					12 42							13 19									13 42	
Holton Heath	d												13 23										
Wareham	d					12 49							13 28									13 49	
Wool	d												13 35										
Moreton (Dorset)	d												13 41										
Dorchester South	d					13 05							13 49									14 05	
Dorchester West	d																				13 54		
Upwey	d												13 55								14 02		
Weymouth	a					13 13							14 00								14 09	14 13	

A ☕ to Bournemouth

London - Basingstoke, Southampton, Romsey Lymington, Bournemouth and Weymouth

Network Diagram - see first Page of Table 158

		GW		GW	SW	SW	XC	SW	SW	SW	SW	SW		SW	XC	SW	SW	GW	GW	SW	SW	SW		SW	GW
		◇		◇	■	■	◇■	◇■	■	■	■	■		■	◇■	◇■	■	◇	◇	■	■	◇■		■	■
								A								A						A			
		🍴		🍴			🍴	🍴							🍴	🍴		🍴	🍴			🍴			🍴
London Waterloo 15 ⊖	d					11 39		12 05			12 09					12 35					12 39	13 05			
Clapham Junction 10	d					11u46		12u12													12u46	13u12			
	d																								
Woking	d										12 35					13 00									
Farnborough (Main)	d					12 13					12 45										13 13				
Fleet	d					12 19															13 19				
Reading 7	d						12 15								12 46										
Basingstoke	a					12 31	12 39	12 47			12 58				13 08						13 31	13 47			
	d					12 33	12 40	12 49			13 00				13 10						13 33	13 49			
Micheldever	d										13 10														
Winchester	d					12 49	12 55	13 05			13 19				13 25	13 33					13 49	14 05			
Shawford	d					12 54															13 54				
Romsey	d			12 50						13 07		13 19							13 50						14 19
Chandlers Ford	d									13 14															
Eastleigh 8	a					12 59				13 20	13 27	13 49									13 59				
	d					13 00				13 21	13 28	13 50									14 00				
Hedge End	d										13 34														
Botley	d										13 38														
Fareham	d	12 47		13 27							13 48							13 47	14 27						
Portchester	d										13 53														
Cosham	d			13 35							13 58								14 35						
Hilsea	a										14 03														
Fratton	a			13 42							14 07								14 42						
Portsmouth & Southsea	a			13 46							14 11								14 46						
Portsmouth Harbour ⛴	a			13 54							14 18								14 54						
Southampton Airport Pkwy ✈	d					13 05	13 09	13 14		13 25					13 33	13 42					14 05	14 14			
Swaythling	d									13 27															
St Denys	d								←	13 30														←	
Southampton Central ⛴	a	13 08				13 15	13 17	13 22	13 15	13 35					13 41	13 49		14 08			14 12	14 22		14 12	14 32
	d	13 10				13 30		13 24	13 30	13 37					13 43	13 51		14 10			14 30	14 24		14 30	
Millbrook (Hants)	d					→				13 40											→				
Redbridge	d									13 43															
Romsey	d	13 21								13 51		14a03						14 21							
Mottisfont & Dunbridge	d									13 56															
Dean	d									14 02															
Salisbury	a	13 39								14 15								14 39							
Totton	d								13 35															14 35	
Ashurst New Forest	d								13 40															14 40	
Beaulieu Road	d																←								
Brockenhurst 3	a							13 37	13 51						13 56	14 04	13 51					14 37		14 51	
	d				13 12			13 38	14 16					13 42	13 57	14 05	14 16			14 12		14 38		15 16	
Lymington Town	d				13 20				→					13 50						14 20				→	
Lymington Pier	a				13 23									13 53						14 23					
Sway	d																14 20								
New Milton	d							13 45									14 25					14 45			
Hinton Admiral	d																14 29								
Christchurch	d							13 52									14 34					14 52			
Pokesdown	d							13 56									14 38					14 56			
Bournemouth	a							14 00							14 10	14 20	14 42					15 00			
	d							14 04								14 24	14 43					15 04			
Branksome	d															14 29	14 48								
Parkstone (Dorset)	d															14 32	14 51								
Poole 4	a							14 13								14 36	14 55					15 13			
	d							14 14								14 37						15 14			
Hamworthy	d							14 19								14 42						15 19			
Holton Heath	d							14 23														15 23			
Wareham	d							14 28								14 49						15 28			
Wool	d							14 35														15 35			
Moreton (Dorset)	d							14 41														15 41			
Dorchester South	d							14 49								15 05						15 49			
Dorchester West	d																								
Upwey	d							14 55														15 55			
Weymouth	a							15 00								15 13						16 00			

A 🍴 to Bournemouth

Mondays to Fridays

London - Basingstoke, Southampton, Romsey Lymington, Bournemouth and Weymouth

Network Diagram - see first Page of Table 158

		SW	SW	SW	XC	SW	SW	GW		SN	SW	GW	SW	SW	XC	SW	SW	SW		SW	SW	SW	XC	GW	SW
		■	■	■	◇■	◇■	■	■		■	■	◇	■	■	◇■	◇■	■	■		■	■	■	◇■	◇	◇■
						A										A									A
					🍴	🍴		🍴				🍴			🍴	🍴							🍴		🍴
London Waterloo 15 ⊖	d		13 09			13 35								13 39		14 05				14 09					14 35
Clapham Junction 10	d													13u46		14u12									
	d																								
Woking	d		13 35			14 00														14 35					15 00
Farnborough (Main)	d		13 45											14 13						14 45					
Fleet	d													14 19											
Reading 7	d				13 46										14 15								14 46		
Basingstoke	a		13 58		14 08									14 31	14 39	14 47				14 58			15 08		
	d		14 00		14 10									14 33	14 40	14 49				15 00			15 10		
Micheldever	d		14 10																	15 10					
Winchester	d		14 19		14 25	14 33								14 49	14 55	15 05				15 19			15 25		15 33
Shawford	d													14 54											
Romsey	d	14 07									14 13	14 50						15 07			15 19				
Chandlers Ford	d	14 14																15 14							
Eastleigh 8	a	14 20	14 27								14 49			14 59				15 20		15 27	15 49				
	d	14 21	14 28							14 41	14 50			15 00				15 21		15 28	15 50				
Hedge End	d		14 34																	15 34					
Botley	d		14 38																	15 38					
Fareham	d		14 48					14 47		14a59		15 27								15 48					
Portchester	d		14 53																	15 53					
Cosham	d		14 58									15 35								15 58					
Hilsea	a		15 03																	16 03					
Fratton	a		15 07									15 42								16 07					
Portsmouth & Southsea	a		15 11									15 46								16 11					
Portsmouth Harbour ⛴	a		15 18									15 54								16 18					
Southampton Airport Pkwy ✈	d	14 25			14 35	14 42								15 05	15 09	15 14		15 25					15 33		15 42
Swaythling	d	14 27																15 27							
St Denys	d	14 30															←	15 30							
Southampton Central ⛴	a	14 35			14 42	14 49		15 08						15 12	15 17	15 22	15 12	15 35					15 41		15 49
	d	14 37			14 43	14 51		15 10						15 30		15 24	15 30	15 37					15 43		15 51
Millbrook (Hants)	d	14 40												→				15 40							
Redbridge	d	14 43																15 43							
Romsey	d	14 51						15 21			15a04							15 51			16a03				
Mottisfont & Dunbridge	d	14 56																15 56							
Dean	d	15 02																16 02							
Salisbury	a	15 15						15 39										16 15							
Totton	d																15 35								
Ashurst New Forest	d																15 40								
Beaulieu Road	d						←																		
Brockenhurst 3	a				14 56	15 04	14 51									15 37	15 51						15 56		16 04
	d			14 42	14 57	15 05	15 16						15 12			15 38	16 28					15 42	15 57		16 05
Lymington Town	d			14 50									15 20				→					15 50			
Lymington Pier	a			14 53									15 23									15 53			
Sway	d						15 20																		
New Milton	d						15 25									15 45									
Hinton Admiral	d						15 29																		
Christchurch	d						15 34									15 52									
Pokesdown	d						15 38									15 56									
Bournemouth	a				15 11	15 20	15 42									16 00							16 10		16 20
	d					15 24	15 43									16 04									16 24
Branksome	d					15 29	15 48																		16 29
Parkstone (Dorset)	d					15 32	15 51																		16 32
Poole 4	a					15 36	15 55									16 13									16 36
	d					15 37										16 14									16 37
Hamworthy	d					15 42										16 19									16 42
Holton Heath	d															16 23									
Wareham	d					15 49										16 28									16 49
Wool	d															16 35									16 55
Moreton (Dorset)	d															16 41									
Dorchester South	d					16 05										16 49									17 06
Dorchester West	d																							16 58	
Upwey	d															16 55								17 05	
Weymouth	a					16 13										17 00								17 10	17 15

A 🍴 to Bournemouth

London - Basingstoke, Southampton, Romsey Lymington, Bournemouth and Weymouth

Network Diagram - see first Page of Table 158

		SW	GW	GW	SW	SW	SW	SW	SW	SW	SW	XC	SW	SW		SW	SW	GW	SW	GW	SW	XC
		1	■ ⌶	◇ ⌶	1	1	◇1 A ⌶	1	1	1	1	◇1 ⌶	1	◇1 A ⌶		1	1	■ ⌶	1	◇ ⌶	1	◇1 ⌶
London Waterloo 15 ⊖	d					14 39	15 05				15 09			15 35							15 39	
Clapham Junction 10	d					14u46	15u12														15u46	
	d																					
Woking	d										15 35			16 00								
Farnborough (Main)	d					15 13					15 45										16 13	
Fleet	d					15 19															16 19	
Reading 7	d											15 46										16 15
Basingstoke	a					15 31	15 47				15 58	16 08									16 31	16 39
	d					15 33	15 49				16 00	16 10							16 24		16 33	16 40
Micheldever	d										16 10											
Winchester	d					15 49	16 05				16 19	16 25		16 33		16 38			16 45		16 50	17 00
Shawford	d					15 54										16 43					16 54	
Romsey	d			15 50						16 07							16 19			16 50		
Chandlers Ford	d									16 14												
Eastleigh 3	a					15 59				16 20	16 27					16 48	16 49		16 53		17 00	
	d					16 00				16 21	16 28					16 49	16 50		16 54		17 01	
Hedge End	d										16 34								17 00			
Botley	d										16 38								17 04			
Fareham	d		15 47	16 27							16 48							16 47	17 12	17 27		
Portchester	d										16 53								17 17			
Cosham	d			16 35							16 58								17 22	17 35		
Hilsea	a										17 03											
Fratton	a			16 42							17 07								17 31	17 42		
Portsmouth & Southsea	a			16 46							17 11								17 35	17 46		
Portsmouth Harbour ⛴	a			16 54							17 18								17 40	17 54		
Southampton Airport Pkwy ✈	d					16 05	16 14			16 25		16 33		16 42		16 54					17 05	
Swaythling	d									16 27						16 56						
St Denys	d								←	16 30						16 59						
Southampton Central ⛴	a		16 08			16 15	16 22		16 15	16 35		16 41		16 49		17 04		17 08			17 13	17 17
	d		16 10			16 30	16 24		16 30	16 37		16 43		16 54	16 56	17 06		17 10			17 30	
Millbrook (Hants)	d					→				16 40											→	
Redbridge	d									16 43												
Romsey	d		16 21							16 51							17a03	17 21				
Mottisfont & Dunbridge	d									16 56												
Dean	d									17 02												
Salisbury	a		16 39							17 15								17 39				
Totton	d								16 35						17 01	17a11						
Ashurst New Forest	d								16 40						17 06							
Beaulieu Road	d	←							16 44													
Brockenhurst 3	a	15 51					16 37		16 51			16 56		17 07	17 14							
	d	16 28			16 12		16 38	16 42				16 57	17 12	17 08	17 16							
Lymington Town	d				16 20			16 50					17 20									
Lymington Pier	a				16 23			16 53					17 23									
Sway	d	16 32					16 43								17 20							
New Milton	d	16 37					16 48								17 25							
Hinton Admiral	d	16 41					16 52								17 29							
Christchurch	d	16 46					16 57								17 34							
Pokesdown	d	16 50					17 00								17 38							
Bournemouth	a	16 54					17 04					17 10		17 23	17 42							
	d	16 55					17 07							17 24	17 43							
Branksome	d	17 00												17 29	17 48							
Parkstone (Dorset)	d	17 03												17 32	17 51							
Poole 4	a	17 07					17 16							17 36	17 55							
	d						17 17							17 37								
Hamworthy	d						17 22							17 42								
Holton Heath	d						17 26															
Wareham	d						17 31							17 49								
Wool	d						17 37							17 55								
Moreton (Dorset)	d						17 43															
Dorchester South	d						17 51							18 06								
Dorchester West	d																					
Upwey	d						17 58															
Weymouth	a						18 02							18 15								

A ⌶ to Bournemouth

London - Basingstoke, Southampton, Romsey Lymington, Bournemouth and Weymouth

Network Diagram - see first Page of Table 158

		SW	SN	SW	SW	SW	SW	XC	SW	GW	SW	SW		SW	GW	SW	SW		GW	SW	GW	SW	SW
		◇1 A ⌶	1	1	1	1	1	◇1 ⌶	1	◇	1	◇1 A ⌶		1	◇ ⌶	1	◇1 A ⌶		◇ ⌶	1	◇ ⌶	1	1
London Waterloo 15 ⊖	d	16 05					16 09					16 35				16 39	17 05					17 09	
Clapham Junction 10	d	16u12														16u46							
	d																						
Woking	d						16 35					17u00										17 34	
Farnborough (Main)	d						16 45									17 13							
Fleet	d															17 19							
Reading 7	d							16 46															
Basingstoke	a	16 47					16 58	17 08								17 31						17 52	
	d	16 49					17 00	17 10						17 24		17 33						17 54	
Micheldever	d						17 10							17 34								18 04	
Winchester	d	17 05					17 19	17 25				17 33		17 44		17 49	18 00					18 14	
Shawford	d													17 49		17 54						18 18	
Romsey	d					17 07			17 19										17 50	18 07			18 19
Chandlers Ford	d					17 14														18 14			
Eastleigh 3	a					17 20	17 27		17 49					17 54		17 59				18 20		18 24	18 49
	d		17 16			17 21	17 28		17 50					17 55		18 01				18 21		18 25	18 50
Hedge End	d						17 34									18 07						18 31	
Botley	d						17 39									18 11						18 36	
Fareham	d						17 48								17 47	18 23			18 27		18 13	18 45	
Portchester	d						17 53									18 28						18 50	
Cosham	d						17 58									18 33			18 35			18 55	
Hilsea	a						18 04															19 05	
Fratton	a						18 08									18 40			18 48			19 09	
Portsmouth & Southsea	a						18 12									18 43			18 52			19 12	
Portsmouth Harbour ⛴	a						18 20									18 51			19 00			19 20	
Southampton Airport Pkwy ✈	d	17 14	17 20			17 25		17 33				17 42		18 00			18 09			18 25			
Swaythling	d					17 27								18 02						18 27			
St Denys	d				←	17 30								18 05						18 30			
Southampton Central ⛴	a	17 22	17 28		17 13	17 35		17 41				17 49		18 10	18 08		18 16			18 35	18 40		
	d	17 24			17 30	17 37		17 43				17 53	17 56		18 10		18 21	18 24		18 37	18 42		
Millbrook (Hants)	d					17 40														18 40			
Redbridge	d					17 43														18 44			
Romsey	d					17 51			18a03						18 21					19 00	18 54		19a04
Mottisfont & Dunbridge	d					17 56														19 05			
Dean	d					18 02														19 10			
Salisbury	a					18 15									18 39					19 23	19 12		
Totton	d				17 35								18 01					18 29					
Ashurst New Forest	d				17 40								18 06					18 34					
Beaulieu Road	d				17 44																		
Brockenhurst 3	a	17 37			17 51			17 56				18 07	18 14					18 42					
	d	17 38		17 42				17 57			18 12	18 08	18 16					18 43					
Lymington Town	d			17 50							18 20												
Lymington Pier	a			17 53							18 23												
Sway	d	17 43											18 20					18 47					
New Milton	d	17 48											18 25					18 52					
Hinton Admiral	d	17 52											18 29					18 57					
Christchurch	d	17 57											18 34					19 01					
Pokesdown	d	18 00											18 38					19 05					
Bournemouth	a	18 04						18 15				18 22	18 42				18 48	19 09					
	d	18 09										18 24					18 50	19 10					
Branksome	d											18 29					18 55	19 15					
Parkstone (Dorset)	d											18 32					18 58	19 18					
Poole 4	a	18 18										18 36					19 02	19 26					
	d	18 19										18 37					19 03						
Hamworthy	d	18 24										18 42					19 08						
Holton Heath	d	18 28															19 12						
Wareham	d	18 33										18 49					19 17						
Wool	d	18 39										18 55					19 23						
Moreton (Dorset)	d	18 45															19 29						
Dorchester South	d	18 53										19 06					19 37						
Dorchester West	d									18 58													
Upwey	d	19 00								19 06							19 44						
Weymouth	a	19 06								19 14		19 17					19 50						

A ⌶ to Bournemouth

London - Basingstoke, Southampton, Romsey Lymington, Bournemouth and Weymouth

Network Diagram - see first Page of Table 158

		SW	XC	GW	SW		GW	SW	SW	GW	SW	SW	SW	XC	SW	SW	SW	SW	XC	SW		GW	SW
		■1	◇■1 ✠	◇	◇■1 A ✠		◇ ✠	■1	■1	■ ✠	■1	◇■1 A ✠	■1	◇■1 ✠	■1	■1	■1	■1	◇■1 ✠	◇■1 A ✠		◇	■1
London Waterloo ■15 ⊖	d				17 35			17 39	17 48			18 05				18 09				18 35			
Clapham Junction ■10	d																						
	d																						
Woking	d							18 04	18 13							18 35							
Farnborough (Main)	d																						
Fleet	d																						
Reading ■7	d		17 46											18 15					18 46				
Basingstoke	a		18 08					18 22	18 31					18 47		18 53			19 08				
	d		18 10					18 24	18 33					18 48		18 55			19 10				19 24
Micheldever	d							18 34								19 05							
Winchester	d		18 25		18 30			18 44	18 50			19 00	19 05	19 09		19 14			19 25	19 30			19 40
Shawford	d							18 49					19 09			19 19							19 45
Romsey	d									18 54					19 07		19 19						
Chandlers Ford	d														19 14								
Eastleigh ■8	a							18 54	18 58				19 15	19 27	19 20	19 25	19 49						19 50
	d							18 55	18 59				19 16		19 21	19 29	19 50						19 51
Hedge End	d							19 01								19 35							19 57
Botley	d							19 05								19 38							20 01
Fareham	d						18 47	19 14		19 27						19 48						19 47	20a09
Portchester	d							19 19								19 53							
Cosham	d							19 24		19 35						19 58							
Hilsea	a							19 28								20 02							
Fratton	a							19 32		19 42						20 06							
Portsmouth & Southsea	a							19 36		19 46						20 11							
Portsmouth Harbour ⛴	a							19 43		19 54						20 20							
Southampton Airport Pkwy ✈	d		18 33		18 39				19 03			19 09	19 20		19 25				19 33	19 39			
Swaythling	d								19 06				19 23		19 27								
St Denys	d								19 09				19 26		19 30								
Southampton Central ⛴	a		18 44		18 46		19 08		19 18			19 18	19 33		19 35				19 41	19 46		20 08	
	d		18 45		18 51	18 54	19 10					19 19			19 37				19 43	19 51	19 54	20 10	
Millbrook (Hants)	d														19 40								
Redbridge	d														19 43								
Romsey	d						19 21								19 51		20a03					20 21	
Mottisfont & Dunbridge	d														19 56								
Dean	d														20 02								
Salisbury	a						19 39								20 15							20 39	
Totton	d					18 59						19 25									19 59		
Ashurst New Forest	d					19 04															20 04		
Beaulieu Road	d																						
Brockenhurst ■3	a		18 58			19 12						19 35							19 56		20 12		
	d	18 48	18 59			19 13					19 18	19 36						19 48	19 57		20 13		
Lymington Town	d	18 56									19 26							19 56					
Lymington Pier	a	18 59									19 29							19 59					
Sway	d					19 17						19 41									20 17		
New Milton	d					19 22						19 46									20 22		
Hinton Admiral	d					19 26						19 50									20 26		
Christchurch	d					19 31						19 55									20 31		
Pokesdown	d					19 35						19 58									20 35		
Bournemouth	a		19 13		19 20	19 39						20 02							20 12	20 20	20 39		
	d				19 21	19 40						20 07								20 21	20 40		
Branksome	d				19 26	19 45						20 12								20 26	20 45		
Parkstone (Dorset)	d				19 29	19 48						20 15								20 29	20 48		
Poole ■4	a				19 33	19 56						20 18								20 33	20 56		
	d				19 34							20 19								20 34			
Hamworthy	d				19 39							20 24								20 39			
Holton Heath	d											20 28											
Wareham	d				19 46							20 33								20 46			
Wool	d											20 40											
Moreton (Dorset)	d											20 46											
Dorchester South	d				20 02							20 54								21 02			
Dorchester West	d			19 54																			
Upwey	d			20 02								21 00											
Weymouth	a			20 10	20 15							21 07								21 13			

A ✠ to Bournemouth

London - Basingstoke, Southampton, Romsey Lymington, Bournemouth and Weymouth

Network Diagram - see first Page of Table 158

		GW	SW	SW	SW	SW	SW	SW	SW	SW	XC	GW	SW	SW	GW	SW	GW	SW	GW	SW	SW	SW
		■ ✠	■1	■1	◇■1 A ✠	■1	■1	■1	■1	■1	◇■1 ✠	◇	◇■1 A ✠	■1	◇	■1	◇ ✠	■1		◇■1 ✠	■1	■1
London Waterloo ■15 ⊖	d			18 39	19 05			19 09					19 35			19 39				20 05		20 09
Clapham Junction ■10	d			18u46	19u12											19u46				20u12		
	d																					
Woking	d			19 06				19 35					20 00									20 35
Farnborough (Main)	d							19 45								20 13						20 45
Fleet	d															20 19						
Reading ■7	d										19 46											
Basingstoke	a			19 28	19 47			19 58			20 09					20 31				20 47		20 58
	d			19 30	19 49			20 00			20 10					20 33				20 49		21 00
Micheldever	d			19 40				20 10														21 10
Winchester	d			19 49	20 05			20 19			20 25		20 33			20 49				21 05		21 19
Shawford	d			19 54				20 24								20 54						21 24
Romsey	d	19 50					20 07		20 19			20 35					20 50				21 07	
Chandlers Ford	d						20 14														21 14	
Eastleigh ■8	a			19 59			20 20	20 29	20 49							20 59					21 20	21 30
	d			20 00			20 21	20 30	20 50							21 00					21 21	21 30
Hedge End	d							20 36														21 36
Botley	d							20 40														21 40
Fareham	d	20 27						20 49							20 47		21 27					21 48
Portchester	d							20 54														21 53
Cosham	d							20 59														21 58
Hilsea	a							21 03														22 03
Fratton	a	20 42						21 07									21 41					22 08
Portsmouth & Southsea	a	20 46						21 11									21 45					22 11
Portsmouth Harbour ⛴	a	20 54						21 16									21 52					22 16
Southampton Airport Pkwy ✈	d			20 05	20 14		20 25				20 33		20 42			21 05				21 15	21 24	
Swaythling	d						20 27														21 27	
St Denys	d					←	20 30														21 30	
Southampton Central ⛴	a			20 16	20 22	20 16	20 35				20 41	20 48	20 49		21 08	21 12				21 24	21 35	
	d			20 30	20 24	20 30	20 37				20 43		20 51		21 10				21 20	21 25	21 37	
Millbrook (Hants)	d			→			20 40														21 40	
Redbridge	d						20 43														21 43	
Romsey	d						20 51		21a03						21 21				21 31		21 51	
Mottisfont & Dunbridge	d						20 56														21 56	
Dean	d						21 02														22 02	
Salisbury	a						21 15								21 39				21 51		22 15	
Totton	d					20 35							20 56							21 31		
Ashurst New Forest	d					20 40														21 35		
Beaulieu Road	d					20 44								←								
Brockenhurst ■3	a				20 37	20 51					20 58		21 07	20 51						21 43		
	d		20 18		20 38	21 16				20 48	20 59		21 08	21 16				21 18		21 44		
Lymington Town	d		20 26			→				20 56								21 26				
Lymington Pier	a		20 29							20 59								21 29				
Sway	d													21 20						21 49		
New Milton	d				20 45									21 25						21 54		
Hinton Admiral	d													21 29						21 58		
Christchurch	d				20 52									21 34						22 03		
Pokesdown	d				20 56									21 38						22 06		
Bournemouth	a				21 00						21 15		21 22	21 42						22 10		
	d				21 04								21 27	21 43						22 12		
Branksome	d												21 32	21 48						22 17		
Parkstone (Dorset)	d												21 35	21 51						22 20		
Poole ■4	a				21 13								21 38	21 57						22 23		
	d				21 15								21 39									
Hamworthy	d				21 20								21 44									
Holton Heath	d																					
Wareham	d				21 27								21 51									
Wool	d				21 33								21 58									
Moreton (Dorset)	d				21 39								22 04									
Dorchester South	d				21 47								22 12									
Dorchester West	d																					
Upwey	d				21 54								22 18									
Weymouth	a				21 58								22 23									

A ✠ to Bournemouth

London - Basingstoke, Southampton, Romsey Lymington, Bournemouth and Weymouth

Network Diagram - see first Page of Table 158

		SW 1	SW 1	XC ◇1	GW	SW ◇1 A ✠	SW 1	GW	SW 1	SW ◇1 ✠	SW 1	XC ◇1	SW ◇1 A ✠	GW ◇	SW 1	SW 1	SW 1	SW 1	SW ◇1 ✠	GW ◇	SW 1	SW 1	XC ◇1
London Waterloo 15 ⊖	d					20 35	20 39			21 05			21 35				21 39	21 42	22 05				
Clapham Junction 10	d						20u46			21u12							21u46		22u12				
	d																						
Woking	d					21 00				21 32			22 00					22 29	22 32				
Farnborough (Main)	d						21 13										22 13	22 33					
Fleet	d						21 19										22 19	22 38					
Reading 7	d			20 46								21 46										←	22 48
Basingstoke	a			21 09			21 31			21 51		22 09					22 31	22 58	22 51			22 58	23 06
	d			21 10			21 33			21 52		22 10				22 21	22 33	23 00	22 52			23 00	23 10
Micheldever	d						21 43									22 31	22s43	→				23 10	
Winchester	d			21 25		21 33	21 52			22 09		22 25	22 33			22 40	22 52		23 09			23 19	23 25
Shawford	d						21 57									22 45	22 57					23 24	
Romsey	d	21 19									22 07			21 50	22 19					22 53	23 07		
Chandlers Ford	d										22 14										23 14		
Eastleigh 3	a	21 49					22 02			22 17	22 21			22 14	22 49	22 50	23 02		23 17		23 22	23 29	
	d	21 50					22 03	22 11		22 18	22 22			22 24	22 50	22 51	23 03		23 18		23 22	23 30	
Hedge End	d															22 57						23 36	
Botley	d													22 35		23 01						23 40	
Fareham	d													22 42		23 10				23 27		23 49	
Portchester	d															23 15						23 54	
Cosham	d															23 20						23 59	
Hilsea	a															23 24						00 03	
Fratton	a													22 56		23 32				23 44		00 08	
Portsmouth & Southsea	a													22 59		23 36				23 48		00 13	
Portsmouth Harbour ⛴	a													23 04		23 40				23 54		00 16	
Southampton Airport Pkwy ✈	d			21 33		21 42	22 08			22 22	22 26	22 33	22 42				23 08		23 22		23 26		23 37
Swaythling	d										22 28										23 28		
St Denys	d										22 31										23 31		
Southampton Central ⛴	a			21 41		21 49	22 18	22 21		22 29	22 36	22 42	22 49				23 17		23 29		23 36		23 43
	d			21 43		21 51		22 22		22 31	22 38	22 43	22 51						23 31		23 38		
Millbrook (Hants)	d										22 40										23 40		
Redbridge	d										22 44										23 44		
Romsey	d	22a03						22 34			22a52				23a03						23 56		
Mottisfont & Dunbridge	d																				00 01		
Dean	d																				00 07		
Salisbury	a							22 58													00 19		
Totton	d									22 36									23 36				
Ashurst New Forest	d									22 41									23 41				
Beaulieu Road	d																						
Brockenhurst 3	a			21 56		22 04				22 49		22 56	23 04						23 49				
	d		21 48	21 57		22 05			22 18	22 50		22 59	23 05						23 50				
Lymington Town	d		21 56						22 26														
Lymington Pier	a		21 59						22 29														
Sway	d									22 54									23 54				
New Milton	d									22 59									23 59				
Hinton Admiral	d									23 03									00 03				
Christchurch	d									23 08									00 08				
Pokesdown	d									23 12									00 11				
Bournemouth	a			22 16		22 20				23 16		23 21	23 25						00 15				
	d					22 24				23 17			23 29						00 17				
Branksome	d					22 29				23 22			23 35						00 22				
Parkstone (Dorset)	d					22 32				23 25			23 38						00 25				
Poole 4	a					22 36				23 29			23 41						00 29				
	d					22 37							23 42										
Hamworthy	d					22 42							23 47										
Holton Heath	d																						
Wareham	d					22 49							23 54										
Wool	d					22 55							00 01										
Moreton (Dorset)	d					23 01							00 07										
Dorchester South	d					23 09							00 15										
Dorchester West	d				22 54																		
Upwey	d				23 02	23 16							00 21										
Weymouth	a				23 10	23 20							00 26										

A ✠ to Bournemouth

London - Basingstoke, Southampton, Romsey Lymington, Bournemouth and Weymouth

Network Diagram - see first Page of Table 158

		SW ◇1 ✠	SW 1	SW 1	SW ◇1	SW 1
London Waterloo 15 ⊖	d	22 35		22 39	23 05	23 35
Clapham Junction 10	d			22u46	23u12	23u42
	d					
Woking	d	23 00			23 32	00 03
Farnborough (Main)	d			23 16		00 14
Fleet	d			23 21		00 20
Reading 7	d					
Basingstoke	a			23 33	23 53	00 33
	d			23 34	23 53	00 35
Micheldever	d				00 03	
Winchester	d	23 33		23 51	00 14	00 51
Shawford	d			23 55		
Romsey	d		22 58			
Chandlers Ford	d					
Eastleigh 3	a		23 34	00 01	00 22	00 59
	d		23 36	00 02	00 23	01 00
Hedge End	d					
Botley	d					
Fareham	d					
Portchester	d					
Cosham	d					
Hilsea	a					
Fratton	a					
Portsmouth & Southsea	a					
Portsmouth Harbour ⛴	a					
Southampton Airport Pkwy ✈	d	23 42		00 06	00 28	01 05
Swaythling	d					
St Denys	d				00s32	
Southampton Central ⛴	a	23 49		00 13	00 37	01 12
	d	23 51			00 38	
Millbrook (Hants)	d					
Redbridge	d					
Romsey	d		23a48			
Mottisfont & Dunbridge	d					
Dean	d					
Salisbury	a					
Totton	d				00s43	
Ashurst New Forest	d					
Beaulieu Road	d					
Brockenhurst 3	a	00 04			00s54	
	d	00 05				
Lymington Town	d					
Lymington Pier	a					
Sway	d					
New Milton	d				01s02	
Hinton Admiral	d					
Christchurch	d				01s09	
Pokesdown	d				01s13	
Bournemouth	a	00 21			01 17	
	d	00 22			01 18	
Branksome	d	00 27			01s23	
Parkstone (Dorset)	d	00 30			01s26	
Poole 4	a	00 35			01 30	
	d					
Hamworthy	d					
Holton Heath	d					
Wareham	d					
Wool	d					
Moreton (Dorset)	d					
Dorchester South	d					
Dorchester West	d					
Upwey	d					
Weymouth	a					

London - Basingstoke, Southampton, Romsey Lymington, Bournemouth and Weymouth

Network Diagram - see first Page of Table 158

		SW ◇1 A ✠	SW ◇1 ✠	SW 1	SW ◇1 ✠	SW 1	SW ◇1	SW 1	SW 1	SW 1	SW 1	SW 1	SW 1	SW 1	SW 1	SW 1	GW ◇	SW 1	SW 1	GW	SW 1	SW 1	GW
London Waterloo 15 ⊖	d	21p35	22p05		22p35	22p39	23p05		23p35	00 05	01 05												
Clapham Junction 10	d		22b12			22b46	23b12		23b42	00u12	01 15												
	d																						
Woking	d	22p00	22p32		23p00		23p32		00 03	00 37	01 42												
Farnborough (Main)	d					23p16			00 14		01s51												
Fleet	d					23p21			00 20		01s57												
Reading 7	d																						
Basingstoke	a		22p51			23p33	23p53		00 33	00 55	02s09												
	d		22p52			23p34	23p53		00 35	00 56													
Micheldever	d						00 03																
Winchester	d	22p33	23p09		23p33	23p51	00 14		00 51	01 13	02s26												
Shawford	d					23p55																	
Romsey	d			23p07												05 58				06 50			
Chandlers Ford	d			23p14												06 06							
Eastleigh 8	a		23p17	23p22		00 01	00 22		00 59	01 21	02s35					06 11							
	d		23p18	23p22		00 02	00 23	00 30	01 00	01 22						06 13		06 28			06 50		
Hedge End	d							00s36										06 34					
Botley	d							00s39										06 38					
Fareham	d							00s47									06 28	06 48		07 27			
Portchester	d							00s53										06 53					
Cosham	d							00s57										06 58		07 35			
Hilsea	a																	07 03					
Fratton	a							01s05										07 07		07 42			
Portsmouth & Southsea	a							01s08										07 11		07 46			
Portsmouth Harbour ⛴	a							01 12										07 16		07 52			
Southampton Airport Pkwy ✈	d	22p42	23p22	23p26	23p42	00 06	00 28		01 05	01 26	02s39					06 17							
Swaythling	d			23p28												06 20							
St Denys	d			23p31			00s32				02s44					06 23							
Southampton Central ⛴	a	22p49	23p29	23p36	23p49	00 13	00 37		01 12	01 35	02 49					06 28	06 49						
	d	22p51	23p31	23p38	23p51		00 38			01 37					06 21	06 30	06 53						
Millbrook (Hants)	d			23p40												06 32							
Redbridge	d			23p44												06 36							
Romsey	d			23p56												06 44	07 11				07a03		
Mottisfont & Dunbridge	d			00 01												06 49							
Dean	d			00 07												06 54							
Salisbury	a			00 19												07 07	07 29						
Totton	d		23p36				00s43			01s42					06 26								
Ashurst New Forest	d		23p41												06 31								
Beaulieu Road	d																						
Brockenhurst 8	a	23p04	23p49		00 04		00s54			01s53					06 39								
	d	23p05	23p50		00 05								06 12	06 16	06 40				06 42			07 12	
Lymington Town	d												06 20						06 50			07 20	
Lymington Pier	a												06 22						06 52			07 22	
Sway	d		23p54											06 20	06 44								
New Milton	d		23p59				01s02			02s00				06 25	06 49								
Hinton Admiral	d		00 03											06 29	06 53								
Christchurch	d		00 08				01s09			02s07				06 34	06 58								
Pokesdown	d		00 11				01s13			02s11				06 38	07 02								
Bournemouth	a	23p25	00 15		00 21		01 17			02 15				06 42	07 06								
	d	23p29	00 17		00 22		01 18					06 11		06 44	07 11								
Branksome	d	23p35	00 22		00 27		01s23					06 16		06 49	07 16								
Parkstone (Dorset)	d	23p38	00 25		00 30		01s26					06 19		06 52	07 19								
Poole 4	a	23p41	00 29		00 35		01 30					06 23		06 55	07 23								
	d	23p42										06 24		06 57	07 24								
Hamworthy	d	23p47										06 29		07 02	07 29								
Holton Heath	d											06 33		07 06	07 33								
Wareham	d	23p54										06 38		07 11	07 38								
Wool	d	00 01										06 44		07 17	07 44								
Moreton (Dorset)	d	00 07										06 50		07 23	07 50								
Dorchester South	d	00 15										06 58		07 31	07 58								
Dorchester West	d																						08 03
Upwey	d	00 21										07 05		07 38	08 05								08 11
Weymouth	a	00 26										07 09		07 42	08 09								08 17

A ✠ to Bournemouth

b Previous night, stops to pick up only

London - Basingstoke, Southampton, Romsey Lymington, Bournemouth and Weymouth

Network Diagram - see first Page of Table 158

		SW ◇1	SW 1	SW 1	SN 1	SW 1	SW 1	SW 1	SW ◇1	SW 1	SW 1	GW ◇ ✠	GW ◇	GW	SW 1	GW ◇	SN 1	SW 1	SW 1	XC ◇1 ✠	SW 1	SW ◇1	SW 1	GW ◇ ✠	GW ◇
London Waterloo 15 ⊖	d	05 30							06 30	06 42												07 35			
Clapham Junction 10	d	05u37							06u37	06 49															
	d																								
Woking	d	06 01	06 19						06 57	07 19												08 00			
Farnborough (Main)	d		06 33							07 33															
Fleet	d		06 38							07 38															
Reading 7	d																			07 46					
Basingstoke	a	06 20	06 58						07 16	07 56										08 08		08 20			
	d	06 21	07 00						07 18	08 00										08 10		08 21			
Micheldever	d	06 31	07 10							08 10															
Winchester	d	06 41	07 19						07 34	08 19										08 25		08 38			
Shawford	d																								
Romsey	d					07 07					07 13		07 44	07 55				08 07					08 19		08 50
Chandlers Ford	d					07 14												08 14							
Eastleigh 8	a	06 50	07 27			07 20			07 42	08 30	07 49							08 20				08 46	08 49		
	d	06 51	07 28		07 14	07 21			07 43	08 31	07 50						08 14	08 21				08 47	08 50		
Hedge End	d		07 34							08 37															
Botley	d		07 38							08 42															
Fareham	d		07 48							08 51		07 47	08 27											08 47	09 27
Portchester	d		07 53							08 56															
Cosham	d		07 58							09 00			08 35												09 35
Hilsea	a		08 03							09 05															
Fratton	a		08 07							09 09			08 42												09 42
Portsmouth & Southsea	a		08 11							09 13			08 46												09 46
Portsmouth Harbour ⛴	a		08 16							09 18			08 52												09 52
Southampton Airport Pkwy ✈	d	06 56			07 18	07 25			07 48								08 18	08 25		08 33		08 51			
Swaythling	d					07 27												08 27							
St Denys	d					07 30												08 30							
Southampton Central ⛴	a	07 03			07 28	07 35			07 56			08 07		08 07			08 28	08 35		08 41		08 58		09 08	
	d	07 05		07 21		07 37			08 00			08 10			08 19	08 27		08 37		08 43		09 00		09 10	
Millbrook (Hants)	d					07 40												08 40							
Redbridge	d					07 43												08 43							
Romsey	d					07 51					08a03	08 21				08 38		08 51					09a03	09 21	
Mottisfont & Dunbridge	d					07 56												08 56							
Dean	d					08 02												09 02							
Salisbury	a					08 15						08 40				09 02		09 15						09 39	
Totton	d	07 10		07 26					08 05						08 24							09 05			
Ashurst New Forest	d			07 31											08 29										
Beaulieu Road	d														08 33										
Brockenhurst 8	a	07 21		07 39					08 16						08 39					08 56		09 16			
	d	07 22		07 40			07 42	08 12	08 17						08 40				08 42	08 58	09 12	09 17			
Lymington Town	d						07 50	08 20											08 50		09 20				
Lymington Pier	a						07 52	08 22											08 52		09 22				
Sway	d	07 26		07 44					08 21						08 45							09 21			
New Milton	d	07 31		07 49					08 26						08 50							09 26			
Hinton Admiral	d	07 35		07 53					08 30						08 54							09 30			
Christchurch	d	07 40		07 58					08 35						08 59							09 35			
Pokesdown	d	07 44		08 02					08 39						09 02							09 39			
Bournemouth	a	07 48		08 06					08 43						09 06					09 14		09 43			
	d	07 49		08 11					08 44						09 11							09 44			
Branksome	d	07 54		08 16					08 49						09 16							09 49			
Parkstone (Dorset)	d	07 57		08 19					08 52						09 19							09 52			
Poole 4	a	08 01		08 23					08 56						09 23							09 56			
	d	08 02		08 24					08 57						09 24							09 57			
Hamworthy	d	08 07		08 29					09 02						09 29							10 02			
Holton Heath	d			08 33											09 33										
Wareham	d	08 14		08 38					09 09						09 38							10 09			
Wool	d	08 20		08 44					09 15						09 44										
Moreton (Dorset)	d	08 26		08 50					09 21						09 50										
Dorchester South	d	08 34		08 58					09 29						09 58							10 27			
Dorchester West	d																								
Upwey	d	08 41		09 05					09 36						10 05										
Weymouth	a	08 45		09 09					09 40						10 09							10 35			

Table 158

Saturdays

London - Basingstoke, Southampton, Romsey Lymington, Bournemouth and Weymouth

Network Diagram - see first Page of Table 158

		GW		SW	XC	SW	SW	SW	SW	SW	SW	XC		SW	SW	GW	GW	SW	SW	SW	SW	SN		SW	GW
		◇		1	◇1	◇1	1	1	1	1	1	◇1		◇1	1	◇	◇	1	1	◇1	1	1		1	◇
														A						A					
												🍴		🍴		🍴				🍴					
London Waterloo 15 ⊖	d			07 39		08 05			08 09					08 35					08 39	09 05					
Clapham Junction 10	d			07u46		08u12													08u46	09u12					
	d																								
Woking	d								08 35					09 00											
Farnborough (Main)	d			08 13					08 45										09 13						
Fleet	d			08 19															09 19						
Reading 7	d				08 23							08 46													
Basingstoke	a			08 31	08 40	08 47			08 58			09 08							09 31	09 47					
	d			08 33	08 41	08 49			09 00			09 10							09 33	09 49					
Micheldever	d								09 10																
Winchester	d			08 49	08 56	09 05			09 19			09 25		09 33					09 49	10 05					
Shawford	d			08 54															09 54						
Romsey	d							09 07		09 19							09 50							10 07	
Chandlers Ford	d							09 14																10 14	
Eastleigh 8	a			08 59				09 20	09 27	09 49									09 59					10 20	
	d			09 00				09 21	09 28	09 50									10 00			10 14		10 21	
Hedge End	d								09 34																
Botley	d								09 38																
Fareham	d								09 48							09 47	10 27								10 16
Portchester	d								09 53																
Cosham	d								09 58								10 35								
Hilsea	a								10 03																
Fratton	a								10 07								10 42								
Portsmouth & Southsea	a								10 11								10 46								
Portsmouth Harbour ⛴	a								10 18								10 52								
Southampton Airport Pkwy ✈	d			09 05	09 09	09 14		09 25				09 33		09 42					10 05	10 14		10 18		10 25	
Swaythling	d							09 27																10 27	
St Denys	d						←	09 30													←			10 30	
Southampton Central ⛴	a			09 12	09 17	09 22	09 12	09 35				09 40		09 49		10 08			10 12	10 22	10 12	10 28		10 35	10 40
	d			09 30		09 24	09 30	09 37				09 42		09 51		10 10			10 30	10 24	10 30			10 37	10 42
Millbrook (Hants)	d			→				09 40											→					10 40	
Redbridge	d							09 43																10 44	
Romsey	d							09 51		10a03						10 21								10 59	10 53
Mottisfont & Dunbridge	d							09 56																11 04	
Dean	d							10 02																11 10	
Salisbury	a							10 15								10 39								11 22	11 12
Totton	d						09 35														10 35				
Ashurst New Forest	d						09 40														10 40				
Beaulieu Road	d						09 44								←										
Brockenhurst 3	a					09 37	09 51					09 57		10 04	09 51					10 37	10 51				
	d					09 38	10 16				09 42	09 58		10 05	10 16			10 12		10 38	11 16				
Lymington Town	d						→				09 50							10 20			→				
Lymington Pier	a										09 52							10 22							
Sway	d														10 20										
New Milton	d					09 45									10 25					10 45					
Hinton Admiral	d														10 29										
Christchurch	d					09 52									10 34					10 52					
Pokesdown	d					09 56									10 38					10 56					
Bournemouth	a					10 00						10 11		10 20	10 42					11 00					
	d					10 04								10 24	10 43					11 04					
Branksome	d													10 29	10 48										
Parkstone (Dorset)	d													10 32	10 51										
Poole 4	a					10 13								10 36	10 55					11 13					
	d					10 14								10 37						11 14					
Hamworthy	d					10 19								10 42						11 19					
Holton Heath	d					10 23														11 23					
Wareham	d					10 28								10 49						11 28					
Wool	d					10 35														11 35					
Moreton (Dorset)	d					10 41														11 41					
Dorchester South	d					10 49								11 05						11 49					
Dorchester West	d	10 38																							
Upwey	d	10 49				10 55														11 55					
Weymouth	a	10 57				11 00								11 13						12 00					

A 🍴 to Bournemouth

Table 158

Saturdays

London - Basingstoke, Southampton, Romsey Lymington, Bournemouth and Weymouth

Network Diagram - see first Page of Table 158

		SW	SW	SW	XC	GW	SW	SW		GW	GW	SW	SW	XC	SW	SW	SW	SW		SW	SW	XC	SW	SW	GW
		1	1	1	◇1	◇	◇1	1		◇	◇	1	1	◇1	◇1	1	1	1		1	1	◇1	◇1	1	◇
							A								A								A		
					🍴		🍴							🍴	🍴							🍴	🍴		
London Waterloo 15 ⊖	d	09 09					09 35						09 39		10 05			10 09					10 35		
Clapham Junction 10	d												09u46		10u12										
	d																								
Woking	d	09 35					10 00											10 35					11 00		
Farnborough (Main)	d	09 45											10 13					10 45							
Fleet	d												10 19												
Reading 7	d				09 46									10 15								10 46			
Basingstoke	a	09 58			10 08								10 31	10 39	10 47			10 58				11 08			
	d	10 00			10 10								10 33	10 40	10 49			11 00				11 10			
Micheldever	d	10 10																11 10							
Winchester	d	10 19			10 25		10 33						10 49	10 55	11 06			11 19				11 25	11 33		
Shawford	d												10 54												
Romsey	d		10 19								10 50						11 07			11 19					
Chandlers Ford	d																11 14								
Eastleigh 8	a	10 27	10 49										10 59				11 20	11 27		11 49					
	d	10 28	10 50										11 00				11 21	11 28		11 50					
Hedge End	d	10 34																11 34							
Botley	d	10 38																11 38							
Fareham	d	10 48								10 47	11 27							11 48							11 47
Portchester	d	10 53																11 53							
Cosham	d	10 58									11 35							11 58							
Hilsea	a	11 03																12 03							
Fratton	a	11 07									11 42							12 07							
Portsmouth & Southsea	a	11 11									11 46							12 11							
Portsmouth Harbour ⛴	a	11 18									11 52							12 18							
Southampton Airport Pkwy ✈	d				10 33		10 42						11 05	11 09	11 15		11 25					11 33	11 42		
Swaythling	d																11 27								
St Denys	d															←	11 30								
Southampton Central ⛴	a				10 43		10 49			11 08			11 12	11 17	11 22	11 12	11 35					11 41	11 49		12 08
	d				10 45		10 51			11 10			11 30		11 24	11 30	11 37					11 43	11 51		12 10
Millbrook (Hants)	d												→				11 40								
Redbridge	d																11 43								
Romsey	d		11a03							11 21							11 51			12a03					12 21
Mottisfont & Dunbridge	d																11 56								
Dean	d																12 02								
Salisbury	a									11 39							12 15								12 39
Totton	d															11 35									
Ashurst New Forest	d															11 40									
Beaulieu Road	d							←								11 44								←	
Brockenhurst 3	a				10 58		11 04	10 51							11 37	11 51						11 57	12 04	11 51	
	d			10 42	10 59		11 05	11 16				11 12			11 38	12 16					11 42	11 58	12 05	12 16	
Lymington Town	d			10 50								11 20				→					11 50				
Lymington Pier	a			10 52								11 22									11 52				
Sway	d							11 20																12 20	
New Milton	d							11 25							11 45									12 25	
Hinton Admiral	d							11 29																12 29	
Christchurch	d							11 34							11 52									12 34	
Pokesdown	d							11 38							11 56									12 38	
Bournemouth	a				11 12		11 20	11 42							12 00							12 11	12 20	12 42	
	d						11 24	11 43							12 04								12 24	12 43	
Branksome	d						11 29	11 48															12 29	12 48	
Parkstone (Dorset)	d						11 32	11 51															12 32	12 51	
Poole 4	a						11 36	11 55							12 13								12 36	12 55	
	d						11 37								12 14								12 37		
Hamworthy	d						11 42								12 19								12 42		
Holton Heath	d														12 23										
Wareham	d						11 49								12 28								12 49		
Wool	d														12 35										
Moreton (Dorset)	d														12 41										
Dorchester South	d						12 05								12 49								13 05		
Dorchester West	d					11 54																			
Upwey	d					12 02									12 55										
Weymouth	a					12 09	12 13								13 00								13 13		

A 🍴 to Bournemouth

London - Basingstoke, Southampton, Romsey Lymington, Bournemouth and Weymouth

Network Diagram - see first Page of Table 158

		GW ◇ ⌶	GW	SW 1	SW 1	SW ◇1 A ⌶	SW 1	GW ◇	SN 1	SW 1	SW 1	SW 1	SW 1	XC ◇1 ⌶	GW ◇	SW ◇1 A ⌶	SW 1	GW ◇	GW ◇ ⌶	SW 1	SW 1	XC ◇1 ⌶
London Waterloo 15 ⊖	d				10 39	11 05					11 09					11 35					11 39	
Clapham Junction 10	d				10u46	11u12															11u46	
	d																					
Woking	d										11 35					12 00						
Farnborough (Main)	d				11 13						11 45										12 13	
Fleet	d				11 19																12 19	
Reading 7	d													11 46								12 15
Basingstoke	a				11 31	11 47					11 58			12 08							12 31	12 40
	d				11 33	11 49					12 00			12 10							12 33	12 41
Micheldever	d										12 10											
Winchester	d				11 49	12 05					12 19			12 25		12 33					12 49	12 56
Shawford	d				11 54																12 54	
Romsey	d	11 50	12 04							12 07		12 19							12 50			
Chandlers Ford	d									12 14												
Eastleigh 8	a				11 59					12 20	12 27	12 49									12 59	
	d				12 00				12 14	12 21	12 28	12 50									13 00	
Hedge End	d										12 34											
Botley	d										12 38											
Fareham	d	12 27									12 48							12 47	13 27			
Portchester	d										12 53											
Cosham	d	12 35									12 58								13 35			
Hilsea	a										13 03											
Fratton	a	12 42									13 07								13 42			
Portsmouth & Southsea	a	12 46									13 11								13 46			
Portsmouth Harbour ⛴	a	12 52									13 18								13 52			
Southampton Airport Pkwy ✈	d				12 05	12 14			12 19	12 25				12 33		12 42					13 05	13 09
Swaythling	d									12 27												
St Denys	d						←			12 30												
Southampton Central ⛴	a		12 20		12 12	12 22	12 12		12 28	12 35				12 41		12 49		13 08			13 12	13 17
	d				12 30	12 24	12 30	12 27		12 37				12 43		12 51		13 10			13 30	
Millbrook (Hants)	d				→					12 40											→	
Redbridge	d									12 43												
Romsey	d							12 38		12 51		13a03						13 21				
Mottisfont & Dunbridge	d									12 56												
Dean	d									13 02												
Salisbury	a							13 02		13 15								13 39				
Totton	d						12 35															
Ashurst New Forest	d						12 40															
Beaulieu Road	d																←					
Brockenhurst 3	a					12 37	12 51							12 57		13 04	12 51					
	d			12 12		12 38	13 16						12 42	12 58		13 05	13 16			13 12		
Lymington Town	d			12 20			→						12 50							13 20		
Lymington Pier	a			12 22									12 52							13 22		
Sway	d																13 20					
New Milton	d					12 45											13 25					
Hinton Admiral	d																13 29					
Christchurch	d					12 52											13 34					
Pokesdown	d					12 56											13 38					
Bournemouth	a					13 00								13 11		13 20	13 42					
	d					13 04										13 24	13 43					
Branksome	d															13 29	13 48					
Parkstone (Dorset)	d															13 32	13 51					
Poole 4	a					13 13										13 36	13 55					
	d					13 14										13 37						
Hamworthy	d					13 19										13 42						
Holton Heath	d					13 23																
Wareham	d					13 28										13 49						
Wool	d					13 35																
Moreton (Dorset)	d					13 41																
Dorchester South	d					13 49										14 05						
Dorchester West	d														13 54							
Upwey	d					13 55									14 02							
Weymouth	a					14 00									14 08	14 13						

A ⌶ to Bournemouth

London - Basingstoke, Southampton, Romsey Lymington, Bournemouth and Weymouth

Network Diagram - see first Page of Table 158

		SW ◇1 A ⌶	SW 1	SW 1	SW 1	SW 1	SW 1	XC ◇1 ⌶	SW ◇1 A ⌶	SW 1	GW ◇	GW ◇ ⌶	SW 1	SW 1	SW ◇1 A ⌶	SW 1	GW ◇	SW 1	SW 1	SW 1	XC ◇1 ⌶	SW ◇1 A ⌶	SW 1
London Waterloo 15 ⊖	d	12 05			12 09				12 35					12 39	13 05				13 09			13 35	
Clapham Junction 10	d	12u12												12u46	13u12								
	d																						
Woking	d				12 35				13 00										13 35			14 00	
Farnborough (Main)	d				12 45									13 13					13 45				
Fleet	d													13 19									
Reading 7	d							12 46													13 46		
Basingstoke	a	12 47			12 58			13 08						13 31	13 47				13 58		14 08		
	d	12 49			13 00			13 10						13 33	13 49				14 00		14 10		
Micheldever	d				13 10														14 10				
Winchester	d	13 05			13 19			13 25	13 33					13 49	14 05				14 19		14 25	14 33	
Shawford	d													13 54									
Romsey	d			13 07		13 19						13 50					14 20	14 07					
Chandlers Ford	d			13 14														14 14					
Eastleigh 8	a			13 20	13 27	13 49								13 59				14 20	14 27				
	d			13 21	13 28	13 50								14 00				14 21	14 28				
Hedge End	d				13 34														14 34				
Botley	d				13 38														14 38				
Fareham	d				13 48						13 47	14 27							14 48				
Portchester	d				13 53														14 53				
Cosham	d				13 58							14 35							14 58				
Hilsea	a				14 03														15 03				
Fratton	a				14 07							14 42							15 07				
Portsmouth & Southsea	a				14 11							14 46							15 11				
Portsmouth Harbour ⛴	a				14 18							14 52							15 18				
Southampton Airport Pkwy ✈	d	13 14		13 25				13 33	13 42					14 05	14 14			14 25			14 33	14 42	
Swaythling	d			13 27														14 27					
St Denys	d		←	13 30												←		14 30					
Southampton Central ⛴	a	13 22	13 12	13 35				13 41	13 49		14 08			14 12	14 22	14 12	14 32	14 35			14 41	14 49	
	d	13 24	13 30	13 37				13 43	13 51		14 10			14 30	14 24	14 30		14 37			14 43	14 51	
Millbrook (Hants)	d			13 40										→				14 40					
Redbridge	d			13 43														14 43					
Romsey	d			13 51		14a03					14 21							14 51					
Mottisfont & Dunbridge	d			13 56														14 56					
Dean	d			14 02														15 02					
Salisbury	a			14 15							14 39							15 15					
Totton	d		13 35													14 35							
Ashurst New Forest	d		13 40													14 40							
Beaulieu Road	d		13 44							←													←
Brockenhurst 3	a	13 37	13 51					13 57	14 04	13 51					14 37	14 51					14 57	15 04	14 51
	d	13 38	14 16				13 42	13 58	14 05	14 16			14 12		14 38	15 16				14 42	14 58	15 05	15 16
Lymington Town	d		→				13 50						14 20			→				14 50			
Lymington Pier	a						13 52						14 22							14 52			
Sway	d									14 20													15 20
New Milton	d	13 45								14 25					14 45								15 25
Hinton Admiral	d									14 29													15 29
Christchurch	d	13 52								14 34					14 52								15 34
Pokesdown	d	13 56								14 38					14 56								15 38
Bournemouth	a	14 00						14 11	14 20	14 42					15 00						15 11	15 20	15 42
	d	14 04							14 24	14 43					15 04							15 24	15 43
Branksome	d								14 29	14 48												15 29	15 48
Parkstone (Dorset)	d								14 32	14 51												15 32	15 51
Poole 4	a	14 13							14 36	14 55					15 13							15 36	15 55
	d	14 14							14 37						15 14							15 37	
Hamworthy	d	14 19							14 42						15 19							15 42	
Holton Heath	d	14 23													15 23								
Wareham	d	14 28							14 49						15 28							15 49	
Wool	d	14 35													15 35								
Moreton (Dorset)	d	14 41													15 41								
Dorchester South	d	14 49							15 05						15 49							16 05	
Dorchester West	d																						
Upwey	d	14 55													15 55								
Weymouth	a	15 00							15 13						16 00							16 13	

A ⌶ to Bournemouth

London - Basingstoke, Southampton, Romsey Lymington, Bournemouth and Weymouth

Network Diagram - see first Page of Table 158

		GW	SN	SW	GW	SW	SW	XC	SW	SW	SW	SW	SW	SW	XC	GW	SW	SW	GW	GW	SW	SW	SW
		◇	1	1	◇	1	1	◇1 ⌶	◇1 ⌶	1	1	1	1	1	◇1 ⌶	◇	◇1 A ⌶	1	◇	◇	1	1	◇1 A ⌶
London Waterloo 15 ⊖	d						13 39		14 05			14 09					14 35					14 39	15 05
Clapham Junction 10	d						13u46		14u12													14u46	15u12
	d																						
Woking	d											14 35					15 00						
Farnborough (Main)	d						14 13					14 45										15 13	
Fleet	d						14 19															15 19	
Reading 7	d							14 15							14 46								
Basingstoke	a						14 31	14 40	14 47			14 58			15 08							15 31	15 47
	d						14 33	14 41	14 49			15 00			15 10							15 33	15 49
Micheldever	d											15 10											
Winchester	d						14 49	14 56	15 05			15 19			15 25		15 33					15 49	16 05
Shawford	d						14 54															15 54	
Romsey	d			14 13	14 50						15 07		15 19							15 50			
Chandlers Ford	d										15 14												
Eastleigh 8	a			14 49			14 59				15 20	15 27	15 49									15 59	
	d		14 41	14 50			15 00				15 21	15 28	15 50									16 00	
Hedge End	d											15 34											
Botley	d											15 38											
Fareham	d	14 47	14a59		15 27							15 48							15 47	16 27			
Portchester	d											15 53											
Cosham	d				15 35							15 58								16 35			
Hilsea	a											16 03											
Fratton	a				15 42							16 07								16 42			
Portsmouth & Southsea	a				15 46							16 11								16 46			
Portsmouth Harbour ⛴	a				15 52							16 18								16 52			
Southampton Airport Pkwy ✈	d						15 05	15 09	15 14		15 25				15 33		15 42					16 05	16 14
Swaythling	d										15 27												
St Denys	d									←	15 30												
Southampton Central ⛴	a	15 08					15 12	15 17	15 22	15 12	15 35				15 41		15 49		16 08			16 12	16 22
	d	15 10					15 30		15 24	15 30	15 37				15 43		15 51		16 10			16 30	16 24
Millbrook (Hants)	d						→				15 40											→	
Redbridge	d										15 43												
Romsey	d	15 21		15a04							15 51		16a03						16 21				
Mottisfont & Dunbridge	d										15 56												
Dean	d										16 02												
Salisbury	a	15 39									16 15								16 39				
Totton	d									15 35													
Ashurst New Forest	d									15 40													
Beaulieu Road	d									15 44								←					
Brockenhurst 5	a								15 37	15 51					15 57		16 04	15 51					16 37
	d					15 12			15 38	16 16				15 42	15 58		16 05	16 16			16 12		16 38
Lymington Town	d					15 20				→				15 50							16 20		
Lymington Pier	a					15 22								15 52							16 22		
Sway	d																	16 20					
New Milton	d								15 45									16 25					16 45
Hinton Admiral	d																	16 29					
Christchurch	d								15 52									16 34					16 52
Pokesdown	d								15 56									16 38					16 56
Bournemouth	a								16 00						16 11		16 20	16 42					17 00
	d								16 04								16 24	16 43					17 04
Branksome	d																16 29	16 48					
Parkstone (Dorset)	d																16 32	16 51					
Poole 4	a								16 13								16 36	16 55					17 13
	d								16 14								16 37						17 14
Hamworthy	d								16 19								16 42						17 19
Holton Heath	d								16 23														17 23
Wareham	d								16 28								16 49						17 28
Wool	d								16 35														17 35
Moreton (Dorset)	d								16 41														17 41
Dorchester South	d								16 49								17 06						17 49
Dorchester West	d															16 58							
Upwey	d								16 55							17 05							17 55
Weymouth	a								17 00							17 10	17 15						18 00

A ⌶ to Bournemouth

Table 158

Saturdays

London - Basingstoke, Southampton, Romsey Lymington, Bournemouth and Weymouth

Network Diagram - see first Page of Table 158

		SW	SN	SW	SW	SW	SW	XC	SW	SW	GW	GW	SW	SW	XC	SW	SW	SW	SW	SW	SW	XC
		1	1	1	1	1	1	◇1 ⌶	◇1 A ⌶	1	■	◇	1	1	◇1 ⌶	◇1 A ⌶	1	1	1	1	1	◇1 ⌶
London Waterloo 15 ⊖	d				15 09				15 35					15 39		16 05			16 09			
Clapham Junction 10	d													15u46		16u12						
	d																					
Woking	d				15 35				16 00										16 35			
Farnborough (Main)	d				15 45									16 13					16 45			
Fleet	d													16 19								
Reading 7	d							15 46							16 15							16 46
Basingstoke	a				15 58			16 08						16 31	16 40	16 47			16 58			17 08
	d				16 00			16 10						16 33	16 41	16 49			17 00			17 10
Micheldever	d				16 10														17 10			
Winchester	d				16 19			16 25	16 33					16 49	16 56	17 05			17 19			17 25
Shawford	d													16 54								
Romsey	d			16 07		16 19						16 50						17 07		17 19		
Chandlers Ford	d			16 14														17 14				
Eastleigh 8	a			16 20	16 27	16 49								16 59				17 20	17 27	17 49		
	d		16 14	16 21	16 28	16 50								17 00				17 21	17 28	17 50		
Hedge End	d				16 34														17 34			
Botley	d				16 38														17 38			
Fareham	d				16 48						16 47	17 27							17 48			
Portchester	d				16 53														17 53			
Cosham	d				16 58							17 35							17 58			
Hilsea	a				17 03														18 03			
Fratton	a				17 07							17 42							18 07			
Portsmouth & Southsea	a				17 11							17 46							18 11			
Portsmouth Harbour ⛴	a				17 18							17 52							18 18			
Southampton Airport Pkwy ✈	d		16 18	16 25				16 33	16 42					17 05	17 09	17 14		17 25				17 33
Swaythling	d			16 27														17 27				
St Denys	d	←		16 30													←	17 30				
Southampton Central ⛴	a	16 12	16 28	16 35				16 41	16 49		17 08			17 12	17 17	17 22	17 12	17 35				17 41
	d	16 30		16 37				16 43	16 51		17 10			17 30		17 24	17 30	17 37				17 43
Millbrook (Hants)	d			16 40										→				17 40				
Redbridge	d			16 43														17 43				
Romsey	d			16 51		17a03					17 21							17 51		18a03		
Mottisfont & Dunbridge	d			16 56														17 56				
Dean	d			17 02														18 02				
Salisbury	a			17 15							17 39							18 15				
Totton	d	16 35															17 35					
Ashurst New Forest	d	16 40															17 40					
Beaulieu Road	d									←							17 44					
Brockenhurst 5	a	16 51						16 57	17 04	16 51						17 37	17 51					17 57
	d	17 16					16 42	16 58	17 05	17 16			17 12			17 38	18 16				17 42	17 58
Lymington Town	d	→					16 50						17 20				→				17 50	
Lymington Pier	a						16 52						17 22								17 52	
Sway	d									17 20												
New Milton	d									17 25						17 45						
Hinton Admiral	d									17 29												
Christchurch	d									17 34						17 52						
Pokesdown	d									17 38						17 56						
Bournemouth	a							17 11	17 20	17 42						18 00						18 11
	d								17 24	17 43						18 04						
Branksome	d								17 29	17 48												
Parkstone (Dorset)	d								17 32	17 51												
Poole 4	a								17 36	17 55						18 13						
	d								17 37							18 14						
Hamworthy	d								17 42							18 19						
Holton Heath	d															18 23						
Wareham	d								17 49							18 28						
Wool	d															18 35						
Moreton (Dorset)	d															18 41						
Dorchester South	d								18 05							18 49						
Dorchester West	d																					
Upwey	d															18 55						
Weymouth	a								18 13							19 00						

A ⌶ to Bournemouth

London - Basingstoke, Southampton, Romsey Lymington, Bournemouth and Weymouth

Network Diagram - see first Page of Table 158

		GW	SW	SW	SW	GW	GW	SW	SW	SW	SW	SN	SW	SW	SW	XC	GW	SW	GW	SW	SW	GW	GW
		◇	◇1 A ✕	1	1	◇	◇	1	1	◇1 B	1	1	1	1	1	◇1 ✕	◇	1	◇	◇1 A ✕	1	◇	1
London Waterloo 15 ⊖	d		16 35						16 39	17 05				17 09						17 35			
Clapham Junction 10	d								16u46	17u12													
	d																						
Woking	d		17 00											17 35						18 00			
Farnborough (Main)	d								17 13					17 45									
Fleet	d								17 19														
Reading 7	d															17 46							
Basingstoke	a								17 31	17 47				17 58		18 08							
	d				17 24				17 33	17 49				18 00		18 10							
Micheldever	d				17 34									18 10									
Winchester	d		17 33		17 43				17 49	18 05				18 19		18 25				18 33			
Shawford	d				17 48				17 54														
Romsey	d						17 50						18 07					18 19					18 50
Chandlers Ford	d												18 14										
Eastleigh 3	a				17 53				17 59				18 20	18 27				18 49					
	d				17 54				18 00			18 14	18 21	18 28				18 50					
Hedge End	d													18 34									
Botley	d													18 38									
Fareham	d					17 47	18 27							18 48			18 15					18 47	19 27
Portchester	d													18 53									
Cosham	d						18 35							18 58									19 35
Hilsea	a													19 03									
Fratton	a						18 42							19 07									19 42
Portsmouth & Southsea	a						18 46							19 11									19 46
Portsmouth Harbour ⛴	a						18 52							19 18									19 52
Southampton Airport Pkwy ✈	d		17 42		17 59				18 05	18 14		18 18	18 25			18 33				18 42			
Swaythling	d				18 01								18 27										
St Denys	d				18 04						←		18 30										
Southampton Central ⛴	a		17 49		18 10	18 08			18 14	18 22	18 14	18 28	18 35			18 40	18 43			18 49		19 08	
	d		17 51			18 10			18 30	18 24	18 30		18 37			18 43	18 45			18 51		19 10	
Millbrook (Hants)	d								→				18 40										
Redbridge	d												18 44										
Romsey	d					18 21							19 00				18 56	19a04				19 21	
Mottisfont & Dunbridge	d												19 05										
Dean	d												19 10										
Salisbury	a					18 39							19 23				19 14					19 39	
Totton	d										18 35												
Ashurst New Forest	d										18 40												
Beaulieu Road	d			←																	←		
Brockenhurst 3	a		18 04	17 51						18 37	18 51					18 57				19 04	18 51		
	d		18 05	18 16				18 12		18 38	19 16				18 42	18 58				19 05	19 16		
Lymington Town	d							18 20			→				18 50								
Lymington Pier	a							18 22							18 52								
Sway	d			18 20																	19 20		
New Milton	d			18 25						18 45											19 25		
Hinton Admiral	d			18 29																	19 29		
Christchurch	d			18 34						18 52											19 34		
Pokesdown	d			18 38						18 56											19 38		
Bournemouth	a		18 20	18 42						19 00						19 11				19 20	19 42		
	d		18 24	18 43						19 04										19 24	19 43		
Branksome	d		18 29	18 48																19 29	19 48		
Parkstone (Dorset)	d		18 32	18 51																19 32	19 51		
Poole 4	a		18 36	18 55						19 13										19 36	19 55		
	d		18 37							19 14										19 37			
Hamworthy	d		18 42							19 19										19 42			
Holton Heath	d									19 23													
Wareham	d		18 49							19 28										19 49			
Wool	d									19 35													
Moreton (Dorset)	d									19 41													
Dorchester South	d		19 05							19 49										20 05			
Dorchester West	d	18 54																	19 54				
Upwey	d	19 02								19 55									20 01				
Weymouth	a	19 10	19 13							20 00									20 09	20 13			

A ✕ to Bournemouth

B ☕ to Bournemouth

London - Basingstoke, Southampton, Romsey Lymington, Bournemouth and Weymouth

Network Diagram - see first Page of Table 158

		SW	SW	XC	SW	SW	SW	SW	SW	SW	XC	SW	SW	GW	GW	GW	SW	SW	SW	SW	SN	SW
		1	1	◇1 ✕	◇1 A ✕	1	1	1	1	1	◇1 ✕	◇1 A ✕	1	◇	◇		1	1	◇1 A ✕	1	1	1
London Waterloo 15 ⊖	d		17 39		18 05			18 09				18 35						18 39	19 05			
Clapham Junction 10	d		17u46		18u12													18u46	19u12			
	d																					
Woking	d							18 35				19 00										
Farnborough (Main)	d		18 13					18 45										19 13				
Fleet	d		18 19															19 19				
Reading 7	d			18 15							18 46											
Basingstoke	a		18 31	18 40	18 47			18 58			19 08							19 31	19 47			
	d		18 33	18 41	18 49			19 00			19 10							19 33	19 49			
Micheldever	d							19 10														
Winchester	d		18 49	18 56	19 05			19 19			19 25	19 33						19 49	20 05			
Shawford	d		18 54															19 54				
Romsey	d						19 07		19 19						19 50	20 04						20 07
Chandlers Ford	d						19 14															20 14
Eastleigh 3	a		18 59				19 20	19 27	19 49									19 59				20 20
	d		19 00				19 21	19 28	19 50									20 00			20 14	20 21
Hedge End	d							19 34														
Botley	d							19 38														
Fareham	d							19 48						19 47	20 28							
Portchester	d							19 53														
Cosham	d							19 58														
Hilsea	a							20 03														
Fratton	a							20 07							20 42							
Portsmouth & Southsea	a							20 11							20 46							
Portsmouth Harbour ⛴	a							20 18							20 52							
Southampton Airport Pkwy ✈	d		19 05	19 09	19 14		19 25				19 33	19 42						20 05	20 14		20 18	20 25
Swaythling	d						19 27															20 27
St Denys	d					←	19 30													←		20 30
Southampton Central ⛴	a		19 12	19 17	19 22	19 12	19 35				19 41	19 49		20 09		20 18		20 14	20 22	20 14	20 28	20 35
	d		19 30		19 24	19 30	19 37				19 43	19 51		20 10				20 30	20 24	20 30		20 37
Millbrook (Hants)	d		→				19 40											→				20 40
Redbridge	d						19 43															20 43
Romsey	d						19 51		20a03					20 21								20 51
Mottisfont & Dunbridge	d						19 56															20 56
Dean	d						20 02															21 02
Salisbury	a						20 15							20 39								21 15
Totton	d					19 35														20 35		
Ashurst New Forest	d					19 40														20 40		
Beaulieu Road	d					19 44							←									
Brockenhurst 3	a				19 37	19 51					19 57	20 04	19 51						20 37	20 51		
	d	19 12			19 38	20 16				19 42	19 58	20 05	20 16				20 12		20 38	21 16		
Lymington Town	d	19 20				→				19 50							20 20			→		
Lymington Pier	a	19 22								19 52							20 22					
Sway	d												20 20									
New Milton	d				19 45								20 25						20 45			
Hinton Admiral	d												20 29									
Christchurch	d				19 52								20 34						20 52			
Pokesdown	d				19 56								20 38						20 56			
Bournemouth	a				20 00						20 11	20 20	20 42						21 00			
	d				20 04							20 24	20 43						21 04			
Branksome	d											20 29	20 48									
Parkstone (Dorset)	d											20 32	20 51									
Poole 4	a				20 13							20 36	20 55						21 13			
	d				20 14							20 37							21 14			
Hamworthy	d				20 19							20 42							21 19			
Holton Heath	d				20 23																	
Wareham	d				20 28							20 49							21 28			
Wool	d				20 35														21 35			
Moreton (Dorset)	d				20 41														21 41			
Dorchester South	d				20 49							21 05							21 49			
Dorchester West	d																					
Upwey	d				20 55														21 55			
Weymouth	a				21 00							21 13							22 00			

A ✕ to Bournemouth

Table 158

Saturdays

London - Basingstoke, Southampton, Romsey Lymington, Bournemouth and Weymouth

Network Diagram - see first Page of Table 158

		SW	SW	SW	XC	SW	SW	GW	SW	GW	SW	SW	GW	SW	SW	SW	SW	XC	GW	GW	SW	SW	SW	SW
		■	■	■	◇■	◇■	■	◇	■	◇	■	◇■		■	■	■	■	◇■	◇		◇■	■	■	■
						A															A			
					✠	✠						✠									✠			
London Waterloo ■ ⊖	d	19 09				19 35			19 39			20 05			20 09						20 35	20 39	20 42	
Clapham Junction ■	d								19u46			20u12										20u46		
	d																							
Woking	d	19 35				20 00									20 35						21 00		21 19	
Farnborough (Main)	d	19 45							20 13						20 45							21 13	21 33	
Fleet	d								20 19													21 19	21 38	
Reading ■	d				19 46													20 46						
Basingstoke	a	19 58			20 08				20 31			20 47			20 58			21 08				21 31	21 58	
	d	20 00			20 10				20 33			20 49			21 00			21 10				21 33	22 00	
Micheldever	d	20 10													21 10							21 43	22 10	
Winchester	d	20 19			20 25	20 33			20 49			21 05			21 19			21 25			21 33	21 52	22 19	
Shawford	d								20 54													21 57		
Romsey	d		20 19							20 50				21 07		21 19			21 50					
Chandlers Ford	d													21 14										
Eastleigh ■	a	20 27	20 49						20 59					21 20	21 27	21 49						22 02	22 27	
	d	20 28	20 50						21 00					21 21	21 28	21 50						22 03	22 28	
Hedge End	d	20 34													21 34								22 34	
Botley	d	20 38													21 38								22 38	
Fareham	d	20 48						20 47		21 27					21 48				22 27				22 48	
Portchester	d	20 53													21 53								22 53	
Cosham	d	20 58													21 58								22 58	
Hilsea	a	21 03													22 03								23 03	
Fratton	a	21 07								21 42					22 07				22 42				23 07	
Portsmouth & Southsea	a	21 11								21 46					22 11				22 46				23 11	
Portsmouth Harbour ⛴	a	21 18								21 52					22 18				22 52				23 18	
Southampton Airport Pkwy ✈	d				20 33	20 42			21 05			21 14		21 25				21 33			21 42	22 08		
Swaythling	d													21 27										
St Denys	d													21 30										
Southampton Central ⛴	a				20 41	20 49		21 10	21 12			21 22		21 35				21 41			21 49	22 17		
	d				20 43	20 51		21 10				21 24	21 27	21 37				21 43			21 51			
Millbrook (Hants)	d													21 40										
Redbridge	d													21 43										
Romsey	d		21a03					21 21					21 38	21 51		22a03								
Mottisfont & Dunbridge	d													21 56										
Dean	d													22 02										
Salisbury	a							21 40					22 02	22 15										
Totton	d											21 29												
Ashurst New Forest	d											21 34												
Beaulieu Road	d						←																	
Brockenhurst ■	a				20 57	21 04	20 51					21 42						21 57			22 04			
	d			20 42	20 58	21 05	21 16				21 12	21 43					21 48	21 58			22 05			22 18
Lymington Town	d			20 50							21 20						21 56							22 26
Lymington Pier	a			20 52							21 22						21 58							22 28
Sway	d						21 20					21 47												
New Milton	d						21 25					21 52												
Hinton Admiral	d						21 29					21 56												
Christchurch	d						21 34					22 01												
Pokesdown	d						21 38					22 05												
Bournemouth	a				21 11	21 20	21 42					22 09						22 15			22 20			
	d					21 24	21 43					22 10									22 24			
Branksome	d					21 29	21 48					22 15									22 29			
Parkstone (Dorset)	d					21 32	21 51					22 18									22 32			
Poole ■	a					21 36	21 55					22 23									22 36			
	d					21 37															22 37			
Hamworthy	d					21 42															22 42			
Holton Heath	d																							
Wareham	d					21 49															22 49			
Wool	d					21 55															22 55			
Moreton (Dorset)	d					22 01															23 01			
Dorchester South	d					22 09															23 09			
Dorchester West	d																			22 54				
Upwey	d					22 16														23 02	23 16			
Weymouth	a					22 20														23 10	23 20			

A ✠ to Bournemouth

Table 158

Saturdays

London - Basingstoke, Southampton, Romsey Lymington, Bournemouth and Weymouth

Network Diagram - see first Page of Table 158

		SW	SW	XC	SW	SW	GW	SW	SW	SW	SW	XC	SW	SW	SW	SW	SW
		◇■	■	◇■	◇■	■	◇	■	■	◇■	■	◇■	◇■	■	■	◇■	■
					A												
		✠			✠					✠			✠				
London Waterloo ■ ⊖	d	21 05			21 35			21 39	21 42	22 05			22 35		22 39	23 05	23 35
Clapham Junction ■	d	21u12						21u46		22u12					22u46	23u12	23u42
	d																
Woking	d	21 32			22 00				22 19	22 32			23 00			23 32	00 03
Farnborough (Main)	d							22 13	22 33						23 16		00 14
Fleet	d							22 19	22 38						23 21		00 20
Reading ■	d			21 47								22 49					
Basingstoke	a	21 51		22 09				22 31	22 58	22 51		23 06			23 34	23 51	00 33
	d	21 52		22 10				22 33	23 00	22 52		23 10			23 36	23 52	00 35
Micheldever	d							22s43	23 10							00 02	
Winchester	d	22 09		22 25	22 33			22 53	23 19	23 09		23 25	23 33		23 52	00 12	00 51
Shawford	d							22 57							23 57		
Romsey	d		22 07			22 19	22 50				23 09			23 00			
Chandlers Ford	d		22 14								23 16						
Eastleigh ■	a	22 17	22 21			22 49		23 03	23 27	23 17	23 22			23 35	00 02	00 20	00 59
	d	22 18	22 22			22 50		23 04	23 28	23 18	23 23			23 37	00 03	00 21	01 00
Hedge End	d								23 34								
Botley	d								23 38								
Fareham	d						23 27		23 48								
Portchester	d								23 53								
Cosham	d								23 58								
Hilsea	a								00 03								
Fratton	a						23 40		00 07								
Portsmouth & Southsea	a						23 44		00 11								
Portsmouth Harbour ⛴	a						23 52		00 16								
Southampton Airport Pkwy ✈	d	22 22	22 26	22 34	22 42			23 08		23 22	23 27	23 33	23 42		00 08	00 25	01 05
Swaythling	d		22 29								23 30						
St Denys	d		22 32								23 33					00s29	
Southampton Central ⛴	a	22 29	22 36	22 41	22 49			23 17		23 29	23 38	23 41	23 49		00 15	00 34	01 12
	d	22 31	22 38	22 43	22 51					23 31	23 40		23 51			00 36	
Millbrook (Hants)	d		22 41								23 42						
Redbridge	d		22 45								23 46						
Romsey	d		22a52			23a03					23 57			23a49			
Mottisfont & Dunbridge	d										00 02						
Dean	d										00 08						
Salisbury	a										00 20						
Totton	d	22 36								23 36						00s41	
Ashurst New Forest	d	22 41								23 41							
Beaulieu Road	d																
Brockenhurst ■	a	22 49		22 56	23 04					23 49			00 04			00s52	
	d	22 50		22 59	23 05					23 50			00 05				
Lymington Town	d																
Lymington Pier	a																
Sway	d	22 54								23 54							
New Milton	d	22 59								23 59						01s00	
Hinton Admiral	d	23 03								00 03							
Christchurch	d	23 08								00 08						01s07	
Pokesdown	d	23 12								00 11						01s11	
Bournemouth	a	23 16		23 21	23 25					00 15			00 21			01 15	
	d	23 17			23 29					00 17			00 22			01 16	
Branksome	d	23 22			23 35					00 23			00 27			01s21	
Parkstone (Dorset)	d	23 25			23 38					00 26			00 30			01s24	
Poole ■	a	23 29			23 41					00 30			00 35			01 29	
	d				23 42												
Hamworthy	d				23 47												
Holton Heath	d																
Wareham	d				23 54												
Wool	d				00 01												
Moreton (Dorset)	d				00 07												
Dorchester South	d				00 15												
Dorchester West	d																
Upwey	d				00 21												
Weymouth	a				00 26												

A ✠ to Bournemouth

London - Basingstoke, Southampton, Romsey Lymington, Bournemouth and Weymouth

Network Diagram - see first Page of Table 158

		SW ◇■ A 🍴	SW ◇■ B 🍴	SW ■ B	SW ◇■ B 🍴	SW ■ B	SW ◇■ B	SW ■	SW ■ B	SW ■	SW ■	SW ■	GW	SW ■	SW ■		SN ◇■	SW ■	SW ■	SW ■	SW ■	SW ■	GW ■
London Waterloo ⊖	d	21p35	22p05		22p35	22p39	23p05		23p35	00 05	01 05												
Clapham Junction	d		22b12			22b46	23b12		23b42	00u12													
	d										01 15												
Woking	d	22p00	22p32		23p00		23p32		00 03	00 37	01 49												
Farnborough (Main)	d					23p16			00 14		01s58												
Fleet	d					23p21			00 20		02s04												
Reading	d																						
Basingstoke	a		22p51			23p34	23p51		00 33	00 55	02s16												
	d		22p52			23p36	23p52		00 35	00 56					07 48								
Micheldever	d						00 02								07 58								
Winchester	d	22p33	23p09		23p33	23p52	00 12		00 51	01 13	02s33				08 08								
Shawford	d					23p57									08 12								
Romsey	d			23p09									08 19							08 35	08 39		
Chandlers Ford	d			23p16																08 42			
Eastleigh	a		23p17	23p22		00 02	00 20		00 59	01 21	02s42				08 18					08 47	09 13		
	d		23p18	23p23		00 03	00 21	00 30	01 00	01 22					08 22	08 26	08 48			08 54	09 15		
Hedge End	d							00s36								08 32							
Botley	d							00s39								08 36							
Fareham	d							00s47				07 44				08 44	09 02						09 32
Portchester	d							00s53				07 49				08 49							
Cosham	d							00s57				07 54				08 54	09a10						
Hilsea	a											08 00				09 00							
Fratton	a							01s05				08 04				09 04							
Portsmouth & Southsea	a							01s08				08 08				09 08							
Portsmouth Harbour ⛴	a							01 12				08 13				09 13							
Southampton Airport Pkwy ✈	d	22p42	23p22	23p27	23p42	00 08	00 25		01 05	01 26	02s46				08 27					08 58			
Swaythling	d			23p30																09 01			
St Denys	d			23p33			00s29				02s51									09 04			
Southampton Central ⛴	a	22p49	23p29	23p38	23p49	00 15	00 34		01 12	01 35	02 56		08 29		08 34					09 09			09 53
	d	22p51	23p31	23p40	23p51		00 36			01 37					08 35				09 03	09 10			09 54
Millbrook (Hants)	d			23p42																09 13			
Redbridge	d			23p46																09 16			
Romsey	d			23p57																09 24	09a28		10 06
Mottisfont & Dunbridge	d			00 02																09 29			
Dean	d			00 08																09 35			
Salisbury	a			00 20																09 49			10 24
Totton	d		23p36				00s41			01s42					08 41								
Ashurst New Forest	d		23p41												08 45								
Beaulieu Road	d														08 50								
Brockenhurst	a	23p04	23p49		00 04		00s52			01s53					08 56				09 16				
	d	23p05	23p50		00 05										08 57			08 59	09 17			09 29	
Lymington Town	d																	09 07				09 37	
Lymington Pier	a																	09 09				09 39	
Sway	d		23p54												09 01								
New Milton	d		23p59				01s00			02s00					09 06				09 24				
Hinton Admiral	d		00 03												09 10								
Christchurch	d		00 08				01s07			02s07					09 15								
Pokesdown	d		00 11				01s11			02s11					09 19								
Bournemouth	a	23p25	00 15		00 21		01 15			02 15					09 23				09 34				
	d	23p29	00 17		00 22		01 16							08 39	09 24				09 39				
Branksome	d	23p35	00 23		00 27		01s21							08 44					09 44				
Parkstone (Dorset)	d	23p38	00 26		00 30		01s24							08 47					09 47				
Poole	a	23p41	00 30		00 35		01 29							08 50	09 33				09 50				
	d	23p42												08 51					09 51				
Hamworthy	d	23p47												08 56					09 56				
Holton Heath	d																						
Wareham	d	23p54												09 03					10 03				
Wool	d	00 01												09 10					10 10				
Moreton (Dorset)	d	00 07												09 16					10 16				
Dorchester South	d	00 15												09 24					10 24				
Dorchester West	d																						
Upwey	d	00 21												09 31					10 31				
Weymouth	a	00 26												09 35					10 35				

A not 11 December. 🍴 to Bournemouth

B not 11 December

b Previous night, stops to pick up only

London - Basingstoke, Southampton, Romsey Lymington, Bournemouth and Weymouth

Network Diagram - see first Page of Table 158

		SW ◇■		SW ■	SW ◇■	SW ■	SW ■	SW ■	SW ◇■		SW ■	XC ◇■ 🍴	SW ◇■	SW ■	SW ■	GW ◇	SW ■	SW ◇■		SW ■	XC ◇■ 🍴	GW ◇	SW ◇■ A 🍴
London Waterloo ⊖	d	07 54			08 35				08 54				09 35					09 54					10 35
Clapham Junction	d	08u03			08u45				09u03				09u45					10u03					10u45
	d																						
Woking	d	08 28			09 09				09 28				10 09					10 28					11 07
Farnborough (Main)	d																						
Fleet	d																						
Reading	d											09 53									10 53		
Basingstoke	a	08 46			09 28				09 46			10 09	10 28					10 46			11 09		11 26
	d	08 48			09 29				09 48			10 10	10 29					10 48			11 10		11 28
Micheldever	d	08 58							09 58									10 58					
Winchester	d	09 08			09 46				10 08			10 25	10 46					11 08			11 25		11 44
Shawford	d								10 12														
Romsey	d					09 35	09 32							10 35	10 32	10 51							
Chandlers Ford	d					09 42								10 42									
Eastleigh	a	09 18				09 48	10 13		10 18					10 48	11 13			11 18					
	d	09 22	09 26			09 54	10 15		10 22	10 26				10 54	11 15			11 22	11 26				
Hedge End	d		09 32							10 32									11 32				
Botley	d		09 36							10 36									11 36				
Fareham	d		09 44							10 44						11 27			11 44			11 32	
Portchester	d		09 49							10 49									11 49				
Cosham	d		09 54							10 54						11 35			11 54				
Hilsea	a		10 04							11 04									12 00				
Fratton	a		10 08							11 08						11 41			12 04				
Portsmouth & Southsea	a		10 11							11 11						11 46			12 08				
Portsmouth Harbour ⛴	a		10 15							11 15						11 52			12 13				
Southampton Airport Pkwy ✈	d	09 27			09 55	09 58			10 27			10 34	10 55	10 58				11 27			11 34		11 53
Swaythling	d					10 01								11 01									
St Denys	d					10 04								11 04									
Southampton Central ⛴	a	09 34			10 02	10 09			10 34			10 42	11 02	11 09				11 34			11 42	11 53	11 59
	d	09 35			10 03	10 10			10 35			10 45	11 03	11 10				11 35			11 45	11 54	12 03
Millbrook (Hants)	d					10 13								11 13									
Redbridge	d					10 16								11 16									
Romsey	d					10 24	10a28							11 24	11a28							12 06	
Mottisfont & Dunbridge	d													11 29									
Dean	d													11 35									
Salisbury	a					10 42								11 48								12 24	
Totton	d	09 41							10 41									11 41					
Ashurst New Forest	d	09 45							10 45									11 45					
Beaulieu Road	d	09 50							10 50									11 50					
Brockenhurst	a	09 56			10 17				10 56			11 02	11 17					11 56			12 02		12 16
	d	09 57		09 59	10 18			10 29	10 57		10 59	11 03	11 18				11 29	11 57		11 59	12 03		12 17
Lymington Town	d			10 07				10 37			11 07						11 37			12 07			
Lymington Pier	a			10 09				10 39			11 09						11 39			12 09			
Sway	d	10 01							11 01									12 01					
New Milton	d	10 06			10 25				11 06				11 25					12 06					12 24
Hinton Admiral	d	10 10							11 10									12 10					
Christchurch	d	10 15							11 15									12 15					
Pokesdown	d	10 19							11 19									12 19					
Bournemouth	a	10 23			10 35				11 23			11 26	11 35					12 23			12 26		12 34
	d	10 24			10 39				11 24				11 39					12 24					12 39
Branksome	d				10 44								11 44										12 44
Parkstone (Dorset)	d				10 47								11 47										12 47
Poole	a	10 33			10 50				11 33				11 50					12 33					12 50
	d				10 51								11 51										12 51
Hamworthy	d				10 56								11 56										12 56
Holton Heath	d																						
Wareham	d				11 03								12 03										13 03
Wool	d				11 10								12 10										13 10
Moreton (Dorset)	d				11 16								12 16										13 16
Dorchester South	d				11 24								12 24										13 24
Dorchester West	d																						
Upwey	d				11 31								12 31										13 31
Weymouth	a				11 35								12 35										13 35

A 🍴 to Bournemouth

Table 158

Sundays
until 12 February

London - Basingstoke, Southampton, Romsey Lymington, Bournemouth and Weymouth

Network Diagram - see first Page of Table 158

		SW	SW	GW	SW	SW	SW	XC	GW	SW	GW	SW	SW	SW	SW	SW	XC	GW	SW	SW
		■	■	◇	■	◇■	■	◇■	◇	◇■	◇	■	■	■	◇■	■	◇■	◇	◇■	■
										A									A	
						⊼		⊐		⊼					⊼		⊐		⊼	
London Waterloo ⊖	d					10 54				11 35					11 54				12 35	
Clapham Junction	d					11u04				11u45					12u04				12u42	
	d																			
Woking	d					11 28				12 07					12 28				13 07	
Farnborough (Main)	d																			
Fleet	d																			
Reading	d							11 53									12 53			
Basingstoke	a					11 46		12 09		12 26					12 46		13 09		13 26	
	d					11 48		12 10		12 28					12 48		13 10		13 28	
Micheldever	d					11 58									12 58					
Winchester	d					12 08		12 25		12 44					13 08		13 25		13 44	
Shawford	d					12 12														
Romsey	d	11 35	11 32	11 51							12 52	12 35	12 32							13 35
Chandlers Ford	d	11 42										12 42								13 42
Eastleigh	a	11 48	12 13			12 18						12 48	13 13		13 18					13 48
	d	11 54	12 15			12 22 / 12 26						12 54	13 15		13 22 / 13 26					13 54
Hedge End	d					12 32									13 32					
Botley	d					12 36									13 36					
Fareham	d			12 28		12 44			12 32						13 44			13 32		
Portchester	d					12 49									13 49					
Cosham	d			12 36		12 54									13 54					
Hilsea	a					13 00									14 00					
Fratton	a			12 42		13 04									14 04					
Portsmouth & Southsea	a			12 46		13 08									14 08					
Portsmouth Harbour ⛴	a			12 52		13 13									14 13					
Southampton Airport Pkwy ✈	d	11 58				12 27		12 34		12 53		12 58			13 27		13 34		13 53	13 58
Swaythling	d	12 01										13 01								14 01
St Denys	d	12 04										13 04								14 04
Southampton Central ⛴	a	12 09				12 34		12 42	12 53	13 00	13 05	13 09			13 34		13 42	13 53	14 00	14 09
	d	12 10				12 35		12 45	12 54	13 03		13 10			13 35		13 45	13 54	14 03	14 10
Millbrook (Hants)	d	12 13										13 13								14 13
Redbridge	d	12 16										13 16								14 16
Romsey	d	12 24	12a28						13 06			13 24	13a28					14 06		14 24
Mottisfont & Dunbridge	d											13 29								
Dean	d											13 35								
Salisbury	a	12 42							13 24			13 48						14 24		14 42
Totton	d					12 41									13 41					
Ashurst New Forest	d					12 45									13 45					
Beaulieu Road	d					12 50									13 50					
Brockenhurst	a					12 56		13 02		13 16					13 56		14 01		14 16	
	d				12 29	12 57	12 59	13 03		13 17				13 29	13 57	13 59	14 02		14 17	
Lymington Town	d				12 37		13 07							13 37		14 07				
Lymington Pier	a				12 39		13 09							13 39		14 09				
Sway	d					13 01									14 01					
New Milton	d					13 06				13 24					14 06				14 24	
Hinton Admiral	d					13 10									14 10					
Christchurch	d					13 15									14 15					
Pokesdown	d					13 19									14 19					
Bournemouth	a					13 23		13 26		13 34					14 23		14 26		14 34	
	d					13 24				13 39					14 24				14 39	
Branksome	d									13 44									14 44	
Parkstone (Dorset)	d									13 47									14 47	
Poole	a					13 33				13 50					14 33				14 50	
	d									13 51									14 51	
Hamworthy	d									13 56									14 56	
Holton Heath	d																			
Wareham	d									14 03									15 03	
Wool	d									14 10									15 10	
Moreton (Dorset)	d									14 16									15 16	
Dorchester South	d									14 24									15 24	
Dorchester West	d																			
Upwey	d									14 31									15 31	
Weymouth	a									14 35									15 35	

A ⊼ to Bournemouth

Table 158

Sundays
until 12 February

London - Basingstoke, Southampton, Romsey Lymington, Bournemouth and Weymouth

Network Diagram - see first Page of Table 158

		SW	GW	SW	SW	SW	XC	GW	GW	SW	SW	SW	GW	SW	SW	SW	XC	GW	SW	SW	SW
		■	◇	■	◇■	■	◇■	◇		◇■	■	■	◇	■	◇■	■	◇■	■	◇■	■	■
										A									A		
			⊼		⊼		⊐			⊼					⊼		⊐		⊼		
London Waterloo ⊖	d				12 54					13 35					13 54				14 35		
Clapham Junction	d				13u03					13u42					14u03				14u42		
	d																				
Woking	d				13 28					14 07					14 28				15 07		
Farnborough (Main)	d																				
Fleet	d																				
Reading	d						13 53										14 53				
Basingstoke	a				13 46		14 09			14 26					14 46		15 09		15 26		
	d				13 48		14 10			14 28					14 48		15 10		15 28		
Micheldever	d				13 58										14 58						
Winchester	d				14 08		14 25			14 44					15 08		15 25		15 44		
Shawford	d				14 12																
Romsey	d	13 32	13 51								14 35	14 32	15 10							15 35	15 32
Chandlers Ford	d										14 42									15 42	
Eastleigh	a	14 13			14 18						14 48	15 13			15 18					15 48	16 13
	d	14 15			14 22 / 14 26						14 54	15 15			15 22 / 15 26					15 54	16 15
Hedge End	d				14 32										15 32						
Botley	d				14 36										15 36						
Fareham	d		14 27		14 44			14 32							15 44			15 32			
Portchester	d				14 49										15 49						
Cosham	d		14 35		14 54										15 54						
Hilsea	a				15 00										16 00						
Fratton	a		14 41		15 04										16 04						
Portsmouth & Southsea	a		14 45		15 08										16 08						
Portsmouth Harbour ⛴	a		14 55		15 13										16 13						
Southampton Airport Pkwy ✈	d				14 27		14 34			14 53	14 58				15 27		15 34		15 53	15 58	
Swaythling	d										15 01									16 01	
St Denys	d										15 04									16 04	
Southampton Central ⛴	a				14 34		14 42	14 53		15 00	15 09		15 21		15 34		15 42	15 53	16 00	16 09	
	d				14 35		14 45	14 54		15 03	15 10				15 35		15 45	15 54	16 03	16 10	
Millbrook (Hants)	d										15 13									16 13	
Redbridge	d										15 16									16 16	
Romsey	d	14a28						15 06			15 24	15a28						16 06		16 24	16a28
Mottisfont & Dunbridge	d										15 29										
Dean	d										15 35										
Salisbury	a							15 24			15 48							16 24		16 42	
Totton	d				14 41										15 41						
Ashurst New Forest	d				14 45										15 45						
Beaulieu Road	d				14 50										15 50						
Brockenhurst	a				14 56		15 02			15 16					15 56		16 02		16 16		
	d			14 29	14 57	14 59	15 03			15 17				15 29	15 57	15 59	16 03		16 17		
Lymington Town	d			14 37		15 07								15 37		16 07					
Lymington Pier	a			14 39		15 09								15 39		16 09					
Sway	d				15 01										16 01						
New Milton	d				15 06					15 24					16 06				16 24		
Hinton Admiral	d				15 10										16 10						
Christchurch	d				15 15										16 15						
Pokesdown	d				15 19										16 19						
Bournemouth	a				15 23		15 26			15 34					16 23		16 26		16 34		
	d				15 24					15 39					16 24				16 39		
Branksome	d									15 44									16 44		
Parkstone (Dorset)	d									15 47									16 47		
Poole	a				15 33					15 50					16 33				16 50		
	d									15 51									16 51		
Hamworthy	d									15 56									16 56		
Holton Heath	d																				
Wareham	d									16 03									17 03		
Wool	d									16 10									17 10		
Moreton (Dorset)	d									16 16									17 16		
Dorchester South	d									16 24									17 24		
Dorchester West	d								16 01												
Upwey	d								16 10	16 31									17 31		
Weymouth	a								16 15	16 35									17 35		

A ⊼ to Bournemouth

London - Basingstoke, Southampton, Romsey Lymington, Bournemouth and Weymouth

Network Diagram - see first Page of Table 158

		GW ◇	SW 1	SW ◇1		SW 1	XC ◇1	GW ◇	SW ◇1 A	SW 1	SW 1	SW 1	GW ◇	GW ◇	SW 1	SW ◇1		SW 1	XC ◇1	GW ◇	SW ◇1 A	SW 1	SW 1
London Waterloo 15 ⊖	d			14 54					15 35	15 37						15 54					16 35	16 37	
Clapham Junction 10	d			15u03					15u42	15 46						16u03					16u42	16 46	
	d																						
Woking	d			15 28					16 07	16 23						16 28					17 07	17 23	
Farnborough (Main)	d									16 36												17 36	
Fleet	d									16 41												17 41	
Reading 7	d						15 53												16 53				
Basingstoke	a			15 46			16 09		16 26	16 54						16 46			17 09		17 26	17 54	
	d			15 48			16 10		16 28							16 48			17 10		17 28		
Micheldever	d			15 58												16 58							
Winchester	d			16 08			16 25		16 44							17 08			17 25		17 44		
Shawford	d			16 12																			
Romsey	d	15 50									16 35	16 32		16 51									17 35
Chandlers Ford	d										16 42												17 42
Eastleigh 8	a			16 18							16 48	17 13				17 18							17 48
	d			16 22	16 26						16 54	17 15				17 22	17 26						17 54
Hedge End	d				16 32												17 32						
Botley	d				16 36												17 36						
Fareham	d	16 26			16 44			16 32					17 03	17 27			17 44			17 32			
Portchester	d				16 49												17 49						
Cosham	d	16 34			16 54									17 35			17 54						
Hilsea	a				17 00												18 00						
Fratton	a	16 41			17 03									17 41			18 04						
Portsmouth & Southsea	a	16 45			17 08									17 46			18 08						
Portsmouth Harbour ⛴	a	16 52			17 13									17 52			18 13						
Southampton Airport Pkwy ✈	d			16 27			16 34		16 53		16 58					17 27			17 34		17 53		17 58
Swaythling	d										17 01												18 01
St Denys	d										17 04												18 04
Southampton Central ⛴	a			16 34			16 42	16 53	17 00		17 09		17 24			17 34			17 40	17 53	18 00		18 09
	d			16 35			16 45	16 54	17 03		17 10		17 26			17 35			17 45	17 54	18 03		18 10
Millbrook (Hants)	d										17 13												18 13
Redbridge	d										17 16												18 16
Romsey	d							17 06			17 24	17a28	17 39							18 06			18 24
Mottisfont & Dunbridge	d										17 29												
Dean	d										17 35												
Salisbury	a							17 24			17 48		18 00							18 24			18 42
Totton	d			16 41												17 41							
Ashurst New Forest	d			16 45												17 45							
Beaulieu Road	d			16 50												17 50							
Brockenhurst 3	a			16 56			17 02		17 16							17 56			18 02		18 16		
	d		16 29	16 57		16 59	17 03		17 17						17 29	17 57		17 59	18 03		18 17		
Lymington Town	d		16 37			17 07									17 37			18 07					
Lymington Pier	a		16 39			17 09									17 39			18 09					
Sway	d			17 01												18 01							
New Milton	d			17 06					17 24							18 06					18 24		
Hinton Admiral	d			17 10												18 10							
Christchurch	d			17 15												18 15							
Pokesdown	d			17 19												18 19							
Bournemouth	a			17 23			17 26		17 34							18 23			18 26		18 34		
	d			17 24					17 39							18 24					18 39		
Branksome	d								17 44												18 44		
Parkstone (Dorset)	d								17 47												18 47		
Poole 4	a			17 33					17 50							18 33					18 50		
	d								17 51												18 51		
Hamworthy	d								17 56												18 56		
Holton Heath	d																						
Wareham	d								18 03												19 03		
Wool	d								18 10												19 10		
Moreton (Dorset)	d								18 16												19 16		
Dorchester South	d								18 24												19 24		
Dorchester West	d																						
Upwey	d								18 31												19 31		
Weymouth	a								18 35												19 35		

A to Bournemouth

Sundays

until 12 February

London - Basingstoke, Southampton, Romsey Lymington, Bournemouth and Weymouth

Network Diagram - see first Page of Table 158

		SW 1	GW ◇	SW 1	SW ◇1		SW 1	XC ◇1	GW ◇	GW ◇	SW ◇1 A	SW 1	SW 1	SW 1	GW ◇	GW ◇	GW ◇	SW 1	SW ◇1		SW 1	XC ◇1
London Waterloo 15 ⊖	d				16 54						17 35	17 37							17 54			
Clapham Junction 10	d				17u03						17u42	17 46							18u03			
	d																					
Woking	d				17 28						18 07	18 23							18 28			
Farnborough (Main)	d											18 36										
Fleet	d											18 41										
Reading 7	d							17 53														18 53
Basingstoke	a				17 46			18 09			18 26	18 54							18 46			19 09
	d				17 48			18 10			18 28								18 48			19 10
Micheldever	d				17 58														18 58			
Winchester	d				18 08			18 25			18 44								19 08			19 25
Shawford	d				18 12																	
Romsey	d	17 32	17 51										18 35	18 32		18 50	19 14					
Chandlers Ford	d												18 42									
Eastleigh 8	a	18 13			18 18								18 48	19 13					19 18			
	d	18 15			18 22	18 26							18 54	19 15					19 22	19 26		
Hedge End	d					18 32														19 32		
Botley	d					18 36														19 36		
Fareham	d		18 27			18 44			18 32						19 03	19 27				19 44		
Portchester	d					18 49														19 49		
Cosham	d		18 35			18 54										19 35				19 54		
Hilsea	a					19 00														20 00		
Fratton	a		18 41			19 03										19 42				20 04		
Portsmouth & Southsea	a		18 45			19 08										19 46				20 08		
Portsmouth Harbour ⛴	a		18 52			19 13										19 52				20 13		
Southampton Airport Pkwy ✈	d				18 27			18 34			18 53		18 58						19 27			19 34
Swaythling	d												19 01									
St Denys	d												19 04									
Southampton Central ⛴	a				18 34			18 42	18 53		19 00		19 09		19 24		19 25		19 34			19 40
	d				18 35			18 45	18 54		19 03		19 10		19 30				19 35			19 45
Millbrook (Hants)	d												19 13									
Redbridge	d												19 16									
Romsey	d	18a28							19 06				19 24	19a28	19 42							
Mottisfont & Dunbridge	d												19 29									
Dean	d												19 35									
Salisbury	a								19 24				19 48		20 00							
Totton	d				18 41														19 41			
Ashurst New Forest	d				18 45														19 45			
Beaulieu Road	d				18 50														19 50			
Brockenhurst 3	a				18 56			19 01			19 16								19 56			20 02
	d			18 29	18 57		18 59	19 02			19 17							19 29	19 57		19 59	20 03
Lymington Town	d			18 37			19 07											19 37			20 07	
Lymington Pier	a			18 39			19 09											19 39			20 09	
Sway	d				19 01														20 01			
New Milton	d				19 06						19 24								20 06			
Hinton Admiral	d				19 10														20 10			
Christchurch	d				19 15														20 15			
Pokesdown	d				19 19														20 19			
Bournemouth	a				19 23			19 26			19 34								20 23			20 26
	d				19 24						19 39								20 24			
Branksome	d										19 44											
Parkstone (Dorset)	d										19 47											
Poole 4	a				19 33						19 50								20 33			
	d										19 51											
Hamworthy	d										19 56											
Holton Heath	d																					
Wareham	d										20 03											
Wool	d										20 10											
Moreton (Dorset)	d										20 17											
Dorchester South	d										20 25											
Dorchester West	d									19 47												
Upwey	d									19 55	20 32											
Weymouth	a									20 01	20 36											

A to Bournemouth

Sundays until 12 February

London - Basingstoke, Southampton, Romsey Lymington, Bournemouth and Weymouth

Network Diagram - see first Page of Table 158

		GW	SW	SW	SN	SW	SW	GW	SW	SW		SW	XC	GW	SW	SW	GW	SN	SW	SW	GW	SW
		◇	◇■ A 🍴	■	◇■	■	■	◇	■	◇■ 🍴		■	◇■ 🛒	◇	◇■ A 🍴	■	■	◇■	■	■	◇	■
London Waterloo ⊖	d		18 35	18 37						18 54					19 35	19 37						
Clapham Junction	d		18u42	18 46						19u03					19u42	19 46						
	d																					
Woking	d		19 07	19 23						19 28					20 07	20 23						
Farnborough (Main)	d			19 36												20 36						
Fleet	d			19 41												20 41						
Reading	d												19 53									
Basingstoke	a		19 26	19 54						19 46			20 09		20 26	20 54						
	d		19 28							19 48			20 10		20 28							
Micheldever	d									19 58												
Winchester	d		19 44							20 08			20 25		20 44							
Shawford	d									20 12												
Romsey	d					19 35	19 32	19 50									20 19		20 35	20 32	20 48	
Chandlers Ford	d					19 42													20 42			
Eastleigh	a					19 48	20 13			20 18									20 48	21 13		
	d				19 46	19 54	20 15			20 22	20 26							20 46	20 54	21 15		
Hedge End	d										20 32											
Botley	d										20 36											
Fareham	d	19 32			20 03			20 26			20 44			20 32			20 55	21 02			21 25	
Portchester	d										20 49											
Cosham	d				20a11						20 54							21a10				
Hilsea	a										21 00											
Fratton	a							20 41			21 04						21 09				21 38	
Portsmouth & Southsea	a							20 45			21 08						21 15				21 41	
Portsmouth Harbour ⛴	a							20 51			21 13						21 26				21 48	
Southampton Airport Pkwy ✈	d		19 53			19 58				20 27			20 34		20 53				20 58			
Swaythling	d					20 01													21 01			
St Denys	d					20 04													21 04			
Southampton Central ⛴	a	19 53	20 00			20 09				20 34			20 42	20 53	21 00				21 09			
	d	19 54	20 03			20 10				20 35			20 45	20 54	21 03				21 10			
Millbrook (Hants)	d					20 13													21 13			
Redbridge	d					20 16													21 16			
Romsey	d	20 06				20 24	20a28							21 06					21 24	21a28		
Mottisfont & Dunbridge	d																		21 29			
Dean	d																		21 35			
Salisbury	a	20 24				20 42								21 24					21 48			
Totton	d									20 41												
Ashurst New Forest	d									20 45												
Beaulieu Road	d									20 50												
Brockenhurst	a		20 16							20 56			21 02		21 16							
	d		20 17						20 29	20 57		20 59	21 03		21 17							21 29
Lymington Town	d								20 37			21 07										21 37
Lymington Pier	a								20 39			21 09										21 39
Sway	d									21 01												
New Milton	d		20 24							21 06					21 24							
Hinton Admiral	d									21 10												
Christchurch	d									21 15												
Pokesdown	d									21 19												
Bournemouth	a		20 34							21 23			21 26		21 34							
	d		20 39							21 24					21 39							
Branksome	d		20 44												21 44							
Parkstone (Dorset)	d		20 47												21 47							
Poole	a		20 50							21 33					21 50							
	d		20 51												21 51							
Hamworthy	d		20 56												21 56							
Holton Heath	d																					
Wareham	d		21 03												22 03							
Wool	d		21 10												22 10							
Moreton (Dorset)	d		21 17												22 17							
Dorchester South	d		21 25												22 25							
Dorchester West	d																					
Upwey	d		21 32												22 32							
Weymouth	a		21 36												22 36							

A 🍴 to Bournemouth

Sundays until 12 February

London - Basingstoke, Southampton, Romsey Lymington, Bournemouth and Weymouth

Network Diagram - see first Page of Table 158

		SW		SW	XC	GW	SW	SW	SW	SW	GW	SW		XC	GW	SW	SW	SW	SW	GW	SW		SW
		◇■		■	◇■		◇■ A 🍴	■	■	■	◇	◇■		◇■		◇■ A 🍴	■	■	■	◇	◇■		■
London Waterloo ⊖	d	19 54					20 35	20 37				20 54				21 35	21 37				21 54		22 37
Clapham Junction	d	20u03					20u42	20 46				21u03				21u42	21 46				22u03		22 46
	d																						
Woking	d	20 28					21 07	21 23				21 28				22 07	22 23				22 28		23 23
Farnborough (Main)	d							21 36									22 36						23 36
Fleet	d							21 41									22 41						23 41
Reading	d				20 53									21 53									
Basingstoke	a	20 46			21 09		21 26	21 54				21 46		22 09		22 26	22 54				22 46		23 54
	d	20 48			21 10		21 28					21 48		22 10		22 28					22 48		
Micheldever	d	20 58										21 58									22 58		
Winchester	d	21 08			21 25		21 44					22 08		22 25		22 44					23 08		
Shawford	d											22 12											
Romsey	d								21 35	21 32	21 51							22 35	22 28	22 54			
Chandlers Ford	d								21 42									22 42					
Eastleigh	a	21 18							21 48	22 13		22 18						22 48	23 19		23 17		
	d	21 22	21 26						21 54	22 15		22 22	22 26					22 54	23 21		23 22	23 26	
Hedge End	d		21 32										22 32									23 32	
Botley	d		21 36										22 36									23 36	
Fareham	d		21 44								22 26		22 44		22 32					23 30		23 44	
Portchester	d		21 49										22 49									23 49	
Cosham	d		21 54										22 54									23 54	
Hilsea	a		22 00										23 00									23 59	
Fratton	a		22 04								22 40		23 04							23 43		00 04	
Portsmouth & Southsea	a		22 08								22 44		23 08							23 46		00 08	
Portsmouth Harbour ⛴	a		22 13								22 50		23 13							23 54		00 13	
Southampton Airport Pkwy ✈	d	21 27			21 34		21 53		21 58			22 27		22 34		22 53		22 58			23 27		
Swaythling	d								22 01									23 01					
St Denys	d								22 04									23 04					
Southampton Central ⛴	a	21 34			21 43		22 00		22 09			22 34		22 42	22 53	23 00		23 09			23 34		
	d	21 35			21 45		22 03		22 10			22 35			22 57	23 03		23 10			23 35		
Millbrook (Hants)	d								22 13									23 13					
Redbridge	d								22 16									23 16					
Romsey	d								22a24	22a31					23 09			23 24	23a33				
Mottisfont & Dunbridge	d																	23 29					
Dean	d																	23 35					
Salisbury	a														23 27			23 51					
Totton	d	21 41										22 41									23 41		
Ashurst New Forest	d	21 45										22 45									23 45		
Beaulieu Road	d	21 50										22 50											
Brockenhurst	a	21 56			22 02		22 16					22 56				23 16					23 53		
	d	21 57		21 59	22 03		22 17					22 57				23 17					23 54		
Lymington Town	d			22 07																			
Lymington Pier	a			22 09																			
Sway	d	22 01										23 01									23 59		
New Milton	d	22 06					22 24					23 06				23 24					00 04		
Hinton Admiral	d	22 10										23 10									00 08		
Christchurch	d	22 15										23 15									00 13		
Pokesdown	d	22 19										23 19									00 16		
Bournemouth	a	22 23			22 26		22 34					23 23				23 34					00 20		
	d	22 24					22 39					23 24				23 39					00 22		
Branksome	d						22 44									23 44					00 27		
Parkstone (Dorset)	d						22 47									23 47					00 30		
Poole	a	22 33					22 50					23 33				23 50					00 34		
	d						22 51									23 51							
Hamworthy	d						22 56									23 56							
Holton Heath	d																						
Wareham	d						23 03									00 03							
Wool	d						23 10									00 10							
Moreton (Dorset)	d						23 17									00 17							
Dorchester South	d						23 25									00 25							
Dorchester West	d					22 53																	
Upwey	d					23 01	23 32									00 32							
Weymouth	a					23 06	23 36									00 36							

A 🍴 to Bournemouth

London - Basingstoke, Southampton, Romsey Lymington, Bournemouth and Weymouth

Network Diagram - see first Page of Table 158

		SW
		◇1 ⊼
London Waterloo 15 ⊖	d	22 54
Clapham Junction 10	d	23u03
	d	
Woking	d	23 28
Farnborough (Main)	d	
Fleet	d	
Reading 7	d	
Basingstoke	a	23 46
	d	23 48
Micheldever	d	23 58
Winchester	d	00 08
Shawford	d	
Romsey	d	
Chandlers Ford	d	
Eastleigh 8	a	00 18
	d	00 22
Hedge End	d	
Botley	d	
Fareham	d	
Portchester	d	
Cosham	d	
Hilsea	a	
Fratton	a	
Portsmouth & Southsea	a	
Portsmouth Harbour ⛴	a	
Southampton Airport Pkwy ✈	d	00 27
Swaythling	d	
St Denys	d	00s31
Southampton Central ⛴	a	00 36
	d	00 37
Millbrook (Hants)	d	
Redbridge	d	
Romsey	d	
Mottisfont & Dunbridge	d	
Dean	d	
Salisbury	a	
Totton	d	00s42
Ashurst New Forest	d	
Beaulieu Road	d	
Brockenhurst 3	a	00s53
	d	
Lymington Town	d	
Lymington Pier	a	
Sway	d	
New Milton	d	01s01
Hinton Admiral	d	
Christchurch	d	01s08
Pokesdown	d	01s12
Bournemouth	a	01 16
	d	01 17
Branksome	d	01s22
Parkstone (Dorset)	d	01s25
Poole 4	a	01 29
	d	
Hamworthy	d	
Holton Heath	d	
Wareham	d	
Wool	d	
Moreton (Dorset)	d	
Dorchester South	d	
Dorchester West	d	
Upwey	d	
Weymouth	a	

London - Basingstoke, Southampton, Romsey Lymington, Bournemouth and Weymouth

Network Diagram - see first Page of Table 158

		SW	SW	SW	SW	SW	SW	SW	SW	SW		SW	SW	GW	SW	SW		SN	SW	SW		SW	SW	SW	GW
		◇1 A ⊼	◇1 ⊼	1	◇1 ⊼	1	◇1	1	1	1		1	1		1	1		◇1	1	1		1	1	1	■
London Waterloo 15 ⊖	d	21p35	22p05		22p35	22p39	23p05		23p35	00 05		01 05													
Clapham Junction 10	d		22b12			22b46	23b12		23b42	00u12															
	d											01 15													
Woking	d	22p00	22p32		23p00		23p32		00 03	00 37		01 49													
Farnborough (Main)	d					23p16			00 14			01s58													
Fleet	d					23p21			00 20			02s04													
Reading 7	d																								
Basingstoke	a		22p51			23p34	23p51		00 33	00 55		02s16													
	d		22p52			23p36	23p52		00 35	00 56						07 48									
Micheldever	d						00 02									07 58									
Winchester	d	22p33	23p09		23p33	23p52	00 12		00 51	01 13		02s33				08 08									
Shawford	d					23p57										08 12									
Romsey	d			23p09										08 19								08 35	08 39		
Chandlers Ford	d			23p16																		08 42			
Eastleigh 8	a		23p17	23p22		00 02	00 20		00 59	01 21		02s42				08 18						08 47	09 13		
	d		23p18	23p23		00 03	00 21	00 30	01 00	01 22						08 22	08 26	08 48				08 54	09 15		
Hedge End	d							00s36									08 32								
Botley	d							00s39									08 36								
Fareham	d							00s47					07 44				08 44	09 02							09 32
Portchester	d							00s53					07 49				08 49								
Cosham	d							00s57					07 54				08 54	09a10							
Hilsea	a												08 00				09 00								
Fratton	a							01s05					08 04				09 04								
Portsmouth & Southsea	a							01s08					08 08				09 08								
Portsmouth Harbour ⛴	a							01 12					08 13				09 13								
Southampton Airport Pkwy ✈	d	22p42	23p22	23p27	23p42	00 08	00 25		01 05	01 26		02s46				08 27						08 58			
Swaythling	d			23p30																		09 01			
St Denys	d			23p33			00s29					02s51										09 04			
Southampton Central ⛴	a	22p49	23p29	23p38	23p49	00 15	00 34		01 12	01 35		02 56		08 29		08 34						09 09			09 53
	d	22p51	23p31	23p40	23p51		00 36			01 37						08 35				09 03		09 10			09 54
Millbrook (Hants)	d			23p42																		09 13			
Redbridge	d			23p46																		09 16			
Romsey	d			23p57																		09 24	09a28		10 05
Mottisfont & Dunbridge	d			00 02																		09 29			
Dean	d			00 08																		09 35			
Salisbury	a			00 20																		09 49			10 23
Totton	d		23p36				00s41			01s42						08 41									
Ashurst New Forest	d		23p41													08 45									
Beaulieu Road	d															08 50									
Brockenhurst 3	a	23p04	23p49		00 04		00s52			01s53						08 56				09 16					
	d	23p05	23p50		00 05											08 57			08 59	09 17				09 29	
Lymington Town	d																		09 07					09 37	
Lymington Pier	a																		09 09					09 39	
Sway	d		23p54													09 01									
New Milton	d		23p59				01s00			02s00						09 06				09 24					
Hinton Admiral	d		00 03													09 10									
Christchurch	d		00 08				01s07			02s07						09 15									
Pokesdown	d		00 11				01s11			02s11						09 19									
Bournemouth	a	23p25	00 15		00 21		01 15			02 15						09 23				09 34					
	d	23p29	00 17		00 22		01 16								08 39	09 24				09 39					
Branksome	d	23p35	00 23		00 27		01s21								08 44					09 44					
Parkstone (Dorset)	d	23p38	00 26		00 30		01s24								08 47					09 47					
Poole 4	a	23p41	00 30		00 35		01 29								08 50	09 33				09 50					
	d	23p42													08 51					09 51					
Hamworthy	d	23p47													08 56					09 56					
Holton Heath	d																								
Wareham	d	23p54													09 03					10 03					
Wool	d	00 01													09 10					10 10					
Moreton (Dorset)	d	00 07													09 16					10 16					
Dorchester South	d	00 15													09 24					10 24					
Dorchester West	d																								
Upwey	d	00 21													09 31					10 31					
Weymouth	a	00 26													09 35					10 35					

A ⊼ to Bournemouth

b Previous night, stops to pick up only

Table 158

Sundays

19 February to 25 March

London - Basingstoke, Southampton, Romsey Lymington, Bournemouth and Weymouth

Network Diagram - see first Page of Table 158

		SW		SW	SW	SW	SW	SW	SW		SW	XC	SW	SW	SW	GW	SW	SW		SW	XC	GW	SW
		◇1		1	◇1	1	1	1	◇1		1	◇1	◇1	1	1	◇	1	◇1		1	◇1	◇	◇1
												ᴫ									ᴫ		A ᴫ
London Waterloo [15] ⊖	d	07 54			08 35				08 54				09 35					09 54					10 35
Clapham Junction [10]	d	08u03			08u45				09u03				09u45					10u03					10u45
	d																						
Woking	d	08 28			09 09				09 28				10 09					10 28					11 07
Farnborough (Main)	d																						
Fleet	d																						
Reading [7]	d											09 53									10 53		
Basingstoke	a	08 46			09 28				09 46			10 09	10 28					10 46			11 09		11 26
	d	08 48			09 29				09 48			10 10	10 29					10 48			11 10		11 28
Micheldever	d	08 58							09 58									10 58					
Winchester	d	09 08			09 46				10 08			10 25	10 46					11 08			11 25		11 44
Shawford	d								10 12														
Romsey	d					09 35	09 32							10 35	10 32	10 50							
Chandlers Ford	d					09 42								10 42									
Eastleigh [8]	a	09 18				09 48	10 13		10 18					10 48	11 13			11 18					
	d	09 22	09 26			09 54	10 15		10 22	10 26				10 54	11 15			11 22	11 26				
Hedge End	d		09 32							10 32									11 32				
Botley	d		09 36							10 36									11 36				
Fareham	d		09 44							10 44						11 26			11 44			11 32	
Portchester	d		09 49							10 49									11 49				
Cosham	d		09 54							10 54						11 34			11 54				
Hilsea	a		10 04							11 04									12 00				
Fratton	a		10 08							11 08						11 40			12 04				
Portsmouth & Southsea	a		10 11							11 11						11 45			12 08				
Portsmouth Harbour ⛴	a		10 15							11 15						11 52			12 13				
Southampton Airport Pkwy ✈	d	09 27			09 55	09 58			10 27			10 34	10 55	10 58				11 27			11 34		11 53
Swaythling	d					10 01								11 01									
St Denys	d					10 04								11 04									
Southampton Central ⛴	a	09 34			10 02	10 09			10 34			10 42	11 02	11 09				11 34			11 42	11 53	11 59
	d	09 35			10 03	10 10			10 35			10 45	11 03	11 10				11 35			11 45	11 54	12 03
Millbrook (Hants)	d					10 13								11 13									
Redbridge	d					10 16								11 16									
Romsey	d					10 24	10a28							11 24	11a28							12 06	
Mottisfont & Dunbridge	d													11 29									
Dean	d													11 35									
Salisbury	a					10 42								11 48								12 24	
Totton	d	09 41							10 41									11 41					
Ashurst New Forest	d	09 45							10 45									11 45					
Beaulieu Road	d	09 50							10 50									11 50					
Brockenhurst [3]	a	09 56			10 17				10 56			11 02	11 17					11 56			12 02		12 16
	d	09 57		09 59	10 18			10 29	10 57		10 59	11 03	11 18				11 29	11 57		11 59	12 03		12 17
Lymington Town	d			10 07				10 37			11 07						11 37			12 07			
Lymington Pier	a			10 09				10 39			11 09						11 39			12 09			
Sway	d	10 01							11 01									12 01					
New Milton	d	10 06			10 25				11 06				11 25					12 06					12 24
Hinton Admiral	d	10 10							11 10									12 10					
Christchurch	d	10 15							11 15									12 15					
Pokesdown	d	10 19							11 19									12 19					
Bournemouth	a	10 23			10 35				11 23			11 26	11 35					12 23			12 26		12 34
	d	10 24			10 39				11 24				11 39					12 24					12 39
Branksome	d				10 44								11 44										12 44
Parkstone (Dorset)	d				10 47								11 47										12 47
Poole [4]	a	10 33			10 50				11 33				11 50					12 33					12 50
	d				10 51								11 51										12 51
Hamworthy	d				10 56								11 56										12 56
Holton Heath	d																						
Wareham	d				11 03								12 03										13 03
Wool	d				11 10								12 10										13 10
Moreton (Dorset)	d				11 16								12 16										13 16
Dorchester South	d				11 24								12 24										13 24
Dorchester West	d																						
Upwey	d				11 31								12 31										13 31
Weymouth	a				11 35								12 35										13 35

A ᴫ to Bournemouth

Table 158

Sundays

19 February to 25 March

London - Basingstoke, Southampton, Romsey Lymington, Bournemouth and Weymouth

Network Diagram - see first Page of Table 158

		SW	SW	GW	SW	SW		SW	XC	GW	SW	GW	SW	SW	SW	SW		SW	XC	GW	SW	SW
		1	1	◇	1	◇1		1	◇1	◇	◇1	◇	1	1	1	◇1		1	◇1	◇	◇1	1
									🚲		A ᴫ					ᴫ			🚲		A ᴫ	
London Waterloo [15] ⊖	d					10 54					11 35					11 54					12 35	
Clapham Junction [10]	d					11u04					11u45					12u04					12u42	
	d																					
Woking	d					11 28					12 07					12 28					13 07	
Farnborough (Main)	d																					
Fleet	d																					
Reading [7]	d								11 53										12 53			
Basingstoke	a					11 46			12 09		12 26					12 46			13 09		13 26	
	d					11 48			12 10		12 28					12 48			13 10		13 28	
Micheldever	d					11 58										12 58						
Winchester	d					12 08			12 25		12 44					13 08			13 25		13 44	
Shawford	d					12 12																
Romsey	d	11 35	11 32	11 51								12 52	12 35	12 32								13 35
Chandlers Ford	d	11 42											12 42									13 42
Eastleigh [8]	a	11 48	12 13			12 18							12 48	13 13		13 18						13 48
	d	11 54	12 15			12 22	12 26						12 54	13 15		13 22	13 26					13 54
Hedge End	d						12 32										13 32					
Botley	d						12 36										13 36					
Fareham	d			12 28			12 44			12 32							13 44			13 32		
Portchester	d						12 49										13 49					
Cosham	d			12 36			12 54										13 54					
Hilsea	a						13 00										14 00					
Fratton	a			12 42			13 04										14 04					
Portsmouth & Southsea	a			12 46			13 08										14 08					
Portsmouth Harbour ⛴	a			12 52			13 13										14 13					
Southampton Airport Pkwy ✈	d	11 58				12 27			12 34		12 53		12 58			13 27			13 34		13 53	13 58
Swaythling	d	12 01											13 01									14 01
St Denys	d	12 04											13 04									14 04
Southampton Central ⛴	a	12 09				12 34			12 42	12 53	13 00	13 05	13 09			13 34			13 42	13 53	14 00	14 09
	d	12 10				12 35			12 45	12 54	13 03		13 10			13 35			13 45	13 54	14 03	14 10
Millbrook (Hants)	d	12 13											13 13									14 13
Redbridge	d	12 16											13 16									14 16
Romsey	d	12 24	12a28							13 06			13 24	13a28						14 06		14 24
Mottisfont & Dunbridge	d												13 29									
Dean	d												13 35									
Salisbury	a	12 42								13 24			13 48							14 24		14 42
Totton	d					12 41										13 41						
Ashurst New Forest	d					12 45										13 45						
Beaulieu Road	d					12 50										13 50						
Brockenhurst [3]	a					12 56			13 02		13 16					13 56			14 01		14 16	
	d				12 29	12 57		12 59	13 03		13 17				13 29	13 57		13 59	14 02		14 17	
Lymington Town	d				12 37			13 07							13 37			14 07				
Lymington Pier	a				12 39			13 09							13 39			14 09				
Sway	d					13 01										14 01						
New Milton	d					13 06					13 24					14 06					14 24	
Hinton Admiral	d					13 10										14 10						
Christchurch	d					13 15										14 15						
Pokesdown	d					13 19										14 19						
Bournemouth	a					13 23			13 26		13 34					14 23			14 26		14 34	
	d					13 24					13 39					14 24					14 39	
Branksome	d										13 44										14 44	
Parkstone (Dorset)	d										13 47										14 47	
Poole [4]	a					13 33					13 50					14 33					14 50	
	d										13 51										14 51	
Hamworthy	d										13 56										14 56	
Holton Heath	d																					
Wareham	d										14 03										15 03	
Wool	d										14 10										15 10	
Moreton (Dorset)	d										14 16										15 16	
Dorchester South	d										14 24										15 24	
Dorchester West	d																					
Upwey	d										14 31										15 31	
Weymouth	a										14 35										15 35	

A ᴫ to Bournemouth

London - Basingstoke, Southampton, Romsey Lymington, Bournemouth and Weymouth

Network Diagram - see first Page of Table 158

		SW	GW	SW	SW		SW	XC	GW	GW	SW	SW	SW	GW	SW	SW		SW	XC	GW	SW	SW	SW
		■	◇ 🍴	■	◇■ 🍴		■	◇■ 🛒	◇		◇■ A 🍴	■	■	◇	■	◇■ 🍴		■	◇■ 🛒	■	◇■ A 🍴	■	■
London Waterloo ⊖	d				12 54						13 35					13 54					14 35		
Clapham Junction	d				13u03						13u42					14u03					14u42		
	d																						
Woking	d				13 28						14 07					14 28					15 07		
Farnborough (Main)	d																						
Fleet	d																						
Reading	d							13 53											14 53				
Basingstoke	a				13 46			14 09			14 26					14 46			15 09		15 26		
	d				13 48			14 10			14 28					14 48			15 10		15 28		
Micheldever	d				13 58											14 58							
Winchester	d				14 08			14 25			14 44					15 08			15 25		15 44		
Shawford	d				14 12																		
Romsey	d	13 32	13 51									14 35	14 32	15 10								15 35	15 32
Chandlers Ford	d											14 42										15 42	
Eastleigh	a	14 13			14 18							14 48	15 13			15 18						15 48	16 13
	d	14 15			14 22	14 26						14 54	15 15			15 22	15 26					15 54	16 15
Hedge End	d					14 32											15 32						
Botley	d					14 36											15 36						
Fareham	d		14 27			14 44			14 32								15 44			15 32			
Portchester	d					14 49											15 49						
Cosham	d		14 35			14 54											15 54						
Hilsea	a					15 00											16 00						
Fratton	a		14 41			15 04											16 04						
Portsmouth & Southsea	a		14 45			15 08											16 08						
Portsmouth Harbour ⛴	a		14 55			15 13											16 13						
Southampton Airport Pkwy ✈	d				14 27			14 34			14 53	14 58				15 27			15 34		15 53	15 58	
Swaythling	d											15 01										16 01	
St Denys	d											15 04										16 04	
Southampton Central ⛴	a				14 34			14 42	14 53		15 00	15 09		15 21		15 34			15 42	15 53	16 00	16 09	
	d				14 35			14 45	14 54		15 03	15 10				15 35			15 45	15 54	16 03	16 10	
Millbrook (Hants)	d											15 13										16 13	
Redbridge	d											15 16										16 16	
Romsey	d	14a28							15 06			15 24	15a28							16 06		16 24	16a28
Mottisfont & Dunbridge	d											15 29											
Dean	d											15 35											
Salisbury	a								15 24			15 48								16 24		16 42	
Totton	d				14 41											15 41							
Ashurst New Forest	d				14 45											15 45							
Beaulieu Road	d				14 50											15 50							
Brockenhurst	a				14 56			15 02			15 16					15 56			16 02		16 16		
	d			14 29	14 57		14 59	15 03			15 17				15 29	15 57		15 59	16 03		16 17		
Lymington Town	d			14 37			15 07								15 37			16 07					
Lymington Pier	a			14 39			15 09								15 39			16 09					
Sway	d				15 01											16 01							
New Milton	d				15 06						15 24					16 06					16 24		
Hinton Admiral	d				15 10											16 10							
Christchurch	d				15 15											16 15							
Pokesdown	d				15 19											16 19							
Bournemouth	a				15 23			15 26			15 34					16 23			16 26		16 34		
	d				15 24						15 39					16 24					16 39		
Branksome	d										15 44										16 44		
Parkstone (Dorset)	d										15 47										16 47		
Poole	a				15 33						15 50					16 33					16 50		
	d										15 51										16 51		
Hamworthy	d										15 56										16 56		
Holton Heath	d																						
Wareham	d										16 03										17 03		
Wool	d										16 10										17 10		
Moreton (Dorset)	d										16 16										17 16		
Dorchester South	d										16 24										17 24		
Dorchester West	d									16 01													
Upwey	d									16 10	16 31										17 31		
Weymouth	a									16 15	16 35										17 35		

A 🍴 to Bournemouth

London - Basingstoke, Southampton, Romsey Lymington, Bournemouth and Weymouth

Network Diagram - see first Page of Table 158

		GW	SW	SW		SW	XC	GW	SW	SW	SW	SW	GW	GW	SW	SW		SW	XC	GW	SW	SW	SW
		◇	■	◇■ 🍴		■	◇■ 🛒	◇	◇■ A 🍴	■	■	■	◇	◇	■	◇■ 🍴		■	◇■ 🛒	◇	◇■ A 🍴	■	■
London Waterloo ⊖	d			14 54					15 35	15 37						15 54					16 35	16 37	
Clapham Junction	d			15u03					15u42	15 46						16u03					16u42	16 46	
	d																						
Woking	d			15 28					16 07	16 23						16 28					17 07	17 23	
Farnborough (Main)	d									16 36												17 36	
Fleet	d									16 41												17 41	
Reading	d						15 53												16 53				
Basingstoke	a			15 46			16 09		16 26	16 54						16 46			17 09		17 26	17 54	
	d			15 48			16 10		16 28							16 48			17 10		17 28		
Micheldever	d			15 58												16 58							
Winchester	d			16 08			16 25		16 44							17 08			17 25		17 44		
Shawford	d			16 12																			
Romsey	d	15 51									16 35	16 32		16 51									17 35
Chandlers Ford	d										16 42												17 42
Eastleigh	a			16 18							16 48	17 13				17 18							17 48
	d			16 22	16 26						16 54	17 15				17 22	17 26						17 54
Hedge End	d				16 32												17 32						
Botley	d				16 36												17 36						
Fareham	d	16 27			16 44			16 32					17 03	17 27			17 44			17 32			
Portchester	d				16 49												17 49						
Cosham	d	16 35			16 54									17 35			17 54						
Hilsea	a				17 00												18 00						
Fratton	a	16 42			17 03									17 41			18 04						
Portsmouth & Southsea	a	16 46			17 08									17 46			18 08						
Portsmouth Harbour ⛴	a	16 52			17 13									17 51			18 13						
Southampton Airport Pkwy ✈	d			16 27			16 34		16 53		16 58					17 27			17 34		17 53		17 58
Swaythling	d										17 01												18 01
St Denys	d										17 04												18 04
Southampton Central ⛴	a			16 34			16 42	16 53	17 00		17 09		17 24			17 34			17 40	17 53	18 00		13 09
	d			16 35			16 45	16 54	17 03		17 10		17 26			17 35			17 45	17 54	18 03		13 10
Millbrook (Hants)	d										17 13												13 13
Redbridge	d										17 16												13 16
Romsey	d							17 06			17 24	17a28	17 39							18 06			13 24
Mottisfont & Dunbridge	d										17 29												
Dean	d										17 35												
Salisbury	a							17 24			17 48		18 00							18 24			18 42
Totton	d			16 41												17 41							
Ashurst New Forest	d			16 45												17 45							
Beaulieu Road	d			16 50												17 50							
Brockenhurst	a			16 56			17 02		17 16							17 56			18 02		18 16		
	d		16 29	16 57		16 59	17 03		17 17						17 29	17 57		17 59	18 03		18 17		
Lymington Town	d		16 37			17 07									17 37			18 07					
Lymington Pier	a		16 39			17 09									17 39			18 09					
Sway	d			17 01												18 01							
New Milton	d			17 06					17 24							18 06					18 24		
Hinton Admiral	d			17 10												18 10							
Christchurch	d			17 15												18 15							
Pokesdown	d			17 19												18 19							
Bournemouth	a			17 23			17 26		17 34							18 23			18 26		18 34		
	d			17 24					17 39							18 24					18 39		
Branksome	d								17 44												18 44		
Parkstone (Dorset)	d								17 47												18 47		
Poole	a			17 33					17 50							18 33					18 50		
	d								17 51												18 51		
Hamworthy	d								17 56												18 56		
Holton Heath	d																						
Wareham	d								18 03												19 03		
Wool	d								18 10												19 10		
Moreton (Dorset)	d								18 16												19 16		
Dorchester South	d								18 24												19 24		
Dorchester West	d																						
Upwey	d								18 31												19 31		
Weymouth	a								18 35												19 35		

A 🍴 to Bournemouth

Table 158

Sundays

19 February to 25 March

London - Basingstoke, Southampton, Romsey Lymington, Bournemouth and Weymouth

Network Diagram - see first Page of Table 158

		SW	GW	SW	SW	SW	XC	GW	GW	SW	SW	SW	SW	GW	GW	GW	SW	SW	SW	XC
		■	◇	■	◇■	■	◇■	◇	◇	◇■	■	■	■	◇	◇	◇	■	◇■	■	◇■
					⊼		☕			A ⊼								⊼		☕
London Waterloo ⊖	d				16 54					17 35	17 37							17 54		
Clapham Junction	d				17u03					17u42	17 46							18u03		
	d																			
Woking	d				17 28					18 07	18 23							18 28		
Farnborough (Main)	d										18 36									
Fleet	d										18 41									
Reading	d						17 53													18 53
Basingstoke	a				17 46		18 09			18 26	18 54							18 46		19 09
	d				17 48		18 10			18 28								18 48		19 10
Micheldever	d				17 58													18 58		
Winchester	d				18 08		18 25			18 44								19 08		19 25
Shawford	d				18 12															
Romsey	d	17 32	17 51									18 35	18 32		18 51	19 14				
Chandlers Ford	d											18 42								
Eastleigh	a	18 13			18 18							18 48	19 13					19 18		
	d	18 15			18 22 18 26							18 54	19 15					19 22 19 26		
Hedge End	d				18 32													19 32		
Botley	d				18 36													19 36		
Fareham	d		18 27		18 44			18 32						19 03	19 28			19 44		
Portchester	d				18 49													19 49		
Cosham	d		18 35		18 54										19 36			19 54		
Hilsea	a				19 00													20 00		
Fratton	a		18 41		19 03										19 42			20 04		
Portsmouth & Southsea	a		18 45		19 08										19 46			20 08		
Portsmouth Harbour ⛴	a		18 52		19 13										19 51			20 13		
Southampton Airport Pkwy ✈	d				18 27		18 34			18 53		18 58						19 27		19 34
Swaythling	d											19 01								
St Denys	d											19 04								
Southampton Central ⛴	a				18 34		18 42	18 53		19 00		19 09		19 24		19 25		19 34		19 40
	d				18 35		18 45	18 54		19 03		19 10		19 30				19 35		19 45
Millbrook (Hants)	d											19 13								
Redbridge	d											19 16								
Romsey	d	18a28						19 06				19 24	19a28	19 42						
Mottisfont & Dunbridge	d											19 29								
Dean	d											19 35								
Salisbury	a							19 24				19 48		20 00						
Totton	d				18 41													19 41		
Ashurst New Forest	d				18 45													19 45		
Beaulieu Road	d				18 50													19 50		
Brockenhurst	a				18 56		19 01			19 16								19 56		20 02
	d			18 29	18 57	18 59	19 02			19 17							19 29	19 57	19 59	20 03
Lymington Town	d			18 37		19 07											19 37		20 07	
Lymington Pier	a			18 39		19 09											19 39		20 09	
Sway	d				19 01													20 01		
New Milton	d				19 06					19 24								20 06		
Hinton Admiral	d				19 10													20 10		
Christchurch	d				19 15													20 15		
Pokesdown	d				19 19													20 19		
Bournemouth	a				19 23		19 26			19 34								20 23		20 26
	d				19 24					19 39								20 24		
Branksome	d									19 44										
Parkstone (Dorset)	d									19 47										
Poole	a				19 33					19 50								20 33		
	d									19 51										
Hamworthy	d									19 56										
Holton Heath	d																			
Wareham	d									20 03										
Wool	d									20 10										
Moreton (Dorset)	d									20 17										
Dorchester South	d									20 25										
Dorchester West	d								19 47											
Upwey	d								19 55	20 32										
Weymouth	a								20 01	20 36										

A ⊼ to Bournemouth

Table 158

Sundays

19 February to 25 March

London - Basingstoke, Southampton, Romsey Lymington, Bournemouth and Weymouth

Network Diagram - see first Page of Table 158

		GW	SW	SW	SN	SW	SW	GW	SW	SW	SW	XC	GW	SW	SW	GW	SN	SW	SW	GW	SW
		◇	◇■	■	◇■	■	■	◇	■	◇■	■	◇■	◇	◇■	■	■	◇■	■	■	◇	■
			A ⊼							⊼		☕		A ⊼							
London Waterloo ⊖	d		18 35	18 37						18 54				19 35	19 37						
Clapham Junction	d		18u42	18 46						19u03				19u42	19 46						
	d																				
Woking	d		19 07	19 23						19 28				20 07	20 23						
Farnborough (Main)	d			19 36											20 36						
Fleet	d			19 41											20 41						
Reading	d											19 53									
Basingstoke	a		19 26	19 54						19 46		20 09		20 26	20 54						
	d		19 28							19 48		20 10		20 28							
Micheldever	d									19 58											
Winchester	d		19 44							20 08		20 25		20 44							
Shawford	d									20 12											
Romsey	d					19 35	19 32	19 50								20 19		20 35	20 32	20 48	
Chandlers Ford	d					19 42												20 42			
Eastleigh	a					19 48	20 13			20 18								20 48	21 13		
	d				19 46	19 54	20 15			20 22 20 26							20 46	20 54	21 15		
Hedge End	d									20 32											
Botley	d									20 36											
Fareham	d	19 32			20 03			20 27		20 44			20 32			20 55	21 02			21 25	
Portchester	d									20 49											
Cosham	d				20a11					20 54							21a10				
Hilsea	a									21 00											
Fratton	a							20 42		21 04						21 09				21 38	
Portsmouth & Southsea	a							20 45		21 08						21 15				21 41	
Portsmouth Harbour ⛴	a							20 49		21 13						21 24				21 46	
Southampton Airport Pkwy ✈	d		19 53			19 58				20 27		20 34		20 53				20 58			
Swaythling	d					20 01												21 01			
St Denys	d					20 04												21 04			
Southampton Central ⛴	a	19 53	20 00			20 09				20 34		20 42	20 53	21 00				21 09			
	d	19 54	20 03			20 10				20 35		20 45	20 54	21 03				21 10			
Millbrook (Hants)	d					20 13												21 13			
Redbridge	d					20 16												21 16			
Romsey	d	20 06				20 24	20a28						21 06					21 24	21a28		
Mottisfont & Dunbridge	d																	21 29			
Dean	d																	21 35			
Salisbury	a	20 24				20 42							21 24					21 48			
Totton	d									20 41											
Ashurst New Forest	d									20 45											
Beaulieu Road	d									20 50											
Brockenhurst	a		20 16							20 56		21 02		21 16							
	d		20 17						20 29	20 57	20 59	21 03		21 17							21 29
Lymington Town	d								20 37		21 07										21 37
Lymington Pier	a								20 39		21 09										21 39
Sway	d									21 01											
New Milton	d		20 24							21 06				21 24							
Hinton Admiral	d									21 10											
Christchurch	d									21 15											
Pokesdown	d									21 19											
Bournemouth	a		20 34							21 23		21 26		21 34							
	d		20 39							21 24				21 39							
Branksome	d		20 44											21 44							
Parkstone (Dorset)	d		20 47											21 47							
Poole	a		20 50							21 33				21 50							
	d		20 51											21 51							
Hamworthy	d		20 56											21 56							
Holton Heath	d																				
Wareham	d		21 03											22 03							
Wool	d		21 10											22 10							
Moreton (Dorset)	d		21 17											22 17							
Dorchester South	d		21 25											22 25							
Dorchester West	d																				
Upwey	d		21 32											22 32							
Weymouth	a		21 36											22 36							

A ⊼ to Bournemouth

London - Basingstoke, Southampton, Romsey Lymington, Bournemouth and Weymouth

Network Diagram - see first Page of Table 158

		SW ◇1		SW 1	XC ◇1	GW	SW ◇1 A ⊼	SW 1	SW 1	SW 1	GW ◇	SW ◇1		XC ◇1	GW	SW ◇1 A ⊼	SW 1	SW 1	SW 1	GW ◇	SW ◇1		SW 1
London Waterloo 15 ⊖	d	19 54					20 35	20 37				20 54				21 35	21 37				21 54		22 37
Clapham Junction 10	d	20u03					20u42	20 46				21u03				21u42	21 46				22u03		22 46
	d																						
Woking	d	20 28					21 07	21 23				21 28				22 07	22 23				22 28		23 23
Farnborough (Main)	d							21 36									22 36						23 36
Fleet	d							21 41									22 41						23 41
Reading 7	d				20 53									21 53									
Basingstoke	a	20 46			21 09		21 26	21 54				21 46		22 09		22 26	22 54				22 46		23 54
	d	20 48			21 10		21 28					21 48		22 10		22 28					22 48		
Micheldever	d	20 58										21 58									22 58		
Winchester	d	21 08			21 25		21 44					22 08		22 25		22 44					23 08		
Shawford	d											22 12											
Romsey	d								21 35	21 32	21 51							22 35	22 28	22 54			
Chandlers Ford	d								21 42									22 42					
Eastleigh 3	a	21 18							21 48	22 13		22 18						22 48	23 19		23 17		
	d	21 22	21 26						21 54	22 15		22 22	22 26					22 54	23 21		23 22	23 26	
Hedge End	d		21 32										22 32									23 32	
Botley	d		21 36										22 36									23 36	
Fareham	d		21 44								22 26		22 44		22 32					23 30		23 44	
Portchester	d		21 49										22 49									23 49	
Cosham	d		21 54										22 54									23 54	
Hilsea	a		22 00										23 00									23 59	
Fratton	a		22 04								22 40		23 04							23 43		00 04	
Portsmouth & Southsea	a		22 08								22 44		23 08							23 46		00 08	
Portsmouth Harbour ⛴	a		22 13								22 50		23 13							23 50		00 13	
Southampton Airport Pkwy ✈	d	21 27			21 34		21 53		21 58			22 27		22 34		22 53		22 58			23 27		
Swaythling	d								22 01									23 01					
St Denys	d								22 04									23 04					
Southampton Central ⛴	a	21 34			21 43		22 00		22 09			22 34		22 42	22 53	23 00		23 09			23 34		
	d	21 35			21 45		22 03		22 10			22 35			22 57	23 03		23 10			23 35		
Millbrook (Hants)	d								22 13									23 13					
Redbridge	d								22 16									23 16					
Romsey	d								22a24	22a31					23 09			23 24	23a33				
Mottisfont & Dunbridge	d																	23 29					
Dean	d																	23 35					
Salisbury	a														23 27			23 51					
Totton	d	21 41										22 41									23 41		
Ashurst New Forest	d	21 45										22 45									23 45		
Beaulieu Road	d	21 50										22 50											
Brockenhurst 3	a	21 56			22 02		22 16					22 56				23 16					23 53		
	d	21 57		21 59	22 03		22 17					22 57				23 17					23 54		
Lymington Town	d			22 07																			
Lymington Pier	a			22 09																			
Sway	d	22 01										23 01									23 59		
New Milton	d	22 06					22 24					23 06				23 24					00 04		
Hinton Admiral	d	22 10										23 10									00 08		
Christchurch	d	22 15										23 15									00 13		
Pokesdown	d	22 19										23 19									00 16		
Bournemouth	a	22 23			22 26		22 34					23 23				23 34					00 20		
	d	22 24					22 39					23 24				23 39					00 22		
Branksome	d						22 44									23 44					00 27		
Parkstone (Dorset)	d						22 47									23 47					00 30		
Poole 4	a	22 33					22 50					23 33				23 50					00 34		
	d						22 51									23 51							
Hamworthy	d						22 56									23 56							
Holton Heath	d																						
Wareham	d						23 03									00 03							
Wool	d						23 10									00 10							
Moreton (Dorset)	d						23 17									00 17							
Dorchester South	d						23 25									00 25							
Dorchester West	d					22 53																	
Upwey	d					23 01	23 32									00 32							
Weymouth	a					23 06	23 36									00 36							

A ⊼ to Bournemouth

London - Basingstoke, Southampton, Romsey Lymington, Bournemouth and Weymouth

Network Diagram - see first Page of Table 158

		SW ◇1 A ⊼
London Waterloo 15 ⊖	d	22 54
Clapham Junction 10	d	23u03
	d	
Woking	d	23 28
Farnborough (Main)	d	
Fleet	d	
Reading 7	d	
Basingstoke	a	23 46
	d	23 48
Micheldever	d	23 58
Winchester	d	00 08
Shawford	d	
Romsey	d	
Chandlers Ford	d	
Eastleigh 3	a	00 18
	d	00 22
Hedge End	d	
Botley	d	
Fareham	d	
Portchester	d	
Cosham	d	
Hilsea	a	
Fratton	a	
Portsmouth & Southsea	a	
Portsmouth Harbour ⛴	a	
Southampton Airport Pkwy ✈	d	00 27
Swaythling	d	
St Denys	d	00s31
Southampton Central ⛴	a	00 36
	d	00 37
Millbrook (Hants)	d	
Redbridge	d	
Romsey	d	
Mottisfont & Dunbridge	d	
Dean	d	
Salisbury	a	
Totton	d	00s42
Ashurst New Forest	d	
Beaulieu Road	d	
Brockenhurst 3	a	00s53
	d	
Lymington Town	d	
Lymington Pier	a	
Sway	d	
New Milton	d	01s01
Hinton Admiral	d	
Christchurch	d	01s08
Pokesdown	d	01s12
Bournemouth	a	01 16
	d	01 17
Branksome	d	01s22
Parkstone (Dorset)	d	01s25
Poole 4	a	01 29
	d	
Hamworthy	d	
Holton Heath	d	
Wareham	d	
Wool	d	
Moreton (Dorset)	d	
Dorchester South	d	
Dorchester West	d	
Upwey	d	
Weymouth	a	

Table 158

Sundays from 1 April

London - Basingstoke, Southampton, Romsey Lymington, Bournemouth and Weymouth

Network Diagram - see first Page of Table 158

		SW	SW	SW	SW	SW	SW	SW	SW	SW	SW	SW	GW	SW	SW		SN	SW	SW	SW	SW	SW	GW
		◇1 A 🛒	◇1 🛒	1	◇1 🛒	1	◇1	1	1	1	1	1		1	1		◇1	1	1	1	1	1	■
London Waterloo 15 ⊖	d	21p35	22p05		22p35	22p39	23p05		23p35	00 05	01 05												
Clapham Junction 10	d		22b12			22b46	23b12		23b42	00u12													
	d										01 15												
Woking	d	22p00	22p32		23p00		23p32		00 03	00 37	01 49												
Farnborough (Main)	d					23p16			00 14		01s58												
Fleet	d					23p21			00 20		02s04												
Reading 7	d																						
Basingstoke	a		22p51			23p34	23p51		00 33	00 55	02s16												
	d		22p52			23p36	23p52		00 35	00 56					07 48								
Micheldever	d						00 02								07 58								
Winchester	d	22p33	23p09		23p33	23p52	00 12		00 51	01 13	02s33				08 08								
Shawford	d					23p57									08 12								
Romsey	d			23p09									08 19							08 35	08 39		
Chandlers Ford	d			23p16																08 42			
Eastleigh 8	a		23p17	23p22		00 02	00 20		00 59	01 21	02s42				08 18					08 47	09 13		
	d		23p18	23p23		00 03	00 21	00 30	01 00	01 22					08 22	08 26	08 48			08 54	09 15		
Hedge End	d							00s36								08 32							
Botley	d							00s39								08 36							
Fareham	d							00s47				07 44				08 44	09 02						09 32
Portchester	d							00s53				07 49				08 49							
Cosham	d							00s57				07 54				08 54	09a10						
Hilsea	a											08 00				09 00							
Fratton	a							01s05				08 04				09 04							
Portsmouth & Southsea	a							01s08				08 08				09 08							
Portsmouth Harbour ⛴	a							01 12				08 13				09 13							
Southampton Airport Pkwy ✈	d	22p42	23p22	23p27	23p42	00 08	00 25		01 05	01 26	02s46				08 27					08 58			
Swaythling	d			23p30																09 01			
St Denys	d			23p33			00s29				02s51									09 04			
Southampton Central ⛴	a	22p49	23p29	23p38	23p49	00 15	00 34		01 12	01 35	02 56		08 29		08 34					09 09			09 53
	d	22p51	23p31	23p40	23p51		00 36			01 37					08 35				09 03	09 10			09 54
Millbrook (Hants)	d			23p42																09 13			
Redbridge	d			23p46																09 16			
Romsey	d			23p57																09 24	09a28		10 06
Mottisfont & Dunbridge	d			00 02																09 29			
Dean	d			00 08																09 35			
Salisbury	a			00 20																09 49			10 24
Totton	d		23p36				00s41			01s42					08 41								
Ashurst New Forest	d		23p41												08 45								
Beaulieu Road	d														08 50								
Brockenhurst 3	a	23p04	23p49		00 04		00s52			01s53					08 56				09 16				
	d	23p05	23p50		00 05										08 57			08 59	09 17			09 29	
Lymington Town	d																	09 07				09 37	
Lymington Pier	a																	09 09				09 39	
Sway	d		23p54												09 01								
New Milton	d		23p59				01s00			02s00					09 06				09 24				
Hinton Admiral	d		00 03												09 10								
Christchurch	d		00 08				01s07			02s07					09 15								
Pokesdown	d		00 11				01s11			02s11					09 19								
Bournemouth	a	23p25	00 15		00 21		01 15			02 15					09 23				09 34				
	d	23p29	00 17		00 22		01 16							08 39	09 24				09 39				
Branksome	d	23p35	00 23		00 27		01s21							08 44					09 44				
Parkstone (Dorset)	d	23p38	00 26		00 30		01s24							08 47					09 47				
Poole 4	a	23p41	00 30		00 35		01 29							08 50	09 33				09 50				
	d	23p42												08 51					09 51				
Hamworthy	d	23p47												08 56					09 56				
Holton Heath	d																						
Wareham	d	23p54												09 03					10 03				
Wool	d	00 01												09 10					10 10				
Moreton (Dorset)	d	00 07												09 16					10 16				
Dorchester South	d	00 15												09 24					10 24				
Dorchester West	d																						
Upwey	d	00 21												09 31					10 31				
Weymouth	a	00 26												09 35					10 35				

A 🛒 to Bournemouth

b Previous night, stops to pick up only

Table 158

Sundays from 1 April

London - Basingstoke, Southampton, Romsey Lymington, Bournemouth and Weymouth

Network Diagram - see first Page of Table 158

		SW		SW	SW	SW	SW	SW	SW		SW	XC	SW	SW	SW	GW	SW	SW		SW	XC	SW	SW
		◇1		1	◇1	1	1	1	◇1		1	◇1 🛒	◇1	1	1	◇	1	◇1		1	◇1 🛒	◇1 A 🛒	1
London Waterloo 15 ⊖	d	07 54			08 35				08 54				09 35					09 54				10 35	
Clapham Junction 10	d	08u03			08u45				09u03				09u45					10u03				10u45	
	d																						
Woking	d	08 28			09 09				09 28				10 09					10 28				11 07	
Farnborough (Main)	d																						
Fleet	d																						
Reading 7	d											09 53									10 53		
Basingstoke	a	08 46			09 28				09 46			10 09	10 28					10 46			11 09	11 26	
	d	08 48			09 29				09 48			10 10	10 29					10 48			11 10	11 28	
Micheldever	d	08 58							09 58									10 58					
Winchester	d	09 08			09 46				10 08			10 25	10 46					11 08			11 25	11 44	
Shawford	d								10 12														
Romsey	d					09 35	09 32							10 35	10 32	10 50							11 35
Chandlers Ford	d					09 42								10 42									11 42
Eastleigh 8	a	09 18				09 48	10 13		10 18					10 48	11 13			11 18					11 48
	d	09 22	09 26			09 54	10 15		10 22	10 26				10 54	11 15			11 22	11 26				11 54
Hedge End	d		09 32							10 32									11 32				
Botley	d		09 36							10 36									11 36				
Fareham	d		09 44							10 44						11 26			11 44				
Portchester	d		09 49							10 49									11 49				
Cosham	d		09 54							10 54						11 34			11 54				
Hilsea	a		10 04							11 04									12 00				
Fratton	a		10 08							11 08						11 40			12 04				
Portsmouth & Southsea	a		10 11							11 11						11 45			12 08				
Portsmouth Harbour ⛴	a		10 15							11 15						11 52			12 13				
Southampton Airport Pkwy ✈	d	09 27			09 55	09 58			10 27			10 34	10 55	10 58				11 27			11 34	11 53	11 58
Swaythling	d					10 01								11 01									12 01
St Denys	d					10 04								11 04									12 04
Southampton Central ⛴	a	09 34			10 02	10 09			10 34			10 42	11 02	11 09				11 34			11 42	11 59	12 09
	d	09 35			10 03	10 10			10 35			10 45	11 03	11 10				11 35			11 45	12 03	12 10
Millbrook (Hants)	d					10 13								11 13									12 13
Redbridge	d					10 16								11 16									12 16
Romsey	d					10 24	10a28							11 24	11a28								12 24
Mottisfont & Dunbridge	d													11 29									
Dean	d													11 35									
Salisbury	a					10 42								11 48									12 42
Totton	d	09 41							10 41									11 41					
Ashurst New Forest	d	09 45							10 45									11 45					
Beaulieu Road	d	09 50							10 50									11 50					
Brockenhurst 3	a	09 56			10 17				10 56			11 02	11 17					11 56			12 02	12 16	
	d	09 57		09 59	10 18			10 29	10 57		10 59	11 03	11 18				11 29	11 57		11 59	12 03	12 17	
Lymington Town	d			10 07				10 37			11 07						11 37			12 07			
Lymington Pier	a			10 09				10 39			11 09						11 39			12 09			
Sway	d	10 01							11 01									12 01					
New Milton	d	10 06			10 25				11 06				11 25					12 06				12 24	
Hinton Admiral	d	10 10							11 10									12 10					
Christchurch	d	10 15							11 15									12 15					
Pokesdown	d	10 19							11 19									12 19					
Bournemouth	a	10 23			10 35				11 23			11 26	11 35					12 23			12 26	12 34	
	d	10 24			10 39				11 24				11 39					12 24				12 39	
Branksome	d				10 44								11 44									12 44	
Parkstone (Dorset)	d				10 47								11 47									12 47	
Poole 4	a	10 33			10 50				11 33				11 50					12 33				12 50	
	d				10 51								11 51									12 51	
Hamworthy	d				10 56								11 56									12 56	
Holton Heath	d																						
Wareham	d				11 03								12 03									13 03	
Wool	d				11 10								12 10									13 10	
Moreton (Dorset)	d				11 16								12 16									13 16	
Dorchester South	d				11 24								12 24									13 24	
Dorchester West	d																						
Upwey	d				11 31								12 31									13 31	
Weymouth	a				11 35								12 35									13 35	

A 🛒 to Bournemouth

London - Basingstoke, Southampton, Romsey Lymington, Bournemouth and Weymouth

Network Diagram - see first Page of Table 158

		SW ■	GW ◇	SW ■	SW ◇■		SW ■	XC ◇■ ⊐	GW ◇	SW ◇■ A ✠	GW ◇	SW ■	SW ■	SW ■	SW ◇■ ✠		SW ■	XC ◇■ ⊐	GW ◇	SW ◇■ A ✠	SW ■	SW ■
London Waterloo ■ ⊖	d				10 54					11 35					11 54					12 35		
Clapham Junction ■	d				11u04					11u45					12u04					12u42		
	d																					
Woking	d				11 28					12 07					12 28					13 07		
Farnborough (Main)	d																					
Fleet	d																					
Reading ■	d							11 53										12 53				
Basingstoke	a				11 46			12 09		12 26					12 46			13 09		13 26		
	d				11 48			12 10		12 28					12 48			13 10		13 28		
Micheldever	d				11 58										12 58							
Winchester	d				12 08			12 25		12 44					13 08			13 25		13 44		
Shawford	d				12 12																	
Romsey	d	11 32	11 51								12 52	12 35	12 32								13 35	13 32
Chandlers Ford	d											12 42									13 42	
Eastleigh ■	a	12 13			12 18							12 48	13 13		13 18						13 48	14 13
	d	12 15			12 22	12 26						12 54	13 15		13 22	13 26					13 54	14 15
Hedge End	d					12 32										13 32						
Botley	d					12 36										13 36						
Fareham	d		12 28			12 44			12 32							13 44			13 32			
Portchester	d					12 49										13 49						
Cosham	d		12 36			12 54										13 54						
Hilsea	a					13 00										14 00						
Fratton	a		12 42			13 04										14 04						
Portsmouth & Southsea	a		12 46			13 08										14 08						
Portsmouth Harbour ⛴	a		12 52			13 13										14 13						
Southampton Airport Pkwy ✈	d				12 27			12 34		12 53		12 58			13 27			13 34		13 53	13 58	
Swaythling	d											13 01									14 01	
St Denys	d											13 04									14 04	
Southampton Central ⛴	a				12 34			12 42	12 53	13 00	13 05	13 09			13 34			13 42	13 53	14 00	14 09	
	d				12 35			12 45	12 54	13 03		13 10			13 35			13 45	13 54	14 03	14 10	
Millbrook (Hants)	d											13 13									14 13	
Redbridge	d											13 16									14 16	
Romsey	d	12a28							13 06			13 24	13a28						14 06		14 24	14a28
Mottisfont & Dunbridge	d											13 29										
Dean	d											13 35										
Salisbury	a								13 24			13 48							14 24		14 42	
Totton	d				12 41										13 41							
Ashurst New Forest	d				12 45										13 45							
Beaulieu Road	d				12 50										13 50							
Brockenhurst ■	a				12 56			13 02		13 16					13 56			14 01		14 16		
	d			12 29	12 57		12 59	13 03		13 17				13 29	13 57		13 59	14 02		14 17		
Lymington Town	d			12 37			13 07							13 37			14 07					
Lymington Pier	a			12 39			13 09							13 39			14 09					
Sway	d				13 01										14 01							
New Milton	d				13 06					13 24					14 06					14 24		
Hinton Admiral	d				13 10										14 10							
Christchurch	d				13 15										14 15							
Pokesdown	d				13 19										14 19							
Bournemouth	a				13 23			13 26		13 34					14 23			14 26		14 34		
	d				13 24					13 39					14 24					14 39		
Branksome	d									13 44										14 44		
Parkstone (Dorset)	d									13 47										14 47		
Poole ■	a				13 33					13 50					14 33					14 50		
	d									13 51										14 51		
Hamworthy	d									13 56										14 56		
Holton Heath	d																					
Wareham	d									14 03										15 03		
Wool	d									14 10										15 10		
Moreton (Dorset)	d									14 16										15 16		
Dorchester South	d									14 24										15 24		
Dorchester West	d																					
Upwey	d									14 31										15 31		
Weymouth	a									14 35										15 35		

A ✠ to Bournemouth

Table 158

Sundays
from 1 April

London - Basingstoke, Southampton, Romsey Lymington, Bournemouth and Weymouth

Network Diagram - see first Page of Table 158

		GW ◇ ✠	SW ■	SW ◇■ ✠		SW ■	XC ◇■ ⊐	GW ◇	GW	SW ◇■ A ✠	SW ■	SW ■	GW ◇	SW ■	SW ◇■ ✠		SW ■	XC ◇■ ⊐	GW ■	SW ◇■ A ✠	SW ■	SW ■	GW ◇
London Waterloo ■ ⊖	d			12 54						13 35					13 54					14 35			
Clapham Junction ■	d			13u03						13u42					14u03					14u42			
	d																						
Woking	d			13 28						14 07					14 28					15 07			
Farnborough (Main)	d																						
Fleet	d																						
Reading ■	d						13 53											14 53					
Basingstoke	a			13 46			14 09			14 26					14 46			15 09		15 26			
	d			13 48			14 10			14 28					14 48			15 10		15 28			
Micheldever	d			13 58											14 58								
Winchester	d			14 08			14 25			14 44					15 08			15 25		15 44			
Shawford	d			14 12																			
Romsey	d	13 51									14 35	14 32	15 10								15 35	15 32	15 50
Chandlers Ford	d										14 42										15 42		
Eastleigh ■	a			14 18							14 48	15 13			15 18						15 48	16 13	
	d			14 22	14 26						14 54	15 15			15 22	15 26					15 54	16 15	
Hedge End	d				14 32											15 32							
Botley	d				14 36											15 36							
Fareham	d	14 27			14 44			14 32								15 44			15 32				16 26
Portchester	d				14 49											15 49							
Cosham	d	14 35			14 54											15 54							16 34
Hilsea	a				15 00											16 00							
Fratton	a	14 41			15 04											16 04							16 41
Portsmouth & Southsea	a	14 45			15 08											16 08							16 45
Portsmouth Harbour ⛴	a	14 55			15 13											16 13							16 52
Southampton Airport Pkwy ✈	d			14 27			14 34			14 53	14 58				15 27			15 34		15 53	15 58		
Swaythling	d										15 01										16 01		
St Denys	d										15 04										16 04		
Southampton Central ⛴	a			14 34			14 42	14 53		15 00	15 09		15 21		15 34			15 42	15 53	16 00	16 09		
	d			14 35			14 45	14 54		15 03	15 10				15 35			15 45	15 54	16 03	16 10		
Millbrook (Hants)	d										15 13										16 13		
Redbridge	d										15 16										16 16		
Romsey	d							15 06			15 24	15a28							16 06		16 24	16a28	
Mottisfont & Dunbridge	d										15 29												
Dean	d										15 35												
Salisbury	a							15 24			15 48								16 24		16 42		
Totton	d			14 41											15 41								
Ashurst New Forest	d			14 45											15 45								
Beaulieu Road	d			14 50											15 50								
Brockenhurst ■	a			14 56			15 02			15 16					15 56			16 02		16 16			
	d		14 29	14 57		14 59	15 03			15 17				15 29	15 57		15 59	16 03		16 17			
Lymington Town	d		14 37			15 07								15 37			16 07						
Lymington Pier	a		14 39			15 09								15 39			16 09						
Sway	d			15 01											16 01								
New Milton	d			15 06						15 24					16 06					16 24			
Hinton Admiral	d			15 10											16 10								
Christchurch	d			15 15											16 15								
Pokesdown	d			15 19											16 19								
Bournemouth	a			15 23			15 26			15 34					16 23			16 26		16 34			
	d			15 24						15 39					16 24					16 39			
Branksome	d									15 44										16 44			
Parkstone (Dorset)	d									15 47										16 47			
Poole ■	a			15 33						15 50					16 33					16 50			
	d									15 51										16 51			
Hamworthy	d									15 56										16 56			
Holton Heath	d																						
Wareham	d									16 03										17 03			
Wool	d									16 10										17 10			
Moreton (Dorset)	d									16 16										17 16			
Dorchester South	d									16 24										17 24			
Dorchester West	d								16 01														
Upwey	d								16 10	16 31										17 31			
Weymouth	a								16 15	16 35										17 35			

A ✠ to Bournemouth

Table 158

Sundays from 1 April

London - Basingstoke, Southampton, Romsey Lymington, Bournemouth and Weymouth

Network Diagram - see first Page of Table 158

		SW ■	SW ◇■ ✠		SW ■	XC ◇■ 🍴	GW ◇	SW ◇■ A ✠	SW ■	SW ■	SW ■	GW ◇	GW ◇	SW ■	SW ◇■ ✠		SW ■	XC ◇■ 🍴	GW ◇	SW ◇■ A ✠	SW ■	SW ■
London Waterloo ■ ⊖	d		14 54					15 35	15 37						15 54					16 35	16 37	
Clapham Junction ■	d		15u03					15u42	15 46						16u03					16u42	16 46	
	d																					
Woking	d		15 28					16 07	16 23						16 28					17 07	17 23	
Farnborough (Main)	d								16 36												17 36	
Fleet	d								16 41												17 41	
Reading ■	d					15 53												16 53				
Basingstoke	a		15 46			16 09		16 26	16 54						16 46			17 09		17 26	17 54	
	d		15 48			16 10		16 28							16 48			17 10		17 28		
Micheldever	d		15 58												16 58							
Winchester	d		16 08			16 25		16 44							17 08			17 25		17 44		
Shawford	d		16 12																			
Romsey	d									16 35	16 32		16 51									17 35
Chandlers Ford	d									16 42												17 42
Eastleigh ■	a		16 18							16 48	17 13				17 18							17 48
	d		16 22	16 26						16 54	17 15				17 22	17 26						17 54
Hedge End	d			16 32												17 32						
Botley	d			16 36												17 36						
Fareham	d			16 44			16 32					17 03	17 27			17 44			17 32			
Portchester	d			16 49												17 49						
Cosham	d			16 54									17 35			17 54						
Hilsea	a			17 00												18 00						
Fratton	a			17 03									17 41			18 04						
Portsmouth & Southsea	a			17 08									17 46			18 08						
Portsmouth Harbour ⛴	a			17 13									17 52			18 13						
Southampton Airport Pkwy ✈	d		16 27			16 34		16 53		16 58					17 27			17 34		17 53		17 58
Swaythling	d									17 01												18 01
St Denys	d									17 04												18 04
Southampton Central ⛴	a		16 34			16 42	16 53	17 00		17 09		17 24			17 34			17 40	17 53	18 00		18 09
	d		16 35			16 45	16 54	17 03		17 10		17 26			17 35			17 45	17 54	18 03		18 10
Millbrook (Hants)	d									17 13												18 13
Redbridge	d									17 16												18 16
Romsey	d						17 06			17 24	17a28	17 39							18 06			18 24
Mottisfont & Dunbridge	d									17 29												
Dean	d									17 35												
Salisbury	a						17 24			17 48		18 00							18 24			18 42
Totton	d		16 41												17 41							
Ashurst New Forest	d		16 45												17 45							
Beaulieu Road	d		16 50												17 50							
Brockenhurst ■	a		16 56			17 02		17 16							17 56			18 02		18 16		
	d	16 29	16 57		16 59	17 03		17 17						17 29	17 57		17 59	18 03		18 17		
Lymington Town	d	16 37			17 07									17 37			18 07					
Lymington Pier	a	16 39			17 09									17 39			18 09					
Sway	d		17 01												18 01							
New Milton	d		17 06					17 24							18 06					18 24		
Hinton Admiral	d		17 10												18 10							
Christchurch	d		17 15												18 15							
Pokesdown	d		17 19												18 19							
Bournemouth	a		17 23			17 26		17 34							18 23			18 26		18 34		
	d		17 24					17 39							18 24					18 39		
Branksome	d							17 44												18 44		
Parkstone (Dorset)	d							17 47												18 47		
Poole ■	a		17 33					17 50							18 33					18 50		
	d							17 51												18 51		
Hamworthy	d							17 56												18 56		
Holton Heath	d																					
Wareham	d							18 03												19 03		
Wool	d							18 10												19 10		
Moreton (Dorset)	d							18 16												19 16		
Dorchester South	d							18 24												19 24		
Dorchester West	d																					
Upwey	d							18 31												19 31		
Weymouth	a							18 35												19 35		

A ✠ to Bournemouth

Table 158

Sundays from 1 April

London - Basingstoke, Southampton, Romsey Lymington, Bournemouth and Weymouth

Network Diagram - see first Page of Table 158

		SW ■	GW ◇	SW ■	SW ◇■ ✠		SW ■	XC ◇■ 🍴	GW ◇	GW ◇	SW ◇■ A ✠	SW ■	SW ■	SW ■	GW ◇	GW ◇	GW ◇	SW ■	SW ◇■ ✠		SW ■	XC ◇■ 🍴	GW ◇
London Waterloo ■ ⊖	d				16 54						17 35	17 37							17 54				
Clapham Junction ■	d				17u03						17u42	17 46							18u03				
	d																						
Woking	d				17 28						18 07	18 23							18 28				
Farnborough (Main)	d											18 36											
Fleet	d											18 41											
Reading ■	d							17 53														18 53	
Basingstoke	a				17 46			18 09			18 26	18 54							18 46			19 09	
	d				17 48			18 10			18 28								18 48			19 10	
Micheldever	d				17 58														18 58				
Winchester	d				18 08			18 25			18 44								19 08			19 25	
Shawford	d				18 12																		
Romsey	d	17 32	17 51										18 35	18 32		18 50	19 14						
Chandlers Ford	d												18 42										
Eastleigh ■	a	18 13			18 18								18 48	19 13					19 18				
	d	18 15			18 22	18 26							18 54	19 15					19 22	19 26			
Hedge End	d					18 32														19 32			
Botley	d					18 36														19 36			
Fareham	d		18 27			18 44			18 32						19 03	19 27				19 44			19 32
Portchester	d					18 49														19 49			
Cosham	d		18 35			18 54										19 35				19 54			
Hilsea	a					19 00														20 00			
Fratton	a		18 41			19 03										19 42				20 04			
Portsmouth & Southsea	a		18 45			19 08										19 46				20 08			
Portsmouth Harbour ⛴	a		18 52			19 13										19 52				20 13			
Southampton Airport Pkwy ✈	d				18 27			18 34			18 53		18 58						19 27			19 34	
Swaythling	d												19 01										
St Denys	d												19 04										
Southampton Central ⛴	a				18 34			18 42	18 53		19 00		19 09		19 24		19 25		19 34			19 40	19 53
	d				18 35			18 45	18 54		19 03		19 10		19 30				19 35			19 45	19 54
Millbrook (Hants)	d												19 13										
Redbridge	d												19 16										
Romsey	d	18a28							19 06				19 24	19a28	19 42								20 06
Mottisfont & Dunbridge	d												19 29										
Dean	d												19 35										
Salisbury	a								19 24				19 48		20 00								20 24
Totton	d				18 41														19 41				
Ashurst New Forest	d				18 45														19 45				
Beaulieu Road	d				18 50														19 50				
Brockenhurst ■	a				18 56			19 01			19 16								19 56			20 02	
	d			18 29	18 57		18 59	19 02			19 17							19 29	19 57		19 59	20 03	
Lymington Town	d			18 37			19 07											19 37			20 07		
Lymington Pier	a			18 39			19 09											19 39			20 09		
Sway	d				19 01														20 01				
New Milton	d				19 06						19 24								20 06				
Hinton Admiral	d				19 10														20 10				
Christchurch	d				19 15														20 15				
Pokesdown	d				19 19														20 19				
Bournemouth	a				19 23			19 26			19 34								20 23			20 26	
	d				19 24						19 39								20 24				
Branksome	d										19 44												
Parkstone (Dorset)	d										19 47												
Poole ■	a				19 33						19 50								20 33				
	d										19 51												
Hamworthy	d										19 56												
Holton Heath	d																						
Wareham	d										20 03												
Wool	d										20 10												
Moreton (Dorset)	d										20 17												
Dorchester South	d										20 25												
Dorchester West	d									19 47													
Upwey	d									19 55	20 32												
Weymouth	a									20 01	20 36												

A ✠ to Bournemouth

London - Basingstoke, Southampton, Romsey Lymington, Bournemouth and Weymouth

Network Diagram - see first Page of Table 158

		SW	SW	SN	SW	SW	GW	SW	SW		SW	XC	GW	SW	SW	GW	SN	SW	SW	GW	SW	SW	
		◇1 A 🛒	1	◇1	1	1	◇	1	◇1 🛒		1	◇1 (bistro)	◇	◇1 A 🛒	1	■	◇1	1	1	◇	1	◇1	
London Waterloo 15 ⊖	d	18 35	18 37						18 54					19 35	19 37							19 54	
Clapham Junction 10	d	18u42	18 46						19u03					19u42	19 46							20u03	
	d																						
Woking	d	19 07	19 23						19 28					20 07	20 23							20 28	
Farnborough (Main)	d		19 36												20 36								
Fleet	d		19 41												20 41								
Reading 7	d											19 53											
Basingstoke	a	19 26	19 54						19 46			20 09		20 26	20 54							20 46	
	d	19 28							19 48			20 10		20 28								20 48	
Micheldever	d								19 58													20 58	
Winchester	d	19 44							20 08			20 25		20 44								21 08	
Shawford	d								20 12														
Romsey	d				19 35	19 32	19 50									20 19		20 35	20 32	20 48			
Chandlers Ford	d				19 42													20 42					
Eastleigh 8	a				19 48	20 13			20 18									20 48	21 13			21 18	
	d			19 46	19 54	20 15			20 22	20 26							20 46	20 54	21 15			21 22	21 26
Hedge End	d									20 32													21 32
Botley	d									20 36													21 36
Fareham	d			20 03			20 26			20 44			20 32			20 55	21 02			21 25			21 44
Portchester	d									20 49													21 49
Cosham	d			20a11						20 54							21a10						21 54
Hilsea	a									21 00													22 00
Fratton	a						20 41			21 04						21 09				21 38			22 04
Portsmouth & Southsea	a						20 45			21 08						21 15				21 41			22 08
Portsmouth Harbour ⛴	a						20 51			21 13						21 26				21 48			22 13
Southampton Airport Pkwy ✈	d	19 53			19 58				20 27			20 34		20 53				20 58				21 27	
Swaythling	d				20 01													21 01					
St Denys	d				20 04													21 04					
Southampton Central ⛴	a	20 00			20 09				20 34			20 42	20 53	21 00				21 09				21 34	
	d	20 03			20 10				20 35			20 45	20 54	21 03				21 10				21 35	
Millbrook (Hants)	d				20 13													21 13					
Redbridge	d				20 16													21 16					
Romsey	d				20 24	20a28							21 06					21 24	21a28				
Mottisfont & Dunbridge	d																	21 29					
Dean	d																	21 35					
Salisbury	a				20 42								21 24					21 48					
Totton	d								20 41													21 41	
Ashurst New Forest	d								20 45													21 45	
Beaulieu Road	d								20 50													21 50	
Brockenhurst 3	a	20 16							20 56			21 02		21 16								21 56	
	d	20 17						20 29	20 57		20 59	21 03		21 17							21 29	21 57	
Lymington Town	d							20 37			21 07										21 37		
Lymington Pier	a							20 39			21 09										21 39		
Sway	d								21 01													22 01	
New Milton	d	20 24							21 06					21 24								22 06	
Hinton Admiral	d								21 10													22 10	
Christchurch	d								21 15													22 15	
Pokesdown	d								21 19													22 19	
Bournemouth	a	20 34							21 23			21 26		21 34								22 23	
	d	20 39							21 24					21 39								22 24	
Branksome	d	20 44												21 44									
Parkstone (Dorset)	d	20 47												21 47									
Poole 4	a	20 50							21 33					21 50								22 33	
	d	20 51												21 51									
Hamworthy	d	20 56												21 56									
Holton Heath	d																						
Wareham	d	21 03												22 03									
Wool	d	21 10												22 10									
Moreton (Dorset)	d	21 17												22 17									
Dorchester South	d	21 25												22 25									
Dorchester West	d																						
Upwey	d	21 32												22 32									
Weymouth	a	21 36												22 36									

A 🛒 to Bournemouth

London - Basingstoke, Southampton, Romsey Lymington, Bournemouth and Weymouth

Network Diagram - see first Page of Table 158

		SW	XC	GW	SW	SW	SW	SW	GW	SW		XC	GW	SW	SW	SW	SW	GW	SW		SW	SW
		1	◇1		◇1 A 🛒	1	1	1	◇	◇1		◇1		◇1 A 🛒	1	1	1	◇	◇1		1	◇1 🛒
London Waterloo 15 ⊖	d				20 35	20 37				20 54				21 35	21 37				21 54		22 37	22 54
Clapham Junction 10	d				20u42	20 46				21u03				21u42	21 46				22u03		22 46	23u03
	d																					
Woking	d				21 07	21 23				21 28				22 07	22 23				22 28		23 23	23 28
Farnborough (Main)	d					21 36									22 36						23 36	
Fleet	d					21 41									22 41						23 41	
Reading 7	d		20 53									21 53										
Basingstoke	a		21 11		21 26	21 54				21 46		22 09		22 26	22 54				22 46		23 54	23 46
	d		21 12		21 28					21 48		22 10		22 28					22 48			23 48
Micheldever	d									21 58									22 58			23 58
Winchester	d		21 27		21 44					22 08		22 25		22 44					23 08			00 08
Shawford	d									22 12												
Romsey	d						21 35	21 32	21 51							22 35	22 28	22 54				
Chandlers Ford	d						21 42									22 42						
Eastleigh 8	a						21 48	22 13		22 18						22 48	23 19		23 17			00 18
	d						21 54	22 15		22 22	22 26					22 54	23 21		23 22	23 26		00 22
Hedge End	d										22 32									23 32		
Botley	d										22 36									23 36		
Fareham	d								22 26		22 44		22 32					23 30		23 44		
Portchester	d										22 49									23 49		
Cosham	d										22 54									23 54		
Hilsea	a										23 00									23 59		
Fratton	a								22 40		23 04							23 43		00 04		
Portsmouth & Southsea	a								22 44		23 08							23 46		00 08		
Portsmouth Harbour ⛴	a								22 50		23 13							23 54		00 13		
Southampton Airport Pkwy ✈	d		21 36		21 53		21 58			22 27		22 34		22 53		22 58			23 27			00 27
Swaythling	d						22 01									23 01						
St Denys	d						22 04									23 04						00s31
Southampton Central ⛴	a		21 45		22 00		22 09			22 34		22 42	22 53	23 00		23 09			23 34			00 36
	d		21 47		22 03		22 10			22 35			22 57	23 03		23 10			23 35			00 37
Millbrook (Hants)	d						22 13									23 13						
Redbridge	d						22 16									23 16						
Romsey	d						22a24	22a31					23 09			23 24	23a33					
Mottisfont & Dunbridge	d															23 29						
Dean	d															23 35						
Salisbury	a												23 27			23 51						
Totton	d									22 41									23 41			00s42
Ashurst New Forest	d									22 45									23 45			
Beaulieu Road	d									22 50												
Brockenhurst 3	a		22 04		22 16					22 56				23 16					23 53			00s53
	d	21 59	22 05		22 17					22 57				23 17					23 54			
Lymington Town	d	22 07																				
Lymington Pier	a	22 09																				
Sway	d									23 01									23 59			
New Milton	d				22 24					23 06				23 24					00 04			01s01
Hinton Admiral	d									23 10									00 08			
Christchurch	d									23 15									00 13			01s08
Pokesdown	d									23 19									00 16			01s12
Bournemouth	a		22 28		22 34					23 23				23 34					00 20			01 16
	d				22 39					23 24				23 39					00 22			01 17
Branksome	d				22 44									23 44					00 27			01s22
Parkstone (Dorset)	d				22 47									23 47					00 30			01s25
Poole 4	a				22 50					23 33				23 50					00 34			01 29
	d				22 51									23 51								
Hamworthy	d				22 56									23 56								
Holton Heath	d																					
Wareham	d				23 03									00 03								
Wool	d				23 10									00 10								
Moreton (Dorset)	d				23 17									00 17								
Dorchester South	d				23 25									00 25								
Dorchester West	d			22 53																		
Upwey	d			23 01	23 32									00 32								
Weymouth	a			23 06	23 36									00 36								

A 🛒 to Bournemouth

Weymouth, Bournemouth, Lymington, Romsey, Southampton and Basingstoke - London

Network Diagram - see first Page of Table 158

Miles	Miles			SW	SW	SW	SW	SW	SW	SW	XC	SW	SW	SW	GW	SW	SW	XC	SW	SW	GW	SW	SW	SW	SW
				MO	MO	MX	MX	MO	MX																
				◇1	1	1	◇1	1	1	1	◇1	1	◇1 ⌶	1	◇	1	1	◇1 ⌶	◇1 ⌶	1	■ ⌶	1	1	1	1
0	—	**Weymouth**	d	20p58			22p10	22p58	23p10						05 33										
2¼	—	Upwey	d	21p02			22p14	23p02	23p14						05 37										
—	—	Dorchester West	a												05 44										
7	—	**Dorchester South**	d	21p10			22p22	23p10	23p22																
12½	—	Moreton (Dorset)	d	21p17			22p28	23p17	23p28																
17	—	Wool	d	21p23			22p34	23p23	23p34																
22	—	Wareham	d	21p30			22p42	23p30	23p42																
24	—	Holton Heath	d																						
26¾	—	Hamworthy	d	21p37			22p48	23p37	23p48																
29	—	**Poole** 4	a	21p41			22p53	23p41	23p53																
—	—		d	21p50			22p54	23p50	23p54				05 00	05 26					05 45						
30¾	—	Parkstone (Dorset)	d	21p54			22p58	23p54					05 04	05 30											
32	—	Branksome	d	21p57			23p01	23p57					05 07	05 33											
34¾	—	**Bournemouth**	a	22p03			23p07	00 03	00 03				05 12	05 38					05 54						
—	—		d	22p06			23p12						05 15	05 40					05 57						
36½	—	Pokesdown	d	22p10			23p16						05 19	05 44											
38½	—	Christchurch	d	22p14			23p20						05 23	05 48											
41¾	—	Hinton Admiral	d	22p19			23p25							05 53											
44¾	—	New Milton	d	22p23			23p29						05 30	05 57											
47¾	—	Sway	d	22p28			23p34							06 02											
—	0	**Lymington Pier**	d																				06 14		
—	0½	Lymington Town	d																				06 16		
50	5¼	**Brockenhurst** 3	a	22p33			23p39						05 37	06 07					06 12				06 25		
—	—		d	22p34			23p40						05 38						06 14						
54¾	—	Beaulieu Road	d	22p39																					
57¼	—	Ashurst New Forest	d	22p43			23p47																		
60¼	—	Totton	d	22p48			23p52						05 49									06 12			
—	0	**Salisbury**	d													05 35									
—	9	Dean	d													05 47									
—	12¾	Mottisfont & Dunbridge	d													05 53									
—	16½	**Romsey**	d													05 58									
60¾	22½	Redbridge	d																			06 14			
62½	—	Millbrook (Hants)	d																			06 17			
63½	—	**Southampton Central** ⛴	a	22p53			23p57						05 54						06 27			06 24			
—	—		d	22p55			23p59			04 52	05 15		05 55				05 42	06 15	06 30			06 35			06 43
65½	—	St Denys	d				00 04			04 57							05 47					06 40			06 48
67	—	Swaythling	d				00 07			05 00							05 50					06 43			06 51
67¾	—	**Southampton Airport Pkwy** ✈	d	23p03			00 10			05 03	05 22		06 03				05 53	06 22	06 38			06 46		06 50	06 54
—	0	**Portsmouth Harbour** ⛴	d		23p17	23p24						05 00								05 43	06 00				
—	0¾	**Portsmouth & Southsea**	d		23p22	23p29						05 05								05 48	06 04				
—	1¾	Fratton	d		23p26	23p33						05 09								05 52	06 08				
—	4	Hilsea	d		23p30	23p37						05 13								05 56					
—	5½	Cosham	d		23p35	23p42						05 19								06 03	06 15				
—	8	Portchester	d		23p40	23p47						05 23								06 08					
—	11¼	Fareham	d		23p46	23p53						05 29								06 19	06 24				
—	16¾	Botley	d		23p54	23p59						05 37								06 27					
—	17¾	Hedge End	d		23p58	00 05						05 41								06 31					
69¼	22¼	Eastleigh 3	a	23p09	00 04	00 11	00 14			05 06		05 49	06 07				05 56			06 37		06 49		06 53	06 58
—	—		d	23p11		00 19				05 07		05 50	06 08							06 43		06 50		06 54	06 59
—	24¼	Chandlers Ford	d													06 06						06 55			
—	29½	**Romsey**	a													06 44					06 59	07 03			
73	—	Shawford	d							05 13		05 56								06 49					07 05
76¼	—	**Winchester**	d	23p23		00a28				05 19	05 31	06 02	06 18					06 31	06 48	06 55				07 05	07 10
84¾	—	Micheldever	d	23p32						05 27		06 10								07 04					
95	—	**Basingstoke**	a	23p42						05 38	05 46	06 20	06 34					06 46		07 14					07 27
—	—		d	23p44						05 39	05 47		06 35					06 47		07 17					07 36
—	—	Reading 7	a								06 04							07 04							
106¾	—	Fleet	d							05 50															07 52
109½	—	Farnborough (Main)	d							05 56															07 58
118½	—	**Woking**	a	00 02						06 06			06 53											07 40	08 09
—	—	**Clapham Junction**	a																						
138¾	—	**Clapham Junction** 10	a	00 23						06 26			07 14												
142¾	—	**London Waterloo** 15 ⊖	a	00 33						06 34			07 24						07 47	08 01				08 08	08 39

Weymouth, Bournemouth, Lymington, Romsey, Southampton and Basingstoke - London

Network Diagram - see first Page of Table 158

		GW	SW	SW	SW	SW	XC	SW	SW	SW	SW	SW	GW	GW	SW	XC	SW	SW	SW	GW	SW	XC	GW	SW	SW
			◇1 ⌶	◇1 ⌶	1	1	◇1 ⌶	1	◇1 ⌶	◇1 A ⌶	1	1	◇ ⌶	◇	1	◇1 ⌶	1	◇1 ⌶	◇1 A ⌶	◇	1	◇1 ⌶		1	1 ⌶
Weymouth	d									05 55									06 25	06 40					
Upwey	d									05 59									06 29	06 45					
Dorchester West	a																			06 52					
Dorchester South	d									06 07									06 37						
Moreton (Dorset)	d									06 14									06 44						
Wool	d									06 20									06 50						
Wareham	d									06 27									06 57						
Holton Heath	d									06 31															
Hamworthy	d									06 36									07 04						
Poole 4	a									06 40									07 08						
	d			06 11						06 41									07 11						07 20
Parkstone (Dorset)	d			06 15						06 45									07 15						07 24
Branksome	d			06 18						06 49									07 19						07 27
Bournemouth	a			06 23						06 54									07 24						07 32
	d		06 04	06 25			06 30		06 34	06 56								07 04	07 26			07 30			07 34
Pokesdown	d		06 08						06 38									07 08							07 38
Christchurch	d		06 12						06 42									07 12							07 42
Hinton Admiral	d		06 17						06 47									07 17							07 47
New Milton	d		06 21						06 51									07 21							07 51
Sway	d		06 26						06 56									07 26							07 56
Lymington Pier	d							06 44							07 14									07 44	
Lymington Town	d							06 46							07 16									07 46	
Brockenhurst 3	a		06 31				06 46	06 55	07 01						07 25			07 31				07 46		07 55	08 01
	d		06 33				06 49		07 03									07 33				07 49			08 03
Beaulieu Road	d																								08 08
Ashurst New Forest	d		06 41						07 11									07 41							08 12
Totton	d		06 46						07 16									07 46							08 17
Salisbury	d	06 19										06 50		07 11									07 36		
Dean	d											07 02													
Mottisfont & Dunbridge	d											07 08													
Romsey	d	06 38										07 13		07 30									07 56		
Redbridge	d											07 23													
Millbrook (Hants)	d											07 26													
Southampton Central ⛴	a	06 49	06 51	06 55			07 01		07 21	07 25		07 29		07 40				07 51	07 55			08 03	08 09		08 23
	d	06 53	07 00			07 10	07 15		07 30			07 35		07 42			07 38	08 00				08 15			08 48
St Denys	d											07 40													→
Swaythling	d											07 43					07 46								
Southampton Airport Pkwy ✈	d		07 08			07 18	07 22		07 38			07 46					07 49	08 08				08 22			
Portsmouth Harbour ⛴	d				06 23						06 50		07 05								07 24				
Portsmouth & Southsea	d				06 28						06 55		07 09								07 29				
Fratton	d				06 32						06 59		07 13								07 33				
Hilsea	d				06 36						07 03										07 37				
Cosham	d				06 42						07 08		07 21								07 43				
Portchester	d				06 46						07 13										07 48				
Fareham	d	07a14			06 53						07 20		07 29	08a05							07 54				
Botley	d				07 01						07 28										08 01				
Hedge End	d				07 05						07 32										08 06				
Eastleigh 3	a				07 11	07 21					07 38	07 49					07 53				08 12				
	d				07 13	07 30					07 43	07 50					07 54				08 13				
Chandlers Ford	d											07 55													
Romsey	a											08 03	08 10												
Shawford	d					07 36					07 49						08 00				08 20				
Winchester	d		07 18		07 22	07 42	07 31		07 48		07 55					08 01	08 06	08 18			08 26	08 31			
Micheldever	d				07 31						08 02														
Basingstoke	a				07 41	07 58	07 46				08 14					08 16	08 22	08 34			08 42	08 46			
	d				07 47	08 05	07 47				08 16					08 18	08 24	08 35			08 43	08 47			
Reading 7	a						08 04									08 36						09 04			
Fleet	d					08 22											08 40				08 54				
Farnborough (Main)	d					08 28											08 46				09 00				
Woking	a				08 05	08 38					08 34						08 58	08 53							
Clapham Junction	a																								
Clapham Junction 10	a																	09 14			09 26				
London Waterloo 15 ⊖	a		08 16		08 34	09 10			08 50		09 03						09 29	09 25			09 38				

A ⌶ from Bournemouth

Weymouth, Bournemouth, Lymington, Romsey, Southampton and Basingstoke - London

Network Diagram - see first Page of Table 158

		SW	SW	SW	SW	SW	SW	SW	SW	SW	GW	SW	GW	SW	XC	SW	SW	SW	SW	GW	SW	XC	SW	SW
		◇1 A 🛒	1	1	1	1 🛒	1	◇1 🛒	1 🛒	1	◇ 🛒	1	◇ 🛒	1	◇1 🛒	◇1 A 🛒	1	1	1	◇ 🛒	1	◇1 🛒	1	◇1 A 🛒
Weymouth	d	06 55								07 25						07 55								08 20
Upwey	d	06 59								07 29						07 59								08 24
Dorchester West	a																							
Dorchester South	d	07 07								07 37						08 07								08 33
Moreton (Dorset)	d	07 14								07 44						08 14								08 39
Wool	d	07 20								07 50						08 20								08 45
Wareham	d	07 27								07 57						08 27								08 53
Holton Heath	d	07 31								08 01						08 31								08 56
Hamworthy	d	07 36								08 06						08 36								09 01
Poole 4	a	07 40								08 10						08 40								09 06
	d	07 41						07 55		08 11						08 41							08 50	09 07
Parkstone (Dorset)	d	07 45						07 59		08 15						08 45							08 54	
Branksome	d	07 49						08 02		08 19						08 49							08 57	
Bournemouth	a	07 54						08 07		08 24						08 54							09 02	09 16
	d	07 59						08 10		08 25					08 45	08 59							09 05	09 18
Pokesdown	d							08 14		08 29													09 09	09 22
Christchurch	d							08 18		08 33													09 13	09 26
Hinton Admiral	d							08 24		08 38													09 18	
New Milton	d							08 29		08 42													09 22	09 33
Sway	d							08 34		08 47													09 27	
Lymington Pier	d						08 14							08 44					09 14					
Lymington Town	d						08 16							08 46					09 16					
Brockenhurst 3	a	08 14					08 25	08 39		08 52				08 55	08 58	09 14			09 25				09 32	09 40
	d	08 15						08 41							09 00	09 15							09 33	09 41
Beaulieu Road	d																							
Ashurst New Forest	d							08 48															09 40	
Totton	d							08 53															09 45	
Salisbury	d			07 50									08 32					08 56						
Dean	d			08 02														09 08						
Mottisfont & Dunbridge	d			08 08														09 14						
Romsey	d			08 13									08 50					09 19						
Redbridge	d			08 21														09 27						
Millbrook (Hants)	d			08 25		←												09 31						
Southampton Central ⛴	a	08 28		08 27		08 23		08 58					09 04		09 12	09 28		09 34					09 52	09 55
	d			08 35		08 48		09 00					09 05		09 15	09 30		09 36				09 46	09 55	10 00
St Denys	d	08 30		08 40		08 53												09 41						
Swaythling	d			08 43		08 56												09 44						
Southampton Airport Pkwy ✈	d	08 38		08 46		08 59		09 08							09 22	09 38		09 46				09 53	10 03	10 08
Portsmouth Harbour ⛴	d		07 55		08 05						08 23	08 33					08 59			09 23	09 33			
Portsmouth & Southsea	d		08 00		08 10						08 27	08 38					09 04			09 27	09 38			
Fratton	d		08 04		08 13						08 31	08 42					09 08			09 31	09 42			
Hilsea	d		08 08		08 17							08 46					09 12				09 46			
Cosham	d		08 13		08 22						08 39	08 51					09 17			09 39	09 51			
Portchester	d		08 18		08 27							08 56					09 22				09 56			
Fareham	d		08 24		08 33						08 47	09a01	09a27				09 28			09 47	10a01			
Botley	d		08 31		08 41												09 35							
Hedge End	d		08 36		08 45												09 40							
Eastleigh 3	a		08 42	08 49	08 51	09 03											09 46	09 50					10 06	
	d		08 43	08 50	08 54	09 14											09 47	09 51					10 14	
Chandlers Ford	d			08 55														09 56						
Romsey	a			09 03							09 21							10 03		10 21				
Shawford	d		08 49			09 19			←														10 19	
Winchester	d	08 48	08 56		09 03	09 25		09 18	09 25						09 31	09 48	09 56					10 03	10 25	10 18
Micheldever	d		09 04			→											10 05						→	
Basingstoke	a		09 15		09 19			09 35	09 41						09 46		10 15					10 18		10 34
	d		09 17					09 36	09 43						09 47		10 17					10 19		10 35
Reading 7	a														10 04							10 36		
Fleet	d								09 54															
Farnborough (Main)	d		09 30						10 00								10 30							
Woking	a	09 22	09 39					09 54								10 20	10 39							
Clapham Junction	a																							
Clapham Junction 10	a	09 43						10 15	10 25															11 12
London Waterloo 15 ⊖	a	09 43	10 08					10 23	10 34							10 49	11 08							11 20

A 🛒 from Bournemouth

Weymouth, Bournemouth, Lymington, Romsey, Southampton and Basingstoke - London

Network Diagram - see first Page of Table 158

		SW	GW	GW	SW	SW	XC	SW	SW	SW	GW	SW	SW	SW	SW	SW	GW	XC	SW	SW	SW	SW
		1	◇	1 🛒	1	1	◇1 🛒	◇1 A 🛒	1	1	◇ 🛒	1	1	1	◇1 A 🛒	1	◇ 🛒	◇1 🛒	1	◇1 A 🛒	1	1
Weymouth	d		08 53					09 03							09 20					10 03		
Upwey	d		08 58												09 24							
Dorchester West	a		09 05																			
Dorchester South	d							09 13							09 33					10 13		
Moreton (Dorset)	d														09 39							
Wool	d														09 45							
Wareham	d							09 28							09 53					10 28		
Holton Heath	d														09 56							
Hamworthy	d							09 35							10 01					10 35		
Poole 4	a							09 39							10 06					10 39		
	d				09 13			09 40					09 50		10 07					10 40		
Parkstone (Dorset)	d				09 17			09 44					09 54							10 44		
Branksome	d				09 20			09 48					09 57							10 48		
Bournemouth	a				09 25			09 53					10 02		10 17					10 54		
	d				09 27		09 45	09 55					10 05		10 22			10 45		10 59		
Pokesdown	d				09 30								10 09		10 26							
Christchurch	d				09 34								10 13		10 30							
Hinton Admiral	d				09 39								10 18									
New Milton	d				09 44								10 22		10 37							
Sway	d				09 48								10 27									
Lymington Pier	d					09 44								10 27					10 57			
Lymington Town	d					09 46								10 29					10 59			
Brockenhurst 3	a				09 53	09 55	09 59	10 10					10 32	10 38	10 44			10 58	11 08	11 14		
	d				09 54		10 00	10 11					10 33		10 45			11 00		11 15		
Beaulieu Road	d																					
Ashurst New Forest	d												10 40									
Totton	d												10 45									
Salisbury	d			09 32						09 56							10 30					10 56
Dean	d									10 08												11 08
Mottisfont & Dunbridge	d									10 14												11 14
Romsey	d			09 50						10 19							10 50					11 20
Redbridge	d									10 27												11 27
Millbrook (Hants)	d									10 31												11 31
Southampton Central ⛴	a			10 04	10 09		10 12	10 26		10 34			10 53		10 58		11 04	11 12		11 28		11 34
	d			10 05			10 15	10 30		10 35			10 55		11 00		11 05	11 15		11 30		11 35
St Denys	d									10 40												11 40
Swaythling	d									10 43												11 43
Southampton Airport Pkwy ✈	d						10 22	10 38		10 46			11 03		11 08			11 22		11 38		11 46
Portsmouth Harbour ⛴	d								09 59		10 23	10 33									10 59	
Portsmouth & Southsea	d								10 04		10 27	10 38									11 04	
Fratton	d								10 08		10 31	10 42									11 08	
Hilsea	d								10 12			10 46									11 12	
Cosham	d								10 17		10 39	10 51									11 17	
Portchester	d								10 22			10 56									11 22	
Fareham	d			10a27					10 28		10 47	11a01					11a27				11 28	
Botley	d								10 35												11 35	
Hedge End	d								10 40												11 40	
Eastleigh 3	a								10 46	10 49			11 06								11 46	11 49
	d								10 47	10 50			11 14								11 47	11 50
Chandlers Ford	d									10 55												11 55
Romsey	a									11 03	11 21											12 03
Shawford	d	←											11 19			←						
Winchester	d	10 25					10 31	10 48	10 56				11 25		11 18	11 25		11 31		11 48	11 56	
Micheldever	d								11 05				→								12 05	
Basingstoke	a	10 41					10 46		11 15						11 34	11 41		11 46			12 15	
	d	10 43					10 47		11 17						11 35	11 43		11 47			12 17	
Reading 7	a						11 04											12 04				
Fleet	d	10 54														11 54						
Farnborough (Main)	d	11 00							11 30							12 00					12 30	
Woking	a							11 19	11 39											12 19	12 39	
Clapham Junction	a																					
Clapham Junction 10	a	11 25													12 12	12 25						
London Waterloo 15 ⊖	a	11 34						11 49	12 08						12 20	12 34				12 49	13 07	

A 🛒 from Bournemouth

Table 158

Mondays to Fridays

Weymouth, Bournemouth, Lymington, Romsey, Southampton and Basingstoke - London

Network Diagram - see first Page of Table 158

		GW	XC	SW	SW	SW	SW	GW	XC	GW	SW	SW	GW	SW	SW	GW	SW	SW	SW	SW	GW	XC	SW
		◇ ⌶	◇[1] ⌶	[1]	[1]	◇[1] A ⌶	[1]	◇ ⌶	◇[1] ⌶		[1]	◇[1] A ⌶		[1]	[1]	◇ ⌶	[1]	[1]	◇[1] A ⌶	[1]	◇ ⌶	◇[1] ⌶	[1]
Weymouth	d					10 20						11 03	11 10						11 20				
Upwey	d					10 24							11 15						11 24				
Dorchester West	a												11 22										
Dorchester South	d					10 33						11 13							11 33				
Moreton (Dorset)	d					10 39													11 39				
Wool	d					10 45													11 45				
Wareham	d					10 53						11 28							11 53				
Holton Heath	d					10 56													11 56				
Hamworthy	d					11 01						11 35							12 01				
Poole [4]	a					11 06						11 39							12 06				
	d			10 50		11 07						11 40					11 50		12 07				
Parkstone (Dorset)	d			10 54								11 44					11 54						
Branksome	d			10 57								11 48					11 57						
Bournemouth	a			11 02		11 17						11 54					12 02		12 17				
	d			11 05		11 22			11 45			11 59					12 05		12 22			12 45	
Pokesdown	d			11 09		11 26											12 09		12 26				
Christchurch	d			11 13		11 30											12 13		12 30				
Hinton Admiral	d			11 18													12 18						
New Milton	d			11 22		11 37											12 22		12 37				
Sway	d			11 27													12 27						
Lymington Pier	d				11 27						11 57							12 27					12 57
Lymington Town	d				11 29						11 59							12 29					12 59
Brockenhurst [3]	a			11 32	11 38	11 44			11 58		12 08	12 14					12 32	12 38	12 44			12 58	13 08
	d			11 33		11 45			12 00			12 15					12 33		12 45			13 00	
Beaulieu Road	d			11 38																			
Ashurst New Forest	d			11 42													12 40						
Totton	d			11 47													12 45						
Salisbury	d							11 32		11 42					11 56						12 32		
Dean	d														12 08								
Mottisfont & Dunbridge	d														12 14								
Romsey	d							11 50		12 10					12 19						12 50		
Redbridge	d														12 27								
Millbrook (Hants)	d														12 31								
Southampton Central ⛴	a			11 53		11 58		12 04	12 12	12 22		12 28			12 34		12 52		12 58		13 04	13 12	
	d		11 46	11 55		12 00		12 05	12 15			12 30			12 35		12 55		13 00		13 05	13 15	
St Denys	d														12 40								
Swaythling	d														12 43								
Southampton Airport Pkwy ✈	d		11 53	12 03		12 08			12 22			12 38			12 46		13 03		13 08			13 22	
Portsmouth Harbour ⛴	d	11 23												11 59		12 23							
Portsmouth & Southsea	d	11 27												12 04		12 27							
Fratton	d	11 31												12 08		12 31							
Hilsea	d													12 12									
Cosham	d	11 39												12 17		12 39							
Portchester	d													12 22									
Fareham	d	11 47						12a27						12 28		12 47					13a27		
Botley	d													12 35									
Hedge End	d													12 40									
Eastleigh [3]	a			12 06										12 46	12 49		13 06						
	d			12 14										12 47	12 50		13 14						
Chandlers Ford	d														12 55								
Romsey	a	12 21													13 03	13 21							
Shawford	d			12 19			←										13 19			←			
Winchester	d		12 02	12 25		12 18	12 25		12 31			12 48		12 56			13 25		13 18	13 25		13 31	
Micheldever	d			→										13 05			→						
Basingstoke	a		12 17			12 34	12 41		12 46					13 15					13 34	13 41		13 46	
	d		12 18			12 35	12 43		12 47					13 17					13 35	13 43		13 47	
Reading [7]	a		12 36						13 04													14 04	
Fleet	d						12 54													13 54			
Farnborough (Main)	d						13 00							13 30						14 00			
Woking	a											13 19		13 39									
Clapham Junction	a																						
Clapham Junction [10]	a					13 12	13 25												14 12	14 25			
London Waterloo [15] ⊖	a					13 20	13 34					13 49		14 07					14 20	14 34			

A ⌶ from Bournemouth

Table 158

Mondays to Fridays

Weymouth, Bournemouth, Lymington, Romsey, Southampton and Basingstoke - London

Network Diagram - see first Page of Table 158

		SW	SW	SW	GW	XC	SW	SW	SW	SW	GW	XC	SW	SW	GW	SW	GW	GW	SW	SW	SW	SW
		◇[1] A ⌶	[1]	[1]	◇ ⌶	◇[1]	[1]	[1]	◇[1] A ⌶	[1]	◇ ⌶	◇[1] ⌶	[1]	◇[1] A ⌶	◇	[1]	[1] ⌶	[1] ⌶	[1]	[1]	[1]	◇[1] A ⌶
Weymouth	d	12 03							12 20					13 03	13 10							13 20
Upwey	d								12 24						13 15							13 24
Dorchester West	a														13 22							
Dorchester South	d	12 13							12 33					13 13								13 33
Moreton (Dorset)	d								12 39													13 39
Wool	d								12 45													13 45
Wareham	d	12 28							12 53					13 28								13 53
Holton Heath	d								12 56													13 56
Hamworthy	d	12 35							13 01					13 35								14 01
Poole [4]	a	12 39							13 06					13 39								14 06
	d	12 40					12 50		13 07					13 40						13 50		14 07
Parkstone (Dorset)	d	12 44					12 54							13 44						13 54		
Branksome	d	12 48					12 57							13 48						13 57		
Bournemouth	a	12 54					13 02		13 17					13 54						14 02		14 17
	d	12 59					13 05		13 22			13 45		13 59						14 05		14 22
Pokesdown	d						13 09		13 26											14 09		14 26
Christchurch	d						13 13		13 30											14 13		14 30
Hinton Admiral	d						13 18													14 18		
New Milton	d						13 22		13 37											14 22		14 37
Sway	d						13 27													14 27		
Lymington Pier	d							13 27					13 57								14 27	
Lymington Town	d							13 29					13 59								14 29	
Brockenhurst [3]	a	13 14					13 32	13 38	13 44			13 58	14 08	14 14						14 32	14 38	14 44
	d	13 15					13 33		13 45			14 00		14 15						14 33		14 45
Beaulieu Road	d																					
Ashurst New Forest	d						13 40													14 40		
Totton	d						13 45													14 45		
Salisbury	d			12 56							13 32							13 59	13 50			
Dean	d			13 08															14 02			
Mottisfont & Dunbridge	d			13 14															14 08			
Romsey	d			13 19							13 50							14 19	14 13			
Redbridge	d			13 27															14 21			
Millbrook (Hants)	d			13 31															14 24			
Southampton Central ⛴	a	13 28		13 34			13 53		13 58		14 04	14 12		14 28				14 32	14 28	14 53		14 58
	d	13 30		13 35		13 46	13 55		14 00		14 05	14 15		14 30				14 34	14 35	14 55		15 00
St Denys	d			13 40															14 40			
Swaythling	d			13 43															14 43			
Southampton Airport Pkwy ✈	d	13 38		13 46		13 53	14 03		14 08			14 22		14 38					14 46	15 03		15 08
Portsmouth Harbour ⛴	d		12 59		13 23											13 59	14 23					
Portsmouth & Southsea	d		13 04		13 27											14 04	14 27					
Fratton	d		13 08		13 31											14 08	14 31					
Hilsea	d		13 12													14 12						
Cosham	d		13 17		13 39											14 17	14 39					
Portchester	d		13 22													14 22						
Fareham	d		13 28		13 47						14a27					14 28	14 47	14a55				
Botley	d		13 35													14 35						
Hedge End	d		13 40													14 40						
Eastleigh [3]	a		13 46	13 49			14 06									14 46			14 49	15 06		
	d		13 47	13 50			14 14									14 47			14 50	15 14		
Chandlers Ford	d			13 55															14 55			
Romsey	a			14 03	14 21												15 21		15 04			
Shawford	d						14 19			←										15 19		
Winchester	d	13 48	13 56			14 03	14 25		14 18	14 25		14 31		14 48		14 56				15 25		15 18
Micheldever	d		14 05				→									15 05				→		
Basingstoke	a		14 15			14 18			14 34	14 41		14 46				15 15						15 34
	d		14 17			14 19			14 35	14 43		14 47				15 17						15 35
Reading [7]	a					14 36						15 04										
Fleet	d									14 54												
Farnborough (Main)	d		14 30							15 00						15 30						
Woking	a	14 19	14 39											15 19		15 39						
Clapham Junction	a																					
Clapham Junction [10]	a								15 12	15 25												16 12
London Waterloo [15] ⊖	a	14 49	15 08						15 20	15 34				15 49		16 07						16 20

A ⌶ from Bournemouth

Weymouth, Bournemouth, Lymington, Romsey, Southampton and Basingstoke - London

Network Diagram - see first Page of Table 158

		SW	GW	XC	SW	SW	SW	SW	GW	XC	SW	SW	SW	SW	GW	XC	SW	SW	GW	SW	SW	GW	SW
		[1]	◇ 🍴	◇[1] 🍴	[1]	◇[1] A 🍴	[1]	[1]	■ 🍴	◇[1] 🍴	[1]	[1]	◇[1] A 🍴	[1]	◇ 🍴	◇[1] 🍴	[1]	◇[1] A 🍴	◇	[1]	[1]	■ 🍴	[1]
Weymouth	d					14 03							14 20					15 03	15 08				
Upwey	d												14 24						15 13				
Dorchester West	a																		15 20				
Dorchester South	d					14 13							14 33					15 13					
Moreton (Dorset)	d												14 39										
Wool	d												14 45										
Wareham	d					14 28							14 53					15 28					
Holton Heath	d												14 56										
Hamworthy	d					14 35							15 01					15 35					
Poole [4]	a					14 39							15 06					15 39					
	d					14 40					14 50		15 07					15 40					
Parkstone (Dorset)	d					14 44					14 54							15 44					
Branksome	d					14 48					14 57							15 48					
Bournemouth	a					14 54					15 02		15 17					15 54					
	d			14 45		14 59					15 05		15 22			15 45		15 59					
Pokesdown	d										15 09		15 26										
Christchurch	d										15 13		15 30										
Hinton Admiral	d										15 18												
New Milton	d										15 22		15 37										
Sway	d										15 27												
Lymington Pier	d				14 57							15 27					15 57						
Lymington Town	d				14 59							15 29					15 59						
Brockenhurst [3]	a			14 58	15 08	15 14					15 32	15 38	15 44			15 58	16 08	16 14					
	d			15 00		15 15					15 33		15 45			16 00		16 15					
Beaulieu Road	d																						
Ashurst New Forest	d										15 40												
Totton	d										15 45												
Salisbury	d		14 32					14 56							15 32						15 56		
Dean	d							15 08													16 08		
Mottisfont & Dunbridge	d							15 14													16 14		
Romsey	d		14 50					15 19							15 50						16 19		
Redbridge	d							15 27													16 27		
Millbrook (Hants)	d							15 31													16 31		
Southampton Central ⛴	a		15 04	15 12		15 28		15 34			15 51		15 58		16 04	16 12		16 28			16 34		
	d		15 05	15 15		15 30		15 35		15 47	15 55		16 00		16 05	16 15		16 30			16 35		
St Denys	d							15 40													16 40		
Swaythling	d							15 43													16 43		
Southampton Airport Pkwy ✈	d			15 22		15 38		15 46			16 03		16 08			16 22		16 38			16 46		
Portsmouth Harbour ⛴	d						14 59		15 23											15 59		16 23	16 49
Portsmouth & Southsea	d						15 04		15 27											16 04		16 27	16 55
Fratton	d						15 08		15 31											16 08		16 31	16 59
Hilsea	d						15 12													16 12			17 03
Cosham	d						15 17		15 39											16 17		16 39	17 08
Portchester	d						15 22													16 22			17 13
Fareham	d		15a27				15 28		15 47						16a27					16 28		16 47	17a18
Botley	d						15 35													16 35			
Hedge End	d						15 40													16 40			
Eastleigh [3]	a						15 46	15 49			16 07									16 46	16 49		
	d						15 47	15 50			16 14									16 47	16 50		
Chandlers Ford	d							15 55													16 55		
Romsey	a							16 03	16 21												17 03	17 21	
Shawford	d	←									16 19			←									
Winchester	d	15 25		15 31		15 48	15 56				16 25		16 18	16 25		16 31		16 48		16 56			
Micheldever	d						16 05				→									17 05			
Basingstoke	a	15 41		15 46			16 15			16 17			16 34	16 41		16 46				17 15			
	d	15 43		15 47			16 17			16 18			16 35	16 43		16 47				17 17			
Reading [7]	a			16 04						16 35						17 03							
Fleet	d	15 54												16 54									
Farnborough (Main)	d	16 00					16 30							17 00						17 30			
Woking	a					16 19	16 39											17 20		17 39			
Clapham Junction	a																						
Clapham Junction [10]	a	16 25											17 12	17 25									
London Waterloo [15] ⊖	a	16 34				16 49	17 08						17 20	17 36				17 50		18 08			

A 🍴 from Bournemouth

Weymouth, Bournemouth, Lymington, Romsey, Southampton and Basingstoke - London

Network Diagram - see first Page of Table 158

		SW	SW	SW	SW	GW	XC	SW	SW	SW	SW	SW	GW	SW	XC	SW	SW	SW	SW	GW	XC	SW	SW	SW
		[1]	[1]	◇[1] A 🍴	[1]	◇ 🍴	◇[1] 🍴	[1]	◇[1] A 🍴	[1]	[1]	[1]	◇ 🍴	[1]	◇[1] 🍴	[1]	[1]	◇[1] A 🍴	[1]	◇ 🍴	◇[1] 🍴	[1]	[1]	◇[1] A 🍴
Weymouth	d			15 20					16 03									16 20						17 04
Upwey	d			15 24														16 24						
Dorchester West	a																							
Dorchester South	d			15 33					16 13									16 33						17 14
Moreton (Dorset)	d			15 39														16 39						
Wool	d			15 45														16 45						
Wareham	d			15 53					16 28									16 53						17 29
Holton Heath	d			15 56														16 56						
Hamworthy	d			16 01					16 35									17 01						17 36
Poole [4]	a			16 06					16 39									17 06						17 40
	d	15 50		16 07					16 40							16 50		17 07						17 41
Parkstone (Dorset)	d	15 54							16 44							16 54								17 45
Branksome	d	15 57							16 48							16 57								17 49
Bournemouth	a	16 02		16 17					16 54							17 02		17 17						17 54
	d	16 05		16 22			16 45		16 59							17 05		17 22			17 45			17 59
Pokesdown	d	16 09		16 26												17 09		17 26						
Christchurch	d	16 13		16 30												17 13		17 30						
Hinton Admiral	d	16 18														17 18								
New Milton	d	16 22		16 37												17 22		17 37						
Sway	d	16 27														17 27								
Lymington Pier	d		16 27					16 57									17 27					17 57		
Lymington Town	d		16 29					16 59									17 29					17 59		
Brockenhurst [3]	a	16 32	16 38	16 44			16 58	17 08	17 14							17 32	17 38	17 44			17 58	18 08		18 14
	d	16 33		16 45			17 00		17 15			17 20				17 33		17 45			18 00			18 15
Beaulieu Road	d																							
Ashurst New Forest	d	16 40										17 27				17 40								
Totton	d	16 45										17 32				17 45								
Salisbury	d					16 32					16 56									17 32				
Dean	d										17 08													
Mottisfont & Dunbridge	d										17 14													
Romsey	d					16 50					17 19									17 50				
Redbridge	d										17 27													
Millbrook (Hants)	d										17 31													
Southampton Central ⛴	a	16 51		16 58		17 04	17 12		17 28		17 34	17 41				17 53		17 58		18 04	18 12			18 28
	d	16 52		17 00		17 05	17 15		17 30		17 35				17 46	17 55		18 00		18 05	18 15		18 17	18 30
St Denys	d	16 57									17 40												18 22	
Swaythling	d	17 00									17 43												18 25	
Southampton Airport Pkwy ✈	d	17 04		17 08			17 22		17 38		17 46				17 53	18 03		18 08			18 22		18 28	18 38
Portsmouth Harbour ⛴	d									16 59			17 23	17 33										
Portsmouth & Southsea	d									17 04			17 27	17 38										
Fratton	d									17 08			17 31	17 42										
Hilsea	d									17 12				17 46										
Cosham	d									17 17			17 39	17 51										
Portchester	d									17 22				17 56										
Fareham	d					17a27				17 28			17 47	18a01						18a27				
Botley	d									17 35														
Hedge End	d									17 40														
Eastleigh [3]	a	17 07								17 46	17 49					18 06							18 32	
	d	17 14								17 47	17 50					18 14							18 33	
Chandlers Ford	d										17 55													
Romsey	a										18 03		18 21											
Shawford	d	17 19			←											18 19			←					
Winchester	d	17 25		17 18	17 25		17 31		17 48	17 56					18 02	18 25		18 18	18 25		18 31		18 41	18 48
Micheldever	d	→								18 05						→								
Basingstoke	a			17 34	17 42		17 46			18 15					18 17			18 34	18 41		18 46			
	d			17 36	17 43		17 47			18 17					18 18			18 35	18 43		18 47			
Reading [7]	a						18 04								18 36						19 04			
Fleet	d				17 54														18 54					
Farnborough (Main)	d				18 00					18 30									19 00					
Woking	a								18 19	18 39														19 24
Clapham Junction	a																							
Clapham Junction [10]	a			18 12	18 25													19 12	19 26					
London Waterloo [15] ⊖	a			18 23	18 34				18 47	19 08								19 20	19 34					19 51

A 🍴 from Bournemouth

Table 158

Mondays to Fridays

Weymouth, Bournemouth, Lymington, Romsey, Southampton and Basingstoke - London

Network Diagram - see first Page of Table 158

		SW	SW	GW	SW	SW	SW	SW	GW	GW	XC	SW	SW	SW	SW	GW	SW	SW	SW	GW	SW	XC
		■	■	◇	■	■	◇■	■	◇	■	◇■	◇■	■	■	■	◇	■	◇■	■	■	■	◇■
							A					A						A				
				⌶			⌶			⌶	⌶	⌶						⌶		⌶		
Weymouth	d						17 20		17 30			18 06						18 20				
Upwey	d						17 24		17 35									18 24				
Dorchester West	a								17 42													
Dorchester South	d						17 33					18 16						18 33				
Moreton (Dorset)	d						17 39											18 39				
Wool	d						17 45											18 45				
Wareham	d						17 53					18 31						18 53				
Holton Heath	d						17 56											18 56				
Hamworthy	d						18 01					18 38						19 01				
Poole ■	a						18 06					18 42						19 06				
	d				17 50		18 07					18 43					18 50	19 07				
Parkstone (Dorset)	d				17 54							18 47					18 54					
Branksome	d				17 57							18 51					18 57					
Bournemouth	a				18 02		18 17					18 56					19 02	19 17				
	d				18 05		18 22				18 45	18 59					19 05	19 22				19 45
Pokesdown	d				18 09		18 26										19 09	19 26				
Christchurch	d				18 13		18 30										19 13	19 30				
Hinton Admiral	d				18 18												19 18					
New Milton	d				18 22		18 37										19 22	19 37				
Sway	d				18 27												19 27					
Lymington Pier	d					18 27									19 03						19 33	
Lymington Town	d					18 29									19 05						19 35	
Brockenhurst ■	a				18 32	18 38	18 44				18 58	19 14			19 14		19 32	19 44			19 44	19 58
	d				18 33		18 45				19 00	19 15					19 33	19 45				20 00
Beaulieu Road	d				18 38																	
Ashurst New Forest	d				18 42												19 41					
Totton	d				18 47												19 46					
Salisbury	d		17 56							18 35				18 56						19 32		
Dean	d		18 08											19 08								
Mottisfont & Dunbridge	d		18 14											19 14								
Romsey	d		18 19							18 54				19 19						19 50		
Redbridge	d		18 27											19 27								
Millbrook (Hants)	d		18 31											19 31								
Southampton Central ⛴	a		18 34		18 53		18 58			19 04	19 12	19 28		19 34			19 52	19 58		20 04		20 12
	d		18 35		18 55		19 00			19 05	19 15	19 30		19 35			19 55	20 00		20 05		20 15
St Denys	d		18 40											19 40								
Swaythling	d		18 43											19 43								
Southampton Airport Pkwy ✈	d		18 46		19 03		19 08				19 22	19 38		19 46			20 03	20 08				20 22
Portsmouth Harbour ⛴	d	17 59		18 23									18 59			19 23						
Portsmouth & Southsea	d	18 04		18 27									19 04			19 27						
Fratton	d	18 08		18 31									19 08			19 31						
Hilsea	d	18 12											19 12									
Cosham	d	18 17		18 39									19 17			19 39						
Portchester	d	18 22											19 22									
Fareham	d	18 28		18 47						19a27			19 28			19 47				20a27		
Botley	d	18 35											19 35									
Hedge End	d	18 40											19 40									
Eastleigh ■	a	18 46	18 49		19 06								19 46	19 49			20 06					
	d	18 47	18 50		19 14								19 47	19 50			20 14					
Chandlers Ford	d		18 55											19 55								
Romsey	a		19 04	19 21										20 03		20 21						
Shawford	d				19 19			←									20 19		←			
Winchester	d	18 56			19 25		19 18	19 25			19 31	19 48	19 56				20 25	20 18	20 25			20 31
Micheldever	d	19 05			→								20 05				→					
Basingstoke	a	19 15					19 34	19 41			19 46		20 15					20 34	20 41			20 46
	d	19 17					19 35	19 43			19 47		20 17					20 36	20 43			20 47
Reading ■	a										20 04											21 04
Fleet	d							19 54											20 54			
Farnborough (Main)	d	19 30						20 00					20 30						21 00			
Woking	a	19 39										20 19	20 39						21 09			
Clapham Junction	a																					
Clapham Junction ■	a						20 12	20 25										21 16	21 29			
London Waterloo ■ ⊖	a	20 08					20 20	20 34				20 49	21 07					21 24	21 38			

A ⌶ from Bournemouth

Table 158

Mondays to Fridays

Weymouth, Bournemouth, Lymington, Romsey, Southampton and Basingstoke - London

Network Diagram - see first Page of Table 158

		SW	SW	SW	SW	GW	GW	SW	SW	SW	GW	SW	SW	SW	SW	SW	SW	SW	GW	GW	GW	SW	SW	SW	SW
		◇■	■	■	■	◇	◇	■	◇■	■	◇	■	■	■	■	■	■	◇■			◇	■	■	■	■
		A																							
		⌶									⌶														
Weymouth	d	19 06							19 20									20 10	20 21						
Upwey	d								19 24									20 14	20 26						
Dorchester West	a																		20 33						
Dorchester South	d	19 16							19 37									20 22							
Moreton (Dorset)	d								19 43									20 28							
Wool	d								19 49									20 34							
Wareham	d	19 31							19 57									20 42							
Holton Heath	d																								
Hamworthy	d	19 38							20 03									20 48							
Poole ■	a	19 42							20 08									20 53							
	d	19 43						19 50	20 09									20 54							
Parkstone (Dorset)	d	19 47						19 54										20 58							
Branksome	d	19 51						19 57										21 01							
Bournemouth	a	19 56						20 02	20 18									21 07							
	d	19 59						20 05	20 22									21 12							
Pokesdown	d							20 09	20 26									21 16							
Christchurch	d							20 13	20 30									21 20							
Hinton Admiral	d							20 18										21 25							
New Milton	d							20 22	20 37									21 29							
Sway	d							20 27										21 34							
Lymington Pier	d				20 03							20 33				21 03						21 33			
Lymington Town	d				20 05							20 35				21 05						21 35			
Brockenhurst ■	a	20 14			20 14			20 32	20 44			20 44				21 14		21 39				21 44			
	d	20 15						20 33	20 45									21 40							
Beaulieu Road	d																								
Ashurst New Forest	d							20 40										21 47							
Totton	d							20 45										21 52							
Salisbury	d			19 56		20 14					20 32				20 56						21 32				21 56
Dean	d			20 08											21 08										22 08
Mottisfont & Dunbridge	d			20 14											21 14										22 14
Romsey	d			20 19		20 35					20 50				21 19						21 50				22 19
Redbridge	d			20 27											21 27										22 27
Millbrook (Hants)	d			20 31											21 31										22 31
Southampton Central ⛴	a	20 28		20 34		20 48		20 51	20 58		21 04				21 34			21 57			22 02				22 34
	d	20 30		20 35				20 55	21 00		21 05			21 30	21 35		21 55	22 00			22 04			22 30	22 35
St Denys	d			20 40											21 40										22 40
Swaythling	d			20 43											21 43										22 43
Southampton Airport Pkwy ✈	d	20 38		20 46				21 03	21 08					21 38	21 46		22 03	22 08						22 38	22 46
Portsmouth Harbour ⛴	d		19 59				20 23						20 59							21 23			21 54		
Portsmouth & Southsea	d		20 04				20 27						21 04							21 27			21 59		
Fratton	d		20 08				20 31						21 08							21 31			22 03		
Hilsea	d		20 12										21 12										22 07		
Cosham	d		20 17										21 17										22 12		
Portchester	d		20 22										21 22										22 17		
Fareham	d		20 28				20 47				21a27		21 28							21 48			22 26		
Botley	d		20 35										21 35										22 33		
Hedge End	d		20 40										21 40										22 37		
Eastleigh ■	a		20 46	20 49				21 06					21 46		21 49		22 06			22 06	22 14		22 43		22 49
	d		20 47	20 50				21 14					21 47		21 50		22 14			22 11					22 50
Chandlers Ford	d			20 55											21 55										22 55
Romsey	a			21 03			21 21								22 03					22 33					23 03
Shawford	d		20 53					21 19		←							22 19								
Winchester	d	20 48	20 59					21 25	21 18	21 25			21 56	21 48			22 25	22 18						22 55	
Micheldever	d		21 07					→					22 05												
Basingstoke	a		21 21						21 34	21 41			22 15				22 41	22 34						23 11	
	d		21 24						21 35	21 43			22 24				22 43	22 36						23 13	
Reading ■	a																								
Fleet	d		21 40							21 54			22 40				22 54								
Farnborough (Main)	d		21 46							22 00			22 46				23 00								
Woking	a	21 19	21 58							22 09			22 59	22 19			23 09	22 54						23 31	
Clapham Junction	a																								
Clapham Junction ■	a								22 14	22 29							23 29	23 14						23 55	
London Waterloo ■ ⊖	a	21 49	22 34						22 22	22 38			23 32	22 49			23 42	23 23						00 09	

A ⌶ from Bournemouth

Weymouth, Bournemouth, Lymington, Romsey, Southampton and Basingstoke - London

Network Diagram - see first Page of Table 158

		SW 1	SW 1	SW 1	SW 1	GW ◇	SW 1	SW 1		SW ◇1	SW 1
Weymouth	d		21 10							22 10	23 10
Upwey	d		21 14							22 14	23 14
Dorchester West	a										
Dorchester South	d									22 22	23 22
Moreton (Dorset)	d		21 28							22 28	23 28
Wool	d		21 34							22 34	23 34
Wareham	d		21 42							22 42	23 42
Holton Heath	d										
Hamworthy	d		21 48							22 48	23 48
Poole 4	a		21 53							22 53	23 53
	d		21 54							22 54	23 54
Parkstone (Dorset)	d		21 58							22 58	
Branksome	d		22 01							23 01	
Bournemouth	a		22 07							23 07	00 03
	d		22 12							23 12	
Pokesdown	d		22 16							23 16	
Christchurch	d		22 20							23 20	
Hinton Admiral	d		22 25							23 25	
New Milton	d		22 29							23 29	
Sway	d		22 34							23 34	
Lymington Pier	d	22 03		22 33							
Lymington Town	d	22 05		22 35							
Brockenhurst 3	a	22 14	22 39	22 44						23 39	
	d		22 40							23 40	
Beaulieu Road	d										
Ashurst New Forest	d		22 47							23 47	
Totton	d		22 52							23 52	
Salisbury	d					22 32					
Dean	d										
Mottisfont & Dunbridge	d										
Romsey	d					22 53	22 58				
Redbridge	d						23 05				
Millbrook (Hants)	d						23 09				
Southampton Central ⛴	a		22 57			23 04	23 11			23 57	
	d		23 00			23 05	23 20			23 59	
St Denys	d		23 04				23 25			00 04	
Swaythling	d						23 28			00 07	
Southampton Airport Pkwy ✈	d		23 08				23 31			00 10	
Portsmouth Harbour ⛴	d				22 33			23 24			
Portsmouth & Southsea	d				22 38			23 29			
Fratton	d				22 42			23 33			
Hilsea	d				22 46			23 37			
Cosham	d				22 51			23 42			
Portchester	d				22 56			23 47			
Fareham	d				23a01	23a27		23 53			
Botley	d							23 59			
Hedge End	d							00 05			
Eastleigh 8	a		23 11				23 34	00 11		00 14	
	d		23 12				23 36	00 19			
Chandlers Ford	d						23 41				
Romsey	a						23 48				
Shawford	d		23 18								
Winchester	d		23 24					00a28			
Micheldever	d		23 33								
Basingstoke	a		23 43								
	d		23 44								
Reading 7	a										
Fleet	d		00 01								
Farnborough (Main)	d		00 06								
Woking	a		00 18								
Clapham Junction	a										
Clapham Junction 10	a		00 53								
London Waterloo 15 ⊖	a		01 04								

Weymouth, Bournemouth, Lymington, Romsey, Southampton and Basingstoke - London

Network Diagram - see first Page of Table 158

		SW 1	SW ◇1	SW 1	XC ◇1	SW 1	SW 1	SW 1	SW 1	SW 1	XC ◇1 🛒	SW ◇1 🛒	SW 1	SW 1	GW ◇	SW 1	XC ◇1 🛒	SW 1	GW	XC ◇1 🛒	GW ◇	SW 1	SW ◇1 A 🛒	SW 1	SW 1
Weymouth	d		22p10	23p10																	06 38				
Upwey	d		22p14	23p14																	06 43				
Dorchester West	a																				06 50				
Dorchester South	d		22p22	23p22																					
Moreton (Dorset)	d		22p28	23p28																					
Wool	d		22p34	23p34																					
Wareham	d		22p42	23p42																			06 10		
Holton Heath	d																						06 13		
Hamworthy	d		22p48	23p48																			06 18		
Poole 4	a		22p53	23p53																			06 23		
	d		22p54	23p54								05 28											06 24		
Parkstone (Dorset)	d		22p58									05 32											06 28		
Branksome	d		23p01									05 35											06 31		
Bournemouth	a		23p07	00 03								05 40											06 37		
	d		23p12									05 42					06 25			06 37			06 42		
Pokesdown	d		23p16									05 46											06 46		
Christchurch	d		23p20									05 50											06 50		
Hinton Admiral	d		23p25									05 55											06 55		
New Milton	d		23p29									05 59											06 59		
Sway	d		23p34									06 04											07 04		
Lymington Pier	d															06 27						06 57			
Lymington Town	d															06 29						06 59			
Brockenhurst 3	a		23p39									06 09				06 37	06 38			06 52		07 07	07 09		
	d		23p40									06 10					06 39			06 55			07 10		
Beaulieu Road	d																								
Ashurst New Forest	d		23p47									06 17											07 17		
Totton	d		23p52									06 22		06 12									07 22		
Salisbury	d								05 35										06 32						06 50
Dean	d								05 47																07 02
Mottisfont & Dunbridge	d								05 53																07 08
Romsey	d								05 58										06 50						07 13
Redbridge	d													06 14											07 21
Millbrook (Hants)	d													06 18											07 24
Southampton Central ⛴	a		23p57									06 27		06 21			06 52		07 02	07 07			07 27		07 27
	d		23p59		05 09	05 12		05 30		06 00	06 15	06 30		06 35			06 53	07 00	07 05	07 15			07 30		07 35
St Denys	d		00 04											06 40											07 40
Swaythling	d		00 07											06 43											07 43
Southampton Airport Pkwy ✈	d		00 10		05 16	05 19		05 41		06 08	06 22	06 38		06 46			07 01	07 08		07 22			07 38		07 46
Portsmouth Harbour ⛴	d	23p24											05 50		06 00									06 59	
Portsmouth & Southsea	d	23p29											05 55		06 04									07 04	
Fratton	d	23p33											05 59		06 08									07 08	
Hilsea	d	23p37											06 03											07 12	
Cosham	d	23p42					05 09						06 08		06 19									07 17	
Portchester	d	23p47					05 14						06 13											07 22	
Fareham	d	23p53					05 20						06 19		06 28				07a27					07 28	
Botley	d	23p59					05 27						06 26											07 35	
Hedge End	d	00 05					05 32						06 31											07 40	
Eastleigh 8	a	00 11	00 14			05 23	05 38	05 45		06 11		06 41	06 39	06 49				07 11						07 46	07 49
	d	00 19				05 24		05 46		06 13		06 42	06 47	06 50				07 14						07 47	07 50
Chandlers Ford	d								06 06					06 55											07 55
Romsey	a								06 43					07 03	07 10										08 03
Shawford	d												06 53					07 19							
Winchester	d	00a28			05 25	05 34		06 00		06 22	06 31	06 52	07 00				07 09	07 25		07 31			07 48	07 56	
Micheldever	d							06 08					07 08											08 05	
Basingstoke	a				05 40	05 50		06 19		06 39	06 46	07 08	07 19				07 24	07 41		07 46				08 15	
	d				05 41	05 54		06 24		06 40	06 47	07 09	07 24				07 25	07 43		07 47				08 17	
Reading 7	a				05 59						07 04						07 42			08 04					
Fleet	d					06 10		06 40					07 40					07 54							
Farnborough (Main)	d					06 16		06 46					07 46					08 00						08 30	
Woking	a					06 28		06 58		06 58		07 27	07 58					08 09					08 21	08 39	
Clapham Junction	a																								
Clapham Junction 10	a					06 57						07 24						08 30							
London Waterloo 15 ⊖	a					07 05		07 33		07 31		07 53	08 34					08 39					08 49	09 08	

A 🛒 from Bournemouth

Table 158

Saturdays

Weymouth, Bournemouth, Lymington, Romsey, Southampton and Basingstoke - London

Network Diagram - see first Page of Table 158

		GW	XC	SW	SW	SW	SW	SW	GW	GW	XC	SW	SW	SW	SW	GW	SW	SW	SW	SW	GW	XC	SW	SW	SW
		◇	◇1	1	1	1	◇1	1	◇		◇1	1	◇1	1	1	◇	1	1	◇1	1	◇	◇1	1	◇1	1
													A						A					A	
		🍴	🍴				🍴				🍴		🍴			🍴			🍴			🍴		🍴	
Weymouth	d												06 55						07 20					08 03	
Upwey	d												06 59						07 24						
Dorchester West	a																								
Dorchester South	d												07 07						07 33					08 13	
Moreton (Dorset)	d												07 14						07 39						
Wool	d												07 20						07 45						
Wareham	d												07 27						07 53					08 28	
Holton Heath	d												07 31						07 56						
Hamworthy	d												07 36						08 01					08 35	
Poole 4	a												07 40						08 06					08 39	
	d				06 50		07 07						07 41				07 50		08 07					08 40	
Parkstone (Dorset)	d				06 54								07 45				07 54							08 44	
Branksome	d				06 57								07 49				07 57							08 48	
Bournemouth	a				07 02		07 17						07 54				08 02		08 17					08 54	
	d				07 05		07 22				07 45		07 59				08 05		08 22			08 45		08 59	
Pokesdown	d				07 09		07 26										08 09		08 26						
Christchurch	d				07 13		07 30										08 13		08 30						
Hinton Admiral	d				07 18												08 18								
New Milton	d				07 22		07 37										08 22		08 37						
Sway	d				07 27												08 27								
Lymington Pier	d					07 27						07 57						08 27					08 57		
Lymington Town	d					07 29						07 59						08 29					08 59		
Brockenhurst 3	a				07 32	07 37	07 44				07 58	08 07	08 14				08 32	08 37	08 44			08 58	09 07	09 14	
	d				07 33		07 45				08 00		08 15				08 33		08 45			09 00		09 15	
Beaulieu Road	d																								
Ashurst New Forest	d				07 40												08 40								
Totton	d				07 45												08 45								
Salisbury	d								07 24	07 36					07 56						08 32				
Dean	d														08 08										
Mottisfont & Dunbridge	d														08 14										
Romsey	d								07 44	07 55					08 19						08 50				
Redbridge	d														08 27										
Millbrook (Hants)	d														08 31										
Southampton Central ⛴	a				07 52		07 58		08 02	08 07	08 12		08 28		08 34		08 52		08 58		09 03	09 12		09 28	
	d		07 47		07 55		08 00		08 05		08 15		08 30		08 35		08 55		09 00		09 05	09 15		09 30	
St Denys	d														08 40										
Swaythling	d														08 43										
Southampton Airport Pkwy ✈	d		07 54		08 03		08 08				08 22		08 38		08 46		09 03		09 08			09 22		09 38	
Portsmouth Harbour ⛴	d	07 23												07 59		08 23									08 59
Portsmouth & Southsea	d	07 27												08 04		08 27									09 04
Fratton	d	07 31												08 08		08 31									09 08
Hilsea	d													08 12											09 12
Cosham	d	07 39												08 17		08 39									09 17
Portchester	d													08 22											09 22
Fareham	d	07 47							08a27					08 28		08 47					09a27				09 28
Botley	d													08 35											09 35
Hedge End	d													08 40											09 40
Eastleigh 3	a				08 06									08 46	08 49		09 06								09 46
	d				08 14									08 47	08 50		09 14								09 47
Chandlers Ford	d														08 55										
Romsey	a	08 21													09 03	09 21									
Shawford	d				08 19			←									09 19			←					
Winchester	d		08 03		08 25		08 18	08 25			08 31		08 48	08 56			09 25		09 18	09 25		09 31		09 48	09 56
Micheldever	d				→									09 05			→								10 05
Basingstoke	a		08 17				08 34	08 41			08 46			09 15					09 34	09 41		09 46			10 15
	d		08 19				08 35	08 43			08 47			09 17					09 35	09 43		09 47			10 17
Reading 7	a		08 35								09 04											10 04			
Fleet	d							08 54												09 54					
Farnborough (Main)	d							09 00						09 30						10 00					10 30
Woking	a												09 19	09 39										10 19	10 39
Clapham Junction	a																								
Clapham Junction 10	a						09 12	09 25											10 12	10 25					
London Waterloo 15 ⊖	a						09 20	09 34					09 49	10 07					10 20	10 34				10 49	11 07

A 🍴 from Bournemouth

Table 158

Saturdays

Weymouth, Bournemouth, Lymington, Romsey, Southampton and Basingstoke - London

Network Diagram - see first Page of Table 158

		SW	GW	XC	SW	SW	SW	SW	GW	GW	XC	SW	SW	SW	SW	GW	SW	SW	SW	SW	GW	XC	SW	SW	SW
		1	◇	◇1	1	1	◇1	1	◇	◇	◇1	1	◇1	1	1	◇	1	1	◇1	1	◇	◇1	1	◇1	1
							A						A						A					A	
			🍴	🍴			🍴				🍴		🍴						🍴			🍴		🍴	
Weymouth	d						08 20		08 46				09 03						09 20					10 03	
Upwey	d						08 24		08 51										09 24						
Dorchester West	a								08 58																
Dorchester South	d						08 33						09 13						09 33					10 13	
Moreton (Dorset)	d						08 39												09 39						
Wool	d						08 45												09 45						
Wareham	d						08 53						09 28						09 53					10 28	
Holton Heath	d						08 56												09 56						
Hamworthy	d						09 01						09 35						10 01					10 35	
Poole 4	a						09 07						09 39						10 06					10 39	
	d				08 50		09 07						09 40				09 50		10 07					10 40	
Parkstone (Dorset)	d				08 54								09 44				09 54							10 44	
Branksome	d				08 57								09 48				09 57							10 48	
Bournemouth	a				09 02		09 17						09 54				10 02		10 17					10 54	
	d				09 05		09 22				09 45		09 59				10 05		10 22			10 45		10 59	
Pokesdown	d				09 09		09 26										10 09		10 26						
Christchurch	d				09 13		09 30										10 13		10 30						
Hinton Admiral	d				09 18												10 18								
New Milton	d				09 22		09 37										10 22		10 37						
Sway	d				09 27												10 27								
Lymington Pier	d					09 27						09 57						10 27					10 57		
Lymington Town	d					09 29						09 59						10 29					10 59		
Brockenhurst 3	a				09 32	09 37	09 44				09 58	10 07	10 14				10 32	10 37	10 44			10 58	11 07	11 14	
	d				09 33		09 45				10 00		10 15				10 33		10 45			11 00		11 15	
Beaulieu Road	d				09 38																				
Ashurst New Forest	d				09 42												10 40								
Totton	d				09 47												10 45								
Salisbury	d	08 56								09 32					09 56						10 32				
Dean	d	09 08													10 08										
Mottisfont & Dunbridge	d	09 14													10 14										
Romsey	d	09 19								09 50					10 19						10 50				
Redbridge	d	09 27													10 27										
Millbrook (Hants)	d	09 31													10 31										
Southampton Central ⛴	a	09 34			09 53		09 58			10 03	10 12		10 28		10 34		10 53		10 58		11 03	11 12		11 28	
	d	09 35		09 47	09 55		10 00			10 05	10 15		10 30		10 35		10 55		11 00		11 05	11 15		11 30	
St Denys	d	09 40													10 40										
Swaythling	d	09 43													10 43										
Southampton Airport Pkwy ✈	d	09 46		09 54	10 03		10 08				10 22		10 38		10 46		11 03		11 08			11 22		11 38	
Portsmouth Harbour ⛴	d		09 23											09 59		10 23									10 59
Portsmouth & Southsea	d		09 27											10 04		10 27									11 04
Fratton	d		09 31											10 08		10 31									11 08
Hilsea	d													10 12											11 12
Cosham	d		09 39											10 17		10 39									11 17
Portchester	d													10 22											11 22
Fareham	d		09 47							10a27				10 28		10 47					11a27				11 28
Botley	d													10 35											11 35
Hedge End	d													10 40											11 40
Eastleigh 3	a	09 49			10 06									10 46	10 49		11 06								11 46
	d	09 50			10 14									10 47	10 50		11 14								11 47
Chandlers Ford	d	09 55													10 55										
Romsey	a	10 03	10 21												11 03	11 21									
Shawford	d				10 19			←									11 19			←					
Winchester	d			10 03	10 25		10 18	10 25			10 31		10 48	10 56			11 25		11 18	11 25		11 31		11 48	11 56
Micheldever	d				→									11 05			→								12 05
Basingstoke	a			10 17			10 34	10 41			10 46			11 15					11 34	11 41		11 46			12 15
	d			10 19			10 35	10 43			10 47			11 17					11 35	11 43		11 47			12 17
Reading 7	a			10 34							11 04											12 04			
Fleet	d							10 54												11 54					
Farnborough (Main)	d							11 00						11 30						12 00					12 30
Woking	a												11 19	11 39										12 19	12 39
Clapham Junction	a																								
Clapham Junction 10	a						11 12	11 25											12 12	12 25					
London Waterloo 15 ⊖	a						11 20	11 34					11 49	12 07					12 21	12 34				12 51	13 07

A 🍴 from Bournemouth

Weymouth, Bournemouth, Lymington, Romsey, Southampton and Basingstoke - London

Network Diagram - see first Page of Table 158

		SW ■	GW ◇	XC ◇■ ⊼	SW ■	SW ■	SW ◇■ A ⊼	SW ■	GW ◇ ⊼	XC ◇■ ⊼	GW	SW ■	SW ◇■ A ⊼	GW ◇	SW ■	SW ■	GW ◇	SW ■	SW ■	SW ◇■ A ⊼	SW ■	GW ◇ ⊼	XC ◇■ ⊼
Weymouth	d						10 20						11 03	11 10						11 20			
Upwey	d						10 24							11 15						11 24			
Dorchester West	a													11 23									
Dorchester South	d						10 33						11 13							11 33			
Moreton (Dorset)	d						10 39													11 39			
Wool	d						10 45													11 45			
Wareham	d						10 53						11 28							11 53			
Holton Heath	d						10 56													11 56			
Hamworthy	d						11 01						11 35							12 01			
Poole	a						11 06						11 39							12 06			
	d				10 50		11 07						11 40					11 50		12 07			
Parkstone (Dorset)	d				10 54								11 44					11 54					
Branksome	d				10 57								11 48					11 57					
Bournemouth	a				11 02		11 17						11 54					12 02		12 17			
	d				11 05		11 22			11 45			11 59					12 05		12 22			12 45
Pokesdown	d				11 09		11 26											12 09		12 26			
Christchurch	d				11 13		11 30											12 13		12 30			
Hinton Admiral	d				11 18													12 18					
New Milton	d				11 22		11 37											12 22		12 37			
Sway	d				11 27													12 27					
Lymington Pier	d					11 27						11 57							12 27				
Lymington Town	d					11 29						11 59							12 29				
Brockenhurst	a				11 32	11 37	11 44			11 58		12 07	12 14					12 32	12 37	12 44			12 58
	d				11 33		11 45			12 00			12 15					12 33		12 45			13 00
Beaulieu Road	d				11 38																		
Ashurst New Forest	d				11 42													12 40					
Totton	d				11 47													12 45					
Salisbury	d	10 56							11 32		11 43					11 56						12 32	
Dean	d	11 08														12 08							
Mottisfont & Dunbridge	d	11 14														12 14							
Romsey	d	11 19							11 50		12 04					12 19						12 50	
Redbridge	d	11 27														12 27							
Millbrook (Hants)	d	11 31														12 31							
Southampton Central ⛴	a	11 34			11 53		11 58		12 03	12 12	12 20		12 28			12 34		12 51		12 58		13 03	13 12
	d	11 35		11 47	11 55		12 00		12 05	12 15			12 30			12 35		12 55		13 00		13 05	13 15
St Denys	d	11 40														12 40							
Swaythling	d	11 43														12 43							
Southampton Airport Pkwy ✈	d	11 46		11 54	12 03		12 08			12 22			12 38			12 46		13 03		13 08			13 22
Portsmouth Harbour ⛴	d		11 23												11 59		12 23						
Portsmouth & Southsea	d		11 27												12 04		12 27						
Fratton	d		11 31												12 08		12 31						
Hilsea	d														12 12								
Cosham	d		11 39												12 17		12 39						
Portchester	d														12 22								
Fareham	d		11 47						12a27						12 28		12 47					13a27	
Botley	d														12 35								
Hedge End	d														12 40								
Eastleigh	a	11 49			12 06										12 46	12 49		13 06					
	d	11 50			12 14										12 47	12 50		13 14					
Chandlers Ford	d	11 55														12 55							
Romsey	a	12 03	12 21													13 03	13 21						
Shawford	d				12 19			←										13 19			←		
Winchester	d			12 03	12 25		12 18	12 25		12 31			12 48		12 56			13 25		13 18	13 25		13 31
Micheldever	d				→										13 05			→					
Basingstoke	a			12 17			12 34	12 41		12 46					13 15					13 34	13 41		13 46
	d			12 19			12 35	12 43		12 47					13 17					13 35	13 43		13 47
Reading	a			12 35						13 04													14 04
Fleet	d							12 54													13 54		
Farnborough (Main)	d							13 00							13 30						14 00		
Woking	a												13 19		13 39								
Clapham Junction	a																						
Clapham Junction	a						13 12	13 25												14 12	14 25		
London Waterloo ⊖	a						13 21	13 34					13 51		14 07					14 21	14 34		

A ⊼ from Bournemouth

Weymouth, Bournemouth, Lymington, Romsey, Southampton and Basingstoke - London

Network Diagram - see first Page of Table 158

		SW ■	SW ◇■ A ⊼	SW ■	SW ■	GW ◇	XC ◇■ ⊼	SW ■	SW ■	SW ◇■ A ⊼	SW ■	GW ◇ ⊼	XC ◇■ ⊼	SW ■	SW ◇■ A ⊼	GW ◇	SW ■	GW ◇	GW ◇	SW ■	SW ■	SW ■
Weymouth	d		12 03							12 20					13 03	13 10						
Upwey	d									12 24						13 15						
Dorchester West	a															13 22						
Dorchester South	d		12 13							12 33					13 13							
Moreton (Dorset)	d									12 39												
Wool	d									12 45												
Wareham	d		12 28							12 53					13 28							
Holton Heath	d									12 56												
Hamworthy	d		12 35							13 01					13 35							
Poole	a		12 39							13 06					13 39							
	d		12 40					12 50		13 07					13 40						13 50	
Parkstone (Dorset)	d		12 44					12 54							13 44						13 54	
Branksome	d		12 48					12 57							13 48						13 57	
Bournemouth	a		12 54					13 02		13 17					13 54						14 02	
	d		12 59					13 05		13 22			13 45		13 59						14 05	
Pokesdown	d							13 09		13 26											14 09	
Christchurch	d							13 13		13 30											14 13	
Hinton Admiral	d							13 18													14 18	
New Milton	d							13 22		13 37											14 22	
Sway	d							13 27													14 27	
Lymington Pier	d	12 57							13 27					13 57								14 27
Lymington Town	d	12 59							13 29					13 59								14 29
Brockenhurst	a	13 07	13 14					13 32	13 37	13 44			13 58	14 07	14 14						14 32	14 37
	d		13 15					13 33		13 45			14 00		14 15						14 33	
Beaulieu Road	d							13 38														
Ashurst New Forest	d							13 42													14 40	
Totton	d							13 47													14 45	
Salisbury	d				12 56							13 32							14 00	13 50		
Dean	d				13 08															14 02		
Mottisfont & Dunbridge	d				13 14															14 08		
Romsey	d				13 19							13 50							14 20	14 13		
Redbridge	d				13 27															14 21		
Millbrook (Hants)	d				13 31															14 24		
Southampton Central ⛴	a		13 28		13 34			13 53		13 58		14 03	14 12		14 28				14 32	14 28	14 51	
	d		13 30		13 35		13 47	13 55		14 00		14 05	14 15		14 30				14 34	14 35	14 55	
St Denys	d				13 40															14 40		
Swaythling	d				13 43															14 43		
Southampton Airport Pkwy ✈	d		13 38		13 46		13 54	14 03		14 08			14 22		14 38					14 46	15 03	
Portsmouth Harbour ⛴	d			12 59		13 23											13 59	14 23				
Portsmouth & Southsea	d			13 04		13 27											14 04	14 27				
Fratton	d			13 08		13 31											14 08	14 31				
Hilsea	d			13 12													14 12					
Cosham	d			13 17		13 39											14 17	14 39				
Portchester	d			13 22													14 22					
Fareham	d			13 28		13 47						14a27					14 28	14 47	14a54			
Botley	d			13 35													14 35					
Hedge End	d			13 40													14 40					
Eastleigh	a			13 46	13 49			14 06									14 46			14 49	15 06	
	d			13 47	13 50			14 14									14 47			14 50	15 14	
Chandlers Ford	d				13 55															14 55		
Romsey	a				14 03	14 21												15 21		15 04		
Shawford	d							14 19			←										15 19	
Winchester	d		13 48	13 56			14 03	14 25		14 18	14 25		14 31		14 48		14 56				15 25	
Micheldever	d			14 05				→									15 05				→	
Basingstoke	a			14 15			14 17			14 34	14 41		14 46				15 15					
	d			14 17			14 19			14 35	14 43		14 47				15 17					
Reading	a						14 35						15 04									
Fleet	d										14 54											
Farnborough (Main)	d			14 30							15 00						15 30					
Woking	a		14 19	14 39											15 19		15 39					
Clapham Junction	a																					
Clapham Junction	a									15 12	15 25											
London Waterloo ⊖	a		14 51	15 07						15 21	15 34				15 51		16 07					

A ⊼ from Bournemouth

Table 158

Saturdays

Weymouth, Bournemouth, Lymington, Romsey, Southampton and Basingstoke - London

Network Diagram - see first Page of Table 158

		SW	SW	GW	XC	SW	SW	SW	SW	GW	XC	SW	SW	SW	SW	GW	XC	SW	SW	GW	SW	SW	GW
		◇[1]	[1]	◇	◇[1]	[1]	◇[1]	[1]	[1]	◇	◇[1]	[1]	[1]	◇[1]	[1]	◇	◇[1]	[1]	◇[1]	◇	[1]	[1]	[1]
		A					A							A					A				
		🚌			🚌		🚌				🚌			🚌			🚌		🚌				
Weymouth	d	13 20					14 03							14 20					15 03	15 08			
Upwey	d	13 24												14 24						15 13			
Dorchester West	a																			15 20			
Dorchester South	d	13 33					14 13							14 33					15 13				
Moreton (Dorset)	d	13 39												14 39									
Wool	d	13 45												14 45									
Wareham	d	13 53					14 28							14 53					15 28				
Holton Heath	d	13 56												14 56									
Hamworthy	d	14 01					14 35							15 01					15 35				
Poole [4]	a	14 06					14 39							15 06					15 39				
	d	14 07					14 40					14 50		15 07					15 40				
Parkstone (Dorset)	d						14 44					14 54							15 44				
Branksome	d						14 48					14 57							15 48				
Bournemouth	a	14 17					14 54					15 02		15 17					15 54				
	d	14 22			14 45		14 59					15 05		15 22			15 45		15 59				
Pokesdown	d	14 26										15 09		15 26									
Christchurch	d	14 30										15 13		15 30									
Hinton Admiral	d											15 18											
New Milton	d	14 37										15 22		15 37									
Sway	d											15 27											
Lymington Pier	d					14 57							15 27					15 57					
Lymington Town	d					14 59							15 29					15 59					
Brockenhurst [3]	a	14 44			14 58	15 07	15 14					15 32	15 37	15 44			15 58	16 07	16 14				
	d	14 45			15 00		15 15					15 33		15 45			16 00		16 15				
Beaulieu Road	d											15 38											
Ashurst New Forest	d											15 42											
Totton	d											15 47											
Salisbury	d			14 32					14 56							15 32						15 56	
Dean	d								15 08													16 08	
Mottisfont & Dunbridge	d								15 14													16 14	
Romsey	d			14 50					15 19							15 50						16 19	
Redbridge	d								15 27													16 27	
Millbrook (Hants)	d								15 31													16 31	
Southampton Central ⛴	a	14 58		15 03	15 12		15 28		15 34			15 53		15 58		16 03	16 12		16 28			16 34	
	d	15 00		15 05	15 15		15 30		15 35		15 47	15 55		16 00		16 05	16 15		16 30			16 35	
St Denys	d								15 40													16 40	
Swaythling	d								15 43													16 43	
Southampton Airport Pkwy ✈	d	15 08			15 22		15 38		15 46		15 54	16 03		16 08			16 22		16 38			16 46	
Portsmouth Harbour ⛴	d							14 59		15 23											15 59		16 23
Portsmouth & Southsea	d							15 04		15 27											16 04		16 27
Fratton	d							15 08		15 31											16 08		16 31
Hilsea	d							15 12													16 12		
Cosham	d							15 17		15 39											16 17		16 39
Portchester	d							15 22													16 22		
Fareham	d			15a27				15 28		15 47						16a27					16 28		16 47
Botley	d							15 35													16 35		
Hedge End	d							15 40													16 40		
Eastleigh [8]	a							15 46	15 49			16 06									16 46	16 49	
	d							15 47	15 50			16 14									16 47	16 50	
Chandlers Ford	d								15 55													16 55	
Romsey	a								16 03	16 21												17 03	17 21
Shawford	d		←									16 19			←								
Winchester	d	15 18	15 25		15 31		15 48	15 56			16 03	16 25		16 18	16 25		16 31		16 48		16 56		
Micheldever	d							16 05				→									17 05		
Basingstoke	a	15 34	15 41		15 46			16 15			16 17			16 34	16 41		16 46				17 15		
	d	15 35	15 43		15 47			16 17			16 19			16 35	16 43		16 47				17 17		
Reading [7]	a				16 05						16 35						17 04						
Fleet	d		15 54												16 54								
Farnborough (Main)	d		16 00					16 30							17 00						17 30		
Woking	a						16 19	16 39											17 19		17 39		
Clapham Junction	a																						
Clapham Junction [10]	a	16 12	16 25											17 12	17 25								
London Waterloo [15] ⊖	a	16 20	16 34				16 49	17 07						17 20	17 34				17 49		18 07		

A 🚌 from Bournemouth

Table 158

Saturdays

Weymouth, Bournemouth, Lymington, Romsey, Southampton and Basingstoke - London

Network Diagram - see first Page of Table 158

		SW	SW	SW	SW	GW	XC	SW	SW	SW	SW	GW	SW	XC	SW	SW	SW	SW	GW	XC	SW	SW	SW
		[1]	[1]	◇[1]	[1]	◇	◇[1]	[1]	◇[1]	[1]	[1]	◇	[1]	◇[1]	[1]	[1]	◇[1]	[1]	◇	◇[1]	[1]	◇[1]	[1]
				A					A								A					A	
				🚌			🚌		🚌					🚌			🚌			🚌		🚌	
Weymouth	d			15 20					16 03								16 20					17 03	
Upwey	d			15 24													16 24						
Dorchester West	a																						
Dorchester South	d			15 33					16 13								16 33					17 13	
Moreton (Dorset)	d			15 39													16 39						
Wool	d			15 45													16 45						
Wareham	d			15 53					16 28								16 53					17 28	
Holton Heath	d			15 56													16 56						
Hamworthy	d			16 01					16 35								17 01					17 35	
Poole [4]	a			16 06					16 39								17 06					17 39	
	d	15 50		16 07					16 40						16 50		17 07					17 40	
Parkstone (Dorset)	d	15 54							16 44						16 54							17 44	
Branksome	d	15 57							16 48						16 57							17 48	
Bournemouth	a	16 02		16 17					16 54						17 02		17 17					17 54	
	d	16 05		16 22			16 45		16 59						17 05		17 22			17 45		17 59	
Pokesdown	d	16 09		16 26											17 09		17 26						
Christchurch	d	16 13		16 30											17 13		17 30						
Hinton Admiral	d	16 18													17 18								
New Milton	d	16 22		16 37											17 22		17 37						
Sway	d	16 27													17 27								
Lymington Pier	d		16 27					16 57								17 27					17 57		
Lymington Town	d		16 29					16 59								17 29					17 59		
Brockenhurst [3]	a	16 32	16 37	16 44			16 58	17 07	17 14						17 32	17 37	17 44			17 58	18 07	18 14	
	d	16 33		16 45			17 00		17 15						17 33		17 45			18 00		18 15	
Beaulieu Road	d														17 38								
Ashurst New Forest	d	16 40													17 42								
Totton	d	16 45													17 47								
Salisbury	d					16 32					16 56								17 32				
Dean	d										17 08												
Mottisfont & Dunbridge	d										17 14												
Romsey	d					16 50					17 19								17 50				
Redbridge	d										17 27												
Millbrook (Hants)	d										17 31												
Southampton Central ⛴	a	16 51		16 58		17 03	17 12		17 28		17 34				17 53		17 58		18 03	18 12		18 28	
	d	16 55		17 00		17 05	17 15		17 30		17 35			17 47	17 55		18 00		18 05	18 15		18 30	
St Denys	d										17 40												
Swaythling	d										17 43												
Southampton Airport Pkwy ✈	d	17 03		17 08			17 22		17 38		17 46			17 54	18 03		18 08			18 22		18 38	
Portsmouth Harbour ⛴	d									16 59		17 23	17 33										17 59
Portsmouth & Southsea	d									17 04		17 27	17 38										18 04
Fratton	d									17 08		17 31	17 42										18 08
Hilsea	d									17 12			17 46										18 12
Cosham	d									17 17		17 39	17 51										18 17
Portchester	d									17 22			17 56										18 22
Fareham	d					17a27				17 28		17 47	18a01						18a27				18 28
Botley	d									17 35													18 35
Hedge End	d									17 40													18 40
Eastleigh [8]	a	17 06								17 46	17 49				18 06								18 46
	d	17 14								17 47	17 50				18 14								18 47
Chandlers Ford	d										17 55												
Romsey	a										18 03	18 21											
Shawford	d	17 19			←										18 19			←					
Winchester	d	17 25		17 18	17 25		17 31		17 48	17 56				18 03	18 25		18 18	18 25		18 31		18 48	18 56
Micheldever	d	→								18 05					→								19 05
Basingstoke	a			17 34	17 41		17 46			18 15				18 17			18 34	18 41		18 46			19 15
	d			17 35	17 43		17 47			18 17				18 19			18 35	18 43		18 47			19 17
Reading [7]	a						18 04							18 35						19 04			
Fleet	d				17 54													18 54					
Farnborough (Main)	d				18 00					18 30								19 00					19 30
Woking	a								18 19	18 39												19 19	19 39
Clapham Junction	a																						
Clapham Junction [10]	a			18 12	18 25												19 12	19 25					
London Waterloo [15] ⊖	a			18 20	18 34				18 49	19 07							19 20	19 34				19 49	20 07

A 🚌 from Bournemouth

Weymouth, Bournemouth, Lymington, Romsey, Southampton and Basingstoke - London

Network Diagram - see first Page of Table 158

		SW	GW	SW	SW	SW	SW	GW	GW	XC	SW	SW	SW	SW	GW	SW	SW	SW	SW	GW	XC	GW
		1	◇	1	1	◇1 A [trolley]	1	◇	■	◇1 [trolley]	1	◇1 A [trolley]	1	1	◇	1	1	◇1 A [trolley]	1	◇	◇1	
Weymouth	d					17 20		17 28				18 06						18 20				
Upwey	d					17 24		17 33										18 24				
Dorchester West	a							17 40														
Dorchester South	d					17 33						18 16						18 33				
Moreton (Dorset)	d					17 39												18 39				
Wool	d					17 45												18 45				
Wareham	d					17 53						18 31						18 53				
Holton Heath	d					17 56												18 56				
Hamworthy	d					18 01						18 38						19 01				
Poole 4	a					18 06						18 42						19 06				
	d			17 50		18 07						18 43				18 50		19 07				
Parkstone (Dorset)	d			17 54								18 47				18 54						
Branksome	d			17 57								18 51				18 57						
Bournemouth	a			18 02		18 17						18 56				19 02		19 17				
	d			18 05		18 22				18 45		18 59				19 05		19 22			19 45	
Pokesdown	d			18 09		18 26										19 09		19 26				
Christchurch	d			18 13		18 30										19 13		19 30				
Hinton Admiral	d			18 18												19 18						
New Milton	d			18 22		18 37										19 22		19 37				
Sway	d			18 27												19 27						
Lymington Pier	d				18 27						18 57						19 27					
Lymington Town	d				18 29						18 59						19 29					
Brockenhurst 3	a			18 32	18 37	18 44				18 58	19 07	19 14				19 32	19 37	19 44			19 58	
	d			18 33		18 45				19 00		19 15				19 33		19 45			20 00	
Beaulieu Road	d																					
Ashurst New Forest	d			18 40												19 40						
Totton	d			18 45												19 45						
Salisbury	d	17 56							18 32					18 56						19 32		19 41
Dean	d	18 08												19 08								
Mottisfont & Dunbridge	d	18 14												19 14								
Romsey	d	18 19							18 50					19 19						19 50		20 04
Redbridge	d	18 27												19 27								
Millbrook (Hants)	d	18 31												19 31								
Southampton Central ⛴	a	18 34		18 51		18 58			19 03	19 12		19 28		19 34		19 51		19 58		20 02	20 12	20 18
	d	18 35		18 55		19 00			19 05	19 15		19 30		19 35		19 55		20 00		20 05	20 15	
St Denys	d	18 40												19 40								
Swaythling	d	18 43												19 43								
Southampton Airport Pkwy ✈	d	18 46		19 03		19 08				19 22		19 38		19 46		20 03		20 08			20 22	
Portsmouth Harbour ⛴	d		18 23										18 59		19 23							
Portsmouth & Southsea	d		18 27										19 04		19 27							
Fratton	d		18 31										19 08		19 31							
Hilsea	d												19 12									
Cosham	d		18 39										19 17		19 39							
Portchester	d												19 22									
Fareham	d		18 47						19a27				19 28		19 47					20a27		
Botley	d												19 35									
Hedge End	d												19 40									
Eastleigh 3	a	18 49		19 06									19 46	19 49		20 06						
	d	18 50		19 14									19 47	19 50		20 14						
Chandlers Ford	d	18 55												19 55								
Romsey	a	19 04	19 21											20 03	20 21							
Shawford	d			19 19			←									20 19			←			
Winchester	d			19 25		19 18	19 25			19 31		19 48	19 56			20 25		20 18	20 25		20 31	
Micheldever	d			→									20 05			→						
Basingstoke	a					19 34	19 41			19 46			20 15					20 34	20 41		20 46	
	d					19 35	19 43			19 47			20 17					20 35	20 43		20 47	
Reading 7	a									20 04											21 04	
Fleet	d						19 54												20 54			
Farnborough (Main)	d						20 00						20 30						21 00			
Woking	a											20 19	20 39						21 09			
Clapham Junction	a																					
Clapham Junction 10	a					20 12	20 25											21 16	21 29			
London Waterloo 15 ⊖	a					20 20	20 34					20 49	21 07					21 24	21 38			

A [trolley] from Bournemouth

Weymouth, Bournemouth, Lymington, Romsey, Southampton and Basingstoke - London

Network Diagram - see first Page of Table 158

		SW	SW	SW	GW	SW	SW	SW	SW	SW	GW	SW	SW	SW	SW	SW	SW	SW	GW	SW	GW
		1	◇1 A [trolley]	1	◇	1	1	◇1	1	1	◇	1	1	1	1	1	◇1	1		1	◇
Weymouth	d		19 03					19 20									20 10		20 21		
Upwey	d							19 24									20 14		20 26		
Dorchester West	a																		20 33		
Dorchester South	d		19 13					19 33									20 22				
Moreton (Dorset)	d							19 39									20 28				
Wool	d							19 45									20 34				
Wareham	d		19 28					19 53									20 42				
Holton Heath	d																				
Hamworthy	d		19 35					20 01									20 48				
Poole 4	a		19 39					20 06									20 53				
	d		19 40			19 50		20 07									20 54				
Parkstone (Dorset)	d		19 44			19 54											20 58				
Branksome	d		19 48			19 57											21 01				
Bournemouth	a		19 54			20 02		20 17									21 07				
	d		19 59			20 05		20 22									21 12				
Pokesdown	d					20 09		20 26									21 16				
Christchurch	d					20 13		20 30									21 20				
Hinton Admiral	d					20 18											21 25				
New Milton	d					20 22		20 37									21 29				
Sway	d					20 27											21 34				
Lymington Pier	d	19 57					20 27							20 57	21 27						
Lymington Town	d	19 59					20 29							20 59	21 29						
Brockenhurst 3	a	20 07	20 14			20 32	20 37	20 44						21 07	21 37		21 39				
	d		20 15			20 33		20 45									21 40				
Beaulieu Road	d																				
Ashurst New Forest	d					20 40											21 47				
Totton	d					20 45											21 52				
Salisbury	d			19 56							20 32		20 56								21 32
Dean	d			20 08									21 08								
Mottisfont & Dunbridge	d			20 14									21 14								
Romsey	d			20 19							20 50		21 19								21 50
Redbridge	d			20 27									21 27								
Millbrook (Hants)	d			20 31									21 31								
Southampton Central ⛴	a		20 28	20 34		20 51		20 58			21 03		21 34				21 57				22 03
	d		20 30	20 35		20 55		21 00			21 05	21 30	21 35			21 55	22 00				22 05
St Denys	d			20 40									21 40								
Swaythling	d			20 43									21 43								
Southampton Airport Pkwy ✈	d		20 38	20 46		21 03		21 08				21 38	21 46			21 03	22 08				
Portsmouth Harbour ⛴	d				20 23				19 59									20 59		21 54	
Portsmouth & Southsea	d				20 27				20 04									21 04		21 59	
Fratton	d				20 31				20 08									21 08		22 03	
Hilsea	d								20 12									21 12		22 07	
Cosham	d								20 17									21 17		22 12	
Portchester	d								20 22									21 22		22 17	
Fareham	d				20 47				20 28		21a27							21 28		22 23	22a26
Botley	d								20 35									21 35		22 30	
Hedge End	d								20 40									21 40		22 35	
Eastleigh 3	a			20 49		21 06			20 46				21 49					21 46		22 41	
	d			20 50		21 14			20 47				21 50					21 47			
Chandlers Ford	d			20 55									21 55								
Romsey	a			21 03	21 21								22 03								
Shawford	d					21 19				←						22 19					
Winchester	d		20 48			21 25		21 18	20 56	21 25		21 47				22 25	22 18	21 56			
Micheldever	d					→			21 05									22 05			
Basingstoke	a							21 34	21 17	21 41						22 41	22 34	22 15			
	d							21 35	21 24	21 43						22 43	22 35	22 24			
Reading 7	a																				
Fleet	d								21 40	21 54						22 54		22 40			
Farnborough (Main)	d								21 46	22 00								22 46			
Woking	a		21 19						21 58	22 09		21 19				23 09	22 53	22 58			
Clapham Junction	a																				
Clapham Junction 10	a							22 14		22 29						23 29	23 14				
London Waterloo 15 ⊖	a		21 49					22 22	22 34	22 38		22 49				23 39	23 22	23 32			

A [trolley] from Bournemouth

Table 158

Weymouth, Bournemouth, Lymington, Romsey, Southampton and Basingstoke - London

Network Diagram - see first Page of Table 158

		SW 1	SW 1	SW 1	SW 1	SW 1	SW 1	GW ◇	SW 1	SW 1	SW 1	SW 1	SW 1
Weymouth	d					21 10						22 10	23 10
Upwey	d					21 14						22 14	23 14
Dorchester West	a												
Dorchester South	d					21 22						22 22	23 22
Moreton (Dorset)	d					21 28						22 28	23 28
Wool	d					21 34						22 34	23 34
Wareham	d					21 42						22 42	23 42
Holton Heath	d												
Hamworthy	d					21 48						22 48	23 48
Poole 4	a					21 53						22 53	23 53
	d					21 54						22 54	23 54
Parkstone (Dorset)	d					21 58						22 58	
Branksome	d					22 01						23 01	
Bournemouth	a					22 07						23 07	00 03
	d					22 12						23 12	
Pokesdown	d					22 16						23 16	
Christchurch	d					22 20						23 20	
Hinton Admiral	d					22 25						23 25	
New Milton	d					22 29						23 29	
Sway	d					22 34						23 34	
Lymington Pier	d			22 03	22 33								
Lymington Town	d			22 05	22 35								
Brockenhurst 3	a			22 13	22 43	22 39						23 39	
	d					22 40						23 40	
Beaulieu Road	d												
Ashurst New Forest	d					22 47						23 47	
Totton	d					22 52						23 52	
Salisbury	d		21 56					22 32					
Dean	d		22 08										
Mottisfont & Dunbridge	d		22 14										
Romsey	d		22 19					22 50		23 00			
Redbridge	d		22 27							23 08			
Millbrook (Hants)	d		22 31							23 12			
Southampton Central ⛴	a		22 34			22 57		23 03		23 15		23 57	
	d	22 30	22 35			23 00		23 05		23 21		23 59	
St Denys	d		22 40							23 26		00 04	
Swaythling	d		22 43							23 29		00 07	
Southampton Airport Pkwy ✈	d	22 38	22 46			23 08				23 32		00 10	
Portsmouth Harbour ⛴	d						22 33				23 24		
Portsmouth & Southsea	d						22 38				23 29		
Fratton	d						22 42				23 33		
Hilsea	d						22 46				23 37		
Cosham	d						22 51				23 42		
Portchester	d						22 56				23 47		
Fareham	d						23a01	23a26			23 53		
Botley	d										23 59		
Hedge End	d										00 05		
Eastleigh 8	a	22 41	22 49			23 11				23 35	00 11	00 14	
	d	22 46	22 50			23 12				23 37	00 21		
Chandlers Ford	d		22 55							23 42			
Romsey	a		23 03							23 49			
Shawford	d					23 18							
Winchester	d	22 55				23 24					00a30		
Micheldever	d					23 33							
Basingstoke	a	23 11				23 43							
	d	23 13				23 44							
Reading 7	a												
Fleet	d					00 01							
Farnborough (Main)	d					00 06							
Woking	a	23 31				00 18							
Clapham Junction	a												
Clapham Junction 10	a	23 52				00 53							
London Waterloo 15 ⊖	a	00 03				01 03							

Table 158

Weymouth, Bournemouth, Lymington, Romsey, Southampton and Basingstoke - London

Network Diagram - see first Page of Table 158

		SW 1 A	SW 1 A	SW 1 A	SW 1	SW 1	SW ◇1 B ⚒	SW 1	SW 1	SW ◇1 C	SW 1	GW ■	XC ◇1 ⚒	SW ◇1 D ⚒	SW 1	SW 1 ⚒	SW ◇1 E ⚒	SW 1	XC ◇1 ⚒	SW 1	SW ◇1 D ⚒	SW 1
Weymouth	d		22p10	23p10										07 48							08 48	
Upwey	d		22p14	23p14										07 52							08 52	
Dorchester West	a																					
Dorchester South	d		22p22	23p22										08 00							09 00	
Moreton (Dorset)	d		22p28	23p28										08 07							09 07	
Wool	d		22p34	23p34										08 13							09 13	
Wareham	d		22p42	23p42										08 20							09 20	
Holton Heath	d																					
Hamworthy	d		22p48	23p48										08 27							09 27	
Poole 4	a		22p53	23p53										08 31							09 31	
	d		22p54	23p54			06 50			07 50				08 32			08 55				09 32	
Parkstone (Dorset)	d		22p58				06 54			07 54				08 36							09 36	
Branksome	d		23p01				06 57			07 57				08 40							09 40	
Bournemouth	a		23p07	00 03			07 02			08 02				08 46			09 04				09 46	
	d		23p12				07 06			08 06				08 50			09 06		09 40		09 50	
Pokesdown	d		23p16				07 10			08 10							09 10					
Christchurch	d		23p20				07 14			08 14							09 14					
Hinton Admiral	d		23p25				07 19			08 19							09 19					
New Milton	d		23p29				07 23			08 23				09 01			09 23				10 01	
Sway	d		23p34				07 28			08 28							09 28					
Lymington Pier	d														09 14					09 44		10 14
Lymington Town	d														09 16					09 46		10 16
Brockenhurst 3	a		23p39				07 33			08 33				09 08	09 24		09 33		09 53	09 54	10 08	10 24
	d		23p40				07 34			08 34				09 09			09 34		09 57		10 09	
Beaulieu Road	d									08 39							09 39					
Ashurst New Forest	d		23p47				07 43			08 43							09 43					
Totton	d		23p52				07 48			08 48							09 48					
Salisbury	d							08 08			08 20							09 08				
Dean	d							08 20										09 20				
Mottisfont & Dunbridge	d							08 26										09 26				
Romsey	d							08 35			08 39							09 32				
Redbridge	d										08 46							09 39				
Millbrook (Hants)	d										08 50							09 43				
Southampton Central ⛴	a		23p57				07 53			08 53	08 52			09 23			09 53	09 45	10 10		10 23	
	d		23p59				07 55			08 55	08 59		09 15	09 25			09 55	09 59	10 15		10 25	
St Denys	d		00 04								09 04							10 04				
Swaythling	d		00 07								09 07							10 07				
Southampton Airport Pkwy ✈	d		00 10				08 03			09 03	09 10		09 22	09 33			10 03	10 10	10 22		10 33	
Portsmouth Harbour ⛴	d	23p24			06 37	07 17			08 17			09 08				09 17						
Portsmouth & Southsea	d	23p29			06 42	07 22			08 22			09 12				09 22						
Fratton	d	23p33			06 46	07 26			08 26			09 16				09 26						
Hilsea	d	23p37			06 50	07 30			08 30							09 30						
Cosham	d	23p42			06 55	07 35			08 35			09 23				09 35						
Portchester	d	23p47			07 00	07 40			08 40							09 40						
Fareham	d	23p53			07a05	07 46			08 46			09 32				09 46						
Botley	d	23p59				07 54			08 54							09 54						
Hedge End	d	00 05				07 58			08 58							09 58						
Eastleigh 8	a	00 11	00 14			08 04	08 07		09 04	09 07	09 13					10 04	10 07	10 13				
	d	00 21					08 11			09 11	09 15						10 11	10 15				
Chandlers Ford	d							08 42			09 20							10 20				
Romsey	a							09 24			09 28	10 05						10 28				
Shawford	d									09 17												
Winchester	d	00a30					08 23			09 23			09 31	09 42			10 23		10 31		10 42	
Micheldever	d						08 32			09 32							10 32					
Basingstoke	a						08 42			09 42			09 46	09 58			10 42		10 46		10 58	
	d						08 44			09 44			09 47	10 00			10 44		10 47		11 00	
Reading 7	a												10 04						11 03			
Fleet	d																					
Farnborough (Main)	d																					
Woking	a						09 02			10 02				10 19			11 02				11 18	
Clapham Junction	a																					
Clapham Junction 10	a						09 30			10 27				10 40			11 27				11 39	
London Waterloo 15 ⊖	a						09 43			10 42				10 54			11 42				11 54	

A not 11 December
B ⚒ to Eastleigh ◇ to Eastleigh
C ◇ to Eastleigh
D ⚒ from Bournemouth
E ⚒ from Eastleigh ◇ to Eastleigh

Weymouth, Bournemouth, Lymington, Romsey, Southampton and Basingstoke - London

Network Diagram - see first Page of Table 158

		SW	SW	SW	GW	XC	SW	SW	GW	SW	SW	SW	SW	GW	XC	XC	SW	SW	SW	SW	SW	SW	SW
		1	◇1	1	◇	◇1	1	◇1	◇	1	1	◇1	1	◇	◇1	◇1	1	◇1	1	1	◇1	1	1
			A					B				C			D	E		B			A		
		⊼	⊼			⊼		⊼			⊼	⊼			⊼	⊼		⊼		⊼	⊼		
Weymouth	d							09 48										10 48					
Upwey	d							09 52										10 52					
Dorchester West	a																						
Dorchester South	d							10 00										11 00					
Moreton (Dorset)	d							10 07										11 07					
Wool	d							10 13										11 13					
Wareham	d							10 20										11 20					
Holton Heath	d																						
Hamworthy	d							10 27										11 27					
Poole 4	a							10 31										11 31					
	d		09 55					10 32				10 55						11 32			11 55		
Parkstone (Dorset)	d							10 36										11 36					
Branksome	d							10 40										11 40					
Bournemouth	a		10 04					10 46				11 04						11 46			12 04		
	d		10 06			10 40		10 50				11 06			11 40	11 40		11 50			12 06		
Pokesdown	d		10 10									11 10									12 10		
Christchurch	d		10 14									11 14									12 14		
Hinton Admiral	d		10 19									11 19									12 19		
New Milton	d		10 23					11 01				11 23						12 01			12 23		
Sway	d		10 28									11 28									12 28		
Lymington Pier	d						10 44			11 14							11 44		12 14				12 44
Lymington Town	d						10 46			11 16							11 46		12 16				12 46
Brockenhurst 3	a		10 33			10 53	10 54	11 08		11 24		11 33			11 53	11 53	11 54	12 08	12 24		12 33		12 54
	d		10 34			10 57		11 09				11 34			11 57	11 57		12 09			12 34		
Beaulieu Road	d		10 39									11 39									12 39		
Ashurst New Forest	d		10 43									11 43									12 43		
Totton	d		10 48									11 48									12 48		
Salisbury	d			10 13	10 33								11 08	11 33								12 13	
Dean	d												11 20										
Mottisfont & Dunbridge	d												11 26										
Romsey	d			10 32	10 51								11 32	11 51								12 32	
Redbridge	d			10 39									11 39									12 39	
Millbrook (Hants)	d			10 43									11 43									12 43	
Southampton Central ⛴	a		10 53	10 45	11 03	11 10		11 23				11 53	11 45	12 03	12 10	12 10		12 23			12 53	12 45	
	d		10 55	10 59	11 04	11 15		11 25				11 55	11 59	12 04	12 15	12 15		12 25			12 55	12 59	
St Denys	d			11 04									12 04									13 04	
Swaythling	d			11 07									12 07									13 07	
Southampton Airport Pkwy ✈	d		11 03	11 10		11 22		11 33				12 03	12 10		12 22	12 22		12 33			13 03	13 10	
Portsmouth Harbour ⛴	d	10 17							11 08		11 17									12 17			
Portsmouth & Southsea	d	10 22							11 12		11 22									12 22			
Fratton	d	10 26							11 16		11 26									12 26			
Hilsea	d	10 30									11 30									12 30			
Cosham	d	10 35							11 23		11 35									12 35			
Portchester	d	10 40									11 40									12 40			
Fareham	d	10 46			11a27				11 32		11 46			12a28						12 46			
Botley	d	10 54									11 54									12 54			
Hedge End	d	10 58									11 58									12 58			
Eastleigh 3	a	11 04	11 07	11 13							12 04	12 07	12 13							13 04	13 07	13 13	
	d		11 11	11 15								12 11	12 15								13 11	13 15	
Chandlers Ford	d			11 20									12 20									13 20	
Romsey	a			11 28					12 05				12 28									13 28	
Shawford	d		11 17																		13 17		
Winchester	d		11 23			11 31		11 42				12 23			12 31	12 31		12 42			13 23		
Micheldever	d		11 32									12 32									13 32		
Basingstoke	a		11 42			11 46		11 58				12 42			12 46	12 46		12 58			13 42		
	d		11 44			11 47		12 00				12 44			12 47	12 47		13 00			13 44		
Reading 7	a					12 03									13 02	13 03							
Fleet	d																						
Farnborough (Main)	d																						
Woking	a		12 02					12 18				13 02						13 18			14 02		
Clapham Junction	a																						
Clapham Junction 10	a		12 27					12 39				13 27						13 39			14 27		
London Waterloo 15 ⊖	a		12 42					12 49				13 37						13 49			14 37		

A ⊼ from Bournemouth ◇ to Eastleigh
B ⊼ from Bournemouth
C ⊼ from Eastleigh ◇ to Eastleigh
D until 1 January
E from 8 January until 12 February

Weymouth, Bournemouth, Lymington, Romsey, Southampton and Basingstoke - London

Network Diagram - see first Page of Table 158

		GW	GW	XC	SW	SW	SW	SW	SW	GW	XC	SW	SW	GW	SW	SW	SW	SW	XC	SW	GW	GW
		◇	◇	◇1	◇1	1	1	◇1	1	◇	◇1	1	◇1	◇	1	1	◇1	1	◇1	1	1	◇
					A			B					A				B					
				⊼	⊼		⊼	⊼		⊼	⊼		⊼			⊼	⊼		⊼			
Weymouth	d				11 48								12 48									
Upwey	d				11 52								12 52									
Dorchester West	a																					
Dorchester South	d				12 00								13 00									
Moreton (Dorset)	d				12 07								13 07									
Wool	d				12 13								13 13									
Wareham	d				12 20								13 20									
Holton Heath	d																					
Hamworthy	d				12 27								13 27									
Poole 4	a				12 31								13 31									
	d				12 32			12 55					13 32				13 55					
Parkstone (Dorset)	d				12 36								13 36									
Branksome	d				12 40								13 40									
Bournemouth	a				12 46			13 04					13 46				14 04					
	d			12 40	12 50			13 06			13 40		13 50				14 06		14 40			
Pokesdown	d							13 10									14 10					
Christchurch	d							13 14									14 14					
Hinton Admiral	d							13 19									14 19					
New Milton	d				13 01			13 23					14 01				14 23					
Sway	d							13 28									14 28					
Lymington Pier	d					13 14						13 44			14 14					14 44		
Lymington Town	d					13 16						13 46			14 16					14 46		
Brockenhurst 3	a			12 53	13 08	13 24		13 33			13 53	13 54	14 08		14 24		14 33		14 53	14 54		
	d			12 57	13 09			13 34			13 57		14 09				14 34		14 57			
Beaulieu Road	d							13 39									14 39					
Ashurst New Forest	d							13 43									14 43					
Totton	d							13 48									14 48					
Salisbury	d		12 33						13 08	13 33								14 13				14 48
Dean	d								13 20													
Mottisfont & Dunbridge	d								13 26													
Romsey	d		12 52						13 32	13 51								14 32				15 10
Redbridge	d								13 39									14 39				
Millbrook (Hants)	d								13 43									14 43				
Southampton Central ⛴	a		13 05	13 10	13 23			13 53	13 45	14 03	14 10		14 23				14 53	14 45	15 10			15 21
	d		13 07	13 15	13 25			13 55	13 59	14 04	14 15		14 25				14 55	14 59	15 15			15 22
St Denys	d								14 04									15 04				
Swaythling	d								14 07									15 07				
Southampton Airport Pkwy ✈	d			13 22	13 33			14 03	14 10		14 22		14 33				15 03	15 10	15 22			
Portsmouth Harbour ⛴	d	13 08					13 17							14 08		14 17					15 08	
Portsmouth & Southsea	d	13 12					13 22							14 12		14 22					15 12	
Fratton	d	13 16					13 26							14 16		14 26					15 16	
Hilsea	d						13 30									14 30						
Cosham	d	13 23					13 35							14 23		14 35					15 23	
Portchester	d						13 40									14 40						
Fareham	d	13 32	13a33				13 46			14a26				14 32		14 46					15 32	15a50
Botley	d						13 54									14 54						
Hedge End	d						13 58									14 58						
Eastleigh 3	a						14 04	14 07	14 13							15 04	15 07	15 13				
	d							14 11	14 15								15 11	15 15				
Chandlers Ford	d								14 20									15 20				
Romsey	a	14 05							14 28					15 05				15 28			16 05	
Shawford	d																15 17					
Winchester	d			13 31	13 42			14 23			14 31		14 42				15 23		15 31			
Micheldever	d							14 32									15 32					
Basingstoke	a			13 46	13 58			14 42			14 46		14 58				15 42		15 46			
	d			13 47	14 00			14 44			14 47		15 00				15 44		15 47			
Reading 7	a			14 03							15 04								16 03			
Fleet	d																					
Farnborough (Main)	d																					
Woking	a				14 18			15 02					15 18				16 02					
Clapham Junction	a																					
Clapham Junction 10	a				14 39			15 27					15 39				16 27					
London Waterloo 15 ⊖	a				14 49			15 37					15 49				16 37					

A ⊼ from Bournemouth
B ⊼ from Eastleigh ◇ to Eastleigh

Table 158

Sundays until 12 February

Weymouth, Bournemouth, Lymington, Romsey, Southampton and Basingstoke - London

Network Diagram - see first Page of Table 158

		SW ◇1 A ⌶	GW ◇	SW 1	SW 1 ⌶	SW ◇1 B ⌶	SW 1	GW ◇	XC ◇1 ⌶		SW 1	SW ◇1 A ⌶	GW ◇	SW 1	SW 1 ⌶	SW ◇1 B ⌶	SW 1	GW ◇	XC ◇1 C ⌶		XC ◇1 D ⌶	SW 1	SW ◇1 A ⌶	GW ◇	SW 1
Weymouth	d	13 48	14 00									14 48											15 48		
Upwey	d	13 52	14 05									14 52											15 52		
Dorchester West	a		14 12																						
Dorchester South	d	14 00										15 00											16 00		
Moreton (Dorset)	d	14 07										15 07											16 07		
Wool	d	14 13										15 13											16 13		
Wareham	d	14 20										15 20											16 20		
Holton Heath	d																								
Hamworthy	d	14 27										15 27											16 27		
Poole 4	a	14 31										15 31											16 31		
	d	14 32				14 55						15 32				15 55							16 32		
Parkstone (Dorset)	d	14 36										15 36											16 36		
Branksome	d	14 40										15 40											16 40		
Bournemouth	a	14 46				15 04						15 46				16 04							16 46		
	d	14 50				15 06			15 40			15 50				16 06			16 40		16 40		16 50		
Pokesdown	d					15 10										16 10									
Christchurch	d					15 14										16 14									
Hinton Admiral	d					15 19										16 19									
New Milton	d	15 01				15 23						16 01				16 23							17 01		
Sway	d					15 28										16 28									
Lymington Pier	d			15 14							15 44			16 14								16 44			17 14
Lymington Town	d			15 16							15 46			16 16								16 46			17 16
Brockenhurst 3	a	15 08		15 24		15 33			15 53		15 54	16 08		16 24		16 33			16 53		16 53	16 54	17 08		17 24
	d	15 09				15 34			15 57			16 09				16 34			16 57		16 57		17 09		
Beaulieu Road	d					15 39										16 39									
Ashurst New Forest	d					15 43										16 43									
Totton	d					15 48										16 48									
Salisbury	d						15 08	15 32									16 13	16 33							
Dean	d						15 20																		
Mottisfont & Dunbridge	d						15 26																		
Romsey	d						15 32	15 50									16 32	16 51							
Redbridge	d						15 39										16 39								
Millbrook (Hants)	d						15 43										16 43								
Southampton Central ⛴	a	15 23				15 53	15 45	16 02	16 10			16 23				16 53	16 45	17 03	17 10		17 10		17 23		
	d	15 25				15 55	15 59	16 04	16 15			16 25				16 55	16 59	17 04	17 15		17 15		17 25		
St Denys	d						16 04										17 04								
Swaythling	d						16 07										17 07								
Southampton Airport Pkwy ✈	d	15 33				16 03	16 10		16 22			16 33				17 03	17 10		17 22		17 22		17 33		
Portsmouth Harbour ⛴	d				15 17								16 08		16 17									17 08	
Portsmouth & Southsea	d				15 22								16 12		16 22									17 12	
Fratton	d				15 26								16 16		16 26									17 16	
Hilsea	d				15 30										16 30										
Cosham	d				15 35								16 23		16 35									17 23	
Portchester	d				15 40										16 40										
Fareham	d				15 46			16a26					16 32		16 46			17a27						17 32	
Botley	d				15 54										16 54										
Hedge End	d				15 58										16 58										
Eastleigh 3	a				16 04	16 07	16 13								17 04	17 07	17 13								
	d					16 11	16 15									17 11	17 15								
Chandlers Ford	d						16 20										17 20								
Romsey	a						16 28						17 05				17 28							18 05	
Shawford	d															17 17									
Winchester	d	15 42				16 23			16 31			16 42				17 23			17 31		17 31		17 42		
Micheldever	d					16 32										17 32									
Basingstoke	a	15 58				16 42			16 46			16 58				17 42			17 46		17 46		17 58		
	d	16 00				16 44			16 47			17 00				17 44			17 47		17 47		18 00		
Reading 7	a								17 03										18 03		18 04				
Fleet	d																								
Farnborough (Main)	d																								
Woking	a	16 18				17 02						17 18				18 02							18 18		
Clapham Junction	a																								
Clapham Junction 10	a	16 39				17 27						17 39				18 27							18 39		
London Waterloo 15 ⊖	a	16 49				17 37						17 49				18 37							18 49		

A ⌶ from Bournemouth

B ⌶ from Eastleigh ◇ to Eastleigh

C from 8 January until 12 February

D until 1 January

Table 158

Sundays until 12 February

Weymouth, Bournemouth, Lymington, Romsey, Southampton and Basingstoke - London

Network Diagram - see first Page of Table 158

		SW 1	SW ◇1 A	SW 1	GW ◇		XC ◇1 ⌶	SW 1	SW ◇1 B ⌶	GW ◇	SW 1	SW 1	SW ◇1 A	SW 1	GW ◇		XC ◇1 ⌶	SW 1	SW ◇1 B ⌶	GW ◇	GW ◇	SW 1	GW ◇	SW 1	SW ◇1 A
Weymouth	d								16 48										17 48	17 56					
Upwey	d								16 52										17 52	18 01					
Dorchester West	a																			18 08					
Dorchester South	d								17 00										18 00						
Moreton (Dorset)	d								17 07										18 07						
Wool	d								17 13										18 13						
Wareham	d								17 20										18 20						
Holton Heath	d																								
Hamworthy	d								17 27										18 27						
Poole 4	a								17 31										18 31						
	d		16 55						17 32				17 55						18 32						18 55
Parkstone (Dorset)	d								17 36										18 36						
Branksome	d								17 40										18 40						
Bournemouth	a		17 04						17 46				18 04						18 46						19 04
	d		17 06				17 40		17 50				18 06				18 40		18 50						19 06
Pokesdown	d		17 10										18 10												19 10
Christchurch	d		17 14										18 14												19 14
Hinton Admiral	d		17 19										18 19												19 19
New Milton	d		17 23						18 01				18 23						19 01						19 23
Sway	d		17 28										18 28												19 28
Lymington Pier	d							17 44			18 14							18 44				19 14			
Lymington Town	d							17 46			18 16							18 46				19 16			
Brockenhurst 3	a		17 33				17 53	17 54	18 08		18 24		18 33				18 53	18 54	19 08			19 24			19 33
	d		17 34				17 57		18 09				18 34				18 57		19 09						19 34
Beaulieu Road	d		17 39										18 39												19 39
Ashurst New Forest	d		17 43										18 43												19 43
Totton	d		17 48										18 48												19 48
Salisbury	d			17 08	17 33									18 13	18 32								18 56		
Dean	d			17 20																					
Mottisfont & Dunbridge	d			17 26																					
Romsey	d			17 32	17 51									18 32	18 50								19 14		
Redbridge	d			17 39										18 39											
Millbrook (Hants)	d			17 43										18 43											
Southampton Central ⛴	a		17 53	17 45	18 03		18 10		18 23				18 53	18 45	19 02		19 10		19 23				19 25		19 53
	d		17 55	17 59	18 04		18 15		18 25				18 55	18 59	19 04		19 15		19 25				19 26		19 55
St Denys	d			18 04										19 04											
Swaythling	d			18 07										19 07											
Southampton Airport Pkwy ✈	d		18 03	18 10			18 22		18 33				19 03	19 10			19 22		19 33						20 03
Portsmouth Harbour ⛴	d	17 17								18 08		18 17									19 08			19 17	
Portsmouth & Southsea	d	17 22								18 12		18 22									19 12			19 22	
Fratton	d	17 26								18 16		18 26									19 16			19 26	
Hilsea	d	17 30										18 30												19 30	
Cosham	d	17 35								18 23		18 35									19 23			19 35	
Portchester	d	17 40										18 40												19 40	
Fareham	d	17 46			18a27					18 32		18 46			19a27						19 32		19a48	19 46	
Botley	d	17 54										18 54												19 54	
Hedge End	d	17 58										18 58												19 58	
Eastleigh 3	a	18 04	18 07	18 13								19 04	19 07	19 13										20 04	20 07
	d		18 11	18 15									19 11	19 15											20 11
Chandlers Ford	d			18 20										19 20											
Romsey	a			18 28						19 05				19 28							20 05				
Shawford	d												19 17												
Winchester	d		18 23				18 31		18 42				19 23				19 31		19 42						20 23
Micheldever	d		18 32										19 32												20 32
Basingstoke	a		18 42				18 46		18 58				19 42				19 46		19 58						20 42
	d		18 44				18 47		19 00				19 44				19 47		20 00						20 44
Reading 7	a						19 03										20 03								
Fleet	d																								
Farnborough (Main)	d																								
Woking	a		19 02						19 18				20 02						20 18						21 02
Clapham Junction	a																								
Clapham Junction 10	a		19 27						19 39				20 27						20 39						21 27
London Waterloo 15 ⊖	a		19 37						19 49				20 37						20 49						21 37

A ◇ to Eastleigh

B ⌶ from Bournemouth

Weymouth, Bournemouth, Lymington, Romsey, Southampton and Basingstoke - London

Network Diagram - see first Page of Table 158

		SW	GW	XC	SW	SW	GW	SW	GW	SW	SW	SW	GW	SW	SW	SW	SW	GW	SW	GW	SW	GW
		■	◇	◇■	■	◇■ A ✠	◇	■	■	■	◇■ B	■	◇	■	■	■	◇■ B		■	◇	■	
Weymouth	d					18 48											19 58	20 09				
Upwey	d					18 52											20 02	20 14				
Dorchester West	a																	20 21				
Dorchester South	d					19 00											20 10					
Moreton (Dorset)	d					19 07											20 17					
Wool	d					19 13											20 23					
Wareham	d					19 20											20 30					
Holton Heath	d																					
Hamworthy	d					19 27											20 37					
Poole ■	a					19 31											20 41					
	d					19 32					19 55						20 50					
Parkstone (Dorset)	d					19 36											20 54					
Branksome	d					19 40											20 57					
Bournemouth	a					19 46					20 04						21 03					
	d			19 40		19 50					20 06						21 06					
Pokesdown	d										20 10						21 10					
Christchurch	d										20 14						21 14					
Hinton Admiral	d										20 19						21 19					
New Milton	d					20 01					20 23						21 23					
Sway	d										20 28						21 28					
Lymington Pier	d				19 44			20 14						20 44	21 14						21 44	
Lymington Town	d				19 46			20 16						20 46	21 16						21 46	
Brockenhurst ■	a			19 53	19 54	20 08		20 24			20 33			20 54	21 24		21 33				21 54	
	d			19 57		20 09					20 34						21 34					
Beaulieu Road	d										20 39						21 39					
Ashurst New Forest	d										20 43						21 43					
Totton	d										20 48						21 48					
Salisbury	d	19 08	19 32						20 01			20 13	20 30						21 08	21 33		
Dean	d	19 20																	21 20			
Mottisfont & Dunbridge	d	19 26																	21 26			
Romsey	d	19 32	19 50						20 19			20 32	20 48						21 32	21 51		
Redbridge	d	19 39										20 39							21 39			
Millbrook (Hants)	d	19 43										20 43							21 43			
Southampton Central ⛴	a	19 45	20 02	20 10		20 23			20 29		20 53	20 45	20 59				21 53		21 45	22 03		
	d	19 59	20 04	20 15		20 25			20 31		20 55	20 59	21 02				21 55		21 59	22 04		
St Denys	d	20 04										21 04							22 04			
Swaythling	d	20 07										21 07							22 07			
Southampton Airport Pkwy ✈	d	20 10		20 22		20 33					21 03	21 10					22 03		22 10			
Portsmouth Harbour ⛴	d						20 08			20 17						21 17						22 03
Portsmouth & Southsea	d						20 12			20 22						21 22						22 12
Fratton	d						20 16			20 26						21 26						22 16
Hilsea	d									20 30						21 30						
Cosham	d									20 35						21 35						
Portchester	d									20 40						21 40						
Fareham	d		20a26				20 32		20a54	20 46			21a24			21 46				22a26		22 32
Botley	d									20 54						21 54						
Hedge End	d									20 58						21 58						
Eastleigh ■	a	20 13								21 04	21 07	21 13				22 04	22 07		22 13			
	d	20 15								21 11		21 15				22 11			22 15			
Chandlers Ford	d	20 20										21 20							22 20			
Romsey	a	20 28					21 05					21 28							22 31			23 08
Shawford	d									21 17												
Winchester	d			20 31		20 42				21 23						22 23						
Micheldever	d									21 32						22 32						
Basingstoke	a			20 46		20 58				21 42						22 42						
	d			20 47		21 00				21 44						22 44						
Reading ■	a			21 03																		
Fleet	d																					
Farnborough (Main)	d																					
Woking	a					21 18				22 02						23 02						
Clapham Junction	a																					
Clapham Junction ■	a					21 39				22 27						23 27						
London Waterloo ■ ⊖	a					21 49				22 37						23 37						

A ✠ from Bournemouth

B ◇ to Eastleigh

Weymouth, Bournemouth, Lymington, Romsey, Southampton and Basingstoke - London

Network Diagram - see first Page of Table 158

		SW	SW	SW	SW	GW	SW	SW	SW
		■	■	◇■	■	◇	■	■	■
Weymouth	d			20 58			21 58	22 58	
Upwey	d			21 02			22 02	23 02	
Dorchester West	a								
Dorchester South	d			21 10			22 10	23 10	
Moreton (Dorset)	d			21 17			22 17	23 17	
Wool	d			21 23			22 23	23 23	
Wareham	d			21 30			22 30	23 30	
Holton Heath	d								
Hamworthy	d			21 37			22 37	23 37	
Poole ■	a			21 41			22 41	23 41	
	d			21 50			22 50	23 50	
Parkstone (Dorset)	d			21 54			22 54	23 54	
Branksome	d			21 57			22 57	23 57	
Bournemouth	a			22 03			23 03	00 03	
	d			22 06			23 06		
Pokesdown	d			22 10			23 10		
Christchurch	d			22 14			23 14		
Hinton Admiral	d			22 19			23 19		
New Milton	d			22 23			23 23		
Sway	d			22 28			23 28		
Lymington Pier	d	22 14							
Lymington Town	d	22 16							
Brockenhurst ■	a	22 24		22 33			23 33		
	d			22 34			23 34		
Beaulieu Road	d			22 39					
Ashurst New Forest	d			22 43			23 43		
Totton	d			22 48			23 48		
Salisbury	d					22 36			
Dean	d								
Mottisfont & Dunbridge	d								
Romsey	d				22 28	22 54			
Redbridge	d				22 35				
Millbrook (Hants)	d				22 39				
Southampton Central ⛴	a			22 53	22 41	23 05	23 53		
	d			22 55	23 05	23 08			
St Denys	d				23 10				
Swaythling	d				23 13				
Southampton Airport Pkwy ✈	d			23 03	23 16				
Portsmouth Harbour ⛴	d		22 17						23 17
Portsmouth & Southsea	d		22 22						23 22
Fratton	d		22 26						23 26
Hilsea	d		22 30						23 30
Cosham	d		22 35						23 35
Portchester	d		22 40						23 40
Fareham	d		22 46			23a29			23 46
Botley	d		22 54						23 54
Hedge End	d		22 58						23 58
Eastleigh ■	a		23 04	23 09	23 19				00 04
	d			23 11	23 21				
Chandlers Ford	d				23 26				
Romsey	a				23 33				
Shawford	d								
Winchester	d			23 23					
Micheldever	d			23 32					
Basingstoke	a			23 42					
	d			23 44					
Reading ■	a								
Fleet	d								
Farnborough (Main)	d								
Woking	a			00 02					
Clapham Junction	a								
Clapham Junction ■	a			00 23					
London Waterloo ■ ⊖	a			00 33					

Table 158

Sundays

19 February to 25 March

Weymouth, Bournemouth, Lymington, Romsey, Southampton and Basingstoke - London

Network Diagram - see first Page of Table 158

		SW ■	SW ■	SW ■	SW ■	SW ■	SW ◇■ A 🚲	SW ■	SW ■	SW ◇■ B	SW ■	GW ■	XC ◇■ 🚲	SW ◇■ C 🚲	SW ■	SW ■ 🚲	SW ◇■ D 🚲	SW ■	XC ◇■ 🚲	SW ■	SW ◇■ C 🚲	SW ■
Weymouth	d		22p10	23p10										07 48							08 48	
Upwey	d		22p14	23p14										07 52							08 52	
Dorchester West	a																					
Dorchester South	d		22p22	23p22										08 00							09 00	
Moreton (Dorset)	d		22p28	23p28										08 07							09 07	
Wool	d		22p34	23p34										08 13							09 13	
Wareham	d		22p42	23p42										08 20							09 20	
Holton Heath	d																					
Hamworthy	d		22p48	23p48										08 27							09 27	
Poole 4	a		22p53	23p53										08 31							09 31	
	d		22p54	23p54			06 50			07 50				08 32			08 55				09 32	
Parkstone (Dorset)	d		22p58				06 54			07 54				08 36							09 36	
Branksome	d		23p01				06 57			07 57				08 40							09 40	
Bournemouth	a		23p07	00 03			07 02			08 02				08 46			09 04				09 46	
	d		23p12				07 06			08 06				08 50			09 06		09 40		09 50	
Pokesdown	d		23p16				07 10			08 10							09 10					
Christchurch	d		23p20				07 14			08 14							09 14					
Hinton Admiral	d		23p25				07 19			08 19							09 19					
New Milton	d		23p29				07 23			08 23				09 01			09 23				10 01	
Sway	d		23p34				07 28			08 28							09 28					
Lymington Pier	d														09 14					09 44		10 14
Lymington Town	d														09 16					09 46		10 16
Brockenhurst 3	a		23p39				07 33			08 33				09 08	09 24		09 33		09 53	09 54	10 08	10 24
	d		23p40				07 34			08 34				09 09			09 34		09 57		10 09	
Beaulieu Road	d									08 39							09 39					
Ashurst New Forest	d		23p47				07 43			08 43							09 43					
Totton	d		23p52				07 48			08 48							09 48					
Salisbury	d							08 08			08 20							09 08				
Dean	d							08 20										09 20				
Mottisfont & Dunbridge	d							08 26										09 26				
Romsey	d							08 35			08 39							09 32				
Redbridge	d										08 46							09 39				
Millbrook (Hants)	d										08 50							09 43				
Southampton Central ⛴	a		23p57				07 53			08 53	08 52			09 23			09 53	09 45	10 10		10 23	
	d		23p59				07 55			08 55	08 59		09 15	09 25			09 55	09 59	10 15		10 25	
St Denys	d		00 04								09 04							10 04				
Swaythling	d		00 07								09 07							10 07				
Southampton Airport Pkwy ✈	d		00 10				08 03			09 03	09 10		09 22	09 33			10 03	10 10	10 22		10 33	
Portsmouth Harbour ⛴	d	23p24			06 37	07 17			08 17			09 08				09 17						
Portsmouth & Southsea	d	23p29			06 42	07 22			08 22			09 12				09 22						
Fratton	d	23p33			06 46	07 26			08 26			09 16				09 26						
Hilsea	d	23p37			06 50	07 30			08 30							09 30						
Cosham	d	23p42			06 55	07 35			08 35			09 23				09 35						
Portchester	d	23p47			07 00	07 40			08 40							09 40						
Fareham	d	23p53			07a05	07 46			08 46			09 32				09 46						
Botley	d	23p59				07 54			08 54							09 54						
Hedge End	d	00 05				07 58			08 58							09 58						
Eastleigh 5	a	00 11	00 14			08 04	08 07		09 04	09 07	09 13					10 04	10 07	10 13				
	d	00 21					08 11			09 11	09 15						10 11	10 15				
Chandlers Ford	d							08 42			09 20							10 20				
Romsey	a							09 24			09 28	10 05						10 28				
Shawford	d									09 17												
Winchester	d	00a30					08 23			09 23			09 31	09 42			10 23		10 31		10 42	
Micheldever	d						08 32			09 32							10 32					
Basingstoke	a						08 42			09 42			09 46	09 58			10 42		10 46		10 58	
	d						08 44			09 44			09 47	10 00			10 44		10 47		11 00	
Reading 7	a												10 04						11 03			
Fleet	d																					
Farnborough (Main)	d																					
Woking	a						09 02			10 02				10 19			11 02				11 18	
Clapham Junction	a																					
Clapham Junction 10	a						09 30			10 27				10 40			11 27				11 39	
London Waterloo 15 ⊖	a						09 43			10 42				10 54			11 42				11 54	

A 🚲 to Eastleigh ◇ to Eastleigh

B ◇ to Eastleigh

C 🚲 from Bournemouth

D 🚲 from Eastleigh ◇ to Eastleigh

Table 158

Sundays

19 February to 25 March

Weymouth, Bournemouth, Lymington, Romsey, Southampton and Basingstoke - London

Network Diagram - see first Page of Table 158

		SW ■ 🚲	SW ◇■ A 🚲	SW ■	GW ◇	XC ◇■ 🚲	SW ■	SW ◇■ B 🚲	GW ◇	SW ■	SW ■ 🚲	SW ◇■ C 🚲	SW ■	GW ◇	XC ◇■ 🚲	SW ■	SW ◇■ B 🚲	SW ■	SW ■ 🚲	SW ◇■ A 🚲	SW ■	SW ■	GW ◇
Weymouth	d							09 48									10 48						
Upwey	d							09 52									10 52						
Dorchester West	a																						
Dorchester South	d							10 00									11 00						
Moreton (Dorset)	d							10 07									11 07						
Wool	d							10 13									11 13						
Wareham	d							10 20									11 20						
Holton Heath	d																						
Hamworthy	d							10 27									11 27						
Poole 4	a							10 31									11 31						
	d		09 55					10 32				10 55					11 32			11 55			
Parkstone (Dorset)	d							10 36									11 36						
Branksome	d							10 40									11 40						
Bournemouth	a		10 04					10 46				11 04					11 46			12 04			
	d		10 06			10 40		10 50				11 06			11 40		11 50			12 06			
Pokesdown	d		10 10									11 10								12 10			
Christchurch	d		10 14									11 14								12 14			
Hinton Admiral	d		10 19									11 19								12 19			
New Milton	d		10 23					11 01				11 23					12 01			12 23			
Sway	d		10 28									11 28								12 28			
Lymington Pier	d						10 44			11 14						11 44		12 14				12 44	
Lymington Town	d						10 46			11 16						11 46		12 16				12 46	
Brockenhurst 3	a		10 33			10 53	10 54	11 08		11 24		11 33			11 53	11 54	12 08	12 24		12 33		12 54	
	d		10 34			10 57		11 09				11 34			11 57		12 09			12 34			
Beaulieu Road	d		10 39									11 39								12 39			
Ashurst New Forest	d		10 43									11 43								12 43			
Totton	d		10 48									11 48								12 48			
Salisbury	d			10 13	10 32								11 08	11 33							12 13		
Dean	d												11 20										
Mottisfont & Dunbridge	d												11 26										
Romsey	d			10 32	10 50								11 32	11 51							12 32		
Redbridge	d			10 39									11 39								12 39		
Millbrook (Hants)	d			10 43									11 43								12 43		
Southampton Central ⛴	a		10 53	10 45	11 02	11 10		11 23				11 53	11 45	12 03	12 10		12 23			12 53	12 45		
	d		10 55	10 59	11 04	11 15		11 25				11 55	11 59	12 04	12 15		12 25			12 55	12 59		
St Denys	d			11 04									12 04								13 04		
Swaythling	d			11 07									12 07								13 07		
Southampton Airport Pkwy ✈	d		11 03	11 10		11 22		11 33				12 03	12 10		12 22		12 33			13 03	13 10		
Portsmouth Harbour ⛴	d	10 17							11 08		11 17								12 17				13 08
Portsmouth & Southsea	d	10 22							11 12		11 22								12 22				13 12
Fratton	d	10 26							11 16		11 26								12 26				13 16
Hilsea	d	10 30									11 30								12 30				
Cosham	d	10 35							11 23		11 35								12 35				13 23
Portchester	d	10 40									11 40								12 40				
Fareham	d	10 46			11a26				11 32		11 46			12a28					12 46				13 32
Botley	d	10 54									11 54								12 54				
Hedge End	d	10 58									11 58								12 58				
Eastleigh 5	a	11 04	11 07	11 13							12 04	12 07	12 13						13 04	13 07	13 13		
	d		11 11	11 15								12 11	12 15							13 11	13 15		
Chandlers Ford	d			11 20									12 20								13 20		
Romsey	a			11 28					12 05				12 28								13 28		14 05
Shawford	d		11 17																	13 17			
Winchester	d		11 23			11 31		11 42				12 23			12 31		12 42			13 23			
Micheldever	d		11 32									12 32								13 32			
Basingstoke	a		11 42			11 46		11 58				12 42			12 46		12 58			13 42			
	d		11 44			11 47		12 00				12 44			12 47		13 00			13 44			
Reading 7	a					12 03									13 03								
Fleet	d																						
Farnborough (Main)	d																						
Woking	a		12 02					12 18				13 02					13 18			14 02			
Clapham Junction	a																						
Clapham Junction 10	a		12 27					12 39				13 27					13 39			14 27			
London Waterloo 15 ⊖	a		12 42					12 49				13 37					13 49			14 37			

A 🚲 from Bournemouth ◇ to Eastleigh

B 🚲 from Bournemouth

C 🚲 from Eastleigh ◇ to Eastleigh

Weymouth, Bournemouth, Lymington, Romsey, Southampton and Basingstoke - London

Network Diagram - see first Page of Table 158

		GW ◇	XC ◇ 1 ⌶	SW ◇ 1 A ⌶	SW 1	SW 1 ⌶	SW ◇ 1 B ⌶	SW 1	GW ◇ ⌶	XC ◇ 1 ⌶	SW 1	SW ◇ 1 A ⌶	GW ◇	SW 1	SW 1 ⌶	SW ◇ 1 B ⌶	SW 1	XC ◇ 1 ⌶	SW 1	GW ■	GW ◇	SW ◇ 1 A ⌶
Weymouth	d			11 48								12 48										13 48
Upwey	d			11 52								12 52										13 52
Dorchester West	a																					
Dorchester South	d			12 00								13 00										14 00
Moreton (Dorset)	d			12 07								13 07										14 07
Wool	d			12 13								13 13										14 13
Wareham	d			12 20								13 20										14 20
Holton Heath	d																					
Hamworthy	d			12 27								13 27										14 27
Poole 4	a			12 31								13 31										14 31
	d			12 32			12 55					13 32				13 55						14 32
Parkstone (Dorset)	d			12 36								13 36										14 36
Branksome	d			12 40								13 40										14 40
Bournemouth	a			12 46			13 04					13 46				14 04						14 46
	d		12 40	12 50			13 06			13 40		13 50				14 06		14 40				14 50
Pokesdown	d						13 10									14 10						
Christchurch	d						13 14									14 14						
Hinton Admiral	d						13 19									14 19						
New Milton	d			13 01			13 23					14 01				14 23						15 01
Sway	d						13 28									14 28						
Lymington Pier	d				13 14						13 44			14 14					14 44			
Lymington Town	d				13 16						13 46			14 16					14 46			
Brockenhurst 3	a		12 53	13 08	13 24		13 33			13 53	13 54	14 08		14 24		14 33		14 53	14 54			15 08
	d		12 57	13 09			13 34			13 57		14 09				14 34		14 57				15 09
Beaulieu Road	d						13 39									14 39						
Ashurst New Forest	d						13 43									14 43						
Totton	d						13 48									14 48						
Salisbury	d	12 33						13 08	13 33								14 13				14 48	
Dean	d							13 20														
Mottisfont & Dunbridge	d							13 26														
Romsey	d	12 52						13 32	13 51								14 32				15 10	
Redbridge	d							13 39									14 39					
Millbrook (Hants)	d							13 43									14 43					
Southampton Central ⛴	a	13 05	13 10	13 23			13 53	13 45	14 03	14 10		14 23				14 53	14 45	15 10			15 21	15 23
	d	13 07	13 15	13 25			13 55	13 59	14 04	14 15		14 25				14 55	14 59	15 15			15 22	15 25
St Denys	d							14 04									15 04					
Swaythling	d							14 07									15 07					
Southampton Airport Pkwy ✈	d		13 22	13 33			14 03	14 10		14 22		14 33				15 03	15 10	15 22				15 33
Portsmouth Harbour ⛴	d					13 17							14 08		14 17					15 08		
Portsmouth & Southsea	d					13 22							14 12		14 22					15 12		
Fratton	d					13 26							14 16		14 26					15 16		
Hilsea	d					13 30									14 30							
Cosham	d					13 35							14 23		14 35					15 23		
Portchester	d					13 40									14 40							
Fareham	d	13a33				13 46			14a26				14 32		14 46					15 32	15a50	
Botley	d					13 54									14 54							
Hedge End	d					13 58									14 58							
Eastleigh 3	a					14 04	14 07	14 13							15 04	15 07	15 13					
	d						14 11	14 15								15 11	15 15					
Chandlers Ford	d							14 20									15 20					
Romsey	a							14 28					15 05				15 28			16 05		
Shawford	d															15 17						
Winchester	d		13 31	13 42			14 23			14 31		14 42				15 23		15 31				15 42
Micheldever	d						14 32									15 32						
Basingstoke	a		13 46	13 58			14 42			14 46		14 58				15 42		15 46				15 58
	d		13 47	14 00			14 44			14 47		15 00				15 44		15 47				16 00
Reading 7	a		14 03							15 04								16 03				
Fleet	d																					
Farnborough (Main)	d																					
Woking	a			14 18			15 02					15 18				16 02						16 18
Clapham Junction	a																					
Clapham Junction 10	a			14 39			15 27					15 39				16 27						16 39
London Waterloo 15 ⊖	a			14 49			15 37					15 49				16 37						16 49

A ⌶ from Bournemouth

B ⌶ from Eastleigh ◇ to Eastleigh

Weymouth, Bournemouth, Lymington, Romsey, Southampton and Basingstoke - London

Network Diagram - see first Page of Table 158

		GW ◇	SW 1	SW 1 ⌶	SW ◇ 1 A ⌶	SW 1	GW ◇	XC ◇ 1 ⌶	SW 1	SW ◇ 1 B ⌶	GW ◇	SW 1	SW 1 ⌶	SW ◇ 1 A ⌶	SW 1	GW ◇	XC ◇ 1 ⌶	SW 1	SW ◇ 1 B ⌶	GW ◇	SW 1	SW 1	SW ◇ 1 C
Weymouth	d	14 00								14 48									15 48				
Upwey	d	14 05								14 52									15 52				
Dorchester West	a	14 12																					
Dorchester South	d									15 00									16 00				
Moreton (Dorset)	d									15 07									16 07				
Wool	d									15 13									16 13				
Wareham	d									15 20									16 20				
Holton Heath	d																						
Hamworthy	d									15 27									16 27				
Poole 4	a									15 31									16 31				
	d				14 55					15 32				15 55					16 32				16 55
Parkstone (Dorset)	d									15 36									16 36				
Branksome	d									15 40									16 40				
Bournemouth	a				15 04					15 46				16 04					16 46				17 04
	d				15 06			15 40		15 50				16 06			16 40		16 50				17 06
Pokesdown	d				15 10									16 10									17 10
Christchurch	d				15 14									16 14									17 14
Hinton Admiral	d				15 19									16 19									17 19
New Milton	d				15 23					16 01				16 23					17 01				17 23
Sway	d				15 28									16 28									17 28
Lymington Pier	d		15 14						15 44			16 14						16 44			17 14		
Lymington Town	d		15 16						15 46			16 16						16 46			17 16		
Brockenhurst 3	a		15 24		15 33			15 53	15 54	16 08		16 24		16 33			16 53	16 54	17 08		17 24		17 33
	d				15 34			15 57		16 09				16 34			16 57		17 09				17 34
Beaulieu Road	d				15 39									16 39									17 39
Ashurst New Forest	d				15 43									16 43									17 43
Totton	d				15 48									16 48									17 48
Salisbury	d					15 08	15 33								16 13	16 33							
Dean	d					15 20																	
Mottisfont & Dunbridge	d					15 26																	
Romsey	d					15 32	15 51								16 32	16 51							
Redbridge	d					15 39									16 39								
Millbrook (Hants)	d					15 43									16 43								
Southampton Central ⛴	a				15 53	15 45	16 03	16 10		16 23				16 53	16 45	17 03	17 10		17 23				17 53
	d				15 55	15 59	16 05	16 15		16 25				16 55	16 59	17 04	17 15		17 25				17 55
St Denys	d					16 04									17 04								
Swaythling	d					16 07									17 07								
Southampton Airport Pkwy ✈	d				16 03	16 10		16 22		16 33				17 03	17 10		17 22		17 33				18 03
Portsmouth Harbour ⛴	d			15 17							16 08		16 17							17 08		17 17	
Portsmouth & Southsea	d			15 22							16 12		16 22							17 12		17 22	
Fratton	d			15 26							16 16		16 26							17 16		17 26	
Hilsea	d			15 30									16 30									17 30	
Cosham	d			15 35							16 23		16 35							17 23		17 35	
Portchester	d			15 40									16 40									17 40	
Fareham	d			15 46			16a27				16 32		16 46			17a27				17 32		17 46	
Botley	d			15 54									16 54									17 54	
Hedge End	d			15 58									16 58									17 58	
Eastleigh 3	a			16 04	16 07	16 13							17 04	17 07	17 13							18 04	18 07
	d				16 11	16 15								17 11	17 15								18 11
Chandlers Ford	d					16 20									17 20								
Romsey	a					16 28					17 05				17 28					18 05			
Shawford	d													17 17									
Winchester	d				16 23			16 31		16 42				17 23			17 31		17 42				18 23
Micheldever	d				16 32									17 32									18 32
Basingstoke	a				16 42			16 46		16 58				17 42			17 46		17 58				18 42
	d				16 44			16 47		17 00				17 44			17 47		18 00				18 44
Reading 7	a							17 02									18 03						
Fleet	d																						
Farnborough (Main)	d																						
Woking	a				17 02					17 18				18 02					18 18				19 02
Clapham Junction	a																						
Clapham Junction 10	a				17 27					17 39				18 27					18 39				19 27
London Waterloo 15 ⊖	a				17 37					17 49				18 37					18 49				19 37

A ⌶ from Eastleigh ◇ to Eastleigh

B ⌶ from Bournemouth

C ◇ to Eastleigh

Table 158

Sundays

19 February to 25 March

Weymouth, Bournemouth, Lymington, Romsey, Southampton and Basingstoke - London

Network Diagram - see first Page of Table 158

		SW	GW	XC	SW	SW	GW	SW	SW	SW	SW	GW	XC	SW	SW	GW	GW	SW	GW	SW	SW	SW	GW
		■	◇	◇■ 🍴	■	◇■ A 🍴	◇	■	■	◇■ B	■	◇	◇■ 🍴	■	◇■ A 🍴	◇	◇	■	◇	■	◇■ B	■	◇
Weymouth	d					16 48									17 48	17 56							
Upwey	d					16 52									17 52	18 01							
Dorchester West	a															18 08							
Dorchester South	d					17 00									18 00								
Moreton (Dorset)	d					17 07									18 07								
Wool	d					17 13									18 13								
Wareham	d					17 20									18 20								
Holton Heath	d																						
Hamworthy	d					17 27									18 27								
Poole ■	a					17 31									18 31								
	d					17 32				17 55					18 32						18 55		
Parkstone (Dorset)	d					17 36									18 36								
Branksome	d					17 40									18 40								
Bournemouth	a					17 46				18 04					18 46						19 04		
	d			17 40		17 50				18 06			18 40		18 50						19 06		
Pokesdown	d									18 10											19 10		
Christchurch	d									18 14											19 14		
Hinton Admiral	d									18 19											19 19		
New Milton	d					18 01				18 23					19 01						19 23		
Sway	d									18 28											19 28		
Lymington Pier	d				17 44			18 14						18 44				19 14					
Lymington Town	d				17 46			18 16						18 46				19 16					
Brockenhurst ■	a			17 53	17 54	18 08		18 24		18 33			18 53	18 54	19 08			19 24			19 33		
	d			17 57		18 09				18 34			18 57		19 09						19 34		
Beaulieu Road	d									18 39											19 39		
Ashurst New Forest	d									18 43											19 43		
Totton	d									18 48											19 48		
Salisbury	d	17 08	17 33								18 13	18 33							18 56			19 08	19 32
Dean	d	17 20																				19 20	
Mottisfont & Dunbridge	d	17 26																				19 26	
Romsey	d	17 32	17 51								18 32	18 51							19 14			19 32	19 50
Redbridge	d	17 39									18 39											19 39	
Millbrook (Hants)	d	17 43									18 43											19 43	
Southampton Central ⛴	a	17 45	18 03	18 10		18 23				18 53	18 45	19 03	19 10		19 23				19 25		19 53	19 45	20 02
	d	17 59	18 04	18 15		18 25				18 55	18 59	19 04	19 15		19 25				19 26		19 55	19 59	20 04
St Denys	d	18 04									19 04											20 04	
Swaythling	d	18 07									19 07											20 07	
Southampton Airport Pkwy ✈	d	18 10		18 22		18 33				19 03	19 10		19 22		19 33						20 03	20 10	
Portsmouth Harbour ⛴	d						18 08		18 17								19 08			19 17			
Portsmouth & Southsea	d						18 12		18 22								19 12			19 22			
Fratton	d						18 16		18 26								19 16			19 26			
Hilsea	d								18 30											19 30			
Cosham	d						18 23		18 35								19 23			19 35			
Portchester	d								18 40											19 40			
Fareham	d		18a27				18 32		18 46			19a28					19 32		19a48	19 46			20a27
Botley	d								18 54											19 54			
Hedge End	d								18 58											19 58			
Eastleigh ■	a	18 13							19 04	19 07	19 13									20 04	20 07	20 13	
	d	18 15							19 11		19 15									20 11		20 15	
Chandlers Ford	d	18 20									19 20											20 20	
Romsey	a	18 28					19 05				19 28						20 05					20 28	
Shawford	d								19 17														
Winchester	d			18 31		18 42			19 23				19 31		19 42					20 23			
Micheldever	d								19 32											20 32			
Basingstoke	a			18 46		18 58			19 42				19 46		19 58					20 42			
	d			18 47		19 00			19 44				19 47		20 00					20 44			
Reading ■	a			19 03									20 03										
Fleet	d																						
Farnborough (Main)	d																						
Woking	a					19 18			20 02						20 18					21 02			
Clapham Junction	a																						
Clapham Junction ■	a					19 39			20 27						20 39					21 27			
London Waterloo ■ ⊖	a					19 49			20 37						20 49					21 37			

A 🍴 from Bournemouth

B ◇ to Eastleigh

Table 158

Sundays

19 February to 25 March

Weymouth, Bournemouth, Lymington, Romsey, Southampton and Basingstoke - London

Network Diagram - see first Page of Table 158

		XC	SW	SW	GW	SW	GW	SW	SW	SW	GW	SW	SW	SW	SW	GW	SW	GW	SW	GW	SW	SW
		◇■	■	◇■ A 🍴	◇	■	■	■	◇■ B	■	◇	■	■	■	◇■ B		■	◇	■		■	■
Weymouth	d			18 48											19 58	20 09						
Upwey	d			18 52											20 02	20 14						
Dorchester West	a															20 21						
Dorchester South	d			19 00											20 10							
Moreton (Dorset)	d			19 07											20 17							
Wool	d			19 13											20 23							
Wareham	d			19 20											20 30							
Holton Heath	d																					
Hamworthy	d			19 27											20 37							
Poole ■	a			19 31											20 41							
	d			19 32					19 55						20 50							
Parkstone (Dorset)	d			19 36											20 54							
Branksome	d			19 40											20 57							
Bournemouth	a			19 46					20 04						21 03							
	d	19 40		19 50					20 06						21 06							
Pokesdown	d								20 10						21 10							
Christchurch	d								20 14						21 14							
Hinton Admiral	d								20 19						21 19							
New Milton	d			20 01					20 23						21 23							
Sway	d								20 28						21 28							
Lymington Pier	d		19 44			20 14						20 44	21 14						21 44		22 14	
Lymington Town	d		19 46			20 16						20 46	21 16						21 46		22 16	
Brockenhurst ■	a	19 53	19 54	20 08		20 24			20 33			20 54	21 24		21 33				21 54		22 24	
	d	19 57		20 09					20 34						21 34							
Beaulieu Road	d								20 39						21 39							
Ashurst New Forest	d								20 43						21 43							
Totton	d								20 48						21 48							
Salisbury	d						20 01			20 13	20 30						21 08	21 33				
Dean	d																21 20					
Mottisfont & Dunbridge	d																21 26					
Romsey	d						20 19			20 32	20 48						21 32	21 51				
Redbridge	d									20 39							21 39					
Millbrook (Hants)	d									20 43							21 43					
Southampton Central ⛴	a	20 10		20 23			20 29		20 53	20 45	20 59				21 53		21 45	22 03				
	d	20 15		20 25			20 31		20 55	20 59	21 02				21 55		21 59	22 04				
St Denys	d									21 04							22 04					
Swaythling	d									21 07							22 07					
Southampton Airport Pkwy ✈	d	20 22		20 33					21 03	21 10					22 03		22 10					
Portsmouth Harbour ⛴	d				20 08			20 17						21 17						22 03		22 17
Portsmouth & Southsea	d				20 12			20 22						21 22						22 12		22 22
Fratton	d				20 16			20 26						21 26						22 16		22 26
Hilsea	d							20 30						21 30								22 30
Cosham	d							20 35						21 35								22 35
Portchester	d							20 40						21 40								22 40
Fareham	d				20 32		20a54	20 46			21a24			21 46				22a26		22 32		22 46
Botley	d							20 54						21 54								22 54
Hedge End	d							20 58						21 58								22 58
Eastleigh ■	a							21 04	21 07	21 13				22 04	22 07		22 13					23 04
	d							21 11		21 15				22 11			22 15					
Chandlers Ford	d									21 20							22 20					
Romsey	a				21 05					21 28							22 31			23 08		
Shawford	d							21 17														
Winchester	d	20 31		20 42				21 23						22 23								
Micheldever	d							21 32						22 32								
Basingstoke	a	20 46		20 58				21 42						22 42								
	d	20 47		21 00				21 44						22 44								
Reading ■	a	21 03																				
Fleet	d																					
Farnborough (Main)	d																					
Woking	a			21 18				22 02						23 02								
Clapham Junction	a																					
Clapham Junction ■	a			21 39				22 27						23 27								
London Waterloo ■ ⊖	a			21 49				22 37						23 37								

A 🍴 from Bournemouth

B ◇ to Eastleigh

Weymouth, Bournemouth, Lymington, Romsey, Southampton and Basingstoke - London

Sundays
19 February to 25 March

Network Diagram - see first Page of Table 158

		SW ◇[1]	SW [1]	GW ◇	SW [1]	SW [1]	SW [1]	SW [1]	SW [1]	SW [1]
Weymouth	d	20 58			21 58	22 58				
Upwey	d	21 02			22 02	23 02				
Dorchester West	a									
Dorchester South	d	21 10			22 10	23 10				
Moreton (Dorset)	d	21 17			22 17	23 17				
Wool	d	21 23			22 23	23 23				
Wareham	d	21 30			22 30	23 30				
Holton Heath	d									
Hamworthy	d	21 37			22 37	23 37				
Poole [4]	a	21 41			22 41	23 41				
	d	21 50			22 50	23 50				
Parkstone (Dorset)	d	21 54			22 54	23 54				
Branksome	d	21 57			22 57	23 57				
Bournemouth	a	22 03			23 03	00 03				
	d	22 06			23 06					
Pokesdown	d	22 10			23 10					
Christchurch	d	22 14			23 14					
Hinton Admiral	d	22 19			23 19					
New Milton	d	22 23			23 23					
Sway	d	22 28			23 28					
Lymington Pier	d									
Lymington Town	d									
Brockenhurst [3]	a	22 33			23 33					
	d	22 34			23 34					
Beaulieu Road	d	22 39								
Ashurst New Forest	d	22 43			23 43					
Totton	d	22 48			23 48					
Salisbury	d			22 36						
Dean	d									
Mottisfont & Dunbridge	d									
Romsey	d		22 28	22 54						22 28
Redbridge	d		22 35							22 35
Millbrook (Hants)	d		22 39							22 39
Southampton Central ⛴	a	22 53	22 41	23 05	23 53					22 41
	d	22 55	23 05	23 08						23 05
St Denys	d		23 10							23 10
Swaythling	d		23 13							23 13
Southampton Airport Pkwy ✈	d	23 03	23 16							23 16
Portsmouth Harbour ⛴	d						23 17			
Portsmouth & Southsea	d						23 22			
Fratton	d						23 26			
Hilsea	d						23 30			
Cosham	d						23 35			
Portchester	d						23 40			
Fareham	d			23a29			23 46			
Botley	d						23 54			
Hedge End	d						23 58			
Eastleigh [3]	a	23 09	23 19				00 04			23 19
	d	23 11	23 21							23 21
Chandlers Ford	d		23 26							23 26
Romsey	a		23 33							23 33
Shawford	d									
Winchester	d	23 23								
Micheldever	d	23 32								
Basingstoke	a	23 42								
	d	23 44								
Reading [7]	a									
Fleet	d									
Farnborough (Main)	d									
Woking	a	00 02								
Clapham Junction	a									
Clapham Junction [10]	a	00 23								
London Waterloo [15] ⊖	a	00 33								

Weymouth, Bournemouth, Lymington, Romsey, Southampton and Basingstoke - London

Sundays
from 1 April

Network Diagram - see first Page of Table 158

		SW [1]	SW [1]	SW [1]	SW [1]	SW [1]	SW ◇[1] A 🍴	SW [1]	SW [1]	SW ◇[1] B		SW [1]	GW ■	XC ◇[1] 🍴	SW ◇[1] C 🍴	SW [1]	SW [1] 🍴	SW ◇[1] D 🍴	SW [1]	XC ◇[1] 🍴		SW [1]	SW ◇[1] C 🍴	SW [1]
Weymouth	d		22p10	23p10											07 48								08 48	
Upwey	d		22p14	23p14											07 52								08 52	
Dorchester West	a																							
Dorchester South	d		22p22	23p22											08 00								09 00	
Moreton (Dorset)	d		22p28	23p28											08 07								09 07	
Wool	d		22p34	23p34											08 13								09 13	
Wareham	d		22p42	23p42											08 20								09 20	
Holton Heath	d																							
Hamworthy	d		22p48	23p48											08 27								09 27	
Poole [4]	a		22p53	23p53											08 31								09 31	
	d		22p54	23p54			06 50			07 50					08 32			08 55					09 32	
Parkstone (Dorset)	d		22p58				06 54			07 54					08 36								09 36	
Branksome	d		23p01				06 57			07 57					08 40								09 40	
Bournemouth	a		23p07	00 03			07 02			08 02					08 46			09 04					09 46	
	d		23p12				07 06			08 06					08 50			09 06		09 40			09 50	
Pokesdown	d		23p16				07 10			08 10								09 10						
Christchurch	d		23p20				07 14			08 14								09 14						
Hinton Admiral	d		23p25				07 19			08 19								09 19						
New Milton	d		23p29				07 23			08 23					09 01			09 23					10 01	
Sway	d		23p34				07 28			08 28								09 28						
Lymington Pier	d															09 14						09 44		10 14
Lymington Town	d															09 16						09 46		10 16
Brockenhurst [3]	a		23p39				07 33			08 33					09 08	09 24		09 33		09 53		09 54	10 08	10 24
	d		23p40				07 34			08 34					09 09			09 34		09 57			10 09	
Beaulieu Road	d									08 39								09 39						
Ashurst New Forest	d		23p47				07 43			08 43								09 43						
Totton	d		23p52				07 48			08 48								09 48						
Salisbury	d							08 08				08 20							09 08					
Dean	d							08 20											09 20					
Mottisfont & Dunbridge	d							08 26											09 26					
Romsey	d							08 35				08 39							09 32					
Redbridge	d											08 46							09 39					
Millbrook (Hants)	d											08 50							09 43					
Southampton Central ⛴	a		23p57				07 53			08 53		08 52			09 23			09 53	09 45	10 10			10 23	
	d		23p59				07 55			08 55		08 59		09 15	09 25			09 55	09 59	10 15			10 25	
St Denys	d		00 04									09 04							10 04					
Swaythling	d		00 07									09 07							10 07					
Southampton Airport Pkwy ✈	d		00 10				08 03			09 03		09 10		09 22	09 33			10 03	10 10	10 22			10 33	
Portsmouth Harbour ⛴	d	23p24			06 37	07 17			08 17				09 08				09 17							
Portsmouth & Southsea	d	23p29			06 42	07 22			08 22				09 12				09 22							
Fratton	d	23p33			06 46	07 26			08 26				09 16				09 26							
Hilsea	d	23p37			06 50	07 30			08 30								09 30							
Cosham	d	23p42			06 55	07 35			08 35				09 23				09 35							
Portchester	d	23p47			07 00	07 40			08 40								09 40							
Fareham	d	23p53			07a05	07 46			08 46				09 32				09 46							
Botley	d	23p59				07 54			08 54								09 54							
Hedge End	d	00 05				07 58			08 58								09 58							
Eastleigh [3]	a	00 11	00 14			08 04	08 07		09 04	09 07		09 13					10 04	10 07	10 13					
	d	00 21				08 11			09 11			09 15					10 11		10 15					
Chandlers Ford	d							08 42				09 20							10 20					
Romsey	a							09 24				09 28	10 05						10 28					
Shawford	d								09 17															
Winchester	d	00a30				08 23			09 23					09 31	09 42		10 23			10 31			10 42	
Micheldever	d					08 32			09 32								10 32							
Basingstoke	a					08 42			09 42					09 46	09 58		10 42			10 46			10 58	
	d					08 44			09 44					09 47	10 00		10 44			10 47			11 00	
Reading [7]	a													10 03						11 03				
Fleet	d																							
Farnborough (Main)	d																							
Woking	a					09 02			10 02						10 19		11 02						11 18	
Clapham Junction	a																							
Clapham Junction [10]	a					09 30			10 27						10 40		11 27						11 39	
London Waterloo [15] ⊖	a					09 43			10 42						10 54		11 42						11 54	

A 🍴 to Eastleigh ◇ to Eastleigh
B ◇ to Eastleigh
C 🍴 from Bournemouth
D 🍴 from Eastleigh ◇ to Eastleigh

Table 158

Sundays from 1 April

Weymouth, Bournemouth, Lymington, Romsey, Southampton and Basingstoke - London

Network Diagram - see first Page of Table 158

		SW	SW	SW	GW	XC	SW	SW	SW	SW	SW	SW	GW	XC	SW	SW	SW	SW	SW	SW	SW	GW	GW
		[1] ⌶	◇[1] A ⌶	[1]	◇	◇[1] ⌶	[1]	◇[1] B ⌶	[1]	[1] ⌶	◇[1] C ⌶	[1]	◇	◇[1] ⌶	[1]	◇[1] B ⌶	[1]	[1] ⌶	◇[1] A ⌶	[1]	[1]	◇	◇
Weymouth	d							09 48								10 48							
Upwey	d							09 52								10 52							
Dorchester West	a																						
Dorchester South	d							10 00								11 00							
Moreton (Dorset)	d							10 07								11 07							
Wool	d							10 13								11 13							
Wareham	d							10 20								11 20							
Holton Heath	d																						
Hamworthy	d							10 27								11 27							
Poole [4]	a							10 31								11 31							
	d		09 55					10 32			10 55					11 32			11 55				
Parkstone (Dorset)	d							10 36								11 36							
Branksome	d							10 40								11 40							
Bournemouth	a		10 04					10 46			11 04					11 46			12 04				
	d		10 06			10 40		10 50			11 06			11 40		11 50			12 06				
Pokesdown	d		10 10								11 10								12 10				
Christchurch	d		10 14								11 14								12 14				
Hinton Admiral	d		10 19								11 19								12 19				
New Milton	d		10 23					11 01			11 23					12 01			12 23				
Sway	d		10 28								11 28								12 28				
Lymington Pier	d						10 44		11 14						11 44		12 14				12 44		
Lymington Town	d						10 46		11 16						11 46		12 16				12 46		
Brockenhurst [3]	a		10 33			10 53	10 54	11 08	11 24		11 33			11 53	11 54	12 08	12 24		12 33		12 54		
	d		10 34			10 57		11 09			11 34			11 57		12 09			12 34				
Beaulieu Road	d		10 39								11 39								12 39				
Ashurst New Forest	d		10 43								11 43								12 43				
Totton	d		10 48								11 48								12 48				
Salisbury	d			10 13	10 32							11 08	11 33							12 13			12 33
Dean	d											11 20											
Mottisfont & Dunbridge	d											11 26											
Romsey	d			10 32	10 50							11 32	11 51							12 32			12 52
Redbridge	d			10 39								11 39								12 39			
Millbrook (Hants)	d			10 43								11 43								12 43			
Southampton Central ⛴	a		10 53	10 45	11 02	11 10		11 23			11 53	11 45	12 03	12 10		12 23			12 53	12 45			13 05
	d		10 55	10 59	11 04	11 15		11 25			11 55	11 59	12 04	12 15		12 25			12 55	12 59			13 07
St Denys	d			11 04								12 04								13 04			
Swaythling	d			11 07								12 07								13 07			
Southampton Airport Pkwy ✈	d		11 03	11 10		11 22		11 33			12 03	12 10		12 22		12 33			13 03	13 10			
Portsmouth Harbour ⛴	d	10 17								11 17								12 17				13 08	
Portsmouth & Southsea	d	10 22								11 22								12 22				13 12	
Fratton	d	10 26								11 26								12 26				13 16	
Hilsea	d	10 30								11 30								12 30					
Cosham	d	10 35								11 35								12 35				13 23	
Portchester	d	10 40								11 40								12 40					
Fareham	d	10 46			11a26					11 46			12a28					12 46				13 32	13a33
Botley	d	10 54								11 54								12 54					
Hedge End	d	10 58								11 58								12 58					
Eastleigh [8]	a	11 04	11 07	11 13						12 04	12 07	12 13						13 04	13 07	13 13			
	d		11 11	11 15							12 11	12 15							13 11	13 15			
Chandlers Ford	d			11 20								12 20								13 20			
Romsey	a			11 28								12 28								13 28		14 05	
Shawford	d		11 17																13 17				
Winchester	d		11 23			11 31		11 42			12 23			12 31		12 42			13 23				
Micheldever	d		11 32								12 32								13 32				
Basingstoke	a		11 42			11 46		11 58			12 42			12 46		12 58			13 42				
	d		11 44			11 47		12 00			12 44			12 47		13 00			13 44				
Reading [7]	a					12 04								13 02									
Fleet	d																						
Farnborough (Main)	d																						
Woking	a		12 02					12 18			13 02					13 18			14 02				
Clapham Junction	a																						
Clapham Junction [10]	a		12 27					12 39			13 27					13 39			14 27				
London Waterloo [15] ⊖	a		12 42					12 49			13 37					13 49			14 37				

A ⌶ from Bournemouth ◇ to Eastleigh

B ⌶ from Bournemouth

C ⌶ from Eastleigh ◇ to Eastleigh

Table 158

Sundays from 1 April

Weymouth, Bournemouth, Lymington, Romsey, Southampton and Basingstoke - London

Network Diagram - see first Page of Table 158

		XC	SW	SW	SW	SW	SW	GW	XC	SW	SW	GW	SW	SW	SW	SW	XC	SW	GW	GW	SW	GW
		◇[1] ⌶	◇[1] A ⌶	[1]	[1] ⌶	◇[1] B ⌶	[1]	◇ ⌶	◇[1] ⌶	[1]	◇[1] A ⌶	◇	[1]	[1] ⌶	◇[1] B ⌶	[1]	◇[1] ⌶	[1]	■	◇	◇[1] A ⌶	◇
Weymouth	d		11 48								12 48										13 48	14 00
Upwey	d		11 52								12 52										13 52	14 05
Dorchester West	a																					14 12
Dorchester South	d		12 00								13 00										14 00	
Moreton (Dorset)	d		12 07								13 07										14 07	
Wool	d		12 13								13 13										14 13	
Wareham	d		12 20								13 20										14 20	
Holton Heath	d																					
Hamworthy	d		12 27								13 27										14 27	
Poole [4]	a		12 31								13 31										14 31	
	d		12 32			12 55					13 32				13 55						14 32	
Parkstone (Dorset)	d		12 36								13 36										14 36	
Branksome	d		12 40								13 40										14 40	
Bournemouth	a		12 46			13 04					13 46				14 04						14 46	
	d	12 40	12 50			13 06			13 40		13 50				14 06		14 40				14 50	
Pokesdown	d					13 10									14 10							
Christchurch	d					13 14									14 14							
Hinton Admiral	d					13 19									14 19							
New Milton	d		13 01			13 23					14 01				14 23						15 01	
Sway	d					13 28									14 28							
Lymington Pier	d			13 14						13 44			14 14					14 44				
Lymington Town	d			13 16						13 46			14 16					14 46				
Brockenhurst [3]	a	12 53	13 08	13 24		13 33			13 53	13 54	14 08		14 24		14 33		14 53	14 54			15 08	
	d	12 57	13 09			13 34			13 57		14 09				14 34		14 57				15 09	
Beaulieu Road	d					13 39									14 39							
Ashurst New Forest	d					13 43									14 43							
Totton	d					13 48									14 48							
Salisbury	d						13 08	13 33								14 13				14 48		
Dean	d						13 20															
Mottisfont & Dunbridge	d						13 26															
Romsey	d						13 32	13 51								14 32				15 10		
Redbridge	d						13 39									14 39						
Millbrook (Hants)	d						13 43									14 43						
Southampton Central ⛴	a	13 10	13 23			13 53	13 45	14 03	14 10		14 23				14 53	14 45	15 10			15 21	15 23	
	d	13 15	13 25			13 55	13 59	14 04	14 15		14 25				14 55	14 59	15 15			15 22	15 25	
St Denys	d						14 04									15 04						
Swaythling	d						14 07									15 07						
Southampton Airport Pkwy ✈	d	13 22	13 33			14 03	14 10		14 22		14 33				15 03	15 10	15 22				15 33	
Portsmouth Harbour ⛴	d				13 17							14 08		14 17					15 08			
Portsmouth & Southsea	d				13 22							14 12		14 22					15 12			
Fratton	d				13 26							14 16		14 26					15 16			
Hilsea	d				13 30									14 30								
Cosham	d				13 35							14 23		14 35					15 23			
Portchester	d				13 40									14 40								
Fareham	d				13 46			14a26				14 32		14 46					15 32	15a50		
Botley	d				13 54									14 54								
Hedge End	d				13 58									14 58								
Eastleigh [8]	a				14 04	14 07	14 13							15 04	15 07	15 13						
	d					14 11	14 15								15 11	15 15						
Chandlers Ford	d						14 20									15 20						
Romsey	a						14 28					15 05				15 28			16 05			
Shawford	d														15 17							
Winchester	d	13 31	13 42			14 23			14 31		14 42				15 23		15 31				15 42	
Micheldever	d					14 32									15 32							
Basingstoke	a	13 46	13 58			14 42			14 46		14 58				15 42		15 46				15 58	
	d	13 47	14 00			14 44			14 47		15 00				15 44		15 47				16 00	
Reading [7]	a	14 03							15 04								16 03					
Fleet	d																					
Farnborough (Main)	d																					
Woking	a		14 18			15 02					15 18				16 02						16 18	
Clapham Junction	a																					
Clapham Junction [10]	a		14 39			15 27					15 39				16 27						16 39	
London Waterloo [15] ⊖	a		14 49			15 37					15 49				16 37						16 49	

A ⌶ from Bournemouth

B ⌶ from Eastleigh ◇ to Eastleigh

Weymouth, Bournemouth, Lymington, Romsey, Southampton and Basingstoke - London

Network Diagram - see first Page of Table 158

		SW	SW	SW	SW	GW	XC	SW	SW	GW	SW	SW	SW	SW	GW	XC	SW	SW	GW	SW	SW	SW	SW
		1	1	◇1	1	◇	◇1	1	◇1	◇	1	1	◇1	1	◇	◇1	1	◇1	◇	1	1	◇1	1
				A					B				A					B				C	
			bus	bus			bus		bus			bus	bus			bus		bus					
Weymouth	d								14 48									15 48					
Upwey	d								14 52									15 52					
Dorchester West	a																						
Dorchester South	d								15 00									16 00					
Moreton (Dorset)	d								15 07									16 07					
Wool	d								15 13									16 13					
Wareham	d								15 20									16 20					
Holton Heath	d																						
Hamworthy	d								15 27									16 27					
Poole 4	a								15 31									16 31					
	d			14 55					15 32				15 55					16 32				16 55	
Parkstone (Dorset)	d								15 36									16 36					
Branksome	d								15 40									16 40					
Bournemouth	a			15 04					15 46				16 04					16 46				17 04	
	d			15 06			15 40		15 50				16 06			16 40		16 50				17 06	
Pokesdown	d			15 10									16 10									17 10	
Christchurch	d			15 14									16 14									17 14	
Hinton Admiral	d			15 19									16 19									17 19	
New Milton	d			15 23					16 01				16 23					17 01				17 23	
Sway	d			15 28									16 28									17 28	
Lymington Pier	d	15 14						15 44			16 14						16 44			17 14			
Lymington Town	d	15 16						15 46			16 16						16 46			17 16			
Brockenhurst 3	a	15 24		15 33			15 53	15 54	16 08		16 24		16 33			16 53	16 54	17 08		17 24		17 33	
	d			15 34			15 57		16 09				16 34			16 57		17 09				17 34	
Beaulieu Road	d			15 39									16 39									17 39	
Ashurst New Forest	d			15 43									16 43									17 43	
Totton	d			15 48									16 48									17 48	
Salisbury	d				15 08	15 32								16 13	16 33								17 08
Dean	d				15 20																		17 20
Mottisfont & Dunbridge	d				15 26																		17 26
Romsey	d				15 32	15 50								16 32	16 51								17 32
Redbridge	d				15 39									16 39									17 39
Millbrook (Hants)	d				15 43									16 43									17 43
Southampton Central ⛴	a			15 53	15 45	16 02	16 10		16 23				16 53	16 45	17 03	17 10		17 23				17 53	17 45
	d			15 55	15 59	16 04	16 15		16 25				16 55	16 59	17 04	17 15		17 25				17 55	17 59
St Denys	d				16 04									17 04									18 04
Swaythling	d				16 07									17 07									18 07
Southampton Airport Pkwy ✈	d			16 03	16 10		16 22		16 33				17 03	17 10		17 22		17 33				18 03	18 10
Portsmouth Harbour ⛴	d		15 17							16 08		16 17							17 08		17 17		
Portsmouth & Southsea	d		15 22							16 12		16 22							17 12		17 22		
Fratton	d		15 26							16 16		16 26							17 16		17 26		
Hilsea	d		15 30									16 30									17 30		
Cosham	d		15 35							16 23		16 35							17 23		17 35		
Portchester	d		15 40									16 40									17 40		
Fareham	d		15 46			16a26				16 32		16 46			17a27				17 32		17 46		
Botley	d		15 54									16 54									17 54		
Hedge End	d		15 58									16 58									17 58		
Eastleigh 3	a		16 04	16 07	16 13							17 04	17 07	17 13							18 04	18 07	18 13
	d		16 11		16 15							17 11		17 15							18 11		18 15
Chandlers Ford	d				16 20									17 20									18 20
Romsey	a				16 28					17 05				17 28					18 05				18 28
Shawford	d											17 17											
Winchester	d		16 23				16 31		16 42			17 23				17 31		17 42			18 23		
Micheldever	d		16 32									17 32									18 32		
Basingstoke	a		16 42				16 46		16 58			17 42				17 46		17 58			18 42		
	d		16 44				16 47		17 00			17 44				17 47		18 00			18 44		
Reading 7	a						17 03									18 04							
Fleet	d																						
Farnborough (Main)	d																						
Woking	a		17 02						17 18			18 02						18 18			19 02		
Clapham Junction	a																						
Clapham Junction 10	a		17 27						17 39			18 27						18 39			19 27		
London Waterloo 15 ⊖	a		17 37						17 49			18 37						18 49			19 37		

A bus from Eastleigh ◇ to Eastleigh

B bus from Bournemouth

C ◇ to Eastleigh

Table 158

Sundays from 1 April

Weymouth, Bournemouth, Lymington, Romsey, Southampton and Basingstoke - London

Network Diagram - see first Page of Table 158

		GW	XC	SW	SW	GW	SW	SW	SW	SW	GW	XC	SW	SW	GW	GW	SW	GW	SW	SW	SW	GW	XC
		◇	◇1	1	◇1	◇	1	1	◇1	1	◇	◇1	1	◇1	◇	◇	1	◇	1	◇1	1	◇	◇1
					A				B					A						B			
			bus		bus							bus		bus									
Weymouth	d				16 48									17 48	17 56								
Upwey	d				16 52									17 52	18 01								
Dorchester West	a														18 08								
Dorchester South	d				17 00									18 00									
Moreton (Dorset)	d				17 07									18 07									
Wool	d				17 13									18 13									
Wareham	d				17 20									18 20									
Holton Heath	d																						
Hamworthy	d				17 27									18 27									
Poole 4	a				17 31									18 31									
	d				17 32				17 55					18 32						18 55			
Parkstone (Dorset)	d				17 36									18 36									
Branksome	d				17 40									18 40									
Bournemouth	a				17 46				18 04					18 46						19 04			
	d		17 40		17 50				18 06			18 40		18 50						19 06			19 40
Pokesdown	d								18 10											19 10			
Christchurch	d								18 14											19 14			
Hinton Admiral	d								18 19											19 19			
New Milton	d				18 01				18 23					19 01						19 23			
Sway	d								18 28											19 28			
Lymington Pier	d			17 44			18 14						18 44				19 14						
Lymington Town	d			17 46			18 16						18 46				19 16						
Brockenhurst 3	a		17 53	17 54	18 08		18 24		18 33			18 53	18 54	19 08			19 24			19 33			19 53
	d		17 57		18 09				18 34			18 57		19 09						19 34			19 57
Beaulieu Road	d								18 39											19 39			
Ashurst New Forest	d								18 43											19 43			
Totton	d								18 48											19 48			
Salisbury	d	17 33								18 13	18 32							18 56			19 08	19 32	
Dean	d																				19 20		
Mottisfont & Dunbridge	d																				19 26		
Romsey	d	17 51								18 32	18 50							19 14			19 32	19 50	
Redbridge	d									18 39											19 39		
Millbrook (Hants)	d									18 43											19 43		
Southampton Central ⛴	a	18 03	18 10		18 23				18 53	18 45	19 02	19 10		19 23				19 25		19 53	19 45	20 02	20 10
	d	18 04	18 15		18 25				18 55	18 59	19 04	19 15		19 25				19 26		19 55	19 59	20 04	20 15
St Denys	d									19 04											20 04		
Swaythling	d									19 07											20 07		
Southampton Airport Pkwy ✈	d		18 22		18 33				19 03	19 10		19 22		19 33						20 03	20 10		20 22
Portsmouth Harbour ⛴	d					18 08		18 17								19 08			19 17				
Portsmouth & Southsea	d					18 12		18 22								19 12			19 22				
Fratton	d					18 16		18 26								19 16			19 26				
Hilsea	d							18 30											19 30				
Cosham	d					18 23		18 35								19 23			19 35				
Portchester	d							18 40											19 40				
Fareham	d	18a27				18 32		18 46			19a27					19 32		19a48	19 46			20a26	
Botley	d							18 54											19 54				
Hedge End	d							18 58											19 58				
Eastleigh 3	a							19 04	19 07	19 13									20 04	20 07	20 13		
	d							19 11		19 15									20 11		20 15		
Chandlers Ford	d									19 20											20 20		
Romsey	a					19 05				19 28						20 05					20 28		
Shawford	d							19 17															
Winchester	d		18 31		18 42			19 23				19 31		19 42					20 23				20 31
Micheldever	d							19 32											20 32				
Basingstoke	a		18 46		18 58			19 42				19 46		19 58					20 42				20 46
	d		18 47		19 00			19 44				19 47		20 00					20 44				20 47
Reading 7	a		19 03									20 03											21 03
Fleet	d																						
Farnborough (Main)	d																						
Woking	a				19 18			20 02						20 18					21 02				
Clapham Junction	a																						
Clapham Junction 10	a				19 39			20 27						20 39					21 27				
London Waterloo 15 ⊖	a				19 49			20 37						20 49					21 37				

A bus from Bournemouth

B ◇ to Eastleigh

Table 158

Sundays
from 1 April

Weymouth, Bournemouth, Lymington, Romsey, Southampton and Basingstoke - London

Network Diagram - see first Page of Table 158

		SW	SW	GW	SW	GW	SW	SW	SW	GW	SW	SW	SW	SW	GW	SW	GW	SW	GW	SW	SW
		■1	◇■1 A ⌶	◇	■1	■	■1	◇■1 B	■1	◇	■1	■1	■1	◇■1 B		■1	◇	■1		■1	■1
Weymouth	d		18 48											19 58	20 09						
Upwey	d		18 52											20 02	20 14						
Dorchester West	a														20 21						
Dorchester South	d		19 00											20 10							
Moreton (Dorset)	d		19 07											20 17							
Wool	d		19 13											20 23							
Wareham	d		19 20											20 30							
Holton Heath	d																				
Hamworthy	d		19 27											20 37							
Poole ■4	a		19 31											20 41							
	d		19 32					19 55						20 50							
Parkstone (Dorset)	d		19 36											20 54							
Branksome	d		19 40											20 57							
Bournemouth	a		19 46					20 04						21 03							
	d		19 50					20 06						21 06							
Pokesdown	d							20 10						21 10							
Christchurch	d							20 14						21 14							
Hinton Admiral	d							20 19						21 19							
New Milton	d		20 01					20 23						21 23							
Sway	d							20 28						21 28							
Lymington Pier	d	19 44			20 14						20 44	21 14						21 44		22 14	
Lymington Town	d	19 46			20 16						20 46	21 16						21 46		22 16	
Brockenhurst ■3	a	19 54	20 08		20 24			20 33			20 54	21 24		21 33				21 54		22 24	
	d		20 09					20 34						21 34							
Beaulieu Road	d							20 39						21 39							
Ashurst New Forest	d							20 43						21 43							
Totton	d							20 48						21 48							
Salisbury	d					20 01			20 13	20 30						21 08	21 33				
Dean	d															21 20					
Mottisfont & Dunbridge	d															21 26					
Romsey	d					20 19			20 32	20 48						21 32	21 51				
Redbridge	d								20 39							21 39					
Millbrook (Hants)	d								20 43							21 43					
Southampton Central ⛴	a		20 23			20 29		20 53	20 45	20 59				21 53		21 45	22 03				
	d		20 25			20 31		20 55	20 59	21 02				21 55		21 59	22 04				
St Denys	d								21 04							22 04					
Swaythling	d								21 07							22 07					
Southampton Airport Pkwy ✈	d		20 33					21 03	21 10					22 03		22 10					
Portsmouth Harbour ⛴	d			20 08			20 17						21 17						22 03		22 17
Portsmouth & Southsea	d			20 12			20 22						21 22						22 12		22 22
Fratton	d			20 16			20 26						21 26						22 16		22 26
Hilsea	d						20 30						21 30								22 30
Cosham	d						20 35						21 35								22 35
Portchester	d						20 40						21 40								22 40
Fareham	d			20 32		20a54	20 46			21a24			21 46				22a26		22 32		22 46
Botley	d						20 54						21 54								22 54
Hedge End	d						20 58						21 58								22 58
Eastleigh ■3	a						21 04	21 07	21 13				22 04	22 07		22 13					23 04
	d						21 11		21 15				22 11			22 15					
Chandlers Ford	d								21 20							22 20					
Romsey	a			21 05					21 28							22 31			23 08		
Shawford	d						21 17														
Winchester	d		20 42				21 23						22 23								
Micheldever	d						21 32						22 32								
Basingstoke	a		20 58				21 42						22 42								
	d		21 00				21 44						22 44								
Reading ■7	a																				
Fleet	d																				
Farnborough (Main)	d																				
Woking	a		21 18				22 02						23 02								
Clapham Junction	a																				
Clapham Junction ■10	a		21 39				22 27						23 27								
London Waterloo ■15 ⊖	a		21 49				22 37						23 37								

A ⌶ from Bournemouth

B ◇ to Eastleigh

Table 158

Sundays
from 1 April

Weymouth, Bournemouth, Lymington, Romsey, Southampton and Basingstoke - London

Network Diagram - see first Page of Table 158

		SW	SW	GW	SW	SW	SW
		◇■1	■1	◇	■1	■1	■1
Weymouth	d	20 58			21 58	22 58	
Upwey	d	21 02			22 02	23 02	
Dorchester West	a						
Dorchester South	d	21 10			22 10	23 10	
Moreton (Dorset)	d	21 17			22 17	23 17	
Wool	d	21 23			22 23	23 23	
Wareham	d	21 30			22 30	23 30	
Holton Heath	d						
Hamworthy	d	21 37			22 37	23 37	
Poole ■4	a	21 41			22 41	23 41	
	d	21 50			22 50	23 50	
Parkstone (Dorset)	d	21 54			22 54	23 54	
Branksome	d	21 57			22 57	23 57	
Bournemouth	a	22 03			23 03	00 03	
	d	22 06			23 06		
Pokesdown	d	22 10			23 10		
Christchurch	d	22 14			23 14		
Hinton Admiral	d	22 19			23 19		
New Milton	d	22 23			23 23		
Sway	d	22 28			23 28		
Lymington Pier	d						
Lymington Town	d						
Brockenhurst ■3	a	22 33			23 33		
	d	22 34			23 34		
Beaulieu Road	d	22 39					
Ashurst New Forest	d	22 43			23 43		
Totton	d	22 48			23 48		
Salisbury	d			22 36			
Dean	d						
Mottisfont & Dunbridge	d						
Romsey	d		22 28	22 54			
Redbridge	d		22 35				
Millbrook (Hants)	d		22 39				
Southampton Central ⛴	a	22 53	22 41	23 05	23 53		
	d	22 55	23 05	23 08			
St Denys	d		23 10				
Swaythling	d		23 13				
Southampton Airport Pkwy ✈	d	23 03	23 16				
Portsmouth Harbour ⛴	d						23 17
Portsmouth & Southsea	d						23 22
Fratton	d						23 26
Hilsea	d						23 30
Cosham	d						23 35
Portchester	d						23 40
Fareham	d			23a29			23 46
Botley	d						23 54
Hedge End	d						23 58
Eastleigh ■3	a	23 09	23 19				00 04
	d		23 21				
Chandlers Ford	d		23 26				
Romsey	a	23 11	23 33				
Shawford	d						
Winchester	d						
Micheldever	d	23 23					
Basingstoke	a	23 32					
	d	23 42					
Reading ■7	a	23 44					
Fleet	d						
Farnborough (Main)	d						
Woking	a						
Clapham Junction	a	00 02					
Clapham Junction ■10	a						
London Waterloo ■15 ⊖	a	00 23					

Table 158A

Mondays to Saturdays

Woking - Heathrow Railair

Express Coach Service

	SW SX 🚌	SW SX 🚌	SW SX 🚌	SW SX 🚌	SW 🚌	SW 🚌	SW 🚌	SW SO 🚌	SW SX 🚌		SW 🚌	SW SO 🚌	SW SX 🚌	SW SO 🚌	SW 🚌	SW SX 🚌	SW SO 🚌	SW 🚌	SW SX 🚌		SW SO 🚌	SW 🚌	SW SX 🚌	SW 🚌
Woking d		05 20		05 50		06 20		06 50	06 50			07 20	07 20	07 50		07 50	08 20		08 20		08 50		08 50	
Heathrow Terminal 5 Bus d		05 45		06 15		06 45		07 15	07 25			07 45	08 05	08 15		08 35	08 45		09 05		09 15		09 35	
Heathrow Central Bus Stn. a		06 00		06 30		07 00		07 30	07 40			08 00	08 20	08 30		08 50	09 00		09 20		09 30		09 50	
d	05 45		06 15		06 45		07 15				07 45				08 30			09 00				09 30		10 00
Heathrow Terminal 5 Bus a	06 00		06 30		07 00		07 30				08 00				08 45			09 15				09 45		10 15
Woking a	06 30		07 00		07 30		08 05				08 40				09 25			09 55				10 25		10 50

	SW SO 🚌	SW SX 🚌	SW 🚌	SW 🚌	SW 🚌		SW 🚌	SW 🚌	SW 🚌	SW 🚌	SW 🚌	SW 🚌	SW 🚌	SW 🚌	SW 🚌		SW 🚌	SW 🚌	SW 🚌	SW 🚌	SW 🚌	SW 🚌	SW 🚌	SW 🚌
Woking d	09 35	09 35		10 05			10 35		11 05		11 35		12 05		12 35			13 05		13 35		14 05		14 35
Heathrow Terminal 5 Bus d	10 00	10 10		10 30			11 00		11 30		12 00		12 30		13 00			13 30		14 00		14 30		15 00
Heathrow Central Bus Stn. a	10 15	10 25		10 45			11 15		11 45		12 15		12 45		13 15			13 45		14 15		14 45		15 15
d			10 30		11 00			11 30		12 00		12 30		13 00			13 30		14 00		14 30		15 00	
Heathrow Terminal 5 Bus a			10 45		11 15			11 45		12 15		12 45		13 15			13 45		14 15		14 45		15 15	
Woking a			11 15		11 45			12 15		12 45		13 15		13 45			14 15		14 45		15 15		15 45	

	SW 🚌		SW 🚌	SW 🚌	SW 🚌	SW 🚌	SW SO 🚌	SW SX 🚌	SW 🚌	SW SO 🚌	SW SX 🚌		SW 🚌	SW SO 🚌	SW SX 🚌	SW 🚌	SW SO 🚌	SW SX 🚌	SW 🚌	SW SO 🚌	SW SX 🚌		SW 🚌	SW 🚌
Woking d			15 05		15 35		16 05	16 05		16 35	16 35			17 05	17 05		17 35	17 35		18 05	18 05			18 35
Heathrow Terminal 5 Bus d			15 30		16 00		16 30	16 35		17 00	17 10			17 30	17 40		18 00	18 10		18 30	18 40			19 00
Heathrow Central Bus Stn. a			15 45		16 15		16 45	16 50		17 15	17 25			17 45	17 55		18 15	18 25		18 45	18 55			19 15
d	15 30			16 00		16 30			17 00				17 30			18 00			18 30				19 00	
Heathrow Terminal 5 Bus a	15 45			16 15		16 45			17 15				17 45			18 15			18 45				19 15	
Woking a	16 15			16 45		17 25			18 05				18 35			19 05			19 35				19 55	

	SW 🚌	SW SO 🚌	SW SX 🚌	SW 🚌	SW SO 🚌	SW SX 🚌	SW 🚌		SW SO 🚌	SW SX 🚌	SW SO 🚌	SW SX 🚌	SW 🚌	SW SO 🚌	SW SX 🚌	SW SO 🚌	SW SX 🚌		SW SO 🚌	SW SX 🚌	SW SO 🚌	SW SX 🚌		
Woking d		19 05	19 05		19 35	19 35			20 05	20 05	20 35	20 35		21 05	21 05				22 05	22 05				
Heathrow Terminal 5 Bus d		19 30	19 35		20 00	20 05			20 30	20 35	21 00	21 05		21 30	21 35				22 30	22 35				
Heathrow Central Bus Stn. a		19 45	19 45		20 15	20 15			20 45	20 45	21 15	21 15		21 45	21 45				22 45	22 45				
d	19 30			20 00			20 30						21 15			22 15	22 15				23 15	23 15		
Heathrow Terminal 5 Bus a	19 45			20 15			20 45						21 30			22 30	22 30				23 30	23 30		
Woking a	20 15			20 45			21 15						22 00			22 55	23 00				23 55	23 59		

Sundays

	SW 🚌	SW 🚌	SW 🚌	SW 🚌	SW 🚌	SW 🚌	SW 🚌	SW 🚌	SW 🚌		SW 🚌	SW 🚌	SW 🚌	SW 🚌	SW 🚌	SW 🚌	SW 🚌	SW 🚌	SW 🚌		SW 🚌	SW 🚌	SW 🚌	SW 🚌
Woking d		06 20		06 50		07 20	07 50		08 20			08 50			09 35		10 05		10 35			11 05		11 35
Heathrow Terminal 5 Bus d		06 45		07 15		07 45	08 15		08 45			09 15			10 00		10 30		11 00			11 30		12 00
Heathrow Central Bus Stn. a		07 00		07 30		08 00	08 30		09 00			09 30			10 15		10 45		11 15			11 45		12 15
d	06 45		07 15		07 45			08 30			09 00		09 30	10 00		10 30		11 00			11 30		12 00	
Heathrow Terminal 5 Bus a	07 00		07 30		08 00			08 45			09 15		09 45	10 15		10 45		11 15			11 45		12 15	
Woking a	07 30		08 00		08 25			09 15			09 45		10 15	10 45		11 15		11 45			12 15		12 45	

	SW 🚌	SW 🚌	SW 🚌	SW 🚌	SW 🚌		SW 🚌	SW 🚌	SW 🚌	SW 🚌	SW 🚌	SW 🚌	SW 🚌	SW 🚌	SW 🚌		SW 🚌	SW 🚌	SW 🚌	SW 🚌	SW 🚌	SW 🚌	SW 🚌	SW 🚌
Woking d		12 05		12 35			13 05		13 35		14 05		14 35		15 05			15 35		16 05		16 35		17 05
Heathrow Terminal 5 Bus d		12 30		13 00			13 30		14 00		14 30		15 00		15 30			16 00		16 30		17 00		17 30
Heathrow Central Bus Stn. a		12 45		13 15			13 45		14 15		14 45		15 15		15 45			16 15		16 45		17 15		17 45
d	12 30		13 00		13 30			14 00		14 30		15 00		15 30			16 00		16 30		17 00		17 30	
Heathrow Terminal 5 Bus a	12 45		13 15		13 45			14 15		14 45		15 15		15 45			16 15		16 45		17 15		17 45	
Woking a	13 15		13 45		14 15			14 45		15 15		15 45		16 15			16 45		17 15		17 45		18 15	

	SW 🚌		SW 🚌	SW 🚌	SW 🚌	SW 🚌	SW 🚌	SW 🚌	SW 🚌	SW 🚌	SW 🚌		SW 🚌	SW 🚌	SW 🚌	SW 🚌	SW 🚌	SW 🚌	SW 🚌	SW 🚌				
Woking d			17 35		18 05		18 35		19 05		19 35			20 05	20 35		21 05		22 05					
Heathrow Terminal 5 Bus d			18 00		18 30		19 00		19 30		20 00			20 30	21 00		21 30		22 30					
Heathrow Central Bus Stn. a			18 15		18 45		19 15		19 45		20 15			20 45	21 15		21 45		22 45					
d	18 00			18 30		19 00		19 30		20 00			20 30			21 15		22 15		23 15				
Heathrow Terminal 5 Bus a	18 15			18 45		19 15		19 45		20 15			20 45			21 30		22 30		23 30				
Woking a	18 45			19 15		19 45		20 15		20 45			21 15			22 00		23 00		23 59				

Network Diagram for Table 160

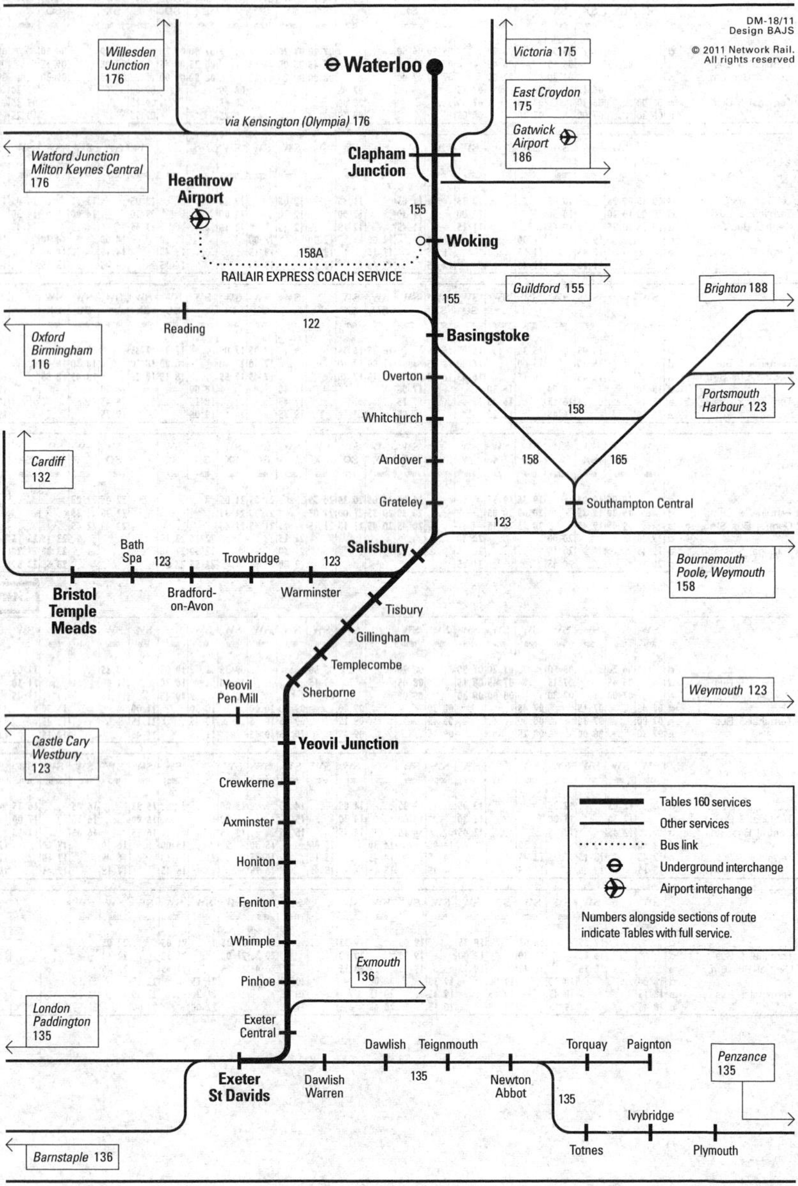

Table 160

Mondays to Fridays

London - Salisbury and Exeter

Network Diagram - see first Page of Table 160

Miles			SW MX ◇1	SW MO ◇1	SW MO 1	SW MX 1	SW 1		SW 1	SW 1	SW 1		SW ◇1	SW ◇1	SW ◇1	SW ◇1	SW ◇1	SW ◇1	SW ◇1		SW ◇1		SW ◇1	SW ◇1	SW ◇1
0	**London Waterloo** 15 ⊖	d	20p20	21p15	23p35	23p40									07 10	07 50	08 20	08 50	09 20		09 50		10 20	10 50	11 20
4	Clapham Junction 10	d	20b27	21b22	23b44	23b47									07u17	07u57	08u27		09u27				10u27		11u27
24½	Woking	d	20p46	21p46	00 08	00 08									07 36	08 16	08 46	09 16	09 46		10 16		10 46	11 16	11 46
47¾	**Basingstoke**	d	21p07	22p07	00 40	00 28								07 22	07 57	08 38	09 07	09 38	10 07		10 38		11 07	11 38	12 07
55½	Overton	d	21p15		00s49	00s37								07 30	08 05	08 47		09 46			10 46			11 46	
59¼	Whitchurch (Hants)	d	21p20		00s54	00s42								07 35	08 10	08 52		09 51			10 51			11 51	
66½	Andover	d	21p29	22p26	01 02	00 50								07 44	08 19	09 00	09 24	10 00	10 24		11 00		11 24	12 00	12 24
72¾	Grateley	d	21p36	22p33	01s10	00s58								07 51	08 26	09 08		10 07			11 07			12 07	
83¾	**Salisbury**	a	21p48	22p45	01 22	01 10								08 03	08 39	09 20	09 43	10 19	10 42		11 19		11 42	12 19	12 42
—																									
—		d	22p06	22p51						06 08	06 40		07 40	08 08	08 47		09 47		10 47	10 52			11 47		12 47
—	Warminster	d									07 00									11 12					
—	Westbury	d									07 09									11 21					
—	Trowbridge	d									07 15									11 27					
—	Bradford-on-Avon	d									07 21									11 33					
—	Bath Spa 7	a									07 33									11 46					
—	Bristol Temple Meads 10	a									07 52									12 05					
96¼	Tisbury	d	22p24	23p10						06 29			07 59	08 27	09 06		10 06		11 06				12 06		13 06
105¼	Gillingham (Dorset)	a	22p34	23p20						06 39			08 09	08 37	09 16		10 16		11 16				12 16		13 16
—		d	22p35	23p21						06 42			08 11		09 17		10 17		11 17				12 17		13 17
112¼	Templecombe	d	22p42	23p28						06 50			08 19		09 25		10 25		11 25				12 25		13 25
118¼	Sherborne	d	22p50	23p36						06 57			08 26		09 32		10 32		11 32				12 32		13 32
122¾	Yeovil Junction	a	22p55	23p41						07 03			08 32		09 38		10 38		11 38				12 38		13 38
—		d	22p57	23p43					06 15	07 07			08 39		09 39		10 39		11 39				12 39		13 39
131¾	Crewkerne	d	23p06	23p52					06 24	07 16			08 49		09 49		10 49		11 49				12 49		13 49
144¾	Axminster	a	23p19	00 05					06 43	07 35			09 02		10 02		11 02		12 02				13 02		14 02
—		d	23p20	00 06			05 52		06 56	07 36			09 03		10 03		11 03		12 03				13 03		14 03
155	Honiton	a	23p31	00 18			06 03		07 07	07 49			09 15		10 15		11 15		12 15				13 15		14 15
—		d	23p32	00 19			06 08		07 12	07 50			09 16		10 16		11 16		12 16				13 16		14 16
159½	Feniton	d	23p38	00 24			06 13		07 18	07 56			09 21				11 21						13 21		
163¼	Whimple	d	23p43	00 29			06 18		07 23	08 01			09 26				11 26						13 26		
169	Pinhoe	d	23p49				06 25		07 30	08 08			09 33		10 28				12 28						14 28
171¾	**Exeter Central**	a	23p56				06 29		07 37	08 12			09 37		10 37		11 37		12 37				13 37		14 37
172¾	**Exeter St Davids** 6	a	00 01	00 40			06 35		07 42	08 18			09 42		10 42		11 42		12 42				13 42		14 42

		SW ◇1	SW ◇1		SW ◇1	SW ◇1	SW ◇1		SW ◇1	SW ◇1	SW ◇1	SW ◇1	SW ◇1	SW ◇1	SW ◇1	SW ◇1	SW ◇1	SW ◇1	SW ◇1		SW ◇1	SW ◇1	SW ◇1	SW 1	SW 1
London Waterloo 15 ⊖	d	11 50	12 20		12 50	13 20	13 50		14 20	14 50	15 20	15 50	16 20	16 50	17 20	17 50	18 20	18 50	19 20		19 50	20 20	21 20	22 20	23 40
Clapham Junction 10	d		12u27			13u27			14u27		15u27	15u57	16u27	16u57			18u27		19u27			20u27	21u27	22u27	23u47
Woking	d	12 16	12 46		13 16	13 46	14 16		14 46	15 16	15 46	16 16	16 46	17u16	17u46		18 46	19 18	19 46		20 16	20 46	21 49	22 49	00 08
Basingstoke	d	12 38	13 07		13 38	14 07	14 38		15 07	15 38	16 07	16 38	17 07	17 38	18 07	18 38	19 07	19 39	20 07		20 38	21 07	22 14	23 11	00 28
Overton	d	12 46			13 46		14 46			15 46		16 46	17 15	17 46	18 15	18 47	19 15	19 47	20 15		20 46	21 15	22 22	23 19	00s37
Whitchurch (Hants)	d	12 51			13 51		14 51			15 51		16 51	17 20	17 51	18 20	18 52	19 20	19 52	20 20		20 51	21 20	22 27	23 24	00s42
Andover	d	13 00	13 24		14 00	14 24	15 00		15 24	16 00	16 24	17 00	17 29	18 00	18 29	19 00	19 29	20 01	20 29		21 00	21 29	22 36	23 33	00 50
Grateley	d	13 07			14 07		15 07			16 07		17 07	17 36	18 07	18 36	19 08	19 36	20 08	20 36		21 07	21 36	22 43	23 40	00s58
Salisbury	a	13 19	13 43		14 19	14 42	15 19		15 42	16 19	16 42	17 19	17 48	18 19	18 48	19 20	19 48	20 22	20 49		21 19	21 48	22 55	23 52	01 10
	d		13 47	13 52		14 47	15 23		15 47		16 47	17 23	17 53	18 23	18 53	19 23	19 53		20 53	20 57		22 06	23 03		
Warminster	d			14 12																21 17					
Westbury	d			14 21																21 25					
Trowbridge	d			14 27																21 31					
Bradford-on-Avon	d			14 33																21 37					
Bath Spa 7	a			14 46																21 50					
Bristol Temple Meads 10	a			15 05																22 06					
Tisbury	d		14 06			15 06	15 37		16 06		17 06	17 37	18 08	18 37	19 08	19 37	20 08		21 08			22 24	23s16		
Gillingham (Dorset)	a		14 16			15 16	15 47		16 16		17 16	17 47	18 18	18 47	19 18	19 48	20 18		21 18			22 34	23s27		
	d		14 17			15 17			16 17		17 17		18 19	18 51	19 19	19 51	20 19		21 19			22 35			
Templecombe	d		14 25			15 25			16 25		17 25		18 26	18 58	19 26	19 58	20 26		21 26			22 42	23s35		
Sherborne	d		14 32			15 32			16 32		17 32		18 34	19 06	19 34	20 06	20 34		21 34			22 50	23s42		
Yeovil Junction	a		14 38			15 38			16 38		17 38		18 39	19 14	19 39	20 14	20 39		21 39			22 55	23 49		
	d		14 39			15 39			16 39		17 39		18 41		19 41		20 41		21 41			22 57			
Crewkerne	d		14 49			15 49			16 49		17 49		18 50		19 50		20 50		21 50			23 06			
Axminster	a		15 02			16 02			17 02		18 02		19 03		20 03		21 03		22 03			23 19			
	d		15 03			16 03			17 03		18 03		19 04		20 04		21 04		22 04			23 20			
Honiton	a		15 15			16 15			17 15		18 15		19 16		20 16		21 16		22 16			23 31			
	d		15 16			16 16			17 16		18 18		19 17		20 17		21 17		22 17			23 32			
Feniton	d		15 21						17 21				19 22				21 22		22 22			23 38			
Whimple	d		15 26						17 26				19 27				21 27		22 27			23 43			
Pinhoe	d					16 28					18 31				20 29				22 34			23 49			
Exeter Central	a		15 37			16 35			17 35		18 38		19 38		20 39		21 37		22 40			23 56			
Exeter St Davids 6	a		15 42			16 42			17 42		18 42		19 45		20 44		21 44		22 45			00 01			

b Previous night, stops to pick up only

For Bus Connections for either to or from Yeovil Junction and Yeovil Pen Mill please see Table 123A

London - Salisbury and Exeter

Network Diagram - see first Page of Table 160

		SW	SW	SW	SW	SW	SW	SW	SW	SW	SW	SW	SW	SW		SW	SW	SW	SW	SW	SW	
		◇1 ⚲	1	1	1	1	1	◇1	◇1	◇1 ⚲	◇1 ⚲	◇1 ⚲	◇1 ⚲	◇1 ⚲		◇1 ⚲	◇1 ⚲	◇1 ⚲	◇1 ⚲	◇1 ⚲	◇1 ⚲	
London Waterloo 15 ⊖	d	20p20	23p40							07 10	07 50	08 20	08 50	09 20		09 50	10 20	10 50	11 20	11 50	12 20	
Clapham Junction 10	d	20b27	23b47							07u17	07u57	08u27		09u27			10u27		11u27		12u27	
Woking	d	20p46	00 08							07 36	08 16	08 46	09 16	09 46		10 16	10 46	11 16	11 46	12 16	12 46	
Basingstoke	d	21p07	00 28					07 22		07 59	08 38	09 07	09 38	10 07		10 38	11 07	11 38	12 07	12 38	13 07	
Overton	d	21p15	00s37					07 30		08 07	08 46		09 46			10 46		11 46		12 46		
Whitchurch (Hants)	d	21p20	00s42					07 35		08 12	08 51		09 51			10 51		11 51		12 51		
Andover	d	21p29	00 50					07 44		08 21	09 00	09 24	10 00	10 24		11 00	11 24	12 00	12 24	13 00	13 24	
Grateley	d	21p36	00s58					07 51		08 28	09 07		10 07			11 07		12 07		13 07		
Salisbury	a	21p48	01 10					08 05		08 42	09 19	09 42	10 19	10 42		11 19	11 42	12 19	12 42	13 19	13 42	
	d	22p06				06 15	06 40		07 45	08 47		09 47		10 47	10 52		11 47		12 47		13 47	13 52
Warminster	d						07 00								11 12							14 12
Westbury	d						07 09								11 21							14 21
Trowbridge	d						07 15								11 27							14 27
Bradford-on-Avon	d						07 21								11 33							14 33
Bath Spa 7	a						07 33								11 46							14 46
Bristol Temple Meads 10	a						07 53								12 05							15 05
Tisbury	d	22p24				06 29			07 59	09 06		10 06		11 06			12 06		13 06		14 06	
Gillingham (Dorset)	a	22p34				06 39			08 09	09 16		10 16		11 16			12 16		13 16		14 16	
	d	22p35				06 42			08 11	09 17		10 17		11 17			12 17		13 17		14 17	
Templecombe	d	22p42				06 50			08 19	09 25		10 25		11 25			12 25		13 25		14 25	
Sherborne	d	22p50				06 57			08 26	09 32		10 32		11 32			12 32		13 32		14 32	
Yeovil Junction	a	22p55				07 03			08 32	09 38		10 38		11 38			12 38		13 38		14 38	
	d	22p57			06 15	07 07			08 39	09 39		10 39		11 39			12 39		13 39		14 39	
Crewkerne	d	23p06			06 24	07 16			08 49	09 49		10 49		11 49			12 49		13 49		14 49	
Axminster	a	23p19			06 43	07 36			09 02	10 02		11 02		12 02			13 02		14 02		15 02	
	d	23p20		05 52	06 56	07 38			09 03	10 03		11 03		12 03			13 03		14 03		15 03	
Honiton	a	23p31		06 03	07 07	07 51			09 15	10 15		11 15		12 15			13 15		14 15		15 15	
	d	23p32		06 08	07 12	07 52			09 16	10 16		11 16		12 16			13 16		14 16		15 16	
Feniton	d	23p38		06 13	07 18	07 57			09 21			11 21					13 21				15 21	
Whimple	d	23p43		06 18	07 23	08 02			09 26			11 26					13 26				15 26	
Pinhoe	d	23p49		06 25	07 30	08 09			09 33	10 28				12 28					14 28			
Exeter Central	a	23p56		06 29	07 37	08 13			09 37	10 37		11 37		12 37			13 37		14 37		15 37	
Exeter St Davids 6	a	00 01		06 35	07 42	08 18			09 42	10 42		11 42		12 42			13 42		14 42		15 42	

b Previous night, stops to pick up only

		SW	SW	SW	SW	SW	SW	SW	SW	SW	SW	SW	SW	SW	SW		SW	SW	SW	SW	SW
		◇1 ⚲	◇1 ⚲	◇1 ⚲	◇1 ⚲	◇1 ⚲	◇1 ⚲	◇1 ⚲	◇1 ⚲	◇1 ⚲	◇1 ⚲	◇1 ⚲	◇1 ⚲	◇1 ⚲	◇1 ⚲		◇1 ⚲	◇1 ⚲	◇1 ⚲	1 ⚲	1
London Waterloo 15 ⊖	d	12 50	13 20	13 50	14 20	14 50	15 20	15 50	16 20	16 50	17 20	17 50	18 20	18 50	19 20		19 50	20 20	21 20	22 20	23 40
Clapham Junction 10	d		13u27		14u27		15u27		16u27		17u27		18u27		19u27			20u27	21u27	22u27	23u47
Woking	d	13 16	13 46	14 16	14 46	15 16	15 46	16 16	16 46	17 16	17 46	18 16	18 46	19 16	19 46		20 16	20 46	21 49	22 49	00 08
Basingstoke	d	13 38	14 07	14 38	15 07	15 38	16 07	16 38	17 07	17 38	18 07	18 38	19 07	19 38	20 07		20 38	21 07	22 14	23 11	00 28
Overton	d	13 46		14 46		15 46		16 46		17 46		18 46		19 46			20 46	21 15	22 22	23 20	00s37
Whitchurch (Hants)	d	13 51		14 51		15 51		16 51		17 51		18 51		19 51			20 51	21 20	22 27	23 25	00s42
Andover	d	14 00	14 24	15 00	15 24	16 00	16 24	17 00	17 24	18 00	18 24	19 00	19 24	20 00	20 24		21 00	21 29	22 36	23 33	00 50
Grateley	d	14 07		15 07		16 07		17 07		18 07		19 07		20 07			21 07	21 36	22 43	23 41	00s58
Salisbury	a	14 19	14 42	15 19	15 42	16 19	16 42	17 19	17 42	18 19	18 43	19 19	19 43	20 19	20 42		21 19	21 48	22 55	23 53	01 10
	d		14 47		15 47		16 47		17 47		18 47		19 47		20 47	20 57		21 53	23 03		
Warminster	d															21 17					
Westbury	d															21 25					
Trowbridge	d															21 31					
Bradford-on-Avon	d															21 37					
Bath Spa 7	a															21 50					
Bristol Temple Meads 10	a															22 06					
Tisbury	d		15 06		16 06		17 06		18 06		19 06		20 06		21 06			22 06	23s16		
Gillingham (Dorset)	a		15 16		16 16		17 16		18 16		19 16		20 16		21 16			22 16	23s27		
	d		15 17		16 17		17 17		18 17		19 17		20 17		21 17			22 17			
Templecombe	d		15 25		16 25		17 25		18 25		19 25		20 25		21 25			22 24	23s35		
Sherborne	d		15 32		16 32		17 32		18 32		19 32		20 32		21 32			22 32	23s42		
Yeovil Junction	a		15 38		16 38		17 38		18 38		19 38		20 38		21 38			22 40	23 49		
	d		15 39		16 39		17 39		18 39		19 39		20 39		21 39						
Crewkerne	d		15 49		16 49		17 49		18 49		19 49		20 49		21 49						
Axminster	a		16 02		17 02		18 02		19 02		20 02		21 02		22 02						
	d		16 03		17 03		18 03		19 03		20 03		21 03		22 03						
Honiton	a		16 15		17 15		18 15		19 15		20 15		21 15		22 15						
	d		16 16		17 16		18 16		19 16		20 16		21 16		22 16						
Feniton	d				17 21				19 21				21 21		22 21						
Whimple	d				17 26				19 26				21 26		22 26						
Pinhoe	d		16 28				18 28				20 28				22 33						
Exeter Central	a		16 35		17 37		18 35		19 37		20 39		21 37		22 41						
Exeter St Davids 6	a		16 42		17 42		18 42		19 42		20 43		21 42		22 45						

For Bus Connections for either to or from Yeovil Junction and Yeovil Pen Mill please see Table 123A

Table 160

Sundays

London - Salisbury and Exeter

Network Diagram - see first Page of Table 160

		SW	SW	SW	SW	SW	SW	SW	SW		SW	SW	SW	SW	SW	SW		SW	SW	SW	SW	SW
		[1]	[1]	◇[1]	◇[1]	◇[1]	◇[1]	◇[1]	◇[1]		◇[1]	◇[1]	◇[1]	◇[1]	◇[1]	◇[1]		◇[1]	◇[1]	◇[1]	[1]	[1]
		A																				
					[trolley]	[trolley]	[trolley]	[trolley]	[trolley]		[trolley]	[trolley]	[trolley]	[trolley]	[trolley]	[trolley]		[trolley]	[trolley]	[trolley]	[trolley]	
London Waterloo [15] ⊖	d	23p40			08 15	09 15	10 15	11 15	12 15		13 15	14 15	15 15	16 15	17 15	18 15		19 15	20 15	21 15	22 15	23 35
Clapham Junction [10]	d	23b47			08u22	09u22	10u22	11u22	12u22		13u22	14u22	15u22	16u22	17u22	18u22		19u22	20u22	21u22	22u22	23u44
Woking	d	00 08			08 47	09 47	10 46	11 46	12 46		13 46	14 46	15 46	16 46	17 46	18 46		19 46	20 46	21 46	22 46	00 08
Basingstoke	d	00 28		08 05	09 08	10 08	11 07	12 07	13 07		14 07	15 07	16 07	17 07	18 07	19 07		20 07	21 07	22 07	23 07	00 40
Overton	d	00s37		08 13	09 16		11 15		13 15			15 15		17 15		19 15			21 15		23 15	00s49
Whitchurch (Hants)	d	00s42		08 18	09 21		11 20		13 20			15 20		17 20		19 20			21 20		23 20	00s54
Andover	d	00 50		08 27	09 30	10 25	11 29	12 24	13 29		14 24	15 29	16 24	17 29	18 24	19 29		20 24	21 29	22 26	23 29	01 02
Grateley	d	00s58		08 34		10 32		12 31			14 31		16 31		18 31			20 31		22 33	23 36	01s10
Salisbury	a	01 10		08 46	09 46	10 45	11 45	12 45	13 45		14 45	15 45	16 45	17 45	18 45	19 45		20 45	21 45	22 45	23 48	01 22
	d		07 10	08 51	09 51	10 51	11 51	12 51	13 51	13 55	14 51	15 51	16 51	17 51	18 51	19 51	19 55	20 51	21 51	22 51		
Warminster	d									14 15							20 15					
Westbury	d									14 24							20 23					
Trowbridge	d									14 30							20 29					
Bradford-on-Avon	d									14 36							20 35					
Bath Spa [7]	a									14 49							20 48					
Bristol Temple Meads [10]	a									15 05							21 04					
Tisbury	d		07 24	09 10	10 10	11 10	12 10	13 10	14 10		15 10	16 10	17 10	18 10	19 10	20 10		21 10	22 10	23 10		
Gillingham (Dorset)	a		07 34	09 20	10 20	11 20	12 20	13 20	14 20		15 20	16 20	17 20	18 20	19 20	20 20		21 20	22 20	23 20		
	d		07 35	09 21	10 21	11 21	12 21	13 21	14 21		15 21	16 21	17 21	18 21	19 21	20 21		21 21	22 21	23 21		
Templecombe	d		07 42	09 28	10 28	11 28	12 28	13 28	14 28		15 28	16 28	17 28	18 28	19 28	20 28		21 28	22 28	23 28		
Sherborne	d		07 50	09 36	10 36	11 36	12 36	13 36	14 36		15 36	16 36	17 36	18 36	19 36	20 36		21 36	22 36	23 36		
Yeovil Junction	a		07 55	09 41	10 41	11 41	12 41	13 41	14 41		15 41	16 41	17 41	18 41	19 41	20 41		21 41	22 42	23 41		
	d		07 57	09 43	10 43	11 43	12 43	13 43	14 43		15 43	16 43	17 43	18 43	19 43	20 43		21 43		23 43		
Crewkerne	d		08 06	09 52	10 52	11 52	12 52	13 52	14 52		15 52	16 52	17 52	18 52	19 52	20 52		21 52		23 52		
Axminster	a		08 19	10 05	11 05	12 05	13 05	14 05	15 05		16 05	17 05	18 05	19 05	20 05	21 05		22 05		00 05		
	d		08 20	10 06	11 06	12 06	13 06	14 06	15 06		16 06	17 06	18 06	19 06	20 06	21 06		22 06		00 06		
Honiton	a		08 31	10 18	11 18	12 18	13 18	14 18	15 18		16 18	17 18	18 18	19 18	20 18	21 18		22 18		00 18		
	d		08 35	10 19	11 19	12 19	13 19	14 19	15 19		16 19	17 19	18 19	19 19	20 19	21 19		22 19		00 19		
Feniton	d		08 40		11 24		13 24		15 24			17 24		19 24		21 24		22 24		00 24		
Whimple	d		08 45		11 29		13 29		15 29			17 29		19 29		21 29		22 29		00 29		
Pinhoe	d			10 31		12 31		14 31			16 31		18 31		20 31			22 36				
Exeter Central	a		08 56	10 40	11 40	12 40	13 40	14 40	15 40		16 40	17 40	18 40	19 40	20 40	21 40		22 40				
Exeter St Davids [6]	a		09 01	10 45	11 45	12 45	13 45	14 45	15 45		16 45	17 45	18 45	19 45	20 45	21 45		22 45		00 40		

A not 11 December

b Previous night, stops to pick up only

For Bus Connections for either to or from Yeovil Junction and Yeovil Pen Mill please see Table 123A

Exeter and Salisbury - London

Network Diagram - see first Page of Table 160

Miles			SW MX	SW MO	SW	SW	SW	SW	SW	SW	SW	SW	SW	SW	SW	SW	SW	SW	SW	SW	SW	SW
			1	1	◇1	◇1	◇1	◇1	◇1	◇1	◇1	◇1	◇1	◇1	◇1	◇1	◇1	◇1	◇1	◇1	◇1	◇1
															A							
					🍴	🍴	🍴	🍴	🍴	🍴	🍴	🍴	🍴	🍴	🍴	🍴	🍴	🍴	🍴	🍴	🍴	🍴
0	**Exeter St Davids** 6	d	22p57	23p15					05 10			06 41	07 26			08 26		09 26		10 26		11 26
0¾	**Exeter Central**	d	23p01	23p19					05 14			06 45	07 30			08 30		09 30		10 30		11 30
3½	Pinhoe	d	23p06						05 19			06 50	07 35			08 35		09 35				11 35
9¼	Whimple	d	23p13						05 26			06 57				08 42				10 39		
13	Feniton	d	23p18						05 31			07 02				08 47				10 45		
17½	Honiton	a	23p25	23b34					05 38			07 10	07 47			08 54		09 47		10 51		11 48
—		d	23p32						05 39	06 19		07 11	07 49			08 55		09 53		10 53		11 53
27¾	Axminster	a	23p42	23b45					05 49	06 29		07 21	07 59			09 05		10 03		11 03		12 03
—		d	23p43						05 51	06 30		07 22	08 00			09 06		10 06		11 06		12 06
40¾	Crewkerne	d	23p56	00s11					06 04	06 43		07 35	08 13			09 19		10 19		11 19		12 19
49¾	Yeovil Junction	a	00 04	00s20					06 12	06 52		07 44	08 22			09 27		10 27		11 27		12 27
—		d	00 09				05 15	05 50	06 20	06 53	07 22	07 50	08 29			09 29		10 29		11 29		12 29
54¼	Sherborne	d					05 21	05 56	06 26	07 00	07 28	07 56	08 35			09 35		10 35		11 35		12 35
60¼	Templecombe	d					05 29	06 04	06 34	07 07	07 36	08 04	08 43			09 43		10 43		11 43		12 43
67¾	Gillingham (Dorset)	a					05 36	06 11	06 41	07 14	07 43	08 11	08 50			09 50		10 50		11 50		12 50
—		d					05 37	06 12	06 42	07 15	07 44	08 12	08 51	09 18		09 51		10 51		11 51		12 51
76¼	Tisbury	d					05 47	06 24	06 52	07 26	07 54	08 22	09 01	09 28		10 01		11 01		12 01		13 01
—	Bristol Temple Meads 10	d													08 51							
—	Bath Spa 7	d													09 07							
—	Bradford-on-Avon	d													09 20							
—	Trowbridge	d													09 27							
—	Westbury	d													09 39							
—	Warminster	d													09 46							
88¾	**Salisbury**	a	00 43	00 56			06 02	06 39	07 07	07 40	08 09	08 37	09 16	09 42	10 09	10 16		11 16		12 16		13 16
—																						
—		d			05 15	05 43	06 06	06 45	07 15	07 45	08 15	08 47	09 21	09 47	10 21		10 47	11 21	11 47	12 21	12 47	13 21
99¾	Grateley	d			05 27	05 55	06 19	06 57	07 27	07 57	08 27	08 59		09 59			10 59		11 59		12 59	
106	Andover	d			05 35	06 03	06 26	07 05	07 35	08 05	08 35	09 06	09 38	10 06	10 38		11 06	11 38	12 06	12 38	13 06	13 38
113¼	Whitchurch (Hants)	d			05 43	06 11	06 35	07 13	07 43	08 13	08 43	09 14		10 14			11 14		12 14		13 14	
117	Overton	d			05 49	06 17	06 41	07 19	07 49	08 19	08 49	09 20		10 20			11 20		12 20		13 20	
124¾	**Basingstoke**	a			05 58	06 26	06 49	07 28	07 58	08 28	08 58	09 28	09 55	10 28	10 55		11 28	11 55	12 28	12 55	13 28	13 55
148¼	Woking	a			06 18	06 46			08 18	08 48	09 18	09 49	10 15	10 49	11 15		11 49	12 15	12 49	13 15	13 49	14 15
168¼	Clapham Junction 10	a			06 38		07 28				09 38	10 09	10 36		11 36			12 36		13 36		14 36
172½	**London Waterloo** 15 ⊖	a			06 49	07 14	07 39	08 14	08 46	09 17	09 51	10 19	10 49	11 19	11 49		12 19	12 49	13 19	13 49	14 19	14 49

		SW	SW	SW	SW	SW	SW	SW	SW	SW	SW	SW	SW	SW	SW	SW	SW	SW	SW	SW	SW	SW	SW
		◇1	◇1	◇1	◇1	◇1	◇1	◇1	◇1	◇1	◇1	◇1	◇1	◇1	◇1	◇1	1	◇1	◇1	◇1	1	1	1
				B							A												
		🍴	🍴	🍴	🍴	🍴	🍴	🍴	🍴	🍴	🍴	🍴	🍴	🍴	🍴	🍴		🍴		🍴			
Exeter St Davids 6	d				12 26		13 26		14 26			15 26		16 26		17 26	17 46	18 26	19 26	20 26	21 23		22 57
Exeter Central	d				12 30		13 30		14 30			15 30		16 30		17 30	17 50	18 30	19 30	20 30	21 30		23 01
Pinhoe	d						13 35					15 35				17 35	17 56		19 35		21 35		23 06
Whimple	d				12 39				14 39					16 39			18 02	18 39		20 39			23 13
Feniton	d				12 45				14 45					16 45			18 08	18 45		20 45			23 18
Honiton	a				12 51		13 48		14 51			15 48		16 51		17 48	18 18	18 51	19 48	20 51	21 47		23 25
	d				12 53		13 53		14 53			15 53		16 53		17 53	18 19	18 53	19 53	20 53	21 53		23 32
Axminster	a				13 03		14 03		15 03			16 03		17 03		18 03	18 29	19 03	20 03	21 03	22 03		23 42
	d				13 06		14 06		15 06			16 06		17 06		18 06		19 06	20 06	21 06	22 06		23 43
Crewkerne	d				13 19		14 19		15 19			16 19		17 19		18 19		19 19	20 19	21 19	22 19		23 56
Yeovil Junction	a				13 27		14 27		15 27			16 27		17 27		18 27		19 27	20 27	21 27	22 27		00 04
	d				13 29		14 29		15 29			16 29		17 29		18 29		19 29	20 29	21 29	22 29		00 09
Sherborne	d				13 35		14 35		15 35			16 35		17 35		18 35		19 35	20 35	21 35	22 35		
Templecombe	d				13 43		14 43		15 43			16 43		17 43		18 43		19 43	20 43	21 43	22 47		
Gillingham (Dorset)	a				13 50		14 50		15 50			16 50		17 50		18 50		19 50	20 50	21 50	22 54		
	d				13 51		14 51		15 51	16 18		16 51		17 51		18 51		19 51	20 51	21 51	22 55		
Tisbury	d				14 01		15 01		16 01	16 28		17 01		18 01		19 01		20 01	21 01	22 01	23 05		
Bristol Temple Meads 10	d	12 51		12 51							15 51											22 25	
Bath Spa 7	d	13 07		13 07							16 07											22 38	
Bradford-on-Avon	d	13 20		13 20							16 22											22 51	
Trowbridge	d	13 27		13 27							16 28											22 57	
Westbury	d	13 39		13e39							16 39											23 08	
Warminster	d	13 46		13 46							16 47											23 15	
Salisbury	a	14 10		14 10	14 16		15 16		16 16	16 43	17 09	17 16		18 21		19 23		20 21	21 21	22 16	23 29	23 35	00 43
	d		13 47	14 21		14 47	15 21	15 47	16 21	16 47	17 21		17 47	18 26	18 47	19 26		20 26	21 26	22 26			
Grateley	d		13 59			14 59		15 59		16 59			17 59		18 59	19 38		20 38	21 38	22 38			
Andover	d		14 06	14 38		15 06	15 38	16 06	16 38	17 06	17 38		18 06	18 43	19 06	19 45		20 45	21 45	22 45			
Whitchurch (Hants)	d		14 14			15 14		16 14		17 14			18 14		19 14	19 53		20 53	21 53	22 53			
Overton	d		14 20			15 20		16 20		17 20			18 20		19 20	19 59		20 59	21 59	22 59			
Basingstoke	a		14 28	14 55		15 28	15 55	16 28	16 55	17 29	17 55		18 28	19 00	19 28	20 08		21 08	22 07	23 07			
Woking	a		14 49	15 15		15 49	16 15	16 49	17 15	17 49	18 15		18 49	19 20	19 49	20 29		21 29	22 28				
Clapham Junction 10	a			15 36			16 36		17 36		18 36			19 41		20 52		21 52	22 48				
London Waterloo 15 ⊖	a		15 19	15 49		16 19	16 49	17 19	17 44	18 21	18 45		19 19	19 49	20 19	21 00		22 04	22 58				

A 🍴 from Salisbury

B not from 26 December until 2 January

b Previous night, stops to set down only

For Bus Connections for either to or from Yeovil Junction and Yeovil Pen Mill please see Table 123A

Table 160

Saturdays

Exeter and Salisbury - London

Network Diagram - see first Page of Table 160

		SW	SW	SW	SW	SW	SW	SW	SW	SW	SW	SW	SW	SW	SW	SW	SW	SW	SW	SW	SW
		1	◇1	◇1	◇1	◇1	◇1	◇1	◇1	◇1	◇1	◇1	◇1	◇1	◇1	◇1	◇1	◇1	◇1	◇1	◇1
													A								
			✕	✕	✕	✕	✕	✕	✕	✕	✕	✕	✕	✕	✕	✕	✕	✕	✕	✕	✕
Exeter St Davids 6	d	22p57					05 10			06 41	07 26			08 26		09 26		10 26		11 26	
Exeter Central	d	23p01					05 14			06 45	07 30			08 30		09 30		10 30		11 30	
Pinhoe	d	23p06					05 19			06 50	07 35			08 35		09 35				11 35	
Whimple	d	23p13					05 26			06 57				08 42				10 39			
Feniton	d	23p18					05 31			07 02				08 47				10 45			
Honiton	a	23p25					05 38			07 11	07 48			08 54		09 48		10 51		11 48	
	d	23p32					05 39	06 19		07 13	07 53			08 55		09 53		10 53		11 53	
Axminster	a	23p42					05 49	06 29		07 23	08 03			09 05		10 03		11 03		12 03	
	d	23p43					05 51	06 30		07 24	08 06			09 06		10 06		11 06		12 06	
Crewkerne	d	23p56					06 04	06 43		07 37	08 19			09 19		10 19		11 19		12 19	
Yeovil Junction	a	00 04					06 12	06 52		07 45	08 27			09 27		10 27		11 27		12 27	
	d	00 09					06 20	06 53		07 50	08 29			09 29		10 29		11 29		12 29	
Sherborne	d						06 26	07 00		07 56	08 35			09 35		10 35		11 35		12 35	
Templecombe	d						06 34	07 07		08 04	08 43			09 43		10 43		11 43		12 43	
Gillingham (Dorset)	a						06 41	07 14		08 11	08 50			09 50		10 50		11 50		12 50	
	d						06 42	07 15		08 12	08 51			09 51		10 51		11 51		12 51	
Tisbury	d						06 52	07 26		08 22	09 01			10 01		11 01		12 01		13 01	
Bristol Temple Meads 10	d												08 51								
Bath Spa 7	d												09 07								
Bradford-on-Avon	d												09 20								
Trowbridge	d												09 27								
Westbury	d												09 39								
Warminster	d												09 46								
Salisbury	a	00 43					07 07	07 40		08 37	09 16		10 09	10 16		11 16		12 16		13 16	
	d		05 15	05 47	06 21	06 47	07 21	07 47	08 21	08 47	09 21	09 47	10 21		10 47	11 21	11 47	12 21	12 47	13 21	13 47
Grateley	d		05 27	05 59		06 59		07 59		08 59		09 59			10 59		11 59		12 59		13 59
Andover	d		05 35	06 06	06 38	07 06	07 38	08 06	08 38	09 06	09 38	10 06	10 38		11 06	11 38	12 06	12 38	13 06	13 38	14 06
Whitchurch (Hants)	d		05 43	06 14		07 14		08 14		09 14		10 14			11 14		12 14		13 14		14 14
Overton	d		05 49	06 20		07 20		08 20		09 20		10 20			11 20		12 20		13 20		14 20
Basingstoke	a		05 58	06 28	06 55	07 28	07 55	08 28	08 55	09 28	09 55	10 28	10 55		11 28	11 55	12 28	12 55	13 28	13 55	14 28
Woking	a		06 18	06 49	07 15	07 49	08 17	08 49	09 15	09 49	10 15	10 49	11 15		11 49	12 15	12 49	13 15	13 49	14 15	14 49
Clapham Junction 10	a		06 38		07 36		08 37		09 36		10 36		11 36			12 36		13 36		14 36	
London Waterloo 15 ⊖	a		06 49	07 19	07 49	08 19	08 49	09 19	09 49	10 19	10 49	11 19	11 49		12 19	12 49	13 19	13 49	14 19	14 49	15 19

		SW	SW	SW	SW	SW	SW	SW	SW	SW	SW	SW	SW	SW	SW	SW	SW	SW	SW	SW
		◇1	◇1	◇1	◇1	◇1	◇1	◇1	◇1	◇1	◇1	◇1	◇1	◇1	◇1	◇1	◇1	1	1	1
									A											
		✕	✕	✕	✕	✕	✕	✕	✕	✕	✕	✕	✕	✕	✕		✕			
Exeter St Davids 6	d		12 26		13 26		14 26			15 26		16 26		17 26	18 26	19 26	20 26	21 26		22 57
Exeter Central	d		12 30		13 30		14 30			15 30		16 30		17 30	18 30	19 30	20 30	21 30		23 01
Pinhoe	d				13 35					15 35				17 35		19 35		21 35		23 06
Whimple	d		12 39				14 39					16 39		17 42	18 39		20 39			23 13
Feniton	d		12 45				14 45					16 45		17 47	18 45		20 45			23 18
Honiton	a		12 51		13 48		14 51			15 48		16 51		17 54	18 51	19 48	20 51	21 48		23 25
	d		12 53		13 53		14 53			15 53		16 53		17 55	18 53	19 53	20 53	21 53		23 32
Axminster	a		13 03		14 03		15 03			16 03		17 03		18 05	19 03	20 03	21 03	22 03		23 42
	d		13 06		14 06		15 06			16 06		17 06		18 06	19 06	20 06	21 06	22 06		23 43
Crewkerne	d		13 19		14 19		15 19			16 19		17 19		18 19	19 19	20 19	21 19	22 19		23 56
Yeovil Junction	a		13 27		14 27		15 27			16 27		17 27		18 27	19 27	20 27	21 27	22 27		00 04
	d		13 29		14 29		15 29			16 29		17 29		18 29	19 29	20 29	21 29	22 29		00 16
Sherborne	d		13 35		14 35		15 35			16 35		17 35		18 35	19 35	20 35	21 35	22 35		
Templecombe	d		13 43		14 43		15 43			16 43		17 43		18 43	19 43	20 43	21 43	22 43		
Gillingham (Dorset)	a		13 50		14 50		15 50			16 50		17 50		18 50	19 50	20 50	21 50	22 50		
	d		13 51		14 51		15 51			16 51		17 51		18 51	19 51	20 51	21 51	22 51		
Tisbury	d		14 01		15 01		16 01			17 01		18 01		19 01	20 01	21 01	22 01	23 01		
Bristol Temple Meads 10	d	12 51							15 51										22 23	
Bath Spa 7	d	13 07							16 07										22 36	
Bradford-on-Avon	d	13 20							16 24										22 47	
Trowbridge	d	13 27							16 30										22 53	
Westbury	d	13 39							16 39										23 04	
Warminster	d	13 46							16 47										23 11	
Salisbury	a	14 10	14 16		15 16		16 16		17 09	17 16		18 16		19 16	20 16	21 16	22 21	23 29	23 34	00 50
	d	14 21		14 47	15 21	15 47	16 21	16 47	17 21		17 47	18 21	18 47	19 26	20 26	21 26	22 26			
Grateley	d			14 59		15 59		16 59			17 59		18 59	19 38	20 38	21 38	22 38			
Andover	d	14 38		15 06	15 38	16 06	16 38	17 06	17 38		18 06	18 38	19 06	19 45	20 45	21 45	22 45			
Whitchurch (Hants)	d			15 14		16 14		17 14			18 14		19 14	19 53	20 53	21 53	22 53			
Overton	d			15 20		16 20		17 20			18 20		19 20	19 59	20 59	21 59	22 59			
Basingstoke	a	14 55		15 28	15 55	16 28	16 55	17 28	17 55		18 28	18 55	19 28	20 08	21 08	22 07	23 07			
Woking	a	15 15		15 49	16 15	16 49	17 15	17 49	18 15		18 49	19 15	19 49	20 29	21 29	22 28				
Clapham Junction 10	a	15 36			16 36		17 36		18 36			19 36		20 52	21 52	22 48				
London Waterloo 15 ⊖	a	15 49		16 19	16 49	17 19	17 49	18 19	18 49		19 19	19 49	20 19	21 04	22 04	22 57				

A ✕ from Salisbury

For Bus Connections for either to or from Yeovil Junction and Yeovil Pen Mill please see Table 123A

Table 160

Sundays

Exeter and Salisbury - London

Network Diagram - see first Page of Table 160

		SW	SW	SW	SW	SW	SW	SW	SW	SW	SW	SW	SW	SW	SW	SW	SW	SW	SW	SW	SW	SW	SW
		1	◇1	◇1	◇1	◇1	◇1	◇1	◇1	◇1	◇1	◇1	◇1	◇1	◇1	◇1	◇1	◇1	◇1	◇1	1	1	1
		A												B									
			☕	☕	☕	☕	☕	☕	☕	☕	☕	☕	☕	☕	☕	☕	☕	☕					
Exeter St Davids 6	d	22p57						09 26	10 26	11 26	12 26	13 26	14 26		15 26	16 26	17 26	18 26	19 26	20 26		21 26	23 15
Exeter Central	d	23p01						09 30	10 30	11 30	12 30	13 30	14 30		15 30	16 30	17 30	18 30	19 30	20 30		21 30	23 19
Pinhoe	d	23p06						09 35		11 35		13 35			15 35		17 35		19 35			21 35	
Whimple	d	23p13						09 42	10 39		12 39		14 39			16 39		18 39		20 39		21 42	
Feniton	d	23p18						09 47	10 45		12 45		14 45			16 45		18 45		20 45		21 47	
Honiton	a	23p25						09 54	10 51	11 48	12 51	13 48	14 51		15 48	16 51	17 48	18 51	19 48	20 51		21 54	23s34
	d	23p32					08 58	09 55	10 53	11 53	12 53	13 53	14 53		15 53	16 53	17 53	18 53	19 53	20 53		21 55	
Axminster	a	23p42					09 08	10 05	11 03	12 03	13 03	14 03	15 03		16 03	17 03	18 03	19 03	20 03	21 03		22 05	23s45
	d	23p43					09 09	10 09	11 09	12 09	13 09	14 09	15 09		16 09	17 09	18 09	19 09	20 09	21 09		22 09	
Crewkerne	d	23p56					09 22	10 22	11 22	12 22	13 22	14 22	15 22		16 22	17 22	18 22	19 22	20 22	21 22		22 22	00s11
Yeovil Junction	a	00 04					09 30	10 30	11 30	12 30	13 30	14 30	15 30		16 30	17 30	18 30	19 30	20 30	21 30		22 30	00s20
	d	00 16			07 32		09 32	10 32	11 32	12 32	13 32	14 32	15 32		16 32	17 32	18 32	19 32	20 32	21 32		22 32	
Sherborne	d				07 38		09 38	10 38	11 38	12 38	13 38	14 38	15 38		16 38	17 38	18 38	19 38	20 38	21 38		22 38	
Templecombe	d				07 46		09 46	10 46	11 46	12 46	13 46	14 46	15 46		16 46	17 46	18 46	19 46	20 46	21 46		22 46	
Gillingham (Dorset)	a				07 53		09 53	10 53	11 53	12 53	13 53	14 53	15 53		16 53	17 53	18 53	19 53	20 53	21 53		22 53	
	d				07 54	08 54	09 54	10 54	11 54	12 54	13 54	14 54	15 54		16 54	17 54	18 54	19 54	20 54	21 54		22 54	
Tisbury	d				08 05	09 05	10 05	11 05	12 05	13 05	14 05	15 05	16 05		17 05	18 05	19 05	20 05	21 05	22 05		23 05	
Bristol Temple Meads 10	d													16 04							21 35		
Bath Spa 7	d													16 20							21 49		
Bradford-on-Avon	d													16 31							22 00		
Trowbridge	d													16 37							22 06		
Westbury	d													16 46							22 15		
Warminster	d													16 53							22 22		
Salisbury	a	00 50			08 20	09 20	10 20	11 20	12 20	13 20	14 20	15 20	16 20	17 16	17 20	18 20	19 20	20 20	21 20	22 20	22 46	23 19	00 56
	d		06 45	07 27	08 27	09 27	10 27	11 27	12 27	13 27	14 27	15 27	16 27	17 27		18 27	19 27	20 27	21 27	22 27			
Grateley	d				08 39	09 39		11 39		13 39		15 39		17 39			19 39		21 39	22 39			
Andover	d		07 02	07 44	08 46	09 46	10 44	11 46	12 44	13 46	14 44	15 46	16 44	17 46		18 44	19 46	20 44	21 46	22 46			
Whitchurch (Hants)	d			07 52	08 54		10 52		12 52		14 52		16 52			18 52		20 52		22 54			
Overton	d			07 58	09 00		10 58		12 58		14 58		16 58			18 58		20 58		23 00			
Basingstoke	a		07 19	08 06	09 08	10 02	11 06	12 02	13 06	14 02	15 06	16 02	17 06	18 02		19 06	20 02	21 06	22 03	23 08			
Woking	a		07 39	08 28	09 28	10 28	11 28	12 28	13 28	14 28	15 28	16 28	17 28	18 28		19 28	20 28	21 28	22 28				
Clapham Junction 10	a		08 05	08 57	09 57	10 49	11 49	12 49	13 49	14 49	15 49	16 49	17 49	18 49		19 49	20 49	21 49	22 49				
London Waterloo 15 ⊖	a		08 19	09 09	10 08	11 04	12 03	13 04	13 59	14 59	15 59	16 59	17 59	18 59		19 59	20 59	21 59	22 59				

A not 11 December

B ☕ from Salisbury

For Bus Connections for either to or from Yeovil Junction and Yeovil Pen Mill please see Table 123A

Network Diagram for Tables 165, 167

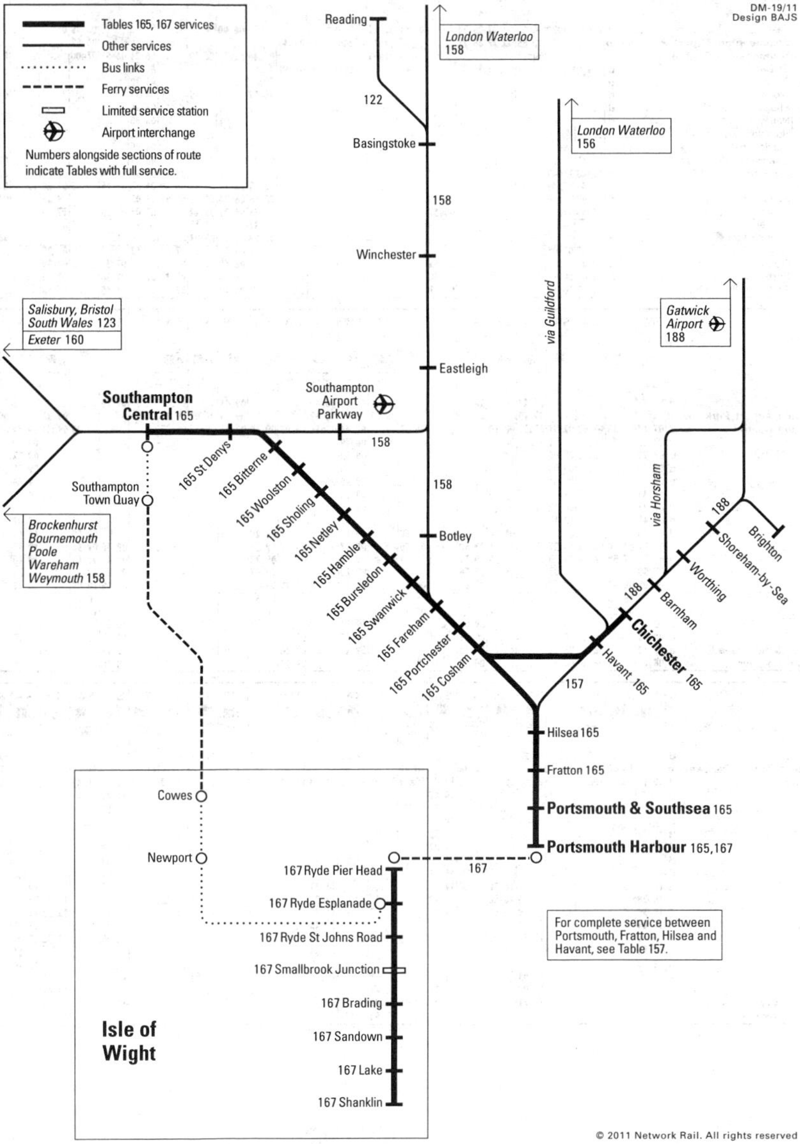

Southampton - Fareham and Portsmouth

Network Diagram - see first Page of Table 165

Miles	Miles			SW	SW	SW	SW	SW	SW	SW	SW	SW		SW	SN	SW	SN	SW	SW	GW	SW	SW		SN	SW
				MO	MX	MX	MO	MX		MX	MX	MO		MX											
				■1	■1	■1	◇■1 🛒	◇■1	■1	■1	■1	■1		■1	■1	■1		■1	■1		◇■1	■1		◇■1	■1
0	—	Eastleigh	d	23p26	23p30	00 02	00 22	00 23	00 30	01 00	01 22					06 00		06 29			06 48	07 02			07 28
1¼	—	**Southampton Airport Parkway**	d			00 06	00 27	00 28		01 05	01 26	02s46		02s46							06 53				
—	—	**Southampton Central** ⛴	d			00a13				01a12	01a35				05 48		06 10		06 21	06 53	07a00			07 06	
3¼	—	St Denys	d				00s31	00s32				02s51		02s51					06 28						
3¾	—	Bitterne	d																06 30						
5½	—	Woolston	d												05 57		06 19		06 34					07 15	
6¼	—	Sholing	d																06 36						
8	—	Netley	d																06 40						
8¾	—	Hamble	d																06 42						
10	—	Bursledon	d																06 45						
12	—	Swanwick	d												06 06		06 27		06 49					07 24	
15¾	—	**Fareham**	a	23p43	23p48				00s47						06 12	06 17	06 33	06 49	06 57	07 14		07 19		07 30	07 46
—	—		d	23p44	23p49										06 13	06 19	06 34	06 50	06 58	07 15		07 20		07 31	07 48
19	—	Portchester	d	23p49	23p54				00s53						06 18	06 24	06 40	06 55	07 03			07 25		07 36	07 53
21½	0	Cosham	d	23p54	23p59				00s57						06 23	06 29	06 44	07 00	07 08	07 23		07 29		07 40	07 58
—	4	Havant	a												06 37		06 53							07 46	
—	12¾	**Chichester ■4**	a												06 58		07 07							08 08	
23	—	Hilsea	a	23p59	00 03											06 33		07 05	07 13			07 35			08 03
25¼	—	Fratton	a	00 04	00 07				01s05							06 40		07 09	07 17	07 34		07 39			08 07
26¼	—	**Portsmouth & Southsea**	a	00 08	00 11				01s08							06 44		07 12	07 22	07 38		07 42			08 11
27	—	**Portsmouth Harbour** ⛴	a	00 13	00 16				01 12							06 49		07 17		07 45		07 48			08 16

		SW	SN	GW	SW	SW	SN	SW		SN	XC	SW	SW	GW	SN	SW	XC	SW		SW	SN	XC	SW	SW	GW
		■1	■1	◇	■1	◇■1	◇■1	■1		■1	◇■1 🛒	■1	◇■1 🛒	◇ 🛒	◇■1	■1 🛒	◇■1 🛒	◇■1 🛒		■1	■1	◇■1 🛒	■1	◇■1 🛒	■ 🛒
Eastleigh	d					07 44		08 31					08 48			09 01				09 28					
Southampton Airport Parkway	d					07 49					08 33		08 52			09 05	09 09	09 14				09 33		09 42	
Southampton Central ⛴	d	07 17	07 33	07 42	07 51	07a57	08 10			08 33	08a44	08 44	08a59	09 05	09 10	09a15	09a17	09a22			09 33	09a41	09 44	09a49	10 05
St Denys	d	07 23			07 57		08 15					08 49											09 49		
Bitterne	d	07 25			08 00							08 52											09 52		
Woolston	d	07 29			08 03							08 55											09 55		
Sholing	d	07 31			08 06							08 58											09 58		
Netley	d	07 35			08 10							09 02											10 02		
Hamble	d	07 37			08 12							09 04											10 04		
Bursledon	d	07 40			08 15							09 07											10 07		
Swanwick	d	07 44	07 51		08 20		08 28			08 50		09 11			09 28						09 50		10 11		
Fareham	a	07 52	07 58	08 05	08 27		08 34	08 50		08 56		09 17		09 27	09 36					09 46	09 56		10 17		10 27
	d	07 53	07 58	08 06	08 28		08 35	08 51		08 57		09 18		09 27	09 37					09 48	09 56		10 18		10 27
Portchester	d	07 58			08 33		08 40	08 56				09 23			09 42					09 53			10 23		
Cosham	d	08 03	08 07	08 14	08 38		08 44	09 01		09 05		09 28		09 35	09 46					09 58	10 05		10 28		10 35
Havant	a		08 13				08 50			09 11					09 53						10 11				
Chichester ■4	a		08 27				09 11			09 24					10 10						10 23				
Hilsea	a	08 09			08 45			09 05				09 33								10 03			10 33		
Fratton	a	08 13		08 20	08 49			09 09				09 37		09 42						10 07			10 37		10 42
Portsmouth & Southsea	a	08 19		08 24	08 52			09 13				09 42		09 46						10 11			10 42		10 46
Portsmouth Harbour ⛴	a	08 24		08 30	08 57			09 18						09 55						10 18					10 54

		SN	SW	SW		SW	SN	XC	SW	SW	GW	SW	SN	XC		SW	SW	SN	XC	SW	SW	GW	SN	SW	
		◇■1	■1	◇■1 🛒		■1	■1	◇■1 🛒	■1	◇■1 🛒	◇ 🛒	■1	◇■1	◇■1 🛒		◇■1 🛒	■1	■1	◇■1 🛒	■1	◇■1 🛒	◇ 🛒	◇■1	■1	
Eastleigh	d		10 03			10 28						11 00					11 28							12 00	
Southampton Airport Parkway	d		10 08	10 14				10 33		10 42		11 05		11 09		11 14			11 33		11 42			12 05	
Southampton Central ⛴	d	10 13	10a18	10a22			10 33	10a43	10 44	10a49	11 05	11a12	11 13	11a16		11a22		11 33	11a43	11 44	11a49	12 05	12 13	12a15	
St Denys	d								10 49											11 49					
Bitterne	d								10 52											11 52					
Woolston	d								10 55											11 55					
Sholing	d								10 58											11 58					
Netley	d								11 02											12 02					
Hamble	d								11 04											12 04					
Bursledon	d								11 07											12 07					
Swanwick	d	10 32					10 50		11 11				11 33					11 50		12 11			12 33		
Fareham	a	10 38				10 46	10 56		11 17		11 27		11 39				11 46	11 56		12 17		12 27	12 39		
	d	10 39				10 48	10 57		11 18		11 27		11 40				11 48	11 57		12 18		12 27	12 40		
Portchester	d	10 44				10 53			11 23				11 45				11 53			12 23			12 45		
Cosham	d	10 48				10 58	11 05		11 28		11 35		11 49				11 58	12 05		12 28		12 35	12 49		
Havant	a	10 55					11 11						11 55					12 11					12 55		
Chichester ■4	a	11 10					11 24						12 10					12 24					13 10		
Hilsea	a					11 03			11 33								12 03			12 33					
Fratton	a					11 07			11 37		11 42						12 07			12 37		12 42			
Portsmouth & Southsea	a					11 11			11 42		11 46						12 11			12 42		12 46			
Portsmouth Harbour ⛴	a					11 18					11 54						12 18					12 54			

Southampton - Fareham and Portsmouth

Network Diagram - see first Page of Table 165

		SW	SW	SN	XC	SW	SW	GW	SN	SW		XC	SW	SW	SN	XC	SW	SW	GW	SW		SN	SW	SW	GW
		◇[1] 🛒	[1]	[1]	◇[1] 🛒	[1]	◇[1] 🛒	◇ 🛒	◇[1]	[1]		◇[1] 🛒	◇[1] 🛒	[1]	[1]	◇[1] 🛒	[1]	◇[1] 🛒	◇ 🛒	[1]		◇[1]	◇[1] 🛒	[1]	[R] 🛒
Eastleigh	d		12 28							13 00				13 28						14 00				14 28	
Southampton Airport Parkway	d	12 14			12 33		12 42			13 05		13 09	13 14			13 33		13 42		14 05			14 14		
Southampton Central ⛴	d	12a22		12 33	12a41	12 44	12a49	13 05	13 13	13a15		13a17	13a22		13 33	13a41	13 44	13a49	14 05	14a12		14 13	14a22		14 34
St Denys	d					12 49											13 49								
Bitterne	d					12 52											13 52								
Woolston	d					12 55											13 55								
Sholing	d					12 58											13 58								
Netley	d					13 02											14 02								
Hamble	d					13 04											14 04								
Bursledon	d					13 07											14 07								
Swanwick	d			12 50		13 11			13 33						13 50		14 11					14 33			
Fareham	a		12 46	12 56		13 17		13 27	13 39					13 46	13 56		14 17		14 27			14 39		14 46	14 55
	d		12 48	12 56		13 18		13 27	13 40					13 48	13 56		14 18		14 27			14 40		14 48	14 56
Portchester	d		12 53			13 23			13 45					13 53			14 23					14 45		14 53	
Cosham	d		12 58	13 05		13 28		13 35	13 49					13 58	14 05		14 28		14 35			14 49		14 58	15 04
Havant	a			13 11					13 55						14 11							14 55			15 10
Chichester [4]	a			13 23					14 10						14 23							15 10			15 21
Hilsea	a		13 03			13 33								14 03			14 33							15 03	
Fratton	a		13 07			13 37		13 42						14 07			14 37		14 42					15 07	
Portsmouth & Southsea	a		13 11			13 42		13 46						14 11			14 42		14 46					15 11	
Portsmouth Harbour ⛴	a		13 18					13 54						14 18					14 54					15 18	

		XC	SN	SW	SW	GW		SW	SN	XC	SW	SW	SN	XC	SW	SW		GW	SN	SW	SW	SW	SW	SN	XC
		◇[1] 🛒	[1]	[1]	◇[1] 🛒	◇ 🛒		[1]	◇[1]	◇[1] 🛒	◇[1] 🛒	[1]	[1]	◇[1] 🛒	[1]	◇[1] 🛒		◇ 🛒	◇[1]	[1]	◇[1] 🛒	[1]	[1]	[1]	◇[1] 🛒
			A																						
Eastleigh	d		14 41					15 00				15 28								16 00			16 28		
Southampton Airport Parkway	d		14 35		14 42			15 05		15 09	15 14			15 33		15 42				16 05	16 14				16 33
Southampton Central ⛴	d		14a42	14 44	14a49	15 05		15a12	15 13	15a17	15a22		15 33	15a41	15 44	15a49		16 05	16 12	16a15	16a22			16 33	16a41
St Denys	d			14 49											15 49										
Bitterne	d			14 52											15 52										
Woolston	d			14 55											15 55										
Sholing	d			14 58											15 58										
Netley	d			15 02											16 02										
Hamble	d			15 04											16 04										
Bursledon	d			15 07											16 07										
Swanwick	d			15 11					15 33				15 50		16 11				16 29					16 50	
Fareham	a		14 59	15 17		15 27			15 39			15 46	15 56		16 17			16 27	16 35				16 46	16 56	
	d		15 00	15 18		15 27			15 40			15 48	15 57		16 18			16 27	16 36			16 43	16 48	16 57	
Portchester	d			15 23					15 45			15 53			16 23				16 41				16 53		
Cosham	d			15 28		15 35			15 49			15 58	16 05		16 28			16 35	16 45				16 58	17 05	
Havant	a		15 14						15 57				16 11						16 51			16 55		17 11	
Chichester [4]	a		15 25						16 12				16 24						17 08					17 25	
Hilsea	a			15 33								16 03			16 33								17 03		
Fratton	a			15 37		15 42						16 07			16 37			16 42					17 07		
Portsmouth & Southsea	a			15 42		15 46						16 11			16 40			16 46					17 11		
Portsmouth Harbour ⛴	a					15 54						16 18			16 44			16 54					17 18		

		SW		SW	SW	GW	SW	SN	SW	SN	SW	SN		XC	SW	SW	SW	GW	SN	SW	SW	SN		XC	SW
		[1]		[1]	◇[1] 🛒	◇ 🛒	[1]	◇[1]	◇[1] 🛒	[1]	[1]	[1]		◇[1] 🛒	[1]	◇[1] 🛒	[1]	◇ 🛒	◇[1]	◇[1] 🛒	[1]	[1]		◇[1] 🛒	[1]
Eastleigh	d	16 54					17 01			17 16	17 28						18 01				18 25				18 55
Southampton Airport Parkway	d				16 42		17 05		17 14	17 20				17 33		17 42				18 09				18 33	
Southampton Central ⛴	d			16 44	16a49	17 05	17a13	17 13	17a22	17a28		17 33		17a41	17 44	17a49		18 05	18 11	18a16		18 33		18a44	
St Denys	d			16 49											17 49										
Bitterne	d			16 52											17 52										
Woolston	d			16 55											17 55										
Sholing	d			16 58											17 58										
Netley	d			17 02											18 02										
Hamble	d			17 04											18 04										
Bursledon	d			17 07											18 07										
Swanwick	d			17 11				17 33				17 50			18 11				18 28			18 50			
Fareham	a	17 11		17 17		17 27		17 39			17 46	17 56			18 17		18 22	18 27	18 34		18 44	18 56			19 13
	d	17 12		17 18		17 27		17 40			17 48	17 56			18 18		18 23	18 27	18 35		18 45	18 56			19 14
Portchester	d	17 17		17 23				17 45			17 53				18 23		18 28		18 40		18 50				19 19
Cosham	d	17 22		17 28		17 35		17 49			17 58	18 05			18 28		18 33	18 35	18 44		18 55	19 05			19 24
Havant	a							17 55				18 11							18 50			19 11			
Chichester [4]	a							18 10				18 24							19 05			19 22			
Hilsea	a			17 33							18 04				18 33						19 05				19 28
Fratton	a	17 31		17 37		17 42					18 08				18 37		18 40	18 48			19 09				19 32
Portsmouth & Southsea	a	17 35		17 42		17 46					18 12				18 41		18 43	18 52			19 12				19 36
Portsmouth Harbour ⛴	a	17 40				17 54					18 20						18 51	19 00			19 20				19 43

A Stops at these stations before Eastleigh

Southampton - Fareham and Portsmouth

Network Diagram - see first Page of Table 165

		SW	SW	GW	SN	SW	SW	SN		XC	SW	SW	SW	GW	SN	SW	SW	SW		SN	XC	SW	SW	GW	SW
		1	◇1 🚲	R 🚲	◇1	◇1 🚲	1	1		◇1 🚲	1	1	◇1 🚲	R 🚲	◇1	1	◇1 🚲	1		1	◇1 🚲	1	◇1 🚲	◇ 🚲	1
Eastleigh	d						19 28				19 51					20 00		20 30							21 00
Southampton Airport Parkway	d		18 39			19 09				19 33			19 39			20 05	20 14				20 33		20 42		21 05
Southampton Central ⛴	d	18 44	18a46	19 05	19 12	19a18		19 33		19a41		19 44	19a46	20 05	20 11	20a16	20a22			20 33	20a41	20 44	20a49	21 05	21a12
St Denys	d	18 49										19 49										20 49			
Bitterne	d	18 52										19 52										20 52			
Woolston	d	18 55										19 55										20 55			
Sholing	d	18 58										19 58										20 58			
Netley	d	19 02										20 02										21 02			
Hamble	d	19 04										20 04										21 04			
Bursledon	d	19 07										20 07										21 07			
Swanwick	d	19 11			19 29			19 51				20 11			20 28					20 50		21 11			
Fareham	a	19 17		19 27	19 35		19 45	19 57			20 09	20 17		20 27	20 34			20 48		20 56		21 17		21 27	
	d	19 18		19 27	19 36		19 48	19 57			20 09	20 18		20 27	20 35			20 49		20 57		21 18		21 27	
Portchester	d	19 23			19 41		19 53					20 23			20 40			20 54				21 23			
Cosham	d	19 28		19 35	19 46		19 58	20 06				20 28			20 44			20 59		21 06		21 28			
Havant	a				19 52			20 12			20 21				20 50					21 12					
Chichester 4	a				20 06			20 24							21 05					21 24					
Hilsea	a	19 33					20 02					20 33						21 03				21 33			
Fratton	a	19 37		19 42			20 06					20 37		20 42				21 07				21 37		21 41	
Portsmouth & Southsea	a	19 42		19 46			20 11					20 42		20 46				21 11				21 40		21 45	
Portsmouth Harbour ⛴	a			19 54			20 20							20 54				21 16				21 45		21 52	

		SN	SW	SW		SN	XC	SW	SW	SN	SW	SW	GW	SN		XC	SW	SW	SW	GW	SW	SW	SW	XC	
		1	◇1 🚲	1		1	◇1	1	◇1 🚲	1	1	◇1 🚲	◇	1		◇1	1	1	◇1 🚲	◇	1	◇1 🚲	1	◇1	
Eastleigh	d			21 30							22 03	22 18	22 24				22 51				23 03	23 18	23 30		
Southampton Airport Parkway	d		21 15				21 33		21 42		22 08	22 22				22 33			22 42		23 08	23 22		23 37	
Southampton Central ⛴	d	21 13	21a24			21 33	21a41	21 44	21a49	22 13	22a18	22a29		22 33		22a42		22 44	22a49	23 05	23a17	23a29		23a43	
St Denys	d							21 49										22 49							
Bitterne	d							21 52										22 52							
Woolston	d							21 55										22 55							
Sholing	d							21 58										22 58							
Netley	d							22 02										23 02							
Hamble	d							22 04										23 04							
Bursledon	d							22 07										23 07							
Swanwick	d	21 33				21 51		22 11		22 30				22 50				23 11							
Fareham	a	21 39		21 48		21 57		22 17		22 36			22 42	22 56			23 09	23 17		23 27			23 48		
	d	21 40		21 48		21 58		22 18		22 37			22 42	22 57			23 10	23 18		23 27			23 49		
Portchester	d	21 45		21 53		22 03		22 23		22 42							23 15	23 23					23 54		
Cosham	d	21 49		21 58		22 07		22 28		22 47				23 05			23 20	23 28					23 59		
Havant	a	21 55				22 13				22 56				23 11											
Chichester 4	a	22 06				22 34				23 11				23 22											
Hilsea	a			22 03				22 33									23 24	23 33					00 03		
Fratton	a			22 08				22 37					22 56				23 32	23 37		23 44			00 07		
Portsmouth & Southsea	a			22 11				22 42					22 59				23 36	23 40		23 48			00 11		
Portsmouth Harbour ⛴	a			22 16									23 04				23 40			23 54			00 16		

		SW
		◇1 🚲
Eastleigh	d	
Southampton Airport Parkway	d	23 42
Southampton Central ⛴	d	23a49
St Denys	d	
Bitterne	d	
Woolston	d	
Sholing	d	
Netley	d	
Hamble	d	
Bursledon	d	
Swanwick	d	
Fareham	a	
	d	
Portchester	d	
Cosham	d	
Havant	a	
Chichester 4	a	
Hilsea	a	
Fratton	a	
Portsmouth & Southsea	a	
Portsmouth Harbour ⛴	a	

Table 165

Saturdays

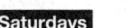

Southampton - Fareham and Portsmouth

Network Diagram - see first Page of Table 165

		SW	SW	SW	SW	SW	SW	SW	SW	SN		SW	SN	SW	SW	GW	SN	SN	SW	SN		SW	SW	GW	SN
		1	1	◇1	1	1	1	1	1	◇1		1	1	1	◇1		◇1	1	1	1		1	◇1	◇	◇1
Eastleigh	d	23p30	00 02	00 23	00 30	01 00	01 22					06 28			06 51			07 14	07 30				07 43		
Southampton Airport Parkway	d		00 06	00 28		01 05	01 26	02s39							06 56			07 18					07 48		
Southampton Central ⛴	d		00a13			01a12	01a35		05 44	06 13			06 33	06 44	07a03	07 05	07 13	07a28		07 33		07 44	07a56	08 05	08 13
St Denys	d			00s32				02s44	05 49					06 49								07 49			
Bitterne	d								05 52					06 52								07 52			
Woolston	d								05 55					06 55								07 55			
Sholing	d								05 58					06 58								07 58			
Netley	d								06 02					07 02								08 02			
Hamble	d								06 04					07 04								08 04			
Bursledon	d								06 07					07 07								08 07			
Swanwick	d								06 11	06 33			06 50	07 11			07 33			07 50		08 11			08 33
Fareham	a	23p48			00s47				06 17	06 39		06 46	06 56	07 17		07 27	07 39		07 48	07 56		08 17		08 27	08 39
	d	23p49							06 18	06 40		06 48	06 56	07 18		07 27	07 40		07 49	07 56		08 18		08 27	08 40
Portchester	d	23p54			00s53				06 23	06 45		06 53		07 23			07 45		07 54			08 23			08 45
Cosham	d	23p59			00s57				06 28	06 49		06 58	07 05	07 28		07 35	07 49		07 59	08 05		08 28		08 35	08 49
Havant	a									06 55			07 11				07 55			08 11					08 55
Chichester 4	a									07 10			07 23				08 10			08 23					09 10
Hilsea	a	00 03							06 33			07 03		07 33					08 03			08 33			
Fratton	a	00 07			01s05				06 37			07 07		07 37		07 42			08 07			08 37		08 42	
Portsmouth & Southsea	a	00 11			01s08				06 42			07 11		07 42		07 46			08 11			08 42		08 46	
Portsmouth Harbour ⛴	a	00 16			01 12							07 16				07 52			08 18					08 52	

		SN	SW	SN	XC	SW		SW	GW	SW	SN	XC	SW	SW	SN	XC		SW	SW	GW	SW	SN	SW	SN	SW
		1	1	1	◇1 🍴	1		◇1	◇	1	◇1	◇1 🍴	◇1	1	1	◇1 🍴		1	◇1 🍴	◇	1	◇1	◇1 🍴	1	1
Eastleigh	d	08 14	08 31					08 47		09 00				09 28							10 00			10 14	10 28
Southampton Airport Parkway	d	08 18			08 33			08 51		09 05		09 09	09 14			09 33			09 42		10 05		10 14	10 18	
Southampton Central ⛴	d	08a28		08 33	08a41	08 44		08a58	09 05	09a12	09 13	09a17	09a22		09 33	09a40		09 44	09a49	10 05	10a12	10 13	10a22	10a28	
St Denys	d					08 49												09 49							
Bitterne	d					08 52												09 52							
Woolston	d					08 55												09 55							
Sholing	d					08 58												09 58							
Netley	d					09 02												10 02							
Hamble	d					09 04												10 04							
Bursledon	d					09 07												10 07							
Swanwick	d			08 50		09 11					09 33				09 50			10 11				10 33			
Fareham	a		08 48	08 56		09 17			09 27		09 39			09 46	09 56			10 17		10 27		10 39			10 46
	d		08 49	08 56		09 18			09 27		09 40			09 48	09 56			10 18		10 27		10 40			10 48
Portchester	d		08 54			09 23					09 45			09 53				10 23				10 45			10 53
Cosham	d		08 59	09 05		09 28			09 35		09 49			09 58	10 05			10 28		10 35		10 49			10 58
Havant	a			09 11							09 55				10 11							10 55			
Chichester 4	a			09 23							10 10				10 23							11 10			
Hilsea	a		09 04			09 33								10 03				10 33							11 03
Fratton	a		09 08			09 37			09 42					10 07				10 37		10 42					11 07
Portsmouth & Southsea	a		09 12			09 42			09 46					10 11				10 42		10 46					11 11
Portsmouth Harbour ⛴	a		09 18						09 52					10 18						10 52					11 18

		SN		XC	SW	SW	GW	SW	SN	XC	SW	SW		SN	XC	SW	SW	GW	SW	SN	SW	SN		SW	SN
		1		◇1 🍴	1	◇1 🍴	◇	1	◇1	◇1 🍴	◇1 🍴	1		1	◇1 🍴	1	◇1 🍴	◇ 🍴	1	◇1	◇1 🍴	1		1	1
Eastleigh	d							11 00				11 28							12 00			12 14		12 28	
Southampton Airport Parkway	d			10 33		10 42		11 05		11 09	11 15				11 33		11 42		12 05		12 14	12 19			
Southampton Central ⛴	d	10 33		10a43	10 44	10a49	11 05	11a12	11 13	11a17	11a22			11 33	11a41	11 44	11a49	12 05	12a12	12 13	12a22	12a28			12 33
St Denys	d				10 49											11 49									
Bitterne	d				10 52											11 52									
Woolston	d				10 55											11 55									
Sholing	d				10 58											11 58									
Netley	d				11 02											12 02									
Hamble	d				11 04											12 04									
Bursledon	d				11 07											12 07									
Swanwick	d	10 50			11 11				11 33					11 50		12 11				12 33					12 50
Fareham	a	10 56			11 17		11 27		11 39			11 46		11 56		12 17		12 27		12 39				12 46	12 56
	d	10 56			11 18		11 27		11 40			11 48		11 56		12 18		12 27		12 40				12 48	12 56
Portchester	d				11 23				11 45			11 53				12 23				12 45				12 53	
Cosham	d	11 05			11 28		11 35		11 49			11 58		12 05		12 28		12 35		12 49				12 58	13 05
Havant	a	11 11							11 55					12 11						12 55					13 11
Chichester 4	a	11 23							12 10					12 23						13 10					13 23
Hilsea	a				11 33							12 03				12 33								13 03	
Fratton	a				11 37		11 42					12 07				12 37		12 42						13 07	
Portsmouth & Southsea	a				11 42		11 46					12 11				12 42		12 46						13 11	
Portsmouth Harbour ⛴	a						11 52					12 18						12 52						13 18	

Table 165

Southampton - Fareham and Portsmouth

Network Diagram - see first Page of Table 165

		XC	SW	SW	GW	SW	SN	XC		SW	SW	SN	XC	SW	SW	GW	SW	SN		SW	SW	GW	XC	SN	SW
		◇1 🛒	1	◇1 🛒	◇ 🛒	1	◇1	◇1 🛒		◇1 🛒	1	1	◇1 🛒	1	◇1 🛒	◇ 🛒	1	◇1		◇1 🛒	1	◇	◇1 🛒	1	1
Eastleigh	d					13 00					13 28						14 00				14 28			14 41	
Southampton Airport Parkway	d	12 33		12 42		13 05		13 09		13 14			13 33		13 42		14 05			14 14			14 33		
Southampton Central ⛴	d	12a41	12 44	12a49	13 05	13a12	13 13	13a17		13a22		13 33	13a41	13 44	13a49	14 05	14a12	14 13		14a22		14 34	14a41		14 44
St Denys	d		12 49											13 49											14 49
Bitterne	d		12 52											13 52											14 52
Woolston	d		12 55											13 55											14 55
Sholing	d		12 58											13 58											14 58
Netley	d		13 02											14 02											15 02
Hamble	d		13 04											14 04											15 04
Bursledon	d		13 07											14 07											15 07
Swanwick	d		13 11				13 33					13 50		14 11				14 33							15 11
Fareham	a		13 17		13 27		13 39				13 46	13 56		14 17		14 27		14 39			14 46	14 54		14 59	15 17
	d		13 18		13 27		13 40				13 48	13 56		14 18		14 27		14 40			14 48	14 55		15 00	15 18
Portchester	d		13 23				13 45				13 53			14 23				14 45			14 53				15 23
Cosham	d		13 28		13 35		13 49				13 58	14 05		14 28		14 35		14 49			14 58	15 03			15 28
Havant	a						13 55					14 11						14 55				15 10		15 14	
Chichester 4	a						14 10					14 23						15 10				15 21		15 25	
Hilsea	a		13 33								14 03			14 33							15 03				15 33
Fratton	a		13 37		13 42						14 07			14 37		14 42					15 07				15 37
Portsmouth & Southsea	a		13 42		13 46						14 11			14 42		14 46					15 11				15 42
Portsmouth Harbour ⛴	a				13 52						14 18					14 52					15 18				

		SW	GW	SW		SN	XC	SW	SW	SN	XC	SW	SW	GW		SW	SN	SW	SN	SW	SN	XC	SW	SW	
		◇1 🛒 A	◇	1		◇1	◇1 🛒	◇1 🛒	1	1	◇1 🛒	1	◇1 🛒	◇		1	◇1	◇1 🛒	1	1	1	◇1 🛒	1	◇1 🛒	
Eastleigh	d			15 00					15 28							16 00			16 14	16 28					
Southampton Airport Parkway	d	14 42		15 05			15 09	15 14			15 33		15 42			16 05		16 14	16 18			16 33		16 42	
Southampton Central ⛴	d	14a49	15 05	15a12		15 13	15a17	15a22		15 33	15a41	15 44	15a49	16 05		16a12	16 13	16a22	16a28		16 33	16a41	16 44	16a49	
St Denys	d											15 49											16 49		
Bitterne	d											15 52											16 52		
Woolston	d											15 55											16 55		
Sholing	d											15 58											16 58		
Netley	d											16 02											17 02		
Hamble	d											16 04											17 04		
Bursledon	d											16 07											17 07		
Swanwick	d					15 33				15 50		16 11					16 33				16 50		17 11		
Fareham	a		15 27			15 39			15 46	15 56		16 17		16 27			16 39			16 46	16 56		17 17		
	d		15 27			15 40			15 48	15 56		16 18		16 27			16 40			16 48	16 56		17 18		
Portchester	d					15 45			15 53			16 23					16 45			16 53			17 23		
Cosham	d		15 35			15 49			15 58	16 05		16 28		16 35			16 49			16 58	17 05		17 28		
Havant	a					15 55				16 11							16 55				17 11				
Chichester 4	a					16 10				16 23							17 10				17 23				
Hilsea	a								16 03			16 33								17 03			17 33		
Fratton	a		15 42						16 07			16 37		16 42						17 07			17 37		
Portsmouth & Southsea	a		15 46						16 11			16 40		16 46						17 11			17 42		
Portsmouth Harbour ⛴	a		15 52						16 18			16 44		16 52						17 18					

		GW	SW	SN	XC	SW	SW	SN	XC	SW		SW	GW	SN	SW	SW	SN	SW	SN	XC		SW	SW	GW	SN
		◇	1	◇1	◇1 🛒	◇1 🛒	1	1	◇1 🛒	1		◇1 🛒	◇	◇1	1	◇1 ☕	1	1	1	◇1 🛒		1	◇1 🛒	R	◇1
Eastleigh	d		17 00				17 28								18 00		18 14	18 28							
Southampton Airport Parkway	d		17 05		17 09	17 14			17 33			17 42			18 05	18 14	18 18			18 33			18 42		
Southampton Central ⛴	d	17 05	17a12	17 13	17a17	17a22		17 33	17a41	17 44		17a49	18 05	18 11	18a14	18a22	18a28		18 33	18a40		18 44	18a49	19 05	19 09
St Denys	d									17 49												18 49			
Bitterne	d									17 52												18 52			
Woolston	d									17 55												18 55			
Sholing	d									17 58												18 58			
Netley	d									18 02												19 02			
Hamble	d									18 04												19 04			
Bursledon	d									18 07												19 07			
Swanwick	d			17 33				17 50		18 11				18 28					18 50			19 11			19 28
Fareham	a	17 27		17 39			17 46	17 56		18 17			18 27	18 34				18 46	18 56			19 17		19 27	19 34
	d	17 27		17 40			17 48	17 56		18 18			18 27	18 35				18 48	18 56			19 18		19 27	19 35
Portchester	d			17 45			17 53			18 23				18 40				18 53				19 23			19 40
Cosham	d	17 35		17 49			17 58	18 05		18 28			18 35	18 44				18 58	19 05			19 28		19 35	19 44
Havant	a			17 55				18 11						18 50					19 11						19 51
Chichester 4	a			18 10				18 23						19 05					19 23						20 06
Hilsea	a						18 03			18 33								19 03				19 33			
Fratton	a	17 42					18 07			18 37			18 42					19 07				19 37		19 42	
Portsmouth & Southsea	a	17 46					18 11			18 42			18 46					19 11				19 42		19 46	
Portsmouth Harbour ⛴	a	17 52					18 18						18 52					19 18						19 52	

A Stops at these stations before Eastleigh

Table 165

Saturdays

Southampton - Fareham and Portsmouth

Network Diagram - see first Page of Table 165

		SW	XC	SW	SW	SN	XC	SW	SW	GW	SN	SW	SW	SN	SW	SN	XC	SW	SW	GW	SW	SN	SW
		1	◇1	◇1	1	1	◇1	1	◇1	◇	◇1	1	◇1	1	1	1	◇1	1	◇1	◇	1	1	◇1
Eastleigh	d	19 00			19 28							20 00		20 14	20 28						21 00		
Southampton Airport Parkway	d	19 05	19 09	19 14			19 33		19 42			20 05	20 14	20 18			20 33		20 42		21 05		21 14
Southampton Central	d	19a12	19a17	19a22		19 33	19a41	19 44	19a49	20 05	20 11	20a14	20a22	20a28		20 33	20a41	20 44	20a49	21 05	21a12	21 13	21a22
St Denys	d							19 49										20 49					
Bitterne	d							19 52										20 52					
Woolston	d							19 55										20 55					
Sholing	d							19 58										20 58					
Netley	d							20 02										21 02					
Hamble	d							20 04										21 04					
Bursledon	d							20 07										21 07					
Swanwick	d					19 50		20 11			20 28					20 50		21 11				21 33	
Fareham	a				19 46	19 56		20 17		20 27	20 34				20 46	20 56		21 17		21 27		21 39	
	d				19 48	19 56		20 18		20 28	20 35				20 48	20 56		21 18		21 27		21 40	
Portchester	d				19 53			20 23			20 40				20 53			21 23				21 45	
Cosham	d				19 58	20 05		20 28			20 44				20 58	21 05		21 28				21 49	
Havant	a					20 11					20 50					21 11						21 55	
Chichester 4	a					20 23					21 05					21 23						22 06	
Hilsea	a				20 03			20 37							21 03			21 33					
Fratton	a				20 07			20 41		20 42					21 07			21 37		21 42			
Portsmouth & Southsea	a				20 11			20 44		20 46					21 11			21 40		21 46			
Portsmouth Harbour	a				20 18					20 52					21 18			21 45		21 52			

		SW	SN	XC	SW	SW	GW	SN	SW	SW	SW	SN	XC	SW	SW	GW	SW	SW	SW	XC	SW
		1	1	◇1	1	◇1	◇	1	1	◇1	1	1	◇1	1	◇1	◇	1	◇1	1	◇1	◇1
Eastleigh	d	21 28							22 03	22 18	22 28						23 04	23 18	23 28		
Southampton Airport Parkway	d			21 33		21 42			22 08	22 22			22 34		22 42		23 08	23 22		23 33	23 42
Southampton Central	d		21 33	21a41	21 44	21a49	22 05	22 13	22a17	22a29		22 33	22a41	22 44	22a49	23 05	23a17	23a29		23a41	23a49
St Denys	d				21 49									22 49							
Bitterne	d				21 52									22 52							
Woolston	d				21 55									22 55							
Sholing	d				21 58									22 58							
Netley	d				22 02									23 02							
Hamble	d				22 04									23 04							
Bursledon	d				22 07									23 07							
Swanwick	d		21 50		22 11			22 31				22 50		23 11							
Fareham	a	21 46	21 56		22 17		22 26	22 38			22 46	22 56		23 17		23 26			23 46		
	d	21 48	21 57		22 18		22 27	22 39			22 48	23 00		23 18		23 27			23 48		
Portchester	d	21 53	22 02		22 23			22 44			22 53			23 23					23 53		
Cosham	d	21 58	22 06		22 28			22 48			22 58	23 08		23 28					23 58		
Havant	a		22 12					22 54				23 14									
Chichester 4	a		22 33					23 09				23 25									
Hilsea	a	22 03			22 33						23 03			23 33					00 03		
Fratton	a	22 07			22 37		22 42				23 07			23 37		23 40			00 07		
Portsmouth & Southsea	a	22 11			22 40		22 46				23 11			23 40		23 44			00 11		
Portsmouth Harbour	a	22 18			22 47		22 52				23 18					23 52			00 16		

Sundays

until 12 February

		SW	SW	SW	SW	SW	SW	SW	SW	SW	SN	SW	SW	SW	GW	SN	SW	SW	SW	SN	SW	SW	SW
		1	1	◇1	1	1	1	1	1	1	◇1	1	1	1		◇1	1	◇1	1	◇1	1	◇1	◇1
		A	A	A		A																B	
Eastleigh	d	23p28	00 03	00 21	00 30	01 00	01 22						08 22	08 26		08 48		09 22	09 26				10 22
Southampton Airport Parkway	d		00 08	00 25		01 05	01 26	02s46					08 27					09 27				09 55	10 27
Southampton Central	d		00a15			01a12	01a35		06 35		07 29	07 35	08a34		08 31		08 35	09a34		09 29	09 35	10a02	10a34
St Denys	d			00s29				02s51	06 41			07 41					08 41				09 41		
Bitterne	d								06 43			07 43					08 43				09 43		
Woolston	d								06 47			07 47					08 47				09 47		
Sholing	d								06 49			07 49					08 49				09 49		
Netley	d								06 53			07 53					08 53				09 53		
Hamble	d								06 55			07 55					08 55				09 55		
Bursledon	d								06 58			07 58					08 58				09 58		
Swanwick	d								07 02		07 46	08 02					09 02			09 46	10 02		
Fareham	a	23p46			00s47				07 09		07 52	08 09		08 43	08 51	09 02	09 09		09 43	09 52	10 09		
	d	23p48							07 10	07 44	07 53	08 10		08 44	08 52	09 02	09 10		09 44	09 53	10 10		
Portchester	d	23p53			00s53				07 15	07 49		08 15		08 49			09 15		09 49		10 15		
Cosham	d	23p58			00s57				07 20	07 54	08 02	08 20		08 54	09 00	09 11	09 20		09 54	10 02	10 20		
Havant	a										08 10				09 11	09 17				10 10			
Chichester 4	a										08 23				09 22	09 29				10 23			
Hilsea	a	00 03							07 26	08 00		08 26		09 00			09 26		10 04		10 26		
Fratton	a	00 07			01s05				07 30	08 04		08 30		09 04			09 30		10 08		10 30		
Portsmouth & Southsea	a	00 11			01s08				07 33	08 08		08 33		09 08			09 33		10 11		10 33		
Portsmouth Harbour	a	00 16			01 12					08 13				09 13					10 15				

A not 11 December

B Stops at these stations before Eastleigh

Table 165

Sundays

until 12 February

Southampton - Fareham and Portsmouth

Network Diagram - see first Page of Table 165

		SW	SN	SW	XC	SW		GW	SW	SW	SN	SW	XC	SW	GW	SW		SW	SN	SW	XC	SW	GW	SW	SW
		1	◇1	1	◇1	◇1		◇	◇1	1	◇1	1	◇1	◇1	◇	◇1		1	◇1	1	◇1	◇1	◇	◇1	1
					🛒								🛒	🛒							🍴	🛒		🛒	
Eastleigh	d	10 26							11 22	11 26						12 22		12 26						13 22	13 26
Southampton Airport Parkway	d				10 34	10 55			11 27				11 34	11 53		12 27					12 34	12 53		13 27	
Southampton Central ⛴	d		10 29	10 35	10a42	11a02		11 04	11a34		11 28	11 35	11a42	11a59	12 04	12a34			12 29	12 35	12a42	13a00	13 07	13a34	
St Denys	d			10 41								11 41								12 41					
Bitterne	d			10 43								11 43								12 43					
Woolston	d			10 47								11 47								12 47					
Sholing	d			10 49								11 49								12 49					
Netley	d			10 53								11 53								12 53					
Hamble	d			10 55								11 55								12 55					
Bursledon	d			10 58								11 58								12 58					
Swanwick	d		10 46	11 02							11 46	12 02							12 46	13 02					
Fareham	a	10 43	10 52	11 09				11 26		11 43	11 52	12 09			12 27			12 43	12 52	13 09			13 33		13 43
	d	10 44	10 53	11 10				11 26		11 44	11 53	12 10			12 27			12 44	12 53	13 10			13 34		13 44
Portchester	d	10 49		11 15						11 49		12 15						12 49		13 15					13 49
Cosham	d	10 54	11 02	11 20				11 34		11 54	12 02	12 20			12 35			12 54	13 02	13 20			13 42		13 54
Havant	a		11 10								12 10								13 10				14 03		
Chichester 4	a		11 23								12 23								13 23				14 19		
Hilsea	a	11 04		11 26						12 00		12 26						13 00		13 26					14 00
Fratton	a	11 08		11 30				11 41		12 04		12 30			12 42			13 04		13 30					14 04
Portsmouth & Southsea	a	11 11		11 33				11 45		12 08		12 33			12 45			13 08		13 33					14 08
Portsmouth Harbour ⛴	a	11 15						11 52		12 13					12 52			13 13							14 13

		SN		SW	XC	SW	GW	SW	SW	SN	SW	XC		SW	SW	SW	GW	SN	SW	XC	SW	GW		SW	SW
		◇1		1	◇1	◇1	◇	◇1	1	◇1	1	◇1		◇1	◇1	1	◇	◇1	1	◇1	◇1	◇		◇1	1
					🍴	🛒	🛒	🛒				🍴		🛒	🛒					🍴	🛒			🛒	
Eastleigh	d							14 22	14 26						15 22	15 26								16 22	16 26
Southampton Airport Parkway	d				13 34	13 53		14 27				14 34		14 53	15 27					15 34	15 53			16 27	
Southampton Central ⛴	d	13 29		13 35	13a42	14a00	14 04	14a34		14 29	14 35	14a42		15a00	15a34		15 22	15 29	15 35	15a42	16a00	16 04		16a34	
St Denys	d			13 41							14 41								15 41						
Bitterne	d			13 43							14 43								15 43						
Woolston	d			13 47							14 47								15 47						
Sholing	d			13 49							14 49								15 49						
Netley	d			13 53							14 53								15 53						
Hamble	d			13 55							14 55								15 55						
Bursledon	d			13 58							14 58								15 58						
Swanwick	d	13 46		14 02						14 46	15 02							15 46	16 02						
Fareham	a	13 52		14 09			14 25		14 43	14 52	15 09					15 43	15 50	15 57	16 09			16 26			16 43
	d	13 53		14 10			14 26		14 44	14 53	15 10					15 44	15 51	15 58	16 10			16 26			16 44
Portchester	d			14 15					14 49		15 15					15 49			16 15						16 49
Cosham	d	14 02		14 20			14 34		14 54	15 02	15 20					15 54	16 01	16 07	16 20			16 34			16 54
Havant	a	14 10								15 10							16 11	16 15							
Chichester 4	a	14 23								15 23							16 22	16 28							
Hilsea	a			14 26					15 00		15 26					16 00			16 26						17 00
Fratton	a			14 30			14 41		15 04		15 30					16 04			16 30			16 41			17 03
Portsmouth & Southsea	a			14 33			14 45		15 08		15 33					16 08			16 33			16 45			17 08
Portsmouth Harbour ⛴	a						14 55		15 13							16 13						16 52			17 13

		SN	SW	XC	SW	GW	SW	SW		SN	SW	XC	SW	GW	SW	SW	SN	SW		XC	SW	GW	SW	SW	GW
		◇1	1	◇1	◇1	◇	◇1	1		◇1	1	◇1	◇1	◇	◇1	1	◇1	1		◇1	◇1	◇	◇1	1	◇
				🍴	🛒		🛒					🍴	🛒		🛒					🍴	🛒		🛒		
Eastleigh	d						17 22	17 26							18 22	18 26							19 22	19 26	
Southampton Airport Parkway	d			16 34	16 53		17 27					17 34	17 53		18 27					18 34	18 53		19 27		
Southampton Central ⛴	d	16 29	16 35	16a42	17a00	17 04	17a34			17 29	17 35	17a40	18a00	18 04	18a34		18 29	18 35		18a42	19a00	19 04	19a34		19 27
St Denys	d		16 41								17 41							18 41							
Bitterne	d		16 43								17 43							18 43							
Woolston	d		16 47								17 47							18 47							
Sholing	d		16 49								17 49							18 49							
Netley	d		16 53								17 53							18 53							
Hamble	d		16 55								17 55							18 55							
Bursledon	d		16 58								17 58							18 58							
Swanwick	d	16 46	17 02							17 46	18 02						18 46	19 02							
Fareham	a	16 52	17 09			17 26		17 43		17 52	18 09			18 26		18 43	18 52	19 09				19 27		19 43	19 49
	d	16 53	17 10			17 26		17 44		17 53	18 10			18 26		18 44	18 53	19 10				19 27		19 44	19 50
Portchester	d		17 15					17 49			18 15					18 49		19 15						19 49	
Cosham	d	17 02	17 20			17 34		17 54		18 02	18 20			18 34		18 54	19 02	19 20				19 35		19 54	19 59
Havant	a	17 10								18 10							19 10								20 10
Chichester 4	a	17 23								18 23							19 23								20 21
Hilsea	a		17 26					18 00			18 26					19 00		19 26						20 00	
Fratton	a		17 30			17 41		18 04			18 30			18 41		19 03		19 30				19 42		20 04	
Portsmouth & Southsea	a		17 33			17 45		18 08			18 33			18 45		19 08		19 33				19 46		20 08	
Portsmouth Harbour ⛴	a					17 52		18 13						18 52		19 13						19 52		20 13	

Table 165

Sundays

until 12 February

Southampton - Fareham and Portsmouth

Network Diagram - see first Page of Table 165

		SN	SW	XC	SW	GW	SW	SW	GW	SN	SW	XC	SW	GW	SW	SW	SN	SW	XC	SW	GW	SN
		◇1	1	◇1	◇1	◇	◇1	1	R	◇1	1	◇1	◇1	◇	◇1	1	◇1	1	◇1	◇1	◇	1
Eastleigh	d	19 46					20 22	20 26		20 46					21 22	21 26						
Southampton Airport Parkway	d			19 34	19 53		20 27					20 34	20 53		21 27				21 34	21 53		
Southampton Central ⛴	d		19 35	19a40	20a00	20 04	20a34		20 31		20 35	20a42	21a00	21 01	21a34		21 30	21 35	21a43	22a00	22 04	22 15
St Denys	d		19 41								20 41							21 41				
Bitterne	d		19 43								20 43							21 43				
Woolston	d		19 47								20 47							21 47				
Sholing	d		19 49								20 49							21 49				
Netley	d		19 53								20 53							21 53				
Hamble	d		19 55								20 55							21 55				
Bursledon	d		19 58								20 58							21 58				
Swanwick	d		20 02								21 02						21 47	22 02				22 32
Fareham	a	20 02	20 09			20 26		20 43	20 54	21 02	21 10			21 23		21 43	21 53	22 09			22 26	22 38
	d	20 03	20 10			20 26		20 44	20 55	21 02	21 10			21 24		21 44	21 54	22 10			22 26	22 39
Portchester	d		20 15					20 49			21 15					21 49		22 15				
Cosham	d	20 12	20 20					20 54		21 11	21 20					21 54	22 03	22 20				22 48
Havant	a	20 18								21 17							22 10					22 54
Chichester 4	a	20 30								21 29							22 23					23 06
Hilsea	a		20 26					21 00			21 26					22 00		22 26				
Fratton	a		20 30			20 41		21 04	21 09		21 30			21 37		22 04		22 30			22 40	
Portsmouth & Southsea	a		20 33			20 45		21 08	21 15		21 33			21 41		22 08		22 33			22 44	
Portsmouth Harbour ⛴	a					20 52		21 13	21 26					21 48		22 13					22 50	

		SW	SW	SW	XC	SN	SW	GW	SW	SW
		◇1	1	1	◇1	1	◇1	◇	◇1	1
Eastleigh	d	22 22	22 26						23 22	23 26
Southampton Airport Parkway	d	22 27			22 34		22 53		23 27	
Southampton Central ⛴	d	22a34		22 35	22a42	22 52	23a00	23 07	23a34	
St Denys	d			22 41						
Bitterne	d			22 43						
Woolston	d			22 47						
Sholing	d			22 49						
Netley	d			22 53						
Hamble	d			22 55						
Bursledon	d			22 58						
Swanwick	d			23 02		23 11				
Fareham	a		22 43	23 09		23 17		23 28		23 43
	d		22 44	23 10		23 17		23 29		23 44
Portchester	d		22 49	23 15						23 49
Cosham	d		22 54	23 20		23 26				23 54
Havant	a					23 32				
Chichester 4	a					23 44				
Hilsea	a		23 00	23 24						23 59
Fratton	a		23 04	23 28				23 42		00 04
Portsmouth & Southsea	a		23 08	23 32				23 46		00 08
Portsmouth Harbour ⛴	a		23 13					23 54		00 13

Sundays

19 February to 25 March

		SW	SW	SW	SW	SW	SW	SW	SW	SW	SN	SW	SW	SW	GW	SN	SW	SW	SW	SN	SW	SW	SW
		1	1	◇1	1	1	1	1	1	1	◇1	1	1	1		◇1	1	◇1	1	◇1	1	◇1	◇1
Eastleigh	d	23p28	00 03	00 21	00 30	01 00	01 22						08 22	08 26		08 48		09 22	09 26				10 22
Southampton Airport Parkway	d		00 08	00 25		01 05	01 26	02s46					08 27					09 27				09 55	10 27
Southampton Central ⛴	d		00a15			01a12	01a35		06 35		07 29	07 35	08a34		08 31		08 35	09a34		09 29	09 35	10a02	10a34
St Denys	d			00s29				02s51	06 41			07 41					08 41				09 41		
Bitterne	d								06 43			07 43					08 43				09 43		
Woolston	d								06 47			07 47					08 47				09 47		
Sholing	d								06 49			07 49					08 49				09 49		
Netley	d								06 53			07 53					08 53				09 53		
Hamble	d								06 55			07 55					08 55				09 55		
Bursledon	d								06 58			07 58					08 58				09 58		
Swanwick	d								07 02		07 46	08 02					09 02			09 46	10 02		
Fareham	a	23p46			00s47				07 09		07 52	08 09		08 43	08 51	09 02	09 09		09 43	09 52	10 09		
	d	23p48							07 10	07 44	07 53	08 10		08 44	08 52	09 02	09 10		09 44	09 53	10 10		
Portchester	d	23p53			00s53				07 15	07 49		08 15		08 49			09 15		09 49		10 15		
Cosham	d	23p58			00s57				07 20	07 54	08 02	08 20		08 54	09 00	09 11	09 20		09 54	10 02	10 20		
Havant	a										08 10				09 11	09 17				10 10			
Chichester 4	a										08 23				09 22	09 29				10 23			
Hilsea	a	00 03							07 26	08 00		08 26		09 00			09 26		10 04		10 26		
Fratton	a	00 07			01s05				07 30	08 04		08 30		09 04			09 30		10 08		10 30		
Portsmouth & Southsea	a	00 11			01s08				07 33	08 08		08 33		09 08			09 33		10 11		10 33		
Portsmouth Harbour ⛴	a	00 16			01 12					08 13				09 13					10 15				

Table 165

Sundays

19 February to 25 March

Southampton - Fareham and Portsmouth

Network Diagram - see first Page of Table 165

		SW	SN	SW	XC	SW		GW	SW	SW	SN	SW	XC	SW	GW	SW		SW	SN	SW	XC	SW	GW	SW	SW
		1	◇1	1	◇1	◇1		◇	◇1	1	◇1	1	◇1	◇1	◇	◇1		1	◇1	1	◇1	◇1	◇	◇1	1
					🍴								🍴	🍴							☕	🍴		🍴	
Eastleigh	d	10 26							11 22	11 26						12 22		12 26						13 22	13 26
Southampton Airport Parkway	d				10 34	10 55			11 27				11 34	11 53		12 27					12 34	12 53		13 27	
Southampton Central ⛴	d		10 29	10 35	10a42	11a02		11 04	11a34		11 28	11 35	11a42	11a59	12 04	12a34			12 29	12 35	12a42	13a00	13 07	13a34	
St Denys	d			10 41								11 41								12 41					
Bitterne	d			10 43								11 43								12 43					
Woolston	d			10 47								11 47								12 47					
Sholing	d			10 49								11 49								12 49					
Netley	d			10 53								11 53								12 53					
Hamble	d			10 55								11 55								12 55					
Bursledon	d			10 58								11 58								12 58					
Swanwick	d		10 46	11 02							11 46	12 02							12 46	13 02					
Fareham	a	10 43	10 52	11 09				11 28		11 43	11 52	12 09			12 28			12 43	12 52	13 09			13 33		13 43
	d	10 44	10 53	11 10				11 28		11 44	11 53	12 10			12 28			12 44	12 53	13 10			13 34		13 44
Portchester	d	10 49		11 15						11 49		12 15						12 49		13 15					13 49
Cosham	d	10 54	11 02	11 20				11 36		11 54	12 02	12 20			12 36			12 54	13 02	13 20			13 42		13 54
Havant	a		11 10								12 10								13 10				14 03		
Chichester 4	a		11 23								12 23								13 23				14 19		
Hilsea	a	11 04		11 26						12 00		12 26						13 00		13 26					14 00
Fratton	a	11 08		11 30				11 42		12 04		12 30			12 42			13 04		13 30					14 04
Portsmouth & Southsea	a	11 11		11 33				11 46		12 08		12 33			12 46			13 08		13 33					14 08
Portsmouth Harbour ⛴	a	11 15						11 51		12 13					12 52			13 13							14 13

		SN		SW	XC	SW	GW	SW	SW	SN	SW	XC		SW	SW	SW	GW	SN	SW	XC	SW	GW		SW	SW
		◇1		1	◇1	◇1	◇	◇1	1	◇1	1	◇1		◇1	◇1	1	◇	◇1	1	◇1	◇1	◇		◇1	1
					☕	🍴	🍴	🍴				☕		🍴	🍴					☕	🍴			🍴	
Eastleigh	d							14 22	14 26						15 22	15 26								16 22	16 26
Southampton Airport Parkway	d				13 34	13 53		14 27				14 34		14 53	15 27					15 34	15 53			16 27	
Southampton Central ⛴	d	13 29		13 35	13a42	14a00	14 04	14a34		14 29	14 35	14a42		15a00	15a34		15 22	15 29	15 35	15a42	16a00	16 05		16a34	
St Denys	d			13 41							14 41								15 41						
Bitterne	d			13 43							14 43								15 43						
Woolston	d			13 47							14 47								15 47						
Sholing	d			13 49							14 49								15 49						
Netley	d			13 53							14 53								15 53						
Hamble	d			13 55							14 55								15 55						
Bursledon	d			13 58							14 58								15 58						
Swanwick	d	13 46		14 02						14 46	15 02							15 46	16 02						
Fareham	a	13 52		14 09			14 26		14 43	14 52	15 09					15 43	15 50	15 57	16 09			16 27			16 43
	d	13 53		14 10			14 27		14 44	14 53	15 10					15 44	15 51	15 58	16 10			16 27			16 44
Portchester	d			14 15					14 49		15 15					15 49			16 15						16 49
Cosham	d	14 02		14 20			14 35		14 54	15 02	15 20					15 54	16 01	16 07	16 20			16 35			16 54
Havant	a	14 10								15 10							16 11	16 15							
Chichester 4	a	14 23								15 23							16 22	16 28							
Hilsea	a			14 26					15 00		15 26					16 00			16 26						17 00
Fratton	a			14 30			14 41		15 04		15 30					16 04			16 30			16 42			17 03
Portsmouth & Southsea	a			14 33			14 45		15 08		15 33					16 08			16 33			16 46			17 08
Portsmouth Harbour ⛴	a						14 55		15 13							16 13						16 52			17 13

		SN	SW	XC	SW	GW	SW	SW		SN	SW	XC	SW	GW	SW	SW	SN	SW		XC	SW	GW	SW	SW	SN
		◇1	1	◇1	◇1	◇	◇1	1		◇1	1	◇1	◇1	◇	◇1	1	◇1	1		◇1	◇1	◇	◇1	1	◇1
				☕	🍴		🍴					☕	🍴		🍴					☕	🍴		🍴		
Eastleigh	d						17 22	17 26							18 22	18 26							19 22	19 26	19 46
Southampton Airport Parkway	d			16 34	16 53		17 27					17 34	17 53		18 27					18 34	18 53		19 27		
Southampton Central ⛴	d	16 29	16 35	16a42	17a00	17 04	17a34			17 29	17 35	17a40	18a00	18 04	18a34		18 29	18 35		18a42	19a00	19 04	19a34		
St Denys	d		16 41								17 41							18 41							
Bitterne	d		16 43								17 43							18 43							
Woolston	d		16 47								17 47							18 47							
Sholing	d		16 49								17 49							18 49							
Netley	d		16 53								17 53							18 53							
Hamble	d		16 55								17 55							18 55							
Bursledon	d		16 58								17 58							18 58							
Swanwick	d	16 46	17 02							17 46	18 02						18 46	19 02							
Fareham	a	16 52	17 09			17 27		17 43		17 52	18 09			18 27		18 43	18 52	19 09				19 28		19 43	20 02
	d	16 53	17 10			17 27		17 44		17 53	18 10			18 27		18 44	18 53	19 10				19 28		19 44	20 03
Portchester	d		17 15					17 49			18 15					18 49		19 15						19 49	
Cosham	d	17 02	17 20			17 35		17 54		18 02	18 20			18 35		18 54	19 02	19 20				19 36		19 54	20 12
Havant	a	17 10								18 10							19 10								20 18
Chichester 4	a	17 23								18 23							19 23								20 30
Hilsea	a		17 26					18 00			18 26					19 00		19 26						20 00	
Fratton	a		17 30			17 41		18 04			18 30			18 41		19 03		19 30				19 42		20 04	
Portsmouth & Southsea	a		17 33			17 46		18 08			18 33			18 45		19 08		19 33				19 46		20 08	
Portsmouth Harbour ⛴	a					17 51		18 13						18 52		19 13						19 51		20 13	

B Stops at these stations before Eastleigh

Table 165

Sundays

19 February to 25 March

Southampton - Fareham and Portsmouth

Network Diagram - see first Page of Table 165

		SW	XC	SW	GW	SW	SW	GW	SN	SW	XC	SW	GW	SW	SW	SN	SW	XC	SW	GW	SN	SW
		[1]	◇[1] ☕ B	◇[1] 🛒 B	◇	◇[1] 🛒	[1]	R	◇[1]	[1]	◇[1] ☕	◇[1] 🛒	◇	◇[1]	[1]	◇[1]	[1]	◇[1]	◇[1] 🛒	◇	[1]	◇[1]
Eastleigh	d					20 22	20 26		20 46					21 22	21 26							22 22
Southampton Airport Parkway	d		19 34	19 53		20 27					20 34	20 53		21 27				21 34	21 53			22 27
Southampton Central ⛴	d	19 35	19a40	20a00	20 04	20a34		20 31		20 35	20a42	21a00	21 02	21a34		21 30	21 35	21a43	22a00	22 04	22 15	22a34
St Denys	d	19 41								20 41							21 41					
Bitterne	d	19 43								20 43							21 43					
Woolston	d	19 47								20 47							21 47					
Sholing	d	19 49								20 49							21 49					
Netley	d	19 53								20 53							21 53					
Hamble	d	19 55								20 55							21 55					
Bursledon	d	19 58								20 58							21 58					
Swanwick	d	20 02								21 02						21 47	22 02				22 32	
Fareham	a	20 09			20 27		20 43	20 54	21 02	21 10			21 24		21 43	21 53	22 09			22 26	22 38	
	d	20 10			20 27		20 44	20 55	21 02	21 10			21 25		21 44	21 54	22 10			22 26	22 39	
Portchester	d	20 15					20 49			21 15					21 49		22 15					
Cosham	d	20 20					20 54		21 11	21 20					21 54	22 03	22 20				22 48	
Havant	a								21 17							22 10					22 54	
Chichester [4]	a								21 29							22 23					23 06	
Hilsea	a	20 26					21 00			21 26					22 00		22 26					
Fratton	a	20 30			20 42		21 04	21 09		21 30			21 38		22 04		22 30			22 40		
Portsmouth & Southsea	a	20 33			20 45		21 08	21 15		21 33			21 41		22 08		22 33			22 44		
Portsmouth Harbour ⛴	a				20 49		21 13	21 24					21 46		22 13					22 50		

		SW	SW	XC	SN	SW	GW	SW	SW
		[1]	[1]	◇[1]	[1]	◇[1] 🛒	◇	◇[1]	[1]
Eastleigh	d	22 26						23 22	23 26
Southampton Airport Parkway	d			22 34		22 53		23 27	
Southampton Central ⛴	d		22 35	22a42	22 52	23a00	23 08	23a34	
St Denys	d		22 41						
Bitterne	d		22 43						
Woolston	d		22 47						
Sholing	d		22 49						
Netley	d		22 53						
Hamble	d		22 55						
Bursledon	d		22 58						
Swanwick	d		23 02		23 11				
Fareham	a	22 43	23 09		23 17		23 29		23 43
	d	22 44	23 10		23 17		23 30		23 44
Portchester	d	22 49	23 15						23 49
Cosham	d	22 54	23 20		23 26				23 54
Havant	a				23 32				
Chichester [4]	a				23 44				
Hilsea	a	23 00	23 24						23 59
Fratton	a	23 04	23 28				23 43		00 04
Portsmouth & Southsea	a	23 08	23 32				23 46		00 08
Portsmouth Harbour ⛴	a	23 13					23 50		00 13

Sundays

from 1 April

		SW	SW	SW	SW	SW	SW	SW	SW	SW	SN	SW	SW	SW	GW	SN	SW	SW	SW	SN	SW	SW	SW
		[1]	[1]	◇[1]	[1]	[1]	[1]	[1]	[1]	[1]	◇[1]	[1]	[1]	[1]		◇[1]	[1]	◇[1]	[1]	◇[1]	[1]	◇[1]	◇[1]
Eastleigh	d	23p28	00 03	00 21	00 30	01 00	01 22						08 22	08 26		08 48		09 22	09 26				10 22
Southampton Airport Parkway	d		00 08	00 25		01 05	01 26	02s46					08 27					09 27				09 55	10 27
Southampton Central ⛴	d		00a15			01a12	01a35		06 35		07 29	07 35	08a34		08 31		08 35	09a34		09 29	09 35	10a02	10a34
St Denys	d			00s29				02s51	06 41			07 41					08 41				09 41		
Bitterne	d								06 43			07 43					08 43				09 43		
Woolston	d								06 47			07 47					08 47				09 47		
Sholing	d								06 49			07 49					08 49				09 49		
Netley	d								06 53			07 53					08 53				09 53		
Hamble	d								06 55			07 55					08 55				09 55		
Bursledon	d								06 58			07 58					08 58				09 58		
Swanwick	d								07 02		07 46	08 02					09 02			09 46	10 02		
Fareham	a	23p46			00s47				07 09		07 52	08 09		08 43	08 51	09 02	09 09		09 43	09 52	10 09		
	d	23p48							07 10	07 44	07 53	08 10		08 44	08 52	09 02	09 10		09 44	09 53	10 10		
Portchester	d	23p53			00s53				07 15	07 49		08 15		08 49			09 15		09 49		10 15		
Cosham	d	23p58			00s57				07 20	07 54	08 02	08 20		08 54	09 00	09 11	09 20		09 54	10 02	10 20		
Havant	a										08 10				09 11	09 17				10 10			
Chichester [4]	a										08 23				09 22	09 29				10 23			
Hilsea	a	00 03							07 26	08 00		08 26		09 00			09 26		10 04		10 26		
Fratton	a	00 07			01s05				07 30	08 04		08 30		09 04			09 30		10 08		10 30		
Portsmouth & Southsea	a	00 11			01s08				07 33	08 08		08 33		09 08			09 33		10 11		10 33		
Portsmouth Harbour ⛴	a	00 16			01 12					08 13				09 13					10 15				

A Stops at these stations before Eastleigh

Table 165

Sundays

from 1 April

Southampton - Fareham and Portsmouth

Network Diagram - see first Page of Table 165

		SW	SN	SW	XC	SW		GW	SW	SW	SN	SW	XC	SW	GW	SW		SW	SN	SW	XC	SW	GW	SW	SW
		1	◇1	1	◇1 trolley	◇1		◇	◇1	1	◇1	1	◇1 trolley	◇1 trolley	◇	◇1		1	◇1	1	◇1 buffet	◇1 trolley	◇	◇1 trolley	1
Eastleigh	d	10 26							11 22	11 26						12 22		12 26						13 22	13 26
Southampton Airport Parkway	d				10 34	10 55			11 27				11 34	11 53		12 27					12 34	12 53		13 27	
Southampton Central ⛴	d		10 29	10 35	10a42	11a02		11 04	11a34		11 28	11 35	11a42	11a59	12 04	12a34			12 29	12 35	12a42	13a00	13 07	13a34	
St Denys	d			10 41								11 41								12 41					
Bitterne	d			10 43								11 43								12 43					
Woolston	d			10 47								11 47								12 47					
Sholing	d			10 49								11 49								12 49					
Netley	d			10 53								11 53								12 53					
Hamble	d			10 55								11 55								12 55					
Bursledon	d			10 58								11 58								12 58					
Swanwick	d		10 46	11 02							11 46	12 02							12 46	13 02					
Fareham	a	10 43	10 52	11 09				11 27		11 43	11 52	12 09			12 28			12 43	12 52	13 09			13 33		13 43
	d	10 44	10 53	11 10				11 27		11 44	11 53	12 10			12 28			12 44	12 53	13 10			13 34		13 44
Portchester	d	10 49		11 15						11 49		12 15						12 49		13 15					13 49
Cosham	d	10 54	11 02	11 20				11 35		11 54	12 02	12 20			12 36			12 54	13 02	13 20			13 42		13 54
Havant	a		11 10								12 10								13 10				14 03		
Chichester 4	a		11 23								12 23								13 23				14 19		
Hilsea	a	11 04		11 26						12 00		12 26						13 00		13 26					14 00
Fratton	a	11 08		11 30				11 41		12 04		12 30			12 42			13 04		13 30					14 04
Portsmouth & Southsea	a	11 11		11 33				11 46		12 08		12 33			12 46			13 08		13 33					14 08
Portsmouth Harbour ⛴	a	11 15						11 52		12 13					12 52			13 13							14 13

		SN		SW	XC	SW	GW	SW	SW	SN	SW	XC		SW	SW	SW	GW	SN	SW	XC	SW	GW		SW	SW
		◇1		1	◇1 buffet	◇1 trolley	◇ trolley	◇1 trolley	1	◇1	1	◇1 buffet		◇1 trolley	◇1 trolley	1	◇	◇1	1	◇1 buffet	◇1 trolley	◇		◇1 trolley	1
Eastleigh	d							14 22	14 26						15 22	15 26								16 22	16 26
Southampton Airport Parkway	d				13 34	13 53		14 27				14 34		14 53	15 27					15 34	15 53			16 27	
Southampton Central ⛴	d	13 29		13 35	13a42	14a00	14 04	14a34		14 29	14 35	14a42		15a00	15a34		15 22	15 29	15 35	15a42	16a00	16 04		16a34	
St Denys	d			13 41							14 41								15 41						
Bitterne	d			13 43							14 43								15 43						
Woolston	d			13 47							14 47								15 47						
Sholing	d			13 49							14 49								15 49						
Netley	d			13 53							14 53								15 53						
Hamble	d			13 55							14 55								15 55						
Bursledon	d			13 58							14 58								15 58						
Swanwick	d	13 46		14 02						14 46	15 02							15 46	16 02						
Fareham	a	13 52		14 09			14 25		14 43	14 52	15 09					15 43	15 50	15 57	16 09			16 26			16 43
	d	13 53		14 10			14 26		14 44	14 53	15 10					15 44	15 51	15 58	16 10			16 26			16 44
Portchester	d			14 15					14 49		15 15					15 49			16 15						16 49
Cosham	d	14 02		14 20			14 34		14 54	15 02	15 20					15 54	16 01	16 07	16 20			16 34			16 54
Havant	a	14 10								15 10							16 11	16 15							
Chichester 4	a	14 23								15 23							16 22	16 28							
Hilsea	a			14 26					15 00		15 26					16 00			16 26						17 00
Fratton	a			14 30			14 41		15 04		15 30					16 04			16 30			16 41			17 03
Portsmouth & Southsea	a			14 33			14 45		15 08		15 33					16 08			16 33			16 45			17 08
Portsmouth Harbour ⛴	a						14 55		15 13							16 13						16 52			17 13

		SN	SW	XC	SW	GW	SW	SW		SN	SW	XC	SW	GW	SW	SW	SN	SW		XC	SW	GW	SW	SW	GW
		◇1	1	◇1 buffet	◇1 trolley	◇	◇1 trolley	1		◇1	1	◇1 buffet	◇1 trolley	◇	◇1 trolley	1	◇1	1		◇1 buffet	◇1 trolley	◇	◇1 trolley	1	◇
Eastleigh	d						17 22	17 26							18 22	18 26							19 22	19 26	
Southampton Airport Parkway	d			16 34	16 53		17 27					17 34	17 53		18 27					18 34	18 53		19 27		
Southampton Central ⛴	d	16 29	16 35	16a42	17a00	17 04	17a34			17 29	17 35	17a40	18a00	18 04	18a34		18 29	18 35		18a42	19a00	19 04	19a34		19 27
St Denys	d		16 41								17 41							18 41							
Bitterne	d		16 43								17 43							18 43							
Woolston	d		16 47								17 47							18 47							
Sholing	d		16 49								17 49							18 49							
Netley	d		16 53								17 53							18 53							
Hamble	d		16 55								17 55							18 55							
Bursledon	d		16 58								17 58							18 58							
Swanwick	d	16 46	17 02							17 46	18 02						18 46	19 02							
Fareham	a	16 52	17 09			17 26		17 43		17 52	18 09			18 26		18 43	18 52	19 09				19 27		19 43	19 49
	d	16 53	17 10			17 26		17 44		17 53	18 10			18 26		18 44	18 53	19 10				19 27		19 44	19 50
Portchester	d		17 15					17 49			18 15					18 49		19 15						19 49	
Cosham	d	17 02	17 20			17 34		17 54		18 02	18 20			18 34		18 54	19 02	19 20				19 35		19 54	19 59
Havant	a	17 10								18 10							19 10								20 10
Chichester 4	a	17 23								18 23							19 23								20 21
Hilsea	a		17 26					18 00			18 26					19 00		19 26						20 00	
Fratton	a		17 30			17 41		18 04			18 30			18 41		19 03		19 30				19 42		20 04	
Portsmouth & Southsea	a		17 33			17 45		18 08			18 33			18 45		19 08		19 33				19 46		20 08	
Portsmouth Harbour ⛴	a					17 52		18 13						18 52		19 13						19 52		20 13	

Table 165

Sundays
from 1 April

Southampton - Fareham and Portsmouth

Network Diagram - see first Page of Table 165

		SN	SW	XC	SW	GW	SW	SW	GW	SN	SW	XC	SW	GW	SW	SW	SN	SW	XC	SW	GW	SN
		◇1	1	◇1	◇1	◇	◇1	1		◇1	1	◇1	◇1	◇	◇1	1	◇1	1	◇1	◇1	◇	1
Eastleigh	d	19 46					20 22	20 26		20 46					21 22	21 26						
Southampton Airport Parkway	d			19 34	19 53		20 27					20 34	20 53		21 27				21 36	21 53		
Southampton Central ⛴	d		19 35	19a40	20a00	20 04	20a34		20 31		20 35	20a42	21a00	21 01	21a34		21 30	21 35	21a45	22a00	22 04	22 15
St Denys	d		19 41								20 41							21 41				
Bitterne	d		19 43								20 43							21 43				
Woolston	d		19 47								20 47							21 47				
Sholing	d		19 49								20 49							21 49				
Netley	d		19 53								20 53							21 53				
Hamble	d		19 55								20 55							21 55				
Bursledon	d		19 58								20 58							21 58				
Swanwick	d		20 02								21 02						21 47	22 02				22 32
Fareham	a	20 02	20 09			20 26		20 43	20 54	21 02	21 10			21 23		21 43	21 53	22 09			22 26	22 38
	d	20 03	20 10			20 26		20 44	20 55	21 02	21 10			21 24		21 44	21 54	22 10			22 26	22 39
Portchester	d		20 15					20 49			21 15					21 49		22 15				
Cosham	d	20 12	20 20					20 54		21 11	21 20					21 54	22 03	22 20				22 48
Havant	a	20 18								21 17							22 10					22 54
Chichester 4	a	20 30								21 29							22 23					23 06
Hilsea	a		20 26					21 00			21 26					22 00		22 26				
Fratton	a		20 30			20 41		21 04	21 09		21 30			21 37		22 04		22 30			22 40	
Portsmouth & Southsea	a		20 33			20 45		21 08	21 15		21 33			21 41		22 08		22 33			22 44	
Portsmouth Harbour ⛴	a					20 52		21 13	21 26					21 48		22 13					22 50	

		SW	SW	SW	XC	SN	SW	GW	SW	SW
		◇1	1	1	◇1	1	◇1	◇	◇1	1
Eastleigh	d	22 22	22 26						23 22	23 26
Southampton Airport Parkway	d	22 27			22 34		22 53		23 27	
Southampton Central ⛴	d	22a34		22 35	22a42	22 52	23a00	23 07	23a34	
St Denys	d			22 41						
Bitterne	d			22 43						
Woolston	d			22 47						
Sholing	d			22 49						
Netley	d			22 53						
Hamble	d			22 55						
Bursledon	d			22 58						
Swanwick	d			23 02		23 11				
Fareham	a		22 43	23 09		23 17		23 28		23 43
	d		22 44	23 10		23 17		23 29		23 44
Portchester	d		22 49	23 15						23 49
Cosham	d		22 54	23 20		23 26				23 54
Havant	a					23 32				
Chichester 4	a					23 44				
Hilsea	a		23 00	23 24						23 59
Fratton	a		23 04	23 28				23 42		00 04
Portsmouth & Southsea	a		23 08	23 32				23 46		00 08
Portsmouth Harbour ⛴	a		23 13					23 54		00 13

A Stops at these stations before Eastleigh

Portsmouth and Fareham - Southampton

Network Diagram - see first Page of Table 165

Miles	Miles			SW	SW	SW	SW	SW	SW	SN	SW	SW		GW	SN	SW	SW	SN	SW	GW	SN	SN		SW	SW
				MO	MX	MO	MX																		
				■1	■1	◇■1 trolley	◇■1	■1	■1		■1	■1		■R trolley	■1	■1	■1	■1	■1	◇ trolley	■1	■1		■1	■1
0	—	**Portsmouth Harbour** ⛴	d	23p17	23p24				05 00			05 43		06 00			06 23		06 50	07 05				07 24	
0¾	—	**Portsmouth & Southsea**	d	23p22	23p29				05 05		05 16	05 48		06 04		06 23	06 28		06 55	07 09				07 29	07 38
1¾	—	Fratton	d	23p26	23p33				05 09		05 20	05 52		06 08		06 27	06 32		06 59	07 13				07 33	07 42
4	—	Hilsea	d	23p30	23p37				05 13		05 24	05 56				06 31	06 36		07 03					07 37	07 46
—	0	**Chichester ■4**	d							05 06					06 09			06 26			07 08	07 13			
—	8¾	Havant	d							05 17					06 20			06 40			07 19	07 31			
5½	12¾	Cosham	d	23p35	23p42				05 19	05 24	05 29	06 03		06 15	06 27	06 36	06 42	06 50	07 08	07 21	07 26	07 38		07 43	07 51
8	—	Portchester	d	23p40	23p47				05 23	05 28	05 34	06 08				06 41	06 46	06 54	07 13		07 30			07 48	07 56
11¼	—	**Fareham**	a	23p45	23p52				05 28	05 33	05 39	06 13		06 23	06 36	06 46	06 51	06 59	07 18	07 28	07 35	07 46		07 53	08 01
—	—		d	23p46	23p53				05 29	05 34	05 40	06 19		06 24	06 37	06 47	06 53	07 00	07 20	07 29	07 36	07 47		07 54	08 03
15	—	Swanwick	d							05 40	05 46				06 43	06 53		07 06			07 42	07 53			08 09
17	—	Bursledon	d								05 50					06 57									08 13
18¼	—	Hamble	d								05 53					07 00									08 16
19	—	Netley	d							05 46	05 55					07 02					07 48	07 59			08 18
20¾	—	Sholing	d								05 59					07 06									08 22
21½	—	Woolston	d							05 50	06 01					07 08					07 52	08 04			08 24
23¼	—	Bitterne	d								06 05					07 12									08 28
—	—	Eastleigh	a	00 04	00 11				05 49			06 37					07 11		07 38					08 12	
—	—	Southampton Airport Parkway	a																						
23¾	—	St Denys	d								06 08					07 15						08 08			08 31
25¾	—	**Southampton Central** ⛴	a			00 36	00 37	02 56		05 59	06 13			06 45	07 02	07 21		07 25		07 50	08 01	08 13			08 38

		SN	SW	SW	GW	SN	SW	SW		SN	GW	SN	SW	GW	SW	SN	GW	SN		SW	SW	SN	GW	SN	SW
		■1	■1	■1	◇ trolley	■1	■1	■1		◇■1	◇ trolley	■1	■1	◇ trolley	■1	◇■1	◇ trolley			■1	■1	◇■1	◇ trolley		■1
Portsmouth Harbour ⛴	d		07 55	08 05	08 23		08 33	08 59			09 23		09 33		09 59		10 23			10 33	10 59		11 23		
Portsmouth & Southsea	d		08 00	08 10	08 27		08 38	09 04			09 27		09 38		10 04		10 27			10 38	11 04		11 27		11 38
Fratton	d		08 04	08 13	08 31		08 42	09 08			09 31		09 42		10 08		10 31			10 42	11 08		11 31		11 42
Hilsea	d		08 08	08 17			08 46	09 12					09 46		10 12					10 46	11 12				11 46
Chichester ■4	d	07 52				08 22				09 08		09 25		09 47		10 06		10 25				11 05		11 25	
Havant	d	08 03				08 37				09 23		09 39		09 59		10 20		10 37				11 19		11 37	
Cosham	d	08 09	08 13	08 22	08 39	08 45	08 51	09 17		09 30	09 39	09 46	09 51	10 05	10 17	10 28	10 39	10 46		10 51	11 17	11 26	11 39	11 46	11 51
Portchester	d	08 13	08 18	08 27		08 49	08 56	09 22					09 56		10 22	10 32				10 56	11 22	11 30			11 56
Fareham	a	08 18	08 23	08 32	08 46	08 54	09 01	09 27		09 37	09 46	09 53	10 01	10 14	10 27	10 37	10 46	10 53		11 01	11 27	11 35	11 46	11 53	12 01
	d	08 19	08 24	08 33	08 47	08 55	09 03	09 28		09 38	09 47	09 54	10 03	10 14	10 28	10 38	10 47	10 54		11 03	11 28	11 36	11 47	11 54	12 03
Swanwick	d	08 26				09 01	09 09			09 44		10 00	10 09			10 44		11 00		11 09		11 42		12 00	12 09
Bursledon	d	08 29					09 13						10 13							11 13					12 13
Hamble	d	08 32					09 16						10 16							11 16					12 16
Netley	d	08 34					09 18						10 18							11 18					12 18
Sholing	d	08 38					09 22						10 22							11 22					12 22
Woolston	d	08 40					09 24						10 24							11 24					12 24
Bitterne	d	08 43					09 28						10 28							11 28					12 28
Eastleigh	a		08 42	08 51				09 46							10 46						11 46				
Southampton Airport Parkway	a																								
St Denys	d	08 46					09 31						10 31							11 31					12 31
Southampton Central ⛴	a	08 52			09 08	09 19	09 38			10 01	10 08	10 20	10 38	10 40		11 01	11 08	11 19		11 38		12 01	12 08	12 19	12 38

		SW	SN	GW		SN	SW	SW	SN	GW	SN	SW	SW	SN		GW	SN	SW	SW	SN	GW	SN	SW	SW	
		■1	◇■1	◇ trolley			■1	■1	◇■1	◇ trolley	■1	■1	■1	◇■1		■R trolley		■1	■1	◇■1	■R trolley		■1	■1	
Portsmouth Harbour ⛴	d	11 59		12 23				12 59		13 23			13 59			14 23			14 59		15 23			15 59	
Portsmouth & Southsea	d	12 04		12 27			12 38	13 04		13 27		13 38	14 04			14 27		14 38	15 04		15 27		15 38	16 04	
Fratton	d	12 08		12 31			12 42	13 08		13 31		13 42	14 08			14 31		14 42	15 08		15 31		15 42	16 08	
Hilsea	d	12 12					12 46	13 12				13 46	14 12					14 46	15 12				15 46	16 12	
Chichester ■4	d		12 05			12 25			13 05		13 25			14 05			14 25			15 05		15 25			
Havant	d		12 19			12 37			13 19		13 37			14 19			14 37			15 19		15 37			
Cosham	d	12 17	12 26	12 39		12 46	12 51	13 17	13 26	13 39	13 46	13 51	14 17	14 26		14 39	14 46	14 51	15 17	15 26	15 39	15 46	15 51	16 17	
Portchester	d	12 22	12 30				12 56	13 22	13 30			13 56	14 22	14 30				14 56	15 22	15 30			15 56	16 22	
Fareham	a	12 27	12 35	12 46		12 53	13 01	13 27	13 35	13 46	13 53	14 01	14 27	14 35		14 46	14 53	15 01	15 27	15 35	15 46	15 53	16 01	16 27	
	d	12 28	12 36	12 47		12 54	13 03	13 28	13 36	13 47	13 56	14 03	14 28	14 36		14 47	14 54	15 03	15 28	15 36	15 47	15 54	16 03	16 28	
Swanwick	d		12 42			13 00	13 09		13 42		14 02	14 09		14 42			15 00	15 09		15 42		16 00	16 09		
Bursledon	d						13 13					14 13						15 13					16 13		
Hamble	d						13 16					14 16						15 16					16 16		
Netley	d						13 18					14 18						15 18					16 18		
Sholing	d						13 22					14 22						15 22					16 22		
Woolston	d						13 24					14 24						15 24					16 24		
Bitterne	d						13 28					14 28						15 28					16 28		
Eastleigh	a	12 46						13 46					14 46						15 46					16 46	
Southampton Airport Parkway	a																								
St Denys	d						13 31					14 31						15 31					16 31		
Southampton Central ⛴	a		12 59	13 08		13 19	13 38		13 59	14 08	14 19	14 39		14 59		15 08	15 19	15 38		15 59	16 08	16 20	16 38		

Portsmouth and Fareham - Southampton

Network Diagram - see first Page of Table 165

		SN	GW	SN	SW	SW	SW	SN	GW	SN		SW	GW	SW	SN	GW	SN	SW	SW	SN		GW	SN	SW	SW
		◇1	R 🛒	1	1	1	1	◇1	◇ 🛒	1		1	◇ 🛒	1	◇1	◇ 🛒	1	1	1	◇1		◇		1	1
Portsmouth Harbour ⛴	d		16 23			16 49	16 59		17 23			17 33		17 59		18 23			18 59			19 23			19 59
Portsmouth & Southsea	d		16 27		16 38	16 55	17 04		17 27			17 38		18 04		18 27		18 38	19 04			19 27		19 38	20 04
Fratton	d		16 31		16 42	16 59	17 08		17 31			17 42		18 08		18 31		18 42	19 08			19 31		19 42	20 08
Hilsea	d				16 46	17 03	17 12					17 46		18 12				18 46	19 12					19 46	20 12
Chichester 4	d	16 05		16 25				17 05		17 25			17 47		18 05		18 25			19 02			19 20		
Havant	d	16 19		16 37				17 19		17 37			17 58		18 23		18 37			19 20			19 37		
Cosham	d	16 26	16 39	16 46	16 51	17 08	17 17	17 27	17 39	17 46		17 51	18 05	18 17	18 30	18 39	18 44	18 51	19 17	19 29		19 39	19 46	19 51	20 17
Portchester	d	16 30			16 56	17 13	17 22	17 31				17 56		18 22	18 34			18 56	19 22	19 33				19 56	20 22
Fareham	a	16 35	16 46	16 53	17 01	17 18	17 27	17 36	17 46	17 53		18 01	18 12	18 27	18 39	18 46	18 52	19 01	19 27	19 38		19 46	19 54	20 01	20 27
	d	16 36	16 47	16 57	17 03		17 28	17 37	17 47	17 54		18 03	18 13	18 28	18 40	18 47	18 53	19 03	19 28	19 39		19 47	19 55	20 03	20 28
Swanwick	d	16 42			17 09			17 43		18 00		18 09			18 46		18 59	19 09		19 45			20 01	20 09	
Bursledon	d				17 13							18 13						19 13						20 13	
Hamble	d				17 16							18 16						19 16						20 16	
Netley	d				17 18			17 49				18 18						19 18						20 18	
Sholing	d				17 22							18 22						19 22						20 22	
Woolston	d				17 24			17 53				18 24						19 24						20 24	
Bitterne	d				17 28							18 28						19 28						20 28	
Eastleigh	a			17 11			17 46							18 46					19 46						20 46
Southampton Airport Parkway	a			17 20																					
St Denys	d				17 31			17 58				18 31						19 31						20 31	
Southampton Central ⛴	a	17 01	17 08	17 28	17 38			18 03	18 08	18 20		18 38	18 40		19 05	19 08	19 20	19 38		20 03		20 08	20 18	20 38	

		SN	GW	SN	SW	SW		SN	GW	SN	SW	SW	SW	SN	SW	SW		SW							
		◇1	◇	1	1	1		◇1		1	1	1	1	◇1	1	1		1							
Portsmouth Harbour ⛴	d		20 23			20 59			21 23				21 54		22 33			23 24							
Portsmouth & Southsea	d		20 27		20 38	21 04			21 27		21 38		21 59		22 38			23 29							
Fratton	d		20 31		20 42	21 08			21 31		21 42		22 03		22 42			23 33							
Hilsea	d				20 46	21 12					21 46		22 07		22 46			23 37							
Chichester 4	d	20 01		20 26				21 05		21 26				22 05											
Havant	d	20 22		20 37				21 26		21 37		21 58		22 26		22 59									
Cosham	d	20 29		20 45	20 51	21 17		21 34		21 44	21 51	22 05	22 12	22 34	22 51	23 08		23 42							
Portchester	d			20 49	20 56	21 22		21 38			21 56		22 17		22 56	23 13		23 47							
Fareham	a	20 36	20 46	20 54	21 01	21 27		21 43	21 47	21 51	22 01	22 12	22 25	22 42	23 01	23 18		23 52							
	d	20 37	20 47	20 55	21 03	21 28		21 43	21 48	21 52	22 03		22 26	22 43	23 03			23 53							
Swanwick	d	20 43		21 01	21 09			21 49		21 58	22 09			22 49	23 09										
Bursledon	d				21 13						22 13				23 13										
Hamble	d				21 16						22 16				23 16										
Netley	d				21 18						22 18				23 18										
Sholing	d				21 22						22 22				23 22										
Woolston	d				21 24			21 58			22 24				23 24										
Bitterne	d				21 28						22 28				23 28										
Eastleigh	a					21 46			22 06				22 43					00 11							
Southampton Airport Parkway	a																								
St Denys	d				21 31			22 02			22 31				23 31										
Southampton Central ⛴	a	21 01	21 08	21 19	21 38			22 07	22 21	22 16	22 39			23 07	23 39										

Saturdays

		SW	SW	SW	SW	SN	SW	SN	SW	GW		SN	SN	SW	SW	SN	GW	SN	SW	SW		SN	GW	SN	SW
		1	◇1	1	1	1	1	1	1	◇		1	1	1	1	1	◇ 🛒	1	1	1		1	◇ 🛒		1
Portsmouth Harbour ⛴	d	23p24							05 50	06 00					06 55		07 23			07 59			08 23		
Portsmouth & Southsea	d	23p29					05 16		05 55	06 04				06 38	07 00		07 27		07 38	08 04			08 27		08 38
Fratton	d	23p33					05 20		05 59	06 08				06 42	07 04		07 31		07 42	08 08			08 31		08 42
Hilsea	d	23p37					05 24		06 03					06 46	07 08				07 46	08 12					08 46
Chichester 4	d					05 05		05 28				06 06	06 23			07 07		07 25				08 05		08 25	
Havant	d					05 16		05 39				06 24	06 37			07 23		07 37				08 20		08 37	
Cosham	d	23p42			05 09	05 23	05 29	05 49	06 08	06 19		06 30	06 46	06 51	07 13	07 30	07 39	07 46	07 51	08 17		08 28	08 39	08 46	08 51
Portchester	d	23p47			05 14	05 27	05 34		06 13			06 34		06 56	07 18	07 34			07 56	08 22		08 32			08 56
Fareham	a	23p52			05 19	05 32	05 39	05 57	06 18	06 27		06 39	06 53	07 01	07 23	07 39	07 46	07 53	08 01	08 27		08 37	08 46	08 53	09 01
	d	23p53			05 20	05 33	05 40	05 58	06 19	06 28		06 40	06 57	07 03	07 24	07 39	07 47	07 57	08 03	08 28		08 38	08 47	08 54	09 03
Swanwick	d					05 39	05 46	06 04				06 46		07 09		07 45			08 09			08 44		09 00	09 09
Bursledon	d						05 50							07 13					08 13						09 13
Hamble	d						05 53							07 16					08 16						09 16
Netley	d					05 45	05 55							07 18					08 18						09 18
Sholing	d						05 59							07 22					08 22						09 22
Woolston	d					05 49	06 01							07 24					08 24						09 24
Bitterne	d						06 05							07 28					08 28						09 28
Eastleigh	a	00 11			05 38				06 39				07 10		07 42			08 10		08 46					
Southampton Airport Parkway	a												07 17					08 17							
St Denys	d						06 08							07 31					08 31						09 31
Southampton Central ⛴	a		00 37	02 49		05 58	06 13	06 24		06 49		07 05	07 28	07 38		08 03	08 07	08 28	08 38			09 01	09 08	09 19	09 38

Portsmouth and Fareham - Southampton

Network Diagram - see first Page of Table 165

		SW 1	SN ◇1	GW ◇ 🚲	SN 1	SW 1		GW ◇	SW 1	SN ◇1	GW ◇	SN	SW 1	SW 1	SN ◇1	GW ◇		SN 1	SW 1	SW 1	SN ◇1	GW ◇	SN	SW 1	SW 1
Portsmouth Harbour ⛴	d	08 59		09 23					09 59		10 23			10 59		11 23				11 59		12 23			12 59
Portsmouth & Southsea	d	09 04		09 27		09 38			10 04		10 27		10 38	11 04		11 27			11 38	12 04		12 27		12 38	13 04
Fratton	d	09 08		09 31		09 42			10 08		10 31		10 42	11 08		11 31			11 42	12 08		12 31		12 42	13 08
Hilsea	d	09 12				09 46			10 12				10 46	11 12					11 46	12 12				12 46	13 12
Chichester 4	d		09 05		09 25			09 49		10 05		10 25			11 05			11 25			12 05		12 25		
Havant	d		09 19		09 37			10 00		10 19		10 37			11 19			11 37			12 19		12 37		
Cosham	d	09 17	09 26	09 39	09 46	09 51		10 06	10 17	10 26	10 39	10 46	10 51	11 17	11 26	11 39		11 46	11 51	12 17	12 26	12 39	12 46	12 51	13 17
Portchester	d	09 22	09 30			09 56			10 22	10 30			10 56	11 22	11 30				11 56	12 22	12 30			12 56	13 22
Fareham	a	09 27	09 35	09 46	09 53	10 01		10 15	10 27	10 35	10 46	10 53	11 01	11 27	11 35	11 46		11 53	12 01	12 27	12 35	12 46	12 53	13 01	13 27
	d	09 28	09 36	09 47	09 57	10 03		10 16	10 28	10 36	10 47	10 54	11 03	11 28	11 36	11 47		11 57	12 03	12 28	12 36	12 47	12 54	13 03	13 28
Swanwick	d		09 42			10 09				10 42		11 00	11 09		11 42				12 09		12 42		13 00	13 09	
Bursledon	d					10 13							11 13						12 13					13 13	
Hamble	d					10 16							11 16						12 16					13 16	
Netley	d					10 18							11 18						12 18					13 18	
Sholing	d					10 22							11 22						12 22					13 22	
Woolston	d					10 24							11 24						12 24					13 24	
Bitterne	d					10 28							11 28						12 28					13 28	
Eastleigh	a	09 46			10 10				10 46					11 46				12 10		12 46					13 46
Southampton Airport Parkway	a				10 17													12 18							
St Denys	d					10 31							11 31						12 31					13 31	
Southampton Central ⛴	a		09 59	10 08	10 28	10 38		10 40		10 59	11 08	11 19	11 38		11 59	12 08		12 28	12 38		12 59	13 08	13 19	13 38	

		SN ◇1		GW ◇	SN 1	SW 1	SW 1	SN ◇1	GW ◇	SN	SW 1	SW 1		SN ◇1	GW ◇	SN 1	SW 1	SW 1	SN ◇1	GW R	SN	SW 1		SW 1	SN ◇1
Portsmouth Harbour ⛴	d			13 23			13 59		14 23			14 59			15 23			15 59		16 23				16 59	
Portsmouth & Southsea	d			13 27		13 38	14 04		14 27		14 38	15 04			15 27		15 38	16 04		16 27		16 38		17 04	
Fratton	d			13 31		13 42	14 08		14 31		14 42	15 08			15 31		15 42	16 08		16 31		16 42		17 08	
Hilsea	d					13 46	14 12				14 46	15 12					15 46	16 12				16 46		17 12	
Chichester 4	d	13 05			13 25			14 05		14 25				15 05		15 25			16 05		16 25				17 05
Havant	d	13 19			13 37			14 19		14 37				15 19		15 37			16 19		16 37				17 19
Cosham	d	13 26		13 39	13 46	13 51	14 17	14 26	14 39	14 46	14 51	15 17		15 26	15 39	15 46	15 51	16 17	16 26	16 39	16 46	16 51		17 17	17 26
Portchester	d	13 30				13 56	14 22	14 30			14 56	15 22		15 30			15 56	16 22	16 30			16 56		17 22	17 30
Fareham	a	13 35		13 46	13 53	14 01	14 27	14 35	14 46	14 53	15 01	15 27		15 35	15 46	15 53	16 01	16 27	16 35	16 46	16 53	17 01		17 27	17 35
	d	13 36		13 47	13 56	14 03	14 28	14 36	14 47	14 54	15 03	15 28		15 36	15 47	15 57	16 03	16 28	16 36	16 47	16 54	17 03		17 28	17 36
Swanwick	d	13 42			14 02	14 09		14 42		15 00	15 09			15 42			16 09		16 42		17 00	17 09			17 42
Bursledon	d					14 13					15 13						16 13					17 13			
Hamble	d					14 16					15 16						16 16					17 16			
Netley	d					14 18					15 18						16 18					17 18			
Sholing	d					14 22					15 22						16 22					17 22			
Woolston	d					14 24					15 24						16 24					17 24			
Bitterne	d					14 28					15 28						16 28					17 28			
Eastleigh	a						14 46					15 46				16 10		16 46						17 46	
Southampton Airport Parkway	a															16 17									
St Denys	d					14 31					15 31						16 31					17 31			
Southampton Central ⛴	a	13 59		14 08	14 19	14 39		14 59	15 08	15 19	15 38			15 59	16 08	16 28	16 38		16 59	17 08	17 19	17 38			17 59

		GW ◇	SN 1	SW 1	GW ◇	SW 1	SN ◇1	GW ◇		SN	SW 1	SW 1	SN ◇1	GW ◇	SN 1	SW 1	SW 1	SN ◇1		GW ◇	SN 1	SW 1	SW 1	SN ◇1	SN 1
Portsmouth Harbour ⛴	d	17 23		17 33		17 59		18 23				18 59		19 23			19 59			20 23			20 59		
Portsmouth & Southsea	d	17 27		17 38		18 04		18 27			18 38	19 04		19 27		19 38	20 04			20 27		20 38	21 04		
Fratton	d	17 31		17 42		18 08		18 31			18 42	19 08		19 31		19 42	20 08			20 31		20 42	21 08		
Hilsea	d			17 46		18 12					18 46	19 12				19 46	20 12					20 46	21 12		
Chichester 4	d		17 25		17 46		18 05			18 25			19 05		19 25			20 05			20 25			21 05	21 28
Havant	d		17 37		18 00		18 19			18 37			19 19		19 37			20 26			20 37			21 23	21 40
Cosham	d	17 39	17 46	17 51	18 06	18 17	18 26	18 39		18 46	18 51	19 17	19 26	19 39	19 46	19 51	20 17	20 32			20 46	20 51	21 17	21 29	21 47
Portchester	d			17 56		18 22	18 30				18 56	19 22	19 30			19 56	20 22	20 36				20 56	21 22	21 33	
Fareham	a	17 46	17 53	18 01	18 14	18 27	18 35	18 46		18 53	19 01	19 27	19 35	19 46	19 53	20 01	20 27	20 41		20 45	20 53	21 01	21 27	21 38	21 54
	d	17 47	17 57	18 03	18 15	18 28	18 36	18 47		18 54	19 03	19 28	19 36	19 47	19 57	20 03	20 28	20 42		20 47	20 54	21 03	21 28	21 39	21 55
Swanwick	d			18 09			18 42			19 00	19 09		19 42			20 09		20 48			21 00	21 09		21 45	22 01
Bursledon	d			18 13							19 13					20 13						21 13			
Hamble	d			18 16							19 16					20 16						21 16			
Netley	d			18 18							19 18					20 18						21 18			
Sholing	d			18 22							19 22					20 22						21 22			
Woolston	d			18 24							19 24					20 24						21 24			
Bitterne	d			18 28							19 28					20 28						21 28			
Eastleigh	a		18 10			18 46						19 46			20 10		20 46						21 46		
Southampton Airport Parkway	a		18 17												20 17										
St Denys	d			18 31							19 31					20 31						21 31			
Southampton Central ⛴	a	18 08	18 28	18 38	18 43		18 59	19 08		19 19	19 38		19 59	20 09	20 28	20 38		21 05		21 10	21 19	21 38		22 02	22 20

Table 165

Saturdays

Portsmouth and Fareham - Southampton

Network Diagram - see first Page of Table 165

		SW	SW	SN		SW	SW
		1	1	◇1		1	1
Portsmouth Harbour ⛴	d		21 54			22 33	23 24
Portsmouth & Southsea	d	21 38	21 59			22 38	23 29
Fratton	d	21 42	22 03			22 42	23 33
Hilsea	d	21 46	22 07			22 46	23 37
Chichester 4	d			22 05			
Havant	d			22 26			
Cosham	d	21 51	22 12	22 34		22 51	23 42
Portchester	d	21 56	22 17			22 56	23 47
Fareham	a	22 01	22 22	22 41		23 01	23 52
	d	22 03	22 23	22 42		23 03	23 53
Swanwick	d	22 09		22 48		23 09	
Bursledon	d	22 13				23 13	
Hamble	d	22 16				23 16	
Netley	d	22 18				23 18	
Sholing	d	22 22				23 22	
Woolston	d	22 24				23 24	
Bitterne	d	22 28				23 28	
Eastleigh	a		22 41				00 11
Southampton Airport Parkway	a						
St Denys	d	22 31				23 31	
Southampton Central ⛴	a	22 39		23 05		23 36	

Sundays

until 12 February

		SW	SW	SW	SW	SW	SW	SN	SW	SW		SN	GW	SW	SW	SN	SW	SW	SN	GW		SW	SW	SN	GW
		1 A	◇1 A	1	1	1	1	◇1	1	1		◇1	R	1 ⊼	1	◇1	1 ⊼	1	◇1	◇		1 ⊼	1	◇1	◇
Portsmouth Harbour ⛴	d	23p24			06 37	07 17			08 17				09 08	09 17			10 17			11 08		11 17			
Portsmouth & Southsea	d	23p29			06 42	07 22	07 42		08 22	08 42			09 12	09 22	09 42		10 22	10 42		11 12		11 22	11 42		
Fratton	d	23p33			06 46	07 26	07 46		08 26	08 46			09 16	09 26	09 46		10 26	10 46		11 16		11 26	11 46		
Hilsea	d	23p37			06 50	07 30	07 50		08 30	08 50				09 30	09 50		10 30	10 50				11 30	11 50		
Chichester 4	d							07 45				08 45				09 45			10 45					11 45	11 54
Havant	d							07 58				08 58				09 58			10 58					11 58	12 10
Cosham	d	23p42			06 55	07 35	07 55	08 05	08 35	08 55		09 05	09 23	09 35	09 55	10 06	10 35	10 55	11 06	11 23		11 35	11 55	12 05	12 23
Portchester	d	23p47			07 00	07 40	08 00		08 40	09 00				09 40	10 00		10 40	11 00				11 40	12 00		
Fareham	a	23p52			07 05	07 45	08 05	08 13	08 45	09 05		09 13	09 31	09 45	10 05	10 14	10 45	11 05	11 14	11 31		11 45	12 05	12 13	12 31
	d	23p53			07 06	07 46	08 06	08 14	08 46	09 06		09 14	09 32	09 46	10 06	10 15	10 46	11 06	11 15	11 32		11 46	12 06	12 14	12 32
Swanwick	d				07 12		08 12	08 20		09 12		09 20			10 12	10 21		11 12	11 21				12 12	12 20	
Bursledon	d				07 16		08 16			09 16					10 16			11 16					12 16		
Hamble	d				07 19		08 19			09 19					10 19			11 19					12 19		
Netley	d				07 21		08 21			09 21					10 21			11 21					12 21		
Sholing	d				07 25		08 25			09 25					10 25			11 25					12 25		
Woolston	d				07 27		08 27			09 27					10 27			11 27					12 27		
Bitterne	d				07 31		08 31			09 31					10 31			11 31					12 31		
Eastleigh	a	00 11				08 04			09 04					10 04			11 04					12 04			
Southampton Airport Parkway	a																								
St Denys	d				07 34		08 34			09 34					10 34			11 34					12 34		
Southampton Central ⛴	a		00 34	02 56	07 40		08 40	08 44		09 40		09 44	09 53		10 40	10 44		11 40	11 45	11 53			12 40	12 44	12 53

		SW	SW	SN	GW	SW		SW	SN	GW	SW	SW	SN	GW	SW	SW		SN	GW	SW	GW	SW	SN	GW	SW
		1 ⊼	1	◇1	◇	1 ⊼		1	◇1	◇	1 ⊼	1	◇1	R	1 ⊼	1		◇1	◇	1 ⊼	◇	1	◇1	◇	1
Portsmouth Harbour ⛴	d	12 17			13 08	13 17				14 08	14 17			15 08	15 17				16 08	16 17				17 08	17 17
Portsmouth & Southsea	d	12 22	12 42		13 12	13 22		13 42		14 12	14 22	14 42		15 12	15 22	15 42			16 12	16 22		16 42		17 12	17 22
Fratton	d	12 26	12 46		13 16	13 26		13 46		14 16	14 26	14 46		15 16	15 26	15 46			16 16	16 26		16 46		17 16	17 26
Hilsea	d	12 30	12 50			13 30		13 50			14 30	14 50			15 30	15 50				16 30		16 50			17 30
Chichester 4	d			12 45					13 45				14 45					15 45			16 34		16 45		
Havant	d			12 58					13 58				14 58					15 58			16 48		16 58		
Cosham	d	12 35	12 55	13 05	13 23	13 35		13 55	14 05	14 23	14 35	14 55	15 05	15 23	15 35	15 55		16 05	16 23	16 35	16 55	16 59	17 05	17 23	17 35
Portchester	d	12 40	13 00			13 40		14 00			14 40	15 00			15 40	16 00				16 40		17 03			17 40
Fareham	a	12 45	13 05	13 13	13 31	13 45		14 05	14 13	14 31	14 45	15 05	15 13	15 31	15 45	16 05		16 13	16 31	16 45	17 02	17 08	17 14	17 31	17 45
	d	12 46	13 06	13 14	13 32	13 46		14 06	14 14	14 32	14 46	15 06	15 14	15 32	15 46	16 06		16 14	16 32	16 46	17 03	17 09	17 15	17 32	17 46
Swanwick	d		13 12	13 20				14 12	14 20			15 12	15 20			16 12		16 20				17 16	17 22		
Bursledon	d		13 16					14 16				15 16				16 16						17 19			
Hamble	d		13 19					14 19				15 19				16 19						17 23			
Netley	d		13 21					14 21				15 21				16 21						17 25			
Sholing	d		13 25					14 25				15 25				16 25						17 29			
Woolston	d		13 27					14 27				15 27				16 27						17 31			
Bitterne	d		13 31					14 31				15 31				16 31						17 34			
Eastleigh	a	13 04				14 04					15 04				16 04					17 04					18 04
Southampton Airport Parkway	a																								
St Denys	d		13 34					14 34				15 34				16 34						17 38			
Southampton Central ⛴	a		13 40	13 44	13 53			14 40	14 44	14 53		15 40	15 44	15 53		16 40		16 44	16 53		17 24	17 43	17 48	17 53	

A not 11 December

Table 165

Sundays

until 12 February

Portsmouth and Fareham - Southampton

Network Diagram - see first Page of Table 165

		SW 1		SN ◇1	GW ◇	SW 1	GW ◇	SW 1	SN ◇1	GW ◇	SW 1	SW 1		SN ◇1	GW ◇	SW 1	SW 1	SN ◇1	SW 1	SW 1	SN ◇1	GW		SW 1	SW 1
Portsmouth Harbour ⛴	d				18 08	18 17				19 08	19 17				20 08	20 17			21 17			22 03		22 17	
Portsmouth & Southsea	d	17 42			18 12	18 22		18 42		19 12	19 22	19 42			20 12	20 22	20 42		21 22	21 42		22 12		22 22	22 42
Fratton	d	17 46			18 16	18 26		18 46		19 16	19 26	19 46			20 16	20 26	20 46		21 26	21 46		22 16		22 26	22 46
Hilsea	d	17 50				18 30		18 50			19 30	19 50				20 30	20 50		21 30	21 50				22 30	22 50
Chichester 4	d			17 45			18 34		18 45					19 45				20 45			21 45				
Havant	d			17 58			18 48		18 58					19 58				20 58			21 58				
Cosham	d	17 55		18 05	18 23	18 35	18 55	18 59	19 05	19 23	19 35	19 55		20 05		20 35	20 55	21 07	21 35	21 55	22 05			22 35	22 55
Portchester	d	18 00				18 40		19 03			19 40	20 00				20 40	21 00		21 40	22 00				22 40	23 00
Fareham	a	18 05		18 13	18 31	18 45	19 02	19 08	19 13	19 31	19 45	20 05		20 13	20 31	20 45	21 05	21 15	21 45	22 05	22 13	22 31		22 45	23 05
	d	18 06		18 14	18 32	18 46	19 03	19 09	19 14	19 32	19 46	20 06		20 14	20 32	20 46	21 06	21 16	21 46	22 06	22 14	22 32		22 46	23 06
Swanwick	d	18 12		18 20				19 16	19 22			20 12		20 20			21 12	21 22		22 12	22 20				23 12
Bursledon	d	18 16						19 19				20 16					21 16			22 16					23 16
Hamble	d	18 19						19 23				20 19					21 19			22 19					23 19
Netley	d	18 21						19 25				20 21					21 21			22 21					23 21
Sholing	d	18 25						19 29				20 25					21 25			22 25					23 25
Woolston	d	18 27						19 31				20 27					21 27			22 27					23 27
Bitterne	d	18 31						19 34				20 31					21 31			22 31					23 31
Eastleigh	a					19 04					20 04					21 04			22 04					23 04	
Southampton Airport Parkway	a																								
St Denys	d	18 34						19 38				20 34					21 34			22 34					23 34
Southampton Central ⛴	a	18 40		18 42	18 53		19 24	19 43	19 48	19 53		20 40		20 46	20 53		21 40	21 45		22 40	22 44	22 53			23 40

		SW 1
Portsmouth Harbour ⛴	d	23 17
Portsmouth & Southsea	d	23 22
Fratton	d	23 26
Hilsea	d	23 30
Chichester 4	d	
Havant	d	
Cosham	d	23 35
Portchester	d	23 40
Fareham	a	23 45
	d	23 46
Swanwick	d	
Bursledon	d	
Hamble	d	
Netley	d	
Sholing	d	
Woolston	d	
Bitterne	d	
Eastleigh	a	00 04
Southampton Airport Parkway	a	
St Denys	d	
Southampton Central ⛴	a	

Sundays

19 February to 25 March

		SW 1	SW ◇1	SW 1	SW 1	SW 1	SW 1	SN ◇1	SW 1	SW 1		SN ◇1	GW R	SW 1 (trolley)	SW 1	SN ◇1	SW 1 (trolley)	SW 1	SN ◇1	GW ◇		SW 1 (trolley)	SW 1	SN ◇1	SW 1 (trolley)
Portsmouth Harbour ⛴	d	23p24			06 37	07 17			08 17				09 08	09 17			10 17			11 08		11 17			12 17
Portsmouth & Southsea	d	23p29			06 42	07 22	07 42		08 22	08 42			09 12	09 22	09 42		10 22	10 42		11 12		11 22	11 42		12 22
Fratton	d	23p33			06 46	07 26	07 46		08 26	08 46			09 16	09 26	09 46		10 26	10 46		11 16		11 26	11 46		12 26
Hilsea	d	23p37			06 50	07 30	07 50		08 30	08 50				09 30	09 50		10 30	10 50				11 30	11 50		12 30
Chichester 4	d							07 45				08 45				09 45			10 45					11 45	
Havant	d							07 58				08 58				09 58			10 58					11 58	
Cosham	d	23p42			06 55	07 35	07 55	08 05	08 35	08 55		09 05	09 23	09 35	09 55	10 06	10 35	10 55	11 06	11 23		11 35	11 55	12 05	12 35
Portchester	d	23p47			07 00	07 40	08 00		08 40	09 00				09 40	10 00		10 40	11 00				11 40	12 00		12 40
Fareham	a	23p52			07 05	07 45	08 05	08 13	08 45	09 05		09 13	09 31	09 45	10 05	10 14	10 45	11 05	11 14	11 31		11 45	12 05	12 13	12 45
	d	23p53			07 06	07 46	08 06	08 14	08 46	09 06		09 14	09 32	09 46	10 06	10 15	10 46	11 06	11 15	11 32		11 46	12 06	12 14	12 46
Swanwick	d				07 12		08 12	08 20		09 12		09 20			10 12	10 21		11 12	11 21				12 12	12 20	
Bursledon	d				07 16		08 16			09 16					10 16			11 16					12 16		
Hamble	d				07 19		08 19			09 19					10 19			11 19					12 19		
Netley	d				07 21		08 21			09 21					10 21			11 21					12 21		
Sholing	d				07 25		08 25			09 25					10 25			11 25					12 25		
Woolston	d				07 27		08 27			09 27					10 27			11 27					12 27		
Bitterne	d				07 31		08 31			09 31					10 31			11 31					12 31		
Eastleigh	a	00 11				08 04			09 04					10 04			11 04					12 04			13 04
Southampton Airport Parkway	a																								
St Denys	d				07 34		08 34			09 34					10 34			11 34					12 34		
Southampton Central ⛴	a		00 34	02 56	07 40		08 40	08 44		09 40		09 44	09 53		10 40	10 44		11 40	11 45	11 53			12 40	12 44	

Table 165

Sundays

19 February to 25 March

Portsmouth and Fareham - Southampton

Network Diagram - see first Page of Table 165

		SW	SN	GW	SW	SW		SN	GW	SW	SW	SN	GW	SW	SW	SN		GW	SW	GW	SW	SN	GW	SW	SW
		1	◇1	◇	1 trolley	1		◇1	◇	1 trolley	1	◇1	R	1 trolley	1	◇1		◇	1 trolley	◇	1	◇1	◇	1	1
Portsmouth Harbour ⛴	d			13 08	13 17				14 08	14 17			15 08	15 17				16 08	16 17				17 08	17 17	
Portsmouth & Southsea	d	12 42		13 12	13 22	13 42			14 12	14 22	14 42		15 12	15 22	15 42			16 12	16 22		16 42		17 12	17 22	17 42
Fratton	d	12 46		13 16	13 26	13 46			14 16	14 26	14 46		15 16	15 26	15 46			16 16	16 26		16 46		17 16	17 26	17 46
Hilsea	d	12 50			13 30	13 50				14 30	14 50			15 30	15 50				16 30		16 50			17 30	17 50
Chichester 4	d		12 45					13 45				14 45				15 45				16 34		16 45			
Havant	d		12 58					13 58				14 58				15 58				16 48		16 58			
Cosham	d	12 55	13 05	13 23	13 35	13 55		14 05	14 23	14 35	14 55	15 05	15 23	15 35	15 55	16 05		16 23	16 35	16 55	16 59	17 05	17 23	17 35	17 55
Portchester	d	13 00			13 40	14 00				14 40	15 00			15 40	16 00				16 40		17 03			17 40	18 00
Fareham	a	13 05	13 13	13 31	13 45	14 05		14 13	14 31	14 45	15 05	15 13	15 31	15 45	16 05	16 13		16 31	16 45	17 02	17 08	17 14	17 31	17 45	18 05
	d	13 06	13 14	13 32	13 46	14 06		14 14	14 32	14 46	15 06	15 14	15 32	15 46	16 06	16 14		16 32	16 46	17 03	17 09	17 15	17 32	17 46	18 06
Swanwick	d	13 12	13 20			14 12		14 20			15 12	15 20			16 12	16 20					17 16	17 22			18 12
Bursledon	d	13 16				14 16					15 16				16 16						17 19				18 16
Hamble	d	13 19				14 19					15 19				16 19						17 23				18 19
Netley	d	13 21				14 21					15 21				16 21						17 25				18 21
Sholing	d	13 25				14 25					15 25				16 25						17 29				18 25
Woolston	d	13 27				14 27					15 27				16 27						17 31				18 27
Bitterne	d	13 31				14 31					15 31				16 31						17 34				18 31
Eastleigh	a				14 04					15 04				16 04					17 04					18 04	
Southampton Airport Parkway	a																								
St Denys	d	13 34				14 34					15 34				16 34						17 38				18 34
Southampton Central ⛴	a	13 40	13 44	13 53		14 40		14 44	14 53		15 40	15 44	15 53		16 40	16 44		16 53		17 24	17 43	17 48	17 53		18 40

		SN		GW	SW	GW	SW	SN	GW	SW	SW	SN		GW	SW	SW	SN	SW	SW	SN	GW	SW		SW	SW
		◇1		◇	1	◇	1	◇1	◇	1	1	◇1		◇	1	1	◇1	1	1	◇1		1		1	1
Portsmouth Harbour ⛴	d			18 08	18 17				19 08	19 17				20 08	20 17			21 17			22 03	22 17			23 17
Portsmouth & Southsea	d			18 12	18 22		18 42		19 12	19 22	19 42			20 12	20 22	20 42		21 22	21 42		22 12	22 22		22 42	23 22
Fratton	d			18 16	18 26		18 46		19 16	19 26	19 46			20 16	20 26	20 46		21 26	21 46		22 16	22 26		22 46	23 26
Hilsea	d				18 30		18 50			19 30	19 50				20 30	20 50		21 30	21 50			22 30		22 50	23 30
Chichester 4	d	17 45				18 34		18 45				19 45					20 45			21 45					
Havant	d	17 58				18 48		18 58				19 58					20 58			21 58					
Cosham	d	18 05		18 23	18 35	18 55	18 59	19 05	19 23	19 35	19 55	20 05			20 35	20 55	21 07	21 35	21 55	22 05		22 35		22 55	23 35
Portchester	d				18 40		19 03			19 40	20 00				20 40	21 00		21 40	22 00			22 40		23 00	23 40
Fareham	a	18 13		18 31	18 45	19 02	19 08	19 13	19 31	19 45	20 05	20 13		20 31	20 45	21 05	21 15	21 45	22 05	22 13	22 31	22 45		23 05	23 45
	d	18 14		18 32	18 46	19 03	19 09	19 14	19 32	19 46	20 06	20 14		20 32	20 46	21 06	21 16	21 46	22 06	22 14	22 32	22 46		23 06	23 46
Swanwick	d	18 20					19 16	19 22			20 12	20 20				21 12	21 22		22 12	22 20				23 12	
Bursledon	d						19 19				20 16					21 16			22 16					23 16	
Hamble	d						19 23				20 19					21 19			22 19					23 19	
Netley	d						19 25				20 21					21 21			22 21					23 21	
Sholing	d						19 29				20 25					21 25			22 25					23 25	
Woolston	d						19 31				20 27					21 27			22 27					23 27	
Bitterne	d						19 34				20 31					21 31			22 31					23 31	
Eastleigh	a				19 04					20 04					21 04			22 04				23 04			00 04
Southampton Airport Parkway	a																								
St Denys	d						19 38				20 34					21 34			22 34					23 34	
Southampton Central ⛴	a	18 42		18 53		19 24	19 43	19 48	19 53		20 40	20 46		20 53		21 40	21 45		22 40	22 44	22 53			23 40	

Sundays

from 1 April

		SW	SW	SW	SW	SW	SW	SN	SW	SW		SN	GW	SW	SW	SN	SW	SW	SN	GW		SW	SW	SN	SW
		1	◇1	1	1	1	1	◇1	1	1		◇1	R	1 trolley	1	◇1	1 trolley	1	◇1	◇		1 trolley	1	◇1	1 trolley
Portsmouth Harbour ⛴	d	23p24			06 37	07 17			08 17				09 08	09 17			10 17			11 08		11 17			12 17
Portsmouth & Southsea	d	23p29			06 42	07 22	07 42		08 22	08 42			09 12	09 22	09 42		10 22	10 42		11 12		11 22	11 42		12 22
Fratton	d	23p33			06 46	07 26	07 46		08 26	08 46			09 16	09 26	09 46		10 26	10 46		11 16		11 26	11 46		12 26
Hilsea	d	23p37			06 50	07 30	07 50		08 30	08 50				09 30	09 50		10 30	10 50				11 30	11 50		12 30
Chichester 4	d							07 45				08 45				09 45			10 45					11 45	
Havant	d							07 58				08 58				09 58			10 58					11 58	
Cosham	d	23p42			06 55	07 35	07 55	08 05	08 35	08 55		09 05	09 23	09 35	09 55	10 06	10 35	10 55	11 06	11 23		11 35	11 55	12 05	12 35
Portchester	d	23p47			07 00	07 40	08 00		08 40	09 00				09 40	10 00		10 40	11 00				11 40	12 00		12 40
Fareham	a	23p52			07 05	07 45	08 05	08 13	08 45	09 05		09 13	09 31	09 45	10 05	10 14	10 45	11 05	11 14	11 31		11 45	12 05	12 13	12 45
	d	23p53			07 06	07 46	08 06	08 14	08 46	09 06		09 14	09 32	09 46	10 06	10 15	10 46	11 06	11 15	11 32		11 46	12 06	12 14	12 46
Swanwick	d				07 12		08 12	08 20		09 12		09 20			10 12	10 21		11 12	11 21				12 12	12 20	
Bursledon	d				07 16		08 16			09 16					10 16			11 16					12 16		
Hamble	d				07 19		08 19			09 19					10 19			11 19					12 19		
Netley	d				07 21		08 21			09 21					10 21			11 21					12 21		
Sholing	d				07 25		08 25			09 25					10 25			11 25					12 25		
Woolston	d				07 27		08 27			09 27					10 27			11 27					12 27		
Bitterne	d				07 31		08 31			09 31					10 31			11 31					12 31		
Eastleigh	a	00 11				08 04			09 04					10 04			11 04					12 04			13 04
Southampton Airport Parkway	a																								
St Denys	d				07 34		08 34			09 34					10 34			11 34					12 34		
Southampton Central ⛴	a		00 34	02 56	07 40		08 40	08 44		09 40		09 44	09 53		10 40	10 44		11 40	11 45	11 53			12 40	12 44	

Table 165

Sundays

from 1 April

Portsmouth and Fareham - Southampton

Network Diagram - see first Page of Table 165

		SW 1	SN ◇1	GW ◇	SW 1 🛒	SW 1		SN ◇1	GW ◇	SW 1 🛒	SW 1	SN ◇1	GW R	SW 1 🛒	SW 1	SN ◇1		GW ◇	SW 1 🛒	GW ◇	SW 1	SN ◇1	GW ◇	SW 1	SW 1
Portsmouth Harbour ⛴	d			13 08	13 17				14 08	14 17			15 08	15 17				16 08	16 17				17 08	17 17	
Portsmouth & Southsea	d	12 42		13 12	13 22	13 42			14 12	14 22	14 42		15 12	15 22	15 42			16 12	16 22		16 42		17 12	17 22	17 42
Fratton	d	12 46		13 16	13 26	13 46			14 16	14 26	14 46		15 16	15 26	15 46			16 16	16 26		16 46		17 16	17 26	17 46
Hilsea	d	12 50			13 30	13 50				14 30	14 50			15 30	15 50				16 30		16 50			17 30	17 50
Chichester 4	d		12 45					13 45				14 45				15 45				16 34		16 45			
Havant	d		12 58					13 58				14 58				15 58				16 48		16 58			
Cosham	d	12 55	13 05	13 23	13 35	13 55		14 05	14 23	14 35	14 55	15 05	15 23	15 35	15 55	16 05		16 23	16 35	16 55	16 59	17 05	17 23	17 35	17 55
Portchester	d	13 00			13 40	14 00				14 40	15 00			15 40	16 00				16 40		17 03			17 40	18 00
Fareham	a	13 05	13 13	13 31	13 45	14 05		14 13	14 31	14 45	15 05	15 13	15 31	15 45	16 05	16 13		16 31	16 45	17 02	17 08	17 14	17 31	17 45	18 05
	d	13 06	13 14	13 32	13 46	14 06		14 14	14 32	14 46	15 06	15 14	15 32	15 46	16 06	16 14		16 32	16 46	17 03	17 09	17 15	17 32	17 46	18 06
Swanwick	d	13 12	13 20			14 12		14 20			15 12	15 20			16 12	16 20					17 16	17 22			18 12
Bursledon	d	13 16				14 16					15 16				16 16						17 19				18 16
Hamble	d	13 19				14 19					15 19				16 19						17 23				18 19
Netley	d	13 21				14 21					15 21				16 21						17 25				18 21
Sholing	d	13 25				14 25					15 25				16 25						17 29				18 25
Woolston	d	13 27				14 27					15 27				16 27						17 31				18 27
Bitterne	d	13 31				14 31					15 31				16 31						17 34				18 31
Eastleigh	a				14 04					15 04				16 04					17 04					18 04	
Southampton Airport Parkway	a																								
St Denys	d	13 34				14 34					15 34				16 34						17 38				18 34
Southampton Central ⛴	a	13 40	13 44	13 53		14 40		14 44	14 53		15 40	15 44	15 53		16 40	16 44		16 53		17 24	17 43	17 48	17 53		18 40

		SN ◇1		GW ◇	SW 1	GW ◇	SW 1	SN ◇1	GW ◇	SW 1	SW 1	SN ◇1		GW ◇	SW 1	SW 1	SN ◇1	SW 1	SW 1	SN ◇1	GW	SW 1		SW 1	SW 1
Portsmouth Harbour ⛴	d			18 08	18 17				19 08	19 17				20 08	20 17			21 17			22 03	22 17			23 17
Portsmouth & Southsea	d			18 12	18 22		18 42		19 12	19 22	19 42			20 12	20 22	20 42		21 22	21 42		22 12	22 22		22 42	23 22
Fratton	d			18 16	18 26		18 46		19 16	19 26	19 46			20 16	20 26	20 46		21 26	21 46		22 16	22 26		22 46	23 26
Hilsea	d				18 30		18 50			19 30	19 50				20 30	20 50		21 30	21 50			22 30		22 50	23 30
Chichester 4	d	17 45				18 34		18 45				19 45					20 45			21 45					
Havant	d	17 58				18 48		18 58				19 58					20 58			21 58					
Cosham	d	18 05		18 23	18 35	18 55	18 59	19 05	19 23	19 35	19 55	20 05			20 35	20 55	21 07	21 35	21 55	22 05		22 35		22 55	23 35
Portchester	d				18 40		19 03			19 40	20 00				20 40	21 00		21 40	22 00			22 40		23 00	23 40
Fareham	a	18 13		18 31	18 45	19 02	19 08	19 13	19 31	19 45	20 05	20 13		20 31	20 45	21 05	21 15	21 45	22 05	22 13	22 31	22 45		23 05	23 45
	d	18 14		18 32	18 46	19 03	19 09	19 14	19 32	19 46	20 06	20 14		20 32	20 46	21 06	21 16	21 46	22 06	22 14	22 32	22 46		23 06	23 46
Swanwick	d	18 20					19 16	19 22			20 12	20 20				21 12	21 22		22 12	22 20				23 12	
Bursledon	d						19 19				20 16					21 16			22 16					23 16	
Hamble	d						19 23				20 19					21 19			22 19					23 19	
Netley	d						19 25				20 21					21 21			22 21					23 21	
Sholing	d						19 29				20 25					21 25			22 25					23 25	
Woolston	d						19 31				20 27					21 27			22 27					23 27	
Bitterne	d						19 34				20 31					21 31			22 31					23 31	
Eastleigh	a				19 04					20 04					21 04			22 04				23 04			00 04
Southampton Airport Parkway	a																								
St Denys	d						19 38				20 34					21 34			22 34					23 34	
Southampton Central ⛴	a	18 42		18 53		19 24	19 43	19 48	19 53		20 40	20 46		20 53		21 40	21 45		22 40	22 44	22 53			23 40	

Mondays to Fridays

To and from the Isle of Wight via Portsmouth and Ryde

Network Diagram - see first Page of Table 165

Miles			IL	IL	IL	IL	IL	IL	IL	IL	IL		IL	IL	IL	IL	IL	IL	IL	IL	IL		IL	IL	IL
—	**Portsmouth Harbour** ⛴	d																							
0	**Ryde Pier Head**	d	05 49	06 07	06 49	07 07	07 49	08 07	08 49	09 07	09 49		10 07	10 49	11 07	11 49	12 07	12 49	13 07	13 49	14 07		14 49	15 07	15 49
—	**Ryde Esplanade**	d	05 51	06 09	06 52	07 09	07 52	08 09	08 52	09 09	09 52		10 09	10 52	11 09	11 52	12 09	12 52	13 09	13 52	14 09		14 52	15 09	15 52
1¼	Ryde St Johns Road	d	05 55	06 13	06 55	07 13	07 55	08 13	08 55	09 13	09 55		10 13	10 55	11 13	11 55	12 13	12 55	13 13	13 55	14 13		14 55	15 13	15 55
2¼	Smallbrook Junction §	d												10 58		11 58	12 15	12 58	13 15				14 58	15 15	15 58
4¾	Brading	d	06 02	06 20	07 03	07 20	08 03	08 20	09 03	09 20	10 03		10 20	11 03	11 20	12 03	12 20	13 03	13 20	14 03	14 20		15 03	15 20	16 03
6½	Sandown	d	06 07	06 25	07 07	07 25	08 07	08 25	09 07	09 25	10 07		10 25	11 07	11 25	12 07	12 25	13 07	13 25	14 07	14 25		15 07	15 25	16 07
7¼	Lake	d	06 09	06 27	07 10	07 27	08 10	08 27	09 10	09 27	10 10		10 27	11 10	11 27	12 10	12 27	13 10	13 27	14 10	14 27		15 10	15 27	16 10
8½	**Shanklin**	a	06 12	06 30	07 13	07 30	08 13	08 30	09 13	09 30	10 13		10 30	11 13	11 30	12 13	12 30	13 13	13 30	14 13	14 30		15 13	15 30	16 13

		IL	IL	IL	IL	IL	IL		IL	IL	IL	IL	IL	IL
Portsmouth Harbour ⛴	d													
Ryde Pier Head	d	16 07	16 49	17 07	17 49	18 07	18 49		19 07	19 49	20 07	20 45	21 45	22 45
Ryde Esplanade	d	16 09	16 52	17 09	17 52	18 09	18 52		19 09	19 52	20 09	20 47	21 47	22 47
Ryde St Johns Road	d	16 13	16 55	17 13	17 55	18 13	18 55		19 13	19 55	20 13	20 51	21 51	22a51
Smallbrook Junction §	d	16 15												
Brading	d	16 20	17 03	17 20	18 03	18 20	19 03		19 20	20 03	20 20	20 57	21 57	
Sandown	d	16 25	17 07	17 25	18 07	18 25	19 07		19 25	20 07	20 25	21 01	22 01	
Lake	d	16 27	17 10	17 27	18 10	18 27	19 10		19 27	20 10	20 27	21 04	22 04	
Shanklin	a	16 30	17 13	17 30	18 13	18 30	19 13		19 30	20 13	20 30	21 07	22 07	

Saturdays

		IL	IL	IL	IL	IL	IL	IL	IL	IL		IL	IL	IL	IL	IL	IL	IL	IL	IL		IL	IL	IL	IL
Portsmouth Harbour ⛴	d																								
Ryde Pier Head	d	05 49	06 07	06 49	07 07	07 49	08 07	08 49	09 07	09 49		10 07	10 49	11 07	11 49	12 07	12 49	13 07	13 49	14 07		14 49	15 07	15 49	16 07
Ryde Esplanade	d	05 51	06 09	06 52	07 09	07 52	08 09	08 52	09 09	09 52		10 09	10 52	11 09	11 52	12 09	12 52	13 09	13 52	14 09		14 52	15 09	15 52	16 09
Ryde St Johns Road	d	05 55	06 13	06 55	07 13	07 55	08 13	08 55	09 13	09 55		10 13	10 55	11 13	11 55	12 13	12 55	13 13	13 55	14 13		14 55	15 13	15 55	16 13
Smallbrook Junction §	d												10 58		11 58	12 15	12 58	13 15				14 58	15 15	15 58	16 15
Brading	d	06 02	06 20	07 03	07 20	08 03	08 20	09 03	09 20	10 03		10 20	11 03	11 20	12 03	12 20	13 03	13 20	14 03	14 20		15 03	15 20	16 03	16 20
Sandown	d	06 07	06 25	07 07	07 25	08 07	08 25	09 07	09 25	10 07		10 25	11 07	11 25	12 07	12 25	13 07	13 25	14 07	14 25		15 07	15 25	16 07	16 25
Lake	d	06 09	06 27	07 10	07 27	08 10	08 27	09 10	09 27	10 10		10 27	11 10	11 27	12 10	12 27	13 10	13 27	14 10	14 27		15 10	15 27	16 10	16 27
Shanklin	a	06 12	06 30	07 13	07 30	08 13	08 30	09 13	09 30	10 13		10 30	11 13	11 30	12 13	12 30	13 13	13 30	14 13	14 30		15 13	15 30	16 13	16 30

		IL	IL	IL	IL	IL		IL	IL	IL	IL	IL	IL
Portsmouth Harbour ⛴	d												
Ryde Pier Head	d	16 49	17 07	17 49	18 07	18 49		19 07	19 49	20 07	20 45	21 45	22 45
Ryde Esplanade	d	16 52	17 09	17 52	18 09	18 52		19 09	19 52	20 09	20 47	21 47	22 47
Ryde St Johns Road	d	16 55	17 13	17 55	18 13	18 55		19 13	19 55	20 13	20 51	21 51	22a51
Smallbrook Junction §	d												
Brading	d	17 03	17 20	18 03	18 20	19 03		19 20	20 03	20 20	20 57	21 57	
Sandown	d	17 07	17 25	18 07	18 25	19 07		19 25	20 07	20 25	21 01	22 01	
Lake	d	17 10	17 27	18 10	18 27	19 10		19 27	20 10	20 27	21 04	22 04	
Shanklin	a	17 13	17 30	18 13	18 30	19 13		19 30	20 13	20 30	21 07	22 07	

Sundays

		IL	IL	IL A	IL	IL A	IL	IL A	IL	IL A		IL	IL A	IL	IL	IL	IL	IL	IL	IL		IL	IL	IL	IL
Portsmouth Harbour ⛴	d																								
Ryde Pier Head	d	06 49	07 49		08 49	09⌇07	09 49	10⌇07	10 49	11⌇07		11 49	12⌇07	12 49	13 07	13 49	14 07	14 49	15 07	15 49		16 07	16 49	17 07	17 49
Ryde Esplanade	d	06 52	07 52		08 52	09⌇09	09 52	10⌇09	10 52	11⌇09		11 52	12⌇09	12 52	13 09	13 52	14 09	14 52	15 09	15 52		16 09	16 52	17 09	17 52
Ryde St Johns Road	d	06 55	07 55	08⌇13	08 55	09⌇13	09 55	10⌇13	10 55	11⌇13		11 55	12⌇13	12 55	13 13	13 55	14 13	14 55	15 13	15 55		16 13	16 55	17 13	17 55
Smallbrook Junction §	d			⌇		⌇		⌇	10 58	⌇		11 58	12⌇15	12 58	13 15			14 58	15 15	15 58		16 15			
Brading	d	07 03	08 03	08⌇20	09 03	09⌇20	10 03	10⌇20	11 03	11⌇20		12 03	12⌇20	13 03	13 20	14 03	14 20	15 03	15 20	16 03		16 20	17 03	17 20	18 03
Sandown	d	07 07	08 07	08⌇25	09 07	09⌇25	10 07	10⌇25	11 07	11⌇25		12 07	12⌇25	13 07	13 25	14 07	14 25	15 07	15 25	16 07		16 25	17 07	17 25	18 07
Lake	d	07 10	08 10	08⌇27	09 10	09⌇27	10 10	10⌇27	11 10	11⌇27		12 10	12⌇27	13 10	13 27	14 10	14 27	15 10	15 27	16 10		16 27	17 10	17 27	18 10
Shanklin	a	07 13	08 13	08⌇30	09 13	09⌇30	10 13	10⌇30	11 13	11⌇30		12 13	12⌇30	13 13	13 30	14 13	14 30	15 13	15 30	16 13		16 30	17 13	17 30	18 13

		IL	IL	IL A	IL	IL A		IL	IL	IL
Portsmouth Harbour ⛴	d									
Ryde Pier Head	d	18 07	18 49	19⌇07	19 49	20⌇07		20 45	21 45	22 45
Ryde Esplanade	d	18 09	18 52	19⌇09	19 52	20⌇09		20 47	21 47	22 47
Ryde St Johns Road	d	18 13	18 55	19⌇13	19 55	20a13		20 51	21 51	22a51
Smallbrook Junction §	d			⌇						
Brading	d	18 20	19 03	19⌇20	20 03			20 57	21 57	
Sandown	d	18 25	19 07	19⌇25	20 07			21 01	22 01	
Lake	d	18 27	19 10	19⌇27	20 10			21 04	22 04	
Shanklin	a	18 30	19 13	19⌇30	20 13			21 07	22 07	

Mondays to Fridays

		IL	IL	IL	IL	IL	IL	IL	IL	IL		IL	IL	IL	IL	IL	IL	IL	IL	IL		IL	IL	IL	IL
Shanklin	d			06 18	06 38	07 18	07 38	08 18	08 38	09 18		09 38	10 18	10 38	11 18	11 38	12 18	12 38	13 18	13 38		14 18	14 38	15 18	15 38
Lake	d			06 21	06 41	07 21	07 41	08 21	08 41	09 21		09 41	10 21	10 41	11 21	11 41	12 21	12 41	13 21	13 41		14 21	14 41	15 21	15 41
Sandown	d			06 24	06 44	07 24	07 44	08 24	08 44	09 24		09 44	10 24	10 44	11 24	11 44	12 24	12 44	13 24	13 44		14 24	14 44	15 24	15 44
Brading	d			06 28	06 48	07 28	07 48	08 28	08 48	09 28		09 48	10 28	10 48	11 28	11 48	12 28	12 48	13 28	13 48		14 28	14 48	15 28	15 48
Smallbrook Junction §	d													10 53		11 53	12 33	12 53	13 33				14 53	15 33	15 53
Ryde St Johns Road	d	05 35	05 56	06 35	06 55	07 35	07 55	08 35	08 55	09 35		09 55	10 35	10 55	11 35	11 55	12 35	12 55	13 35	13 55		14 35	14 55	15 35	15 55
Ryde Esplanade	d	05 40	06 00	06 40	07 00	07 40	08 00	08 40	09 00	09 40		10 00	10 40	11 00	11 40	12 00	12 40	13 00	13 40	14 00		14 40	15 00	15 40	16 00
Ryde Pier Head	a	05 42	06 02	06 42	07 02	07 42	08 02	08 42	09 02	09 41		10 02	10 42	11 02	11 42	12 02	12 42	13 02	13 42	14 02		14 42	15 02	15 42	16 02
Portsmouth Harbour ⛴	a																								

§ Smallbrook Jn. is only open for access to the I.O.W Steam Railway. For days of operation please enquire locally.

A from 8 April

To and from the Isle of Wight via Portsmouth and Ryde

Network Diagram - see first Page of Table 165

Mondays to Fridays

		IL	IL	IL	IL	IL		IL	IL	IL	IL	IL	IL	IL
Shanklin	d	16 18	16 38	17 18	17 38	18 18		18 38	19 18	19 38	20 18	20 38	21 18	22 18
Lake	d	16 21	16 41	17 21	17 41	18 21		18 41	19 21	19 41	20 21	20 41	21 21	22 21
Sandown	d	16 24	16 44	17 24	17 44	18 24		18 44	19 24	19 44	20 24	20 44	21 24	22 24
Brading	d	16 28	16 48	17 28	17 48	18 28		18 48	19 28	19 48	20 28	20 48	21 28	22 28
Smallbrook Junction §	d	16 33												
Ryde St Johns Road	d	16 35	16 55	17 35	17 55	18 35		18 55	19 35	19 55	20 34	20a54	21 34	22 34
Ryde Esplanade	d	16 40	17 00	17 40	18 00	18 40		19 00	19 40	20 00	20 38		21 38	22 38
Ryde Pier Head	a	16 42	17 02	17 42	18 02	18 42		19 02	19 42	20 02	20 41		21 41	22 41
Portsmouth Harbour ⛴	a													

Saturdays

		IL	IL	IL	IL	IL	IL	IL	IL	IL		IL	IL	IL	IL	IL	IL	IL	IL	IL		IL	IL	IL	IL
Shanklin	d			06 18	06 38	07 18	07 38	08 18	08 38	09 18		09 38	10 18	10 38	11 18	11 38	12 18	12 38	13 18	13 38		14 18	14 38	15 18	15 38
Lake	d			06 21	06 41	07 21	07 41	08 21	08 41	09 21		09 41	10 21	10 41	11 21	11 41	12 21	12 41	13 21	13 41		14 21	14 41	15 21	15 41
Sandown	d			06 24	06 44	07 24	07 44	08 24	08 44	09 24		09 44	10 24	10 44	11 24	11 44	12 24	12 44	13 24	13 44		14 24	14 44	15 24	15 44
Brading	d			06 28	06 48	07 28	07 48	08 28	08 48	09 28		09 48	10 28	10 48	11 28	11 48	12 28	12 48	13 28	13 48		14 28	14 48	15 28	15 48
Smallbrook Junction §	d													10 53		11 53	12 33	12 53	13 33				14 53	15 33	15 53
Ryde St Johns Road	d	05 35	05 56	06 35	06 55	07 35	07 55	08 35	08 55	09 35		09 55	10 35	10 55	11 35	11 55	12 35	12 55	13 35	13 55		14 35	14 55	15 35	15 55
Ryde Esplanade	d	05 40	06 00	06 40	07 00	07 40	08 00	08 40	09 00	09 40		10 00	10 40	11 00	11 40	12 00	12 40	13 00	13 40	14 00		14 40	15 00	15 40	16 00
Ryde Pier Head	a	05 42	06 02	06 42	07 02	07 42	08 02	08 42	09 02	09 42		10 02	10 42	11 02	11 42	12 02	12 42	13 02	13 42	14 02		14 42	15 02	15 42	16 02
Portsmouth Harbour ⛴	a																								

		IL	IL	IL	IL	IL		IL	IL	IL	IL	IL	IL	IL
Shanklin	d	16 18	16 38	17 18	17 38	18 18		18 38	19 18	19 38	20 18	20 38	21 18	22 18
Lake	d	16 21	16 41	17 21	17 41	18 21		18 41	19 21	19 41	20 21	20 41	21 21	22 21
Sandown	d	16 24	16 44	17 24	17 44	18 24		18 44	19 24	19 44	20 24	20 44	21 24	22 24
Brading	d	16 28	16 48	17 28	17 48	18 28		18 48	19 28	19 48	20 28	20 48	21 28	22 28
Smallbrook Junction §	d	16 33												
Ryde St Johns Road	d	16 35	16 55	17 35	17 55	18 35		18 55	19 35	19 55	20 34	20a54	21 34	22 34
Ryde Esplanade	d	16 40	17 00	17 40	18 00	18 40		19 00	19 40	20 00	20 38		21 38	22 38
Ryde Pier Head	a	16 42	17 02	17 42	18 02	18 42		19 02	19 42	20 02	20 41		21 41	22 41
Portsmouth Harbour ⛴	a													

Sundays

		IL	IL	IL	IL A	IL	IL A	IL	IL A	IL		IL A	IL	IL A	IL	IL	IL	IL	IL	IL		IL	IL	IL	IL
Shanklin	d		07 18	08 18	08 38	09 18	09 38	10 18	10 38	11 18		11 38	12 18	12 38	13 18	13 38	14 18	14 38	15 18	15 38		16 18	16 38	17 18	17 38
Lake	d		07 21	08 21	08 41	09 21	09 41	10 21	10 41	11 21		11 41	12 21	12 41	13 21	13 41	14 21	14 41	15 21	15 41		16 21	16 41	17 21	17 41
Sandown	d		07 24	08 24	08 44	09 24	09 44	10 24	10 44	11 24		11 44	12 24	12 44	13 24	13 44	14 24	14 44	15 24	15 44		16 24	16 44	17 24	17 44
Brading	d		07 28	08 28	08 48	09 28	09 48	10 28	10 48	11 28		11 48	12 28	12 48	13 28	13 48	14 28	14 48	15 28	15 48		16 28	16 48	17 28	17 48
Smallbrook Junction §	d								10 53			11 53	12 33	12 53	13 33			14 53	15 33	15 53		16 33			
Ryde St Johns Road	d	06 35	07 35	08 35	08 55	09 35	09 55	10 35	10 55	11 35		11 55	12 35	12 55	13 35	13 55	14 35	14 55	15 35	15 55		16 35	16 55	17 35	17 55
Ryde Esplanade	d	06 40	07 40	08 40	09 00	09 40	10 00	10 40	11 00	11 40		12 00	12 40	13 00	13 40	14 00	14 40	15 00	15 40	16 00		16 40	17 00	17 40	18 00
Ryde Pier Head	a	06 42	07 42	08 42	09 02	09 42	10 02	10 42	11 02	11 42		12 02	12 42	13 02	13 42	14 02	14 42	15 02	15 42	16 02		16 42	17 02	17 42	18 02
Portsmouth Harbour ⛴	a																								

		IL	IL B	IL A	IL	IL A		IL	IL	IL
Shanklin	d	18 18	18 38	18 38	19 18	19 38		20 18	21 18	22 18
Lake	d	18 21	18 41	18 41	19 21	19 41		20 21	21 21	22 21
Sandown	d	18 24	18 44	18 44	19 24	19 44		20 24	21 24	22 24
Brading	d	18 28	18 48	18 48	19 28	19 48		20 28	21 28	22 28
Smallbrook Junction §	d									
Ryde St Johns Road	d	18 35	18a54	18 55	19 35	19 55		20 34	21 34	22 34
Ryde Esplanade	d	18 40		18 59	19 40	20 00		20 38	21 38	22 38
Ryde Pier Head	a	18 42		19 02	19 42	20 02		20 41	21 41	22 41
Portsmouth Harbour ⛴	a									

§ Smallbrook Jn. is only open for access to the I.O.W Steam Railway. For days of operation please enquire locally.

A from 8 April

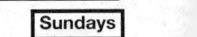

B until 1 April

London - East Croydon and Purley

COMPLETE SERVICE

	SN	SN	SN	SN	SN	SN	SN	SN	SN		SN	FC	SN	SN	SN	FC	SN	SN	SN		FC	FC	SN	FC
	MX 1	MO	MX	MX 1	MO	MO	MX 1	MO	MO 1		MX ◇1		1	MX			MX		◇1		1	1	1	1
London Victoria 15 ⊖ d				23p47	23p47		23p49	23p50			00 05		00 14		00 16			00 42	01 00				02 00	
Clapham Junction 10 d	23p40			23p53	23p53		23p56	23p56	00 05		00 11		00 20		00 24			00 50	01 08				02 08	
St Pancras International 15 ⊖ d																								
Farringdon 3 ⊖ d																								
City Thameslink 3 d																								
London Blackfriars 3 ⊖ d																								
London Bridge 4 ⊖ d		23p21	23p36			23p39						00 12		00 06		00 42	00 36				01 08	01 35		02 05
New Cross Gate d			23p41			23p44								00 11			00 41							
Norwood Junction 2 a			23p59			00 02								00 29			00 59							
East Croydon a	00 01	00 01	00 03	00 05	00 06	00 06	00 09	00 17	00 22		00 26	00 26	00 31	00 33	00 44	00 56	01 03	01 10	01 23		01 31	02 01	02 23	02 31
South Croydon 4 a			00 06			00 09		00 20						00 37										
Purley Oaks a			00 09			00 12		00 23						00 40										
Purley 4 a			00 12	00 11		00 15		00 26					00 37	00 43					01 29				02 29	

	SN	FC	FC	SN	FC		FC	SN	FC	FC	SN	SN	FC	SN	SN		SN	SN	FC	SN	SN	SN	SN	SN
	1		1	◇1	1		1	◇1	1	1	1	◇1	1	1	◇1		1		1		◇1	1	1	1
London Victoria 15 ⊖ d	03 00			04 00				05 02			05 25	05 32		05 53	06 02					06 13	06 21	06 24	06 32	
Clapham Junction 10 d	03 08			04 08				05 08			05 33	05 38		05 59	06 08					06 21	06 27	06 30	06 38	
St Pancras International 15 ⊖ d									04 54	05 12			05 32						06 02					
Farringdon 3 ⊖ d									04 59	05 18			05 38						06 08					
City Thameslink 3 d										05 21			05 41						06 11					
London Blackfriars 3 ⊖ d									05 04	05 24			05 44						06 14					
London Bridge 4 ⊖ d		03 05	03 35		04 05		04 35			05 30			05 50				06 08	06 06	06 20					06 38
New Cross Gate d																		06 11						
Norwood Junction 2 a											05 50							06 29						
East Croydon a	03 23	03 31	04 01	04 23	04 31		05 01	05 20	05 29	05 47	05 54	05 48	06 05	06 09	06 17		06 22	06 33	06 33	06 43	06 38	06 40	06 48	06 52
South Croydon 4 a											05 57							06 36						
Purley Oaks a																		06 40						
Purley 4 a	03 29			04 29				05 25				05 53			06 23			06 43		06 51	06 43		06 55	

	FC		SN	SN	SN	SN	SN	FC	SN	SN	SN		SN	FC	SN	SN	SN	SN	SN	SN	SN		SN	SN
	1				◇1	1	1	1	1	1			1	1	◇1	1		1			1		1	1
London Victoria 15 ⊖ d				06 44	06 47	06 51	06 54			07 02			07 10		07 17				07 20	07 23				07 32
Clapham Junction 10 d				06 50	06 53	06 57	07 00			07 08			07 16		07 23				07 28	07 30				07 38
St Pancras International 15 ⊖ d	06 22							06 38						06 58										
Farringdon 3 ⊖ d	06 28							06 44						07 04										
City Thameslink 3 d	06 31							06 47						07 07										
London Blackfriars 3 ⊖ d	06 34							06 50						07 09										
London Bridge 4 ⊖ d	06 42		06 36					07 00	07 03		06 54			07 16		07 19	07 06	07 27			07 30		07 33	
New Cross Gate d			06 41								06 59						07 11						07 38	
Norwood Junction 2 a			06 59								07 17					07 29	07 29	07 38			07 41			
East Croydon a	06 54		07 03	07 12	07 03	07 06	07 10	07 14	07 16	07 17	07 21		07 26	07 30	07 33	07 33	07 37	07 42	07 49	07 44	07 45		07 48	07 52
South Croydon 4 a			07 06								07 24						07 40		07 52					
Purley Oaks a			07 09								07 28						07 43		07 55					
Purley 4 a			07 12							07 23	07 31						07 46		07 58	07 52				

	SN	FC	SN	SN	SN	SN	SN		SN	SN	SN	SN	SN	SN	SN	FC	SN		SN	SN	SN	SN	FC	SN
	1	1			◇1		1		◇1	1	1	◇1	1	◇1	1	1	1					◇1	1	1
London Victoria 15 ⊖ d	07 36			07 45	07 47				07 52			08 02		08 07			08 10				08 15	08 17		
Clapham Junction 10 d	07 42			07 51	07 53				07 58			08 08		08 13			08 16				08 23	08 23		
St Pancras International 15 ⊖ d		07 20														07 44							07 56	
Farringdon 3 ⊖ d		07 26														07 50							08 02	
City Thameslink 3 d		07 29														07 53							08 05	
London Blackfriars 3 ⊖ d		07 32														07 56							08 08	
London Bridge 4 ⊖ d		07 42	07 44			07 36	07 53			07 56	08 02		08 00		08 08				08 14	08 06			08 18	08 23
New Cross Gate d			07 49			07 41							08 08							08 11				
Norwood Junction 2 a						07 59				08 07			08 16						08 27	08 29				
East Croydon a	07 51	07 54	08 00	08 12	08 02	08 03	08 05		08 09	08 10	08 15	08 18	08 20	08 22	08 22	08 26	08 26		08 30	08 33	08 44	08 33	08 37	08 37
South Croydon 4 a				08 15		08 06									08 26					08 36	08 47			
Purley Oaks a				08 18		08 09														08 39	08 50			
Purley 4 a	07 57			08 21		08 12							08 25						08 38	08 42	08 54			

	SN	SN	SN		SN	SN	SN	FC	SN	SN	SN	SN	SN		SN	SN	SN	SN	SN	SN	SN	FC	SN	
	◇1	1			◇1 (trolley)	1	◇1 (trolley)	1	1			◇1 (trolley)	1			◇1	1	◇1 (trolley)	1	◇1 (trolley)	1	1	1	
London Victoria 15 ⊖ d	08 21				08 32		08 36				08 43	08 47				08 51	08 53	09 02		09 06				
Clapham Junction 10 d	08 27				08 38		08 43				08 51	08 53	08 36				08 59	09 08		09 12				
St Pancras International 15 ⊖ d								08 20														08 48		
Farringdon 3 ⊖ d								08 26														08 54		
City Thameslink 3 d								08 29														08 57		
London Blackfriars 3 ⊖ d								08 32														09 00		
London Bridge 4 ⊖ d		08 25	08 27			08 30			08 45	08 47					08 36				09 03		09 08	09 12	09 15	
New Cross Gate d						08 36									08 41				09 08					
Norwood Junction 2 a		08 36				08 43			08 55						08 59				09 16				09 25	
East Croydon a	08 40	08 40	08 42		08 48	08 48	08 52	08 57	08 59	09 02	09 12	09 03	09 04		09 06	09 07	09 09	09 18	09 20	09 22	09 22	09 24	09 29	
South Croydon 4 a											09 15				09 09									
Purley Oaks a											09 18				09 12									
Purley 4 a						08 58			09 05	09 09	09 22				09 15				09 26				09 35	

London - East Croydon and Purley

COMPLETE SERVICE

	SN	SN	SN	SN	FC	SN	SN	SN	SN		FC	SN	SN	SN	SN	SN	SN	SN	FC		SN	SN	SN	SN
		◇1 🚲			1	1	◇1 🚲	1	◇1		1	1	1		◇1 🚲			◇1	1		1	◇1 🚲	1	◇1 🚲
London Victoria 15 ⊖ d	09 13	09 17				09 23	09 32		09 36					09 43	09 47			09 51			09 53	10 02		10 06
Clapham Junction 10 d	09 21	09 23				09 29	09 38		09 42			09 34		09 51	09 53						09 59	10 08		10 12
St Pancras International 15 ⊖ d					09 04						09 22								09 40					
Farringdon 3 ⊖ d					09 10						09 28								09 45					
City Thameslink 3 d					09 13						09 31								09 48					
London Blackfriars 3 ⊖ d					09 16						09 34								09 50					
London Bridge 4 ⊖ d			09 06	09 20	09 27			09 32			09 42		09 45			09 36	09 50		09 57				10 03	
New Cross Gate d			09 12					09 37								09 41							10 08	
Norwood Junction 2 a			09 30	09 32				09 45					09 55			09 59	10 02						10 16	
East Croydon a	09 42	09 32	09 33	09 36	09 39	09 39	09 48	09 49	09 52		09 54	09 57	09 59	10 12	10 02	10 03	10 06	10 07	10 09		10 09	10 17	10 20	10 22
South Croydon 4 a	09 45		09 36									10 01		10 15		10 06								
Purley Oaks a	09 48		09 39											10 18		10 09								
Purley 4 a	09 52		09 42	09 45				09 56					10 05	10 22		10 12	10 15						10 26	

	SN	FC	SN	SN	SN		SN	SN	FC	SN	SN	SN	SN	FC	SN		SN	SN	SN	SN	SN	SN	FC	SN
	1	1	1		◇1 🚲				1	1	◇1 🚲	1	◇1	1	1		1		◇1 🚲			◇1	1	1
London Victoria 15 ⊖ d				10 13	10 17					10 23	10 32		10 36					10 43	10 47			10 51		10 53
Clapham Junction 10 d				10 21	10 23					10 29	10 38		10 42		10 34			10 51	10 53					10 59
St Pancras International 15 ⊖ d		09 54							10 09					10 24									10 39	
Farringdon 3 ⊖ d		09 59							10 14					10 29									10 44	
City Thameslink 3 d		10 03							10 18					10 33									10 48	
London Blackfriars 3 ⊖ d		10 05							10 20					10 35									10 50	
London Bridge 4 ⊖ d	10 08	10 12	10 15				10 06	10 20	10 27			10 33		10 42			10 45			10 36	10 50		10 57	
New Cross Gate d							10 11					10 38								10 41				
Norwood Junction 2 a			10 25				10 29	10 32				10 46					10 55			10 59	11 02			
East Croydon a	10 22	10 24	10 29	10 42	10 32		10 33	10 36	10 39	10 39	10 48	10 50	10 52	10 54	10 57		10 59	11 12	11 02	11 03	11 06	11 07	11 09	11 09
South Croydon 4 a				10 45			10 36								11 01			11 15		11 06				
Purley Oaks a				10 48			10 39											11 18		11 09				
Purley 4 a			10 35	10 52			10 42	10 45				10 56					11 06	11 22		11 12	11 15			

	SN		SN	SN	SN	FC	SN	SN	SN	SN	SN		FC	SN	SN	SN	SN	FC	SN	SN	SN		SN	SN
	◇1		1	◇1	1	1	1		◇1				1	1	◇1	1	◇1 🚲	1	1	1			◇1	
London Victoria 15 ⊖ d	11 02			11 06				11 13	11 17					11 23	11 32		11 36				11 43		11 47	
Clapham Junction 10 d	11 08			11 12				11 21	11 23					11 29	11 38		11 42		11 34		11 51		11 53	
St Pancras International 15 ⊖ d						10 54							11 09					11 24						
Farringdon 3 ⊖ d						10 59							11 14					11 29						
City Thameslink 3 d						11 03							11 18					11 33						
London Blackfriars 3 ⊖ d						11 05							11 20					11 35						
London Bridge 4 ⊖ d			11 03		11 08	11 12	11 15			11 06	11 20		11 27			11 33		11 42		11 45				11 36
New Cross Gate d			11 08							11 11						11 38								11 41
Norwood Junction 2 a			11 16				11 25			11 29	11 32					11 46				11 55				11 59
East Croydon a	11 17		11 20	11 22	11 23	11 24	11 29	11 42	11 32	11 33	11 36		11 39	11 39	11 48	11 50	11 52	11 54	11 57	11 59	12 12		12 02	12 03
South Croydon 4 a								11 45		11 36									12 01		12 15			12 06
Purley Oaks a								11 48		11 39											12 18			12 09
Purley 4 a			11 26				11 35	11 52		11 42	11 45					11 56				12 05	12 22			12 12

	SN	SN	FC	SN	SN	SN	SN		SN	FC	SN	SN	SN	SN	SN	FC	SN		SN	SN	SN	FC	SN	SN
		◇1	1	1	◇1	1	◇1 🚲		1	1	1		◇1			1	1		◇1	1	◇1 🚲	1	1	1
London Victoria 15 ⊖ d		11 51		11 53	12 02		12 06					12 13	12 17				12 23		12 32		12 36			
Clapham Junction 10 d				11 59	12 08		12 12					12 21	12 23				12 29		12 38		12 42		12 34	
St Pancras International 15 ⊖ d			11 39							11 54						12 09						12 24		
Farringdon 3 ⊖ d			11 44							11 59						12 14						12 29		
City Thameslink 3 d			11 48							12 03						12 18						12 33		
London Blackfriars 3 ⊖ d			11 50							12 05						12 20						12 35		
London Bridge 4 ⊖ d	11 50		11 57			12 03			12 08	12 12	12 15			12 06	12 20	12 27				12 33		12 42		12 45
New Cross Gate d						12 08								12 11						12 38				
Norwood Junction 2 a	12 02					12 16					12 25			12 29	12 32					12 46				12 55
East Croydon a	12 06	12 07	12 09	12 09	12 17	12 20	12 22		12 22	12 24	12 29	12 42	12 32	12 33	12 36	12 39	12 39		12 48	12 50	12 52	12 54	12 57	12 59
South Croydon 4 a												12 45		12 36									13 01	
Purley Oaks a												12 48		12 39										
Purley 4 a	12 15					12 26					12 35	12 52		12 42	12 45					12 57				13 05

	SN	SN	SN		SN	SN	FC	SN	SN	SN	SN	SN	FC		SN	SN	SN	SN	SN	FC	SN	SN	SN	
		◇1				◇1	1	1	◇1	1	◇1 🚲	1	1		1		◇1			1	1	◇1 🚲	1	
London Victoria 15 ⊖ d	12 43	12 47				12 51		12 53	13 02		13 06					13 13	13 17				13 23	13 32		
Clapham Junction 10 d	12 51	12 53						12 59	13 08		13 12					13 21	13 23				13 29	13 38		
St Pancras International 15 ⊖ d							12 39						12 54							13 09				
Farringdon 3 ⊖ d							12 44						12 59							13 14				
City Thameslink 3 d							12 48						13 03							13 18				
London Blackfriars 3 ⊖ d							12 50						13 05							13 20				
London Bridge 4 ⊖ d			12 36		12 50		12 57			13 03		13 08	13 12		13 15			13 06	13 20	13 27			13 33	
New Cross Gate d			12 41							13 08								13 11					13 38	
Norwood Junction 2 a			12 59		13 02					13 16		13 19			13 25			13 29	13 32				13 46	
East Croydon a	13 12	13 02	13 03		13 06	13 07	13 09	13 09	13 17	13 20	13 22	13 23	13 24		13 29	13 42	13 32	13 33	13 36	13 39	13 39	13 48	13 50	
South Croydon 4 a	13 15		13 06													13 45		13 36						
Purley Oaks a	13 18		13 09													13 48		13 39						
Purley 4 a	13 22		13 12		13 15					13 26					13 35	13 52		13 42	13 45				13 56	

London - East Croydon and Purley

COMPLETE SERVICE

	SN	FC	SN	SN	SN	SN	SN	SN	SN		FC	SN	SN	SN	SN	SN	FC	SN	SN		SN	SN	SN	FC
	◇1	1	1	1		◇1			◇1		1	1	◇1	1	◇1	1	1	1			◇1			1
	🚲														🚲									
London Victoria 15 ⊖ d	13 36				13 43	13 47			13 51			13 53	14 02		14 06				14 13		14 17			
Clapham Junction 10 d	13 42		13 34		13 51	13 53						13 59	14 08		14 12				14 21		14 23			
St Pancras International 15 ⊖ d		13 24									13 39						13 54							14 09
Farringdon 3 ⊖ d		13 29									13 44						13 59							14 14
City Thameslink 3 d		13 33									13 48						14 03							14 18
London Blackfriars 3 ⊖ d		13 35									13 50						14 05							14 20
London Bridge 4 ⊖ d		13 42		13 45			13 36	13 50			13 57			14 03		14 08	14 12	14 15				14 06	14 20	14 27
New Cross Gate d							13 41							14 08								14 11		
Norwood Junction 2 a				13 55			13 59	14 02						14 16		14 19		14 25				14 29	14 32	
East Croydon a	13 52	13 54	13 57	13 59	14 12	14 02	14 03	14 06	14 07		14 09	14 09	14 17	14 20	14 22	14 23	14 25	14 29	14 42		14 32	14 33	14 36	14 39
South Croydon 4 a			14 01		14 15		14 06												14 45			14 36		
Purley Oaks a					14 18		14 09												14 48			14 39		
Purley 4 a				14 05	14 22		14 12	14 15						14 26				14 35	14 52			14 42	14 45	

	SN	SN	SN	SN	FC		SN	SN	SN	SN	SN	SN	SN	FC	SN		SN	SN	SN	SN	FC	SN	SN	SN
	1	◇1	1	◇1	1		1	1		◇1			◇1	1	1		◇1	1	◇1	1	1	1		◇1
		🚲		🚲															🚲					
London Victoria 15 ⊖ d	14 23	14 32		14 36					14 43	14 47			14 51		14 53		15 02		15 06				15 13	15 17
Clapham Junction 10 d	14 29	14 38		14 42			14 34		14 51	14 53					14 59		15 08		15 12				15 21	15 23
St Pancras International 15 ⊖ d					14 24									14 39							14 54			
Farringdon 3 ⊖ d					14 29									14 44							14 59			
City Thameslink 3 d					14 33									14 48							15 03			
London Blackfriars 3 ⊖ d					14 35									14 50							15 05			
London Bridge 4 ⊖ d			14 33		14 42			14 45			14 36	14 50		14 57				15 03		15 08	15 12	15 15		
New Cross Gate d			14 38								14 41							15 08						
Norwood Junction 2 a			14 46					14 55			14 59	15 02						15 16		15 19		15 25		
East Croydon a	14 40	14 48	14 50	14 52	14 54		14 57	14 59	15 12	15 02	15 03	15 06	15 07	15 09	15 09		15 17	15 20	15 22	15 23	15 24	15 29	15 42	15 32
South Croydon 4 a							15 01		15 15		15 06												15 45	
Purley Oaks a									15 18		15 09												15 48	
Purley 4 a			14 56					15 05	15 22		15 12	15 15						15 26				15 35	15 52	

	SN		SN	FC	SN	SN	SN	SN	SN	FC	SN		SN	SN	SN	SN	SN	SN	FC	SN	SN		SN	SN
				1	1	◇1	1	◇1	1	1	1		1		◇1			◇1	1	1	◇1		1	1
								🚲																🚲
London Victoria 15 ⊖ d					15 23	15 32		15 36						15 43	15 47			15 51		15 53	16 02			16 06
Clapham Junction 10 d					15 29	15 38		15 42			15 34			15 51	15 53					15 59	16 08			16 12
St Pancras International 15 ⊖ d				15 09						15 24									15 39					
Farringdon 3 ⊖ d				15 14						15 29									15 44					
City Thameslink 3 d				15 18						15 33									15 48					
London Blackfriars 3 ⊖ d				15 20						15 35									15 50					
London Bridge 4 ⊖ d	15 06		15 20	15 27			15 33		15 38	15 42			15 45			15 36	15 50		15 57				16 03	
New Cross Gate d	15 11						15 38									15 41							16 08	
Norwood Junction 2 a	15 29		15 32				15 46						15 55			15 59	16 02						16 16	
East Croydon a	15 33		15 36	15 39	15 40	15 47	15 50	15 52	15 52	15 54	15 57		15 59	16 12	16 02	16 03	16 06	16 07	16 09	16 09	16 17		16 20	16 22
South Croydon 4 a	15 36				15 43						16 01			16 15		16 06				16 12				
Purley Oaks a	15 39													16 18		16 09								
Purley 4 a	15 42		15 45				15 56						16 05	16 22		16 12	16 15						16 26	

	SN	FC	SN	SN	SN	SN	SN		SN	FC	SN	SN	SN	SN	SN	SN	SN		FC	SN	SN	SN	SN	SN
	1	1	1			◇1	1			1	1	◇1	1	1	1		1		1		◇1		1	1
						🚲						🚲		🚲							🚲			
London Victoria 15 ⊖ d					16 13	16 17	16 19				16 23	16 32		16 36		16 39				16 43	16 47		16 49	16 53
Clapham Junction 10 d					16 21	16 23	16 26				16 29	16 38		16 42		16 45	16 34			16 51	16 53		16 56	16 59
St Pancras International 15 ⊖ d		15 54								16 09									16 22					
Farringdon 3 ⊖ d		15 59								16 14									16 27					
City Thameslink 3 d		16 03								16 18									16 31					
London Blackfriars 3 ⊖ d		16 05								16 20									16 36					
London Bridge 4 ⊖ d	16 08	16 12	16 15	16 06					16 20	16 27			16 33		16 38				16 43			16 48		
New Cross Gate d				16 11																				
Norwood Junction 2 a	16 19		16 25	16 29					16 32				16 44									17 01		
East Croydon a	16 23	16 24	16 29	16 33	16 42	16 33	16 36		16 36	16 39	16 39	16 47	16 48	16 52	16 52	16 55	16 58		16 59	17 12	17 03	17 05	17 06	17 09
South Croydon 4 a				16 36	16 45						16 42					16 58	17 02			17 19		17 08		17 12
Purley Oaks a				16 39	16 48											17 01				17 22		17 11		
Purley 4 a			16 35	16 42	16 52				16 45				16 55			17 05				17 25		17 14		

	SN	SN	SN		SN	SN	FC	SN	SN	SN	SN	SN	SN		SN	FC	SN	SN	SN	SN	SN	SN	SN	
	1	1	◇1		1	1	1		1	◇1		1	1		1	1	◇1	1	◇1	1		1	1	
			🚲																🚲					
London Victoria 15 ⊖ d			17 02		17 06			17 09		17 17			17 21		17 23		17 32		17 35		17 39			
Clapham Junction 10 d			17 08		17 12			17 15		17 23			17 27		17 30		17 38		17 42		17 45			
St Pancras International 15 ⊖ d							16 46									17 10								
Farringdon 3 ⊖ d							16 51									17 15								
City Thameslink 3 d							16 55									17 19								
London Blackfriars 3 ⊖ d							16 58									17 22								
London Bridge 4 ⊖ d	16 57	16 59				17 09			17 15		17 17	17 23						17 32		17 42		17 44	17 47	
New Cross Gate d																								
Norwood Junction 2 a		17 10									17 30							17 43						
East Croydon a	17 09	17 14	17 17		17 22	17 22	17 26	17 27	17 29	17 32	17 34	17 35	17 36		17 40	17 47	17 48	17 49	17 51	17 54	17 55	17 57	17 58	
South Croydon 4 a								17 30	17 32		17 37										17 58	18 01		
Purley Oaks a								17 33			17 40										18 01			
Purley 4 a		17 20						17 36			17 44							17 55			18 04			

London - East Croydon and Purley

COMPLETE SERVICE

	SN	SN	SN	SN	FC	SN	SN	SN	SN		SN	SN	FC	SN	SN	SN	SN	SN	SN		SN	SN	SN	FC
	1	◇1	1		1	1	1	1	◇1		1	◇1 ⊥	1	1		1		◇1			1	1	1	1
London Victoria 15 ⊖ d		17 47	17 49			17 53			18 02			18 06			18 09			18 17				18 19	18 23	
Clapham Junction 10 d	17 33	17 53	17 56			18 00			18 08			18 12			18 15		18 02	18 23				18 26	18 30	
St Pancras International 15 ⊖ d					17 28								17 40											18 08
Farringdon 3 ⊖ d					17 33								17 45											18 13
City Thameslink 3 d					17 37								17 49											18 17
London Blackfriars 3 ⊖ d					17 40								17 51											18 20
London Bridge 4 ⊖ d				17 49			17 57	17 59			18 08			18 12		18 16			18 18		18 23			18 27
New Cross Gate d																								
Norwood Junction 2 a				18 01				18 11											18 30					
East Croydon a	17 59	18 02	18 05	18 05	18 07	18 10	18 11	18 15	18 17		18 21	18 22	18 24	18 24	18 27	18 30	18 32	18 33	18 35		18 36	18 37	18 40	18 41
South Croydon 4 a				18 08											18 30	18 33	18 35		18 39					
Purley Oaks a				18 11											18 33		18 38		18 45					
Purley 4 a				18 14				18 20							18 36		18 40		18 48			18 42		

	SN	SN	SN	SN	FC		SN	SN	SN	SN	SN	SN	FC	SN	SN		SN	SN	SN	FC	SN	SN	SN	SN
	1	◇1	1		1		1	1		◇1 ⊥		1	1	1	1		◇1 ⊥	⊥	1	1	1			◇1 ⊥
London Victoria 15 ⊖ d		18 32	18 36	18 39					18 45	18 47		18 51		18 53			19 02	19 06			19 10		19 15	19 17
Clapham Junction 10 d		18 38	18 42	18 45				18 34	18 53	18 53		18 57		19 00			19 08	19 12			19 16		19 23	19 23
St Pancras International 15 ⊖ d					18 20								18 34							18 54				
Farringdon 3 ⊖ d					18 25								18 40							18 59				
City Thameslink 3 d					18 29								18 43							19 03				
London Blackfriars 3 ⊖ d					18 32								18 46							19 05				
London Bridge 4 ⊖ d	18 30						18 47				18 49		18 57		18 59				19 08	19 12		19 06		
New Cross Gate d															19 06							19 11		
Norwood Junction 2 a	18 41										19 01				19 13							19 29		
East Croydon a	18 45	18 48	18 52	18 57	19 00		19 00	19 02	19 13	19 03	19 05	19 07	19 10	19 10	19 17		19 18	19 22	19 22	19 24	19 27	19 33	19 44	19 33
South Croydon 4 a				19 00			19 03		19 16		19 08											19 36	19 47	
Purley Oaks a				19 03					19 19		19 11											19 39	19 50	
Purley 4 a	18 50			19 06					19 22		19 14				19 24						19 33	19 42	19 53	

	FC		SN	SN	SN	SN	FC	SN	SN	SN	SN		SN	FC	SN	SN	SN	SN	FC	SN	SN		SN	SN
	1		1	◇1 ⊥	1		1	1			◇1 ⊥		1	1	1	◇1 ⊥	1	◇1	1	1				◇1
London Victoria 15 ⊖ d			19 23	19 32		19 36		19 40		19 45	19 47				19 53	20 02		20 06		20 10			20 15	20 17
Clapham Junction 10 d			19 29	19 38		19 42		19 46		19 53	19 53				19 59	20 08		20 12		20 16			20 23	20 23
St Pancras International 15 ⊖ d	19 09						19 24							19 39					19 54					
Farringdon 3 ⊖ d	19 14						19 29							19 44					19 59					
City Thameslink 3 d	19 18						19 33							19 48					20 03					
London Blackfriars 3 ⊖ d	19 20						19 35							19 50					20 05					
London Bridge 4 ⊖ d	19 27				19 33		19 42		19 36				19 52	19 57			20 04		20 12		20 06			
New Cross Gate d					19 39				19 41												20 11			
Norwood Junction 2 a					19 46				19 59				20 03				20 16				20 29			
East Croydon a	19 39		19 39	19 48	19 50	19 52	19 54	19 57	20 03	20 14	20 03		20 06	20 09	20 09	20 19	20 19	20 22	20 24	20 27	20 33		20 44	20 33
South Croydon 4 a									20 06	20 17											20 36		20 47	
Purley Oaks a									20 09	20 21											20 39		20 50	
Purley 4 a					19 56			20 03	20 12	20 24			20 12							20 33	20 42		20 53	

	SN	SN	SN	SN	SN	FC	SN		SN	SN	SN	SN	SN	SN	SN	SN	FC		SN	SN	SN	SN	SN	SN
	1	1	◇1	1	◇1	1	1				◇1	1	1	1	1	◇1	1		1			◇1	1	1
London Victoria 15 ⊖ d	20 23		20 32		20 36		20 40			20 45	20 47	20 53		21 02		21 06			21 10		21 15	21 17	21 23	
Clapham Junction 10 d	20 29		20 38		20 42		20 46			20 53	20 53	20 59		21 08		21 12			21 16		21 23	21 23	21 29	
St Pancras International 15 ⊖ d						20 24											20 54							
Farringdon 3 ⊖ d						20 29											20 59							
City Thameslink 3 d						20 33											21 03							
London Blackfriars 3 ⊖ d						20 35											21 05							
London Bridge 4 ⊖ d		20 28		20 34		20 42			20 36				20 58		21 04		21 12			21 06				21 26
New Cross Gate d									20 41											21 11				
Norwood Junction 2 a				20 45					20 59						21 15					21 29				21 37
East Croydon a	20 39	20 40	20 48	20 49	20 52	20 54	20 57		21 03	21 14	21 03	21 09	21 10	21 18	21 19	21 22	21 24		21 27	21 33	21 44	21 33	21 39	21 41
South Croydon 4 a									21 06	21 17										21 36	21 47			
Purley Oaks a									21 09	21 20										21 39	21 50			
Purley 4 a							21 03		21 12	21 23									21 33	21 42	21 53			

	SN	SN	FC		SN	SN	SN	SN	SN	SN	SN	SN	FC		SN	SN	SN	SN	SN	SN	SN	SN	FC	
	1	◇1	1		1			◇1	1	◇1	1	◇1	1		1		◇1		1		1		1	
London Victoria 15 ⊖ d	21 32	21 36			21 40		21 45	21 47	21 53	22 02		22 06			22 10	22 15	22 17		22 23		22 32	22 36		
Clapham Junction 10 d	21 38	21 42			21 46		21 53	21 53	21 59	22 08		22 12			22 16	22 23	22 23		22 29		22 38	22 42		
St Pancras International 15 ⊖ d			21 24										21 54											
Farringdon 3 ⊖ d			21 29										21 59											
City Thameslink 3 d			21 33										22 03											
London Blackfriars 3 ⊖ d			21 35										22 05											
London Bridge 4 ⊖ d			21 42			21 36					22 04		22 12					22 08		22 26			22 42	
New Cross Gate d						21 41												22 13						
Norwood Junction 2 a						21 59					22 15							22 31		22 38				
East Croydon a	21 48	21 52	21 54		21 57	22 03	22 14	22 03	22 09	22 18	22 19	22 22	22 24		22 26	22 44	22 33	22 35	22 39	22 42	22 48	22 52	22 54	
South Croydon 4 a						22 06	22 17									22 47		22 38						
Purley Oaks a						22 09	22 20									22 50		22 41						
Purley 4 a					22 03	22 12	22 23								22 33	22 53		22 44						

London - East Croydon and Purley

COMPLETE SERVICE

		SN	SN	SN	SN	SN	SN	SN	SN	SN		FC	SN	SN	SN	SN	SN	SN	FC	SN		SN	SN	SN	SN
		1		◇1		1		◇1	1	◇1		1	1			◇1	1	◇1	1	1			FO	1	1
London Victoria 15 ⊖	d	22 40	22 45	22 47		22 53		23 02		23 06			23 10		23 15	23 17	23 24	23 32					23 45	23 47	23 49
Clapham Junction 10	d	22 46	22 53	22 53		22 59		23 08		23 12			23 16		23 23	23 23	23 30	23 38		23 40			23 53	23 53	23 56
St Pancras International 15 ⊖	d																								
Farringdon 3 ⊖	d																								
City Thameslink 3	d																								
London Blackfriars 3 ⊖	d																								
London Bridge 4 ⊖	d				22 38		22 56		23 04			23 12		23 06					23 42			23 36			
New Cross Gate	d				22 43									23 11								23 41			
Norwood Junction 2	a				23 01		23 07		23 15					23 29								23 59			
East Croydon	a	22 57	23 14	23 03	23 06	23 09	23 11	23 19	23 19	23 22		23 24	23 27	23 33	23 44	23 33	23 40	23 51	23 56	00 01		00 03	00 14	00 05	00 09
South Croydon 4	a		23 17		23 09									23 36	23 47							00 06	00 17		
Purley Oaks	a		23 20		23 12									23 39	23 50							00 09	00 20		
Purley 4	a	23 03	23 23		23 15								23 33	23 42	23 54							00 12	00 23	00 11	

Saturdays

		SN	SN	SN	SN	SN	SN	FC	SN	SN		SN	FC	SN	SN	SN	FC	FC	SN	FC		SN	FC	FC	SN
		1			1	1	◇1		1							◇1	1	1	1	1		1	1	1	◇1
London Victoria 15 ⊖	d			23p45	23p47	23p49	00 05		00 14			00 16			00 42	01 00			02 00			03 00			04 00
Clapham Junction 10	d	23p40		23p53	23p53	23p56	00 11		00 20			00 24			00 50	01 08			02 08			03 08			04 08
St Pancras International 15 ⊖	d																								
Farringdon 3 ⊖	d																								
City Thameslink 3	d																								
London Blackfriars 3 ⊖	d																								
London Bridge 4 ⊖	d		23p36					00 12		00 06			00 42	00 36			01 08	01 35		02 05			03 05	03 35	
New Cross Gate	d		23p41							00 11				00 41											
Norwood Junction 2	a		23p59							00 29				00 59											
East Croydon	a	00 01	00 03	00 14	00 05	00 09	00 24	00 26	00 31	00 33		00 44	00 56	01 03	01 10	01 21	01 31	02 02	02 21	02 31		03 21	03 31	04 01	04 21
South Croydon 4	a		00 06	00 17						00 37		00 50													
Purley Oaks	a		00 09	00 20						00 40		00 53													
Purley 4	a		00 12	00 23	00 11				00 37	00 43		00 56				01 27			02 27			03 27			04 27

		FC	FC	SN	FC	SN		SN	FC	SN	SN	SN	FC	SN	FC	SN		SN	SN	FC	SN	SN	SN	SN	SN
		1	1	◇1	1	1		◇1	1	1	1	1	1	1	1	1				1		1	1	◇1	1
London Victoria 15 ⊖	d			05 02		05 23		05 32		06 02		06 23		06 32							06 43	06 53		07 06	
Clapham Junction 10	d			05 08		05 29		05 38		06 08		06 29		06 38		06 34					06 51	06 59		07 12	
St Pancras International 15 ⊖	d																								
Farringdon 3 ⊖	d																								
City Thameslink 3	d																								
London Blackfriars 3 ⊖	d																								
London Bridge 4 ⊖	d	04 05	04 35		05 05				05 52		06 08		06 27		06 42			06 36	06 50	06 57			07 03		07 08
New Cross Gate	d																	06 41					07 08		
Norwood Junction 2	a					05 46												06 59	07 02				07 16		
East Croydon	a	04 31	05 01	05 21	05 31	05 49		05 47	06 04	06 17	06 22	06 39	06 39	06 47	06 54	06 57		07 03	07 06	07 09	07 12	07 09	07 20	07 22	07 22
South Croydon 4	a					05 52										07 01		07 06			07 15				
Purley Oaks	a																	07 09			07 18				
Purley 4	a			05 26				05 53		06 23				06 53				07 12	07 15		07 21		07 26		

		FC		SN	SN	FC	SN	SN	SN	SN	SN	FC		SN	SN	SN	SN	SN	SN	SN	SN	FC		SN	SN
		1				1		1	◇1	1	◇1	1		1	1		◇1			◇1	1	1		◇1	1
London Victoria 15 ⊖	d						07 13	07 23	07 32		07 36					07 43	07 47			07 51	07 53			08 02	
Clapham Junction 10	d						07 21	07 29	07 38		07 42			07 34		07 51	07 53				07 59			08 08	
St Pancras International 15 ⊖	d																								
Farringdon 3 ⊖	d																								
City Thameslink 3	d																								
London Blackfriars 3 ⊖	d																								
London Bridge 4 ⊖	d	07 12		07 06	07 20	07 27				07 33		07 42			07 45			07 36	07 50			07 57			08 03
New Cross Gate	d			07 11						07 38								07 41							08 08
Norwood Junction 2	a			07 29	07 32					07 46					07 55			07 59	08 02						08 16
East Croydon	a	07 24		07 33	07 36	07 39	07 42	07 39	07 47	07 50	07 52	07 54		07 57	07 59	08 12	08 02	08 03	08 06	08 07	08 09	08 09		08 17	08 20
South Croydon 4	a			07 36			07 45							08 01		08 15		08 06							
Purley Oaks	a			07 39			07 48									08 18		08 09							
Purley 4	a			07 42	07 45		07 51			07 56					08 05	08 21		08 12	08 15						08 26

		SN	SN	FC	SN	SN	SN	SN		SN	SN	FC	SN	SN	SN	FC	SN	SN		SN	SN	SN	SN	SN	SN
		◇1	1	1	1		◇1				1	1	◇1	1	◇1	1	1	1			◇1			◇1	1
London Victoria 15 ⊖	d	08 06				08 13	08 17				08 23		08 32		08 36					08 43	08 47			08 51	08 53
Clapham Junction 10	d	08 12				08 21	08 23				08 29		08 38		08 42		08 34			08 51	08 53				08 59
St Pancras International 15 ⊖	d																								
Farringdon 3 ⊖	d																								
City Thameslink 3	d																								
London Blackfriars 3 ⊖	d																								
London Bridge 4 ⊖	d		08 08	08 12	08 15			08 06		08 20		08 27		08 33		08 42		08 45				08 36	08 50		
New Cross Gate	d							08 11						08 38								08 41			
Norwood Junction 2	a				08 25			08 29		08 32				08 46				08 55				08 59	09 02		
East Croydon	a	08 22	08 22	08 24	08 29	08 42	08 32	08 33		08 36	08 39	08 39	08 47	08 50	08 52	08 54	08 57	08 59		09 12	09 02	09 03	09 06	09 07	09 09
South Croydon 4	a					08 45		08 36									09 01			09 15		09 06			
Purley Oaks	a					08 48		08 39												09 18		09 09			
Purley 4	a				08 35	08 52		08 42		08 45				08 56				09 05		09 21		09 12	09 15		

London - East Croydon and Purley

COMPLETE SERVICE

		FC ■1	SN ◇■1	SN ■1		SN ◇■1 🛒	SN ■1	FC ■1	SN ■1	SN	and at the same minutes past each hour until	SN	SN ◇■1		SN	SN	SN ■1	FC ■1	SN ◇■1	SN ■1	SN ◇■1 🛒	FC ■1	SN ■1	
London Victoria 15 ⊖	d		09 02			09 06				09 13		13 13	13 17				13 23		13 32		13 36			
Clapham Junction 10	d		09 08			09 12				09 21		13 21	13 23				13 29		13 38		13 42		13 34	
St Pancras International 15 ⊖	d																							
Farringdon 3 ⊖	d																							
City Thameslink 3	d																							
London Blackfriars 3 ⊖	d																							
London Bridge 4 ⊖	d	08 57		09 03			09 08	09 12	09 15						13 06	13 20		13 27		13 33		13 42		
New Cross Gate	d			09 08											13 11					13 38				
Norwood Junction 2	a			09 16					09 25						13 29	13 32				13 46				
East Croydon 🚊	a	09 09	09 17	09 20		09 22	09 22	09 24	09 29	09 42		13 42	13 32		13 33	13 36	13 39	13 39	13 47	13 50	13 52	13 54	13 57	
South Croydon 4	a									09 45		13 45			13 36								14 01	
Purley Oaks	a									09 48		13 48			13 39									
Purley 4	a			09 26					09 35	09 51		13 51			13 42	13 45				13 56				

		SN ■1	SN	SN ◇■1	SN	SN	SN ◇■1	SN ■1	FC ■1	SN ◇■1 🛒		SN ■1	SN ◇■1 🛒	SN ■1	FC ■1	SN ■1	SN	SN ◇■1	SN	SN		SN ■1	FC ■1	SN ◇■1	SN ■1
London Victoria 15 ⊖	d		13 43	13 47			13 51	13 53		14 02			14 06				14 13	14 17				14 23		14 32	
Clapham Junction 10	d		13 51	13 53				13 59		14 08			14 12				14 21	14 23				14 29		14 38	
St Pancras International 15 ⊖	d																								
Farringdon 3 ⊖	d																								
City Thameslink 3	d																								
London Blackfriars 3 ⊖	d																								
London Bridge 4 ⊖	d	13 45			13 36	13 50			13 57			14 03		14 08	14 12	14 15			14 06	14 20			14 27		14 33
New Cross Gate	d				13 41							14 08							14 11						14 38
Norwood Junction 2	a	13 55			13 59	14 02						14 16				14 25			14 29	14 32					14 46
East Croydon 🚊	a	13 59	14 12	14 02	14 03	14 06	14 07	14 09	14 09	14 17		14 20	14 22	14 22	14 24	14 29	14 42	14 32	14 33	14 36		14 39	14 39	14 47	14 50
South Croydon 4	a		14 15		14 06												14 45		14 36						
Purley Oaks	a		14 18		14 09												14 48		14 39						
Purley 4	a	14 05	14 22		14 12	14 15						14 26				14 35	14 52		14 42	14 45					14 56

		SN ◇■1 🛒	FC ■1	SN ■1	SN ■1	SN		SN ◇■1	SN	SN	SN ◇■1	SN ■1	FC ■1	SN ◇■1 🛒	SN ■1	SN ◇■1 🛒		SN ■1	FC ■1	SN ■1	SN	SN ◇■1	SN	SN	SN ■1
London Victoria 15 ⊖	d	14 36				14 43		14 47			14 51	14 53		15 02		15 06					15 13	15 17			15 23
Clapham Junction 10	d	14 42		14 34		14 51		14 53				14 59		15 08		15 12					15 21	15 23			15 29
St Pancras International 15 ⊖	d																								
Farringdon 3 ⊖	d																								
City Thameslink 3	d																								
London Blackfriars 3 ⊖	d																								
London Bridge 4 ⊖	d		14 42		14 45				14 36	14 50			14 57		15 03			15 08	15 12	15 15			15 06	15 20	
New Cross Gate	d								14 41						15 08								15 11		
Norwood Junction 2	a				14 55				14 59	15 02					15 16					15 25			15 29	15 32	
East Croydon 🚊	a	14 52	14 54	14 57	14 59	15 12		15 02	15 03	15 06	15 07	15 09	15 09	15 17	15 20	15 22		15 22	15 24	15 29	15 42	15 32	15 33	15 36	15 39
South Croydon 4	a			15 01		15 15			15 06												15 45		15 36		
Purley Oaks	a					15 18			15 09												15 48		15 39		
Purley 4	a				15 05	15 21			15 12	15 15					15 26					15 35	15 51		15 42	15 45	

		FC ■1		SN ◇■1	SN ■1	SN ◇■1 🛒	FC ■1	SN ■1	SN ■1	SN	SN ◇■1	SN		SN	SN ◇■1	SN ■1	FC ■1	SN ◇■1 🛒	SN ■1	SN ◇■1 🛒	SN ■1	FC ■1		SN ■1	SN
London Victoria 15 ⊖	d			15 32		15 36				15 43	15 47				15 51	15 53		16 02		16 06					16 13
Clapham Junction 10	d			15 38		15 42		15 34		15 51	15 53					15 59		16 08		16 12					16 21
St Pancras International 15 ⊖	d																								
Farringdon 3 ⊖	d																								
City Thameslink 3	d																								
London Blackfriars 3 ⊖	d																								
London Bridge 4 ⊖	d	15 27			15 33		15 42		15 45			15 36		15 50			15 57		16 03		16 08	16 12		16 15	
New Cross Gate	d				15 38							15 41							16 08						
Norwood Junction 2	a				15 46				15 55			15 59		16 02					16 16					16 25	
East Croydon 🚊	a	15 39		15 47	15 50	15 52	15 54	15 57	15 59	16 12	16 02	16 03		16 06	16 07	16 09	16 09	16 17	16 20	16 22	16 22	16 24		16 29	16 42
South Croydon 4	a							16 01		16 15		16 06													16 45
Purley Oaks	a									16 18		16 09													16 48
Purley 4	a				15 56				16 05	16 21		16 12		16 15					16 26					16 35	16 51

		SN ◇■1	SN	SN	SN ■1	FC ■1	SN ◇■1	SN ■1		SN ◇■1 🛒	FC ■1	SN ■1	SN ■1	SN	SN ◇■1	SN	SN	SN ◇■1		SN ■1	FC ■1	SN ◇■1 🛒	SN ■1	SN ◇■1 🛒	SN ■1
London Victoria 15 ⊖	d	16 17			16 23		16 32			16 36				16 43	16 47			16 51		16 53		17 02		17 06	
Clapham Junction 10	d	16 23			16 29		16 38			16 42		16 34		16 51	16 53					16 59		17 08		17 12	
St Pancras International 15 ⊖	d																								
Farringdon 3 ⊖	d																								
City Thameslink 3	d																								
London Blackfriars 3 ⊖	d																								
London Bridge 4 ⊖	d		16 06	16 20		16 27		16 33			16 42		16 45			16 36	16 50				16 57		17 03		17 08
New Cross Gate	d		16 11					16 38								16 41							17 08		
Norwood Junction 2	a		16 29	16 32				16 46					16 55			16 59	17 02						17 16		
East Croydon 🚊	a	16 32	16 33	16 36	16 39	16 39	16 47	16 50		16 52	16 54	16 57	16 59	17 12	17 02	17 03	17 06	17 07		17 09	17 09	17 17	17 20	17 22	17 22
South Croydon 4	a		16 36									17 01		17 15		17 06									
Purley Oaks	a		16 39											17 18		17 09									
Purley 4	a		16 42	16 45				16 56					17 05	17 21		17 12	17 15						17 26		

Table 175

Saturdays

London - East Croydon and Purley

COMPLETE SERVICE

	FC	SN	SN		SN	SN	SN	SN	FC	SN	SN	SN	FC		SN	SN	SN	SN	SN	SN	SN	SN	FC	
	1	1			◇1			1	1	◇1	1	◇1	1		1	1		◇1			◇1	1	1	
												🚲												
London Victoria 15 ⊖ d			17 13		17 17			17 23		17 32		17 36					17 43	17 47			17 51	17 53		
Clapham Junction 10 d			17 21		17 23			17 29		17 38		17 42			17 34		17 51	17 53				17 59		
St Pancras International 15 ⊖ d																								
Farringdon 3 ⊖ d																								
City Thameslink 3 d																								
London Blackfriars 3 ⊖ d																								
London Bridge 4 ⊖ d	17 12	17 15				17 06	17 20		17 27		17 33		17 42			17 45			17 36	17 50			17 57	
New Cross Gate d						17 11					17 38								17 41					
Norwood Junction 2 a		17 25				17 29	17 32				17 46					17 56			17 59	18 02				
East Croydon a	17 24	17 29	17 42		17 32	17 33	17 36	17 39	17 39	17 47	17 50	17 52	17 54		17 57	18 00	18 12	18 02	18 03	18 06	18 07	18 09	18 09	
South Croydon 4 a			17 45			17 36									18 01		18 15		18 06					
Purley Oaks a			17 48			17 39											18 18		18 09					
Purley 4 a		17 35	17 51			17 42	17 45				17 56					18 06	18 21		18 12	18 15				

	SN	SN	SN	SN	FC	SN	SN	SN	SN		SN	SN	FC	SN	SN	SN	FC	SN	SN		SN	SN	SN	SN
	◇1	1	◇1	1	1	1		◇1				1	1	◇1	1	◇1	1	1	1			◇1		
	🚲		🚲													🚲								
London Victoria 15 ⊖ d	18 02		18 06				18 13	18 17				18 23		18 32		18 36					18 43	18 47		
Clapham Junction 10 d	18 08		18 12				18 21	18 23				18 29		18 38		18 42		18 34			18 51	18 53		
St Pancras International 15 ⊖ d																								
Farringdon 3 ⊖ d																								
City Thameslink 3 d																								
London Blackfriars 3 ⊖ d																								
London Bridge 4 ⊖ d		18 03		18 08	18 12	18 15			18 06		18 20		18 27		18 33		18 42		18 45				18 36	18 50
New Cross Gate d		18 08							18 11						18 38								18 41	
Norwood Junction 2 a		18 16				18 25			18 29		18 32				18 46				18 55				18 59	19 02
East Croydon a	18 17	18 20	18 22	18 22	18 24	18 29	18 42	18 32	18 33		18 36	18 39	18 39	18 47	18 50	18 52	18 54	18 57	18 59		19 12	19 02	19 03	19 06
South Croydon 4 a							18 45		18 36									19 01			19 15		19 06	
Purley Oaks a							18 48		18 39												19 18		19 09	
Purley 4 a		18 26				18 35	18 51		18 42		18 45				18 56				19 05		19 21		19 12	19 15

	SN	SN	FC	SN	SN		SN	SN	FC	SN	SN	SN	SN	SN	FC		SN	SN	SN	FC	SN	SN	SN	SN
	◇1	1	1	◇1	1		◇1	1	1			◇1		1	1		◇1	1	◇1	1	1		◇1	
				🚲			🚲																	
London Victoria 15 ⊖ d	18 51	18 53		19 02			19 06				19 13	19 17		19 23			19 32		19 36			19 43	19 47	
Clapham Junction 10 d		18 59		19 08			19 12				19 21	19 23		19 29			19 38		19 42		19 34	19 51	19 53	
St Pancras International 15 ⊖ d																								
Farringdon 3 ⊖ d																								
City Thameslink 3 d																								
London Blackfriars 3 ⊖ d																								
London Bridge 4 ⊖ d			18 57		19 03			19 08	19 12	19 06			19 20		19 27			19 33		19 42				19 36
New Cross Gate d					19 08					19 11								19 38						19 41
Norwood Junction 2 a					19 16					19 29			19 32					19 46						19 59
East Croydon a	19 07	19 09	19 09	19 17	19 20		19 22	19 22	19 24	19 33	19 42	19 33	19 36	19 39	19 39		19 47	19 50	19 52	19 54	19 57	20 12	20 02	20 03
South Croydon 4 a										19 36	19 45											20 15		20 06
Purley Oaks a										19 39	19 48											20 18		20 09
Purley 4 a					19 26					19 42	19 51		19 45					19 56				20 21		20 12

	SN		SN	SN	FC	SN	SN	SN	FC	SN	SN		SN	SN	SN	SN	SN	SN	SN	FC	SN		SN	SN
			◇1	1	1	◇1	◇1	1	1	1			◇1			◇1	1	◇1	◇1	1	1		1	
London Victoria 15 ⊖ d			19 51	19 53		20 02	20 06			20 10	20 13		20 17			20 21	20 23	20 32	20 36		20 40			20 43
Clapham Junction 10 d				19 59		20 08	20 12			20 16	20 21		20 23				20 29	20 38	20 42		20 46		20 34	20 51
St Pancras International 15 ⊖ d																								
Farringdon 3 ⊖ d																								
City Thameslink 3 d																								
London Blackfriars 3 ⊖ d																								
London Bridge 4 ⊖ d	19 50				19 57			20 08	20 12					20 06	20 20					20 42				
New Cross Gate d														20 11										
Norwood Junction 2 a	20 02							20 19						20 29	20 32									
East Croydon a	20 06		20 07	20 09	20 09	20 17	20 22	20 22	20 24	20 29	20 42		20 32	20 33	20 36	20 37	20 39	20 47	20 52	20 53	20 57		20 59	21 12
South Croydon 4 a											20 45			20 36										21 15
Purley Oaks a											20 48			20 39										21 18
Purley 4 a	20 15									20 34	20 51			20 42	20 45						21 03			21 21

	SN	SN	SN	SN	SN	SN	SN		FC	SN	SN	SN	SN	SN	SN	SN	SN		FC	SN	SN	SN	SN	SN
	◇1			1	◇1	◇1	1		1	1			◇1		1		◇1		1	1		◇1		
London Victoria 15 ⊖ d	20 47			20 53	21 02	21 06				21 10		21 13	21 17		21 23	21 32	21 36			21 40	21 43	21 47		
Clapham Junction 10 d	20 53			20 59	21 08	21 12				21 16		21 21	21 23		21 29	21 38	21 42			21 46	21 51	21 53		
St Pancras International 15 ⊖ d																								
Farringdon 3 ⊖ d																								
City Thameslink 3 d																								
London Blackfriars 3 ⊖ d																								
London Bridge 4 ⊖ d		20 36	20 50				21 08		21 12		21 06			21 20					21 42				21 36	21 50
New Cross Gate d		20 41									21 11												21 41	
Norwood Junction 2 a		20 59	21 02				21 19				21 29			21 32									21 59	22 02
East Croydon a	21 02	21 03	21 06	21 09	21 17	21 22	21 22		21 24	21 27	21 33	21 42	21 33	21 36	21 39	21 47	21 52		21 54	21 57	22 12	22 03	22 04	22 07
South Croydon 4 a		21 06									21 36	21 45									22 15		22 07	
Purley Oaks a		21 09									21 39	21 48									22 18		22 10	
Purley 4 a		21 12	21 15							21 33	21 42	21 51		21 45						22 03	22 21		22 13	22 16

Table 175

Saturdays

London - East Croydon and Purley

COMPLETE SERVICE

	SN 1	SN ◇1	SN ◇1	SN 1	FC 1	SN 1	SN	SN ◇1	SN	SN	SN 1	SN 1	SN ◇1	FC 1	SN 1	SN	SN	SN ◇1	SN	SN 1	SN ◇1
London Victoria 15 ⊖ d	21 53	22 02	22 06			22 10	22 13	22 17			22 23	22 32	22 36		22 40		22 43	22 47		22 53	23 02
Clapham Junction 10 d	21 59	22 08	22 12			22 16	22 21	22 23			22 29	22 38	22 42		22 46		22 51	22 53		22 59	23 08
St Pancras International 15 ⊖ d																					
Farringdon 3 ⊖ d																					
City Thameslink 3 d																					
London Blackfriars 3 ⊖ d																					
London Bridge 4 ⊖ d				22 08	22 12				22 06	22 20				22 42		22 36			22 50		
New Cross Gate d									22 11							22 41					
Norwood Junction 2 a				22 19					22 29	22 32						22 59			23 02		
East Croydon a	22 09	22 17	22 22	22 22	22 24	22 27	22 42	22 33	22 35	22 37	22 39	22 47	22 52	22 54	22 57	23 03	23 13	23 03	23 06	23 09	23 17
South Croydon 4 a							22 46		22 38							23 06	23 16				
Purley Oaks a							22 49		22 41							23 09	23 19				
Purley 4 a						22 33	22 52		22 44	22 47					23 03	23 12	23 22		23 15		

	SN 1	SN ◇1	FC 1	SN 1	SN	SN ◇1	SN	SN 1	SN 1	FC 1	SN	SN	SN 1	SN 1
London Victoria 15 ⊖ d		23 06		23 10	23 15	23 17		23 24	23 32			23 45	23 47	23 49
Clapham Junction 10 d		23 12		23 16	23 23	23 23		23 30	23 38			23 53	23 53	23 56
St Pancras International 15 ⊖ d														
Farringdon 3 ⊖ d														
City Thameslink 3 d														
London Blackfriars 3 ⊖ d														
London Bridge 4 ⊖ d	23 04		23 12				23 06			23 42	23 36			
New Cross Gate d							23 11				23 41			
Norwood Junction 2 a	23 15						23 29				23 59			
East Croydon a	23 19	23 22	23 24	23 27	23 44	23 32	23 33	23 40	23 52	23 56	00 03	00 14	00 05	00 09
South Croydon 4 a					23 47		23 36				00 06	00 17		
Purley Oaks a					23 50		23 39				00 09	00 20		
Purley 4 a				23 33	23 53		23 42				00 13	00 23	00 11	

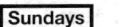

Sundays

	SN A	SN A	SN 1 A	SN 1 A	SN ◇1	FC 1	SN 1	SN	SN	FC 1	SN	SN	SN 1	FC 1	SN 1	SN 1	SN 1	SN 1	SN ◇1	SN ◇1	SN	SN ◇1
London Victoria 15 ⊖ d		23p45	23p47	23p49	00 05		00 14		00 16			00 42	01 00		02 00	03 00	04 00	05 02	05 47	06 32	06 36	07 02
Clapham Junction 10 d		23p53	23p53	23p56	00 11		00 20		00 24			00 50	01 08		02 08	03 08	04 08	05 08	05 53	06 38	06 42	07 08
St Pancras International 15 ⊖ d																						
Farringdon 3 ⊖ d																						
City Thameslink 3 d																						
London Blackfriars 3 ⊖ d																						
London Bridge 4 ⊖ d	23p36					00 12		00 06		00 42	00 36			01 08								
New Cross Gate d	23p41							00 11			00 41											
Norwood Junction 2 a	23p59							00 29			00 59											
East Croydon a	00 03	00 14	00 05	00 09	00 24	00 27	00 31	00 33	00 44	00 56	01 03	01 10	01 21	01 32	02 21	03 21	04 21	05 21	06 05	06 51	07 03	07 23
South Croydon 4 a	00 06	00 17						00 37	00 50													
Purley Oaks a	00 09	00 20						00 40	00 53													
Purley 4 a	00 13	00 23	00 11				00 37	00 43	00 56				01 26		02 27	03 27	04 26	05 28		06 56	07 10	07 29

	FC 1	SN	SN ◇1	SN 1	FC 1	SN 1	SN	SN	SN	SN ◇1	FC 1	SN	SN	SN ◇1	SN	SN ◇1	SN 1	FC 1	SN 1	SN	SN	SN ◇1 🛒
London Victoria 15 ⊖ d		07 06	07 32			07 34		07 36		08 04			08 06	08 17		08 32			08 34		08 36	08 47
Clapham Junction 10 d		07 12	07 38			07 40		07 42		08 10			08 12	08 23		08 38			08 40		08 42	08 53
St Pancras International 15 ⊖ d																						
Farringdon 3 ⊖ d																						
City Thameslink 3 d																						
London Blackfriars 3 ⊖ d																						
London Bridge 4 ⊖ d	07 12			07 37	07 42		07 21		07 39		08 12	07 51			08 09		08 37	08 42		08 21		
New Cross Gate d									07 44						08 14							
Norwood Junction 2 a				07 47					08 02						08 32		08 47					
East Croydon a	07 26	07 33	07 50	07 54	07 56	07 57	08 01	08 03	08 07	08 23	08 27	08 30	08 33	08 36	08 37	08 50	08 54	08 56	08 57	09 01	09 03	09 06
South Croydon 4 a									08 10						08 40							
Purley Oaks a									08 13						08 43							
Purley 4 a		07 40		08 00				08 10	08 16	08 30			08 40		08 46		09 00				09 10	

	SN	SN ◇1		SN ◇1	SN ◇1	FC 1	SN	SN	SN ◇1	SN	SN ◇1	SN 1	FC 1	SN 1	SN	SN	SN ◇1	SN	SN ◇1	FC 1
London Victoria 15 ⊖ d		09 02		21 02	21 04			21 06	21 17		21 32			21 34		21 36	21 47		22 04	
Clapham Junction 10 d		09 08	and at the same minutes past each hour until	21 08	21 10			21 12	21 23		21 38			21 40		21 42	21 53		22 10	
St Pancras International 15 ⊖ d																				
Farringdon 3 ⊖ d																				
City Thameslink 3 d																				
London Blackfriars 3 ⊖ d																				
London Bridge 4 ⊖ d	08 39					21 12	20 51			21 09		21 37	21 42		21 21			21 39		22 12
New Cross Gate d	08 44									21 14								21 44		
Norwood Junction 2 a	09 02									21 32		21 47						22 02		
East Croydon a	09 07	09 21		21 21	21 23	21 27	21 30	21 33	21 36	21 37	21 50	21 54	21 56	21 57	22 01	22 03	22 06	22 07	22 23	22 27
South Croydon 4 a	09 10									21 40								22 10		
Purley Oaks a	09 13									21 43								22 13		
Purley 4 a	09 16				21 30			21 40		21 46		22 00				22 10		22 16	22 30	

A not 11 December

Table 175

Sundays

London - East Croydon and Purley

COMPLETE SERVICE

		SN	SN	SN ◇1	SN	SN ◇1	SN 1	FC 1		SN 1	SN	SN	SN ◇1	SN	SN 1	FC 1	SN	SN		SN ◇1	SN	SN ◇1	FC 1	SN	SN
London Victoria 15 ⊖	d		22 06	22 17		22 32				22 34		22 36	22 47		23 04			23 06		23 17		23 32			23 47
Clapham Junction 10	d		22 12	22 23		22 38				22 40		22 42	22 53		23 10			23 12		23 23		23 38			23 53
St Pancras International 15 ⊖	d																								
Farringdon 3 ⊖	d																								
City Thameslink 3	d																								
London Blackfriars 3 ⊖	d																								
London Bridge 4 ⊖	d	21 51			22 09		22 37	22 42			22 21			22 39		23 12	22 51				23 09		23 42	23 21	
New Cross Gate	d				22 14									22 44							23 14				
Norwood Junction 2	a				22 32		22 47							23 02							23 32				
East Croydon	a	22 30	22 33	22 36	22 37	22 50	22 54	22 56		22 57	23 00	23 03	23 06	23 07	23 22	23 27	23 30	23 34		23 37	23 38	23 52	23 56	00 01	00 06
South Croydon 4	a				22 40									23 10				23 37							
Purley Oaks	a				22 43									23 13				23 40							
Purley 4	a		22 40		22 46		23 00					23 10		23 16	23 28			23 43							

		SN	SN
London Victoria 15 ⊖	d		23 50
Clapham Junction 10	d		23 56
St Pancras International 15 ⊖	d		
Farringdon 3 ⊖	d		
City Thameslink 3	d		
London Blackfriars 3 ⊖	d		
London Bridge 4 ⊖	d	23 39	
New Cross Gate	d	23 44	
Norwood Junction 2	a	00 02	
East Croydon	a	00 06	00 17
South Croydon 4	a	00 09	00 20
Purley Oaks	a	00 12	00 23
Purley 4	a	00 15	00 26

Purley and East Croydon - London

COMPLETE SERVICE

		SN MO 1	SN MO 1	SN MX 1	FC 1	SN MO ◇1	SN MX ◇1	FC 1	SN	SN 1		FC 1	SN 1	FC 1	SN 1	FC 1	SN 1	FC	SN	FC 1		SN 1	SN	FC 1	SN
Purley 4	d		23p50	23p49		00 11	00 11			01 22			02 22		03 22		04 26		05 07			05 23			05 39
Purley Oaks	d																								05 42
South Croydon 4	d																								05 45
East Croydon	d	23p50	23p56	23p58	00 04	00 16	00 17	00 36	00 49	01 28		01 49	02 28	02 47	03 28	03 47	04 32	04 47	05 13	05 17		05 29	05 33	05 47	05 48
Norwood Junction 2	d																		05 17				05 37		
New Cross Gate	d																		05 34						
London Bridge 4 ⊖	a				00 19			00 52				02 14		03 12		04 12			05 41	05 34				06 02	
London Blackfriars 3 ⊖	a																	05 13		05 41				06 10	
City Thameslink 3	a																	05 16		05 44				06 14	
Farringdon 3 ⊖	a																	05 20		05 47				06 18	
St Pancras International 15 ⊖	a																	05 24		05 52				06 22	
Clapham Junction 10	a	00 01	00 11	00 11		00 29	00 29		01 01	01 40			02 40		03 40		04 51					05 48	05 57		06 09
London Victoria 15 ⊖	a	00 08	00 19	00 18		00 37	00 37		01 09	01 49			02 49		03 49		04 58					05 58	06 06		06 18

		SN	FC 1	SN 1	SN	SN		SN ◇1	SN	SN 1	SN 1	SN	SN 1	FC 1	SN	SN 1		SN 1	FC 1	SN	SN 1	SN	SN 1	SN 1	SN 1
Purley 4	d			06 00		06 04						06 22	06 25		06 27							06 47		06 54	06 59
Purley Oaks	d					06 07						06 25			06 30							06 50			
South Croydon 4	d					06 10						06 28			06 33					06 42	06 50	06 53			
East Croydon	d	05 51	06 02	06 06	06 11	06 13		06 15	06 17	06 23	06 27	06 31	06 31	06 32	06 36	06 39		06 42	06 44	06 45	06 54	06 57	06 59	07 00	07 05
Norwood Junction 2	d	05 55				06 18						06 37			06 40										
New Cross Gate	d					06 35																			
London Bridge 4 ⊖	a	06 25	06 15			06 44				06 39		06 49		06 46	06 52	06 55			06 58		07 11		07 14	07 16	
London Blackfriars 3 ⊖	a		06 23											06 52					07 04						
City Thameslink 3	a		06 26											06 54					07 08						
Farringdon 3 ⊖	a		06 30											06 58					07 12						
St Pancras International 15 ⊖	a		06 34											07 02					07 16						
Clapham Junction 10	a			06 18	06 21			06 25	06 37		06 38		06 41					06 51		07 05		07 06			07 16
London Victoria 15 ⊖	a			06 25	06 28			06 32	06 48		06 45		06 48					07 00		07 16		07 15			07 25

		FC 1		SN	SN ◇1	SN 1	SN	FC 1	SN	SN 1	SN 1	SN ◇1 trolley		SN 1	SN 1	SN ◇1 trolley	SN	SN 1	SN 1	SN 1	SN	SN		FC 1	SN
Purley 4	d			07 01					07 17						07 29		07 31	07 37			07 39				07 47
Purley Oaks	d			07 04					07 20								07 34				07 42				07 50
South Croydon 4	d			07 07					07 23		07 25						07 37				07 45				07 53
East Croydon	d	07 09		07 10	07 15	07 15	07 18	07 23	07 26	07 28	07 28	07 31		07 32	07 35	07 39	07 40	07 42	07 45	07 46	07 48	07 50		07 54	07 56
Norwood Junction 2	d			07 14													07 44								
New Cross Gate	d																								
London Bridge 4 ⊖	a	07 23		07 28						07 43	07 47			07 49	07 51		07 58			08 01					
London Blackfriars 3 ⊖	a	07 30						07 51																08 20	
City Thameslink 3	a	07 32						07 56																08 23	
Farringdon 3 ⊖	a	07 36						08 00																08 27	
St Pancras International 15 ⊖	a	07 40						08 04																08 31	
Clapham Junction 10	a				07 24	07 27	07 38		07 36			07 40				07 48		07 51	07 55		08 08	08 13			08 06
London Victoria 15 ⊖	a				07 33	07 36	07 48		07 46			07 49				07 57		08 00	08 04		08 19				08 15

		SN 1	SN 1	SN ◇1 trolley	SN 1	SN 1	SN 1	SN 1		SN ◇1	SN	SN 1	SN ◇1 trolley	SN 1	SN	SN 1	FC 1	SN 1		SN	SN 1	SN 1	SN ◇1	SN 1	SN 1
Purley 4	d				07 55						08 01					08 15				08 17					
Purley Oaks	d										08 04									08 20					
South Croydon 4	d		07 54								08 07									08 23		08 26			
East Croydon	d	07 57	07 59	08 01	08 02	08 03	08 05	08 07		08 08	08 10	08 11	08 13	08 15	08 18	08 21	08 23	08 25		08 26	08 27	08 29	08 30	08 32	08 33
Norwood Junction 2	d										08 16														
New Cross Gate	d																								
London Bridge 4 ⊖	a	08 13	08 16		08 19	08 21	08 23				08 28					08 37		08 40			08 45	08 47		08 52	08 51
London Blackfriars 3 ⊖	a																08 53								
City Thameslink 3	a																08 56								
Farringdon 3 ⊖	a																09 00								
St Pancras International 15 ⊖	a																09 04								
Clapham Junction 10	a			08 10				08 36		08 17		08 20	08 23	08 26	08 38					08 36			08 39		
London Victoria 15 ⊖	a			08 19						08 26		08 29	08 32	08 35	08 48					08 45			08 48		

		SN 1	SN	FC 1		SN	SN ◇1 trolley	SN 1	SN	SN ◇1 trolley	SN 1	SN	FC 1	SN 1		SN ◇1	SN 1	SN 1	SN	SN 1	FC 1	SN 1	SN ◇1 trolley	SN 1	
Purley 4	d	08 31				08 33						08 45					08 52		08 56			09 05			
Purley Oaks	d					08 36						08 48							08 59						
South Croydon 4	d		08 35			08 39		08 42				08 51		08 52					09 02						
East Croydon	d	08 37	08 39	08 39		08 42	08 43	08 45	08 48	08 50	08 51	08 54	08 54	08 56		08 58	08 59	09 02	09 05	09 08	09 09	09 11	09 14	09 14	
Norwood Junction 2	d					08 47													09 09						
New Cross Gate	d																								
London Bridge 4 ⊖	a					09 01					09 06		09 08	09 13			09 15	09 20	09 23						
London Blackfriars 3 ⊖	a			09 09									09 21								09 37				
City Thameslink 3	a			09 12									09 24								09 40				
Farringdon 3 ⊖	a			09 16									09 27								09 44				
St Pancras International 15 ⊖	a			09 20									09 32								09 48				
Clapham Junction 10	a	08 48	09 04				08 52	08 55	09 08	09 00		09 04				09 07				09 34		09 20	09 23	09 26	
London Victoria 15 ⊖	a	08 56					09 01	09 04	09 18	09 09		09 13				09 16						09 27	09 32	09 35	

Table 175

Purley and East Croydon - London

COMPLETE SERVICE

	SN	SN	SN ◇1 (trolley)	SN 1	SN	SN 1	FC 1	SN 1	SN 1		SN ◇1 (trolley)	SN ◇1	SN 1	SN	FC 1	SN	SN ◇1 (trolley)	SN 1	SN		SN ◇1 (trolley)	FC 1	SN 1	SN ◇1
Purley 4 d	09 08	09 14			09 21				09 32					09 38		09 45		09 49	09 51				10 02	
Purley Oaks d	09 11				09 24									09 41					09 54					
South Croydon 4 d	09 14				09 27									09 44					09 57					
East Croydon d	09 17	09 20	09 23	09 26	09 30	09 31	09 32	09 33	09 37		09 39	09 43	09 44	09 47	09 47	09 51	09 53	09 55	10 00		10 00	10 02	10 07	10 08
Norwood Junction 2 d		09 25			09 35				09 42							09 55		09 59	10 05				10 13	
New Cross Gate d		09 33			09 52													10 07	10 22					
London Bridge 4 ⊖ a		09 41			10 00		09 46	09 51	09 55						10 00	10 09		10 13	10 29			10 15	10 25	
London Blackfriars 3 ⊖ a							09 53								10 08							10 23		
City Thameslink 3 a							09 56								10 10							10 26		
Farringdon 3 ⊖ a							10 00								10 14							10 30		
St Pancras International 15 ⊖ a							10 04								10 18							10 34		
Clapham Junction 10 a	09 38		09 32	09 36		09 41					09 48	09 52	09 55	10 07			10 02				10 09			10 17
London Victoria 15 ⊖ a	09 48		09 42	09 43		09 50					09 58	09 59	10 05	10 16			10 11				10 16			10 26

	SN 1	SN ◇1 (trolley)	SN 1	SN	FC 1		SN	SN ◇1 (trolley)	SN 1	SN ◇1	SN	FC 1	SN 1	SN 1	SN ◇1 (trolley)		SN 1	SN	FC 1	SN	SN ◇1 (trolley)	SN 1	SN	SN ◇1
Purley 4 d				10 08			10 15		10 19		10 21			10 33				10 38		10 45		10 49	10 51	
Purley Oaks d				10 11							10 24							10 41					10 54	
South Croydon 4 d	10 07			10 14							10 27							10 44					10 57	
East Croydon d	10 10	10 12	10 14	10 17	10 17		10 21	10 23	10 25	10 28	10 30	10 32	10 33	10 38	10 42		10 44	10 47	10 47	10 51	10 53	10 55	11 00	11 00
Norwood Junction 2 d							10 25		10 29		10 35			10 43						10 55		10 59	11 05	
New Cross Gate d									10 37		10 52											11 07	11 22	
London Bridge 4 ⊖ a					10 30		10 39		10 43		10 59	10 45	10 49	10 55					11 00	11 09		11 13	11 29	
London Blackfriars 3 ⊖ a					10 37							10 52							11 07					
City Thameslink 3 a					10 40							10 56							11 10					
Farringdon 3 ⊖ a					10 44							11 00							11 14					
St Pancras International 15 ⊖ a					10 48							11 04							11 18					
Clapham Junction 10 a	10 35	10 21	10 25	10 37				10 32		10 37					10 51		10 55	11 07			11 02			11 09
London Victoria 15 ⊖ a		10 28	10 35	10 46				10 41		10 45					10 58		11 05	11 16			11 10			11 16

	FC 1		SN 1	SN ◇1	SN 1	SN ◇1	SN 1	SN	FC 1	SN	SN ◇1 (trolley)		SN 1	SN ◇1	SN	FC 1	SN 1	SN 1	SN ◇1	SN 1	SN		FC 1	SN
Purley 4 d			11 01					11 08		11 15			11 19		11 21			11 32			11 38			11 45
Purley Oaks d								11 11							11 24						11 41			
South Croydon 4 d					11 07			11 14							11 27						11 44			
East Croydon d	11 02		11 07	11 08	11 11	11 12	11 14	11 17	11 17	11 21	11 23		11 25	11 28	11 30	11 32	11 33	11 37	11 41	11 44	11 47		11 47	11 51
Norwood Junction 2 d			11 13							11 25			11 29		11 35			11 43						11 55
New Cross Gate d													11 37		11 52									
London Bridge 4 ⊖ a	11 15		11 25						11 30	11 39			11 43		11 59	11 45	11 49	11 55					12 00	12 09
London Blackfriars 3 ⊖ a	11 22								11 37							11 52							12 07	
City Thameslink 3 a	11 26								11 40							11 56							12 10	
Farringdon 3 ⊖ a	11 30								11 44							12 00							12 14	
St Pancras International 15 ⊖ a	11 34								11 48							12 04							12 18	
Clapham Junction 10 a				11 17	11 33	11 21	11 25	11 37			11 32			11 37					11 50	11 55	12 07			
London Victoria 15 ⊖ a				11 24		11 28	11 32				11 40			11 44					11 57	12 02				

	SN ◇1 (trolley)	SN 1	SN	SN ◇1	FC 1	SN 1	SN ◇1		SN 1	SN ◇1	SN 1	SN	FC 1	SN	SN ◇1 (trolley)	SN 1	SN ◇1		SN	FC 1	SN 1	SN 1	SN ◇1	SN 1
Purley 4 d		11 49	11 51			12 02						12 08		12 15		12 19			12 21			12 32		
Purley Oaks d			11 54									12 11							12 24					
South Croydon 4 d			11 57						12 07			12 14							12 27					
East Croydon d	11 53	11 55	12 00	12 00	12 02	12 07	12 08		12 10	12 12	12 14	12 17	12 17	12 21	12 23	12 25	12 28		12 30	12 32	12 33	12 37	12 41	12 44
Norwood Junction 2 d		11 59	12 05			12 13								12 25		12 29			12 35			12 43		
New Cross Gate d		12 07	12 22													12 37			12 52					
London Bridge 4 ⊖ a		12 13	12 29		12 15	12 25							12 30	12 39		12 43			12 59	12 45	12 49	12 55		
London Blackfriars 3 ⊖ a					12 22								12 37							12 52				
City Thameslink 3 a					12 26								12 40							12 56				
Farringdon 3 ⊖ a					12 30								12 44							13 00				
St Pancras International 15 ⊖ a					12 34								12 48							13 04				
Clapham Junction 10 a	12 02			12 09			12 17		12 34	12 21	12 25	12 37			12 32		12 37						12 50	12 55
London Victoria 15 ⊖ a	12 10			12 18			12 24			12 28	12 32				12 40		12 44						12 57	13 02

	SN	FC 1	SN		SN ◇1 (trolley)	SN 1	SN	SN ◇1	FC 1	SN 1	SN ◇1	SN 1	SN ◇1		SN 1	SN	FC 1	SN	SN ◇1 (trolley)	SN 1	SN ◇1	SN	FC 1	
Purley 4 d	12 38		12 45			12 49	12 51			13 02						13 08		13 15		13 19		13 21		
Purley Oaks d	12 41						12 54									13 11						13 24		
South Croydon 4 d	12 44						12 57					13 07				13 14						13 27		
East Croydon d	12 47	12 47	12 51		12 53	12 55	13 00	13 00	13 02	13 07	13 08	13 10	13 12		13 14	13 17	13 17	13 21	13 23	13 25	13 28	13 30	13 32	
Norwood Junction 2 d			12 55			12 59	13 05			13 13								13 25		13 29		13 35		
New Cross Gate d						13 07	13 22													13 37		13 52		
London Bridge 4 ⊖ a		13 00	13 09			13 13	13 29		13 15	13 25							13 30	13 39		13 43		13 59	13 45	
London Blackfriars 3 ⊖ a		13 07							13 22								13 37						13 52	
City Thameslink 3 a		13 10							13 26								13 40						13 56	
Farringdon 3 ⊖ a		13 14							13 30								13 44						14 00	
St Pancras International 15 ⊖ a		13 18							13 34								13 48						14 04	
Clapham Junction 10 a	13 07				13 02			13 09			13 17	13 34	13 21		13 25	13 37			13 32		13 37			
London Victoria 15 ⊖ a	13 16				13 10			13 16			13 24		13 28		13 32				13 40		13 44			

Purley and East Croydon - London

COMPLETE SERVICE

	SN	SN	SN	SN	SN	FC	SN	SN	SN		SN	SN	FC	SN	SN	SN	SN	SN	SN		FC	SN	SN	SN
	1	1	◇1	1		1		◇1 trolley	1			◇1	1	1	◇1	1	◇1	1			1		◇1 trolley	1
Purley 4 d		13 32			13 38		13 45		13 49		13 51			14 02					14 08			14 15		14 19
Purley Oaks d					13 41						13 54								14 11					
South Croydon 4 d					13 44						13 57					14 07			14 14					
East Croydon d	13 33	13 37	13 41	13 44	13 47	13 47	13 51	13 53	13 55		14 00	14 00	14 02	14 08	14 08	14 10	14 12	14 14	14 17		14 17	14 21	14 23	14 25
Norwood Junction 2 d		13 43					13 55		13 59		14 05			14 13								14 25		14 29
New Cross Gate d									14 07		14 22													14 37
London Bridge 4 ⊖ a	13 49	13 55				14 00	14 09		14 13		14 29		14 15	14 25							14 30	14 39		14 43
London Blackfriars 3 ⊖ a						14 07							14 22								14 37			
City Thameslink 3 a						14 10							14 26								14 40			
Farringdon 3 ⊖ a						14 14							14 29								14 44			
St Pancras International 15 ⊖ a						14 18							14 34								14 48			
Clapham Junction 10 a			13 50	13 55	14 07			14 02				14 09			14 17	14 34	14 21	14 25	14 37				14 32	
London Victoria 15 ⊖ a			13 57	14 03				14 10				14 16			14 24		14 28	14 32					14 40	

	SN	SN	FC	SN	SN		SN	SN	SN	FC	SN	SN	SN	SN	SN		FC	SN	SN	SN	SN	SN	SN	FC
	◇1		1	1	1		◇1	1		1		◇1 trolley	1		◇1		1	1	◇1	1	◇1	1		1
Purley 4 d		14 21			14 32				14 38		14 45		14 49	14 51				15 02					15 08	
Purley Oaks d		14 24							14 41					14 54									15 11	
South Croydon 4 d		14 27							14 44					14 57						15 07			15 14	
East Croydon d	14 28	14 30	14 32	14 33	14 37		14 41	14 44	14 47	14 47	14 51	14 53	14 55	15 00	15 00		15 02	15 07	15 08	15 10	15 12	15 14	15 17	15 17
Norwood Junction 2 d		14 35			14 43						14 55		14 59	15 05				15 13						
New Cross Gate d		14 52											15 07	15 22										
London Bridge 4 ⊖ a		14 59	14 45	14 49	14 55					15 00	15 09		15 13	15 29			15 15	15 25						15 30
London Blackfriars 3 ⊖ a			14 52							15 07							15 22							15 37
City Thameslink 3 a			14 56							15 10							15 26							15 40
Farringdon 3 ⊖ a			15 00							15 14							15 29							15 44
St Pancras International 15 ⊖ a			15 04							15 18							15 34							15 48
Clapham Junction 10 a	14 37						14 50	14 55	15 07			15 02			15 09				15 17	15 35	15 21	15 25	15 37	
London Victoria 15 ⊖ a	14 44						14 57	15 02	15 16			15 10			15 20				15 24		15 28	15 35	15 46	

	SN		SN	SN	SN	SN	FC	SN	SN	SN	SN		SN	FC	SN	SN	SN	SN	SN	FC	SN		SN	SN
			◇1 trolley	1	◇1		1	1	1	◇1 trolley	1			1		◇1 trolley	1		◇1 trolley	1	1		◇1	1
Purley 4 d	15 15			15 19		15 21			15 32				15 38		15 45		15 49	15 51			16 02			
Purley Oaks d						15 24							15 41					15 54						
South Croydon 4 d						15 27							15 44					15 57						16 07
East Croydon d	15 21		15 23	15 25	15 28	15 30	15 32	15 33	15 37	15 41	15 44		15 47	15 47	15 51	15 53	15 55	16 00	16 00	16 02	16 07		16 08	16 10
Norwood Junction 2 d	15 25			15 29		15 35			15 43						15 55		15 59	16 05			16 13			
New Cross Gate d				15 37		15 52											16 07	16 22						
London Bridge 4 ⊖ a	15 39			15 43		15 59	15 45	15 49	15 55					16 00	16 09		16 13	16 29		16 15	16 25			
London Blackfriars 3 ⊖ a							15 52							16 07						16 25				
City Thameslink 3 a							15 56							16 10						16 28				
Farringdon 3 ⊖ a							15 59							16 13						16 31				
St Pancras International 15 ⊖ a							16 04							16 17						16 35				
Clapham Junction 10 a			15 32		15 37					15 50	15 55		16 07			16 02			16 09				16 17	16 34
London Victoria 15 ⊖ a			15 40		15 46					15 57	16 05		16 16			16 10			16 16				16 24	

	SN	SN	SN	FC	SN	SN	SN		FC	SN	SN	SN	SN	SN	SN	SN	SN		FC	SN	SN	SN	FC	SN
	◇1 trolley	1		1		1	◇1 trolley		1		◇1 trolley	1	◇1	1	◇1 trolley	1			1		1 trolley	1	1	
Purley 4 d			16 08		16 15	16 18				16 21				16 34			16 38			16 45		16 49		16 51
Purley Oaks d			16 11							16 24							16 41							16 54
South Croydon 4 d			16 14							16 27							16 44							16 57
East Croydon d	16 12	16 14	16 17	16 17	16 21	16 24	16 24		16 28	16 30	16 30	16 33	16 38	16 40	16 41	16 44	16 47		16 47	16 51	16 54	16 55	16 58	17 00
Norwood Junction 2 d					16 25	16 28				16 35				16 45						16 55		16 59		17 05
New Cross Gate d						16 36				16 52												17 06		17 22
London Bridge 4 ⊖ a					16 39	16 43				17 02		16 47		17 00						17 08		17 14		17 35
London Blackfriars 3 ⊖ a				16 47					16 55										17 19				17 25	
City Thameslink 3 a				16 54					16 58										17 24				17 28	
Farringdon 3 ⊖ a				16 57					17 01										17 27				17 31	
St Pancras International 15 ⊖ a				17 01					17 05										17 31				17 35	
Clapham Junction 10 a	16 21	16 25	16 37				16 33				16 39		16 47		16 50	16 55	17 07				17 03			
London Victoria 15 ⊖ a	16 28	16 35	16 46				16 42				16 46		16 54		16 58	17 05	17 16				17 10			

	SN	SN	FC		SN	SN	SN	SN	SN	FC	SN	SN	SN		SN	SN	SN	SN	SN	SN	SN	FC	SN	
	◇1	1	1		1	◇1 trolley	1			1	1	1 trolley			◇1 trolley	1	1	◇1 trolley	1	1		1		
Purley 4 d		17 02						17 08	17 15		17 19		17 21								17 38		17 45	
Purley Oaks d								17 11					17 24								17 41			
South Croydon 4 d					17 07			17 14					17 27								17 44			
East Croydon d	17 01	17 07	17 09		17 10	17 13	17 14	17 17	17 21	17 23	17 25	17 26	17 30		17 30	17 36	17 38	17 41	17 41	17 44	17 47	17 47	17 51	
Norwood Junction 2 d		17 12							17 25		17 31		17 35						17 45				17 55	
New Cross Gate d											17 38		17 52											
London Bridge 4 ⊖ a		17 26	17 27						17 37		17 45		17 59			17 52			17 58			18 13	18 09	
London Blackfriars 3 ⊖ a			17 35							17 49												18 21		
City Thameslink 3 a			17 38							17 54												18 24		
Farringdon 3 ⊖ a			17 41							17 57												18 27		
St Pancras International 15 ⊖ a			17 45							18 01												18 31		
Clapham Junction 10 a	17 10				17 34	17 22	17 25	17 37				17 35			17 39		17 47	17 50		17 55	18 07			
London Victoria 15 ⊖ a	17 17					17 29	17 35	17 48				17 42			17 46		17 54	17 58		18 05	18 16			

Purley and East Croydon - London

COMPLETE SERVICE

		SN	SN	SN	FC	SN	SN	SN	SN	SN		SN	FC	SN	SN	SN	SN	SN	SN	FC		SN	SN	SN	SN
		1	1	1 ⊥	1	◇1 ⊥		1	1	◇1 ⊥		1	1			1 ⊥	1		◇1 ⊥	1		1	1	◇1 ⊥	1
Purley 4	d		17 49				17 59							18 08	18 15		18 19	18 21							
Purley Oaks	d						18 02							18 11				18 24							
South Croydon 4	d						18 05							18 14				18 27							
East Croydon	d	17 53	17 55	17 57	17 58	18 02	18 08	18 09	18 10	18 12		18 14	18 16	18 17	18 21	18 26	18 27	18 30	18 30	18 32		18 36	18 40	18 43	18 44
Norwood Junction 2	d		17 59				18 12								18 29			18 35							
New Cross Gate	d		18 07															18 52							
London Bridge 4 ⊖	a		18 16				18 26								18 41			18 59		18 46		18 50			
London Blackfriars 3 ⊖	a				18 25								18 51							18 55					
City Thameslink 3	a				18 28								18 54							18 58					
Farringdon 3 ⊖	a				18 31								18 57							19 01					
St Pancras International 15 ⊖	a				18 35								19 01							19 05					
Clapham Junction 10	a	18 02		18 06		18 13		18 18	18 35	18 21		18 25		18 39		18 35	18 38		18 41				18 49	18 52	18 55
London Victoria 15 ⊖	a	18 09		18 14		18 20		18 26		18 29		18 35		18 46		18 42	18 45		18 48				18 56	18 59	19 05

		SN	FC	SN	SN	SN		SN	SN	SN	FC	SN	SN	SN	SN	SN		FC	SN	SN	SN	SN	FC	SN	SN
			1	1	1	1		1		◇1	1	1	1	◇1 ⊥	1			1	◇1	1	◇1		1	1	1
Purley 4	d	18 37			18 49				18 51							19 08				19 19		19 21			
Purley Oaks	d	18 40							18 54							19 11						19 24			
South Croydon 4	d	18 44							18 57							19 14						19 27			
East Croydon	d	18 47	18 47	18 53	18 55	18 57		18 57	19 00	19 00	19 02	19 10	19 10	19 12	19 14	19 17		19 17	19 24	19 25	19 29	19 30	19 32	19 33	19 40
Norwood Junction 2	d					19 02			19 05			19 13										19 35			
New Cross Gate	d								19 22													19 52			
London Bridge 4 ⊖	a		19 00			19 15			19 29		19 15	19 25						19 30				19 59	19 45	19 49	
London Blackfriars 3 ⊖	a		19 09								19 22							19 37					19 52		
City Thameslink 3	a		19 12								19 26							19 40					19 56		
Farringdon 3 ⊖	a		19 15								19 30							19 44					20 00		
St Pancras International 15 ⊖	a		19 19								19 34							19 48					20 04		
Clapham Junction 10	a	19 08		19 02	19 05			19 08		19 11			19 34	19 21	19 25	19 37			19 33	19 37	19 40				19 49
London Victoria 15 ⊖	a	19 15		19 09	19 13			19 15		19 18				19 29	19 35	19 48			19 41	19 44	19 47				19 56

		SN		SN	SN	FC	SN	SN	SN	SN	FC	SN		SN	SN	SN	FC	SN	SN	SN	SN	FC		SN	SN
		◇1		1		1	◇1	1		1	1	1		◇1	1		1	◇1	1	◇1		1		1	◇1
Purley 4	d				19 38			19 53	19 51							20 08			20 18		20 22				
Purley Oaks	d				19 41				19 54							20 11					20 25				
South Croydon 4	d				19 44				19 57							20 14					20 28				
East Croydon	d	19 43		19 44	19 47	19 47	19 54	19 59	20 00	20 01	20 02	20 07		20 11	20 14	20 17	20 17	20 24	20 26	20 30	20 31	20 32		20 34	20 41
Norwood Junction 2	d								20 05												20 35				
New Cross Gate	d								20 22												20 52				
London Bridge 4 ⊖	a					20 00			20 29		20 15	20 21					20 30				20 59	20 45		20 48	
London Blackfriars 3 ⊖	a					20 07					20 22						20 37					20 52			
City Thameslink 3	a					20 10					20 26						20 40					20 56			
Farringdon 3 ⊖	a					20 14					20 30						20 44					21 00			
St Pancras International 15 ⊖	a					20 18					20 34						20 48					21 04			
Clapham Junction 10	a	19 52		19 55	20 07		20 03	20 08		20 11				20 20	20 25	20 37		20 33	20 37	20 40					20 50
London Victoria 15 ⊖	a	19 59		20 05			20 10	20 15		20 20				20 28	20 32	20 46		20 40	20 44	20 50					20 59

		SN	SN	FC	SN	SN	SN	SN		SN	FC	SN	SN	SN	FC	SN	SN	SN		SN	FC	SN	SN	SN	SN
		1		1	1	◇1	1			◇1	1	◇1	1		1	◇1	1			◇1	1	1	◇1	1	
Purley 4	d		20 38				20 49	20 51						21 08			21 19	21 21							21 38
Purley Oaks	d		20 41					20 54						21 11				21 24							21 41
South Croydon 4	d		20 44					20 57						21 14				21 27							21 44
East Croydon	d	20 44	20 47	20 47	20 54	20 54	20 57	21 00		21 00	21 02	21 09	21 14	21 17	21 17	21 24	21 26	21 30		21 30	21 32	21 33	21 42	21 44	21 47
Norwood Junction 2	d							21 05										21 35							
New Cross Gate	d							21 22										21 52							
London Bridge 4 ⊖	a			21 00	21 09			21 29			21 15				21 30			21 59			21 45	21 49			
London Blackfriars 3 ⊖	a			21 07							21 22				21 37						21 52				
City Thameslink 3	a			21 10							21 26				21 40						21 56				
Farringdon 3 ⊖	a			21 14							21 30				21 44						22 00				
St Pancras International 15 ⊖	a			21 18							21 34				21 48						22 04				
Clapham Junction 10	a	20 55	21 07			21 03	21 07			21 11		21 18	21 25	21 37		21 33	21 37			21 40			21 51	21 55	22 07
London Victoria 15 ⊖	a	21 03	21 18			21 10	21 15			21 18		21 28	21 32	21 48		21 40	21 45			21 49			21 58	22 05	22 18

		SN	SN	SN		SN	FC	SN	SN	SN	SN	SN	SN	SN		SN	FC	SN	SN	SN	SN	SN	SN	SN	
		◇1	1			◇1	1	◇1	1		1	◇1	1			◇1	1	1	◇1 ⊥	1		◇1	1	◇1	
Purley 4	d		21 49	21 51						22 08			22 19	22 21							22 38		22 50		
Purley Oaks	d			21 54						22 11				22 24							22 41				
South Croydon 4	d			21 57						22 14				22 27							22 44				
East Croydon	d	21 54	21 57	22 00		22 00	22 02	22 09	22 14	22 17	22 18	22 24	22 25	22 30		22 30	22 32	22 34	22 41	22 44	22 47	22 54	22 56	23 00	
Norwood Junction 2	d			22 05										22 35											
New Cross Gate	d			22 22										22 52											
London Bridge 4 ⊖	a			22 29			22 17				22 33			22 59			22 47	22 49							
London Blackfriars 3 ⊖	a																								
City Thameslink 3	a																								
Farringdon 3 ⊖	a																								
St Pancras International 15 ⊖	a																								
Clapham Junction 10	a	22 03	22 07			22 10		22 18	22 25	22 37		22 33	22 37			22 40			22 50	22 55	23 07	23 03	23 06	23 10	
London Victoria 15 ⊖	a	22 11	22 14			22 20		22 26	22 35	22 48		22 41	22 44			22 50			22 57	23 05	23 16	23 13	23 15	23 20	

Purley and East Croydon - London

COMPLETE SERVICE

Mondays to Fridays

	SN	FC 1	SN 1	SN	SN 1	SN ◇1	FC 1	SN	SN 1
Purley 4 d	22 52			23 08				23 34	23 49
Purley Oaks d	22 55			23 11				23 37	
South Croydon 4 d	22 58			23 14				23 40	
East Croydon d	23 01	23 02	23 14	23 17	23 20	23 30	23 32	23 43	23 58
Norwood Junction 2 d	23 06							23a47	
New Cross Gate d	23 23								
London Bridge 4 ⊖ a	23 30	23 17					23 47		
London Blackfriars 3 ⊖ a									
City Thameslink 3 a									
Farringdon 3 ⊖ a									
St Pancras International 15 ⊖ a									
Clapham Junction 10 a			23 25	23 37	23 32	23 42			00 11
London Victoria 15 ⊖ a			23 35	23 48	23 40	23 52			00 18

Saturdays

	SN 1	FC 1	SN ◇1	FC 1	SN	SN 1	FC 1	SN 1	FC 1		SN 1	FC 1	SN 1	FC 1	FC 1	SN 1	FC 1	SN ◇1	SN 1		SN ◇1	FC 1	SN 1	SN
Purley 4 d	23p49		00 11			01 22		02 22			03 22		04 22			05 24		05 58					06 19	06 21
Purley Oaks d																								06 24
South Croydon 4 d																								06 27
East Croydon d	23p58	00 04	00 17	00 36	00 49	01 28	01 50	02 28	02 47		03 28	03 47	04 28	04 47	05 17	05 29	05 47	06 07	06 10		06 11	06 17	06 25	06 30
Norwood Junction 2 d																							06 29	06 35
New Cross Gate d																							06 37	06 52
London Bridge 4 ⊖ a		00 19		00 52			02 14		03 12			04 12		05 12	05 42		06 01					06 32	06 43	06 59
London Blackfriars 3 ⊖ a																								
City Thameslink 3 a																								
Farringdon 3 ⊖ a																								
St Pancras International 15 ⊖ a																								
Clapham Junction 10 a	00 11		00 29		01 01	01 41		02 41			03 41		04 41			05 49		06 18	06 34		06 21			
London Victoria 15 ⊖ a	00 18		00 37		01 09	01 49		02 49			03 49		04 50			05 58		06 26			06 30			

	SN ◇1	SN	SN	FC 1	SN ◇1		SN 1	SN	SN 1	SN ◇1	SN 1	SN 1	SN	FC 1	SN ◇1		SN 1	SN	SN ◇1	FC 1	SN 1	SN 1	SN ◇1	SN 1
Purley 4 d			06 38				06 49	06 51	07 02				07 08				07 19	07 21				07 34		
Purley Oaks d			06 41					06 54					07 11					07 24						
South Croydon 4 d			06 44					06 57			07 07		07 14					07 27						
East Croydon d	06 41	06 43	06 47	06 47	06 53		06 55	07 00	07 07	07 10	07 10	07 14	07 17	07 17	07 23		07 25	07 30	07 30	07 32	07 33	07 39	07 42	07 44
Norwood Junction 2 d		06 50					06 59	07 05	07 13								07 29	07 35				07 45		
New Cross Gate d		07 04					07 07	07 22									07 37	07 52						
London Bridge 4 ⊖ a		07 11		07 02			07 13	07 29	07 25					07 32			07 43	07 59		07 47	07 49	07 57		
London Blackfriars 3 ⊖ a																								
City Thameslink 3 a																								
Farringdon 3 ⊖ a																								
St Pancras International 15 ⊖ a																								
Clapham Junction 10 a	06 50		07 07		07 02					07 19	07 34	07 25	07 37		07 32				07 39				07 51	07 55
London Victoria 15 ⊖ a	06 57		07 16		07 09					07 27		07 32	07 46		07 40				07 46				07 58	08 02

	SN		FC 1	SN	SN ◇1	SN 1	SN	SN ◇1	FC 1	SN 1	SN ◇1		SN 1	SN ◇1	SN 1	SN	FC 1	SN	SN ◇1 (trolley)	SN 1	SN ◇1		SN	FC 1
Purley 4 d	07 38			07 45		07 49	07 51			08 02						08 08		08 15		08 19			08 21	
Purley Oaks d	07 41						07 54									08 11							08 24	
South Croydon 4 d	07 44						07 57						08 07			08 14							08 27	
East Croydon d	07 47		07 47	07 51	07 53	07 55	08 00	08 00	08 01	08 07	08 08		08 10	08 12	08 14	08 17	08 17	08 21	08 23	08 25	08 28		08 30	08 32
Norwood Junction 2 d				07 55		07 59	08 05			08 13								08 25		08 29			08 35	
New Cross Gate d						08 07	08 22													08 37			08 52	
London Bridge 4 ⊖ a			08 02	08 09		08 13	08 29		08 17	08 25							08 32	08 39		08 43			08 59	08 47
London Blackfriars 3 ⊖ a																								
City Thameslink 3 a																								
Farringdon 3 ⊖ a																								
St Pancras International 15 ⊖ a																								
Clapham Junction 10 a	08 07				08 02			08 09			08 17		08 34	08 21	08 25	08 37			08 32		08 37			
London Victoria 15 ⊖ a	08 16				08 10			08 16			08 24			08 28	08 32	08 46			08 40		08 44			

	SN 1	SN 1	SN ◇1		SN ◇1	SN 1		SN	FC 1	SN	SN ◇1 (trolley)	SN 1	SN	SN ◇1	FC 1	SN 1		SN ◇1	SN 1	SN ◇1	SN 1	SN	FC 1
Purley 4 d		08 32						11 38		11 45		11 49	11 51			12 02						12 08	
Purley Oaks d				and at				11 41					11 54									12 11	
South Croydon 4 d				the same				11 44					11 57						12 07			12 14	
East Croydon d	08 33	08 37	08 40	minutes	11 40	11 44		11 47	11 47	11 51	11 53	11 55	12 00	12 00	12 01	12 07		12 08	12 10	12 12	12 14	12 17	12 17
Norwood Junction 2 d		08 43		past						11 55		11 59	12 05			12 13							
New Cross Gate d				each								12 07	12 22										
London Bridge 4 ⊖ a	08 49	08 55		hour until					12 02	12 09		12 13	12 29		12 17	12 25							12 32
London Blackfriars 3 ⊖ a																							
City Thameslink 3 a																							
Farringdon 3 ⊖ a																							
St Pancras International 15 ⊖ a																							
Clapham Junction 10 a			08 50		11 50	11 55		12 07			12 02			12 09				12 17	12 34	12 21	12 25	12 37	
London Victoria 15 ⊖ a			08 57		11 57	12 02		12 16			12 10			12 16				12 24		12 28	12 32	12 46	

Table 175

Saturdays

Purley and East Croydon - London

COMPLETE SERVICE

		SN	SN	SN		SN	SN	FC	SN	SN	SN	SN	SN	FC		SN	SN	SN	SN	SN	FC	SN	SN	SN	
			◇1 🚲	1		◇1 🚲		1	1	1	◇1	1		1			◇1 🚲	1		◇1	1	1	◇1	1	
Purley 4	d	12 15		12 19			12 21			12 32			12 38			12 45		12 49	12 51			13 02			
Purley Oaks	d						12 24						12 41						12 54						
South Croydon 4	d						12 27						12 44						12 57					13 07	
East Croydon	d	12 21	12 23	12 25		12 28	12 30	12 32	12 33	12 38	12 40	12 44	12 47	12 47		12 51	12 53	12 55	13 00	13 00	13 01	13 07	13 08	13 10	
Norwood Junction 2	d	12 25		12 29			12 35			12 43						12 55		12 59	13 05			13 13			
New Cross Gate	d			12 37			12 52											13 07	13 22						
London Bridge 4 ⊖	a	12 39		12 43			12 59	12 47	12 49	12 55				13 02		13 09		13 13	13 29		13 17	13 25			
London Blackfriars 3 ⊖	a																								
City Thameslink 3	a																								
Farringdon 3 ⊖	a																								
St Pancras International 15 ⊖	a																								
Clapham Junction 10	a		12 32			12 37					12 50	12 55	13 07				13 02			13 09			13 17	13 34	
London Victoria 15 ⊖	a		12 40			12 44					12 57	13 02	13 16				13 10			13 16			13 24		

		SN	SN	SN	FC	SN	SN	SN	SN	SN		FC	SN	SN		SN	SN	SN	SN		FC	SN	SN	SN
		◇1	1		1		◇1 🚲	1	◇1 🚲			1	1	1	and at the same minutes past each hour until	1	◇1	1			1		◇1 🚲	1
Purley 4	d			13 08		13 15		13 19		13 21				13 32		16 32			16 38			16 45		16 49
Purley Oaks	d			13 11						13 24									16 41					
South Croydon 4	d			13 14						13 27									16 44					
East Croydon	d	13 12	13 14	13 17	13 17	13 21	13 23	13 25	13 28	13 30		13 32	13 33	13 37		16 37	16 40	16 44	16 47		16 47	16 51	16 53	16 55
Norwood Junction 2	d					13 25		13 29		13 35				13 43		16 43						16 55		16 59
New Cross Gate	d							13 37		13 52														17 07
London Bridge 4 ⊖	a				13 32	13 39		13 43		13 59		13 47	13 49	13 55		16 55					17 02	17 09		17 13
London Blackfriars 3 ⊖	a																							
City Thameslink 3	a																							
Farringdon 3 ⊖	a																							
St Pancras International 15 ⊖	a																							
Clapham Junction 10	a	13 21	13 25	13 37			13 32		13 37								16 50	16 55	17 07				17 02	
London Victoria 15 ⊖	a	13 28	13 32	13 46			13 40		13 44								16 57	17 02	17 16				17 10	

		SN	SN	FC	SN	SN		SN	SN	SN	SN	FC	SN	SN	SN	SN		SN	FC	SN	SN	SN	SN	SN	FC
			◇1	1	1	◇1		1	◇1	1		1		◇1 🚲	1	◇1 🚲			1	1	1	◇1	1		1
Purley 4	d	16 51			17 02						17 08		17 15		17 19			17 21			17 32			17 38	
Purley Oaks	d	16 54									17 11							17 24						17 41	
South Croydon 4	d	16 57						17 07			17 14							17 27						17 44	
East Croydon	d	17 00	17 00	17 01	17 07	17 08		17 10	17 12	17 14	17 17	17 17	17 21	17 23	17 25	17 28		17 30	17 32	17 33	17 37	17 40	17 44	17 47	17 47
Norwood Junction 2	d	17 05			17 13								17 25		17 29			17 35			17 43				
New Cross Gate	d	17 22													17 37			17 52							
London Bridge 4 ⊖	a	17 30		17 17	17 25							17 32	17 39		17 43			17 59	17 47	17 49	17 55				18 02
London Blackfriars 3 ⊖	a																								
City Thameslink 3	a																								
Farringdon 3 ⊖	a																								
St Pancras International 15 ⊖	a																								
Clapham Junction 10	a		17 09			17 17		17 34	17 21	17 25	17 38			17 32		17 37						17 50	17 55	18 07	
London Victoria 15 ⊖	a		17 16			17 24			17 28	17 32	17 47			17 40		17 44						17 57	18 02	18 16	

		SN		SN	SN	SN	SN	FC	SN	SN	SN	SN		SN	SN	FC	SN	SN	SN	SN	SN	FC		SN	SN
				◇1 🚲	1		◇1	1	1	◇1	1	◇1		1		1		◇1 🚲	1	◇1 🚲		1		1	1
Purley 4	d	17 45			17 49	17 51			18 02						18 08		18 15		18 19		18 21				18 32
Purley Oaks	d					17 54									18 11						18 24				
South Croydon 4	d					17 57					18 07				18 14						18 27				
East Croydon	d	17 51		17 53	17 55	18 00	18 00	18 01	18 07	18 08	18 10	18 12		18 14	18 17	18 17	18 21	18 23	18 25	18 28	18 30	18 32		18 33	18 37
Norwood Junction 2	d	17 55			17 59	18 05			18 13								18 25		18 29		18 35				18 43
New Cross Gate	d				18 07	18 22													18 37		18 52				
London Bridge 4 ⊖	a	18 09			18 13	18 29		18 17	18 25							18 32	18 39		18 43		18 59	18 47		18 49	18 55
London Blackfriars 3 ⊖	a																								
City Thameslink 3	a																								
Farringdon 3 ⊖	a																								
St Pancras International 15 ⊖	a																								
Clapham Junction 10	a			18 02			18 09			18 17	18 34	18 21		18 25	18 37			18 32		18 37					
London Victoria 15 ⊖	a			18 10			18 16			18 24		18 28		18 32	18 46			18 40		18 44					

		SN	SN	SN	FC	SN	SN	SN		SN	SN	FC	SN	SN	SN	SN	SN	SN		FC	SN	SN	SN	SN	SN
		◇1	1		1		◇1	1			◇1	1	1	◇1	1	◇1	1			1		◇1	1	◇1	
Purley 4	d			18 38		18 45		18 49		18 51			19 02					19 08			19 15		19 19		19 21
Purley Oaks	d			18 41						18 54								19 11							19 24
South Croydon 4	d			18 44						18 57					19 07			19 14							19 27
East Croydon	d	18 40	18 44	18 47	18 47	18 51	18 53	18 55		19 00	19 00	19 01	19 07	19 08	19 10	19 12	19 14	19 17		19 17	19 21	19 23	19 25	19 29	19 30
Norwood Junction 2	d					18 55		18 59		19 05			19 13								19 25				19 35
New Cross Gate	d							19 07		19 22															19 52
London Bridge 4 ⊖	a				19 02	19 09		19 13		19 29		19 17	19 25							19 32	19 39				19 59
London Blackfriars 3 ⊖	a																								
City Thameslink 3	a																								
Farringdon 3 ⊖	a																								
St Pancras International 15 ⊖	a																								
Clapham Junction 10	a	18 50	18 55	19 07			19 02				19 09			19 17	19 34	19 21	19 25	19 37				19 32	19 37	19 40	
London Victoria 15 ⊖	a	18 57	19 02	19 16			19 10				19 16			19 24		19 28	19 32	19 46				19 40	19 44	19 50	

Table 175

Saturdays

Purley and East Croydon - London

COMPLETE SERVICE

	FC	SN	SN		SN	SN	SN	FC	SN	SN	SN	SN	SN		FC	SN	SN	SN	FC	SN	SN	SN	SN	
	1	1	◇1		◇1	1		1		◇1	1		1		1	◇1	1		1		◇1	1		
Purley 4 d							19 38		19 45		19 49	19 51						20 08		20 15		20 19	20 21	
Purley Oaks d							19 41					19 54						20 11					20 24	
South Croydon 4 d							19 44					19 57						20 14					20 27	
East Croydon d	19 32	19 33	19 38		19 42	19 44	19 47	19 47	19 51	19 53	19 57	20 00	20 00		20 01	20 12	20 14	20 17	20 17	20 21	20 23	20 26	20 30	
Norwood Junction 2 d									19 55			20 05								20 25			20 35	
New Cross Gate d												20 22											20 52	
London Bridge 4 ⊖ a	19 47	19 49						20 02	20 09			20 29			20 17				20 32	20 39			20 59	
London Blackfriars 3 ⊖ a																								
City Thameslink 3 a																								
Farringdon 3 ⊖ a																								
St Pancras International 15 ⊖ a																								
Clapham Junction 10 a			19 47		19 51	19 55	20 07			20 02	20 08		20 11			20 21	20 25	20 37			20 32	20 37		
London Victoria 15 ⊖ a			19 54		19 58	20 05	20 16			20 10	20 15		20 20			20 28	20 32	20 46			20 40	20 44		

	SN	FC	SN	SN	SN	SN	FC	SN	SN		SN	SN	SN	FC	SN	SN	SN	FC	SN		SN	SN	SN	SN
	◇1	1	1	◇1	1		1		◇1		1		◇1	1	◇1	1		1			◇1	1		◇1
Purley 4 d						20 38		20 45			20 49	20 51					21 08		21 15			21 19	21 21	
Purley Oaks d						20 41						20 54					21 11						21 24	
South Croydon 4 d						20 44						20 57					21 14						21 27	
East Croydon d	20 30	20 32	20 33	20 42	20 44	20 47	20 47	20 51	20 53		20 56	21 00	21 00	21 01	21 09	21 14	21 17	21 17	21 21		21 23	21 26	21 30	21 31
Norwood Junction 2 d								20 55				21 05							21 25				21 35	
New Cross Gate d												21 22											21 52	
London Bridge 4 ⊖ a		20 47	20 49				21 02	21 09				21 29		21 17				21 32	21 39				21 59	
London Blackfriars 3 ⊖ a																								
City Thameslink 3 a																								
Farringdon 3 ⊖ a																								
St Pancras International 15 ⊖ a																								
Clapham Junction 10 a	20 40			20 51	20 55	21 07			21 02		21 07		21 10		21 18	21 25	21 37				21 32	21 37		21 40
London Victoria 15 ⊖ a	20 50			20 58	21 02	21 16			21 10		21 14		21 17		21 26	21 32	21 46				21 40	21 44		21 50

	FC	SN	SN	SN	SN		SN	SN	SN	SN	SN	FC	SN	SN	SN		SN	SN	SN	SN	SN	FC	SN	SN
	1	1	◇1	1				◇1	1		◇1	1	◇1	1				◇1	1		◇1	1	1	◇1 trolley
Purley 4 d					21 38		21 45		21 49	21 51					22 08		22 15		22 19	22 21				
Purley Oaks d					21 41					21 54					22 11					22 24				
South Croydon 4 d					21 44					21 57					22 14					22 27				
East Croydon d	21 32	21 33	21 42	21 44	21 47		21 51	21 53	21 56	22 00	22 00	22 01	22 09	22 14	22 17		22 21	22 23	22 26	22 30	22 31	22 32	22 33	22 40
Norwood Junction 2 d							21 55			22 05							22 25			22 35				
New Cross Gate d										22 22										22 52				
London Bridge 4 ⊖ a	21 47	21 49					22 09			22 29		22 17					22 39			22 59		22 47	22 49	
London Blackfriars 3 ⊖ a																								
City Thameslink 3 a																								
Farringdon 3 ⊖ a																								
St Pancras International 15 ⊖ a																								
Clapham Junction 10 a			21 51	21 55	22 07			22 02	22 07		22 10		22 18	22 25	22 37			22 32	22 37		22 40			22 49
London Victoria 15 ⊖ a			21 58	22 02	22 16			22 13	22 15		22 20		22 26	22 35	22 46			22 40	22 44		22 50			22 57

	SN		SN	SN	SN	SN	FC	SN	SN	SN	SN		SN	FC	SN	SN								
	1				1	◇1	1		1				◇1	1		1								
Purley 4 d			22 38	22 45	22 50			22 52		23 08	23 15				23 34	23 49								
Purley Oaks d			22 41					22 55		23 11					23 37									
South Croydon 4 d			22 44					22 58		23 14					23 40									
East Croydon d	22 44		22 47	22 51	22 56	23 00	23 01	23 01	23 14	23 17	23 21		23 30	23 32	23 43	23 56								
Norwood Junction 2 d				22 55				23 06			23 25				23a47									
New Cross Gate d								23 23																
London Bridge 4 ⊖ a				23 09			23 17	23 30			23 39			23 47										
London Blackfriars 3 ⊖ a																								
City Thameslink 3 a																								
Farringdon 3 ⊖ a																								
St Pancras International 15 ⊖ a																								
Clapham Junction 10 a	22 55		23 07		23 06	23 10			23 25	23 37			23 41			00 11								
London Victoria 15 ⊖ a	23 05		23 16		23 14	23 20			23 35	23 48			23 52			00 18								

Sundays

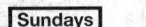

	SN	FC	SN	FC	SN	SN	SN	SN	SN		SN	FC	SN	FC	SN	SN	FC	SN	SN		SN	SN	FC	SN
	1	1	◇1	1		1	1	1	1		◇1	1	1	1			1	◇1				1	1	
	A	A	A	A																				
Purley 4 d	23p49		00 11			01 37	02 33	03 33	04 33		05 22		05 56			06 38					07 08	07 20		
Purley Oaks d																06 41					07 11			
South Croydon 4 d																06 44					07 14	07 24		
East Croydon d	23p56	00 04	00 17	00 36	00 49	01 43	02 40	03 40	04 40		05 28	05 32	06 02	06 32	06 40	06 47	07 02	07 10	07 12		07 17	07 27	07 32	07 42
Norwood Junction 2 d												05 36		06 36		06 52					07 22			
New Cross Gate d																07 09					07 39			
London Bridge 4 ⊖ a		00 19		00 52								05 59		06 59		07 17	07 15		07 50		07 48		07 45	08 19
London Blackfriars 3 ⊖ a																								
City Thameslink 3 a																								
Farringdon 3 ⊖ a																								
St Pancras International 15 ⊖ a																								
Clapham Junction 10 a	00 11		00 29		01 03	01 54	02 53	03 53	04 53		05 47		06 14		07 00			07 24				07 41		
London Victoria 15 ⊖ a	00 18		00 37		01 10	02 05	03 05	04 05	05 05		05 56		06 22		07 09			07 31				07 48		

A not 11 December

Table 175

Sundays

Purley and East Croydon - London

COMPLETE SERVICE

		SN	SN	SN 1	SN ◇1	FC 1		SN ◇1 (trolley)	SN	SN	SN	SN ◇1	FC 1	SN ◇1	SN	SN		SN 1	SN	SN 1	SN ◇1	FC 1	SN ◇1 (trolley)	SN	SN ◇1 (trolley)
Purley 4	d	07 38	07 47	07 50						08 08	08 17	08 20				08 38			08 47	08 50					
Purley Oaks	d	07 41								08 11						08 41									
South Croydon 4	d	07 44								08 14						08 44									
East Croydon	d	07 47	07 53	07 56	08 00	08 02		08 10	08 12	08 17	08 23	08 26	08 32	08 41	08 42	08 47		08 50	08 53	08 56	09 00	09 02	09 10	09 12	09 13
Norwood Junction 2	d	07 52		08 01						08 22						08 52				09 01					
New Cross Gate	d	08 09								08 39						09 09									
London Bridge 4 ⊖	a	08 17		08 12		08 15			08 49	08 48			08 45		09 19	09 18				09 12		09 15		09 49	
London Blackfriars 3 ⊖	a																								
City Thameslink 3	a																								
Farringdon 3 ⊖	a																								
St Pancras International 15 ⊖	a																								
Clapham Junction 10	a		08 12		08 11			08 23			08 42	08 37		08 54				09 01	09 12		09 11		09 24		09 27
London Victoria 15 ⊖	a		08 20		08 18			08 30			08 50	08 46		09 01				09 08	09 20		09 18		09 31		09 35

		SN		SN	SN ◇1 (trolley)	FC 1	SN ◇1	SN	SN	SN 1	SN	SN 1		SN ◇1	FC 1	SN ◇1 (trolley)	SN	SN ◇1 (trolley)	SN	SN	SN ◇1 (trolley)	FC 1		SN ◇1	SN
Purley 4	d	09 08		09 17	09 20				09 38		09 47	09 50							10 08	10 17	10 20				
Purley Oaks	d	09 11							09 41										10 11						
South Croydon 4	d	09 14							09 44										10 14						
East Croydon	d	09 17		09 23	09 26	09 32	09 41	09 42	09 47	09 50	09 53	09 56		10 00	10 02	10 10	10 12	10 14	10 17	10 23	10 26	10 32		10 40	10 42
Norwood Junction 2	d	09 22							09 52			10 01							10 22						
New Cross Gate	d	09 39							10 09										10 39						
London Bridge 4 ⊖	a	09 48				09 45		10 19	10 18			10 12			10 15		10 49		10 48			10 45			11 19
London Blackfriars 3 ⊖	a																								
City Thameslink 3	a																								
Farringdon 3 ⊖	a																								
St Pancras International 15 ⊖	a																								
Clapham Junction 10	a			09 42	09 37		09 54			10 01	10 12			10 11		10 24		10 27		10 42	10 37			10 54	
London Victoria 15 ⊖	a			09 50	09 46		10 01			10 08	10 20			10 18		10 31		10 35		10 50	10 46			11 01	

		SN	SN 1	SN	SN 1	SN ◇1	FC 1	SN ◇1 (trolley)		SN	SN ◇1 (trolley)	SN	SN	SN ◇1 (trolley)	FC 1	SN ◇1	SN	SN		SN 1	SN	SN 1	SN ◇1	FC 1	SN ◇1 (trolley)
Purley 4	d	10 38		10 47	10 50							11 08	11 17	11 20				11 38			11 47	11 50			
Purley Oaks	d	10 41										11 11						11 41							
South Croydon 4	d	10 44										11 14						11 44							
East Croydon	d	10 47	10 50	10 53	10 56	11 00	11 02	11 10		11 12	11 14	11 17	11 23	11 26	11 32	11 41	11 42	11 47		11 50	11 53	11 56	12 00	12 02	12 10
Norwood Junction 2	d	10 52			11 01							11 22						11 52				12 01			
New Cross Gate	d	11 09										11 39						12 09							
London Bridge 4 ⊖	a	11 18			11 12		11 15			11 49		11 48			11 45		12 19	12 18				12 12		12 15	
London Blackfriars 3 ⊖	a																								
City Thameslink 3	a																								
Farringdon 3 ⊖	a																								
St Pancras International 15 ⊖	a																								
Clapham Junction 10	a		11 01	11 12		11 11		11 24			11 27		11 42	11 37		11 54				12 01	12 12		12 11		12 24
London Victoria 15 ⊖	a		11 08	11 20		11 18		11 31			11 35		11 50	11 46		12 01				12 08	12 20		12 18		12 31

		SN	SN ◇1 (trolley)	SN		SN	SN ◇1 (trolley)	FC 1	SN ◇1	SN	SN	SN 1	SN	SN 1		SN ◇1	FC 1	SN ◇1 (trolley)	SN	SN ◇1 (trolley)	SN	SN	SN ◇1 (trolley)	FC 1	
Purley 4	d			12 08		12 17	12 20				12 38		12 47	12 50							13 08	13 17	13 19		
Purley Oaks	d			12 11							12 41										13 11				
South Croydon 4	d			12 14							12 44										13 14				
East Croydon	d	12 12	12 14	12 17		12 23	12 26	12 32	12 40	12 42	12 47	12 50	12 53	12 56		13 00	13 02	13 10	13 12	13 14	13 17	13 23	13 26	13 32	
Norwood Junction 2	d			12 22							12 52			13 01							13 22				
New Cross Gate	d			12 39							13 09										13 39				
London Bridge 4 ⊖	a	12 49		12 48				12 45		13 19	13 18			13 12			13 15		13 49		13 48			13 45	
London Blackfriars 3 ⊖	a																								
City Thameslink 3	a																								
Farringdon 3 ⊖	a																								
St Pancras International 15 ⊖	a																								
Clapham Junction 10	a		12 27			12 42	12 37		12 54			13 01	13 12			13 11		13 24		13 27		13 42	13 37		
London Victoria 15 ⊖	a		12 35			12 50	12 46		13 01			13 08	13 20			13 18		13 31		13 35		13 50	13 46		

		SN ◇1	SN	SN	SN 1	SN	SN 1	SN ◇1	FC 1	SN ◇1 (trolley)		SN	SN ◇1 (trolley)	SN	SN	SN ◇1 (trolley)	FC 1	SN ◇1	SN	SN		SN 1	SN	SN 1	SN ◇1
Purley 4	d			13 38		13 47	13 50							14 08	14 17	14 20				14 38			14 47	14 50	
Purley Oaks	d			13 41										14 11						14 41					
South Croydon 4	d			13 44										14 14						14 44					
East Croydon	d	13 40	13 42	13 47	13 50	13 53	13 56	14 00	14 02	14 10		14 12	14 14	14 17	14 23	14 26	14 32	14 41	14 42	14 47		14 50	14 53	14 56	15 00
Norwood Junction 2	d			13 52			14 01							14 22						14 52				15 01	
New Cross Gate	d			14 09										14 39						15 09					
London Bridge 4 ⊖	a		14 19	14 18			14 12		14 15			14 49		14 48			14 45		15 19	15 18				15 12	
London Blackfriars 3 ⊖	a																								
City Thameslink 3	a																								
Farringdon 3 ⊖	a																								
St Pancras International 15 ⊖	a																								
Clapham Junction 10	a	13 54			14 01	14 12		14 11		14 24			14 27		14 42	14 37		14 54				15 01	15 12		15 11
London Victoria 15 ⊖	a	14 01			14 08	14 20		14 18		14 31			14 35		14 50	14 46		15 01				15 08	15 20		15 18

Table 175

Sundays

Purley and East Croydon - London

COMPLETE SERVICE

		FC 1	SN ◇1 🛒	SN	SN ◇1 🛒	SN		SN	SN ◇1 🛒	FC 1	SN ◇1	SN	SN	SN 1	SN	SN 1		SN ◇1	FC 1	SN ◇1 🛒	SN	SN ◇1 🛒	SN	SN	SN ◇1 🛒
Purley 4	d					15 08		15 17	15 20				15 38		15 47	15 50							16 08	16 17	16 20
Purley Oaks	d					15 11							15 41										16 11		
South Croydon 4	d					15 14							15 44										16 14		
East Croydon	d	15 02	15 10	15 12	15 14	15 17		15 23	15 26	15 32	15 40	15 42	15 47	15 50	15 53	15 56		16 00	16 02	16 10	16 12	16 14	16 17	16 23	16 26
Norwood Junction 2	d					15 22							15 52			16 01							16 22		
New Cross Gate	d					15 39							16 09										16 39		
London Bridge 4 ⊖	a	15 15		15 49		15 48				15 45		16 19	16 18			16 12			16 15		16 49		16 48		
London Blackfriars 3 ⊖	a																								
City Thameslink 3	a																								
Farringdon 3 ⊖	a																								
St Pancras International 15 ⊖	a																								
Clapham Junction 10	a		15 24		15 27			15 42	15 37		15 54			16 01	16 12			16 11		16 24		16 27		16 42	16 37
London Victoria 15 ⊖	a		15 31		15 35			15 50	15 46		16 01			16 08	16 20			16 18		16 31		16 35		16 50	16 46

		FC 1		SN ◇1	SN	SN	SN 1	SN	SN 1	SN ◇1	FC 1	SN ◇1 🛒		SN	SN ◇1 🛒	SN	SN	SN ◇1 🛒	FC 1	SN ◇1	SN	SN		SN 1	SN
Purley 4	d					16 38		16 47	16 50							17 08	17 17	17 20				17 38			17 47
Purley Oaks	d					16 41										17 11						17 41			
South Croydon 4	d					16 44										17 14						17 44			
East Croydon	d	16 32		16 41	16 42	16 47	16 50	16 53	16 56	17 00	17 02	17 10		17 12	17 14	17 17	17 23	17 26	17 32	17 41	17 42	17 47		17 50	17 53
Norwood Junction 2	d					16 52			17 01							17 22						17 52			
New Cross Gate	d					17 09										17 39						18 09			
London Bridge 4 ⊖	a	16 45			17 19	17 18			17 12		17 15			17 49		17 48			17 45		18 19	18 18			
London Blackfriars 3 ⊖	a																								
City Thameslink 3	a																								
Farringdon 3 ⊖	a																								
St Pancras International 15 ⊖	a																								
Clapham Junction 10	a			16 54			17 01	17 12		17 11		17 24			17 27		17 42	17 37		17 54				18 01	18 12
London Victoria 15 ⊖	a			17 01			17 08	17 20		17 18		17 31			17 35		17 50	17 46		18 01				18 08	18 20

		SN 1	SN ◇1	FC 1	SN ◇1 🛒	SN	SN ◇1 🛒	SN		SN	SN ◇1 🛒	FC 1	SN ◇1	SN	SN	SN 1	SN	SN 1		SN ◇1	FC 1	SN ◇1 🛒	SN	SN ◇1	SN
Purley 4	d	17 50						18 08		18 17	18 20				18 38		18 47	18 50							19 08
Purley Oaks	d							18 11							18 41										19 11
South Croydon 4	d							18 14							18 44										19 14
East Croydon	d	17 56	18 00	18 02	18 10	18 12	18 14	18 17		18 23	18 26	18 32	18 41	18 42	18 47	18 50	18 53	18 56		19 00	19 02	19 10	19 12	19 14	19 17
Norwood Junction 2	d	18 01						18 22							18 52			19 01							19 22
New Cross Gate	d							18 40							19 09										19 39
London Bridge 4 ⊖	a	18 12		18 15		18 49		18 48				18 45		19 19	19 18			19 12			19 15		19 49		19 48
London Blackfriars 3 ⊖	a																								
City Thameslink 3	a																								
Farringdon 3 ⊖	a																								
St Pancras International 15 ⊖	a																								
Clapham Junction 10	a		18 11		18 24		18 27			18 42	18 37		18 54			19 01	19 12			19 11		19 24		19 27	
London Victoria 15 ⊖	a		18 18		18 31		18 35			18 50	18 46		19 01			19 08	19 20			19 18		19 31		19 35	

		SN	SN ◇1	FC 1		SN ◇1	SN	SN	SN 1	SN	SN 1	SN ◇1	FC 1	SN ◇1		SN	SN ◇1	SN	SN	SN ◇1	FC 1	SN ◇1	SN	SN	
Purley 4	d	19 17	19 20					19 38		19 47	19 50							20 08	20 17	20 20				20 38	
Purley Oaks	d							19 41										20 11						20 41	
South Croydon 4	d							19 44										20 14						20 44	
East Croydon	d	19 23	19 26	19 32		19 41	19 42	19 47	19 50	19 53	19 56	20 00	20 02	20 10		20 12	20 14	20 17	20 23	20 26	20 32	20 41	20 42	20 47	
Norwood Junction 2	d							19 52			20 01							20 22						20 52	
New Cross Gate	d							20 09										20 39						21 09	
London Bridge 4 ⊖	a			19 45			20 19	20 18			20 12		20 15			20 49		20 48			20 45		21 19	21 18	
London Blackfriars 3 ⊖	a																								
City Thameslink 3	a																								
Farringdon 3 ⊖	a																								
St Pancras International 15 ⊖	a																								
Clapham Junction 10	a	19 42	19 37			19 54			20 01	20 12		20 11		20 24			20 27		20 42	20 37		20 54			
London Victoria 15 ⊖	a	19 50	19 46			20 01			20 08	20 20		20 18		20 31			20 35		20 50	20 46		21 01			

		SN 1	SN	SN 1	SN ◇1	FC 1	SN ◇1	SN	SN ◇1	SN		SN	SN ◇1	FC 1	SN ◇1	SN	SN	SN 1	SN	SN 1		SN ◇1	FC 1	SN ◇1	SN
Purley 4	d		20 47	20 50						21 08		21 17	21 20				21 38		21 47	21 50					
Purley Oaks	d									21 11							21 41								
South Croydon 4	d									21 14							21 44								
East Croydon	d	20 50	20 53	20 56	21 00	21 02	21 10	21 12	21 14	21 17		21 23	21 26	21 32	21 41	21 42	21 47	21 50	21 53	21 56		22 00	22 02	22 10	22 12
Norwood Junction 2	d			21 01						21 22							21 52			22 01					
New Cross Gate	d									21 39							22 09								
London Bridge 4 ⊖	a			21 12		21 15		21 49		21 48				21 45		22 19	22 18			22 12			22 15		22 49
London Blackfriars 3 ⊖	a																								
City Thameslink 3	a																								
Farringdon 3 ⊖	a																								
St Pancras International 15 ⊖	a																								
Clapham Junction 10	a	21 01	21 12		21 11		21 24		21 27			21 42	21 37		21 54			22 01	22 12			22 11		22 24	
London Victoria 15 ⊖	a	21 08	21 20		21 18		21 31		21 35			21 50	21 46		22 01			22 08	22 20			22 18		22 31	

Table 175

Sundays

Purley and East Croydon - London

COMPLETE SERVICE

		SN	SN	SN	FC	SN		SN	SN	SN	SN	SN	FC	SN	SN	SN		FC	SN	SN					
				◇1	1				1		1	◇1	1			◇1		1	1	1					
Purley 4	d	22 08	22 17	22 20				22 38		22 47	22 50			23 08	23 17	23 20				23 50					
Purley Oaks	d	22 11						22 41						23 11	23 20										
South Croydon 4	d	22 14						22 44						23 14	23 23										
East Croydon	d	22 17	22 23	22 26	22 32	22 42		22 47	22 50	22 53	22 56	23 00	23 02	23 17	23a25	23 27		23 32	23 50	23 56					
Norwood Junction 2	d	22 22						22 52						23a21											
New Cross Gate	d	22 39						23 09																	
London Bridge 4 ⊖	a	22 48			22 45	23 19		23 18					23 15					23 45							
London Blackfriars 3 ⊖	a																								
City Thameslink 3	a																								
Farringdon 3 ⊖	a																								
St Pancras International 15 ⊖	a																								
Clapham Junction 10	a		22 42	22 37					23 01	23 12	23 07	23 12				23 38			00 01	00 11					
London Victoria 15 ⊖	a		22 50	22 46					23 08	23 20	23 14	23 20				23 46			00 08	00 19					

Network Diagram for Table 176

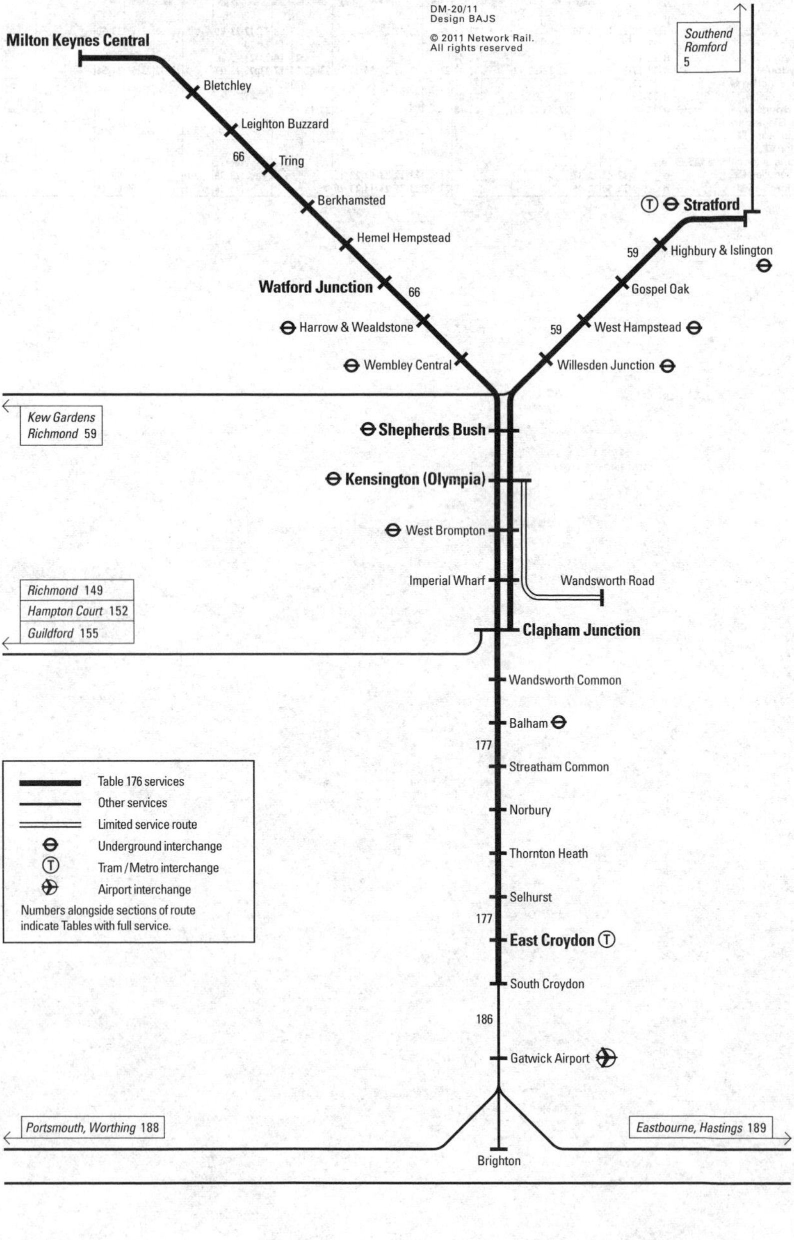

East Croydon, Clapham Junction, Kensington (Olympia) - Watford Junction and Milton Keynes Central

Miles	Miles			SN 1	SN 1	LO	SN 1	LO	LO	SN 1	LO	LO		LO	LO	SN 1	LO	LO	LO	SN	LO	SN 1		LO	SN
—	—	**South Croydon**	d																						
0	—	**East Croydon**	d																	07 50		08 07			
1	—	Selhurst 4	d																	07 54		08 13			
1¾	—	Thornton Heath	d																	07 56		08 16			
3	—	Norbury	d																	07 59		08 20			
4	—	Streatham Common 4	d																	08 02		08 23			
5¾	—	Balham 4	d		05 25															08 06		08 28			
6½	—	Wandsworth Common	d																	08 08		08 31			
—	—	Wandsworth Road	d																						
7¾	—	**Clapham Junction 10**	a		05 29															08 13		08 36			
—	—		d	05 03	05 30		05 55			06 38						07 39				08 14		08 39			08 48
8¾	—	Imperial Wharf	d	05 07	05 39	05 51	06 00	06 18	06 33	06 42	06 48	07 03		07 18	07 33	07 44	07 48	08 03	08 13	08 18	08 33	08 44		08 48	08 52
9½	—	West Brompton ⊖	d	05 10	05 41	05 54	06 03	06 21	06 36	06 45	06 51	07 06		07 21	07 36	07 47	07 51	08 06	08 16	08 21	08 36	08 47		08 51	08 55
11½	—	**Kensington (Olympia)** ⊖	d	05 14	05 44	05 57	06 07	06 24	06 39	06 49	06 54	07 09		07 24	07 39	07 50	07 54	08 09	08 19	08 25	08 39	08 50		08 54	08 59
12¾	0	**Shepherd's Bush** ⊖	d	05 17	05 47	05 59	06 10	06 26	06 41	06 52	06 56	07 11		07 26	07 41	07 53	07 56	08 11	08 21	08a27	08 41	08 53		08 56	09a01
—	1½	Willesden Jn. High Level ⊖	a			06 09		06 34	06 50		07 04	07 19		07 35	07 49		08 05	08 19	08 36		08 49			09 05	
—	4	West Hampstead ⊖	a					06 43	06 58		07 13	07 28		07 43	07 58		08 14	08 28	08 44		08 58			09 14	
—	6	Gospel Oak	a					06 49	07 04		07 19	07 34		07 49	08 04		08 20	08 34	08 52		09 04			09 20	
—	8¾	Highbury & Islington ⊖	a					07 00	07 15		07 30	07 45		08 00	08 15		08 31	08 45	09 02		09 15			09 31	
—	13½	Stratford	a					07 18	07 33		07 48	08 03		08 18	08 33		08 49	09 03	09 19		09 33			09 51	
17	—	Wembley Central ⊖	a		06 00		06 24			07 07						08 08						09 08			
20½	—	Harrow & Wealdstone ⊖	a	05 33	06 07		06 29			07 12						08 13						09 13			
25	—	**Watford Junction**	a	05 40	06 14		06 36			07 19						08 20						09 20			
32	—	Hemel Hempstead	a		06 22					07 27						08 28						09 28			
35½	—	Berkhamsted	a		06 26					07 31						08 32						09 32			
39¼	—	Tring	a		06 33					07 39						08 39						09 39			
47¾	—	Leighton Buzzard	a		06 41					07 50						08 47						09 47			
54¼	—	Bletchley	a		06 48					07 57						08 55						09 55			
57¼	—	**Milton Keynes Central 10**	a		06 55					08 03						09 01						10 01			

		LO	SN	LO	SN	LO	SN 1	LO		LO	LO	LO	SN 1	LO	LO	LO	LO	SN 1		LO	LO	LO	LO	SN 1	LO
South Croydon	d		08 35										10 07					11 07						12 07	
East Croydon	d		08 39				09 08						10 10					11 11						12 10	
Selhurst 4	d		08 43				09 13						10 14					11 16						12 14	
Thornton Heath	d		08 46				09 16						10 16					11 18						12 16	
Norbury	d		08 49				09 19						10 19					11 21						12 19	
Streatham Common 4	d		08 52				09 21						10 22					11 24						12 22	
Balham 4	d		08 58				09 28						10 29					11 28						12 28	
Wandsworth Common	d		09 00				09 30						10 31					11 30						12 30	
Wandsworth Road	d																								
Clapham Junction 10	a		09 04				09 34						10 35					11 33						12 34	
	d		09 05		09 24		09 39						10 39					11 39						12 39	
Imperial Wharf	d	09 03	09 09	09 19	09 28	09 34	09 44	09 49		10 04	10 19	10 36	10 44	10 49	11 04	11 19	11 34	11 44		11 49	12 04	12 19	12 35	12 44	12 49
West Brompton ⊖	d	09 06	09 12	09 22	09 31	09 37	09 47	09 52		10 07	10 22	10 39	10 47	10 52	11 07	11 22	11 37	11 47		11 52	12 07	12 22	12 38	12 47	12 52
Kensington (Olympia) ⊖	d	09 09	09 15	09 25	09 35	09 40	09 50	09 55		10 10	10 25	10 42	10 50	10 55	11 10	11 25	11 40	11 50		11 55	12 10	12 25	12 41	12 50	12 55
Shepherd's Bush ⊖	d	09 11	09a18	09 27	09a37	09 42	09 53	09 57		10 12	10 27	10 44	10 53	10 57	11 12	11 27	11 42	11 53		11 57	12 12	12 27	12 43	12 53	12 57
Willesden Jn. High Level ⊖	a	09 19		09 35		09 52		10 05		10 22	10 35	10 53		11 05	11 22	11 35	11 52			12 05	12 22	12 35	12 52		13 05
West Hampstead ⊖	a	09 29		09 44				10 14			10 44			11 14		11 44				12 14		12 44			13 14
Gospel Oak	a	09 36		09 50				10 20			10 50			11 20		11 50				12 20		12 50			13 20
Highbury & Islington ⊖	a	09 47		10 01				10 31			11 01			11 31		12 01				12 31		13 01			13 31
Stratford	a	10 05		10 20				10 50			11 20			11 49		12 20				12 50		13 20			13 50
Wembley Central ⊖	a						10 08						11 08					12 08						13 08	
Harrow & Wealdstone ⊖	a						10 13						11 13					12 13						13 13	
Watford Junction	a						10 20						11 20					12 20						13 20	
Hemel Hempstead	a						10 28						11 28					12 28						13 28	
Berkhamsted	a						10 32						11 32					12 32						13 32	
Tring	a						10 39						11 39					12 39						13 39	
Leighton Buzzard	a						10 47						11 48					12 48						13 48	
Bletchley	a						10 57						11 55					12 55						13 55	
Milton Keynes Central 10	a						11 02						12 01					13 01						14 01	

East Croydon, Clapham Junction, Kensington (Olympia) - Watford Junction and Milton Keynes Central

		LO	LO	LO		SN ■1	LO	LO	LO	LO	SN ■1	LO	LO	LO		LO	SN ■1	LO	LO	LO	SN	LO	SN ■1	LO	
South Croydon	d					13 07					14 07						15 07						16 07		
East Croydon 🚌	d					13 10					14 10						15 10						16 10		
Selhurst ■4	d					13 13					14 13						15 13						16 13		
Thornton Heath	d					13 16					14 16						15 16						16 16		
Norbury	d					13 19					14 19						15 19						16 19		
Streatham Common ■4	d					13 21					14 21						15 21						16 21		
Balham ■4	d					13 28					14 28						15 29						16 28		
Wandsworth Common	d					13 30					14 30						15 31						16 30		
Wandsworth Road	d																				16 12				
Clapham Junction ■10	a					13 34					14 34						15 35						16 34		
	d					13 39					14 39						15 39						16 39		
Imperial Wharf	d	13 04	13 19	13 36		13 44	13 49	14 04	14 19	14 34	14 44	14 55	15 04	15 19		15 34	15 44	15 49	16 03	16 18	16 24	16 33	16 44	16 48	
West Brompton ⊖	d	13 07	13 22	13 39		13 47	13 52	14 07	14 22	14 37	14 47	14 58	15 07	15 22		15 37	15 47	15 52	16 06	16 21	16 26	16 36	16 47	16 51	
Kensington (Olympia) ⊖	d	13 10	13 25	13 42		13 50	13 55	14 10	14 25	14 40	14 50	15 01	15 10	15 25		15 40	15 50	15 55	16 09	16 24	16a29	16 39	16 50	16 54	
Shepherd's Bush ⊖	d	13 12	13 27	13 44		13 53	13 57	14 12	14 27	14 42	14 53	15 03	15 12	15 27		15 42	15 53	15 57	16 11	16 26		16 41	16 53	16 56	
Willesden Jn. High Level ⊖	a	13 22	13 35	13 53			14 05	14 22	14 35	14 52		15 10	15 22	15 35		15 52		16 05	16 20	16 34		16 49		17 04	
West Hampstead ⊖	a		13 44				14 14		14 44			15 19		15 44				16 14	16 28	16 43		16 58		17 13	
Gospel Oak	a		13 50				14 20		14 50			15 26		15 50				16 20	16 34	16 49		17 04		17 19	
Highbury & Islington ⊖	a		14 01				14 31		15 01			15 37		16 01				16 31	16 45	17 00		17 15		17 30	
Stratford	a		14 20				14 50		15 20			15 56		16 20				16 49	17 05	17 20		17 35		17 50	
Wembley Central ⊖	a					14 08					15 08						16 08						17 08		
Harrow & Wealdstone ⊖	a					14 13					15 13						16 13						17 13		
Watford Junction	a					14 20					15 20						16 20						17 20		
Hemel Hempstead	a					14 28					15 28						16 28						17 28		
Berkhamsted	a					14 32					15 32						16 32						17 33		
Tring	a					14 39					15 39						16 39						17 38		
Leighton Buzzard	a					14 48					15 48						16 47						17 47		
Bletchley	a					14 55					15 55						16 55						17 54		
Milton Keynes Central ■10	a					15 01					16 01						17 00						17 59		

		SN	LO	LO	SN	LO	SN ■1	LO	LO	LO		LO	SN ■1	LO	LO	LO	LO	SN ■1	LO	LO		LO	LO	SN ■1	LO
South Croydon	d						17 07																		
East Croydon 🚌	d						17 10						18 10					19 10							
Selhurst ■4	d						17 13						18 13					19 13							
Thornton Heath	d						17 16						18 16					19 16							
Norbury	d						17 19						18 19					19 19							
Streatham Common ■4	d						17 21						18 21					19 21							
Balham ■4	d						17 28						18 29					19 28							
Wandsworth Common	d						17 30						18 31					19 30							
Wandsworth Road	d																								
Clapham Junction ■10	a						17 34						18 35					19 34							
	d	16 49			17 20		17 39						18 39					19 39						20 39	
Imperial Wharf	d	16 53	17 03	17 18	17 24	17 33	17 44	17 48	18 03	18 18		18 33	18 44	18 48	19 03	19 19	19 34	19 44	19 49	20 04		20 19	20 34	20 44	20 49
West Brompton ⊖	d	16 56	17 06	17 21	17 27	17 36	17 47	17 51	18 06	18 21		18 36	18 47	18 51	19 06	19 22	19 37	19 47	19 52	20 07		20 22	20 37	20 47	20 52
Kensington (Olympia) ⊖	d	16a59	17 09	17 24	17 30	17 39	17 50	17 54	18 09	18 24		18 39	18 50	18 54	19 09	19 25	19 40	19 50	19 55	20 10		20 25	20 40	20 50	20 55
Shepherd's Bush ⊖	d		17 11	17 26	17a32	17 41	17 53	17 56	18 11	18 26		18 41	18 53	18 56	19 11	19 27	19 42	19 53	19 57	20 12		20 27	20 42	20 53	20 57
Willesden Jn. High Level ⊖	a		17 19	17 34		17 49		18 04	18 19	18 34		18 49		19 04	19 19	19 35	19 52		20 05	20 22		20 35	20 52		21 05
West Hampstead ⊖	a		17 28	17 43		17 58		18 13	18 28	18 43		18 58		19 13	19 28	19 44			20 14			20 44			21 14
Gospel Oak	a		17 34	17 49		18 04		18 19	18 34	18 49		19 04		19 19	19 34	19 50			20 20			20 50			21 20
Highbury & Islington ⊖	a		17 45	18 00		18 15		18 30	18 45	19 00		19 15		19 30	19 45	20 01			20 32			21 01			21 31
Stratford	a		18 05	18 20		18 35		18 50	19 05	19 21		19 35		19 50	20 04	20 20			20 51			21 20			21 50
Wembley Central ⊖	a						18 08						19 08					20 08						21 08	
Harrow & Wealdstone ⊖	a						18 13						19 13					20 13						21 13	
Watford Junction	a						18 20						19 20					20 20						21 20	
Hemel Hempstead	a						18 28						19 28					20 28						21 28	
Berkhamsted	a						18 32						19 33					20 32						21 32	
Tring	a						18 38						19 40					20 39						21 39	
Leighton Buzzard	a						18 46						19 51					20 48						21 50	
Bletchley	a						18 53						20 00					20 55						21 58	
Milton Keynes Central ■10	a						19 00						20 06					21 01						22 05	

Table 176

East Croydon, Clapham Junction, Kensington (Olympia) - Watford Junction and Milton Keynes Central

	LO	LO	LO	SN 1	LO		LO	LO	LO	SN 1	LO	LO	LO
South Croydon d													
East Croydon d													
Selhurst 4 d													
Thornton Heath d													
Norbury d													
Streatham Common 4 d													
Balham 4 d													
Wandsworth Common d													
Wandsworth Road d													
Clapham Junction 10 a													
d				21 39						22 39			
Imperial Wharf d	21 04	21 19	21 34	21 44	21 49		22 04	22 19	22 34	22 44	22 49	23 04	23 34
West Brompton ⊖ d	21 07	21 22	21 37	21 47	21 52		22 07	22 22	22 37	22 47	22 52	23 07	23 37
Kensington (Olympia) ⊖ d	21 10	21 25	21 40	21 50	21 55		22 10	22 25	22 40	22 50	22 55	23 10	23 40
Shepherd's Bush ⊖ d	21 12	21 27	21 42	21 53	21 57		22 12	22 27	22 42	22 53	22 57	23 12	23 42
Willesden Jn. High Level ⊖ a	21 22	21 35	21 52		22 05		22 22	22 37	22 52		23 07	23 24	23 52
West Hampstead ⊖ a		21 44			22 14								
Gospel Oak a		21 50			22 20								
Highbury & Islington ⊖ a		22 01			22 31								
Stratford a		22 20			22 50								
Wembley Central ⊖ a													
Harrow & Wealdstone ⊖ a				22 16						23 16			
Watford Junction a				22 23						23 23			
Hemel Hempstead a													
Berkhamsted a													
Tring a													
Leighton Buzzard a													
Bletchley a													
Milton Keynes Central 10 a													

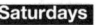

Saturdays

	SN 1	SN 1	LO	SN 1	LO	LO	SN 1	LO	LO		LO	LO	SN 1	LO	LO	LO	LO	SN 1	LO		LO	LO	LO	SN 1
South Croydon d													07 07					08 07						09 07
East Croydon d							06 10						07 10					08 10						09 10
Selhurst 4 d							06 13						07 13					08 13						09 13
Thornton Heath d							06 16						07 16					08 16						09 16
Norbury d							06 19						07 19					08 19						09 19
Streatham Common 4 d							06 21						07 21					08 21						09 21
Balham 4 d		05 33					06 28						07 28					08 28						09 28
Wandsworth Common d							06 30						07 30					08 30						09 30
Wandsworth Road d																								
Clapham Junction 10 a		05 37					06 34						07 34					08 34						09 34
d	05 08	05 38		06 09			06 39						07 39					08 39						09 39
Imperial Wharf d	05 12	05 42	05 51	06 13	06 19	06 34	06 44	06 49	07 04		07 19	07 34	07 44	07 49	08 04	08 19	08 34	08 44	08 49		09 04	09 19	09 34	09 44
West Brompton ⊖ d	05 15	05 45	05 54	06 16	06 22	06 37	06 47	06 52	07 07		07 22	07 37	07 47	07 52	08 07	08 22	08 37	08 47	08 52		09 07	09 22	09 37	09 47
Kensington (Olympia) ⊖ d	05 19	05 49	05 57	06 20	06 25	06 40	06 50	06 55	07 10		07 25	07 40	07 50	07 55	08 10	08 25	08 40	08 50	08 55		09 10	09 25	09 40	09 50
Shepherd's Bush ⊖ d	05 22	05 52	05 59	06 23	06 27	06 42	06 53	06 57	07 12		07 27	07 42	07 53	07 57	08 12	08 27	08 42	08 53	08 57		09 12	09 27	09 42	09 53
Willesden Jn. High Level ⊖ a			06 09		06 35	06 54		07 05	07 22		07 35	07 52		08 05	08 22	08 35	08 52		09 05		09 22	09 35	09 52	
West Hampstead ⊖ a					06 44			07 14			07 44			08 14		08 44			09 14			09 44		
Gospel Oak a					06 50			07 20			07 50			08 20		08 50			09 20			09 50		
Highbury & Islington ⊖ a					07 01			07 31			08 01			08 31		09 01			09 31			10 01		
Stratford a					07 20			07 50			08 20			08 50		09 20			09 50			10 20		
Wembley Central ⊖ a		06 07		06 38			07 07						08 07					09 07						10 07
Harrow & Wealdstone ⊖ a	05 40	06 12		06 43			07 12						08 12					09 12						10 12
Watford Junction a	05 47	06 19		06 50			07 19						08 19					09 19						10 19
Hemel Hempstead a		06 27					07 27						08 27					09 27						10 27
Berkhamsted a		06 31					07 32						08 31					09 33						10 31
Tring a		06 37					07 39						08 37					09 38						10 37
Leighton Buzzard a		06 46					07 47						08 46					09 47						10 47
Bletchley a		06 54					07 54						08 54					09 54						10 54
Milton Keynes Central 10 a		07 00					08 00						09 00					10 00						11 00

Table 176

Saturdays

East Croydon, Clapham Junction, Kensington (Olympia) - Watford Junction and Milton Keynes Central

		LO	LO	LO	LO	SN 1		LO	LO	LO	LO	SN 1	LO	LO	LO	LO		SN 1	LO	LO	LO	LO	SN 1	LO	LO
South Croydon	d					10 07						11 07						12 07					13 07		
East Croydon	d					10 10						11 10						12 10					13 10		
Selhurst 4	d					10 13						11 13						12 13					13 13		
Thornton Heath	d					10 16						11 16						12 16					13 16		
Norbury	d					10 19						11 19						12 19					13 19		
Streatham Common 4	d					10 21						11 21						12 21					13 21		
Balham 4	d					10 28						11 28						12 28					13 28		
Wandsworth Common	d					10 30						11 30						12 30					13 30		
Wandsworth Road	d																								
Clapham Junction 10	a					10 34						11 34						12 34					13 34		
	d					10 39						11 39						12 39					13 39		
Imperial Wharf	d	09 49	10 04	10 19	10 34	10 44		10 49	11 04	11 19	11 34	11 44	11 49	12 04	12 19	12 34		12 44	12 49	13 04	13 19	13 34	13 44	13 49	14 04
West Brompton ⊖	d	09 52	10 07	10 22	10 37	10 47		10 52	11 07	11 22	11 37	11 47	11 52	12 07	12 22	12 37		12 47	12 52	13 07	13 22	13 37	13 47	13 52	14 07
Kensington (Olympia) ⊖	d	09 55	10 10	10 25	10 40	10 50		10 55	11 10	11 25	11 40	11 50	11 55	12 10	12 25	12 40		12 50	12 55	13 10	13 25	13 40	13 50	13 55	14 10
Shepherd's Bush ⊖	d	09 57	10 12	10 27	10 42	10 53		10 57	11 12	11 27	11 42	11 53	11 57	12 12	12 27	12 42		12 53	12 57	13 12	13 27	13 42	13 53	13 57	14 12
Willesden Jn. High Level ⊖	a	10 05	10 22	10 35	10 52			11 05	11 22	11 35	11 52		12 05	12 22	12 35	12 52			13 05	13 22	13 35	13 52		14 05	14 22
West Hampstead ⊖	a	10 14		10 44				11 14		11 44			12 14		12 44				13 14		13 44			14 14	
Gospel Oak	a	10 20		10 50				11 20		11 50			12 20		12 50				13 20		13 50			14 20	
Highbury & Islington ⊖	a	10 31		11 01				11 31		12 01			12 31		13 01				13 31		14 01			14 31	
Stratford	a	10 50		11 20				11 50		12 20			12 50		13 20				13 50		14 20			14 50	
Wembley Central ⊖	a					11 08						12 07						13 07					14 08		
Harrow & Wealdstone ⊖	a					11 13						12 13						13 12					14 13		
Watford Junction	a					11 20						12 20						13 19					14 20		
Hemel Hempstead	a					11 28						12 28						13 27					14 28		
Berkhamsted	a					11 33						12 32						13 32					14 32		
Tring	a					11 38						12 37						13 37					14 37		
Leighton Buzzard	a					11 47						12 47						13 47					14 47		
Bletchley	a					11 54						12 54						13 54					14 54		
Milton Keynes Central 10	a					12 00						13 00						14 00					15 00		

		LO		LO	SN 1	LO	LO	LO	LO	SN 1	LO	LO		LO	LO	SN 1	LO	LO	LO	LO	SN 1	LO		LO	LO
South Croydon	d				14 07					15 07						16 07					17 07				
East Croydon	d				14 10					15 10						16 10					17 10				
Selhurst 4	d				14 13					15 13						16 13					17 13				
Thornton Heath	d				14 16					15 16						16 16					17 16				
Norbury	d				14 19					15 19						16 19					17 19				
Streatham Common 4	d				14 21					15 21						16 21					17 21				
Balham 4	d				14 28					15 28						16 28					17 28				
Wandsworth Common	d				14 30					15 30						16 30					17 30				
Wandsworth Road	d																								
Clapham Junction 10	a				14 34					15 34						16 34					17 34				
	d				14 39					15 39						16 39					17 39				
Imperial Wharf	d	14 19		14 34	14 44	14 49	15 04	15 19	15 34	15 44	15 49	16 04		16 19	16 34	16 44	16 49	17 04	17 19	17 34	17 44	17 49		18 04	18 19
West Brompton ⊖	d	14 22		14 37	14 47	14 52	15 07	15 22	15 37	15 47	15 52	16 07		16 22	16 37	16 47	16 52	17 07	17 22	17 37	17 47	17 52		18 07	18 22
Kensington (Olympia) ⊖	d	14 25		14 40	14 50	14 55	15 10	15 25	15 40	15 50	15 55	16 10		16 25	16 40	16 50	16 55	17 10	17 25	17 40	17 50	17 55		18 10	18 25
Shepherd's Bush ⊖	d	14 27		14 42	14 53	14 57	15 12	15 27	15 42	15 53	15 57	16 12		16 27	16 42	16 53	16 57	17 12	17 27	17 42	17 53	17 57		18 12	18 27
Willesden Jn. High Level ⊖	a	14 35		14 52		15 05	15 22	15 35	15 52		16 05	16 22		16 35	16 54		17 05	17 22	17 35	17 52		18 05		18 22	18 35
West Hampstead ⊖	a	14 44				15 14		15 44			16 14			16 44			17 14		17 44			18 14			18 44
Gospel Oak	a	14 50				15 20		15 50			16 20			16 50			17 20		17 50			18 20			18 50
Highbury & Islington ⊖	a	15 01				15 31		16 01			16 31			17 01			17 31		18 01			18 31			19 01
Stratford	a	15 20				15 50		16 20			16 50			17 20			17 50		18 20			18 50			19 20
Wembley Central ⊖	a				15 07					16 07						17 07					18 07				
Harrow & Wealdstone ⊖	a				15 12					16 12						17 12					18 12				
Watford Junction	a				15 19					16 19						17 19					18 19				
Hemel Hempstead	a				15 27					16 27						17 27					18 27				
Berkhamsted	a				15 32					16 32						17 32					18 32				
Tring	a				15 37					16 37						17 37					18 37				
Leighton Buzzard	a				15 47					16 47						17 46					18 46				
Bletchley	a				15 54					16 54						17 54					18 54				
Milton Keynes Central 10	a				16 00					17 00						18 00					19 00				

Table 176

Saturdays

East Croydon, Clapham Junction, Kensington (Olympia) - Watford Junction and Milton Keynes Central

		LO	SN 1	LO	LO	LO	LO	SN 1	LO	LO	LO	SN 1	LO	LO	LO	LO	LO	SN 1	LO	LO	LO	LO	SN 1
South Croydon	d		18 07					19 07															
East Croydon	d		18 10					19 10															
Selhurst 4	d		18 13					19 13															
Thornton Heath	d		18 16					19 16															
Norbury	d		18 19					19 19															
Streatham Common 4	d		18 21					19 21															
Balham 4	d		18 28					19 28															
Wandsworth Common	d		18 30					19 30															
Wandsworth Road	d																						
Clapham Junction 10	a		18 34					19 34															
	d		18 39					19 38				20 25						21 39					22 39
Imperial Wharf	d	18 34	18 44	18 49	19 04	19 19	19 34	19 42	19 49	20 04	20 19	20 29	20 34	20 49	21 04	21 19	21 34	21 44	21 49	22 04	22 19	22 34	22 44
West Brompton ⊖	d	18 37	18 47	18 52	19 07	19 22	19 37	19 45	19 52	20 07	20 22	20 32	20 37	20 52	21 07	21 22	21 37	21 47	21 52	22 07	22 22	22 37	22 47
Kensington (Olympia) ⊖	d	18 40	18 50	18 55	19 10	19 25	19 40	19 48	19 55	20 10	20 25	20 36	20 40	20 55	21 10	21 25	21 40	21 50	21 55	22 10	22 25	22 40	22 50
Shepherd's Bush ⊖	d	18 42	18 53	18 57	19 12	19 27	19 42	19 50	19 57	20 12	20 27	20 39	20 42	20 57	21 12	21 27	21 42	21 53	21 57	22 12	22 27	22 42	22 53
Willesden Jn. High Level ⊖	a	18 52		19 05	19 22	19 35	19 52		20 05	20 22	20 35		20 52	21 05	21 22	21 35	21 53		22 05	22 22	22 37	22 53	
West Hampstead ⊖	a			19 14		19 44			20 14		20 44			21 14		21 44			22 14				
Gospel Oak	a			19 20		19 50			20 20		20 50			21 20		21 50			22 20				
Highbury & Islington ⊖	a			19 31		20 01			20 31		21 01			21 31		22 01			22 31				
Stratford	a			19 50		20 20			20 50		21 20			21 50		22 20			22 50				
Wembley Central ⊖	a		19 08																				
Harrow & Wealdstone ⊖	a		19 13					20 08				21 02						22 13					23 12
Watford Junction	a		19 21					20 15				21 09						22 20					23 19
Hemel Hempstead	a																						
Berkhamsted	a																						
Tring	a																						
Leighton Buzzard	a																						
Bletchley	a																						
Milton Keynes Central 10	a																						

		LO	LO	LO
South Croydon	d			
East Croydon	d			
Selhurst 4	d			
Thornton Heath	d			
Norbury	d			
Streatham Common 4	d			
Balham 4	d			
Wandsworth Common	d			
Wandsworth Road	d			
Clapham Junction 10	a			
	d			
Imperial Wharf	d	22 51	23 04	23 34
West Brompton ⊖	d	22 54	23 07	23 37
Kensington (Olympia) ⊖	d	22 59	23 10	23 40
Shepherd's Bush ⊖	d	23 01	23 12	23 42
Willesden Jn. High Level ⊖	a	23 09	23 22	23 52
West Hampstead ⊖	a			
Gospel Oak	a			
Highbury & Islington ⊖	a			
Stratford	a			
Wembley Central ⊖	a			
Harrow & Wealdstone ⊖	a			
Watford Junction	a			
Hemel Hempstead	a			
Berkhamsted	a			
Tring	a			
Leighton Buzzard	a			
Bletchley	a			
Milton Keynes Central 10	a			

Table 176

Sundays

East Croydon, Clapham Junction, Kensington (Olympia) - Watford Junction and Milton Keynes Central

		SN 1	SN 1	LO	LO	SN 1	LO	LO	SN 1	LO		LO	LO	LO	SN 1	LO	LO	LO	LO	SN 1		LO	LO	LO	LO
South Croydon	d																								
East Croydon	d																								
Selhurst 4	d																								
Thornton Heath	d																								
Norbury	d																								
Streatham Common 4	d																								
Balham 4	d																								
Wandsworth Common	d																								
Wandsworth Road	d																								
Clapham Junction 10	a																								
	d	07 24	08 15			09 15			10 15						11 15					12 05					
Imperial Wharf	d	07 28	08 19	08 34	09 04	09 19	09 34	10 04	10 19	10 24		10 34	10 49	11 04	11 19	11 24	11 34	11 49	12 04	12 09		12 19	12 34	12 49	13 04
West Brompton ⊖	d	07 31	08 22	08 37	09 07	09 22	09 37	10 07	10 22	10 27		10 37	10 52	11 07	11 22	11 27	11 37	11 52	12 07	12 12		12 22	12 37	12 52	13 07
Kensington (Olympia) ⊖	d	07 34	08 26	08 40	09 10	09 26	09 40	10 10	10 26	10 30		10 40	10 55	11 10	11 26	11 30	11 40	11 55	12 10	12 16		12 25	12 40	12 55	13 10
Shepherd's Bush ⊖	d	07a36	08 29	08 42	09 12	09 29	09 42	10 12	10 29	10 32		10 42	10 57	11 12	11 29	11 32	11 42	11 57	12 12	12 19		12 27	12 42	12 57	13 12
Willesden Jn. High Level ⊖	a			08 52	09 22		09 52	10 22		10 40		10 52	11 05	11 22		11 40	11 54	12 05	12 22			12 35	12 52	13 05	13 22
West Hampstead ⊖	a									10 49			11 14			11 49		12 14				12 44		13 14	
Gospel Oak	a									10 55			11 20			11 55		12 20				12 50		13 20	
Highbury & Islington ⊖	a									11 06			11 31			12 06		12 31				13 01		13 31	
Stratford	a									11 25			11 50			12 25		12 50				13 20		13 50	
Wembley Central ⊖	a																								
Harrow & Wealdstone ⊖	a		08 48			09 48			10 48						11 48					12 36					
Watford Junction	a		08 56			09 58			10 56						11 56					12 44					
Hemel Hempstead	a																								
Berkhamsted	a																								
Tring	a																								
Leighton Buzzard	a																								
Bletchley	a																								
Milton Keynes Central 10	a																								

		SN 1	LO	LO	LO	LO		SN 1	LO	LO	LO	LO	SN 1	LO	LO	LO		LO	SN 1	LO	LO	LO	LO	SN 1	LO
South Croydon	d																								
East Croydon	d																								
Selhurst 4	d																								
Thornton Heath	d																								
Norbury	d																								
Streatham Common 4	d																								
Balham 4	d																								
Wandsworth Common	d																								
Wandsworth Road	d																								
Clapham Junction 10	a																								
	d	13 05						14 05					15 05						16 05					17 05	
Imperial Wharf	d	13 09	13 19	13 34	13 49	14 04		14 09	14 19	14 34	14 49	15 04	15 09	15 19	15 34	15 49		16 04	16 09	16 19	16 34	16 49	17 04	17 09	17 19
West Brompton ⊖	d	13 12	13 22	13 37	13 52	14 07		14 12	14 22	14 37	14 52	15 07	15 12	15 22	15 37	15 52		16 07	16 12	16 22	16 37	16 52	17 07	17 12	17 22
Kensington (Olympia) ⊖	d	13 16	13 25	13 40	13 55	14 10		14 16	14 25	14 40	14 55	15 10	15 16	15 25	15 40	15 55		16 10	16 16	16 25	16 40	16 55	17 10	17 16	17 25
Shepherd's Bush ⊖	d	13 19	13 27	13 42	13 57	14 12		14 19	14 27	14 42	14 57	15 12	15 19	15 27	15 42	15 57		16 12	16 19	16 27	16 42	16 57	17 12	17 19	17 27
Willesden Jn. High Level ⊖	a		13 35	13 52	14 05	14 24			14 35	14 52	15 05	15 22		15 35	15 52	16 05		16 22		16 35	16 52	17 05	17 22		17 35
West Hampstead ⊖	a		13 44		14 14				14 44		15 14			15 44		16 14				16 44		17 14			17 44
Gospel Oak	a		13 50		14 20				14 50		15 20			15 50		16 20				16 50		17 20			17 50
Highbury & Islington ⊖	a		14 01		14 31				15 01		15 31			16 01		16 31				17 01		17 31			18 01
Stratford	a		14 20		14 50				15 20		15 50			16 20		16 50				17 20		17 50			18 20
Wembley Central ⊖	a																								
Harrow & Wealdstone ⊖	a	13 36						14 36					15 36						16 36					17 36	
Watford Junction	a	13 44						14 44					15 44						16 44					17 44	
Hemel Hempstead	a																								
Berkhamsted	a																								
Tring	a																								
Leighton Buzzard	a																								
Bletchley	a																								
Milton Keynes Central 10	a																								

Table 176

Sundays

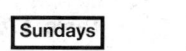

East Croydon, Clapham Junction, Kensington (Olympia) - Watford Junction and Milton Keynes Central

		LO		LO	LO	SN [1]	LO	LO	LO	LO	SN [1]	LO		LO	LO	LO	SN [1]	LO	LO	LO	LO	SN [1]		LO	LO
South Croydon	d																								
East Croydon 🚋	d																								
Selhurst [4]	d																								
Thornton Heath	d																								
Norbury	d																								
Streatham Common [4]	d																								
Balham [4]	d																								
Wandsworth Common	d																								
Wandsworth Road	d																								
Clapham Junction [10]	a																								
	d					18 05					19 05						20 05					21 15			
Imperial Wharf	d	17 34		17 49	18 04	18 09	18 19	18 34	18 49	19 04	19 09	19 19		19 34	19 49	20 04	20 09	20 19	20 34	20 49	21 04	21 19		21 24	21 34
West Brompton ⊖	d	17 37		17 52	18 07	18 12	18 22	18 37	18 52	19 07	19 12	19 22		19 37	19 52	20 07	20 12	20 22	20 37	20 52	21 07	21 22		21 27	21 37
Kensington (Olympia) ⊖	d	17 40		17 55	18 10	18 16	18 25	18 40	18 55	19 10	19 16	19 25		19 40	19 55	20 10	20 16	20 25	20 40	20 55	21 10	21 26		21 30	21 40
Shepherd's Bush ⊖	d	17 42		17 57	18 12	18 19	18 27	18 42	18 57	19 12	19 19	19 27		19 42	19 57	20 12	20 19	20 27	20 42	20 57	21 12	21 29		21 32	21 42
Willesden Jn. High Level ⊖	a	17 52		18 05	18 22		18 35	18 52	19 05	19 22		19 35		19 52	20 05	20 22		20 37	20 53	21 10	21 22			21 42	21 52
West Hampstead ⊖	a			18 14			18 44		19 14			19 44			20 14										
Gospel Oak	a			18 20			18 50		19 20			19 50			20 20										
Highbury & Islington ⊖	a			18 31			19 01		19 31			20 01			20 31										
Stratford	a			18 50			19 20		19 50			20 20			20 49										
Wembley Central ⊖	a																								
Harrow & Wealdstone ⊖	a					18 36					19 36						20 36					21 47			
Watford Junction	a					18 44					19 43						20 44					21 54			
Hemel Hempstead	a																								
Berkhamsted	a																								
Tring	a																								
Leighton Buzzard	a																								
Bletchley	a																								
Milton Keynes Central [10]	a																								

		LO	LO	SN [1]	LO	LO	LO
South Croydon	d						
East Croydon 🚋	d						
Selhurst [4]	d						
Thornton Heath	d						
Norbury	d						
Streatham Common [4]	d						
Balham [4]	d						
Wandsworth Common	d						
Wandsworth Road	d						
Clapham Junction [10]	a						
	d			22 15			
Imperial Wharf	d	21 49	22 04	22 19	22 24	22 48	23 19
West Brompton ⊖	d	21 52	22 07	22 22	22 27	22 51	23 22
Kensington (Olympia) ⊖	d	21 55	22 10	22 26	22 30	22 54	23 25
Shepherd's Bush ⊖	d	21 57	22 12	22 29	22 32	22 56	23 27
Willesden Jn. High Level ⊖	a	22 10	22 25		22 43	23 10	23 37
West Hampstead ⊖	a						
Gospel Oak	a						
Highbury & Islington ⊖	a						
Stratford	a						
Wembley Central ⊖	a						
Harrow & Wealdstone ⊖	a			22 48			
Watford Junction	a			22 56			
Hemel Hempstead	a						
Berkhamsted	a						
Tring	a						
Leighton Buzzard	a						
Bletchley	a						
Milton Keynes Central [10]	a						

Milton Keynes Central, Watford Junction, Kensington (Olympia) - Clapham Junction and East Croydon

Miles	Miles			SN MX 1	SN MO 1	SN MX 1	LO	SN 1	LO	LO	LO	SN 1		LO	LO	LO	SN 1	LO	LO	SN	LO	LO		SN	LO
0	—	**Milton Keynes Central** 10	d	22p11													07 01								
3	—	Bletchley	d	22p15													07 05								
9½	—	Leighton Buzzard	d	22p22													07 13								
18	—	Tring	d	22p34													07 22								
21¾	—	Berkhamsted	d	22p39													07 26								
25¼	—	Hemel Hempstead	d	22p43													07 31								
32¼	—	**Watford Junction**	d	22p53	23p17	23p29		05 54				06 53					07 38								
36¾	—	Harrow & Wealdstone ⊖	d	23p00	23p23	23p35		06 00				06 59					07 45								
40¼	—	Wembley Central ⊖	d					06 05				07 04					07 49								
—	0	Stratford 7 ⊖	d							06 05	06 20			06 35	06 50	07 00		07 20	07 35		07 50	08 05			08 20
—	4¾	Highbury & Islington ⊖	d							06 19	06 35			06 50	07 05	07 15		07 35	07 50		08 05	08 20			08 35
—	7½	Gospel Oak	d							06 30	06 45			07 00	07 15	07 25		07 45	08 00		08 15	08 30			08 45
—	9½	West Hampstead ⊖	d							06 36	06 51			07 06	07 21	07 31		07 51	08 06		08 21	08 36			08 51
—	12	Willesden Jn. High Level ⊖	d				06 01		06 33	06 46	07 01			07 16	07 31	07 41		08 01	08 16		08 31	08 46			09 01
44½	13½	**Shepherd's Bush** ⊖	d	23p21	23p45	23p54	06 08	06 19	06 40	06 54	07 09	07 19		07 24	07 39	07 49	08 04	08 09	08 24	08 31	08 39	08 54		09 06	09 09
45¾	—	**Kensington (Olympia)** ⊖	d	23p23	23p48	23p56	06 10	06 22	06 42	06 56	07 11	07 22		07 26	07 41	07 51	08 07	08 11	08 26	08 33	08 41	08 56		09 09	09 11
47¾	—	West Brompton ⊖	d	23p26	23p50	23p59	06 13	06 25	06 45	06 58	07 13	07 25		07 28	07 43	07 53	08 10	08 13	08 28	08 36	08 43	08 58		09 12	09 13
48½	—	Imperial Wharf	d	23p28	23p53	00 02	06a16	06 27	06a48	07a01	07a16	07 27		07a31	07a46	07a56	08 13	08a16	08a31	08 38	08a46	09a01		09 15	09a16
49½	—	**Clapham Junction** 10	a	23p33	23p58	00 07		06 32				07 32					08 17			08 43				09 19	
—	—		d	23p40	00 05												08 36								
—	—	Wandsworth Road	a																						
50¾	—	Wandsworth Common	a														08 39								
51½	—	Balham 4	a	23p44													08 42								
53¼	—	Streatham Common 4	a	23p48													08 46								
54¼	—	Norbury	a	23p51													08 48								
55½	—	Thornton Heath	a	23p54													08 51								
56¼	—	Selhurst 4	a	23p56	00 18												08 54								
57¼	—	**East Croydon**	a	00 01	00 22												09 04								
—	—	**South Croydon**	a																						

		SN 1	LO	SN	LO	LO	SN	LO		SN 1	LO	LO	LO	LO	SN 1	LO	LO	LO		LO	SN 1	LO	LO	LO	LO
Milton Keynes Central 10	d	08 13								09 13					10 13						11 13				
Bletchley	d	08 17								09 17					10 17						11 17				
Leighton Buzzard	d	08 24								09 24					10 24						11 24				
Tring	d	08 34								09 34					10 34						11 34				
Berkhamsted	d	08 39								09 39					10 39						11 39				
Hemel Hempstead	d	08 43								09 43					10 43						11 43				
Watford Junction	d	08 51								09 51					10 51						11 51				
Harrow & Wealdstone ⊖	d	08 58								09 58					10 59						11 59				
Wembley Central ⊖	d	09 05								10 05					11 04						12 04				
Stratford 7 ⊖	d		08 35		08 50	09 03					09 35		10 05			10 35		11 05				11 37		12 05	
Highbury & Islington ⊖	d		08 50		09 05	09 18					09 50		10 20			10 50		11 20				11 52		12 20	
Gospel Oak	d		09 02		09 15	09 27					10 00		10 30			11 00		11 30				12 02		12 30	
West Hampstead ⊖	d		09 08		09 21	09 33					10 06		10 36			11 06		11 36				12 08		12 36	
Willesden Jn. High Level ⊖	d		09 17		09 31	09 44		10 01			10 16	10 31	10 46	11 01		11 16	11 31	11 45		12 01		12 17	12 31	12 46	13 01
Shepherd's Bush ⊖	d	09 18	09 25	09 33	09 39	09 54		10 09		10 21	10 26	10 39	10 54	11 09	11 19	11 24	11 39	11 54		12 09	12 19	12 25	12 39	12 54	13 09
Kensington (Olympia) ⊖	d	09 21	09 27	09 35	09 41	09 56	10 02	10 11		10 24	10 28	10 41	10 56	11 11	11 21	11 26	11 41	11 56		12 11	12 22	12 27	12 41	12 56	13 11
West Brompton ⊖	d	09 23	09 29	09 37	09 43	09 58	10 04	10 13		10 27	10 30	10 43	10 58	11 13	11 23	11 28	11 43	11 58		12 13	12 25	12 29	12 43	12 58	13 13
Imperial Wharf	d	09 26	09a32	09 40	09a46	10a01	10 07	10a16		10 29	10a33	10a46	11a01	11a16	11 26	11a31	11a46	12a01		12a16	12 27	12a32	12a46	13a01	13a16
Clapham Junction 10	a	09 31		09 45						10 34					11 30						12 32				
	d	09 34								10 34					11 34						12 34				
Wandsworth Road	a						10 20																		
Wandsworth Common	a	09 37								10 37					11 37						12 37				
Balham 4	a	09 41								10 40					11 40						12 40				
Streatham Common 4	a	09 45								10 45					11 45						12 45				
Norbury	a	09 48								10 48					11 48						12 48				
Thornton Heath	a	09 51								10 51					11 51						12 51				
Selhurst 4	a	09 53								10 53					11 53						12 53				
East Croydon	a	09 57								10 57					11 57						12 57				
South Croydon	a	10 01								11 01					12 01						13 01				

Milton Keynes Central, Watford Junction, Kensington (Olympia) - Clapham Junction and East Croydon

		SN [1]	LO	LO		LO	LO	SN [1]	LO	LO	LO	LO	SN [1]	LO		LO	LO	LO	SN [1]	LO	SN	LO	LO	SN	
Milton Keynes Central [10]	d	12 13						13 13					14 13						15 13						
Bletchley	d	12 17						13 17					14 17						15 17						
Leighton Buzzard	d	12 24						13 24					14 24						15 24						
Tring	d	12 34						13 34					14 34						15 34						
Berkhamsted	d	12 39						13 39					14 39						15 39						
Hemel Hempstead	d	12 43						13 43					14 43						15 43						
Watford Junction	d	12 51						13 51					14 51						15 51						
Harrow & Wealdstone ⊖	d	12 59						13 59					14 59						15 59						
Wembley Central ⊖	d	13 04						14 04					15 04						16 05						
Stratford [7] ⊖	d		12 35			13 05			13 35		14 05			14 35			15 05			15 35		15 50			
Highbury & Islington ⊖	d		12 50			13 20			13 50		14 20			14 50			15 20			15 50		16 05			
Gospel Oak	d		13 00			13 30			14 00		14 30			15 00			15 30			16 02		16 15			
West Hampstead ⊖	d		13 06			13 36			14 06		14 36			15 06			15 36			16 08		16 21			
Willesden Jn. High Level ⊖	d		13 16	13 31		13 46	14 01		14 16	14 31	14 46	15 01		15 16		15 31	15 46	16 01		16 17		16 31	16 46		
Shepherd's Bush ⊖	d	13 19	13 24	13 39		13 54	14 09	14 19	14 24	14 39	14 54	15 09	15 22	15 26		15 39	15 54	16 09	16 19	16 25		16 39	16 53		
Kensington (Olympia) ⊖	d	13 22	13 26	13 41		13 56	14 11	14 22	14 26	14 41	14 56	15 11	15 24	15 28		15 41	15 56	16 11	16 22	16 27	16 34	16 41	16 55	17 04	
West Brompton ⊖	d	13 25	13 28	13 43		13 58	14 13	14 25	14 28	14 43	14 58	15 13	15 26	15 30		15 43	15 58	16 13	16 25	16 29	16 36	16 43	16 58	17 06	
Imperial Wharf	d	13 28	13a31	13a46		14a01	14a16	14 28	14a31	14a46	15a01	15a16	15 29	15a33		15a46	16a01	16a16	16 27	16a32	16 39	16a46	17a01	17 09	
Clapham Junction [10]	a	13 32						14 32					15 33						16 32		16 43			17 13	
	d	13 34						14 34					15 34						16 34						
Wandsworth Road	a																								
Wandsworth Common	a	13 37						14 37					15 37						16 37						
Balham [4]	a	13 40						14 40					15 40						16 40						
Streatham Common [4]	a	13 45						14 45					15 45						16 45						
Norbury	a	13 48						14 48					15 48						16 48						
Thornton Heath	a	13 51						14 51					15 51						16 51						
Selhurst [4]	a	13 53						14 53					15 53						16 54						
East Croydon	a	13 57						14 57					15 57						16 58						
South Croydon	a	14 01						15 01					16 01						17 02						

		LO	SN [1]	LO	LO	SN	LO	LO	SN [1]	LO		LO	LO	LO	SN [1]	LO	LO	LO	LO	SN [1]		LO	LO	LO	LO
Milton Keynes Central [10]	d		16 13						17 13						18 13					19 15					
Bletchley	d		16 17						17 17						18 17					19 19					
Leighton Buzzard	d		16 24						17 24						18 24					19 26					
Tring	d		16 34						17 34						18 34					19 36					
Berkhamsted	d		16 39						17 39						18 39					19 41					
Hemel Hempstead	d		16 43						17 43						18 43					19 45					
Watford Junction	d		16 51						17 51						18 51					19 54					
Harrow & Wealdstone ⊖	d		16 59						17 59						18 59					20 01					
Wembley Central ⊖	d		17 05						18 05						19 05					20 06					
Stratford [7] ⊖	d	16 20		16 35	16 50		17 05	17 21		17 36		17 51	18 05	18 20		18 35	18 48	19 05				19 37		20 05	
Highbury & Islington ⊖	d	16 35		16 49	17 05		17 20	17 35		17 50		18 06	18 20	18 35		18 50	19 03	19 20				19 52		20 20	
Gospel Oak	d	16 45		17 03	17 17		17 30	17 45		18 02		18 18	18 30	18 45		19 00	19 13	19 30				20 01		20 30	
West Hampstead ⊖	d	16 51		17 09	17 23		17 36	17 51		18 08		18 24	18 36	18 51		19 06	19 19	19 36				20 07		20 36	
Willesden Jn. High Level ⊖	d	17 01		17 19	17 32		17 46	18 01		18 18		18 33	18 46	19 01		19 16	19 31	19 46	20 01			20 17	20 31	20 46	21 01
Shepherd's Bush ⊖	d	17 09	17 19	17 26	17 40	17 45	17 54	18 09	18 19	18 25		18 41	18 54	19 09	19 18	19 23	19 39	19 54	20 09	20 21		20 26	20 39	20 54	21 09
Kensington (Olympia) ⊖	d	17 11	17 22	17 28	17 42	17 47	17 56	18 11	18 22	18 27		18 43	18 56	19 11	19 20	19 25	19 41	19 56	20 11	20 23		20 28	20 41	20 56	21 11
West Brompton ⊖	d	17 13	17 25	17 31	17 44	17 50	17 58	18 13	18 25	18 30		18 45	18 58	19 13	19 23	19 28	19 43	19 58	20 13	20 25		20 30	20 43	20 58	21 13
Imperial Wharf	d	17a16	17 28	17a34	17a47	17 53	18a01	18a16	18 27	18a33		18a48	19a01	19a16	19 25	19a31	19a46	20a01	20a16	20 28		20a33	20a46	21a01	21a16
Clapham Junction [10]	a		17 32			17 57			18 32						19 30					20 33					
	d		17 33			18 02			18 34						19 34										
Wandsworth Road	a																								
Wandsworth Common	a		17 36			18 05			18 37						19 37										
Balham [4]	a		17 39			18 08			18 40						19 40										
Streatham Common [4]	a		17 46			18 15			18 46						19 45										
Norbury	a		17 48			18 18			18 49						19 48										
Thornton Heath	a		17 51			18 21			18 52						19 51										
Selhurst [4]	a		17 54			18 24			18 54						19 53										
East Croydon	a		17 59			18 32			19 02																
South Croydon	a					18 35																			

Milton Keynes Central, Watford Junction, Kensington (Olympia) - Clapham Junction and East Croydon

		SN 1	LO	LO	LO	LO		SN 1	LO	LO	SN 1	LO	SN 1	LO	SN 1
Milton Keynes Central 10	d	20 13						21 13					22 11		
Bletchley	d	20 17						21 17					22 15		
Leighton Buzzard	d	20 24						21 24					22 22		
Tring	d	20 34						21 34					22 34		
Berkhamsted	d	20 39						21 39					22 39		
Hemel Hempstead	d	20 43						21 43					22 43		
Watford Junction	d	20 51						21 51			22 27		22 53		23 29
Harrow & Wealdstone ⊖	d	20 59						21 59			22 33		23 00		23 35
Wembley Central ⊖	d	21 04													
Stratford 7 ⊖	d		20 35		21 05				21 35						
Highbury & Islington ⊖	d		20 50		21 20				21 50						
Gospel Oak	d		21 00		21 30				22 00						
West Hampstead ⊖	d		21 06		21 36				22 06						
Willesden Jn. High Level ⊖	d		21 16	21 31	21 46	22 01			22 16	22 31		23 01		23 40	
Shepherd's Bush ⊖	d	21 22	21 26	21 39	21 54	22 09		22 23	22 26	22 39	22 49	23 09	23 21	23 48	23 54
Kensington (Olympia) ⊖	d	21 24	21 28	21 41	21 56	22 11		22 25	22 28	22 41	22 51	23 11	23 23	23 50	23 56
West Brompton ⊖	d	21 27	21 31	21 43	21 58	22 13		22 27	22 30	22 43	22 54	23 13	23 26	23 52	23 59
Imperial Wharf	d	21 29	21a34	21a46	22a01	22a16		22 30	22a33	22a46	22 56	23a16	23 28	23a55	00 02
Clapham Junction 10	a	21 34						22 34			23 01		23 33		00 07
	d												23 40		
Wandsworth Road	a														
Wandsworth Common	a														
Balham 4	a												23 44		
Streatham Common 4	a												23 48		
Norbury	a												23 51		
Thornton Heath	a												23 54		
Selhurst 4	a												23 56		
East Croydon	a												00 01		
South Croydon	a														

Saturdays

		SN 1	SN 1	LO	SN 1	LO	LO	LO	SN 1	LO		LO	LO	LO	SN 1	LO	LO	LO	LO	SN 1		LO	LO	LO	LO
Milton Keynes Central 10	d	22p11													07 13					08 13					
Bletchley	d	22p15													07 17					08 17					
Leighton Buzzard	d	22p22													07 24					08 24					
Tring	d	22p34													07 34					08 34					
Berkhamsted	d	22p39													07 39					08 39					
Hemel Hempstead	d	22p43													07 43					08 43					
Watford Junction	d	22p53	23p29		05 52				06 55						07 52					08 52					
Harrow & Wealdstone ⊖	d	23p00	23p35		05 58				07 01						07 59					08 59					
Wembley Central ⊖	d								07 06						08 04					09 04					
Stratford 7 ⊖	d						06 05			06 35			07 05			07 35		08 05				08 35		09 05	
Highbury & Islington ⊖	d						06 20			06 50			07 20			07 50		08 20				08 50		09 20	
Gospel Oak	d						06 30			07 00			07 30			08 00		08 30				09 00		09 30	
West Hampstead ⊖	d						06 36			07 06			07 36			08 06		08 36				09 06		09 36	
Willesden Jn. High Level ⊖	d			06 02		06 31	06 46	07 01		07 16		07 31	07 46	08 01		08 16	08 31	08 46	09 01			09 16	09 31	09 46	10 01
Shepherd's Bush ⊖	d	23p21	23p54	06 10	06 20	06 39	06 54	07 09	07 19	07 24		07 39	07 54	08 09	08 19	08 24	08 39	08 54	09 09	09 19		09 24	09 39	09 54	10 09
Kensington (Olympia) ⊖	d	23p23	23p56	06 12	06 23	06 41	06 56	07 11	07 22	07 26		07 41	07 56	08 11	08 22	08 26	08 41	08 56	09 11	09 22		09 26	09 41	09 56	10 11
West Brompton ⊖	d	23p26	23p59	06 14	06 26	06 43	06 58	07 13	07 25	07 28		07 43	07 58	08 13	08 25	08 28	08 43	08 58	09 13	09 25		09 28	09 43	09 58	10 13
Imperial Wharf	d	23p28	00 02	06a17	06 28	06a46	07a01	07a16	07 27	07a31		07a46	08a01	08a16	08 27	08a31	08a46	09a01	09a16	09 27		09a31	09a46	10a01	10a16
Clapham Junction 10	a	23p33	00 07		06 33				07 33						08 33					09 33					
	d	23p40			06 34				07 34						08 34					09 34					
Wandsworth Road	a																								
Wandsworth Common	a				06 37				07 37						08 37					09 37					
Balham 4	a	23p44			06 40				07 40						08 40					09 40					
Streatham Common 4	a	23p48			06 45				07 45						08 45					09 45					
Norbury	a	23p51			06 48				07 48						08 48					09 48					
Thornton Heath	a	23p54			06 51				07 51						08 51					09 51					
Selhurst 4	a	23p56			06 53				07 53						08 53					09 53					
East Croydon	a	00 01			06 57				07 57						08 57					09 57					
South Croydon	a				07 01				08 01						09 01					10 01					

Table 176

Saturdays

Milton Keynes Central, Watford Junction, Kensington (Olympia) - Clapham Junction and East Croydon

		SN 1	LO	LO	LO	LO		SN 1	LO	LO	LO	LO	SN 1	LO	LO	LO		LO	SN 1	LO	LO	LO	LO	SN 1	LO
Milton Keynes Central 10	d	09 13						10 13					11 13						12 13					13 13	
Bletchley	d	09 17						10 17					11 17						12 17					13 17	
Leighton Buzzard	d	09 24						10 24					11 24						12 24					13 24	
Tring	d	09 34						10 34					11 34						12 34					13 34	
Berkhamsted	d	09 39						10 39					11 39						12 39					13 39	
Hemel Hempstead	d	09 43						10 43					11 43						12 43					13 43	
Watford Junction	d	09 52						10 52					11 52						12 52					13 52	
Harrow & Wealdstone ⊖	d	09 59						10 59					11 59						12 59					13 59	
Wembley Central ⊖	d	10 04						11 04					12 04						13 04					14 04	
Stratford 7 ⊖	d		09 35		10 05				10 35		11 05			11 35		12 05				12 35		13 05			13 35
Highbury & Islington ⊖	d		09 50		10 20				10 50		11 20			11 50		12 20				12 50		13 20			13 50
Gospel Oak	d		10 00		10 30				11 00		11 30			12 00		12 30				13 00		13 30			14 00
West Hampstead ⊖	d		10 06		10 36				11 06		11 36			12 06		12 36				13 06		13 36			14 06
Willesden Jn. High Level ⊖	d		10 16	10 31	10 46	11 01			11 16	11 31	11 46	12 01		12 16	12 31	12 46		13 01		13 16	13 31	13 46	14 01		14 16
Shepherd's Bush ⊖	d	10 19	10 24	10 39	10 54	11 09		11 19	11 24	11 39	11 54	12 09	12 19	12 24	12 39	12 54		13 09	13 19	13 24	13 39	13 54	14 09	14 19	14 24
Kensington (Olympia) ⊖	d	10 22	10 26	10 41	10 56	11 11		11 22	11 26	11 41	11 56	12 11	12 22	12 26	12 41	12 56		13 11	13 22	13 26	13 41	13 56	14 11	14 22	14 26
West Brompton ⊖	d	10 25	10 28	10 43	10 58	11 13		11 25	11 28	11 43	11 58	12 13	12 25	12 28	12 43	12 58		13 13	13 25	13 28	13 43	13 58	14 13	14 25	14 28
Imperial Wharf	d	10 27	10a31	10a46	11a01	11a16		11 27	11a31	11a46	12a01	12a16	12 27	12a31	12a46	13a01		13a16	13 27	13a31	13a46	14a01	14a16	14 27	14a31
Clapham Junction 10	a	10 33						11 33					12 33						13 33					14 33	
	d	10 34						11 34					12 34						13 34					14 34	
Wandsworth Road	a																								
Wandsworth Common	a	10 37						11 37					12 37						13 37					14 37	
Balham 4	a	10 40						11 40					12 40						13 40					14 40	
Streatham Common 4	a	10 45						11 45					12 45						13 45					14 45	
Norbury	a	10 48						11 48					12 48						13 48					14 48	
Thornton Heath	a	10 51						11 51					12 51						13 51					14 51	
Selhurst 4	a	10 53						11 53					12 53						13 53					14 53	
East Croydon	a	10 57						11 57					12 57						13 57					14 57	
South Croydon	a	11 01						12 01					13 01						14 01					15 01	

		LO		LO	LO	SN 1	LO	LO	LO	LO	SN 1	LO		LO	LO	LO	SN 1	LO	LO	LO	LO	SN 1		LO	LO
Milton Keynes Central 10	d					14 13					15 13						16 13					17 13			
Bletchley	d					14 17					15 17						16 17					17 17			
Leighton Buzzard	d					14 24					15 24						16 24					17 24			
Tring	d					14 34					15 34						16 34					17 34			
Berkhamsted	d					14 39					15 39						16 39					17 39			
Hemel Hempstead	d					14 43					15 43						16 43					17 43			
Watford Junction	d					14 52					15 52						16 52					17 52			
Harrow & Wealdstone ⊖	d					14 59					15 59						16 59					17 59			
Wembley Central ⊖	d					15 04					16 04						17 04					18 04			
Stratford 7 ⊖	d			14 05			14 35		15 05			15 35			16 05			16 35		17 05				17 35	
Highbury & Islington ⊖	d			14 20			14 50		15 20			15 50			16 20			16 50		17 20				17 50	
Gospel Oak	d			14 30			15 00		15 30			16 00			16 30			17 00		17 30				18 00	
West Hampstead ⊖	d			14 36			15 06		15 36			16 06			16 36			17 06		17 36				18 06	
Willesden Jn. High Level ⊖	d	14 31		14 46	15 01		15 16	15 31	15 46	16 01		16 16		16 31	16 46	17 01		17 16	17 31	17 46	18 01			18 16	18 31
Shepherd's Bush ⊖	d	14 39		14 54	15 09	15 19	15 24	15 39	15 54	16 09	16 19	16 24		16 39	16 54	17 09	17 19	17 24	17 39	17 54	18 09	18 19		18 24	18 39
Kensington (Olympia) ⊖	d	14 41		14 56	15 11	15 22	15 26	15 41	15 56	16 11	16 22	16 26		16 41	16 56	17 11	17 22	17 26	17 41	17 56	18 11	18 22		18 26	18 41
West Brompton ⊖	d	14 43		14 58	15 13	15 25	15 28	15 43	15 58	16 13	16 25	16 28		16 43	16 58	17 13	17 25	17 28	17 43	17 58	18 13	18 25		18 28	18 43
Imperial Wharf	d	14a46		15a01	15a16	15 27	15a31	15a46	16a01	16a16	16 27	16a31		16a46	17a01	17a16	17 27	17a31	17a46	18a01	18a16	18 27		18a31	18a46
Clapham Junction 10	a					15 33					16 33						17 32					18 32			
	d					15 34					16 34						17 34					18 34			
Wandsworth Road	a																								
Wandsworth Common	a					15 37					16 37						17 37					18 37			
Balham 4	a					15 40					16 40						17 40					18 40			
Streatham Common 4	a					15 45					16 45						17 45					18 45			
Norbury	a					15 48					16 48						17 48					18 48			
Thornton Heath	a					15 51					16 51						17 51					18 51			
Selhurst 4	a					15 53					16 53						17 53					18 53			
East Croydon	a					15 57					16 57						17 57					18 57			
South Croydon	a					16 01					17 01						18 01					19 01			

Milton Keynes Central, Watford Junction, Kensington (Olympia) - Clapham Junction and East Croydon

		LO	LO	SN [1]	LO	LO	LO	SN [1]		LO	SN [1]	LO	LO	LO	SN [1]	LO	LO	LO		LO	SN [1]	LO	LO	LO	LO
Milton Keynes Central [10]	d			18 13							19 13														
Bletchley	d			18 17							19 17														
Leighton Buzzard	d			18 24							19 24														
Tring	d			18 34							19 34														
Berkhamsted	d			18 39							19 39														
Hemel Hempstead	d			18 43							19 43														
Watford Junction	d			18 52				19 31			19 51				20 43						21 43				
Harrow & Wealdstone ⊖	d			18 59				19 38			19 58				20 50						21 50				
Wembley Central ⊖	d			19 04				19 43																	
Stratford [7] ⊖	d	18 05			18 35		19 05					19 35		20 05			20 35			21 05			21 35		
Highbury & Islington ⊖	d	18 20			18 50		19 20					19 50		20 20			20 50			21 20			21 50		
Gospel Oak	d	18 30			19 00		19 30					20 00		20 30			21 00			21 30			22 00		
West Hampstead ⊖	d	18 36			19 06		19 36					20 06		20 36			21 06			21 36			22 06		
Willesden Jn. High Level ⊖	d	18 46	19 01		19 16	19 31	19 46			20 01		20 16	20 31	20 46		21 01	21 16	21 31		21 46		22 01	22 16	22 31	23 01
Shepherd's Bush ⊖	d	18 54	19 09	19 19	19 24	19 39	19 54	19 57		20 09	20 19	20 24	20 39	20 54	21 07	21 11	21 24	21 39		21 54	22 07	22 11	22 24	22 39	23 09
Kensington (Olympia) ⊖	d	18 56	19 11	19 22	19 26	19 41	19 56	20 00		20 11	20 22	20 26	20 41	20 56	21 10	21 13	21 26	21 41		21 56	22 10	22 13	22 26	22 41	23 11
West Brompton ⊖	d	18 58	19 13	19 25	19 28	19 43	19 58	20 03		20 13	20 25	20 28	20 43	20 58	21 13	21 15	21 28	21 43		21 58	22 13	22 15	22 28	22 43	23 13
Imperial Wharf	d	19a01	19a16	19 27	19a31	19a46	20a01	20 05		20a16	20 27	20a31	20a46	21a01	21 15	21a18	21a31	21a46		22a01	22 15	22a18	22a31	22a46	23a16
Clapham Junction [10]	a			19 32				20 10			20 32				21 20						22 20				
	d			19 34							20 34														
Wandsworth Road	a																								
Wandsworth Common	a			19 37							20 37														
Balham [4]	a			19 40							20 40														
Streatham Common [4]	a			19 45							20 45														
Norbury	a			19 48							20 48														
Thornton Heath	a			19 51							20 51														
Selhurst [4]	a			19 53							20 53														
East Croydon	a			19 57							20 59														
South Croydon	a																								

		SN [1]	LO	SN [1]
Milton Keynes Central [10]	d			
Bletchley	d			
Leighton Buzzard	d			
Tring	d			
Berkhamsted	d			
Hemel Hempstead	d			
Watford Junction	d	22 48		23 25
Harrow & Wealdstone ⊖	d	22 55		23 31
Wembley Central ⊖	d			
Stratford [7] ⊖	d			
Highbury & Islington ⊖	d			
Gospel Oak	d			
West Hampstead ⊖	d			
Willesden Jn. High Level ⊖	d		23 31	
Shepherd's Bush ⊖	d	23 14	23 39	23 49
Kensington (Olympia) ⊖	d	23 16	23 41	23 51
West Brompton ⊖	d	23 19	23 43	23 54
Imperial Wharf	d	23 21	23 46	23 57
Clapham Junction [10]	a	23 26	23 53	00 02
	d			
Wandsworth Road	a			
Wandsworth Common	a			
Balham [4]	a			
Streatham Common [4]	a			
Norbury	a			
Thornton Heath	a			
Selhurst [4]	a			
East Croydon	a			
South Croydon	a			

Table 176

Sundays

Milton Keynes Central, Watford Junction, Kensington (Olympia) - Clapham Junction and East Croydon

		SN ■1 A	SN ■1	LO	SN ■1	LO	LO	SN ■1	LO	LO		LO	LO	SN ■1	LO	LO	LO	LO	SN ■1	LO		LO	LO	LO	SN ■1
Milton Keynes Central ■10	d																								
Bletchley	d																								
Leighton Buzzard	d																								
Tring	d																								
Berkhamsted	d																								
Hemel Hempstead	d																								
Watford Junction	d	23p25						09 17						10 17					11 22						12 22
Harrow & Wealdstone ⊖	d	23p31						09 23						10 23					11 28						12 29
Wembley Central ⊖	d	⌇																							
Stratford ■7 ⊖	d	⌇															10 35			11 05			11 35		
Highbury & Islington ⊖	d	⌇															10 50			11 20			11 50		
Gospel Oak	d	⌇															11 00			11 30			12 00		
West Hampstead ⊖	d	⌇															11 06			11 36			12 06		
Willesden Jn. High Level ⊖	d	⌇		08 32		09 02	09 32		09 48	10 02		10 16	10 32		10 46	11 02	11 16	11 32		11 46		12 02	12 16	12 32	
Shepherd's Bush ⊖	d	23p49	07 47	08 40	08 50	09 10	09 40	09 45	09 54	10 10		10 24	10 40	10 45	10 55	11 10	11 24	11 40	11 45	11 54		12 10	12 24	12 40	12 45
Kensington (Olympia) ⊖	d	23p51	07 49	08 42	08 53	09 12	09 42	09 48	09 56	10 12		10 26	10 42	10 48	10 56	11 12	11 26	11 42	11 48	11 56		12 12	12 26	12 42	12 48
West Brompton ⊖	d	23p54	07 51	08 44	08 56	09 14	09 44	09 50	09 58	10 14		10 28	10 44	10 50	10 58	11 14	11 28	11 44	11 50	11 58		12 14	12 28	12 44	12 50
Imperial Wharf	d	23p57	07 54	08a47	08 58	09a17	09a47	09 53	10a01	10a17		10a31	10a47	10 53	11a01	11a17	11a31	11a47	11 53	12a01		12a17	12a31	12a47	12 53
Clapham Junction ■10	a	00⌇02	07 58		09 03			09 58						10 58					11 58						12 58
	d																								
Wandsworth Road	a																								
Wandsworth Common	a																								
Balham ■4	a																								
Streatham Common ■4	a																								
Norbury	a																								
Thornton Heath	a																								
Selhurst ■4	a																								
East Croydon 🚌	a																								
South Croydon	a																								

		LO	LO	LO	LO	SN ■1		LO	LO	LO	LO	SN ■1	LO	LO	LO	LO		SN ■1	LO	LO	LO	LO	SN ■1	LO	LO
Milton Keynes Central ■10	d																								
Bletchley	d																								
Leighton Buzzard	d																								
Tring	d																								
Berkhamsted	d																								
Hemel Hempstead	d																								
Watford Junction	d					13 22						14 22						15 22					16 22		
Harrow & Wealdstone ⊖	d					13 28						14 28						15 28					16 28		
Wembley Central ⊖	d																								
Stratford ■7 ⊖	d	12 05		12 35				13 05		13 35			14 05		14 35				15 05		15 35			16 05	
Highbury & Islington ⊖	d	12 20		12 50				13 20		13 50			14 20		14 50				15 20		15 50			16 20	
Gospel Oak	d	12 30		13 00				13 30		14 00			14 30		15 00				15 30		16 00			16 30	
West Hampstead ⊖	d	12 36		13 06				13 36		14 06			14 36		15 06				15 36		16 06			16 36	
Willesden Jn. High Level ⊖	d	12 46	13 02	13 16	13 32			13 46	14 02	14 16	14 32		14 46	15 02	15 16	15 32			15 46	16 02	16 16	16 32		16 46	17 02
Shepherd's Bush ⊖	d	12 54	13 10	13 24	13 40	13 45		13 54	14 10	14 24	14 40	14 45	14 54	15 10	15 24	15 40		15 45	15 54	16 10	16 24	16 40	16 45	16 54	17 10
Kensington (Olympia) ⊖	d	12 56	13 12	13 26	13 42	13 48		13 56	14 12	14 26	14 42	14 48	14 56	15 12	15 26	15 42		15 48	15 56	16 12	16 26	16 42	16 48	16 56	17 12
West Brompton ⊖	d	12 58	13 14	13 28	13 44	13 50		13 58	14 14	14 28	14 44	14 50	14 58	15 14	15 28	15 44		15 50	15 58	16 14	16 28	16 44	16 50	16 58	17 14
Imperial Wharf	d	13a01	13a17	13a31	13a47	13 53		14a01	14a17	14a31	14a47	14 53	15a01	15a17	15a31	15a47		15 53	16a01	16a17	16a31	16a47	16 53	17a01	17a17
Clapham Junction ■10	a					13 58						14 58						15 58					16 58		
	d																								
Wandsworth Road	a																								
Wandsworth Common	a																								
Balham ■4	a																								
Streatham Common ■4	a																								
Norbury	a																								
Thornton Heath	a																								
Selhurst ■4	a																								
East Croydon 🚌	a																								
South Croydon	a																								

A not 11 December

Table 176

Sundays

Milton Keynes Central, Watford Junction, Kensington (Olympia) - Clapham Junction and East Croydon

		LO		LO	SN 1	LO	LO	LO	LO	SN 1	LO	LO		LO	LO	SN 1	LO	LO	LO	LO	SN 1	LO		LO	LO
Milton Keynes Central 10	d																								
Bletchley	d																								
Leighton Buzzard	d																								
Tring	d																								
Berkhamsted	d																								
Hemel Hempstead	d																								
Watford Junction	d				17 22					18 22						19 22					20 22				
Harrow & Wealdstone ⊖	d				17 28					18 28						19 28					20 28				
Wembley Central ⊖	d																								
Stratford 7 ⊖	d	16 35				17 05		17 35			18 05			18 35			19 05		19 35			20 05			20 35
Highbury & Islington ⊖	d	16 50				17 20		17 50			18 20			18 50			19 20		19 50			20 20			20 50
Gospel Oak	d	17 01				17 31		18 02			18 30			19 00			19 30		20 00			20 30			21 00
West Hampstead ⊖	d	17 06				17 36		18 06			18 36			19 06			19 36		20 06			20 36			21 06
Willesden Jn. High Level ⊖	d	17 16		17 32		17 46	18 02	18 16	18 32		18 46	19 02		19 16	19 32		19 46	20 02	20 16	20 32		20 46		21 02	21 16
Shepherd's Bush ⊖	d	17 24		17 40	17 45	17 54	18 10	18 24	18 40	18 45	18 54	19 10		19 24	19 40	19 45	19 54	20 10	20 24	20 40	20 45	20 54		21 10	21 24
Kensington (Olympia) ⊖	d	17 26		17 42	17 48	17 56	18 12	18 26	18 42	18 48	18 56	19 12		19 26	19 42	19 48	19 56	20 12	20 26	20 42	20 48	20 56		21 12	21 26
West Brompton ⊖	d	17 28		17 44	17 50	17 58	18 14	18 28	18 44	18 50	18 58	19 14		19 28	19 44	19 50	19 58	20 14	20 28	20 44	20 50	20 58		21 14	21 28
Imperial Wharf	d	17a31		17a47	17 53	18a01	18a17	18a31	18a47	18 53	19a01	19a17		19a31	19a47	19 53	20a01	20a17	20a31	20a47	20 53	21a01		21a17	21a31
Clapham Junction 10	a				17 58					18 58						19 58					20 58				
	d																								
Wandsworth Road	a																								
Wandsworth Common	a																								
Balham 4	a																								
Streatham Common 4	a																								
Norbury	a																								
Thornton Heath	a																								
Selhurst 4	a																								
East Croydon ⇌	a																								
South Croydon	a																								

		LO	SN 1	LO	LO	LO	SN 1	LO		LO	SN 1
Milton Keynes Central 10	d										
Bletchley	d										
Leighton Buzzard	d										
Tring	d										
Berkhamsted	d										
Hemel Hempstead	d										
Watford Junction	d		21 17				22 17				23 17
Harrow & Wealdstone ⊖	d		21 23				22 23				23 23
Wembley Central ⊖	d										
Stratford 7 ⊖	d			21 05							
Highbury & Islington ⊖	d			21 20							
Gospel Oak	d			21 30							
West Hampstead ⊖	d			21 36							
Willesden Jn. High Level ⊖	d	21 32		21 46	22 02	22 32		22 46		23 16	
Shepherd's Bush ⊖	d	21 40	21 45	21 54	22 10	22 40	22 45	22 54		23 24	23 45
Kensington (Olympia) ⊖	d	21 42	21 48	21 56	22 12	22 42	22 48	22 56		23 26	23 48
West Brompton ⊖	d	21 44	21 50	21 58	22 14	22 44	22 50	22 58		23 28	23 50
Imperial Wharf	d	21a47	21 53	22a01	22a17	22a47	22 53	23a01		23 31	23 53
Clapham Junction 10	a		21 58				22 58			23 40	23 58
	d										00 05
Wandsworth Road	a										
Wandsworth Common	a										
Balham 4	a										
Streatham Common 4	a										
Norbury	a										
Thornton Heath	a										
Selhurst 4	a										00 18
East Croydon ⇌	a										00 22
South Croydon	a										

Network Diagram for Tables 177, 178, 179, 181, 182 | also 175 ⊙

DM-21/11
Design BAJS

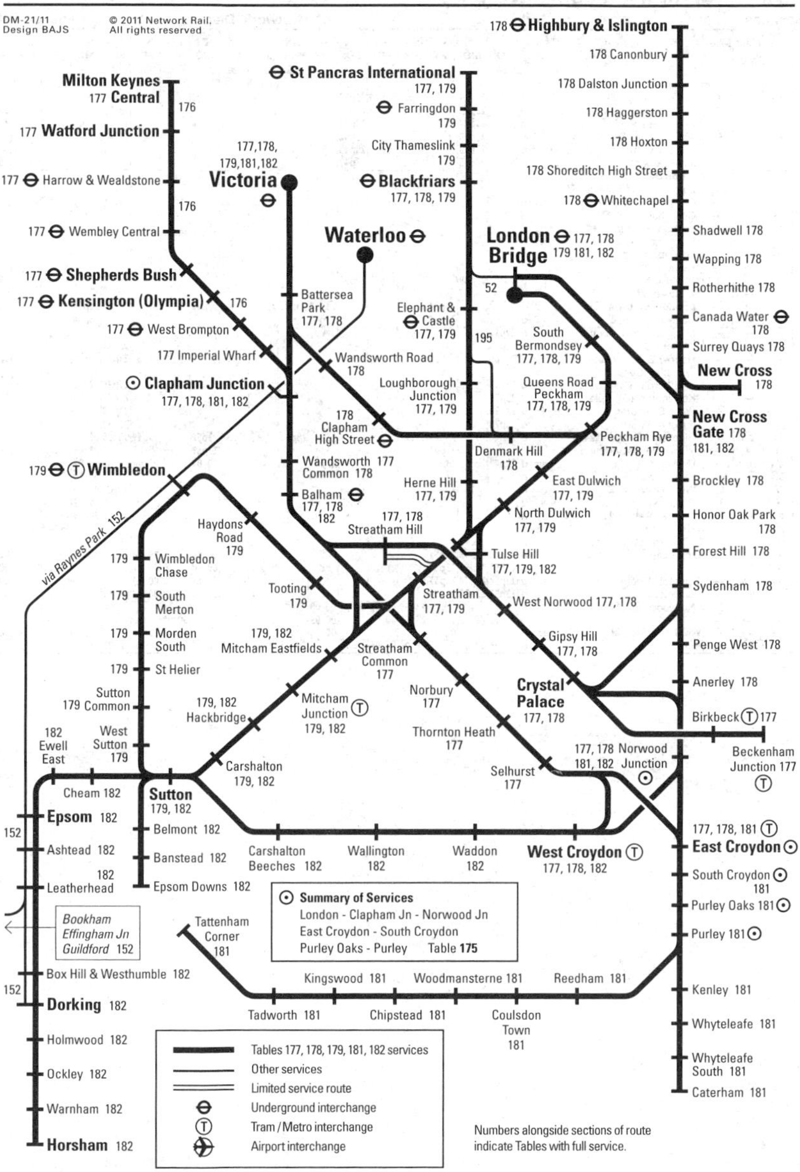

Luton, Milton Keynes Central and London East and West Croydon via Tulse Hill - Crystal Palace - Norbury

Local Services

Network Diagram - see first Page of Table 177

Miles	Miles	Miles	Miles	Miles			SN MX 1	SN MO	SN MX	SN MX	SN MO	SN MX	SN MX	SN MX 1	SN MO	SN MX 1	SN MO	LO MO	SN MX	SN MO 1	SN MX		LO MX	SN MX	SN MO
—	0	—	—	0	**London Bridge** 4 ⊖	d		23p21		23p36	23p39	23p33												23p48	
—	1¾	—	—	1¾	South Bermondsey	d		23p25				23p37												23p52	
—	2¾	—	—	2¾	Queens Rd Peckham	d		23p27				23p39												23p54	
—	3½	—	—	3½	Peckham Rye 4	d		23p30				23p42												23p57	
—	4¼	—	—	4¼	East Dulwich	d		23p33				23p45												00 01	
—	4¾	—	—	4¾	North Dulwich	d		23p35				23p47												00 03	
—	—	—	—	—	**Luton** 10	d																			
—	—	—	—	—	Luton Airport Parkway 7	d																			
—	—	—	—	—	St Pancras International 15 ⊖	d																			
—	—	—	—	—	City Thameslink 3	d																			
—	—	—	—	—	London Blackfriars 3 ⊖	d																			
—	—	—	—	—	Elephant & Castle ⊖	d																			
—	—	—	—	—	Loughborough Jn	d																			
—	—	—	—	—	Herne Hill 4	d																			
—	6	—	—	6	Tulse Hill 3	d		23p39				23p51												00 06	
—	7½	—	—	—	Streatham 4	d		23p42																00 10	
0	—	0	0	—	**London Victoria** 15 ⊖	d			23p34				23p38	23p47	23p47	23p49	23p50		23p51		23p54				23p54
1¼	—	1¼	1¼	—	Battersea Park 4	d			23p38				23p42						23p55		23p58				23p58
—	—	—	—	—	Milton Keynes Central	d	22p11																		
—	—	—	—	—	Watford Junction	d	22p53													23p17					
—	—	—	—	—	Harrow & Wealdstone ⊖	d	23p00													23p23					
—	—	—	—	—	Wembley Central ⊖	d																			
—	—	—	—	—	Shepherd's Bush ⊖	d	23p21													23p45					
—	—	—	—	—	Kensington (Olympia) ⊖	d	23p23													23p48					
—	—	—	—	—	West Brompton ⊖	d	23p26													23p50					
—	—	—	—	—	Imperial Wharf	d	23p28													23p53					
2¾	—	2¾	2¾	—	Clapham Junction 10	d	23b40		23p42				23p46	23p53	23p53	23p56	23p56		23p59	00 05	00 02				00 02
4	—	4	4	—	Wandsworth Common	d			23p45				23p49				23p59		00 02		00 05				00 05
4¾	—	4¾	4¾	—	Balham 4 ⊖	d	23p44		23p47				23p51				00 02		00 04		00 07				00 07
5¾	—	5¾	—	—	Streatham Hill	d							23p54								00 10				00 11
7	—	7	—	6½	West Norwood 4	d						23p54	23p58								00 14				00 14
8	—	8	—	7½	Gipsy Hill	d						23p57	00 01								00 17				00 17
8¾	—	8¾	—	8¼	**Crystal Palace** 4	d						23p59	00 03								00a19				00 20
—	—	10¼	—	—	Birkbeck 🚋	d																			
—	—	11¾	—	—	Beckenham Junction 4 🚋	a																			
—	8	—	6½	—	Streatham Common 4	d	23p48	23p48	23p51								00 06		00 08					00 13	
—	9	—	7½	—	Norbury	d	23p51	23p51	23p54								00 08		00 11					00 15	
—	10¼	—	8¾	—	Thornton Heath	d	23p54	23p54	23p57								00 11		00 14					00 18	
—	11	—	9½	—	Selhurst 4	d	23p57	23p57	23p59								00 14		00 17	00 19				00 21	
10¼	—	—	—	9¾	Norwood Junction 2	a				23p59	00 02	00 04	00 08												00 25
—	—	—	—	—		d				23p59	00 03		00 09					00 08					00 20		
—	12	—	—	—	**West Croydon** 4 🚋	a			00 03				00 14					00 15	00 21				00 27	00 28	
11½	—	—	10½	11	**East Croydon** 🚋	a	00 01	00 01		00 03	00 06			00 05	00 06	00 09	00 17			00 22					

b Previous night, arr. 2333

Luton, Milton Keynes Central and London East and West Croydon via Tulse Hill - Crystal Palace - Norbury

Local Services

Network Diagram - see first Page of Table 177

	FC MX	SN MX ◇1	SN MX	SN MX	FC	SN 1	SN	SN MX	FC	SN	SN ◇1	FC 1		FC 1	SN 1	FC 1	SN 1	FC	FC 1	SN ◇1	FC 1	FC 1	SN ◇1	FC 1
London Bridge 4 ⊖ d	23p59		00 06	00 03	00 12			00 36	00 42			01 08		01 35		02 05		03 05	03 35		04 05	04 35		
South Bermondsey d				00 07																				
Queens Rd Peckham d				00 09																				
Peckham Rye 4 d				00 12																				
East Dulwich d				00 15																				
North Dulwich d				00 17																				
Luton 10 d																								04 06
Luton Airport Parkway 7 d																								04 09
St Pancras International 15 ⊖ d																								04 54
City Thameslink 3 d																								
London Blackfriars 3 ⊖ d																								05 04
Elephant & Castle ⊖ d																								
Loughborough Jn. d																								
Herne Hill 4 d																								
Tulse Hill 3 d	00 09			00 21																				
Streatham 4 d	00a13																							
London Victoria 15 ⊖ d		00 05				00 14	00 16			00 42	01 00				02 00		03 00			04 00			05 02	
Battersea Park 4 d							00 20			00 46														
Milton Keynes Central d																								
Watford Junction d																								
Harrow & Wealdstone ⊖ d																								
Wembley Central ⊖ d																								
Shepherd's Bush ⊖ d																								
Kensington (Olympia) ⊖ d																								
West Brompton ⊖ d																								
Imperial Wharf d																								
Clapham Junction 10 d		00 11				00 20	00 24			00 50	01 08				02 08		03 08			04 08			05 08	
Wandsworth Common d							00 27			00 53														
Balham 4 ⊖ d							00 29			00 55														
Streatham Hill d																								
West Norwood 4 d				00 24																				
Gipsy Hill d				00 27																				
Crystal Palace 4 d				00 29																				
Birkbeck 🚋 d																								
Beckenham Junction 4 🚋 a																								
Streatham Common 4 d							00 33			00 59														
Norbury d							00 36			01 02														
Thornton Heath d							00 39			01 05														
Selhurst 4 d		00 22					00 41			01 07		01 27		01 54		02 24		03 24	03 54		04 24	04 54		05 27
Norwood Junction 2 a			00 29	00 34				00 59																
d			00 30					01 00																
West Croydon 4 🚋 a																								
East Croydon 🚋 a		00 26	00 33		00 26	00 31	00 44	01 03	00 56	01 10	01 23	01 31		02 01	02 23	02 31	03 23	03 31	04 01	04 23	04 31	05 01	05 20	05 29

Table 177

Mondays to Fridays

Luton, Milton Keynes Central and London East and West Croydon via Tulse Hill - Crystal Palace - Norbury

Local Services

Network Diagram - see first Page of Table 177

Station		FC	FC	SN	FC		FC	FC	SN	SN	SN	LO	LO	SN	SN	FC	SN	LO	SN	SN	SN		SN	SN	SN
		■1	■1	◇■1	■1		■1								◇■1	■1									
		A	B		A		B																		
London Bridge ■4 ⊖	d									05 36	06 00						06 06						06 11	06 18	06 19
South Bermondsey	d										06 04												06 15	06 22	
Queens Rd Peckham	d										06 06												06 18	06 24	
Peckham Rye ■4	d										06 09												06 20	06 27	
East Dulwich	d										06 12													06 30	
North Dulwich	d										06 14													06 32	
Luton ■10	d	04 32	04 33		04 44		04 45									05 24									
Luton Airport Parkway ■7	d	04 35	04 35		04 47		04 47									05 27									
St Pancras International ■15 ⊖	d	05 12	05 12		05 32		05 32	05 36								06 02									
City Thameslink ■3	d	05 21	05 21		05 41		05 41	05 44								06 11									
London Blackfriars ■3 ⊖	d	05 24	05 24		05 44		05 44	05 47								06 14									
Elephant & Castle ⊖	d							05 50																	
Loughborough Jn.	d																								
Herne Hill ■4	d							05 57																	
Tulse Hill ■3	d							06 02			06 18													06 36	
Streatham ■4	d							06a05			06a21													06 39	
London Victoria ■15 ⊖	d			05 32										06 00	06 02				06 07	06 13	06 19				
Battersea Park ■4	d													06 04					06 11	06 17	06 23		06a32		
Milton Keynes Central	d																								
Watford Junction	d																								
Harrow & Wealdstone ⊖	d																								
Wembley Central ⊖	d																								
Shepherd's Bush ⊖	d																								
Kensington (Olympia) ⊖	d																								
West Brompton ⊖	d																								
Imperial Wharf	d																								
Clapham Junction ■10	d			05 38										06 08	06 08				06 15	06 21	06 27				
Wandsworth Common	d													06 11					06 18	06 24	06 30				
Balham ■4 ⊖	d													06 13					06 20	06 26	06 32				
Streatham Hill	d																		06 23		06 35				
West Norwood ■4	d																		06 27		06 39				
Gipsy Hill	d																		06 30		06 42				06a41
Crystal Palace ■4	d																		06 32		06a44				
Birkbeck 🚊	d																								
Beckenham Junction ■4 🚊	a																								
Streatham Common ■4	d													06 17						06 30				06 42	
Norbury	d													06 20						06 33				06 45	
Thornton Heath	d													06 23						06 36				06 48	
Selhurst ■4	d													06 26						06 39				06 51	
Norwood Junction ■2	a									06 00							06 29		06 37						
	d								05 53	06 00		06 05	06 20				06 30	06 35	06 39						
West Croydon ■4 🚊	a								05 57	06 05		06 13	06 30	06 31				06 41	06 44					06 56	
East Croydon 🚊	a	05 47	05 47	05 48	06 05		06 05								06 17	06 33	06 33			06 43					

A until 23 March

B from 26 March

Luton, Milton Keynes Central and London East and West Croydon via Tulse Hill - Crystal Palace - Norbury

Local Services

Network Diagram - see first Page of Table 177

Station		SN ◇1	SN	SN	SN	LO	SN	SN 1	FC 1	FC	SN	LO	SN		SN	SN	SN ◇1	SN	SN	SN	SN	SN 1	FC 1	SN	SN
London Bridge 4 ⊖	d		06 30		06 33						06 36								06 41	06 48	06 51			06 54	06 58
South Bermondsey	d		06 34		06 37														06 45	06 52					07 02
Queens Rd Peckham	d		06 36		06 39														06 48	06 54					07 04
Peckham Rye 4	d		06 39		06 42														06 50	06 57					07 07
East Dulwich	d		06 42		06 45															07 00					07 10
North Dulwich	d		06 44		06 47															07 02					07 12
Luton 10	d								05 44	05 48													06 04		
Luton Airport Parkway 7	d								05 46	05 50													06 06		
St Pancras International 15 ⊖	d								06 22	06 34													06 38		
City Thameslink 3	d								06 31	06 43													06 47		
London Blackfriars 3 ⊖	d								06 34	06 46													06 50		
Elephant & Castle ⊖	d									06 49															
Loughborough Jn.	d									06 53															
Herne Hill 4	d									06 57															
Tulse Hill 3	d		06 48		06 50					07 02										07 07					07 16
Streatham 4	d		06a51							07a05										07 10					07a19
London Victoria 15 ⊖	d	06 21					06 30	06 32					06 36		06 41	06 44	06 47	06 49				06 51			
Battersea Park 4	d						06 34						06 40		06a45			06 53	07a02						
Milton Keynes Central	d																								
Watford Junction	d																								
Harrow & Wealdstone ⊖	d																								
Wembley Central ⊖	d																								
Shepherd's Bush ⊖	d																								
Kensington (Olympia) ⊖	d																								
West Brompton ⊖	d																								
Imperial Wharf	d																								
Clapham Junction 10	d	06 27					06 38	06 38					06 44			06 50	06 53	06 57				06 57			
Wandsworth Common	d						06 41						06 47			06 53		07 00							
Balham 4 ⊖	d						06 44						06 49			06 56		07 02							
Streatham Hill	d			06 42									06 53					07 05							
West Norwood 4	d			06 45	06 53								06 56					07 09							
Gipsy Hill	d			06 48	06 56								06 59					07 12			07a15				
Crystal Palace 4	d			06a51	06 59								07 02					07a14							
Birkbeck 🚊	d				07 03																				
Beckenham Junction 4 🚊	a				07 06																				
Streatham Common 4	d						06 48									07 00				07 13					
Norbury	d						06 50									07 02				07 16					
Thornton Heath	d						06 53									07 05				07 19					
Selhurst 4	d						06 56									07 09				07 21					
Norwood Junction 2	a										06 59		07 07											07 17	
	d					06 50					07 00	07 05	07 09											07 18	
West Croydon 4 🚊	a					07 00	07 02					07 11	07 13							07 26					
East Croydon 🚊	a	06 38						06 48	06 54		07 03					07 12	07 03					07 06	07 14	07 21	

Station		SN	SN	LO	SN		SN 1	FC 1	FC 1	SN	LO	SN	SN	SN ◇1	SN	SN	SN	SN	SN	SN 1	SN		SN	SN 1	SN
London Bridge 4 ⊖	d		07 03							07 06							07 11	07 16	07 21	07 27			07 29	07 30	07 33
South Bermondsey	d		07 07														07 15	07 20					07 33		07 37
Queens Rd Peckham	d		07 09														07 17	07 22					07 35		07 39
Peckham Rye 4	d		07 12														07 20	07 25					07 38		07 42
East Dulwich	d		07 15															07 28					07 41		07 45
North Dulwich	d		07 17															07 30					07 43		07 47
Luton 10	d							06 22	06 34																
Luton Airport Parkway 7	d							06 24																	
St Pancras International 15 ⊖	d							06 58	07 04																
City Thameslink 3	d							07 07	07 13																
London Blackfriars 3 ⊖	d							07 09	07 16																
Elephant & Castle ⊖	d								07 19																
Loughborough Jn.	d								07 23																
Herne Hill 4	d								07 27																
Tulse Hill 3	d		07 20						07 31									07 34					07 47		07 50
Streatham 4	d								07a34									07 37					07a51		
London Victoria 15 ⊖	d				07 00		07 02					07 06	07 11	07 17	07 17	07 20					07 23				
Battersea Park 4	d				07 04							07 10	07a15		07 21	07 24	07a32								
Milton Keynes Central	d																								
Watford Junction	d																								
Harrow & Wealdstone ⊖	d																								
Wembley Central ⊖	d																								
Shepherd's Bush ⊖	d																								
Kensington (Olympia) ⊖	d																								
West Brompton ⊖	d																								
Imperial Wharf	d																								
Clapham Junction 10	d				07 08		07 08					07 14		07 23	07 25	07 28					07 30				
Wandsworth Common	d				07 11							07 17				07 31									
Balham 4 ⊖	d				07 13							07 20			07 29	07 33									
Streatham Hill	d	07 12										07 23			07 32										
West Norwood 4	d	07 15	07 23									07 27			07 38										07 53
Gipsy Hill	d	07 18	07 26									07 30			07 41				07a45						07 56
Crystal Palace 4	d	07a21	07 29									07 32			07a43										07 59
Birkbeck 🚊	d		07 33																						08 03
Beckenham Junction 4 🚊	a		07 36																						08 06
Streatham Common 4	d				07 18											07 37		07 40							
Norbury	d				07 21											07 40		07 43							
Thornton Heath	d				07 24											07 43		07 46							
Selhurst 4	d				07 27											07 46		07 51							
Norwood Junction 2	a									07 29		07 38								07 38				07 41	
	d			07 20						07 31	07 35	07 39								07 38				07 42	
West Croydon 4 🚊	a			07 30	07 32						07 42	07 44						07 56							
East Croydon 🚊	a						07 17	07 30		07 37				07 33		07 49				07 42	07 44			07 45	

Luton, Milton Keynes Central and London East and West Croydon via Tulse Hill - Crystal Palace - Norbury

Local Services

Network Diagram - see first Page of Table 177

		SN ■1	LO	SN	SN ■1	FC ■1	FC ■1	FC	SN	SN	SN	LO	SN ■1		SN	SN	SN	SN	FC	SN ◇■1	SN	SN	SN ■1	SN ◇■1	SN ■1
London Bridge 4 ⊖	d	07 33							07 36	07 41	07 44		07 56					07 47				07 51	07 53		08 00
South Bermondsey	d									07 45															
Queens Rd Peckham	d									07 47															
Peckham Rye 4	d									07 50								07 53							
East Dulwich	d																	07 56							
North Dulwich	d																	07 58							
Luton 10	d					06 46	06 54	06 43											06 50						
Luton Airport Parkway 7	d					06 48		06 45											06 52						
St Pancras International 15 ⊖	d					07 20	07 24	07 28											07 32						
City Thameslink 3	d					07 29	07 33	07 37											07 41						
London Blackfriars 3 ⊖	d					07 32	07 36	07 40											07 44						
Elephant & Castle ⊖	d						07a39	07a43											07 47						
Loughborough Jn.	d																		07 51						
Herne Hill 4	d																		07 57						
Tulse Hill 3	d																	08 02	08 05						
Streatham 4	d																	08 05	08a08						
London Victoria 15 ⊖	d			07 30	07 36										07 36	07 41	07 45			07 47	07 52			07 52	
Battersea Park 4	d			07 34						08a02					07 40	07a45									
Milton Keynes Central	d																								
Watford Junction	d																								
Harrow & Wealdstone ⊖	d																								
Wembley Central ⊖	d																								
Shepherd's Bush ⊖	d																								
Kensington (Olympia) ⊖	d																								
West Brompton ⊖	d																								
Imperial Wharf	d																								
Clapham Junction 10	d			07 38	07 42										07 44		07 51			07 53	07 58			07 58	
Wandsworth Common	d			07 41											07 47		07 54								
Balham 4 ⊖	d			07 44											07 50		07 57				08 03				
Streatham Hill	d														07 53						08 06				
West Norwood 4	d														07 58						08 09				
Gipsy Hill	d														08 01						08 12	08a15			
Crystal Palace 4	d														08 04						08a15				
Birkbeck 🚊	d																								
Beckenham Junction 4 🚊	a																								
Streatham Common 4	d			07 48													08 01	08 08							
Norbury	d			07 50													08 03	08 11							
Thornton Heath	d			07 53													08 06	08 14							
Selhurst 4	d			07 56													08 09	08 17							
Norwood Junction 2	a								07 59				08 07		08 08										08 16
	d		07 50						08 00			08 05	08 07		08 09										08 16
West Croydon 4 🚊	a		08 00	08 02								08 12			08 14			08 23							
East Croydon 🚊	a	07 48			07 51	07 54			08 03		08 00		08 10				08 12			08 02			08 05	08 09	08 20

		SN	LO	SN	SN ◇■1		FC ■1	SN	SN	SN	SN	SN ■1	LO	SN	SN	SN	SN ◇■1	FC ■1	SN ◇■1	SN	SN		SN	SN	FC
London Bridge 4 ⊖	d							08 03	08 06	08 14	08 06	08 08											08 10	08 17	
South Bermondsey	d							08 07	08 11														08 14		
Queens Rd Peckham	d							08 09	08 13														08 16		
Peckham Rye 4	d							08 12	08 16														08 19	08 23	
East Dulwich	d							08 15	08 19															08 26	
North Dulwich	d							08 17	08 21															08 28	
Luton 10	d						07 14											07 22							07 30
Luton Airport Parkway 7	d																	07 25							07 32
St Pancras International 15 ⊖	d						07 44											07 56							08 12
City Thameslink 3	d						07 53											08 05							08 21
London Blackfriars 3 ⊖	d						07 56											08 08							08 24
Elephant & Castle ⊖	d																								08 27
Loughborough Jn.	d																								08 31
Herne Hill 4	d																								08 36
Tulse Hill 3	d						08 10	08 21	08 25															08 32	08 40
Streatham 4	d								08a28															08 36	08a44
London Victoria 15 ⊖	d			08 03	08 07									08 07	08 11	08 15	08 17		08 21		08 22				
Battersea Park 4	d			08 07										08 11	08a15	08 19					08 26		08a32		
Milton Keynes Central	d																								
Watford Junction	d																								
Harrow & Wealdstone ⊖	d																								
Wembley Central ⊖	d																								
Shepherd's Bush ⊖	d																								
Kensington (Olympia) ⊖	d																								
West Brompton ⊖	d																								
Imperial Wharf	d																								
Clapham Junction 10	d			08 11	08 13									08 16		08 23	08 23		08 27		08 30				
Wandsworth Common	d			08 14										08 19		08 26					08 33				
Balham 4 ⊖	d			08 16										08 21		08 28					08 35				
Streatham Hill	d	08 15												08 24						08 35	08 38				
West Norwood 4	d	08 19						08 24						08 28						08 38	08 42				
Gipsy Hill	d	08 22						08 27						08 31						08 41	08 45				
Crystal Palace 4	d	08a24						08 29						08 34						08a44	08a47				
Birkbeck 🚊	d							08 33																	
Beckenham Junction 4 🚊	a							08 37																	
Streatham Common 4	d			08 20												08 32								08 39	
Norbury	d			08 23												08 35								08 41	
Thornton Heath	d			08 26												08 38								08 44	
Selhurst 4	d			08 32												08 41								08 47	
Norwood Junction 2	a									08 27	08 29			08 38											
	d		08 20							08 27	08 30		08 35	08 39											
West Croydon 4 🚊	a		08 30	08 36									08 43	08 44										08 53	
East Croydon 🚊	a				08 22		08 26			08 30	08 33	08 22				08 44	08 33	08 37	08 40						

Luton, Milton Keynes Central and London East and West Croydon via Tulse Hill - Crystal Palace - Norbury

Local Services

Network Diagram - see first Page of Table 177

		SN	SN	SN	SN	SN	SN	SN	SN	LO	SN	SN	SN		FC	FC	SN	SN	LO	SN	SN	SN	SN	SN	SN
			1				1	1				◇1 ⚲	◇1 ⚲		1	1	1						◇1 ⚲		◇1
London Bridge 4 ⊖	d	08 21	08 23	08 24		08 27	08 30		08 33								08 45	08 36							
South Bermondsey	d			08 28					08 37																
Queens Rd Peckham	d			08 30					08 39																
Peckham Rye 4	d			08 33					08 42																
East Dulwich	d			08 36					08 45																
North Dulwich	d			08 38					08 47																
Luton 10	d														07 50	07 57									
Luton Airport Parkway 7	d															07 59									
St Pancras International 15 ⊖	d														08 20	08 32									
City Thameslink 3	d														08 29	08 41									
London Blackfriars 3 ⊖	d														08 32	08 44									
Elephant & Castle ⊖	d															08 47									
Loughborough Jn.	d															08 51									
Herne Hill 4	d															08 57									
Tulse Hill 3	d			08 47					08 50							09 01									
Streatham 4	d			08a50												09a05									
London Victoria 15 ⊖	d				08 26						08 31	08 32	08 36							08 36	08 41	08 43	08 47	08 49	08 51
Battersea Park 4	d										08 36									08 40	08a45	08 47		08 53	
Milton Keynes Central	d							07 01																	
Watford Junction	d							07 38																	
Harrow & Wealdstone ⊖	d							07 45																	
Wembley Central ⊖	d							07 49																	
Shepherd's Bush ⊖	d							08 04																	
Kensington (Olympia) ⊖	d							08 07																	
West Brompton ⊖	d							08 10																	
Imperial Wharf	d							08 13																	
Clapham Junction 10	d				08 33			08 36			08 40	08 38	08 43							08 44		08 51	08 53	08 57	
Wandsworth Common	d				08 36			08 39			08 43									08 47		08 54		09 00	
Balham 4 ⊖	d				08 38			08 42			08 46									08 50		08 56		09 02	
Streatham Hill	d																			08 53				09 05	
West Norwood 4	d								08 53											08 57				09 09	
Gipsy Hill	d	08a43							08 56											09 00				09 12	
Crystal Palace 4	d								08 59											09 02				09a14	
Birkbeck 🚋	d								09 03																
Beckenham Junction 4 🚋	a								09 06																
Streatham Common 4	d				08 42			08 46			08 51											09 00			
Norbury	d				08 45			08 48			08 54											09 03			
Thornton Heath	d				08 48			08 51			08 57											09 06			
Selhurst 4	d				08 51			08 54			09 00											09 09			
Norwood Junction 2	a						08 43										08 55	08 59		09 07					
	d						08 44			08 50							08 56	09 00	09 05	09 09					
West Croydon 4 🚋	a				08 55					09 00	09 05								09 12	09 13					
East Croydon 🚋	a		08 37			08 42	08 48	09 04				08 48	08 52		08 57		08 59	09 06				09 12	09 03		09 07

Luton, Milton Keynes Central and London East and West Croydon via Tulse Hill - Crystal Palace - Norbury

Local Services

Network Diagram - see first Page of Table 177

		SN	SN	SN	SN		SN	SN	SN 1	LO	SN	SN 1	SN	SN	SN	LO	SN	SN ◇1 🚲	FC 1	FC	SN		SN	SN ◇1 🚲	FC 1
London Bridge 4 ⊖	d		08 41	08 47	08 48		08 51	09 03	09 03			09 15	09 06	09 11	09 20										
South Bermondsey	d		08 45		08 52			09 07						09 15											
Queens Rd Peckham	d		08 48		08 54			09 09						09 18											
Peckham Rye 4	d		08 50		08 57			09 12						09 20											
East Dulwich	d				09 00			09 15																	
North Dulwich	d				09 02			09 17																	
Luton 10	d																		08 12						08 28
Luton Airport Parkway 7	d																		08 15						08 30
St Pancras International 15 ⊖	d																		08 48	08 56					09 04
City Thameslink 3	d																		08 57	09 05					09 13
London Blackfriars 3 ⊖	d																		09 00	09 08					09 16
Elephant & Castle ⊖	d																			09 12					
Loughborough Jn	d																			09 16					
Herne Hill 4	d																			09 25					
Tulse Hill 3	d				09 05			09 20												09 31					
Streatham 4	d				09 09															09a35					
London Victoria 15 ⊖	d	08 52									09 03						09 05	09 06			09 11		09 13	09 17	
Battersea Park 4	d	08 56	09a02								09 07			09a32			09 10				09a15		09 17		
Milton Keynes Central	d																								
Watford Junction	d																								
Harrow & Wealdstone ⊖	d																								
Wembley Central ⊖	d																								
Shepherd's Bush ⊖	d																								
Kensington (Olympia) ⊖	d																								
West Brompton ⊖	d																								
Imperial Wharf	d																								
Clapham Junction 10	d	09 00									09 11						09 14	09 12					09 21	09 23	
Wandsworth Common	d	09 03									09 14						09 17						09 24		
Balham 4 ⊖	d	09 05									09 16						09 20						09 26		
Streatham Hill	d																09 23								
West Norwood 4	d							09 23									09 27								
Gipsy Hill	d						09a14	09 26									09 30								
Crystal Palace 4	d							09 29									09 32								
Birkbeck 🚋	d							09 33																	
Beckenham Junction 4 🚋	a							09 36																	
Streatham Common 4	d	09 09			09 13						09 20												09 30		
Norbury	d	09 12			09 15						09 23												09 33		
Thornton Heath	d	09 15			09 18						09 26												09 36		
Selhurst 4	d	09 18			09 21						09 29												09 39		
Norwood Junction 2	a								09 16			09 25	09 30		09 32		09 37								
	d								09 16	09 20		09 26	09 30		09 33	09 35	09 39								
West Croydon 4 🚋	a	09 22			09 26					09 30	09 33					09 42	09 43								
East Croydon 🚋	a			09 02					09 20			09 29	09 33		09 36			09 22	09 24				09 42	09 32	09 39

Table 177

Mondays to Fridays

Luton, Milton Keynes Central and London East and West Croydon via Tulse Hill - Crystal Palace - Norbury

Local Services

Network Diagram - see first Page of Table 177

		SN	SN	SN	SN	SN	SN	SN	SN	LO	SN	SN	SN		SN	SN	LO	SN	SN	FC	FC	SN	SN	SN	SN
					1		◇1 🚲	1				1							◇1	1				◇1 🚲	
London Bridge 4 ⊖	d			09 18		09 22		09 32	09 33			09 45	09 36		09 41	09 50									
South Bermondsey	d			09 22					09 37						09 45										
Queens Rd Peckham	d			09 24					09 39						09 48										
Peckham Rye 4	d			09 27					09 42						09 50										
East Dulwich	d			09 30					09 45																
North Dulwich	d			09 32					09 47																
Luton 10	d																			08 48	08 54				
Luton Airport Parkway 7	d																			08 50	08 56				
St Pancras International 15 ⊖	d																			09 22	09 34				
City Thameslink 3	d																			09 31	09 43				
London Blackfriars 3 ⊖	d																			09 34	09 46				
Elephant & Castle ⊖	d																				09 49				
Loughborough Jn.	d																				09 53				
Herne Hill 4	d																				09 57				
Tulse Hill 3	d			09 35					09 50												10 01				
Streatham 4	d			09 39																	10a05				
London Victoria 15 ⊖	d	09 19	09 22				09 32				09 33							09 35	09 36			09 41	09 43	09 47	09 49
Battersea Park 4	d	09 23									09 37				10a02			09 40				09a45	09 47		09 53
Milton Keynes Central	d				08 13																				
Watford Junction	d				08 51																				
Harrow & Wealdstone ⊖	d				08 58																				
Wembley Central ⊖	d				09 05																				
Shepherd's Bush ⊖	d				09 18																				
Kensington (Olympia) ⊖	d				09 21																				
West Brompton ⊖	d				09 23																				
Imperial Wharf	d				09 26																				
Clapham Junction 10	d	09 27	09 30		09 34		09 38				09 41							09 44	09 42				09 51	09 53	09 57
Wandsworth Common	d	09 30	09 33		09 37						09 44							09 47					09 54		10 00
Balham 4 ⊖	d	09 32	09 35		09 41						09 46							09 50					09 56		10 02
Streatham Hill	d	09 35																09 53							10 05
West Norwood 4	d	09 40							09 53									09 57							10 10
Gipsy Hill	d	09 43				09a46			09 56									10 00							10 13
Crystal Palace 4	d	09a46							09 59									10 02							10a16
Birkbeck 🚋	d								10 03																
Beckenham Junction 4 🚋	a								10 06																
Streatham Common 4	d		09 39	09 42	09 45						09 50												10 00		
Norbury	d		09 42	09 45	09 48						09 53												10 03		
Thornton Heath	d		09 45	09 48	09 51						09 56												10 06		
Selhurst 4	d		09 48	09 51	09 54						09 59												10 09		
Norwood Junction 2	a							09 45				09 55	09 59			10 02		10 07							
	d							09 45		09 50		09 56	10 00			10 03	10 05	10 09							
West Croydon 4 🚋	a		09 52	09 56						10 00	10 03						10 12	10 13							
East Croydon 🚋	a				09 57		09 48	09 49				09 59	10 03			10 06			09 52	09 54			10 12	10 02	

Luton, Milton Keynes Central and London East and West Croydon via Tulse Hill - Crystal Palace - Norbury

Local Services

Network Diagram - see first Page of Table 177

		SN	FC	SN	SN		SN	SN	SN	LO	SN	SN	FC	FC	SN	SN	SN	SN	LO	SN	SN		SN	SN	FC
		◇1	1						1			◇1 🛒	1		1									◇1 🛒	1
London Bridge 4 ⊖	d				09 48		09 52	10 03	10 03						10 15	10 06	10 11	10 20							
South Bermondsey	d				09 52			10 07									10 15								
Queens Rd Peckham	d				09 54			10 09									10 18								
Peckham Rye 4	d				09 57			10 12									10 20								
East Dulwich	d				10 00			10 15																	
North Dulwich	d				10 02			10 17																	
Luton 10	d		09 04										09 18	09 14											09 34
Luton Airport Parkway 7	d		09 06										09 20	09 16											09 36
St Pancras International 15 ⊖	d		09 40										09 54	10 04											10 09
City Thameslink 3	d		09 48										10 03	10 13											10 18
London Blackfriars 3 ⊖	d		09 50										10 05	10 16											10 20
Elephant & Castle ⊖	d													10 19											
Loughborough Jn.	d													10 23											
Herne Hill 4	d													10 27											
Tulse Hill 3	d				10 05			10 20						10 31											
Streatham 4	d				10 09									10a35											
London Victoria 15 ⊖	d	09 51		09 53							10 03	10 06								10 06	10 11		10 13	10 17	
Battersea Park 4	d										10 07						10a32			10 10	10a15		10 17		
Milton Keynes Central	d																								
Watford Junction	d																								
Harrow & Wealdstone ⊖	d																								
Wembley Central ⊖	d																								
Shepherd's Bush ⊖	d																								
Kensington (Olympia) ⊖	d																								
West Brompton ⊖	d																								
Imperial Wharf	d																								
Clapham Junction 10	d			10 00							10 11	10 12								10 14			10 21	10 23	
Wandsworth Common	d			10 03							10 14									10 17			10 24		
Balham 4 ⊖	d			10 05							10 16									10 20			10 26		
Streatham Hill	d																			10 23					
West Norwood 4	d							10 23												10 27					
Gipsy Hill	d						10a15	10 26												10 30					
Crystal Palace 4	d							10 29												10 32					
Birkbeck 🚊	d							10 33																	
Beckenham Junction 4 🚊	a							10 36																	
Streatham Common 4	d			10 09	10 12						10 20												10 30		
Norbury	d			10 12	10 15						10 23												10 33		
Thornton Heath	d			10 15	10 18						10 26												10 36		
Selhurst 4	d			10 18	10 21						10 29												10 39		
Norwood Junction 2	a								10 16						10 25	10 29		10 32		10 37					
	d								10 16	10 20					10 26	10 30		10 33	10 35	10 39					
West Croydon 4 🚊	a			10 22	10 26					10 30	10 33								10 42	10 43					
East Croydon 🚊	a	10 07	10 09						10 20			10 22	10 24		10 29	10 33		10 36					10 42	10 32	10 39

Luton, Milton Keynes Central and London East and West Croydon via Tulse Hill - Crystal Palace - Norbury

Local Services

Network Diagram - see first Page of Table 177

Station		SN	SN	SN	SN 1	SN	SN ◇1	SN	SN 1	LO	SN	SN ◇1	FC 1		FC	SN 1	SN	SN	SN	LO	SN	SN	SN	SN ◇1	SN
London Bridge 4 ⊖	d			10 18		10 22		10 33	10 33							10 45	10 36	10 41	10 50						
South Bermondsey	d			10 22				10 37										10 45							
Queens Rd Peckham	d			10 24				10 39										10 48							
Peckham Rye 4	d			10 27				10 42										10 50							
East Dulwich	d			10 30				10 45																	
North Dulwich	d			10 32				10 47																	
Luton 10	d												09 48		09 44										
Luton Airport Parkway 7	d												09 50		09 46										
St Pancras International 15 ⊖	d												10 24		10 34										
City Thameslink 3	d												10 33		10 43										
London Blackfriars 3 ⊖	d												10 35		10 46										
Elephant & Castle ⊖	d														10 49										
Loughborough Jn.	d														10 53										
Herne Hill 4	d														10 57										
Tulse Hill 3	d			10 35				10 50							11 01										
Streatham 4	d			10 39											11a05										
London Victoria 15 ⊖	d	10 19	10 23				10 32				10 33	10 36									10 36	10 41	10 43	10 47	10 49
Battersea Park 4	d	10 23									10 37							11a02			10 40	10a45	10 47		10 53
Milton Keynes Central	d				09 13																				
Watford Junction	d				09 51																				
Harrow & Wealdstone ⊖	d				09 58																				
Wembley Central ⊖	d				10 05																				
Shepherd's Bush ⊖	d				10 21																				
Kensington (Olympia) ⊖	d				10 24																				
West Brompton ⊖	d				10 27																				
Imperial Wharf	d				10 29																				
Clapham Junction 10	d	10 27	10 30		10 34		10 38				10 41	10 42									10 44		10 51	10 53	10 57
Wandsworth Common	d	10 30	10 33		10 37						10 44										10 47		10 54		11 00
Balham 4 ⊖	d	10 32	10 35		10 40						10 46										10 50		10 56		11 02
Streatham Hill	d	10 35																			10 53				11 05
West Norwood 4	d	10 40						10 53													10 57				11 10
Gipsy Hill	d	10 43				10a45		10 56													11 00				11 13
Crystal Palace 4	d	10a46						10 59													11 02				11a16
Birkbeck 🚊	d							11 03																	
Beckenham Junction 4 🚊	a							11 06																	
Streatham Common 4	d		10 39	10 42	10 45						10 50												11 00		
Norbury	d		10 42	10 45	10 48						10 53												11 03		
Thornton Heath	d		10 45	10 48	10 51						10 56												11 06		
Selhurst 4	d		10 48	10 51	10 54						10 59												11 09		
Norwood Junction 2	a								10 46							10 55	10 59		11 02		11 07				
	d								10 46	10 50						10 56	11 00		11 03	11 05	11 09				
West Croydon 4 🚊	a		10 52	10 56						11 00	11 03									11 12	11 13				
East Croydon 🚊	a				10 57		10 48		10 50			10 52	10 54			10 59	11 03		11 06				11 12	11 02	

Station		SN ◇1	FC 1	SN	SN		SN	SN	SN 1	LO	SN	SN ◇1	FC 1	FC	SN 1	SN	SN	SN	LO	SN	SN		SN	SN ◇1	FC 1
London Bridge 4 ⊖	d				10 48		10 52	11 03	11 03						11 15	11 06	11 11	11 20							
South Bermondsey	d				10 52			11 07									11 15								
Queens Rd Peckham	d				10 54			11 09									11 18								
Peckham Rye 4	d				10 57			11 12									11 20								
East Dulwich	d				11 00			11 15																	
North Dulwich	d				11 02			11 17																	
Luton 10	d		10 04										10 18	10 14											10 34
Luton Airport Parkway 7	d		10 06										10 20	10 16											10 36
St Pancras International 15 ⊖	d		10 39										10 54	11 04											11 09
City Thameslink 3	d		10 48										11 03	11 13											11 18
London Blackfriars 3 ⊖	d		10 50										11 05	11 16											11 20
Elephant & Castle ⊖	d													11 19											
Loughborough Jn.	d													11 23											
Herne Hill 4	d													11 27											
Tulse Hill 3	d				11 05			11 20						11 31											
Streatham 4	d				11 09									11a35											
London Victoria 15 ⊖	d	10 51		10 53							11 03	11 06								11 06	11 11		11 13	11 17	
Battersea Park 4	d										11 07						11a32			11 10	11a15		11 17		
Milton Keynes Central	d																								
Watford Junction	d																								
Harrow & Wealdstone ⊖	d																								
Wembley Central ⊖	d																								
Shepherd's Bush ⊖	d																								
Kensington (Olympia) ⊖	d																								
West Brompton ⊖	d																								
Imperial Wharf	d																								
Clapham Junction 10	d			11 00							11 11	11 12								11 14			11 21	11 23	
Wandsworth Common	d			11 03							11 14									11 17			11 24		
Balham 4 ⊖	d			11 05							11 16									11 20			11 26		
Streatham Hill	d																			11 23					
West Norwood 4	d							11 23												11 27					
Gipsy Hill	d						11a15	11 26												11 30					
Crystal Palace 4	d							11 29												11 32					
Birkbeck 🚊	d							11 33																	
Beckenham Junction 4 🚊	a							11 36																	
Streatham Common 4	d			11 09	11 12						11 20												11 30		
Norbury	d			11 12	11 15						11 23												11 33		
Thornton Heath	d			11 15	11 18						11 26												11 36		
Selhurst 4	d			11 18	11 21						11 29												11 39		
Norwood Junction 2	a								11 16						11 25	11 29		11 32		11 37					
	d								11 16	11 20					11 26	11 30		11 33	11 35	11 39					
West Croydon 4 🚊	a			11 22	11 26					11 30	11 33								11 42	11 43					
East Croydon 🚊	a	11 07	11 09						11 20			11 22	11 24		11 29	11 33		11 36					11 42	11 32	11 39

Luton, Milton Keynes Central and London East and West Croydon via Tulse Hill - Crystal Palace - Norbury

Local Services

Network Diagram - see first Page of Table 177

		SN	SN	SN	SN 1	SN	SN ◇1	SN	SN 1	LO	SN	SN ◇1	FC 1		FC	SN 1	SN	SN	SN	LO	SN	SN	SN	SN ◇1	SN
London Bridge 4 ⊖	d			11 18		11 22		11 33	11 33							11 45	11 36	11 41	11 50						
South Bermondsey	d			11 22				11 37										11 45							
Queens Rd Peckham	d			11 24				11 39										11 48							
Peckham Rye 4	d			11 27				11 42										11 50							
East Dulwich	d			11 30				11 45																	
North Dulwich	d			11 32				11 47																	
Luton 10	d												10 49		10 44										
Luton Airport Parkway 7	d												10 51		10 46										
St Pancras International 15 ⊖	d												11 24		11 34										
City Thameslink 3	d												11 33		11 43										
London Blackfriars 3 ⊖	d												11 35		11 46										
Elephant & Castle ⊖	d														11 49										
Loughborough Jn.	d														11 53										
Herne Hill 4	d														11 57										
Tulse Hill 3	d			11 35				11 50							12 01										
Streatham 4	d			11 39											12a05										
London Victoria 15 ⊖	d	11 19	11 23				11 32				11 33	11 36									11 36	11 41	11 43	11 47	11 49
Battersea Park 4	d	11 23									11 37							12a02			11 40	11a45	11 47		11 53
Milton Keynes Central	d				10 13																				
Watford Junction	d				10 51																				
Harrow & Wealdstone ⊖	d				10 59																				
Wembley Central ⊖	d				11 04																				
Shepherd's Bush ⊖	d				11 19																				
Kensington (Olympia) ⊖	d				11 21																				
West Brompton ⊖	d				11 23																				
Imperial Wharf	d				11 26																				
Clapham Junction 10	d	11 27	11 30		11 34		11 38				11 41	11 42									11 44		11 51	11 53	11 57
Wandsworth Common	d	11 30	11 33		11 37						11 44										11 47		11 54		12 00
Balham 4 ⊖	d	11 32	11 35		11 40						11 46										11 50		11 56		12 02
Streatham Hill	d	11 35																			11 53				12 05
West Norwood 4	d	11 40						11 53													11 57				12 10
Gipsy Hill	d	11 43				11a45		11 56													12 00				12 13
Crystal Palace 4	d	11a46						11 59													12 02				12a16
Birkbeck 🚋	d							12 03																	
Beckenham Junction 4 🚋	a							12 06																	
Streatham Common 4	d		11 39	11 42	11 45						11 50												12 00		
Norbury	d		11 42	11 45	11 48						11 53												12 03		
Thornton Heath	d		11 45	11 48	11 51						11 56												12 06		
Selhurst 4	d		11 48	11 51	11 54						11 59												12 09		
Norwood Junction 2	a								11 46							11 55	11 59		12 02		12 07				
	d								11 46	11 50						11 56	12 00		12 03	12 05	12 09				
West Croydon 4 🚋	a		11 52	11 56						12 00	12 03									12 12	12 13				
East Croydon 🚋	a				11 57		11 48		11 50			11 52	11 54			11 59	12 03		12 06				12 12	12 02	

Luton, Milton Keynes Central and London East and West Croydon via Tulse Hill - Crystal Palace - Norbury

Local Services

Network Diagram - see first Page of Table 177

		SN ◇1	FC 1	SN	SN		SN	SN	SN 1	LO	SN	SN ◇1 🚲	FC 1	FC	SN 1	SN	SN	SN	LO	SN	SN		SN	SN ◇1	FC 1
London Bridge 4 ⊖	d				11 48		11 52	12 03	12 03						12 15	12 06	12 11	12 20							
South Bermondsey	d				11 52			12 07									12 15								
Queens Rd Peckham	d				11 54			12 09									12 18								
Peckham Rye 4	d				11 57			12 12									12 20								
East Dulwich	d				12 00			12 15																	
North Dulwich	d				12 02			12 17																	
Luton 10	d		11 04										11 18	11 14											11 34
Luton Airport Parkway 7	d		11 06										11 20	11 16											11 36
St Pancras International 15 ⊖	d		11 39										11 54	12 04											12 09
City Thameslink 3	d		11 48										12 03	12 13											12 18
London Blackfriars 3 ⊖	d		11 50										12 05	12 16											12 20
Elephant & Castle ⊖	d													12 19											
Loughborough Jn.	d													12 23											
Herne Hill 4	d													12 27											
Tulse Hill 3	d				12 05			12 20						12 31											
Streatham 4	d				12 09									12a35											
London Victoria 15 ⊖	d	11 51									12 03	12 06								12 06	12 11		12 13	12 17	
Battersea Park 4	d										12 07						12a32			12 10	12a15		12 17		
Milton Keynes Central	d																								
Watford Junction	d																								
Harrow & Wealdstone ⊖	d																								
Wembley Central ⊖	d																								
Shepherd's Bush ⊖	d																								
Kensington (Olympia) ⊖	d																								
West Brompton ⊖	d																								
Imperial Wharf	d																								
Clapham Junction 10	d			12 00							12 11	12 12								12 14			12 21	12 23	
Wandsworth Common	d			12 03							12 14									12 17			12 24		
Balham 4 ⊖	d			12 05							12 16									12 20			12 26		
Streatham Hill	d																			12 23					
West Norwood 4	d							12 23												12 27					
Gipsy Hill	d						12a15	12 26												12 30					
Crystal Palace 4	d							12 29												12 32					
Birkbeck 🚊	d							12 33																	
Beckenham Junction 4 🚊	a							12 36																	
Streatham Common 4	d			12 09	12 12						12 20												12 30		
Norbury	d			12 12	12 15						12 23												12 33		
Thornton Heath	d			12 15	12 18						12 26												12 36		
Selhurst 4	d			12 18	12 21						12 29												12 39		
Norwood Junction 2	a								12 16						12 25	12 29		12 32		12 37					
	d								12 16	12 20					12 26	12 30		12 33	12 35	12 39					
West Croydon 4 🚊	a			12 22	12 26					12 30	12 33								12 42	12 43					
East Croydon 🚊	a	12 07	12 09						12 20			12 22	12 24		12 29	12 33		12 36					12 42	12 32	12 39

Table 177

Mondays to Fridays

Luton, Milton Keynes Central and London East and West Croydon via Tulse Hill - Crystal Palace - Norbury

Local Services

Network Diagram - see first Page of Table 177

		SN	SN	SN	SN	SN	SN	SN	SN	LO	SN	SN	FC		FC	SN	SN	SN	SN	LO	SN	SN	SN	SN	SN
					1		◇1		1			◇1 [trolley]	1			1								◇1	
London Bridge 4 ⊖	d			12 18		12 22		12 33	12 33							12 45	12 36	12 41	12 50						
South Bermondsey	d			12 22				12 37										12 45							
Queens Rd Peckham	d			12 24				12 39										12 48							
Peckham Rye 4	d			12 27				12 42										12 50							
East Dulwich	d			12 30				12 45																	
North Dulwich	d			12 32				12 47																	
Luton 10	d												11 48		11 44										
Luton Airport Parkway 7	d												11 50		11 46										
St Pancras International 15 ⊖	d												12 24		12 34										
City Thameslink 3	d												12 33		12 43										
London Blackfriars 3 ⊖	d												12 35		12 46										
Elephant & Castle ⊖	d														12 49										
Loughborough Jn.	d														12 53										
Herne Hill 4	d														12 57										
Tulse Hill 3	d			12 35				12 50							13 01										
Streatham 4	d			12 39											13a05										
London Victoria 15 ⊖	d	12 19					12 32				12 33	12 36									12 36	12 41	12 43	12 47	12 49
Battersea Park 4	d	12 23									12 37							13a02			12 40	12a45	12 47		12 53
Milton Keynes Central	d				11 13																				
Watford Junction	d				11 51																				
Harrow & Wealdstone ⊖	d				11 59																				
Wembley Central ⊖	d				12 04																				
Shepherd's Bush ⊖	d				12 19																				
Kensington (Olympia) ⊖	d				12 22																				
West Brompton ⊖	d				12 25																				
Imperial Wharf	d				12 27																				
Clapham Junction 10	d	12 27	12 30		12 34		12 38				12 41	12 42									12 44		12 51	12 53	12 57
Wandsworth Common	d	12 30	12 33		12 37						12 44										12 47		12 54		13 00
Balham 4 ⊖	d	12 32	12 35		12 40						12 46										12 50		12 56		13 02
Streatham Hill	d	12 35																			12 53				13 05
West Norwood 4	d	12 40						12 53													12 57				13 10
Gipsy Hill	d	12 43				12a45		12 56													13 00				13 13
Crystal Palace 4	d	12a46						12 59													13 02				13a16
Birkbeck 🚌	d							13 03																	
Beckenham Junction 4 🚌	a							13 06																	
Streatham Common 4	d		12 39	12 42	12 45						12 50												13 00		
Norbury	d		12 42	12 45	12 48						12 53												13 03		
Thornton Heath	d		12 45	12 48	12 51						12 56												13 06		
Selhurst 4	d		12 48	12 51	12 54						12 59												13 09		
Norwood Junction 2	a								12 46							12 55	12 59		13 02		13 07				
	d								12 46	12 50						12 56	13 00		13 03	13 05	13 09				
West Croydon 4 🚌	a		12 52	12 56						13 00	13 03									13 12	13 13				
East Croydon 🚌	a				12 57		12 48		12 50			12 52	12 54			12 59	13 03		13 06				13 12	13 02	

Luton, Milton Keynes Central and London East and West Croydon via Tulse Hill - Crystal Palace - Norbury

Local Services Network Diagram - see first Page of Table 177

		SN	FC	SN	SN		SN	SN	SN	LO	SN	SN	FC	FC	SN	SN	SN	SN	LO	SN	SN		SN	SN	FC
		◇1	1						1			◇1 🚲	1		1									◇1	1
London Bridge 4 ⊖	d				12 48		12 52	13 03	13 03						13 15	13 06	13 11	13 20							
South Bermondsey	d				12 52			13 07									13 15								
Queens Rd Peckham	d				12 54			13 09									13 18								
Peckham Rye 4	d				12 57			13 12									13 20								
East Dulwich	d				13 00			13 15																	
North Dulwich	d				13 02			13 17																	
Luton 10	d		12 04										12 18	12 14											12 34
Luton Airport Parkway 7	d		12 06										12 20	12 16											12 36
St Pancras International 15 ⊖	d		12 39										12 54	13 04											13 09
City Thameslink 3	d		12 48										13 03	13 13											13 18
London Blackfriars 3 ⊖	d		12 50										13 05	13 16											13 20
Elephant & Castle ⊖	d													13 19											
Loughborough Jn.	d													13 23											
Herne Hill 4	d													13 27											
Tulse Hill 3	d				13 05			13 20						13 31											
Streatham 4	d				13 09									13a35											
London Victoria 15 ⊖	d	12 51									13 03	13 06								13 06	13 11		13 13	13 17	
Battersea Park 4	d										13 07						13a32			13 10	13a15		13 17		
Milton Keynes Central	d																								
Watford Junction	d																								
Harrow & Wealdstone ⊖	d																								
Wembley Central ⊖	d																								
Shepherd's Bush ⊖	d																								
Kensington (Olympia) ⊖	d																								
West Brompton ⊖	d																								
Imperial Wharf	d																								
Clapham Junction 10	d			13 00							13 11	13 12								13 14			13 21	13 23	
Wandsworth Common	d			13 03							13 14									13 17			13 24		
Balham 4 ⊖	d			13 05							13 16									13 20			13 26		
Streatham Hill	d																			13 23					
West Norwood 4	d							13 23												13 27					
Gipsy Hill	d						13a15	13 26												13 30					
Crystal Palace 4	d							13 29												13 32					
Birkbeck	d							13 33																	
Beckenham Junction 4	a							13 36																	
Streatham Common 4	d			13 09	13 12						13 20												13 30		
Norbury	d			13 12	13 15						13 23												13 33		
Thornton Heath	d			13 15	13 18						13 26												13 36		
Selhurst 4	d			13 18	13 21						13 29												13 39		
Norwood Junction 2	a								13 16						13 25	13 29		13 32		13 37					
	d								13 16	13 20					13 26	13 30		13 33	13 35	13 39					
West Croydon 4	a			13 22	13 26					13 30	13 33								13 42	13 43					
East Croydon	a	13 07	13 09						13 20			13 22	13 24		13 29	13 33		13 36					13 42	13 32	13 39

Table 177

Mondays to Fridays

Luton, Milton Keynes Central and London East and West Croydon via Tulse Hill - Crystal Palace - Norbury

Local Services

Network Diagram - see first Page of Table 177

		SN	SN	SN	SN ■1	SN	SN ◇■1 🚲	SN	SN ■1	LO	SN	SN ◇■1 🚲	FC ■1		FC	SN ■1	SN	SN	SN	LO	SN	SN	SN	SN ◇■1	SN
London Bridge ■4 ⊖	d			13 18		13 22		13 33	13 33							13 45	13 36	13 41	13 50						
South Bermondsey	d			13 22				13 37										13 45							
Queens Rd Peckham	d			13 24				13 39										13 48							
Peckham Rye ■4	d			13 27				13 42										13 50							
East Dulwich	d			13 30				13 45																	
North Dulwich	d			13 32				13 47																	
Luton ■10	d												12 48		12 44										
Luton Airport Parkway ■7	d												12 50		12 46										
St Pancras International ■15 ⊖	d												13 24		13 34										
City Thameslink ■3	d												13 33		13 43										
London Blackfriars ■3 ⊖	d												13 35		13 46										
Elephant & Castle ⊖	d														13 49										
Loughborough Jn.	d														13 53										
Herne Hill ■4	d														13 57										
Tulse Hill ■3	d			13 35				13 50							14 01										
Streatham ■4	d			13 39											14a05										
London Victoria ■15 ⊖	d	13 19	13 23				13 32				13 33	13 36									13 36	13 41	13 43	13 47	13 49
Battersea Park ■4	d	13 23									13 37							14a02			13 40	13a45	13 47		13 53
Milton Keynes Central	d				12 13																				
Watford Junction	d				12 51																				
Harrow & Wealdstone ⊖	d				12 59																				
Wembley Central ⊖	d				13 04																				
Shepherd's Bush ⊖	d				13 19																				
Kensington (Olympia) ⊖	d				13 22																				
West Brompton ⊖	d				13 25																				
Imperial Wharf	d				13 28																				
Clapham Junction ■10	d	13 27	13 30		13 34		13 38				13 41	13 42									13 44		13 51	13 53	13 57
Wandsworth Common	d	13 30	13 33		13 37						13 44										13 47		13 54		14 00
Balham ■4 ⊖	d	13 32	13 35		13 40						13 46										13 50		13 56		14 02
Streatham Hill	d	13 35																			13 53				14 05
West Norwood ■4	d	13 40						13 53													13 57				14 10
Gipsy Hill	d	13 43				13a45		13 56													14 00				14 13
Crystal Palace ■4	d	13a46						13 59													14 02				14a16
Birkbeck 🚊	d							14 03																	
Beckenham Junction ■4 🚊	a							14 06																	
Streatham Common ■4	d		13 39	13 42	13 45						13 50												14 00		
Norbury	d		13 42	13 45	13 48						13 53												14 03		
Thornton Heath	d		13 45	13 48	13 51						13 56												14 06		
Selhurst ■4	d		13 48	13 51	13 54						13 59												14 09		
Norwood Junction ■2	a								13 46							13 55	13 59		14 02		14 07				
	d								13 46	13 50						13 56	14 00		14 03	14 05	14 09				
West Croydon ■4 🚊	a		13 52	13 56						14 00	14 03									14 12	14 13				
East Croydon 🚊	a				13 57		13 48		13 50			13 52	13 54			13 59	14 03		14 06				14 12	14 02	

Luton, Milton Keynes Central and London East and West Croydon via Tulse Hill - Crystal Palace - Norbury

Local Services

Network Diagram - see first Page of Table 177

		SN ◇[1]	FC [1]	SN	SN		SN	SN	SN [1]	LO	SN	SN ◇[1]	FC [1]	FC	SN [1]	SN	SN	SN	LO	SN	SN		SN	SN ◇[1]	FC [1]
London Bridge [4] ⊖	d				13 48		13 52	14 03	14 03						14 15	14 06	14 11	14 20							
South Bermondsey	d				13 52			14 07									14 15								
Queens Rd Peckham	d				13 54			14 09									14 18								
Peckham Rye [4]	d				13 57			14 12									14 20								
East Dulwich	d				14 00			14 15																	
North Dulwich	d				14 02			14 17																	
Luton [10]	d		13 04										13 18	13 14											13 34
Luton Airport Parkway [7]	d		13 06										13 20	13 16											13 36
St Pancras International [15] ⊖	d		13 39										13 54	14 04											14 09
City Thameslink [3]	d		13 48										14 03	14 13											14 18
London Blackfriars [3] ⊖	d		13 50										14 05	14 16											14 20
Elephant & Castle ⊖	d													14 19											
Loughborough Jn.	d													14 23											
Herne Hill [4]	d													14 27											
Tulse Hill [3]	d				14 05			14 20						14 31											
Streatham [4]	d				14 09									14a35											
London Victoria [15] ⊖	d	13 51									14 03	14 06								14 06	14 11		14 13	14 17	
Battersea Park [4]	d										14 07						14a32			14 10	14a15		14 17		
Milton Keynes Central	d																								
Watford Junction	d																								
Harrow & Wealdstone ⊖	d																								
Wembley Central ⊖	d																								
Shepherd's Bush ⊖	d																								
Kensington (Olympia) ⊖	d																								
West Brompton ⊖	d																								
Imperial Wharf	d																								
Clapham Junction [10]	d			14 00							14 11	14 12								14 14			14 21	14 23	
Wandsworth Common	d			14 03							14 14									14 17			14 24		
Balham [4] ⊖	d			14 05							14 16									14 20			14 26		
Streatham Hill	d																			14 23					
West Norwood [4]	d							14 23												14 27					
Gipsy Hill	d						14a15	14 26												14 30					
Crystal Palace [4]	d							14 29												14 32					
Birkbeck 🚋	d							14 33																	
Beckenham Junction [4] 🚋	a							14 36																	
Streatham Common [4]	d			14 09	14 12						14 20												14 30		
Norbury	d			14 12	14 15						14 23												14 33		
Thornton Heath	d			14 15	14 18						14 26												14 36		
Selhurst [4]	d			14 18	14 21						14 29												14 39		
Norwood Junction [2]	a								14 16						14 25	14 29		14 32		14 37					
	d								14 16	14 20					14 26	14 30		14 33	14 35	14 39					
West Croydon [4] 🚋	a			14 22	14 26					14 30	14 33								14 42	14 43					
East Croydon 🚋	a	14 07	14 09						14 20			14 22	14 25		14 29	14 33		14 36					14 42	14 32	14 39

Luton, Milton Keynes Central and London East and West Croydon via Tulse Hill - Crystal Palace - Norbury

Local Services

Network Diagram - see first Page of Table 177

		SN	SN	SN	SN	SN	SN	SN	SN	LO	SN	SN	FC		FC	SN	SN	SN	SN	LO	SN	SN	SN	SN	SN
					1		◇1 ⚒		1			◇1 ⚒	1			1								◇1	
London Bridge 4 ⊖	d			14 18		14 22		14 33	14 33							14 45	14 36	14 41	14 50						
South Bermondsey	d			14 22				14 37										14 45							
Queens Rd Peckham	d			14 24				14 39										14 48							
Peckham Rye 4	d			14 27				14 42										14 50							
East Dulwich	d			14 30				14 45																	
North Dulwich	d			14 32				14 47																	
Luton 10	d												13 48		13 44										
Luton Airport Parkway 7	d												13 50		13 46										
St Pancras International 15 ⊖	d												14 24		14 34										
City Thameslink 3	d												14 33		14 43										
London Blackfriars 3 ⊖	d												14 35		14 46										
Elephant & Castle ⊖	d														14 49										
Loughborough Jn.	d														14 53										
Herne Hill 4	d														14 57										
Tulse Hill 3	d			14 35				14 50							15 01										
Streatham 4	d			14 39											15a05										
London Victoria 15 ⊖	d	14 19					14 32				14 33	14 36									14 36	14 41	14 43	14 47	14 49
Battersea Park 4	d	14 23									14 37							15a02			14 40	14a45	14 47		14 53
Milton Keynes Central	d				13 13																				
Watford Junction	d				13 51																				
Harrow & Wealdstone ⊖	d				13 59																				
Wembley Central ⊖	d				14 04																				
Shepherd's Bush ⊖	d				14 19																				
Kensington (Olympia) ⊖	d				14 22																				
West Brompton ⊖	d				14 25																				
Imperial Wharf	d				14 28																				
Clapham Junction 10	d	14 27	14 30		14 34		14 38				14 41	14 42									14 44		14 51	14 53	14 57
Wandsworth Common	d	14 30	14 33		14 37						14 44										14 47		14 54		15 00
Balham 4 ⊖	d	14 32	14 35		14 40						14 46										14 50		14 56		15 02
Streatham Hill	d	14 35																			14 53				15 05
West Norwood 4	d	14 40						14 53													14 57				15 10
Gipsy Hill	d	14 43				14a45		14 56													15 00				15 13
Crystal Palace 4	d	14a46						14 59													15 02				15a16
Birkbeck 🚊	d							15 03																	
Beckenham Junction 4 🚊	a							15 06																	
Streatham Common 4	d		14 39	14 42	14 45						14 50												15 00		
Norbury	d		14 42	14 45	14 48						14 53												15 03		
Thornton Heath	d		14 45	14 48	14 51						14 56												15 06		
Selhurst 4	d		14 48	14 51	14 54						14 59												15 09		
Norwood Junction 2	a								14 46							14 55	14 59		15 02		15 07				
	d								14 46	14 50						14 56	15 00		15 03	15 05	15 09				
West Croydon 4 🚊	a		14 52	14 56						15 00	15 03									15 12	15 13				
East Croydon 🚊	a				14 57		14 48		14 50			14 52	14 54			14 59	15 03		15 06				15 12	15 02	

Luton, Milton Keynes Central and London
East and West Croydon via
Tulse Hill - Crystal Palace - Norbury

Local Services

Network Diagram - see first Page of Table 177

		SN ◇1	FC 1	SN	SN		SN	SN	SN 1	LO	SN	SN ◇1	FC 1	FC	SN 1	SN	SN	SN	LO	SN	SN		SN	SN ◇1	FC 1
London Bridge 4 ⊖	d				14 48		14 52	15 03	15 03						15 15	15 06	15 11	15 20							
South Bermondsey	d				14 52			15 07									15 15								
Queens Rd Peckham	d				14 54			15 09									15 18								
Peckham Rye 4	d				14 57			15 12									15 20								
East Dulwich	d				15 00			15 15																	
North Dulwich	d				15 02			15 17																	
Luton 10	d		14 04										14 18	14 14											14 34
Luton Airport Parkway 7	d		14 06										14 20	14 16											14 36
St Pancras International 15 ⊖	d		14 39										14 54	15 04											15 09
City Thameslink 3	d		14 48										15 03	15 13											15 18
London Blackfriars 3 ⊖	d		14 50										15 05	15 16											15 20
Elephant & Castle ⊖	d													15 19											
Loughborough Jn.	d													15 23											
Herne Hill 4	d													15 27											
Tulse Hill 3	d				15 05			15 20						15 31											
Streatham 4	d				15 09									15a35											
London Victoria 15 ⊖	d	14 51									15 03	15 06								15 06	15 11		15 13	15 17	
Battersea Park 4	d										15 07						15a32			15 10	15a15		15 17		
Milton Keynes Central	d																								
Watford Junction	d																								
Harrow & Wealdstone ⊖	d																								
Wembley Central ⊖	d																								
Shepherd's Bush ⊖	d																								
Kensington (Olympia) ⊖	d																								
West Brompton ⊖	d																								
Imperial Wharf	d																								
Clapham Junction 10	d			15 00							15 11	15 12								15 14			15 21	15 23	
Wandsworth Common	d			15 03							15 14									15 17			15 24		
Balham 4 ⊖	d			15 05							15 16									15 20			15 26		
Streatham Hill	d																			15 23					
West Norwood 4	d							15 23												15 27					
Gipsy Hill	d						15a15	15 26												15 30					
Crystal Palace 4	d							15 29												15 32					
Birkbeck	d							15 33																	
Beckenham Junction 4	a							15 36																	
Streatham Common 4	d			15 09	15 12						15 20												15 30		
Norbury	d			15 12	15 15						15 23												15 33		
Thornton Heath	d			15 15	15 18						15 26												15 36		
Selhurst 4	d			15 18	15 21						15 29												15 39		
Norwood Junction 2	a								15 16						15 25	15 29		15 32		15 37					
	d								15 16	15 20					15 26	15 30		15 33	15 35	15 39					
West Croydon 4	a			15 22	15 26					15 30	15 33								15 42	15 43					
East Croydon	a	15 07	15 09						15 20			15 22	15 24		15 29	15 33		15 36					15 42	15 32	15 39

Table 177

Mondays to Fridays

Luton, Milton Keynes Central and London East and West Croydon via Tulse Hill - Crystal Palace - Norbury

Local Services

Network Diagram - see first Page of Table 177

		SN	SN	SN	SN 1	SN	SN ◇1	SN	SN 1	LO	SN	SN ◇1	FC 1		FC	SN 1	SN	SN	SN	LO	SN	SN	SN	SN ◇1	SN
London Bridge 4 ⊖	d			15 18		15 22		15 33	15 33							15 45	15 36	15 41	15 50						
South Bermondsey	d			15 22				15 37										15 45							
Queens Rd Peckham	d			15 24				15 39										15 48							
Peckham Rye 4	d			15 27				15 42										15 50							
East Dulwich	d			15 30				15 45																	
North Dulwich	d			15 32				15 47																	
Luton 10	d												14 48		14 44										
Luton Airport Parkway 7	d												14 50		14 46										
St Pancras International 15 ⊖	d												15 24		15 34										
City Thameslink 3	d												15 33		15 43										
London Blackfriars 3 ⊖	d												15 35		15 46										
Elephant & Castle ⊖	d														15 49										
Loughborough Jn.	d														15 53										
Herne Hill 4	d														15 57										
Tulse Hill 3	d			15 35				15 50							16 01										
Streatham 4	d			15 39											16a05										
London Victoria 15 ⊖	d	15 19	15 23				15 32				15 33	15 36									15 36	15 41	15 43	15 47	15 49
Battersea Park 4	d	15 23									15 37							16a02			15 40	15a45	15 47		15 53
Milton Keynes Central	d				14 13																				
Watford Junction	d				14 51																				
Harrow & Wealdstone ⊖	d				14 59																				
Wembley Central ⊖	d				15 04																				
Shepherd's Bush ⊖	d				15 22																				
Kensington (Olympia) ⊖	d				15 24																				
West Brompton ⊖	d				15 26																				
Imperial Wharf	d				15 29																				
Clapham Junction 10	d	15 27	15 30		15 34		15 38				15 41	15 42									15 44		15 51	15 53	15 57
Wandsworth Common	d	15 30	15 33		15 37						15 44										15 47		15 54		16 00
Balham 4 ⊖	d	15 32	15 35		15 40						15 46										15 50		15 56		16 02
Streatham Hill	d	15 35																			15 53				16 05
West Norwood 4	d	15 40						15 53													15 57				16 10
Gipsy Hill	d	15 43				15a45		15 56													16 00				16 13
Crystal Palace 4	d	15a46						15 59													16 02				16a16
Birkbeck	d							16 03																	
Beckenham Junction 4	a							16 06																	
Streatham Common 4	d		15 39	15 42	15 45						15 50												16 00		
Norbury	d		15 42	15 45	15 48						15 53												16 03		
Thornton Heath	d		15 45	15 48	15 51						15 56												16 06		
Selhurst 4	d		15 48	15 51	15 54						15 59												16 09		
Norwood Junction 2	a								15 46							15 55	15 59		16 02		16 07				
	d								15 46	15 50						15 56	16 00		16 03	16 05	16 09				
West Croydon 4	a		15 52	15 56						16 00	16 03									16 12	16 13				
East Croydon	a				15 57		15 47		15 50			15 52	15 54			15 59	16 03		16 06				16 12	16 02	

Table 177

Mondays to Fridays

Luton, Milton Keynes Central and London East and West Croydon via Tulse Hill - Crystal Palace - Norbury

Local Services

Network Diagram - see first Page of Table 177

		SN	FC	SN	SN		SN	SN	SN	LO	SN	SN	FC	FC	SN	SN	SN	SN	LO	SN	SN		SN	SN	SN
		◇1	1						1			1 🚲	1		1									◇1 🚲	
London Bridge 4 ⊖	d				15 48		15 52	16 03	16 03						16 15	16 06	16 11	16 20							16 18
South Bermondsey	d				15 52			16 07									16 15								16 22
Queens Rd Peckham	d				15 54			16 09									16 18								16 24
Peckham Rye 4	d				15 57			16 12									16 20								16 27
East Dulwich	d				16 00			16 15																	16 30
North Dulwich	d				16 02			16 17																	16 32
Luton 10	d		15 04										15 18	15 14											
Luton Airport Parkway 7	d		15 06										15 20	15 16											
St Pancras International 15 ⊖	d		15 39										15 54	16 04											
City Thameslink 3	d		15 48										16 03	16 13											
London Blackfriars 3 ⊖	d		15 50										16 05	16 16											
Elephant & Castle ⊖	d													16 19											
Loughborough Jn	d													16 23											
Herne Hill 4	d													16 27											
Tulse Hill 3	d				16 05			16 20						16 32											16 35
Streatham 4	d				16 09									16a35											16 39
London Victoria 15 ⊖	d	15 51		15 53							16 03	16 06								16 07	16 11		16 13	16 17	
Battersea Park 4	d										16 07						16a32			16 11	16a15		16 17		
Milton Keynes Central	d																								
Watford Junction	d																								
Harrow & Wealdstone ⊖	d																								
Wembley Central ⊖	d																								
Shepherd's Bush ⊖	d																								
Kensington (Olympia) ⊖	d																								
West Brompton ⊖	d																								
Imperial Wharf	d																								
Clapham Junction 10	d			16 00							16 11	16 12								16 15			16 21	16 23	
Wandsworth Common	d			16 03							16 14									16 18			16 24		
Balham 4 ⊖	d			16 05							16 16									16 20			16 26		
Streatham Hill	d																			16 23					
West Norwood 4	d							16 23												16 27					
Gipsy Hill	d						16a15	16 26												16 30					
Crystal Palace 4	d							16 29												16 32					
Birkbeck 🚊	d							16 33																	
Beckenham Junction 4 🚊	a							16 38																	
Streatham Common 4	d			16 09	16 12						16 20												16 30		16 42
Norbury	d			16 12	16 15						16 23												16 33		16 45
Thornton Heath	d			16 15	16 18						16 26												16 36		16 48
Selhurst 4	d			16 18	16 21						16 29												16 39		16 51
Norwood Junction 2	a								16 16						16 25	16 29		16 32		16 37					
	d								16 16	16 20					16 26	16 30		16 33	16 35	16 39					
West Croydon 4 🚊	a			16 22	16 26					16 30	16 33								16 42	16 43					16 57
East Croydon 🚊	a	16 07	16 09						16 20			16 22	16 24		16 29	16 33		16 36					16 42	16 33	

Luton, Milton Keynes Central and London East and West Croydon via Tulse Hill - Crystal Palace - Norbury

Local Services

Network Diagram - see first Page of Table 177

		SN ■1	FC ■1	SN	SN ■1	SN	SN ◇■1 🛒	SN	SN ■1	LO	SN	SN	SN ■1 🛒		SN	SN	LO	SN	SN	FC ■1	FC	FC ■1	SN	SN	SN ◇■1 🛒
London Bridge ■4	⊖ d					16 22		16 33	16 33			16 36			16 41	16 48									
South Bermondsey	d							16 37							16 45										
Queens Rd Peckham	d							16 39							16 48										
Peckham Rye ■4	d							16 42							16 50										
East Dulwich	d							16 45																	
North Dulwich	d							16 47																	
Luton ■10	d		15 34																	15 48	15 44	16 04			
Luton Airport Parkway ■7	d		15 36																	15 50	15 46	16 06			
St Pancras International ■15	⊖ d		16 09																	16 22	16 34	16 40			
City Thameslink ■3	d		16 18																	16 31	16 43	16 49			
London Blackfriars ■3	⊖ d		16 20																	16 36	16 46	16 52			
Elephant & Castle	⊖ d																				16 49	16 56			
Loughborough Jn.	d																				16 53	17 00			
Herne Hill ■4	d																				16 57	17a04			
Tulse Hill ■3	d							16 50													17 02				
Streatham ■4	d																				17a05				
London Victoria ■15	⊖ d	16 19		16 19			16 32				16 33		16 36					16 37	16 39				16 41	16 43	16 47
Battersea Park ■4	d			16 23							16 37				17a02			16 41					16a45	16 47	
Milton Keynes Central	d				15 13																				
Watford Junction	d				15 51																				
Harrow & Wealdstone	⊖ d				15 59																				
Wembley Central	⊖ d				16 05																				
Shepherd's Bush	⊖ d				16 19																				
Kensington (Olympia)	⊖ d				16 22																				
West Brompton	⊖ d				16 25																				
Imperial Wharf	d				16 27																				
Clapham Junction ■10	d	16 26		16 27	16 34		16 38				16 41		16 42					16 45	16 45					16 51	16 53
Wandsworth Common	d			16 30	16 37						16 44							16 48						16 54	
Balham ■4	⊖ d			16 32	16 40						16 46							16 50						16 56	
Streatham Hill	d			16 35														16 53							
West Norwood ■4	d			16 39				16 53										16 57							
Gipsy Hill	d			16 44		16a45		16 56										17 00							
Crystal Palace ■4	d			16a46				16 59										17 03							
Birkbeck	🚊 d							17 03																	
Beckenham Junction ■4	🚊 a							17 08																	
Streatham Common ■4	d				16 45						16 50													17 00	
Norbury	d				16 48						16 53													17 03	
Thornton Heath	d				16 51						16 56													17 06	
Selhurst ■4	d				16 55						16 59													17 09	
Norwood Junction ■2	a								16 44			16 59				17 01		17 07							
	d								16 44	16 50		17 00				17 02	17 05	17 09							
West Croydon ■4	🚊 a									17 00	17 03	17 07					17 12	17 13							
East Croydon	🚊 a	16 36	16 39		16 58		16 47		16 48				16 52			17 05			16 55	16 59				17 12	17 03

		SN	SN ■1	SN	SN		SN ■1	SN	SN ■1	SN	LO	SN	SN	SN ■1	FC ■1	FC	SN	SN	LO	SN	SN		SN	SN	SN ◇■1
London Bridge ■4	⊖ d	16 48			16 52		16 57	16 58	16 59	17 03			17 05				17 11	17 17							
South Bermondsey	d	16 52						17 02									17 15								
Queens Rd Peckham	d	16 54						17 04									17 18								
Peckham Rye ■4	d	16 57						17 07									17 20								
East Dulwich	d	17 00						17 10																	
North Dulwich	d	17 02						17 12																	
Luton ■10	d														16 14	16 16									
Luton Airport Parkway ■7	d														16 17	16 18									
St Pancras International ■15	⊖ d														16 46	17 02									
City Thameslink ■3	d														16 55	17 11									
London Blackfriars ■3	⊖ d														16 58	17 14									
Elephant & Castle	⊖ d														17 02	17 18									
Loughborough Jn.	d															17 22									
Herne Hill ■4	d															17 26									
Tulse Hill ■3	d	17 05						17 17								17 31									
Streatham ■4	d	17 09														17a35									
London Victoria ■15	⊖ d		16 49	16 49								17 01		17 06						17 06	17 09		17 11	17 13	17 17
Battersea Park ■4	d			16 53								17 05					17a32			17 10			17a15	17 17	
Milton Keynes Central	d																								
Watford Junction	d																								
Harrow & Wealdstone	⊖ d																								
Wembley Central	⊖ d																								
Shepherd's Bush	⊖ d																								
Kensington (Olympia)	⊖ d																								
West Brompton	⊖ d																								
Imperial Wharf	d																								
Clapham Junction ■10	d		16 56	16 57								17 09		17 12						17 14	17 15			17 21	17 23
Wandsworth Common	d			17 00								17 12								17 17				17 24	
Balham ■4	⊖ d			17 03								17 14								17 19				17 26	
Streatham Hill	d			17 06																17 22					
West Norwood ■4	d			17 09				17 20												17 27					
Gipsy Hill	d			17 12	17a15			17 23												17 30					
Crystal Palace ■4	d			17a15				17 26												17 33					
Birkbeck	🚊 d							17 30																	
Beckenham Junction ■4	🚊 a							17 35																	
Streatham Common ■4	d	17 12										17 18												17 30	
Norbury	d	17 15										17 21												17 33	
Thornton Heath	d	17 18										17 24												17 36	
Selhurst ■4	d	17 21										17 27												17a40	
Norwood Junction ■2	a								17 10	17 16			17 29					17 30		17 37					
	d								17 10	17 16	17 20		17 30					17 30	17 35	17 38					
West Croydon ■4	🚊 a	17 27								17 21	17 30	17 32	17 37						17 42	17 43					
East Croydon	🚊 a		17 06				17 09		17 14					17 22	17 26			17 34			17 27				17 32

Luton, Milton Keynes Central and London East and West Croydon via Tulse Hill - Crystal Palace - Norbury

Local Services

Network Diagram - see first Page of Table 177

		SN	SN ■1	SN	SN	SN ■1	FC ■1	SN ■1	SN	SN	SN ◇■1	SN ■1	LO		SN	SN ◇■1 🚲	SN	SN	SN ■1	FC ■1	FC	SN	SN	LO	SN
London Bridge ■4 ⊖	d	17 18			17 19	17 23			17 28	17 29		17 32					17 36	17 41	17 42			17 48	17 49		
South Bermondsey	d	17 22							17 32									17 45				17 52			
Queens Rd Peckham	d	17 24							17 35									17 47				17 54			
Peckham Rye ■4	d	17 27							17 37									17 50				17 57			
East Dulwich	d	17 30							17 40													18 00			
North Dulwich	d	17 32							17 42													18 02			
Luton ■10	d						16 34													16 50	16 46				
Luton Airport Parkway ■7	d						16 36													16 52	16 48				
St Pancras International ■15 ⊖	d						17 10													17 28	17 32				
City Thameslink ■3	d						17 19													17 37	17 41				
London Blackfriars ■3 ⊖	d						17 22													17 40	17 44				
Elephant & Castle ⊖	d																				17 48				
Loughborough Jn	d																				17 52				
Herne Hill ■4	d																				17 57				
Tulse Hill ■3	d	17 36							17 46												18 02	18 05			
Streatham ■4	d	17 39																			18a05	18 09			
London Victoria ■15 ⊖	d		17 21	17 22							17 32				17 33	17 35									17 37
Battersea Park ■4	d			17 26											17 37			18a02							17 41
Milton Keynes Central	d							16 13																	
Watford Junction	d							16 51																	
Harrow & Wealdstone ⊖	d							16 59																	
Wembley Central ⊖	d							17 05																	
Shepherd's Bush ⊖	d							17 19																	
Kensington (Olympia) ⊖	d							17 22																	
West Brompton ⊖	d							17 25																	
Imperial Wharf	d							17 28																	
Clapham Junction ■10	d		17 27	17 30				17 33			17 38				17 41	17 42									17 45
Wandsworth Common	d			17 33				17 36							17 44										17 48
Balham ■4 ⊖	d			17 35				17 39							17 46										17 50
Streatham Hill	d			17 38																					17 53
West Norwood ■4	d			17 42					17 49																17 57
Gipsy Hill	d			17 45	17a46				17 52																18 00
Crystal Palace ■4	d			17a47					17 54																18 02
Birkbeck 🚋	d								17 58																
Beckenham Junction ■4 🚋	a								18 04																
Streatham Common ■4	d	17 42						17 46							17 50							18 12			
Norbury	d	17 45						17 48							17 53							18 14			
Thornton Heath	d	17 48						17 51							17 56							18 17			
Selhurst ■4	d	17 50						17 55							17 59							18 21			
Norwood Junction ■2	a									17 41		17 43					17 59						18 01		18 08
	d									17 43		17 44	17 50				18 00						18 02	18 05	18 09
West Croydon ■4 🚋	a	17 57								17 47			18 01		18 03		18 08					18 27		18 12	18 14
East Croydon 🚋	a		17 36			17 35	17 47	17 59			17 48	17 49				17 51			17 54	18 07			18 05		

Luton, Milton Keynes Central and London East and West Croydon via Tulse Hill - Crystal Palace - Norbury

Local Services

Network Diagram - see first Page of Table 177

		SN	SN	SN	SN ◇1		SN 1	SN	SN	SN 1	SN	SN 1	SN	SN	LO	SN	SN	SN ◇1	FC 1	FC	FC		SN	SN 1	SN
London Bridge 4 ⊖	d							17 53		17 57	17 58	17 59		18 02			18 06						18 11	18 12	18 18
South Bermondsey	d										18 02												18 15		
Queens Rd Peckham	d										18 04												18 18		
Peckham Rye 4	d										18 07												18 20		
East Dulwich	d										18 10														
North Dulwich	d										18 12														
Luton 10	d																			17 10	17 22				
Luton Airport Parkway 7	d																			17 12	17 24				
St Pancras International 15 ⊖	d																		17 40	17 44	18 04				
City Thameslink 3	d																		17 49	17 53	18 13				
London Blackfriars 3 ⊖	d																		17 51	17 56	18 16				
Elephant & Castle ⊖	d																		17 55	18 00	18 20				
Loughborough Jn.	d																				18 24				
Herne Hill 4	d																			18a06	18 28				
Tulse Hill 3	d										18 17										18 32				
Streatham 4	d																				18a35				
London Victoria 15 ⊖	d	17 39	17 41	17 45	17 47		17 49		17 52							18 03		18 06							
Battersea Park 4	d		17a45	17 49					17 56							18 07							18a32		
Milton Keynes Central	d																								
Watford Junction	d																								
Harrow & Wealdstone ⊖	d																								
Wembley Central ⊖	d																								
Shepherd's Bush ⊖	d												17 45												
Kensington (Olympia) ⊖	d												17 47												
West Brompton ⊖	d												17 50												
Imperial Wharf	d												17 53												
Clapham Junction 10	d	17 45		17 53	17 53		17 56		18 00				18 02			18 11		18 12							
Wandsworth Common	d			17 56					18 03				18 05			18 14									
Balham 4 ⊖	d			17 58					18 05				18 08			18 16									
Streatham Hill	d								18 08																
West Norwood 4	d								18 14		18 20														
Gipsy Hill	d							18a15	18 17		18 23														
Crystal Palace 4	d								18a19		18 26														
Birkbeck	d										18 30														
Beckenham Junction 4	a										18 35														
Streatham Common 4	d			18 02									18 15			18 20									
Norbury	d			18 05									18 18			18 23									
Thornton Heath	d			18 08									18 21			18 26									
Selhurst 4	d			18a12									18 26			18 29									
Norwood Junction 2	a											18 11		18 15			18 29								18 30
	d											18 11		18 16	18 20		18 32								18 31
West Croydon 4	a													18 20	18 30	18 34	18 39								
East Croydon	a	17 55			18 02		18 05			18 11		18 15	18 32					18 22	18 24					18 24	18 35

		LO	SN	SN	SN	SN	SN ◇1	SN	SN	SN 1	SN 1	FC 1	SN		SN	SN 1	SN 1	SN	SN ◇1	LO	SN	SN	SN 1	SN	SN
London Bridge 4 ⊖	d							18 18	18 21	18 23					18 28	18 30		18 32				18 36		18 41	18 49
South Bermondsey	d							18 22							18 32									18 45	
Queens Rd Peckham	d							18 24							18 34									18 48	
Peckham Rye 4	d							18 27							18 37									18 50	
East Dulwich	d							18 30							18 40										
North Dulwich	d							18 32							18 42										
Luton 10	d											17 30													
Luton Airport Parkway 7	d											17 33													
St Pancras International 15 ⊖	d											18 08													
City Thameslink 3	d											18 17													
London Blackfriars 3 ⊖	d											18 20													
Elephant & Castle ⊖	d																								
Loughborough Jn.	d																								
Herne Hill 4	d																								
Tulse Hill 3	d							18 35							18 48										
Streatham 4	d							18 39																	
London Victoria 15 ⊖	d		18 07	18 09	18 11	18 13	18 17				18 19		18 22						18 32		18 32		18 36		
Battersea Park 4	d		18 11		18a15	18 17							18 26								18 36			19a02	
Milton Keynes Central	d																17 13								
Watford Junction	d																17 51								
Harrow & Wealdstone ⊖	d																17 59								
Wembley Central ⊖	d																18 05								
Shepherd's Bush ⊖	d																18 19								
Kensington (Olympia) ⊖	d																18 22								
West Brompton ⊖	d																18 25								
Imperial Wharf	d																18 27								
Clapham Junction 10	d		18 15	18 15		18 21	18 23				18 26		18 30				18 34		18 38		18 40		18 42		
Wandsworth Common	d		18 18			18 24							18 33				18 37				18 43				
Balham 4 ⊖	d		18 20			18 26							18 35				18 40				18 45				
Streatham Hill	d		18 23										18 38												
West Norwood 4	d		18 27										18 42		18 51										
Gipsy Hill	d		18 30						18a45				18 45		18 54										
Crystal Palace 4	d		18 33										18a47		18 57										
Birkbeck	d														19 01										
Beckenham Junction 4	a														19 06										
Streatham Common 4	d					18 30		18 42									18 46				18 50				
Norbury	d					18 33		18 44									18 49				18 52				
Thornton Heath	d					18 36		18 47									18 52				18 55				
Selhurst 4	d					18a40		18 51									18 56				19 00				
Norwood Junction 2	a		18 37													18 41		18 45				18 59			19 01
	d	18 35	18 39													18 42		18 46		18 50		19 02			19 02
West Croydon 4	a	18 42	18 44					18 57										18 50		19 01	19 04	19 09			
East Croydon	a			18 27			18 33			18 36	18 37	18 41				18 45	19 02		18 48				18 52		19 05

Table 177

Mondays to Fridays

Luton, Milton Keynes Central and London East and West Croydon via Tulse Hill - Crystal Palace - Norbury

Local Services

Network Diagram - see first Page of Table 177

		LO	SN	SN	FC		SN	SN	SN	SN	SN	SN	FC	FC	SN	SN	LO	SN	SN	SN	FC		SN	LO	SN
					1				◇1			1	1			1					1				
									🚲											🚲					
London Bridge 4 ⊖	d									18 48	18 51					18 59			18 57				19 06		
South Bermondsey	d									18 52									19 01						
Queens Rd Peckham	d									18 54									19 03						
Peckham Rye 4	d									18 57									19 06						
East Dulwich	d									19 00									19 09						
North Dulwich	d									19 02									19 11						
Luton 10	d				17 46								18 00								18 18				
Luton Airport Parkway 7	d				17 48								18 02								18 20				
St Pancras International 15 ⊖	d				18 20								18 34	18 38							18 54				
City Thameslink 3	d				18 29								18 43	18 47							19 03				
London Blackfriars 3 ⊖	d				18 32								18 46	18 50							19 05				
Elephant & Castle ⊖	d				18 36									18 54											
Loughborough Jn.	d													18 58											
Herne Hill 4	d													19 02											
Tulse Hill 3	d									19 05				19 09					19 14						
Streatham 4	d									19 09				19a13											
London Victoria 15 ⊖	d		18 36	18 39			18 41	18 45	18 47			18 51			18 52			18 59		19 06					19 06
Battersea Park 4	d		18 40				18a45	18 49							18 56			19 04							19 10
Milton Keynes Central	d																								
Watford Junction	d																								
Harrow & Wealdstone ⊖	d																								
Wembley Central ⊖	d																								
Shepherd's Bush ⊖	d																								
Kensington (Olympia) ⊖	d																								
West Brompton ⊖	d																								
Imperial Wharf	d																								
Clapham Junction 10	d		18 44	18 45				18 53	18 53			18 57			19 00			19 08		19 12					19 14
Wandsworth Common	d		18 47					18 56							19 03			19 11							19 17
Balham 4 ⊖	d		18 49					18 58							19 05			19 14							19 20
Streatham Hill	d		18 52												19 08										19 23
West Norwood 4	d		18 56												19 12				19 17						19 27
Gipsy Hill	d		18 59								19a15				19 15				19 20						19 30
Crystal Palace 4	d		19 01												19a19				19 23						19 32
Birkbeck 🚊	d																								
Beckenham Junction 4 🚊	a																								
Streatham Common 4	d							19 02		19 12								19 18							
Norbury	d							19 05		19 15								19 20							
Thornton Heath	d							19 08		19 18								19 23							
Selhurst 4	d							19 10		19 21								19 27							
Norwood Junction 2	a		19 06													19 13			19 27				19 29		19 37
	d	19 05	19 09													19 14	19 20		19 28				19 30	19 35	19 39
West Croydon 4 🚊	a	19 12	19 14							19 27							19 30	19 32	19 35					19 42	19 44
East Croydon 🚊	a			18 57	19 00			19 13	19 03			19 07	19 10			19 17				19 22	19 24		19 33		

Luton, Milton Keynes Central and London East and West Croydon via Tulse Hill - Crystal Palace - Norbury

Local Services

Network Diagram - see first Page of Table 177

	SN	FC	SN	SN	SN	SN	FC	SN	SN	SN	SN	SN		SN	LO	SN	SN	SN	SN	FC	SN	SN	LO	SN
			1			◇1 ⚲	1							1				◇1 ⚲		1		1		
London Bridge 4 ⊖ d	19 08								19 11	19 18	19 22	19 31		19 33			19 28				19 36	19 52		
South Bermondsey d	19 12								19 15	19 22							19 32							
Queens Rd Peckham d	19 14								19 18	19 24							19 34							
Peckham Rye 4 d	19 17								19 20	19 27							19 37							
East Dulwich d	19 20									19 30							19 40							
North Dulwich d	19 22									19 32							19 42							
Luton 10 d		18 22					18 34													18 48				
Luton Airport Parkway 7 d		18 24					18 36													18 50				
St Pancras International 15 ⊖ d		19 04					19 09													19 24				
City Thameslink 3 d		19 13					19 18													19 33				
London Blackfriars 3 ⊖ d		19 16					19 20													19 35				
Elephant & Castle ⊖ d		19 19																						
Loughborough Jn d		19 23																						
Herne Hill 4 d		19 27																						
Tulse Hill 3 d	19 27	19 31								19 35							19 46							
Streatham 4 d		19a35								19 39														
London Victoria 15 ⊖ d			19 10	19 11	19 15	19 17		19 22								19 30		19 32	19 36					19 36
Battersea Park 4 d				19a15	19 19			19 26	19a32							19 34								19 40
Milton Keynes Central d																								
Watford Junction d																								
Harrow & Wealdstone ⊖ d																								
Wembley Central ⊖ d																								
Shepherd's Bush ⊖ d																								
Kensington (Olympia) ⊖ d																								
West Brompton ⊖ d																								
Imperial Wharf d																								
Clapham Junction 10 d			19 16		19 23	19 23		19 30								19 38		19 38	19 42					19 44
Wandsworth Common d					19 26			19 33								19 41								19 47
Balham 4 ⊖ d					19 28			19 35								19 44								19 50
Streatham Hill d								19 38																19 53
West Norwood 4 d	19 30							19 42									19 49							19 57
Gipsy Hill d	19 33							19 45			19a45						19 52							20 00
Crystal Palace 4 d	19 35							19a47									19 54							20 02
Birkbeck 🚋 d	19 39																							
Beckenham Junction 4 🚋 a	19 43																							
Streatham Common 4 d					19 32					19 42						19 48								
Norbury d					19 35					19 45						19 51								
Thornton Heath d					19 38					19 48						19 54								
Selhurst 4 d					19 41					19 51						19 57								
Norwood Junction 2 a												19 44		19 46			19 59				19 59	20 03		20 07
d												19 44		19 47	19 50		20 02				20 00	20 03	20 05	20 09
West Croydon 4 🚋 a										19 56		19 49			20 00	20 02	20 07						20 12	20 13
East Croydon 🚋 a			19 27		19 44	19 33	19 39							19 50				19 48	19 52	19 54	20 03	20 06		

Luton, Milton Keynes Central and London East and West Croydon via Tulse Hill - Crystal Palace - Norbury

Local Services

Network Diagram - see first Page of Table 177

		SN	FC	SN 1	SN		SN	SN ◇1	FC 1	SN	SN	SN	SN	SN	LO	SN	SN ◇1	FC 1	FC	SN	LO		SN	SN 1	SN
London Bridge 4 ⊖	d	19 38									19 41	19 48	19 54	20 03						20 06					
South Bermondsey	d	19 42									19 45	19 52		20 07											
Queens Rd Peckham	d	19 44									19 48	19 54		20 09											
Peckham Rye 4	d	19 47									19 50	19 57		20 12											
East Dulwich	d	19 50										20 00		20 15											
North Dulwich	d	19 52										20 02		20 17											
Luton 10	d		18 54						19 04									19 18	19 24						
Luton Airport Parkway 7	d		18 57						19 06									19 20	19 27						
St Pancras International 15 ⊖	d		19 34						19 39									19 54	20 04						
City Thameslink 3	d		19 43						19 48									20 03	20 13						
London Blackfriars 3 ⊖	d		19 46						19 50									20 05	20 16						
Elephant & Castle ⊖	d		19 49																20 19						
Loughborough Jn.	d		19 53																20 23						
Herne Hill 4	d		19 57																20 27						
Tulse Hill 3	d	19 57	20 01									20 05		20 21					20 31						
Streatham 4	d		20a05									20 09							20a35						
London Victoria 15 ⊖	d			19 40	19 41		19 45	19 47		19 52						20 00	20 06						20 06	20 10	20 11
Battersea Park 4	d				19a45		19 49			19 56	20a02					20 04							20 10		20a15
Milton Keynes Central	d																								
Watford Junction	d																								
Harrow & Wealdstone ⊖	d																								
Wembley Central ⊖	d																								
Shepherd's Bush ⊖	d																								
Kensington (Olympia) ⊖	d																								
West Brompton ⊖	d																								
Imperial Wharf	d																								
Clapham Junction 10	d			19 46			19 53	19 53		20 00						20 08	20 12						20 14	20 16	
Wandsworth Common	d						19 56			20 03						20 11							20 17		
Balham 4 ⊖	d						19 59			20 05						20 14							20 20		
Streatham Hill	d									20 08													20 23		
West Norwood 4	d	20 00								20 12				20 24									20 27		
Gipsy Hill	d	20 03								20 15			20a16	20 27									20 30		
Crystal Palace 4	d	20 05								20a17				20 29									20 33		
Birkbeck	d	20 09												20 33											
Beckenham Junction 4	a	20 13												20 37											
Streatham Common 4	d						20 03					20 12				20 18									
Norbury	d						20 05					20 15				20 20									
Thornton Heath	d						20 08					20 18				20 23									
Selhurst 4	d						20 11					20 21				20 27									
Norwood Junction 2	a																			20 29			20 37		
	d														20 20					20 30	20 35		20 39		
West Croydon 4	a											20 26			20 29	20 32					20 42		20 43		
East Croydon	a			19 57			20 14	20 03	20 09								20 22	20 24		20 33				20 27	

		SN	SN ◇1	SN	SN	SN	SN	SN 1	SN	SN 1	LO	SN	SN ◇1		SN ◇1	FC 1	FC	SN	LO	SN	SN 1	SN	SN	SN ◇1	SN
London Bridge 4 ⊖	d				20 11	20 18	20 22	20 28	20 33	20 34								20 36							
South Bermondsey	d				20 15	20 22			20 37																
Queens Rd Peckham	d				20 18	20 24			20 39																
Peckham Rye 4	d				20 20	20 27			20 42																
East Dulwich	d					20 30			20 45																
North Dulwich	d					20 32			20 47																
Luton 10	d															19 50	19 46								
Luton Airport Parkway 7	d															19 52	19 48								
St Pancras International 15 ⊖	d															20 24	20 34								
City Thameslink 3	d															20 33	20 43								
London Blackfriars 3 ⊖	d															20 35	20 46								
Elephant & Castle ⊖	d																20 49								
Loughborough Jn.	d																20 53								
Herne Hill 4	d																20 57								
Tulse Hill 3	d					20 35			20 51								21 01								
Streatham 4	d					20 39											21a05								
London Victoria 15 ⊖	d	20 15	20 17	20 22								20 30	20 32		20 36					20 36	20 40	20 41	20 45	20 47	20 52
Battersea Park 4	d	20 19		20 26	20a32							20 34								20 40		20a45	20 49		20 56
Milton Keynes Central	d																								
Watford Junction	d																								
Harrow & Wealdstone ⊖	d																								
Wembley Central ⊖	d																								
Shepherd's Bush ⊖	d																								
Kensington (Olympia) ⊖	d																								
West Brompton ⊖	d																								
Imperial Wharf	d																								
Clapham Junction 10	d	20 23	20 23	20 30								20 38	20 38		20 42					20 44	20 46		20 53	20 53	21 00
Wandsworth Common	d	20 26		20 33								20 41								20 47			20 56		21 03
Balham 4 ⊖	d	20 28		20 35								20 44								20 50			20 58		21 05
Streatham Hill	d			20 38																20 53					21 08
West Norwood 4	d			20 42					20 54											20 57					21 12
Gipsy Hill	d			20 45			20a45		20 57											21 00					21 15
Crystal Palace 4	d			20a47					20 59											21 03					21a17
Birkbeck	d								21 03																
Beckenham Junction 4	a								21 07																
Streatham Common 4	d	20 32				20 42						20 48											21 02		
Norbury	d	20 35				20 45						20 50											21 05		
Thornton Heath	d	20 38				20 48						20 53											21 08		
Selhurst 4	d	20 41				20 51						20 57											21 11		
Norwood Junction 2	a									20 45								20 59		21 07					
	d									20 45	20 50							21 00	21 05	21 09					
West Croydon 4	a					20 56					21 00	21 02							21 12	21 13					
East Croydon	a	20 44	20 33					20 40		20 49			20 48		20 52	20 54		21 03			20 57		21 14	21 03	

Table 177

Mondays to Fridays

Luton, Milton Keynes Central and London East and West Croydon via Tulse Hill - Crystal Palace - Norbury

Local Services

Network Diagram - see first Page of Table 177

		SN	SN	SN	SN 1		SN	LO	SN	SN 1	SN ◇1	FC 1	FC	SN	LO	SN	SN 1	SN	SN	SN ◇1	SN		SN	SN	SN
London Bridge 4 ⊖	d	20 41	20 48	20 52	20 58		21 03							21 06									21 11	21 18	21 22
South Bermondsey	d	20 45	20 52				21 07																21 15	21 22	
Queens Rd Peckham	d	20 48	20 54				21 09																21 18	21 24	
Peckham Rye 4	d	20 50	20 57				21 12																21 20	21 27	
East Dulwich	d		21 00				21 15																	21 30	
North Dulwich	d		21 02				21 17																	21 32	
Luton 10	d											20 16	20 20												
Luton Airport Parkway 7	d											20 18	20 22												
St Pancras International 15 ⊖	d											20 54	21 06												
City Thameslink 3	d											21 03	21 13												
London Blackfriars 3 ⊖	d											21 05	21 16												
Elephant & Castle ⊖	d												21 19												
Loughborough Jn.	d												21 23												
Herne Hill 4	d												21 27												
Tulse Hill 3	d		21 05				21 21						21 31											21 35	
Streatham 4	d		21 09										21a35											21 39	
London Victoria 15 ⊖	d								21 00	21 02	21 06					21 06	21 10	21 11	21 15	21 17	21 23				
Battersea Park 4	d	21a02							21 04							21 10		21a15	21 19		21 27		21a32		
Milton Keynes Central	d																								
Watford Junction	d																								
Harrow & Wealdstone ⊖	d																								
Wembley Central ⊖	d																								
Shepherd's Bush ⊖	d																								
Kensington (Olympia) ⊖	d																								
West Brompton ⊖	d																								
Imperial Wharf	d																								
Clapham Junction 10	d								21 08	21 08	21 12					21 14	21 16		21 23	21 23	21 31				
Wandsworth Common	d								21 11							21 17			21 26		21 34				
Balham 4 ⊖	d								21 14							21 20			21 29		21 36				
Streatham Hill	d															21 23					21 39				
West Norwood 4	d						21 24									21 27					21 43				
Gipsy Hill	d			21a15			21 27									21 30					21 46				21a45
Crystal Palace 4	d						21 29									21 33					21a48				
Birkbeck	d						21 33																		
Beckenham Junction 4	a						21 37																		
Streatham Common 4	d		21 12						21 18										21 33					21 42	
Norbury	d		21 15						21 20										21 35					21 45	
Thornton Heath	d		21 18						21 23										21 38					21 48	
Selhurst 4	d		21 21						21 27										21 41					21 51	
Norwood Junction 2	a													21 29		21 37									
	d							21 20						21 30	21 35	21 39									
West Croydon 4	a		21 26					21 30	21 32						21 42	21 43								21 56	
East Croydon	a				21 10					21 18	21 22	21 24		21 33			21 27		21 44	21 33					

		SN 1	SN	LO	SN	SN ◇1	FC 1	FC	SN	LO	SN	SN 1	SN		SN	SN ◇1	SN	SN	SN	SN	SN	LO	SN	SN ◇1	SN ◇1
London Bridge 4 ⊖	d	21 26	21 33						21 36									21 41	21 48	21 52	22 03				
South Bermondsey	d		21 37															21 45	21 52		22 07				
Queens Rd Peckham	d		21 39															21 48	21 54		22 09				
Peckham Rye 4	d		21 42															21 50	21 57		22 12				
East Dulwich	d		21 45																22 00		22 15				
North Dulwich	d		21 47																22 02		22 17				
Luton 10	d						20 46	20 50																	
Luton Airport Parkway 7	d						20 48	20 52																	
St Pancras International 15 ⊖	d						21 24	21 36																	
City Thameslink 3	d						21 33	21 43																	
London Blackfriars 3 ⊖	d						21 35	21 46																	
Elephant & Castle ⊖	d							21 49																	
Loughborough Jn.	d							21 53																	
Herne Hill 4	d							21 57																	
Tulse Hill 3	d		21 51					22 01											22 05		22 21				
Streatham 4	d							22a05											22 09						
London Victoria 15 ⊖	d				21 30	21 36					21 36	21 40	21 41		21 45	21 47	21 52						22 00	22 02	22 06
Battersea Park 4	d				21 34						21 40		21a45		21 49		21 56	22a02					22 04		
Milton Keynes Central	d																								
Watford Junction	d																								
Harrow & Wealdstone ⊖	d																								
Wembley Central ⊖	d																								
Shepherd's Bush ⊖	d																								
Kensington (Olympia) ⊖	d																								
West Brompton ⊖	d																								
Imperial Wharf	d																								
Clapham Junction 10	d				21 38	21 42					21 44	21 46			21 53	21 53	22 00						22 08	22 08	22 12
Wandsworth Common	d				21 41						21 47				21 56		22 03						22 11		
Balham 4 ⊖	d				21 44						21 50				21 58		22 05						22 14		
Streatham Hill	d										21 53						22 08								
West Norwood 4	d		21 54								21 57						22 12				22 24				
Gipsy Hill	d		21 57								22 00						22 15			22a15	22 27				
Crystal Palace 4	d		21 59								22 03						22a17				22 29				
Birkbeck	d		22 03																		22 35				
Beckenham Junction 4	a		22 07																		22 38				
Streatham Common 4	d				21 48										22 02				22 12				22 18		
Norbury	d				21 50										22 05				22 15				22 20		
Thornton Heath	d				21 53										22 08				22 18				22 23		
Selhurst 4	d				21 57										22 11				22 21				22 27		
Norwood Junction 2	a	21 37							21 59		22 07														
	d	21 38		21 50					22 00	22 05	22 09											22 20			
West Croydon 4	a			22 00	22 02					22 12	22 13								22 26			22 30	22 32		
East Croydon	a	21 41				21 52	21 54		22 03			21 57			22 14	22 03								22 18	22 22

Luton, Milton Keynes Central and London East and West Croydon via Tulse Hill - Crystal Palace - Norbury

Local Services

Network Diagram - see first Page of Table 177

Station	FC	FC	SN	LO		SN	SN	SN	SN	SN	SN	SN	SN	SN	SN	LO	SN	SN	SN	SN		SN	FC	SN
	1						1											1					1	
London Bridge 4 ⊖ d			22 08								22 11	22 18	22 23	22 26	22 33					22 38		22 41	22 42	22 56
South Bermondsey d											22 15	22 22			22 37							22 45		
Queens Rd Peckham d											22 18	22 24			22 39							22 48		
Peckham Rye 4 d											22 20	22 27			22 42							22 50		
East Dulwich d												22 30			22 45									
North Dulwich d												22 32			22 47									
Luton 10 d	21 16	21 20																						
Luton Airport Parkway 7 d	21 18	21 22																						
St Pancras International 15 ⊖ d	21 54	22 06																						
City Thameslink 3 d	22 03	22 13																						
London Blackfriars 3 ⊖ d	22 05	22 16																						
Elephant & Castle ⊖ d		22 19																						
Loughborough Jn. d		22 23																						
Herne Hill 4 d		22 27																						
Tulse Hill 3 d		22 31										22 35			22 51									
Streatham 4 d		22a35										22 39												
London Victoria 15 ⊖ d						22 06	22 10	22 11	22 15	22 22							22 30	22 32	22 36					
Battersea Park 4 d						22 10		22a15	22 19	22 26	22a32						22 34					23a02		
Milton Keynes Central d																								
Watford Junction d																								
Harrow & Wealdstone ⊖ d																								
Wembley Central ⊖ d																								
Shepherd's Bush ⊖ d																								
Kensington (Olympia) ⊖ d																								
West Brompton ⊖ d																								
Imperial Wharf d																								
Clapham Junction 10 d						22 14	22 16		22 23	22 30							22 38	22 38	22 42					
Wandsworth Common d						22 17			22 26	22 33							22 41							
Balham 4 ⊖ d						22 20			22 28	22 35							22 44							
Streatham Hill d						22 23				22 38														
West Norwood 4 d						22 27				22 42					22 54									
Gipsy Hill d						22 30				22 45			22a45		22 57									
Crystal Palace 4 d						22 33				22a47					22 59									
Birkbeck d															23 03									
Beckenham Junction 4 a															23 07									
Streatham Common 4 d									22 32			22 42					22 48							
Norbury d									22 35			22 45					22 50							
Thornton Heath d									22 38			22 48					22 53							
Selhurst 4 d									22 41			22 51					22 57							
Norwood Junction 2 a			22 31			22 37								22 38						23 01				23 07
d			22 32	22 35		22 39								22 38		22 50				23 02				23 07
West Croydon 4 a				22 42		22 43						22 56				23 00	23 02							
East Croydon a	22 24		22 35				22 26		22 44					22 42				22 48	22 52	23 06			22 54	23 11

Station	SN	SN	SN	SN	SN	SN	SN	SN	FC	LO	SN	SN		SN	SN	SN	SN	SN	SN	SN	SN	SN	SN	FC
		1			◇1							◇1		◇1				1			◇1			1
London Bridge 4 ⊖ d						22 48	22 52		23 01						23 06	23 05							23 11	23 12
South Bermondsey d						22 52										23 09							23 15	
Queens Rd Peckham d						22 54										23 11							23 18	
Peckham Rye 4 d						22 57										23 14							23 20	
East Dulwich d						23 00										23 17								
North Dulwich d						23 02										23 19								
Luton 10 d																								
Luton Airport Parkway 7 d																								
St Pancras International 15 ⊖ d																								
City Thameslink 3 d																								
London Blackfriars 3 ⊖ d																								
Elephant & Castle ⊖ d																								
Loughborough Jn. d																								
Herne Hill 4 d																								
Tulse Hill 3 d						23 05			23 11							23 23								
Streatham 4 d						23 09			23a15															
London Victoria 15 ⊖ d	22 36	22 40	22 41	22 45	22 47			22 52			23 00	23 02		23 06			23 06	23 10	23 11	23 15	23 17	23 22		
Battersea Park 4 d	22 40		22a45	22 49				22 56			23 04						23 10		23a15	23 19		23 26	23a32	
Milton Keynes Central d																								
Watford Junction d																								
Harrow & Wealdstone ⊖ d																								
Wembley Central ⊖ d																								
Shepherd's Bush ⊖ d																								
Kensington (Olympia) ⊖ d																								
West Brompton ⊖ d																								
Imperial Wharf d																								
Clapham Junction 10 d	22 46	22 46		22 53	22 53			23 00			23 08	23 08		23 12			23 14	23 16		23 23	23 23	23 30		
Wandsworth Common d	22 49			22 56				23 03			23 11						23 17			23 26		23 33		
Balham 4 ⊖ d	22 52			22 58				23 05			23 14						23 20			23 28		23 35		
Streatham Hill d	22 55							23 08									23 23					23 38		
West Norwood 4 d	22 58							23 12								23 26	23 29					23 42		
Gipsy Hill d	23 01						23a15	23 15								23 29	23 32					23 45		
Crystal Palace 4 d	23 04							23a17								23 31	23 35					23a47		
Birkbeck d																								
Beckenham Junction 4 a																								
Streatham Common 4 d				23 02		23 12					23 18									23 32				
Norbury d				23 05		23 15					23 20									23 35				
Thornton Heath d				23 08		23 18					23 23									23 38				
Selhurst 4 d				23 11		23 21					23 27									23 41				
Norwood Junction 2 a	23 08														23 29	23 36	23 39							
d	23 09									23 20					23 30		23 40							
West Croydon 4 a	23 13					23 26				23 30	23 32						23 44							
East Croydon a		22 57		23 14	23 03							23 19		23 22	23 33			23 27		23 44	23 33			23 24

Luton, Milton Keynes Central and London East and West Croydon via Tulse Hill - Crystal Palace - Norbury

Local Services Network Diagram - see first Page of Table 177

		SN	SN	FC	SN		LO	SN	SN	FC	SN	SN	SN	SN	SN	SN	SN	SN	SN	SN	SN		FC		
														FO			FX				FO				
					◇1					1	1				1	1									
London Bridge 4 ⊖	d	23 18	23 22	23 29				23 36	23 33	23 42								23 48	23 52				23 59		
South Bermondsey	d	23 22							23 37									23 52							
Queens Rd Peckham	d	23 24							23 39									23 54							
Peckham Rye 4	d	23 27							23 42									23 57							
East Dulwich	d	23 30							23 45									00 01							
North Dulwich	d	23 32							23 47									00 03							
Luton 10	d																								
Luton Airport Parkway 7	d																								
St Pancras International 15 ⊖	d																								
City Thameslink 3	d																								
London Blackfriars 3 ⊖	d																								
Elephant & Castle ⊖	d																								
Loughborough Jn.	d																								
Herne Hill 4	d																								
Tulse Hill 3	d	23 35		23 41					23 51									00 06					00 09		
Streatham 4	d	23 39		23a45														00 10					00a13		
London Victoria 15 ⊖	d				23 32							23 34	23 38	23 45	23 47	23 49	23 51			23 54	23 59				
Battersea Park 4	d											23 38	23 42	23 49			23 55			23 58	00 03				
Milton Keynes Central	d										22 11														
Watford Junction	d										22 53														
Harrow & Wealdstone ⊖	d										23 00														
Wembley Central ⊖	d																								
Shepherd's Bush ⊖	d										23 21														
Kensington (Olympia) ⊖	d										23 23														
West Brompton ⊖	d										23 26														
Imperial Wharf	d										23 28														
Clapham Junction 10	d				23 38						23 40	23 42	23 46	23 53	23 53	23 56	23 59			00 02	00 07				
Wandsworth Common	d											23 45	23 49	23 56			00 02			00 05	00 10				
Balham 4 ⊖	d										23 44	23 47	23 51	23 58			00 04			00 07	00 12				
Streatham Hill	d												23 54							00 10					
West Norwood 4	d								23 54				23 58							00 14					
Gipsy Hill	d		23a45						23 57				00 01						00a15	00 17					
Crystal Palace 4	d								23 59				00 03							00a19					
Birkbeck 🚋	d																								
Beckenham Junction 4 🚋	a																								
Streatham Common 4	d	23 42									23 48	23 51		00 02			00 08	00 13			00 16				
Norbury	d	23 45									23 51	23 54		00 05			00 11	00 15			00 19				
Thornton Heath	d	23 48									23 54	23 57		00 08			00 14	00 18			00 22				
Selhurst 4	d	23 51									23 57	23 59		00 11			00 17	00 21			00 25				
Norwood Junction 2	a							23 59	00 04				00 08												
	d						23 50	23 59					00 09												
West Croydon 4 🚋	a	23 56					23 59					00 03	00 14				00 21	00 28			00 30				
East Croydon 🚋	a				23 51			00 03		23 56	00 01			00 14	00 05	00 09									

Table 177

Saturdays

Luton, Milton Keynes Central and London East and West Croydon via Tulse Hill - Crystal Palace - Norbury

Local Services

Network Diagram - see first Page of Table 177

Station		SN 1	SN	SN	SN	SN	SN	SN 1	SN 1	SN	LO	SN	SN	FC	SN ◇1	SN		SN	SN	FC	SN 1	SN	SN	SN	SN
London Bridge 4 ⊖	d			23p36	23p33							23p48		23p59		00 06		00 03		00 12			00 18		
South Bermondsey	d				23p37							23p52						00 07					00 22		
Queens Rd Peckham	d				23p39							23p54						00 09					00 24		
Peckham Rye 4	d				23p42							23p57						00 12					00 27		
East Dulwich	d				23p45							00 01						00 15					00 30		
North Dulwich	d				23p47							00 03						00 17					00 32		
Luton 10	d																								
Luton Airport Parkway 7	d																								
St Pancras International 15 ⊖	d																								
City Thameslink 3	d																								
London Blackfriars 3 ⊖	d																								
Elephant & Castle ⊖	d																								
Loughborough Jn.	d																								
Herne Hill 4	d																								
Tulse Hill 3	d				23p51							00 06		00 09				00 21					00 35		
Streatham 4	d											00 10		00a13									00 39		
London Victoria 15 ⊖	d		23p34			23p38	23p45	23p47	23p49	23p54			23p59		00 05				00 07		00 14	00 16		00 22	00 34
Battersea Park 4	d		23p38			23p42	23p49			23p58			00 03						00 11			00 20		00 26	00 38
Milton Keynes Central	d	22p11																							
Watford Junction	d	22p53																							
Harrow & Wealdstone ⊖	d	23p00																							
Wembley Central ⊖	d																								
Shepherd's Bush ⊖	d	23p21																							
Kensington (Olympia) ⊖	d	23p23																							
West Brompton ⊖	d	23p26																							
Imperial Wharf	d	23p28																							
Clapham Junction 10	d	23b40	23p42			23p46	23p53	23p53	23p56	00 02			00 07		00 11				00 15		00 20	00 24		00 30	00 42
Wandsworth Common	d		23p45			23p49	23p56			00 05			00 10						00 18			00 27		00 33	00 45
Balham 4 ⊖	d	23p44	23p47			23p51	23p58			00 07			00 12						00 20			00 29		00 35	00 47
Streatham Hill	d					23p54				00 10									00 23					00 38	
West Norwood 4	d				23p54	23p58				00 14								00 24	00 28					00 42	
Gipsy Hill	d				23p57	00 01				00 17								00 27	00 31					00 45	
Crystal Palace 4	d				23p59	00 03				00a19								00 29	00 33					00 47	
Birkbeck	d																								
Beckenham Junction 4	a																								
Streatham Common 4	d	23p48	23p51				00 02					00 13	00 16									00 33	00 42		00 51
Norbury	d	23p51	23p54				00 05					00 15	00 19									00 36	00 45		00 54
Thornton Heath	d	23p54	23p57				00 08					00 18	00 22									00 39	00 48		00 57
Selhurst 4	d	23p57	23p59				00 11					00 21	00 25		00 21							00 41	00 51		01 00
Norwood Junction 2	a			23p59	00 04	00 08										00 29		00 34	00 38					00 52	
	d			23p59		00 09					00 20					00 30			00 38					00 52	
West Croydon 4	a		00 03			00 14					00 27	00 28	00 30						00 43				00 55	00 58	01 04
East Croydon	a	00 01		00 03			00 14	00 05	00 09						00 24	00 33				00 26	00 31	00 44			

Station		SN	SN	SN	FC	SN	SN ◇1	FC 1		FC 1	SN 1	FC 1	SN 1	FC 1	FC 1	SN ◇1	FC 1	FC 1	SN ◇1	FC 1	SN ◇1	FC 1	SN 1	LO	
London Bridge 4 ⊖	d	00 36	00 33		00 42			01 08		01 35		02 05		03 05	03 35		04 05	04 35		05 05		05 52			
South Bermondsey	d		00 37																						
Queens Rd Peckham	d		00 39																						
Peckham Rye 4	d		00 42																						
East Dulwich	d		00 45																						
North Dulwich	d		00 47																						
Luton 10	d																								
Luton Airport Parkway 7	d																								
St Pancras International 15 ⊖	d																								
City Thameslink 3	d																								
London Blackfriars 3 ⊖	d																								
Elephant & Castle ⊖	d																								
Loughborough Jn.	d																								
Herne Hill 4	d																								
Tulse Hill 3	d		00 51																						
Streatham 4	d																								
London Victoria 15 ⊖	d			00 37		00 42	01 00				02 00		03 00			04 00			05 02		05 32		06 02		
Battersea Park 4	d			00 41		00 46																			
Milton Keynes Central	d																								
Watford Junction	d																								
Harrow & Wealdstone ⊖	d																								
Wembley Central ⊖	d																								
Shepherd's Bush ⊖	d																								
Kensington (Olympia) ⊖	d																								
West Brompton ⊖	d																								
Imperial Wharf	d																								
Clapham Junction 10	d			00 45		00 50	01 08				02 08		03 08			04 08			05 08		05 38		06 08		
Wandsworth Common	d			00 48		00 53																			
Balham 4 ⊖	d			00 50		00 55																			
Streatham Hill	d			00 53																					
West Norwood 4	d		00 54	00 58																					
Gipsy Hill	d		00 57	01 01																					
Crystal Palace 4	d		00 59	01 03																					
Birkbeck	d																								
Beckenham Junction 4	a																								
Streatham Common 4	d					00 59																			
Norbury	d					01 02																			
Thornton Heath	d					01 05																			
Selhurst 4	d					01 07		01 27		01 54		02 24		03 24	03 54		04 24	04 54		05 27					
Norwood Junction 2	a	00 59	01 04	01 08																					
	d	01 00		01 08																				06 05	
West Croydon 4	a			01 13																				06 12	
East Croydon	a	01 03			00 56	01 10	01 21	01 31		02 02	02 21	02 31	03 21	03 31	04 01	04 21	04 31	05 01	05 21	05 31	05 47	06 04	06 17		

b Previous night, arr. 2333

Table 177

Saturdays

Luton, Milton Keynes Central and London East and West Croydon via Tulse Hill - Crystal Palace - Norbury

Local Services — Network Diagram - see first Page of Table 177

		SN	LO	FC	SN	FC ■1	LO	SN	SN ■1	SN ■1	SN	LO	SN	SN	SN	FC ■1		FC	SN	SN	SN	FC ■1	LO	SN	SN ■1
London Bridge ■4 ⊖	d	06 11		06 21		06 27							06 36		06 41	06 42		06 45		06 48	06 50	06 57			07 03
South Bermondsey	d	06 15													06 45					06 52					
Queens Rd Peckham	d	06 18													06 48					06 54					
Peckham Rye ■4	d	06 20													06 50					06 57					
East Dulwich	d																			07 00					
North Dulwich	d																			07 02					
Luton ■10	d																								
Luton Airport Parkway ■7	d																								
St Pancras International ■15 ⊖	d																								
City Thameslink ■3	d																								
London Blackfriars ■3 ⊖	d																								
Elephant & Castle ⊖	d																								
Loughborough Jn.	d																								
Herne Hill ■4	d																								
Tulse Hill ■3	d			06 31														07 01		07 05					
Streatham ■4	d			06a35														07a05		07 09					
London Victoria ■15 ⊖	d							06 23		06 32	06 41			06 43					06 53						
Battersea Park ■4	d	06a32									06a45			06 47	07a02										
Milton Keynes Central	d																								
Watford Junction	d								05 52																
Harrow & Wealdstone ⊖	d								05 58																
Wembley Central ⊖	d																								
Shepherd's Bush ⊖	d								06 20																
Kensington (Olympia) ⊖	d								06 23																
West Brompton ⊖	d								06 26																
Imperial Wharf	d								06 28																
Clapham Junction ■10	d							06 30	06 34	06 38				06 51					07 00						
Wandsworth Common	d							06 33	06 37					06 54					07 03						
Balham ■4 ⊖	d							06 35	06 40					06 56					07 05						
Streatham Hill	d																							06 53	
West Norwood ■4	d																							06 57	
Gipsy Hill	d																							07 00	
Crystal Palace ■4	d																							07 02	
Birkbeck (tram)	d																								
Beckenham Junction ■4 (tram)	a																								
Streatham Common ■4	d							06 39	06 45					07 00					07 09	07 12					
Norbury	d							06 42	06 48					07 03					07 12	07 15					
Thornton Heath	d							06 45	06 51					07 06					07 15	07 18					
Selhurst ■4	d							06 48	06 54					07 09					07 18	07 21					
Norwood Junction ■2	a												06 59								07 02			07 07	07 16
	d		06 18		06 33		06 35					06 50	07 00								07 03		07 05	07 09	07 16
West Croydon ■4 (tram)	a		06 30				06 41	06 52				07 00							07 22	07 26			07 11	07 14	
East Croydon (tram)	a				06 36	06 39			06 57	06 47			07 03	07 12		06 54					07 06	07 09			07 20

		SN ◇■1	LO	SN	SN	FC ■1	FC	SN		LO	SN	SN	SN	SN	SN	FC ■1	SN ■1	SN ◇■1	SN	SN ■1	LO	SN	SN ◇■1	SN ■1	
London Bridge ■4 ⊖	d			07 06	07 11	07 12	07 15	07 20							07 18	07 27			07 33	07 33				07 45	
South Bermondsey	d				07 15										07 22				07 37						
Queens Rd Peckham	d				07 18										07 24				07 39						
Peckham Rye ■4	d				07 20										07 27				07 42						
East Dulwich	d														07 30				07 45						
North Dulwich	d														07 32				07 47						
Luton ■10	d																								
Luton Airport Parkway ■7	d																								
St Pancras International ■15 ⊖	d																								
City Thameslink ■3	d																								
London Blackfriars ■3 ⊖	d																								
Elephant & Castle ⊖	d																								
Loughborough Jn.	d																								
Herne Hill ■4	d																								
Tulse Hill ■3	d						07 31								07 35				07 50						
Streatham ■4	d						07a35								07 39										
London Victoria ■15 ⊖	d	07 06									07 06	07 11	07 13	07 23				07 32				07 33	07 36		
Battersea Park ■4	d				07a32						07 10	07a15	07 17									07 37			
Milton Keynes Central	d																								
Watford Junction	d																06 55								
Harrow & Wealdstone ⊖	d																07 01								
Wembley Central ⊖	d																07 06								
Shepherd's Bush ⊖	d																07 19								
Kensington (Olympia) ⊖	d																07 22								
West Brompton ⊖	d																07 25								
Imperial Wharf	d																07 27								
Clapham Junction ■10	d	07 12									07 14		07 21	07 30			07 34	07 38				07 41	07 42		
Wandsworth Common	d										07 17		07 24	07 33			07 37					07 44			
Balham ■4 ⊖	d										07 20		07 26	07 35			07 40					07 46			
Streatham Hill	d										07 23														
West Norwood ■4	d										07 27								07 53						
Gipsy Hill	d										07 30								07 56						
Crystal Palace ■4	d										07 32								07 59						
Birkbeck (tram)	d																		08 03						
Beckenham Junction ■4 (tram)	a																		08 06						
Streatham Common ■4	d												07 30	07 39	07 42		07 45					07 50			
Norbury	d												07 33	07 42	07 45		07 48					07 53			
Thornton Heath	d												07 36	07 45	07 48		07 51					07 56			
Selhurst ■4	d												07 39	07 48	07 51		07 54					07 59			
Norwood Junction ■2	a			07 29				07 32			07 37									07 46				07 55	
	d		07 20	07 30				07 33		07 35	07 39									07 46	07 50			07 56	
West Croydon ■4 (tram)	a		07 30							07 41	07 43			07 52	07 56						08 00	08 03			
East Croydon (tram)	a	07 22		07 33		07 24		07 36					07 42			07 39	07 57	07 47		07 50			07 52	07 59	

Table 177

Saturdays

Luton, Milton Keynes Central and London East and West Croydon via Tulse Hill - Crystal Palace - Norbury

Local Services

Network Diagram - see first Page of Table 177

		SN	SN	FC	FC	SN	LO	SN	SN	SN	SN	SN	SN	SN	SN	FC		SN	SN	LO	SN	SN	SN	SN	SN
				[1]							◇[1]		◇[1]			[1]			[1]			◇[1]	[1]		
London Bridge [4] ⊖	d	07 36	07 41	07 42	07 45	07 50									07 48	07 57		08 03	08 03				08 15	08 06	08 11
South Bermondsey	d		07 45												07 52			08 07							08 15
Queens Rd Peckham	d		07 48												07 54			08 09							08 18
Peckham Rye [4]	d		07 50												07 57			08 12							08 20
East Dulwich	d														08 00			08 15							
North Dulwich	d														08 02			08 17							
Luton [10]	d																								
Luton Airport Parkway [7]	d																								
St Pancras International [15] ⊖	d																								
City Thameslink [3]	d																								
London Blackfriars [3] ⊖	d																								
Elephant & Castle ⊖	d																								
Loughborough Jn.	d																								
Herne Hill [4]	d																								
Tulse Hill [3]	d				08 01										08 05			08 20							
Streatham [4]	d				08a05										08 09										
London Victoria [15] ⊖	d							07 36	07 41	07 43	07 47	07 49	07 51	07 53							08 03	08 06			
Battersea Park [4]	d		08a02					07 40	07a45	07 47		07 53									08 07				08a32
Milton Keynes Central	d																								
Watford Junction	d																								
Harrow & Wealdstone ⊖	d																								
Wembley Central ⊖	d																								
Shepherd's Bush ⊖	d																								
Kensington (Olympia) ⊖	d																								
West Brompton ⊖	d																								
Imperial Wharf	d																								
Clapham Junction [10]	d							07 44		07 51	07 53	07 57		08 00							08 11	08 12			
Wandsworth Common	d							07 47		07 54		08 00		08 03							08 14				
Balham [4] ⊖	d							07 50		07 56		08 02		08 05							08 16				
Streatham Hill	d							07 53				08 05													
West Norwood [4]	d							07 57				08 10						08 23							
Gipsy Hill	d							08 00				08 13						08 26							
Crystal Palace [4]	d							08 02				08a16						08 29							
Birkbeck	d																	08 33							
Beckenham Junction [4]	a																	08 36							
Streatham Common [4]	d									08 00				08 09	08 12						08 20				
Norbury	d									08 03				08 12	08 15						08 23				
Thornton Heath	d									08 06				08 15	08 18						08 26				
Selhurst [4]	d									08 09				08 18	08 21						08 29				
Norwood Junction [2]	a	07 59				08 02		08 07											08 16				08 25	08 29	
	d	08 00				08 03	08 05	08 09											08 16	08 20			08 26	08 30	
West Croydon [4]	a						08 11	08 13						08 22	08 26					08 30	08 33				
East Croydon	a	08 03		07 54		08 06				08 12	08 02		08 07			08 09			08 20			08 22	08 29	08 33	

		FC	FC	SN	LO	SN	SN	SN		SN	SN	SN	SN	SN	FC	SN	SN	SN	SN	LO	SN	SN	SN	SN	
		[1]								◇[1]					[1]	[1]	◇[1]		[1]			◇[1]	[1]		
London Bridge [4] ⊖	d	08 12	08 15	08 20									08 18	08 22	08 27			08 33	08 33				08 45	08 36	
South Bermondsey	d												08 22					08 37							
Queens Rd Peckham	d												08 24					08 39							
Peckham Rye [4]	d												08 27					08 42							
East Dulwich	d												08 30					08 45							
North Dulwich	d												08 32					08 47							
Luton [10]	d																								
Luton Airport Parkway [7]	d																								
St Pancras International [15] ⊖	d																								
City Thameslink [3]	d																								
London Blackfriars [3] ⊖	d																								
Elephant & Castle ⊖	d																								
Loughborough Jn.	d																								
Herne Hill [4]	d																								
Tulse Hill [3]	d		08 31										08 35					08 50							
Streatham [4]	d		08a35										08 39												
London Victoria [15] ⊖	d					08 06	08 11	08 13		08 17	08 19	08 23					08 32				08 33	08 36			
Battersea Park [4]	d					08 10	08a15	08 17			08 23										08 37				
Milton Keynes Central	d															07 13									
Watford Junction	d															07 52									
Harrow & Wealdstone ⊖	d															07 59									
Wembley Central ⊖	d															08 04									
Shepherd's Bush ⊖	d															08 19									
Kensington (Olympia) ⊖	d															08 22									
West Brompton ⊖	d															08 25									
Imperial Wharf	d															08 27									
Clapham Junction [10]	d					08 14		08 21		08 23	08 27	08 30				08 34	08 38				08 41	08 42			
Wandsworth Common	d					08 17		08 24			08 30	08 33				08 37					08 44				
Balham [4] ⊖	d					08 20		08 26			08 32	08 35				08 40					08 46				
Streatham Hill	d					08 23					08 35														
West Norwood [4]	d					08 27					08 40							08 53							
Gipsy Hill	d					08 30					08 43			08a45				08 56							
Crystal Palace [4]	d					08 32					08a46							08 59							
Birkbeck	d																	09 03							
Beckenham Junction [4]	a																	09 06							
Streatham Common [4]	d							08 30				08 39	08 42			08 45					08 50				
Norbury	d							08 33				08 42	08 45			08 48					08 53				
Thornton Heath	d							08 36				08 45	08 48			08 51					08 56				
Selhurst [4]	d							08 39				08 48	08 51			08 54					08 59				
Norwood Junction [2]	a			08 32		08 37													08 46				08 55	08 59	
	d			08 33	08 35	08 39													08 46	08 50			08 56	09 00	
West Croydon [4]	a				08 41	08 43						08 52	08 56							09 00	09 03				
East Croydon	a	08 24		08 36				08 42		08 32					08 39	08 57	08 47		08 50			08 52	08 59	09 03	

Table 177

Saturdays

Luton, Milton Keynes Central and London East and West Croydon via Tulse Hill - Crystal Palace - Norbury

Local Services

Network Diagram - see first Page of Table 177

		SN	FC 1	FC	SN	LO	SN	SN	SN	SN ◇1	SN	SN ◇1	SN	SN	SN	FC 1		SN	SN 1	LO	SN	SN ◇1 🚲	SN 1	SN	SN
London Bridge 4 ⊖	d	08 41	08 42	08 45	08 50									08 48	08 52	08 57		09 03	09 03				09 15	09 06	09 11
South Bermondsey	d	08 45												08 52				09 07							09 15
Queens Rd Peckham	d	08 48												08 54				09 09							09 18
Peckham Rye 4	d	08 50												08 57				09 12							09 20
East Dulwich	d													09 00				09 15							
North Dulwich	d													09 02				09 17							
Luton 10	d																								
Luton Airport Parkway 7	d																								
St Pancras International 15 ⊖	d																								
City Thameslink 3	d																								
London Blackfriars 3 ⊖	d																								
Elephant & Castle ⊖	d																								
Loughborough Jn.	d																								
Herne Hill 4	d																								
Tulse Hill 3	d			09 01										09 05				09 20							
Streatham 4	d			09a05										09 09											
London Victoria 15 ⊖	d						08 36	08 41	08 43	08 47	08 49	08 51	08 53								09 03	09 06			
Battersea Park 4	d	09a02					08 40	08a45	08 47		08 53										09 07				09a32
Milton Keynes Central	d																								
Watford Junction	d																								
Harrow & Wealdstone ⊖	d																								
Wembley Central ⊖	d																								
Shepherd's Bush ⊖	d																								
Kensington (Olympia) ⊖	d																								
West Brompton ⊖	d																								
Imperial Wharf	d																								
Clapham Junction 10	d						08 44		08 51	08 53	08 57		09 00								09 11	09 12			
Wandsworth Common	d						08 47		08 54		09 00		09 03								09 14				
Balham 4 ⊖	d						08 50		08 56		09 02		09 05								09 16				
Streatham Hill	d						08 53				09 05														
West Norwood 4	d						08 57				09 10							09 23							
Gipsy Hill	d						09 00				09 13				09a15			09 26							
Crystal Palace 4	d						09 02				09a16							09 29							
Birkbeck 🚋	d																	09 33							
Beckenham Junction 4 🚋	a																	09 36							
Streatham Common 4	d								09 00				09 09	09 12							09 20				
Norbury	d								09 03				09 12	09 15							09 23				
Thornton Heath	d								09 06				09 15	09 18							09 26				
Selhurst 4	d								09 09				09 18	09 21							09 29				
Norwood Junction 2	a				09 02		09 07												09 16				09 25	09 29	
	d				09 03	09 05	09 09												09 16	09 20			09 26	09 30	
West Croydon 4 🚋	a					09 12	09 13						09 22	09 26						09 30	09 33				
East Croydon 🚋	a		08 54		09 06				09 12	09 02		09 07				09 09			09 20			09 22	09 29	09 33	

		FC 1	FC	SN	LO		LO		SN	SN	SN	SN ◇1	SN	SN	SN	SN	FC 1	SN 1	SN ◇1	SN	SN 1	LO	SN
London Bridge 4 ⊖	d	09 12	09 15	09 20											17 18	17 22	17 27			17 33	17 33		
South Bermondsey	d														17 22					17 37			
Queens Rd Peckham	d														17 24					17 39			
Peckham Rye 4	d														17 27					17 42			
East Dulwich	d														17 30					17 45			
North Dulwich	d														17 32					17 47			
Luton 10	d																						
Luton Airport Parkway 7	d																						
St Pancras International 15 ⊖	d																						
City Thameslink 3	d																						
London Blackfriars 3 ⊖	d																						
Elephant & Castle ⊖	d																						
Loughborough Jn.	d																						
Herne Hill 4	d																						
Tulse Hill 3	d		09 31												17 35					17 50			
Streatham 4	d		09a35												17 39								
London Victoria 15 ⊖	d					and at			17 06	17 11	17 13	17 17	17 19	17 23					17 32				17 33
Battersea Park 4	d					the same			17 10	17a15	17 17		17 23										17 37
Milton Keynes Central	d					minutes												16 13					
Watford Junction	d					past												16 52					
Harrow & Wealdstone ⊖	d					each												16 59					
Wembley Central ⊖	d					hour until												17 04					
Shepherd's Bush ⊖	d																	17 19					
Kensington (Olympia) ⊖	d																	17 22					
West Brompton ⊖	d																	17 25					
Imperial Wharf	d																	17 27					
Clapham Junction 10	d								17 14		17 21	17 23	17 27	17 30				17 34	17 38				17 41
Wandsworth Common	d								17 17		17 24		17 30	17 33				17 37					17 44
Balham 4 ⊖	d								17 20		17 26		17 32	17 35				17 40					17 46
Streatham Hill	d								17 23				17 35										
West Norwood 4	d								17 27				17 40							17 53			
Gipsy Hill	d								17 30				17 43			17a45				17 56			
Crystal Palace 4	d								17 32				17a46							17 59			
Birkbeck 🚋	d																			18 03			
Beckenham Junction 4 🚋	a																			18 06			
Streatham Common 4	d										17 30			17 39	17 42			17 45					17 50
Norbury	d										17 33			17 42	17 45			17 48					17 53
Thornton Heath	d										17 36			17 45	17 48			17 51					17 56
Selhurst 4	d										17 39			17 48	17 51			17 54					17 59
Norwood Junction 2	a			09 32					17 37												17 46		
	d			09 33	09 35		17 35		17 39												17 46	17 50	
West Croydon 4 🚋	a				09 42		17 42		17 43					17 52	17 56							18 00	18 03
East Croydon 🚋	a	09 24		09 36							17 42	17 32					17 39	17 57	17 47		17 50		

Luton, Milton Keynes Central and London East and West Croydon via Tulse Hill - Crystal Palace - Norbury

Local Services

Network Diagram - see first Page of Table 177

		SN ◇1	SN 1	SN	SN	FC 1	FC	SN	LO	SN	SN	SN	SN ◇1	SN	SN ◇1	SN		SN	SN	FC 1	SN	SN 1	LO	SN	SN ◇1
London Bridge 4 ⊖	d		17 45	17 36	17 41	17 42	17 45	17 50										17 48	17 52	17 57	18 03	18 03			
South Bermondsey	d				17 45													17 52			18 07				
Queens Rd Peckham	d				17 48													17 54			18 09				
Peckham Rye 4	d				17 50													17 57			18 12				
East Dulwich	d																	18 00			18 15				
North Dulwich	d																	18 02			18 17				
Luton 10	d																								
Luton Airport Parkway 7	d																								
St Pancras International 15 ⊖	d																								
City Thameslink 3	d																								
London Blackfriars 3 ⊖	d																								
Elephant & Castle ⊖	d																								
Loughborough Jn.	d																								
Herne Hill 4	d																								
Tulse Hill 3	d						18 01											18 05			18 20				
Streatham 4	d						18a05											18 09							
London Victoria 15 ⊖	d	17 36								17 36	17 41	17 43	17 47	17 49	17 51	17 53								18 03	18 06
Battersea Park 4	d				18a02					17 40	17a45	17 47		17 53										18 07	
Milton Keynes Central	d																								
Watford Junction	d																								
Harrow & Wealdstone ⊖	d																								
Wembley Central ⊖	d																								
Shepherd's Bush ⊖	d																								
Kensington (Olympia) ⊖	d																								
West Brompton ⊖	d																								
Imperial Wharf	d																								
Clapham Junction 10	d	17 42								17 44		17 51	17 53	17 57		18 00								18 11	18 12
Wandsworth Common	d									17 47		17 54		18 00		18 03								18 14	
Balham 4 ⊖	d									17 50		17 56		18 02		18 05								18 16	
Streatham Hill	d									17 53				18 05											
West Norwood 4	d									17 57				18 10							18 23				
Gipsy Hill	d									18 00				18 13					18a15		18 26				
Crystal Palace 4	d									18 02				18a16							18 29				
Birkbeck	d																				18 33				
Beckenham Junction 4	a																				18 36				
Streatham Common 4	d											18 00				18 09		18 12						18 20	
Norbury	d											18 03				18 12		18 15						18 23	
Thornton Heath	d											18 06				18 15		18 18						18 26	
Selhurst 4	d											18 09				18 18		18 21						18 29	
Norwood Junction 2	a		17 56	17 59				18 02		18 07												18 16			
	d		17 56	18 00				18 03	18 05	18 09												18 16	18 20		
West Croydon 4	a								18 11	18 13						18 22		18 26					18 30	18 33	
East Croydon	a	17 52	18 00	18 03		17 54		18 06				18 12	18 02		18 07					18 09		18 20			18 22

		SN 1	SN	SN	FC 1	FC	SN	LO		SN	SN	SN	SN ◇1	SN	SN	SN	SN	FC 1	SN 1	SN ◇1	SN	SN 1	LO	SN	
London Bridge 4 ⊖	d	18 15	18 06	18 11	18 12	18 15	18 20									18 18	18 22	18 27			18 33	18 33			
South Bermondsey	d			18 15												18 22					18 37				
Queens Rd Peckham	d			18 18												18 24					18 39				
Peckham Rye 4	d			18 20												18 27					18 42				
East Dulwich	d															18 30					18 45				
North Dulwich	d															18 32					18 47				
Luton 10	d																								
Luton Airport Parkway 7	d																								
St Pancras International 15 ⊖	d																								
City Thameslink 3	d																								
London Blackfriars 3 ⊖	d																								
Elephant & Castle ⊖	d																								
Loughborough Jn.	d																								
Herne Hill 4	d																								
Tulse Hill 3	d					18 31										18 35					18 50				
Streatham 4	d					18a35										18 39									
London Victoria 15 ⊖	d									18 06	18 11	18 13	18 17	18 19	18 23					18 32				18 33	
Battersea Park 4	d			18a32						18 10	18a15	18 17		18 23										18 37	
Milton Keynes Central	d																		17 13						
Watford Junction	d																		17 52						
Harrow & Wealdstone ⊖	d																		17 59						
Wembley Central ⊖	d																		18 04						
Shepherd's Bush ⊖	d																		18 19						
Kensington (Olympia) ⊖	d																		18 22						
West Brompton ⊖	d																		18 25						
Imperial Wharf	d																		18 27						
Clapham Junction 10	d									18 14		18 21	18 23	18 27	18 30				18 34	18 38				18 41	
Wandsworth Common	d									18 17		18 24		18 30	18 33				18 37					18 44	
Balham 4 ⊖	d									18 20		18 26		18 32	18 35				18 40					18 46	
Streatham Hill	d									18 23				18 35											
West Norwood 4	d									18 27				18 40							18 53				
Gipsy Hill	d									18 30				18 43			18a45				18 56				
Crystal Palace 4	d									18 32				18a46							18 59				
Birkbeck	d																				19 03				
Beckenham Junction 4	a																				19 06				
Streatham Common 4	d											18 30			18 39	18 42			18 45					18 50	
Norbury	d											18 33			18 42	18 45			18 48					18 53	
Thornton Heath	d											18 36			18 45	18 48			18 51					18 56	
Selhurst 4	d											18 39			18 48	18 51			18 54					18 59	
Norwood Junction 2	a	18 25	18 29				18 32			18 37												18 46			
	d	18 26	18 30				18 33	18 35		18 39												18 46	18 50		
West Croydon 4	a							18 41		18 43					18 52	18 56							19 00	19 03	
East Croydon	a	18 29	18 33		18 24		18 36					18 42	18 32					18 39	18 57	18 47		18 50			

Table 177

Saturdays

Luton, Milton Keynes Central and London East and West Croydon via Tulse Hill - Crystal Palace - Norbury

Local Services

Network Diagram - see first Page of Table 177

	SN	SN	SN	SN	FC	FC	SN	LO	SN	SN	SN	SN	SN	SN	SN		SN	SN	FC	SN	SN	LO	SN	SN
	◇1	1			1							◇1		◇1					1		1			◇1
London Bridge 4 ⊖ d		18 45	18 36	18 41	18 42	18 45	18 50										18 48	18 52	18 57	19 03	19 03			
South Bermondsey d				18 45													18 52			19 07				
Queens Rd Peckham d				18 48													18 54			19 09				
Peckham Rye 4 d				18 50													18 57			19 12				
East Dulwich d																	19 00			19 15				
North Dulwich d																	19 02			19 17				
Luton 10 d																								
Luton Airport Parkway 7 d																								
St Pancras International 15 ⊖ d																								
City Thameslink 3 d																								
London Blackfriars 3 ⊖ d																								
Elephant & Castle ⊖ d																								
Loughborough Jn. d																								
Herne Hill 4 d																								
Tulse Hill 3 d						19 01											19 05			19 20				
Streatham 4 d						19a05											19 09							
London Victoria 15 ⊖ d	18 36								18 36	18 41	18 43	18 47	18 49	18 51	18 53								19 03	19 06
Battersea Park 4 d				19a02					18 40	18a45	18 47		18 53										19 07	
Milton Keynes Central d																								
Watford Junction d																								
Harrow & Wealdstone ⊖ d																								
Wembley Central ⊖ d																								
Shepherd's Bush ⊖ d																								
Kensington (Olympia) ⊖ d																								
West Brompton ⊖ d																								
Imperial Wharf d																								
Clapham Junction 10 d	18 42								18 44		18 51	18 53	18 57		19 00								19 11	19 12
Wandsworth Common d									18 47		18 54		19 00		19 03								19 14	
Balham 4 ⊖ d									18 50		18 56		19 02		19 05								19 16	
Streatham Hill d									18 53				19 05											
West Norwood 4 d									18 57				19 10							19 23				
Gipsy Hill d									19 00				19 13					19a15		19 26				
Crystal Palace 4 d									19 02				19a16							19 29				
Birkbeck d																				19 33				
Beckenham Junction 4 a																				19 36				
Streatham Common 4 d											19 00				19 09		19 12						19 20	
Norbury d											19 03				19 12		19 15						19 23	
Thornton Heath d											19 06				19 15		19 18						19 26	
Selhurst 4 d											19 09				19 18		19 21						19 29	
Norwood Junction 2 a		18 55	18 59				19 02		19 07												19 16			
d		18 56	19 00				19 03	19 05	19 09												19 16	19 20		
West Croydon 4 a								19 11	19 13						19 22		19 26					19 30	19 33	
East Croydon a	18 52	18 59	19 03		18 54		19 06				19 12	19 02		19 07					19 09		19 20			19 22

	SN	SN	FC	FC	SN	LO	SN		SN	SN	SN	SN	SN	SN	SN	FC	SN	SN	SN	SN	LO	SN	SN	
			1								◇1					1	1	◇1		1			◇1	
London Bridge 4 ⊖ d	19 06	19 11	19 12	19 15	19 20									19 18	19 22	19 27			19 33	19 33				
South Bermondsey d		19 15												19 22					19 37					
Queens Rd Peckham d		19 18												19 24					19 39					
Peckham Rye 4 d		19 20												19 27					19 42					
East Dulwich d														19 30					19 45					
North Dulwich d														19 32					19 47					
Luton 10 d																								
Luton Airport Parkway 7 d																								
St Pancras International 15 ⊖ d																								
City Thameslink 3 d																								
London Blackfriars 3 ⊖ d																								
Elephant & Castle ⊖ d																								
Loughborough Jn. d																								
Herne Hill 4 d																								
Tulse Hill 3 d				19 31										19 35					19 50					
Streatham 4 d				19a35										19 39										
London Victoria 15 ⊖ d							19 06		19 11	19 13	19 17	19 19	19 23					19 32				19 33	19 36	
Battersea Park 4 d		19a32					19 10		19a15	19 17		19 23										19 37		
Milton Keynes Central d																	18 13							
Watford Junction d																	18 52							
Harrow & Wealdstone ⊖ d																	18 59							
Wembley Central ⊖ d																	19 04							
Shepherd's Bush ⊖ d																	19 19							
Kensington (Olympia) ⊖ d																	19 22							
West Brompton ⊖ d																	19 25							
Imperial Wharf d																	19 27							
Clapham Junction 10 d							19 14			19 21	19 23	19 27	19 30				19 34	19 38				19 41	19 42	
Wandsworth Common d							19 17			19 24		19 30	19 33				19 37					19 44		
Balham 4 ⊖ d							19 20			19 26		19 32	19 35				19 40					19 46		
Streatham Hill d							19 23					19 35												
West Norwood 4 d							19 27					19 40							19 53					
Gipsy Hill d							19 30					19 43			19a45				19 56					
Crystal Palace 4 d							19 32					19a46							19 59					
Birkbeck d																			20 03					
Beckenham Junction 4 a																			20 06					
Streatham Common 4 d										19 30			19 39	19 42			19 45					19 50		
Norbury d										19 33			19 42	19 45			19 48					19 53		
Thornton Heath d										19 36			19 45	19 48			19 51					19 56		
Selhurst 4 d										19 39			19 48	19 51			19 54					19 59		
Norwood Junction 2 a	19 29				19 32		19 37													19 46				
d	19 30				19 33	19 35	19 39													19 46	19 50			
West Croydon 4 a						19 41	19 43						19 52	19 56							20 00	20 03		
East Croydon a	19 33		19 24		19 36					19 42	19 33					19 39	19 57	19 47		19 50			19 52	

Table 177

Luton, Milton Keynes Central and London East and West Croydon via Tulse Hill - Crystal Palace - Norbury

Local Services

Network Diagram - see first Page of Table 177

		SN	SN	FC	FC	SN	LO	SN	SN	SN	SN	SN	SN	SN	SN	SN		FC	SN	LO	SN	SN	SN	SN	FC
				1							◇1		◇1					1				◇1			1
London Bridge 4 ⊖	d	19 36	19 41	19 42	19 45	19 50									19 48	19 52		19 57	20 03				20 06	20 11	20 12
South Bermondsey	d		19 45												19 52				20 07					20 15	
Queens Rd Peckham	d		19 48												19 54				20 09					20 18	
Peckham Rye 4	d		19 50												19 57				20 12					20 20	
East Dulwich	d														20 00				20 15						
North Dulwich	d														20 02				20 17						
Luton 10	d																								
Luton Airport Parkway 7	d																								
St Pancras International 15 ⊖	d																								
City Thameslink 3	d																								
London Blackfriars 3 ⊖	d																								
Elephant & Castle ⊖	d																								
Loughborough Jn.	d																								
Herne Hill 4	d																								
Tulse Hill 3	d				20 01										20 05				20 20						
Streatham 4	d				20a05										20 09										
London Victoria 15 ⊖	d							19 36	19 41	19 43	19 47	19 49	19 51	19 53							20 03	20 06			
Battersea Park 4	d		20a02					19 40	19a45	19 47		19 53									20 07			20a32	
Milton Keynes Central	d																								
Watford Junction	d																								
Harrow & Wealdstone ⊖	d																								
Wembley Central ⊖	d																								
Shepherd's Bush ⊖	d																								
Kensington (Olympia) ⊖	d																								
West Brompton ⊖	d																								
Imperial Wharf	d																								
Clapham Junction 10	d							19 44		19 51	19 53	19 57		20 00							20 11	20 12			
Wandsworth Common	d							19 47		19 54		20 00		20 03							20 14				
Balham 4 ⊖	d							19 50		19 56		20 02		20 05							20 16				
Streatham Hill	d							19 53				20 05													
West Norwood 4	d							19 57				20 10							20 23						
Gipsy Hill	d							20 00				20 13				20a15			20 26						
Crystal Palace 4	d							20 02				20a16							20 29						
Birkbeck 🚋	d																		20 33						
Beckenham Junction 4 🚋	a																		20 36						
Streatham Common 4	d									20 00				20 09	20 12						20 20				
Norbury	d									20 03				20 12	20 15						20 23				
Thornton Heath	d									20 06				20 15	20 18						20 26				
Selhurst 4	d									20 09				20 18	20 21						20 29				
Norwood Junction 2	a	19 59				20 02		20 07															20 29		
	d	20 00				20 03	20 05	20 09												20 20			20 30		
West Croydon 4 🚋	a						20 15	20 14						20 24	20 27					20 30	20 33				
East Croydon 🚋	a	20 03		19 54		20 06				20 12	20 02		20 07					20 09				20 22	20 33		20 24

		FC	SN	LO	SN	SN	SN	SN		SN	SN	SN	SN	SN	SN	SN	SN	SN	LO	SN	SN	SN	SN	FC	
						1				◇1		◇1			1		◇1				◇1			1	
London Bridge 4 ⊖	d	20 15	20 20											20 18		20 22		20 33				20 36	20 41	20 42	
South Bermondsey	d													20 22				20 37					20 45		
Queens Rd Peckham	d													20 24				20 39					20 48		
Peckham Rye 4	d													20 27				20 42					20 50		
East Dulwich	d													20 30				20 45							
North Dulwich	d													20 32				20 47							
Luton 10	d																								
Luton Airport Parkway 7	d																								
St Pancras International 15 ⊖	d																								
City Thameslink 3	d																								
London Blackfriars 3 ⊖	d																								
Elephant & Castle ⊖	d																								
Loughborough Jn.	d																								
Herne Hill 4	d																								
Tulse Hill 3	d	20 31												20 35				20 50							
Streatham 4	d	20a35												20 39											
London Victoria 15 ⊖	d				20 06	20 10	20 11	20 13		20 17	20 19	20 21	20 23				20 32			20 33	20 36				
Battersea Park 4	d				20 10		20a15	20 17			20 23									20 37			21a02		
Milton Keynes Central	d														19 13										
Watford Junction	d														19 51										
Harrow & Wealdstone ⊖	d														19 58										
Wembley Central ⊖	d																								
Shepherd's Bush ⊖	d														20 19										
Kensington (Olympia) ⊖	d														20 22										
West Brompton ⊖	d														20 25										
Imperial Wharf	d														20 27										
Clapham Junction 10	d				20 14	20 16		20 21		20 23	20 27		20 30		20 34		20 38			20 41	20 42				
Wandsworth Common	d				20 17			20 24			20 30		20 33		20 37					20 44					
Balham 4 ⊖	d				20 20			20 26			20 32		20 35		20 40					20 46					
Streatham Hill	d				20 23						20 35														
West Norwood 4	d				20 27						20 40							20 53							
Gipsy Hill	d				20 30						20 43					20a45		20 56							
Crystal Palace 4	d				20 32						20a46							20 59							
Birkbeck 🚋	d																	21 03							
Beckenham Junction 4 🚋	a																	21 06							
Streatham Common 4	d							20 30					20 39	20 42	20 45					20 50					
Norbury	d							20 33					20 42	20 45	20 48					20 53					
Thornton Heath	d							20 36					20 45	20 48	20 51					20 56					
Selhurst 4	d							20 39					20 48	20 51	20 55					20 59					
Norwood Junction 2	a		20 32		20 37																	20 59			
	d		20 33	20 35	20 39														20 50			21 00			
West Croydon 4 🚋	a			20 45	20 44								20 54	20 56					21 00	21 03					
East Croydon 🚋	a		20 36			20 29		20 42		20 32		20 37			20 59		20 47				20 52	21 03		20 53	

Table 177

Saturdays

Luton, Milton Keynes Central and London East and West Croydon via Tulse Hill - Crystal Palace - Norbury

Local Services

Network Diagram - see first Page of Table 177

Station		FC	SN	LO	SN	SN ■1	SN	SN	SN ◇■1	SN	SN	SN	SN	SN ◇■1	SN	LO		SN	SN ◇■1	SN	SN	FC ■1	FC	SN	LO
London Bridge ■4 ⊖	d	20 45	20 50									20 48	20 52		21 03					21 06	21 11	21 12	21 15	21 20	
South Bermondsey	d											20 52			21 07						21 15				
Queens Rd Peckham	d											20 54			21 09						21 18				
Peckham Rye ■4	d											20 57			21 12						21 20				
East Dulwich	d											21 00			21 15										
North Dulwich	d											21 02			21 17										
Luton ■10	d																								
Luton Airport Parkway ■7	d																								
St Pancras International ■15 ⊖	d																								
City Thameslink ■3	d																								
London Blackfriars ■3 ⊖	d																								
Elephant & Castle ⊖	d																								
Loughborough Jn.	d																								
Herne Hill ■4	d																								
Tulse Hill ■3	d	21 01										21 05			21 20								21 31		
Streatham ■4	d	21a05										21 09											21a35		
London Victoria ■15 ⊖	d				20 36	20 40	20 41	20 43	20 47	20 49	20 53			21 02				21 03	21 06						
Battersea Park ■4	d				20 40		20a45	20 47		20 53								21 07			21a32				
Milton Keynes Central	d																								
Watford Junction	d																								
Harrow & Wealdstone ⊖	d																								
Wembley Central ⊖	d																								
Shepherd's Bush ⊖	d																								
Kensington (Olympia) ⊖	d																								
West Brompton ⊖	d																								
Imperial Wharf	d																								
Clapham Junction ■10	d				20 44	20 46		20 51	20 53	20 57	21 00			21 08				21 11	21 12						
Wandsworth Common	d				20 47			20 54		21 00	21 03							21 14							
Balham ■4 ⊖	d				20 50			20 56		21 02	21 05							21 16							
Streatham Hill	d				20 53					21 05															
West Norwood ■4	d				20 57					21 10					21 23										
Gipsy Hill	d				21 00					21 13			21a15		21 26										
Crystal Palace ■4	d				21 02					21a16					21 29										
Birkbeck 🚋	d														21 33										
Beckenham Junction ■4 🚋	a														21 36										
Streatham Common ■4	d							21 00			21 09	21 12						21 20							
Norbury	d							21 03			21 12	21 15						21 23							
Thornton Heath	d							21 06			21 15	21 18						21 26							
Selhurst ■4	d							21 09			21 18	21 21						21 29							
Norwood Junction ■2	a		21 02		21 07															21 29				21 32	
	d		21 03	21 05	21 09											21 20				21 30				21 33	21 35
West Croydon ■4 🚋	a			21 15	21 14						21 24	21 26				21 30		21 33							21 45
East Croydon 🚋	a		21 06			20 57		21 12	21 02					21 17					21 22	21 33		21 24		21 36	

Station		SN	SN ■1	SN	SN	SN ◇■1	SN	SN		SN	SN	SN	LO	SN	SN ◇■1	SN	SN	FC ■1	FC	SN	LO	SN	SN ■1	SN	
London Bridge ■4 ⊖	d									21 18	21 22	21 33				21 36	21 41	21 42	21 45	21 50					
South Bermondsey	d									21 22		21 37					21 45								
Queens Rd Peckham	d									21 24		21 39					21 48								
Peckham Rye ■4	d									21 27		21 42					21 50								
East Dulwich	d									21 30		21 45													
North Dulwich	d									21 32		21 47													
Luton ■10	d																								
Luton Airport Parkway ■7	d																								
St Pancras International ■15 ⊖	d																								
City Thameslink ■3	d																								
London Blackfriars ■3 ⊖	d																								
Elephant & Castle ⊖	d																								
Loughborough Jn.	d																								
Herne Hill ■4	d																								
Tulse Hill ■3	d									21 35		21 50							22 01						
Streatham ■4	d									21 39									22a05						
London Victoria ■15 ⊖	d	21 06	21 10	21 11	21 13	21 17	21 19	21 23						21 33	21 36							21 36	21 40	21 41	
Battersea Park ■4	d	21 10		21a15	21 17		21 23							21 37			22a02					21 40		21a45	
Milton Keynes Central	d																								
Watford Junction	d																								
Harrow & Wealdstone ⊖	d																								
Wembley Central ⊖	d																								
Shepherd's Bush ⊖	d																								
Kensington (Olympia) ⊖	d																								
West Brompton ⊖	d																								
Imperial Wharf	d																								
Clapham Junction ■10	d	21 14	21 16		21 21	21 23	21 27	21 30						21 41	21 42							21 44	21 46		
Wandsworth Common	d	21 17			21 24		21 30	21 33						21 44								21 47			
Balham ■4 ⊖	d	21 20			21 26		21 32	21 35						21 46								21 50			
Streatham Hill	d	21 23					21 35															21 53			
West Norwood ■4	d	21 27					21 40					21 53										21 57			
Gipsy Hill	d	21 30					21 43				21a45	21 56										22 00			
Crystal Palace ■4	d	21 32					21a46					21 59										22 02			
Birkbeck 🚋	d											22 03													
Beckenham Junction ■4 🚋	a											22 06													
Streatham Common ■4	d				21 30			21 39		21 42				21 50											
Norbury	d				21 33			21 42		21 45				21 53											
Thornton Heath	d				21 36			21 45		21 48				21 56											
Selhurst ■4	d				21 39			21 48		21 51				21 59											
Norwood Junction ■2	a	21 37														21 59				22 02		22 07			
	d	21 39											21 50			22 00				22 03	22 05	22 09			
West Croydon ■4 🚋	a	21 44						21 54		21 56			22 00	22 03							22 12	22 13			
East Croydon 🚋	a		21 27		21 42	21 33									21 52	22 04		21 54		22 07			21 57		

Table 177

Saturdays

Luton, Milton Keynes Central and London East and West Croydon via Tulse Hill - Crystal Palace - Norbury

Local Services

Network Diagram - see first Page of Table 177

		SN	SN ◇1	SN	SN	SN	SN	SN ◇1	SN	LO	SN	SN ◇1	SN	SN	FC 1	FC		SN	LO	SN	SN 1	SN	SN	SN	SN
London Bridge 4 ⊖	d					21 48	21 52		22 03				22 06	22 11	22 12	22 15		22 20							
South Bermondsey	d					21 52			22 07					22 15											
Queens Rd Peckham	d					21 54			22 09					22 18											
Peckham Rye 4	d					21 57			22 12					22 20											
East Dulwich	d					22 00			22 15																
North Dulwich	d					22 02			22 17																
Luton 10	d																								
Luton Airport Parkway 7	d																								
St Pancras International 15 ⊖	d																								
City Thameslink 3	d																								
London Blackfriars 3 ⊖	d																								
Elephant & Castle ⊖	d																								
Loughborough Jn	d																								
Herne Hill 4	d																								
Tulse Hill 3	d					22 05			22 20							22 31									
Streatham 4	d					22 09										22a35									
London Victoria 15 ⊖	d	21 43	21 47	21 49	21 53			22 02			22 03	22 06								22 06	22 10	22 11	22 13	22 19	22 23
Battersea Park 4	d	21 47		21 53							22 07			22a32						22 10		22a15	22 17	22 23	
Milton Keynes Central	d																								
Watford Junction	d																								
Harrow & Wealdstone ⊖	d																								
Wembley Central ⊖	d																								
Shepherd's Bush ⊖	d																								
Kensington (Olympia) ⊖	d																								
West Brompton ⊖	d																								
Imperial Wharf	d																								
Clapham Junction 10	d	21 51	21 53	21 57	22 00			22 08			22 11	22 12								22 14	22 16		22 21	22 27	22 30
Wandsworth Common	d	21 54		22 00	22 03						22 14									22 17			22 24	22 30	22 33
Balham 4 ⊖	d	21 56		22 02	22 05						22 16									22 20			22 26	22 32	22 35
Streatham Hill	d			22 05																22 23				22 35	
West Norwood 4	d			22 10					22 23											22 27				22 40	
Gipsy Hill	d			22 13			22a15		22 26											22 30				22 43	
Crystal Palace 4	d			22a16					22 29											22 32				22a46	
Birkbeck 🚋	d								22 33																
Beckenham Junction 4 🚋	a								22 36																
Streatham Common 4	d	22 00			22 09	22 12					22 20												22 30		22 39
Norbury	d	22 03			22 12	22 15					22 23												22 33		22 42
Thornton Heath	d	22 06			22 15	22 18					22 26												22 36		22 45
Selhurst 4	d	22 09			22 18	22 21					22 29												22 39		22 48
Norwood Junction 2	a												22 29					22 32		22 37					
	d									22 20			22 30					22 33	22 35	22 39					
West Croydon 4 🚋	a				22 22	22 26				22 30	22 33								22 42	22 43					22 52
East Croydon 🚋	a	22 12	22 03					22 17				22 22	22 35		22 24			22 37			22 27		22 42		

		SN	SN	SN 1	SN	LO	SN	SN ◇1		SN	SN	FC 1	FC	SN	SN	SN 1	SN	SN	SN ◇1	SN	SN	SN	SN	SN ◇1	
London Bridge 4 ⊖	d	22 18	22 22		22 33					22 36	22 41	22 42	22 45	22 50								22 48	22 52		
South Bermondsey	d	22 22			22 37						22 45											22 52			
Queens Rd Peckham	d	22 24			22 39						22 48											22 54			
Peckham Rye 4	d	22 27			22 42						22 50											22 57			
East Dulwich	d	22 30			22 45																	23 00			
North Dulwich	d	22 32			22 47																	23 02			
Luton 10	d																								
Luton Airport Parkway 7	d																								
St Pancras International 15 ⊖	d																								
City Thameslink 3	d																								
London Blackfriars 3 ⊖	d																								
Elephant & Castle ⊖	d																								
Loughborough Jn	d																								
Herne Hill 4	d																								
Tulse Hill 3	d	22 35			22 50								23 01									23 05			
Streatham 4	d	22 39											23a05									23 09			
London Victoria 15 ⊖	d			22 32			22 33	22 36							22 36	22 40	22 41	22 43	22 47	22 49	22 53			23 02	
Battersea Park 4	d						22 37				23a02				22 40		22a45	22 47		22 53					
Milton Keynes Central	d																								
Watford Junction	d																								
Harrow & Wealdstone ⊖	d																								
Wembley Central ⊖	d																								
Shepherd's Bush ⊖	d																								
Kensington (Olympia) ⊖	d																								
West Brompton ⊖	d																								
Imperial Wharf	d																								
Clapham Junction 10	d			22 38			22 41	22 42							22 44	22 46		22 51	22 53	22 57	23 00			23 08	
Wandsworth Common	d						22 44								22 47			22 54		23 00	23 03				
Balham 4 ⊖	d						22 46								22 50			22 56		23 02	23 05				
Streatham Hill	d														22 53					23 05					
West Norwood 4	d				22 53										22 57					23 10					
Gipsy Hill	d		22a45		22 56										23 00					23 13			23a15		
Crystal Palace 4	d				22 59										23 03					23a16					
Birkbeck 🚋	d				23 03																				
Beckenham Junction 4 🚋	a				23 06																				
Streatham Common 4	d	22 42					22 50											23 00			23 09	23 12			
Norbury	d	22 45					22 53											23 03			23 12	23 15			
Thornton Heath	d	22 48					22 56											23 06			23 15	23 18			
Selhurst 4	d	22 51					22 59											23 09			23 18	23 21			
Norwood Junction 2	a									22 59				23 02	23 07										
	d					22 50				23 00				23 03	23 09										
West Croydon 4 🚋	a	22 56				23 00	23 03								23 13						23 22	23 26			
East Croydon 🚋	a			22 47				22 52		23 03		22 54		23 06		22 57		23 13	23 03					23 17	

Table 177

Saturdays

Luton, Milton Keynes Central and London East and West Croydon via Tulse Hill - Crystal Palace - Norbury

Local Services

Network Diagram - see first Page of Table 177

		LO	SN	SN ◇1	SN	SN	SN	SN 1	SN	SN	SN ◇1	SN	SN	FC 1	FC	SN		SN	SN 1	LO	SN	SN	SN	SN	FC 1
London Bridge 4	⊖ d				23 06	23 03							23 11	23 12	23 15	23 18		23 22				23 36	23 33		23 42
South Bermondsey	d					23 07							23 15			23 22							23 37		
Queens Rd Peckham	d					23 09							23 18			23 24							23 39		
Peckham Rye 4	d					23 12							23 20			23 27							23 42		
East Dulwich	d					23 15										23 30							23 45		
North Dulwich	d					23 17										23 32							23 47		
Luton 10	d																								
Luton Airport Parkway 7	d																								
St Pancras International 15	⊖ d																								
City Thameslink 3	d																								
London Blackfriars 3	⊖ d																								
Elephant & Castle	⊖ d																								
Loughborough Jn.	d																								
Herne Hill 4	d																								
Tulse Hill 3	d					23 21									23 31	23 35							23 51		
Streatham 4	d														23a35	23 39									
London Victoria 15	⊖ d		23 03	23 06			23 06	23 10	23 11	23 15	23 17	23 19							23 32		23 34			23 38	
Battersea Park 4	d		23 07				23 10		23a15	23 19		23 23	23a32								23 38			23 42	
Milton Keynes Central	d																								
Watford Junction	d																								
Harrow & Wealdstone	⊖ d																								
Wembley Central	⊖ d																								
Shepherd's Bush	⊖ d																								
Kensington (Olympia)	⊖ d																								
West Brompton	⊖ d																								
Imperial Wharf	d																								
Clapham Junction 10	d		23 11	23 12			23 14	23 16		23 23	23 23	23 27							23 38		23 42			23 46	
Wandsworth Common	d		23 14				23 17			23 26		23 30									23 45			23 49	
Balham 4	⊖ d		23 16				23 20			23 28		23 32									23 47			23 51	
Streatham Hill	d						23 23					23 35												23 54	
West Norwood 4	d					23 24	23 27					23 40											23 54	23 58	
Gipsy Hill	d					23 27	23 30					23 43						23a45					23 57	00 01	
Crystal Palace 4	d					23 29	23 32					23a46											23 59	00 03	
Birkbeck	d																								
Beckenham Junction 4	a																								
Streatham Common 4	d		23 20							23 32						23 42					23 51				
Norbury	d		23 23							23 35						23 45					23 54				
Thornton Heath	d		23 26							23 38						23 48					23 57				
Selhurst 4	d		23 29							23 41						23 51					23 59				
Norwood Junction 2	a				23 29	23 34	23 37															23 59	00 04	00 08	
	d	23 20			23 30		23 39													23 50		23 59		00 09	
West Croydon 4	a	23 30	23 33				23 43									23 56				23 59	00 03			00 14	
East Croydon	a			23 22	23 33			23 27		23 44	23 32			23 24					23 52			00 03			23 56

		FC	SN	SN 1	SN	SN 1	SN	SN		SN
London Bridge 4	⊖ d	23 45			23 48		23 52			
South Bermondsey	d				23 52					
Queens Rd Peckham	d				23 54					
Peckham Rye 4	d				23 57					
East Dulwich	d				00 01					
North Dulwich	d				00 03					
Luton 10	d									
Luton Airport Parkway 7	d									
St Pancras International 15	⊖ d									
City Thameslink 3	d									
London Blackfriars 3	⊖ d									
Elephant & Castle	⊖ d									
Loughborough Jn.	d									
Herne Hill 4	d									
Tulse Hill 3	d	00 01			00 06					
Streatham 4	d	00a05			00 10					
London Victoria 15	⊖ d		23 45	23 47		23 49		23 54		23 59
Battersea Park 4	d		23 49					23 58		00 03
Milton Keynes Central	d									
Watford Junction	d									
Harrow & Wealdstone	⊖ d									
Wembley Central	⊖ d									
Shepherd's Bush	⊖ d									
Kensington (Olympia)	⊖ d									
West Brompton	⊖ d									
Imperial Wharf	d									
Clapham Junction 10	d		23 53	23 53		23 56		00 02		00 07
Wandsworth Common	d		23 56					00 05		00 10
Balham 4	⊖ d		23 58					00 07		00 12
Streatham Hill	d							00 10		
West Norwood 4	d							00 14		
Gipsy Hill	d						00a15	00 17		
Crystal Palace 4	d							00a19		
Birkbeck	d									
Beckenham Junction 4	a									
Streatham Common 4	d		00 02		00 13					00 16
Norbury	d		00 05		00 15					00 19
Thornton Heath	d		00 08		00 18					00 22
Selhurst 4	d		00 11	00 02	00 21					00 25
Norwood Junction 2	a									
	d									
West Croydon 4	a				00 27					00 30
East Croydon	a		00 14	00 05		00 09				

Table 177

Sundays

Luton, Milton Keynes Central and London East and West Croydon via Tulse Hill - Crystal Palace - Norbury

Local Services

Network Diagram - see first Page of Table 177

		SN	SN	SN	SN	FC	SN	SN	SN	SN	LO	SN	SN	SN	SN	SN	SN	FC	SN	SN	SN	SN	SN	SN
								1	1				◇1					1	1					
		A	A	A	A	A	A	A	A	A	A	A		A										
London Bridge 4 ⊖	d		23p36	23p33		23p45								23p48	00 06	00 03		00 12			00 18			00 36
South Bermondsey	d			23p37										23p52		00 07					00 22			
Queens Rd Peckham	d			23p39										23p54		00 09					00 24			
Peckham Rye 4	d			23p42										23p57		00 12					00 27			
East Dulwich	d			23p45										00 01		00 15					00 30			
North Dulwich	d			23p47										00 03		00 17					00 32			
Luton 10	d																							
Luton Airport Parkway 7	d																							
St Pancras International 15 ⊖	d																							
City Thameslink 3	d																							
London Blackfriars 3 ⊖	d																							
Elephant & Castle ⊖	d																							
Loughborough Jn.	d																							
Herne Hill 4	d																							
Tulse Hill 3	d			23p51		00 01								00 06		00 21					00 35			
Streatham 4	d					00a05								00 10							00 39			
London Victoria 15 ⊖	d	23p34			23p38		23p45	23p47	23p49	23p54		23p59	00 05				00 07		00 14	00 16		00 22	00 34	
Battersea Park 4	d	23p38			23p42		23p49			23p58		00 03					00 11			00 20		00 26	00 38	
Milton Keynes Central	d																							
Watford Junction	d																							
Harrow & Wealdstone ⊖	d																							
Wembley Central ⊖	d																							
Shepherd's Bush ⊖	d																							
Kensington (Olympia) ⊖	d																							
West Brompton ⊖	d																							
Imperial Wharf	d																							
Clapham Junction 10	d	23p42			23p46		23p53	23p53	23p56	00 02		00 07	00 11				00 15		00 20	00 24		00 30	00 42	
Wandsworth Common	d	23p45			23p49		23p56			00 05		00 10					00 18			00 27		00 33	00 45	
Balham 4 ⊖	d	23p47			23p51		23p58			00 07		00 12					00 20			00 29		00 35	00 47	
Streatham Hill	d				23p54					00 10							00 23					00 38		
West Norwood 4	d			23p54	23p58					00 14						00 24	00 28					00 42		
Gipsy Hill	d			23p57	00 01					00 17						00 27	00 31					00 45		
Crystal Palace 4	d			23p59	00 03					00a19						00 29	00 33					00 47		
Birkbeck 🚋	d																							
Beckenham Junction 4 🚋	a																							
Streatham Common 4	d	23p51					00 02					00 16		00 13						00 33	00 42		00 51	
Norbury	d	23p54					00 05					00 19		00 15						00 36	00 45		00 54	
Thornton Heath	d	23p57					00 08					00 22		00 18						00 39	00 48		00 57	
Selhurst 4	d	23p59					00 11	00 02				00 25	00 20	00 21						00 41	00 51		01 00	
Norwood Junction 2	a		23p59	00 04	00 08										00 29	00 34	00 38					00 52		00 59
	d		23p59		00 09						00 20				00 30		00 38					00 52		01 00
West Croydon 4 🚋	a	00 03			00 14						00 27	00 30		00 27			00 43				00 55	00 58	01 04	
East Croydon 🚋	a		00 03				00 14	00 05	00 09				00 24		00 33			00 27	00 31	00 44				01 03

A not 11 December

Table 177

Sundays

Luton, Milton Keynes Central and London East and West Croydon via Tulse Hill - Crystal Palace - Norbury

Local Services

Network Diagram - see first Page of Table 177

		SN	SN	FC 1	SN	SN 1	FC 1	SN 1		SN 1	SN 1	SN 1	SN ◇1	SN ◇1	SN	SN	SN	FC 1	SN	LO	SN	SN	SN	SN 1	
London Bridge 4 ⊖	d	00 33		00 42			01 08										07 11	07 12				07 21	07 24	07 37	
South Bermondsey	d	00 37															07 15					07 25			
Queens Rd Peckham	d	00 39															07 18					07 27			
Peckham Rye 4	d	00 42															07 20					07 30			
East Dulwich	d	00 45																				07 33			
North Dulwich	d	00 47																				07 35			
Luton 10	d																								
Luton Airport Parkway 7	d																								
St Pancras International 15 ⊖	d																								
City Thameslink 3	d																								
London Blackfriars 3 ⊖	d																								
Elephant & Castle ⊖	d																								
Loughborough Jn.	d																								
Herne Hill 4	d																								
Tulse Hill 3	d	00 51																				07 39			
Streatham 4	d																					07 42			
London Victoria 15 ⊖	d		00 37		00 42	01 00		02 00		03 00	04 00	05 02	05 47	06 32	06 36	06 49			07 06		07 19				
Battersea Park 4	d		00 41		00 46											06 53	07a32								
Milton Keynes Central	d																								
Watford Junction	d																								
Harrow & Wealdstone ⊖	d																								
Wembley Central ⊖	d																								
Shepherd's Bush ⊖	d																								
Kensington (Olympia) ⊖	d																								
West Brompton ⊖	d																								
Imperial Wharf	d																								
Clapham Junction 10	d		00 45		00 50	01 08		02 08		03 08	04 08	05 08	05 53	06 38	06 42	06 57			07 12		07 26				
Wandsworth Common	d		00 48		00 53											07 00									
Balham 4 ⊖	d		00 50		00 55										06 47	07 02			07 17		07 30				
Streatham Hill	d		00 53																						
West Norwood 4	d	00 54	00 58																						
Gipsy Hill	d	00 57	01 01																						
Crystal Palace 4	d	00 59	01 03																						
Birkbeck 🚊	d																								
Beckenham Junction 4 🚊	a																								
Streatham Common 4	d				00 59										06 51	07 06			07 21		07 34	07 48			
Norbury	d				01 02										06 54	07 09			07 24		07 37	07 51			
Thornton Heath	d				01 05										06 57	07 12			07 27		07 40	07 54			
Selhurst 4	d				01 07		01 27								07 00	07 16			07 30		07 43	07 57			
Norwood Junction 2	a	01 04	01 08																				07 44	07 47	
	d		01 08																	07 22			07 48	07 48	
West Croydon 4 🚊	a		01 13													07 20				07 29	07 48		07 55		
East Croydon 🚊	a			00 56	01 10	01 21	01 32	02 21		03 21	04 21	05 21	06 05	06 51	07 03			07 26	07 33			08 01		07 54	

		LO	SN	SN ◇1	SN	SN	SN	SN	SN	FC 1	SN	SN	SN	LO	SN	SN		SN	SN	SN	SN	FC 1	SN ◇1	SN	SN
London Bridge 4 ⊖	d				07 36		07 39		07 41	07 42		07 51	07 54			08 06			08 09		08 11	08 12			08 21
South Bermondsey	d				07 40				07 45			07 55				08 10					08 15				08 25
Queens Rd Peckham	d				07 42				07 48			07 57				08 12					08 18				08 27
Peckham Rye 4	d				07 45				07 50			08 00				08 15					08 20				08 30
East Dulwich	d				07 48							08 03				08 18									08 33
North Dulwich	d				07 50							08 05				08 20									08 35
Luton 10	d																								
Luton Airport Parkway 7	d																								
St Pancras International 15 ⊖	d																								
City Thameslink 3	d																								
London Blackfriars 3 ⊖	d																								
Elephant & Castle ⊖	d																								
Loughborough Jn.	d																								
Herne Hill 4	d																								
Tulse Hill 3	d				07 54							08 09				08 24									08 39
Streatham 4	d											08 12													08 42
London Victoria 15 ⊖	d		07 24	07 32		07 36		07 41			07 49				07 54			08 06		08 11			08 17	08 19	
Battersea Park 4	d		07 28					07a45	08a02						07 58					08a15	08a32				
Milton Keynes Central	d																								
Watford Junction	d																								
Harrow & Wealdstone ⊖	d																								
Wembley Central ⊖	d																								
Shepherd's Bush ⊖	d																								
Kensington (Olympia) ⊖	d																								
West Brompton ⊖	d																								
Imperial Wharf	d																								
Clapham Junction 10	d		07 32	07 38		07 42					07 56				08 02			08 12					08 23	08 26	
Wandsworth Common	d		07 35												08 05										
Balham 4 ⊖	d		07 37			07 47					08 00				08 07			08 17						08 30	
Streatham Hill	d		07 41												08 11										
West Norwood 4	d		07 46		07 57										08 16	08 27									
Gipsy Hill	d		07 49		08 00										08 19	08 30									
Crystal Palace 4	d		07 51		08a02										08 21	08a32									
Birkbeck 🚊	d																								
Beckenham Junction 4 🚊	a																								
Streatham Common 4	d					07 51					08 04	08 18						08 21						08 34	08 48
Norbury	d					07 54					08 07	08 21						08 24						08 37	08 51
Thornton Heath	d					07 57					08 10	08 24						08 27						08 40	08 54
Selhurst 4	d					08 00					08 13	08 27						08 30						08 43	08 57
Norwood Junction 2	a		07 56				08 02						08 14		08 26				08 32						
	d	07 52	07 57				08 03						08 16	08 22	08 27				08 33						
West Croydon 4 🚊	a	07 59	08 01								08 18		08 24	08 28	08 31									08 48	
East Croydon 🚊	a			07 50		08 03	08 07			07 56		08 30						08 33	08 37			08 27	08 36		09 01

Table 177

Sundays

Luton, Milton Keynes Central and London East and West Croydon via Tulse Hill - Crystal Palace - Norbury

Local Services

Network Diagram - see first Page of Table 177

Station		SN	SN 1	LO	SN	SN ◇1	SN	SN		SN	SN	SN	FC 1	SN ◇1	SN	SN	SN	LO	SN	SN ◇1	SN	SN	SN	SN	
London Bridge 4 ⊖	d	08 24	08 37				08 36			08 39		08 41	08 42			08 51	08 54				09 06		09 09		
South Bermondsey	d						08 40					08 45				08 55					09 10				
Queens Rd Peckham	d						08 42					08 48				08 57					09 12				
Peckham Rye 4	d						08 45					08 50				09 00					09 15				
East Dulwich	d						08 48									09 03					09 18				
North Dulwich	d						08 50									09 05					09 20				
Luton 10	d																								
Luton Airport Parkway 7	d																								
St Pancras International 15 ⊖	d																								
City Thameslink 3	d																								
London Blackfriars 3 ⊖	d																								
Elephant & Castle ⊖	d																								
Loughborough Jn.	d																								
Herne Hill 4	d																								
Tulse Hill 3	d						08 54									09 09					09 24				
Streatham 4	d															09 12									
London Victoria 15 ⊖	d				08 24	08 32		08 36			08 41			08 47	08 49				08 54	09 02		09 06		09 11	
Battersea Park 4	d				08 28						08a45	09a02							08 58					09a15	
Milton Keynes Central	d																								
Watford Junction	d																								
Harrow & Wealdstone ⊖	d																								
Wembley Central ⊖	d																								
Shepherd's Bush ⊖	d																								
Kensington (Olympia) ⊖	d																								
West Brompton ⊖	d																								
Imperial Wharf	d																								
Clapham Junction 10	d				08 32	08 38		08 42						08 53	08 56				09 02	09 08		09 12			
Wandsworth Common	d				08 35														09 05						
Balham 4 ⊖	d				08 37			08 47							09 00				09 07			09 17			
Streatham Hill	d				08 41														09 11						
West Norwood 4	d				08 46		08 57												09 16		09 27				
Gipsy Hill	d				08 49		09 00												09 19		09 30				
Crystal Palace 4	d				08 51		09a02												09 21		09a32				
Birkbeck 🚊	d																								
Beckenham Junction 4 🚊	a																								
Streatham Common 4	d							08 51							09 04	09 18						09 21			
Norbury	d							08 54							09 07	09 21						09 24			
Thornton Heath	d							08 57							09 10	09 24						09 27			
Selhurst 4	d							09 00							09 13	09 27						09 30			
Norwood Junction 2	a	08 44	08 47		08 56					09 02							09 14		09 26				09 32		
	d	08 46	08 48	08 52	08 57					09 03							09 16	09 22	09 27				09 33		
West Croydon 4 🚊	a	08 54		08 58	09 01										09 18		09 24	09 28	09 31						
East Croydon 🚊	a		08 54			08 50		09 03		09 07			08 56	09 06		09 30				09 21		09 33	09 37		

Table 177

Sundays

Luton, Milton Keynes Central and London East and West Croydon via Tulse Hill - Crystal Palace - Norbury

Local Services

Network Diagram - see first Page of Table 177

		SN	FC	SN	SN	SN	SN	FC	SN	LO	SN	SN	SN	SN	SN	SN		SN	FC	SN	SN	SN	SN	FC	LO
			1	◇1					1			◇1							1	◇1 ⚲					
London Bridge 4 ⊖	d	09 11	09 12			09 21	09 24	09 32	09 37				09 36		09 39			09 41	09 42			09 51	09 54	10 02	
South Bermondsey	d	09 15				09 25							09 40					09 45				09 55			
Queens Rd Peckham	d	09 18				09 27							09 42					09 48				09 57			
Peckham Rye 4	d	09 20				09 30							09 45					09 50				10 00			
East Dulwich	d					09 33							09 48									10 03			
North Dulwich	d					09 35							09 50									10 05			
Luton 10	d																								
Luton Airport Parkway 7	d																								
St Pancras International 15 ⊖	d																								
City Thameslink 3	d																								
London Blackfriars 3 ⊖	d																								
Elephant & Castle ⊖	d																								
Loughborough Jn.	d																								
Herne Hill 4	d																								
Tulse Hill 3	d					09 39		09 43					09 54									10 09		10 13	
Streatham 4	d					09 42		09a46														10 12		10a16	
London Victoria 15 ⊖	d			09 17	09 19						09 24	09 32		09 36		09 41				09 47	09 49				
Battersea Park 4	d	09a32									09 28					09a45		10a02							
Milton Keynes Central	d																								
Watford Junction	d																								
Harrow & Wealdstone ⊖	d																								
Wembley Central ⊖	d																								
Shepherd's Bush ⊖	d																								
Kensington (Olympia) ⊖	d																								
West Brompton ⊖	d																								
Imperial Wharf	d																								
Clapham Junction 10	d			09 23	09 26						09 32	09 38		09 42						09 53	09 56				
Wandsworth Common	d										09 35														
Balham 4 ⊖	d				09 30						09 37			09 47							10 00				
Streatham Hill	d										09 41														
West Norwood 4	d										09 46		09 57												
Gipsy Hill	d										09 49		10 00												
Crystal Palace 4	d										09 51		10a02												
Birkbeck 🚋	d																								
Beckenham Junction 4 🚋	a																								
Streatham Common 4	d				09 34	09 48								09 51							10 04	10 18			
Norbury	d				09 37	09 51								09 54							10 07	10 21			
Thornton Heath	d				09 40	09 54								09 57							10 10	10 24			
Selhurst 4	d				09 43	09 57								10 00							10 13	10 27			
Norwood Junction 2	a						09 44		09 47		09 56				10 02								10 14		
	d						09 46		09 48	09 52	09 57				10 03								10 16		10 22
West Croydon 4 🚋	a				09 48		09 54			09 58	10 01										10 18		10 24		10 28
East Croydon 🚋	a		09 27	09 36		10 01			09 54			09 50		10 03	10 07				09 56	10 06		10 30			

Table 177

Sundays

Luton, Milton Keynes Central and London East and West Croydon via Tulse Hill - Crystal Palace - Norbury

Local Services

Network Diagram - see first Page of Table 177

		SN	SN	SN	SN	SN	SN	SN		FC	SN	SN	SN	SN	FC	SN	LO	SN	SN	SN	SN	SN	SN	SN	
			◇1							1	◇1					1			◇1						
London Bridge 4	⊖ d			10 06		10 09		10 11		10 12			10 21	10 24	10 32	10 37				10 36		10 39		10 41	
South Bermondsey	d			10 10				10 15					10 25							10 40				10 45	
Queens Rd Peckham	d			10 12				10 18					10 27							10 42				10 48	
Peckham Rye 4	d			10 15				10 20					10 30							10 45				10 50	
East Dulwich	d			10 18									10 33							10 48					
North Dulwich	d			10 20									10 35							10 50					
Luton 10	d																								
Luton Airport Parkway 7	d																								
St Pancras International 15	⊖ d																								
City Thameslink 3	d																								
London Blackfriars 3	⊖ d																								
Elephant & Castle	⊖ d																								
Loughborough Jn	d																								
Herne Hill 4	d																								
Tulse Hill 3	d			10 24									10 39		10 43					10 54					
Streatham 4	d												10 42		10a46										
London Victoria 15	⊖ d	09 54	10 02		10 06		10 11				10 17	10 19						10 24	10 32		10 36		10 41		
Battersea Park 4	d	09 58					10a15	10a32										10 28					10a45	11a02	
Milton Keynes Central	d																								
Watford Junction	d																								
Harrow & Wealdstone	⊖ d																								
Wembley Central	⊖ d																								
Shepherd's Bush	⊖ d																								
Kensington (Olympia)	⊖ d																								
West Brompton	⊖ d																								
Imperial Wharf	d																								
Clapham Junction 10	d	10 02	10 08		10 12						10 23	10 26						10 32	10 38		10 42				
Wandsworth Common	d	10 05																10 35							
Balham 4	⊖ d	10 07			10 17							10 30						10 37			10 47				
Streatham Hill	d	10 11																10 41							
West Norwood 4	d	10 16		10 27														10 46		10 57					
Gipsy Hill	d	10 19		10 30														10 49		11 00					
Crystal Palace 4	d	10 21		10a32														10 51		11a02					
Birkbeck	🚋 d																								
Beckenham Junction 4	🚋 a																								
Streatham Common 4	d				10 21							10 34	10 48								10 51				
Norbury	d				10 24							10 37	10 51								10 54				
Thornton Heath	d				10 27							10 40	10 54								10 57				
Selhurst 4	d				10 30							10 43	10 57								11 00				
Norwood Junction 2	a	10 26				10 32								10 44		10 47		10 56				11 02			
	d	10 27				10 33								10 46		10 48	10 52	10 57				11 03			
West Croydon 4	🚋 a	10 31										10 48		10 54			10 58	11 01							
East Croydon	🚋 a		10 21		10 33	10 37				10 27	10 36		11 01			10 54			10 50		11 03	11 07			

Table 177

Sundays

Luton, Milton Keynes Central and London East and West Croydon via Tulse Hill - Crystal Palace - Norbury

Local Services

Network Diagram - see first Page of Table 177

		FC	SN	SN	SN	SN	FC	LO	SN	SN	SN	SN	SN	SN	SN	FC		SN	SN	SN	SN	FC	SN	LO	SN
		1	◇1 🛒							◇1 🛒						1		◇1					1		
London Bridge 4 ⊖	d	10 42			10 51	10 54	11 02				11 06		11 09		11 11	11 12				11 21	11 24	11 32	11 37		
South Bermondsey	d				10 55						11 10				11 15					11 25					
Queens Rd Peckham	d				10 57						11 12				11 18					11 27					
Peckham Rye 4	d				11 00						11 15				11 20					11 30					
East Dulwich	d				11 03						11 18									11 33					
North Dulwich	d				11 05						11 20									11 35					
Luton 10	d																								
Luton Airport Parkway 7	d																								
St Pancras International 15 ⊖	d																								
City Thameslink 3	d																								
London Blackfriars 3 ⊖	d																								
Elephant & Castle ⊖	d																								
Loughborough Jn	d																								
Herne Hill 4	d																								
Tulse Hill 3	d				11 09		11 13				11 24									11 39		11 43			
Streatham 4	d				11 12		11a16													11 42		11a46			
London Victoria 15 ⊖	d		10 47	10 49					10 54	11 02		11 06		11 11				11 17	11 19						11 24
Battersea Park 4	d								10 58					11a15	11a32										11 28
Milton Keynes Central	d																								
Watford Junction	d																								
Harrow & Wealdstone ⊖	d																								
Wembley Central ⊖	d																								
Shepherd's Bush ⊖	d																								
Kensington (Olympia) ⊖	d																								
West Brompton ⊖	d																								
Imperial Wharf	d																								
Clapham Junction 10	d		10 53	10 56					11 02	11 08		11 12						11 23	11 26						11 32
Wandsworth Common	d								11 05																11 35
Balham 4 ⊖	d			11 00					11 07			11 17							11 30						11 37
Streatham Hill	d								11 11																11 41
West Norwood 4	d								11 16		11 27														11 46
Gipsy Hill	d								11 19		11 30														11 49
Crystal Palace 4	d								11 21		11a32														11 51
Birkbeck 🚊	d																								
Beckenham Junction 4 🚊	a																								
Streatham Common 4	d			11 04	11 18							11 21							11 34	11 48					
Norbury	d			11 07	11 21							11 24							11 37	11 51					
Thornton Heath	d			11 10	11 24							11 27							11 40	11 54					
Selhurst 4	d			11 13	11 27							11 30							11 43	11 57					
Norwood Junction 2	a					11 14			11 26				11 32								11 44		11 47		11 56
	d					11 16		11 22	11 27				11 33								11 46		11 48	11 52	11 57
West Croydon 4 🚊	a			11 18		11 24		11 28	11 31										11 48		11 54			11 58	12 01
East Croydon 🚊	a	10 56	11 06		11 30					11 21		11 33	11 37			11 27		11 36		12 01			11 54		

Table 177

Sundays

Luton, Milton Keynes Central and London East and West Croydon via Tulse Hill - Crystal Palace - Norbury

Local Services

Network Diagram - see first Page of Table 177

		SN ◇1	SN	SN	SN	SN	SN	FC 1		SN ◇1 🚲	SN	SN	SN	FC	LO	SN	SN ◇1 🚲	SN	SN	SN	SN	SN	FC 1	SN ◇1	
London Bridge 4 ⊖	d		11 36		11 39		11 41	11 42				11 51	11 54	12 02				12 06		12 09		12 11	12 12		
South Bermondsey	d		11 40				11 45					11 55						12 10				12 15			
Queens Rd Peckham	d		11 42				11 48					11 57						12 12				12 18			
Peckham Rye 4	d		11 45				11 50					12 00						12 15				12 20			
East Dulwich	d		11 48									12 03						12 18							
North Dulwich	d		11 50									12 05						12 20							
Luton 10	d																								
Luton Airport Parkway 7	d																								
St Pancras International 15 ⊖	d																								
City Thameslink 3	d																								
London Blackfriars 3 ⊖	d																								
Elephant & Castle ⊖	d																								
Loughborough Jn.	d																								
Herne Hill 4	d																								
Tulse Hill 3	d		11 54									12 09		12 13				12 24							
Streatham 4	d											12 12		12a16											
London Victoria 15 ⊖	d	11 32		11 36		11 41				11 47	11 49					11 54	12 02		12 06		12 11			12 17	
Battersea Park 4	d					11a45	12a02									11 58					12a15	12a32			
Milton Keynes Central	d																								
Watford Junction	d																								
Harrow & Wealdstone ⊖	d																								
Wembley Central ⊖	d																								
Shepherd's Bush ⊖	d																								
Kensington (Olympia) ⊖	d																								
West Brompton ⊖	d																								
Imperial Wharf	d																								
Clapham Junction 10	d	11 38		11 42						11 53	11 56					12 02	12 08		12 12					12 23	
Wandsworth Common	d															12 05									
Balham 4 ⊖	d			11 47							12 00					12 07			12 17						
Streatham Hill	d															12 11									
West Norwood 4	d		11 57													12 16		12 27							
Gipsy Hill	d		12 00													12 19		12 30							
Crystal Palace 4	d		12a02													12 21		12a32							
Birkbeck 🚊	d																								
Beckenham Junction 4 🚊	a																								
Streatham Common 4	d			11 51							12 04	12 18							12 21						
Norbury	d			11 54							12 07	12 21							12 24						
Thornton Heath	d			11 57							12 10	12 24							12 27						
Selhurst 4	d			12 00							12 13	12 27							12 30						
Norwood Junction 2	a				12 02								12 14			12 26				12 32					
	d				12 03								12 16		12 22	12 27				12 33					
West Croydon 4 🚊	a										12 18		12 24		12 28	12 31									
East Croydon 🚊	a	11 50		12 03	12 07			11 56		12 06		12 30					12 21		12 33	12 37			12 27	12 36	

Table 177

Sundays

Luton, Milton Keynes Central and London East and West Croydon via Tulse Hill - Crystal Palace - Norbury

Local Services

Network Diagram - see first Page of Table 177

		LO	SN	SN	SN	FC	SN 1	LO	SN	SN ◇1	SN	SN	SN	SN	SN	FC 1		SN ◇1 ⚲	LO	SN	SN	SN	FC		
London Bridge 4 ⊖	d			12 21	12 24	12 32	12 37				12 36		12 39		12 41	12 42					12 51	12 54	13 02		
South Bermondsey	d			12 25							12 40				12 45						12 55				
Queens Rd Peckham	d			12 27							12 42				12 48						12 57				
Peckham Rye 4	d			12 30							12 45				12 50						13 00				
East Dulwich	d			12 33							12 48										13 03				
North Dulwich	d			12 35							12 50										13 05				
Luton 10	d																								
Luton Airport Parkway 7	d																								
St Pancras International 15 ⊖	d																								
City Thameslink 3	d																								
London Blackfriars 3 ⊖	d																								
Elephant & Castle ⊖	d																								
Loughborough Jn.	d																								
Herne Hill 4	d																								
Tulse Hill 3	d			12 39		12 43					12 54										13 09		13 13		
Streatham 4	d			12 42		12a46															13 12		13a16		
London Victoria 15 ⊖	d		12 19						12 24	12 32		12 36		12 41				12 47		12 49					
Battersea Park 4	d								12 28					12a45	13a02										
Milton Keynes Central	d																								
Watford Junction	d																								
Harrow & Wealdstone ⊖	d																								
Wembley Central ⊖	d																								
Shepherd's Bush ⊖	d																								
Kensington (Olympia) ⊖	d																								
West Brompton ⊖	d																								
Imperial Wharf	d																								
Clapham Junction 10	d		12 26						12 32	12 38		12 42						12 53		12 56					
Wandsworth Common	d								12 35																
Balham 4 ⊖	d		12 30						12 37			12 47								13 00					
Streatham Hill	d								12 41																
West Norwood 4	d								12 46		12 57														
Gipsy Hill	d								12 49		13 00														
Crystal Palace 4	d								12 51		13a02														
Birkbeck 🚋	d																								
Beckenham Junction 4 🚋	a																								
Streatham Common 4	d		12 34	12 48								12 51								13 04	13 18				
Norbury	d		12 37	12 51								12 54								13 07	13 21				
Thornton Heath	d		12 40	12 54								12 57								13 10	13 24				
Selhurst 4	d		12 43	12 57								13 00								13 13	13 27				
Norwood Junction 2	a				12 44		12 47		12 56				13 02									13 14			
	d	12 38			12 46		12 48	12 53	12 57				13 03						13 08			13 16			
West Croydon 4 🚋	a	12 45	12 48		12 54			12 59	13 01										13 15	13 18		13 24			
East Croydon 🚋	a			13 01			12 54			12 50		13 03	13 07			12 56		13 06			13 30				

Table 177

Sundays

Luton, Milton Keynes Central and London East and West Croydon via Tulse Hill - Crystal Palace - Norbury

Local Services

Network Diagram - see first Page of Table 177

Station		LO		LO	SN	SN ◇1	SN	SN	SN		SN	SN	FC 1	SN ◇1	LO	SN	SN	SN	FC	SN 1	LO	SN	SN ◇1	SN
London Bridge 4 ⊖	d						17 06		17 09			17 11	17 12				17 21	17 24	17 32	17 37				17 36
South Bermondsey	d						17 10					17 15					17 25							17 40
Queens Rd Peckham	d						17 12					17 18					17 27							17 42
Peckham Rye 4	d						17 15					17 20					17 30							17 45
East Dulwich	d						17 18										17 33							17 48
North Dulwich	d						17 20										17 35							17 50
Luton 10	d																							
Luton Airport Parkway 7	d																							
St Pancras International 15 ⊖	d																							
City Thameslink 3	d																							
London Blackfriars 3 ⊖	d																							
Elephant & Castle ⊖	d																							
Loughborough Jn.	d																							
Herne Hill 4	d																							
Tulse Hill 3	d						17 24										17 39		17 43					17 54
Streatham 4	d																17 42		17a46					
London Victoria 15 ⊖	d		and at the same minutes past each hour until		16 54	17 02		17 06			17 11			17 17		17 19						17 24	17 32	
Battersea Park 4	d				16 58						17a15	17a32										17 28		
Milton Keynes Central	d																							
Watford Junction	d																							
Harrow & Wealdstone ⊖	d																							
Wembley Central ⊖	d																							
Shepherd's Bush ⊖	d																							
Kensington (Olympia) ⊖	d																							
West Brompton ⊖	d																							
Imperial Wharf	d																							
Clapham Junction 10	d				17 02	17 08		17 12						17 23		17 26						17 32	17 38	
Wandsworth Common	d				17 05																	17 35		
Balham 4 ⊖	d				17 07			17 17								17 30						17 37		
Streatham Hill	d				17 11																	17 41		
West Norwood 4	d				17 16		17 27															17 46		17 57
Gipsy Hill	d				17 19		17 30															17 49		18 00
Crystal Palace 4	d				17 21		17a32															17 51		18a02
Birkbeck 🚊	d																							
Beckenham Junction 4 🚊	a																							
Streatham Common 4	d							17 21								17 34	17 48							
Norbury	d							17 24								17 37	17 51							
Thornton Heath	d							17 27								17 40	17 54							
Selhurst 4	d							17 30								17 43	17 57							
Norwood Junction 2	a				17 26				17 32									17 44		17 47		17 56		
	d	13 23		17 23	17 27				17 33						17 38			17 46		17 48	17 53	17 57		
West Croydon 4 🚊	a	13 29		17 29	17 31										17 45	17 48		17 54			17 59	18 01		
East Croydon 🚊	a					17 21		17 33	17 37				17 27	17 36			18 01			17 54			17 50	

Table 177

Sundays

Luton, Milton Keynes Central and London East and West Croydon via Tulse Hill - Crystal Palace - Norbury

Local Services — Network Diagram - see first Page of Table 177

		SN		SN	SN	SN	FC	SN	LO	SN	SN	SN	FC	LO	SN	SN	SN	SN		SN	SN	SN	FC	SN	LO
							1	◇1 🚲								◇1 🚲							1	◇1	
London Bridge 4 ⊖	d			17 39		17 41	17 42				17 51	17 54	18 02				18 06			18 09		18 11	18 12		
South Bermondsey	d					17 45					17 55						18 10					18 15			
Queens Rd Peckham	d					17 48					17 57						18 12					18 18			
Peckham Rye 4	d					17 50					18 00						18 15					18 20			
East Dulwich	d										18 03						18 18								
North Dulwich	d										18 05						18 20								
Luton 10	d																								
Luton Airport Parkway 7	d																								
St Pancras International 15 ⊖	d																								
City Thameslink 3	d																								
London Blackfriars 3 ⊖	d																								
Elephant & Castle ⊖	d																								
Loughborough Jn.	d																								
Herne Hill 4	d																								
Tulse Hill 3	d										18 09		18 13				18 24								
Streatham 4	d										18 12		18a16												
London Victoria 15 ⊖	d	17 36			17 41			17 47		17 49					17 54	18 02		18 06			18 11			18 17	
Battersea Park 4	d				17a45	18a02									17 58						18a15	18a32			
Milton Keynes Central	d																								
Watford Junction	d																								
Harrow & Wealdstone ⊖	d																								
Wembley Central ⊖	d																								
Shepherd's Bush ⊖	d																								
Kensington (Olympia) ⊖	d																								
West Brompton ⊖	d																								
Imperial Wharf	d																								
Clapham Junction 10	d	17 42						17 53		17 56					18 02	18 08		18 12						18 23	
Wandsworth Common	d														18 05										
Balham 4 ⊖	d	17 47								18 00					18 07			18 17							
Streatham Hill	d														18 11										
West Norwood 4	d														18 16		18 27								
Gipsy Hill	d														18 19		18 30								
Crystal Palace 4	d														18 21		18a32								
Birkbeck 🚋	d																								
Beckenham Junction 4 🚋	a																								
Streatham Common 4	d	17 51								18 04	18 18							18 21							
Norbury	d	17 54								18 07	18 21							18 24							
Thornton Heath	d	17 57								18 10	18 24							18 27							
Selhurst 4	d	18 00								18 13	18 27							18 30							
Norwood Junction 2	a			18 02								18 14			18 26					18 32					
	d			18 03					18 08			18 16		18 23	18 27					18 33					18 38
West Croydon 4 🚋	a								18 14	18 18		18 24		18 29	18 31										18 44
East Croydon 🚋	a	18 03		18 07			17 56	18 06			18 30					18 21		18 33		18 37			18 27	18 36	

Table 177

Sundays

Luton, Milton Keynes Central and London East and West Croydon via Tulse Hill - Crystal Palace - Norbury

Local Services

Network Diagram - see first Page of Table 177

		SN	SN	SN	FC	SN	LO	SN	SN	SN		SN	SN	SN	SN	FC	SN	LO	SN	SN	SN	FC	LO	SN	SN
						1			◇1							1	◇1 🚲								◇1 🚲
London Bridge 4 ⊖	d		18 21	18 24	18 32	18 37				18 36			18 39		18 41	18 42				18 51	18 54	19 02			
South Bermondsey	d		18 25							18 40					18 45					18 55					
Queens Rd Peckham	d		18 27							18 42					18 48					18 57					
Peckham Rye 4	d		18 30							18 45					18 50					19 00					
East Dulwich	d		18 33							18 48										19 03					
North Dulwich	d		18 35							18 50										19 05					
Luton 10	d																								
Luton Airport Parkway 7	d																								
St Pancras International 15 ⊖	d																								
City Thameslink 3	d																								
London Blackfriars 3 ⊖	d																								
Elephant & Castle ⊖	d																								
Loughborough Jn.	d																								
Herne Hill 4	d																								
Tulse Hill 3	d		18 39		18 43					18 54										19 09		19 13			
Streatham 4	d		18 42		18a46															19 12		19a16			
London Victoria 15 ⊖	d	18 19						18 24	18 32			18 36		18 41			18 47		18 49					18 54	19 02
Battersea Park 4	d							18 28						18a45	19a02									18 58	
Milton Keynes Central	d																								
Watford Junction	d																								
Harrow & Wealdstone ⊖	d																								
Wembley Central ⊖	d																								
Shepherd's Bush ⊖	d																								
Kensington (Olympia) ⊖	d																								
West Brompton ⊖	d																								
Imperial Wharf	d																								
Clapham Junction 10	d	18 26						18 32	18 38			18 42					18 53		18 56					19 02	19 08
Wandsworth Common	d							18 35																19 05	
Balham 4 ⊖	d	18 30						18 37				18 47							19 00					19 07	
Streatham Hill	d							18 41																19 11	
West Norwood 4	d							18 46		18 57														19 16	
Gipsy Hill	d							18 49		19 00														19 19	
Crystal Palace 4	d							18 51		19a02														19 21	
Birkbeck 🚊	d																								
Beckenham Junction 4 🚊	a																								
Streatham Common 4	d	18 34	18 48									18 51							19 04	19 18					
Norbury	d	18 37	18 51									18 54							19 07	19 21					
Thornton Heath	d	18 40	18 54									18 57							19 10	19 24					
Selhurst 4	d	18 43	18 57									19 00							19 13	19 27					
Norwood Junction 2	a			18 44		18 47		18 56					19 02								19 14			19 26	
	d			18 46		18 48	18 53	18 57					19 03					19 08			19 16		19 23	19 27	
West Croydon 4 🚊	a	18 48		18 54			18 59	19 01										19 14	19 18		19 24		19 29	19 31	
East Croydon 🚊	a		19 01			18 54			18 50			19 03	19 07			18 56	19 06			19 30					19 21

		SN		SN	SN	SN	SN	FC	SN	LO	SN	SN	SN	FC	SN	LO	SN	SN		SN	SN	SN	SN	SN	FC
								1	◇1						1			◇1							1
London Bridge 4 ⊖	d	19 06			19 09		19 11	19 12				19 21	19 24	19 32	19 37					19 36		19 39		19 41	19 42
South Bermondsey	d	19 10					19 15					19 25								19 40				19 45	
Queens Rd Peckham	d	19 12					19 18					19 27								19 42				19 48	
Peckham Rye 4	d	19 15					19 20					19 30								19 45				19 50	
East Dulwich	d	19 18										19 33								19 48					
North Dulwich	d	19 20										19 35								19 50					
Luton 10	d																								
Luton Airport Parkway 7	d																								
St Pancras International 15 ⊖	d																								
City Thameslink 3	d																								
London Blackfriars 3 ⊖	d																								
Elephant & Castle ⊖	d																								
Loughborough Jn.	d																								
Herne Hill 4	d																								
Tulse Hill 3	d	19 24										19 39		19 43						19 54					
Streatham 4	d											19 42		19a46											
London Victoria 15 ⊖	d			19 06		19 11			19 17		19 19						19 24	19 32			19 36		19 41		
Battersea Park 4	d					19a15	19a32										19 28						19a45	20a02	
Milton Keynes Central	d																								
Watford Junction	d																								
Harrow & Wealdstone ⊖	d																								
Wembley Central ⊖	d																								
Shepherd's Bush ⊖	d																								
Kensington (Olympia) ⊖	d																								
West Brompton ⊖	d																								
Imperial Wharf	d																								
Clapham Junction 10	d			19 12					19 23		19 26						19 32	19 38			19 42				
Wandsworth Common	d																19 35								
Balham 4 ⊖	d			19 17							19 30						19 37				19 47				
Streatham Hill	d																19 41								
West Norwood 4	d	19 27															19 46			19 57					
Gipsy Hill	d	19 30															19 49			20 00					
Crystal Palace 4	d	19a32															19 51			20a02					
Birkbeck 🚊	d																								
Beckenham Junction 4 🚊	a																								
Streatham Common 4	d			19 21							19 34	19 48									19 51				
Norbury	d			19 24							19 37	19 51									19 54				
Thornton Heath	d			19 27							19 40	19 54									19 57				
Selhurst 4	d			19 30							19 43	19 57									20 00				
Norwood Junction 2	a				19 32								19 44		19 47		19 56					20 02			
	d				19 33					19 38			19 46		19 48	19 53	19 57					20 03			
West Croydon 4 🚊	a									19 44	19 48		19 54			19 59	20 01								
East Croydon 🚊	a			19 33	19 37			19 27	19 36			20 01			19 54			19 50			20 03	20 07			19 56

Table 177

Sundays

Luton, Milton Keynes Central and London East and West Croydon via Tulse Hill - Crystal Palace - Norbury

Local Services

Network Diagram - see first Page of Table 177

		SN	LO	SN	SN	SN	FC	LO	SN	SN		SN	SN	SN	SN	SN	FC	SN	LO	SN	SN	SN	FC	SN	LO
		◇1								◇1							1	◇1						1	
London Bridge 4	⊖ d				19 51	19 54	20 02					20 06		20 09		20 11	20 12				20 21	20 24	20 32	20 37	
South Bermondsey	d				19 55							20 10				20 15					20 25				
Queens Rd Peckham	d				19 57							20 12				20 18					20 27				
Peckham Rye 4	d				20 00							20 15				20 20					20 30				
East Dulwich	d				20 03							20 18									20 33				
North Dulwich	d				20 05							20 20									20 35				
Luton 10	d																								
Luton Airport Parkway 7	d																								
St Pancras International 15	⊖ d																								
City Thameslink 3	d																								
London Blackfriars 3	⊖ d																								
Elephant & Castle	⊖ d																								
Loughborough Jn.	d																								
Herne Hill 4	d																								
Tulse Hill 3	d				20 09		20 13					20 24									20 39		20 43		
Streatham 4	d				20 12		20a16														20 42		20a46		
London Victoria 15	⊖ d	19 47		19 49					19 54	20 02			20 06		20 11			20 17		20 19					
Battersea Park 4	d								19 58						20a15	20a32									
Milton Keynes Central	d																								
Watford Junction	d																								
Harrow & Wealdstone	⊖ d																								
Wembley Central	⊖ d																								
Shepherd's Bush	⊖ d																								
Kensington (Olympia)	⊖ d																								
West Brompton	⊖ d																								
Imperial Wharf	d																								
Clapham Junction 10	d	19 53		19 56					20 02	20 08			20 12					20 23		20 26					
Wandsworth Common	d								20 05																
Balham 4	⊖ d			20 00					20 07				20 17							20 30					
Streatham Hill	d								20 11																
West Norwood 4	d								20 16			20 27													
Gipsy Hill	d								20 19			20 30													
Crystal Palace 4	d								20 21			20a32													
Birkbeck	🚋 d																								
Beckenham Junction 4	🚋 a																								
Streatham Common 4	d			20 04	20 18								20 21							20 34	20 48				
Norbury	d			20 07	20 21								20 24							20 37	20 51				
Thornton Heath	d			20 10	20 24								20 27							20 40	20 54				
Selhurst 4	d			20 13	20 27								20 30							20 43	20 57				
Norwood Junction 2	a					20 14			20 26					20 32								20 44		20 47	
	d		20 08			20 16		20 23	20 27					20 33					20 38			20 46		20 48	20 53
West Croydon 4	🚋 a		20 15	20 18		20 24		20 29	20 31										20 45	20 48		20 54			20 59
East Croydon	🚋 a	20 06			20 30					20 21			20 33	20 37			20 27	20 36			21 01			20 54	

		SN		SN	SN	SN	SN	SN	SN	FC	SN	LO	SN	SN	SN	FC	LO	SN		SN	SN	SN	SN	SN	SN
				◇1						1	◇1									◇1					
London Bridge 4	⊖ d				20 36		20 39		20 41	20 42				20 51	20 54	21 02					21 06		21 09		21 11
South Bermondsey	d				20 40				20 45					20 55							21 10				21 15
Queens Rd Peckham	d				20 42				20 48					20 57							21 12				21 18
Peckham Rye 4	d				20 45				20 50					21 00							21 15				21 20
East Dulwich	d				20 48									21 03							21 18				
North Dulwich	d				20 50									21 05							21 20				
Luton 10	d																								
Luton Airport Parkway 7	d																								
St Pancras International 15	⊖ d																								
City Thameslink 3	d																								
London Blackfriars 3	⊖ d																								
Elephant & Castle	⊖ d																								
Loughborough Jn.	d																								
Herne Hill 4	d																								
Tulse Hill 3	d				20 54									21 09		21 13					21 24				
Streatham 4	d													21 12		21a16									
London Victoria 15	⊖ d	20 24		20 32		20 36		20 41			20 47		20 49					20 54		21 02		21 06		21 11	
Battersea Park 4	d	20 28						20a45	21a02									20 58						21a15	21a32
Milton Keynes Central	d																								
Watford Junction	d																								
Harrow & Wealdstone	⊖ d																								
Wembley Central	⊖ d																								
Shepherd's Bush	⊖ d																								
Kensington (Olympia)	⊖ d																								
West Brompton	⊖ d																								
Imperial Wharf	d																								
Clapham Junction 10	d	20 32		20 38		20 42					20 53		20 56					21 02		21 08		21 12			
Wandsworth Common	d	20 35																21 05							
Balham 4	⊖ d	20 37				20 47							21 00					21 07				21 17			
Streatham Hill	d	20 41																21 11							
West Norwood 4	d	20 46			20 57													21 16			21 27				
Gipsy Hill	d	20 49			21 00													21 19			21 30				
Crystal Palace 4	d	20 51			21a02													21 21			21a32				
Birkbeck	🚋 d																								
Beckenham Junction 4	🚋 a																								
Streatham Common 4	d					20 51							21 04	21 18								21 21			
Norbury	d					20 54							21 07	21 21								21 24			
Thornton Heath	d					20 57							21 10	21 24								21 27			
Selhurst 4	d					21 00							21 13	21 27								21 30			
Norwood Junction 2	a	20 56					21 02								21 14			21 26					21 32		
	d	20 57					21 03					21 08			21 16		21 23	21 27					21 33		
West Croydon 4	🚋 a	21 01										21 15	21 18		21 24		21 29	21 31							
East Croydon	🚋 a			20 50		21 03	21 07			20 56	21 06			21 30						21 21		21 33	21 37		

Table 177

Sundays

Luton, Milton Keynes Central and London East and West Croydon via Tulse Hill - Crystal Palace - Norbury

Local Services

Network Diagram - see first Page of Table 177

		FC 1	SN ◇1	LO	SN	SN	SN	SN 1	LO	SN		SN ◇1	SN	SN	SN	SN	SN	FC 1	SN ◇1	LO	SN	SN	SN	LO	SN
London Bridge 4 ⊖	d	21 12				21 21	21 24	21 37					21 36		21 39		21 41	21 42				21 51	21 54		
South Bermondsey	d					21 25							21 40				21 45					21 55			
Queens Rd Peckham	d					21 27							21 42				21 48					21 57			
Peckham Rye 4	d					21 30							21 45				21 50					22 00			
East Dulwich	d					21 33							21 48									22 03			
North Dulwich	d					21 35							21 50									22 05			
Luton 10	d																								
Luton Airport Parkway 7	d																								
St Pancras International 15 ⊖	d																								
City Thameslink 3	d																								
London Blackfriars 3 ⊖	d																								
Elephant & Castle ⊖	d																								
Loughborough Jn.	d																								
Herne Hill 4	d																								
Tulse Hill 3	d					21 39							21 54									22 09			
Streatham 4	d					21 42																22 12			
London Victoria 15 ⊖	d		21 17		21 19					21 24		21 32		21 36		21 41			21 47		21 49				21 54
Battersea Park 4	d									21 28						21a45	22a02								21 58
Milton Keynes Central	d																								
Watford Junction	d																								
Harrow & Wealdstone ⊖	d																								
Wembley Central ⊖	d																								
Shepherd's Bush ⊖	d																								
Kensington (Olympia) ⊖	d																								
West Brompton ⊖	d																								
Imperial Wharf	d																								
Clapham Junction 10	d		21 23		21 26					21 32		21 38		21 42					21 53		21 56				22 02
Wandsworth Common	d									21 35															22 05
Balham 4 ⊖	d				21 30					21 38				21 47							22 00				22 07
Streatham Hill	d									21 41															22 11
West Norwood 4	d									21 46			21 57												22 16
Gipsy Hill	d									21 49			22 00												22 19
Crystal Palace 4	d									21 51			22a02												22 21
Birkbeck 🚊	d																								
Beckenham Junction 4 🚊	a																								
Streatham Common 4	d				21 34	21 48								21 51							22 04	22 18			
Norbury	d				21 37	21 51								21 54							22 07	22 21			
Thornton Heath	d				21 40	21 54								21 57							22 10	22 24			
Selhurst 4	d				21 43	21 57								22 00							22 13	22 27			
Norwood Junction 2	a						21 44	21 47		21 56					22 02								22 14		22 26
	d			21 38			21 46	21 48	21 53	21 57					22 03					22 08			22 16	22 23	22 27
West Croydon 4 🚊	a			21 45	21 48		21 54		21 59	22 01										22 15	22 18		22 24	22 29	22 31
East Croydon 🚊	a	21 27	21 36			22 01		21 54				21 50		22 03	22 07			21 56	22 06			22 30			

		SN		SN	SN	SN	SN	FC 1	SN ◇1	LO	SN	SN	SN 1	SN	SN ◇1	SN	SN	SN		SN ◇1	SN	LO	SN	SN	SN
London Bridge 4 ⊖	d	22 06			22 09		22 11	22 12				22 21	22 37			22 36					22 39				22 41
South Bermondsey	d	22 10					22 15					22 25				22 40									22 45
Queens Rd Peckham	d	22 12					22 18					22 27				22 42									22 48
Peckham Rye 4	d	22 15					22 20					22 30				22 45									22 50
East Dulwich	d	22 18										22 33				22 48									
North Dulwich	d	22 20										22 35				22 50									
Luton 10	d																								
Luton Airport Parkway 7	d																								
St Pancras International 15 ⊖	d																								
City Thameslink 3	d																								
London Blackfriars 3 ⊖	d																								
Elephant & Castle ⊖	d																								
Loughborough Jn.	d																								
Herne Hill 4	d																								
Tulse Hill 3	d	22 24										22 39				22 54									
Streatham 4	d											22 42													
London Victoria 15 ⊖	d			22 06		22 11			22 17		22 19			22 24	22 32		22 36	22 41		22 47			22 49	22 54	
Battersea Park 4	d					22a15	22a32							22 28				22a45						22 58	23a02
Milton Keynes Central	d																								
Watford Junction	d																								
Harrow & Wealdstone ⊖	d																								
Wembley Central ⊖	d																								
Shepherd's Bush ⊖	d																								
Kensington (Olympia) ⊖	d																								
West Brompton ⊖	d																								
Imperial Wharf	d																								
Clapham Junction 10	d			22 12					22 23		22 26			22 32	22 38		22 42			22 53			22 56	23 02	
Wandsworth Common	d													22 35										23 05	
Balham 4 ⊖	d			22 17							22 30			22 38			22 47						23 00	23 07	
Streatham Hill	d													22 41										23 11	
West Norwood 4	d	22 27												22 46		22 57								23 16	
Gipsy Hill	d	22 30												22 49		23 00								23 19	
Crystal Palace 4	d	22a32												22 51		23a02								23 21	
Birkbeck 🚊	d																								
Beckenham Junction 4 🚊	a																								
Streatham Common 4	d			22 21							22 34	22 48					22 51						23 04		
Norbury	d			22 24							22 37	22 51					22 54						23 07		
Thornton Heath	d			22 27							22 40	22 54					22 57						23 10		
Selhurst 4	d			22 30							22 43	22 57					23 00						23 13		
Norwood Junction 2	a				22 32								22 47	22 56							23 02			23 26	
	d				22 33					22 38			22 48	22 57							23 03	23 08		23 27	
West Croydon 4 🚊	a									22 45	22 48			23 01								23 14	23 18	23 31	
East Croydon 🚊	a			22 33	22 37			22 27	22 36			23 00	22 54		22 50		23 03			23 06	23 07				

Table 177

Sundays

Luton, Milton Keynes Central and London East and West Croydon via Tulse Hill - Crystal Palace - Norbury

Local Services

Network Diagram - see first Page of Table 177

		FC [1]	SN [1]	SN	SN	SN	SN	SN ◇[1]	SN	LO		SN	SN	SN	FC [1]	SN ◇[1]	SN	SN	SN	FC [1]	SN	SN	SN [1]	SN	
London Bridge [4] ⊖	d	22 42		22 51	23 06				23 09					23 11	23 12		23 21		23 39	23 42					
South Bermondsey	d			22 55	23 10									23 15			23 25								
Queens Rd Peckham	d			22 57	23 12									23 18			23 27								
Peckham Rye [4]	d			23 00	23 15									23 20			23 30								
East Dulwich	d			23 03	23 18												23 33								
North Dulwich	d			23 05	23 20												23 35								
Luton [10]	d																								
Luton Airport Parkway [7]	d																								
St Pancras International [15] ⊖	d																								
City Thameslink [3]	d																								
London Blackfriars [3] ⊖	d																								
Elephant & Castle ⊖	d																								
Loughborough Jn	d																								
Herne Hill [4]	d																								
Tulse Hill [3]	d			23 09	23 24												23 39								
Streatham [4]	d			23 12													23 42								
London Victoria [15] ⊖	d		23 04			23 06	23 11	23 17				23 19	23 24			23 32		23 36			23 47	23 50		23 54	
Battersea Park [4]	d						23a15					23 23	23 28	23a32				23 40						23 58	
Milton Keynes Central	d																								
Watford Junction	d																						23 17		
Harrow & Wealdstone ⊖	d																						23 23		
Wembley Central ⊖	d																								
Shepherd's Bush ⊖	d																						23 45		
Kensington (Olympia) ⊖	d																						23 48		
West Brompton ⊖	d																						23 50		
Imperial Wharf	d																						23 53		
Clapham Junction [10]	d		23 10			23 12		23 23				23 27	23 32			23 38		23 44			23 53	23 56	00b05	00 02	
Wandsworth Common	d											23 30	23 35					23 47				23 59		00 05	
Balham [4] ⊖	d					23 17						23 32	23 37					23 49				00 02		00 07	
Streatham Hill	d												23 41											00 11	
West Norwood [4]	d				23 27								23 44											00 14	
Gipsy Hill	d				23 30								23 47											00 17	
Crystal Palace [4]	d				23a32								23 50											00 20	
Birkbeck 🚊	d																								
Beckenham Junction [4] 🚊	a																								
Streatham Common [4]	d			23 18		23 21						23 36					23 48	23 53				00 06			
Norbury	d			23 21		23 24						23 39					23 51	23 56				00 08			
Thornton Heath	d			23 24		23 27						23 42					23 54	23 59				00 11			
Selhurst [4]	d			23 27		23 30						23 45				23 48	23 57	00a01				00 14	00 19		
Norwood Junction [2]	a								23 32				23 54						00 02					00 25	
	d								23 33	23 38			23 55						00 03						
West Croydon [4] 🚊	a									23 44		23 49	23 59												
East Croydon 🚊	a	22 56	23 22	23 30		23 34		23 37	23 38						23 27	23 52	00 01		00 06	23 56	00 06	00 17	00 22		

b Arr. 2358

East and West Croydon, London
Milton Keynes Central and Luton via Norbury
Crystal Palace - Tulse Hill

Local Services Network Diagram - see first Page of Table 177

Miles	Miles	Miles	Miles	Miles			SN MO	SN MO	SN MX	SN MX	SN MO	SN MO [1]	SN MX [1]	SN MX	SN MX	SN	SN [1]	FC [1]	SN [1]	FC [1]	SN [1]		FC [1]	SN [1]	FC
0	—	—	0	0	**East Croydon** 🚊	d						23p56	23p58			00 49	01 28	01 49	02 28	02 47	03 28		03 47	04 32	04 47
—	0	—	—	—	**West Croydon** [4] 🚊	d	23p37				23p52														
1¼	—	—	—	1¾	Norwood Junction [2]	a																			
—	—	—	—	—		d																			
—	1	—	1	—	Selhurst [4]	d	23p41				23p56	00 01	00 02					01 52		02 50			03 50		04 50
—	1¾	—	1¾	—	Thornton Heath	d	23p43				23p58														
—	3	—	3	—	Norbury	d	23p46				00 01														
—	4	—	4	—	Streatham Common [4]	d	23p49				00 04														
—	—	0	—	—	Beckenham Junction [4] 🚊	d																			
—	—	1½	—	—	Birkbeck 🚊	d																			
2¾	—	3	—	2¾	**Crystal Palace** [4]	d		23p37	23p43	23p51				00 13	00 21										
3½	—	3¾	—	3½	Gipsy Hill	d		23p39	23p45					00 15											
4½	—	4¾	—	4½	West Norwood [4]	d		23p42	23p48					00 18											
5¾	—	6	—	—	Streatham Hill	d			23p52					00 22											
6¾	—	7	5¾	—	Balham [4] ⊖	d	23p53		23p55		00 08			00 25											
7½	—	7¾	6½	—	Wandsworth Common	d			23p58					00 27											
8¾	—	9	7¾	—	Clapham Junction [10]	d	23p58		00 02		00 12	00 12	00 12	00 31		01 01	01 41		02 41		03 41			04 51	
—	—	—	—	—	Imperial Wharf	d																			
—	—	—	—	—	West Brompton ⊖	d																			
—	—	—	—	—	Kensington (Olympia) ⊖	d																			
—	—	—	—	—	Shepherd's Bush ⊖	d																			
—	—	—	—	—	Wembley Central ⊖	d																			
—	—	—	—	—	Harrow & Wealdstone ⊖	d																			
—	—	—	—	—	Watford Junction	d																			
—	—	—	—	—	Milton Keynes Central [10]	a																			
10¼	—	10½	9¼	—	Battersea Park [4]	d			00 05					00 35											
11½	—	11¾	10¼	—	**London Victoria** [15] ⊖	a	00 04		00 10		00 19	00 19	00 18	00 42		01 09	01 49		02 49		03 49			04 58	
—	4½	—	—	—	Streatham [4]	d																			
—	6	—	—	5	Tulse Hill [3]	d		23p46																	
—	—	—	—	—	Herne Hill [4]	a																			
—	—	—	—	—	Loughborough Jn	a																			
—	—	—	—	—	Elephant & Castle ⊖	a																			
—	—	—	—	—	London Blackfriars [3] ⊖	a																			05 13
—	—	—	—	—	City Thameslink [3]	a																			05 16
—	—	—	—	—	St Pancras International [15] ⊖	a																			05 24
—	—	—	—	—	Luton Airport Parkway [7]	a																			06 09
—	—	—	—	—	**Luton** [10]	a																			06 12
—	7¼	—	—	6¼	North Dulwich	d		23p49																	
—	7¾	—	—	6¾	East Dulwich	d		23p51																	
—	8½	—	—	7½	Peckham Rye [4]	d		23p53																	
—	9¼	—	—	8¼	Queens Rd Peckham	d		23p56																	
—	10¼	—	—	9¼	South Bermondsey	d		23p58																	
—	12	—	—	11	**London Bridge** [4] ⊖	a		00 03		00 11					00 41			02 14		03 12			04 12		

		SN	SN	FC [1]	SN	FC	LO	SN	FC [1]	SN	SN	LO	FC		SN	SN [1]	LO	SN	SN ◇[1]	SN	SN	SN	SN [1]	SN [1]	FC
East Croydon 🚊	d		05 13	05 17	05 33				05 47	05 48	05 51					06 06		06 13	06 15			06 17	06 23	06 31	
West Croydon [4] 🚊	d						05 39	05 45				05 52			06 01		06 09			06 15					
Norwood Junction [2]	a		05 17		05 37		05 43	05 50			05 55	05 58					06 13	06 17		06 19					
	d		05 17		05 37			05 50			05 55							06 18		06 20					
Selhurst [4]	d					05 36				05 52			05 56		06 06	06 09						06 20			
Thornton Heath	d					05 38				05 54			05 58		06 08							06 22			
Norbury	d					05 40				05 57			06 00		06 11							06 25			
Streatham Common [4]	d					05 43				05 59			06 03		06 13							06 27			
Beckenham Junction [4] 🚊	d																								
Birkbeck 🚊	d																								
Crystal Palace [4]	d				05 41						05 59														
Gipsy Hill	d				05 43						06 01														
West Norwood [4]	d				05 46						06 04														
Streatham Hill	d				05 50																				
Balham [4] ⊖	d				05 53					06 03					06 17							06 31			
Wandsworth Common	d									06 05					06 19							06 33			
Clapham Junction [10]	d	05 02			05 57					06 09					06 23	06 18			06 25			06 37		06 41	
Imperial Wharf	d																								
West Brompton ⊖	d																								
Kensington (Olympia) ⊖	d																								
Shepherd's Bush ⊖	d																								
Wembley Central ⊖	d																								
Harrow & Wealdstone ⊖	d																								
Watford Junction	d																								
Milton Keynes Central [10]	a																								
Battersea Park [4]	d	05 05			06 01					06 13					06 27						06 32	06 41			
London Victoria [15] ⊖	a	05 10			06 06					06 18					06 31	06 25			06 32		06 36	06 48		06 48	
Streatham [4]	d					05 46							06 06												06 38
Tulse Hill [3]	d					05 50					06 08		06 10												06 42
Herne Hill [4]	a					05 54							06 14												06 46
Loughborough Jn	a												06 19												06 49
Elephant & Castle ⊖	a					06 00							06 23												06 53
London Blackfriars [3] ⊖	a			05 41		06 03			06 10				06 27												06 57
City Thameslink [3]	a			05 44		06 06			06 14				06 32												07 00
St Pancras International [15] ⊖	a			05 52		06 14			06 22				06 40												07 08
Luton Airport Parkway [7]	a			06 35		07 00			06 55				07 23												07 49
Luton [10]	a			06 38		07 03			06 58				07 26												07 53
North Dulwich	d										06 11														
East Dulwich	d										06 13														
Peckham Rye [4]	d										06 15														
Queens Rd Peckham	d										06 18														
South Bermondsey	d										06 20														
London Bridge [4] ⊖	a		05 41					06 14			06 25							06 44		06 33			06 39		

East and West Croydon, London Milton Keynes Central and Luton via Norbury Crystal Palace - Tulse Hill

Local Services

Network Diagram - see first Page of Table 177

		SN	SN	LO	SN		SN	SN	SN ■1	SN	SN	SN	LO	SN	SN	SN	SN	SN	SN ■1	SN	SN ■1		SN	SN	LO
East Croydon 🚊	d						06 31	06 36	06 42								06 57	06 45	06 59		07 00				
West Croydon ■4 🚊	d			06 22	06 26							06 31	06 39		06 45										06 52
Norwood Junction ■2	a			06 28			06 35	06 40					06 43		06 49										06 58
	d		06 23				06 37	06 40						06 47	06 50									06 53	
Selhurst ■4	d				06 31							06 35						06 48							
Thornton Heath	d				06 33							06 37						06 50							
Norbury	d				06 36							06 40						06 53							
Streatham Common ■4	d				06 38							06 43						06 56							
Beckenham Junction ■4 🚊	d																								
Birkbeck 🚊	d																								
Crystal Palace ■4	d		06 27							06 39	06 44			06 51						06 51				06 57	
Gipsy Hill	d		06 29							06 41				06 53										06 59	
West Norwood ■4	d		06 32							06 44				06 56										07 02	
Streatham Hill	d		06 36							06 48														07 06	
Balham ■4 ⊖	d		06 39		06 42					06 51								07 00						07 09	
Wandsworth Common	d		06 41		06 44													07 02						07 11	
Clapham Junction ■10	d		06 45		06 48				06 51	06 56							07 07	07 06						07 15	
Imperial Wharf	d																								
West Brompton ⊖	d																								
Kensington (Olympia) ⊖	d																								
Shepherd's Bush ⊖	d																								
Wembley Central ⊖	d																								
Harrow & Wealdstone ⊖	d																								
Watford Junction	d																								
Milton Keynes Central ■10	a																								
Battersea Park ■4	d	06 45	06 48		06 52											07 02		07 09					07 15	07 18	
London Victoria ■15 ⊖	a		06 53		06 58				07 00	07 05						07 08	07 15	07 16						07 25	
Streatham ■4	d											06 46													
Tulse Hill ■3	d											06 50		07 00											
Herne Hill ■4	a																								
Loughborough Jn.	a																								
Elephant & Castle ⊖	a																								
London Blackfriars ■3 ⊖	a																								
City Thameslink ■3	a																								
St Pancras International ■15 ⊖	a																								
Luton Airport Parkway ■7	a																								
Luton ■10	a																								
North Dulwich	d											06 53		07 03											
East Dulwich	d											06 55		07 05											
Peckham Rye ■4	d	06 56										06 59		07 08									07 26		
Queens Rd Peckham	d	06 59										07 02		07 10									07 29		
South Bermondsey	d	07 01										07 04		07 13									07 31		
London Bridge ■4 ⊖	a	07 08					06 49	06 52			07 06	07 11		07 19	07 04				07 14	07 16	07 16		07 38		

		SN ■1	SN	FC	SN	LO	SN	SN	SN ◇■1	SN	SN	SN	SN		SN	SN ■1	SN	SN	SN ◇■1 🛒	SN ■1	FC	SN	SN	LO	SN ◇■1 🛒
East Croydon 🚊	d	07 05					07 10		07 15				07 26		07 18	07 28			07 31	07 35					07 39
West Croydon ■4 🚊	d		06 58		07 01	07 09		07 13															07 17	07 22	
Norwood Junction ■2	a					07 13	07 14	07 17															07 21	07 28	
	d						07 14	07 18															07 22		
Selhurst ■4	d		07 02		07 05										07 21										
Thornton Heath	d		07 04		07 07										07 23										
Norbury	d		07 07		07 10										07 26										
Streatham Common ■4	d		07 10		07 13										07 28										
Beckenham Junction ■4 🚊	d																07 13								
Birkbeck 🚊	d																07 16								
Crystal Palace ■4	d										07 13	07 14					07 20	07 21					07 26		
Gipsy Hill	d										07 15						07 22						07 28		
West Norwood ■4	d										07 18						07 25						07 31		
Streatham Hill	d										07 22												07 35		
Balham ■4 ⊖	d		07 14								07 25				07 32								07 39		
Wandsworth Common	d		07 16								07 27				07 34								07 41		
Clapham Junction ■10	d	07 17	07 20						07 24		07 31		07 37		07 38				07 41				07 45		07 48
Imperial Wharf	d																								
West Brompton ⊖	d																								
Kensington (Olympia) ⊖	d																								
Shepherd's Bush ⊖	d																								
Wembley Central ⊖	d																								
Harrow & Wealdstone ⊖	d																								
Watford Junction	d																								
Milton Keynes Central ■10	a																								
Battersea Park ■4	d		07 23							07 32	07 35				07 42							07 45	07 48		
London Victoria ■15 ⊖	a	07 25	07 30						07 33	07 38	07 41		07 46		07 48				07 49				07 57		07 57
Streatham ■4	d			07 16	07 19																07 38				
Tulse Hill ■3	d			07 20	07 24												07 29				07 43				
Herne Hill ■4	a			07 23																	07 46				
Loughborough Jn.	a			07 27																	07 50				
Elephant & Castle ⊖	a			07 31																	07 54				
London Blackfriars ■3 ⊖	a			07 35																	07 58				
City Thameslink ■3	a			07 38																	08 00				
St Pancras International ■15 ⊖	a			07 46																	08 08				
Luton Airport Parkway ■7	a			08 20																					
Luton ■10	a			08 23																					
North Dulwich	d				07 27												07 32								
East Dulwich	d				07 29												07 34								
Peckham Rye ■4	d				07 31												07 36					07 56			
Queens Rd Peckham	d				07 34												07 39					07 59			
South Bermondsey	d				07 36												07 41					08 01			
London Bridge ■4 ⊖	a				07 43		07 28	07 32				07 36				07 43	07 48	07 45		07 51		08 08			

Table 177

Mondays to Fridays

East and West Croydon, London
Milton Keynes Central and Luton via Norbury
Crystal Palace - Tulse Hill

Local Services

Network Diagram - see first Page of Table 177

		SN	SN	LO	SN		SN	SN	SN	SN	SN	SN	SN	SN	SN	SN	SN	SN	SN	SN	SN		SN	FC	SN
							1		1								1			◇1	1		1		
East Croydon	d				07 40		07 42		07 46					07 56	07 48	07 50	07 57			08 01	08 02		08 03		
West Croydon 4	d	07 28	07 31	07 39				07 34		07 44															
Norwood Junction 2	a			07 43	07 44					07 48															
	d				07 44					07 49															
Selhurst 4	d	07 32	07 35					07 38							07 51	07 54									
Thornton Heath	d	07 34	07 37					07 40							07 53	07 56									
Norbury	d	07 37	07 40					07 43							07 56	07 59									
Streatham Common 4	d	07 40	07 43					07 46							07 59	08 02									
Beckenham Junction 4	d																	07 42							
Birkbeck	d																	07 45							
Crystal Palace 4	d											07 43	07 44					07 49	07 52						
Gipsy Hill	d											07 45						07 51							
West Norwood 4	d											07 48						07 54							
Streatham Hill	d											07 52													
Balham 4 ⊖	d	07 44						07 50				07 55			08 03	08 06									
Wandsworth Common	d	07 46						07 52				07 57			08 05	08 08									
Clapham Junction 10	d	07 50					07 51	07 56				08 01		08 07	08 09	08 14				08 11					
Imperial Wharf	d															08 18									
West Brompton ⊖	d															08 21									
Kensington (Olympia) ⊖	d															08 25									
Shepherd's Bush ⊖	d															08a27									
Wembley Central ⊖	d																								
Harrow & Wealdstone ⊖	d																								
Watford Junction	d																								
Milton Keynes Central 10	a																								
Battersea Park 4	d	07 53						07 59			08 02	08 05			08 12										08 15
London Victoria 15 ⊖	a	08 00					08 00	08 06			08 08	08 11		08 15	08 19					08 19					
Streatham 4	d		07 46																					08 09	
Tulse Hill 3	d		07 52															07 59						08 13	
Herne Hill 4	a																							08 17	
Loughborough Jn.	a																							08 23	
Elephant & Castle ⊖	a																							08 27	
London Blackfriars 3 ⊖	a																							08 32	
City Thameslink 3	a																							08 35	
St Pancras International 15 ⊖	a																							08 43	
Luton Airport Parkway 7	a																							09 29	
Luton 10	a																							09 34	
North Dulwich	d		07 55															08 02							
East Dulwich	d		07 57															08 04							
Peckham Rye 4	d		07 59															08 06							08 26
Queens Rd Peckham	d		08 02															08 09							08 29
South Bermondsey	d		08 04															08 11							08 31
London Bridge 4 ⊖	a		08 11		07 58				08 01	08 05			08 07				08 13	08 18	08 15		08 19		08 21		08 38

East and West Croydon, London Milton Keynes Central and Luton via Norbury Crystal Palace - Tulse Hill

Local Services

Network Diagram - see first Page of Table 177

		SN	LO	SN	SN	SN	SN	SN	SN	LO	SN	SN	SN		SN	SN	SN	SN	SN	SN	SN	SN	SN	SN	SN
				◇1	1			◇1					1		1						1	1			◇1
													A		B										
East Croydon	d			08 08	08 11			08 13					08 07		08 07	08 10			08 26	08 18	08 21	08 27			08 30
West Croydon 4	d	07 47	07 52			07 58	08 01		08 05	08 09							08 15								
Norwood Junction 2	a	07 51	07 58							08 13						08 16	08 20								
	d	07 52														08 16	08 20								
Selhurst 4	d					08 02	08 05		08 09				08 13		08 13					08 21					
Thornton Heath	d					08 04	08 07		08 11				08 16		08 16					08 23					
Norbury	d					08 07	08 10		08 14				08 20		08 20					08 26					
Streatham Common 4	d					08 10	08 13		08 17				08 23		08 23					08 28					
Beckenham Junction 4	d																						08 12		
Birkbeck	d																						08 15		
Crystal Palace 4	d	07 56										08 13						08 15					08 19	08 24	
Gipsy Hill	d	07 58										08 15											08 21		
West Norwood 4	d	08 01										08 18											08 24		
Streatham Hill	d	08 05										08 22													
Balham 4	d	08 09				08 14			08 21			08 25	08 28		08 28					08 32					
Wandsworth Common	d	08 11				08 16						08 27	08 31		08 31					08 34					
Clapham Junction 10	d	08 16		08 18	08 21	08 20		08 24	08 26			08 31	08 39		08 39				08 37	08 38					08 40
Imperial Wharf	d												08 44		08 44										
West Brompton	d												08 47		08 47										
Kensington (Olympia)	d												08 50		08 50										
Shepherd's Bush	d												08 53		08 53										
Wembley Central	d												09s08		09 08										
Harrow & Wealdstone	d												09 13		09 13										
Watford Junction	d												09 20		09 20										
Milton Keynes Central 10	a												10 01		10 01										
Battersea Park 4	d	08 19				08 23					08 32	08 35								08 42					
London Victoria 15	a	08 26		08 26	08 29	08 30		08 32	08 36		08 39	08 41							08 45	08 48					08 48
Streatham 4	d						08 16																		
Tulse Hill 3	d						08 22																08 28		
Herne Hill 4	a																								
Loughborough Jn	a																								
Elephant & Castle	a																								
London Blackfriars 3	a																								
City Thameslink 3	a																								
St Pancras International 15	a																								
Luton Airport Parkway 7	a																								
Luton 10	a																								
North Dulwich	d						08 25																08 31		
East Dulwich	d						08 27																08 33		
Peckham Rye 4	d						08 29																08 36		
Queens Rd Peckham	d						08 32																08 38		
South Bermondsey	d						08 34																08 41		
London Bridge 4	a						08 41									08 28	08 35	08 37			08 37	08 45	08 48	08 47	

A until 30 March

B from 2 April

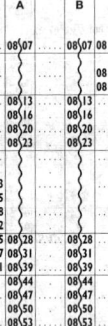

Table 177

Mondays to Fridays

East and West Croydon, London
Milton Keynes Central and Luton via Norbury
Crystal Palace - Tulse Hill

Local Services — Network Diagram - see first Page of Table 177

		SN 1	SN 1	FC	SN		SN	LO	SN	SN	SN	LO	SN	SN ◇1	SN	SN	SN ◇1	SN	SN	SN	SN ◇1		SN	SN 1	SN
East Croydon	d	08 33	08 37								08 39		08 42	08 43			08 50			08 54	08 58		08 48	08 51	
West Croydon 4	d						08 19	08 23	08 26	08 31		08 39			08 44										
Norwood Junction 2	a						08 24	08 28				08 43	08 46		08 49										
	d						08 25						08 47		08 49										
Selhurst 4	d								08 31	08 35	08 43												08 51		
Thornton Heath	d								08 33	08 37	08 46												08 53		
Norbury	d								08 36	08 40	08 49												08 56		
Streatham Common 4	d								08 38	08 43	08 52												08 58		
Beckenham Junction 4	d																								08 43
Birkbeck	d																								08 46
Crystal Palace 4	d						08 29											08 40	08 44						08 50
Gipsy Hill	d						08 31											08 43							08 52
West Norwood 4	d						08 34											08 46							08 55
Streatham Hill	d						08 38											08 49							
Balham 4	d						08 41		08 43		08 58							08 55					09 02		
Wandsworth Common	d						08 43		08 45		09 00							08 57					09 04		
Clapham Junction 10	d		08 48				08 47		08 50		09 05			08 53			09 01	09 01		09 04	09 08		09 08		
Imperial Wharf	d										09 09														
West Brompton	d										09 12														
Kensington (Olympia)	d										09 15														
Shepherd's Bush	d										09a18														
Wembley Central	d																								
Harrow & Wealdstone	d																								
Watford Junction	d																								
Milton Keynes Central 10	a																								
Battersea Park 4	d				08 45		08 50		08 53							09 02		09 05					09 12		
London Victoria 15	a		08 56				08 57		09 00					09 01		09 08	09 09	09 11		09 13	09 16		09 18		
Streatham 4	d			08 39						08 50															
Tulse Hill 3	d			08 43						08 55															08 59
Herne Hill 4	a			08 47																					
Loughborough Jn.	a			08 50																					
Elephant & Castle	a			08 57																					
London Blackfriars 3	a			09 01																					
City Thameslink 3	a			09 04																					
St Pancras International 15	a			09 12																					
Luton Airport Parkway 7	a			09 58																					
Luton 10	a			10 03																					
North Dulwich	d									08 58															09 02
East Dulwich	d									09 00															09 04
Peckham Rye 4	d				08 56					09 02															09 07
Queens Rd Peckham	d				08 59					09 05															09 09
South Bermondsey	d				09 01					09 07															09 12
London Bridge 4	a	08 51			09 08					09 14			09 01		09 04				09 06					09 06	09 19

East and West Croydon, London
Milton Keynes Central and Luton via Norbury
Crystal Palace - Tulse Hill

Local Services **Network Diagram - see first Page of Table 177**

		SN	SN 1	FC	SN	SN	LO	SN	SN 1	SN	SN	SN 1 A	SN 1 B		LO	SN ◇1	SN	SN	SN	SN	SN ◇1	SN	SN 1	SN	SN
East Croydon	d		08 59					09 05	09 11			09 08	09 08			09 14					09 23	09 17	09 31		
West Croydon 4	d					08 49	08 53			08 57	09 01				09 09										09 15
Norwood Junction 2	a					08 53	08 58	09 09							09 13										09 19
	d					08 54		09 09																	09 22
Selhurst 4	d									09 01	09 05	09 13	09 13									09 21			
Thornton Heath	d									09 03	09 07	09 16	09 16									09 23			
Norbury	d									09 06	09 10	09 19	09 19									09 26			
Streatham Common 4	d									09 09	09 13	09 21	09 21									09 28			
Beckenham Junction 4	d																								
Birkbeck	d																								
Crystal Palace 4	d	08 51				08 58												09 11	09 14	09 21					09 26
Gipsy Hill	d					09 00												09 14							09 28
West Norwood 4	d					09 03												09 17							09 31
Streatham Hill	d					09 07												09 21							09 35
Balham 4 ⊖	d					09 10				09 13		09 28	09 28					09 25				09 32			09 41
Wandsworth Common	d					09 12				09 15		09 30	09 30					09 27				09 34			09 43
Clapham Junction 10	d					09 16			09 21	09 19		09 39	09 39			09 24		09 31			09 33	09 38	09 41		09 47
Imperial Wharf	d											09 44	09 44												
West Brompton ⊖	d											09 47	09 47												
Kensington (Olympia) ⊖	d											09 50	09 50												
Shepherd's Bush ⊖	d											09 53	09 53												
Wembley Central ⊖	d											10s08	10 08												
Harrow & Wealdstone ⊖	d											10 13	10 13												
Watford Junction	d											10 20	10 20												
Milton Keynes Central 10	a											11 02	11 02												
Battersea Park 4	d				09 15	09 19				09 22							09 32	09 35				09 42		09 45	09 50
London Victoria 15 ⊖	a					09 27			09 27	09 31						09 32	09 38	09 42			09 42	09 48	09 50		09 58
Streatham 4	d			09 08							09 20														
Tulse Hill 3	d			09 16							09 26														
Herne Hill 4	a			09 19																					
Loughborough Jn.	a			09 23																					
Elephant & Castle ⊖	a			09 29																					
London Blackfriars 3 ⊖	a			09 33																					
City Thameslink 3	a			09 36																					
St Pancras International 15 ⊖	a			09 44																					
Luton Airport Parkway 7	a			10 29																					
Luton 10	a			10 33																					
North Dulwich	d										09 29														
East Dulwich	d										09 31														
Peckham Rye 4	d				09 26						09 33													09 56	
Queens Rd Peckham	d				09 29						09 36													09 59	
South Bermondsey	d				09 31						09 38													10 01	
London Bridge 4 ⊖	a	09 14	09 15		09 38			09 23			09 44								09 37	09 43				10 06	

A until 30 March **B** from 2 April

East and West Croydon, London
Milton Keynes Central and Luton via Norbury
Crystal Palace - Tulse Hill

Local Services

Network Diagram - see first Page of Table 177

		SN	LO	SN	SN		SN	SN	FC	SN	SN	SN	SN	SN	LO	SN	SN	SN	SN	SN	SN		SN	SN	LO
					■1					◇■1 🚲			◇■1							◇■1 🚲					
East Croydon 🚊	d	09 20		09 30	09 37					09 39			09 43					09 47		10 00				09 51	
West Croydon ■4 🚊	d		09 22								09 28	09 31		09 35	09 39								09 45		09 52
Norwood Junction ■2	a	09 24	09 28	09 34	09 41										09 43								09 50	09 55	09 58
	d	09 25		09 35	09 42																		09 52	09 55	
Selhurst ■4	d										09 32	09 35		09 39				09 50							
Thornton Heath	d										09 34	09 37		09 41				09 52							
Norbury	d										09 37	09 40		09 44				09 55							
Streatham Common ■4	d										09 40	09 43		09 47				09 58							
Beckenham Junction ■4 🚊	d						09 23																		
Birkbeck 🚊	d						09 26																		
Crystal Palace ■4	d						09 30	09 36									09 43		09 51				09 56		
Gipsy Hill	d						09 32										09 46						09 58		
West Norwood ■4	d						09 35										09 49						10 01		
Streatham Hill	d																09 52						10 05		
Balham ■4 ⊖	d										09 44			09 52			09 56	10 02					10 09		
Wandsworth Common	d										09 46			09 54			09 58	10 04					10 11		
Clapham Junction ■10	d									09 48	09 50		09 52	09 58			10 02	10 08		10 09			10 15		
Imperial Wharf	d																								
West Brompton ⊖	d																								
Kensington (Olympia) ⊖	d																								
Shepherd's Bush ⊖	d																								
Wembley Central ⊖	d																								
Harrow & Wealdstone ⊖	d																								
Watford Junction	d																								
Milton Keynes Central ■10	a																								
Battersea Park ■4	d										09 53					10 03	10 05	10 11			10 15		10 19		
London Victoria ■15 ⊖	a									09 58	09 58		09 59	10 05		10 07	10 11	10 16		10 16			10 24		
Streatham ■4	d								09 38			09 46													
Tulse Hill ■3	d						09 39		09 42			09 54													
Herne Hill ■4	a								09 46																
Loughborough Jn.	a								09 50																
Elephant & Castle ⊖	a								09 54																
London Blackfriars ■3 ⊖	a								09 59																
City Thameslink ■3	a								10 02																
St Pancras International ■15 ⊖	a								10 10																
Luton Airport Parkway ■7	a								10 58																
Luton ■10	a								11 03																
North Dulwich	d						09 42					09 57													
East Dulwich	d						09 44					09 59													
Peckham Rye ■4	d						09 47					10 01									10 26				
Queens Rd Peckham	d						09 49					10 04									10 29				
South Bermondsey	d						09 52					10 06									10 31				
London Bridge ■4 ⊖	a	09 41		10 00	09 55		09 58	09 59				10 11							10 11		10 36			10 09	

East and West Croydon, London
Milton Keynes Central and Luton via Norbury
Crystal Palace - Tulse Hill

Local Services

Network Diagram - see first Page of Table 177

		SN 1	SN	SN	SN 1	SN	FC	SN	SN ◇1	SN	LO	SN	SN		SN 1 A	SN 1 B	SN	SN ◇1	SN	SN	SN	SN	LO	SN 1	SN
East Croydon	d	09 55		10 00	10 07				10 12						10 10	10 10		10 28	10 17			10 21		10 25	
West Croydon 4	d		09 58					10 01		10 04	10 09										10 15		10 22		10 28
Norwood Junction 2	a	09 59		10 04	10 12						10 13										10 19	10 25	10 28	10 29	
	d	09 59		10 05	10 13																10 22	10 25		10 29	
Selhurst 4	d		10 02					10 05		10 09					10 14	10 14			10 20						10 32
Thornton Heath	d		10 04					10 07		10 11					10 16	10 16			10 22						10 34
Norbury	d		10 07					10 10		10 14					10 19	10 19			10 25						10 37
Streatham Common 4	d		10 10					10 13		10 17					10 22	10 22			10 28						10 40
Beckenham Junction 4	d					09 53																			
Birkbeck	d					09 56																			
Crystal Palace 4	d					10 00							10 13				10 21				10 26				
Gipsy Hill	d					10 02							10 15								10 29				
West Norwood 4	d					10 05							10 18								10 32				
Streatham Hill	d												10 22								10 35				
Balham 4	d		10 14							10 21			10 25		10 29	10 29			10 32		10 39				10 44
Wandsworth Common	d		10 16							10 23			10 27		10 31	10 31			10 34		10 41				10 46
Clapham Junction 10	d		10 20						10 21	10 27			10 31		10 39	10 39		10 38	10 38		10 45				10 50
Imperial Wharf	d														10 44	10 44									
West Brompton	d														10 47	10 47									
Kensington (Olympia)	d														10 50	10 50									
Shepherd's Bush	d														10 53	10 53									
Wembley Central	d														11s08	11 08									
Harrow & Wealdstone	d														11 13	11 13									
Watford Junction	d														11 20	11 20									
Milton Keynes Central 10	a														12 01	12 01									
Battersea Park 4	d		10 23									10 32	10 35						10 41	10 45	10 49				10 53
London Victoria 15	a		10 28						10 28	10 34		10 36	10 39					10 45	10 46		10 53				10 58
Streatham 4	d						10 08	10 16																	
Tulse Hill 3	d					10 09	10 12	10 24																	
Herne Hill 4	a						10 16																		
Loughborough Jn.	a						10 19																		
Elephant & Castle	a						10 23																		
London Blackfriars 3	a						10 27																		
City Thameslink 3	a						10 32																		
St Pancras International 15	a						10 40																		
Luton Airport Parkway 7	a						11 27																		
Luton 10	a						11 31																		
North Dulwich	d					10 12		10 27																	
East Dulwich	d					10 14		10 29																	
Peckham Rye 4	d					10 17		10 31												10 56					
Queens Rd Peckham	d					10 19		10 34												10 59					
South Bermondsey	d					10 22		10 36												11 01					
London Bridge 4	a	10 13		10 29	10 25	10 26		10 41									10 41			11 06		10 39		10 43	

A until 30 March

B from 2 April

East and West Croydon, London
Milton Keynes Central and Luton via Norbury
Crystal Palace - Tulse Hill

Local Services

Network Diagram - see first Page of Table 177

		SN	SN	SN	FC		SN	SN	SN	LO	SN	SN	SN	SN	SN	SN	SN	SN	LO	SN	SN		SN	SN	SN
			1					◇1 ✠							◇1					1				1	
East Croydon	d	10 30	10 38					10 42					10 47		11 00			10 51		10 55			11 00	11 07	
West Croydon 4	d						10 31		10 34	10 39							10 45		10 52		10 58				
Norwood Junction 2	a	10 34	10 42							10 43							10 49	10 55	10 58	10 59			11 04	11 12	
	d	10 35	10 43														10 52	10 55		10 59			11 05	11 13	
Selhurst 4	d						10 35		10 39				10 50								11 02				
Thornton Heath	d						10 37		10 41				10 52								11 04				
Norbury	d						10 40		10 44				10 55								11 07				
Streatham Common 4	d						10 43		10 47				10 58								11 10				
Beckenham Junction 4	d			10 23																					10 53
Birkbeck	d			10 26																					10 56
Crystal Palace 4	d			10 30								10 43		10 51			10 56								11 00
Gipsy Hill	d			10 32								10 45					10 59								11 02
West Norwood 4	d			10 35								10 48					11 02								11 05
Streatham Hill	d											10 52					11 05								
Balham 4 ⊖	d								10 51			10 55	11 02				11 09				11 14				
Wandsworth Common	d								10 53			10 57	11 04				11 11				11 16				
Clapham Junction 10	d							10 51	10 57			11 01	11 08		11 10		11 15				11 20				
Imperial Wharf	d																								
West Brompton ⊖	d																								
Kensington (Olympia) ⊖	d																								
Shepherd's Bush ⊖	d																								
Wembley Central ⊖	d																								
Harrow & Wealdstone ⊖	d																								
Watford Junction	d																								
Milton Keynes Central 10	a																								
Battersea Park 4	d										11 02	11 05	11 11			11 15	11 18				11 23				
London Victoria 15 ⊖	a							10 58	11 04		11 06	11 09	11 16		11 16		11 23				11 28				
Streatham 4	d				10 38		10 46																		
Tulse Hill 3	d			10 39	10 42		10 54																		11 09
Herne Hill 4	a				10 46																				
Loughborough Jn.	a				10 49																				
Elephant & Castle ⊖	a				10 53																				
London Blackfriars 3 ⊖	a				10 57																				
City Thameslink 3	a				11 02																				
St Pancras International 15 ⊖	a				11 10																				
Luton Airport Parkway 7	a				11 55																				
Luton 10	a				11 59																				
North Dulwich	d			10 42			10 57																		11 12
East Dulwich	d			10 44			10 59																		11 14
Peckham Rye 4	d			10 47			11 01									11 26									11 17
Queens Rd Peckham	d			10 49			11 04									11 29									11 19
South Bermondsey	d			10 52			11 06									11 31									11 22
London Bridge 4 ⊖	a	10 59	10 55	10 56			11 11							11 11		11 36		11 09		11 13			11 29	11 25	11 26

Table 177

Mondays to Fridays

East and West Croydon, London
Milton Keynes Central and Luton via Norbury
Crystal Palace - Tulse Hill

Local Services

Network Diagram - see first Page of Table 177

	FC	SN	SN ◇1	SN	LO	SN	SN	SN 1 A	SN 1 B	SN	SN	SN ◇1		SN	SN	SN	LO	SN 1	SN	SN 1	SN	FC	SN ◇1	SN
East Croydon d			11 12					11 11	11 11	11 17		11 28				11 21		11 25	11 30	11 37			11 41	
West Croydon 4 d		11 01		11 04	11 09										11 15		11 22							11 28
Norwood Junction 2 a					11 13										11 19	11 25	11 28	11 29	11 34	11 42				
d															11 22	11 25		11 29	11 35	11 43				
Selhurst 4 d		11 05		11 09				11 16	11 16	11 20														11 32
Thornton Heath d		11 07		11 11				11 18	11 18	11 22														11 34
Norbury d		11 10		11 14				11 21	11 21	11 25														11 37
Streatham Common 4 d		11 13		11 17				11 24	11 24	11 28														11 40
Beckenham Junction 4 d																					11 23			
Birkbeck d																					11 26			
Crystal Palace 4 d							11 13				11 21				11 26						11 30			
Gipsy Hill d							11 15								11 29						11 32			
West Norwood 4 d							11 18								11 32						11 35			
Streatham Hill d							11 22								11 35									
Balham 4 ⊖ d				11 21			11 25	11 28	11 28	11 32					11 40									11 44
Wandsworth Common d				11 23			11 27	11 30	11 30	11 34					11 42									11 46
Clapham Junction 10 d			11 21	11 27			11 31	11b39	11b39	11 38		11 37			11 46								11 50	11 50
Imperial Wharf d								11 44	11 44															
West Brompton ⊖ d								11 47	11 47															
Kensington (Olympia) ⊖ d								11 50	11 50															
Shepherd's Bush ⊖ d								11 53	11 53															
Wembley Central ⊖ d								12s08	12 08															
Harrow & Wealdstone ⊖ d								12 13	12 13															
Watford Junction d								12 20	12 20															
Milton Keynes Central 10 a								13 01	13 01															
Battersea Park 4 d						11 32	11 35			11a41				11 45	11 49									11 53
London Victoria 15 ⊖ a			11 28	11 34		11 36	11 39					11 44			11 54								11 57	11 58
Streatham 4 d	11 08	11 16																				11 38		
Tulse Hill 3 d	11 12	11 24																			11 39	11 42		
Herne Hill 4 a	11 16																					11 46		
Loughborough Jn. a	11 19																					11 49		
Elephant & Castle ⊖ a	11 23																					11 53		
London Blackfriars 3 ⊖ a	11 27																					11 57		
City Thameslink 3 a	11 32																					12 02		
St Pancras International 15 ⊖ a	11 40																					12 10		
Luton Airport Parkway 7 a	12 25																					12 55		
Luton 10 a	12 29																					12 57		
North Dulwich d		11 27																			11 42			
East Dulwich d		11 29																			11 44			
Peckham Rye 4 d		11 31												11 56							11 47			
Queens Rd Peckham d		11 34												11 59							11 49			
South Bermondsey d		11 36												12 01							11 52			
London Bridge 4 ⊖ a		11 41									11 41			12 06		11 39		11 43	11 59	11 55	11 56			

A until 30 March

B from 2 April

b Arr. 1133

Table 177

Mondays to Fridays

East and West Croydon, London
Milton Keynes Central and Luton via Norbury
Crystal Palace - Tulse Hill

Local Services

Network Diagram - see first Page of Table 177

		SN	SN	LO	SN		SN	SN	SN	SN ◇1	SN	SN	SN	LO	SN 1	SN	SN	SN 1	SN	FC	SN		SN ◇1	SN	LO
East Croydon	d							11 47		12 00			11 51		11 55		12 00	12 07					12 12		
West Croydon 4	d	11 31	11 34	11 39								11 45		11 52		11 58					12 01			12 04	12 09
Norwood Junction 2	a			11 43								11 49	11 55	11 58	11 59		12 04	12 12							12 13
	d											11 52	11 55		11 59		12 05	12 13							
Selhurst 4	d	11 35	11 39					11 50								12 02					12 05			12 09	
Thornton Heath	d	11 37	11 41					11 52								12 04					12 07			12 11	
Norbury	d	11 40	11 44					11 55								12 07					12 10			12 14	
Streatham Common 4	d	11 43	11 47					11 58								12 10					12 13			12 17	
Beckenham Junction 4	d																		11 53						
Birkbeck	d																		11 56						
Crystal Palace 4	d						11 43		11 51			11 56							12 00						
Gipsy Hill	d						11 45					11 59							12 02						
West Norwood 4	d						11 48					12 02							12 05						
Streatham Hill	d						11 52					12 05													
Balham 4	d		11 51				11 55	12 02				12 09				12 14								12 21	
Wandsworth Common	d		11 53				11 57	12 04				12 11				12 16								12 23	
Clapham Junction 10	d		11 57				12 01	12 08		12 12		12 15				12 20							12 22	12 27	
Imperial Wharf	d																								
West Brompton	d																								
Kensington (Olympia)	d																								
Shepherd's Bush	d																								
Wembley Central	d																								
Harrow & Wealdstone	d																								
Watford Junction	d																								
Milton Keynes Central 10	a																								
Battersea Park 4	d				12 02		12 05	12a11			12 15	12 18				12 23									
London Victoria 15	a		12 04		12 07		12 09			12 18		12 23				12 28							12 28	12 34	
Streatham 4	d	11 46																		12 08	12 16				
Tulse Hill 3	d	11 54																	12 09	12 12	12 24				
Herne Hill 4	a																			12 16					
Loughborough Jn.	a																			12 19					
Elephant & Castle	a																			12 23					
London Blackfriars 3	a																			12 27					
City Thameslink 3	a																			12 32					
St Pancras International 15	a																			12 40					
Luton Airport Parkway 7	a																			13 25					
Luton 10	a																			13 29					
North Dulwich	d	11 57																	12 12		12 27				
East Dulwich	d	11 59																	12 14		12 29				
Peckham Rye 4	d	12 01									12 26								12 17		12 31				
Queens Rd Peckham	d	12 04									12 29								12 19		12 34				
South Bermondsey	d	12 06									12 31								12 22		12 36				
London Bridge 4	a	12 11							12 14		12 36		12 09		12 13		12 29	12 25	12 26		12 41				

East and West Croydon, London Milton Keynes Central and Luton via Norbury Crystal Palace - Tulse Hill

Local Services

Network Diagram - see first Page of Table 177

		SN	SN	SN 1 A	SN 1 B	SN	SN	SN ◇1	SN	SN	SN	LO	SN 1		SN	SN 1	SN	FC	SN ◇1	SN	SN	SN	LO	SN	SN
East Croydon	d			12 10	12 10	12 17		12 28			12 21		12 25		12 30	12 37			12 41						
West Croydon 4	d									12 15		12 22								12 28	12 31	12 34	12 39		
Norwood Junction 2	a									12 19	12 25	12 28	12 29		12 34	12 42							12 43		
	d									12 22	12 25		12 29		12 35	12 43									
Selhurst 4	d			12 14	12 14	12 20														12 32	12 35	12 39			
Thornton Heath	d			12 16	12 16	12 22														12 34	12 37	12 41			
Norbury	d			12 19	12 19	12 25														12 37	12 40	12 44			
Streatham Common 4	d			12 22	12 22	12 28														12 40	12 43	12 47			
Beckenham Junction 4	d																12 23								
Birkbeck	d																12 26								
Crystal Palace 4	d		12 13				12 21			12 26							12 30								12 43
Gipsy Hill	d		12 15							12 29							12 32								12 45
West Norwood 4	d		12 18							12 32							12 35								12 48
Streatham Hill	d		12 22							12 35															12 52
Balham 4	⊖ d		12 25	12 28	12 28	12 32				12 39										12 44		12 51			12 55
Wandsworth Common	d		12 27	12 30	12 30	12 34				12 41										12 46		12 53			12 57
Clapham Junction 10	d		12 31	12 39	12 39	12 38		12 37		12 45									12 50	12 50		12 57			13 01
Imperial Wharf	d			12 44	12 44																				
West Brompton	⊖ d			12 47	12 47																				
Kensington (Olympia)	⊖ d			12 50	12 50																				
Shepherd's Bush	⊖ d			12 53	12 53																				
Wembley Central	⊖ d			13s08	13 08																				
Harrow & Wealdstone	⊖ d			13 13	13 13																				
Watford Junction	d			13 20	13 20																				
Milton Keynes Central 10	a			14 01	14 01																				
Battersea Park 4	d	12 32	12 35			12a41			12 45	12 48										12 53				13 02	13 05
London Victoria 15	⊖ a	12 36	12 39					12 44		12 53									12 57	12 58		13 04		13 06	13 09
Streatham 4	d																	12 38			12 46				
Tulse Hill 3	d																12 39	12 42			12 54				
Herne Hill 4	a																	12 46							
Loughborough Jn.	a																	12 49							
Elephant & Castle	⊖ a																	12 53							
London Blackfriars 3	⊖ a																	12 57							
City Thameslink 3	a																	13 02							
St Pancras International 15	⊖ a																	13 10							
Luton Airport Parkway 7	a																	13 55							
Luton 10	a																	13 59							
North Dulwich	d																12 42				12 57				
East Dulwich	d																12 44				12 59				
Peckham Rye 4	d								12 56								12 47				13 01				
Queens Rd Peckham	d								12 59								12 49				13 04				
South Bermondsey	d								13 01								12 52				13 06				
London Bridge 4	⊖ a						12 41		13 06		12 39		12 43		12 59	12 55	12 56				13 11				

A until 30 March

B from 2 April

Table 177

Mondays to Fridays

East and West Croydon, London
Milton Keynes Central and Luton via Norbury
Crystal Palace - Tulse Hill

Local Services

Network Diagram - see first Page of Table 177

		SN	SN	SN ◇1	SN		SN	SN	LO	SN 1	SN	SN	SN 1	SN	FC	SN	SN ◇1	SN	LO	SN	SN		SN 1 A	SN 1 B	SN
East Croydon	d	12 47		13 00				12 51		12 55		13 00	13 07				13 12						13 10	13 10	13 17
West Croydon 4	d						12 45		12 52		12 58					13 01		13 04	13 09						
Norwood Junction 2	a						12 49	12 55	12 58	12 59		13 04	13 12						13 13						
	d						12 52	12 55		12 59		13 05	13 13												
Selhurst 4	d	12 50									13 02					13 05		13 09					13 13	13 13	13 20
Thornton Heath	d	12 52									13 04					13 07		13 11					13 16	13 16	13 22
Norbury	d	12 55									13 07					13 10		13 14					13 19	13 19	13 25
Streatham Common 4	d	12 58									13 10					13 13		13 17					13 21	13 21	13 28
Beckenham Junction 4	d													12 53											
Birkbeck	d													12 56											
Crystal Palace 4	d		12 51				12 56							13 00							13 13				
Gipsy Hill	d						12 59							13 02							13 15				
West Norwood 4	d						13 02							13 05							13 18				
Streatham Hill	d						13 05														13 22				
Balham 4 ⊖	d	13 02					13 09				13 14							13 21			13 25		13 28	13 28	13 32
Wandsworth Common	d	13 04					13 11				13 16							13 23			13 27		13 30	13 30	13 34
Clapham Junction 10	d	13 08		13 10			13 15				13 20						13 21	13 27			13 31		13 39	13 39	13 38
Imperial Wharf	d																						13 44	13 44	
West Brompton ⊖	d																						13 47	13 47	
Kensington (Olympia) ⊖	d																						13 50	13 50	
Shepherd's Bush ⊖	d																						13 53	13 53	
Wembley Central ⊖	d																						14s08	14 08	
Harrow & Wealdstone ⊖	d																						14 13	14 13	
Watford Junction	d																						14 20	14 20	
Milton Keynes Central 10	a																						15 01	15 01	
Battersea Park 4	d	13 11			13 15		13 18				13 23									13 32	13 35				13a41
London Victoria 15 ⊖	a	13 16		13 16			13 23				13 28						13 28	13 34		13 36	13 39				
Streatham 4	d														13 08	13 16									
Tulse Hill 3	d													13 09	13 12	13 24									
Herne Hill 4	a														13 16										
Loughborough Jn.	a														13 19										
Elephant & Castle ⊖	a														13 23										
London Blackfriars 3 ⊖	a														13 27										
City Thameslink 3	a														13 32										
St Pancras International 15 ⊖	a														13 40										
Luton Airport Parkway 7	a														14 25										
Luton 10	a														14 29										
North Dulwich	d													13 12		13 27									
East Dulwich	d													13 14		13 29									
Peckham Rye 4	d				13 26									13 17		13 31									
Queens Rd Peckham	d				13 29									13 19		13 34									
South Bermondsey	d				13 31									13 22		13 36									
London Bridge 4 ⊖	a		13 11		13 36			13 09		13 13		13 29	13 25	13 26		13 41									

A until 30 March

B from 2 April

Table 177

Mondays to Fridays

East and West Croydon, London
Milton Keynes Central and Luton via Norbury
Crystal Palace - Tulse Hill

Local Services

Network Diagram - see first Page of Table 177

		SN	SN ◇1	SN	SN	SN	LO	SN 1	SN	SN 1	SN	FC	SN ◇1		SN	SN	SN	LO	SN	SN	SN	SN	SN ◇1	SN	SN
East Croydon 🚊	d		13 28			13 21		13 25	13 30	13 37			13 41								13 47		14 00		
West Croydon 4 🚊	d				13 15		13 22								13 28	13 31	13 34	13 39							13 45
Norwood Junction 2	a				13 19	13 25	13 28	13 29	13 34	13 42								13 43							13 49
	d				13 22	13 25		13 29	13 35	13 43															13 52
Selhurst 4	d														13 32	13 35	13 39				13 50				
Thornton Heath	d														13 34	13 37	13 41				13 52				
Norbury	d														13 37	13 40	13 44				13 55				
Streatham Common 4	d														13 40	13 43	13 47				13 58				
Beckenham Junction 4 🚊	d										13 23														
Birkbeck 🚊	d										13 26														
Crystal Palace 4	d	13 21			13 26						13 30									13 43		13 51			13 56
Gipsy Hill	d				13 29						13 32									13 45					13 59
West Norwood 4	d				13 32						13 35									13 48					14 02
Streatham Hill	d				13 35															13 52					14 05
Balham 4 ⊖	d				13 39										13 44		13 51			13 55	14 02				14 09
Wandsworth Common	d				13 41										13 46		13 53			13 57	14 04				14 11
Clapham Junction 10	d		13 37		13 45								13 50		13 50		13 57			14 01	14 08		14 10		14 15
Imperial Wharf	d																								
West Brompton ⊖	d																								
Kensington (Olympia) ⊖	d																								
Shepherd's Bush ⊖	d																								
Wembley Central ⊖	d																								
Harrow & Wealdstone ⊖	d																								
Watford Junction	d																								
Milton Keynes Central 10	a																								
Battersea Park 4	d			13 45	13 48										13 53				14 02	14 05	14a11			14 15	14 18
London Victoria 15 ⊖	a		13 44		13 53								13 57		13 58		14 04		14 06	14 09			14 16		14 23
Streatham 4	d											13 38				13 46									
Tulse Hill 3	d										13 39	13 42				13 54									
Herne Hill 4	a											13 46													
Loughborough Jn.	a											13 49													
Elephant & Castle ⊖	a											13 53													
London Blackfriars 3 ⊖	a											13 57													
City Thameslink 3	a											14 02													
St Pancras International 15 ⊖	a											14 10													
Luton Airport Parkway 7	a											14 55													
Luton 10	a											14 59													
North Dulwich	d										13 42					13 57									
East Dulwich	d										13 44					13 59									
Peckham Rye 4	d			13 56							13 47					14 01								14 26	
Queens Rd Peckham	d			13 59							13 49					14 04								14 29	
South Bermondsey	d			14 01							13 52					14 06								14 31	
London Bridge 4 ⊖	a	13 44		14 06		13 39		13 43	13 59	13 55	13 56					14 11						14 11		14 36	

Table 177

Mondays to Fridays

East and West Croydon, London
Milton Keynes Central and Luton via Norbury
Crystal Palace - Tulse Hill

Local Services

Network Diagram - see first Page of Table 177

		SN	LO	SN 1	SN		SN	SN 1	SN	FC	SN	SN ◇1	SN	LO	SN	SN	SN 1 A	SN 1 B	SN	SN	SN ◇1		SN	SN	SN
East Croydon	d	13 51		13 55			14 00	14 08				14 12					14 10	14 10	14 17		14 28				14 21
West Croydon 4	d		13 52		13 58						14 01		14 04	14 09										14 15	
Norwood Junction 2	a	13 55	13 58	13 59			14 04	14 12						14 13										14 19	14 25
	d	13 55		13 59			14 05	14 13																14 22	14 25
Selhurst 4	d				14 02						14 05		14 09				14 13	14 13	14 20						
Thornton Heath	d				14 04						14 07		14 11				14 16	14 16	14 22						
Norbury	d				14 07						14 10		14 14				14 19	14 19	14 25						
Streatham Common 4	d				14 10						14 13		14 17				14 21	14 21	14 28						
Beckenham Junction 4	d								13 53																
Birkbeck	d								13 56																
Crystal Palace 4	d								14 00							14 13				14 21				14 26	
Gipsy Hill	d								14 02							14 15								14 29	
West Norwood 4	d								14 05							14 18								14 32	
Streatham Hill	d															14 22								14 35	
Balham 4 ⊖	d				14 14								14 21			14 25	14 28	14 28	14 32					14 39	
Wandsworth Common	d				14 16								14 23			14 27	14 30	14 30	14 34					14 41	
Clapham Junction 10	d				14 20							14 21	14 27			14 31	14 39	14 39	14 38		14 37			14 45	
Imperial Wharf	d																14 44	14 44							
West Brompton ⊖	d																14 47	14 47							
Kensington (Olympia) ⊖	d																14 50	14 50							
Shepherd's Bush ⊖	d																14 53	14 53							
Wembley Central ⊖	d																15s08	15 08							
Harrow & Wealdstone ⊖	d																15 13	15 13							
Watford Junction	d																15 20	15 20							
Milton Keynes Central 10	a																16 01	16 01							
Battersea Park 4	d				14 23										14 32	14 35			14a41				14 45	14 48	
London Victoria 15 ⊖	a				14 28							14 28	14 34		14 36	14 39					14 44			14 53	
Streatham 4	d									14 08	14 16														
Tulse Hill 3	d								14 09	14 12	14 24														
Herne Hill 4	a									14 16															
Loughborough Jn.	a									14 19															
Elephant & Castle ⊖	a									14 23															
London Blackfriars 3 ⊖	a									14 27															
City Thameslink 3	a									14 32															
St Pancras International 15 ⊖	a									14 40															
Luton Airport Parkway 7	a									15 25															
Luton 10	a									15 29															
North Dulwich	d								14 12		14 27														
East Dulwich	d								14 14		14 29														
Peckham Rye 4	d								14 17		14 31												14 56		
Queens Rd Peckham	d								14 19		14 34												14 59		
South Bermondsey	d								14 22		14 36												15 01		
London Bridge 4 ⊖	a	14 09		14 13			14 29	14 25	14 26		14 41									14 41			15 06		14 39

A until 30 March

B from 2 April

Table 177

Mondays to Fridays

East and West Croydon, London
Milton Keynes Central and Luton via Norbury
Crystal Palace - Tulse Hill

Local Services

Network Diagram - see first Page of Table 177

		LO	SN	SN	SN	SN	FC	SN	SN	SN	SN	LO	SN	SN	SN	SN	SN	SN	SN	SN	LO	SN	SN	SN
			■1		■1			◇■1									◇■1					■1		
East Croydon 🚊	d		14 25	14 30	14 37			14 41							14 47		15 00			14 51		14 55		15 00
West Croydon ■4 🚊	d	14 22							14 28	14 31	14 34	14 39							14 45		14 52		14 58	
Norwood Junction ■2	a	14 28	14 29	14 34	14 42							14 43							14 49	14 55	14 58	14 59		15 04
	d		14 29	14 35	14 43														14 52	14 55		14 59		15 05
Selhurst ■4	d								14 32	14 35	14 39				14 50								15 02	
Thornton Heath	d								14 34	14 37	14 41				14 52								15 04	
Norbury	d								14 37	14 40	14 44				14 55								15 07	
Streatham Common ■4	d								14 40	14 43	14 47				14 58								15 10	
Beckenham Junction ■4 🚊	d					14 23																		
Birkbeck 🚊	d					14 26																		
Crystal Palace ■4	d					14 30								14 43		14 51			14 56					
Gipsy Hill	d					14 32								14 45					14 59					
West Norwood ■4	d					14 35								14 48					15 02					
Streatham Hill	d													14 52					15 05					
Balham ■4 ⊖	d								14 44		14 51			14 55	15 02				15 09				15 14	
Wandsworth Common	d								14 46		14 53			14 57	15 04				15 11				15 16	
Clapham Junction ■10	d							14 50	14 50		14 57			15 01	15 08		15 10		15 15				15 20	
Imperial Wharf	d																							
West Brompton ⊖	d																							
Kensington (Olympia) ⊖	d																							
Shepherd's Bush ⊖	d																							
Wembley Central ⊖	d																							
Harrow & Wealdstone ⊖	d																							
Watford Junction	d																							
Milton Keynes Central ■10	a																							
Battersea Park ■4	d								14 53				15 02	15 05	15 11			15 15	15 18				15 23	
London Victoria ■15 ⊖	a							14 57	14 58		15 04		15 06	15 09	15 16		15 20		15 24				15 28	
Streatham ■4	d						14 38			14 46														
Tulse Hill ■3	d					14 39	14 42			14 54														
Herne Hill ■4	a						14 46																	
Loughborough Jn.	a						14 49																	
Elephant & Castle ⊖	a						14 53																	
London Blackfriars ■3 ⊖	a						14 57																	
City Thameslink ■3	a						15 02																	
St Pancras International ■15 ⊖	a						15 10																	
Luton Airport Parkway ■7	a						15 55																	
Luton ■10	a						15 59																	
North Dulwich	d					14 42				14 57														
East Dulwich	d					14 44				14 59														
Peckham Rye ■4	d					14 47				15 01								15 26						
Queens Rd Peckham	d					14 49				15 04								15 29						
South Bermondsey	d					14 52				15 06								15 31						
London Bridge ■4 ⊖	a		14 43	14 59	14 55	14 56				15 11						15 11		15 36		15 09		15 13		15 29

Table 177

Mondays to Fridays

East and West Croydon, London
Milton Keynes Central and Luton via Norbury
Crystal Palace - Tulse Hill

Local Services

Network Diagram - see first Page of Table 177

		SN	SN	FC	SN		SN	SN	LO	SN	SN	SN	SN	SN	SN	SN	SN	SN	SN	LO	SN		SN	SN	SN
		1					◇1					1	1			◇1					1			1	
												A	B												
East Croydon	d	15 07					15 12					15 10	15 10	15 17		15 28			15 21		15 25		15 30	15 37	
West Croydon 4	d				15 01			15 04	15 09									15 15		15 22					
Norwood Junction 2	a	15 12							15 13									15 19	15 25	15 28	15 29		15 34	15 42	
	d	15 13																15 22	15 25		15 29		15 35	15 43	
Selhurst 4	d				15 05			15 09				15 13	15 13	15 20											
Thornton Heath	d				15 07			15 11				15 16	15 16	15 22											
Norbury	d				15 10			15 14				15 19	15 19	15 25											
Streatham Common 4	d				15 13			15 17				15 21	15 21	15 28											
Beckenham Junction 4	d		14 53																						15 23
Birkbeck	d		14 56																						15 26
Crystal Palace 4	d		15 00								15 13				15 21			15 26							15 30
Gipsy Hill	d		15 02								15 15							15 29							15 32
West Norwood 4	d		15 05								15 18							15 32							15 35
Streatham Hill	d										15 22							15 35							
Balham 4 ⊖	d							15 21			15 25	15 29	15 29	15 32				15 39							
Wandsworth Common	d							15 23			15 27	15 31	15 31	15 34				15 41							
Clapham Junction 10	d						15 21	15 27			15 31	15 39	15 39	15 38		15 38		15 45							
Imperial Wharf	d											15 44	15 44												
West Brompton ⊖	d											15 47	15 47												
Kensington (Olympia) ⊖	d											15 50	15 50												
Shepherd's Bush ⊖	d											15 53	15 53												
Wembley Central ⊖	d											16s08	16 08												
Harrow & Wealdstone ⊖	d											16 13	16 13												
Watford Junction	d											16 20	16 20												
Milton Keynes Central 10	a											17 00	17 00												
Battersea Park 4	d									15 32	15 35			15 41			15 45	15 49							
London Victoria 15 ⊖	a						15 28	15 34		15 36	15 39			15 46		15 46		15 54							
Streatham 4	d			15 08	15 16																				
Tulse Hill 3	d		15 09	15 12	15 24																				15 39
Herne Hill 4	a			15 16																					
Loughborough Jn.	a			15 19																					
Elephant & Castle ⊖	a			15 23																					
London Blackfriars 3 ⊖	a			15 27																					
City Thameslink 3	a			15 32																					
St Pancras International 15 ⊖	a			15 40																					
Luton Airport Parkway 7	a			16 25																					
Luton 10	a			16 29																					
North Dulwich	d		15 12		15 27																				15 42
East Dulwich	d		15 14		15 29																				15 44
Peckham Rye 4	d		15 17		15 31												15 56								15 47
Queens Rd Peckham	d		15 19		15 34												15 59								15 49
South Bermondsey	d		15 22		15 36												16 01								15 52
London Bridge 4 ⊖	a	15 25	15 26		15 41										15 41		16 06		15 39		15 43		15 59	15 55	15 56

A until 30 March

B from 2 April

East and West Croydon, London Milton Keynes Central and Luton via Norbury Crystal Palace - Tulse Hill

Local Services

Network Diagram - see first Page of Table 177

		FC	SN ◇1 ⚒	SN	SN	SN	LO	SN	SN	SN	SN	SN	SN ◇1 ⚒		SN	SN	SN	LO	SN 1	SN	SN	SN 1	SN	FC	SN
East Croydon 🚌	d		15 41							15 47			16 00				15 51		15 55		16 00	16 07			
West Croydon 4 🚌	d			15 28	15 31	15 34	15 39									15 45		15 52		15 58					16 01
Norwood Junction 2	a						15 43									15 49	15 55	15 58	15 59		16 04	16 12			
	d															15 52	15 55		15 59		16 05	16 13			
Selhurst 4	d			15 32	15 35	15 39				15 50										16 02					16 05
Thornton Heath	d			15 34	15 37	15 41				15 52										16 04					16 07
Norbury	d			15 37	15 40	15 44				15 55										16 07					16 10
Streatham Common 4	d			15 40	15 43	15 47				15 58										16 10					16 13
Beckenham Junction 4 🚌	d																						15 53		
Birkbeck 🚌	d																						15 56		
Crystal Palace 4	d								15 43		15 51					15 56							16 00		
Gipsy Hill	d								15 45							15 59							16 02		
West Norwood 4	d								15 48							16 02							16 05		
Streatham Hill	d								15 52			15 56				16 05									
Balham 4 ⊖	d			15 44		15 51			15 55	16 02						16 09				16 14					
Wandsworth Common	d			15 46		15 53			15 57	16 04						16 11				16 16					
Clapham Junction 10	d		15 50	15 50		15 57			16 01	16 08			16 09			16 15				16 20					
Imperial Wharf	d																								
West Brompton ⊖	d																								
Kensington (Olympia) ⊖	d																								
Shepherd's Bush ⊖	d																								
Wembley Central ⊖	d																								
Harrow & Wealdstone ⊖	d																								
Watford Junction	d																								
Milton Keynes Central 10	a																								
Battersea Park 4	d			15 53				16 02	16 05	16 11					16 15	16 18				16 23					
London Victoria 15 ⊖	a		15 57	15 58		16 04		16 06	16 10	16 16			16 16			16 23				16 28					
Streatham 4	d	15 38			15 46																			16 08	16 16
Tulse Hill 3	d	15 42			15 54							16 00											16 09	16 12	16 24
Herne Hill 4	a	15 46																						16 16	
Loughborough Jn.	a	15 49																						16 19	
Elephant & Castle ⊖	a	15 53																						16 23	
London Blackfriars 3 ⊖	a	15 57																						16 29	
City Thameslink 3	a	16 02																						16 32	
St Pancras International 15 ⊖	a	16 10																						16 39	
Luton Airport Parkway 7	a	16 57																						17 25	
Luton 10	a	17 01																						17 29	
North Dulwich	d				15 57							16 03											16 12		16 27
East Dulwich	d				15 59							16 05											16 14		16 29
Peckham Rye 4	d				16 01							16 07			16 26								16 17		16 31
Queens Rd Peckham	d				16 04							16 10			16 29								16 19		16 34
South Bermondsey	d				16 06							16 12			16 31								16 22		16 36
London Bridge 4 ⊖	a				16 11						16 11	16 17			16 38		16 09		16 13		16 29	16 25	16 26		16 41

Table 177 | **Mondays to Fridays**

East and West Croydon, London Milton Keynes Central and Luton via Norbury Crystal Palace - Tulse Hill

Local Services | **Network Diagram - see first Page of Table 177**

		SN ◇1 🍴	SN	LO	SN		SN	SN 1 A	SN 1 B	SN	SN	SN ◇1 🍴	SN	SN	SN	LO	SN 1	SN	SN	SN	FC		SN	LO	SN 1
East Croydon 🚌	d	16 12						16 10	16 10	16 17		16 30			16 21		16 24			16 30					16 40
West Croydon 4 🚌	d		16 04	16 09										16 15		16 22			16 28				16 31	16 39	
Norwood Junction 2	a			16 13										16 20	16 25	16 28	16 28			16 34				16 43	16 44
	d													16 22	16 25		16 28			16 35					16 45
Selhurst 4	d		16 09					16 13	16 13	16 20									16 32				16 35		
Thornton Heath	d		16 11					16 16	16 16	16 22									16 34				16 37		
Norbury	d		16 14					16 19	16 19	16 25									16 37				16 40		
Streatham Common 4	d		16 17					16 21	16 21	16 28									16 40				16 43		
Beckenham Junction 4 🚌	d																	16 23							
Birkbeck 🚌	d																	16 26							
Crystal Palace 4	d						16 13				16 21			16 26				16 30							
Gipsy Hill	d						16 15							16 29				16 32							
West Norwood 4	d						16 18							16 32				16 35							
Streatham Hill	d						16 22							16 35											
Balham 4 ⊖	d		16 21				16 25	16 28	16 28	16 32				16 39					16 44						
Wandsworth Common	d		16 23				16 27	16 30	16 30	16 34				16 41					16 46						
Clapham Junction 10	d	16 21	16 27				16 31	16 39	16 39	16 38		16 40		16 45					16 50						
Imperial Wharf	d							16 44	16 44																
West Brompton ⊖	d							16 47	16 47																
Kensington (Olympia) ⊖	d							16 50	16 50																
Shepherd's Bush ⊖	d							16 53	16 53																
Wembley Central ⊖	d							17s08	17 08																
Harrow & Wealdstone ⊖	d							17 13	17 13																
Watford Junction	d							17 21	17 21																
Milton Keynes Central 10	a							17 59	17 59																
Battersea Park 4	d				16 32		16 35			16 41			16 45	16 49					16 53						
London Victoria 15 ⊖	a	16 28	16 34		16 38		16 40			16 46		16 46		16 55					16 58						
Streatham 4	d																				16 40		16 46		
Tulse Hill 3	d																	16 39			16 46		16 53		
Herne Hill 4	a																				16 50				
Loughborough Jn.	a																				16 53				
Elephant & Castle ⊖	a																				16 59				
London Blackfriars 3 ⊖	a																				17 03				
City Thameslink 3	a																				17 06				
St Pancras International 15 ⊖	a																				17 13				
Luton Airport Parkway 7	a																								
Luton 10	a																								
North Dulwich	d																	16 42					16 56		
East Dulwich	d																	16 44					16 58		
Peckham Rye 4	d												16 56					16 47					17 00		
Queens Rd Peckham	d												16 59					16 49					17 03		
South Bermondsey	d												17 01					16 52					17 05		
London Bridge 4 ⊖	a										16 41		17 08		16 39		16 43	16 56		17 02			17 10		17 00

A until 30 March

B from 2 April

East and West Croydon, London Milton Keynes Central and Luton via Norbury Crystal Palace - Tulse Hill

Local Services

Network Diagram - see first Page of Table 177

		SN	SN	SN	SN	SN	SN	SN	SN	SN	SN	LO	SN		SN	SN	SN	SN	FC	SN	SN	SN	LO	SN	SN
		◇1						◇1					1				1				◇1				
East Croydon	d	16 41				16 47		17 01			16 51		16 55			17 00	17 07				17 13				
West Croydon 4	d		16 34							16 45		16 52			16 58					17 01		17 04	17 09	17 12	
Norwood Junction 2	a									16 50	16 55	16 58	16 59			17 04	17 11						17 13		
	d									16 52	16 55		16 59			17 05	17 12								
Selhurst 4	d		16 39			16 50									17 02					17 05		17 09			
Thornton Heath	d		16 41			16 52									17 04					17 07		17 11			
Norbury	d		16 44			16 55									17 07					17 10		17 14			
Streatham Common 4	d		16 47			16 58									17 10					17 13		17 17			
Beckenham Junction 4	d																	16 53							
Birkbeck	d																	16 56							
Crystal Palace 4	d				16 43		16 50			16 56								17 00							
Gipsy Hill	d				16 45					16 59								17 02							
West Norwood 4	d				16 48					17 02								17 05							
Streatham Hill	d				16 52					17 05															
Balham 4 ⊖	d		16 51		16 55	17 02				17 09					17 14							17 21			
Wandsworth Common	d		16 53		16 57	17 04				17 11					17 16							17 23			
Clapham Junction 10	d	16 51	16 57		17 01	17 08		17 11		17 15					17 20						17 23	17 27			
Imperial Wharf	d																								
West Brompton ⊖	d																								
Kensington (Olympia) ⊖	d																								
Shepherd's Bush ⊖	d																								
Wembley Central ⊖	d																								
Harrow & Wealdstone ⊖	d																								
Watford Junction	d																								
Milton Keynes Central 10	a																								
Battersea Park 4	d			17 02	17 05	17 11			17 15	17 18					17 23										17 32
London Victoria 15 ⊖	a	16 58	17 04	17 08	17 10	17 16		17 17		17 23					17 28						17 29	17 34			17 38
Streatham 4	d																		17 10	17 16					
Tulse Hill 3	d																	17 09	17 16	17 22					
Herne Hill 4	a																		17 20						
Loughborough Jn.	a																		17 24						
Elephant & Castle ⊖	a																		17 28						
London Blackfriars 3 ⊖	a																		17 31						
City Thameslink 3	a																		17 34						
St Pancras International 15 ⊖	a																		17 41						
Luton Airport Parkway 7	a																		18 27						
Luton 10	a																		18 31						
North Dulwich	d																	17 12		17 25					
East Dulwich	d																	17 14		17 27					
Peckham Rye 4	d								17 26									17 17		17 29					
Queens Rd Peckham	d								17 29									17 19		17 32					
South Bermondsey	d								17 31									17 22		17 34					
London Bridge 4 ⊖	a						17 12		17 38		17 08		17 14			17 35	17 26	17 27		17 40				17 28	

East and West Croydon, London
Milton Keynes Central and Luton via Norbury
Crystal Palace - Tulse Hill

Local Services

Network Diagram - see first Page of Table 177

		SN	SN	SN	SN		SN	SN	SN	SN	FC	SN	SN	SN	LO	SN	SN	SN	SN	SN	LO		SN	SN	SN
			1	1				◇1		1						1							◇1	1	
			A	B																					
East Croydon	d		17 10	17 10				17 30	17 17	17 38				17 21		17 25			17 30				17 41	17 41	
West Croydon 4	d												17 18		17 22		17 28			17 31	17 39				17 42
Norwood Junction 2	a												17 22	17 25	17 28	17 30			17 34		17 43			17 45	
	d												17 23	17 25		17 31		17 32	17 35					17 45	
Selhurst 4	d		17 13	17 13					17 20								17 32			17 35					
Thornton Heath	d		17 16	17 16					17 22								17 34			17 37					
Norbury	d		17 19	17 19					17 25								17 37			17 40					
Streatham Common 4	d		17 21	17 21					17 28								17 40			17 43					
Beckenham Junction 4	d				17 11																				
Birkbeck	d				17 14																				
Crystal Palace 4	d	17 13			17 18		17 21						17 27					17 36							
Gipsy Hill	d	17 15			17 20								17 29					17 38							
West Norwood 4	d	17 18			17 23								17 32					17 41							
Streatham Hill	d	17 22											17 36												
Balham 4 ⊖	d	17 25	17 28	17 28					17 32				17 39				17 44								
Wandsworth Common	d	17 27	17 30	17 30					17 34				17 41				17 46								
Clapham Junction 10	d	17 31	17 39	17 39				17 40	17 38	17 48			17 45				17 50						17 51		
Imperial Wharf	d		17 44	17 44																					
West Brompton ⊖	d		17 47	17 47																					
Kensington (Olympia) ⊖	d		17 50	17 50																					
Shepherd's Bush ⊖	d		17 53	17 53																					
Wembley Central ⊖	d		18s08	18 08																					
Harrow & Wealdstone ⊖	d		18 13	18 13																					
Watford Junction	d		18 20	18 20																					
Milton Keynes Central 10	a		19 00	19 00																					
Battersea Park 4	d	17 35							17 41			17 45	17 48				17 53								
London Victoria 15 ⊖	a	17 42						17 46	17 48	17 54			17 55				17 58						17 58		
Streatham 4	d										17 40									17 46					
Tulse Hill 3	d				17 27						17 44							17 45		17 54					
Herne Hill 4	a										17 47														
Loughborough Jn	a										17 51														
Elephant & Castle ⊖	a										17 55														
London Blackfriars 3 ⊖	a										17 59														
City Thameslink 3	a										18 02														
St Pancras International 15 ⊖	a										18 09														
Luton Airport Parkway 7	a										18 58														
Luton 10	a										19 01														
North Dulwich	d				17 30													17 48		17 57					
East Dulwich	d				17 32													17 50		17 59					
Peckham Rye 4	d				17 35							17 57						17 53		18 01					
Queens Rd Peckham	d				17 37							17 59						17 55		18 04					
South Bermondsey	d				17 40							18 02						17 58		18 06					
London Bridge 4 ⊖	a				17 44		17 43					18 08		17 37		17 45		18 02	17 59	18 11				17 58	18 00

A until 30 March

B from 2 April

East and West Croydon, London
Milton Keynes Central and Luton via Norbury
Crystal Palace - Tulse Hill

Local Services

Network Diagram - see first Page of Table 177

		SN	SN	SN	SN	SN	SN	SN ◇1 🚲	FC	SN	SN	LO	SN 1		SN	SN 1	SN	SN	LO	SN 1 A	SN 1 B	SN ◇1 🚲	SN	SN	SN
East Croydon	d			17 47	17 51			18 02					17 55		18 08	18 09				18 10	18 10	18 12			
West Croydon 4	d										17 48	17 52					17 58	18 01	18 09				18 13		
Norwood Junction 2	a				17 55						17 54	17 58	17 59		18 12				18 13						
	d				17 55						17 55		17 59		18 12										
Selhurst 4	d			17 50													18 02	18 05		18 13	18 13				
Thornton Heath	d			17 52													18 04	18 07		18 16	18 16				
Norbury	d			17 55													18 07	18 10		18 19	18 19				
Streatham Common 4	d			17 58													18 10	18 13		18 21	18 21				
Beckenham Junction 4	d						17 48																		
Birkbeck	d						17 51																		
Crystal Palace 4	d		17 44			17 48	17 55				17 59														
Gipsy Hill	d		17 46				17 57				18 01														
West Norwood 4	d		17 49				18 00				18 04														
Streatham Hill	d		17 53								18 08														
Balham 4 ⊖	d		17 56	18 02							18 11						18 14			18 29	18 29				
Wandsworth Common	d		17 58	18 04							18 13						18 16			18 31	18 31				
Clapham Junction 10	d		18 02	18 08				18 13			18 17					18 19	18 20			18 39	18 39	18 22			
Imperial Wharf	d																			18 44	18 44				
West Brompton ⊖	d																			18 47	18 47				
Kensington (Olympia) ⊖	d																			18 50	18 50				
Shepherd's Bush ⊖	d																			18 53	18 53				
Wembley Central ⊖	d																			19s08	19 08				
Harrow & Wealdstone ⊖	d																			19 13	19 13				
Watford Junction	d																			19 21	19 21				
Milton Keynes Central 10	a																			20 06	20 06				
Battersea Park 4	d	18 02	18 06	18 11						18 15	18 20						18 23								18 32
London Victoria 15 ⊖	a	18 08	18 12	18 16				18 20			18 25					18 26	18 28					18 29			18 39
Streatham 4	d								18 10									18 16						18 20	
Tulse Hill 3	d						18 05		18 16									18 20						18 24	
Herne Hill 4	a								18 19																
Loughborough Jn.	a								18 23																
Elephant & Castle ⊖	a								18 27																
London Blackfriars 3 ⊖	a								18 31																
City Thameslink 3	a								18 34																
St Pancras International 15 ⊖	a								18 41																
Luton Airport Parkway 7	a								19 30																
Luton 10	a								19 33																
North Dulwich	d						18 08											18 23						18 27	
East Dulwich	d						18 10											18 25						18 29	
Peckham Rye 4	d						18 12			18 26								18 29						18 32	
Queens Rd Peckham	d						18 15			18 29								18 32						18 35	
South Bermondsey	d						18 17			18 31								18 34						18 37	
London Bridge 4 ⊖	a				18 09	18 13	18 22			18 38			18 16		18 26			18 39					18 29	18 42	

A until 30 March

B from 2 April

East and West Croydon, London Milton Keynes Central and Luton via Norbury Crystal Palace - Tulse Hill

Local Services

Network Diagram - see first Page of Table 177

		SN	SN	SN	SN [1]		SN	SN ◇[1] (bus)	FC	SN	SN	SN	LO	SN	SN [1]	SN	SN	LO	SN ◇[1] (bus)	SN	SN		SN	SN [1]	SN
East Croydon (train)	d				18 27		18 17	18 30				18 21		18 30	18 40				18 43					18 55	18 47
West Croydon [4] (train)	d										18 18		18 22			18 28	18 31	18 39							
Norwood Junction [2]	a										18 23	18 28	18 28	18 34				18 43							
	d										18 24	18 29		18 35											
Selhurst [4]	d						18 20									18 32	18 36								18 51
Thornton Heath	d						18 22									18 34	18 38								18 53
Norbury	d						18 25									18 37	18 41								18 56
Streatham Common [4]	d						18 28									18 40	18 44								18 58
Beckenham Junction [4] (train)	d		18 11																						
Birkbeck (train)	d		18 14																						
Crystal Palace [4]	d	18 13	18 18	18 20							18 28										18 43		18 51		
Gipsy Hill	d	18 15	18 20								18 30										18 45				
West Norwood [4]	d	18 18	18 23								18 33										18 48				
Streatham Hill	d	18 22									18 37										18 52				
Balham [4] (U)	d	18 25					18 33				18 40					18 44					18 55				19 02
Wandsworth Common	d	18 27					18 35				18 42					18 46					18 57				19 04
Clapham Junction [10]	d	18 32			18 38		18 39	18 41			18 46				18 50	18 50			18 53		19 01			19 06	19 08
Imperial Wharf	d																								
West Brompton (U)	d																								
Kensington (Olympia) (U)	d																								
Shepherd's Bush (U)	d																								
Wembley Central (U)	d																								
Harrow & Wealdstone (U)	d																								
Watford Junction	d																								
Milton Keynes Central [10]	a																								
Battersea Park [4]	d	18 35								18 45	18 49									19 02	19 05				
London Victoria [15] (U)	a	18 42			18 45		18 46	18 48			18 54				18 56	18 57			18 59	19 08	19 12			19 13	19 15
Streatham [4]	d								18 40								18 47								
Tulse Hill [3]	d		18 28						18 44								18 54								
Herne Hill [4]	a								18 47																
Loughborough Jn.	a								18 51																
Elephant & Castle (U)	a								18 55																
London Blackfriars [3] (U)	a								18 59																
City Thameslink [3]	a								19 02																
St Pancras International [15] (U)	a								19 09																
Luton Airport Parkway [7]	a								19 54																
Luton [10]	a								19 57																
North Dulwich	d		18 31														18 57								
East Dulwich	d		18 33														18 59								
Peckham Rye [4]	d		18 36							18 57							19 01								
Queens Rd Peckham	d		18 38							19 00							19 04								
South Bermondsey	d		18 41							19 02							19 06								
London Bridge [4] (U)	a		18 45	18 45						19 09		18 41		18 59			19 11						19 13		

East and West Croydon, London
Milton Keynes Central and Luton via Norbury
Crystal Palace - Tulse Hill

Local Services

Network Diagram - see first Page of Table 177

Station		SN	SN	SN ◇1	FC	SN	SN	LO	SN	SN	SN 1	SN	LO		SN 1 A	SN 1 B	SN ◇1 🚂	SN	SN	SN	SN 1	SN	SN ◇1	SN	SN
East Croydon 🚆	d			19 00						19 00	19 10				19 10	19 10	19 12				19 25		19 29	19 17	
West Croydon 4 🚆	d						18 47	18 52	18 58			19 01	19 09												
Norwood Junction 2	a						18 51	18 58		19 04	19 13		19 13												
	d						18 52			19 05	19 13														
Selhurst 4	d								19 02			19 05			19 13	19 13								19 20	
Thornton Heath	d								19 04			19 07			19 16	19 16								19 22	
Norbury	d								19 07			19 10			19 19	19 19								19 25	
Streatham Common 4	d								19 10			19 13			19 21	19 21								19 28	
Beckenham Junction 4 🚆	d		18 44																						
Birkbeck 🚆	d		18 47																						
Crystal Palace 4	d		18 51				18 56												19 13	19 21					
Gipsy Hill	d		18 53				18 59												19 15						
West Norwood 4	d		18 56				19 02												19 18						
Streatham Hill	d						19 05												19 22						
Balham 4 ⊖	d						19 09		19 14						19 28	19 28			19 25					19 32	
Wandsworth Common	d						19 11		19 16						19 30	19 30			19 27					19 34	
Clapham Junction 10	d			19 12			19 15		19 20						19 39	19 39	19 22		19 31		19 38		19 41	19 38	
Imperial Wharf	d														19 44	19 44									
West Brompton ⊖	d														19 47	19 47									
Kensington (Olympia) ⊖	d														19 50	19 50									
Shepherd's Bush ⊖	d														19 53	19 53									
Wembley Central ⊖	d														20s08	20 08									
Harrow & Wealdstone ⊖	d														20 13	20 13									
Watford Junction	d														20 20	20 20									
Milton Keynes Central 10	a														21 01	21 01									
Battersea Park 4	d					19 15	19 18		19 23									19 32	19 35					19 41	19 45
London Victoria 15 ⊖	a			19 18			19 25		19 28								19 29	19 36	19 41		19 44		19 47	19 48	
Streatham 4	d	18 56			19 10							19 16										19 26			
Tulse Hill 3	d	19 00	19 07		19 14							19 22										19 31			
Herne Hill 4	a				19 17																				
Loughborough Jn.	a				19 20																				
Elephant & Castle ⊖	a				19 24																				
London Blackfriars 3 ⊖	a				19 28																				
City Thameslink 3	a				19 32																				
St Pancras International 15 ⊖	a				19 40																				
Luton Airport Parkway 7	a				20 25																				
Luton 10	a				20 29																				
North Dulwich	d	19 03	19 10									19 25										19 34			
East Dulwich	d	19 05	19 12									19 27										19 36			
Peckham Rye 4	d	19 07	19 14			19 26						19 29										19 38			19 56
Queens Rd Peckham	d	19 10	19 17			19 29						19 32										19 41			19 59
South Bermondsey	d	19 12	19 19			19 31						19 34										19 43			20 01
London Bridge 4 ⊖	a	19 17	19 24			19 36				19 29	19 25	19 41								19 41		19 51			20 06

A until 30 March

B from 2 April

East and West Croydon, London
Milton Keynes Central and Luton via Norbury
Crystal Palace - Tulse Hill

Local Services **Network Diagram - see first Page of Table 177**

		SN	LO	SN	SN		SN	SN	FC	SN	FC	SN	SN	SN	SN	LO	SN	SN	SN	SN	SN		LO	SN	SN
							■1			◇■1	■1							■1	■1						
East Croydon	d				19 30		19 40			19 43	19 47						19 47	19 59	20 01						
West Croydon ■4	d	19 17	19 22					19 28							19 31	19 39					19 47		19 52		19 58
Norwood Junction ■2	a	19 21	19 28		19 34											19 43					19 51		19 58		
	d	19 22			19 35																19 52				
Selhurst ■4	d							19 32							19 35		19 50								20 02
Thornton Heath	d							19 34							19 37		19 52								20 04
Norbury	d							19 37							19 40		19 55								20 07
Streatham Common ■4	d							19 40							19 43		19 58								20 10
Beckenham Junction ■4	d			19 25																				19 54	
Birkbeck	d			19 28																				19 57	
Crystal Palace ■4	d	19 26		19 32									19 43	19 51							19 56			20 01	
Gipsy Hill	d	19 29		19 34									19 45								19 58			20 03	
West Norwood ■4	d	19 32		19 37									19 48								20 01			20 06	
Streatham Hill	d	19 35											19 52								20 05				
Balham ■4 ⊖	d	19 39						19 45					19 55				20 02				20 08				20 14
Wandsworth Common	d	19 41						19 47					19 57				20 04				20 10				20 16
Clapham Junction ■10	d	19 45					19 50	19 51		19 53			20 01				20 08	20 08	20 11		20 14				20 20
Imperial Wharf	d																								
West Brompton ⊖	d																								
Kensington (Olympia) ⊖	d																								
Shepherd's Bush ⊖	d																								
Wembley Central ⊖	d																								
Harrow & Wealdstone ⊖	d																								
Watford Junction	d																								
Milton Keynes Central ■10	a																								
Battersea Park ■4	d	19 48						19 54				20 02	20 05				20a11			20 15	20 18				20 23
London Victoria ■15 ⊖	a	19 54					19 56	19 59		19 59		20 06	20 09					20 15	20 20		20 22				20 28
Streatham ■4	d								19 40						19 46										
Tulse Hill ■3	d			19 41					19 44						19 54									20 11	
Herne Hill ■4	a								19 47																
Loughborough Jn	a								19 50																
Elephant & Castle ⊖	a								19 54																
London Blackfriars ■3 ⊖	a								19 58		20 07														
City Thameslink ■3	a								20 02		20 10														
St Pancras International ■15 ⊖	a								20 10		20 18														
Luton Airport Parkway ■7	a								20 55		20 50														
Luton ■10	a								20 59		20 53														
North Dulwich	d			19 44											19 57									20 14	
East Dulwich	d			19 46											19 59									20 16	
Peckham Rye ■4	d			19 49											20 01					20 26				20 18	
Queens Rd Peckham	d			19 51											20 04					20 29				20 21	
South Bermondsey	d			19 54											20 06					20 31				20 23	
London Bridge ■4 ⊖	a			19 58	19 59									20 11	20 14					20 36				20 28	

		SN	FC	SN	LO	SN	SN	SN	SN	SN	SN	SN	SN		SN	LO	SN	SN	FC	SN	SN	SN	LO	SN	SN
						◇■1				■1		◇■1									◇■1				
East Croydon	d	20 00				20 11				20 26	20 17	20 30						20 31			20 41				
West Croydon ■4	d			20 01	20 09										20 18	20 22				20 31		20 35	20 39		
Norwood Junction ■2	a	20 04			20 13										20 22	20 28		20 35					20 43		
	d	20 05													20 23			20 35							
Selhurst ■4	d			20 05							20 20									20 35		20 39			
Thornton Heath	d			20 07							20 22									20 37		20 41			
Norbury	d			20 10							20 25									20 40		20 44			
Streatham Common ■4	d			20 13							20 28									20 43		20 47			
Beckenham Junction ■4	d																20 24								
Birkbeck	d																20 27								
Crystal Palace ■4	d							20 13	20 21						20 27		20 31								20 43
Gipsy Hill	d							20 16							20 29		20 33								20 45
West Norwood ■4	d							20 19							20 32		20 36								20 48
Streatham Hill	d							20 22							20 36										20 52
Balham ■4 ⊖	d							20 25			20 32				20 39							20 51			20 56
Wandsworth Common	d							20 27			20 34				20 41							20 53			20 58
Clapham Junction ■10	d					20 21		20 31		20 37	20 38	20 41			20 45						20 51	20 57			21 03
Imperial Wharf	d																								
West Brompton ⊖	d																								
Kensington (Olympia) ⊖	d																								
Shepherd's Bush ⊖	d																								
Wembley Central ⊖	d																								
Harrow & Wealdstone ⊖	d																								
Watford Junction	d																								
Milton Keynes Central ■10	a																								
Battersea Park ■4	d						20 32	20 35			20 41		20 45		20 48									21 02	21 06
London Victoria ■15 ⊖	a					20 28	20 36	20 39		20 44	20 46	20 50			20 53						20 59	21 04		21 06	21 11
Streatham ■4	d		20 06	20 17															20 36	20 46					
Tulse Hill ■3	d		20 12	20 24													20 40		20 42	20 54					
Herne Hill ■4	a		20 16																20 46						
Loughborough Jn	a		20 19																20 49						
Elephant & Castle ⊖	a		20 23																20 53						
London Blackfriars ■3 ⊖	a		20 27																20 57						
City Thameslink ■3	a		20 32																21 02						
St Pancras International ■15 ⊖	a		20 40																21 10						
Luton Airport Parkway ■7	a		21 25																21 55						
Luton ■10	a		21 29																21 59						
North Dulwich	d			20 27													20 43			20 57					
East Dulwich	d			20 29													20 45			20 59					
Peckham Rye ■4	d			20 31									20 56				20 48			21 01					
Queens Rd Peckham	d			20 34									20 59				20 50			21 04					
South Bermondsey	d			20 36									21 01				20 53			21 06					
London Bridge ■4 ⊖	a	20 29		20 41					20 41				21 06				20 57	20 59		21 11					

East and West Croydon, London
Milton Keynes Central and Luton via Norbury
Crystal Palace - Tulse Hill

Local Services

Network Diagram - see first Page of Table 177

		SN	SN 1	SN	SN		SN	LO	SN	SN	FC	SN	SN ◇1	SN	LO	SN	SN	SN	SN 1	SN	SN ◇1		SN	SN	LO
East Croydon	d		20 57	20 47						21 00			21 09						21 26	21 17	21 30				
West Croydon 4	d						20 45	20 52				21 01		21 04	21 09									21 18	21 22
Norwood Junction 2	a						20 49	20 58		21 04					21 13									21 22	21 28
	d						20 52			21 05														21 23	
Selhurst 4	d			20 50								21 05		21 09						21 20					
Thornton Heath	d			20 52								21 07		21 11						21 22					
Norbury	d			20 55								21 10		21 14						21 25					
Streatham Common 4	d			20 58								21 13		21 17						21 28					
Beckenham Junction 4	d								20 53																
Birkbeck	d								20 56																
Crystal Palace 4	d	20 51					20 56		21 00								21 13	21 21						21 27	
Gipsy Hill	d						20 59		21 02								21 15							21 29	
West Norwood 4	d						21 02		21 05								21 18							21 32	
Streatham Hill	d						21 05										21 22							21 36	
Balham 4 ⊖	d			21 02			21 08							21 21			21 26			21 32				21 39	
Wandsworth Common	d			21 04			21 10							21 23			21 28			21 34				21 41	
Clapham Junction 10	d		21 08	21 08			21 14						21 18	21 27			21 33		21 38	21 38	21 41			21 45	
Imperial Wharf	d																								
West Brompton ⊖	d																								
Kensington (Olympia) ⊖	d																								
Shepherd's Bush ⊖	d																								
Wembley Central ⊖	d																								
Harrow & Wealdstone ⊖	d																								
Watford Junction	d																								
Milton Keynes Central 10	a																								
Battersea Park 4	d			21 11	21 15		21 18									21 32	21 36			21 41			21 45	21 48	
London Victoria 15 ⊖	a		21 15	21 18			21 22						21 28	21 34		21 36	21 41		21 45	21 48	21 49			21 53	
Streatham 4	d										21 06	21 16													
Tulse Hill 3	d								21 09		21 12	21 24													
Herne Hill 4	a										21 16														
Loughborough Jn.	a										21 19														
Elephant & Castle ⊖	a										21 23														
London Blackfriars 3 ⊖	a										21 27														
City Thameslink 3	a										21 32														
St Pancras International 15 ⊖	a										21 40														
Luton Airport Parkway 7	a										22 25														
Luton 10	a										22 29														
North Dulwich	d								21 12			21 27													
East Dulwich	d								21 14			21 29													
Peckham Rye 4	d				21 26				21 17			21 31											21 56		
Queens Rd Peckham	d				21 29				21 19			21 34											21 59		
South Bermondsey	d				21 31				21 22			21 36											22 01		
London Bridge 4 ⊖	a	21 11			21 36				21 26	21 29		21 41						21 43					22 06		

		SN	SN	SN ◇1	FC	SN	SN	LO	SN	SN	SN	SN 1	SN		SN	SN	LO	SN	SN	SN	SN ◇1	SN	LO	SN	SN
East Croydon	d		21 30	21 42								21 57	21 47						22 00		22 09				
West Croydon 4	d					21 31	21 34	21 39								21 48	21 52			22 01		22 04	22 09		
Norwood Junction 2	a		21 34					21 43								21 52	21 58		22 04				22 13		
	d		21 35													21 53			22 05						
Selhurst 4	d					21 35	21 39						21 50							22 05		22 09			
Thornton Heath	d					21 37	21 41						21 52							22 07		22 11			
Norbury	d					21 40	21 44						21 55							22 10		22 14			
Streatham Common 4	d					21 43	21 47						21 58							22 13		22 17			
Beckenham Junction 4	d	21 23																21 53							
Birkbeck	d	21 26																21 56							
Crystal Palace 4	d	21 30								21 43	21 51					21 57		22 00							22 13
Gipsy Hill	d	21 32								21 45						21 59		22 02							22 15
West Norwood 4	d	21 35								21 48						22 02		22 05							22 18
Streatham Hill	d									21 52						22 06									22 22
Balham 4 ⊖	d						21 51			21 56			22 02			22 09						22 21			22 26
Wandsworth Common	d						21 53			21 58			22 04			22 11						22 23			22 28
Clapham Junction 10	d			21 51			21 57			22 03		22 08	22 08			22 15					22 18	22 27			22 33
Imperial Wharf	d																								
West Brompton ⊖	d																								
Kensington (Olympia) ⊖	d																								
Shepherd's Bush ⊖	d																								
Wembley Central ⊖	d																								
Harrow & Wealdstone ⊖	d																								
Watford Junction	d																								
Milton Keynes Central 10	a																								
Battersea Park 4	d								22 02	22 06			22 11		22 15	22 18								22 32	22 36
London Victoria 15 ⊖	a			21 58			22 04		22 06	22 11		22 14	22 18			22 23					22 26	22 34		22 36	22 41
Streatham 4	d				21 49	21 46														22 16					
Tulse Hill 3	d	21 39			21 53	21 54												22 09		22 24					
Herne Hill 4	a				21 56																				
Loughborough Jn.	a				22 00																				
Elephant & Castle ⊖	a				22 04																				
London Blackfriars 3 ⊖	a				22 07																				
City Thameslink 3	a				22 10																				
St Pancras International 15 ⊖	a				22 17																				
Luton Airport Parkway 7	a				23 01																				
Luton 10	a				23 04																				
North Dulwich	d	21 42				21 57												22 12		22 27					
East Dulwich	d	21 44				21 59												22 14		22 29					
Peckham Rye 4	d	21 47				22 01									22 26			22 17		22 31					
Queens Rd Peckham	d	21 49				22 04									22 29			22 19		22 34					
South Bermondsey	d	21 52				22 06									22 31			22 22		22 36					
London Bridge 4 ⊖	a	21 56	21 59			22 11					22 13				22 36			22 26	22 29	22 41					

Table 177

Mondays to Fridays

East and West Croydon, London
Milton Keynes Central and Luton via Norbury
Crystal Palace - Tulse Hill

Local Services

Network Diagram - see first Page of Table 177

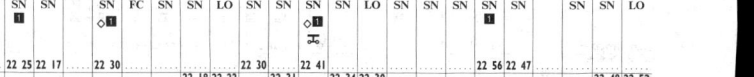

		SN	SN	SN 1	SN		SN ◇1	FC	SN	SN	LO	SN	SN	SN ◇1	SN	LO	SN	SN	SN	SN 1	SN		SN	SN	LO
East Croydon	d			22 25	22 17		22 30					22 30		22 41						22 56	22 47				
West Croydon 4	d									22 18	22 22		22 31		22 34	22 39								22 48	22 52
Norwood Junction 2	a									22 22	22 28	22 34				22 43								22 52	22 58
	d									22 23		22 35												22 53	
Selhurst 4	d				22 20								22 35		22 39						22 50				
Thornton Heath	d				22 22								22 37		22 41						22 52				
Norbury	d				22 25								22 40		22 44						22 55				
Streatham Common 4	d				22 28								22 43		22 47						22 58				
Beckenham Junction 4	d		22 15																						
Birkbeck	d		22 18																						
Crystal Palace 4	d	22 21	22 22							22 27								22 43	22 51					22 57	
Gipsy Hill	d		22 24							22 29								22 45						22 59	
West Norwood 4	d		22 27							22 32								22 48						23 02	
Streatham Hill	d									22 36								22 52						23 06	
Balham 4 ⊖	d				22 32					22 39					22 51			22 56			23 02			23 09	
Wandsworth Common	d				22 34					22 41					22 53			22 58			23 04			23 11	
Clapham Junction 10	d			22 38	22 38		22 41			22 45				22 51	22 57			23 03		23 07	23 08			23 15	
Imperial Wharf	d																								
West Brompton ⊖	d																								
Kensington (Olympia) ⊖	d																								
Shepherd's Bush ⊖	d																								
Wembley Central ⊖	d																								
Harrow & Wealdstone ⊖	d																								
Watford Junction	d																								
Milton Keynes Central 10	a																								
Battersea Park 4	d				22 41				22 45	22 48							23 02	23 07			23 11		23 15	23 19	
London Victoria 15 ⊖	a			22 44	22 48		22 50			22 53				22 57	23 04		23 06	23 14		23 15	23 16			23 25	
Streatham 4	d							22 40					22 46												
Tulse Hill 3	d		22 35					22 44					22 54												
Herne Hill 4	a																								
Loughborough Jn.	a																								
Elephant & Castle ⊖	a																								
London Blackfriars 3 ⊖	a																								
City Thameslink 3	a																								
St Pancras International 15 ⊖	a																								
Luton Airport Parkway 7	a																								
Luton 10	a																								
North Dulwich	d		22 38										22 57												
East Dulwich	d		22 40										22 59												
Peckham Rye 4	d		22 43						22 56				23 01										23 26		
Queens Rd Peckham	d		22 45						22 59				23 04										23 29		
South Bermondsey	d		22 48						23 01				23 06										23 31		
London Bridge 4 ⊖	a	22 45	22 52					22 55	23 06			22 59	23 11						23 11				23 36		

		SN	SN	SN	SN	SN	SN	SN	SN	SN ◇1	SN	LO	SN		SN	SN	SN	SN 1							
East Croydon	d		23 01					23 17		23 30					23 43			23 58							
West Croydon 4	d			23 01	23 04						23 18	23 22													
Norwood Junction 2	a		23 05								23 22	23 28			23 47										
	d		23 06								23 23														
Selhurst 4	d			23 05	23 09			23 20										00 02							
Thornton Heath	d			23 07	23 11			23 22																	
Norbury	d			23 10	23 14			23 25																	
Streatham Common 4	d			23 13	23 17			23 28																	
Beckenham Junction 4	d	22 53											23 23												
Birkbeck	d	22 56											23 26												
Crystal Palace 4	d	23 00					23 13		23 21		23 27		23 30			23 43	23 51								
Gipsy Hill	d	23 02					23 15				23 29		23 32			23 45									
West Norwood 4	d	23 05					23 18				23 32		23 35			23 48									
Streatham Hill	d						23 22				23 36					23 52									
Balham 4 ⊖	d				23 21		23 26	23 32			23 40					23 55									
Wandsworth Common	d				23 23		23 28	23 34			23 42					23 58									
Clapham Junction 10	d				23 27		23 33	23 38		23 42	23 46					00 02		00 12							
Imperial Wharf	d																								
West Brompton ⊖	d																								
Kensington (Olympia) ⊖	d																								
Shepherd's Bush ⊖	d																								
Wembley Central ⊖	d																								
Harrow & Wealdstone ⊖	d																								
Watford Junction	d																								
Milton Keynes Central 10	a																								
Battersea Park 4	d					23 32	23 37	23 41			23 49					00 05									
London Victoria 15 ⊖	a				23 34	23 37	23 41	23 48		23 52	23 54					00 10		00 18							
Streatham 4	d			23 16																					
Tulse Hill 3	d	23 09		23 24									23 39												
Herne Hill 4	a																								
Loughborough Jn.	a																								
Elephant & Castle ⊖	a																								
London Blackfriars 3 ⊖	a																								
City Thameslink 3	a																								
St Pancras International 15 ⊖	a																								
Luton Airport Parkway 7	a																								
Luton 10	a																								
North Dulwich	d	23 12		23 27									23 42												
East Dulwich	d	23 14		23 29									23 44												
Peckham Rye 4	d	23 17		23 31									23 47												
Queens Rd Peckham	d	23 19		23 34									23 49												
South Bermondsey	d	23 22		23 36									23 52												
London Bridge 4 ⊖	a	23 26	23 30	23 41					23 45				23 56				00 11								

Table 177

Saturdays

East and West Croydon, London Milton Keynes Central and Luton via Norbury Crystal Palace - Tulse Hill

Local Services

Network Diagram - see first Page of Table 177

		SN	SN	SN 1	SN	SN	SN	SN 1	FC 1	SN 1	FC 1	SN 1	FC 1	SN 1	FC 1	SN		FC 1	LO	FC 1	FC	SN	LO	SN	FC
East Croydon	d			23p58			00 49	01 28	01 50	02 28	02 47	03 28	03 47	04 28	04 47			05 17		05 47					
West Croydon 4	d																		05 39				05 52		
Norwood Junction 2	a																		05 43				05 58		
	d																					05 52			
Selhurst 4	d			00 02			00 52	01 30	01 53		02 50		03 50		04 50			05 20			05 39			06 01	06 09
Thornton Heath	d																				05 41			06 03	06 11
Norbury	d																				05 43			06 06	06 13
Streatham Common 4	d																				05 46			06 08	06 16
Beckenham Junction 4	d																								
Birkbeck	d																								
Crystal Palace 4	d	23p43	23p51		00 13	00 21																05 56			
Gipsy Hill	d	23p45			00 15																	05 59			
West Norwood 4	d	23p48			00 18																	06 02			
Streatham Hill	d	23p52			00 22																	06 05			
Balham 4 ⊖	d	23p55			00 25																	06 09		06 12	
Wandsworth Common	d	23p58			00 27																	06 11		06 14	
Clapham Junction 10	d	00 02		00 12	00 31		01 01	01 41		02 41		03 41		04 41		05 00						06 15		06 18	
Imperial Wharf	d																								
West Brompton ⊖	d																								
Kensington (Olympia) ⊖	d																								
Shepherd's Bush ⊖	d																								
Wembley Central ⊖	d																								
Harrow & Wealdstone ⊖	d																								
Watford Junction	d																								
Milton Keynes Central 10	a																								
Battersea Park 4	d	00 05			00 35											05 03						06 18		06 22	
London Victoria 15 ⊖	a	00 10		00 18	00 42		01 09	01 49		02 49		03 49		04 50		05 08						06 23		06 26	
Streatham 4	d																				05 49				06 19
Tulse Hill 3	d																				05 55				06 23
Herne Hill 4	a																								
Loughborough Jn.	a																								
Elephant & Castle ⊖	a																								
London Blackfriars 3 ⊖	a																								
City Thameslink 3	a																								
St Pancras International 15 ⊖	a																								
Luton Airport Parkway 7	a																								
Luton 10	a																								
North Dulwich	d																								
East Dulwich	d																								
Peckham Rye 4	d																								
Queens Rd Peckham	d																								
South Bermondsey	d																								
London Bridge 4 ⊖	a		00 11			00 41			02 14		03 12		04 12		05 12			05 42		06 01	06 09				06 35

Table 177

Saturdays

East and West Croydon, London
Milton Keynes Central and Luton via Norbury
Crystal Palace - Tulse Hill

Local Services

Network Diagram - see first Page of Table 177

		SN	LO	SN	SN	SN	SN	SN	LO	SN	SN	SN	SN	FC	LO	SN	SN	SN	SN	SN	LO	SN	SN
		◇1		1	1					1		◇1										1	
				A	B																		
East Croydon 🚌	d	06 07		06 10	06 10					06 25	06 30	06 41				06 43		06 47				06 55	07 00
West Croydon 4 🚌	d		06 09					06 18	06 22						06 39					06 45	06 52		
Norwood Junction 2	a		06 13					06 22	06 28	06 29	06 34				06 43	06 49				06 52	06 58	06 59	07 04
	d							06 23		06 29	06 35		06 41			06 50				06 53		06 59	07 05
Selhurst 4	d			06 13	06 13									06 39				06 50					
Thornton Heath	d			06 16	06 16									06 41				06 52					
Norbury	d			06 19	06 19									06 43				06 55					
Streatham Common 4	d			06 21	06 21									06 46				06 58					
Beckenham Junction 4 🚌	d																						
Birkbeck 🚌	d																						
Crystal Palace 4	d							06 27					06 45							06 57			
Gipsy Hill	d							06 29					06 47							06 59			
West Norwood 4	d							06 32					06 50							07 02			
Streatham Hill	d							06 36												07 06			
Balham 4 ⊖	d			06 28	06 28			06 39										07 02		07 09			
Wandsworth Common	d			06 30	06 30			06 41										07 04		07 11			
Clapham Junction 10	d	06 19		06 39	06 39			06 45				06 50						07 08		07 15			
Imperial Wharf	d			06 44	06 44																		
West Brompton ⊖	d			06 47	06 47																		
Kensington (Olympia) ⊖	d			06 50	06 50																		
Shepherd's Bush ⊖	d			06 53	06 53																		
Wembley Central ⊖	d			07s07	07 07																		
Harrow & Wealdstone ⊖	d			07 12	07 12																		
Watford Junction	d			07 19	07 19																		
Milton Keynes Central 10	a			08 00	08 00																		
Battersea Park 4	d					06 32	06 45	06 48									07 02	07 11	07 15	07 19			
London Victoria 15 ⊖	a	06 26				06 36		06 53				06 57					07 06	07 16		07 24			
Streatham 4	d													06 49									
Tulse Hill 3	d												06 54	06 57									
Herne Hill 4	a													07 01									
Loughborough Jn.	a																						
Elephant & Castle ⊖	a																						
London Blackfriars 3 ⊖	a																						
City Thameslink 3	a																						
St Pancras International 15 ⊖	a																						
Luton Airport Parkway 7	a																						
Luton 10	a																						
North Dulwich	d												06 57										
East Dulwich	d												06 59										
Peckham Rye 4	d						06 56						07 01						07 26				
Queens Rd Peckham	d						06 59						07 04						07 29				
South Bermondsey	d						07 01						07 06						07 31				
London Bridge 4 ⊖	a						07 06			06 43	06 59		07 14			07 11			07 36			07 13	07 29

A until 31 March

B from 7 April

Table 177

Saturdays

East and West Croydon, London
Milton Keynes Central and Luton via Norbury
Crystal Palace - Tulse Hill

Local Services

Network Diagram - see first Page of Table 177

		SN	SN	SN	FC	SN	LO	SN	SN	SN	SN	SN	SN	SN	SN	LO		SN	SN	SN	FC	SN	LO	SN	SN
		■1	◇■1					■1	■1				◇■1					■1						■1	◇■1
								A	B																
East Croydon 🚌	d	07 07	07 10					07 10	07 10			07 17	07 30					07 25		07 30				07 39	07 42
West Croydon ■4 🚌	d			06 58		07 01	07 09			07 15						07 22			07 28			07 31	07 39		
Norwood Junction ■2	a	07 12					07 13			07 19						07 28		07 29		07 34			07 43	07 44	
	d	07 13								07 20					07 23			07 29		07 35				07 45	
Selhurst ■4	d			07 02		07 05		07 13	07 13			07 20							07 32			07 35			
Thornton Heath	d			07 04		07 07		07 16	07 16			07 22							07 34			07 37			
Norbury	d			07 07		07 10		07 19	07 19			07 25							07 37			07 40			
Streatham Common ■4	d			07 10		07 13		07 21	07 21			07 28							07 40			07 43			
Beckenham Junction ■4 🚌	d																								
Birkbeck 🚌	d																								
Crystal Palace ■4	d														07 27										
Gipsy Hill	d														07 29										
West Norwood ■4	d														07 32										
Streatham Hill	d														07 36										
Balham ■4 ⊖	d			07 14				07 28	07 28			07 32			07 39				07 44						
Wandsworth Common	d			07 16				07 30	07 30			07 34			07 41				07 46						
Clapham Junction ■10	d		07 19	07 20				07 39	07 39			07 38	07 39		07 45				07 50						07 51
Imperial Wharf	d							07 44	07 44																
West Brompton ⊖	d							07 47	07 47																
Kensington (Olympia) ⊖	d							07 50	07 50																
Shepherd's Bush ⊖	d							07 53	07 53																
Wembley Central ⊖	d							08s07	08 07																
Harrow & Wealdstone ⊖	d							08 12	08 12																
Watford Junction	d							08 19	08 19																
Milton Keynes Central ■10	a							09 00	09 00																
Battersea Park ■4	d			07 23							07 32	07 41		07 45	07 48				07 53						
London Victoria ■15 ⊖	a		07 27	07 28							07 36	07 46	07 46		07 53				07 58						07 58
Streatham ■4	d				07 10	07 16															07 40	07 46			
Tulse Hill ■3	d				07 17	07 24															07 47	07 54			
Herne Hill ■4	a																								
Loughborough Jn.	a																								
Elephant & Castle ⊖	a																								
London Blackfriars ■3 ⊖	a																								
City Thameslink ■3	a																								
St Pancras International ■15 ⊖	a																								
Luton Airport Parkway ■7	a																								
Luton ■10	a																								
North Dulwich	d					07 27																07 57			
East Dulwich	d					07 29																07 59			
Peckham Rye ■4	d					07 31								07 56								08 01			
Queens Rd Peckham	d					07 34								07 59								08 04			
South Bermondsey	d					07 36								08 01								08 06			
London Bridge ■4 ⊖	a	07 25			07 30	07 41				07 41				08 06				07 43		07 59	08 00	08 11		07 57	

A until 31 March

B from 7 April

Table 177

Saturdays

East and West Croydon, London
Milton Keynes Central and Luton via Norbury
Crystal Palace - Tulse Hill

Local Services

Network Diagram - see first Page of Table 177

		SN	SN	SN	SN	SN ◇1	SN	SN		SN	LO	SN 1	SN	SN	SN 1	FC	SN	LO	SN 1 A	SN 1 B	SN ◇1	SN	SN	SN	
East Croydon	d				07 47	08 00				07 51		07 55		08 00	08 07				08 10	08 10	08 12				
West Croydon 4	d	07 45									07 52		07 58				08 01	08 09							
Norwood Junction 2	a	07 49								07 55	07 58	07 59		08 04	08 12			08 13							
	d	07 50						07 53		07 55		07 59		08 05	08 13										
Selhurst 4	d				07 50								08 02				08 05		08 13	08 13					
Thornton Heath	d				07 52								08 04				08 07		08 16	08 16					
Norbury	d				07 55								08 07				08 10		08 19	08 19					
Streatham Common 4	d				07 58								08 10				08 13		08 21	08 21					
Beckenham Junction 4	d																								
Birkbeck	d																								
Crystal Palace 4	d			07 43				07 57															08 13	08 21	
Gipsy Hill	d			07 45				07 59															08 15		
West Norwood 4	d			07 48				08 02															08 18		
Streatham Hill	d			07 52				08 06															08 22		
Balham 4	⊖ d			07 55	08 02			08 09					08 14						08 28	08 28			08 25		
Wandsworth Common	d			07 57	08 04			08 11					08 16						08 30	08 30			08 27		
Clapham Junction 10	d			08 01	08 08	08 10		08 15					08 20						08 39	08 39	08 21		08 31		
Imperial Wharf	d																		08 44	08 44					
West Brompton	⊖ d																		08 47	08 47					
Kensington (Olympia)	⊖ d																		08 50	08 50					
Shepherd's Bush	⊖ d																		08 53	08 53					
Wembley Central	⊖ d																		09s07	09 07					
Harrow & Wealdstone	⊖ d																		09 12	09 12					
Watford Junction	d																		09 19	09 19					
Milton Keynes Central 10	a																		10 00	10 00					
Battersea Park 4	d		08 02	08 05	08 11		08 15	08 18					08 23									08 32	08 35		
London Victoria 15	⊖ a		08 06	08 09	08 16	08 16		08 23					08 28								08 28	08 36	08 39		
Streatham 4	d															08 10	08 16								
Tulse Hill 3	d															08 17	08 24								
Herne Hill 4	a																								
Loughborough Jn.	a																								
Elephant & Castle	⊖ a																								
London Blackfriars 3	⊖ a																								
City Thameslink 3	a																								
St Pancras International 15	⊖ a																								
Luton Airport Parkway 7	a																								
Luton 10	a																								
North Dulwich	d																08 27								
East Dulwich	d																08 29								
Peckham Rye 4	d						08 26										08 31								
Queens Rd Peckham	d						08 29										08 34								
South Bermondsey	d						08 31										08 36								
London Bridge 4	⊖ a	08 11					08 36			08 09		08 13		08 29	08 25	08 30	08 41							08 41	

A until 31 March

B from 7 April

Table 177

Saturdays

East and West Croydon, London Milton Keynes Central and Luton via Norbury Crystal Palace - Tulse Hill

Local Services | **Network Diagram - see first Page of Table 177**

		SN	SN	SN	SN	SN	LO	SN	SN	SN	SN	SN	SN	FC	SN	SN		LO	SN	SN	SN	SN	SN	SN	SN
		◇1						1		1		◇1											◇1		
East Croydon	d	08 28	08 17			08 21		08 25	08 30	08 37		08 40									08 47		09 00		
West Croydon 4	d				08 15		08 22						08 28		08 31	08 34		08 39							08 45
Norwood Junction 2	a				08 19	08 25	08 28	08 29	08 34	08 42								08 43							08 49
	d				08 22	08 25		08 29	08 35	08 43															08 52
Selhurst 4	d		08 20										08 32		08 35	08 39					08 50				
Thornton Heath	d		08 22										08 34		08 37	08 41					08 52				
Norbury	d		08 25										08 37		08 40	08 44					08 55				
Streatham Common 4	d		08 28										08 40		08 43	08 47					08 58				
Beckenham Junction 4	d										08 23														
Birkbeck	d										08 26														
Crystal Palace 4	d				08 26						08 30									08 43		08 51			08 56
Gipsy Hill	d				08 29						08 32									08 45					08 58
West Norwood 4	d				08 32						08 35									08 48					09 01
Streatham Hill	d				08 35															08 52					09 06
Balham 4 ⊖	d		08 32		08 39								08 44			08 51				08 55	09 02				09 09
Wandsworth Common	d		08 34		08 41								08 46			08 53				08 57	09 04				09 11
Clapham Junction 10	d	08 37	08 38		08 45							08 50	08 50			08 57				09 01	09 08		09 10		09 15
Imperial Wharf	d																								
West Brompton ⊖	d																								
Kensington (Olympia) ⊖	d																								
Shepherd's Bush ⊖	d																								
Wembley Central ⊖	d																								
Harrow & Wealdstone ⊖	d																								
Watford Junction	d																								
Milton Keynes Central 10	a																								
Battersea Park 4	d		08 41	08 45	08 48								08 53						09 02	09 05	09 11			09 15	09 18
London Victoria 15 ⊖	a	08 44	08 46		08 53							08 57	08 58			09 04			09 06	09 09	09 16		09 16		09 23
Streatham 4	d													08 40	08 46										
Tulse Hill 3	d										08 39			08 47	08 54										
Herne Hill 4	a																								
Loughborough Jn.	a																								
Elephant & Castle ⊖	a																								
London Blackfriars 3 ⊖	a																								
City Thameslink 3	a																								
St Pancras International 15 ⊖	a																								
Luton Airport Parkway 7	a																								
Luton 10	a																								
North Dulwich	d										08 42				08 57										
East Dulwich	d										08 44				08 59										
Peckham Rye 4	d			08 56							08 46				09 01									09 26	
Queens Rd Peckham	d			08 59							08 49				09 04									09 29	
South Bermondsey	d			09 01							08 51				09 06									09 31	
London Bridge 4 ⊖	a			09 06		08 39		08 43	08 59	08 55	08 56			09 00	09 11							09 11		09 36	

Table 177

Saturdays

East and West Croydon, London
Milton Keynes Central and Luton via Norbury
Crystal Palace - Tulse Hill

Local Services — Network Diagram - see first Page of Table 177

Station		SN	LO	SN	SN	SN	SN	SN		FC	SN	SN	SN	LO	SN	SN	SN	SN	SN	SN	SN	SN	SN	SN	
				1			1					◇1					1	1		◇1					
																	A	B							
																				🚲					
East Croydon 🚊	d	08 51		08 55		09 00	09 07					09 12					09 10	09 10		09 28	09 17			09 21	
West Croydon 4 🚊	d		08 52		08 58						09 01		09 04	09 09									09 15		
Norwood Junction 2	a	08 55	08 58	08 59		09 04	09 12							09 13									09 19	09 25	
	d	08 55		08 59		09 05	09 13																09 22	09 25	
Selhurst 4	d				09 02						09 05		09 09				09 13	09 13			09 20				
Thornton Heath	d				09 04						09 07		09 11				09 16	09 16			09 22				
Norbury	d				09 07						09 10		09 14				09 19	09 19			09 25				
Streatham Common 4	d				09 10						09 13		09 17				09 21	09 21			09 28				
Beckenham Junction 4 🚊	d							08 53																	
Birkbeck 🚊	d							08 56																	
Crystal Palace 4	d							09 00								09 13			09 21				09 26		
Gipsy Hill	d							09 02								09 15							09 29		
West Norwood 4	d							09 05								09 18							09 32		
Streatham Hill	d															09 22							09 35		
Balham 4 ⊖	d				09 14								09 21			09 25	09 28	09 28			09 32		09 39		
Wandsworth Common	d				09 16								09 23			09 27	09 30	09 30			09 34		09 41		
Clapham Junction 10	d				09 20							09 21	09 27			09 32	09 39	09 39		09 37	09 38		09 45		
Imperial Wharf	d																09 44	09 44							
West Brompton ⊖	d																09 47	09 47							
Kensington (Olympia) ⊖	d																09 50	09 50							
Shepherd's Bush ⊖	d																09 53	09 53							
Wembley Central ⊖	d																10s07	10 07							
Harrow & Wealdstone ⊖	d																10 12	10 12							
Watford Junction	d																10 19	10 19							
Milton Keynes Central 10	a																11 00	11 00							
Battersea Park 4	d				09 23										09 32	09 36					09 41	09 45	09 48		
London Victoria 15 ⊖	a				09 28							09 28	09 34		09 36	09 40				09 44	09 46		09 53		
Streatham 4	d									09 10	09 16														
Tulse Hill 3	d							09 09		09 17	09 24														
Herne Hill 4	a																								
Loughborough Jn.	a																								
Elephant & Castle ⊖	a																								
London Blackfriars 3 ⊖	a																								
City Thameslink 3	a																								
St Pancras International 15 ⊖	a																								
Luton Airport Parkway 7	a																								
Luton 10	a																								
North Dulwich	d							09 12			09 27														
East Dulwich	d							09 14			09 29														
Peckham Rye 4	d							09 16			09 31											09 56			
Queens Rd Peckham	d							09 19			09 34											09 59			
South Bermondsey	d							09 21			09 36											10 01			
London Bridge 4 ⊖	a	09 09		09 13		09 29	09 25	09 26		09 30	09 41								09 41			10 06		09 39	

A until 31 March

B from 7 April

Table 177

Saturdays

East and West Croydon, London
Milton Keynes Central and Luton via Norbury
Crystal Palace - Tulse Hill

Local Services

Network Diagram - see first Page of Table 177

		LO	SN 1	SN	SN 1	SN	SN ◇1	SN	FC	SN	SN	LO	SN	SN	SN	SN		SN ◇1	SN	SN	SN	LO	SN 1	SN	SN
East Croydon 🚋	d		09 25	09 30	09 37		09 40								09 47			10 00			09 51		09 55		10 00
West Croydon 4 🚋	d	09 22						09 28		09 31	09 34	09 39								09 45		09 52		09 58	
Norwood Junction 2	a	09 28	09 29	09 34	09 42							09 43								09 49	09 55	09 58	09 59		10 04
	d		09 29	09 35	09 43															09 52	09 55		09 59		10 05
Selhurst 4	d							09 32		09 35	09 39				09 50									10 02	
Thornton Heath	d							09 34		09 37	09 41				09 52									10 04	
Norbury	d							09 37		09 40	09 44				09 55									10 07	
Streatham Common 4	d							09 40		09 43	09 47				09 58									10 10	
Beckenham Junction 4 🚋	d					09 23																			
Birkbeck 🚋	d					09 26																			
Crystal Palace 4	d					09 30								09 43		09 51				09 56					
Gipsy Hill	d					09 32								09 45						09 59					
West Norwood 4	d					09 35								09 48						10 02					
Streatham Hill	d													09 52						10 05					
Balham 4 ⊖	d							09 44			09 51			09 55	10 02					10 09				10 14	
Wandsworth Common	d							09 46			09 53			09 57	10 04					10 11				10 16	
Clapham Junction 10	d						09 50	09 50			09 57			10 01	10 08			10 10		10 15				10 20	
Imperial Wharf	d																								
West Brompton ⊖	d																								
Kensington (Olympia) ⊖	d																								
Shepherd's Bush ⊖	d																								
Wembley Central ⊖	d																								
Harrow & Wealdstone ⊖	d																								
Watford Junction	d																								
Milton Keynes Central 10	a																								
Battersea Park 4	d							09 53					10 02	10 05	10 11				10 15	10 18				10 23	
London Victoria 15 ⊖	a						09 57	09 58			10 04		10 06	10 09	10 16			10 16		10 23				10 28	
Streatham 4	d								09 40	09 46															
Tulse Hill 3	d					09 39			09 47	09 54															
Herne Hill 4	a																								
Loughborough Jn.	a																								
Elephant & Castle ⊖	a																								
London Blackfriars 3 ⊖	a																								
City Thameslink 3	a																								
St Pancras International 15 ⊖	a																								
Luton Airport Parkway 7	a																								
Luton 10	a																								
North Dulwich	d					09 42				09 57															
East Dulwich	d					09 44				09 59															
Peckham Rye 4	d					09 46				10 01									10 26						
Queens Rd Peckham	d					09 49				10 04									10 29						
South Bermondsey	d					09 51				10 06									10 31						
London Bridge 4 ⊖	a		09 43	09 59	09 55	09 56			10 00	10 11						10 11			10 36		10 09		10 13		10 29

Table 177

Saturdays

East and West Croydon, London
Milton Keynes Central and Luton via Norbury
Crystal Palace - Tulse Hill

Local Services

Network Diagram - see first Page of Table 177

		SN	SN	FC	SN	SN	SN	LO		SN	SN	SN	SN	SN	SN	SN	SN	SN	SN	LO	SN	SN	SN	SN
		1				◇1						1	1		◇1						1		1	
												A	B											
															🚲									
East Croydon 🚌	d	10 07				10 12						10 10	10 10		10 28	10 17			10 21		10 25	10 30	10 37	
West Croydon 4 🚌	d				10 01		10 04	10 09										10 15		10 22				
Norwood Junction 2	a	10 12						10 13										10 19	10 25	10 28	10 29	10 34	10 42	
	d	10 13																10 22	10 25		10 29	10 35	10 43	
Selhurst 4	d				10 05		10 09					10 13	10 13			10 20								
Thornton Heath	d				10 07		10 11					10 16	10 16			10 22								
Norbury	d				10 10		10 14					10 19	10 19			10 25								
Streatham Common 4	d				10 13		10 17					10 21	10 21			10 28								
Beckenham Junction 4 🚌	d		09 53																					10 23
Birkbeck 🚌	d		09 56																					10 26
Crystal Palace 4	d		10 00								10 13			10 21				10 26						10 30
Gipsy Hill	d		10 02								10 15							10 29						10 32
West Norwood 4	d		10 05								10 18							10 32						10 35
Streatham Hill	d										10 22							10 35						
Balham 4 ⊖	d						10 21				10 25	10 28	10 28			10 32		10 39						
Wandsworth Common	d						10 23				10 27	10 30	10 30			10 34		10 41						
Clapham Junction 10	d					10 21	10 27				10 31	10 39	10 39		10 37	10 38		10 45						
Imperial Wharf	d											10 44	10 44											
West Brompton ⊖	d											10 47	10 47											
Kensington (Olympia) ⊖	d											10 50	10 50											
Shepherd's Bush ⊖	d											10 53	10 53											
Wembley Central ⊖	d											11s08	11 08											
Harrow & Wealdstone ⊖	d											11 13	11 13											
Watford Junction	d											11 20	11 20											
Milton Keynes Central 10	a											12 00	12 00											
Battersea Park 4	d									10 32	10 35					10 41	10 45	10 48						
London Victoria 15 ⊖	a					10 28	10 34			10 36	10 39				10 44	10 46		10 53						
Streatham 4	d			10 10	10 16																			
Tulse Hill 3	d		10 09	10 17	10 24																			10 39
Herne Hill 4	a																							
Loughborough Jn.	a																							
Elephant & Castle ⊖	a																							
London Blackfriars 3 ⊖	a																							
City Thameslink 3	a																							
St Pancras International 15 ⊖	a																							
Luton Airport Parkway 7	a																							
Luton 10	a																							
North Dulwich	d		10 12		10 27																			10 42
East Dulwich	d		10 14		10 29																			10 44
Peckham Rye 4	d		10 16		10 31												10 56							10 46
Queens Rd Peckham	d		10 19		10 34												10 59							10 49
South Bermondsey	d		10 21		10 36												11 01							10 51
London Bridge 4 ⊖	a	10 25	10 26	10 30	10 41									10 41			11 06		10 39		10 43	10 59	10 55	10 56

A until 31 March

B from 7 April

East and West Croydon, London
Milton Keynes Central and Luton via Norbury
Crystal Palace - Tulse Hill

Local Services

Network Diagram - see first Page of Table 177

		SN ◇1	SN	FC	SN	SN	LO	SN	SN	SN	SN	SN ◇1	SN	SN	SN	LO		SN 1	SN	SN	SN 1	SN	FC	SN	SN ◇1
East Croydon 🚊	d	10 40								10 47		11 00			10 51			10 55		11 00	11 07				11 12
West Croydon 4 🚊	d		10 28		10 31	10 34	10 39							10 45		10 52			10 58					11 01	
Norwood Junction 2	a						10 43							10 49	10 55	10 58		10 59		11 04	11 12				
	d													10 52	10 55			10 59		11 05	11 13				
Selhurst 4	d		10 32		10 35	10 39				10 50									11 02					11 05	
Thornton Heath	d		10 34		10 37	10 41				10 52									11 04					11 07	
Norbury	d		10 37		10 40	10 44				10 55									11 07					11 10	
Streatham Common 4	d		10 40		10 43	10 47				10 58									11 10					11 13	
Beckenham Junction 4 🚊	d																					10 53			
Birkbeck 🚊	d																					10 56			
Crystal Palace 4	d								10 43		10 51			10 56								11 00			
Gipsy Hill	d								10 45					10 59								11 02			
West Norwood 4	d								10 48					11 02								11 05			
Streatham Hill	d								10 52					11 05											
Balham 4 ⊖	d		10 44			10 51			10 55	11 02				11 09					11 14						
Wandsworth Common	d		10 46			10 53			10 57	11 04				11 11					11 16						
Clapham Junction 10	d	10 50	10 50			10 57			11 01	11 08		11 10		11 15					11 20						11 21
Imperial Wharf	d																								
West Brompton ⊖	d																								
Kensington (Olympia) ⊖	d																								
Shepherd's Bush ⊖	d																								
Wembley Central ⊖	d																								
Harrow & Wealdstone ⊖	d																								
Watford Junction	d																								
Milton Keynes Central 10	a																								
Battersea Park 4	d		10 53					11 02	11 05	11 11			11 15	11 18					11 23						
London Victoria 15 ⊖	a	10 57	10 58			11 04		11 06	11 09	11 16		11 16		11 23					11 28						11 28
Streatham 4	d			10 40	10 46																		11 10	11 16	
Tulse Hill 3	d			10 47	10 54																	11 09	11 17	11 24	
Herne Hill 4	a																								
Loughborough Jn.	a																								
Elephant & Castle ⊖	a																								
London Blackfriars 3 ⊖	a																								
City Thameslink 3	a																								
St Pancras International 15 ⊖	a																								
Luton Airport Parkway 7	a																								
Luton 10	a																								
North Dulwich	d				10 57																	11 12		11 27	
East Dulwich	d				10 59																	11 14		11 29	
Peckham Rye 4	d				11 01								11 26									11 16		11 31	
Queens Rd Peckham	d				11 04								11 29									11 19		11 34	
South Bermondsey	d				11 06								11 31									11 21		11 36	
London Bridge 4 ⊖	a			11 00	11 11						11 11		11 36		11 09			11 13		11 29	11 25	11 26	11 30	11 41	

Table 177

Saturdays

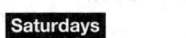

East and West Croydon, London
Milton Keynes Central and Luton via Norbury
Crystal Palace - Tulse Hill

Local Services — Network Diagram - see first Page of Table 177

Station		SN	LO	SN	SN	SN	SN	SN	SN	SN	SN	SN	SN	LO	SN	SN	SN	SN	SN	SN	FC	SN	SN
						1 A	1 B		◇1						1		1		◇1				
East Croydon	d					11 10	11 10		11 28	11 17			11 21		11 25	11 30	11 37		11 40				
West Croydon 4	d	11 04	11 09									11 15		11 22						11 28		11 31	11 34
Norwood Junction 2	a		11 13									11 19	11 25	11 28	11 29	11 34	11 42						
	d											11 22	11 25		11 29	11 35	11 43						
Selhurst 4	d	11 09				11 13	11 13			11 20										11 32		11 35	11 39
Thornton Heath	d	11 11				11 16	11 16			11 22										11 34		11 37	11 41
Norbury	d	11 14				11 19	11 19			11 25										11 37		11 40	11 44
Streatham Common 4	d	11 17				11 21	11 21			11 28										11 40		11 43	11 47
Beckenham Junction 4	d																	11 23					
Birkbeck	d																	11 26					
Crystal Palace 4	d				11 13			11 21				11 26						11 30					
Gipsy Hill	d				11 15							11 29						11 32					
West Norwood 4	d				11 18							11 32						11 35					
Streatham Hill	d				11 22							11 35											
Balham 4 ⊖	d	11 21			11 25	11 28	11 28			11 32		11 39								11 44			11 51
Wandsworth Common	d	11 23			11 27	11 30	11 30			11 34		11 41								11 46			11 53
Clapham Junction 10	d	11 27			11 31	11 39	11 39		11 37	11 38		11 45							11 50	11 50			11 57
Imperial Wharf	d					11 44	11 44																
West Brompton ⊖	d					11 47	11 47																
Kensington (Olympia) ⊖	d					11 50	11 50																
Shepherd's Bush ⊖	d					11 53	11 53																
Wembley Central ⊖	d					12s07	12 07																
Harrow & Wealdstone ⊖	d					12 13	12 13																
Watford Junction	d					12 20	12 20																
Milton Keynes Central 10	a					13 00	13 00																
Battersea Park 4	d			11 32	11 35					11 41	11 45	11 48								11 53			
London Victoria 15 ⊖	a	11 34		11 36	11 39				11 44	11 46		11 53							11 57	11 58			12 04
Streatham 4	d																				11 40	11 46	
Tulse Hill 3	d																	11 39			11 47	11 54	
Herne Hill 4	a																						
Loughborough Jn.	a																						
Elephant & Castle ⊖	a																						
London Blackfriars 3 ⊖	a																						
City Thameslink 3	a																						
St Pancras International 15 ⊖	a																						
Luton Airport Parkway 7	a																						
Luton 10	a																						
North Dulwich	d																	11 42				11 57	
East Dulwich	d																	11 44				11 59	
Peckham Rye 4	d										11 56							11 46				12 01	
Queens Rd Peckham	d										11 59							11 49				12 04	
South Bermondsey	d										12 01							11 51				12 06	
London Bridge 4 ⊖	a							11 41			12 06		11 39		11 43	11 59	11 55	11 56			12 00	12 11	

A until 31 March

B from 7 April

Table 177

Saturdays

East and West Croydon, London
Milton Keynes Central and Luton via Norbury
Crystal Palace - Tulse Hill

Local Services Network Diagram - see first Page of Table 177

		LO	SN	SN	SN	SN	SN	SN	SN	SN	LO	SN	SN	SN	SN	SN		FC	SN	SN	SN	LO	SN	SN	SN
							◇1					1			1					◇1					1
																									A
East Croydon	d				11 47		12 00			11 51		11 55		12 00	12 07					12 12					12 10
West Croydon 4	d	11 39							11 45		11 52		11 58						12 01		12 04	12 09			
Norwood Junction 2	a	11 43							11 49	11 55	11 58	11 59		12 04	12 12							12 13			
	d								11 52	11 55		11 59		12 05	12 13										
Selhurst 4	d				11 50								12 02						12 05		12 09				12 13
Thornton Heath	d				11 52								12 04						12 07		12 11				12 16
Norbury	d				11 55								12 07						12 10		12 14				12 19
Streatham Common 4	d				11 58								12 10						12 13		12 17				12 21
Beckenham Junction 4	d															11 53									
Birkbeck	d															11 56									
Crystal Palace 4	d			11 43		11 51			11 56							12 00								12 13	
Gipsy Hill	d			11 45					11 59							12 02								12 15	
West Norwood 4	d			11 48					12 02							12 05								12 18	
Streatham Hill	d			11 52					12 05															12 22	
Balham 4 ⊖	d			11 55	12 02				12 09				12 14								12 21			12 25	12 28
Wandsworth Common	d			11 57	12 04				12 11				12 16								12 23			12 27	12 30
Clapham Junction 10	d			12 01	12 08		12 10		12 15				12 20							12 21	12 27			12 31	12 39
Imperial Wharf	d																								12 44
West Brompton ⊖	d																								12 47
Kensington (Olympia) ⊖	d																								12 50
Shepherd's Bush ⊖	d																								12 53
Wembley Central ⊖	d																								13s07
Harrow & Wealdstone ⊖	d																								13 12
Watford Junction	d																								13 19
Milton Keynes Central 10	a																								14 00
Battersea Park 4	d		12 02	12 05	12 11			12 15	12 18				12 23										12 32	12 35	
London Victoria 15 ⊖	a		12 06	12 09	12 16		12 16		12 23				12 28							12 28	12 34		12 36	12 39	
Streatham 4	d																	12 10	12 16						
Tulse Hill 3	d															12 09		12 17	12 24						
Herne Hill 4	a																								
Loughborough Jn.	a																								
Elephant & Castle ⊖	a																								
London Blackfriars 3 ⊖	a																								
City Thameslink 3	a																								
St Pancras International 15 ⊖	a																								
Luton Airport Parkway 7	a																								
Luton 10	a																								
North Dulwich	d															12 12			12 27						
East Dulwich	d															12 14			12 29						
Peckham Rye 4	d							12 26								12 16			12 31						
Queens Rd Peckham	d							12 29								12 19			12 34						
South Bermondsey	d							12 31								12 21			12 36						
London Bridge 4 ⊖	a					12 11		12 36		12 09		12 13		12 29	12 25	12 26		12 30	12 41						

A until 31 March

Table 177

Saturdays

East and West Croydon, London
Milton Keynes Central and Luton via Norbury
Crystal Palace - Tulse Hill

Local Services

Network Diagram - see first Page of Table 177

		SN 1 A	SN	SN ◇1	SN	SN	SN	SN		LO	SN 1	SN	SN 1	SN	SN ◇1	SN	FC	SN	SN	LO	SN	SN	SN	SN	
East Croydon	d	12 10		12 28	12 17			12 21			12 25	12 30	12 38		12 40								12 47		
West Croydon 4	d						12 15			12 22						12 28		12 31	12 34	12 39					
Norwood Junction 2	a						12 19	12 25		12 28	12 29	12 34	12 42							12 43					
	d						12 22	12 25			12 29	12 35	12 43												
Selhurst 4	d	12 13			12 20											12 32		12 35	12 39				12 50		
Thornton Heath	d	12 16			12 22											12 34		12 37	12 41				12 52		
Norbury	d	12 19			12 25											12 37		12 40	12 44				12 55		
Streatham Common 4	d	12 21			12 28											12 40		12 43	12 47				12 57		
Beckenham Junction 4	d													12 23											
Birkbeck	d													12 26											
Crystal Palace 4	d		12 21				12 26							12 30								12 43		12 51	
Gipsy Hill	d						12 29							12 32								12 45			
West Norwood 4	d						12 32							12 35								12 48			
Streatham Hill	d						12 35															12 52			
Balham 4 ⊖	d	12 28			12 32		12 39									12 44			12 51			12 55	13 01		
Wandsworth Common	d	12 30			12 34		12 41									12 46			12 53			12 57	13 03		
Clapham Junction 10	d	12 39		12 37	12 38		12 45								12 50	12 50			12 57			13 01	13 07		
Imperial Wharf	d	12 44																							
West Brompton ⊖	d	12 47																							
Kensington (Olympia) ⊖	d	12 50																							
Shepherd's Bush ⊖	d	12 53																							
Wembley Central ⊖	d	13 07																							
Harrow & Wealdstone ⊖	d	13 12																							
Watford Junction	d	13 19																							
Milton Keynes Central 10	a	14 00																							
Battersea Park 4	d				12 41	12 45	12 48									12 53					13 02	13 05	13 11		
London Victoria 15 ⊖	a			12 44	12 46		12 53								12 57	12 58			13 04		13 06	13 09	13 16		
Streatham 4	d																12 40	12 46							
Tulse Hill 3	d													12 39			12 47	12 54							
Herne Hill 4	a																								
Loughborough Jn.	a																								
Elephant & Castle ⊖	a																								
London Blackfriars 3 ⊖	a																								
City Thameslink 3	a																								
St Pancras International 15 ⊖	a																								
Luton Airport Parkway 7	a																								
Luton 10	a																								
North Dulwich	d													12 42				12 57							
East Dulwich	d													12 44				12 59							
Peckham Rye 4	d					12 56								12 46				13 01							
Queens Rd Peckham	d					12 59								12 49				13 04							
South Bermondsey	d					13 01								12 51				13 06							
London Bridge 4 ⊖	a		12 44			13 06		12 39			12 43	12 59	12 55	12 56			13 00	13 11						13 11	

A from 7 April

Table 177

Saturdays

East and West Croydon, London Milton Keynes Central and Luton via Norbury Crystal Palace - Tulse Hill

Local Services

Network Diagram - see first Page of Table 177

		SN	SN	SN	SN	LO	SN	SN	SN	SN	SN	FC	SN	SN	SN	LO		SN	SN	SN	SN	SN	SN	SN	SN
		◇1					1			1				◇1						1 A	1 B		◇1 bike		
East Croydon	d	13 00			12 51		12 55		13 00	13 07				13 12						13 10	13 10		13 28	13 17	
West Croydon 4	d			12 45		12 52		12 58					13 01		13 04	13 09									
Norwood Junction 2	a			12 49	12 55	12 58	12 59		13 04	13 12						13 13									
	d			12 52	12 55		12 59		13 05	13 13															
Selhurst 4	d							13 02					13 05		13 09					13 13	13 13			13 20	
Thornton Heath	d							13 04					13 07		13 11					13 16	13 16			13 22	
Norbury	d							13 07					13 10		13 14					13 19	13 19			13 25	
Streatham Common 4	d							13 10					13 13		13 17					13 21	13 21			13 28	
Beckenham Junction 4	d										12 53														
Birkbeck	d										12 56														
Crystal Palace 4	d			12 56							13 00								13 13			13 21			
Gipsy Hill	d			12 59							13 02								13 15						
West Norwood 4	d			13 02							13 05								13 18						
Streatham Hill	d			13 05															13 22						
Balham 4	d			13 09				13 14							13 21				13 25	13 28	13 28			13 32	
Wandsworth Common	d			13 11				13 16							13 23				13 27	13 30	13 30			13 34	
Clapham Junction 10	d	13 10		13 15				13 20						13 21	13 27				13 31	13 39	13 39		13 37	13 38	
Imperial Wharf	d																			13 44	13 44				
West Brompton	d																			13 47	13 47				
Kensington (Olympia)	d																			13 50	13 50				
Shepherd's Bush	d																			13 53	13 53				
Wembley Central	d																			14s08	14 08				
Harrow & Wealdstone	d																			14 13	14 13				
Watford Junction	d																			14 20	14 20				
Milton Keynes Central 10	a																			15 00	15 00				
Battersea Park 4	d		13 15	13 18				13 23										13 32	13 35					13 41	13 45
London Victoria 15	a	13 16		13 23				13 28						13 28	13 34			13 36	13 39				13 44	13 46	
Streatham 4	d											13 10	13 16												
Tulse Hill 3	d										13 09	13 17	13 24												
Herne Hill 4	a																								
Loughborough Jn.	a																								
Elephant & Castle	a																								
London Blackfriars 3	a																								
City Thameslink 3	a																								
St Pancras International 15	a																								
Luton Airport Parkway 7	a																								
Luton 10	a																								
North Dulwich	d										13 12		13 27												
East Dulwich	d										13 14		13 29												
Peckham Rye 4	d		13 26								13 16		13 31												13 56
Queens Rd Peckham	d		13 29								13 19		13 34												13 59
South Bermondsey	d		13 31								13 21		13 36												14 01
London Bridge 4	a		13 36		13 09		13 13		13 29	13 25	13 26	13 30	13 41									13 44			14 06

A until 31 March

B from 7 April

Table 177

Saturdays

East and West Croydon, London
Milton Keynes Central and Luton via Norbury
Crystal Palace - Tulse Hill

Local Services

Network Diagram - see first Page of Table 177

		SN	SN	LO	SN 1	SN	SN 1	SN		SN ◇1	SN	FC	SN	SN	LO	SN	SN	SN	SN	SN ◇1	SN	SN	SN	LO	
East Croydon 🚋	d		13 21		13 25	13 30	13 37			13 40								13 47		14 00			13 51		
West Croydon 4 🚋	d	13 15		13 22							13 28		13 31	13 34	13 39							13 45		13 52	
Norwood Junction 2	a	13 19	13 25	13 28	13 29	13 34	13 42								13 43							13 49	13 55	13 58	
	d	13 22	13 25		13 29	13 35	13 43															13 52	13 55		
Selhurst 4	d										13 32		13 35	13 39				13 50							
Thornton Heath	d										13 34		13 37	13 41				13 52							
Norbury	d										13 37		13 40	13 44				13 55							
Streatham Common 4	d										13 40		13 43	13 47				13 58							
Beckenham Junction 4 🚋	d							13 23																	
Birkbeck 🚋	d							13 26																	
Crystal Palace 4	d	13 26						13 30									13 43		13 51			13 56			
Gipsy Hill	d	13 29						13 32									13 45					13 59			
West Norwood 4	d	13 32						13 35									13 48					14 02			
Streatham Hill	d	13 35															13 52					14 05			
Balham 4 ⊖	d	13 39									13 44			13 51			13 55	14 02				14 09			
Wandsworth Common	d	13 41									13 46			13 53			13 57	14 04				14 11			
Clapham Junction 10	d	13 45								13 50	13 50			13 57			14 01	14 08		14 10		14 15			
Imperial Wharf	d																								
West Brompton ⊖	d																								
Kensington (Olympia) ⊖	d																								
Shepherd's Bush ⊖	d																								
Wembley Central ⊖	d																								
Harrow & Wealdstone ⊖	d																								
Watford Junction	d																								
Milton Keynes Central 10	a																								
Battersea Park 4	d	13 48									13 53					14 02	14 05	14 11			14 15	14 18			
London Victoria 15 ⊖	a	13 53								13 57	13 58			14 04		14 06	14 09	14 16		14 16		14 23			
Streatham 4	d											13 40	13 46												
Tulse Hill 3	d							13 39				13 47	13 54												
Herne Hill 4	a																								
Loughborough Jn.	a																								
Elephant & Castle ⊖	a																								
London Blackfriars 3 ⊖	a																								
City Thameslink 3	a																								
St Pancras International 15 ⊖	a																								
Luton Airport Parkway 7	a																								
Luton 10	a																								
North Dulwich	d							13 42					13 57												
East Dulwich	d							13 44					13 59												
Peckham Rye 4	d							13 46					14 01								14 26				
Queens Rd Peckham	d							13 49					14 04								14 29				
South Bermondsey	d							13 51					14 06								14 31				
London Bridge 4 ⊖	a		13 39		13 43	13 59	13 55	13 56				14 00	14 11						14 11		14 36		14 09		

Table 177

Saturdays

East and West Croydon, London Milton Keynes Central and Luton via Norbury Crystal Palace - Tulse Hill

Local Services

Network Diagram - see first Page of Table 177

		SN	SN	SN	SN	SN	FC	SN	SN	SN	LO	SN	SN	SN	SN	SN		SN	SN	SN	SN	SN	LO	SN	SN
		1			1				◇1					1	1			◇1						1	
														A	B										
																		🚲							
East Croydon 🚋	d	13 55		14 00	14 07				14 12					14 10	14 10			14 28	14 17			14 21		14 25	14 30
West Croydon 4 🚋	d		13 58					14 01		14 04	14 09										14 15		14 22		
Norwood Junction 2	a	13 59		14 04	14 12						14 13										14 19	14 25	14 28	14 29	14 34
	d	13 59		14 05	14 13																14 22	14 25		14 29	14 35
Selhurst 4	d		14 02					14 05		14 09				14 13	14 13				14 20						
Thornton Heath	d		14 04					14 07		14 11				14 16	14 16				14 22						
Norbury	d		14 07					14 10		14 14				14 19	14 19				14 25						
Streatham Common 4	d		14 10					14 13		14 17				14 21	14 21				14 28						
Beckenham Junction 4 🚋	d					13 53																			
Birkbeck 🚋	d					13 56																			
Crystal Palace 4	d					14 00							14 13			14 21					14 26				
Gipsy Hill	d					14 02							14 15								14 29				
West Norwood 4	d					14 05							14 18								14 32				
Streatham Hill	d												14 22								14 35				
Balham 4 ⊖	d		14 14							14 21			14 25	14 28	14 28				14 32		14 39				
Wandsworth Common	d		14 16							14 23			14 27	14 30	14 30				14 34		14 41				
Clapham Junction 10	d		14 20						14 21	14 27			14 31	14 39	14 39			14 37	14 38		14 45				
Imperial Wharf	d													14 44	14 44										
West Brompton ⊖	d													14 47	14 47										
Kensington (Olympia) ⊖	d													14 50	14 50										
Shepherd's Bush ⊖	d													14 53	14 53										
Wembley Central ⊖	d													15s07	15 07										
Harrow & Wealdstone ⊖	d													15 12	15 12										
Watford Junction	d													15 19	15 19										
Milton Keynes Central 10	a													16 00	16 00										
Battersea Park 4	d		14 23									14 32	14 35						14 41	14 45	14 48				
London Victoria 15 ⊖	a		14 28						14 28	14 34		14 36	14 39					14 44	14 46		14 53				
Streatham 4	d						14 10	14 16																	
Tulse Hill 3	d					14 09	14 17	14 24																	
Herne Hill 4	a																								
Loughborough Jn.	a																								
Elephant & Castle ⊖	a																								
London Blackfriars 3 ⊖	a																								
City Thameslink 3	a																								
St Pancras International 15 ⊖	a																								
Luton Airport Parkway 7	a																								
Luton 10	a																								
North Dulwich	d					14 12		14 27																	
East Dulwich	d					14 14		14 29																	
Peckham Rye 4	d					14 16		14 31												14 56					
Queens Rd Peckham	d					14 19		14 34												14 59					
South Bermondsey	d					14 21		14 36												15 01					
London Bridge 4 ⊖	a	14 13		14 29	14 25	14 26	14 30	14 41								14 44				15 06		14 39		14 43	14 59

A until 31 March

B from 7 April

Table 177

Saturdays

East and West Croydon, London
Milton Keynes Central and Luton via Norbury
Crystal Palace - Tulse Hill

Local Services

Network Diagram - see first Page of Table 177

		SN ■1	SN	SN ◇■1	SN	FC	SN	SN		LO	SN	SN	SN	SN	SN ◇■1	SN	SN	SN	LO	SN ■1	SN	SN	SN ■1	SN	
East Croydon 🚌	d	14 37		14 40									14 47		15 00			14 51		14 55		15 00	15 07		
West Croydon ■4 🚌	d				14 28		14 31	14 34		14 39							14 45		14 52		14 58				
Norwood Junction ■2	a	14 42								14 43							14 49	14 55	14 58	14 59		15 04	15 12		
	d	14 43															14 52	14 55		14 59		15 05	15 13		
Selhurst ■4	d				14 32		14 35	14 39					14 50								15 02				
Thornton Heath	d				14 34		14 37	14 41					14 52								15 04				
Norbury	d				14 37		14 40	14 44					14 55								15 07				
Streatham Common ■4	d				14 40		14 43	14 47					14 58								15 10				
Beckenham Junction ■4 🚌	d		14 23																					14 53	
Birkbeck 🚌	d		14 26																					14 56	
Crystal Palace ■4	d		14 30									14 43		14 51			14 56							15 00	
Gipsy Hill	d		14 32									14 45					14 59							15 02	
West Norwood ■4	d		14 35									14 48					15 02							15 05	
Streatham Hill	d											14 52					15 05								
Balham ■4 ⊖	d				14 44			14 51				14 55	15 02				15 09				15 14				
Wandsworth Common	d				14 46			14 53				14 57	15 04				15 11				15 16				
Clapham Junction ■10	d			14 50	14 50			14 57				15 01	15 08		15 10		15 15				15 20				
Imperial Wharf	d																								
West Brompton ⊖	d																								
Kensington (Olympia) ⊖	d																								
Shepherd's Bush ⊖	d																								
Wembley Central ⊖	d																								
Harrow & Wealdstone ⊖	d																								
Watford Junction	d																								
Milton Keynes Central ■10	a																								
Battersea Park ■4	d				14 53						15 02	15 05	15 11			15 15	15 18				15 23				
London Victoria ■15 ⊖	a			14 57	14 58			15 04			15 06	15 09	15 16		15 16		15 23				15 28				
Streatham ■4	d					14 40	14 46																		
Tulse Hill ■3	d		14 39			14 47	14 54																	15 09	
Herne Hill ■4	a																								
Loughborough Jn.	a																								
Elephant & Castle ⊖	a																								
London Blackfriars ■3 ⊖	a																								
City Thameslink ■3	a																								
St Pancras International ■15 ⊖	a																								
Luton Airport Parkway ■7	a																								
Luton ■10	a																								
North Dulwich	d		14 42				14 57																	15 12	
East Dulwich	d		14 44				14 59																	15 14	
Peckham Rye ■4	d		14 46				15 01									15 26								15 16	
Queens Rd Peckham	d		14 49				15 04									15 29								15 19	
South Bermondsey	d		14 51				15 06									15 31								15 21	
London Bridge ■4 ⊖	a	14 55	14 56			15 00	15 11							15 11		15 36		15 09		15 13		15 29	15 25	15 26	

Table 177

East and West Croydon, London Milton Keynes Central and Luton via Norbury Crystal Palace - Tulse Hill

Local Services

Network Diagram - see first Page of Table 177

		FC	SN	SN	SN	LO	SN	SN	SN	SN	SN	SN	SN	SN	SN	SN		LO	SN	SN	SN	SN	SN	SN	FC
				◇1					1	1		◇1							1		1		◇1		
									A	B															
East Croydon	d			15 12					15 10	15 10		15 28	15 17			15 21			15 25	15 30	15 37		15 40		
West Croydon 4	d		15 01		15 04	15 09									15 15			15 22						15 28	
Norwood Junction 2	a					15 13									15 19	15 25		15 28	15 29	15 34	15 42				
	d														15 22	15 25			15 29	15 35	15 43				
Selhurst 4	d		15 05		15 09				15 13	15 13			15 20											15 32	
Thornton Heath	d		15 07		15 11				15 16	15 16			15 22											15 34	
Norbury	d		15 10		15 14				15 19	15 19			15 25											15 37	
Streatham Common 4	d		15 13		15 17				15 21	15 21			15 28											15 40	
Beckenham Junction 4	d																					15 23			
Birkbeck	d																					15 26			
Crystal Palace 4	d							15 13			15 21				15 26							15 30			
Gipsy Hill	d							15 15							15 29							15 32			
West Norwood 4	d							15 18							15 32							15 35			
Streatham Hill	d							15 22							15 35										
Balham 4 ⊖	d				15 21			15 25	15 28	15 28			15 32		15 39									15 44	
Wandsworth Common	d				15 23			15 27	15 30	15 30			15 34		15 41									15 46	
Clapham Junction 10	d			15 21	15 27			15 31	15 39	15 39		15 37	15 38		15 45								15 50	15 50	
Imperial Wharf	d								15 44	15 44															
West Brompton ⊖	d								15 47	15 47															
Kensington (Olympia) ⊖	d								15 50	15 50															
Shepherd's Bush ⊖	d								15 53	15 53															
Wembley Central ⊖	d								16s07	16 07															
Harrow & Wealdstone ⊖	d								16 12	16 12															
Watford Junction	d								16 19	16 19															
Milton Keynes Central 10	a								17 00	17 00															
Battersea Park 4	d						15 32	15 35					15 41	15 45	15 48									15 53	
London Victoria 15 ⊖	a			15 28	15 34		15 36	15 39				15 44	15 46		15 53								15 57	15 58	
Streatham 4	d	15 10	15 16																						15 40
Tulse Hill 3	d	15 17	15 24																			15 39			15 47
Herne Hill 4	a																								
Loughborough Jn.	a																								
Elephant & Castle ⊖	a																								
London Blackfriars 3 ⊖	a																								
City Thameslink 3	a																								
St Pancras International 15 ⊖	a																								
Luton Airport Parkway 7	a																								
Luton 10	a																								
North Dulwich	d		15 27																			15 42			
East Dulwich	d		15 29																			15 44			
Peckham Rye 4	d		15 31											15 56								15 46			
Queens Rd Peckham	d		15 34											15 59								15 49			
South Bermondsey	d		15 36											16 01								15 51			
London Bridge 4 ⊖	a	15 30	15 41								15 44			16 06		15 39			15 43	15 59	15 55	15 56			16 00

A until 31 March

B from 7 April

Table 177

Saturdays

East and West Croydon, London
Milton Keynes Central and Luton via Norbury
Crystal Palace - Tulse Hill

Local Services

Network Diagram - see first Page of Table 177

		SN	SN	LO	SN	SN	SN	SN		SN	SN	SN	SN	LO	SN	SN	SN	SN	SN	FC	SN	SN	SN	LO	
										◇1					1			1				◇1			
East Croydon	d						15 47			16 00			15 51		15 55		16 00	16 07				16 12			
West Croydon 4	d	15 31	15 34	15 39								15 45		15 52		15 58					16 01		16 04	16 09	
Norwood Junction 2	a			15 43								15 49	15 55	15 58	15 59		16 04	16 12						16 13	
	d											15 52	15 55		15 59		16 05	16 13							
Selhurst 4	d	15 35	15 39				15 50									16 02					16 05		16 09		
Thornton Heath	d	15 37	15 41				15 52									16 04					16 07		16 11		
Norbury	d	15 40	15 44				15 55									16 07					16 10		16 14		
Streatham Common 4	d	15 43	15 47				15 58									16 10					16 13		16 17		
Beckenham Junction 4	d																		15 53						
Birkbeck	d																		15 56						
Crystal Palace 4	d					15 43		15 51				15 56							16 00						
Gipsy Hill	d					15 45						15 59							16 02						
West Norwood 4	d					15 48						16 02							16 05						
Streatham Hill	d					15 52						16 05													
Balham 4 ⊖	d		15 51			15 55	16 02					16 09				16 14							16 21		
Wandsworth Common	d		15 53			15 57	16 04					16 11				16 16							16 23		
Clapham Junction 10	d		15 57			16 01	16 08			16 10		16 15				16 20						16 21	16 27		
Imperial Wharf	d																								
West Brompton ⊖	d																								
Kensington (Olympia) ⊖	d																								
Shepherd's Bush ⊖	d																								
Wembley Central ⊖	d																								
Harrow & Wealdstone ⊖	d																								
Watford Junction	d																								
Milton Keynes Central 10	a																								
Battersea Park 4	d				16 02	16 05	16 11				16 15	16 18				16 23									
London Victoria 15 ⊖	a		16 04		16 06	16 09	16 16			16 16		16 23				16 28						16 28	16 34		
Streatham 4	d	15 46																		16 10	16 16				
Tulse Hill 3	d	15 54																	16 09	16 17	16 24				
Herne Hill 4	a																								
Loughborough Jn	a																								
Elephant & Castle ⊖	a																								
London Blackfriars 3 ⊖	a																								
City Thameslink 3	a																								
St Pancras International 15 ⊖	a																								
Luton Airport Parkway 7	a																								
Luton 10	a																								
North Dulwich	d	15 57																	16 12		16 27				
East Dulwich	d	15 59																	16 14		16 29				
Peckham Rye 4	d	16 01									16 26								16 16		16 31				
Queens Rd Peckham	d	16 04									16 29								16 19		16 34				
South Bermondsey	d	16 06									16 31								16 21		16 36				
London Bridge 4 ⊖	a	16 11						16 11			16 36		16 09		16 13		16 29	16 25	16 26	16 30	16 41				

Table 177

Saturdays

East and West Croydon, London
Milton Keynes Central and Luton via Norbury
Crystal Palace - Tulse Hill

Local Services — Network Diagram - see first Page of Table 177

		SN	SN	SN	SN	SN	SN	SN	SN	SN	SN	LO	SN	SN	SN	SN		SN	SN	FC	SN	SN	LO	SN	SN
				■1	■1		◇■1						■1		■1			◇■1							
				A	B																				
							🛒																		
East Croydon 🚊	d			16 10	16 10		16 28	16 17			16 21		16 25	16 30	16 37			16 40							
West Croydon ■4 🚊	d									16 15		16 22							16 28		16 31	16 34	16 39		
Norwood Junction ■2	a									16 19	16 25	16 28	16 29	16 34	16 42								16 43		
	d									16 22	16 25		16 29	16 35	16 43										
Selhurst ■4	d			16 13	16 13			16 20											16 32		16 35	16 39			
Thornton Heath	d			16 16	16 16			16 22											16 34		16 37	16 41			
Norbury	d			16 19	16 19			16 25											16 37		16 40	16 44			
Streatham Common ■4	d			16 21	16 21			16 28											16 40		16 43	16 47			
Beckenham Junction ■4 🚊	d															16 23									
Birkbeck 🚊	d															16 26									
Crystal Palace ■4	d		16 13			16 21				16 26						16 30									16 43
Gipsy Hill	d		16 15							16 29						16 32									16 45
West Norwood ■4	d		16 18							16 32						16 35									16 48
Streatham Hill	d		16 22							16 35															16 52
Balham ■4 ⊖	d		16 25	16 28	16 28			16 32		16 39									16 44			16 51			16 55
Wandsworth Common	d		16 27	16 30	16 30			16 34		16 41									16 46			16 53			16 57
Clapham Junction ■10	d		16 31	16 39	16 39		16 37	16 38		16 45								16 50	16 50			16 57			17 01
Imperial Wharf	d			16 44	16 44																				
West Brompton ⊖	d			16 47	16 47																				
Kensington (Olympia) ⊖	d			16 50	16 50																				
Shepherd's Bush ⊖	d			16 53	16 53																				
Wembley Central ⊖	d			17s07	17 07																				
Harrow & Wealdstone ⊖	d			17 12	17 12																				
Watford Junction	d			17 19	17 19																				
Milton Keynes Central ■10	a			18 00	18 00																				
Battersea Park ■4	d	16 32	16 35					16 41	16 45	16 48									16 53					17 02	17 05
London Victoria ■15 ⊖	a	16 36	16 39				16 44	16 46		16 53								16 57	16 58			17 04		17 06	17 09
Streatham ■4	d																			16 40	16 46				
Tulse Hill ■3	d															16 39				16 47	16 54				
Herne Hill ■4	a																								
Loughborough Jn.	a																								
Elephant & Castle ⊖	a																								
London Blackfriars ■3 ⊖	a																								
City Thameslink ■3	a																								
St Pancras International ■15 ⊖	a																								
Luton Airport Parkway ■7	a																								
Luton ■10	a																								
North Dulwich	d															16 42					16 57				
East Dulwich	d															16 44					16 59				
Peckham Rye ■4	d								16 56							16 46					17 01				
Queens Rd Peckham	d								16 59							16 49					17 04				
South Bermondsey	d								17 01							16 51					17 06				
London Bridge ■4 ⊖	a					16 41			17 06		16 39		16 43	16 59	16 55	16 56				17 00	17 11				

A until 31 March

B from 7 April

Table 177

Saturdays

East and West Croydon, London
Milton Keynes Central and Luton via Norbury
Crystal Palace - Tulse Hill

Local Services — Network Diagram - see first Page of Table 177

		SN	SN	SN	SN	SN	SN	LO		SN	SN	SN	SN	SN	FC	SN	SN	SN	LO	SN	SN	SN	SN	SN	
				◇1						1			1				◇1					1	1		
																						A	B		
East Croydon (tram)	d	16 47		17 00			16 51			16 55		17 00	17 07				17 12					17 10	17 10		
West Croydon 4 (tram)	d					16 45		16 52			16 58					17 01		17 04	17 09						
Norwood Junction 2	a					16 50	16 55	16 58		16 59		17 04	17 12						17 13						
	d					16 52	16 55			16 59		17 05	17 13												
Selhurst 4	d	16 50									17 02					17 05		17 09				17 13	17 13		
Thornton Heath	d	16 52									17 04					17 07		17 11				17 16	17 16		
Norbury	d	16 55									17 07					17 10		17 14				17 19	17 19		
Streatham Common 4	d	16 58									17 10					17 13		17 17				17 21	17 21		
Beckenham Junction 4 (tram)	d													16 53											
Birkbeck (tram)	d													16 56											
Crystal Palace 4	d		16 51			16 56								17 00							17 13			17 21	
Gipsy Hill	d					16 59								17 02							17 15				
West Norwood 4	d					17 02								17 05							17 18				
Streatham Hill	d					17 05															17 22				
Balham 4 ⊖	d	17 02				17 09					17 14							17 21			17 25	17 28	17 28		
Wandsworth Common	d	17 04				17 11					17 16							17 23			17 27	17 30	17 30		
Clapham Junction 10	d	17 08		17 10		17 15					17 20						17 21	17 27			17 31	17 39	17 39		
Imperial Wharf	d																					17 44	17 44		
West Brompton ⊖	d																					17 47	17 47		
Kensington (Olympia) ⊖	d																					17 50	17 50		
Shepherd's Bush ⊖	d																					17 53	17 53		
Wembley Central ⊖	d																					18s07	18 07		
Harrow & Wealdstone ⊖	d																					18 12	18 12		
Watford Junction	d																					18 19	18 19		
Milton Keynes Central 10	a																					19 00	19 00		
Battersea Park 4	d	17 11			17 15	17 18					17 23									17 32	17 35				
London Victoria 15 ⊖	a	17 16		17 16		17 23					17 28						17 28	17 34		17 36	17 39				
Streatham 4	d														17 10	17 16									
Tulse Hill 3	d													17 09	17 17	17 24									
Herne Hill 4	a																								
Loughborough Jn.	a																								
Elephant & Castle ⊖	a																								
London Blackfriars 3 ⊖	a																								
City Thameslink 3	a																								
St Pancras International 15 ⊖	a																								
Luton Airport Parkway 7	a																								
Luton 10	a																								
North Dulwich	d													17 12		17 27									
East Dulwich	d													17 14		17 29									
Peckham Rye 4	d				17 26									17 16		17 31									
Queens Rd Peckham	d				17 29									17 19		17 34									
South Bermondsey	d				17 31									17 21		17 36									
London Bridge 4 ⊖	a		17 11		17 36		17 09			17 13		17 30	17 25	17 26	17 30	17 41								17 41	

A until 31 March

B from 7 April

Table 177

Saturdays

East and West Croydon, London
Milton Keynes Central and Luton via Norbury
Crystal Palace - Tulse Hill

Local Services — Network Diagram - see first Page of Table 177

		SN	SN	SN	SN	SN	LO	SN	SN	SN	SN	SN	SN	FC	SN	SN		LO	SN	SN	SN	SN	SN	SN	SN
		◇1						1		1		◇1											◇1		
East Croydon	d	17 28	17 17			17 21		17 25	17 30	17 37		17 40									17 47		18 00		
West Croydon 4	d				17 15		17 22						17 28		17 31	17 34		17 39							17 45
Norwood Junction 2	a				17 19	17 25	17 28	17 29	17 34	17 42								17 43							17 49
	d				17 22	17 25		17 29	17 35	17 43															17 52
Selhurst 4	d		17 20										17 32		17 35	17 39					17 50				
Thornton Heath	d		17 22										17 34		17 37	17 41					17 52				
Norbury	d		17 25										17 37		17 40	17 44					17 55				
Streatham Common 4	d		17 28										17 40		17 43	17 47					17 58				
Beckenham Junction 4	d										17 23														
Birkbeck	d										17 26														
Crystal Palace 4	d				17 26						17 30									17 43		17 51			17 56
Gipsy Hill	d				17 29						17 32									17 45					17 59
West Norwood 4	d				17 32						17 35									17 48					18 02
Streatham Hill	d				17 35															17 52					18 05
Balham 4 ⊖	d		17 33		17 39								17 44			17 51				17 55	18 02				18 09
Wandsworth Common	d		17 35		17 41								17 46			17 53				17 57	18 04				18 11
Clapham Junction 10	d	17 37	17 39		17 45							17 50	17 50			17 57				18 01	18 08		18 10		18 15
Imperial Wharf	d																								
West Brompton ⊖	d																								
Kensington (Olympia) ⊖	d																								
Shepherd's Bush ⊖	d																								
Wembley Central ⊖	d																								
Harrow & Wealdstone ⊖	d																								
Watford Junction	d																								
Milton Keynes Central 10	a																								
Battersea Park 4	d		17 42	17 45	17 48								17 53						18 02	18 05	18 11			18 15	18 18
London Victoria 15 ⊖	a	17 44	17 47		17 53							17 57	17 58			18 04			18 06	18 09	18 16		18 16		18 23
Streatham 4	d													17 40	17 46										
Tulse Hill 3	d										17 39			17 47	17 54										
Herne Hill 4	a																								
Loughborough Jn.	a																								
Elephant & Castle ⊖	a																								
London Blackfriars 3 ⊖	a																								
City Thameslink 3	a																								
St Pancras International 15 ⊖	a																								
Luton Airport Parkway 7	a																								
Luton 10	a																								
North Dulwich	d										17 42				17 57										
East Dulwich	d										17 44				17 59										
Peckham Rye 4	d			17 56							17 46				18 01									18 26	
Queens Rd Peckham	d			17 59							17 49				18 04									18 29	
South Bermondsey	d			18 01							17 51				18 06									18 31	
London Bridge 4 ⊖	a			18 06		17 39		17 43	17 59	17 55	17 56			18 00	18 11							18 11		18 36	

Table 177

Saturdays

East and West Croydon, London
Milton Keynes Central and Luton via Norbury
Crystal Palace - Tulse Hill

Local Services

Network Diagram - see first Page of Table 177

		SN	LO	SN 1	SN	SN	SN 1	SN		FC	SN	SN ◇1	SN	LO	SN	SN	SN 1	SN	SN ◇1	SN	SN	SN	SN	LO	
East Croydon	d	17 51		17 55		18 00	18 07					18 12					18 10		18 28	18 17			18 21		
West Croydon 4	d		17 52		17 58						18 01		18 04	18 09								18 15		18 22	
Norwood Junction 2	a	17 55	17 58	17 59		18 04	18 12							18 13								18 19	18 25	18 28	
	d	17 55		17 59		18 05	18 13															18 22	18 25		
Selhurst 4	d				18 02						18 05		18 09				18 13			18 20					
Thornton Heath	d				18 04						18 07		18 11				18 16			18 22					
Norbury	d				18 07						18 10		18 14				18 19			18 25					
Streatham Common 4	d				18 10						18 13		18 17				18 21			18 28					
Beckenham Junction 4	d							17 53																	
Birkbeck	d							17 56																	
Crystal Palace 4	d							18 00								18 13		18 21				18 26			
Gipsy Hill	d							18 02								18 15						18 29			
West Norwood 4	d							18 05								18 18						18 32			
Streatham Hill	d															18 22						18 35			
Balham 4 ⊖	d				18 14								18 21			18 25	18 28			18 32		18 39			
Wandsworth Common	d				18 16								18 23			18 27	18 30			18 34		18 41			
Clapham Junction 10	d				18 20							18 21	18 27			18 31	18 39		18 37	18 38		18 45			
Imperial Wharf	d																18 44								
West Brompton ⊖	d																18 47								
Kensington (Olympia) ⊖	d																18 50								
Shepherd's Bush ⊖	d																18 53								
Wembley Central ⊖	d																19 08								
Harrow & Wealdstone ⊖	d																19 13								
Watford Junction	d																19a21								
Milton Keynes Central 10	a																								
Battersea Park 4	d				18 23										18 32	18 35				18 41	18 45	18 48			
London Victoria 15 ⊖	a				18 28							18 28	18 34		18 36	18 39			18 44	18 46		18 53			
Streatham 4	d									18 10	18 16														
Tulse Hill 3	d							18 09		18 17	18 24														
Herne Hill 4	a																								
Loughborough Jn.	a																								
Elephant & Castle ⊖	a																								
London Blackfriars 3 ⊖	a																								
City Thameslink 3	a																								
St Pancras International 15 ⊖	a																								
Luton Airport Parkway 7	a																								
Luton 10	a																								
North Dulwich	d							18 12			18 27														
East Dulwich	d							18 14			18 29														
Peckham Rye 4	d							18 16			18 31										18 56				
Queens Rd Peckham	d							18 19			18 34										18 59				
South Bermondsey	d							18 21			18 36										19 01				
London Bridge 4 ⊖	a	18 09		18 13		18 29	18 25	18 26		18 30	18 41							18 41			19 06		18 39		

		SN 1	SN	SN 1	SN	SN ◇1	SN	FC	SN	SN	LO	SN	SN	SN	SN	SN ◇1		SN	SN	SN	LO	SN 1	SN	SN	SN 1
East Croydon	d	18 25	18 30	18 37		18 40								18 47		19 00				18 51		18 55		19 00	19 07
West Croydon 4	d						18 28		18 31	18 34	18 39								18 45		18 52		18 58		
Norwood Junction 2	a	18 29	18 34	18 42							18 43								18 49	18 55	18 58	18 59		19 04	19 12
	d	18 29	18 35	18 43															18 52	18 55		18 59		19 05	19 13
Selhurst 4	d						18 32		18 35	18 39				18 50									19 02		
Thornton Heath	d						18 34		18 37	18 41				18 52									19 04		
Norbury	d						18 37		18 40	18 44				18 55									19 07		
Streatham Common 4	d						18 40		18 43	18 47				18 58									19 10		
Beckenham Junction 4	d				18 23																				
Birkbeck	d				18 26																				
Crystal Palace 4	d				18 30								18 43		18 51				18 56						
Gipsy Hill	d				18 32								18 45						18 59						
West Norwood 4	d				18 35								18 48						19 02						
Streatham Hill	d												18 52						19 05						
Balham 4 ⊖	d						18 44			18 51			18 55	19 02					19 09				19 14		
Wandsworth Common	d						18 46			18 53			18 57	19 04					19 11				19 16		
Clapham Junction 10	d					18 50	18 50			18 57			19 01	19 08		19 10			19 15				19 20		
Imperial Wharf	d																								
West Brompton ⊖	d																								
Kensington (Olympia) ⊖	d																								
Shepherd's Bush ⊖	d																								
Wembley Central ⊖	d																								
Harrow & Wealdstone ⊖	d																								
Watford Junction	d																								
Milton Keynes Central 10	a																								
Battersea Park 4	d						18 53					19 02	19 05	19 11				19 15	19 18				19 23		
London Victoria 15 ⊖	a					18 57	18 58			19 04		19 06	19 09	19 16		19 16			19 23				19 28		
Streatham 4	d							18 40	18 46																
Tulse Hill 3	d				18 39			18 47	18 54																
Herne Hill 4	a																								
Loughborough Jn.	a																								
Elephant & Castle ⊖	a																								
London Blackfriars 3 ⊖	a																								
City Thameslink 3	a																								
St Pancras International 15 ⊖	a																								
Luton Airport Parkway 7	a																								
Luton 10	a																								
North Dulwich	d				18 42				18 57																
East Dulwich	d				18 44				18 59																
Peckham Rye 4	d				18 46				19 01									19 26							
Queens Rd Peckham	d				18 49				19 04									19 29							
South Bermondsey	d				18 51				19 06									19 31							
London Bridge 4 ⊖	a	18 43	18 59	18 55	18 56			19 00	19 11						19 11			19 36		19 09		19 13		19 29	19 25

East and West Croydon, London Milton Keynes Central and Luton via Norbury Crystal Palace - Tulse Hill

Local Services

Network Diagram - see first Page of Table 177

		SN	FC	SN	SN	SN	LO	SN		SN	SN	SN	SN	SN	SN	SN	SN	SN	LO	SN	SN	SN	FC	SN	
					◇[1]						[1]		[1]		◇[1]										
East Croydon	d				19 12						19 10		19 25	19 17	19 29			19 21				19 30			
West Croydon [4]	d			19 01		19 04	19 09										19 15		19 22		19 28			19 31	
Norwood Junction [2]	a						19 13										19 19	19 25	19 28			19 34			
	d																19 22	19 25				19 35			
Selhurst [4]	d			19 05		19 09					19 13			19 20							19 32			19 35	
Thornton Heath	d			19 07		19 11					19 16			19 22							19 34			19 37	
Norbury	d			19 10		19 14					19 19			19 25							19 37			19 40	
Streatham Common [4]	d			19 13		19 17					19 21			19 28							19 40			19 43	
Beckenham Junction [4]	d	18 53																		19 23					
Birkbeck	d	18 56																		19 26					
Crystal Palace [4]	d	19 00								19 13		19 21					19 26			19 30					
Gipsy Hill	d	19 02								19 15							19 29			19 32					
West Norwood [4]	d	19 05								19 18							19 32			19 35					
Streatham Hill	d									19 22							19 35								
Balham [4] ⊖	d					19 21				19 25	19 28			19 32			19 39				19 44				
Wandsworth Common	d					19 23				19 27	19 30			19 34			19 41				19 46				
Clapham Junction [10]	d				19 21	19 27				19 31	19 38		19 37	19 38	19 40		19 45				19 50				
Imperial Wharf	d										19 42														
West Brompton ⊖	d										19 45														
Kensington (Olympia) ⊖	d										19 48														
Shepherd's Bush ⊖	d										19 50														
Wembley Central ⊖	d																								
Harrow & Wealdstone ⊖	d										20 08														
Watford Junction	d										20a15														
Milton Keynes Central [10]	a																								
Battersea Park [4]	d							19 32		19 35				19 41		19 45	19 48				19 53				
London Victoria [15] ⊖	a				19 28	19 34		19 36		19 39			19 44	19 46	19 50		19 53				19 58				
Streatham [4]	d		19 10	19 16																			19 40	19 46	
Tulse Hill [3]	d	19 09	19 17	19 24																19 39			19 47	19 54	
Herne Hill [4]	a																								
Loughborough Jn.	a																								
Elephant & Castle ⊖	a																								
London Blackfriars [3] ⊖	a																								
City Thameslink [3]	a																								
St Pancras International [15] ⊖	a																								
Luton Airport Parkway [7]	a																								
Luton [10]	a																								
North Dulwich	d	19 12		19 27																19 42				19 57	
East Dulwich	d	19 14		19 29																19 44				19 59	
Peckham Rye [4]	d	19 16		19 31												19 56				19 46				20 01	
Queens Rd Peckham	d	19 19		19 34												19 59				19 49				20 04	
South Bermondsey	d	19 21		19 36												20 01				19 51				20 06	
London Bridge [4] ⊖	a	19 26	19 30	19 41								19 41				20 06		19 39		19 56		19 59	20 00	20 11	

		SN	SN	LO	SN	SN	SN	SN	SN	SN	SN	SN	SN	LO	SN	SN		SN	FC	SN	SN	SN	LO	SN	SN
		◇[1]						[1]		[1]											◇[1]				
East Croydon	d	19 42						19 57	19 47	20 00			19 51					20 00			20 12				
West Croydon [4]	d		19 34	19 39								19 45		19 52		19 58				20 01		20 04	20 09		
Norwood Junction [2]	a			19 43								19 49	19 55	19 58				20 04					20 13		
	d											19 52	19 55					20 05							
Selhurst [4]	d		19 39						19 50							20 02				20 05		20 09			
Thornton Heath	d		19 41						19 52							20 04				20 07		20 11			
Norbury	d		19 44						19 55							20 07				20 10		20 14			
Streatham Common [4]	d		19 47						19 58							20 10				20 13		20 17			
Beckenham Junction [4]	d														19 53										
Birkbeck	d														19 56										
Crystal Palace [4]	d					19 43	19 51					19 56			20 00										20 13
Gipsy Hill	d					19 45						19 59			20 03										20 15
West Norwood [4]	d					19 48						20 02			20 06										20 18
Streatham Hill	d					19 52						20 05													20 22
Balham [4] ⊖	d		19 51			19 55			20 02			20 09				20 14						20 21			20 25
Wandsworth Common	d		19 53			19 57			20 04			20 11				20 16						20 23			20 27
Clapham Junction [10]	d	19 51	19 57			20 01		20 09	20 08	20 12		20 15				20 20					20 21	20 27			20 31
Imperial Wharf	d																								
West Brompton ⊖	d																								
Kensington (Olympia) ⊖	d																								
Shepherd's Bush ⊖	d																								
Wembley Central ⊖	d																								
Harrow & Wealdstone ⊖	d																								
Watford Junction	d																								
Milton Keynes Central [10]	a																								
Battersea Park [4]	d				20 02	20 05			20 11		20 15	20 18				20 23								20 32	20 35
London Victoria [15] ⊖	a	19 58	20 04		20 06	20 09		20 15	20 16	20 20		20 23				20 28					20 28	20 34		20 36	20 39
Streatham [4]	d																		20 10	20 16					
Tulse Hill [3]	d														20 09				20 17	20 24					
Herne Hill [4]	a																								
Loughborough Jn.	a																								
Elephant & Castle ⊖	a																								
London Blackfriars [3] ⊖	a																								
City Thameslink [3]	a																								
St Pancras International [15] ⊖	a																								
Luton Airport Parkway [7]	a																								
Luton [10]	a																								
North Dulwich	d														20 12					20 27					
East Dulwich	d														20 14					20 29					
Peckham Rye [4]	d										20 26				20 16					20 31					
Queens Rd Peckham	d										20 29				20 19					20 34					
South Bermondsey	d										20 31				20 21					20 36					
London Bridge [4] ⊖	a						20 11				20 36		20 09		20 26			20 29	20 30	20 41					

Table 177

Saturdays

East and West Croydon, London
Milton Keynes Central and Luton via Norbury
Crystal Palace - Tulse Hill

Local Services

Network Diagram - see first Page of Table 177

		SN	SN ■1	SN	SN ◇■1	SN	SN	SN		LO	SN	SN	SN	FC	SN	SN ◇■1	SN	LO	SN	SN	SN	SN ■1	SN	SN	
East Croydon	d		20 26	20 17	20 30			20 21					20 30			20 42						20 56	20 47		
West Croydon ■4	d						20 15			20 22		20 28			20 31		20 34	20 39							
Norwood Junction ■2	a						20 19	20 25		20 28			20 34					20 43							
	d						20 22	20 25					20 35												
Selhurst ■4	d			20 20								20 32			20 35		20 39						20 50		
Thornton Heath	d			20 22								20 34			20 37		20 41						20 52		
Norbury	d			20 25								20 37			20 40		20 44						20 55		
Streatham Common ■4	d			20 28								20 40			20 43		20 47						20 58		
Beckenham Junction ■4	d										20 23														
Birkbeck	d										20 26														
Crystal Palace ■4	d	20 21					20 26				20 30									20 43	20 51				
Gipsy Hill	d						20 29				20 33									20 45					
West Norwood ■4	d						20 32				20 36									20 48					
Streatham Hill	d						20 35													20 52					
Balham ■4 ⊖	d			20 32			20 39					20 44					20 51			20 55			21 02		
Wandsworth Common	d			20 34			20 41					20 46					20 53			20 57			21 04		
Clapham Junction ■10	d		20 37	20 38	20 41		20 45					20 50				20 51	20 57			21 01		21 07	21 08		
Imperial Wharf	d																								
West Brompton ⊖	d																								
Kensington (Olympia) ⊖	d																								
Shepherd's Bush ⊖	d																								
Wembley Central ⊖	d																								
Harrow & Wealdstone ⊖	d																								
Watford Junction	d																								
Milton Keynes Central ■10	a																								
Battersea Park ■4	d			20 41		20 45	20 48					20 53							21 02	21 05			21 11	21 15	
London Victoria ■15 ⊖	a		20 44	20 46	20 50		20 53					20 58				20 58	21 04		21 06	21 09		21 14	21 16		
Streatham ■4	d													20 40	20 46										
Tulse Hill ■3	d										20 39			20 47	20 54										
Herne Hill ■4	a																								
Loughborough Jn.	a																								
Elephant & Castle ⊖	a																								
London Blackfriars ■3 ⊖	a																								
City Thameslink ■3	a																								
St Pancras International ■15 ⊖	a																								
Luton Airport Parkway ■7	a																								
Luton ■10	a																								
North Dulwich	d										20 42				20 57										
East Dulwich	d										20 44				20 59										
Peckham Rye ■4	d					20 56					20 46				21 01									21 26	
Queens Rd Peckham	d					20 59					20 49				21 04									21 29	
South Bermondsey	d					21 01					20 51				21 06									21 31	
London Bridge ■4 ⊖	a	20 41				21 06		20 39			20 56		20 59	21 00	21 11						21 13			21 36	

		SN	SN	LO	SN	SN	SN ◇■1	SN	FC	SN	SN	LO	SN	SN	SN	SN ■1		SN	SN ◇■1	SN	SN	SN	LO	SN	SN
East Croydon	d		20 51			21 00	21 09									21 26		21 17	21 31			21 21			
West Croydon ■4	d	20 45		20 52				20 58		21 02	21 04	21 09									21 15		21 22		21 28
Norwood Junction ■2	a	20 49	20 55	20 58		21 04						21 13									21 19	21 25	21 28		
	d	20 52	20 55			21 05															21 22	21 25			
Selhurst ■4	d							21 02		21 06	21 09							21 20							21 32
Thornton Heath	d							21 04		21 08	21 11							21 22							21 34
Norbury	d							21 07		21 11	21 14							21 25							21 37
Streatham Common ■4	d							21 10		21 14	21 17							21 28							21 40
Beckenham Junction ■4	d				20 53																			21 23	
Birkbeck	d				20 56																			21 26	
Crystal Palace ■4	d	20 56			21 00									21 13	21 21						21 26			21 30	
Gipsy Hill	d	20 59			21 02									21 15							21 29			21 32	
West Norwood ■4	d	21 02			21 05									21 18							21 32			21 35	
Streatham Hill	d	21 05												21 22							21 35				
Balham ■4 ⊖	d	21 09						21 14			21 21			21 25				21 32			21 39				21 44
Wandsworth Common	d	21 11						21 16			21 23			21 27				21 34			21 41				21 46
Clapham Junction ■10	d	21 15					21 18	21 20			21 27			21 31		21 37		21 38	21 41		21 45				21 50
Imperial Wharf	d																								
West Brompton ⊖	d																								
Kensington (Olympia) ⊖	d																								
Shepherd's Bush ⊖	d																								
Wembley Central ⊖	d																								
Harrow & Wealdstone ⊖	d																								
Watford Junction	d																								
Milton Keynes Central ■10	a																								
Battersea Park ■4	d	21 18						21 23					21 32	21 35				21 41		21 45	21 48				21 53
London Victoria ■15 ⊖	a	21 23					21 26	21 28			21 34		21 36	21 39		21 44		21 46	21 50		21 53				21 58
Streatham ■4	d								21 10	21 17															
Tulse Hill ■3	d				21 09				21 17	21 24														21 39	
Herne Hill ■4	a																								
Loughborough Jn.	a																								
Elephant & Castle ⊖	a																								
London Blackfriars ■3 ⊖	a																								
City Thameslink ■3	a																								
St Pancras International ■15 ⊖	a																								
Luton Airport Parkway ■7	a																								
Luton ■10	a																								
North Dulwich	d				21 12					21 27														21 42	
East Dulwich	d				21 14					21 29														21 44	
Peckham Rye ■4	d				21 16					21 31										21 56				21 46	
Queens Rd Peckham	d				21 19					21 34										21 59				21 49	
South Bermondsey	d				21 21					21 36										22 01				21 51	
London Bridge ■4 ⊖	a		21 09		21 26	21 29			21 30	21 41					21 43					22 06		21 39		21 56	

Table 177

Saturdays

East and West Croydon, London
Milton Keynes Central and Luton via Norbury
Crystal Palace - Tulse Hill

Local Services

Network Diagram - see first Page of Table 177

Station		SN	FC	SN	SN ◇1	SN	LO	SN		SN	SN	SN 1	SN	SN	SN	SN	LO	SN	SN	SN ◇1	SN	FC	SN	SN	
East Croydon	d	21 30			21 42							21 56	21 47			21 51			22 00	22 09					
West Croydon 4	d			21 31		21 34	21 39								21 45		21 52				21 58		22 01	22 04	
Norwood Junction 2	a	21 34					21 43								21 49	21 55	21 58		22 04						
	d	21 35													21 52	21 55			22 05						
Selhurst 4	d			21 35		21 39							21 50								22 02		22 05	22 10	
Thornton Heath	d			21 37		21 41							21 52								22 04		22 07	22 12	
Norbury	d			21 40		21 44							21 55								22 07		22 10	22 15	
Streatham Common 4	d			21 43		21 47							21 58								22 10		22 13	22 17	
Beckenham Junction 4	d																	21 53							
Birkbeck	d																	21 56							
Crystal Palace 4	d									21 43	21 51				21 56			22 00							
Gipsy Hill	d									21 45					21 59			22 02							
West Norwood 4	d									21 48					22 02			22 05							
Streatham Hill	d									21 52					22 05										
Balham 4 ⊖	d					21 51				21 55			22 02		22 09						22 14			22 22	
Wandsworth Common	d					21 53				21 57			22 04		22 11						22 16			22 24	
Clapham Junction 10	d				21 51	21 57				22 01		22 07	22 08		22 15					22 18	22 20			22 27	
Imperial Wharf	d																								
West Brompton ⊖	d																								
Kensington (Olympia) ⊖	d																								
Shepherd's Bush ⊖	d																								
Wembley Central ⊖	d																								
Harrow & Wealdstone ⊖	d																								
Watford Junction	d																								
Milton Keynes Central 10	a																								
Battersea Park 4	d							22 02		22 05			22 11	22 15	22 18						22 23				
London Victoria 15 ⊖	a				21 58	22 04		22 06		22 09		22 15	22 16		22 23					22 26	22 28			22 34	
Streatham 4	d		21 40	21 46																		22 10	22 16		
Tulse Hill 3	d		21 47	21 54														22 09				22 17	22 24		
Herne Hill 4	a																								
Loughborough Jn.	a																								
Elephant & Castle ⊖	a																								
London Blackfriars 3 ⊖	a																								
City Thameslink 3	a																								
St Pancras International 15 ⊖	a																								
Luton Airport Parkway 7	a																								
Luton 10	a																								
North Dulwich	d			21 57														22 12					22 27		
East Dulwich	d			21 59														22 14					22 29		
Peckham Rye 4	d			22 01										22 26				22 16					22 31		
Queens Rd Peckham	d			22 04										22 29				22 19					22 34		
South Bermondsey	d			22 06										22 31				22 21					22 36		
London Bridge 4 ⊖	a	21 59	22 00	22 11							22 13			22 36		22 09		22 26	22 29			22 30	22 41		

Station		LO	SN	SN	SN	SN 1	SN	SN ◇1	SN	SN	SN	LO	SN	SN	SN ◇1 ✈	SN		FC	SN	SN	LO	SN	SN	SN	SN 1
East Croydon	d					22 26	22 17	22 31			22 21			22 30	22 40										22 56
West Croydon 4	d	22 09								22 15		22 22				22 28			22 31	22 34	22 39				
Norwood Junction 2	a	22 13								22 19	22 25	22 28		22 34							22 43				
	d									22 22	22 25			22 35											
Selhurst 4	d						22 20									22 32			22 35	22 39					
Thornton Heath	d						22 22									22 34			22 37	22 41					
Norbury	d						22 25									22 37			22 40	22 44					
Streatham Common 4	d						22 28									22 40			22 43	22 47					
Beckenham Junction 4	d												22 23												
Birkbeck	d												22 26												
Crystal Palace 4	d			22 13	22 21					22 26			22 30										22 43	22 51	
Gipsy Hill	d			22 15						22 29			22 32										22 45		
West Norwood 4	d			22 18						22 32			22 35										22 48		
Streatham Hill	d			22 22						22 35													22 52		
Balham 4 ⊖	d			22 25			22 32			22 39						22 44				22 51			22 55		
Wandsworth Common	d			22 27			22 34			22 41						22 46				22 53			22 57		
Clapham Junction 10	d			22 31		22 37	22 38	22 41		22 45					22 50	22 50				22 57			23 01		23 07
Imperial Wharf	d																								
West Brompton ⊖	d																								
Kensington (Olympia) ⊖	d																								
Shepherd's Bush ⊖	d																								
Wembley Central ⊖	d																								
Harrow & Wealdstone ⊖	d																								
Watford Junction	d																								
Milton Keynes Central 10	a																								
Battersea Park 4	d		22 32	22 35			22 41		22 45	22 48						22 53						23 02	23 05		
London Victoria 15 ⊖	a		22 36	22 39		22 44	22 46	22 50		22 53					22 57	22 58				23 04		23 06	23 09		23 14
Streatham 4	d																	22 40	22 46						
Tulse Hill 3	d												22 39					22 47	22 54						
Herne Hill 4	a																								
Loughborough Jn.	a																								
Elephant & Castle ⊖	a																								
London Blackfriars 3 ⊖	a																								
City Thameslink 3	a																								
St Pancras International 15 ⊖	a																								
Luton Airport Parkway 7	a																								
Luton 10	a																								
North Dulwich	d												22 42						22 57						
East Dulwich	d												22 44						22 59						
Peckham Rye 4	d								22 56				22 46						23 01						
Queens Rd Peckham	d								22 59				22 49						23 04						
South Bermondsey	d								23 01				22 51						23 06						
London Bridge 4 ⊖	a				22 43				23 06		22 39		22 56	22 59				23 00	23 11					23 13	

East and West Croydon, London
Milton Keynes Central and Luton via Norbury
Crystal Palace - Tulse Hill

Local Services

Network Diagram - see first Page of Table 177

		SN	SN	SN	SN	LO	SN	SN	SN	SN	SN	SN	SN	SN	SN	SN ◇1	SN	SN	LO	SN	SN	SN	SN
East Croydon (tram)	d	22 47			22 51				23 01					23 17		23 30		23 21					23 43
West Croydon 4 (tram)	d			22 45		22 52		22 58		23 01	23 04						23 15		23 22		23 28	23 34	
Norwood Junction 2	a			22 49	22 55	22 58			23 05								23 19	23 25	23 28				23 47
	d			22 52	22 55				23 06								23 22	23 25					
Selhurst 4	d	22 50						23 02		23 05	23 09			23 20							23 32	23 39	
Thornton Heath	d	22 52						23 04		23 07	23 11			23 22							23 34	23 41	
Norbury	d	22 55						23 07		23 10	23 14			23 25							23 37	23 44	
Streatham Common 4	d	22 58						23 10		23 13	23 17			23 28							23 40	23 46	
Beckenham Junction 4 (tram)	d						22 53													23 23			
Birkbeck (tram)	d						22 56													23 26			
Crystal Palace 4	d			22 56			23 00						23 13		23 21		23 26			23 30			
Gipsy Hill	d			22 59			23 02						23 15				23 29			23 32			
West Norwood 4	d			23 02			23 05						23 18				23 32			23 35			
Streatham Hill	d			23 05									23 22				23 35						
Balham 4 ⊖	d	23 02		23 09				23 14			23 21		23 25	23 32			23 39				23 44	23 50	
Wandsworth Common	d	23 04		23 11				23 16			23 23		23 27	23 34			23 41				23 46	23 52	
Clapham Junction 10	d	23 08		23 15				23 20			23 27		23 31	23 38		23 42	23 45				23 50	23 56	
Imperial Wharf	d																						
West Brompton ⊖	d																						
Kensington (Olympia) ⊖	d																						
Shepherd's Bush ⊖	d																						
Wembley Central ⊖	d																						
Harrow & Wealdstone ⊖	d																						
Watford Junction	d																						
Milton Keynes Central 10	a																						
Battersea Park 4	d	23 11	23 15	23 18				23 23				23 32	23 35	23 41			23 49				23 53		
London Victoria 15 ⊖	a	23 16		23 24				23 29			23 34	23 37	23 41	23 48		23 52	23 53				23 58	00 04	
Streatham 4	d									23 19													
Tulse Hill 3	d						23 09			23 24										23 39			
Herne Hill 4	a																						
Loughborough Jn	a																						
Elephant & Castle ⊖	a																						
London Blackfriars 3 ⊖	a																						
City Thameslink 3	a																						
St Pancras International 15 ⊖	a																						
Luton Airport Parkway 7	a																						
Luton 10	a																						
North Dulwich	d						23 12			23 27										23 42			
East Dulwich	d						23 14			23 29										23 44			
Peckham Rye 4	d		23 26				23 16			23 31										23 46			
Queens Rd Peckham	d		23 29				23 19			23 34										23 49			
South Bermondsey	d		23 31				23 21			23 36										23 51			
London Bridge 4 ⊖	a		23 36		23 09		23 26		23 30	23 41					23 43			23 39		23 56			

		SN	SN	SN 1
East Croydon (tram)	d			23 56
West Croydon 4 (tram)	d			
Norwood Junction 2	a			
	d			
Selhurst 4	d			00 02
Thornton Heath	d			
Norbury	d			
Streatham Common 4	d			
Beckenham Junction 4 (tram)	d			
Birkbeck (tram)	d			
Crystal Palace 4	d	23 43	23 51	
Gipsy Hill	d	23 45		
West Norwood 4	d	23 48		
Streatham Hill	d	23 52		
Balham 4 ⊖	d	23 55		
Wandsworth Common	d	23 57		
Clapham Junction 10	d	00 02		00 12
Imperial Wharf	d			
West Brompton ⊖	d			
Kensington (Olympia) ⊖	d			
Shepherd's Bush ⊖	d			
Wembley Central ⊖	d			
Harrow & Wealdstone ⊖	d			
Watford Junction	d			
Milton Keynes Central 10	a			
Battersea Park 4	d	00 05		
London Victoria 15 ⊖	a	00 10		00 18
Streatham 4	d			
Tulse Hill 3	d			
Herne Hill 4	a			
Loughborough Jn	a			
Elephant & Castle ⊖	a			
London Blackfriars 3 ⊖	a			
City Thameslink 3	a			
St Pancras International 15 ⊖	a			
Luton Airport Parkway 7	a			
Luton 10	a			
North Dulwich	d			
East Dulwich	d			
Peckham Rye 4	d			
Queens Rd Peckham	d			
South Bermondsey	d			
London Bridge 4 ⊖	a		00 11	

Table 177

Sundays

East and West Croydon, London
Milton Keynes Central and Luton via Norbury
Crystal Palace - Tulse Hill

Local Services

Network Diagram - see first Page of Table 177

		SN	SN	SN	SN	SN	SN	SN	SN	SN	SN	SN	FC	SN	SN	LO		SN	SN	SN	SN	SN	SN	LO	SN
					1				1	1	1	1	1	1											
		A	A	A	A	A	A																		
East Croydon	d				23p56			00 49	01 43	02 40	03 40	04 40	05 32	06 02	06 40			06 47					07 12		07 17
West Croydon 4	d	23p34														06 42					07 07			07 12	
Norwood Junction 2	a												05 36			06 47		06 51						07 17	07 21
	d												05 36					06 52		06 57					07 22
Selhurst 4	d	23p39			00 02			00 53	01 45						06 43				06 47		07 11		07 15		
Thornton Heath	d	23p41													06 45				06 49		07 13		07 17		
Norbury	d	23p44													06 48				06 52		07 16		07 20		
Streatham Common 4	d	23p46													06 51				06 55		07 19		07 23		
Beckenham Junction 4	d																								
Birkbeck	d																								
Crystal Palace 4	d		23p43	23p51		00 13	00 21													07 01		07 07			
Gipsy Hill	d		23p45			00 15														07 03		07 09			
West Norwood 4	d		23p48			00 18														07 06		07 12			
Streatham Hill	d		23p52			00 22														07 10					
Balham 4 ⊖	d	23p50	23p55			00 26									06 55					07 13	07 23				
Wandsworth Common	d	23p52	23p57			00 28									06 57					07 15					
Clapham Junction 10	d	23p56	00 02		00 12	00 32		01 03	01 54	02 53	03 53	04 53		06 15	07 00					07 19	07 27				
Imperial Wharf	d																								
West Brompton ⊖	d																								
Kensington (Olympia) ⊖	d																								
Shepherd's Bush ⊖	d																								
Wembley Central ⊖	d																								
Harrow & Wealdstone ⊖	d																								
Watford Junction	d																								
Milton Keynes Central 10	a																								
Battersea Park 4	d		00 05			00 35									07 04					07 23					
London Victoria 15 ⊖	a	00 04	00 10		00 18	00 42		01 10	02 05	03 05	04 05	05 05		06 22	07 09					07 27	07 34				
Streatham 4	d																		06 58				07 28		
Tulse Hill 3	d																		07 02			07 16	07 32		
Herne Hill 4	a																								
Loughborough Jn.	a																								
Elephant & Castle ⊖	a																								
London Blackfriars 3 ⊖	a																								
City Thameslink 3	a																								
St Pancras International 15 ⊖	a																								
Luton Airport Parkway 7	a																								
Luton 10	a																								
North Dulwich	d																		07 05			07 19	07 35		
East Dulwich	d																		07 07			07 21	07 37		
Peckham Rye 4	d																		07 09			07 23	07 39		
Queens Rd Peckham	d																		07 12			07 26	07 42		
South Bermondsey	d																		07 14			07 28	07 44		
London Bridge 4 ⊖	a			00 11			00 41						05 59					07 17	07 19			07 33	07 50		07 48

A not 11 December

Table 177

Sundays

East and West Croydon, London Milton Keynes Central and Luton via Norbury Crystal Palace - Tulse Hill

Local Services

Network Diagram - see first Page of Table 177

		SN	SN ■1	SN	SN	SN	SN	SN		SN	LO	SN	SN	SN	SN	SN	SN ■1	SN	SN	SN ◇■1 🚲	SN	SN	LO	SN	
East Croydon 🚊	d		07 27							07 42		07 47		07 53			07 56			08 10		08 12		08 17	
West Croydon ■4 🚊	d				07 22	07 34	07 37				07 42					07 52		08 04			08 07		08 12		
Norwood Junction ■2	a				07 26	07 39					07 47	07 51				07 56	08 00	08 09					08 17	08 21	
	d				07 27	07 40						07 52				07 57	08 01	08 10						08 22	
Selhurst ■4	d		07 31				07 41			07 46				07 57							08 11	08 16			
Thornton Heath	d						07 43			07 48				07 59							08 13	08 18			
Norbury	d						07 46			07 51				08 02							08 16	08 21			
Streatham Common ■4	d						07 49			07 53				08 04							08 19	08 23			
Beckenham Junction ■4 🚊	d																								
Birkbeck 🚊	d																								
Crystal Palace ■4	d				07 31			07 37								08 01			08 07						
Gipsy Hill	d				07 33			07 39								08 03			08 09						
West Norwood ■4	d				07 36			07 42								08 06			08 12						
Streatham Hill	d				07 40											08 10									
Balham ■4 ⊖	d				07 43		07 53							08 08		08 13					08 23				
Wandsworth Common	d				07 45											08 15									
Clapham Junction ■10	d		07 41		07 49		07 57							08 13		08 19				08 24	08 27				
Imperial Wharf	d																								
West Brompton ⊖	d																								
Kensington (Olympia) ⊖	d																								
Shepherd's Bush ⊖	d																								
Wembley Central ⊖	d																								
Harrow & Wealdstone ⊖	d																								
Watford Junction	d																								
Milton Keynes Central ■10	a																								
Battersea Park ■4	d	07 32		07 45	07 53								08 02		08 15	08 23									
London Victoria ■15 ⊖	a	07 36	07 48		07 57		08 04						08 06	08 20		08 27				08 30	08 34				
Streatham ■4	d									07 58												08 28			
Tulse Hill ■3	d							07 46		08 02									08 16			08 32			
Herne Hill ■4	a																								
Loughborough Jn.	a																								
Elephant & Castle ⊖	a																								
London Blackfriars ■3 ⊖	a																								
City Thameslink ■3	a																								
St Pancras International ■15 ⊖	a																								
Luton Airport Parkway ■7	a																								
Luton ■10	a																								
North Dulwich	d							07 49		08 05									08 19			08 35			
East Dulwich	d							07 51		08 07									08 21			08 37			
Peckham Rye ■4	d			07 56				07 53		08 10					08 26				08 23			08 40			
Queens Rd Peckham	d			07 59				07 56		08 12					08 29				08 26			08 42			
South Bermondsey	d			08 01				07 58		08 15					08 31				08 28			08 45			
London Bridge ■4 ⊖	a			08 06		08 01		08 03		08 19		08 17			08 36		08 12	08 31	08 33			08 49		08 48	

Table 177 | **Sundays**

East and West Croydon, London
Milton Keynes Central and Luton via Norbury
Crystal Palace - Tulse Hill

Local Services | **Network Diagram - see first Page of Table 177**

		SN	SN	SN	SN	SN	SN	SN	SN	SN	SN	LO	SN	SN	SN	SN		SN	SN	SN	SN	SN	SN	SN	LO
			◇1						◇1										1			◇1 ⚲			
East Croydon ⇌	d		08 26	08 23					08 41		08 42		08 47		08 53				08 56			09 10		09 12	
West Croydon 4 ⇌	d					08 22	08 34			08 37		08 42						08 52		09 04			09 07		09 12
Norwood Junction 2	a					08 26	08 39					08 47	08 51					08 56	09 00	09 09					09 17
	d					08 27	08 40						08 52					08 57	09 01	09 10					
Selhurst 4	d			08 26						08 41	08 46				08 57								09 11	09 16	
Thornton Heath	d			08 28						08 43	08 48				08 59								09 13	09 18	
Norbury	d			08 31						08 46	08 51				09 02								09 16	09 21	
Streatham Common 4	d			08 34						08 49	08 53				09 04								09 19	09 23	
Beckenham Junction 4 ⇌	d																								
Birkbeck ⇌	d																								
Crystal Palace 4	d					08 31		08 37										09 01			09 07				
Gipsy Hill	d					08 33		08 39										09 03			09 09				
West Norwood 4	d					08 36		08 42										09 06			09 12				
Streatham Hill	d					08 40												09 10							
Balham 4 ⊖	d			08 38		08 43				08 53					09 08			09 13					09 23		
Wandsworth Common	d					08 45												09 15							
Clapham Junction 10	d		08 38	08 42		08 49			08 55	08 57					09 13			09 19				09 25	09 27		
Imperial Wharf	d																								
West Brompton ⊖	d																								
Kensington (Olympia) ⊖	d																								
Shepherd's Bush ⊖	d																								
Wembley Central ⊖	d																								
Harrow & Wealdstone ⊖	d																								
Watford Junction	d																								
Milton Keynes Central 10	a																								
Battersea Park 4	d	08 32			08 45	08 52								09 02		09 15		09 23							
London Victoria 15 ⊖	a	08 36	08 46	08 50		08 57			09 01	09 04				09 06	09 20			09 27				09 31	09 34		
Streatham 4	d										08 58													09 28	
Tulse Hill 3	d							08 46			09 02										09 16			09 32	
Herne Hill 4	a																								
Loughborough Jn.	a																								
Elephant & Castle ⊖	a																								
London Blackfriars 3 ⊖	a																								
City Thameslink 3	a																								
St Pancras International 15 ⊖	a																								
Luton Airport Parkway 7	a																								
Luton 10	a																								
North Dulwich	d							08 49			09 05										09 19			09 35	
East Dulwich	d							08 51			09 07										09 21			09 37	
Peckham Rye 4	d				08 56			08 53			09 10					09 26					09 23			09 40	
Queens Rd Peckham	d				08 59			08 56			09 12					09 29					09 26			09 42	
South Bermondsey	d				09 01			08 58			09 15					09 31					09 28			09 45	
London Bridge 4 ⊖	a				09 06		09 01	09 03			09 19		09 18			09 36			09 12	09 31	09 33			09 49	

Table 177

Sundays

East and West Croydon, London Milton Keynes Central and Luton via Norbury Crystal Palace - Tulse Hill

Local Services

Network Diagram - see first Page of Table 177

		SN	SN	SN	SN	SN	SN	SN		SN	SN	SN	SN	LO	SN	SN	SN	SN	SN	SN	SN	SN	SN	SN	
				◇1							◇1									1			◇1		
East Croydon	d	09 17		09 26	09 23						09 41		09 42		09 47		09 53			09 56			10 10		
West Croydon 4	d						09 22	09 34				09 37		09 42					09 52		10 04			10 07	
Norwood Junction 2	a	09 21					09 26	09 39						09 47	09 51				09 56	10 00	10 09				
	d	09 22					09 27	09 40							09 52				09 57	10 01	10 10				
Selhurst 4	d				09 26							09 41	09 46				09 57							10 11	
Thornton Heath	d				09 28							09 43	09 48				09 59							10 13	
Norbury	d				09 31							09 46	09 51				10 02							10 16	
Streatham Common 4	d				09 34							09 49	09 53				10 04							10 19	
Beckenham Junction 4	d																								
Birkbeck	d																								
Crystal Palace 4	d						09 31			09 37									10 01			10 07			
Gipsy Hill	d						09 33			09 39									10 03			10 09			
West Norwood 4	d						09 36			09 42									10 06			10 12			
Streatham Hill	d						09 40												10 10						
Balham 4 ⊖	d				09 38		09 43					09 53					10 08		10 13					10 23	
Wandsworth Common	d						09 45												10 15						
Clapham Junction 10	d			09 38	09 42		09 49				09 55	09 57					10 13		10 19				10 25	10 27	
Imperial Wharf	d																								
West Brompton ⊖	d																								
Kensington (Olympia) ⊖	d																								
Shepherd's Bush ⊖	d																								
Wembley Central ⊖	d																								
Harrow & Wealdstone ⊖	d																								
Watford Junction	d																								
Milton Keynes Central 10	a																								
Battersea Park 4	d		09 32			09 45	09 53									10 02		10 15	10 22						
London Victoria 15 ⊖	a		09 36	09 46	09 50		09 57				10 01	10 04				10 06	10 20		10 27				10 31	10 34	
Streatham 4	d												09 58												
Tulse Hill 3	d									09 46			10 02									10 16			
Herne Hill 4	a																								
Loughborough Jn	a																								
Elephant & Castle ⊖	a																								
London Blackfriars 3 ⊖	a																								
City Thameslink 3	a																								
St Pancras International 15 ⊖	a																								
Luton Airport Parkway 7	a																								
Luton 10	a																								
North Dulwich	d									09 49			10 05									10 19			
East Dulwich	d									09 51			10 07									10 21			
Peckham Rye 4	d					09 56				09 53			10 10					10 26				10 23			
Queens Rd Peckham	d					09 59				09 56			10 12					10 29				10 26			
South Bermondsey	d					10 01				09 58			10 15					10 31				10 28			
London Bridge 4 ⊖	a	09 48				10 06		10 01		10 03			10 19		10 18			10 36		10 12	10 31	10 33			

Table 177

Sundays

East and West Croydon, London
Milton Keynes Central and Luton via Norbury
Crystal Palace - Tulse Hill

Local Services

Network Diagram - see first Page of Table 177

		SN	LO	SN	SN	SN	SN	SN	SN	SN	SN	SN	SN	LO	FC	SN		SN	SN	SN	SN	SN	SN	SN	SN
						◇1						◇1											1		
East Croydon	d	10 12		10 17		10 26	10 23					10 40				10 42		10 47		10 53			10 56		
West Croydon 4	d		10 12						10 22	10 34			10 37	10 42								10 52		11 04	
Norwood Junction 2	a		10 17	10 21					10 26	10 39				10 47				10 51				10 56	11 00	11 09	
	d			10 22					10 27	10 40								10 52				10 57	11 01	11 10	
Selhurst 4	d	10 16					10 26						10 41			10 46				10 57					
Thornton Heath	d	10 18					10 28						10 43			10 48				10 59					
Norbury	d	10 21					10 31						10 46			10 51				11 02					
Streatham Common 4	d	10 23					10 34						10 49			10 53				11 04					
Beckenham Junction 4	d																								
Birkbeck	d																								
Crystal Palace 4	d								10 31		10 37											11 01			11 07
Gipsy Hill	d								10 33		10 39											11 03			11 09
West Norwood 4	d								10 36		10 42											11 06			11 12
Streatham Hill	d								10 40													11 10			
Balham 4 ⊖	d						10 38		10 43				10 53							11 08		11 13			
Wandsworth Common	d								10 45													11 15			
Clapham Junction 10	d					10 38	10 42		10 49			10 55	10 57							11 13		11 19			
Imperial Wharf	d																								
West Brompton ⊖	d																								
Kensington (Olympia) ⊖	d																								
Shepherd's Bush ⊖	d																								
Wembley Central ⊖	d																								
Harrow & Wealdstone ⊖	d																								
Watford Junction	d																								
Milton Keynes Central 10	a																								
Battersea Park 4	d				10 32			10 45	10 52										11 02		11 15	11 22			
London Victoria 15 ⊖	a				10 36	10 46	10 50		10 57			11 01	11 04						11 06	11 20		11 27			
Streatham 4	d	10 28													10 55	10 58									
Tulse Hill 3	d	10 32									10 46				10 59	11 02									11 16
Herne Hill 4	a																								
Loughborough Jn.	a																								
Elephant & Castle ⊖	a																								
London Blackfriars 3 ⊖	a																								
City Thameslink 3	a																								
St Pancras International 15 ⊖	a																								
Luton Airport Parkway 7	a																								
Luton 10	a																								
North Dulwich	d	10 35									10 49					11 05									11 19
East Dulwich	d	10 37									10 51					11 07									11 21
Peckham Rye 4	d	10 40						10 56			10 53					11 10					11 26				11 23
Queens Rd Peckham	d	10 42						10 59			10 56					11 12					11 29				11 26
South Bermondsey	d	10 45						11 01			10 58					11 15					11 31				11 28
London Bridge 4 ⊖	a	10 49		10 48				11 06		11 01	11 03				11 10	11 19		11 18			11 36		11 12	11 31	11 33

Table 177

Sundays

East and West Croydon, London
Milton Keynes Central and Luton via Norbury
Crystal Palace - Tulse Hill

Local Services

Network Diagram - see first Page of Table 177

		SN ◇1 🚲	SN	LO	FC	SN	SN	SN		SN ◇1 🚲	SN	SN	SN	SN	SN	SN ◇1	SN	LO	FC	SN	SN	SN	SN	SN
East Croydon 🚋	d	11 10				11 12	11 17			11 26	11 23					11 41				11 42	11 47		11 53	
West Croydon 4 🚋	d		11 07	11 12									11 22	11 34			11 37	11 42						
Norwood Junction 2	a			11 17			11 21						11 26	11 39				11 47			11 51			
	d						11 22						11 27	11 40							11 52			
Selhurst 4	d		11 11			11 16					11 26						11 41			11 46			11 57	
Thornton Heath	d		11 13			11 18					11 28						11 43			11 48			11 59	
Norbury	d		11 16			11 21					11 31						11 46			11 51			12 02	
Streatham Common 4	d		11 19			11 23					11 34						11 49			11 53			12 04	
Beckenham Junction 4 🚋	d																							
Birkbeck 🚋	d																							
Crystal Palace 4	d												11 31		11 37									
Gipsy Hill	d												11 33		11 39									
West Norwood 4	d												11 36		11 42									
Streatham Hill	d												11 40											
Balham 4 ⊖	d		11 23								11 38		11 43				11 53						12 08	
Wandsworth Common	d												11 45											
Clapham Junction 10	d	11 25	11 27							11 38	11 42		11 49			11 55	11 57						12 13	
Imperial Wharf	d																							
West Brompton ⊖	d																							
Kensington (Olympia) ⊖	d																							
Shepherd's Bush ⊖	d																							
Wembley Central ⊖	d																							
Harrow & Wealdstone ⊖	d																							
Watford Junction	d																							
Milton Keynes Central 10	a																							
Battersea Park 4	d							11 32				11 45	11 52									12 02		12 15
London Victoria 15 ⊖	a	11 31	11 34					11 36		11 46	11 50		11 57			12 01	12 04					12 06	12 20	
Streatham 4	d				11 25	11 28													11 55	11 58				
Tulse Hill 3	d				11 29	11 32									11 46				11 59	12 02				
Herne Hill 4	a																							
Loughborough Jn.	a																							
Elephant & Castle ⊖	a																							
London Blackfriars 3 ⊖	a																							
City Thameslink 3	a																							
St Pancras International 15 ⊖	a																							
Luton Airport Parkway 7	a																							
Luton 10	a																							
North Dulwich	d					11 35									11 49					12 05				
East Dulwich	d					11 37									11 51					12 07				
Peckham Rye 4	d					11 40						11 56			11 53					12 10				12 26
Queens Rd Peckham	d					11 42						11 59			11 56					12 12				12 29
South Bermondsey	d					11 45						12 01			11 58					12 15				12 31
London Bridge 4 ⊖	a				11 40	11 49	11 48					12 06		12 01	12 03				12 10	12 19	12 18			12 36

Table 177

Sundays

East and West Croydon, London Milton Keynes Central and Luton via Norbury Crystal Palace - Tulse Hill

Local Services

Network Diagram - see first Page of Table 177

		SN	SN	SN	SN	SN	SN	LO	FC	SN	SN	SN	SN	SN	SN	SN		SN	SN	SN	SN	LO	FC	SN	SN
			■1			◇■1 ⊼							◇■1 ⊼							◇■1					
East Croydon 🚌	d		11 56			12 10				12 12	12 17		12 26	12 23						12 40				12 42	12 47
West Croydon ■4 🚌	d	11 52		12 04			12 07	12 12								12 22		12 34			12 37	12 42			
Norwood Junction ■2	a	11 56	12 00	12 09				12 16			12 21					12 26		12 39				12 46			12 51
	d	11 57	12 01	12 10							12 22					12 27		12 40							12 52
Selhurst ■4	d						12 11			12 16				12 26							12 41			12 46	
Thornton Heath	d						12 13			12 18				12 28							12 43			12 48	
Norbury	d						12 16			12 21				12 31							12 46			12 51	
Streatham Common ■4	d						12 19			12 23				12 34							12 49			12 53	
Beckenham Junction ■4 🚌	d																								
Birkbeck 🚌	d																								
Crystal Palace ■4	d	12 01			12 07											12 31			12 37						
Gipsy Hill	d	12 03			12 09											12 33			12 39						
West Norwood ■4	d	12 06			12 12											12 36			12 42						
Streatham Hill	d	12 10														12 40									
Balham ■4 ⊖	d	12 13					12 23							12 38		12 43					12 53				
Wandsworth Common	d	12 15														12 45									
Clapham Junction ■10	d	12 19				12 25	12 27						12 38	12 42		12 49				12 55	12 57				
Imperial Wharf	d																								
West Brompton ⊖	d																								
Kensington (Olympia) ⊖	d																								
Shepherd's Bush ⊖	d																								
Wembley Central ⊖	d																								
Harrow & Wealdstone ⊖	d																								
Watford Junction	d																								
Milton Keynes Central ■10	a																								
Battersea Park ■4	d	12 22										12 32			12 45	12 52									
London Victoria ■15 ⊖	a	12 27				12 31	12 34					12 36	12 46	12 50		12 57				13 01	13 04				
Streatham ■4	d								12 25	12 28													12 55	12 58	
Tulse Hill ■3	d				12 16				12 29	12 32									12 46				12 59	13 02	
Herne Hill ■4	a																								
Loughborough Jn.	a																								
Elephant & Castle ⊖	a																								
London Blackfriars ■3 ⊖	a																								
City Thameslink ■3	a																								
St Pancras International ■15 ⊖	a																								
Luton Airport Parkway ■7	a																								
Luton ■10	a																								
North Dulwich	d				12 19					12 35									12 49					13 05	
East Dulwich	d				12 21					12 37									12 51					13 07	
Peckham Rye ■4	d				12 23					12 40					12 56				12 53					13 10	
Queens Rd Peckham	d				12 26					12 42					12 59				12 56					13 12	
South Bermondsey	d				12 28					12 45					13 01				12 58					13 15	
London Bridge ■4 ⊖	a		12 12	12 31	12 33				12 40	12 49	12 48				13 06			13 01	13 03				13 10	13 19	13 18

Table 177

Sundays

East and West Croydon, London
Milton Keynes Central and Luton via Norbury
Crystal Palace - Tulse Hill

Local Services

Network Diagram - see first Page of Table 177

		SN	SN	SN	SN	SN	LO	SN		SN	SN	SN	LO	FC	SN	SN	SN	SN	SN	SN	SN	LO	SN	SN	
						1					◇1 ⚲							◇1 ⚲							
East Croydon	d		12 53			12 56					13 10				13 12	13 17		13 26	13 23						
West Croydon 4	d				12 52		12 57	13 04				13 07	13 12								13 22	13 27	13 34		
Norwood Junction 2	a				12 56	13 00	13 01	13 09					13 16			13 21					13 26	13 31	13 39		
	d				12 57	13 01		13 10								13 22					13 27		13 40		
Selhurst 4	d		12 57									13 11			13 16				13 26						
Thornton Heath	d		12 59									13 13			13 18				13 28						
Norbury	d		13 02									13 16			13 21				13 31						
Streatham Common 4	d		13 04									13 19			13 23				13 34						
Beckenham Junction 4	d																								
Birkbeck	d																								
Crystal Palace 4	d				13 01					13 07											13 31			13 37	
Gipsy Hill	d				13 03					13 09											13 33			13 39	
West Norwood 4	d				13 06					13 12											13 36			13 42	
Streatham Hill	d				13 10																13 40				
Balham 4 ⊖	d		13 08		13 13							13 23							13 38		13 43				
Wandsworth Common	d				13 15																13 45				
Clapham Junction 10	d		13 13		13 19						13 25	13 27						13 38	13 42		13 49				
Imperial Wharf	d																								
West Brompton ⊖	d																								
Kensington (Olympia) ⊖	d																								
Shepherd's Bush ⊖	d																								
Wembley Central ⊖	d																								
Harrow & Wealdstone ⊖	d																								
Watford Junction	d																								
Milton Keynes Central 10	a																								
Battersea Park 4	d	13 02		13 15	13 23												13 32			13 45	13 52				
London Victoria 15 ⊖	a	13 06	13 20		13 27						13 31	13 34					13 36	13 46	13 50		13 57				
Streatham 4	d													13 25	13 28										
Tulse Hill 3	d									13 16				13 29	13 32									13 46	
Herne Hill 4	a																								
Loughborough Jn.	a																								
Elephant & Castle ⊖	a																								
London Blackfriars 3 ⊖	a																								
City Thameslink 3	a																								
St Pancras International 15 ⊖	a																								
Luton Airport Parkway 7	a																								
Luton 10	a																								
North Dulwich	d									13 19					13 35									13 49	
East Dulwich	d									13 21					13 37									13 51	
Peckham Rye 4	d			13 26						13 23					13 40					13 56				13 53	
Queens Rd Peckham	d			13 29						13 26					13 42					13 59				13 56	
South Bermondsey	d			13 31						13 28					13 45					14 01				13 58	
London Bridge 4 ⊖	a			13 36		13 12		13 31		13 33				13 40	13 49	13 48				14 06			14 01	14 03	

Table 177

Sundays

East and West Croydon, London
Milton Keynes Central and Luton via Norbury
Crystal Palace - Tulse Hill

Local Services

Network Diagram - see first Page of Table 177

		SN ◇1	SN	LO	FC	SN	SN	SN	SN	SN	SN	SN 1	LO	SN	SN	SN ◇1 ⚲		SN	LO	FC	SN	SN	SN	SN ◇1 ⚲	SN
East Croydon 🚊	d	13 40				13 42	13 47		13 53			13 56				14 10					14 12	14 17		14 26	14 23
West Croydon 4 🚊	d		13 37	13 42							13 52		13 57	14 04				14 07	14 12						
Norwood Junction 2	a			13 46			13 51				13 56	14 00	14 01	14 09					14 16			14 21			
	d						13 52				13 57	14 01		14 10								14 22			
Selhurst 4	d		13 41			13 46			13 57									14 11			14 16				14 26
Thornton Heath	d		13 43			13 48			13 59									14 13			14 18				14 28
Norbury	d		13 46			13 51			14 02									14 16			14 21				14 31
Streatham Common 4	d		13 49			13 53			14 04									14 19			14 23				14 34
Beckenham Junction 4 🚊	d																								
Birkbeck 🚊	d																								
Crystal Palace 4	d										14 01				14 07										
Gipsy Hill	d										14 03				14 09										
West Norwood 4	d										14 06				14 12										
Streatham Hill	d										14 10														
Balham 4 ⊖	d		13 53						14 08		14 13							14 23							14 38
Wandsworth Common	d										14 15														
Clapham Junction 10	d	13 55	13 57						14 13		14 19					14 25		14 27						14 38	14 42
Imperial Wharf	d																								
West Brompton ⊖	d																								
Kensington (Olympia) ⊖	d																								
Shepherd's Bush ⊖	d																								
Wembley Central ⊖	d																								
Harrow & Wealdstone ⊖	d																								
Watford Junction	d																								
Milton Keynes Central 10	a																								
Battersea Park 4	d							14 02		14 15	14 23												14 32		
London Victoria 15 ⊖	a	14 01	14 04					14 06	14 20		14 27					14 31		14 34					14 36	14 46	14 50
Streatham 4	d				13 55	13 58														14 25	14 28				
Tulse Hill 3	d				13 59	14 02									14 16					14 29	14 32				
Herne Hill 4	a																								
Loughborough Jn	a																								
Elephant & Castle ⊖	a																								
London Blackfriars 3 ⊖	a																								
City Thameslink 3	a																								
St Pancras International 15 ⊖	a																								
Luton Airport Parkway 7	a																								
Luton 10	a																								
North Dulwich	d					14 05									14 19						14 35				
East Dulwich	d					14 07									14 21						14 37				
Peckham Rye 4	d					14 10				14 26					14 23						14 40				
Queens Rd Peckham	d					14 12				14 29					14 26						14 42				
South Bermondsey	d					14 15				14 31					14 28						14 45				
London Bridge 4 ⊖	a				14 10	14 19	14 18			14 36		14 12		14 31	14 33					14 40	14 49	14 48			

Table 177

Sundays

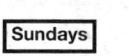

East and West Croydon, London Milton Keynes Central and Luton via Norbury Crystal Palace - Tulse Hill

Local Services

Network Diagram - see first Page of Table 177

		SN	SN	LO	SN	SN	SN	SN		LO	FC	SN	SN	SN	SN	SN	SN	SN	LO	SN	SN	SN	SN	LO	
							◇1											1				◇1 🚲			
East Croydon 🚊	d						14 41					14 42	14 47		14 53			14 56				15 10			
West Croydon 4 🚊	d		14 22	14 27	14 34			14 37		14 42							14 52		14 57	15 04			15 07	15 12	
Norwood Junction 2	a		14 26	14 31	14 39					14 46			14 51				14 56	15 00	15 01	15 09				15 16	
	d		14 27		14 40								14 52				14 57	15 01		15 10					
Selhurst 4	d							14 41				14 46			14 57								15 11		
Thornton Heath	d							14 43				14 48			14 59								15 13		
Norbury	d							14 46				14 51			15 02								15 16		
Streatham Common 4	d							14 49				14 53			15 04								15 19		
Beckenham Junction 4 🚊	d																								
Birkbeck 🚊	d																								
Crystal Palace 4	d		14 31			14 37											15 01				15 07				
Gipsy Hill	d		14 33			14 39											15 03				15 09				
West Norwood 4	d		14 36			14 42											15 06				15 12				
Streatham Hill	d		14 40														15 10								
Balham 4 ⊖	d		14 43					14 53							15 08		15 13						15 23		
Wandsworth Common	d		14 45														15 15								
Clapham Junction 10	d		14 49				14 55	14 57							15 13		15 19					15 25	15 27		
Imperial Wharf	d																								
West Brompton ⊖	d																								
Kensington (Olympia) ⊖	d																								
Shepherd's Bush ⊖	d																								
Wembley Central ⊖	d																								
Harrow & Wealdstone ⊖	d																								
Watford Junction	d																								
Milton Keynes Central 10	a																								
Battersea Park 4	d	14 45	14 52											15 02		15 15	15 23								
London Victoria 15 ⊖	a		14 57				15 01	15 04						15 06	15 20		15 27					15 31	15 34		
Streatham 4	d										14 55	14 58													
Tulse Hill 3	d					14 46					14 59	15 02									15 16				
Herne Hill 4	a																								
Loughborough Jn.	a																								
Elephant & Castle ⊖	a																								
London Blackfriars 3 ⊖	a																								
City Thameslink 3	a																								
St Pancras International 15 ⊖	a																								
Luton Airport Parkway 7	a																								
Luton 10	a																								
North Dulwich	d					14 49						15 05									15 19				
East Dulwich	d					14 51						15 07									15 21				
Peckham Rye 4	d	14 56				14 53						15 10				15 26					15 23				
Queens Rd Peckham	d	14 59				14 56						15 12				15 29					15 26				
South Bermondsey	d	15 01				14 58						15 15				15 31					15 28				
London Bridge 4 ⊖	a	15 06			15 01	15 03					15 10	15 19	15 18			15 36		15 12		15 31	15 33				

Table 177

Sundays

East and West Croydon, London
Milton Keynes Central and Luton via Norbury
Crystal Palace - Tulse Hill

Local Services

Network Diagram - see first Page of Table 177

		FC	SN	SN	SN	SN	SN	SN	SN	LO	SN	SN	SN	SN	LO	FC		SN	SN	SN	SN	SN	SN	SN	LO
						◇1 trolley							◇1											1	
East Croydon	d		15 12	15 17		15 26	15 23						15 40					15 42	15 47		15 53			15 56	
West Croydon 4	d								15 22	15 27	15 34			15 37	15 42								15 52		15 57
Norwood Junction 2	a			15 21					15 26	15 31	15 39				15 46				15 51				15 56	16 00	16 01
	d			15 22					15 27		15 40								15 52				15 57	16 01	
Selhurst 4	d		15 16				15 26							15 41				15 46			15 57				
Thornton Heath	d		15 18				15 28							15 43				15 48			15 59				
Norbury	d		15 21				15 31							15 46				15 51			16 02				
Streatham Common 4	d		15 23				15 34							15 49				15 53			16 04				
Beckenham Junction 4	d																								
Birkbeck	d																								
Crystal Palace 4	d								15 31			15 37											16 01		
Gipsy Hill	d								15 33			15 39											16 03		
West Norwood 4	d								15 36			15 42											16 06		
Streatham Hill	d								15 40														16 10		
Balham 4 ⊖	d						15 38		15 43					15 53							16 08		16 13		
Wandsworth Common	d								15 45														16 15		
Clapham Junction 10	d					15 38	15 42		15 49				15 55	15 57							16 13		16 19		
Imperial Wharf	d																								
West Brompton ⊖	d																								
Kensington (Olympia) ⊖	d																								
Shepherd's Bush ⊖	d																								
Wembley Central ⊖	d																								
Harrow & Wealdstone ⊖	d																								
Watford Junction	d																								
Milton Keynes Central 10	a																								
Battersea Park 4	d				15 32			15 45	15 52											16 02		16 15	16 23		
London Victoria 15 ⊖	a				15 36	15 46	15 50		15 57				16 01	16 04						16 06	16 20		16 27		
Streatham 4	d	15 25	15 28													15 55		15 58							
Tulse Hill 3	d	15 29	15 32									15 46				15 59		16 02							
Herne Hill 4	a																								
Loughborough Jn.	a																								
Elephant & Castle ⊖	a																								
London Blackfriars 3 ⊖	a																								
City Thameslink 3	a																								
St Pancras International 15 ⊖	a																								
Luton Airport Parkway 7	a																								
Luton 10	a																								
North Dulwich	d		15 35									15 49						16 05							
East Dulwich	d		15 37									15 51						16 07							
Peckham Rye 4	d		15 40					15 56				15 53						16 10				16 26			
Queens Rd Peckham	d		15 42					15 59				15 56						16 12				16 29			
South Bermondsey	d		15 45					16 01				15 58						16 15				16 31			
London Bridge 4 ⊖	a	15 40	15 49	15 48				16 06			16 01	16 03				16 10		16 19	16 18			16 36		16 12	

Table 177

Sundays

East and West Croydon, London
Milton Keynes Central and Luton via Norbury
Crystal Palace - Tulse Hill

Local Services

Network Diagram - see first Page of Table 177

		SN	SN	SN ◇1	SN	LO	FC	SN		SN	SN	SN ◇1	SN	SN	SN	LO	SN	SN	SN ◇1		SN ◇1	SN	LO	
East Croydon	d			16 10				16 12		16 17		16 26	16 23						16 41		19 41			
West Croydon 4	d	16 04			16 07	16 12									16 22	16 27	16 34					19 37	19 42	
Norwood Junction 2	a	16 09				16 16				16 21					16 26	16 31	16 39						19 46	
	d	16 10								16 22					16 27		16 40							
Selhurst 4	d				16 11			16 16					16 26									19 41		
Thornton Heath	d				16 13			16 18					16 28									19 43		
Norbury	d				16 16			16 21					16 31									19 46		
Streatham Common 4	d				16 19			16 23					16 34									19 49		
Beckenham Junction 4	d																							
Birkbeck	d																							
Crystal Palace 4	d		16 07												16 31			16 37						
Gipsy Hill	d		16 09												16 33			16 39						
West Norwood 4	d		16 12												16 36			16 42						
Streatham Hill	d														16 40									
Balham 4 ⊖	d				16 23								16 38		16 43							19 53		
Wandsworth Common	d														16 45									
Clapham Junction 10	d			16 25	16 27							16 38	16 42		16 49				16 55	and at the same minutes past each hour until	19 55	19 57		
Imperial Wharf	d																							
West Brompton ⊖	d																							
Kensington (Olympia) ⊖	d																							
Shepherd's Bush ⊖	d																							
Wembley Central ⊖	d																							
Harrow & Wealdstone ⊖	d																							
Watford Junction	d																							
Milton Keynes Central 10	a																							
Battersea Park 4	d										16 32			16 45	16 52									
London Victoria 15 ⊖	a			16 31	16 34						16 36	16 46	16 50		16 57				17 01		20 01	20 04		
Streatham 4	d						16 25	16 28																
Tulse Hill 3	d		16 16				16 29	16 32										16 46						
Herne Hill 4	a																							
Loughborough Jn.	a																							
Elephant & Castle ⊖	a																							
London Blackfriars 3 ⊖	a																							
City Thameslink 3	a																							
St Pancras International 15 ⊖	a																							
Luton Airport Parkway 7	a																							
Luton 10	a																							
North Dulwich	d		16 19					16 35										16 49						
East Dulwich	d		16 21					16 37										16 51						
Peckham Rye 4	d		16 23					16 40						16 56				16 53						
Queens Rd Peckham	d		16 26					16 42						16 59				16 56						
South Bermondsey	d		16 28					16 45						17 01				16 58						
London Bridge 4 ⊖	a	16 31	16 33				16 40	16 49		16 48				17 06			17 01	17 03						

		FC	SN	SN	SN	SN	SN	SN	SN 1	LO	SN	SN	SN ◇1	SN	LO	FC		SN	SN	SN	SN ◇1	SN	SN	SN	LO
East Croydon	d		19 42	19 47		19 53			19 56				20 10					20 12	20 17		20 26	20 23			
West Croydon 4	d							19 52		19 57	20 04			20 07	20 12									20 22	20 27
Norwood Junction 2	a			19 51				19 56	20 00	20 01	20 09				20 16				20 21					20 26	20 31
	d			19 52				19 57	20 01		20 10								20 22					20 27	
Selhurst 4	d		19 46			19 57								20 11				20 16				20 26			
Thornton Heath	d		19 48			19 59								20 13				20 18				20 28			
Norbury	d		19 51			20 02								20 16				20 21				20 31			
Streatham Common 4	d		19 53			20 04								20 19				20 23				20 34			
Beckenham Junction 4	d																								
Birkbeck	d																								
Crystal Palace 4	d							20 01				20 07												20 31	
Gipsy Hill	d							20 03				20 09												20 33	
West Norwood 4	d							20 06				20 12												20 36	
Streatham Hill	d							20 10																20 40	
Balham 4 ⊖	d					20 08		20 13						20 23								20 38		20 43	
Wandsworth Common	d							20 15																20 45	
Clapham Junction 10	d					20 13		20 19					20 25	20 27							20 38	20 42		20 49	
Imperial Wharf	d																								
West Brompton ⊖	d																								
Kensington (Olympia) ⊖	d																								
Shepherd's Bush ⊖	d																								
Wembley Central ⊖	d																								
Harrow & Wealdstone ⊖	d																								
Watford Junction	d																								
Milton Keynes Central 10	a																								
Battersea Park 4	d				20 02		20 15	20 22												20 32			20 45	20 52	
London Victoria 15 ⊖	a				20 06	20 20		20 27					20 31	20 34						20 36	20 46	20 50		20 57	
Streatham 4	d	19 55	19 58													20 25		20 28							
Tulse Hill 3	d	19 59	20 02									20 16				20 29		20 32							
Herne Hill 4	a																								
Loughborough Jn.	a																								
Elephant & Castle ⊖	a																								
London Blackfriars 3 ⊖	a																								
City Thameslink 3	a																								
St Pancras International 15 ⊖	a																								
Luton Airport Parkway 7	a																								
Luton 10	a																								
North Dulwich	d		20 05									20 19						20 35							
East Dulwich	d		20 07									20 21						20 37							
Peckham Rye 4	d		20 10				20 26					20 23						20 40					20 56		
Queens Rd Peckham	d		20 12				20 29					20 26						20 42					20 59		
South Bermondsey	d		20 15				20 31					20 28						20 45					21 01		
London Bridge 4 ⊖	a	20 10	20 19	20 18			20 36		20 12		20 31	20 33				20 40		20 49	20 48				21 06		

Table 177

Sundays

East and West Croydon, London
Milton Keynes Central and Luton via Norbury
Crystal Palace - Tulse Hill

Local Services

Network Diagram - see first Page of Table 177

		SN	SN	SN ◇1	SN	LO	FC	SN		SN	SN	SN	SN	SN	SN 1	LO	SN	SN	SN ◇1	SN	LO	FC	SN	SN
East Croydon	d			20 41				20 42		20 47		20 53			20 56				21 10				21 12	21 17
West Croydon 4	d	20 34			20 37	20 42								20 52		20 57	21 04			21 07	21 12			
Norwood Junction 2	a	20 39				20 46				20 51				20 56	21 00	21 01	21 09				21 16			21 21
	d	20 40								20 52				20 57	21 01		21 10							21 22
Selhurst 4	d				20 41			20 46				20 57								21 11			21 16	
Thornton Heath	d				20 43			20 48				20 59								21 13			21 18	
Norbury	d				20 46			20 51				21 02								21 16			21 21	
Streatham Common 4	d				20 49			20 53				21 04								21 19			21 23	
Beckenham Junction 4	d																							
Birkbeck	d																							
Crystal Palace 4	d		20 37											21 01				21 07						
Gipsy Hill	d		20 39											21 03				21 09						
West Norwood 4	d		20 42											21 06				21 12						
Streatham Hill	d													21 10										
Balham 4 ⊖	d				20 53							21 08		21 13						21 23				
Wandsworth Common	d													21 15										
Clapham Junction 10	d			20 55	20 57							21 13		21 19					21 25	21 27				
Imperial Wharf	d																							
West Brompton ⊖	d																							
Kensington (Olympia) ⊖	d																							
Shepherd's Bush ⊖	d																							
Wembley Central ⊖	d																							
Harrow & Wealdstone ⊖	d																							
Watford Junction	d																							
Milton Keynes Central 10	a																							
Battersea Park 4	d										21 02		21 15	21 23										
London Victoria 15 ⊖	a			21 01	21 04						21 06	21 20		21 27					21 31	21 34				
Streatham 4	d						20 55	20 58														21 25	21 28	
Tulse Hill 3	d		20 46				20 59	21 02										21 16				21 29	21 32	
Herne Hill 4	a																							
Loughborough Jn.	a																							
Elephant & Castle ⊖	a																							
London Blackfriars 3 ⊖	a																							
City Thameslink 3	a																							
St Pancras International 15 ⊖	a																							
Luton Airport Parkway 7	a																							
Luton 10	a																							
North Dulwich	d		20 49					21 05										21 19					21 35	
East Dulwich	d		20 51					21 07										21 21					21 37	
Peckham Rye 4	d		20 53					21 10					21 26					21 23					21 40	
Queens Rd Peckham	d		20 56					21 12					21 29					21 26					21 42	
South Bermondsey	d		20 58					21 15					21 31					21 28					21 45	
London Bridge 4 ⊖	a	21 01	21 03				21 10	21 19		21 18			21 36		21 12		21 31	21 33				21 40	21 49	21 48

		SN	SN ◇1	SN	SN	SN	LO	SN	SN	SN ◇1	SN	LO	FC	SN	SN	SN		SN	SN	SN	SN 1	LO	SN	SN	SN ◇1
East Croydon	d		21 26	21 23						21 41				21 42	21 47			21 53			21 56				22 10
West Croydon 4	d					21 22	21 27	21 34			21 37	21 42								21 52		21 57	22 04		
Norwood Junction 2	a					21 26	21 31	21 39				21 46			21 51					21 56	22 00	22 01	22 09		
	d					21 27		21 40							21 52					21 57	22 01		22 10		
Selhurst 4	d			21 26							21 41			21 46				21 56							
Thornton Heath	d			21 28							21 43			21 48				21 58							
Norbury	d			21 31							21 46			21 51				22 01							
Streatham Common 4	d			21 34							21 49			21 53				22 04							
Beckenham Junction 4	d																								
Birkbeck	d																								
Crystal Palace 4	d					21 31			21 37											22 01				22 07	
Gipsy Hill	d					21 33			21 39											22 03				22 09	
West Norwood 4	d					21 36			21 42											22 06				22 12	
Streatham Hill	d					21 40														22 10					
Balham 4 ⊖	d			21 38		21 43					21 53							22 08		22 13					
Wandsworth Common	d					21 45														22 15					
Clapham Junction 10	d		21 38	21 42		21 49				21 55	21 57							22 12		22 19					22 25
Imperial Wharf	d																								
West Brompton ⊖	d																								
Kensington (Olympia) ⊖	d																								
Shepherd's Bush ⊖	d																								
Wembley Central ⊖	d																								
Harrow & Wealdstone ⊖	d																								
Watford Junction	d																								
Milton Keynes Central 10	a																								
Battersea Park 4	d	21 32			21 45	21 53										22 02			22 15	22 23					
London Victoria 15 ⊖	a	21 36	21 46	21 50		21 57				22 01	22 04					22 06		22 20		22 27					22 31
Streatham 4	d												21 55	21 58											
Tulse Hill 3	d								21 46				21 59	22 02										22 16	
Herne Hill 4	a																								
Loughborough Jn.	a																								
Elephant & Castle ⊖	a																								
London Blackfriars 3 ⊖	a																								
City Thameslink 3	a																								
St Pancras International 15 ⊖	a																								
Luton Airport Parkway 7	a																								
Luton 10	a																								
North Dulwich	d								21 49					22 05										22 19	
East Dulwich	d								21 51					22 07										22 21	
Peckham Rye 4	d				21 56				21 53					22 10					22 26					22 23	
Queens Rd Peckham	d				21 59				21 56					22 12					22 29					22 26	
South Bermondsey	d				22 01				21 58					22 15					22 31					22 28	
London Bridge 4 ⊖	a				22 06			22 01	22 03				22 10	22 19	22 18				22 36		22 12		22 31	22 33	

Table 177

Sundays

East and West Croydon, London Milton Keynes Central and Luton via Norbury Crystal Palace - Tulse Hill

Local Services

Network Diagram - see first Page of Table 177

		SN	SN	LO	SN	SN	SN	SN		SN	SN	LO	SN	SN	SN	SN	LO	SN	SN	SN	SN	SN	SN	LO
							◇1														1			
East Croydon	d		22 12		22 17		22 26	22 23								22 42		22 47		22 53	22 56			
West Croydon 4	d	22 07		22 12							22 22	22 27	22 34	22 37			22 42						22 52	22 57
Norwood Junction 2	a			22 16	22 21						22 26	22 31	22 39				22 46	22 51					22 56	23 01
	d				22 22						22 27		22 40					22 52					22 57	
Selhurst 4	d	22 11	22 16					22 26						22 41		22 46				22 57	22 59			
Thornton Heath	d	22 13	22 18					22 28						22 43		22 48				22 59				
Norbury	d	22 16	22 21					22 31						22 46		22 51				23 02				
Streatham Common 4	d	22 19	22 23					22 34						22 49		22 53				23 04				
Beckenham Junction 4	d																							
Birkbeck	d																							
Crystal Palace 4	d										22 31				22 37								23 01	
Gipsy Hill	d										22 33				22 39								23 03	
West Norwood 4	d										22 36				22 42								23 06	
Streatham Hill	d										22 40												23 10	
Balham 4 ⊖	d	22 23						22 38			22 43			22 53						23 08			23 13	
Wandsworth Common	d										22 45												23 15	
Clapham Junction 10	d	22 27					22 38	22 42			22 49			22 57						23 13	23 08		23 19	
Imperial Wharf	d																							
West Brompton ⊖	d																							
Kensington (Olympia) ⊖	d																							
Shepherd's Bush ⊖	d																							
Wembley Central ⊖	d																							
Harrow & Wealdstone ⊖	d																							
Watford Junction	d																							
Milton Keynes Central 10	a																							
Battersea Park 4	d					22 32				22 45	22 53								23 02			23 15	23 23	
London Victoria 15 ⊖	a	22 34				22 36	22 46	22 50			22 57			23 04					23 06	23 20	23 14		23 27	
Streatham 4	d		22 28													22 58								
Tulse Hill 3	d		22 32												22 46	23 02								
Herne Hill 4	a																							
Loughborough Jn.	a																							
Elephant & Castle ⊖	a																							
London Blackfriars 3 ⊖	a																							
City Thameslink 3	a																							
St Pancras International 15 ⊖	a																							
Luton Airport Parkway 7	a																							
Luton 10	a																							
North Dulwich	d		22 35												22 49	23 05								
East Dulwich	d		22 37												22 51	23 07								
Peckham Rye 4	d		22 40							22 56					22 53	23 10						23 26		
Queens Rd Peckham	d		22 42							22 59					22 56	23 12						23 29		
South Bermondsey	d		22 45							23 01					22 58	23 15						23 31		
London Bridge 4 ⊖	a		22 49		22 48					23 06			23 01		23 03	23 19		23 18				23 36		

		SN	SN	SN	SN	SN	SN	SN	SN	SN	SN	SN
							◇1					1
East Croydon	d			23 17	23 26		23 27					23 56
West Croydon 4	d	23 07						23 22	23 37		23 52	
Norwood Junction 2	a			23 21				23 26				
	d							23 27				
Selhurst 4	d	23 11			23a29				23 41		23 56	00 01
Thornton Heath	d	23 13							23 43		23 58	
Norbury	d	23 16							23 46		00 01	
Streatham Common 4	d	23 19							23 49		00 04	
Beckenham Junction 4	d											
Birkbeck	d											
Crystal Palace 4	d		23 07					23 31		23 37		
Gipsy Hill	d		23 09					23 33		23 39		
West Norwood 4	d		23 12					23 36		23 42		
Streatham Hill	d							23 40				
Balham 4 ⊖	d	23 23						23 43	23 53		00 08	
Wandsworth Common	d							23 45				
Clapham Junction 10	d	23 27					23 39	23 49	23 58		00 12	00 12
Imperial Wharf	d											
West Brompton ⊖	d											
Kensington (Olympia) ⊖	d											
Shepherd's Bush ⊖	d											
Wembley Central ⊖	d											
Harrow & Wealdstone ⊖	d											
Watford Junction	d											
Milton Keynes Central 10	a											
Battersea Park 4	d					23 32		23 53				
London Victoria 15 ⊖	a	23 34				23 37	23 46	23 57	00 04		00 19	00 19
Streatham 4	d											
Tulse Hill 3	d		23 16							23 46		
Herne Hill 4	a											
Loughborough Jn.	a											
Elephant & Castle ⊖	a											
London Blackfriars 3 ⊖	a											
City Thameslink 3	a											
St Pancras International 15 ⊖	a											
Luton Airport Parkway 7	a											
Luton 10	a											
North Dulwich	d		23 19							23 49		
East Dulwich	d		23 21							23 51		
Peckham Rye 4	d		23 23							23 53		
Queens Rd Peckham	d		23 26							23 56		
South Bermondsey	d		23 28							23 58		
London Bridge 4 ⊖	a		23 33							00 03		

London Bridge to London Victoria - Croydon and East London Line

Network Diagram - see first Page of Table 177

Miles	Miles	Miles	Miles	Miles			SN MX	SN MX	SN MO	SN MX	LO MO	LO MX	SN MX	LO MX	LO MX		SN MX	SN MX	LO MX	LO MX	SN MX
0	0	0	—	—	**London Bridge** 4 ⊖	d	23p22	23p36	23p39				23p52				00 03	00 06			00 36
—	—	—	—	—	**Highbury & Islington**	d					23p23	23p25		23p35	23p42				23p56	00 10	
—	—	—	—	—	Canonbury	d					23p25	23p27		23p37	23p44				23p58	00 12	
—	—	—	0	—	Dalston Junction Stn ELL	d					23p28	23p30		23p40	23p47				00 02	00 15	
—	—	—	0½	—	Haggerston	d					23p29	23p31		23p41	23p48				00 03	00 16	
—	—	—	1	—	Hoxton	d					23p31	23p33		23p43	23p50				00 05	00 18	
—	—	—	1¾	—	Shoreditch High Street	d					23p34	23p36		23p46	23p53				00 08	00 21	
—	—	—	2½	—	Whitechapel	d					23p36	23p38		23p48	23p55				00 10	00 23	
—	—	—	3¼	—	Shadwell	d					23p38	23p40		23p50	23p57				00 12	00 25	
—	—	—	3¾	—	Wapping	d					23p40	23p42		23p52	23p59				00 14	00 27	
—	—	—	4	—	Rotherhithe	d					23p42	23p44		23p54	00 01				00 16	00 29	
—	—	—	4¼	—	Canada Water	d					23p44	23p46		23p56	00 03				00 18	00 31	
—	—	—	4½	—	Surrey Quays	d					23p45	23p47		23p57	00 05				00 19	00 32	
—	—	—	5¼	—	**New Cross ELL**	a															
—	2¾	2¾	5¾	—	**New Cross Gate** 4	a	23p27	23p41	23p44		23p49	23p51	23p57	00 01	00 08			00 11	00 23	00 36	00 41
—	—	—	—	—		d	23p27	23p41	23p44		23p50	23p52	23p57	00 02				00 11			00 41
—	3¾	3¾	—	—	Brockley	d	23p30	23p44	23p47		23p52	23p54	00 01	00 04				00 14			00 44
—	4¾	4¾	—	—	Honor Oak Park	d	23p33	23p47	23p50		23p55	23p57	00 04	00 07				00 17			00 47
—	5¾	5¾	—	—	Forest Hill 4	d	23p35	23p49	23p52		23p58	23p59	00 06	00 10				00 19			00 49
—	6½	6½	—	—	Sydenham	d	23p38	23p52	23p55		00 01	00 02	00 09	00 12				00 22			00 52
—	7¼	—	—	—	**Crystal Palace** 4	d	23p43			00 03		00a07	00 13								
—	8½	—	—	—	Gipsy Hill	d	23p45						00 15								
—	9½	—	—	—	West Norwood 4	d	23p48						00 18								
—	10¾	—	—	—	Streatham Hill	d	23p52						00 22								
—	11¾	—	—	—	Balham 4 ⊖	d	23p55						00 25								
—	12½	—	—	—	Wandsworth Common	d	23p58						00 27								
—	13¾	—	—	—	Clapham Junction 10	d	00 02						00 31								
1¾	—	—	—	—	South Bermondsey	d											00 07				
2¾	—	—	—	—	Queens Rd Peckham	d											00 09				
3½	—	—	0	0	Peckham Rye 4	d											00 12				
4¼	—	—	0¾	0¾	Denmark Hill 4	d															
—	—	—	—	4½	**London Blackfriars** 3 ⊖	a															
6¼	—	—	—	—	Clapham High Street ⊖	d															
6¾	—	—	—	—	Wandsworth Road	d															
7½	15¼	—	—	—	Battersea Park 4	d	00 05						00 35								
8¾	16½	—	5	—	**London Victoria** 15 ⊖	a	00 10						00 42								
—	—	7¼	—	—	Penge West	d		23p54	23p57		00 03			00 15				00 24			00 54
—	—	7½	—	—	Anerley	d		23p56	23p59		00 05			00 17				00 26			00 56
—	—	8¾	—	0	Norwood Junction 2	d		23p59	00 03	00 09	00 08			00 20			00a34	00 30			01 00
—	—	—	—	1¾	**West Croydon** 4	a				00 14	00 15			00 27							
—	—	10	—	—	**East Croydon**	a		00 03	00 06									00 33			01 03

					SE	SE	SN	SN	LO	LO	LO	LO		LO	SN	SN	LO	LO	SN	LO	LO	SN		SN	SE	SN
London Bridge 4 ⊖	d					06 00								06 06	06 11			06 19			06 30		06 33		
Highbury & Islington	d								05 35							05 55		06 05						
Canonbury	d								05 37							05 57		06 07						
Dalston Junction Stn ELL	d								05 40	05 50						06 00		06 10	06 20					
Haggerston	d								05 41	05 51						06 01		06 11	06 21					
Hoxton	d								05 43	05 53						06 03		06 13	06 23					
Shoreditch High Street	d								05 46	05 56						06 06		06 16	06 26					
Whitechapel	d								05 48	05 58						06 08		06 18	06 28					
Shadwell	d								05 50	06 00						06 10		06 20	06 30					
Wapping	d								05 52	06 02						06 12		06 22	06 32					
Rotherhithe	d								05 54	06 04						06 14		06 24	06 34					
Canada Water	d								05 56	06 06						06 16		06 26	06 36					
Surrey Quays	d								05 57	06 07						06 17		06 27	06 37					
New Cross ELL	a									06 13									06 43					
New Cross Gate 4	a								06 01				06 11			06 21	06 25	06 31						
	d						05 47	05 52	06 02			06 07	06 11		06 17	06 22	06 25	06 32						
Brockley	d						05 49	05 54	06 04			06 09	06 14		06 19	06 24	06 27	06 34						
Honor Oak Park	d						05 52	05 57	06 07			06 12	06 17		06 22	06 27	06 30	06 37						
Forest Hill 4	d						05 55	06 00	06 10			06 15	06 19		06 25	06 30	06 33	06 40						
Sydenham	d						05 57	06 02	06 12			06 17	06 22		06 27	06 32	06 35	06 42						
Crystal Palace 4	d					05 59		06a07				06a22				06a37	06 39							06 51
Gipsy Hill	d					06 01											06 41							06 53
West Norwood 4	d					06 04											06 44							06 56
Streatham Hill	d																06 48							
Balham 4 ⊖	d																06 51							
Wandsworth Common	d																							
Clapham Junction 10	d																06 56							
South Bermondsey	d				06 04									06 15						06 34		06 37		
Queens Rd Peckham	d				06 06									06 18						06 36		06 39		
Peckham Rye 4	d			05 04	06 04	06a09	06a15								06 20						06a39		06a42	06 47	07a08
Denmark Hill 4	d			05 07	06 07										06 23									06 50	
London Blackfriars 3 ⊖	a			05 17	06 17																				
Clapham High Street ⊖	d														06 28										
Wandsworth Road	d														06 29										
Battersea Park 4	d														06 32										
London Victoria 15 ⊖	a														06 36			07 05						07 04	
Penge West	d							06 00		06 15				06 24		06 30			06 45						
Anerley	d							06 02		06 17				06 26		06 32			06 47						
Norwood Junction 2	d							06 05		06 20				06 30		06 35			06 50						
West Croydon 4	a							06 13		06 30						06 41			07 00						
East Croydon	a													06 33											

London Bridge to London Victoria - Croydon and East London Line

Network Diagram - see first Page of Table 177

		LO	SN	SN	LO	LO	LO		SN	SN	LO	SN	SN	SN	LO	LO	SN		LO	LO	LO	SN	SE	SN	LO
London Bridge 4 ⊖	d		06 36	06 41					06 51	06 54		06 58	07 03				07 06					07 11		07 21	
Highbury & Islington	d					06 25					06 33				06 40				06 48	06 55					07 03
Canonbury	d					06 27					06 35				06 42				06 50	06 57					07 05
Dalston Junction Stn ELL	d					06 30	06 35				06 40				06 45	06 50			06 55	07 00	07 05				07 10
Haggerston	d					06 31	06 36				06 41				06 46	06 51			06 56	07 01	07 06				07 11
Hoxton	d					06 33	06 38				06 43				06 48	06 53			06 58	07 03	07 08				07 13
Shoreditch High Street	d					06 36	06 41				06 46				06 51	06 56			07 01	07 06	07 11				07 16
Whitechapel	d					06 38	06 43				06 48				06 53	06 58			07 03	07 08	07 13				07 18
Shadwell	d					06 40	06 45				06 50				06 55	07 00			07 05	07 10	07 15				07 20
Wapping	d					06 42	06 47				06 52				06 57	07 02			07 07	07 12	07 17				07 22
Rotherhithe	d					06 44	06 49				06 54				06 59	07 04			07 09	07 14	07 19				07 24
Canada Water	d					06 46	06 51				06 56				07 01	07 06			07 11	07 16	07 21				07 26
Surrey Quays	d					06 47	06 52				06 57				07 02	07 07			07 12	07 17	07 22				07 27
New Cross ELL	a						06 58									07 13					07 28				
New Cross Gate 4	a		06 41			06 51			06 56	06 59	07 00				07 06		07 11		07 15	07 21				07 26	07 31
	d	06 37	06 41		06 47	06 52			06 56	06 59	07 02				07 07		07 11		07 17	07 22				07 26	07 32
Brockley	d	06 39	06 44		06 49	06 54			06 59	07 02	07 04				07 09		07 14		07 19	07 24				07 29	07 34
Honor Oak Park	d	06 42	06 47		06 52	06 57			07 02	07 05	07 07				07 12		07 17		07 22	07 27				07 32	07 37
Forest Hill 4	d	06 45	06 49		06 55	07 00			07 04	07 07	07 10				07 15		07 19		07 25	07 30				07 34	07 40
Sydenham	d	06 47	06 52		06 57	07 02			07 07	07 10	07 12				07 17		07 22		07 27	07 32				07 37	07 42
Crystal Palace 4	d	06a52				07a07			07 13					07 20	07a22					07a37				07 43	
Gipsy Hill	d								07 15					07 22										07 45	
West Norwood 4	d								07 18					07 25										07 48	
Streatham Hill	d								07 22															07 52	
Balham 4 ⊖	d								07 25															07 55	
Wandsworth Common	d								07 27															07 57	
Clapham Junction 10	d								07 31															08 01	
South Bermondsey	d			06 45								07 02	07 07									07 15			
Queens Rd Peckham	d			06 48								07 04	07 09									07 17			
Peckham Rye 4	d			06 50								07a07	07a12	07a36								07 20	07 23		
Denmark Hill 4	d			06 53																		07 23	07 29		
London Blackfriars 3 ⊖	a																								
Clapham High Street ⊖	d			06 58																		07 28			
Wandsworth Road	d			06 59																		07 29			
Battersea Park 4	d			07 02					07 35													07 32		08 05	
London Victoria 15 ⊖	a			07 08					07 41													07 38	07 42	08 11	
Penge West	d		06 54		07 00					07 12	07 15						07 24		07 30						07 45
Anerley	d		06 56		07 02					07 14	07 17						07 26		07 32						07 47
Norwood Junction 2	d		07 00		07 05					07 18	07 20						07 31		07 35						07 50
West Croydon 4	a				07 11						07 30								07 42						08 00
East Croydon	a		07 03							07 21							07 37								

		SN	SN		SN	LO	LO	SN	LO	SN	SN	LO	LO		SE	SN	LO	SN	SE	SN	SN	LO	LO		SN
London Bridge 4 ⊖	d	07 29	07 33					07 36		07 41	07 44					07 51		08 03		08 06					08 06
Highbury & Islington	d					07 10			07 18			07 25					07 33					07 40			
Canonbury	d					07 12			07 20			07 27					07 35					07 42			
Dalston Junction Stn ELL	d					07 15	07 20		07 25			07 30	07 35				07 40					07 45	07 50		
Haggerston	d					07 16	07 21		07 26			07 31	07 36				07 41					07 46	07 51		
Hoxton	d					07 18	07 23		07 28			07 33	07 38				07 43					07 48	07 53		
Shoreditch High Street	d					07 21	07 26		07 31			07 36	07 41				07 46					07 51	07 56		
Whitechapel	d					07 23	07 28		07 33			07 38	07 43				07 48					07 53	07 58		
Shadwell	d					07 25	07 30		07 35			07 40	07 45				07 50					07 55	08 00		
Wapping	d					07 27	07 32		07 37			07 42	07 47				07 52					07 57	08 02		
Rotherhithe	d					07 29	07 34		07 39			07 44	07 49				07 54					07 59	08 04		
Canada Water	d					07 31	07 36		07 41			07 46	07 51				07 56					08 01	08 06		
Surrey Quays	d					07 32	07 37		07 42			07 47	07 52				07 57					08 02	08 07		
New Cross ELL	a						07 43						07 58										08 13		
New Cross Gate 4	a					07 36		07 41	07 45		07 49	07 51				07 56	08 01					08 06			08 11
	d					07 37		07 41	07 47		07 49	07 52				07 56	08 02					08 07			08 11
Brockley	d					07 39		07 44	07 49			07 54				07 59	08 04					08 09			08 14
Honor Oak Park	d					07 42		07 47	07 52			07 57				08 02	08 07					08 12			08 17
Forest Hill 4	d					07 45		07 49	07 55			08 00				08 04	08 10					08 15			08 19
Sydenham	d					07 47		07 52	07 57			08 02				08 07	08 12					08 17			08 22
Crystal Palace 4	d				07 49	07a52						08a07				08 13					08 19	08a22			
Gipsy Hill	d				07 51											08 15					08 21				
West Norwood 4	d				07 54											08 18					08 24				
Streatham Hill	d															08 22									
Balham 4 ⊖	d															08 25									
Wandsworth Common	d															08 27									
Clapham Junction 10	d															08 31									
South Bermondsey	d	07 33	07 37							07 45								08 07		08 11					
Queens Rd Peckham	d	07 35	07 39							07 47								08 09		08 13					
Peckham Rye 4	d	07a38	07a42		08a06					07 50					07 54			08a12	08 13	08a16	08a36				
Denmark Hill 4	d									07 53					07 59				08 17						
London Blackfriars 3 ⊖	a																								
Clapham High Street ⊖	d									07 58															
Wandsworth Road	d									07 59															
Battersea Park 4	d									08 02						08 35									
London Victoria 15 ⊖	a									08 08					08 11	08 41			08 29						
Penge West	d							07 54	08 00								08 15								08 24
Anerley	d							07 56	08 02								08 17								08 26
Norwood Junction 2	d							08 00	08 05								08 20								08 30
West Croydon 4	a								08 12								08 30								
East Croydon	a							08 03			08 00														08 33

London Bridge to London Victoria - Croydon and East London Line

Network Diagram - see first Page of Table 177

		LO	LO	LO	SN	SE 1	SE	SN	LO		SN	SN	LO	LO	SN	LO	LO	LO	SN		SE	SN	LO	LO	LO
London Bridge 4 ⊖	d				08 10			08 21			08 33				08 36				08 41			08 51			
Highbury & Islington	d	07 48	07 55						08 03				08 10			08 18	08 25						08 33	08 40	
Canonbury	d	07 50	07 57						08 05				08 12			08 20	08 27						08 35	08 42	
Dalston Junction Stn ELL	d	07 55	08 00	08 05					08 10				08 15	08 20		08 25	08 30	08 35					08 40	08 46	08 50
Haggerston	d	07 56	08 01	08 06					08 11				08 16	08 21		08 26	08 31	08 36					08 41	08 47	08 51
Hoxton	d	07 58	08 03	08 08					08 13				08 18	08 23		08 28	08 33	08 38					08 43	08 49	08 53
Shoreditch High Street	d	08 01	08 06	08 11					08 16				08 21	08 26		08 31	08 36	08 41					08 46	08 52	08 56
Whitechapel	d	08 03	08 08	08 13					08 18				08 23	08 28		08 33	08 38	08 43					08 48	08 54	08 58
Shadwell	d	08 05	08 10	08 15					08 20				08 25	08 30		08 35	08 40	08 45					08 50	08 56	09 00
Wapping	d	08 07	08 12	08 17					08 22				08 27	08 32		08 37	08 42	08 47					08 52	08 58	09 02
Rotherhithe	d	08 09	08 14	08 19					08 24				08 29	08 34		08 39	08 44	08 49					08 54	09 00	09 04
Canada Water	d	08 11	08 16	08 21					08 26				08 31	08 36		08 41	08 46	08 51					08 56	09 02	09 06
Surrey Quays	d	08 12	08 17	08 22					08 27				08 32	08 37		08 42	08 47	08 52					08 57	09 03	09 07
New Cross ELL	a			08 28										08 43				08 58							09 13
New Cross Gate 4	a	08 16	08 21					08 26	08 31				08 36		08 41	08 46	08 51					08 57	09 01	09 07	
	d	08 17	08 22					08 26	08 32				08 37		08 41	08 47	08 52					08 57	09 02	09 08	
Brockley	d	08 19	08 24					08 29	08 34				08 39		08 44	08 49	08 54					09 00	09 04	09 10	
Honor Oak Park	d	08 22	08 27					08 32	08 37				08 42		08 47	08 52	08 57					09 03	09 07	09 13	
Forest Hill 4	d	08 25	08 30					08 34	08 40				08 45		08 49	08 55	09 00					09 05	09 10	09 16	
Sydenham	d	08 27	08 32					08 37	08 42				08 47		08 52	08 57	09 02					09 08	09 12	09 18	
Crystal Palace 4	d		08a37					08 40				08 50	08a52				09a07					09 11		09a23	
Gipsy Hill	d							08 43				08 52										09 14			
West Norwood 4	d							08 46				08 55										09 17			
Streatham Hill	d							08 49														09 21			
Balham 4 ⊖	d							08 55														09 25			
Wandsworth Common	d							08 57														09 27			
Clapham Junction 10	d							09 01														09 31			
South Bermondsey	d				08 14						08 37								08 45						
Queens Rd Peckham	d				08 16						08 39								08 48						
Peckham Rye 4	d				08 19		08 33				08a42	09a07							08 50		08 55				
Denmark Hill 4	d				08 22	08 30	08 36												08 53		09 02				
London Blackfriars 3 ⊖	a																								
Clapham High Street ⊖	d				08 27														08 58						
Wandsworth Road	d				08 29														08 59						
Battersea Park 4	d				08 32			09 05											09 02			09 35			
London Victoria 15 ⊖	a				08 39	08 42	08 49	09 11											09 08		09 11	09 42			
Penge West	d	08 30							08 45						08 54	09 00							09 15		
Anerley	d	08 32							08 47						08 56	09 02							09 17		
Norwood Junction 2	d	08 35							08 50						09 00	09 05							09 20		
West Croydon 4	a	08 43							09 00							09 12							09 30		
East Croydon	a														09 06										

		SN	SN	LO	SE		SN	SN	LO	LO	SN	LO	LO	LO	SN		SN	LO	SE	SN	SN	LO	LO	SN	LO
London Bridge 4 ⊖	d	09 03	09 06				09 11				09 22				09 33		09 36			09 41				09 52	
Highbury & Islington	d			08 48					08 55			09 03	09 10					09 18				09 25			09 33
Canonbury	d			08 50					08 57			09 05	09 12					09 20				09 27			09 35
Dalston Junction Stn ELL	d			08 55					09 01	09 05		09 10	09 15	09 20				09 25				09 30	09 35		09 40
Haggerston	d			08 56					09 02	09 06		09 11	09 16	09 21				09 26				09 31	09 36		09 41
Hoxton	d			08 58					09 04	09 08		09 13	09 18	09 23				09 28				09 33	09 38		09 43
Shoreditch High Street	d			09 01					09 07	09 11		09 16	09 21	09 26				09 31				09 36	09 41		09 46
Whitechapel	d			09 03					09 09	09 13		09 18	09 23	09 28				09 33				09 38	09 43		09 48
Shadwell	d			09 05					09 11	09 15		09 20	09 25	09 30				09 35				09 40	09 45		09 50
Wapping	d			09 07					09 13	09 17		09 22	09 27	09 32				09 37				09 42	09 47		09 52
Rotherhithe	d			09 09					09 15	09 19		09 24	09 29	09 34				09 39				09 44	09 49		09 54
Canada Water	d			09 11					09 17	09 21		09 26	09 31	09 36				09 41				09 46	09 51		09 56
Surrey Quays	d			09 12					09 18	09 22		09 27	09 32	09 37				09 42				09 47	09 52		09 57
New Cross ELL	a									09 28				09 43									09 58		
New Cross Gate 4	a		09 12	09 16					09 22		09 28	09 30	09 36				09 41	09 46				09 51		09 57	10 01
	d		09 12	09 17					09 23		09 28	09 32	09 37				09 41	09 47				09 52		09 57	10 02
Brockley	d		09 14	09 19					09 25		09 30	09 34	09 39				09 44	09 49				09 54		10 00	10 04
Honor Oak Park	d		09 17	09 22					09 28		09 33	09 37	09 42				09 47	09 52				09 57		10 03	10 07
Forest Hill 4	d		09 20	09 25					09 31		09 36	09 40	09 45				09 49	09 55				10 00		10 05	10 10
Sydenham	d		09 22	09 27					09 33		09 38	09 42	09 47				09 52	09 57				10 02		10 08	10 12
Crystal Palace 4	d							09 30	09a38		09 43		09a52								10 00	10a07		10 13	
Gipsy Hill	d							09 32			09 46										10 02			10 15	
West Norwood 4	d							09 35			09 49										10 05			10 18	
Streatham Hill	d										09 52													10 22	
Balham 4 ⊖	d										09 56													10 25	
Wandsworth Common	d										09 58													10 27	
Clapham Junction 10	d										10 02													10 31	
South Bermondsey	d	09 07					09 15								09 37					09 45					
Queens Rd Peckham	d	09 09					09 18								09 39					09 48					
Peckham Rye 4	d	09a12			09 14		09 20	09a47							09a42				09 45	09 50	10a17				
Denmark Hill 4	d				09 17		09 23												09 49	09 53					
London Blackfriars 3 ⊖	a																								
Clapham High Street ⊖	d						09 28													09 58					
Wandsworth Road	d						09 29													09 59					
Battersea Park 4	d						09 32				10 05									10 03				10 35	
London Victoria 15 ⊖	a				09 29		09 38				10 11								10 00	10 07				10 39	
Penge West	d		09 25	09 30								09 45					09 54	10 00							10 15
Anerley	d		09 27	09 32								09 47					09 56	10 02							10 17
Norwood Junction 2	d		09 30	09 35								09 50					10 00	10 05							10 20
West Croydon 4	a			09 42								10 00						10 12							10 30
East Croydon	a		09 33														10 03								

London Bridge to London Victoria - Croydon and East London Line

Network Diagram - see first Page of Table 177

Station		LO	LO	SN	SN	LO	SE	SN	SN	LO	LO	SN	LO	LO	LO	SN	SN	LO	SE	SN	SN	LO
London Bridge 4 ⊖	d			10 03	10 06			10 11				10 22				10 33	10 36			10 41		
Highbury & Islington	d	09 40				09 48				09 55			10 03	10 10				10 18				10 25
Canonbury	d	09 42				09 50				09 57			10 05	10 12				10 20				10 27
Dalston Junction Stn ELL	d	09 45	09 50			09 55				10 00	10 05		10 10	10 15	10 20			10 25				10 30
Haggerston	d	09 46	09 51			09 56				10 01	10 06		10 11	10 16	10 21			10 26				10 31
Hoxton	d	09 48	09 53			09 58				10 03	10 08		10 13	10 18	10 23			10 28				10 33
Shoreditch High Street	d	09 51	09 56			10 01				10 06	10 11		10 16	10 21	10 26			10 31				10 36
Whitechapel	d	09 53	09 58			10 03				10 08	10 13		10 18	10 23	10 28			10 33				10 38
Shadwell	d	09 55	10 00			10 05				10 10	10 15		10 20	10 25	10 30			10 35				10 40
Wapping	d	09 57	10 02			10 07				10 12	10 17		10 22	10 27	10 32			10 37				10 42
Rotherhithe	d	09 59	10 04			10 09				10 14	10 19		10 24	10 29	10 34			10 39				10 44
Canada Water	d	10 01	10 06			10 11				10 16	10 21		10 26	10 31	10 36			10 41				10 46
Surrey Quays	d	10 02	10 07			10 12				10 17	10 22		10 27	10 32	10 37			10 42				10 47
New Cross ELL	a		10 13								10 28				10 43							
New Cross Gate 4	a	10 06			10 11	10 16				10 21		10 27	10 31	10 36			10 41	10 46				10 51
	d	10 07			10 11	10 17				10 22		10 27	10 32	10 37			10 41	10 47				10 52
Brockley	d	10 09			10 14	10 19				10 24		10 30	10 34	10 39			10 44	10 49				10 54
Honor Oak Park	d	10 12			10 17	10 22				10 27		10 33	10 37	10 42			10 47	10 52				10 57
Forest Hill 4	d	10 15			10 19	10 25				10 30		10 35	10 40	10 45			10 49	10 55				11 00
Sydenham	d	10 17			10 22	10 27				10 32		10 38	10 42	10 47			10 52	10 57				11 02
Crystal Palace 4	d	10a22							10 30	10a37		10 43		10a52							11 00	11a07
Gipsy Hill	d								10 32			10 45									11 02	
West Norwood 4	d								10 35			10 48									11 05	
Streatham Hill	d											10 52										
Balham 4 ⊖	d											10 55										
Wandsworth Common	d											10 57										
Clapham Junction 10	d											11 01										
South Bermondsey	d			10 07				10 15								10 37				10 45		
Queens Rd Peckham	d			10 09				10 18								10 39				10 48		
Peckham Rye 4	d			10a12			10 15	10 20	10a47							10a42			10 45	10 50	11a17	
Denmark Hill 4	d						10 19	10 23											10 49	10 53		
London Blackfriars 3 ⊖	a																					
Clapham High Street ⊖	d							10 28												10 58		
Wandsworth Road	d							10 29												10 59		
Battersea Park 4	d							10 32				11 05								11 02		
London Victoria 15 ⊖	a						10 28	10 36				11 09							10 58	11 06		
Penge West	d				10 24	10 30							10 45				10 54	11 00				
Anerley	d				10 26	10 32							10 47				10 56	11 02				
Norwood Junction 2	d				10 30	10 35							10 50				11 00	11 05				
West Croydon 4	a					10 42							11 00					11 12				
East Croydon	a				10 33												11 03					

Station		LO	SN	LO	LO	LO	SN	SN	LO	SE	SN	SN	LO	LO	SN	LO	LO	LO	SN	SN	LO	SE	SN
London Bridge 4 ⊖	d		10 52				11 03	11 06			11 11				11 22				11 33	11 36			11 41
Highbury & Islington	d			10 33	10 40				10 48				10 55			11 03	11 10				11 18		
Canonbury	d			10 35	10 42				10 50				10 57			11 05	11 12				11 20		
Dalston Junction Stn ELL	d	10 35		10 40	10 45	10 50			10 55				11 00	11 05		11 10	11 15	11 20			11 25		
Haggerston	d	10 36		10 41	10 46	10 51			10 56				11 01	11 06		11 11	11 16	11 21			11 26		
Hoxton	d	10 38		10 43	10 48	10 53			10 58				11 03	11 08		11 13	11 18	11 23			11 28		
Shoreditch High Street	d	10 41		10 46	10 51	10 56			11 01				11 06	11 11		11 16	11 21	11 26			11 31		
Whitechapel	d	10 43		10 48	10 53	10 58			11 03				11 08	11 13		11 18	11 23	11 28			11 33		
Shadwell	d	10 45		10 50	10 55	11 00			11 05				11 10	11 15		11 20	11 25	11 30			11 35		
Wapping	d	10 47		10 52	10 57	11 02			11 07				11 12	11 17		11 22	11 27	11 32			11 37		
Rotherhithe	d	10 49		10 54	10 59	11 04			11 09				11 14	11 19		11 24	11 29	11 34			11 39		
Canada Water	d	10 51		10 56	11 01	11 06			11 11				11 16	11 21		11 26	11 31	11 36			11 41		
Surrey Quays	d	10 52		10 57	11 02	11 07			11 12				11 17	11 22		11 27	11 32	11 37			11 42		
New Cross ELL	a	10 58				11 13								11 28				11 43					
New Cross Gate 4	a		10 57	11 01	11 06			11 11	11 16				11 21		11 27	11 31	11 36			11 41	11 46		
	d		10 57	11 02	11 07			11 11	11 17				11 22		11 27	11 32	11 37			11 41	11 47		
Brockley	d		11 00	11 04	11 09			11 14	11 19				11 24		11 30	11 34	11 39			11 44	11 49		
Honor Oak Park	d		11 03	11 07	11 12			11 17	11 22				11 27		11 33	11 37	11 42			11 47	11 52		
Forest Hill 4	d		11 05	11 10	11 15			11 19	11 25				11 30		11 35	11 40	11 45			11 49	11 55		
Sydenham	d		11 08	11 12	11 17			11 22	11 27				11 32		11 38	11 42	11 47			11 52	11 57		
Crystal Palace 4	d		11 13		11a22							11 30	11a37		11 43		11a52						
Gipsy Hill	d		11 15									11 32			11 45								
West Norwood 4	d		11 18									11 35			11 48								
Streatham Hill	d		11 22												11 52								
Balham 4 ⊖	d		11 25												11 55								
Wandsworth Common	d		11 27												11 57								
Clapham Junction 10	d		11 31												12 01								
South Bermondsey	d						11 07				11 15								11 37				11 45
Queens Rd Peckham	d						11 09				11 18								11 39				11 48
Peckham Rye 4	d						11a12			11 15	11 20	11a47							11a42			11 45	11 50
Denmark Hill 4	d									11 19	11 23											11 49	11 54
London Blackfriars 3 ⊖	a																						
Clapham High Street ⊖	d										11 28												11 58
Wandsworth Road	d										11 29												12 00
Battersea Park 4	d		11 35								11 32				12 05								12 02
London Victoria 15 ⊖	a		11 39							11 28	11 36				12 09							11 58	12 07
Penge West	d			11 15				11 24	11 30							11 45				11 54	12 00		
Anerley	d			11 17				11 26	11 32							11 47				11 56	12 02		
Norwood Junction 2	d			11 20				11 30	11 35							11 50				12 00	12 05		
West Croydon 4	a			11 30					11 42							12 00					12 12		
East Croydon	a							11 33												12 03			

London Bridge to London Victoria - Croydon and East London Line

Network Diagram - see first Page of Table 177

		SN	LO		LO	SN	LO	LO	LO	SN	SN	LO	SE		SN	SN	LO	LO	SN	LO	LO	LO	SN		SN
London Bridge 4 ⊖	d					11 52				12 03	12 06				12 11				12 22				12 33		12 36
Highbury & Islington	d		11 25				11 33	11 40				11 48					11 55			12 03	12 10				
Canonbury	d		11 27				11 35	11 42				11 50					11 57			12 05	12 12				
Dalston Junction Stn ELL	d		11 30		11 35		11 40	11 45	11 50			11 55					12 00	12 05		12 10	12 15	12 20			
Haggerston	d		11 31		11 36		11 41	11 46	11 51			11 56					12 01	12 06		12 11	12 16	12 21			
Hoxton	d		11 33		11 38		11 43	11 48	11 53			11 58					12 03	12 08		12 13	12 18	12 23			
Shoreditch High Street	d		11 36		11 41		11 46	11 51	11 56			12 01					12 06	12 11		12 16	12 21	12 26			
Whitechapel	d		11 38		11 43		11 48	11 53	11 58			12 03					12 08	12 13		12 18	12 23	12 28			
Shadwell	d		11 40		11 45		11 50	11 55	12 00			12 05					12 10	12 15		12 20	12 25	12 30			
Wapping	d		11 42		11 47		11 52	11 57	12 02			12 07					12 12	12 17		12 22	12 27	12 32			
Rotherhithe	d		11 44		11 49		11 54	11 59	12 04			12 09					12 14	12 19		12 24	12 29	12 34			
Canada Water	d		11 46		11 51		11 56	12 01	12 06			12 11					12 16	12 21		12 26	12 31	12 36			
Surrey Quays	d		11 47		11 52		11 57	12 02	12 07			12 12					12 17	12 22		12 27	12 32	12 37			
New Cross ELL	a				11 58				12 13									12 28				12 43			
New Cross Gate 4	a		11 51			11 57	12 01	12 06			12 11	12 16					12 21		12 27	12 31	12 36				12 41
	d		11 52			11 57	12 02	12 07			12 11	12 17					12 22		12 27	12 32	12 37				12 41
Brockley	d		11 54			12 00	12 04	12 09			12 14	12 19					12 24		12 30	12 34	12 39				12 44
Honor Oak Park	d		11 57			12 03	12 07	12 12			12 17	12 22					12 27		12 33	12 37	12 42				12 47
Forest Hill 4	d		12 00			12 05	12 10	12 15			12 19	12 25					12 30		12 35	12 40	12 45				12 49
Sydenham	d		12 02			12 08	12 12	12 17			12 22	12 27					12 32		12 38	12 42	12 47				12 52
Crystal Palace 4	d	12 00	12a07			12 13		12a22								12 30	12a37		12 43		12a52				
Gipsy Hill	d	12 02				12 15										12 32			12 45						
West Norwood 4	d	12 05				12 18										12 35			12 48						
Streatham Hill	d					12 22													12 52						
Balham 4 ⊖	d					12 25													12 55						
Wandsworth Common	d					12 27													12 57						
Clapham Junction 10	d					12 31													13 01						
South Bermondsey	d									12 07					12 15								12 37		
Queens Rd Peckham	d									12 09					12 18								12 39		
Peckham Rye 4	d	12a17								12a12			12 15		12 20	12a47							12a42		
Denmark Hill 4	d												12 19		12 23										
London Blackfriars 3 ⊖	a																								
Clapham High Street ⊖	d														12 28										
Wandsworth Road	d														12 29										
Battersea Park 4	d					12 35									12 32				13 05						
London Victoria 15 ⊖	a					12 39							12 28		12 36				13 09						
Penge West	d						12 15				12 24	12 30								12 45					12 54
Anerley	d						12 17				12 26	12 32								12 47					12 56
Norwood Junction 2	d						12 20				12 30	12 35								12 50					13 00
West Croydon 4	a						12 30					12 42								13 00					
East Croydon	a										12 33														13 03

		LO	SE	SN	SN	LO	LO	SN	LO		LO	LO	SN	SN	LO	SE	SN	SN	LO		LO	SN	LO	LO	LO
London Bridge 4 ⊖	d			12 41				12 52					13 03	13 06			13 11					13 22			
Highbury & Islington	d	12 18				12 25			12 33		12 40				12 48				12 55				13 03	13 10	
Canonbury	d	12 20				12 27			12 35		12 42				12 50				12 57				13 05	13 12	
Dalston Junction Stn ELL	d	12 25				12 30	12 35		12 40		12 45	12 50			12 55				13 00		13 05		13 10	13 15	13 20
Haggerston	d	12 26				12 31	12 36		12 41		12 46	12 51			12 56				13 01		13 06		13 11	13 16	13 21
Hoxton	d	12 28				12 33	12 38		12 43		12 48	12 53			12 58				13 03		13 08		13 13	13 18	13 23
Shoreditch High Street	d	12 31				12 36	12 41		12 46		12 51	12 56			13 01				13 06		13 11		13 16	13 21	13 26
Whitechapel	d	12 33				12 38	12 43		12 48		12 53	12 58			13 03				13 08		13 13		13 18	13 23	13 28
Shadwell	d	12 35				12 40	12 45		12 50		12 55	13 00			13 05				13 10		13 15		13 20	13 25	13 30
Wapping	d	12 37				12 42	12 47		12 52		12 57	13 02			13 07				13 12		13 17		13 22	13 27	13 32
Rotherhithe	d	12 39				12 44	12 49		12 54		12 59	13 04			13 09				13 14		13 19		13 24	13 29	13 34
Canada Water	d	12 41				12 46	12 51		12 56		13 01	13 06			13 11				13 16		13 21		13 26	13 31	13 36
Surrey Quays	d	12 42				12 47	12 52		12 57		13 02	13 07			13 12				13 17		13 22		13 27	13 32	13 37
New Cross ELL	a						12 58					13 13									13 28				13 43
New Cross Gate 4	a	12 46				12 51		12 57	13 01		13 06			13 11	13 16				13 21			13 27	13 31	13 36	
	d	12 47				12 52		12 57	13 02		13 07			13 11	13 17				13 22			13 27	13 32	13 37	
Brockley	d	12 49				12 54		13 00	13 04		13 09			13 14	13 19				13 24			13 30	13 34	13 39	
Honor Oak Park	d	12 52				12 57		13 03	13 07		13 12			13 17	13 22				13 27			13 33	13 37	13 42	
Forest Hill 4	d	12 55				13 00		13 05	13 10		13 15			13 19	13 25				13 30			13 35	13 40	13 45	
Sydenham	d	12 57				13 02		13 08	13 12		13 17			13 22	13 27				13 32			13 38	13 42	13 47	
Crystal Palace 4	d				13 00	13a07		13 13			13a22							13 30	13a37			13 43		13a52	
Gipsy Hill	d				13 02			13 15										13 32				13 45			
West Norwood 4	d				13 05			13 18										13 35				13 48			
Streatham Hill	d							13 22														13 52			
Balham 4 ⊖	d							13 25														13 55			
Wandsworth Common	d							13 27														13 57			
Clapham Junction 10	d							13 31														14 01			
South Bermondsey	d			12 45									13 07				13 15								
Queens Rd Peckham	d			12 48									13 09				13 18								
Peckham Rye 4	d		12 45	12 50	13a17								13a12			13 15	13 20	13a47							
Denmark Hill 4	d		12 49	12 53												13 19	13 23								
London Blackfriars 3 ⊖	a																								
Clapham High Street ⊖	d			12 58													13 28								
Wandsworth Road	d			12 59													13 29								
Battersea Park 4	d			13 02				13 35									13 32					14 05			
London Victoria 15 ⊖	a		12 58	13 06				13 39								13 28	13 36					14 09			
Penge West	d	13 00							13 15					13 24	13 30								13 45		
Anerley	d	13 02							13 17					13 26	13 32								13 47		
Norwood Junction 2	d	13 05							13 20					13 30	13 35								13 50		
West Croydon 4	a	13 12							13 30						13 42								14 00		
East Croydon	a													13 33											

London Bridge to London Victoria - Croydon and East London Line

Network Diagram - see first Page of Table 177

		SN	SN	LO	SE		SN	SN	LO	LO	SN	LO	LO	LO	SN		SN	LO	SE	SN	SN	LO	LO	SN	LO
London Bridge 4 ⊖	d	13 33	13 36				13 41				13 52				14 03		14 06			14 11				14 22	
Highbury & Islington	d			13 18					13 25			13 33	13 40					13 48				13 55			14 03
Canonbury	d			13 20					13 27			13 35	13 42					13 50				13 57			14 05
Dalston Junction Stn ELL	d			13 25					13 30	13 35		13 40	13 45	13 50				13 55				14 00	14 05		14 10
Haggerston	d			13 26					13 31	13 36		13 41	13 46	13 51				13 56				14 01	14 06		14 11
Hoxton	d			13 28					13 33	13 38		13 43	13 48	13 53				13 58				14 03	14 08		14 13
Shoreditch High Street	d			13 31					13 36	13 41		13 46	13 51	13 56				14 01				14 06	14 11		14 16
Whitechapel	d			13 33					13 38	13 43		13 48	13 53	13 58				14 03				14 08	14 13		14 18
Shadwell	d			13 35					13 40	13 45		13 50	13 55	14 00				14 05				14 10	14 15		14 20
Wapping	d			13 37					13 42	13 47		13 52	13 57	14 02				14 07				14 12	14 17		14 22
Rotherhithe	d			13 39					13 44	13 49		13 54	13 59	14 04				14 09				14 14	14 19		14 24
Canada Water	d			13 41					13 46	13 51		13 56	14 01	14 06				14 11				14 16	14 21		14 26
Surrey Quays	d			13 42					13 47	13 52		13 57	14 02	14 07				14 12				14 17	14 22		14 27
New Cross ELL	a									13 58				14 13									14 28		
New Cross Gate 4	a		13 41	13 46					13 51		13 57	14 01	14 06				14 11	14 16				14 21		14 27	14 31
	d		13 41	13 47					13 52		13 57	14 02	14 07				14 11	14 17				14 22		14 27	14 32
Brockley	d		13 44	13 49					13 54		14 00	14 04	14 09				14 14	14 19				14 24		14 30	14 34
Honor Oak Park	d		13 47	13 52					13 57		14 03	14 07	14 12				14 17	14 22				14 27		14 33	14 37
Forest Hill 4	d		13 49	13 55					14 00		14 05	14 10	14 15				14 19	14 25				14 30		14 35	14 40
Sydenham	d		13 52	13 57					14 02		14 08	14 12	14 17				14 22	14 27				14 32		14 38	14 42
Crystal Palace 4	d							14 00	14a07		14 13		14a22								14 30	14a37		14 43	
Gipsy Hill	d							14 02			14 15										14 32			14 45	
West Norwood 4	d							14 05			14 18										14 35			14 48	
Streatham Hill	d										14 22													14 52	
Balham 4 ⊖	d										14 25													14 55	
Wandsworth Common	d										14 27													14 57	
Clapham Junction 10	d										14 31													15 01	
South Bermondsey	d	13 37					13 45								14 07					14 15					
Queens Rd Peckham	d	13 39					13 48								14 09					14 18					
Peckham Rye 4	d	13a42			13 45		13 50	14a17							14a12				14 15	14 20	14a47				
Denmark Hill 4	d				13 49		13 53												14 19	14 23					
London Blackfriars 3 ⊖	a																								
Clapham High Street ⊖	d						13 58													14 28					
Wandsworth Road	d						13 59													14 29					
Battersea Park 4	d						14 02				14 35									14 32				15 05	
London Victoria 15 ⊖	a				13 58		14 06				14 39								14 28	14 36				15 09	
Penge West	d		13 54	14 00								14 15					14 24	14 30							14 45
Anerley	d		13 56	14 02								14 17					14 26	14 32							14 47
Norwood Junction 2	d		14 00	14 05								14 20					14 30	14 35							14 50
West Croydon 4	a			14 12								14 30						14 42							15 00
East Croydon	a		14 03														14 33								

			LO	LO	SN	SN	LO	SE	SN	SN	LO		LO	SN	LO	LO	LO	SN	SN	LO	SE		SN	SN	LO
London Bridge 4 ⊖	d				14 33	14 36			14 41					14 52				15 03	15 06				15 11		
Highbury & Islington	d		14 10				14 18				14 25				14 33	14 40				14 48					14 55
Canonbury	d		14 12				14 20				14 27				14 35	14 42				14 50					14 57
Dalston Junction Stn ELL	d		14 15	14 20			14 25				14 30		14 35		14 40	14 45	14 50			14 55					15 00
Haggerston	d		14 16	14 21			14 26				14 31		14 36		14 41	14 46	14 51			14 56					15 01
Hoxton	d		14 18	14 23			14 28				14 33		14 38		14 43	14 48	14 53			14 58					15 03
Shoreditch High Street	d		14 21	14 26			14 31				14 36		14 41		14 46	14 51	14 56			15 01					15 06
Whitechapel	d		14 23	14 28			14 33				14 38		14 43		14 48	14 53	14 58			15 03					15 08
Shadwell	d		14 25	14 30			14 35				14 40		14 45		14 50	14 55	15 00			15 05					15 10
Wapping	d		14 27	14 32			14 37				14 42		14 47		14 52	14 57	15 02			15 07					15 12
Rotherhithe	d		14 29	14 34			14 39				14 44		14 49		14 54	14 59	15 04			15 09					15 14
Canada Water	d		14 31	14 36			14 41				14 46		14 51		14 56	15 01	15 06			15 11					15 16
Surrey Quays	d		14 32	14 37			14 42				14 47		14 52		14 57	15 02	15 07			15 12					15 17
New Cross ELL	a			14 43									14 58				15 13								
New Cross Gate 4	a		14 36			14 41	14 46				14 51			14 57	15 01	15 06			15 11	15 16					15 21
	d		14 37			14 41	14 47				14 52			14 57	15 02	15 07			15 11	15 17					15 22
Brockley	d		14 39			14 44	14 49				14 54			15 00	15 04	15 09			15 14	15 19					15 24
Honor Oak Park	d		14 42			14 47	14 52				14 57			15 03	15 07	15 12			15 17	15 22					15 27
Forest Hill 4	d		14 45			14 49	14 55				15 00			15 05	15 10	15 15			15 19	15 25					15 30
Sydenham	d		14 47			14 52	14 57				15 02			15 08	15 12	15 17			15 22	15 27					15 32
Crystal Palace 4	d		14a52							15 00	15a07			15 13		15a22								15 30	15a37
Gipsy Hill	d									15 02				15 15										15 32	
West Norwood 4	d									15 05				15 18										15 35	
Streatham Hill	d													15 22											
Balham 4 ⊖	d													15 25											
Wandsworth Common	d													15 27											
Clapham Junction 10	d													15 31											
South Bermondsey	d				14 37				14 45									15 07					15 15		
Queens Rd Peckham	d				14 39				14 48									15 09					15 18		
Peckham Rye 4	d				14a42			14 45	14 50	15a17								15a12			15 15		15 20	15a47	
Denmark Hill 4	d							14 49	14 53												15 19		15 23		
London Blackfriars 3 ⊖	a																								
Clapham High Street ⊖	d								14 58														15 28		
Wandsworth Road	d								14 59														15 29		
Battersea Park 4	d								15 02					15 35									15 32		
London Victoria 15 ⊖	a							14 58	15 06					15 39							15 28		15 36		
Penge West	d					14 54	15 00								15 15				15 24	15 30					
Anerley	d					14 56	15 02								15 17				15 26	15 32					
Norwood Junction 2	d					15 00	15 05								15 20				15 30	15 35					
West Croydon 4	a						15 12								15 30					15 42					
East Croydon	a					15 03													15 33						

London Bridge to London Victoria - Croydon and East London Line

Network Diagram - see first Page of Table 177

		LO	SN	LO	LO	LO	SN		SN	LO	SE	SN	SN	SN	LO	LO	SN		LO	LO	LO	SN	SN	LO	SE
London Bridge [4] ⊖	d		15 22				15 33		15 36			15 41					15 52					16 03	16 06		
Highbury & Islington	d			15 03	15 10					15 18					15 25				15 33	15 40				15 48	
Canonbury	d			15 05	15 12					15 20					15 27				15 35	15 42				15 50	
Dalston Junction Stn ELL	d	15 05		15 10	15 15	15 20				15 25					15 30	15 35			15 40	15 45	15 50			15 55	
Haggerston	d	15 06		15 11	15 16	15 21				15 26					15 31	15 36			15 41	15 46	15 51			15 56	
Hoxton	d	15 08		15 13	15 18	15 23				15 28					15 33	15 38			15 43	15 48	15 53			15 58	
Shoreditch High Street	d	15 11		15 16	15 21	15 26				15 31					15 36	15 41			15 46	15 51	15 56			16 01	
Whitechapel	d	15 13		15 18	15 23	15 28				15 33					15 38	15 43			15 48	15 53	15 58			16 03	
Shadwell	d	15 15		15 20	15 25	15 30				15 35					15 40	15 45			15 50	15 55	16 00			16 05	
Wapping	d	15 17		15 22	15 27	15 32				15 37					15 42	15 47			15 52	15 57	16 02			16 07	
Rotherhithe	d	15 19		15 24	15 29	15 34				15 39					15 44	15 49			15 54	15 59	16 04			16 09	
Canada Water	d	15 21		15 26	15 31	15 36				15 41					15 46	15 51			15 56	16 01	16 06			16 11	
Surrey Quays	d	15 22		15 27	15 32	15 37				15 42					15 47	15 52			15 57	16 02	16 07			16 12	
New Cross ELL	a	15 28				15 43										15 58					16 13				
New Cross Gate [4]	a		15 27	15 31	15 36				15 41	15 46					15 51		15 57		16 01	16 06			16 11	16 16	
	d		15 27	15 32	15 37				15 41	15 47					15 52		15 57		16 02	16 07			16 11	16 17	
Brockley	d		15 30	15 34	15 39				15 44	15 49					15 54		16 00		16 04	16 09			16 14	16 19	
Honor Oak Park	d		15 33	15 37	15 42				15 47	15 52					15 57		16 03		16 07	16 12			16 17	16 22	
Forest Hill [4]	d		15 35	15 40	15 45				15 49	15 55					16 00		16 05		16 10	16 15			16 19	16 25	
Sydenham	d		15 38	15 42	15 47				15 52	15 57					16 02		16 08		16 12	16 17			16 22	16 27	
Crystal Palace [4]	d		15 43		15a52									16 00	16a07		16 13			16a22					
Gipsy Hill	d		15 45											16 02			16 15								
West Norwood [4]	d		15 48											16 05			16 18								
Streatham Hill	d		15 52										15 56				16 22								
Balham [4] ⊖	d		15 55														16 25								
Wandsworth Common	d		15 57														16 27								
Clapham Junction [10]	d		16 01														16 31								
South Bermondsey	d						15 37					15 45										16 07			
Queens Rd Peckham	d						15 39					15 48										16 09			
Peckham Rye [4]	d						15a42				15 45	15 50	16a07	16a17								16a12			16 15
Denmark Hill [4]	d										15 49	15 53													16 19
London Blackfriars [3] ⊖	a																								
Clapham High Street ⊖	d											15 58													
Wandsworth Road	d											15 59													
Battersea Park [4]	d		16 05									16 02					16 35								
London Victoria [15] ⊖	a		16 10								15 58	16 06					16 40								16 28
Penge West	d			15 45					15 54	16 00									16 15				16 24	16 30	
Anerley	d			15 47					15 56	16 02									16 17				16 26	16 32	
Norwood Junction [2]	d			15 50					16 00	16 05									16 20				16 30	16 35	
West Croydon [4] 🚋	a			16 00						16 12									16 30					16 42	
East Croydon 🚋	a								16 03														16 33		

		SN	SN		LO	LO	SN	LO	LO	LO	SN	SN	LO		SE	SN	SN	LO	LO	SN	LO	SN	SE		SN
London Bridge [4] ⊖	d	16 11					16 22				16 33	16 36				16 41				16 52		16 58			
Highbury & Islington	d				15 55			16 03	16 10				16 18					16 25			16 33				
Canonbury	d				15 57			16 05	16 12				16 20					16 27			16 35				
Dalston Junction Stn ELL	d				16 00	16 05		16 10	16 15	16 20			16 25					16 30	16 35		16 40				
Haggerston	d				16 01	16 06		16 11	16 16	16 21			16 26					16 31	16 36		16 41				
Hoxton	d				16 03	16 08		16 13	16 18	16 23			16 28					16 33	16 38		16 43				
Shoreditch High Street	d				16 06	16 11		16 16	16 21	16 26			16 31					16 36	16 41		16 46				
Whitechapel	d				16 08	16 13		16 18	16 23	16 28			16 33					16 38	16 43		16 48				
Shadwell	d				16 10	16 15		16 20	16 25	16 30			16 35					16 40	16 45		16 50				
Wapping	d				16 12	16 17		16 22	16 27	16 32			16 37					16 42	16 47		16 52				
Rotherhithe	d				16 14	16 19		16 24	16 29	16 34			16 39					16 44	16 49		16 54				
Canada Water	d				16 16	16 21		16 26	16 31	16 36			16 41					16 46	16 51		16 56				
Surrey Quays	d				16 17	16 22		16 27	16 32	16 37			16 42					16 47	16 52		16 57				
New Cross ELL	a					16 28				16 43									16 58						
New Cross Gate [4]	a				16 21		16 27	16 31	16 36			16 41	16 46					16 51		16 57	17 01				
	d				16 22		16 27	16 32	16 37			16 41	16 47					16 52		16 57	17 02				
Brockley	d				16 24		16 30	16 34	16 39			16 44	16 49					16 54		17 00	17 04				
Honor Oak Park	d				16 27		16 33	16 37	16 42			16 47	16 52					16 57		17 03	17 07				
Forest Hill [4]	d				16 30		16 35	16 40	16 45			16 49	16 55					17 00		17 05	17 10				
Sydenham	d				16 32		16 38	16 42	16 47			16 52	16 57					17 02		17 08	17 12				
Crystal Palace [4]	d		16 30		16a37		16 43		16a52								17 00	17a07		17 13					17 18
Gipsy Hill	d		16 32				16 45										17 02			17 15					17 20
West Norwood [4]	d		16 35				16 48										17 05			17 18					17 23
Streatham Hill	d						16 52													17 22					
Balham [4] ⊖	d						16 55													17 25					
Wandsworth Common	d						16 57													17 27					
Clapham Junction [10]	d						17 01													17 31					
South Bermondsey	d	16 15									16 37					16 45						17 02			
Queens Rd Peckham	d	16 18									16 39					16 48						17 04			
Peckham Rye [4]	d	16 20	16a47								16a42				16 45	16 50	17a17					17a07	17 15		17a35
Denmark Hill [4]	d	16 23													16 49	16 53							17 19		
London Blackfriars [3] ⊖	a																								
Clapham High Street ⊖	d	16 28														16 58									
Wandsworth Road	d	16 29														16 59									
Battersea Park [4]	d	16 32					17 05									17 02				17 35					
London Victoria [15] ⊖	a	16 38					17 10								17 01	17 08				17 42			17 28		
Penge West	d							16 45				16 54	17 00								17 15				
Anerley	d							16 47				16 56	17 02								17 17				
Norwood Junction [2]	d							16 50				17 00	17 05								17 20				
West Croydon [4] 🚋	a							17 00				17 07	17 12								17 30				
East Croydon 🚋	a																								

London Bridge to London Victoria - Croydon and East London Line

Network Diagram - see first Page of Table 177

		LO	LO	SN	LO	SN	SN	LO	LO		SN	LO	LO	LO	SN	SN	LO	SE	SN		SN	LO	LO	SN	LO
London Bridge 4 ⊖	d			17 05		17 11					17 19				17 28	17 36			17 41					17 53	
Highbury & Islington	d	16 40			16 48			16 55				17 03	17 10				17 18					17 25			17 33
Canonbury	d	16 42			16 50			16 57				17 05	17 12				17 20					17 27			17 35
Dalston Junction Stn ELL	d	16 45	16 50		16 55			17 00	17 05			17 10	17 15	17 20			17 25					17 30	17 35		17 40
Haggerston	d	16 46	16 51		16 56			17 01	17 06			17 11	17 16	17 21			17 26					17 31	17 36		17 41
Hoxton	d	16 48	16 53		16 58			17 03	17 08			17 13	17 18	17 23			17 28					17 33	17 38		17 43
Shoreditch High Street	d	16 51	16 56		17 01			17 06	17 11			17 16	17 21	17 26			17 31					17 36	17 41		17 46
Whitechapel	d	16 53	16 58		17 03			17 08	17 13			17 18	17 23	17 28			17 33					17 38	17 43		17 48
Shadwell	d	16 55	17 00		17 05			17 10	17 15			17 20	17 25	17 30			17 35					17 40	17 45		17 50
Wapping	d	16 57	17 02		17 07			17 12	17 17			17 22	17 27	17 32			17 37					17 42	17 47		17 52
Rotherhithe	d	16 59	17 04		17 09			17 14	17 19			17 24	17 29	17 34			17 39					17 44	17 49		17 54
Canada Water	d	17 01	17 06		17 11			17 16	17 21			17 26	17 31	17 36			17 41					17 46	17 51		17 56
Surrey Quays	d	17 02	17 07		17 12			17 17	17 22			17 27	17 32	17 37			17 42					17 47	17 52		17 57
New Cross ELL	a		17 13						17 28					17 43									17 58		
New Cross Gate 4	a	17 06		17 11	17 16			17 21			17 26	17 30	17 36			17 41	17 46					17 51		17 58	18 01
	d	17 07		17 11	17 17			17 22			17 26	17 32	17 37			17 41	17 47					17 52		17 58	18 02
Brockley	d	17 09		17 14	17 19			17 24			17 29	17 34	17 39			17 44	17 49					17 54		18 01	18 04
Honor Oak Park	d	17 12		17 17	17 22			17 27			17 32	17 37	17 42			17 47	17 52					17 57		18 04	18 07
Forest Hill 4	d	17 15		17 19	17 25			17 30			17 34	17 40	17 45			17 49	17 55					18 00		18 06	18 10
Sydenham	d	17 17		17 22	17 27			17 32			17 37	17 42	17 47			17 52	17 57					18 02		18 09	18 12
Crystal Palace 4	d	17a22					17 36	17a37			17 44		17a52								17 55	18a07		18 13	
Gipsy Hill	d						17 38				17 46										17 57			18 15	
West Norwood 4	d						17 41				17 49										18 00			18 18	
Streatham Hill	d										17 53													18 22	
Balham 4 ⊖	d										17 56													18 25	
Wandsworth Common	d										17 58													18 27	
Clapham Junction 10	d										18 02													18 32	
South Bermondsey	d					17 15									17 32				17 45						
Queens Rd Peckham	d					17 18									17 35				17 47						
Peckham Rye 4	d					17 20	17a53								17a37			17 45	17 50		18a12				
Denmark Hill 4	d					17 23												17 49	17 53						
London Blackfriars 3 ⊖	a																								
Clapham High Street ⊖	d					17 28													17 58						
Wandsworth Road	d					17 29													17 59						
Battersea Park 4	d					17 32					18 06								18 02					18 35	
London Victoria 15 ⊖	a					17 38					18 12							17 59	18 08					18 42	
Penge West	d			17 24	17 30							17 45				17 54	18 00								18 15
Anerley	d			17 26	17 32							17 47				17 56	18 02								18 17
Norwood Junction 2	d			17 30	17 35							17 50				18 00	18 05								18 20
West Croydon 4	a			17 37	17 42							18 01				18 08	18 12								18 30
East Croydon	a																								

		SN	SE	SN	LO		LO	SN	LO	LO	LO	SN	SN	LO	SN		SE	SN	LO	LO	SN	LO	LO	LO	SN
London Bridge 4 ⊖	d	17 58						18 06				18 11	18 21		18 28						18 36				18 41
Highbury & Islington	d				17 40				17 48	17 55				18 03					18 10			18 18	18 25		
Canonbury	d				17 42				17 50	17 57				18 05					18 12			18 20	18 27		
Dalston Junction Stn ELL	d				17 45		17 50		17 55	18 00	18 05			18 10					18 15	18 20		18 25	18 30	18 35	
Haggerston	d				17 46		17 51		17 56	18 01	18 06			18 11					18 16	18 21		18 26	18 31	18 36	
Hoxton	d				17 48		17 53		17 58	18 03	18 08			18 13					18 18	18 23		18 28	18 33	18 38	
Shoreditch High Street	d				17 51		17 56		18 01	18 06	18 11			18 16					18 21	18 26		18 31	18 36	18 41	
Whitechapel	d				17 53		17 58		18 03	18 08	18 13			18 18					18 23	18 28		18 33	18 38	18 43	
Shadwell	d				17 55		18 00		18 05	18 10	18 15			18 20					18 25	18 30		18 35	18 40	18 45	
Wapping	d				17 57		18 02		18 07	18 12	18 17			18 22					18 27	18 32		18 37	18 42	18 47	
Rotherhithe	d				17 59		18 04		18 09	18 14	18 19			18 24					18 29	18 34		18 39	18 44	18 49	
Canada Water	d				18 01		18 06		18 11	18 16	18 21			18 26					18 31	18 36		18 41	18 46	18 51	
Surrey Quays	d				18 02		18 07		18 12	18 17	18 22			18 27					18 32	18 37		18 42	18 47	18 52	
New Cross ELL	a						18 13				18 28									18 43				18 58	
New Cross Gate 4	a				18 06			18 11	18 16	18 21			18 26	18 30					18 36		18 41	18 46	18 51		
	d				18 07			18 11	18 17	18 22			18 26	18 32					18 37		18 41	18 47	18 52		
Brockley	d				18 09			18 14	18 19	18 24			18 29	18 34					18 39		18 44	18 49	18 54		
Honor Oak Park	d				18 12			18 17	18 22	18 27			18 32	18 37					18 42		18 47	18 52	18 57		
Forest Hill 4	d				18 15			18 19	18 25	18 30			18 34	18 40					18 45		18 49	18 55	19 00		
Sydenham	d				18 17			18 22	18 27	18 32			18 37	18 42					18 47		18 52	18 57	19 02		
Crystal Palace 4	d			18 18	18a22					18a37			18 43					18 51	18a52				19a07		
Gipsy Hill	d			18 20									18 45					18 53							
West Norwood 4	d			18 23									18 48					18 56							
Streatham Hill	d												18 52												
Balham 4 ⊖	d												18 55												
Wandsworth Common	d												18 57												
Clapham Junction 10	d												19 01												
South Bermondsey	d	18 02										18 15			18 32										18 45
Queens Rd Peckham	d	18 04										18 18			18 34										18 48
Peckham Rye 4	d	18a07	18 15	18a36								18 20			18a37		18 45	19a14							18 50
Denmark Hill 4	d		18 19									18 23					18 49								18 53
London Blackfriars 3 ⊖	a																								
Clapham High Street ⊖	d											18 28													18 58
Wandsworth Road	d											18 29													18 59
Battersea Park 4	d											18 32	19 05												19 02
London Victoria 15 ⊖	a		18 29									18 39	19 12				18 58								19 08
Penge West	d							18 24	18 30					18 45							18 54	19 00			
Anerley	d							18 26	18 32					18 47							18 56	19 02			
Norwood Junction 2	d							18 32	18 35					18 50							19 02	19 05			
West Croydon 4	a							18 39	18 42					19 01							19 09	19 12			
East Croydon	a																								

London Bridge to London Victoria - Croydon and East London Line

Network Diagram - see first Page of Table 177

Station			SE	SN	LO	LO	LO	SN	SN	LO	SE		SN	SN	SE	SN	LO	LO	SN	LO	LO		LO	SN	SN
London Bridge 4 ⊖	d			18 51				18 57	19 06				19 08	19 11					19 22					19 28	19 36
Highbury & Islington	d				18 33	18 40				18 48							18 55			19 03	19 10				
Canonbury	d				18 35	18 42				18 50							18 57			19 05	19 12				
Dalston Junction Stn ELL	d				18 40	18 45	18 50			18 55							19 00	19 05		19 10	19 15		19 20		
Haggerston	d				18 41	18 46	18 51			18 56							19 01	19 06		19 11	19 16		19 21		
Hoxton	d				18 43	18 48	18 53			18 58							19 03	19 08		19 13	19 18		19 23		
Shoreditch High Street	d				18 46	18 51	18 56			19 01							19 06	19 11		19 16	19 21		19 26		
Whitechapel	d				18 48	18 53	18 58			19 03							19 08	19 13		19 18	19 23		19 28		
Shadwell	d				18 50	18 55	19 00			19 05							19 10	19 15		19 20	19 25		19 30		
Wapping	d				18 52	18 57	19 02			19 07							19 12	19 17		19 22	19 27		19 32		
Rotherhithe	d				18 54	18 59	19 04			19 09							19 14	19 19		19 24	19 29		19 34		
Canada Water	d				18 56	19 01	19 06			19 11							19 16	19 21		19 26	19 31		19 36		
Surrey Quays	d				18 57	19 02	19 07			19 12							19 17	19 22		19 27	19 32		19 37		
New Cross ELL	a						19 13											19 28					19 43		
New Cross Gate 4	a			18 56	19 01	19 06			19 11	19 16							19 21		19 27	19 31	19 36				19 41
	d			18 56	19 02	19 07			19 11	19 17							19 22		19 27	19 32	19 37				19 41
Brockley	d			18 59	19 04	19 09			19 14	19 19							19 24		19 30	19 34	19 39				19 44
Honor Oak Park	d			19 02	19 07	19 12			19 17	19 22							19 27		19 33	19 37	19 42				19 47
Forest Hill 4	d			19 04	19 10	19 15			19 19	19 25							19 30		19 35	19 40	19 45				19 49
Sydenham	d			19 07	19 12	19 17			19 22	19 27							19 32		19 38	19 42	19 47				19 52
Crystal Palace 4	d			19 13		19a22										19 32	19a37		19 43		19a52				
Gipsy Hill	d			19 15												19 34			19 45						
West Norwood 4	d			19 18												19 37			19 48						
Streatham Hill	d			19 22															19 52						
Balham 4 ⊖	d			19 25															19 55						
Wandsworth Common	d			19 27															19 57						
Clapham Junction 10	d			19 31															20 01						
South Bermondsey	d							19 01					19 12	19 15										19 32	
Queens Rd Peckham	d							19 03					19 14	19 18										19 34	
Peckham Rye 4	d							19 06			19 15		19a17	19 20		19a49								19 37	
Denmark Hill 4	d		18 59								19 19			19 23	19 28										
London Blackfriars 3 ⊖	a																								
Clapham High Street ⊖	d													19 28											
Wandsworth Road	d													19 29											
Battersea Park 4	d			19 35										19 32					20 05						
London Victoria 15 ⊖	a		19 13	19 41							19 28			19 36	19 43				20 09						
Penge West	d				19 15				19 24	19 30										19 45					19 54
Anerley	d				19 17				19 26	19 32										19 47					19 56
Norwood Junction 2	d				19 20			19 28	19 30	19 35										19 50				20 02	20 00
West Croydon 4	a				19 30			19 35		19 42										20 00				20 07	
East Croydon	a								19 33																20 03

Station		LO	SN	SN	SN	LO	LO		SN	LO	LO	LO	SN	SN	LO	SN	SN		LO	LO	SN	LO	LO	LO	SN
London Bridge 4 ⊖	d		19 38	19 41					19 54				20 03	20 06		20 11					20 22				20 33
Highbury & Islington	d	19 18				19 25				19 33	19 40				19 48				19 55			20 03	20 10		
Canonbury	d	19 20				19 27				19 35	19 42				19 50				19 57			20 05	20 12		
Dalston Junction Stn ELL	d	19 25				19 30	19 35			19 40	19 45	19 50			19 55				20 00	20 05		20 10	20 15	20 20	
Haggerston	d	19 26				19 31	19 36			19 41	19 46	19 51			19 56				20 01	20 06		20 11	20 16	20 21	
Hoxton	d	19 28				19 33	19 38			19 43	19 48	19 53			19 58				20 03	20 08		20 13	20 18	20 23	
Shoreditch High Street	d	19 31				19 36	19 41			19 46	19 51	19 56			20 01				20 06	20 11		20 16	20 21	20 26	
Whitechapel	d	19 33				19 38	19 43			19 48	19 53	19 58			20 03				20 08	20 13		20 18	20 23	20 28	
Shadwell	d	19 35				19 40	19 45			19 50	19 55	20 00			20 05				20 10	20 15		20 20	20 25	20 30	
Wapping	d	19 37				19 42	19 47			19 52	19 57	20 02			20 07				20 12	20 17		20 22	20 27	20 32	
Rotherhithe	d	19 39				19 44	19 49			19 54	19 59	20 04			20 09				20 14	20 19		20 24	20 29	20 34	
Canada Water	d	19 41				19 46	19 51			19 56	20 01	20 06			20 11				20 16	20 21		20 26	20 31	20 36	
Surrey Quays	d	19 42				19 47	19 52			19 57	20 02	20 07			20 12				20 17	20 22		20 27	20 32	20 37	
New Cross ELL	a						19 58					20 13								20 28				20 43	
New Cross Gate 4	a	19 46				19 51			19 59	20 00	20 06			20 11	20 16				20 21		20 27	20 31	20 36		
	d	19 47				19 52			19 59	20 02	20 07			20 11	20 17				20 22		20 27	20 32	20 37		
Brockley	d	19 49				19 54			20 02	20 04	20 09			20 14	20 19				20 24		20 30	20 34	20 39		
Honor Oak Park	d	19 52				19 57			20 05	20 07	20 12			20 17	20 22				20 27		20 33	20 37	20 42		
Forest Hill 4	d	19 55				20 00			20 07	20 10	20 15			20 19	20 25				20 30		20 35	20 40	20 45		
Sydenham	d	19 57				20 02			20 10	20 12	20 17			20 22	20 27				20 32		20 38	20 42	20 47		
Crystal Palace 4	d				20 01	20a07			20 13		20a22						20 31		20a37		20 43		20a52		
Gipsy Hill	d				20 03				20 16								20 33				20 45				
West Norwood 4	d				20 06				20 19								20 36				20 48				
Streatham Hill	d								20 22												20 52				
Balham 4 ⊖	d								20 25												20 56				
Wandsworth Common	d								20 27												20 58				
Clapham Junction 10	d								20 31												21 03				
South Bermondsey	d		19 42	19 45									20 07			20 15									20 37
Queens Rd Peckham	d		19 44	19 48									20 09			20 18									20 39
Peckham Rye 4	d		19a47	19 50	20a18								20a12			20 20	20a48								20a42
Denmark Hill 4	d			19 53												20 23									
London Blackfriars 3 ⊖	a																								
Clapham High Street ⊖	d			19 58												20 28									
Wandsworth Road	d			19 59												20 29									
Battersea Park 4	d			20 02					20 35							20 32					21 06				
London Victoria 15 ⊖	a			20 06					20 39							20 36					21 11				
Penge West	d	20 00								20 15				20 24	20 30							20 45			
Anerley	d	20 02								20 17				20 26	20 32							20 47			
Norwood Junction 2	d	20 05								20 20				20 30	20 35							20 50			
West Croydon 4	a	20 12								20 29					20 42							21 00			
East Croydon	a													20 33											

London Bridge to London Victoria - Croydon and East London Line

Network Diagram - see first Page of Table 177

		SN	LO		SN	SN	LO	LO	SN	LO	LO	LO	SN		SN	LO	SE	SN	SN	LO	LO	SN	LO		LO
London Bridge 4 ⊖	d	20 36			20 41				20 52				21 03		21 06			21 11				21 22			
Highbury & Islington	d		20 18				20 25			20 33	20 40					20 48				20 55			21 03		21 10
Canonbury	d		20 20				20 27			20 35	20 42					20 50				20 57			21 05		21 12
Dalston Junction Stn ELL	d		20 25				20 30	20 35		20 40	20 45	20 50				20 55				21 00	21 05		21 10		21 15
Haggerston	d		20 26				20 31	20 36		20 41	20 46	20 51				20 56				21 01	21 06		21 11		21 16
Hoxton	d		20 28				20 33	20 38		20 43	20 48	20 53				20 58				21 03	21 08		21 13		21 18
Shoreditch High Street	d		20 31				20 36	20 41		20 46	20 51	20 56				21 01				21 06	21 11		21 16		21 21
Whitechapel	d		20 33				20 38	20 43		20 48	20 53	20 58				21 03				21 08	21 13		21 18		21 23
Shadwell	d		20 35				20 40	20 45		20 50	20 55	21 00				21 05				21 10	21 15		21 20		21 25
Wapping	d		20 37				20 42	20 47		20 52	20 57	21 02				21 07				21 12	21 17		21 22		21 27
Rotherhithe	d		20 39				20 44	20 49		20 54	20 59	21 04				21 09				21 14	21 19		21 24		21 29
Canada Water	d		20 41				20 46	20 51		20 56	21 01	21 06				21 11				21 16	21 21		21 26		21 31
Surrey Quays	d		20 42				20 47	20 52		20 57	21 02	21 07				21 12				21 17	21 22		21 27		21 32
New Cross ELL	a							20 58				21 13									21 28				
New Cross Gate 4	a	20 41	20 46				20 51		20 57	21 01	21 06				21 11	21 16				21 21		21 27	21 31		21 36
	d	20 41	20 47				20 52		20 57	21 02	21 07				21 11	21 17				21 22		21 27	21 32		21 37
Brockley	d	20 44	20 49				20 54		21 00	21 04	21 09				21 14	21 19				21 24		21 30	21 34		21 39
Honor Oak Park	d	20 47	20 52				20 57		21 03	21 07	21 12				21 17	21 22				21 27		21 33	21 37		21 42
Forest Hill 4	d	20 49	20 55				21 00		21 05	21 10	21 15				21 19	21 25				21 30		21 35	21 40		21 45
Sydenham	d	20 52	20 57				21 02		21 08	21 12	21 17				21 22	21 27				21 32		21 38	21 42		21 47
Crystal Palace 4	d					21 00	21a07		21 13		21a22								21 30	21a37		21 43			21a52
Gipsy Hill	d					21 02			21 15										21 32			21 45			
West Norwood 4	d					21 05			21 18										21 35			21 48			
Streatham Hill	d								21 22													21 52			
Balham 4 ⊖	d								21 26													21 56			
Wandsworth Common	d								21 28													21 58			
Clapham Junction 10	d								21 33													22 03			
South Bermondsey	d				20 45								21 07					21 15							
Queens Rd Peckham	d				20 48								21 09					21 18							
Peckham Rye 4	d				20 50	21a17							21a12				21 20	21 20	21a47						
Denmark Hill 4	d				20 53												21 23	21 23							
London Blackfriars 3 ⊖	a																								
Clapham High Street ⊖	d				20 58													21 28							
Wandsworth Road	d				20 59													21 29							
Battersea Park 4	d				21 02				21 36									21 32				22 06			
London Victoria 15 ⊖	a				21 06				21 41								21 33	21 36				22 11			
Penge West	d	20 54	21 00							21 15					21 24	21 30							21 45		
Anerley	d	20 56	21 02							21 17					21 26	21 32							21 47		
Norwood Junction 2	d	21 00	21 05							21 20					21 30	21 35							21 50		
West Croydon 4	a		21 12							21 30						21 42							22 00		
East Croydon	a	21 03													21 33										

		LO	SN	SN	LO	SE	SN	SN	LO		LO	SN	LO	LO	LO	SN	SN	LO	SE		SN	SN	LO	SN	LO
London Bridge 4 ⊖	d		21 33	21 36			21 41					21 52				22 03	22 08				22 11			22 23	
Highbury & Islington	d				21 18				21 25				21 33	21 40				21 48					21 55		22 05
Canonbury	d				21 20				21 27				21 35	21 42				21 50					21 57		22 07
Dalston Junction Stn ELL	d	21 20			21 25				21 30		21 35		21 40	21 45	21 50			21 55					22 00		22 10
Haggerston	d	21 21			21 26				21 31		21 36		21 41	21 46	21 51			21 56					22 01		22 11
Hoxton	d	21 23			21 28				21 33		21 38		21 43	21 48	21 53			21 58					22 03		22 13
Shoreditch High Street	d	21 26			21 31				21 36		21 41		21 46	21 51	21 56			22 01					22 06		22 16
Whitechapel	d	21 28			21 33				21 38		21 43		21 48	21 53	21 58			22 03					22 08		22 18
Shadwell	d	21 30			21 35				21 40		21 45		21 50	21 55	22 00			22 05					22 10		22 20
Wapping	d	21 32			21 37				21 42		21 47		21 52	21 57	22 02			22 07					22 12		22 22
Rotherhithe	d	21 34			21 39				21 44		21 49		21 54	21 59	22 04			22 09					22 14		22 24
Canada Water	d	21 36			21 41				21 46		21 51		21 56	22 01	22 06			22 11					22 16		22 26
Surrey Quays	d	21 37			21 42				21 47		21 52		21 57	22 02	22 07			22 12					22 17		22 27
New Cross ELL	a	21 43									21 58				22 13										
New Cross Gate 4	a			21 41	21 46				21 51			21 57	22 01	22 06			22 13	22 16					22 21	22 28	22 31
	d			21 41	21 47				21 52			21 57	22 02	22 07			22 13	22 17					22 22	22 28	22 32
Brockley	d			21 44	21 49				21 54			22 00	22 04	22 09			22 16	22 19					22 24	22 31	22 34
Honor Oak Park	d			21 47	21 52				21 57			22 03	22 07	22 12			22 19	22 22					22 27	22 34	22 37
Forest Hill 4	d			21 49	21 55				22 00			22 05	22 10	22 15			22 21	22 25					22 30	22 36	22 40
Sydenham	d			21 52	21 57				22 02			22 08	22 12	22 17			22 24	22 27					22 32	22 39	22 42
Crystal Palace 4	d							22 00	22a07			22 13		22a22								22 22	22a37	22 43	
Gipsy Hill	d							22 02				22 15										22 24		22 45	
West Norwood 4	d							22 05				22 18										22 27		22 48	
Streatham Hill	d											22 22												22 52	
Balham 4 ⊖	d											22 26												22 56	
Wandsworth Common	d											22 28												22 58	
Clapham Junction 10	d											22 33												23 03	
South Bermondsey	d		21 37				21 45									22 07					22 15				
Queens Rd Peckham	d		21 39				21 48									22 09					22 18				
Peckham Rye 4	d		21a42			21 50	21 50	22a17								22a12			22 20		22 20	22a43			
Denmark Hill 4	d					21 53	21 53												22 23		22 23				
London Blackfriars 3 ⊖	a																								
Clapham High Street ⊖	d						21 58														22 28				
Wandsworth Road	d						21 59														22 29				
Battersea Park 4	d						22 02					22 36									22 32			23 07	
London Victoria 15 ⊖	a					22 03	22 06					22 41							22 33		22 36			23 14	
Penge West	d			21 54	22 00								22 15				22 26	22 30							22 45
Anerley	d			21 56	22 02								22 17				22 28	22 32							22 47
Norwood Junction 2	d			22 00	22 05								22 20				22 32	22 35							22 50
West Croydon 4	a				22 12								22 30					22 42							23 00
East Croydon	a			22 03													22 35								

London Bridge to London Victoria - Croydon and East London Line

Network Diagram - see first Page of Table 177

		LO	SN	SN	SE		SN	SN	LO	SN	LO	LO	SN	SN	SE		SN	SN	LO	SN	LO	LO	SN	SN	LO
London Bridge 4 ⊖	d		22 33	22 38			22 41			22 52			23 05	23 06			23 11			23 22			23 33	23 36	
Highbury & Islington	d								22 25		22 35								22 55		23 05				23 25
Canonbury	d								22 27		22 37								22 57		23 07				23 27
Dalston Junction Stn ELL	d	22 20							22 30		22 40	22 50							23 00		23 10	23 20			23 30
Haggerston	d	22 21							22 31		22 41	22 51							23 01		23 11	23 21			23 31
Hoxton	d	22 23							22 33		22 43	22 53							23 03		23 13	23 23			23 33
Shoreditch High Street	d	22 26							22 36		22 46	22 56							23 06		23 16	23 26			23 36
Whitechapel	d	22 28							22 38		22 48	22 58							23 08		23 18	23 28			23 38
Shadwell	d	22 30							22 40		22 50	23 00							23 10		23 20	23 30			23 40
Wapping	d	22 32							22 42		22 52	23 02							23 12		23 22	23 32			23 42
Rotherhithe	d	22 34							22 44		22 54	23 04							23 14		23 24	23 34			23 44
Canada Water	d	22 36							22 46		22 56	23 06							23 16		23 26	23 36			23 46
Surrey Quays	d	22 37							22 47		22 57	23 07							23 17		23 27	23 37			23 47
New Cross ELL	a	22 43										23 13										23 43			
New Cross Gate 4	a			22 43					22 51	22 57	23 01			23 11					23 21	23 27	23 31			23 41	23 51
	d			22 43					22 52	22 57	23 02			23 11					23 22	23 27	23 32			23 41	23 52
Brockley	d			22 46					22 54	23 00	23 04			23 14					23 24	23 30	23 34			23 44	23 54
Honor Oak Park	d			22 49					22 57	23 03	23 07			23 17					23 27	23 33	23 37			23 47	23 57
Forest Hill 4	d			22 51					23 00	23 05	23 10			23 19					23 30	23 35	23 40			23 49	23 59
Sydenham	d			22 54					23 02	23 08	23 12			23 22					23 32	23 38	23 42			23 52	00 02
Crystal Palace 4	d							23 00	23a07	23 13								23 30	23a37	23 43					00a07
Gipsy Hill	d							23 02		23 15								23 32		23 45					
West Norwood 4	d							23 05		23 18								23 35		23 48					
Streatham Hill	d									23 22										23 52					
Balham 4 ⊖	d									23 26										23 55					
Wandsworth Common	d									23 28										23 58					
Clapham Junction 10	d									23 33										00 02					
South Bermondsey	d		22 37				22 45						23 09				23 15						23 37		
Queens Rd Peckham	d		22 39				22 48						23 11				23 18						23 39		
Peckham Rye 4	d		22a42		22 50		22 50	23a17					23 14		23 20		23 20	23a47					23 42		
Denmark Hill 4	d				22 53		22 53								23 23		23 23								
London Blackfriars 3 ⊖	a																								
Clapham High Street ⊖	d						22 58										23 28								
Wandsworth Road	d						22 59										23 29								
Battersea Park 4	d						23 02			23 37							23 32			00 05					
London Victoria 15 ⊖	a				23 03		23 06			23 41					23 33		23 37			00 10					
Penge West	d			22 56							23 15			23 24							23 45			23 54	
Anerley	d			22 58							23 17			23 26							23 47			23 56	
Norwood Junction 2	d			23 02							23 20		23a36	23 30							23 50		00a04	23 59	
West Croydon 4	a										23 30										23 59				
East Croydon	a			23 06										23 33										00 03	

			SN	LO	LO	LO
London Bridge 4 ⊖	d		23 52			
Highbury & Islington	d			23 35	23 42	23 56
Canonbury	d			23 37	23 44	23 58
Dalston Junction Stn ELL	d			23 40	23 47	00 02
Haggerston	d			23 41	23 48	00 03
Hoxton	d			23 43	23 50	00 05
Shoreditch High Street	d			23 46	23 53	00 08
Whitechapel	d			23 48	23 55	00 10
Shadwell	d			23 50	23 57	00 12
Wapping	d			23 52	23 59	00 14
Rotherhithe	d			23 54	00 01	00 16
Canada Water	d			23 56	00 03	00 18
Surrey Quays	d			23 57	00 05	00 19
New Cross ELL	a					
New Cross Gate 4	a		23 57	00 01	00 08	00 23
	d		23 57	00 02		
Brockley	d		00 01	00 04		
Honor Oak Park	d		00 04	00 07		
Forest Hill 4	d		00 06	00 10		
Sydenham	d		00 09	00 12		
Crystal Palace 4	d		00 13			
Gipsy Hill	d		00 15			
West Norwood 4	d		00 18			
Streatham Hill	d		00 22			
Balham 4 ⊖	d		00 25			
Wandsworth Common	d		00 27			
Clapham Junction 10	d		00 31			
South Bermondsey	d					
Queens Rd Peckham	d					
Peckham Rye 4	d					
Denmark Hill 4	d					
London Blackfriars 3 ⊖	a					
Clapham High Street ⊖	d					
Wandsworth Road	d					
Battersea Park 4	d		00 35			
London Victoria 15 ⊖	a		00 42			
Penge West	d			00 15		
Anerley	d			00 17		
Norwood Junction 2	d			00 20		
West Croydon 4	a			00 27		
East Croydon	a					

Table 178

Saturdays

London Bridge to London Victoria - Croydon and East London Line

Network Diagram - see first Page of Table 177

		SN	SN	SN	LO	SN	LO	LO	SN	SN		LO	LO	SN	SN	SN	SN		SN						SE
London Bridge 4	⊖ d	23p22	23p36			23p52			00 03	00 06						00 33	00 36								
Highbury & Islington	d				23p25		23p35	23p42				23p56	00 10												
Canonbury	d				23p27		23p37	23p44				23p58	00 12												
Dalston Junction Stn ELL	d				23p30		23p40	23p47				00 02	00 15												
Haggerston	d				23p31		23p41	23p48				00 03	00 16												
Hoxton	d				23p33		23p43	23p50				00 05	00 18												
Shoreditch High Street	d				23p36		23p46	23p53				00 08	00 21												
Whitechapel	d				23p38		23p48	23p55				00 10	00 23												
Shadwell	d				23p40		23p50	23p57				00 12	00 25												
Wapping	d				23p42		23p52	23p59				00 14	00 27												
Rotherhithe	d				23p44		23p54	00 01				00 16	00 29												
Canada Water	d				23p46		23p56	00 03				00 18	00 31												
Surrey Quays	d				23p47		23p57	00 05				00 19	00 32												
New Cross ELL	a																								
New Cross Gate 4	a	23p27	23p41		23p51	23p57	00 01	00 08		00 11		00 23	00 36				00 41								
	d	23p27	23p41		23p52	23p57	00 02			00 11							00 41								
Brockley	d	23p30	23p44		23p54	00 01	00 04			00 14							00 44								
Honor Oak Park	d	23p33	23p47		23p57	00 04	00 07			00 17							00 47								
Forest Hill 4	d	23p35	23p49		23p59	00 06	00 10			00 19							00 49								
Sydenham	d	23p38	23p52		00 02	00 09	00 12			00 22							00 52								
Crystal Palace 4	d	23p43		00 03	00a07	00 13								00 33	00 47				01 03						
Gipsy Hill	d	23p45				00 15																			
West Norwood 4	d	23p48				00 18																			
Streatham Hill	d	23p52				00 22																			
Balham 4	⊖ d	23p55				00 25																			
Wandsworth Common	d	23p58				00 27																			
Clapham Junction 10	d	00 02				00 31																			
South Bermondsey	d								00 07							00 37									
Queens Rd Peckham	d								00 09							00 39									
Peckham Rye 4	d								00 12							00 42									06 13
Denmark Hill 4	d																								06 17
London Blackfriars 3	⊖ a																								
Clapham High Street	⊖ d																								
Wandsworth Road	d																								
Battersea Park 4	d	00 05				00 35																			
London Victoria 15	⊖ a	00 10				00 42																			06 26
Penge West	d		23p54				00 15			00 24							00 54								
Anerley	d		23p56				00 17			00 26							00 56								
Norwood Junction 2	d		23p59	00 09			00 20		00a34	00 30				00 38	00 52	01a04	01 00		01 08						
West Croydon 4	a			00 14			00 27							00 43	00 58				01 13						
East Croydon	a		00 03							00 33							01 03								

		SN	LO	LO	LO	LO		SE	LO	LO	LO	LO	LO	SN	LO	SN		SN	SE	SE	LO	LO	LO	LO	LO
London Bridge 4	⊖ d	06 11														06 36		06 41							
Highbury & Islington	d				05 35						05 55	06 05										06 25		06 33	06 40
Canonbury	d				05 37						05 57	06 07										06 27		06 35	06 42
Dalston Junction Stn ELL	d				05 40	05 50					06 00	06 10	06 20									06 30	06 35	06 40	06 45
Haggerston	d				05 41	05 51					06 01	06 11	06 21									06 31	06 36	06 41	06 46
Hoxton	d				05 43	05 53					06 03	06 13	06 23									06 33	06 38	06 43	06 48
Shoreditch High Street	d				05 46	05 56					06 06	06 16	06 26									06 36	06 41	06 46	06 51
Whitechapel	d				05 48	05 58					06 08	06 18	06 28									06 38	06 43	06 48	06 53
Shadwell	d				05 50	06 00					06 10	06 20	06 30									06 40	06 45	06 50	06 55
Wapping	d				05 52	06 02					06 12	06 22	06 32									06 42	06 47	06 52	06 57
Rotherhithe	d				05 54	06 04					06 14	06 24	06 34									06 44	06 49	06 54	06 59
Canada Water	d				05 56	06 06					06 16	06 26	06 36									06 46	06 51	06 56	07 01
Surrey Quays	d				05 57	06 07					06 17	06 27	06 37									06 47	06 52	06 57	07 02
New Cross ELL	a					06 13							06 43										06 58		
New Cross Gate 4	a				06 01						06 21	06 31				06 41						06 51		07 01	07 06
	d		05 47	05 52	06 02				06 07	06 17	06 22	06 32			06 37	06 41					06 47	06 52		07 02	07 07
Brockley	d		05 49	05 54	06 04				06 09	06 19	06 24	06 34			06 39	06 44					06 49	06 54		07 04	07 09
Honor Oak Park	d		05 52	05 57	06 07				06 12	06 22	06 27	06 37			06 42	06 47					06 52	06 57		07 07	07 12
Forest Hill 4	d		05 55	06 00	06 10				06 15	06 25	06 30	06 40			06 45	06 49					06 55	07 00		07 10	07 15
Sydenham	d		05 57	06 02	06 12				06 17	06 27	06 32	06 42			06 47	06 52					06 57	07 02		07 12	07 17
Crystal Palace 4	d			06a07					06a22		06a37			06 45	06a52							07a07			07a22
Gipsy Hill	d													06 47											
West Norwood 4	d													06 50											
Streatham Hill	d																								
Balham 4	⊖ d																								
Wandsworth Common	d																								
Clapham Junction 10	d																								
South Bermondsey	d	06 15																06 45							
Queens Rd Peckham	d	06 18																06 48							
Peckham Rye 4	d	06 20						06 43						07a01				06 50	07 13	07 17					
Denmark Hill 4	d	06 23						06 47										06 53	07 17	07 21					
London Blackfriars 3	⊖ a																								
Clapham High Street	⊖ d	06 28																06 58							
Wandsworth Road	d	06 29																06 59							
Battersea Park 4	d	06 32																07 02							
London Victoria 15	⊖ a	06 36						06 56										07 06	07 26	07 30					
Penge West	d		06 00		06 15					06 30		06 45				06 54					07 00			07 15	
Anerley	d		06 02		06 17					06 32		06 47				06 56					07 02			07 17	
Norwood Junction 2	d		06 05		06 18					06 35		06 50				07 00					07 05			07 20	
West Croydon 4	a		06 12		06 30					06 41		07 00									07 11			07 30	
East Croydon	a															07 03									

London Bridge to London Victoria - Croydon and East London Line

Network Diagram - see first Page of Table 177

		LO		SN	LO	LO	LO	LO	LO	SN	LO	SN		SN	LO	LO	LO	LO	LO	LO	SE	SE		SN	SN
London Bridge [4] ⊖	d			07 06						07 11		07 33		07 36										07 41	08 03
Highbury & Islington	d				06 48	06 55		07 03	07 10						07 18	07 25		07 33	07 40						
Canonbury	d				06 50	06 57		07 05	07 12						07 20	07 27		07 35	07 42						
Dalston Junction Stn ELL	d	06 50			06 55	07 00	07 05	07 10	07 15		07 20				07 25	07 30	07 35	07 40	07 45	07 50					
Haggerston	d	06 51			06 56	07 01	07 06	07 11	07 16		07 21				07 26	07 31	07 36	07 41	07 46	07 51					
Hoxton	d	06 53			06 58	07 03	07 08	07 13	07 18		07 23				07 28	07 33	07 38	07 43	07 48	07 53					
Shoreditch High Street	d	06 56			07 01	07 06	07 11	07 16	07 21		07 26				07 31	07 36	07 41	07 46	07 51	07 56					
Whitechapel	d	06 58			07 03	07 08	07 13	07 18	07 23		07 28				07 33	07 38	07 43	07 48	07 53	07 58					
Shadwell	d	07 00			07 05	07 10	07 15	07 20	07 25		07 30				07 35	07 40	07 45	07 50	07 55	08 00					
Wapping	d	07 02			07 07	07 12	07 17	07 22	07 27		07 32				07 37	07 42	07 47	07 52	07 57	08 02					
Rotherhithe	d	07 04			07 09	07 14	07 19	07 24	07 29		07 34				07 39	07 44	07 49	07 54	07 59	08 04					
Canada Water	d	07 06			07 11	07 16	07 21	07 26	07 31		07 36				07 41	07 46	07 51	07 56	08 01	08 06					
Surrey Quays	d	07 07			07 12	07 17	07 22	07 27	07 32		07 37				07 42	07 47	07 52	07 57	08 02	08 07					
New Cross ELL	a	07 13					07 28				07 43						07 58			08 13					
New Cross Gate [4]	a			07 11	07 16	07 21		07 31	07 36					07 41	07 46	07 51		08 01	08 06						
	d			07 11	07 17	07 22		07 32	07 37					07 41	07 47	07 52		08 02	08 07						
Brockley	d			07 14	07 19	07 24		07 34	07 39					07 44	07 49	07 54		08 04	08 09						
Honor Oak Park	d			07 17	07 22	07 27		07 37	07 42					07 47	07 52	07 57		08 07	08 12						
Forest Hill [4]	d			07 19	07 25	07 30		07 40	07 45					07 49	07 55	08 00		08 10	08 15						
Sydenham	d			07 22	07 27	07 32		07 42	07 47					07 52	07 57	08 02		08 12	08 17						
Crystal Palace [4]	d					07a37			07a52							08a07			08a22						
Gipsy Hill	d																								
West Norwood [4]	d																								
Streatham Hill	d																								
Balham [4] ⊖	d																								
Wandsworth Common	d																								
Clapham Junction [10]	d																								
South Bermondsey	d									07 15		07 37												07 45	08 07
Queens Rd Peckham	d									07 18		07 39												07 48	08 09
Peckham Rye [4]	d									07 20		07a42									07 43	07 47		07 50	08a12
Denmark Hill [4]	d									07 23											07 47	07 51		07 53	
London Blackfriars [3] ⊖	a																								
Clapham High Street ⊖	d									07 28														07 58	
Wandsworth Road	d									07 29														07 59	
Battersea Park [4]	d									07 32														08 02	
London Victoria [15] ⊖	a									07 36											07 56	08 00		08 06	
Penge West	d			07 24	07 30			07 45						07 54	08 00			08 15							
Anerley	d			07 26	07 32			07 47						07 56	08 02			08 17							
Norwood Junction [2]	d			07 30	07 35			07 50						08 00	08 05			08 20							
West Croydon [4]	a				07 41			08 00							08 11			08 30							
East Croydon	a			07 33										08 03											

		SN	LO	SE	SE	SN	SN	LO		LO	SN	LO	LO	LO	SN	SN	LO	SE		SE	SN	SN	LO	LO	SN
London Bridge [4] ⊖	d	08 06				08 11					08 22				08 33	08 36					08 41				08 52
Highbury & Islington	d		07 48					07 55				08 03	08 10				08 18						08 25		
Canonbury	d		07 50					07 57				08 05	08 12				08 20						08 27		
Dalston Junction Stn ELL	d		07 55					08 00		08 05		08 10	08 15	08 20			08 25						08 30	08 35	
Haggerston	d		07 56					08 01		08 06		08 11	08 16	08 21			08 26						08 31	08 36	
Hoxton	d		07 58					08 03		08 08		08 13	08 18	08 23			08 28						08 33	08 38	
Shoreditch High Street	d		08 01					08 06		08 11		08 16	08 21	08 26			08 31						08 36	08 41	
Whitechapel	d		08 03					08 08		08 13		08 18	08 23	08 28			08 33						08 38	08 43	
Shadwell	d		08 05					08 10		08 15		08 20	08 25	08 30			08 35						08 40	08 45	
Wapping	d		08 07					08 12		08 17		08 22	08 27	08 32			08 37						08 42	08 47	
Rotherhithe	d		08 09					08 14		08 19		08 24	08 29	08 34			08 39						08 44	08 49	
Canada Water	d		08 11					08 16		08 21		08 26	08 31	08 36			08 41						08 46	08 51	
Surrey Quays	d		08 12					08 17		08 22		08 27	08 32	08 37			08 42						08 47	08 52	
New Cross ELL	a									08 28				08 43										08 58	
New Cross Gate [4]	a	08 11	08 16					08 21			08 27	08 31	08 36			08 41	08 46						08 51		08 57
	d	08 11	08 17					08 22			08 27	08 32	08 37			08 41	08 47						08 52		08 57
Brockley	d	08 14	08 19					08 24			08 30	08 34	08 39			08 44	08 49						08 54		09 00
Honor Oak Park	d	08 17	08 22					08 27			08 33	08 37	08 42			08 47	08 52						08 57		09 03
Forest Hill [4]	d	08 19	08 25					08 30			08 35	08 40	08 45			08 49	08 55						09 00		09 05
Sydenham	d	08 22	08 27					08 32			08 38	08 42	08 47			08 52	08 57						09 02		09 08
Crystal Palace [4]	d						08 30	08a37			08 43		08a52									09 00	09a07		09 13
Gipsy Hill	d						08 32				08 45											09 02			09 15
West Norwood [4]	d						08 35				08 48											09 05			09 18
Streatham Hill	d										08 52														09 22
Balham [4] ⊖	d										08 55														09 25
Wandsworth Common	d										08 57														09 27
Clapham Junction [10]	d										09 01														09 32
South Bermondsey	d					08 15									08 37						08 45				
Queens Rd Peckham	d					08 18									08 39						08 48				
Peckham Rye [4]	d			08 13	08 17	08 20	08a46								08a42			08 43		08 47	08 50	09a16			
Denmark Hill [4]	d			08 17	08 21	08 23												08 47		08 51	08 53				
London Blackfriars [3] ⊖	a																								
Clapham High Street ⊖	d					08 28															08 58				
Wandsworth Road	d					08 29															08 59				
Battersea Park [4]	d					08 32					09 05										09 02				09 36
London Victoria [15] ⊖	a			08 26	08 30	08 36					09 09							08 56		09 00	09 06				09 40
Penge West	d	08 24	08 30									08 45				08 54	09 00								
Anerley	d	08 26	08 32									08 47				08 56	09 02								
Norwood Junction [2]	d	08 30	08 35									08 50				09 00	09 05								
West Croydon [4]	a		08 41									09 00					09 12								
East Croydon	a	08 33														09 03									

Table 178

Saturdays

London Bridge to London Victoria - Croydon and East London Line

Network Diagram - see first Page of Table 177

		LO	LO	LO	SN	SN	LO	SE	SE	SN	SN	LO	LO	SN	LO	LO	LO	SN	SN	LO	SE	SE
London Bridge [4] ⊖	d				09 03	09 06				09 11				09 22				09 33	09 36			
Highbury & Islington	d	08 33	08 40				08 48					08 55			09 03	09 10				09 18		
Canonbury	d	08 35	08 42				08 50					08 57			09 05	09 12				09 20		
Dalston Junction Stn ELL	d	08 40	08 45	08 50			08 55					09 00	09 05		09 10	09 15	09 20			09 25		
Haggerston	d	08 41	08 46	08 51			08 56					09 01	09 06		09 11	09 16	09 21			09 26		
Hoxton	d	08 43	08 48	08 53			08 58					09 03	09 08		09 13	09 18	09 23			09 28		
Shoreditch High Street	d	08 46	08 51	08 56			09 01					09 06	09 11		09 16	09 21	09 26			09 31		
Whitechapel	d	08 48	08 53	08 58			09 03					09 08	09 13		09 18	09 23	09 28			09 33		
Shadwell	d	08 50	08 55	09 00			09 05					09 10	09 15		09 20	09 25	09 30			09 35		
Wapping	d	08 52	08 57	09 02			09 07					09 12	09 17		09 22	09 27	09 32			09 37		
Rotherhithe	d	08 54	08 59	09 04			09 09					09 14	09 19		09 24	09 29	09 34			09 39		
Canada Water	d	08 56	09 01	09 06			09 11					09 16	09 21		09 26	09 31	09 36			09 41		
Surrey Quays	d	08 57	09 02	09 07			09 12					09 17	09 22		09 27	09 32	09 37			09 42		
New Cross ELL	a			09 13									09 28				09 43					
New Cross Gate [4]	a	09 01	09 06			09 11	09 16					09 21		09 27	09 31	09 36			09 41	09 46		
	d	09 02	09 07			09 11	09 17					09 22		09 27	09 32	09 37			09 41	09 47		
Brockley	d	09 04	09 09			09 14	09 19					09 24		09 30	09 34	09 39			09 44	09 49		
Honor Oak Park	d	09 07	09 12			09 17	09 22					09 27		09 33	09 37	09 42			09 47	09 52		
Forest Hill [4]	d	09 10	09 15			09 19	09 25					09 30		09 35	09 40	09 45			09 49	09 55		
Sydenham	d	09 12	09 17			09 22	09 27					09 32		09 38	09 42	09 47			09 52	09 57		
Crystal Palace [4]	d		09a22								09 30	09a37		09 43		09a52						
Gipsy Hill	d										09 32			09 45								
West Norwood [4]	d										09 35			09 48								
Streatham Hill	d													09 52								
Balham [4] ⊖	d													09 55								
Wandsworth Common	d													09 57								
Clapham Junction [10]	d													10 01								
South Bermondsey	d				09 07					09 15								09 37				
Queens Rd Peckham	d				09 09					09 18								09 39				
Peckham Rye [4]	d				09a12			09 13	09 17	09 20	09a46							09a42			09 43	09 47
Denmark Hill [4]	d							09 17	09 21	09 23											09 47	09 51
London Blackfriars [3] ⊖	a																					
Clapham High Street ⊖	d									09 28												
Wandsworth Road	d									09 29												
Battersea Park [4]	d									09 32				10 05								
London Victoria [15] ⊖	a							09 26	09 30	09 36				10 09							09 56	10 00
Penge West	d	09 15				09 24	09 30								09 45				09 54	10 00		
Anerley	d	09 17				09 26	09 32								09 47				09 56	10 02		
Norwood Junction [2]	d	09 20				09 30	09 35								09 50				10 00	10 05		
West Croydon [4] 🚋	a	09 30					09 42								10 00					10 12		
East Croydon 🚋	a					09 33													10 03			

		SN	SN	LO	LO	SN		SN	LO	LO	LO	SN	SN	LO	SE	SE	SN	SN	LO	LO	SN	LO
London Bridge [4] ⊖	d	09 41				09 52		16 52				17 03	17 06				17 11				17 22	
Highbury & Islington	d			09 25					16 33	16 40				16 48					16 55			17 03
Canonbury	d			09 27					16 35	16 42				16 50					16 57			17 05
Dalston Junction Stn ELL	d			09 30	09 35				16 40	16 45	16 50			16 55					17 00	17 05		17 10
Haggerston	d			09 31	09 36				16 41	16 46	16 51			16 56					17 01	17 06		17 11
Hoxton	d			09 33	09 38				16 43	16 48	16 53			16 58					17 03	17 08		17 13
Shoreditch High Street	d			09 36	09 41				16 46	16 51	16 56			17 01					17 06	17 11		17 16
Whitechapel	d			09 38	09 43				16 48	16 53	16 58			17 03					17 08	17 13		17 18
Shadwell	d			09 40	09 45				16 50	16 55	17 00			17 05					17 10	17 15		17 20
Wapping	d			09 42	09 47				16 52	16 57	17 02			17 07					17 12	17 17		17 22
Rotherhithe	d			09 44	09 49				16 54	16 59	17 04			17 09					17 14	17 19		17 24
Canada Water	d			09 46	09 51				16 56	17 01	17 06			17 11					17 16	17 21		17 26
Surrey Quays	d			09 47	09 52				16 57	17 02	17 07			17 12					17 17	17 22		17 27
New Cross ELL	a				09 58						17 13									17 28		
New Cross Gate [4]	a			09 51		09 57		16 57	17 01	17 06			17 11	17 16					17 21		17 27	17 31
	d			09 52		09 57		16 57	17 02	17 07			17 11	17 17					17 22		17 27	17 32
Brockley	d			09 54		10 00	and at the same minutes past each hour until	17 00	17 04	17 09			17 14	17 19					17 24		17 30	17 34
Honor Oak Park	d			09 57		10 03		17 03	17 07	17 12			17 17	17 22					17 27		17 33	17 37
Forest Hill [4]	d			10 00		10 05		17 05	17 10	17 15			17 19	17 25					17 30		17 35	17 40
Sydenham	d			10 02		10 08		17 08	17 12	17 17			17 22	17 27					17 32		17 38	17 42
Crystal Palace [4]	d		10 00	10a07		10 13		17 13		17a22								17 30	17a37		17 43	
Gipsy Hill	d		10 02			10 15		17 15										17 32			17 45	
West Norwood [4]	d		10 05			10 18		17 18										17 35			17 48	
Streatham Hill	d					10 22		17 22													17 52	
Balham [4] ⊖	d					10 25		17 25													17 55	
Wandsworth Common	d					10 27		17 27													17 57	
Clapham Junction [10]	d					10 31		17 31													18 01	
South Bermondsey	d	09 45										17 07					17 15					
Queens Rd Peckham	d	09 48										17 09					17 18					
Peckham Rye [4]	d	09 50	10a16									17a12			17 13	17 17	17 20	17a46				
Denmark Hill [4]	d	09 53													17 17	17 21	17 23					
London Blackfriars [3] ⊖	a																					
Clapham High Street ⊖	d	09 58															17 28					
Wandsworth Road	d	09 59															17 29					
Battersea Park [4]	d	10 02				10 35		17 35									17 32				18 05	
London Victoria [15] ⊖	a	10 06				10 39		17 39							17 26	17 30	17 36				18 09	
Penge West	d								17 15				17 24	17 30								17 45
Anerley	d								17 17				17 26	17 32								17 47
Norwood Junction [2]	d								17 20				17 30	17 35								17 50
West Croydon [4] 🚋	a								17 30					17 42								18 00
East Croydon 🚋	a												17 33									

Table 178

Saturdays

London Bridge to London Victoria - Croydon and East London Line

Network Diagram - see first Page of Table 177

Station		LO	LO	SN	SN	LO		SE	SE	SN	SN	LO	LO	SN	LO	LO		LO	SN	SN	LO	SE	SE	SN	SN
London Bridge 4 ⊖	d			17 33	17 36					17 41				17 52					18 03	18 06				18 11	
Highbury & Islington	d	17 10				17 18						17 25			17 33	17 40					17 48				
Canonbury	d	17 12				17 20						17 27			17 35	17 42					17 50				
Dalston Junction Stn ELL	d	17 15	17 20			17 25						17 30	17 35		17 40	17 45		17 50			17 55				
Haggerston	d	17 16	17 21			17 26						17 31	17 36		17 41	17 46		17 51			17 56				
Hoxton	d	17 18	17 23			17 28						17 33	17 38		17 43	17 48		17 53			17 58				
Shoreditch High Street	d	17 21	17 26			17 31						17 36	17 41		17 46	17 51		17 56			18 01				
Whitechapel	d	17 23	17 28			17 33						17 38	17 43		17 48	17 53		17 58			18 03				
Shadwell	d	17 25	17 30			17 35						17 40	17 45		17 50	17 55		18 00			18 05				
Wapping	d	17 27	17 32			17 37						17 42	17 47		17 52	17 57		18 02			18 07				
Rotherhithe	d	17 29	17 34			17 39						17 44	17 49		17 54	17 59		18 04			18 09				
Canada Water	d	17 31	17 36			17 41						17 46	17 51		17 56	18 01		18 06			18 11				
Surrey Quays	d	17 32	17 37			17 42						17 47	17 52		17 57	18 02		18 07			18 12				
New Cross ELL	a		17 43										17 58					18 13							
New Cross Gate 4	a	17 36			17 41	17 46						17 51		17 57	18 01	18 06				18 11	18 16				
	d	17 37			17 41	17 47						17 52		17 57	18 02	18 07				18 11	18 17				
Brockley	d	17 39			17 44	17 49						17 54		18 00	18 04	18 09				18 14	18 19				
Honor Oak Park	d	17 42			17 47	17 52						17 57		18 03	18 07	18 12				18 17	18 22				
Forest Hill 4	d	17 45			17 49	17 55						18 00		18 05	18 10	18 15				18 19	18 25				
Sydenham	d	17 47			17 52	17 57						18 02		18 08	18 12	18 17				18 22	18 27				
Crystal Palace 4	d	17a52									18 00	18a07		18 13		18a22									18 30
Gipsy Hill	d										18 02			18 15											18 32
West Norwood 4	d										18 05			18 18											18 35
Streatham Hill	d													18 22											
Balham 4 ⊖	d													18 25											
Wandsworth Common	d													18 27											
Clapham Junction 10	d													18 31											
South Bermondsey	d			17 37						17 45									18 07					18 15	
Queens Rd Peckham	d			17 39						17 48									18 09					18 18	
Peckham Rye 4	d			17a42				17 43	17 47	17 50	18a16								18a12			18 13	18 17	18 20	18a46
Denmark Hill 4	d							17 47	17 51	17 53												18 17	18 21	18 23	
London Blackfriars 3 ⊖	a																								
Clapham High Street ⊖	d									17 58														18 28	
Wandsworth Road	d									17 59														18 29	
Battersea Park 4	d									18 02				18 35										18 32	
London Victoria 15 ⊖	a							17 56	18 00	18 06				18 39								18 26	18 30	18 36	
Penge West	d				17 54	18 00									18 15					18 24	18 30				
Anerley	d				17 56	18 02									18 17					18 26	18 32				
Norwood Junction 2	d				18 00	18 05									18 20					18 30	18 35				
West Croydon 4	a					18 11									18 30						18 41				
East Croydon	a				18 03															18 33					

Station		LO		LO	SN	LO	LO	LO	SN	SN	LO	SE		SE	SN	SN	LO	LO	SN	LO	LO	LO		SN	SN
London Bridge 4 ⊖	d				18 22				18 33	18 36					18 41				18 52					19 03	19 06
Highbury & Islington	d	17 55				18 03	18 10				18 18						18 25			18 33	18 40				
Canonbury	d	17 57				18 05	18 12				18 20						18 27			18 35	18 42				
Dalston Junction Stn ELL	d	18 00		18 05		18 10	18 15	18 20			18 25						18 30	18 35		18 40	18 45	18 50			
Haggerston	d	18 01		18 06		18 11	18 16	18 21			18 26						18 31	18 36		18 41	18 46	18 51			
Hoxton	d	18 03		18 08		18 13	18 18	18 23			18 28						18 33	18 38		18 43	18 48	18 53			
Shoreditch High Street	d	18 06		18 11		18 16	18 21	18 26			18 31						18 36	18 41		18 46	18 51	18 56			
Whitechapel	d	18 08		18 13		18 18	18 23	18 28			18 33						18 38	18 43		18 48	18 53	18 58			
Shadwell	d	18 10		18 15		18 20	18 25	18 30			18 35						18 40	18 45		18 50	18 55	19 00			
Wapping	d	18 12		18 17		18 22	18 27	18 32			18 37						18 42	18 47		18 52	18 57	19 02			
Rotherhithe	d	18 14		18 19		18 24	18 29	18 34			18 39						18 44	18 49		18 54	18 59	19 04			
Canada Water	d	18 16		18 21		18 26	18 31	18 36			18 41						18 46	18 51		18 56	19 01	19 06			
Surrey Quays	d	18 17		18 22		18 27	18 32	18 37			18 42						18 47	18 52		18 57	19 02	19 07			
New Cross ELL	a			18 28				18 43										18 58				19 13			
New Cross Gate 4	a	18 21			18 27	18 31	18 36			18 41	18 46						18 51		18 57	19 01	19 06				19 11
	d	18 22			18 27	18 32	18 37			18 41	18 47						18 52		18 57	19 02	19 07				19 11
Brockley	d	18 24			18 30	18 34	18 39			18 44	18 49						18 54		19 00	19 04	19 09				19 14
Honor Oak Park	d	18 27			18 33	18 37	18 42			18 47	18 52						18 57		19 03	19 07	19 12				19 17
Forest Hill 4	d	18 30			18 35	18 40	18 45			18 49	18 55						19 00		19 05	19 10	19 15				19 19
Sydenham	d	18 32			18 38	18 42	18 47			18 52	18 57						19 02		19 08	19 12	19 17				19 22
Crystal Palace 4	d	18a37			18 43		18a52									19 00	19a07		19 13		19a22				
Gipsy Hill	d				18 45											19 02			19 15						
West Norwood 4	d				18 48											19 05			19 18						
Streatham Hill	d				18 52														19 22						
Balham 4 ⊖	d				18 55														19 25						
Wandsworth Common	d				18 57														19 27						
Clapham Junction 10	d				19 01														19 31						
South Bermondsey	d								18 37						18 45									19 07	
Queens Rd Peckham	d								18 39						18 48									19 09	
Peckham Rye 4	d								18a42			18 43		18 47	18 50	19a16								19a12	
Denmark Hill 4	d											18 47		18 51	18 53										
London Blackfriars 3 ⊖	a																								
Clapham High Street ⊖	d														18 58										
Wandsworth Road	d														18 59										
Battersea Park 4	d				19 05										19 02				19 35						
London Victoria 15 ⊖	a				19 09							18 56		19 00	19 06				19 39						
Penge West	d					18 45				18 54	19 00									19 15					19 24
Anerley	d					18 47				18 56	19 02									19 17					19 26
Norwood Junction 2	d					18 50				19 00	19 05									19 20					19 30
West Croydon 4	a					19 00					19 11									19 30					
East Croydon	a									19 03															19 33

Table 178

Saturdays

London Bridge to London Victoria - Croydon and East London Line

Network Diagram - see first Page of Table 177

		LO	SE	SE	SN	SN	LO	LO		SN	LO	LO	LO	SN	SN	LO	SE	SN		SN	LO	LO	SN	LO	LO
London Bridge 4 ⊖	d				19 11					19 22				19 33	19 36			19 41					19 52		
Highbury & Islington	d	18 48					18 55				19 03	19 10				19 18					19 25			19 33	19 40
Canonbury	d	18 50					18 57				19 05	19 12				19 20					19 27			19 35	19 42
Dalston Junction Stn ELL	d	18 55					19 00	19 05			19 10	19 15	19 20			19 25					19 30	19 35		19 40	19 45
Haggerston	d	18 56					19 01	19 06			19 11	19 16	19 21			19 26					19 31	19 36		19 41	19 46
Hoxton	d	18 58					19 03	19 08			19 13	19 18	19 23			19 28					19 33	19 38		19 43	19 48
Shoreditch High Street	d	19 01					19 06	19 11			19 16	19 21	19 26			19 31					19 36	19 41		19 46	19 51
Whitechapel	d	19 03					19 08	19 13			19 18	19 23	19 28			19 33					19 38	19 43		19 48	19 53
Shadwell	d	19 05					19 10	19 15			19 20	19 25	19 30			19 35					19 40	19 45		19 50	19 55
Wapping	d	19 07					19 12	19 17			19 22	19 27	19 32			19 37					19 42	19 47		19 52	19 57
Rotherhithe	d	19 09					19 14	19 19			19 24	19 29	19 34			19 39					19 44	19 49		19 54	19 59
Canada Water	d	19 11					19 16	19 21			19 26	19 31	19 36			19 41					19 46	19 51		19 56	20 01
Surrey Quays	d	19 12					19 17	19 22			19 27	19 32	19 37			19 42					19 47	19 52		19 57	20 02
New Cross ELL	a							19 28					19 43									19 58			
New Cross Gate 4	a	19 16					19 21			19 27	19 31	19 36			19 41	19 46					19 51		19 57	20 01	20 06
	d	19 17					19 22			19 27	19 32	19 37			19 41	19 47					19 52		19 57	20 02	20 07
Brockley	d	19 19					19 24			19 30	19 34	19 39			19 44	19 49					19 54		20 00	20 04	20 09
Honor Oak Park	d	19 22					19 27			19 33	19 37	19 42			19 47	19 52					19 57		20 03	20 07	20 12
Forest Hill 4	d	19 25					19 30			19 35	19 40	19 45			19 49	19 55					20 00		20 05	20 10	20 15
Sydenham	d	19 27					19 32			19 38	19 42	19 47			19 52	19 57					20 02		20 08	20 12	20 17
Crystal Palace 4	d					19 30	19a37			19 43		19a52								20 00	20a07		20 13		20a22
Gipsy Hill	d					19 32				19 45										20 03			20 15		
West Norwood 4	d					19 35				19 48										20 06			20 18		
Streatham Hill	d									19 52													20 22		
Balham 4 ⊖	d									19 55													20 25		
Wandsworth Common	d									19 57													20 27		
Clapham Junction 10	d									20 01													20 31		
South Bermondsey	d				19 15									19 37				19 45							
Queens Rd Peckham	d				19 18									19 39				19 48							
Peckham Rye 4	d		19 13	19 17	19 20	19a46								19a42			19 43	19 50		20a16					
Denmark Hill 4	d		19 17	19 21	19 23												19 47	19 53							
London Blackfriars 3 ⊖	a																								
Clapham High Street ⊖	d				19 28													19 58							
Wandsworth Road	d				19 29													19 59							
Battersea Park 4	d				19 32					20 05								20 02					20 35		
London Victoria 15 ⊖	a		19 26	19 30	19 36					20 09							19 56	20 06					20 39		
Penge West	d	19 30									19 45				19 54	20 00								20 15	
Anerley	d	19 32									19 47				19 56	20 02								20 17	
Norwood Junction 2	d	19 35									19 50				20 00	20 05								20 20	
West Croydon 4	a	19 41									20 00					20 15								20 30	
East Croydon	a														20 03										

		LO	SN	SN		LO	SE	SN	SN	LO	LO	SN	LO	LO		LO	SN	SN	LO	SE	SN	SN	LO	LO	
London Bridge 4 ⊖	d		20 03	20 06				20 11				20 22					20 33	20 36			20 41				
Highbury & Islington	d					19 48				19 55			20 03	20 10					20 18				20 25		
Canonbury	d					19 50				19 57			20 05	20 12					20 20				20 27		
Dalston Junction Stn ELL	d	19 50				19 55				20 00	20 05		20 10	20 15		20 20			20 25				20 30	20 35	
Haggerston	d	19 51				19 56				20 01	20 06		20 11	20 16		20 21			20 26				20 31	20 36	
Hoxton	d	19 53				19 58				20 03	20 08		20 13	20 18		20 23			20 28				20 33	20 38	
Shoreditch High Street	d	19 56				20 01				20 06	20 11		20 16	20 21		20 26			20 31				20 36	20 41	
Whitechapel	d	19 58				20 03				20 08	20 13		20 18	20 23		20 28			20 33				20 38	20 43	
Shadwell	d	20 00				20 05				20 10	20 15		20 20	20 25		20 30			20 35				20 40	20 45	
Wapping	d	20 02				20 07				20 12	20 17		20 22	20 27		20 32			20 37				20 42	20 47	
Rotherhithe	d	20 04				20 09				20 14	20 19		20 24	20 29		20 34			20 39				20 44	20 49	
Canada Water	d	20 06				20 11				20 16	20 21		20 26	20 31		20 36			20 41				20 46	20 51	
Surrey Quays	d	20 07				20 12				20 17	20 22		20 27	20 32		20 37			20 42				20 47	20 52	
New Cross ELL	a	20 13									20 28					20 43								20 58	
New Cross Gate 4	a			20 11		20 16				20 21		20 27	20 31	20 36				20 41	20 46				20 51		
	d			20 11		20 17				20 22		20 27	20 32	20 37				20 41	20 47				20 52		
Brockley	d			20 14		20 19				20 24		20 30	20 34	20 39				20 44	20 49				20 54		
Honor Oak Park	d			20 17		20 22				20 27		20 33	20 37	20 42				20 47	20 52				20 57		
Forest Hill 4	d			20 19		20 25				20 30		20 35	20 40	20 45				20 49	20 55				21 00		
Sydenham	d			20 22		20 27				20 32		20 38	20 42	20 47				20 52	20 57				21 02		
Crystal Palace 4	d								20 30	20a37		20 43		20a52								21 00	21a07		
Gipsy Hill	d								20 33			20 45										21 02			
West Norwood 4	d								20 36			20 48										21 05			
Streatham Hill	d											20 52													
Balham 4 ⊖	d											20 55													
Wandsworth Common	d											20 57													
Clapham Junction 10	d											21 01													
South Bermondsey	d		20 07					20 15									20 37				20 45				
Queens Rd Peckham	d		20 09					20 18									20 39				20 48				
Peckham Rye 4	d		20a12				20 13	20 20	20a46								20a42			20 43	20 50	21a16			
Denmark Hill 4	d						20 17	20 23												20 47	20 53				
London Blackfriars 3 ⊖	a																								
Clapham High Street ⊖	d							20 28													20 58				
Wandsworth Road	d							20 29													20 59				
Battersea Park 4	d							20 32				21 05									21 02				
London Victoria 15 ⊖	a						20 26	20 36				21 09								20 56	21 06				
Penge West	d			20 24		20 30							20 45					20 54	21 00						
Anerley	d			20 26		20 32							20 47					20 56	21 02						
Norwood Junction 2	d			20 30		20 35							20 50					21 00	21 05						
West Croydon 4	a					20 45							21 00						21 15						
East Croydon	a			20 33														21 03							

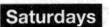

London Bridge to London Victoria - Croydon and East London Line

Network Diagram - see first Page of Table 177

		SN	LO	LO	LO	SN	SN	LO	SE	SN		SN	LO	LO	SN	LO	LO	LO	SN	SN		LO	SE	SN	SN
London Bridge 4 ⊖	d	20 52				21 03	21 06			21 11					21 22				21 33	21 36				21 41	
Highbury & Islington	d		20 33	20 40				20 48					20 55			21 03	21 10					21 18			
Canonbury	d		20 35	20 42				20 50					20 57			21 05	21 12					21 20			
Dalston Junction Stn ELL	d		20 40	20 45	20 50			20 55					21 00	21 05		21 10	21 15	21 20				21 25			
Haggerston	d		20 41	20 46	20 51			20 56					21 01	21 06		21 11	21 16	21 21				21 26			
Hoxton	d		20 43	20 48	20 53			20 58					21 03	21 08		21 13	21 18	21 23				21 28			
Shoreditch High Street	d		20 46	20 51	20 56			21 01					21 06	21 11		21 16	21 21	21 26				21 31			
Whitechapel	d		20 48	20 53	20 58			21 03					21 08	21 13		21 18	21 23	21 28				21 33			
Shadwell	d		20 50	20 55	21 00			21 05					21 10	21 15		21 20	21 25	21 30				21 35			
Wapping	d		20 52	20 57	21 02			21 07					21 12	21 17		21 22	21 27	21 32				21 37			
Rotherhithe	d		20 54	20 59	21 04			21 09					21 14	21 19		21 24	21 29	21 34				21 39			
Canada Water	d		20 56	21 01	21 06			21 11					21 16	21 21		21 26	21 31	21 36				21 41			
Surrey Quays	d		20 57	21 02	21 07			21 12					21 17	21 22		21 27	21 32	21 37				21 42			
New Cross ELL	a				21 13									21 28				21 43							
New Cross Gate 4	a	20 57	21 01	21 06			21 11	21 16					21 21		21 27	21 31	21 36			21 41		21 46			
	d	20 57	21 02	21 07			21 11	21 17					21 22		21 27	21 32	21 37			21 41		21 47			
Brockley	d	21 00	21 04	21 09			21 14	21 19					21 24		21 30	21 34	21 39			21 44		21 49			
Honor Oak Park	d	21 03	21 07	21 12			21 17	21 22					21 27		21 33	21 37	21 42			21 47		21 52			
Forest Hill 4	d	21 05	21 10	21 15			21 19	21 25					21 30		21 35	21 40	21 45			21 49		21 55			
Sydenham	d	21 08	21 12	21 17			21 22	21 27					21 32		21 38	21 42	21 47			21 52		21 57			
Crystal Palace 4	d	21 13		21a22								21 30	21a37		21 43		21a52								22 00
Gipsy Hill	d	21 15										21 32			21 45										22 02
West Norwood 4	d	21 18										21 35			21 48										22 05
Streatham Hill	d	21 22													21 52										
Balham 4 ⊖	d	21 25													21 55										
Wandsworth Common	d	21 27													21 57										
Clapham Junction 10	d	21 31													22 01										
South Bermondsey	d					21 07				21 15									21 37					21 45	
Queens Rd Peckham	d					21 09				21 18									21 39					21 48	
Peckham Rye 4	d					21a12			21 13	21 20		21a46							21a42				21 43	21 50	22a16
Denmark Hill 4	d								21 17	21 23													21 47	21 53	
London Blackfriars 3 ⊖	a																								
Clapham High Street ⊖	d									21 28														21 58	
Wandsworth Road	d									21 29														21 59	
Battersea Park 4	d	21 35								21 32					22 05									22 02	
London Victoria 15 ⊖	a	21 39							21 26	21 36					22 09								21 56	22 06	
Penge West	d		21 15				21 24	21 30								21 45				21 54		22 00			
Anerley	d		21 17				21 26	21 32								21 47				21 56		22 02			
Norwood Junction 2	d		21 20				21 30	21 35								21 50				22 00		22 05			
West Croydon 4 🚌	a		21 30					21 45								22 00						22 12			
East Croydon 🚌	a						21 33													22 04					

		LO	LO	SN	LO	LO		LO	SN	SN	LO	SE	SN	SN	LO	SN		LO	LO	SN	SN	SE	SN	SN	LO
London Bridge 4 ⊖	d			21 52					22 03	22 06			22 11			22 22				22 33	22 36		22 41		
Highbury & Islington	d	21 25			21 33	21 40					21 48				21 55			22 05							22 25
Canonbury	d	21 27			21 35	21 42					21 50				21 57			22 07							22 27
Dalston Junction Stn ELL	d	21 30	21 35		21 40	21 45		21 50			21 55				22 00			22 10	22 20						22 30
Haggerston	d	21 31	21 36		21 41	21 46		21 51			21 56				22 01			22 11	22 21						22 31
Hoxton	d	21 33	21 38		21 43	21 48		21 53			21 58				22 03			22 13	22 23						22 33
Shoreditch High Street	d	21 36	21 41		21 46	21 51		21 56			22 01				22 06			22 16	22 26						22 36
Whitechapel	d	21 38	21 43		21 48	21 53		21 58			22 03				22 08			22 18	22 28						22 38
Shadwell	d	21 40	21 45		21 50	21 55		22 00			22 05				22 10			22 20	22 30						22 40
Wapping	d	21 42	21 47		21 52	21 57		22 02			22 07				22 12			22 22	22 32						22 42
Rotherhithe	d	21 44	21 49		21 54	21 59		22 04			22 09				22 14			22 24	22 34						22 44
Canada Water	d	21 46	21 51		21 56	22 01		22 06			22 11				22 16			22 26	22 36						22 46
Surrey Quays	d	21 47	21 52		21 57	22 02		22 07			22 12				22 17			22 27	22 37						22 47
New Cross ELL	a		21 58					22 13											22 43						
New Cross Gate 4	a	21 51		21 57	22 01	22 06				22 11	22 16				22 21	22 27		22 31			22 41				22 51
	d	21 52		21 57	22 02	22 07				22 11	22 17				22 22	22 27		22 32			22 41				22 52
Brockley	d	21 54		22 00	22 04	22 09				22 14	22 19				22 24	22 30		22 34			22 44				22 54
Honor Oak Park	d	21 57		22 03	22 07	22 12				22 17	22 22				22 27	22 33		22 37			22 47				22 57
Forest Hill 4	d	22 00		22 05	22 10	22 15				22 19	22 25				22 30	22 35		22 40			22 49				23 00
Sydenham	d	22 02		22 08	22 12	22 17				22 22	22 27				22 32	22 38		22 42			22 52				23 02
Crystal Palace 4	d	22a07		22 13		22a22								22 30	22a37	22 43								23 00	23a07
Gipsy Hill	d			22 15										22 32		22 45								23 02	
West Norwood 4	d			22 18										22 35		22 48								23 05	
Streatham Hill	d			22 22												22 52									
Balham 4 ⊖	d			22 25												22 55									
Wandsworth Common	d			22 27												22 57									
Clapham Junction 10	d			22 31												23 01									
South Bermondsey	d								22 07				22 15							22 37			22 45		
Queens Rd Peckham	d								22 09				22 18							22 39			22 48		
Peckham Rye 4	d								22a12			22 13	22 20	22a46						22a42		22 43	22 50	23a16	
Denmark Hill 4	d											22 17	22 23									22 47	22 53		
London Blackfriars 3 ⊖	a																								
Clapham High Street ⊖	d												22 28										22 58		
Wandsworth Road	d												22 29										22 59		
Battersea Park 4	d			22 35									22 32			23 05							23 02		
London Victoria 15 ⊖	a			22 39								22 26	22 36			23 09						22 56	23 06		
Penge West	d				22 15					22 24	22 30							22 45			22 54				
Anerley	d				22 17					22 26	22 32							22 47			22 56				
Norwood Junction 2	d				22 20					22 30	22 35							22 50			23 00				
West Croydon 4 🚌	a				22 30						22 42							23 00							
East Croydon 🚌	a									22 35											23 03				

Table 178

Saturdays

London Bridge to London Victoria - Croydon and East London Line

Network Diagram - see first Page of Table 177

		SN		LO	LO	SN	SN	SE	SN	SN	LO	SN		LO	LO	SN	SN	LO	SN	LO	LO	LO			
London Bridge 4 ⊖	d	22 52				23 03	23 06		23 11			23 22				23 33	23 36		23 52						
Highbury & Islington	d			22 35							22 55			23 05				23 25		23 35	23 42	23 56			
Canonbury	d			22 37							22 57			23 07				23 27		23 37	23 44	23 58			
Dalston Junction Stn ELL	d			22 40	22 50						23 00			23 10	23 20			23 30		23 40	23 47	00 02			
Haggerston	d			22 41	22 51						23 01			23 11	23 21			23 31		23 41	23 48	00 03			
Hoxton	d			22 43	22 53						23 03			23 13	23 23			23 33		23 43	23 50	00 05			
Shoreditch High Street	d			22 46	22 56						23 06			23 16	23 26			23 36		23 46	23 53	00 08			
Whitechapel	d			22 48	22 58						23 08			23 18	23 28			23 38		23 48	23 55	00 10			
Shadwell	d			22 50	23 00						23 10			23 20	23 30			23 40		23 50	23 57	00 12			
Wapping	d			22 52	23 02						23 12			23 22	23 32			23 42		23 52	23 59	00 14			
Rotherhithe	d			22 54	23 04						23 14			23 24	23 34			23 44		23 54	00 01	00 16			
Canada Water	d			22 56	23 06						23 16			23 26	23 36			23 46		23 56	00 03	00 18			
Surrey Quays	d			22 57	23 07						23 17			23 27	23 37			23 47		23 57	00 05	00 19			
New Cross ELL	a				23 13										23 43										
New Cross Gate 4	a	22 57		23 01			23 11				23 21	23 27		23 31			23 41	23 51	23 57	00 02	00 08	00 23			
	d	22 57		23 02			23 11				23 22	23 27		23 32			23 41	23 52	23 57	00 02					
Brockley	d	23 00		23 04			23 14				23 24	23 30		23 34			23 44	23 54	00 01	00 04					
Honor Oak Park	d	23 03		23 07			23 17				23 27	23 33		23 37			23 47	23 57	00 04	00 07					
Forest Hill 4	d	23 05		23 10			23 19				23 30	23 35		23 40			23 49	23 59	00 06	00 10					
Sydenham	d	23 08		23 12			23 22				23 32	23 38		23 42			23 52	00 02	00 09	00 12					
Crystal Palace 4	d	23 13								23 30	23a37	23 43						00a07	00 13						
Gipsy Hill	d	23 15								23 32		23 45							00 15						
West Norwood 4	d	23 18								23 35		23 48							00 18						
Streatham Hill	d	23 22										23 52							00 22						
Balham 4 ⊖	d	23 25										23 55							00 26						
Wandsworth Common	d	23 27										23 57							00 28						
Clapham Junction 10	d	23 31										00 02							00 32						
South Bermondsey	d					23 07			23 15							23 37									
Queens Rd Peckham	d					23 09			23 18							23 39									
Peckham Rye 4	d					23 12		23 13	23 20	23a46						23 42									
Denmark Hill 4	d							23 17	23 23																
London Blackfriars 3 ⊖	a																								
Clapham High Street ⊖	d								23 28																
Wandsworth Road	d								23 29																
Battersea Park 4	d	23 35							23 32			00 05							00 35						
London Victoria 15 ⊖	a	23 41						23 26	23 37			00 10							00 42						
Penge West	d			23 15			23 24							23 45			23 54			00 15					
Anerley	d			23 17			23 26							23 47			23 56			00 17					
Norwood Junction 2	d			23 20		23a34	23 30							23 50		00a04	23 59			00 20					
West Croydon 4	a			23 30										23 59						00 27					
East Croydon	a						23 33										00 03								

Sundays

		SN A	SN A	SN A	LO A	SN A	LO A	LO A	SN	SN		LO A	LO	SN	SN	SN	SN		SN			SE	SN	SN	LO
London Bridge 4 ⊖	d	23p22	23p36			23p52			00 03	00 06						00 33	00 36						07 11		
Highbury & Islington	d				23p25		23p35	23p42				23p56	00 10												
Canonbury	d				23p27		23p37	23p44				23p58	00 12												
Dalston Junction Stn ELL	d				23p30		23p40	23p47				00 02	00 15												
Haggerston	d				23p31		23p41	23p48				00 03	00 16												
Hoxton	d				23p33		23p43	23p50				00 05	00 18												
Shoreditch High Street	d				23p36		23p46	23p53				00 08	00 21												
Whitechapel	d				23p38		23p48	23p55				00 10	00 23												
Shadwell	d				23p40		23p50	23p57				00 12	00 25												
Wapping	d				23p42		23p52	23p59				00 14	00 27												
Rotherhithe	d				23p44		23p54	00 01				00 16	00 29												
Canada Water	d				23p46		23p56	00 03				00 18	00 31												
Surrey Quays	d				23p47		23p57	00 05				00 19	00 32												
New Cross ELL	a																								
New Cross Gate 4	a	23p27	23p41		23p51	23p57	00 02	00 08		00 11		00 23	00 36				00 41								
	d	23p27	23p41		23p52	23p57	00 02			00 11							00 41								07 04
Brockley	d	23p30	23p44		23p54	00 01	00 04			00 14							00 44								07 06
Honor Oak Park	d	23p33	23p47		23p57	00 04	00 07			00 17							00 47								07 09
Forest Hill 4	d	23p35	23p49		23p59	00 06	00 10			00 19							00 49								07 12
Sydenham	d	23p38	23p52		00 02	00 09	00 12			00 22							00 52								07 14
Crystal Palace 4	d	23p43		00 03	00a07	00 13								00 33	00 47				01 03					07 07	
Gipsy Hill	d	23p45				00 15																		07 09	
West Norwood 4	d	23p48				00 18																		07 12	
Streatham Hill	d	23p52				00 22																			
Balham 4 ⊖	d	23p55				00 26																			
Wandsworth Common	d	23p57				00 28																			
Clapham Junction 10	d	00 02				00 32																			
South Bermondsey	d								00 07							00 37							07 15		
Queens Rd Peckham	d								00 09							00 39							07 18		
Peckham Rye 4	d								00 12							00 42						07 12	07 20	07a23	
Denmark Hill 4	d																					07 16	07 23		
London Blackfriars 3 ⊖	a																								
Clapham High Street ⊖	d																						07 28		
Wandsworth Road	d																						07 29		
Battersea Park 4	d	00 05				00 35																	07 32		
London Victoria 15 ⊖	a	00 10				00 42																07 25	07 36		
Penge West	d		23p54				00 15			00 24							00 54								07 17
Anerley	d		23p56				00 17			00 26							00 56								07 19
Norwood Junction 2	d		23p59	00 09			00 20		00a34	00 30				00 38	00 52	01a04	01 00		01 08						07 22
West Croydon 4	a			00 14			00 27							00 43	00 58				01 13						07 29
East Croydon	a		00 03							00 33							01 03								

A not 11 December

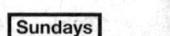

London Bridge to London Victoria - Croydon and East London Line

Network Diagram - see first Page of Table 177

		LO	SN	LO	SE	SN		SN	SN	SN	LO	SN	LO	SE	SN	SN		SN	SN	LO	SN	LO	LO	SE	SN
London Bridge 4 ⊖	d		07 24			07 36		07 39	07 41			07 54			08 06	08 09		08 11			08 24				08 36
Highbury & Islington	d	06 51		07 05							07 21		07 35							07 51		08 05	08 15		
Canonbury	d	06 53		07 07							07 23		07 37							07 53		08 07	08 17		
Dalston Junction Stn ELL	d	06 56		07 12							07 26		07 42							07 56		08 12	08 22		
Haggerston	d	06 57		07 13							07 27		07 43							07 57		08 13	08 23		
Hoxton	d	06 59		07 15							07 29		07 45							07 59		08 15	08 25		
Shoreditch High Street	d	07 02		07 18							07 32		07 48							08 02		08 18	08 28		
Whitechapel	d	07 04		07 20							07 34		07 50							08 04		08 20	08 30		
Shadwell	d	07 06		07 22							07 36		07 52							08 06		08 22	08 32		
Wapping	d	07 08		07 24							07 38		07 54							08 08		08 24	08 34		
Rotherhithe	d	07 10		07 26							07 40		07 56							08 10		08 26	08 36		
Canada Water	d	07 12		07 28							07 42		07 58							08 12		08 28	08 38		
Surrey Quays	d	07 13		07 29							07 43		07 59							08 13		08 29	08 39		
New Cross ELL	a																						08 45		
New Cross Gate 4	a	07 17	07 29	07 33				07 44			07 47	07 59	08 03			08 14				08 17	08 29	08 33			
	d	07 18	07 29	07 34				07 44			07 48	07 59	08 03			08 14				08 18	08 29	08 34			
Brockley	d	07 20	07 32	07 36				07 47			07 50	08 02	08 06			08 17				08 20	08 32	08 36			
Honor Oak Park	d	07 23	07 35	07 39				07 50			07 53	08 05	08 09			08 20				08 23	08 35	08 39			
Forest Hill 4	d	07 26	07 37	07 42				07 52			07 56	08 07	08 12			08 22				08 26	08 37	08 42			
Sydenham	d	07 28	07 40	07 44				07 55			07 58	08 10	08 14			08 25				08 28	08 40	08 44			
Crystal Palace 4	d	07a33								07 37	08a03								08 07	08a33					
Gipsy Hill	d									07 39									08 09						
West Norwood 4	d									07 42									08 12						
Streatham Hill	d																								
Balham 4 ⊖	d																								
Wandsworth Common	d																								
Clapham Junction 10	d																								
South Bermondsey	d					07 40			07 45						08 10			08 15							08 40
Queens Rd Peckham	d					07 42			07 48						08 12			08 18							08 42
Peckham Rye 4	d				07 42	07a45			07 50	07a53				08 12	08a15			08 20	08a23					08 42	08a45
Denmark Hill 4	d				07 46				07 53					08 16				08 23						08 46	
London Blackfriars 3 ⊖	a																								
Clapham High Street ⊖	d								07 58									08 28							
Wandsworth Road	d								07 59									08 29							
Battersea Park 4	d								08 02									08 32							
London Victoria 15 ⊖	a				07 55				08 06					08 25				08 36						08 55	
Penge West	d			07 47				07 57					08 17			08 27						08 47			
Anerley	d			07 49				07 59					08 19			08 29						08 49			
Norwood Junction 2	d		07 48	07 52				08 03				08 16	08 22			08 33					08 46	08 52			
West Croydon 4	a		07 55	07 59								08 24	08 28								08 54	08 58			
East Croydon	a							08 07								08 37									

		SN		SN	SN	LO	LO	SN	LO	LO	SE	SN		SN	SN	SN	LO	LO	SN	LO	LO	SE		SN	SN
London Bridge 4 ⊖	d	08 39		08 41				08 54				09 06		09 09	09 11				09 24					09 36	09 39
Highbury & Islington	d					08 21	08 30		08 35	08 45							08 51	09 00		09 05	09 15				
Canonbury	d					08 23	08 32		08 37	08 47							08 53	09 02		09 07	09 17				
Dalston Junction Stn ELL	d					08 26	08 37		08 42	08 52							08 56	09 07		09 12	09 22				
Haggerston	d					08 27	08 38		08 43	08 53							08 57	09 08		09 13	09 23				
Hoxton	d					08 29	08 40		08 45	08 55							08 59	09 10		09 15	09 25				
Shoreditch High Street	d					08 32	08 43		08 48	08 58							09 02	09 13		09 18	09 28				
Whitechapel	d					08 34	08 45		08 50	09 00							09 04	09 15		09 20	09 30				
Shadwell	d					08 36	08 47		08 52	09 02							09 06	09 17		09 22	09 32				
Wapping	d					08 38	08 49		08 54	09 04							09 08	09 19		09 24	09 34				
Rotherhithe	d					08 40	08 51		08 56	09 06							09 10	09 21		09 26	09 36				
Canada Water	d					08 42	08 53		08 58	09 08							09 12	09 23		09 28	09 38				
Surrey Quays	d					08 43	08 54		08 59	09 09							09 13	09 24		09 29	09 39				
New Cross ELL	a						09 00			09 15								09 30			09 45				
New Cross Gate 4	a	08 44				08 47		08 59	09 03					09 14			09 17		09 29	09 33					09 44
	d	08 44				08 48		08 59	09 04					09 14			09 18		09 29	09 34					09 44
Brockley	d	08 47				08 50		09 02	09 06					09 17			09 20		09 32	09 36					09 47
Honor Oak Park	d	08 50				08 53		09 05	09 09					09 20			09 23		09 35	09 39					09 50
Forest Hill 4	d	08 52				08 56		09 07	09 12					09 22			09 26		09 37	09 42					09 52
Sydenham	d	08 55				08 58		09 10	09 14					09 25			09 28		09 40	09 44					09 55
Crystal Palace 4	d				08 37	09a03										09 07	09a33								
Gipsy Hill	d				08 39											09 09									
West Norwood 4	d				08 42											09 12									
Streatham Hill	d																								
Balham 4 ⊖	d																								
Wandsworth Common	d																								
Clapham Junction 10	d																								
South Bermondsey	d			08 45								09 10			09 15									09 40	
Queens Rd Peckham	d			08 48								09 12			09 18									09 42	
Peckham Rye 4	d			08 50	08a53						09 12	09a15			09 20	09a23						09 42		09a45	
Denmark Hill 4	d			08 53							09 16				09 23							09 46			
London Blackfriars 3 ⊖	a																								
Clapham High Street ⊖	d			08 58											09 28										
Wandsworth Road	d			08 59											09 29										
Battersea Park 4	d			09 02											09 32										
London Victoria 15 ⊖	a			09 06							09 25				09 36							09 55			
Penge West	d	08 57							09 17					09 27						09 47					09 57
Anerley	d	08 59							09 19					09 29						09 49					09 59
Norwood Junction 2	d	09 03						09 16	09 22					09 33					09 46	09 52					10 03
West Croydon 4	a							09 24	09 28										09 54	09 58					
East Croydon	a	09 07												09 37											10 07

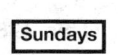

London Bridge to London Victoria - Croydon and East London Line

Network Diagram - see first Page of Table 177

		SN	SN	LO	LO	SN	LO	LO		SE	SN	SN	SN	SN	LO	LO	SN	LO		LO	SE	SN	SN	SN	SN
London Bridge 4 ⊖	d	09 41				09 54					10 06	10 09	10 11				10 24					10 36	10 39	10 41	
Highbury & Islington	d			09 21	09 30		09 35	09 45							09 51	10 00		10 05		10 15					
Canonbury	d			09 23	09 32		09 37	09 47							09 53	10 02		10 07		10 17					
Dalston Junction Stn ELL	d			09 26	09 37		09 42	09 52							09 56	10 07		10 12		10 22					
Haggerston	d			09 27	09 38		09 43	09 53							09 57	10 08		10 13		10 23					
Hoxton	d			09 29	09 40		09 45	09 55							09 59	10 10		10 15		10 25					
Shoreditch High Street	d			09 32	09 43		09 48	09 58							10 02	10 13		10 18		10 28					
Whitechapel	d			09 34	09 45		09 50	10 00							10 04	10 15		10 20		10 30					
Shadwell	d			09 36	09 47		09 52	10 02							10 06	10 17		10 22		10 32					
Wapping	d			09 38	09 49		09 54	10 04							10 08	10 19		10 24		10 34					
Rotherhithe	d			09 40	09 51		09 56	10 06							10 10	10 21		10 26		10 36					
Canada Water	d			09 42	09 53		09 58	10 08							10 12	10 23		10 28		10 38					
Surrey Quays	d			09 43	09 54		09 59	10 09							10 13	10 24		10 29		10 39					
New Cross ELL	a				10 00			10 15								10 30				10 45					
New Cross Gate 4	a			09 47		09 59	10 03					10 14			10 17		10 29	10 33					10 44		
	d			09 48		09 59	10 04					10 14			10 18		10 29	10 34					10 44		
Brockley	d			09 50		10 02	10 06					10 17			10 20		10 32	10 36					10 47		
Honor Oak Park	d			09 53		10 05	10 09					10 20			10 23		10 35	10 39					10 50		
Forest Hill 4	d			09 56		10 07	10 12					10 22			10 26		10 37	10 42					10 52		
Sydenham	d			09 58		10 10	10 14					10 25			10 28		10 40	10 44					10 55		
Crystal Palace 4	d		09 37	10a03										10 07	10a33										10 37
Gipsy Hill	d		09 39											10 09											10 39
West Norwood 4	d		09 42											10 12											10 42
Streatham Hill	d																								
Balham 4 ⊖	d																								
Wandsworth Common	d																								
Clapham Junction 10	d																								
South Bermondsey	d	09 45									10 10		10 15									10 40		10 45	
Queens Rd Peckham	d	09 48									10 12		10 18									10 42		10 48	
Peckham Rye 4	d	09 50	09a53							10 12	10a15		10 20	10a23							10 42	10a45		10 50	10a53
Denmark Hill 4	d	09 53								10 16			10 23								10 46			10 53	
London Blackfriars 3 ⊖	a																								
Clapham High Street ⊖	d	09 58											10 28											10 58	
Wandsworth Road	d	09 59											10 29											10 59	
Battersea Park 4	d	10 02											10 32											11 02	
London Victoria 15 ⊖	a	10 06								10 25			10 36								10 55			11 06	
Penge West	d						10 17					10 27						10 47					10 57		
Anerley	d						10 19					10 29						10 49					10 59		
Norwood Junction 2	d					10 16	10 22					10 33					10 46	10 52					11 03		
West Croydon 4	a					10 24	10 28										10 54	10 58							
East Croydon	a											10 37											11 07		

		LO	LO	SN		LO	LO	SE	SN	SN	SN	SN	LO	LO		SN	LO	LO	SE	SN	SN	SN	SN	LO	
London Bridge 4 ⊖	d			10 54					11 06	11 09	11 11					11 24				11 36	11 39	11 41			
Highbury & Islington	d	10 21	10 30			10 35	10 45						10 51	11 00			11 05	11 15						11 21	
Canonbury	d	10 23	10 32			10 37	10 47						10 53	11 02			11 07	11 17						11 23	
Dalston Junction Stn ELL	d	10 26	10 37			10 42	10 52						10 56	11 07			11 12	11 22						11 26	
Haggerston	d	10 27	10 38			10 43	10 53						10 57	11 08			11 13	11 23						11 27	
Hoxton	d	10 29	10 40			10 45	10 55						10 59	11 10			11 15	11 25						11 29	
Shoreditch High Street	d	10 32	10 43			10 48	10 58						11 02	11 13			11 18	11 28						11 32	
Whitechapel	d	10 34	10 45			10 50	11 00						11 04	11 15			11 20	11 30						11 34	
Shadwell	d	10 36	10 47			10 52	11 02						11 06	11 17			11 22	11 32						11 36	
Wapping	d	10 38	10 49			10 54	11 04						11 08	11 19			11 24	11 34						11 38	
Rotherhithe	d	10 40	10 51			10 56	11 06						11 10	11 21			11 26	11 36						11 40	
Canada Water	d	10 42	10 53			10 58	11 08						11 12	11 23			11 28	11 38						11 42	
Surrey Quays	d	10 43	10 54			10 59	11 09						11 13	11 24			11 29	11 39						11 43	
New Cross ELL	a		11 00				11 15							11 30				11 45							
New Cross Gate 4	a	10 47		10 59		11 03				11 14			11 17			11 29	11 33				11 44			11 47	
	d	10 48		10 59		11 04				11 14			11 18			11 29	11 34				11 44			11 48	
Brockley	d	10 50		11 02		11 06				11 17			11 20			11 32	11 36				11 47			11 50	
Honor Oak Park	d	10 53		11 05		11 09				11 20			11 23			11 35	11 39				11 50			11 53	
Forest Hill 4	d	10 56		11 07		11 12				11 22			11 26			11 37	11 42				11 52			11 56	
Sydenham	d	10 58		11 10		11 14				11 25			11 28			11 40	11 44				11 55			11 58	
Crystal Palace 4	d	11a03										11 07	11a33										11 37	12a03	
Gipsy Hill	d											11 09											11 39		
West Norwood 4	d											11 12											11 42		
Streatham Hill	d																								
Balham 4 ⊖	d																								
Wandsworth Common	d																								
Clapham Junction 10	d																								
South Bermondsey	d								11 10		11 15									11 40		11 45			
Queens Rd Peckham	d								11 12		11 18									11 42		11 48			
Peckham Rye 4	d							11 12	11a15		11 20	11a23							11 42	11a45		11 50	11a53		
Denmark Hill 4	d							11 16			11 23								11 46			11 53			
London Blackfriars 3 ⊖	a																								
Clapham High Street ⊖	d										11 28											11 58			
Wandsworth Road	d										11 29											11 59			
Battersea Park 4	d										11 32											12 02			
London Victoria 15 ⊖	a							11 25			11 36								11 55			12 06			
Penge West	d					11 17				11 27							11 47				11 57				
Anerley	d					11 19				11 29							11 49				11 59				
Norwood Junction 2	d			11 16		11 22				11 33						11 46	11 52				12 03				
West Croydon 4	a			11 24		11 28										11 54	11 58								
East Croydon	a									11 37											12 07				

Table 178

Sundays

London Bridge to London Victoria - Croydon and East London Line

Network Diagram - see first Page of Table 177

		LO	SN	LO	SE	SN	SN	LO	LO	SN		LO	SN	SE	SN	LO	LO	SN	LO	LO		LO	SN	SN	LO
London Bridge [4] ⊖	d		11 54			12 06				12 09			12 11					12 24					12 36	12 39	
Highbury & Islington	d	11 30		11 35				11 43				11 51				11 58			12 06	12 13					12 21
Canonbury	d	11 32		11 37				11 45				11 53				12 00			12 08	12 15					12 23
Dalston Junction Stn ELL	d	11 37		11 42				11 48	11 52			11 58				12 03	12 08		12 13	12 18		12 23			12 28
Haggerston	d	11 38		11 43				11 49	11 53			11 59				12 04	12 09		12 14	12 19		12 24			12 29
Hoxton	d	11 40		11 45				11 51	11 55			12 01				12 06	12 11		12 16	12 21		12 26			12 31
Shoreditch High Street	d	11 43		11 48				11 54	11 58			12 04				12 09	12 14		12 19	12 24		12 29			12 34
Whitechapel	d	11 45		11 50				11 56	12 00			12 06				12 11	12 16		12 21	12 26		12 31			12 36
Shadwell	d	11 47		11 52				11 58	12 02			12 08				12 13	12 18		12 23	12 28		12 33			12 38
Wapping	d	11 49		11 54				12 00	12 04			12 10				12 15	12 20		12 25	12 30		12 35			12 40
Rotherhithe	d	11 51		11 56				12 02	12 06			12 12				12 17	12 22		12 27	12 32		12 37			12 42
Canada Water	d	11 53		11 58				12 04	12 08			12 14				12 19	12 24		12 29	12 34		12 39			12 44
Surrey Quays	d	11 54		11 59				12 05	12 09			12 15				12 20	12 25		12 30	12 35		12 40			12 45
New Cross ELL	a	12 00							12 15								12 31					12 46			
New Cross Gate [4]	a		11 59	12 03				12 09		12 14		12 19				12 24		12 29	12 34	12 39				12 44	12 49
	d		11 59	12 04				12 10		12 14		12 20				12 25		12 29	12 35	12 40				12 44	12 50
Brockley	d		12 02	12 06				12 12		12 17		12 22				12 27		12 32	12 37	12 42				12 47	12 52
Honor Oak Park	d		12 05	12 09				12 15		12 20		12 25				12 30		12 35	12 40	12 45				12 50	12 55
Forest Hill [4]	d		12 07	12 12				12 18		12 22		12 28				12 33		12 37	12 43	12 48				12 52	12 58
Sydenham	d		12 10	12 14				12 20		12 25		12 30				12 35		12 40	12 45	12 50				12 55	13 00
Crystal Palace [4]	d						12 07	12a25							12 37	12a40				12a55					
Gipsy Hill	d						12 09								12 39										
West Norwood [4]	d						12 12								12 42										
Streatham Hill	d																								
Balham [4] ⊖	d																								
Wandsworth Common	d																								
Clapham Junction [10]	d																								
South Bermondsey	d					12 10							12 15										12 40		
Queens Rd Peckham	d					12 12							12 18										12 42		
Peckham Rye [4]	d				12 12	12a15	12a23						12 20	12 42	12a53								12a45		
Denmark Hill [4]	d				12 16								12 23	12 46											
London Blackfriars [3] ⊖	a																								
Clapham High Street ⊖	d												12 28												
Wandsworth Road	d												12 29												
Battersea Park [4]	d												12 32												
London Victoria [15] ⊖	a				12 25								12 36	12 55											
Penge West	d			12 17						12 27		12 33							12 48					12 57	13 03
Anerley	d			12 19						12 29		12 35							12 50					12 59	13 05
Norwood Junction [2]	d		12 16	12 22						12 33		12 38						12 46	12 53					13 03	13 08
West Croydon [4]	a		12 24	12 28								12 45						12 54	12 59						13 15
East Croydon	a									12 37														13 07	

		SN	SE	SN	LO	LO		SN	LO	LO	LO	SN		SN	SN		LO	SN	SE	SN	LO	LO	SN	LO
London Bridge [4] ⊖	d	12 41						12 54				13 06		17 06	17 09			17 11					17 24	
Highbury & Islington	d				12 28				12 36	12 43							16 51				16 58			17 06
Canonbury	d				12 30				12 38	12 45							16 53				17 00			17 08
Dalston Junction Stn ELL	d				12 33	12 38			12 43	12 48	12 53						16 58				17 03	17 08		17 13
Haggerston	d				12 34	12 39			12 44	12 49	12 54						16 59				17 04	17 09		17 14
Hoxton	d				12 36	12 41			12 46	12 51	12 56						17 01				17 06	17 11		17 16
Shoreditch High Street	d				12 39	12 44			12 49	12 54	12 59						17 04				17 09	17 14		17 19
Whitechapel	d				12 41	12 46			12 51	12 56	13 01						17 06				17 11	17 16		17 21
Shadwell	d				12 43	12 48			12 53	12 58	13 03						17 08				17 13	17 18		17 23
Wapping	d				12 45	12 50			12 55	13 00	13 05						17 10				17 15	17 20		17 25
Rotherhithe	d				12 47	12 52			12 57	13 02	13 07						17 12				17 17	17 22		17 27
Canada Water	d				12 49	12 54			12 59	13 04	13 09						17 14				17 19	17 24		17 29
Surrey Quays	d				12 50	12 55			13 00	13 05	13 10						17 15				17 20	17 25		17 30
New Cross ELL	a					13 01					13 16											17 31		
New Cross Gate [4]	a				12 54			12 59	13 04	13 09					17 14		17 19				17 24		17 29	17 34
	d				12 55			12 59	13 05	13 10					17 14		17 20				17 25		17 29	17 35
Brockley	d				12 57			13 02	13 07	13 12			and at the same minutes past each hour until		17 17		17 22				17 27		17 32	17 37
Honor Oak Park	d				13 00			13 05	13 10	13 15					17 20		17 25				17 30		17 35	17 40
Forest Hill [4]	d				13 03			13 07	13 13	13 18					17 22		17 28				17 33		17 37	17 43
Sydenham	d				13 05			13 10	13 15	13 20					17 25		17 30				17 35		17 40	17 45
Crystal Palace [4]	d			13 07	13a10					13a25										17 37	17a40			
Gipsy Hill	d			13 09																17 39				
West Norwood [4]	d			13 12																17 42				
Streatham Hill	d																							
Balham [4] ⊖	d																							
Wandsworth Common	d																							
Clapham Junction [10]	d																							
South Bermondsey	d	12 45										13 10		17 10				17 15						
Queens Rd Peckham	d	12 48										13 12		17 12				17 18						
Peckham Rye [4]	d	12 50	13 12	13a23								13a15		17a15				17 20	17 42	17a53				
Denmark Hill [4]	d	12 53	13 16															17 23	17 46					
London Blackfriars [3] ⊖	a																							
Clapham High Street ⊖	d	12 58																17 28						
Wandsworth Road	d	12 59																17 29						
Battersea Park [4]	d	13 02																17 32						
London Victoria [15] ⊖	a	13 06	13 25															17 36	17 55					
Penge West	d								13 18						17 27		17 33							17 48
Anerley	d								13 20						17 29		17 35							17 50
Norwood Junction [2]	d							13 16	13 23						17 33		17 38						17 46	17 53
West Croydon [4]	a							13 24	13 29								17 45						17 54	17 59
East Croydon	a														17 37									

London Bridge to London Victoria - Croydon and East London Line

Network Diagram - see first Page of Table 177

		LO		LO	SN	SN	LO	SN	SE	SN	LO	LO		SN	LO	LO	LO	SN	SN	LO	SN	SE		SN	LO
London Bridge 4 ⊖	d				17 36	17 39		17 41						17 54				18 06	18 09		18 11				
Highbury & Islington	d	17 13					17 21				17 28				17 36	17 43				17 51					17 58
Canonbury	d	17 15					17 23				17 30				17 38	17 45				17 53					18 00
Dalston Junction Stn ELL	d	17 18		17 23			17 28				17 33	17 38			17 43	17 48	17 53			17 58					18 03
Haggerston	d	17 19		17 24			17 29				17 34	17 39			17 44	17 49	17 54			17 59					18 04
Hoxton	d	17 21		17 26			17 31				17 36	17 41			17 46	17 51	17 56			18 01					18 06
Shoreditch High Street	d	17 24		17 29			17 34				17 39	17 44			17 49	17 54	17 59			18 04					18 09
Whitechapel	d	17 26		17 31			17 36				17 41	17 46			17 51	17 56	18 01			18 06					18 11
Shadwell	d	17 28		17 33			17 38				17 43	17 48			17 53	17 58	18 03			18 08					18 13
Wapping	d	17 30		17 35			17 40				17 45	17 50			17 55	18 00	18 05			18 10					18 15
Rotherhithe	d	17 32		17 37			17 42				17 47	17 52			17 57	18 02	18 07			18 12					18 17
Canada Water	d	17 34		17 39			17 44				17 49	17 54			17 59	18 04	18 09			18 14					18 19
Surrey Quays	d	17 35		17 40			17 45				17 50	17 55			18 00	18 05	18 10			18 15					18 20
New Cross ELL	a			17 46								18 01					18 16								
New Cross Gate 4	a	17 39				17 44	17 49				17 54			17 59	18 04	18 09			18 14	18 19					18 24
	d	17 40				17 44	17 50				17 55			17 59	18 05	18 10			18 14	18 20					18 25
Brockley	d	17 42				17 47	17 52				17 57			18 02	18 07	18 12			18 17	18 22					18 27
Honor Oak Park	d	17 45				17 50	17 55				18 00			18 05	18 10	18 15			18 20	18 25					18 30
Forest Hill 4	d	17 48				17 52	17 58				18 03			18 07	18 13	18 18			18 22	18 28					18 33
Sydenham	d	17 50				17 55	18 00				18 05			18 10	18 15	18 20			18 25	18 30					18 35
Crystal Palace 4	d	17a55								18 07	18a10					18a25								18 37	18a40
Gipsy Hill	d									18 09														18 39	
West Norwood 4	d									18 12														18 42	
Streatham Hill	d																								
Balham 4 ⊖	d																								
Wandsworth Common	d																								
Clapham Junction 10	d																								
South Bermondsey	d				17 40			17 45										18 10			18 15				
Queens Rd Peckham	d				17 42			17 48										18 12			18 18				
Peckham Rye 4	d				17a45			17 50	18 12	18a23								18a15			18 20	18 42		18a53	
Denmark Hill 4	d							17 53	18 16												18 23	18 46			
London Blackfriars 3 ⊖	a																								
Clapham High Street ⊖	d							17 58													18 28				
Wandsworth Road	d							17 59													18 29				
Battersea Park 4	d							18 02													18 32				
London Victoria 15 ⊖	a							18 06	18 25												18 36	18 55			
Penge West	d					17 57	18 03								18 18				18 27	18 33					
Anerley	d					17 59	18 05								18 20				18 29	18 35					
Norwood Junction 2	d					18 03	18 08							18 16	18 23				18 33	18 38					
West Croydon 4	a						18 14							18 24	18 29					18 44					
East Croydon	a					18 07													18 37						

		LO	SN	LO	LO	LO	SN	SN		LO	SN	SE	SN	LO	LO	SN	LO	LO		LO	SN	SN	LO	SN	SE
London Bridge 4 ⊖	d		18 24				18 36	18 39			18 41					18 54					19 06	19 09		19 11	
Highbury & Islington	d			18 06	18 13					18 21				18 28			18 36	18 43					18 51		
Canonbury	d			18 08	18 15					18 23				18 30			18 38	18 45					18 53		
Dalston Junction Stn ELL	d	18 08		18 13	18 18	18 23				18 28				18 33	18 38		18 43	18 48		18 53			18 58		
Haggerston	d	18 09		18 14	18 19	18 24				18 29				18 34	18 39		18 44	18 49		18 54			18 59		
Hoxton	d	18 11		18 16	18 21	18 26				18 31				18 36	18 41		18 46	18 51		18 56			19 01		
Shoreditch High Street	d	18 14		18 19	18 24	18 29				18 34				18 39	18 44		18 49	18 54		18 59			19 04		
Whitechapel	d	18 16		18 21	18 26	18 31				18 36				18 41	18 46		18 51	18 56		19 01			19 06		
Shadwell	d	18 18		18 23	18 28	18 33				18 38				18 43	18 48		18 53	18 58		19 03			19 08		
Wapping	d	18 20		18 25	18 30	18 35				18 40				18 45	18 50		18 55	19 00		19 05			19 10		
Rotherhithe	d	18 22		18 27	18 32	18 37				18 42				18 47	18 52		18 57	19 02		19 07			19 12		
Canada Water	d	18 24		18 29	18 34	18 39				18 44				18 49	18 54		18 59	19 04		19 09			19 14		
Surrey Quays	d	18 25		18 30	18 35	18 40				18 45				18 50	18 55		19 00	19 05		19 10			19 15		
New Cross ELL	a	18 31				18 46									19 01					19 16					
New Cross Gate 4	a		18 29	18 34	18 39			18 44		18 49				18 54		18 59	19 04	19 09				19 14	19 19		
	d		18 29	18 35	18 40			18 44		18 50				18 55		18 59	19 05	19 10				19 14	19 20		
Brockley	d		18 32	18 37	18 42			18 47		18 52				18 57		19 02	19 07	19 12				19 17	19 22		
Honor Oak Park	d		18 35	18 40	18 45			18 50		18 55				19 00		19 05	19 10	19 15				19 20	19 25		
Forest Hill 4	d		18 37	18 43	18 48			18 52		18 58				19 03		19 07	19 13	19 18				19 22	19 28		
Sydenham	d		18 40	18 45	18 50			18 55		19 00				19 05		19 10	19 15	19 20				19 25	19 30		
Crystal Palace 4	d				18a55								19 07	19a10				19a25							
Gipsy Hill	d												19 09												
West Norwood 4	d												19 12												
Streatham Hill	d																								
Balham 4 ⊖	d																								
Wandsworth Common	d																								
Clapham Junction 10	d																								
South Bermondsey	d						18 40				18 45										19 10			19 15	
Queens Rd Peckham	d						18 42				18 48										19 12			19 18	
Peckham Rye 4	d						18a45				18 50	19 12	19a23								19a15			19 20	19 42
Denmark Hill 4	d										18 53	19 16												19 23	19 46
London Blackfriars 3 ⊖	a																								
Clapham High Street ⊖	d										18 58													19 28	
Wandsworth Road	d										18 59													19 29	
Battersea Park 4	d										19 02													19 32	
London Victoria 15 ⊖	a										19 06	19 25												19 36	19 55
Penge West	d			18 48				18 57		19 03								19 18				19 27	19 33		
Anerley	d			18 50				18 59		19 05								19 20				19 29	19 35		
Norwood Junction 2	d		18 46	18 53				19 03		19 08							19 16	19 23				19 33	19 38		
West Croydon 4	a		18 54	18 59						19 14							19 24	19 29					19 44		
East Croydon	a							19 07														19 37			

Table 178

Sundays

London Bridge to London Victoria - Croydon and East London Line

Network Diagram - see first Page of Table 177

Station		SN	LO	LO		SN	LO	LO	LO	SN	SN	LO	SN	SE		SN	LO	LO	SN	LO	LO	LO	SN	SN	
London Bridge 4 ⊖	d					19 24				19 36	19 39		19 41						19 54				20 06	20 09	
Highbury & Islington	d		18 58				19 06	19 13				19 21					19 28			19 36	19 43				
Canonbury	d		19 00				19 08	19 15				19 23					19 30			19 38	19 45				
Dalston Junction Stn ELL	d		19 03	19 08			19 13	19 18	19 23			19 28					19 33	19 38		19 43	19 48	19 53			
Haggerston	d		19 04	19 09			19 14	19 19	19 24			19 29					19 34	19 39		19 44	19 49	19 54			
Hoxton	d		19 06	19 11			19 16	19 21	19 26			19 31					19 36	19 41		19 46	19 51	19 56			
Shoreditch High Street	d		19 09	19 14			19 19	19 24	19 29			19 34					19 39	19 44		19 49	19 54	19 59			
Whitechapel	d		19 11	19 16			19 21	19 26	19 31			19 36					19 41	19 46		19 51	19 56	20 01			
Shadwell	d		19 13	19 18			19 23	19 28	19 33			19 38					19 43	19 48		19 53	19 58	20 03			
Wapping	d		19 15	19 20			19 25	19 30	19 35			19 40					19 45	19 50		19 55	20 00	20 05			
Rotherhithe	d		19 17	19 22			19 27	19 32	19 37			19 42					19 47	19 52		19 57	20 02	20 07			
Canada Water	d		19 19	19 24			19 29	19 34	19 39			19 44					19 49	19 54		19 59	20 04	20 09			
Surrey Quays	d		19 20	19 25			19 30	19 35	19 40			19 45					19 50	19 55		20 00	20 05	20 10			
New Cross ELL	a			19 31					19 46									20 01				20 16			
New Cross Gate 4	a		19 24			19 29	19 34	19 39			19 44	19 49					19 54		19 59	20 04	20 09			20 14	
	d		19 25			19 29	19 35	19 40			19 44	19 50					19 55		19 59	20 05	20 10			20 14	
Brockley	d		19 27			19 32	19 37	19 42			19 47	19 52					19 57		20 02	20 07	20 12			20 17	
Honor Oak Park	d		19 30			19 35	19 40	19 45			19 50	19 55					20 00		20 05	20 10	20 15			20 20	
Forest Hill 4	d		19 33			19 37	19 43	19 48			19 52	19 58					20 03		20 07	20 13	20 18			20 22	
Sydenham	d		19 35			19 40	19 45	19 50			19 55	20 00					20 05		20 10	20 15	20 20			20 25	
Crystal Palace 4	d	19 37	19a40					19a55								20 07	20a10				20a25				
Gipsy Hill	d	19 39														20 09									
West Norwood 4	d	19 42														20 12									
Streatham Hill	d																								
Balham 4 ⊖	d																								
Wandsworth Common	d																								
Clapham Junction 10	d																								
South Bermondsey	d									19 40			19 45										20 10		
Queens Rd Peckham	d									19 42			19 48										20 12		
Peckham Rye 4	d	19a53								19a45			19 50	20 12		20a23							20a15		
Denmark Hill 4	d												19 53	20 16											
London Blackfriars 3 ⊖	a																								
Clapham High Street ⊖	d												19 58												
Wandsworth Road	d												19 59												
Battersea Park 4	d												20 02												
London Victoria 15 ⊖	a												20 06	20 25											
Penge West	d						19 48				19 57	20 03								20 18				20 27	
Anerley	d						19 50				19 59	20 05								20 20				20 29	
Norwood Junction 2	d					19 46	19 53				20 03	20 08							20 16	20 23				20 33	
West Croydon 4	a					19 54	19 59					20 15							20 24	20 29					
East Croydon	a										20 07													20 37	

Station		LO	SN	SE	SN	LO	LO	SN	LO	LO		LO	SN	SN	LO	SN	SE	SN	LO	LO		SN	LO	LO	LO
London Bridge 4 ⊖	d		20 11					20 24					20 36	20 39		20 41						20 54			
Highbury & Islington	d	19 51				19 58			20 06	20 13					20 21				20 28				20 36	20 43	
Canonbury	d	19 53				20 00			20 08	20 15					20 23				20 30				20 38	20 45	
Dalston Junction Stn ELL	d	19 58				20 03	20 08		20 13	20 18		20 23			20 28				20 33	20 38			20 43	20 48	20 53
Haggerston	d	19 59				20 04	20 09		20 14	20 19		20 24			20 29				20 34	20 39			20 44	20 49	20 54
Hoxton	d	20 01				20 06	20 11		20 16	20 21		20 26			20 31				20 36	20 41			20 46	20 51	20 56
Shoreditch High Street	d	20 04				20 09	20 14		20 19	20 24		20 29			20 34				20 39	20 44			20 49	20 54	20 59
Whitechapel	d	20 06				20 11	20 16		20 21	20 26		20 31			20 36				20 41	20 46			20 51	20 56	21 01
Shadwell	d	20 08				20 13	20 18		20 23	20 28		20 33			20 38				20 43	20 48			20 53	20 58	21 03
Wapping	d	20 10				20 15	20 20		20 25	20 30		20 35			20 40				20 45	20 50			20 55	21 00	21 05
Rotherhithe	d	20 12				20 17	20 22		20 27	20 32		20 37			20 42				20 47	20 52			20 57	21 02	21 07
Canada Water	d	20 14				20 19	20 24		20 29	20 34		20 39			20 44				20 49	20 54			20 59	21 04	21 09
Surrey Quays	d	20 15				20 20	20 25		20 30	20 35		20 40			20 45				20 50	20 55			21 00	21 05	21 10
New Cross ELL	a						20 31					20 46								21 01					21 16
New Cross Gate 4	a	20 19				20 24		20 29	20 34	20 39				20 44	20 49				20 54			20 59	21 04	21 09	
	d	20 20				20 25		20 29	20 35	20 40				20 44	20 50				20 55			20 59	21 05	21 10	
Brockley	d	20 22				20 27		20 32	20 37	20 42				20 47	20 52				20 57			21 02	21 07	21 12	
Honor Oak Park	d	20 25				20 30		20 35	20 40	20 45				20 50	20 55				21 00			21 05	21 10	21 15	
Forest Hill 4	d	20 28				20 33		20 37	20 43	20 48				20 52	20 58				21 03			21 07	21 13	21 18	
Sydenham	d	20 30				20 35		20 40	20 45	20 50				20 55	21 00				21 05			21 10	21 15	21 20	
Crystal Palace 4	d				20 37	20a40				20a55								21 07	21a10					21a25	
Gipsy Hill	d				20 39													21 09							
West Norwood 4	d				20 42													21 12							
Streatham Hill	d																								
Balham 4 ⊖	d																								
Wandsworth Common	d																								
Clapham Junction 10	d																								
South Bermondsey	d		20 15										20 40			20 45									
Queens Rd Peckham	d		20 18										20 42			20 48									
Peckham Rye 4	d		20 20	20 42	20a53								20a45			20 50	21 12	21a23							
Denmark Hill 4	d		20 23	20 46												20 53	21 16								
London Blackfriars 3 ⊖	a																								
Clapham High Street ⊖	d		20 28													20 58									
Wandsworth Road	d		20 29													20 59									
Battersea Park 4	d		20 32													21 02									
London Victoria 15 ⊖	a		20 36	20 55												21 06	21 25								
Penge West	d	20 33							20 48					20 57	21 03								21 18		
Anerley	d	20 35							20 50					20 59	21 05								21 20		
Norwood Junction 2	d	20 38						20 46	20 53					21 03	21 08							21 16	21 23		
West Croydon 4	a	20 45						20 54	20 59						21 15							21 24	21 29		
East Croydon	a													21 07											

Table 178

Sundays

London Bridge to London Victoria - Croydon and East London Line

Network Diagram - see first Page of Table 177

	SN	SN	LO	SN	SE		SN	LO	LO	SN	LO	LO	LO	SN	SN		LO	SN	SE	SN	LO	LO	SN	LO
London Bridge 4 ⊖ d	21 06	21 09		21 11						21 24				21 36	21 39			21 41					21 54	
Highbury & Islington d			20 51					20 58			21 06	21 13					21 21				21 28			21 36
Canonbury d			20 53					21 00			21 08	21 15					21 23				21 30			21 38
Dalston Junction Stn ELL d			20 58					21 03	21 08		21 13	21 18	21 23				21 28				21 33	21 38		21 43
Haggerston d			20 59					21 04	21 09		21 14	21 19	21 24				21 29				21 34	21 39		21 44
Hoxton d			21 01					21 06	21 11		21 16	21 21	21 26				21 31				21 36	21 41		21 46
Shoreditch High Street d			21 04					21 09	21 14		21 19	21 24	21 29				21 34				21 39	21 44		21 49
Whitechapel d			21 06					21 11	21 16		21 21	21 26	21 31				21 36				21 41	21 46		21 51
Shadwell d			21 08					21 13	21 18		21 23	21 28	21 33				21 38				21 43	21 48		21 53
Wapping d			21 10					21 15	21 20		21 25	21 30	21 35				21 40				21 45	21 50		21 55
Rotherhithe d			21 12					21 17	21 22		21 27	21 32	21 37				21 42				21 47	21 52		21 57
Canada Water d			21 14					21 19	21 24		21 29	21 34	21 39				21 44				21 49	21 54		21 59
Surrey Quays d			21 15					21 20	21 25		21 30	21 35	21 40				21 45				21 50	21 55		22 00
New Cross ELL a									21 31				21 46									22 01		
New Cross Gate 4 a		21 14	21 19					21 24		21 29	21 34	21 39			21 44		21 49				21 54		21 59	22 04
d		21 14	21 20					21 25		21 29	21 35	21 40			21 44		21 50				21 55		21 59	22 05
Brockley d		21 17	21 22					21 27		21 32	21 37	21 42			21 47		21 52				21 57		22 02	22 07
Honor Oak Park d		21 20	21 25					21 30		21 35	21 40	21 45			21 50		21 55				22 00		22 05	22 10
Forest Hill 4 d		21 22	21 28					21 33		21 37	21 43	21 48			21 52		21 58				22 03		22 07	22 13
Sydenham d		21 25	21 30					21 35		21 40	21 45	21 50			21 55		22 00				22 05		22 10	22 15
Crystal Palace 4 d							21 37	21a40				21a55								22 07	22a10			
Gipsy Hill d							21 39													22 09				
West Norwood 4 d							21 42													22 12				
Streatham Hill d																								
Balham 4 ⊖ d																								
Wandsworth Common d																								
Clapham Junction 10 d																								
South Bermondsey d	21 10			21 15										21 40				21 45						
Queens Rd Peckham d	21 12			21 18										21 42				21 48						
Peckham Rye 4 d	21a15			21 20	21 42		21a53							21a45				21 50	22 12	22a23				
Denmark Hill 4 d				21 23	21 46													21 53	22 16					
London Blackfriars 3 ⊖ a																								
Clapham High Street ⊖ d				21 28														21 58						
Wandsworth Road d				21 29														21 59						
Battersea Park 4 d				21 32														22 02						
London Victoria 15 ⊖ a				21 36	21 55													22 06	22 25					
Penge West d		21 27	21 33								21 48				21 57		22 03							22 18
Anerley d		21 29	21 35								21 50				21 59		22 05							22 20
Norwood Junction 2 d		21 33	21 38							21 46	21 53				22 03		22 08						22 16	22 23
West Croydon 4 a			21 45							21 54	21 59						22 15						22 24	22 29
East Croydon a		21 37													22 07									

	LO		LO	SN	SN	LO	LO	SN	SE	SN	SN		LO	SN	LO	LO	SN	SE	SN	SN	LO		SN	LO
London Bridge 4 ⊖ d				22 06	22 09			22 11		22 36				22 39			22 41		23 06				23 09	
Highbury & Islington d	21 43					21 51							22 13		22 23						22 43			22 53
Canonbury d	21 45					21 53							22 15		22 25						22 45			22 55
Dalston Junction Stn ELL d	21 48		21 53			21 58	22 08						22 18		22 28	22 38					22 48			22 58
Haggerston d	21 49		21 54			21 59	22 09						22 19		22 29	22 39					22 49			22 59
Hoxton d	21 51		21 56			22 01	22 11						22 21		22 31	22 41					22 51			23 01
Shoreditch High Street d	21 54		21 59			22 04	22 14						22 24		22 34	22 44					22 54			23 04
Whitechapel d	21 56		22 01			22 06	22 16						22 26		22 36	22 46					22 56			23 06
Shadwell d	21 58		22 03			22 08	22 18						22 28		22 38	22 48					22 58			23 08
Wapping d	22 00		22 05			22 10	22 20						22 30		22 40	22 50					23 00			23 10
Rotherhithe d	22 02		22 07			22 12	22 22						22 32		22 42	22 52					23 02			23 12
Canada Water d	22 04		22 09			22 14	22 24						22 34		22 44	22 54					23 04			23 14
Surrey Quays d	22 05		22 10			22 15	22 25						22 35		22 45	22 55					23 05			23 15
New Cross ELL a			22 17				22 31									23 01								
New Cross Gate 4 a	22 09				22 14	22 19							22 39	22 44	22 49						23 09		23 14	23 19
d	22 10				22 14	22 20							22 40	22 44	22 50						23 10		23 14	23 20
Brockley d	22 12				22 17	22 22							22 42	22 47	22 52						23 12		23 17	23 22
Honor Oak Park d	22 15				22 20	22 25							22 45	22 50	22 55						23 15		23 20	23 25
Forest Hill 4 d	22 18				22 22	22 28							22 48	22 52	22 58						23 18		23 22	23 28
Sydenham d	22 20				22 25	22 30							22 50	22 55	23 00						23 20		23 25	23 30
Crystal Palace 4 d	22a25										22 37		22a55							23 07	23a25			
Gipsy Hill d											22 39									23 09				
West Norwood 4 d											22 42									23 12				
Streatham Hill d																								
Balham 4 ⊖ d																								
Wandsworth Common d																								
Clapham Junction 10 d																								
South Bermondsey d				22 10				22 15		22 40							22 45		23 10					
Queens Rd Peckham d				22 12				22 18		22 42							22 48		23 12					
Peckham Rye 4 d				22a15				22 20	22 42	22a45	22a53						22 50	23 12	23a15	23a23				
Denmark Hill 4 d								22 23	22 46								22 53	23 16						
London Blackfriars 3 ⊖ a																								
Clapham High Street ⊖ d								22 28									22 58							
Wandsworth Road d								22 29									22 59							
Battersea Park 4 d								22 32									23 02							
London Victoria 15 ⊖ a								22 36	22 55								23 06	23 25						
Penge West d					22 27	22 33								22 57	23 03								23 27	23 33
Anerley d					22 29	22 35								22 59	23 05								23 29	23 35
Norwood Junction 2 d					22 33	22 38								23 03	23 08								23 33	23 38
West Croydon 4 a						22 45									23 14									23 44
East Croydon a					22 37									23 07									23 38	

Table 178

Sundays

London Bridge to London Victoria - Croydon and East London Line

Network Diagram - see first Page of Table 177

Station		LO	SN	SE	SN	SN	LO	SN		LO
London Bridge 4 ⊖	d		23 11					23 39		
Highbury & Islington	d						23 13			23 23
Canonbury	d						23 15			23 25
Dalston Junction Stn ELL	d	23 08					23 18			23 28
Haggerston	d	23 09					23 19			23 29
Hoxton	d	23 11					23 21			23 31
Shoreditch High Street	d	23 14					23 24			23 34
Whitechapel	d	23 16					23 26			23 36
Shadwell	d	23 18					23 28			23 38
Wapping	d	23 20					23 30			23 40
Rotherhithe	d	23 22					23 32			23 42
Canada Water	d	23 24					23 34			23 44
Surrey Quays	d	23 25					23 35			23 45
New Cross ELL	a	23 31								
New Cross Gate 4	a						23 39	23 44		23 49
	d						23 40	23 44		23 50
Brockley	d						23 42	23 47		23 52
Honor Oak Park	d						23 45	23 50		23 55
Forest Hill 4	d						23 48	23 52		23 58
Sydenham	d						23 50	23 55		00 01
Crystal Palace 4	d				23 37	23 50	23a55			
Gipsy Hill	d				23 39					
West Norwood 4	d				23 42					
Streatham Hill	d									
Balham 4 ⊖	d									
Wandsworth Common	d									
Clapham Junction 10	d									
South Bermondsey	d		23 15							
Queens Rd Peckham	d		23 18							
Peckham Rye 4	d		23 20	23 42	23a53					
Denmark Hill 4	d		23 23	23 46						
London Blackfriars 3 ⊖	a									
Clapham High Street ⊖	d		23 28							
Wandsworth Road	d		23 29							
Battersea Park 4	d		23 32							
London Victoria 15 ⊖	a		23 37	23 55						
Penge West	d							23 57		00 03
Anerley	d							23 59		00 05
Norwood Junction 2	d					23 55		00 03		00 08
West Croydon 4 🚌	a					23 59				00 15
East Croydon 🚌	a							00 06		

East London Line and Croydon - London Victoria to London Bridge

Network Diagram - see first Page of Table 177

Miles	Miles	Miles	Miles	Miles			LO MX	LO MX	SN MO	SN MX	SN MX	SN MX						SN	SE	LO	SN	LO	LO		
—	—	0	—	—	**East Croydon**	d												05 13			05 51				
—	—	—	—	0	**West Croydon** [4]	d	23p22													05 39					
—	—	1¼	—	1¾	Norwood Junction [2]	d	23p28											05 17		05 43	05 55				
—	—	2½	—	—	Anerley	d	23p31											05 20		05 46					
—	—	2¾	—	—	Penge West	d	23p33											05 22		05 48					
0	0	—	0	—	**London Victoria** [15]	⊖ d				23p22	23p54														
1¼	1¼	—	—	—	Battersea Park [4]	d				23p26	23p58														
2	—	—	—	—	Wandsworth Road	d																			
2½	—	—	—	—	Clapham High Street	⊖ d																			
—	—	—	—	0	**London Blackfriars** [3]	⊖ d													05 28						
4½	—	—	4¼	3¾	Denmark Hill [4]	d													05 39						
5¼	—	—	5	4¼	Peckham Rye [4]	d			23p53			00 12							05a41		06 15				
6	—	—	—	—	Queens Rd Peckham	d			23p56												06 18				
7	—	—	—	—	South Bermondsey	d			23p58												06 20				
—	2¾	—	—	—	Clapham Junction [10]	d				23p30	00 02														
—	4	—	—	—	Wandsworth Common	d				23p33	00 05														
—	4¾	—	—	—	Balham [4]	⊖ d				23p35	00 07														
—	5¾	—	—	—	Streatham Hill	d				23p38	00 10														
—	7	—	—	—	West Norwood [4]	d				23p42	00 14	00 24													
—	8	—	—	—	Gipsy Hill	d				23p45	00 17	00 27													
—	8¾	—	—	—	**Crystal Palace** [4]	d		23p43		23p51	00 21	00a29											05 58		
—	10	3½	—	—	Sydenham	d	23p36	23p46		23p54	00 24							05 24		05 51			06 01		
—	10¾	4¼	—	—	Forest Hill [4]	d	23p38	23p49		23p57	00 27							05 27		05 53			06 04		
—	11¾	5¼	—	—	Honor Oak Park	d	23p41	23p51		23p59	00 29							05 29		05 56			06 06		
—	12¾	6¼	—	—	Brockley	d	23p43	23p54		00 02	00 32							05 32		05 58			06 09		
—	13¾	7¼	—	—	**New Cross Gate** [4]	a	23p46	23p56		00 04	00 34							05 34		06 01			06 11		
—	—	—	—	—		d	23p46	23p56		00 04	00 34							05 34		06 01			06 11		
—	—	—	0	—	**New Cross ELL**	d																06 06			
—	—	—	1¼	—	Surrey Quays	d	23p49	23p59												06 05		06 10	06 15		
—	—	—	1½	—	Canada Water	d	23p51	00 02												06 07		06 12	06 17		
—	—	—	1¾	—	Rotherhithe	d	23p53	00 03												06 08		06 13	06 18		
—	—	—	2	—	Wapping	d	23p54	00 05												06 10		06 15	06 20		
—	—	—	2½	—	Shadwell	d	23p56	00 07												06 12		06 17	06 22		
—	—	—	3¼	—	Whitechapel	d	23p59	00 09												06 14		06 19	06 24		
—	—	—	4	—	Shoreditch High Street	d	00 01	00 11												06 16		06 21	06 26		
—	—	—	4¾	—	Hoxton	d	00 03	00 13												06 18		06 23	06 28		
—	—	—	5¼	—	Haggerston	d	00 05	00 15												06 20		06 25	06 30		
—	—	—	5¾	—	Dalston Junction Stn ELL	a	00 07	00 17												06 22		06 29	06 32		
—	—	—	—	—	Canonbury	d	00 12	00 20												06 27			06 35		
—	—	—	—	—	**Highbury & Islington**	a	00 16	00 25												06 32			06 40		
—	—	—	—	—		d																			
8¾	16½	10	—	—	**London Bridge** [4]	⊖ a			00 03	00 11	00 41							05 41			06 25				

		LO	LO	LO		LO	SN	LO	LO	LO	SN	LO	LO	SN		SN	LO	SN	SE	SN	SN	LO	SN	LO	
East Croydon	d						06 13																		
West Croydon [4]	d	05 52				06 09				06 22											06 31	06 39			
Norwood Junction [2]	d	05 58				06 13	06 18			06 28	06 32											06 43	06 47		
Anerley	d	06 01				06 16	06 21			06 31	06 35											06 46			
Penge West	d	06 03				06 18	06 23			06 33	06 37											06 48			
London Victoria [15]	⊖ d													06 19						06 41					
Battersea Park [4]	d													06 23						06 45					
Wandsworth Road	d																			06 47					
Clapham High Street	⊖ d																			06 49					
London Blackfriars [3]	⊖ d																		06 42						
Denmark Hill [4]	d																		06 52	06 54					
Peckham Rye [4]	d																	06 42	06a55	06 56	06 59		07 08		
Queens Rd Peckham	d																			06 59	07 02		07 10		
South Bermondsey	d																			07 01	07 04		07 13		
Clapham Junction [10]	d													06 27											
Wandsworth Common	d													06 30											
Balham [4]	⊖ d													06 32											
Streatham Hill	d													06 35		06 42									
West Norwood [4]	d													06 39		06 45		06 53							
Gipsy Hill	d													06 42		06 48		06 56							
Crystal Palace [4]	d			06 13					06 28				06 41	06 44		06 51	06 58	06a59							
Sydenham	d	06 06		06 16		06 21	06 25		06 31	06 36	06 39		06 44	06 48		06 54	07 01					06 51			
Forest Hill [4]	d	06 08		06 19		06 23	06 28		06 34	06 38	06 42		06 47	06 50		06 57	07 04					06 53			
Honor Oak Park	d	06 11		06 21		06 26	06 30		06 36	06 41	06 44		06 49	06 53		06 59	07 06					06 56			
Brockley	d	06 13		06 24		06 28	06 33		06 39	06 43	06 47		06 52	06 55		07 02	07 09					06 58			
New Cross Gate [4]	a	06 16		06 26		06 31	06 35		06 41	06 46	06 49		06 54	06 58		07 04	07 11					07 01			
	d	06 16		06 26		06 31	06 35		06 41	06 46	06 49		06 54	06 58		07 04	07 11					07 01			
New Cross ELL	d		06 21					06 36				06 51												07 06	
Surrey Quays	d	06 19	06 25	06 30		06 35		06 40	06 45	06 49		06 55	07 00				07 15					07 05		07 10	
Canada Water	d	06 21	06 27	06 32		06 37		06 42	06 47	06 51		06 57	07 02				07 17					07 07		07 12	
Rotherhithe	d	06 23	06 28	06 33		06 38		06 43	06 48	06 53		06 58	07 03				07 18					07 08		07 13	
Wapping	d	06 24	06 30	06 35		06 40		06 45	06 50	06 54		07 00	07 05				07 20					07 10		07 15	
Shadwell	d	06 26	06 32	06 37		06 42		06 47	06 52	06 56		07 02	07 07				07 22					07 12		07 17	
Whitechapel	d	06 29	06 34	06 39		06 44		06 49	06 54	06 59		07 04	07 09				07 24					07 14		07 19	
Shoreditch High Street	d	06 31	06 36	06 41		06 46		06 51	06 56	07 01		07 06	07 11				07 26					07 16		07 21	
Hoxton	d	06 33	06 38	06 43		06 48		06 53	06 58	07 03		07 08	07 13				07 28					07 18		07 23	
Haggerston	d	06 35	06 40	06 45		06 50		06 55	07 00	07 05		07 10	07 15				07 30					07 20		07 25	
Dalston Junction Stn ELL	a	06 37	06 44	06 47		06 52		06 59	07 02	07 07		07 14	07 17				07 32					07 23		07 29	
Canonbury	d	06 42		06 50		06 57			07 05	07 12			07 20				07 35					07 27			
Highbury & Islington	a	06 46		06 56		07 02			07 10	07 16			07 25				07 40					07 32			
	d																								
London Bridge [4]	⊖ a						06 44				07 00			07 06		07 16				07 08	07 11		07 19		

East London Line and Croydon - London Victoria to London Bridge

Network Diagram - see first Page of Table 177

		LO	SN	LO	LO	SN	SN	SN	SN	SN		LO	SN	SN	LO	LO	LO	SN	LO	LO		SN	SN	SN	SN
East Croydon ⇌	d																								
West Croydon 4 ⇌	d	06 52								07 01		07 09	07 17				07 22								
Norwood Junction 2	d	06 58	07 02									07 13	07 22				07 28	07 32							
Anerley	d	07 01	07 05									07 16					07 31	07 35							
Penge West	d	07 03	07 07									07 18					07 33	07 37							
London Victoria 15 ⊖	d					06 49			07 11													07 17			07 41
Battersea Park 4	d					06 53			07 15													07 21			07 45
Wandsworth Road	d								07 17																07 47
Clapham High Street ⊖	d								07 19																07 49
London Blackfriars 3 ⊖	d																								
Denmark Hill 4	d								07 24																07 54
Peckham Rye 4	d							07 12	07 26	07 31				07 36										07 42	07 56
Queens Rd Peckham	d								07 29	07 34				07 39											07 59
South Bermondsey	d								07 31	07 36				07 41											08 01
Clapham Junction 10	d					06 57																07 25			
Wandsworth Common	d					07 00																			
Balham 4 ⊖	d					07 02																07 29			
Streatham Hill	d					07 05	07 12															07 32			
West Norwood 4	d					07 09	07 15	07 23														07 38		07 53	
Gipsy Hill	d					07 12	07 18	07 26														07 41		07 56	
Crystal Palace 4	d				07 11	07 14	07 21	07a29					07a26			07 28				07 41		07 44	07 52	07a59	
Sydenham	d	07 06	07 09		07 14	07 18	07 24					07 21				07 31	07 36	07 39		07 44		07 48	07 56		
Forest Hill 4	d	07 08	07 12		07 17	07 20	07 27					07 23				07 34	07 38	07 42		07 47		07 50	07 58		
Honor Oak Park	d	07 11	07 14		07 19	07 23	07 29					07 26				07 36	07 41	07 44		07 49		07 53	08 01		
Brockley	d	07 13	07 17		07 22	07 25	07 32					07 28				07 39	07 43	07 47		07 52		07 55	08 03		
New Cross Gate 4	a	07 16	07 19		07 24	07 28	07 34					07 31				07 41	07 46	07 49		07 54		07 58	08 06		
	d	07 16	07 19		07 24	07 28	07 34					07 31				07 41	07 46	07 49		07 54		07 58	08 06		
New Cross ELL	d			07 21											07 36				07 51						
Surrey Quays	d	07 19		07 25	07 30							07 35			07 40	07 45	07 49		07 55	08 00					
Canada Water	d	07 21		07 27	07 32							07 37			07 42	07 47	07 51		07 57	08 02					
Rotherhithe	d	07 23		07 28	07 33							07 38			07 43	07 48	07 53		07 58	08 03					
Wapping	d	07 24		07 30	07 35							07 40			07 45	07 50	07 54		08 00	08 05					
Shadwell	d	07 26		07 32	07 37							07 42			07 47	07 52	07 56		08 02	08 07					
Whitechapel	d	07 29		07 34	07 39							07 44			07 49	07 54	07 59		08 04	08 09					
Shoreditch High Street	d	07 31		07 36	07 41							07 46			07 51	07 56	08 01		08 06	08 11					
Hoxton	d	07 33		07 38	07 43							07 48			07 53	07 58	08 03		08 08	08 13					
Haggerston	d	07 35		07 40	07 45							07 50			07 55	08 00	08 05		08 10	08 15					
Dalston Junction Stn ELL	a	07 37		07 44	07 47							07 53			07 59	08 02	08 07		08 14	08 17					
Canonbury	d	07 42			07 50							07 57				08 05	08 12			08 20					
Highbury & Islington	a	07 46			07 55							08 02				08 10	08 16			08 25					
	d																								
London Bridge 4 ⊖	a		07 30			07 36	07 45		07 38	07 43				07 48				07 58				08 07	08 15		08 08

		SE	SN	LO	SN	SN		LO	LO	LO	LO	SN	LO	LO	SN	SN		LO	LO	SN	SE	SN	SN	LO	SN
East Croydon ⇌	d																								
West Croydon 4 ⇌	d		07 31	07 39	07 47						07 52												08 01	08 09	08 19
Norwood Junction 2	d			07 43	07 52						07 58	08 02												08 13	08 25
Anerley	d			07 46							08 01	08 05												08 16	
Penge West	d			07 48							08 03	08 07												08 18	
London Victoria 15 ⊖	d	07 43													07 52						08 09	08 11			
Battersea Park 4	d																					08 15			
Wandsworth Road	d																					08 17			
Clapham High Street ⊖	d																					08 19			
London Blackfriars 3 ⊖	d																								
Denmark Hill 4	d	07 53																			08 18	08 24			
Peckham Rye 4	d	07a56	07 59			08 06														08 12	08a21	08 26	08 29		
Queens Rd Peckham	d		08 02			08 09																08 29	08 32		
South Bermondsey	d		08 04			08 11																08 31	08 34		
Clapham Junction 10	d														07 58										
Wandsworth Common	d																								
Balham 4 ⊖	d														08 03										
Streatham Hill	d														08 06	08 15									
West Norwood 4	d														08 09	08 19				08 24					
Gipsy Hill	d														08 12	08 22				08 27					
Crystal Palace 4	d				07a56				07 58					08 11	08 15	08 24			08 28	08a29					08a29
Sydenham	d			07 51					08 01		08 06	08 09		08 14	08 18	08 28			08 31					08 21	
Forest Hill 4	d			07 53					08 04		08 08	08 12		08 17	08 21	08 30			08 34					08 23	
Honor Oak Park	d			07 56					08 06		08 11	08 14		08 19	08 23	08 33			08 36					08 26	
Brockley	d			07 58					08 09		08 13	08 17		08 22	08 26	08 35			08 39					08 28	
New Cross Gate 4	a			08 01					08 11		08 16	08 19		08 24	08 28	08 38			08 41					08 31	
	d			08 01					08 11		08 16	08 19		08 24	08 28	08 38			08 41					08 31	
New Cross ELL	d							08 06					08 21												
Surrey Quays	d			08 05				08 10	08 15	08 19	08 21		08 25	08 30				08 34	08 45					08 37	
Canada Water	d			08 07				08 12	08 17	08 21	08 23		08 27	08 32				08 36	08 47					08 39	
Rotherhithe	d			08 08				08 13	08 18	08 22	08 25		08 28	08 33				08 37	08 48					08 40	
Wapping	d			08 10				08 15	08 20	08 24	08 26		08 30	08 35				08 39	08 50					08 42	
Shadwell	d			08 12				08 17	08 22	08 26	08 28		08 32	08 37				08 41	08 52					08 44	
Whitechapel	d			08 14				08 19	08 24	08 28	08 31		08 34	08 39				08 43	08 54					08 46	
Shoreditch High Street	d			08 16				08 21	08 26	08 30	08 33		08 36	08 41				08 45	08 56					08 48	
Hoxton	d			08 18				08 23	08 28	08 32	08 35		08 38	08 43				08 47	08 58					08 50	
Haggerston	d			08 20				08 25	08 30	08 34	08 37		08 40	08 45				08 49	09 00					08 52	
Dalston Junction Stn ELL	a			08 23				08 29	08 32	08 36	08 39		08 44	08 47				08 51	09 02					08 55	
Canonbury	d			08 27					08 35		08 42			08 50					09 05					08 57	
Highbury & Islington	a			08 32					08 40		08 46			08 55					09 10					09 02	
	d																								
London Bridge 4 ⊖	a		08 11			08 18						08 28			08 37	08 47						08 38	08 41		

East London Line and Croydon - London Victoria to London Bridge

Network Diagram - see first Page of Table 177

		SN		LO	LO	SN	LO	LO	SN	SN	LO	SN		SE	SN	SN	LO	SN	LO	LO	SN	SN		LO	LO
East Croydon	d																								
West Croydon 4	d				08 23											08 31	08 39	08 49		08 53					
Norwood Junction 2	d				08 28	08 32											08 43	08 54		08 58		09 02			
Anerley	d				08 31	08 35											08 46			09 01		09 05			
Penge West	d				08 33	08 37											08 48			09 03		09 07			
London Victoria 15 ⊖	d									08 22				08 39	08 41										
Battersea Park 4	d									08 26					08 45										
Wandsworth Road	d														08 47										
Clapham High Street ⊖	d														08 49										
London Blackfriars 3 ⊖	d																								
Denmark Hill 4	d													08 48	08 54										
Peckham Rye 4	d	08 36										08 42		08a51	08 56	09 02					09 07				
Queens Rd Peckham	d	08 38													08 59	09 05					09 09				
South Bermondsey	d	08 41													09 01	09 07					09 12				
Clapham Junction 10	d									08 30															
Wandsworth Common	d									08 33															
Balham 4 ⊖	d									08 35															
Streatham Hill	d								08 35	08 38															
West Norwood 4	d								08 38	08 42		08 53													
Gipsy Hill	d								08 41	08 45		08 56													
Crystal Palace 4	d							08 41	08 44	08 51	08 58	08a59						08a58							09 11
Sydenham	d				08 36	08 39		08 44	08 47	08 54	09 01						08 51			09 06		09 09			09 14
Forest Hill 4	d				08 38	08 42		08 47	08 50	08 57	09 04						08 53			09 08		09 12			09 17
Honor Oak Park	d				08 41	08 44		08 49	08 52	08 59	09 06						08 56			09 11		09 14			09 19
Brockley	d				08 43	08 47		08 52	08 55	09 02	09 09						08 58			09 13		09 17			09 22
New Cross Gate 4	a				08 46	08 49		08 54	08 57	09 04	09 11						09 01			09 16		09 19			09 24
	d				08 46	08 49		08 54	08 57	09 04	09 11						09 01			09 16		09 19			09 24
New Cross ELL	d			08 36			08 51												09 06					09 21	
Surrey Quays	d			08 40	08 49		08 55	09 00			09 15						09 05		09 10	09 19				09 25	09 30
Canada Water	d			08 42	08 51		08 57	09 02			09 17						09 07		09 12	09 21				09 27	09 32
Rotherhithe	d			08 43	08 53		08 58	09 03			09 18						09 08		09 13	09 23				09 28	09 33
Wapping	d			08 45	08 54		09 00	09 05			09 20						09 10		09 15	09 24				09 30	09 35
Shadwell	d			08 47	08 56		09 02	09 07			09 22						09 12		09 17	09 26				09 32	09 37
Whitechapel	d			08 49	08 59		09 04	09 09			09 24						09 14		09 19	09 29				09 34	09 39
Shoreditch High Street	d			08 51	09 01		09 06	09 11			09 26						09 16		09 21	09 31				09 36	09 41
Hoxton	d			08 53	09 03		09 08	09 13			09 28						09 18		09 23	09 33				09 38	09 43
Haggerston	d			08 55	09 05		09 10	09 15			09 30						09 20		09 25	09 35				09 40	09 45
Dalston Junction Stn ELL	a			08 59	09 07		09 14	09 17			09 32						09 23		09 29	09 37				09 44	09 47
Canonbury	d				09 12			09 20			09 35						09 27			09 42					09 50
Highbury & Islington	a				09 16			09 25			09 40						09 32			09 46					09 55
	d																								
London Bridge 4 ⊖	a	08 48				08 58			09 06	09 14					09 08	09 14					09 19	09 29			

		SN	SN	LO	SN	SE	SN	SN		LO	SN	LO	LO	SN	SN	LO	LO	SN		LO	SN	SN	SE	SN	SN
East Croydon	d										09 20				09 30										
West Croydon 4	d							09 01		09 09			09 22												09 31
Norwood Junction 2	d									09 14	09 25		09 28		09 35										
Anerley	d									09 17			09 31		09 38										
Penge West	d									09 19			09 33		09 40										
London Victoria 15 ⊖	d	08 49				09 09	09 11											09 19					09 39	09 41	
Battersea Park 4	d	08 53					09 15											09 23						09 45	
Wandsworth Road	d						09 17																	09 47	
Clapham High Street ⊖	d						09 19																	09 49	
London Blackfriars 3 ⊖	d																								
Denmark Hill 4	d					09 18	09 24																09 48	09 54	
Peckham Rye 4	d				09 12	09a21	09 26	09 33													09 42	09 47	09a51	09 56	10 01
Queens Rd Peckham	d						09 29	09 36														09 49		09 59	10 04
South Bermondsey	d						09 31	09 38														09 52		10 01	10 06
Clapham Junction 10	d	08 57																09 27							
Wandsworth Common	d	09 00																09 30							
Balham 4 ⊖	d	09 02																09 32							
Streatham Hill	d	09 05																09 35							
West Norwood 4	d	09 09			09 23													09 40			09 53				
Gipsy Hill	d	09 12			09 26													09 43			09 56				
Crystal Palace 4	d	09 14	09 21	09 28	09a29									09 36			09 43	09 51		09 58	09a59				
Sydenham	d	09 18	09 24	09 31						09 21			09 36	09 39	09 42		09 46	09 54		10 01					
Forest Hill 4	d	09 20	09 27	09 34						09 23			09 38	09 42	09 45		09 49	09 57		10 04					
Honor Oak Park	d	09 23	09 29	09 36						09 26			09 41	09 44	09 47		09 51	09 59		10 06					
Brockley	d	09 25	09 32	09 39						09 28			09 43	09 47	09 50		09 54	10 02		10 09					
New Cross Gate 4	a	09 28	09 34	09 41						09 31	09 32		09 46	09 49	09 52		09 56	10 04		10 11					
	d	09 28	09 34	09 41						09 31	09 33		09 46	09 49	09 52		09 56	10 04		10 11					
New Cross ELL	d											09 36				09 51									
Surrey Quays	d			09 45						09 35		09 40	09 49			09 55	10 00			10 15					
Canada Water	d			09 47						09 37		09 42	09 51			09 57	10 02			10 17					
Rotherhithe	d			09 48						09 38		09 43	09 53			09 58	10 03			10 18					
Wapping	d			09 50						09 40		09 45	09 54			10 00	10 05			10 20					
Shadwell	d			09 52						09 42		09 47	09 56			10 02	10 07			10 22					
Whitechapel	d			09 54						09 44		09 49	09 59			10 04	10 09			10 24					
Shoreditch High Street	d			09 56						09 46		09 51	10 01			10 06	10 11			10 26					
Hoxton	d			09 58						09 48		09 53	10 03			10 08	10 13			10 28					
Haggerston	d			10 00						09 50		09 55	10 05			10 10	10 15			10 30					
Dalston Junction Stn ELL	a			10 02						09 53		09 59	10 07			10 14	10 17			10 32					
Canonbury	d			10 05						09 57			10 12				10 20			10 35					
Highbury & Islington	a			10 10						10 02			10 16				10 25			10 40					
	d																								
London Bridge 4 ⊖	a	09 37	09 43				09 38	09 44			09 41			09 59	10 00			10 11				09 58		10 06	10 11

East London Line and Croydon - London Victoria to London Bridge

Network Diagram - see first Page of Table 177

		LO	LO	LO	SN	LO	LO	SN	LO	SN	SN	SE	SN	SN	LO	LO	LO	SN	LO	LO	SN	LO
East Croydon 🚊	d				10 00													10 30				
West Croydon 4 🚊	d	09 39		09 52										10 01	10 09		10 22					
Norwood Junction 2	d	09 43		09 58	10 05										10 13		10 28	10 35				
Anerley	d	09 46		10 01	10 08										10 16		10 31	10 38				
Penge West	d	09 48		10 03	10 10										10 18		10 33	10 40				
London Victoria 15 ⊖	d							09 49				10 09	10 11								10 19	
Battersea Park 4	d							09 53					10 15								10 23	
Wandsworth Road	d												10 17									
Clapham High Street ⊖	d												10 19									
London Blackfriars 3 ⊖	d																					
Denmark Hill 4	d											10 18	10 24									
Peckham Rye 4	d									10 12	10 17	10a21	10 26	10 31								
Queens Rd Peckham	d										10 19		10 29	10 34								
South Bermondsey	d										10 22		10 31	10 36								
Clapham Junction 10	d							09 57													10 27	
Wandsworth Common	d							10 00													10 30	
Balham 4 ⊖	d							10 02													10 32	
Streatham Hill	d							10 05													10 35	
West Norwood 4	d							10 10		10 23											10 40	
Gipsy Hill	d							10 13		10 26											10 43	
Crystal Palace 4	d						10 13	10 21	10 28	10a29										10 43	10 51	10 58
Sydenham	d	09 51		10 06	10 12		10 16	10 24	10 31						10 21		10 36	10 42		10 46	10 54	11 01
Forest Hill 4	d	09 53		10 08	10 15		10 19	10 27	10 34						10 23		10 38	10 45		10 49	10 57	11 04
Honor Oak Park	d	09 56		10 11	10 17		10 21	10 29	10 36						10 26		10 41	10 47		10 51	10 59	11 06
Brockley	d	09 58		10 13	10 20		10 24	10 32	10 39						10 28		10 43	10 50		10 54	11 02	11 09
New Cross Gate 4	a	10 01		10 16	10 22		10 26	10 34	10 41						10 31		10 46	10 52		10 56	11 04	11 11
	d	10 01		10 16	10 22		10 26	10 34	10 41						10 31		10 46	10 52		10 56	11 04	11 11
New Cross ELL	d		10 06			10 21										10 36			10 51			
Surrey Quays	d	10 05	10 10	10 19		10 25	10 30		10 45						10 35	10 40	10 49		10 55	11 00		11 15
Canada Water	d	10 07	10 12	10 21		10 27	10 32		10 47						10 37	10 42	10 51		10 57	11 02		11 17
Rotherhithe	d	10 08	10 13	10 23		10 28	10 33		10 48						10 38	10 43	10 53		10 58	11 03		11 18
Wapping	d	10 10	10 15	10 24		10 30	10 35		10 50						10 40	10 45	10 54		11 00	11 05		11 20
Shadwell	d	10 12	10 17	10 26		10 32	10 37		10 52						10 42	10 47	10 56		11 02	11 07		11 22
Whitechapel	d	10 14	10 19	10 29		10 34	10 39		10 54						10 44	10 49	10 59		11 04	11 09		11 24
Shoreditch High Street	d	10 16	10 21	10 31		10 36	10 41		10 56						10 46	10 51	11 01		11 06	11 11		11 26
Hoxton	d	10 18	10 23	10 33		10 38	10 43		10 58						10 48	10 53	11 03		11 08	11 13		11 28
Haggerston	d	10 20	10 25	10 35		10 40	10 45		11 00						10 50	10 55	11 05		11 10	11 15		11 30
Dalston Junction Stn ELL	a	10 22	10 29	10 37		10 44	10 47		11 02						10 52	10 59	11 07		11 14	11 17		11 32
Canonbury	d	10 27		10 42			10 50		11 05						10 57		11 12			11 20		11 35
Highbury & Islington	a	10 32		10 46			10 55		11 10						11 02		11 16			11 25		11 40
	d																					
London Bridge 4 ⊖	a				10 29			10 41			10 26		10 36	10 41				10 59			11 11	

		SN	SN	SE	SN	SN	LO	LO	LO	SN	LO	LO	SN	LO	SN	SN	SE	SN	SN	LO	LO	LO	SN
East Croydon 🚊	d									11 00													11 30
West Croydon 4 🚊	d					10 31	10 39		10 52										11 01	11 09		11 22	
Norwood Junction 2	d						10 43		10 58	11 05										11 13		11 28	11 35
Anerley	d						10 46		11 01	11 08										11 16		11 31	11 38
Penge West	d						10 48		11 03	11 10										11 18		11 33	11 40
London Victoria 15 ⊖	d			10 39	10 41								10 49				11 09	11 11					
Battersea Park 4	d				10 45								10 53					11 15					
Wandsworth Road	d				10 47													11 17					
Clapham High Street ⊖	d				10 49													11 19					
London Blackfriars 3 ⊖	d																						
Denmark Hill 4	d			10 48	10 54												11 18	11 24					
Peckham Rye 4	d	10 42	10 47	10a51	10 56	11 01									11 12	11 17	11a21	11 26	11 31				
Queens Rd Peckham	d		10 49		10 59	11 04										11 19		11 29	11 34				
South Bermondsey	d		10 52		11 01	11 06										11 22		11 31	11 36				
Clapham Junction 10	d												10 57										
Wandsworth Common	d												11 00										
Balham 4 ⊖	d												11 02										
Streatham Hill	d												11 05										
West Norwood 4	d	10 53											11 10		11 23								
Gipsy Hill	d	10 56											11 13		11 26								
Crystal Palace 4	d	10a59										11 13	11 21	11 28	11a29								
Sydenham	d						10 51		11 06	11 12		11 16	11 24	11 31						11 21		11 36	11 42
Forest Hill 4	d						10 53		11 08	11 15		11 19	11 27	11 34						11 23		11 38	11 45
Honor Oak Park	d						10 56		11 11	11 17		11 21	11 29	11 36						11 26		11 41	11 47
Brockley	d						10 58		11 13	11 20		11 24	11 32	11 39						11 28		11 43	11 50
New Cross Gate 4	a						11 01		11 16	11 22		11 26	11 34	11 41						11 31		11 46	11 52
	d						11 01		11 16	11 22		11 26	11 34	11 41						11 31		11 46	11 52
New Cross ELL	d							11 06			11 21										11 36		
Surrey Quays	d						11 05	11 10	11 19		11 25	11 30		11 45						11 35	11 40	11 49	
Canada Water	d						11 07	11 12	11 21		11 27	11 32		11 47						11 37	11 42	11 51	
Rotherhithe	d						11 08	11 13	11 23		11 28	11 33		11 48						11 38	11 43	11 53	
Wapping	d						11 10	11 15	11 24		11 30	11 35		11 50						11 40	11 45	11 54	
Shadwell	d						11 12	11 17	11 26		11 32	11 37		11 52						11 42	11 47	11 56	
Whitechapel	d						11 14	11 19	11 29		11 34	11 39		11 54						11 44	11 49	11 59	
Shoreditch High Street	d						11 16	11 21	11 31		11 36	11 41		11 56						11 46	11 51	12 01	
Hoxton	d						11 18	11 23	11 33		11 38	11 43		11 58						11 48	11 53	12 03	
Haggerston	d						11 20	11 25	11 35		11 40	11 45		12 00						11 50	11 55	12 05	
Dalston Junction Stn ELL	a						11 22	11 29	11 37		11 44	11 47		12 02						11 52	11 59	12 07	
Canonbury	d						11 27		11 42			11 50		12 05						11 57		12 12	
Highbury & Islington	a						11 32		11 46			11 55		12 10						12 02		12 16	
	d																						
London Bridge 4 ⊖	a		10 56		11 06	11 11				11 29			11 41			11 26		11 36	11 41				11 59

East London Line and Croydon - London Victoria to London Bridge

Network Diagram - see first Page of Table 177

Station		LO	LO	SN	LO	SN		SN	SE	SN	SN	LO	LO	LO	SN	LO		LO	SN	LO	SN	SN	SE	SN	SN
East Croydon	d														12 00										
West Croydon 4	d										11 31	11 39		11 52											12 01
Norwood Junction 2	d											11 43		11 58	12 05										
Anerley	d											11 46		12 01	12 08										
Penge West	d											11 48		12 03	12 10										
London Victoria 15 ⊖	d			11 19					11 39	11 41									11 49				12 09	12 11	
Battersea Park 4	d			11 23						11 45									11 53					12 15	
Wandsworth Road	d									11 47														12 17	
Clapham High Street ⊖	d									11 49														12 19	
London Blackfriars 3 ⊖	d																								
Denmark Hill 4	d								11 48	11 54													12 18	12 24	
Peckham Rye 4	d					11 42		11 47	11a51	11 56	12 01										12 12	12 17	12a21	12 26	12 31
Queens Rd Peckham	d							11 49		11 59	12 04											12 19		12 29	12 34
South Bermondsey	d							11 52		12 01	12 06											12 22		12 31	12 36
Clapham Junction 10	d			11 27															11 57						
Wandsworth Common	d			11 30															12 00						
Balham 4 ⊖	d			11 32															12 02						
Streatham Hill	d			11 35															12 05						
West Norwood 4	d			11 40		11 53													12 10		12 23				
Gipsy Hill	d			11 43		11 56													12 13		12 26				
Crystal Palace 4	d		11 43	11 51	11 58	11a59												12 13	12 21	12 28	12a29				
Sydenham	d		11 46	11 54	12 01							11 51		12 06	12 12			12 16	12 24	12 31					
Forest Hill 4	d		11 49	11 57	12 04							11 53		12 08	12 15			12 19	12 27	12 34					
Honor Oak Park	d		11 51	11 59	12 06							11 56		12 11	12 17			12 21	12 29	12 36					
Brockley	d		11 54	12 02	12 09							11 58		12 13	12 20			12 24	12 32	12 39					
New Cross Gate 4	a		11 56	12 04	12 11							12 01		12 16	12 22			12 26	12 34	12 41					
	d		11 56	12 04	12 11							12 01		12 16	12 22			12 26	12 34	12 41					
New Cross ELL	d	11 51											12 06			12 21									
Surrey Quays	d	11 55	12 00		12 15							12 05	12 10	12 19		12 25		12 30		12 45					
Canada Water	d	11 57	12 02		12 17							12 07	12 12	12 21		12 27		12 32		12 47					
Rotherhithe	d	11 58	12 03		12 18							12 08	12 13	12 23		12 28		12 33		12 48					
Wapping	d	12 00	12 05		12 20							12 10	12 15	12 24		12 30		12 35		12 50					
Shadwell	d	12 02	12 07		12 22							12 12	12 17	12 26		12 32		12 37		12 52					
Whitechapel	d	12 04	12 09		12 24							12 14	12 19	12 29		12 34		12 39		12 54					
Shoreditch High Street	d	12 06	12 11		12 26							12 16	12 21	12 31		12 36		12 41		12 56					
Hoxton	d	12 08	12 13		12 28							12 18	12 23	12 33		12 38		12 43		12 58					
Haggerston	d	12 10	12 15		12 30							12 20	12 25	12 35		12 40		12 45		13 00					
Dalston Junction Stn ELL	a	12 14	12 17		12 32							12 22	12 29	12 37		12 44		12 47		13 02					
Canonbury	d		12 20		12 35							12 27		12 42				12 50		13 05					
Highbury & Islington	a		12 25		12 40							12 32		12 46				12 55		13 10					
	d																								
London Bridge 4 ⊖	a			12 14				11 56		12 06	12 11				12 29				12 41			12 26		12 36	12 41

Station		LO		LO	LO	SN	LO	LO	SN	LO	SN	SN		SE	SN	SN	LO	LO	LO	SN	LO	LO		SN	LO
East Croydon	d					12 30														13 00					
West Croydon 4	d	12 09			12 22											12 31	12 39		12 52						
Norwood Junction 2	d	12 13			12 28	12 35											12 43		12 58	13 05					
Anerley	d	12 16			12 31	12 38											12 46		13 01	13 08					
Penge West	d	12 18			12 33	12 40											12 48		13 03	13 10					
London Victoria 15 ⊖	d								12 19					12 39	12 41									12 49	
Battersea Park 4	d								12 23						12 45									12 53	
Wandsworth Road	d														12 47										
Clapham High Street ⊖	d														12 49										
London Blackfriars 3 ⊖	d																								
Denmark Hill 4	d													12 48	12 54										
Peckham Rye 4	d										12 42	12 47		12a51	12 56	13 01									
Queens Rd Peckham	d											12 49			12 59	13 04									
South Bermondsey	d											12 52			13 01	13 06									
Clapham Junction 10	d								12 27															12 57	
Wandsworth Common	d								12 30															13 00	
Balham 4 ⊖	d								12 32															13 02	
Streatham Hill	d								12 35															13 05	
West Norwood 4	d								12 40		12 53													13 10	
Gipsy Hill	d								12 43		12 56													13 13	
Crystal Palace 4	d							12 43	12 51	12 58	12a59											13 13		13 21	13 28
Sydenham	d	12 21			12 36	12 42		12 46	12 54	13 01							12 51		13 06	13 12		13 16		13 24	13 31
Forest Hill 4	d	12 23			12 38	12 45		12 49	12 57	13 04							12 53		13 08	13 15		13 19		13 27	13 34
Honor Oak Park	d	12 26			12 41	12 47		12 51	12 59	13 06							12 56		13 11	13 17		13 21		13 29	13 36
Brockley	d	12 28			12 43	12 50		12 54	13 02	13 09							12 58		13 13	13 20		13 24		13 32	13 39
New Cross Gate 4	a	12 31			12 46	12 52		12 56	13 04	13 11							13 01		13 16	13 22		13 26		13 34	13 41
	d	12 31			12 46	12 52		12 56	13 04	13 11							13 01		13 16	13 22		13 26		13 34	13 41
New Cross ELL	d			12 36			12 51											13 06			13 21				
Surrey Quays	d	12 35		12 40	12 49		12 55	13 00		13 15							13 05	13 10	13 19		13 25	13 30			13 45
Canada Water	d	12 37		12 42	12 51		12 57	13 02		13 17							13 07	13 12	13 21		13 27	13 32			13 47
Rotherhithe	d	12 38		12 43	12 53		12 58	13 03		13 18							13 08	13 13	13 23		13 28	13 33			13 48
Wapping	d	12 40		12 45	12 54		13 00	13 05		13 20							13 10	13 15	13 24		13 30	13 35			13 50
Shadwell	d	12 42		12 47	12 56		13 02	13 07		13 22							13 12	13 17	13 26		13 32	13 37			13 52
Whitechapel	d	12 44		12 49	12 59		13 04	13 09		13 24							13 14	13 19	13 29		13 34	13 39			13 54
Shoreditch High Street	d	12 46		12 51	13 01		13 06	13 11		13 26							13 16	13 21	13 31		13 36	13 41			13 56
Hoxton	d	12 48		12 53	13 03		13 08	13 13		13 28							13 18	13 23	13 33		13 38	13 43			13 58
Haggerston	d	12 50		12 55	13 05		13 10	13 15		13 30							13 20	13 25	13 35		13 40	13 45			14 00
Dalston Junction Stn ELL	a	12 52		12 59	13 07		13 14	13 17		13 32							13 22	13 29	13 37		13 44	13 47			14 02
Canonbury	d	12 57			13 12			13 20		13 35							13 27		13 42			13 50			14 05
Highbury & Islington	a	13 02			13 16			13 25		13 40							13 32		13 46			13 55			14 10
	d																								
London Bridge 4 ⊖	a					12 59			13 11			12 56			13 06	13 11				13 29				13 44	

East London Line and Croydon - London Victoria to London Bridge

Network Diagram - see first Page of Table 177

		SN	SN	SE	SN	SN	LO	LO		LO	SN	LO	LO	SN	LO	SN	SN	SE		SN	SN	LO	LO	LO	SN
East Croydon	d										13 30														14 00
West Croydon 4	d					13 01	13 09			13 22											13 31	13 39		13 52	
Norwood Junction 2	d						13 13			13 28	13 35											13 43		13 58	14 05
Anerley	d						13 16			13 31	13 38											13 46		14 01	14 08
Penge West	d						13 18			13 33	13 40											13 48		14 03	14 10
London Victoria 15	d			13 09	13 11									13 19				13 39		13 41					
Battersea Park 4	d				13 15									13 23						13 45					
Wandsworth Road	d				13 17															13 47					
Clapham High Street	d				13 19															13 49					
London Blackfriars 3	d																								
Denmark Hill 4	d			13 18	13 24													13 48		13 54					
Peckham Rye 4	d	13 12	13 17	13a21	13 26	13 31										13 42	13 47	13a51		13 56	14 01				
Queens Rd Peckham	d		13 19		13 29	13 34											13 49			13 59	14 04				
South Bermondsey	d		13 22		13 31	13 36											13 52			14 01	14 06				
Clapham Junction 10	d													13 27											
Wandsworth Common	d													13 30											
Balham 4	d													13 32											
Streatham Hill	d													13 35											
West Norwood 4	d	13 23												13 40		13 53									
Gipsy Hill	d	13 26												13 43		13 56									
Crystal Palace 4	d	13a29											13 43	13 51	13 58	13a59									
Sydenham	d						13 21			13 36	13 42		13 46	13 54	14 01							13 51		14 06	14 12
Forest Hill 4	d						13 23			13 38	13 45		13 49	13 57	14 04							13 53		14 08	14 15
Honor Oak Park	d						13 26			13 41	13 47		13 51	13 59	14 06							13 56		14 11	14 17
Brockley	d						13 28			13 43	13 50		13 54	14 02	14 09							13 58		14 13	14 20
New Cross Gate 4	a						13 31			13 46	13 52		13 56	14 04	14 11							14 01		14 16	14 22
	d						13 31			13 46	13 52		13 56	14 04	14 11							14 01		14 16	14 22
New Cross ELL	d							13 36				13 51											14 06		
Surrey Quays	d						13 35	13 40		13 49		13 55	14 00		14 15							14 05	14 10	14 19	
Canada Water	d						13 37	13 42		13 51		13 57	14 02		14 17							14 07	14 12	14 21	
Rotherhithe	d						13 38	13 43		13 53		13 58	14 03		14 18							14 08	14 13	14 23	
Wapping	d						13 40	13 45		13 54		14 00	14 05		14 20							14 10	14 15	14 24	
Shadwell	d						13 42	13 47		13 56		14 02	14 07		14 22							14 12	14 17	14 26	
Whitechapel	d						13 44	13 49		13 59		14 04	14 09		14 24							14 14	14 19	14 29	
Shoreditch High Street	d						13 46	13 51		14 01		14 06	14 11		14 26							14 16	14 21	14 31	
Hoxton	d						13 48	13 53		14 03		14 08	14 13		14 28							14 18	14 23	14 33	
Haggerston	d						13 50	13 55		14 05		14 10	14 15		14 30							14 20	14 25	14 35	
Dalston Junction Stn ELL	a						13 52	13 59		14 07		14 14	14 17		14 32							14 22	14 29	14 37	
Canonbury	d						13 57			14 12			14 20		14 35							14 27		14 42	
Highbury & Islington	a						14 02			14 16			14 25		14 40							14 32		14 46	
	d																								
London Bridge 4	a		13 26		13 36	13 41					13 59			14 11			13 56			14 06	14 11				14 29

		LO	LO	SN		LO	SN	SN	SE	SN	SN	LO	LO	LO		SN	LO	LO	SN	LO	SN	SN	SE	SN	
East Croydon	d															14 30									
West Croydon 4	d										14 01	14 09		14 22											
Norwood Junction 2	d											14 13		14 28		14 35									
Anerley	d											14 16		14 31		14 38									
Penge West	d											14 18		14 33		14 40									
London Victoria 15	d			13 49					14 09	14 11									14 19				14 39	14 41	
Battersea Park 4	d			13 53						14 15									14 23					14 45	
Wandsworth Road	d									14 17														14 47	
Clapham High Street	d									14 19														14 49	
London Blackfriars 3	d																								
Denmark Hill 4	d								14 18	14 24													14 48	14 54	
Peckham Rye 4	d						14 12	14 17	14a21	14 26	14 31										14 42	14 47	14a51	14 56	
Queens Rd Peckham	d							14 19		14 29	14 34											14 49		14 59	
South Bermondsey	d							14 22		14 31	14 36											14 52		15 01	
Clapham Junction 10	d			13 57															14 27						
Wandsworth Common	d			14 00															14 30						
Balham 4	d			14 02															14 32						
Streatham Hill	d			14 05															14 35						
West Norwood 4	d			14 10			14 23												14 40		14 53				
Gipsy Hill	d			14 13			14 26												14 43		14 56				
Crystal Palace 4	d		14 13	14 21		14 28	14a29											14 43	14 51	14 58	14a59				
Sydenham	d		14 16	14 24		14 31						14 21		14 36		14 42		14 46	14 54	15 01					
Forest Hill 4	d		14 19	14 27		14 34						14 23		14 38		14 45		14 49	14 57	15 04					
Honor Oak Park	d		14 21	14 29		14 36						14 26		14 41		14 47		14 51	14 59	15 06					
Brockley	d		14 24	14 32		14 39						14 28		14 43		14 50		14 54	15 02	15 09					
New Cross Gate 4	a		14 26	14 34		14 41						14 31		14 46		14 52		14 56	15 04	15 11					
	d		14 26	14 34		14 41						14 31		14 46		14 52		14 56	15 04	15 11					
New Cross ELL	d	14 21											14 36				14 51								
Surrey Quays	d	14 25	14 30			14 45						14 35	14 40	14 49			14 55	15 00		15 15					
Canada Water	d	14 27	14 32			14 47						14 37	14 42	14 51			14 57	15 02		15 17					
Rotherhithe	d	14 28	14 33			14 48						14 38	14 43	14 53			14 58	15 03		15 18					
Wapping	d	14 30	14 35			14 50						14 40	14 45	14 54			15 00	15 05		15 20					
Shadwell	d	14 32	14 37			14 52						14 42	14 47	14 56			15 02	15 07		15 22					
Whitechapel	d	14 34	14 39			14 54						14 44	14 49	14 59			15 04	15 09		15 24					
Shoreditch High Street	d	14 36	14 41			14 56						14 46	14 51	15 01			15 06	15 11		15 26					
Hoxton	d	14 38	14 43			14 58						14 48	14 53	15 03			15 08	15 13		15 28					
Haggerston	d	14 40	14 45			15 00						14 50	14 55	15 05			15 10	15 15		15 30					
Dalston Junction Stn ELL	a	14 44	14 47			15 02						14 52	14 59	15 07			15 14	15 17		15 32					
Canonbury	d		14 50			15 05						14 57		15 12				15 20		15 35					
Highbury & Islington	a		14 55			15 10						15 02		15 16				15 25		15 40					
	d																								
London Bridge 4	a			14 41				14 26		14 36	14 41					14 59			15 11			14 56		15 06	

East London Line and Croydon - London Victoria to London Bridge

Network Diagram - see first Page of Table 177

		SN	LO	LO	LO	SN	LO	LO	SN	LO		SN	SN	SE	SN	SN	LO	LO	LO	SN		LO	LO	SN	LO
East Croydon	d					15 00														15 30					
West Croydon 4	d	14 31	14 39		14 52											15 01	15 09		15 22						
Norwood Junction 2	d		14 43		14 58	15 05											15 13		15 28	15 35					
Anerley	d		14 46		15 01	15 08											15 16		15 31	15 38					
Penge West	d		14 48		15 03	15 10											15 18		15 33	15 40					
London Victoria 15 ⊖	d								14 49					15 09	15 11									15 19	
Battersea Park 4	d								14 53						15 15									15 23	
Wandsworth Road	d														15 17										
Clapham High Street ⊖	d														15 19										
London Blackfriars 3 ⊖	d																								
Denmark Hill 4	d													15 18	15 24										
Peckham Rye 4	d	15 01										15 12	15 17	15a21	15 26	15 31									
Queens Rd Peckham	d	15 04											15 19		15 29	15 34									
South Bermondsey	d	15 06											15 22		15 31	15 36									
Clapham Junction 10	d								14 57															15 27	
Wandsworth Common	d								15 00															15 30	
Balham 4 ⊖	d								15 02															15 32	
Streatham Hill	d								15 05															15 35	
West Norwood 4	d								15 10			15 23												15 40	
Gipsy Hill	d								15 13			15 26												15 43	
Crystal Palace 4	d							15 13	15 21	15 28		15a29											15 43	15 51	15 58
Sydenham	d		14 51		15 06	15 12		15 16	15 24	15 31							15 21		15 36	15 42			15 46	15 54	16 01
Forest Hill 4	d		14 53		15 08	15 15		15 19	15 27	15 34							15 23		15 38	15 45			15 49	15 57	16 04
Honor Oak Park	d		14 56		15 11	15 17		15 21	15 29	15 36							15 26		15 41	15 47			15 51	15 59	16 06
Brockley	d		14 58		15 13	15 20		15 24	15 32	15 39							15 28		15 43	15 50			15 54	16 02	16 09
New Cross Gate 4	a		15 01		15 16	15 22		15 26	15 34	15 41							15 31		15 46	15 52			15 56	16 04	16 11
	d		15 01		15 16	15 22		15 26	15 34	15 41							15 31		15 46	15 52			15 56	16 04	16 11
New Cross ELL	d			15 06			15 21											15 36				15 51			
Surrey Quays	d		15 05	15 10	15 19		15 25	15 30		15 45							15 35	15 40	15 49			15 55	16 00		16 15
Canada Water	d		15 07	15 12	15 21		15 27	15 32		15 47							15 37	15 42	15 51			15 57	16 02		16 17
Rotherhithe	d		15 08	15 13	15 23		15 28	15 33		15 48							15 38	15 43	15 53			15 58	16 03		16 18
Wapping	d		15 10	15 15	15 24		15 30	15 35		15 50							15 40	15 45	15 54			16 00	16 05		16 20
Shadwell	d		15 12	15 17	15 26		15 32	15 37		15 52							15 42	15 47	15 56			16 02	16 07		16 22
Whitechapel	d		15 14	15 19	15 29		15 34	15 39		15 54							15 44	15 49	15 59			16 04	16 09		16 24
Shoreditch High Street	d		15 16	15 21	15 31		15 36	15 41		15 56							15 46	15 51	16 01			16 06	16 11		16 26
Hoxton	d		15 18	15 23	15 33		15 38	15 43		15 58							15 48	15 53	16 03			16 08	16 13		16 28
Haggerston	d		15 20	15 25	15 35		15 40	15 45		16 00							15 50	15 55	16 05			16 10	16 15		16 30
Dalston Junction Stn ELL	a		15 22	15 29	15 37		15 44	15 47		16 02							15 52	15 59	16 07			16 14	16 17		16 32
Canonbury	d		15 27		15 42			15 50		16 05							15 57		16 12				16 20		16 35
Highbury & Islington	a		15 32		15 46			15 55		16 10							16 02		16 16				16 25		16 40
	d																								
London Bridge 4 ⊖	a	15 11				15 29			15 41				15 26		15 36	15 41				15 59				16 11	

		SN	SN	SE	SN	SN		LO	LO	LO	SN	SN	LO	LO	SN	LO		SN	SN	SE	SN	SN	LO	LO	LO
East Croydon	d											16 00													
West Croydon 4	d					15 31		15 39		15 52												16 01	16 09		16 22
Norwood Junction 2	d							15 43		15 58		16 05											16 13		16 28
Anerley	d							15 46		16 01		16 08											16 16		16 31
Penge West	d							15 48		16 03		16 10											16 18		16 33
London Victoria 15 ⊖	d			15 39	15 41										15 49					16 09	16 11				
Battersea Park 4	d				15 45										15 53						16 15				
Wandsworth Road	d				15 47																16 17				
Clapham High Street ⊖	d				15 49																16 19				
London Blackfriars 3 ⊖	d																								
Denmark Hill 4	d			15 48	15 54															16 18	16 24				
Peckham Rye 4	d	15 42	15 47	15a51	15 56	16 01					16 07							16 12	16 17	16a21	16 26	16 31			
Queens Rd Peckham	d		15 49		15 59	16 04					16 10								16 19		16 29	16 34			
South Bermondsey	d		15 52		16 01	16 06					16 12								16 22		16 31	16 36			
Clapham Junction 10	d														15 57										
Wandsworth Common	d														16 00										
Balham 4 ⊖	d														16 02										
Streatham Hill	d														16 05										
West Norwood 4	d	15 53													16 10			16 23							
Gipsy Hill	d	15 56													16 13			16 26							
Crystal Palace 4	d	15a59												16 13	16 21	16 28		16a29							
Sydenham	d							15 51		16 06		16 12		16 16	16 24	16 31							16 21		16 36
Forest Hill 4	d							15 53		16 08		16 15		16 19	16 27	16 34							16 23		16 38
Honor Oak Park	d							15 56		16 11		16 17		16 21	16 29	16 36							16 26		16 41
Brockley	d							15 58		16 13		16 20		16 24	16 32	16 39							16 28		16 43
New Cross Gate 4	a							16 01		16 16		16 22		16 26	16 34	16 41							16 31		16 46
	d							16 01		16 16		16 22		16 26	16 34	16 41							16 31		16 46
New Cross ELL	d								16 06				16 21											16 36	
Surrey Quays	d							16 05	16 10	16 19			16 25	16 30		16 45							16 35	16 40	16 49
Canada Water	d							16 07	16 12	16 21			16 27	16 32		16 47							16 37	16 42	16 51
Rotherhithe	d							16 08	16 13	16 23			16 28	16 33		16 48							16 38	16 43	16 53
Wapping	d							16 10	16 15	16 24			16 30	16 35		16 50							16 40	16 45	16 54
Shadwell	d							16 12	16 17	16 26			16 32	16 37		16 52							16 42	16 47	16 56
Whitechapel	d							16 14	16 19	16 29			16 34	16 39		16 54							16 44	16 49	16 59
Shoreditch High Street	d							16 16	16 21	16 31			16 36	16 41		16 56							16 46	16 51	17 01
Hoxton	d							16 18	16 23	16 33			16 38	16 43		16 58							16 48	16 53	17 03
Haggerston	d							16 20	16 25	16 35			16 40	16 45		17 00							16 50	16 55	17 05
Dalston Junction Stn ELL	a							16 22	16 29	16 37			16 44	16 47		17 02							16 52	16 59	17 07
Canonbury	d							16 27		16 42				16 50		17 05							16 57		17 12
Highbury & Islington	a							16 32		16 46				16 55		17 10							17 02		17 16
	d																								
London Bridge 4 ⊖	a		15 56		16 06	16 11					16 17	16 29			16 41				16 26		16 38	16 41			

East London Line and Croydon - London Victoria to London Bridge

Network Diagram - see first Page of Table 177

		SN		LO	LO	SN	LO	SN	SN	SE	SN	SN		LO	LO	LO	SN	LO	LO	SN	SN	SE		SN	SN
East Croydon	d	16 30															17 00								
West Croydon 4	d											16 31		16 39		16 52									
Norwood Junction 2	d	16 35												16 43		16 58	17 05								
Anerley	d	16 38												16 46		17 01	17 08								
Penge West	d	16 40												16 48		17 03	17 10								
London Victoria 15	d					16 19				16 39	16 41									16 49		17 04			17 11
Battersea Park 4	d					16 23					16 45									16 53					17 15
Wandsworth Road	d										16 47														17 17
Clapham High Street	d										16 49														17 19
London Blackfriars 3	d																								
Denmark Hill 4	d									16 48	16 54											17 13			17 24
Peckham Rye 4	d							16 42	16 47	16a51	16 56	17 00									17 07	17a16		17 17	17 26
Queens Rd Peckham	d								16 49		16 59	17 03												17 19	17 29
South Bermondsey	d								16 52		17 01	17 05												17 22	17 31
Clapham Junction 10	d					16 27														16 57					
Wandsworth Common	d					16 30														17 00					
Balham 4	d					16 32														17 03					
Streatham Hill	d					16 35														17 06					
West Norwood 4	d					16 39		16 53												17 09	17 20				
Gipsy Hill	d					16 44		16 56												17 12	17 23				
Crystal Palace 4	d				16 43	16 50	16 58	16a59											17 13	17b21	17a26				
Sydenham	d	16 42			16 46	16 54	17 01							16 51		17 06	17 12		17 16	17 24					
Forest Hill 4	d	16 45			16 49	16 56	17 04							16 53		17 08	17 15		17 19	17 27					
Honor Oak Park	d	16 47			16 51	16 59	17 06							16 56		17 11	17 17		17 21	17 29					
Brockley	d	16 50			16 54	17 01	17 09							16 58		17 13	17 20		17 24	17 32					
New Cross Gate 4	a	16 52			16 56	17 04	17 11							17 01		17 16	17 22		17 26	17 34					
	d	16 52			16 56	17 04	17 11							17 01		17 16	17 22		17 26	17 34					
New Cross ELL	d			16 51											17 06			17 21							
Surrey Quays	d			16 55	17 00		17 15							17 05	17 10	17 19		17 25	17 30						
Canada Water	d			16 57	17 02		17 17							17 07	17 12	17 21		17 27	17 32						
Rotherhithe	d			16 58	17 03		17 18							17 08	17 13	17 23		17 28	17 33						
Wapping	d			17 00	17 05		17 20							17 10	17 15	17 24		17 30	17 35						
Shadwell	d			17 02	17 07		17 22							17 12	17 17	17 26		17 32	17 37						
Whitechapel	d			17 04	17 09		17 24							17 14	17 19	17 29		17 34	17 39						
Shoreditch High Street	d			17 06	17 11		17 26							17 16	17 21	17 31		17 36	17 41						
Hoxton	d			17 08	17 13		17 28							17 18	17 23	17 33		17 38	17 43						
Haggerston	d			17 10	17 15		17 30							17 20	17 25	17 35		17 40	17 45						
Dalston Junction Stn ELL	a			17 14	17 17		17 32							17 22	17 29	17 37		17 44	17 47						
Canonbury	d				17 20		17 35							17 27		17 42			17 50						
Highbury & Islington	a				17 25		17 40							17 32		17 46			17 55						
	d																								
London Bridge 4	a	17 02				17 12			16 56		17 08	17 10					17 35			17 43				17 27	17 38

		SN	LO	SN	SN	LO	LO	LO		LO	LO	SN	SN	SE	SN	SN	SN	SN		LO	SN	LO	LO	LO	SN
East Croydon	d															17 30									
West Croydon 4	d	17 01	17 09	17 12				17 22										17 31		17 39	17 42			17 52	
Norwood Junction 2	d		17 13					17 28							17 32	17 35				17 43				17 58	18 04
Anerley	d		17 16					17 31								17 38				17 46				18 01	18 07
Penge West	d		17 18					17 33								17 40				17 48				18 03	18 09
London Victoria 15	d											17 22		17 34			17 41								
Battersea Park 4	d											17 26					17 45								
Wandsworth Road	d																17 47								
Clapham High Street	d																17 49								
London Blackfriars 3	d																								
Denmark Hill 4	d													17 43			17 54								
Peckham Rye 4	d	17 29			17 35								17 37	17a46	17 53		17 57	18 01							
Queens Rd Peckham	d	17 32			17 37										17 55		17 59	18 04							
South Bermondsey	d	17 34			17 40										17 58		18 02	18 06							
Clapham Junction 10	d											17 30													
Wandsworth Common	d											17 33													
Balham 4	d											17 35													
Streatham Hill	d											17 38													
West Norwood 4	d											17 42	17 49												
Gipsy Hill	d											17 45	17 52												
Crystal Palace 4	d						17 28				17 43	17 48	17a54										17 58		
Sydenham	d		17 21				17 31	17 36			17 46	17 54				17 42				17 51			18 01	18 06	18 11
Forest Hill 4	d		17 23				17 34	17 38			17 49	17 57				17 45				17 53			18 04	18 08	18 14
Honor Oak Park	d		17 26				17 36	17 41			17 51	17 59				17 47				17 56			18 06	18 11	18 16
Brockley	d		17 28				17 39	17 43			17 54	18 02				17 50				17 58			18 09	18 13	18 19
New Cross Gate 4	a		17 31				17 41	17 46			17 56	18 04				17 52				18 01			18 11	18 16	18 21
	d		17 31				17 41	17 46			17 56	18 04				17 52				18 01			18 11	18 16	18 21
New Cross ELL	d					17 36				17 51												18 06			
Surrey Quays	d		17 35			17 40	17 45	17 49		17 55	18 00									18 05		18 10	18 15	18 19	
Canada Water	d		17 37			17 42	17 47	17 51		17 57	18 02									18 07		18 12	18 17	18 21	
Rotherhithe	d		17 38			17 43	17 48	17 53		17 58	18 03									18 08		18 13	18 18	18 23	
Wapping	d		17 40			17 45	17 50	17 54		18 00	18 05									18 10		18 15	18 20	18 24	
Shadwell	d		17 42			17 47	17 52	17 56		18 02	18 07									18 12		18 17	18 22	18 26	
Whitechapel	d		17 44			17 49	17 54	17 59		18 04	18 09									18 14		18 19	18 24	18 29	
Shoreditch High Street	d		17 46			17 51	17 56	18 01		18 06	18 11									18 16		18 21	18 26	18 31	
Hoxton	d		17 48			17 53	17 58	18 03		18 08	18 13									18 18		18 23	18 28	18 33	
Haggerston	d		17 50			17 55	18 00	18 05		18 10	18 15									18 20		18 25	18 30	18 35	
Dalston Junction Stn ELL	a		17 52			17 59	18 02	18 07		18 14	18 17									18 23		18 29	18 32	18 37	
Canonbury	d		17 57				18 05	18 12			18 20									18 27			18 35	18 42	
Highbury & Islington	a		18 02				18 10	18 16			18 25									18 32			18 40	18 46	
	d																								
London Bridge 4	a	17 40		17 28	17 44							18 13			18 02	17 59	18 08	18 11			18 00				18 31

b Arr. 1715

East London Line and Croydon - London Victoria to London Bridge

Network Diagram - see first Page of Table 177

		LO	LO	SN		SN	SE	SN	SN	SN	LO	SN	LO	LO		LO	LO	SE	SN	SN	SN	LO	SN	SN	
East Croydon 🚊	d																				18 30				
West Croydon 4 🚊	d									18 01	18 09	18 13				18 22									
Norwood Junction 2	d										18 13					18 28					18 35				
Anerley	d										18 16					18 31					18 38				
Penge West	d										18 18					18 33					18 40				
London Victoria 15 ⊖	d			17 52			17 56		18 11									18 18					18 22		
Battersea Park 4	d			17 56					18 15														18 26		
Wandsworth Road	d								18 17																
Clapham High Street ⊖	d								18 19																
London Blackfriars 3 ⊖	d																								
Denmark Hill 4	d						18 06		18 24									18 28							
Peckham Rye 4	d					18 07	18a08	18 12	18 26	18 29								18a31	18 32	18 36				18 37	
Queens Rd Peckham	d							18 15	18 29	18 32									18 35	18 38					
South Bermondsey	d							18 17	18 31	18 34									18 37	18 41					
Clapham Junction 10	d			18 00																			18 30		
Wandsworth Common	d			18 03																			18 33		
Balham 4 ⊖	d			18 05																			18 35		
Streatham Hill	d			18 08																			18 38		
West Norwood 4	d			18 14		18 20																	18 42	18 51	
Gipsy Hill	d			18 17		18 23																	18 45	18 54	
Crystal Palace 4	d		18 13	18 20		18a26								18 28								18 43	18 51	18a57	
Sydenham	d		18 16	18 24							18 21			18 31		18 36					18 42	18 46	18 54		
Forest Hill 4	d		18 19	18 27							18 23			18 34		18 38					18 45	18 49	18 57		
Honor Oak Park	d		18 21	18 29							18 26			18 36		18 41					18 47	18 51	18 59		
Brockley	d		18 24	18 32							18 28			18 39		18 43					18 50	18 54	19 02		
New Cross Gate 4	a		18 26	18 34							18 31			18 41		18 46					18 52	18 56	19 04		
	d		18 26	18 34							18 31			18 41		18 46					18 52	18 56	19 04		
New Cross ELL	d	18 21											18 36				18 51								
Surrey Quays	d	18 25	18 30								18 35		18 40	18 45		18 49	18 55					19 00			
Canada Water	d	18 27	18 32								18 37		18 42	18 47		18 51	18 57					19 02			
Rotherhithe	d	18 28	18 33								18 38		18 43	18 48		18 53	18 58					19 03			
Wapping	d	18 30	18 35								18 40		18 45	18 50		18 54	19 00					19 05			
Shadwell	d	18 32	18 37								18 42		18 47	18 52		18 56	19 02					19 07			
Whitechapel	d	18 34	18 39								18 44		18 49	18 54		18 59	19 04					19 09			
Shoreditch High Street	d	18 36	18 41								18 46		18 51	18 56		19 01	19 06					19 11			
Hoxton	d	18 38	18 43								18 48		18 53	18 58		19 03	19 08					19 13			
Haggerston	d	18 40	18 45								18 50		18 55	19 00		19 05	19 10					19 15			
Dalston Junction Stn ELL	a	18 44	18 47								18 52		18 59	19 02		19 07	19 14					19 17			
Canonbury	d		18 50								18 57			19 05		19 12						19 20			
Highbury & Islington	a		18 55								19 02			19 10		19 16						19 25			
	d																								
London Bridge 4 ⊖	a			18 45				18 22	18 38	18 39		18 29							18 42	18 45	18 59		19 13		

		SE	SN	SN	LO	LO	LO	LO	SN	LO		LO	SN	SN	SN	SN	LO	SN	SE	SN		SN	LO	LO	LO
East Croydon 🚊	d								19 00																
West Croydon 4 🚊	d			18 31	18 39			18 52														19 01	19 09		19 22
Norwood Junction 2	d				18 43			18 58	19 05														19 13		19 28
Anerley	d				18 46			19 01	19 08														19 16		19 31
Penge West	d				18 48			19 03	19 10														19 18		19 33
London Victoria 15 ⊖	d	18 39	18 41										18 52						19 09	19 11					
Battersea Park 4	d		18 45										18 56							19 15					
Wandsworth Road	d		18 47																	19 17					
Clapham High Street ⊖	d		18 49																	19 19					
London Blackfriars 3 ⊖	d																								
Denmark Hill 4	d	18 48	18 54																19 18	19 24					
Peckham Rye 4	d	18a51	18 57	19 01										19 06	19 07	19 14		19 17	19a21	19 26		19 29			
Queens Rd Peckham	d		19 00	19 04											19 10	19 17				19 29		19 32			
South Bermondsey	d		19 02	19 06											19 12	19 19				19 31		19 34			
Clapham Junction 10	d												19 00												
Wandsworth Common	d												19 03												
Balham 4 ⊖	d												19 05												
Streatham Hill	d												19 08												
West Norwood 4	d												19 12	19 17				19 30							
Gipsy Hill	d												19 15	19 20				19 33							
Crystal Palace 4	d						18 58					19 13	19 21	19a23			19 28	19a35							
Sydenham	d				18 51		19 01	19 06	19 12			19 16	19 24				19 31						19 21		19 36
Forest Hill 4	d				18 53		19 04	19 08	19 15			19 19	19 27				19 34						19 23		19 38
Honor Oak Park	d				18 56		19 06	19 11	19 17			19 21	19 29				19 36						19 26		19 41
Brockley	d				18 58		19 09	19 13	19 20			19 24	19 32				19 39						19 28		19 43
New Cross Gate 4	a				19 01		19 11	19 16	19 22			19 26	19 34				19 41						19 31		19 46
	d				19 01		19 11	19 16	19 22			19 26	19 34				19 41						19 31		19 46
New Cross ELL	d					19 06				19 21														19 36	
Surrey Quays	d				19 05	19 10	19 15	19 19		19 25		19 30					19 45						19 35	19 40	19 49
Canada Water	d				19 07	19 12	19 17	19 21		19 27		19 32					19 47						19 37	19 42	19 51
Rotherhithe	d				19 08	19 13	19 18	19 23		19 28		19 33					19 48						19 38	19 43	19 53
Wapping	d				19 10	19 15	19 20	19 24		19 30		19 35					19 50						19 40	19 45	19 54
Shadwell	d				19 12	19 17	19 22	19 26		19 32		19 37					19 52						19 42	19 47	19 56
Whitechapel	d				19 14	19 19	19 24	19 29		19 34		19 39					19 54						19 44	19 49	19 59
Shoreditch High Street	d				19 16	19 21	19 26	19 31		19 36		19 41					19 56						19 46	19 51	20 01
Hoxton	d				19 18	19 23	19 28	19 33		19 38		19 43					19 58						19 48	19 53	20 03
Haggerston	d				19 20	19 25	19 30	19 35		19 40		19 45					20 00						19 50	19 55	20 05
Dalston Junction Stn ELL	a				19 22	19 29	19 32	19 37		19 44		19 47					20 02						19 52	19 59	20 07
Canonbury	d				19 27		19 35	19 42				19 50					20 05						19 57		20 12
Highbury & Islington	a				19 32		19 40	19 46				19 55					20 10						20 02		20 16
	d																								
London Bridge 4 ⊖	a		19 09	19 11					19 29				19 41		19 17	19 24				19 36		19 41			

East London Line and Croydon - London Victoria to London Bridge

Network Diagram - see first Page of Table 177

Station		SN	LO	LO	SN	SN		SN	LO	SN	SN	SE	SN	SN	LO	LO		LO	SN	LO	LO	SN	LO	SN	SN
East Croydon	d	19 30																	20 00						
West Croydon 4	d													19 31	19 39			19 52							
Norwood Junction 2	d	19 35													19 43			19 58	20 05						
Anerley	d	19 38													19 46			20 01	20 08						
Penge West	d	19 40													19 48			20 03	20 10						
London Victoria 15 ⊖	d				19 22							19 39	19 41									19 52			
Battersea Park 4	d				19 26								19 45									19 56			
Wandsworth Road	d												19 47												
Clapham High Street ⊖	d												19 49												
London Blackfriars 3 ⊖	d																								
Denmark Hill 4	d											19 48	19 54												
Peckham Rye 4	d					19 37		19 38		19 47	19 49	19a51	19 56	20 01										20 12	20 18
Queens Rd Peckham	d							19 41			19 51		19 59	20 04											20 21
South Bermondsey	d							19 43			19 54		20 01	20 06											20 23
Clapham Junction 10	d				19 30																	20 00			
Wandsworth Common	d				19 33																	20 03			
Balham 4 ⊖	d				19 35																	20 05			
Streatham Hill	d				19 38																	20 08			
West Norwood 4	d				19 42	19 49				20 00												20 12		20 24	
Gipsy Hill	d				19 45	19 52				20 03												20 15		20 27	
Crystal Palace 4	d			19 43	19 51	19a54			19 58	20a05											20 13	20 21	20 28	20a29	
Sydenham	d	19 42		19 46	19 54				20 01						19 51			20 06	20 12		20 16	20 24	20 31		
Forest Hill 4	d	19 45		19 49	19 57				20 04						19 53			20 08	20 15		20 19	20 27	20 34		
Honor Oak Park	d	19 47		19 51	19 59				20 06						19 56			20 11	20 17		20 21	20 29	20 36		
Brockley	d	19 50		19 54	20 02				20 09						19 58			20 13	20 20		20 24	20 32	20 39		
New Cross Gate 4	a	19 52		19 56	20 04				20 11						20 01			20 16	20 22		20 26	20 34	20 41		
	d	19 52		19 56	20 04				20 11						20 01			20 16	20 22		20 26	20 34	20 41		
New Cross ELL	d		19 51													20 06				20 21					
Surrey Quays	d		19 55	20 00					20 15						20 05	20 10		20 19		20 25	20 30		20 45		
Canada Water	d		19 57	20 02					20 17						20 07	20 12		20 21		20 27	20 32		20 47		
Rotherhithe	d		19 58	20 03					20 18						20 08	20 13		20 23		20 28	20 33		20 48		
Wapping	d		20 00	20 05					20 20						20 10	20 15		20 24		20 30	20 35		20 50		
Shadwell	d		20 02	20 07					20 22						20 12	20 17		20 26		20 32	20 37		20 52		
Whitechapel	d		20 04	20 09					20 24						20 14	20 19		20 29		20 34	20 39		20 54		
Shoreditch High Street	d		20 06	20 11					20 26						20 16	20 21		20 31		20 36	20 41		20 56		
Hoxton	d		20 08	20 13					20 28						20 18	20 23		20 33		20 38	20 43		20 58		
Haggerston	d		20 10	20 15					20 30						20 20	20 25		20 35		20 40	20 45		21 00		
Dalston Junction Stn ELL	a		20 14	20 17					20 32						20 22	20 29		20 37		20 44	20 47		21 02		
Canonbury	d			20 20					20 35						20 27			20 42			20 50		21 05		
Highbury & Islington	a			20 25					20 40						20 32			20 46			20 55		21 10		
	d																								
London Bridge 4 ⊖	a	19 59			20 11			19 51			19 58		20 06	20 14					20 29			20 41			20 28

Station		SN		SN	LO	LO	LO	SN	LO	LO	SN	LO		SN	SN	SN	SN	LO	LO	LO	SN	LO		LO	SN
East Croydon	d							20 31													21 00				
West Croydon 4	d			20 01	20 09		20 22										20 31	20 39		20 52					
Norwood Junction 2	d				20 13		20 28	20 35										20 43		20 58	21 05				
Anerley	d				20 16		20 31	20 38										20 46		21 01	21 08				
Penge West	d				20 18		20 33	20 40										20 48		21 03	21 10				
London Victoria 15 ⊖	d	20 11									20 22					20 41									20 52
Battersea Park 4	d	20 15									20 26					20 45									20 56
Wandsworth Road	d	20 17														20 47									
Clapham High Street ⊖	d	20 19														20 49									
London Blackfriars 3 ⊖	d																								
Denmark Hill 4	d	20 24														20 54									
Peckham Rye 4	d	20 26		20 31										20 42	20 48	20 56	21 01								
Queens Rd Peckham	d	20 29		20 34											20 50	20 59	21 04								
South Bermondsey	d	20 31		20 36											20 53	21 01	21 06								
Clapham Junction 10	d										20 30														21 00
Wandsworth Common	d										20 33														21 03
Balham 4 ⊖	d										20 35														21 05
Streatham Hill	d										20 38														21 08
West Norwood 4	d										20 42			20 54											21 12
Gipsy Hill	d										20 45			20 57											21 15
Crystal Palace 4	d									20 43	20 51	20 58		20a59										21 13	21 21
Sydenham	d				20 21		20 36	20 42		20 46	20 54	21 01						20 51		21 06	21 12			21 16	21 27
Forest Hill 4	d				20 23		20 38	20 45		20 49	20 57	21 04						20 53		21 08	21 15			21 19	21 29
Honor Oak Park	d				20 26		20 41	20 47		20 51	20 59	21 06						20 56		21 11	21 17			21 21	21 32
Brockley	d				20 28		20 43	20 50		20 54	21 02	21 09						20 58		21 13	21 20			21 24	21 34
New Cross Gate 4	a				20 31		20 46	20 52		20 56	21 04	21 11						21 01		21 16	21 22			21 26	21 37
	d				20 31		20 46	20 52		20 56	21 04	21 11						21 01		21 16	21 22			21 26	21 37
New Cross ELL	d					20 36			20 51										21 06			21 21			
Surrey Quays	d				20 35	20 40	20 49		20 55	21 00		21 15						21 05	21 10	21 19		21 25		21 30	
Canada Water	d				20 37	20 42	20 51		20 57	21 02		21 17						21 07	21 12	21 21		21 27		21 32	
Rotherhithe	d				20 38	20 43	20 53		20 58	21 03		21 18						21 08	21 13	21 23		21 28		21 33	
Wapping	d				20 40	20 45	20 54		21 00	21 05		21 20						21 10	21 15	21 24		21 30		21 35	
Shadwell	d				20 42	20 47	20 56		21 02	21 07		21 22						21 12	21 17	21 26		21 32		21 37	
Whitechapel	d				20 44	20 49	20 59		21 04	21 09		21 24						21 14	21 19	21 29		21 34		21 39	
Shoreditch High Street	d				20 46	20 51	21 01		21 06	21 11		21 26						21 16	21 21	21 31		21 36		21 41	
Hoxton	d				20 48	20 53	21 03		21 08	21 13		21 28						21 18	21 23	21 33		21 38		21 43	
Haggerston	d				20 50	20 55	21 05		21 10	21 15		21 30						21 20	21 25	21 35		21 40		21 45	
Dalston Junction Stn ELL	a				20 52	20 59	21 07		21 14	21 17		21 32						21 22	21 29	21 37		21 44		21 47	
Canonbury	d				20 57		21 12			21 20		21 35						21 27		21 42				21 50	
Highbury & Islington	a				21 02		21 16			21 25		21 40						21 32		21 46				21 55	
	d																								
London Bridge 4 ⊖	a	20 36		20 41				20 59			21 11				20 57	21 06	21 11				21 29				21 43

East London Line and Croydon - London Victoria to London Bridge

Network Diagram - see first Page of Table 177

Station		LO	SN	SN	SN	SN	LO	LO		LO	SN	LO	LO	SN	LO	SN	SN	SN		SE	SN	LO	LO	LO	SN
East Croydon	d										21 30														22 00
West Croydon 4	d					21 01	21 09			21 22											21 31	21 39		21 52	
Norwood Junction 2	d						21 13			21 28	21 35											21 43		21 58	22 05
Anerley	d						21 16			21 31	21 38											21 46		22 01	22 08
Penge West	d						21 18			21 33	21 40											21 48		22 03	22 10
London Victoria 15 ⊖	d				21 11									21 23				21 41		21 43					
Battersea Park 4	d				21 15									21 27				21 45							
Wandsworth Road	d				21 17													21 47							
Clapham High Street ⊖	d				21 19													21 49							
London Blackfriars 3 ⊖	d																								
Denmark Hill 4	d				21 24													21 54		21 52					
Peckham Rye 4	d		21 12	21 17	21 26	21 31										21 42	21 47	21 56		21a55	22 01				
Queens Rd Peckham	d			21 19	21 29	21 34											21 49	21 59			22 04				
South Bermondsey	d			21 22	21 31	21 36											21 52	22 01			22 06				
Clapham Junction 10	d													21 31											
Wandsworth Common	d													21 34											
Balham 4 ⊖	d													21 36											
Streatham Hill	d													21 39											
West Norwood 4	d		21 24											21 43		21 54									
Gipsy Hill	d		21 27											21 46		21 57									
Crystal Palace 4	d	21 28	21a29										21 43	21 51	21 58	21a59									
Sydenham	d	21 31					21 21			21 36	21 42		21 46	21 54	22 01							21 51		22 06	22 12
Forest Hill 4	d	21 34					21 23			21 38	21 45		21 49	21 57	22 04							21 53		22 08	22 15
Honor Oak Park	d	21 36					21 26			21 41	21 47		21 51	21 59	22 06							21 56		22 11	22 17
Brockley	d	21 39					21 28			21 43	21 50		21 54	22 02	22 09							21 58		22 13	22 20
New Cross Gate 4	a	21 41					21 31			21 46	21 52		21 56	22 04	22 11							22 01		22 16	22 22
	d	21 41					21 31			21 46	21 52		21 56	22 04	22 11							22 01		22 16	22 22
New Cross ELL	d							21 36				21 51											22 06		
Surrey Quays	d	21 45					21 35	21 40		21 49		21 55	22 00		22 15							22 05	22 10	22 19	
Canada Water	d	21 47					21 37	21 42		21 51		21 57	22 02		22 17							22 07	22 12	22 21	
Rotherhithe	d	21 48					21 38	21 43		21 53		21 58	22 03		22 18							22 08	22 13	22 23	
Wapping	d	21 50					21 40	21 45		21 54		22 00	22 05		22 20							22 10	22 15	22 24	
Shadwell	d	21 52					21 42	21 47		21 56		22 02	22 07		22 22							22 12	22 17	22 26	
Whitechapel	d	21 54					21 44	21 49		21 59		22 04	22 09		22 24							22 14	22 19	22 29	
Shoreditch High Street	d	21 56					21 46	21 51		22 01		22 06	22 11		22 26							22 16	22 21	22 31	
Hoxton	d	21 58					21 48	21 53		22 03		22 08	22 13		22 28							22 18	22 23	22 33	
Haggerston	d	22 00					21 50	21 55		22 05		22 10	22 15		22 30							22 20	22 25	22 35	
Dalston Junction Stn ELL	a	22 02					21 52	21 59		22 07		22 14	22 17		22 32							22 22	22 29	22 37	
Canonbury	d	22 05					21 57			22 12			22 20		22 35							22 27		22 42	
Highbury & Islington	a	22 10					22 02			22 16			22 25		22 40							22 32		22 46	
	d																								
London Bridge 4 ⊖	a			21 26	21 36	21 41					21 59			22 13			21 56	22 06			22 11				22 29

Station		LO	SN	LO		SN	SN	SN	SE	SN	LO	LO	LO	SN		LO	SN	SN	SN	SN	SE	SN	LO	LO	
East Croydon	d													22 30											
West Croydon 4	d									22 01	22 09		22 22									22 31	22 39		
Norwood Junction 2	d										22 13		22 28	22 35									22 43		
Anerley	d										22 16		22 31	22 38									22 46		
Penge West	d										22 18		22 33	22 40									22 48		
London Victoria 15 ⊖	d		21 52					22 11	22 13								22 22			22 41	22 43				
Battersea Park 4	d		21 56					22 15									22 26			22 45					
Wandsworth Road	d							22 17												22 47					
Clapham High Street ⊖	d							22 19												22 49					
London Blackfriars 3 ⊖	d																								
Denmark Hill 4	d							22 24	22 22											22 54	22 52				
Peckham Rye 4	d					22 12	22 17	22 26	22a25	22 31								22 42	22 43	22 56	22a55	23 01			
Queens Rd Peckham	d						22 19	22 29		22 34									22 45	22 59		23 04			
South Bermondsey	d						22 22	22 31		22 36									22 48	23 01		23 06			
Clapham Junction 10	d		22 00														22 30								
Wandsworth Common	d		22 03														22 33								
Balham 4 ⊖	d		22 05														22 35								
Streatham Hill	d		22 08														22 38								
West Norwood 4	d		22 12			22 24											22 42	22 54							
Gipsy Hill	d		22 15			22 27											22 45	22 57							
Crystal Palace 4	d	22 13	22 21	22 28		22a29										22 43	22 51	22a59							
Sydenham	d	22 16	22 24	22 31							22 21		22 36	22 42		22 46	22 54						22 51		
Forest Hill 4	d	22 19	22 27	22 34							22 23		22 38	22 45		22 49	22 57						22 53		
Honor Oak Park	d	22 21	22 29	22 36							22 26		22 41	22 47		22 51	22 59						22 56		
Brockley	d	22 24	22 32	22 39							22 28		22 43	22 50		22 54	23 02						22 58		
New Cross Gate 4	a	22 26	22 34	22 41							22 31		22 46	22 52		22 56	23 04						23 01		
	d	22 26	22 34	22 41							22 31		22 46	22 52		22 56	23 04						23 01		
New Cross ELL	d											22 36												23 06	
Surrey Quays	d	22 30		22 45							22 35	22 40	22 49			23 00							23 05	23 10	
Canada Water	d	22 32		22 47							22 37	22 42	22 51			23 02							23 07	23 12	
Rotherhithe	d	22 33		22 48							22 38	22 43	22 53			23 03							23 08	23 13	
Wapping	d	22 35		22 50							22 40	22 45	22 54			23 05							23 10	23 15	
Shadwell	d	22 37		22 52							22 42	22 47	22 56			23 07							23 12	23 17	
Whitechapel	d	22 39		22 54							22 44	22 49	22 59			23 09							23 14	23 19	
Shoreditch High Street	d	22 41		22 56							22 46	22 51	23 01			23 11							23 16	23 21	
Hoxton	d	22 43		22 58							22 48	22 53	23 03			23 13							23 18	23 23	
Haggerston	d	22 45		23 00							22 50	22 55	23 05			23 15							23 20	23 25	
Dalston Junction Stn ELL	a	22 47		23 02							22 52	22 59	23 07			23 17							23 22	23 29	
Canonbury	d	22 50		23 05							22 57		23 12			23 20							23 27		
Highbury & Islington	a	22 55		23 10							23 02		23 16			23 25							23 32		
	d																								
London Bridge 4 ⊖	a		22 45				22 26	22 36		22 41				22 59			23 11		22 52	23 06		23 11			

East London Line and Croydon - London Victoria to London Bridge

Network Diagram - see first Page of Table 177

		LO	SN	LO	SN	SN	SN	SN	LO	SE	SN	LO	LO	SN	SN	SN	SE	SN
East Croydon	d		23 01															
West Croydon 4	d	22 52									23 01	23 22						
Norwood Junction 2	d	22 58	23 06									23 28						
Anerley	d	23 01	23 09									23 31						
Penge West	d	23 03	23 11									23 33						
London Victoria 15 ⊖	d				22 52			23 11		23 13				23 22			23 43	23 54
Battersea Park 4	d				22 56			23 15						23 26				23 58
Wandsworth Road	d							23 17										
Clapham High Street ⊖	d							23 19										
London Blackfriars 3 ⊖	d																	
Denmark Hill 4	d							23 24		23 22							23 52	
Peckham Rye 4	d					23 14	23 17	23 26		23a25	23 31				23 42	23 47	23a55	
Queens Rd Peckham	d						23 19	23 29			23 34					23 49		
South Bermondsey	d						23 22	23 31			23 36					23 52		
Clapham Junction 10	d				23 00									23 30				00 02
Wandsworth Common	d				23 03									23 33				00 05
Balham 4 ⊖	d				23 05									23 35				00 07
Streatham Hill	d				23 08									23 38				00 10
West Norwood 4	d				23 12	23 26								23 42	23 54			00 14
Gipsy Hill	d				23 15	23 29								23 45	23 57			00 17
Crystal Palace 4	d			23 13	23 21	23a31							23 43	23 51	23a59			00 21
Sydenham	d	23 06	23 13	23 16	23 24							23 36	23 46	23 54				00 24
Forest Hill 4	d	23 08	23 16	23 19	23 27							23 38	23 49	23 57				00 27
Honor Oak Park	d	23 11	23 18	23 21	23 29							23 41	23 51	23 59				00 29
Brockley	d	23 13	23 21	23 24	23 32							23 43	23 54	00 02				00 32
New Cross Gate 4	a	23 16	23 23	23 26	23 34							23 46	23 56	00 04				00 34
	d	23 16	23 23	23 26	23 34							23 46	23 56	00 04				00 34
New Cross ELL	d								23 36									
Surrey Quays	d	23 19		23 30					23 40			23 49	23 59					
Canada Water	d	23 21		23 32					23 42			23 51	00 02					
Rotherhithe	d	23 23		23 33					23 43			23 53	00 03					
Wapping	d	23 24		23 35					23 45			23 54	00 05					
Shadwell	d	23 26		23 37					23 47			23 56	00 07					
Whitechapel	d	23 29		23 39					23 49			23 59	00 09					
Shoreditch High Street	d	23 31		23 41					23 51			00 01	00 11					
Hoxton	d	23 33		23 43					23 53			00 03	00 13					
Haggerston	d	23 35		23 45					23 55			00 05	00 15					
Dalston Junction Stn ELL	a	23 37		23 47					23 59			00 07	00 17					
Canonbury	d	23 42		23 50								00 12	00 20					
Highbury & Islington	a	23 46		23 55								00 16	00 25					
	d																	
London Bridge 4 ⊖	a		23 30		23 45		23 26	23 36			23 41			00 11		23 56		00 41

Saturdays

		LO	LO	SN	SN	SN	SN	LO	LO	LO	LO	LO	LO	LO	SN	LO	LO
East Croydon	d																
West Croydon 4	d	23p22						05 39			05 52			06 09	06 18		
Norwood Junction 2	d	23p28						05 43			05 58			06 13	06 23		
Anerley	d	23p31						05 46			06 01			06 16			
Penge West	d	23p33						05 48			06 03			06 18			
London Victoria 15 ⊖	d			23p22	23p54												
Battersea Park 4	d			23p26	23p58												
Wandsworth Road	d																
Clapham High Street ⊖	d																
London Blackfriars 3 ⊖	d																
Denmark Hill 4	d																
Peckham Rye 4	d					00 12	00 42										
Queens Rd Peckham	d																
South Bermondsey	d																
Clapham Junction 10	d			23p30	00 02												
Wandsworth Common	d			23p33	00 05												
Balham 4 ⊖	d			23p35	00 07												
Streatham Hill	d			23p38	00 10												
West Norwood 4	d			23p42	00 14	00 24	00 54										
Gipsy Hill	d			23p45	00 17	00 27	00 57										
Crystal Palace 4	d		23p43	23p51	00 21	00a29	00a59			05 58			06 13		06a27		06 28
Sydenham	d	23p36	23p46	23p54	00 24			05 51		06 01	06 06		06 16	06 21			06 31
Forest Hill 4	d	23p38	23p49	23p57	00 27			05 53		06 04	06 08		06 19	06 23			06 34
Honor Oak Park	d	23p41	23p51	23p59	00 29			05 56		06 06	06 11		06 21	06 26			06 36
Brockley	d	23p43	23p54	00 02	00 32			05 58		06 09	06 13		06 24	06 28			06 39
New Cross Gate 4	a	23p46	23p56	00 04	00 34			06 01		06 11	06 16		06 26	06 31			06 41
	d	23p46	23p56	00 04	00 34			06 01		06 11	06 16		06 26	06 31			06 41
New Cross ELL	d								06 06			06 21				06 36	
Surrey Quays	d	23p49	23p59					06 05	06 10	06 15	06 19	06 25	06 30	06 35		06 40	06 45
Canada Water	d	23p51	00 02					06 07	06 12	06 17	06 21	06 27	06 32	06 37		06 42	06 47
Rotherhithe	d	23p53	00 03					06 08	06 13	06 18	06 23	06 28	06 33	06 38		06 43	06 48
Wapping	d	23p54	00 05					06 10	06 15	06 20	06 24	06 30	06 35	06 40		06 45	06 50
Shadwell	d	23p56	00 07					06 12	06 17	06 22	06 26	06 32	06 37	06 42		06 47	06 52
Whitechapel	d	23p59	00 09					06 14	06 19	06 24	06 29	06 34	06 39	06 44		06 49	06 54
Shoreditch High Street	d	00 01	00 11					06 16	06 21	06 26	06 31	06 36	06 41	06 46		06 51	06 56
Hoxton	d	00 03	00 13					06 18	06 23	06 28	06 33	06 38	06 43	06 48		06 53	06 58
Haggerston	d	00 05	00 15					06 20	06 25	06 30	06 35	06 40	06 45	06 50		06 55	07 00
Dalston Junction Stn ELL	a	00 07	00 17					06 22	06 29	06 32	06 37	06 44	06 47	06 52		06 59	07 02
Canonbury	d	00 12	00 20					06 27		06 35	06 42		06 50	06 57			07 05
Highbury & Islington	a	00 16	00 25					06 32		06 40	06 46		06 56	07 02			07 10
	d																
London Bridge 4 ⊖	a			00 11	00 41												

Table 178

Saturdays

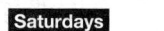

East London Line and Croydon - London Victoria to London Bridge

Network Diagram - see first Page of Table 177

Station		LO	SN	LO	LO	SE	SN	SE	SN		LO	SN	SN	LO	LO	LO	SN	SN	LO		LO	SE	SN	LO	LO
East Croydon	d		06 30									06 43					07 00								
West Croydon 4	d	06 22									06 39		06 45			06 52							07 01	07 09	
Norwood Junction 2	d	06 28	06 35						06 41		06 43	06 50	06 53			06 58	07 05							07 13	
Anerley	d	06 31	06 38								06 46					07 01	07 08							07 16	
Penge West	d	06 33	06 40								06 48					07 03	07 10							07 18	
London Victoria 15 ⊖	d					06 13	06 41	06 43										07 11				07 13			
Battersea Park 4	d						06 45											07 15							
Wandsworth Road	d						06 47											07 17							
Clapham High Street ⊖	d						06 49											07 19							
London Blackfriars 3 ⊖	d																								
Denmark Hill 4	d					06 22	06 54	06 52										07 24				07 22			
Peckham Rye 4	d					06a25	06 56	06a55	07 01									07 26				07a25	07 31		
Queens Rd Peckham	d						06 59		07 04									07 29					07 34		
South Bermondsey	d						07 01		07 06									07 31					07 36		
Clapham Junction 10	d																								
Wandsworth Common	d																								
Balham 4 ⊖	d																								
Streatham Hill	d																								
West Norwood 4	d																								
Gipsy Hill	d																								
Crystal Palace 4	d				06 43								06a57		06 58						07 13				
Sydenham	d	06 36	06 42		06 46						06 51	06 54			07 01	07 06	07 12				07 16			07 21	
Forest Hill 4	d	06 38	06 45		06 49						06 53	06 57			07 04	07 08	07 15				07 19			07 23	
Honor Oak Park	d	06 41	06 47		06 51						06 56	06 59			07 06	07 11	07 17				07 21			07 26	
Brockley	d	06 43	06 50		06 54						06 58	07 02			07 09	07 13	07 20				07 24			07 28	
New Cross Gate 4	a	06 46	06 52		06 56						07 01	07 04			07 11	07 16	07 22				07 26			07 31	
	d	06 46	06 52		06 56						07 01	07 04			07 11	07 16	07 22				07 26			07 31	
New Cross ELL	d			06 51										07 06					07 21						07 36
Surrey Quays	d	06 49		06 55	07 00						07 05			07 10	07 15	07 19			07 25		07 30			07 35	07 40
Canada Water	d	06 51		06 57	07 02						07 07			07 12	07 17	07 21			07 27		07 32			07 37	07 42
Rotherhithe	d	06 53		06 58	07 03						07 08			07 13	07 18	07 23			07 28		07 33			07 38	07 43
Wapping	d	06 54		07 00	07 05						07 10			07 15	07 20	07 24			07 30		07 35			07 40	07 45
Shadwell	d	06 56		07 02	07 07						07 12			07 17	07 22	07 26			07 32		07 37			07 42	07 47
Whitechapel	d	06 59		07 04	07 09						07 14			07 19	07 24	07 29			07 34		07 39			07 44	07 49
Shoreditch High Street	d	07 01		07 06	07 11						07 16			07 21	07 26	07 31			07 36		07 41			07 46	07 51
Hoxton	d	07 03		07 08	07 13						07 18			07 23	07 28	07 33			07 38		07 43			07 48	07 53
Haggerston	d	07 05		07 10	07 15						07 20			07 25	07 30	07 35			07 40		07 45			07 50	07 55
Dalston Junction Stn ELL	a	07 07		07 14	07 17						07 22			07 29	07 32	07 37			07 44		07 47			07 52	07 59
Canonbury	d	07 12			07 20						07 27				07 35	07 42					07 50			07 57	
Highbury & Islington	a	07 16			07 25						07 32				07 40	07 46					07 55			08 02	
	d																								
London Bridge 4 ⊖	a		06 59				07 06		07 14			07 11					07 29	07 36					07 41		

Station		LO	LO	SN	LO		LO	LO	SN	SE	SN	SE	SN	LO	LO		LO	SN	LO	LO	SN	LO	SN	SE	SN
East Croydon	d			07 30														08 00							
West Croydon 4	d		07 22										07 31	07 39			07 52								
Norwood Junction 2	d		07 28	07 35										07 43			07 58	08 05							
Anerley	d		07 31	07 38										07 46			08 01	08 08							
Penge West	d		07 33	07 40										07 48			08 03	08 10							
London Victoria 15 ⊖	d									07 39	07 41	07 43									07 49			08 09	08 11
Battersea Park 4	d										07 45										07 53				08 15
Wandsworth Road	d										07 47														08 17
Clapham High Street ⊖	d										07 49														08 19
London Blackfriars 3 ⊖	d																								
Denmark Hill 4	d									07 48	07 54	07 52												08 18	08 24
Peckham Rye 4	d								07 42	07a51	07 56	07a55	08 01										08 12	08a21	08 26
Queens Rd Peckham	d										07 59		08 04												08 29
South Bermondsey	d										08 01		08 06												08 31
Clapham Junction 10	d																				07 57				
Wandsworth Common	d																				08 00				
Balham 4 ⊖	d																				08 02				
Streatham Hill	d																				08 05				
West Norwood 4	d								07 53												08 10		08 23		
Gipsy Hill	d								07 56												08 13		08 26		
Crystal Palace 4	d	07 28					07 43	07 58	07a59											08 13	08 21	08 28	08a29		
Sydenham	d	07 31	07 36	07 42			07 46	08 01						07 51			08 06	08 12		08 16	08 24	08 31			
Forest Hill 4	d	07 34	07 38	07 45			07 49	08 04						07 53			08 08	08 15		08 19	08 27	08 34			
Honor Oak Park	d	07 36	07 41	07 47			07 51	08 06						07 56			08 11	08 17		08 21	08 29	08 36			
Brockley	d	07 39	07 43	07 50			07 54	08 09						07 58			08 13	08 20		08 24	08 32	08 39			
New Cross Gate 4	a	07 41	07 46	07 52			07 56	08 11						08 01			08 16	08 22		08 26	08 34	08 41			
	d	07 41	07 46	07 52			07 56	08 11						08 01			08 16	08 22		08 26	08 34	08 41			
New Cross ELL	d				07 51										08 06				08 21						
Surrey Quays	d	07 45	07 49		07 55		08 00	08 15						08 05	08 10		08 19		08 25	08 30		08 45			
Canada Water	d	07 47	07 51		07 57		08 02	08 17						08 07	08 12		08 21		08 27	08 32		08 47			
Rotherhithe	d	07 48	07 53		07 58		08 03	08 18						08 08	08 13		08 23		08 28	08 33		08 48			
Wapping	d	07 50	07 54		08 00		08 05	08 20						08 10	08 15		08 24		08 30	08 35		08 50			
Shadwell	d	07 52	07 56		08 02		08 07	08 22						08 12	08 17		08 26		08 32	08 37		08 52			
Whitechapel	d	07 54	07 59		08 04		08 09	08 24						08 14	08 19		08 29		08 34	08 39		08 54			
Shoreditch High Street	d	07 56	08 01		08 06		08 11	08 26						08 16	08 21		08 31		08 36	08 41		08 56			
Hoxton	d	07 58	08 03		08 08		08 13	08 28						08 18	08 23		08 33		08 38	08 43		08 58			
Haggerston	d	08 00	08 05		08 10		08 15	08 30						08 20	08 25		08 35		08 40	08 45		09 00			
Dalston Junction Stn ELL	a	08 02	08 07		08 14		08 17	08 32						08 22	08 29		08 37		08 44	08 47		09 02			
Canonbury	d	08 05	08 12				08 20	08 35						08 27			08 42			08 50		09 05			
Highbury & Islington	a	08 10	08 16				08 25	08 40						08 32			08 46			08 55		09 10			
	d																								
London Bridge 4 ⊖	a			07 59							08 06		08 11					08 29			08 41				08 36

Table 178

Saturdays

East London Line and Croydon - London Victoria to London Bridge

Network Diagram - see first Page of Table 177

Station			SE	SN	LO	LO	LO	SN	LO	LO	SN		LO	SN	SN	SE	SN	SE	SN	LO	LO		LO	SN	LO
East Croydon	d							08 30																09 00	
West Croydon [4]	d			08 01	08 09		08 22												08 31	08 39			08 52		
Norwood Junction [2]	d				08 13		08 28	08 35												08 43			08 58	09 05	
Anerley	d				08 16		08 31	08 38												08 46			09 01	09 08	
Penge West	d				08 18		08 33	08 40												08 48			09 03	09 10	
London Victoria [15] ⊖	d		08 13								08 19					08 39	08 41	08 43							
Battersea Park [4]	d										08 23						08 45								
Wandsworth Road	d																08 47								
Clapham High Street ⊖	d																08 49								
London Blackfriars [3] ⊖	d																								
Denmark Hill [4]	d		08 22													08 48	08 54	08 52							
Peckham Rye [4]	d		08a25	08 31										08 42	08 46	08a51	08 56	08a55	09 01						
Queens Rd Peckham	d			08 34											08 49		08 59		09 04						
South Bermondsey	d			08 36											08 51		09 01		09 06						
Clapham Junction [10]	d										08 27														
Wandsworth Common	d										08 30														
Balham [4] ⊖	d										08 32														
Streatham Hill	d										08 35														
West Norwood [4]	d										08 40			08 53											
Gipsy Hill	d										08 43			08 56											
Crystal Palace [4]	d									08 43	08 51		08 58	08a59											
Sydenham	d				08 21		08 36	08 42		08 46	08 54		09 01							08 51			09 06	09 12	
Forest Hill [4]	d				08 23		08 38	08 45		08 49	08 57		09 04							08 53			09 08	09 15	
Honor Oak Park	d				08 26		08 41	08 47		08 51	08 59		09 06							08 56			09 11	09 17	
Brockley	d				08 28		08 43	08 50		08 54	09 02		09 09							08 58			09 13	09 20	
New Cross Gate [4]	a				08 31		08 46	08 52		08 56	09 04		09 11							09 01			09 16	09 22	
	d				08 31		08 46	08 52		08 56	09 04		09 11							09 01			09 16	09 22	
New Cross ELL	d					08 36			08 51												09 06				09 21
Surrey Quays	d				08 35	08 40	08 49		08 55	09 00			09 15							09 05	09 10		09 19		09 25
Canada Water	d				08 37	08 42	08 51		08 57	09 02			09 17							09 07	09 12		09 21		09 27
Rotherhithe	d				08 38	08 43	08 53		08 58	09 03			09 18							09 08	09 13		09 23		09 28
Wapping	d				08 40	08 45	08 54		09 00	09 05			09 20							09 10	09 15		09 24		09 30
Shadwell	d				08 42	08 47	08 56		09 02	09 07			09 22							09 12	09 17		09 26		09 32
Whitechapel	d				08 44	08 49	08 59		09 04	09 09			09 24							09 14	09 19		09 29		09 34
Shoreditch High Street	d				08 46	08 51	09 01		09 06	09 11			09 26							09 16	09 21		09 31		09 36
Hoxton	d				08 48	08 53	09 03		09 08	09 13			09 28							09 18	09 23		09 33		09 38
Haggerston	d				08 50	08 55	09 05		09 10	09 15			09 30							09 20	09 25		09 35		09 40
Dalston Junction Stn ELL	a				08 52	08 59	09 07		09 14	09 17			09 32							09 22	09 29		09 37		09 44
Canonbury	d				08 57		09 12			09 20			09 35							09 27			09 42		
Highbury & Islington	a				09 02		09 16			09 25			09 40							09 32			09 46		
	d																								
London Bridge [4] ⊖	a			08 41				08 59			09 11				08 56		09 06		09 11					09 29	

Station		LO	SN	LO	SN	SN	SE		SN	SE	SN	LO	LO	LO	SN	LO	LO		SN	LO	SN	SN	SE	SN	SE
East Croydon	d														09 30										
West Croydon [4]	d										09 01	09 09		09 22											
Norwood Junction [2]	d											09 13		09 28	09 35										
Anerley	d											09 16		09 31	09 38										
Penge West	d											09 18		09 33	09 40										
London Victoria [15] ⊖	d		08 49				09 09		09 11	09 13									09 19				09 39	09 41	09 43
Battersea Park [4]	d		08 53						09 15										09 23					09 45	
Wandsworth Road	d								09 17															09 47	
Clapham High Street ⊖	d								09 19															09 49	
London Blackfriars [3] ⊖	d																								
Denmark Hill [4]	d						09 18		09 24	09 22													09 48	09 54	09 52
Peckham Rye [4]	d				09 12	09 16	09a21		09 26	09a25	09 31										09 42	09 46	09a51	09 56	09a55
Queens Rd Peckham	d					09 19			09 29		09 34											09 49		09 59	
South Bermondsey	d					09 21			09 31		09 36											09 51		10 01	
Clapham Junction [10]	d		08 57																09 27						
Wandsworth Common	d		09 00																09 30						
Balham [4] ⊖	d		09 02																09 32						
Streatham Hill	d		09 05																09 35						
West Norwood [4]	d		09 10		09 23														09 40		09 53				
Gipsy Hill	d		09 13		09 26														09 43		09 56				
Crystal Palace [4]	d	09 13	09 21	09 28	09a29												09 43		09 51	09 58	09a59				
Sydenham	d	09 16	09 24	09 31								09 21		09 36	09 42		09 46		09 54	10 01					
Forest Hill [4]	d	09 19	09 27	09 34								09 23		09 38	09 45		09 49		09 57	10 04					
Honor Oak Park	d	09 21	09 29	09 36								09 26		09 41	09 47		09 51		09 59	10 06					
Brockley	d	09 24	09 32	09 39								09 28		09 43	09 50		09 54		10 02	10 09					
New Cross Gate [4]	a	09 26	09 34	09 41								09 31		09 46	09 52		09 56		10 04	10 11					
	d	09 26	09 34	09 41								09 31		09 46	09 52		09 56		10 04	10 11					
New Cross ELL	d												09 36			09 51									
Surrey Quays	d	09 30		09 45								09 35	09 40	09 49		09 55	10 00			10 15					
Canada Water	d	09 32		09 47								09 37	09 42	09 51		09 57	10 02			10 17					
Rotherhithe	d	09 33		09 48								09 38	09 43	09 53		09 58	10 03			10 18					
Wapping	d	09 35		09 50								09 40	09 45	09 54		10 00	10 05			10 20					
Shadwell	d	09 37		09 52								09 42	09 47	09 56		10 02	10 07			10 22					
Whitechapel	d	09 39		09 54								09 44	09 49	09 59		10 04	10 09			10 24					
Shoreditch High Street	d	09 41		09 56								09 46	09 51	10 01		10 06	10 11			10 26					
Hoxton	d	09 43		09 58								09 48	09 53	10 03		10 08	10 13			10 28					
Haggerston	d	09 45		10 00								09 50	09 55	10 05		10 10	10 15			10 30					
Dalston Junction Stn ELL	a	09 47		10 02								09 52	09 59	10 07		10 14	10 17			10 32					
Canonbury	d	09 50		10 05								09 57		10 12			10 20			10 35					
Highbury & Islington	a	09 55		10 10								10 02		10 16			10 25			10 40					
	d																								
London Bridge [4] ⊖	a		09 41			09 26			09 36		09 41				09 59				10 11			09 56		10 06	

East London Line and Croydon - London Victoria to London Bridge

Network Diagram - see first Page of Table 177

		SN	LO		LO	LO	SN	LO	LO	SN	LO	SN	SN		SE	SN	SE	SN	LO	LO	LO	SN	LO		LO
East Croydon	d						10 00															10 30			
West Croydon 4	d	09 31	09 39			09 52												10 01	10 09		10 22				
Norwood Junction 2	d		09 43			09 58	10 05												10 13		10 28	10 35			
Anerley	d		09 46			10 01	10 08												10 16		10 31	10 38			
Penge West	d		09 48			10 03	10 10												10 18		10 33	10 40			
London Victoria 15 ⊖	d									09 49					10 09	10 11	10 13								
Battersea Park 4	d									09 53						10 15									
Wandsworth Road	d															10 17									
Clapham High Street ⊖	d															10 19									
London Blackfriars 3 ⊖	d																								
Denmark Hill 4	d														10 18	10 24	10 22								
Peckham Rye 4	d	10 01										10 12	10 16		10a21	10 26	10a25	10 31							
Queens Rd Peckham	d	10 04											10 19			10 29		10 34							
South Bermondsey	d	10 06											10 21			10 31		10 36							
Clapham Junction 10	d									09 57															
Wandsworth Common	d									10 00															
Balham 4 ⊖	d									10 02															
Streatham Hill	d									10 05															
West Norwood 4	d									10 10		10 23													
Gipsy Hill	d									10 13		10 26													
Crystal Palace 4	d								10 13	10 21	10 28	10a29													10 43
Sydenham	d		09 51			10 06	10 12		10 16	10 24	10 31								10 21		10 36	10 42			10 46
Forest Hill 4	d		09 53			10 08	10 15		10 19	10 27	10 34								10 23		10 38	10 45			10 49
Honor Oak Park	d		09 56			10 11	10 17		10 21	10 29	10 36								10 26		10 41	10 47			10 51
Brockley	d		09 58			10 13	10 20		10 24	10 32	10 39								10 28		10 43	10 50			10 54
New Cross Gate 4	a		10 01			10 16	10 22		10 26	10 34	10 41								10 31		10 46	10 52			10 56
	d		10 01			10 16	10 22		10 26	10 34	10 41								10 31		10 46	10 52			10 56
New Cross ELL	d				10 06			10 21												10 36			10 51		
Surrey Quays	d		10 05		10 10	10 19		10 25	10 30		10 45								10 35	10 40	10 49		10 55		11 00
Canada Water	d		10 07		10 12	10 21		10 27	10 32		10 47								10 37	10 42	10 51		10 57		11 02
Rotherhithe	d		10 08		10 13	10 23		10 28	10 33		10 48								10 38	10 43	10 53		10 58		11 03
Wapping	d		10 10		10 15	10 24		10 30	10 35		10 50								10 40	10 45	10 54		11 00		11 05
Shadwell	d		10 12		10 17	10 26		10 32	10 37		10 52								10 42	10 47	10 56		11 02		11 07
Whitechapel	d		10 14		10 19	10 29		10 34	10 39		10 54								10 44	10 49	10 59		11 04		11 09
Shoreditch High Street	d		10 16		10 21	10 31		10 36	10 41		10 56								10 46	10 51	11 01		11 06		11 11
Hoxton	d		10 18		10 23	10 33		10 38	10 43		10 58								10 48	10 53	11 03		11 08		11 13
Haggerston	d		10 20		10 25	10 35		10 40	10 45		11 00								10 50	10 55	11 05		11 10		11 15
Dalston Junction Stn ELL	a		10 22		10 29	10 37		10 44	10 47		11 02								10 52	10 59	11 07		11 14		11 17
Canonbury	d		10 27			10 42			10 50		11 05								10 57		11 12				11 20
Highbury & Islington	a		10 32			10 46			10 55		11 10								11 02		11 16				11 25
	d																								
London Bridge 4 ⊖	a	10 11					10 29			10 41			10 26			10 36		10 41				10 59			

		SN	LO	SN	SN	SE	SN	SE	SN		LO	LO	LO	SN	LO	LO	SN	LO	SN		SN	SE	SN	SE	SN
East Croydon	d													11 00											
West Croydon 4	d								10 31		10 39		10 52												11 01
Norwood Junction 2	d										10 43		10 58	11 05											
Anerley	d										10 46		11 01	11 08											
Penge West	d										10 48		11 03	11 10											
London Victoria 15 ⊖	d	10 19				10 39	10 41	10 43									10 49					11 09	11 11	11 13	
Battersea Park 4	d	10 23					10 45										10 53						11 15		
Wandsworth Road	d						10 47																11 17		
Clapham High Street ⊖	d						10 49																11 19		
London Blackfriars 3 ⊖	d																								
Denmark Hill 4	d					10 48	10 54	10 52														11 18	11 24	11 22	
Peckham Rye 4	d			10 42	10 46	10a51	10 56	10a55	11 01										11 12		11 16	11a21	11 26	11a25	11 31
Queens Rd Peckham	d				10 49		10 59		11 04												11 19		11 29		11 34
South Bermondsey	d				10 51		11 01		11 06												11 21		11 31		11 36
Clapham Junction 10	d	10 27															10 57								
Wandsworth Common	d	10 30															11 00								
Balham 4 ⊖	d	10 32															11 02								
Streatham Hill	d	10 35															11 05								
West Norwood 4	d	10 40		10 53													11 10		11 23						
Gipsy Hill	d	10 43		10 56													11 13		11 26						
Crystal Palace 4	d	10 51	10 58	10a59												11 13	11 21	11 28	11a29						
Sydenham	d	10 54	11 01								10 51		11 06	11 12		11 16	11 24	11 31							
Forest Hill 4	d	10 57	11 04								10 53		11 08	11 15		11 19	11 27	11 34							
Honor Oak Park	d	10 59	11 06								10 56		11 11	11 17		11 21	11 29	11 36							
Brockley	d	11 02	11 09								10 58		11 13	11 20		11 24	11 32	11 39							
New Cross Gate 4	a	11 04	11 11								11 01		11 16	11 22		11 26	11 34	11 41							
	d	11 04	11 11								11 01		11 16	11 22		11 26	11 34	11 41							
New Cross ELL	d											11 06			11 21										
Surrey Quays	d		11 15								11 05	11 10	11 19		11 25	11 30		11 45							
Canada Water	d		11 17								11 07	11 12	11 21		11 27	11 32		11 47							
Rotherhithe	d		11 18								11 08	11 13	11 23		11 28	11 33		11 48							
Wapping	d		11 20								11 10	11 15	11 24		11 30	11 35		11 50							
Shadwell	d		11 22								11 12	11 17	11 26		11 32	11 37		11 52							
Whitechapel	d		11 24								11 14	11 19	11 29		11 34	11 39		11 54							
Shoreditch High Street	d		11 26								11 16	11 21	11 31		11 36	11 41		11 56							
Hoxton	d		11 28								11 18	11 23	11 33		11 38	11 43		11 58							
Haggerston	d		11 30								11 20	11 25	11 35		11 40	11 45		12 00							
Dalston Junction Stn ELL	a		11 32								11 22	11 29	11 37		11 44	11 47		12 02							
Canonbury	d		11 35								11 27		11 42			11 50		12 05							
Highbury & Islington	a		11 40								11 32		11 46			11 55		12 10							
	d																								
London Bridge 4 ⊖	a	11 11			10 56		11 06		11 11					11 29			11 41				11 26		11 36		11 41

Table 178

Saturdays

East London Line and Croydon - London Victoria to London Bridge

Network Diagram - see first Page of Table 177

		LO	LO	LO	SN		LO	LO	SN	LO	SN	SN	SE	SN	SE		SN	LO	LO	LO	SN	LO	LO	SN	LO
East Croydon 🚊	d				11 30																12 00				
West Croydon 4 🚊	d	11 09		11 22													11 31	11 39		11 52					
Norwood Junction 2	d	11 13		11 28	11 35													11 43		11 58	12 05				
Anerley	d	11 16		11 31	11 38													11 46		12 01	12 08				
Penge West	d	11 18		11 33	11 40													11 48		12 03	12 10				
London Victoria 15 ⊖	d								11 19				11 39	11 41	11 43									11 49	
Battersea Park 4	d								11 23					11 45										11 53	
Wandsworth Road	d													11 47											
Clapham High Street ⊖	d													11 49											
London Blackfriars 3 ⊖	d																								
Denmark Hill 4	d												11 48	11 54	11 52										
Peckham Rye 4	d										11 42	11 46	11a51	11 56	11a55		12 01								
Queens Rd Peckham	d											11 49		11 59			12 04								
South Bermondsey	d											11 51		12 01			12 06								
Clapham Junction 10	d								11 27															11 57	
Wandsworth Common	d								11 30															12 00	
Balham 4 ⊖	d								11 32															12 02	
Streatham Hill	d								11 35															12 05	
West Norwood 4	d								11 40		11 53													12 10	
Gipsy Hill	d								11 43		11 56													12 13	
Crystal Palace 4	d							11 43	11 51	11 58	11a59												12 13	12 21	12 28
Sydenham	d	11 21		11 36	11 42			11 46	11 54	12 01								11 51		12 06	12 12		12 16	12 24	12 31
Forest Hill 4	d	11 23		11 38	11 45			11 49	11 57	12 04								11 53		12 08	12 15		12 19	12 27	12 34
Honor Oak Park	d	11 26		11 41	11 47			11 51	11 59	12 06								11 56		12 11	12 17		12 21	12 29	12 36
Brockley	d	11 28		11 43	11 50			11 54	12 02	12 09								11 58		12 13	12 20		12 24	12 32	12 39
New Cross Gate 4	a	11 31		11 46	11 52			11 56	12 04	12 11								12 01		12 16	12 22		12 26	12 34	12 41
	d	11 31		11 46	11 52			11 56	12 04	12 11								12 01		12 16	12 22		12 26	12 34	12 41
New Cross ELL	d		11 36				11 51												12 06			12 21			
Surrey Quays	d	11 35	11 40	11 49			11 55	12 00		12 15								12 05	12 10	12 19		12 25	12 30		12 45
Canada Water	d	11 37	11 42	11 51			11 57	12 02		12 17								12 07	12 12	12 21		12 27	12 32		12 47
Rotherhithe	d	11 38	11 43	11 53			11 58	12 03		12 18								12 08	12 13	12 23		12 28	12 33		12 48
Wapping	d	11 40	11 45	11 54			12 00	12 05		12 20								12 10	12 15	12 24		12 30	12 35		12 50
Shadwell	d	11 42	11 47	11 56			12 02	12 07		12 22								12 12	12 17	12 26		12 32	12 37		12 52
Whitechapel	d	11 44	11 49	11 59			12 04	12 09		12 24								12 14	12 19	12 29		12 34	12 39		12 54
Shoreditch High Street	d	11 46	11 51	12 01			12 06	12 11		12 26								12 16	12 21	12 31		12 36	12 41		12 56
Hoxton	d	11 48	11 53	12 03			12 08	12 13		12 28								12 18	12 23	12 33		12 38	12 43		12 58
Haggerston	d	11 50	11 55	12 05			12 10	12 15		12 30								12 20	12 25	12 35		12 40	12 45		13 00
Dalston Junction Stn ELL	a	11 52	11 59	12 07			12 14	12 17		12 32								12 22	12 29	12 37		12 44	12 47		13 02
Canonbury	d	11 57		12 12				12 20		12 35								12 27		12 42			12 50		13 05
Highbury & Islington	a	12 02		12 16				12 25		12 40								12 32		12 46			12 55		13 10
	d																								
London Bridge 4 ⊖	a				11 59				12 11			11 56		12 06			12 11				12 29			12 44	

			SN	SN	SE	SN	SE	SN	LO	LO	LO		SN	LO	LO	SN	LO	SN	SN	SE	SN		SE	SN	LO
East Croydon 🚊	d												12 30												
West Croydon 4 🚊	d							12 01	12 09		12 22													12 31	12 39
Norwood Junction 2	d								12 13		12 28		12 35												12 43
Anerley	d								12 16		12 31		12 38												12 46
Penge West	d								12 18		12 33		12 40												12 48
London Victoria 15 ⊖	d				12 09	12 11	12 13									12 19				12 39	12 41		12 43		
Battersea Park 4	d					12 15										12 23					12 45				
Wandsworth Road	d					12 17															12 47				
Clapham High Street ⊖	d					12 19															12 49				
London Blackfriars 3 ⊖	d																								
Denmark Hill 4	d				12 18	12 24	12 22													12 48	12 54		12 52		
Peckham Rye 4	d		12 12	12 16	12a21	12 26	12a25	12 31										12 42	12 46	12a51	12 56		12a55	13 01	
Queens Rd Peckham	d			12 19		12 29		12 34											12 49		12 59			13 04	
South Bermondsey	d			12 21		12 31		12 36											12 51		13 01			13 06	
Clapham Junction 10	d															12 27									
Wandsworth Common	d															12 30									
Balham 4 ⊖	d															12 32									
Streatham Hill	d															12 35									
West Norwood 4	d		12 23													12 40		12 53							
Gipsy Hill	d		12 26													12 43		12 56							
Crystal Palace 4	d		12a29												12 43	12 51	12 58	12a59							
Sydenham	d								12 21		12 36		12 42		12 46	12 54	13 01								12 51
Forest Hill 4	d								12 23		12 38		12 45		12 49	12 57	13 04								12 53
Honor Oak Park	d								12 26		12 41		12 47		12 51	12 59	13 06								12 56
Brockley	d								12 28		12 43		12 50		12 54	13 02	13 09								12 58
New Cross Gate 4	a								12 31		12 46		12 52		12 56	13 04	13 11								13 01
	d								12 31		12 46		12 52		12 56	13 04	13 11								13 01
New Cross ELL	d									12 36				12 51											
Surrey Quays	d								12 35	12 40	12 49			12 55	13 00		13 15								13 05
Canada Water	d								12 37	12 42	12 51			12 57	13 02		13 17								13 07
Rotherhithe	d								12 38	12 43	12 53			12 58	13 03		13 18								13 08
Wapping	d								12 40	12 45	12 54			13 00	13 05		13 20								13 10
Shadwell	d								12 42	12 47	12 56			13 02	13 07		13 22								13 12
Whitechapel	d								12 44	12 49	12 59			13 04	13 09		13 24								13 14
Shoreditch High Street	d								12 46	12 51	13 01			13 06	13 11		13 26								13 16
Hoxton	d								12 48	12 53	13 03			13 08	13 13		13 28								13 18
Haggerston	d								12 50	12 55	13 05			13 10	13 15		13 30								13 20
Dalston Junction Stn ELL	a								12 52	12 59	13 07			13 14	13 17		13 32								13 22
Canonbury	d								12 57		13 12				13 20		13 35								13 27
Highbury & Islington	a								13 02		13 16				13 25		13 40								13 32
	d																								
London Bridge 4 ⊖	a			12 26		12 36		12 41					12 59			13 11			12 56		13 06			13 11	

Table 178

Saturdays

East London Line and Croydon - London Victoria to London Bridge

Network Diagram - see first Page of Table 177

		LO	LO	SN	LO	LO	SN		LO	SN	SN	SE	SN	SE	SN	LO	LO		LO	SN	LO	LO	SN	LO	SN
East Croydon	d			13 00																13 30					
West Croydon 4	d		12 52												13 01	13 09			13 22						
Norwood Junction 2	d		12 58	13 05												13 13			13 28	13 35					
Anerley	d		13 01	13 08												13 16			13 31	13 38					
Penge West	d		13 03	13 10												13 18			13 33	13 40					
London Victoria 15 ⊖	d						12 49					13 09	13 11	13 13									13 19		
Battersea Park 4	d						12 53						13 15										13 23		
Wandsworth Road	d												13 17												
Clapham High Street ⊖	d												13 19												
London Blackfriars 3 ⊖	d																								
Denmark Hill 4	d											13 18	13 24	13 22											
Peckham Rye 4	d									13 12	13 16	13a21	13 26	13a25	13 31										13 42
Queens Rd Peckham	d										13 19		13 29		13 34										
South Bermondsey	d										13 21		13 31		13 36										
Clapham Junction 10	d						12 57																13 27		
Wandsworth Common	d						13 00																13 30		
Balham 4 ⊖	d						13 02																13 32		
Streatham Hill	d						13 05																13 35		
West Norwood 4	d						13 10			13 23													13 40		13 53
Gipsy Hill	d						13 13			13 26													13 43		13 56
Crystal Palace 4	d					13 13	13 21		13 28	13a29												13 43	13 51	13 58	13a59
Sydenham	d		13 06	13 12		13 16	13 24		13 31							13 21			13 36	13 42		13 46	13 54	14 01	
Forest Hill 4	d		13 08	13 15		13 19	13 27		13 34							13 23			13 38	13 45		13 49	13 57	14 04	
Honor Oak Park	d		13 11	13 17		13 21	13 29		13 36							13 26			13 41	13 47		13 51	13 59	14 06	
Brockley	d		13 13	13 20		13 24	13 32		13 39							13 28			13 43	13 50		13 54	14 02	14 09	
New Cross Gate 4	a		13 16	13 22		13 26	13 34		13 41							13 31			13 46	13 52		13 56	14 04	14 11	
	d		13 16	13 22		13 26	13 34		13 41							13 31			13 46	13 52		13 56	14 04	14 11	
New Cross ELL	d	13 06			13 21												13 36				13 51				
Surrey Quays	d	13 10	13 19		13 25	13 30			13 45							13 35	13 40		13 49		13 55	14 00		14 15	
Canada Water	d	13 12	13 21		13 27	13 32			13 47							13 37	13 42		13 51		13 57	14 02		14 17	
Rotherhithe	d	13 13	13 23		13 28	13 33			13 48							13 38	13 43		13 53		13 58	14 03		14 18	
Wapping	d	13 15	13 24		13 30	13 35			13 50							13 40	13 45		13 54		14 00	14 05		14 20	
Shadwell	d	13 17	13 26		13 32	13 37			13 52							13 42	13 47		13 56		14 02	14 07		14 22	
Whitechapel	d	13 19	13 29		13 34	13 39			13 54							13 44	13 49		13 59		14 04	14 09		14 24	
Shoreditch High Street	d	13 21	13 31		13 36	13 41			13 56							13 46	13 51		14 01		14 06	14 11		14 26	
Hoxton	d	13 23	13 33		13 38	13 43			13 58							13 48	13 53		14 03		14 08	14 13		14 28	
Haggerston	d	13 25	13 35		13 40	13 45			14 00							13 50	13 55		14 05		14 10	14 15		14 30	
Dalston Junction Stn ELL	a	13 29	13 37		13 44	13 47			14 02							13 52	13 59		14 07		14 14	14 17		14 32	
Canonbury	d		13 42			13 50			14 05							13 57			14 12			14 20		14 35	
Highbury & Islington	a		13 46			13 55			14 10							14 02			14 16			14 25		14 40	
	d																								
London Bridge 4 ⊖	a			13 29			13 44				13 26		13 36		13 41					13 59			14 11		

		SN	SE		SN	SE	SN	LO	LO	LO	SN	LO	LO		SN	LO	SN	SN	SE	SN	SE	SN	LO		LO
East Croydon	d										14 00														
West Croydon 4	d						13 31	13 39		13 52												14 01	14 09		
Norwood Junction 2	d							13 43		13 58	14 05												14 13		
Anerley	d							13 46		14 01	14 08												14 16		
Penge West	d							13 48		14 03	14 10												14 18		
London Victoria 15 ⊖	d		13 39		13 41	13 43									13 49				14 09	14 11	14 13				
Battersea Park 4	d				13 45										13 53					14 15					
Wandsworth Road	d				13 47															14 17					
Clapham High Street ⊖	d				13 49															14 19					
London Blackfriars 3 ⊖	d																								
Denmark Hill 4	d		13 48		13 54	13 52													14 18	14 24	14 22				
Peckham Rye 4	d	13 46	13a51		13 56	13a55	14 01										14 12	14 16	14a21	14 26	14a25	14 31			
Queens Rd Peckham	d	13 49			13 59		14 04											14 19		14 29		14 34			
South Bermondsey	d	13 51			14 01		14 06											14 21		14 31		14 36			
Clapham Junction 10	d														13 57										
Wandsworth Common	d														14 00										
Balham 4 ⊖	d														14 02										
Streatham Hill	d														14 05										
West Norwood 4	d														14 10		14 23								
Gipsy Hill	d														14 13		14 26								
Crystal Palace 4	d												14 13		14 21	14 28	14a29								
Sydenham	d							13 51		14 06	14 12		14 16		14 24	14 31							14 21		
Forest Hill 4	d							13 53		14 08	14 15		14 19		14 27	14 34							14 23		
Honor Oak Park	d							13 56		14 11	14 17		14 21		14 29	14 36							14 26		
Brockley	d							13 58		14 13	14 20		14 24		14 32	14 39							14 28		
New Cross Gate 4	a							14 01		14 16	14 22		14 26		14 34	14 41							14 31		
	d							14 01		14 16	14 22		14 26		14 34	14 41							14 31		
New Cross ELL	d								14 06			14 21													14 36
Surrey Quays	d							14 05	14 10	14 19		14 25	14 30			14 45							14 35		14 40
Canada Water	d							14 07	14 12	14 21		14 27	14 32			14 47							14 37		14 42
Rotherhithe	d							14 08	14 13	14 23		14 28	14 33			14 48							14 38		14 43
Wapping	d							14 10	14 15	14 24		14 30	14 35			14 50							14 40		14 45
Shadwell	d							14 12	14 17	14 26		14 32	14 37			14 52							14 42		14 47
Whitechapel	d							14 14	14 19	14 29		14 34	14 39			14 54							14 44		14 49
Shoreditch High Street	d							14 16	14 21	14 31		14 36	14 41			14 56							14 46		14 51
Hoxton	d							14 18	14 23	14 33		14 38	14 43			14 58							14 48		14 53
Haggerston	d							14 20	14 25	14 35		14 40	14 45			15 00							14 50		14 55
Dalston Junction Stn ELL	a							14 22	14 29	14 37		14 44	14 47			15 02							14 52		14 59
Canonbury	d							14 27		14 42			14 50			15 05							14 57		
Highbury & Islington	a							14 32		14 46			14 55			15 10							15 02		
	d																								
London Bridge 4 ⊖	a	13 56			14 06		14 11				14 29				14 44			14 26		14 36		14 41			

East London Line and Croydon - London Victoria to London Bridge

Network Diagram - see first Page of Table 177

		LO	SN	LO	LO	SN	LO	SN	SN		SE	SN	SE	SN	LO	LO	LO	SN	LO		LO	SN	LO	SN	SN
East Croydon	d		14 30															15 00							
West Croydon 4	d	14 22												14 31	14 39		14 52								
Norwood Junction 2	d	14 28	14 35												14 43		14 58	15 05							
Anerley	d	14 31	14 38												14 46		15 01	15 08							
Penge West	d	14 33	14 40												14 48		15 03	15 10							
London Victoria 15 ⊖	d					14 19					14 39	14 41	14 43									14 49			
Battersea Park 4	d					14 23						14 45										14 53			
Wandsworth Road	d											14 47													
Clapham High Street ⊖	d											14 49													
London Blackfriars 3 ⊖	d																								
Denmark Hill 4	d										14 48	14 54	14 52												
Peckham Rye 4	d							14 42	14 46		14a51	14 56	14a55	15 01										15 12	15 16
Queens Rd Peckham	d								14 49			14 59		15 04											15 19
South Bermondsey	d								14 51			15 01		15 06											15 21
Clapham Junction 10	d					14 27																14 57			
Wandsworth Common	d					14 30																15 00			
Balham 4 ⊖	d					14 32																15 02			
Streatham Hill	d					14 35																15 05			
West Norwood 4	d					14 40		14 53														15 10		15 23	
Gipsy Hill	d					14 43		14 56														15 13		15 26	
Crystal Palace 4	d				14 43	14 51	14 58	14a59													15 13	15 21	15 28	15a29	
Sydenham	d	14 36	14 42		14 46	14 54	15 01								14 51		15 06	15 12			15 16	15 24	15 31		
Forest Hill 4	d	14 38	14 45		14 49	14 57	15 04								14 53		15 08	15 15			15 19	15 27	15 34		
Honor Oak Park	d	14 41	14 47		14 51	14 59	15 06								14 56		15 11	15 17			15 21	15 29	15 36		
Brockley	d	14 43	14 50		14 54	15 02	15 09								14 58		15 13	15 20			15 24	15 32	15 39		
New Cross Gate 4	a	14 46	14 52		14 56	15 04	15 11								15 01		15 16	15 22			15 26	15 34	15 41		
	d	14 46	14 52		14 56	15 04	15 11								15 01		15 16	15 22			15 26	15 34	15 41		
New Cross ELL	d			14 51												15 06			15 21						
Surrey Quays	d	14 49		14 55	15 00		15 15								15 05	15 10	15 19		15 25		15 30		15 45		
Canada Water	d	14 51		14 57	15 02		15 17								15 07	15 12	15 21		15 27		15 32		15 47		
Rotherhithe	d	14 53		14 58	15 03		15 18								15 08	15 13	15 23		15 28		15 33		15 48		
Wapping	d	14 54		15 00	15 05		15 20								15 10	15 15	15 24		15 30		15 35		15 50		
Shadwell	d	14 56		15 02	15 07		15 22								15 12	15 17	15 26		15 32		15 37		15 52		
Whitechapel	d	14 59		15 04	15 09		15 24								15 14	15 19	15 29		15 34		15 39		15 54		
Shoreditch High Street	d	15 01		15 06	15 11		15 26								15 16	15 21	15 31		15 36		15 41		15 56		
Hoxton	d	15 03		15 08	15 13		15 28								15 18	15 23	15 33		15 38		15 43		15 58		
Haggerston	d	15 05		15 10	15 15		15 30								15 20	15 25	15 35		15 40		15 45		16 00		
Dalston Junction Stn ELL	a	15 07		15 14	15 17		15 32								15 22	15 29	15 37		15 44		15 47		16 02		
Canonbury	d	15 12			15 20		15 35								15 27		15 42				15 50		16 05		
Highbury & Islington	a	15 16			15 25		15 40								15 32		15 46				15 55		16 10		
	d																								
London Bridge 4 ⊖	a		14 59			15 11			14 56			15 06		15 11				15 29				15 44			15 26

		SE	SN	SE	SN		LO	LO	LO	SN	LO	LO	SN	LO	SN		SN	SE	SN	SE	SN	LO	LO	LO	SN
East Croydon	d									15 30															16 00
West Croydon 4	d				15 01		15 09		15 22												15 31	15 39		15 52	
Norwood Junction 2	d						15 13		15 28	15 35												15 43		15 58	16 05
Anerley	d						15 16		15 31	15 38												15 46		16 01	16 08
Penge West	d						15 18		15 33	15 40												15 48		16 03	16 10
London Victoria 15 ⊖	d	15 09	15 11	15 13									15 19					15 39	15 41	15 43					
Battersea Park 4	d		15 15										15 23						15 45						
Wandsworth Road	d		15 17																15 47						
Clapham High Street ⊖	d		15 19																15 49						
London Blackfriars 3 ⊖	d																								
Denmark Hill 4	d	15 18	15 24	15 22														15 48	15 54	15 52					
Peckham Rye 4	d	15a21	15 26	15a25	15 31										15 42		15 46	15a51	15 56	15a55	16 01				
Queens Rd Peckham	d		15 29		15 34												15 49		15 59		16 04				
South Bermondsey	d		15 31		15 36												15 51		16 01		16 06				
Clapham Junction 10	d												15 27												
Wandsworth Common	d												15 30												
Balham 4 ⊖	d												15 32												
Streatham Hill	d												15 35												
West Norwood 4	d												15 40		15 53										
Gipsy Hill	d												15 43		15 56										
Crystal Palace 4	d											15 43	15 51	15 58	15a59										
Sydenham	d						15 21		15 36	15 42		15 46	15 54	16 01								15 51		16 06	16 12
Forest Hill 4	d						15 23		15 38	15 45		15 49	15 57	16 04								15 53		16 08	16 15
Honor Oak Park	d						15 26		15 41	15 47		15 51	15 59	16 06								15 56		16 11	16 17
Brockley	d						15 28		15 43	15 50		15 54	16 02	16 09								15 58		16 13	16 20
New Cross Gate 4	a						15 31		15 46	15 52		15 56	16 04	16 11								16 01		16 16	16 22
	d						15 31		15 46	15 52		15 56	16 04	16 11								16 01		16 16	16 22
New Cross ELL	d							15 36			15 51												16 06		
Surrey Quays	d						15 35	15 40	15 49		15 55	16 00		16 15								16 05	16 10	16 19	
Canada Water	d						15 37	15 42	15 51		15 57	16 02		16 17								16 07	16 12	16 21	
Rotherhithe	d						15 38	15 43	15 53		15 58	16 03		16 18								16 08	16 13	16 23	
Wapping	d						15 40	15 45	15 54		16 00	16 05		16 20								16 10	16 15	16 24	
Shadwell	d						15 42	15 47	15 56		16 02	16 07		16 22								16 12	16 17	16 26	
Whitechapel	d						15 44	15 49	15 59		16 04	16 09		16 24								16 14	16 19	16 29	
Shoreditch High Street	d						15 46	15 51	16 01		16 06	16 11		16 26								16 16	16 21	16 31	
Hoxton	d						15 48	15 53	16 03		16 08	16 13		16 28								16 18	16 23	16 33	
Haggerston	d						15 50	15 55	16 05		16 10	16 15		16 30								16 20	16 25	16 35	
Dalston Junction Stn ELL	a						15 52	15 59	16 07		16 14	16 17		16 32								16 22	16 29	16 37	
Canonbury	d						15 57		16 12			16 20		16 35								16 27		16 42	
Highbury & Islington	a						16 02		16 16			16 25		16 40								16 32		16 46	
	d																								
London Bridge 4 ⊖	a		15 36		15 41					15 59			16 11				15 56		16 06		16 11				16 29

Table 178

Saturdays

East London Line and Croydon - London Victoria to London Bridge

Network Diagram - see first Page of Table 177

			LO	LO	SN	LO	SN	SN	SE	SN	SE		SN	LO	LO	LO	SN	LO	LO	SN	LO		SN	SN	SE
East Croydon	d																16 30								
West Croydon 4	d												16 01	16 09		16 22									
Norwood Junction 2	d													16 13		16 28	16 35								
Anerley	d													16 16		16 31	16 38								
Penge West	d													16 18		16 33	16 40								
London Victoria 15 ⊖	d				15 49				16 09	16 11	16 13									16 19					16 39
Battersea Park 4	d				15 53					16 15										16 23					
Wandsworth Road	d									16 17															
Clapham High Street ⊖	d									16 19															
London Blackfriars 3 ⊖	d																								
Denmark Hill 4	d								16 18	16 24	16 22														16 48
Peckham Rye 4	d						16 12	16 16	16a21	16 26	16a25		16 31										16 42	16 46	16a51
Queens Rd Peckham	d							16 19		16 29			16 34											16 49	
South Bermondsey	d							16 21		16 31			16 36											16 51	
Clapham Junction 10	d				15 57															16 27					
Wandsworth Common	d				16 00															16 30					
Balham 4 ⊖	d				16 02															16 32					
Streatham Hill	d				16 05															16 35					
West Norwood 4	d				16 10		16 23													16 40			16 53		
Gipsy Hill	d				16 13		16 26													16 43			16 56		
Crystal Palace 4	d			16 13	16 21	16 28	16a29												16 43	16 51	16 58		16a59		
Sydenham	d			16 16	16 24	16 31								16 21		16 36	16 42		16 46	16 54	17 01				
Forest Hill 4	d			16 19	16 27	16 34								16 23		16 38	16 45		16 49	16 57	17 04				
Honor Oak Park	d			16 21	16 29	16 36								16 26		16 41	16 47		16 51	16 59	17 06				
Brockley	d			16 24	16 32	16 39								16 28		16 43	16 50		16 54	17 02	17 09				
New Cross Gate 4	a			16 26	16 34	16 41								16 31		16 46	16 52		16 56	17 04	17 11				
	d			16 26	16 34	16 41								16 31		16 46	16 52		16 56	17 04	17 11				
New Cross ELL	d		16 21												16 36			16 51							
Surrey Quays	d		16 25	16 30		16 45								16 35	16 40	16 49		16 55	17 00		17 15				
Canada Water	d		16 27	16 32		16 47								16 37	16 42	16 51		16 57	17 02		17 17				
Rotherhithe	d		16 28	16 33		16 48								16 38	16 43	16 53		16 58	17 03		17 18				
Wapping	d		16 30	16 35		16 50								16 40	16 45	16 54		17 00	17 05		17 20				
Shadwell	d		16 32	16 37		16 52								16 42	16 47	16 56		17 02	17 07		17 22				
Whitechapel	d		16 34	16 39		16 54								16 44	16 49	16 59		17 04	17 09		17 24				
Shoreditch High Street	d		16 36	16 41		16 56								16 46	16 51	17 01		17 06	17 11		17 26				
Hoxton	d		16 38	16 43		16 58								16 48	16 53	17 03		17 08	17 13		17 28				
Haggerston	d		16 40	16 45		17 00								16 50	16 55	17 05		17 10	17 15		17 30				
Dalston Junction Stn ELL	a		16 44	16 47		17 02								16 52	16 59	17 07		17 14	17 17		17 32				
Canonbury	d			16 50		17 05								16 57		17 12			17 20		17 35				
Highbury & Islington	a			16 55		17 10								17 02		17 16			17 25		17 40				
	d																								
London Bridge 4 ⊖	a				16 41			16 26		16 36			16 41				16 59			17 11				16 56	

		SN	SE	SN	LO	LO	LO		SN	LO	LO	SN	LO	SN	SN	SE	SN		SE	SN	LO	LO	LO	SN	LO
East Croydon	d								17 00															17 30	
West Croydon 4	d			16 31	16 39		16 52													17 01	17 09		17 22		
Norwood Junction 2	d				16 43		16 58		17 05												17 13		17 28	17 35	
Anerley	d				16 46		17 01		17 08												17 16		17 31	17 38	
Penge West	d				16 48		17 03		17 10												17 18		17 33	17 40	
London Victoria 15 ⊖	d	16 41	16 43									16 49				17 09	17 11		17 13						
Battersea Park 4	d	16 45										16 53					17 15								
Wandsworth Road	d	16 47															17 17								
Clapham High Street ⊖	d	16 49															17 19								
London Blackfriars 3 ⊖	d																								
Denmark Hill 4	d	16 54	16 52													17 18	17 24		17 22						
Peckham Rye 4	d	16 56	16a55	17 01										17 12	17 16	17a21	17 26		17a25	17 31					
Queens Rd Peckham	d	16 59		17 04											17 19		17 29			17 34					
South Bermondsey	d	17 01		17 06											17 21		17 31			17 36					
Clapham Junction 10	d											16 57													
Wandsworth Common	d											17 00													
Balham 4 ⊖	d											17 02													
Streatham Hill	d											17 05													
West Norwood 4	d											17 10		17 23											
Gipsy Hill	d											17 13		17 26											
Crystal Palace 4	d										17 13	17 21	17 28	17a29											
Sydenham	d				16 51		17 06		17 12		17 16	17 24	17 31								17 21		17 36	17 42	
Forest Hill 4	d				16 53		17 08		17 15		17 19	17 27	17 34								17 23		17 38	17 45	
Honor Oak Park	d				16 56		17 11		17 17		17 21	17 29	17 36								17 26		17 41	17 47	
Brockley	d				16 58		17 13		17 20		17 24	17 32	17 39								17 28		17 43	17 50	
New Cross Gate 4	a				17 01		17 16		17 22		17 26	17 34	17 41								17 31		17 46	17 52	
	d				17 01		17 16		17 22		17 26	17 34	17 41								17 31		17 46	17 52	
New Cross ELL	d					17 06				17 21												17 36			17 51
Surrey Quays	d				17 05	17 10	17 19			17 25	17 30		17 45								17 35	17 40	17 49		17 55
Canada Water	d				17 07	17 12	17 21			17 27	17 32		17 47								17 37	17 42	17 51		17 57
Rotherhithe	d				17 08	17 13	17 23			17 28	17 33		17 48								17 38	17 43	17 53		17 58
Wapping	d				17 10	17 15	17 24			17 30	17 35		17 50								17 40	17 45	17 54		18 00
Shadwell	d				17 12	17 17	17 26			17 32	17 37		17 52								17 42	17 47	17 56		18 02
Whitechapel	d				17 14	17 19	17 29			17 34	17 39		17 54								17 44	17 49	17 59		18 04
Shoreditch High Street	d				17 16	17 21	17 31			17 36	17 41		17 56								17 46	17 51	18 01		18 06
Hoxton	d				17 18	17 23	17 33			17 38	17 43		17 58								17 48	17 53	18 03		18 08
Haggerston	d				17 20	17 25	17 35			17 40	17 45		18 00								17 50	17 55	18 05		18 10
Dalston Junction Stn ELL	a				17 22	17 29	17 37			17 44	17 47		18 02								17 52	17 59	18 07		18 14
Canonbury	d				17 27		17 42				17 50		18 05								17 57		18 12		
Highbury & Islington	a				17 32		17 46				17 55		18 10								18 02		18 16		
	d																								
London Bridge 4 ⊖	a	17 06		17 11					17 30			17 41			17 26		17 36			17 41				17 59	

Table 178

Saturdays

East London Line and Croydon - London Victoria to London Bridge

Network Diagram - see first Page of Table 177

Station		LO	SN		LO	SN	SN	SE	SN	SE	SN	LO	LO		LO	SN	LO	LO	SN	LO	SN	SN	SE		SN
East Croydon	d															18 00									
West Croydon 4	d										17 31	17 39			17 52										
Norwood Junction 2	d											17 43			17 58	18 05									
Anerley	d											17 46			18 01	18 08									
Penge West	d											17 48			18 03	18 10									
London Victoria 15 ⊖	d		17 19					17 39	17 41	17 43									17 49				18 09		18 11
Battersea Park 4	d		17 23						17 45										17 53						18 15
Wandsworth Road	d								17 47																18 17
Clapham High Street ⊖	d								17 49																18 19
London Blackfriars 3 ⊖	d																								
Denmark Hill 4	d							17 48	17 54	17 52													18 18		18 24
Peckham Rye 4	d					17 42	17 46	17a51	17 56	17a55	18 01										18 12	18 16	18a21		18 26
Queens Rd Peckham	d						17 49		17 59		18 04											18 19			18 29
South Bermondsey	d						17 51		18 01		18 06											18 21			18 31
Clapham Junction 10	d		17 27																17 57						
Wandsworth Common	d		17 30																18 00						
Balham 4 ⊖	d		17 32																18 02						
Streatham Hill	d		17 35																18 05						
West Norwood 4	d		17 40			17 53													18 10		18 23				
Gipsy Hill	d		17 43			17 56													18 13		18 26				
Crystal Palace 4	d	17 43	17 51		17 58	17a59												18 13	18 21	18 28	18a29				
Sydenham	d	17 46	17 54		18 01							17 51			18 06	18 12		18 16	18 24	18 31					
Forest Hill 4	d	17 49	17 57		18 04							17 53			18 08	18 15		18 19	18 27	18 34					
Honor Oak Park	d	17 51	17 59		18 06							17 56			18 11	18 17		18 21	18 29	18 36					
Brockley	d	17 54	18 02		18 09							17 58			18 13	18 20		18 24	18 32	18 39					
New Cross Gate 4	a	17 56	18 04		18 11							18 01			18 16	18 22		18 26	18 34	18 41					
	d	17 56	18 04		18 11							18 01			18 16	18 22		18 26	18 34	18 41					
New Cross ELL	d												18 06				18 21								
Surrey Quays	d	18 00			18 15							18 05	18 10		18 19		18 25	18 30		18 45					
Canada Water	d	18 02			18 17							18 07	18 12		18 21		18 27	18 32		18 47					
Rotherhithe	d	18 03			18 18							18 08	18 13		18 23		18 28	18 33		18 48					
Wapping	d	18 05			18 20							18 10	18 15		18 24		18 30	18 35		18 50					
Shadwell	d	18 07			18 22							18 12	18 17		18 26		18 32	18 37		18 52					
Whitechapel	d	18 09			18 24							18 14	18 19		18 29		18 34	18 39		18 54					
Shoreditch High Street	d	18 11			18 26							18 16	18 21		18 31		18 36	18 41		18 56					
Hoxton	d	18 13			18 28							18 18	18 23		18 33		18 38	18 43		18 58					
Haggerston	d	18 15			18 30							18 20	18 25		18 35		18 40	18 45		19 00					
Dalston Junction Stn ELL	a	18 17			18 32							18 22	18 29		18 37		18 44	18 47		19 02					
Canonbury	d	18 20			18 35							18 27			18 42			18 50		19 05					
Highbury & Islington	a	18 25			18 40							18 32			18 46			18 55		19 10					
	d																								
London Bridge 4 ⊖	a		18 11				17 56		18 06		18 11					18 29			18 41			18 26			18 36

Station		SE	SN	LO	LO	LO	SN	LO	LO		SN	LO	SN	SN	SE	SN	SE	SN	LO		LO	LO	SN	LO	LO
East Croydon	d						18 30																19 00		
West Croydon 4	d		18 01	18 09		18 22												18 31	18 39			18 52			
Norwood Junction 2	d			18 13		18 28	18 35												18 43			18 58	19 05		
Anerley	d			18 16		18 31	18 38												18 46			19 01	19 08		
Penge West	d			18 18		18 33	18 40												18 48			19 03	19 10		
London Victoria 15 ⊖	d	18 13									18 19				18 39	18 41	18 43								
Battersea Park 4	d										18 23					18 45									
Wandsworth Road	d															18 47									
Clapham High Street ⊖	d															18 49									
London Blackfriars 3 ⊖	d																								
Denmark Hill 4	d	18 22													18 48	18 54	18 52								
Peckham Rye 4	d	18a25	18 31										18 42	18 46	18a51	18 56	18a55	19 01							
Queens Rd Peckham	d		18 34											18 49		18 59		19 04							
South Bermondsey	d		18 36											18 51		19 01		19 06							
Clapham Junction 10	d										18 27														
Wandsworth Common	d										18 30														
Balham 4 ⊖	d										18 32														
Streatham Hill	d										18 35														
West Norwood 4	d										18 40		18 53												
Gipsy Hill	d										18 43		18 56												
Crystal Palace 4	d								18 43		18 51	18 58	18a59												19 13
Sydenham	d			18 21		18 36	18 42		18 46		18 54	19 01							18 51			19 06	19 12		19 16
Forest Hill 4	d			18 23		18 38	18 45		18 49		18 57	19 04							18 53			19 08	19 15		19 19
Honor Oak Park	d			18 26		18 41	18 47		18 51		18 59	19 06							18 56			19 11	19 17		19 21
Brockley	d			18 28		18 43	18 50		18 54		19 02	19 09							18 58			19 13	19 20		19 24
New Cross Gate 4	a			18 31		18 46	18 52		18 56		19 04	19 11							19 01			19 16	19 22		19 26
	d			18 31		18 46	18 52		18 56		19 04	19 11							19 01			19 16	19 22		19 26
New Cross ELL	d				18 36			18 51													19 06			19 21	
Surrey Quays	d			18 35	18 40	18 49		18 55	19 00			19 15							19 05		19 10	19 19		19 25	19 30
Canada Water	d			18 37	18 42	18 51		18 57	19 02			19 17							19 07		19 12	19 21		19 27	19 32
Rotherhithe	d			18 38	18 43	18 53		18 58	19 03			19 18							19 08		19 13	19 23		19 28	19 33
Wapping	d			18 40	18 45	18 54		19 00	19 05			19 20							19 10		19 15	19 24		19 30	19 35
Shadwell	d			18 42	18 47	18 56		19 02	19 07			19 22							19 12		19 17	19 26		19 32	19 37
Whitechapel	d			18 44	18 49	18 59		19 04	19 09			19 24							19 14		19 19	19 29		19 34	19 39
Shoreditch High Street	d			18 46	18 51	19 01		19 06	19 11			19 26							19 16		19 21	19 31		19 36	19 41
Hoxton	d			18 48	18 53	19 03		19 08	19 13			19 28							19 18		19 23	19 33		19 38	19 43
Haggerston	d			18 50	18 55	19 05		19 10	19 15			19 30							19 20		19 25	19 35		19 40	19 45
Dalston Junction Stn ELL	a			18 52	18 59	19 07		19 14	19 17			19 32							19 22		19 29	19 37		19 44	19 47
Canonbury	d			18 57		19 12			19 20			19 35							19 27			19 42			19 50
Highbury & Islington	a			19 02		19 16			19 25			19 40							19 32			19 46			19 55
	d																								
London Bridge 4 ⊖	a		18 41				18 59				19 11			18 56		19 06		19 11					19 29		

Table 178

Saturdays

East London Line and Croydon - London Victoria to London Bridge

Network Diagram - see first Page of Table 177

Station		SN	LO	SN	SN		SE	SN	SE	SN	LO	LO	LO	SN	LO		LO	SN	LO	SN	SN	SE	SN	SE	SN
East Croydon	d													19 30											
West Croydon 4	d									19 01	19 09		19 22												19 31
Norwood Junction 2	d										19 13		19 28	19 35											
Anerley	d										19 16		19 31	19 38											
Penge West	d										19 18		19 33	19 40											
London Victoria 15 ⊖	d	18 49					19 09	19 11	19 13									19 19				19 39	19 41	19 43	
Battersea Park 4	d	18 53						19 15										19 23					19 45		
Wandsworth Road	d							19 17															19 47		
Clapham High Street ⊖	d							19 19															19 49		
London Blackfriars 3 ⊖	d																								
Denmark Hill 4	d						19 18	19 24	19 22													19 48	19 54	19 52	
Peckham Rye 4	d			19 12	19 16		19a21	19 26	19a25	19 31										19 42	19 46	19a51	19 56	19a55	20 01
Queens Rd Peckham	d				19 19			19 29		19 34											19 49		19 59		20 04
South Bermondsey	d				19 21			19 31		19 36											19 51		20 01		20 06
Clapham Junction 10	d	18 57																19 27							
Wandsworth Common	d	19 00																19 30							
Balham 4 ⊖	d	19 02																19 32							
Streatham Hill	d	19 05																19 35							
West Norwood 4	d	19 10		19 23														19 40		19 53					
Gipsy Hill	d	19 13		19 26														19 43		19 56					
Crystal Palace 4	d	19 21	19 28	19a29													19 43	19 51	19 58	19a59					
Sydenham	d	19 24	19 31								19 21		19 36	19 42			19 46	19 54	20 01						
Forest Hill 4	d	19 27	19 34								19 23		19 38	19 45			19 49	19 57	20 04						
Honor Oak Park	d	19 29	19 36								19 26		19 41	19 47			19 51	19 59	20 06						
Brockley	d	19 32	19 39								19 28		19 43	19 50			19 54	20 02	20 09						
New Cross Gate 4	a	19 34	19 41								19 31		19 46	19 52			19 56	20 04	20 11						
	d	19 34	19 41								19 31		19 46	19 52			19 56	20 04	20 11						
New Cross ELL	d											19 36			19 51										
Surrey Quays	d		19 45								19 35	19 40	19 49		19 55		20 00		20 15						
Canada Water	d		19 47								19 37	19 42	19 51		19 57		20 02		20 17						
Rotherhithe	d		19 48								19 38	19 43	19 53		19 58		20 03		20 18						
Wapping	d		19 50								19 40	19 45	19 54		20 00		20 05		20 20						
Shadwell	d		19 52								19 42	19 47	19 56		20 02		20 07		20 22						
Whitechapel	d		19 54								19 44	19 49	19 59		20 04		20 09		20 24						
Shoreditch High Street	d		19 56								19 46	19 51	20 01		20 06		20 11		20 26						
Hoxton	d		19 58								19 48	19 53	20 03		20 08		20 13		20 28						
Haggerston	d		20 00								19 50	19 55	20 05		20 10		20 15		20 30						
Dalston Junction Stn ELL	a		20 02								19 52	19 59	20 07		20 14		20 17		20 32						
Canonbury	d		20 05								19 57		20 12				20 20		20 35						
Highbury & Islington	a		20 10								20 02		20 16				20 25		20 40						
	d																								
London Bridge 4 ⊖	a	19 41			19 26			19 36		19 41				19 59				20 11			19 56		20 06		20 11

Station			LO	LO	LO	SN	LO	LO	SN	LO	SN		SN	SN	SE	SN	LO	LO	LO	SN	LO		LO	SN	LO
East Croydon	d					20 00														20 30					
West Croydon 4	d		19 39		19 52											20 01	20 09		20 22						
Norwood Junction 2	d		19 43		19 58	20 05											20 13		20 28	20 35					
Anerley	d		19 46		20 01	20 08											20 16		20 31	20 38					
Penge West	d		19 48		20 03	20 10											20 18		20 33	20 40					
London Victoria 15 ⊖	d								19 49					20 11	20 13									20 19	
Battersea Park 4	d								19 53					20 15										20 23	
Wandsworth Road	d													20 17											
Clapham High Street ⊖	d													20 19											
London Blackfriars 3 ⊖	d																								
Denmark Hill 4	d													20 24	20 22										
Peckham Rye 4	d										20 12		20 16	20 26	20a25	20 31									
Queens Rd Peckham	d												20 19	20 29		20 34									
South Bermondsey	d												20 21	20 31		20 36									
Clapham Junction 10	d								19 57															20 27	
Wandsworth Common	d								20 00															20 30	
Balham 4 ⊖	d								20 02															20 32	
Streatham Hill	d								20 05															20 35	
West Norwood 4	d								20 10		20 23													20 40	
Gipsy Hill	d								20 13		20 26													20 43	
Crystal Palace 4	d							20 13	20 21	20 28	20a29												20 43	20 51	20 58
Sydenham	d		19 51		20 06	20 12		20 16	20 24	20 31							20 21		20 36	20 42			20 46	20 54	21 01
Forest Hill 4	d		19 53		20 08	20 15		20 19	20 27	20 34							20 23		20 38	20 45			20 49	20 57	21 04
Honor Oak Park	d		19 56		20 11	20 17		20 21	20 29	20 36							20 26		20 41	20 47			20 51	20 59	21 06
Brockley	d		19 58		20 13	20 20		20 24	20 32	20 39							20 28		20 43	20 50			20 54	21 02	21 09
New Cross Gate 4	a		20 01		20 16	20 22		20 26	20 34	20 41							20 31		20 46	20 52			20 56	21 04	21 11
	d		20 01		20 16	20 22		20 26	20 34	20 41							20 31		20 46	20 52			20 56	21 04	21 11
New Cross ELL	d			20 06			20 21											20 36			20 51				
Surrey Quays	d		20 05	20 10	20 19		20 25	20 30		20 45							20 35	20 40	20 49		20 55		21 00		21 15
Canada Water	d		20 07	20 12	20 21		20 27	20 32		20 47							20 37	20 42	20 51		20 57		21 02		21 17
Rotherhithe	d		20 08	20 13	20 23		20 28	20 33		20 48							20 38	20 43	20 53		20 58		21 03		21 18
Wapping	d		20 10	20 15	20 24		20 30	20 35		20 50							20 40	20 45	20 54		21 00		21 05		21 20
Shadwell	d		20 12	20 17	20 26		20 32	20 37		20 52							20 42	20 47	20 56		21 02		21 07		21 22
Whitechapel	d		20 14	20 19	20 29		20 34	20 39		20 54							20 44	20 49	20 59		21 04		21 09		21 24
Shoreditch High Street	d		20 16	20 21	20 31		20 36	20 41		20 56							20 46	20 51	21 01		21 06		21 11		21 26
Hoxton	d		20 18	20 23	20 33		20 38	20 43		20 58							20 48	20 53	21 03		21 08		21 13		21 28
Haggerston	d		20 20	20 25	20 35		20 40	20 45		21 00							20 50	20 55	21 05		21 10		21 15		21 30
Dalston Junction Stn ELL	a		20 22	20 29	20 37		20 44	20 47		21 02							20 52	20 59	21 07		21 14		21 17		21 32
Canonbury	d		20 27		20 42			20 50		21 05							20 57		21 12				21 20		21 35
Highbury & Islington	a		20 32		20 46			20 55		21 10							21 02		21 16				21 25		21 40
	d																								
London Bridge 4 ⊖	a					20 29			20 41				20 26	20 36		20 41				20 59				21 13	

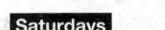

East London Line and Croydon - London Victoria to London Bridge

Network Diagram - see first Page of Table 177

		SN	SN	SN	SE	SN	LO		LO	LO	SN	LO	LO	SN	LO	SN	SN		SN	SE	SN	LO	LO	LO	SN
East Croydon	d										21 00														21 30
West Croydon 4	d					20 31	20 39			20 52											21 02	21 09		21 22	
Norwood Junction 2	d						20 43			20 58	21 05											21 13		21 28	21 35
Anerley	d						20 46			21 01	21 08											21 16		21 31	21 38
Penge West	d						20 48			21 03	21 10											21 18		21 33	21 40
London Victoria 15 ⊖	d			20 41	20 43									20 49					21 11	21 13					
Battersea Park 4	d			20 45										20 53					21 15						
Wandsworth Road	d			20 47															21 17						
Clapham High Street ⊖	d			20 49															21 19						
London Blackfriars 3 ⊖	d																								
Denmark Hill 4	d			20 54	20 52														21 24	21 22					
Peckham Rye 4	d	20 42	20 46	20 56	20a55	21 01										21 12	21 16		21 26	21a25	21 31				
Queens Rd Peckham	d		20 49	20 59		21 04											21 19		21 29		21 34				
South Bermondsey	d		20 51	21 01		21 06											21 21		21 31		21 36				
Clapham Junction 10	d													20 57											
Wandsworth Common	d													21 00											
Balham 4 ⊖	d													21 02											
Streatham Hill	d													21 05											
West Norwood 4	d	20 53												21 10		21 23									
Gipsy Hill	d	20 56												21 13		21 26									
Crystal Palace 4	d	20a59											21 13	21 21	21 28	21a29									
Sydenham	d						20 51			21 06	21 12		21 16	21 24	21 31							21 21		21 36	21 42
Forest Hill 4	d						20 53			21 08	21 15		21 19	21 27	21 34							21 23		21 38	21 45
Honor Oak Park	d						20 56			21 11	21 17		21 21	21 29	21 36							21 26		21 41	21 47
Brockley	d						20 58			21 13	21 20		21 24	21 32	21 39							21 28		21 43	21 50
New Cross Gate 4	a						21 01			21 16	21 22		21 26	21 34	21 41							21 31		21 46	21 52
	d						21 01			21 16	21 22		21 26	21 34	21 41							21 31		21 46	21 52
New Cross ELL	d								21 06			21 21											21 36		
Surrey Quays	d						21 05		21 10	21 19		21 25	21 30		21 45							21 35	21 40	21 49	
Canada Water	d						21 07		21 12	21 21		21 27	21 32		21 47							21 37	21 42	21 51	
Rotherhithe	d						21 08		21 13	21 23		21 28	21 33		21 48							21 38	21 43	21 53	
Wapping	d						21 10		21 15	21 24		21 30	21 35		21 50							21 40	21 45	21 54	
Shadwell	d						21 12		21 17	21 26		21 32	21 37		21 52							21 42	21 47	21 56	
Whitechapel	d						21 14		21 19	21 29		21 34	21 39		21 54							21 44	21 49	21 59	
Shoreditch High Street	d						21 16		21 21	21 31		21 36	21 41		21 56							21 46	21 51	22 01	
Hoxton	d						21 18		21 23	21 33		21 38	21 43		21 58							21 48	21 53	22 03	
Haggerston	d						21 20		21 25	21 35		21 40	21 45		22 00							21 50	21 55	22 05	
Dalston Junction Stn ELL	a						21 22		21 29	21 37		21 44	21 47		22 02							21 52	21 59	22 07	
Canonbury	d						21 27			21 42			21 50		22 05							21 57		22 12	
Highbury & Islington	a						21 32			21 46			21 55		22 10							22 02		22 16	
	d																								
London Bridge 4 ⊖	a		20 56	21 06		21 11					21 29			21 43			21 26		21 36		21 41				21 59

		LO	LO		SN	LO	SN	SN	SN	SE	SN	LO	LO		LO	SN	LO	SN	LO	SN	SN	SN	SE		SN
East Croydon	d															22 00									
West Croydon 4	d										21 31	21 39			21 52										22 01
Norwood Junction 2	d											21 43			21 58	22 05									
Anerley	d											21 46			22 01	22 08									
Penge West	d											21 48			22 03	22 10									
London Victoria 15 ⊖	d				21 19				21 41	21 43								21 49				22 11	22 13		
Battersea Park 4	d				21 23				21 45									21 53				22 15			
Wandsworth Road	d								21 47													22 17			
Clapham High Street ⊖	d								21 49													22 19			
London Blackfriars 3 ⊖	d																								
Denmark Hill 4	d								21 54	21 52												22 24	22 22		
Peckham Rye 4	d						21 42	21 46	21 56	21a55	22 01									22 12	22 16	22 26	22a25		22 31
Queens Rd Peckham	d							21 49	21 59		22 04										22 19	22 29			22 34
South Bermondsey	d							21 51	22 01		22 06										22 21	22 31			22 36
Clapham Junction 10	d				21 27													21 57							
Wandsworth Common	d				21 30													22 00							
Balham 4 ⊖	d				21 32													22 02							
Streatham Hill	d				21 35													22 05							
West Norwood 4	d				21 40		21 53											22 10		22 23					
Gipsy Hill	d				21 43		21 56											22 13		22 26					
Crystal Palace 4	d		21 43		21 51	21 58	21a59										22 13	22 21	22 28	22a29					
Sydenham	d		21 46		21 54	22 01						21 51			22 06	22 12	22 16	22 24	22 31						
Forest Hill 4	d		21 49		21 57	22 04						21 53			22 08	22 15	22 19	22 27	22 34						
Honor Oak Park	d		21 51		21 59	22 06						21 56			22 11	22 17	22 21	22 29	22 36						
Brockley	d		21 54		22 02	22 09						21 58			22 13	22 20	22 24	22 32	22 39						
New Cross Gate 4	a		21 56		22 04	22 11						22 01			22 16	22 22	22 26	22 34	22 41						
	d		21 56		22 04	22 11						22 01			22 16	22 22	22 26	22 34	22 41						
New Cross ELL	d	21 51											22 06												
Surrey Quays	d	21 55	22 00			22 15						22 05	22 10		22 19		22 30		22 45						
Canada Water	d	21 57	22 02			22 17						22 07	22 12		22 21		22 32		22 47						
Rotherhithe	d	21 58	22 03			22 18						22 08	22 13		22 23		22 33		22 48						
Wapping	d	22 00	22 05			22 20						22 10	22 15		22 24		22 35		22 50						
Shadwell	d	22 02	22 07			22 22						22 12	22 17		22 26		22 37		22 52						
Whitechapel	d	22 04	22 09			22 24						22 14	22 19		22 29		22 39		22 54						
Shoreditch High Street	d	22 06	22 11			22 26						22 16	22 21		22 31		22 41		22 56						
Hoxton	d	22 08	22 13			22 28						22 18	22 23		22 33		22 43		22 58						
Haggerston	d	22 10	22 15			22 30						22 20	22 25		22 35		22 45		23 00						
Dalston Junction Stn ELL	a	22 14	22 17			22 32						22 22	22 29		22 37		22 47		23 02						
Canonbury	d		22 20			22 35						22 27			22 42		22 50		23 05						
Highbury & Islington	a		22 25			22 40						22 32			22 46		22 55		23 10						
	d																								
London Bridge 4 ⊖	a				22 13			21 56	22 06		22 11					22 29		22 43			22 26	22 36			22 41

Table 178

Saturdays

East London Line and Croydon - London Victoria to London Bridge

Network Diagram - see first Page of Table 177

		LO	LO	LO	SN	LO	SN	SN	SN		SN	SE	SN	LO	LO	LO	SN	LO	SN		SN	SN	SN	LO	SE
East Croydon	d				22 30												23 01								
West Croydon 4	d	22 09		22 22									22 31	22 39		22 52									
Norwood Junction 2	d	22 13		22 28	22 35									22 43		22 58	23 06								
Anerley	d	22 16		22 31	22 38									22 46		23 01	23 09								
Penge West	d	22 18		22 33	22 40									22 48		23 03	23 11								
London Victoria 15 ⊖	d						22 19				22 41	22 43							22 49				23 11		23 13
Battersea Park 4	d						22 23				22 45								22 53				23 15		
Wandsworth Road	d										22 47												23 17		
Clapham High Street ⊖	d										22 49												23 19		
London Blackfriars 3 ⊖	d																								
Denmark Hill 4	d										22 54	22 52											23 24		23 22
Peckham Rye 4	d							22 42	22 46		22 56	22a55	23 01								23 12	23 16	23 26		23a25
Queens Rd Peckham	d								22 49		22 59		23 04									23 19	23 29		
South Bermondsey	d								22 51		23 01		23 06									23 21	23 31		
Clapham Junction 10	d						22 27												22 57						
Wandsworth Common	d						22 30												23 00						
Balham 4 ⊖	d						22 32												23 02						
Streatham Hill	d						22 35												23 05						
West Norwood 4	d						22 40	22 53											23 10		23 24				
Gipsy Hill	d						22 43	22 56											23 13		23 27				
Crystal Palace 4	d					22 43	22 51	22a59										23 13	23 21		23a29				
Sydenham	d	22 21		22 36	22 42	22 46	22 54							22 51		23 06	23 13	23 16	23 24						
Forest Hill 4	d	22 23		22 38	22 45	22 49	22 57							22 53		23 08	23 16	23 19	23 27						
Honor Oak Park	d	22 26		22 41	22 47	22 51	22 59							22 56		23 11	23 18	23 21	23 29						
Brockley	d	22 28		22 43	22 50	22 54	23 02							22 58		23 13	23 21	23 24	23 32						
New Cross Gate 4	a	22 31		22 46	22 52	22 56	23 04							23 01		23 16	23 23	23 26	23 34						
	d	22 31		22 46	22 52	22 56	23 04							23 01		23 16	23 23	23 26	23 34						
New Cross ELL	d		22 36												23 06									23 36	
Surrey Quays	d	22 35	22 40	22 49		23 00								23 05	23 10	23 19		23 30						23 40	
Canada Water	d	22 37	22 42	22 51		23 02								23 07	23 12	23 21		23 32						23 42	
Rotherhithe	d	22 38	22 43	22 53		23 03								23 08	23 13	23 23		23 33						23 43	
Wapping	d	22 40	22 45	22 54		23 05								23 10	23 15	23 24		23 35						23 45	
Shadwell	d	22 42	22 47	22 56		23 07								23 12	23 17	23 26		23 37						23 47	
Whitechapel	d	22 44	22 49	22 59		23 09								23 14	23 19	23 29		23 39						23 49	
Shoreditch High Street	d	22 46	22 51	23 01		23 11								23 16	23 21	23 31		23 41						23 51	
Hoxton	d	22 48	22 53	23 03		23 13								23 18	23 23	23 33		23 43						23 53	
Haggerston	d	22 50	22 55	23 05		23 15								23 20	23 25	23 35		23 45						23 55	
Dalston Junction Stn ELL	a	22 52	22 59	23 07		23 17								23 22	23 29	23 37		23 47						23 59	
Canonbury	d	22 57		23 12		23 20								23 27		23 42		23 50							
Highbury & Islington	a	23 02		23 16		23 25								23 32		23 46		23 55							
	d																								
London Bridge 4 ⊖	a				22 59		23 13		22 56		23 06		23 11				23 30		23 43			23 26	23 36		

		SN	LO	LO	SN		SN	SN	SE	SN
East Croydon	d									
West Croydon 4	d	23 01	23 22							
Norwood Junction 2	d		23 28							
Anerley	d		23 31							
Penge West	d		23 33							
London Victoria 15 ⊖	d				23 19				23 43	23 54
Battersea Park 4	d				23 23					23 58
Wandsworth Road	d									
Clapham High Street ⊖	d									
London Blackfriars 3 ⊖	d									
Denmark Hill 4	d								23 52	
Peckham Rye 4	d	23 31					23 42	23 46	23a55	
Queens Rd Peckham	d	23 34						23 49		
South Bermondsey	d	23 36						23 51		
Clapham Junction 10	d				23 27					00 02
Wandsworth Common	d				23 30					00 05
Balham 4 ⊖	d				23 32					00 07
Streatham Hill	d				23 35					00 10
West Norwood 4	d				23 40		23 54			00 14
Gipsy Hill	d				23 43		23 57			00 17
Crystal Palace 4	d			23 43	23 51		23a59			00 21
Sydenham	d		23 36	23 46	23 54					00 24
Forest Hill 4	d		23 38	23 49	23 57					00 27
Honor Oak Park	d		23 41	23 51	23 59					00 29
Brockley	d		23 43	23 54	00 02					00 32
New Cross Gate 4	a		23 46	23 56	00 04					00 35
	d		23 46	23 56	00 04					00 35
New Cross ELL	d									
Surrey Quays	d		23 49	23 59						
Canada Water	d		23 51	00 02						
Rotherhithe	d		23 53	00 03						
Wapping	d		23 54	00 05						
Shadwell	d		23 56	00 07						
Whitechapel	d		23 59	00 09						
Shoreditch High Street	d		00 01	00 11						
Hoxton	d		00 03	00 13						
Haggerston	d		00 05	00 15						
Dalston Junction Stn ELL	a		00 07	00 17						
Canonbury	d		00 12	00 20						
Highbury & Islington	a		00 16	00 25						
	d									
London Bridge 4 ⊖	a	23 41			00 11			23 56		00 41

Table 178

Sundays

East London Line and Croydon - London Victoria to London Bridge

Network Diagram - see first Page of Table 177

		LO A	LO A	SN A	SN A	SN	SN	LO	SN	LO		SN	LO	SN	SN	SN	SN	LO	SN	LO		SN	SE	SN	SN
East Croydon	d								06 47						07 12	07 17									
West Croydon 4	d	23p22						06 42					07 12				07 22		07 34	07 42					
Norwood Junction 2	d	23p28						06 47	06 52				07 17			07 22	07 27		07 40	07 47					
Anerley	d	23p31						06 50	06 55				07 20			07 25				07 50					
Penge West	d	23p33						06 52	06 57				07 22			07 27				07 52					
London Victoria 15 ⊖	d			23p19	23p54																		07 39		07 41
Battersea Park 4	d			23p23	23p58																				07 45
Wandsworth Road	d																								07 47
Clapham High Street ⊖	d																								07 49
London Blackfriars 3 ⊖	d																								
Denmark Hill 4	d																						07 48		07 54
Peckham Rye 4	d					00 12	00 42					07 09		07 23	07 39							07 45	07a51	07 53	07 56
Queens Rd Peckham	d											07 12		07 26	07 42									07 56	07 59
South Bermondsey	d											07 14		07 28	07 44									07 58	08 01
Clapham Junction 10	d			23p27	00 02																				
Wandsworth Common	d			23p30	00 05																				
Balham 4 ⊖	d			23p32	00 07																				
Streatham Hill	d			23p35	00 10																				
West Norwood 4	d			23p40	00 14	00 24	00 54															07 57			
Gipsy Hill	d			23p43	00 17	00 27	00 57															08 00			
Crystal Palace 4	d		23p43	23p51	00 21	00a29	00a59			07 07							07a31	07 37				08a02			
Sydenham	d	23p36	23p46	23p54	00 24			06 55	06 59	07 10			07 25			07 29		07 40	07 44	07 55					
Forest Hill 4	d	23p38	23p49	23p57	00 27			06 57	07 02	07 13			07 27			07 32		07 43	07 47	07 57					
Honor Oak Park	d	23p41	23p51	23p59	00 29			07 00	07 04	07 15			07 30			07 34		07 45	07 49	08 00					
Brockley	d	23p43	23p54	00 02	00 32			07 02	07 07	07 18			07 32			07 37		07 48	07 52	08 02					
New Cross Gate 4	a	23p46	23p56	00 04	00 35			07 05	07 09	07 20			07 35			07 39		07 50	07 54	08 05					
	d	23p46	23p56	00 04	00 35			07 05	07 09	07 20			07 35			07 39		07 50	07 54	08 05					
New Cross ELL	d																								
Surrey Quays	d	23p49	23p59					07 09		07 24			07 39					07 54		08 09					
Canada Water	d	23p51	00 02					07 11		07 26			07 41					07 56		08 11					
Rotherhithe	d	23p53	00 03					07 12		07 27			07 42					07 57		08 12					
Wapping	d	23p54	00 05					07 14		07 29			07 44					07 59		08 14					
Shadwell	d	23p56	00 07					07 16		07 31			07 46					08 01		08 16					
Whitechapel	d	23p59	00 09					07 18		07 33			07 48					08 03		08 18					
Shoreditch High Street	d	00 01	00 11					07 20		07 35			07 50					08 05		08 20					
Hoxton	d	00 03	00 13					07 22		07 37			07 52					08 07		08 22					
Haggerston	d	00 05	00 15					07 24		07 39			07 54					08 09		08 24					
Dalston Junction Stn ELL	a	00 07	00 17					07 26		07 41			07 56					08 11		08 26					
Canonbury	d	00 12	00 20					07 31		07 44			08 01					08 14		08 31					
Highbury & Islington	a	00 16	00 25					07 36		07 49			08 06					08 21		08 36					
	d																								
London Bridge 4 ⊖	a			00 11	00 41				07 17			07 19		07 33	07 50	07 48			08 01					08 03	08 06

		SN	SN	SN	LO	SN		LO	SN	SE	SN	SN	SN	SN	LO	SN		SN	LO	LO	LO	SE	SN	SN	SN
East Croydon	d	07 42	07 47										08 12	08 17											08 42
West Croydon 4	d			07 52		08 04		08 12								08 34				08 42					
Norwood Junction 2	d		07 52	07 57		08 10		08 17						08 22		08 40				08 47					
Anerley	d		07 55					08 20						08 25						08 50					
Penge West	d		07 57					08 22						08 27						08 52					
London Victoria 15 ⊖	d									08 09		08 11										08 39		08 41	
Battersea Park 4	d											08 15												08 45	
Wandsworth Road	d											08 17												08 47	
Clapham High Street ⊖	d											08 19												08 49	
London Blackfriars 3 ⊖	d																								
Denmark Hill 4	d									08 18		08 24										08 48		08 54	
Peckham Rye 4	d	08 10							08 15	08a21	08 23	08 26	08 40					08 45				08a51	08 53	08 56	09 10
Queens Rd Peckham	d	08 12									08 26	08 29	08 42										08 56	08 59	09 12
South Bermondsey	d	08 15									08 28	08 31	08 45										08 58	09 01	09 15
Clapham Junction 10	d																								
Wandsworth Common	d																								
Balham 4 ⊖	d																								
Streatham Hill	d																								
West Norwood 4	d								08 27									08 57							
Gipsy Hill	d								08 30									09 00							
Crystal Palace 4	d			08a01	08 07				08a32						08 37			09a02							
Sydenham	d		07 59		08 10	08 14		08 25						08 29	08 40	08 44				08 55					
Forest Hill 4	d		08 02		08 13	08 17		08 27						08 32	08 43	08 47				08 57					
Honor Oak Park	d		08 04		08 15	08 19		08 30						08 34	08 45	08 49				09 00					
Brockley	d		08 07		08 18	08 22		08 32						08 37	08 48	08 52				09 02					
New Cross Gate 4	a		08 09		08 20	08 24		08 35						08 39	08 50	08 54				09 05					
	d		08 09		08 20	08 24		08 35						08 39	08 50	08 54				09 05					
New Cross ELL	d																		08 54		09 09				
Surrey Quays	d				08 24			08 39							08 54				08 58	09 09	09 13				
Canada Water	d				08 26			08 41							08 56				09 00	09 11	09 15				
Rotherhithe	d				08 27			08 42							08 57				09 01	09 12	09 16				
Wapping	d				08 29			08 44							08 59				09 03	09 14	09 18				
Shadwell	d				08 31			08 46							09 01				09 05	09 16	09 20				
Whitechapel	d				08 33			08 48							09 03				09 07	09 18	09 22				
Shoreditch High Street	d				08 35			08 50							09 05				09 09	09 20	09 24				
Hoxton	d				08 37			08 52							09 07				09 11	09 22	09 26				
Haggerston	d				08 39			08 54							09 09				09 13	09 24	09 28				
Dalston Junction Stn ELL	a				08 41			08 56							09 11				09 15	09 26	09 31				
Canonbury	d				08 44			09 01							09 14				09 20	09 31	09 36				
Highbury & Islington	a				08 51			09 06							09 21				09 27	09 36	09 41				
	d																								
London Bridge 4 ⊖	a	08 19	08 17			08 31					08 33	08 36	08 49	08 48		09 01							09 03	09 06	09 19

A not 11 December

Table 178

Sundays

East London Line and Croydon - London Victoria to London Bridge

Network Diagram - see first Page of Table 177

		SN		LO	SN	SN	LO	LO	LO	SE	SN	SN		SN	SN	LO	SN	SN	LO	LO	LO	SE		SN	SN
East Croydon	d	08 47												09 12	09 17										
West Croydon 4	d				09 04			09 12									09 34			09 42					
Norwood Junction 2	d	08 52			09 10			09 17							09 22		09 40			09 47					
Anerley	d	08 55						09 20							09 25					09 50					
Penge West	d	08 57						09 22							09 27					09 52					
London Victoria 15 ⊖	d									09 09		09 11										09 39			09 41
Battersea Park 4	d											09 15													09 45
Wandsworth Road	d											09 17													09 47
Clapham High Street ⊖	d											09 19													09 49
London Blackfriars 3 ⊖	d																								
Denmark Hill 4	d									09 18		09 24										09 48			09 54
Peckham Rye 4	d					09 15				09a21	09 23	09 26		09 40				09 45				09a51		09 53	09 56
Queens Rd Peckham	d										09 26	09 29		09 42										09 56	09 59
South Bermondsey	d										09 28	09 31		09 45										09 58	10 01
Clapham Junction 10	d																								
Wandsworth Common	d																								
Balham 4 ⊖	d																								
Streatham Hill	d																								
West Norwood 4	d					09 27												09 57							
Gipsy Hill	d					09 30												10 00							
Crystal Palace 4	d			09 07		09a32										09 37		10a02							
Sydenham	d	08 59		09 10	09 14			09 25							09 29	09 40	09 44			09 55					
Forest Hill 4	d	09 02		09 13	09 17			09 27							09 32	09 43	09 47			09 57					
Honor Oak Park	d	09 04		09 15	09 19			09 30							09 34	09 45	09 49			10 00					
Brockley	d	09 07		09 18	09 22			09 32							09 37	09 48	09 52			10 02					
New Cross Gate 4	a	09 09		09 20	09 24			09 35							09 39	09 50	09 54			10 05					
	d	09 09		09 20	09 24			09 35							09 39	09 50	09 54			10 05					
New Cross ELL	d						09 24		09 39										09 54		10 09				
Surrey Quays	d			09 24			09 28	09 39	09 43							09 54			09 58	10 09	10 13				
Canada Water	d			09 26			09 30	09 41	09 45							09 56			10 00	10 11	10 15				
Rotherhithe	d			09 27			09 31	09 42	09 46							09 57			10 01	10 12	10 16				
Wapping	d			09 29			09 33	09 44	09 48							09 59			10 03	10 14	10 18				
Shadwell	d			09 31			09 35	09 46	09 50							10 01			10 05	10 16	10 20				
Whitechapel	d			09 33			09 37	09 48	09 52							10 03			10 07	10 18	10 22				
Shoreditch High Street	d			09 35			09 39	09 50	09 54							10 05			10 09	10 20	10 24				
Hoxton	d			09 37			09 41	09 52	09 56							10 07			10 11	10 22	10 26				
Haggerston	d			09 39			09 43	09 54	09 58							10 09			10 13	10 24	10 28				
Dalston Junction Stn ELL	a			09 41			09 45	09 56	10 01							10 11			10 15	10 26	10 31				
Canonbury	d			09 44			09 50	10 01	10 06							10 14			10 20	10 31	10 36				
Highbury & Islington	a			09 51			09 57	10 06	10 11							10 21			10 27	10 36	10 41				
	d																								
London Bridge 4 ⊖	a	09 18			09 31						09 33	09 36		09 49	09 48		10 01							10 03	10 06

		SN	SN	LO	SN	SN	LO	LO		LO	SE	SN	SN	SN	SN	LO	SN	SN		LO	LO	LO	SE	SN	SN
East Croydon	d	09 42	09 47											10 12	10 17										
West Croydon 4	d				10 04			10 12									10 34				10 42				
Norwood Junction 2	d		09 52		10 10			10 17							10 22		10 40				10 47				
Anerley	d		09 55					10 20							10 25						10 50				
Penge West	d		09 57					10 22							10 27						10 52				
London Victoria 15 ⊖	d										10 09		10 11										10 39		10 41
Battersea Park 4	d												10 15												10 45
Wandsworth Road	d												10 17												10 47
Clapham High Street ⊖	d												10 19												10 49
London Blackfriars 3 ⊖	d																								
Denmark Hill 4	d										10 18		10 24										10 48		10 54
Peckham Rye 4	d	10 10				10 15					10a21	10 23	10 26	10 40				10 45					10a51	10 53	10 56
Queens Rd Peckham	d	10 12										10 26	10 29	10 42										10 56	10 59
South Bermondsey	d	10 15										10 28	10 31	10 45										10 58	11 01
Clapham Junction 10	d																								
Wandsworth Common	d																								
Balham 4 ⊖	d																								
Streatham Hill	d																								
West Norwood 4	d					10 27												10 57							
Gipsy Hill	d					10 30												11 00							
Crystal Palace 4	d			10 07		10a32										10 37		11a02							
Sydenham	d		09 59	10 10	10 14			10 25							10 29	10 40	10 44				10 55				
Forest Hill 4	d		10 02	10 13	10 17			10 27							10 32	10 43	10 47				10 57				
Honor Oak Park	d		10 04	10 15	10 19			10 30							10 34	10 45	10 49				11 00				
Brockley	d		10 07	10 18	10 22			10 32							10 37	10 48	10 52				11 02				
New Cross Gate 4	a		10 09	10 20	10 24			10 35							10 39	10 50	10 54				11 05				
	d		10 09	10 20	10 24			10 35							10 39	10 50	10 54				11 05				
New Cross ELL	d						10 24			10 39										10 54		11 09			
Surrey Quays	d			10 24			10 28	10 39		10 43						10 54				10 58	11 09	11 13			
Canada Water	d			10 26			10 30	10 41		10 45						10 56				11 00	11 11	11 15			
Rotherhithe	d			10 27			10 31	10 42		10 46						10 57				11 01	11 12	11 16			
Wapping	d			10 29			10 33	10 44		10 48						10 59				11 03	11 14	11 18			
Shadwell	d			10 31			10 35	10 46		10 50						11 01				11 05	11 16	11 20			
Whitechapel	d			10 33			10 37	10 48		10 52						11 03				11 07	11 18	11 22			
Shoreditch High Street	d			10 35			10 39	10 50		10 54						11 05				11 09	11 20	11 24			
Hoxton	d			10 37			10 41	10 52		10 56						11 07				11 11	11 22	11 26			
Haggerston	d			10 39			10 43	10 54		10 58						11 09				11 13	11 24	11 28			
Dalston Junction Stn ELL	a			10 41			10 45	10 56		11 01						11 11				11 15	11 26	11 31			
Canonbury	d			10 44			10 50	11 01		11 06						11 14				11 20	11 31	11 36			
Highbury & Islington	a			10 51			10 57	11 06		11 11						11 21				11 27	11 36	11 41			
	d																								
London Bridge 4 ⊖	a	10 19	10 18		10 31							10 33	10 36	10 49	10 48		11 01							11 03	11 06

Table 178

Sundays

East London Line and Croydon - London Victoria to London Bridge

Network Diagram - see first Page of Table 177

		SN	SN	LO		SN	SN	LO	LO	LO	LO	LO	SE	SN		SN	SN	SN	LO	SN	SN	LO	LO	LO	
East Croydon	d	10 42	10 47														11 12	11 17							
West Croydon 4	d					11 04				11 12										11 34				11 42	
Norwood Junction 2	d		10 52			11 10				11 17								11 22		11 40				11 47	
Anerley	d		10 55							11 20								11 25						11 50	
Penge West	d		10 57							11 22								11 27						11 52	
London Victoria 15 ⊖	d												11 09			11 11									
Battersea Park 4	d															11 15									
Wandsworth Road	d															11 17									
Clapham High Street ⊖	d															11 19									
London Blackfriars 3 ⊖	d																								
Denmark Hill 4	d												11 18			11 24									
Peckham Rye 4	d	11 10					11 15						11a21	11 23		11 26	11 40				11 45				
Queens Rd Peckham	d	11 12												11 26		11 29	11 42								
South Bermondsey	d	11 15												11 28		11 31	11 45								
Clapham Junction 10	d																								
Wandsworth Common	d																								
Balham 4 ⊖	d																								
Streatham Hill	d																								
West Norwood 4	d						11 27														11 57				
Gipsy Hill	d						11 30														12 00				
Crystal Palace 4	d			11 07			11a32												11 37		12a02				
Sydenham	d		10 59	11 10		11 14				11 25								11 29	11 40	11 44				11 55	
Forest Hill 4	d		11 02	11 13		11 17				11 27								11 32	11 43	11 47				11 57	
Honor Oak Park	d		11 04	11 15		11 19				11 30								11 34	11 45	11 49				12 00	
Brockley	d		11 07	11 18		11 22				11 32								11 37	11 48	11 52				12 02	
New Cross Gate 4	a		11 09	11 20		11 24				11 35								11 39	11 50	11 54				12 05	
	d		11 09	11 20		11 24				11 35								11 39	11 50	11 54				12 05	
New Cross ELL	d							11 24			11 39											11 54			
Surrey Quays	d			11 24				11 28	11 35	11 39	11 43	11 51							11 54			11 58	12 05	12 09	
Canada Water	d			11 26				11 30	11 37	11 41	11 45	11 53							11 56			12 00	12 07	12 11	
Rotherhithe	d			11 27				11 31	11 38	11 42	11 46	11 54							11 57			12 01	12 08	12 12	
Wapping	d			11 29				11 33	11 40	11 44	11 48	11 56							11 59			12 03	12 10	12 14	
Shadwell	d			11 31				11 35	11 42	11 46	11 50	11 58							12 01			12 05	12 12	12 16	
Whitechapel	d			11 33				11 37	11 44	11 48	11 52	12 00							12 03			12 07	12 14	12 18	
Shoreditch High Street	d			11 35				11 39	11 46	11 50	11 54	12 02							12 05			12 09	12 16	12 20	
Hoxton	d			11 37				11 41	11 48	11 52	11 56	12 04							12 07			12 11	12 18	12 22	
Haggerston	d			11 39				11 43	11 50	11 54	11 58	12 06							12 09			12 13	12 20	12 24	
Dalston Junction Stn ELL	a			11 41				11 47	11 52	11 56	12 02	12 08							12 11			12 17	12 22	12 26	
Canonbury	d			11 44					11 55	12 01		12 11							12 14				12 25	12 31	
Highbury & Islington	a			11 49					12 00	12 06		12 16							12 19				12 30	12 36	
	d																								
London Bridge 4 ⊖	a	11 19	11 18			11 31								11 33		11 36	11 49	11 48		12 01					

		LO	LO	SE	SN	SN	SN	SN	LO	SN		LO	LO	LO	LO	LO	SN	LO	LO	SE		SN	SN	SN	SN
East Croydon	d						11 42	11 47																12 12	12 17
West Croydon 4	d									12 04				12 12											
Norwood Junction 2	d							11 52		12 10				12 16											12 22
Anerley	d							11 55						12 19											12 25
Penge West	d							11 57						12 21											12 27
London Victoria 15 ⊖	d			11 39		11 41														12 09			12 11		
Battersea Park 4	d					11 45																	12 15		
Wandsworth Road	d					11 47																	12 17		
Clapham High Street ⊖	d					11 49																	12 19		
London Blackfriars 3 ⊖	d																								
Denmark Hill 4	d			11 48		11 54														12 18			12 24		
Peckham Rye 4	d			11a51	11 53	11 56	12 10										12 15			12a21		12 23	12 26	12 40	
Queens Rd Peckham	d				11 56	11 59	12 12															12 26	12 29	12 42	
South Bermondsey	d				11 58	12 01	12 15															12 28	12 31	12 45	
Clapham Junction 10	d																								
Wandsworth Common	d																								
Balham 4 ⊖	d																								
Streatham Hill	d																								
West Norwood 4	d																12 27								
Gipsy Hill	d																12 30								
Crystal Palace 4	d								12 07							12 31	12a32								
Sydenham	d							11 59	12 10	12 14				12 24		12 34									12 29
Forest Hill 4	d							12 02	12 13	12 17				12 26		12 37									12 32
Honor Oak Park	d							12 04	12 15	12 19				12 29		12 39									12 34
Brockley	d							12 07	12 18	12 22				12 31		12 42									12 37
New Cross Gate 4	a							12 09	12 20	12 24				12 34		12 44									12 39
	d							12 09	12 20	12 24				12 34		12 44									12 39
New Cross ELL	d	12 09										12 24			12 39				12 54						
Surrey Quays	d	12 13	12 21						12 24			12 28	12 35	12 38	12 43	12 48		12 53	12 58						
Canada Water	d	12 15	12 23						12 26			12 30	12 37	12 40	12 45	12 50		12 55	13 00						
Rotherhithe	d	12 16	12 24						12 27			12 31	12 38	12 41	12 46	12 51		12 56	13 01						
Wapping	d	12 18	12 26						12 29			12 33	12 40	12 43	12 48	12 53		12 58	13 03						
Shadwell	d	12 20	12 28						12 31			12 35	12 42	12 45	12 50	12 55		13 00	13 05						
Whitechapel	d	12 22	12 30						12 33			12 37	12 44	12 47	12 52	12 57		13 02	13 07						
Shoreditch High Street	d	12 24	12 32						12 35			12 39	12 46	12 49	12 54	12 59		13 04	13 09						
Hoxton	d	12 26	12 34						12 37			12 41	12 48	12 51	12 56	13 01		13 06	13 11						
Haggerston	d	12 28	12 36						12 39			12 43	12 50	12 53	12 58	13 03		13 08	13 13						
Dalston Junction Stn ELL	a	12 32	12 38						12 41			12 47	12 52	12 55	13 02	13 05		13 10	13 17						
Canonbury	d		12 41						12 44				12 55	13 00		13 08		13 15							
Highbury & Islington	a		12 46						12 49				13 00	13 05		13 13		13 20							
	d																								
London Bridge 4 ⊖	a				12 03	12 06	12 19	12 18		12 31												12 33	12 36	12 49	12 48

Table 178

Sundays

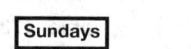

East London Line and Croydon - London Victoria to London Bridge

Network Diagram - see first Page of Table 177

		SN	LO	LO	LO	LO		SN	SE	SN	SN	SN	SN	LO	SN	LO		LO	LO	LO	LO	SN	SE	SN	SN
East Croydon	d											12 42	12 47												
West Croydon 4	d	12 34		12 42										12 57	13 04				13 12						
Norwood Junction 2	d	12 40		12 46									12 52	13 01	13 10				13 16						
Anerley	d			12 49									12 55	13 04					13 19						
Penge West	d			12 51									12 57	13 06					13 21						
London Victoria 15 ⊖	d								12 39		12 41												13 09		13 11
Battersea Park 4	d										12 45														13 15
Wandsworth Road	d										12 47														13 17
Clapham High Street ⊖	d										12 49														13 19
London Blackfriars 3 ⊖	d																								
Denmark Hill 4	d								12 48		12 54												13 18		13 24
Peckham Rye 4	d							12 45	12a51	12 53	12 56	13 10										13 15	13a21	13 23	13 26
Queens Rd Peckham	d									12 56	12 59	13 12												13 26	13 29
South Bermondsey	d									12 58	13 01	13 15												13 28	13 31
Clapham Junction 10	d																								
Wandsworth Common	d																								
Balham 4 ⊖	d																								
Streatham Hill	d																								
West Norwood 4	d							12 57														13 27			
Gipsy Hill	d							13 00														13 30			
Crystal Palace 4	d		12 46			13 01		13a02										13 16			13 31	13a32			
Sydenham	d	12 44	12 49	12 54		13 04							12 59	13 09	13 14			13 19	13 24		13 34				
Forest Hill 4	d	12 47	12 52	12 56		13 07							13 02	13 11	13 17			13 22	13 26		13 37				
Honor Oak Park	d	12 49	12 54	12 59		13 09							13 04	13 14	13 19			13 24	13 29		13 39				
Brockley	d	12 52	12 57	13 01		13 12							13 07	13 16	13 22			13 27	13 31		13 42				
New Cross Gate 4	a	12 54	12 59	13 04		13 14							13 09	13 19	13 24			13 29	13 34		13 44				
	d	12 54	12 59	13 04		13 14							13 09	13 19	13 24			13 29	13 34		13 44				
New Cross ELL	d				13 09											13 24				13 39					
Surrey Quays	d		13 03	13 08	13 13	13 18								13 23		13 28		13 33	13 38	13 43	13 48				
Canada Water	d		13 05	13 10	13 15	13 20								13 25		13 30		13 35	13 40	13 45	13 50				
Rotherhithe	d		13 06	13 11	13 16	13 21								13 26		13 31		13 36	13 41	13 46	13 51				
Wapping	d		13 08	13 13	13 18	13 23								13 28		13 33		13 38	13 43	13 48	13 53				
Shadwell	d		13 10	13 15	13 20	13 25								13 30		13 35		13 40	13 45	13 50	13 55				
Whitechapel	d		13 12	13 17	13 22	13 27								13 32		13 37		13 42	13 47	13 52	13 57				
Shoreditch High Street	d		13 14	13 19	13 24	13 29								13 34		13 39		13 44	13 49	13 54	13 59				
Hoxton	d		13 16	13 21	13 26	13 31								13 36		13 41		13 46	13 51	13 56	14 01				
Haggerston	d		13 18	13 23	13 28	13 33								13 38		13 43		13 48	13 53	13 58	14 03				
Dalston Junction Stn ELL	a		13 20	13 25	13 32	13 35								13 40		13 47		13 50	13 55	14 02	14 05				
Canonbury	d		13 23	13 30		13 38								13 45				13 53	14 00		14 08				
Highbury & Islington	a		13 28	13 35		13 43								13 50				13 58	14 05		14 13				
	d																								
London Bridge 4 ⊖	a	13 01								13 03	13 06	13 19	13 18		13 31									13 33	13 36

		SN		SN	LO	SN	LO	LO	LO	LO	LO	SN		SE	SN	SN	SN	SN	LO	SN	LO	LO		LO	LO
East Croydon	d	13 12		13 17													13 42	13 47							
West Croydon 4	d				13 27	13 34			13 42										13 57	14 04				14 12	
Norwood Junction 2	d			13 22	13 31	13 40			13 46									13 52	14 01	14 10				14 16	
Anerley	d			13 25	13 34				13 49									13 55	14 04					14 19	
Penge West	d			13 27	13 36				13 51									13 57	14 06					14 21	
London Victoria 15 ⊖	d													13 39		13 41									
Battersea Park 4	d															13 45									
Wandsworth Road	d															13 47									
Clapham High Street ⊖	d															13 49									
London Blackfriars 3 ⊖	d																								
Denmark Hill 4	d													13 48		13 54									
Peckham Rye 4	d	13 40										13 45		13a51	13 53	13 56	14 10								
Queens Rd Peckham	d	13 42													13 56	13 59	14 12								
South Bermondsey	d	13 45													13 58	14 01	14 15								
Clapham Junction 10	d																								
Wandsworth Common	d																								
Balham 4 ⊖	d																								
Streatham Hill	d																								
West Norwood 4	d											13 57													
Gipsy Hill	d											14 00													
Crystal Palace 4	d							13 46			14 01	14a02										14 16			
Sydenham	d			13 29	13 39	13 44		13 49	13 54		14 04							13 59	14 09	14 14		14 19		14 24	
Forest Hill 4	d			13 32	13 41	13 47		13 52	13 56		14 07							14 02	14 11	14 17		14 22		14 26	
Honor Oak Park	d			13 34	13 44	13 49		13 54	13 59		14 09							14 04	14 14	14 19		14 24		14 29	
Brockley	d			13 37	13 46	13 52		13 57	14 01		14 12							14 07	14 16	14 22		14 27		14 31	
New Cross Gate 4	a			13 39	13 49	13 54		13 59	14 04		14 14							14 09	14 19	14 24		14 29		14 34	
	d			13 39	13 49	13 54		13 59	14 04		14 14							14 09	14 19	14 24		14 29		14 34	
New Cross ELL	d						13 54			14 09											14 24				14 39
Surrey Quays	d				13 53		13 58	14 03	14 08	14 13	14 18								14 23		14 28	14 33		14 38	14 43
Canada Water	d				13 55		14 00	14 05	14 10	14 15	14 20								14 25		14 30	14 35		14 40	14 45
Rotherhithe	d				13 56		14 01	14 06	14 11	14 16	14 21								14 26		14 31	14 36		14 41	14 46
Wapping	d				13 58		14 03	14 08	14 13	14 18	14 23								14 28		14 33	14 38		14 43	14 48
Shadwell	d				14 00		14 05	14 10	14 15	14 20	14 25								14 30		14 35	14 40		14 45	14 50
Whitechapel	d				14 02		14 07	14 12	14 17	14 22	14 27								14 32		14 37	14 42		14 47	14 52
Shoreditch High Street	d				14 04		14 09	14 14	14 19	14 24	14 29								14 34		14 39	14 44		14 49	14 54
Hoxton	d				14 06		14 11	14 16	14 21	14 26	14 31								14 36		14 41	14 46		14 51	14 56
Haggerston	d				14 08		14 13	14 18	14 23	14 28	14 33								14 38		14 43	14 48		14 53	14 58
Dalston Junction Stn ELL	a				14 10		14 17	14 20	14 25	14 32	14 35								14 40		14 47	14 50		14 55	15 02
Canonbury	d				14 15			14 23	14 30		14 38								14 45			14 53		15 00	
Highbury & Islington	a				14 20			14 28	14 35		14 43								14 50			14 58		15 05	
	d																								
London Bridge 4 ⊖	a	13 49		13 48		14 01									14 03	14 06	14 19	14 18		14 31					

Table 178

Sundays

East London Line and Croydon - London Victoria to London Bridge

Network Diagram - see first Page of Table 177

		LO	SN	SE	SN	SN	SN	SN		LO	SN	LO	LO	LO	LO	LO	SN	SE		SN	SN	SN	SN	LO	SN
East Croydon	d						14 12	14 17													14 42	14 47		
West Croydon 4	d									14 27	14 34			14 42										14 57	15 04
Norwood Junction 2	d							14 22		14 31	14 40			14 46									14 52	15 01	15 10
Anerley	d							14 25		14 34				14 49									14 55	15 04	
Penge West	d							14 27		14 36				14 51									14 57	15 06	
London Victoria 15 ⊖	d			14 09		14 11												14 39			14 41				
Battersea Park 4	d					14 15															14 45				
Wandsworth Road	d					14 17															14 47				
Clapham High Street ⊖	d					14 19															14 49				
London Blackfriars 3 ⊖	d																								
Denmark Hill 4	d			14 18		14 24												14 48			14 54				
Peckham Rye 4	d		14 15	14a21	14 23	14 26	14 40										14 45	14a51		14 53	14 56	15 10			
Queens Rd Peckham	d				14 26	14 29	14 42													14 56	14 59	15 12			
South Bermondsey	d				14 28	14 31	14 45													14 58	15 01	15 15			
Clapham Junction 10	d																								
Wandsworth Common	d																								
Balham 4 ⊖	d																								
Streatham Hill	d																								
West Norwood 4	d		14 27														14 57								
Gipsy Hill	d		14 30														15 00								
Crystal Palace 4	d	14 31	14a32										14 46			15 01	15a02								
Sydenham	d	14 34						14 29		14 39	14 44		14 49	14 54		15 04							14 59	15 09	15 14
Forest Hill 4	d	14 37						14 32		14 41	14 47		14 52	14 56		15 07							15 02	15 11	15 17
Honor Oak Park	d	14 39						14 34		14 44	14 49		14 54	14 59		15 09							15 04	15 14	15 19
Brockley	d	14 42						14 37		14 46	14 52		14 57	15 01		15 12							15 07	15 16	15 22
New Cross Gate 4	a	14 44						14 39		14 49	14 54		14 59	15 04		15 14							15 09	15 19	15 24
	d	14 44						14 39		14 49	14 54		14 59	15 04		15 14							15 09	15 19	15 24
New Cross ELL	d											14 54			15 09										
Surrey Quays	d	14 48								14 53		14 58	15 03	15 08	15 13	15 18								15 23	
Canada Water	d	14 50								14 55		15 00	15 05	15 10	15 15	15 20								15 25	
Rotherhithe	d	14 51								14 56		15 01	15 06	15 11	15 16	15 21								15 26	
Wapping	d	14 53								14 58		15 03	15 08	15 13	15 18	15 23								15 28	
Shadwell	d	14 55								15 00		15 05	15 10	15 15	15 20	15 25								15 30	
Whitechapel	d	14 57								15 02		15 07	15 12	15 17	15 22	15 27								15 32	
Shoreditch High Street	d	14 59								15 04		15 09	15 14	15 19	15 24	15 29								15 34	
Hoxton	d	15 01								15 06		15 11	15 16	15 21	15 26	15 31								15 36	
Haggerston	d	15 03								15 08		15 13	15 18	15 23	15 28	15 33								15 38	
Dalston Junction Stn ELL	a	15 05								15 10		15 17	15 20	15 25	15 32	15 35								15 40	
Canonbury	d	15 08								15 15			15 23	15 30		15 38								15 45	
Highbury & Islington	a	15 13								15 20			15 28	15 35		15 43								15 50	
	d																								
London Bridge 4 ⊖	a				14 33	14 36	14 49	14 48			15 01									15 03	15 06	15 19	15 18		15 31

		LO	LO	LO		LO	LO	SN	SE	SN	SN	SN	SN	LO		SN	LO	LO	LO	LO	LO	SN	SE	SN	
East Croydon	d											15 12	15 17												
West Croydon 4	d			15 12										15 27		15 34			15 42						
Norwood Junction 2	d			15 16									15 22	15 31		15 40			15 46						
Anerley	d			15 19									15 25	15 34					15 49						
Penge West	d			15 21									15 27	15 36					15 51						
London Victoria 15 ⊖	d								15 09		15 11												15 39		
Battersea Park 4	d										15 15														
Wandsworth Road	d										15 17														
Clapham High Street ⊖	d										15 19														
London Blackfriars 3 ⊖	d																								
Denmark Hill 4	d								15 18		15 24												15 48		
Peckham Rye 4	d							15 15	15a21	15 23	15 26	15 40										15 45	15a51	15 53	
Queens Rd Peckham	d									15 26	15 29	15 42												15 56	
South Bermondsey	d									15 28	15 31	15 45												15 58	
Clapham Junction 10	d																								
Wandsworth Common	d																								
Balham 4 ⊖	d																								
Streatham Hill	d																								
West Norwood 4	d							15 27														15 57			
Gipsy Hill	d							15 30														16 00			
Crystal Palace 4	d		15 16				15 31	15a32										15 46			16 01	16a02			
Sydenham	d		15 19	15 24			15 34						15 29	15 39		15 44		15 49	15 54		16 04				
Forest Hill 4	d		15 22	15 26			15 37						15 32	15 41		15 47		15 52	15 56		16 07				
Honor Oak Park	d		15 24	15 29			15 39						15 34	15 44		15 49		15 54	15 59		16 09				
Brockley	d		15 27	15 31			15 42						15 37	15 46		15 52		15 57	16 01		16 12				
New Cross Gate 4	a		15 29	15 34			15 44						15 39	15 49		15 54		15 59	16 04		16 14				
	d		15 29	15 34			15 44						15 39	15 49		15 54		15 59	16 04		16 14				
New Cross ELL	d	15 24				15 39											15 54			16 09					
Surrey Quays	d	15 28	15 33	15 38		15 43	15 48							15 53			15 58	16 03	16 08	16 13	16 18				
Canada Water	d	15 30	15 35	15 40		15 45	15 50							15 55			16 00	16 05	16 10	16 15	16 20				
Rotherhithe	d	15 31	15 36	15 41		15 46	15 51							15 56			16 01	16 06	16 11	16 16	16 21				
Wapping	d	15 33	15 38	15 43		15 48	15 53							15 58			16 03	16 08	16 13	16 18	16 23				
Shadwell	d	15 35	15 40	15 45		15 50	15 55							16 00			16 05	16 10	16 15	16 20	16 25				
Whitechapel	d	15 37	15 42	15 47		15 52	15 57							16 02			16 07	16 12	16 17	16 22	16 27				
Shoreditch High Street	d	15 39	15 44	15 49		15 54	15 59							16 04			16 09	16 14	16 19	16 24	16 29				
Hoxton	d	15 41	15 46	15 51		15 56	16 01							16 06			16 11	16 16	16 21	16 26	16 31				
Haggerston	d	15 43	15 48	15 53		15 58	16 03							16 08			16 13	16 18	16 23	16 28	16 33				
Dalston Junction Stn ELL	a	15 47	15 50	15 55		16 02	16 05							16 10			16 17	16 20	16 25	16 32	16 35				
Canonbury	d		15 53	16 00			16 08							16 15				16 23	16 30		16 38				
Highbury & Islington	a		15 58	16 05			16 13							16 20				16 28	16 35		16 43				
	d																								
London Bridge 4 ⊖	a									15 33	15 36	15 49	15 48			16 01								16 03	

Table 178

Sundays

East London Line and Croydon - London Victoria to London Bridge

Network Diagram - see first Page of Table 177

		SN	SN	SN	LO	SN	LO	LO	LO	LO		LO	SN	SE	SN	SN	SN	SN	LO	SN		LO	LO	LO	LO
East Croydon	d		15 42	15 47													16 12	16 17							
West Croydon 4	d				15 57	16 04			16 12										16 27	16 34				16 42	
Norwood Junction 2	d			15 52	16 01	16 10			16 16									16 22	16 31	16 40				16 46	
Anerley	d			15 55	16 04				16 19									16 25	16 34					16 49	
Penge West	d			15 57	16 06				16 21									16 27	16 36					16 51	
London Victoria 15 ⊖	d	15 41												16 09		16 11									
Battersea Park 4	d	15 45														16 15									
Wandsworth Road	d	15 47														16 17									
Clapham High Street ⊖	d	15 49														16 19									
London Blackfriars 3 ⊖	d																								
Denmark Hill 4	d	15 54												16 18		16 24									
Peckham Rye 4	d	15 56	16 10										16 15	16a21	16 23	16 26	16 40								
Queens Rd Peckham	d	15 59	16 12												16 26	16 29	16 42								
South Bermondsey	d	16 01	16 15												16 28	16 31	16 45								
Clapham Junction 10	d																								
Wandsworth Common	d																								
Balham 4 ⊖	d																								
Streatham Hill	d																								
West Norwood 4	d												16 27												
Gipsy Hill	d												16 30												
Crystal Palace 4	d							16 16				16 31	16a32										16 46		
Sydenham	d			15 59	16 09	16 14		16 19	16 24			16 34						16 29	16 39	16 44			16 49	16 54	
Forest Hill 4	d			16 02	16 11	16 17		16 22	16 26			16 37						16 32	16 41	16 47			16 52	16 56	
Honor Oak Park	d			16 04	16 14	16 19		16 24	16 29			16 39						16 34	16 44	16 49			16 54	16 59	
Brockley	d			16 07	16 16	16 22		16 27	16 31			16 42						16 37	16 46	16 52			16 57	17 01	
New Cross Gate 4	a			16 09	16 19	16 24		16 29	16 34			16 44						16 39	16 49	16 54			16 59	17 04	
	d			16 09	16 19	16 24		16 29	16 34			16 44						16 39	16 49	16 54			16 59	17 04	
New Cross ELL	d						16 24			16 39												16 54			17 09
Surrey Quays	d				16 23		16 28	16 33	16 38	16 43		16 48							16 53			16 58	17 03	17 08	17 13
Canada Water	d				16 25		16 30	16 35	16 40	16 45		16 50							16 55			17 00	17 05	17 10	17 15
Rotherhithe	d				16 26		16 31	16 36	16 41	16 46		16 51							16 56			17 01	17 06	17 11	17 16
Wapping	d				16 28		16 33	16 38	16 43	16 48		16 53							16 58			17 03	17 08	17 13	17 18
Shadwell	d				16 30		16 35	16 40	16 45	16 50		16 55							17 00			17 05	17 10	17 15	17 20
Whitechapel	d				16 32		16 37	16 42	16 47	16 52		16 57							17 02			17 07	17 12	17 17	17 22
Shoreditch High Street	d				16 34		16 39	16 44	16 49	16 54		16 59							17 04			17 09	17 14	17 19	17 24
Hoxton	d				16 36		16 41	16 46	16 51	16 56		17 01							17 06			17 11	17 16	17 21	17 26
Haggerston	d				16 38		16 43	16 48	16 53	16 58		17 03							17 08			17 13	17 18	17 23	17 28
Dalston Junction Stn ELL	a				16 40		16 47	16 50	16 55	17 02		17 05							17 10			17 17	17 20	17 25	17 32
Canonbury	d				16 45			16 53	17 00			17 08							17 15				17 23	17 30	
Highbury & Islington	a				16 50			16 58	17 05			17 13							17 20				17 28	17 35	
	d																								
London Bridge 4 ⊖	a	16 06	16 19	16 18		16 31									16 33	16 36	16 49	16 48		17 01					

		LO	SN	SE	SN	SN		SN	SN	LO	SN	LO	LO	LO	LO	LO		SN	SE	SN	SN	SN	SN	LO	SN
East Croydon	d							16 42	16 47													17 12	17 17		
West Croydon 4	d									16 57	17 04			17 12										17 27	17 34
Norwood Junction 2	d								16 52	17 01	17 10			17 16									17 22	17 31	17 40
Anerley	d								16 55	17 04				17 19									17 25	17 34	
Penge West	d								16 57	17 06				17 21									17 27	17 36	
London Victoria 15 ⊖	d			16 39		16 41													17 09		17 11				
Battersea Park 4	d					16 45															17 15				
Wandsworth Road	d					16 47															17 17				
Clapham High Street ⊖	d					16 49															17 19				
London Blackfriars 3 ⊖	d																								
Denmark Hill 4	d			16 48		16 54													17 18		17 24				
Peckham Rye 4	d		16 45	16a51	16 53	16 56		17 10										17 15	17a21	17 23	17 26	17 40			
Queens Rd Peckham	d				16 56	16 59		17 12												17 26	17 29	17 42			
South Bermondsey	d				16 58	17 01		17 15												17 28	17 31	17 45			
Clapham Junction 10	d																								
Wandsworth Common	d																								
Balham 4 ⊖	d																								
Streatham Hill	d																								
West Norwood 4	d		16 57															17 27							
Gipsy Hill	d		17 00															17 30							
Crystal Palace 4	d	17 01	17a02										17 16			17 31		17a32							
Sydenham	d	17 04							16 59	17 09	17 14		17 19	17 24		17 34							17 29	17 39	17 44
Forest Hill 4	d	17 07							17 02	17 11	17 17		17 22	17 26		17 37							17 32	17 41	17 47
Honor Oak Park	d	17 09							17 04	17 14	17 19		17 24	17 29		17 39							17 34	17 44	17 49
Brockley	d	17 12							17 07	17 16	17 22		17 27	17 31		17 42							17 37	17 46	17 52
New Cross Gate 4	a	17 14							17 09	17 19	17 24		17 29	17 34		17 44							17 39	17 49	17 54
	d	17 14							17 09	17 19	17 24		17 29	17 34		17 44							17 39	17 49	17 54
New Cross ELL	d											17 24			17 39										
Surrey Quays	d	17 18								17 23		17 28	17 33	17 38	17 43	17 48								17 53	
Canada Water	d	17 20								17 25		17 30	17 35	17 40	17 45	17 50								17 55	
Rotherhithe	d	17 21								17 26		17 31	17 36	17 41	17 46	17 51								17 56	
Wapping	d	17 23								17 28		17 33	17 38	17 43	17 48	17 53								17 58	
Shadwell	d	17 25								17 30		17 35	17 40	17 45	17 50	17 55								18 00	
Whitechapel	d	17 27								17 32		17 37	17 42	17 47	17 52	17 57								18 02	
Shoreditch High Street	d	17 29								17 34		17 39	17 44	17 49	17 54	17 59								18 04	
Hoxton	d	17 31								17 36		17 41	17 46	17 51	17 56	18 01								18 06	
Haggerston	d	17 33								17 38		17 43	17 48	17 53	17 58	18 03								18 08	
Dalston Junction Stn ELL	a	17 35								17 40		17 47	17 50	17 55	18 02	18 05								18 10	
Canonbury	d	17 38								17 45			17 53	18 00		18 08								18 15	
Highbury & Islington	a	17 43								17 50			17 58	18 05		18 13								18 20	
	d																								
London Bridge 4 ⊖	a				17 03	17 06		17 19	17 18		17 31									17 33	17 36	17 49	17 48		18 01

East London Line and Croydon - London Victoria to London Bridge

Network Diagram - see first Page of Table 177

Station		LO		LO	LO	LO	LO	SN	SE	SN	SN	SN		SN	LO	SN	LO	LO	LO	LO	LO	SN		SE	SN
East Croydon	d											17 42		17 47											
West Croydon 4	d				17 42										17 57	18 04			18 12						
Norwood Junction 2	d				17 46									17 52	18 01	18 10			18 16						
Anerley	d				17 49									17 55	18 04				18 19						
Penge West	d				17 51									17 57	18 06				18 21						
London Victoria 15	⊖ d								17 39		17 41													18 09	
Battersea Park 4	d										17 45														
Wandsworth Road	d										17 47														
Clapham High Street	⊖ d										17 49														
London Blackfriars 3	⊖ d																								
Denmark Hill 4	d								17 48		17 54													18 18	
Peckham Rye 4	d							17 45	17a51	17 53	17 56	18 10										18 15		18a21	18 23
Queens Rd Peckham	d									17 56	17 59	18 12													18 26
South Bermondsey	d									17 58	18 01	18 15													18 28
Clapham Junction 10	d																								
Wandsworth Common	d																								
Balham 4	⊖ d																								
Streatham Hill	d																								
West Norwood 4	d							17 57														18 27			
Gipsy Hill	d							18 00														18 30			
Crystal Palace 4	d			17 46			18 01	18a02										18 16			18 31	18a32			
Sydenham	d			17 49	17 54		18 04							17 59	18 09	18 14		18 19	18 24		18 34				
Forest Hill 4	d			17 52	17 56		18 07							18 02	18 11	18 17		18 22	18 26		18 37				
Honor Oak Park	d			17 54	17 59		18 09							18 04	18 14	18 19		18 24	18 29		18 39				
Brockley	d			17 57	18 01		18 12							18 07	18 16	18 22		18 27	18 31		18 42				
New Cross Gate 4	a			17 59	18 04		18 14							18 09	18 19	18 24		18 29	18 34		18 44				
	d			17 59	18 04		18 14							18 09	18 19	18 24		18 29	18 34		18 44				
New Cross ELL	d	17 54				18 09											18 24			18 39					
Surrey Quays	d	17 58		18 03	18 08	18 13	18 18								18 23		18 28	18 33	18 38	18 43	18 48				
Canada Water	d	18 00		18 05	18 10	18 15	18 20								18 25		18 30	18 35	18 40	18 45	18 50				
Rotherhithe	d	18 01		18 06	18 11	18 16	18 21								18 26		18 31	18 36	18 41	18 46	18 51				
Wapping	d	18 03		18 08	18 13	18 18	18 23								18 28		18 33	18 38	18 43	18 48	18 53				
Shadwell	d	18 05		18 10	18 15	18 20	18 25								18 30		18 35	18 40	18 45	18 50	18 55				
Whitechapel	d	18 07		18 12	18 17	18 22	18 27								18 32		18 37	18 42	18 47	18 52	18 57				
Shoreditch High Street	d	18 09		18 14	18 19	18 24	18 29								18 34		18 39	18 44	18 49	18 54	18 59				
Hoxton	d	18 11		18 16	18 21	18 26	18 31								18 36		18 41	18 46	18 51	18 56	19 01				
Haggerston	d	18 13		18 18	18 23	18 28	18 33								18 38		18 43	18 48	18 53	18 58	19 03				
Dalston Junction Stn ELL	a	18 17		18 20	18 25	18 32	18 35								18 40		18 47	18 50	18 55	19 02	19 05				
Canonbury	d			18 23	18 30		18 38								18 45			18 53	19 00		19 08				
Highbury & Islington	a			18 28	18 35		18 43								18 50			18 58	19 05		19 13				
	d																								
London Bridge 4	⊖ a									18 03	18 06	18 19		18 18		18 31									18 33

Station		SN	SN	SN	LO	SN	LO	LO		LO	LO	LO	SN	SE	SN	SN	SN	SN		LO	SN	LO	LO	LO	LO
East Croydon	d		18 12	18 17													18 42	18 47							
West Croydon 4	d				18 27	18 34				18 42										18 57	19 04			19 12	
Norwood Junction 2	d			18 22	18 31	18 40				18 46								18 52		19 01	19 10			19 16	
Anerley	d			18 25	18 34					18 49								18 55		19 04				19 19	
Penge West	d			18 27	18 36					18 51								18 57		19 06				19 21	
London Victoria 15	⊖ d	18 11												18 39		18 41									
Battersea Park 4	d	18 15														18 45									
Wandsworth Road	d	18 17														18 47									
Clapham High Street	⊖ d	18 19														18 49									
London Blackfriars 3	⊖ d																								
Denmark Hill 4	d	18 24												18 48		18 54									
Peckham Rye 4	d	18 26	18 40										18 45	18a51	18 53	18 56	19 10								
Queens Rd Peckham	d	18 29	18 42												18 56	18 59	19 12								
South Bermondsey	d	18 31	18 45												18 58	19 01	19 15								
Clapham Junction 10	d																								
Wandsworth Common	d																								
Balham 4	⊖ d																								
Streatham Hill	d																								
West Norwood 4	d												18 57												
Gipsy Hill	d												19 00												
Crystal Palace 4	d							18 46				19 01	19a02										19 16		
Sydenham	d			18 29	18 39	18 44		18 49		18 54		19 04						18 59		19 09	19 14		19 19	19 24	
Forest Hill 4	d			18 32	18 41	18 47		18 52		18 56		19 07						19 02		19 11	19 17		19 22	19 26	
Honor Oak Park	d			18 34	18 44	18 49		18 54		18 59		19 09						19 04		19 14	19 19		19 24	19 29	
Brockley	d			18 37	18 46	18 52		18 57		19 01		19 12						19 07		19 16	19 22		19 27	19 31	
New Cross Gate 4	a			18 39	18 49	18 54		18 59		19 04		19 14						19 09		19 19	19 24		19 29	19 34	
	d			18 40	18 49	18 54		18 59		19 04		19 14						19 09		19 19	19 24		19 29	19 34	
New Cross ELL	d						18 54				19 09											19 24			19 39
Surrey Quays	d				18 53		18 58	19 03		19 08	19 13	19 18								19 23		19 28	19 33	19 38	19 43
Canada Water	d				18 55		19 00	19 05		19 10	19 15	19 20								19 25		19 30	19 35	19 40	19 45
Rotherhithe	d				18 56		19 01	19 06		19 11	19 16	19 21								19 26		19 31	19 36	19 41	19 46
Wapping	d				18 58		19 03	19 08		19 13	19 18	19 23								19 28		19 33	19 38	19 43	19 48
Shadwell	d				19 00		19 05	19 10		19 15	19 20	19 25								19 30		19 35	19 40	19 45	19 50
Whitechapel	d				19 02		19 07	19 12		19 17	19 22	19 27								19 32		19 37	19 42	19 47	19 52
Shoreditch High Street	d				19 04		19 09	19 14		19 19	19 24	19 29								19 34		19 39	19 44	19 49	19 54
Hoxton	d				19 06		19 11	19 16		19 21	19 26	19 31								19 36		19 41	19 46	19 51	19 56
Haggerston	d				19 08		19 13	19 18		19 23	19 28	19 33								19 38		19 43	19 48	19 53	19 58
Dalston Junction Stn ELL	a				19 10		19 17	19 20		19 25	19 32	19 35								19 40		19 47	19 50	19 55	20 02
Canonbury	d				19 15			19 23		19 30		19 38								19 45			19 53	20 00	
Highbury & Islington	a				19 20			19 28		19 35		19 43								19 50			19 58	20 05	
	d																								
London Bridge 4	⊖ a	18 36	18 49	18 48		19 01									19 03	19 06	19 19	19 18			19 31				

Table 178

Sundays

East London Line and Croydon - London Victoria to London Bridge

Network Diagram - see first Page of Table 177

		LO	SN	SE		SN	SN	SN	SN	LO	SN	LO	LO	LO		LO	LO	SN	SE	SN	SN	SN	SN	LO	
East Croydon	d							19 12	19 17													19 42	19 47		
West Croydon 4	d									19 27	19 34			19 42										19 57	
Norwood Junction 2	d								19 22	19 31	19 40			19 46									19 52	20 01	
Anerley	d								19 25	19 34				19 49									19 55	20 04	
Penge West	d								19 27	19 36				19 51									19 57	20 06	
London Victoria 15 ⊖	d			19 09			19 11												19 39		19 41				
Battersea Park 4	d						19 15														19 45				
Wandsworth Road	d						19 17														19 47				
Clapham High Street ⊖	d						19 19														19 49				
London Blackfriars 3 ⊖	d																								
Denmark Hill 4	d			19 18			19 24												19 48		19 54				
Peckham Rye 4	d		19 15	19a21		19 23	19 26	19 40										19 45	19a51	19 53	19 56	20 10			
Queens Rd Peckham	d					19 26	19 29	19 42												19 56	19 59	20 12			
South Bermondsey	d					19 28	19 31	19 45												19 58	20 01	20 15			
Clapham Junction 10	d																								
Wandsworth Common	d																								
Balham 4 ⊖	d																								
Streatham Hill	d																								
West Norwood 4	d		19 27															19 57							
Gipsy Hill	d		19 30															20 00							
Crystal Palace 4	d	19 31	19a32										19 46				20 01	20a02							
Sydenham	d	19 34							19 29	19 39	19 44		19 49	19 54			20 04						19 59	20 09	
Forest Hill 4	d	19 37							19 32	19 41	19 47		19 52	19 56			20 07						20 02	20 11	
Honor Oak Park	d	19 39							19 34	19 44	19 49		19 54	19 59			20 09						20 04	20 14	
Brockley	d	19 42							19 37	19 46	19 52		19 57	20 01			20 12						20 07	20 16	
New Cross Gate 4	a	19 44							19 39	19 49	19 54		19 59	20 04			20 14						20 09	20 19	
	d	19 44							19 39	19 49	19 54		19 59	20 04			20 14						20 09	20 19	
New Cross ELL	d											19 54				20 09									
Surrey Quays	d	19 48								19 53		19 58	20 03	20 08		20 13	20 18							20 23	
Canada Water	d	19 50								19 55		20 00	20 05	20 10		20 15	20 20							20 25	
Rotherhithe	d	19 51								19 56		20 01	20 06	20 11		20 16	20 21							20 26	
Wapping	d	19 53								19 58		20 03	20 08	20 13		20 18	20 23							20 28	
Shadwell	d	19 55								20 00		20 05	20 10	20 15		20 20	20 25							20 30	
Whitechapel	d	19 57								20 02		20 07	20 12	20 17		20 22	20 27							20 32	
Shoreditch High Street	d	19 59								20 04		20 09	20 14	20 19		20 24	20 29							20 34	
Hoxton	d	20 01								20 06		20 11	20 16	20 21		20 26	20 31							20 36	
Haggerston	d	20 03								20 08		20 13	20 18	20 23		20 28	20 33							20 38	
Dalston Junction Stn ELL	a	20 05								20 10		20 17	20 20	20 25		20 32	20 35							20 40	
Canonbury	d	20 08								20 15			20 23	20 30			20 38							20 45	
Highbury & Islington	a	20 13								20 20			20 28	20 35			20 43							20 50	
	d																								
London Bridge 4 ⊖	a					19 33	19 36	19 49	19 48		20 01									20 03	20 06	20 19	20 18		

		SN	LO	LO	LO	LO	LO	SN	SE	SN		SN	SN	SN	LO	SN	LO	LO	LO	LO		LO	SN	SE	SN
East Croydon	d												20 12	20 17											
West Croydon 4	d	20 04			20 12										20 27	20 34			20 42						
Norwood Junction 2	d	20 10			20 16									20 22	20 31	20 40			20 46						
Anerley	d				20 19									20 25	20 34				20 49						
Penge West	d				20 21									20 27	20 36				20 51						
London Victoria 15 ⊖	d								20 09			20 11												20 39	
Battersea Park 4	d											20 15													
Wandsworth Road	d											20 17													
Clapham High Street ⊖	d											20 19													
London Blackfriars 3 ⊖	d																								
Denmark Hill 4	d								20 18			20 24												20 48	
Peckham Rye 4	d							20 15	20a21	20 23		20 26	20 40										20 45	20a51	20 53
Queens Rd Peckham	d									20 26		20 29	20 42												20 56
South Bermondsey	d									20 28		20 31	20 45												20 58
Clapham Junction 10	d																								
Wandsworth Common	d																								
Balham 4 ⊖	d																								
Streatham Hill	d																								
West Norwood 4	d							20 27															20 57		
Gipsy Hill	d							20 30															21 00		
Crystal Palace 4	d			20 16			20 31	20a32										20 46				21 01	21a02		
Sydenham	d	20 14		20 19	20 24		20 34							20 29	20 39	20 44		20 49	20 54			21 04			
Forest Hill 4	d	20 17		20 22	20 26		20 37							20 32	20 41	20 47		20 52	20 56			21 07			
Honor Oak Park	d	20 19		20 24	20 29		20 39							20 34	20 44	20 49		20 54	20 59			21 09			
Brockley	d	20 22		20 27	20 31		20 42							20 37	20 46	20 52		20 57	21 01			21 12			
New Cross Gate 4	a	20 24		20 29	20 34		20 44							20 39	20 49	20 54		20 59	21 04			21 14			
	d	20 24		20 29	20 34		20 44							20 39	20 49	20 54		20 59	21 04			21 14			
New Cross ELL	d		20 24			20 39											20 54			21 09					
Surrey Quays	d		20 28	20 33	20 38	20 43	20 48								20 53		20 58	21 03	21 08	21 13		21 18			
Canada Water	d		20 30	20 35	20 40	20 45	20 50								20 55		21 00	21 05	21 10	21 15		21 20			
Rotherhithe	d		20 31	20 36	20 41	20 46	20 51								20 56		21 01	21 06	21 11	21 16		21 21			
Wapping	d		20 33	20 38	20 43	20 48	20 53								20 58		21 03	21 08	21 13	21 18		21 23			
Shadwell	d		20 35	20 40	20 45	20 50	20 55								21 00		21 05	21 10	21 15	21 20		21 25			
Whitechapel	d		20 37	20 42	20 47	20 52	20 57								21 02		21 07	21 12	21 17	21 22		21 27			
Shoreditch High Street	d		20 39	20 44	20 49	20 54	20 59								21 04		21 09	21 14	21 19	21 24		21 29			
Hoxton	d		20 41	20 46	20 51	20 56	21 01								21 06		21 11	21 16	21 21	21 26		21 31			
Haggerston	d		20 43	20 48	20 53	20 58	21 03								21 08		21 13	21 18	21 23	21 28		21 33			
Dalston Junction Stn ELL	a		20 47	20 50	20 55	21 02	21 05								21 10		21 17	21 20	21 25	21 32		21 35			
Canonbury	d			20 53	21 00		21 08								21 15			21 23	21 30			21 38			
Highbury & Islington	a			20 58	21 05		21 13								21 20			21 28	21 35			21 43			
	d																								
London Bridge 4 ⊖	a	20 31								20 33		20 36	20 49	20 48		21 01									21 03

Table 178

Sundays

East London Line and Croydon - London Victoria to London Bridge

Network Diagram - see first Page of Table 177

		SN	SN	SN	LO	SN		LO	LO	LO	LO	LO	SN	SE	SN	SN		SN	SN	LO	SN	LO	LO	LO	LO
East Croydon	d		20 42	20 47														21 12	21 17						
West Croydon 4	d				20 57	21 04				21 12										21 27	21 34			21 42	
Norwood Junction 2	d			20 52	21 01	21 10				21 16									21 22	21 31	21 40			21 46	
Anerley	d			20 55	21 04					21 19									21 25	21 34				21 49	
Penge West	d			20 57	21 06					21 21									21 27	21 36				21 51	
London Victoria 15 ⊖	d	20 41												21 09		21 11									
Battersea Park 4	d	20 45														21 15									
Wandsworth Road	d	20 47														21 17									
Clapham High Street ⊖	d	20 49														21 19									
London Blackfriars 3 ⊖	d																								
Denmark Hill 4	d	20 54												21 18		21 24									
Peckham Rye 4	d	20 56	21 10										21 15	21a21	21 23	21 26		21 40							
Queens Rd Peckham	d	20 59	21 12												21 26	21 29		21 42							
South Bermondsey	d	21 01	21 15												21 28	21 31		21 45							
Clapham Junction 10	d																								
Wandsworth Common	d																								
Balham 4 ⊖	d																								
Streatham Hill	d																								
West Norwood 4	d												21 27												
Gipsy Hill	d												21 30												
Crystal Palace 4	d								21 16			21 31	21a32										21 46		
Sydenham	d			20 59	21 09	21 14			21 19	21 24		21 34							21 29	21 39	21 44		21 49	21 54	
Forest Hill 4	d			21 02	21 11	21 17			21 22	21 26		21 37							21 32	21 41	21 47		21 52	21 56	
Honor Oak Park	d			21 04	21 14	21 19			21 24	21 29		21 39							21 34	21 44	21 49		21 54	21 59	
Brockley	d			21 07	21 16	21 22			21 27	21 31		21 42							21 37	21 46	21 52		21 57	22 01	
New Cross Gate 4	a			21 09	21 19	21 24			21 29	21 34		21 44							21 39	21 49	21 54		21 59	22 04	
	d			21 09	21 19	21 24			21 29	21 34		21 44							21 39	21 49	21 54		21 59	22 04	
New Cross ELL	d							21 24			21 39											21 54			22 09
Surrey Quays	d				21 23			21 28	21 33	21 38	21 43	21 48								21 53		21 58	22 03	22 08	22 13
Canada Water	d				21 25			21 30	21 35	21 40	21 45	21 50								21 55		22 00	22 05	22 10	22 15
Rotherhithe	d				21 26			21 31	21 36	21 41	21 46	21 51								21 56		22 01	22 06	22 11	22 16
Wapping	d				21 28			21 33	21 38	21 43	21 48	21 53								21 58		22 03	22 08	22 13	22 18
Shadwell	d				21 30			21 35	21 40	21 45	21 50	21 55								22 00		22 05	22 10	22 15	22 20
Whitechapel	d				21 32			21 37	21 42	21 47	21 52	21 57								22 02		22 07	22 12	22 17	22 22
Shoreditch High Street	d				21 34			21 39	21 44	21 49	21 54	21 59								22 04		22 09	22 14	22 19	22 24
Hoxton	d				21 36			21 41	21 46	21 51	21 56	22 01								22 06		22 11	22 16	22 21	22 26
Haggerston	d				21 38			21 43	21 48	21 53	21 58	22 03								22 08		22 13	22 18	22 23	22 28
Dalston Junction Stn ELL	a				21 40			21 47	21 50	21 55	22 02	22 05								22 10		22 17	22 20	22 25	22 32
Canonbury	d				21 45				21 53	22 00		22 08								22 15			22 23	22 30	
Highbury & Islington	a				21 50				21 58	22 05		22 13								22 20			22 28	22 35	
	d																								
London Bridge 4 ⊖	a	21 06	21 19	21 18		21 31									21 33	21 36		21 49	21 48		22 01				

		LO		SN	SE	SN	SN	SN	SN	LO	SN	LO		LO	SN	LO	SE	SN	SN	SN	SN	LO		SN	LO
East Croydon	d							21 42	21 47											22 12	22 17				
West Croydon 4	d									21 57	22 04			22 12								22 27		22 34	
Norwood Junction 2	d								21 52	22 01	22 10			22 16							22 22	22 31		22 40	
Anerley	d								21 55	22 04				22 19							22 25	22 34			
Penge West	d								21 57	22 06				22 21							22 27	22 36			
London Victoria 15 ⊖	d				21 39		21 41										22 09		22 11						
Battersea Park 4	d						21 45												22 15						
Wandsworth Road	d						21 47												22 17						
Clapham High Street ⊖	d						21 49												22 19						
London Blackfriars 3 ⊖	d																								
Denmark Hill 4	d				21 48		21 54										22 18		22 24						
Peckham Rye 4	d			21 45	21a51	21 53	21 56	22 10							22 15		22a21	22 23	22 26	22 40					
Queens Rd Peckham	d					21 56	21 59	22 12										22 26	22 29	22 42					
South Bermondsey	d					21 58	22 01	22 15										22 28	22 31	22 45					
Clapham Junction 10	d																								
Wandsworth Common	d																								
Balham 4 ⊖	d																								
Streatham Hill	d																								
West Norwood 4	d			21 57											22 27										
Gipsy Hill	d			22 00											22 30										
Crystal Palace 4	d	22 01		22a02								22 16			22a32										22 46
Sydenham	d	22 04							21 59	22 09	22 14	22 19		22 24							22 29	22 39		22 44	22 49
Forest Hill 4	d	22 07							22 02	22 11	22 17	22 22		22 26							22 32	22 41		22 47	22 52
Honor Oak Park	d	22 09							22 04	22 14	22 19	22 24		22 29							22 34	22 44		22 49	22 54
Brockley	d	22 12							22 07	22 16	22 22	22 27		22 31							22 37	22 46		22 52	22 57
New Cross Gate 4	a	22 14							22 09	22 19	22 24	22 29		22 34							22 39	22 49		22 54	22 59
	d	22 14							22 09	22 19	22 24	22 29		22 34							22 39	22 49		22 54	22 59
New Cross ELL	d															22 39									
Surrey Quays	d	22 18								22 23		22 33		22 38		22 43						22 53			23 03
Canada Water	d	22 20								22 25		22 35		22 40		22 45						22 55			23 05
Rotherhithe	d	22 21								22 26		22 36		22 41		22 46						22 56			23 06
Wapping	d	22 23								22 28		22 38		22 43		22 48						22 58			23 08
Shadwell	d	22 25								22 30		22 40		22 45		22 50						23 00			23 10
Whitechapel	d	22 27								22 32		22 42		22 47		22 52						23 02			23 12
Shoreditch High Street	d	22 29								22 34		22 44		22 49		22 54						23 04			23 14
Hoxton	d	22 31								22 36		22 46		22 51		22 56						23 06			23 16
Haggerston	d	22 33								22 38		22 48		22 53		22 58						23 08			23 18
Dalston Junction Stn ELL	a	22 35								22 40		22 50		22 55		23 02						23 10			23 20
Canonbury	d	22 38								22 45		22 53		23 00								23 15			23 23
Highbury & Islington	a	22 43								22 50		22 58		23 05								23 20			23 28
	d																								
London Bridge 4 ⊖	a					22 03	22 06	22 19	22 18		22 31							22 33	22 36	22 49	22 48			23 01	

Table 178

Sundays

East London Line and Croydon - London Victoria to London Bridge

Network Diagram - see first Page of Table 177

		LO	SN	LO	SE	SN	SN	SN		SN	LO	LO	SN	SE	SN	SN	SN
East Croydon 🚋	d							22 42		22 47							
West Croydon 4 🚋	d	22 42									22 57						
Norwood Junction 2	d	22 46								22 52	23 01						
Anerley	d	22 49								22 55	23 04						
Penge West	d	22 51								22 57	23 06						
London Victoria 15 ⊖	d				22 39		22 41							23 09		23 11	
Battersea Park 4	d						22 45									23 15	
Wandsworth Road	d						22 47									23 17	
Clapham High Street ⊖	d						22 49									23 19	
London Blackfriars 3 ⊖	d																
Denmark Hill 4	d				22 48		22 54							23 18		23 24	
Peckham Rye 4	d		22 45		22a51	22 53	22 56	23 10					23 15	23a21	23 23	23 26	23 53
Queens Rd Peckham	d					22 56	22 59	23 12							23 26	23 29	23 56
South Bermondsey	d					22 58	23 01	23 15							23 28	23 31	23 58
Clapham Junction 10	d																
Wandsworth Common	d																
Balham 4 ⊖	d																
Streatham Hill	d																
West Norwood 4	d		22 57										23 27				
Gipsy Hill	d		23 00										23 30				
Crystal Palace 4	d		23a02									23 16	23a32				
Sydenham	d	22 54								22 59	23 09	23 19					
Forest Hill 4	d	22 56								23 02	23 11	23 22					
Honor Oak Park	d	22 59								23 04	23 14	23 24					
Brockley	d	23 01								23 07	23 16	23 27					
New Cross Gate 4	a	23 04								23 09	23 19	23 29					
	d	23 04								23 09	23 19	23 29					
New Cross ELL	d			23 09													
Surrey Quays	d	23 08		23 13							23 23	23 33					
Canada Water	d	23 10		23 15							23 25	23 35					
Rotherhithe	d	23 11		23 16							23 26	23 36					
Wapping	d	23 13		23 18							23 28	23 38					
Shadwell	d	23 15		23 20							23 30	23 40					
Whitechapel	d	23 17		23 22							23 32	23 42					
Shoreditch High Street	d	23 19		23 24							23 34	23 44					
Hoxton	d	23 21		23 26							23 36	23 46					
Haggerston	d	23 23		23 28							23 38	23 48					
Dalston Junction Stn ELL	a	23 25		23 32							23 40	23 50					
Canonbury	d	23 30									23 45	23 53					
Highbury & Islington	a	23 35									23 50	23 58					
	d																
London Bridge 4 ⊖	a					23 03	23 06	23 19		23 18					23 33	23 36	00 03

Luton and London - Wimbledon and Sutton via Streatham

Network Diagram - see first Page of Table 177

Miles	Miles			FC MX	FC MX	SN	FC	SN	FC		FC	SN			FC	SN	FC		FC	FC	SN			FC	FC
																			1	1 A					
—	—	**Luton** 10	d						05 08						05 48		06 06		06 34	06 39				06 50	07 10
—	—	Luton Airport Parkway 7	d						05 10						05 50		06 08			06 41				06 52	07 12
—	—	St Pancras International 15 ⊖	d				05 36		05 54		06 12				06 34		06 52		07 04	07 16				07 32	07 52
—	—	Farringdon 3 ⊖	d				05 42		06 00		06 18				06 40		06 58		07 10	07 22				07 38	07 58
—	0	City Thameslink 3	d				05 44		06 03		06 21				06 43		07 01		07 13	07 25				07 41	08 01
—	0½	**London Blackfriars** 3 ⊖	d				05 47		06 06		06 24				06 46		07 04		07 16	07 28				07 44	08 04
—	1½	Elephant & Castle ⊖	d				05 50		06 09		06 27				06 49		07 07		07 19	07 33				07 47	08 07
—	3½	Loughborough Jn	d						06 13		06 31				06 53		07 11		07 23	07 37				07 51	08 11
—	4½	Herne Hill 4	d				05 57		06 17		06 35				06 57		07 15		07 27	07 41				07 57	08 17
0	—	**London Bridge** 4 ⊖	d	23p29	23p59			06 00				06 30				06 58					07 29				
1¾	—	South Bermondsey	d					06 04				06 34				07 02					07 33				
2¾	—	Queens Rd Peckham	d					06 06				06 36				07 04					07 35				
3½	—	Peckham Rye 4	d					06 09				06 39				07 07					07 38				
4½	—	East Dulwich	d					06 12				06 42				07 10					07 41				
4¾	—	North Dulwich	d					06 14				06 44				07 12					07 43				
6	5½	Tulse Hill 3	d	23p41	00 09		06 02	06 18	06 22		06 42	06 48			07 02	07 16	07 20		07 31	07 45	07 47			08 05	08 21
7½	7	Streatham 4	d	23p45	00 13		06 05	06 21	06 25		06 45	06 51			07 05	07 19	07 23		07 34	07 48	07 51			08 08	08 24
—	8	Mitcham Eastfields	d						06 29		06 49						07 27			07 52					08 28
—	9	Mitcham Junction 🚋	d						06 32		06 52						07 30			07 55					08 31
—	11	Hackbridge	d						06 35		06 55						07 33			07 58					08 34
—	11¾	Carshalton	d						06 38		06 58						07 36			08 01					08 37
9	—	Tooting	d	23p50	00 18		06 10	06 25				06 55			07 10	07 23			07 38		07 55			08 12	
10¼	—	Haydons Road	d	23p53	00 21		06 13	06 28				06 58			07 13	07 26			07 41		07 58			08 15	
11½	—	**Wimbledon** 6 ⊖ 🚋	a	23p56	00 24		06 15	06 31				07 01			07 16	07 30			07 44		08 01			08 18	
—	—		d	23p57	00 25	05 56	06 16	06 32				07 02			07 16	07 31			07 47		08 02			08 19	
12½	—	Wimbledon Chase	d	00 01	00 28	05 59	06 19	06 35				07 05			07 19	07 34			07 50		08 05			08 22	
13	—	South Merton	d	00 03	00 30	06 01	06 21	06 37				07 07			07 21	07 36			07 52		08 07			08 24	
13½	—	Morden South	d	00 05	00 32	06 03	06 23	06 39				07 09			07 23	07 38			07 54		08 09			08 26	
14	—	St Helier	d	00 07	00 34	06 05	06 25	06 41				07 11			07 25	07 40			07 56		08 11			08 28	
15	—	Sutton Common	d	00 09	00 36	06 07	06 27	06 43				07 13			07 27	07 42			07 58		08 13			08 30	
16	—	West Sutton	d	00 12	00 39	06 10	06 30	06 46				07 16			07 30	07 45			08 01		08 16			08 33	
17	13	**Sutton (Surrey)** 4	a	00 15	00 43	06 13	06 33	06 49	06 43		07 03	07 19			07 35	07 48	07 39		08 07	08 04	08 19			08 37	08 40

		SN		FC	SN	FC	FC	FC		FC	FC	FC	FC	FC	FC	FC	FC	FC		FC	FC	FC	FC		
						1 A	1																		
Luton 10	d			07 30			07 57	08 02				08 54		09 14		09 44		10 14			10 44		11 14		
Luton Airport Parkway 7	d			07 32			07 59	08 04				08 56		09 16		09 46		10 16			10 46		11 16		
St Pancras International 15 ⊖	d			08 12		08 24	08 32	08 44		08 56	09 16	09 34	09 48	10 04	10 18	10 34	10 48	11 04		11 18	11 34	11 48	12 04		
Farringdon 3 ⊖	d			08 18		08 30	08 38	08 50		09 02	09 22	09 40	09 53	10 09	10 24	10 39	10 54	11 09		11 24	11 39	11 53	12 09		
City Thameslink 3	d			08 21		08 33	08 41	08 53		09 05	09 25	09 43	09 57	10 13	10 27	10 43	10 57	11 13		11 27	11 43	11 57	12 13		
London Blackfriars 3 ⊖	d			08 24		08 36	08 44	08 56		09 08	09 28	09 46	10 00	10 16	10 30	10 46	11 00	11 16		11 30	11 46	12 00	12 16		
Elephant & Castle ⊖	d			08 27			08 47	09 00		09 12	09 31	09 49	10 03	10 19	10 33	10 49	11 03	11 19		11 33	11 49	12 03	12 19		
Loughborough Jn	d			08 31			08 51	09 04		09 16	09 35	09 53	10 07	10 23	10 37	10 53	11 07	11 23		11 37	11 53	12 07	12 23		
Herne Hill 4	d			08 36		08 46	08 57	09 11		09 25	09 41	09 57	10 11	10 27	10 41	10 57	11 11	11 27		11 41	11 57	12 11	12 27		
London Bridge 4 ⊖	d	08 06			08 24																				
South Bermondsey	d	08 11			08 28																				
Queens Rd Peckham	d	08 13			08 30																				
Peckham Rye 4	d	08 16			08 33																				
East Dulwich	d	08 19			08 36																				
North Dulwich	d	08 21			08 38																				
Tulse Hill 3	d	08 25		08 40	08 47	08 50	09 01	09 16		09 31	09 46	10 01	10 16	10 31	10 46	11 01	11 16	11 31		11 46	12 01	12 16	12 31		
Streatham 4	d	08 28		08 44	08 50	08 54	09 05	09 20		09 35	09 50	10 05	10 20	10 35	10 50	11 05	11 20	11 35		11 50	12 05	12 20	12 35		
Mitcham Eastfields	d					08 58		09 24			09 54		10 24		10 54		11 24			11 54		12 24			
Mitcham Junction 🚋	d					09 01		09 27			09 57		10 27		10 57		11 27			11 57		12 27			
Hackbridge	d					09 04		09 30			10 00		10 30		11 00		11 30			12 00		12 30			
Carshalton	d					09 07		09 33			10 03		10 33		11 03		11 33			12 03		12 33			
Tooting	d	08 33		08 48			09 10			09 40		10 10		10 40		11 10		11 40			12 10		12 40		
Haydons Road	d	08 36		08 51			09 13			09 43		10 13		10 43		11 13		11 43			12 13		12 43		
Wimbledon 6 ⊖ 🚋	a	08 38		08 54			09 16			09 46		10 16		10 46		11 16		11 46			12 16		12 46		
	d	08 39		08 55			09 17			09 47		10 17		10 47		11 17		11 47			12 17		12 47		
Wimbledon Chase	d	08 42		08 58			09 20			09 50		10 20		10 50		11 20		11 50			12 20		12 50		
South Merton	d	08 44		09 00			09 22			09 52		10 22		10 52		11 22		11 52			12 22		12 52		
Morden South	d	08 46		09 02			09 24			09 54		10 24		10 54		11 24		11 54			12 24		12 54		
St Helier	d	08 48		09 04			09 26			09 56		10 26		10 56		11 26		11 56			12 26		12 56		
Sutton Common	d	08 50		09 06			09 28			09 58		10 28		10 58		11 28		11 58			12 28		12 58		
West Sutton	d	08 53		09 09			09 31			10 01		10 31		11 01		11 31		12 01			12 31		13 01		
Sutton (Surrey) 4	a	08 56		09 12	09 02	09 10	09 37	09 36		10 05	10 06	10 35	10 36	11 05	11 06	11 35	11 36	12 05		12 06	12 35	12 36	13 05		

A 1 from London Blackfriars

Luton and London - Wimbledon and Sutton via Streatham

Network Diagram - see first Page of Table 177

		FC		FC	FC		FC	FC	FC	FC	FC 1	FC	SN	FC	FC 1		FC	SN	FC	FC	FC	FC 1	SN	FC
Luton 10	d				14 44			15 14		15 44	16 04			16 16	16 42				16 46	17 10		17 18		17 22
Luton Airport Parkway 7	d				14 46			15 16		15 46	16 06			16 18	16 44				16 48	17 12		17 20		17 24
St Pancras International 15 ⊖	d	12 18		15 18	15 34		15 48	16 04	16 18	16 34	16 40	16 52		17 02	17 14		17 18		17 32	17 44	17 52	17 56		18 04
Farringdon 3 ⊖	d	12 23		15 23	15 39		15 53	16 09	16 23	16 39	16 45	16 57		17 07	17 19		17 23		17 37	17 49	17 57	18 01		18 09
City Thameslink 3	d	12 27		15 27	15 43		15 57	16 13	16 27	16 43	16 49	17 01		17 11	17 23		17 27		17 41	17 53	18 01	18 05		18 13
London Blackfriars 3 ⊖	d	12 30		15 30	15 46		16 00	16 16	16 30	16 46	16 52	17 04		17 14	17 25		17 30		17 44	17 56	18 04	18 10		18 16
Elephant & Castle ⊖	d	12 33		15 33	15 49		16 03	16 19	16 33	16 49	16 56	17 08		17 18	17 29		17 34		17 48	18 00	18 08	18 14		18 20
Loughborough Jn	d	12 37		15 37	15 53		16 07	16 23	16 37	16 53	17 00	17 12		17 22			17 38		17 52		18 12			18 24
Herne Hill 4	d	12 41		15 41	15 57		16 11	16 27	16 41	16 57	17a04	17 16		17 26	17a36		17 43		17 57	18a06	18 17	18a21		18 28
London Bridge 4 ⊖	d												17 06					17 37					18 08	
South Bermondsey	d												17 10					17 41					18 12	
Queens Rd Peckham	d		and at										17 12					17 43					18 14	
Peckham Rye 4	d		the same										17 15					17 46					18 17	
East Dulwich	d		minutes										17 18					17 49					18 20	
North Dulwich	d		past										17 20					17 51					18 22	
Tulse Hill 3	d	12 46	each	15 46	16 01		16 16	16 32	16 46	17 02		17 20	17 24	17 31			17 48	17 55	18 02		18 22		18 27	18 32
Streatham 4	d	12 50	hour until	15 50	16 05		16 20	16 36	16 50	17 06		17 24	17 28	17 36			17 52	17 58	18 06		18 26		18 30	18 36
Mitcham Eastfields	d	12 54		15 54			16 24		16 55			17 28	17 32				17 55	18 02			18 29		18 34	
Mitcham Junction	d	12 57		15 57			16 27		16 58			17 31	17 35				17 58	18 05			18 32		18 37	
Hackbridge	d	13 00		16 00			16 30		17 01			17 34	17 38				18 02	18 09			18 36		18 41	
Carshalton	d	13 03		16 03			16 33		17 04			17 37	17 41				18 04	18 11			18 38		18 43	
Tooting	d				16 10			16 40		17 10				17 40					18 10					18 40
Haydons Road	d				16 13			16 43		17 13				17 43					18 13					18 43
Wimbledon 6 ⊖	a				16 16			16 46		17 16				17 46					18 16					18 46
	d				16 17			16 47		17 19				17 49					18 19					18 49
Wimbledon Chase	d				16 20			16 50		17 22				17 52					18 22					18 52
South Merton	d				16 22			16 52		17 24				17 54					18 24					18 54
Morden South	d				16 24			16 54		17 26				17 56					18 26					18 56
St Helier	d				16 26			16 56		17 28				17 58					18 28					18 58
Sutton Common	d				16 28			16 58		17 30				18 00					18 30					19 00
West Sutton	d				16 31			17 01		17 33				18 03					18 33					19 03
Sutton (Surrey) 4	a	13 06		16 06	16 35		16 36	17 05	17 08	17 37		17 40	17 44	18 07			18 08	18 15	18 37		18 42		18 47	19 07

		FC		SN	FC	FC	FC	FC	FC	FC	FC	FC		FC	FC	FC	FC	FC	FC	FC
Luton 10	d	17 38				18 06	18 22		18 54		19 24			19 46	20 20	20 50	21 20			
Luton Airport Parkway 7	d	17 40				18 08	18 24		18 57		19 27			19 48	20 22	20 52	21 22			
St Pancras International 15 ⊖	d	18 24			18 38	18 48	19 04	19 18	19 34	19 48	20 04	20 18		20 34	21 06	21 36	22 06			
Farringdon 3 ⊖	d	18 29			18 43	18 53	19 09	19 23	19 39	19 53	20 09	20 23		20 39	21 10	21 40	22 10			
City Thameslink 3	d	18 33			18 47	18 57	19 13	19 27	19 43	19 57	20 13	20 27		20 43	21 13	21 43	22 13			
London Blackfriars 3 ⊖	d	18 36			18 50	19 00	19 16	19 30	19 46	20 00	20 16	20 30		20 46	21 16	21 46	22 16			
Elephant & Castle ⊖	d	18 40			18 54	19 04	19 19	19 33	19 49	20 03	20 19	20 33		20 49	21 19	21 49	22 19			
Loughborough Jn	d	18 44			18 58	19 08	19 23	19 37	19 53	20 07	20 23	20 37		20 53	21 23	21 53	22 23			
Herne Hill 4	d	18 48			19 02	19 12	19 27	19 41	19 57	20 11	20 27	20 41		20 57	21 27	21 57	22 27			
London Bridge 4 ⊖	d			18 38														23 01	23 29	23 59
South Bermondsey	d			18 42																
Queens Rd Peckham	d			18 44																
Peckham Rye 4	d			18 47																
East Dulwich	d			18 50																
North Dulwich	d			18 52																
Tulse Hill 3	d	18 52		18 56	19 09	19 16	19 31	19 46	20 01	20 16	20 31	20 50		21 01	21 31	22 01	22 31	23 11	23 41	00 09
Streatham 4	d	18 56		18 59	19 13	19 20	19 35	19 50	20 05	20 20	20 35	20 53		21 05	21 35	22 05	22 35	23 15	23 45	00 13
Mitcham Eastfields	d	18 59		19 03		19 24		19 54		20 24		20 57								
Mitcham Junction	d	19 02		19 06		19 27		19 57		20 27		21 00								
Hackbridge	d	19 06		19 10		19 30		20 00		20 30		21 03								
Carshalton	d	19 08		19 12		19 33		20 03		20 33		21 06								
Tooting	d				19 18		19 40		20 10		20 40			21 10	21 40	22 10	22 40	23 20	23 50	00 18
Haydons Road	d				19 21		19 43		20 13		20 43			21 13	21 43	22 13	22 43	23 23	23 53	00 21
Wimbledon 6 ⊖	a				19 23		19 46		20 16		20 46			21 16	21 46	22 16	22 46	23 26	23 56	00 24
	d				19 24		19 49		20 19		20 49			21 19	21 49	22 19	22 49	23 27	23 57	00 25
Wimbledon Chase	d				19 27		19 52		20 22		20 52			21 22	21 52	22 22	22 52	23 30	00 01	00 28
South Merton	d				19 29		19 54		20 24		20 54			21 24	21 54	22 24	22 54	23 32	00 03	00 30
Morden South	d				19 31		19 56		20 26		20 56			21 26	21 56	22 26	22 56	23 34	00 05	00 32
St Helier	d				19 33		19 58		20 28		20 58			21 28	21 58	22 28	22 58	23 36	00 07	00 34
Sutton Common	d				19 35		20 00		20 30		21 00			21 30	22 00	22 30	23 00	23 38	00 09	00 36
West Sutton	d				19 38		20 03		20 33		21 03			21 33	22 03	22 33	23 03	23 41	00 12	00 39
Sutton (Surrey) 4	a	19 12		19 16	19 41	19 36	20 07	20 06	20 39	20 36	21 09	21 10		21 39	22 09	22 39	23 09	23 45	00 15	00 43

Table 179

Saturdays

Luton and London - Wimbledon and Sutton via Streatham

Network Diagram - see first Page of Table 177

		FC	FC	FC	FC	FC	FC	FC		FC		FC	FC	FC	FC	FC	FC	FC	FC	FC		FC	FC	FC
Luton 10	d																							
Luton Airport Parkway 7	d																							
St Pancras International 15 ⊖	d																							
Farringdon 3 ⊖	d																							
City Thameslink 3	d																							
London Blackfriars 3 ⊖	d																							
Elephant & Castle ⊖	d																							
Loughborough Jn	d																							
Herne Hill 4	d				06 42		07 12					18 42		19 12		19 42								
London Bridge 4 ⊖	d	23p29	23p59	06 21		06 45		07 15		18 15			18 45		19 15		19 45	20 15	20 45	21 15		21 45	22 15	22 45
South Bermondsey	d																							
Queens Rd Peckham	d																							
Peckham Rye 4	d								and at the same minutes past each hour until															
East Dulwich	d																							
North Dulwich	d																							
Tulse Hill 3	d	23p41	00 09	06 31	06 46	07 01	07 16	07 31		18 31		18 46	19 01	19 16	19 31	19 46	20 01	20 31	21 01	21 31		22 01	22 31	23 01
Streatham 4	d	23p45	00 13	06 35	06 50	07 05	07 20	07 35		18 35		18 50	19 05	19 20	19 35	19 51	20 05	20 35	21 05	21 35		22 05	22 35	23 05
Mitcham Eastfields	d				06 54		07 24					18 54		19 24		19 55								
Mitcham Junction 🚋	d				06 57		07 27					18 57		19 27		19 58								
Hackbridge	d				07 00		07 30					19 00		19 30		20 01								
Carshalton	d				07 03		07 33					19 03		19 33		20 04								
Tooting	d	23p50	00 18	06 40		07 10		07 40		18 40			19 10		19 40		20 10	20 40	21 10	21 40		22 10	22 40	23 10
Haydons Road	d	23p53	00 21	06 43		07 13		07 43		18 43			19 13		19 43		20 13	20 43	21 13	21 43		22 13	22 43	23 13
Wimbledon 6 ⊖ 🚋	a	23p56	00 24	06 46		07 16		07 46		18 46			19 16		19 46		20 16	20 46	21 16	21 46		22 16	22 46	23 16
	d	23p57	00 25	06 47		07 17		07 47		18 47			19 17		19 47		20 17	20 47	21 17	21 47		22 17	22 47	23 17
Wimbledon Chase	d	00 01	00 28	06 50		07 20		07 50		18 50			19 20		19 50		20 20	20 50	21 20	21 50		22 20	22 50	23 20
South Merton	d	00 03	00 30	06 52		07 22		07 52		18 52			19 22		19 52		20 22	20 52	21 22	21 52		22 22	22 52	23 22
Morden South	d	00 05	00 32	06 54		07 24		07 54		18 54			19 24		19 54		20 24	20 54	21 24	21 54		22 24	22 54	23 24
St Helier	d	00 07	00 34	06 56		07 26		07 56		18 56			19 26		19 56		20 26	20 56	21 26	21 56		22 26	22 56	23 26
Sutton Common	d	00 09	00 36	06 58		07 28		07 58		18 58			19 28		19 58		20 28	20 58	21 28	21 58		22 28	22 58	23 28
West Sutton	d	00 12	00 39	07 01		07 31		08 01		19 01			19 31		20 01		20 31	21 01	21 31	22 01		22 31	23 01	23 31
Sutton (Surrey) 4	a	00 15	00 43	07 05	07 06	07 35	07 36	08 05		19 05		19 06	19 39	19 36	20 05	20 07	20 37	21 05	21 37	22 05		22 39	23 05	23 35

		FC	FC
Luton 10	d		
Luton Airport Parkway 7	d		
St Pancras International 15 ⊖	d		
Farringdon 3 ⊖	d		
City Thameslink 3	d		
London Blackfriars 3 ⊖	d		
Elephant & Castle ⊖	d		
Loughborough Jn	d		
Herne Hill 4	d		
London Bridge 4 ⊖	d	23 15	23 45
South Bermondsey	d		
Queens Rd Peckham	d		
Peckham Rye 4	d		
East Dulwich	d		
North Dulwich	d		
Tulse Hill 3	d	23 31	00 01
Streatham 4	d	23 35	00 05
Mitcham Eastfields	d		
Mitcham Junction 🚋	d		
Hackbridge	d		
Carshalton	d		
Tooting	d	23 40	00 10
Haydons Road	d	23 43	00 13
Wimbledon 6 ⊖ 🚋	a	23 46	00 16
	d	23 47	00 17
Wimbledon Chase	d	23 50	00 20
South Merton	d	23 52	00 22
Morden South	d	23 54	00 24
St Helier	d	23 56	00 26
Sutton Common	d	23 58	00 28
West Sutton	d	00 01	00 31
Sutton (Surrey) 4	a	00 05	00 35

Table 179

Sundays

Luton and London - Wimbledon and Sutton via Streatham

Network Diagram - see first Page of Table 177

		FC A	FC A	FC		FC
Luton 10	d					
Luton Airport Parkway 7	d					
St Pancras International 15 ⊖	d					
Farringdon 3 ⊖	d					
City Thameslink 3	d					
London Blackfriars 3 ⊖	d					
Elephant & Castle ⊖	d					
Loughborough Jn	d					
Herne Hill 4	d					
London Bridge 4 ⊖	d	23p15	23p45	09 32		21 02
South Bermondsey	d					
Queens Rd Peckham	d					
Peckham Rye 4	d					
East Dulwich	d				and every 30 minutes until	
North Dulwich	d					
Tulse Hill 3	d	23p31	00 01	09 43		21 13
Streatham 4	d	23p35	00 05	09 46		21 16
Mitcham Eastfields	d					
Mitcham Junction	d					
Hackbridge	d					
Carshalton	d					
Tooting	d	23p40	00 10	09 50		21 20
Haydons Road	d	23p43	00 13	09 53		21 23
Wimbledon 6 ⊖	a	23p46	00 16	09 57		21 27
	d	23p47	00 17	09 58		21 28
Wimbledon Chase	d	23p50	00 20	10 01		21 31
South Merton	d	23p52	00 22	10 03		21 33
Morden South	d	23p54	00 24	10 05		21 35
St Helier	d	23p56	00 26	10 07		21 37
Sutton Common	d	23p58	00 28	10 09		21 39
West Sutton	d	00 01	00 31	10 12		21 42
Sutton (Surrey) 4	a	00 05	00 35	10 16		21 46

A not 11 December

Sutton and Wimbledon - London and Luton via Streatham

Network Diagram - see first Page of Table 177

Miles	Miles			SE	SN	SN	FC	FC	SN	FC	SN	SE		FC	SE	FC	SN	SE 1	FC	FC	SN	FC		SE 1	FC
0	0	**Sutton (Surrey) 4**	d		05 37	06 14	06 05	06 34	06 50	06 45	07 20			07 05		07 37	07 49		07 40	08 08	08 20	08 08			08 39
1	—	West Sutton	d				06 08			06 48				07 08					07 43			08 11			
2	—	Sutton Common	d				06 10			06 50				07 10					07 45			08 13			
3	—	St Helier	d				06 13			06 53				07 13					07 48			08 16			
3½	—	Morden South	d				06 15			06 55				07 15					07 50			08 18			
4	—	South Merton	d				06 17			06 57				07 17					07 52			08 20			
4½	—	Wimbledon Chase	d				06 19			06 59				07 19					07 54			08 22			
5½	—	Wimbledon 6 ⊖	a				06 22			07 05				07 22					07 57			08 25			
—	—		d				06 28			07 06				07 26					07 58			08 28			
6¾	—	Haydons Road	d				06 30			07 08				07 28					08 00			08 30			
8	—	Tooting	d				06 33			07 11				07 31					08 03			08 33			
—	1¼	Carshalton	d		05 40	06 17		06 37	06 53		07 23					07 40	07 52			08 11	08 23				08 42
—	2	Hackbridge	d		05 42	06 19		06 39	06 55		07 25					07 42	07 54			08 13	08 25				08 44
—	4	Mitcham Junction	d		05 46	06 23		06 42	06 59		07 29					07 45	07 58			08 16	08 29				08 47
—	5	Mitcham Eastfields	d		05 49	06 26		06 45	07 02		07 32					07 48	08 01			08 19	08 32				08 50
9½	6	Streatham 4	d		05 53	06 30	06 38	06 49	07 05	07 16	07 35			07 38		07 52	08 05		08 09	08 23	08 36	08 39			08 54
11	7½	Tulse Hill 3	d		05 57	06 34	06 42	06 53	07 10	07 20	07 41			07 43		07 57	08 10		08 13	08 28	08 40	08 43			08 58
12¼	—	North Dulwich	d			06 37			07 13		07 44						08 13				08 43				
12½	—	East Dulwich	d			06 39			07 15		07 46						08 15				08 45				
13½	—	Peckham Rye 4	d		06 02	06 42			07 17		07 48						08 18				08 48				
14¼	—	Queens Rd Peckham	d			06 44			07 20		07 51						08 20				08 50				
15¼	—	South Bermondsey	d			06 47			07 22		07 53						08 23				08 53				
17	—	**London Bridge 4** ⊖	a		06 08	06 51			07 28		07 59						08 28				08 57				
—	8½	Herne Hill 4	d	05 23			06 46	06 57		07 24		07 31		07 47	07 57	08 01		08 13	08 20	08 32		08 47		08 52	09 02
—	9½	Loughborough Jn	d				06 49	07 00		07 27		07 34		07 50	08 00	08 04		08 16	08 23	08 36		08 50		08 55	09 05
—	11½	Elephant & Castle ⊖	d	05 29			06 54	07 06		07 32		07 38		07 54	08 05	08 09		08 21	08 28	08 40		08 58		09 02	09 10
—	12½	**London Blackfriars 3** ⊖	a	05 32			06 57	07 09		07 35		07 42		07 58	08 08	08 12		08 25	08 32	08 45		09 01		09 06	09 13
—	13	City Thameslink 3	a	05 35			07 00	07 14		07 38		07 44		08 00	08 11	08 15		08 27	08 35	08 48		09 04		09 08	09 16
—	—	Farringdon 3 ⊖	a	05 38			07 04	07 18		07 42		07 48		08 03	08 15	08 19		08 30	08 39	08 52		09 08		09 12	09 20
—	—	St Pancras International 15 ⊖	a	05 42			07 08	07 22		07 46		07 52		08 08	08 19	08 23		08 35	08 43	08 56		09 12		09 16	09 24
—	—	Luton Airport Parkway 7	a				07 49			08 20					09 01			09 09	09 29			09 58		09 43	
—	—	**Luton 10**	a				07 53			08 23					09 04			09 12	09 34			10 03		09 46	

		FC	SN	FC	FC	FC	FC	FC		FC	FC	FC	FC	FC	FC	FC	FC	FC		FC	FC	FC	FC	FC	FC
Sutton (Surrey) 4	d	08 41	08 57	09 13	09 11	09 38	09 37	10 08		10 07	10 38	10 37	11 08	11 07	11 38	11 37	12 08	12 07		12 38	12 37	13 08	13 07	13 38	13 37
West Sutton	d	08 44			09 14		09 40			10 10		10 40		11 10		11 40		12 10			12 40		13 10		13 40
Sutton Common	d	08 46			09 16		09 42			10 12		10 42		11 12		11 42		12 12			12 42		13 12		13 42
St Helier	d	08 49			09 19		09 45			10 15		10 45		11 15		11 45		12 15			12 45		13 15		13 45
Morden South	d	08 51			09 21		09 47			10 17		10 47		11 17		11 47		12 17			12 47		13 17		13 47
South Merton	d	08 53			09 23		09 49			10 19		10 49		11 19		11 49		12 19			12 49		13 19		13 49
Wimbledon Chase	d	08 55			09 25		09 51			10 21		10 51		11 21		11 51		12 21			12 51		13 21		13 51
Wimbledon 6 ⊖	a	08 58			09 28		09 54			10 24		10 54		11 24		11 54		12 24			12 54		13 24		13 54
	d	08 58			09 28		09 58			10 28		10 58		11 28		11 58		12 28			12 58		13 28		13 58
Haydons Road	d	09 00			09 30		10 00			10 30		11 00		11 30		12 00		12 30			13 00		13 30		14 00
Tooting	d	09 03			09 33		10 03			10 33		11 03		11 33		12 03		12 33			13 03		13 33		14 03
Carshalton	d		09 00	09 16		09 41		10 11			10 41		11 11		11 41		12 11			12 41		13 11		13 41	
Hackbridge	d		09 02	09 18		09 43		10 13			10 43		11 13		11 43		12 13			12 43		13 13		13 43	
Mitcham Junction	d		09 06	09 21		09 46		10 16			10 46		11 16		11 46		12 16			12 46		13 16		13 46	
Mitcham Eastfields	d		09 09	09 24		09 49		10 19			10 49		11 19		11 49		12 19			12 49		13 19		13 49	
Streatham 4	d	09 08	09 12	09 28	09 38	09 53	10 08	10 23		10 38	10 53	11 08	11 23	11 38	11 53	12 08	12 23	12 38		12 53	13 08	13 23	13 38	13 53	14 08
Tulse Hill 3	d	09 16	09 16	09 32	09 42	09 57	10 12	10 27		10 42	10 57	11 12	11 27	11 42	11 57	12 12	12 27	12 42		12 57	13 12	13 27	13 42	13 57	14 12
North Dulwich	d		09 19																						
East Dulwich	d		09 21																						
Peckham Rye 4	d		09 23																						
Queens Rd Peckham	d		09 26																						
South Bermondsey	d		09 28																						
London Bridge 4 ⊖	a		09 35																						
Herne Hill 4	d	09 20		09 36	09 46	10 01	10 16	10 31		10 46	11 01	11 16	11 31	11 46	12 01	12 16	12 31	12 46		13 01	13 16	13 31	13 46	14 01	14 16
Loughborough Jn	d	09 23		09 40	09 50	10 04	10 19	10 34		10 49	11 04	11 19	11 34	11 49	12 04	12 19	12 34	12 49		13 04	13 19	13 34	13 49	14 04	14 19
Elephant & Castle ⊖	d	09 30		09 45	09 55	10 09	10 24	10 39		10 54	11 09	11 24	11 39	11 54	12 09	12 24	12 39	12 54		13 09	13 24	13 39	13 54	14 09	14 24
London Blackfriars 3 ⊖	a	09 33		09 49	09 59	10 12	10 27	10 42		10 57	11 12	11 27	11 42	11 57	12 12	12 27	12 42	12 57		13 12	13 27	13 42	13 57	14 12	14 27
City Thameslink 3	a	09 36		09 52	10 02	10 16	10 32	10 46		11 02	11 16	11 32	11 46	12 02	12 16	12 32	12 46	13 02		13 16	13 32	13 46	14 02	14 16	14 32
Farringdon 3 ⊖	a	09 40		09 56	10 06	10 19	10 35	10 49		11 06	11 19	11 36	11 49	12 06	12 19	12 36	12 49	13 06		13 19	13 36	13 49	14 06	14 19	14 36
St Pancras International 15 ⊖	a	09 44		10 00	10 10	10 23	10 40	10 53		11 10	11 23	11 40	11 53	12 10	12 23	12 40	12 53	13 10		13 23	13 40	13 53	14 10	14 23	14 40
Luton Airport Parkway 7	a	10 29			10 58		11 27			11 55		12 25		12 55		13 25		13 55			14 25		14 55		15 25
Luton 10	a	10 33			11 03		11 31			11 59		12 29		12 57		13 29		13 59			14 29		14 59		15 29

Table 179

Mondays to Fridays

Sutton and Wimbledon - London and Luton via Streatham

Network Diagram - see first Page of Table 177

		FC	FC	FC		FC	FC	FC	FC	FC	FC	FC	FC 1 A	FC		FC	SE 1	FC	FC	FC		SN	FC	FC	
Sutton (Surrey) 4	d	14 08	14 07	14 38		14 37	15 08	15 07	15 38	15 37	16 08	16 07	16 38	16 37		17 08		17 11	17 42	17 41		17 48	18 08	18 09	
West Sutton	d		14 10			14 40		15 10		15 40		16 10		16 40				17 14		17 44		17 52		18 12	
Sutton Common	d		14 12			14 42		15 12		15 42		16 12		16 42				17 16		17 46		17 54		18 14	
St Helier	d		14 15			14 45		15 15		15 45		16 15		16 45				17 19		17 49		17 57		18 17	
Morden South	d		14 17			14 47		15 17		15 47		16 17		16 47				17 21		17 51		17 59		18 19	
South Merton	d		14 19			14 49		15 19		15 49		16 19		16 49				17 23		17 53		18 01		18 21	
Wimbledon Chase	d		14 21			14 51		15 21		15 51		16 21		16 51				17 25		17 55		18 03		18 23	
Wimbledon 6 ⊖	a		14 24			14 54		15 24		15 54		16 24		16 54				17 28		17 58		18 06		18 26	
	d		14 28			14 58		15 28		15 58		16 30		17 00				17 30		18 00		18 10		18 28	
Haydons Road	d		14 30			15 00		15 30		16 00		16 32		17 02				17 32		18 02		18 12		18 30	
Tooting	d		14 33			15 03		15 33		16 03		16 35		17 05				17 35		18 05		18 15		18 33	
Carshalton	d	14 11		14 41			15 11		15 41		16 11		16 41			17 11			17 45				18 11		
Hackbridge	d	14 13		14 43			15 13		15 43		16 13		16 43			17 13			17 47				18 13		
Mitcham Junction	d	14 16		14 46			15 16		15 46		16 16		16 46			17 16			17 50				18 16		
Mitcham Eastfields	d	14 19		14 49			15 19		15 49		16 19		16 49			17 19			17 53				18 19		
Streatham 4	d	14 23	14 38	14 53		15 08	15 23	15 38	15 53	16 08	16 23	16 40	16 53	17 10		17 23		17 40	17 57	18 10		18 20	18 23	18 40	
Tulse Hill 3	d	14 27	14 42	14 57		15 12	15 27	15 42	15 57	16 12	16 27	16 46	16 57	17 16		17 27		17 44	18 01	18 16		18 24	18 28	18 44	
North Dulwich	d																					18 27			
East Dulwich	d																					18 29			
Peckham Rye 4	d																					18 32			
Queens Rd Peckham	d																					18 35			
South Bermondsey	d																					18 37			
London Bridge 4 ⊖	a																					18 42			
Herne Hill 4	d	14 31	14 46	15 01		15 16	15 31	15 46	16 01	16 16	16 31	16 50	17 01	17 21		17 31	17 44	17 48	18 06	18 20			18 32	18 48	
Loughborough Jn	d	14 34	14 49	15 04		15 19	15 34	15 49	16 04	16 19	16 34	16 53		17 24		17 34	17 47	17 51	18 09	18 23			18 35	18 51	
Elephant & Castle ⊖	d	14 39	14 54	15 09		15 24	15 39	15 54	16 09	16 24	16 39	17 00	17 08	17 28		17 39	17 52	17 56	18 14	18 28			18 40	18 56	
London Blackfriars 3 ⊖	a	14 42	14 57	15 12		15 27	15 42	15 57	16 12	16 29	16 42	17 03	17 11	17 31		17 43	17 55	17 59	18 17	18 31			18 43	18 59	
City Thameslink 3	a	14 46	15 02	15 16		15 32	15 46	16 02	16 16	16 32	16 46	17 06	17 14	17 34		17 48	17 58	18 02	18 20	18 34			18 46	19 02	
Farringdon 3 ⊖	a	14 49	15 06	15 19		15 36	15 49	16 06	16 19	16 35	16 49	17 09	17 17	17 37		17 51	18 01	18 05	18 23	18 37			18 49	19 05	
St Pancras International 15 ⊖	a	14 53	15 10	15 23		15 40	15 53	16 10	16 23	16 39	16 53	17 13	17 21	17 41		17 55	18 05	18 09	18 27	18 41			18 53	19 09	
Luton Airport Parkway 7	a		15 55			16 25		16 57		17 25			17 57	18 27			18 38	18 58		19 30			19 33	19 54	
Luton 10	a		15 59			16 29		17 01		17 29			18 00	18 31			18 41	19 01		19 33			19 36	19 57	

		SN	FC	SN	FC	SN	FC	SN	FC	FC		FC	FC	FC	FC	FC	FC	FC	FC						
Sutton (Surrey) 4	d	18 16	18 38		18 43	18 48	19 08		19 13	19 42		19 37	20 12	20 07	20 42	20 37	21 12	21 17	22 12						
West Sutton	d	18 20			18 46	18 54			19 16			19 40		20 10		20 40		21 20	22 15						
Sutton Common	d	18 22			18 48	18 56			19 18			19 42		20 12		20 42		21 22	22 17						
St Helier	d	18 25			18 51	18 59			19 21			19 45		20 15		20 45		21 25	22 20						
Morden South	d	18 27			18 53	19 01			19 23			19 47		20 17		20 47		21 27	22 22						
South Merton	d	18 29			18 55	19 03			19 25			19 49		20 19		20 49		21 29	22 24						
Wimbledon Chase	d	18 31			18 57	19 05			19 27			19 51		20 21		20 51		21 31	22 26						
Wimbledon 6 ⊖	a	18 34			19 00	19 08			19 30			19 54		20 24		20 54		21 34	22 29						
	d			18 43	19 00			19 17	19 30			19 56		20 26		20 56		21 38	22 30						
Haydons Road	d			18 45	19 02			19 19	19 32			19 58		20 28		20 58		21 40	22 32						
Tooting	d			18 48	19 05			19 22	19 35			20 01		20 31		21 01		21 43	22 35						
Carshalton	d		18 41				19 11			19 45			20 15		20 45		21 15								
Hackbridge	d		18 43				19 13			19 47			20 17		20 47		21 17								
Mitcham Junction	d		18 46				19 16			19 50			20 20		20 50		21 20								
Mitcham Eastfields	d		18 49				19 19			19 53			20 23		20 53		21 23								
Streatham 4	d		18 53	18 56	19 10		19 23	19 26	19 40	19 57		20 06	20 27	20 36	20 57	21 06	21 27	21 49	22 40						
Tulse Hill 3	d		18 57	19 00	19 14		19 27	19 31	19 44	20 01		20 12	20 31	20 42	21 01	21 12	21 31	21 53	22 44						
North Dulwich	d			19 03				19 34																	
East Dulwich	d			19 05				19 36																	
Peckham Rye 4	d			19 07				19 38																	
Queens Rd Peckham	d			19 10				19 41																	
South Bermondsey	d			19 12				19 43																	
London Bridge 4 ⊖	a			19 17				19 51											22 55						
Herne Hill 4	d		19 02		19 17		19 31		19 47	20 05		20 16	20 35	20 46	21 05	21 16	21 35	21 57							
Loughborough Jn	d		19 05		19 20		19 34		19 50	20 08		20 19	20 38	20 49	21 08	21 19	21 38	22 00							
Elephant & Castle ⊖	d		19 10		19 25		19 39		19 55	20 13		20 24	20 43	20 54	21 13	21 24	21 43	22 04							
London Blackfriars 3 ⊖	a		19 13		19 28		19 42		19 58	20 16		20 27	20 46	20 57	21 16	21 27	21 46	22 07							
City Thameslink 3	a		19 20		19 32		19 48		20 02	20 20		20 32	20 50	21 02	21 20	21 32	21 50	22 10							
Farringdon 3 ⊖	a		19 23		19 36		19 51		20 06	20 23		20 36	20 53	21 06	21 23	21 36	21 53	22 13							
St Pancras International 15 ⊖	a		19 27		19 40		19 55		20 10	20 27		20 40	20 57	21 10	21 27	21 40	21 57	22 17							
Luton Airport Parkway 7	a				20 25				20 55			21 25		21 55		22 25	22 41	23 01							
Luton 10	a				20 29				20 59			21 29		21 59		22 29	22 44	23 04							

A 1 to Farringdon

Table 179

Saturdays

Sutton and Wimbledon - London and Luton via Streatham

Network Diagram - see first Page of Table 177

		FC	FC	FC	FC	FC		FC	FC		FC	FC	FC	FC		FC
Sutton (Surrey) 4	d		07 08	07 07	07 38	07 37		18 37	19 08		19 07	19 37	20 08	20 37		22 07
West Sutton	d			07 10		07 40		18 40			19 10	19 40	20 11	20 40		22 10
Sutton Common	d			07 12		07 42		18 42			19 12	19 42	20 13	20 42		22 12
St Helier	d			07 15		07 45		18 45			19 15	19 45	20 16	20 45		22 15
Morden South	d			07 17		07 47		18 47			19 17	19 47	20 18	20 47		22 17
South Merton	d			07 19		07 49		18 49			19 19	19 49	20 20	20 49		22 19
Wimbledon Chase	d			07 21		07 51		18 51			19 21	19 51	20 22	20 51		22 21
Wimbledon 6 ⊖	a			07 25		07 55		18 55			19 25	19 55	20 25	20 55		22 25
	d	07 00		07 30		08 00		19 00			19 30	20 00	20 30	21 00		22 30
Haydons Road	d	07 02		07 32		08 02		19 02			19 32	20 02	20 32	21 02		22 32
Tooting	d	07 05		07 35		08 05		19 05			19 35	20 05	20 35	21 05		22 35
Carshalton	d		07 11		07 41				19 11							
Hackbridge	d		07 13		07 43		and at the same minutes past each hour until		19 13							
Mitcham Junction	d		07 16		07 46				19 16						and every 30 minutes until	
Mitcham Eastfields	d		07 19		07 49				19 19							
Streatham 4	d	07 10	07 23	07 40	07 53	08 10		19 10	19 23		19 40	20 10	20 40	21 10		22 40
Tulse Hill 3	d	07 17	07 27	07 47	07 57	08 17		19 17	19 27		19 47	20 17	20 47	21 17		22 47
North Dulwich	d															
East Dulwich	d															
Peckham Rye 4	d															
Queens Rd Peckham	d															
South Bermondsey	d															
London Bridge 4 ⊖	a	07 30		08 00		08 30		19 30			20 00	20 30	21 00	21 30		23 00
Herne Hill 4	d		07a31		08a01				19a31							
Loughborough Jn.	d															
Elephant & Castle ⊖	d															
London Blackfriars 3 ⊖	a															
City Thameslink 3	a															
Farringdon 3 ⊖	a															
St Pancras International 15 ⊖	a															
Luton Airport Parkway 7	a															
Luton 10	a															

Sundays

		FC		FC
Sutton (Surrey) 4	d	10 28		21 28
West Sutton	d	10 31		21 31
Sutton Common	d	10 33		21 33
St Helier	d	10 36		21 36
Morden South	d	10 38		21 38
South Merton	d	10 40		21 40
Wimbledon Chase	d	10 42		21 42
Wimbledon 6 ⊖	a	10 45		21 45
	d	10 45		21 45
Haydons Road	d	10 48		21 48
Tooting	d	10 51		21 51
Carshalton	d			
Hackbridge	d			
Mitcham Junction	d		and every 30 minutes until	
Mitcham Eastfields	d			
Streatham 4	d	10 55		21 55
Tulse Hill 3	d	10 59		21 59
North Dulwich	d			
East Dulwich	d			
Peckham Rye 4	d			
Queens Rd Peckham	d			
South Bermondsey	d			
London Bridge 4 ⊖	a	11 10		22 10
Herne Hill 4	d			
Loughborough Jn.	d			
Elephant & Castle ⊖	d			
London Blackfriars 3 ⊖	a			
City Thameslink 3	a			
Farringdon 3 ⊖	a			
St Pancras International 15 ⊖	a			
Luton Airport Parkway 7	a			
Luton 10	a			

London and Croydon - Caterham and Tattenham Corner

Network Diagram - see first Page of Table 177

Miles	Miles			SN MX	SN MX	SN MO	SN MO	SN MX	SN	SN	SN	SN			SN	SN	SN	SN		SN	SN	SN	SN		SN
0	—	**London Victoria** 15	⊖ d	23p15			23p50			06 13						07 23	07 20			07 45			08 15		
2¾	—	Clapham Junction 10	d	23p23			23p56			06 21						07 30	07 28			07 51			08 23		
—	0	**London Bridge** 4	⊖ d		23p36	23p39		00 06	06 06		06 36	06 54			07 06			07 36			08 14	08 06			08 47
—	2¾	New Cross Gate 4	⊖ d		23p41	23p44		00 11	06 11		06 41	06 59			07 11			07 41				08 11			
—	8¾	Norwood Junction 2	d		23p59	00 03		00 30	06 30		07 00	07 18			07 31			08 00			08 27	08 30			
10½	10	**East Croydon**	d	23p45	00 04	00 07	00 18	00 35	06 34	06 44	07 04	07 22			07 38	07 45	07 49	08 04		08 13	08 31	08 34	08 45		09 03
11½	11	South Croydon 4	d	23p47	00 06	00 09	00 20	00 37	06 37		07 06	07 25			07 40		07 52	08 06		08 15		08 36	08 47		
12½	12	Purley Oaks	d	23p50	00 09	00 12	00 23	00 40	06 40		07 09	07 28			07 43		07 55	08 09		08 18		08 39	08 50		
13½	13	Purley 4	a	23p54	00 12	00 15	00 26	00 43	06 43	06 51	07 12	07 31			07 46	07 52	07 58	08 12		08 21	08 38	08 42	08 54		09 09
—	—																								
—	—		d	23p55	00 15	00 16	00 27	00 46	06 45	06 54	07 13	07 34	07 36		07 49	07 53	07 58	08 16	08 18	08 24	08 39	08 45	08 54		09 11
—	14¼	Kenley	d		00 18	00 19	00 30	00 49	06 48		07 16	07 37			07 52	08 00		08 19		08 27		08 48	08 57		
—	15½	Whyteleafe	d		00 21	00 22	00 33	00 52	06 52		07 19	07 40			07 55	08 04		08 22		08 30		08 51	09 01		
—	16	Whyteleafe South	d		00 23	00 24	00 35	00 54	06 54		07 21	07 42			07 57	08 06		08 24		08 32		08 53	09 03		
—	17¾	**Caterham**	a		00 28	00 29	00 40	00 59	06 58		07 26	07 48			08 02	08 10		08 29		08 37		08 58	09 07		
14¼	—	Reedham	d	23p57						06 56			07 38				08 00		08 20		08 42				09 14
15	—	Coulsdon Town	d	23p59						06 59			07 41				08 03		08 23		08 44				09 16
15¾	—	Woodmansterne	d	00 03						07 02			07 44				08 06		08 26		08 47				09 19
16¾	—	Chipstead	d	00 06						07 05			07 47				08 09		08 29		08 50				09 22
19¼	—	Kingswood	d	00 11						07 10			07 52				08 14		08 34		08 56				09 28
20½	—	Tadworth	d	00 15						07 14			07 56				08 18		08 38		08 59				09 31
21¾	—	**Tattenham Corner**	a	00 18						07 18			07 59				08 21		08 41		09 03				09 36

		SN	SN	SN	SN	SN	SN	SN	SN		SN	SN		SN	SN	SN	SN	SN		SN	SN	SN	SN	SN
London Victoria 15	⊖ d		08 43			09 13					09 43		and at the same minutes past each hour until			14 13					14 43			15 13
Clapham Junction 10	d		08 51			09 21					09 51					14 21					14 51			15 21
London Bridge 4	⊖ d	08 36		09 06	09 20			09 36	09 50			10 06		14 06	14 20			14 36		14 50		15 06	15 20	
New Cross Gate 4	⊖ d	08 41		09 12				09 41				10 11		14 11				14 41				15 11		
Norwood Junction 2	d	09 00		09 30	09 33			10 00	10 03			10 30		14 30	14 33			15 00		15 03		15 30	15 33	
East Croydon	d	09 07	09 13	09 34	09 37	09 43		10 04	10 07		10 13	10 34		14 34	14 37	14 43		15 04		15 07	15 13	15 34	15 37	15 43
South Croydon 4	d	09 09	09 15	09 36		09 45		10 06			10 15	10 36		14 36		14 45		15 06			15 15	15 36		15 45
Purley Oaks	d	09 12	09 18	09 39		09 48		10 09			10 18	10 39		14 39		14 48		15 09			15 18	15 39		15 48
Purley 4	a	09 15	09 22	09 42	09 45	09 52		10 12	10 15		10 22	10 42		14 42	14 45	14 52		15 12		15 15	15 22	15 42	15 45	15 52
	d	09 18	09 26	09 43	09 46	09 52	10 02	10 13	10 16		10 22	10 43		14 43	14 46	14 54	15 02	15 13		15 16	15 22	15 43	15 46	15 52
Kenley	d	09 21	09 29	09 46		09 55		10 16			10 25	10 46		14 46		14 57		15 16			15 25	15 46		15 55
Whyteleafe	d	09 24	09 32	09 49		09 59		10 19			10 29	10 49		14 49		15 01		15 19			15 29	15 49		15 59
Whyteleafe South	d	09 26	09 34	09 51		10 01		10 21			10 31	10 51		14 51		15 03		15 21			15 31	15 51		16 01
Caterham	a	09 31	09 40	09 56		10 05		10 26			10 35	10 56		14 56		15 07		15 26			15 35	15 56		16 05
Reedham	d				09 48		10 04		10 18						14 48		15 04			15 18			15 48	
Coulsdon Town	d				09 51		10 07		10 21						14 51		15 07			15 21			15 51	
Woodmansterne	d				09 54		10 10		10 24						14 54		15 10			15 24			15 54	
Chipstead	d				09 57		10 13		10 27						14 57		15 13			15 27			15 57	
Kingswood	d				10 02		10 18		10 32						15 02		15 18			15 32			16 02	
Tadworth	d				10 06		10 22		10 36						15 06		15 22			15 36			16 06	
Tattenham Corner	a				10 09		10 25		10 39						15 09		15 25			15 39			16 09	

		SN	SN	SN	SN		SN	SN	SN	SN	SN		SN	SN			SN		SN		SN		SN		
London Victoria 15	⊖ d				15 43				16 13	16 39			16 43	17 09					17 39				18 09		
Clapham Junction 10	d				15 51				16 21	16 45			16 51	17 15					17 45				18 15		
London Bridge 4	⊖ d		15 36	15 50			16 06	16 20			16 48						17 17				17 49				
New Cross Gate 4	⊖ d		15 41				16 11																		
Norwood Junction 2	d		16 00	16 03			16 30	16 33			17 02						17 30				18 02				
East Croydon	d		16 04	16 07	16 13		16 34	16 37	16 43	16 56	17 06		17 17	17 27			17 35		17 56		18 06		18 28		
South Croydon 4	d		16 06		16 15		16 36		16 45	16 58	17 08		17 19	17 30			17 37		17 58		18 08		18 30		
Purley Oaks	d		16 09		16 18		16 39		16 48	17 01	17 11		17 22	17 33			17 40		18 01		18 11		18 33		
Purley 4	a		16 12	16 15	16 22		16 42	16 45	16 52	17 05	17 14		17 25	17 36			17 44		18 04		18 14		18 36		
	d	16 02	16 13	16 16	16 24		16 43	16 48	16 52	17 05	17 18	17 22	17 28	17 40	17 42		17 48	17 50	18 08	18 10	18 18	18 21	18 40	18 42	
Kenley	d		16 16		16 27		16 46		16 55	17 08	17 21		17 31	17 43			17 51		18 11		18 21		18 43		
Whyteleafe	d		16 19		16 31		16 49		16 59	17 12	17 24		17 34	17 46			17 54		18 14		18 24		18 46		
Whyteleafe South	d		16 21		16 33		16 51		17 01	17 14	17 26		17 36	17 48			17 56		18 16		18 26		18 48		
Caterham	a		16 26		16 37		16 58		17 07	17 20	17 33		17 43	17 55			18 03		18 23		18 33		18 55		
Reedham	d	16 04		16 18				16 50				17 24			17 44			17 52		18 12		18 23		18 44	
Coulsdon Town	d	16 07		16 21				16 53				17 27			17 47			17 55		18 15		18 26		18 47	
Woodmansterne	d	16 10		16 24				16 56				17 30			17 50			17 58		18 18		18 29		18 50	
Chipstead	d	16 13		16 27				16 59				17 33			17 53			18 01		18 21		18 32		18 53	
Kingswood	d	16 18		16 32				17 04				17 38			17 58			18 06		18 26		18 37		18 58	
Tadworth	d	16 22		16 36				17 08				17 42			18 02			18 10		18 30		18 41		19 02	
Tattenham Corner	a	16 25		16 39				17 11				17 47			18 05			18 15		18 33		18 45		19 05	

		SN			SN		SN		SN		SN	SN	SN		SN	SN	SN	SN	SN	SN	SN	SN	SN		SN
London Victoria 15	⊖ d				18 39				18 45			19 15			19 45		20 15		20 45		21 15		21 45		
Clapham Junction 10	d				18 45				18 53			19 23			19 53		20 23		20 53		21 23		21 53		
London Bridge 4	⊖ d	18 18					18 49				19 06		19 36			20 06		20 36		21 06		21 36			22 08
New Cross Gate 4	⊖ d										19 11		19 41			20 11		20 41		21 11		21 41			22 13
Norwood Junction 2	d	18 31					19 02				19 30		20 00			20 30		21 00		21 30		22 00			22 32
East Croydon	d	18 37			18 57		19 06		19 14		19 34	19 44	20 04		20 15	20 34	20 44	21 04	21 14	21 34	21 45	22 04	22 14		22 36
South Croydon 4	d	18 42			19 00		19 08		19 16		19 36	19 47	20 06		20 17	20 36	20 47	21 06	21 17	21 36	21 47	22 06	22 17		22 38
Purley Oaks	d	18 45			19 03		19 11		19 19		19 39	19 50	20 09		20 21	20 39	20 50	21 09	21 20	21 39	21 50	22 09	22 20		22 41
Purley 4	a	18 48			19 16		19 14		19 22		19 42	19 53	20 12		20 24	20 42	20 53	21 12	21 23	21 42	21 53	22 12	22 23		22 44
	d	18 51	18 54		19 10	19 12	19 18	19 20	19 26	19 28	19 45	19 53	20 15		20 24	20 45	20 53	21 15	21 23	21 45	21 54	22 15	22 23		22 47
Kenley	d	18 54			19 13		19 21		19 29		19 48		20 18			20 48		21 18		21 48		22 18			22 50
Whyteleafe	d	18 57			19 16		19 24		19 32		19 51		20 21			20 51		21 21		21 51		22 21			22 53
Whyteleafe South	d	18 59			19 18		19 26		19 34		19 53		20 23			20 53		21 23		21 53		22 23			22 55
Caterham	a	19 06			19 25		19 33		19 41		19 58		20 28			20 58		21 28		21 58		22 28			23 00
Reedham	d		18 56			19 14		19 22		19 31		19 56			20 27		20 56		21 26		21 56		22 26		
Coulsdon Town	d		18 59			19 17		19 25		19 34		19 58			20 29		20 58		21 28		21 59		22 28		
Woodmansterne	d		19 02			19 20		19 28		19 37		20 01			20 32		21 01		21 31		22 02		22 31		
Chipstead	d		19 05			19 23		19 31		19 40		20 04			20 35		21 04		21 34		22 05		22 34		
Kingswood	d		19 10			19 28		19 36		19 45		20 10			20 41		21 10		21 40		22 10		22 40		
Tadworth	d		19 14			19 32		19 40		19 49		20 13			20 44		21 13		21 43		22 14		22 43		
Tattenham Corner	a		19 17			19 35		19 45		19 52		20 17			20 48		21 17		21 47		22 17		22 47		

London and Croydon - Caterham and Tattenham Corner

Network Diagram - see first Page of Table 177

Station		SN	SN	SN	SN	SN	SN	SN FO
London Victoria 15 ⊖	d	22 15		22 45		23 15		23 45
Clapham Junction 10	d	22 23		22 53		23 23		23 53
London Bridge 4 ⊖	d		22 38		23 06		23 36	
New Cross Gate 4 ⊖	d		22 43		23 11		23 41	
Norwood Junction 2	d		23 02		23 30		23 59	
East Croydon	d	22 45	23 07	23 14	23 34	23 45	00 04	00 14
South Croydon 4	d	22 47	23 09	23 17	23 36	23 47	00 06	00 17
Purley Oaks	d	22 50	23 12	23 20	23 39	23 50	00 09	00 20
Purley 4	a	22 53	23 15	23 23	23 42	23 54	00 12	00 23
	d	22 54	23 15	23 24	23 45	23 55	00 15	00 23
Kenley	d		23 18		23 48		00 18	
Whyteleafe	d		23 22		23 51		00 21	
Whyteleafe South	d		23 24		23 53		00 23	
Caterham	a		23 28		23 58		00 28	
Reedham	d	22 56		23 26		23 57		00 26
Coulsdon Town	d	22 59		23 29		23 59		00 28
Woodmansterne	d	23 02		23 32		00 03		00 31
Chipstead	d	23 05		23 35		00 06		00 34
Kingswood	d	23 10		23 40		00 11		00 40
Tadworth	d	23 14		23 44		00 15		00 43
Tattenham Corner	a	23 17		23 47		00 18		00 47

Saturdays

Station		SN	SN	SN	SN	SN	SN	SN	SN	SN		SN	SN	SN	SN	SN	SN	SN	SN	SN		SN	SN	SN	SN
London Victoria 15 ⊖	d	23p15		23p45		00 16				06 43				07 13				07 43				08 13			
Clapham Junction 10	d	23p23		23p53		00 24				06 51				07 21				07 51				08 21			
London Bridge 4 ⊖	d		23p36		00 06			06 36	06 50			07 06	07 20			07 36	07 50		08 06	08 20				08 36	08 50
New Cross Gate 4 ⊖	d		23p41		00 11			06 41				07 11				07 41			08 11					08 41	
Norwood Junction 2	d		23p59		00 30		06 33	07 00	07 03			07 30	07 33			08 00	08 03		08 30	08 33				09 00	09 03
East Croydon	d	23p45	00 04	00 14	00 34	00 48	06 37	07 04	07 07	07 13		07 34	07 37	07 43		08 04	08 07	08 13	08 34	08 37		08 43		09 04	09 07
South Croydon 4	d	23p47	00 06	00 17	00 36	00 50		07 06		07 15		07 36		07 45		08 06		08 15	08 36			08 45		09 06	
Purley Oaks	d	23p50	00 09	00 20	00 39	00 53		07 09		07 18		07 39		07 48		08 09		08 18	08 39			08 48		09 09	
Purley 4	a	23p54	00 12	00 23	00 42	00 56	06 45	07 12	07 15	07 21		07 42	07 45	07 51		08 12	08 15	08 21	08 42	08 45		08 52		09 12	09 15
	d	23p55	00 15	00 23	00 45	00 57	06 46	07 13	07 16	07 22		07 43	07 46	07 52	08 02	08 13	08 16	08 22	08 43	08 46		08 52	09 02	09 13	09 16
Kenley	d		00 18		00 48			07 16		07 25		07 46		07 55		08 16		08 25	08 46			08 55		09 16	
Whyteleafe	d		00 21		00 51			07 19		07 28		07 49		07 58		08 19		08 28	08 49			08 59		09 19	
Whyteleafe South	d		00 23		00 53			07 21		07 30		07 51		08 00		08 21		08 30	08 51			09 01		09 21	
Caterham	a		00 28		00 58			07 26		07 35		07 56		08 05		08 26		08 35	08 56			09 05		09 26	
Reedham	d	23p57		00 26		00 59	06 48		07 18				07 48		08 04		08 18			08 48			09 04		09 18
Coulsdon Town	d	23p59		00 28		01 02	06 51		07 21				07 51		08 07		08 21			08 51			09 07		09 21
Woodmansterne	d	00 03		00 31		01 05	06 54		07 24				07 54		08 10		08 24			08 54			09 10		09 24
Chipstead	d	00 06		00 34		01 08	06 57		07 27				07 57		08 13		08 27			08 57			09 13		09 27
Kingswood	d	00 11		00 40		01 13	07 02		07 32				08 02		08 18		08 32			09 02			09 18		09 32
Tadworth	d	00 15		00 43		01 17	07 06		07 36				08 06		08 22		08 36			09 06			09 22		09 36
Tattenham Corner	a	00 18		00 47		01 20	07 09		07 39				08 09		08 25		08 39			09 09			09 25		09 39

Station		SN	SN	SN	SN	and at the same minutes past each hour until		SN		SN	SN	SN	SN	SN	SN	SN	SN	SN		SN	SN	SN	SN		
London Victoria 15 ⊖	d	08 43			09 13			13 13					13 43			14 13					14 43				
Clapham Junction 10	d	08 51			09 21			13 21					13 51			14 21					14 51				
London Bridge 4 ⊖	d		09 06	09 20							13 36	13 50		14 06	14 20			14 36		14 50		15 06	15 20		
New Cross Gate 4 ⊖	d		09 11								13 41			14 11				14 41				15 11			
Norwood Junction 2	d		09 30	09 33							14 00	14 03		14 30	14 33			15 00		15 03		15 30	15 33		
East Croydon	d	09 13	09 34	09 37	09 43			13 43			14 04	14 07	14 13	14 34	14 37	14 43		15 04		15 07	15 13	15 34	15 37		
South Croydon 4	d	09 15	09 36		09 45			13 45			14 06		14 15	14 36		14 45		15 06			15 15	15 36			
Purley Oaks	d	09 18	09 39		09 48			13 48			14 09		14 18	14 39		14 48		15 09			15 18	15 39			
Purley 4	a	09 21	09 42	09 45	09 51			13 51			14 12	14 15	14 22	14 42	14 45	14 52		15 12		15 15	15 21	15 42	15 45		
	d	09 22	09 43	09 46	09 52			13 52		14 02	14 13	14 16	14 22	14 43	14 46	14 52	15 02	15 13		15 16	15 22	15 43	15 46		
Kenley	d	09 25	09 46		09 55			13 55			14 16		14 25	14 46		14 55		15 16			15 25	15 46			
Whyteleafe	d	09 28	09 49		09 58			13 58			14 19		14 29	14 49		14 59		15 19			15 28	15 49			
Whyteleafe South	d	09 30	09 51		10 00			14 00			14 21		14 31	14 51		15 01		15 21			15 30	15 51			
Caterham	a	09 35	09 56		10 05			14 05			14 26		14 35	14 56		15 05		15 26			15 35	15 56			
Reedham	d			09 48						14 04		14 18			14 48		15 04			15 18			15 48		
Coulsdon Town	d			09 51						14 07		14 21			14 51		15 07			15 21			15 51		
Woodmansterne	d			09 54						14 10		14 24			14 54		15 10			15 24			15 54		
Chipstead	d			09 57						14 13		14 27			14 57		15 13			15 27			15 57		
Kingswood	d			10 02						14 18		14 32			15 02		15 18			15 32			16 02		
Tadworth	d			10 06						14 22		14 36			15 06		15 22			15 36			16 06		
Tattenham Corner	a			10 09						14 25		14 39			15 09		15 25			15 39			16 09		

Station		SN	and at the same minutes past each hour until		SN	SN		SN	SN	SN	SN	SN	SN	SN	SN	SN		SN	SN	SN	SN	SN	SN	SN	SN
London Victoria 15 ⊖	d	15 13			20 13					20 43			21 13					21 43			22 13			22 43	
Clapham Junction 10	d	15 21			20 21					20 51			21 21					21 51			22 21			22 51	
London Bridge 4 ⊖	d							20 36	20 50		21 06	21 20			21 36	21 50			22 06	22 20		22 36	22 50		23 06
New Cross Gate 4 ⊖	d							20 41			21 11				21 41				22 11			22 41			23 11
Norwood Junction 2	d							21 00	21 03		21 30	21 33			22 00	22 03			22 30	22 33		23 00	23 03		23 30
East Croydon	d	15 43			20 43			21 04	21 07	21 13	21 34	21 37	21 43		22 05	22 07		22 13	22 36	22 38	22 43	23 04	23 07	23 14	23 34
South Croydon 4	d	15 45			20 45			21 06		21 15	21 36		21 45		22 07			22 15	22 38		22 46	23 06		23 16	23 36
Purley Oaks	d	15 48			20 48			21 09		21 18	21 39		21 48		22 10			22 18	22 41		22 49	23 09		23 19	23 39
Purley 4	a	15 51			20 51			21 12	21 15	21 21	21 42	21 45	21 51		22 13	22 16		22 21	22 44	22 47	22 52	23 12	23 15	23 22	23 42
	d	15 52			20 52	21 04		21 13	21 16	21 22	21 43	21 46	21 52	22 04	22 14	22 17		22 22	22 45	22 48	22 52	23 13	23 16	23 23	23 43
Kenley	d	15 55			20 55			21 16		21 25	21 46		21 55		22 17			22 25	22 48		22 55	23 16		23 26	23 46
Whyteleafe	d	15 58			20 58			21 19		21 28	21 49		21 58		22 20			22 28	22 51		22 59	23 19		23 29	23 49
Whyteleafe South	d	16 00			21 00			21 21		21 30	21 51		22 00		22 22			22 30	22 53		23 01	23 21		23 31	23 51
Caterham	a	16 05			21 05			21 26		21 35	21 56		22 05		22 27			22 36	22 58		23 06	23 26		23 36	23 56
Reedham	d					21 06			21 18			21 48		22 06		22 19				22 50			23 18		
Coulsdon Town	d					21 09			21 21			21 51		22 09		22 22				22 53			23 21		
Woodmansterne	d					21 12			21 24			21 54		22 12		22 25				22 56			23 24		
Chipstead	d					21 15			21 27			21 57		22 15		22 28				22 59			23 27		
Kingswood	d					21 20			21 32			22 02		22 20		22 33				23 04			23 32		
Tadworth	d					21 24			21 36			22 06		22 24		22 37				23 08			23 36		
Tattenham Corner	a					21 27			21 39			22 09		22 27		22 40				23 11			23 39		

Table 181

Saturdays

London and Croydon - Caterham and Tattenham Corner

Network Diagram - see first Page of Table 177

		SN		SN	SN
London Victoria 15 ⊖	d	23 15			23 45
Clapham Junction 10	d	23 23			23 53
London Bridge 4 ⊖	d			23 36	
New Cross Gate 4 ⊖	d			23 41	
Norwood Junction 2	d			23 59	
East Croydon	d	23 44		00 04	00 14
South Croydon 4	d	23 47		00 06	00 17
Purley Oaks	d	23 50		00 09	00 20
Purley 4	a	23 53		00 13	00 23
	d	23 53		00 16	00 23
Kenley	d			00 19	
Whyteleafe	d			00 22	
Whyteleafe South	d			00 24	
Caterham	a			00 29	
Reedham	d	23 56			00 26
Coulsdon Town	d	23 58			00 28
Woodmansterne	d	00 01			00 31
Chipstead	d	00 04			00 34
Kingswood	d	00 10			00 40
Tadworth	d	00 13			00 43
Tattenham Corner	a	00 17			00 47

Sundays

		SN A	SN A	SN A	SN	SN	SN	SN	SN	SN	SN	SN		SN	SN	SN	SN	SN	SN
London Victoria 15 ⊖	d	23p15		23p45		00 16	06 36	07 06	07 36		08 06				22 36		23 06		23 50
Clapham Junction 10	d	23p23		23p53		00 24	06 42	07 12	07 42		08 12				22 42		23 12		23 56
London Bridge 4 ⊖	d		23p36		00 06					07 39		08 09		22 09		22 39		23 39	
New Cross Gate 4 ⊖	d		23p41		00 11					07 44		08 14		22 14		22 44		23 44	
Norwood Junction 2	d		23p59		00 30					08 03		08 33		22 33		23 03		00 03	
East Croydon	d	23p44	00 04	00 14	00 34	00 48	07 04	07 34	08 04	08 08	08 34	08 38		22 38	23 04	23 08	23 35	00 07	00 18
South Croydon 4	d	23p47	00 06	00 17	00 36	00 50				08 10		08 40	and at the same minutes past each hour until	22 40		23 10	23 37	00 09	00 20
Purley Oaks	d	23p50	00 09	00 20	00 39	00 53				08 13		08 43		22 43		23 13	23 40	00 12	00 23
Purley 4	a	23p53	00 13	00 23	00 42	00 56	07 10	07 40	08 10	08 16	08 40	08 46		22 46	23 10	23 16	23 43	00 15	00 26
	d	23p53	00 16	00 23	00 45	00 57	07 10	07 40	08 10	08 17	08 40	08 47		22 47	23 10	23 32	23 44	00 16	00 27
Kenley	d		00 19		00 48		07 13	07 43	08 13		08 43				23 13		23 47	00 19	00 30
Whyteleafe	d		00 22		00 51		07 17	07 47	08 17		08 47				23 17		23 50	00 22	00 33
Whyteleafe South	d		00 24		00 53		07 19	07 49	08 19		08 49				23 19		23 52	00 24	00 35
Caterham	a		00 29		00 58		07 23	07 53	08 23		08 53				23 23		23 57	00 29	00 40
Reedham	d	23p56		00 26		00 59				08 19		08 49		22 49		23 34			
Coulsdon Town	d	23p58		00 28		01 02				08 22		08 52		22 52		23 37			
Woodmansterne	d	00 01		00 31		01 05				08 25		08 55		22 55		23 40			
Chipstead	d	00 04		00 34		01 08				08 28		08 58		22 58		23 43			
Kingswood	d	00 10		00 40		01 13				08 33		09 03		23 03		23 48			
Tadworth	d	00 13		00 43		01 17				08 37		09 07		23 07		23 52			
Tattenham Corner	a	00 17		00 47		01 20				08 40		09 10		23 10		23 55			

A not 11 December

Tattenham Corner and Caterham - Croydon and London

Network Diagram - see first Page of Table 177

Miles	Miles			SN	SN	SN	SN	SN	SN	SN	SN	SN	SN		SN	SN	SN	SN	SN	SN	SN	SN	SN		
0	—	**Tattenham Corner**	d		05 56			06 32		06 48		07 02				07 18		07 32		07 48		08 04			
1¼	—	Tadworth	d		05 59			06 35		06 51		07 05				07 21		07 35		07 51		08 07			
2½	—	Kingswood	d		06 02			06 38		06 54		07 08				07 24		07 38		07 54		08 10			
5	—	Chipstead	d		06 08			06 44		07 00		07 14				07 30		07 44		08 00		08 16			
6	—	Woodmansterne	d		06 11			06 47		07 03		07 17				07 33		07 47		08 03		08 19			
6¾	—	Coulsdon Town	d		06 14			06 50		07 06		07 20			07 31	07 36		07 50		08 06		08 22			
7½	—	Reedham	d		06 16			06 52		07 08		07 22			07 34	07 38		07 52		08 08		08 24			
—	0	**Caterham**	d	05 52		06 15	06 35		06 45		07 01		07 15				07 31		07 45		08 01		08 17		
—	1¾	Whyteleafe South	d	05 55		06 18	06 38		06 48		07 04		07 18				07 34		07 48		08 04		08 20		
—	2¼	Whyteleafe	d	05 57		06 20	06 40		06 50		07 06		07 20				07 36		07 50		08 06		08 22		
—	3½	Kenley	d	06 00		06 23	06 43		06 53		07 09		07 23				07 39		07 53		08 09		08 25		
8¼	4¾	Purley 4	a	06 03	06 19	06 26	06 46	06 55	06 57	07 11	07 13	07 25	07 27		07 37	07 41	07 43	07 55	07 57	08 11	08 13	08 27	08 29		
—	—																								
—	—		d	06 04	06 22	06 27	06 47	07 01		07 17		07 31			07 39	07 47		08 01		08 17		08 33			
9¼	5¾	Purley Oaks	d	06 07	06 25	06 30	06 50	07 04		07 20		07 34			07 42	07 50		08 04		08 20		08 36			
10¼	6¾	South Croydon 4	d	06 10	06 28	06 33	06 53	07 07		07 23		07 37			07 45	07 53		08 07		08 23		08 39			
11¼	7¾	**East Croydon**	d	06 13	06 31	06 36	06 57	07 10		07 26		07 40			07 48	07 56		08 10		08 26		08 42			
—	9	Norwood Junction 2	d	06 18	06 37	06 40		07 14				07 44						08 16				08 47			
—	15	New Cross Gate 4 ⊖	a	06 35																					
—	17¾	**London Bridge 4** ⊖	a	06 44	06 49	06 52		07 28				07 58						08 28				09 01			
19	—	Clapham Junction 10	a				07 06			07 36					08 08	08 06				08 36					
21¾	—	**London Victoria 15** ⊖	a				07 15			07 46					08 19	08 15				08 45					

		SN	SN	SN	SN	SN	SN	SN	SN	SN		SN	SN	SN	SN	SN	SN	SN	SN	SN		SN	SN	SN	SN
Tattenham Corner	d	08 16		08 27			08 51			09 21			09 33		09 49			10 21		10 33			10 51		
Tadworth	d	08 19		08 30			08 54			09 24			09 36		09 52			10 24		10 36			10 54		
Kingswood	d	08 22		08 33			08 57			09 27			09 39		09 55			10 27		10 39			10 57		
Chipstead	d	08 28		08 39			09 03			09 33			09 45		10 01			10 33		10 45			11 03		
Woodmansterne	d	08 31		08 42			09 06			09 36			09 48		10 04			10 36		10 48			11 06		
Coulsdon Town	d	08 34		08 45			09 09			09 39			09 51		10 07			10 39		10 51			11 09		
Reedham	d	08 36		08 47			09 11			09 41			09 53		10 09			10 41		10 53			11 11		
Caterham	d		08 29		08 40	08 56		09 07	09 26			09 37		09 56		10 09	10 26		10 39			10 56		11 09	11 26
Whyteleafe South	d		08 32		08 43	08 59		09 10	09 29			09 40		09 59		10 12	10 29		10 42			10 59		11 12	11 29
Whyteleafe	d		08 34		08 45	09 01		09 12	09 31			09 42		10 01		10 14	10 31		10 44			11 01		11 14	11 31
Kenley	d		08 37		08 48	09 04		09 15	09 34			09 45		10 04		10 17	10 34		10 47			11 04		11 17	11 34
Purley 4	a	08 39	08 41	08 50	08 52	09 07	09 14	09 18	09 37	09 44		09 48	09 56	10 07	10 12	10 20	10 37	10 44	10 50	10 56		11 07	11 14	11 20	11 37
	d	08 45		08 56		09 08	09 14	09 21	09 38	09 45		09 51		10 08	10 15	10 21	10 38	10 45	10 51			11 08	11 15	11 21	11 38
Purley Oaks	d	08 48		08 59		09 11		09 24	09 41			09 54		10 11		10 24	10 41		10 54			11 11		11 24	11 41
South Croydon 4	d	08 51		09 02		09 14		09 27	09 44			09 57		10 14		10 27	10 44		10 57			11 14		11 27	11 44
East Croydon	d	08 54		09 05		09 17	09 20	09 30	09 47	09 51		10 00		10 17	10 21	10 30	10 47	10 51	11 00			11 17	11 21	11 30	11 47
Norwood Junction 2	d			09 09			09 25	09 35		09 55		10 05			10 25	10 35		10 55	11 05				11 25	11 35	
New Cross Gate 4 ⊖	a						09 32	09 52				10 22				10 52			11 22					11 52	
London Bridge 4 ⊖	a			09 23			09 41	10 00		10 09		10 29			10 39	10 59		11 09	11 29				11 39	11 59	
Clapham Junction 10	a	09 04				09 38			10 07					10 37			11 07					11 37			12 07
London Victoria 15 ⊖	a	09 13				09 48			10 16					10 46			11 16					11 46			12 16

		SN	SN	SN	SN	SN		SN	SN	SN	SN	SN	SN	SN	SN	SN		SN	SN	SN	SN	SN	SN	SN	SN
Tattenham Corner	d	11 21		11 33		11 51				12 21		12 33		12 51				13 21		13 33		13 51			14 21
Tadworth	d	11 24		11 36		11 54				12 24		12 36		12 54				13 24		13 36		13 54			14 24
Kingswood	d	11 27		11 39		11 57				12 27		12 39		12 57				13 27		13 39		13 57			14 27
Chipstead	d	11 33		11 45		12 03				12 33		12 45		13 03				13 33		13 45		14 03			14 33
Woodmansterne	d	11 36		11 48		12 06				12 36		12 48		13 06				13 36		13 48		14 06			14 36
Coulsdon Town	d	11 39		11 51		12 09				12 39		12 51		13 09				13 39		13 51		14 09			14 39
Reedham	d	11 41		11 53		12 11				12 41		12 53		13 11				13 41		13 53		14 11			14 41
Caterham	d		11 39		11 56			12 09	12 26		12 39		12 56		13 09	13 26			13 39		13 56		14 09	14 26	
Whyteleafe South	d		11 42		11 59			12 12	12 29		12 42		12 59		13 12	13 29			13 42		13 59		14 12	14 29	
Whyteleafe	d		11 44		12 01			12 14	12 31		12 44		13 01		13 14	13 31			13 44		14 01		14 14	14 31	
Kenley	d		11 47		12 04			12 17	12 34		12 47		13 04		13 17	13 34			13 47		14 04		14 17	14 34	
Purley 4	a	11 44	11 50	11 56	12 07	12 14		12 20	12 37	12 44	12 50	12 56	13 07	13 14	13 20	13 37		13 44	13 50	13 56	14 07	14 14	14 20	14 37	14 44
	d	11 45	11 51		12 08	12 15		12 21	12 38	12 45	12 51		13 08	13 15	13 21	13 38		13 45	13 51		14 08	14 15	14 21	14 38	14 45
Purley Oaks	d		11 54		12 11			12 24	12 41		12 54		13 11		13 24	13 41			13 54		14 11		14 24	14 41	
South Croydon 4	d		11 57		12 14			12 27	12 44		12 57		13 14		13 27	13 44			13 57		14 14		14 27	14 44	
East Croydon	d	11 51	12 00		12 17	12 21		12 30	12 47	12 51	13 00		13 17	13 21	13 30	13 47		13 51	14 00		14 17	14 21	14 30	14 47	14 51
Norwood Junction 2	d	11 55	12 05			12 25		12 35		12 55	13 05			13 25	13 35			13 55	14 05			14 25	14 35		14 55
New Cross Gate 4 ⊖	a		12 22					12 52			13 22				13 52				14 22				14 52		
London Bridge 4 ⊖	a	12 09	12 29			12 39		12 59		13 09	13 29			13 39	13 59			14 09	14 29			14 39	14 59		15 09
Clapham Junction 10	a				12 37				13 07				13 37			14 07					14 37			15 07	
London Victoria 15 ⊖	a				12 46				13 16				13 46			14 16					14 46			15 16	

		SN		SN	SN	SN	SN	SN	SN	SN	SN	SN		SN	SN	SN	SN	SN	SN	SN	SN	SN		SN	SN
Tattenham Corner	d			14 33		14 51			15 21		15 33			15 51			16 20		16 33		16 51				17 19
Tadworth	d			14 36		14 54			15 24		15 36			15 54			16 23		16 36		16 54				17 22
Kingswood	d			14 39		14 57			15 27		15 39			15 57			16 27		16 39		16 57				17 25
Chipstead	d			14 45		15 03			15 33		15 45			16 03			16 32		16 45		17 03				17 31
Woodmansterne	d			14 48		15 06			15 36		15 48			16 06			16 35		16 48		17 06				17 34
Coulsdon Town	d			14 51		15 09			15 39		15 51			16 09			16 38		16 51		17 09				17 37
Reedham	d			14 53		15 11			15 41		15 53			16 11			16 41		16 53		17 11				17 39
Caterham	d	14 39			14 56		15 09	15 24		15 39		15 56			16 09	16 26		16 39		16 52		17 09		17 26	
Whyteleafe South	d	14 42			14 59		15 12	15 27		15 42		15 59			16 12	16 29		16 42		16 55		17 12		17 29	
Whyteleafe	d	14 44			15 01		15 14	15 29		15 44		16 01			16 14	16 31		16 44		16 57		17 14		17 31	
Kenley	d	14 47			15 04		15 17	15 32		15 47		16 04			16 17	16 34		16 47		17 00		17 17		17 34	
Purley 4	a	14 50		14 56	15 07	15 14	15 20	15 35	15 44	15 50	15 56	16 07		16 14	16 20	16 37	16 44	16 50	16 56	17 04	17 14	17 20		17 37	17 42
	d	14 51			15 08	15 15	15 21	15 38	15 45	15 51		16 08		16 15	16 21	16 38	16 44	16 51	17 08		17 15	17 21		17 38	17 45
Purley Oaks	d	14 54			15 11		15 24	15 41		15 54		16 11			16 24	16 41		16 54	17 11			17 24		17 41	
South Croydon 4	d	14 57			15 14		15 27	15 44		15 57		16 14			16 27	16 44		16 57	17 14			17 27		17 44	
East Croydon	d	15 00			15 17	15 21	15 30	15 47	15 51	16 00		16 17		16 21	16 30	16 47	16 50	17 00	17 17		17 21	17 30		17 47	17 51
Norwood Junction 2	d	15 05				15 25	15 35		15 55	16 05				16 25	16 35		16 55	17 05			17 25	17 35			17 55
New Cross Gate 4 ⊖	a	15 22					15 52			16 22					16 52			17 22				17 52			
London Bridge 4 ⊖	a	15 29				15 39	15 59		16 09	16 29				16 39	17 02		17 08	17 35			17 37	17 59			18 09
Clapham Junction 10	a				15 37			16 07				16 37				17 07			17 37					18 07	
London Victoria 15 ⊖	a				15 46			16 16				16 46				17 16			17 48					18 16	

Tattenham Corner and Caterham - Croydon and London

Network Diagram - see first Page of Table 177

		SN	SN	SN	SN	SN	SN	SN		SN	SN	SN	SN	SN	SN	SN	SN	SN		SN	SN	SN	SN	SN	SN
Tattenham Corner	d			17 51		18 12		18 42			19 14		19 42	19 53		20 12		20 42			21 12		21 42		22 12
Tadworth	d			17 54		18 15		18 45			19 17		19 45	19 56		20 15		20 45			21 15		21 45		22 15
Kingswood	d			17 57		18 18		18 48			19 20		19 48	19 59		20 18		20 48			21 18		21 48		22 18
Chipstead	d			18 03		18 24		18 54			19 26		19 54	20 05		20 24		20 54			21 24		21 54		22 24
Woodmansterne	d			18 06		18 27		18 57			19 29		19 57	20 08		20 27		20 57			21 27		21 57		22 27
Coulsdon Town	d			18 09		18 30		19 00			19 32		20 00	20 11		20 30		21 00			21 30		22 00		22 30
Reedham	d			18 11		18 32		19 02			19 34		20 02	20 13		20 32		21 02			21 32		22 02		22 32
Caterham	d	17 45	17 56		18 09		18 39			19 07		19 39			20 08		20 37			21 07		21 39		22 09	
Whyteleafe South	d	17 48	17 59		18 12		18 42			19 10		19 42			20 11		20 40			21 10		21 42		22 12	
Whyteleafe	d	17 50	18 01		18 14		18 44			19 12		19 44			20 13		20 42			21 12		21 44		22 14	
Kenley	d	17 53	18 04		18 17		18 47			19 15		19 47			20 16		20 45			21 15		21 47		22 17	
Purley 4	a	17 56	18 07	18 14	18 20	18 35	18 50	19 05		19 18	19 37	19 50	20 05	20 16	20 19	20 35	20 48	21 05		21 18	21 35	21 50	22 05	22 20	22 35
	d	17 59	18 08	18 15	18 21	18 37	18 51	19 08		19 21	19 38	19 51	20 08		20 22	20 38	20 51	21 08		21 21	21 38	21 51	22 08	22 21	22 38
Purley Oaks	d	18 02	18 11		18 24	18 40	18 54	19 11		19 24	19 41	19 54	20 11		20 25	20 41	20 54	21 11		21 24	21 41	21 54	22 11	22 24	22 41
South Croydon 4	d	18 05	18 14		18 27	18 44	18 57	19 14		19 27	19 44	19 57	20 14		20 28	20 44	20 57	21 14		21 27	21 44	21 57	22 14	22 27	22 44
East Croydon	d	18 08	18 17	18 21	18 30	18 47	19 00	19 17		19 30	19 47	20 00	20 17		20 31	20 47	21 00	21 17		21 30	21 47	22 00	22 17	22 30	22 47
Norwood Junction 2	d	18 12		18 29	18 35		19 05			19 35		20 05			20 35		21 05			21 35		22 05		22 35	
New Cross Gate 4 ⊖	a				18 52		19 22			19 52		20 22			20 52		21 22			21 52		22 22		22 52	
London Bridge 4 ⊖	a	18 26		18 41	18 59		19 29			19 59		20 29			20 59		21 29			21 59		22 29		22 59	
Clapham Junction 10	a		18 39			19 08		19 37			20 07		20 37			21 07		21 37			22 07		22 37		23 07
London Victoria 15 ⊖	a		18 46			19 15		19 48			20 18		20 46			21 18		21 48			22 18		22 48		23 18

		SN	SN	SN
Tattenham Corner	d		22 42	
Tadworth	d		22 45	
Kingswood	d		22 48	
Chipstead	d		22 54	
Woodmansterne	d		22 57	
Coulsdon Town	d		23 00	
Reedham	d		23 02	
Caterham	d	22 38		23 20
Whyteleafe South	d	22 41		23 23
Whyteleafe	d	22 43		23 25
Kenley	d	22 46		23 28
Purley 4	a	22 49	23 05	23 31
	d	22 52	23 08	23 34
Purley Oaks	d	22 55	23 11	23 37
South Croydon 4	d	22 58	23 14	23 40
East Croydon	d	23 01	23 17	23 43
Norwood Junction 2	d	23 06		23a47
New Cross Gate 4 ⊖	a	23 23		
London Bridge 4 ⊖	a	23 30		
Clapham Junction 10	a		23 37	
London Victoria 15 ⊖	a		23 46	

Saturdays

		SN	SN	SN	SN	SN	SN	SN	SN	SN		SN	SN	SN	SN	SN	SN	SN	SN	SN		SN	SN	SN	
Tattenham Corner	d		06 12		06 42			07 21				07 51			08 21		08 35		08 51				09 21		
Tadworth	d		06 15		06 45			07 24				07 54			08 24		08 38		08 54				09 24		
Kingswood	d		06 18		06 48			07 27				07 57			08 27		08 41		08 57				09 27		
Chipstead	d		06 24		06 54			07 33				08 03			08 33		08 47		09 03				09 33		
Woodmansterne	d		06 27		06 57			07 36				08 06			08 36		08 50		09 06				09 36		
Coulsdon Town	d		06 30		07 00			07 39				08 09			08 39		08 53		09 09				09 39		
Reedham	d		06 32		07 02			07 41				08 11			08 41		08 55		09 11				09 41		
Caterham	d	06 07		06 39		07 09	07 26		07 39	07 56			08 09	08 26		08 39		08 56		09 09		09 26		09 39	
Whyteleafe South	d	06 10		06 42		07 12	07 29		07 42	07 59			08 12	08 29		08 42		08 59		09 12		09 29		09 42	
Whyteleafe	d	06 12		06 44		07 14	07 31		07 44	08 01			08 14	08 31		08 44		09 01		09 14		09 31		09 44	
Kenley	d	06 15		06 47		07 17	07 34		07 47	08 04			08 17	08 34		08 47		09 04		09 17		09 34		09 47	
Purley 4	a	06 18	06 35	06 50	07 05	07 20	07 37	07 44	07 50	08 07		08 14	08 20	08 37	08 44	08 50	08 58	09 07	09 14	09 20		09 37	09 44	09 50	
	d	06 21	06 38	06 51	07 08	07 21	07 38	07 45	07 51	08 08		08 15	08 21	08 38	08 45	08 51		09 08	09 15	09 21		09 38	09 45	09 51	
Purley Oaks	d	06 24	06 41	06 54	07 11	07 24	07 41		07 54	08 11			08 24	08 41		08 54		09 11		09 24		09 41		09 54	
South Croydon 4	d	06 27	06 44	06 57	07 14	07 27	07 44		07 57	08 14			08 27	08 44		08 57		09 14		09 27		09 44		09 57	
East Croydon	d	06 30	06 47	07 00	07 17	07 30	07 47	07 51	08 00	08 17		08 21	08 30	08 47	08 51	09 00		09 17	09 21	09 30		09 47	09 51	10 00	
Norwood Junction 2	d	06 35		07 05		07 35		07 55	08 05			08 25	08 35		08 55	09 05			09 25	09 35			09 55	10 05	
New Cross Gate 4 ⊖	a	06 52		07 22		07 52			08 22				08 52			09 22				09 52				10 22	
London Bridge 4 ⊖	a	06 59		07 29		07 59		08 09	08 29			08 39	08 59		09 09	09 29			09 39	09 59			10 09	10 29	
Clapham Junction 10	a		07 07		07 37		08 07			08 37				09 07				09 37				10 07			
London Victoria 15 ⊖	a		07 16		07 46		08 16			08 46				09 16				09 46				10 16			

		SN		SN	SN	SN		SN	SN	SN	SN	SN	SN	SN	SN	SN		SN	SN	SN	SN		SN
Tattenham Corner	d	09 33	and at the same minutes past each hour until	15 33		15 51				16 21		16 33		16 51				17 21		17 33		and at the same minutes past each hour until	
Tadworth	d	09 36		15 36		15 54				16 24		16 36		16 54				17 24		17 36			
Kingswood	d	09 39		15 39		15 57				16 27		16 39		16 57				17 27		17 39			
Chipstead	d	09 45		15 45		16 03				16 33		16 45		17 03				17 33		17 45			
Woodmansterne	d	09 48		15 48		16 06				16 36		16 48		17 06				17 36		17 48			
Coulsdon Town	d	09 51		15 51		16 09				16 39		16 51		17 09				17 39		17 51			
Reedham	d	09 53		15 53		16 11				16 41		16 53		17 11				17 41		17 53			
Caterham	d				15 56			16 09	16 26		16 39		16 56		17 09	17 26			17 39		17 56		21 56
Whyteleafe South	d				15 59			16 12	16 29		16 42		16 59		17 12	17 29			17 42		17 59		21 59
Whyteleafe	d				16 01			16 14	16 31		16 44		17 01		17 14	17 31			17 44		18 01		22 01
Kenley	d				16 04			16 17	16 34		16 47		17 04		17 17	17 34			17 47		18 04		22 04
Purley 4	a	09 56		15 56	16 07	16 14		16 20	16 37	16 44	16 50	16 56	17 07	17 14	17 20	17 37		17 44	17 50	17 56	18 07		22 07
	d				16 08	16 15		16 21	16 38	16 45	16 51		17 08	17 15	17 21	17 38		17 45	17 51		18 08		22 08
Purley Oaks	d				16 11			16 24	16 41		16 54		17 11		17 24	17 41			17 54		18 11		22 11
South Croydon 4	d				16 14			16 27	16 44		16 57		17 14		17 27	17 44			17 57		18 14		22 14
East Croydon	d				16 17	16 21		16 30	16 47	16 51	17 00		17 17	17 21	17 30	17 47		17 51	18 00		18 17		22 17
Norwood Junction 2	d					16 25		16 35		16 55	17 05			17 25	17 35			17 55	18 05				
New Cross Gate 4 ⊖	a							16 52			17 22				17 52				18 22				
London Bridge 4 ⊖	a					16 39		16 59		17 09	17 30			17 39	17 59			18 09	18 29				
Clapham Junction 10	a				16 37				17 07				17 38			18 07					18 37		22 37
London Victoria 15 ⊖	a				16 46				17 16				17 47			18 16					18 46		22 46

Table 181

Saturdays

Tattenham Corner and Caterham - Croydon and London

Network Diagram - see first Page of Table 177

		SN	SN		SN	SN	SN	SN	SN	SN	SN
Tattenham Corner	d	21 51				22 21		22 33		22 51	
Tadworth	d	21 54				22 24		22 36		22 54	
Kingswood	d	21 57				22 27		22 39		22 57	
Chipstead	d	22 03				22 33		22 45		23 03	
Woodmansterne	d	22 06				22 36		22 48		23 06	
Coulsdon Town	d	22 09				22 39		22 51		23 09	
Reedham	d	22 11				22 41		22 53		23 11	
Caterham	d		22 09		22 26		22 39		22 56		23 20
Whyteleafe South	d		22 12		22 29		22 42		22 59		23 23
Whyteleafe	d		22 14		22 31		22 44		23 01		23 25
Kenley	d		22 17		22 34		22 47		23 04		23 28
Purley 4	a	22 14	22 20		22 37	22 44	22 50	22 56	23 07	23 14	23 31
	d	22 15	22 21		22 38	22 45	22 52		23 08	23 15	23 34
Purley Oaks	d		22 24		22 41		22 55		23 11		23 37
South Croydon 4	d		22 27		22 44		22 58		23 14		23 40
East Croydon	d	22 21	22 30		22 47	22 51	23 01		23 17	23 21	23 43
Norwood Junction 2	d	22 25	22 35			22 55	23 06			23 25	23a47
New Cross Gate 4 ⊖	a		22 52				23 23				
London Bridge 4 ⊖	a	22 39	22 59			23 09	23 30			23 39	
Clapham Junction 10	a				23 07				23 37		
London Victoria 15 ⊖	a				23 16				23 48		

Sundays

		SN	SN	SN	SN	SN		SN	SN		SN	SN
Tattenham Corner	d			07 45		08 15	and at the same minutes past each hour until	22 15			22 45	
Tadworth	d			07 48		08 18		22 18			22 48	
Kingswood	d			07 51		08 21		22 21			22 51	
Chipstead	d			07 57		08 27		22 27			22 57	
Woodmansterne	d			08 00		08 30		22 30			23 00	
Coulsdon Town	d			08 03		08 33		22 33			23 03	
Reedham	d			08 05		08 35		22 35			23 05	
Caterham	d	07 24	07 35		08 05				22 35			23 05
Whyteleafe South	d	07 27	07 38		08 08				22 38			23 08
Whyteleafe	d	07 29	07 40		08 10				22 40			23 10
Kenley	d	07 32	07 43		08 13				22 43			23 13
Purley 4	a	07 35	07 46	08 08	08 16	08 38		22 38	22 46		23 08	23 16
	d	07 38	07 47	08 08	08 17	08 38		22 38	22 47		23 08	23 17
Purley Oaks	d	07 41		08 11		08 41		22 41			23 11	23 20
South Croydon 4	d	07 44		08 14		08 44		22 44			23 14	23 23
East Croydon	d	07 47	07 53	08 17	08 23	08 47		22 47	22 53		23 17	23a25
Norwood Junction 2	d	07 52		08 22		08 52		22 52			23a21	
New Cross Gate 4 ⊖	a	08 09		08 39		09 09		23 09				
London Bridge 4 ⊖	a	08 17		08 48		09 18		23 18				
Clapham Junction 10	a		08 12		08 42				23 12			
London Victoria 15 ⊖	a		08 20		08 50				23 20			

London - Sutton, Epsom, Guildford, Dorking and Horsham

Network Diagram - see first Page of Table 177

Miles	Miles	Miles			SN MO	SN MO	SN MX	SW MO	FC MX	SN MX	SW MX	SN MX	SW MX		SW	FC MX	SN	SN	SN	SN	SN	FC	FC	SN	SN
—	0	—	**London Victoria 15** ⊖	d	23p08	23p19	23p26			23p34		23p51									05 52			06 00	
—	—	—	**London Waterloo 15** ⊖	d				23p32			23p42		00 15		05 47										
—	2¾	—	Clapham Junction 10	d	23p16	23p27	23p34	23p41		23p42	23p51	23p59	00 25		05 56						05 58			06 08	
—	4¾	—	Balham 4 ⊖	d	23p21	23p32	23p40			23p47		00 04									06 03			06 13	
—	—	—	**London Bridge 4** ⊖	d					23p29							23p59			05 36	06 00					
—	—	6	Tulse Hill 3	d					23p41							00 09				06 18		06 02	06 22		
—	—	6	New Cross Gate 4 ⊖	d															05 42						
8¾	—	—	Norwood Junction 2	d														05 53	06 00						
10½	—	12	**West Croydon 4**	d		23p50				00 04		00 21					05 45	05 58	06 05					06 32	
11½	—	—	Waddon	d		23p52				00 06		00 24					05 47	06 00	06 08					06 34	
13	—	—	Wallington	d		23p56				00 10		00 27					05 51	06 04	06 11					06 38	
13¾	—	—	Carshalton Beeches	d		23p58				00 12		00 30					05 53	06 06	06 14					06 40	
—	8	—	Mitcham Eastfields	d	23p28		23p46														06 12		06 29		
—	9	—	Mitcham Junction	d	23p31		23p49														06 15		06 32		
—	9¾	—	Hackbridge	d	23p34		23p53														06 19		06 35		
—	10¾	—	Carshalton	d	23p37		23p55														06 21		06 38		
14¾	12	0	**Sutton (Surrey) 4**	a	23p40	00 02	23p59		00 15	00 16		00 33				00 43	05 57	06 10	06 17		06 25	06 33	06 43	06 44	
—	—	—		d	23p41	00 04	00 01											06 11			06 25			06 48	06 39
—	13	—	Belmont	d														06 14						06 51	
—	14½	—	Banstead	d														06 18						06 55	
—	16	—	**Epsom Downs**	a														06 21						06 58	
15¾	—	—	Cheam	d	23p43	00 06	00 03														06 28				06 41
17¼	—	—	Ewell East	d	23p47	00 10	00 07														06 31				06 45
18¾	—	—	**Epsom 3**	a	23p51	00 14	00 11	00 06			00 15		00 50		06 20						06 35				06 49
—	—	—		d	23p51		00 11				00 19				06 21						06 36				06 50
20½	—	—	Ashtead	d	23p55		00 15				00 23				06 25						06 40				
22½	—	0	Leatherhead	d	23p58		00 18				00 26				06 28						06 43				06 56
25	—	—	Bookham	d							00 31				06 33										07 01
26¾	—	—	Effingham Junction 6	d							00 36				06 37										07 05
35	—	—	**Guildford**	a							00 53				06 50										07 17
—	—	3¼	Box Hill & Westhumble	d	00 03		00 23														06 48				
—	—	4	**Dorking 4**	a	00 06		00 26														06 50				
—	—	—		d			00 26														06 51				
—	—	9	Holmwood	d			00s33														06 58				
—	—	11¼	Ockley	d			00s37														07 02				
—	—	15¾	Warnham	d			00s43														07 08				
—	—	17¾	**Horsham 4**	a			00 47														07 12				

		SN	SN	SN	SW	FC	SN	SN	SW	SN	SW	FC	FC	SN	SN	SW	SN	SN	SW	FC 1	FC 1	SN	SN	SW	SN
London Victoria 15 ⊖	d	06 07	06 17				06 30	06 36						07 00	07 06		07 15					07 30	07 36		07 47
London Waterloo 15 ⊖	d				06 24				06 39		06 54					07 09			07 24					07 39	
Clapham Junction 10	d	06 15	06 24		06 33		06 38	06 44	06 48		07 03			07 08	07 14	07 18	07 21		07 33			07 38	07 44	07 48	07 55
Balham 4 ⊖	d	06 20	06 30				06 44	06 49						07 13	07 20		07 26					07 44	07 50		08 00
London Bridge 4 ⊖	d			06 30						06 58								07 29							
Tulse Hill 3	d			06 48		06 42				07 16		07 02	07 20					07 47		07 31	07 45				
New Cross Gate 4 ⊖	d																								
Norwood Junction 2	d	06 39						07 09							07 39								08 09		
West Croydon 4	d	06 46					07 03	07 14						07 32	07 46							08 04	08 15		
Waddon	d	06 48					07 05	07 16						07 35	07 48							08 06	08 17		
Wallington	d	06 52					07 09	07 20						07 38	07 52							08 10	08 21		
Carshalton Beeches	d	06 54					07 11	07 22						07 41	07 54							08 12	08 23		
Mitcham Eastfields	d		06 38			06 49							07 27								07 52				08 07
Mitcham Junction	d		06 41			06 52							07 30				07 34				07 55				08 10
Hackbridge	d		06 45			06 55							07 33				07 37				07 58				08 13
Carshalton	d		06 47			06 58							07 36				07 40				08 01				08 16
Sutton (Surrey) 4	a	06 58	06 51			07 03	07 15	07 26				07 35	07 39	07 44	07 58		07 43			08 07	08 04	08 16	08 27		08 19
	d	07 00	06 52				07 18	07 26						07 45	07 59		07 44					08 16	08 27		
Belmont	d						07 21							07 48								08 20			
Banstead	d						07 25							07 52								08 23			
Epsom Downs	a						07 28							07 55								08 27			
Cheam	d	07 02	06 54					07 29							08 01		07 46						08 30		
Ewell East	d	07 06	06 58					07 32							08 05		07 50						08 33		
Epsom 3	a	07 10	07 02		06 57			07 36	07 11		07 27				08 09	07 42	07 54		07 58				08 37	08 13	
	d		07 02		06 58			07 37	07 12		07 28						07 54		07 58				08 38	08 17	
Ashtead	d		07 06		07 02			07 41	07 16		07 32						07 58		08 02				08 42	08 21	
Leatherhead	d		07 09		07 05			07 44	07 19		07 35						08 01		08 05				08 45	08 24	
Bookham	d							07 49	07 24															08 29	
Effingham Junction 6	d							07 53	07a28															08 33	
Guildford	a							08 06																08 50	
Box Hill & Westhumble	d																08 06						08 50		
Dorking 4	a		07 15		07 11						07 41						08 09		08 12				08 52		
	d		07 16														08 09								
Holmwood	d		07 23														08 17								
Ockley	d		07 27														08 21								
Warnham	d		07 33														08 26								
Horsham 4	a		07 37														08 30								

London - Sutton, Epsom, Guildford, Dorking and Horsham

Network Diagram - see first Page of Table 177

		SN	SW	FC	SN	FC	SN	SN	SW	SN	SW	FC	SN	SN	FC ■1	SN	SN	SW	SN	SN	SW	SN	FC ■1	FC	SN
London Victoria ■15 ⊖	d	07 55					08 03	08 07		08 19				08 26		08 31	08 36		08 47	08 52		09 01			09 03
London Waterloo ■15 ⊖	d		07 54						08 09		08 24							08 39			08 54				
Clapham Junction ■10	d	08 02	08 03				08 11	08 16	08 18	08 26	08 33			08 33		08 40	08 44	08 48	08 54	09 00	09 03	09 08			09 11
Balham ■4 ⊖	d						08 16	08 21		08 31				08 38		08 46	08 50		09 00	09 05					09 16
London Bridge ■4 ⊖	d				08 06								08 24												
Tulse Hill ■3	d			08 05	08 25	08 21						08 40	08 47		08 50								09 01	09 16	
New Cross Gate ■4 ⊖	d																								
Norwood Junction ■2	d							08 39									09 09								
West Croydon ■4	d						08 36	08 45						08 56		09 06	09 14			09 24					09 34
Waddon	d						08 39	08 47						08 58		09 08	09 16			09 26					09 36
Wallington	d						08 42	08 51						09 02		09 12	09 20			09 30					09 40
Carshalton Beeches	d						08 45	08 53						09 04		09 14	09 22			09 32					09 42
Mitcham Eastfields	d					08 28				08 37					08 58				09 06					09 24	
Mitcham Junction	d					08 31				08 40					09 01				09 09					09 27	
Hackbridge	d					08 34				08 44					09 04				09 13					09 30	
Carshalton	d					08 37				08 46					09 07				09 15					09 33	
Sutton (Surrey) ■4	a	08 22		08 37		08 40	08 48	08 57		08 50		09 12	09 02	09 08	09 10	09 18	09 26		09 19	09 39		09 28	09 37	09 36	09 46
	d	08 23					08 53			08 50			09 02			09 19			09 19	09 40		09 29			
Belmont	d						08 56									09 22									
Banstead	d						09 00									09 26									
Epsom Downs	a						09 03									09 29									
Cheam	d	08 25								08 53			09 05						09 22	09 42		09 31			
Ewell East	d	08 29								08 56			09 08						09 25	09 46					
Epsom ■3	a	08 33	08 27						08 42	09 00	08 57		09 12					09 16	09 29	09 50	09 27	09 37			
	d	08 33	08 28						08 47	09 01	08 58							09 17			09 28	09 37			
Ashtead	d	08 37	08 32						08 51	09 05	09 02							09 21			09 32	09 41			
Leatherhead	d	08 40	08 35						08 54	09 08	09 05							09 24			09 35	09 44			
Bookham	d								08 59									09 29							
Effingham Junction ■6	d								09 03									09 33							
Guildford	a								09 20									09 50							
Box Hill & Westhumble	d									09 13												09 49			
Dorking ■4	a	08 46	08 41							09 15	09 11										09 41	09 52			
	d	08 47								09 16															
Holmwood	d									09 23															
Ockley	d									09 27															
Warnham	d									09 33															
Horsham ■4	a	09 03								09 37															

			SN	SW	SN	SN	SW	SN	FC	FC	SN		SN	SW	SN	SN	SW	SN	FC	FC	SN		SN	SW	SN
London Victoria ■15 ⊖	d		09 05		09 17	09 22		09 31			09 33		09 35		09 47	09 53		10 01			10 03		10 06		10 17
London Waterloo ■15 ⊖	d			09 09			09 24							09 39			09 54							10 09	
Clapham Junction ■10	d		09 14	09 18	09 24	09 30	09 33	09 38			09 41		09 44	09 48	09 54	10 00	10 03	10 08			10 11		10 14	10 18	10 24
Balham ■4 ⊖	d		09 20		09 30	09 35					09 46		09 50		10 00	10 05					10 16		10 20		10 30
London Bridge ■4 ⊖	d																								
Tulse Hill ■3	d								09 31	09 46									10 01	10 16					
New Cross Gate ■4 ⊖	d																								
Norwood Junction ■2	d		09 39										10 09										10 39		
West Croydon ■4	d		09 44			09 54					10 04		10 14			10 24					10 34		10 44		
Waddon	d		09 46			09 56					10 06		10 16			10 26					10 36		10 46		
Wallington	d		09 50			10 00					10 10		10 20			10 30					10 40		10 50		
Carshalton Beeches	d		09 52			10 02					10 12		10 22			10 32					10 42		10 52		
Mitcham Eastfields	d				09 36					09 54					10 06					10 24					10 36
Mitcham Junction	d				09 39					09 57					10 09					10 27					10 39
Hackbridge	d				09 43					10 00					10 13					10 30					10 43
Carshalton	d				09 45					10 03					10 15					10 33					10 45
Sutton (Surrey) ■4	a		09 56		09 49	10 06		09 58	10 05	10 06	10 16		10 26		10 19	10 39		10 28	10 35	10 36	10 46		10 56		10 49
	d				09 49	10 07		09 59							10 19	10 40		10 29							10 49
Belmont	d					10 10																			
Banstead	d					10 14																			
Epsom Downs	a					10 17																			
Cheam	d				09 52			10 01							10 22	10 42		10 31							10 52
Ewell East	d				09 55			10 05							10 25	10 46									10 55
Epsom ■3	a			09 42	09 59		09 57	10 09						10 16	10 29	10 52	10 27	10 37						10 46	10 59
	d			09 47			09 58	10 09						10 17			10 28	10 37						10 47	
Ashtead	d			09 51			10 02	10 13						10 21			10 32	10 41						10 51	
Leatherhead	d			09 54			10 05	10 16						10 24			10 35	10 44						10 54	
Bookham	d			09 59										10 29										10 59	
Effingham Junction ■6	d			10 03										10 33										11 03	
Guildford	a			10 20										10 50										11 20	
Box Hill & Westhumble	d							10 21																	
Dorking ■4	a						10 11	10 24									10 41	10 50							
	d							10 24																	
Holmwood	d							10 32																	
Ockley	d							10 36																	
Warnham	d							10 41																	
Horsham ■4	a							10 45																	

London - Sutton, Epsom, Guildford, Dorking and Horsham

Network Diagram - see first Page of Table 177

		SN	SW	SN	FC	FC	SN		SN	SW	SN	SN	SW	SN	FC	FC	SN		SN	SW	SN	SN	SW	SN	FC
London Victoria 15 ⊖	d	10 23		10 31			10 33		10 36		10 47	10 53		11 01			11 03		11 06		11 17	11 23		11 31	
London Waterloo 15 ⊖	d		10 24							10 39			10 54							11 09			11 24		
Clapham Junction 10	d	10 30	10 33	10 38			10 41		10 44	10 48	10 54	11 00	11 03	11 08			11 11		11 14	11 18	11 24	11 30	11 33	11 38	
Balham 4 ⊖	d	10 35					10 46		10 50		11 00	11 05					11 16		11 20		11 30	11 35			
London Bridge 4 ⊖	d																								
Tulse Hill 3	d				10 31	10 46									11 01	11 16									11 31
New Cross Gate 4 ⊖	d																								
Norwood Junction 2	d								11 09										11 39						
West Croydon 4	d	10 54					11 04		11 14			11 24					11 34		11 44			11 54			
Waddon	d	10 56					11 06		11 16			11 26					11 36		11 46			11 56			
Wallington	d	11 00					11 10		11 20			11 30					11 40		11 50			12 00			
Carshalton Beeches	d	11 02					11 12		11 22			11 32					11 42		11 52			12 02			
Mitcham Eastfields	d					10 54					11 06					11 24					11 36				
Mitcham Junction	d					10 57					11 09					11 27					11 39				
Hackbridge	d					11 00					11 13					11 30					11 43				
Carshalton	d					11 03					11 15					11 33					11 45				
Sutton (Surrey) 4	a	11 06		10 58	11 05	11 06	11 16		11 26		11 19	11 39		11 28	11 35	11 36	11 46		11 56		11 49	12 06		11 58	12 05
	d	11 07		10 59							11 19	11 40		11 29							11 49	12 07		11 59	
Belmont	d	11 10																				12 10			
Banstead	d	11 14																				12 14			
Epsom Downs	a	11 17																				12 17			
Cheam	d			11 01							11 22	11 42		11 31							11 52			12 01	
Ewell East	d			11 05							11 25	11 46									11 55			12 05	
Epsom 3	a		10 57	11 09						11 16	11 29	11 52	11 27	11 37						11 46	11 59		11 57	12 09	
	d		10 58	11 09						11 17			11 28	11 37						11 47			11 58	12 09	
Ashtead	d		11 02	11 13						11 21			11 32	11 41						11 51			12 02	12 13	
Leatherhead	d		11 05	11 16						11 24			11 35	11 44						11 54			12 05	12 16	
Bookham	d									11 29										11 59					
Effingham Junction 6	d									11 33										12 03					
Guildford	a									11 50										12 20					
Box Hill & Westhumble	d			11 21																				12 21	
Dorking 4	a		11 11	11 24									11 41	11 50									12 11	12 24	
	d			11 24																				12 24	
Holmwood	d			11 32																				12 32	
Ockley	d			11 36																				12 36	
Warnham	d			11 41																				12 41	
Horsham 4	a			11 45																				12 45	

		FC	SN		SN	SW	SN	SN	SW	SN	FC	FC	SN		SN	SW	SN	SN	SW	SN	FC	FC	SN		SN
London Victoria 15 ⊖	d		11 33		11 36		11 47	11 53		12 01			12 03		12 06		12 17	12 23		12 31			12 33		12 36
London Waterloo 15 ⊖	d					11 39			11 54							12 09			12 24						
Clapham Junction 10	d		11 41		11 44	11 48	11 54	12 00	12 03	12 08			12 11		12 14	12 18	12 24	12 30	12 33	12 38			12 41		12 44
Balham 4 ⊖	d		11 46		11 50		12 00	12 05					12 16		12 20		12 30	12 35					12 46		12 50
London Bridge 4 ⊖	d																								
Tulse Hill 3	d	11 46									12 01	12 16									12 31	12 46			
New Cross Gate 4 ⊖	d																								
Norwood Junction 2	d				12 09										12 39										13 09
West Croydon 4	d		12 04		12 14			12 24					12 34		12 44			12 54					13 04		13 14
Waddon	d		12 06		12 16			12 26					12 36		12 46			12 56					13 06		13 16
Wallington	d		12 10		12 20			12 30					12 40		12 50			13 00					13 10		13 20
Carshalton Beeches	d		12 12		12 22			12 32					12 42		12 52			13 02					13 12		13 22
Mitcham Eastfields	d	11 54					12 06					12 24					12 36					12 54			
Mitcham Junction	d	11 57					12 09					12 27					12 39					12 57			
Hackbridge	d	12 00					12 13					12 30					12 43					13 00			
Carshalton	d	12 03					12 15					12 33					12 45					13 03			
Sutton (Surrey) 4	a	12 06	12 16		12 26		12 19	12 39		12 28	12 35	12 36	12 46		12 56		12 49	13 06		12 58	13 05	13 06	13 16		13 26
	d						12 19	12 40		12 29							12 49	13 07		12 59					
Belmont	d																	13 10							
Banstead	d																	13 14							
Epsom Downs	a																	13 17							
Cheam	d						12 22	12 42		12 31							12 52			13 01					
Ewell East	d						12 25	12 46									12 55			13 05					
Epsom 3	a					12 16	12 29	12 52	12 27	12 37						12 46	12 59		12 57	13 09					
	d					12 17			12 28	12 37						12 47			12 58	13 09					
Ashtead	d					12 21			12 32	12 41						12 51			13 02	13 13					
Leatherhead	d					12 24			12 35	12 44						12 54			13 05	13 16					
Bookham	d					12 29										12 59									
Effingham Junction 6	d					12 33										13 03									
Guildford	a					12 50										13 20									
Box Hill & Westhumble	d																			13 21					
Dorking 4	a								12 41	12 50									13 11	13 24					
	d																			13 24					
Holmwood	d																			13 32					
Ockley	d																			13 36					
Warnham	d																			13 41					
Horsham 4	a																			13 45					

London - Sutton, Epsom, Guildford, Dorking and Horsham

Network Diagram - see first Page of Table 177

		SW	SN	SN	SW	SN	FC	FC	SN		SN	SW	SN	SN	SW	SN	FC	FC	SN		SN	SW	SN	SN	SW
London Victoria 15 ⊖	d		12 47	12 53		13 01			13 03		13 06		13 17	13 23		13 31			13 33		13 36		13 47	13 53	
London Waterloo 15 ⊖	d	12 39			12 54							13 09			13 24							13 39			13 54
Clapham Junction 10	d	12 48	12 54	13 00	13 03	13 08			13 11		13 14	13 18	13 24	13 30	13 33	13 38			13 41		13 44	13 48	13 54	14 00	14 03
Balham 4 ⊖	d		13 00	13 05					13 16		13 20		13 30	13 35					13 46		13 50		14 00	14 05	
London Bridge 4 ⊖	d																								
Tulse Hill 3	d						13 01	13 16									13 31	13 46							
New Cross Gate 4 ⊖	d																								
Norwood Junction 2	d										13 39										14 09				
West Croydon 4	d			13 24					13 34		13 44			13 54					14 04		14 14			14 24	
Waddon	d			13 26					13 36		13 46			13 56					14 06		14 16			14 26	
Wallington	d			13 30					13 40		13 50			14 00					14 10		14 20			14 30	
Carshalton Beeches	d			13 32					13 42		13 52			14 02					14 12		14 22			14 32	
Mitcham Eastfields	d		13 06					13 24					13 36					13 54					14 06		
Mitcham Junction	d		13 09					13 27					13 39					13 57					14 09		
Hackbridge	d		13 13					13 30					13 43					14 00					14 13		
Carshalton	d		13 15					13 33					13 45					14 03					14 15		
Sutton (Surrey) 4	a		13 19	13 39		13 28	13 35	13 36	13 46		13 56		13 49	14 06		13 58	14 05	14 06	14 16		14 26		14 19	14 39	
	d		13 19	13 40		13 29							13 49	14 07		13 59							14 19	14 40	
Belmont	d													14 10											
Banstead	d													14 14											
Epsom Downs	a													14 17											
Cheam	d		13 22	13 42		13 31							13 52			14 01							14 22	14 42	
Ewell East	d		13 25	13 46									13 55			14 05							14 25	14 46	
Epsom 3	a	13 16	13 29	13 52	13 27	13 37						13 46	13 59		13 57	14 09						14 16	14 29	14 52	14 27
	d	13 17			13 28	13 37						13 47			13 58	14 09						14 17			14 28
Ashtead	d	13 21			13 32	13 41						13 51			14 02	14 13						14 21			14 32
Leatherhead	d	13 24			13 35	13 44						13 54			14 05	14 16						14 24			14 35
Bookham	d	13 29										13 59										14 29			
Effingham Junction 6	d	13 33										14 03										14 33			
Guildford	a	13 50										14 20										14 50			
Box Hill & Westhumble	d															14 21									
Dorking 4	a				13 41	13 50									14 11	14 24									14 41
	d															14 24									
Holmwood	d															14 32									
Ockley	d															14 36									
Warnham	d															14 41									
Horsham 4	a															14 45									

		SN	FC	FC	SN		SN	SW	SN	SN	SW	SN	FC	FC	SN		SN	SW	SN	SN	SW	SN	FC	FC	SN
London Victoria 15 ⊖	d	14 01			14 03		14 06		14 17	14 23		14 31			14 33		14 36		14 47	14 53		15 01			15 03
London Waterloo 15 ⊖	d							14 09			14 24							14 39			14 54				
Clapham Junction 10	d	14 08			14 11		14 14	14 18	14 24	14 30	14 33	14 38			14 41		14 44	14 48	14 54	15 00	15 03	15 08			15 11
Balham 4 ⊖	d				14 16		14 20		14 30	14 35					14 46		14 50		15 00	15 05					15 16
London Bridge 4 ⊖	d																								
Tulse Hill 3	d		14 01	14 16									14 31	14 46									15 01	15 16	
New Cross Gate 4 ⊖	d																								
Norwood Junction 2	d						14 39										15 09								
West Croydon 4	d				14 34		14 44			14 54					15 04		15 14			15 24					15 34
Waddon	d				14 36		14 46			14 56					15 06		15 16			15 26					15 36
Wallington	d				14 40		14 50			15 00					15 10		15 20			15 30					15 40
Carshalton Beeches	d				14 42		14 52			15 02					15 12		15 22			15 32					15 42
Mitcham Eastfields	d			14 24					14 36					14 54					15 06					15 24	
Mitcham Junction	d			14 27					14 39					14 57					15 09					15 27	
Hackbridge	d			14 30					14 43					15 00					15 13					15 30	
Carshalton	d			14 33					14 45					15 03					15 15					15 33	
Sutton (Surrey) 4	a	14 28	14 35	14 36	14 46		14 56		14 49	15 06		14 58	15 05	15 06	15 16		15 26		15 19	15 39		15 28	15 35	15 36	15 46
	d	14 29							14 49	15 07		14 59							15 19	15 40		15 29			
Belmont	d									15 10															
Banstead	d									15 14															
Epsom Downs	a									15 17															
Cheam	d	14 31							14 52			15 01							15 22	15 42		15 31			
Ewell East	d								14 55			15 05							15 25	15 46					
Epsom 3	a	14 37						14 46	14 59		14 57	15 09						15 16	15 29	15 52	15 27	15 37			
	d	14 37						14 47			14 58	15 09						15 17			15 28	15 37			
Ashtead	d	14 41						14 51			15 02	15 13						15 21			15 32	15 41			
Leatherhead	d	14 44						14 54			15 05	15 16						15 24			15 35	15 44			
Bookham	d							14 59										15 29							
Effingham Junction 6	d							15 03										15 33							
Guildford	a							15 20										15 50							
Box Hill & Westhumble	d											15 21													
Dorking 4	a	14 50									15 11	15 24									15 41	15 50			
	d											15 24													
Holmwood	d											15 32													
Ockley	d											15 36													
Warnham	d											15 41													
Horsham 4	a											15 45													

London - Sutton, Epsom, Guildford, Dorking and Horsham

Network Diagram - see first Page of Table 177

Station		SN	SW	SN	SN	SW	SN	FC	FC	SN	SN	SW	SN	SN	SW	SN	FC	FC	SN	SN	SW	SN
London Victoria 15 ⊖	d	15 06		15 17	15 23		15 31			15 33	15 36		15 47	15 53		16 01			16 03	16 07		16 17
London Waterloo 15 ⊖	d		15 09			15 24						15 39			15 54						16 09	
Clapham Junction 10	d	15 14	15 18	15 24	15 30	15 33	15 38			15 41	15 44	15 48	15 54	16 00	16 03	16 08			16 11	16 15	16 18	16 24
Balham 4 ⊖	d	15 20		15 30	15 35					15 46	15 50		16 00	16 05					16 16	16 20		16 30
London Bridge 4 ⊖	d																					
Tulse Hill 3	d							15 31	15 46								16 01	16 16				
New Cross Gate 4 ⊖	d																					
Norwood Junction 2	d	15 39									16 09									16 39		
West Croydon 4	d	15 44			15 54					16 04	16 14			16 24					16 34	16 44		
Waddon	d	15 46			15 56					16 06	16 16			16 26					16 36	16 46		
Wallington	d	15 50			16 00					16 10	16 20			16 30					16 40	16 50		
Carshalton Beeches	d	15 52			16 02					16 12	16 22			16 32					16 42	16 52		
Mitcham Eastfields	d			15 36					15 54				16 06					16 24				16 36
Mitcham Junction	d			15 39					15 57				16 09			16 22		16 27				16 39
Hackbridge	d			15 43					16 00				16 13					16 30				16 43
Carshalton	d			15 45					16 03				16 15					16 33				16 45
Sutton (Surrey) 4	a	15 56		15 49	16 06		15 58	16 05	16 06	16 16	16 26		16 19	16 36		16 29	16 35	16 36	16 47	16 58		16 49
	d			15 49	16 07		15 59						16 19	16 37		16 30						16 49
Belmont	d				16 10									16 40								
Banstead	d				16 14									16 44								
Epsom Downs	a				16 17									16 47								
Cheam	d			15 52			16 01						16 22			16 32						16 52
Ewell East	d			15 55			16 05						16 25			16 36						16 55
Epsom 3	a		15 46	15 59		15 57	16 09					16 15	16 29		16 27	16 40					16 46	17 01
	d		15 47			15 58	16 09					16 17			16 28	16 40					16 47	17 02
Ashtead	d		15 51			16 02	16 13					16 21			16 32	16 44					16 51	17 06
Leatherhead	d		15 54			16 05	16 16					16 24			16 35	16 47					16 54	17 09
Bookham	d		15 59									16 29									16 59	
Effingham Junction 6	d		16 03									16 33									17 03	
Guildford	a		16 20									16 50									17 22	
Box Hill & Westhumble	d						16 21									16 52						17 14
Dorking 4	a					16 11	16 24								16 41	16 57						17 16
	d						16 24															17 17
Holmwood	d						16 32															17 24
Ockley	d						16 36															17 28
Warnham	d						16 41															17 34
Horsham 4	a						16 45															17 40

Station		SW	SN	FC	FC	SN	SN	SW	SN	SW	SN	FC	FC	SN	SN	SN	SW	SN	SW	SN	SN	SW	FC
London Victoria 15 ⊖	d		16 31			16 33	16 37		16 47						17 01	17 06		17 20			17 31		
London Waterloo 15 ⊖	d	16 24						16 39		16 54							17 09		17 24			17 30	
Clapham Junction 10	d	16 33	16 38			16 41	16 45	16 48	16 54	17 03					17 09	17 14	17 18	17 26	17 33		17 37	17 39	
Balham 4 ⊖	d					16 46	16 50		17 00						17 14	17 19		17 32			17 42		
London Bridge 4 ⊖	d										17 03			17 06						17 29			
Tulse Hill 3	d			16 32	16 46							17 02	17 20	17 24									17 31
New Cross Gate 4 ⊖	d																						
Norwood Junction 2	d						17 09				17 16					17 38				17 43			
West Croydon 4	d					17 04	17 14				17 22				17 33	17 44				17 48			
Waddon	d					17 06	17 16				17 24				17 35	17 46				17 51			
Wallington	d					17 10	17 20				17 28				17 39	17 50				17 54			
Carshalton Beeches	d					17 12	17 22				17 30				17 41	17 52				17 57			
Mitcham Eastfields	d		16 51		16 55				17 07				17 28	17 32				17 38			17 48		
Mitcham Junction	d		16 54		16 58				17 10				17 31	17 35				17 41			17 51		
Hackbridge	d		16 57		17 01				17 13				17 34	17 38				17 45			17 55		
Carshalton	d		17 00		17 04				17 16				17 37	17 41				17 47			17 57		
Sutton (Surrey) 4	a		17 03	17 05	17 08	17 16	17 26		17 19		17 34	17 37	17 40	17 44	17 45	17 58		17 51		18 00	18 03		18 07
	d		17 04			17 16	17 27		17 20		17 34				17 45			17 51		18 01	18 05		
Belmont	d					17 20									17 49								
Banstead	d					17 23									17 52								
Epsom Downs	a					17 28									17 58								
Cheam	d		17 06				17 29		17 22		17 37							17 54		18 03	18 07		
Ewell East	d		17 10				17 33		17 26		17 40							17 57		18 07	18 11		
Epsom 3	a	16 57	17 16				17 37	17 12	17 30	17 27	17 46						17 42	18 01	17 54	18 11	18 17	18 07	
	d	16 58					17 37	17 17	17 31	17 28							17 47	18 02	17 54	18 12			
Ashtead	d	17 02					17 41	17 21	17 35	17 32							17 51	18 06	17 58	18 16			
Leatherhead	d	17 05					17 44	17 24	17 38	17 35							17 54	18 09	18 01	18 19			
Bookham	d						17 50	17 29									17 59			18 24			
Effingham Junction 6	d						17 53	17 33									18a05			18 28			
Guildford	a						18 13	17 52												18 46			
Box Hill & Westhumble	d	17 10							17 43	17 40								18 14	18 06				
Dorking 4	a	17 14							17 45	17 44								18 16	18 11				
	d								17 46									18 19					
Holmwood	d								17 53									18 26					
Ockley	d								17 57									18 30					
Warnham	d								18 03									18 36					
Horsham 4	a								18 09									18 42					

London - Sutton, Epsom, Guildford, Dorking and Horsham

Network Diagram - see first Page of Table 177

		FC	SN		SN	SN	SW	SN	SW	SN	SN	SW	FC		FC	SN	SN	SN	SW	SN	SW	SW	SN		FC
London Victoria 15 ⊖	d				17 33	17 37		17 50			18 01					18 03		18 07		18 20					
London Waterloo 15 ⊖	d						17 39		17 54			18 00							18 09		18 24	18 30			
Clapham Junction 10	d				17 41	17 45	17 48	17 56	18 03		18 08	18 09				18 11		18 15	18 18	18 26	18 33	18 39			
Balham 4 ⊖	d				17 46	17 50		18 02			18 12					18 16		18 20		18 32					
London Bridge 4 ⊖	d		17 37							18 02							18 08						18 32		
Tulse Hill 3	d	17 48	17 55										18 02		18 22		18 27								18 32
New Cross Gate 4 ⊖	d																								
Norwood Junction 2	d					18 09				18 16								18 39					18 46		
West Croydon 4	d				18 04	18 15				18 21						18 35		18 45					18 51		
Waddon	d				18 06	18 17				18 23						18 37		18 47					18 53		
Wallington	d				18 10	18 21				18 27						18 41		18 51					18 57		
Carshalton Beeches	d				18 12	18 23				18 29						18 43		18 53					18 59		
Mitcham Eastfields	d	17 55	18 02					18 08			18 19				18 29		18 34			18 38					
Mitcham Junction	d	17 58	18 05					18 11			18 22				18 32		18 37			18 41					
Hackbridge	d	18 02	18 09					18 15			18 25				18 36		18 41			18 45					
Carshalton	d	18 04	18 11					18 17			18 28				18 38		18 43			18 47					
Sutton (Surrey) 4	a	18 08	18 15		18 18	18 29		18 21		18 33	18 36		18 37		18 42	18 47	18 47	18 58		18 51			19 03		19 07
	d				18 19			18 21		18 33	18 36					18 48				18 51			19 03		
Belmont	d				18 22											18 51									
Banstead	d				18 26											18 55									
Epsom Downs	a				18 31											19 00									
Cheam	d							18 24		18 36	18 39									18 54			19 06		
Ewell East	d							18 27		18 39	18 42									18 57			19 09		
Epsom 3	a						18 15	18 31	18 24	18 43	18 48	18 35							18 46	19 01	18 54	19 07	19 13		
	d						18 17	18 34	18 24	18 44									18 47	19 02	18 54		19 14		
Ashtead	d						18 21	18 38	18 28	18 48									18 51	19 06	18 58		19 18		
Leatherhead	d						18 24	18 41	18 31	18 51									18 54	19 09	19 01		19 21		
Bookham	d						18 29												18 59						
Effingham Junction 6	d						18a42												19 03						
Guildford	a																		19 22						
Box Hill & Westhumble	d							18 46	18 36	18 56										19 14	19 06		19 26		
Dorking 4	a							18 48	18 41	19 00										19 16	19 11		19 30		
	d							18 49												19 19					
Holmwood	d							18 56												19 26					
Ockley	d							19 00												19 30					
Warnham	d							19 06												19 36					
Horsham 4	a							19 12												19 42					

		FC	SN	SN	SN	SW	SN	SW	FC		FC	SN	SW	SN	SW	SN	SW	SN	FC		FC	SN	SN	SN	SW
London Victoria 15 ⊖	d		18 32		18 36		18 50					18 59		19 06		19 20						19 30	19 34	19 36	
London Waterloo 15 ⊖	d					18 39		18 54					19 00		19 09		19 24								19 39
Clapham Junction 10	d		18 40		18 44	18 48	18 56	19 03				19 08	19 09	19 14	19 18	19 26	19 33					19 38	19 41	19 44	19 48
Balham 4 ⊖	d		18 45		18 49		19 02					19 14		19 20		19 32						19 44	19 46	19 50	
London Bridge 4 ⊖	d			18 38														19 31							
Tulse Hill 3	d	18 52		18 56					19 09		19 16								19 31		19 46				
New Cross Gate 4 ⊖	d																								
Norwood Junction 2	d				19 09									19 39				19 44						20 09	
West Croydon 4	d		19 04		19 15							19 32		19 45				19 49				20 02		20 14	
Waddon	d		19 07		19 17							19 35		19 47				19 52				20 05		20 16	
Wallington	d		19 10		19 21							19 38		19 51				19 55				20 08		20 20	
Carshalton Beeches	d		19 13		19 23							19 41		19 53				19 58				20 11		20 22	
Mitcham Eastfields	d	18 59		19 03			19 08				19 24					19 38					19 54		19 57		
Mitcham Junction	d	19 02		19 06			19 11				19 27					19 41					19 57		20 00		
Hackbridge	d	19 06		19 10			19 15				19 30					19 45					20 00		20 03		
Carshalton	d	19 08		19 12			19 17				19 33					19 47					20 03		20 06		
Sutton (Surrey) 4	a	19 12	19 16	19 16	19 28		19 21		19 41		19 36	19 44		19 57		19 51		20 01	20 07		20 06	20 14	20 09	20 26	
	d		19 17	19 16			19 21					19 45		19 58		19 51		20 02					20 10	20 27	
Belmont	d		19 20											20 01										20 30	
Banstead	d		19 24											20 05										20 34	
Epsom Downs	a		19 29											20 08										20 37	
Cheam	d			19 19			19 24					19 47				19 54		20 04					20 12		
Ewell East	d			19 22			19 27					19 51				19 57		20 08					20 16		
Epsom 3	a			19 26		19 16	19 31	19 24				19 55	19 35		19 44	20 01	19 57	20 12					20 20		20 16
	d					19 17	19 34	19 24							19 47	20 02	19 58	20 12							20 17
Ashtead	d					19 21	19 38	19 28							19 51	20 06	20 02	20 16							20 21
Leatherhead	d					19 24	19 41	19 31							19 54	20 09	20 05	20 19							20 24
Bookham	d					19 29									19 59										20 29
Effingham Junction 6	d					19 33									20 03										20 33
Guildford	a					19 52									20 20										20 50
Box Hill & Westhumble	d						19 46	19 36								20 14	20 10								
Dorking 4	a						19 50	19 41								20 16	20 14	20 25							
	d															20 17									
Holmwood	d															20 24									
Ockley	d															20 28									
Warnham	d															20 34									
Horsham 4	a															20 38									

London - Sutton, Epsom, Guildford, Dorking and Horsham

Network Diagram - see first Page of Table 177

		SN	SW	FC	FC		SN	SN	SN	SW	SN	SW	SN	SN	FC		FC	SN	SW	SN	SW	SN	SN	FC	SN
London Victoria 15 ⊖	d	19 50					20 00	20 03	20 06		20 20		20 30	20 33				20 36		20 50		21 00	21 03		21 06
London Waterloo 15 ⊖	d		19 54							20 09		20 24							20 39		20 54				
Clapham Junction 10	d	19 56	20 03				20 08	20 11	20 14	20 18	20 26	20 33	20 38	20 41				20 44	20 48	20 56	21 03	21 08	21 11		21 14
Balham 4 ⊖	d	20 02					20 14	20 16	20 20		20 31		20 44	20 46				20 50		21 02		21 14	21 16		21 20
London Bridge 4 ⊖	d																								
Tulse Hill 3	d			20 01	20 16										20 31		20 50							21 01	
New Cross Gate 4 ⊖	d																								
Norwood Junction 2	d								20 39									21 09							21 39
West Croydon 4	d						20 32		20 44				21 02					21 14				21 32			21 44
Waddon	d						20 35		20 46				21 05					21 16				21 35			21 46
Wallington	d						20 38		20 50				21 08					21 20				21 38			21 50
Carshalton Beeches	d						20 41		20 52				21 11					21 22				21 41			21 52
Mitcham Eastfields	d	20 08			20 24			20 27			20 38			20 53			20 57			21 08			21 23		
Mitcham Junction	d	20 11			20 27			20 30			20 41			20 56			21 00			21 11			21 26		
Hackbridge	d	20 15			20 30			20 34			20 45			20 59			21 03			21 15			21 30		
Carshalton	d	20 17			20 33			20 36			20 47			21 02			21 06			21 17			21 32		
Sutton (Surrey) 4	a	20 21		20 39	20 36		20 44	20 40	20 56		20 51		21 14	21 05	21 09		21 10	21 26		21 21		21 44	21 36	21 39	21 56
	d	20 21						20 40	20 57		20 51			21 06				21 27		21 21			21 36		21 57
Belmont	d																	21 30							
Banstead	d																	21 34							
Epsom Downs	a																	21 37							
Cheam	d	20 24						20 43	20 59		20 54			21 08						21 24			21 39		21 59
Ewell East	d	20 27						20 46	21 03		20 57			21 12						21 27			21 42		22 03
Epsom 3	a	20 31	20 27					20 50	21 07	20 42	21 01	20 57		21 16					21 12	21 31	21 27		21 46		22 07
	d	20 32								20 43	21 02								21 13	21 32					
Ashtead	d	20 36								20 47	21 06								21 17	21 36					
Leatherhead	d	20 39								20 50	21 09								21 20	21 39					
Bookham	d																		21 25						
Effingham Junction 6	d																		21 29						
Guildford	a																		21 46						
Box Hill & Westhumble	d	20 44								20 55	21 14									21 44					
Dorking 4	a	20 46								20 57	21 16									21 46					
	d																								
Holmwood	d																								
Ockley	d																								
Warnham	d																								
Horsham 4	a																								

			SW	SN	SW	SN	SN	FC	SN	SW	SN		SW	SN	SN	FC	SN	SW	SN	SN	SN		FC	SN	SW
London Victoria 15 ⊖	d			21 20		21 30	21 33		21 36		21 50			22 00	22 03		22 06		22 20	22 30	22 33			22 36	
London Waterloo 15 ⊖	d		21 09		21 24					21 39			21 54					22 09							22 39
Clapham Junction 10	d		21 18	21 26	21 33	21 38	21 41		21 44	21 48	21 56		22 03	22 08	22 11		22 14	22 18	22 26	22 38	22 41			22 46	22 48
Balham 4 ⊖	d			21 31		21 44	21 46		21 50		22 02			22 14	22 16		22 20		22 32	22 44	22 46			22 52	
London Bridge 4 ⊖	d																								
Tulse Hill 3	d							21 31								22 01							22 31		
New Cross Gate 4 ⊖	d																								
Norwood Junction 2	d								22 09								22 39							23 09	
West Croydon 4	d					22 02			22 14					22 32			22 44			23 02				23 14	
Waddon	d					22 05			22 16					22 35			22 46			23 05				23 16	
Wallington	d					22 08			22 20					22 38			22 50			23 08				23 20	
Carshalton Beeches	d					22 11			22 22					22 41			22 52			23 11				23 22	
Mitcham Eastfields	d			21 38			21 53				22 08				22 23				22 38		22 53				
Mitcham Junction	d			21 41			21 56				22 11				22 26				22 41		22 56				
Hackbridge	d			21 45			21 59				22 15				22 29				22 45		22 59				
Carshalton	d			21 47			22 02				22 17				22 32				22 47		23 02				
Sutton (Surrey) 4	a			21 51		22 14	22 05	22 09	22 26		22 21			22 44	22 35	22 39	22 56		22 51	23 14	23 05		23 09	23 26	
	d			21 51			22 06		22 27		22 21				22 36		22 57		22 51		23 06			23 27	
Belmont	d								22 30															23 30	
Banstead	d								22 34															23 34	
Epsom Downs	a								22 37															23 37	
Cheam	d			21 54			22 08				22 24				22 38		22 59		22 54		23 08				
Ewell East	d			21 57			22 12				22 27				22 42		23 03		22 57		23 12				
Epsom 3	a		21 42	22 01	21 57		22 16			22 12	22 31		22 27		22 46		23 07	22 42	23 01		23 16				23 12
	d		21 43	22 02						22 13	22 32							22 43	23 02						23 13
Ashtead	d		21 47	22 06						22 17	22 36							22 47	23 06						23 17
Leatherhead	d		21 50	22 09						22 20	22 39							22 50	23 09						23 20
Bookham	d									22 25															23 25
Effingham Junction 6	d									22 29															23 29
Guildford	a									22 46															23 46
Box Hill & Westhumble	d		21 55								22 44							22 55							
Dorking 4	a		21 57	22 15							22 46							22 57	23 15						
	d																								
Holmwood	d																								
Ockley	d																								
Warnham	d																								
Horsham 4	a																								

London - Sutton, Epsom, Guildford, Dorking and Horsham

Network Diagram - see first Page of Table 177

		SN	SN	SN	FC	SN	SW	SN	FC	SN	SW	SN FX	SN FO	FC
London Victoria 15 ⊖	d	22 50	23 00	23 03		23 06		23 26		23 34		23 51	23 59	
London Waterloo 15 ⊖	d						23 09				23 42			
Clapham Junction 10	d	22 56	23 08	23 11		23 14	23 18	23 34		23 42	23 51	23 59	00 07	
Balham 4 ⊖	d	23 01	23 14	23 16		23 20		23 40		23 47		00 04	00 12	
London Bridge 4 ⊖	d				23 01				23 29					23 59
Tulse Hill 3	d				23 11				23 41					00 09
New Cross Gate 4 ⊖	d													
Norwood Junction 2	d					23 40								
West Croydon 4	d		23 32			23 45				00 04		00 21	00 31	
Waddon	d		23 35			23 47				00 06		00 24	00 33	
Wallington	d		23 38			23 51				00 10		00 27	00 37	
Carshalton Beeches	d		23 41			23 53				00 12		00 30	00 39	
Mitcham Eastfields	d	23 07		23 23				23 46						
Mitcham Junction	d	23 10		23 26				23 49						
Hackbridge	d	23 14		23 29				23 53						
Carshalton	d	23 16		23 32				23 55						
Sutton (Surrey) 4	a	23 20	23 44	23 35	23 45	23 57		23 59	00 15	00 16		00 33	00 43	00 43
	d	23 20	23 45	23 36				00 01						
Belmont	d													
Banstead	d													
Epsom Downs	a													
Cheam	d	23 23	23 47	23 38				00 03						
Ewell East	d	23 26	23 51	23 42				00 07						
Epsom 3	a	23 30	23 55	23 46			23 42	00 11			00 15			
	d	23 31					23 43	00 11			00 19			
Ashtead	d	23 35					23 47	00 15			00 23			
Leatherhead	d	23 38					23 50	00 18			00 26			
Bookham	d										00 31			
Effingham Junction 6	d										00 36			
Guildford	a										00 53			
Box Hill & Westhumble	d	23 43					23 55	00 23						
Dorking 4	a	23 45					23 57	00 26						
	d							00 26						
Holmwood	d							00s33						
Ockley	d							00s37						
Warnham	d							00s43						
Horsham 4	a							00 47						

Saturdays

		SN	FC	SN	SW	SN	SW	FC	SN	SN	SN	FC	SN	SW	FC	SN	SN	FC	FC	SN	SN	SW	SN
London Victoria 15 ⊖	d	23p26		23p34		23p59			00 20	00 34			06 23			06 47				06 53	07 06		07 17
London Waterloo 15 ⊖	d				23p42		00 15							06 39								07 09	
Clapham Junction 10	d	23p34		23p42	23p51	00 07	00 25		00 27	00 42			06 30	06 48		06 54				07 00	07 14	07 18	07 24
Balham 4 ⊖	d	23p40		23p47		00 12			00 32	00 47			06 35			07 00				07 05	07 20		07 30
London Bridge 4 ⊖	d		23p29					23p59				06 21						06 45					
Tulse Hill 3	d		23p41					00 09				06 31			06 46			07 01	07 16				
New Cross Gate 4 ⊖	d																						
Norwood Junction 2	d																07 09				07 39		
West Croydon 4	d			00 04		00 31				01 04	06 45		06 54				07 15			07 24	07 44		
Waddon	d			00 06		00 33				01 07	06 47		06 56				07 17			07 26	07 46		
Wallington	d			00 10		00 37				01 10	06 51		07 00				07 21			07 30	07 50		
Carshalton Beeches	d			00 12		00 39				01 13	06 53		07 02				07 23			07 32	07 52		
Mitcham Eastfields	d	23p46							00 38						06 54	07 06			07 24				07 36
Mitcham Junction	d	23p49							00 41						06 57	07 09			07 27				07 39
Hackbridge	d	23p53							00 45						07 00	07 13			07 30				07 43
Carshalton	d	23p55							00 47						07 03	07 15			07 33				07 45
Sutton (Surrey) 4	a	23p59	00 15	00 16		00 43		00 43	00 51	01 16	06 57	07 05	07 06		07 06	07 19	07 27	07 35	07 36	07 39	07 56		07 49
	d	00 01									06 57		07 07			07 19				07 40			07 49
Belmont	d												07 10										
Banstead	d												07 14										
Epsom Downs	a												07 17										
Cheam	d	00 03									07 00					07 22				07 42			07 52
Ewell East	d	00 07									07 03					07 25				07 46			07 55
Epsom 3	a	00 11			00 15		00 50				07 07			07 16		07 29				07 52		07 46	07 59
	d	00 11			00 19						07 08			07 17		07 30						07 47	
Ashtead	d	00 15			00 23						07 12			07 21		07 34						07 51	
Leatherhead	d	00 18			00 26						07 15			07 24		07 37						07 54	
Bookham	d				00 31									07 29								07 59	
Effingham Junction 6	d				00 36									07 33								08 03	
Guildford	a				00 53									07 50								08 20	
Box Hill & Westhumble	d	00 23														07 42							
Dorking 4	a	00 26									07 21					07 44							
	d	00 26																					
Holmwood	d	00s33																					
Ockley	d	00s37																					
Warnham	d	00s43																					
Horsham 4	a	00 47																					

Table 182

Saturdays

London - Sutton, Epsom, Guildford, Dorking and Horsham

Network Diagram - see first Page of Table 177

		SN	SW	SN	FC	FC	SN	SN	SW	SN	SN	SW	SN	FC	FC	SN	SN	SW	SN	SN	SW	SN	FC
London Victoria 15 ⊖	d	07 23		07 31			07 33	07 36		07 47	07 53		08 01			08 03	08 06		08 17	08 23		08 31	
London Waterloo 15 ⊖	d		07 24						07 39			07 54						08 09			08 24		
Clapham Junction 10	d	07 30	07 33	07 38			07 41	07 44	07 48	07 54	08 00	08 03	08 08			08 11	08 14	08 18	08 24	08 30	08 33	08 38	
Balham 4 ⊖	d	07 35					07 46	07 50		08 00	08 05					08 16	08 20		08 30	08 35			
London Bridge 4 ⊖	d				07 15									07 45									08 15
Tulse Hill 3	d				07 31	07 46								08 01	08 16								08 31
New Cross Gate 4 ⊖	d																						
Norwood Junction 2	d							08 09									08 39						
West Croydon 4	d	07 54					08 04	08 14			08 24					08 34	08 44			08 54			
Waddon	d	07 56					08 06	08 16			08 26					08 36	08 46			08 56			
Wallington	d	08 00					08 10	08 20			08 30					08 40	08 50			09 00			
Carshalton Beeches	d	08 02					08 12	08 22			08 32					08 42	08 52			09 02			
Mitcham Eastfields	d					07 54				08 06					08 24				08 36				
Mitcham Junction	d					07 57				08 09					08 27				08 39				
Hackbridge	d					08 00				08 13					08 30				08 43				
Carshalton	d					08 03				08 15					08 33				08 45				
Sutton (Surrey) 4	a	08 06		07 58	08 05	08 06	08 16	08 26		08 19	08 39		08 28	08 35	08 36	08 46	08 56		08 49	09 06		08 58	09 05
	d	08 07		07 59						08 19	08 40		08 29						08 49	09 07		08 59	
Belmont	d	08 10																		09 10			
Banstead	d	08 14																		09 14			
Epsom Downs	a	08 17																		09 17			
Cheam	d			08 01						08 22	08 42		08 31						08 52			09 01	
Ewell East	d			08 05						08 25	08 46								08 55			09 05	
Epsom 3	a		07 57	08 09					08 16	08 29	08 52	08 27	08 37					08 46	08 59		08 57	09 09	
	d		07 58	08 09					08 17			08 28	08 37					08 47			08 58	09 09	
Ashtead	d		08 02	08 13					08 21			08 32	08 41					08 51			09 02	09 13	
Leatherhead	d		08 05	08 16					08 24			08 35	08 44					08 54			09 05	09 16	
Bookham	d								08 29									08 59					
Effingham Junction 6	d								08 33									09 03					
Guildford	a								08 50									09 20					
Box Hill & Westhumble	d			08 21																		09 21	
Dorking 4	a		08 11	08 24								08 41	08 50								09 11	09 24	
	d			08 24																		09 24	
Holmwood	d			08 32																		09 32	
Ockley	d			08 36																		09 36	
Warnham	d			08 41																		09 41	
Horsham 4	a			08 45																		09 45	

		FC	SN	SN	SW	SN	SN	SW	SN	FC	FC	SN	SN	SW	SN	SN	SW	SN	FC	FC	SN	SN
London Victoria 15 ⊖	d		08 33	08 36		08 47	08 53		09 01			09 03	09 06		09 17	09 23		09 31			09 33	09 36
London Waterloo 15 ⊖	d				08 39			08 54						09 09			09 24					
Clapham Junction 10	d		08 41	08 44	08 48	08 54	09 00	09 03	09 08			09 11	09 14	09 18	09 24	09 30	09 33	09 38			09 41	09 44
Balham 4 ⊖	d		08 46	08 50		09 00	09 05					09 16	09 20		09 30	09 35					09 46	09 50
London Bridge 4 ⊖	d									08 45									09 15			
Tulse Hill 3	d	08 46								09 01	09 16								09 31	09 46		
New Cross Gate 4 ⊖	d																					
Norwood Junction 2	d			09 09									09 39									10 09
West Croydon 4	d		09 04	09 14			09 24					09 34	09 44			09 54					10 04	10 14
Waddon	d		09 06	09 16			09 26					09 36	09 46			09 56					10 06	10 16
Wallington	d		09 10	09 20			09 30					09 40	09 50			10 00					10 10	10 20
Carshalton Beeches	d		09 12	09 22			09 32					09 42	09 52			10 02					10 12	10 22
Mitcham Eastfields	d	08 54				09 06					09 24				09 36					09 54		
Mitcham Junction	d	08 57				09 09					09 27				09 39					09 57		
Hackbridge	d	09 00				09 13					09 30				09 43					10 00		
Carshalton	d	09 03				09 15					09 33				09 45					10 03		
Sutton (Surrey) 4	a	09 06	09 16	09 26		09 19	09 39		09 28	09 35	09 36	09 46	09 56		09 49	10 06		09 58	10 05	10 06	10 16	10 26
	d					09 19	09 40		09 29						09 49	10 07		09 59				
Belmont	d															10 10						
Banstead	d															10 14						
Epsom Downs	a															10 17						
Cheam	d					09 22	09 42		09 31						09 52			10 01				
Ewell East	d					09 25	09 46								09 55			10 05				
Epsom 3	a				09 16	09 29	09 52	09 27	09 37					09 46	09 59		09 57	10 09				
	d				09 17			09 28	09 37					09 47			09 58	10 09				
Ashtead	d				09 21			09 32	09 41					09 51			10 02	10 13				
Leatherhead	d				09 24			09 35	09 44					09 54			10 05	10 16				
Bookham	d				09 29									09 59								
Effingham Junction 6	d				09 33									10 03								
Guildford	a				09 50									10 20								
Box Hill & Westhumble	d																	10 21				
Dorking 4	a							09 41	09 50								10 11	10 24				
	d																	10 24				
Holmwood	d																	10 32				
Ockley	d																	10 36				
Warnham	d																	10 41				
Horsham 4	a																	10 45				

London - Sutton, Epsom, Guildford, Dorking and Horsham

Network Diagram - see first Page of Table 177

		SW	SN	SN	SW	SN	FC	FC		SN	SN	SW	SN	SN	SW	SN	FC	FC		SN	SN	SW	SN	SN	SW
London Victoria 15 ⊖	d		09 47	09 53		10 01				10 03	10 06		10 17	10 23		10 31				10 33	10 36		10 47	10 53	
London Waterloo 15 ⊖	d	09 39			09 54							10 09			10 24							10 39			10 54
Clapham Junction 10	d	09 48	09 54	10 00	10 03	10 08				10 11	10 14	10 18	10 24	10 30	10 33	10 38				10 41	10 44	10 48	10 54	11 00	11 03
Balham 4 ⊖	d		10 00	10 05						10 16	10 20		10 30	10 35						10 46	10 50		11 00	11 05	
London Bridge 4 ⊖	d						09 45										10 15								
Tulse Hill 3	d						10 01	10 16									10 31	10 46							
New Cross Gate 4 ⊖	d																								
Norwood Junction 2	d										10 39										11 09				
West Croydon 4	d			10 24						10 34	10 44			10 54						11 04	11 14			11 24	
Waddon	d			10 26						10 36	10 46			10 56						11 06	11 16			11 26	
Wallington	d			10 30						10 40	10 50			11 00						11 10	11 20			11 30	
Carshalton Beeches	d			10 32						10 42	10 52			11 02						11 12	11 22			11 32	
Mitcham Eastfields	d		10 06					10 24					10 36					10 54					11 06		
Mitcham Junction	d		10 09					10 27					10 39					10 57					11 09		
Hackbridge	d		10 13					10 30					10 43					11 00					11 13		
Carshalton	d		10 15					10 33					10 45					11 03					11 15		
Sutton (Surrey) 4	a		10 19	10 39		10 28	10 35	10 36		10 46	10 56		10 49	11 06		10 58	11 05	11 06		11 16	11 26		11 19	11 39	
	d		10 19	10 40		10 29							10 49	11 07		10 59							11 19	11 40	
Belmont	d													11 10											
Banstead	d													11 14											
Epsom Downs	a													11 17											
Cheam	d		10 22	10 42		10 31							10 52			11 01							11 22	11 42	
Ewell East	d		10 25	10 46									10 55			11 05							11 25	11 46	
Epsom 3	a	10 16	10 29	10 52	10 27	10 37						10 46	10 59		10 57	11 09						11 16	11 29	11 52	11 27
	d	10 17			10 28	10 37						10 47			10 58	11 09						11 17			11 28
Ashtead	d	10 21			10 32	10 41						10 51			11 02	11 13						11 21			11 32
Leatherhead	d	10 24			10 35	10 44						10 54			11 05	11 16						11 24			11 35
Bookham	d	10 29										10 59										11 29			
Effingham Junction 6	d	10 33										11 03										11 33			
Guildford	a	10 50										11 20										11 50			
Box Hill & Westhumble	d															11 21									
Dorking 4	a				10 41	10 50									11 11	11 24									11 41
	d															11 24									
Holmwood	d															11 32									
Ockley	d															11 36									
Warnham	d															11 41									
Horsham 4	a															11 45									

		SN	FC	FC		SN	SN	SW	SN	SN	SW	SN	FC	FC		SN	SN	SW	SN	SN	SW	SN	FC	FC	
London Victoria 15 ⊖	d	11 01				11 03	11 06		11 17	11 23		11 31				11 33	11 36		11 47	11 53		12 01			
London Waterloo 15 ⊖	d							11 09			11 24							11 39			11 54				
Clapham Junction 10	d	11 08				11 11	11 14	11 18	11 24	11 30	11 33	11 38				11 41	11 44	11 48	11 54	12 00	12 03	12 08			
Balham 4 ⊖	d					11 16	11 20		11 30	11 35						11 46	11 50		12 00	12 05					
London Bridge 4 ⊖	d		10 45										11 15										11 45		
Tulse Hill 3	d		11 01	11 16									11 31	11 46									12 01	12 16	
New Cross Gate 4 ⊖	d																								
Norwood Junction 2	d						11 39										12 09								
West Croydon 4	d					11 34	11 44			11 54						12 04	12 14			12 24					
Waddon	d					11 36	11 46			11 56						12 06	12 16			12 26					
Wallington	d					11 40	11 50			12 00						12 10	12 20			12 30					
Carshalton Beeches	d					11 42	11 52			12 02						12 12	12 22			12 32					
Mitcham Eastfields	d			11 24					11 36					11 54					12 06					12 24	
Mitcham Junction	d			11 27					11 39					11 57					12 09					12 27	
Hackbridge	d			11 30					11 43					12 00					12 13					12 30	
Carshalton	d			11 33					11 45					12 03					12 15					12 33	
Sutton (Surrey) 4	a	11 28	11 35	11 36		11 46	11 56		11 49	12 06		11 58	12 05	12 06		12 16	12 26		12 19	12 39		12 28	12 35	12 36	
	d	11 29							11 49	12 07		11 59							12 19	12 40		12 29			
Belmont	d									12 10															
Banstead	d									12 14															
Epsom Downs	a									12 17															
Cheam	d	11 31							11 52			12 01							12 22	12 42		12 31			
Ewell East	d								11 55			12 05							12 25	12 46					
Epsom 3	a	11 37						11 46	11 59		11 57	12 09						12 16	12 29	12 52	12 27	12 37			
	d	11 37						11 47			11 58	12 09						12 17			12 28	12 37			
Ashtead	d	11 41						11 51			12 02	12 13						12 21			12 32	12 41			
Leatherhead	d	11 44						11 54			12 05	12 16						12 24			12 35	12 44			
Bookham	d							11 59										12 29							
Effingham Junction 6	d							12 03										12 33							
Guildford	a							12 20										12 50							
Box Hill & Westhumble	d											12 21													
Dorking 4	a	11 50									12 11	12 24									12 41	12 50			
	d											12 24													
Holmwood	d											12 32													
Ockley	d											12 36													
Warnham	d											12 41													
Horsham 4	a											12 45													

Table 182

Saturdays

London - Sutton, Epsom, Guildford, Dorking and Horsham

Network Diagram - see first Page of Table 177

Station		SN	SN	SW	SN	SN	SW	SN	FC	FC		SN	SN	SW	SN	SN	SW	SN	FC	FC		SN	SN	SW	SN
London Victoria 15 ⊖	d	12 03	12 06		12 17	12 23		12 31				12 33	12 36		12 47	12 53		13 01				13 03	13 06		13 17
London Waterloo 15 ⊖	d			12 09			12 24							12 39			12 54							13 09	
Clapham Junction 10	d	12 11	12 14	12 18	12 24	12 30	12 33	12 38				12 41	12 44	12 48	12 54	13 00	13 03	13 08				13 11	13 14	13 18	13 24
Balham 4 ⊖	d	12 16	12 20		12 30	12 35						12 46	12 50		13 00	13 05						13 16	13 20		13 30
London Bridge 4 ⊖	d								12 15										12 45						
Tulse Hill 3	d								12 31	12 46									13 01	13 16					
New Cross Gate 4 ⊖	d																								
Norwood Junction 2	d		12 39										13 09										13 39		
West Croydon 4	d	12 34	12 44			12 54						13 04	13 14			13 24						13 34	13 44		
Waddon	d	12 36	12 46			12 56						13 06	13 16			13 26						13 36	13 46		
Wallington	d	12 40	12 50			13 00						13 10	13 20			13 30						13 40	13 50		
Carshalton Beeches	d	12 42	12 52			13 02						13 12	13 22			13 32						13 42	13 52		
Mitcham Eastfields	d				12 36					12 54					13 06					13 24					13 36
Mitcham Junction	d				12 39					12 57					13 09					13 27					13 39
Hackbridge	d				12 43					13 00					13 13					13 30					13 43
Carshalton	d				12 45					13 03					13 15					13 33					13 45
Sutton (Surrey) 4	a	12 46	12 56		12 49	13 06		12 58	13 05	13 06		13 16	13 26		13 19	13 39		13 28	13 35	13 36		13 46	13 56		13 49
	d				12 49	13 07		12 59							13 19	13 40		13 29							13 49
Belmont	d					13 10																			
Banstead	d					13 14																			
Epsom Downs	a					13 17																			
Cheam	d				12 52			13 01							13 22	13 42		13 31							13 52
Ewell East	d				12 55			13 05							13 25	13 46									13 55
Epsom 3	a			12 46	12 59		12 57	13 09						13 16	13 29	13 52	13 27	13 37						13 46	13 59
	d			12 47			12 58	13 09						13 17			13 28	13 37						13 47	
Ashtead	d			12 51			13 02	13 13						13 21			13 32	13 41						13 51	
Leatherhead	d			12 54			13 05	13 16						13 24			13 35	13 44						13 54	
Bookham	d			12 59										13 29										13 59	
Effingham Junction 6	d			13 03										13 33										14 03	
Guildford	a			13 20										13 50										14 20	
Box Hill & Westhumble	d							13 21																	
Dorking 4	a						13 11	13 24									13 41	13 50							
	d							13 24																	
Holmwood	d							13 32																	
Ockley	d							13 36																	
Warnham	d							13 41																	
Horsham 4	a							13 45																	

Station		SN	SW	SN	FC	FC		SN	SN	SW	SN	SN	SW	SN	FC	FC		SN	SN	SW	SN	SN	SW	SN	FC
London Victoria 15 ⊖	d	13 23		13 31				13 33	13 36		13 47	13 53		14 01				14 03	14 06		14 17	14 23		14 31	
London Waterloo 15 ⊖	d		13 24							13 39			13 54							14 09			14 24		
Clapham Junction 10	d	13 30	13 33	13 38				13 41	13 44	13 48	13 54	14 00	14 03	14 08				14 11	14 14	14 18	14 24	14 30	14 33	14 38	
Balham 4 ⊖	d	13 35						13 46	13 50		14 00	14 05						14 16	14 20		14 30	14 35			
London Bridge 4 ⊖	d				13 15										13 45										14 15
Tulse Hill 3	d				13 31	13 46									14 01	14 16									14 31
New Cross Gate 4 ⊖	d																								
Norwood Junction 2	d								14 09										14 39						
West Croydon 4	d	13 54						14 04	14 14			14 24						14 34	14 44			14 54			
Waddon	d	13 56						14 06	14 16			14 26						14 36	14 46			14 56			
Wallington	d	14 00						14 10	14 20			14 30						14 40	14 50			15 00			
Carshalton Beeches	d	14 02						14 12	14 22			14 32						14 42	14 52			15 02			
Mitcham Eastfields	d					13 54					14 06					14 24					14 36				
Mitcham Junction	d					13 57					14 09					14 27					14 39				
Hackbridge	d					14 00					14 13					14 30					14 43				
Carshalton	d					14 03					14 15					14 33					14 45				
Sutton (Surrey) 4	a	14 06		13 58	14 05	14 06		14 16	14 26		14 19	14 39		14 28	14 35	14 36		14 46	14 56		14 49	15 06		14 58	15 05
	d	14 07		13 59							14 19	14 40		14 29							14 49	15 07		14 59	
Belmont	d	14 10																				15 10			
Banstead	d	14 14																				15 14			
Epsom Downs	a	14 17																				15 17			
Cheam	d			14 01							14 22	14 42		14 31							14 52			15 01	
Ewell East	d			14 05							14 25	14 46									14 55			15 05	
Epsom 3	a		13 57	14 09						14 16	14 29	14 52	14 27	14 37						14 46	14 59		14 57	15 09	
	d		13 58	14 09						14 17			14 28	14 37						14 47			14 58	15 09	
Ashtead	d		14 02	14 13						14 21			14 32	14 41						14 51			15 02	15 13	
Leatherhead	d		14 05	14 16						14 24			14 35	14 44						14 54			15 05	15 16	
Bookham	d									14 29										14 59					
Effingham Junction 6	d									14 33										15 03					
Guildford	a									14 50										15 20					
Box Hill & Westhumble	d			14 21																				15 21	
Dorking 4	a		14 11	14 24									14 41	14 50									15 11	15 24	
	d			14 24																				15 24	
Holmwood	d			14 32																				15 32	
Ockley	d			14 36																				15 36	
Warnham	d			14 41																				15 41	
Horsham 4	a			14 45																				15 45	

London - Sutton, Epsom, Guildford, Dorking and Horsham

Network Diagram - see first Page of Table 177

		FC		SN	SN	SW	SN	SN	SW	SN	FC	FC		SN	SN	SW	SN	SN	SW	SN	FC	FC		SN	SN
London Victoria 15 ⊖	d			14 33	14 36		14 47	14 53		15 01				15 03	15 06		15 17	15 23		15 31				15 33	15 36
London Waterloo 15 ⊖	d					14 39			14 54							15 09			15 24						
Clapham Junction 10	d			14 41	14 44	14 48	14 54	15 00	15 03	15 08				15 11	15 14	15 18	15 24	15 30	15 33	15 38				15 41	15 44
Balham 4 ⊖	d			14 46	14 50		15 00	15 05						15 16	15 20		15 30	15 35						15 46	15 50
London Bridge 4 ⊖	d										14 45										15 15				
Tulse Hill 3	d	14 46									15 01	15 16									15 31	15 46			
New Cross Gate 4 ⊖	d																								
Norwood Junction 2	d				15 09										15 39										16 09
West Croydon 4	d			15 04	15 14			15 24						15 34	15 44			15 54						16 04	16 14
Waddon	d			15 06	15 16			15 26						15 36	15 46			15 56						16 06	16 16
Wallington	d			15 10	15 20			15 30						15 40	15 50			16 00						16 10	16 20
Carshalton Beeches	d			15 12	15 22			15 32						15 42	15 52			16 02						16 12	16 22
Mitcham Eastfields	d	14 54					15 06					15 24					15 36					15 54			
Mitcham Junction	d	14 57					15 09					15 27					15 39					15 57			
Hackbridge	d	15 00					15 13					15 30					15 43					16 00			
Carshalton	d	15 03					15 15					15 33					15 45					16 03			
Sutton (Surrey) 4	a	15 06		15 16	15 26		15 19	15 39		15 28	15 35	15 36		15 46	15 56		15 49	16 06		15 58	16 05	16 06		16 16	16 26
	d						15 19	15 40		15 29							15 49	16 07		15 59					
Belmont	d																	16 10							
Banstead	d																	16 14							
Epsom Downs	a																	16 17							
Cheam	d						15 22	15 42		15 31							15 52			16 01					
Ewell East	d						15 25	15 46									15 55			16 05					
Epsom 3	a					15 16	15 29	15 52	15 27	15 37						15 46	15 59		15 57	16 09					
	d					15 17			15 28	15 37						15 47			15 58	16 09					
Ashtead	d					15 21			15 32	15 41						15 51			16 02	16 13					
Leatherhead	d					15 24			15 35	15 44						15 54			16 05	16 16					
Bookham	d					15 29										15 59									
Effingham Junction 6	d					15 33										16 03									
Guildford	a					15 50										16 20									
Box Hill & Westhumble	d																			16 21					
Dorking 4	a								15 41	15 50									16 11	16 24					
	d																			16 24					
Holmwood	d																			16 32					
Ockley	d																			16 36					
Warnham	d																			16 41					
Horsham 4	a																			16 45					

		SW	SN	SN	SW	SN	FC	FC		SN	SN	SW	SN	SN	SW	SN	FC	FC		SN	SN	SW	SN	SN	SW
London Victoria 15 ⊖	d		15 47	15 53		16 01				16 03	16 06		16 17	16 23		16 31				16 33	16 36		16 47	16 53	
London Waterloo 15 ⊖	d	15 39			15 54							16 09			16 24							16 39			16 54
Clapham Junction 10	d	15 48	15 54	16 00	16 03	16 08				16 11	16 14	16 18	16 24	16 30	16 33	16 38				16 41	16 44	16 48	16 54	17 00	17 03
Balham 4 ⊖	d		16 00	16 05						16 16	16 20		16 30	16 35						16 46	16 50		17 00	17 05	
London Bridge 4 ⊖	d						15 45										16 15								
Tulse Hill 3	d						16 01	16 16									16 31	16 46							
New Cross Gate 4 ⊖	d																								
Norwood Junction 2	d										16 39										17 09				
West Croydon 4	d			16 24						16 34	16 44			16 54						17 04	17 14			17 24	
Waddon	d			16 26						16 36	16 46			16 56						17 06	17 16			17 26	
Wallington	d			16 30						16 40	16 50			17 00						17 10	17 20			17 30	
Carshalton Beeches	d			16 32						16 42	16 52			17 02						17 12	17 22			17 32	
Mitcham Eastfields	d		16 06					16 24					16 36					16 54					17 06		
Mitcham Junction	d		16 09					16 27					16 39					16 57					17 09		
Hackbridge	d		16 13					16 30					16 43					17 00					17 13		
Carshalton	d		16 15					16 33					16 45					17 03					17 15		
Sutton (Surrey) 4	a		16 19	16 39		16 28	16 35	16 36		16 46	16 56		16 49	17 06		16 58	17 05	17 06		17 16	17 26		17 19	17 39	
	d		16 19	16 40		16 29							16 49	17 07		16 59							17 19	17 40	
Belmont	d													17 10											
Banstead	d													17 14											
Epsom Downs	a													17 17											
Cheam	d		16 22	16 42		16 31							16 52			17 01							17 22	17 42	
Ewell East	d		16 25	16 46									16 55			17 05							17 25	17 46	
Epsom 3	a	16 16	16 29	16 52	16 27	16 37						16 46	16 59		16 57	17 09						17 16	17 29	17 52	17 27
	d	16 17			16 28	16 37						16 47			16 58	17 09						17 17			17 28
Ashtead	d	16 21			16 32	16 41						16 51			17 02	17 13						17 21			17 32
Leatherhead	d	16 24			16 35	16 44						16 54			17 05	17 16						17 24			17 35
Bookham	d	16 29										16 59										17 29			
Effingham Junction 6	d	16 33										17 03										17 33			
Guildford	a	16 50										17 20										17 50			
Box Hill & Westhumble	d															17 21									
Dorking 4	a				16 41	16 50									17 11	17 24									17 41
	d															17 24									
Holmwood	d															17 32									
Ockley	d															17 36									
Warnham	d															17 41									
Horsham 4	a															17 45									

London - Sutton, Epsom, Guildford, Dorking and Horsham

Network Diagram - see first Page of Table 177

		SN	FC	FC		SN	SN	SW	SN	SN	SW	SN	FC	FC		SN	SN	SW	SN	SN	SW	SN	FC	FC	
London Victoria 15 ⊖	d	17 01				17 03	17 06		17 17	17 23		17 31				17 33	17 36		17 47	17 53		18 01			
London Waterloo 15 ⊖	d							17 09			17 24							17 39			17 54				
Clapham Junction 10	d	17 08				17 11	17 14	17 18	17 24	17 30	17 33	17 38				17 41	17 44	17 48	17 54	18 00	18 03	18 08			
Balham 4 ⊖	d					17 16	17 20		17 30	17 35						17 46	17 50		18 00	18 05					
London Bridge 4 ⊖	d		16 45										17 15										17 45		
Tulse Hill 3	d		17 01	17 16									17 31	17 46									18 01	18 16	
New Cross Gate 4 ⊖	d																								
Norwood Junction 2	d						17 39										18 09								
West Croydon 4	d					17 34	17 44			17 54						18 04	18 14			18 24					
Waddon	d					17 36	17 46			17 56						18 06	18 16			18 26					
Wallington	d					17 40	17 50			18 00						18 10	18 20			18 30					
Carshalton Beeches	d					17 42	17 52			18 02						18 12	18 22			18 32					
Mitcham Eastfields	d			17 24					17 36					17 54					18 06					18 24	
Mitcham Junction	d			17 27					17 39					17 57					18 09					18 27	
Hackbridge	d			17 30					17 43					18 00					18 13					18 30	
Carshalton	d			17 33					17 45					18 03					18 15					18 33	
Sutton (Surrey) 4	a	17 28	17 35	17 36		17 46	17 56		17 49	18 06		17 58	18 05	18 06		18 16	18 26		18 19	18 39		18 28	18 35	18 36	
	d	17 29							17 49	18 07		17 59							18 19	18 40		18 29			
Belmont	d									18 10															
Banstead	d									18 14															
Epsom Downs	a									18 17															
Cheam	d	17 31							17 52			18 01							18 22	18 42		18 31			
Ewell East	d								17 55			18 05							18 25	18 46					
Epsom 3	a	17 37						17 46	17 59		17 57	18 09						18 16	18 29	18 52	18 27	18 37			
	d	17 37						17 47			17 58	18 09						18 17			18 28	18 37			
Ashtead	d	17 41						17 51			18 02	18 13						18 21			18 32	18 41			
Leatherhead	d	17 44						17 54			18 05	18 16						18 24			18 35	18 44			
Bookham	d							17 59										18 29							
Effingham Junction 6	d							18 03										18 33							
Guildford	a							18 20										18 50							
Box Hill & Westhumble	d											18 21										18 49			
Dorking 4	a	17 50									18 11	18 24									18 41	18 52			
	d											18 24													
Holmwood	d											18 32													
Ockley	d											18 36													
Warnham	d											18 41													
Horsham 4	a											18 45													

		SN	SN	SW	SN	SN	SW	SN	FC	FC		SN	SN	SW	SN	SN	SW	SN	FC	FC		SN	SN	SW	SN
London Victoria 15 ⊖	d	18 03	18 06		18 17	18 23		18 31				18 33	18 36		18 47	18 53		19 01				19 03	19 06		19 17
London Waterloo 15 ⊖	d			18 09			18 24							18 39			18 54							19 09	
Clapham Junction 10	d	18 11	18 14	18 18	18 24	18 30	18 33	18 38				18 41	18 44	18 48	18 54	19 00	19 03	19 08				19 11	19 14	19 18	19 24
Balham 4 ⊖	d	18 16	18 20		18 30	18 35						18 46	18 50		19 00	19 05						19 16	19 20		19 30
London Bridge 4 ⊖	d								18 15										18 45						
Tulse Hill 3	d								18 31	18 46									19 01	19 16					
New Cross Gate 4 ⊖	d																								
Norwood Junction 2	d		18 39										19 09										19 39		
West Croydon 4	d	18 34	18 44			18 54						19 04	19 14			19 24						19 34	19 44		
Waddon	d	18 36	18 46			18 56						19 06	19 16			19 26						19 36	19 46		
Wallington	d	18 40	18 50			19 00						19 10	19 20			19 30						19 40	19 50		
Carshalton Beeches	d	18 42	18 52			19 02						19 12	19 22			19 32						19 42	19 52		
Mitcham Eastfields	d				18 36					18 54					19 06					19 24					19 36
Mitcham Junction	d				18 39					18 57					19 09					19 27					19 39
Hackbridge	d				18 43					19 00					19 13					19 30					19 43
Carshalton	d				18 45					19 03					19 15					19 33					19 45
Sutton (Surrey) 4	a	18 46	18 56		18 49	19 06		18 58	19 05	19 06		19 16	19 26		19 19	19 39		19 28	19 39	19 36		19 46	19 56		19 49
	d				18 49	19 07		18 59							19 19	19 40		19 29							19 49
Belmont	d					19 10																			
Banstead	d					19 14																			
Epsom Downs	a					19 17																			
Cheam	d				18 52			19 01							19 22	19 42		19 31							19 52
Ewell East	d				18 55			19 05							19 25	19 46									19 55
Epsom 3	a			18 46	18 59		18 57	19 09						19 16	19 29	19 52	19 27	19 37						19 46	19 59
	d			18 47			18 58	19 09						19 17			19 28	19 37						19 47	
Ashtead	d			18 51			19 02	19 13						19 21			19 32	19 41						19 51	
Leatherhead	d			18 54			19 05	19 16						19 24			19 35	19 44						19 54	
Bookham	d			18 59										19 29										19 59	
Effingham Junction 6	d			19 03										19 33										20 03	
Guildford	a			19 20										19 50										20 20	
Box Hill & Westhumble	d																	19 49							
Dorking 4	a						19 11	19 22									19 41	19 52							
	d																								
Holmwood	d																								
Ockley	d																								
Warnham	d																								
Horsham 4	a																								

London - Sutton, Epsom, Guildford, Dorking and Horsham

Network Diagram - see first Page of Table 177

		SN	SW	SN	FC	FC		SN	SN	SW	SN	SN	SW	SN	FC	SN		SN	SW	SN	SN	SW	SN	FC	SN
London Victoria 15 ⊖	d	19 23		19 31				19 33	19 36		19 47	19 53		20 01		20 03		20 06		20 17	20 23		20 31		20 33
London Waterloo 15 ⊖	d		19 24							19 39			19 54						20 09			20 24			
Clapham Junction 10	d	19 30	19 33	19 38				19 41	19 44	19 48	19 54	20 00	20 03	20 08		20 11		20 14	20 18	20 24	20 30	20 33	20 38		20 41
Balham 4 ⊖	d	19 35						19 46	19 50		20 00	20 05				20 16		20 20		20 30	20 35				20 46
London Bridge 4 ⊖	d				19 15										19 45									20 15	
Tulse Hill 3	d				19 31	19 46									20 01									20 31	
New Cross Gate 4 ⊖	d																								
Norwood Junction 2	d								20 09									20 39							
West Croydon 4	d	19 54						20 04	20 15			20 25				20 34		20 45			20 55				21 04
Waddon	d	19 56						20 06	20 17			20 27				20 36		20 47			20 57				21 06
Wallington	d	20 00						20 10	20 21			20 31				20 40		20 51			21 01				21 10
Carshalton Beeches	d	20 02						20 12	20 23			20 33				20 42		20 53			21 03				21 12
Mitcham Eastfields	d					19 55					20 06									20 36					
Mitcham Junction	d					19 58					20 09									20 39					
Hackbridge	d					20 01					20 13									20 43					
Carshalton	d					20 04					20 15									20 45					
Sutton (Surrey) 4	a	20 06		19 58	20 05	20 07		20 16	20 27		20 19	20 39		20 28	20 37	20 46		20 57		20 49	21 07		20 58	21 05	21 16
	d	20 07		19 59							20 19	20 40		20 29						20 49	21 08		20 59		
Belmont	d	20 10																			21 11				
Banstead	d	20 14																			21 15				
Epsom Downs	a	20 17																			21 18				
Cheam	d			20 01							20 22	20 42		20 31						20 52			21 01		
Ewell East	d			20 05							20 25	20 46								20 55			21 05		
Epsom 3	a		19 57	20 09						20 16	20 29	20 52	20 27	20 37					20 46	20 59		20 57	21 09		
	d		19 58	20 09						20 17				20 37					20 47				21 09		
Ashtead	d		20 02	20 13						20 21				20 41					20 51				21 13		
Leatherhead	d		20 05	20 16						20 24				20 44					20 54				21 16		
Bookham	d									20 29															
Effingham Junction 6	d									20 33															
Guildford	a									20 50															
Box Hill & Westhumble	d													20 49											
Dorking 4	a		20 11	20 22										20 52					21 00				21 22		
	d																								
Holmwood	d																								
Ockley	d																								
Warnham	d																								
Horsham 4	a																								

		SN		SW	SN	SN	SW	SN	FC	SN	SN	SW		SN	SN	SW	SN	FC	SN	SN	SW	SN		SN	SW
London Victoria 15 ⊖	d	20 36			20 47	20 53		21 01		21 03	21 06			21 17	21 23		21 31		21 33	21 36		21 47		21 53	
London Waterloo 15 ⊖	d			20 39			20 54					21 09				21 24					21 39				21 54
Clapham Junction 10	d	20 44		20 48	20 54	21 00	21 03	21 08		21 11	21 14	21 18		21 24	21 30	21 33	21 38		21 41	21 44	21 48	21 54		22 00	22 03
Balham 4 ⊖	d	20 50			21 00	21 05				21 16	21 20			21 30	21 35				21 46	21 50		22 00		22 05	
London Bridge 4 ⊖	d								20 45									21 15							
Tulse Hill 3	d								21 01									21 31							
New Cross Gate 4 ⊖	d																								
Norwood Junction 2	d	21 09									21 39									22 09					
West Croydon 4	d	21 15				21 25				21 34	21 45				21 55				22 04	22 14				22 24	
Waddon	d	21 17				21 27				21 36	21 47				21 57				22 06	22 16				22 26	
Wallington	d	21 21				21 31				21 40	21 51				22 01				22 10	22 20				22 30	
Carshalton Beeches	d	21 23				21 33				21 42	21 53				22 03				22 12	22 22				22 32	
Mitcham Eastfields	d				21 06									21 36								22 06			
Mitcham Junction	d				21 09									21 39								22 09			
Hackbridge	d				21 13									21 43								22 13			
Carshalton	d				21 15									21 45								22 15			
Sutton (Surrey) 4	a	21 27			21 19	21 39		21 28	21 37	21 46	21 57			21 49	22 07		21 58	22 05	22 16	22 26		22 19		22 39	
	d				21 19	21 40		21 29						21 49	22 08		21 59					22 19		22 40	
Belmont	d														22 11										
Banstead	d														22 15										
Epsom Downs	a														22 18										
Cheam	d				21 22	21 42		21 31						21 52			22 01					22 22		22 42	
Ewell East	d				21 25	21 46								21 55			22 05					22 25		22 46	
Epsom 3	a			21 16	21 29	21 52	21 27	21 37				21 46		21 59		21 57	22 09				22 16	22 29		22 52	22 27
	d			21 17				21 37				21 47					22 09				22 17				
Ashtead	d			21 21				21 41				21 51					22 13				22 21				
Leatherhead	d			21 24				21 44				21 54					22 16				22 24				
Bookham	d			21 29																	22 29				
Effingham Junction 6	d			21 33																	22 33				
Guildford	a			21 50																	22 50				
Box Hill & Westhumble	d							21 49																	
Dorking 4	a							21 52				22 00					22 22								
	d																								
Holmwood	d																								
Ockley	d																								
Warnham	d																								
Horsham 4	a																								

Table 182

Saturdays

London - Sutton, Epsom, Guildford, Dorking and Horsham

Network Diagram - see first Page of Table 177

		SN	FC	SN	SN	SW	SN	SN		SN	FC	SN	SN	SW	SN	SN	SN	FC		SN	SN	SW	SN	FC	SN
London Victoria 15 ⊖	d	22 01		22 03	22 06		22 17	22 23		22 31		22 33	22 36		22 47	22 53	23 01			23 03	23 06		23 26		23 34
London Waterloo 15 ⊖	d					22 09								22 39								23 09			
Clapham Junction 10	d	22 08		22 11	22 14	22 18	22 24	22 30		22 38		22 41	22 44	22 48	22 54	23 00	23 08			23 11	23 14	23 18	23 32		23 42
Balham 4 ⊖	d			22 16	22 20		22 30	22 35				22 46	22 50		23 00	23 05				23 16	23 20		23 37		23 47
London Bridge 4 ⊖	d		21 45								22 15							22 45						23 15	
Tulse Hill 3	d		22 01								22 31							23 01						23 31	
New Cross Gate 4 ⊖	d																								
Norwood Junction 2	d				22 39								23 09								23 39				
West Croydon 4	d			22 34	22 44			22 54				23 04	23 14			23 24				23 34	23 44				00 04
Waddon	d			22 36	22 46			22 56				23 06	23 16			23 26				23 36	23 46				00 06
Wallington	d			22 40	22 50			23 00				23 10	23 20			23 30				23 40	23 50				00 10
Carshalton Beeches	d			22 42	22 52			23 02				23 12	23 22			23 32				23 42	23 52				00 12
Mitcham Eastfields	d						22 36								23 06								23 43		
Mitcham Junction	d						22 39								23 09								23 46		
Hackbridge	d						22 43								23 13								23 50		
Carshalton	d						22 45								23 15								23 52		
Sutton (Surrey) 4	a	22 28	22 39	22 46	22 56		22 49	23 06		22 58	23 05	23 16	23 26		23 19	23 39	23 28	23 35		23 46	23 56		23 59	00 05	00 16
	d	22 29					22 49	23 07		22 59			23 33		23 19	23 40	23 29						00 01		
Belmont	d							23 10					23 36												
Banstead	d							23 14					23 40												
Epsom Downs	a							23 17					23 43												
Cheam	d	22 31					22 52			23 01					23 22	23 42	23 31						00 03		
Ewell East	d						22 55			23 05					23 25	23 46							00 07		
Epsom 3	a	22 37				22 46	22 59			23 09				23 12	23 29	23 52	23 37					23 42	00 11		
	d	22 37				22 47				23 09				23 17			23 37					23 47	00 11		
Ashtead	d	22 41				22 51				23 13				23 21			23 41					23 51	00 15		
Leatherhead	d	22 44				22 54				23 16				23 24			23 44					23 54	00 18		
Bookham	d													23 29											
Effingham Junction 6	d													23 33											
Guildford	a													23 50											
Box Hill & Westhumble	d	22 49								23 21													00 23		
Dorking 4	a	22 52				23 00				23 24							23 50					00 01	00 26		
	d																								
Holmwood	d																								
Ockley	d																								
Warnham	d																								
Horsham 4	a																								

		SW	FC	SN
London Victoria 15 ⊖	d			23 59
London Waterloo 15 ⊖	d	23 42		
Clapham Junction 10	d	23 51		00 07
Balham 4 ⊖	d			00 12
London Bridge 4 ⊖	d		23 45	
Tulse Hill 3	d		00 01	
New Cross Gate 4 ⊖	d			
Norwood Junction 2	d			
West Croydon 4	d			00 31
Waddon	d			00 33
Wallington	d			00 37
Carshalton Beeches	d			00 39
Mitcham Eastfields	d			
Mitcham Junction	d			
Hackbridge	d			
Carshalton	d			
Sutton (Surrey) 4	a		00 35	00 43
	d			
Belmont	d			
Banstead	d			
Epsom Downs	a			
Cheam	d			
Ewell East	d			
Epsom 3	a	00 15		
	d	00 19		
Ashtead	d	00 23		
Leatherhead	d	00 26		
Bookham	d	00 31		
Effingham Junction 6	d	00 36		
Guildford	a	00 53		
Box Hill & Westhumble	d			
Dorking 4	a			
	d			
Holmwood	d			
Ockley	d			
Warnham	d			
Horsham 4	a			

Table 182

Sundays

London - Sutton, Epsom, Guildford, Dorking and Horsham

Network Diagram - see first Page of Table 177

		SW A	SN A	FC A	SN A	SW A	FC A	SN A	SW	SN		SN	SN	SN	SN	SN	SW	SN	SN	SW		SN	SN	SN	SN
London Victoria 15 ⊖	d		23p26		23p34			23p59		00 34		06 49	07 19	07 22	07 24	07 49		07 52	07 54			08 08	08 19	08 22	08 24
London Waterloo 15 ⊖	d	23p09				23p42			00 15											08 02					
Clapham Junction 10	d	23p18	23p32		23p42	23p51		00 07	00 25	00 42		06 57	07 26	07 29	07 32	07 56		07 59	08 02	08 11		08 16	08 26	08 29	08 32
Balham 4 ⊖	d		23p37		23p47			00 12		00 47		07 02	07 30	07 33	07 37	08 00		08 03	08 07			08 22	08 30	08 33	08 37
London Bridge 4 ⊖	d			23p15			23p45																		
Tulse Hill 3	d			23p31			00 01																		
New Cross Gate 4 ⊖	d																								
Norwood Junction 2	d														07 57				08 27						08 57
West Croydon 4	d				00 04			00 31		01 04		07 21	07 49		08 04	08 19			08 34				08 49		09 04
Waddon	d				00 06			00 33		01 07		07 23	07 51		08 06	08 21			08 36				08 51		09 06
Wallington	d				00 10			00 37		01 10		07 27	07 55		08 10	08 25			08 40				08 55		09 10
Carshalton Beeches	d				00 12			00 39		01 13		07 29	07 57		08 12	08 27			08 42				08 57		09 12
Mitcham Eastfields	d		23p43											07 40				08 10				08 28		08 40	
Mitcham Junction	d		23p46											07 43				08 13				08 31		08 43	
Hackbridge	d		23p50											07 46				08 16				08 35		08 46	
Carshalton	d		23p52											07 49				08 19				08 37		08 49	
Sutton (Surrey) 4	a		23p59	00 05	00 16		00 35	00 43		01 16		07 33	08 01	07 52	08 16	08 31		08 22	08 46			08 41	09 01	08 52	09 16
	d		00 01									07 41	08 11	07 53				08 23				08 41		08 53	
Belmont	d																								
Banstead	d																								
Epsom Downs	a																								
Cheam	d		00 03									07 43	08 13	07 55				08 25				08 44		08 55	
Ewell East	d		00 07									07 47	08 17	07 59				08 29				08 47		08 59	
Epsom 3	a	23p42	00 11			00 15			00 50			07 52	08 22	08 03				08 33		08 36		08 51		09 03	
	d	23p47	00 11			00 19						07 53	08 23				08 08			08 38		08 52			
Ashtead	d	23p51	00 15			00 23						07 57	08 27				08 12			08 42		08 56			
Leatherhead	d	23p54	00 18			00 26						08 00	08 30				08 15			08 45		08 59			
Bookham	d					00 31											08 21								
Effingham Junction 6	d					00 36											08 25								
Guildford	a					00 53											08 41								
Box Hill & Westhumble	d		00 23									08 05	08 35									09 04			
Dorking 4	a	00 01	00 26									08 07	08 37							08 51		09 06			
	d																								
Holmwood	d																								
Ockley	d																								
Warnham	d																								
Horsham 4	a																								

		SW	SN	SN	SN	SN		SW	SN	SN	SN	SN	SW	SN	FC	SN		SN	SN	SW	SN	FC	SN	SN	SN
London Victoria 15 ⊖	d		08 38	08 49	08 52	08 54			09 08	09 19	09 22	09 24		09 38		09 49		09 52	09 54		10 08		10 19	10 22	10 24
London Waterloo 15 ⊖	d	08 32						09 02					09 32							10 02					
Clapham Junction 10	d	08 41	08 46	08 56	08 59	09 02		09 11	09 16	09 26	09 29	09 32	09 41	09 46		09 56		09 59	10 02	10 11	10 16		10 26	10 29	10 32
Balham 4 ⊖	d		08 51	09 00	09 03	09 07			09 21	09 30	09 33	09 37		09 51		10 00		10 03	10 07		10 21		10 30	10 33	10 37
London Bridge 4 ⊖	d														09 32							10 02			
Tulse Hill 3	d														09 43							10 13			
New Cross Gate 4 ⊖	d																								
Norwood Junction 2	d					09 27						09 57							10 27						10 57
West Croydon 4	d			09 19		09 34				09 49		10 04				10 19			10 34				10 49		11 04
Waddon	d			09 21		09 36				09 51		10 06				10 21			10 36				10 51		11 06
Wallington	d			09 25		09 40				09 55		10 10				10 25			10 40				10 55		11 10
Carshalton Beeches	d			09 27		09 42				09 57		10 12				10 27			10 42				10 57		11 12
Mitcham Eastfields	d		08 58		09 10				09 28		09 40			09 58				10 10			10 28			10 40	
Mitcham Junction	d		09 01		09 13				09 31		09 43			10 01				10 13			10 31			10 43	
Hackbridge	d		09 04		09 16				09 34		09 46			10 04				10 16			10 34			10 46	
Carshalton	d		09 07		09 19				09 37		09 49			10 07				10 19			10 37			10 49	
Sutton (Surrey) 4	a		09 10	09 31	09 22	09 46			09 40	10 01	09 52	10 16		10 10	10 16	10 31		10 22	10 46		10 40	10 46	11 01	10 52	11 16
	d		09 11		09 23				09 41		09 53			10 11				10 23			10 41			10 53	
Belmont	d																								
Banstead	d																								
Epsom Downs	a																								
Cheam	d		09 13		09 25				09 43		09 55			10 13				10 25			10 43			10 55	
Ewell East	d		09 17		09 29				09 47		09 59			10 17				10 29			10 47			10 59	
Epsom 3	a	09 06	09 21		09 33			09 36	09 51		10 03		10 06	10 21				10 33		10 36	10 51			11 03	
	d	09 08	09 21					09 38	09 51				10 08	10 21						10 38	10 51				
Ashtead	d	09 12	09 25					09 42	09 55				10 12	10 25						10 42	10 55				
Leatherhead	d	09 15	09 28					09 45	09 58				10 15	10 28						10 45	10 58				
Bookham	d	09 21											10 21												
Effingham Junction 6	d	09 25											10 25												
Guildford	a	09 41											10 41												
Box Hill & Westhumble	d		09 33						10 03					10 33							11 03				
Dorking 4	a		09 36					09 51	10 06					10 36						10 51	11 06				
	d																								
Holmwood	d																								
Ockley	d																								
Warnham	d																								
Horsham 4	a																								

A not 11 December

Table 182

Sundays

London - Sutton, Epsom, Guildford, Dorking and Horsham

Network Diagram - see first Page of Table 177

		SW		SN	FC	SN	SN	SN	SW	SN	FC	SN		SN	SN	SW	SN	FC	SN	SN	SN	SW		SN	FC
London Victoria 15 ⊖	d			10 38		10 49	10 52	10 54		11 08		11 19		11 22	11 24		11 38		11 49	11 52	11 54			12 08	
London Waterloo 15 ⊖	d	10 32							11 02							11 32						12 02			
Clapham Junction 10	d	10 41		10 46		10 56	10 59	11 02	11 11	11 16		11 26		11 29	11 32	11 41	11 46		11 56	11 59	12 02	12 11		12 16	
Balham 4 ⊖	d			10 51		11 00	11 03	11 07		11 21		11 30		11 33	11 37		11 51		12 00	12 03	12 07			12 21	
London Bridge 4 ⊖	d				10 32						11 02							11 32							12 02
Tulse Hill 3	d				10 43						11 13							11 43							12 13
New Cross Gate 4 ⊖	d																								
Norwood Junction 2	d							11 27							11 57						12 27				
West Croydon 4	d					11 19		11 34				11 49			12 04				12 19		12 34				
Waddon	d					11 21		11 36				11 51			12 06				12 21		12 36				
Wallington	d					11 25		11 40				11 55			12 10				12 25		12 40				
Carshalton Beeches	d					11 27		11 42				11 57			12 12				12 27		12 42				
Mitcham Eastfields	d			10 58			11 10			11 28				11 40			11 58			12 10				12 28	
Mitcham Junction	d			11 01			11 13			11 31				11 43			12 01			12 13				12 31	
Hackbridge	d			11 04			11 16			11 34				11 46			12 04			12 16				12 34	
Carshalton	d			11 07			11 19			11 37				11 49			12 07			12 19				12 37	
Sutton (Surrey) 4	a			11 10	11 16	11 31	11 22	11 46		11 40	11 46	12 01		11 52	12 16		12 10	12 16	12 31	12 22	12 46			12 40	12 46
	d			11 11			11 23			11 41				11 53			12 11			12 23				12 41	
Belmont	d																								
Banstead	d																								
Epsom Downs	a																								
Cheam	d			11 13			11 25			11 43				11 55			12 13			12 25				12 43	
Ewell East	d			11 17			11 29			11 47				11 59			12 17			12 29				12 47	
Epsom 3	a	11 06		11 21			11 33		11 36	11 51				12 03		12 06	12 21			12 33		12 36		12 51	
	d	11 08		11 21					11 38	11 51						12 08	12 21					12 38		12 51	
Ashtead	d	11 12		11 25					11 42	11 55						12 12	12 25					12 42		12 55	
Leatherhead	d	11 15		11 28					11 45	11 58						12 15	12 28					12 45		12 58	
Bookham	d	11 21														12 21									
Effingham Junction 6	d	11 25														12 25									
Guildford	a	11 41														12 41									
Box Hill & Westhumble	d			11 33						12 03							12 33							13 03	
Dorking 4	a			11 36					11 51	12 06							12 36					12 51		13 06	
	d																								
Holmwood	d																								
Ockley	d																								
Warnham	d																								
Horsham 4	a																								

		SN	SN	SN	SW	SN	FC	SN		SN	SN	SW	SN	FC	SN	SN	SN	SW		SN	FC	SN	SN	SN	SW
London Victoria 15 ⊖	d	12 19	12 22	12 24		12 38		12 49		12 52	12 54		13 08		13 19	13 22	13 24			13 38		13 49	13 52	13 54	
London Waterloo 15 ⊖	d				12 32							13 02						13 32							14 02
Clapham Junction 10	d	12 26	12 29	12 32	12 41	12 46		12 56		12 59	13 02	13 11	13 16		13 26	13 29	13 32	13 41		13 46		13 56	13 59	14 02	14 11
Balham 4 ⊖	d	12 30	12 33	12 37		12 51		13 00		13 03	13 07		13 21		13 30	13 33	13 37			13 51		14 00	14 03	14 07	
London Bridge 4 ⊖	d						12 32							13 02							13 32				
Tulse Hill 3	d						12 43							13 13							13 43				
New Cross Gate 4 ⊖	d																								
Norwood Junction 2	d			12 57							13 27						13 57							14 27	
West Croydon 4	d	12 49		13 04				13 19			13 34				13 49		14 04					14 19		14 34	
Waddon	d	12 51		13 06				13 21			13 36				13 51		14 06					14 21		14 36	
Wallington	d	12 55		13 10				13 25			13 40				13 55		14 10					14 25		14 40	
Carshalton Beeches	d	12 57		13 12				13 27			13 42				13 57		14 12					14 27		14 42	
Mitcham Eastfields	d		12 40			12 58				13 10			13 28			13 40				13 58			14 10		
Mitcham Junction	d		12 43			13 01				13 13			13 31			13 43				14 01			14 13		
Hackbridge	d		12 46			13 04				13 16			13 34			13 46				14 04			14 16		
Carshalton	d		12 49			13 07				13 19			13 37			13 49				14 07			14 19		
Sutton (Surrey) 4	a	13 01	12 52	13 16		13 10	13 16	13 31		13 22	13 46		13 40	13 46	14 01	13 52	14 16			14 10	14 16	14 31	14 22	14 46	
	d		12 53			13 11				13 23			13 41			13 53				14 11			14 23		
Belmont	d																								
Banstead	d																								
Epsom Downs	a																								
Cheam	d		12 55			13 13				13 25			13 43			13 55				14 13			14 25		
Ewell East	d		12 59			13 17				13 29			13 47			13 59				14 17			14 29		
Epsom 3	a		13 05		13 06	13 21				13 33		13 36	13 51			14 03		14 06		14 21			14 33		14 36
	d				13 08	13 21						13 38	13 51					14 08		14 21					14 38
Ashtead	d				13 12	13 25						13 42	13 55					14 12		14 25					14 42
Leatherhead	d				13 15	13 28						13 45	13 58					14 15		14 28					14 45
Bookham	d				13 21													14 21							
Effingham Junction 6	d				13 25													14 25							
Guildford	a				13 41													14 41							
Box Hill & Westhumble	d					13 33							14 03							14 33					
Dorking 4	a					13 36						13 51	14 06							14 36					14 51
	d																								
Holmwood	d																								
Ockley	d																								
Warnham	d																								
Horsham 4	a																								

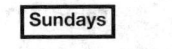

London - Sutton, Epsom, Guildford, Dorking and Horsham

Network Diagram - see first Page of Table 177

		SN	FC	SN		SN	SN	SW	SN	FC	SN	SN	SN	SW		SN	FC	SN	SN	SN	SW	SN	FC	SN	
London Victoria 15 ⊖	d	14 08		14 19		14 22	14 24		14 38		14 49	14 52	14 54			15 08		15 19	15 22	15 24		15 38		15 49	
London Waterloo 15 ⊖	d							14 32						15 02							15 32				
Clapham Junction 10	d	14 16		14 26		14 29	14 32	14 41	14 46		14 56	14 59	15 02	15 11		15 16		15 26	15 29	15 32	15 41	15 46		15 56	
Balham 4 ⊖	d	14 21		14 30		14 33	14 37		14 51		15 00	15 03	15 07			15 21		15 30	15 33	15 37		15 51		16 00	
London Bridge 4 ⊖	d		14 02							14 32							15 02						15 32		
Tulse Hill 3	d		14 13							14 43							15 13						15 43		
New Cross Gate 4 ⊖	d																								
Norwood Junction 2	d						14 57						15 27							15 57					
West Croydon 4	d			14 49			15 04				15 19		15 34					15 49		16 04				16 19	
Waddon	d			14 51			15 06				15 21		15 36					15 51		16 06				16 21	
Wallington	d			14 55			15 10				15 25		15 40					15 55		16 10				16 25	
Carshalton Beeches	d			14 57			15 12				15 27		15 42					15 57		16 12				16 27	
Mitcham Eastfields	d	14 28				14 40			14 58			15 10				15 28			15 40			15 58			
Mitcham Junction	d	14 31				14 43			15 01			15 13				15 31			15 43			16 01			
Hackbridge	d	14 34				14 46			15 04			15 16				15 34			15 46			16 04			
Carshalton	d	14 37				14 49			15 07			15 19				15 37			15 49			16 07			
Sutton (Surrey) 4	a	14 40	14 46	15 01		14 52	15 16		15 10	15 16	15 31	15 22	15 46			15 40	15 46	16 01	15 52	16 16		16 10	16 16	16 31	
	d	14 41				14 53			15 11			15 23				15 41			15 53			16 11			
Belmont	d																								
Banstead	d																								
Epsom Downs	a																								
Cheam	d	14 43				14 55			15 13			15 25				15 43			15 55			16 13			
Ewell East	d	14 47				14 59			15 17			15 29				15 47			15 59			16 17			
Epsom 3	a	14 51				15 03		15 06	15 21			15 33		15 36		15 51			16 03		16 06	16 21			
	d	14 51						15 08	15 21					15 38		15 51					16 08	16 21			
Ashtead	d	14 55						15 12	15 25					15 42		15 55					16 12	16 25			
Leatherhead	d	14 58						15 15	15 28					15 45		15 58					16 15	16 28			
Bookham	d							15 21													16 21				
Effingham Junction 6	d							15 25													16 25				
Guildford	a							15 41													16 41				
Box Hill & Westhumble	d	15 03							15 33							16 03						16 33			
Dorking 4	a	15 06							15 36					15 51		16 06						16 36			
	d																								
Holmwood	d																								
Ockley	d																								
Warnham	d																								
Horsham 4	a																								

		SN	SN	SW	SN	FC	SN	SN	SN	SW		SN	FC	SN	SN	SN	SW	SN	FC	SN		SN	SN	SW	SN
London Victoria 15 ⊖	d	15 52	15 54		16 08		16 19	16 22	16 24			16 38		16 49	16 52	16 54		17 08		17 19		17 22	17 24		17 38
London Waterloo 15 ⊖	d			16 02						16 32							17 02							17 32	
Clapham Junction 10	d	15 59	16 02	16 11	16 16		16 26	16 29	16 32	16 41		16 46		16 56	16 59	17 02	17 11	17 16		17 26		17 29	17 32	17 41	17 46
Balham 4 ⊖	d	16 03	16 07		16 21		16 30	16 33	16 37			16 51		17 00	17 03	17 07		17 21		17 30		17 33	17 37		17 51
London Bridge 4 ⊖	d					16 02							16 32						17 02						
Tulse Hill 3	d					16 13							16 43						17 13						
New Cross Gate 4 ⊖	d																								
Norwood Junction 2	d		16 27						16 57							17 27							17 57		
West Croydon 4	d		16 34				16 49		17 04					17 19		17 34				17 49			18 04		
Waddon	d		16 36				16 51		17 06					17 21		17 36				17 51			18 06		
Wallington	d		16 40				16 55		17 10					17 25		17 40				17 55			18 10		
Carshalton Beeches	d		16 42				16 57		17 12					17 27		17 42				17 57			18 12		
Mitcham Eastfields	d	16 10			16 28			16 40				16 58			17 10			17 28				17 40			17 58
Mitcham Junction	d	16 13			16 31			16 43				17 01			17 13			17 31				17 43			18 01
Hackbridge	d	16 16			16 34			16 46				17 04			17 16			17 34				17 46			18 04
Carshalton	d	16 19			16 37			16 49				17 07			17 19			17 37				17 49			18 07
Sutton (Surrey) 4	a	16 22	16 46		16 40	16 46	17 01	16 52	17 16			17 10	17 16	17 31	17 22	17 46		17 40	17 46	18 01		17 52	18 16		18 10
	d	16 23			16 41			16 53				17 11			17 23			17 41				17 53			18 11
Belmont	d																								
Banstead	d																								
Epsom Downs	a																								
Cheam	d	16 25			16 43			16 55				17 13			17 25			17 43				17 55			18 13
Ewell East	d	16 29			16 47			16 59				17 17			17 29			17 47				17 59			18 17
Epsom 3	a	16 33		16 36	16 51			17 03		17 06		17 21			17 33		17 36	17 51				18 03		18 06	18 21
	d			16 38	16 51					17 08		17 21					17 38	17 51						18 08	18 21
Ashtead	d			16 42	16 55					17 12		17 25					17 42	17 55						18 12	18 25
Leatherhead	d			16 45	16 58					17 15		17 28					17 45	17 58						18 15	18 28
Bookham	d									17 21														18 21	
Effingham Junction 6	d									17 25														18 25	
Guildford	a									17 41														18 41	
Box Hill & Westhumble	d				17 03							17 33						18 03							18 33
Dorking 4	a			16 51	17 06							17 36					17 51	18 06							18 36
	d																								
Holmwood	d																								
Ockley	d																								
Warnham	d																								
Horsham 4	a																								

Table 182

Sundays

London - Sutton, Epsom, Guildford, Dorking and Horsham

Network Diagram - see first Page of Table 177

		FC	SN	SN	SN	SW		SN	FC	SN	SN	SW	SN	FC	SN	SN		SW	SN	FC	SN	SN	SW	SN	FC
London Victoria 15 ⊖	d		17 49	17 52	17 54			18 08		18 19	18 24		18 38		18 49	18 54			19 08		19 19	19 24		19 38	
London Waterloo 15 ⊖	d					18 02						18 32						19 02					19 32		
Clapham Junction 10	d		17 56	17 59	18 02	18 11		18 16		18 26	18 32	18 41	18 46		18 56	19 02		19 11	19 16		19 26	19 32	19 41	19 46	
Balham 4 ⊖	d		18 00	18 03	18 07			18 21		18 30	18 37		18 51		19 00	19 07			19 21		19 30	19 37		19 51	
London Bridge 4 ⊖	d	17 32							18 02					18 32						19 02					19 32
Tulse Hill 3	d	17 43							18 13					18 43						19 13					19 43
New Cross Gate 4 ⊖	d																								
Norwood Junction 2	d				18 27						18 57					19 27						19 57			
West Croydon 4	d		18 19		18 34					18 49	19 04				19 19	19 34					19 49	20 04			
Waddon	d		18 21		18 36					18 51	19 06				19 21	19 36					19 51	20 06			
Wallington	d		18 25		18 40					18 55	19 10				19 25	19 40					19 55	20 10			
Carshalton Beeches	d		18 27		18 42					18 57	19 12				19 27	19 42					19 57	20 12			
Mitcham Eastfields	d			18 10				18 28					18 58						19 28					19 58	
Mitcham Junction	d			18 13				18 31					19 01						19 31					20 01	
Hackbridge	d			18 16				18 34					19 04						19 34					20 04	
Carshalton	d			18 19				18 37					19 07						19 37					20 07	
Sutton (Surrey) 4	a	18 16	18 31	18 22	18 46			18 40	18 46	19 01	19 16		19 10	19 16	19 31	19 46			19 40	19 46	20 01	20 16		20 10	20 16
	d			18 23				18 41					19 11						19 41					20 11	
Belmont	d																								
Banstead	d																								
Epsom Downs	a																								
Cheam	d			18 25				18 43					19 13						19 43					20 13	
Ewell East	d			18 29				18 47					19 17						19 47					20 17	
Epsom 3	a			18 33		18 36		18 51				19 06	19 21					19 36	19 51				20 06	20 21	
	d					18 38		18 51				19 08	19 21					19 38	19 51				20 08	20 21	
Ashtead	d					18 42		18 55				19 12	19 25					19 42	19 55				20 12	20 25	
Leatherhead	d					18 45		18 58				19 15	19 28					19 45	19 58				20 15	20 28	
Bookham	d											19 21											20 21		
Effingham Junction 6	d											19 25											20 25		
Guildford	a											19 41											20 41		
Box Hill & Westhumble	d							19 03					19 33						20 03					20 33	
Dorking 4	a					18 51		19 06					19 36					19 51	20 06					20 36	
	d																								
Holmwood	d																								
Ockley	d																								
Warnham	d																								
Horsham 4	a																								

		SN		SN	SW	SN	FC	SN	SN	SW	SN	FC		SN	SN	SW	SN	FC	SN	SN	SW	SN		SN	SN
London Victoria 15 ⊖	d	19 49		19 54		20 08		20 19	20 24		20 38			20 49	20 54		21 08		21 19	21 24		21 38		21 49	21 54
London Waterloo 15 ⊖	d				20 02					20 32						21 02					21 32				
Clapham Junction 10	d	19 56		20 02	20 11	20 16		20 26	20 32	20 41	20 46			20 56	21 02	21 11	21 16		21 26	21 32	21 41	21 46		21 56	22 02
Balham 4 ⊖	d	20 00		20 07		20 21		20 30	20 37		20 51			21 00	21 07		21 21		21 30	21 38		21 51		22 00	22 07
London Bridge 4 ⊖	d						20 02					20 32						21 02							
Tulse Hill 3	d						20 13					20 43						21 13							
New Cross Gate 4 ⊖	d																								
Norwood Junction 2	d			20 27					20 57						21 27					21 57					22 27
West Croydon 4	d	20 19		20 34				20 49	21 04					21 19	21 34				21 49	22 04				22 19	22 34
Waddon	d	20 21		20 36				20 51	21 06					21 21	21 36				21 51	22 06				22 21	22 36
Wallington	d	20 25		20 40				20 55	21 10					21 25	21 40				21 55	22 10				22 25	22 40
Carshalton Beeches	d	20 27		20 42				20 57	21 12					21 27	21 42				21 57	22 12				22 27	22 42
Mitcham Eastfields	d					20 28					20 58						21 28					21 58			
Mitcham Junction	d					20 31					21 01						21 31					22 01			
Hackbridge	d					20 34					21 04						21 34					22 04			
Carshalton	d					20 37					21 07						21 37					22 07			
Sutton (Surrey) 4	a	20 31		20 46		20 40	20 46	21 01	21 16		21 10	21 16		21 31	21 46		21 40	21 46	22 01	22 16		22 10		22 31	22 46
	d					20 41					21 11						21 41					22 11			
Belmont	d																								
Banstead	d																								
Epsom Downs	a																								
Cheam	d					20 43					21 13						21 43					22 13			
Ewell East	d					20 47					21 17						21 47					22 17			
Epsom 3	a				20 36	20 51				21 06	21 21					21 36	21 51				22 06	22 21			
	d				20 38	20 51				21 08	21 21					21 38	21 51				22 08	22 21			
Ashtead	d				20 42	20 55				21 12	21 25					21 42	21 55				22 12	22 25			
Leatherhead	d				20 45	20 58				21 15	21 28					21 45	21 58				22 15	22 28			
Bookham	d									21 21											22 21				
Effingham Junction 6	d									21 25											22 25				
Guildford	a									21 41											22 41				
Box Hill & Westhumble	d					21 03					21 33						22 03					22 33			
Dorking 4	a				20 51	21 06					21 36					21 51	22 06					22 36			
	d																								
Holmwood	d																								
Ockley	d																								
Warnham	d																								
Horsham 4	a																								

Table 182

Sundays

London - Sutton, Epsom, Guildford, Dorking and Horsham

Network Diagram - see first Page of Table 177

		SW	SN	SN	SN	SW	SN	SN		SN	SW	SN	SN	SW
London Victoria 15 ⊖	d		22 08	22 19	22 24		22 38	22 49		22 54		23 08	23 19	
London Waterloo 15 ⊖	d	22 02				22 32					23 02			23 32
Clapham Junction 10	d	22 11	22 16	22 26	22 32	22 41	22 46	22 56		23 02	23 11	23 16	23 27	23 41
Balham 4 ⊖	d		22 21	22 30	22 38		22 51	23 00		23 07		23 21	23 32	
London Bridge 4 ⊖	d													
Tulse Hill 3	d													
New Cross Gate 4 ⊖	d													
Norwood Junction 2	d				22 57					23 27				
West Croydon 4	d			22 49	23 04			23 19		23 34			23 50	
Waddon	d			22 51	23 06			23 21		23 36			23 52	
Wallington	d			22 55	23 10			23 25		23 40			23 56	
Carshalton Beeches	d			22 57	23 12			23 27		23 42			23 58	
Mitcham Eastfields	d		22 28				22 58					23 28		
Mitcham Junction	d		22 31				23 01					23 31		
Hackbridge	d		22 34				23 04					23 34		
Carshalton	d		22 37				23 07					23 37		
Sutton (Surrey) 4	a		22 40	23 01	23 16		23 10	23 31		23 46		23 40	00 02	
	d		22 41				23 11					23 41	00 04	
Belmont	d													
Banstead	d													
Epsom Downs	a													
Cheam	d		22 43				23 13					23 43	00 06	
Ewell East	d		22 47				23 17					23 47	00 10	
Epsom 3	a	22 36	22 51			23 06	23 21				23 36	23 51	00 14	00 06
	d	22 38	22 51			23 08	23 21					23 51		
Ashtead	d	22 42	22 55			23 12	23 25					23 55		
Leatherhead	d	22 45	22 58			23 15	23 28					23 58		
Bookham	d					23 21								
Effingham Junction 6	d					23 25								
Guildford	a					23 41								
Box Hill & Westhumble	d		23 03				23 33					00 03		
Dorking 4	a	22 51	23 06				23 36					00 06		
	d													
Holmwood	d													
Ockley	d													
Warnham	d													
Horsham 4	a													

Horsham, Dorking, Guildford, Epsom and Sutton - London

Network Diagram - see first Page of Table 177

Miles	Miles	Miles			SN MO	SN MO	SN MO	SN MX	SN	SW	SN	SN	SN		FC	SN	SW	SN	SW	SN	SN	FC	SN		SW
—	—	0	**Horsham 4**	d																			05 49		
—	—	2	Warnham	d																			05 53		
—	—	6½	Ockley	d																			06 00		
—	—	8¾	Holmwood	d																			06 04		
—	—	13¾	**Dorking 4**	a																			06 10		
—	—	—		d			23p16										05 48						06 11		
—	—	14½	Box Hill & Westhumble	d			23p18										05 50						06 13		
0	—	—	**Guildford**	d						04 58															05 58
8¼	—	—	Effingham Junction 6	d						05 16															06 16
10	—	—	Bookham	d						05 19															06 19
12½	—	17¾	Leatherhead	d			23p23			05 24							05 56						06 18		06 24
14½	—	—	Ashtead	d			23p27			05 28							05 59						06 22		06 28
16¼	—	—	**Epsom 3**	a			23p31			05 32							06 04						06 26		06 32
—	—	—		d			23p32		05 23	05 34		05 39				05 57	06 04		06 18				06 27		06 34
17¾	—	—	Ewell East	d			23p36		05 27			05 43				06 01							06 31		
19¼	—	—	Cheam	d			23p39		05 30			05 46				06 04							06 34		
—	0	—	**Epsom Downs**	d				23p43																	
—	1½	—	Banstead	d				23p46																	
—	3	—	Belmont	d				23p49																	
20¼	4	5½	**Sutton (Surrey) 4**	a			23p42	23p52	05 33			05 49				06 07							06 37		
—	—	—		d	23p25	23p40	23p43	23p53	05 33		05 37	05 49	06 03		06 05	06 08		06 14		06 14	06 33	06 34	06 37		
—	5¼	—	Carshalton	d			23p46				05 40					06 11		06 17				06 37	06 40		
—	6¼	—	Hackbridge	d			23p48				05 42					06 13		06 19				06 39	06 43		
—	7	—	Mitcham Junction	d			23p52				05 46					06 17		06 23				06 42	06 46		
—	8	—	Mitcham Eastfields	d			23p55				05 49					06 20		06 26				06 45	06 49		
21¼	—	—	Carshalton Beeches	d	23p28	23p43		23p56	05 36			05 52	06 06							06 17	06 36				
22	—	—	Wallington	d	23p30	23p45		23p58	05 39			05 55	06 08							06 20	06 38				
23½	—	—	Waddon	d	23p33	23p48		00 01	05 42			05 58	06 11							06 23	06 41				
24½	—	0	**West Croydon 4**	d	23p37	23p52		00a04	05 45			06 01	06 15							06 26	06 45				
26¼	—	—	Norwood Junction 2	d					05 50				06 20								06 50				
32¼	—	—	New Cross Gate 4 ⊖	d					06 08																
—	—	6	Tulse Hill 3	a							05 57				06 42			06 34				06 53			
—	—	—		d							05 57							06 34							
35	—	12	**London Bridge 4** ⊖	a					06 14		06 08		06 33					06 51			07 04				
—	11¼	—	Balham 4 ⊖	d	23p53	00 08	00 01					06 17				06 27				06 42			06 57		
—	13¼	—	Clapham Junction 10	a	23p57	00 12	00 06			06 00		06 23				06 31	06 30		06 45	06 48			07 01		07 00
—	—	—	**London Waterloo 15** ⊖	a						06 11							06 40		06 55						07 12
—	16	—	**London Victoria 15** ⊖	a	00 04	00 19	00 15					06 31				06 38				06 58			07 08		

		SW	SN	FC	SN	SN	FC	SN	SW		SN	SN	SN	SN	SW	SN	SW	FC	SN		SW	SW	FC	SN	SN
Horsham 4	d							06 20											06 55						
Warnham	d							06 24											06 59						
Ockley	d							06 31											07 06						
Holmwood	d							06 35											07 10						
Dorking 4	a							06 41											07 16						
	d	06 32						06 44						06 59	07 02				07 17			07 32			
Box Hill & Westhumble	d	06 34						06 46						07 01	07 04							07 34			
Guildford	d								06 28												06 58				
Effingham Junction 6	d								06 48												07 16				
Bookham	d								06 51												07 19				
Leatherhead	d	06 39						06 51	06 56					07 06	07 09				07 23		07 26	07 39			
Ashtead	d	06 43						06 55	06 59					07 10	07 13				07 26		07 29	07 43			
Epsom 3	a	06 47						06 59	07 04					07 14	07 17				07 31		07 34	07 47			
	d	06 48				06 49		07 00	07 04					07 15	07 18	07 21	07 22		07 31		07 34	07 48			
Ewell East	d					06 53		07 04						07 19		07 25									
Cheam	d					06 56		07 07						07 22		07 28			07 37						
Epsom Downs	d		06 34								07 05													07 34	
Banstead	d		06 37								07 08													07 37	
Belmont	d		06 40								07 11													07 40	
Sutton (Surrey) 4	a		06 43			06 59		07 10			07 14			07 25		07 31			07 40					07 43	
	d		06 44	06 45	06 50	07 00	07 05	07 10			07 15	07 20	07 22	07 26		07 32		07 37	07 42				07 40	07 45	07 49
Carshalton	d				06 53			07 13				07 23		07 29				07 40	07 45						07 52
Hackbridge	d				06 55			07 16				07 25		07 31				07 42							07 54
Mitcham Junction	d				06 59			07 19				07 29		07 35				07 45	07 49						07 58
Mitcham Eastfields	d				07 02			07 22				07 32		07 38				07 48	07 52						08 01
Carshalton Beeches	d		06 47			07 03					07 18		07 25			07 35								07 48	
Wallington	d		06 50			07 05					07 20		07 27			07 37								07 50	
Waddon	d		06 53			07 08					07 23		07 30			07 40								07 53	
West Croydon 4	d		06 58			07 13					07 28		07 34			07 44								07 58	
Norwood Junction 2	d					07 18										07 49									
New Cross Gate 4 ⊖	d																								
Tulse Hill 3	a			07 20	07 09		07 43					07 39						07 56					08 13		08 09
	d				07 10							07 41													08 10
London Bridge 4 ⊖	a				07 28	07 32						07 59				08 05									08 28
Balham 4 ⊖	d		07 14					07 29			07 44		07 50	07 47					07 59					08 14	
Clapham Junction 10	a	07 15	07 19					07 34	07 30		07 49		07 55	07 51	07 42		07 48		08 04		08 01	08 12		08 19	
London Waterloo 15 ⊖	a	07 27							07 42						07 54		08 00				08 13	08 24			
London Victoria 15 ⊖	a		07 30					07 41			08 00		08 06	08 00					08 11					08 30	

Horsham, Dorking, Guildford, Epsom and Sutton - London

Network Diagram - see first Page of Table 177

		SN	SN	SW	SN		FC	FC	SN	SW	SW	SW	SN	SN	SN		SN	SW	FC	FC	SN	SN	SW	SN	SN
Horsham 4	d								07 21													07 56			
Warnham	d								07 25													08 00			
Ockley	d								07 32													08 07			
Holmwood	d								07 36													08 11			
Dorking 4	a								07 42													08 17			
	d								07 46		08 02											08 22	08 31		
Box Hill & Westhumble	d										08 04											08 24	08 33		
Guildford	d				07 25													07 58							08 16
Effingham Junction 6	d				07 37					07 46								08 16							08 32
Bookham	d				07 40					07 49								08 19							08 35
Leatherhead	d				07 45				07 52	07 56	08 09							08 25				08 29	08 38		08 41
Ashtead	d				07 49				07 55	07 59	08 13							08 28				08 33	08 42		08 45
Epsom 3	a				07 53				08 00	08 04	08 17							08 33				08 37	08 46		08 49
	d		07 49	07 52	07 54				08 02	08 04	08 18	08 22					08 22	08 34				08 38	08 48		08 50
Ewell East	d		07 53		07 58				08 06								08 26					08 42			08 54
Cheam	d		07 56		08 01				08 09								08 29					08 45			08 57
Epsom Downs	d												08 04								08 34				
Banstead	d												08 07								08 37				
Belmont	d												08 10								08 40				
Sutton (Surrey) 4	a		07 59		08 04				08 12				08 13				08 32				08 43	08 48			09 00
	d	07 53	07 59		08 05		08 08	08 08	08 12				08 14	08 20	08 29		08 32		08 39	08 41	08 45	08 48		08 57	09 00
Carshalton	d		08 02				08 11		08 15					08 23	08 32				08 42			08 51		09 00	09 03
Hackbridge	d		08 05				08 13		08 18					08 25	08 34				08 44			08 54		09 02	09 06
Mitcham Junction	d		08 08				08 16		08 21					08 29	08 38				08 47			08 57		09 06	09 09
Mitcham Eastfields	d		08 11				08 19		08 24					08 32	08 41				08 50			09 00		09 09	09 12
Carshalton Beeches	d	07 56			08 08								08 17				08 35				08 48				
Wallington	d	07 58			08 10								08 19				08 38				08 50				
Waddon	d	08 01											08 22				08 41				08 53				
West Croydon 4	d	08 05			08 15								08 26				08 44				08 57				
Norwood Junction 2	d				08 20												08 49								
New Cross Gate 4 ⊖	d																								
Tulse Hill 3	a						08 27	08 43						08 40					08 58	09 12				09 16	
	d													08 40										09 16	
London Bridge 4 ⊖	a				08 35									08 57			09 04							09 35	
Balham 4 ⊖	d	08 21	08 18										08 43		08 49						09 13	09 07			09 18
Clapham Junction 10	a	08 25	08 22	08 18					08 32	08 31	08 42	08 48	08 49		08 54			09 00			09 18	09 11	09 15		09 22
London Waterloo 15 ⊖	a			08 30						08 43	08 54	09 00						09 12					09 27		
London Victoria 15 ⊖	a	08 36	08 30						08 39				09 00		09 04						09 31	09 20			09 33

			SW	SN	FC	FC	SN	SN	SW	SN	SN		SW	SN	FC	FC	SN	SN	SN	SN	SW		SW	SN	FC
Horsham 4	d																			09 09					
Warnham	d																			09 13					
Ockley	d																			09 20					
Holmwood	d																			09 24					
Dorking 4	a																			09 30					
	d							08 57	09 02											09 31	09 35				
Box Hill & Westhumble	d							08 59	09 04											09 33					
Guildford	d												08 58										09 28		
Effingham Junction 6	d		08 48										09 16										09 46		
Bookham	d		08 51										09 19										09 49		
Leatherhead	d		08 56					09 04	09 09				09 24							09 38	09 41		09 54		
Ashtead	d		08 59					09 08	09 13				09 28							09 42	09 45		09 58		
Epsom 3	a		09 04					09 12	09 17				09 32							09 46	09 49		10 02		
	d		09 04					09 13	09 18		09 19		09 35					09 42		09 49	09 50		10 05		
Ewell East	d							09 17			09 23							09 46		09 53					
Cheam	d							09 20			09 26							09 49		09 56					
Epsom Downs	d									09 09							09 35								
Banstead	d									09 12							09 38								
Belmont	d									09 15							09 41								
Sutton (Surrey) 4	a							09 23		09 18	09 29						09 44	09 52		09 59					
	d			09 03	09 11	09 13	09 15	09 23		09 23	09 29			09 33	09 37	09 38	09 45	09 52	09 52	09 59				10 03	10 07
Carshalton	d					09 16					09 32					09 41				10 02					
Hackbridge	d					09 18					09 35					09 43				10 05					
Mitcham Junction	d					09 21					09 38					09 46				10 08					
Mitcham Eastfields	d					09 24		09 32			09 41					09 49				10 11					
Carshalton Beeches	d			09 06			09 18			09 26				09 36			09 48		09 55					10 06	
Wallington	d			09 08			09 20			09 28				09 38			09 50		09 57					10 08	
Waddon	d			09 11			09 23			09 31				09 41			09 53		10 00					10 11	
West Croydon 4	d			09 15			09 28			09 35				09 45			09 58		10 04					10 15	
Norwood Junction 2	d			09 22										09 52										10 22	
New Cross Gate 4 ⊖	d																								
Tulse Hill 3	a				09 42	09 32									10 12	09 57									10 42
	d																								
London Bridge 4 ⊖	a																								
Balham 4 ⊖	d			09 41			09 44			09 52	09 49			10 09			10 14		10 21	10 18				10 39	
Clapham Junction 10	a		09 30	09 46			09 49	09 42	09 45	09 57	09 53		10 00	10 15			10 19	10 11	10 26	10 22	10 15		10 30	10 45	
London Waterloo 15 ⊖	a		09 42						09 57				10 10								10 25		10 40		
London Victoria 15 ⊖	a			09 58			09 58	09 52		10 05	10 00			10 24			10 28	10 20	10 34	10 31				10 53	

Horsham, Dorking, Guildford, Epsom and Sutton - London

Network Diagram - see first Page of Table 177

Station		FC	SN	SN	SN	SW	SN		SW	SN	FC	FC	SN	SN	SW	SN	SN		SW	SN	FC	FC	SN	SN	SW
Horsham 4	d													10 04											
Warnham	d													10 08											
Ockley	d													10 15											
Holmwood	d													10 19											
Dorking 4	a													10 25											
	d				09 57	10 05								10 26	10 35									10 58	11 05
Box Hill & Westhumble	d				09 59									10 28											
Guildford	d								09 58										10 28						
Effingham Junction 6	d								10 16										10 46						
Bookham	d								10 19										10 49						
Leatherhead	d				10 04	10 11			10 24					10 33	10 41				10 54					11 04	11 11
Ashtead	d				10 08	10 14			10 28					10 37	10 44				10 58					11 07	11 14
Epsom 3	a				10 12	10 19			10 32					10 41	10 49				11 02					11 12	11 19
	d		10 04		10 13	10 20	10 19		10 35					10 42	10 50		10 49		11 05				11 04	11 13	11 20
Ewell East	d		10 08		10 17		10 23							10 46			10 53						11 08		
Cheam	d		10 11		10 20		10 26							10 49			10 56						11 11	11 18	
Epsom Downs	d												10 35												
Banstead	d												10 38												
Belmont	d												10 41												
Sutton (Surrey) 4	a		10 14		10 23		10 29						10 44	10 52			10 59						11 14	11 21	
	d	10 08	10 15	10 22	10 23		10 29			10 33	10 37	10 38	10 45	10 52		10 52	10 59			11 03	11 07	11 08	11 15	11 22	
Carshalton	d	10 11					10 32					10 41					11 02					11 11			
Hackbridge	d	10 13					10 35					10 43					11 05					11 13			
Mitcham Junction	d	10 16					10 38					10 46					11 08					11 16			
Mitcham Eastfields	d	10 19					10 41					10 49					11 11					11 19			
Carshalton Beeches	d		10 18	10 25						10 36			10 48			10 55				11 06			11 18		
Wallington	d		10 20	10 27						10 38			10 50			10 57				11 08			11 20		
Waddon	d		10 23	10 30						10 41			10 53			11 00				11 11			11 23		
West Croydon 4	d		10 28	10 34						10 45			10 58			11 04				11 15			11 28		
Norwood Junction 2	d									10 52										11 22					
New Cross Gate 4 ⊖	d																								
Tulse Hill 3	a	10 27									11 12	10 57									11 42	11 27			
	d																								
London Bridge 4 ⊖	a																								
Balham 4 ⊖	d		10 44	10 51			10 48			11 09			11 14			11 21	11 18			11 40			11 44		
Clapham Junction 10	a		10 49	10 56	10 40	10 45	10 52		11 00	11 14			11 19	11 10	11 15	11 26	11 22		11 30	11 45			11 49	11 40	11 45
London Waterloo 15 ⊖	a					10 55			11 10						11 25				11 40						11 55
London Victoria 15 ⊖	a		10 58	11 04	10 48		11 00			11 23			11 28	11 20		11 34	11 30			11 54			11 58	11 50	

Station		SN	SN		SW	SN	FC	FC	SN	SN	SW	SN	SN		SW	SN	FC	FC	SN	SN	SW	SN	SN		SW
Horsham 4	d									11 04															
Warnham	d									11 08															
Ockley	d									11 15															
Holmwood	d									11 19															
Dorking 4	a									11 25															
	d									11 26	11 35									11 58	12 05				
Box Hill & Westhumble	d									11 28															
Guildford	d				10 58										11 28										11 58
Effingham Junction 6	d				11 16										11 46										12 16
Bookham	d				11 19										11 49										12 19
Leatherhead	d				11 24					11 33	11 41				11 54					12 04	12 11				12 24
Ashtead	d				11 28					11 37	11 44				11 58					12 07	12 14				12 28
Epsom 3	a				11 32					11 41	11 49				12 02					12 12	12 19				12 32
	d		11 19		11 35					11 42	11 50		11 49		12 05				12 04	12 13	12 20		12 19		12 35
Ewell East	d		11 23							11 46			11 53						12 08				12 23		
Cheam	d		11 26							11 49			11 56						12 11	12 18			12 26		
Epsom Downs	d								11 35																
Banstead	d								11 38																
Belmont	d								11 41																
Sutton (Surrey) 4	a		11 29						11 44	11 52			11 59						12 14	12 21			12 29		
	d	11 22	11 29			11 33	11 37	11 38	11 45	11 52		11 52	11 59			12 03	12 07	12 08	12 15	12 22		12 22	12 29		
Carshalton	d		11 32					11 41					12 02					12 11					12 32		
Hackbridge	d		11 35					11 43					12 05					12 13					12 35		
Mitcham Junction	d		11 38					11 46					12 08					12 16					12 38		
Mitcham Eastfields	d		11 41					11 49					12 11					12 19					12 41		
Carshalton Beeches	d	11 25				11 36			11 48			11 55				12 06			12 18			12 25			
Wallington	d	11 27				11 38			11 50			11 57				12 08			12 20			12 27			
Waddon	d	11 30				11 41			11 53			12 00				12 11			12 23			12 30			
West Croydon 4	d	11 34				11 45			11 58			12 04				12 15			12 28			12 34			
Norwood Junction 2	d					11 52										12 22									
New Cross Gate 4 ⊖	d																								
Tulse Hill 3	a						12 12	11 57									12 42	12 27							
	d																								
London Bridge 4 ⊖	a																								
Balham 4 ⊖	d	11 51	11 48			12 09			12 14			12 21	12 18			12 39			12 44			12 51	12 48		
Clapham Junction 10	a	11 56	11 52		12 00	12 14			12 19	12 10	12 15	12 26	12 22		12 30	12 44			12 49	12 40	12 45	12 56	12 52		13 00
London Waterloo 15 ⊖	a				12 10						12 25				12 40						12 55				13 10
London Victoria 15 ⊖	a	12 04	12 00			12 23			12 28	12 18		12 34	12 30			12 53			12 58	12 48		13 04	13 00		

Horsham, Dorking, Guildford, Epsom and Sutton - London

Network Diagram - see first Page of Table 177

		SN	FC	FC	SN	SN	SW	SN	SN		SW	SN	FC	FC	SN	SN	SW	SN	SN		SW	SN	FC	FC	SN
Horsham 4	d					12 04																			
Warnham	d					12 08																			
Ockley	d					12 15																			
Holmwood	d					12 19																			
Dorking 4	a					12 25																			
	d					12 26	12 35									12 58	13 05								
Box Hill & Westhumble	d					12 28																			
Guildford	d										12 28										12 58				
Effingham Junction 6	d										12 46										13 16				
Bookham	d										12 49										13 19				
Leatherhead	d					12 33	12 41				12 54					13 04	13 11				13 24				
Ashtead	d					12 37	12 44				12 58					13 07	13 14				13 28				
Epsom 3	a					12 41	12 49				13 02					13 12	13 19				13 32				
	d					12 42	12 50		12 49		13 05				13 04	13 13	13 20		13 19		13 35				
Ewell East	d					12 46			12 53						13 08				13 23						
Cheam	d					12 49			12 56						13 11	13 18			13 26						
Epsom Downs	d				12 35																				13 35
Banstead	d				12 38																				13 38
Belmont	d				12 41																				13 41
Sutton (Surrey) 4	a				12 44	12 52			12 59						13 14	13 21			13 29						13 44
	d	12 33	12 37	12 38	12 45	12 52		12 52	12 59			13 03	13 07	13 08	13 15	13 22		13 22	13 29			13 33	13 37	13 38	13 45
Carshalton	d			12 41					13 02					13 11					13 32					13 41	
Hackbridge	d			12 43					13 05					13 13					13 35					13 43	
Mitcham Junction	d			12 46					13 08					13 16					13 38					13 46	
Mitcham Eastfields	d			12 49					13 11					13 19					13 41					13 49	
Carshalton Beeches	d	12 36			12 48			12 55				13 06			13 18			13 25				13 36			13 48
Wallington	d	12 38			12 50			12 57				13 08			13 20			13 27				13 38			13 50
Waddon	d	12 41			12 53			13 00				13 11			13 23			13 30				13 41			13 53
West Croydon 4	d	12 45			12 58			13 04				13 15			13 28			13 34				13 45			13 58
Norwood Junction 2	d	12 52										13 22										13 52			
New Cross Gate 4 ⊖	d																								
Tulse Hill 3	a		13 12	12 57									13 42	13 27									14 12	13 57	
	d																								
London Bridge 4 ⊖	a																								
Balham 4 ⊖	d	13 09			13 14			13 21	13 18			13 39			13 44			13 51	13 48			14 09			14 14
Clapham Junction 10	a	13 14			13 19	13 10	13 15	13 26	13 22		13 30	13 44			13 49	13 40	13 45	13 56	13 52		14 00	14 14			14 19
London Waterloo 15 ⊖	a						13 25				13 40						13 55				14 10				
London Victoria 15 ⊖	a	13 23			13 28	13 18		13 34	13 30			13 53			13 58	13 48		14 04	14 00			14 23			14 28

		SN	SW	SN	SN		SW	SN	FC	FC	SN	SN	SW	SN	SN		SW	SN	FC	FC	SN	SN	SW	SN	SN
Horsham 4	d	13 04																				14 04			
Warnham	d	13 08																				14 08			
Ockley	d	13 15																				14 15			
Holmwood	d	13 19																				14 19			
Dorking 4	a	13 25																				14 25			
	d	13 26	13 35									13 58	14 05									14 26	14 35		
Box Hill & Westhumble	d	13 28																				14 28			
Guildford	d						13 28										13 58								
Effingham Junction 6	d						13 46										14 16								
Bookham	d						13 49										14 19								
Leatherhead	d	13 33	13 41				13 54					14 04	14 11				14 24					14 33	14 41		
Ashtead	d	13 37	13 44				13 58					14 07	14 14				14 28					14 37	14 44		
Epsom 3	a	13 41	13 49				14 02					14 12	14 19				14 32					14 41	14 49		
	d	13 42	13 50		13 49		14 05				14 04	14 13	14 20		14 19		14 35					14 42	14 50		14 49
Ewell East	d	13 46			13 53						14 08				14 23							14 46			14 53
Cheam	d	13 49			13 56						14 11	14 18			14 26							14 49			14 56
Epsom Downs	d																				14 35				
Banstead	d																				14 38				
Belmont	d																				14 41				
Sutton (Surrey) 4	a	13 52			13 59						14 14	14 21			14 29						14 44	14 52			14 59
	d	13 52		13 52	13 59			14 03	14 07	14 08	14 15	14 22		14 22	14 29			14 33	14 37	14 38	14 45	14 52		14 52	14 59
Carshalton	d				14 02					14 11					14 32					14 41					15 02
Hackbridge	d				14 05					14 13					14 35					14 43					15 05
Mitcham Junction	d				14 08					14 16					14 38					14 46					15 08
Mitcham Eastfields	d				14 11					14 19					14 41					14 49					15 11
Carshalton Beeches	d			13 55				14 06			14 18			14 25				14 36			14 48			14 55	
Wallington	d			13 57				14 08			14 20			14 27				14 38			14 50			14 57	
Waddon	d			14 00				14 11			14 23			14 30				14 41			14 53			15 00	
West Croydon 4	d			14 04				14 15			14 28			14 34				14 45			14 58			15 04	
Norwood Junction 2	d							14 22										14 52							
New Cross Gate 4 ⊖	d																								
Tulse Hill 3	a								14 42	14 27									15 12	14 57					
	d																								
London Bridge 4 ⊖	a																								
Balham 4 ⊖	d			14 21	14 18			14 39			14 44			14 51	14 48			15 09			15 14			15 21	15 18
Clapham Junction 10	a	14 10	14 15	14 26	14 22		14 30	14 44			14 49	14 40	14 45	14 56	14 52		15 00	15 14			15 19	15 10	15 15	15 26	15 22
London Waterloo 15 ⊖	a		14 25				14 40						14 55				15 10						15 25		
London Victoria 15 ⊖	a	14 18		14 34	14 30			14 53			14 58	14 48		15 04	15 00			15 24			15 28	15 22		15 34	15 30

Horsham, Dorking, Guildford, Epsom and Sutton - London

Network Diagram - see first Page of Table 177

			SW	SN	FC	FC	SN	SN	SW	SN	SN		SW	SN	FC	FC	SN	SN	SW	SN	SN		SW	SN	FC
Horsham 4	d																	15 04							
Warnham	d																	15 08							
Ockley	d																	15 15							
Holmwood	d																	15 19							
Dorking 4	a																	15 25							
	d							14 58	15 05									15 26	15 35						
Box Hill & Westhumble	d																	15 28							
Guildford	d		14 28										14 58										15 28		
Effingham Junction 6	d		14 46										15 16										15 46		
Bookham	d		14 49										15 19										15 49		
Leatherhead	d		14 54					15 04	15 11				15 24					15 33	15 41				15 54		
Ashtead	d		14 58					15 07	15 14				15 28					15 37	15 44				15 58		
Epsom 3	a		15 02					15 12	15 19				15 32					15 41	15 49				16 02		
	d		15 05				15 04	15 13	15 20		15 19		15 35					15 42	15 50		15 49		16 05		
Ewell East	d						15 08				15 23							15 46			15 53				
Cheam	d						15 11	15 18			15 26							15 49			15 56				
Epsom Downs	d																15 35								
Banstead	d																15 38								
Belmont	d																15 41								
Sutton (Surrey) 4	a						15 14	15 21			15 29						15 44	15 52			15 59				
	d			15 03	15 07	15 08	15 15	15 22		15 22	15 29			15 33	15 37	15 38	15 45	15 52		15 52	15 59			16 03	16 07
Carshalton	d					15 11					15 32					15 41					16 02				
Hackbridge	d					15 13					15 35					15 43					16 05				
Mitcham Junction	d					15 16					15 38					15 46					16 08				
Mitcham Eastfields	d					15 19					15 41					15 49					16 11				
Carshalton Beeches	d			15 06			15 18			15 25				15 36			15 48			15 55				16 06	
Wallington	d			15 08			15 20			15 27				15 38			15 50			15 57				16 08	
Waddon	d			15 11			15 23			15 30				15 41			15 53			16 00				16 11	
West Croydon 4	d			15 15			15 28			15 34				15 45			15 58			16 04				16 15	
Norwood Junction 2	d			15 22										15 52										16 22	
New Cross Gate 4 ⊖	d																								
Tulse Hill 3	a				15 42	15 27									16 12	15 57									16 46
	d																								
London Bridge 4 ⊖	a																								
Balham 4 ⊖	d			15 39			15 44			15 51	15 48			16 09			16 14			16 21	16 18			16 39	
Clapham Junction 10	a		15 30	15 44			15 49	15 40	15 45	15 56	15 52		16 00	16 14			16 19	16 10	16 15	16 26	16 23		16 30	16 45	
London Waterloo 15 ⊖	a		15 40						15 55				16 10						16 25				16 40		
London Victoria 15 ⊖	a			15 54			15 58	15 52		16 04	16 00			16 23			16 28	16 18		16 34	16 30			16 55	

		FC	SN	SN	SW	SN	SN		SW	SN	SN	FC	FC 1	SN	SW	SN	SN		SW	SN	FC	SN	FC	SN	SW
Horsham 4	d													16 04											
Warnham	d													16 08											
Ockley	d													16 15											
Holmwood	d													16 19											
Dorking 4	a													16 25											
	d			15 56	16 05									16 26	16 35									17 00	17 05
Box Hill & Westhumble	d			15 58										16 28										17 02	
Guildford	d								15 58										16 28						
Effingham Junction 6	d								16 16										16 46						
Bookham	d								16 19										16 49						
Leatherhead	d			16 03	16 11				16 24					16 33	16 41				16 54					17 07	17 11
Ashtead	d			16 07	16 14				16 28					16 37	16 44				16 58					17 11	17 14
Epsom 3	a			16 11	16 19				16 32					16 41	16 49				17 02					17 15	17 19
	d		16 04	16 12	16 20		16 19		16 35					16 42	16 50		16 49		17 05					17 19	17 20
Ewell East	d		16 08	16 16			16 23							16 46			16 53							17 23	
Cheam	d		16 11	16 19			16 26							16 49			16 56							17 26	
Epsom Downs	d										16 26											17 02			
Banstead	d										16 29											17 05			
Belmont	d										16 32											17 08			
Sutton (Surrey) 4	a		16 14	16 22			16 29				16 35			16 52			16 59					17 11		17 29	
	d	16 08	16 15	16 22		16 22	16 29			16 33	16 45	16 37	16 38	16 52		16 52	16 59			17 03	17 08	17 15	17 11	17 29	
Carshalton	d	16 11					16 32						16 41				17 02				17 11			17 32	
Hackbridge	d	16 13					16 35						16 43				17 05				17 13			17 35	
Mitcham Junction	d	16 16					16 38						16 46				17 08				17 16			17 38	
Mitcham Eastfields	d	16 19					16 41						16 49				17 11				17 19			17 41	
Carshalton Beeches	d		16 18			16 25				16 36	16 48					16 55				17 06		17 18			
Wallington	d		16 20			16 27				16 38	16 50					16 57				17 08		17 20			
Waddon	d		16 23			16 30				16 41	16 53					17 00				17 11		17 23			
West Croydon 4	d		16 28			16 34				16 45	16 58					17 04				17 18		17 28			
Norwood Junction 2	d									16 52										17 23					
New Cross Gate 4 ⊖	d																								
Tulse Hill 3	a	16 27										17 15	16 57								17 27		17 44		
	d																								
London Bridge 4 ⊖	a																								
Balham 4 ⊖	d		16 44			16 51	16 48			17 09	17 14					17 21	17 18			17 39		17 44		17 48	
Clapham Junction 10	a		16 49	16 40	16 45	16 56	16 53		17 00	17 14	17 19			17 10	17 15	17 26	17 23		17 30	17 44		17 49		17 52	17 45
London Waterloo 15 ⊖	a				16 55				17 10						17 25				17 40						17 55
London Victoria 15 ⊖	a		16 58	16 48		17 04	17 00			17 23	17 28			17 18		17 34	17 30			17 55		17 58		18 00	

Horsham, Dorking, Guildford, Epsom and Sutton - London

Network Diagram - see first Page of Table 177

		SN	SW		FC	FC	SN	SN	SW	SN	SW	SN	FC	FC	SN	SN	SW	SN	SW	FC	SN	FC	SN	SN	SW
Horsham [4]	d							17 07								17 34								18 04	
Warnham	d							17 11								17 38								18 08	
Ockley	d							17 18								17 45								18 15	
Holmwood	d							17 22								17 49								18 19	
Dorking [4]	a							17 28								17 55								18 25	
	d							17 31	17 35							17 56	18 05							18 26	18 35
Box Hill & Westhumble	d							17 33								17 58								18 28	
Guildford	d		16 58								17 28								17 58						
Effingham Junction [6]	d		17 16								17 46								18 16						
Bookham	d		17 19								17 49								18 19						
Leatherhead	d		17 24					17 38	17 41		17 54					18 03	18 11		18 24					18 33	18 41
Ashtead	d		17 28					17 42	17 45		17 58					18 07	18 14		18 28					18 37	18 45
Epsom [3]	a		17 32					17 46	17 49		18 02					18 14	18 19		18 32					18 43	18 49
	d	17 23	17 35					17 49	17 50	17 52	18 05					18 17	18 20	18 22	18 35					18 49	18 50
Ewell East	d	17 27						17 53		17 56						18 23		18 26						18 53	
Cheam	d	17 30						17 56		17 59						18 26		18 29						18 56	
Epsom Downs	d						17 35								18 02								18 35		
Banstead	d						17 38								18 05								18 38		
Belmont	d						17 41								18 08								18 41		
Sutton (Surrey) [4]	a	17 33					17 44	17 59		18 02					18 11	18 29		18 32					18 44	18 59	
	d	17 33			17 41	17 42	17 45	17 59		18 04			18 08	18 09	18 12	18 29		18 33		18 38		18 43	18 45	18 59	
Carshalton	d					17 45		18 02					18 11			18 32				18 41				19 02	
Hackbridge	d					17 47		18 05					18 13			18 35				18 43				19 05	
Mitcham Junction	d					17 50		18 08					18 16			18 38				18 46				19 08	
Mitcham Eastfields	d					17 53		18 11					18 19			18 41				18 49				19 11	
Carshalton Beeches	d	17 36					17 48			18 07					18 15			18 36					18 48		
Wallington	d	17 39					17 50			18 09					18 17			18 38					18 50		
Waddon	d	17 42					17 53			18 12					18 20			18 41					18 53		
West Croydon [4]	d	17 48					17 58			18 18					18 28			18 47					18 58		
Norwood Junction [2]	d	17 55								18 24								18 52							
New Cross Gate [4] ⊖	d																								
Tulse Hill [3]	a				18 15	18 01						18 24	18 28	18 44						18 57	19 00	19 14			
	d											18 43									19 18				
London Bridge [4] ⊖	a																								
Balham [4] ⊖	d	18 11					18 14	18 18		18 40					18 44	18 48		19 09					19 14	19 18	
Clapham Junction [10]	a	18 16	18 00				18 19	18 22	18 15	18 45	18 30				18 49	18 52	18 45	19 14	19 00				19 19	19 22	19 16
London Waterloo [15] ⊖	a		18 10						18 25		18 40						18 55		19 10						19 27
London Victoria [15] ⊖	a	18 25					18 28	18 33		18 54					18 57	19 01		19 25					19 28	19 30	

		SN	SW	FC	FC	SN	SN	SN	SW	SN	SW	FC	FC	SN	SN	SN	SW	SN	SW		FC	FC	SN	SN	SW
Horsham [4]	d							18 34								19 04									
Warnham	d							18 38								19 08									
Ockley	d							18 45								19 15									
Holmwood	d							18 49								19 19									
Dorking [4]	a							18 55								19 25									
	d		18 50					18 56		19 05						19 28	19 33	19 37						19 57	20 05
Box Hill & Westhumble	d							18 58								19 30								19 59	
Guildford	d	18 22													19 04				19 28						
Effingham Junction [6]	d	18 39							18 59						19 20				19 46						
Bookham	d	18 42							19 02						19 23				19 49						
Leatherhead	d	18 47	18 56					19 03	19 08	19 11					19 28	19 35	19 39	19 43	19 54					20 04	20 11
Ashtead	d	18 51	18 59					19 07	19 12	19 15					19 32	19 39	19 42	19 46	19 58					20 08	20 14
Epsom [3]	a	18 57	19 04					19 11	19 16	19 19					19 36	19 43	19 47	19 51	20 02					20 12	20 19
	d	18 57	19 05					19 12	19 20	19 20	19 35				19 37	19 46	19 50	19 52	20 05					20 13	20 20
Ewell East	d							19 16		19 24					19 41	19 50		19 56						20 17	
Cheam	d							19 19		19 27					19 44	19 53		19 59						20 20	
Epsom Downs	d					19 06								19 36									20 13		
Banstead	d					19 09								19 39									20 16		
Belmont	d					19 12								19 42									20 19		
Sutton (Surrey) [4]	a	19 04				19 15		19 22		19 30				19 45	19 47	19 56		20 02					20 22	20 23	
	d	19 05		19 08	19 13	19 16		19 22		19 33		19 37	19 42	19 46		19 56		20 03			20 07	20 12	20 23	20 25	
Carshalton	d			19 11				19 25					19 45			19 59						20 15		20 28	
Hackbridge	d			19 13				19 28					19 47			20 02						20 17		20 31	
Mitcham Junction	d			19 16				19 31					19 50			20 05						20 20		20 34	
Mitcham Eastfields	d			19 19				19 34					19 53			20 08						20 23		20 37	
Carshalton Beeches	d	19 08				19 19				19 36				19 49				20 06					20 26		
Wallington	d	19 10				19 21				19 38				19 51				20 08					20 28		
Waddon	d	19 13				19 24				19 41				19 54				20 11					20 31		
West Croydon [4]	d	19 17				19 28				19 47				19 58				20 18					20 35		
Norwood Junction [2]	d	19 22								19 52								20 23							
New Cross Gate [4] ⊖	d																								
Tulse Hill [3]	a			19 27	19 44		19 31					20 10	20 01								20 40	20 31			
	d																								
London Bridge [4] ⊖	a						19 52																		
Balham [4] ⊖	d	19 39				19 45		19 42		20 08				20 14		20 17		20 39					20 51	20 44	
Clapham Junction [10]	a	19 44	19 30			19 50		19 47	19 45	20 14	20 00			20 19		20 22	20 15	20 44	20 30				20 56	20 48	20 45
London Waterloo [15] ⊖	a		19 41						19 55		20 10						20 25		20 41						20 55
London Victoria [15] ⊖	a	19 54				19 59		19 56		20 22				20 28		20 30		20 53					21 04	20 56	

Horsham, Dorking, Guildford, Epsom and Sutton - London

Network Diagram - see first Page of Table 177

Station		SN	SN	SW	FC		FC	SN	SN	SW	SN	SW	SN	FC	FC		SN	SN	SW	SN	SN	SW	SN	SN	SW
Horsham 4	d								20 06																
Warnham	d								20 10																
Ockley	d								20 17																
Holmwood	d								20 21																
Dorking 4	a								20 27																
	d								20 30	20 35								20 59						21 30	21 35
Box Hill & Westhumble	d																	21 01							
Guildford	d			19 58															20 46						
Effingham Junction 6	d			20 16															21 03						
Bookham	d			20 19															21 06						
Leatherhead	d			20 24					20 36	20 41								21 06	21 11					21 36	21 41
Ashtead	d			20 28					20 39	20 44								21 10	21 14					21 40	21 44
Epsom 3	a			20 32					20 44	20 49								21 14	21 19					21 44	21 49
	d	20 22	20 25	20 35					20 45	20 50	20 55	21 05						21 15	21 20	21 21	21 25	21 35		21 45	21 50
Ewell East	d	20 26	20 29						20 49		20 59							21 19		21 25	21 29			21 49	
Cheam	d	20 29	20 32						20 52		21 02							21 22		21 28	21 32			21 52	
Epsom Downs	d												20 54												
Banstead	d												20 57												
Belmont	d												21 00												
Sutton (Surrey) 4	a	20 32	20 35						20 55		21 05		21 03					21 25		21 31	21 35			21 55	
	d	20 33	20 36		20 37		20 42	20 52	20 55		21 06		21 06	21 12	21 17		21 22	21 25		21 32	21 36		21 52	21 55	
Carshalton	d		20 39				20 45		20 58		21 09			21 15				21 28			21 39			21 58	
Hackbridge	d		20 41				20 47		21 01		21 11			21 17				21 31			21 41			22 01	
Mitcham Junction	d		20 45				20 50		21 04		21 15			21 20				21 34			21 45			22 04	
Mitcham Eastfields	d		20 48				20 53		21 07		21 18			21 23				21 37			21 48			22 07	
Carshalton Beeches	d	20 36						20 55					21 09				21 25			21 35			21 55		
Wallington	d	20 38						20 57					21 11				21 27			21 37			21 57		
Waddon	d	20 41						21 00					21 14				21 30			21 40			22 00		
West Croydon 4	d	20 45						21 04					21 18				21 34			21 48			22 04		
Norwood Junction 2	d	20 52											21 23							21 53					
New Cross Gate 4 ⊖	d																								
Tulse Hill 3	a				21 10		21 01							21 31	21 53										
	d																								
London Bridge 4 ⊖	a																								
Balham 4 ⊖	d	21 08	20 54					21 21	21 14		21 24		21 39				21 51	21 44		22 09	21 54		22 21	22 14	
Clapham Junction 10	a	21 14	20 59	21 00				21 26	21 18	21 15	21 29	21 30	21 44				21 56	21 49	21 45	22 14	21 59	22 00	22 26	22 19	22 15
London Waterloo 15 ⊖	a			21 10						21 25		21 40							21 55			22 10			22 25
London Victoria 15 ⊖	a	21 22	21 09					21 34	21 26		21 39		21 53				22 04	21 58		22 23	22 09		22 34	22 27	

Station			SN	SN	FC	SN	SN	SW	SN	SN	SN		SN	SW	SN	SN	SN	SN	SW	SN	SN		SN		
Horsham 4	d																								
Warnham	d																								
Ockley	d																								
Holmwood	d																								
Dorking 4	a																								
	d						21 59						22 30	22 35				23 00			23 30				
Box Hill & Westhumble	d						22 01											23 02							
Guildford	d							21 46											22 46						
Effingham Junction 6	d							22 03											23 03						
Bookham	d							22 06											23 06						
Leatherhead	d						22 06	22 11					22 36	22 41				23 07	23 11		23 36				
Ashtead	d						22 10	22 14					22 40	22 44				23 11	23 14		23 39				
Epsom 3	a						22 14	22 19					22 44	22 49				23 15	23 19		23 45				
	d		21 55				22 15	22 20	22 21	22 25			22 45	22 50	22 55			23 16	23 20	23 27					
Ewell East	d		21 59				22 19		22 25	22 29			22 49		22 59			23 20		23 31					
Cheam	d		22 02				22 22		22 28	22 32			22 52		23 02			23 23		23 35					
Epsom Downs	d			21 54												22 54							23 43		
Banstead	d			21 57												22 57							23 46		
Belmont	d			22 00												23 00							23 49		
Sutton (Surrey) 4	a		22 05	22 03			22 25		22 31	22 35			22 55		23 05	23 03		23 26		23 40			23 52		
	d		22 06	22 06	22 12	22 22	22 25		22 32	22 36	22 52		22 55		23 06	23 06	23 20	23 30		23 41			23 53		
Carshalton	d		22 09				22 28			22 39			22 58		23 09										
Hackbridge	d		22 11				22 31			22 41			23 01		23 11										
Mitcham Junction	d		22 15				22 34			22 45			23 04		23 15										
Mitcham Eastfields	d		22 18				22 37			22 48			23 07		23 18										
Carshalton Beeches	d			22 09		22 25			22 35		22 55					23 09	23 23	23 33		23 44			23 56		
Wallington	d			22 11		22 27			22 37		22 57					23 11	23 25	23 35		23 46			23 58		
Waddon	d			22 14		22 30			22 40		23 00					23 14	23 28	23 38		23 49			00 01		
West Croydon 4	d			22 18		22 34			22 48		23 04					23 18	23a31	23a41		23a52			00a04		
Norwood Junction 2	d			22 23					22 53							23 23									
New Cross Gate 4 ⊖	d																								
Tulse Hill 3	a				22 44																				
	d				22 44																				
London Bridge 4 ⊖	a				22 55																				
Balham 4 ⊖	d		22 24	22 39		22 51	22 44		23 09	22 54	23 21		23 14		23 24	23 40									
Clapham Junction 10	a		22 29	22 44		22 56	22 48	22 45	23 15	22 59	23 26		23 18	23 15	23 29	23 45			23 48						
London Waterloo 15 ⊖	a							22 55						23 27					23 58						
London Victoria 15 ⊖	a		22 39	22 53		23 04	22 56		23 25	23 09	23 34		23 27		23 39	23 54									

Horsham, Dorking, Guildford, Epsom and Sutton - London

Network Diagram - see first Page of Table 177

		SN	SW	SW	SW	SN	SN	SN	SW	SN		FC	FC	SN	SN	SN	SW	SN	FC	FC		SN	SN	SN	SW
Horsham 4	d																								
Warnham	d																								
Ockley	d																								
Holmwood	d																								
Dorking 4	a																								
	d						06 28								06 57								07 26		
Box Hill & Westhumble	d														06 59								07 28		
Guildford	d								06 28								06 58								07 28
Effingham Junction 6	d								06 46								07 16								07 46
Bookham	d								06 49								07 19								07 49
Leatherhead	d						06 34		06 54						07 04		07 24						07 33		07 54
Ashtead	d						06 37		06 58						07 08		07 28						07 37		07 58
Epsom 3	a						06 42		07 02						07 12		07 32						07 41		08 02
	d		05 35	06 05	06 35		06 42	06 49	07 05					07 04	07 13	07 19	07 35						07 42	07 49	08 05
Ewell East	d						06 46	06 53						07 08		07 23							07 46	07 53	
Cheam	d						06 49	06 56						07 11	07 18	07 26							07 49	07 56	
Epsom Downs	d	23p43																				07 35			
Banstead	d	23p46																				07 38			
Belmont	d	23p49																				07 41			
Sutton (Surrey) 4	a	23p52					06 52	06 59						07 14	07 22	07 29						07 44	07 52	07 59	
	d	23p53				06 45	06 53	06 59		07 03		07 07	07 08	07 15	07 22	07 29		07 33	07 37	07 38		07 45	07 52	07 59	
Carshalton	d							07 02					07 11			07 32				07 41				08 02	
Hackbridge	d							07 05					07 13			07 35				07 43				08 05	
Mitcham Junction	d							07 08					07 16			07 38				07 46				08 08	
Mitcham Eastfields	d							07 11					07 19			07 41				07 49				08 11	
Carshalton Beeches	d	23p56				06 48				07 06				07 18				07 36				07 48			
Wallington	d	23p58				06 50				07 08				07 20				07 38				07 50			
Waddon	d	00 01				06 53				07 11				07 23				07 41				07 53			
West Croydon 4	d	00a04				06 58				07 15				07 28				07 45				07 58			
Norwood Junction 2	d									07 20								07 50							
New Cross Gate 4 ⊖	d									07 34								08 04							
Tulse Hill 3	a											07 44	07 27						08 14	07 57					
	d											07 47							08 17						
London Bridge 4 ⊖	a									07 41		08 00						08 11	08 30						
Balham 4 ⊖	d					07 14		07 18						07 44		07 48						08 14		08 18	
Clapham Junction 10	a		06 01	06 30	07 00	07 19	07 10	07 22	07 30					07 49	07 40	07 52	08 00					08 19	08 10	08 22	08 30
London Waterloo 15 ⊖	a		06 11	06 40	07 10				07 40								08 10								08 40
London Victoria 15 ⊖	a					07 28	07 18	07 30						07 58	07 48	08 00						08 28	08 18	08 30	

		SN	FC	FC	SN	SN		SW	SN	SN	SW	SN	FC	FC	SN	SN		SW	SN	SN	SW	SN	FC	FC	SN
Horsham 4	d															08 04									
Warnham	d															08 08									
Ockley	d															08 15									
Holmwood	d															08 19									
Dorking 4	a															08 25									
	d					07 58		08 05								08 26		08 35							
Box Hill & Westhumble	d															08 28									
Guildford	d										07 58										08 28				
Effingham Junction 6	d										08 16										08 46				
Bookham	d										08 19										08 49				
Leatherhead	d					08 04		08 11			08 24					08 33		08 41			08 54				
Ashtead	d					08 07		08 14			08 28					08 37		08 44			08 58				
Epsom 3	a					08 12		08 19			08 32					08 41		08 49			09 02				
	d				08 04	08 13		08 20		08 19	08 35					08 42		08 50		08 49	09 05				09 04
Ewell East	d				08 08					08 23						08 46				08 53					09 08
Cheam	d				08 11	08 18				08 26						08 49				08 56					09 11
Epsom Downs	d														08 35										
Banstead	d														08 38										
Belmont	d														08 41										
Sutton (Surrey) 4	a				08 14	08 21				08 29					08 44	08 52				08 59					09 14
	d	08 03	08 07	08 08	08 15	08 22			08 22	08 29		08 33	08 37	08 38	08 45	08 52			08 52	08 59		09 03	09 07	09 08	09 15
Carshalton	d			08 11						08 32				08 41						09 02				09 11	
Hackbridge	d			08 13						08 35				08 43						09 05				09 13	
Mitcham Junction	d			08 16						08 38				08 46						09 08				09 16	
Mitcham Eastfields	d			08 19						08 41				08 49						09 11				09 19	
Carshalton Beeches	d	08 06			08 18				08 25			08 36			08 48				08 55			09 06			09 18
Wallington	d	08 08			08 20				08 27			08 38			08 50				08 57			09 08			09 20
Waddon	d	08 11			08 23				08 30			08 41			08 53				09 00			09 11			09 23
West Croydon 4	d	08 15			08 28				08 34			08 45			08 58				09 04			09 15			09 28
Norwood Junction 2	d	08 22										08 52										09 22			
New Cross Gate 4 ⊖	d																								
Tulse Hill 3	a		08 44	08 27									09 14	08 57									09 44	09 27	
	d		08 47										09 17										09 47		
London Bridge 4 ⊖	a		09 00										09 30										10 00		
Balham 4 ⊖	d	08 39			08 44				08 51	08 48		09 09			09 14				09 21	09 18		09 39			09 44
Clapham Junction 10	a	08 44			08 49	08 40		08 45	08 56	08 52	09 00	09 14			09 19	09 10		09 15	09 26	09 22	09 30	09 44			09 49
London Waterloo 15 ⊖	a							08 55			09 10							09 25			09 40				
London Victoria 15 ⊖	a	08 53			08 58	08 48			09 04	09 00		09 23			09 28	09 18			09 34	09 30		09 53			09 58

Table 182

Saturdays

Horsham, Dorking, Guildford, Epsom and Sutton - London

Network Diagram - see first Page of Table 177

		SN		SW	SN	SN	SW	SN	FC	FC	SN	SN		SW	SN	SN	SW	SN	FC	FC	SN	SN		SW	SN
Horsham 4	d											09 04													
Warnham	d											09 08													
Ockley	d											09 15													
Holmwood	d											09 19													
Dorking 4	a											09 25													
	d	08 58		09 05								09 26		09 35								09 58		10 05	
Box Hill & Westhumble	d											09 28													
Guildford	d						08 58										09 28								
Effingham Junction 6	d						09 16										09 46								
Bookham	d						09 19										09 49								
Leatherhead	d	09 04		09 11			09 24					09 33		09 41			09 54					10 04		10 11	
Ashtead	d	09 07		09 14			09 28					09 37		09 44			09 58					10 07		10 14	
Epsom 3	a	09 12		09 19			09 32					09 41		09 49			10 02					10 12		10 19	
	d	09 13		09 20		09 19	09 35					09 42		09 50		09 49	10 05				10 04	10 12		10 20	
Ewell East	d					09 23						09 46				09 53					10 08				
Cheam	d	09 18				09 26						09 49				09 56					10 11	10 18			
Epsom Downs	d										09 35														
Banstead	d										09 38														
Belmont	d										09 41														
Sutton (Surrey) 4	a	09 21				09 29					09 44	09 52				09 59					10 14	10 22			
	d	09 22			09 22	09 29		09 33	09 37	09 38	09 45	09 52			09 52	09 59		10 03	10 07	10 08	10 15	10 22			10 22
Carshalton	d					09 32				09 41						10 02				10 11					
Hackbridge	d					09 35				09 43						10 05				10 13					
Mitcham Junction	d					09 38				09 46						10 08				10 16					
Mitcham Eastfields	d					09 41				09 49						10 11				10 19					
Carshalton Beeches	d				09 25			09 36			09 48				09 55			10 06			10 18				10 25
Wallington	d				09 27			09 38			09 50				09 57			10 08			10 20				10 27
Waddon	d				09 30			09 41			09 53				10 00			10 11			10 23				10 30
West Croydon 4	d				09 34			09 45			09 58				10 04			10 15			10 28				10 34
Norwood Junction 2	d							09 52										10 22							
New Cross Gate 4 ⊖	d																								
Tulse Hill 3	a								10 14	09 57									10 44	10 27					
	d								10 17										10 47						
London Bridge 4 ⊖	a								10 30										11 00						
Balham 4 ⊖	d				09 51	09 48		10 09			10 14				10 21	10 18		10 39			10 44				10 51
Clapham Junction 10	a	09 40		09 45	09 56	09 52	10 00	10 14			10 19	10 10		10 15	10 26	10 22	10 30	10 44			10 49	10 40		10 45	10 56
London Waterloo 15 ⊖	a			09 55			10 10							10 25			10 40							10 55	
London Victoria 15 ⊖	a	09 48			10 04	10 00		10 23			10 28	10 18			10 34	10 30		10 53			10 58	10 48			11 04

		SN	SW	SN	FC	FC	SN	SN		SW	SN	SN	SW	SN	FC	FC	SN	SN		SW	SN	SN	SW	SN	FC
Horsham 4	d							10 04																	
Warnham	d							10 08																	
Ockley	d							10 15																	
Holmwood	d							10 19																	
Dorking 4	a							10 25																	
	d							10 26		10 35								10 58		11 05					
Box Hill & Westhumble	d							10 28																	
Guildford	d		09 58										10 28										10 58		
Effingham Junction 6	d		10 16										10 46										11 16		
Bookham	d		10 19										10 49										11 19		
Leatherhead	d		10 24					10 33		10 41			10 54					11 04		11 11			11 24		
Ashtead	d		10 28					10 37		10 44			10 58					11 07		11 14			11 28		
Epsom 3	a		10 32					10 41		10 49			11 02					11 12		11 19			11 32		
	d	10 19	10 35					10 42		10 50		10 49	11 05				11 04	11 13		11 20		11 19	11 35		
Ewell East	d	10 23						10 46				10 53					11 08					11 23			
Cheam	d	10 26						10 49				10 56					11 11	11 18				11 26			
Epsom Downs	d						10 35																		
Banstead	d						10 38																		
Belmont	d						10 41																		
Sutton (Surrey) 4	a	10 29					10 44	10 52				10 59					11 14	11 21				11 29			
	d	10 29		10 33	10 37	10 38	10 45	10 53			10 52	10 59		11 03	11 07	11 08	11 15	11 22			11 22	11 29		11 33	11 37
Carshalton	d	10 32				10 41						11 02				11 11						11 32			
Hackbridge	d	10 35				10 43						11 05				11 13						11 35			
Mitcham Junction	d	10 38				10 46						11 08				11 16						11 38			
Mitcham Eastfields	d	10 41				10 49						11 11				11 19						11 41			
Carshalton Beeches	d			10 36			10 48				10 55			11 06			11 18				11 25			11 36	
Wallington	d			10 38			10 50				10 57			11 08			11 20				11 27			11 38	
Waddon	d			10 41			10 53				11 00			11 11			11 23				11 30			11 41	
West Croydon 4	d			10 45			10 58				11 04			11 15			11 28				11 34			11 45	
Norwood Junction 2	d			10 52										11 22										11 52	
New Cross Gate 4 ⊖	d																								
Tulse Hill 3	a				11 14	10 57									11 44	11 27									12 14
	d				11 17										11 47										12 17
London Bridge 4 ⊖	a				11 30										12 00										12 30
Balham 4 ⊖	d	10 48		11 09			11 14				11 21	11 18		11 39			11 44				11 51	11 48		12 09	
Clapham Junction 10	a	10 52	11 00	11 14			11 19	11 10		11 15	11 26	11 22	11 30	11 44			11 49	11 40		11 45	11 56	11 52	12 00	12 14	
London Waterloo 15 ⊖	a		11 10							11 25			11 40							11 55			12 10		
London Victoria 15 ⊖	a	11 00		11 23			11 28	11 18			11 34	11 30		11 53			11 58	11 48			12 04	12 00		12 23	

Table 182

Saturdays

Horsham, Dorking, Guildford, Epsom and Sutton - London

Network Diagram - see first Page of Table 177

		FC	SN	SN		SW	SN	SN	SW	SN	FC	FC	SN	SN		SW	SN	SN	SW	SN	FC	FC	SN	SN	
Horsham 4	d			11 04																				12 04	
Warnham	d			11 08																				12 08	
Ockley	d			11 15																				12 15	
Holmwood	d			11 19																				12 19	
Dorking 4	a			11 25																				12 25	
	d			11 26		11 35								11 58		12 05								12 26	
Box Hill & Westhumble	d			11 28																				12 28	
Guildford	d								11 28										11 58						
Effingham Junction 6	d								11 46										12 16						
Bookham	d								11 49										12 19						
Leatherhead	d			11 33		11 41			11 54					12 04		12 11			12 24					12 33	
Ashtead	d			11 37		11 44			11 58					12 07		12 14			12 28					12 37	
Epsom 3	a			11 41		11 49			12 02					12 12		12 19			12 32					12 41	
	d			11 42		11 50		11 49	12 05				12 04	12 13		12 20		12 19	12 35					12 42	
Ewell East	d			11 46				11 53					12 08					12 23						12 46	
Cheam	d			11 49				11 56					12 11	12 18				12 26						12 49	
Epsom Downs	d		11 35																				12 35		
Banstead	d		11 38																				12 38		
Belmont	d		11 41																				12 41		
Sutton (Surrey) 4	a		11 44	11 52				11 59					12 14	12 21				12 29					12 44	12 52	
	d	11 38	11 45	11 52			11 52	11 59		12 03	12 07	12 08	12 15	12 22			12 22	12 29		12 33	12 37	12 38	12 45	12 52	
Carshalton	d	11 41						12 02				12 11						12 32				12 41			
Hackbridge	d	11 43						12 05				12 13						12 35				12 43			
Mitcham Junction	d	11 46						12 08				12 16						12 38				12 46			
Mitcham Eastfields	d	11 49						12 11				12 19						12 41				12 49			
Carshalton Beeches	d		11 48				11 55			12 06			12 18				12 25			12 36			12 48		
Wallington	d		11 50				11 57			12 08			12 20				12 27			12 38			12 50		
Waddon	d		11 53				12 00			12 11			12 23				12 30			12 41			12 53		
West Croydon 4	d		11 58				12 04			12 15			12 28				12 34			12 45			12 58		
Norwood Junction 2	d									12 22										12 52					
New Cross Gate 4 ⊖	d																								
Tulse Hill 3	a	11 57									12 44	12 27									13 14	12 57			
	d										12 47										13 17				
London Bridge 4 ⊖	a										13 00										13 30				
Balham 4 ⊖	d		12 14				12 21	12 18		12 39			12 44				12 51	12 48		13 09			13 14		
Clapham Junction 10	a		12 19	12 10		12 15	12 26	12 22	12 30	12 44			12 49	12 40		12 45	12 56	12 52	13 00	13 14			13 19	13 10	
London Waterloo 15 ⊖	a					12 25			12 40							12 55			13 10						
London Victoria 15 ⊖	a		12 28	12 18			12 34	12 30		12 53			12 58	12 48			13 04	13 00		13 23			13 28	13 18	

		SW	SN	SN	SW	SN	FC	FC	SN	SN		SW	SN	SN	SW	SN	FC	FC	SN	SN		SW	SN	SN	SW
Horsham 4	d																			13 04					
Warnham	d																			13 08					
Ockley	d																			13 15					
Holmwood	d																			13 19					
Dorking 4	a																			13 25					
	d	12 35								12 58		13 05								13 26		13 35			
Box Hill & Westhumble	d																			13 28					
Guildford	d				12 28										12 58										13 28
Effingham Junction 6	d				12 46										13 16										13 46
Bookham	d				12 49										13 19										13 49
Leatherhead	d	12 41			12 54					13 04		13 11			13 24					13 33		13 41			13 54
Ashtead	d	12 44			12 58					13 07		13 14			13 28					13 37		13 44			13 58
Epsom 3	a	12 49			13 02					13 12		13 19			13 32					13 41		13 49			14 02
	d	12 50		12 49	13 05				13 04	13 13		13 20		13 19	13 35					13 42		13 50		13 49	14 05
Ewell East	d			12 53					13 08					13 23						13 46				13 53	
Cheam	d			12 56					13 11	13 18				13 26						13 49				13 56	
Epsom Downs	d																		13 35						
Banstead	d																		13 38						
Belmont	d																		13 41						
Sutton (Surrey) 4	a			12 59					13 14	13 21				13 29					13 44	13 52				13 59	
	d		12 52	12 59		13 03	13 07	13 08	13 15	13 22			13 22	13 29		13 33	13 37	13 38	13 45	13 52			13 52	13 59	
Carshalton	d			13 02				13 11						13 32				13 41						14 02	
Hackbridge	d			13 05				13 13						13 35				13 43						14 05	
Mitcham Junction	d			13 08				13 16						13 38				13 46						14 08	
Mitcham Eastfields	d			13 11				13 19						13 41				13 49						14 11	
Carshalton Beeches	d		12 55			13 06			13 18				13 25			13 36			13 48				13 55		
Wallington	d		12 57			13 08			13 20				13 27			13 38			13 50				13 57		
Waddon	d		13 00			13 11			13 23				13 30			13 41			13 53				14 00		
West Croydon 4	d		13 04			13 15			13 28				13 34			13 45			13 58				14 04		
Norwood Junction 2	d					13 22										13 52									
New Cross Gate 4 ⊖	d																								
Tulse Hill 3	a						13 44	13 27									14 14	13 57							
	d						13 47										14 17								
London Bridge 4 ⊖	a						14 00										14 30								
Balham 4 ⊖	d		13 21	13 18		13 39			13 44				13 51	13 48		14 09			14 14				14 21	14 18	
Clapham Junction 10	a	13 15	13 26	13 22	13 30	13 44			13 49	13 40		13 45	13 56	13 52	14 00	14 14			14 19	14 10		14 15	14 26	14 22	14 30
London Waterloo 15 ⊖	a	13 25			13 40							13 55			14 10							14 25			14 40
London Victoria 15 ⊖	a		13 34	13 30		13 53			13 58	13 48			14 04	14 00		14 23			14 28	14 18			14 34	14 30	

Horsham, Dorking, Guildford, Epsom and Sutton - London

Network Diagram - see first Page of Table 177

		SN	FC	FC	SN	SN		SW	SN	SN	SW	SN	FC	FC	SN	SN		SW	SN	SN	SW	SN	FC	FC	SN
Horsham 4	d															14 04									
Warnham	d															14 08									
Ockley	d															14 15									
Holmwood	d															14 19									
Dorking 4	a															14 25									
	d					13 58		14 05								14 26		14 35							
Box Hill & Westhumble	d															14 28									
Guildford	d										13 58										14 28				
Effingham Junction 6	d										14 16										14 46				
Bookham	d										14 19										14 49				
Leatherhead	d					14 04		14 11			14 24					14 33		14 41			14 54				
Ashtead	d					14 07		14 14			14 28					14 37		14 44			14 58				
Epsom 3	a					14 12		14 19			14 32					14 41		14 49			15 02				
	d				14 04	14 13		14 20		14 19	14 35					14 42		14 50		14 49	15 05				15 04
Ewell East	d				14 08					14 23						14 46				14 53					15 08
Cheam	d				14 11	14 18				14 26						14 49				14 56					15 11
Epsom Downs	d														14 35										
Banstead	d														14 38										
Belmont	d														14 41										
Sutton (Surrey) 4	a				14 14	14 21				14 29					14 44	14 52				14 59					15 14
	d	14 03	14 07	14 08	14 15	14 22			14 22	14 29		14 33	14 37	14 38	14 45	14 52			14 52	14 59		15 03	15 07	15 08	15 15
Carshalton	d			14 11						14 32				14 41						15 02				15 11	
Hackbridge	d			14 13						14 35				14 43						15 05				15 13	
Mitcham Junction	d			14 16						14 38				14 46						15 08				15 16	
Mitcham Eastfields	d			14 19						14 41				14 49						15 11				15 19	
Carshalton Beeches	d	14 06			14 18				14 25			14 36			14 48				14 55			15 06			15 18
Wallington	d	14 08			14 20				14 27			14 38			14 50				14 57			15 08			15 20
Waddon	d	14 11			14 23				14 30			14 41			14 53				15 00			15 11			15 23
West Croydon 4	d	14 15			14 28				14 34			14 45			14 58				15 04			15 15			15 28
Norwood Junction 2	d	14 22										14 52										15 22			
New Cross Gate 4 ⊖	d																								
Tulse Hill 3	a		14 44	14 27									15 14	14 57									15 44	15 27	
	d		14 47										15 17										15 47		
London Bridge 4 ⊖	a		15 00										15 30										16 00		
Balham 4 ⊖	d	14 39			14 44				14 51	14 48		15 09			15 14				15 21	15 18		15 39			15 44
Clapham Junction 10	a	14 44			14 49	14 40		14 45	14 56	14 52	15 00	15 14			15 19	15 10		15 15	15 26	15 22	15 30	15 44			15 49
London Waterloo 15 ⊖	a							14 55			15 10							15 25			15 40				
London Victoria 15 ⊖	a	14 53			14 58	14 48			15 04	15 00		15 23			15 28	15 18			15 34	15 30		15 53			15 58

		SN		SW	SN	SN	SW	SN	FC	FC	SN	SN		SW	SN	SN	SW	SN	FC	FC	SN	SN		SW	SN
Horsham 4	d											15 04													
Warnham	d											15 08													
Ockley	d											15 15													
Holmwood	d											15 19													
Dorking 4	a											15 25													
	d	14 58		15 05								15 26		15 35								15 58		16 05	
Box Hill & Westhumble	d											15 28													
Guildford	d						14 58										15 28								
Effingham Junction 6	d						15 16										15 46								
Bookham	d						15 19										15 49								
Leatherhead	d	15 04		15 11			15 24					15 33		15 41			15 54					16 04		16 11	
Ashtead	d	15 07		15 14			15 28					15 37		15 44			15 58					16 07		16 14	
Epsom 3	a	15 12		15 19			15 32					15 41		15 49			16 02					16 12		16 19	
	d	15 13		15 20		15 19	15 35					15 42		15 50		15 49	16 05				16 04	16 13		16 20	
Ewell East	d					15 23						15 46				15 53					16 08				
Cheam	d	15 18				15 26						15 49				15 56					16 11	16 18			
Epsom Downs	d										15 35														
Banstead	d										15 38														
Belmont	d										15 41														
Sutton (Surrey) 4	a	15 21				15 29					15 44	15 52				15 59					16 14	16 21			
	d	15 22			15 22	15 29		15 33	15 37	15 38	15 45	15 52			15 52	15 59		16 03	16 07	16 08	16 15	16 22			16 22
Carshalton	d					15 32				15 41						16 02				16 11					
Hackbridge	d					15 35				15 43						16 05				16 13					
Mitcham Junction	d					15 38				15 46						16 08				16 16					
Mitcham Eastfields	d					15 41				15 49						16 11				16 19					
Carshalton Beeches	d				15 25			15 36			15 48				15 55			16 06			16 18				16 25
Wallington	d				15 27			15 38			15 50				15 57			16 08			16 20				16 27
Waddon	d				15 30			15 41			15 53				16 00			16 11			16 23				16 30
West Croydon 4	d				15 34			15 45			15 58				16 04			16 15			16 28				16 34
Norwood Junction 2	d							15 52										16 22							
New Cross Gate 4 ⊖	d																								
Tulse Hill 3	a								16 14	15 57									16 44	16 27					
	d								16 17										16 47						
London Bridge 4 ⊖	a								16 30										17 00						
Balham 4 ⊖	d				15 51	15 48		16 09			16 14				16 21	16 18		16 39			16 44				16 51
Clapham Junction 10	a	15 40		15 45	15 56	15 52	16 00	16 14			16 19	16 10		16 15	16 26	16 22	16 30	16 44			16 49	16 40		16 45	16 56
London Waterloo 15 ⊖	a			15 55			16 10							16 25			16 40							16 55	
London Victoria 15 ⊖	a	15 48			16 04	16 00		16 23			16 28	16 18			16 34	16 30		16 53			16 58	16 48			17 04

Horsham, Dorking, Guildford, Epsom and Sutton - London

Network Diagram - see first Page of Table 177

		SN	SW	SN	FC	FC	SN	SN		SW	SN	SN	SW	SN	FC	FC	SN	SN		SW	SN	SN	SW	SN	FC
Horsham 4	d							16 04																	
Warnham	d							16 08																	
Ockley	d							16 15																	
Holmwood	d							16 19																	
Dorking 4	a							16 25																	
	d							16 26		16 35								16 58		17 05					
Box Hill & Westhumble	d							16 28																	
Guildford	d		15 58										16 28										16 58		
Effingham Junction 6	d		16 16										16 46										17 16		
Bookham	d		16 19										16 49										17 19		
Leatherhead	d		16 24					16 33		16 41			16 54					17 04		17 11			17 24		
Ashtead	d		16 28					16 37		16 44			16 58					17 07		17 14			17 28		
Epsom 3	a		16 32					16 41		16 49			17 02					17 12		17 19			17 32		
	d	16 19	16 35					16 42		16 50		16 49	17 05				17 04	17 13		17 20		17 19	17 35		
Ewell East	d	16 23						16 46				16 53					17 08					17 23			
Cheam	d	16 26						16 49				16 56					17 11	17 18				17 26			
Epsom Downs	d						16 35																		
Banstead	d						16 38																		
Belmont	d						16 41																		
Sutton (Surrey) 4	a	16 29					16 44	16 52				16 59					17 14	17 21				17 29			
	d	16 29		16 33	16 37	16 38	16 45	16 52			16 52	16 59		17 03	17 07	17 08	17 15	17 22			17 22	17 29		17 33	17 37
Carshalton	d	16 32				16 41						17 02				17 11						17 32			
Hackbridge	d	16 35				16 43						17 05				17 13						17 35			
Mitcham Junction	d	16 38				16 46						17 08				17 16						17 38			
Mitcham Eastfields	d	16 41				16 49						17 11				17 19						17 41			
Carshalton Beeches	d			16 36			16 48				16 55			17 06			17 18				17 25			17 36	
Wallington	d			16 38			16 50				16 57			17 08			17 20				17 27			17 38	
Waddon	d			16 41			16 53				17 00			17 11			17 23				17 30			17 41	
West Croydon 4	d			16 45			16 58				17 04			17 15			17 28				17 34			17 45	
Norwood Junction 2	d			16 52										17 22										17 52	
New Cross Gate 4 ⊖	d																								
Tulse Hill 3	a				17 14	16 57									17 44	17 27									18 14
	d				17 17										17 47										18 17
London Bridge 4 ⊖	a				17 30										18 00										18 30
Balham 4 ⊖	d	16 48		17 09			17 14				17 21	17 18		17 39			17 44				17 51	17 48		18 09	
Clapham Junction 10	a	16 52	17 00	17 14			17 19	17 10		17 15	17 26	17 22	17 30	17 44			17 49	17 41		17 45	17 56	17 52	18 00	18 14	
London Waterloo 15 ⊖	a		17 10							17 25			17 40							17 55			18 10		
London Victoria 15 ⊖	a	17 00		17 23			17 28	17 18			17 34	17 30		17 53			17 58	17 49			18 04	18 00		18 23	

		FC	SN	SN		SW	SN	SN	SW	SN	FC	FC	SN	SN		SW	SN	SN	SW	SN	FC	FC	SN	SN	
Horsham 4	d			17 04																				18 04	
Warnham	d			17 08																				18 08	
Ockley	d			17 15																				18 15	
Holmwood	d			17 19																				18 19	
Dorking 4	a			17 25																				18 25	
	d			17 26		17 35								17 58		18 05								18 26	
Box Hill & Westhumble	d			17 28																				18 28	
Guildford	d								17 28										17 58						
Effingham Junction 6	d								17 46										18 16						
Bookham	d								17 49										18 19						
Leatherhead	d			17 33		17 41			17 54					18 04		18 11			18 24					18 33	
Ashtead	d			17 37		17 44			17 58					18 07		18 14			18 28					18 37	
Epsom 3	a			17 41		17 49			18 02					18 12		18 19			18 32					18 41	
	d			17 42		17 50		17 49	18 05				18 04	18 13		18 20		18 19	18 35					18 42	
Ewell East	d			17 46				17 53					18 08					18 23						18 46	
Cheam	d			17 49				17 56					18 11	18 18				18 26						18 49	
Epsom Downs	d		17 35																				18 35		
Banstead	d		17 38																				18 38		
Belmont	d		17 41																				18 41		
Sutton (Surrey) 4	a		17 44	17 52				17 59					18 14	18 21				18 29					18 44	18 52	
	d	17 38	17 45	17 52			17 52	17 59		18 03	18 07	18 08	18 15	18 22			18 22	18 29		18 33	18 37	18 38	18 45	18 52	
Carshalton	d	17 41						18 02				18 11						18 32				18 41			
Hackbridge	d	17 43						18 05				18 13						18 35				18 43			
Mitcham Junction	d	17 46						18 08				18 16						18 38				18 46			
Mitcham Eastfields	d	17 49						18 11				18 19						18 41				18 49			
Carshalton Beeches	d		17 48				17 55			18 06			18 18				18 25			18 36			18 48		
Wallington	d		17 50				17 57			18 08			18 20				18 27			18 38			18 50		
Waddon	d		17 53				18 00			18 11			18 23				18 30			18 41			18 53		
West Croydon 4	d		17 58				18 04			18 15			18 28				18 34			18 45			18 58		
Norwood Junction 2	d									18 22										18 52					
New Cross Gate 4 ⊖	d																								
Tulse Hill 3	a	17 57									18 44	18 27									19 14	18 57			
	d										18 47										19 17				
London Bridge 4 ⊖	a										19 00										19 30				
Balham 4 ⊖	d		18 14				18 21	18 18		18 39			18 44				18 51	18 48		19 09			19 14		
Clapham Junction 10	a		18 19	18 10		18 15	18 26	18 22	18 30	18 44			18 49	18 40		18 45	18 56	18 52	19 00	19 14			19 19	19 10	
London Waterloo 15 ⊖	a					18 25			18 40							18 55			19 10						
London Victoria 15 ⊖	a		18 28	18 18			18 34	18 30		18 53			18 58	18 48			19 04	19 00		19 23			19 28	19 18	

Table 182

Saturdays

Horsham, Dorking, Guildford, Epsom and Sutton - London

Network Diagram - see first Page of Table 177

		SW	SN	SN	SW	SN	FC	FC	SN	SN		SW	SN	SN	SW	SN	FC	SN	SN	SW		SN	SN	SW	SN
Horsham 4	d																								
Warnham	d																								
Ockley	d																								
Holmwood	d																								
Dorking 4	a																								
	d	18 35								18 58		19 05							19 28	19 35					
Box Hill & Westhumble	d									19 00															
Guildford	d				18 28										18 58									19 28	
Effingham Junction 6	d				18 46										19 16									19 46	
Bookham	d				18 49										19 19									19 49	
Leatherhead	d	18 41			18 54					19 05		19 11			19 24				19 34	19 41				19 54	
Ashtead	d	18 44			18 58					19 09		19 14			19 28				19 37	19 44				19 58	
Epsom 3	a	18 49			19 02					19 13		19 19			19 32				19 42	19 49				20 02	
	d	18 50		18 49	19 05				19 04	19 14		19 20		19 19	19 35				19 42	19 50			19 49	20 05	
Ewell East	d			18 53					19 08					19 23					19 46				19 53		
Cheam	d			18 56					19 11	19 19				19 26					19 49				19 56		
Epsom Downs	d																	19 35							
Banstead	d																	19 38							
Belmont	d																	19 41							
Sutton (Surrey) 4	a			18 59					19 14	19 22				19 29				19 44	19 52				19 59		
	d		18 52	18 59		19 03	19 07	19 08	19 15	19 23			19 22	19 29		19 33	19 37	19 45	19 53			19 52	19 59		20 03
Carshalton	d			19 02				19 11						19 32									20 02		
Hackbridge	d			19 05				19 13						19 35									20 05		
Mitcham Junction	d			19 08				19 16						19 38									20 08		
Mitcham Eastfields	d			19 11				19 19						19 41									20 11		
Carshalton Beeches	d		18 55			19 06			19 18				19 25			19 36		19 48				19 55			20 06
Wallington	d		18 57			19 08			19 20				19 27			19 38		19 50				19 57			20 08
Waddon	d		19 00			19 11			19 23				19 30			19 41		19 53				20 00			20 11
West Croydon 4	d		19 04			19 15			19 28				19 34			19 45		19 58				20 04			20 15
Norwood Junction 2	d					19 22										19 52									20 22
New Cross Gate 4 ⊖	d																								
Tulse Hill 3	a						19 44	19 27									20 14								
	d						19 47										20 17								
London Bridge 4 ⊖	a						20 00										20 30								
Balham 4 ⊖	d		19 21	19 18		19 39			19 44				19 51	19 48		20 09		20 14				20 21	20 18		20 39
Clapham Junction 10	a	19 15	19 26	19 22	19 30	19 44			19 49	19 40		19 45	19 56	19 52	20 00	20 14		20 19	20 10	20 15		20 26	20 22	20 30	20 44
London Waterloo 15 ⊖	a	19 25			19 40							19 55			20 10					20 25				20 40	
London Victoria 15 ⊖	a		19 34	19 30		19 53			19 58	19 48			20 04	20 00		20 23		20 28	20 18			20 34	20 30		20 53

		FC	SN	SN	SW	SN		SN	SW	SN	FC	SN	SN	SW	SN	SN		SN	FC	SN	SW	SN	SW	SN	SN
Horsham 4	d																								
Warnham	d																								
Ockley	d																								
Holmwood	d																								
Dorking 4	a																								
	d			19 58	20 05								20 28	20 35								20 58			
Box Hill & Westhumble	d			20 00																		21 00			
Guildford	d								19 58														20 46		
Effingham Junction 6	d								20 16														21 03		
Bookham	d								20 19														21 06		
Leatherhead	d			20 05	20 11				20 24				20 34	20 41								21 05	21 11		
Ashtead	d			20 09	20 14				20 28				20 37	20 44								21 09	21 14		
Epsom 3	a			20 13	20 19				20 32				20 42	20 49								21 13	21 19		
	d		20 04	20 14	20 20			20 19	20 35				20 42	20 50		20 49				21 03	21 05	21 14	21 20		21 19
Ewell East	d		20 08					20 23					20 46			20 53				21 08					21 23
Cheam	d		20 11	20 19				20 26					20 49			20 56				21 11		21 19			21 26
Epsom Downs	d											20 35													
Banstead	d											20 38													
Belmont	d											20 41													
Sutton (Surrey) 4	a		20 14	20 22				20 29				20 44	20 52			20 59				21 14		21 22			21 29
	d	20 08	20 15	20 23		20 22		20 29		20 33	20 37	20 45	20 53		20 52	20 59		21 03	21 07	21 15		21 23		21 22	21 29
Carshalton	d							20 32								21 02									21 32
Hackbridge	d							20 35								21 05									21 35
Mitcham Junction	d							20 38								21 08									21 38
Mitcham Eastfields	d							20 41								21 11									21 41
Carshalton Beeches	d		20 18			20 25				20 36		20 48			20 55			21 06		21 18				21 25	
Wallington	d		20 20			20 27				20 38		20 50			20 57			21 08		21 20				21 27	
Waddon	d		20 23			20 30				20 41		20 53			21 00			21 11		21 23				21 30	
West Croydon 4	d		20 28			20 34				20 45		20 58			21 04			21 15		21 28				21 34	
Norwood Junction 2	d									20 52								21 22							
New Cross Gate 4 ⊖	d																								
Tulse Hill 3	a	20 44									21 14								21 44						
	d	20 47									21 17								21 47						
London Bridge 4 ⊖	a	21 00									21 30								22 00						
Balham 4 ⊖	d		20 44			20 51		20 48		21 09		21 14			21 21	21 18		21 39		21 44				21 51	21 48
Clapham Junction 10	a		20 49	20 40	20 45	20 56		20 52	21 00	21 14		21 19	21 10	21 15	21 26	21 22		21 44		21 49	21 30	21 40	21 45	21 56	21 52
London Waterloo 15 ⊖	a				20 55				21 10					21 25							21 40		21 55		
London Victoria 15 ⊖	a		20 58	20 48		21 04		21 00		21 23		21 28	21 18		21 34	21 30		21 53		21 58		21 48		22 04	22 00

Table 182

Saturdays

Horsham, Dorking, Guildford, Epsom and Sutton - London

Network Diagram - see first Page of Table 177

			SW		SN	FC	SN	SN	SW	SN	SN	SN	FC		SN	SN	SW	SN	SN	SN	SN	SN	SW		SN	SN
Horsham 4		d																								
Warnham		d																								
Ockley		d																								
Holmwood		d																								
Dorking 4		a																								
		d						21 28	21 35							21 58						22 28	22 35			
Box Hill & Westhumble		d														22 00										
Guildford		d															21 46									
Effingham Junction 6		d															22 03									
Bookham		d															22 06									
Leatherhead		d						21 34	21 41							22 05	22 11					22 34	22 41			
Ashtead		d						21 37	21 44							22 09	22 14					22 37	22 44			
Epsom 3		a						21 42	21 49							22 13	22 19					22 42	22 49			
		d	21 35					21 42	21 50		21 49				22 04	22 14	22 20		22 19			22 42	22 50			22 49
Ewell East		d						21 46			21 53				22 08				22 23			22 46				22 53
Cheam		d						21 49			21 56				22 11	22 19			22 26			22 49				22 56
Epsom Downs		d					21 35														22 35					
Banstead		d					21 38														22 38					
Belmont		d					21 41														22 41					
Sutton (Surrey) 4		a					21 44	21 52			21 59				22 14	22 22			22 29		22 44	22 52				22 59
		d			21 33	21 37	21 45	21 53		21 52	21 59	22 03	22 07		22 15	22 23		22 22	22 29	22 33	22 45	22 53			22 52	22 59
Carshalton		d									22 02								22 32							23 02
Hackbridge		d									22 05								22 35							23 05
Mitcham Junction		d									22 08								22 38							23 08
Mitcham Eastfields		d									22 11								22 41							23 11
Carshalton Beeches		d			21 36		21 48			21 55		22 06			22 18			22 25		22 36	22 48				22 55	
Wallington		d			21 38		21 50			21 57		22 08			22 20			22 27		22 38	22 51				22 57	
Waddon		d			21 41		21 53			22 00		22 11			22 23			22 30		22 41	22 54				23 00	
West Croydon 4		d			21 45		21 58			22 04		22 15			22 28			22 34		22 45	22 58				23 04	
Norwood Junction 2		d			21 52							22 22								22 52						
New Cross Gate 4	⊖	d																								
Tulse Hill 3		a				22 14							22 44													
		d				22 17							22 47													
London Bridge 4	⊖	a				22 30							23 00													
Balham 4	⊖	d			22 09		22 14			22 22	22 18	22 39			22 44			22 51	22 48	23 09	23 14				23 21	23 18
Clapham Junction 10		a	22 00		22 14		22 19	22 10	22 15	22 27	22 22	22 44			22 49	22 40	22 45	22 56	22 52	23 14	23 19	23 10	23 15		23 26	23 22
London Waterloo 15	⊖	a	22 10						22 25								22 55						23 25			
London Victoria 15	⊖	a			22 23		22 28	22 18		22 34	22 30	22 53			22 58	22 48		23 04	23 00	23 24	23 29	23 22			23 34	23 31

			SN	SN	SN	SN	SW	SN	SN		SN	SN
Horsham 4		d										
Warnham		d										
Ockley		d										
Holmwood		d										
Dorking 4		a										
		d				23 00					23 30	
Box Hill & Westhumble		d				23 02						
Guildford		d					22 46					
Effingham Junction 6		d					23 03					
Bookham		d					23 06					
Leatherhead		d				23 07	23 11				23 36	
Ashtead		d				23 11	23 14				23 39	
Epsom 3		a				23 15	23 19				23 45	
		d		23 04		23 16	23 20		23 35			
Ewell East		d		23 08		23 20			23 39			
Cheam		d		23 11		23 23			23 42			
Epsom Downs		d						23 23				23 50
Banstead		d						23 26				23 53
Belmont		d						23 29				23 56
Sutton (Surrey) 4		a		23 14		23 26		23 32	23 45			23 59
		d	23 03	23 15	23 22	23 30		23 34	23 46			00 01
Carshalton		d										
Hackbridge		d										
Mitcham Junction		d										
Mitcham Eastfields		d										
Carshalton Beeches		d	23 06	23 18	23 25	23 33		23 37	23 49			00 04
Wallington		d	23 08	23 20	23 27	23 35		23 39	23 51			00 06
Waddon		d	23 11	23 23	23 30	23 38		23 42	23 54			00 09
West Croydon 4		d	23 15	23 28	23 34	23a41		23a45	23a57			00a12
Norwood Junction 2		d	23 22									
New Cross Gate 4	⊖	d										
Tulse Hill 3		a										
		d										
London Bridge 4	⊖	a										
Balham 4	⊖	d	23 39	23 44	23 50							
Clapham Junction 10		a	23 45	23 49	23 56		23 48					
London Waterloo 15	⊖	a					23 58					
London Victoria 15	⊖	a	23 53	23 58	00 04							

Table 182

Sundays

Horsham, Dorking, Guildford, Epsom and Sutton - London

Network Diagram - see first Page of Table 177

		SN A	SN A	SN	SN	SN	SW	SN	SN	SN		SW	SN	SN	SN	SN	SW	SN	SN	SN		SN	SW	SN	SN
Horsham 4	d																								
Warnham	d																								
Ockley	d																								
Holmwood	d																								
Dorking 4	a																								
	d							07 16						07 46					08 16						08 46
Box Hill & Westhumble	d							07 18						07 48					08 18						08 48
Guildford	d																						08 20		
Effingham Junction 6	d																						08 36		
Bookham	d																						08 39		
Leatherhead	d							07 23						07 53					08 23				08 45		08 53
Ashtead	d							07 27						07 57					08 27				08 48		08 57
Epsom 3	a							07 31						08 01					08 31				08 53		09 01
	d			06 44		07 17	07 24	07 32		07 47		07 54		08 02		08 17	08 24		08 32			08 47	08 54		09 02
Ewell East	d			06 48		07 21		07 36		07 51				08 06		08 21			08 36			08 51			09 06
Cheam	d			06 51		07 24		07 39		07 54				08 09		08 24			08 39			08 54			09 09
Epsom Downs	d		23p50																						
Banstead	d		23p53																						
Belmont	d		23p56																						
Sutton (Surrey) 4	a		23p59	06 54		07 27		07 42		07 57				08 12		08 27			08 42			08 57			09 12
	d	23p22	00 01	06 55	07 25	07 28		07 43	07 55	07 58			08 10	08 13	08 25	08 28		08 40	08 43	08 55		08 58		09 10	09 13
Carshalton	d					07 31		07 46		08 01				08 16		08 31			08 46			09 01			09 16
Hackbridge	d					07 33		07 48		08 03				08 18		08 33			08 48			09 03			09 18
Mitcham Junction	d					07 37		07 52		08 07				08 22		08 37			08 52			09 07			09 22
Mitcham Eastfields	d					07 40		07 55		08 10				08 25		08 40			08 55			09 10			09 25
Carshalton Beeches	d	23p25	00 04	06 58	07 28				07 58				08 13		08 28			08 43		08 58				09 13	
Wallington	d	23p27	00 06	07 00	07 30				08 00				08 15		08 30			08 45		09 00				09 15	
Waddon	d	23p30	00 09	07 03	07 33				08 03				08 18		08 33			08 48		09 03				09 18	
West Croydon 4	d	23p34	00a12	07 07	07 37				08 07				08 22		08 37			08 52		09 07				09 22	
Norwood Junction 2	d												08 27					08 57						09 27	
New Cross Gate 4 ⊖	d																								
Tulse Hill 3	a																								
	d																								
London Bridge 4 ⊖	a																								
Balham 4 ⊖	d	23p50		07 23	07 53	07 48		08 01	08 23	08 18			08 43	08 31	08 53	08 48		09 13	09 01	09 23		09 18		09 43	09 31
Clapham Junction 10	a	23p56		07 27	07 57	07 52	07 49	08 06	08 27	08 22		08 19	08 48	08 36	08 57	08 52	08 49	09 19	09 06	09 27		09 22	09 19	09 49	09 36
London Waterloo 15 ⊖	a						08 04					08 34					09 04						09 34		
London Victoria 15 ⊖	a	00 04		07 34	08 04	07 59		08 15	08 34	08 29			08 57	08 45	09 04	08 59		09 27	09 15	09 34		09 29		09 57	09 45

		SN	SN	SW	SN	SN		SN	SN	SW	SN	SN	SN	SN	SW	FC		SN	SN	SN	SN	SW	FC	SN	SN
Horsham 4	d																								
Warnham	d																								
Ockley	d																								
Holmwood	d																								
Dorking 4	a																								
	d			09 08		09 16						09 46			10 08				10 16						10 46
Box Hill & Westhumble	d					09 18						09 48							10 18						10 48
Guildford	d									09 20												10 20			
Effingham Junction 6	d									09 36												10 36			
Bookham	d									09 39												10 39			
Leatherhead	d			09 15		09 23				09 45		09 53			10 15				10 23			10 45			10 53
Ashtead	d			09 18		09 27				09 48		09 57			10 18				10 27			10 48			10 57
Epsom 3	a			09 23		09 31				09 53		10 01			10 23				10 31			10 53			11 01
	d		09 17	09 24		09 32			09 47	09 54		10 02		10 17	10 24				10 32		10 47	10 54			11 02
Ewell East	d		09 21			09 36			09 51			10 06		10 21					10 36		10 51				11 06
Cheam	d		09 24			09 39			09 54			10 09		10 24					10 39		10 54				11 09
Epsom Downs	d																								
Banstead	d																								
Belmont	d																								
Sutton (Surrey) 4	a		09 27			09 42			09 57			10 12		10 27					10 42		10 57				11 12
	d	09 25	09 28		09 40	09 43		09 55	09 58		10 10	10 13	10 25	10 28		10 28		10 40	10 43	10 55	10 58		10 58	11 10	11 13
Carshalton	d		09 31			09 46			10 01			10 16		10 31					10 46		11 01				11 16
Hackbridge	d		09 33			09 48			10 03			10 18		10 33					10 48		11 03				11 18
Mitcham Junction	d		09 37			09 52			10 07			10 22		10 37					10 52		11 07				11 22
Mitcham Eastfields	d		09 40			09 55			10 10			10 25		10 40					10 55		11 10				11 25
Carshalton Beeches	d	09 28			09 43			09 58			10 13		10 28					10 43		10 58				11 13	
Wallington	d	09 30			09 45			10 00			10 15		10 30					10 45		11 00				11 15	
Waddon	d	09 33			09 48			10 03			10 18		10 33					10 48		11 03				11 18	
West Croydon 4	d	09 37			09 52			10 07			10 22		10 37					10 52		11 07				11 22	
Norwood Junction 2	d				09 57						10 27							10 57						11 27	
New Cross Gate 4 ⊖	d																								
Tulse Hill 3	a															10 59							11 29		
	d															10 59							11 29		
London Bridge 4 ⊖	a															11 10							11 40		
Balham 4 ⊖	d	09 53	09 48		10 13	10 01		10 23	10 18		10 43	10 31	10 53	10 48				11 13	11 01	11 23	11 18			11 43	11 31
Clapham Junction 10	a	09 57	09 52	09 49	10 18	10 06		10 27	10 22	10 19	10 48	10 36	10 57	10 52	10 49			11 18	11 06	11 27	11 22	11 19		11 48	11 36
London Waterloo 15 ⊖	a			10 04						10 34					11 04							11 34			
London Victoria 15 ⊖	a	10 04	09 59		10 27	10 15		10 34	10 29		10 57	10 45	11 04	10 59				11 27	11 15	11 34	11 29			11 57	11 45

A not 11 December

Horsham, Dorking, Guildford, Epsom and Sutton - London

Network Diagram - see first Page of Table 177

		SN		SN	SW	FC	SN	SN	SN	SN	SW	FC		SN	SN	SN	SN	SW	FC	SN	SN	SN		SN	SW
Horsham ■4	d																								
Warnham	d																								
Ockley	d																								
Holmwood	d																								
Dorking ■4	a																								
	d				11 08			11 16							11 46			12 08			12 16				
Box Hill & Westhumble	d							11 18							11 48						12 18				
Guildford	d										11 20														12 20
Effingham Junction ■6	d										11 36														12 36
Bookham	d										11 39														12 39
Leatherhead	d				11 15			11 23			11 45				11 53			12 15			12 23				12 45
Ashtead	d				11 18			11 27			11 48				11 57			12 18			12 27				12 48
Epsom ■3	a				11 23			11 31			11 53				12 01			12 23			12 31				12 53
	d			11 17	11 24			11 32		11 47	11 54				12 02		12 17	12 24			12 32			12 47	12 54
Ewell East	d			11 21				11 36		11 51					12 06		12 21				12 36			12 51	
Cheam	d			11 24				11 39		11 54					12 09		12 24				12 39			12 54	
Epsom Downs	d																								
Banstead	d																								
Belmont	d																								
Sutton (Surrey) ■4	a			11 27				11 42		11 57					12 12		12 27				12 42			12 57	
	d	11 25		11 28		11 28	11 40	11 43	11 55	11 58		11 58		12 10	12 13	12 25	12 28		12 28	12 40	12 43	12 55		12 58	
Carshalton	d			11 31				11 46		12 01					12 16		12 31				12 46			13 01	
Hackbridge	d			11 33				11 48		12 03					12 18		12 33				12 48			13 03	
Mitcham Junction	d			11 37				11 52		12 07					12 22		12 37				12 52			13 07	
Mitcham Eastfields	d			11 40				11 55		12 10					12 25		12 40				12 55			13 10	
Carshalton Beeches	d	11 28					11 43		11 58					12 13		12 28				12 43		12 58			
Wallington	d	11 30					11 45		12 00					12 15		12 30				12 45		13 00			
Waddon	d	11 33					11 48		12 03					12 18		12 33				12 48		13 03			
West Croydon ■4	d	11 37					11 52		12 07					12 22		12 37				12 52		13 07			
Norwood Junction ■2	d						11 57							12 27						12 57					
New Cross Gate ■4 ⊖	d																								
Tulse Hill ■3	a					11 59						12 29							12 59						
	d					11 59						12 29							12 59						
London Bridge ■4 ⊖	a					12 10						12 40							13 10						
Balham ■4 ⊖	d	11 53		11 48			12 13	12 01	12 23	12 18				12 43	12 31	12 53	12 48			13 13	13 01	13 23		13 18	
Clapham Junction ■10	a	11 57		11 52	11 49		12 18	12 06	12 27	12 22	12 19			12 48	12 36	12 57	12 52	12 49		13 19	13 06	13 27		13 22	13 19
London Waterloo ■15 ⊖	a				12 04						12 34							13 04							13 34
London Victoria ■15 ⊖	a	12 04		11 59			12 27	12 15	12 34	12 29				12 57	12 45	13 04	12 59			13 27	13 15	13 34		13 29	

		FC	SN	SN	SN	SN	SW	FC		SN	SN	SN	SN	SW	FC	SN	SN	SN		SN	SW	FC	SN	SN	SN
Horsham ■4	d																								
Warnham	d																								
Ockley	d																								
Holmwood	d																								
Dorking ■4	a																								
	d			12 46			13 08				13 16						13 46				14 08			14 16	
Box Hill & Westhumble	d			12 48							13 18						13 48							14 18	
Guildford	d													13 20											
Effingham Junction ■6	d													13 36											
Bookham	d													13 39											
Leatherhead	d			12 53			13 15				13 23			13 45			13 53				14 15			14 23	
Ashtead	d			12 57			13 18				13 27			13 48			13 57				14 18			14 27	
Epsom ■3	a			13 01			13 23				13 31			13 53			14 01				14 23			14 31	
	d			13 02		13 17	13 24				13 32		13 47	13 54			14 02			14 17	14 24			14 32	
Ewell East	d			13 06		13 21					13 36		13 51				14 06			14 21				14 36	
Cheam	d			13 09		13 24					13 39		13 54				14 09			14 24				14 39	
Epsom Downs	d																								
Banstead	d																								
Belmont	d																								
Sutton (Surrey) ■4	a			13 12		13 27					13 42		13 57				14 12			14 27				14 42	
	d	12 58	13 10	13 13	13 25	13 28		13 28		13 40	13 43	13 55	13 58		13 58	14 10	14 13	14 25		14 28		14 28	14 40	14 43	14 55
Carshalton	d			13 16		13 31					13 46		14 01				14 16			14 31				14 46	
Hackbridge	d			13 18		13 33					13 48		14 03				14 18			14 33				14 48	
Mitcham Junction	d			13 22		13 37					13 52		14 07				14 22			14 37				14 52	
Mitcham Eastfields	d			13 25		13 40					13 55		14 10				14 25			14 40				14 55	
Carshalton Beeches	d		13 13		13 28					13 43		13 58				14 13		14 28					14 43		14 58
Wallington	d		13 15		13 30					13 45		14 00				14 15		14 30					14 45		15 00
Waddon	d		13 18		13 33					13 48		14 03				14 18		14 33					14 48		15 03
West Croydon ■4	d		13 22		13 37					13 52		14 07				14 22		14 37					14 52		15 07
Norwood Junction ■2	d		13 27							13 57						14 27							14 57		
New Cross Gate ■4 ⊖	d																								
Tulse Hill ■3	a	13 29						13 59							14 29							14 59			
	d	13 29						13 59							14 29							14 59			
London Bridge ■4 ⊖	a	13 40						14 10							14 40							15 10			
Balham ■4 ⊖	d		13 43	13 31	13 53	13 48				14 13	14 01	14 23	14 18			14 43	14 31	14 53		14 48			15 13	15 01	15 23
Clapham Junction ■10	a		13 48	13 36	13 57	13 52	13 49			14 19	14 06	14 27	14 22	14 19		14 48	14 36	14 57		14 52	14 49		15 19	15 06	15 27
London Waterloo ■15 ⊖	a						14 04							14 34							14 59				
London Victoria ■15 ⊖	a		13 57	13 45	14 04	13 59				14 27	14 15	14 34	14 29			14 57	14 45	15 04		14 59			15 27	15 15	15 34

Table 182

Sundays

Horsham, Dorking, Guildford, Epsom and Sutton - London

Network Diagram - see first Page of Table 177

		SN	SW	FC		SN	SN	SN	SN	SW	FC	SN	SN	SN		SN	SW	FC	SN	SN	SN	SN	SW	FC	
Horsham 4	d																								
Warnham	d																								
Ockley	d																								
Holmwood	d																								
Dorking 4	a																								
	d						14 46			15 08			15 16							15 46			16 08		
Box Hill & Westhumble	d						14 48						15 18							15 48					
Guildford	d		14 20														15 20								
Effingham Junction 6	d		14 36														15 36								
Bookham	d		14 39														15 39								
Leatherhead	d		14 45				14 53			15 15			15 23				15 45			15 53			16 15		
Ashtead	d		14 48				14 57			15 18			15 27				15 48			15 57			16 18		
Epsom 3	a		14 53				15 01			15 23			15 31				15 53			16 01			16 23		
	d	14 47	14 54				15 02		15 17	15 24			15 32			15 47	15 54			16 02		16 17	16 24		
Ewell East	d	14 51					15 06		15 21				15 36			15 51				16 06		16 21			
Cheam	d	14 54					15 09		15 24				15 39			15 54				16 09		16 24			
Epsom Downs	d																								
Banstead	d																								
Belmont	d																								
Sutton (Surrey) 4	a	14 57					15 12		15 27				15 42			15 57				16 12		16 27			
	d	14 58		14 58		15 10	15 13	15 25	15 28		15 28	15 40	15 43	15 55		15 58		15 58	16 10	16 13	16 25	16 28		16 28	
Carshalton	d	15 01					15 16		15 31				15 46			16 01				16 16		16 31			
Hackbridge	d	15 03					15 18		15 33				15 48			16 03				16 18		16 33			
Mitcham Junction	d	15 07					15 22		15 37				15 52			16 07				16 22		16 37			
Mitcham Eastfields	d	15 10					15 25		15 40				15 55			16 10				16 25		16 40			
Carshalton Beeches	d					15 13		15 28				15 43		15 58					16 13		16 28				
Wallington	d					15 15		15 30				15 45		16 00					16 15		16 30				
Waddon	d					15 18		15 33				15 48		16 03					16 18		16 33				
West Croydon 4	d					15 22		15 37				15 52		16 07					16 22		16 37				
Norwood Junction 2	d					15 27						15 57							16 27						
New Cross Gate 4 ⊖	d																								
Tulse Hill 3	a			15 29							15 59							16 29						16 59	
	d			15 29							15 59							16 29						16 59	
London Bridge 4 ⊖	a			15 40							16 10							16 40						17 10	
Balham 4 ⊖	d	15 18				15 43	15 31	15 53	15 48			16 13	16 01	16 23		16 18			16 43	16 31	16 53	16 48			
Clapham Junction 10	a	15 22	15 19			15 48	15 36	15 57	15 52	15 49		16 19	16 06	16 27		16 22	16 19		16 48	16 36	16 57	16 52	16 49		
London Waterloo 15 ⊖	a		15 29							15 59							16 29						16 59		
London Victoria 15 ⊖	a	15 29				15 57	15 45	16 04	15 59			16 27	16 15	16 34		16 29			16 57	16 45	17 04	16 59			

		SN	SN	SN	SN	SW	FC	SN	SN	SN		SN	SW	FC	SN	SN	SN	SN	SW	FC		SN	SN	SN	SN
Horsham 4	d																								
Warnham	d																								
Ockley	d																								
Holmwood	d																								
Dorking 4	a																								
	d		16 16						16 46				17 08			17 16							17 46		
Box Hill & Westhumble	d		16 18						16 48							17 18							17 48		
Guildford	d					16 20													17 20						
Effingham Junction 6	d					16 36													17 36						
Bookham	d					16 39													17 39						
Leatherhead	d		16 23			16 45			16 53				17 15			17 23			17 45				17 53		
Ashtead	d		16 27			16 48			16 57				17 18			17 27			17 48				17 57		
Epsom 3	a		16 31			16 53			17 01				17 23			17 31			17 53				18 01		
	d		16 32		16 47	16 54			17 02			17 17	17 24			17 32		17 47	17 54				18 02		18 17
Ewell East	d		16 36		16 51				17 06			17 21				17 36		17 51					18 06		18 21
Cheam	d		16 39		16 54				17 09			17 24				17 39		17 54					18 09		18 24
Epsom Downs	d																								
Banstead	d																								
Belmont	d																								
Sutton (Surrey) 4	a		16 42		16 57				17 12			17 27				17 42		17 57					18 12		18 27
	d	16 40	16 43	16 55	16 58		16 58	17 10	17 13	17 25		17 28		17 28	17 40	17 43	17 55	17 58		17 58		18 10	18 13	18 25	18 28
Carshalton	d		16 46		17 01				17 16			17 31				17 46		18 01					18 16		18 31
Hackbridge	d		16 48		17 03				17 18			17 33				17 48		18 03					18 18		18 33
Mitcham Junction	d		16 52		17 07				17 22			17 37				17 52		18 07					18 22		18 37
Mitcham Eastfields	d		16 55		17 10				17 25			17 40				17 55		18 10					18 25		18 40
Carshalton Beeches	d	16 43		16 58				17 13		17 28					17 43		17 58					18 13		18 28	
Wallington	d	16 45		17 00				17 15		17 30					17 45		18 00					18 15		18 30	
Waddon	d	16 48		17 03				17 18		17 33					17 48		18 03					18 18		18 33	
West Croydon 4	d	16 52		17 07				17 22		17 37					17 52		18 07					18 22		18 37	
Norwood Junction 2	d	16 57						17 27							17 57							18 27			
New Cross Gate 4 ⊖	d																								
Tulse Hill 3	a						17 29							17 59						18 29					
	d						17 29							17 59						18 29					
London Bridge 4 ⊖	a						17 40							18 10						18 40					
Balham 4 ⊖	d	17 13	17 01	17 23	17 18			17 43	17 31	17 53		17 48			18 13	18 01	18 23	18 18				18 43	18 31	18 53	18 48
Clapham Junction 10	a	17 19	17 06	17 27	17 22	17 19		17 48	17 36	17 57		17 52	17 49		18 19	18 06	18 27	18 22	18 19			18 48	18 36	18 57	18 52
London Waterloo 15 ⊖	a					17 29							17 59						18 29						
London Victoria 15 ⊖	a	17 27	17 15	17 34	17 29			17 57	17 45	18 04		17 59			18 27	18 15	18 34	18 29				18 57	18 45	19 04	18 59

Table 182

Sundays

Horsham, Dorking, Guildford, Epsom and Sutton - London

Network Diagram - see first Page of Table 177

		SW	FC	SN	SN	SN		SN	SW	FC	SN	SN	SW	SN	FC	SN		SN	SW	SN	FC	SN	SN	SW	SN
Horsham 4	d																								
Warnham	d																								
Ockley	d																								
Holmwood	d																								
Dorking 4	a																								
	d	18 08			18 16							18 46	19 08					19 16					19 46	20 08	
Box Hill & Westhumble	d				18 18							18 48						19 18					19 48		
Guildford	d								18 20										19 20						
Effingham Junction 6	d								18 36										19 36						
Bookham	d								18 39										19 39						
Leatherhead	d	18 15			18 23				18 45			18 53	19 15					19 23	19 45				19 53	20 15	
Ashtead	d	18 18			18 27				18 48			18 57	19 18					19 27	19 48				19 57	20 18	
Epsom 3	a	18 23			18 31				18 53			19 01	19 23					19 31	19 53				20 01	20 23	
	d	18 24			18 32			18 47	18 54			19 02	19 24					19 32	19 54				20 02	20 24	
Ewell East	d				18 36			18 51				19 06						19 36					20 06		
Cheam	d				18 39			18 54				19 09						19 39					20 09		
Epsom Downs	d																								
Banstead	d																								
Belmont	d																								
Sutton (Surrey) 4	a				18 42			18 57				19 12						19 42					20 12		
	d		18 28	18 40	18 43	18 55		18 58		18 58	19 10	19 13		19 25	19 28	19 40		19 43		19 55	19 58	20 10	20 13		20 25
Carshalton	d				18 46			19 01				19 16						19 46					20 16		
Hackbridge	d				18 48			19 03				19 18						19 48					20 18		
Mitcham Junction	d				18 52			19 07				19 22						19 52					20 22		
Mitcham Eastfields	d				18 55			19 10				19 25						19 55					20 25		
Carshalton Beeches	d			18 43		18 58					19 13			19 28		19 43				19 58		20 13			20 28
Wallington	d			18 45		19 00					19 15			19 30		19 45				20 00		20 15			20 30
Waddon	d			18 48		19 03					19 18			19 33		19 48				20 03		20 18			20 33
West Croydon 4	d			18 52		19 07					19 22			19 37		19 52				20 07		20 22			20 37
Norwood Junction 2	d			18 57							19 27					19 57						20 27			
New Cross Gate 4 ⊖	d																								
Tulse Hill 3	a		18 59							19 29					19 59						20 29				
	d		18 59							19 29					19 59						20 29				
London Bridge 4 ⊖	a		19 10							19 40					20 10						20 40				
Balham 4 ⊖	d			19 13	19 01	19 23		19 18			19 43	19 31		19 53		20 13		20 01		20 23		20 43	20 31		20 53
Clapham Junction 10	a	18 49		19 19	19 06	19 27		19 22	19 19		19 48	19 36	19 49	19 57		20 18		20 06	20 19	20 27		20 48	20 36	20 49	20 57
London Waterloo 15 ⊖	a	18 59							19 29				19 59						20 29					21 00	
London Victoria 15 ⊖	a			19 27	19 15	19 34		19 29			19 57	19 45		20 04		20 27		20 15		20 34		20 57	20 45		21 04

		FC		SN	SN	SW	SN	FC	SN	SN	SW	SN		FC	SN	SN	SW	SN	SN	SN	SW	SN		SN	SN
Horsham 4	d																								
Warnham	d																								
Ockley	d																								
Holmwood	d																								
Dorking 4	a																								
	d				20 16					20 46	21 08					21 16				21 46	22 08				22 16
Box Hill & Westhumble	d				20 18					20 48						21 18				21 48					22 18
Guildford	d					20 20											21 20								
Effingham Junction 6	d					20 36											21 36								
Bookham	d					20 39											21 39								
Leatherhead	d				20 23	20 45				20 53	21 15					21 23	21 45			21 53	22 15				22 23
Ashtead	d				20 27	20 48				20 57	21 18					21 27	21 48			21 57	22 18				22 27
Epsom 3	a				20 31	20 53				21 01	21 23					21 31	21 53			22 01	22 23				22 31
	d				20 32	20 54				21 02	21 24					21 32	21 54			22 02	22 24				22 32
Ewell East	d				20 36					21 06						21 36				22 06					22 36
Cheam	d				20 39					21 09						21 39				22 09					22 39
Epsom Downs	d																								
Banstead	d																								
Belmont	d																								
Sutton (Surrey) 4	a				20 42					21 12						21 42				22 12					22 42
	d	20 28		20 40	20 43		20 55	20 58	21 10	21 13		21 25		21 28	21 40	21 43		21 55	22 10	22 13		22 25		22 40	22 43
Carshalton	d				20 46					21 16						21 46				22 16					22 46
Hackbridge	d				20 48					21 18						21 48				22 18					22 48
Mitcham Junction	d				20 52					21 22						21 52				22 22					22 52
Mitcham Eastfields	d				20 55					21 25						21 55				22 25					22 55
Carshalton Beeches	d			20 43			20 58		21 13			21 28			21 43			21 58	22 13			22 28		22 43	
Wallington	d			20 45			21 00		21 15			21 30			21 45			22 00	22 15			22 30		22 45	
Waddon	d			20 48			21 03		21 18			21 33			21 48			22 03	22 18			22 33		22 48	
West Croydon 4	d			20 52			21 07		21 22			21 37			21 52			22 07	22 22			22 37		22 52	
Norwood Junction 2	d			20 57					21 27						21 57				22 27					22 57	
New Cross Gate 4 ⊖	d																								
Tulse Hill 3	a	20 59						21 29						21 59											
	d	20 59						21 29						21 59											
London Bridge 4 ⊖	a	21 10						21 40						22 10											
Balham 4 ⊖	d			21 13	21 01		21 23		21 43	21 31		21 53			22 13	22 01		22 23	22 43	22 31		22 53		23 13	23 01
Clapham Junction 10	a			21 19	21 06	21 19	21 27		21 49	21 36	21 49	21 57			22 19	22 06	22 19	22 27	22 49	22 36	22 49	22 57		23 19	23 06
London Waterloo 15 ⊖	a					21 29					22 00						22 29				23 00				
London Victoria 15 ⊖	a			21 27	21 15		21 34		21 57	21 45		22 04			22 27	22 15		22 34	22 57	22 45		23 04		23 27	23 15

Table 182

Sundays

Horsham, Dorking, Guildford, Epsom and Sutton - London

Network Diagram - see first Page of Table 177

		SW	SN	SN	SN	SW	SN	SN		SN
Horsham 4	d									
Warnham	d									
Ockley	d									
Holmwood	d									
Dorking 4	a									
	d				22 46	23 08				23 16
Box Hill & Westhumble	d				22 48					23 18
Guildford	d	22 20								
Effingham Junction 6	d	22 36								
Bookham	d	22 39								
Leatherhead	d	22 45			22 53	23 15				23 23
Ashtead	d	22 48			22 57	23 18				23 27
Epsom 3	a	22 53			23 01	23 23				23 31
	d	22 54			23 02	23 24				23 32
Ewell East	d				23 06					23 36
Cheam	d				23 09					23 39
Epsom Downs	d									
Banstead	d									
Belmont	d									
Sutton (Surrey) 4	a				23 12					23 42
	d		22 55	23 10	23 13		23 25	23 40		23 43
Carshalton	d				23 16					23 46
Hackbridge	d				23 18					23 48
Mitcham Junction	d				23 22					23 52
Mitcham Eastfields	d				23 25					23 55
Carshalton Beeches	d		22 58	23 13			23 28	23 43		
Wallington	d		23 00	23 15			23 30	23 45		
Waddon	d		23 03	23 18			23 33	23 48		
West Croydon 4	d		23 07	23 22			23 37	23 52		
Norwood Junction 2	d			23 27						
New Cross Gate 4 ⊖	d									
Tulse Hill 3	a									
	d									
London Bridge 4 ⊖	a									
Balham 4 ⊖	d		23 23	23 43	23 31		23 53	00 08		00 01
Clapham Junction 10	a	23 19	23 27	23 49	23 36	23 49	23 57	00 12		00 06
London Waterloo 15 ⊖	a	23 29				23 59				
London Victoria 15 ⊖	a		23 34	23 57	23 45		00 04	00 19		00 15

Network Diagram for Tables 184, 189

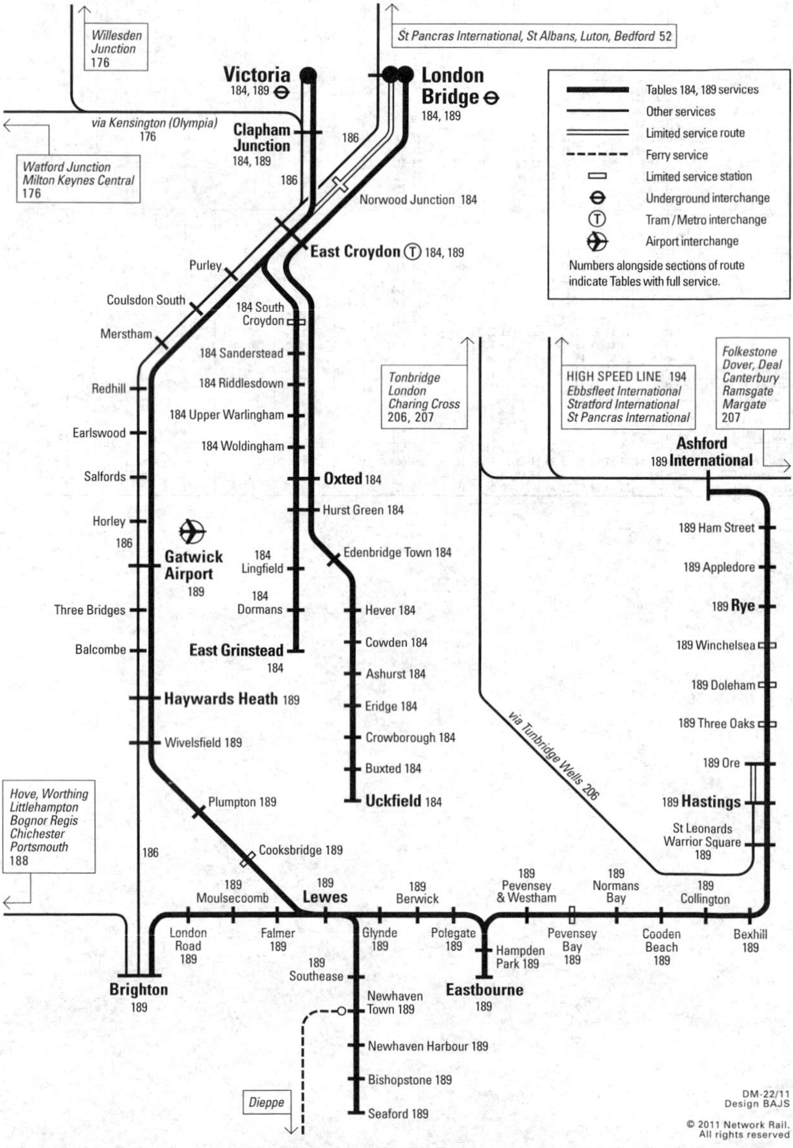

London - Oxted, East Grinstead and Uckfield

Network Diagram - see first Page of Table 184

Miles	Miles		SN MX 1	SN MX 1	SN MX 1	SN 1	SN 1	SN 1	SN 1	SN 1	SN 1	SN 1	SN 1	SN 1	SN 1	SN 1	SN 1	SN 1	SN 1	SN 1	SN 1	SN 1
0	—	**London Victoria** 15 ⊖175,177 d		23p24	23p49		05 23	05 53		06 24		06 54		07 10		07 32		08 10		08 53		09 23
2¾	—	Clapham Junction 10 175,177 d		23p30	23p56		05 33	05 59		06 30		07 00		07 16		07 38		08 16		08 59		09 29
—	0	**London Bridge** 4 ⊖175,177 d	23p04						06 08		06 38		07 03		07 19		08 00		08 25		09 08	
—	8¾	Norwood Junction 2 175,177 d	23p15				05 50								07 30				08 36			
10½	10¼	**East Croydon** 175,177 ⛴ d	23p19	23p41	00 10	05 26	05 55	06 10	06 22	06 41	06 53	07 11	07 17	07 27	07 34	07 52	08 16	08 27	08 41	09 10	09 23	09 40
11½	—	South Croydon 4 175 d					05 57															
12½	—	Sanderstead d	23p24	23p46	00s14			06 14		06 45		07 15	07 21	07 31	07 38	07 57	08 20	08 31	08 45	09 14		09 44
13¾	—	Riddlesdown d		23p49	00s17			06 17		06 48			07 24		07 41	08 00	08 23		08 48	09 17		09 47
15½	—	Upper Warlingham d	23p29	23p53	00s21			06 21		06 52			07 28		07 45	08 04	08 27		08 52	09 21		09 51
17¼	—	Woldingham d		23p57	00s25			06 25		06 56			07 32		07 49	08 08	08 31		08 56	09 25		09 55
20½	—	**Oxted** 3 a	23p36	00 02	00 30	05 41	06 09	06 30	06 36	07 01	07 06	07 26	07 37	07 43	07 54	08 13	08 36	08 42	09 01	09 30	09 36	10 00
—	—	d	23p37	00 02		05 41	06 09	06 31	06 36	07 02	07 07	07 26	07 38	07 43	07 55	08 13	08 37	08 42	09 02	09 31	09 37	10 00
21½	0	Hurst Green d	23p39	00 05		05 44	06 11	06 33	06 39	07 04	07 09	07 29	07 40	07 46	07 57	08 16	08 39	08 46	09 04	09 33	09 39	10 03
26¼	—	Lingfield d		00 11			06 17	06 39		07 10		07 35		07 52	08 03	08 22		08 52	09 10	09 39		10 09
28	—	Dormans d		00 14			06 21	06 43		07 14		07 38		07 55	08 07	08 25		08 55	09 14	09 43		10 12
30¼	—	**East Grinstead** a		00 19			06 25	06 47		07 18		07 43		08 00	08 12	08 30		09 00	09 18	09 47		10 17
—	4¼	Edenbridge Town d	23b45			05 50			06 45		07 15		07 46				08 45				09 45	
—	6	Hever d							06 48		07 19		07 50				08 49				09 49	
—	8	Cowden d							06 52		07 23		07 54				08 53				09 53	
—	10¾	Ashurst d							06 57		07 27		07 58				08 57				09 57	
—	14½	Eridge d	23b58			06 11			07 02		07 35		08 04				09 03				10 03	
—	17¾	Crowborough d	00s04			06 17			07 13		07 41		08 10				09 09				10 09	
—	22½	Buxted d	00s10			06 23			07 19		07 47		08 16				09 15				10 15	
—	25	**Uckfield** a	00 16			06 29			07 25		07 53		08 22				09 21				10 21	

	SN 1	SN 1	SN 1	SN 1	SN 1	SN 1	SN 1	SN 1	SN 1	SN 1	SN 1	SN 1	SN 1	SN 1	SN 1	SN 1	SN 1	SN 1	SN 1	SN 1	SN 1	SN 1
London Victoria 15 ⊖175,177 d	09 53		10 23	10 53		11 23	11 53		12 23	12 53		13 23	13 53		14 23	14 53		15 23		15 53		16 23
Clapham Junction 10 175,177 d	09 59		10 29	10 59		11 29	11 59		12 29	12 59		13 29	13 59		14 29	14 59		15 29		15 59		16 29
London Bridge 4 ⊖175,177 d		10 08			11 08			12 08			13 08			14 08			15 08		15 38		16 08	
Norwood Junction 2 175,177 d																						
East Croydon 175,177 ⛴ d	10 10	10 23	10 40	11 10	11 24	11 40	12 10	12 23	12 40	13 10	13 24	13 40	14 10	14 23	14 40	15 10	15 23	15 40	15 53	16 10	16 23	16 40
South Croydon 4 175 d																		15 43		16 12		16 42
Sanderstead d	10 14		10 44	11 14		11 44	12 14		12 44	13 14		13 44	14 14		14 45	15 14		15 46		16 15		16 45
Riddlesdown d	10 17		10 47	11 17		11 47	12 17		12 47	13 17		13 47	14 17		14 48	15 17		15 49		16 18		16 48
Upper Warlingham d	10 21		10 51	11 21		11 51	12 21		12 51	13 21		13 51	14 21		14 52	15 21		15 53		16 22		16 52
Woldingham d	10 25		10 55	11 25		11 55	12 25		12 55	13 25		13 55	14 25		14 56	15 25		15 57		16 26		16 56
Oxted 3 a	10 30	10 36	11 00	11 30	11 36	12 00	12 30	12 36	13 00	13 30	13 36	14 00	14 30	14 36	15 01	15 30	15 36	16 02	16 06	16 31	16 36	17 01
d	10 30	10 37	11 00	11 30	11 37	12 00	12 30	12 37	13 00	13 30	13 37	14 00	14 30	14 37	15 01	15 30	15 37	16 02	16 07	16 31	16 37	17 02
Hurst Green d	10 33	10 39	11 03	11 33	11 39	12 03	12 33	12 39	13 03	13 33	13 39	14 03	14 33	14 39	15 03	15 33	15 39	16 04	16 09	16 34	16 39	17 04
Lingfield d	10 39		11 09	11 39		12 09	12 39		13 09	13 39		14 09	14 39		15 09	15 39		16 10		16 40		17 10
Dormans d	10 42		11 12	11 42		12 12	12 42		13 12	13 42		14 12	14 42		15 13	15 42		16 14		16 43		17 14
East Grinstead a	10 47		11 17	11 47		12 17	12 47		13 17	13 47		14 17	14 47		15 17	15 47		16 18		16 48		17 20
Edenbridge Town d		10 45			11 45			12 45			13 45			14 45			15 45		16 15		16 45	
Hever d		10 49			11 49			12 49			13 49			14 49			15 49		16 19		16 49	
Cowden d		10 53			11 53			12 53			13 53			14 53			15 53		16 23		16 53	
Ashurst d		10 57			11 57			12 57			13 57			14 57			15 57		16 27		16 57	
Eridge d		11 03			12 03			13 03			14 03			15 03			16 03		16 33		17 03	
Crowborough d		11 09			12 09			13 09			14 09			15 09			16 09		16 39		17 09	
Buxted d		11 15			12 15			13 15			14 15			15 15			16 15		16 45		17 15	
Uckfield a		11 21			12 21			13 21			14 21			15 21			16 21		16 51		17 21	

	SN 1	SN 1	SN 1	SN 1	SN 1	SN 1	SN 1	SN 1	SN 1	SN 1	SN 1	SN 1	SN 1	SN 1	SN 1	SN 1	SN 1	SN 1	SN 1	SN 1	SN 1
London Victoria 15 ⊖175,177 d		16 53			17 23			17 53			18 23			18 53		19 23	19 53		20 23	20 53	
Clapham Junction 10 175,177 d		16 59			17 30			18 00			18 30			19 00		19 29	19 59		20 29	20 59	
London Bridge 4 ⊖175,177 d	16 38		17 09	17 15			17 44		18 08	18 16			18 47		19 08			20 04			21 04
Norwood Junction 2 175,177 d																		20 16			21 15
East Croydon 175,177 ⛴ d	16 53	17 10	17 23	17 30	17 41		17 58	18 11	18 22	18 31	18 41		19 01	19 11	19 23	19 40	20 10	20 20	20 40	21 10	21 19
South Croydon 4 175 d		17 12		17 32			18 01			18 33			19 03								
Sanderstead d		17 15		17 35	17 45		18 04	18 15		18 36	18 46		19 06	19 15		19 44	20 14	20 24	20 44	21 14	21 24
Riddlesdown d		17 18		17 38	17 48		18 07	18 18		18 39	18 49		19 09	19 18		19 47	20 17		20 47	21 17	
Upper Warlingham d		17 22		17 42	17 52		18 11	18 22		18 43	18 53		19 13	19 22		19 51	20 21	20 30	20 51	21 21	21 29
Woldingham d		17 26		17 46	17 56		18 15	18 26		18 47	18 57		19 17	19 26		19 55	20 25		20 55	21 25	
Oxted 3 a	17 06	17 31	17 36	17 51	18 01		18 20	18 31	18 36	18 52	19 02		19 22	19 31	19 36	20 00	20 30	20 37	21 00	21 30	21 36
d	17 07	17 32	17 37	17 52	18 02	18 07	18 20	18 32	18 37	18 53	19 03	19 07	19 23	19 32	19 37	20 00	20 30	20 37	21 00	21 30	21 37
Hurst Green d	17 09	17 34	17 40	17 54	18 04	18 09	18 23	18 34	18 39	18 55	19 05	19 09	19 25	19 34	19 39	20 03	20 33	20 40	21 03	21 33	21 39
Lingfield d		17 40		18 00	18 10		18 29	18 40		19 01	19 11		19 31	19 40		20 09	20 39		21 09	21 39	
Dormans d		17 44		18 04	18 14		18 32	18 44		19 05	19 15		19 35	19 44		20 12	20 42		21 12	21 42	
East Grinstead a		17 50		18 12	18 22		18 40	18 52		19 12	19 22		19 42	19 52		20 17	20 47		21 17	21 47	
Edenbridge Town d	17 15		17 46			18 15			18 45			19 15			19 45			20 46			21 45
Hever d	17 19					18 19						19 19			19 49			20 49			21 49
Cowden d	17 23					18 23			18 51			19 23			19 53			20 53			21 53
Ashurst d	17 27					18 27						19 27			19 57			20 58			21 57
Eridge d	17 33		17 58			18 33			18 59			19 33			20 03			21 03			22 03
Crowborough d	17 39		18 04			18 39			19 05			19 39			20 09			21 09			22 09
Buxted d	17 45		18 10			18 45			19 11			19 45			20 15			21 15			22 15
Uckfield a	17 51		18 18			18 51			19 19			19 51			20 21			21 21			22 21

b Previous night, stops to set down only

London - Oxted, East Grinstead and Uckfield

Network Diagram - see first Page of Table 184

Mondays to Fridays

		SN 1	SN 1	SN 1	SN 1	SN 1	SN 1	SN 1	SN 1
London Victoria 15 ⊖175,177	d	21 23	21 53		22 23	22 53		23 24	23 49
Clapham Junction 10 175,177	d	21 29	21 59		22 29	22 59		23 30	23 56
London Bridge 4 ⊖175,177	d			22 04			23 04		
Norwood Junction 2 175,177	d			22 15			23 15		
East Croydon 175,177 ⛴	d	21 40	22 10	22 19	22 40	23 10	23 19	23 41	00 10
South Croydon 4 175	d								
Sanderstead	d	21 44	22 14	22 24	22 44	23 14	23 24	23 46	00s14
Riddlesdown	d	21 47	22 17		22 47	23 17		23 49	00s17
Upper Warlingham	d	21 51	22 21	22 29	22 51	23 21	23 29	23 53	00s21
Woldingham	d	21 55	22 25		22 55	23 25		23 57	00s25
Oxted 3	a	22 00	22 30	22 36	23 00	23 30	23 36	00 02	00 30
	d	22 00	22 30	22 37	23 00	23 30	23 37	00 02	
Hurst Green	d	22 03	22 33	22 39	23 03	23 33	23 39	00 05	
Lingfield	d	22 09	22 39		23 09	23 39		00 11	
Dormans	d	22 12	22 42		23 12	23 42		00 14	
East Grinstead	a	22 17	22 47		23 17	23 47		00 19	
Edenbridge Town	d			22 45			23s45		
Hever	d			22s49					
Cowden	d			22s53					
Ashurst	d			22s57					
Eridge	d			23 03			23s58		
Crowborough	d			23 09			00s04		
Buxted	d			23 15			00s10		
Uckfield	a			23 21			00 16		

Saturdays

		SN 1	SN 1	SN 1	SN 1	SN 1	SN 1	SN 1		SN 1	SN 1	SN 1	SN 1	SN 1	SN 1	SN 1	SN 1	SN 1	SN 1	SN 1	SN 1	SN 1
London Victoria 15 ⊖175,177	d		23p24	23p49	05 23		06 23	06 53		19 53		20 23	20 53		21 23	21 53		22 23	22 53		23 24	23 49
Clapham Junction 10 175,177	d		23p30	23p56	05 29		06 29	06 59		19 59		20 29	20 59		21 29	21 59		22 29	22 59		23 30	23 56
London Bridge 4 ⊖175,177	d	23p04				06 08					20 08			21 08			22 08			23 04		
Norwood Junction 2 175,177	d	23p15			05 46						20 19			21 19			22 19			23 15		
East Croydon 175,177 ⛴	d	23p19	23p41	00 10	05 50	06 23	06 40	07 10		20 10	20 23	20 40	21 10	21 23	21 40	22 10	22 23	22 40	23 10	23 19	23 41	00 10
South Croydon 4 175	d				05 52																	
Sanderstead	d	23p24	23p46	00s14			06 44	07 14		20 14		20 44	21 14		21 44	22 14		22 44	23 14	23 24	23 46	00s14
Riddlesdown	d		23p49	00s17			06 47	07 17	and at	20 17		20 47	21 17		21 47	22 17		22 47	23 17		23 49	00s17
Upper Warlingham	d	23p29	23p53	00s21			06 51	07 21	the same	20 21		20 51	21 21		21 51	22 21		22 51	23 21	23 29	23 53	00s21
Woldingham	d		23p57	00s25			06 55	07 25	minutes	20 25		20 55	21 25		21 55	22 25		22 55	23 25		23 57	00s25
Oxted 3	a	23p36	00 02	00 30	06 04	06 36	07 00	07 30	past	20 30	20 36	21 00	21 30	21 36	22 00	22 30	22 36	23 00	23 30	23 36	00 02	00 30
	d	23p37	00 02		06 04	06 37	07 01	07 31	each	20 31	20 37	21 01	21 31	21 37	22 01	22 31	22 37	23 01	23 31	23 37	00 02	
Hurst Green	d	23p39	00 05		06 07	06 39	07 03	07 33	hour until	20 33	20 39	21 03	21 33	21 39	22 03	22 33	22 39	23 03	23 33	23 39	00 05	
Lingfield	d		00 11		06 13		07 09	07 39		20 39		21 09	21 39		22 09	22 39		23 09	23 39		00 11	
Dormans	d		00 14		06 16		07 13	07 43		20 43		21 13	21 43		22 13	22 43		23 13	23 43		00 14	
East Grinstead	a		00 19		06 21		07 17	07 47		20 47		21 17	21 47		22 17	22 47		23 17	23 47		00 19	
Edenbridge Town	d	23b45				06 45					20 45			21 45			22 45			23s45		
Hever	d					06 49					20 49			21 49			22s49					
Cowden	d					06 53					20 53			21 53			22s53					
Ashurst	d					06 57					20 57			21 57			22s57					
Eridge	d	23b58				07 03					21 03			22 03			23 03			23s58		
Crowborough	d	00s04				07 09					21 09			22 09			23 09			00s04		
Buxted	d	00s10				07 15					21 15			22 15			23 15			00s10		
Uckfield	a	00 16				07 21					21 21			22 21			23 21			00 16		

Sundays

		SN 1 A	SN 1 A	SN 1 A	SN 1	SN 1	SN 1	SN 1	SN 1	SN 1	SN 1		SN 1	SN 1	SN 1	SN 1	SN 1	SN 1	SN 1	SN 1
London Victoria 15 ⊖175,177	d		23p24	23p49	07 34	08 34		09 34		10 34				19 34		20 34		21 34		22 34
Clapham Junction 10 175,177	d		23p30	23p56	07 40	08 40		09 40		10 40				19 40		20 40		21 40		22 40
London Bridge 4 ⊖175,177	d	23p04																		
Norwood Junction 2 175,177	d	23p15																		
East Croydon 175,177 ⛴	d	23p19	23p41	00 10	07 58	08 58	09 15	09 58	10 15	10 58				19 58		20 58		21 58		22 58
South Croydon 4 175	d																			
Sanderstead	d	23p24	23p46	00s14	08 02	09 02		10 02		11 02				20 02		21 02		22 02		23 02
Riddlesdown	d		23p49	00s17	08 05	09 05		10 05		11 05		and at		20 05		21 05		22 05		23 05
Upper Warlingham	d	23p29	23p53	00s21	08 09	09 09		10 09		11 09		the same		20 09		21 09		22 09		23 09
Woldingham	d		23p57	00s25	08 13	09 13		10 13		11 13		minutes		20 13		21 13		22 13		23 13
Oxted 3	a	23p36	00 02	00 30	08 18	09 18	09 27	10 18	10 27	11 18		past		20 18		21 18		22 18		23 18
	d	23p37	00 02		08 18	09 18	09 33	10 18	10 33	11 18	11 33	each	19 33	20 19	20 33	21 18	21 33	22 18	22 33	23 18
Hurst Green	d	23p39	00 05		08 21	09 21	09 36	10 21	10 36	11 21	11 36	hour until	19 36	20 21	20 36	21 21	21 36	22 21	22 36	23 21
Lingfield	d		00 11		08 27	09 27		10 27		11 27				20 27		21 27		22 27		23 27
Dormans	d		00 14		08 30	09 30		10 30		11 30				20 31		21 30		22 30		23 30
East Grinstead	a		00 19		08 35	09 35		10 35		11 35				20 35		21 35		22 35		23 35
Edenbridge Town	d	23b45					09 42		10 42		11 42		19 42		20 42		21 42		22 42	
Hever	d						09 46		10 46		11 46		19 46		20 46		21 46		22 46	
Cowden	d						09 50		10 50		11 50		19 50		20 50		21 50		22 50	
Ashurst	d						09 54		10 54		11 54		19 54		20 54		21 54		22 54	
Eridge	d	23b58					10 00		11 00		12 00		20 00		21 00		22 00		23 00	
Crowborough	d	00s04					10 06		11 06		12 06		20 06		21 06		22 06		23 06	
Buxted	d	00s10					10 12		11 12		12 12		20 12		21 12		22 12		23 12	
Uckfield	a	00 16					10 18		11 18		12 18		20 18		21 18		22 18		23 18	

A not 11 December

b Previous night, stops to set down only

Table 184

Mondays to Fridays

Uckfield, East Grinstead and Oxted - London

Network Diagram - see first Page of Table 184

Miles	Miles			SN MO 1	SN 1	SN 1	SN 1	SN 1	SN 1	SN 1	SN 1	SN 1		SN 1	SN 1	SN 1	SN 1	SN 1	SN 1	SN 1	SN 1	SN 1		SN 1	SN 1
—	0	**Uckfield**	d				05 45				06 34				07 08			07 34			08 04			08 34	
—	2½	Buxted	d				05 50				06 39				07 14			07 39			08 09			08 39	
—	7¼	Crowborough	d				05 57				06 46				07 21			07 46			08 16			08 46	
—	10½	Eridge	d				06 02				06 51				07 27			07 51			08 21			08 51	
—	14¼	Ashurst	d								06 56							07 56			08 26			08 56	
—	17	Cowden	d				06 10				07 01							08 01			08 31			09 01	
—	19	Hever	d								07 05							08 05			08 35			09 05	
—	20¾	Edenbridge Town	d				06 15				07 09				07 39			08 09			08 39			09 08	
0	—	**East Grinstead**	d	23p12		05 58		06 14	06 37	06 49		07 07		07 19		07 37	07 49		08 07	08 17		08 37			09 07
2¼	—	Dormans	d	23p16		06 02		06 18	06 41	06 53		07 11		07 23		07 41	07 53		08 11	08 21		08 41			09 11
4	—	Lingfield	d	23p19		06 05		06 21	06 44	06 56		07 14		07 26		07 44	07 56		08 14	08 24		08 44			09 14
8¾	—	Hurst Green	d	23p26	06 00	06 12	06 22	06 28	06 51	07 03	07 17	07 21		07 33	07 47	07 51	08 03	08 16	08 21	08 31	08 46	08 51		09 15	09 21
9¾	25	**Oxted** 3	a	23p28	06 02	06 14	06 24	06 30	06 53	07 05	07 19	07 23		07 35	07 49	07 53	08 05	08 19	08 23	08 33	08 48	08 53		09 18	09 23
—	—		d	23p28	06 03	06 15	06 25	06 30	06 54	07 06	07 20	07 24		07 36	07 50	07 54	08 06	08 20	08 24	08 34	08 49	08 53		09 19	09 23
13	—	Woldingham	d	23p34	06 08			06 36	06 59	07 11		07 29		07 41		07 59	08 11		08 29	08 39		08 59			09 29
14¾	—	Upper Warlingham	d	23p37	06 12			06 39	07 03	07 15		07 33		07 45		08 03	08 15		08 33	08 43		09 02			09 32
16½	—	Riddlesdown	d	23p41	06 15			06 43	07 06	07 18		07 36		07 48		08 06	08 18		08 36	08 46		09 06			09 36
17¾	—	Sanderstead	d	23p44	06 18			06 46	07 10	07 22		07 40		07 51		08 10	08 22		08 39	08 49		09 09			09 39
18¾	—	South Croydon 4 175	d					06 50		07 25				07 54			08 26		08 42	08 52					
19¾	0	**East Croydon** 175,177 ⛴	a	23p49	06 23	06 27	06 38	06 53	07 15	07 27	07 31	07 44		07 58	08 04	08 14	08 29	08 32	08 45	08 55	09 01	09 13		09 32	09 43
—	1½	Norwood Junction 2 175,177	a																						
—	10¼	**London Bridge** 4 ⊖175,177	a		06 39		06 55	07 11		07 47	07 49			08 16	08 23		08 47	08 52		09 13	09 20			09 51	
27½	—	Clapham Junction 10 175,177	a	00 01		06 38			07 27			07 55				08 26			08 55			09 26			09 55
30¼	—	**London Victoria** 15 ⊖175,177	a	00 08		06 45			07 36			08 04				08 35			09 04			09 35			10 05

		SN 1	SN 1	SN 1	SN 1	SN 1	SN 1	SN 1		SN 1	SN 1	SN 1	SN 1	SN 1	SN 1	SN 1	SN 1	SN 1		SN 1	SN 1	SN 1	SN 1	SN 1	SN 1
Uckfield	d		09 34			10 34				11 34			12 34			13 34				14 34			15 34		
Buxted	d		09 39			10 39				11 39			12 39			13 39				14 39			15 39		
Crowborough	d		09 46			10 46				11 46			12 46			13 46				14 46			15 46		
Eridge	d		09 51			10 51				11 51			12 51			13 51				14 51			15 51		
Ashurst	d		09 56			10 56				11 56			12 56			13 56				14 56			15 56		
Cowden	d		10 01			11 01				12 01			13 01			14 01				15 01			16 01		
Hever	d		10 05			11 05				12 05			13 05			14 05				15 05			16 05		
Edenbridge Town	d		10 08			11 08				12 08			13 08			14 08				15 08			16 08		
East Grinstead	d	09 37		10 07	10 37		11 07	11 37			12 07	12 37		13 07	13 37		14 07	14 37			15 07	15 37		16 07	16 37
Dormans	d	09 41		10 11	10 41		11 11	11 41			12 11	12 41		13 11	13 41		14 11	14 41			15 11	15 41		16 11	16 41
Lingfield	d	09 44		10 14	10 44		11 14	11 44			12 14	12 44		13 14	13 44		14 14	14 44			15 14	15 44		16 14	16 44
Hurst Green	d	09 51	10 15	10 21	10 51	11 15	11 21	11 51		12 15	12 21	12 51	13 15	13 21	13 51	14 15	14 21	14 51		15 15	15 21	15 51	16 15	16 21	16 51
Oxted 3	a	09 53	10 17	10 23	10 53	11 17	11 23	11 53		12 17	12 23	12 53	13 17	13 23	13 53	14 17	14 23	14 53		15 17	15 23	15 53	16 17	16 23	16 53
	d	09 53	10 18	10 23	10 53	11 18	11 23	11 53		12 18	12 23	12 53	13 18	13 23	13 53	14 18	14 23	14 53		15 18	15 23	15 53	16 18	16 23	16 53
Woldingham	d	09 59		10 29	10 59		11 29	11 59			12 29	12 59		13 29	13 59		14 29	14 59			15 29	15 59		16 29	16 59
Upper Warlingham	d	10 02		10 32	11 02		11 32	12 02			12 32	13 02		13 32	14 02		14 32	15 02			15 32	16 02		16 32	17 02
Riddlesdown	d	10 06		10 36	11 06		11 36	12 06			12 36	13 06		13 36	14 06		14 36	15 06			15 36	16 06		16 36	17 06
Sanderstead	d	10 09		10 39	11 09		11 39	12 09			12 39	13 09		13 39	14 09		14 39	15 09			15 39	16 09		16 39	17 09
South Croydon 4 175	d																								
East Croydon 175,177 ⛴	a	10 13	10 32	10 43	11 13	11 32	11 43	12 13		12 32	12 43	13 13	13 32	13 43	14 13	14 32	14 43	15 13		15 32	15 43	16 13	16 32	16 43	17 13
Norwood Junction 2 175,177	a																								
London Bridge 4 ⊖175,177	a		10 49			11 49				12 49			13 49			14 49				15 49			16 47		
Clapham Junction 10 175,177	a	10 25		10 55	11 25		11 55	12 25			12 55	13 25		13 55	14 25		14 55	15 25			15 55	16 25		16 55	17 25
London Victoria 15 ⊖175,177	a	10 35		11 05	11 32		12 02	12 32			13 02	13 32		14 03	14 32		15 02	15 35			16 05	16 35		17 05	17 35

		SN 1	SN 1	SN 1		SN 1	SN 1	SN 1	SN 1	SN 1	SN 1	SN 1	SN 1	SN 1		SN 1	SN 1	SN 1	SN 1	SN 1	SN 1	SN 1	SN 1	SN 1	
Uckfield	d	16 33		17 03			17 32			17 58			18 32				18 57			19 33		20 04		20 34	
Buxted	d	16 38		17 08			17 37			18 03			18 37				19 02			19 38		20 09		20 39	
Crowborough	d	16 46		17 16			17 44			18 16			18 45				19 16			19 46		20 16		20 46	
Eridge	d	16 51		17 21			17 49			18 21			18 50				19 21			19 51		20 21		20 51	
Ashurst	d	16 56					17 54						18 55				19 26			19 56				20 56	
Cowden	d	17 01					17 59						18 59				19 31			20 01				21 01	
Hever	d	17 05					18 03						19 03				19 35			20 05				21 05	
Edenbridge Town	d	17 08		17 34			18 06			18 34			19 07				19 38			20 08		20 33		21 08	
East Grinstead	d		17 07			17 37		18 07	18 17		18 37	18 47		19 07		19 17		19 37	19 47		20 07		20 37		
Dormans	d		17 11			17 41		18 11	18 21		18 41	18 51		19 11		19 21		19 41	19 51		20 11		20 41		
Lingfield	d		17 14			17 44		18 14	18 24		18 44	18 54		19 14		19 24		19 44	19 54		20 14		20 44		
Hurst Green	d	17 15	17 21	17 40		17 51	18 13	18 21	18 31	18 40	18 51	19 01	19 13	19 21		19 31	19 45	19 51	20 01	20 15	20 21	20 39	20 51	21 15	
Oxted 3	a	17 17	17 23	17 43		17 53	18 15	18 23	18 33	18 43	18 53	19 03	19 16	19 23		19 33	19 47	19 53	20 03	20 17	20 23	20 42	20 53	21 17	
	d	17 18	17 23			17 53	18 18	18 23	18 34		18 53	19 04	19 18	19 23		19 34	19 48	19 53	20 04	20 18	20 23	20 42	20 53	21 18	
Woldingham	d		17 29			17 59		18 29	18 39		18 59	19 09		19 29		19 39		19 59	20 09		20 29		20 59		
Upper Warlingham	d		17 32			18 02		18 32	18 43		19 02	19 13		19 32		19 43		20 02	20 13		20 32		21 02		
Riddlesdown	d		17 36			18 06		18 36	18 46		19 06	19 16		19 36		19 46		20 06	20 16		20 36		21 06		
Sanderstead	d		17 39			18 09		18 39	18 49		19 09	19 19		19 39		19 49		20 09	20 19		20 39		21 09		
South Croydon 4 175	d																								
East Croydon 175,177 ⛴	a	17 35	17 43			18 13	18 35	18 43	18 56		19 13	19 25	19 33	19 43		19 57	20 06	20 13	20 25	20 33	20 43	20 54	21 13	21 30	
Norwood Junction 2 175,177	a								19 01																
London Bridge 4 ⊖175,177	a	17 52					18 50		19 15				19 49				20 21			20 48		21 09		21 49	
Clapham Junction 10 175,177	a		17 55			18 25		18 55			19 25			19 55				20 25			20 55		21 25		
London Victoria 15 ⊖175,177	a		18 05			18 35		19 05			19 32			20 02				20 32			21 03		21 35		

Uckfield, East Grinstead and Oxted - London

Network Diagram - see first Page of Table 184

		SN 1	SN 1	SN 1	SN 1	SN 1	SN 1	SN 1
Uckfield	d			21 34				22 34
Buxted	d			21 39				22 39
Crowborough	d			21 46				22 46
Eridge	d			21 51				22 51
Ashurst	d			21 56				
Cowden	d			22 01				
Hever	d			22 05				
Edenbridge Town	d			22 08				23 04
East Grinstead	d	21 07	21 37		22 07	22 37	22 54	
Dormans	d	21 11	21 41		22 11	22 41		
Lingfield	d	21 14	21 44		22 14	22 44		
Hurst Green	d	21 21	21 51	22 15	22 21	22 51		23 10
Oxted 3	a	21 23	21 53	22 17	22 23	22 53	23 06	23 13
	d	21 23	21 53	22 18	22 23	22 53	23 07	23 13
Woldingham	d	21 29	21 59		22 29	22 59		
Upper Warlingham	d	21 32	22 02		22 32	23 02		
Riddlesdown	d	21 36	22 06		22 36	23 06		
Sanderstead	d	21 39	22 09		22 39	23 09		
South Croydon 4 175	d							
East Croydon 175,177	a	21 43	22 13	22 33	22 43	23 13	23 19	23 28
Norwood Junction 2 175,177	a							
London Bridge 4 ⊖175,177	a			22 49				
Clapham Junction 10 175,177	a	21 55	22 25		22 55	23 25	23 32	
London Victoria 15 ⊖175,177	a	22 05	22 35		23 05	23 35	23 40	

Saturdays

		SN 1	SN 1	SN 1	SN 1	SN 1	SN 1	SN 1	SN 1		SN 1	SN 1	SN 1	SN 1	SN 1	SN 1	SN 1	SN 1	SN 1	SN 1	SN 1	SN 1
Uckfield	d		06 34			07 34			08 34		18 34			19 34			20 34			21 34		
Buxted	d		06 39			07 39			08 39		18 39			19 39			20 39			21 39		
Crowborough	d		06 46			07 46			08 46		18 46			19 46			20 46			21 46		
Eridge	d		06 51			07 51			08 51		18 51			19 51			20 51			21 51		
Ashurst	d		06 56			07 56			08 56		18 56			19 56			20 56			21 56		
Cowden	d		07 01			08 01			09 01		19 01			20 01			21 01			22 01		
Hever	d		07 05			08 05			09 05		19 05			20 05			21 05			22 05		
Edenbridge Town	d		07 08			08 08			09 08	and at the same minutes past each hour until	19 08			20 08			21 08			22 08		
East Grinstead	d	06 37		07 07	07 37		08 07	08 37				19 07	19 37		20 07	20 37		21 07	21 37		22 07	22 37
Dormans	d	06 41		07 11	07 41		08 11	08 41				19 11	19 41		20 11	20 41		21 11	21 41		22 11	22 41
Lingfield	d	06 44		07 14	07 44		08 14	08 44				19 14	19 44		20 14	20 44		21 14	21 44		22 14	22 44
Hurst Green	d	06 51	07 15	07 21	07 51	08 15	08 21	08 51	09 15		19 15	19 21	19 51	20 15	20 21	20 51	21 15	21 21	21 51	22 15	22 21	22 51
Oxted 3	a	06 53	07 18	07 23	07 53	08 18	08 23	08 53	09 17		19 17	19 23	19 53	20 17	20 23	20 53	21 17	21 23	21 53	22 17	22 23	22 53
	d	06 53	07 19	07 23	07 53	08 19	08 23	08 53	09 18		19 18	19 23	19 53	20 18	20 23	20 53	21 18	21 23	21 53	22 18	22 23	22 53
Woldingham	d	06 59		07 29	07 59		08 29	08 59				19 29	19 59		20 29	20 59		21 29	21 59		22 29	22 59
Upper Warlingham	d	07 02		07 32	08 02		08 32	09 02				19 32	20 02		20 32	21 02		21 32	22 02		22 32	23 02
Riddlesdown	d	07 06		07 36	08 06		08 36	09 06				19 36	20 06		20 36	21 06		21 36	22 06		22 36	23 06
Sanderstead	d	07 09		07 39	08 09		08 39	09 09				19 39	20 09		20 39	21 09		21 39	22 09		22 39	23 09
South Croydon 4 175	d																					
East Croydon 175,177	a	07 13	07 33	07 43	08 13	08 32	08 43	09 13	09 32		19 32	19 43	20 13	20 32	20 43	21 13	21 32	21 43	22 13	22 32	22 43	23 13
Norwood Junction 2 175,177	a																					
London Bridge 4 ⊖175,177	a		07 49			08 49			09 49		19 49			20 49			21 49			22 49		
Clapham Junction 10 175,177	a	07 25		07 55	08 25		08 55	09 25				19 55	20 25		20 55	21 25		21 55	22 25		22 55	23 25
London Victoria 15 ⊖175,177	a	07 32		08 02	08 32		09 02	09 32				20 05	20 32		21 02	21 32		22 02	22 35		23 05	23 35

		SN 1
Uckfield	d	22 34
Buxted	d	22 39
Crowborough	d	22 46
Eridge	d	22 51
Ashurst	d	
Cowden	d	
Hever	d	
Edenbridge Town	d	23 04
East Grinstead	d	
Dormans	d	
Lingfield	d	
Hurst Green	d	23 10
Oxted 3	a	23 13
	d	23 13
Woldingham	d	
Upper Warlingham	d	
Riddlesdown	d	
Sanderstead	d	
South Croydon 4 175	d	
East Croydon 175,177	a	23 26
Norwood Junction 2 175,177	a	
London Bridge 4 ⊖175,177	a	
Clapham Junction 10 175,177	a	
London Victoria 15 ⊖175,177	a	

Table 184

Sundays

Uckfield, East Grinstead and Oxted - London

Network Diagram - see first Page of Table 184

		SN 1	SN 1	SN 1	SN 1		SN 1	SN 1	SN 1	SN 1
Uckfield	d				10 32		21 32		22 32	
Buxted	d				10 37		21 37		22 37	
Crowborough	d				10 44		21 44		22 44	
Eridge	d				10 49		21 49		22 49	
Ashurst	d				10 54		21 54		22 54	
Cowden	d				10 59		21 59		22 59	
Hever	d				11 03		22 03		23 03	
Edenbridge Town	d				11 06	and at	22 06		23 06	
East Grinstead	d	08 12	09 12	10 12		the same		22 12		23 12
Dormans	d	08 16	09 16	10 16		minutes		22 16		23 16
Lingfield	d	08 19	09 19	10 19		past		22 19		23 19
Hurst Green	d	08 26	09 26	10 26	11 13	each	22 13	22 26	23 13	23 26
Oxted 3	a	08 28	09 28	10 28	11 16	hour until	22 16	22 28	23 16	23 28
	d	08 28	09 28	10 28				22 28	23 17	23 28
Woldingham	d	08 34	09 34	10 34				22 34		23 34
Upper Warlingham	d	08 37	09 37	10 37				22 37		23 37
Riddlesdown	d	08 41	09 41	10 41				22 41		23 41
Sanderstead	d	08 44	09 44	10 44				22 44		23 44
South Croydon 4 175	d									
East Croydon 175,177 ⇌	a	08 49	09 49	10 49				22 49	23 29	23 49
Norwood Junction 2 175,177	a									
London Bridge 4 ⊖175,177	a									
Clapham Junction 10 175,177	a	09 01	10 01	11 01				23 01		00 01
London Victoria 15 ⊖175,177	a	09 08	10 08	11 08				23 08		00 08

Network Diagram for Tables 186, 188

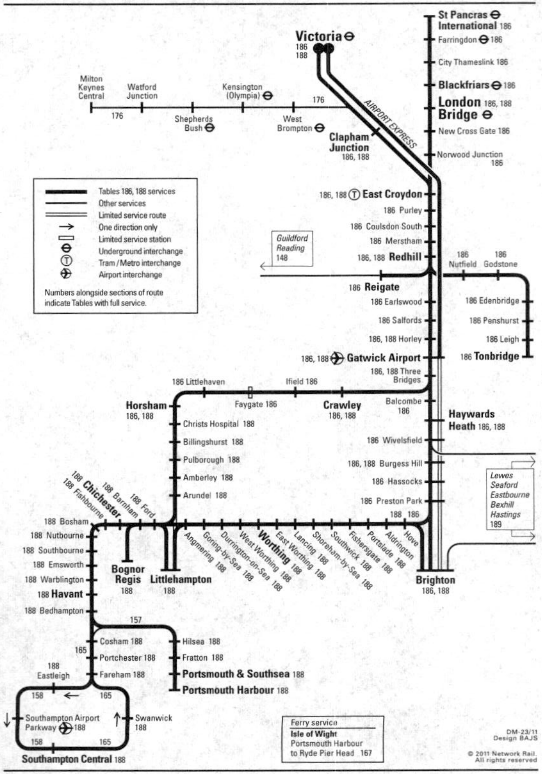

Bedford and London - Brighton

Network Diagram - see first Page of Table 186

Miles	Miles	Miles			SN MX ◇1	SN MO 1	SN MX ◇1	FC MX 1	FC MO 1	SN MX 1	SN MX ◇1		SN MO 1	SN MX 1	SN MO ◇1	GX 1	SN MX 1	GW MX 1	SN MX ◇1		SN MO ◇1	FC 1	GX 1	SN MO	SN MX 1
0	—	—	**London Victoria** 15 ⊖	d	23p02	23p04	23p06			23p10	23p17				23p17	23p30			23p32		23p32		23p45	23p47	23p47
2¾	50¾	6¼	Clapham Junction 10	d	23p08	23p10	23p12			23p16	23p23				23p23				23p38		23p38			23p53	23p53
—	—	—	**Bedford**	d																					
—	—	—	Luton 10	d																					
—	—	—	Luton Airport Parkway 7 ✈	d																					
—	—	—	St Albans City	d																					
—	—	—	St Pancras International 15 ⊖	d																					
—	—	—	Farringdon 3 ⊖	d																					
—	—	—	City Thameslink 3	d																					
—	—	—	**London Blackfriars** 3 ⊖	d																					
—	0	—	**London Bridge** 4 ⊖	d				23p12	23p12													23p42			
—	—	—	New Cross Gate	d																					
—	9	—	Norwood Junction 2	d																					
10½	10¼	—	**East Croydon**	a	23p19	23p22	23p22	23p24	23p27	23p27	23p33				23p37				23p51		23p52	23p56		00 06	00 05
—	—	—		d	23p20	23p22	23p23	23p25	23p27	23p28	23p33				23p38				23p52		23p53	23p57			00 06
13½	—	—	Purley 4	d		23p29				23p33															00 12
15½	—	—	Coulsdon South	d		23p33				23p37															00 15
19	—	—	Merstham	d		23p38				23p42															00 21
21	0	0	**Redhill**	a	23p31	23p42				23p46									00 03		00 05				00 24
—	—	—		d	23p31	23p42				23p46							23p55	00 01	00 05		00 05				00 25
—	1¾	—	**Reigate**	a																					
—	—	2	Nutfield	d																					
—	—	5¾	Godstone	d																					
—	—	10½	Edenbridge	d													00 06								
—	—	15½	Penshurst	d																					
—	—	17¼	Leigh (Kent)	d																					
—	—	19¾	**Tonbridge** 4	a													00 15								
21¼	—	—	Earlswood (Surrey)	d						23p49															
23¾	—	—	Salfords	d						23p52															
26	—	—	Horley 4	d		23p50				23p56			←	←											00 31
26¾	—	—	**Gatwick Airport** 10 ✈	a	23p38	23p54		23p40	23p48	23p58	23p50		23p54	23p58	23p59	00 05		00 11	00 14		00 14	00 18	00 20		00 33
—	—	—		d	23p39	23p55		23p41	23p50	23p59	23p51		23p55	23p59	00 01				00 15		00 15	00 19			00 34
29½	0	—	Three Bridges 15	a	23p44	→		23p47	23p54	→	23p55		00 01	00 04	00 05				00 20		00 19	00 24			00 39
—	—	—		d	23p44			23p47	23p54		23p56		00 01	00 04	00 06				00 20		00 20				00 39
—	1½	—	Crawley	d									00 05	00 07											00 43
—	2¾	—	Ifield	d									00 07	00 10											00 46
—	5¼	—	Faygate	d																					
—	7½	—	Littlehaven	d									00 14	00 16											00 52
—	8½	—	**Horsham** 4	a									00 17	00 19											00 55
34	—	—	Balcombe	d				23p53											00 26		00 26				
38	—	—	**Haywards Heath**	a	23p53		23p46	23p58	00 03		00 05				00 15				00 31		00 31				
—	—	—		d	23p53		23p46	23p59	00 03		00 05				00 15				00 31		00 31				
41	0	—	Wivelsfield	d	23p57			00 03											00 35		00 35				
—	9¼	—	Lewes 4	a																					
41¾	—	—	Burgess Hill 4	d	23p59			00 05	00 08		00 11				00 20				00 37		00 37				
43¾	—	—	Hassocks 4	d	00 03			00 08	00 12										00 41		00 41				
49½	0	—	Preston Park	d	00 09			00 15											00 48		00 48				
—	1½	—	Hove 2	a							00 21				00 31										
51	—	—	Brighton 10	a	00 15		00 01	00 19	00 22										00 52		00 52				

Bedford and London - Brighton

Network Diagram - see first Page of Table 186

		SN MX 1	GX 1	GW MO 1	SN MX ◇1	FC	SN 1	GW MX 1	GX 1	FC	SN ◇1	FC 1	FC 1	SN 1	FC 1	SN 1	FC	GX 1	FC 1	SN ◇1	FC 1
London Victoria 15 ⊖	d	23p49	00 02		00 05		00 14		00 30		01 00			02 00		03 00		03 30		04 00	
Clapham Junction 10	d	23p56			00 11		00 20				01 08			02 08		03 08				04 08	
Bedford	d																				
Luton 10	d																				
Luton Airport Parkway 7 ✈	d																				
St Albans City	d																				
St Pancras International 15 ⊖	d																				
Farringdon 3 ⊖	d																				
City Thameslink 3	d																				
London Blackfriars 3 ⊖	d																				
London Bridge 4 ⊖	d					00 12				00 42		01 08	01 35		02 05		03 05		03 35		04 05
New Cross Gate	d																				
Norwood Junction 2	d																				
East Croydon	a	00 09			00 26	00 26	00 31			00 56	01 23	01 31	02 01	02 23	02 31	03 23	03 31		04 01	04 23	04 31
	d				00 27	00 27	00 32			00 57	01 24	01 32	02 02	02 24	02 32	03 24	03 32		04 02	04 24	04 32
Purley 4	d						00 37				01 29			02 29		03 29				04 29	
Coulsdon South	d						00 41														
Merstham	d						00 47														
Redhill	a						00 50														
	d			00 34			00 51	00 54													
Reigate	a																				
Nutfield	d																				
Godstone	d																				
Edenbridge	d																				
Penshurst	d																				
Leigh (Kent)	d																				
Tonbridge 4	a																				
Earlswood (Surrey)	d																				
Salfords	d																				
Horley 4	d						00 57				01 44			02 44		03 44				04 44	
Gatwick Airport 10 ✈	a		00 37	00 41	00 43	00 48	00 59	01 03	01 05	01 18	01 46	01 51	02 21	02 46	02 51	03 46	03 51	04 05	04 24	04 46	04 51
	d				00 44	00 49				01 22	01 48	01 52	02 22	02 48	02 52	03 48	03 52		04 24	04 48	04 52
Three Bridges 15	a				00 48	00 54				01 28	01 52	01 58	02 28	02 53	02 58	03 53	03 58		04 30	04 52	04 58
	d				00 49						01 53									04 53	05 00
Crawley	d																				
Ifield	d																				
Faygate	d																				
Littlehaven	d																				
Horsham 4	a																				
Balcombe	d																				
Haywards Heath	a				00 58						02 05									05 02	05 10
	d				01 02 01 06						02 06									05 02	05 11
Wivelsfield	d																				
Lewes 4	a				01 20																
Burgess Hill 4	d																				05 16
Hassocks 4	d																				05 19
Preston Park	d																				
Hove 2	a																				
Brighton 10	a				01s16						02 23									05 18	05 29

Bedford and London - Brighton

Network Diagram - see first Page of Table 186

		GX 1	FC 1	GX 1	SN 1	SN ◇1	GX 1	GW 1	GW 1	SN 1	SN	FC 1	SN 1	GX 1	FC 1 A	FC 1 B	SN ◇1	GX 1	FC 1 A	FC 1 B	GX 1	GW 1
London Victoria 15 ⊖	d	04 30		05 00		05 02	05 15							05 30			05 32	05 45			06 00	
Clapham Junction 10	d					05 08											05 38					
Bedford	d											03 42			04 08	04 08			04 20	04 20		
Luton 10	d											04 06			04 33	04 32			04 45	04 44		
Luton Airport Parkway 7 ✈	d											04 09			04 35	04 35			04 47	04 47		
St Albans City	d											04 21			04 47	04 47			04 59	04 59		
St Pancras International 15 ⊖	d											04 54			05 12	05 12			05 32	05 32		
Farringdon 3 ⊖	d											04 59			05 18	05 18			05 38	05 38		
City Thameslink 3	d														05 21	05 21			05 41	05 41		
London Blackfriars 3 ⊖	d											05 04			05 24	05 24			05 44	05 44		
London Bridge 4 ⊖	d		04 35												05 30	05 30			05 50	05 50		
New Cross Gate	d																					
Norwood Junction 2	d																					
East Croydon	a		05 01			05 20						05 29			05 47	05 47	05 48		06 05	06 05		
	d		05 02			05 20						05 32			05 47	05 47	05 49		06 05	06 05		
Purley 4	d					05 25											05 53					
Coulsdon South	d					05 28											05 57					
Merstham	d					05 34											06 02					
Redhill	a					05 37											06 06					
	d				05 35	05 38		05 43	05 44	05 56							06 06					06 13
Reigate	a							05 48														06 18
Nutfield	d				05 39					06 00												
Godstone	d				05 45					06 06												
Edenbridge	d				05 50					06 11												
Penshurst	d				05 57					06 18												
Leigh (Kent)	d				06 00					06 21												
Tonbridge 4	a				06 05					06 26												
Earlswood (Surrey)	d																06 09					
Salfords	d																06 12					
Horley 4	d					05 44											06 16					
Gatwick Airport 10 ✈	a	05 05	05 21	05 35		05 46	05 50		05 54			05 53		06 00	06 02	06 02	06 18	06 15	06 21	06 21	06 30	
	d		05 21			05 47						05 54	05 56		06 04	06 04	06 20		06 22	06 22		
Three Bridges 15	a		05 26			05 52						05 59	06 00		06 08	06 08	06 24		06 26	06 26		
	d		05 27			05 52						06 00	06 01		06 08	06 08	06 25		06 26	06 26		
Crawley	d												06 05									
Ifield	d												06 07									
Faygate	d																					
Littlehaven	d												06 14									
Horsham 4	a												06 17									
Balcombe	d					05 58									06 14	06 14			06 33	06 33		
Haywards Heath	a		05 36			06 03						06 09			06 19	06 19	06 34		06 39	06 39		
	d		05 36			06 04					06 07	06 11			06 19	06 19	06 34		06 39	06 39		
Wivelsfield	d		05 40			06 08					06 11				06 23	06 23	06 38		06 43	06 43		
Lewes 4	a										06 22						06 50					
Burgess Hill 4	d		05 43			06 10						06 16			06 25	06 25			06 45	06 45		
Hassocks 4	d		05 46			06 13						06 20			06 29	06 29			06 49	06 49		
Preston Park	d		05 53			06 20						06 27			06 35	06 35			06 55	06 55		
Hove 2	a																					
Brighton 10	a		05 57			06 26						06 31			06 40	06 40			06 59	06 59		

A from 26 March

B until 23 March

Bedford and London - Brighton

Network Diagram - see first Page of Table 186

Station		GW 1	GW 1	SN 1	SN ◇1		SN 1 A 🛒	FC 1	SN ◇1	SN 1	SN 1	SN ◇1	SN 1 B 🛒	SN ◇1	SN 1	GW 1	SN 1		FC 1	GW 1	SN 1 🛒	SN ◇1
London Victoria 15 ⊖	d				06 02		06 15					06 21	06 30				06 32				06 45	06 47
Clapham Junction 10	d				06 08							06 27					06 38					06 53
Bedford	d							05 00											05 20			
Luton 10	d							05 24											05 44			
Luton Airport Parkway 7 ✈	d							05 27											05 46			
St Albans City	d							05 39											05 58			
St Pancras International 15 ⊖	d							06 02											06 22			
Farringdon 3 ⊖	d							06 08											06 28			
City Thameslink 3	d							06 11											06 31			
London Blackfriars 3 ⊖	d							06 14											06 34			
London Bridge 4 ⊖	d							06 20											06 42			
New Cross Gate	d																					
Norwood Junction 2	d																					
East Croydon ⇌	a				06 17			06 33				06 38					06 48		06 54			07 03
	d				06 18			06 35				06 38					06 49		06 55			07 04
Purley 4	d				06 23							06 43					06 55					
Coulsdon South	d				06 26							06 47					06 58					
Merstham	d				06 32							06 52					07 04					
Redhill	a				06 35							06 56					07 08					
	d	06 24	06 33	06 39	06 39	06 41						06 57			07 00	07 10	07 12	07 14		07 28		
Reigate	a	06 28		06 43											07 04	07 15				07 32		
Nutfield	d					06 45												07 18				
Godstone	d					06 51												07 24				
Edenbridge	d					06 56												07 29				
Penshurst	d					07 03												07 36				
Leigh (Kent)	d					07 06												07 39				
Tonbridge 4	a					07 11												07 44				
Earlswood (Surrey)	d				06 41												07 14					
Salfords	d				06 45												07 18					
Horley 3	d				06 48				←			07 03		←			07 21					
Gatwick Airport 10 ✈	a		06 40		06 54		06 45	06 51	06 54			07 05	06 59	07 05			07 24		07 10		07 16	07 19
	d				06 55		06 48	06 52	06 55			07 06	07 04	07 06			07 25		07 11		07 25	07 20
Three Bridges 15	a				→			06 56	06 59			→		07 11			→		07 15		→	07 24
	d							06 56	07 00	07 05				07 11					07 15			07 24
Crawley	d								07 03	07 08												
Ifield	d									07 11												
Faygate	d									07 15												
Littlehaven	d									07 19												
Horsham 4	a								07 11	07 22												
Balcombe	d																		07 21			
Haywards Heath	a						06 58	07 05					07 14	07 20					07 26			07 33
	d						07 00	07 06			07 10		07 16	07 21					07 26			07 33
Wivelsfield	d							07 10			07 14			07 25								07 37
Lewes 4	a										07 29											07 52
Burgess Hill 4	d							07 12						07 27					07 31			
Hassocks 4	d							07 16						07 30					07 35			
Preston Park	d							07 22						07 37								
Hove 2	a																					
Brighton 10	a						07 13	07 27					07 35	07 41					07 44			

A 🛒 to Gatwick Airport

B 🛒 to Gatwick Airport

Bedford and London - Brighton

Network Diagram - see first Page of Table 186

Station		SN 1	SN 1	SN 1		FC 1	GX 1 🛒	SN 1	GW 1	SN 1	GX 1 🛒	FC 1	SN ◇1	GX 1 🛒	SN 1	SN 1	SN 1	GW 1	SN 1	FC 1	GX 1 🛒	SN ◇1
London Victoria 15 ⊖	d			06 51			07 00			07 02	07 15		07 17	07 30					07 36		07 45	07 47
Clapham Junction 10	d			06 57						07 08			07 23						07 42			07 53
Bedford	d					05 40						05 58								06 22		
Luton 10	d					06 04						06 22								06 46		
Luton Airport Parkway 7 ✈	d					06 06						06 24								06 48		
St Albans City	d					06 18						06 36								07 00		
St Pancras International 15 ⊖	d					06 38						06 58								07 20		
Farringdon 3 ⊖	d					06 44						07 04								07 26		
City Thameslink 3	d					06 47						07 07								07 29		
London Blackfriars 3 ⊖	d					06 50						07 09								07 32		
London Bridge 4 ⊖	d					07 00						07 16				07 30	07 33			07 42		
New Cross Gate	d																07 38					
Norwood Junction 2	d															07 42						
East Croydon ⇌	a			07 06		07 14				07 17		07 30	07 33			07 45	07 48		07 51	07 54		08 02
	d			07 07		07 15				07 18		07 31	07 34			07 46	07 49		07 52	07 55		08 03
Purley 4	d									07 23									07 57			
Coulsdon South	d			07 13						07 26						07 52			08 01			
Merstham	d			07 19						07 32						07 58			08 07			
Redhill	a			07 23						07 35			07 47			08 01			08 10			
	d			07 28	07 30				07 41	07 44			07 47		08 00	08 02		08 08	08 11			
Reigate	a									07 48					08 04			08 13				
Nutfield	d				07 34											08 06						
Godstone	d				07 40											08 12						
Edenbridge	d				07 45											08 17						
Penshurst	d				07 52											08 24						
Leigh (Kent)	d				07 55											08 27						
Tonbridge 4	a				08 02											08 32						
Earlswood (Surrey)	d			07 30									07 50						08 13			
Salfords	d			07 34									07 53						08 17			
Horley 3	d	←	←	07 37				←					07 57						08 21			
Gatwick Airport 10 ✈	a	07 24	07 16	07 40		07 30	07 31	07 40	07 50		07 45	07 46	07 59	08 02			08 03		08 23	08 11	08 15	08 18
	d	07 25	07 25	07 41		07 31		07 41				07 47	08 00				08 05		08 24	08 12		08 20
Three Bridges 15	a	07 29		→		07 35		07 45				07 51	08 05				08 09		→	08 16		
	d	07 30				07 35		07 46				07 51	08 05				08 09			08 16		
Crawley	d	07 34						07 50					08 09									
Ifield	d	07 36						07 53					08 11									
Faygate	d												08 15									
Littlehaven	d	07 43						07 59					08 19									
Horsham 4	a	07 46						08 02					08 22									
Balcombe	d											07 57								08 22		
Haywards Heath	a					07 44						08 02					08 18			08 27		08 30
	d					07 46						08 02					08 19			08 27		08 31
Wivelsfield	d					07 50						08 06								08 31		08 35
Lewes 4	a																					08 50
Burgess Hill 4	d					07 52						08 08					08 24			08 33		
Hassocks 4	d					07 55						08 12								08 37		
Preston Park	d					08 02						08 18								08 43		
Hove 2	a																					
Brighton 10	a		07 53			08 06						08 23					08 36			08 48		

Bedford and London - Brighton

Network Diagram - see first Page of Table 186

Station		SN	SN	SN	SN	SN	SN	GX	SN	GW	SN	SN	FC	GX	SN	SN	FC	SN	GW	SN	SN	SN
		1	1	1		◇1	1	1	◇1	1	1	◇1	1	1	◇1		1	1	1	1		◇1
								⌶						⌶								
London Victoria 15 ⊖	d					07 52		08 00	08 02			08 07		08 15	08 17							08 21
Clapham Junction 10	d					07 58			08 08			08 13			08 23							08 27
Bedford	d												06 54				06 58					
Luton 10	d												07 14				07 22					
Luton Airport Parkway 7 ✈	d																07 25					
St Albans City	d												07 26				07 38					
St Pancras International 15 ⊖	d												07 44				07 56					
Farringdon 3 ⊖	d												07 50				08 02					
City Thameslink 3	d												07 53				08 05					
London Blackfriars 3 ⊖	d												07 56				08 08					
London Bridge 4 ⊖	d			07 53							08 00						08 18			08 23		
New Cross Gate	d										08 08											
Norwood Junction 2	d										08 16											
East Croydon	a			08 05		08 09			08 18		08 20	08 22	08 26		08 33		08 37			08 37		08 40
	d			08 06		08 09			08 18		08 20	08 23	08 26		08 34		08 37			08 38		08 40
Purley 4	d										08 26											
Coulsdon South	d										08 29									08 47		
Merstham	d										08 35											
Redhill	a			08 18					08 30		08 38									08 54		
	d		08 17	08 22	08 24				08 30	08 33	08 41								08 50	08 58	09 00	
Reigate	a		08 21							08 37											09 04	
Nutfield	d				08 28															09 02		
Godstone	d				08 34															09 08		
Edenbridge	d				08 39															09 13		
Penshurst	d				08 46															09 20		
Leigh (Kent)	d				08 49															09 23		
Tonbridge 4	a				08 54															09 28		
Earlswood (Surrey)	d										08 43											
Salfords	d										08 47											
Horley 4	d	←					←				08 50							←				
Gatwick Airport 10 ✈	a	08 23		08 29		08 24	08 29	08 31	08 37		08 53		08 41	08 45	08 48		08 52	08 53	08 59			08 56
	d	08 24		08 30		08 26	08 30		08 40		08 54		08 42		08 49		08 53	08 54				08 57
Three Bridges 15	a	08 29		→			08 34		08 44		→	08 41	08 46				08 57	08 59				09 01
	d	08 30					08 35		08 45			08 42	08 46				08 58	08 59				09 01
Crawley	d	08 34							08 48									09 03				
Ifield	d	08 36																09 06				
Faygate	d	08 40																09 10				
Littlehaven	d	08 44																09 14				
Horsham 4	a	08 48							08 56									09 17				
Balcombe	d												08 52									
Haywards Heath	a					08 36	08 44					08 51	08 57		09 00		09 07					09 12
	d					08 37	08 44					08 51	08 58		09 04	09 10	09 08					09 21
Wivelsfield	d						08 48						09 02			09 14						09 25
Lewes 4	a															09 25						
Burgess Hill 4	d						08 50						09 04		09 09		09 13					09 27
Hassocks 4	d						08 54						09 07									09 30
Preston Park	d						09 00						09 14		09 18							09 37
Hove 2	a					08 53									09 21							
Brighton 10	a						09 05					09 08	09 18				09 25					09 41

Bedford and London - Brighton

Network Diagram - see first Page of Table 186

Station		SN	SN	SN	SN	FC	SN	SN	SN		SN	SN	GX	SN	GW	SN	GW	SN	SN	FC	GX	GW
		1	◇1	1	◇1	1	1	1	◇1		◇1	1	1		1	◇1	1	1	◇1	1	1	1
		⌶	⌶		⌶		⌶		⌶				⌶			⌶			⌶		⌶	
London Victoria 15 ⊖	d	08 30	08 32		08 36		08 45		08 47		08 51		09 00	09 01		09 02			09 06		09 15	
Clapham Junction 10	d		08 38		08 43				08 53					09 08		09 08			09 12			
Bedford	d					07 30														07 48		
Luton 10	d					07 50														08 12		
Luton Airport Parkway 7 ✈	d																			08 15		
St Albans City	d					08 02														08 27		
St Pancras International 15 ⊖	d					08 20														08 48		
Farringdon 3 ⊖	d					08 26														08 54		
City Thameslink 3	d					08 29														08 57		
London Blackfriars 3 ⊖	d					08 32														09 00		
London Bridge 4 ⊖	d			08 30				08 45										09 03		09 12		
New Cross Gate	d			08 36														09 08				
Norwood Junction 2	d			08 44				08 56										09 16				
East Croydon	a		08 48	08 48	08 52	08 57		08 59	09 03		09 07					09 18		09 20	09 22	09 24		
	d		08 48	08 51	08 53	08 58		09 00	09 04		09 08					09 19		09 21	09 23	09 25		
Purley 4	d			08 59				09 06										09 27				
Coulsdon South	d			09 02				09 09										09 30				
Merstham	d			09 08														09 36				
Redhill	a		09 02	09 12				09 17								09 30		09 39				
	d		09 03	09 12				09 17							09 23	09 30	09 34	09 40				09 51
Reigate	a														09 28		09 38					
Nutfield	d							09 22														
Godstone	d							09 27														
Edenbridge	d							09 33														
Penshurst	d							09 39														
Leigh (Kent)	d							09 43														
Tonbridge 4	a							09 48														
Earlswood (Surrey)	d			09 15														09 42				
Salfords	d			09 18														09 46				
Horley 4	d			09 22								←				09 36		09 50				
Gatwick Airport 10 ✈	a	09 00	09 10	09 24		09 12	09 15		09 18		09 22	09 24	09 30			09 39		09 53		09 40	09 45	09 59
	d		09 11	09 25		09 13			09 20		09 23	09 25				09 40		09 54		09 41		
Three Bridges 15	a		09 16	→		09 17						09 30				09 44		→		09 45		
	d		09 16			09 17						09 30				09 45				09 45		
Crawley	d		09 19									09 34				09 48						
Ifield	d											09 36										
Faygate	d																					
Littlehaven	d											09 43										
Horsham 4	a		09 27									09 46				09 56						
Balcombe	d																			09 51		
Haywards Heath	a					09 26			09 30											09 56		
	d					09 27			09 35	09 37										09 56		
Wivelsfield	d																			10 00		
Lewes 4	a								09 53													
Burgess Hill 4	d					09 32					09 38									10 02		
Hassocks 4	d					09 35					09 41									10 06		
Preston Park	d					09 42														10 12		
Hove 2	a									09 53												
Brighton 10	a				09 28	09 46					09 52								09 58	10 17		

Bedford and London - Brighton

Network Diagram - see first Page of Table 186

		SN	SN	SN	FC	SN	SN	SN	SN	FC	GX	GW	SN	SN	SN	SN	FC	GX	SN	SN
		1	◇1 A 🚌	1	1	1 🚌	◇1 🚌	1	◇1	1	1 🚌	1	1	◇1 🚌	◇1	1	1	1 🚌		◇1 🚌
London Victoria [15] ⊖	d		09 17			09 30	09 32		09 36		09 45			09 47	09 51			10 00	10 01	10 02
Clapham Junction [10]	d		09 23				09 38		09 42					09 53					10 08	10 08
Bedford	d				08 04					08 24							08 40			
Luton [10]	d				08 28					08 48							09 04			
Luton Airport Parkway [7] ✈	d				08 30					08 50							09 06			
St Albans City	d				08 44					09 02							09 18			
St Pancras International [15] ⊖	d				09 04					09 22							09 40			
Farringdon [3] ⊖	d				09 10					09 28							09 45			
City Thameslink [3]	d				09 13					09 31							09 48			
London Blackfriars [3] ⊖	d				09 16					09 34							09 50			
London Bridge [4] ⊖	d	09 15			09 27			09 32		09 42			09 45				09 57			
New Cross Gate	d							09 37												
Norwood Junction [2]	d	09 26						09 45					09 56							
East Croydon ⇌	a	09 29	09 32		09 39		09 48	09 49	09 52	09 54			09 59	10 02	10 07		10 09			10 17
	d	09 30	09 33		09 41		09 48	09 51	09 53	09 55			10 00	10 03	10 08		10 11			10 18
Purley [4]	d	09 36						09 57					10 06							
Coulsdon South	d	09 39						10 00					10 09							
Merstham	d	09 45						10 06												
Redhill	a	09 49					10 00	10 09					10 17							10 30
	d	09 53					10 00	10 10				10 13	10 17							10 30
Reigate	a	09 57										10 18								
Nutfield	d												10 22							
Godstone	d												10 27							
Edenbridge	d												10 33							
Penshurst	d												10 39							
Leigh (Kent)	d												10 43							
Tonbridge [4]	a												10 48							
Earlswood (Surrey)	d							10 12												
Salfords	d							10 16												
Horley [4]	d			←				10 19								←				10 36
Gatwick Airport [10] ✈	a		09 48	09 53	09 56	10 00	10 08	10 23		10 10	10 15			10 18	10 22	10 23	10 26	10 30		10 39
	d		09 50	09 54	09 57		10 09	10 24		10 11				10 20	10 23	10 24	10 27			10 40
Three Bridges [15]	a			09 59	10 01		10 14	→		10 15						10 29	10 31			10 44
	d			10 00	10 02		10 14			10 15						10 30	10 32			10 45
Crawley	d			10 03			10 18									10 33				10 48
Ifield	d			10 06												10 36				
Faygate	d																			
Littlehaven	d			10 12												10 42				
Horsham [4]	a			10 15			10 26									10 47				10 56
Balcombe	d									10 21										
Haywards Heath	a		10 00		10 11					10 26				10 30			10 41			
	d		10 05 / 10 07		10 11					10 27				10 35 / 10 37			10 41			
Wivelsfield	d		10 11							10 31										
Lewes [4]	a		10 22											10 52						
Burgess Hill [4]	d		10 10							10 33					10 38					
Hassocks [4]	d									10 36					10 41					
Preston Park	d		10 18							10 43										
Hove [2]	a		10 22											10 53						
Brighton [10]	a				10 25				10 28	10 47					10 52		10 55			

A 🚌 to Haywards Heath

Bedford and London - Brighton

Network Diagram - see first Page of Table 186

		GW	GW	SN	SN	FC	GX	SN	SN	SN	FC	GX	SN	SN	SN	FC	GX	GW	SN	SN
		1	1	1	◇1 🚌	1	1 🚌	1	◇1 A 🚌	1	1	1 🚌	◇1 🚌	1	◇1	1	1 🚌	1	1	◇1 🚌
London Victoria [15] ⊖	d				10 06		10 15		10 17			10 30	10 32		10 36		10 45			10 47
Clapham Junction [10]	d				10 12				10 23				10 38		10 42					10 53
Bedford	d					08 54					09 10					09 24				
Luton [10]	d					09 18					09 34					09 48				
Luton Airport Parkway [7] ✈	d					09 20					09 36					09 50				
St Albans City	d					09 32					09 48					10 02				
St Pancras International [15] ⊖	d					09 54					10 09					10 24				
Farringdon [3] ⊖	d					09 59					10 14					10 29				
City Thameslink [3]	d					10 03					10 18					10 33				
London Blackfriars [3] ⊖	d					10 05					10 20					10 35				
London Bridge [4] ⊖	d			10 03		10 12		10 15			10 27			10 33		10 42			10 45	
New Cross Gate	d			10 08										10 38						
Norwood Junction [2]	d			10 16				10 26						10 46					10 56	
East Croydon ⇌	a			10 20	10 22	10 24		10 29	10 32		10 39		10 48	10 50	10 52	10 54			10 59	11 02
	d			10 21	10 23	10 25		10 30	10 33		10 41		10 48	10 51	10 53	10 55			11 00	11 03
Purley [4]	d			10 26				10 36						10 57					11 07	
Coulsdon South	d			10 30				10 39						11 00					11 10	
Merstham	d			10 35				10 45						11 06						
Redhill	a			10 39				10 49					11 00	11 09					11 18	
	d	10 34	10 41	10 45				10 52					11 00	11 10				11 13	11 18	
Reigate	a	10 38						10 56										11 18		
Nutfield	d																		11 23	
Godstone	d																		11 28	
Edenbridge	d																		11 34	
Penshurst	d																		11 40	
Leigh (Kent)	d																		11 44	
Tonbridge [4]	a																		11 48	
Earlswood (Surrey)	d													11 12						
Salfords	d													11 16						
Horley [4]	d			10 53						←				11 19						
Gatwick Airport [10] ✈	a		10 50	10 55		10 40	10 45		10 48	10 55	10 56	11 00	11 08	11 23		11 10	11 15			11 18
	d			10 56		10 41			10 50	10 56	10 57		11 09	11 24		11 11				11 20
Three Bridges [15]	a			→		10 45				11 01	11 01		11 14	→		11 15				
	d					10 45				11 01	11 02		11 14			11 15				
Crawley	d									11 05			11 18							
Ifield	d									11 07										
Faygate	d																			
Littlehaven	d									11 14										
Horsham [4]	a									11 17			11 26							
Balcombe	d															11 21				
Haywards Heath	a					10 54			11 00		11 11					11 26				11 30
	d					10 55			11 04 / 11 07		11 11					11 27				11 35 / 11 37
Wivelsfield	d					10 59			11 11							11 31				
Lewes [4]	a								11 22											11 52
Burgess Hill [4]	d					11 01			11 09							11 33				
Hassocks [4]	d					11 04										11 36				
Preston Park	d					11 11			11 18							11 43				
Hove [2]	a								11 22											11 53
Brighton [10]	a				10 58	11 15					11 25				11 28	11 47				

A 🚌 to Haywards Heath

Bedford and London - Brighton

Network Diagram - see first Page of Table 186

		SN ◇1	SN 1	FC 1	GX 1	SN	SN ◇1	GW 1	GW 1	SN 1	SN ◇1	FC 1	GX 1	SN 1	SN ◇1		SN 1	FC 1	GX 1	SN ◇1	SN 1	SN ◇1
London Victoria 15 ⊖	d	10 51			11 00	11 01	11 02				11 06		11 15		11 17				11 30	11 32		11 36
Clapham Junction 10	d					11 08	11 08				11 12				11 23					11 38		11 42
Bedford	d			09 40								09 54						10 10				
Luton 10	d			10 04								10 18						10 34				
Luton Airport Parkway 7 ✈	d			10 06								10 20						10 36				
St Albans City	d			10 18								10 32						10 48				
St Pancras International 15 ⊖	d			10 39								10 54						11 09				
Farringdon 3 ⊖	d			10 44								10 59						11 14				
City Thameslink 3	d			10 48								11 03						11 18				
London Blackfriars 3 ⊖	d			10 50								11 05						11 20				
London Bridge 4 ⊖	d			10 57						11 03		11 12		11 15				11 27			11 33	
New Cross Gate	d									11 08											11 38	
Norwood Junction 2	d									11 16				11 26							11 46	
East Croydon	a	11 07		11 09			11 17			11 20	11 22	11 24		11 29	11 32			11 39		11 48	11 50	11 52
	d	11 08		11 11			11 18			11 21	11 23	11 25		11 30	11 33			11 41		11 48	11 51	11 53
Purley 4	d									11 27				11 36							11 57	
Coulsdon South	d									11 30				11 39							12 00	
Merstham	d									11 36				11 45							12 06	
Redhill	a						11 30			11 39				11 49						12 00	12 09	
	d						11 30	11 34	11 41	11 45				11 52						12 00	12 10	
Reigate	a							11 38						11 56								
Nutfield	d																					
Godstone	d																					
Edenbridge	d																					
Penshurst	d																					
Leigh (Kent)	d																					
Tonbridge 4	a																					
Earlswood (Surrey)	d																				12 12	
Salfords	d																				12 16	
Horley 4	d		←				11 36			11 53							←				12 19	
Gatwick Airport 10 ✈	a	11 22	11 23	11 26	11 30		11 39		11 50	11 55		11 40	11 45		11 48		11 55	11 56	12 00	12 08	12 23	
	d	11 23	11 24	11 27			11 40			11 56		11 41			11 50		11 56	11 57		12 09	12 24	
Three Bridges 15	a		11 29	11 31			11 44			→		11 45					12 01	12 01		12 14	→	
	d		11 30	11 32			11 45					11 45					12 01	12 02		12 14		
Crawley	d		11 33				11 48										12 05			12 18		
Ifield	d		11 36														12 07					
Faygate	d																12 11					
Littlehaven	d		11 42														12 15					
Horsham 4	a		11 45				11 56										12 18			12 26		
Balcombe	d																					
Haywards Heath	a			11 41								11 54			12 00			12 11				
	d			11 41								11 55			12 04	12 07		12 11				
Wivelsfield	d											11 59				12 11						
Lewes 4	a															12 22						
Burgess Hill 4	d	11 38										12 01			12 09							
Hassocks 4	d	11 41										12 04										
Preston Park	d											12 11			12 18							
Hove 2	a														12 22							
Brighton 10	a	11 52		11 55							11 58	12 15						12 25				12 28

Bedford and London - Brighton

Network Diagram - see first Page of Table 186

		FC 1	GX 1	GW 1	SN 1	SN ◇1		SN ◇1	SN 1	FC 1	GX 1	SN	SN ◇1	GW 1	GW 1	SN 1	SN ◇1	FC 1	GX 1	SN 1	SN ◇1	
London Victoria 15 ⊖	d		11 45			11 47		11 51			12 00	12 01	12 02				12 06		12 15		12 17	
Clapham Junction 10	d					11 53						12 08	12 08				12 12				12 23	
Bedford	d	10 25								10 40								10 54				
Luton 10	d	10 49								11 04								11 18				
Luton Airport Parkway 7 ✈	d	10 51								11 06								11 20				
St Albans City	d	11 03								11 18								11 32				
St Pancras International 15 ⊖	d	11 24								11 39								11 54				
Farringdon 3 ⊖	d	11 29								11 44								11 59				
City Thameslink 3	d	11 33								11 48								12 03				
London Blackfriars 3 ⊖	d	11 35								11 50								12 05				
London Bridge 4 ⊖	d	11 42			11 45					11 57						12 03		12 12		12 15		
New Cross Gate	d															12 08						
Norwood Junction 2	d				11 56											12 16				12 26		
East Croydon	a	11 54			11 59	12 02		12 07		12 09			12 17			12 20	12 22	12 24		12 29	12 32	
	d	11 55			12 00	12 03		12 08		12 11			12 18			12 21	12 23	12 25		12 30	12 33	
Purley 4	d				12 06											12 27				12 36		
Coulsdon South	d				12 09											12 30				12 39		
Merstham	d															12 36				12 45		
Redhill	a				12 17								12 30			12 39				12 49		
	d			12 13	12 17								12 30	12 34	12 41	12 45				12 52		
Reigate	a			12 18										12 38						12 56		
Nutfield	d				12 22																	
Godstone	d				12 27																	
Edenbridge	d				12 33																	
Penshurst	d				12 39																	
Leigh (Kent)	d				12 43																	
Tonbridge 4	a				12 48																	
Earlswood (Surrey)	d																					
Salfords	d																					
Horley 4	d								←				12 36			12 53						
Gatwick Airport 10 ✈	a	12 10	12 15			12 18		12 22	12 23	12 26	12 30		12 39		12 50	12 55		12 40	12 45		12 48	
	d	12 11				12 20		12 23	12 24	12 27			12 40			12 56		12 41			12 50	
Three Bridges 15	a	12 15							12 29	12 31			12 44			→		12 45				
	d	12 15							12 30	12 32			12 45					12 45				
Crawley	d								12 33				12 48									
Ifield	d								12 36													
Faygate	d																					
Littlehaven	d								12 42													
Horsham 4	a								12 45				12 56									
Balcombe	d	12 21																				
Haywards Heath	a	12 26				12 30				12 41								12 54			13 00	
	d	12 27				12 35	12 37			12 41								12 55			13 04	13 07
Wivelsfield	d	12 31																12 59				13 11
Lewes 4	a					12 52																13 22
Burgess Hill 4	d	12 33						12 38										13 01			13 09	
Hassocks 4	d	12 36						12 41										13 04				
Preston Park	d	12 43																13 11			13 18	
Hove 2	a						12 53														13 22	
Brighton 10	a	12 47						12 52		12 55							12 58	13 15				

Table 186

Mondays to Fridays

Bedford and London - Brighton

Network Diagram - see first Page of Table 186

		SN 1	FC 1	GX 1	SN ◇1	SN 1	SN ◇1	FC 1	GX 1	GW 1	SN 1	SN ◇1		SN ◇1	SN 1	FC 1	GX 1	SN	SN ◇1	GW 1	GW 1	SN 1
London Victoria 15 ⊖	d			12 30	12 32		12 36		12 45			12 47		12 51			13 00	13 01	13 02			
Clapham Junction 10	d				12 38		12 42					12 53						13 08	13 08			
Bedford	d		11 10					11 24								11 40						
Luton 10	d		11 34					11 48								12 04						
Luton Airport Parkway 7 ✈	d		11 36					11 50								12 06						
St Albans City	d		11 48					12 02								12 18						
St Pancras International 15 ⊖	d		12 09					12 24								12 39						
Farringdon 3 ⊖	d		12 14					12 29								12 44						
City Thameslink 3	d		12 18					12 33								12 48						
London Blackfriars 3 ⊖	d		12 20					12 35								12 50						
London Bridge 4 ⊖	d		12 27			12 33		12 42			12 45					12 57						13 03
New Cross Gate	d					12 38																13 08
Norwood Junction 2	d					12 46					12 56											13 16
East Croydon	a		12 39		12 48	12 50	12 52	12 54			12 59	13 02		13 07		13 09			13 17			13 20
	d		12 41		12 48	12 51	12 53	12 55			13 00	13 03		13 08		13 11			13 18			13 21
Purley 4	d					12 58					13 06											13 27
Coulsdon South	d					13 01					13 09											13 30
Merstham	d					13 07																13 36
Redhill	a				13 00	13 10					13 17								13 30			13 39
	d				13 00	13 11				13 13	13 17								13 30	13 34	13 41	13 45
Reigate	a									13 18										13 38		
Nutfield	d										13 22											
Godstone	d										13 27											
Edenbridge	d										13 33											
Penshurst	d										13 39											
Leigh (Kent)	d										13 43											
Tonbridge 4	a										13 48											
Earlswood (Surrey)	d					13 13																
Salfords	d					13 17																
Horley 4	d	←				13 20									←				13 36			13 53
Gatwick Airport 10 ✈	a	12 55	12 56	13 00	13 08	13 23		13 10	13 15			13 18		13 22	13 23	13 26	13 30		13 39		13 50	13 55
	d	12 56	12 57		13 09	13 24		13 11				13 20		13 23	13 24	13 27			13 40			13 56
Three Bridges 15	a	13 01	13 01		13 14	→		13 15							13 29	13 31			13 44			→
	d	13 01	13 02		13 14			13 15							13 30	13 32			13 45			
Crawley	d	13 05			13 18										13 33				13 48			
Ifield	d	13 07													13 36							
Faygate	d																					
Littlehaven	d	13 14													13 42							
Horsham 4	a	13 17			13 26										13 45				13 56			
Balcombe	d							13 21														
Haywards Heath	a		13 11					13 26				13 30				13 41						
	d		13 11					13 27				13 35	13 37			13 41						
Wivelsfield	d							13 31														
Lewes 4	a											13 52										
Burgess Hill 4	d							13 33						13 38								
Hassocks 4	d							13 36						13 41								
Preston Park	d							13 43														
Hove 2	a												13 53									
Brighton 10	a		13 25				13 28	13 47						13 52		13 55						

Table 186

Mondays to Fridays

Bedford and London - Brighton

Network Diagram - see first Page of Table 186

		SN ◇1	FC 1	GX 1	SN 1	SN ◇1		SN 1	FC 1	GX 1	SN ◇1	SN 1	SN ◇1	FC 1	GX 1	GW 1	SN 1	SN ◇1		SN ◇1	SN 1	FC 1
London Victoria 15 ⊖	d	13 06		13 15		13 17				13 30	13 32		13 36		13 45			13 47		13 51		
Clapham Junction 10	d	13 12				13 23					13 38		13 42					13 53				
Bedford	d		11 54						12 10					12 24								12 40
Luton 10	d		12 18						12 34					12 48								13 04
Luton Airport Parkway 7 ✈	d		12 20						12 36					12 50								13 06
St Albans City	d		12 32						12 48					13 02								13 18
St Pancras International 15 ⊖	d		12 54						13 09					13 24								13 39
Farringdon 3 ⊖	d		12 59						13 14					13 29								13 44
City Thameslink 3	d		13 03						13 18					13 33								13 48
London Blackfriars 3 ⊖	d		13 05						13 20					13 35								13 50
London Bridge 4 ⊖	d		13 12		13 15				13 27			13 33		13 42			13 45					13 57
New Cross Gate	d											13 38										
Norwood Junction 2	d				13 26							13 46					13 56					
East Croydon	a	13 22	13 24		13 29	13 32			13 39		13 48	13 50	13 52	13 54			13 59	14 02		14 07		14 09
	d	13 23	13 25		13 30	13 33			13 41		13 48	13 51	13 53	13 55			14 00	14 03		14 08		14 11
Purley 4	d				13 36							13 57					14 06					
Coulsdon South	d				13 39							14 00					14 09					
Merstham	d				13 45							14 06										
Redhill	a				13 49						14 00	14 09					14 17					
	d				13 52						14 00	14 10				14 13	14 17					
Reigate	a				13 56											14 18						
Nutfield	d																14 22					
Godstone	d																14 27					
Edenbridge	d																14 33					
Penshurst	d																14 39					
Leigh (Kent)	d																14 43					
Tonbridge 4	a																14 48					
Earlswood (Surrey)	d											14 12										
Salfords	d											14 16										
Horley 4	d							←				14 19									←	
Gatwick Airport 10 ✈	a		13 40	13 45		13 48		13 55	13 56	14 00	14 08	14 23		14 10	14 15			14 18		14 22	14 23	14 26
	d		13 41			13 50		13 56	13 57		14 09	14 24		14 11				14 20		14 23	14 24	14 27
Three Bridges 15	a		13 45					14 01	14 01		14 14	→		14 15							14 29	14 31
	d		13 45					14 01	14 02		14 14			14 15							14 30	14 32
Crawley	d							14 05			14 18										14 33	
Ifield	d							14 07													14 36	
Faygate	d																					
Littlehaven	d							14 14													14 42	
Horsham 4	a							14 17			14 26										14 45	
Balcombe	d													14 21								
Haywards Heath	a		13 54			14 00			14 11					14 26				14 30				14 41
	d		13 55			14 04	14 07		14 11					14 27				14 35	14 37			14 41
Wivelsfield	d		13 59				14 11							14 31								
Lewes 4	a						14 22											14 52				
Burgess Hill 4	d		14 01			14 09								14 33						14 38		
Hassocks 4	d		14 04											14 36						14 41		
Preston Park	d		14 11			14 18								14 43								
Hove 2	a					14 22													14 53			
Brighton 10	a	13 58	14 15						14 25				14 28	14 47						14 52		14 55

Bedford and London - Brighton

Network Diagram - see first Page of Table 186

		GX 1 ⌶	SN	SN ◇1	GW 1	GW 1	SN 1		SN ◇1 ⌶	FC 1	GX 1 ⌶	SN 1	SN ◇1		SN 1		FC 1	GX 1 ⌶	SN ◇1 ⌶	SN 1	SN ◇1 ⌶	FC 1	GX 1 ⌶		GW 1
London Victoria 15 Θ	d	14 00	14 01	14 02					14 06		14 15		14 17					14 30	14 32		14 36		14 45		
Clapham Junction 10	d		14 08	14 08					14 12				14 23						14 38		14 42				
Bedford	d									12 54							13 10					13 24			
Luton 10	d									13 18							13 34					13 48			
Luton Airport Parkway 7 ✈	d									13 20							13 36					13 50			
St Albans City	d									13 32							13 48					14 02			
St Pancras International 15 Θ	d									13 54							14 09					14 24			
Farringdon 3 Θ	d									13 59							14 14					14 29			
City Thameslink 3	d									14 03							14 18					14 33			
London Blackfriars 3 Θ	d									14 05							14 20					14 35			
London Bridge 4 Θ	d						14 03			14 12		14 15					14 27			14 33		14 42			
New Cross Gate	d						14 08													14 38					
Norwood Junction 2	d						14 16					14 26								14 46					
East Croydon ⇌	a			14 17			14 20		14 22	14 25		14 29	14 32				14 39		14 48	14 50	14 52	14 54			
	d			14 18			14 21		14 23	14 25		14 30	14 33				14 41		14 48	14 51	14 53	14 55			
Purley 4	d						14 27					14 36								14 57					
Coulsdon South	d						14 30					14 39								15 00					
Merstham	d						14 36					14 45								15 06					
Redhill	a			14 30			14 39					14 49							15 00	15 09					
	d			14 30	14 34	14 41	14 45					14 52							15 00	15 10					15 13
Reigate	a				14 38							14 56													15 18
Nutfield	d																								
Godstone	d																								
Edenbridge	d																								
Penshurst	d																								
Leigh (Kent)	d																								
Tonbridge 4	a																								
Earlswood (Surrey)	d																			15 12					
Salfords	d																			15 16					
Horley 4	d			14 36			14 53								←					15 19					
Gatwick Airport 10 ✈	a	14 30		14 39		14 50	14 55			14 40	14 45		14 48		14 55		14 56	15 00	15 08	15 23		15 10	15 15		
	d			14 40			14 56			14 41			14 50		14 56		14 57		15 09	15 24		15 11			
Three Bridges 15	a			14 44			→			14 45					15 01		15 01		15 14	→		15 15			
	d			14 45						14 45					15 01		15 02		15 14			15 15			
Crawley	d			14 48											15 05				15 18						
Ifield	d														15 07										
Faygate	d																								
Littlehaven	d														15 14										
Horsham 4	a			14 56											15 17				15 26						
Balcombe	d																					15 21			
Haywards Heath	a									14 54			15 00				15 11					15 26			
	d									14 55			15 04	15 07			15 11					15 27			
Wivelsfield	d									14 59				15 11								15 31			
Lewes 4	a													15 22											
Burgess Hill 4	d									15 01			15 09									15 33			
Hassocks 4	d									15 04												15 36			
Preston Park	d									15 11			15 18									15 43			
Hove 2	a												15 22												
Brighton 10	a								14 58	15 15							15 25				15 28	15 47			

Bedford and London - Brighton

Network Diagram - see first Page of Table 186

		SN 1	SN ◇1		SN ◇1	SN 1	FC 1		GX 1 ⌶	SN	GW 1	SN ◇1	GW 1	SN 1	SN ◇1 ⌶		FC 1	GX 1 ⌶	SN 1	SN ◇1		FC 1	SN 1		GX 1 ⌶
London Victoria 15 Θ	d		14 47		14 51				15 00	15 01		15 02			15 06			15 15		15 17					15 30
Clapham Junction 10	d		14 53							15 08		15 08			15 12					15 23					
Bedford	d						13 40										13 54					14 10			
Luton 10	d						14 04										14 18					14 34			
Luton Airport Parkway 7 ✈	d						14 06										14 20					14 36			
St Albans City	d						14 18										14 32					14 48			
St Pancras International 15 Θ	d						14 39										14 54					15 09			
Farringdon 3 Θ	d						14 44										14 59					15 14			
City Thameslink 3	d						14 48										15 03					15 18			
London Blackfriars 3 Θ	d						14 50										15 05					15 20			
London Bridge 4 Θ	d	14 45					14 57							15 03			15 12		15 15			15 27			
New Cross Gate	d													15 08											
Norwood Junction 2	d	14 56												15 16					15 26						
East Croydon ⇌	a	14 59	15 02		15 07		15 09					15 17		15 20	15 22		15 24		15 29	15 32		15 39			
	d	15 00	15 03		15 08		15 11					15 18		15 21	15 23		15 25		15 30	15 33		15 41			
Purley 4	d	15 06												15 27					15 36						
Coulsdon South	d	15 09												15 30					15 39						
Merstham	d													15 36					15 45						
Redhill	a	15 17										15 30		15 39					15 49						
	d	15 17									15 29	15 30	15 41	15 45					15 52						
Reigate	a										15 33								15 56						
Nutfield	d	15 22																							
Godstone	d	15 27																							
Edenbridge	d	15 33																							
Penshurst	d	15 39																							
Leigh (Kent)	d	15 43																							
Tonbridge 4	a	15 48																							
Earlswood (Surrey)	d													15 48											
Salfords	d													15 51											
Horley 4	d					←						15 36		15 55									←		
Gatwick Airport 10 ✈	a		15 18		15 22	15 23	15 26		15 30			15 39	15 50	15 57			15 40	15 45		15 48		15 56	15 57		16 00
	d		15 20		15 23	15 24	15 27					15 40		15 58			15 41			15 50		15 57	15 58		
Three Bridges 15	a					15 29	15 31					15 44		→			15 45					16 01	16 03		
	d					15 30	15 32					15 45					15 45					16 02	16 03		
Crawley	d					15 33						15 48											16 07		
Ifield	d					15 36																	16 10		
Faygate	d																						16 14		
Littlehaven	d					15 42																	16 18		
Horsham 4	a					15 48						15 56											16 21		
Balcombe	d																								
Haywards Heath	a		15 30				15 41										15 54			16 00		16 11			
	d		15 35	15 37			15 41										15 55			16 04	16 07	16 11			
Wivelsfield	d		15 39														15 59				16 11				
Lewes 4	a		15 52																		16 22				
Burgess Hill 4	d				15 38												16 01			16 09					
Hassocks 4	d				15 41												16 04								
Preston Park	d																16 11			16 18					
Hove 2	a			15 53																16 22					
Brighton 10	a				15 52		15 55								15 58		16 15					16 25			

Bedford and London - Brighton

Network Diagram - see first Page of Table 186

	SN ◇1	SN 1	SN ◇1 ✠	FC 1	GX 1 ✠	GW 1		SN 1	SN ◇1		SN ◇1	SN 1	FC 1	GX 1 ✠		SN	SN ◇1	GW 1	SN 1		SN 1 ✠	FC 1		GX 1
London Victoria 15 ⊖ d	15 32		15 36		15 45				15 47		15 51			16 00		16 01	16 02				16 06			16 15
Clapham Junction 10 d	15 38		15 42						15 53							16 08	16 08				16 12			
Bedford d				14 24									14 40									14 54		
Luton 10 d				14 48									15 04									15 18		
Luton Airport Parkway 7 ✈ d				14 50									15 06									15 20		
St Albans City d				15 02									15 18									15 32		
St Pancras International 15 ⊖ d				15 24									15 39									15 54		
Farringdon 3 ⊖ d				15 29									15 44									15 59		
City Thameslink 3 d				15 33									15 48									16 03		
London Blackfriars 3 ⊖ d				15 35									15 50									16 05		
London Bridge 4 ⊖ d		15 33		15 42				15 45					15 57						16 03			16 12		
New Cross Gate d		15 38																	16 08					
Norwood Junction 2 d		15 46						15 56											16 16					
East Croydon a	15 47	15 50	15 52	15 54				15 59	16 02		16 07		16 09				16 17		16 20		16 22	16 24		
d	15 48	15 51	15 53	15 55				16 00	16 03		16 08		16 11				16 18		16 21		16 23	16 25		
Purley 4 d		15 57						16 06											16 27					
Coulsdon South d		16 00						16 09											16 30					
Merstham d		16 06						16 15											16 36					
Redhill a	16 00	16 09						16 19									16 30		16 39					
d	16 00	16 10				16 13		16 20									16 30	16 32	16 43	16 45				
Reigate a						16 18												16 36						
Nutfield d								16 24												16 49				
Godstone d								16 30												16 55				
Edenbridge d								16 35												17 00				
Penshurst d								16 42												17 07				
Leigh (Kent) d								16 45												17 10				
Tonbridge 4 a								16 52												17 15				
Earlswood (Surrey) d		16 12																	16 45					
Salfords d		16 16																	16 49					
Horley 4 d		16 19										←					16 36		16 52					
Gatwick Airport 10 ✈ a	16 08	16 23		16 10	16 15				16 18		16 22	16 23	16 26	16 30			16 39		16 55			16 40		16 45
d	16 09	16 24		16 11					16 20		16 23	16 24	16 27				16 40		16 56			16 41		
Three Bridges 15 a	16 14	→		16 15								16 29	16 31				16 44		→			16 45		
d	16 14			16 15								16 30	16 32				16 45					16 45		
Crawley d	16 18											16 34					16 48							
Ifield d												16 36												
Faygate d												16 40												
Littlehaven d												16 44												
Horsham 4 a	16 26											16 47					16 56							
Balcombe d				16 21																				
Haywards Heath a				16 26					16 30				16 41									16 54		
d				16 27					16 35	16 37			16 41									16 55		
Wivelsfield d				16 31					16 39													16 59		
Lewes 4 a									16 54															
Burgess Hill 4 d				16 33							16 38											17 01		
Hassocks 4 d				16 36							16 41											17 04		
Preston Park d				16 43																		17 11		
Hove 2 a										16 53														
Brighton 10 a			16 28	16 47							16 52		16 55								17 00	17 15		

Table 186 Mondays to Fridays

Bedford and London - Brighton

Network Diagram - see first Page of Table 186

	GW 1	SN 1	SN ◇1 A ✠		SN 1	SN 1		FC 1	GX 1 ✠	SN	SN ◇1 B ✠		SN 1	SN 1 ✠			FC 1	GX 1 ✠	SN 1	GW 1	SN ◇1 ✠	SN 1	SN 1	
London Victoria 15 ⊖ d			16 17		16 19				16 30	16 31	16 32			16 36				16 45			16 47		16 49	
Clapham Junction 10 d			16 23		16 26					16a37	16 38			16 42							16 53		16 56	
Bedford d								15 10									15 24							
Luton 10 d								15 34									15 48							
Luton Airport Parkway 7 ✈ d								15 36									15 50							
St Albans City d								15 48									16 02							
St Pancras International 15 ⊖ d								16 09									16 22							
Farringdon 3 ⊖ d								16 14									16 27							
City Thameslink 3 d								16 18									16 31							
London Blackfriars 3 ⊖ d								16 20									16 36							
London Bridge 4 ⊖ d		16 15						16 27					16 33				16 43							
New Cross Gate d																								
Norwood Junction 2 d		16 26											16 44											
East Croydon a		16 29	16 33		16 36			16 39			16 47		16 48	16 52			16 59				17 03		17 06	
d		16 30	16 33		16 36			16 41			16 48		16 49	16 52			17 00				17 03		17 07	
Purley 4 d		16 36											16 55											
Coulsdon South d		16 39											16 59										17 13	
Merstham d		16 45											17 04										17 19	
Redhill a		16 49									16 59		17 08										17 22	
d	16 51	16 53									17 00		17 08						17 12	17 13			17 27	17 29
Reigate a		16 59																		17 18				17 35
Nutfield d																			17 16					
Godstone d																			17 22					
Edenbridge d																			17 27					
Penshurst d																			17 34					
Leigh (Kent) d																			17 37					
Tonbridge 4 a																			17 42					
Earlswood (Surrey) d													17 11										17 29	
Salfords d													17 14										17 33	
Horley 4 d						←					17 06		17 18									←	17 36	
Gatwick Airport 10 ✈ a	16 59		16 48		16 52	16 55		16 56	17 00		17 08		17 20				17 15	17 15			17 19	17 20	17 39	
d			16 49		16 53	16 56		16 57			17 09		17 21				17 16				17 20	17 21	17 40	
Three Bridges 15 a					16 57	17 00		17 01			17 14		→	17 09			17 20				17 24	17 26	17 46	
d					16 58	17 02		17 02			17 18	17 22		17 10			17 21				17 25	17 26		
Crawley d					17 02	17 06					17 22	17 26										17 30		
Ifield d						17 08						17 28										17 33		
Faygate d						17 12																17 37		
Littlehaven d						17 16						17 35										17 41		
Horsham 4 a					17 12	17 19					17 30	17 38										17 44		
Balcombe d																	17 27							
Haywards Heath a			17 00					17 11						17 19			17 32				17 35			
d			17 04	17 06				17 11						17 23	17 26		17 32				17 36			
Wivelsfield d				17 10											17 30		17 37				17 41			
Lewes 4 a				17 21																	17 56			
Burgess Hill 4 d			17 09					17 17							17 32		17 39							
Hassocks 4 d								17 21							17 35		17 43							
Preston Park d															17 42		17 50							
Hove 2 a			17 20																					
Brighton 10 a								17 30						17 39	17 46		17 54							

A ✠ to Haywards Heath

B ✠ to Three Bridges

Bedford and London - Brighton

Network Diagram - see first Page of Table 186

		FC 1		SN ◇1	SN 1	GW 1	GW 1	SN 1	SN 1			FC 1	SN 1 ⚲	SN 1		SN ◇1	SN 1	SN 1		SN 1 ⚲	FC 1	SN 1	SN ◇1 ⚲		SN 1
London Victoria 15 ⊖	d			18 17					18 19				18 30			18 32		18 36		18 45			18 47		18 51
Clapham Junction 10	d			18 23					18 26							18 38		18 42					18 53		18 57
Bedford	d											17 06									17 22				
Luton 10	d											17 30									17 46				
Luton Airport Parkway 7 ✈	d											17 33									17 48				
St Albans City	d											17 45									18 00				
St Pancras International 15 ⊖	d	17 40										18 08									18 20				
Farringdon 3 ⊖	d	17 45										18 13									18 25				
City Thameslink 3	d	17 49										18 17									18 29				
London Blackfriars 3 ⊖	d	17 51										18 20									18 32				
London Bridge 4 ⊖	d				18 23							18 27		18 30											
New Cross Gate	d																								
Norwood Junction 2	d													18 42											
East Croydon	a	18 24		18 33	18 36				18 37			18 41		18 45		18 48		18 52			19 00		19 03		19 07
	d	18 25		18 33	18 37				18 38			18 41		18 46		18 48		18 53			19 01		19 04		19 08
Purley 4	d								18 43					18 51											
Coulsdon South	d								18 46					18 54											19 14
Merstham	d								18 52					19 00											19 20
Redhill	a	18 37							18 55					19 03											19 23
	d	18 38				18 43	18 51	18 54	18 59	19 01				19 07	19 09										19 24
Reigate	a					18 47		18 58							19 15										
Nutfield	d									19 05															
Godstone	d									19 11															
Edenbridge	d									19 16															
Penshurst	d									19 23															
Leigh (Kent)	d									19 26															
Tonbridge 4	a									19 34															
Earlswood (Surrey)	d								19 01					19 09											19 26
Salfords	d								19 05					19 13											19 30
Horley 4	d			18 48					19 08					19 16			←					←			19 33
Gatwick Airport 10 ✈	a	18 49					19 00		19 13			18 56	19 00	19 19			19 13			19 12	19 16	19 19	19 20		19 36
	d	18 50							19 14			18 57	19 05	19 20			19 14			19 15	19 18	19 20	19 21		19 37
Three Bridges 15	a	18 56			18 56				→			19 01		→		19 06	19 19					19 24			→
	d				18 57							19 02				19 07	19 19					19 25			
Crawley	d															19 11	19 23					19 29			
Ifield	d																19 26					19 31			
Faygate	d																					19 35			
Littlehaven	d															19 19	19 32					19 39			
Horsham 4	a															19 22	19 37					19 43			
Balcombe	d			18 57								19 08													
Haywards Heath	a			19 02	19 05							19 13	19 16					19 19		19 25	19 29		19 32		
	d			19 03	19 06							19 14	19 17					19 21		19 26	19 30		19 35	19 38	
Wivelsfield	d				19 11													19 25					19 39		
Lewes 4	a				19 27																		19 54		
Burgess Hill 4	d			19 09								19 19	19 23								19 35			19 43	
Hassocks 4	d			19 13								19 23	19 27								19 39			19 47	
Preston Park	d																			19 41	19 46				
Hove 2	a			19 22																				19 57	
Brighton 10	a											19 33	19 39					19 42		19 47	19 52				

Table 186 Mondays to Fridays

Bedford and London - Brighton

Network Diagram - see first Page of Table 186

		FC 1		GX 1 ⚲	SN 1	GW 1	SN ◇1 ⚲	SN 1	SN 1	SN ⚲		FC 1	GW 1	SN 1	GX 1 ⚲	SN ◇1 A ⚲		SN 1		FC 1	SN 1	GX 1 ⚲	SN 1	SN ◇1 ⚲	SN 1
London Victoria 15 ⊖	d			19 00			19 02			19 06				19 10	19 15	19 17						19 30		19 32	
Clapham Junction 10	d						19 08			19 12				19 16		19 23								19 38	
Bedford	d	17 36										17 54								18 10					
Luton 10	d	18 00										18 18								18 34					
Luton Airport Parkway 7 ✈	d	18 02										18 20								18 36					
St Albans City	d	18 14										18 32								18 48					
St Pancras International 15 ⊖	d	18 34										18 54								19 09					
Farringdon 3 ⊖	d	18 40										18 59								19 14					
City Thameslink 3	d	18 43										19 03								19 18					
London Blackfriars 3 ⊖	d	18 46										19 05								19 20					
London Bridge 4 ⊖	d	18 57							18 59			19 12								19 27					
New Cross Gate	d								19 06																
Norwood Junction 2	d								19 14																
East Croydon	a	19 10					19 18		19 17	19 22		19 24		19 27		19 33				19 39				19 48	
	d	19 11					19 18		19 19	19 23		19 25		19 28		19 33				19 41				19 48	
Purley 4	d								19 24					19 33											
Coulsdon South	d								19 28					19 36											
Merstham	d								19 33					19 42											
Redhill	a						19 30		19 37					19 45										20 00	
	d					19 26	19 31	19 36	19 37				19 43	19 46									19 51	20 00	20 05
Reigate	a					19 30		19 40																	20 10
Nutfield	d																						19 55		
Godstone	d																						20 01		
Edenbridge	d																						20 06		
Penshurst	d																						20 13		
Leigh (Kent)	d																						20 16		
Tonbridge 4	a																						20 21		
Earlswood (Surrey)	d								19 40					19 48											
Salfords	d								19 43					19 52											
Horley 4	d				←				19 47					19 55				←			←				
Gatwick Airport 10 ✈	a	19 25		19 30	19 36		19 39		19 49			19 40	19 55	19 58	19 45	19 48		19 49		19 55	19 58	20 00		20 08	
	d	19 26			19 37		19 40		19 50			19 41		19 59		19 49		19 50		19 57	19 59			20 09	
Three Bridges 15	a	19 30			19 41		19 45		→			19 45		→				19 55		20 01	20 03			20 14	
	d	19 31					19 45					19 45						19 55		20 02	20 04			20 14	
Crawley	d						19 49											19 59			20 08			20 18	
Ifield	d																	20 02			20 10				
Faygate	d																				20 14				
Littlehaven	d																	20 08			20 18				
Horsham 4	a						19 57											20 11			20 21			20 26	
Balcombe	d	19 37										19 51													
Haywards Heath	a	19 42								19 46		19 56				20 00				20 11					
	d	19 42								19 47		19 57				20 04	20 07			20 11					
Wivelsfield	d											20 01					20 11								
Lewes 4	a																20 22								
Burgess Hill 4	d	19 48										20 03				20 09				20 16					
Hassocks 4	d	19 51										20 06								20 20					
Preston Park	d											20 13													
Hove 2	a															20 21									
Brighton 10	a	20 01								20 03		20 17								20 29					

A ⚲ to Haywards Heath

Bedford and London - Brighton

Network Diagram - see first Page of Table 186

		SN 1	GX 1 ⊼	SN 1		SN ◇1 ⊼	SN 1	FC 1	GX 1 ⊼	SN ◇1	SN 1	SN 1	GW 1	GW 1	SN 1		SN 1 ⊼	FC 1	SN ◇1	SN 1		SN ◇1 ⊼
London Victoria ⊖	d		17 00			17 02	17 06		17 15	17 17					17 21		17 30		17 32			17 35
Clapham Junction	d					17 08	17 12			17 23					17 27				17 38			17 42
Bedford	d							15 52										16 10				
Luton	d							16 14										16 34				
Luton Airport Parkway ✈	d							16 17										16 36				
St Albans City	d							16 25										16 48				
St Pancras International ⊖	d							16 46										17 10				
Farringdon ⊖	d							16 51										17 15				
City Thameslink	d							16 55										17 19				
London Blackfriars ⊖	d							16 58										17 22				
London Bridge ⊖	d	16 57		16 59								17 23								17 32		
New Cross Gate	d																					
Norwood Junction	d			17 10																17 44		
East Croydon	a	17 09		17 14		17 17	17 22	17 26		17 32		17 35			17 36			17 47	17 48	17 49		17 51
	d	17 10		17 15		17 18	17 23	17 26		17 33		17 36			17 38			17 47	17 49	17 49		17 52
Purley	d			17 21																17 55		
Coulsdon South	d			17 24											17 44					17 58		
Merstham	d			17 30											17 50					18 04		
Redhill	a			17 33											17 53			18 02		18 07		
	d			17 37	17 39								17 41	17 43	17 57	17 59		18 03		18 11	18 13	
Reigate	a													17 48		18 05						
Nutfield	d				17 43																18 17	
Godstone	d				17 49																18 23	
Edenbridge	d				17 54																18 28	
Penshurst	d				18 01																18 35	
Leigh (Kent)	d				18 04																18 38	
Tonbridge	a				18 09																18 45	
Earlswood (Surrey)	d			17 39											17 59					18 13		
Salfords	d			17 43											18 03					18 17		
Horley	d			17 46							←	17 50			18 06					18 20		
Gatwick Airport ✈	a		17 30	17 49				17 41	17 45	17 47	17 49		17 54		18 09		17 57	18 13		18 23		18 06
	d			17 50				17 42		17 48	17 50				18 10		18 00	18 14		18 24		18 07
Three Bridges	a	17 29		→		17 36		17 46			17 54	17 55			→			→	18 06	→		
	d	17 29				17 37		17 46			17 55	17 56							18 07			
Crawley	d					17 41					17 59								18 11			
Ifield	d										18 01											
Faygate	d																					
Littlehaven	d										18 08								18 19			
Horsham	a					17 49					18 11								18 22			
Balcombe	d							17 52														
Haywards Heath	a	17 38					17 46	17 57		18 00		18 05					18 10					18 18
	d	17 39					17 47	17 58		18 01		18 05					18 11					18 18
Wivelsfield	d						17 52					18 10										18 23
Lewes	a											18 21										18 38
Burgess Hill	d	17 46					17 55	18 03		18 07							18 17					
Hassocks	d	17 49					17 59	18 07		18 11							18 22					
Preston Park	d	17 56					18 06	18 14														
Hove	a	18 00								18 21												
Brighton	a						18 12	18 18									18 34					

Bedford and London - Brighton

Network Diagram - see first Page of Table 186

		SN 1	SN 1	FC 1	SN 1 ⊼	SN 1	SN ◇1	SN 1	GW 1	SN 1		FC 1	SN 1	SN 1 ⊼	SN 1	SN 1	SN 1	SN ◇1	SN ◇1 ⊼	SN 1	SN 1 ⊼	SN 1
London Victoria ⊖	d				17 45		17 47			17 49				18 00				18 02	18 06		18 15	
Clapham Junction	d						17 53			17 56								18 08	18 12			
Bedford	d											16 26										
Luton	d											16 50										
Luton Airport Parkway ✈	d											16 52										
St Albans City	d											17 04										
St Pancras International ⊖	d											17 28										
Farringdon ⊖	d											17 33										
City Thameslink	d											17 37										
London Blackfriars ⊖	d											17 40										
London Bridge ⊖	d		17 42			17 47							17 57				17 59			18 12		
New Cross Gate	d																					
Norwood Junction	d																18 11					
East Croydon	a		17 54			17 58	18 02			18 05		18 07	18 11				18 15	18 17	18 22	18 24		
	d		17 55			18 00	18 03			18 06		18 09	18 16				18 15	18 19	18 22	18 25		
Purley	d																18 21					
Coulsdon South	d									18 12							18 24					
Merstham	d									18 18							18 30					
Redhill	a									18 21							18 33					
	d								18 13	18 25	18 27					18 32	18 34					
Reigate	a								18 18		18 33											
Nutfield	d															18 36						
Godstone	d															18 42						
Edenbridge	d															18 47						
Penshurst	d															18 54						
Leigh (Kent)	d															18 57						
Tonbridge	a															19 02						
Earlswood (Surrey)	d									18 27							18 36					
Salfords	d									18 31							18 40					
Horley	d	←		←			18 18	←		18 34					←		18 43					←
Gatwick Airport ✈	a	18 09		18 13	18 12		18 20	18 23		18 37		18 24		18 28	18 37		18 46		18 37		18 44	18 46
	d	18 10		18 14	18 15		18 21	18 24		18 38		18 25		18 35	18 38		18 47		18 38		18 46	18 47
Three Bridges	a	18 16		18 18		18 21		18 28		→		18 29	18 34		18 42		→	18 37		18 44		18 51
	d			18 19		18 22		18 29				18 30	18 35					18 38		18 45		18 52
Crawley	d					18 26		18 33										18 42				18 56
Ifield	d					18 28		18 35														18 58
Faygate	d							18 39														
Littlehaven	d					18 35		18 43														19 05
Horsham	a					18 38		18 48										18 50				19 08
Balcombe	d			18 25																		
Haywards Heath	a		18 22	18 30	18 25		18 33					18 39	18 44	18 46					18 49	18 54	18 57	
	d		18 22	18 31	18 26		18 34					18 39	18 45	18 47					18 50	18 54	18 58	
Wivelsfield	d											18 44							18 54			
Lewes	a																		19 09			
Burgess Hill	d		18 28	18 36			18 41					18 46	18 50	18 54						19 00		
Hassocks	d		18 32	18 40			18 45					18 50	18 54	18 59						19 04		
Preston Park	d		18 39	18 47	18 43		18 53					18 57	19 01							19 11	19 15	
Hove	a		18 43				18 57													19 17		
Brighton	a			18 53	18 49							19 02	19 07	19 10							19 22	

Bedford and London - Brighton

Network Diagram - see first Page of Table 186

		SN 1		SN	FC 1	GW 1	SN 1	GX 1 ⚲	SN 1	SN ◇1 A ⚲			SN 1	FC 1	SN 1	GX 1 ⚲	SN ◇1 ⚲	SN ◇1	FC 1		GW 1	GW 1	SN 1	SN 1	
London Victoria 15 ⊖	d			19 36			19 40	19 45		19 47						20 00	20 02	20 06					20 10	20 15	
Clapham Junction 10	d			19 42			19 46			19 53							20 08	20 12					20 16		
Bedford	d				18 24									18 40					18 54						
Luton 10	d				18 48									19 04					19 18						
Luton Airport Parkway 7 ✈	d				18 50									19 06					19 20						
St Albans City	d				19 02									19 18					19 32						
St Pancras International 15 ⊖	d				19 24									19 39					19 54						
Farringdon 3 ⊖	d				19 29									19 44					19 59						
City Thameslink 3	d				19 33									19 48					20 03						
London Blackfriars 3 ⊖	d				19 35									19 50					20 05						
London Bridge 4 ⊖	d	19 33			19 42								19 52	19 57					20 12						
New Cross Gate	d	19 39																							
Norwood Junction 2	d	19 47											20 03												
East Croydon 🚌	a	19 50		19 52	19 54		19 57			20 03			20 06	20 09			20 19	20 22	20 24				20 27		
	d	19 51		19 53	19 55		19 58			20 03			20 07	20 11			20 19	20 23	20 25				20 28		
Purley 4	d	19 57					20 03						20 12										20 33		
Coulsdon South	d	20 00					20 06						20 15										20 36		
Merstham	d	20 06					20 12						20 21										20 42		
Redhill	a	20 09					20 15						20 24				20 30						20 45		
	d	20 10				20 13	20 16						20 25				20 31				20 34	20 41	20 46		
Reigate	a					20 18							20 30								20 38				
Nutfield	d																								
Godstone	d																								
Edenbridge	d																								
Penshurst	d																								
Leigh (Kent)	d																								
Tonbridge 4	a																								
Earlswood (Surrey)	d						20 18																20 48		
Salfords	d						20 22																		
Horley 4	d	20 16					20 25		←						←								20 54		
Gatwick Airport 10 ✈	a	20 18			20 10		20 28	20 15	20 18	20 18				20 25	20 28	20 30	20 38		20 40			20 50	20 56	20 45	
	d	20 19			20 11		20 29		20 19	20 19				20 27	20 29		20 39		20 41				20 57		
Three Bridges 15	a	→			20 15		→		20 24					20 31	20 33		20 44		20 45				→		
	d				20 15				20 24					20 32	20 34		20 44		20 45						
Crawley	d								20 28						20 37		20 48								
Ifield	d								20 31						20 40										
Faygate	d																								
Littlehaven	d								20 37						20 46										
Horsham 4	a								20 40						20 49		20 56								
Balcombe	d																		20 51						
Haywards Heath	a			20 16	20 24					20 30				20 41				20 47	20 56						
	d			20 17	20 25					20 34	20 36			20 41				20 47	20 57						
Wivelsfield	d				20 29						20 40								21 01						
Lewes 4	a										20 55														
Burgess Hill 4	d				20 31					20 39				20 46					21 03						
Hassocks 4	d				20 34					20 42									21 06						
Preston Park	d				20 41					20 49									21 13						
Hove 2	a									20 53															
Brighton 10	a			20 33	20 45									20 57				21 01	21 17						

A ⚲ to Haywards Heath

Bedford and London - Brighton

Network Diagram - see first Page of Table 186

		SN ◇1		SN 1		SN 1	GX 1	SN 1	SN ◇1	SN ◇1	FC 1	SN 1		GW 1	SN 1	SN 1	SN ◇1		SN 1	SN 1		GX 1	SN 1	SN 1	SN ◇1
London Victoria 15 ⊖	d	20 17					20 30		20 32	20 36					20 40	20 45	20 47					21 00		21 02	21 06
Clapham Junction 10	d	20 23							20 38	20 42					20 46		20 53							21 08	21 12
Bedford	d										19 26														
Luton 10	d										19 50														
Luton Airport Parkway 7 ✈	d										19 52														
St Albans City	d										20 04														
St Pancras International 15 ⊖	d										20 24														
Farringdon 3 ⊖	d										20 29														
City Thameslink 3	d										20 33														
London Blackfriars 3 ⊖	d										20 35														
London Bridge 4 ⊖	d			20 28							20 42								20 58						
New Cross Gate	d																								
Norwood Junction 2	d																								
East Croydon 🚌	a	20 33		20 40					20 48	20 52	20 54				20 57		21 03		21 10					21 18	21 22
	d	20 33		20 41					20 48	20 53	20 55				20 58		21 04		21 11					21 18	21 23
Purley 4	d														21 03										
Coulsdon South	d														21 06										
Merstham	d														21 12										
Redhill	a								21 00						21 15									21 30	
	d							20 51	21 00			21 05		21 13	21 16								21 22	21 31	
Reigate	a											21 09		21 18									21 26		
Nutfield	d							20 55																	
Godstone	d							21 01																	
Edenbridge	d							21 06																	
Penshurst	d							21 13																	
Leigh (Kent)	d							21 16																	
Tonbridge 4	a							21 21																	
Earlswood (Surrey)	d														21 18										
Salfords	d														21 22										
Horley 4	d					←									21 25					←					
Gatwick Airport 10 ✈	a	20 48		20 55		20 56	21 00		21 08		21 10				21 28	21 15	21 18		21 26	21 28		21 30		21 38	
	d	20 49		20 56		20 57			21 09		21 11				21 29		21 19		21 27	21 29				21 39	
Three Bridges 15	a			21 00		21 02			21 14		21 15				→				21 31	21 33				21 44	
	d			21 01		21 03			21 14		21 15								21 31	21 34				21 44	
Crawley	d					21 06			21 18											21 37					
Ifield	d					21 09														21 40					
Faygate	d																								
Littlehaven	d					21 15														21 46					
Horsham 4	a					21 18			21 26											21 49					
Balcombe	d																								
Haywards Heath	a	21 00		21 10						21 16	21 24						21 30		21 40					21 53	21 46
	d	21 04	21 07	21 11						21 16	21 25						21 34	21 37	21 41					21 53	21 46
Wivelsfield	d		21 11								21 29							21 41						21 57	
Lewes 4	a		21 22															21 54							
Burgess Hill 4	d	21 09									21 31						21 39							21 59	
Hassocks 4	d										21 34						21 42							22 03	
Preston Park	d										21 41						21 49							22 09	
Hove 2	a	21 21															21 53								
Brighton 10	a			21 26						21 30	21 45								21 56					22 15	22 00

Bedford and London - Brighton

Network Diagram - see first Page of Table 186

		FC 1	GW 1	SN 1	GX 1	SN ◇1	SN 1	GX 1	GW 1	SN 1	SN 1	SN ◇1	FC 1	SN 1	SN 1	GX 1	SN ◇1	SN 1	GX 1	SN 1
London Victoria 15 ⊖	d			21 10	21 15	21 17		21 30			21 32	21 36			21 40	21 45	21 47		22 00	
Clapham Junction 10	d			21 16		21 23					21 38	21 42			21 46		21 53			
Bedford	d	19 52											20 22							
Luton 10	d	20 16											20 46							
Luton Airport Parkway 7 ✈	d	20 18											20 48							
St Albans City	d	20 30											21 00							
St Pancras International 15 ⊖	d	20 54											21 24							
Farringdon 3 ⊖	d	20 59											21 29							
City Thameslink 3	d	21 03											21 33							
London Blackfriars 3 ⊖	d	21 05											21 35							
London Bridge 4 ⊖	d	21 12											21 42							
New Cross Gate	d																			
Norwood Junction 2	d																			
East Croydon	a	21 24		21 27		21 33					21 48	21 52	21 54		21 57		22 03			
	d	21 25		21 28		21 33					21 48	21 53	21 55		21 58		22 03			
Purley 4	d			21 33											22 03					
Coulsdon South	d			21 36											22 06					
Merstham	d			21 42											22 12					
Redhill	a			21 45							21 59				22 15					
	d		21 35	21 46					21 53	21 55	22 00			22 05	22 16					22 22
Reigate	a		21 39											22 09						22 26
Nutfield	d									21 59										
Godstone	d									22 05										
Edenbridge	d									22 10										
Penshurst	d									22 17										
Leigh (Kent)	d									22 20										
Tonbridge 4	a									22 28										
Earlswood (Surrey)	d			21 48											22 18					
Salfords	d														22 22					
Horley 4	d			21 54			←								22 25			←		
Gatwick Airport 10 ✈	a	21 40		21 56	21 45	21 48	21 56	22 00	22 06		22 08		22 10		22 28	22 15	22 18	22 28	22 30	
	d	21 41		21 57		21 49	21 57				22 09		22 11		22 29		22 19	22 29		
Three Bridges 15	a	21 45		→		21 53	22 02				22 14		22 15		→			22 33		
	d	21 45				21 53	22 03				22 14		22 15					22 36		
Crawley	d						22 06				22 18							22 39		
Ifield	d						22 09											22 42		
Faygate	d																			
Littlehaven	d						22 15											22 48		
Horsham 4	a						22 18				22 26							22 51		
Balcombe	d	21 53																		
Haywards Heath	a	21 58				22 02						22 16	22 24				22 30			
	d	21 59				22 06 / 22 08						22 16	22 25				22 34 / 22 37			
Wivelsfield	d	22 03				22 12							22 29				22 38			
Lewes 4	a					22 23											22 53			
Burgess Hill 4	d	22 05				22 11							22 31							
Hassocks 4	d	22 08											22 34							
Preston Park	d	22 15											22 41							
Hove 2	a					22 22											22 51			
Brighton 10	a	22 19										22 30	22 45							

Bedford and London - Brighton

Network Diagram - see first Page of Table 186

		SN ◇1	SN ◇1	FC 1	GW 1	SN 1	SN 1	SN ◇1	SN 1	GX 1	GW 1	SN 1	SN 1	SN	FC 1	SN 1	SN 1	GX 1	SN ◇1	SN 1	SN 1
London Victoria 15 ⊖	d	22 02	22 06			22 10	22 15	22 17		22 30			22 32	22 36			22 40	22 45	22 47		23 00
Clapham Junction 10	d	22 08	22 12			22 16		22 23					22 38	22 42			22 46		22 53		
Bedford	d			20 52																	
Luton 10	d			21 16																	
Luton Airport Parkway 7 ✈	d			21 18																	
St Albans City	d			21 30																	
St Pancras International 15 ⊖	d			21 54																	
Farringdon 3 ⊖	d			21 59																	
City Thameslink 3	d			22 03																	
London Blackfriars 3 ⊖	d			22 05																	
London Bridge 4 ⊖	d			22 12											22 42						
New Cross Gate	d																				
Norwood Junction 2	d																				
East Croydon	a	22 18	22 22	22 24		22 26		22 33					22 48	22 52	22 54		22 57		23 03		
	d	22 18	22 23	22 25		22 28		22 34					22 48	22 53	22 55		22 58		23 03		
Purley 4	d					22 33											23 03				
Coulsdon South	d					22 36											23 06				
Merstham	d					22 42											23 12				
Redhill	a	22 30				22 45							23 00				23 15				
	d	22 31			22 33	22 46					22 52	22 55	23 01			23 05	23 16				
Reigate	a				22 38											23 09					
Nutfield	d											22 59									
Godstone	d											23 05									
Edenbridge	d											23 10									
Penshurst	d											23 17									
Leigh (Kent)	d											23 20									
Tonbridge 4	a											23 25									
Earlswood (Surrey)	d					22 48											23 18				
Salfords	d																23 22				
Horley 4	d					22 54			←								23 25			←	
Gatwick Airport 10 ✈	a	22 38		22 40		22 56	22 45	22 48	22 56	23 00	23 06		23 08		23 10		23 28	23 15	23 18	23 28	23 30
	d	22 39		22 41		22 57		22 49	22 57				23 09		23 11		23 29		23 19	23 29	
Three Bridges 15	a	22 44		22 45		→		22 53	23 02				23 15		23 15		→			23 33	
	d	22 44		22 45				22 53	23 03				23 16		23 15					23 38	
Crawley	d								23 06				23 19							23 41	
Ifield	d								23 09											23 44	
Faygate	d																				
Littlehaven	d								23 15											23 50	
Horsham 4	a								23 18				23 27							23 53	
Balcombe	d			22 53																	
Haywards Heath	a	22 53	22 46	22 58				23 02						23 16	23 24				23 30		
	d	22 53	22 46	22 59				23 03						23 16	23 25				23 34 / 23 37		
Wivelsfield	d	22 57		23 03											23 29				23 38		
Lewes 4	a																		23 51		
Burgess Hill 4	d	22 59		23 05				23 08							23 31						
Hassocks 4	d	23 03		23 08											23 34						
Preston Park	d	23 09		23 15											23 41						
Hove 2	a							23 21											23 51		
Brighton 10	a	23 15	23 00	23 19										23 30	23 45						

Mondays to Fridays

Bedford and London - Brighton

Network Diagram - see first Page of Table 186

		GW ■	SN ◇■	SN ◇■	FC ■	SN ■	GX ■	SN ◇■	SN ■	GX ■	SN ■	SN ◇■	FC ■	SN ■	SN ■	SN ■
London Victoria 15 ⊖	d		23 02	23 06		23 10	23 15	23 17		23 30		23 32		23 45	23 47	23 49
Clapham Junction 10	d		23 08	23 12		23 16		23 23				23 38			23 53	23 56
Bedford	d															
Luton 10	d															
Luton Airport Parkway 7 ✈	d															
St Albans City	d															
St Pancras International 15 ⊖	d															
Farringdon 3 ⊖	d															
City Thameslink 3	d															
London Blackfriars 3 ⊖	d															
London Bridge 4 ⊖	d				23 12								23 42			
New Cross Gate	d															
Norwood Junction 2	d															
East Croydon	a		23 19	23 22	23 24	23 27		23 33				23 51	23 56		00 05	00 09
	d		23 20	23 23	23 25	23 28		23 33				23 52	23 57		00 06	
Purley 4	d					23 33									00 12	
Coulsdon South	d					23 37									00 15	
Merstham	d					23 42									00 21	
Redhill	a		23 31			23 46						00 03			00 24	
	d	23 28	23 31			23 46					23 55	00 05			00 25	
Reigate	a	23 33														
Nutfield	d															
Godstone	d															
Edenbridge	d										00 06					
Penshurst	d															
Leigh (Kent)	d															
Tonbridge 4	a										00 15					
Earlswood (Surrey)	d					23 49										
Salfords	d					23 52										
Horley 4	d					23 56			←						00 31	
Gatwick Airport 10 ✈	a		23 38		23 40	23 58	23 45	23 50	23 58	00 05		00 14	00 18	00 20	00 33	
	d		23 39		23 41	23 59		23 51	23 59			00 15	00 19		00 34	
Three Bridges 15	a		23 44		23 47	→		23 55	00 04			00 20	00 24		00 39	
	d		23 44		23 47			23 56	00 04			00 20			00 39	
Crawley	d								00 07						00 43	
Ifield	d								00 10						00 46	
Faygate	d															
Littlehaven	d								00 16						00 52	
Horsham 4	a								00 19						00 55	
Balcombe	d				23 53							00 26				
Haywards Heath	a		23 53	23 46	23 58			00 05				00 31				
	d		23 53	23 46	23 59			00 05				00 31				
Wivelsfield	d		23 57		00 03							00 35				
Lewes 4	a															
Burgess Hill 4	d		23 59		00 05			00 11				00 37				
Hassocks 4	d		00 03		00 08							00 41				
Preston Park	d		00 09		00 15							00 48				
Hove 2	a							00 21								
Brighton 10	a		00 15	00 01	00 19							00 52				

Table 186

Saturdays

Bedford and London - Brighton

Network Diagram - see first Page of Table 186

		SN ◇■	SN ◇■	FC ■	SN ■	SN ◇■	SN ■	GX ■	SN ■	GW ■	SN ◇■	FC ■	SN ■	SN ■	SN ■	GX ■	SN ◇■	FC	SN ■	GW ■	SN ■
London Victoria 15 ⊖	d	23p02	23p06		23p10	23p17		23p30			23p32		23p45	23p47	23p49	00 02	00 05		00 14		00 30
Clapham Junction 10	d	23p08	23p12		23p16	23p23					23p38			23p53	23p56		00 11		00 20		
Bedford	d																				
Luton 10	d																				
Luton Airport Parkway 7 ✈	d																				
St Albans City	d																				
St Pancras International 15 ⊖	d																				
Farringdon 3 ⊖	d																				
City Thameslink 3	d																				
London Blackfriars 3 ⊖	d																				
London Bridge 4 ⊖	d			23p12								23p42						00 12			
New Cross Gate	d																				
Norwood Junction 2	d																				
East Croydon	a	23p19	23p22	23p24	23p27	23p33					23p51	23p56		00 05	00 09		00 24	00 26	00 31		
	d	23p20	23p23	23p25	23p28	23p33					23p52	23p57		00 06			00 24	00 27	00 32		
Purley 4	d				23p33									00 12					00 37		
Coulsdon South	d				23p37									00 15					00 41		
Merstham	d				23p42									00 21					00 47		
Redhill	a	23p31			23p46						00 03			00 24					00 50		
	d	23p31			23p46				23p55	00 01	00 05			00 25					00 51	00 54	
Reigate	a																				
Nutfield	d																				
Godstone	d																				
Edenbridge	d								00 06												
Penshurst	d																				
Leigh (Kent)	d																				
Tonbridge 4	a								00 15												
Earlswood (Surrey)	d				23p49																
Salfords	d				23p52																
Horley 4	d				23p56		←							00 31					00 57		
Gatwick Airport 10 ✈	a	23p38		23p40	23p58	23p50	23p58	00 05		00 11	00 14	00 18	00 20	00 33		00 37	00 41	00 48	00 59	01 03	01 20
	d	23p39		23p41	23p59	23p51	23p59				00 15	00 19		00 34			00 42	00 49			
Three Bridges 15	a	23p44		23p47	→	23p55	00 04				00 20	00 24		00 39			00 47	00 54			
	d	23p44		23p47		23p56	00 04				00 20			00 39			00 47				
Crawley	d						00 07							00 43							
Ifield	d						00 10							00 46							
Faygate	d																				
Littlehaven	d						00 16							00 52							
Horsham 4	a						00 19							00 55							
Balcombe	d			23p53							00 26										
Haywards Heath	a	23p53	23p46	23p58		00 05					00 31						00 58				
	d	23p53	23p46	23p59		00 05					00 31						01 02 / 01 06				
Wivelsfield	d	23p57		00 03							00 35										
Lewes 4	a																01 20				
Burgess Hill 4	d	23p59		00 05		00 11					00 37										
Hassocks 4	d	00 03		00 08							00 41										
Preston Park	d	00 09		00 15							00 48										
Hove 2	a					00 21															
Brighton 10	a	00 15	00 01	00 19							00 52						01s16				

Table 186

Saturdays

Bedford and London - Brighton

Network Diagram - see first Page of Table 186

		FC	SN ◇	FC	FC	SN	FC	SN	FC	GX	FC	SN ◇	FC	GX	FC	SN	SN ◇	GX	FC	GW	GW	SN
London Victoria ⊖	d		01 00			02 00		03 00		03 30		04 00		04 30		05 00	05 02	05 15				
Clapham Junction	d		01 08			02 08		03 08				04 08					05 08					
Bedford	d																					
Luton	d																					
Luton Airport Parkway ✈	d																					
St Albans City	d																					
St Pancras International ⊖	d																					
Farringdon ⊖	d																					
City Thameslink	d																					
London Blackfriars ⊖	d																					
London Bridge ⊖	d	00 42		01 08	01 35		02 05		03 05		03 35		04 05		04 35				05 05			
New Cross Gate	d																					
Norwood Junction	d																					
East Croydon	a	00 56	01 21	01 31	02 02	02 21	02 31	03 21	03 31		04 01	04 21	04 31		05 01		05 21		05 31			
	d	00 57	01 22	01 32	02 02	02 22	02 32	03 22	03 32		04 02	04 22	04 32		05 02		05 22		05 32			
Purley	d		01 27			02 27		03 27				04 27					05 26					
Coulsdon South	d																05 30					
Merstham	d																05 35					
Redhill	a											04 35					05 39					
	d											04 38					05 40			05 41	05 49	
Reigate	a																			05 47		
Nutfield	d																					
Godstone	d																					
Edenbridge	d																					
Penshurst	d																					
Leigh (Kent)	d																					
Tonbridge	a																					
Earlswood (Surrey)	d																					
Salfords	d																					
Horley	d		01 43			02 42		03 42				04 44					05 46					
Gatwick Airport ✈	a	01 18	01 46	01 51	02 21	02 44	02 51	03 44	03 51	04 05	04 24	04 46	04 51	05 05	05 21	05 35	05 48	05 50	05 53		05 58	
	d	01 22	01 48	01 52	02 22	02 46	02 52	03 46	03 52		04 24	04 47	04 52		05 22		05 49		05 54			05 58
Three Bridges	a	01 28	01 52	01 58	02 28	02 50	02 58	03 50	03 58		04 30	04 51	04 58		05 26		05 54		05 59			06 02
	d		01 53									04 52			05 27		05 54		06 00			06 03
Crawley	d																					06 06
Ifield	d																					06 09
Faygate	d																					
Littlehaven	d																					06 15
Horsham	a																					06 18
Balcombe	d														05 33				06 06			
Haywards Heath	a		02 06									05 01			05 38		06 03		06 11			
	d		02 06									05 01			05 39		06 04		06 11			
Wivelsfield	d														05 43		06 08		06 15			
Lewes	a																					
Burgess Hill	d														05 45		06 10		06 17			
Hassocks	d														05 48		06 13		06 21			
Preston Park	d														05 55		06 20		06 27			
Hove	a																					
Brighton	a		02 23									05 16			05 59		06 24		06 31			

Table 186

Saturdays

Bedford and London - Brighton

Network Diagram - see first Page of Table 186

		GX	SN	SN ◇	GX	FC	SN ◇		GX	GW	SN	GW	GW	SN		GX	FC	SN	GX	SN		GW
London Victoria ⊖	d	05 30		05 32	05 45				06 00					06 02		06 15			06 30	06 32		
Clapham Junction	d			05 38										06 08						06 38		
Bedford	d																					
Luton	d																					
Luton Airport Parkway ✈	d																					
St Albans City	d																					
St Pancras International ⊖	d																					
Farringdon ⊖	d																					
City Thameslink	d																					
London Blackfriars ⊖	d																					
London Bridge ⊖	d					05 52											06 27					
New Cross Gate	d																					
Norwood Junction	d																					
East Croydon	a			05 47		06 04								06 17			06 39			06 47		
	d			05 48		06 05								06 18			06 41			06 48		
Purley	d			05 53										06 23						06 53		
Coulsdon South	d			05 57										06 27						06 57		
Merstham	d			06 03										06 32						07 02		
Redhill	a			06 07										06 36						07 06		
	d			06 07						06 13	06 22	06 34	06 41	06 46	06 52					07 10	07 22	07 13
Reigate	a									06 18		06 38			06 56							07 18
Nutfield	d										06 26										07 26	
Godstone	d										06 32										07 32	
Edenbridge	d										06 37										07 37	
Penshurst	d										06 44										07 44	
Leigh (Kent)	d										06 47										07 47	
Tonbridge	a										06 52										07 52	
Earlswood (Surrey)	d			06 11										06 48						07 12		
Salfords	d			06 15										06 52						07 16		
Horley	d			06 18			←							06 55				←		07 19		
Gatwick Airport ✈	a	06 00		06 21	06 15	06 19	06 21		06 30				06 50	06 58		06 45	06 56	06 58	07 00	07 23		
	d		06 11	06 22		06 20	06 22							06 59			06 57	06 59		07 24		
Three Bridges	a		06 15	→		06 24	06 26							→			07 01	07 03		→		
	d		06 16			06 25	06 30	06 34									07 02	07 04				
Crawley	d							06 37										07 07				
Ifield	d							06 40										07 10				
Faygate	d																					
Littlehaven	d							06 46										07 16				
Horsham	a							06 49										07 19				
Balcombe	d					06 31	06 36															
Haywards Heath	a		06 26			06 36	06 41										07 11					
	d		06 26			06 37	06 41										07 11					
Wivelsfield	d		06 30			06 41	06 45															
Lewes	a		06 41																			
Burgess Hill	d					06 43	06 47															
Hassocks	d					06 46	06 51															
Preston Park	d					06 53	06 57															
Hove	a																					
Brighton	a					06 57	07 03										07 25					

Bedford and London - Brighton

Network Diagram - see first Page of Table 186

		FC ■1	GX ■1 🛒	SN ■1	SN ■1	GW ■1	SN ◇■1	FC ■1	GX ■1 🛒	GW ■1	SN ■1		SN ◇■1	FC ■1	GX ■1 🛒	SN ■1	FC ■1	GX ■1 🛒	SN ◇■1	SN ■1	SN ◇■1	FC ■1
London Victoria 15 ⊖	d		06 45						07 00				07 06		07 15			07 30	07 32		07 36	
Clapham Junction 10	d												07 12						07 38		07 42	
Bedford	d																					
Luton 10	d																					
Luton Airport Parkway 7 ✈	d																					
St Albans City	d																					
St Pancras International 15 ⊖	d																					
Farringdon 3 ⊖	d																					
City Thameslink 3	d																					
London Blackfriars 3 ⊖	d																					
London Bridge 4 ⊖	d	06 42						06 57			07 03			07 12			07 27			07 33		07 42
New Cross Gate	d										07 08									07 38		
Norwood Junction 2	d										07 16									07 46		
East Croydon 🚊	a	06 54						07 09			07 20		07 22	07 24			07 39		07 47	07 50	07 52	07 54
	d	06 55						07 11			07 21		07 23	07 25			07 41		07 48	07 51	07 53	07 55
Purley 4	d										07 26									07 56		
Coulsdon South	d										07 30									08 00		
Merstham	d										07 35									08 05		
Redhill	a										07 39								08 00	08 09		
	d					07 34				07 41	07 44	07 52							08 00	08 10		
Reigate	a					07 38						07 56										
Nutfield	d																					
Godstone	d																					
Edenbridge	d																					
Penshurst	d																					
Leigh (Kent)	d																					
Tonbridge 4	a																					
Earlswood (Surrey)	d																			08 12		
Salfords	d																			08 16		
Horley 4	d			←							07 51					←				08 19		
Gatwick Airport 10 ✈	a	07 10	07 15	07 23				07 26	07 30	07 50	07 55			07 40	07 45	07 55	07 56	08 00	08 08	08 23		08 10
	d	07 11		07 24				07 27			07 56			07 41		07 56	07 57		08 09	08 24		08 11
Three Bridges 15	a	07 15		07 29				07 31			→			07 45		08 01	08 01		08 14	→		08 15
	d	07 15		07 30				07 32						07 45		08 01	08 02		08 14			08 15
Crawley	d			07 33												08 05			08 18			
Ifield	d			07 36												08 07						
Faygate	d																					
Littlehaven	d			07 42												08 14						
Horsham 4	a			07 45												08 17			08 26			
Balcombe	d	07 21																				08 21
Haywards Heath	a	07 26						07 41						07 54			08 11					08 26
	d	07 27			07 33		07 37	07 41						07 55			08 11					08 27
Wivelsfield	d	07 31			07 37									07 59								08 31
Lewes 4	a				07 48																	
Burgess Hill 4	d	07 33												08 01								08 33
Hassocks 4	d	07 36												08 04								08 36
Preston Park	d	07 43												08 11								08 43
Hove 2	a						07 51															
Brighton 10	a	07 47						07 55					07 57	08 15			08 25				08 27	08 47

Bedford and London - Brighton

Network Diagram - see first Page of Table 186

		GX ■1 🛒	GW ■1	SN ■1	SN ◇■1		SN ◇■1	SN ■1	FC ■1	GX ■1 🛒	SN	SN ◇■1	GW ■1	GW ■1	SN ■1	SN ◇■1	FC ■1	GX ■1 🛒	SN ■1	SN ◇■1		SN ■1
London Victoria 15 ⊖	d	07 45			07 47		07 51			08 00	08 01	08 02				08 06		08 15		08 17		
Clapham Junction 10	d				07 53						08 08	08 08				08 12				08 23		
Bedford	d																					
Luton 10	d																					
Luton Airport Parkway 7 ✈	d																					
St Albans City	d																					
St Pancras International 15 ⊖	d																					
Farringdon 3 ⊖	d																					
City Thameslink 3	d																					
London Blackfriars 3 ⊖	d																					
London Bridge 4 ⊖	d			07 45					07 57						08 03		08 12		08 15			
New Cross Gate	d														08 08							
Norwood Junction 2	d			07 56											08 16				08 26			
East Croydon 🚊	a			07 59	08 02		08 07		08 09			08 17			08 20	08 22	08 24		08 29	08 32		
	d			08 00	08 03		08 08		08 11			08 18			08 21	08 23	08 25		08 30	08 33		
Purley 4	d			08 06											08 26				08 36			
Coulsdon South	d			08 09											08 30				08 39			
Merstham	d														08 35				08 45			
Redhill	a			08 17								08 30			08 39				08 49			
	d		08 13	08 17								08 30	08 34	08 41	08 44				08 52			
Reigate	a		08 18										08 38						08 56			
Nutfield	d			08 22																		
Godstone	d			08 27																		
Edenbridge	d			08 33																		
Penshurst	d			08 39																		
Leigh (Kent)	d			08 43																		
Tonbridge 4	a			08 48																		
Earlswood (Surrey)	d																					
Salfords	d																					
Horley 4	d							←				08 36			08 51							←
Gatwick Airport 10 ✈	a	08 15			08 18		08 22	08 23	08 26	08 30		08 39		08 50	08 55		08 40	08 45		08 48		08 55
	d				08 20		08 23	08 24	08 27			08 40			08 56		08 41			08 50		08 56
Three Bridges 15	a							08 29	08 31			08 44			→		08 45					09 01
	d							08 30	08 32			08 45					08 45					09 01
Crawley	d							08 33				08 48										09 05
Ifield	d							08 36														09 07
Faygate	d																					
Littlehaven	d							08 42														09 14
Horsham 4	a							08 45				08 56										09 17
Balcombe	d																					
Haywards Heath	a				08 30				08 41								08 54			09 00		
	d				08 35	08 37			08 41								08 55			09 05	09 07	
Wivelsfield	d																08 59				09 11	
Lewes 4	a				08 49																09 22	
Burgess Hill 4	d						08 38										09 01			09 10		
Hassocks 4	d						08 41										09 04					
Preston Park	d																09 11			09 18		
Hove 2	a					08 53														09 22		
Brighton 10	a						08 52		08 55							08 57	09 15					

Table 186

Bedford and London - Brighton

Network Diagram - see first Page of Table 186

Station		FC	SN	SN	SN	SN	FC	GX	GW	SN	SN	SN	SN	SN	FC	GX	SN	SN	GW	GW	SN	SN
		1	1	◇1	1	◇1	1	1	1	1	◇1		◇1	1	1	1		◇1	1	1	1	◇1
London Victoria 15 ⊖	d		08 30	08 32		08 36		08 45			08 47		08 51			09 00	09 01	09 02				09 06
Clapham Junction 10	d			08 38		08 42					08 53						09 08	09 08				09 12
Bedford	d																					
Luton 10	d																					
Luton Airport Parkway 7 ✈	d																					
St Albans City	d																					
St Pancras International 15 ⊖	d																					
Farringdon 3 ⊖	d																					
City Thameslink 3	d																					
London Blackfriars 3 ⊖	d																					
London Bridge 4 ⊖	d	08 27			08 33		08 42			08 45					08 57						09 03	
New Cross Gate	d				08 38																09 08	
Norwood Junction 2	d				08 46					08 56											09 16	
East Croydon	a	08 39		08 47	08 50	08 52	08 54			08 59	09 02		09 07		09 09			09 17			09 20	09 22
	d	08 40		08 48	08 51	08 53	08 55			09 00	09 03		09 08		09 11			09 18			09 21	09 23
Purley 4	d				08 56					09 06											09 26	
Coulsdon South	d				09 00					09 09											09 30	
Merstham	d				09 05																09 35	
Redhill	a			09 00	09 09					09 17								09 30			09 39	
	d			09 00	09 10				09 13	09 17								09 30	09 34	09 41	09 44	
Reigate	a								09 18										09 38			
Nutfield	d									09 22												
Godstone	d									09 27												
Edenbridge	d									09 33												
Penshurst	d									09 39												
Leigh (Kent)	d									09 43												
Tonbridge 4	a									09 48												
Earlswood (Surrey)	d				09 12																	
Salfords	d				09 16																	
Horley 4	d				09 19									←				09 36			09 51	
Gatwick Airport 10 ✈	a	08 56	09 00	09 08	09 23		09 10	09 15			09 18		09 22	09 23	09 26	09 30		09 39		09 50	09 55	
	d	08 57		09 09	09 24		09 11				09 20		09 23	09 24	09 27			09 40			09 56	
Three Bridges 15	a	09 01		09 14	→		09 15							09 29	09 31			09 44			→	
	d	09 02		09 14			09 15							09 30	09 32			09 45				
Crawley	d			09 18										09 33				09 48				
Ifield	d													09 36								
Faygate	d																					
Littlehaven	d													09 42								
Horsham 4	a			09 26										09 45				09 56				
Balcombe	d						09 21															
Haywards Heath	a	09 11					09 26				09 30				09 41							
	d	09 11					09 27				09 35	09 37			09 41							
Wivelsfield	d						09 31															
Lewes 4	a										09 52											
Burgess Hill 4	d						09 33						09 38									
Hassocks 4	d						09 36						09 41									
Preston Park	d						09 43															
Hove 2	a											09 53										
Brighton 10	a	09 25				09 27	09 47						09 52		09 55							09 57

Table 186

Saturdays

Bedford and London - Brighton

Network Diagram - see first Page of Table 186

Station		FC	GX	SN	SN	SN	SN	FC	GX	SN	SN	SN	FC	GX	GW	SN	SN	SN	SN	SN	FC	GX
		1	1	1	◇1		1	1	1	◇1	1	◇1	1	1	1	1	◇1		◇1	1	1	1
London Victoria 15 ⊖	d		09 15		09 17				09 30	09 32		09 36		09 45			09 47		09 51			10 00
Clapham Junction 10	d				09 23					09 38		09 42					09 53					
Bedford	d																					
Luton 10	d																					
Luton Airport Parkway 7 ✈	d																					
St Albans City	d																					
St Pancras International 15 ⊖	d																					
Farringdon 3 ⊖	d																					
City Thameslink 3	d																					
London Blackfriars 3 ⊖	d																					
London Bridge 4 ⊖	d	09 12		09 15				09 27			09 33		09 42			09 45					09 57	
New Cross Gate	d										09 38											
Norwood Junction 2	d			09 26							09 46					09 56						
East Croydon	a	09 24		09 29	09 32			09 39		09 47	09 50	09 52	09 54			09 59	10 02		10 07		10 09	
	d	09 25		09 30	09 33			09 41		09 48	09 51	09 53	09 55			10 00	10 03		10 08		10 11	
Purley 4	d			09 36							09 56					10 06						
Coulsdon South	d			09 39							10 00					10 09						
Merstham	d			09 45							10 05											
Redhill	a			09 49						10 00	10 09					10 17						
	d			09 52						10 00	10 10				10 13	10 17						
Reigate	a			09 56											10 18							
Nutfield	d															10 22						
Godstone	d															10 27						
Edenbridge	d															10 33						
Penshurst	d															10 39						
Leigh (Kent)	d															10 43						
Tonbridge 4	a															10 48						
Earlswood (Surrey)	d										10 12											
Salfords	d										10 16											
Horley 4	d						←				10 19									←		
Gatwick Airport 10 ✈	a	09 40	09 45		09 48		09 55	09 56	10 00	10 08	10 23		10 10	10 15			10 18		10 22	10 23	10 26	10 30
	d	09 41			09 50		09 56	09 57		10 09	10 24		10 11				10 20		10 23	10 24	10 27	
Three Bridges 15	a	09 45					10 01	10 01		10 14	→		10 15							10 29	10 31	
	d	09 45					10 01	10 02		10 14			10 15							10 30	10 32	
Crawley	d						10 05			10 18										10 33		
Ifield	d						10 07													10 36		
Faygate	d																					
Littlehaven	d						10 14													10 42		
Horsham 4	a						10 17			10 26										10 45		
Balcombe	d												10 21									
Haywards Heath	a	09 54			10 00			10 11					10 26				10 30				10 41	
	d	09 55			10 04	10 07		10 11					10 27				10 35	10 37			10 41	
Wivelsfield	d	09 59				10 11							10 31									
Lewes 4	a					10 22											10 52					
Burgess Hill 4	d	10 01			10 09								10 33						10 38			
Hassocks 4	d	10 04											10 36						10 41			
Preston Park	d	10 11			10 18								10 43									
Hove 2	a				10 22													10 53				
Brighton 10	a	10 15						10 25				10 27	10 47						10 52		10 55	

Bedford and London - Brighton

Network Diagram - see first Page of Table 186

Station			SN	SN ◇1 ⌶	GW 1	GW 1	SN 1	SN ◇1 ⌶	FC 1		GX 1 ⌶	SN 1	SN ◇1		SN 1	FC 1	GX 1 ⌶		SN ◇1	SN 1	SN ◇1 ⌶	FC 1	GX 1 ⌶	GW 1	SN 1
London Victoria 15 ⊖	d		10 01	10 02				10 06			10 15		10 17				10 30		10 32		10 36		10 45		
Clapham Junction 10	d		10 08	10 08				10 12					10 23						10 38		10 42				
Bedford	d																								
Luton 10	d																								
Luton Airport Parkway 7 ✈	d																								
St Albans City	d																								
St Pancras International 15 ⊖	d																								
Farringdon 3 ⊖	d																								
City Thameslink 3	d																								
London Blackfriars 3 ⊖	d																								
London Bridge 4 ⊖	d						10 03		10 12			10 15				10 27				10 33		10 42			10 45
New Cross Gate	d						10 08													10 38					
Norwood Junction 2	d						10 16					10 26								10 46					10 56
East Croydon 🚊	a			10 17			10 20	10 22	10 24			10 29	10 32			10 39			10 47	10 50	10 52	10 54			10 59
	d			10 18			10 21	10 23	10 25			10 30	10 33			10 41			10 48	10 51	10 53	10 55			11 00
Purley 4	d						10 26					10 36								10 56					11 06
Coulsdon South	d						10 30					10 39								11 00					11 09
Merstham	d						10 35					10 45								11 05					
Redhill	a			10 30			10 39					10 49							11 00	11 09					11 17
	d			10 30	10 34	10 41	10 44					10 52							11 00	11 10				11 13	11 17
Reigate	a				10 38							10 56												11 18	
Nutfield	d																								11 22
Godstone	d																								11 27
Edenbridge	d																								11 33
Penshurst	d																								11 39
Leigh (Kent)	d																								11 43
Tonbridge 4	a																								11 48
Earlswood (Surrey)	d																			11 12					
Salfords	d																			11 16					
Horley 4	d			10 36			10 51								←					11 19					
Gatwick Airport 10 ✈	a			10 39		10 50	10 55		10 40		10 45		10 48		10 55	10 56	11 00		11 08	11 23		11 10	11 15		
	d			10 40			10 56		10 41				10 50		10 56	10 57			11 09	11 24		11 11			
Three Bridges 15	a			10 44			→		10 45						11 01	11 01			11 14	→		11 15			
	d			10 45					10 45						11 01	11 02			11 14			11 15			
Crawley	d			10 48											11 05				11 18						
Ifield	d														11 07										
Faygate	d																								
Littlehaven	d														11 14										
Horsham 4	a			10 56											11 17				11 26						
Balcombe	d																					11 21			
Haywards Heath	a								10 54				11 00			11 11						11 26			
	d								10 55				11 04	11 07		11 11						11 27			
Wivelsfield	d								10 59					11 11								11 31			
Lewes 4	a													11 22											
Burgess Hill 4	d								11 01				11 09									11 33			
Hassocks 4	d								11 04													11 36			
Preston Park	d								11 11				11 18									11 43			
Hove 2	a												11 22												
Brighton 10	a							10 57	11 15							11 25					11 27	11 47			

Bedford and London - Brighton

Network Diagram - see first Page of Table 186

Station			SN ◇1		SN ◇1	SN 1	FC 1	GX 1 ⌶	SN		SN ◇1 ⌶	GW 1	GW 1	SN 1	SN ◇1 ⌶	FC 1	GX 1 ⌶		SN 1	SN ◇1		SN 1	FC 1	GX 1 ⌶	SN ◇1
London Victoria 15 ⊖	d		10 47		10 51			11 00	11 01		11 02				11 06		11 15			11 17				11 30	11 32
Clapham Junction 10	d		10 53						11 08		11 08				11 12					11 23					11 38
Bedford	d																								
Luton 10	d																								
Luton Airport Parkway 7 ✈	d																								
St Albans City	d																								
St Pancras International 15 ⊖	d																								
Farringdon 3 ⊖	d																								
City Thameslink 3	d																								
London Blackfriars 3 ⊖	d																								
London Bridge 4 ⊖	d						10 57							11 03		11 12			11 15				11 27		
New Cross Gate	d													11 08											
Norwood Junction 2	d													11 16					11 26						
East Croydon 🚊	a		11 02		11 07		11 09				11 17			11 20	11 22	11 24			11 29	11 32			11 39		11 47
	d		11 03		11 08		11 11				11 18			11 21	11 23	11 25			11 30	11 33			11 41		11 48
Purley 4	d													11 26					11 36						
Coulsdon South	d													11 30					11 39						
Merstham	d													11 35					11 45						
Redhill	a										11 30			11 39					11 49						12 00
	d										11 30	11 34	11 41	11 44					11 52						12 00
Reigate	a											11 38							11 56						
Nutfield	d																								
Godstone	d																								
Edenbridge	d																								
Penshurst	d																								
Leigh (Kent)	d																								
Tonbridge 4	a																								
Earlswood (Surrey)	d																								
Salfords	d																								
Horley 4	d					←					11 36			11 51								←			
Gatwick Airport 10 ✈	a		11 18		11 22	11 23	11 26	11 30			11 39		11 50	11 55		11 40	11 45			11 48		11 55	11 56	12 00	12 08
	d		11 20		11 23	11 24	11 27				11 40			11 56		11 41				11 50		11 56	11 57		12 09
Three Bridges 15	a					11 29	11 31				11 44			→		11 45						12 01	12 01		12 14
	d					11 30	11 32				11 45					11 45						12 01	12 02		12 14
Crawley	d					11 33					11 48											12 05			12 18
Ifield	d					11 36																12 07			
Faygate	d																								
Littlehaven	d					11 42																12 14			
Horsham 4	a					11 45					11 56											12 17			12 26
Balcombe	d																								
Haywards Heath	a		11 30				11 41									11 54				12 00			12 11		
	d		11 35	11 37			11 41									11 55				12 04	12 07		12 11		
Wivelsfield	d															11 59					12 11				
Lewes 4	a		11 52																		12 22				
Burgess Hill 4	d				11 38											12 01				12 09					
Hassocks 4	d				11 41											12 04									
Preston Park	d															12 11				12 18					
Hove 2	a			11 53																12 22					
Brighton 10	a				11 52		11 55								11 57	12 15							12 25		

Table 186

Bedford and London - Brighton

Network Diagram - see first Page of Table 186

		SN	SN	FC	GX	GW	SN	SN		SN	SN	FC	GX	SN	SN	GW	GW	SN	SN	FC	GX	SN
		1	◇1	1	1	1	1	◇1		◇1	1	1	1		◇1	1	1	1	◇1	1	1	1
London Victoria 15 ⊖	d		11 36		11 45			11 47		11 51			12 00	12 01	12 02				12 06		12 15	
Clapham Junction 10	d		11 42					11 53						12 08	12 08				12 12			
Bedford	d																					
Luton 10	d																					
Luton Airport Parkway 7 ✈	d																					
St Albans City	d																					
St Pancras International 15 ⊖	d																					
Farringdon 3 ⊖	d																					
City Thameslink 3	d																					
London Blackfriars 3 ⊖	d																					
London Bridge 4 ⊖	d	11 33		11 42			11 45					11 57						12 03		12 12		12 15
New Cross Gate	d	11 38																12 08				
Norwood Junction 2	d	11 46					11 56											12 16				12 26
East Croydon	a	11 50	11 52	11 54			11 59	12 02		12 07		12 09			12 17			12 20	12 22	12 24		12 29
	d	11 51	11 53	11 55			12 00	12 03		12 08		12 11			12 18			12 21	12 23	12 25		12 30
Purley 4	d	11 56					12 06											12 26				12 36
Coulsdon South	d	12 00					12 09											12 30				12 39
Merstham	d	12 05																12 35				12 45
Redhill	a	12 09					12 17								12 30			12 39				12 49
	d	12 10				12 13	12 17								12 30	12 34	12 41	12 44				12 52
Reigate	a					12 18										12 38						12 56
Nutfield	d						12 22															
Godstone	d						12 27															
Edenbridge	d						12 33															
Penshurst	d						12 39															
Leigh (Kent)	d						12 43															
Tonbridge 4	a						12 48															
Earlswood (Surrey)	d	12 12																				
Salfords	d	12 16																				
Horley 4	d	12 19									←				12 36			12 51				
Gatwick Airport 10 ✈	a	12 23		12 10	12 15			12 18		12 22	12 23	12 26	12 30		12 39		12 50	12 55		12 40	12 45	
	d	12 24		12 11				12 20		12 23	12 24	12 27			12 40			12 56		12 41		
Three Bridges 15	a	→		12 15							12 29	12 31			12 44			→		12 45		
	d			12 15							12 30	12 32			12 45					12 45		
Crawley	d										12 33				12 48							
Ifield	d										12 36											
Faygate	d																					
Littlehaven	d										12 42											
Horsham 4	a										12 45				12 56							
Balcombe	d			12 21																		
Haywards Heath	a			12 26				12 30				12 41								12 54		
	d			12 27				12 35	12 37			12 41								12 55		
Wivelsfield	d			12 31																12 59		
Lewes 4	a							12 52														
Burgess Hill 4	d			12 33						12 38										13 01		
Hassocks 4	d			12 36						12 41										13 04		
Preston Park	d			12 43																13 11		
Hove 2	a								12 53													
Brighton 10	a		12 27	12 47						12 52		12 55							12 57	13 15		

Table 186

Bedford and London - Brighton

Network Diagram - see first Page of Table 186

		SN		SN	FC	GX	SN	SN	SN	FC	GX	GW	SN	SN		SN	SN	FC	GX	SN	SN	GW
		◇1		1	1	1	◇1	1	◇1	1	1	1	1	◇1		◇1	1	1	1		◇1	1
London Victoria 15 ⊖	d	12 17				12 30	12 32		12 36		12 45			12 47		12 51			13 00	13 01	13 02	
Clapham Junction 10	d	12 23					12 38		12 42					12 53						13 08	13 08	
Bedford	d																					
Luton 10	d																					
Luton Airport Parkway 7 ✈	d																					
St Albans City	d																					
St Pancras International 15 ⊖	d																					
Farringdon 3 ⊖	d																					
City Thameslink 3	d																					
London Blackfriars 3 ⊖	d																					
London Bridge 4 ⊖	d				12 27			12 33		12 42			12 45					12 57				
New Cross Gate	d							12 38														
Norwood Junction 2	d							12 46					12 56									
East Croydon	a	12 32			12 39		12 47	12 50	12 52	12 54			12 59	13 02		13 07		13 09			13 17	
	d	12 33			12 41		12 48	12 51	12 53	12 55			13 00	13 03		13 08		13 11			13 18	
Purley 4	d							12 56					13 06									
Coulsdon South	d							13 00					13 09									
Merstham	d							13 05														
Redhill	a						13 00	13 09					13 17								13 30	
	d						13 00	13 10				13 13	13 17								13 30	13 34
Reigate	a											13 18										13 38
Nutfield	d												13 22									
Godstone	d												13 27									
Edenbridge	d												13 33									
Penshurst	d												13 39									
Leigh (Kent)	d												13 43									
Tonbridge 4	a												13 48									
Earlswood (Surrey)	d							13 12														
Salfords	d							13 16														
Horley 4	d			←				13 19									←				13 36	
Gatwick Airport 10 ✈	a	12 48		12 55	12 56	13 00	13 08	13 23		13 10	13 15			13 18		13 22	13 23	13 26	13 30		13 39	
	d	12 50		12 56	12 57		13 09	13 24		13 11				13 20		13 23	13 24	13 27			13 40	
Three Bridges 15	a			13 01	13 01		13 14	→		13 15							13 29	13 31			13 44	
	d			13 01	13 02		13 14			13 15							13 30	13 32			13 45	
Crawley	d			13 05			13 18										13 33				13 48	
Ifield	d			13 07													13 36					
Faygate	d																					
Littlehaven	d			13 14													13 42					
Horsham 4	a			13 17			13 26										13 45				13 56	
Balcombe	d									13 21												
Haywards Heath	a	13 00			13 11					13 26				13 30				13 41				
	d	13 04	13 07		13 11					13 27				13 35	13 37			13 41				
Wivelsfield	d		13 11							13 31												
Lewes 4	a		13 22											13 52								
Burgess Hill 4	d	13 09								13 33						13 38						
Hassocks 4	d									13 36						13 41						
Preston Park	d	13 18								13 43												
Hove 2	a	13 22													13 53							
Brighton 10	a				13 25				13 27	13 47						13 52		13 55				

Bedford and London - Brighton

Network Diagram - see first Page of Table 186

		GW	SN	SN	FC	GX	SN	SN	SN	SN	FC	GX	SN	SN	SN	FC	GX	GW	SN	SN	SN	SN
		1	1	◇1 🍴	1	1 🍴	1	◇1		1	1	1 🍴	◇1	1	◇1 🍴	1	1 🍴	1	1	◇1		◇1
London Victoria ⊖	d			13 06		13 15		13 17				13 30	13 32		13 36		13 45			13 47		13 51
Clapham Junction	d			13 12				13 23					13 38		13 42					13 53		
Bedford	d																					
Luton	d																					
Luton Airport Parkway ✈	d																					
St Albans City	d																					
St Pancras International ⊖	d																					
Farringdon ⊖	d																					
City Thameslink	d																					
London Blackfriars ⊖	d																					
London Bridge ⊖	d		13 03		13 12		13 15				13 27			13 33		13 42			13 45			
New Cross Gate	d		13 08											13 38								
Norwood Junction	d		13 16				13 26							13 46					13 56			
East Croydon	a		13 20	13 22	13 24		13 29	13 32			13 39		13 47	13 50	13 52	13 54			13 59	14 02		14 07
	d		13 21	13 23	13 25		13 30	13 33			13 41		13 48	13 51	13 53	13 55			14 00	14 03		14 08
Purley	d		13 26				13 36							13 56					14 06			
Coulsdon South	d		13 30				13 39							14 00					14 09			
Merstham	d		13 35				13 45							14 05								
Redhill	a		13 39				13 49						14 00	14 09					14 17			
	d	13 41	13 44				13 52						14 00	14 10				14 13	14 17			
Reigate	a						13 56											14 18				
Nutfield	d																		14 22			
Godstone	d																		14 27			
Edenbridge	d																		14 33			
Penshurst	d																		14 39			
Leigh (Kent)	d																		14 43			
Tonbridge	a																		14 48			
Earlswood (Surrey)	d													14 12								
Salfords	d													14 16								
Horley	d		13 51							←				14 19								
Gatwick Airport ✈	a	13 50	13 55		13 40	13 45		13 48		13 55	13 56	14 00	14 08	14 23		14 10	14 15			14 18		14 22
	d		13 56		13 41			13 50		13 56	13 57		14 09	14 24		14 11				14 20		14 23
Three Bridges	a		→		13 45					14 01	14 01		14 14	→		14 15						
	d				13 45					14 01	14 02		14 14			14 15						
Crawley	d									14 05			14 18									
Ifield	d									14 07												
Faygate	d																					
Littlehaven	d									14 14												
Horsham	a									14 17			14 26									
Balcombe	d															14 21						
Haywards Heath	a				13 54			14 00			14 11					14 26				14 30		
	d				13 55			14 04	14 07		14 11					14 27				14 35	14 37	
Wivelsfield	d				13 59				14 11							14 31						
Lewes	a								14 22											14 52		
Burgess Hill	d				14 01			14 09								14 33						14 38
Hassocks	d				14 04											14 36						14 41
Preston Park	d				14 11			14 18								14 43						
Hove	a							14 22													14 53	
Brighton	a			13 57	14 15						14 25				14 27	14 47						14 52

Bedford and London - Brighton

Network Diagram - see first Page of Table 186

		SN	FC	GX	SN	SN	GW	GW	SN	SN	FC	GX	SN	SN	SN	SN	FC	GX	SN	SN	SN	FC
		1	1	1 🍴		◇1 🍴	1	1	1	◇1 🍴	1	1 🍴	1	◇1		1	1	1 🍴	◇1	1	◇1 🍴	1
London Victoria ⊖	d			14 00	14 01	14 02				14 06		14 15		14 17				14 30	14 32		14 36	
Clapham Junction	d				14 08	14 08				14 12				14 23					14 38		14 42	
Bedford	d																					
Luton	d																					
Luton Airport Parkway ✈	d																					
St Albans City	d																					
St Pancras International ⊖	d																					
Farringdon ⊖	d																					
City Thameslink	d																					
London Blackfriars ⊖	d																					
London Bridge ⊖	d		13 57						14 03		14 12		14 15				14 27			14 33		14 42
New Cross Gate	d								14 08											14 38		
Norwood Junction	d								14 16				14 26							14 46		
East Croydon	a		14 09			14 17			14 20	14 22	14 24		14 29	14 32			14 39		14 47	14 50	14 52	14 54
	d		14 11			14 18			14 21	14 23	14 25		14 30	14 33			14 41		14 48	14 51	14 53	14 55
Purley	d								14 26				14 36							14 56		
Coulsdon South	d								14 30				14 39							15 00		
Merstham	d								14 35				14 45							15 05		
Redhill	a					14 30			14 39				14 49						15 00	15 09		
	d					14 30	14 34	14 41	14 44				14 52						15 00	15 10		
Reigate	a						14 38						14 56									
Nutfield	d																					
Godstone	d																					
Edenbridge	d																					
Penshurst	d																					
Leigh (Kent)	d																					
Tonbridge	a																					
Earlswood (Surrey)	d																			15 12		
Salfords	d																			15 16		
Horley	d	←				14 36			14 51							←				15 19		
Gatwick Airport ✈	a	14 23	14 26	14 30		14 39		14 50	14 55		14 40	14 45		14 48		14 55	14 56	15 00	15 08	15 23		15 10
	d	14 24	14 27			14 40			14 56		14 41			14 50		14 56	14 57		15 09	15 24		15 11
Three Bridges	a	14 29	14 31			14 44			→		14 45					15 01	15 01		15 14	→		15 15
	d	14 30	14 32			14 45					14 45					15 01	15 02		15 14			15 15
Crawley	d	14 33				14 48										15 05			15 18			
Ifield	d	14 36														15 07						
Faygate	d																					
Littlehaven	d	14 42														15 14						
Horsham	a	14 45				14 56										15 17			15 26			
Balcombe	d																					15 21
Haywards Heath	a		14 41								14 54			15 00			15 11					15 26
	d		14 41								14 55			15 04	15 07		15 11					15 27
Wivelsfield	d										14 59				15 11							15 31
Lewes	a														15 22							
Burgess Hill	d										15 01			15 09								15 33
Hassocks	d										15 04											15 36
Preston Park	d										15 11			15 18								15 43
Hove	a													15 22								
Brighton	a		14 55							14 57	15 15						15 25				15 27	15 47

Table 186

Saturdays

Bedford and London - Brighton

Network Diagram - see first Page of Table 186

		GX	GW		SN	SN		SN	SN	FC	GX		SN	SN	GW	GW	SN	SN	FC		GX	SN	SN		SN
		1 H	1		1	◇1		◇1	1	1	1 H			◇1 H	1	1	1	◇1 H	1		1 H	1	◇1		1
London Victoria 15 ⊖	d	14 45				14 47		14 51			15 00		15 01	15 02				15 06			15 15		15 17		
Clapham Junction 10	d					14 53							15 08	15 08				15 12					15 23		
Bedford	d																								
Luton 10	d																								
Luton Airport Parkway 7 ✈	d																								
St Albans City	d																								
St Pancras International 15 ⊖	d																								
Farringdon 3 ⊖	d																								
City Thameslink 3	d																								
London Blackfriars 3 ⊖	d																								
London Bridge 4 ⊖	d				14 45					14 57							15 03		15 12			15 15			
New Cross Gate	d																15 08								
Norwood Junction 2	d				14 56												15 16					15 26			
East Croydon ⇌	a				14 59	15 02		15 07		15 09				15 17			15 20	15 22	15 24			15 29	15 32		
	d				15 00	15 03		15 08		15 11				15 18			15 21	15 23	15 25			15 30	15 33		
Purley 4	d				15 06												15 26					15 36			
Coulsdon South	d				15 09												15 30					15 39			
Merstham	d																15 35					15 45			
Redhill	a				15 17									15 30			15 39					15 49			
	d		15 13		15 17									15 30	15 34	15 41	15 44					15 52			
Reigate	a		15 18												15 38							15 56			
Nutfield	d				15 22																				
Godstone	d				15 27																				
Edenbridge	d				15 33																				
Penshurst	d				15 39																				
Leigh (Kent)	d				15 43																				
Tonbridge 4	a				15 48																				
Earlswood (Surrey)	d																								
Salfords	d																								
Horley 4	d								←					15 36			15 51								←
Gatwick Airport 10 ✈	a	15 15				15 18		15 22	15 23	15 26	15 30			15 39		15 50	15 55		15 40		15 45		15 48		15 55
	d					15 20		15 23	15 24	15 27				15 40			15 56		15 41				15 50		15 56
Three Bridges 15	a								15 29	15 31				15 44			→		15 45						16 01
	d								15 30	15 32				15 45					15 45						16 01
Crawley	d								15 33					15 48											16 05
Ifield	d								15 36																16 07
Faygate	d																								
Littlehaven	d								15 42																16 14
Horsham 4	a								15 45					15 56											16 17
Balcombe	d																								
Haywards Heath	a					15 30				15 41									15 54				16 00		
	d					15 35	15 37			15 41									15 55				16 04	16 07	
Wivelsfield	d																		15 59					16 11	
Lewes 4	a					15 52																		16 22	
Burgess Hill 4	d							15 38											16 01				16 09		
Hassocks 4	d							15 41											16 04						
Preston Park	d																		16 11				16 18		
Hove 2	a						15 53																16 22		
Brighton 10	a							15 52		15 55								15 57	16 15						

Table 186

Saturdays

Bedford and London - Brighton

Network Diagram - see first Page of Table 186

		FC	GX		SN	SN	SN	FC	GX	GW	SN		SN		SN	SN	FC	GX	SN		SN	GW	GW	SN	SN
		1	1 H		◇1	1	◇1 H	1	1 H	1	1		◇1		◇1	1	1	1 H			◇1 H	1	1	1	◇1 H
London Victoria 15 ⊖	d		15 30		15 32		15 36		15 45				15 47		15 51			16 00	16 01		16 02				16 06
Clapham Junction 10	d				15 38		15 42						15 53						16 08		16 08				16 12
Bedford	d																								
Luton 10	d																								
Luton Airport Parkway 7 ✈	d																								
St Albans City	d																								
St Pancras International 15 ⊖	d																								
Farringdon 3 ⊖	d																								
City Thameslink 3	d																								
London Blackfriars 3 ⊖	d																								
London Bridge 4 ⊖	d	15 27				15 33		15 42			15 45						15 57							16 03	
New Cross Gate	d					15 38																		16 08	
Norwood Junction 2	d					15 46					15 56													16 16	
East Croydon ⇌	a	15 39			15 47	15 50	15 52	15 54			15 59		16 02		16 07		16 09				16 17			16 20	16 22
	d	15 41			15 48	15 51	15 53	15 55			16 00		16 03		16 08		16 11				16 18			16 21	16 23
Purley 4	d					15 56					16 06													16 26	
Coulsdon South	d					16 00					16 09													16 30	
Merstham	d					16 05																		16 35	
Redhill	a				16 00	16 09					16 17										16 30			16 39	
	d				16 00	16 10				16 13	16 17										16 30	16 34	16 41	16 44	
Reigate	a									16 18												16 38			
Nutfield	d										16 22														
Godstone	d										16 27														
Edenbridge	d										16 33														
Penshurst	d										16 39														
Leigh (Kent)	d										16 43														
Tonbridge 4	a										16 48														
Earlswood (Surrey)	d					16 12																			
Salfords	d					16 16																			
Horley 4	d					16 19										←					16 36			16 51	
Gatwick Airport 10 ✈	a	15 56	16 00		16 08	16 23		16 10	16 15				16 18		16 22	16 23	16 26	16 30			16 39		16 50	16 55	
	d	15 57			16 09	16 24		16 11					16 20		16 23	16 24	16 27				16 40			16 56	
Three Bridges 15	a	16 01			16 14	→		16 15								16 29	16 31				16 44			→	
	d	16 02			16 14			16 15								16 30	16 32				16 45				
Crawley	d				16 18											16 33					16 48				
Ifield	d															16 36									
Faygate	d																								
Littlehaven	d															16 42									
Horsham 4	a				16 26											16 45					16 56				
Balcombe	d							16 21																	
Haywards Heath	a	16 11						16 26					16 30				16 41								
	d	16 11						16 27					16 35	16 37			16 41								
Wivelsfield	d							16 31																	
Lewes 4	a												16 52												
Burgess Hill 4	d							16 33							16 38										
Hassocks 4	d							16 36							16 41										
Preston Park	d							16 43																	
Hove 2	a													16 53											
Brighton 10	a	16 25					16 27	16 47							16 52		16 55								16 57

Bedford and London - Brighton

Network Diagram - see first Page of Table 186

		FC [1]	GX [1] ⊤		SN [1]	SN ◇[1]		SN [1]	FC [1]	GX [1] ⊤	SN ◇[1]		SN [1]	SN ◇[1] ⊤	FC [1]	GX [1] ⊤	GW [1]	SN [1]	SN ◇[1]			SN ◇[1]	SN [1]	FC [1]	GX [1] ⊤
London Victoria [15] ⊖	d		16 15			16 17				16 30	16 32			16 36		16 45			16 47			16 51			17 00
Clapham Junction [10]	d					16 23					16 38			16 42					16 53						
Bedford	d																								
Luton [10]	d																								
Luton Airport Parkway [7] ✈	d																								
St Albans City	d																								
St Pancras International [15] ⊖	d																								
Farringdon [3] ⊖	d																								
City Thameslink [3]	d																								
London Blackfriars [3] ⊖	d																								
London Bridge [4] ⊖	d	16 12			16 15				16 27				16 33		16 42			16 45						16 57	
New Cross Gate	d												16 38												
Norwood Junction [2]	d				16 26								16 46					16 56							
East Croydon 🚋	a	16 24			16 29	16 32			16 39		16 47		16 50	16 52	16 54			16 59	17 02			17 07		17 09	
	d	16 25			16 30	16 33			16 41		16 48		16 51	16 53	16 55			17 00	17 03			17 08		17 11	
Purley [4]	d				16 36								16 56					17 06							
Coulsdon South	d				16 39								17 00					17 09							
Merstham	d				16 45								17 05												
Redhill	a				16 49						17 00		17 09					17 17							
	d				16 52						17 00		17 10				17 13	17 17							
Reigate	a				16 56												17 18								
Nutfield	d																	17 22							
Godstone	d																	17 27							
Edenbridge	d																	17 33							
Penshurst	d																	17 39							
Leigh (Kent)	d																	17 43							
Tonbridge [4]	a																	17 48							
Earlswood (Surrey)	d												17 12												
Salfords	d												17 16												
Horley [4]	d							←					17 19										←		
Gatwick Airport [10] ✈	a	16 40	16 45			16 48		16 55	16 56	17 00	17 08		17 23		17 10	17 15			17 18			17 22	17 23	17 26	17 30
	d	16 41				16 50		16 56	16 57		17 09		17 24		17 11				17 20			17 23	17 24	17 27	
Three Bridges [15]	a	16 45						17 01	17 01		17 14		→		17 15								17 29	17 31	
	d	16 45						17 01	17 02		17 14				17 15								17 30	17 32	
Crawley	d							17 05			17 18												17 33		
Ifield	d							17 07															17 36		
Faygate	d																								
Littlehaven	d							17 14															17 42		
Horsham [4]	a							17 17			17 26												17 45		
Balcombe	d														17 21										
Haywards Heath	a	16 54				17 00			17 11						17 26				17 30					17 41	
	d	16 55				17 04	17 07		17 11						17 27				17 35	17 37				17 41	
Wivelsfield	d	16 59					17 11								17 31										
Lewes [4]	a						17 22												17 52						
Burgess Hill [4]	d	17 01				17 09									17 33							17 38			
Hassocks [4]	d	17 04													17 36							17 41			
Preston Park	d	17 11				17 18									17 43										
Hove [2]	a					17 22														17 53					
Brighton [10]	a	17 15							17 25					17 27	17 47							17 52		17 55	

Bedford and London - Brighton

Network Diagram - see first Page of Table 186

		SN	SN ◇[1] ⊤	GW [1]		GW [1]	SN [1]	SN ◇[1] ⊤	FC [1]	GX [1] ⊤	SN [1]	SN ◇[1]			SN [1]	FC [1]	GX [1] ⊤	SN ◇[1]	SN [1]	SN ◇[1] ⊤	FC [1]		GX [1] ⊤	GW [1]	SN [1]
London Victoria [15] ⊖	d	17 01	17 02					17 06		17 15		17 17					17 30	17 32		17 36			17 45		
Clapham Junction [10]	d	17 08	17 08					17 12				17 23						17 38		17 42					
Bedford	d																								
Luton [10]	d																								
Luton Airport Parkway [7] ✈	d																								
St Albans City	d																								
St Pancras International [15] ⊖	d																								
Farringdon [3] ⊖	d																								
City Thameslink [3]	d																								
London Blackfriars [3] ⊖	d																								
London Bridge [4] ⊖	d						17 03		17 12		17 15					17 27			17 33		17 42				17 45
New Cross Gate	d						17 08												17 38						
Norwood Junction [2]	d						17 16				17 26								17 46						17 56
East Croydon 🚋	a		17 17				17 20	17 22	17 24		17 29	17 32				17 39		17 47	17 50	17 52	17 54				18 00
	d		17 18				17 21	17 23	17 25		17 30	17 33				17 41		17 48	17 51	17 53	17 55				18 00
Purley [4]	d						17 26				17 36								17 56						18 06
Coulsdon South	d						17 30				17 39								18 00						18 09
Merstham	d						17 35				17 45								18 05						
Redhill	a		17 30				17 39				17 49							18 00	18 09						18 17
	d		17 30	17 34		17 41	17 44				17 52							18 00	18 10					18 13	18 17
Reigate	a			17 38							17 56													18 18	
Nutfield	d																								18 22
Godstone	d																								18 27
Edenbridge	d																								18 33
Penshurst	d																								18 39
Leigh (Kent)	d																								18 43
Tonbridge [4]	a																								18 48
Earlswood (Surrey)	d																		18 12						
Salfords	d																		18 16						
Horley [4]	d		17 36				17 51								←				18 19						
Gatwick Airport [10] ✈	a		17 39			17 50	17 55		17 40	17 45		17 48			17 55	17 56	18 00	18 08	18 23		18 10		18 15		
	d		17 40				17 56		17 41			17 50			17 56	17 57		18 09	18 24		18 11				
Three Bridges [15]	a		17 44				→		17 45						18 01	18 01		18 14	→		18 15				
	d		17 45						17 45						18 01	18 02		18 14			18 15				
Crawley	d		17 48												18 05			18 18							
Ifield	d														18 07										
Faygate	d																								
Littlehaven	d														18 14										
Horsham [4]	a		17 56												18 17			18 26							
Balcombe	d																				18 21				
Haywards Heath	a								17 54			18 00				18 11					18 26				
	d								17 55			18 04	18 07			18 11					18 27				
Wivelsfield	d								17 59				18 11								18 31				
Lewes [4]	a												18 22												
Burgess Hill [4]	d								18 01			18 09									18 33				
Hassocks [4]	d								18 04												18 36				
Preston Park	d								18 11			18 18									18 43				
Hove [2]	a											18 22													
Brighton [10]	a							17 57	18 15							18 25				18 27	18 47				

Table 186

Saturdays

Bedford and London - Brighton

Network Diagram - see first Page of Table 186

		SN		SN	SN		FC	GX	SN	SN	GW	GW	SN		SN	FC	GX	SN	SN		SN		FC	GX	SN
		◇1		◇1	1		1	1		◇1	1	1	1		◇1	1	1	1	◇1		1		1	1	
London Victoria 15	d	17 47		17 51				18 00	18 01	18 02					18 06		18 15		18 17					18 30	18 31
Clapham Junction 10	d	17 53							18 08	18 08					18 12				18 23						18 38
Bedford	d																								
Luton 10	d																								
Luton Airport Parkway 7	d																								
St Albans City	d																								
St Pancras International 15	d																								
Farringdon 3	d																								
City Thameslink 3	d																								
London Blackfriars 3	d																								
London Bridge 4	d						17 57						18 03			18 12		18 15					18 27		
New Cross Gate	d												18 08												
Norwood Junction 2	d												18 16					18 26							
East Croydon	a	18 02		18 07			18 09			18 17			18 20		18 22	18 24		18 29	18 32				18 39		
	d	18 03		18 08			18 11			18 18			18 21		18 23	18 25		18 30	18 33				18 41		
Purley 4	d												18 26					18 36							
Coulsdon South	d												18 30					18 39							
Merstham	d												18 35					18 45							
Redhill	a									18 30			18 39					18 49							
	d									18 30	18 34	18 41	18 44					18 52							
Reigate	a										18 38							18 56							
Nutfield	d																								
Godstone	d																								
Edenbridge	d																								
Penshurst	d																								
Leigh (Kent)	d																								
Tonbridge 4	a																								
Earlswood (Surrey)	d																								
Salfords	d																								
Horley 4	d				←					18 36			18 51								←				
Gatwick Airport 10	a	18 18		18 22	18 23		18 26	18 30		18 39		18 50	18 55			18 40	18 45		18 48		18 55		18 56	19 00	
	d	18 20		18 23	18 24		18 27			18 40			18 56			18 41			18 50		18 56		18 57		
Three Bridges 15	a				18 29		18 31			18 44			→			18 45					19 01		19 01		
	d				18 30		18 32			18 45						18 45					19 01		19 02		
Crawley	d				18 33					18 48											19 05				
Ifield	d				18 36																19 07				
Faygate	d																								
Littlehaven	d				18 42																19 14				
Horsham 4	a				18 47					18 56											19 17				
Balcombe	d																								
Haywards Heath	a	18 30					18 41									18 54			19 00				19 11		
	d	18 35	18 37				18 41									18 55			19 04	19 07			19 11		
Wivelsfield	d															18 59				19 11					
Lewes 4	a	18 52																		19 22					
Burgess Hill 4	d			18 38												19 01			19 09						
Hassocks 4	d			18 41												19 04									
Preston Park	d															19 11			19 18						
Hove 2	a		18 53																19 22						
Brighton 10	a			18 52			18 55								18 57	19 15							19 25		

Table 186

Saturdays

Bedford and London - Brighton

Network Diagram - see first Page of Table 186

		SN	SN	SN	FC		GX	GW	SN	SN		SN	SN		FC	GX	SN	SN	GW	GW	SN		SN	FC	GX
		◇1	1	◇1	1		1	1	1	◇1		◇1	1		1	1		◇1	1	1	1		◇1	1	1
London Victoria 15	d	18 32		18 36			18 45			18 47		18 51				19 00	19 01	19 02					19 06		19 15
Clapham Junction 10	d	18 38		18 42						18 53							19 08	19 08					19 12		
Bedford	d																								
Luton 10	d																								
Luton Airport Parkway 7	d																								
St Albans City	d																								
St Pancras International 15	d																								
Farringdon 3	d																								
City Thameslink 3	d																								
London Blackfriars 3	d																								
London Bridge 4	d		18 33		18 42				18 45						18 57						19 03			19 12	
New Cross Gate	d		18 38																		19 08				
Norwood Junction 2	d		18 46						18 56												19 16				
East Croydon	a	18 47	18 50	18 52	18 54				18 59	19 02		19 07			19 09			19 17			19 20		19 22	19 24	
	d	18 48	18 51	18 53	18 55				19 00	19 03		19 08			19 11			19 18			19 21		19 23	19 25	
Purley 4	d		18 56						19 06												19 26				
Coulsdon South	d		19 00						19 09												19 30				
Merstham	d		19 05																		19 35				
Redhill	a	19 00	19 09						19 17									19 30			19 39				
	d	19 00	19 10					19 13	19 17									19 30	19 34	19 41	19 46				
Reigate	a							19 18											19 38						
Nutfield	d								19 22																
Godstone	d								19 27																
Edenbridge	d								19 33																
Penshurst	d								19 39																
Leigh (Kent)	d								19 43																
Tonbridge 4	a								19 48																
Earlswood (Surrey)	d		19 12																						
Salfords	d		19 16																						
Horley 4	d		19 19										←					19 36			19 52				
Gatwick Airport 10	a	19 08	19 23		19 10		19 15			19 18		19 22	19 23		19 26	19 30		19 39		19 50	19 55			19 40	19 45
	d	19 09	19 24		19 11					19 20		19 23	19 24		19 27			19 40			19 56			19 41	
Three Bridges 15	a	19 14	→		19 15								19 28		19 31			19 44			→			19 45	
	d	19 14			19 15								19 30		19 32			19 45						19 45	
Crawley	d	19 18											19 33					19 48							
Ifield	d												19 36												
Faygate	d																								
Littlehaven	d												19 42												
Horsham 4	a	19 26											19 45					19 56							
Balcombe	d				19 21																				
Haywards Heath	a				19 26					19 30					19 41									19 54	
	d				19 27					19 35	19 37				19 41									19 55	
Wivelsfield	d				19 31																			19 59	
Lewes 4	a									19 52															
Burgess Hill 4	d				19 33							19 38												20 01	
Hassocks 4	d				19 36							19 41												20 04	
Preston Park	d				19 43																			20 11	
Hove 2	a										19 52														
Brighton 10	a			19 27	19 47							19 52			19 55								19 57	20 15	

Bedford and London - Brighton

Network Diagram - see first Page of Table 186

		SN ◇1		SN 1	FC 1	GX 1	SN	SN 1	SN ◇1	SN 1	SN ◇1	FC 1	GX 1	SN ◇1		SN ◇1	SN 1	FC 1	GX 1	SN	GW 1	SN ◇1
London Victoria 15 ⊖	d	19 17				19 30	19 31		19 32		19 36		19 45	19 47		19 51			20 00	20 01		20 02
Clapham Junction 10	d	19 23					19 38		19 38		19 42			19 53						20 08		20 08
Bedford	d																					
Luton 10	d																					
Luton Airport Parkway 7 ✈	d																					
St Albans City	d																					
St Pancras International 15 ⊖	d																					
Farringdon 3 ⊖	d																					
City Thameslink 3	d																					
London Blackfriars 3 ⊖	d																					
London Bridge 4 ⊖	d				19 27					19 33		19 42						19 57				
New Cross Gate	d									19 38												
Norwood Junction 2	d									19 46												
East Croydon	a	19 33			19 39				19 47	19 50	19 52	19 54		20 02		20 07		20 09				20 17
	d	19 33			19 41				19 48	19 51	19 53	19 55		20 03		20 08		20 11				20 18
Purley 4	d									19 56												
Coulsdon South	d									20 00												
Merstham	d									20 05												
Redhill	a								20 00	20 09												20 30
	d							19 51	20 00	20 10											20 13	20 30
Reigate	a																				20 18	
Nutfield	d							19 55														
Godstone	d							20 01														
Edenbridge	d							20 06														
Penshurst	d							20 13														
Leigh (Kent)	d							20 16														
Tonbridge 4	a							20 21														
Earlswood (Surrey)	d									20 12												
Salfords	d									20 16												
Horley 4	d			←						20 19							←					
Gatwick Airport 10 ✈	a	19 48		19 55	19 56	20 00			20 08	20 23		20 10	20 15	20 18		20 22	20 23	20 26	20 30			20 38
	d	19 50		19 56	19 57				20 09	20 24		20 11		20 20		20 23	20 24	20 27				20 40
Three Bridges 15	a			20 01	20 01				20 14	→		20 15					20 29	20 31				20 44
	d			20 01	20 02				20 14			20 15					20 33	20 32				20 45
Crawley	d			20 05					20 18								20 36					20 48
Ifield	d			20 07													20 39					
Faygate	d																					
Littlehaven	d			20 14													20 45					
Horsham 4	a			20 17					20 26								20 48					20 56
Balcombe	d											20 21										
Haywards Heath	a	20 00			20 11							20 26		20 30				20 41				
	d	20 04	20 07		20 11							20 27		20 35	20 37			20 41				
Wivelsfield	d		20 11									20 31		20 39								
Lewes 4	a		20 22											20 52								
Burgess Hill 4	d	20 09										20 33				20 38						
Hassocks 4	d											20 36				20 41						
Preston Park	d	20 18										20 43										
Hove 2	a	20 22													20 53							
Brighton 10	a				20 25						20 27	20 47				20 52		20 55				

Bedford and London - Brighton

Network Diagram - see first Page of Table 186

		SN ◇1	FC 1	GW 1	GW 1	SN 1	GX 1	SN ◇1		SN ◇1	SN 1	GX 1	SN	SN 1	SN ◇1	SN ◇1	FC 1	GW 1	SN 1	GX 1	SN ◇1	
London Victoria 15 ⊖	d	20 06				20 10	20 15	20 17		20 21		20 30	20 31		20 32	20 36			20 40	20 45	20 47	
Clapham Junction 10	d	20 12				20 16		20 23					20 38		20 38	20 42			20 46		20 53	
Bedford	d																					
Luton 10	d																					
Luton Airport Parkway 7 ✈	d																					
St Albans City	d																					
St Pancras International 15 ⊖	d																					
Farringdon 3 ⊖	d																					
City Thameslink 3	d																					
London Blackfriars 3 ⊖	d																					
London Bridge 4 ⊖	d		20 12														20 42					
New Cross Gate	d																					
Norwood Junction 2	d																					
East Croydon	a	20 22	20 24			20 29		20 32		20 37					20 47	20 52	20 53		20 57		21 02	
	d	20 23	20 25			20 29		20 33		20 38					20 48	20 53	20 54		20 58		21 03	
Purley 4	d					20 34													21 03			
Coulsdon South	d					20 38													21 06			
Merstham	d					20 44													21 12			
Redhill	a					20 47									21 00				21 15			
	d			20 34	20 41	20 48								20 51	21 00			21 13	21 16			
Reigate	a			20 38														21 18				
Nutfield	d													20 55								
Godstone	d													21 01								
Edenbridge	d													21 06								
Penshurst	d													21 13								
Leigh (Kent)	d													21 16								
Tonbridge 4	a													21 21								
Earlswood (Surrey)	d																		21 18			
Salfords	d																		21 22			
Horley 4	d					20 54					←								21 25			
Gatwick Airport 10 ✈	a		20 40		20 50	20 58	20 45	20 48		20 52	20 58	21 00			21 08		21 10		21 28	21 15	21 18	
	d		20 41			20 59		20 50		20 53	20 59				21 09		21 11		21 29		21 20	
Three Bridges 15	a		20 45			→					21 03				21 14		21 15		→			
	d		20 45								21 04				21 14		21 15					
Crawley	d										21 07				21 18							
Ifield	d										21 10											
Faygate	d																					
Littlehaven	d										21 16											
Horsham 4	a										21 19				21 26							
Balcombe	d		20 51																			
Haywards Heath	a		20 56					21 00									21 24				21 30	
	d		20 57					21 05	21 07								21 25				21 34	21 37
Wivelsfield	d		21 01						21 11								21 29				21 38	
Lewes 4	a								21 22												21 51	
Burgess Hill 4	d		21 03					21 10									21 31					
Hassocks 4	d		21 06							21 10							21 34					
Preston Park	d		21 13					21 19									21 41					
Hove 2	a							21 22														21 51
Brighton 10	a	20 57	21 17							21 22						21 27	21 45					

Table 186

Saturdays

Bedford and London - Brighton

Network Diagram - see first Page of Table 186

		SN 1	GX 1	SN	SN ◇1		SN ◇1	FC 1	GW 1	SN 1	GX 1	SN ◇1			SN 1	GW 1	GX 1	SN	SN 1	SN	SN ◇1		FC 1	SN 1	GX 1
London Victoria 15 ⊖	d		21 00	21 01	21 02		21 06			21 10	21 15	21 17					21 30	21 31		21 32	21 36			21 40	21 45
Clapham Junction 10	d			21 08	21 08		21 12			21 16		21 23						21 38		21 38	21 42			21 46	
Bedford	d																								
Luton 10	d																								
Luton Airport Parkway 7 ✈	d																								
St Albans City	d																								
St Pancras International 15 ⊖	d																								
Farringdon 3 ⊖	d																								
City Thameslink 3	d																								
London Blackfriars 3 ⊖	d																								
London Bridge 4 ⊖	d							21 12															21 42		
New Cross Gate	d																								
Norwood Junction 2	d																								
East Croydon	a				21 17		21 22	21 24		21 27		21 33								21 47	21 52		21 54	21 57	
	d				21 18		21 23	21 25		21 28		21 33								21 48	21 53		21 55	21 58	
Purley 4	d									21 33														22 03	
Coulsdon South	d									21 37														22 06	
Merstham	d									21 42														22 12	
Redhill	a				21 30					21 46										22 00				22 15	
	d				21 31				21 36	21 46						21 49			21 51	22 00				22 16	
Reigate	a								21 40																
Nutfield	d																		21 55						
Godstone	d																		22 01						
Edenbridge	d																		22 06						
Penshurst	d																		22 13						
Leigh (Kent)	d																		22 16						
Tonbridge 4	a																		22 21						
Earlswood (Surrey)	d																							22 18	
Salfords	d																							22 22	
Horley 4	d	←								21 52					←									22 25	
Gatwick Airport 10 ✈	a	21 28	21 30		21 38			21 40		21 55	21 45	21 48			21 55	21 59	22 00			22 08			22 10	22 28	22 15
	d	21 29			21 39			21 41		21 56		21 49			21 56					22 09			22 11	22 29	
Three Bridges 15	a	21 33			21 44			21 45		→		21 53			22 00					22 14			22 15	→	
	d	21 36			21 44			21 45				21 53			22 01					22 14			22 15		
Crawley	d	21 39													22 04					22 18					
Ifield	d	21 42													22 07										
Faygate	d																								
Littlehaven	d	21 48													22 13										
Horsham 4	a	21 52													22 16					22 26					
Balcombe	d							21 53																	
Haywards Heath	a				21 53		21 46	21 58				22 02									22 16		22 24		
	d				21 53		21 46	21 59				22 06	22 08								22 16		22 25		
Wivelsfield	d				21 57			22 03					22 12										22 29		
Lewes 4	a												22 23												
Burgess Hill 4	d				21 59			22 05				22 11											22 31		
Hassocks 4	d				22 03			22 08															22 34		
Preston Park	d				22 09			22 15															22 41		
Hove 2	a											22 22													
Brighton 10	a				22 15		22 00	22 19													22 30		22 45		

Table 186

Saturdays

Bedford and London - Brighton

Network Diagram - see first Page of Table 186

		SN ◇1		SN 1	GX 1		SN	SN ◇1	SN ◇1	FC 1	GW 1	SN 1	GX 1		SN ◇1	SN 1	GX 1	SN	SN 1	GW 1	SN 1		SN ◇1	FC 1	SN 1
London Victoria 15 ⊖	d	21 47			22 00		22 01	22 02	22 06			22 10	22 15		22 17		22 30	22 31			22 32		22 36		22 40
Clapham Junction 10	d	21 53					22 08	22 08	22 12			22 16			22 23			22 38			22 38		22 42		22 46
Bedford	d																								
Luton 10	d																								
Luton Airport Parkway 7 ✈	d																								
St Albans City	d																								
St Pancras International 15 ⊖	d																								
Farringdon 3 ⊖	d																								
City Thameslink 3	d																								
London Blackfriars 3 ⊖	d																								
London Bridge 4 ⊖	d									22 12														22 42	
New Cross Gate	d																								
Norwood Junction 2	d																								
East Croydon	a	22 03						22 17	22 22	22 24		22 27			22 33						22 47		22 52	22 54	22 57
	d	22 03						22 18	22 23	22 25		22 28			22 33						22 48		22 53	22 55	22 58
Purley 4	d											22 33													23 03
Coulsdon South	d											22 37													23 07
Merstham	d											22 42													23 12
Redhill	a							22 30				22 46									23 00				23 16
	d							22 31			22 33	22 46							22 55	22 56	23 00				23 16
Reigate	a										22 38														
Nutfield	d																		22 59						
Godstone	d																		23 05						
Edenbridge	d																		23 10						
Penshurst	d																		23 17						
Leigh (Kent)	d																		23 20						
Tonbridge 4	a																		23 25						
Earlswood (Surrey)	d																								23 19
Salfords	d																								23 22
Horley 4	d			←								22 52				←									23 26
Gatwick Airport 10 ✈	a	22 18		22 28	22 30			22 38		22 40		22 55	22 45		22 48	22 55	23 00			23 05	23 08			23 10	23 28
	d	22 20		22 29				22 39		22 41		22 56			22 50	22 56					23 09			23 11	23 29
Three Bridges 15	a			22 33				22 44		22 45		→			22 54	23 00					23 14			23 15	→
	d			22 36				22 44		22 45					22 54	23 01					23 15			23 15	
Crawley	d			22 39												23 04					23 18				
Ifield	d			22 42												23 07									
Faygate	d																								
Littlehaven	d			22 48												23 13									
Horsham 4	a			22 52												23 16					23 26				
Balcombe	d									22 53															
Haywards Heath	a	22 30						22 53	22 46	22 58					23 03								23 16	23 24	
	d	22 34	22 37					22 53	22 46	22 59					23 03								23 16	23 25	
Wivelsfield	d	22 38						22 57		23 03														23 29	
Lewes 4	a	22 51																							
Burgess Hill 4	d							22 59		23 05					23 09									23 31	
Hassocks 4	d							23 03		23 08														23 34	
Preston Park	d							23 09		23 15														23 41	
Hove 2	a		22 51												23 21										
Brighton 10	a							23 15	23 00	23 19													23 30	23 45	

Bedford and London - Brighton

Network Diagram - see first Page of Table 186

		GX	SN		SN		GX	SN	GW	SN	SN	FC	SN		GX	SN	SN	GX	SN	SN	FC		GX	SN	SN
		1	◇1		1		1		1	◇1	◇1	1	1		1	◇1	1	1	1	1	1		1	1	1
London Victoria 15 ⊖	d	22 45	22 47				23 00	23 01		23 02	23 06		23 10		23 15	23 17		23 30		23 32			23 45	23 47	23 49
Clapham Junction 10	d		22 53					23 08		23 08	23 12		23 16			23 23				23 38				23 53	23 56
Bedford	d																								
Luton 10	d																								
Luton Airport Parkway 7 ✈	d																								
St Albans City	d																								
St Pancras International 15 ⊖	d																								
Farringdon 3 ⊖	d																								
City Thameslink 3	d																								
London Blackfriars 3 ⊖	d																								
London Bridge 4 ⊖	d											23 12									23 42				
New Cross Gate	d																								
Norwood Junction 2	d																								
East Croydon	a		23 03							23 17	23 22	23 24	23 27			23 32				23 52	23 56			00 05	00 09
	d		23 03							23 18	23 23	23 25	23 28			23 33				23 52	23 57			00 06	
Purley 4	d												23 33											00 12	
Coulsdon South	d												23 37											00 15	
Merstham	d												23 42											00 21	
Redhill	a									23 30			23 46							00 03				00 24	
	d								23 28	23 31			23 46						23 55	00 05				00 25	
Reigate	a								23 33																
Nutfield	d																								
Godstone	d																								
Edenbridge	d																		00 06						
Penshurst	d																								
Leigh (Kent)	d																								
Tonbridge 4	a																		00 15						
Earlswood (Surrey)	d												23 49												
Salfords	d												23 52												
Horley 4	d				←								23 56				←							00 31	
Gatwick Airport 10 ✈	a	23 15	23 18		23 28		23 30			23 38		23 40	23 58		23 45	23 49	23 58	00 05		00 14	00 18		00 20	00 33	
	d		23 20		23 29					23 39		23 41	23 59			23 50	23 59			00 15	00 19			00 34	
Three Bridges 15	a				23 34					23 44		23 47	→			23 54	00 04			00 20	00 24			00 39	
	d				23 38					23 44		23 47				23 55	00 04			00 20				00 39	
Crawley	d				23 41												00 07							00 43	
Ifield	d				23 44												00 10							00 46	
Faygate	d																								
Littlehaven	d				23 50												00 16							00 52	
Horsham 4	a				23 53												00 19							00 55	
Balcombe	d											23 53								00 28					
Haywards Heath	a		23 30							23 53	23 46	23 58				00 04				00 34					
	d		23 34	23 37						23 53	23 46	23 59				00 05				00 35					
Wivelsfield	d		23 38							23 57		00 03								00 39					
Lewes 4	a		23 51																						
Burgess Hill 4	d									23 59		00 05				00 10				00 41					
Hassocks 4	d									00 03		00 08								00 44					
Preston Park	d									00 09		00 15								00 51					
Hove 2	a			23 51												00 23									
Brighton 10	a									00 15	00 01	00 19								00 55					

Bedford and London - Brighton

Network Diagram - see first Page of Table 186

		SN	SN	FC	SN	SN	SN	GX		SN	GW	SN	FC	GX	SN	SN		GX	SN		FC	SN	GW	GX	
		◇1	◇1	1	1	◇1	1	1		1	1	1	1	1	1	1		1	◇1		1	1	1	1	
London Victoria 15 ⊖	d	23p02	23p06		23p10	23p17		23p30				23p32		23p45	23p47	23p49		00 02	00 05			00 14		00 30	
Clapham Junction 10	d	23p08	23p12		23p16	23p23						23p38			23p53	23p56			00 11			00 20			
Bedford	d																								
Luton 10	d																								
Luton Airport Parkway 7 ✈	d																								
St Albans City	d																								
St Pancras International 15 ⊖	d																								
Farringdon 3 ⊖	d																								
City Thameslink 3	d																								
London Blackfriars 3 ⊖	d																								
London Bridge 4 ⊖	d			23p12									23p42								00 12				
New Cross Gate	d																								
Norwood Junction 2	d																								
East Croydon	a	23p17	23p22	23p24	23p27	23p32						23p52	23p56		00 05	00 09			00 24		00 27	00 31			
	d	23p18	23p23	23p25	23p28	23p33						23p52	23p57		00 06				00 24		00 27	00 32			
Purley 4	d				23p33										00 12							00 37			
Coulsdon South	d				23p37										00 15							00 41			
Merstham	d				23p42										00 21							00 47			
Redhill	a	23p30			23p46							00 03			00 24							00 50			
	d	23p31			23p46					23p55	00 03	00 05			00 25							00 51	00 54		
Reigate	a																								
Nutfield	d																								
Godstone	d																								
Edenbridge	d									00 06															
Penshurst	d																								
Leigh (Kent)	d																								
Tonbridge 4	a									00 15															
Earlswood (Surrey)	d				23p49																				
Salfords	d				23p52																				
Horley 4	d				23p56		←								00 31							00 57			
Gatwick Airport 10 ✈	a	23p38		23p40	23p58	23p49	23p58	00 05			00 10	00 14	00 18	00 20	00 33			00 38	00 42		00 48	00 59	01 02	01 05	
	d	23p39		23p41	23p59	23p50	23p59					00 15	00 19		00 34				00 43		00 49	01 00			
Three Bridges 15	a	23p44		23p47	→	23p54	00 04					00 20	00 24		00 39				00 48		00 54	01 05			
	d	23p44		23p47		23p55	00 04					00 20			00 39				00 48						
Crawley	d						00 07								00 43										
Ifield	d						00 10								00 46										
Faygate	d																								
Littlehaven	d						00 16								00 52										
Horsham 4	a						00 19								00 55										
Balcombe	d			23p53								00 28													
Haywards Heath	a	23p53	23p46	23p58		00 04						00 34							00 58						
	d	23p53	23p46	23p59		00 05						00 35							01 02	01 06					
Wivelsfield	d	23p57		00 03								00 39													
Lewes 4	a																			01 20					
Burgess Hill 4	d	23p59		00 05		00 10						00 41													
Hassocks 4	d	00 03		00 08								00 44													
Preston Park	d	00 09		00 15								00 51													
Hove 2	a					00 23																			
Brighton 10	a	00 15	00 01	00 19								00 55							01s16						

Table 186

Sundays

Bedford and London - Brighton

Network Diagram - see first Page of Table 186

		FC	SN	FC	SN	SN	GX	SN	GX	GX	SN	GX	GX	GX	SN	SN	GX	GX	GW	GX	SN	GX
		1	1	1	1	1	1	1	1	1	1	1	1	1	1	◇1	1	1	1	1	◇1	1
London Victoria 15 ⊖	d		01 00		02 00	03 00	03 30	04 00	04 30	05 00	05 02	05 15	05 30	05 45		05 47	06 00	06 15		06 30	06 32	06 45
Clapham Junction 10	d		01 08		02 08	03 08		04 08			05 08					05 53					06 38	
Bedford	d																					
Luton 10	d																					
Luton Airport Parkway 7 ✈	d																					
St Albans City	d																					
St Pancras International 15 ⊖	d																					
Farringdon 3 ⊖	d																					
City Thameslink 3	d																					
London Blackfriars 3 ⊖	d																					
London Bridge 4 ⊖	d	00 42		01 08																		
New Cross Gate	d																					
Norwood Junction 2	d																					
East Croydon	a	00 56	01 21	01 32	02 21	03 21		04 21			05 21					06 05					06 51	
	d	00 57	01 21	01 32	02 22	03 22		04 21			05 23					06 06					06 52	
Purley 4	d		01 26		02 27	03 27		04 26			05 28										06 56	
Coulsdon South	d																				07 00	
Merstham	d																				07 05	
Redhill	a							04 35			05 37					06 18					07 09	
	d							04 35			05 37					06 19			06 20		07 09	
Reigate	a																		06 24			
Nutfield	d																					
Godstone	d																					
Edenbridge	d																					
Penshurst	d																					
Leigh (Kent)	d																					
Tonbridge 4	a																					
Earlswood (Surrey)	d																					
Salfords	d																					
Horley 4	d		01 42		02 42	03 42		04 42								06 25					07 15	
Gatwick Airport 10 ✈	a	01 19	01 45	01 51	02 44	03 44	04 05	04 45	05 05	05 35	05 44	05 50	06 05	06 20		06 31	06 35	06 47		07 05	07 18	07 20
	d	01 20	01 46	01 52	02 46	03 46		04 46			05 45				06 29	06 32					07 19	
Three Bridges 15	a	01 24	01 51	01 58	03 00	04 00		04 54			05 50				06 33	06 36					07 23	
	d		01 51					04 54			05 50				06 40	06 36					07 24	
Crawley	d														06 43							
Ifield	d														06 46							
Faygate	d																					
Littlehaven	d														06 52							
Horsham 4	a														06 56							
Balcombe	d																				07 30	
Haywards Heath	a		02 05					05 06			05 59					06 47					07 35	
	d		02 06					05 07			06 00					06 47					07 36	
Wivelsfield	d															06 51					07 40	
Lewes 4	a																					
Burgess Hill 4	d															06 53					07 42	
Hassocks 4	d															06 57					07 45	
Preston Park	d															07 03					07 52	
Hove 2	a																					
Brighton 10	a		02 23					05 21			06 18					07 08					07 58	

Table 186

Sundays

Bedford and London - Brighton

Network Diagram - see first Page of Table 186

		GW	GX	GW	SN	FC	GX	GX	SN	GX	SN	SN	FC	SN	GW	GW	GX	SN	FC	GX	SN	GX
		1	1	1	◇1	1	1	1	◇1	1	1	1	1	1	1	1	1	◇1	1	1	◇1	1
London Victoria 15 ⊖	d		07 00		07 02		07 15	07 30	07 32	07 45							08 00	08 04		08 15	08 17	08 30
Clapham Junction 10	d				07 08				07 38									08 10			08 23	
Bedford	d																					
Luton 10	d																					
Luton Airport Parkway 7 ✈	d																					
St Albans City	d																					
St Pancras International 15 ⊖	d																					
Farringdon 3 ⊖	d																					
City Thameslink 3	d																					
London Blackfriars 3 ⊖	d																					
London Bridge 4 ⊖	d					07 12						07 37	07 42						08 12			
New Cross Gate	d																					
Norwood Junction 2	d											07 48										
East Croydon	a				07 23	07 26			07 50			07 54	07 56					08 23	08 27		08 36	
	d				07 23	07 27			07 51			07 55	07 57					08 24	08 27		08 37	
Purley 4	d				07 29							08 00						08 30				
Coulsdon South	d											08 04										
Merstham	d											08 09										
Redhill	a				07 37				08 03			08 13						08 38				
	d	07 15		07 20	07 37				08 04		08 10	08 13			08 19	08 21		08 39				
Reigate	a			07 24											08 23							
Nutfield	d										08 14											
Godstone	d										08 20											
Edenbridge	d										08 25											
Penshurst	d										08 32											
Leigh (Kent)	d										08 35											
Tonbridge 4	a										08 40											
Earlswood (Surrey)	d																					
Salfords	d																					
Horley 4	d				07 43							08 22		←				08 45				
Gatwick Airport 10 ✈	a	07 27	07 35		07 46	07 48	07 50	08 05	08 11	08 20		08 24	08 18	08 24		08 31	08 35	08 47	08 48	08 50	08 54	09 05
	d				07 47	07 50			08 12			08 25	08 20	08 25				08 48	08 50		08 56	
Three Bridges 15	a				07 51	07 54			08 16			→	08 24	08 30				08 53	08 54			
	d				07 52	07 54			08 17				08 24	08 33				08 53	08 54			
Crawley	d				07 55									08 36				08 56				
Ifield	d				07 58									08 39								
Faygate	d																					
Littlehaven	d				08 04									08 45								
Horsham 4	a				08 07									08 49				09 04				
Balcombe	d								08 23													
Haywards Heath	a					08 03			08 28				08 33						09 03		09 06	
	d					08 03			08 28				08 33						09 03		09 07	
Wivelsfield	d								08 32													
Lewes 4	a																					
Burgess Hill 4	d					08 08			08 34				08 38						09 08		09 12	
Hassocks 4	d					08 12			08 38				08 42						09 12			
Preston Park	d								08 44													
Hove 2	a																				09 24	
Brighton 10	a					08 22			08 48				08 52						09 22			

Bedford and London - Brighton

Network Diagram - see first Page of Table 186

		SN ◇1	GX 1 ✠	SN 1	SN 1	FC 1	SN 1	SN ◇1 ✠	GW 1	GW 1	GX 1 ✠	SN ◇1	SN ◇1	FC 1	GX 1 ✠	SN ◇1	GX 1 ✠	SN ◇1	GX 1 ✠	SN 1	SN 1	FC 1
London Victoria 15 ⊖	d	08 32	08 45					08 47			09 00	09 02	09 04		09 15	09 17	09 30	09 32	09 45			
Clapham Junction 10	d	08 38						08 53				09 08	09 10			09 23		09 38				
Bedford	d																					
Luton 10	d																					
Luton Airport Parkway 7 ✈	d																					
St Albans City	d																					
St Pancras International 15 ⊖	d																					
Farringdon 3 ⊖	d																					
City Thameslink 3	d																					
London Blackfriars 3 ⊖	d																					
London Bridge 4 ⊖	d				08 37	08 42								09 12							09 37	09 42
New Cross Gate	d																					
Norwood Junction 2	d				08 48																09 48	
East Croydon	a	08 50			08 54	08 56		09 06				09 21	09 23	09 27		09 36		09 50			09 54	09 56
	d	08 51			08 55	08 57		09 07				09 22	09 24	09 27		09 37		09 51			09 55	09 57
Purley 4	d				09 00								09 30								10 00	
Coulsdon South	d				09 04																10 04	
Merstham	d				09 09																10 09	
Redhill	a	09 03			09 13								09 38					10 03			10 13	
	d	09 04		09 10	09 16				09 20	09 21			09 39					10 04		10 10	10 16	
Reigate	a								09 24													
Nutfield	d			09 14																10 14		
Godstone	d			09 20																10 20		
Edenbridge	d			09 25																10 25		
Penshurst	d			09 32																10 32		
Leigh (Kent)	d			09 35																10 35		
Tonbridge 4	a			09 40																10 40		
Earlswood (Surrey)	d																					
Salfords	d																					
Horley 4	d				09 22		←						09 45								10 22	
Gatwick Airport 10 ✈	a	09 11	09 20		09 24	09 18	09 24	09 27		09 31	09 35	09 39	09 47	09 48	09 50	09 54	10 05	10 11	10 20		10 24	10 18
	d	09 12			09 25	09 20	09 25	09 29				09 40	09 48	09 50		09 56		10 12			10 25	10 20
Three Bridges 15	a	09 16			→	09 24	09 30						09 53	09 54				10 16			→	10 24
	d	09 17				09 24	09 33						09 53	09 54				10 17				10 24
Crawley	d						09 37						09 56									
Ifield	d						09 39															
Faygate	d																					
Littlehaven	d						09 46															
Horsham 4	a						09 49						10 04									
Balcombe	d	09 23																10 23				
Haywards Heath	a	09 28				09 33		09 40						10 03		10 06		10 28				10 33
	d	09 28				09 33		09 41						10 03		10 07		10 28				10 33
Wivelsfield	d	09 32						09 45										10 32				
Lewes 4	a							09 58														
Burgess Hill 4	d	09 34				09 38								10 08		10 12		10 34				10 38
Hassocks 4	d	09 38				09 42								10 12				10 38				10 42
Preston Park	d	09 44																10 44				
Hove 2	a															10 24						
Brighton 10	a	09 48				09 52						10 03		10 22				10 48				10 52

Sundays

Bedford and London - Brighton

Network Diagram - see first Page of Table 186

		SN 1	SN ◇1 ✠	GW 1	GW 1	SN 1 ✠	SN ◇1 ✠	SN ◇1 ✠	FC 1	GX 1 ✠	SN ◇1	GX 1 ✠	SN ◇1	GX 1 ✠	SN 1	SN 1	FC 1	SN 1	SN ◇1 ✠	GW 1	GW 1	GX 1 ✠
London Victoria 15 ⊖	d		09 47			10 00	10 02	10 04		10 15	10 17	10 30	10 32	10 45					10 47			11 00
Clapham Junction 10	d		09 53				10 08	10 10			10 23		10 38						10 53			
Bedford	d																					
Luton 10	d																					
Luton Airport Parkway 7 ✈	d																					
St Albans City	d																					
St Pancras International 15 ⊖	d																					
Farringdon 3 ⊖	d																					
City Thameslink 3	d																					
London Blackfriars 3 ⊖	d																					
London Bridge 4 ⊖	d								10 12							10 37	10 42					
New Cross Gate	d																					
Norwood Junction 2	d															10 48						
East Croydon	a		10 06				10 21	10 23	10 27		10 36		10 50			10 54	10 56		11 06			
	d		10 07				10 22	10 24	10 27		10 37		10 51			10 55	10 57		11 07			
Purley 4	d							10 30								11 00						
Coulsdon South	d															11 04						
Merstham	d															11 09						
Redhill	a							10 38					11 03			11 13						
	d			10 19	10 21			10 39					11 04		11 10	11 16				11 20	11 21	
Reigate	a			10 23																11 24		
Nutfield	d														11 14							
Godstone	d														11 20							
Edenbridge	d														11 25							
Penshurst	d														11 32							
Leigh (Kent)	d														11 35							
Tonbridge 4	a														11 40							
Earlswood (Surrey)	d																					
Salfords	d																					
Horley 4	d	←						10 45								11 22		←				
Gatwick Airport 10 ✈	a	10 24	10 27		10 30	10 35	10 39	10 47	10 48	10 50	10 54	11 05	11 11	11 20		11 24	11 18	11 24	11 27		11 30	11 35
	d	10 25	10 29				10 40	10 48	10 50		10 56		11 12			11 25	11 20	11 25	11 29			
Three Bridges 15	a	10 30						10 53	10 54				11 16			→	11 24	11 30				
	d	10 33						10 53	10 54				11 17				11 24	11 33				
Crawley	d	10 37						10 56										11 37				
Ifield	d	10 39																11 39				
Faygate	d																					
Littlehaven	d	10 46																11 46				
Horsham 4	a	10 49						11 04										11 49				
Balcombe	d												11 23									
Haywards Heath	a		10 40						11 03		11 06		11 28				11 33		11 40			
	d		10 41						11 03		11 07		11 28				11 33		11 41			
Wivelsfield	d		10 45										11 32						11 45			
Lewes 4	a		10 58																11 58			
Burgess Hill 4	d								11 08		11 12		11 34				11 38					
Hassocks 4	d								11 12				11 38				11 42					
Preston Park	d												11 44									
Hove 2	a										11 24											
Brighton 10	a						11 03		11 22				11 48				11 52					

Table 186

Sundays

Bedford and London - Brighton

Network Diagram - see first Page of Table 186

		SN ◇1 trolley	SN ◇1 trolley	FC 1	GX 1 trolley	SN ◇1	SN 1 trolley	SN ◇1	GX 1 trolley	SN 1	SN 1	FC 1	SN 1	SN ◇1 trolley	GW 1	GW 1	GX 1 trolley	SN ◇1 trolley	SN ◇1 trolley	FC 1	GX 1 trolley	SN ◇1
London Victoria 15 ⊖	d	11 02	11 04		11 15	11 17	11 30	11 32	11 45					11 47			12 00	12 02	12 04		12 15	12 17
Clapham Junction 10	d	11 08	11 10			11 23		11 38						11 53				12 08	12 10			12 23
Bedford	d																					
Luton 10	d																					
Luton Airport Parkway 7 ✈	d																					
St Albans City	d																					
St Pancras International 15 ⊖	d																					
Farringdon 3 ⊖	d																					
City Thameslink 3	d																					
London Blackfriars 3 ⊖	d																					
London Bridge 4 ⊖	d			11 12							11 37	11 42								12 12		
New Cross Gate	d																					
Norwood Junction 2	d										11 48											
East Croydon	a	11 21	11 23	11 27		11 36		11 50			11 54	11 56		12 06				12 21	12 23	12 27		12 36
	d	11 22	11 24	11 27		11 37		11 51			11 55	11 57		12 07				12 22	12 24	12 27		12 37
Purley 4	d		11 30								12 00								12 30			
Coulsdon South	d										12 04											
Merstham	d										12 09											
Redhill	a		11 38					12 03			12 13								12 38			
	d		11 39					12 04		12 10	12 16				12 19	12 21			12 39			
Reigate	a														12 23							
Nutfield	d									12 14												
Godstone	d									12 20												
Edenbridge	d									12 25												
Penshurst	d									12 32												
Leigh (Kent)	d									12 35												
Tonbridge 4	a									12 40												
Earlswood (Surrey)	d																					
Salfords	d																					
Horley 4	d		11 45								12 22		←						12 45			
Gatwick Airport 10 ✈	a	11 39	11 47	11 48	11 50	11 54	12 05	12 11	12 20		12 24	12 18	12 24	12 27		12 30	12 35	12 39	12 47	12 48	12 50	12 54
	d	11 40	11 48	11 50		11 56		12 12			12 25	12 20	12 25	12 29				12 40	12 48	12 50		12 56
Three Bridges 15	a		11 53	11 54				12 16			→	12 24	12 30						12 53	12 54		
	d		11 53	11 54				12 17				12 24	12 33						12 53	12 54		
Crawley	d		11 56										12 37						12 56			
Ifield	d												12 39									
Faygate	d																					
Littlehaven	d												12 46									
Horsham 4	a		12 04										12 49						13 04			
Balcombe	d							12 23														
Haywards Heath	a			12 03		12 06		12 28				12 33		12 40						13 03		13 06
	d			12 03		12 07		12 28				12 33		12 41						13 03		13 07
Wivelsfield	d							12 32						12 45								
Lewes 4	a													12 58								
Burgess Hill 4	d			12 08		12 12		12 34				12 38								13 08		13 12
Hassocks 4	d			12 12				12 38				12 42								13 12		
Preston Park	d							12 44														
Hove 2	a					12 24																13 24
Brighton 10	a	12 03		12 22				12 48				12 52						13 03		13 22		

Table 186

Sundays

Bedford and London - Brighton

Network Diagram - see first Page of Table 186

		GX 1 trolley	SN ◇1	GX 1 trolley	SN 1	SN 1	FC 1	SN 1	SN ◇1 trolley	GW 1	GW 1	GX 1 trolley	SN ◇1 trolley	SN ◇1 trolley	FC 1	GX 1 trolley	SN ◇1	GX 1 trolley	SN ◇1	GX 1 trolley	SN 1	SN 1
London Victoria 15 ⊖	d	12 30	12 32	12 45					12 47			13 00	13 02	13 04		13 15	13 17	13 30	13 32	13 45		
Clapham Junction 10	d		12 38						12 53				13 08	13 10			13 23		13 38			
Bedford	d																					
Luton 10	d																					
Luton Airport Parkway 7 ✈	d																					
St Albans City	d																					
St Pancras International 15 ⊖	d																					
Farringdon 3 ⊖	d																					
City Thameslink 3	d																					
London Blackfriars 3 ⊖	d																					
London Bridge 4 ⊖	d					12 37	12 42								13 12							13 37
New Cross Gate	d																					
Norwood Junction 2	d					12 48																13 48
East Croydon	a		12 50			12 54	12 56		13 06				13 21	13 23	13 27		13 36		13 50			13 54
	d		12 51			12 55	12 57		13 07				13 22	13 24	13 27		13 37		13 51			13 55
Purley 4	d					13 00								13 30								14 00
Coulsdon South	d					13 04																14 04
Merstham	d					13 09																14 09
Redhill	a		13 03			13 13								13 38					14 03			14 13
	d		13 04		13 10	13 16				13 20	13 21			13 39					14 04		14 10	14 16
Reigate	a									13 24												
Nutfield	d				13 14																14 14	
Godstone	d				13 20																14 20	
Edenbridge	d				13 25																14 25	
Penshurst	d				13 32																14 32	
Leigh (Kent)	d				13 35																14 35	
Tonbridge 4	a				13 40																14 40	
Earlswood (Surrey)	d																					
Salfords	d																					
Horley 4	d					13 22		←						13 45								14 22
Gatwick Airport 10 ✈	a	13 05	13 11	13 20		13 24	13 18	13 24	13 27		13 30	13 35	13 39	13 47	13 48	13 50	13 54	14 05	14 11	14 20		14 24
	d		13 12			13 25	13 20	13 25	13 29				13 40	13 48	13 50		13 56		14 12			14 25
Three Bridges 15	a		13 16			→	13 24	13 30						13 53	13 54				14 16			→
	d		13 17				13 24	13 33						13 53	13 54				14 17			
Crawley	d							13 37						13 56								
Ifield	d							13 39														
Faygate	d																					
Littlehaven	d							13 46														
Horsham 4	a							13 49						14 04								
Balcombe	d		13 23																14 23			
Haywards Heath	a		13 28				13 33		13 40						14 03		14 06		14 28			
	d		13 28				13 33		13 41						14 03		14 07		14 28			
Wivelsfield	d		13 32						13 45										14 32			
Lewes 4	a								13 56													
Burgess Hill 4	d		13 34				13 38								14 08		14 12		14 34			
Hassocks 4	d		13 38				13 42								14 12				14 38			
Preston Park	d		13 44																14 44			
Hove 2	a																14 24					
Brighton 10	a		13 48				13 52						14 03		14 22				14 48			

Bedford and London - Brighton

Network Diagram - see first Page of Table 186

		FC 1	SN 1	SN ◇1 🍴	GW 1	GW 1	GX 1 🍴	SN ◇1 🍴	SN ◇1 🍴	FC 1	GX 1 🍴	SN ◇1	GX 1 🍴	SN ◇1	GX 1 🍴	SN 1	SN 1	FC 1	SN 1	SN ◇1 🍴	GW 1	GW 1
London Victoria 15 ⊖	d			13 47			14 00	14 02	14 04		14 15	14 17	14 30	14 32	14 45					14 47		
Clapham Junction 10	d			13 53				14 08	14 10			14 23		14 38						14 53		
Bedford	d																					
Luton 10	d																					
Luton Airport Parkway 7 ✈	d																					
St Albans City	d																					
St Pancras International 15 ⊖	d																					
Farringdon 3 ⊖	d																					
City Thameslink 3	d																					
London Blackfriars 3 ⊖	d																					
London Bridge 4 ⊖	d	13 42								14 12							14 37	14 42				
New Cross Gate	d																					
Norwood Junction 2	d																14 48					
East Croydon ⇌	a	13 56		14 06				14 21	14 23	14 27		14 36		14 50			14 54	14 56		15 06		
	d	13 57		14 07				14 22	14 24	14 27		14 37		14 51			14 55	14 57		15 07		
Purley 4	d								14 30								15 00					
Coulsdon South	d																15 04					
Merstham	d																15 09					
Redhill	a								14 38					15 03			15 13					
	d				14 19	14 21			14 39					15 04		15 10	15 16				15 20	15 21
Reigate	a				14 23																15 24	
Nutfield	d															15 14						
Godstone	d															15 20						
Edenbridge	d															15 25						
Penshurst	d															15 32						
Leigh (Kent)	d															15 35						
Tonbridge 4	a															15 40						
Earlswood (Surrey)	d																					
Salfords	d																					
Horley 4	d		←						14 45								15 22		←			
Gatwick Airport 10 ✈	a	14 18	14 24	14 27		14 30	14 35	14 39	14 47	14 48	14 50	14 54	15 05	15 11	15 20		15 24	15 18	15 24	15 27		15 30
	d	14 20	14 25	14 29				14 40	14 48	14 50		14 56		15 12			15 25	15 20	15 25	15 29		
Three Bridges 15	a	14 24	14 30						14 53	14 54				15 16			→	15 24	15 30			
	d	14 24	14 33						14 53	14 54				15 17				15 24	15 33			
Crawley	d		14 37						14 56										15 37			
Ifield	d		14 39																15 39			
Faygate	d																					
Littlehaven	d		14 46																15 46			
Horsham 4	a		14 49						15 04										15 49			
Balcombe	d													15 23								
Haywards Heath	a	14 33		14 40						15 03		15 06		15 28				15 33		15 40		
	d	14 33		14 41						15 03		15 07		15 28				15 33		15 41		
Wivelsfield	d			14 45										15 32						15 45		
Lewes 4	a			14 56																15 56		
Burgess Hill 4	d	14 38								15 08		15 12		15 34				15 38				
Hassocks 4	d	14 42								15 12				15 38				15 42				
Preston Park	d													15 44								
Hove 2	a											15 24										
Brighton 10	a	14 52						15 03		15 22				15 48				15 52				

Bedford and London - Brighton

Network Diagram - see first Page of Table 186

		GX 1 🍴	SN ◇1 🍴	SN ◇1 🍴	FC 1	GX 1 🍴	SN ◇1	GX 1 🍴	SN ◇1	GX 1 🍴	SN 1	SN 1	FC 1	SN 1	SN ◇1 🍴	GW 1	GW 1	GX 1 🍴	SN ◇1 🍴	SN ◇1 🍴	FC 1	GX 1 🍴
London Victoria 15 ⊖	d	15 00	15 02	15 04		15 15	15 17	15 30	15 32	15 45					15 47			16 00	16 02	16 04		16 15
Clapham Junction 10	d		15 08	15 10			15 23		15 38						15 53				16 08	16 10		
Bedford	d																					
Luton 10	d																					
Luton Airport Parkway 7 ✈	d																					
St Albans City	d																					
St Pancras International 15 ⊖	d																					
Farringdon 3 ⊖	d																					
City Thameslink 3	d																					
London Blackfriars 3 ⊖	d																					
London Bridge 4 ⊖	d				15 12							15 37	15 42								16 12	
New Cross Gate	d																					
Norwood Junction 2	d											15 48										
East Croydon ⇌	a		15 21	15 23	15 27		15 36		15 50			15 54	15 56		16 06				16 21	16 23	16 27	
	d		15 22	15 24	15 27		15 37		15 51			15 55	15 57		16 07				16 22	16 24	16 27	
Purley 4	d			15 30								16 00								16 30		
Coulsdon South	d											16 04										
Merstham	d											16 09										
Redhill	a			15 38					16 03			16 13								16 38		
	d			15 39					16 04		16 10	16 16				16 19	16 21			16 39		
Reigate	a															16 23						
Nutfield	d										16 14											
Godstone	d										16 20											
Edenbridge	d										16 25											
Penshurst	d										16 32											
Leigh (Kent)	d										16 35											
Tonbridge 4	a										16 40											
Earlswood (Surrey)	d																					
Salfords	d																					
Horley 4	d			15 45								16 22		←						16 45		
Gatwick Airport 10 ✈	a	15 35	15 39	15 47	15 48	15 50	15 54	16 05	16 11	16 20		16 24	16 18	16 24	16 27		16 30	16 35	16 39	16 47	16 48	16 50
	d		15 40	15 48	15 50		15 56		16 12			16 25	16 20	16 25	16 29				16 40	16 48	16 50	
Three Bridges 15	a			15 53	15 54				16 16			→	16 24	16 30						16 53	16 54	
	d			15 53	15 54				16 17				16 24	16 33						16 53	16 54	
Crawley	d			15 56										16 37						16 56		
Ifield	d													16 39								
Faygate	d																					
Littlehaven	d													16 46								
Horsham 4	a			16 04										16 49						17 04		
Balcombe	d								16 23													
Haywards Heath	a				16 03		16 06		16 28				16 33		16 40						17 03	
	d				16 03		16 07		16 28				16 33		16 41						17 03	
Wivelsfield	d								16 32						16 45							
Lewes 4	a														16 58							
Burgess Hill 4	d				16 08		16 12		16 34				16 38								17 08	
Hassocks 4	d				16 12				16 38				16 42								17 12	
Preston Park	d								16 44													
Hove 2	a						16 24															
Brighton 10	a		16 03		16 22				16 48				16 52						17 03		17 22	

Table 186

Sundays

Bedford and London - Brighton

Network Diagram - see first Page of Table 186

		SN ◇1	GX 1 ✠	SN ◇1	GX 1 ✠	SN 1	SN 1	FC 1	SN 1	SN ◇1 ✠	GW 1	GW 1	GX 1 ✠	SN ◇1 ✠	SN ◇1 ✠	FC 1	GX 1 ✠	SN ◇1	GX 1 ✠	SN ◇1	GX 1 ✠	SN 1
London Victoria 15 ⊖	d	16 17	16 30	16 32	16 45					16 47			17 00	17 02	17 04		17 15	17 17	17 30	17 32	17 45	
Clapham Junction 10	d	16 23		16 38						16 53				17 08	17 10			17 23		17 38		
Bedford	d																					
Luton 10	d																					
Luton Airport Parkway 7 ✈	d																					
St Albans City	d																					
St Pancras International 15 ⊖	d																					
Farringdon 3 ⊖	d																					
City Thameslink 3	d																					
London Blackfriars 3 ⊖	d																					
London Bridge 4 ⊖	d						16 37	16 42								17 12						
New Cross Gate	d																					
Norwood Junction 2	d						16 48															
East Croydon	a	16 36		16 50			16 54	16 56		17 06				17 21	17 23	17 27		17 36		17 50		
	d	16 37		16 51			16 55	16 57		17 07				17 22	17 24	17 27		17 37		17 51		
Purley 4	d						17 00								17 30							
Coulsdon South	d						17 04															
Merstham	d						17 09															
Redhill	a			17 03			17 13								17 38					18 03		
	d			17 04		17 10	17 16				17 20	17 21			17 39					18 04		18 10
Reigate	a										17 24											
Nutfield	d					17 14																18 14
Godstone	d					17 20																18 20
Edenbridge	d					17 25																18 25
Penshurst	d					17 32																18 32
Leigh (Kent)	d					17 35																18 35
Tonbridge 4	a					17 40																18 40
Earlswood (Surrey)	d																					
Salfords	d																					
Horley 4	d						17 22		←						17 45							
Gatwick Airport 10 ✈	a	16 54	17 05	17 11	17 20		17 24	17 18	17 24	17 27		17 30	17 35	17 39	17 47	17 48	17 50	17 54	18 05	18 11	18 20	
	d	16 56		17 12			17 25	17 20	17 25	17 29				17 40	17 48	17 50		17 56		18 12		
Three Bridges 15	a			17 16			→	17 24	17 30						17 53	17 54				18 16		
	d			17 17				17 24	17 33						17 53	17 54				18 17		
Crawley	d								17 37						17 56							
Ifield	d								17 39													
Faygate	d																					
Littlehaven	d								17 46													
Horsham 4	a								17 49						18 04							
Balcombe	d			17 23																18 23		
Haywards Heath	a	17 06		17 28				17 33		17 40						18 03		18 06		18 28		
	d	17 07		17 28				17 33		17 41						18 03		18 07		18 28		
Wivelsfield	d			17 32						17 45										18 32		
Lewes 4	a									17 58												
Burgess Hill 4	d	17 12		17 34				17 38								18 08		18 12		18 34		
Hassocks 4	d			17 38				17 42								18 12				18 38		
Preston Park	d			17 44																18 44		
Hove 2	a	17 24																18 24				
Brighton 10	a			17 48				17 52						18 03		18 22				18 48		

Table 186

Sundays

Bedford and London - Brighton

Network Diagram - see first Page of Table 186

		SN 1	FC 1	SN 1	SN ◇1 ✠	GW 1	GW 1	GX 1 ✠	SN ◇1 ✠	SN ◇1 ✠	FC 1	GX 1 ✠	SN ◇1	GX 1 ✠	SN ◇1	GX 1 ✠	SN 1	SN 1	FC 1	SN 1	SN ◇1 ✠	GW 1
London Victoria 15 ⊖	d				17 47			18 00	18 02	18 04		18 15	18 17	18 30	18 32	18 45					18 47	
Clapham Junction 10	d				17 53				18 08	18 10			18 23		18 38						18 53	
Bedford	d																					
Luton 10	d																					
Luton Airport Parkway 7 ✈	d																					
St Albans City	d																					
St Pancras International 15 ⊖	d																					
Farringdon 3 ⊖	d																					
City Thameslink 3	d																					
London Blackfriars 3 ⊖	d																					
London Bridge 4 ⊖	d	17 37	17 42								18 12							18 37	18 42			
New Cross Gate	d																					
Norwood Junction 2	d	17 48																18 48				
East Croydon	a	17 54	17 56		18 06				18 21	18 23	18 27		18 36		18 50			18 54	18 56		19 06	
	d	17 55	17 57		18 07				18 22	18 24	18 27		18 37		18 51			18 55	18 57		19 07	
Purley 4	d	18 00								18 30								19 00				
Coulsdon South	d	18 04																19 04				
Merstham	d	18 09																19 09				
Redhill	a	18 13								18 38					19 03			19 13				
	d	18 16				18 19	18 21			18 39					19 04		19 10	19 16				19 20
Reigate	a					18 23																19 24
Nutfield	d																19 14					
Godstone	d																19 20					
Edenbridge	d																19 25					
Penshurst	d																19 32					
Leigh (Kent)	d																19 35					
Tonbridge 4	a																19 40					
Earlswood (Surrey)	d																					
Salfords	d																					
Horley 4	d	18 22		←						18 45								19 22		←		
Gatwick Airport 10 ✈	a	18 24	18 18	18 24	18 27		18 30	18 35	18 39	18 47	18 48	18 50	18 54	19 05	19 11	19 20		19 24	19 18	19 24	19 27	
	d	18 25	18 20	18 25	18 29				18 40	18 48	18 50		18 56		19 12			19 25	19 20	19 25	19 29	
Three Bridges 15	a	→	18 24	18 30						18 53	18 54				19 16			→	19 24	19 30		
	d		18 24	18 33						18 53	18 54				19 17				19 24	19 33		
Crawley	d			18 37						18 56										19 37		
Ifield	d			18 39																19 39		
Faygate	d																					
Littlehaven	d			18 46																19 46		
Horsham 4	a			18 49						19 04										19 49		
Balcombe	d														19 23							
Haywards Heath	a		18 33		18 40						19 03		19 06		19 28				19 33		19 40	
	d		18 33		18 41						19 03		19 07		19 28				19 33		19 41	
Wivelsfield	d				18 45										19 32						19 45	
Lewes 4	a				18 58																19 58	
Burgess Hill 4	d		18 38								19 08		19 12		19 34				19 38			
Hassocks 4	d		18 42								19 12				19 38				19 42			
Preston Park	d														19 44							
Hove 2	a												19 24									
Brighton 10	a		18 52						19 03		19 22				19 48				19 52			

Bedford and London - Brighton

Network Diagram - see first Page of Table 186

Station		GW 1	GX 1 ✠	SN ◇1 ✠	SN ◇1 ✠	FC 1	GX 1	SN ◇1	GX 1	SN ◇1	GX 1	SN 1	SN 1	FC 1	SN 1	SN ◇1 ✠	GW 1	GW 1	GX 1	SN ◇1	SN ◇1	FC 1
London Victoria 15 ⊖	d		19 00	19 02	19 04		19 15	19 17	19 30	19 32	19 45					19 47			20 00	20 02	20 04	
Clapham Junction 10	d			19 08	19 10			19 23		19 38						19 53				20 08	20 10	
Bedford	d																					
Luton 10	d																					
Luton Airport Parkway 7 ✈	d																					
St Albans City	d																					
St Pancras International 15 ⊖	d																					
Farringdon 3 ⊖	d																					
City Thameslink 3	d																					
London Blackfriars 3 ⊖	d																					
London Bridge 4 ⊖	d					19 12							19 37	19 42								20 12
New Cross Gate	d																					
Norwood Junction 2	d												19 48									
East Croydon	a			19 21	19 23	19 27		19 36		19 50			19 54	19 56		20 06				20 21	20 23	20 27
	d			19 22	19 24	19 27		19 37		19 51			19 55	19 57		20 07				20 22	20 24	20 27
Purley 4	d				19 30								20 00								20 30	
Coulsdon South	d												20 04									
Merstham	d												20 09									
Redhill	a				19 38					20 03			20 13								20 38	
	d	19 21			19 39					20 04		20 10	20 16				20 19	20 21			20 39	
Reigate	a																20 23					
Nutfield	d											20 14										
Godstone	d											20 20										
Edenbridge	d											20 25										
Penshurst	d											20 32										
Leigh (Kent)	d											20 35										
Tonbridge 4	a											20 40										
Earlswood (Surrey)	d																					
Salfords	d																					
Horley 4	d				19 45								20 22		←						20 45	
Gatwick Airport 10 ✈	a	19 30	19 35	19 39	19 47	19 48	19 50	19 54	20 05	20 11	20 20		20 24	20 18	20 24	20 27		20 30	20 35	20 39	20 47	20 48
	d			19 40	19 48	19 50		19 56		20 12			20 25	20 20	20 25	20 29				20 40	20 48	20 50
Three Bridges 15	a				19 53	19 54				20 16			→	20 24	20 30						20 53	20 54
	d				19 53	19 54				20 17				20 24	20 33						20 53	20 54
Crawley	d				19 56										20 37						20 56	
Ifield	d														20 39							
Faygate	d																					
Littlehaven	d														20 46							
Horsham 4	a				20 04										20 49						21 04	
Balcombe	d									20 23												
Haywards Heath	a					20 03		20 06		20 28				20 33		20 40						21 03
	d					20 03		20 07		20 28				20 33		20 41						21 03
Wivelsfield	d									20 32						20 45						
Lewes 4	a															20 58						
Burgess Hill 4	d					20 08		20 12		20 34				20 38								21 08
Hassocks 4	d					20 12				20 38				20 42								21 12
Preston Park	d									20 44												
Hove 2	a							20 24														
Brighton 10	a			20 03		20 22				20 48				20 52						21 03		21 22

Bedford and London - Brighton

Network Diagram - see first Page of Table 186

Station		GX 1	SN ◇1	GX 1	SN ◇1	GX 1	SN 1	SN 1	FC 1	SN 1	SN ◇1	GW 1	GW 1	GX 1	SN ◇1	SN ◇1	FC 1	GX 1	SN ◇1	GX 1	SN ◇1	GX 1
London Victoria 15 ⊖	d	20 15	20 17	20 30	20 32	20 45					20 47			21 00	21 02	21 04		21 15	21 17	21 30	21 32	21 45
Clapham Junction 10	d		20 23		20 38						20 53				21 08	21 10			21 23		21 38	
Bedford	d																					
Luton 10	d																					
Luton Airport Parkway 7 ✈	d																					
St Albans City	d																					
St Pancras International 15 ⊖	d																					
Farringdon 3 ⊖	d																					
City Thameslink 3	d																					
London Blackfriars 3 ⊖	d																					
London Bridge 4 ⊖	d							20 37	20 42								21 12					
New Cross Gate	d																					
Norwood Junction 2	d							20 48														
East Croydon	a		20 36		20 50			20 54	20 56		21 06				21 21	21 23	21 27		21 36		21 50	
	d		20 37		20 51			20 55	20 57		21 07				21 22	21 24	21 27		21 37		21 51	
Purley 4	d							21 00								21 30						
Coulsdon South	d							21 04														
Merstham	d							21 09														
Redhill	a				21 03			21 13								21 38					22 03	
	d				21 03		21 10	21 16				21 20	21 21			21 38					22 04	
Reigate	a											21 24										
Nutfield	d						21 14															
Godstone	d						21 20															
Edenbridge	d						21 25															
Penshurst	d						21 32															
Leigh (Kent)	d						21 35															
Tonbridge 4	a						21 40															
Earlswood (Surrey)	d																					
Salfords	d																					
Horley 4	d							21 22		←						21 44						
Gatwick Airport 10 ✈	a	20 50	20 54	21 05	21 10	21 20		21 24	21 18	21 24	21 27		21 30	21 35	21 39	21 47	21 48	21 50	21 55	22 05	22 12	22 20
	d		20 56		21 11			21 25	21 20	21 25	21 29				21 40	21 48	21 50		21 56		22 13	
Three Bridges 15	a				21 16			→	21 24	21 30						21 53	21 54				22 18	
	d				21 16				21 24	21 33						21 53	21 54				22 18	
Crawley	d									21 37						21 56						
Ifield	d									21 39												
Faygate	d																					
Littlehaven	d									21 46												
Horsham 4	a									21 49						22 04						
Balcombe	d				21 22																22 24	
Haywards Heath	a		21 06		21 27				21 33		21 40						22 03		22 06		22 29	
	d		21 07		21 28				21 33		21 41						22 03		22 07		22 30	
Wivelsfield	d				21 32						21 45										22 34	
Lewes 4	a										21 58											
Burgess Hill 4	d		21 12		21 34				21 38								22 08		22 12		22 36	
Hassocks 4	d				21 37				21 42								22 12				22 39	
Preston Park	d				21 44																22 46	
Hove 2	a		21 24																22 24			
Brighton 10	a				21 49				21 52						22 03		22 22				22 50	

Table 186

Sundays

Bedford and London - Brighton

Network Diagram - see first Page of Table 186

		SN ■	SN ■	FC ■	SN ■	SN ◇■	GW ■	GW ■	GX ■	SN ◇■	FC ■	GX ■	SN ◇■	GX ■	SN ◇■	GX ■	SN ■	SN ■	FC ■	SN ■	SN ◇■	GW ■
London Victoria [15] ⊖	d					21 47			22 00	22 04		22 15	22 17	22 30	22 32	22 45					22 47	
Clapham Junction [10]	d					21 53				22 10			22 23		22 38						22 53	
Bedford	d																					
Luton [10]	d																					
Luton Airport Parkway [7] ✈	d																					
St Albans City	d																					
St Pancras International [15] ⊖	d																					
Farringdon [3] ⊖	d																					
City Thameslink [3]	d																					
London Blackfriars [3] ⊖	d																					
London Bridge [4] ⊖	d		21 37	21 42							22 12							22 37	22 42			
New Cross Gate	d																					
Norwood Junction [2]	d		21 48															22 48				
East Croydon ⇌	a		21 54	21 56		22 06				22 23	22 27		22 36		22 50			22 54	22 56		23 06	
	d		21 55	21 57		22 07				22 24	22 27		22 37		22 51			22 55	22 57		23 07	
Purley [4]	d		22 00							22 30								23 00				
Coulsdon South	d		22 04															23 04				
Merstham	d		22 09															23 09				
Redhill	a		22 13							22 38					23 03			23 13				
	d	22 10	22 16				22 19	22 21		22 39					23 04		23 10	23 16				23 20
Reigate	a						22 23															23 24
Nutfield	d	22 14															23 14					
Godstone	d	22 20															23 20					
Edenbridge	d	22 25															23 25					
Penshurst	d	22 32															23 32					
Leigh (Kent)	d	22 35															23 35					
Tonbridge [4]	a	22 40															23 40					
Earlswood (Surrey)	d																					
Salfords	d																					
Horley [4]	d		22 22		←					22 45								23 22		←		
Gatwick Airport [10] ✈	a		22 24	22 18	22 24	22 27		22 30	22 35	22 47	22 48	22 50	22 54	23 05	23 11	23 20		23 24	23 18	23 24	23 27	
	d		22 25	22 20	22 25	22 29				22 48	22 50		22 56		23 12			23 25	23 20	23 25	23 29	
Three Bridges [15]	a		→	22 24	22 30					22 53	22 54				23 16			→	23 24	23 30		
	d			22 24	22 33					22 53	22 54				23 17				23 24	23 33		
Crawley	d				22 37					22 56										23 37		
Ifield	d				22 39															23 39		
Faygate	d																					
Littlehaven	d				22 46															23 46		
Horsham [4]	a				22 49					23 04										23 49		
Balcombe	d														23 23							
Haywards Heath	a			22 33		22 40					23 03		23 06		23 28				23 33		23 40	
	d			22 33		22 41					23 03		23 07		23 28				23 33		23 41	
Wivelsfield	d					22 45									23 32						23 45	
Lewes [4]	a					22 58															23 58	
Burgess Hill [4]	d			22 38							23 08		23 12		23 34				23 38			
Hassocks [4]	d			22 42							23 12				23 38				23 42			
Preston Park	d														23 44							
Hove [2]	a												23 24									
Brighton [10]	a			22 52							23 22				23 48				23 52			

Table 186

Sundays

Bedford and London - Brighton

Network Diagram - see first Page of Table 186

		GW ■	GX ■	SN ■	FC ■	GX ■	SN ■	SN ◇■	GX ■	SN ◇■	FC ■	GX ■	SN
London Victoria [15] ⊖	d		23 00	23 04		23 15		23 17	23 30	23 32		23 45	23 47
Clapham Junction [10]	d			23 10				23 23		23 38			23 53
Bedford	d												
Luton [10]	d												
Luton Airport Parkway [7] ✈	d												
St Albans City	d												
St Pancras International [15] ⊖	d												
Farringdon [3] ⊖	d												
City Thameslink [3]	d												
London Blackfriars [3] ⊖	d												
London Bridge [4] ⊖	d				23 12						23 42		
New Cross Gate	d												
Norwood Junction [2]	d												
East Croydon ⇌	a			23 22	23 27			23 37		23 52	23 56		00 06
	d			23 22	23 27			23 38		23 53	23 57		
Purley [4]	d			23 29									
Coulsdon South	d			23 33									
Merstham	d			23 38									
Redhill	a			23 42						00 05			
	d	23 21		23 42						00 05			
Reigate	a												
Nutfield	d												
Godstone	d												
Edenbridge	d												
Penshurst	d												
Leigh (Kent)	d												
Tonbridge [4]	a												
Earlswood (Surrey)	d												
Salfords	d												
Horley [4]	d			23 50			←						
Gatwick Airport [10] ✈	a	23 31	23 35	23 54	23 48	23 50	23 54	23 59	00 05	00 14	00 18	00 20	
	d			23 55	23 50		23 55	00 01		00 15	00 19		
Three Bridges [15]	a			→	23 54		00 01	00 05		00 19	00 24		
	d				23 54		00 01	00 06		00 20			
Crawley	d						00 05						
Ifield	d						00 07						
Faygate	d												
Littlehaven	d						00 14						
Horsham [4]	a						00 17						
Balcombe	d									00 26			
Haywards Heath	a				00 03			00 15		00 31			
	d				00 03			00 15		00 31			
Wivelsfield	d									00 35			
Lewes [4]	a												
Burgess Hill [4]	d				00 08			00 20		00 37			
Hassocks [4]	d				00 12					00 41			
Preston Park	d									00 48			
Hove [2]	a							00 31					
Brighton [10]	a				00 22					00 52			

Brighton - London and Bedford

Network Diagram - see first Page of Table 186

Miles	Miles	Miles			SN MO 1	SN MX 1	SN MO 1	SN 1	SN MX 1	SN MO ◇1	SN MX ◇1	FC MX 1	FC MO 1	SN MO ◇1	SN 1	SN MX ◇1	SN 1	FC MX 1	FC MO 1	SN 1	GW MO 1	GW MX 1	SN
0	—	—	**Brighton** 10	d						23p02	23p02	23p11	23p14					23p37	23p45				
—	0	—	Hove 2	d																			
1½	1½	—	Preston Park	d						23p06	23p06							23p41					
7¼	—	—	Hassocks 4	d						23p12	23p12	23p20	23p23					23p47	23p53				
9¾	—	—	Burgess Hill 4	d						23p16	23p16	23p23	23p26					23p51	23p57				
—	—	—	Lewes 4	d																			
10	9¼	—	Wivelsfield 4	d						23p18	23p19							23p53					
13	—	—	**Haywards Heath** 3	a						23p23	23p23	23p28	23p31					23p58	00 02				
—	—	—		d						23p23	23p24	23p29	23p32					23p59	00 02				
17	—	—	Balcombe	d						23p29								00 04					
—	0	—	**Horsham** 4	d		23p02	23p03																
—	1	—	Littlehaven	d		23p05	23p06																
—	3¼	—	Faygate	d																			
—	5¾	—	Ifield	d		23p11	23p12																
—	7	—	Crawley	d		23p14	23p16							←		←							
21½	8½	—	Three Bridges 4	a		23p18	23p19			23p36	23p33	23p38	23p40	23p36		23p33		00 10	00 11				
—	—	—		d		23p18	23p20			23p41	23p47	23p38	23p40	23p41		23p47		00 10	00 11				
24¼	—	—	**Gatwick Airport** 10 ✈	a		23p22	23p24			→	→	23p42	23p44	23p45		23p52		00 14	00 15				
—	—	—		d		23p23	23p25	23p35				23p43	23p45	23p46	23p50	23p53	00 05	00 15	00 16	00 20			
25	—	—	Horley 4	d		23p26	23p28							23p49		23p56							
27¼	—	—	Salfords	d		23p30																	
29¼	—	—	Earlswood (Surrey)	d		23p33																	
—	—	0	**Tonbridge** 4	d																			
—	—	2½	Leigh (Kent)	d																			
—	—	4¼	Penshurst	d																			
—	—	9¼	Edenbridge	d																			
—	—	14	Godstone	d																			
—	—	17¾	Nutfield	d																			
—	0	—	**Reigate**	d					←												00 26	00 45	
30	1¾	19¾	**Redhill** 5	a		23p36	23p34		23p36					23p57		00 03		00 22	00 23		00 30	00 49	
—	—	—		d		23p37	23p35		23p37					00 01		00 03		00 23	00 23				
32	—	—	Merstham	d		→	23p39		23p41														
35½	—	—	Coulsdon South	d			23p44		23p46														
37½	—	—	Purley 4	d			23p50		23p49					00 11		00 11							
40½	0	—	**East Croydon**	a			23p55		23p54			00 01	00 02	00 16		00 16		00 35	00 35				
—	—	—		d	23p50		23p56		23p58			00 04	00 04	00 16		00 17		00 36	00 36				00 49
—	1¼	—	Norwood Junction 2	a																			
—	—	—	New Cross Gate	d																			
—	10¼	—	**London Bridge** 4 ⊖	a								00 19	00 19					00 52	00 52				
—	—	—	**London Blackfriars** 3 ⊖	a																			
—	—	—	City Thameslink 3	a																			
—	—	—	Farringdon 3 ⊖	a																			
—	—	—	St Pancras International 15 ⊖	a																			
—	—	—	St Albans City	a																			
—	—	—	Luton Airport Parkway 4 ✈	a																			
—	—	—	Luton 7	a																			
—	—	—	**Bedford** 10	a																			
48¼	0	0	Clapham Junction 10	a	00 01		00 11		00 11					00 29		00 29							01 01
—	—	—		d	00 02		00 12		00 12					00 30		00 30							01 01
51	—	—	**London Victoria** 15 ⊖	a	00 08		00 19	00 10	00 18					00 37	00 25	00 37	00 40			00 55			01 09

Brighton - London and Bedford

Network Diagram - see first Page of Table 186

		GX 1	GX 1	SN 1	FC 1	GX 1	SN 1	FC 1	SN 1	FC 1	FC	SN 1	SN	GX 1	FC 1	GX 1	FC 1	GW 1	GW 1	SN 1	FC 1	SN 1	GX 1
Brighton 10	d																				05 10		
Hove 2	d																						
Preston Park	d																				05 14		
Hassocks 4	d																				05 20		
Burgess Hill 4	d																				05 24		
Lewes 4	d																						
Wivelsfield 4	d																				05 26		
Haywards Heath 3	a																				05 30		
	d																				05 31		
Balcombe	d																				05 36		
Horsham 4	d																			05 17			
Littlehaven	d																			05 20			
Faygate	d																						
Ifield	d																			05 26			
Crawley	d																			05 29			
Three Bridges 4	a																			05 33	05 42		
	d				01 25		01 59	02 25	02 59	03 25	04 25				04 55					05 33	05 42		
Gatwick Airport 10 ✈	a				01 29		02 03	02 29	03 03	03 29	04 29				04 59					05 37	05 46		
	d	00 36	00 50	01 05	01 30	01 35	02 05	02 30	03 05	03 30	04 30			04 35	05 00	05 20	05 27		05 31	05 38	05 47		05 50
Horley 4	d			01 07			02 07		03 07											05 40			
Salfords	d																						
Earlswood (Surrey)	d																						
Tonbridge 4	d											04 59										05 20	
Leigh (Kent)	d											05 03										05 24	
Penshurst	d											05 07										05 28	
Edenbridge	d											05 13										05 34	
Godstone	d											05 20										05 41	
Nutfield	d											05 25										05 46	
Reigate	d																	05 34					
Redhill 5	a											05 30					05 34	05 39	05 41	05 47		05 51	
	d																05 35			05 48			
Merstham	d																			05 52			
Coulsdon South	d																			05 57			
Purley 4	d			01 22			02 22		03 22											06 00			
East Croydon	a			01 27	01 49		02 27	02 47	03 27	03 47	04 47				05 17		05 47			06 06	06 01		
	d			01 28	01 49		02 28	02 47	03 28	03 47	04 47				05 17		05 47			06 06	06 02		
Norwood Junction 2	a																			→			
New Cross Gate	d																						
London Bridge 4 ⊖	a				02 14			03 12		04 12					05 34		06 02				06 15		
London Blackfriars 3 ⊖	a										05 13				05 41		06 10				06 23		
City Thameslink 3	a										05 16				05 44		06 14				06 26		
Farringdon 3 ⊖	a										05 20				05 47		06 18				06 30		
St Pancras International 15 ⊖	a										05 24				05 52		06 22				06 34		
St Albans City	a										05 57				06 23		06 43				06 57		
Luton Airport Parkway 4 ✈	a										06 09				06 35		06 55				07 09		
Luton 7	a										06 12				06 38		06 58				07 12		
Bedford 10	a										06 39				07 04		07 24				07 40		
Clapham Junction 10	a			01 40			02 40		03 40														
	d			01 41			02 41		03 41				05 02										
London Victoria 15 ⊖	a	01 11	01 25	01 49		02 10	02 49		03 49				05 10	05 12		05 55							06 20

Brighton - London and Bedford

Network Diagram - see first Page of Table 186

		SN 1	SN	GW 1	SN ◇1	SN 1	SN 1	GX 1 ⊼	FC 1	GX 1 ⊼	GW 1	FC 1	SN 1	FC 1	SN 1	SN 1	GX 1 ⊼	SN 1	SN 1	SN 1	SN 1	SN 1	FC 1
Brighton 10	d		05 23						05 40			05 50						06 01					06 08
Hove 2	d												05 57										
Preston Park	d								05 44			05 54											06 12
Hassocks 4	d								05 50			06 00						06 09					06 19
Burgess Hill 4	d		05 33						05 54			06 04						06 13					06 23
Lewes 4	d				05 29														06 05				
Wivelsfield 4	d								05 56			06 06						06 15					06 25
Haywards Heath 3	a		05 38		05 46				06 00			06 10	06 12					06 19	06 23				06 30
	d		05 39		05 47				06 01			06 11	06 13					06 27					06 30
Balcombe	d		05 44						06 06														06 36
Horsham 4	d						05 38									06 10							
Littlehaven	d						05 41									06 13							
Faygate	d																						
Ifield	d						05 47									06 19							
Crawley	d						05 50									06 23							
Three Bridges 4	a		05 50				05 54		06 12			06 19	06 21			06 26		06 36					06 41
	d		05 50				05 54		06 12			06 20	06 22			06 27		06 37					06 42
Gatwick Airport 10 ✈	a		05 54		05 58		05 58		06 16			06 24	06 26			06 31		06 41					06 46
	d		05 55	05 56	05 59		05 59	06 06	06 17	06 20		06 25	06 27			06 32	06 35	06 42					06 47
Horley 4	d						06 02									06 35							
Salfords	d						06 06									06 39							
Earlswood (Surrey)	d						06 09									06 42							
Tonbridge 4	d														06 10								
Leigh (Kent)	d														06 14								
Penshurst	d														06 18								
Edenbridge	d														06 24								
Godstone	d														06 31								
Nutfield	d														06 36								
Reigate	d										06 24											06 49	
Redhill 5	a			06 07			06 12				06 29	06 32			06 42	06 46						06 53	06 54
	d						06 13					06 33			06 43	06 46							06 56
Merstham	d						06 17									06 50							
Coulsdon South	d						06 22								06 50	06 55							
Purley 4	d	←					06 25							←	06 54	06 59				←	←		
East Croydon ⇌	a	06 06	06 10		06 14		06 30		06 32			06 44	06 41	06 44	06 59	07 04		06 58		06 59	07 04		07 08
	d	06 06	06 11		06 15	06 27	06 31		06 32			06 44	06 42	06 44	07 00	07 05		06 59		07 00	07 05		07 09
Norwood Junction 2	a											→			→	→							
New Cross Gate	d																						
London Bridge 4 ⊖	a								06 46					06 58				07 14		07 16			07 23
London Blackfriars 3 ⊖	a								06 52					07 04									07 30
City Thameslink 3	a								06 54					07 08									07 32
Farringdon 3 ⊖	a								06 58					07 12									07 36
St Pancras International 15 ⊖	a								07 02					07 16									07 40
St Albans City	a								07 22					07 41									
Luton Airport Parkway 4 ✈	a								07 34					07 53									08 06
Luton 7	a								07 37					07 57									08 10
Bedford 10	a								08 03					08 23									
Clapham Junction 10	a	06 18	06 21		06 25	06 38	06 41						06 51								07 16		
	d	06 18	06 21		06 25	06 38	06 41						06 51								07 17		
London Victoria 15 ⊖	a	06 25	06 28		06 32	06 45	06 48	06 35		06 50			07 00				07 05				07 25		

Brighton - London and Bedford

Network Diagram - see first Page of Table 186

		GX 1 ⊼	SN ◇1 A	SN ◇1	GW 1	SN 1	FC 1	SN 1	SN 1 ⊼	SN 1	SN 1	SN 1	SN 1	SN ◇1 ⊼	SN 1	SN 1 ⊼	GW 1	SN 1	SN 1	SN ◇1 ⊼	SN ◇1 B ⊼	SN 1
Brighton 10	d		06 17				06 24		06 30				06 37			06 40				06 51		
Hove 2	d											06 31										
Preston Park	d						06 28						06 41			06 44						
Hassocks 4	d		06 26				06 35					06 43				06 52						
Burgess Hill 4	d		06 30				06 39		06 43			06 47				06 56				07 01		
Lewes 4	d																					
Wivelsfield 4	d								06 46				06 52									
Haywards Heath 3	a		06 35				06 44		06 50			06 53	06 56			07 01				07 06		
	d		06 36				06 45		06 51			07 00				07 03				07 07		
Balcombe	d						06 51															
Horsham 4	d			06 24				06 38						06 50							07 04	
Littlehaven	d			06 27				06 41						06 53								
Faygate	d							06 45														
Ifield	d			06 33				06 49						07 00								
Crawley	d			06 37				06 52						07 04							07 13	
Three Bridges 4	a		06 45	06 40			06 56	06 56						07 07						07 16	07 18	
	d		06 48				06 57	06 56			07 04			07 08				07 14		07 22		
Gatwick Airport 10 ✈	a		06 52				07 01	07 01	07 04		07 08	07 11		07 12		07 15		07 21				
	d	06 50	06 53		06 58		07 02	07 02	07 06		07 09	07 12		07 14		07 20		07 22				
Horley 4	d		06 56					07 04			07 12			07 16				07 25				
Salfords	d							07 08			07 16							07 29				
Earlswood (Surrey)	d							07 12			07 19							07 32				
Tonbridge 4	d									06 47												
Leigh (Kent)	d									06 51												
Penshurst	d									06 55												
Edenbridge	d									07 01												
Godstone	d									07 08												
Nutfield	d									07 13												
Reigate	d																07 18		07 27			
Redhill 5	a		07 02		07 07		07 10	07 15		07 18	07 22						07 24	07 36	07 31			
	d		07 03				07 11	07 15			07 23							07 40				
Merstham	d							07 19			07 27							07 44				
Coulsdon South	d							07 25			07 33							07 50				
Purley 4	d							07 29			07 37				←			07 55				←
East Croydon ⇌	a		07 14				07 22	07 34			07 41	07 26		07 31	07 34			08 01		07 38		07 41
	d		07 15			07 15	07 23	07 35			07 42	07 28		07 31	07 35			08 02		07 39		07 42
Norwood Junction 2	a							→			→							→				
New Cross Gate	d																					
London Bridge 4 ⊖	a											07 43			07 51							
London Blackfriars 3 ⊖	a						07 51															
City Thameslink 3	a						07 56															
Farringdon 3 ⊖	a						08 00															
St Pancras International 15 ⊖	a						08 04															
St Albans City	a						08 24															
Luton Airport Parkway 4 ✈	a						08 37															
Luton 7	a						08 40															
Bedford 10	a						09 05															
Clapham Junction 10	a		07 24			07 27								07 40						07 48		07 51
	d		07 24			07 27								07 41						07 48		07 51
London Victoria 15 ⊖	a	07 20	07 33			07 36			07 37					07 49		07 50				07 57		08 00

A ◇ from Three Bridges

B ⊼ from Three Bridges

Brighton - London and Bedford

Network Diagram - see first Page of Table 186

		SN 1	SN 1	GW 1	SN 1	SN 1	SN 1 🚲	FC 1	SN 1	SN 1	SN ◇1 🚲	SN 1	SN 1	SN 1	SN 1	SN 1	SN 1	SN 1	SN 1 🚲	SN ◇1	SN 1	SN ◇1 🚲
Brighton 10	d						06 56	07 02											07 14			
Hove 2	d								07 11											07 21		
Preston Park	d						07 00	07 06											07 19			
Hassocks 4	d							07 13	07 20											07 30		
Burgess Hill 4	d						07 10	07 17											07 28			
Lewes 4	d	06 51																				07 22
Wivelsfield 4	d	07 08					07 14	07 20	07 25											07 35		07 39
Haywards Heath 3	a	07 12					07 18	07 24	07 30										07 34	07 40		07 44
	d	07 13					07 20	07 25	07 31										07 35	07 40		07 44
Balcombe	d	07 19																				
Horsham 4	d				07 09					07 17	07 25											
Littlehaven	d				07 12					07 20	07 29											
Faygate	d				07 16																	
Ifield	d				07 20					07 27												
Crawley	d				07 23					07 31	07 37											
Three Bridges 4	a	07 24			07 27			07 33		07 34	07 40											
	d	07 25			07 28			07 34		07 35	07 41											
Gatwick Airport 10 ✈	a	07 29			07 32		07 32	07 38		07 39									07 47			
	d	07 30			07 33		07 35	07 39		07 40							07 44		07 50			
Horley 4	d				07 36					07 43							07 47					07 58
Salfords	d				07 40					07 47							07 51					
Earlswood (Surrey)	d				07 43					07 50							07 54					
Tonbridge 4	d																	07 25				
Leigh (Kent)	d																	07 29				
Penshurst	d																	07 33				
Edenbridge	d																	07 39				
Godstone	d																	07 46				
Nutfield	d																	07 51				
Reigate	d			07 34		07 40										07 52						
Redhill 5	a			07 38	07 47	07 45				07 53						07 56	07 58	07 56				
	d				07 51					07 54							08 02					
Merstham	d									07 59							08 06					
Coulsdon South	d									08 04							08 11					
Purley 4	d											←	←	←	←		08 15				←	
East Croydon	a	07 45			08 02			07 53	07 56	08 11	07 59	08 01	08 01	08 02	08 02		08 20			08 08	08 11	08 13
	d	07 46	07 45		08 03			07 54	07 57	08 11	08 01	08 02	08 02	08 03	08 03		08 21			08 08	08 11	08 13
Norwood Junction 2	a				→					→							→					
New Cross Gate	d																					
London Bridge 4 ⊖	a	08 01							08 13			08 19	08 19	08 21	08 21							
London Blackfriars 3 ⊖	a							08 20														
City Thameslink 3	a							08 23														
Farringdon 3 ⊖	a							08 27														
St Pancras International 15 ⊖	a							08 31														
St Albans City	a							08 51														
Luton Airport Parkway 4 ✈	a							09 00														
Luton 7	a							09 04														
Bedford 10	a							09 26														
Clapham Junction 10	a		07 55								08 10									08 17	08 20	08 23
	d		07 56								08 11									08 18	08 21	08 24
London Victoria 15 ⊖	a		08 04				08 06				08 19								08 20	08 26	08 29	08 32

Table 186

Brighton - London and Bedford

Network Diagram - see first Page of Table 186

		SN 1	SN 1	GW 1	FC 1	SN 1 🚲	SN 1	SN 1	SN 1	SN 1	SN ◇1	SN 1	SN 1	GX 1 🚲	SN 1 🚲	SN 1	FC 1	SN ◇1 🚲	GW 1	GX 1 🚲	SN ◇1 🚲	SN 1
Brighton 10	d				07 24	07 29			07 33						07 44		07 50					
Hove 2	d										07 41											
Preston Park	d				07 28				07 37						07 48		07 54					
Hassocks 4	d				07 35	07 39									07 56		08 01					
Burgess Hill 4	d				07 39				07 47		07 52				08 00							
Lewes 4	d											07 42									07 55	
Wivelsfield 4	d					07 46			07 49												08 11	
Haywards Heath 3	a				07 46	07 50			07 54		07 58	08 03			08 05		08 09				08 16	
	d				07 47	07 51			07 54		07 59	08 04			08 06		08 09				08 16	
Balcombe	d								08 00								08 15				08 22	
Horsham 4	d							07 40		07 46			07 51					08 09				
Littlehaven	d							07 43		07 49			07 54									
Faygate	d												07 58									
Ifield	d							07 50		07 56			08 02									
Crawley	d							07 53		08 00			08 06					08 18				
Three Bridges 4	a				07 55			07 57	08 05	08 05			08 09					08 22			08 28	
	d				07 56			07 58	08 06	08 06			08 10					08 22			08 28	
Gatwick Airport 10 ✈	a				08 00	08 02		08 04			08 12		08 14		08 18		08 23					
	d			07 58	08 01	08 05		08 05			08 13		08 15	08 18	08 20		08 24			08 35		
Horley 4	d							08 07					08 18					08 28				
Salfords	d							08 11					08 22									
Earlswood (Surrey)	d							08 15					08 25									
Tonbridge 4	d																					
Leigh (Kent)	d																					
Penshurst	d																					
Edenbridge	d																					
Godstone	d																					
Nutfield	d																					
Reigate	d						08 09												08 24			
Redhill 5	a			08 05	08 08		08 13	08 18					08 28						08 30			
	d				08 09			08 18					08 29									
Merstham	d							08 22														
Coulsdon South	d							08 27					08 36									
Purley 4	d		←					08 31								←						←
East Croydon	a		08 20		08 22			08 36	08 24	08 27	08 29	08 31	08 50			08 36	08 38	08 43			08 46	08 50
	d	08 15	08 21		08 23			08 37	08 25	08 27	08 30	08 33	08 51			08 37	08 39	08 43			08 50	08 51
Norwood Junction 2	a							→					→									
New Cross Gate	d																					
London Bridge 4 ⊖	a		08 37						08 40	08 45		08 51										09 06
London Blackfriars 3 ⊖	a				08 53												09 09					
City Thameslink 3	a				08 56												09 12					
Farringdon 3 ⊖	a				09 00												09 16					
St Pancras International 15 ⊖	a				09 04												09 20					
St Albans City	a				09 25												09 40					
Luton Airport Parkway 4 ✈	a				09 37												09 51					
Luton 7	a				09 40												09 54					
Bedford 10	a				10 08												10 20					
Clapham Junction 10	a	08 26									08 39					08 48		08 52			09 00	
	d	08 27									08 40					08 48		08 53			09 01	
London Victoria 15 ⊖	a	08 35				08 35					08 48			08 50	08 52	08 56		09 01		09 05	09 09	

Table 186

Mondays to Fridays

Brighton - London and Bedford

Network Diagram - see first Page of Table 186

		SN 1	SN 1	GW 1	SN 1	SN 1	FC 1	SN ◇1	SN 1	SN 1	SN ◇1 H	FC 1	SN 1	SN 1	SN 1	SN ◇1 H	GX 1 H	SN 1	SN ◇1 H	GW 1	FC 1	SN 1	SN 1
Brighton 10	d						08 02				08 13	08 16									08 34	08 45	
Hove 2	d							08 08															
Preston Park	d						08 06	08 12				08 20									08 38		
Hassocks 4	d						08 13	08 19				08 27									08 44		
Burgess Hill 4	d						08 17	08 23				08 31									08 48		
Lewes 4	d															08 23							
Wivelsfield 4	d						08 20					08 34				08 39					08 50		
Haywards Heath 3	a						08 24	08 28				08 38				08 44					08 55	08 58	
	d						08 25	08 29				08 39				08 44					09 00	08 58	
Balcombe	d																				09 06		
Horsham 4	d				08 12									08 35					08 49				
Littlehaven	d				08 15									08 38									
Faygate	d				08 19																		
Ifield	d				08 23									08 44									
Crawley	d				08 26									08 47					08 58				
Three Bridges 4	a				08 29		08 33	08 38				08 47		08 51					09 01		09 11		
	d				08 30		08 34	08 39				08 48		08 51					09 02		09 12		
Gatwick Airport 10 ✈	a				08 34		08 38				08 46	08 52		08 55		08 56			09 06		09 16	09 09	
	d				08 35		08 39				08 50	08 53		08 56		08 57	09 05		09 07	09 07	09 17	09 10	
Horley 4	d				08 38									08 59		08 59							
Salfords	d				08 42									09 03									
Earlswood (Surrey)	d				08 45									09 06									
Tonbridge 4	d	07 59				08 16									08 37								
Leigh (Kent)	d	08 03				08 20									08 41								
Penshurst	d	08 07				08 24									08 45								
Edenbridge	d	08 13				08 30									08 51								
Godstone	d	08 20				08 37									08 58								
Nutfield	d	08 25				08 42									09 03								
Reigate	d		08 27	08 42																			
Redhill 5	a	08 34	08 32	08 46	08 49	08 47								09 10	09 08					09 15			
	d		08 38			08 53									09 14								
Merstham	d		08 43			08 57									09 18								
Coulsdon South	d		08 48			09 02									09 23								
Purley 4	d		08 52			09 05			←	←			←										←
East Croydon	a		08 58			09 10	08 53	08 57	08 58	08 58		09 08	09 10		09 30	09 14			09 22		09 32	09 25	09 30
	d		08 59			09 11	08 54	08 58	08 59	08 59		09 09	09 11		09 31	09 14		09 14	09 23		09 32	09 26	09 31
Norwood Junction 2	a		→			→									→						→		
New Cross Gate	d																						
London Bridge 4 ⊖	a						09 08		09 15	09 15													
London Blackfriars 3 ⊖	a						09 21					09 37											
City Thameslink 3	a						09 24					09 40											
Farringdon 3 ⊖	a						09 27					09 44											
St Pancras International 15 ⊖	a						09 32					09 48											
St Albans City	a						09 51					10 10											
Luton Airport Parkway 4 ✈	a						10 00					10 21											
Luton 7	a						10 03					10 24											
Bedford 10	a						10 24					10 50											
Clapham Junction 10	a							09 07					09 20			09 23		09 26	09 32			09 36	09 41
	d							09 08					09 21			09 24		09 27	09 33			09 36	09 41
London Victoria 15 ⊖	a							09 16			09 20		09 27			09 32	09 35	09 35	09 42			09 43	09 50

Table 186

Mondays to Fridays

Brighton - London and Bedford

Network Diagram - see first Page of Table 186

		SN 1	FC 1	SN 1	GX 1 H	SN ◇1 H	GW 1	SN 1	SN ◇1	GW 1	SN 1	FC 1	GX 1 H	SN ◇1 H	FC 1	SN ◇1 H	SN 1	SN ◇1 H	FC 1	SN 1	GX 1 H	SN
Brighton 10	d											09 00			09 07	09 19						
Hove 2	d								08 52													
Preston Park	d								08 57						09 11							
Hassocks 4	d								09 04			09 09			09 17							
Burgess Hill 4	d								09 08			09 12			09 21							
Lewes 4	d					08 48																
Wivelsfield 4	d					09 01									09 23							
Haywards Heath 3	a					09 05			09 13			09 17			09 28							
	d					09 08			09 14			09 18			09 32							
Balcombe	d														09 37							
Horsham 4	d							09 00						09 20								
Littlehaven	d							09 03														
Faygate	d																					
Ifield	d							09 09														
Crawley	d							09 13						09 29								
Three Bridges 4	a					09 17		09 16				09 26		09 32	09 43							
	d					09 17		09 18				09 27		09 33	09 43							
Gatwick Airport 10 ✈	a					09 22		09 22	09 26			09 31		09 37	09 47							
	d				09 20	09 23		09 23	09 27			09 32	09 35	09 38	09 47						09 50	
Horley 4	d							09 26						09 41								
Salfords	d							09 30														
Earlswood (Surrey)	d							09 33														
Tonbridge 4	d																			09 19		
Leigh (Kent)	d																			09 23		
Penshurst	d																			09 27		
Edenbridge	d																			09 33		
Godstone	d																			09 40		
Nutfield	d																			09 45		
Reigate	d			09 14			09 24			09 37												
Redhill 5	a			09 18			09 30	09 36		09 42				09 47						09 50		
	d			09 19				09 37						09 48						09 51		
Merstham	d			09 23				09 41														
Coulsdon South	d			09 28				09 46												09 58		
Purley 4	d	←	←	09 32				09 49									←	←	←	10 02		
East Croydon	a	09 30	09 32	09 37		09 38		09 54	09 42			09 46		09 59	10 02	09 52	09 54	09 59	10 02	10 07		
	d	09 31	09 32	09 37		09 39		09 55	09 43		09 44	09 47		10 00	10 02	09 53	09 55	10 00	10 02	10 07		
Norwood Junction 2	a			09 41				→						→	→		09 59			10 12		
New Cross Gate	d																10 07					
London Bridge 4 ⊖	a		09 46	09 55								10 00					10 13		10 15	10 25		
London Blackfriars 3 ⊖	a		09 53									10 08							10 23			
City Thameslink 3	a		09 56									10 10							10 26			
Farringdon 3 ⊖	a		10 00									10 14							10 30			
St Pancras International 15 ⊖	a		10 04									10 18							10 34			
St Albans City	a		10 23									10 38							10 54			
Luton Airport Parkway 4 ✈	a		10 37									10 50							11 06			
Luton 7	a		10 40									10 53							11 09			
Bedford 10	a		11 05									11 19							11 35			
Clapham Junction 10	a	09 41				09 48			09 52		09 55					10 02		10 09				
	d	09 41				09 48			09 52		09 56					10 03		10 09				10 11
London Victoria 15 ⊖	a	09 50			09 50	09 58			09 59		10 05		10 05			10 11		10 16			10 20	10 20

Brighton - London and Bedford

Network Diagram - see first Page of Table 186

		SN ◇1	SN 1	SN ◇1 ✕	SN ◇1 A ✕	SN 1	FC 1	GW 1	GX 1 ✕	SN ◇1	FC 1	SN ◇1 ✕	SN 1	SN ◇1	FC 1	SN 1	GW 1	GX 1 ✕	SN 1	SN ◇1 ✕	SN ◇1 A ✕	GW 1
Brighton 10	d	09 25					09 34				09 37	09 49										
Hove 2	d				09 22																09 51	
Preston Park	d										09 41										09 55	
Hassocks 4	d	09 34			09 31						09 47											
Burgess Hill 4	d	09 38									09 51										10 04	
Lewes 4	d			09 18																09 48		
Wivelsfield 4	d			09 34							09 53											
Haywards Heath 3	a			09 38	09 40		09 47				09 58									10 07	10 10	
	d			09 44			09 48				10 02									10 14		
Balcombe	d																					
Horsham 4	d		09 30							09 51									10 00			
Littlehaven	d		09 33																10 03			
Faygate	d		09 37																			
Ifield	d		09 41																10 09			
Crawley	d		09 44							10 00									10 13			
Three Bridges 4	a		09 48				09 56			10 03	10 11								10 16			
	d		09 48				09 57			10 04	10 12								10 18			
Gatwick Airport 10 ✈	a	09 51	09 53	09 56			10 01			10 08	10 16								10 22	10 25		
	d	09 53	09 54	09 57			10 02	10 03	10 05	10 09	10 17							10 20	10 23	10 26		
Horley 4	d		09 56																10 26			
Salfords	d																		10 30			
Earlswood (Surrey)	d																		10 33			
Tonbridge 4	d																					
Leigh (Kent)	d																					
Penshurst	d																					
Edenbridge	d																					
Godstone	d																					
Nutfield	d																					
Reigate	d															10 14	10 19					10 34
Redhill 5	a		10 03					10 10		10 16						10 18	10 25		10 36			10 38
	d		10 07							10 17						10 20			10 37			
Merstham	d		10 11													10 24			10 41			
Coulsdon South	d		10 16													10 29			10 46			
Purley 4	d		10 19										←	←	←	10 33			10 49			
East Croydon	a	10 08	10 24	10 11			10 16			10 28	10 31	10 22	10 24	10 28	10 31	10 38			10 54	10 41		
	d	10 08	10 25	10 12		10 14	10 17			10 28	10 32	10 23	10 25	10 28	10 32	10 38			10 55	10 42		
Norwood Junction 2	a		→							→	→		10 29			10 42			→			
New Cross Gate	d												10 37									
London Bridge 4 ⊖	a						10 30						10 43		10 45	10 55						
London Blackfriars 3 ⊖	a						10 37								10 52							
City Thameslink 3	a						10 40								10 56							
Farringdon 3 ⊖	a						10 44								11 00							
St Pancras International 15 ⊖	a						10 48								11 04							
St Albans City	a						11 10								11 23							
Luton Airport Parkway 4 ✈	a						11 21								11 37							
Luton 7	a						11 24								11 40							
Bedford 10	a						11 50								12 05							
Clapham Junction 10	a	10 17		10 21		10 25						10 32		10 37						10 51		
	d	10 18		10 21		10 26						10 33		10 38						10 51		
London Victoria 15 ⊖	a	10 26		10 28		10 35			10 35			10 41		10 45				10 50		10 58		

A ✕ from Haywards Heath

Brighton - London and Bedford

Network Diagram - see first Page of Table 186

		SN 1	FC 1	GX 1 ✕	SN ◇1	FC 1	SN ◇1 ✕	SN 1	SN ◇1	FC 1	SN 1	GX 1 ✕	SN ◇1	SN 1	SN ◇1	SN ◇1	SN 1	FC 1	GW 1	GX 1 ✕	SN ◇1	FC 1	SN ◇1 ✕
Brighton 10	d		10 04			10 07	10 19						10 25					10 34				10 37	10 49
Hove 2	d														10 21								
Preston Park	d					10 11																10 41	
Hassocks 4	d					10 17							10 34									10 47	
Burgess Hill 4	d					10 21							10 38									10 51	
Lewes 4	d															10 19							
Wivelsfield 4	d					10 23										10 35						10 53	
Haywards Heath 3	a		10 17			10 28									10 35	10 40		10 47				10 58	
	d		10 18			10 32									10 44			10 48				11 02	
Balcombe	d					10 37																	
Horsham 4	d				10 20									10 30							10 50		
Littlehaven	d													10 33									
Faygate	d																						
Ifield	d													10 39									
Crawley	d				10 29									10 43							10 59		
Three Bridges 4	a		10 26		10 32	10 43								10 46				10 56			11 02	11 11	
	d		10 27		10 33	10 43								10 48				10 57			11 03	11 12	
Gatwick Airport 10 ✈	a		10 31		10 37	10 47							10 51	10 52	10 55			11 01			11 07	11 16	
	d		10 32	10 35	10 38	10 47						10 50	10 53	10 53	10 56			11 02	11 03	11 05	11 08	11 17	
Horley 4	d				10 41									10 56									
Salfords	d																						
Earlswood (Surrey)	d																						
Tonbridge 4	d										10 19												
Leigh (Kent)	d										10 23												
Penshurst	d										10 27												
Edenbridge	d										10 33												
Godstone	d										10 40												
Nutfield	d										10 45												
Reigate	d																						
Redhill 5	a				10 47						10 50			11 02					11 10		11 15		
	d				10 48						10 51			11 07							11 16		
Merstham	d													11 11									
Coulsdon South	d										10 58			11 16									
Purley 4	d							←	←	←	11 01			11 19									
East Croydon	a		10 46		10 59	11 02	10 52	10 54	10 59	11 02	11 06		11 08	11 24	11 11			11 16			11 27	11 31	11 22
	d	10 44	10 47		11 00	11 02	10 53	10 55	11 00	11 02	11 07		11 08	11 25	11 12		11 14	11 17			11 28	11 32	11 23
Norwood Junction 2	a				→	→		10 59			11 12			→							→	→	
New Cross Gate	d							11 07															
London Bridge 4 ⊖	a		11 00					11 13		11 15	11 25							11 30					
London Blackfriars 3 ⊖	a		11 07							11 22								11 37					
City Thameslink 3	a		11 10							11 26								11 40					
Farringdon 3 ⊖	a		11 14							11 30								11 44					
St Pancras International 15 ⊖	a		11 18							11 34								11 48					
St Albans City	a		11 38							11 53								12 08					
Luton Airport Parkway 4 ✈	a		11 50							12 07								12 20					
Luton 7	a		11 53							12 10								12 23					
Bedford 10	a		12 19							12 35								12 49					
Clapham Junction 10	a	10 55					11 02		11 09				11 17		11 21		11 25						11 32
	d	10 56					11 03		11 10				11 18		11 21		11 26						11 33
London Victoria 15 ⊖	a	11 05		11 05			11 10		11 16			11 20	11 24		11 28		11 32			11 35			11 40

Table 186

Mondays to Fridays

Brighton - London and Bedford

Network Diagram - see first Page of Table 186

		SN 1	SN ◇1		FC 1	SN 1	GW 1	GX 1	SN 1	SN ◇1	SN ◇1	GW 1	SN 1		FC 1	GX 1	SN ◇1	FC 1	SN ◇1	SN 1	SN ◇1	FC 1	SN 1		GX 1
Brighton 10	d														11 04			11 07	11 19						
Hove 2	d										10 51														
Preston Park	d										10 55							11 11							
Hassocks 4	d																	11 17							
Burgess Hill 4	d										11 04							11 21							
Lewes 4	d									10 50															
Wivelsfield 4	d																	11 23							
Haywards Heath 3	a									11 05	11 09				11 17			11 28							
	d									11 13					11 18			11 32							
Balcombe	d																	11 37							
Horsham 4	d								11 00								11 20								
Littlehaven	d								11 03																
Faygate	d																								
Ifield	d								11 09																
Crawley	d								11 13								11 29								
Three Bridges 4	a								11 16						11 26		11 32	11 43							
	d								11 18						11 27		11 33	11 43							
Gatwick Airport 10 ✈	a								11 22	11 24					11 31		11 37	11 47							
	d							11 20	11 23	11 25					11 32	11 35	11 38	11 47							11 50
Horley 4	d								11 26								11 41								
Salfords	d								11 30																
Earlswood (Surrey)	d								11 33																
Tonbridge 4	d																						11 19		
Leigh (Kent)	d																						11 23		
Penshurst	d																						11 27		
Edenbridge	d																						11 33		
Godstone	d																						11 40		
Nutfield	d																						11 45		
Reigate	d					11 14	11 19					11 34													
Redhill 5	a					11 18	11 25		11 36			11 38					11 47						11 50		
	d					11 19			11 37								11 48						11 51		
Merstham	d					11 23			11 41																
Coulsdon South	d					11 28			11 46														11 58		
Purley 4	d	←	←		←	11 32			11 49											←	←	←	12 02		
East Croydon ⇌	a	11 24	11 27		11 31	11 37			11 54	11 40					11 46		11 59	12 02	11 52	11 54	11 59	12 02	12 07		
	d	11 25	11 28		11 32	11 37			11 55	11 41			11 44		11 47		12 00	12 02	11 53	11 55	12 00	12 02	12 07		
Norwood Junction 2	a	11 29				11 42			→								→	→		11 59			12 12		
New Cross Gate	d	11 37																		12 07					
London Bridge 4 ⊖	a	11 43			11 45	11 55									12 00					12 13		12 15	12 25		
London Blackfriars 3 ⊖	a				11 52										12 07							12 22			
City Thameslink 3	a				11 56										12 10							12 26			
Farringdon 3 ⊖	a				12 00										12 14							12 30			
St Pancras International 15 ⊖	a				12 04										12 18							12 34			
St Albans City	a				12 24										12 38							12 53			
Luton Airport Parkway 4 ✈	a				12 37										12 50							13 06			
Luton 7	a				12 40										12 53							13 09			
Bedford 10	a				13 05										13 19							13 35			
Clapham Junction 10	a		11 37							11 50			11 55						12 02		12 09				
	d		11 37							11 50			11 56						12 03		12 12				
London Victoria 15 ⊖	a		11 44					11 50		11 57			12 02			12 05			12 10		12 18				12 20

Table 186

Mondays to Fridays

Brighton - London and Bedford

Network Diagram - see first Page of Table 186

		SN ◇1	SN 1	SN ◇1	SN ◇1	SN 1	FC 1	GW 1	GX 1		SN ◇1	FC 1	SN ◇1	SN 1	SN ◇1	FC 1	SN 1	GW 1	GX 1		SN 1	SN ◇1	SN ◇1	GW 1	SN 1
Brighton 10	d	11 25					11 34					11 37	11 49												
Hove 2	d			11 21																			11 51		
Preston Park	d											11 41											11 55		
Hassocks 4	d	11 34										11 47													
Burgess Hill 4	d	11 38										11 51											12 04		
Lewes 4	d				11 20																	11 50			
Wivelsfield 4	d				11 35							11 53													
Haywards Heath 3	a			11 35	11 40		11 47					11 58										12 05	12 09		
	d			11 44			11 48					12 02										12 13			
Balcombe	d																								
Horsham 4	d		11 30								11 50										12 00				
Littlehaven	d		11 33																		12 03				
Faygate	d																								
Ifield	d		11 39																		12 09				
Crawley	d		11 43								11 59										12 13				
Three Bridges 4	a		11 46				11 56				12 02	12 11									12 16				
	d		11 48				11 57				12 03	12 12									12 18				
Gatwick Airport 10 ✈	a	11 51	11 52	11 55			12 01				12 07	12 16									12 22	12 24			
	d	11 53	11 53	11 56			12 02	12 03	12 05		12 08	12 17							12 20		12 23	12 25			
Horley 4	d		11 56																		12 26				
Salfords	d																				12 30				
Earlswood (Surrey)	d																				12 33				
Tonbridge 4	d																								
Leigh (Kent)	d																								
Penshurst	d																								
Edenbridge	d																								
Godstone	d																								
Nutfield	d																								
Reigate	d																12 14	12 19						12 34	
Redhill 5	a		12 02					12 10			12 15						12 18	12 25			12 36			12 38	
	d		12 07								12 16						12 19				12 37				
Merstham	d		12 11														12 23				12 41				
Coulsdon South	d		12 16														12 28				12 46				
Purley 4	d		12 19											←	←	←	12 32				12 49				
East Croydon ⇌	a	12 08	12 24	12 11			12 16				12 27	12 31	12 22	12 24	12 27	12 31	12 37				12 54	12 40			
	d	12 08	12 25	12 12		12 14	12 17				12 28	12 32	12 23	12 25	12 28	12 32	12 37				12 55	12 41			12 44
Norwood Junction 2	a		→								→	→		12 29			12 42				→				
New Cross Gate	d													12 37											
London Bridge 4 ⊖	a						12 30							12 43		12 45	12 55								
London Blackfriars 3 ⊖	a						12 37									12 52									
City Thameslink 3	a						12 40									12 56									
Farringdon 3 ⊖	a						12 44									13 00									
St Pancras International 15 ⊖	a						12 48									13 04									
St Albans City	a						13 08									13 24									
Luton Airport Parkway 4 ✈	a						13 20									13 37									
Luton 7	a						13 23									13 40									
Bedford 10	a						13 49									14 05									
Clapham Junction 10	a	12 17		12 21		12 25							12 32		12 37							12 50			12 55
	d	12 18		12 22		12 26							12 33		12 37							12 50			12 56
London Victoria 15 ⊖	a	12 24		12 28		12 32			12 35				12 40		12 44				12 50			12 57			13 02

Brighton - London and Bedford

Network Diagram - see first Page of Table 186

		FC 1	GX 1	SN ◇1	FC 1		SN ◇1	SN 1	SN ◇1	FC 1	SN 1	GX 1	SN ◇1	SN 1	SN ◇1	SN ◇1		SN 1	FC 1	GW 1	GX 1	SN ◇1	FC 1	SN ◇1	SN 1
Brighton 10	d	12 04			12 07		12 19						12 25						12 34				12 37	12 49	
Hove 2	d														12 21										
Preston Park	d				12 11																		12 41		
Hassocks 4	d				12 17								12 34										12 47		
Burgess Hill 4	d				12 21								12 38										12 51		
Lewes 4	d															12 20									
Wivelsfield 4	d				12 23											12 35							12 53		
Haywards Heath 3	a	12 17			12 28										12 35	12 40			12 47				12 58		
	d	12 18			12 32										12 44				12 48				13 02		
Balcombe	d				12 37																				
Horsham 4	d			12 20										12 30								12 50			
Littlehaven	d													12 33											
Faygate	d													12 37											
Ifield	d													12 41											
Crawley	d			12 29										12 44								12 59			
Three Bridges 4	a	12 26		12 32	12 43									12 47					12 56			13 02	13 11		
	d	12 27		12 33	12 43									12 48					12 57			13 03	13 12		
Gatwick Airport 10 ✈	a	12 31		12 37	12 47								12 51	12 52	12 55				13 01			13 07	13 16		
	d	12 32	12 35	12 38	12 47							12 50	12 53	12 53	12 56				13 02	13 03	13 05	13 08	13 17		
Horley 4	d			12 41										12 56											
Salfords	d																								
Earlswood (Surrey)	d																								
Tonbridge 4	d										12 19														
Leigh (Kent)	d										12 23														
Penshurst	d										12 27														
Edenbridge	d										12 33														
Godstone	d										12 40														
Nutfield	d										12 45														
Reigate	d																								
Redhill 5	a			12 47							12 50			13 02						13 10		13 15			
	d			12 48							12 51			13 07								13 16			
Merstham	d													13 11											
Coulsdon South	d										12 58			13 16											
Purley 4	d							←	←	←	13 02			13 19											←
East Croydon	a	12 46		12 59	13 02		12 52	12 54	12 59	13 02	13 07		13 08	13 24	13 11				13 16			13 27	13 31	13 22	13 24
	d	12 47		13 00	13 02		12 53	12 55	13 00	13 02	13 07		13 08	13 25	13 12			13 14	13 17			13 28	13 32	13 23	13 25
Norwood Junction 2	a			→	→			12 59			13 12			→								→	→		13 29
New Cross Gate	d							13 07																	13 37
London Bridge 4 ⊖	a	13 00						13 13		13 15	13 25								13 30						13 43
London Blackfriars 3 ⊖	a	13 07								13 22									13 37						
City Thameslink 3	a	13 10								13 26									13 40						
Farringdon 3 ⊖	a	13 14								13 30									13 44						
St Pancras International 15 ⊖	a	13 18								13 34									13 48						
St Albans City	a	13 38								13 53									14 08						
Luton Airport Parkway 4 ✈	a	13 50								14 07									14 20						
Luton 7	a	13 53								14 10									14 23						
Bedford 10	a	14 19								14 35									14 49						
Clapham Junction 10	a						13 02		13 09				13 17		13 21			13 25						13 32	
	d						13 03		13 10				13 18		13 21			13 26						13 33	
London Victoria 15 ⊖	a		13 05				13 10		13 16			13 20	13 24		13 28			13 32			13 35			13 40	

Brighton - London and Bedford

Network Diagram - see first Page of Table 186

		SN ◇1		FC 1	SN 1	GW 1	GX 1	SN 1	SN ◇1	SN ◇1	GW 1	SN 1		FC 1	GX 1	SN ◇1	FC 1	SN ◇1	SN 1	SN ◇1	FC 1	SN 1		GX 1	SN ◇1
Brighton 10	d													13 04			13 07	13 19							13 25
Hove 2	d									12 51															
Preston Park	d									12 55							13 11								
Hassocks 4	d																13 17								13 34
Burgess Hill 4	d									13 04							13 21								13 38
Lewes 4	d								12 50																
Wivelsfield 4	d																13 23								
Haywards Heath 3	a								13 05	13 09				13 17			13 28								
	d								13 13					13 18			13 32								
Balcombe	d																13 37								
Horsham 4	d							13 00								13 20									
Littlehaven	d							13 03																	
Faygate	d																								
Ifield	d							13 09																	
Crawley	d							13 13								13 29									
Three Bridges 4	a							13 16						13 26		13 32	13 43								
	d							13 18						13 27		13 33	13 43								
Gatwick Airport 10 ✈	a							13 22	13 24					13 31		13 37	13 47								13 51
	d						13 20	13 23	13 25					13 32	13 35	13 38	13 47							13 50	13 53
Horley 4	d							13 26								13 41									
Salfords	d							13 30																	
Earlswood (Surrey)	d							13 33																	
Tonbridge 4	d																					13 19			
Leigh (Kent)	d																					13 23			
Penshurst	d																					13 27			
Edenbridge	d																					13 33			
Godstone	d																					13 40			
Nutfield	d																					13 45			
Reigate	d				13 14	13 19					13 34														
Redhill 5	a				13 18	13 25		13 36			13 38					13 47						13 50			
	d				13 19			13 37								13 48						13 51			
Merstham	d				13 23			13 41																	
Coulsdon South	d				13 28			13 46														13 58			
Purley 4	d	←		←	13 32			13 49											←	←	←	14 02			
East Croydon	a	13 27		13 31	13 37			13 54	13 40					13 46		13 59	14 02	13 52	13 54	13 59	14 02	14 07			14 08
	d	13 28		13 32	13 37			13 55	13 41			13 44		13 47		14 00	14 02	13 53	13 55	14 00	14 02	14 08			14 08
Norwood Junction 2	a				13 42			→								→	→		13 59			14 12			
New Cross Gate	d																		14 07						
London Bridge 4 ⊖	a			13 45	13 55									14 00					14 13		14 15	14 25			
London Blackfriars 3 ⊖	a			13 52										14 07							14 22				
City Thameslink 3	a			13 56										14 10							14 26				
Farringdon 3 ⊖	a			14 00										14 14							14 29				
St Pancras International 15 ⊖	a			14 04										14 18							14 34				
St Albans City	a			14 23										14 38							14 54				
Luton Airport Parkway 4 ✈	a			14 37										14 50							15 07				
Luton 7	a			14 40										14 53							15 10				
Bedford 10	a			15 05										15 19							15 35				
Clapham Junction 10	a	13 37							13 50			13 55						14 02		14 09					14 17
	d	13 37							13 50			13 56						14 03		14 10					14 18
London Victoria 15 ⊖	a	13 44					13 50		13 57			14 03			14 05			14 10		14 16				14 20	14 24

Table 186

Mondays to Fridays

Brighton - London and Bedford

Network Diagram - see first Page of Table 186

		SN 1	SN ◇1	SN ◇1	SN 1	FC 1	GW 1	GX 1 (trolley)		SN ◇1	FC 1	SN ◇1 (trolley)	SN 1	SN ◇1	FC 1	SN 1	GW 1	GX 1 (trolley)		SN 1	SN ◇1	SN ◇1	GW 1	SN 1	FC 1
Brighton 10	d					13 34					13 37	13 49													14 04
Hove 2	d		13 21																			13 51			
Preston Park	d										13 41											13 55			
Hassocks 4	d										13 47														
Burgess Hill 4	d										13 51											14 04			
Lewes 4	d			13 20																	13 50				
Wivelsfield 4	d			13 35							13 53														
Haywards Heath 3	a		13 35	13 40		13 47					13 58										14 05	14 09			14 17
	d		13 44			13 48					14 02										14 13				14 18
Balcombe	d																								
Horsham 4	d	13 30								13 50										14 00					
Littlehaven	d	13 33																		14 03					
Faygate	d																								
Ifield	d	13 39																		14 09					
Crawley	d	13 43								13 59										14 13					
Three Bridges 4	a	13 46				13 56				14 02	14 11									14 16					14 26
	d	13 48				13 57				14 03	14 12									14 18					14 27
Gatwick Airport 10 ✈	a	13 52	13 55			14 01				14 07	14 16									14 22	14 24				14 31
	d	13 53	13 56			14 02	14 03	14 05		14 08	14 17							14 20		14 23	14 25				14 32
Horley 4	d	13 56																		14 26					
Salfords	d																			14 30					
Earlswood (Surrey)	d																			14 33					
Tonbridge 4	d																								
Leigh (Kent)	d																								
Penshurst	d																								
Edenbridge	d																								
Godstone	d																								
Nutfield	d																								
Reigate	d															14 14	14 19						14 34		
Redhill 5	a	14 02					14 10			14 15						14 18	14 25			14 36			14 38		
	d	14 07								14 16						14 19				14 37					
Merstham	d	14 11														14 23				14 41					
Coulsdon South	d	14 16														14 28				14 46					
Purley 4	d	14 19											←	←	←	14 32				14 49					
East Croydon	a	14 24	14 11			14 16				14 27	14 31	14 22	14 24	14 27	14 31	14 37				14 54	14 40				14 46
	d	14 25	14 12		14 14	14 17				14 28	14 32	14 23	14 25	14 28	14 32	14 37				14 55	14 41			14 44	14 47
Norwood Junction 2	a	→								→	→		14 29			14 42				→					
New Cross Gate	d												14 37												
London Bridge 4 ⊖	a					14 30							14 43		14 45	14 55									15 00
London Blackfriars 3 ⊖	a					14 37									14 52										15 07
City Thameslink 3	a					14 40									14 56										15 10
Farringdon 3 ⊖	a					14 44									15 00										15 14
St Pancras International 15 ⊖	a					14 48									15 04										15 18
St Albans City	a					15 08									15 24										15 38
Luton Airport Parkway 4 ✈	a					15 20									15 37										15 50
Luton 7	a					15 23									15 40										15 53
Bedford 10	a					15 49									16 05										16 19
Clapham Junction 10	a		14 21		14 25							14 32		14 37							14 50			14 55	
	d		14 21		14 26							14 33		14 37							14 50			14 56	
London Victoria 15 ⊖	a		14 28		14 32			14 35				14 40		14 44				14 50			14 57			15 02	

Table 186

Mondays to Fridays

Brighton - London and Bedford

Network Diagram - see first Page of Table 186

		GX 1 (trolley)	SN ◇1	FC 1		SN ◇1 (trolley)	SN 1	SN ◇1	FC 1	SN 1	GX 1 (trolley)	SN ◇1	SN 1	SN ◇1	SN ◇1		SN 1	FC 1	GW 1	GX 1 (trolley)	SN ◇1	FC 1	SN ◇1 (trolley)	SN 1	SN ◇1
Brighton 10	d			14 07		14 19						14 25						14 34				14 37	14 49		
Hove 2	d													14 21											
Preston Park	d			14 11																		14 41			
Hassocks 4	d			14 17								14 34										14 47			
Burgess Hill 4	d			14 21								14 38										14 51			
Lewes 4	d														14 20										
Wivelsfield 4	d			14 23											14 35							14 53			
Haywards Heath 3	a			14 28										14 35	14 40			14 47				14 58			
	d			14 32										14 44				14 48				15 02			
Balcombe	d			14 37																					
Horsham 4	d		14 20										14 30								14 50				
Littlehaven	d												14 33												
Faygate	d																								
Ifield	d												14 39												
Crawley	d		14 29										14 43								14 59				
Three Bridges 4	a		14 32	14 43									14 46					14 56			15 02	15 11			
	d		14 33	14 43									14 48					14 57			15 03	15 12			
Gatwick Airport 10 ✈	a		14 37	14 47								14 51	14 52	14 55				15 01			15 07	15 16			
	d	14 35	14 38	14 47							14 50	14 53	14 53	14 56				15 02	15 03	15 05	15 08	15 17			
Horley 4	d		14 41										14 56												
Salfords	d																								
Earlswood (Surrey)	d																								
Tonbridge 4	d									14 19															
Leigh (Kent)	d									14 23															
Penshurst	d									14 27															
Edenbridge	d									14 33															
Godstone	d									14 40															
Nutfield	d									14 45															
Reigate	d																								
Redhill 5	a		14 47							14 50			15 02						15 10		15 16				
	d		14 48							14 51			15 07								15 17				
Merstham	d												15 11												
Coulsdon South	d									14 58			15 16												
Purley 4	d						←	←	←	15 02			15 19											←	←
East Croydon	a		14 59	15 02		14 52	14 54	14 59	15 02	15 07		15 08	15 24	15 11				15 16			15 28	15 31	15 22	15 24	15 28
	d		15 00	15 02		14 53	14 55	15 00	15 02	15 07		15 08	15 25	15 12			15 14	15 17			15 28	15 32	15 23	15 25	15 28
Norwood Junction 2	a		→	→			14 59			15 12			→								→	→		15 29	
New Cross Gate	d						15 07																	15 37	
London Bridge 4 ⊖	a						15 13		15 15	15 25								15 30						15 43	
London Blackfriars 3 ⊖	a								15 22									15 37							
City Thameslink 3	a								15 26									15 40							
Farringdon 3 ⊖	a								15 29									15 44							
St Pancras International 15 ⊖	a								15 34									15 48							
St Albans City	a								15 52									16 08							
Luton Airport Parkway 4 ✈	a								16 04									16 20							
Luton 7	a								16 07									16 23							
Bedford 10	a								16 33									16 49							
Clapham Junction 10	a					15 02		15 09				15 17		15 21			15 25						15 32		15 37
	d					15 03		15 10				15 18		15 21			15 26						15 33		15 38
London Victoria 15 ⊖	a	15 05				15 10		15 20			15 20	15 24		15 28			15 35			15 35			15 40		15 46

Brighton - London and Bedford

Network Diagram - see first Page of Table 186

		FC 1	SN 1	GW 1	GX 1 🛒	SN 1	SN ◇1 🛒	SN ◇1 A 🛒	GW 1	SN 1	FC 1	GX 1 🛒	SN ◇1 🛒	FC 1	SN ◇1 🛒	SN 1	SN ◇1 🛒	FC 1	SN 1	GX 1 🛒	SN ◇1	SN 1
Brighton 10	d										15 04			15 07	15 19						15 25	
Hove 2	d							14 51														
Preston Park	d							14 55						15 11								
Hassocks 4	d													15 17							15 34	
Burgess Hill 4	d							15 04						15 21							15 38	
Lewes 4	d						14 50															
Wivelsfield 4	d													15 23								
Haywards Heath 3	a						15 05	15 09			15 17			15 28								
	d						15 13				15 18			15 32								
Balcombe	d													15 37								
Horsham 4	d					15 00							15 20									15 30
Littlehaven	d					15 03																15 33
Faygate	d																					
Ifield	d					15 09																15 39
Crawley	d					15 13							15 29									15 43
Three Bridges 4	a					15 16					15 26		15 32	15 43								15 46
	d					15 18					15 27		15 33	15 43								15 48
Gatwick Airport 10 ✈	a					15 22	15 24				15 31		15 37	15 47							15 51	15 52
	d				15 20	15 23	15 25				15 32	15 35	15 38	15 47						15 50	15 53	15 53
Horley 4	d					15 26							15 41									15 56
Salfords	d					15 30																
Earlswood (Surrey)	d					15 33																
Tonbridge 4	d																		15 19			
Leigh (Kent)	d																		15 23			
Penshurst	d																		15 27			
Edenbridge	d																		15 33			
Godstone	d																		15 40			
Nutfield	d																		15 45			
Reigate	d		15 14	15 19					15 34													
Redhill 5	a		15 18	15 25		15 36			15 38				15 47						15 50			16 02
	d		15 19			15 37							15 48						15 51			16 06
Merstham	d		15 23			15 41																16 10
Coulsdon South	d		15 28			15 46													15 58			16 15
Purley 4	d	←	15 32			15 49										←	←	←	16 02			16 18
East Croydon 🚌	a	15 31	15 37			15 54	15 40				15 46		15 59	16 02	15 52	15 54	15 59	16 02	16 07		16 08	16 23
	d	15 32	15 37			15 55	15 41			15 44	15 47		16 00	16 02	15 53	15 55	16 00	16 02	16 07		16 08	16 24
Norwood Junction 2	a		15 42			→							→	→		15 59			16 12			→
New Cross Gate	d															16 07						
London Bridge 4 ⊖	a	15 45	15 55								16 00					16 13		16 15	16 25			
London Blackfriars 3 ⊖	a	15 52									16 07							16 25				
City Thameslink 3	a	15 56									16 10							16 28				
Farringdon 3 ⊖	a	15 59									16 13							16 31				
St Pancras International 15 ⊖	a	16 04									16 17							16 35				
St Albans City	a	16 24									16 38							16 55				
Luton Airport Parkway 4 ✈	a	16 37									16 51							17 08				
Luton 7	a	16 40									16 54							17 11				
Bedford 10	a	17 05									17 19							17 36				
Clapham Junction 10	a						15 50			15 55					16 02		16 09				16 17	
	d						15 50			15 56					16 03		16 09				16 18	
London Victoria 15 ⊖	a				15 50		15 57			16 05		16 05			16 10		16 16			16 22	16 24	

A 🛒 from Haywards Heath

Brighton - London and Bedford

Network Diagram - see first Page of Table 186

		SN ◇1 A 🛒	SN ◇1 🛒	SN 1	FC 1	SN 1	GW 1	GX 1 🛒	SN ◇1 🛒	FC 1	SN ◇1 🛒	FC 1	SN ◇1 🛒	SN 1 🛒	SN ◇1	SN 1	GW 1	SN 1	SN ◇1 🛒	SN ◇1 A 🛒	GW 1	SN 1	FC 1
Brighton 10	d				15 34					15 37	15 49				15 55								16 04
Hove 2	d	15 21																		15 52			
Preston Park	d									15 41										15 56			
Hassocks 4	d									15 47					16 06								
Burgess Hill 4	d									15 51										16 05			
Lewes 4	d		15 19																15 50				
Wivelsfield 4	d		15 35							15 53													
Haywards Heath 3	a	15 35	15 40		15 47					15 57									16 05	16 10			16 17
	d	15 44			15 48					15 58									16 14				16 18
Balcombe	d																						
Horsham 4	d								15 50									16 00					
Littlehaven	d																	16 03					
Faygate	d																						
Ifield	d																	16 09					
Crawley	d								15 59									16 13					
Three Bridges 4	a				15 56				16 02	16 06								16 16					16 26
	d				15 57				16 03	16 07								16 18					16 27
Gatwick Airport 10 ✈	a	15 55			16 01				16 07	16 11					16 21			16 22	16 25				16 31
	d	15 56			16 02		16 03	16 05	16 08	16 12				16 20	16 23			16 23	16 26				16 32
Horley 4	d																	16 26					
Salfords	d																	16 30					
Earlswood (Surrey)	d																	16 33					
Tonbridge 4	d																						
Leigh (Kent)	d																						
Penshurst	d																						
Edenbridge	d																						
Godstone	d																						
Nutfield	d																						
Reigate	d															16 14	16 21				16 38		
Redhill 5	a						16 10		16 17							16 18	16 27	16 36			16 42		
	d								16 18							16 21		16 37					
Merstham	d															16 25		16 41					
Coulsdon South	d															16 30		16 46					
Purley 4	d					←						←	←			16 34		16 49					
East Croydon 🚌	a	16 11			16 16	16 23			16 30	16 27	16 24	16 27	16 30		16 38	16 39		16 54	16 40				16 46
	d	16 12		16 14	16 17	16 24			16 30	16 28	16 24	16 28	16 30		16 38	16 40		16 55	16 41			16 44	16 47
Norwood Junction 2	a					16 28			→	→						16 44		→					
New Cross Gate	d					16 36																	
London Bridge 4 ⊖	a					16 43										17 00							
London Blackfriars 3 ⊖	a				16 47							16 55											17 19
City Thameslink 3	a				16 54							16 58											17 24
Farringdon 3 ⊖	a				16 57							17 01											17 27
St Pancras International 15 ⊖	a				17 01							17 05											17 31
St Albans City	a				17 19							17 25											17 49
Luton Airport Parkway 4 ✈	a											17 38											
Luton 7	a				17 32							17 41											18 02
Bedford 10	a				17 53							18 06											18 23
Clapham Junction 10	a	16 21		16 25							16 33		16 39		16 47				16 50			16 55	
	d	16 21		16 26							16 34		16 40		16 48				16 51			16 56	
London Victoria 15 ⊖	a	16 28		16 35				16 35			16 42		16 46	16 52	16 54				16 58			17 05	

A 🛒 from Haywards Heath

Table 186

Mondays to Fridays

Brighton - London and Bedford

Network Diagram - see first Page of Table 186

		SN	GX	SN	FC	SN	FC	SN	SN	GX	SN	SN	SN	SN	FC	GW	SN	GX	FC	SN	SN	SN
		[1]	[1]	◇[1]	[1]	[1]	[1]	◇[1]	[1]	[1]	[1]	[1]	◇[1]	◇[1]	[1]	[1]	[1]	[1]	[1]	[1]	[1]	◇[1]
													A									
			⌶			⌶				⌶			⌶	⌶				⌶			⌶	⌶
Brighton [10]	d				16 07	16 19									16 24				16 30		16 49	
Hove [2]	d												16 21									
Preston Park	d				16 11														16 34			
Hassocks [4]	d				16 17														16 40			
Burgess Hill [4]	d				16 21														16 44			
Lewes [4]	d													16 20								
Wivelsfield [4]	d													16 38					16 46			
Haywards Heath [3]	a				16 26								16 35	16 42	16 38				16 50			
	d				16 26									16 46	16 38				16 51			
Balcombe	d				16 32														16 56			
Horsham [4]	d			16 20								16 30										16 52
Littlehaven	d											16 33										
Faygate	d											16 37										
Ifield	d											16 41										
Crawley	d			16 29								16 44										17 01
Three Bridges [4]	a			16 32	16 37							16 47			16 47				17 02			17 04
	d			16 33	16 37							16 48			16 47				17 02			17 05
Gatwick Airport [10] ✈	a			16 37	16 41							16 52		16 57	16 52				17 07			17 09
	d		16 35	16 38	16 42					16 50		16 53		16 58	16 53	17 03		17 05	17 08			17 10
Horley [4]	d											16 56										
Salfords	d											17 00										
Earlswood (Surrey)	d											17 03										
Tonbridge [4]	d								16 19													
Leigh (Kent)	d								16 23													
Penshurst	d								16 27													
Edenbridge	d								16 33													
Godstone	d								16 40													
Nutfield	d								16 45													
Reigate	d										17 03											
Redhill [5]	a			16 46					16 50		17 07	17 06				17 10						17 17
	d			16 47					16 51			17 07										17 18
Merstham	d											17 11										
Coulsdon South	d								16 58			17 16										
Purley [4]	d	←					←	←	17 02			17 19								←		
East Croydon 🚋	a	16 54		17 01	16 57	16 54	16 57	17 01	17 07			17 24		17 13	17 07				17 22	17 24	17 26	17 30
	d	16 55		17 01	16 58	16 54	16 58	17 01	17 07			17 25		17 13	17 09		17 14		17 23	17 25	17 26	17 30
Norwood Junction [2]	a	16 59		→	→				17 11			→		→						17 30		
New Cross Gate	d	17 06																		17 38		
London Bridge [4] ⊖	a	17 14							17 26						17 27					17 45		
London Blackfriars [3] ⊖	a						17 25								17 35				17 49			
City Thameslink [3]	a						17 28								17 38				17 54			
Farringdon [3] ⊖	a						17 31								17 41				17 57			
St Pancras International [15] ⊖	a						17 35								17 45				18 01			
St Albans City	a						17 55								18 06				18 19			
Luton Airport Parkway [4] ✈	a						18 08								18 20							
Luton [7]	a						18 11								18 23				18 32			
Bedford [10]	a						18 36								18 48				18 55			
Clapham Junction [10]	a					17 03		17 10									17 25				17 35	17 39
	d					17 04		17 11									17 26				17 36	17 40
London Victoria [15] ⊖	a		17 05			17 10		17 17		17 20							17 35	17 38			17 42	17 46

A ⌶ from Haywards Heath

Table 186

Mondays to Fridays

Brighton - London and Bedford

Network Diagram - see first Page of Table 186

		GX	SN	SN	GW	SN	SN	SN	GW	SN	SN	FC	GX	SN	SN	FC	SN	FC	SN	GX	SN	SN	SN
		[1]	[1]	[1]	[1]	[1]	◇[1]	◇[1]	[1]	[1]	[1]	[1]	[1]	[1]	[1]	[1]	[1]	[1]	◇[1]	[1]	[1]	[1]	[1]
								A															
		⌶					⌶	⌶					⌶				⌶		⌶	⌶			
Brighton [10]	d										16 55	17 02				17 07	17 19						
Hove [2]	d							16 51															
Preston Park	d										16 58					17 11							
Hassocks [4]	d										17 05					17 17							
Burgess Hill [4]	d							17 02			17 08	17 13				17 21							
Lewes [4]	d						16 50																
Wivelsfield [4]	d										17 11												
Haywards Heath [3]	a						17 06	17 09			17 15	17 18				17 26							
	d							17 14			17 21	17 18				17 26							
Balcombe	d										17 26												
Horsham [4]	d					17 00													17 22				17 30
Littlehaven	d					17 03																	17 33
Faygate	d					17 07																	17 37
Ifield	d					17 11																	17 41
Crawley	d					17 14								←					17 31				17 44
Three Bridges [4]	a					17 17					17 32	17 27		17 32					17 34				17 47
	d					17 18					17 32	17 27		17 32					17 36				17 48
Gatwick Airport [10] ✈	a					17 22		17 25			→	17 31		17 36		17 38			17 41				17 52
	d	17 20				17 23		17 26				17 32	17 35	17 38		17 39			17 42	17 50			17 53
Horley [4]	d					17 26																	17 56
Salfords	d					17 30																	18 00
Earlswood (Surrey)	d					17 33																	18 03
Tonbridge [4]	d		16 49	17 03																	17 21		
Leigh (Kent)	d		16 53																		17 25		
Penshurst	d		16 57																		17 29		
Edenbridge	d		17 03	17 13																	17 35		
Godstone	d		17 10																		17 42		
Nutfield	d		17 15																		17 47		
Reigate	d				17 26				17 34													17 44	
Redhill [5]	a		17 20	17 25	17 32	17 36			17 38										17 49		17 53	17 48	18 06
	d		17 21	17 28		17 37													17 49			17 57	18 07
Merstham	d		17 25			17 41																	18 11
Coulsdon South	d		17 30			17 46																	18 16
Purley [4]	d					17 49									←			←					18 19
East Croydon 🚋	a		17 38	17 40		17 54		17 41				17 46		17 53	17 54	17 57	17 56	17 57	18 01			18 08	18 24
	d		17 38	17 41		17 55		17 41		17 44		17 47		17 53	17 55	17 58	17 57	17 58	18 02			18 09	18 27
Norwood Junction [2]	a			17 45		→									17 59	→							→
New Cross Gate	d														18 07								
London Bridge [4] ⊖	a			17 58								18 13			18 16								
London Blackfriars [3] ⊖	a											18 21						18 25					
City Thameslink [3]	a											18 24						18 28					
Farringdon [3] ⊖	a											18 27						18 31					
St Pancras International [15] ⊖	a											18 31						18 35					
St Albans City	a											18 49						18 57					
Luton Airport Parkway [4] ✈	a																	19 09					
Luton [7]	a											19 02						19 12					
Bedford [10]	a											19 23						19 38					
Clapham Junction [10]	a		17 47					17 50		17 55				18 02			18 06		18 13			18 18	
	d		17 48					17 51		17 56				18 03			18 07		18 13			18 19	
London Victoria [15] ⊖	a	17 52	17 54					17 58		18 05			18 05	18 09			18 14		18 20	18 22		18 26	

A ⌶ from Haywards Heath

Brighton - London and Bedford

Network Diagram - see first Page of Table 186

		SN ◇1 A ✠	SN ◇1 ✠	SN 1	FC 1		GW 1	GX 1 ✠	SN ◇1 ✠	SN 1	FC 1	SN 1 ✠	SN 1	SN ◇1 ✠	FC 1		GX 1 ✠	SN 1	GW 1	SN 1	SN ◇1 ✠	SN ◇1 A ✠	SN 1	GW 1	SN 1
Brighton 10	d				17 24						17 37	17 49													
Hove 2	d	17 21																				17 51			
Preston Park	d				17 28						17 41														
Hassocks 4	d				17 34						17 47														
Burgess Hill 4	d				17 38						17 51											18 04			
Lewes 4	d		17 19																		17 50				
Wivelsfield 4	d		17 35		17 40						17 53														
Haywards Heath 3	a	17 35	17 39		17 45						17 58										18 07	18 11			
	d	17 43			17 46						18 02										18 15				
Balcombe	d										18 07														
Horsham 4	d								17 52											18 00					
Littlehaven	d																			18 03					
Faygate	d																			18 07					
Ifield	d																			18 11					
Crawley	d								18 01											18 14					
Three Bridges 4	a				17 54				18 04		18 13									18 17					
	d				17 55				18 05		18 13									18 18					
Gatwick Airport 10 ✈	a	17 54			17 59				18 09		18 17									18 22	18 26				
	d	17 55			18 00		18 03	18 05	18 10		18 17						18 20			18 23	18 27				
Horley 4	d																			18 26					
Salfords	d																			18 30					
Earlswood (Surrey)	d																			18 33					
Tonbridge 4	d									17 49															
Leigh (Kent)	d									17 53															
Penshurst	d									17 57															
Edenbridge	d									18 03															
Godstone	d									18 10															
Nutfield	d									18 15															
Reigate	d																	18 14	18 26				18 38	18 42	
Redhill 5	a						18 10		18 17	18 21								18 19	18 32	18 36			18 42	18 47	
	d								18 18									18 24		18 37					
Merstham	d																	18 28		18 41					
Coulsdon South	d																	18 33		18 46					
Purley 4	d												←	←	←					18 49					
East Croydon 🚋	a	18 11			18 15				18 29		18 32	18 25	18 24	18 29	18 32			18 40		18 54	18 42				
	d	18 12		18 14	18 16				18 30		18 32	18 26	18 27	18 30	18 32			18 40		18 55	18 43				18 44
Norwood Junction 2	a								→		→									→					
New Cross Gate	d																								
London Bridge 4 ⊖	a														18 46										
London Blackfriars 3 ⊖	a				18 51										18 55										
City Thameslink 3	a				18 54										18 58										
Farringdon 3 ⊖	a				18 57										19 01										
St Pancras International 15 ⊖	a				19 01										19 05										
St Albans City	a				19 19										19 25										
Luton Airport Parkway 4 ✈	a														19 38										
Luton 7	a				19 32										19 41										
Bedford 10	a				19 55										20 06										
Clapham Junction 10	a	18 21		18 25								18 35	18 38	18 41				18 49			18 52				18 55
	d	18 22		18 26								18 35	18 38	18 41				18 50			18 53				18 56
London Victoria 15 ⊖	a	18 29		18 35				18 35				18 42	18 45	18 48			18 50	18 56			18 59				19 05

A ✠ from Haywards Heath

Mondays to Fridays

Brighton - London and Bedford

Network Diagram - see first Page of Table 186

			SN 1	FC 1	GX 1 ✠	SN 1	SN 1	SN ◇1	FC 1	SN 1	SN ◇1		FC 1	SN 1	GX 1 ✠	SN 1	SN 1	SN ◇1 ✠	SN ◇1 A ✠	SN 1	FC 1		GX 1 ✠	SN ◇1	GW 1
Brighton 10	d		17 55	18 02					18 07	18 19											18 34				
Hove 2	d																		18 21						
Preston Park	d		17 59						18 11																
Hassocks 4	d		18 05						18 17																
Burgess Hill 4	d		18 09	18 13					18 21										18 34						
Lewes 4	d																	18 18							
Wivelsfield 4	d		18 11						18 23									18 34							
Haywards Heath 3	a		18 16	18 18					18 28									18 38	18 41		18 47				
	d		18 22	18 18					18 32									18 45			18 48				
Balcombe	d								18 37																
Horsham 4	d							18 22									18 30							18 52	
Littlehaven	d																18 33								
Faygate	d																18 37								
Ifield	d																18 41								
Crawley	d					←		18 31									18 44							19 01	
Three Bridges 4	a		18 31	18 27		18 31		18 34	18 43								18 47				18 56			19 04	
	d		18 31	18 27		18 31		18 35	18 43								18 48				18 57			19 05	
Gatwick Airport 10 ✈	a		→	18 31		18 36		18 39	18 47								18 52	18 56			19 01			19 09	
	d			18 32	18 35	18 38		18 40	18 47						18 50		18 53	18 57			19 02		19 05	19 10	19 16
Horley 4	d																18 56								
Salfords	d																19 00								
Earlswood (Surrey)	d																19 03								
Tonbridge 4	d													18 23											
Leigh (Kent)	d													18 27											
Penshurst	d													18 31											
Edenbridge	d													18 37											
Godstone	d													18 44											
Nutfield	d													18 49											
Reigate	d															19 02									
Redhill 5	a							18 47						18 54		19 06	19 06							19 17	19 23
	d							18 48						18 57			19 07							19 18	
Merstham	d																19 11								
Coulsdon South	d																19 16								
Purley 4	d						←				←		←				19 19								
East Croydon 🚋	a			18 47		18 53	18 54	18 59	19 02	18 56	18 59		19 02	19 09			19 24	19 12			19 16			19 29	
	d			18 47		18 53	18 55	19 00	19 02	18 57	19 00		19 02	19 10			19 25	19 12		19 14	19 17			19 29	
Norwood Junction 2	a							→	→					19 13			→							→	
New Cross Gate	d																								
London Bridge 4 ⊖	a			19 00									19 15	19 25							19 30				
London Blackfriars 3 ⊖	a			19 09									19 22								19 37				
City Thameslink 3	a			19 12									19 26								19 40				
Farringdon 3 ⊖	a			19 15									19 30								19 44				
St Pancras International 15 ⊖	a			19 19									19 34								19 48				
St Albans City	a			19 45									19 55								20 08				
Luton Airport Parkway 4 ✈	a			19 57									20 06								20 20				
Luton 7	a			20 00									20 09								20 23				
Bedford 10	a			20 26									20 35								20 49				
Clapham Junction 10	a					19 02	19 05			19 08	19 11							19 21		19 25					
	d					19 03	19 06			19 09	19 12							19 22		19 26					
London Victoria 15 ⊖	a				19 05	19 09	19 13			19 15	19 18				19 20			19 29		19 35			19 35		

A ✠ from Haywards Heath

Table 186

Brighton - London and Bedford

Network Diagram - see first Page of Table 186

		FC 1	SN ◇1	SN 1	SN ◇1	FC 1	GX 1	SN 1	SN 1	GW 1	SN 1	SN ◇1	SN ◇1	GW 1	SN 1	SN 1	FC 1	GX 1	SN ◇1 A	SN 1	SN 1	FC 1	SN ◇1
Brighton 10	d	18 37	18 49																18 59			19 07	19 19
Hove 2	d											18 52											
Preston Park	d	18 41																	19 03			19 11	
Hassocks 4	d	18 47																	19 09			19 17	
Burgess Hill 4	d	18 51																	19 13			19 21	
Lewes 4	d												18 50										
Wivelsfield 4	d	18 53											19 06						19 15			19 23	
Haywards Heath 3	a	18 58										19 07	19 10						19 20			19 28	
	d	19 02										19 14							19 21			19 32	
Balcombe	d																					19 37	
Horsham 4	d										19 02									19 17			
Littlehaven	d										19 05												
Faygate	d																						
Ifield	d										19 11												
Crawley	d										19 14									19 26			
Three Bridges 4	a	19 11									19 18								19 31	19 29		19 43	
	d	19 12									19 18						19 27		19 35			19 43	
Gatwick Airport 10 ✈	a	19 16									19 22	19 25					19 31		19 39			19 47	
	d	19 17					19 20				19 23	19 26					19 32	19 35	19 40			19 47	
Horley 4	d										19 26												
Salfords	d										19 30												
Earlswood (Surrey)	d										19 33												
Tonbridge 4	d							18 50							19 10								
Leigh (Kent)	d							18 54							19 14								
Penshurst	d							18 58							19 18								
Edenbridge	d							19 04							19 24								
Godstone	d							19 11							19 31								
Nutfield	d							19 16							19 36								
Reigate	d								19 21	19 30				19 36							19 51		
Redhill 5	a							19 21	19 25	19 35	19 38			19 40	19 41				19 47		19 55		
	d							19 23			19 39								19 48				
Merstham	d							19 27			19 43												
Coulsdon South	d							19 32			19 48												
Purley 4	d			←	←	←					19 53												
East Croydon	a	19 31	19 23	19 24	19 29	19 31		19 40			19 58	19 43					19 46		20 00			20 02	19 53
	d	19 32	19 24	19 25	19 29	19 32		19 40			19 59	19 43				19 44	19 47		20 01			20 02	19 54
Norwood Junction 2	a	→									→								→			→	
New Cross Gate	d																						
London Bridge 4 ⊖	a					19 45											20 00						
London Blackfriars 3 ⊖	a					19 52											20 07						
City Thameslink 3	a					19 56											20 10						
Farringdon 3 ⊖	a					20 00											20 14						
St Pancras International 15 ⊖	a					20 04											20 18						
St Albans City	a					20 25											20 38						
Luton Airport Parkway 4 ✈	a					20 37											20 50						
Luton 7	a					20 40											20 53						
Bedford 10	a					21 05											21 19						
Clapham Junction 10	a		19 33	19 37	19 40			19 49				19 52				19 55							20 03
	d		19 34	19 38	19 41			19 50				19 53				19 56							20 04
London Victoria 15 ⊖	a		19 41	19 44	19 47		19 50	19 56				19 59				20 05		20 05					20 10

A ◇ to Three Bridges

Table 186

Mondays to Fridays

Brighton - London and Bedford

Network Diagram - see first Page of Table 186

		SN 1	SN 1	SN 1	FC 1	GX 1	SN ◇1	SN ◇1	SN 1	SN 1	FC 1	GW 1	GX 1	SN 1	SN ◇1	FC 1	SN ◇1	SN 1	SN ◇1	FC 1	GX 1	SN 1
Brighton 10	d										19 34					19 37	19 49					
Hove 2	d						19 22															
Preston Park	d															19 41						
Hassocks 4	d															19 47						
Burgess Hill 4	d						19 32									19 51						
Lewes 4	d							19 21														
Wivelsfield 4	d															19 53						
Haywards Heath 3	a						19 37	19 40			19 47					19 58						
	d						19 44				19 48					20 02						
Balcombe	d																					
Horsham 4	d									19 32					19 52							20 02
Littlehaven	d									19 35												20 05
Faygate	d																					
Ifield	d									19 41												20 11
Crawley	d									19 45					20 01							20 14
Three Bridges 4	a									19 49	19 56				20 04	20 11						20 18
	d									19 51	19 57				20 05	20 12						20 18
Gatwick Airport 10 ✈	a						19 55			19 55	20 01				20 10	20 16						20 22
	d					19 50	19 56			19 56	20 02	20 03	20 05		20 11	20 17					20 20	20 23
Horley 4	d									19 59												20 26
Salfords	d																					20 30
Earlswood (Surrey)	d																					20 33
Tonbridge 4	d																					
Leigh (Kent)	d																					
Penshurst	d																					
Edenbridge	d																					
Godstone	d																					
Nutfield	d																					
Reigate	d													20 14								
Redhill 5	a									20 05		20 11		20 18	20 18							20 36
	d									20 06					20 18							20 37
Merstham	d									20 10												20 41
Coulsdon South	d									20 15												20 46
Purley 4	d	←	←	←	←					20 18								←	←	←		20 49
East Croydon	a	19 58	20 00	20 00	20 02		20 11			20 23	20 16				20 30	20 32	20 23	20 23	20 30	20 32		20 57
	d	19 59	20 01	20 01	20 02		20 11		20 14	20 26	20 17				20 30	20 32	20 24	20 26	20 30	20 32		20 57
Norwood Junction 2	a									→					→	→						→
New Cross Gate	d																					
London Bridge 4 ⊖	a				20 15						20 30									20 45		
London Blackfriars 3 ⊖	a				20 22						20 37									20 52		
City Thameslink 3	a				20 26						20 40									20 56		
Farringdon 3 ⊖	a				20 30						20 44									21 00		
St Pancras International 15 ⊖	a				20 34						20 48									21 04		
St Albans City	a				20 55						21 08									21 25		
Luton Airport Parkway 4 ✈	a				21 07						21 20									21 37		
Luton 7	a				21 10						21 23									21 40		
Bedford 10	a				21 35						21 49									22 05		
Clapham Junction 10	a	20 08	20 11	20 11			20 20		20 25								20 33	20 37	20 40			
	d	20 08	20 11	20 11			20 21		20 26								20 34	20 37	20 41			
London Victoria 15 ⊖	a	20 15	20 20	20 20		20 20	20 28		20 32				20 35				20 40	20 44	20 50		20 50	

Brighton - London and Bedford

Network Diagram - see first Page of Table 186

		SN ◇1	SN ◇1	GW 1	SN 1	SN 1	SN ◇1	FC 1	GX 1	SN ◇1	SN 1	FC 1	SN ◇1	SN 1	SN ◇1	FC 1	GX 1	SN ◇1	SN 1	SN 1	FC 1	GW 1	GX 1
Brighton 10	d						19 55	20 02				20 07	20 19								20 34		
Hove 2	d	19 52																20 22					
Preston Park	d						19 58					20 11											
Hassocks 4	d						20 05					20 17											
Burgess Hill 4	d						20 08	20 13				20 21						20 33					
Lewes 4	d		19 50																				
Wivelsfield 4	d		20 05				20 11					20 23											
Haywards Heath 3	a	20 05	20 10				20 15	20 18				20 28						20 38			20 47		
	d	20 14					20 22	20 19				20 32						20 38			20 48		
Balcombe	d											20 37											
Horsham 4	d																			20 32			
Littlehaven	d																			20 35			
Faygate	d																						
Ifield	d																			20 41			
Crawley	d									←										20 45			
Three Bridges 4	a						20 32	20 27		20 32		20 43						20 47		20 48	20 56		
	d						20 32	20 27		20 32		20 43						20 47		20 51	20 57		
Gatwick Airport 10 ✈	a	20 25					→	20 31		20 37		20 47						20 51		20 56	21 01		
	d	20 26						20 32	20 35	20 38		20 47					20 50	20 53		20 57	21 02	21 03	21 05
Horley 4	d																			20 59			
Salfords	d																						
Earlswood (Surrey)	d																						
Tonbridge 4	d				20 10																		
Leigh (Kent)	d				20 14																		
Penshurst	d				20 18																		
Edenbridge	d				20 24																		
Godstone	d				20 31																		
Nutfield	d				20 36																		
Reigate	d			20 34							20 50												
Redhill 5	a			20 38	20 45					20 47	20 54									21 06		21 10	
	d									20 48										21 07			
Merstham	d																			21 11			
Coulsdon South	d																			21 16			
Purley 4	d													←	←	←				21 19			
East Croydon	a	20 41						20 47		20 59		21 02	20 53	20 57	20 59	21 02		21 08		21 25	21 16		
	d	20 41				20 44		20 47		21 00		21 02	20 54	20 57	21 00	21 02		21 09	21 14	21 26	21 17		
Norwood Junction 2	a									→		→								→			
New Cross Gate	d																						
London Bridge 4 ⊖	a							21 00								21 15					21 30		
London Blackfriars 3 ⊖	a							21 07								21 22					21 37		
City Thameslink 3	a							21 10								21 26					21 40		
Farringdon 3 ⊖	a							21 14								21 30					21 44		
St Pancras International 15 ⊖	a							21 18								21 34					21 48		
St Albans City	a							21 38								21 55					22 08		
Luton Airport Parkway 4 ✈	a							21 50								22 07					22 20		
Luton 7	a							21 53								22 10					22 23		
Bedford 10	a							22 19								22 35					22 49		
Clapham Junction 10	a	20 50				20 55							21 03	21 07	21 11			21 18	21 25				
	d	20 51				20 57							21 04	21 08	21 11			21 18	21 26				
London Victoria 15 ⊖	a	20 59				21 03			21 05				21 10	21 15	21 18		21 20	21 28	21 32				21 35

Mondays to Fridays

Brighton - London and Bedford

Network Diagram - see first Page of Table 186

		SN 1	SN ◇1	GW 1	FC 1	SN ◇1	SN 1	SN ◇1	FC 1	GX 1	SN 1	SN ◇1	SN ◇1	SN 1	GX 1	SN 1	SN ◇1	GW 1	SN 1	FC 1	SN ◇1	SN 1	SN ◇1
Brighton 10	d				20 37	20 49											21 02			21 11	21 19		
Hove 2	d											20 52											
Preston Park	d				20 41												21 06						
Hassocks 4	d				20 47												21 12			21 20			
Burgess Hill 4	d				20 51												21 16			21 23			
Lewes 4	d												20 50										
Wivelsfield 4	d				20 53								21 05				21 18						
Haywards Heath 3	a				20 58							21 05	21 09				21 23			21 28			
	d				21 02							21 13					21 23			21 32			
Balcombe	d																			21 37			
Horsham 4	d		20 52								21 02												
Littlehaven	d										21 05												
Faygate	d																						
Ifield	d										21 11												
Crawley	d		21 01								21 14												
Three Bridges 4	a		21 05		21 11						21 18						21 32			21 43			
	d		21 05		21 12						21 18						21 33			21 43			
Gatwick Airport 10 ✈	a		21 10		21 16						21 22	21 25					21 37			21 47			
	d		21 11		21 17					21 20	21 23	21 26			21 35		21 38			21 47			
Horley 4	d										21 26												
Salfords	d										21 30												
Earlswood (Surrey)	d										21 33												
Tonbridge 4	d													21 10									
Leigh (Kent)	d													21 14									
Penshurst	d													21 18									
Edenbridge	d													21 24									
Godstone	d													21 31									
Nutfield	d													21 36									
Reigate	d	21 13		21 24														21 45	21 52				
Redhill 5	a	21 17	21 18	21 30							21 36			21 42			21 45	21 49	21 57				
	d		21 18								21 37						21 46						
Merstham	d										21 41												
Coulsdon South	d										21 46												
Purley 4	d						←	←	←		21 49											←	←
East Croydon	a		21 30		21 32	21 23	21 25	21 30	21 32		21 54	21 41					21 59			22 02	21 53	21 54	21 59
	d		21 30		21 32	21 24	21 26	21 30	21 32		21 57	21 42				21 44	22 00			22 02	21 54	21 57	22 00
Norwood Junction 2	a		→		→						→						→			→			
New Cross Gate	d																						
London Bridge 4 ⊖	a								21 45														
London Blackfriars 3 ⊖	a								21 52														
City Thameslink 3	a								21 56														
Farringdon 3 ⊖	a								22 00														
St Pancras International 15 ⊖	a								22 04														
St Albans City	a								22 25														
Luton Airport Parkway 4 ✈	a								22 37														
Luton 7	a								22 40														
Bedford 10	a								23 05														
Clapham Junction 10	a					21 33	21 37	21 40				21 51				21 55					22 03	22 07	22 10
	d					21 34	21 38	21 41				21 51				21 56					22 04	22 08	22 11
London Victoria 15 ⊖	a					21 40	21 45	21 49		21 50		21 58			22 05	22 05					22 11	22 14	22 20

Brighton - London and Bedford

Network Diagram - see first Page of Table 186

		FC 1	SN 1	SN ◇1	SN 1	SN 1	SN 1	GX 1	SN 1	SN ◇1	FC 1	SN ◇1	SN 1	SN ◇1	FC 1	GX 1	GW 1	SN 1	SN 1	SN ◇1 bus	SN ◇1 A bus	SN 1
Brighton 10	d						21 34				21 37	21 49										
Hove 2	d			21 22																	21 52	
Preston Park	d										21 41											
Hassocks 4	d										21 47											
Burgess Hill 4	d			21 33							21 51										22 04	
Lewes 4	d																			21 50		
Wivelsfield 4	d										21 53									22 02		
Haywards Heath 3	a			21 38			21 47				21 58									22 06	22 10	
	d			21 38			21 47				22 02									22 14		
Balcombe	d																					
Horsham 4	d					21 32				21 52									22 02			
Littlehaven	d					21 35													22 05			
Faygate	d																					
Ifield	d					21 41													22 11			
Crawley	d					21 45				22 01									22 14			
Three Bridges 4	a			21 47		21 48	21 56			22 05	22 11								22 18			
	d			21 47		21 51	21 56			22 05	22 12								22 19			
Gatwick Airport 10 ✈	a			21 51		21 55	22 00			22 10	22 16								22 23	22 25		
	d		21 50	21 53		21 56	22 02	22 05		22 11	22 17					22 20	22 22		22 24	22 26		
Horley 4	d					21 59													22 27			
Salfords	d																		22 31			
Earlswood (Surrey)	d																		22 34			
Tonbridge 4	d																					22 10
Leigh (Kent)	d																					22 14
Penshurst	d																					22 18
Edenbridge	d																					22 24
Godstone	d																					22 31
Nutfield	d																					22 36
Reigate	d								22 13									22 33				
Redhill 5	a					22 05			22 17	22 18							22 30	22 37	22 37			22 42
	d					22 06				22 18									22 38			
Merstham	d					22 10													22 42			
Coulsdon South	d					22 15													22 47			
Purley 4	d	←				22 19							←	←	←				22 50			
East Croydon	a	22 02		22 08		22 24	22 17			22 30	22 32	22 23	22 24	22 30	22 32				22 55	22 41		
	d	22 02		22 09	22 14	22 25	22 18			22 30	22 32	22 24	22 25	22 30	22 32				22 56	22 41		
Norwood Junction 2	a					→				→	→								→			
New Cross Gate	d																					
London Bridge 4 ⊖	a	22 17					22 33								22 47							
London Blackfriars 3 ⊖	a																					
City Thameslink 3	a																					
Farringdon 3 ⊖	a																					
St Pancras International 15 ⊖	a																					
St Albans City	a																					
Luton Airport Parkway 4 ✈	a																					
Luton 7	a																					
Bedford 10	a																					
Clapham Junction 10	a			22 18	22 25							22 33	22 37	22 40						22 50		
	d			22 18	22 26							22 34	22 38	22 41						22 51		
London Victoria 15 ⊖	a		22 20	22 26	22 35			22 35				22 41	22 44	22 50		22 50				22 57		

A bus from Haywards Heath

Brighton - London and Bedford

Network Diagram - see first Page of Table 186

		GX 1	SN 1	SN ◇1	GW 1	FC 1	SN ◇1	SN 1	SN ◇1	FC 1	GX 1	GX 1	SN 1	SN 1	FC 1	SN ◇1	FC 1	GW 1	GX 1	SN 1	SN 1	GX 1	GW 1
Brighton 10	d			22 03		22 07	22 19								22 33								
Hove 2	d																						
Preston Park	d			22 06		22 11									22 37								
Hassocks 4	d			22 13		22 17									22 43								
Burgess Hill 4	d			22 16		22 21									22 47								
Lewes 4	d															22 40							
Wivelsfield 4	d			22 18		22 23									22 49	22 54							
Haywards Heath 3	a			22 23		22 28									22 53	22 58							
	d			22 23		22 32									22 54	22 59							
Balcombe	d					22 37									22 59								
Horsham 4	d																			23 02			
Littlehaven	d																			23 05			
Faygate	d																						
Ifield	d																			23 11			
Crawley	d																←			23 14			
Three Bridges 4	a			22 32		22 43									23 05	23 08	23 05			23 18			
	d			22 33		22 43									23 12	23 08	23 12			23 18			
Gatwick Airport 10 ✈	a			22 37		22 47									→	23 12	23 16			23 22			
	d	22 35		22 38		22 47					22 50	23 05				23 13	23 17	23 18	23 20	23 23		23 35	
Horley 4	d																			23 26			
Salfords	d																			23 30			
Earlswood (Surrey)	d																			23 33			
Tonbridge 4	d																				23 17		
Leigh (Kent)	d																				23 21		
Penshurst	d																				23 25		
Edenbridge	d																				23 31		
Godstone	d																				23 38		
Nutfield	d																				23 43		
Reigate	d				22 44																		23 54
Redhill 5	a			22 45	22 48													23 25		23 36	23 49		23 58
	d			22 46																23 37			
Merstham	d																			23 41			
Coulsdon South	d																			23 46			
Purley 4	d							←	←	←										23 49			
East Croydon	a			22 59		23 02	22 53	22 55	22 59	23 02						23 30	23 32			23 54			
	d		22 44	23 00		23 02	22 54	22 56	23 00	23 02			23 14	23 20		23 30	23 32			23 58			
Norwood Junction 2	a			→		→																	
New Cross Gate	d																						
London Bridge 4 ⊖	a									23 17							23 47						
London Blackfriars 3 ⊖	a																						
City Thameslink 3	a																						
Farringdon 3 ⊖	a																						
St Pancras International 15 ⊖	a																						
St Albans City	a																						
Luton Airport Parkway 4 ✈	a																						
Luton 7	a																						
Bedford 10	a																						
Clapham Junction 10	a		22 55				23 03	23 06	23 10				23 25	23 32		23 42				00 11			
	d		22 56				23 04	23 07	23 11				23 26	23 33		23 42				00 12			
London Victoria 15 ⊖	a	23 05	23 05				23 13	23 15	23 20		23 20	23 35	23 35	23 40		23 52			23 55	00 18		00 10	

Brighton - London and Bedford

Network Diagram - see first Page of Table 186

		SN ◇1	FC 1	GX 1	SN ◇1	FC 1
Brighton 10	d	23 02	23 11			23 37
Hove 2	d					
Preston Park	d	23 06				23 41
Hassocks 4	d	23 12	23 20			23 47
Burgess Hill 4	d	23 16	23 23			23 51
Lewes 4	d					
Wivelsfield 4	d	23 19				23 53
Haywards Heath 3	a	23 23	23 28			23 58
	d	23 24	23 29			23 59
Balcombe	d					00 04
Horsham 4	d					
Littlehaven	d					
Faygate	d					
Ifield	d					
Crawley	d				←	
Three Bridges 4	a	23 33	23 38		23 33	00 10
	d	23 47	23 38		23 47	00 10
Gatwick Airport 10 ✈	a	→	23 42		23 52	00 14
	d		23 43	23 50	23 53	00 15
Horley 4	d				23 56	
Salfords	d					
Earlswood (Surrey)	d					
Tonbridge 4	d					
Leigh (Kent)	d					
Penshurst	d					
Edenbridge	d					
Godstone	d					
Nutfield	d					
Reigate	d					
Redhill 5	a				00 03	00 22
	d				00 03	00 23
Merstham	d					
Coulsdon South	d					
Purley 4	d				00 11	
East Croydon	a		00 01		00 16	00 35
	d		00 04		00 17	00 36
Norwood Junction 2	a					
New Cross Gate	d					
London Bridge 4 ⊖	a		00 19			00 52
London Blackfriars 3 ⊖	a					
City Thameslink 3	a					
Farringdon 3 ⊖	a					
St Pancras International 15 ⊖	a					
St Albans City	a					
Luton Airport Parkway 4 ✈	a					
Luton 7	a					
Bedford 10	a					
Clapham Junction 10	a				00 29	
	d				00 30	
London Victoria 15 ⊖	a			00 25	00 37	

Brighton - London and Bedford

Network Diagram - see first Page of Table 186

		SN 1	GX 1	SN ◇1	FC 1	GX 1	SN ◇1	SN 1	FC 1	GX 1	GW 1	SN	GX 1	GX 1	SN 1	FC 1	SN 1	SN 1	FC 1	SN 1	FC 1	SN 1	FC 1
Brighton 10	d			23p02	23p11				23p37														
Hove 2	d																						
Preston Park	d			23p06					23p41														
Hassocks 4	d			23p12	23p20				23p47														
Burgess Hill 4	d			23p16	23p23				23p51														
Lewes 4	d																						
Wivelsfield 4	d			23p19					23p53														
Haywards Heath 3	a			23p23	23p28				23p58														
	d			23p24	23p29				23p59														
Balcombe	d								00 04														
Horsham 4	d	23p02																					
Littlehaven	d	23p05																					
Faygate	d																						
Ifield	d	23p11																					
Crawley	d	23p14					←																
Three Bridges 4	a	23p18		23p33	23p38		23p33		00 10														
	d	23p18		23p47	23p38		23p47		00 10							01 25		01 59	02 25	02 55	03 25	03 55	04 25
Gatwick Airport 10 ✈	a	23p22		→	23p42		23p52		00 14							01 29		02 03	02 29	02 59	03 29	03 59	04 29
	d	23p23	23p35		23p43	23p50	23p53	00 05	00 15	00 20			00 35	00 50	01 05	01 30	01 35	02 05	02 30	03 05	03 30	04 05	04 30
Horley 4	d	23p26					23p56								01 07			02 07		03 07		04 07	
Salfords	d	23p30																					
Earlswood (Surrey)	d	23p33																					
Tonbridge 4	d																						
Leigh (Kent)	d																						
Penshurst	d																						
Edenbridge	d																						
Godstone	d																						
Nutfield	d																						
Reigate	d										00 45												
Redhill 5	a	23p36					00 03		00 22		00 49											04 14	
	d	23p37					00 03		00 23													04 14	
Merstham	d	23p41																					
Coulsdon South	d	23p46																					
Purley 4	d	23p49					00 11								01 22			02 22		03 22		04 22	
East Croydon	a	23p54			00 01		00 16		00 35						01 27	01 49		02 27	02 47	03 27	03 47	04 27	04 47
	d	23p58			00 04		00 17		00 36			00 49			01 28	01 50		02 28	02 47	03 28	03 47	04 28	04 47
Norwood Junction 2	a																						
New Cross Gate	d																						
London Bridge 4 ⊖	a				00 19				00 52							02 14			03 12		04 12		05 12
London Blackfriars 3 ⊖	a																						
City Thameslink 3	a																						
Farringdon 3 ⊖	a																						
St Pancras International 15 ⊖	a																						
St Albans City	a																						
Luton Airport Parkway 4 ✈	a																						
Luton 7	a																						
Bedford 10	a																						
Clapham Junction 10	a	00 11					00 29					01 01			01 41			02 41		03 41		04 41	
	d	00 12					00 30					01 01			01 41			02 41		03 41		04 41	
London Victoria 15 ⊖	a	00 18	00 10			00 25	00 37	00 40		00 55		01 09	01 11	01 25	01 49		02 10	02 49		03 49		04 50	

Table 186

Saturdays

Brighton - London and Bedford

Network Diagram - see first Page of Table 186

		GX 1	FC 1	GX 1	FC 1	GW 1		GW 1	SN ◇1	SN 1	GX 1	SN ◇1	SN 1	SN 1	FC 1	SN 1		SN 1	GW 1	GX 1	GX 1	SN 1	SN ◇1	SN ◇1	GW 1
Brighton 10	d											05 21			05 25								05 50		
Hove 2	d																							05 54	
Preston Park	d														05 29										
Hassocks 4	d														05 35										
Burgess Hill 4	d											05 31			05 39										
Lewes 4	d												05 26												
Wivelsfield 4	d														05 41										
Haywards Heath 3	a											05 36	05 41		05 45								06 03	06 08	
	d											05 37	05 49		05 46								06 12		
Balcombe	d														05 51										
Horsham 4	d													05 30								06 00			
Littlehaven	d													05 33								06 03			
Faygate	d																								
Ifield	d													05 39								06 09			
Crawley	d													05 43		←						06 13			
Three Bridges 4	a											05 46	05 59	05 46	05 57	05 59						06 16	06 20		
	d		04 55		05 21				05 33			05 46	05 59	05 48	05 57	05 59						06 18	06 21		
Gatwick Airport 10 ✈	a		04 59		05 25				05 37			05 50	→	05 52	06 01	06 03						06 22	06 25		
	d	04 35	05 00	05 20	05 27	05 31			05 38		05 50	05 53		05 53	06 02				06 03	06 05	06 20	06 23	06 26		
Horley 4	d								05 40					05 56								06 26			
Salfords	d													06 00								06 30			
Earlswood (Surrey)	d													06 03								06 33			
Tonbridge 4	d									05 24															
Leigh (Kent)	d									05 28															
Penshurst	d									05 32															
Edenbridge	d									05 38															
Godstone	d									05 45															
Nutfield	d									05 50															
Reigate	d							05 34																	06 34
Redhill 5	a				05 34	05 38		05 39	05 47	05 55				06 06					06 12			06 36			06 39
	d				05 35				05 48					06 07								06 37			
Merstham	d													06 11								06 41			
Coulsdon South	d													06 16								06 46			
Purley 4	d								05 58					06 19				←				06 49			
East Croydon	a		05 17		05 47				06 02			06 10		06 24	06 16			06 24				06 54	06 40		
	d		05 17		05 47				06 07			06 11		06 25	06 17			06 25				06 55	06 41		
Norwood Junction 2	a													→				06 29				→			
New Cross Gate	d																	06 37							
London Bridge 4 ⊖	a		05 42		06 01										06 32			06 43							
London Blackfriars 3 ⊖	a																								
City Thameslink 3	a																								
Farringdon 3 ⊖	a																								
St Pancras International 15 ⊖	a																								
St Albans City	a																								
Luton Airport Parkway 4 ✈	a																								
Luton 7	a																								
Bedford 10	a																								
Clapham Junction 10	a								06 18			06 21											06 50		
	d								06 19			06 22											06 50		
London Victoria 15 ⊖	a	05 10		05 55					06 26		06 20	06 30								06 35	06 50		06 57		

Table 186

Saturdays

Brighton - London and Bedford

Network Diagram - see first Page of Table 186

		SN ◇1		FC 1	GX 1	SN ◇1	SN 1	SN 1	GX 1	SN 1	SN ◇1	SN ◇1		SN 1	FC 1	GW 1	GX 1	SN ◇1	FC 1	SN ◇1	SN 1	SN ◇1		FC 1	SN 1
Brighton 10	d	05 56		06 02							06 11				06 25				06 37	06 49					
Hove 2	d											06 21													
Preston Park	d	06 00									06 15				06 29				06 41						
Hassocks 4	d	06 06									06 21				06 35				06 47						
Burgess Hill 4	d			06 12							06 25				06 39				06 51						
Lewes 4	d																								
Wivelsfield 4	d	06 11									06 27				06 41				06 53						
Haywards Heath 3	a	06 15		06 17							06 31	06 35			06 45				06 58						
	d	06 16		06 17							06 40				06 46				07 02						
Balcombe	d														06 51										
Horsham 4	d									06 30								06 52							
Littlehaven	d									06 33															
Faygate	d																								
Ifield	d									06 39															
Crawley	d					←				06 43								07 01							
Three Bridges 4	a	06 24		06 26		06 24				06 46	06 48				06 57			07 04	07 11						
	d	06 31		06 27		06 31				06 48	06 49				06 57			07 05	07 12						
Gatwick Airport 10 ✈	a	→		06 31		06 37				06 52	06 53				07 01			07 09	07 16						
	d			06 32	06 35	06 38			06 50	06 53	06 55				07 02	07 03	07 05	07 10	07 16						
Horley 4	d									06 56															
Salfords	d																								
Earlswood (Surrey)	d																								
Tonbridge 4	d							06 19																	
Leigh (Kent)	d							06 23																	
Penshurst	d							06 27																	
Edenbridge	d							06 33																	
Godstone	d							06 40																	
Nutfield	d							06 45																	
Reigate	d																								07 14
Redhill 5	a							06 50		07 02						07 10		07 17							07 18
	d							06 51		07 07								07 18							07 21
Merstham	d									07 11															07 25
Coulsdon South	d							06 58		07 16															07 30
Purley 4	d						←	07 02		07 19											←	←		←	07 34
East Croydon	a			06 46		06 53	06 54	07 07		07 24	07 09				07 16			07 29	07 31	07 22	07 24	07 29		07 31	07 39
	d			06 47		06 53	06 55	07 07		07 25	07 10			07 14	07 17			07 30	07 32	07 23	07 25	07 30		07 32	07 39
Norwood Junction 2	a						06 59	07 12		→								→	→		07 29				07 44
New Cross Gate	d						07 07														07 37				
London Bridge 4 ⊖	a			07 02			07 13	07 25							07 32						07 43			07 47	07 57
London Blackfriars 3 ⊖	a																								
City Thameslink 3	a																								
Farringdon 3 ⊖	a																								
St Pancras International 15 ⊖	a																								
St Albans City	a																								
Luton Airport Parkway 4 ✈	a																								
Luton 7	a																								
Bedford 10	a																								
Clapham Junction 10	a					07 02					07 19			07 25						07 32		07 39			
	d					07 03					07 19			07 26						07 33		07 39			
London Victoria 15 ⊖	a				07 05	07 09			07 20		07 27			07 32			07 35			07 40		07 46			

Brighton - London and Bedford

Network Diagram - see first Page of Table 186

		GW	GX	SN	SN	SN	GW	SN	FC	GX	SN	FC	SN	SN	SN	FC	SN	GX	SN	SN	SN	SN	SN
		1	1	1	◇1	◇1	1	1	1	1	◇1	1	◇1	1	◇1	1	1	1	◇1	1	◇1	◇1	1
Brighton 10	d								07 04			07 07	07 19						07 24				
Hove 2	d					06 51															07 22		
Preston Park	d					06 55						07 11											
Hassocks 4	d											07 17							07 34				
Burgess Hill 4	d					07 04						07 21							07 38				
Lewes 4	d				06 50																	07 20	
Wivelsfield 4	d											07 23										07 35	
Haywards Heath 3	a				07 05	07 09			07 17			07 28									07 35	07 40	
	d				07 14				07 18			07 32									07 44		
Balcombe	d											07 37											
Horsham 4	d			07 00							07 20									07 30			
Littlehaven	d			07 03																07 33			
Faygate	d																						
Ifield	d			07 09																07 39			
Crawley	d			07 13							07 29									07 43			
Three Bridges 4	a			07 16					07 26		07 32	07 42								07 46			
	d			07 18					07 27		07 33	07 42								07 48			
Gatwick Airport 10 ✈	a			07 22	07 25				07 31		07 37	07 46							07 51	07 52	07 55		
	d		07 20	07 23	07 26				07 32	07 35	07 38	07 46						07 50	07 53	07 53	07 56		
Horley 4	d			07 26							07 41									07 56			
Salfords	d			07 30																			
Earlswood (Surrey)	d			07 33																			
Tonbridge 4	d																07 19						
Leigh (Kent)	d																07 23						
Penshurst	d																07 27						
Edenbridge	d																07 33						
Godstone	d																07 40						
Nutfield	d																07 45						
Reigate	d	07 18					07 34																
Redhill 5	a	07 25		07 36			07 39				07 47						07 50			08 02			
	d			07 37							07 48						07 51			08 07			
Merstham	d			07 41																08 11			
Coulsdon South	d			07 46													07 58			08 16			
Purley 4	d			07 49										←	←	←	08 02			08 19			
East Croydon	a			07 54	07 41				07 46		07 59	08 01	07 52	07 54	07 59	08 01	08 07		08 08	08 24	08 11		
	d			07 55	07 42			07 44	07 47		08 00	08 01	07 53	07 55	08 00	08 01	08 07		08 08	08 25	08 12		08 14
Norwood Junction 2	a			→							→	→		07 59			08 12			→			
New Cross Gate	d													08 07									
London Bridge 4 ⊖	a								08 02					08 13		08 17	08 25						
London Blackfriars 3 ⊖	a																						
City Thameslink 3	a																						
Farringdon 3 ⊖	a																						
St Pancras International 15 ⊖	a																						
St Albans City	a																						
Luton Airport Parkway 4 ✈	a																						
Luton 7	a																						
Bedford 10	a																						
Clapham Junction 10	a				07 51			07 55					08 02		08 09				08 17		08 21		08 25
	d				07 51			07 56					08 03		08 10				08 18		08 21		08 26
London Victoria 15 ⊖	a		07 50		07 58			08 02		08 05			08 10		08 16			08 20	08 24		08 28		08 32

Brighton - London and Bedford

Network Diagram - see first Page of Table 186

		FC	GW	GX	SN	FC	SN	SN	SN	FC	SN	GW	GX	SN	SN	SN	GW	SN	FC	GX	SN	FC
		1	1	1	◇1	1	◇1	1	◇1	1	1	1	1	1	◇1	◇1	1	1	1	1	◇1	1
Brighton 10	d	07 34				07 37	07 49												08 04			08 07
Hove 2	d															07 51						
Preston Park	d					07 41										07 55						08 11
Hassocks 4	d					07 47																08 17
Burgess Hill 4	d					07 51										08 04						08 21
Lewes 4	d														07 50							
Wivelsfield 4	d					07 53																08 23
Haywards Heath 3	a	07 47				07 58									08 05	08 09			08 17			08 28
	d	07 48				08 02									08 13				08 18			08 32
Balcombe	d																					08 37
Horsham 4	d				07 50									08 00							08 20	
Littlehaven	d													08 03								
Faygate	d																					
Ifield	d													08 09								
Crawley	d				07 59									08 13							08 29	
Three Bridges 4	a	07 56			08 02	08 11								08 16					08 26		08 32	08 42
	d	07 57			08 03	08 12								08 18					08 27		08 33	08 42
Gatwick Airport 10 ✈	a	08 01			08 07	08 16								08 22	08 24				08 31		08 37	08 46
	d	08 02	08 03	08 05	08 08	08 16							08 20	08 23	08 25				08 32	08 35	08 38	08 46
Horley 4	d													08 26							08 41	
Salfords	d													08 30								
Earlswood (Surrey)	d													08 33								
Tonbridge 4	d																					
Leigh (Kent)	d																					
Penshurst	d																					
Edenbridge	d																					
Godstone	d																					
Nutfield	d																					
Reigate	d										08 14	08 19					08 34					
Redhill 5	a		08 10		08 15						08 18	08 25		08 36			08 38				08 47	
	d				08 16						08 19			08 37							08 48	
Merstham	d										08 23			08 41								
Coulsdon South	d										08 28			08 46								
Purley 4	d							←	←	←	08 32			08 49								
East Croydon	a	08 16			08 27	08 31	08 22	08 24	08 27	08 31	08 37			08 54	08 40				08 46		08 59	09 01
	d	08 17			08 28	08 32	08 23	08 25	08 28	08 32	08 37			08 55	08 40			08 44	08 47		09 00	09 01
Norwood Junction 2	a				→	→		08 29			08 42			→							→	→
New Cross Gate	d							08 37														
London Bridge 4 ⊖	a	08 32						08 43		08 47	08 55								09 02			
London Blackfriars 3 ⊖	a																					
City Thameslink 3	a																					
Farringdon 3 ⊖	a																					
St Pancras International 15 ⊖	a																					
St Albans City	a																					
Luton Airport Parkway 4 ✈	a																					
Luton 7	a																					
Bedford 10	a																					
Clapham Junction 10	a						08 32		08 37						08 50			08 55				
	d						08 33		08 37						08 50			08 56				
London Victoria 15 ⊖	a			08 35			08 40		08 44				08 50		08 57			09 02		09 05		

Table 186

Saturdays

Brighton - London and Bedford

Network Diagram - see first Page of Table 186

		SN ◇1 ⊼	SN 1	SN ◇1	FC 1	SN 1	GX 1 ⊼	SN ◇1	SN 1	SN ◇1	SN ◇1		SN 1	FC 1	GW 1	GX 1 ⊼	SN ◇1 ⊼	FC 1	SN ◇1 ⊼	SN 1	SN ◇1 ⊼		FC 1	SN 1	GW 1
Brighton [10]	d	08 19						08 24						08 34				08 37	08 49						
Hove [2]	d									08 21															
Preston Park	d																	08 41							
Hassocks [4]	d							08 34										08 47							
Burgess Hill [4]	d							08 38										08 51							
Lewes [4]	d										08 20														
Wivelsfield [4]	d										08 35							08 53							
Haywards Heath [3]	a									08 35	08 40			08 47				08 58							
	d										08 44			08 48				09 02							
Balcombe	d																								
Horsham [4]	d								08 30								08 50								
Littlehaven	d								08 33																
Faygate	d																								
Ifield	d								08 39																
Crawley	d								08 43								08 59								
Three Bridges [4]	a								08 46					08 56			09 02	09 11							
	d								08 48					08 57			09 03	09 12							
Gatwick Airport [10] ✈	a							08 51	08 52		08 55			09 01			09 07	09 16							
	d						08 50	08 53	08 53		08 56			09 02	09 03	09 05	09 08	09 16							
Horley [4]	d								08 56																
Salfords	d																								
Earlswood (Surrey)	d																								
Tonbridge [4]	d					08 19																			
Leigh (Kent)	d					08 23																			
Penshurst	d					08 27																			
Edenbridge	d					08 33																			
Godstone	d					08 40																			
Nutfield	d					08 45																			
Reigate	d																							09 14	09 18
Redhill [5]	a					08 50			09 02						09 10		09 15							09 18	09 25
	d					08 51			09 07								09 16							09 19	
Merstham	d								09 11															09 23	
Coulsdon South	d					08 58			09 16															09 28	
Purley [4]	d		←	←	←	09 02			09 19											←	←		←	09 32	
East Croydon	a	08 52	08 54	08 59	09 01	09 07		09 08	09 24		09 11			09 16			09 27	09 31	09 22	09 24	09 27		09 31	09 37	
	d	08 53	08 55	09 00	09 01	09 07		09 08	09 25		09 12		09 14	09 17			09 28	09 32	09 23	09 25	09 28		09 32	09 37	
Norwood Junction [2]	a		08 59			09 12			→								→	→		09 29				09 42	
New Cross Gate	d		09 07																	09 37					
London Bridge [4] ⊖	a		09 13		09 17	09 25								09 32						09 43			09 47	09 55	
London Blackfriars [3] ⊖	a																								
City Thameslink [3]	a																								
Farringdon [3] ⊖	a																								
St Pancras International [15] ⊖	a																								
St Albans City	a																								
Luton Airport Parkway [4] ✈	a																								
Luton [7]	a																								
Bedford [10]	a																								
Clapham Junction [10]	a	09 02		09 09				09 17			09 21		09 25						09 32		09 37				
	d	09 03		09 10				09 18			09 21		09 26						09 33		09 37				
London Victoria [15] ⊖	a	09 10		09 16			09 20	09 24			09 28		09 32			09 35			09 40		09 44				

Table 186

Saturdays

Brighton - London and Bedford

Network Diagram - see first Page of Table 186

		GX 1 ⊼	SN 1	SN ◇1	SN ◇1	GW 1	SN 1		FC 1	GX 1 ⊼	SN ◇1	FC 1	SN ◇1 ⊼	SN 1	SN ◇1	FC 1	SN 1		GX 1 ⊼	SN ◇1	SN 1	SN ◇1	SN ◇1	SN 1	FC 1
Brighton [10]	d								09 04			09 07	09 19							09 24					09 34
Hove [2]	d				08 51																	09 21			
Preston Park	d				08 55							09 11													
Hassocks [4]	d											09 17								09 34					
Burgess Hill [4]	d				09 04							09 21								09 38					
Lewes [4]	d			08 50																			09 20		
Wivelsfield [4]	d											09 23											09 35		
Haywards Heath [3]	a			09 05	09 09				09 17			09 28										09 35	09 40		09 47
	d				09 13				09 18			09 32											09 44		09 48
Balcombe	d											09 37													
Horsham [4]	d		09 00								09 20										09 30				
Littlehaven	d		09 03																		09 33				
Faygate	d																								
Ifield	d		09 09																		09 39				
Crawley	d		09 13								09 29										09 43				
Three Bridges [4]	a		09 16						09 26		09 32	09 42									09 46				09 56
	d		09 18						09 27		09 33	09 42									09 48				09 57
Gatwick Airport [10] ✈	a		09 22		09 24				09 31		09 37	09 46								09 51	09 52		09 55		10 01
	d	09 20	09 23		09 25				09 32	09 35	09 38	09 46							09 50	09 53	09 53		09 56		10 02
Horley [4]	d		09 26								09 41										09 56				
Salfords	d		09 30																						
Earlswood (Surrey)	d		09 33																						
Tonbridge [4]	d																09 19								
Leigh (Kent)	d																09 23								
Penshurst	d																09 27								
Edenbridge	d																09 33								
Godstone	d																09 40								
Nutfield	d																09 45								
Reigate	d					09 34																			
Redhill [5]	a		09 36			09 38					09 47						09 50				10 02				
	d		09 37								09 48						09 51				10 07				
Merstham	d		09 41																		10 11				
Coulsdon South	d		09 46														09 58				10 16				
Purley [4]	d		09 49											←	←	←	10 02				10 19				
East Croydon	a		09 54		09 40				09 46		09 59	10 01	09 52	09 54	09 59	10 01	10 07			10 08	10 24		10 11		10 16
	d		09 55		09 40		09 44		09 47		10 00	10 01	09 53	09 55	10 00	10 01	10 07			10 08	10 25		10 12	10 14	10 17
Norwood Junction [2]	a		→								→	→		09 59			10 12				→				
New Cross Gate	d													10 07											
London Bridge [4] ⊖	a								10 02					10 13		10 17	10 25								10 32
London Blackfriars [3] ⊖	a																								
City Thameslink [3]	a																								
Farringdon [3] ⊖	a																								
St Pancras International [15] ⊖	a																								
St Albans City	a																								
Luton Airport Parkway [4] ✈	a																								
Luton [7]	a																								
Bedford [10]	a																								
Clapham Junction [10]	a				09 50		09 55						10 02		10 09					10 17			10 21	10 25	
	d				09 50		09 56						10 03		10 10					10 18			10 21	10 26	
London Victoria [15] ⊖	a	09 50			09 57		10 02			10 05			10 10		10 16				10 20	10 24			10 28	10 32	

Brighton - London and Bedford

Network Diagram - see first Page of Table 186

Station		GW 1	GX 1 ⊼	SN ◇1 ⊼	FC 1	SN ◇1 ⊼	SN 1	SN ◇1 ⊼	FC 1	SN 1	GW 1	GX 1 ⊼	SN 1	SN ◇1	SN ◇1	GW 1	SN 1	FC 1	GX 1 ⊼	SN ◇1	FC 1	SN ◇1 ⊼
Brighton 10	d				09 37	09 49												10 04			10 07	10 19
Hove 2	d														09 51							
Preston Park	d				09 41										09 55						10 11	
Hassocks 4	d				09 47																10 17	
Burgess Hill 4	d				09 51										10 04						10 21	
Lewes 4	d													09 50								
Wivelsfield 4	d				09 53																10 23	
Haywards Heath 3	a				09 58									10 05	10 09			10 17			10 28	
	d				10 02									10 13				10 18			10 32	
Balcombe	d																				10 37	
Horsham 4	d			09 50									10 00							10 20		
Littlehaven	d												10 03									
Faygate	d																					
Ifield	d												10 09									
Crawley	d			09 59									10 13							10 29		
Three Bridges 4	a			10 02	10 11								10 16					10 26		10 32	10 42	
	d			10 03	10 12								10 18					10 27		10 33	10 42	
Gatwick Airport 10 ✈	a			10 07	10 16								10 22	10 24				10 31		10 37	10 46	
	d	10 03	10 05	10 08	10 16							10 20	10 23	10 25				10 32	10 35	10 38	10 46	
Horley 4	d												10 26							10 41		
Salfords	d												10 30									
Earlswood (Surrey)	d												10 33									
Tonbridge 4	d																					
Leigh (Kent)	d																					
Penshurst	d																					
Edenbridge	d																					
Godstone	d																					
Nutfield	d																					
Reigate	d									10 14	10 19					10 34						
Redhill 5	a	10 10		10 15						10 18	10 25		10 36			10 38				10 47		
	d			10 16						10 19			10 37							10 48		
Merstham	d									10 23			10 41									
Coulsdon South	d									10 28			10 46									
Purley 4	d						←	←	←	10 32			10 49									
East Croydon ⇋	a			10 27	10 31	10 22	10 24	10 27	10 31	10 37			10 54	10 40				10 46		10 59	11 01	10 52
	d			10 28	10 32	10 23	10 25	10 28	10 32	10 37			10 55	10 40			10 44	10 47		11 00	11 01	10 53
Norwood Junction 2	a			→	→		10 29			10 42			→							→	→	
New Cross Gate	d						10 37																
London Bridge 4 ⊖	a						10 43		10 47	10 55								11 02				
London Blackfriars 3 ⊖	a																					
City Thameslink 3	a																					
Farringdon 3 ⊖	a																					
St Pancras International 15 ⊖	a																					
St Albans City	a																					
Luton Airport Parkway 4 ✈	a																					
Luton 7	a																					
Bedford 10	a																					
Clapham Junction 10	a					10 32		10 37						10 50			10 55					11 02
	d					10 33		10 37						10 50			10 56					11 03
London Victoria 15 ⊖	a		10 35			10 40		10 44				10 50		10 57			11 02		11 05			11 10

Brighton - London and Bedford

Network Diagram - see first Page of Table 186

Station		SN 1	SN ◇1	FC 1	SN 1	GX 1 ⊼	SN ◇1	SN 1	SN ◇1	SN ◇1	SN 1	FC 1	GW 1	GX 1 ⊼	SN ◇1 ⊼	FC 1	SN ◇1 ⊼	SN 1	SN ◇1 ⊼	FC 1	SN 1	GW 1	GX 1 ⊼
Brighton 10	d						10 24					10 34				10 37	10 49						
Hove 2	d								10 21														
Preston Park	d															10 41							
Hassocks 4	d						10 34									10 47							
Burgess Hill 4	d						10 38									10 51							
Lewes 4	d									10 20													
Wivelsfield 4	d									10 35						10 53							
Haywards Heath 3	a								10 35	10 40		10 47				10 58							
	d								10 44			10 48				11 02							
Balcombe	d																						
Horsham 4	d							10 30							10 50								
Littlehaven	d							10 33															
Faygate	d																						
Ifield	d							10 39															
Crawley	d							10 43							10 59								
Three Bridges 4	a							10 46				10 56			11 02	11 11							
	d							10 48				10 57			11 03	11 12							
Gatwick Airport 10 ✈	a						10 51	10 52	10 55			11 01			11 07	11 16							
	d					10 50	10 53	10 53	10 56			11 02	11 03	11 05	11 08	11 16							11 20
Horley 4	d							10 56															
Salfords	d																						
Earlswood (Surrey)	d																						
Tonbridge 4	d				10 19																		
Leigh (Kent)	d				10 23																		
Penshurst	d				10 27																		
Edenbridge	d				10 33																		
Godstone	d				10 40																		
Nutfield	d				10 45																		
Reigate	d																				11 14	11 18	
Redhill 5	a				10 50			11 02					11 10		11 15						11 18	11 25	
	d				10 51			11 07							11 16						11 19		
Merstham	d							11 11													11 23		
Coulsdon South	d				10 58			11 16													11 28		
Purley 4	d	←	←	←	11 02			11 19										←	←	←	11 32		
East Croydon ⇋	a	10 54	10 59	11 01	11 07		11 08	11 24	11 11			11 16			11 27	11 31	11 22	11 24	11 27	11 31	11 37		
	d	10 55	11 00	11 01	11 07		11 08	11 25	11 12		11 14	11 17			11 28	11 32	11 23	11 25	11 28	11 32	11 37		
Norwood Junction 2	a	10 59			11 12			→							→	→		11 29			11 42		
New Cross Gate	d	11 07																11 37					
London Bridge 4 ⊖	a	11 13		11 17	11 25							11 32						11 43		11 47	11 55		
London Blackfriars 3 ⊖	a																						
City Thameslink 3	a																						
Farringdon 3 ⊖	a																						
St Pancras International 15 ⊖	a																						
St Albans City	a																						
Luton Airport Parkway 4 ✈	a																						
Luton 7	a																						
Bedford 10	a																						
Clapham Junction 10	a		11 09				11 17		11 21		11 25						11 32		11 37				
	d		11 10				11 18		11 21		11 26						11 33		11 37				
London Victoria 15 ⊖	a		11 16			11 20	11 24		11 28		11 32			11 35			11 40		11 44				11 50

Table 186

Brighton - London and Bedford

Network Diagram - see first Page of Table 186

		SN ■	SN ◇■	SN ◇■	GW ■	SN ■		FC ■	GX ■ ⌶	SN ◇■	FC ■	SN ◇■ ⌶	SN ■	SN ◇■	FC ■	SN ■		GX ■ ⌶	SN ◇■	SN ■	SN ◇■	SN ◇■	SN ■	FC ■	GW ■
Brighton 10	d							11 04			11 07	11 19							11 24					11 34	
Hove 2	d			10 51																	11 21				
Preston Park	d			10 55							11 11														
Hassocks 4	d										11 17								11 34						
Burgess Hill 4	d			11 04							11 21								11 38						
Lewes 4	d		10 50																			11 20			
Wivelsfield 4	d										11 23											11 35			
Haywards Heath 3	a		11 05	11 09				11 17			11 28										11 35	11 40		11 47	
	d			11 13				11 18			11 32											11 44		11 48	
Balcombe	d										11 37														
Horsham 4	d	11 00								11 20										11 30					
Littlehaven	d	11 03																		11 33					
Faygate	d																								
Ifield	d	11 09																		11 39					
Crawley	d	11 13								11 29										11 43					
Three Bridges 4	a	11 16						11 26		11 32	11 42									11 46				11 56	
	d	11 18						11 27		11 33	11 42									11 48				11 57	
Gatwick Airport 10 ✈	a	11 22		11 24				11 31		11 37	11 46								11 51	11 52		11 55		12 01	
	d	11 23		11 25				11 32	11 35	11 38	11 46							11 50	11 53	11 53		11 56		12 02	12 03
Horley 4	d	11 26								11 41										11 56					
Salfords	d	11 30																							
Earlswood (Surrey)	d	11 33																							
Tonbridge 4	d															11 19									
Leigh (Kent)	d															11 23									
Penshurst	d															11 27									
Edenbridge	d															11 33									
Godstone	d															11 40									
Nutfield	d															11 45									
Reigate	d				11 34																				
Redhill 5	a	11 36			11 38					11 47						11 50				12 02					12 10
	d	11 37								11 48						11 51				12 07					
Merstham	d	11 41																		12 11					
Coulsdon South	d	11 46														11 58				12 16					
Purley 4	d	11 49											←	←	←	12 02				12 19					
East Croydon ⇌	a	11 54		11 40				11 46		11 59	12 01	11 52	11 54	11 59	12 01	12 07			12 08	12 24		12 11		12 16	
	d	11 55		11 40		11 44		11 47		12 00	12 01	11 53	11 55	12 00	12 01	12 07			12 08	12 25		12 12	12 14	12 17	
Norwood Junction 2	a	→								→	→		11 59			12 12				→					
New Cross Gate	d												12 07												
London Bridge 4 ⊖	a							12 02					12 13		12 17	12 25								12 32	
London Blackfriars 3 ⊖	a																								
City Thameslink 3	a																								
Farringdon 3 ⊖	a																								
St Pancras International 15 ⊖	a																								
St Albans City	a																								
Luton Airport Parkway 4 ✈	a																								
Luton 7	a																								
Bedford 10	a																								
Clapham Junction 10	a			11 50		11 55						12 02		12 09					12 17			12 21	12 25		
	d			11 50		11 56						12 03		12 10					12 18			12 21	12 26		
London Victoria 15 ⊖	a			11 57		12 02			12 05			12 10		12 16				12 20	12 24			12 28	12 32		

Table 186

Saturdays

Brighton - London and Bedford

Network Diagram - see first Page of Table 186

		GX ■ ⌶		SN ◇■ ⌶	FC ■	SN ◇■ ⌶	SN ■	SN ◇■ ⌶	FC ■	SN ■	GW ■	GX ■ ⌶		SN ■	SN ◇■	SN ◇■	GW ■	SN ■	FC ■	GX ■ ⌶	SN ◇■	FC ■		SN ◇■ ⌶	SN ■
Brighton 10	d				11 37	11 49													12 04			12 07		12 19	
Hove 2	d															11 51									
Preston Park	d				11 41											11 55						12 11			
Hassocks 4	d				11 47																	12 17			
Burgess Hill 4	d				11 51											12 04						12 21			
Lewes 4	d														11 50										
Wivelsfield 4	d				11 53																	12 23			
Haywards Heath 3	a				11 58										12 05	12 09			12 17			12 28			
	d				12 02											12 13			12 18			12 32			
Balcombe	d																					12 37			
Horsham 4	d			11 50										12 00							12 20				
Littlehaven	d													12 03											
Faygate	d																								
Ifield	d													12 09											
Crawley	d			11 59										12 13							12 29				
Three Bridges 4	a			12 02	12 11									12 16					12 26		12 32	12 42			
	d			12 03	12 12									12 18					12 27		12 33	12 42			
Gatwick Airport 10 ✈	a			12 07	12 16									12 22		12 24			12 31		12 37	12 46			
	d	12 05		12 08	12 16							12 20		12 23		12 25			12 32	12 35	12 38	12 46			
Horley 4	d													12 26							12 41				
Salfords	d													12 30											
Earlswood (Surrey)	d													12 33											
Tonbridge 4	d																								
Leigh (Kent)	d																								
Penshurst	d																								
Edenbridge	d																								
Godstone	d																								
Nutfield	d																								
Reigate	d									12 14	12 19						12 34								
Redhill 5	a			12 15						12 18	12 25			12 36			12 38				12 47				
	d			12 16						12 19				12 37							12 48				
Merstham	d									12 23				12 41											
Coulsdon South	d									12 28				12 46											
Purley 4	d						←	←	←	12 32				12 49											←
East Croydon ⇌	a			12 27	12 31	12 22	12 24	12 27	12 31	12 37				12 54		12 40			12 46		12 59	13 01		12 52	12 54
	d			12 28	12 32	12 23	12 25	12 28	12 32	12 38				12 55		12 40		12 44	12 47		13 00	13 01		12 53	12 55
Norwood Junction 2	a			→	→		12 29			12 42				→							→	→			12 59
New Cross Gate	d						12 37																		13 07
London Bridge 4 ⊖	a						12 43		12 47	12 55									13 02						13 13
London Blackfriars 3 ⊖	a																								
City Thameslink 3	a																								
Farringdon 3 ⊖	a																								
St Pancras International 15 ⊖	a																								
St Albans City	a																								
Luton Airport Parkway 4 ✈	a																								
Luton 7	a																								
Bedford 10	a																								
Clapham Junction 10	a					12 32		12 37								12 50		12 55						13 02	
	d					12 33		12 37								12 50		12 56						13 03	
London Victoria 15 ⊖	a	12 35				12 40		12 44				12 50				12 57		13 02		13 05				13 10	

Brighton - London and Bedford

Network Diagram - see first Page of Table 186

		SN ◇1	FC 1	SN 1	GX 1 ⊥	SN ◇1	SN 1	SN ◇1	SN ◇1	SN 1	FC 1	GW 1	GX 1 ⊥	SN ◇1 ⊥	FC 1	SN ◇1 ⊥	SN 1	SN ◇1 ⊥	FC 1	SN 1	GW 1	GX 1 ⊥	SN 1
Brighton 10	d					12 24					12 34				12 37	12 49							
Hove 2	d							12 21															
Preston Park	d														12 41								
Hassocks 4	d					12 34									12 47								
Burgess Hill 4	d					12 38									12 51								
Lewes 4	d								12 20														
Wivelsfield 4	d								12 35						12 53								
Haywards Heath 3	a							12 35	12 40		12 47				12 58								
	d								12 44		12 48				13 02								
Balcombe	d																						
Horsham 4	d						12 30							12 50									13 00
Littlehaven	d						12 33																13 03
Faygate	d																						
Ifield	d						12 39																13 09
Crawley	d						12 43							12 59									13 13
Three Bridges 4	a						12 46				12 56			13 02	13 11								13 16
	d						12 48				12 57			13 03	13 12								13 18
Gatwick Airport 10 ✈	a					12 51	12 52		12 55		13 01			13 07	13 16								13 22
	d				12 50	12 53	12 53		12 56		13 02	13 03	13 05	13 08	13 16							13 20	13 23
Horley 4	d						12 56																13 26
Salfords	d																						13 30
Earlswood (Surrey)	d																						13 33
Tonbridge 4	d			12 19																			
Leigh (Kent)	d			12 23																			
Penshurst	d			12 27																			
Edenbridge	d			12 33																			
Godstone	d			12 40																			
Nutfield	d			12 45																			
Reigate	d																			13 14	13 18		
Redhill 5	a			12 50			13 02					13 10		13 15						13 18	13 25		13 36
	d			12 51			13 07							13 16						13 19			13 37
Merstham	d						13 11													13 23			13 41
Coulsdon South	d			12 58			13 16													13 28			13 46
Purley 4	d	←	←	13 02			13 19										←	←	←	13 32			13 49
East Croydon ⇌	a	12 59	13 01	13 07		13 08	13 24		13 11		13 16			13 27	13 31	13 22	13 24	13 27	13 31	13 37			13 54
	d	13 00	13 01	13 07		13 08	13 25		13 12	13 14	13 17			13 28	13 32	13 23	13 25	13 28	13 32	13 37			13 55
Norwood Junction 2	a			13 12			→							→	→		13 29			13 42			→
New Cross Gate	d																13 37						
London Bridge 4 ⊖	a		13 17	13 25							13 32						13 43		13 47	13 55			
London Blackfriars 3 ⊖	a																						
City Thameslink 3	a																						
Farringdon 3 ⊖	a																						
St Pancras International 15 ⊖	a																						
St Albans City	a																						
Luton Airport Parkway 4 ✈	a																						
Luton 7	a																						
Bedford 10	a																						
Clapham Junction 10	a	13 09				13 17			13 21	13 25						13 32		13 37					
	d	13 10				13 18			13 21	13 26						13 33		13 37					
London Victoria 15 ⊖	a	13 16			13 20	13 24			13 28	13 32			13 35			13 40		13 44				13 50	

Brighton - London and Bedford

Network Diagram - see first Page of Table 186

		SN ◇1	SN ◇1	GW 1	SN 1	FC 1	GX 1 ⊥	SN ◇1	FC 1	SN ◇1 ⊥	SN 1	SN ◇1	FC 1	SN 1	GX 1 ⊥	SN ◇1	SN 1	SN ◇1	SN ◇1	SN 1	FC 1	GW 1	GX 1 ⊥
Brighton 10	d					13 04			13 07	13 19						13 24					13 34		
Hove 2	d		12 51															13 21					
Preston Park	d		12 55						13 11														
Hassocks 4	d								13 17							13 34							
Burgess Hill 4	d		13 04						13 21							13 38							
Lewes 4	d	12 50																	13 20				
Wivelsfield 4	d								13 23										13 35				
Haywards Heath 3	a	13 05	13 09			13 17			13 28									13 35	13 40		13 47		
	d		13 13			13 18			13 32										13 44		13 48		
Balcombe	d								13 37														
Horsham 4	d							13 20									13 30						
Littlehaven	d																13 33						
Faygate	d																						
Ifield	d																13 39						
Crawley	d							13 29									13 43						
Three Bridges 4	a					13 26		13 32	13 42								13 46				13 56		
	d					13 27		13 33	13 42								13 48				13 57		
Gatwick Airport 10 ✈	a		13 24			13 31		13 37	13 46							13 51	13 52		13 55		14 01		
	d		13 25			13 32	13 35	13 38	13 46						13 50	13 53	13 53		13 56		14 02	14 03	14 05
Horley 4	d							13 41									13 56						
Salfords	d																						
Earlswood (Surrey)	d																						
Tonbridge 4	d													13 19									
Leigh (Kent)	d													13 23									
Penshurst	d													13 27									
Edenbridge	d													13 33									
Godstone	d													13 40									
Nutfield	d													13 45									
Reigate	d			13 34																			
Redhill 5	a			13 38				13 47						13 50			14 02					14 10	
	d							13 48						13 51			14 07						
Merstham	d																14 11						
Coulsdon South	d													13 58			14 16						
Purley 4	d										←	←	←	14 02			14 19						
East Croydon ⇌	a		13 40			13 46		13 59	14 01	13 52	13 54	13 59	14 01	14 07		14 08	14 24		14 11		14 16		
	d		13 40		13 44	13 47		14 00	14 01	13 53	13 55	14 00	14 01	14 07		14 08	14 25		14 12	14 14	14 17		
Norwood Junction 2	a							→	→		13 59			14 12			→						
New Cross Gate	d										14 07												
London Bridge 4 ⊖	a					14 02					14 13		14 17	14 25							14 32		
London Blackfriars 3 ⊖	a																						
City Thameslink 3	a																						
Farringdon 3 ⊖	a																						
St Pancras International 15 ⊖	a																						
St Albans City	a																						
Luton Airport Parkway 4 ✈	a																						
Luton 7	a																						
Bedford 10	a																						
Clapham Junction 10	a		13 50		13 55					14 02		14 09				14 17			14 21	14 25			
	d		13 50		13 56					14 03		14 10				14 18			14 21	14 26			
London Victoria 15 ⊖	a		13 57		14 02		14 05			14 10		14 16			14 20	14 24			14 28	14 32			14 35

Table 186

Saturdays

Brighton - London and Bedford

Network Diagram - see first Page of Table 186

		SN	FC	SN	SN	SN	FC	SN	GW	GX	SN	SN	SN	GW	SN	FC	GX	SN	FC	SN	SN	SN
		◇1	1	◇1	1	◇1	1	1	1	1	1	◇1	◇1	1	1	1	1	◇1	1	◇1	1	◇1
		H		H		H				H							H			H		
Brighton 10	d		13 37	13 49												14 04			14 07	14 19		
Hove 2	d												13 51									
Preston Park	d		13 41										13 55						14 11			
Hassocks 4	d		13 47																14 17			
Burgess Hill 4	d		13 51										14 04						14 21			
Lewes 4	d											13 50										
Wivelsfield 4	d		13 53																14 23			
Haywards Heath 3	a		13 58									14 05	14 09			14 17			14 28			
	d		14 02									14 13				14 18			14 32			
Balcombe	d																		14 37			
Horsham 4	d	13 50									14 00							14 20				
Littlehaven	d										14 03											
Faygate	d																					
Ifield	d										14 09											
Crawley	d	13 59									14 13							14 29				
Three Bridges 4	a	14 02	14 11								14 16					14 26		14 32	14 42			
	d	14 03	14 12								14 18					14 27		14 33	14 42			
Gatwick Airport 10 ✈	a	14 07	14 16								14 22	14 24				14 31		14 37	14 46			
	d	14 08	14 16							14 20	14 23	14 25				14 32	14 35	14 38	14 46			
Horley 4	d										14 26							14 41				
Salfords	d										14 30											
Earlswood (Surrey)	d										14 33											
Tonbridge 4	d																					
Leigh (Kent)	d																					
Penshurst	d																					
Edenbridge	d																					
Godstone	d																					
Nutfield	d																					
Reigate	d							14 14	14 19					14 34								
Redhill 5	a	14 15						14 18	14 25		14 36			14 38				14 47				
	d	14 16						14 19			14 37							14 48				
Merstham	d							14 23			14 41											
Coulsdon South	d							14 28			14 46											
Purley 4	d				←	←	←	14 32			14 49										←	←
East Croydon ⇌	a	14 27	14 31	14 22	14 24	14 27	14 31	14 37			14 54	14 40				14 46		14 59	15 01	14 52	14 54	14 59
	d	14 28	14 32	14 23	14 25	14 28	14 32	14 37			14 55	14 40			14 44	14 47		15 00	15 01	14 53	14 55	15 00
Norwood Junction 2	a	→	→		14 29			14 42			→							→	→		14 59	
New Cross Gate	d				14 37																15 07	
London Bridge 4 ⊖	a				14 43		14 47	14 55								15 02					15 13	
London Blackfriars 3 ⊖	a																					
City Thameslink 3	a																					
Farringdon 3 ⊖	a																					
St Pancras International 15 ⊖	a																					
St Albans City	a																					
Luton Airport Parkway 4 ✈	a																					
Luton 7	a																					
Bedford 10	a																					
Clapham Junction 10	a			14 32		14 37						14 50			14 55					15 02		15 09
	d			14 33		14 37						14 50			14 56					15 03		15 10
London Victoria 15 ⊖	a			14 40		14 44				14 50		14 57			15 02		15 05			15 10		15 16

Table 186

Saturdays

Brighton - London and Bedford

Network Diagram - see first Page of Table 186

		FC	SN	GX	SN	SN	SN	SN	SN	FC	GW	GX	SN	FC	SN	SN	SN	FC	SN	GW	GX	SN
		1	1	1	◇1	1	◇1	◇1	1	1	1	1	◇1	1	◇1	1	◇1	1	1	1	1	1
				H								H	H		H		H				H	
Brighton 10	d				14 24					14 34				14 37	14 49							
Hove 2	d						14 21															
Preston Park	d													14 41								
Hassocks 4	d				14 34									14 47								
Burgess Hill 4	d				14 38									14 51								
Lewes 4	d							14 20														
Wivelsfield 4	d							14 35						14 53								
Haywards Heath 3	a						14 35	14 40		14 47				14 58								
	d						14 44			14 48				15 02								
Balcombe	d																					
Horsham 4	d					14 30							14 50									15 00
Littlehaven	d					14 33																15 03
Faygate	d																					
Ifield	d					14 39																15 09
Crawley	d					14 43							14 59									15 13
Three Bridges 4	a					14 46				14 56			15 02	15 11								15 16
	d					14 48				14 57			15 03	15 12								15 18
Gatwick Airport 10 ✈	a				14 51	14 52	14 55			15 01			15 07	15 16								15 22
	d			14 50	14 53	14 53	14 56			15 02	15 03	15 05	15 08	15 16							15 20	15 23
Horley 4	d					14 56																15 26
Salfords	d																					15 30
Earlswood (Surrey)	d																					15 33
Tonbridge 4	d		14 19																			
Leigh (Kent)	d		14 23																			
Penshurst	d		14 27																			
Edenbridge	d		14 33																			
Godstone	d		14 40																			
Nutfield	d		14 45																			
Reigate	d																		15 14	15 18		
Redhill 5	a		14 50			15 02					15 10		15 15						15 18	15 25		15 36
	d		14 51			15 07							15 16						15 19			15 37
Merstham	d					15 11													15 23			15 41
Coulsdon South	d		14 58			15 16													15 28			15 46
Purley 4	d	←	15 02			15 19										←	←	←	15 32			15 49
East Croydon ⇌	a	15 01	15 07		15 08	15 24	15 11			15 16			15 27	15 31	15 22	15 24	15 27	15 31	15 37			15 54
	d	15 01	15 07		15 08	15 25	15 12		15 14	15 17			15 28	15 32	15 23	15 25	15 28	15 32	15 37			15 55
Norwood Junction 2	a		15 12			→							→	→		15 29			15 42			→
New Cross Gate	d															15 37						
London Bridge 4 ⊖	a	15 17	15 25							15 32						15 43		15 47	15 55			
London Blackfriars 3 ⊖	a																					
City Thameslink 3	a																					
Farringdon 3 ⊖	a																					
St Pancras International 15 ⊖	a																					
St Albans City	a																					
Luton Airport Parkway 4 ✈	a																					
Luton 7	a																					
Bedford 10	a																					
Clapham Junction 10	a				15 17		15 21		15 25						15 32		15 37					
	d				15 18		15 21		15 26						15 33		15 37					
London Victoria 15 ⊖	a			15 20	15 24		15 28		15 32			15 35			15 40		15 44				15 50	

Brighton - London and Bedford

Network Diagram - see first Page of Table 186

		SN	SN	GW	SN		FC	GX	SN	FC	SN	SN	SN	FC	SN		GX	SN	SN	SN	SN	SN	FC	GW	GX
		◇1	◇1	1	1		1	1 ✕	◇1	1	◇1 ✕	1	◇1	1	1		1 ✕	◇1	1	◇1	◇1	1	1	1	1 ✕
Brighton 10	d						15 04			15 07	15 19							15 24					15 34		
Hove 2	d		14 51																	15 21					
Preston Park	d		14 55							15 11															
Hassocks 4	d									15 17								15 34							
Burgess Hill 4	d		15 04							15 21								15 38							
Lewes 4	d	14 50																			15 20				
Wivelsfield 4	d									15 23											15 35				
Haywards Heath 3	a	15 05	15 09				15 17			15 28										15 35	15 40		15 47		
	d		15 13				15 18			15 32											15 44		15 48		
Balcombe	d									15 37															
Horsham 4	d								15 20										15 30						
Littlehaven	d																		15 33						
Faygate	d																								
Ifield	d																		15 39						
Crawley	d								15 29										15 43						
Three Bridges 4	a						15 26		15 32	15 42									15 46				15 56		
	d						15 27		15 33	15 42									15 48				15 57		
Gatwick Airport 10 ✈	a		15 24				15 31		15 37	15 46								15 51	15 52		15 55		16 01		
	d		15 25				15 32	15 35	15 38	15 46							15 50	15 53	15 53		15 56		16 02	16 03	16 05
Horley 4	d								15 41										15 56						
Salfords	d																								
Earlswood (Surrey)	d																								
Tonbridge 4	d														15 19										
Leigh (Kent)	d														15 23										
Penshurst	d														15 27										
Edenbridge	d														15 33										
Godstone	d														15 40										
Nutfield	d														15 45										
Reigate	d			15 34																					
Redhill 5	a			15 38					15 47						15 50				16 02					16 10	
	d								15 48						15 51				16 07						
Merstham	d																		16 11						
Coulsdon South	d														15 58				16 16						
Purley 4	d											←	←	←	16 02				16 19						
East Croydon 🚊	a		15 40				15 46		15 59	16 01	15 52	15 54	15 59	16 01	16 07			16 08	16 24		16 11		16 16		
	d		15 40		15 44		15 47		16 00	16 01	15 53	15 55	16 00	16 01	16 07			16 08	16 25		16 12	16 14	16 17		
Norwood Junction 2	a								→	→		15 59			16 12				→						
New Cross Gate	d											16 07													
London Bridge 4 ⊖	a						16 02					16 13		16 17	16 25								16 32		
London Blackfriars 3 ⊖	a																								
City Thameslink 3	a																								
Farringdon 3 ⊖	a																								
St Pancras International 15 ⊖	a																								
St Albans City	a																								
Luton Airport Parkway 4 ✈	a																								
Luton 7	a																								
Bedford 10	a																								
Clapham Junction 10	a		15 50		15 55						16 02		16 09					16 17			16 21	16 25			
	d		15 50		15 56						16 03		16 10					16 18			16 21	16 26			
London Victoria 15 ⊖	a		15 57		16 02			16 05			16 10		16 16				16 20	16 24			16 28	16 32			16 35

Brighton - London and Bedford

Network Diagram - see first Page of Table 186

			SN	FC	SN	SN	SN	FC	SN	GW	GX		SN	SN	SN	GW	SN	FC	GX	SN	FC		SN	SN	SN
			◇1 ✕	1	◇1 ✕	1	◇1 ✕	1	1	1	1 ✕		1	◇1	◇1	1	1	1	1 ✕	◇1	1		◇1 ✕	1	◇1
Brighton 10	d			15 37	15 49													16 04			16 07		16 19		
Hove 2	d														15 51										
Preston Park	d			15 41											15 55						16 11				
Hassocks 4	d			15 47																	16 17				
Burgess Hill 4	d			15 51											16 04						16 21				
Lewes 4	d												15 50												
Wivelsfield 4	d			15 53																	16 23				
Haywards Heath 3	a			15 58									16 05	16 09			16 17			16 28					
	d			16 02											16 13			16 18			16 32				
Balcombe	d																				16 37				
Horsham 4	d		15 50									16 00							16 20						
Littlehaven	d											16 03													
Faygate	d																								
Ifield	d											16 09													
Crawley	d		15 59									16 13							16 29						
Three Bridges 4	a		16 02	16 11									16 16					16 26		16 32	16 42				
	d		16 03	16 12									16 18					16 27		16 33	16 42				
Gatwick Airport 10 ✈	a		16 07	16 16									16 22		16 24			16 31		16 37	16 46				
	d		16 08	16 16							16 20		16 23		16 25			16 32	16 35	16 38	16 46				
Horley 4	d												16 26							16 41					
Salfords	d												16 30												
Earlswood (Surrey)	d												16 33												
Tonbridge 4	d																								
Leigh (Kent)	d																								
Penshurst	d																								
Edenbridge	d																								
Godstone	d																								
Nutfield	d																								
Reigate	d								16 14	16 19						16 34									
Redhill 5	a		16 15						16 18	16 25			16 36			16 38				16 47					
	d		16 16						16 19				16 37							16 48					
Merstham	d								16 23				16 41												
Coulsdon South	d								16 28				16 46												
Purley 4	d					←	←	←	16 32				16 49											←	←
East Croydon 🚊	a		16 27	16 31	16 22	16 24	16 27	16 31	16 37				16 54		16 40			16 46		16 59	17 01		16 52	16 54	16 59
	d		16 28	16 32	16 23	16 25	16 28	16 32	16 37				16 55		16 40		16 44	16 47		17 00	17 01		16 53	16 55	17 00
Norwood Junction 2	a		→	→		16 29			16 42				→							→	→			16 59	
New Cross Gate	d					16 37																		17 07	
London Bridge 4 ⊖	a					16 43		16 47	16 55									17 02						17 13	
London Blackfriars 3 ⊖	a																								
City Thameslink 3	a																								
Farringdon 3 ⊖	a																								
St Pancras International 15 ⊖	a																								
St Albans City	a																								
Luton Airport Parkway 4 ✈	a																								
Luton 7	a																								
Bedford 10	a																								
Clapham Junction 10	a				16 32		16 37								16 50		16 55						17 02		17 09
	d				16 33		16 37								16 50		16 56						17 03		17 10
London Victoria 15 ⊖	a				16 40		16 44				16 50				16 57		17 02		17 05				17 10		17 16

Table 186

Saturdays

Brighton - London and Bedford

Network Diagram - see first Page of Table 186

		FC ■	SN ■	GX ■	SN ◇■	SN ■	SN ◇■	SN ◇■	SN ■	FC ■	GW ■	GX ■	SN ◇■	FC ■	SN ◇■	SN ■	SN ◇■	FC ■	SN ■	GW ■	GX ■	SN ■
Brighton 10	d				16 24					16 34				16 37	16 49							
Hove 2	d						16 21															
Preston Park	d													16 41								
Hassocks 4	d				16 34									16 47								
Burgess Hill 4	d				16 38									16 51								
Lewes 4	d							16 20														
Wivelsfield 4	d							16 35						16 53								
Haywards Heath 3	a						16 35	16 40		16 47				16 58								
	d						16 44			16 48				17 02								
Balcombe	d																					
Horsham 4	d					16 30							16 50									17 00
Littlehaven	d					16 33																17 03
Faygate	d																					
Ifield	d					16 39																17 09
Crawley	d					16 43							16 59									17 13
Three Bridges 4	a					16 46				16 56			17 02	17 11								17 16
	d					16 48				16 57			17 03	17 12								17 18
Gatwick Airport 10 ✈	a				16 51	16 52	16 55			17 01			17 07	17 16								17 22
	d			16 50	16 53	16 53	16 56			17 02	17 03	17 05	17 08	17 16							17 20	17 23
Horley 4	d					16 56																17 26
Salfords	d																					17 30
Earlswood (Surrey)	d																					17 33
Tonbridge 4	d		16 19																			
Leigh (Kent)	d		16 23																			
Penshurst	d		16 27																			
Edenbridge	d		16 33																			
Godstone	d		16 40																			
Nutfield	d		16 45																			
Reigate	d																		17 14	17 18		
Redhill 5	a		16 50			17 02					17 10		17 15						17 18	17 25		17 36
	d		16 51			17 07							17 16						17 19			17 37
Merstham	d					17 11													17 23			17 41
Coulsdon South	d		16 58			17 16													17 28			17 46
Purley 4	d	←	17 02			17 19										←	←	←	17 32			17 49
East Croydon	a	17 01	17 07		17 08	17 24	17 11			17 16			17 27	17 31	17 22	17 24	17 27	17 31	17 37			17 54
	d	17 01	17 07		17 08	17 25	17 12		17 14	17 17			17 28	17 32	17 23	17 25	17 28	17 32	17 37			17 55
Norwood Junction 2	a		17 12			→							→	→		17 29			17 42			→
New Cross Gate	d															17 37						
London Bridge 4 ⊖	a	17 17	17 25							17 32						17 43		17 47	17 55			
London Blackfriars 3 ⊖	a																					
City Thameslink 3	a																					
Farringdon 3 ⊖	a																					
St Pancras International 15 ⊖	a																					
St Albans City	a																					
Luton Airport Parkway 4 ✈	a																					
Luton 7	a																					
Bedford 10	a																					
Clapham Junction 10	a				17 17		17 21		17 25						17 32		17 37					
	d				17 18		17 21		17 26						17 33		17 37					
London Victoria 15 ⊖	a			17 20	17 24		17 28		17 32			17 35			17 40		17 44				17 50	

Table 186

Saturdays

Brighton - London and Bedford

Network Diagram - see first Page of Table 186

		SN ◇■	SN ◇■	GW ■	SN ■	FC ■	GX ■	SN ◇■	FC ■	SN ◇■	SN ■	SN ◇■	FC ■	SN ■	GX ■	SN ◇■	SN ■	SN ◇■	SN ◇■	SN ■	FC ■	GW ■	GX ■
Brighton 10	d					17 04			17 07	17 19						17 24					17 34		
Hove 2	d		16 51															17 21					
Preston Park	d		16 55						17 11														
Hassocks 4	d								17 17							17 34							
Burgess Hill 4	d		17 04						17 21							17 38							
Lewes 4	d	16 50																	17 20				
Wivelsfield 4	d								17 23										17 35				
Haywards Heath 3	a	17 05	17 09			17 17			17 28									17 35	17 40		17 47		
	d	17 13				17 18			17 32									17 44			17 48		
Balcombe	d								17 37														
Horsham 4	d							17 20									17 30						
Littlehaven	d																17 33						
Faygate	d																						
Ifield	d																17 39						
Crawley	d							17 29									17 43						
Three Bridges 4	a					17 26		17 32	17 42								17 46				17 56		
	d					17 27		17 33	17 42								17 48				17 57		
Gatwick Airport 10 ✈	a	17 24				17 31		17 37	17 46							17 51	17 52	17 55			18 01		
	d	17 25				17 32	17 35	17 38	17 46						17 50	17 53	17 53	17 56			18 02	18 03	18 05
Horley 4	d							17 41									17 56						
Salfords	d																						
Earlswood (Surrey)	d																						
Tonbridge 4	d													17 19									
Leigh (Kent)	d													17 23									
Penshurst	d													17 27									
Edenbridge	d													17 33									
Godstone	d													17 40									
Nutfield	d													17 45									
Reigate	d			17 34																			
Redhill 5	a			17 38				17 47						17 50			18 02					18 10	
	d							17 48						17 51			18 07						
Merstham	d																18 11						
Coulsdon South	d													17 58			18 16						
Purley 4	d										←	←	←	18 02			18 19						
East Croydon	a	17 40				17 46		17 59	18 01	17 52	17 54	17 59	18 01	18 07		18 08	18 24	18 11			18 16		
	d	17 40			17 44	17 47		18 00	18 01	17 53	17 55	18 00	18 01	18 07		18 08	18 25	18 12		18 14	18 17		
Norwood Junction 2	a							→	→		17 59			18 12			→						
New Cross Gate	d										18 07												
London Bridge 4 ⊖	a					18 02					18 13		18 17	18 25							18 32		
London Blackfriars 3 ⊖	a																						
City Thameslink 3	a																						
Farringdon 3 ⊖	a																						
St Pancras International 15 ⊖	a																						
St Albans City	a																						
Luton Airport Parkway 4 ✈	a																						
Luton 7	a																						
Bedford 10	a																						
Clapham Junction 10	a	17 50			17 55					18 02		18 09				18 17		18 21		18 25			
	d	17 50			17 56					18 03		18 10				18 18		18 21		18 26			
London Victoria 15 ⊖	a	17 57			18 02		18 05			18 10		18 16			18 20	18 24		18 28		18 32			18 35

Brighton - London and Bedford

Network Diagram - see first Page of Table 186

Station		SN ◇1 🍴	FC 1	SN ◇1 🍴	SN 1	SN ◇1 🍴	FC 1	SN 1	GW 1	GX 1 🍴	SN 1	SN ◇1	SN ◇1	GW 1	SN 1	FC 1	GX 1 🍴	SN ◇1	FC 1	SN ◇1	SN 1	SN ◇1
Brighton 10	d		17 37	17 49												18 04			18 07	18 19		
Hove 2	d												17 51									
Preston Park	d		17 41										17 55						18 11			
Hassocks 4	d		17 47																18 17			
Burgess Hill 4	d		17 51										18 04						18 21			
Lewes 4	d											17 50										
Wivelsfield 4	d		17 53																18 23			
Haywards Heath 3	a		17 58									18 05	18 09			18 17			18 28			
	d		18 02									18 13				18 18			18 32			
Balcombe	d																		18 37			
Horsham 4	d	17 50									18 00							18 20				
Littlehaven	d										18 03											
Faygate	d																					
Ifield	d										18 09											
Crawley	d	17 59									18 13							18 29				
Three Bridges 4	a	18 02	18 11								18 16					18 26		18 32	18 42			
	d	18 03	18 12								18 18					18 27		18 33	18 42			
Gatwick Airport 10 ✈	a	18 07	18 16								18 22	18 24				18 31		18 37	18 46			
	d	18 08	18 16							18 20	18 23	18 25				18 32	18 35	18 38	18 46			
Horley 4	d										18 26							18 41				
Salfords	d										18 30											
Earlswood (Surrey)	d										18 33											
Tonbridge 4	d																					
Leigh (Kent)	d																					
Penshurst	d																					
Edenbridge	d																					
Godstone	d																					
Nutfield	d																					
Reigate	d							18 14	18 19					18 34								
Redhill 5	a	18 15						18 18	18 25		18 36			18 38				18 47				
	d	18 16						18 19			18 37							18 48				
Merstham	d							18 23			18 41											
Coulsdon South	d							18 28			18 46											
Purley 4	d				←	←	←	18 32			18 49										←	←
East Croydon 🚊	a	18 27	18 31	18 22	18 24	18 27	18 31	18 37			18 54	18 40				18 46		18 59	19 01	18 52	18 54	18 59
	d	18 28	18 32	18 23	18 25	18 28	18 32	18 37			18 55	18 40			18 44	18 47		19 00	19 01	18 53	18 55	19 00
Norwood Junction 2	a	→	→		18 29			18 42			→							→	→		18 59	
New Cross Gate	d				18 37																19 07	
London Bridge 4 ⊖	a				18 43		18 47	18 55								19 02					19 13	
London Blackfriars 3 ⊖	a																					
City Thameslink 3	a																					
Farringdon 3 ⊖	a																					
St Pancras International 15 ⊖	a																					
St Albans City	a																					
Luton Airport Parkway 4 ✈	a																					
Luton 7	a																					
Bedford 10	a																					
Clapham Junction 10	a			18 32		18 37						18 50			18 55					19 02		19 09
	d			18 33		18 37						18 50			18 56					19 03		19 10
London Victoria 15 ⊖	a			18 40		18 44				18 50		18 57			19 02		19 05			19 10		19 16

Brighton - London and Bedford

Network Diagram - see first Page of Table 186

Station		FC 1	SN 1	GX 1 🍴	SN ◇1	SN 1	SN ◇1	SN ◇1	SN 1	FC 1	GW 1	GX 1 🍴	SN	SN ◇1	GW 1	FC 1	SN ◇1	SN 1	SN ◇1	FC 1	GX 1 🍴	SN ◇1	SN 1
Brighton 10	d				18 24					18 34						18 37	18 49					18 54	
Hove 2	d						18 21																
Preston Park	d															18 41							
Hassocks 4	d				18 34											18 47						19 06	
Burgess Hill 4	d				18 38											18 51							
Lewes 4	d							18 20															
Wivelsfield 4	d							18 35								18 53							
Haywards Heath 3	a						18 35	18 40		18 47						18 58							
	d						18 44			18 48						19 02							
Balcombe	d																						
Horsham 4	d					18 32								18 50									19 02
Littlehaven	d					18 35																	19 05
Faygate	d																						
Ifield	d					18 41																	19 11
Crawley	d					18 45								18 59									19 14
Three Bridges 4	a					18 48				18 56				19 02		19 11							19 18
	d					18 50				18 57				19 03		19 12							19 18
Gatwick Airport 10 ✈	a				18 51	18 54	18 55			19 01				19 07		19 16						19 21	19 22
	d			18 50	18 53	18 55	18 56			19 02	19 03	19 05		19 08		19 16					19 20	19 23	19 23
Horley 4	d					18 58								19 11									19 26
Salfords	d																						19 30
Earlswood (Surrey)	d																						19 33
Tonbridge 4	d		18 19																				
Leigh (Kent)	d		18 23																				
Penshurst	d		18 27																				
Edenbridge	d		18 33																				
Godstone	d		18 40																				
Nutfield	d		18 45																				
Reigate	d												19 14		19 18								
Redhill 5	a		18 50			19 04					19 10		19 18	19 17	19 25								19 36
	d		18 51			19 07								19 18									19 37
Merstham	d					19 11																	19 41
Coulsdon South	d		18 58			19 16																	19 46
Purley 4	d	←	19 02			19 19												←	←	←			19 49
East Croydon 🚊	a	19 01	19 07		19 08	19 24	19 11			19 16				19 29		19 31	19 22	19 24	19 29	19 31		19 38	19 54
	d	19 01	19 07		19 08	19 25	19 12		19 14	19 17				19 29		19 32	19 23	19 25	19 29	19 32		19 38	19 57
Norwood Junction 2	a		19 12			→								→		→							→
New Cross Gate	d																						
London Bridge 4 ⊖	a	19 17	19 25							19 32										19 47			
London Blackfriars 3 ⊖	a																						
City Thameslink 3	a																						
Farringdon 3 ⊖	a																						
St Pancras International 15 ⊖	a																						
St Albans City	a																						
Luton Airport Parkway 4 ✈	a																						
Luton 7	a																						
Bedford 10	a																						
Clapham Junction 10	a				19 17		19 21		19 25								19 32	19 37	19 40			19 47	
	d				19 18		19 21		19 26								19 33	19 37	19 40			19 48	
London Victoria 15 ⊖	a			19 20	19 24		19 28		19 32			19 35					19 40	19 44	19 50		19 50	19 54	

Brighton - London and Bedford

Network Diagram - see first Page of Table 186

		SN ◇1	SN ◇1	GW 1	SN 1	SN 1	FC 1	GX 1	SN 1	FC 1	SN ◇1	SN 1	SN 1	FC 1	GX 1	SN 1	SN ◇1	SN ◇1	SN 1	FC 1	GW 1	GX 1
Brighton 10	d						19 04			19 07	19 19									19 34		
Hove 2	d		18 51														19 21					
Preston Park	d		18 55							19 11												
Hassocks 4	d									19 17												
Burgess Hill 4	d		19 04							19 21												
Lewes 4	d	18 50																19 20				
Wivelsfield 4	d									19 23								19 35				
Haywards Heath 3	a	19 05	19 09				19 17			19 28							19 35	19 40		19 47		
	d		19 14				19 18			19 32								19 44		19 48		
Balcombe	d									19 37												
Horsham 4	d								19 21							19 32						
Littlehaven	d															19 35						
Faygate	d																					
Ifield	d															19 41						
Crawley	d								19 30							19 45						
Three Bridges 4	a						19 26		19 33	19 42						19 48				19 56		
	d						19 27		19 34	19 42						19 50				19 57		
Gatwick Airport 10 ✈	a		19 25				19 31		19 38	19 46						19 54		19 55		20 01		
	d		19 26				19 32	19 35	19 39	19 46					19 50	19 55		19 56		20 02	20 03	20 05
Horley 4	d															19 58						
Salfords	d																					
Earlswood (Surrey)	d																					
Tonbridge 4	d				19 10																	
Leigh (Kent)	d				19 14																	
Penshurst	d				19 18																	
Edenbridge	d				19 24																	
Godstone	d				19 31																	
Nutfield	d				19 36																	
Reigate	d			19 34																		
Redhill 5	a			19 38	19 45				19 47							20 04					20 10	
	d								19 48							20 07						
Merstham	d															20 11						
Coulsdon South	d															20 16						
Purley 4	d											←	←	←		20 19						
East Croydon ⇌	a		19 41				19 46		20 00	20 01	19 52	19 54	20 00	20 01		20 24		20 11		20 16		
	d		19 42			19 44	19 47		20 00	20 01	19 53	19 57	20 00	20 01		20 26		20 12	20 14	20 17		
Norwood Junction 2	a								→	→						→						
New Cross Gate	d																					
London Bridge 4 ⊖	a						20 02							20 17						20 32		
London Blackfriars 3 ⊖	a																					
City Thameslink 3	a																					
Farringdon 3 ⊖	a																					
St Pancras International 15 ⊖	a																					
St Albans City	a																					
Luton Airport Parkway 4 ✈	a																					
Luton 7	a																					
Bedford 10	a																					
Clapham Junction 10	a		19 51			19 55					20 02	20 08	20 11					20 21	20 25			
	d		19 51			19 56					20 03	20 09	20 12					20 21	20 26			
London Victoria 15 ⊖	a		19 58			20 05		20 05			20 10	20 15	20 20		20 20			20 28	20 32			20 35

Brighton - London and Bedford

Network Diagram - see first Page of Table 186

		SN ◇1	GW 1	FC 1	SN ◇1	SN 1	SN ◇1	FC 1	GX 1	SN 1	SN ◇1	SN ◇1	GW 1	SN 1	SN 1	SN ◇1	FC 1	GX 1	SN ◇1	FC 1	SN ◇1	SN 1	SN ◇1
Brighton 10	d			19 37	19 49											19 54	20 04			20 07	20 19		
Hove 2	d											19 52											
Preston Park	d			19 41												19 58				20 11			
Hassocks 4	d			19 47												20 04				20 17			
Burgess Hill 4	d			19 51								20 02				20 08				20 21			
Lewes 4	d										19 50												
Wivelsfield 4	d			19 53							20 02					20 10				20 23			
Haywards Heath 3	a			19 58							20 07	20 10				20 14	20 17			20 28			
	d			20 02								20 14				20 22	20 18			20 32			
Balcombe	d																			20 37			
Horsham 4	d	19 52								20 02													
Littlehaven	d									20 05													
Faygate	d																						
Ifield	d									20 11													
Crawley	d	20 01								20 14									←				
Three Bridges 4	a	20 05		20 11						20 18						20 32	20 26		20 32	20 42			
	d	20 05		20 12						20 18						20 32	20 26		20 32	20 42			
Gatwick Airport 10 ✈	a	20 10		20 16						20 22		20 25				→	20 31		20 37	20 46			
	d	20 11		20 16					20 20	20 23		20 26					20 31	20 35	20 38	20 46			
Horley 4	d									20 26													
Salfords	d									20 30													
Earlswood (Surrey)	d									20 33													
Tonbridge 4	d													20 10									
Leigh (Kent)	d													20 14									
Penshurst	d													20 18									
Edenbridge	d													20 24									
Godstone	d													20 31									
Nutfield	d													20 36									
Reigate	d		20 19										20 34										
Redhill 5	a	20 18	20 25							20 36			20 38	20 45					20 47				
	d	20 18								20 37									20 48				
Merstham	d									20 41													
Coulsdon South	d									20 46													
Purley 4	d					←	←	←		20 49												←	←
East Croydon ⇌	a	20 29		20 31	20 22	20 24	20 29	20 31		20 54		20 41					20 46		20 59	21 01	20 52	20 54	20 59
	d	20 30		20 32	20 23	20 26	20 30	20 32		20 56		20 42			20 44		20 47		21 00	21 01	20 53	20 56	21 00
Norwood Junction 2	a	→		→						→									→	→			
New Cross Gate	d																						
London Bridge 4 ⊖	a							20 47									21 02						
London Blackfriars 3 ⊖	a																						
City Thameslink 3	a																						
Farringdon 3 ⊖	a																						
St Pancras International 15 ⊖	a																						
St Albans City	a																						
Luton Airport Parkway 4 ✈	a																						
Luton 7	a																						
Bedford 10	a																						
Clapham Junction 10	a				20 32	20 37	20 40					20 51			20 55						21 02	21 07	21 10
	d				20 33	20 37	20 41					20 51			20 56						21 03	21 07	21 11
London Victoria 15 ⊖	a				20 40	20 44	20 50		20 50			20 58			21 02			21 05			21 10	21 14	21 17

Brighton - London and Bedford

Network Diagram - see first Page of Table 186

		FC 1	GX 1	SN ◇1	SN 1	SN 1		FC 1	GW 1	GX 1	SN ◇1	GW 1	FC 1	SN ◇1	SN 1	SN ◇1		FC 1	GX 1	SN 1	SN ◇1	SN ◇1	SN 1	GW 1	SN 1
Brighton 10	d							20 34					20 37	20 49											
Hove 2	d			20 22																		20 52			
Preston Park	d												20 41												
Hassocks 4	d												20 47												
Burgess Hill 4	d												20 51									21 04			
Lewes 4	d																				20 50				
Wivelsfield 4	d												20 53								21 04				
Haywards Heath 3	a			20 36				20 47					20 58								21 09	21 11			
	d			20 39				20 48					21 02								21 15				
Balcombe	d																								
Horsham 4	d					20 32					20 52									21 02					
Littlehaven	d					20 35														21 05					
Faygate	d																								
Ifield	d					20 41														21 11					
Crawley	d					20 45					21 01									21 14					
Three Bridges 4	a			20 47		20 48		20 56			21 05		21 11							21 18					
	d			20 48		20 51		20 57			21 05		21 12							21 18					
Gatwick Airport 10 ✈	a			20 52		20 56		21 01			21 10		21 16							21 22	21 26				
	d		20 50	20 53		20 57		21 02	21 03	21 05	21 11		21 16						21 20	21 23	21 27				
Horley 4	d					20 59														21 26					
Salfords	d																			21 30					
Earlswood (Surrey)	d																			21 33					
Tonbridge 4	d																						21 10		
Leigh (Kent)	d																						21 14		
Penshurst	d																						21 18		
Edenbridge	d																						21 24		
Godstone	d																						21 31		
Nutfield	d																						21 36		
Reigate	d											21 18												21 40	
Redhill 5	a					21 06			21 10		21 18	21 25								21 36			21 41	21 44	
	d					21 07					21 18									21 37					
Merstham	d					21 11														21 41					
Coulsdon South	d					21 16														21 46					
Purley 4	d	←				21 19									←	←		←		21 49					
East Croydon	a	21 01		21 08		21 24		21 16			21 30		21 31	21 22	21 24	21 30		21 31		21 54	21 41				
	d	21 01		21 09	21 14	21 26		21 17			21 31		21 32	21 23	21 26	21 31		21 32		21 56	21 42				21 44
Norwood Junction 2	a					→					→		→							→					
New Cross Gate	d																								
London Bridge 4 ⊖	a	21 17						21 32										21 47							
London Blackfriars 3 ⊖	a																								
City Thameslink 3	a																								
Farringdon 3 ⊖	a																								
St Pancras International 15 ⊖	a																								
St Albans City	a																								
Luton Airport Parkway 4 ✈	a																								
Luton 7	a																								
Bedford 10	a																								
Clapham Junction 10	a			21 18	21 25									21 32	21 37	21 40					21 51				21 55
	d			21 18	21 26									21 33	21 37	21 41					21 51				21 56
London Victoria 15 ⊖	a		21 20	21 26	21 32					21 35				21 40	21 44	21 50			21 50		21 58				22 02

Table 186

Brighton - London and Bedford

Network Diagram - see first Page of Table 186

		SN 1		SN ◇1	FC 1	SN ◇1	SN 1	SN ◇1	FC 1	GX 1	SN ◇1	SN 1		SN 1	GX 1	SN ◇1	FC 1	SN ◇1	SN 1	SN ◇1	FC 1	GX 1		GW 1	SN 1
Brighton 10	d			21 00	21 07	21 19											21 37	21 49							
Hove 2	d										21 22														
Preston Park	d			21 04	21 11												21 41								
Hassocks 4	d			21 10	21 17												21 47								
Burgess Hill 4	d			21 14	21 21												21 51								
Lewes 4	d																								
Wivelsfield 4	d			21 16	21 23												21 53								
Haywards Heath 3	a			21 21	21 28						21 36						21 58								
	d			21 22	21 32						21 39						22 02								
Balcombe	d				21 37																				
Horsham 4	d													21 32		21 52									22 02
Littlehaven	d													21 35											22 05
Faygate	d																								
Ifield	d													21 41											22 11
Crawley	d													21 45		22 01									22 14
Three Bridges 4	a			21 31	21 42						21 47			21 48		22 05	22 11								22 18
	d			21 32	21 42						21 48			21 52		22 05	22 12								22 19
Gatwick Airport 10 ✈	a			21 37	21 46						21 52			21 56		22 10	22 16								22 23
	d	21 35		21 38	21 46					21 50	21 53			21 57	22 05	22 11	22 16					22 20		22 22	22 24
Horley 4	d													22 00											22 27
Salfords	d																								22 31
Earlswood (Surrey)	d																								22 34
Tonbridge 4	d																								
Leigh (Kent)	d																								
Penshurst	d																								
Edenbridge	d																								
Godstone	d																								
Nutfield	d																								
Reigate	d																								
Redhill 5	a			21 47										22 06		22 18								22 30	22 37
	d			21 47										22 07		22 18									22 38
Merstham	d													22 11											22 42
Coulsdon South	d													22 16											22 47
Purley 4	d						←	←	←					22 19					←	←	←				22 50
East Croydon	a			21 59	22 01	21 52	21 54	21 59	22 01		22 08			22 24		22 30	22 31	22 22	22 24	22 30	22 31				22 55
	d			22 00	22 01	21 53	21 56	22 00	22 01		22 09	22 14		22 26		22 31	22 32	22 23	22 26	22 31	22 32				22 56
Norwood Junction 2	a			→	→									→		→	→								→
New Cross Gate	d																								
London Bridge 4 ⊖	a								22 17												22 47				
London Blackfriars 3 ⊖	a																								
City Thameslink 3	a																								
Farringdon 3 ⊖	a																								
St Pancras International 15 ⊖	a																								
St Albans City	a																								
Luton Airport Parkway 4 ✈	a																								
Luton 7	a																								
Bedford 10	a																								
Clapham Junction 10	a					22 02	22 07	22 10			22 18	22 25						22 32	22 37	22 40					
	d					22 03	22 07	22 11			22 18	22 26						22 33	22 37	22 41					
London Victoria 15 ⊖	a	22 05				22 13	22 15	22 20		22 20	22 26	22 35			22 35			22 40	22 44	22 50		22 50			

Table 186

Brighton - London and Bedford

Network Diagram - see first Page of Table 186

		SN ◇1 🍴	SN ◇1 A 🍴	SN 1	GX 1	SN 1	SN 1	SN ◇1		FC 1	GW 1	GX 1	SN 1	SN 1	FC 1	SN ◇1	FC 1	GW 1		GX 1	SN 1	SN 1	GX 1	GW 1	SN ◇1
Brighton 10	d							22 00		22 07					22 33										23 02
Hove 2	d		21 52																						
Preston Park	d							22 04		22 11					22 37										23 06
Hassocks 4	d							22 10		22 17					22 43										23 12
Burgess Hill 4	d		22 04					22 14		22 21					22 47										23 16
Lewes 4	d	21 50														22 40									
Wivelsfield 4	d	22 02						22 16		22 23					22 49	22 54									23 19
Haywards Heath 3	a	22 06	22 09					22 21		22 28					22 53	22 58									23 23
	d	22 13						22 22		22 32					22 54	22 59									23 24
Balcombe	d									22 37					22 59										
Horsham 4	d																				23 02				
Littlehaven	d																				23 05				
Faygate	d																								
Ifield	d																				23 11				
Crawley	d																←				23 14				
Three Bridges 4	a							22 31		22 42					23 05	23 08	23 05				23 18				23 32
	d							22 32		22 42					23 12	23 08	23 12				23 18				23 47
Gatwick Airport 10 ✈	a	22 24						22 37		22 46					→	23 12	23 16				23 22				→
	d	22 25			22 35			22 38		22 46		22 50	23 05			23 13	23 16	23 18		23 20	23 23		23 35		
Horley 4	d																				23 26				
Salfords	d																				23 30				
Earlswood (Surrey)	d																				23 33				
Tonbridge 4	d			22 10																		23 17			
Leigh (Kent)	d			22 14																		23 21			
Penshurst	d			22 18																		23 25			
Edenbridge	d			22 24																		23 31			
Godstone	d			22 31																		23 38			
Nutfield	d			22 36																		23 43			
Reigate	d										22 48													23 54	
Redhill 5	a			22 42				22 46			22 52							23 25			23 36	23 49		23 58	
	d							22 46													23 37				
Merstham	d																				23 41				
Coulsdon South	d																				23 46				
Purley 4	d						←														23 49				
East Croydon ⇌	a	22 40					22 55	22 59		23 01						23 29	23 32				23 55				
	d	22 40				22 44	22 56	23 00		23 01				23 14		23 30	23 32				23 56				
Norwood Junction 2	a																								
New Cross Gate	d																								
London Bridge 4 ⊖	a									23 17							23 47								
London Blackfriars 3 ⊖	a																								
City Thameslink 3	a																								
Farringdon 3 ⊖	a																								
St Pancras International 15 ⊖	a																								
St Albans City	a																								
Luton Airport Parkway 4 ✈	a																								
Luton 7	a																								
Bedford 10	a																								
Clapham Junction 10	a	22 49				22 55	23 06	23 10						23 25		23 41					00 11				
	d	22 50				22 56	23 07	23 11						23 26		23 42					00 12				
London Victoria 15 ⊖	a	22 57			23 05	23 05	23 14	23 20				23 20	23 35	23 35		23 52				23 55	00 18		00 05		

A 🍴 from Haywards Heath

Table 186

Brighton - London and Bedford

Network Diagram - see first Page of Table 186

		FC 1	GX 1	SN ◇1		FC 1
Brighton 10	d	23 11				23 37
Hove 2	d					
Preston Park	d					23 41
Hassocks 4	d	23 20				23 47
Burgess Hill 4	d	23 23				23 51
Lewes 4	d					
Wivelsfield 4	d					23 53
Haywards Heath 3	a	23 28				23 58
	d	23 29				23 59
Balcombe	d					00 04
Horsham 4	d					
Littlehaven	d					
Faygate	d					
Ifield	d					
Crawley	d			←		
Three Bridges 4	a	23 37		23 32		00 10
	d	23 38		23 47		00 10
Gatwick Airport 10 ✈	a	23 42		23 52		00 14
	d	23 43	23 50	23 53		00 15
Horley 4	d			23 56		
Salfords	d					
Earlswood (Surrey)	d					
Tonbridge 4	d					
Leigh (Kent)	d					
Penshurst	d					
Edenbridge	d					
Godstone	d					
Nutfield	d					
Reigate	d					
Redhill 5	a			00 03		00 22
	d			00 03		00 23
Merstham	d					
Coulsdon South	d					
Purley 4	d			00 11		
East Croydon ⇌	a	00 01		00 16		00 35
	d	00 04		00 17		00 36
Norwood Junction 2	a					
New Cross Gate	d					
London Bridge 4 ⊖	a	00 19				00 52
London Blackfriars 3 ⊖	a					
City Thameslink 3	a					
Farringdon 3 ⊖	a					
St Pancras International 15 ⊖	a					
St Albans City	a					
Luton Airport Parkway 4 ✈	a					
Luton 7	a					
Bedford 10	a					
Clapham Junction 10	a			00 29		
	d			00 29		
London Victoria 15 ⊖	a		00 20	00 37		

Brighton - London and Bedford

Network Diagram - see first Page of Table 186

		SN 1 A	GX 1 A	SN ◇1 A	FC 1 A	GX 1 A	SN ◇1 A	SN 1	FC 1 A	GX 1		GW 1 A	SN	GX 1	GX 1	SN 1	GX 1	SN 1	SN 1	SN 1		GX 1	FC 1	GX 1	SN 1
Brighton 10	d			23p02	23p11				23p37																
Hove 2	d																								
Preston Park	d			23p06					23p41																
Hassocks 4	d			23p12	23p20				23p47																
Burgess Hill 4	d			23p16	23p23				23p51																
Lewes 4	d																								
Wivelsfield 4	d			23p19					23p53																
Haywards Heath 3	a			23p23	23p28				23p58																
	d			23p24	23p29				23p59																
Balcombe	d								00 04																
Horsham 4	d	23p02																							
Littlehaven	d	23p05																							
Faygate	d																								
Ifield	d	23p11																							
Crawley	d	23p14					←																		
Three Bridges 4	a	23p18		23p32	23p37		23p32		00 10																
	d	23p18		23p47	23p38		23p47		00 10							01 10		02 10	03 10	04 10			05 10		05 30
Gatwick Airport 10 ✈	a	23p22		→	23p42		23p52		00 14							01 19		02 14	03 14	04 14			05 14		05 34
	d	23p23	23p35		23p43	23p50	23p53	00 07	00 15	00 20				00 35	00 50	01 20	01 35	02 15	03 15	04 15		04 35	05 15	05 20	05 36
Horley 4	d	23p26					23p56									01 22		02 18	03 18	04 18					05 38
Salfords	d	23p30																							
Earlswood (Surrey)	d	23p33																							
Tonbridge 4	d																								
Leigh (Kent)	d																								
Penshurst	d																								
Edenbridge	d																								
Godstone	d																								
Nutfield	d																								
Reigate	d											00 45													
Redhill 5	a	23p36					00 03		00 22			00 49													05 46
	d	23p37					00 03		00 23																05 46
Merstham	d	23p41																							
Coulsdon South	d	23p46																							
Purley 4	d	23p49					00 11									01 37		02 33	03 33	04 33					05 56
East Croydon	a	23p55			00 01		00 16		00 35							01 42		02 39	03 39	04 39			05 31		06 01
	d	23p56			00 04		00 17		00 36				00 49			01 43		02 40	03 40	04 40			05 32		06 02
Norwood Junction 2	a																						05 36		
New Cross Gate	d																								
London Bridge 4 ⊖	a				00 19				00 52														05 59		
London Blackfriars 3 ⊖	a																								
City Thameslink 3	a																								
Farringdon 3 ⊖	a																								
St Pancras International 15 ⊖	a																								
St Albans City	a																								
Luton Airport Parkway 4 ✈	a																								
Luton 7	a																								
Bedford 10	a																								
Clapham Junction 10	a	00 11					00 29						01 03			01 54		02 53	03 53	04 53					06 14
	d	00 12					00 29						01 03			01 54		02 53	03 53	04 53					06 15
London Victoria 15 ⊖	a	00 18	00 05			00 20	00 37	00 42		00 55			01 10	01 11	01 25	02 05	02 10	03 05	04 05	05 05		05 10		05 58	06 22

A not 11 December

Brighton - London and Bedford

Network Diagram - see first Page of Table 186

		GX 1	GX 1 ⌶	GW 1	FC 1	SN 1		GX 1 ⌶	GX 1 ⌶	FC 1	GX 1 ⌶	SN ◇1	GW 1	GX 1 ⌶	GW 1	FC 1		GX 1 ⌶	SN 1	GX 1 ⌶	SN ◇1	FC 1	SN 1	GX 1 ⌶	SN ◇1 ⌶
Brighton 10	d				05 44					06 11		06 19				06 44					07 00	07 14			
Hove 2	d																								
Preston Park	d											06 22									07 03				
Hassocks 4	d				05 52					06 20		06 29				06 53					07 10	07 23			
Burgess Hill 4	d				05 56					06 25		06 32				06 56					07 13	07 26			
Lewes 4	d																								07 20
Wivelsfield 4	d											06 34									07 15				07 32
Haywards Heath 3	a				06 01					06 30		06 39				07 01					07 20	07 31			07 36
	d				06 01					06 31		06 39				07 02					07 20	07 32			07 39
Balcombe	d																				07 26				
Horsham 4	d					06 04													07 03						
Littlehaven	d					06 07													07 06						
Faygate	d																								
Ifield	d					06 13													07 12						
Crawley	d					06 17													07 16						
Three Bridges 4	a				06 10	06 20				06 39		06 48				07 10			07 19		07 31	07 40			
	d				06 11	06 21				06 40		06 48				07 10			07 20		07 32	07 40			
Gatwick Airport 10 ✈	a				06 15	06 25				06 44		06 52				07 14			07 24		07 37	07 44			07 51
	d	05 50	06 05	06 08	06 16			06 20	06 35	06 45	06 50	06 53		07 05	07 08	07 15		07 20	07 25	07 35	07 38	07 45		07 50	07 53
Horley 4	d																		07 28						
Salfords	d																								
Earlswood (Surrey)	d																								
Tonbridge 4	d																						07 29		
Leigh (Kent)	d																						07 33		
Penshurst	d																						07 37		
Edenbridge	d																						07 43		
Godstone	d																						07 50		
Nutfield	d																						07 55		
Reigate	d												07 05												
Redhill 5	a			06 17									07 09		07 16				07 34		07 45		08 00		
	d																		07 35		07 46				
Merstham	d																		07 39						
Coulsdon South	d																		07 44						
Purley 4	d																		07 50						
East Croydon	a				06 32					07 01		07 10				07 31			07 56		07 59	08 01			08 10
	d				06 32					07 02		07 10				07 32			07 56		08 00	08 02			08 10
Norwood Junction 2	a				06 36														08 00						
New Cross Gate	d																								
London Bridge 4 ⊖	a				06 59					07 15						07 45			08 12			08 15			
London Blackfriars 3 ⊖	a																								
City Thameslink 3	a																								
Farringdon 3 ⊖	a																								
St Pancras International 15 ⊖	a																								
St Albans City	a																								
Luton Airport Parkway 4 ✈	a																								
Luton 7	a																								
Bedford 10	a																								
Clapham Junction 10	a											07 24									08 11				08 23
	d											07 24									08 12				08 24
London Victoria 15 ⊖	a	06 25	06 40					06 55	07 10		07 25	07 31		07 40				07 55		08 10	08 18			08 25	08 30

Table 186

Sundays

Brighton - London and Bedford

Network Diagram - see first Page of Table 186

Station		SN ◇1	GX 1	GW 1	FC 1	GW 1	GX 1	SN ◇1	SN 1	SN 1	GX 1	SN ◇1	FC 1	SN 1	GX 1	SN ◇1	SN ◇1	SN ◇1	GX 1	GW 1	FC 1	GW 1
Brighton 10	d				07 44							08 00	08 14				08 34				08 44	
Hove 2	d							07 54														
Preston Park	d											08 03										
Hassocks 4	d				07 53							08 10	08 23								08 53	
Burgess Hill 4	d				07 56			08 04				08 13	08 26								08 56	
Lewes 4	d															08 16						
Wivelsfield 4	d											08 15				08 31						
Haywards Heath 3	a				08 01			08 09				08 20	08 31			08 36					09 01	
	d				08 02			08 10				08 20	08 32			08 39					09 02	
Balcombe	d											08 26										
Horsham 4	d	07 42								08 03								08 42				
Littlehaven	d									08 06												
Faygate	d																					
Ifield	d									08 12												
Crawley	d	07 51								08 16								08 51				
Three Bridges 4	a	07 54			08 10					08 19		08 31	08 40					08 54			09 10	
	d	07 55			08 10					08 20		08 32	08 40					08 55			09 10	
Gatwick Airport 10 ✈	a	07 59			08 14			08 22		08 24		08 37	08 44			08 51	08 55	08 59			09 14	
	d	08 00	08 05	08 08	08 15		08 20	08 23		08 25	08 35	08 38	08 45		08 50	08 53	08 56	09 00	09 05	09 08	09 15	
Horley 4	d	08 02								08 28								09 02				
Salfords	d																					
Earlswood (Surrey)	d																					
Tonbridge 4	d													08 29								
Leigh (Kent)	d													08 33								
Penshurst	d													08 37								
Edenbridge	d													08 43								
Godstone	d													08 50								
Nutfield	d													08 55								
Reigate	d					08 13																09 13
Redhill 5	a	08 09		08 16		08 18				08 34		08 45		09 00				09 09		09 16		09 18
	d	08 09								08 35		08 46						09 10				
Merstham	d									08 39												
Coulsdon South	d									08 44												
Purley 4	d	08 20								08 50								09 20				
East Croydon ⇌	a	08 26			08 31			08 40		08 56		08 59	09 01			09 10	09 12	09 26			09 31	
	d	08 26			08 32			08 41	08 50	08 56		09 00	09 02			09 10	09 13	09 26			09 32	
Norwood Junction 2	a									09 00												
New Cross Gate	d																					
London Bridge 4 ⊖	a				08 45					09 12			09 15								09 45	
London Blackfriars 3 ⊖	a																					
City Thameslink 3	a																					
Farringdon 3 ⊖	a																					
St Pancras International 15 ⊖	a																					
St Albans City	a																					
Luton Airport Parkway 4 ✈	a																					
Luton 7	a																					
Bedford 10	a																					
Clapham Junction 10	a	08 37						08 54	09 01			09 11				09 24	09 27	09 37				
	d	08 38						08 55	09 02			09 12				09 25	09 27	09 38				
London Victoria 15 ⊖	a	08 46	08 40				08 55	09 01	09 08		09 10	09 18			09 25	09 31	09 35	09 46	09 40			

Table 186

Sundays

Brighton - London and Bedford

Network Diagram - see first Page of Table 186

Station		GX 1	SN ◇1	SN 1	SN 1	GX 1	SN ◇1	FC 1	SN 1	GX 1	SN ◇1	SN ◇1	SN ◇1	GX 1	GW 1	FC 1	GW 1	GX 1	SN ◇1	SN 1	SN 1	GX 1	SN ◇1
Brighton 10	d						09 00	09 14				09 34				09 44							10 00
Hove 2	d		08 54																09 54				
Preston Park	d						09 03																10 03
Hassocks 4	d						09 10	09 23								09 53							10 10
Burgess Hill 4	d		09 05				09 13	09 26								09 56			10 05				10 13
Lewes 4	d										09 16												
Wivelsfield 4	d						09 15				09 31												10 15
Haywards Heath 3	a		09 10				09 20	09 31			09 35					10 01			10 10				10 20
	d		09 10				09 20	09 32			09 39					10 02			10 10				10 20
Balcombe	d						09 26																10 26
Horsham 4	d				09 03								09 42								10 03		
Littlehaven	d				09 06																10 06		
Faygate	d																						
Ifield	d				09 12																10 12		
Crawley	d				09 16								09 51								10 16		
Three Bridges 4	a				09 19		09 31	09 40					09 54			10 10					10 19		10 31
	d				09 20		09 32	09 40					09 55			10 10					10 20		10 32
Gatwick Airport 10 ✈	a		09 21		09 24		09 37	09 44			09 52	09 56	09 59			10 14			10 21		10 24		10 37
	d	09 20	09 23		09 25	09 35	09 38	09 45		09 50	09 53	09 57	10 00	10 05	10 08	10 15		10 20	10 23		10 25	10 35	10 38
Horley 4	d				09 28								10 02								10 28		
Salfords	d																						
Earlswood (Surrey)	d																						
Tonbridge 4	d								09 29														
Leigh (Kent)	d								09 33														
Penshurst	d								09 37														
Edenbridge	d								09 43														
Godstone	d								09 50														
Nutfield	d								09 55														
Reigate	d																10 13						
Redhill 5	a				09 34		09 45		10 00				10 09		10 16		10 18				10 34		10 45
	d				09 35		09 46						10 10								10 35		10 46
Merstham	d				09 39																10 39		
Coulsdon South	d				09 44																10 44		
Purley 4	d				09 50								10 20								10 50		
East Croydon ⇌	a		09 40		09 56		09 59	10 01			10 10	10 13	10 26			10 31			10 40		10 56		10 59
	d		09 41	09 50	09 56		10 00	10 02			10 10	10 14	10 26			10 32			10 40	10 50	10 56		11 00
Norwood Junction 2	a				10 00																11 00		
New Cross Gate	d																						
London Bridge 4 ⊖	a				10 12			10 15								10 45					11 12		
London Blackfriars 3 ⊖	a																						
City Thameslink 3	a																						
Farringdon 3 ⊖	a																						
St Pancras International 15 ⊖	a																						
St Albans City	a																						
Luton Airport Parkway 4 ✈	a																						
Luton 7	a																						
Bedford 10	a																						
Clapham Junction 10	a		09 54	10 01			10 11				10 24	10 27	10 37						10 54	11 01			11 11
	d		09 55	10 02			10 12				10 25	10 28	10 38						10 55	11 02			11 12
London Victoria 15 ⊖	a	09 55	10 01	10 08		10 10	10 18			10 25	10 31	10 35	10 46	10 40				10 55	11 01	11 08		11 10	11 18

Brighton - London and Bedford

Network Diagram - see first Page of Table 186

		FC 1	SN 1	GX 1 ⌶	SN ◇1 ⌶	SN ◇1 ⌶	SN ◇1 ⌶	GX 1 ⌶	GW 1	FC 1	GW 1	GX 1 ⌶	SN ◇1	SN 1	SN 1	GX 1 ⌶	SN ◇1	FC 1	SN 1	GX 1 ⌶	SN ◇1 ⌶	SN ◇1 ⌶
Brighton 10	d	10 14				10 34				10 44							11 00	11 14				11 34
Hove 2	d												10 54									
Preston Park	d																11 03					
Hassocks 4	d	10 23								10 53							11 10	11 23				
Burgess Hill 4	d	10 26								10 56			11 05				11 13	11 26				
Lewes 4	d				10 16																11 16	
Wivelsfield 4	d				10 31												11 15				11 31	
Haywards Heath 5	a	10 31			10 35					11 01			11 10				11 20	11 31			11 35	
	d	10 32			10 39					11 02			11 10				11 20	11 32			11 39	
Balcombe	d																11 26					
Horsham 4	d						10 42								11 03							
Littlehaven	d														11 06							
Faygate	d																					
Ifield	d														11 12							
Crawley	d						10 51								11 16							
Three Bridges 4	a	10 40					10 54			11 10					11 19		11 31	11 40				
	d	10 40					10 55			11 10					11 20		11 32	11 40				
Gatwick Airport 10 ✈	a	10 44			10 52	10 56	10 59			11 14			11 21		11 24		11 37	11 44			11 51	11 55
	d	10 45		10 50	10 53	10 57	11 00	11 05	11 08	11 15		11 20	11 23		11 25	11 35	11 38	11 45		11 50	11 52	11 56
Horley 4	d						11 02								11 28							
Salfords	d																					
Earlswood (Surrey)	d																					
Tonbridge 4	d		10 29																11 29			
Leigh (Kent)	d		10 33																11 33			
Penshurst	d		10 37																11 37			
Edenbridge	d		10 43																11 43			
Godstone	d		10 50																11 50			
Nutfield	d		10 55																11 55			
Reigate	d										11 13											
Redhill 5	a		11 00				11 09		11 16		11 18				11 34		11 45		12 00			
	d						11 10								11 35		11 46					
Merstham	d														11 39							
Coulsdon South	d														11 44							
Purley 4	d						11 20								11 50							
East Croydon ⇌	a	11 01			11 10	11 13	11 26			11 31			11 40		11 56		11 59	12 01			12 09	12 13
	d	11 02			11 10	11 14	11 26			11 32			11 41	11 50	11 56		12 00	12 02			12 10	12 14
Norwood Junction 2	a														12 00							
New Cross Gate	d																					
London Bridge 4 ⊖	a	11 15								11 45					12 12			12 15				
London Blackfriars 3 ⊖	a																					
City Thameslink 3	a																					
Farringdon 3 ⊖	a																					
St Pancras International 15 ⊖	a																					
St Albans City	a																					
Luton Airport Parkway 4 ✈	a																					
Luton 7	a																					
Bedford 10	a																					
Clapham Junction 10	a				11 24	11 27	11 37						11 54	12 01			12 11				12 24	12 27
	d				11 25	11 28	11 38						11 55	12 02			12 12				12 25	12 28
London Victoria 15 ⊖	a			11 25	11 31	11 35	11 46	11 40				11 55	12 01	12 08		12 10	12 18			12 25	12 31	12 35

Brighton - London and Bedford

Network Diagram - see first Page of Table 186

		SN ◇1 ⌶	GX 1 ⌶	GW 1	FC 1	GW 1	GX 1 ⌶	SN ◇1	SN 1	SN 1	GX 1 ⌶	SN ◇1	FC 1	SN 1	GX 1 ⌶	SN ◇1 ⌶	SN ◇1 ⌶	SN ◇1 ⌶	GX 1 ⌶	GW 1	FC 1	GW 1	GX 1 ⌶
Brighton 10	d				11 44							12 00	12 14				12 34				12 44		
Hove 2	d							11 54															
Preston Park	d											12 03											
Hassocks 4	d				11 53							12 10	12 23								12 53		
Burgess Hill 4	d				11 56			12 05				12 13	12 26								12 56		
Lewes 4	d															12 16							
Wivelsfield 4	d											12 15				12 31							
Haywards Heath 5	a				12 01			12 10				12 20	12 31			12 35					13 01		
	d				12 02			12 10				12 20	12 32			12 39					13 02		
Balcombe	d											12 26											
Horsham 4	d	11 42								12 03								12 42					
Littlehaven	d									12 06													
Faygate	d																						
Ifield	d									12 12													
Crawley	d	11 51								12 16								12 51					
Three Bridges 4	a	11 54			12 10					12 19		12 31	12 40					12 54			13 10		
	d	11 55			12 10					12 20		12 32	12 40					12 55			13 10		
Gatwick Airport 10 ✈	a	11 59			12 14			12 22		12 24		12 37	12 44			12 51	12 55	12 59			13 14		
	d	12 00	12 05	12 08	12 15		12 20	12 23		12 25	12 35	12 38	12 45		12 50	12 52	12 56	13 00	13 05	13 08	13 15		13 20
Horley 4	d	12 02								12 28								13 02					
Salfords	d																						
Earlswood (Surrey)	d																						
Tonbridge 4	d													12 29									
Leigh (Kent)	d													12 33									
Penshurst	d													12 37									
Edenbridge	d													12 43									
Godstone	d													12 50									
Nutfield	d													12 55									
Reigate	d					12 13																13 13	
Redhill 5	a	12 09		12 16		12 18				12 34		12 45		13 00				13 09		13 16		13 18	
	d	12 10								12 35		12 46						13 10					
Merstham	d									12 39													
Coulsdon South	d									12 44													
Purley 4	d	12 20								12 50								13 19					
East Croydon ⇌	a	12 26			12 31			12 39		12 56		12 59	13 01			13 10	13 13	13 26			13 31		
	d	12 26			12 32			12 40	12 50	12 56		13 00	13 02			13 10	13 14	13 26			13 32		
Norwood Junction 2	a									13 00													
New Cross Gate	d																						
London Bridge 4 ⊖	a				12 45					13 12			13 15								13 45		
London Blackfriars 3 ⊖	a																						
City Thameslink 3	a																						
Farringdon 3 ⊖	a																						
St Pancras International 15 ⊖	a																						
St Albans City	a																						
Luton Airport Parkway 4 ✈	a																						
Luton 7	a																						
Bedford 10	a																						
Clapham Junction 10	a	12 37						12 54	13 01			13 11				13 24	13 27	13 37					
	d	12 38						12 55	13 02			13 12				13 25	13 28	13 38					
London Victoria 15 ⊖	a	12 46	12 40				12 55	13 01	13 08		13 10	13 18			13 25	13 31	13 35	13 46	13 40				13 55

Table 186

Sundays

Brighton - London and Bedford

Network Diagram - see first Page of Table 186

		SN ◇1	SN 1	SN 1	GX 1 🛒	SN ◇1		FC 1	SN 1	GX 1 🛒	SN ◇1 🛒	SN ◇1 🛒	SN ◇1 🛒	GX 1 🛒	GW 1	FC 1		GW 1	GX 1 🛒	SN ◇1	SN 1	SN 1	GX 1 🛒	SN ◇1	FC 1
Brighton 10	d					13 00		13 14				13 34				13 44								14 00	14 14
Hove 2	d	12 54																		13 54					
Preston Park	d					13 03																		14 03	
Hassocks 4	d					13 10		13 23								13 53								14 10	14 23
Burgess Hill 4	d	13 05				13 13		13 26								13 56				14 05				14 13	14 26
Lewes 4	d										13 16														
Wivelsfield 4	d					13 15					13 31													14 15	
Haywards Heath 3	a	13 10				13 20		13 31			13 35					14 01				14 10				14 20	14 31
	d	13 10				13 20		13 32			13 39					14 02				14 10				14 20	14 32
Balcombe	d					13 26																		14 26	
Horsham 4	d			13 03									13 42									14 03			
Littlehaven	d			13 06																		14 06			
Faygate	d																								
Ifield	d			13 12																		14 12			
Crawley	d			13 16									13 51									14 16			
Three Bridges 4	a			13 19		13 31		13 40					13 54			14 10						14 19		14 31	14 40
	d			13 20		13 32		13 40					13 55			14 10						14 20		14 32	14 40
Gatwick Airport 10 ✈	a	13 22		13 24		13 37		13 44			13 52	13 55	13 59			14 14				14 22		14 24		14 37	14 44
	d	13 23		13 25	13 35	13 38		13 45		13 50	13 53	13 56	14 00	14 05	14 08	14 15			14 20	14 23		14 25	14 35	14 38	14 45
Horley 4	d			13 28									14 02									14 28			
Salfords	d																								
Earlswood (Surrey)	d																								
Tonbridge 4	d								13 29																
Leigh (Kent)	d								13 33																
Penshurst	d								13 37																
Edenbridge	d								13 43																
Godstone	d								13 50																
Nutfield	d								13 55																
Reigate	d																	14 13							
Redhill 5	a			13 34		13 45			14 00				14 09		14 16			14 18				14 34		14 45	
	d			13 35		13 46							14 10									14 35		14 46	
Merstham	d			13 39																		14 39			
Coulsdon South	d			13 44																		14 44			
Purley 4	d			13 50									14 20									14 50			
East Croydon	a	13 39		13 56		13 59		14 01			14 10	14 13	14 26			14 31				14 40		14 56		14 59	15 01
	d	13 40	13 50	13 56		14 00		14 02			14 10	14 14	14 26			14 32				14 41	14 50	14 56		15 00	15 02
Norwood Junction 2	a			14 00																		15 00			
New Cross Gate	d																								
London Bridge 4 ⊖	a			14 12				14 15								14 45						15 12			15 15
London Blackfriars 3 ⊖	a																								
City Thameslink 3	a																								
Farringdon 3 ⊖	a																								
St Pancras International 15 ⊖	a																								
St Albans City	a																								
Luton Airport Parkway 4 ✈	a																								
Luton 7	a																								
Bedford 10	a																								
Clapham Junction 10	a	13 54	14 01			14 11					14 24	14 27	14 37							14 54	15 01			15 11	
	d	13 55	14 02			14 12					14 25	14 28	14 38							14 55	15 02			15 12	
London Victoria 15 ⊖	a	14 01	14 08		14 10	14 18				14 25	14 31	14 35	14 46	14 40					14 55	15 01	15 08		15 10	15 18	

Table 186

Sundays

Brighton - London and Bedford

Network Diagram - see first Page of Table 186

		SN 1		GX 1 🛒	SN ◇1 🛒	SN ◇1 🛒	SN ◇1 🛒	GX 1 🛒	GW 1	FC 1	GW 1	GX 1 🛒		SN ◇1	SN 1	SN 1	GX 1 🛒	SN ◇1	FC 1	SN 1	GX 1 🛒	SN ◇1 🛒		SN ◇1 🛒	SN ◇1 🛒
Brighton 10	d					14 34				14 44								15 00	15 14					15 34	
Hove 2	d													14 54											
Preston Park	d																	15 03							
Hassocks 4	d									14 53								15 10	15 23						
Burgess Hill 4	d									14 56				15 05				15 13	15 26						
Lewes 4	d				14 16																	15 16			
Wivelsfield 4	d				14 31													15 15				15 31			
Haywards Heath 3	a				14 35					15 01				15 10				15 20	15 31			15 35			
	d				14 39					15 02				15 10				15 20	15 32			15 39			
Balcombe	d																	15 26							
Horsham 4	d						14 42									15 03									15 42
Littlehaven	d															15 06									
Faygate	d																								
Ifield	d															15 12									
Crawley	d						14 51									15 16									15 51
Three Bridges 4	a						14 54			15 10						15 19		15 31	15 40						15 54
	d						14 55			15 10						15 20		15 32	15 40						15 55
Gatwick Airport 10 ✈	a				14 51	14 55	14 59			15 14				15 22		15 24		15 37	15 44			15 51		15 55	15 59
	d			14 50	14 52	14 56	15 00	15 05	15 08	15 15		15 20		15 23		15 25	15 35	15 38	15 45		15 50	15 52		15 56	16 00
Horley 4	d						15 02									15 28									16 02
Salfords	d																								
Earlswood (Surrey)	d																								
Tonbridge 4	d	14 29																		15 29					
Leigh (Kent)	d	14 33																		15 33					
Penshurst	d	14 37																		15 37					
Edenbridge	d	14 43																		15 43					
Godstone	d	14 50																		15 50					
Nutfield	d	14 55																		15 55					
Reigate	d										15 13														
Redhill 5	a	15 00					15 09		15 16		15 18					15 34		15 45		16 00					16 09
	d						15 10									15 35		15 46							16 10
Merstham	d															15 39									
Coulsdon South	d															15 44									
Purley 4	d						15 20									15 50									16 20
East Croydon	a				15 10	15 13	15 26			15 31				15 40		15 56		15 59	16 01			16 10		16 13	16 26
	d				15 10	15 14	15 26			15 32				15 40	15 50	15 56		16 00	16 02			16 10		16 14	16 26
Norwood Junction 2	a															16 00									
New Cross Gate	d																								
London Bridge 4 ⊖	a									15 45						16 12			16 15						
London Blackfriars 3 ⊖	a																								
City Thameslink 3	a																								
Farringdon 3 ⊖	a																								
St Pancras International 15 ⊖	a																								
St Albans City	a																								
Luton Airport Parkway 4 ✈	a																								
Luton 7	a																								
Bedford 10	a																								
Clapham Junction 10	a				15 24	15 27	15 37							15 54	16 01			16 11				16 24		16 27	16 37
	d				15 25	15 28	15 38							15 55	16 02			16 12				16 25		16 28	16 38
London Victoria 15 ⊖	a			15 25	15 31	15 35	15 46	15 40				15 55		16 01	16 08		16 10	16 18			16 25	16 31		16 35	16 46

Brighton - London and Bedford

Network Diagram - see first Page of Table 186

		GX 1	GW 1	FC 1	GW 1	GX 1	SN ◇1	SN 1	SN 1	GX 1	SN ◇1	FC 1	SN 1	GX 1	SN ◇1	SN ◇1	SN ◇1	GX 1	GW 1	FC 1	GW 1	GX 1	SN ◇1
Brighton 10	d			15 44							16 00	16 14				16 34				16 44			
Hove 2	d						15 54																16 54
Preston Park	d										16 03												
Hassocks 4	d			15 53							16 10	16 23								16 53			
Burgess Hill 4	d			15 56			16 05				16 13	16 26								16 56			17 05
Lewes 4	d														16 16								
Wivelsfield 4	d										16 15				16 31								
Haywards Heath 3	a			16 01			16 10				16 20	16 31			16 35					17 01			17 10
	d			16 02			16 10				16 20	16 32			16 39					17 02			17 10
Balcombe	d										16 26												
Horsham 4	d								16 03								16 42						
Littlehaven	d								16 06														
Faygate	d																						
Ifield	d								16 12														
Crawley	d								16 16								16 51						
Three Bridges 4	a			16 10					16 19		16 31	16 40					16 54			17 10			
	d			16 10					16 20		16 32	16 40					16 55			17 10			
Gatwick Airport 10 ✈	a			16 14			16 22		16 24		16 37	16 44			16 51	16 55	16 59			17 14			17 22
	d	16 05	16 08	16 15		16 20	16 23		16 25	16 35	16 38	16 45		16 50	16 52	16 56	17 00	17 05	17 08	17 15		17 20	17 23
Horley 4	d								16 28								17 02						
Salfords	d																						
Earlswood (Surrey)	d																						
Tonbridge 4	d												16 29										
Leigh (Kent)	d												16 33										
Penshurst	d												16 37										
Edenbridge	d												16 43										
Godstone	d												16 50										
Nutfield	d												16 55										
Reigate	d				16 13																17 13		
Redhill 5	a		16 16		16 18				16 34		16 45		17 00				17 09		17 16		17 18		
	d								16 35		16 46						17 10						
Merstham	d								16 39														
Coulsdon South	d								16 44														
Purley 4	d								16 50								17 20						
East Croydon	a			16 31			16 40		16 56		16 59	17 01			17 10	17 13	17 26			17 31			17 40
	d			16 32			16 41	16 50	16 56		17 00	17 02			17 10	17 14	17 26			17 32			17 41
Norwood Junction 2	a								17 00														
New Cross Gate	d																						
London Bridge 4 ⊖	a			16 45					17 12			17 15								17 45			
London Blackfriars 3 ⊖	a																						
City Thameslink 3	a																						
Farringdon 3 ⊖	a																						
St Pancras International 15 ⊖	a																						
St Albans City	a																						
Luton Airport Parkway 4 ✈	a																						
Luton 7	a																						
Bedford 10	a																						
Clapham Junction 10	a						16 54	17 01			17 11				17 24	17 27	17 37						17 54
	d						16 55	17 02			17 12				17 25	17 28	17 38						17 55
London Victoria 15 ⊖	a	16 40				16 55	17 01	17 08		17 10	17 18			17 25	17 31	17 35	17 46	17 40				17 55	18 01

Brighton - London and Bedford

Network Diagram - see first Page of Table 186

		SN 1	SN 1	GX 1	SN ◇1	FC 1	SN 1	GX 1	SN ◇1	SN ◇1	SN ◇1	GX 1	GW 1	FC 1	GW 1	GX 1	SN ◇1	SN 1	SN 1	GX 1	SN ◇1	FC 1
Brighton 10	d				17 00	17 14				17 34				17 44							18 00	18 14
Hove 2	d																17 54					
Preston Park	d				17 03																18 03	
Hassocks 4	d				17 10	17 23								17 53							18 10	18 23
Burgess Hill 4	d				17 13	17 26								17 56			18 05				18 13	18 26
Lewes 4	d								17 16													
Wivelsfield 4	d				17 15				17 31												18 15	
Haywards Heath 3	a				17 20	17 31			17 35					18 01			18 10				18 20	18 31
	d				17 20	17 32			17 39					18 02			18 10				18 20	18 32
Balcombe	d				17 26																18 26	
Horsham 4	d		17 03								17 42								18 03			
Littlehaven	d		17 06																18 06			
Faygate	d																					
Ifield	d		17 12																18 12			
Crawley	d		17 16								17 51								18 16			
Three Bridges 4	a		17 19		17 31	17 40					17 54			18 10					18 19		18 31	18 40
	d		17 20		17 32	17 40					17 55			18 10					18 20		18 32	18 40
Gatwick Airport 10 ✈	a		17 24		17 37	17 44			17 51	17 55	17 59			18 14			18 22		18 24		18 37	18 44
	d		17 25	17 35	17 38	17 45		17 50	17 52	17 56	18 00	18 05	18 08	18 15		18 20	18 23		18 25	18 35	18 38	18 45
Horley 4	d		17 28								18 02								18 28			
Salfords	d																					
Earlswood (Surrey)	d																					
Tonbridge 4	d						17 29															
Leigh (Kent)	d						17 33															
Penshurst	d						17 37															
Edenbridge	d						17 43															
Godstone	d						17 50															
Nutfield	d						17 55															
Reigate	d														18 13							
Redhill 5	a		17 34		17 45		18 00				18 09		18 16		18 18				18 34		18 45	
	d		17 35		17 46						18 10								18 35		18 46	
Merstham	d		17 39																18 39			
Coulsdon South	d		17 44																18 44			
Purley 4	d		17 50								18 20								18 50			
East Croydon	a		17 56		17 59	18 01			18 10	18 13	18 26			18 31			18 40		18 56		18 59	19 01
	d	17 50	17 56		18 00	18 02			18 10	18 14	18 26			18 32			18 41	18 50	18 56		19 00	19 02
Norwood Junction 2	a		18 00																19 00			
New Cross Gate	d																					
London Bridge 4 ⊖	a		18 12			18 15								18 45					19 12			19 15
London Blackfriars 3 ⊖	a																					
City Thameslink 3	a																					
Farringdon 3 ⊖	a																					
St Pancras International 15 ⊖	a																					
St Albans City	a																					
Luton Airport Parkway 4 ✈	a																					
Luton 7	a																					
Bedford 10	a																					
Clapham Junction 10	a	18 01			18 11				18 24	18 27	18 37						18 54	19 01			19 11	
	d	18 02			18 12				18 25	18 28	18 38						18 55	19 02			19 12	
London Victoria 15 ⊖	a	18 08		18 10	18 18			18 25	18 31	18 35	18 46	18 40				18 55	19 01	19 08		19 10	19 18	

Table 186

Sundays

Brighton - London and Bedford

Network Diagram - see first Page of Table 186

		SN 1	GX 1	SN ◇1	SN ◇1	SN ◇1	GX 1	GW 1	FC 1	GW 1	GX 1	SN ◇1	SN 1	SN 1	GX 1	SN ◇1	FC 1	SN 1	GX 1	SN ◇1	SN ◇1	SN ◇1	GX 1
Brighton 10	d				18 34				18 44							19 00	19 14				19 34		
Hove 2	d											18 54											
Preston Park	d															19 03							
Hassocks 4	d								18 53							19 10	19 23						
Burgess Hill 4	d								18 56			19 05				19 13	19 26						
Lewes 4	d			18 16																19 16			
Wivelsfield 4	d			18 31												19 15				19 31			
Haywards Heath 3	a			18 35					19 01			19 10				19 20	19 31			19 35			
	d			18 39					19 02			19 10				19 20	19 32			19 39			
Balcombe	d															19 26							
Horsham 4	d					18 42								19 03								19 42	
Littlehaven	d													19 06									
Faygate	d																						
Ifield	d													19 12									
Crawley	d					18 51								19 16								19 51	
Three Bridges 4	a					18 54			19 10					19 19		19 31	19 40					19 54	
	d					18 55			19 10					19 20		19 32	19 40					19 55	
Gatwick Airport 10 ✈	a			18 51	18 55	18 59			19 14			19 22		19 24		19 37	19 44			19 51	19 55	19 59	
	d		18 50	18 52	18 56	19 00	19 05	19 08	19 15		19 20	19 23		19 25	19 35	19 38	19 45		19 50	19 52	19 56	20 00	20 05
Horley 4	d					19 02								19 28								20 02	
Salfords	d																						
Earlswood (Surrey)	d																						
Tonbridge 4	d	18 29																19 29					
Leigh (Kent)	d	18 33																19 33					
Penshurst	d	18 37																19 37					
Edenbridge	d	18 43																19 43					
Godstone	d	18 50																19 50					
Nutfield	d	18 55																19 55					
Reigate	d									19 13													
Redhill 5	a	19 00				19 09		19 16		19 18				19 34		19 45		20 00				20 09	
	d					19 10								19 35		19 46						20 10	
Merstham	d													19 39									
Coulsdon South	d													19 44									
Purley 4	d					19 20								19 50								20 20	
East Croydon 🚌	a			19 10	19 13	19 26			19 31			19 40		19 56		19 59	20 01			20 10	20 13	20 26	
	d			19 10	19 14	19 26			19 32			19 41	19 50	19 56		20 00	20 02			20 10	20 14	20 26	
Norwood Junction 2	a													20 00									
New Cross Gate	d																						
London Bridge 4 ⊖	a								19 45					20 12			20 15						
London Blackfriars 3 ⊖	a																						
City Thameslink 3	a																						
Farringdon 3 ⊖	a																						
St Pancras International 15 ⊖	a																						
St Albans City	a																						
Luton Airport Parkway 4 ✈	a																						
Luton 7	a																						
Bedford 10	a																						
Clapham Junction 10	a			19 24	19 27	19 37						19 54	20 01			20 11				20 24	20 27	20 37	
	d			19 25	19 28	19 38						19 55	20 02			20 12				20 25	20 28	20 38	
London Victoria 15 ⊖	a		19 25	19 31	19 35	19 46	19 40				19 55	20 01	20 08		20 10	20 18			20 25	20 31	20 35	20 46	20 41

Table 186

Sundays

Brighton - London and Bedford

Network Diagram - see first Page of Table 186

		GW 1	FC 1	GW 1	GX 1	SN ◇1	SN 1	SN 1	GX 1	SN ◇1	FC 1	SN 1	GX 1	SN ◇1	SN ◇1	SN ◇1	GX 1	GW 1	FC 1	GW 1	GX 1	SN ◇1	SN 1
Brighton 10	d		19 44							20 00	20 14				20 34				20 44				
Hove 2	d					19 54																20 54	
Preston Park	d									20 03													
Hassocks 4	d		19 53							20 10	20 23								20 53				
Burgess Hill 4	d		19 56			20 05				20 13	20 26								20 56			21 05	
Lewes 4	d													20 16									
Wivelsfield 4	d									20 15				20 31									
Haywards Heath 3	a		20 01			20 10				20 20	20 31			20 35					21 01			21 10	
	d		20 02			20 10				20 20	20 32			20 39					21 02			21 10	
Balcombe	d									20 26													
Horsham 4	d							20 03								20 42							
Littlehaven	d							20 06															
Faygate	d																						
Ifield	d							20 12															
Crawley	d							20 16								20 51							
Three Bridges 4	a		20 10					20 19		20 31	20 40					20 54			21 10				
	d		20 10					20 20		20 32	20 40					20 55			21 10				
Gatwick Airport 10 ✈	a		20 14			20 22		20 24		20 37	20 44			20 51	20 55	20 59			21 14			21 22	
	d	20 08	20 15		20 20	20 23		20 25	20 35	20 38	20 45		20 50	20 52	20 56	21 00	21 05	21 08	21 15		21 20	21 23	
Horley 4	d							20 28								21 02							
Salfords	d																						
Earlswood (Surrey)	d																						
Tonbridge 4	d											20 29											
Leigh (Kent)	d											20 33											
Penshurst	d											20 37											
Edenbridge	d											20 43											
Godstone	d											20 50											
Nutfield	d											20 55											
Reigate	d			20 13																21 13			
Redhill 5	a	20 16		20 18				20 34		20 45		21 00				21 09		21 16		21 18			
	d							20 35		20 46						21 10							
Merstham	d							20 39															
Coulsdon South	d							20 44															
Purley 4	d							20 50								21 20							
East Croydon 🚌	a		20 31			20 40		20 56		20 59	21 01			21 10	21 13	21 26			21 31			21 40	
	d		20 32			20 41	20 50	20 56		21 00	21 02			21 10	21 14	21 26			21 32			21 41	21 50
Norwood Junction 2	a							21 00															
New Cross Gate	d																						
London Bridge 4 ⊖	a		20 45					21 12			21 15								21 45				
London Blackfriars 3 ⊖	a																						
City Thameslink 3	a																						
Farringdon 3 ⊖	a																						
St Pancras International 15 ⊖	a																						
St Albans City	a																						
Luton Airport Parkway 4 ✈	a																						
Luton 7	a																						
Bedford 10	a																						
Clapham Junction 10	a					20 54	21 01			21 11				21 24	21 27	21 37						21 54	22 01
	d					20 55	21 02			21 12				21 25	21 28	21 38						21 55	22 02
London Victoria 15 ⊖	a				20 55	21 01	21 08		21 10	21 18			21 25	21 31	21 35	21 46	21 40				21 55	22 01	22 08

Brighton - London and Bedford

Network Diagram - see first Page of Table 186

		SN 1	GX 1	SN ◇1	FC 1	SN 1	GX 1	SN ◇1	SN ◇1	GX 1	GW 1	FC 1	GW 1	GX 1	SN 1	SN 1	GX 1	SN ◇1	FC 1	SN 1	GX 1	SN ◇1
Brighton 10	d			21 00	21 14							21 44						22 00	22 14			
Hove 2	d																					
Preston Park	d			21 03														22 03				
Hassocks 4	d			21 10	21 23							21 53						22 10	22 23			
Burgess Hill 4	d			21 13	21 26							21 56						22 13	22 26			
Lewes 4	d							21 16														
Wivelsfield 4	d			21 15				21 31										22 15				
Haywards Heath 3	a			21 20	21 31			21 35				22 01						22 20	22 31			
	d			21 20	21 32			21 39				22 02						22 20	22 32			
Balcombe	d			21 26														22 26				
Horsham 4	d	21 03							21 42							22 03						22 42
Littlehaven	d	21 06														22 06						
Faygate	d																					
Ifield	d	21 12														22 12						
Crawley	d	21 16							21 51							22 16						22 51
Three Bridges 4	a	21 19		21 31	21 40				21 54			22 10				22 19		22 31	22 40			22 54
	d	21 20		21 32	21 40				21 55			22 10				22 20		22 32	22 40			22 55
Gatwick Airport 10 ✈	a	21 24		21 37	21 44			21 51	21 59			22 14				22 24		22 37	22 44			22 59
	d	21 25	21 35	21 38	21 45		21 50	21 52	22 00	22 05	22 08	22 15		22 20		22 25	22 35	22 38	22 45		22 50	23 00
Horley 4	d	21 28							22 02							22 28						23 02
Salfords	d																					
Earlswood (Surrey)	d																					
Tonbridge 4	d					21 29														22 29		
Leigh (Kent)	d					21 33														22 33		
Penshurst	d					21 37														22 37		
Edenbridge	d					21 43														22 43		
Godstone	d					21 50														22 50		
Nutfield	d					21 55														22 55		
Reigate	d												22 13									
Redhill 5	a	21 34		21 45		22 00			22 09		22 16		22 18			22 34		22 45		23 00		23 09
	d	21 35		21 46					22 10							22 35		22 46				23 10
Merstham	d	21 39														22 39						
Coulsdon South	d	21 44														22 44						
Purley 4	d	21 50							22 20							22 50						23 20
East Croydon	a	21 56		21 59	22 01			22 10	22 26			22 31				22 55		22 58	23 01			23 26
	d	21 56		22 00	22 02			22 10	22 26			22 32			22 50	22 56		23 00	23 02			23 27
Norwood Junction 2	a	22 00																				
New Cross Gate	d																					
London Bridge 4 ⊖	a	22 12			22 15							22 45							23 15			
London Blackfriars 3 ⊖	a																					
City Thameslink 3	a																					
Farringdon 3 ⊖	a																					
St Pancras International 15 ⊖	a																					
St Albans City	a																					
Luton Airport Parkway 4 ✈	a																					
Luton 7	a																					
Bedford 10	a																					
Clapham Junction 10	a			22 11				22 24	22 37						23 01	23 07		23 12				23 38
	d			22 12				22 25	22 38						23 02	23 08		23 13				23 39
London Victoria 15 ⊖	a		22 10	22 18			22 25	22 31	22 46	22 40				22 55	23 08	23 14	23 10	23 20			23 25	23 46

Brighton - London and Bedford

Network Diagram - see first Page of Table 186

		GX 1	GW 1	FC 1	GW 1	GX 1	SN 1	SN 1	GX 1	SN ◇1	FC 1	SN ◇1	GX 1	FC 1
Brighton 10	d			22 44						23 02	23 14			23 45
Hove 2	d													
Preston Park	d									23 06				
Hassocks 4	d			22 53						23 12	23 23			23 53
Burgess Hill 4	d			22 56						23 16	23 26			23 57
Lewes 4	d													
Wivelsfield 4	d									23 18				
Haywards Heath 3	a			23 01						23 23	23 31			00 02
	d			23 02						23 23	23 32			00 02
Balcombe	d									23 29				
Horsham 4	d							23 03						
Littlehaven	d							23 06						
Faygate	d													
Ifield	d							23 12						
Crawley	d							23 16				←		
Three Bridges 4	a			23 10				23 19		23 36	23 40	23 36		00 11
	d			23 10				23 20		23 41	23 40	23 41		00 11
Gatwick Airport 10 ✈	a			23 14				23 24		→	23 44	23 45		00 15
	d	23 05	23 08	23 15		23 20		23 25	23 35		23 45	23 46	23 50	00 16
Horley 4	d							23 28				23 49		
Salfords	d													
Earlswood (Surrey)	d													
Tonbridge 4	d													
Leigh (Kent)	d													
Penshurst	d													
Edenbridge	d													
Godstone	d													
Nutfield	d													
Reigate	d				23 13									
Redhill 5	a		23 16		23 18			23 34				23 57		00 23
	d							23 35				00 01		00 23
Merstham	d							23 39						
Coulsdon South	d							23 44						
Purley 4	d							23 50				00 11		
East Croydon	a			23 31				23 55			00 02	00 16		00 35
	d			23 32			23 50	23 56			00 04	00 16		00 36
Norwood Junction 2	a													
New Cross Gate	d													
London Bridge 4 ⊖	a			23 45							00 19			00 52
London Blackfriars 3 ⊖	a													
City Thameslink 3	a													
Farringdon 3 ⊖	a													
St Pancras International 15 ⊖	a													
St Albans City	a													
Luton Airport Parkway 4 ✈	a													
Luton 7	a													
Bedford 10	a													
Clapham Junction 10	a						00 01	00 11				00 29		
	d						00 02	00 12				00 30		
London Victoria 15 ⊖	a	23 40				23 55	00 08	00 19	00 10			00 37	00 25	

Table 188

London, Gatwick Airport, Brighton - Sussex Coast, Portsmouth and Southampton

Network Diagram - see first Page of Table 186

Miles	Miles	Miles			SN MX ◇1	SN MX 1	SN MX ◇1	SN MX ◇1	SN MX	SN	SN MX ◇1	SN MO 1	SN MX 1	SN MO ◇1	SN MX 1	SN MX ◇1	SN 1	SN	SN	SN	SN	SN 1	SN 1
0	—	0	**London Victoria** 15 ⊖	d	22p17	22p32		22p47			23p17	23p04	23p10	23p17	23p47	00 05							
2¾	—	—	Clapham Junction 10	d	22p23	22p38		22p53			23p23	23p10	23p16	23p23	23p53	00 11							
—	0	—	London Bridge 4 ⊖	d																			
10½	10¼	—	**East Croydon** ⇌	d	22p34	22p48		23p03			23p33	23p22	23p28	23p38	00 06	00 27							
21	—	—	Redhill 5	d		23p01						23p42	23p46		00 25								
26	—	—	Horley	d								23p50	23p56		00 31								
26¾	—	—	**Gatwick Airport** 10 ✈	d	22p49	23p09		23p19			23p51	23p55	23p59	00 01	00 34	00 44							
29½	—	29½	**Three Bridges** 4	a	22p53	23p15					23p55	00 01	00 04	00 05	00 39	00 48							
—	—	—		d	22p53	23p16					23p56	00 01	00 04	00 06	00 39	00 49							
—	—	31	Crawley	d		23p19						00 05	00 07		00 43								
—	—	38	**Horsham** 4	a		23p27						00 17	00 19		00 55								
—	—	—		d		23p28																	
—	—	40½	Christs Hospital	d		23p31																	
—	—	45¼	Billingshurst	d		23p37																	
—	—	50¼	Pulborough	d		23p44																	
—	—	55	Amberley	d		23p50																	
—	—	58¾	Arundel	d		23p55																	
38	—	—	Haywards Heath 3	d	23p03			23b37			00 05			00 15		01 02							
41¾	—	—	Burgess Hill	d	23p08						00 11			00 20									
—	—	—	Preston Park	d																			
—	0	—	**Brighton** 10	d					00 04	00 10						01s16							
51	1½	—	Hove 2	a	23p21			23p51	00 07	00 14	00 21			00 31		01s24							
—	—	—		d	23p22			23p52	00 08		00 22			00 31									
—	2	—	Aldrington	d					00 10														
—	3	—	Portslade	d	23p25			23p55	00 12		00s25			00s34		01s27							
—	3½	—	Fishersgate	d					00 14														
—	4½	—	Southwick	d	23p28			23p58	00 16		00s28			00s37		01s30							
—	5½	—	Shoreham-by-Sea	d	23p31			00 01	00 19		00s31			00s40		01s33							
—	8¼	—	Lancing	d	23p35			00 05	00 23		00s35			00s44		01s37							
—	9¾	—	East Worthing	d					00 26														
—	10½	—	**Worthing** 4	a	23p39			00 09	00 29		00 39			00 48		01 42							
—	—	—		d	23p39				00 29														
—	11½	—	West Worthing	d	23p41				00a31														
—	12¼	—	Durrington-on-Sea	d	23p44																		
—	13	—	Goring-by-Sea	d	23p46																		
0	15½	—	Angmering 3	d	23p50																		
6	—	—	**Littlehampton** 4	a																			
—	—	—		d																			05 35
8	19¾	61	Ford 4	d	23p56	00 01																	05 39
—	—	—	Bognor Regis 4	d			←												05 13			05 35	
0	22½	—	Barnham	a	00 01	00 06	00 01												05 19			05 41	05 43
—	—	—		d	00 09	00 06	00 09										04 58	05 02		05 21	05 36		05 44
3½	—	—	**Bognor Regis**	a	→		00 15														05 43		
—	28¾	—	**Chichester** 4	a		00 14											05 05	05 09		05 28			05 51
—	—	—		d													05 06	05 10		05 29			05 52
—	30½	—	Fishbourne (Sussex)	d																			05 55
—	31¼	—	Bosham	d																			05 58
—	33¼	—	Nutbourne	d																			06 01
—	34¼	—	Southbourne	d																			06 04
—	35¾	—	Emsworth	d																			06 07
—	37	—	Warblington	d																			06 10
0	37½	—	**Havant**	d													05 17	05 21		05 40			06 13
—	38¾	—	Bedhampton	a																			06 15
—	41¼	—	Hilsea	a																			06 20
—	44	—	Fratton	a														05 29		05 48			06 24
—	44¾	—	Portsmouth & Southsea	a														05 33		05 52			06 28
—	45½	—	**Portsmouth Harbour** ⛴	a														05 37		05 56			06 32
4	—	—	Cosham	a													05 23						
6½	—	—	Portchester	a													05 28						
9¾	—	—	Fareham	a													05 33						
13½	—	—	Swanwick	a													05 40						
—	—	—	Eastleigh	a																			
—	—	—	Southampton Airport Parkway	a																			
24¼	—	—	**Southampton Central** ⛴	a													05 59						

b Previous night, arr. 2330

Table 188

London, Gatwick Airport, Brighton - Sussex Coast, Portsmouth and Southampton

Network Diagram - see first Page of Table 186

		SN	SN 1	SN	SN	SN ◇1 H	SN 1	SN	SN	SN	SN	SN	SN	SN	SN	SN ◇1 H	SN	SN 1	SN 1	SN	SN 1		SN 1
London Victoria 15 ⊖	d																						
Clapham Junction 10	d																						
London Bridge 4 ⊖	d																						
East Croydon ⇌	d																						
Redhill 5	d																						
Horley	d																						
Gatwick Airport 10 ✈	d																				05 56		
Three Bridges 4	a																				06 00		
	d																				06 01		
Crawley	d																				06 05		
Horsham 4	a																				06 17		
	d																				06 17		
Christs Hospital	d																				06 21		
Billingshurst	d																				06 27		
Pulborough	d																				06 34		
Amberley	d																				06 40		
Arundel	d																				06 46		
Haywards Heath 3	d																						
Burgess Hill	d																						
Preston Park	d																						
Brighton 10	d		05 14				05 30	05 44		05 53				05 57	06 14				06 27				06 35
Hove 2	a		05 17				05 33	05 48		05 56				06 00	06 17				06 30				06 38
	d		05 18				05 34			05 57				06 01	06 18				06 31				06 39
Aldrington	d		05 20				05 36							06 03	06 20								
Portslade	d		05 22				05 38							06 05	06 22								06 42
Fishersgate	d		05 24				05 40							06 07	06 24								
Southwick	d		05 26				05 42							06 09	06 26								06 45
Shoreham-by-Sea	d		05 29				05 45			06 03				06 12	06 29				06 37				06 48
Lancing	d		05 33				05 49							06 16	06 33								06 52
East Worthing	d		05 36				05 52							06 19	06 36								
Worthing 4	a		05 39				05 55			06 09				06 22	06 39				06 43				06 56
	d		05 39				05 55			06 09				06 22	06 39				06 43				06 56
West Worthing	d		05 41				05 57							06 24	06a41				06 45				06 58
Durrington-on-Sea	d		05 44				06 00							06 27					06 48				07 01
Goring-by-Sea	d		05 46				06 02							06 29					06 50				07 03
Angmering 3	d		05 50				06 06							06 33					06 54				07 07
Littlehampton 4	a													06 42									
	d				06 04								06 35							06 58			
Ford 4	d		05 56		06 08		06 13						06 39							07 04	06 51		07 13
Bognor Regis 4	d	05 49		05 55		06 06			06 13			06 22				06 41	06 50	06 57					
Barnham	a	05 55	06 01	06 02	06 12	06 12	06 17		06 19	06 24		06 28	06 43			06 47	06 56	07 03	07 04	07 08	06 55		07 18
	d		06 01		06 13		06 18			06 24	06 27		06 48						07 05	07 09	07 00	07 13	07 18
Bognor Regis	a				06 20						06 34		06 55									07 20	
Chichester 4	a		06 09				06 25			06 32									07 12	07 16	07 07		07 26
	d		06 09				06 26			06 32									07 13	07 17	07 08		07 28
Fishbourne (Sussex)	d									06 35										07 20			
Bosham	d									06 38									07 17				
Nutbourne	d									06 42										07 25			
Southbourne	d						06 33			06 44									07 22	07 27			
Emsworth	d						06 36			06 47									07 25	07 30			
Warblington	d									06 50									07 28				
Havant	d		06 20				06 40			06 53									07 31	07 35	07 19		07 41
Bedhampton	a									06 56										07 37			
Hilsea	a									07 01										07 42			
Fratton	a									07 05										07 46			07 49
Portsmouth & Southsea	a									07 08										07 50			07 53
Portsmouth Harbour ⛴	a									07 12													07 58
Cosham	a		06 27				06 49												07 38		07 25		
Portchester	a						06 54														07 30		
Fareham	a		06 36				06 59												07 46		07 35		
Swanwick	a		06 43				07 06												07 53		07 42		
Eastleigh	a																						
Southampton Airport Parkway	a																						
Southampton Central ⛴	a		07 02				07 25												08 13		08 01		

London, Gatwick Airport, Brighton - Sussex Coast, Portsmouth and Southampton

Network Diagram - see first Page of Table 186

	SN ◇1	SN	SN	SN		SN	SN	SN 1	SN ◇1	SN 1	SN	SN	SN ◇1	SN		SN	SN 1	SN	SN 1	SN	SN ◇1	SN 1	SN 1	SN
London Victoria 15 ⊖ d									06 02													06 32	06 51	
Clapham Junction 10 d									06 08													06 38	06 57	
London Bridge 4 ⊖ d																								
East Croydon d									06 18													06 49	07 07	
Redhill 5 d									06 39													07 12	07 28	
Horley d									06 48													07 21	07 37	
Gatwick Airport 10 ✈ d									06 55													07 25	07 41	
Three Bridges 4 a									06 59													07 29	07 45	
d									07 00	07 05												07 30	07 46	
Crawley d									07 03	07 08												07 34	07 50	
Horsham 4 a									07 11	07 22												07 46	08 02	
d									07 12													07 46		
Christs Hospital d									07 15													07 50		
Billingshurst d									07 21													07 56		
Pulborough d									07 28													08 03		
Amberley d									07 34													08 09		
Arundel d									07 39													08 14		
Haywards Heath 3 d																								
Burgess Hill d																								
Preston Park d																								
Brighton 10 d							06 53	07 06			07 15					07 20	07 30		07 37	07 46				07 50
Hove 2 a							06 56	07 09			07 18					07 23	07 33		07 40	07 49				07 53
d							06 57	07 10			07 19					07 24	07 34		07 41	07 50				07 54
Aldrington d							06 59									07 26								07 56
Portslade d							07 01				07 22					07 28	07 37		07 44	07 53				07 58
Fishersgate d							07 03									07 30								08 00
Southwick d							07 05				07 25					07 32	07 40		07 47	07 56				08 02
Shoreham-by-Sea d							07 09	07 16			07 28					07 35	07 43		07 50	08 00				08 06
Lancing d							07 13				07 32					07 39	07 47		07 54	08 04				08 10
East Worthing d							07 16									07 42								08 13
Worthing 4 a							07 18	07 22			07 36					07 45	07 51		07 58	08 08				08 15
d							07 19	07 23			07 36					07 45	07 52		07 59	08 08				08 16
West Worthing d							07 21	07 25								07 47	07 54		08 01					08 18
Durrington-on-Sea d							07 23	07 27								07 50	07 56		08 03	08 12				08 20
Goring-by-Sea d							07 26	07 30								07 52	07 59		08 06					08 23
Angmering 3 d							07 30	07 34								07 56	08 03		08 10	08 17				08 27
Littlehampton 4 a							07 38									08 05						08 21		08 35
d		07 18					07 48							07 56								08 26		
Ford 4 d		07 22					07 52		07 44		07 48			08 00			08 09		08 17			08 30		
Bognor Regis 4 d	07 17		07 27			07 36						←	07 55					08 13			08 26			
Barnham a	07 23	07 26	07 33			07 42	07 56	07 43	07 49		07 53	07 56	08 01	08 04			08 13	08 19	08 21	08 27	08 32	08 34		
d		07 27		07 39			07 57	07 44	07 50		07 53	07 57		08 05			08 14		08 22	08 28		08 35		
Bognor Regis a				07 46			→		07 58					08 11						08 36				
Chichester 4 a		07 34						07 51			08 01	08 05					08 21		08 29			08 42		
d		07 35						07 52			08 01						08 22		08 30					
Fishbourne (Sussex) d		07 38									08 04													
Bosham d		07 41									08 07													
Nutbourne d		07 44									08 11													
Southbourne d		07 47									08 13						08 29		08 37					
Emsworth d		07 50									08 16						08 32		08 40					
Warblington d		07 53									08 19													
Havant d		07 58						08 03			08 22						08 37		08 44					
Bedhampton a		08 00									08 25													
Hilsea a		08 05									08 30													
Fratton a		08 09									08 34								08 53					
Portsmouth & Southsea a		08 15									08 37								08 56					
Portsmouth Harbour ⛴ a		08 20									08 41								09 02					
Cosham a								08 09									08 45							
Portchester a								08 13									08 49							
Fareham a								08 18									08 54							
Swanwick a								08 26									09 01							
Eastleigh a																								
Southampton Airport Parkway a																								
Southampton Central ⛴ a								08 52									09 19							

London, Gatwick Airport, Brighton - Sussex Coast, Portsmouth and Southampton

Network Diagram - see first Page of Table 186

		SN	SN	SN	SN	SN	SN	SN	SN ◇1	SN 1		SN ◇1	SN	SN	SN	SN 1	SN	SN ◇1	SN	SN		SN ◇1	GW ◇	
London Victoria 15 ⊖ d									07 17	07 36								07 52						
Clapham Junction 10 d									07 23	07 42								07 58						
London Bridge 4 ⊖ d																								
East Croydon d									07 34	07 52								08 09						
Redhill 5 d									07 47	08 11														
Horley d									07 57	08 21														
Gatwick Airport 10 ✈ d									08 00	08 24								08 26						
Three Bridges 4 a									08 05	08 29														
d									08 05	08 30														
Crawley d									08 09	08 34														
Horsham 4 a									08 22	08 48														
d									08 23															
Christs Hospital d									08 26															
Billingshurst d									08 32															
Pulborough d									08 39															
Amberley d									08 45															
Arundel d									08 50															
Haywards Heath 3 d																		08 37						
Burgess Hill d																								
Preston Park d																								
Brighton 10 d			08 03		08 07	08 14	08 23									08 33	08 44		08 53				08 59	
Hove 2 a			08 06		08 10	08 18	08 26									08 36	08 48	08 53	08 56				09 02	
d			08 07		08 11		08 27									08 37		08 53	08 57				09 03	
Aldrington d							08 29												08 59					
Portslade d					08 14		08 31									08 40			09 01					
Fishersgate d							08 33												09 03					
Southwick d					08 17		08 35									08 43			09 05					
Shoreham-by-Sea d			08 13		08 20		08 39									08 46		08 59	09 08				09 13	
Lancing d					08 24		08 43									08 50		09 04	09 12					
East Worthing d							08 46												09 15					
Worthing 4 a			08 19		08 28		08 48									08 54		09 08	09 18				09 21	
d			08 20		08 28		08 49									08 55		09 08	09 18				09 22	
West Worthing d			08 22		08 30		08a51									08 57		09 10	09a20					
Durrington-on-Sea d			08 24		08 33											08 59		09 13						
Goring-by-Sea d			08 27		08 35											09 02		09 15						
Angmering 3 d			08 31		08 39											09 06		09 19						
Littlehampton 4 a																		09 28						
d													08 54											
Ford 4 d			08 37		08 45				08 55				08 59											
Bognor Regis 4 d		08 32						08 48				08 56			09 06							09 30		
Barnham a		08 38	08 41		08 50			08 55	08 59			09 02	09 03		09 12	09 16						09 36	09 37	
d			08 42	08 45	08 52				09 00				09 04	09 11		09 17				09 19			09 38	
Bognor Regis a				08 52	08 58									09 18						09 26				
Chichester 4 a			08 49						09 07				09 11			09 24							09 45	
d			08 50						09 08				09 12			09 25							09 47	
Fishbourne (Sussex) d													09 15											
Bosham d													09 18											
Nutbourne d													09 21											
Southbourne d									09 15				09 24			09 32								
Emsworth d									09 18				09 27			09 35								
Warblington d													09 30											
Havant d			09 01						09 23				09 33			09 39							09 59	
Bedhampton a													09 36											
Hilsea a													09 42											
Fratton a			09 11										09 46											
Portsmouth & Southsea a			09 17										09 50											
Portsmouth Harbour ⛴ a			09 21																					
Cosham a									09 29							09 45							10 05	
Portchester a																								
Fareham a									09 37							09 53							10 14	
Swanwick a									09 44							10 00								
Eastleigh a																								
Southampton Airport Parkway a																								
Southampton Central ⛴ a									10 01							10 20							10 40	

Table 188

Mondays to Fridays

London, Gatwick Airport, Brighton - Sussex Coast, Portsmouth and Southampton

Network Diagram - see first Page of Table 186

		SN ◇1		SN	SN	SN ◇1	SN 1	SN	SN	SN	SN	SN ◇1	SN ◇1 A		SN	SN	SN	SN	SN ◇1 B	SN 1	SN	SN ◇1
London Victoria 15 ⊖	d	08 02				08 17							08 32						08 47			
Clapham Junction 10	d	08 08				08 23							08 38						08 53			
London Bridge 4 ⊖	d						08 00													08 30		
East Croydon	d	08 18				08 34	08 20						08 48						09 04	08 51		
Redhill 5	d	08 30					08 41						09 03							09 12		
Horley	d						08 50													09 22		
Gatwick Airport 10	d	08 40				08 49	08 54						09 11						09 20	09 25		
Three Bridges 4	a	08 44					08 59						09 16							09 30		
	d	08 45					08 59						09 16							09 30		
Crawley	d	08 48					09 03						09 19							09 34		
Horsham 4	a	08 56					09 17						09 27							09 46		
	d	09 00	09 05										09 31	09 36								
Christs Hospital	d		09 08											09 39								
Billingshurst	d		09 14											09 45								
Pulborough	d		09 21											09 52								
Amberley	d		09 27											09 58								
Arundel	d		09 32											10 03								
Haywards Heath 3	d					09 04													09 37			
Burgess Hill	d					09 09																
Preston Park	d					09 18																
Brighton 10	d			09 03	09 14			09 23								09 33	09 44				09 53	
Hove 2	a			09 07	09 18	09 21		09 26								09 36	09 48		09 53		09 56	
	d			09 08		09 22		09 27								09 37			09 53		09 57	
Aldrington	d							09 29													09 59	
Portslade	d			09 11		09 25		09 31								09 40					10 01	
Fishersgate	d							09 33													10 03	
Southwick	d			09 14				09 35								09 43					10 05	
Shoreham-by-Sea	d			09 18		09 30		09 39								09 46			10 00		10 09	
Lancing	d			09 22				09 43								09 50			10 04		10 13	
East Worthing	d							09 46													10 16	
Worthing 4	a			09 26		09 36		09 48								09 54			10 08		10 18	
	d			09 26		09 37		09 49								09 55			10 08		10 19	
West Worthing	d					09 39		09a51								09 57			10 10		10a21	
Durrington-on-Sea	d					09 41										09 59			10 13			
Goring-by-Sea	d					09 44										10 02			10 15			
Angmering 3	d			09 34		09 48										10 06			10 19			
Littlehampton 4	a					09 58													10 28			
	d										09 54							10 11				
Ford 4	d		09 37								09 58			10 08		10 12		10 16				
Bognor Regis 4	d								09 39			09 56			10 07							10 30
Barnham	a	09 26	09 41	09 44					09 45		10 02	10 02	09 57	10 12	10 13	10 16		10 20				10 36
	d	09 27	09 42	09 45						09 52	10 03		09 58	10 13		10 17		10 22				
Bognor Regis	a		09 48							09 59				10 19				10 29				
Chichester 4	a	09 34		09 52							10 10		10 05			10 24						
	d	09 35		09 53							10 11		10 06			10 25						
Fishbourne (Sussex)	d										10 14											
Bosham	d										10 17											
Nutbourne	d										10 20											
Southbourne	d			10 00							10 23		10 13									
Emsworth	d			10 03							10 26		10 16			10 33						
Warblington	d										10 29											
Havant	d	09 46		10 07							10 32		10 20			10 37						
Bedhampton	a										10 34											
Hilsea	a										10 42											
Fratton	a	09 54		10 16							10 46											
Portsmouth & Southsea	a	09 58		10 19							10 50											
Portsmouth Harbour	a	10 02		10 23																		
Cosham	a												10 28			10 45						
Portchester	a												10 32									
Fareham	a												10 37			10 53						
Swanwick	a												10 44			11 00						
Eastleigh	a																					
Southampton Airport Parkway	a																					
Southampton Central	a												11 01			11 19						

A to Horsham

B to Haywards Heath

Table 188

Mondays to Fridays

London, Gatwick Airport, Brighton - Sussex Coast, Portsmouth and Southampton

Network Diagram - see first Page of Table 186

		SN ◇1 A		SN	SN	SN ◇1 B	SN 1	SN	SN	SN	SN	SN ◇1	SN ◇1 A		SN	SN	SN	SN	SN ◇1 B	SN 1	SN	SN ◇1
London Victoria 15 ⊖	d	09 02				09 17							09 32						09 47			
Clapham Junction 10	d	09 08				09 23							09 38						09 53			
London Bridge 4 ⊖	d						09 03													09 32		
East Croydon	d	09 19				09 33	09 21						09 48						10 03	09 51		
Redhill 5	d	09 30					09 40						10 00							10 10		
Horley	d	09 36					09 50													10 19		
Gatwick Airport 10	d	09 40				09 50	09 54						10 09						10 20	10 24		
Three Bridges 4	a	09 44					09 59						10 14							10 29		
	d	09 45					10 00						10 14							10 30		
Crawley	d	09 48					10 03						10 18							10 33		
Horsham 4	a	09 56					10 15						10 26							10 47		
	d	10 00	10 05										10 30	10 35								
Christs Hospital	d													10 38								
Billingshurst	d		10 14											10 44								
Pulborough	d		10 20											10 51								
Amberley	d													10 57								
Arundel	d		10 29											11 02								
Haywards Heath 3	d					10 05													10 37			
Burgess Hill	d					10 10																
Preston Park	d					10 18																
Brighton 10	d			10 03	10 14			10 23								10 33	10 44				10 53	
Hove 2	a			10 06	10 18	10 22		10 26								10 36	10 48		10 53		10 56	
	d			10 07		10 23		10 27								10 37			10 53		10 57	
Aldrington	d							10 29													10 59	
Portslade	d			10 10		10 26		10 31								10 40					11 01	
Fishersgate	d							10 33													11 03	
Southwick	d			10 13				10 35								10 43					11 05	
Shoreham-by-Sea	d			10 16		10 31		10 39								10 46			11 00		11 09	
Lancing	d			10 20				10 43								10 50			11 04		11 13	
East Worthing	d							10 46													11 16	
Worthing 4	a			10 24		10 37		10 48								10 54			11 08		11 18	
	d			10 25		10 37		10 49								10 55			11 08		11 19	
West Worthing	d					10 39		10a51								10 57			11 10		11a21	
Durrington-on-Sea	d					10 42										10 59			11 13			
Goring-by-Sea	d					10 44										11 02			11 15			
Angmering 3	d			10 31		10 48										11 06			11 19			
Littlehampton 4	a					10 57													11 28			
	d										10 54							11 11				
Ford 4	d		10 34								10 58			11 07		11 12		11 16				
Bognor Regis 4	d								10 39			10 56			11 07							11 30
Barnham	a	10 26	10 39	10 42					10 45		11 02	11 02	10 56	11 11	11 13	11 16		11 20				11 36
	d	10 27	10 39	10 42						10 52	11 03		10 57	11 12		11 17		11 22				
Bognor Regis	a		10 46							10 59				11 18				11 29				
Chichester 4	a	10 34		10 50							11 10		11 04			11 24						
	d	10 35		10 50							11 11		11 05			11 25						
Fishbourne (Sussex)	d										11 14											
Bosham	d										11 17											
Nutbourne	d										11 20											
Southbourne	d			10 57							11 23		11 12									
Emsworth	d			11 00							11 26		11 15			11 33						
Warblington	d										11 29											
Havant	d	10 46		11 05							11 32		11 19			11 37						
Bedhampton	a										11 34											
Hilsea	a										11 42											
Fratton	a	10 54		11 13							11 46											
Portsmouth & Southsea	a	10 58		11 17							11 50											
Portsmouth Harbour	a	11 02		11 21																		
Cosham	a												11 26			11 45						
Portchester	a												11 30									
Fareham	a												11 35			11 53						
Swanwick	a												11 42			12 00						
Eastleigh	a																					
Southampton Airport Parkway	a																					
Southampton Central	a												12 01			12 19						

A to Horsham

B to Haywards Heath

London, Gatwick Airport, Brighton - Sussex Coast, Portsmouth and Southampton

Network Diagram - see first Page of Table 186

		SN ◇1 A 🚌		SN	SN	SN ◇1 B 🚌	SN 1	SN	SN	SN	SN	SN ◇1	SN ◇1 A 🚌		SN	SN	SN	SN	SN ◇1 B 🚌	SN 1	SN	SN ◇1
London Victoria 15 ⊖	d	10 02				10 17							10 32						10 47			
Clapham Junction 10	d	10 08				10 23							10 38						10 53			
London Bridge 4 ⊖	d						10 03													10 33		
East Croydon	d	10 18				10 33	10 21						10 48						11 03	10 51		
Redhill 5	d	10 30					10 45						11 00							11 10		
Horley	d	10 36					10 53													11 19		
Gatwick Airport 10 ✈	d	10 40				10 50	10 56						11 09						11 20	11 24		
Three Bridges 4	a	10 44					11 01						11 14							11 29		
	d	10 45					11 01						11 14							11 30		
Crawley	d	10 48					11 05						11 18							11 33		
Horsham 4	a	10 56					11 17						11 26							11 45		
	d	11 00	11 05										11 30	11 35								
Christs Hospital	d													11 38								
Billingshurst	d		11 14											11 44								
Pulborough	d		11 20											11 51								
Amberley	d													11 57								
Arundel	d		11 29											12 02								
Haywards Heath 3	d					11 04													11 37			
Burgess Hill	d					11 09																
Preston Park	d					11 18																
Brighton 10	d			11 03	11 14			11 23								11 33	11 44				11 53	
Hove 2	a			11 06	11 18	11 22		11 26								11 36	11 48		11 53		11 56	
	d			11 07		11 22		11 27								11 37			11 53		11 57	
Aldrington	d							11 29													11 59	
Portslade	d			11 10		11 25		11 31								11 40					12 01	
Fishersgate	d							11 33													12 03	
Southwick	d			11 13				11 35								11 43					12 05	
Shoreham-by-Sea	d			11 16		11 30		11 39								11 46			12 00		12 09	
Lancing	d			11 20				11 43								11 50			12 04		12 13	
East Worthing	d							11 46													12 16	
Worthing 4	a			11 24		11 36		11 48								11 54			12 08		12 18	
	d			11 25		11 37		11 49								11 55			12 08		12 19	
West Worthing	d					11 39		11a51								11 57			12 10		12a21	
Durrington-on-Sea	d					11 41										11 59			12 13			
Goring-by-Sea	d					11 44										12 02			12 15			
Angmering 3	d			11 31		11 48										12 06			12 19			
Littlehampton 4	a					11 57													12 28			
	d										11 54							12 11				
Ford 4	d		11 34								11 58			12 07		12 12		12 16				
Bognor Regis 4	d								11 39			11 56			12 07							12 30
Barnham	a	11 26	11 39	11 42					11 45		12 02	12 02	11 56	12 11	12 13	12 16		12 20				12 36
	d	11 27	11 39	11 42						11 52	12 03		11 57	12 12		12 17		12 22				
Bognor Regis	a		11 46							11 59				12 18				12 29				
Chichester 4	a	11 34		11 50							12 10		12 04			12 24						
	d	11 35		11 50							12 11		12 05			12 25						
Fishbourne (Sussex)	d										12 14											
Bosham	d										12 17											
Nutbourne	d										12 20											
Southbourne	d			11 57							12 23		12 12									
Emsworth	d			12 00							12 26		12 15			12 33						
Warblington	d										12 29											
Havant	d	11 46		12 05							12 32		12 19			12 37						
Bedhampton	a										12 34											
Hilsea	a										12 42											
Fratton	a	11 54		12 13							12 46											
Portsmouth & Southsea	a	11 58		12 17							12 50											
Portsmouth Harbour ⛴	a	12 02		12 21																		
Cosham	a												12 26			12 45						
Portchester	a												12 30									
Fareham	a												12 35			12 53						
Swanwick	a												12 42			13 00						
Eastleigh	a																					
Southampton Airport Parkway	a																					
Southampton Central ⛴	a												12 59			13 19						

A 🚌 to Horsham

B 🚌 to Haywards Heath

London, Gatwick Airport, Brighton - Sussex Coast, Portsmouth and Southampton

Network Diagram - see first Page of Table 186

		SN ◇1		SN	SN	SN ◇1	SN 1	SN	SN	SN	SN	SN ◇1	SN ◇1		SN	SN 1	SN	SN	SN ◇1	SN 1	SN	SN ◇1
London Victoria 15 ⊖	d	11 02				11 17							11 32						11 47			
Clapham Junction 10	d	11 08				11 23							11 38						11 53			
London Bridge 4 ⊖	d						11 03													11 33		
East Croydon	d	11 18				11 33	11 21						11 48						12 03	11 51		
Redhill 5	d	11 30					11 45						12 00							12 10		
Horley	d	11 36					11 53													12 19		
Gatwick Airport 10 ✈	d	11 40				11 50	11 56						12 09						12 20	12 24		
Three Bridges 4	a	11 44					12 01						12 14							12 29		
	d	11 45					12 01						12 14							12 30		
Crawley	d	11 48					12 05						12 18							12 33		
Horsham 4	a	11 56					12 18						12 26							12 45		
	d	12 00	12 05										12 30	12 35								
Christs Hospital	d													12 38								
Billingshurst	d		12 14											12 44								
Pulborough	d		12 20											12 51								
Amberley	d													12 57								
Arundel	d		12 29											13 02								
Haywards Heath 3	d					12 04													12 37			
Burgess Hill	d					12 09																
Preston Park	d					12 18																
Brighton 10	d			12 03	12 14			12 23								12 33	12 44				12 53	
Hove 2	a			12 06	12 18	12 22		12 26								12 36	12 48		12 53		12 56	
	d			12 07		12 22		12 27								12 37			12 53		12 57	
Aldrington	d							12 29													12 59	
Portslade	d			12 10		12 25		12 31								12 40					13 01	
Fishersgate	d							12 33													13 03	
Southwick	d			12 13				12 35								12 43					13 05	
Shoreham-by-Sea	d			12 16		12 30		12 39								12 46			13 00		13 09	
Lancing	d			12 20				12 43								12 50			13 04		13 13	
East Worthing	d							12 46													13 16	
Worthing 4	a			12 24		12 36		12 48								12 54			13 08		13 18	
	d			12 25		12 37		12 49								12 55			13 08		13 19	
West Worthing	d					12 39		12a51								12 57			13 10		13a21	
Durrington-on-Sea	d					12 41										12 59			13 13			
Goring-by-Sea	d					12 44										13 02			13 15			
Angmering 3	d			12 31		12 48										13 06			13 19			
Littlehampton 4	a					12 57													13 28			
	d										12 54							13 11				
Ford 4	d		12 34								12 58			13 07		13 12		13 16				
Bognor Regis 4	d								12 39			12 56			13 07							13 30
Barnham	a	12 26	12 39	12 42					12 45		13 02	13 02	12 56	13 11	13 13	13 16		13 20				13 36
	d	12 27	12 39	12 42						12 52	13 03		12 57	13 12		13 17		13 22				
Bognor Regis	a		12 46							12 59				13 18				13 29				
Chichester 4	a	12 34		12 50							13 10		13 04			13 24						
	d	12 35		12 50							13 11		13 05			13 25						
Fishbourne (Sussex)	d										13 14											
Bosham	d										13 17											
Nutbourne	d										13 20											
Southbourne	d			12 57							13 23		13 12									
Emsworth	d			13 00							13 26		13 15			13 33						
Warblington	d										13 29											
Havant	d	12 46		13 05							13 32		13 19			13 37						
Bedhampton	a										13 34											
Hilsea	a										13 42											
Fratton	a	12 54		13 13							13 46											
Portsmouth & Southsea	a	12 58		13 17							13 50											
Portsmouth Harbour ⛴	a	13 02		13 21																		
Cosham	a												13 26			13 45						
Portchester	a												13 30									
Fareham	a												13 35			13 53						
Swanwick	a												13 42			14 02						
Eastleigh	a																					
Southampton Airport Parkway	a																					
Southampton Central ⛴	a												13 59			14 19						

London, Gatwick Airport, Brighton - Sussex Coast, Portsmouth and Southampton

Network Diagram - see first Page of Table 186

		SN ◇1		SN	SN	SN ◇1		SN 1	SN	SN	SN	SN	SN ◇1	SN ◇1		SN		SN	SN	SN	SN ◇1	SN 1	SN	SN ◇1 Bus	
London Victoria 15	d	12 02				12 17								12 32							12 47				
Clapham Junction 10	d	12 08				12 23								12 38							12 53				
London Bridge 4	d							12 03														12 33			
East Croydon	d	12 18				12 33		12 21						12 48							13 03	12 51			
Redhill 5	d	12 30						12 45						13 00								13 11			
Horley	d	12 36						12 53														13 20			
Gatwick Airport 10	d	12 40				12 50		12 56						13 09							13 20	13 24			
Three Bridges 4	a	12 44						13 01						13 14								13 29			
	d	12 45						13 01						13 14								13 30			
Crawley	d	12 48						13 05						13 18								13 33			
Horsham 4	a	12 56						13 17						13 26								13 45			
	d	13 00	13 05											13 30	13 35										
Christs Hospital	d														13 38										
Billingshurst	d		13 14												13 44										
Pulborough	d		13 20												13 51										
Amberley	d														13 57										
Arundel	d		13 29												14 02										
Haywards Heath 3	d					13 04															13 37				
Burgess Hill	d					13 09																			
Preston Park	d					13 18																			
Brighton 10	d			13 03	13 14				13 23									13 33	13 44				13 53		
Hove 2	a			13 06	13 19	13 22			13 26									13 36	13 48		13 53		13 56		
	d			13 07		13 22			13 27									13 37			13 53		13 57		
Aldrington	d								13 29														13 59		
Portslade	d			13 10		13 25			13 31									13 40					14 01		
Fishersgate	d								13 33														14 03		
Southwick	d			13 13					13 35									13 43					14 05		
Shoreham-by-Sea	d			13 16		13 30			13 39									13 46			14 00		14 09		
Lancing	d			13 20					13 43									13 50			14 04		14 13		
East Worthing	d								13 46														14 16		
Worthing 4	a			13 24		13 36			13 48									13 54			14 08		14 18		
	d			13 25		13 37			13 49									13 55			14 08		14 19		
West Worthing	d					13 39			13a51									13 57			14 10		14a21		
Durrington-on-Sea	d					13 41												13 59			14 13				
Goring-by-Sea	d					13 44												14 02			14 15				
Angmering 3	d			13 31		13 48												14 06			14 19				
Littlehampton 4	a					13 57															14 28				
	d											13 54								14 11					
Ford 4	d		13 34									13 58			14 07			14 12		14 16					
Bognor Regis 4	d									13 39			13 56			14 07								14 30	
Barnham	a	13 26	13 39	13 42						13 45		14 02	14 02	13 56	14 11	14 13		14 16		14 20				14 36	
	d	13 27	13 39	13 42							13 52	14 03		13 57	14 12			14 17		14 22					
Bognor Regis	a		13 46								13 59				14 18					14 29					
Chichester 4	a	13 34		13 50								14 10		14 04				14 24							
	d	13 35		13 50								14 11		14 05				14 25							
Fishbourne (Sussex)	d											14 14													
Bosham	d											14 17													
Nutbourne	d											14 20													
Southbourne	d			13 57								14 23		14 12											
Emsworth	d			14 00								14 26		14 15				14 33							
Warblington	d											14 29													
Havant	d	13 46		14 05								14 32		14 19				14 37							
Bedhampton	a											14 34													
Hilsea	a											14 42													
Fratton	a	13 54		14 13								14 46													
Portsmouth & Southsea	a	13 58		14 17								14 50													
Portsmouth Harbour	a	14 02		14 21																					
Cosham	a													14 26				14 45							
Portchester	a													14 30											
Fareham	a													14 35				14 53							
Swanwick	a													14 42				15 00							
Eastleigh	a																								
Southampton Airport Parkway	a																								
Southampton Central	a													14 59				15 19							

London, Gatwick Airport, Brighton - Sussex Coast, Portsmouth and Southampton

Network Diagram - see first Page of Table 186

		SN ◇1			SN	SN	SN ◇1	SN 1	SN	SN	SN	SN	SN ◇1 Bus		SN ◇1 A Bus		SN	SN	SN	SN	SN ◇1	SN 1	SN		SN
London Victoria 15	d	13 02					13 17								13 32						13 47				
Clapham Junction 10	d	13 08					13 23								13 38						13 53				
London Bridge 4	d							13 03														13 33			
East Croydon	d	13 18					13 33	13 21							13 48						14 03	13 51			
Redhill 5	d	13 30						13 45							14 00							14 10			
Horley	d	13 36						13 53														14 19			
Gatwick Airport 10	d	13 40					13 50	13 56							14 09						14 20	14 24			
Three Bridges 4	a	13 44						14 01							14 14							14 29			
	d	13 45						14 01							14 14							14 30			
Crawley	d	13 48						14 05							14 18							14 33			
Horsham 4	a	13 56						14 17							14 26							14 45			
	d	14 00	14 05												14 30	14 35									
Christs Hospital	d															14 38									
Billingshurst	d		14 14													14 44									
Pulborough	d		14 20													14 51									
Amberley	d															14 57									
Arundel	d		14 29													15 02									
Haywards Heath 3	d						14 04														14 37				
Burgess Hill	d						14 09																		
Preston Park	d						14 18																		
Brighton 10	d				14 03	14 14			14 23									14 33	14 44				14 53		
Hove 2	a				14 06	14 18	14 22		14 26									14 36	14 48		14 53		14 56		
	d				14 07		14 22		14 27									14 37			14 53		14 57		
Aldrington	d								14 29														14 59		
Portslade	d				14 10		14 25		14 31									14 40					15 01		
Fishersgate	d								14 33														15 03		
Southwick	d				14 13				14 35									14 43					15 05		
Shoreham-by-Sea	d				14 16		14 30		14 39									14 46			15 00		15 09		
Lancing	d				14 20				14 43									14 50			15 04		15 13		
East Worthing	d								14 46														15 16		
Worthing 4	a				14 24		14 36		14 48									14 54			15 08		15 18		
	d				14 25		14 37		14 49									14 55			15 08		15 19		
West Worthing	d						14 39		14a51									14 57			15 10		15a21		
Durrington-on-Sea	d						14 41											14 59			15 13				
Goring-by-Sea	d						14 44											15 02			15 15				
Angmering 3	d				14 31		14 48											15 06			15 19				
Littlehampton 4	a						14 57														15 30				
	d											14 54								15 11					15 23
Ford 4	d		14 34									14 58				15 07		15 12		15 16					15 27
Bognor Regis 4	d									14 39			14 56				15 07								
Barnham	a	14 26	14 39		14 42					14 45		15 02	15 02		14 56	15 11	15 13	15 16		15 20					15 31
	d	14 27	14 39		14 42						14 52	15 03			14 57	15 12		15 17		15 22					15 33
Bognor Regis	a		14 46								14 59					15 18				15 29					
Chichester 4	a	14 34			14 50							15 10			15 04			15 24							15 40
	d	14 35			14 50							15 11			15 05			15 25							15 41
Fishbourne (Sussex)	d											15 14													15 44
Bosham	d											15 17													15 47
Nutbourne	d											15 20													15 50
Southbourne	d				14 57							15 23			15 12										15 53
Emsworth	d				15 00							15 26			15 15			15 33							15 56
Warblington	d											15 29													15 59
Havant	d	14 46			15 05							15 32			15 19			15 37							16 02
Bedhampton	a											15 34													16 04
Hilsea	a											15 42													
Fratton	a	14 54			15 13							15 46													16 12
Portsmouth & Southsea	a	14 58			15 17							15 50													16 15
Portsmouth Harbour	a	15 02			15 21																				16 21
Cosham	a														15 26			15 45							
Portchester	a														15 30										
Fareham	a														15 35			15 53							
Swanwick	a														15 42			16 00							
Eastleigh	a																								
Southampton Airport Parkway	a																								
Southampton Central	a														15 59			16 20							

A Bus to Horsham

London, Gatwick Airport, Brighton - Sussex Coast, Portsmouth and Southampton

Network Diagram - see first Page of Table 186

		SN ◇1	SN ◇1		SN	SN	SN	SN ◇1	SN 1		SN	SN	SN 1	SN ◇1 ⊼	SN ◇1 A ⊼		SN	SN 1	SN		SN ◇1	SN 1	SN	SN	SN
London Victoria 15 ⊖	d		14 02					14 17							14 32						14 47				
Clapham Junction 10	d		14 08					14 23							14 38						14 53				
London Bridge 4 ⊖	d								14 03													14 33			
East Croydon ⇌	d		14 18					14 33	14 21						14 48						15 03	14 51			
Redhill 5	d		14 30						14 45						15 00							15 10			
Horley	d		14 36						14 53													15 19			
Gatwick Airport 10 ✈	d		14 40					14 50	14 56						15 09						15 20	15 24			
Three Bridges 4	a		14 44						15 01						15 14							15 29			
	d		14 45						15 01						15 14							15 30			
Crawley	d		14 48						15 05						15 18							15 33			
Horsham 4	a		14 56						15 17						15 26							15 48			
	d		15 00	15 05											15 30	15 35									
Christs Hospital	d			15 08												15 38									
Billingshurst	d			15 14												15 44									
Pulborough	d			15 21												15 51									
Amberley	d															15 57									
Arundel	d			15 30												16 02									
Haywards Heath 3	d							15 04													15 37				
Burgess Hill	d							15 09																	
Preston Park	d							15 18																	
Brighton 10	d					15 03	15 14						15 23					15 33	15 44				15 53		
Hove 2	a					15 06	15 18	15 22					15 26					15 36	15 48		15 53		15 56		
	d					15 07		15 22					15 27					15 37			15 53		15 57		
Aldrington	d												15 29										15 59		
Portslade	d					15 10		15 25					15 31					15 40					16 01		
Fishersgate	d												15 33										16 03		
Southwick	d					15 13							15 35					15 43					16 05		
Shoreham-by-Sea	d					15 16		15 30					15 39					15 46			16 00		16 09		
Lancing	d					15 20							15 43					15 50			16 04		16 13		
East Worthing	d							15 35					15 46										16 16		
Worthing 4	a					15 24		15 38					15 48					15 54			16 08		16 18		
	d					15 25		15 38					15 49					15 55			16 08		16 19		
West Worthing	d					15 27		15 40					15 51					15 57			16 10		16a21		
Durrington-on-Sea	d					15 29		15 43					15 53					15 59			16 13				
Goring-by-Sea	d					15 32		15 45					15 56					16 02			16 15				
Angmering 3	d					15 36		15 49					16 00					16 06			16 19				
Littlehampton 4	a							15 58					16 11								16 28				
	d											15 54													
Ford 4	d			15 35		15 42						15 58				16 07		16 13							16 22
Bognor Regis 4	d	15 27			15 39									15 56			16 09								16 26
Barnham	a	15 33	15 26	15 39	15 45	15 46						16 02		16 02	15 56	16 11	16 15	16 17							16 30
	d		15 27	15 40		15 47					15 53	16 03			15 57	16 12		16 18						16 24	16 31
Bognor Regis	a			15 46							16 00					16 18								16 31	
Chichester 4	a		15 34			15 54						16 10			16 04			16 25							16 38
	d		15 35			15 55						16 11			16 05			16 26							16 39
Fishbourne (Sussex)	d											16 14													16 42
Bosham	d											16 17													16 45
Nutbourne	d											16 20													16 48
Southbourne	d					16 02						16 23			16 12										16 51
Emsworth	d					16 05						16 26			16 15			16 34							16 54
Warblington	d											16 29													16 57
Havant	d		15 46			16 09						16 32			16 19			16 38							17 00
Bedhampton	a											16 34													17 02
Hilsea	a											16 42													17 07
Fratton	a		15 54			16 18						16 46													17 11
Portsmouth & Southsea	a		15 58			16 21						16 50													17 16
Portsmouth Harbour ⛴	a		16 02			16 26																			17 20
Cosham	a														16 26			16 45							
Portchester	a														16 30										
Fareham	a														16 35			16 53							
Swanwick	a														16 42										
Eastleigh	a																	17 11							
Southampton Airport Parkway	a																	17 20							
Southampton Central ⛴	a														17 01			17 28							

A ⊼ to Horsham

London, Gatwick Airport, Brighton - Sussex Coast, Portsmouth and Southampton

Network Diagram - see first Page of Table 186

		SN ◇1 ⊼	SN ◇1		SN		SN	SN	SN ◇1	SN 1	SN	SN	SN 1	SN ◇1 ⊼	SN ◇1			SN 1	SN	SN	SN ◇1	SN 1	SN	SN ◇1	SN
London Victoria 15 ⊖	d		15 02						15 17						15 32						15 47				
Clapham Junction 10	d		15 08						15 23						15 38						15 53				
London Bridge 4 ⊖	d									15 03												15 33			
East Croydon ⇌	d		15 18						15 33	15 21					15 48						16 03	15 51			
Redhill 5	d		15 30							15 45					16 00							16 10			
Horley	d		15 36							15 55												16 19			
Gatwick Airport 10 ✈	d		15 40						15 50	15 58					16 09						16 20	16 24			
Three Bridges 4	a		15 44							16 03					16 14							16 29			
	d		15 45							16 03					16 14							16 30			
Crawley	d		15 48							16 07					16 18							16 34			
Horsham 4	a		15 56							16 21					16 26							16 47			
	d		16 00	16 05											16 30	16 35									
Christs Hospital	d			16 08												16 38									
Billingshurst	d			16 14												16 44									
Pulborough	d			16 21												16 51									
Amberley	d															16 57									
Arundel	d			16 30												17 02									
Haywards Heath 3	d								16 04												16 37				
Burgess Hill	d								16 09																
Preston Park	d								16 18																
Brighton 10	d						16 03	16 14			16 24							16 33	16 44						16 53
Hove 2	a						16 06	16 18	16 22		16 27							16 36	16 48		16 53				16 56
	d						16 07		16 22		16 28							16 37			16 53				16 57
Aldrington	d										16 30														16 59
Portslade	d						16 10		16 25		16 32							16 40			16 56				17 01
Fishersgate	d										16 34														17 03
Southwick	d						16 13				16 36							16 43							17 05
Shoreham-by-Sea	d						16 16		16 30		16 40							16 46			17 01				17 08
Lancing	d						16 20				16 44							16 50			17 05				17 12
East Worthing	d										16 47														17 15
Worthing 4	a						16 24		16 36		16 49							16 54			17 09				17 18
	d						16 25		16 37		16 50							16 55			17 10				17 18
West Worthing	d						16 27		16 39		16a52							16 57			17 12				17 20
Durrington-on-Sea	d						16 29		16 41									16 59			17 14				
Goring-by-Sea	d						16 32		16 44									17 02			17 17				
Angmering 3	d						16 36		16 48									17 06			17 21				
Littlehampton 4	a								16 57												17 29				17 33
	d												16 54							17 11					17 41
Ford 4	d			16 35			16 42						16 58			17 07		17 12		17 16					17 46
Bognor Regis 4	d	16 30			16 39									16 56									17 18	17 30	
Barnham	a	16 36	16 26	16 39	16 45		16 46						17 02	17 02	16 56	17 11		17 16		17 20			17 24	17 36	17 50
	d		16 27	16 40			16 47					16 54	17 03		16 57	17 12		17 17		17 24					17 54
Bognor Regis	a			16 46								17 01				17 18				17 31					→
Chichester 4	a		16 34				16 54						17 10		17 04			17 24							
	d		16 35				16 55						17 11		17 05			17 25							
Fishbourne (Sussex)	d												17 14												
Bosham	d												17 17												
Nutbourne	d												17 20												
Southbourne	d						17 02						17 23		17 12										
Emsworth	d						17 05						17 26		17 15			17 33							
Warblington	d												17 29												
Havant	d		16 46				17 09						17 32		17 19			17 37							
Bedhampton	a												17 34												
Hilsea	a												17 42												
Fratton	a		16 54				17 18						17 46												
Portsmouth & Southsea	a		16 58				17 22						17 50												
Portsmouth Harbour ⛴	a		17 02																						
Cosham	a														17 26			17 45							
Portchester	a														17 31										
Fareham	a														17 36			17 53							
Swanwick	a														17 43			18 00							
Eastleigh	a																								
Southampton Airport Parkway	a																								
Southampton Central ⛴	a														18 03			18 20							

London, Gatwick Airport, Brighton - Sussex Coast, Portsmouth and Southampton

Network Diagram - see first Page of Table 186

		GW	SN		SN	SN	SN	SN	SN	SN	SN	SN	SN	SN	SN	SN		SN	SN	SN	SN	SN
		◇ ⊼	◇1					◇1 A ⊼	1	1				◇1		◇1 B ⊼		1	1			1
London Victoria 15 ⊖	d		16 02					16 17	16 19							16 32						
Clapham Junction 10	d		16 08					16 23	16 26							16 38						
London Bridge 4 ⊖	d									16 03								16 33				16 57
East Croydon	d		16 18					16 33	16 36	16 21						16 48		16 49				17 10
Redhill 5	d		16 30							16 43						17 00		17 08				
Horley	d		16 36							16 52						17 06		17 18				
Gatwick Airport 10 ✈	d		16 40					16 49	16 53	16 56						17 09		17 21				
Three Bridges 4	a		16 44						16 57	17 00						17 14		17 26				17 29
	d		16 45						16 58	17 02						17 18	17 22	17 26				17 29
Crawley	d		16 48						17 02	17 06						17 22	17 26	17 30				
Horsham 4	a		16 56						17 12	17 19						17 30	17 38	17 44				
	d		17 00	17 05												17 30	17 38					
Christs Hospital	d			17 08													17 42					
Billingshurst	d			17 15													17 48					
Pulborough	d			17 21													17 54					
Amberley	d			17 27																		
Arundel	d			17 32													18 03					
Haywards Heath 3	d							17 04														17 39
Burgess Hill	d							17 09														17 46
Preston Park	d																					17 56
Brighton 10	d	16 59			17 03		17 14						17 23						17 33	17 45	17 53	
Hove 2	a	17 02			17 06		17 18	17 20					17 26						17 36	17 48	17 57	18 00
	d	17 03			17 07			17 21					17 27						17 37	17 49		18 01
Aldrington	d												17 29							17 51		
Portslade	d				17 10			17 24					17 31						17 40	17 53		18 04
Fishersgate	d												17 33							17 55		
Southwick	d				17 13								17 35						17 43	17 57		
Shoreham-by-Sea	d	17 13			17 16			17 29					17 39						17 46	18 01		18 09
Lancing	d				17 20			17 33					17 43						17 50	18 05		18 13
East Worthing	d												17 46							18 08		
Worthing 4	a	17 21			17 24			17 37					17 48						17 54	18 10		18 17
	d	17 22			17 25			17 38					17 49						17 55	18 11		18 17
West Worthing	d				17 27			17 40					17 51						17 57	18 13		18 19
Durrington-on-Sea	d				17 29			17 42					17 53						17 59	18 15		18 22
Goring-by-Sea	d				17 32			17 45					17 56						18 02	18 18		18 24
Angmering 3	d				17 36			17 49					18 00						18 06	18 22		18 28
Littlehampton 4	a							18 00					18 08							18 30		18 39
	d											17 54										
Ford 4	d			17 37	17 42							17 58					18 08		18 12			
Bognor Regis 4	d					←					17 51			17 57								
Barnham	a	17 38	17 26	17 42	17 46	17 50					17 57	18 02		18 03		17 57	18 13		18 16			
	d	17 39	17 27	17 42	17 47	17 54						18 04			18 08	17 57	18 14		18 17			
Bognor Regis	a			17 49		18 01									18 15		18 22					
Chichester 4	a	17 46	17 34		17 54							18 11				18 05			18 24			
	d	17 47	17 35		17 55							18 12				18 05			18 25			
Fishbourne (Sussex)	d		17 38									18 15										
Bosham	d		17 41									18 18				18 10						
Nutbourne	d											18 21										
Southbourne	d		17 45		18 04							18 24				18 14						
Emsworth	d		17 48		18 07							18 27				18 17			18 33			
Warblington	d				18 10							18 30										
Havant	d	17 58	17 54		18 13							18 34				18 23			18 37			
Bedhampton	a		17 56									18 36										
Hilsea	a		18 01									18 42										
Fratton	a		18 05		18 22							18 46										
Portsmouth & Southsea	a		18 09		18 25							18 49										
Portsmouth Harbour ⛴	a		18 15		18 31																	
Cosham	a	18 04														18 29			18 44			
Portchester	a															18 34						
Fareham	a	18 12														18 39			18 52			
Swanwick	a															18 46			18 59			
Eastleigh	a																					
Southampton Airport Parkway	a																					
Southampton Central ⛴	a	18 40														19 05			19 20			

A ⊼ to Haywards Heath

B ⊼ to Three Bridges

London, Gatwick Airport, Brighton - Sussex Coast, Portsmouth and Southampton

Network Diagram - see first Page of Table 186

		SN	SN	SN		SN	SN	SN	SN	SN	SN	SN	SN	SN		SN	SN	SN	SN	SN	SN	SN	SN
				◇1 A ⊼		◇1			◇1	1				◇1				1	1			◇1	1
London Victoria 15 ⊖	d			17 02					17 17					17 32								17 47	
Clapham Junction 10	d			17 08					17 23					17 38								17 53	
London Bridge 4 ⊖	d									16 59								17 42	17 47				17 32
East Croydon	d			17 18					17 33	17 15				17 49				17 55	18 00			18 03	17 49
Redhill 5	d									17 37													18 11
Horley	d									17 46												18 18	18 20
Gatwick Airport 10 ✈	d								17 48	17 50												18 21	18 24
Three Bridges 4	a			17 36						17 54				18 06					18 21				18 28
	d			17 37						17 55				18 07					18 22				18 29
Crawley	d			17 41						17 59				18 11					18 26				18 33
Horsham 4	a			17 49						18 11				18 22					18 38				18 48
	d			17 53	17 58									18 26	18 31				18 39				
Christs Hospital	d				18 01										18 35				18 42				
Billingshurst	d				18 07										18 41				18 49				
Pulborough	d				18 14										18 48				18 56				
Amberley	d				18 20														19 02				
Arundel	d				18 25										18 57				19 07				
Haywards Heath 3	d								18 01									18 22				18 34	
Burgess Hill	d								18 07									18 28				18 41	
Preston Park	d																	18 39				18 53	
Brighton 10	d						18 00	18 14									18 28			18 48			
Hove 2	a						18 03	18 18	18 21								18 31	18 43		18 53		18 57	
	d						18 04		18 22								18 32	18 44				18 58	
Aldrington	d						18 06										18 34						
Portslade	d						18 08		18 25								18 36	18 47				19 01	
Fishersgate	d						18 10										18 38						
Southwick	d						18 12										18 40						
Shoreham-by-Sea	d						18 16		18 30								18 44	18 52				19 06	
Lancing	d						18 20		18 34								18 48	18 56				19 10	
East Worthing	d						18 23										18 51						
Worthing 4	a						18 25		18 38								18 53	19 00				19 14	
	d						18 27		18 38								18 54	19 00				19 14	
West Worthing	d						18 29		18 40									19 02				19 16	
Durrington-on-Sea	d						18 31		18 43									19 05				19 19	
Goring-by-Sea	d						18 34		18 45									19 07				19 21	
Angmering 3	d						18 38		18 49								19 00	19 11				19 25	
Littlehampton 4	a								19 00									19 24				19 36	
	d		18 18										18 48								19 11		
Ford 4	d		18 22		18 30		18 44						18 53		19 02		19 07				19 15		
Bognor Regis 4	d	18 19				18 33					18 46					19 03							
Barnham	a	18 25	18 26	18 20	18 34	18 39	18 48				18 52		18 57	18 53	19 06	19 09	19 11		19 15		19 19		
	d		18 27	18 21	18 35		18 49					18 55	19 00	18 54	19 07		19 12		19 16		19 24		
Bognor Regis	a		18 34		18 41							19 02			19 13				19 24		19 31		
Chichester 4	a			18 28			18 56						19 07	19 01			19 19						
	d			18 29			18 57						19 11	19 02			19 20						
Fishbourne (Sussex)	d			18 32									19 14	19 05									
Bosham	d			18 35									19 17	19 08									
Nutbourne	d			18 38									19 20										
Southbourne	d			18 41									19 23	19 12									
Emsworth	d			18 44									19 26	19 15			19 30						
Warblington	d			18 47									19 29										
Havant	d			18 54			19 08						19 33	19 20			19 37						
Bedhampton	a			18 57									19 35										
Hilsea	a			19 02									19 43										
Fratton	a			19 06			19 17						19 47										
Portsmouth & Southsea	a			19 09			19 21						19 50										
Portsmouth Harbour ⛴	a						19 26																
Cosham	a													19 29			19 46						
Portchester	a													19 33									
Fareham	a													19 38			19 54						
Swanwick	a													19 45			20 01						
Eastleigh	a																						
Southampton Airport Parkway	a																						
Southampton Central ⛴	a													20 03			20 18						

A ⊼ to Horsham

London, Gatwick Airport, Brighton - Sussex Coast, Portsmouth and Southampton

Network Diagram - see first Page of Table 186

		SN ◇1		SN 1	SN ◇1	SN	SN 1	SN	SN ◇1	SN	SN ◇1		SN 1	SN 1	SN	SN 1	SN	SN	SN ◇1 A ⌶	SN ◇1	SN ◇1 B ⌶	
London Victoria 15 ⊖	d	18 02							18 17		18 32		18 19						18 47		19 02	
Clapham Junction 10	d	18 08							18 23		18 38		18 26						18 53		19 08	
London Bridge 4 ⊖	d			17 59			18 12							18 30								
East Croydon	d	18 19		18 15			18 25		18 33		18 48		18 38	18 46					19 04		19 18	
Redhill 5	d			18 34									18 59	19 07							19 31	
Horley	d			18 43					18 48				19 08	19 16								
Gatwick Airport 10 ✈	d			18 47									19 14	19 20					19 21		19 40	
Three Bridges 4	a	18 37		18 51			18 44				19 06		19 19	19 24							19 45	
	d	18 38		18 52			18 45				19 07		19 19	19 25							19 45	
Crawley	d	18 42		18 56							19 11		19 23	19 29							19 49	
Horsham 4	a	18 50		19 08							19 22		19 37	19 43							19 57	
	d	18 54	18 58								19 26	19 31									20 01	20 06
Christs Hospital	d		19 01									19 34										20 09
Billingshurst	d		19 07									19 41										20 15
Pulborough	d		19 14									19 48										20 22
Amberley	d											19 54										20 28
Arundel	d		19 23									19 59										20 33
Haywards Heath 3	d						18 54		19 03										19 38			
Burgess Hill	d						19 00		19 09										19 43			
Preston Park	d						19 11															
Brighton 10	d					19 00		19 15								19 30	19 44					
Hove 2	a					19 03	19 17	19 19	19 22							19 33	19 48		19 57			
	d					19 04	19 18		19 23							19 34			19 57			
Aldrington	d					19 06										19 36						
Portslade	d					19 08	19 21		19 26							19 38			20 00			
Fishersgate	d					19 10										19 40						
Southwick	d					19 12										19 42						
Shoreham-by-Sea	d					19 16	19 26		19 31							19 46			20 05			
Lancing	d					19 20	19 30		19 36							19 50			20 09			
East Worthing	d					19 23										19 53						
Worthing 4	a					19 25	19 34		19 40							19 55			20 13			
	d					19 26	19 35		19 40							19 56			20 13			
West Worthing	d					19 28	19 37		19 42							19 58			20 15			
Durrington-on-Sea	d					19 30	19 39		19 45							20 00			20 18			
Goring-by-Sea	d					19 33	19 42		19 47							20 03			20 20			
Angmering 3	d					19 37	19 46		19 51							20 07			20 24			
Littlehampton 4	a						19 57		20 03										20 35			
	d									19 35								20 06				
Ford 4	d		19 28			19 43				19 39						20 13		20 10				20 38
Bognor Regis 4	d				19 36										20 05					20 33		
Barnham	a	19 23	19 32		19 42	19 47				19 43	19 52	20 07			20 11	20 18		20 14		20 39	20 27	20 42
	d	19 24	19 33			19 48				19 55	19 53	20 08				20 18		20 22			20 28	20 43
Bognor Regis	a		19 39							20 01		20 14						20 28				20 49
Chichester 4	a	19 31				19 55					20 00					20 26					20 35	
	d	19 32				19 56					20 01					20 26					20 36	
Fishbourne (Sussex)	d										20 04											
Bosham	d										20 07											
Nutbourne	d										20 10											
Southbourne	d	19 39									20 13										20 43	
Emsworth	d	19 42									20 16										20 46	
Warblington	d										20 19											
Havant	d	19 46				20 07					20 22					20 37					20 52	
Bedhampton	a																					
Hilsea	a																					
Fratton	a	19 55				20 15															21 01	
Portsmouth & Southsea	a	20 00				20 19															21 06	
Portsmouth Harbour	a	20 06																				
Cosham	a										20 28					20 44						
Portchester	a															20 49						
Fareham	a										20 36					20 54						
Swanwick	a										20 43					21 01						
Eastleigh	a																					
Southampton Airport Parkway	a																					
Southampton Central	a										21 01					21 19						

A ⌶ to Haywards Heath

B ⌶ to Horsham

London, Gatwick Airport, Brighton - Sussex Coast, Portsmouth and Southampton

Network Diagram - see first Page of Table 186

		SN 1	SN	SN	SN ◇1 A ⌶	SN 1	SN 1	SN	SN ◇1 B ⌶		SN 1	SN 1	SN	SN	SN ◇1 A ⌶	SN 1	SN ◇1 ⌶		SN	SN	SN	SN ◇1	SN 1
London Victoria 15 ⊖	d				19 17		19 10		19 32						19 47	19 40	20 02					20 17	20 10
Clapham Junction 10	d				19 23		19 16		19 38						19 53	19 46	20 08					20 23	20 16
London Bridge 4 ⊖	d					18 59					19 33												
East Croydon	d				19 33	19 19	19 28		19 48		19 51				20 03	19 58	20 19					20 33	20 28
Redhill 5	d					19 37	19 46		20 00		20 10					20 16	20 31						20 46
Horley	d					19 47	19 55				20 16					20 25							20 54
Gatwick Airport 10 ✈	d				19 49	19 50	19 59		20 09		20 19				20 19	20 29	20 39					20 49	20 57
Three Bridges 4	a					19 55	20 03		20 14		20 24					20 33	20 44						21 02
	d					19 55	20 04		20 14		20 24					20 34	20 44						21 03
Crawley	d					19 59	20 08		20 18		20 28					20 37	20 48						21 06
Horsham 4	a					20 11	20 21		20 26		20 40					20 49	20 56						21 18
	d								20 30	20 35							21 00	21 05					
Christs Hospital	d									20 38								21 08					
Billingshurst	d									20 44								21 14					
Pulborough	d									20 51								21 21					
Amberley	d									20 57								21 27					
Arundel	d									21 02								21 32					
Haywards Heath 3	d				20 04										20 34							21 04	
Burgess Hill	d				20 09										20 39							21 09	
Preston Park	d														20 49								
Brighton 10	d	20 03	20 14									20 30	20 47							21 03	21 14		
Hove 2	a	20 06	20 18		20 21							20 33	20 51		20 53					21 06	21 18	21 21	
	d	20 07			20 22							20 34			20 54					21 07		21 22	
Aldrington	d	20 09										20 36								21 09			
Portslade	d	20 11			20 25							20 38			20 57					21 11		21 25	
Fishersgate	d	20 13										20 40								21 13			
Southwick	d	20 15										20 42								21 15			
Shoreham-by-Sea	d	20 19			20 30							20 46			21 01					21 19		21 30	
Lancing	d	20 23			20 34							20 50			21 05					21 23		21 34	
East Worthing	d	20 26										20 53								21 26			
Worthing 4	a	20 28			20 38							20 55			21 09					21 28		21 38	
	d	20 29			20 38							20 56			21 10					21 29		21 38	
West Worthing	d	20 31			20 40							20 58			21 12					21 31		21 40	
Durrington-on-Sea	d	20 33			20 43							21 00			21 14					21 33		21 43	
Goring-by-Sea	d	20 36			20 45							21 03			21 17					21 36		21 45	
Angmering 3	d	20 40			20 49							21 07			21 21					21 40		21 49	
Littlehampton 4	a				20 58										21 29							21 58	
	d			20 37										21 06									
Ford 4	d	20 46		20 42						21 07		21 13		21 10				21 37		21 46			
Bognor Regis 4	d							21 04											21 39				
Barnham	a	20 50		20 46				21 10	20 56	21 11		21 17		21 14			21 26	21 41	21 45	21 50			
	d	20 51		20 52					20 57	21 12		21 18		21 22			21 27	21 42		21 51			
Bognor Regis	a			20 59						21 18				21 28				21 48					
Chichester 4	a	20 58							21 04			21 25					21 34			21 58			
	d	20 59							21 05			21 26					21 35			21 59			
Fishbourne (Sussex)	d								21 08														
Bosham	d								21 11														
Nutbourne	d								21 14														
Southbourne	d								21 17								21 42						
Emsworth	d								21 20								21 45						
Warblington	d								21 23														
Havant	d	21 10							21 26			21 37					21 49			22 10			
Bedhampton	a																						
Hilsea	a																						
Fratton	a	21 18															21 58			22 18			
Portsmouth & Southsea	a	21 23															22 01			22 22			
Portsmouth Harbour	a	21 27															22 05			22 26			
Cosham	a								21 33			21 43											
Portchester	a								21 38														
Fareham	a								21 43			21 51											
Swanwick	a								21 49			21 58											
Eastleigh	a																						
Southampton Airport Parkway	a																						
Southampton Central	a								22 07			22 16											

A ⌶ to Haywards Heath

B ⌶ to Horsham

London, Gatwick Airport, Brighton - Sussex Coast, Portsmouth and Southampton

Network Diagram - see first Page of Table 186

		SN	SN	SN ◇1		SN 1	SN	SN	SN ◇1	SN 1	SN	SN	SN	SN	SN	SN ◇1	SN 1	SN 1	SN ◇1	SN	SN	SN	SN ◇1
London Victoria ⊖	d			20 32					20 47	20 40						21 17	21 10	21 32					21 47
Clapham Junction	d			20 38					20 53	20 46						21 23	21 16	21 38					21 53
London Bridge ⊖	d																						
East Croydon	d			20 48					21 04	20 58						21 33	21 28	21 48					22 03
Redhill	d			21 00						21 16							21 46	22 00					
Horley	d									21 25							21 54						
Gatwick Airport ✈	d			21 09					21 19	21 29						21 49	21 57	22 09					22 19
Three Bridges	a			21 14						21 33						21 53	22 02	22 14					
	d			21 14						21 34						21 53	22 03	22 14					
Crawley	d			21 18						21 37							22 06	22 18					
Horsham	a			21 26						21 49							22 18	22 26					
	d			21 30	21 35													22 27					
Christs Hospital	d				21 38													22 30					
Billingshurst	d				21 44													22 36					
Pulborough	d				21 51													22 43					
Amberley	d				21 57													22 49					
Arundel	d				22 02													22 54					
Haywards Heath	d								21 34							22 06							22 37
Burgess Hill	d								21 39							22 11							
Preston Park	d								21 49														
Brighton	d						21 33	21 44					22 03	22 14							22 33	22 44	
Hove	a						21 36	21 48	21 53				22 06	22 18		22 22					22 36	22 48	22 51
	d						21 37		21 54				22 07			22 23					22 37		22 52
Aldrington	d						21 39						22 09								22 39		
Portslade	d						21 41		21 57				22 11			22 26					22 41		22 55
Fishersgate	d						21 43						22 13								22 43		
Southwick	d						21 45						22 15								22 45		
Shoreham-by-Sea	d						21 49		22 01				22 19			22 31					22 49		23 00
Lancing	d						21 53		22 05				22 23			22 35					22 53		23 04
East Worthing	d						21 56						22 26								22 56		
Worthing	a						21 58		22 09				22 28			22 39					22 58		23 08
	d						21 59		22 10				22 29			22 39					22 59		23 08
West Worthing	d						22 01		22 12				22 31			22 41					23 01		23 10
Durrington-on-Sea	d						22 03		22 14				22 33			22 44					23 03		23 13
Goring-by-Sea	d						22 06		22 17				22 36			22 46					23 06		23 15
Angmering	d						22 10		22 21				22 40			22 50					23 10		23 19
Littlehampton	a								22 30												23 18		23 28
	d					22 08									22 38						23 23		
Ford	d				22 07	22 12	22 16						22 46		22 42	22 56		23 00			23 27		
Bognor Regis	d		22 00									22 30							←	23 15			
Barnham	a		22 06	21 56	22 11	22 16	22 20					22 36	22 50		22 46	23 01		23 04	23 01	23 21	23 31		
	d	21 52		21 57	22 12	22 17	22 21				22 22		22 51		22 52	23 06		23 05	23 06		23 32		
Bognor Regis	a	21 59			22 18						22 29				22 59	→			23 12				
Chichester	a			22 04		22 24	22 28						22 58					23 12			23 39		
	d			22 05			22 29						22 59					23 13					
Fishbourne (Sussex)	d			22 08														23 16					
Bosham	d			22 11														23 19					
Nutbourne	d			22 14														23 22					
Southbourne	d			22 17			22 36											23 25					
Emsworth	d			22 20			22 39											23 28					
Warblington	d			22 23														23 31					
Havant	d			22 26			22 43						23 11					23 34					
Bedhampton	a																						
Hilsea	a																						
Fratton	a						22 52						23 20					23 47					
Portsmouth & Southsea	a						22 55						23 23					23 54					
Portsmouth Harbour ⛴	a						22 59						23 27										
Cosham	a			22 33																			
Portchester	a																						
Fareham	a			22 42																			
Swanwick	a			22 49																			
Eastleigh	a																						
Southampton Airport Parkway	a																						
Southampton Central ⛴	a			23 07																			

London, Gatwick Airport, Brighton - Sussex Coast, Portsmouth and Southampton

Network Diagram - see first Page of Table 186

		SN 1	SN	SN	SN	SN ◇1	SN 1	SN 1	SN ◇1	SN	SN ◇1	SN 1	SN ◇1	SN 1	SN 1
London Victoria ⊖	d	21 40				22 17	22 10	22 32			22 47	22 40	23 17	23 10	23 47
Clapham Junction	d	21 46				22 23	22 16	22 38			22 53	22 46	23 23	23 16	23 53
London Bridge ⊖	d														
East Croydon	d	21 58				22 34	22 28	22 48			23 03	22 58	23 33	23 28	00 06
Redhill	d	22 16					22 46	23 01				23 16		23 46	00 25
Horley	d	22 25					22 54					23 25		23 56	00 31
Gatwick Airport ✈	d	22 29				22 49	22 57	23 09			23 19	23 29	23 51	23 59	00 34
Three Bridges	a	22 33				22 53	23 02	23 15				23 33	23 55	00 04	00 39
	d	22 36				22 53	23 03	23 16				23 38	23 56	00 04	00 39
Crawley	d	22 39					23 06	23 19				23 41		00 07	00 43
Horsham	a	22 51					23 18	23 27				23 53		00 19	00 55
	d							23 28							
Christs Hospital	d							23 31							
Billingshurst	d							23 37							
Pulborough	d							23 44							
Amberley	d							23 50							
Arundel	d							23 55							
Haywards Heath	d					23 03					23b37		00 05		
Burgess Hill	d					23 08							00 11		
Preston Park	d														
Brighton	d		23 04	23 14						23 44					
Hove	a		23 07	23 18		23 21				23 48	23 51		00 21		
	d		23 08			23 22					23 52		00 22		
Aldrington	d		23 10												
Portslade	d		23 12			23 25					23 55		00s25		
Fishersgate	d		23 14												
Southwick	d		23 16			23 28					23 58		00s28		
Shoreham-by-Sea	d		23 19			23 31					00 01		00s31		
Lancing	d		23 23			23 35					00 05		00s35		
East Worthing	d		23 26												
Worthing	a		23 29			23 39					00 09		00 39		
	d		23 29			23 39									
West Worthing	d		23a31			23 41									
Durrington-on-Sea	d					23 44									
Goring-by-Sea	d					23 46									
Angmering	d					23 50									
Littlehampton	a														
	d														
Ford	d					23 56		00 01							
Bognor Regis	d								←						
Barnham	a					00 01		00 06	00 01						
	d				23 36	00 09		00 06	00 09						
Bognor Regis	a				23 43	→			00 15						
Chichester	a							00 14							
	d														
Fishbourne (Sussex)	d														
Bosham	d														
Nutbourne	d														
Southbourne	d														
Emsworth	d														
Warblington	d														
Havant	d														
Bedhampton	a														
Hilsea	a														
Fratton	a														
Portsmouth & Southsea	a														
Portsmouth Harbour ⛴	a														
Cosham	a														
Portchester	a														
Fareham	a														
Swanwick	a														
Eastleigh	a														
Southampton Airport Parkway	a														
Southampton Central ⛴	a														

b Arr. 2330

London, Gatwick Airport, Brighton - Sussex Coast, Portsmouth and Southampton

Network Diagram - see first Page of Table 186

		SN ◇1	SN 1	SN ◇1	SN ◇1	SN	SN	SN ◇1	SN 1	SN 1		SN ◇1	SN 1	SN ◇	SN	SN 1	SN 1	SN 1	SN	SN 1		SN	SN	SN 1	SN
London Victoria 15 ⊖	d	22p17	22p32		22p47			23p17	23p10	23p47		00 05													
Clapham Junction 10	d	22p23	22p38		22p53			23p23	23p16	23p53		00 11													
London Bridge 4 ⊖	d																								
East Croydon	d	22p34	22p48		23p03			23p33	23p28	00 06		00 24													
Redhill 5	d		23p01						23p46	00 25															
Horley	d								23p56	00 31															
Gatwick Airport 10 ✈	d	22p49	23p09		23p19			23p51	23p59	00 34		00 42													
Three Bridges 4	a	22p53	23p15					23p55	00 04	00 39		00 47													
	d	22p53	23p16					23p56	00 04	00 39		00 47													
Crawley	d		23p19						00 07	00 43															
Horsham 4	a		23p27						00 19	00 55															
	d		23p28																						
Christs Hospital	d		23p31																						
Billingshurst	d		23p37																						
Pulborough	d		23p44																						
Amberley	d		23p50																						
Arundel	d		23p55																						
Haywards Heath 3	d	23p03			23b37			00 05				01 02													
Burgess Hill	d	23p08						00 11																	
Preston Park	d																								
Brighton 10	d					00 04	00 10					01s16								05 15				05 27	05 44
Hove 2	a	23p21			23p51	00 07	00 14	00 21				01s24								05 18				05 30	05 48
	d	23p22			23p52	00 08		00 22												05 20				05 31	
Aldrington	d					00 10																		05 33	
Portslade	d	23p25			23p55	00 12		00s25				01s27								05 23				05 35	
Fishersgate	d					00 14																		05 37	
Southwick	d	23p28			23p58	00 16		00s28				01s30												05 39	
Shoreham-by-Sea	d	23p31			00 01	00 19		00s31				01s33								05 27				05 43	
Lancing	d	23p35			00 05	00 23		00s35				01s37								05 31				05 47	
East Worthing	d					00 26																		05 50	
Worthing 4	a	23p39			00 09	00 29		00 39				01 41								05 35				05 52	
	d	23p39				00 29														05 36				05 53	
West Worthing	d	23p41				00a31														05 38				05 55	
Durrington-on-Sea	d	23p44																		05 40				05 57	
Goring-by-Sea	d	23p46																		05 43				06 00	
Angmering 3	d	23p50																		05 47				06 04	
Littlehampton 4	a																								
	d																					05 54			
Ford 4	d	23p56	00 01																	05 53		05 58		06 10	
Bognor Regis 4	d			←											05 13				05 43				06 04		
Barnham	a	00 01	00 06	00 01											05 19				05 49	05 57		06 02	06 10	06 14	
	d	00 09	00 06	00 09									04 57	05 15		05 20	05 30	05 38		05 58		06 03		06 15	
Bognor Regis	a	→		00 15																					
Chichester 4	a		00 14										05 04	05 22		05 27	05 37	05 45		06 05		06 10		06 22	
	d												05 05	05 23		05 28	05 38	05 46		06 06		06 11		06 23	
Fishbourne (Sussex)	d																					06 14			
Bosham	d																			06 10		06 17			
Nutbourne	d																					06 20			
Southbourne	d																			06 15		06 23		06 30	
Emsworth	d																			06 18		06 26		06 33	
Warblington	d																			06 21		06 29			
Havant	d												05 16	05 34		05 39	05 49	05 57		06 24		06 32		06 37	
Bedhampton	a																					06 34			
Hilsea	a																					06 42			
Fratton	a													05 42			05 57	06 05				06 46			
Portsmouth & Southsea	a													05 46			06 01	06 09				06 50			
Portsmouth Harbour ⛴	a																06 05	06 16							
Cosham	a												05 22			05 49				06 30				06 45	
Portchester	a												05 27							06 34					
Fareham	a												05 32			05 57				06 39				06 53	
Swanwick	a												05 39			06 04				06 46					
Eastleigh	a																							07 10	
Southampton Airport Parkway	a																							07 17	
Southampton Central ⛴	a												05 58			06 24				07 05				07 28	

b Previous night, arr. 2330

London, Gatwick Airport, Brighton - Sussex Coast, Portsmouth and Southampton

Network Diagram - see first Page of Table 186

		SN	SN	SN	SN	SN ◇1		SN 1	SN	SN	SN	SN	SN	SN 1	SN ◇1		SN	SN 1	SN	SN	SN ◇1 A	SN	SN	SN ◇1
London Victoria 15 ⊖	d																				05 32			
Clapham Junction 10	d																				05 38			
London Bridge 4 ⊖	d																							
East Croydon	d																				05 48			
Redhill 5	d																				06 07			
Horley	d																				06 18			
Gatwick Airport 10 ✈	d													05 58							06 22			
Three Bridges 4	a													06 02							06 26			
	d													06 03							06 34			
Crawley	d													06 06							06 37			
Horsham 4	a													06 18							06 49			
	d													06 19							06 50			
Christs Hospital	d													06 22							06 53			
Billingshurst	d													06 28							06 59			
Pulborough	d													06 35							07 06			
Amberley	d													06 41							07 12			
Arundel	d													06 46							07 17			
Haywards Heath 3	d																							
Burgess Hill	d																							
Preston Park	d																							
Brighton 10	d	05 53						06 01	06 14	06 23								06 33	06 44			06 48	06 53	
Hove 2	a	05 56						06 04	06 18	06 26								06 36	06 48			06 51	06 56	
	d	05 57						06 05		06 27								06 37				06 52	06 57	
Aldrington	d	05 59								06 29													06 59	
Portslade	d	06 01						06 08		06 31								06 40				06 55	07 01	
Fishersgate	d	06 03								06 33													07 03	
Southwick	d	06 05						06 11		06 35								06 43					07 05	
Shoreham-by-Sea	d	06 09						06 14		06 39								06 46				06 59	07 09	
Lancing	d	06 13						06 18		06 43								06 50				07 03	07 13	
East Worthing	d	06 16								06 46													07 16	
Worthing 4	a	06 18						06 22		06 48								06 54				07 07	07 18	
	d	06 19						06 23		06 49								06 55				07 08	07 19	
West Worthing	d	06a21						06 25		06a51								06 57				07 10	07a21	
Durrington-on-Sea	d							06 27										06 59				07 12		
Goring-by-Sea	d							06 30										07 02				07 15		
Angmering 3	d							06 34										07 06				07 19		
Littlehampton 4	a																					07 27		
	d				06 19								06 54							07 11				
Ford 4	d							06 40					06 58	06 51				07 12		07 16	07 22			
Bognor Regis 4	d		06 13			06 30					06 39				06 56		07 07							07 30
Barnham	a		06 19		06 26	06 36		06 44			06 45		07 02	06 55	07 02		07 13	07 16		07 20	07 27			07 36
	d			06 22	06 27			06 45				06 52	07 03	06 59 / 07 05				07 17		07 22	07 27			
Bognor Regis	a			06 29								06 59		07 12						07 29				
Chichester 4	a				06 34			06 52					07 10	07 06				07 24			07 35			
	d				06 35			06 53					07 11	07 07				07 25			07 35			
Fishbourne (Sussex)	d												07 14											
Bosham	d												07 17											
Nutbourne	d												07 20											
Southbourne	d												07 23	07 14										
Emsworth	d												07 26	07 17				07 33						
Warblington	d												07 29											
Havant	d				06 46			07 04					07 32	07 23				07 37			07 46			
Bedhampton	a												07 34											
Hilsea	a												07 42											
Fratton	a				06 54			07 12					07 46								07 55			
Portsmouth & Southsea	a				06 58			07 16					07 50								07 58			
Portsmouth Harbour ⛴	a				07 02			07 20													08 02			
Cosham	a													07 29				07 45						
Portchester	a													07 34										
Fareham	a													07 39				07 53						
Swanwick	a													07 45										
Eastleigh	a																	08 10						
Southampton Airport Parkway	a																	08 17						
Southampton Central ⛴	a													08 03				08 28						

A 1 to Three Bridges ◇ to Three Bridges

London, Gatwick Airport, Brighton - Sussex Coast, Portsmouth and Southampton

Network Diagram - see first Page of Table 186

		SN		SN	SN	SN	SN	SN 1	SN	SN ◇1	SN	SN		SN	SN	SN 1	SN 1	SN ◇1	SN	SN ◇1	SN	SN		SN	SN
London Victoria 15 ⊖	d							06 02								06 32									
Clapham Junction 10	d							06 08								06 38									
London Bridge 4 ⊖	d																07 03								
East Croydon	d							06 18								06 48	07 21								
Redhill 5	d							06b46								07 10	07 44								
Horley	d							06 55								07 19	07 51								
Gatwick Airport 10 ✈	d							06 59								07 24	07 56								
Three Bridges 4	a							07 03								07 29	08 01								
	d							07 04								07 30	08 01								
Crawley	d							07 07								07 33	08 05								
Horsham 4	a							07 19								07 45	08 17								
	d							07 20								07 50									
Christs Hospital	d							07 23								07 53									
Billingshurst	d							07 29								07 59									
Pulborough	d							07 36								08 06									
Amberley	d							07 42								08 12									
Arundel	d							07 47								08 17									
Haywards Heath 3	d																	07 37							
Burgess Hill	d																								
Preston Park	d																								
Brighton 10	d	07 03		07 14	07 23							07 33		07 44					07 53		08 03	08 14		08 23	
Hove 2	a	07 06		07 18	07 26							07 36		07 48				07 51	07 56		08 06	08 18		08 26	
	d	07 07			07 27							07 37						07 52	07 57		08 07			08 27	
Aldrington	d				07 29														07 59					08 29	
Portslade	d	07 10			07 31							07 40							08 01		08 10			08 31	
Fishersgate	d				07 33														08 03					08 33	
Southwick	d	07 13			07 35							07 43							08 05		08 13			08 35	
Shoreham-by-Sea	d	07 16			07 39							07 46						07 58	08 09		08 16			08 39	
Lancing	d	07 20			07 43							07 50						08 02	08 13		08 20			08 43	
East Worthing	d				07 46														08 16					08 46	
Worthing 4	a	07 24			07 48							07 54						08 06	08 18		08 24			08 48	
	d	07 25			07 49							07 55						08 07	08 19		08 25			08 49	
West Worthing	d				07a51							07 57						08 09	08a21					08a51	
Durrington-on-Sea	d											07 59						08 11							
Goring-by-Sea	d											08 02						08 14							
Angmering 3	d	07 31										08 06						08 18			08 31				
Littlehampton 4	a																	08 27							
	d								07 54						08 11										
Ford 4	d							07 52	07 58			08 12			08 16	08 22									
Bognor Regis 4	d					07 39				07 56	08 07									08 30					08 39
Barnham	a	07 41				07 45		07 57	08 02	08 02	08 13	08 16			08 20	08 27				08 36	08 41				08 45
	d	07 41					07 52	07 57	08 03			08 17			08 22	08 27					08 41				
Bognor Regis	a						07 59								08 29										
Chichester 4	a	07 49						08 05	08 10			08 24				08 35					08 49				
	d	07 49						08 05	08 11			08 25				08 35					08 49				
Fishbourne (Sussex)	d								08 14																
Bosham	d								08 17																
Nutbourne	d								08 20																
Southbourne	d	07 56						08 12	08 23												08 56				
Emsworth	d	07 59						08 15	08 26			08 33									08 59				
Warblington	d								08 29																
Havant	d	08 04						08 20	08 32			08 37				08 46					09 04				
Bedhampton	a								08 34																
Hilsea	a								08 42																
Fratton	a	08 12							08 46							08 55					09 12				
Portsmouth & Southsea	a	08 16							08 50							08 58					09 16				
Portsmouth Harbour ⛴	a	08 20														09 02					09 20				
Cosham	a							08 28				08 45													
Portchester	a							08 32																	
Fareham	a							08 37				08 53													
Swanwick	a							08 44				09 00													
Eastleigh	a																								
Southampton Airport Parkway	a																								
Southampton Central ⛴	a							09 01				09 19													

b Arr. 0636

London, Gatwick Airport, Brighton - Sussex Coast, Portsmouth and Southampton

Network Diagram - see first Page of Table 186

		SN	SN	SN ◇1	SN ◇1		SN	SN 1		SN	SN	SN ◇1	SN 1	SN	SN ◇1	SN ◇1		GW ◇		SN	SN	SN ◇1	SN 1	SN	SN
London Victoria 15 ⊖	d				07 32							07 47				08 02						08 17			
Clapham Junction 10	d				07 38							07 53				08 08						08 23			
London Bridge 4 ⊖	d												07 33										08 03		
East Croydon	d				07 48							08 03	07 51			08 18						08 33	08 21		
Redhill 5	d				08 00								08 10			08 30							08 44		
Horley	d												08 19			08 36							08 51		
Gatwick Airport 10 ✈	d				08 09							08 20	08 24			08 40						08 50	08 56		
Three Bridges 4	a				08 14								08 29			08 44							09 01		
	d				08 14								08 30			08 45							09 01		
Crawley	d				08 18								08 33			08 48							09 05		
Horsham 4	a				08 26								08 45			08 56							09 17		
	d				08 30	08 35										09 00	09 05								
Christs Hospital	d					08 38																			
Billingshurst	d					08 44											09 13								
Pulborough	d					08 51											09 19								
Amberley	d					08 57																			
Arundel	d					09 02											09 28								
Haywards Heath 3	d											08b37										09 05			
Burgess Hill	d																					09 10			
Preston Park	d																					09 18			
Brighton 10	d							08 33		08 44				08 53				09 00		09 03	09 14			09 23	
Hove 2	a							08 36		08 48		08 53		08 56				09 03		09 06	09 18	09 22		09 26	
	d							08 37				08 53		08 57				09 04		09 07		09 22		09 27	
Aldrington	d													08 59										09 29	
Portslade	d							08 40						09 01						09 10		09 25		09 31	
Fishersgate	d													09 03										09 33	
Southwick	d							08 43						09 05						09 13				09 35	
Shoreham-by-Sea	d							08 46				09 00		09 09				09 13		09 17		09 30		09 39	
Lancing	d							08 50				09 04		09 13						09 21				09 43	
East Worthing	d													09 16										09 46	
Worthing 4	a							08 54				09 08		09 18				09 22		09 26		09 36		09 48	
	d							08 55				09 08		09 19				09 22		09 26		09 37		09 49	
West Worthing	d							08 57				09 10		09a21								09 39		09a51	
Durrington-on-Sea	d							08 59				09 13										09 41			
Goring-by-Sea	d							09 02				09 15										09 44			
Angmering 3	d							09 06				09 19								09 34		09 48			
Littlehampton 4	a											09 28										09 57			
	d		08 54								09 11														
Ford 4	d		08 58			09 07		09 12			09 16						09 33								
Bognor Regis 4	d			08 56			09 07								09 30										09 39
Barnham	a		09 02	09 02	08 56	09 11	09 13	09 16			09 20				09 36	09 26	09 38	09 40		09 44					09 45
	d	08 52	09 03		08 57	09 12		09 17			09 22					09 27	09 38	09 41		09 45					
Bognor Regis	a	08 59				09 18					09 29						09 45								
Chichester 4	a		09 10		09 04			09 24								09 34		09 48		09 52					
	d		09 11		09 05			09 25								09 35		09 49		09 53					
Fishbourne (Sussex)	d		09 14																						
Bosham	d		09 17																						
Nutbourne	d		09 20																						
Southbourne	d		09 23		09 12															10 00					
Emsworth	d		09 26		09 15			09 33												10 03					
Warblington	d		09 29																						
Havant	d		09 32		09 19			09 37								09 46		10 00		10 07					
Bedhampton	a		09 34																						
Hilsea	a		09 42																						
Fratton	a		09 46													09 54				10 16					
Portsmouth & Southsea	a		09 50													09 58				10 19					
Portsmouth Harbour ⛴	a															10 02				10 23					
Cosham	a				09 26			09 45										10 06							
Portchester	a				09 30																				
Fareham	a				09 35			09 53										10 15							
Swanwick	a				09 42																				
Eastleigh	a							10 10																	
Southampton Airport Parkway	a							10 17																	
Southampton Central ⛴	a				09 59			10 28										10 40							

b Arr. 0830

London, Gatwick Airport, Brighton - Sussex Coast, Portsmouth and Southampton

Network Diagram - see first Page of Table 186

		SN	SN	SN ◇1 🚌	SN ◇1		SN	SN	SN	SN	SN ◇1	SN 1	SN	SN ◇1	SN ◇1		SN	SN	SN ◇1	SN 1	SN	SN
London Victoria 15 ⊖	d				08 32						08 47				09 02				09 17			
Clapham Junction 10	d				08 38						08 53				09 08				09 23			
London Bridge 4 ⊖	d											08 33								09 03		
East Croydon	d				08 48						09 03	08 51			09 18				09 33	09 21		
Redhill 5	d				09 00							09 10			09 30					09 44		
Horley	d											09 19			09 36					09 51		
Gatwick Airport 10 ✈	d				09 09						09 20	09 24			09 40				09 50	09 56		
Three Bridges 4	a				09 14							09 29			09 44					10 01		
	d				09 14							09 30			09 45					10 01		
Crawley	d				09 18							09 33			09 48					10 05		
Horsham 4	a				09 26							09 45			09 56					10 17		
	d				09 30	09 35									10 00	10 05						
Christs Hospital	d					09 38																
Billingshurst	d					09 44										10 14						
Pulborough	d					09 51										10 20						
Amberley	d					09 57																
Arundel	d					10 02										10 29						
Haywards Heath 3	d										09b37								10 04			
Burgess Hill	d																		10 09			
Preston Park	d																		10 18			
Brighton 10	d							09 33	09 44				09 53				10 03	10 14			10 23	
Hove 2	a							09 36	09 48		09 53		09 56				10 06	10 18	10 22		10 26	
	d							09 37			09 53		09 57				10 07		10 22		10 27	
Aldrington	d												09 59								10 29	
Portslade	d							09 40					10 01				10 10		10 25		10 31	
Fishersgate	d												10 03								10 33	
Southwick	d							09 43					10 05				10 13				10 35	
Shoreham-by-Sea	d							09 46			10 00		10 09				10 16		10 30		10 39	
Lancing	d							09 50			10 04		10 13				10 20				10 43	
East Worthing	d												10 16								10 46	
Worthing 4	a							09 54			10 08		10 18				10 24		10 36		10 48	
	d							09 55			10 08		10 19				10 25		10 37		10 49	
West Worthing	d							09 57			10 10		10a21						10 39		10a51	
Durrington-on-Sea	d							09 59			10 13								10 41			
Goring-by-Sea	d							10 02			10 15								10 44			
Angmering 3	d							10 06			10 19						10 31		10 48			
Littlehampton 4	a										10 28								10 57			
	d		09 54							10 11												
Ford 4	d		09 58			10 07		10 12		10 16						10 34						
Bognor Regis 4	d			09 56			10 07							10 30								10 39
Barnham	a		10 02	10 02	09 56	10 11	10 13	10 16		10 20				10 36	10 26	10 39	10 42					10 45
	d	09 52	10 03		09 57	10 12		10 17		10 22					10 27	10 39	10 42					
Bognor Regis	a	09 59				10 18				10 29						10 46						
Chichester 4	a		10 10		10 04			10 24							10 34		10 50					
	d		10 11		10 05			10 25							10 35		10 50					
Fishbourne (Sussex)	d		10 14																			
Bosham	d		10 17																			
Nutbourne	d		10 20																			
Southbourne	d		10 23		10 12												10 57					
Emsworth	d		10 26		10 15			10 33									11 00					
Warblington	d		10 29																			
Havant	d		10 32		10 19			10 37							10 46		11 05					
Bedhampton	a		10 34																			
Hilsea	a		10 43																			
Fratton	a		10 47												10 54		11 13					
Portsmouth & Southsea	a		10 50												10 58		11 17					
Portsmouth Harbour ⛴	a														11 02		11 21					
Cosham	a				10 26			10 45														
Portchester	a				10 30																	
Fareham	a				10 35			10 53														
Swanwick	a				10 42			11 00														
Eastleigh	a																					
Southampton Airport Parkway	a																					
Southampton Central ⛴	a				10 59			11 19														

b Arr. 0930

London, Gatwick Airport, Brighton - Sussex Coast, Portsmouth and Southampton

Network Diagram - see first Page of Table 186

		SN	SN	SN ◇1 🚌	SN ◇1		SN	SN 1	SN	SN	SN ◇1	SN 1	SN	SN ◇1	SN ◇1 A 🚌		SN	SN	SN ◇1	SN 1	SN	SN	SN
London Victoria 15 ⊖	d				09 32						09 47				10 02				10 17				
Clapham Junction 10	d				09 38						09 53				10 08				10 23				
London Bridge 4 ⊖	d											09 33								10 03			
East Croydon	d				09 48						10 03	09 51			10 18				10 33	10 21			
Redhill 5	d				10 00							10 10			10 30					10 44			
Horley	d											10 19			10 36					10 51			
Gatwick Airport 10 ✈	d				10 09						10 20	10 24			10 40				10 50	10 56			
Three Bridges 4	a				10 14							10 29			10 44					11 01			
	d				10 14							10 30			10 45					11 01			
Crawley	d				10 18							10 33			10 48					11 05			
Horsham 4	a				10 26							10 45			10 56					11 17			
	d				10 30	10 35									11 00	11 05							
Christs Hospital	d					10 38																	
Billingshurst	d					10 44										11 14							
Pulborough	d					10 51										11 20							
Amberley	d					10 57																	
Arundel	d					11 02										11 29							
Haywards Heath 3	d										10b37								11 04				
Burgess Hill	d																		11 09				
Preston Park	d																		11 18				
Brighton 10	d							10 33	10 44				10 53				11 03	11 14			11 23		
Hove 2	a							10 36	10 48		10 53		10 56				11 06	11 18	11 22		11 26		
	d							10 37			10 53		10 57				11 07		11 22		11 27		
Aldrington	d												10 59								11 29		
Portslade	d							10 40					11 01				11 10		11 25		11 31		
Fishersgate	d												11 03								11 33		
Southwick	d							10 43					11 05				11 13				11 35		
Shoreham-by-Sea	d							10 46			11 00		11 09				11 16		11 30		11 39		
Lancing	d							10 50			11 04		11 13				11 20				11 43		
East Worthing	d												11 16								11 46		
Worthing 4	a							10 54			11 08		11 18				11 24		11 36		11 48		
	d							10 55			11 08		11 19				11 25		11 37		11 49		
West Worthing	d							10 57			11 10		11a21						11 39		11a51		
Durrington-on-Sea	d							10 59			11 13								11 41				
Goring-by-Sea	d							11 02			11 15								11 44				
Angmering 3	d							11 06			11 19						11 31		11 48				
Littlehampton 4	a										11 28								11 57				
	d		10 54							11 11													
Ford 4	d		10 58			11 07		11 12		11 16						11 34							
Bognor Regis 4	d			10 56			11 07							11 30								11 39	
Barnham	a		11 02	11 02	10 56	11 11	11 13	11 16		11 20				11 36	11 26	11 39	11 42					11 45	
	d	10 52	11 03		10 57	11 12		11 17		11 22					11 27	11 39	11 42						11 52
Bognor Regis	a	10 59				11 18				11 29						11 46							11 59
Chichester 4	a		11 10		11 04			11 24							11 34		11 50						
	d		11 11		11 05			11 25							11 35		11 50						
Fishbourne (Sussex)	d		11 14																				
Bosham	d		11 17																				
Nutbourne	d		11 20																				
Southbourne	d		11 23		11 12												11 57						
Emsworth	d		11 26		11 15			11 33									12 00						
Warblington	d		11 29																				
Havant	d		11 32		11 19			11 37							11 46		12 05						
Bedhampton	a		11 34																				
Hilsea	a		11 42																				
Fratton	a		11 46												11 54		12 13						
Portsmouth & Southsea	a		11 50												11 58		12 17						
Portsmouth Harbour ⛴	a														12 02		12 21						
Cosham	a				11 26			11 45															
Portchester	a				11 30																		
Fareham	a				11 35			11 53															
Swanwick	a				11 42																		
Eastleigh	a							12 10															
Southampton Airport Parkway	a							12 18															
Southampton Central ⛴	a				11 59			12 28															

A 🚌 to Horsham

b Arr. 1030

London, Gatwick Airport, Brighton - Sussex Coast, Portsmouth and Southampton

Network Diagram - see first Page of Table 186

		SN	SN	SN		SN	SN	SN	SN	SN	SN	SN	SN	SN		SN	SN	SN	SN	SN	SN	SN	SN
			◇1	◇1						◇1	1		◇1	◇1				◇1	1				
														A									
			🚲											🚲									
London Victoria 15 ⊖	d			10 32						10 47				11 02				11 17					
Clapham Junction 10	d			10 38						10 53				11 08				11 23					
London Bridge 4 ⊖	d										10 33								11 03				
East Croydon 🚊	d			10 48						11 03	10 51			11 18				11 33	11 21				
Redhill 5	d			11 00							11 10			11 30					11 44				
Horley	d										11 19			11 36					11 51				
Gatwick Airport 10 ✈	d			11 09						11 20	11 24			11 40				11 50	11 56				
Three Bridges 4	a			11 14							11 29			11 44					12 01				
	d			11 14							11 30			11 45					12 01				
Crawley	d			11 18							11 33			11 48					12 05				
Horsham 4	a			11 26							11 45			11 56					12 17				
	d			11 30	11 35									12 00	12 05								
Christs Hospital	d				11 38																		
Billingshurst	d				11 44										12 14								
Pulborough	d				11 51										12 20								
Amberley	d				11 57																		
Arundel	d				12 02										12 29								
Haywards Heath 3	d									11b37								12 04					
Burgess Hill	d																	12 09					
Preston Park	d																	12 18					
Brighton 10	d						11 33	11 44				11 53				12 03	12 14			12 23			
Hove 2	a						11 36	11 48		11 53		11 56				12 06	12 18	12 22		12 26			
	d						11 37			11 53		11 57				12 07		12 22		12 27			
Aldrington	d											11 59								12 29			
Portslade	d						11 40					12 01				12 10		12 25		12 31			
Fishersgate	d											12 03								12 33			
Southwick	d						11 43					12 05				12 13				12 35			
Shoreham-by-Sea	d						11 46			12 00		12 09				12 16		12 30		12 39			
Lancing	d						11 50			12 04		12 13				12 20				12 43			
East Worthing	d											12 16								12 46			
Worthing 4	a						11 54			12 08		12 18				12 24		12 36		12 48			
	d						11 55			12 08		12 19				12 25		12 37		12 49			
West Worthing	d						11 57			12 10		12a21						12 39		12a51			
Durrington-on-Sea	d						11 59			12 13								12 41					
Goring-by-Sea	d						12 02			12 15								12 44					
Angmering 3	d						12 06			12 19						12 31		12 48					
Littlehampton 4	a									12 28								12 57					
	d	11 54							12 11														12 54
Ford 4	d	11 58			12 07		12 12		12 16						12 34								12 58
Bognor Regis 4	d		11 56			12 07							12 30								12 39		
Barnham	a	12 02	12 02	11 56	12 11	12 13	12 16		12 20				12 36	12 26	12 39	12 42					12 45		13 02
	d	12 03		11 57	12 12		12 17		12 22					12 27	12 39	12 42						12 52	13 03
Bognor Regis	a				12 18				12 29						12 46							12 59	
Chichester 4	a	12 10		12 04			12 24							12 34		12 50							13 10
	d	12 11		12 05			12 25							12 35		12 50							13 11
Fishbourne (Sussex)	d	12 14																					13 14
Bosham	d	12 17																					13 17
Nutbourne	d	12 20																					13 20
Southbourne	d	12 23		12 12												12 57							13 23
Emsworth	d	12 26		12 15			12 33									13 00							13 26
Warblington	d	12 29																					13 29
Havant	d	12 32		12 19			12 37							12 46		13 05							13 32
Bedhampton	a	12 34																					13 34
Hilsea	a	12 42																					13 42
Fratton	a	12 46												12 54		13 13							13 46
Portsmouth & Southsea	a	12 50												12 58		13 17							13 50
Portsmouth Harbour ⛴	a													13 02		13 21							
Cosham	a			12 26			12 45																
Portchester	a			12 30																			
Fareham	a			12 35			12 53																
Swanwick	a			12 42			13 00																
Eastleigh	a																						
Southampton Airport Parkway	a																						
Southampton Central ⛴	a			12 59			13 19																

A 🚲 to Horsham

b Arr. 1130

London, Gatwick Airport, Brighton - Sussex Coast, Portsmouth and Southampton

Network Diagram - see first Page of Table 186

		SN	SN		SN	SN	SN	SN	SN	SN	SN	SN	SN		SN	SN	SN	SN	SN	SN	SN	SN
		◇1	◇1			1			◇1	1		◇1	◇1				◇1	1				
													A									
		🚲											🚲									
London Victoria 15 ⊖	d		11 32						11 47				12 02				12 17					
Clapham Junction 10	d		11 38						11 53				12 08				12 23					
London Bridge 4 ⊖	d									11 33								12 03				
East Croydon 🚊	d		11 48						12 03	11 51			12 18				12 33	12 21				
Redhill 5	d		12 00							12 10			12 30					12 44				
Horley	d									12 19			12 36					12 51				
Gatwick Airport 10 ✈	d		12 09						12 20	12 24			12 40				12 50	12 56				
Three Bridges 4	a		12 14							12 29			12 44					13 01				
	d		12 14							12 30			12 45					13 01				
Crawley	d		12 18							12 33			12 48					13 05				
Horsham 4	a		12 26							12 45			12 56					13 17				
	d		12 30	12 35									13 00	13 05								
Christs Hospital	d			12 38																		
Billingshurst	d			12 44										13 14								
Pulborough	d			12 51										13 20								
Amberley	d			12 57																		
Arundel	d			13 02										13 29								
Haywards Heath 3	d								12b37								13 04					
Burgess Hill	d																13 09					
Preston Park	d																13 18					
Brighton 10	d					12 33	12 44				12 53				13 03	13 14			13 23			
Hove 2	a					12 36	12 48		12 53		12 56				13 06	13 18	13 22		13 26			
	d					12 37			12 53		12 57				13 07		13 22		13 27			
Aldrington	d										12 59								13 29			
Portslade	d					12 40					13 01				13 10		13 25		13 31			
Fishersgate	d										13 03								13 33			
Southwick	d					12 43					13 05				13 13				13 35			
Shoreham-by-Sea	d					12 46			13 00		13 09				13 16		13 30		13 39			
Lancing	d					12 50			13 04		13 13				13 20				13 43			
East Worthing	d										13 16								13 46			
Worthing 4	a					12 54			13 08		13 18				13 24		13 36		13 48			
	d					12 55			13 08		13 19				13 25		13 37		13 49			
West Worthing	d					12 57			13 10		13a21						13 39		13a51			
Durrington-on-Sea	d					12 59			13 13								13 41					
Goring-by-Sea	d					13 02			13 15								13 44					
Angmering 3	d					13 06			13 19						13 31		13 48					
Littlehampton 4	a								13 28								13 57					
	d							13 11														13 54
Ford 4	d			13 07		13 12		13 16						13 34								13 58
Bognor Regis 4	d	12 56			13 07							13 30								13 39		
Barnham	a	13 02	12 56	13 11	13 13	13 16		13 20				13 36	13 26	13 39	13 42					13 45		14 02
	d		12 57	13 12		13 17		13 22					13 27	13 39	13 42						13 52	14 03
Bognor Regis	a			13 18				13 29						13 46							13 59	
Chichester 4	a		13 04			13 24							13 34		13 50							14 10
	d		13 05			13 25							13 35		13 50							14 11
Fishbourne (Sussex)	d																					14 14
Bosham	d																					14 17
Nutbourne	d																					14 20
Southbourne	d		13 12												13 57							14 23
Emsworth	d		13 15			13 33									14 00							14 26
Warblington	d																					14 29
Havant	d		13 19			13 37							13 46		14 05							14 32
Bedhampton	a																					14 34
Hilsea	a																					14 42
Fratton	a												13 54		14 13							14 46
Portsmouth & Southsea	a												13 58		14 17							14 50
Portsmouth Harbour ⛴	a												14 02		14 21							
Cosham	a		13 26			13 45																
Portchester	a		13 30																			
Fareham	a		13 35			13 53																
Swanwick	a		13 42			14 02																
Eastleigh	a																					
Southampton Airport Parkway	a																					
Southampton Central ⛴	a		13 59			14 19																

A 🚲 to Horsham

b Arr. 1230

London, Gatwick Airport, Brighton - Sussex Coast, Portsmouth and Southampton

Network Diagram - see first Page of Table 186

		SN ◇1 🛒	SN ◇1		SN	SN	SN	SN	SN ◇1	SN 1	SN	SN ◇1	SN ◇1 A 🛒		SN	SN	SN ◇1	SN 1	SN	SN	SN	SN	SN ◇1 🛒
London Victoria [15] ⊖	d		12 32						12 47				13 02				13 17						
Clapham Junction [10]	d		12 38						12 53				13 08				13 23						
London Bridge [4] ⊖	d									12 33								13 03					
East Croydon	d		12 48						13 03	12 51			13 18				13 33	13 21					
Redhill [5]	d		13 00							13 10			13 30					13 44					
Horley	d									13 19			13 36					13 51					
Gatwick Airport [10] ✈	d		13 09						13 20	13 24			13 40				13 50	13 56					
Three Bridges [4]	a		13 14							13 29			13 44					14 01					
	d		13 14							13 30			13 45					14 01					
Crawley	d		13 18							13 33			13 48					14 05					
Horsham [4]	a		13 26							13 45			13 56					14 17					
	d		13 30	13 35									14 00	14 05									
Christs Hospital	d			13 38																			
Billingshurst	d			13 44										14 14									
Pulborough	d			13 51										14 20									
Amberley	d			13 57																			
Arundel	d			14 02										14 29									
Haywards Heath [5]	d								13b37								14 04						
Burgess Hill	d																14 09						
Preston Park	d																14 18						
Brighton [10]	d					13 33	13 44				13 53				14 03	14 14			14 23				
Hove [2]	a					13 36	13 48		13 53		13 56				14 06	14 18	14 22		14 26				
	d					13 37			13 53		13 57				14 07		14 22		14 27				
Aldrington	d										13 59								14 29				
Portslade	d					13 40					14 01				14 10		14 25		14 31				
Fishersgate	d										14 03								14 33				
Southwick	d					13 43					14 05				14 13				14 35				
Shoreham-by-Sea	d					13 46			14 00		14 09				14 16		14 30		14 39				
Lancing	d					13 50			14 04		14 13				14 20				14 43				
East Worthing	d										14 16								14 46				
Worthing [4]	a					13 54			14 08		14 18				14 24		14 36		14 48				
	d					13 55			14 08		14 19				14 25		14 37		14 49				
West Worthing	d					13 57			14 10		14a21						14 39		14a51				
Durrington-on-Sea	d					13 59			14 13								14 41						
Goring-by-Sea	d					14 02			14 15								14 44						
Angmering [3]	d					14 06			14 19						14 31		14 48						
Littlehampton [4]	a								14 28								14 57						
	d							14 11														14 54	
Ford [4]	d			14 07		14 12		14 16						14 34								14 58	
Bognor Regis [4]	d	13 56			14 07							14 30								14 39			14 56
Barnham	a	14 02	13 56	14 11	14 13	14 16		14 20				14 36	14 26	14 39	14 42					14 45		15 02	15 02
	d		13 57	14 12		14 17		14 22					14 27	14 39	14 42						14 52	15 03	
Bognor Regis	a			14 18				14 29						14 46							14 59		
Chichester [4]	a		14 04			14 24							14 34		14 50							15 10	
	d		14 05			14 25							14 35		14 50							15 11	
Fishbourne (Sussex)	d																					15 14	
Bosham	d																					15 17	
Nutbourne	d																					15 20	
Southbourne	d		14 12												14 57							15 23	
Emsworth	d		14 15			14 33									15 00							15 26	
Warblington	d																					15 29	
Havant	d		14 19			14 37							14 46		15 05							15 32	
Bedhampton	a																					15 34	
Hilsea	a																					15 42	
Fratton	a												14 54		15 13							15 46	
Portsmouth & Southsea	a												14 58		15 17							15 50	
Portsmouth Harbour ⛴	a												15 02		15 21								
Cosham	a		14 26			14 45																	
Portchester	a		14 30																				
Fareham	a		14 35			14 53																	
Swanwick	a		14 42			15 00																	
Eastleigh	a																						
Southampton Airport Parkway	a																						
Southampton Central ⛴	a		14 59			15 19																	

A 🛒 to Horsham

b Arr. 1330

Table 188

London, Gatwick Airport, Brighton - Sussex Coast, Portsmouth and Southampton

Network Diagram - see first Page of Table 186

		SN ◇1		SN	SN 1	SN	SN	SN ◇1	SN 1	SN	SN ◇1	SN ◇1 A 🛒		SN	SN	SN ◇1	SN 1	SN	SN	SN	SN	SN ◇1 🛒
London Victoria [15] ⊖	d	13 32						13 47				14 02				14 17						
Clapham Junction [10]	d	13 38						13 53				14 08				14 23						
London Bridge [4] ⊖	d								13 33								14 03					
East Croydon	d	13 48						14 03	13 51			14 18				14 33	14 21					
Redhill [5]	d	14 00							14 10			14 30					14 44					
Horley	d								14 19			14 36					14 51					
Gatwick Airport [10] ✈	d	14 09						14 20	14 24			14 40				14 50	14 56					
Three Bridges [4]	a	14 14							14 29			14 44					15 01					
	d	14 14							14 30			14 45					15 01					
Crawley	d	14 18							14 33			14 48					15 05					
Horsham [4]	a	14 26							14 45			14 56					15 17					
	d	14 30	14 35									15 00	15 05									
Christs Hospital	d		14 38																			
Billingshurst	d		14 44										15 14									
Pulborough	d		14 51										15 20									
Amberley	d		14 57																			
Arundel	d		15 02										15 29									
Haywards Heath [5]	d							14b37								15 04						
Burgess Hill	d															15 09						
Preston Park	d															15 18						
Brighton [10]	d				14 33	14 44				14 53				15 03	15 14			15 23				
Hove [2]	a				14 36	14 48		14 53		14 56				15 06	15 18	15 22		15 26				
	d				14 37			14 53		14 57				15 07		15 22		15 27				
Aldrington	d									14 59								15 29				
Portslade	d				14 40					15 01				15 10		15 25		15 31				
Fishersgate	d									15 03								15 33				
Southwick	d				14 43					15 05				15 13				15 35				
Shoreham-by-Sea	d				14 46			15 00		15 09				15 16		15 30		15 39				
Lancing	d				14 50			15 04		15 13				15 20				15 43				
East Worthing	d									15 16								15 46				
Worthing [4]	a				14 54			15 08		15 18				15 24		15 36		15 48				
	d				14 55			15 08		15 19				15 25		15 37		15 49				
West Worthing	d				14 57			15 10		15a21						15 39		15a51				
Durrington-on-Sea	d				14 59			15 13								15 41						
Goring-by-Sea	d				15 02			15 15								15 44						
Angmering [3]	d				15 06			15 19						15 31		15 48						
Littlehampton [4]	a							15 28								15 58						
	d						15 11														15 54	
Ford [4]	d		15 07		15 12		15 16						15 34								15 58	
Bognor Regis [4]	d			15 07							15 30								15 39			15 56
Barnham	a	14 56	15 11	15 13	15 16		15 20				15 36	15 26	15 39	15 42					15 45		16 02	16 02
	d	14 57	15 12		15 17		15 22					15 27	15 39	15 42						15 52	16 03	
Bognor Regis	a		15 18				15 29						15 46							15 59		
Chichester [4]	a	15 04			15 24							15 34		15 50							16 10	
	d	15 05			15 25							15 35		15 50							16 11	
Fishbourne (Sussex)	d																				16 14	
Bosham	d																				16 17	
Nutbourne	d																				16 20	
Southbourne	d	15 12												15 57							16 23	
Emsworth	d	15 15			15 33									16 00							16 26	
Warblington	d																				16 29	
Havant	d	15 19			15 37							15 46		16 05							16 32	
Bedhampton	a																				16 34	
Hilsea	a																				16 42	
Fratton	a											15 54		16 13							16 46	
Portsmouth & Southsea	a											15 58		16 17							16 50	
Portsmouth Harbour ⛴	a											16 02		16 21								
Cosham	a	15 26			15 45																	
Portchester	a	15 30																				
Fareham	a	15 35			15 53																	
Swanwick	a	15 42																				
Eastleigh	a				16 10																	
Southampton Airport Parkway	a				16 17																	
Southampton Central ⛴	a	15 59			16 28																	

A 🛒 to Horsham

b Arr. 1430

London, Gatwick Airport, Brighton - Sussex Coast, Portsmouth and Southampton

Network Diagram - see first Page of Table 186

		SN ◇1		SN	SN	SN	SN	SN ◇1	SN 1	SN		SN ◇1	SN ◇1 A 🚌		SN	SN	SN ◇1	SN 1	SN	SN		SN	SN	SN ◇1 🚌	
London Victoria 15 ⊖	d	14 32						14 47					15 02				15 17								
Clapham Junction 10	d	14 38						14 53					15 08				15 23								
London Bridge 4 ⊖	d								14 33									15 03							
East Croydon ⇌	d	14 48						15 03	14 51				15 18				15 33	15 21							
Redhill 5	d	15 00							15 10				15 30					15 44							
Horley	d								15 19				15 36					15 51							
Gatwick Airport 10 ✈	d	15 09						15 20	15 24				15 40				15 50	15 56							
Three Bridges 4	a	15 14							15 29				15 44					16 01							
	d	15 14							15 30				15 45					16 01							
Crawley	d	15 18							15 33				15 48					16 05							
Horsham 4	a	15 26							15 45				15 56					16 17							
	d	15 30	15 35										16 00	16 05											
Christs Hospital	d		15 38																						
Billingshurst	d		15 44											16 14											
Pulborough	d		15 51											16 20											
Amberley	d		15 57																						
Arundel	d		16 02											16 29											
Haywards Heath 3	d							15b37									16 04								
Burgess Hill	d																16 09								
Preston Park	d																16 18								
Brighton 10	d				15 33	15 44				15 53					16 03	16 14			16 23						
Hove 2	a				15 36	15 48		15 53		15 56					16 06	16 18	16 22		16 26						
	d				15 37			15 53		15 57					16 07		16 22		16 27						
Aldrington	d									15 59									16 29						
Portslade	d				15 40					16 01					16 10		16 25		16 31						
Fishersgate	d									16 03									16 33						
Southwick	d				15 43					16 05					16 13				16 35						
Shoreham-by-Sea	d				15 46			16 00		16 09					16 16		16 30		16 39						
Lancing	d				15 50			16 04		16 13					16 20				16 43						
East Worthing	d									16 16									16 46						
Worthing 4	a				15 54			16 08		16 18					16 24		16 36		16 48						
	d				15 55			16 08		16 19					16 25		16 37		16 49						
West Worthing	d				15 57			16 10		16a21							16 39		16a51						
Durrington-on-Sea	d				15 59			16 13									16 41								
Goring-by-Sea	d				16 02			16 15									16 44								
Angmering 3	d				16 06			16 19							16 31		16 48								
Littlehampton 4	a							16 28									16 57								
	d						16 11																16 54		
Ford 4	d		16 07		16 12		16 16							16 34									16 58		
Bognor Regis 4	d			16 07								16 30								16 39				16 56	
Barnham	a	15 56	16 11	16 13	16 16		16 20					16 36	16 26	16 39	16 42					16 45			17 02	17 02	
	d	15 57	16 12		16 17		16 22						16 27	16 39	16 42							16 52	17 03		
Bognor Regis	a		16 18				16 29							16 46								16 59			
Chichester 4	a	16 04			16 24								16 34		16 50								17 10		
	d	16 05			16 25								16 35		16 50								17 11		
Fishbourne (Sussex)	d																						17 14		
Bosham	d																						17 17		
Nutbourne	d																						17 20		
Southbourne	d	16 12													16 57								17 23		
Emsworth	d	16 15			16 33										17 00								17 26		
Warblington	d																						17 29		
Havant	d	16 19			16 37								16 46		17 05								17 32		
Bedhampton	a																						17 34		
Hilsea	a																						17 42		
Fratton	a												16 54		17 13								17 46		
Portsmouth & Southsea	a												16 58		17 17								17 50		
Portsmouth Harbour ⛴	a												17 02		17 21										
Cosham	a	16 26			16 45																				
Portchester	a	16 30																							
Fareham	a	16 35			16 53																				
Swanwick	a	16 42			17 00																				
Eastleigh	a																								
Southampton Airport Parkway	a																								
Southampton Central ⛴	a	16 59			17 19																				

A 🚌 to Horsham

b Arr. 1530

London, Gatwick Airport, Brighton - Sussex Coast, Portsmouth and Southampton

Network Diagram - see first Page of Table 186

		SN ◇1		SN	SN 1	SN	SN		SN ◇1	SN 1	SN	SN ◇1	GW ◇	SN ◇1 A 🚌		SN	SN		SN ◇1	SN 1	SN	SN	SN	SN	SN ◇1
London Victoria 15 ⊖	d	15 32							15 47					16 02					16 17						
Clapham Junction 10	d	15 38							15 53					16 08					16 23						
London Bridge 4 ⊖	d									15 33										16 03					
East Croydon ⇌	d	15 48							16 03	15 51				16 18					16 33	16 21					
Redhill 5	d	16 00								16 10				16 30						16 44					
Horley	d									16 19				16 36						16 51					
Gatwick Airport 10 ✈	d	16 09							16 20	16 24				16 40					16 50	16 56					
Three Bridges 4	a	16 14								16 29				16 44						17 01					
	d	16 14								16 30				16 45						17 01					
Crawley	d	16 18								16 33				16 48						17 05					
Horsham 4	a	16 26								16 45				16 56						17 17					
	d	16 30	16 35											17 00	17 05										
Christs Hospital	d		16 38																						
Billingshurst	d		16 44												17 14										
Pulborough	d		16 51												17 20										
Amberley	d		16 57																						
Arundel	d		17 02												17 29										
Haywards Heath 3	d								16b37										17 04						
Burgess Hill	d																		17 09						
Preston Park	d																		17 18						
Brighton 10	d				16 33	16 44					16 53		17 00			17 03	17 14				17 23				
Hove 2	a				16 36	16 48			16 53		16 56		17 03			17 06	17 18		17 22		17 26				
	d				16 37				16 53		16 57		17 04			17 07			17 22		17 27				
Aldrington	d										16 59										17 29				
Portslade	d				16 40						17 01					17 10			17 25		17 31				
Fishersgate	d										17 03										17 33				
Southwick	d				16 43						17 05					17 13					17 35				
Shoreham-by-Sea	d				16 46				17 00		17 09		17 13			17 17			17 30		17 39				
Lancing	d				16 50				17 04		17 13					17 21					17 43				
East Worthing	d										17 16										17 46				
Worthing 4	a				16 54				17 08		17 18		17 22			17 25			17 36		17 48				
	d				16 55				17 08		17 19		17 22			17 25			17 37		17 49				
West Worthing	d				16 57				17 10		17a21								17 39		17a51				
Durrington-on-Sea	d				16 59				17 13										17 41						
Goring-by-Sea	d				17 02				17 15										17 44						
Angmering 3	d				17 06				17 19							17 34			17 48						
Littlehampton 4	a								17 28										17 57						
	d						17 11																	17 54	
Ford 4	d		17 07		17 12		17 16								17 36									17 58	
Bognor Regis 4	d			17 07								17 30										17 39			17 56
Barnham	a	16 56	17 11	17 13	17 16		17 20					17 36	17 37	17 26	17 40	17 43						17 45		18 02	18 02
	d	16 57	17 12		17 17		17 22						17 38	17 27	17 41	17 44							17 52	18 03	
Bognor Regis	a		17 18				17 29								17 47								17 59		
Chichester 4	a	17 04			17 24								17 45	17 34		17 51								18 10	
	d	17 05			17 25								17 46	17 35		17 52								18 11	
Fishbourne (Sussex)	d																							18 14	
Bosham	d																							18 17	
Nutbourne	d																							18 20	
Southbourne	d	17 12														17 59								18 23	
Emsworth	d	17 15			17 33											18 02								18 26	
Warblington	d																							18 29	
Havant	d	17 19			17 37								18 00	17 46		18 06								18 32	
Bedhampton	a																							18 34	
Hilsea	a																							18 42	
Fratton	a													17 54		18 15								18 46	
Portsmouth & Southsea	a													17 58		18 18								18 50	
Portsmouth Harbour ⛴	a													18 02		18 22									
Cosham	a	17 26			17 45								18 06												
Portchester	a	17 30																							
Fareham	a	17 35			17 53								18 14												
Swanwick	a	17 42																							
Eastleigh	a				18 10																				
Southampton Airport Parkway	a				18 17																				
Southampton Central ⛴	a	17 59			18 28								18 43												

A 🚌 to Horsham

b Arr. 1630

London, Gatwick Airport, Brighton - Sussex Coast, Portsmouth and Southampton

Network Diagram - see first Page of Table 186

		SN ◇1		SN	SN	SN	SN	SN ◇1	SN 1	SN ◇1 A ⌶		SN	SN ◇1	SN	SN	SN ◇1	SN 1	SN	SN	SN	SN	SN
London Victoria 15 ⊖	d	16 32						16 47		17 02						17 17						
Clapham Junction 10	d	16 38						16 53		17 08						17 23						
London Bridge 4 ⊖	d								16 33								17 03					
East Croydon	d	16 48						17 03	16 51	17 18						17 33	17 21					
Redhill 5	d	17 00							17 10	17 30							17 44					
Horley	d								17 19	17 36							17 51					
Gatwick Airport 10 ✈	d	17 09						17 20	17 24	17 40						17 50	17 56					
Three Bridges 4	a	17 14							17 29	17 44							18 01					
	d	17 14							17 30	17 45							18 01					
Crawley	d	17 18							17 33	17 48							18 05					
Horsham 4	a	17 26							17 45	17 56							18 17					
	d	17 30	17 35							18 00	18 05											
Christs Hospital	d		17 38																			
Billingshurst	d		17 44								18 14											
Pulborough	d		17 51								18 20											
Amberley	d		17 57																			
Arundel	d		18 02								18 29											
Haywards Heath 3	d							17b37								18 04						
Burgess Hill	d															18 09						
Preston Park	d															18 18						
Brighton 10	d				17 33	17 44						17 53		18 03	18 14						18 23	
Hove 2	a				17 36	17 48		17 53				17 56		18 06	18 18	18 22					18 26	
	d				17 37			17 53				17 57		18 07		18 22					18 27	
Aldrington	d											17 59									18 29	
Portslade	d				17 40							18 01		18 10		18 25					18 31	
Fishersgate	d											18 03									18 33	
Southwick	d				17 43							18 05		18 13							18 35	
Shoreham-by-Sea	d				17 46			18 00				18 09		18 16		18 30					18 39	
Lancing	d				17 50			18 04				18 13		18 20							18 43	
East Worthing	d											18 16									18 46	
Worthing 4	a				17 54			18 08				18 18		18 24		18 36					18 48	
	d				17 55			18 08				18 19		18 25		18 37					18 49	
West Worthing	d				17 57			18 10				18a21				18 39					18 51	
Durrington-on-Sea	d				17 59			18 13								18 41					18 53	
Goring-by-Sea	d				18 02			18 15								18 44					18 56	
Angmering 3	d				18 06			18 19						18 31		18 48					19 00	
Littlehampton 4	a							18 28								18 57					19 11	
	d						18 11													18 54		
Ford 4	d		18 07		18 12		18 16				18 34									18 58		
Bognor Regis 4	d			18 07									18 33					18 39				19 03
Barnham	a	17 56	18 11	18 13	18 16		18 20			18 26	18 39		18 40	18 42				18 46		19 02		19 09
	d	17 57	18 12		18 17		18 22			18 27	18 39			18 42					18 52	19 03		
Bognor Regis	a		18 18				18 29				18 46								18 59			
Chichester 4	a	18 04			18 24					18 34				18 50						19 10		
	d	18 05			18 25					18 35				18 50						19 11		
Fishbourne (Sussex)	d																			19 14		
Bosham	d																			19 17		
Nutbourne	d																			19 20		
Southbourne	d	18 12												18 57						19 23		
Emsworth	d	18 15			18 33									19 00						19 26		
Warblington	d																			19 29		
Havant	d	18 19			18 37					18 46				19 05						19 32		
Bedhampton	a																			19 34		
Hilsea	a																			19 42		
Fratton	a									18 54				19 13						19 46		
Portsmouth & Southsea	a									18 58				19 17						19 50		
Portsmouth Harbour ⛴	a									19 02				19 21								
Cosham	a	18 26			18 45																	
Portchester	a	18 30																				
Fareham	a	18 35			18 53																	
Swanwick	a	18 42			19 00																	
Eastleigh	a																					
Southampton Airport Parkway	a																					
Southampton Central ⛴	a	18 59			19 19																	

A ⌶ to Horsham

b Arr. 1730

Table 188

London, Gatwick Airport, Brighton - Sussex Coast, Portsmouth and Southampton

Network Diagram - see first Page of Table 186

		SN ◇1		SN 1	SN	SN	SN ◇1	SN 1	SN ◇1 A ⌶		SN ◇1	SN	SN 1	SN	SN ◇1	SN 1	SN	SN	SN ◇1		SN 1	SN	SN
London Victoria 15 ⊖	d	17 32					17 47		18 02						18 17				18 32				
Clapham Junction 10	d	17 38					17 53		18 08						18 23				18 38				
London Bridge 4 ⊖	d							17 33								18 03							
East Croydon	d	17 48					18 03	17 51	18 18						18 33	18 21			18 48				
Redhill 5	d	18 00						18 10	18 30							18 44			19 00				
Horley	d							18 19	18 36							18 51							
Gatwick Airport 10 ✈	d	18 09					18 20	18 24	18 40						18 50	18 56			19 09				
Three Bridges 4	a	18 14						18 29	18 44							19 01			19 14				
	d	18 14						18 30	18 45							19 01			19 14				
Crawley	d	18 18						18 33	18 48							19 05			19 18				
Horsham 4	a	18 26						18 47	18 56							19 17			19 26				
	d	18 30	18 35						19 00	19 05									19 30	19 35			
Christs Hospital	d		18 38																	19 38			
Billingshurst	d		18 44							19 14										19 44			
Pulborough	d		18 51							19 20										19 51			
Amberley	d		18 57																	19 57			
Arundel	d		19 02							19 29										20 02			
Haywards Heath 3	d						18b37								19 04								
Burgess Hill	d														19 09								
Preston Park	d														19 18								
Brighton 10	d			18 33	18 44								19 03	19 14							19 29	19 44	
Hove 2	a			18 36	18 48		18 53						19 06	19 18	19 22						19 32	19 48	
	d			18 37			18 53						19 07		19 22						19 33		
Aldrington	d												19 09								19 35		
Portslade	d			18 40			18 56						19 11		19 25						19 37		
Fishersgate	d												19 13								19 39		
Southwick	d			18 43									19 15								19 41		
Shoreham-by-Sea	d			18 46			19 01						19 19		19 30						19 45		
Lancing	d			18 50			19 05						19 23		19 34						19 49		
East Worthing	d												19 26								19 52		
Worthing 4	a			18 54			19 09						19 28		19 38						19 54		
	d			18 55			19 10						19 29		19 39						19 55		
West Worthing	d			18 57			19 12						19 31		19 41						19 57		
Durrington-on-Sea	d			18 59			19 14						19 33		19 43						19 59		
Goring-by-Sea	d			19 02			19 17						19 36		19 46						20 02		
Angmering 3	d			19 06			19 21						19 40		19 50						20 06		
Littlehampton 4	a						19 29								19 58								
	d					19 11																	20 11
Ford 4	d		19 07	19 12		19 16				19 34			19 46							20 07	20 12		20 16
Bognor Regis 4	d										19 33	19 39						20 04					
Barnham	a	18 56	19 11	19 16		19 20			19 26	19 39	19 40	19 46	19 50					20 10	19 56	20 11	20 16		20 20
	d	18 57	19 12	19 17		19 22			19 27	19 39			19 51				19 52		19 57	20 12	20 17		20 22
Bognor Regis	a		19 18			19 29				19 46							19 59			20 18			20 29
Chichester 4	a	19 04		19 24					19 34				19 58						20 04		20 24		
	d	19 05		19 25					19 35				19 59						20 05		20 25		
Fishbourne (Sussex)	d																		20 08				
Bosham	d																		20 11				
Nutbourne	d																		20 14				
Southbourne	d	19 12																	20 17				
Emsworth	d	19 15		19 33															20 20		20 33		
Warblington	d																		20 23				
Havant	d	19 19		19 37					19 46				20 10						20 26		20 37		
Bedhampton	a																						
Hilsea	a																						
Fratton	a								19 54				20 18										
Portsmouth & Southsea	a								19 58				20 22										
Portsmouth Harbour ⛴	a								20 02				20 26										
Cosham	a	19 26		19 45															20 32		20 45		
Portchester	a	19 30																	20 36				
Fareham	a	19 35		19 53															20 41		20 53		
Swanwick	a	19 42																	20 48		21 00		
Eastleigh	a			20 10																			
Southampton Airport Parkway	a			20 17																			
Southampton Central ⛴	a	19 59		20 28															21 05		21 19		

A ⌶ to Horsham

b Arr. 1830

London, Gatwick Airport, Brighton - Sussex Coast, Portsmouth and Southampton

Network Diagram - see first Page of Table 186

Station		SN ◇1	SN 1	SN ◇1 A ⊼		SN ◇1	SN 1		SN	SN ◇1	SN 1	SN	SN	SN	SN ◇1		SN 1		SN	SN	SN ◇1	SN 1	SN ◇1		SN
London Victoria 15 ⊖	d	18 47		19 02						19 17					19 32						19 47		20 02		
Clapham Junction 10	d	18 53		19 08						19 23					19 38						19 53		20 08		
London Bridge 4 ⊖	d		18 33								19 03											19 33			
East Croydon	d	19 03	18 51	19 18						19 33	19 21				19 48						20 03	19 51	20 18		
Redhill 5	d		19 10	19 30							19c46				20 00							20 10	20 30		
Horley	d		19 19	19 36							19 52											20 19			
Gatwick Airport 10 ✈	d	19 20	19 24	19 40						19 50	19 56				20 09						20 20	20 24	20 40		
Three Bridges 4	a		19 28	19 44							20 01				20 14							20 29	20 44		
	d		19 30	19 45							20 01				20 14							20 33	20 45		
Crawley	d		19 33	19 48							20 05				20 18							20 36	20 48		
Horsham 4	a		19 45	19 56							20 17				20 26							20 48	20 56		
	d			20 00	20 05										20 30	20 35							21 00	21 05	
Christs Hospital	d															20 38								21 08	
Billingshurst	d				20 14											20 44								21 14	
Pulborough	d				20 20											20 51								21 21	
Amberley	d															20 57								21 27	
Arundel	d				20 29											21 02								21 32	
Haywards Heath 3	d	19b37								20 04											20e37				
Burgess Hill	d									20 09															
Preston Park	d									20 18															
Brighton 10	d						19 56		20 14								20 30		20 44						
Hove 2	a	19 52					19 59		20 18	20 22							20 33		20 48		20 53				
	d	19 53					20 00			20 22							20 34				20 53				
Aldrington	d						20 02										20 36								
Portslade	d	19 56					20 04			20 25							20 38				20 56				
Fishersgate	d						20 06										20 40								
Southwick	d						20 08										20 42								
Shoreham-by-Sea	d	20 01					20 12			20 30							20 46				21 01				
Lancing	d	20 05					20 16			20 34							20 50				21 05				
East Worthing	d						20 19										20 53								
Worthing 4	a	20 09					20 21			20 38							20 55				21 09				
	d	20 09					20 22			20 39							20 56				21 10				
West Worthing	d	20 11					20 24			20 41							20 58				21 12				
Durrington-on-Sea	d	20 14					20 26			20 43							21 00				21 14				
Goring-by-Sea	d	20 16					20 29			20 46							21 03				21 17				
Angmering 3	d	20 20					20 33			20 50							21 07				21 21				
Littlehampton 4	a	20 29								20 58											21 29				
	d																			21 07					
Ford 4	d				20 34		20 39									21 07	21 15			21 11				21 37	
Bognor Regis 4	d					20 33						20 39		21 04											21 39
Barnham	a			20 26	20 39	20 39	20 43					20 45		21 10	20 56	21 11	21 19			21 15			21 26	21 41	21 45
	d			20 27	20 39		20 44						20 52		20 57	21 12	21 20			21 22			21 27	21 42	
Bognor Regis	a				20 46								20 59			21 18				21 29				21 48	
Chichester 4	a			20 34			20 51								21 04		21 27						21 34		
	d			20 35			20 52								21 05		21 28						21 35		
Fishbourne (Sussex)	d						20 55																		
Bosham	d														21 09										
Nutbourne	d						21 00																		
Southbourne	d						21 02								21 14								21 42		
Emsworth	d						21 05								21 17		21 36						21 45		
Warblington	d														21 20										
Havant	d			20 46			21 10								21 23		21 40						21 49		
Bedhampton	a																								
Hilsea	a																								
Fratton	a			20 54			21 18																21 59		
Portsmouth & Southsea	a			20 58			21 22																22 02		
Portsmouth Harbour ⛴	a			21 02			21 26																22 06		
Cosham	a														21 29		21 46								
Portchester	a														21 33										
Fareham	a														21 38		21 54								
Swanwick	a														21 45		22 01								
Eastleigh	a																								
Southampton Airport Parkway	a																								
Southampton Central ⛴	a														22 02		22 20								

A ⊼ to Horsham
b Arr. 1930
c Arr. 1939
e Arr. 2030

London, Gatwick Airport, Brighton - Sussex Coast, Portsmouth and Southampton

Network Diagram - see first Page of Table 186

Station		SN	SN		SN ◇1	SN 1	SN	SN	SN ◇1		SN 1	SN	SN		SN ◇1	SN 1	SN ◇	SN	SN	SN	SN	SN ◇1	SN 1		SN
London Victoria 15 ⊖	d				20 17	20 10			20 32						20 47	20 40						21 17	21 10		21 32
Clapham Junction 10	d				20 23	20 16			20 38						20 53	20 46						21 23	21 16		21 38
London Bridge 4 ⊖	d																								
East Croydon	d				20 33	20 29			20 48						21 03	20 58						21 33	21 28		21 48
Redhill 5	d					20 48			21 00							21 16							21 46		22 00
Horley	d					20 54										21 25							21 52		
Gatwick Airport 10 ✈	d				20 50	20 59			21 09						21 20	21 29						21 49	21 56		22 09
Three Bridges 4	a					21 03			21 14							21 33						21 53	22 00		22 14
	d					21 04			21 14							21 36						21 53	22 01		22 14
Crawley	d					21 07			21 18							21 39							22 04		22 18
Horsham 4	a					21 19			21 26							21 52							22 16		22 26
	d								21 30	21 35															22 27
Christs Hospital	d									21 38															22 30
Billingshurst	d									21 44															22 36
Pulborough	d									21 51															22 43
Amberley	d									21 57															22 49
Arundel	d									22 02															22 54
Haywards Heath 3	d				21 05										21 37							22 06			
Burgess Hill	d				21 10																	22 11			
Preston Park	d				21 19																				
Brighton 10	d	21 03	21 14									21 33	21 44						22 03	22 14					
Hove 2	a	21 06	21 18		21 22							21 36	21 48		21 51				22 06	22 18		22 22			
	d	21 07			21 23							21 37			21 52				22 07			22 23			
Aldrington	d	21 09										21 39							22 09						
Portslade	d	21 11			21 26							21 41			21 55				22 11			22 26			
Fishersgate	d	21 13										21 43							22 13						
Southwick	d	21 15										21 45							22 15						
Shoreham-by-Sea	d	21 19			21 31							21 49			22 00				22 19			22 31			
Lancing	d	21 23			21 35							21 53			22 04				22 23			22 35			
East Worthing	d	21 26										21 56							22 26						
Worthing 4	a	21 28			21 39							21 58			22 08				22 28			22 39			
	d	21 29			21 39							21 59			22 08				22 29			22 39			
West Worthing	d	21 31			21 41							22 01			22 10				22 31			22 41			
Durrington-on-Sea	d	21 33			21 44							22 03			22 13				22 33			22 44			
Goring-by-Sea	d	21 36			21 46							22 06			22 15				22 36			22 46			
Angmering 3	d	21 40			21 50							22 10			22 19				22 40			22 50			
Littlehampton 4	a				21 59										22 28										
	d										22 08										22 38				
Ford 4	d	21 46								22 07	22 12	22 16							22 46		22 42	22 56			23 00
Bognor Regis 4	d							22 00										22 30							
Barnham	a	21 50						22 06	21 56	22 11	22 16	22 20						22 36	22 50		22 46	23 01			23 04
	d	21 51					21 52		21 57	22 12	22 17	22 21					22 22		22 51		22 52	23 06			23 05
Bognor Regis	a						21 59			22 18							22 29				22 59	→			
Chichester 4	a	21 58							22 04		22 24	22 28							22 58						23 12
	d	21 59							22 05			22 29							22 59						23 13
Fishbourne (Sussex)	d								22 08																23 16
Bosham	d								22 11																23 19
Nutbourne	d								22 14																23 22
Southbourne	d								22 17			22 36													23 25
Emsworth	d								22 20			22 39													23 28
Warblington	d								22 23																23 31
Havant	d	22 10							22 26			22 43							23 10						23 36
Bedhampton	a																								
Hilsea	a																								
Fratton	a	22 18										22 52							23 18						23 48
Portsmouth & Southsea	a	22 22										22 55							23 22						23 51
Portsmouth Harbour ⛴	a	22 26										22 59							23 26						
Cosham	a								22 33																
Portchester	a																								
Fareham	a								22 41																
Swanwick	a								22 48																
Eastleigh	a																								
Southampton Airport Parkway	a																								
Southampton Central ⛴	a								23 05																

London, Gatwick Airport, Brighton - Sussex Coast, Portsmouth and Southampton

Network Diagram - see first Page of Table 186

		SN ◇1	SN	SN	SN	SN ◇1	SN 1	SN	SN	SN ◇	SN ◇1	SN 1	SN 1	SN ◇1	SN	SN ◇1	SN 1	SN ◇1	SN 1	SN 1
London Victoria 15 ⊖	d					21 47	21 40				22 17	22 10	22 32			22 47	22 40	23 17	23 10	23 47
Clapham Junction 10	d					21 53	21 46				22 23	22 16	22 38			22 53	22 46	23 23	23 16	23 53
London Bridge 4 ⊖	d																			
East Croydon	d					22 03	21 58				22 33	22 28	22 48			23 03	22 58	23 33	23 28	00 06
Redhill 5	d						22 16					22 46	23 00				23 16		23 46	00 25
Horley	d						22 25					22 52					23 26		23 56	00 31
Gatwick Airport 10 ✈	d					22 20	22 29				22 50	22 56	23 09			23 20	23 29	23 50	23 59	00 34
Three Bridges 4	a						22 33				22 54	23 00	23 14				23 34	23 54	00 04	00 39
	d						22 36				22 54	23 01	23 15				23 38	23 55	00 04	00 39
Crawley	d						22 39					23 04	23 18				23 41		00 07	00 43
Horsham 4	a						22 52					23 16	23 26				23 53		00 19	00 55
	d												23 27							
Christs Hospital	d												23 30							
Billingshurst	d												23 36							
Pulborough	d												23 43							
Amberley	d												23 49							
Arundel	d												23 54							
Haywards Heath 3	d					22 37					23 03					23 37		00 05		
Burgess Hill	d										23 09							00 10		
Preston Park	d																			
Brighton 10	d			22 33	22 44			23 04	23 14						23 44					
Hove 2	a			22 36	22 48	22 51		23 07	23 18		23 21				23 48	23 51		00 23		
	d			22 37		22 52		23 08			23 22					23 52		00 23		
Aldrington	d			22 39				23 10												
Portslade	d			22 41		22 55		23 12			23 25					23 55		00s26		
Fishersgate	d			22 43				23 14												
Southwick	d			22 45				23 16			23 28					23 58		00s29		
Shoreham-by-Sea	d			22 49		23 00		23 19			23 31					00 01		00s32		
Lancing	d			22 53		23 04		23 23			23 35					00 05		00s36		
East Worthing	d			22 56				23 26												
Worthing 4	a			22 58		23 08		23 29			23 39					00 09		00s40		
	d			22 59		23 08		23 29			23 39									
West Worthing	d			23 01		23 10		23a31			23 41							00s43		
Durrington-on-Sea	d			23 03		23 13					23 44							00s45		
Goring-by-Sea	d			23 06		23 15					23 46							00s48		
Angmering 3	d			23 10		23 19					23 50							00s52		
Littlehampton 4	a			23 18		23 28														
	d			23 23																
Ford 4	d			23 27							23 56		23 59					00s58		
Bognor Regis 4	d	←	23 15											←						
Barnham	a	23 01	23 21	23 31							00 01		00 04	00 01				01s02		
	d	23 06		23 32						23 36	00 09		00 05	00 09						
Bognor Regis	a	23 12								23 43	→			00 15						
Chichester 4	a			23 39									00 12					01 10		
	d																			
Fishbourne (Sussex)	d																			
Bosham	d																			
Nutbourne	d																			
Southbourne	d																			
Emsworth	d																			
Warblington	d																			
Havant	d																			
Bedhampton	a																			
Hilsea	a																			
Fratton	a																			
Portsmouth & Southsea	a																			
Portsmouth Harbour ⛴	a																			
Cosham	a																			
Portchester	a																			
Fareham	a																			
Swanwick	a																			
Eastleigh	a																			
Southampton Airport Parkway	a																			
Southampton Central ⛴	a																			

London, Gatwick Airport, Brighton - Sussex Coast, Portsmouth and Southampton

Network Diagram - see first Page of Table 186

		SN ◇1 A	SN 1 A	SN ◇1 A	SN ◇1 A	SN	SN	SN ◇1 A	SN 1 A	SN 1 A	SN ◇1	SN 1	SN	SN 1	SN ◇1	SN 1	SN ◇1	SN 1	SN 1	SN ◇1	SN 1	SN 1	SN ◇1
London Victoria 15 ⊖	d	22p17	22p32		22p47			23p17	23p10	23p47	00 05												
Clapham Junction 10	d	22p23	22p38		22p53			23p23	23p16	23p53	00 11												
London Bridge 4 ⊖	d																						
East Croydon	d	22p33	22p48		23p03			23p33	23p28	00 06	00 24												
Redhill 5	d		23p00						23p46	00 25													
Horley	d								23p56	00 31													
Gatwick Airport 10 ✈	d	22p50	23p09		23p20			23p50	23p59	00 34	00 43	06 29											
Three Bridges 4	a	22p54	23p14					23p54	00 04	00 39	00 48	06 33											
	d	22p54	23p15					23p55	00 04	00 39	00 48	06 40											
Crawley	d		23p18						00 07	00 43		06 43											
Horsham 4	a		23p26						00 19	00 55		06 56											
	d		23p27																				
Christs Hospital	d		23p30																				
Billingshurst	d		23p36																				
Pulborough	d		23p43																				
Amberley	d		23p49																				
Arundel	d		23p54																				
Haywards Heath 3	d	23p03			23b37			00 05			01 02												
Burgess Hill	d	23p09						00 10															
Preston Park	d																						
Brighton 10	d					00 04	00 10				01s16								07 14		07 22		07 50
Hove 2	a	23p21			23p51	00 07	00 14	00 23			01s24								07 17		07 25		07 53
	d	23p22			23p52	00 08		00 23											07 18		07 26		07 54
Aldrington	d					00 10															07 28		07 56
Portslade	d	23p25			23p55	00 12		00s26			01s27										07 30		07 58
Fishersgate	d					00 14															07 32		08 00
Southwick	d	23p28			23p58	00 16		00s29			01s30										07 34		08 02
Shoreham-by-Sea	d	23p31			00 01	00 19		00s32			01s33								07 24		07 37		08 05
Lancing	d	23p35			00 05	00 23		00s36			01s37										07 41		08 09
East Worthing	d					00 26															07 44		08 12
Worthing 4	a	23p39			00 09	00 29		00s40			01 41								07 30		07 47		08 15
	d	23p39				00 29													07 30		07 47		08 15
West Worthing	d	23p41				00a31		00s43													07 49		08 17
Durrington-on-Sea	d	23p44						00s45													07 51		08 20
Goring-by-Sea	d	23p46						00s48													07 54		08 22
Angmering 3	d	23p50						00s52											07 37		07 58		08 26
Littlehampton 4	a																				08 06		
	d													06 42		07 19	07 29				08 11	07 57	
Ford 4	d	23p56	23p59					00s58						06 46		07 23			07 43		08 15	08 01	08 32
Bognor Regis 4	d			←											06 58			07 34		07 58			
Barnham	a	00 01	00 04	00 01				01s02						06 50	07 04	07 27	07 37	07 40	07 48	08 04	08 19	08 08	08 37
	d	00 09	00 05	00 09									06 45	06 51		07 28	07 37		07 48		08 20	08 26	08 37
Bognor Regis	a	→		00 15									06 51			07 34						08 32	
Chichester 4	a		00 12					01 10						06 58			07 45		07 56		08 27		08 45
	d													06 59			07 45		07 56		08 28		08 45
Fishbourne (Sussex)	d																				08 31		
Bosham	d																				08 34		
Nutbourne	d																				08 37		
Southbourne	d																		08 03		08 40		
Emsworth	d																07 53		08 06		08 43		08 53
Warblington	d																				08 46		
Havant	d													07 10			07 58		08 11		08 49		08 58
Bedhampton	a																				08 51		
Hilsea	a																						
Fratton	a													07 18					08 19		08 59		
Portsmouth & Southsea	a													07 22					08 23		09 03		
Portsmouth Harbour ⛴	a													07 26					08 27		09 07		
Cosham	a																08 05						09 05
Portchester	a																						
Fareham	a																08 13						09 13
Swanwick	a																08 20						09 20
Eastleigh	a																						
Southampton Airport Parkway	a																						
Southampton Central ⛴	a																08 44						09 44

A not 11 December

b Previous night, arr. 2330

London, Gatwick Airport, Brighton - Sussex Coast, Portsmouth and Southampton

Network Diagram - see first Page of Table 186

		SN ◇■	SN ■	SN ■	SN ■	SN ◇■ 🚌		SN ■	SN ■	SN ◇■	SN ■	SN ◇■	SN ◇■		SN ■	SN ◇■ 🚌		SN ■	SN ■	SN ◇■	SN ■	SN ◇■	SN ◇■		SN ■
London Victoria ⊖	d	07 02										08 04	08 17									09 04	09 17		
Clapham Junction	d	07 08										08 10	08 23									09 10	09 23		
London Bridge ⊖	d		07 37												08 37										09 37
East Croydon	d	07 23	07 55									08 24	08 37		08 55							09 24	09 37		09 55
Redhill	d	07 37	08 13									08 39			09 16							09 39			10 16
Horley	d	07 43	08 22									08 45			09 22							09 45			10 22
Gatwick Airport ✈	d	07 47	08 25									08 48	08 56		09 25							09 48	09 56		10 25
Three Bridges	a	07 51	08 30									08 53			09 30							09 53			10 30
	d	07 52	08 33									08 53			09 33							09 53			10 33
Crawley	d	07 55	08 36									08 56			09 37							09 56			10 37
Horsham	a	08 07	08 49									09 04			09 49							10 04			10 49
	d	08 08										09 05										10 05			
Christs Hospital	d											09 08										10 08			
Billingshurst	d	08 16										09 15										10 15			
Pulborough	d	08 23										09 21										10 21			
Amberley	d											09 27										10 27			
Arundel	d	08 33										09 33										10 33			
Haywards Heath	d												09 07										10 07		
Burgess Hill	d												09 12										10 12		
Preston Park	d																								
Brighton	d				08 14			08 22		08 50								09 17		09 50					
Hove	a				08 17			08 25		08 53			09 24					09 20		09 53			10 24		
	d				08 18			08 26		08 54			09 24					09 27		09 54			10 24		
Aldrington	d							08 28		08 56								09 29		09 56					
Portslade	d							08 30		08 58								09 32		09 58					
Fishersgate	d							08 32		09 00								09 34		10 00					
Southwick	d							08 34		09 02								09 36		10 02					
Shoreham-by-Sea	d				08 24			08 37		09 05			09 30					09 39		10 05			10 30		
Lancing	d							08 41		09 09								09 43		10 09					
East Worthing	d							08 44		09 12								09 46		10 12					
Worthing	a				08 30			08 47		09 15			09 36					09 48		10 15			10 36		
	d				08 30			08 47		09 15			09 40	09 42				09 49		10 15			10 40	10 42	
West Worthing	d							08 49		09 17				09 44				09 51		10 17				10 44	
Durrington-on-Sea	d							08 51		09 20				09 46				09 53		10 20				10 46	
Goring-by-Sea	d							08 54		09 22				09 49				09 56		10 22				10 49	
Angmering	d				08 37			08 58		09 26				09 53				10 00		10 26				10 53	
Littlehampton	a							09 06						10 02										11 02	
	d							09 11	08 57										09 57						
Ford	d	08 38			08 43			09 15	09 01	09 32		09 39						10 06	10 01	10 32		10 38			
Bognor Regis	d			08 36		08 58					09 36					09 58					10 34				
Barnham	a	08 42		08 42	08 48	09 04		09 19	09 08	09 37	09 42	09 43	09 54			10 04		10 11	10 08	10 37	10 40	10 42	10 54		
	d	08 43			08 48			09 20	09 26	09 37		09 44	09 55					10 12	10 15	10 37		10 43	10 55		
Bognor Regis	a	08 49							09 32			09 50							10 21			10 49			
Chichester	a				08 56			09 27		09 45			10 02					10 19		10 45			11 02		
	d				08 56			09 28		09 45			10 03					10 20		10 45			11 03		
Fishbourne (Sussex)	d							09 31										10 23							
Bosham	d							09 34										10 26							
Nutbourne	d							09 37										10 29							
Southbourne	d				09 03			09 40					10 10					10 32					11 10		
Emsworth	d				09 06			09 43		09 53			10 13					10 35		10 53			11 13		
Warblington	d							09 46										10 38							
Havant	d				09 11			09 49		09 58			10 17					10 41		10 58			11 17		
Bedhampton	a							09 51										10 43							
Hilsea	a																								
Fratton	a				09 19			09 59					10 26					10 51					11 26		
Portsmouth & Southsea	a				09 23			10 03					10 29					10 54					11 29		
Portsmouth Harbour ⛴	a				09 27			10 07					10 35					10 58					11 35		
Cosham	a									10 06										11 06					
Portchester	a																								
Fareham	a									10 14										11 14					
Swanwick	a									10 21										11 21					
Eastleigh	a																								
Southampton Airport Parkway	a																								
Southampton Central ⛴	a									10 44										11 45					

London, Gatwick Airport, Brighton - Sussex Coast, Portsmouth and Southampton

Network Diagram - see first Page of Table 186

		SN ◇■ 🚌		SN ■	SN ■	SN ◇■	SN ■	SN ◇■ 🚌	GW ◇	SN ◇■		SN ■		SN ◇■ 🚌	SN ■	SN ■	SN ◇■	SN ■	SN ◇■ 🚌	SN ◇■		SN ■		SN ◇■ 🚌	SN ■
London Victoria ⊖	d							10 04		10 17									11 04	11 17					
Clapham Junction	d							10 10		10 23									11 10	11 23					
London Bridge ⊖	d											10 37										11 37			
East Croydon	d							10 24		10 37		10 55							11 24	11 37		11 55			
Redhill	d							10 39				11 16							11 39			12 16			
Horley	d							10 45				11 22							11 45			12 22			
Gatwick Airport ✈	d							10 48		10 56		11 25							11 48	11 56		12 25			
Three Bridges	a							10 53				11 30							11 53			12 30			
	d							10 53				11 33							11 53			12 33			
Crawley	d							10 56				11 37							11 56			12 37			
Horsham	a							11 04				11 49							12 04			12 49			
	d							11 05											12 05						
Christs Hospital	d							11 08											12 08						
Billingshurst	d							11 15											12 15						
Pulborough	d							11 21											12 21						
Amberley	d							11 27											12 27						
Arundel	d							11 33											12 33						
Haywards Heath	d									11 07										12 07					
Burgess Hill	d									11 12										12 12					
Preston Park	d																								
Brighton	d			10 17		10 50			11 10						11 17		11 50								12 17
Hove	a			10 20		10 53			11 13	11 24					11 20		11 53			12 24					12 20
	d			10 27		10 54			11 14	11 24					11 27		11 54			12 24					12 27
Aldrington	d			10 29		10 56									11 29		11 56								12 29
Portslade	d			10 32		10 58									11 32		11 58								12 32
Fishersgate	d			10 34		11 00									11 34		12 00								12 34
Southwick	d			10 36		11 02									11 36		12 02								12 36
Shoreham-by-Sea	d			10 39		11 05			11 20	11 30					11 39		12 05			12 30					12 39
Lancing	d			10 43		11 09									11 43		12 09								12 43
East Worthing	d			10 46		11 12									11 46		12 12								12 46
Worthing	a			10 48		11 15			11 26	11 36					11 48		12 15			12 36					12 48
	d			10 49		11 15			11 29	11 40	11 42				11 49		12 15			12 40	12 42				12 49
West Worthing	d			10 51		11 17					11 44				11 51		12 17				12 44				12 51
Durrington-on-Sea	d			10 53		11 20					11 46				11 53		12 20				12 46				12 53
Goring-by-Sea	d			10 56		11 22					11 49				11 56		12 22				12 49				12 56
Angmering	d			11 00		11 26					11 53				12 00		12 26				12 53				13 00
Littlehampton	a										12 02										13 02				
	d				10 57											11 57									
Ford	d			11 06	11 01	11 32		11 38							12 06	12 01	12 32		12 38						13 06
Bognor Regis	d	10 58					11 34							11 58				12 34						12 58	
Barnham	a	11 04		11 11	11 08	11 37	11 40	11 42	11 45	11 54				12 04	12 11	12 08	12 37	12 40	12 42	12 54				13 04	13 11
	d			11 12	11 15	11 37		11 43	11 46	11 55					12 12	12 15	12 37		12 43	12 55					13 12
Bognor Regis	a				11 21			11 49								12 21			12 49						
Chichester	a			11 19		11 45			11 53	12 02					12 19		12 45			13 02					13 19
	d			11 20		11 45			11 54	12 03					12 20		12 45			13 03					13 20
Fishbourne (Sussex)	d			11 23											12 23										13 23
Bosham	d			11 26											12 26										13 26
Nutbourne	d			11 29											12 29										13 29
Southbourne	d			11 32						12 10					12 32					13 10					13 32
Emsworth	d			11 35		11 53				12 13					12 35		12 53			13 13					13 35
Warblington	d			11 38											12 38										13 38
Havant	d			11 44		11 58			12 10	12 17					12 44		12 58			13 17					13 44
Bedhampton	a			11 46											12 46										13 46
Hilsea	a																								
Fratton	a			11 54						12 26					12 54					13 26					13 54
Portsmouth & Southsea	a			11 57						12 29					12 57					13 29					13 57
Portsmouth Harbour ⛴	a			12 01						12 35					13 01					13 35					14 01
Cosham	a					12 05			12 16								13 05								
Portchester	a																								
Fareham	a					12 13			12 31								13 13								
Swanwick	a					12 20											13 20								
Eastleigh	a																								
Southampton Airport Parkway	a																								
Southampton Central ⛴	a					12 44			12 53								13 44								

London, Gatwick Airport, Brighton - Sussex Coast, Portsmouth and Southampton

Network Diagram - see first Page of Table 186

		SN 1	SN ◇1	SN 1	SN ◇1 🛒	SN ◇1		SN 1	SN ◇1 🛒	SN 1	SN 1	SN ◇1	SN 1	SN ◇1 🛒	SN ◇1		SN 1	SN ◇1 🛒	SN 1	SN 1	SN ◇1	SN 1	SN ◇1 🛒
London Victoria 15 ⊖	d				12 04	12 17								13 04	13 17								14 04
Clapham Junction 10	d				12 10	12 23								13 10	13 23								14 10
London Bridge 4 ⊖	d							12 37									13 37						
East Croydon 🚊	d				12 24	12 37		12 55						13 24	13 37		13 55						14 24
Redhill 5	d				12 39			13 16						13 39			14 16						14 39
Horley	d				12 45			13 22						13 45			14 22						14 45
Gatwick Airport 10 ✈	d				12 48	12 56		13 25						13 48	13 56		14 25						14 48
Three Bridges 4	a				12 53			13 30						13 53			14 30						14 53
	d				12 53			13 33						13 53			14 33						14 53
Crawley	d				12 56			13 37						13 56			14 37						14 56
Horsham 4	a				13 04			13 49						14 04			14 49						15 04
	d				13 05									14 05									15 05
Christs Hospital	d				13 08									14 08									15 08
Billingshurst	d				13 15									14 15									15 15
Pulborough	d				13 21									14 21									15 21
Amberley	d				13 27									14 27									15 27
Arundel	d				13 33									14 33									15 33
Haywards Heath 3	d					13 07									14 07								
Burgess Hill	d					13 12									14 12								
Preston Park	d																						
Brighton 10	d		12 50							13 17		13 50							14 17		14 50		
Hove 2	a		12 53			13 24				13 20		13 53			14 24				14 20		14 53		
	d		12 54			13 24				13 27		13 54			14 24				14 27		14 54		
Aldrington	d		12 56							13 29		13 56							14 29		14 56		
Portslade	d		12 58							13 32		13 58							14 32		14 58		
Fishersgate	d		13 00							13 34		14 00							14 34		15 00		
Southwick	d		13 02							13 36		14 02							14 36		15 02		
Shoreham-by-Sea	d		13 05			13 30				13 39		14 05			14 30				14 39		15 05		
Lancing	d		13 09							13 43		14 09							14 43		15 09		
East Worthing	d		13 12							13 46		14 12							14 46		15 12		
Worthing 4	a		13 15			13 36				13 48		14 15			14 36				14 48		15 15		
	d		13 15			13 40	13 42			13 49		14 15			14 40	14 42			14 49		15 15		
West Worthing	d		13 17				13 44			13 51		14 17				14 44			14 51		15 17		
Durrington-on-Sea	d		13 20				13 46			13 53		14 20				14 46			14 53		15 20		
Goring-by-Sea	d		13 22				13 49			13 56		14 22				14 49			14 56		15 22		
Angmering 3	d		13 26				13 53			14 00		14 26				14 53			15 00		15 26		
Littlehampton 4	a						14 02									15 02							
	d	12 57									13 57									14 57			
Ford 4	d	13 01	13 32		13 38					14 06	14 01	14 32		14 38					15 06	15 01	15 32		15 38
Bognor Regis 4	d			13 34					13 58				14 34					14 58				15 34	
Barnham	a	13 08	13 37	13 40	13 42	13 54			14 04	14 11	14 08	14 37	14 40	14 42	14 54			15 04	15 11	15 08	15 37	15 40	15 42
	d	13 15	13 37		13 43	13 55				14 12	14 15	14 37		14 43	14 55				15 12	15 15	15 37		15 43
Bognor Regis	a	13 21			13 49						14 21			14 49						15 21			15 49
Chichester 4	a		13 45			14 02				14 19		14 45			15 02				15 19		15 45		
	d		13 45			14 03				14 20		14 45			15 03				15 20		15 45		
Fishbourne (Sussex)	d									14 23									15 23				
Bosham	d									14 26									15 26				
Nutbourne	d									14 29									15 29				
Southbourne	d					14 10				14 32					15 10				15 32				
Emsworth	d		13 53			14 13				14 35		14 53			15 13				15 35		15 53		
Warblington	d									14 38									15 38				
Havant	d		13 58			14 17				14 44		14 58			15 17				15 44		15 58		
Bedhampton	a									14 46									15 46				
Hilsea	a																						
Fratton	a					14 26				14 54					15 26				15 54				
Portsmouth & Southsea	a					14 29				14 57					15 29				15 57				
Portsmouth Harbour ⛴	a					14 35				15 01					15 35				16 01				
Cosham	a		14 05									15 05									16 05		
Portchester	a																						
Fareham	a		14 13									15 13									16 13		
Swanwick	a		14 20									15 20									16 20		
Eastleigh	a																						
Southampton Airport Parkway	a																						
Southampton Central ⛴	a		14 44									15 44									16 44		

London, Gatwick Airport, Brighton - Sussex Coast, Portsmouth and Southampton

Network Diagram - see first Page of Table 186

		SN ◇1		SN 1	SN ◇1 🛒	SN 1	SN 1	GW ◇	SN ◇1	SN 1	SN ◇1 🛒	SN ◇1		SN 1	SN ◇1 🛒	SN 1	SN 1	SN ◇1	SN 1	SN ◇1 🛒	SN ◇1	
London Victoria 15 ⊖	d	14 17									15 04	15 17								16 04	16 17	
Clapham Junction 10	d	14 23									15 10	15 23								16 10	16 23	
London Bridge 4 ⊖	d			14 37										15 37								
East Croydon 🚊	d	14 37		14 55							15 24	15 37		15 55						16 24	16 37	
Redhill 5	d			15 16							15 39			16 16						16 39		
Horley	d			15 22							15 45			16 22						16 45		
Gatwick Airport 10 ✈	d	14 56		15 25							15 48	15 56		16 25						16 48	16 56	
Three Bridges 4	a			15 30							15 53			16 30						16 53		
	d			15 33							15 53			16 33						16 53		
Crawley	d			15 37							15 56			16 37						16 56		
Horsham 4	a			15 49							16 04			16 49						17 04		
	d										16 05									17 05		
Christs Hospital	d										16 08									17 08		
Billingshurst	d										16 15									17 15		
Pulborough	d										16 21									17 21		
Amberley	d										16 27									17 27		
Arundel	d										16 33									17 33		
Haywards Heath 3	d	15 07										16 07									17 07	
Burgess Hill	d	15 12										16 12									17 12	
Preston Park	d																					
Brighton 10	d					15 17		15 46	15 50							16 17		16 50				
Hove 2	a	15 24				15 20		15 49	15 53			16 24				16 20		16 53			17 24	
	d	15 24				15 27		15 50	15 54			16 24				16 27		16 54			17 24	
Aldrington	d					15 29			15 56							16 29		16 56				
Portslade	d					15 32			15 58							16 32		16 58				
Fishersgate	d					15 34			16 00							16 34		17 00				
Southwick	d					15 36			16 02							16 36		17 02				
Shoreham-by-Sea	d	15 30				15 39		15 56	16 05			16 30				16 39		17 05			17 30	
Lancing	d					15 43			16 09							16 43		17 09				
East Worthing	d					15 46			16 12							16 46		17 12				
Worthing 4	a	15 36				15 48		16 03	16 15			16 36				16 48		17 15			17 36	
	d	15 40	15 42			15 49		16 08	16 15			16 40	16 42			16 49		17 15			17 40	17 42
West Worthing	d		15 44			15 51			16 17				16 44			16 51		17 17				17 44
Durrington-on-Sea	d		15 46			15 53			16 20				16 46			16 53		17 20				17 46
Goring-by-Sea	d		15 49			15 56			16 22				16 49			16 56		17 22				17 49
Angmering 3	d		15 53			16 00			16 26				16 53			17 00		17 26				17 53
Littlehampton 4	a		16 02										17 02									18 02
	d						15 57										16 57					
Ford 4	d					16 06	16 01		16 32		16 39					17 06	17 01	17 32		17 38		
Bognor Regis 4	d				15 58					16 34					16 58				17 34			
Barnham	a	15 54			16 04	16 11	16 08	16 25	16 37	16 40	16 43	16 54			17 04	17 11	17 08	17 37	17 40	17 42	17 54	
	d	15 55				16 12	16 15	16 25	16 37		16 44	16 55				17 12	17 15	17 37		17 43	17 55	
Bognor Regis	a						16 21				16 50						17 21			17 49		
Chichester 4	a	16 02				16 19		16 33	16 45			17 02				17 19		17 45			18 02	
	d	16 03				16 20		16 34	16 45			17 03				17 20		17 45			18 03	
Fishbourne (Sussex)	d					16 23										17 23						
Bosham	d					16 26										17 26						
Nutbourne	d					16 29										17 29						
Southbourne	d	16 10				16 32						17 10				17 32					18 10	
Emsworth	d	16 13				16 35			16 53			17 13				17 35		17 53			18 13	
Warblington	d					16 38										17 38						
Havant	d	16 17				16 44		16 48	16 58			17 17				17 44		17 58			18 17	
Bedhampton	a					16 46										17 46						
Hilsea	a																					
Fratton	a	16 26				16 54						17 26				17 54					18 26	
Portsmouth & Southsea	a	16 29				16 57						17 29				17 57					18 29	
Portsmouth Harbour ⛴	a	16 35				17 01						17 35				18 01					18 35	
Cosham	a							16 54	17 05									18 05				
Portchester	a																					
Fareham	a							17 02	17 14									18 13				
Swanwick	a								17 22									18 20				
Eastleigh	a																					
Southampton Airport Parkway	a																					
Southampton Central ⛴	a							17 24	17 48									18 42				

Table 188

Sundays

London, Gatwick Airport, Brighton - Sussex Coast, Portsmouth and Southampton

Network Diagram - see first Page of Table 186

		SN 1	SN ◇1	SN 1	SN 1	GW ◇	SN ◇1	SN 1	SN ◇1	SN ◇1		SN 1	SN ◇1	SN 1	SN 1	SN ◇1	SN 1	SN ◇1	SN ◇1		SN 1	SN ◇1	SN 1
London Victoria 15 ⊖	d								17 04	17 17								18 04	18 17				
Clapham Junction 10	d								17 10	17 23								18 10	18 23				
London Bridge 4 ⊖	d	16 37										17 37									18 37		
East Croydon	d	16 55							17 24	17 37		17 55						18 24	18 37		18 55		
Redhill 5	d	17 16							17 39			18 16						18 39			19 16		
Horley	d	17 22							17 45			18 22						18 45			19 22		
Gatwick Airport 10 ✈	d	17 25							17 48	17 56		18 25						18 48	18 56		19 25		
Three Bridges 4	a	17 30							17 53			18 30						18 53			19 30		
	d	17 33							17 53			18 33						18 53			19 33		
Crawley	d	17 37							17 56			18 37						18 56			19 37		
Horsham 4	a	17 49							18 04			18 49						19 04			19 49		
	d								18 05									19 05					
Christs Hospital	d								18 08									19 08					
Billingshurst	d								18 15									19 15					
Pulborough	d								18 21									19 21					
Amberley	d								18 27									19 27					
Arundel	d								18 33									19 33					
Haywards Heath 3	d									18 07									19 07				
Burgess Hill	d									18 12									19 12				
Preston Park	d																						
Brighton 10	d			17 17		17 46	17 50							18 17		18 50							19 17
Hove 2	a			17 20		17 49	17 53			18 24				18 20		18 53			19 24				19 20
	d			17 27		17 50	17 54			18 24				18 27		18 54			19 24				19 27
Aldrington	d			17 29			17 56							18 29		18 56							19 29
Portslade	d			17 32			17 58							18 32		18 58							19 32
Fishersgate	d			17 34			18 00							18 34		19 00							19 34
Southwick	d			17 36			18 02							18 36		19 02							19 36
Shoreham-by-Sea	d			17 39		17 56	18 05			18 30				18 39		19 05			19 30				19 39
Lancing	d			17 43			18 09							18 43		19 09							19 43
East Worthing	d			17 46			18 12							18 46		19 12							19 46
Worthing 4	a			17 48		18 03	18 15			18 36				18 48		19 15			19 36				19 48
	d			17 49		18 08	18 15			18 40	18 42			18 49		19 15			19 40	19 42			19 49
West Worthing	d			17 51			18 17				18 44			18 51		19 17				19 44			19 51
Durrington-on-Sea	d			17 53			18 20				18 46			18 53		19 20				19 46			19 53
Goring-by-Sea	d			17 56			18 22				18 49			18 56		19 22				19 49			19 56
Angmering 3	d			18 00			18 26				18 53			19 00		19 26				19 53			20 00
Littlehampton 4	a										19 02									20 02			
	d				17 57										18 57								
Ford 4	d			18 06	18 01		18 32		18 38					19 06	19 01	19 32		19 38					20 06
Bognor Regis 4	d		17 58					18 34					18 58				19 34					19 58	
Barnham	a		18 04	18 11	18 08	18 25	18 37	18 40	18 42	18 54			19 04	19 11	19 08	19 37	19 40	19 42	19 54			20 04	20 11
	d			18 12	18 15	18 25	18 37		18 43	18 55				19 12	19 15	19 37		19 43	19 55				20 12
Bognor Regis	a				18 21				18 49						19 21			19 49					
Chichester 4	a			18 19		18 33	18 45			19 02				19 19		19 45			20 02				20 19
	d			18 20		18 34	18 45			19 03				19 20		19 45			20 03				20 20
Fishbourne (Sussex)	d			18 23										19 23									20 23
Bosham	d			18 26										19 26									20 26
Nutbourne	d			18 29										19 29									20 29
Southbourne	d			18 32						19 10				19 32					20 10				20 32
Emsworth	d			18 35			18 53			19 13				19 35		19 53			20 13				20 35
Warblington	d			18 38										19 38									20 38
Havant	d			18 44		18 48	18 58			19 17				19 44		19 58			20 17				20 44
Bedhampton	a			18 46										19 46									20 46
Hilsea	a																						
Fratton	a			18 54						19 26				19 54					20 26				20 54
Portsmouth & Southsea	a			18 57						19 29				19 57					20 29				20 57
Portsmouth Harbour ⛴	a			19 01						19 35				20 01					20 35				21 01
Cosham	a					18 54	19 05									20 05							
Portchester	a																						
Fareham	a					19 02	19 13									20 13							
Swanwick	a						19 22									20 20							
Eastleigh	a																						
Southampton Airport Parkway	a																						
Southampton Central ⛴	a					19 24	19 48									20 46							

Table 188

Sundays

London, Gatwick Airport, Brighton - Sussex Coast, Portsmouth and Southampton

Network Diagram - see first Page of Table 186

		SN 1	SN ◇1	SN 1	SN ◇1	SN ◇1		SN 1	SN ◇1	SN 1	SN 1	SN ◇1	SN 1	SN ◇1	SN ◇1		SN 1	SN ◇1	SN 1	SN 1	GW	SN 1	SN
London Victoria 15 ⊖	d				19 04	19 17								20 04	20 17								
Clapham Junction 10	d				19 10	19 23								20 10	20 23								
London Bridge 4 ⊖	d							19 37									20 37						
East Croydon	d				19 24	19 37		19 55						20 24	20 37		20 55						
Redhill 5	d				19 39			20 16						20 39			21 16						
Horley	d				19 45			20 22						20 45			21 22						
Gatwick Airport 10 ✈	d				19 48	19 56		20 25						20 48	20 56		21 25						
Three Bridges 4	a				19 53			20 30						20 53			21 30						
	d				19 53			20 33						20 53			21 33						
Crawley	d				19 56			20 37						20 56			21 37						
Horsham 4	a				20 04			20 49						21 04			21 49						
	d				20 05									21 05									
Christs Hospital	d				20 08									21 08									
Billingshurst	d				20 15									21 15									
Pulborough	d				20 21									21 21									
Amberley	d				20 27									21 27									
Arundel	d				20 33									21 33									
Haywards Heath 3	d					20 07									21 07								
Burgess Hill	d					20 12									21 12								
Preston Park	d																						
Brighton 10	d		19 50							20 17		20 50							21 17		21 46	21 50	22 12
Hove 2	a		19 53			20 24				20 20		20 53			21 24				21 20		21 49	21 53	22 15
	d		19 54			20 24				20 27		20 54			21 24				21 27		21 50	21 54	
Aldrington	d		19 56							20 29		20 56							21 29			21 56	
Portslade	d		19 58							20 32		20 58							21 32			21 58	
Fishersgate	d		20 00							20 34		21 00							21 34			22 00	
Southwick	d		20 02							20 36		21 02							21 36			22 02	
Shoreham-by-Sea	d		20 05			20 30				20 39		21 05			21 30				21 39		21 56	22 05	
Lancing	d		20 09							20 43		21 09							21 43			22 09	
East Worthing	d		20 12							20 46		21 12							21 46			22 12	
Worthing 4	a		20 15			20 36				20 48		21 15			21 36				21 48		22 02	22 15	
	d		20 15			20 40	20 42			20 49		21 15			21 40	21 42			21 49		22 03	22 15	
West Worthing	d		20 17				20 44			20 51		21 17				21 44			21 51			22 17	
Durrington-on-Sea	d		20 20				20 46			20 53		21 20				21 46			21 53			22 20	
Goring-by-Sea	d		20 22				20 49			20 56		21 22				21 49			21 56			22 22	
Angmering 3	d		20 26				20 53			21 00		21 26				21 53			22 00			22 26	
Littlehampton 4	a						21 02									22 02						22 36	
	d	19 57									20 57									21 57			
Ford 4	d	20 01	20 32		20 38					21 06	21 01	21 32		21 38					22 06	22 01			
Bognor Regis 4	d			20 34					20 58				21 34					21 58					
Barnham	a	20 08	20 37	20 41	20 42	20 54			21 04	21 11	21 08	21 37	21 40	21 42	21 54			22 04	22 11	22 08	22 17		
	d	20 15	20 37		20 43	20 55				21 12	21 15	21 37		21 43	21 55				22 12	22 15	22 18		
Bognor Regis	a	20 21			20 49						21 21			21 49						22 21			
Chichester 4	a		20 45			21 02				21 19		21 45			22 02				22 19		22 25		
	d		20 45			21 03				21 20		21 45			22 03				22 20		22 26		
Fishbourne (Sussex)	d									21 23									22 23				
Bosham	d									21 26									22 26				
Nutbourne	d									21 29									22 29				
Southbourne	d					21 10				21 32					22 10				22 32				
Emsworth	d		20 53			21 13				21 35		21 53			22 13				22 35				
Warblington	d									21 38									22 38				
Havant	d		20 58			21 17				21 44		21 58			22 17				22 44		22 47		
Bedhampton	a									21 46									22 46				
Hilsea	a																						
Fratton	a					21 26				21 54					22 26				22 54		22 57		
Portsmouth & Southsea	a					21 29				21 57					22 29				22 57		23 00		
Portsmouth Harbour ⛴	a					21 35				22 01					22 35				23 01		23 04		
Cosham	a		21 07									22 05											
Portchester	a																						
Fareham	a		21 15									22 13											
Swanwick	a		21 22									22 20											
Eastleigh	a																						
Southampton Airport Parkway	a																						
Southampton Central ⛴	a		21 45									22 44											

London, Gatwick Airport, Brighton - Sussex Coast, Portsmouth and Southampton

Network Diagram - see first Page of Table 186

		SN	SN ◇1	SN ◇1		SN 1	SN	SN 1	SN ◇1	SN 1	SN	SN ◇1	SN 1	SN 1	SN ◇1
London Victoria 15 ⊖	d		21 04	21 17					22 04			22 17		23 04	23 17
Clapham Junction 10	d		21 10	21 23					22 10			22 23		23 10	23 23
London Bridge 4 ⊖	d					21 37							22 37		
East Croydon	d		21 24	21 37		21 55			22 24			22 37	22 55	23 22	23 38
Redhill 5	d		21 38			22 16			22 39				23 16	23 42	
Horley	d		21 44			22 22			22 45				23 22	23 50	
Gatwick Airport 10 ✈	d		21 48	21 56		22 25			22 48			22 56	23 25	23 55	00 01
Three Bridges 4	a		21 53			22 30			22 53				23 30	00 01	00 05
	d		21 53			22 33			22 53				23 33	00 01	00 06
Crawley	d		21 56			22 37			22 56				23 37	00 05	
Horsham 4	a		22 04			22 49			23 04				23 49	00 17	
	d		22 05						23 05						
Christs Hospital	d		22 08						23 08						
Billingshurst	d		22 15						23 15						
Pulborough	d		22 21						23 21						
Amberley	d		22 27						23 27						
Arundel	d		22 33						23 33						
Haywards Heath 3	d			22 07								23 07			00 15
Burgess Hill	d			22 12								23 12			00 20
Preston Park	d														
Brighton 10	d									22 40	23 15				
Hove 2	a			22 24						22 43	23 18	23 24			00 31
	d			22 25						22 44		23 25			00 31
Aldrington	d									22 46					
Portslade	d									22 48		23 28			00s34
Fishersgate	d									22 50					
Southwick	d									22 52		23 31			00s37
Shoreham-by-Sea	d			22 31						22 55		23 34			00s40
Lancing	d									22 59		23 38			00s44
East Worthing	d									23 02					
Worthing 4	a			22 37						23 05		23 42			00 48
	d			22 41	22 43					23 05					
West Worthing	d				22 45					23 07					
Durrington-on-Sea	d				22 47					23 09					
Goring-by-Sea	d				22 50					23 12					
Angmering 3	d				22 54					23 16					
Littlehampton 4	a				23 02					23 24					
	d							23 06		23 29					
Ford 4	d		22 38					23 10	23 38	23 33					
Bognor Regis 4	d	22 12													
Barnham	a	22 18	22 42	22 55				23 14	23 42	23 37					
	d		22 43	22 56			22 57	23 15	23 43	23 45					
Bognor Regis	a		22 49				23 04	23 21	23 49						
Chichester 4	a			23 03						23 52					
	d			23 04											
Fishbourne (Sussex)	d														
Bosham	d			23 08											
Nutbourne	d			23 12											
Southbourne	d			23 14											
Emsworth	d			23 17											
Warblington	d														
Havant	d			23 22											
Bedhampton	a														
Hilsea	a														
Fratton	a			23 32											
Portsmouth & Southsea	a			23 35											
Portsmouth Harbour ⛴	a			23 39											
Cosham	a														
Portchester	a														
Fareham	a														
Swanwick	a														
Eastleigh	a														
Southampton Airport Parkway	a														
Southampton Central ⛴	a														

Southampton, Portsmouth and Sussex Coast - Brighton, Gatwick Airport and London

Network Diagram - see first Page of Table 186

Miles	Miles	Miles			SN MX	SN MO 1	SN MX 1	SN MO 1	SN MX ◇	SN MX	SW MX 1	SN MX ◇1	SW MO ◇1	SW MX ◇1	SW MX 1	SW MX 1	SW MO 1	SW MX 1	SN 1	SN 1	SN 1	SN 1	SN
—	—	—	Eastleigh	d							00 02		00 22	00 23	01 00	01 22							
—	—	—	Southampton Airport Parkway	d							00 06		00 27	00 28	01 05	01 26	02s46	02s46					
0	—	—	**Southampton Central** ⛴	d		22p52					00a13		00a36	00a37	01a12	01a35	02a56	02a56					
10¾	—	—	Swanwick	d		23p11																	
14½	—	—	Fareham	d		23p17																	
17¾	—	—	Portchester	d																			
20¾	—	—	Cosham	d		23p26																	
—	0	—	**Portsmouth Harbour** ⛴	d	22p44					23p15													
—	0¾	—	Portsmouth & Southsea	d	22p48					23p19													
—	1½	—	Fratton	d	22p52					23p23													
—	4¼	—	Hilsea	d	22p56					23p27													
—	7¼	—	Bedhampton	d	23p01					23p33													
24¼	8	—	**Havant**	d	23p05	23p32				23p36												05 01	
—	8½	—	Warblington	d						23p38													
—	9¾	—	Emsworth	d		23p36				23p41													
—	11¼	—	Southbourne	d						23p44													
—	12¼	—	Nutbourne	d						23p47													
—	14	—	Bosham	d						23p50													
—	15¼	—	Fishbourne (Sussex)	d						23p53													
—	16¾	—	**Chichester** 4	a	23p16	23p44				23p57												05 14	
—	—	—		d	23p17	23p45			23p52	23p57												05 15	
0	—	—	**Bognor Regis** 4	d																			05 13
3½	23	—	Barnham	a	23p24	23p52			23p59	00 05												05 22	05 19
—	—	—		d	23p25	23p53			00 01	00 06		00 09							04 48			05 23	05 27
—	—	—	Bognor Regis	a								00 15											
0	25¾	0	Ford 4	d	23p29				00 05	00 10									04 52				05 31
2	—	2	**Littlehampton** 4	a	23p34	00 01			00 10	00 15									04 57				05 38
—	—	—		d	23p39														05 02				
8	30	—	Angmering 3	d	23p47														05 10			05 33	
—	32½	—	Goring-by-Sea	d	23p51														05 14				
—	33¼	—	Durrington-on-Sea	d	23p53														05 17				
—	34	—	West Worthing	d	23p55														05 19				
—	35	—	**Worthing** 4	a	23p58														05 21			05 40	
—	—	—		d	23p59														05 22			05 41	
—	35¾	—	East Worthing	d	00 01														05 24				
—	37¼	—	Lancing	d	00 04														05 27			05 45	
—	40	—	Shoreham-by-Sea	d	00 08														05 32			05 49	
—	41	—	Southwick	d	00 11														05 35				
—	42	—	Fishersgate	d	00 13														05 37				
—	42½	—	Portslade	d	00 15														05 39			05 53	
—	43½	—	Aldrington	d	00 18														05 41				
0	44	—	Hove 2	a	00 21														05 43			05 57	
—	—	—		d	00 21														05 44			05 57	
—	45½	—	**Brighton** 10	a	00 25														05 48				
—	—	—	Preston Park	d																			
9¼	—	—	Burgess Hill	a																			
13	—	—	Haywards Heath 3	a																		06 12	
—	—	2¼	Arundel	d																			
—	—	6	Amberley	d																			
—	—	10¾	Pulborough	d																			
—	—	15¾	Billingshurst	d																			
—	—	20½	Christs Hospital	d																			
—	—	23	**Horsham** 4	a																			
—	—	—		d			23p02	23p03												05 17	05 38		
—	—	30	Crawley	d			23p14	23p16												05 29	05 50		
21½	—	31½	**Three Bridges** 4	a			23p18	23p19												05 33	05 54	06 21	
24¼	—	—	**Gatwick Airport** 10 ✈	a			23p22	23p24												05 37	05 58	06 26	
—	—	—		d			23p23	23p25												05 38	05 59	06 27	
25	—	—	Horley	a			23p26	23p28												05 40	06 02		
30	—	—	Redhill 5	a			23p36	23p34												05 47	06 12		
40½	0	—	**East Croydon**	a			23p54	23p55												06 06	06 30	06 41	
—	10¾	—	London Bridge 4 ⊖	a																			
48¼	—	—	Clapham Junction 10	a			00 11	00 11												06 18	06 41	06 51	
51	—	61	**London Victoria** 15 ⊖	a			00 18	00 19												06 25	06 48	07 00	

Southampton, Portsmouth and Sussex Coast - Brighton, Gatwick Airport and London

Network Diagram - see first Page of Table 186

		SN	SN	SN ■1	SN ■1	SN ◇■1	SN ■1	SN	SN	SN	SN	SN ■1	SN ◇■1 🚲	SN	SN ■1	SN	SN	SN ◇■1 A 🚲	SN ■1	SN ■1	SN	SN ◇■1	SN
Eastleigh	d																						
Southampton Airport Parkway	d																						
Southampton Central ⛴	d																						
Swanwick	d																						
Fareham	d																						
Portchester	d																						
Cosham	d																						
Portsmouth Harbour ⛴	d														05 33			05 47					06 04
Portsmouth & Southsea	d														05 37			05 51					06 08
Fratton	d														05 41			05 55					06 12
Hilsea	d														05 45			05 59					
Bedhampton	d														05 50			06 04					
Havant	d					05 30									05 53			06 07					06 20
Warblington	d														05 55								
Emsworth	d														05 58			06 11					06 24
Southbourne	d														06 01			06 14					06 27
Nutbourne	d														06 03								
Bosham	d														06 07			06 18					
Fishbourne (Sussex)	d														06 10			06 21					
Chichester ■4	a					05 40									06 13			06 25					06 34
	d					05 41									06 14			06 29					06 35
Bognor Regis ■4	d			05 35				05 49		05 55			06 06	06 13			06 22						
Barnham	a			05 41		05 48		05 55		06 02			06 12	06 19	06 21		06 28	06 36					06 42
	d	05 36		05 42		05 49		05 56		06 02	06 13		06 13		06 22	06 27	06 29	06 37					06 43
Bognor Regis	a	05 43									06 20					06 34							
Ford ■4	d			05 46				06 00		06 07					06 26		06 33						06 47
Littlehampton ■4	a							06 05									06 38						
	d						05 53												06 31			06 41	
Angmering ■3	d			05 53			06 02			06 13					06 32				06 40			06 50	06 56
Goring-by-Sea	d			05 57			06 06			06 17					06 36				06 44			06 54	07 00
Durrington-on-Sea	d			05 59			06 09			06 19					06 39				06 47			06 57	07 03
West Worthing	d			06 01			06 11			06 21					06 41				06 49			07 00	07 05
Worthing ■4	a			06 04			06 13			06 24					06 43				06 52			07 02	07 07
	d			06 04			06 14			06 24					06 44				06 52			07 03	07 08
East Worthing	d			06 07						06 27					06 46								
Lancing	d			06 10			06 18			06 30					06 49				06 57			07 07	07 12
Shoreham-by-Sea	d			06 14			06 22			06 34					06 53				07 01			07 12	07 16
Southwick	d			06 17						06 37					06 56								07 19
Fishersgate	d			06 19						06 39					06 58								
Portslade	d			06 21			06 27			06 41					07 00				07 06			07 17	07 22
Aldrington	d			06 23						06 43					07 03								
Hove ■2	a			06 25			06 30			06 45					07 05				07 10			07 20	07 25
	d		05 59	06 26			06 31		06 38	06 46					07 05				07 11		07 17	07 21	07 26
Brighton ■10	a		06 03	06 30					06 42	06 50					07 09						07 21		07 30
Preston Park	d																						
Burgess Hill	a						06 46																
Haywards Heath ■3	a						06 53												07 30			07 40	
Arundel	d					05 57							06 21										
Amberley	d												06 26										
Pulborough	d					06 06							06 32										
Billingshurst	d					06 13							06 39										
Christs Hospital	d					06 19							06 45										
Horsham ■4	a					06 23							06 49					07 03					
	d				06 10	06 24						06 38	06 50					07 04		07 09			
Crawley	d				06 23	06 37						06 52	07 04					07 13		07 23			
Three Bridges ■4	a				06 26	06 40						06 56	07 07					07 18		07 27			
Gatwick Airport ■10 ✈	a				06 31	06 52	07 11					07 01	07 12							07 32			
	d				06 32	06 53	07 12					07 02	07 14							07 33			
Horley	a				06 35	06 56						07 04	07 16							07 36			
Redhill ■5	a				06 46	07 02						07 15								07 47			
East Croydon 🚋	a				07 04	07 14	07 26					07 34	07 31					07 38	07 56	08 02		08 08	
London Bridge ■4 ⊖	a						07 43					07 51							08 13	08 21			
Clapham Junction ■10	a				07 16	07 24							07 40					07 48				08 17	
London Victoria ■15 ⊖	a				07 25	07 33							07 49					07 57				08 26	

A 🚲 from Three Bridges

Southampton, Portsmouth and Sussex Coast - Brighton, Gatwick Airport and London

Network Diagram - see first Page of Table 186

		SN	SN	SN ■1	SN ◇■1 🚲	SN	SN ■1	SN ■1	SN ■1	SN ◇■1	SN	SN	SN ■1	SW ■1	SW ■1	SN	SN ■1	SN	SN ◇■1 🚲	SN ◇■1 A 🚲	SW ■1	SW ■1	SW ◇■1
Eastleigh	d													06 08	06 13						06 29		06 48
Southampton Airport Parkway	d													06 13	06 17								06 53
Southampton Central ⛴	d							05 48					06 10	06a23	06a29							06 21	07a00
Swanwick	d							06 06					06 27									06 49	
Fareham	d							06 13					06 34								06 50	06 58	
Portchester	d							06 18					06 40								06 55	07 03	
Cosham	d							06 23					06 44								07 00	07 08	
Portsmouth Harbour ⛴	d																			06 46			
Portsmouth & Southsea	d																			06 50			
Fratton	d																			06 54			
Hilsea	d																			06 58	07a05	07a13	
Bedhampton	d							06 34												07 03			
Havant	d							06 37					06 53							07 06			
Warblington	d							06 39												07 08			
Emsworth	d							06 42					06 57							07 11			
Southbourne	d							06 45					07 00							07 14			
Nutbourne	d							06 48												07 16			
Bosham	d							06 51												07 20			
Fishbourne (Sussex)	d							06 54												07 23			
Chichester ■4	a							06 58					07 07							07 26			
	d							06 59					07 08							07 28			
Bognor Regis ■4	d				06 41	06 50			06 57									07 27	07 17				
Barnham	a				06 47	06 56		07 07	07 03				07 15					07 33	07 23	07 35			
	d	06 48			06 48	06 57		07 11			07 13		07 16						07 24	07 36			
Bognor Regis	a	06 55									07 20												
Ford ■4	d				06 52	07 01							07 20										
Littlehampton ■4	a					07 06																	
	d									07 02						07 22							
Angmering ■3	d									07 11			07 26			07 30							
Goring-by-Sea	d									07 15			07 30			07 34							
Durrington-on-Sea	d									07 17			07 33			07 37							
West Worthing	d		07 12							07 20			07 35			07 39							
Worthing ■4	a		07 14							07 22			07 37			07 41							
	d		07 15							07 23			07 38			07 42							
East Worthing	d		07 17													07 44							
Lancing	d		07 20							07 27			07 42			07 47							
Shoreham-by-Sea	d		07 25							07 31			07 46			07 52							
Southwick	d		07 28										07 49			07 55							
Fishersgate	d		07 30													07 57							
Portslade	d		07 32							07 36			07 52			07 59							
Aldrington	d		07 34													08 01							
Hove ■2	a		07 36							07 40			07 55			08 03							
	d		07 37							07 41		07 49	07 56			08 04							
Brighton ■10	a		07 41									07 54	08 01			08 08							
Preston Park	d																						
Burgess Hill	a									07 51													
Haywards Heath ■3	a									07 58													
Arundel	d				06 58			07 18											07 31				
Amberley	d																		07 36				
Pulborough	d				07 07			07 28											07 42				
Billingshurst	d				07 14			07 35											07 49				
Christs Hospital	d				07 20			07 41											07 55				
Horsham ■4	a				07 24			07 45											07 59	08 05			
	d			07 17	07 25		07 40	07 46									07 51		08 09				
Crawley	d			07 31	07 37		07 53	08 00									08 06		08 18				
Three Bridges ■4	a			07 34	07 40		07 57	08 05									08 09		08 22				
Gatwick Airport ■10 ✈	a			07 39			08 04			08 12							08 14						
	d			07 40			08 05			08 13							08 15						
Horley	a			07 42			08 07										08 18		08 28				
Redhill ■5	a			07 53			08 18										08 28						
East Croydon 🚋	a			08 11	07 59		08 36	08 27		08 29							08 50		08 43				
London Bridge ■4 ⊖	a							08 45									09 06						
Clapham Junction ■10	a			08 20	08 10		08 48			08 39									08 52				
London Victoria ■15 ⊖	a			08 29	08 19		08 56			08 48									09 01				

A 🚲 from Horsham

Southampton, Portsmouth and Sussex Coast - Brighton, Gatwick Airport and London

Network Diagram - see first Page of Table 186

		SN	GW	SN	SN	SN	SN	SN	SN	SN	SN	SN	SN	SN	SN	SW	SW	SW	SW	SN	SN	SN
		◇1	🍴		1				◇1			1		◇1 🍴	◇1 A 🍴	1	1	1	1	◇1		
Eastleigh	d															07 21	07 24	07 28				
Southampton Airport Parkway	d															07 25	07 29					
Southampton Central ⛴	d														07 06	07a35	07a39		07 17			
Swanwick	d														07 24				07 44			
Fareham	d														07 31			07 48	07 53			
Portchester	d														07 36			07 53	07 58			
Cosham	d														07 40			07 58	08 03			
Portsmouth Harbour ⛴	d		07 01							07 20												
Portsmouth & Southsea	d		07 05							07 24												
Fratton	d		07 10							07 28												
Hilsea	d																	08a03	08a09			
Bedhampton	d																					
Havant	d		07 20							07 36					07 47							
Warblington	d														07 49							
Emsworth	d														07 52							
Southbourne	d														07 55							
Nutbourne	d														07 58							
Bosham	d														08 01							
Fishbourne (Sussex)	d														08 04							
Chichester 4	a		07 31							07 47					08 08							
	d		07 32							07 47					08 08							
Bognor Regis 4	d							07 36						07 55								08 13
Barnham	a		07 39					07 42		07 55				08 01	08 16							08 19
	d		07 40	07 39				07 45	07 50	07 55			08 05	08 02	08 16							08 20
Bognor Regis	a			07 46					07 58				08 11									
Ford 4	d							07 50		08 00				08 06								08 24
Littlehampton 4	a							07 54														
	d	07 29					07 45				08 01									08 15		
Angmering 3	d	07 38					07 53			08 06	08 10									08 23		08 30
Goring-by-Sea	d	07 42					07 57				08 14									08 27		08 34
Durrington-on-Sea	d	07 45					08 00			08 12	08 17									08 30		08 37
West Worthing	d	07 47					08 02				08 19									08 32		08 39
Worthing 4	a	07 50	07 56				08 04			08 16	08 21									08 34		08 41
	d	07 50	08 00				08 05			08 16	08 22									08 35		08 42
East Worthing	d						08 07				08 24											08 44
Lancing	d	07 54					08 10			08 20	08 27									08 39		08 47
Shoreham-by-Sea	d	07 59	08 06				08 15			08 24	08 32									08 43		08 52
Southwick	d						08 18			08 27	08 35											08 55
Fishersgate	d						08 20				08 37											08 57
Portslade	d	08 04					08 22			08 31	08 39									08 48		08 59
Aldrington	d						08 24				08 41											09 01
Hove 2	a	08 07	08 14				08 26			08 34	08 43									08 51		09 03
	d	08 08	08 14			08 22	08 27			08 34	08 44									08 52	08 54	09 04
Brighton 10	a		08 20			08 26	08 31			08 38	08 48										08 58	09 08
Preston Park	d	08 12																		08 57		
Burgess Hill	a	08 23																		09 07		
Haywards Heath 3	a	08 28																		09 13		
Arundel	d													08 11								
Amberley	d													08 16								
Pulborough	d													08 22								
Billingshurst	d													08 29								
Christs Hospital	d													08 35								
Horsham 4	a													08 39	08 45							
	d				08 12							08 35			08 49							
Crawley	d				08 26							08 47			08 58							
Three Bridges 4	a	08 38			08 29							08 51			09 01							
Gatwick Airport 10 ✈	a				08 34							08 55			09 06					09 26		
	d				08 35							08 56			09 07					09 27		
Horley	a				08 38							08 59										
Redhill 5	a				08 49							09 10										
East Croydon 🚊	a	08 57			09 10							09 30			09 22					09 42		
London Bridge 4 ⊖	a																					
Clapham Junction 10	a	09 07			09 20							09 41			09 32					09 52		
London Victoria 15 ⊖	a	09 16			09 27							09 50			09 42					09 59		

A 🍴 from Horsham

Table 188

Southampton, Portsmouth and Sussex Coast - Brighton, Gatwick Airport and London

Network Diagram - see first Page of Table 186

		SN	SN	SN	SN	SN	SN	SW	SW	SN	SN	SN	SN	SN	SN	SN	SN	SN	SN	SN	SN	SN
		◇		1	1			1	◇1		◇1 🍴	◇1 A 🍴	◇1 B 🍴					1			◇	
Eastleigh	d								07 44													
Southampton Airport Parkway	d								07 49													
Southampton Central ⛴	d				07 33			07 51	07a57													
Swanwick	d				07 51			08 20														
Fareham	d				07 58			08 28														
Portchester	d							08 33														
Cosham	d				08 07			08 38														
Portsmouth Harbour ⛴	d											08 10							08 29			
Portsmouth & Southsea	d						08 03					08 14							08 33			
Fratton	d						08 07					08 18							08 37			
Hilsea	d						08 11	08a45														
Bedhampton	d						08 16															
Havant	d				08 13		08 19					08 27							08 46			
Warblington	d						08 21															
Emsworth	d						08 24					08 31							08 50			
Southbourne	d						08 27												08 53			
Nutbourne	d						08 29															
Bosham	d				08 21																	
Fishbourne (Sussex)	d				08 24																	
Chichester 4	a				08 27		08 35					08 40							09 00			
	d	08 21			08 28		08 36					08 41							09 00		09 06	
Bognor Regis 4	d					08 32					08 26				08 48							09 06
Barnham	a	08 28			08 35	08 38	08 43				08 32	08 48			08 55				09 08		09 14	09 12
	d	08 29	08 28		08 36		08 44			08 45	08 33	08 49		08 52					09 08	09 11		09 15
Bognor Regis	a		08 36							08 52				08 58						09 18		
Ford 4	d	08 33			08 40		08 48				08 37											09 19
Littlehampton 4	a	08 38					08 53															09 24
	d												08 45									
Angmering 3	d				08 46								08 53						09 17			
Goring-by-Sea	d												08 57									
Durrington-on-Sea	d				08 52								09 00									
West Worthing	d												09 02				09 09					
Worthing 4	a				08 56								09 04				09 11		09 24			
	d				08 56								09 05				09 12		09 26			
East Worthing	d																09 14					
Lancing	d				09 00								09 09				09 17		09 30			
Shoreham-by-Sea	d				09 04								09 13				09 22		09 34			
Southwick	d				09 07												09 25		09 37			
Fishersgate	d																09 27					
Portslade	d				09 11								09 18				09 29		09 40			
Aldrington	d																09 31					
Hove 2	a				09 14								09 21				09 33		09 43			
	d				09 14								09 22			09 24	09 34		09 44			
Brighton 10	a				09 18											09 28	09 38		09 48			
Preston Park	d																					
Burgess Hill	a																					
Haywards Heath 3	a												09 40									
Arundel	d										08 42											
Amberley	d										08 47											
Pulborough	d										08 53											
Billingshurst	d										09 00											
Christs Hospital	d										09 06											
Horsham 4	a										09 11	09 16										
	d			09 00								09 20						09 30				
Crawley	d			09 13								09 29						09 44				
Three Bridges 4	a			09 16								09 32						09 48				
Gatwick Airport 10 ✈	a			09 22								09 37	09 56					09 53				
	d			09 23								09 38	09 57					09 54				
Horley	a			09 26								09 41						09 56				
Redhill 5	a			09 36								09 47						10 03				
East Croydon 🚊	a			09 54								09 59	10 11					10 24				
London Bridge 4 ⊖	a			10 13														10 43				
Clapham Junction 10	a											10 09	10 21									
London Victoria 15 ⊖	a											10 16	10 28									

A 🍴 from Horsham

B 🍴 from Haywards Heath

Table 188

Mondays to Fridays

Southampton, Portsmouth and Sussex Coast - Brighton, Gatwick Airport and London

Network Diagram - see first Page of Table 186

		SN ◇1	SN ◇1	SW 1	SN ◇1 A ⌶	SN	SN	SN	SN 1	SW 1	SN 1	SN ◇1	SN	SW 1	SW 1	SW ◇1 ⌶	SN	SN ◇1	SN ◇1	SN ◇1	SN
Eastleigh	d			08 02						08 21				08 31		08 48					
Southampton Airport Parkway	d			08 06						08 25						08 52					
Southampton Central ⛴	d		08 10	08a17					08 33	08a35					08 44	08a59					
Swanwick	d		08 28						08 50						09 11						
Fareham	d		08 35						08 57					08 51	09 18						
Portchester	d		08 40											08 56	09 23						
Cosham	d		08 44						09 05					09 01	09 28						
Portsmouth Harbour ⛴	d												08 51						09 12		
Portsmouth & Southsea	d												08 55						09 16		
Fratton	d												08 59						09 20		
Hilsea	d												09 04	09a05	09a33						
Bedhampton	d												09 13								
Havant	d		08 51						09 12				09 16						09 30		
Warblington	d		08 53										09 18								
Emsworth	d		08 56						09 16				09 21								
Southbourne	d		08 59										09 24								
Nutbourne	d		09 01										09 26								
Bosham	d		09 05										09 30								
Fishbourne (Sussex)	d		09 08										09 33								
Chichester [4]	a		09 11						09 24				09 36						09 40		
	d		09 12						09 25				09 37						09 41		
Bognor Regis [4]	d	08 56															09 39	09 30			
Barnham	a	09 02	09 19						09 32				09 44				09 45	09 36	09 48		
	d	09 03	09 20			09 19			09 33			09 42	09 45					09 37	09 49		09 52
Bognor Regis	a					09 26						09 48									09 59
Ford [4]	d	09 07							09 37				09 49					09 41			
Littlehampton [4]	a												09 54								
	d				09 15															09 45	
Angmering [3]	d				09 23				09 43											09 54	
Goring-by-Sea	d				09 27				09 47											09 58	
Durrington-on-Sea	d				09 30				09 50											10 00	
West Worthing	d				09 32			09 39	09 52											10 02	
Worthing [4]	a				09 34			09 41	09 54											10 05	
	d				09 36			09 42	09 56											10 06	
East Worthing	d							09 44													
Lancing	d							09 47	10 00											10 10	
Shoreham-by-Sea	d				09 42			09 52	10 04											10 14	
Southwick	d							09 55	10 07												
Fishersgate	d							09 57													
Portslade	d				09 47			09 59	10 10												
Aldrington	d							10 01													
Hove [2]	a				09 50			10 03	10 13											10 20	
	d				09 51		09 54	10 04	10 14											10 21	
Brighton [10]	a						09 58	10 08	10 18												
Preston Park	d				09 55																
Burgess Hill	a				10 04																
Haywards Heath [3]	a				10 10															10 35	
Arundel	d	09 12																09 46			
Amberley	d	09 17																			
Pulborough	d	09 23																09 55			
Billingshurst	d	09 29																10 01			
Christs Hospital	d	09 36																			
Horsham [4]	a	09 40	09 47															10 10	10 16		
	d		09 51								10 00								10 20		
Crawley	d		10 00								10 13								10 29		
Three Bridges [4]	a		10 03								10 16								10 32		
Gatwick Airport [10] ✈	a		10 08		10 25						10 22								10 37	10 55	
	d		10 09		10 26						10 23								10 38	10 56	
Horley	a										10 26								10 41		
Redhill [5]	a		10 16								10 36								10 47		
East Croydon 🚋	a		10 28		10 41						10 54								10 59	11 11	
London Bridge [4] ⊖	a										11 13										
Clapham Junction [10]	a		10 37		10 51														11 09	11 21	
London Victoria [15] ⊖	a		10 45		10 58														11 16	11 28	

A ⌶ from Haywards Heath

Table 188

Mondays to Fridays

Southampton, Portsmouth and Sussex Coast - Brighton, Gatwick Airport and London

Network Diagram - see first Page of Table 186

		SN	SN	SN 1	SN	SN	SN ◇1 ⌶	SN ◇1	SN ◇1	SW 1 ⌶	SW ◇1 ⌶	SN ◇1	SN	SN	SN	SN 1	SW 1	SW 1	SN 1	SN ◇1 ⌶	SN
Eastleigh	d									09 01							09 21	09 28			
Southampton Airport Parkway	d									09 05	09 14						09 25				
Southampton Central ⛴	d								09 10	09a15	09a22					09 33	09a35				
Swanwick	d								09 28							09 50					
Fareham	d								09 37							09 56		09 48			
Portchester	d								09 42									09 53			
Cosham	d								09 46							10 05		09 58			
Portsmouth Harbour ⛴	d				09 29																
Portsmouth & Southsea	d				09 33																09 59
Fratton	d				09 37																10 04
Hilsea	d																	10a03			10 08
Bedhampton	d																				10 13
Havant	d				09 46				09 54							10 11					10 16
Warblington	d																				10 18
Emsworth	d				09 50				10 00							10 15					10 21
Southbourne	d				09 53				10 03												10 24
Nutbourne	d																				10 26
Bosham	d																				10 30
Fishbourne (Sussex)	d																				10 33
Chichester [4]	a				10 00				10 10							10 23					10 36
	d				10 00				10 11							10 25					10 37
Bognor Regis [4]	d					10 07		09 56													
Barnham	a				10 08	10 13		10 02	10 18							10 32					10 44
	d				10 08	10 15	10 13	10 03	10 19				10 22			10 33				10 39	10 45
Bognor Regis	a						10 19						10 29							10 46	
Ford [4]	d					10 19		10 07								10 37					10 49
Littlehampton [4]	a					10 24															10 54
	d											10 15									
Angmering [3]	d				10 17							10 23				10 43					
Goring-by-Sea	d											10 27				10 47					
Durrington-on-Sea	d											10 30				10 50					
West Worthing	d		10 09									10 32			10 39	10 52					
Worthing [4]	a		10 11		10 24							10 34			10 41	10 54					
	d		10 12		10 26							10 36			10 42	10 56					
East Worthing	d		10 14												10 44						
Lancing	d		10 17		10 30										10 47	11 00					
Shoreham-by-Sea	d		10 22		10 34							10 42			10 52	11 04					
Southwick	d		10 25		10 37										10 55	11 07					
Fishersgate	d		10 27												10 57						
Portslade	d		10 29		10 40							10 47			10 59	11 10					
Aldrington	d		10 31												11 01						
Hove [2]	a		10 33		10 43							10 50			11 03	11 13					
	d	10 24	10 34		10 44							10 51		10 54	11 04	11 14					
Brighton [10]	a	10 28	10 38		10 48									10 58	11 08	11 18					
Preston Park	d											10 55									
Burgess Hill	a											11 03									
Haywards Heath [3]	a											11 09									
Arundel	d							10 12													
Amberley	d							10 17													
Pulborough	d							10 23													
Billingshurst	d							10 29													
Christs Hospital	d							10 36													
Horsham [4]	a							10 40	10 46												
	d			10 30					10 50										11 00		
Crawley	d			10 43					10 59										11 13		
Three Bridges [4]	a			10 46					11 02										11 16		
Gatwick Airport [10] ✈	a			10 52					11 07			11 24							11 22		
	d			10 53					11 08			11 25							11 23		
Horley	a			10 56															11 26		
Redhill [5]	a			11 02					11 15										11 36		
East Croydon 🚋	a			11 24					11 27			11 40							11 54		
London Bridge [4] ⊖	a			11 43															12 13		
Clapham Junction [10]	a								11 37			11 50									
London Victoria [15] ⊖	a								11 44			11 57									

Southampton, Portsmouth and Sussex Coast - Brighton, Gatwick Airport and London

Network Diagram - see first Page of Table 186

		SW 1	SW ◇1 (trolley)	SN	SN ◇1	SN ◇1	SN ◇1	SN	SN	SN	SN 1	SN	SN ◇1 (trolley)	SN	SN ◇1	SN ◇1	SW 1	SW ◇1 (trolley)	SN ◇1	SN	SN	SN	SN 1
Eastleigh	d																	10 03						
Southampton Airport Parkway	d		09 42															10 08	10 14					
Southampton Central	d	09 44	09a49													10 13	10a18	10a22					10 33
Swanwick	d	10 11															10 32							10 50
Fareham	d	10 18															10 39							10 57
Portchester	d	10 23															10 44							
Cosham	d	10 28															10 48							11 05
Portsmouth Harbour	d					10 12							10 29											
Portsmouth & Southsea	d					10 16							10 33											
Fratton	d					10 20							10 37											
Hilsea	d	10a33																					
Bedhampton	d																						
Havant	d					10 30							10 46				10 56							11 12
Warblington	d																						
Emsworth	d													10 50				11 00							11 16
Southbourne	d													10 53				11 03							
Nutbourne	d																						
Bosham	d																						
Fishbourne (Sussex)	d																						
Chichester 4	a					10 40							11 00				11 10							11 24
	d					10 41							11 00				11 11							11 25
Bognor Regis 4	d			10 39	10 30										11 07	10 56								
Barnham	a			10 45	10 36	10 48						11 08		11 13	11 02	11 18							11 32
	d				10 37	10 49		10 52					11 08	11 12	11 15	11 03	11 19				11 22			11 33
Bognor Regis	a							10 59							11 18							11 29			
Ford 4	d				10 41										11 19	11 07								11 37
Littlehampton 4	a															11 24									
	d						10 45														11 15				
Angmering 3	d						10 53					11 17							11 23				11 43
Goring-by-Sea	d						10 57													11 27				11 47
Durrington-on-Sea	d						11 00													11 30				11 50
West Worthing	d						11 02			11 09											11 32			11 39	11 52
Worthing 4	a						11 04			11 11		11 24							11 34			11 41	11 54
	d						11 06			11 12		11 26							11 36			11 42	11 56
East Worthing	d									11 14												11 44	
Lancing	d						11 10			11 17		11 30										11 47	12 00
Shoreham-by-Sea	d						11 14			11 22		11 34							11 42			11 52	12 04
Southwick	d									11 25		11 37										11 55	12 07
Fishersgate	d									11 27												11 57	
Portslade	d									11 29		11 40							11 47			11 59	12 10
Aldrington	d									11 31												12 01	
Hove 2	a						11 20			11 33		11 43							11 50			12 03	12 13
	d						11 21		11 24	11 34		11 44							11 51		11 54	12 04	12 14
Brighton 10	a								11 28	11 38		11 48									11 58	12 08	12 18
Preston Park	d																			11 55				
Burgess Hill	a																			12 03				
Haywards Heath 3	a						11 35													12 09				
Arundel	d				10 46										11 12									
Amberley	d															11 17									
Pulborough	d				10 55										11 23									
Billingshurst	d				11 01										11 29									
Christs Hospital	d															11 36									
Horsham 4	a				11 10	11 16									11 40	11 46							
	d				11 20						11 30				11 50									
Crawley	d				11 29						11 43				11 59									
Three Bridges 4	a				11 32						11 46				12 02									
Gatwick Airport 10	a				11 37		11 55				11 52				12 07					12 24				
	d				11 38		11 56				11 53				12 08					12 25				
Horley	a				11 41						11 56													
Redhill 5	a				11 47						12 02				12 15									
East Croydon	a				11 59		12 11				12 24				12 27					12 40				
London Bridge 4	a											12 43											
Clapham Junction 10	a				12 09		12 21								12 37					12 50				
London Victoria 15	a				12 18		12 28								12 44					12 57				

Southampton, Portsmouth and Sussex Coast - Brighton, Gatwick Airport and London

Network Diagram - see first Page of Table 186

		SW 1	SW 1	SN 1	SN ◇1 (trolley)	SN	SW 1	SW ◇1 (trolley)	SW 1	SN	SN ◇1	SN ◇1	SN ◇1	SN	SN	SN	SN 1	SN	SN ◇1 (trolley)	SN	SN ◇1	SN ◇1
Eastleigh	d	10 21	10 28							11 00														
Southampton Airport Parkway	d	10 25						10 42	11 05														
Southampton Central	d	10a35						10 44	10a49	11a12														11 13
Swanwick	d						11 11															11 33
Fareham	d		10 48				11 18															11 40
Portchester	d		10 53				11 23															11 45
Cosham	d		10 58				11 28															11 49
Portsmouth Harbour	d											11 12						11 29				
Portsmouth & Southsea	d					10 59						11 16						11 33				
Fratton	d					11 04						11 20						11 37				
Hilsea	d		11a03			11 08	11a33															
Bedhampton	d					11 13															
Havant	d					11 16						11 30						11 46				11 56
Warblington	d					11 18															
Emsworth	d					11 21												11 50				12 00
Southbourne	d					11 24												11 53				12 03
Nutbourne	d					11 26															
Bosham	d					11 30															
Fishbourne (Sussex)	d					11 33															
Chichester 4	a					11 36						11 40						12 00				12 10
	d					11 37						11 41						12 00				12 11
Bognor Regis 4	d									11 39	11 30									12 07	11 56	
Barnham	a					11 44				11 45	11 36	11 48						12 08		12 13	12 02	12 18
	d				11 39	11 45						11 37	11 49		11 52				12 08	12 12	12 15	12 03	12 19
Bognor Regis	a				11 46									11 59						12 18		
Ford 4	d					11 49						11 41									12 19	12 07	
Littlehampton 4	a					11 54														12 24		
	d												11 45										
Angmering 3	d												11 53					12 17				
Goring-by-Sea	d												11 57									
Durrington-on-Sea	d												12 00									
West Worthing	d												12 02			12 09						
Worthing 4	a												12 04			12 11		12 24				
	d												12 06			12 12		12 26				
East Worthing	d															12 14						
Lancing	d												12 10			12 17		12 30				
Shoreham-by-Sea	d												12 14			12 22		12 34				
Southwick	d															12 25		12 37				
Fishersgate	d															12 27						
Portslade	d															12 29		12 40				
Aldrington	d															12 31						
Hove 2	a												12 20			12 33		12 43				
	d												12 21		12 24	12 34		12 44				
Brighton 10	a														12 28	12 38		12 48				
Preston Park	d																					
Burgess Hill	a																					
Haywards Heath 3	a												12 35									
Arundel	d											11 46										12 12	
Amberley	d																					12 17	
Pulborough	d											11 55										12 23	
Billingshurst	d											12 01										12 29	
Christs Hospital	d																					12 36	
Horsham 4	a											12 10	12 16									12 40	12 46
	d			12 00								12 20						12 30				12 50	
Crawley	d			12 13								12 29						12 44				12 59	
Three Bridges 4	a			12 16								12 32						12 47				13 02	
Gatwick Airport 10	a			12 22								12 37		12 55				12 52				13 07	
	d			12 23								12 38		12 56				12 53				13 08	
Horley	a			12 26								12 41						12 56					
Redhill 5	a			12 36								12 47						13 02				13 15	
East Croydon	a			12 54								12 59		13 11				13 24				13 27	
London Bridge 4	a			13 13													13 43					
Clapham Junction 10	a											13 09		13 21									13 37	
London Victoria 15	a											13 16		13 28									13 44	

Southampton, Portsmouth and Sussex Coast - Brighton, Gatwick Airport and London

Network Diagram - see first Page of Table 186

		SW ◇1 ✠	SN ◇1	SN	SN	SN	SN 1	SW 1	SW 1	SN 1	SN ◇1	SN	SW 1	SW ◇1 ✠	SN	SN ◇1	SN ◇1	SN ◇1	SN	SN
Eastleigh	d							11 21	11 28											
Southampton Airport Parkway	d	11 14						11 25						11 42						
Southampton Central	d	11a22					11 33	11a35					11 44	11a49						
Swanwick	d						11 50						12 11							
Fareham	d						11 57		11 48				12 18							
Portchester	d								11 53				12 23							
Cosham	d						12 05		11 58				12 28							
Portsmouth Harbour	d																12 12			
Portsmouth & Southsea	d											11 59					12 16			
Fratton	d											12 04					12 20			
Hilsea	d								12a03			12 08	12a33							
Bedhampton	d											12 13								
Havant	d						12 12					12 16					12 30			
Warblington	d											12 18								
Emsworth	d						12 16					12 21								
Southbourne	d											12 24								
Nutbourne	d											12 26								
Bosham	d											12 30								
Fishbourne (Sussex)	d											12 33								
Chichester 4	a						12 24					12 36					12 40			
	d						12 25					12 37					12 41			
Bognor Regis 4	d														12 39	12 30				
Barnham	a						12 32					12 44			12 45	12 36	12 48			
	d			12 22			12 33				12 39	12 45				12 37	12 49		12 52	
Bognor Regis	a			12 29							12 46								12 59	
Ford 4	d						12 37					12 49				12 41				
Littlehampton 4	a											12 54								
	d		12 15															12 45		
Angmering 3	d		12 23				12 43											12 53		
Goring-by-Sea	d		12 27				12 47											12 57		
Durrington-on-Sea	d		12 30				12 50											13 00		
West Worthing	d		12 32			12 39	12 52											13 02		
Worthing 4	a		12 34			12 41	12 54											13 04		
	d		12 36			12 42	12 56											13 06		
East Worthing	d					12 44														
Lancing	d					12 47	13 00											13 10		
Shoreham-by-Sea	d		12 42			12 52	13 04											13 14		
Southwick	d					12 55	13 07													
Fishersgate	d					12 57														
Portslade	d		12 47			12 59	13 10													
Aldrington	d					13 01														
Hove 2	a		12 50			13 03	13 13											13 20		
	d		12 51		12 54	13 04	13 14											13 21		13 24
Brighton 10	a				12 58	13 08	13 18													13 28
Preston Park	d		12 55																	
Burgess Hill	a		13 03																	
Haywards Heath 3	a		13 09															13 35		
Arundel	d															12 46				
Amberley	d																			
Pulborough	d															12 55				
Billingshurst	d															13 01				
Christs Hospital	d																			
Horsham 4	a															13 10	13 16			
	d									13 00							13 20			
Crawley	d									13 13							13 29			
Three Bridges 4	a									13 16							13 32			
Gatwick Airport 10	a		13 24							13 22							13 37	13 55		
	d		13 25							13 23							13 38	13 56		
Horley	a									13 26							13 41			
Redhill 5	a									13 36							13 47			
East Croydon	a		13 40							13 54							13 59	14 11		
London Bridge 4	a									14 13										
Clapham Junction 10	a		13 50														14 09	14 21		
London Victoria 15	a		13 57														14 16	14 28		

Table 188 Mondays to Fridays

Southampton, Portsmouth and Sussex Coast - Brighton, Gatwick Airport and London

Network Diagram - see first Page of Table 186

		SN	SN 1	SN	SN ◇1	SN	SN ◇1	SN ◇1	SW 1	SW ◇1 ✠	SN ◇1	SN	SN	SN	SN 1	SW 1	SW 1	SN 1	SN ◇1	SN	SW 1	SW ◇1 ✠
Eastleigh	d								12 00							12 21	12 28					
Southampton Airport Parkway	d								12 05	12 14						12 25						12 42
Southampton Central	d							12 13	12a15	12a22					12 33	12a35					12 44	12a49
Swanwick	d							12 33							12 50						13 11	
Fareham	d							12 40							12 56		12 48				13 18	
Portchester	d							12 45									12 53				13 23	
Cosham	d							12 49							13 05		12 58				13 28	
Portsmouth Harbour	d			12 29																		
Portsmouth & Southsea	d			12 33																12 59		
Fratton	d			12 37																13 04		
Hilsea	d																13a03			13 08	13a33	
Bedhampton	d																			13 13		
Havant	d			12 46				12 56							13 11					13 16		
Warblington	d																			13 18		
Emsworth	d			12 50				13 00							13 15					13 21		
Southbourne	d			12 53				13 03												13 24		
Nutbourne	d																			13 26		
Bosham	d																			13 30		
Fishbourne (Sussex)	d																			13 33		
Chichester 4	a			13 00				13 10							13 23					13 36		
	d			13 00				13 11							13 25					13 37		
Bognor Regis 4	d					13 07	12 56															
Barnham	a			13 08		13 13	13 02	13 18							13 32					13 44		
	d			13 08	13 12	13 15	13 03	13 19				13 22			13 33				13 39	13 45		
Bognor Regis	a				13 18							13 29							13 46			
Ford 4	d					13 19	13 07								13 37					13 49		
Littlehampton 4	a					13 24														13 54		
	d										13 15											
Angmering 3	d			13 17							13 23				13 43							
Goring-by-Sea	d										13 27				13 47							
Durrington-on-Sea	d										13 30				13 50							
West Worthing	d	13 09									13 32			13 39	13 52							
Worthing 4	a	13 11		13 24							13 34			13 41	13 54							
	d	13 12		13 26							13 36			13 42	13 56							
East Worthing	d	13 14												13 44								
Lancing	d	13 17		13 30										13 47	14 00							
Shoreham-by-Sea	d	13 22		13 34							13 42			13 52	14 04							
Southwick	d	13 25		13 37										13 55	14 07							
Fishersgate	d	13 27												13 57								
Portslade	d	13 29		13 40							13 47			13 59	14 10							
Aldrington	d	13 31												14 01								
Hove 2	a	13 33		13 43							13 50			14 03	14 13							
	d	13 34		13 44							13 51		13 54	14 04	14 14							
Brighton 10	a	13 38		13 48									13 58	14 08	14 18							
Preston Park	d										13 55											
Burgess Hill	a										14 03											
Haywards Heath 3	a										14 09											
Arundel	d						13 12															
Amberley	d						13 17															
Pulborough	d						13 23															
Billingshurst	d						13 29															
Christs Hospital	d						13 36															
Horsham 4	a						13 40	13 46														
	d		13 30					13 50										14 00				
Crawley	d		13 43					13 59										14 13				
Three Bridges 4	a		13 46					14 02										14 16				
Gatwick Airport 10	a		13 52					14 07			14 24							14 22				
	d		13 53					14 08			14 25							14 23				
Horley	a		13 56															14 26				
Redhill 5	a		14 02					14 15										14 36				
East Croydon	a		14 24					14 27			14 40							14 54				
London Bridge 4	a		14 43															15 13				
Clapham Junction 10	a							14 37			14 50											
London Victoria 15	a							14 44			14 57											

Southampton, Portsmouth and Sussex Coast - Brighton, Gatwick Airport and London

Network Diagram - see first Page of Table 186

		SN	SN ◇1	SN ◇1		SN ◇1	SN	SN	SN	SN 1	SN	SN ◇1	SN	SN ◇1	SN ◇1		SW 1		SW ◇1 ⊼	SN ◇1 A ⊼	SN	SN	SN	SN 1	SW 1
Eastleigh	d																13 00								13 21
Southampton Airport Parkway	d																13 05		13 14						13 25
Southampton Central	d														13 13		13a15		13a22					13 33	13a35
Swanwick	d														13 33									13 50	
Fareham	d														13 40									13 56	
Portchester	d														13 45										
Cosham	d														13 49									14 05	
Portsmouth Harbour	d			13 12							13 29														
Portsmouth & Southsea	d			13 16							13 33														
Fratton	d			13 20							13 37														
Hilsea	d																								
Bedhampton	d																								
Havant	d			13 30							13 46				13 56									14 11	
Warblington	d																								
Emsworth	d										13 50				14 00									14 15	
Southbourne	d										13 53				14 03										
Nutbourne	d																								
Bosham	d																								
Fishbourne (Sussex)	d																								
Chichester 4	a			13 40							14 00				14 10									14 23	
	d			13 41							14 00				14 11									14 25	
Bognor Regis 4	d	13 39	13 30										14 07	13 56											
Barnham	a	13 45	13 36	13 48							14 08		14 13	14 02	14 18									14 32	
	d		13 37	13 49			13 52				14 08	14 12	14 15	14 03	14 19						14 22			14 33	
Bognor Regis	a						13 59					14 18									14 29				
Ford 4	d		13 41										14 19	14 07										14 37	
Littlehampton 4	a												14 24												
	d					13 45														14 15					
Angmering 3	d					13 53					14 17									14 23				14 43	
Goring-by-Sea	d					13 57														14 27				14 47	
Durrington-on-Sea	d					14 00														14 30				14 50	
West Worthing	d					14 02			14 09											14 32			14 39	14 52	
Worthing 4	a					14 04			14 11		14 24									14 34			14 41	14 54	
	d					14 06			14 12		14 26									14 36			14 42	14 56	
East Worthing	d								14 14														14 44		
Lancing	d					14 10			14 17		14 30												14 47	15 00	
Shoreham-by-Sea	d					14 14			14 22		14 34									14 42			14 52	15 04	
Southwick	d								14 25		14 37												14 55	15 07	
Fishersgate	d								14 27														14 57		
Portslade	d								14 29		14 40									14 47			14 59	15 10	
Aldrington	d								14 31														15 01		
Hove 2	a					14 20			14 33		14 43									14 50			15 03	15 13	
	d					14 21		14 24	14 34		14 44									14 51		14 54	15 04	15 14	
Brighton 10	a							14 28	14 38		14 48											14 58	15 08	15 18	
Preston Park	d																			14 55					
Burgess Hill	a																			15 03					
Haywards Heath 3	a					14 35														15 09					
Arundel	d		13 46											14 12											
Amberley	d													14 17											
Pulborough	d		13 55											14 23											
Billingshurst	d		14 01											14 29											
Christs Hospital	d													14 36											
Horsham 4	a		14 10	14 16										14 40	14 46										
	d		14 20							14 30				14 50											
Crawley	d		14 29							14 43				14 59											
Three Bridges 4	a		14 32							14 46				15 02											
Gatwick Airport 10 ✈	a		14 37			14 55				14 52				15 07						15 24					
	d		14 38			14 56				14 53				15 08						15 25					
Horley	a		14 41							14 56															
Redhill 5	a		14 47							15 02				15 16											
East Croydon	a		14 59			15 11				15 24				15 28						15 40					
London Bridge 4 ⊖	a									15 43															
Clapham Junction 10	a		15 09			15 21								15 37						15 50					
London Victoria 15 ⊖	a		15 20			15 28								15 46						15 57					

A ⊼ from Haywards Heath

Southampton, Portsmouth and Sussex Coast - Brighton, Gatwick Airport and London

Network Diagram - see first Page of Table 186

			SW 1		SN 1	SN ◇1	SN	SW 1	SW ◇1 ⊼	SW 1	SN		SN ◇1 ⊼	SN ◇1 A ⊼	SN ◇1 B ⊼	SN	SN	SN	SN 1	SN	SN ◇1		SN	SN ◇1 ⊼	SN ◇1 A ⊼
Eastleigh	d		13 28							14 00															
Southampton Airport Parkway	d								13 42	14 05															
Southampton Central	d							13 44	13a49	14a12															14 13
Swanwick	d							14 11																	14 33
Fareham	d		13 48					14 18																	14 40
Portchester	d		13 53					14 23																	14 45
Cosham	d		13 58					14 28																	14 49
Portsmouth Harbour	d													14 12						14 29					
Portsmouth & Southsea	d						13 59							14 16						14 33					
Fratton	d						14 04							14 20						14 37					
Hilsea	d		14a03				14 08	14a33																	
Bedhampton	d						14 13																		
Havant	d						14 16							14 30						14 46					14 56
Warblington	d						14 18																		
Emsworth	d						14 21													14 50					15 00
Southbourne	d						14 24													14 53					15 03
Nutbourne	d						14 26																		
Bosham	d						14 30																		
Fishbourne (Sussex)	d						14 33																		
Chichester 4	a						14 36							14 40						15 00					15 10
	d						14 37							14 41						15 00					15 11
Bognor Regis 4	d										14 39		14 30										15 07	14 56	
Barnham	a						14 44				14 45		14 36	14 48						15 08			15 13	15 02	15 18
	d					14 39	14 45						14 37	14 49		14 52				15 08	15 12		15 15	15 03	15 19
Bognor Regis	a					14 46										14 59					15 18				
Ford 4	d						14 49						14 41										15 19	15 07	
Littlehampton 4	a						14 54																15 26		
	d														14 45										
Angmering 3	d														14 53					15 17					
Goring-by-Sea	d														14 57										
Durrington-on-Sea	d														15 00										
West Worthing	d														15 02			15 09							
Worthing 4	a														15 04			15 11		15 24					
	d														15 06			15 12		15 26					
East Worthing	d																	15 14							
Lancing	d														15 10			15 17		15 30					
Shoreham-by-Sea	d														15 14			15 22		15 34					
Southwick	d																	15 25		15 37					
Fishersgate	d																	15 27							
Portslade	d																	15 29		15 40					
Aldrington	d																	15 31							
Hove 2	a														15 20			15 33		15 43					
	d														15 21		15 24	15 34		15 44					
Brighton 10	a																15 28	15 38		15 48					
Preston Park	d																								
Burgess Hill	a																								
Haywards Heath 3	a														15 35										
Arundel	d												14 46											15 12	
Amberley	d																							15 17	
Pulborough	d												14 55											15 23	
Billingshurst	d												15 01											15 29	
Christs Hospital	d																							15 36	
Horsham 4	a												15 10	15 16										15 40	15 46
	d				15 00								15 20						15 30					15 50	
Crawley	d				15 13								15 29						15 43					15 59	
Three Bridges 4	a				15 16								15 32						15 46					16 02	
Gatwick Airport 10 ✈	a				15 22								15 37		15 55				15 52					16 07	
	d				15 23								15 38		15 56				15 53					16 08	
Horley	a				15 26								15 41						15 56						
Redhill 5	a				15 36								15 47						16 02					16 17	
East Croydon	a				15 54								15 59		16 11				16 23					16 30	
London Bridge 4 ⊖	a				16 13														16 43						
Clapham Junction 10	a												16 09		16 21									16 39	
London Victoria 15 ⊖	a												16 16		16 28									16 46	

A ⊼ from Horsham

B ⊼ from Haywards Heath

Southampton, Portsmouth and Sussex Coast - Brighton, Gatwick Airport and London

Network Diagram - see first Page of Table 186

		SW ◇1 ⌶	SN ◇1 A ⌶	SN	SN	SN	GW ⌶	SW 1	SW 1	SN 1	SN 1 B	SN ◇1	SN	SW 1	SW ◇1 ⌶	SW 1	SN	SN ◇1	SN ◇1	SN ◇1 A ⌶	SN	SN
Eastleigh	d							14 21	14 28		14 41					15 00						
Southampton Airport Parkway	d	14 14						14 25			14 34				14 42	15 05						
Southampton Central	d	14a22					14 34	14a35			14a26			14 44	14a49	15a12						
Swanwick	d													15 11								
Fareham	d						14 56		14 48		15 00			15 18								
Portchester	d								14 53					15 23								
Cosham	d						15 04		14 58					15 28								
Portsmouth Harbour	d																		15 12			
Portsmouth & Southsea	d												14 59						15 16			
Fratton	d												15 04						15 20			
Hilsea	d								15a03				15 08	15a33								
Bedhampton	d												15 14									
Havant	d						15 11				15 15		15 17						15 30			
Warblington	d												15 19									
Emsworth	d												15 22									
Southbourne	d												15 25									
Nutbourne	d												15 28									
Bosham	d												15 31									
Fishbourne (Sussex)	d												15 34									
Chichester 4	a						15 21				15 25		15 37						15 41			
	d						15 22				15 29		15 38						15 42			
Bognor Regis 4	d																15 39	15 27				
Barnham	a						15 29				15 36		15 45				15 45	15 33	15 49			
	d			15 22			15 30				15 37	15 40	15 46					15 34	15 50		15 53	
Bognor Regis	a			15 29								15 46									16 00	
Ford 4	d										15 41		15 50					15 38				
Littlehampton 4	a												15 55									
	d		15 15																	15 45		
Angmering 3	d		15 23								15 47									15 53		
Goring-by-Sea	d		15 27								15 51									15 57		
Durrington-on-Sea	d		15 30								15 54									16 00		
West Worthing	d		15 32			15 39					15 56									16 02		
Worthing 4	a		15 34			15 41	15 45				15 58									16 04		
	d		15 35			15 42	15 50				15 59									16 06		
East Worthing	d		15 37			15 44																
Lancing	d					15 47					16 03									16 10		
Shoreham-by-Sea	d		15 43			15 52	15 57				16 07									16 14		
Southwick	d					15 55					16 10											
Fishersgate	d					15 57																
Portslade	d		15 48			15 59					16 13											
Aldrington	d					16 01																
Hove 2	a		15 51			16 03	16 07				16 16									16 20		
	d		15 52		15 54	16 04	16 08				16 17									16 21		16 24
Brighton 10	a				15 58	16 08	16 14				16 21											16 28
Preston Park	d		15 56																			
Burgess Hill	a		16 04																			
Haywards Heath 3	a		16 10																	16 35		
Arundel	d																	15 43				
Amberley	d																					
Pulborough	d																	15 52				
Billingshurst	d																	15 58				
Christs Hospital	d																	16 05				
Horsham 4	a																	16 10	16 16			
	d									16 00									16 20			
Crawley	d									16 13									16 29			
Three Bridges 4	a									16 16									16 32			
Gatwick Airport 10 ✈	a		16 25							16 22									16 37	16 57		
	d		16 26							16 23									16 38	16 58		
Horley	a									16 26												
Redhill 5	a									16 36									16 46			
East Croydon	a		16 40							16 54									17 01	17 13		
London Bridge 4 ⊖	a									17 14												
Clapham Junction 10	a		16 50																17 10	17 22		
London Victoria 15 ⊖	a		16 58																17 17	17 29		

A ⌶ from Haywards Heath

B Stops at Southampton Central and Southampton Airport Parkway before Eastleigh

Southampton, Portsmouth and Sussex Coast - Brighton, Gatwick Airport and London

Network Diagram - see first Page of Table 186

		SN	SN 1	SN	SN ◇1	SN	SN ◇1 ⌶	SN ◇1 A ⌶	SW ◇1 ⌶	SN ◇1 B ⌶	SN	SN	SN	SN 1	SW 1	SW 1	SN 1	SN ◇1	SN	SW 1
Eastleigh	d														15 21	15 28				
Southampton Airport Parkway	d								15 14						15 25					
Southampton Central	d							15 13	15a22					15 33	15a35					15 44
Swanwick	d							15 33						15 50						16 11
Fareham	d							15 40						15 57		15 48				16 18
Portchester	d							15 45								15 53				16 23
Cosham	d							15 49						16 05		15 58				16 28
Portsmouth Harbour	d			15 29																
Portsmouth & Southsea	d			15 33															15 59	
Fratton	d			15 37															16 04	
Hilsea	d															16a03			16 08	16a33
Bedhampton	d																		16 13	
Havant	d			15 46				15 58						16 12					16 16	
Warblington	d																		16 18	
Emsworth	d			15 50				16 02						16 16					16 21	
Southbourne	d			15 53				16 05											16 24	
Nutbourne	d																		16 26	
Bosham	d																		16 30	
Fishbourne (Sussex)	d																		16 33	
Chichester 4	a			16 00				16 12						16 24					16 36	
	d			16 00				16 13						16 25					16 37	
Bognor Regis 4	d					16 09	15 56													
Barnham	a			16 08		16 15	16 02	16 20						16 32					16 44	
	d			16 08	16 12		16 03	16 21			16 24			16 33				16 40	16 45	
Bognor Regis	a				16 18						16 31							16 46		
Ford 4	d						16 07							16 37					16 49	
Littlehampton 4	a																		16 54	
	d	15 50								16 15										
Angmering 3	d	16 00		16 17						16 23				16 43						
Goring-by-Sea	d	16 04								16 27				16 47						
Durrington-on-Sea	d	16 07								16 30				16 50						
West Worthing	d	16 09								16 32			16 39	16 52						
Worthing 4	a	16 11		16 24						16 34			16 41	16 54						
	d	16 12		16 26						16 36			16 42	16 56						
East Worthing	d	16 14											16 44							
Lancing	d	16 17		16 30									16 47	17 00						
Shoreham-by-Sea	d	16 22		16 34						16 42			16 52	17 04						
Southwick	d	16 25		16 37									16 55	17 07						
Fishersgate	d	16 27											16 57							
Portslade	d	16 29		16 40						16 47			16 59	17 10						
Aldrington	d	16 31											17 01							
Hove 2	a	16 33		16 43						16 50			17 03	17 13						
	d	16 34		16 44						16 51		16 54	17 04	17 14						
Brighton 10	a	16 38		16 48								16 58	17 08	17 18						
Preston Park	d																			
Burgess Hill	a									17 01										
Haywards Heath 3	a									17 09										
Arundel	d						16 12													
Amberley	d						16 17													
Pulborough	d						16 23													
Billingshurst	d						16 29													
Christs Hospital	d						16 36													
Horsham 4	a						16 40	16 48												
	d		16 30					16 52									17 00			
Crawley	d		16 44					17 01									17 14			
Three Bridges 4	a		16 47					17 04									17 17			
Gatwick Airport 10 ✈	a		16 52					17 09		17 25							17 22			
	d		16 53					17 10		17 26							17 23			
Horley	a		16 56														17 26			
Redhill 5	a		17 06					17 17									17 36			
East Croydon	a		17 24					17 30		17 41							17 54			
London Bridge 4 ⊖	a		17 45														18 16			
Clapham Junction 10	a							17 39		17 50										
London Victoria 15 ⊖	a							17 46		17 58										

A ⌶ from Horsham

B ⌶ from Haywards Heath

Southampton, Portsmouth and Sussex Coast - Brighton, Gatwick Airport and London

Network Diagram - see first Page of Table 186

		SW	SN	SN	SN	SN	SN	SN	SN		SN	SN	SN	SN	SN	SW	SW	SN	SN		SN	SN	SN	SN	SN
		◇1		◇1	◇1	◇1					1		◇1	◇1	◇1	1	◇1	◇1				1			1
					A	B									A			B							
		🍴		🍴	🍴	🍴								🍴	🍴		🍴	🍴							
Eastleigh	d															16 00									
Southampton Airport Parkway	d	15 42														16 05	16 14								
Southampton Central	d	15a49													16 12	16a15	16a22								16 33
Swanwick	d														16 29										16 50
Fareham	d														16 36										16 57
Portchester	d														16 41										
Cosham	d														16 45										17 05
Portsmouth Harbour	d				16 12							16 29												16 40	
Portsmouth & Southsea	d				16 16							16 33												16 46	
Fratton	d				16 20							16 37												16 50	
Hilsea	d																							16 54	
Bedhampton	d																								
Havant	d				16 30							16 46			16 52									17 00	17 12
Warblington	d																							17 02	
Emsworth	d				16 34							16 50			16 56									17 05	17 17
Southbourne	d											16 53			16 59									17 08	
Nutbourne	d																							17 10	
Bosham	d														17 03									17 14	
Fishbourne (Sussex)	d																							17 17	
Chichester 4	a				16 42							17 00			17 08									17 20	17 25
	d				16 43							17 00			17 13									17 21	17 25
Bognor Regis 4	d		16 39	16 30										16 56					17 18						
Barnham	a		16 45	16 36	16 50							17 08		17 02	17 20				17 24					17 28	17 33
	d			16 37	16 51		16 54					17 08	17 12	17 03	17 21				17 25		17 24			17 29	17 33
Bognor Regis	a						17 01						17 18								17 31				
Ford 4	d			16 41										17 07					17 29						17 38
Littlehampton 4	a																		17 37						
	d					16 45												17 15							
Angmering 3	d					16 53						17 17						17 23							17 44
Goring-by-Sea	d					16 57												17 27							17 48
Durrington-on-Sea	d					17 00												17 30							17 50
West Worthing	d					17 02			17 09									17 32							17 52
Worthing 4	a					17 04			17 11			17 24						17 34						17 43	17 55
	d					17 06			17 12			17 26						17 36						17 43	17 56
East Worthing	d								17 14															17 46	
Lancing	d					17 10			17 17			17 30												17 49	18 00
Shoreham-by-Sea	d					17 14			17 22			17 34						17 42						17 53	18 04
Southwick	d								17 25			17 37												17 56	18 07
Fishersgate	d								17 27															17 58	
Portslade	d								17 29			17 40						17 47						18 00	18 10
Aldrington	d								17 31															18 02	
Hove 2	a					17 20			17 33			17 43						17 50						18 04	18 13
	d					17 21		17 24	17 34			17 44						17 51					18 01	18 05	18 14
Brighton 10	a							17 28	17 38			17 48											18 05	18 09	18 18
Preston Park	d																								
Burgess Hill	a																	18 03							
Haywards Heath 3	a					17 35												18 11							
Arundel	d			16 46										17 12											
Amberley	d													17 17											
Pulborough	d			16 55										17 23											
Billingshurst	d			17 01										17 29											
Christs Hospital	d			17 08										17 36											
Horsham 4	a			17 12	17 18									17 40	17 48										
	d				17 22						17 30				17 52							18 00			
Crawley	d				17 31						17 44				18 01							18 14			
Three Bridges 4	a				17 34						17 47				18 04							18 17			
Gatwick Airport 10	a				17 41	17 54					17 52				18 09			18 26				18 22			
	d				17 42	17 55					17 53				18 10			18 27				18 23			
Horley	a										17 56											18 26			
Redhill 5	a				17 49						18 06				18 17							18 36			
East Croydon	a				18 01	18 11					18 24				18 29			18 42				18 54			
London Bridge 4	a																								
Clapham Junction 10	a				18 13	18 21					18 38				18 41			18 52				19 05			
London Victoria 15	a				18 20	18 29					18 45				18 48			18 59				19 13			

A 🍴 from Horsham
B 🍴 from Haywards Heath

Southampton, Portsmouth and Sussex Coast - Brighton, Gatwick Airport and London

Network Diagram - see first Page of Table 186

		SW	SW		SN		SN	SW	SW	SW	SN	SN	SN	SN	SN		SN	SN	SN	SW	SW	SN	SN	SN	SN
		1	1		◇1			1	◇1	1	◇1	◇1	◇1					1		1	1		◇1	◇1	◇1
													A												
									🍴				🍴										🍴		
Eastleigh	d	16 21	16 28							16 49										16 54	17 01				
Southampton Airport Parkway	d	16 25							16 42	16 54											17 05				
Southampton Central	d	16a35						16 44	16a49	17a04											17a13				17 13
Swanwick	d							17 11																	17 33
Fareham	d		16 48					17 18												17 12					17 40
Portchester	d		16 53					17 23												17 17					17 45
Cosham	d		16 58					17 28												17 22					17 49
Portsmouth Harbour	d											17 12							17 29	17a40					
Portsmouth & Southsea	d						17 00					17 16							17 33						
Fratton	d						17 04					17 20							17 37						
Hilsea	d		17a03				17 08	17a33																	
Bedhampton	d						17 14																		
Havant	d						17 17					17 30							17 46						17 56
Warblington	d						17 19																		
Emsworth	d						17 22												17 50						18 00
Southbourne	d						17 25												17 53						18 03
Nutbourne	d						17 28																		
Bosham	d						17 31																		
Fishbourne (Sussex)	d						17 34																		
Chichester 4	a						17 37					17 42							18 00						18 10
	d						17 38					17 43							18 00						18 13
Bognor Regis 4	d										17 30				17 51									17 57	
Barnham	a						17 45				17 36	17 50			17 57				18 08					18 03	18 20
	d				17 42		17 46				17 37	17 51		17 54					18 08			18 08	18 14	18 04	18 21
Bognor Regis	a				17 49									18 01								18 15	18 22		
Ford 4	d						17 50				17 41													18 08	
Littlehampton 4	a						17 55																		
	d												17 45												
Angmering 3	d												17 53						18 18						
Goring-by-Sea	d												17 57												
Durrington-on-Sea	d												18 00												
West Worthing	d												18 02												
Worthing 4	a												18 04						18 25						
	d												18 06						18 25						
East Worthing	d																		18 28						
Lancing	d												18 10						18 31						
Shoreham-by-Sea	d												18 14						18 35						
Southwick	d																		18 38						
Fishersgate	d																		18 40						
Portslade	d																		18 42						
Aldrington	d																		18 44						
Hove 2	a												18 20						18 46						
	d												18 21				18 24		18 47						
Brighton 10	a																18 28		18 51						
Preston Park	d																								
Burgess Hill	a												18 33												
Haywards Heath 3	a												18 41												
Arundel	d										17 46													18 13	
Amberley	d																							18 18	
Pulborough	d										17 55													18 24	
Billingshurst	d										18 01													18 30	
Christs Hospital	d										18 08													18 37	
Horsham 4	a										18 12	18 18												18 42	18 48
	d										18 22							18 30						18 52	
Crawley	d										18 31							18 44						19 01	
Three Bridges 4	a										18 34							18 47						19 04	
Gatwick Airport 10	a										18 39		18 56					18 52						19 09	
	d										18 40		18 57					18 53						19 10	
Horley	a																	18 56							
Redhill 5	a										18 47							19 06						19 17	
East Croydon	a										18 59		19 12					19 24						19 29	
London Bridge 4	a																								
Clapham Junction 10	a										19 11		19 21					19 37						19 40	
London Victoria 15	a										19 18		19 29					19 44						19 47	

A 🍴 from Haywards Heath

Southampton, Portsmouth and Sussex Coast - Brighton, Gatwick Airport and London

Network Diagram - see first Page of Table 186

		SW ◇■ ⌶	SN ■	SN ◇■	SN	SN	SN	SN	SW ■	SW ■	SN ◇■ ⌶	SN ■	SN ◇■	SN ■	SW ■	SW ◇■ ⌶	SW ■	SN	SN	SN
Eastleigh	d		17 16						17 21	17 28							17 55			
Southampton Airport Parkway	d	17 14	17 20						17 25							17 42	18 00			
Southampton Central ⛴	d	17a22	17 33						17a35						17 44	17a49	18a10			
Swanwick	d		17 50												18 11					
Fareham	d		17 56							17 48					18 18					
Portchester	d									17 53					18 23					
Cosham	d		18 05							17 58					18 28					
Portsmouth Harbour ⛴	d																			
Portsmouth & Southsea	d						17 46							17 59						
Fratton	d						17 50							18 04						
Hilsea	d						17 54			18a04				18 08	18a33					
Bedhampton	d													18 13						
Havant	d		18 11				18 00							18 16						
Warblington	d						18 02							18 18						
Emsworth	d		18 15				18 05							18 21						
Southbourne	d						18 08							18 24						
Nutbourne	d						18 10							18 26						
Bosham	d						18 14							18 30						
Fishbourne (Sussex)	d						18 17							18 33						
Chichester ■4	a		18 24				18 20							18 36						
	d		18 25				18 21							18 37						
Bognor Regis ■4	d				18 19								18 33							18 46
Barnham	a		18 32		18 25		18 28						18 39	18 44						18 52
	d		18 33			18 27	18 29				18 35		18 40	18 45						18 53
Bognor Regis	a					18 34					18 41									
Ford ■4	d						18 33						18 44							18 57
Littlehampton ■4	a						18 40													19 02
	d			18 15															18 52	
Angmering ■3	d		18 42	18 23									18 53						19 00	
Goring-by-Sea	d			18 27									18 57						19 04	
Durrington-on-Sea	d		18 48	18 30									19 00						19 07	
West Worthing	d			18 32									19 02						19 09	
Worthing ■4	a		18 52	18 34									19 04						19 11	
	d		18 52	18 35									19 05						19 12	
East Worthing	d		18 55																19 14	
Lancing	d		18 58	18 39									19 09						19 17	
Shoreham-by-Sea	d		19 02	18 43									19 13						19 22	
Southwick	d		19 05																19 25	
Fishersgate	d		19 07																19 27	
Portslade	d		19 09	18 48									19 18						19 29	
Aldrington	d		19 11																19 31	
Hove ■2	a		19 13	18 51									19 21						19 33	
	d		19 14	18 52				19 00					19 22					19 24	19 34	
Brighton ■10	a		19 18					19 04										19 28	19 38	
Preston Park	d																			
Burgess Hill	a												19 32							
Haywards Heath ■3	a			19 07									19 37							
Arundel	d													18 52						
Amberley	d																			
Pulborough	d													19 01						
Billingshurst	d													19 08						
Christs Hospital	d																			
Horsham ■4	a													19 16						
	d											19 02		19 17						
Crawley	d											19 14		19 26						
Three Bridges ■4	a											19 18		19 29						
Gatwick Airport ■10 ✈	a			19 25								19 22	19 55	19 39						
	d			19 26								19 23	19 56	19 40						
Horley	a											19 26								
Redhill ■5	a											19 38		19 47						
East Croydon 🚊	a			19 43								19 58	20 11	20 00						
London Bridge ■4 ⊖	a																			
Clapham Junction ■10	a			19 52								20 08	20 20	20 11						
London Victoria ■15 ⊖	a			19 59								20 15	20 28	20 20						

Southampton, Portsmouth and Sussex Coast - Brighton, Gatwick Airport and London

Network Diagram - see first Page of Table 186

		SN	SN ■	SW ■	SN ◇■	SN	SN ■	SN ◇■	SW ◇■ ⌶	SN ◇■	SN ■	SN	SN	SN	SN ■	SW ■	SW ■	SN ◇■	SN ■	SN ◇■	SN	SN
Eastleigh	d			18 01												18 21	18 25					
Southampton Airport Parkway	d								18 09							18 25						
Southampton Central ⛴	d							18 11	18a16						18 33	18a35						
Swanwick	d							18 28							18 50							
Fareham	d			18 23				18 35							18 56		18 45					
Portchester	d			18 28				18 40									18 50					
Cosham	d			18 33				18 44							19 05		18 55					
Portsmouth Harbour ⛴	d		18 28	18a51									18 37									
Portsmouth & Southsea	d		18 32										18 42									
Fratton	d		18 36										18 46									
Hilsea	d												18 50				19a05					
Bedhampton	d																					
Havant	d		18 44					18 51					18 56		19 11							
Warblington	d												18 58									
Emsworth	d		18 48					18 55					19 01									
Southbourne	d		18 51					18 58					19 04									
Nutbourne	d												19 07									
Bosham	d												19 10									
Fishbourne (Sussex)	d												19 13									
Chichester ■4	a		18 58					19 05					19 17		19 22							
	d		18 59					19 06					19 17		19 22							
Bognor Regis ■4	d					19 03														19 36		
Barnham	a		19 06			19 09		19 13					19 25		19 30					19 42		
	d	18 55	19 07		19 07	19 10		19 14			19 16	19 24	19 25		19 30			19 33		19 43		
Bognor Regis	a	19 02			19 13						19 24	19 31						19 39				
Ford ■4	d					19 14		19 18					19 30							19 47		
Littlehampton ■4	a					19 19							19 38									
	d									19 15												19 52
Angmering ■3	d		19 16							19 23					19 40					19 53		20 00
Goring-by-Sea	d									19 27					19 44					19 57		20 04
Durrington-on-Sea	d									19 30					19 46					20 00		20 07
West Worthing	d									19 32					19 48					20 02		20 09
Worthing ■4	a		19 23							19 34					19 51					20 04		20 11
	d		19 24							19 35					19 52					20 05		20 12
East Worthing	d		19 26												19 55							20 14
Lancing	d		19 29							19 39					19 58					20 09		20 17
Shoreham-by-Sea	d		19 33							19 43					20 02					20 13		20 22
Southwick	d		19 36												20 05							20 25
Fishersgate	d		19 38												20 07							20 27
Portslade	d		19 40							19 48					20 09					20 18		20 29
Aldrington	d		19 43												20 11							20 31
Hove ■2	a		19 45							19 51					20 13					20 21		20 33
	d		19 45							19 52				19 54	20 14					20 22	20 24	20 34
Brighton ■10	a		19 49											19 58	20 18						20 28	20 38
Preston Park	d																					
Burgess Hill	a																			20 32		
Haywards Heath ■3	a									20 05										20 38		
Arundel	d							19 23														
Amberley	d							19 28														
Pulborough	d							19 34														
Billingshurst	d							19 41														
Christs Hospital	d							19 47														
Horsham ■4	a							19 51														
	d						19 32	19 52											20 02			
Crawley	d						19 45	20 01											20 14			
Three Bridges ■4	a						19 49	20 04											20 18	20 47		
Gatwick Airport ■10 ✈	a						19 55	20 10		20 25									20 22	20 51		
	d						19 56	20 11		20 26									20 23	20 53		
Horley	a						19 59												20 26			
Redhill ■5	a						20 05	20 18											20 36			
East Croydon 🚊	a						20 23	20 30		20 41									20 57	21 08		
London Bridge ■4 ⊖	a																					
Clapham Junction ■10	a						20 37	20 40		20 50									21 07	21 18		
London Victoria ■15 ⊖	a						20 44	20 50		20 59									21 15	21 28		

Southampton, Portsmouth and Sussex Coast - Brighton, Gatwick Airport and London

Network Diagram - see first Page of Table 186

		SN	SW 1	SW 1	SW ◇1 Bus	SN	SN 1	SN ◇1	SN	SN 1	SN ◇1	SW 1	SW ◇1 Bus	SW 1	SN ◇1	SN	SN 1	SN	SN 1	SW 1	SW 1
Eastleigh	d		18 55									18 59		19 16						19 21	19 29
Southampton Airport Parkway	d				18 39							19 03	19 09	19 20						19 25	
Southampton Central	d			18 44	18a46						19 12	19a18	19a18	19a33					19 33	19a35	
Swanwick	d			19 11							19 29								19 51		
Fareham	d		19 14	19 18							19 36								19 57		19 48
Portchester	d		19 19	19 23							19 41										19 53
Cosham	d		19 24	19 28							19 46								20 06		19 58
Portsmouth Harbour	d																19 40				
Portsmouth & Southsea	d	18 59					19 32										19 44				
Fratton	d	19 04					19 36										19 48				
Hilsea	d	19 08	19a28	19a33																	20a02
Bedhampton	d	19 13																			
Havant	d	19 16					19 46				19 52						19 57		20 12		
Warblington	d	19 18															19 59				
Emsworth	d	19 21					19 50				19 56						20 02		20 16		
Southbourne	d	19 24					19 53				19 59						20 05				
Nutbourne	d	19 27															20 07				
Bosham	d	19 30															20 11				
Fishbourne (Sussex)	d	19 33															20 14				
Chichester 4	a	19 36					20 00				20 06						20 17		20 24		
	d	19 40					20 01				20 07						20 18		20 25		
Bognor Regis 4	d								20 05												
Barnham	a	19 47					20 08		20 11		20 14						20 25		20 32		
	d	19 48				19 55	20 09	20 08	20 12		20 15					20 22	20 27		20 33		
Bognor Regis	a					20 01		20 14								20 28					
Ford 4	d	19 52							20 16		20 19						20 31				
Littlehampton 4	a	19 58							20 21								20 36				
	d														20 15						
Angmering 3	d						20 18								20 23				20 42		
Goring-by-Sea	d														20 27						
Durrington-on-Sea	d														20 30				20 48		
West Worthing	d														20 32						
Worthing 4	a						20 25								20 34				20 52		
	d						20 25								20 35				20 52		
East Worthing	d						20 28												20 55		
Lancing	d						20 31								20 39				20 58		
Shoreham-by-Sea	d						20 35								20 43				21 02		
Southwick	d						20 38												21 05		
Fishersgate	d						20 40												21 07		
Portslade	d						20 42								20 48				21 09		
Aldrington	d						20 44												21 11		
Hove 2	a						20 46								20 51				21 13		
	d						20 47								20 52			20 55	21 14		
Brighton 10	a						20 51											20 59	21 18		
Preston Park	d																				
Burgess Hill	a																				
Haywards Heath 3	a														21 05						
Arundel	d										20 24										
Amberley	d										20 29										
Pulborough	d										20 35										
Billingshurst	d										20 41										
Christs Hospital	d										20 48										
Horsham 4	a										20 52										
	d									20 32	20 52										
Crawley	d									20 45	21 01										
Three Bridges 4	a									20 48	21 05										
Gatwick Airport 10 ✈	a									20 56	21 10				21 25						
	d									20 57	21 11				21 26						
Horley	a									20 59											
Redhill 5	a									21 06	21 18										
East Croydon	a									21 25	21 30				21 41						
London Bridge 4 ⊖	a																				
Clapham Junction 10	a									21 37	21 40				21 51						
London Victoria 15 ⊖	a									21 45	21 49				21 58						

Southampton, Portsmouth and Sussex Coast - Brighton, Gatwick Airport and London

Network Diagram - see first Page of Table 186

		SN 1	SN ◇1	SN ◇1 Bus	SN	SN	SN	SW 1	SW 1	SW ◇1 Bus	SN	SN	SN	SN ◇1 Bus	SN 1	SN ◇1	SW 1	SW ◇1 Bus	SN ◇1 A Bus	SN	SN 1	SN	SN 1
Eastleigh	d							19 51									20 00						
Southampton Airport Parkway	d									19 39							20 05	20 14					
Southampton Central	d								19 44	19a46						20 11	20a16	20a22					20 33
Swanwick	d								20 11							20 28							20 50
Fareham	d							20 09	20 18							20 35							20 57
Portchester	d								20 23							20 40							
Cosham	d								20 28							20 44							21 06
Portsmouth Harbour	d																				20 40		
Portsmouth & Southsea	d						19 59					20 32									20 44		
Fratton	d						20 04					20 36									20 48		
Hilsea	d						20 08		20a33														
Bedhampton	d						20 14																
Havant	d						20 17	20a21				20 45				20 51					20 57		21 12
Warblington	d						20 19														20 59		
Emsworth	d						20 22					20 49				20 55					21 02		21 16
Southbourne	d						20 25					20 52				20 58					21 05		
Nutbourne	d						20 27														21 07		
Bosham	d						20 31														21 11		
Fishbourne (Sussex)	d						20 34														21 14		
Chichester 4	a						20 37					20 59				21 05					21 17		21 24
	d						20 38					20 59				21 07					21 18		21 25
Bognor Regis 4	d		20 33										21 04										
Barnham	a		20 39				20 45					21 07	21 10			21 14					21 25		21 32
	d		20 40	20 43			20 46				20 52	21 07	21 11	21 12		21 15				21 22	21 26		21 33
Bognor Regis	a			20 49							20 59			21 18						21 28			
Ford 4	d		20 44				20 50						21 15			21 19					21 30		21 37
Littlehampton 4	a						20 55						21 20								21 35		
	d					20 52													21 15				
Angmering 3	d		20 53			21 00						21 16							21 23				21 43
Goring-by-Sea	d		20 57			21 04													21 27				21 47
Durrington-on-Sea	d		21 00			21 07													21 30				21 50
West Worthing	d		21 02			21 09													21 32				21 52
Worthing 4	a		21 04			21 11						21 23							21 34				21 54
	d		21 05			21 12						21 24							21 35				21 55
East Worthing	d					21 14						21 26											21 57
Lancing	d		21 09			21 17						21 29							21 39				22 00
Shoreham-by-Sea	d		21 13			21 22						21 33							21 43				22 04
Southwick	d					21 25						21 36											22 07
Fishersgate	d					21 27						21 38											22 09
Portslade	d		21 18			21 29						21 40							21 48				22 11
Aldrington	d					21 31						21 43											22 14
Hove 2	a		21 21			21 33						21 45							21 51				22 16
	d		21 22		21 24	21 34						21 45							21 52			21 54	22 16
Brighton 10	a				21 28	21 38						21 49										21 58	22 21
Preston Park	d																						
Burgess Hill	a		21 32																22 03				
Haywards Heath 3	a		21 38																22 10				
Arundel	d															21 24							
Amberley	d															21 29							
Pulborough	d															21 35							
Billingshurst	d															21 41							
Christs Hospital	d															21 48							
Horsham 4	a															21 52							
	d	21 02													21 32	21 52							
Crawley	d	21 14													21 45	22 01							
Three Bridges 4	a	21 18	21 47												21 48	22 05							
Gatwick Airport 10 ✈	a	21 22	21 51												21 55	22 10			22 25				
	d	21 23	21 53												21 56	22 11			22 26				
Horley	a	21 26													21 59								
Redhill 5	a	21 36													22 05	22 18							
East Croydon	a	21 54	22 08												22 24	22 30			22 41				
London Bridge 4 ⊖	a																						
Clapham Junction 10	a	22 07	22 18												22 37	22 40			22 50				
London Victoria 15 ⊖	a	22 14	22 26												22 44	22 50			22 57				

A Bus from Haywards Heath

Southampton, Portsmouth and Sussex Coast - Brighton, Gatwick Airport and London

Network Diagram - see first Page of Table 186

		SW	SW	SN	SN	SN	SN	SN	SN	SN	SW	SW	SW	SN	SN	SN	SN	SW	SN	SN	SN	SN
		1	1	◇1 🍴			1			1	1	◇1 🍴	1		◇1		1	◇1 🍴	1			1
Eastleigh	d	20 21	20 30										21 00									
Southampton Airport Parkway	d	20 25										20 42	21 05					21 15				
Southampton Central	d	20a35									20 44	20a49	21a12				21 13	21a24				21 33
Swanwick	d										21 11						21 33					21 51
Fareham	d		20 49								21 18						21 40					21 58
Portchester	d		20 54								21 23						21 45					22 03
Cosham	d		20 59								21 28						21 49					22 07
Portsmouth Harbour	d																		21 40			
Portsmouth & Southsea	d									21 15									21 44			
Fratton	d									21 19									21 48			
Hilsea	d		21a03							21 23	21a33								21 52			
Bedhampton	d									21 28									21 57			
Havant	d									21 31							21 56		22 00			22 14
Warblington	d									21 33												22 16
Emsworth	d									21 36												22 19
Southbourne	d									21 39												22 22
Nutbourne	d									21 41												22 24
Bosham	d									21 45												22 28
Fishbourne (Sussex)	d									21 48												22 31
Chichester 4	a									21 51							22 06		22 10			22 34
	d									21 52							22 07		22 11			22 34
Bognor Regis 4	d				21 39									22 00							22 30	
Barnham	a				21 45					21 59				22 06			22 14		22 18		22 36	22 42
	d			21 42		21 52				22 00					22 12		22 15		22 19	22 22	22 37	
Bognor Regis	a			21 48		21 59									22 18					22 29		
Ford 4	d									22 04							22 19		22 23		22 41	
Littlehampton 4	a																22 24				22 46	
	d								21 52								22 33					
Angmering 3	d								22 00	22 11							22 41					
Goring-by-Sea	d								22 04	22 15							22 45					
Durrington-on-Sea	d								22 07	22 18							22 47					
West Worthing	d								22 09	22 20							22 49					
Worthing 4	a								22 11	22 22							22 52					
	d								22 12	22 23							22 52					
East Worthing	d								22 14	22 25							22 55					
Lancing	d								22 17	22 28							22 58					
Shoreham-by-Sea	d								22 22	22 32							23 02					
Southwick	d								22 25	22 35							23 05					
Fishersgate	d								22 27	22 37							23 07					
Portslade	d								22 29	22 39							23 09					
Aldrington	d								22 31	22 42							23 11					
Hove 2	a								22 33	22 44							23 13					
	d							22 24	22 34	22 44						22 54	23 14					
Brighton 10	a							22 28	22 38	22 48						22 58	23 18					
Preston Park	d																					
Burgess Hill	a																					
Haywards Heath 3	a																					
Arundel	d																		22 28			
Amberley	d																					
Pulborough	d																		22 37			
Billingshurst	d																		22 43			
Christs Hospital	d																		22 50			
Horsham 4	a																		22 54			
	d						22 02												22 55			
Crawley	d						22 14												23 03			
Three Bridges 4	a						22 18												23 07			
Gatwick Airport 10 ✈	a						22 23															
	d						22 24															
Horley	a						22 27															
Redhill 5	a						22 37															
East Croydon	a						22 55															
London Bridge 4 ⊖	a																					
Clapham Junction 10	a						23 06															
London Victoria 15 ⊖	a						23 15															

Southampton, Portsmouth and Sussex Coast - Brighton, Gatwick Airport and London

Network Diagram - see first Page of Table 186

		SW	SW	SN	SN	SN	SN	SN	SW	SW	SN	SN	SW	GW	SW	SN	SN	SN	SN	SW	GW
		1	1	1	1				1	◇1 🍴	◇1	1	1		◇1 🍴				1	1	◇
Eastleigh	d	21 21	21 30										22 03	22 11	22 18					22 22	22 24
Southampton Airport Parkway	d	21 24								21 42			22 08		22 22					22 26	
Southampton Central	d	21a35							21 44	21a49		22 13	22a18	22a21	22a29				22 33	22a36	
Swanwick	d								22 11			22 30							22 50		
Fareham	d		21 48						22 18			22 37							22 57		22 42
Portchester	d		21 53						22 23			22 42									
Cosham	d		21 58						22 28			22 47							23 05		
Portsmouth Harbour	d							22 15										22 44			
Portsmouth & Southsea	d							22 19										22 48			
Fratton	d							22 23										22 52			22a56
Hilsea	d		22a03					22 27	22a33									22 56			
Bedhampton	d							22 32										23 01			
Havant	d							22 35				22 57						23 05	23 12		
Warblington	d																				
Emsworth	d							22 39				23 01									
Southbourne	d							22 42				23 04									
Nutbourne	d																				
Bosham	d																				
Fishbourne (Sussex)	d																				
Chichester 4	a							22 49				23 11						23 16	23 22		
	d				22 40			22 52				23 12						23 17	23 23		
Bognor Regis 4	d															23 15					
Barnham	a				22 47			22 59				23 19				23 21		23 24	23 30		
	d				22 48	22 52		23 00			23 06	23 20						23 25	23 31		
Bognor Regis	a					22 59					23 12										
Ford 4	d				22 52			23 04										23 29			
Littlehampton 4	a											23 31						23 34	23 42		
	d																	23 39			
Angmering 3	d							23 11										23 47			
Goring-by-Sea	d							23 15										23 51			
Durrington-on-Sea	d							23 17										23 53			
West Worthing	d							23 19										23 55			
Worthing 4	a							23 22										23 58			
	d							23 22										23 59			
East Worthing	d							23 25										00 01			
Lancing	d							23 28										00 04			
Shoreham-by-Sea	d							23 32										00 08			
Southwick	d							23 35										00 11			
Fishersgate	d							23 37										00 13			
Portslade	d							23 39										00 15			
Aldrington	d							23 41										00 18			
Hove 2	a							23 43										00 21			
	d						23 24	23 44									23 54	00 21			
Brighton 10	a						23 28	23 48									23 58	00 25			
Preston Park	d																				
Burgess Hill	a																				
Haywards Heath 3	a																				
Arundel	d				22 57																
Amberley	d				23 02																
Pulborough	d				23 08																
Billingshurst	d				23 14																
Christs Hospital	d				23 21																
Horsham 4	a				23 25																
	d			23 02	23 25																
Crawley	d			23 14	23 38																
Three Bridges 4	a			23 18	23 42																
Gatwick Airport 10 ✈	a			23 22																	
	d			23 23																	
Horley	a			23 26																	
Redhill 5	a			23 36																	
East Croydon	a			23 54																	
London Bridge 4 ⊖	a																				
Clapham Junction 10	a			00 11																	
London Victoria 15 ⊖	a			00 18																	

Southampton, Portsmouth and Sussex Coast - Brighton, Gatwick Airport and London

Network Diagram - see first Page of Table 186

		SW ■1	SN	SN ◇	SN	SW ■1	SW ◇■1 ⌘	SW ■1	SW ◇■1 ⌘	SW ■1	SW ■1	SW ◇■1 ⌘
Eastleigh	d	22 51						23 03	23 18	23 22	23 30	
Southampton Airport Parkway	d						22 42	23 08	23 22	23 26		23 42
Southampton Central	d					22 44	22a49	23a17	23a29	23a36		23a49
Swanwick	d					23 11						
Fareham	d	23 10				23 18					23 49	
Portchester	d	23 15				23 23					23 54	
Cosham	d	23 20				23 28					23 59	
Portsmouth Harbour	d				23 15							
Portsmouth & Southsea	d				23 19							
Fratton	d				23 23							
Hilsea	d	23a24			23 27	23a33					00a03	
Bedhampton	d				23 33							
Havant	d				23 36							
Warblington	d				23 38							
Emsworth	d				23 41							
Southbourne	d				23 44							
Nutbourne	d				23 47							
Bosham	d				23 50							
Fishbourne (Sussex)	d				23 53							
Chichester ■4	a				23 57							
	d			23 52	23 57							
Bognor Regis ■4	d											
Barnham	a			23 59	00 05							
	d		23 36	00 01	00 06							
Bognor Regis	a		23 43									
Ford ■4	d			00 05	00 10							
Littlehampton ■4	a			00 10	00 15							
	d											
Angmering ■3	d											
Goring-by-Sea	d											
Durrington-on-Sea	d											
West Worthing	d											
Worthing ■4	a											
	d											
East Worthing	d											
Lancing	d											
Shoreham-by-Sea	d											
Southwick	d											
Fishersgate	d											
Portslade	d											
Aldrington	d											
Hove ■2	a											
	d											
Brighton ■10	a											
Preston Park	d											
Burgess Hill	a											
Haywards Heath ■3	a											
Arundel	d											
Amberley	d											
Pulborough	d											
Billingshurst	d											
Christs Hospital	d											
Horsham ■4	a											
	d											
Crawley	d											
Three Bridges ■4	a											
Gatwick Airport ■10	a											
	d											
Horley	a											
Redhill ■5	a											
East Croydon	a											
London Bridge ■4	a											
Clapham Junction ■10	a											
London Victoria ■15	a											

Southampton, Portsmouth and Sussex Coast - Brighton, Gatwick Airport and London

Network Diagram - see first Page of Table 186

		SN	SN ■1	SN ◇	SN	SW ■1	SN ◇■1	SW ◇■1	SW ■1	SW ■1	SW ■1	SN ■1	SN ■1	SN ◇■1	SN	SN	SN ■1	SN ◇■1	SN	SN	SN	SN ■1	SN ◇■1
Eastleigh	d					00 02		00 23	01 00	01 22													
Southampton Airport Parkway	d					00 06		00 28	01 05	01 26	02s39												
Southampton Central	d					00a13		00a37	01a12	01a35	02a49												
Swanwick	d																						
Fareham	d																						
Portchester	d																						
Cosham	d																						
Portsmouth Harbour	d	22p44			23p15																		
Portsmouth & Southsea	d	22p48			23p19									04 56									
Fratton	d	22p52			23p23									05 00									
Hilsea	d	22p56			23p27																		
Bedhampton	d	23p01			23p33																		
Havant	d	23p05			23p36									05 08									05 52
Warblington	d				23p38																		
Emsworth	d				23p41																		05 56
Southbourne	d				23p44																		05 59
Nutbourne	d				23p47																		
Bosham	d				23p50																		
Fishbourne (Sussex)	d				23p53																		
Chichester ■4	a	23p16			23p57									05 19									06 06
	d	23p17		23p52	23p57									05 19									06 06
Bognor Regis ■4	d														05 13					05 43	06 04		
Barnham	a	23p24		23p59	00 05									05 27	05 19					05 49	06 10		06 14
	d	23p25		00 01	00 06		00 09					04 48		05 27	05 31					05 50			06 14
Bognor Regis	a						00 15																
Ford ■4	d	23p29		00 05	00 10							04 52			05 35					05 54			06 19
Littlehampton ■4	a	23p34		00 10	00 15							04 57			05 40								
	d	23p39										05 02						05 45					
Angmering ■3	d	23p47										05 10						05 53		06 00			
Goring-by-Sea	d	23p51										05 14						05 57		06 04			
Durrington-on-Sea	d	23p53										05 17						06 00		06 07			
West Worthing	d	23p55										05 19						06 02		06 09			
Worthing ■4	a	23p58										05 21		05 41				06 04		06 11			
	d	23p59										05 22		05 42				06 05		06 12			
East Worthing	d	00 01										05 24								06 14			
Lancing	d	00 04										05 27						06 09		06 17			
Shoreham-by-Sea	d	00 08										05 32		05 48				06 13		06 22			
Southwick	d	00 11										05 35								06 25			
Fishersgate	d	00 13										05 37								06 27			
Portslade	d	00 15										05 39						06 17		06 29			
Aldrington	d	00 18										05 41								06 31			
Hove ■2	a	00 21										05 43		05 54				06 21		06 33			
	d	00 21										05 44		05 54		05 56		06 21	06 24	06 34			
Brighton ■10	a	00 25										05 48				06 00			06 28	06 38			
Preston Park	d																						
Burgess Hill	a																						
Haywards Heath ■3	a													06 08				06 35					
Arundel	d																						06 23
Amberley	d																						06 28
Pulborough	d																						06 34
Billingshurst	d																						06 41
Christs Hospital	d																						06 47
Horsham ■4	a																						06 51
	d		23p02										05 30				06 00					06 30	06 52
Crawley	d		23p14										05 43				06 13					06 43	07 01
Three Bridges ■4	a		23p18										05 46	06 20			06 16	06 48				06 46	07 04
Gatwick Airport ■10	a		23p22										05 52	06 25			06 22	06 53				06 52	07 09
	d		23p23										05 53	06 26			06 23	06 55				06 53	07 10
Horley	a		23p26										05 56				06 26					06 56	
Redhill ■5	a		23p36										06 06				06 36					07 02	07 17
East Croydon	a		23p54										06 24	06 40			06 54	07 09				07 24	07 29
London Bridge ■4	a												06 43				07 13					07 43	
Clapham Junction ■10	a		00 11											06 50				07 19					07 39
London Victoria ■15	a		00 18											06 57				07 27					07 46

Southampton, Portsmouth and Sussex Coast - Brighton, Gatwick Airport and London

Network Diagram - see first Page of Table 186

		SN ◇1	SN	SN	SN	SN	SN ◇1	SN 1	SN	SW 1	SN	SN ◇1	SN ◇1	SN ◇1	SN	SN	SN	SN 1	SN	SN 1	SN	SN ◇1	SN ◇1
Eastleigh	d																						
Southampton Airport Parkway	d																						
Southampton Central	d									05 44													06 13
Swanwick	d									06 11													06 33
Fareham	d									06 18													06 40
Portchester	d									06 23													06 45
Cosham	d									06 28													06 49
Portsmouth Harbour	d												06 12							06 29			
Portsmouth & Southsea	d								05 59				06 16							06 33			
Fratton	d								06 04				06 20							06 37			
Hilsea	d								06 08	06a33													
Bedhampton	d								06 13														
Havant	d								06 16				06 30							06 46			06 56
Warblington	d								06 18														
Emsworth	d								06 21											06 50			07 00
Southbourne	d								06 24											06 53			07 03
Nutbourne	d								06 26														
Bosham	d								06 30														
Fishbourne (Sussex)	d								06 33														
Chichester 4	a								06 36				06 40							07 00			07 10
	d						06 25		06 37				06 41							07 00			07 11
Bognor Regis 4	d		06 13								06 39	06 30									07 07	06 56	
Barnham	a		06 19				06 32		06 44		06 45	06 36	06 48							07 08	07 13	07 02	07 18
	d		06 20	06 22			06 33		06 45			06 37	06 49		06 52				07 05	07 08	07 15	07 03	07 19
Bognor Regis	a			06 29											06 59				07 12				
Ford 4	d		06 24				06 37		06 49			06 41									07 19	07 07	
Littlehampton 4	a		06 29						06 54												07 24		
	d	06 15												06 45									
Angmering 3	d	06 23					06 43							06 55						07 17			
Goring-by-Sea	d	06 27					06 47							06 59									
Durrington-on-Sea	d	06 30					06 50							07 02									
West Worthing	d	06 32				06 39	06 52							07 04			07 09						
Worthing 4	a	06 34				06 41	06 54							07 06			07 11			07 24			
	d	06 35				06 42	06 56							07 07			07 12			07 26			
East Worthing	d					06 44											07 14						
Lancing	d	06 39				06 47	07 00							07 11			07 17			07 30			
Shoreham-by-Sea	d	06 43				06 52	07 04							07 15			07 22			07 34			
Southwick	d					06 55	07 07										07 25			07 37			
Fishersgate	d					06 57											07 27						
Portslade	d	06 47				06 59	07 10										07 29			07 40			
Aldrington	d					07 01											07 31						
Hove 2	a	06 51				07 03	07 13							07 21			07 33			07 43			
	d	06 51			06 54	07 04	07 14							07 22		07 24	07 34			07 44			
Brighton 10	a				06 58	07 08	07 18									07 28	07 38			07 48			
Preston Park	d	06 55																					
Burgess Hill	a	07 04																					
Haywards Heath 3	a	07 09												07 35									
Arundel	d											06 46										07 12	
Amberley	d																					07 17	
Pulborough	d											06 55										07 23	
Billingshurst	d											07 01										07 29	
Christs Hospital	d																					07 36	
Horsham 4	a											07 10	07 16									07 40	07 46
	d							07 00					07 20					07 30					07 50
Crawley	d							07 13					07 29					07 43					07 59
Three Bridges 4	a							07 16					07 32					07 46					08 02
Gatwick Airport 10 ✈	a	07 25						07 22					07 37	07 55				07 52					08 07
	d	07 26						07 23					07 38	07 56				07 53					08 08
Horley	a							07 26					07 41					07 56					
Redhill 5	a							07 36					07 47					08 02					08 15
East Croydon	a	07 41						07 54					07 59	08 11				08 24					08 27
London Bridge 4 ⊖	a							08 13										08 43					
Clapham Junction 10	a	07 51											08 09	08 21									08 37
London Victoria 15 ⊖	a	07 58											08 16	08 28									08 44

Table 188 Saturdays

Southampton, Portsmouth and Sussex Coast - Brighton, Gatwick Airport and London

Network Diagram - see first Page of Table 186

		SW 1	SN ◇1	SN	SN	SN	GW	SN 1	SN 1	SN	SW 1	SW ◇1	SN	SN ◇1	SN ◇1	SN ◇1	SN	SN	SN	SN 1	SN	SN
Eastleigh	d	06 13										06 51										
Southampton Airport Parkway	d	06 17										06 56										
Southampton Central	d	06a28						06 33			06 44	07a03										
Swanwick	d							06 50			07 11											
Fareham	d							06 56			07 18											
Portchester	d										07 23											
Cosham	d							07 05			07 28											
Portsmouth Harbour	d						06 48								07 12						07 29	
Portsmouth & Southsea	d						06 54			06 56					07 16						07 33	
Fratton	d						06 58			07 01					07 20						07 37	
Hilsea	d									07 05	07a33											
Bedhampton	d									07 13												
Havant	d						07 08	07 11		07 16					07 30						07 46	
Warblington	d									07 18												
Emsworth	d							07 15		07 21											07 50	
Southbourne	d									07 24											07 53	
Nutbourne	d									07 26												
Bosham	d									07 30												
Fishbourne (Sussex)	d									07 33												
Chichester 4	a						07 19	07 23		07 36					07 40						08 00	
	d						07 20	07 25		07 37					07 41						08 00	
Bognor Regis 4	d												07 39	07 30								08 07
Barnham	a						07 27	07 32		07 44			07 45	07 36	07 48						08 08	08 13
	d			07 22			07 28	07 33		07 45				07 37	07 49		07 52				08 08	08 15
Bognor Regis	a			07 29													07 59					
Ford 4	d							07 37		07 49				07 41								08 19
Littlehampton 4	a									07 54												08 24
	d		07 15													07 45						
Angmering 3	d		07 23					07 43								07 53					08 17	
Goring-by-Sea	d		07 27					07 47								07 57						
Durrington-on-Sea	d		07 30					07 50								08 00						
West Worthing	d		07 32			07 39		07 52								08 02			08 09			
Worthing 4	a		07 34			07 41	07 45	07 54								08 04			08 11		08 24	
	d		07 36			07 42	07 50	07 56								08 06			08 12		08 26	
East Worthing	d					07 44													08 14			
Lancing	d					07 47		08 00								08 10			08 17		08 30	
Shoreham-by-Sea	d		07 42			07 52	07 57	08 04								08 14			08 22		08 34	
Southwick	d					07 55		08 07											08 25		08 37	
Fishersgate	d					07 57													08 27			
Portslade	d		07 47			07 59		08 10											08 29		08 40	
Aldrington	d					08 01													08 31			
Hove 2	a		07 50			08 03	08 07	08 13								08 20			08 33		08 43	
	d		07 51		07 54	08 04	08 08	08 14								08 21		08 24	08 34		08 44	
Brighton 10	a				07 58	08 08	08 15	08 18										08 28	08 38		08 48	
Preston Park	d		07 55																			
Burgess Hill	a		08 03																			
Haywards Heath 3	a		08 09													08 35						
Arundel	d													07 46								
Amberley	d																					
Pulborough	d													07 55								
Billingshurst	d													08 01								
Christs Hospital	d																					
Horsham 4	a													08 10	08 16							
	d								08 00						08 20					08 30		
Crawley	d								08 13						08 29					08 43		
Three Bridges 4	a								08 16						08 32					08 46		
Gatwick Airport 10 ✈	a		08 24						08 22						08 37	08 55				08 52		
	d		08 25						08 23						08 38	08 56				08 53		
Horley	a								08 26						08 41					08 56		
Redhill 5	a								08 36						08 47					09 02		
East Croydon	a		08 40						08 54						08 59	09 11				09 24		
London Bridge 4 ⊖	a								09 13											09 43		
Clapham Junction 10	a		08 50												09 09	09 21						
London Victoria 15 ⊖	a		08 57												09 16	09 28						

Southampton, Portsmouth and Sussex Coast - Brighton, Gatwick Airport and London

Network Diagram - see first Page of Table 186

		SN	SN	SN	SN	SN	SN	SN			SW	SW	SN	SN	SW	SW	SN	SN	SN		SN	SN	SN	SN	SN
		◇1	◇1	1	◇1						1	1	1		1	◇1		◇1	◇1		◇1				1
		✠	A ✠																						
Eastleigh	d			07 14							07 21	07 30				07 43									
Southampton Airport Parkway	d			07 18							07 25					07 48									
Southampton Central	d		07 13	07 33							07a35				07 44	07a56									
Swanwick	d		07 33	07 50											08 11										
Fareham	d		07 40	07 56								07 49			08 18										
Portchester	d		07 45									07 54			08 23										
Cosham	d		07 49	08 05								07 59			08 28										
Portsmouth Harbour	d																		08 12						
Portsmouth & Southsea	d													07 59					08 16						
Fratton	d													08 04					08 20						
Hilsea	d											08a03		08 08	08a33										
Bedhampton	d													08 13											
Havant	d		07 56	08 11										08 16					08 30						
Warblington	d													08 18											
Emsworth	d		08 00	08 15										08 21											
Southbourne	d		08 03											08 24											
Nutbourne	d													08 27											
Bosham	d													08 30											
Fishbourne (Sussex)	d													08 33											
Chichester 4	a		08 10	08 23										08 36					08 40						
	d		08 11	08 25										08 37					08 41						
Bognor Regis 4	d	07 56															08 39	08 30							
Barnham	a	08 02	08 18	08 32										08 44			08 45	08 36	08 48						
	d	08 03	08 19	08 33		08 22								08 45				08 37	08 49			08 52			
Bognor Regis	a					08 29																08 59			
Ford 4	d	08 07		08 37										08 49				08 41							
Littlehampton 4	a													08 54											
	d				08 15																08 45				
Angmering 3	d			08 43	08 23																08 53				
Goring-by-Sea	d			08 47	08 27																08 57				
Durrington-on-Sea	d			08 50	08 30																09 00				
West Worthing	d			08 52	08 32			08 39													09 02			09 09	
Worthing 4	a			08 54	08 34			08 41													09 04			09 11	
	d			08 56	08 36			08 42													09 06			09 12	
East Worthing	d							08 44																09 14	
Lancing	d			09 00				08 47													09 10			09 17	
Shoreham-by-Sea	d			09 04	08 42			08 52													09 14			09 22	
Southwick	d			09 07				08 55																09 25	
Fishersgate	d							08 57																09 27	
Portslade	d			09 10	08 47			08 59																09 29	
Aldrington	d							09 01																09 31	
Hove 2	a			09 13	08 50			09 03													09 20			09 33	
	d			09 14	08 51		08 54	09 04													09 21		09 24	09 34	
Brighton 10	a			09 18			08 58	09 08															09 28	09 38	
Preston Park	d				08 55																				
Burgess Hill	a				09 03																				
Haywards Heath 3	a				09 09																09 35				
Arundel	d	08 12																08 46							
Amberley	d	08 17																							
Pulborough	d	08 23																08 55							
Billingshurst	d	08 29																09 01							
Christs Hospital	d	08 36																							
Horsham 4	a	08 40	08 46															09 10	09 16						
	d		08 50										09 00						09 20						09 30
Crawley	d		08 59										09 13						09 29						09 43
Three Bridges 4	a		09 02										09 16						09 32						09 46
Gatwick Airport 10 ✈	a		09 07		09 24								09 22						09 37		09 55				09 52
	d		09 08		09 25								09 23						09 38		09 56				09 53
Horley	a												09 26						09 41						09 56
Redhill 5	a		09 15										09 36						09 47						10 02
East Croydon	a		09 27		09 40								09 54						09 59		10 11				10 24
London Bridge 4 ⊖	a												10 13												10 43
Clapham Junction 10	a		09 37		09 50														10 09		10 21				
London Victoria 15 ⊖	a		09 44		09 57														10 16		10 28				

A ✠ from Horsham

Southampton, Portsmouth and Sussex Coast - Brighton, Gatwick Airport and London

Network Diagram - see first Page of Table 186

		SN	SN	SN	SN	SN		SN	SN	SN	SN	SN		SW	SW			SN	SN	SN	SW	SW	SW	SN	
			◇1		◇1	◇1		1	◇1					1	1			1	◇1		1	◇1	1		
					✠	A ✠																			
Eastleigh	d							08 14						08 21	08 31							08 47	09 00		
Southampton Airport Parkway	d							08 18						08 25								08 51	09 05		
Southampton Central	d					08 13		08 33						08a35							08 44	08a58	09a12		
Swanwick	d					08 33		08 50													09 11				
Fareham	d					08 40		08 56							08 49						09 18				
Portchester	d					08 45									08 54						09 23				
Cosham	d					08 49		09 05							08 59						09 28				
Portsmouth Harbour	d	08 29																							
Portsmouth & Southsea	d	08 33																		08 59					
Fratton	d	08 37																		09 04					
Hilsea	d														09a04					09 08	09a33				
Bedhampton	d																			09 13					
Havant	d	08 46				08 56		09 11												09 16					
Warblington	d																			09 18					
Emsworth	d	08 50				09 00		09 15												09 21					
Southbourne	d	08 53				09 03														09 24					
Nutbourne	d																			09 26					
Bosham	d																			09 30					
Fishbourne (Sussex)	d																			09 33					
Chichester 4	a	09 00				09 10		09 23												09 36					
	d	09 00				09 11		09 25												09 37					
Bognor Regis 4	d			09 07	08 56																			09 39	
Barnham	a	09 08		09 13	09 02	09 18		09 32												09 44				09 45	
	d	09 08	09 12	09 15	09 03	09 19		09 33		09 22									09 38	09 45					
Bognor Regis	a		09 18							09 29									09 45						
Ford 4	d			09 19	09 07			09 37												09 49					
Littlehampton 4	a			09 24																09 54					
	d								09 15																
Angmering 3	d	09 17						09 43	09 23																
Goring-by-Sea	d							09 47	09 27																
Durrington-on-Sea	d							09 50	09 30																
West Worthing	d							09 52	09 32			09 39													
Worthing 4	a	09 24						09 54	09 34			09 41													
	d	09 26						09 56	09 36			09 42													
East Worthing	d											09 44													
Lancing	d	09 30						10 00				09 47													
Shoreham-by-Sea	d	09 34						10 04	09 42			09 52													
Southwick	d	09 37						10 07				09 55													
Fishersgate	d											09 57													
Portslade	d	09 40						10 10	09 47			09 59													
Aldrington	d											10 01													
Hove 2	a	09 43						10 13	09 50			10 03													
	d	09 44						10 14	09 51		09 54	10 04													
Brighton 10	a	09 48						10 18			09 58	10 08													
Preston Park	d								09 55																
Burgess Hill	a								10 03																
Haywards Heath 3	a								10 09																
Arundel	d				09 12																				
Amberley	d				09 17																				
Pulborough	d				09 23																				
Billingshurst	d				09 29																				
Christs Hospital	d				09 36																				
Horsham 4	a				09 40	09 46																			
	d					09 50												10 00							
Crawley	d					09 59												10 13							
Three Bridges 4	a					10 02												10 16							
Gatwick Airport 10 ✈	a					10 07			10 24									10 22							
	d					10 08			10 25									10 23							
Horley	a																	10 26							
Redhill 5	a					10 15												10 36							
East Croydon	a					10 27			10 40									10 54							
London Bridge 4 ⊖	a																	11 13							
Clapham Junction 10	a					10 37			10 50																
London Victoria 15 ⊖	a					10 44			10 57																

A ✠ from Horsham

Table 188

Saturdays

Southampton, Portsmouth and Sussex Coast - Brighton, Gatwick Airport and London

Network Diagram - see first Page of Table 186

		SN	SN	SN	SN	SN	SN	SN	SN	SN	SN	SN	SN	SW	SN	SN	SN	SN	SN	SW	SW
		◇1	◇1	◇1				1		◇1		◇1 ✠	◇1 A ✠	◇1	◇1				1	1	1
Eastleigh	d																			09 21	09 28
Southampton Airport Parkway	d													09 14						09 25	
Southampton Central ⛴	d												09 13	09a22					09 33	09a35	
Swanwick	d												09 33						09 50		
Fareham	d												09 40						09 56		09 48
Portchester	d												09 45								09 53
Cosham	d												09 49						10 05		09 58
Portsmouth Harbour ⛴	d		09 12						09 29												
Portsmouth & Southsea	d		09 16						09 33												
Fratton	d		09 20						09 37												
Hilsea	d																				10a03
Bedhampton	d																				
Havant	d		09 30						09 46				09 56						10 11		
Warblington	d																				
Emsworth	d								09 50				10 00						10 15		
Southbourne	d								09 53				10 03								
Nutbourne	d																				
Bosham	d																				
Fishbourne (Sussex)	d																				
Chichester 4	a		09 40						10 00				10 10						10 23		
	d		09 41						10 00				10 11						10 25		
Bognor Regis 4	d	09 30									10 07	09 56									
Barnham	a	09 36	09 48						10 08		10 13	10 02	10 18						10 32		
	d	09 37	09 49		09 52				10 08	10 12	10 15	10 03	10 19			10 22			10 33		
Bognor Regis	a				09 59					10 18						10 29					
Ford 4	d	09 41									10 19	10 07							10 37		
Littlehampton 4	a										10 24										
	d			09 45											10 15						
Angmering 3	d			09 53					10 17						10 23				10 43		
Goring-by-Sea	d			09 57											10 27				10 47		
Durrington-on-Sea	d			10 00											10 30				10 50		
West Worthing	d			10 02			10 09								10 32			10 39	10 52		
Worthing 4	a			10 04			10 11		10 24						10 34			10 41	10 54		
	d			10 06			10 12		10 26						10 36			10 42	10 56		
East Worthing	d						10 14											10 44			
Lancing	d			10 10			10 17		10 30									10 47	11 00		
Shoreham-by-Sea	d			10 14			10 22		10 34						10 42			10 52	11 04		
Southwick	d						10 25		10 37									10 55	11 07		
Fishersgate	d						10 27											10 57			
Portslade	d						10 29		10 40						10 47			10 59	11 10		
Aldrington	d						10 31											11 01			
Hove 2	a			10 20			10 33		10 43						10 50			11 03	11 13		
	d			10 21		10 24	10 34		10 44						10 51		10 54	11 04	11 14		
Brighton 10	a					10 28	10 38		10 48								10 58	11 08	11 18		
Preston Park	d														10 55						
Burgess Hill	a														11 03						
Haywards Heath 3	a			10 35											11 09						
Arundel	d	09 46										10 12									
Amberley	d											10 17									
Pulborough	d	09 55										10 23									
Billingshurst	d	10 01										10 29									
Christs Hospital	d											10 36									
Horsham 4	a	10 10	10 16									10 40	10 46								
	d		10 20					10 30					10 50								
Crawley	d		10 29					10 43					10 59								
Three Bridges 4	a		10 32					10 46					11 02								
Gatwick Airport 10 ✈	a		10 37	10 55				10 52					11 07		11 24						
	d		10 38	10 56				10 53					11 08		11 25						
Horley	a		10 41					10 56													
Redhill 5	a		10 47					11 02					11 15								
East Croydon ⇌	a		10 59	11 11				11 24					11 27		11 40						
London Bridge 4 ⊖	a							11 43													
Clapham Junction 10	a		11 09	11 21									11 37		11 50						
London Victoria 15 ⊖	a		11 16	11 28									11 44		11 57						

A ✠ from Horsham

Table 188

Saturdays

Southampton, Portsmouth and Sussex Coast - Brighton, Gatwick Airport and London

Network Diagram - see first Page of Table 186

		SN	SN	SN	SW	SW	SW	SN	SN	SN	SN	SN	SN	SN	SN	SN	SN	SN	SN	SN	SW	SN
		1	◇1		1	◇1 ✠	1		◇1	◇1	◇1				1		◇1		◇1 ✠	◇1 A ✠	◇1 ✠	1
Eastleigh	d						10 00															10 14
Southampton Airport Parkway	d					09 42	10 05														10 14	10 18
Southampton Central ⛴	d				09 44	09a49	10a12													10 13	10a22	10 33
Swanwick	d				10 11															10 33		10 50
Fareham	d				10 18															10 40		10 56
Portchester	d				10 23															10 45		
Cosham	d				10 28															10 49		11 05
Portsmouth Harbour ⛴	d									10 12						10 29						
Portsmouth & Southsea	d			09 59						10 16						10 33						
Fratton	d			10 04						10 20						10 37						
Hilsea	d			10 08	10a33																	
Bedhampton	d			10 13																		
Havant	d			10 16						10 30						10 46				10 56		11 11
Warblington	d			10 18																		
Emsworth	d			10 21												10 50				11 00		11 15
Southbourne	d			10 24												10 53				11 03		
Nutbourne	d			10 26																		
Bosham	d			10 30																		
Fishbourne (Sussex)	d			10 33																		
Chichester 4	a			10 36						10 40						11 00				11 10		11 23
	d			10 37						10 41						11 00				11 11		11 25
Bognor Regis 4	d							10 39	10 30									11 07	10 56			
Barnham	a			10 44				10 45	10 36	10 48						11 08		11 13	11 02	11 18		11 32
	d		10 39	10 45					10 37	10 49		10 52				11 08	11 12	11 15	11 03	11 19		11 33
Bognor Regis	a		10 46									10 59					11 18					
Ford 4	d			10 49					10 41									11 19	11 07			11 37
Littlehampton 4	a			10 54														11 24				
	d										10 45											
Angmering 3	d										10 53					11 17						11 43
Goring-by-Sea	d										10 57											11 47
Durrington-on-Sea	d										11 00											11 50
West Worthing	d										11 02			11 09								11 52
Worthing 4	a										11 04			11 11		11 24						11 54
	d										11 06			11 12		11 26						11 56
East Worthing	d													11 14								
Lancing	d										11 10			11 17		11 30						12 00
Shoreham-by-Sea	d										11 14			11 22		11 34						12 04
Southwick	d													11 25		11 37						12 07
Fishersgate	d													11 27								
Portslade	d													11 29		11 40						12 10
Aldrington	d													11 31								
Hove 2	a										11 20			11 33		11 43						12 13
	d										11 21		11 24	11 34		11 44						12 14
Brighton 10	a												11 28	11 38		11 48						12 18
Preston Park	d																					
Burgess Hill	a																					
Haywards Heath 3	a										11 35											
Arundel	d								10 46										11 12			
Amberley	d																		11 17			
Pulborough	d								10 55										11 23			
Billingshurst	d								11 01										11 29			
Christs Hospital	d																		11 36			
Horsham 4	a								11 10	11 16									11 40	11 46		
	d	11 00								11 20					11 30					11 50		
Crawley	d	11 13								11 29					11 43					11 59		
Three Bridges 4	a	11 16								11 32					11 46					12 02		
Gatwick Airport 10 ✈	a	11 22								11 37	11 55				11 52					12 07		
	d	11 23								11 38	11 56				11 53					12 08		
Horley	a	11 26								11 41					11 56							
Redhill 5	a	11 36								11 47					12 02					12 15		
East Croydon ⇌	a	11 54								11 59	12 11				12 24					12 27		
London Bridge 4 ⊖	a	12 13													12 43							
Clapham Junction 10	a									12 09	12 21									12 37		
London Victoria 15 ⊖	a									12 16	12 28									12 44		

A ✠ from Horsham

Southampton, Portsmouth and Sussex Coast - Brighton, Gatwick Airport and London

Network Diagram - see first Page of Table 186

		SN ◇1	SN	SN	SN	SW 1	SW 1	SN 1	SN ◇1 ⊼	SN	SW 1	SW ◇1 ⊼	SW 1	SN	SN ◇1	SN ◇1	SN ◇1	SN	SN	SN	SN 1
Eastleigh	d					10 21	10 28						11 00								
Southampton Airport Parkway	d					10 25						10 42	11 05								
Southampton Central ⛴	d					10a35					10 44	10a49	11a12								
Swanwick	d										11 11										
Fareham	d						10 48				11 18										
Portchester	d						10 53				11 23										
Cosham	d						10 58				11 28										
Portsmouth Harbour ⛴	d															11 12					
Portsmouth & Southsea	d									10 59						11 16					
Fratton	d									11 04						11 20					
Hilsea	d						11a03			11 08	11a33										
Bedhampton	d									11 13											
Havant	d									11 16						11 30					
Warblington	d									11 18											
Emsworth	d									11 21											
Southbourne	d									11 24											
Nutbourne	d									11 26											
Bosham	d									11 30											
Fishbourne (Sussex)	d									11 33											
Chichester 4	a									11 36						11 40					
	d									11 37						11 41					
Bognor Regis 4	d													11 39	11 30						
Barnham	a									11 44				11 45	11 36	11 48					
	d		11 22						11 39	11 45					11 37	11 49		11 52			
Bognor Regis	a		11 29						11 46									11 59			
Ford 4	d									11 49					11 41						
Littlehampton 4	a									11 54											
	d	11 15															11 45				
Angmering 3	d	11 23															11 53				
Goring-by-Sea	d	11 27															11 57				
Durrington-on-Sea	d	11 30															12 00				
West Worthing	d	11 32			11 39												12 02			12 09	
Worthing 4	a	11 34			11 41												12 04			12 11	
	d	11 36			11 42												12 06			12 12	
East Worthing	d				11 44															12 14	
Lancing	d				11 47												12 10			12 17	
Shoreham-by-Sea	d	11 42			11 52												12 14			12 22	
Southwick	d				11 55															12 25	
Fishersgate	d				11 57															12 27	
Portslade	d	11 47			11 59															12 29	
Aldrington	d				12 01															12 31	
Hove 2	a	11 50			12 03												12 20			12 33	
	d	11 51		11 54	12 04												12 21		12 24	12 34	
Brighton 10	a			11 58	12 08														12 28	12 38	
Preston Park	d	11 55																			
Burgess Hill	a	12 03																			
Haywards Heath 3	a	12 09															12 35				
Arundel	d														11 46						
Amberley	d																				
Pulborough	d														11 55						
Billingshurst	d														12 01						
Christs Hospital	d																				
Horsham 4	a														12 10	12 16					
	d							12 00							12 20						12 30
Crawley	d							12 13							12 29						12 43
Three Bridges 4	a							12 16							12 32						12 46
Gatwick Airport 10 ✈	a	12 24						12 22							12 37		12 55				12 52
	d	12 25						12 23							12 38		12 56				12 53
Horley	a							12 26							12 41						12 56
Redhill 5	a							12 36							12 47						13 02
East Croydon 🚋	a	12 40						12 54							12 59		13 11				13 24
London Bridge 4 ⊖	a							13 13													13 43
Clapham Junction 10	a	12 50													13 09		13 21				
London Victoria 15 ⊖	a	12 57													13 16		13 28				

Southampton, Portsmouth and Sussex Coast - Brighton, Gatwick Airport and London

Network Diagram - see first Page of Table 186

		SN	SN ◇1	SN	SN ◇1 ⊼	SN ◇1 A ⊼	SW ◇1 ⊼	SN ◇1	SN	SN	SN	SN 1	SW 1	SW 1	SN 1	SN ◇1 ⊼	SN	SW 1	SW ◇1 ⊼	SW 1	SN
Eastleigh	d												11 21	11 28						12 00	
Southampton Airport Parkway	d						11 15						11 25						11 42	12 05	
Southampton Central ⛴	d					11 13	11a22					11 33	11a35					11 44	11a49	12a12	
Swanwick	d					11 33						11 50						12 11			
Fareham	d					11 40						11 56		11 48				12 18			
Portchester	d					11 45								11 53				12 23			
Cosham	d					11 49						12 05		11 58				12 28			
Portsmouth Harbour ⛴	d	11 29																			
Portsmouth & Southsea	d	11 33															11 59				
Fratton	d	11 37															12 04				
Hilsea	d													12a03			12 08	12a33			
Bedhampton	d																12 13				
Havant	d	11 46				11 56						12 11					12 16				
Warblington	d																12 18				
Emsworth	d	11 50				12 00						12 15					12 21				
Southbourne	d	11 53				12 03											12 24				
Nutbourne	d																12 26				
Bosham	d																12 30				
Fishbourne (Sussex)	d																12 33				
Chichester 4	a	12 00				12 10						12 23					12 36				
	d	12 00				12 11						12 25					12 37				
Bognor Regis 4	d			12 07	11 56																12 39
Barnham	a	12 08		12 13	12 02	12 18						12 32					12 44				12 45
	d	12 08	12 12	12 15	12 03	12 19			12 22			12 33				12 39	12 45				
Bognor Regis	a		12 18						12 29							12 46					
Ford 4	d			12 19	12 07							12 37					12 49				
Littlehampton 4	a			12 24													12 54				
	d							12 15													
Angmering 3	d	12 17						12 23				12 43									
Goring-by-Sea	d							12 27				12 47									
Durrington-on-Sea	d							12 30				12 50									
West Worthing	d							12 32			12 39	12 52									
Worthing 4	a	12 24						12 34			12 41	12 54									
	d	12 26						12 36			12 42	12 56									
East Worthing	d										12 44										
Lancing	d	12 30									12 47	13 00									
Shoreham-by-Sea	d	12 34						12 42			12 52	13 04									
Southwick	d	12 37									12 55	13 07									
Fishersgate	d										12 57										
Portslade	d	12 40						12 47			12 59	13 10									
Aldrington	d										13 01										
Hove 2	a	12 43						12 50			13 03	13 13									
	d	12 44						12 51		12 54	13 04	13 14									
Brighton 10	a	12 48								12 58	13 08	13 18									
Preston Park	d							12 55													
Burgess Hill	a							13 03													
Haywards Heath 3	a							13 09													
Arundel	d				12 12																
Amberley	d				12 17																
Pulborough	d				12 23																
Billingshurst	d				12 29																
Christs Hospital	d				12 36																
Horsham 4	a				12 40	12 46															
	d				12 50										13 00						
Crawley	d				12 59										13 13						
Three Bridges 4	a				13 02										13 16						
Gatwick Airport 10 ✈	a				13 07			13 24							13 22						
	d				13 08			13 25							13 23						
Horley	a														13 26						
Redhill 5	a				13 15										13 36						
East Croydon 🚋	a				13 27			13 40							13 54						
London Bridge 4 ⊖	a														14 13						
Clapham Junction 10	a				13 37			13 50													
London Victoria 15 ⊖	a				13 44			13 57													

A ⊼ from Horsham

Table 188

Saturdays

Southampton, Portsmouth and Sussex Coast - Brighton, Gatwick Airport and London

Network Diagram - see first Page of Table 186

		SN ◇1	SN ◇1	SN ◇1	SN	SN	SN	SN 1	SN	SN ◇1	SN	SN ◇1 ⊼	SN ◇1 A ⊼	SW ◇1 ⊼	SN 1	SN ◇1	SN	SN	SN	SW 1	SW 1
Eastleigh	d														12 14					12 21	12 28
Southampton Airport Parkway	d													12 14	12 19					12 25	
Southampton Central ⛴	d												12 13	12a22	12 33					12a35	
Swanwick	d												12 33		12 50						
Fareham	d												12 40		12 56						12 48
Portchester	d												12 45								12 53
Cosham	d												12 49		13 05						12 58
Portsmouth Harbour ⛴	d		12 12						12 29												
Portsmouth & Southsea	d		12 16						12 33												
Fratton	d		12 20						12 37												
Hilsea	d																				13a03
Bedhampton	d																				
Havant	d		12 30						12 46				12 56		13 11						
Warblington	d																				
Emsworth	d								12 50				13 00		13 15						
Southbourne	d								12 53				13 03								
Nutbourne	d																				
Bosham	d																				
Fishbourne (Sussex)	d																				
Chichester 4	a		12 40						13 00				13 10		13 23						
	d		12 41						13 00				13 11		13 25						
Bognor Regis 4	d	12 30									13 07	12 56									
Barnham	a	12 36	12 48						13 08		13 13	13 02	13 18		13 32						
	d	12 37	12 49		12 52				13 08	13 12	13 15	13 03	13 19		13 33		13 22				
Bognor Regis	a				12 59					13 18							13 29				
Ford 4	d	12 41									13 19	13 07			13 37						
Littlehampton 4	a										13 24										
	d			12 45												13 15					
Angmering 3	d			12 53					13 17						13 43	13 23					
Goring-by-Sea	d			12 57											13 47	13 27					
Durrington-on-Sea	d			13 00											13 50	13 30					
West Worthing	d			13 02			13 09								13 52	13 32			13 39		
Worthing 4	a			13 04			13 11		13 24						13 54	13 34			13 41		
	d			13 06			13 12		13 26						13 56	13 36			13 42		
East Worthing	d						13 14												13 44		
Lancing	d			13 10			13 17		13 30						14 00				13 47		
Shoreham-by-Sea	d			13 14			13 22		13 34						14 04	13 42			13 52		
Southwick	d						13 25		13 37						14 07				13 55		
Fishersgate	d						13 27												13 57		
Portslade	d						13 29		13 40						14 10	13 47			13 59		
Aldrington	d						13 31												14 01		
Hove 2	a			13 20			13 33		13 43						14 13	13 50			14 03		
	d			13 21		13 24	13 34		13 44						14 14	13 51		13 54	14 04		
Brighton 10	a					13 28	13 38		13 48						14 18			13 58	14 08		
Preston Park	d															13 55					
Burgess Hill	a															14 03					
Haywards Heath 3	a			13 35												14 09					
Arundel	d	12 46										13 12									
Amberley	d											13 17									
Pulborough	d	12 55										13 23									
Billingshurst	d	13 01										13 29									
Christs Hospital	d											13 36									
Horsham 4	a	13 10	13 16									13 40	13 46								
	d		13 20					13 30					13 50								
Crawley	d		13 29					13 43					13 59								
Three Bridges 4	a		13 32					13 46					14 02								
Gatwick Airport 10 ✈	a		13 37	13 55				13 52					14 07			14 24					
	d		13 38	13 56				13 53					14 08			14 25					
Horley	a		13 41					13 56													
Redhill 5	a		13 47					14 02					14 15								
East Croydon 🚋	a		13 59	14 11				14 24					14 27			14 40					
London Bridge 4 ⊖	a							14 43													
Clapham Junction 10	a		14 09	14 21									14 37			14 50					
London Victoria 15 ⊖	a		14 16	14 28									14 44			14 57					

A ⊼ from Horsham

Table 188

Saturdays

Southampton, Portsmouth and Sussex Coast - Brighton, Gatwick Airport and London

Network Diagram - see first Page of Table 186

		SN 1	SN ◇1 ⊼	SN	SW 1	SW ◇1 ⊼	SW 1	SN	SN ◇1	SN ◇1	SN ◇1	SN	SN	SN	SN 1	SN	SN ◇1	SN	SN ◇1 ⊼	SN ◇1 A ⊼	SW ◇1 ⊼
Eastleigh	d						13 00														
Southampton Airport Parkway	d					12 42	13 05														13 14
Southampton Central ⛴	d				12 44	12a49	13a12													13 13	13a22
Swanwick	d				13 11															13 33	
Fareham	d				13 18															13 40	
Portchester	d				13 23															13 45	
Cosham	d				13 28															13 49	
Portsmouth Harbour ⛴	d									13 12						13 29					
Portsmouth & Southsea	d			12 59						13 16						13 33					
Fratton	d			13 04						13 20						13 37					
Hilsea	d			13 08	13a33																
Bedhampton	d			13 13																	
Havant	d			13 16						13 30						13 46				13 56	
Warblington	d			13 18																	
Emsworth	d			13 21												13 50				14 00	
Southbourne	d			13 24												13 53				14 03	
Nutbourne	d			13 26																	
Bosham	d			13 30																	
Fishbourne (Sussex)	d			13 33																	
Chichester 4	a			13 36						13 40						14 00				14 10	
	d			13 37						13 41						14 00				14 11	
Bognor Regis 4	d							13 39	13 30									14 07	13 56		
Barnham	a			13 44				13 45	13 36	13 48						14 08		14 13	14 02	14 18	
	d		13 39	13 45					13 37	13 49		13 52				14 08	14 12	14 15	14 03	14 19	
Bognor Regis	a		13 46									13 59					14 18				
Ford 4	d			13 49					13 41									14 19	14 07		
Littlehampton 4	a			13 54														14 24			
	d										13 45										
Angmering 3	d										13 53					14 17					
Goring-by-Sea	d										13 57										
Durrington-on-Sea	d										14 00										
West Worthing	d										14 02			14 09							
Worthing 4	a										14 04			14 11		14 24					
	d										14 06			14 12		14 26					
East Worthing	d													14 14							
Lancing	d										14 10			14 17		14 30					
Shoreham-by-Sea	d										14 14			14 22		14 34					
Southwick	d													14 25		14 37					
Fishersgate	d													14 27							
Portslade	d													14 29		14 40					
Aldrington	d													14 31							
Hove 2	a										14 20			14 33		14 43					
	d										14 21		14 24	14 34		14 44					
Brighton 10	a												14 28	14 38		14 48					
Preston Park	d																				
Burgess Hill	a																				
Haywards Heath 3	a										14 35										
Arundel	d								13 46										14 12		
Amberley	d																		14 17		
Pulborough	d								13 55										14 23		
Billingshurst	d								14 01										14 29		
Christs Hospital	d																		14 36		
Horsham 4	a								14 10	14 16									14 40	14 46	
	d	14 00								14 20					14 30					14 50	
Crawley	d	14 13								14 29					14 43					14 59	
Three Bridges 4	a	14 16								14 32					14 46					15 02	
Gatwick Airport 10 ✈	a	14 22								14 37	14 55				14 52					15 07	
	d	14 23								14 38	14 56				14 53					15 08	
Horley	a	14 26								14 41					14 56						
Redhill 5	a	14 36								14 47					15 02					15 15	
East Croydon 🚋	a	14 54								14 59	15 11				15 24					15 27	
London Bridge 4 ⊖	a	15 13													15 43						
Clapham Junction 10	a									15 09	15 21									15 37	
London Victoria 15 ⊖	a									15 16	15 28									15 44	

A ⊼ from Horsham

Southampton, Portsmouth and Sussex Coast - Brighton, Gatwick Airport and London

Network Diagram - see first Page of Table 186

		SN	SN	SN	SN	SN	SW	SW			SN	SN	SN	SW	SW	SW	SN	SN	SN		SN	SN	SN	SN	SN
		◇■1				■1	■1	■1			■1	◇■1 ⌶		■1	◇■1 ⌶	■1		◇■1	◇■1		◇■1				■1
Eastleigh	d						13 21	13 28								14 00									
Southampton Airport Parkway	d						13 25								13 42	14 05									
Southampton Central	d					13 33	13a35							13 44	13a49	14a12									
Swanwick	d					13 50								14 11											
Fareham	d					13 56		13 48						14 18											
Portchester	d							13 53						14 23											
Cosham	d					14 05		13 58						14 28											
Portsmouth Harbour	d																		14 12						
Portsmouth & Southsea	d												13 59						14 16						
Fratton	d												14 04						14 20						
Hilsea	d							14a03					14 08	14a33											
Bedhampton	d												14 13												
Havant	d					14 11							14 16						14 30						
Warblington	d												14 18												
Emsworth	d					14 15							14 21												
Southbourne	d												14 24												
Nutbourne	d												14 26												
Bosham	d												14 30												
Fishbourne (Sussex)	d												14 33												
Chichester ■4	a					14 23							14 36						14 40						
	d					14 25							14 37						14 41						
Bognor Regis ■4	d																14 39	14 30							
Barnham	a					14 32							14 44				14 45	14 36	14 48						
	d		14 22			14 33						14 39	14 45					14 37	14 49			14 52			
Bognor Regis	a		14 29									14 46										14 59			
Ford ■4	d					14 37							14 49					14 41							
Littlehampton ■4	a												14 54												
	d	14 15																			14 45				
Angmering ■3	d	14 23				14 43															14 53				
Goring-by-Sea	d	14 27				14 47															14 57				
Durrington-on-Sea	d	14 30				14 50															15 00				
West Worthing	d	14 32			14 39	14 52															15 02			15 09	
Worthing ■4	a	14 34			14 41	14 54															15 04			15 11	
	d	14 36			14 42	14 56															15 06			15 12	
East Worthing	d				14 44																			15 14	
Lancing	d				14 47	15 00															15 10			15 17	
Shoreham-by-Sea	d	14 42			14 52	15 04															15 14			15 22	
Southwick	d				14 55	15 07																		15 25	
Fishersgate	d				14 57																			15 27	
Portslade	d	14 47			14 59	15 10																		15 29	
Aldrington	d				15 01																			15 31	
Hove ■2	a	14 50			15 03	15 13															15 20			15 33	
	d	14 51		14 54	15 04	15 14															15 21		15 24	15 34	
Brighton ■10	a			14 58	15 08	15 18																	15 28	15 38	
Preston Park	d	14 55																							
Burgess Hill	a	15 03																							
Haywards Heath ■3	a	15 09																			15 35				
Arundel	d																	14 46							
Amberley	d																								
Pulborough	d																	14 55							
Billingshurst	d																	15 01							
Christs Hospital	d																								
Horsham ■4	a																	15 10	15 16						
	d										15 00							15 20							15 30
Crawley	d										15 13							15 29							15 43
Three Bridges ■4	a										15 16							15 32							15 46
Gatwick Airport ■10 ✈	a	15 24									15 22							15 37			15 55				15 52
	d	15 25									15 23							15 38			15 56				15 53
Horley	a										15 26							15 41							15 56
Redhill ■5	a										15 36							15 47							16 02
East Croydon	a	15 40									15 54							15 59			16 11				16 24
London Bridge ■4 ⊖	a										16 13														16 43
Clapham Junction ■10	a	15 50																16 09			16 21				
London Victoria ■15 ⊖	a	15 57																16 16			16 28				

Table 188

Southampton, Portsmouth and Sussex Coast - Brighton, Gatwick Airport and London

Network Diagram - see first Page of Table 186

		SN	SN	SN	SN	SN		SW	SN	SN	SN	SN	GW	SW	SW			SN	SN	SN	SN	SW	SW	SW	SN
			◇■1		◇■1 ⌶	◇■1 A ⌶		◇■1 ⌶	◇■1				◇	■1	■1			■1 B	■1	◇■1 ⌶		■1	◇■1 ⌶	■1	
Eastleigh	d													14 21	14 28			14 41						15 00	
Southampton Airport Parkway	d							14 14						14 25				*14 34*					14 42	15 05	
Southampton Central	d					14 13		14a22					14 34	14a35				*14a26*				14 44	14a49	15a12	
Swanwick	d					14 33																15 11			
Fareham	d					14 40							14 55		14 48			15 00				15 18			
Portchester	d					14 45									14 53							15 23			
Cosham	d					14 49							15 03		14 58							15 28			
Portsmouth Harbour	d	14 29																							
Portsmouth & Southsea	d	14 33																			14 59				
Fratton	d	14 37																			15 04				
Hilsea	d														15a03						15 08	15a33			
Bedhampton	d																				15 14				
Havant	d	14 46				14 56							15 10					15 14			15 17				
Warblington	d																				15 19				
Emsworth	d	14 50				15 00															15 22				
Southbourne	d	14 53				15 03															15 25				
Nutbourne	d																				15 28				
Bosham	d																				15 31				
Fishbourne (Sussex)	d																				15 34				
Chichester ■4	a	15 00				15 10							15 21					15 25			15 37				
	d	15 00				15 11							15 21					15 25			15 38				
Bognor Regis ■4	d			15 07	14 56																				15 39
Barnham	a	15 08		15 13	15 02	15 18							15 29					15 33			15 45				15 45
	d	15 08	15 12	15 15	15 03	15 19				15 22			15 29					15 33		15 39	15 46				
Bognor Regis	a		15 18							15 29										15 46					
Ford ■4	d			15 19	15 07													15 38			15 50				
Littlehampton ■4	a			15 24																	15 55				
	d								15 15																
Angmering ■3	d	15 17							15 23									15 44							
Goring-by-Sea	d								15 27									15 48							
Durrington-on-Sea	d								15 30									15 50							
West Worthing	d								15 32			15 39						15 52							
Worthing ■4	a	15 24							15 34			15 41	15 44					15 55							
	d	15 26							15 36			15 42	15 48					15 56							
East Worthing	d											15 44													
Lancing	d	15 30										15 47						16 00							
Shoreham-by-Sea	d	15 34							15 42			15 52	15 56					16 04							
Southwick	d	15 37										15 55						16 07							
Fishersgate	d											15 57													
Portslade	d	15 40							15 47			15 59						16 10							
Aldrington	d											16 01													
Hove ■2	a	15 43							15 50			16 03	16 07					16 13							
	d	15 44							15 51		15 54	16 04	16 08					16 14							
Brighton ■10	a	15 48									15 58	16 08	16 14					16 18							
Preston Park	d								15 55																
Burgess Hill	a								16 03																
Haywards Heath ■3	a								16 09																
Arundel	d				15 12																				
Amberley	d				15 17																				
Pulborough	d				15 23																				
Billingshurst	d				15 29																				
Christs Hospital	d				15 36																				
Horsham ■4	a				15 40	15 46																			
	d					15 50													16 00						
Crawley	d					15 59													16 13						
Three Bridges ■4	a					16 02													16 16						
Gatwick Airport ■10 ✈	a					16 07			16 24										16 22						
	d					16 08			16 25										16 23						
Horley	a																		16 26						
Redhill ■5	a					16 15													16 36						
East Croydon	a					16 27			16 40										16 54						
London Bridge ■4 ⊖	a																		17 13						
Clapham Junction ■10	a					16 37			16 50																
London Victoria ■15 ⊖	a					16 44			16 57																

A ⌶ from Horsham

B Stops at Southampton Central and Southampton Airport Parkway before Eastleigh

Table 188

Saturdays

Southampton, Portsmouth and Sussex Coast - Brighton, Gatwick Airport and London

Network Diagram - see first Page of Table 186

		SN	SN	SN	SN	SN	SN	SN	SN	SN	SN	SN	SN	SW	SN	SN	SN	SN	SN	SW	SW
		◇1	◇1	◇1				1		◇1		◇1 🚌	◇1 A 🚌	◇1 🚌	◇1				1	1	1
Eastleigh	d																			15 21	15 28
Southampton Airport Parkway	d													15 14						15 25	
Southampton Central ⛴	d												15 13	15a22					15 33	15a35	
Swanwick	d												15 33						15 50		
Fareham	d												15 40						15 56		15 48
Portchester	d												15 45								15 53
Cosham	d												15 49						16 05		15 58
Portsmouth Harbour ⛴	d		15 12						15 29												
Portsmouth & Southsea	d		15 16						15 33												
Fratton	d		15 20						15 37												
Hilsea	d																				16a03
Bedhampton	d																				
Havant	d		15 30						15 46				15 56						16 11		
Warblington	d																				
Emsworth	d								15 50				16 00						16 15		
Southbourne	d								15 53				16 03								
Nutbourne	d																				
Bosham	d																				
Fishbourne (Sussex)	d																				
Chichester 4	a		15 41						16 00				16 10						16 23		
	d		15 42						16 00				16 11						16 25		
Bognor Regis 4	d	15 30									16 07	15 56									
Barnham	a	15 36	15 49						16 08		16 13	16 02	16 18						16 32		
	d	15 37	15 50		15 52				16 08	16 12	16 15	16 03	16 19			16 22			16 33		
Bognor Regis	a				15 59					16 18						16 29					
Ford 4	d	15 41									16 19	16 07							16 37		
Littlehampton 4	a										16 24										
	d			15 45											16 15						
Angmering 3	d			15 53					16 17						16 23				16 43		
Goring-by-Sea	d			15 57											16 27				16 47		
Durrington-on-Sea	d			16 00											16 30				16 50		
West Worthing	d			16 02			16 09								16 32			16 39	16 52		
Worthing 4	a			16 04			16 11		16 24						16 34			16 41	16 54		
	d			16 06			16 12		16 26						16 36			16 42	16 56		
East Worthing	d						16 14											16 44			
Lancing	d			16 10			16 17		16 30									16 47	17 00		
Shoreham-by-Sea	d			16 14			16 22		16 34						16 42			16 52	17 04		
Southwick	d						16 25		16 37									16 55	17 07		
Fishersgate	d						16 27											16 57			
Portslade	d						16 29		16 40						16 47			16 59	17 10		
Aldrington	d						16 31											17 01			
Hove 2	a			16 20			16 33		16 43						16 50			17 03	17 13		
	d			16 21		16 24	16 34		16 44						16 51		16 54	17 04	17 14		
Brighton 10	a					16 28	16 38		16 48								16 58	17 08	17 18		
Preston Park	d														16 55						
Burgess Hill	a														17 03						
Haywards Heath 3	a			16 35											17 09						
Arundel	d	15 46										16 12									
Amberley	d											16 17									
Pulborough	d	15 55										16 23									
Billingshurst	d	16 01										16 29									
Christs Hospital	d											16 36									
Horsham 4	a	16 10	16 16									16 40	16 46								
	d		16 20					16 30					16 50								
Crawley	d		16 29					16 43					16 59								
Three Bridges 4	a		16 32					16 46					17 02								
Gatwick Airport 10 ✈	a		16 37	16 55				16 52					17 07		17 24						
	d		16 38	16 56				16 53					17 08		17 25						
Horley	a		16 41					16 56													
Redhill 5	a		16 47					17 02					17 15								
East Croydon	a		16 59	17 11				17 24					17 27		17 40						
London Bridge 4 ⊖	a							17 43													
Clapham Junction 10	a		17 09	17 21									17 37		17 50						
London Victoria 15 ⊖	a		17 16	17 28									17 44		17 57						

A 🚌 from Horsham

Table 188

Saturdays

Southampton, Portsmouth and Sussex Coast - Brighton, Gatwick Airport and London

Network Diagram - see first Page of Table 186

		SN	SN	SN	SW	SW	SW	SN	SN	SN	SN	SN	SN	SN	SN	SN	SN	SN	SN	SN	SW	SN
		1	◇1 🚌		1	◇1 🚌	1		◇1	◇1	◇1				1		◇1		◇1 🚌	◇1 A 🚌	◇1 🚌	1
Eastleigh	d						16 00															16 14
Southampton Airport Parkway	d					15 42	16 05														16 14	16 18
Southampton Central ⛴	d				15 44	15a49	16a12													16 13	16a22	16 33
Swanwick	d				16 11															16 33		16 50
Fareham	d				16 18															16 40		16 56
Portchester	d				16 23															16 45		
Cosham	d				16 28															16 49		17 05
Portsmouth Harbour ⛴	d									16 12						16 29						
Portsmouth & Southsea	d			15 59						16 16						16 33						
Fratton	d			16 04						16 20						16 37						
Hilsea	d			16 08	16a33																	
Bedhampton	d			16 13																		
Havant	d			16 16						16 30						16 46				16 56		17 11
Warblington	d			16 18																		
Emsworth	d			16 21												16 50				17 00		17 15
Southbourne	d			16 24												16 53				17 03		
Nutbourne	d			16 26																		
Bosham	d			16 30																		
Fishbourne (Sussex)	d			16 33																		
Chichester 4	a			16 36						16 40						17 00				17 10		17 23
	d			16 37						16 41						17 00				17 11		17 25
Bognor Regis 4	d							16 39	16 30									17 07	16 56			
Barnham	a			16 44				16 45	16 36	16 48						17 08		17 13	17 02	17 18		17 32
	d		16 39	16 45					16 37	16 49		16 52				17 08	17 12	17 15	17 03	17 19		17 33
Bognor Regis	a		16 46									16 59					17 18					
Ford 4	d			16 49					16 41									17 19	17 07			17 37
Littlehampton 4	a			16 54														17 24				
	d										16 45											
Angmering 3	d										16 53					17 17						17 43
Goring-by-Sea	d										16 57											17 47
Durrington-on-Sea	d										17 00											17 50
West Worthing	d										17 02			17 09								17 52
Worthing 4	a										17 04			17 11		17 24						17 54
	d										17 06			17 12		17 26						17 56
East Worthing	d													17 14								
Lancing	d										17 10			17 17		17 30						18 00
Shoreham-by-Sea	d										17 14			17 22		17 34						18 04
Southwick	d													17 25		17 37						18 07
Fishersgate	d													17 27								
Portslade	d													17 29		17 40						18 10
Aldrington	d													17 31								
Hove 2	a										17 20			17 33		17 43						18 13
	d										17 21		17 24	17 34		17 44						18 14
Brighton 10	a												17 28	17 38		17 48						18 18
Preston Park	d																					
Burgess Hill	a																					
Haywards Heath 3	a										17 35											
Arundel	d								16 46										17 12			
Amberley	d																		17 17			
Pulborough	d								16 55										17 23			
Billingshurst	d								17 01										17 29			
Christs Hospital	d																		17 36			
Horsham 4	a								17 10	17 16									17 40	17 46		
	d	17 00								17 20					17 30					17 50		
Crawley	d	17 13								17 29					17 43					17 59		
Three Bridges 4	a	17 16								17 32					17 46					18 02		
Gatwick Airport 10 ✈	a	17 22								17 37	17 55				17 52					18 07		
	d	17 23								17 38	17 56				17 53					18 08		
Horley	a	17 26								17 41					17 56							
Redhill 5	a	17 36								17 47					18 02					18 15		
East Croydon	a	17 54								17 59	18 11				18 24					18 27		
London Bridge 4 ⊖	a	18 13													18 43							
Clapham Junction 10	a									18 09	18 21									18 37		
London Victoria 15 ⊖	a									18 16	18 28									18 44		

A 🚌 from Horsham

Southampton, Portsmouth and Sussex Coast - Brighton, Gatwick Airport and London

Network Diagram - see first Page of Table 186

		SN	SN	SN	SN	SW	SW	SN	SN	SN	SW	SW	SW	SN	SN	SN	SN	SN	SN	SN	SN
		◇1				1	1	1	◇1 ⌶		1	◇1 ⌶	1		◇1	◇1	◇1				1
Eastleigh	d					16 21	16 28						17 00								
Southampton Airport Parkway	d					16 25						16 42	17 05								
Southampton Central	d					16a35					16 44	16a49	17a12								
Swanwick	d										17 11										
Fareham	d						16 48				17 18										
Portchester	d						16 53				17 23										
Cosham	d						16 58				17 28										
Portsmouth Harbour	d															17 12					
Portsmouth & Southsea	d									16 59						17 16					
Fratton	d									17 04						17 20					
Hilsea	d						17a03			17 08	17a33										
Bedhampton	d									17 13											
Havant	d									17 16						17 30					
Warblington	d									17 18											
Emsworth	d									17 21											
Southbourne	d									17 24											
Nutbourne	d									17 26											
Bosham	d									17 30											
Fishbourne (Sussex)	d									17 33											
Chichester 4	a									17 36						17 40					
	d									17 37						17 41					
Bognor Regis 4	d													17 39	17 30						
Barnham	a									17 44				17 45	17 36	17 48					
	d		17 22						17 41	17 45					17 37	17 49		17 52			
Bognor Regis	a		17 29						17 47									17 59			
Ford 4	d									17 49					17 41						
Littlehampton 4	a									17 54											
	d	17 15															17 45				
Angmering 3	d	17 23															17 53				
Goring-by-Sea	d	17 27															17 57				
Durrington-on-Sea	d	17 30															18 00				
West Worthing	d	17 32			17 39												18 02			18 09	
Worthing 4	a	17 34			17 41												18 04			18 11	
	d	17 36			17 42												18 06			18 12	
East Worthing	d				17 44															18 14	
Lancing	d				17 47												18 10			18 17	
Shoreham-by-Sea	d	17 42			17 52												18 14			18 22	
Southwick	d				17 55															18 25	
Fishersgate	d				17 57															18 27	
Portslade	d	17 47			17 59															18 29	
Aldrington	d				18 01															18 31	
Hove 2	a	17 50			18 03												18 20			18 33	
	d	17 51		17 54	18 04												18 21		18 24	18 34	
Brighton 10	a			17 58	18 08														18 28	18 38	
Preston Park	d	17 55																			
Burgess Hill	a	18 03																			
Haywards Heath 3	a	18 09															18 35				
Arundel	d														17 46						
Amberley	d																				
Pulborough	d														17 55						
Billingshurst	d														18 01						
Christs Hospital	d																				
Horsham 4	a														18 10	18 16					
	d							18 00							18 20						18 32
Crawley	d							18 13							18 29						18 45
Three Bridges 4	a							18 16							18 32						18 48
Gatwick Airport 10	a	18 24						18 22							18 37		18 55				18 54
	d	18 25						18 23							18 38		18 56				18 55
Horley	a							18 26							18 41						18 58
Redhill 5	a							18 36							18 47						19 04
East Croydon	a	18 40						18 54							18 59		19 11				19 24
London Bridge 4	a							19 13													
Clapham Junction 10	a	18 50													19 09		19 21				19 37
London Victoria 15	a	18 57													19 16		19 28				19 44

Southampton, Portsmouth and Sussex Coast - Brighton, Gatwick Airport and London

Network Diagram - see first Page of Table 186

		SN	SN	SN	SN	SN	SW	SN	SN	SN	SN	SN	SW	SW	SN	SN	SN	SN	SW	SW	SW
			◇1		◇1	◇1	◇1 ⌶	◇1				1	1	1	◇1 ⌶	1	◇1	1	1	◇1 ⌶	1
Eastleigh	d												17 21	17 28							17 54
Southampton Airport Parkway	d						17 14						17 25							17 42	17 59
Southampton Central	d					17 13	17a22					17 33	17a35						17 44	17a49	18a10
Swanwick	d					17 33						17 50							18 11		
Fareham	d					17 40						17 56		17 48					18 18		
Portchester	d					17 45								17 53					18 23		
Cosham	d					17 49						18 05		17 58					18 28		
Portsmouth Harbour	d	17 29																			
Portsmouth & Southsea	d	17 33																17 59			
Fratton	d	17 37																18 04			
Hilsea	d													18a03				18 08	18a33		
Bedhampton	d																	18 13			
Havant	d	17 46				17 56						18 11						18 16			
Warblington	d																	18 18			
Emsworth	d	17 50				18 00						18 15						18 21			
Southbourne	d	17 53				18 03												18 24			
Nutbourne	d																	18 26			
Bosham	d																	18 30			
Fishbourne (Sussex)	d																	18 33			
Chichester 4	a	18 00				18 10						18 23						18 36			
	d	18 00				18 11						18 25						18 37			
Bognor Regis 4	d			18 07	17 56												18 33				
Barnham	a	18 08		18 13	18 02	18 18						18 32					18 40	18 44			
	d	18 08	18 12	18 15	18 03	18 19			18 22			18 33			18 39		18 41	18 45			
Bognor Regis	a		18 18						18 29						18 46						
Ford 4	d			18 19	18 07							18 37					18 45	18 49			
Littlehampton 4	a			18 24																	
	d							18 15													
Angmering 3	d	18 17						18 23				18 43					18 53				
Goring-by-Sea	d							18 27				18 47					18 57				
Durrington-on-Sea	d							18 30				18 50					19 00				
West Worthing	d							18 32			18 39	18 52					19 02				
Worthing 4	a	18 24						18 34			18 41	18 54					19 04				
	d	18 26						18 36			18 42	18 56					19 06				
East Worthing	d										18 44										
Lancing	d	18 30									18 47	19 00					19 10				
Shoreham-by-Sea	d	18 34						18 42			18 52	19 04					19 14				
Southwick	d	18 37									18 55	19 07									
Fishersgate	d										18 57										
Portslade	d	18 40						18 47			18 59	19 10									
Aldrington	d										19 01										
Hove 2	a	18 43						18 50			19 03	19 13					19 20				
	d	18 44						18 51		18 54	19 04	19 14					19 21				
Brighton 10	a	18 48								18 58	19 08	19 18									
Preston Park	d							18 55													
Burgess Hill	a							19 03													
Haywards Heath 3	a							19 09									19 35				
Arundel	d				18 12													18 54			
Amberley	d				18 17													18 59			
Pulborough	d				18 23													19 05			
Billingshurst	d				18 29													19 11			
Christs Hospital	d				18 36																
Horsham 4	a				18 40	18 46												19 20			
	d				18 50											19 02		19 21			
Crawley	d				18 59											19 14		19 30			
Three Bridges 4	a				19 02											19 18		19 33			
Gatwick Airport 10	a				19 07			19 25								19 22	19 55	19 38			
	d				19 08			19 26								19 23	19 56	19 39			
Horley	a				19 11											19 26					
Redhill 5	a				19 17											19 36		19 47			
East Croydon	a				19 29			19 41								19 54	20 11	20 00			
London Bridge 4	a																				
Clapham Junction 10	a				19 40			19 51								20 08	20 21	20 11			
London Victoria 15	a				19 50			19 58								20 15	20 28	20 20			

Table 188

Saturdays

Southampton, Portsmouth and Sussex Coast - Brighton, Gatwick Airport and London

Network Diagram - see first Page of Table 186

		SN		SN	SN	SN	SN	SN	SN ◇1	SN 1	SN ◇1	SW 1		SW ◇1	SN 1	SN ◇1	SN	SN	SN		SW 1	SW 1			SN ◇1
Eastleigh	d											18 00			18 14						18 21	18 28			
Southampton Airport Parkway	d											18 05		18 14	18 18						18 25				
Southampton Central ⛴	d										18 11	18a14		18a22	18 33						18a35				
Swanwick	d										18 28				18 50										
Fareham	d										18 35				18 56							18 48			
Portchester	d										18 40											18 53			
Cosham	d										18 44				19 05							18 58			
Portsmouth Harbour ⛴	d						18 12	18 29																	
Portsmouth & Southsea	d						18 16	18 33																	
Fratton	d						18 20	18 37																	
Hilsea	d																					19a03			
Bedhampton	d																								
Havant	d						18 30	18 46			18 51				19 11										
Warblington	d																								
Emsworth	d						18 34	18 50			18 55				19 15										
Southbourne	d						18 37	18 53			18 58														
Nutbourne	d																								
Bosham	d																								
Fishbourne (Sussex)	d																								
Chichester 4	a						18 44	19 00			19 05				19 23										
	d						18 45	19 00			19 07				19 25										
Bognor Regis 4	d	18 39															19 03								
Barnham	a	18 46					18 52	19 08			19 14				19 32		19 09								
	d			18 52			18 53	19 08	19 12		19 15				19 33		19 22	19 22							19 39
Bognor Regis	a			18 59					19 18									19 29							19 46
Ford 4	d						18 57				19 19				19 37		19 26								
Littlehampton 4	a						19 02										19 32								
	d					18 51										19 15									
Angmering 3	d					19 00		19 17							19 43	19 23									
Goring-by-Sea	d					19 04										19 27									
Durrington-on-Sea	d					19 07									19 49	19 30									
West Worthing	d					19 09										19 32									
Worthing 4	a					19 11		19 24							19 53	19 34									
	d					19 12		19 26							19 53	19 35									
East Worthing	d					19 14									19 56										
Lancing	d					19 17		19 30							19 59	19 39									
Shoreham-by-Sea	d					19 22		19 34							20 03	19 43									
Southwick	d					19 25		19 37							20 06										
Fishersgate	d					19 27									20 08										
Portslade	d					19 29		19 40							20 10	19 48									
Aldrington	d					19 31									20 12										
Hove 2	a					19 33		19 43							20 14	19 51									
	d				19 24	19 34		19 44							20 15	19 52			19 54						
Brighton 10	a				19 28	19 38		19 50							20 19				19 59						
Preston Park	d																								
Burgess Hill	a															20 02									
Haywards Heath 3	a															20 10									
Arundel	d										19 24														
Amberley	d										19 29														
Pulborough	d										19 35														
Billingshurst	d										19 41														
Christs Hospital	d										19 48														
Horsham 4	a										19 52														
	d									19 32	19 52														
Crawley	d									19 45	20 01														
Three Bridges 4	a									19 48	20 05														
Gatwick Airport 10 ✈	a									19 54	20 10					20 25									
	d									19 55	20 11					20 26									
Horley	a									19 58															
Redhill 5	a									20 04	20 18														
East Croydon 🚊	a									20 24	20 29					20 41									
London Bridge 4 ⊖	a																								
Clapham Junction 10	a									20 37	20 40					20 51									
London Victoria 15 ⊖	a									20 44	20 50					20 58									

Table 188

Saturdays

Southampton, Portsmouth and Sussex Coast - Brighton, Gatwick Airport and London

Network Diagram - see first Page of Table 186

		SN 1	SN ◇1	SN	SN	SN	SW 1	SW ◇1		SN	SN 1	SN	SN	SN	SN ◇1	SN 1	SN ◇1	SW 1			SW ◇1	SN ◇1	SN	SN	SN 1
Eastleigh	d																	19 00							
Southampton Airport Parkway	d							18 42										19 05			19 14				
Southampton Central ⛴	d						18 44	18a49									19 09	19a12			19a22				19 33
Swanwick	d						19 11										19 28								19 50
Fareham	d						19 18										19 35								19 56
Portchester	d						19 23										19 40								
Cosham	d						19 28										19 44								20 05
Portsmouth Harbour ⛴	d										19 12		19 29												
Portsmouth & Southsea	d					18 59					19 16		19 33												
Fratton	d					19 04					19 20		19 37												
Hilsea	d					19 08	19a33																		
Bedhampton	d					19 13																			
Havant	d					19 16					19 30		19 46				19 52								20 11
Warblington	d					19 18																			
Emsworth	d					19 21					19 34						19 56								20 15
Southbourne	d					19 24					19 37						19 59								
Nutbourne	d					19 26																			
Bosham	d					19 30																			
Fishbourne (Sussex)	d					19 33																			
Chichester 4	a					19 36					19 44		19 57				20 06								20 23
	d					19 37					19 45		19 59				20 07								20 25
Bognor Regis 4	d		19 33							19 39				20 04											
Barnham	a		19 40			19 44				19 46	19 52		20 06	20 10			20 14								20 32
	d		19 41			19 45					19 53	19 52	20 07	20 11	20 12		20 15						20 22		20 33
Bognor Regis	a											19 59			20 18								20 29		
Ford 4	d		19 45			19 49					19 57			20 15			20 19								
Littlehampton 4	a					19 55					20 02			20 20											
	d				19 52																	20 15			
Angmering 3	d		19 53		20 00								20 16									20 23			20 42
Goring-by-Sea	d		19 57		20 04																	20 27			
Durrington-on-Sea	d		20 00		20 07																	20 30			20 48
West Worthing	d		20 02		20 09																	20 32			
Worthing 4	a		20 04		20 11								20 23									20 34			20 52
	d		20 05		20 12								20 23									20 35			20 52
East Worthing	d				20 14								20 26												20 55
Lancing	d		20 09		20 17								20 29									20 39			20 58
Shoreham-by-Sea	d		20 13		20 22								20 33									20 43			21 02
Southwick	d				20 25								20 36												21 05
Fishersgate	d				20 27								20 38												21 07
Portslade	d		20 17		20 29								20 40									20 48			21 09
Aldrington	d				20 31								20 42												21 11
Hove 2	a		20 21		20 33								20 44									20 51			21 13
	d		20 22	20 24	20 34								20 45									20 52		20 54	21 14
Brighton 10	a			20 28	20 38								20 49											20 58	21 18
Preston Park	d																								
Burgess Hill	a																					21 03			
Haywards Heath 3	a		20 36																			21 11			
Arundel	d																20 24								
Amberley	d																20 29								
Pulborough	d																20 35								
Billingshurst	d																20 41								
Christs Hospital	d																20 48								
Horsham 4	a																20 52								
	d	20 02														20 32	20 52								
Crawley	d	20 14														20 45	21 01								
Three Bridges 4	a	20 18	20 47													20 48	21 05								
Gatwick Airport 10 ✈	a	20 22	20 52													20 56	21 10					21 26			
	d	20 23	20 53													20 57	21 11					21 27			
Horley	a	20 26														20 59									
Redhill 5	a	20 36														21 06	21 18								
East Croydon 🚊	a	20 54	21 08													21 24	21 30					21 41			
London Bridge 4 ⊖	a																								
Clapham Junction 10	a	21 07	21 18													21 37	21 40					21 51			
London Victoria 15 ⊖	a	21 14	21 26													21 44	21 50					21 58			

Southampton, Portsmouth and Sussex Coast - Brighton, Gatwick Airport and London

Network Diagram - see first Page of Table 186

		SW 1	SW 1	SN ◇1 ⚒	SN 1	SN ◇1	SN	SN	SN	SN	SW 1	SW ◇1 ⚒	SN	SN 1	SN	SN ◇1	SN 1	SN ◇1	SW 1	SW ◇1 ⚒	SN 1
Eastleigh	d	19 21	19 28																20 00		20 14
Southampton Airport Parkway	d	19 25										19 42							20 05	20 14	20 18
Southampton Central ⛴	d	19a35									19 44	19a49						20 11	20a14	20a22	20 33
Swanwick	d										20 11							20 28			20 50
Fareham	d		19 48								20 18							20 35			20 56
Portchester	d		19 53								20 23							20 40			
Cosham	d		19 58								20 28							20 44			21 05
Portsmouth Harbour ⛴	d													20 28							
Portsmouth & Southsea	d									19 59				20 32							
Fratton	d									20 04				20 36							
Hilsea	d		20a03							20 08	20a37										
Bedhampton	d									20 13											
Havant	d									20 16				20 44				20 51			21 11
Warblington	d									20 18											
Emsworth	d									20 21				20 48				20 55			21 15
Southbourne	d									20 24				20 51				20 58			
Nutbourne	d									20 26											
Bosham	d									20 30											
Fishbourne (Sussex)	d									20 33											
Chichester 4	a									20 36				20 58				21 05			21 23
	d									20 37				20 59				21 07			21 25
Bognor Regis 4	d					20 33	20 39								21 04						
Barnham	a					20 39	20 45			20 44				21 06	21 10			21 14			21 32
	d			20 39		20 40				20 45			20 52	21 07	21 11	21 12		21 15			21 33
Bognor Regis	a			20 46									20 59			21 18					
Ford 4	d					20 44				20 49					21 15			21 19			21 37
Littlehampton 4	a									20 55					21 20						
	d								20 52												
Angmering 3	d					20 53			21 00					21 16							21 43
Goring-by-Sea	d					20 57			21 04												21 47
Durrington-on-Sea	d					21 00			21 07												21 50
West Worthing	d					21 02			21 09												21 52
Worthing 4	a					21 04			21 11					21 23							21 54
	d					21 05			21 12					21 23							21 55
East Worthing	d								21 14					21 26							21 57
Lancing	d					21 09			21 17					21 29							22 00
Shoreham-by-Sea	d					21 13			21 22					21 33							22 04
Southwick	d								21 25					21 36							22 07
Fishersgate	d								21 27					21 38							22 09
Portslade	d					21 18			21 29					21 40							22 11
Aldrington	d								21 31					21 42							22 14
Hove 2	a					21 21			21 33					21 44							22 16
	d					21 22		21 24	21 34					21 45							22 16
Brighton 10	a							21 28	21 38					21 49							22 21
Preston Park	d																				
Burgess Hill	a																				
Haywards Heath 3	a					21 36															
Arundel	d																	21 24			
Amberley	d																	21 29			
Pulborough	d																	21 35			
Billingshurst	d																	21 41			
Christs Hospital	d																	21 48			
Horsham 4	a																	21 52			
	d				21 02												21 32	21 52			
Crawley	d				21 14												21 45	22 01			
Three Bridges 4	a				21 18	21 47											21 48	22 05			
Gatwick Airport 10 ✈	a				21 22	21 52											21 56	22 10			
	d				21 23	21 53											21 57	22 11			
Horley	a				21 26												22 00				
Redhill 5	a				21 36												22 06	22 18			
East Croydon 🚊	a				21 54	22 08											22 24	22 30			
London Bridge 4 ⊖	a																				
Clapham Junction 10	a				22 07	22 18											22 37	22 40			
London Victoria 15 ⊖	a				22 15	22 26											22 44	22 50			

Southampton, Portsmouth and Sussex Coast - Brighton, Gatwick Airport and London

Network Diagram - see first Page of Table 186

		SN ◇1 A ⚒	SN	SN	SN	SW 1	SW 1	SN ◇1	SN	SN	SN 1	SN	SN	SN 1	SW 1	SW ◇1 ⚒	SW 1	SN	SN ◇1	SN	SN 1
Eastleigh	d					20 21	20 28										21 00				
Southampton Airport Parkway	d					20 25										20 42	21 05				
Southampton Central ⛴	d					20a35									20 44	20a49	21a12				21 13
Swanwick	d														21 11						21 33
Fareham	d						20 48								21 18						21 40
Portchester	d						20 53								21 23						21 45
Cosham	d						20 58								21 28						21 49
Portsmouth Harbour ⛴	d			20 40										21 11							
Portsmouth & Southsea	d			20 44										21 15							
Fratton	d			20 48										21 19							
Hilsea	d			20 52			21a03							21 23	21a33						
Bedhampton	d													21 28							
Havant	d			20 58										21 31							21 56
Warblington	d			21 00										21 33							
Emsworth	d			21 03										21 36							
Southbourne	d			21 06										21 39							
Nutbourne	d			21 09										21 41							
Bosham	d			21 12										21 45							
Fishbourne (Sussex)	d			21 15										21 48							
Chichester 4	a			21 18										21 51							22 06
	d			21 19										21 52							22 07
Bognor Regis 4	d								21 39									22 00			
Barnham	a			21 26					21 45					21 59				22 06			22 14
	d		21 22	21 27				21 42		21 52				22 00					22 12		22 15
Bognor Regis	a		21 29					21 48		21 59									22 18		
Ford 4	d			21 31										22 04							22 19
Littlehampton 4	a			21 36																	22 24
	d	21 15											21 52								22 33
Angmering 3	d	21 23											22 00	22 11							22 41
Goring-by-Sea	d	21 27											22 04	22 15							22 45
Durrington-on-Sea	d	21 30											22 07	22 18							22 47
West Worthing	d	21 32											22 09	22 20							22 49
Worthing 4	a	21 34											22 11	22 22							22 52
	d	21 35											22 12	22 23							22 52
East Worthing	d												22 14	22 25							22 55
Lancing	d	21 39											22 17	22 28							22 58
Shoreham-by-Sea	d	21 43											22 22	22 32							23 02
Southwick	d												22 25	22 35							23 05
Fishersgate	d												22 27	22 37							23 07
Portslade	d	21 48											22 29	22 39							23 09
Aldrington	d												22 31	22 42							23 11
Hove 2	a	21 51											22 33	22 44							23 13
	d	21 52			21 54							22 24	22 34	22 44						22 54	23 14
Brighton 10	a				21 58							22 28	22 38	22 48						22 58	23 18
Preston Park	d																				
Burgess Hill	a	22 03																			
Haywards Heath 3	a	22 09																			
Arundel	d																				
Amberley	d																				
Pulborough	d																				
Billingshurst	d																				
Christs Hospital	d																				
Horsham 4	a																				
	d										22 02										
Crawley	d										22 14										
Three Bridges 4	a										22 18										
Gatwick Airport 10 ✈	a	22 24									22 23										
	d	22 25									22 24										
Horley	a										22 27										
Redhill 5	a										22 37										
East Croydon 🚊	a	22 40									22 55										
London Bridge 4 ⊖	a																				
Clapham Junction 10	a	22 49									23 06										
London Victoria 15 ⊖	a	22 57									23 14										

A ⚒ from Haywards Heath

Southampton, Portsmouth and Sussex Coast - Brighton, Gatwick Airport and London

Network Diagram - see first Page of Table 186

		SW ◇1 🍴	SN 1	SN ◇	SN	SN 1	SW 1	SW 1	SN 1	SN 1	SN	SN	SN 1	SW 1	SW ◇1 🍴	SN ◇1	SN 1	SW 1	SW ◇1 🍴	SN	SN	SN
Eastleigh	d						21 21	21 28										22 03	22 18			
Southampton Airport Parkway	d	21 14					21 25								21 42			22 08	22 22			
Southampton Central ⛴	d	21a22				21 33	21a35							21 44	21a49		22 13	22a17	22a29			
Swanwick	d					21 50								22 11			22 31					
Fareham	d					21 57		21 48						22 18			22 39					
Portchester	d					22 02		21 53						22 23			22 44					
Cosham	d					22 06		21 58						22 28			22 48					
Portsmouth Harbour ⛴	d		21 40										22 15									22 44
Portsmouth & Southsea	d		21 44										22 19									22 48
Fratton	d		21 48										22 23									22 52
Hilsea	d		21 52					22a03					22 27	22a33								22 56
Bedhampton	d		21 57										22 32									23 01
Havant	d		22 00			22 13							22 35				22 55					23 05
Warblington	d					22 15																
Emsworth	d					22 18							22 39				22 59					
Southbourne	d					22 21							22 42				23 02					
Nutbourne	d					22 23																
Bosham	d					22 27																
Fishbourne (Sussex)	d					22 30																
Chichester 4	a		22 10			22 33							22 49				23 09					23 16
	d		22 11			22 34				22 40			22 52				23 09					23 18
Bognor Regis 4	d				22 30															23 15		
Barnham	a		22 18		22 36	22 41				22 47			22 59				23 17			23 21		23 26
	d		22 19	22 22	22 37					22 48	22 52		23 00			23 06	23 17					23 26
Bognor Regis	a			22 29							22 59					23 12						
Ford 4	d		22 23		22 41					22 52			23 04									23 31
Littlehampton 4	a				22 46												23 25					23 35
	d																					23 40
Angmering 3	d												23 11									23 48
Goring-by-Sea	d												23 15									23 52
Durrington-on-Sea	d												23 17									23 54
West Worthing	d												23 19									23 56
Worthing 4	a												23 22									23 59
	d												23 22									23 59
East Worthing	d												23 25									00 02
Lancing	d												23 28									00 05
Shoreham-by-Sea	d												23 32									00 09
Southwick	d												23 35									00 12
Fishersgate	d												23 37									00 14
Portslade	d												23 39									00 16
Aldrington	d												23 41									00 18
Hove 2	a												23 43									00 20
	d											23 24	23 44								23 54	00 21
Brighton 10	a											23 28	23 48								23 58	00 25
Preston Park	d																					
Burgess Hill	a																					
Haywards Heath 3	a																					
Arundel	d		22 28							22 57												
Amberley	d									23 02												
Pulborough	d		22 37							23 08												
Billingshurst	d		22 43							23 14												
Christs Hospital	d		22 50							23 21												
Horsham 4	a		22 54							23 25												
	d		22 55						23 02	23 25												
Crawley	d		23 03						23 14	23 38												
Three Bridges 4	a		23 07						23 18	23 42												
Gatwick Airport 10 ✈	a								23 22													
	d								23 23													
Horley	a								23 26													
Redhill 5	a								23 36													
East Croydon 🚌	a								23 55													
London Bridge 4 ⊖	a																					
Clapham Junction 10	a								00 11													
London Victoria 15 ⊖	a								00 18													

Southampton, Portsmouth and Sussex Coast - Brighton, Gatwick Airport and London

Network Diagram - see first Page of Table 186

		SN 1	SW 1	SW 1	SN ◇	SN ◇	SN	SW 1	SW ◇1 🍴	SW 1	SW ◇1 🍴	SW 1	SW 1	SW ◇1 🍴
Eastleigh	d		22 22	22 28						23 04	23 18	23 23	23 28	
Southampton Airport Parkway	d		22 26						22 42	23 08	23 22	23 27		23 42
Southampton Central ⛴	d	22 33	22a36					22 44	22a49	23a17	23a29	23a38		23a49
Swanwick	d	22 50						23 11						
Fareham	d	23 00		22 48				23 18					23 48	
Portchester	d			22 53				23 23					23 53	
Cosham	d	23 08		22 58				23 28					23 58	
Portsmouth Harbour ⛴	d						23 15							
Portsmouth & Southsea	d						23 19							
Fratton	d						23 23							
Hilsea	d			23a03			23 27	23a33					00a03	
Bedhampton	d						23 33							
Havant	d	23 15					23 36							
Warblington	d						23 38							
Emsworth	d						23 41							
Southbourne	d						23 44							
Nutbourne	d						23 47							
Bosham	d						23 50							
Fishbourne (Sussex)	d						23 53							
Chichester 4	a	23 25					23 57							
	d	23 26				23 52	23 57							
Bognor Regis 4	d													
Barnham	a	23 33				23 59	00 05							
	d	23 34			23 36	00 01	00 06							
Bognor Regis	a				23 43									
Ford 4	d					00 05	00 10							
Littlehampton 4	a	23 42				00 10	00 15							
	d													
Angmering 3	d													
Goring-by-Sea	d													
Durrington-on-Sea	d													
West Worthing	d													
Worthing 4	a													
	d													
East Worthing	d													
Lancing	d													
Shoreham-by-Sea	d													
Southwick	d													
Fishersgate	d													
Portslade	d													
Aldrington	d													
Hove 2	a													
	d													
Brighton 10	a													
Preston Park	d													
Burgess Hill	a													
Haywards Heath 3	a													
Arundel	d													
Amberley	d													
Pulborough	d													
Billingshurst	d													
Christs Hospital	d													
Horsham 4	a													
	d													
Crawley	d													
Three Bridges 4	a													
Gatwick Airport 10 ✈	a													
	d													
Horley	a													
Redhill 5	a													
East Croydon 🚌	a													
London Bridge 4 ⊖	a													
Clapham Junction 10	a													
London Victoria 15 ⊖	a													

Southampton, Portsmouth and Sussex Coast - Brighton, Gatwick Airport and London

Network Diagram - see first Page of Table 186

		SN	SN ■	SN ◇	SN	SW ■	SN ◇■	SW ◇■	SW ■	SW ■		SW ■	SN ■	SN ■	SN ■	SW ■	SN	SN ■	SN ◇■	SN ◇■		SN ■	SN	SN	SN ■
		A	A	A	A	A	A	A	A																
Eastleigh	d					00 03		00 21	01 00	01 22															
Southampton Airport Parkway	d					00 08		00 25	01 05	01 26		02s46													
Southampton Central	d					00a15		00a34	01a12	01a35		02a56				06 35									
Swanwick	d															07 02									
Fareham	d															07 10									
Portchester	d															07 15									
Cosham	d															07 20									
Portsmouth Harbour	d	22p44			23p15																				
Portsmouth & Southsea	d	22p48			23p19																				
Fratton	d	22p52			23p23																				
Hilsea	d	22p56			23p27											07a26									
Bedhampton	d	23p01			23p33																				
Havant	d	23p05			23p36																				
Warblington	d				23p38																				
Emsworth	d				23p41																				
Southbourne	d				23p44																				
Nutbourne	d				23p47																				
Bosham	d				23p50																				
Fishbourne (Sussex)	d				23p53																				
Chichester 4	a	23p16			23p57																				
	d	23p18		23p52	23p57																				
Bognor Regis 4	d																		06 58						07 34
Barnham	a	23p26		23p59	00 05														07 04						07 40
	d	23p26		00 01	00 06		00 09							06 06			06 45		07 05			07 28			07 41
Bognor Regis	a						00 15										06 51					07 34			
Ford 4	d	23p31		00 05	00 10														07 09						07 45
Littlehampton 4	a	23p35		00 10	00 15									06 13											07 50
	d	23p40												06 20						07 14				07 40	
Angmering 3	d	23p48																		07 22				07 48	
Goring-by-Sea	d	23p52																		07 26				07 52	
Durrington-on-Sea	d	23p54																		07 29				07 55	
West Worthing	d	23p56																		07 31				07 57	
Worthing 4	a	23p59												06 33						07 33				07 59	
	d	23p59												06 33						07 35				08 00	
East Worthing	d	00 02																						08 02	
Lancing	d	00 05												06 37						07 39				08 05	
Shoreham-by-Sea	d	00 09												06 41						07 43				08 09	
Southwick	d	00 12												06 44						07 46				08 12	
Fishersgate	d	00 14																						08 14	
Portslade	d	00 16												06 48						07 49				08 16	
Aldrington	d	00 18																						08 19	
Hove 2	a	00 20												06 51						07 53				08 21	
	d	00 21												06 51						07 54			07 56	08 21	
Brighton 10	a	00 25												06 55									08 00	08 25	
Preston Park	d																								
Burgess Hill	a																			08 04					
Haywards Heath 3	a																			08 09					
Arundel	d																		07 14						
Amberley	d																		07 19						
Pulborough	d																		07 25						
Billingshurst	d																		07 31						
Christs Hospital	d																		07 38						
Horsham 4	a																		07 42						
	d		23p02										06 04		06 34			07 03	07 42						
Crawley	d		23p14										06 17		06 47			07 16	07 51						
Three Bridges 4	a		23p18										06 20		06 51			07 19	07 54						
Gatwick Airport 10	a		23p22										06 25		06 57			07 24	07 59	08 22					
	d		23p23												06 58			07 25	08 00	08 23					
Horley	a		23p26												07 00			07 28	08 02						
Redhill 5	a		23p36												07 07			07 34	08 09						
East Croydon	a		23p55												07 26			07 56	08 26	08 40					
London Bridge 4	a																	08 12							
Clapham Junction 10	a		00 11												07 41				08 37	08 54					
London Victoria 15	a		00 18												07 48				08 46	09 01					

A not 11 December

Southampton, Portsmouth and Sussex Coast - Brighton, Gatwick Airport and London

Network Diagram - see first Page of Table 186

		SN ■	SN ◇■ ⚒	SN ■	SN ◇■	SN ◇■		SN ■	SN ◇■	SW ■	SN ■	SN ◇■	SN ■	SN ◇■ ⚒	SN ■	SN ◇■	SN ◇■		SN ■	GW	SW ■	SW ■	SN ◇■ A	SW ■	SW ■
Eastleigh	d																				08 22	08 26	08 48		08 54
Southampton Airport Parkway	d																				08 27		*08 36*		08 58
Southampton Central	d								07 29	07 35										08 31	08a34		*08a27*	08 35	09a09
Swanwick	d								07 46	08 02														09 02	
Fareham	d								07 53	08 10										08 52		08 44	09 02	09 10	
Portchester	d									08 15												08 49		09 15	
Cosham	d								08 02	08 20										09 00		08 54	09 11	09 20	
Portsmouth Harbour	d			07 14		07 43									08 14		08 43								
Portsmouth & Southsea	d			07 18		07 47									08 18		08 47								
Fratton	d			07 22		07 51									08 22		08 51								
Hilsea	d									08a26												09a00		09a26	
Bedhampton	d			07 30											08 30										
Havant	d			07 33		08 00			08 11						08 33		09 00			09 11			09 17		
Warblington	d			07 35											08 35										
Emsworth	d			07 38		08 04			08 15						08 38		09 04						09 21		
Southbourne	d			07 41		08 07									08 41		09 07								
Nutbourne	d			07 43											08 43										
Bosham	d			07 47											08 47										
Fishbourne (Sussex)	d			07 50											08 50										
Chichester 4	a			07 53		08 14			08 23						08 53		09 14			09 22			09 29		
	d			07 53		08 14			08 23						08 53		09 14			09 22			09 30		
Bognor Regis 4	d		07 58								08 36			08 58											
Barnham	a		08 04	08 01		08 22			08 31		08 42			09 04	09 01		09 22			09 30			09 37		
	d		08 05	08 08		08 22		08 26	08 38		08 43	08 43		09 05	09 08		09 22		09 26	09 30			09 38		
Bognor Regis	a							08 32				08 49							09 32						
Ford 4	d		08 09	08 12					08 42		08 47			09 09	09 12								09 42		
Littlehampton 4	a										08 52														
	d				08 14											09 14									
Angmering 3	d			08 18	08 22				08 48						09 18	09 22							09 48		
Goring-by-Sea	d			08 22	08 26				08 52						09 22	09 26							09 52		
Durrington-on-Sea	d			08 25	08 29				08 55						09 25	09 29							09 55		
West Worthing	d			08 27	08 31				08 57						09 27	09 31							09 57		
Worthing 4	a			08 29	08 33	08 37			08 59						09 29	09 33	09 37			09 45			09 59		
	d			08 30	08 41				09 00						09 30	09 41				09 45			10 00		
East Worthing	d			08 32					09 02						09 32								10 02		
Lancing	d			08 35					09 05						09 35								10 05		
Shoreham-by-Sea	d			08 39	08 47				09 09						09 39	09 47				09 52			10 09		
Southwick	d			08 42					09 12						09 42								10 12		
Fishersgate	d			08 44					09 14						09 44								10 14		
Portslade	d			08 46					09 16						09 46								10 16		
Aldrington	d			08 49					09 19						09 49								10 19		
Hove 2	a			08 51	08 54				09 21						09 51	09 54				09 59			10 21		
	d			08 56	08 54				09 22						09 56	09 54				09 59			10 21		
Brighton 10	a			09 00					09 26						10 00					10 05			10 25		
Preston Park	d																								
Burgess Hill	a				09 04											10 04									
Haywards Heath 3	a				09 10											10 10									
Arundel	d		08 14											09 14											
Amberley	d		08 19											09 19											
Pulborough	d		08 25											09 25											
Billingshurst	d		08 31											09 31											
Christs Hospital	d		08 38											09 38											
Horsham 4	a		08 42											09 42											
	d	08 03	08 42										09 03	09 42											
Crawley	d	08 16	08 51										09 16	09 51											
Three Bridges 4	a	08 19	08 54										09 19	09 54											
Gatwick Airport 10	a	08 24	08 59		09 21								09 24	09 59		10 21									
	d	08 25	09 00		09 23								09 25	10 00		10 23									
Horley	a	08 28	09 02										09 28	10 02											
Redhill 5	a	08 34	09 09										09 34	10 09											
East Croydon	a	08 56	09 26		09 40								09 56	10 26		10 40									
London Bridge 4	a	09 12											10 12												
Clapham Junction 10	a		09 37		09 54									10 37		10 54									
London Victoria 15	a		09 46		10 01									10 46		11 01									

A Stops at Southampton Central and Southampton Airport Parkway before Eastleigh

Table 188 — Sundays

Southampton, Portsmouth and Sussex Coast - Brighton, Gatwick Airport and London

Network Diagram - see first Page of Table 186

		SN 1	SN ◇1	SN 1	SN ◇1 H	SN 1	SN 1	SN ◇1	SN ◇1	SN ◇1	SW ◇1	SW 1	SW 1	SW ◇1	SW 1	SN 1	SN ◇1	SN 1	SN ◇1 H	SN 1	SN 1
Eastleigh	d										09 22	09 26			09 54						
Southampton Airport Parkway	d										09 27			09 55	09 58						
Southampton Central	d									09 29	09a34		09 35	10a02	10a09						
Swanwick	d									09 46			10 02								
Fareham	d									09 53		09 44	10 10								
Portchester	d											09 49	10 15								
Cosham	d									10 02		09 54	10 20								
Portsmouth Harbour	d					09 14			09 43											10 14	
Portsmouth & Southsea	d					09 18			09 47											10 18	
Fratton	d					09 22			09 51											10 22	
Hilsea	d											10a04	10a26								
Bedhampton	d					09 30														10 30	
Havant	d					09 33			10 00	10 11										10 33	
Warblington	d					09 35														10 35	
Emsworth	d					09 38			10 04	10 15										10 38	
Southbourne	d					09 41			10 07											10 41	
Nutbourne	d					09 43														10 43	
Bosham	d					09 47														10 47	
Fishbourne (Sussex)	d					09 50														10 50	
Chichester 4	a					09 53			10 14	10 23										10 53	
	d					09 53			10 14	10 23										10 53	
Bognor Regis 4	d	09 36			09 58											10 34			10 58		
Barnham	a	09 42			10 04	10 01			10 22	10 31						10 40			11 04	11 01	
	d	09 43	09 44		10 05	10 08	10 15		10 22	10 38						10 41	10 43		11 05	11 08	11 15
Bognor Regis	a		09 50				10 21										10 49				11 21
Ford 4	d	09 47			10 09	10 12				10 42						10 45			11 09	11 12	
Littlehampton 4	a	09 52														10 50					
	d							10 14													
Angmering 3	d					10 18		10 22		10 48										11 18	
Goring-by-Sea	d					10 22		10 26		10 52										11 22	
Durrington-on-Sea	d					10 25		10 29		10 55										11 25	
West Worthing	d					10 27		10 31		10 57										11 27	
Worthing 4	a					10 29		10 33	10 37	10 59										11 29	
	d					10 30		10 41		11 00										11 30	
East Worthing	d					10 32				11 02										11 32	
Lancing	d					10 35				11 05										11 35	
Shoreham-by-Sea	d					10 39		10 47		11 09										11 39	
Southwick	d					10 42				11 12										11 42	
Fishersgate	d					10 44				11 14										11 44	
Portslade	d					10 46				11 16										11 46	
Aldrington	d					10 49				11 19										11 49	
Hove 2	a					10 51		10 54		11 21										11 51	
	d					10 56		10 54		11 22										11 56	
Brighton 10	a					11 00				11 26										12 00	
Preston Park	d																				
Burgess Hill	a							11 04													
Haywards Heath 3	a							11 10													
Arundel	d				10 14														11 14		
Amberley	d				10 19														11 19		
Pulborough	d				10 25														11 25		
Billingshurst	d				10 31														11 31		
Christs Hospital	d				10 38														11 38		
Horsham 4	a				10 42														11 42		
	d			10 03	10 42													11 03	11 42		
Crawley	d			10 16	10 51													11 16	11 51		
Three Bridges 4	a			10 19	10 54													11 19	11 54		
Gatwick Airport 10	a			10 24	10 59			11 21										11 24	11 59		
	d			10 25	11 00			11 23										11 25	12 00		
Horley	a			10 28	11 02													11 28	12 02		
Redhill 5	a			10 34	11 09													11 34	12 09		
East Croydon	a			10 56	11 26			11 40										11 56	12 26		
London Bridge 4	a			11 12														12 12			
Clapham Junction 10	a				11 37			11 54											12 37		
London Victoria 15	a				11 46			12 01											12 46		

Table 188 — Sundays

Southampton, Portsmouth and Sussex Coast - Brighton, Gatwick Airport and London

Network Diagram - see first Page of Table 186

		SN ◇1	SN ◇1	SN ◇1	SW ◇1	SW 1	SW 1	SW ◇1	SW 1	SN 1	SN ◇1 H	SN 1	SN ◇1 H	SN 1	SN 1	SN ◇1	SN ◇1	SN ◇1	SW ◇1	SW 1	SW 1
Eastleigh	d				10 22	10 26			10 54										11 22	11 26	
Southampton Airport Parkway	d				10 27			10 55	10 58										11 27		
Southampton Central	d			10 29	10a34		10 35	11a02	11a09									11 28	11a34		11 35
Swanwick	d			10 46			11 02											11 46			12 02
Fareham	d			10 53		10 44	11 10											11 53		11 44	12 10
Portchester	d					10 49	11 15													11 49	12 15
Cosham	d			11 02		10 54	11 20											12 02		11 54	12 20
Portsmouth Harbour	d		10 43											11 14			11 43				
Portsmouth & Southsea	d		10 47											11 18			11 47				
Fratton	d		10 51											11 22			11 51				
Hilsea	d					11a04	11a26													12a00	12a26
Bedhampton	d													11 32							
Havant	d		11 00	11 11										11 35			12 00	12 11			
Warblington	d													11 37							
Emsworth	d		11 04	11 15										11 40			12 04	12 15			
Southbourne	d		11 07											11 43			12 07				
Nutbourne	d													11 45							
Bosham	d													11 49							
Fishbourne (Sussex)	d													11 52							
Chichester 4	a		11 14	11 23										11 55			12 14	12 23			
	d		11 14	11 23										11 55			12 14	12 23			
Bognor Regis 4	d									11 34			11 58								
Barnham	a		11 22	11 31						11 40			12 04	12 03			12 22	12 31			
	d		11 22	11 38						11 41	11 43		12 05	12 08	12 15		12 22	12 38			
Bognor Regis	a										11 49				12 21						
Ford 4	d			11 42						11 45			12 09	12 12				12 42			
Littlehampton 4	a									11 50											
	d	11 14														12 14					
Angmering 3	d	11 22		11 48										12 18		12 22		12 48			
Goring-by-Sea	d	11 26		11 52										12 22		12 26		12 52			
Durrington-on-Sea	d	11 29		11 55										12 25		12 29		12 55			
West Worthing	d	11 31		11 57										12 27		12 31		12 57			
Worthing 4	a	11 33	11 37	11 59										12 29		12 33	12 37	12 59			
	d	11 41		12 00										12 30		12 41		13 00			
East Worthing	d			12 02										12 32				13 02			
Lancing	d			12 05										12 35				13 05			
Shoreham-by-Sea	d	11 47		12 09										12 39		12 47		13 09			
Southwick	d			12 12										12 42				13 12			
Fishersgate	d			12 14										12 44				13 14			
Portslade	d			12 16										12 46				13 16			
Aldrington	d			12 19										12 49				13 19			
Hove 2	a	11 54		12 21										12 51		12 54		13 21			
	d	11 54		12 22										12 56		12 54		13 22			
Brighton 10	a			12 26										13 00				13 26			
Preston Park	d																				
Burgess Hill	a	12 04														13 04					
Haywards Heath 3	a	12 10														13 10					
Arundel	d												12 14								
Amberley	d												12 19								
Pulborough	d												12 25								
Billingshurst	d												12 31								
Christs Hospital	d												12 38								
Horsham 4	a												12 42								
	d											12 03	12 42								
Crawley	d											12 16	12 51								
Three Bridges 4	a											12 19	12 54								
Gatwick Airport 10	a	12 22										12 24	12 59			13 22					
	d	12 23										12 25	13 00			13 23					
Horley	a											12 28	13 02								
Redhill 5	a											12 34	13 09								
East Croydon	a	12 39										12 56	13 26			13 39					
London Bridge 4	a											13 12									
Clapham Junction 10	a	12 54											13 37			13 54					
London Victoria 15	a	13 01											13 46			14 01					

Sundays

Southampton, Portsmouth and Sussex Coast - Brighton, Gatwick Airport and London

Network Diagram - see first Page of Table 186

		SW	SW	SN	SN	SN		SN	SN	SN	SN	SN	SN	SW	SW	SW			SW	SN	SN	SN	SN	SN	SN
		◇1 ⊼	1	1	◇1 ⊼	1		◇1 ⊼	1	1	◇1	◇1	◇1	◇1	1	1			◇1 ⊼	1	◇1 ⊼	1	◇1 ⊼	1	1
Eastleigh	d		11 54											12 22	12 26										
Southampton Airport Parkway	d	11 53	11 58											12 27					12 53						
Southampton Central	d	11a59	12a09										12 29	12a34		12 35			13a00						
Swanwick	d												12 46			13 02									
Fareham	d												12 53		12 44	13 10									
Portchester	d														12 49	13 15									
Cosham	d												13 02		12 54	13 20									
Portsmouth Harbour	d								12 14			12 43												13 14	
Portsmouth & Southsea	d								12 18			12 47												13 18	
Fratton	d								12 22			12 51												13 22	
Hilsea	d														13a00	13a26									
Bedhampton	d								12 32															13 32	
Havant	d								12 35			13 00	13 11											13 35	
Warblington	d								12 37															13 37	
Emsworth	d								12 40			13 04	13 15											13 40	
Southbourne	d								12 43			13 07												13 43	
Nutbourne	d								12 45															13 45	
Bosham	d								12 49															13 49	
Fishbourne (Sussex)	d								12 52															13 52	
Chichester 4	a								12 55			13 14	13 23											13 55	
	d								12 55			13 14	13 23											13 55	
Bognor Regis 4	d			12 34				12 58												13 34			13 58		
Barnham	a			12 40				13 04	13 03			13 22	13 31							13 40			14 04	14 03	
	d			12 41	12 43			13 05	13 08	13 15		13 22	13 38							13 41	13 43		14 05	14 08	14 15
Bognor Regis	a				12 49					13 21											13 49				14 21
Ford 4	d			12 45				13 09	13 12				13 42							13 45			14 09	14 12	
Littlehampton 4	a			12 50																13 50					
	d										13 14														
Angmering 3	d								13 18		13 22		13 48											14 18	
Goring-by-Sea	d								13 22		13 26		13 52											14 22	
Durrington-on-Sea	d								13 25		13 29		13 55											14 25	
West Worthing	d								13 27		13 31		13 57											14 27	
Worthing 4	a								13 29		13 33	13 37	13 59											14 29	
	d								13 30		13 41		14 00											14 30	
East Worthing	d								13 32				14 02											14 32	
Lancing	d								13 35				14 05											14 35	
Shoreham-by-Sea	d								13 39		13 47		14 09											14 39	
Southwick	d								13 42				14 12											14 42	
Fishersgate	d								13 44				14 14											14 44	
Portslade	d								13 46				14 16											14 46	
Aldrington	d								13 49				14 19											14 49	
Hove 2	a								13 51		13 54		14 21											14 51	
	d								13 56		13 54		14 22											14 56	
Brighton 10	a								14 00				14 26											15 00	
Preston Park	d																								
Burgess Hill	a										14 04														
Haywards Heath 3	a										14 10														
Arundel	d							13 14															14 14		
Amberley	d							13 19															14 19		
Pulborough	d							13 25															14 25		
Billingshurst	d							13 31															14 31		
Christs Hospital	d							13 38															14 38		
Horsham 4	a							13 42															14 42		
	d					13 03		13 42														14 03	14 42		
Crawley	d					13 16		13 51														14 16	14 51		
Three Bridges 4	a					13 19		13 54														14 19	14 54		
Gatwick Airport 10	a					13 24		13 59			14 22											14 24	14 59		
	d					13 25		14 00			14 23											14 25	15 00		
Horley	a					13 28		14 02														14 28	15 02		
Redhill 5	a					13 34		14 09														14 34	15 09		
East Croydon	a					13 56		14 26			14 40											14 56	15 26		
London Bridge 4	a					14 12																15 12			
Clapham Junction 10	a							14 37			14 54												15 37		
London Victoria 15	a							14 46			15 01												15 46		

Sundays

Southampton, Portsmouth and Sussex Coast - Brighton, Gatwick Airport and London

Network Diagram - see first Page of Table 186

		SN	SN		GW	SW	SN	SW	SW	SW		SW	SW		SN	SN	SN	SN	SN	SN	SN	SN	SN		SW
		◇1	◇1		◇	1	◇1	◇1 ⊼	1	1		◇1 ⊼	1		1	◇1 ⊼	1	◇1 ⊼	1	1	◇1	◇1	◇1		◇1 ⊼
Eastleigh	d					12 54		13 22	13 26				13 54												14 22
Southampton Airport Parkway	d					12 58		13 27				13 53	13 58												14 27
Southampton Central	d				13 07	13a09	13 29	13a34		13 35		14a00	14a09										14 29		14a34
Swanwick	d						13 46			14 02													14 46		
Fareham	d				13 34		13 53		13 44	14 10													14 53		
Portchester	d								13 49	14 15															
Cosham	d				13 42		14 02		13 54	14 20													15 02		
Portsmouth Harbour	d		13 43															14 14			14 43				
Portsmouth & Southsea	d		13 47															14 18			14 47				
Fratton	d		13 51															14 22			14 51				
Hilsea	d								14a00	14a26															
Bedhampton	d																	14 30							
Havant	d		14 00		14 04		14 11											14 33			15 00	15 11			
Warblington	d																	14 35							
Emsworth	d		14 04				14 15											14 38			15 04	15 15			
Southbourne	d		14 07															14 41			15 07				
Nutbourne	d																	14 43							
Bosham	d																	14 47							
Fishbourne (Sussex)	d																	14 50							
Chichester 4	a		14 14		14 19		14 23											14 53			15 14	15 23			
	d		14 14		14 20		14 23											14 53			15 14	15 23			
Bognor Regis 4	d														14 34			14 58							
Barnham	a		14 22		14 27		14 31								14 40			15 04	15 01			15 22	15 31		
	d		14 22		14 28		14 38								14 41	14 43		15 05	15 08	15 15		15 22	15 38		
Bognor Regis	a															14 49				15 21					
Ford 4	d						14 42								14 45			15 09	15 12				15 42		
Littlehampton 4	a														14 50										
	d	14 14																			15 14				
Angmering 3	d	14 22					14 48												15 18		15 22		15 48		
Goring-by-Sea	d	14 26					14 52												15 22		15 26		15 52		
Durrington-on-Sea	d	14 29					14 55												15 25		15 29		15 55		
West Worthing	d	14 31					14 57												15 27		15 31		15 57		
Worthing 4	a	14 33	14 37		14 45		14 59												15 29		15 33	15 37	15 59		
	d	14 41			14 45		15 00												15 30		15 41		16 00		
East Worthing	d						15 02												15 32				16 02		
Lancing	d						15 05												15 35				16 05		
Shoreham-by-Sea	d	14 47			14 52		15 09												15 39		15 47		16 09		
Southwick	d						15 12												15 42				16 12		
Fishersgate	d						15 14												15 44				16 14		
Portslade	d						15 16												15 46				16 16		
Aldrington	d						15 19												15 49				16 19		
Hove 2	a	14 54			15 00		15 21												15 51		15 54		16 21		
	d	14 54			15 00		15 22												15 56		15 54		16 22		
Brighton 10	a				15 06		15 26												16 00				16 26		
Preston Park	d																								
Burgess Hill	a	15 04																			16 04				
Haywards Heath 3	a	15 10																			16 10				
Arundel	d																	15 14							
Amberley	d																	15 19							
Pulborough	d																	15 25							
Billingshurst	d																	15 31							
Christs Hospital	d																	15 38							
Horsham 4	a																	15 42							
	d																15 03	15 42							
Crawley	d																15 16	15 51							
Three Bridges 4	a																15 19	15 54							
Gatwick Airport 10	a	15 22															15 24	15 59			16 22				
	d	15 23															15 25	16 00			16 23				
Horley	a																15 28	16 02							
Redhill 5	a																15 34	16 09							
East Croydon	a	15 40															15 56	16 26			16 40				
London Bridge 4	a																16 12								
Clapham Junction 10	a	15 54																16 37			16 54				
London Victoria 15	a	16 01																16 46			17 01				

Table 188

Sundays

Southampton, Portsmouth and Sussex Coast - Brighton, Gatwick Airport and London

Network Diagram - see first Page of Table 186

		SW 1	SW 1	SW ◇1 ⌶	SW 1	SN 1	SN ◇1 ⌶	SN 1	SN ◇1 ⌶	SN 1	SN 1	SN ◇1	SN ◇1	GW ◇	SN ◇1	SW ◇1 ⌶	SW 1	SW 1	SW ◇1 ⌶	SW 1	SN 1
Eastleigh	d	14 26			14 54											15 22	15 26			15 54	
Southampton Airport Parkway	d			14 53	14 58											15 27			15 53	15 58	
Southampton Central ⛴	d		14 35	15a00	15a09									15 22	15 29	15a34		15 35	16a00	16a09	
Swanwick	d		15 02												15 46			16 02			
Fareham	d	14 44	15 10											15 51	15 58		15 44	16 10			
Portchester	d	14 49	15 15														15 49	16 15			
Cosham	d	14 54	15 20											16 01	16 07		15 54	16 20			
Portsmouth Harbour ⛴	d									15 14			15 43								
Portsmouth & Southsea	d									15 18			15 47								
Fratton	d									15 22			15 51								
Hilsea	d	15a00	15a26														16a00	16a26			
Bedhampton	d									15 30											
Havant	d									15 33			16 00	16 12	16 16						
Warblington	d									15 35											
Emsworth	d									15 38			16 04		16 20						
Southbourne	d									15 41			16 07								
Nutbourne	d									15 43											
Bosham	d									15 47											
Fishbourne (Sussex)	d									15 50											
Chichester 4	a									15 53			16 14	16 22	16 28						
	d									15 53			16 14	16 23	16 28						
Bognor Regis 4	d					15 34			15 58												16 34
Barnham	a					15 40			16 04	16 01			16 22	16 30	16 36						16 40
	d					15 41	15 43		16 05	16 08	16 15		16 22	16 31	16 38						16 41
Bognor Regis	a						15 49				16 21										
Ford 4	d					15 45			16 09	16 12					16 42						16 45
Littlehampton 4	a					15 50															16 50
	d											16 14									
Angmering 3	d									16 18		16 22			16 48						
Goring-by-Sea	d									16 22		16 26			16 52						
Durrington-on-Sea	d									16 25		16 29			16 55						
West Worthing	d									16 27		16 31			16 57						
Worthing 4	a									16 29		16 33	16 37	16 45	16 59						
	d									16 30		16 41		16 46	17 00						
East Worthing	d									16 32					17 02						
Lancing	d									16 35					17 05						
Shoreham-by-Sea	d									16 39		16 47		16 52	17 09						
Southwick	d									16 42					17 12						
Fishersgate	d									16 44					17 14						
Portslade	d									16 46					17 16						
Aldrington	d									16 49					17 19						
Hove 2	a									16 51		16 54		16 58	17 21						
	d									16 56		16 54		17 00	17 22						
Brighton 10	a									17 00				17 06	17 26						
Preston Park	d																				
Burgess Hill	a											17 04									
Haywards Heath 3	a											17 10									
Arundel	d								16 14												
Amberley	d								16 19												
Pulborough	d								16 25												
Billingshurst	d								16 31												
Christs Hospital	d								16 38												
Horsham 4	a								16 42												
	d							16 03	16 42												
Crawley	d							16 16	16 51												
Three Bridges 4	a							16 19	16 54												
Gatwick Airport 10 ✈	a							16 24	16 59			17 22									
	d							16 25	17 00			17 23									
Horley	a							16 28	17 02												
Redhill 5	a							16 34	17 09												
East Croydon 🚊	a							16 56	17 26			17 40									
London Bridge 4 ⊖	a							17 12													
Clapham Junction 10	a								17 37			17 54									
London Victoria 15 ⊖	a								17 46			18 01									

Table 188

Sundays

Southampton, Portsmouth and Sussex Coast - Brighton, Gatwick Airport and London

Network Diagram - see first Page of Table 186

		SN ◇1 ⌶	SN 1	SN ◇1 ⌶	SN 1	SN 1	SN ◇1	SN ◇1	SN ◇1	SW ◇1 ⌶	SW 1	SW 1	SW ◇1 ⌶	SW 1	SN 1	SN ◇1 ⌶	SN 1	SN ◇1	SN 1	SN 1	SN ◇1	SN ◇1
Eastleigh	d									16 22	16 26			16 54								
Southampton Airport Parkway	d									16 27			16 53	16 58								
Southampton Central ⛴	d								16 29	16a34		16 35	17a00	17a09								
Swanwick	d								16 46			17 02										
Fareham	d								16 53		16 44	17 10										
Portchester	d										16 49	17 15										
Cosham	d								17 02		16 54	17 20										
Portsmouth Harbour ⛴	d				16 14			16 43											17 14			17 43
Portsmouth & Southsea	d				16 18			16 47											17 18			17 47
Fratton	d				16 22			16 51											17 22			17 51
Hilsea	d										17a00	17a26										
Bedhampton	d				16 30														17 30			
Havant	d				16 33			17 00	17 11										17 33			18 00
Warblington	d				16 35														17 35			
Emsworth	d				16 38			17 04	17 15										17 38			18 04
Southbourne	d				16 41			17 07											17 41			18 07
Nutbourne	d				16 43														17 43			
Bosham	d				16 47														17 47			
Fishbourne (Sussex)	d				16 50														17 50			
Chichester 4	a				16 53			17 14	17 23										17 53			18 14
	d				16 53			17 14	17 23										17 53			18 14
Bognor Regis 4	d			16 58											17 34			17 58				
Barnham	a			17 04	17 01			17 22	17 31						17 40			18 04	18 01			18 22
	d	16 44		17 05	17 08	17 15		17 22	17 38						17 41	17 43		18 05	18 08	18 15		18 22
Bognor Regis	a	16 50				17 21										17 49				18 21		
Ford 4	d			17 09	17 12				17 42						17 45			18 09	18 12			
Littlehampton 4	a														17 50							
	d						17 14														18 14	
Angmering 3	d				17 18		17 22		17 48										18 18		18 22	
Goring-by-Sea	d				17 22		17 26		17 52										18 22		18 26	
Durrington-on-Sea	d				17 25		17 29		17 55										18 25		18 29	
West Worthing	d				17 27		17 31		17 57										18 27		18 31	
Worthing 4	a				17 29		17 33	17 37	17 59										18 29		18 33	18 37
	d				17 30		17 41		18 00										18 30		18 41	
East Worthing	d				17 32				18 02										18 32			
Lancing	d				17 35				18 05										18 35			
Shoreham-by-Sea	d				17 39		17 47		18 09										18 39		18 47	
Southwick	d				17 42				18 12										18 42			
Fishersgate	d				17 44				18 14										18 44			
Portslade	d				17 46				18 16										18 46			
Aldrington	d				17 49				18 19										18 49			
Hove 2	a				17 51		17 54		18 21										18 51		18 54	
	d				17 56		17 54		18 22										18 56		18 54	
Brighton 10	a				18 00				18 26										19 00			
Preston Park	d																					
Burgess Hill	a						18 04														19 04	
Haywards Heath 3	a						18 10														19 10	
Arundel	d			17 14														18 14				
Amberley	d			17 19														18 19				
Pulborough	d			17 25														18 25				
Billingshurst	d			17 31														18 31				
Christs Hospital	d			17 38														18 38				
Horsham 4	a			17 42														18 42				
	d		17 03	17 42													18 03	18 42				
Crawley	d		17 16	17 51													18 16	18 51				
Three Bridges 4	a		17 19	17 54													18 19	18 54				
Gatwick Airport 10 ✈	a		17 24	17 59			18 22										18 24	18 59			19 22	
	d		17 25	18 00			18 23										18 25	19 00			19 23	
Horley	a		17 28	18 02													18 28	19 02				
Redhill 5	a		17 34	18 09													18 34	19 09				
East Croydon 🚊	a		17 56	18 26			18 40										18 56	19 26			19 40	
London Bridge 4 ⊖	a		18 12														19 12					
Clapham Junction 10	a			18 37			18 54											19 37			19 54	
London Victoria 15 ⊖	a			18 46			19 01											19 46			20 01	

Southampton, Portsmouth and Sussex Coast - Brighton, Gatwick Airport and London

Network Diagram - see first Page of Table 186

		SN ◇1	SW ◇1	SW 1	SW 1	SW ◇1	SW 1	SN 1	SN ◇1	SN 1	SN ◇1	SN 1	SN 1	SN ◇1	SN ◇1	SN ◇1	SW ◇1	SW 1	SW 1	SW ◇1
Eastleigh	d		17 22	17 26			17 54										18 22	18 26		
Southampton Airport Parkway	d		17 27			17 53	17 58										18 27			18 53
Southampton Central	d	17 29	17a34		17 35	18a00	18a09									18 29	18a34		18 35	19a00
Swanwick	d	17 46			18 02											18 46			19 02	
Fareham	d	17 53		17 44	18 10											18 53		18 44	19 10	
Portchester	d			17 49	18 15													18 49	19 15	
Cosham	d	18 02		17 54	18 20											19 02		18 54	19 20	
Portsmouth Harbour	d											18 14			18 43					
Portsmouth & Southsea	d											18 18			18 47					
Fratton	d											18 22			18 51					
Hilsea	d			18a00	18a26													19a00	19a26	
Bedhampton	d											18 30								
Havant	d	18 11										18 33			19 00	19 11				
Warblington	d											18 35								
Emsworth	d	18 15										18 38			19 04	19 15				
Southbourne	d											18 41			19 07					
Nutbourne	d											18 43								
Bosham	d											18 47								
Fishbourne (Sussex)	d											18 50								
Chichester 4	a	18 23										18 53			19 14	19 23				
	d	18 23										18 53			19 14	19 23				
Bognor Regis 4	d							18 34			18 58									
Barnham	a	18 31						18 40			19 04	19 01			19 22	19 31				
	d	18 38						18 41	18 43		19 05	19 08	19 15		19 22	19 38				
Bognor Regis	a								18 49				19 21							
Ford 4	d	18 42						18 45			19 09	19 12				19 42				
Littlehampton 4	a							18 50												
	d													19 14						
Angmering 3	d	18 48										19 18		19 22		19 48				
Goring-by-Sea	d	18 52										19 22		19 26		19 52				
Durrington-on-Sea	d	18 55										19 25		19 29		19 55				
West Worthing	d	18 57										19 27		19 31		19 57				
Worthing 4	a	18 59										19 29		19 33	19 37	19 59				
	d	19 00										19 30		19 41		20 00				
East Worthing	d	19 02										19 32				20 02				
Lancing	d	19 05										19 35				20 05				
Shoreham-by-Sea	d	19 09										19 39		19 47		20 09				
Southwick	d	19 12										19 42				20 12				
Fishersgate	d	19 14										19 44				20 14				
Portslade	d	19 16										19 46				20 16				
Aldrington	d	19 19										19 49				20 19				
Hove 2	a	19 21										19 51		19 54		20 21				
	d	19 22										19 56		19 54		20 22				
Brighton 10	a	19 26										20 00				20 26				
Preston Park	d																			
Burgess Hill	a													20 04						
Haywards Heath 3	a													20 10						
Arundel	d										19 14									
Amberley	d										19 19									
Pulborough	d										19 25									
Billingshurst	d										19 31									
Christs Hospital	d										19 38									
Horsham 4	a										19 42									
	d									19 03	19 42									
Crawley	d									19 16	19 51									
Three Bridges 4	a									19 19	19 54									
Gatwick Airport 10	a									19 24	19 59			20 22						
	d									19 25	20 00			20 23						
Horley	a									19 28	20 02									
Redhill 5	a									19 34	20 09									
East Croydon	a									19 56	20 26			20 40						
London Bridge 4	a									20 12										
Clapham Junction 10	a										20 37			20 54						
London Victoria 15	a										20 46			21 01						

Southampton, Portsmouth and Sussex Coast - Brighton, Gatwick Airport and London

Network Diagram - see first Page of Table 186

		SW 1	SN 1	SN ◇1	SN 1	SN ◇1	SN 1	SN 1	SN ◇1	SN ◇1	GW ◇	SW ◇1	SW 1	SN ◇1 A	SW 1	SW ◇1	SW 1	SW ◇1	SW 1	SN 1	SN ◇1	SN 1
Eastleigh	d	18 54										19 22	19 26	19 46			19 54	20 22	20 26			
Southampton Airport Parkway	d	18 58										19 27		*19 38*		19 53	19 58	20 27				
Southampton Central	d	19a09									19 26	19a34		*19a30*	19 35	20a00	20a09	20a34				
Swanwick	d														20 02							
Fareham	d										19 49		19 44	20 03	20 10				20 44			
Portchester	d												19 49		20 15				20 49			
Cosham	d										19 58		19 54	20 12	20 20				20 54			
Portsmouth Harbour	d						19 14			19 43												20 14
Portsmouth & Southsea	d						19 18			19 47												20 18
Fratton	d						19 22			19 51												20 22
Hilsea	d												20a00		20a26				21a00			
Bedhampton	d						19 30															20 30
Havant	d						19 33			20 00	20 10			20 18								20 33
Warblington	d						19 35															20 35
Emsworth	d						19 38			20 04				20 22								20 38
Southbourne	d						19 41			20 07												20 41
Nutbourne	d						19 43															20 43
Bosham	d						19 47															20 47
Fishbourne (Sussex)	d						19 50															20 50
Chichester 4	a						19 53			20 14	20 20			20 30								20 53
	d						19 53			20 14	20 21			20 31								20 53
Bognor Regis 4	d		19 34			19 58														20 34		
Barnham	a		19 40			20 04	20 01			20 22	20 28			20 38						20 41		21 01
	d		19 41	19 43		20 05	20 08	20 15		20 22	20 29			20 39						20 42	20 43	21 02
Bognor Regis	a			19 49				20 21													20 49	
Ford 4	d		19 45			20 09	20 12							20 43						20 46		21 06
Littlehampton 4	a		19 50																	20 51		21 11
	d								20 14													21 15
Angmering 3	d						20 18		20 22					20 49								21 23
Goring-by-Sea	d						20 22		20 26					20 53								21 27
Durrington-on-Sea	d						20 25		20 29					20 56								21 30
West Worthing	d						20 27		20 31					20 58								21 32
Worthing 4	a						20 29		20 33	20 37	20 50			21 00								21 34
	d						20 30		20 41		20 50			21 01								21 35
East Worthing	d						20 32							21 03								21 37
Lancing	d						20 35							21 06								21 40
Shoreham-by-Sea	d						20 39		20 47		20 57			21 10								21 44
Southwick	d						20 42							21 13								21 47
Fishersgate	d						20 44							21 15								21 49
Portslade	d						20 46							21 17								21 51
Aldrington	d						20 49							21 20								21 54
Hove 2	a						20 51		20 54		21 03			21 22								21 56
	d						20 56		20 54		21 04			21 22								21 56
Brighton 10	a						21 00				21 09			21 26								22 00
Preston Park	d																					
Burgess Hill	a								21 04													
Haywards Heath 3	a								21 10													
Arundel	d					20 14																
Amberley	d					20 19																
Pulborough	d					20 25																
Billingshurst	d					20 31																
Christs Hospital	d					20 38																
Horsham 4	a					20 42																
	d				20 03	20 42																
Crawley	d				20 16	20 51																
Three Bridges 4	a				20 19	20 54																
Gatwick Airport 10	a				20 24	20 59			21 22													
	d				20 25	21 00			21 23													
Horley	a				20 28	21 02																
Redhill 5	a				20 34	21 09																
East Croydon	a				20 56	21 26			21 40													
London Bridge 4	a				21 12																	
Clapham Junction 10	a					21 37			21 54													
London Victoria 15	a					21 46			22 01													

A Stops at Southampton Central and Southampton Airport Parkway before Eastleigh

Table 188

Sundays

Southampton, Portsmouth and Sussex Coast - Brighton, Gatwick Airport and London

Network Diagram - see first Page of Table 186

		SN 1	SN ◇1	SN 1	SN 1	SN ◇1 A	SW 1	SW ◇1 🚌	SW 1	SN 1	SN ◇1	SN 1	SN ◇1	SN 1	SN 1	SN	SN 1	SN ◇1	SW ◇1	SW 1	SW 1
Eastleigh	d					20 46			20 54										21 22	21 26	
Southampton Airport Parkway	d					*20 38*		20 53	20 58										21 27		
Southampton Central	d					*20a29*	20 35	21a00	21a09									21 30	21a34		21 35
Swanwick	d						21 02											21 47			22 02
Fareham	d					21 02	21 10											21 54		21 44	22 10
Portchester	d						21 15													21 49	22 15
Cosham	d					21 11	21 20											22 03		21 54	22 20
Portsmouth Harbour	d				20 43									21 14			21 43				
Portsmouth & Southsea	d				20 47									21 18			21 47				
Fratton	d				20 51									21 22			21 51				
Hilsea	d						21a26													22a00	22a26
Bedhampton	d													21 30							
Havant	d				21 00	21 17								21 33			22 00	22 11			
Warblington	d													21 35							
Emsworth	d				21 04	21 21								21 38			22 04	22 15			
Southbourne	d				21 07									21 41			22 07				
Nutbourne	d													21 43							
Bosham	d													21 47							
Fishbourne (Sussex)	d													21 50							
Chichester 4	a				21 14	21 29								21 53			22 14	22 23			
	d				21 14	21 30								21 53			22 14	22 23			
Bognor Regis 4	d		20 58							21 34			21 58			22 12					
Barnham	a		21 04		21 22	21 37				21 40			22 04	22 01		22 18	22 22	22 31			
	d		21 05	21 15	21 22	21 38				21 41	21 43		22 05	22 08	22 15		22 23	22 32			
Bognor Regis	a			21 21							21 49				22 21						
Ford 4	d		21 09		21 27	21 42				21 45			22 09	22 12			22 27	22 36			
Littlehampton 4	a				21 31					21 50							22 32				
	d				21 42												22 42				
Angmering 3	d				21 52	21 48								22 18			22 50	22 42			
Goring-by-Sea	d				21 56	21 52								22 22			22 54	22 46			
Durrington-on-Sea	d				21 59	21 55								22 25			22 57	22 49			
West Worthing	d				22 01	21 57								22 27			22 59	22 51			
Worthing 4	a				22 03	21 59								22 29			23 01	22 53			
	d				22 04	22 00								22 30			23 02	22 54			
East Worthing	d				22 06	22 02								22 32			23 04	22 56			
Lancing	d				22 09	22 05								22 35			23 07	22 59			
Shoreham-by-Sea	d				22 13	22 09								22 39			23 11	23 03			
Southwick	d				22 16	22 12								22 42			23 14	23 06			
Fishersgate	d				22 18	22 14								22 44			23 16	23 08			
Portslade	d				22 20	22 16								22 46			23 18	23 10			
Aldrington	d				22 23	22 19								22 49			23 21	23 13			
Hove 2	a				22 25	22 21								22 51			23 24	23 15			
	d				22 25	22 21								22 51			23 26	23 15			
Brighton 10	a				22 29	22 25								22 56			23 30	23 19			
Preston Park	d																				
Burgess Hill	a																				
Haywards Heath 3	a																				
Arundel	d		21 14										22 14								
Amberley	d		21 19										22 19								
Pulborough	d		21 25										22 25								
Billingshurst	d		21 31										22 31								
Christs Hospital	d		21 38										22 38								
Horsham 4	a		21 42										22 42								
	d	21 03	21 42									22 03	22 42								
Crawley	d	21 16	21 51									22 16	22 51								
Three Bridges 4	a	21 19	21 54									22 19	22 54								
Gatwick Airport 10 ✈	a	21 24	21 59									22 24	22 59								
	d	21 25	22 00									22 25	23 00								
Horley	a	21 28	22 02									22 28	23 02								
Redhill 5	a	21 34	22 09									22 34	23 09								
East Croydon	a	21 56	22 26									22 55	23 26								
London Bridge 4 ⊖	a	22 12																			
Clapham Junction 10	a		22 37									23 07	23 38								
London Victoria 15 ⊖	a		22 46									23 14	23 46								

A Stops at Southampton Central and Southampton Airport Parkway before Eastleigh

Table 188

Sundays

Southampton, Portsmouth and Sussex Coast - Brighton, Gatwick Airport and London

Network Diagram - see first Page of Table 186

		SW ◇1 🚌	SW 1	SN ◇1	SN	SN 1	SN 1	SW ◇1	SW 1	SW 1	SN 1	SN 1	SN 1	SN ◇1	SN ◇1	SN 1	SW ◇1 🚌	SW 1	SW ◇1	SW 1
Eastleigh	d		21 54					22 22	22 26									22 54	23 22	23 26
Southampton Airport Parkway	d	21 53	21 58					22 27									22 53	22 58	23 27	
Southampton Central	d	22a00	22a09				22 15	22a34		22 35						22 52	23a00	23a09	23a34	
Swanwick	d						22 32			23 02						23 11				
Fareham	d						22 39		22 44	23 10						23 17				23 44
Portchester	d								22 49	23 15										23 49
Cosham	d						22 48		22 54	23 20						23 26				23 54
Portsmouth Harbour	d					22 14							22 43							
Portsmouth & Southsea	d					22 18							22 47							
Fratton	d					22 22							22 51							
Hilsea	d								23a00	23a24										23a59
Bedhampton	d					22 32														
Havant	d					22 35	22 54						23 00			23 32				
Warblington	d					22 37														
Emsworth	d					22 40	22 58						23 04			23 36				
Southbourne	d					22 43							23 07							
Nutbourne	d					22 46														
Bosham	d					22 49														
Fishbourne (Sussex)	d					22 52														
Chichester 4	a					22 55	23 06						23 14			23 44				
	d					22 56	23 07						23 14			23 45				
Bognor Regis 4	d																			
Barnham	a					23 03	23 14						23 23			23 52				
	d			22 43	22 57	23 04	23 15					23 15	23 24	23 37	23 43	23 53				
Bognor Regis	a			22 49	23 04							23 21			23 49					
Ford 4	d					23 08	23 20						23 28	23 42						
Littlehampton 4	a					23 13	23 27						23 33	23 46		00 01				
	d																			
Angmering 3	d																			
Goring-by-Sea	d																			
Durrington-on-Sea	d																			
West Worthing	d																			
Worthing 4	a																			
	d																			
East Worthing	d																			
Lancing	d																			
Shoreham-by-Sea	d																			
Southwick	d																			
Fishersgate	d																			
Portslade	d																			
Aldrington	d																			
Hove 2	a																			
	d																			
Brighton 10	a																			
Preston Park	d																			
Burgess Hill	a																			
Haywards Heath 3	a																			
Arundel	d																			
Amberley	d																			
Pulborough	d																			
Billingshurst	d																			
Christs Hospital	d																			
Horsham 4	a																			
	d										23 03									
Crawley	d										23 16									
Three Bridges 4	a										23 19									
Gatwick Airport 10 ✈	a										23 24									
	d										23 25									
Horley	a										23 28									
Redhill 5	a										23 34									
East Croydon	a										23 55									
London Bridge 4 ⊖	a																			
Clapham Junction 10	a										00 11									
London Victoria 15 ⊖	a										00 19									

Table 189

Mondays to Fridays

London, Haywards Heath and Brighton - Lewes, Seaford, Eastbourne, Hastings and Ashford

Network Diagram - see first Page of Table 184

Miles	Miles			SN MX ◇1	SN MX	SN MO ◇1	SN MX ◇1	SN	SN ◇1	SN 1	SN	SN 1		SN 1	SN	SN	SN	SN	SN	SN 1	SN 1	SN 1		SN	SN 1
—	—	**London Victoria** 15 ⊖	d	22p47		22p47	00 05																		
—	—	Clapham Junction 10	d	22p53		22p53	00 11																		
—	—	**London Bridge** 4 ⊖	d																						
—	—	East Croydon	d	23p03		23p07	00 27																		
—	—	**Gatwick Airport** 10 ✈	d	23p19		23p29	00 44																		
—	0	**Haywards Heath** 3	d	23p34		23p41	01 06												06 07						
—	3	Wivelsfield 4	d	23p38		23p45													06 11						
—	6¾	Plumpton	d	23p44		23p51																			
—	9½	Cooksbridge	d																						
0	—	**Brighton** 10	d		23p34							05 12			05 45			06 00							
0¾	—	London Road (Brighton)	d		23p37										05 48			06 03							
1¾	—	Moulsecoomb	d		23p39										05 50			06 05							
3½	—	Falmer	d		23p43										05 54			06 09							
8	12¼	**Lewes** 4	a	23p51	23p49	23p58	01 20					05 23			06 00			06 15	06 22						
—	—		d	23p53	23p56	23p59	01 20					05 23			06 05				06 27						
—	15¾	Southease	d																						
—	18½	Newhaven Town ⛴	d		00 04										06 13				06 35						
—	18¾	Newhaven Harbour	d		00 06										06 15				06 37						
—	20¼	Bishopstone	d		00 09										06 18				06 40						
—	21¼	**Seaford**	a		00 12										06 21				06 43						
11	—	Glynde	d																						
15½	—	Berwick	d	00 02																					
19¾	—	Polegate	d	00 07		00 11	01s32					05 35													
21¾	—	Hampden Park 4	d	00 11		00 15	01s36							05 32						06 08				06 24	
23¾	—	**Eastbourne** 4	a	00 16		00 20	01 41					05 42		05 37						06 13				06 29	
—	—		d	00 22				04 50	05 08	05 15	05 32			05 42			05 53				06 14	06 24			06 33
25¾	—	Hampden Park 4	d						05a12		05a36			05a46							06 18	06a28			
28¾	—	Pevensey & Westham	d	00 29						05 22											06 23				06 40
29½	—	Pevensey Bay	d																						
31½	—	Normans Bay	d																						06 45
33¼	—	Cooden Beach	d	00 35																	06 29				
34¾	—	Collington	d	00 38																	06 32				
35½	—	**Bexhill** 4	d	00 41				05 05		05 31							06 07				06 34				06 51
39¼	—	**St Leonards Warrior Sq** 4	d	00 47				05 12		05 37							06 14				06 41				06 57
40	0	**Hastings** 4	a	00 50				05 15		05 41							06 18				06 44				07 00
—	—		d					05 21								05 47	06 19								
—	1	Ore	d					05 23								05 49									
—	3¾	Three Oaks	d													05 55									
—	5	Doleham	d													05 58									
—	9¼	Winchelsea	d													06 04									
—	11¼	**Rye**	a					05 44								06 08	06 36								
—	—		d					05 44								06 08	06 38								
—	18	Appledore (Kent)	d					05 53								06 17	06 47								
—	21	Ham Street	d					05 58								06 22	06 52								
—	26½	**Ashford International**	a					06 06								06 30	07 00								

London, Haywards Heath and Brighton - Lewes, Seaford, Eastbourne, Hastings and Ashford

Network Diagram - see first Page of Table 184

		SN	SN	SN	SN	SN	SN	SN		SN	SN	SN	SN	SN	SN	SN	SN	SN		SN	SN	SN	SN	SN	SN
		1	◇1			1	1	1		◇1					◇1	◇1	◇1	1		1		1			◇1
London Victoria 15 ⊖	d									05 32															
Clapham Junction 10	d									05 38															
London Bridge 4 ⊖	d																								
East Croydon ⇌	d									05 49															
Gatwick Airport 10 ✈	d									06 20															
Haywards Heath 3	d									06 34								07 10							
Wivelsfield 4	d									06 38								07 14							
Plumpton	d																	07 20							
Cooksbridge	d																	07 24							
Brighton 10	d				06 18		06 26				06 39	06 52	07 00	07 10						07 17	07 25			07 32	
London Road (Brighton)	d						06 29				06 42	06 55	07 03	07 13						07 20					
Moulsecoomb	d						06 31				06 44	06 57	07 05	07 15						07 22					
Falmer	d						06 35				06 48	07 01	07 09	07 19						07 26					
Lewes 4	a				06 29		06 41			06 50	06 54	07 08	07 17	07 26				07 29		07 32	07 38			07 43	
	d				06 30		06 42			06 51	06 55	07 10						07 31		07 34				07 44	
Southease	d																								
Newhaven Town ⛴	d										07 03	07 18								07 42					
Newhaven Harbour	d										07 05	07 23								07 44					
Bishopstone	d										07 08	07 26								07 47					
Seaford	a										07 11	07 29								07 50					
Glynde	d						06 47			06 56								07 36							
Berwick	d						06 53			07 02								07 42							
Polegate	d				06 43		06 58			07 07								07 47						07 57	
Hampden Park 4	d		06 42				07 02			07 11					07 15		07 46	07 51							08 06
Eastbourne 4	a		06 47		06 50		07 07			07 16					07 20		07 51	07 56						08 04	08 11
	d	06 47	06 57		06 54	07 02		07 14		07 21						07 38	07 57					08 04		08 09	
Hampden Park 4	d	06a51	07a01			07 06		07a18		07 25						07 42	08a01					08a08			
Pevensey & Westham	d					07 11				07 30						07 47								08 17	
Pevensey Bay	d															07 49									
Normans Bay	d															07 53									
Cooden Beach	d					07 17				07 36						07 56									
Collington	d					07 20				07 39						07 59									
Bexhill 4	d				07 09	07 22				07 41						08 02								08 25	
St Leonards Warrior Sq 4	d				07 16	07 29				07 48						08 08								08 32	
Hastings 4	a				07 19	07 32				07 51						08 11								08 35	
	d				07 20					07 52						08 12								08 36	
Ore	d									07a55						08a15									
Three Oaks	d				07 28																			08 44	
Doleham	d																								
Winchelsea	d				07 36																				
Rye	a				07 39																			08 54	
	d			07 11	07 41																		08 13	08 56	
Appledore (Kent)	d			07 20	07 50																		08 22	09 05	
Ham Street	d			07 25	07 55																		08 27	09 10	
Ashford International ⇌	a			07 33	08 03																		08 35	09 18	

London, Haywards Heath and Brighton - Lewes, Seaford, Eastbourne, Hastings and Ashford

Network Diagram - see first Page of Table 184

		SN	SN	SN	SN	SN	SN	SN	SN	SN	SN	SN	SN	SN	SN	SN	SN	SN	SN	SN	SN	SN
		◇[1]		[1]	[1]			◇[1]	[1]		◇[1]			◇[1]	[1]	◇[1]			◇[1]	[1]		◇[1]
																						A 🛒
London Victoria [15] ⊖	d	06 47									07 47					08 17						08 47
Clapham Junction [10]	d	06 53									07 53					08 23						08 53
London Bridge [4] ⊖	d																					
East Croydon	d	07 04									08 03					08 34						09 04
Gatwick Airport [10] ✈	d	07 20									08 20					08 49						09 20
Haywards Heath [3]	d	07 33									08 31					09 10						09 35
Wivelsfield [4]	d	07 37									08 35					09 14						
Plumpton	d	07 43									08 41											09 44
Cooksbridge	d	07 48									08 45											09 49
Brighton [10]	d		07 40	07 52	08 03	08 10	08 22			08 32		08 38	08 45		08 52		09 10	09 22			09 32	
London Road (Brighton)	d		07 43	07 55	08 06	08 13	08 25					08 41	08 48		08 55		09 13	09 25				
Moulsecoomb	d		07 45	07 57	08 08	08 15	08 27					08 43	08 50		08 57		09 15	09 27				
Falmer	d		07 49	08 01	08 12	08 19	08 31					08 47	08 54		09 01		09 19	09 31				
Lewes [4]	a	07 52	07 56	08 08	08 18	08 26	08 37			08 43	08 50	08 53	09 00		09 07	09 25	09 25	09 37			09 43	09 53
	d	07 53	07 58	08 09	08 19	08 30				08 44	08 51		09 02		09 09	09 25	09 30				09 44	09 54
Southease	d																09 36					
Newhaven Town ⛴	d		08 06			08 38							09 10				09 40					
Newhaven Harbour	d		08 08			08 40							09 12				09 42					
Bishopstone	d		08 11			08 43							09 15				09 45					
Seaford	a		08 14			08 46							09 18				09 48					
Glynde	d			08 14	08 24										09 14							
Berwick	d			08 20	08 30										09 20							
Polegate	d	08 05		08 25	08 35					08 57	09 03				09 25	09 38					09 57	10 06
Hampden Park [4]	d	08 09		08 29	08 39				08 52		09 07			09 17	09 29	09 42				09 52		
Eastbourne [4]	a	08 14		08 34	08 44				08 57	09 04	09 12			09 22	09 34	09 47				09 58	10 04	10 14
	d	08 21		08 40				08 56	09 04	09 09	09 19				09 40				09 55	10 04	10 09	10 20
Hampden Park [4]	d	08 25		08 44				09a00	09a08		09 23				09 44				09a59	10a08		10 24
Pevensey & Westham	d	08 30		08 49							09 28				09 49							10 29
Pevensey Bay	d	08 32																				
Normans Bay	d	08 36		08 53											09 53							
Cooden Beach	d	08 39		08 57							09 34				09 57							10 35
Collington	d	08 42		09 00							09 37				10 00							10 38
Bexhill [4]	d	08 45		09 02						09 24	09 39				10 02						10 24	10 40
St Leonards Warrior Sq [4]	d	08 51		09 09						09 32	09 46				10 09						10 31	10 47
Hastings [4]	a	08 55		09 12						09 35	09 49				10 12						10 35	10 50
	d	08 56		09 13						09 36	09 50				10 13						10 36	10 51
Ore	d	08a59		09a16							09a53				10a16							10a54
Three Oaks	d																				10 44	
Doleham	d																					
Winchelsea	d									09 50												
Rye	a									09 54											10 54	
	d									09 56											10 56	
Appledore (Kent)	d									10 05											11 05	
Ham Street	d									10 10											11 10	
Ashford International	a									10 18											11 18	

A 🛒 to Lewes

London, Haywards Heath and Brighton - Lewes, Seaford, Eastbourne, Hastings and Ashford

Network Diagram - see first Page of Table 184

		SN	SN	SN	SN	SN	SN	SN	SN	SN		SN	SN	SN	SN	SN	SN	SN	SN	SN		SN	SN	SN	SN
			◇1	1	◇1			◇1	1			◇1		◇1	1	◇1			◇1	1			◇1		◇1
					A 🛒							A 🛒				A 🛒							A 🛒		
London Victoria 15 ⊖	d				09 17							09 47				10 17							10 47		
Clapham Junction 10	d				09 23							09 53				10 23							10 53		
London Bridge 4 ⊖	d																								
East Croydon	d				09 33							10 03				10 33							11 03		
Gatwick Airport 10 ✈	d				09 50							10 20				10 50							11 20		
Haywards Heath 3	d				10 07							10 35				11 07							11 35		
Wivelsfield 4	d				10 11											11 11									
Plumpton	d											10 44											11 44		
Cooksbridge	d																								
Brighton 10	d	09 40		09 52		10 10	10 22			10 32			10 40		10 52		11 10	11 22				11 32		11 40	
London Road (Brighton)	d	09 43		09 55		10 13	10 25						10 43		10 55		11 13	11 25						11 43	
Moulsecoomb	d	09 45		09 57		10 15	10 27						10 45		10 57		11 15	11 27						11 45	
Falmer	d	09 49		10 01		10 19	10 31						10 49		11 01		11 19	11 31						11 49	
Lewes 4	a	09 55		10 07	10 22	10 25	10 37			10 43		10 52	10 55		11 07	11 22	11 25	11 37				11 43	11 52	11 55	
	d	09 58		10 09	10 23	10 28				10 44		10 53	10 58		11 09	11 23	11 28					11 44	11 53	11 58	
Southease	d					10 34											11 34								
Newhaven Town	d	10 06				10 38							11 06				11 38							12 06	
Newhaven Harbour	d	10 08				10 40							11 08				11 40							12 08	
Bishopstone	d	10 11				10 43							11 11				11 43							12 11	
Seaford	a	10 14				10 46							11 14				11 46							12 14	
Glynde	d			10 14											11 14										
Berwick	d			10 20											11 20										
Polegate	d			10 25	10 35					10 57		11 05			11 25	11 35						11 57	12 05		
Hampden Park 4	d		10 20	10 29	10 39				10 52					11 20	11 29	11 39				11 52					12 20
Eastbourne 4	a		10 25	10 34	10 44				10 57	11 04		11 13		11 25	11 34	11 44				11 57		12 04	12 13		12 25
	d			10 40				10 58	11 04	11 09		11 19			11 40				11 58	12 04		12 09	12 19		
Hampden Park 4	d			10 44				11a02	11a08			11 23			11 44				12a02	12a08			12 23		
Pevensey & Westham	d			10 49								11 28			11 49								12 28		
Pevensey Bay	d																								
Normans Bay	d			10 53											11 53										
Cooden Beach	d			10 57								11 34			11 57								12 34		
Collington	d			11 00								11 37			12 00								12 37		
Bexhill 4	d			11 02						11 24		11 39			12 02							12 24	12 39		
St Leonards Warrior Sq 4	d			11 09						11 31		11 46			12 09							12 31	12 46		
Hastings 4	a			11 12						11 35		11 49			12 12							12 35	12 49		
	d			11 13						11 36		11 50			12 13							12 36	12 50		
Ore	d			11a16								11a53			12a16								12a53		
Three Oaks	d																					12 44			
Doleham	d																								
Winchelsea	d									11 50															
Rye	a									11 54												12 54			
	d									11 56												12 56			
Appledore (Kent)	d									12 05												13 05			
Ham Street	d									12 10												13 10			
Ashford International	a									12 18												13 18			

A 🛒 to Lewes

Table 189

Mondays to Fridays

London, Haywards Heath and Brighton - Lewes, Seaford, Eastbourne, Hastings and Ashford

Network Diagram - see first Page of Table 184

		SN 1	SN ◇1	SN	SN	SN ◇1		SN 1	SN	SN ◇1	SN	SN ◇1	SN 1	SN ◇1	SN	SN		SN ◇1	SN 1	SN	SN ◇1	SN	SN ◇1	SN 1	SN ◇1
London Victoria 15 ⊖	d		11 17							11 47				12 17							12 47				13 17
Clapham Junction 10	d		11 23							11 53				12 23							12 53				13 23
London Bridge 4 ⊖	d																								
East Croydon	d		11 33							12 03				12 33							13 03				13 33
Gatwick Airport 10 ✈	d		11 50							12 20				12 50							13 20				13 50
Haywards Heath 3	d		12 07							12 35				13 07							13 35				14 07
Wivelsfield 4	d		12 11											13 11											14 11
Plumpton	d									12 44											13 44				
Cooksbridge	d																								
Brighton 10	d	11 52		12 10	12 22				12 32		12 40		12 52		13 10	13 22				13 32		13 40		13 52	
London Road (Brighton)	d	11 55		12 13	12 25						12 43		12 55		13 13	13 25						13 43		13 55	
Moulsecoomb	d	11 57		12 15	12 27						12 45		12 57		13 15	13 27						13 45		13 57	
Falmer	d	12 01		12 19	12 31						12 49		13 01		13 19	13 31						13 49		14 01	
Lewes 4	a	12 07	12 22	12 25	12 37				12 43	12 52	12 55		13 07	13 22	13 25	13 37				13 43	13 52	13 55		14 07	14 22
	d	12 09	12 23	12 28					12 44	12 53	12 58		13 09	13 23	13 28					13 44	13 53	13 58		14 09	14 23
Southease	d			12 34											13 34										
Newhaven Town ⛴	d			12 38							13 06				13 38							14 06			
Newhaven Harbour	d			12 40							13 08				13 40							14 08			
Bishopstone	d			12 43							13 11				13 43							14 11			
Seaford	a			12 46							13 14				13 46							14 14			
Glynde	d	12 14											13 14											14 14	
Berwick	d	12 20											13 20											14 20	
Polegate	d	12 25	12 35						12 57	13 05			13 25	13 35						13 57	14 05			14 25	14 35
Hampden Park 4	d	12 29	12 39					12 52				13 20	13 29	13 39					13 52				14 20	14 29	14 39
Eastbourne 4	a	12 34	12 44					12 57	13 04	13 13		13 25	13 34	13 44					13 57	14 04	14 13		14 25	14 34	14 44
	d	12 40				12 58		13 04	13 09	13 19			13 40					13 58	14 04	14 09	14 19			14 40	
Hampden Park 4	d	12 44				13a02		13a08		13 23			13 44					14a02	14a08		14 23			14 44	
Pevensey & Westham	d	12 49								13 28			13 49								14 28			14 49	
Pevensey Bay	d																								
Normans Bay	d	12 53											13 53											14 53	
Cooden Beach	d	12 57								13 34			13 57								14 34			14 57	
Collington	d	13 00								13 37			14 00								14 37			15 00	
Bexhill 4	d	13 02							13 24	13 39			14 02							14 24	14 39			15 02	
St Leonards Warrior Sq 4	d	13 09							13 31	13 46			14 09							14 31	14 46			15 09	
Hastings 4	a	13 12							13 35	13 49			14 12							14 35	14 49			15 12	
	d	13 13							13 36	13 50			14 13							14 36	14 50			15 13	
Ore	d	13a16								13a53			14a16								14a53			15a16	
Three Oaks	d																			14 44					
Doleham	d																								
Winchelsea	d								13 50																
Rye	a								13 54											14 54					
	d								13 56											14 56					
Appledore (Kent)	d								14 05											15 05					
Ham Street	d								14 10											15 10					
Ashford International	a								14 18											15 18					

London, Haywards Heath and Brighton - Lewes, Seaford, Eastbourne, Hastings and Ashford

Network Diagram - see first Page of Table 184

		SN		SN	SN ◇1	SN 1	SN	SN ◇1	SN	SN ◇1	SN 1	SN ◇1		SN	SN	SN ◇1	SN 1	SN	SN ◇1	SN	SN ◇1	SN		SN 1	SN ◇1
London Victoria 15 ⊖	d							13 47				14 17							14 47						15 17
Clapham Junction 10	d							13 53				14 23							14 53						15 23
London Bridge 4 ⊖	d																								
East Croydon	d							14 03				14 33							15 03						15 33
Gatwick Airport 10 ✈	d							14 20				14 50							15 20						15 50
Haywards Heath 3	d							14 35				15 07							15 35						16 07
Wivelsfield 4	d											15 11							15 39						16 11
Plumpton	d							14 44											15 45						
Cooksbridge	d																								
Brighton 10	d	14 10		14 22			14 32		14 40		14 52			15 10	15 22			15 32		15 40				15 52	
London Road (Brighton)	d	14 13		14 25					14 43		14 55			15 13	15 25					15 43				15 55	
Moulsecoomb	d	14 15		14 27					14 45		14 57			15 15	15 27					15 45				15 57	
Falmer	d	14 19		14 31					14 49		15 01			15 19	15 31					15 49				16 01	
Lewes 4	a	14 25		14 37			14 43	14 52	14 55		15 07	15 22		15 25	15 37			15 43	15 52	15 55				16 07	16 22
	d	14 28					14 44	14 53	14 58		15 09	15 23		15 28				15 44	15 53	15 58				16 09	16 23
Southease	d	14 34												15 34						16 04					
Newhaven Town ⛴	d	14 38							15 06					15 38						16 08					
Newhaven Harbour	d	14 40							15 08					15 40						16 10					
Bishopstone	d	14 43							15 11					15 43						16 13					
Seaford	a	14 46							15 14					15 46						16 16					
Glynde	d										15 14													16 14	
Berwick	d										15 20													16 20	
Polegate	d						14 57	15 05			15 25	15 35						15 57	16 05					16 25	16 35
Hampden Park 4	d					14 52				15 20	15 29	15 39					15 52				16 20			16 29	16 39
Eastbourne 4	a					14 57	15 04	15 13		15 25	15 34	15 44					15 57	16 04	16 13		16 25			16 34	16 44
	d				14 58	15 04	15 09	15 19			15 40					15 58	16 04	16 09	16 19					16 40	
Hampden Park 4	d				15a02	15a08		15 23			15 44					16a02	16a08		16 23					16 44	
Pevensey & Westham	d							15 28			15 49								16 28					16 49	
Pevensey Bay	d							15 30																	
Normans Bay	d							15 34			15 53													16 53	
Cooden Beach	d							15 37			15 57								16 34					16 57	
Collington	d							15 40			16 00								16 37					17 00	
Bexhill 4	d						15 24	15 43			16 02							16 24	16 39					17 02	
St Leonards Warrior Sq 4	d						15 31	15 49			16 09							16 31	16 46					17 09	
Hastings 4	a						15 35	15 52			16 12							16 35	16 49					17 12	
	d						15 36	15 54			16 13							16 36	16 50			17 09		17 13	
Ore	d							15a57			16a16								16a53			17 12		17a16	
Three Oaks	d																	16 44				17 18			
Doleham	d																					17 21			
Winchelsea	d						15 50															17 27			
Rye	a						15 54											16 54				17 30			
	d						15 56											16 56				17 31			
Appledore (Kent)	d						16 05											17 05				17 40			
Ham Street	d						16 10											17 10				17 45			
Ashford International	a						16 18											17 18				17 53			

Table 189

Mondays to Fridays

London, Haywards Heath and Brighton - Lewes, Seaford, Eastbourne, Hastings and Ashford

Network Diagram - see first Page of Table 184

		SN	SN	SN	SN	SN	SN	SN		SN	SN	SN	SN	SN	SN	SN	SN	SN		SN	SN	SN	SN	SN	SN
					◇1	1		◇1			◇1	1		◇1		◇1	1					◇1		◇1	1
														A								A			
														🚌								🚌			
London Victoria 15 ⊖	d							15 47						16 17								16 47			
Clapham Junction 10	d							15 53						16 23								16 53			
London Bridge 4 ⊖	d																								
East Croydon	d							16 03						16 33								17 03			
Gatwick Airport 10 ✈	d							16 20						16 49								17 20			
Haywards Heath 3	d							16 35						17 06								17 36			
Wivelsfield 4	d							16 39						17 10								17 41			
Plumpton	d							16 45														17 47			
Cooksbridge	d							16 49														17 52			
Brighton 10	d	16 10	16 22				16 32			16 40		16 52	17 02		17 10			17 20			17 32		17 40		17 52
London Road (Brighton)	d	16 13	16 25							16 43		16 55	17 05		17 13			17 23					17 43		17 55
Moulsecoomb	d	16 15	16 27							16 45		16 57	17 07		17 15			17 25					17 45		17 57
Falmer	d	16 19	16 31							16 49		17 01	17 11		!7 19			17 29					17 49		18 01
Lewes 4	a	16 25	16 37				16 43	16 54		16 55		17 07	17 17	17 21	17 25			17 35			17 43	17 56	17 55		18 07
	d	16 28					16 44	16 54		16 58		17 09		17 22	17 28			17 36			17 44	17 57	18 01		18 08
Southease	d	16 34													17 34								18 07		
Newhaven Town ⛴	d	16 38								17 06					17 38								18 11		
Newhaven Harbour	d	16 40								17 08					17 40								18 13		
Bishopstone	d	16 43								17 11					17 43								18 16		
Seaford	a	16 46								17 14					17 46								18 19		
Glynde	d											17 14													18 13
Berwick	d							17 03				17 20		17 31				17 45							18 19
Polegate	d						16 57	17 08				17 25		17 36				17 50			17 57	18 09			18 24
Hampden Park 4	d					16 52					17 20	17 29		17 40			17 52	17 55				18 13		18 20	18 28
Eastbourne 4	a					16 57	17 04	17 16			17 25	17 34		17 48			17 57	18 00			18 04	18 18		18 25	18 34
	d			16 45	16 58	17 04	17 09	17 21				17 40				17 57	18 01				18 09	18 25			18 43
Hampden Park 4	d			16a49	17a02	17a08		17 25				17 44				18a01	18a05					18 29			18 47
Pevensey & Westham	d							17 30				17 49										18 34			18 52
Pevensey Bay	d							17 32				17 51													
Normans Bay	d							17 36				17 55													18 56
Cooden Beach	d							17 39				17 58										18 40			19 00
Collington	d							17 42				18 01										18 43			19 03
Bexhill 4	d						17 25	17 45				18 04									18 24	18 45			19 05
St Leonards Warrior Sq 4	d						17 31	17 53				18 10									18 31	18 56			19 11
Hastings 4	a						17 35	17 57				18 13									18 34	19 00			19 14
	d						17 36	17 58				18 14									18 36				19 15
Ore	d							18a01				18a17													19a18
Three Oaks	d																				18 44				
Doleham	d																								
Winchelsea	d						17 50																		
Rye	a						17 54														18 54				
	d						17 56													18 31	18 56				
Appledore (Kent)	d						18 05													18 40	19 05				
Ham Street	d						18 10													18 45	19 10				
Ashford International	a						18 18													18 53	19 18				

A 🚌 to Lewes

London, Haywards Heath and Brighton - Lewes, Seaford, Eastbourne, Hastings and Ashford

Network Diagram - see first Page of Table 184

		SN 1	SN	SN ◇1		SN 1	SN ◇1 A 🚲	SN	SN	SN	SN	SN ◇1	SN 1	SN ◇1 A 🚲			SN 1	SN	SN	SN 1	SN	SN ◇1 A 🚲	SN	SN ◇1	SN 1
London Victoria 15 ⊖	d						17 35							18 06								18 47			
Clapham Junction 10	d						17 42							18 12								18 53			
London Bridge 4 ⊖	d	17 23															18 23								
East Croydon	d	17 36					17 52							18 22			18 37					19 04			
Gatwick Airport 10 ✈	d						18 07							18 38								19 21			
Haywards Heath 3	d	18 05					18 18							18 50			19 06					19 35			
Wivelsfield 4	d	18 10					18 23							18 54			19 11					19 39			
Plumpton	d						18 29							19 00			19 17					19 45			
Cooksbridge	d						18 33							19 05			19 22					19 50			
Brighton 10	d		18 08					18 17		18 32	18 38		18 51					19 08	19 22		19 32		19 40		19 52
London Road (Brighton)	d		18 11					18 20			18 41		18 54					19 11	19 25				19 43		19 55
Moulsecoomb	d		18 13					18 22			18 43		18 56					19 13	19 27				19 45		19 57
Falmer	d		18 17					18 26			18 47		19 00					19 17	19 31				19 49		20 01
Lewes 4	a	18 21	18 23				18 38	18 32		18 44	18 53		19 06	19 09			19 27	19 23	19 37		19 43	19 54	19 55		20 07
	d	18 21	18 24				18 38	18 42		18 45	18 54		19 07	19 13	19 16		19 27	19 31			19 44	19 55	19 58		20 09
Southease	d										19 00							19 37					20 04		
Newhaven Town	d		18 33					18 50			19 04			19 21				19 41					20 08		
Newhaven Harbour	d										19 09							19 44					20 10		
Bishopstone	d		18 37					18 54			19 12			19 29				19 47					20 13		
Seaford	a		18 40					18 58			19 15			19 34				19 50					20 16		
Glynde	d	18 27													19 21		19 33								20 14
Berwick	d	18 32													19 27		19 39								20 20
Polegate	d	18 38					18 51			18 58			19 19		19 32		19 45				19 57	20 07			20 25
Hampden Park 4	d	18 42				18 52	18 55					19 20			19 36		19 50			19 52				20 20	20 29
Eastbourne 4	a	18 49				18 57	19 01			19 05		19 25	19 28		19 41		19 56			19 57	20 04	20 15		20 25	20 34
	d			18 58		19 04	19 19			19 09					19 51					20 03	20 09	20 19			
Hampden Park 4	d			19a02		19a08	19 23								19 55					20a07		20 23			
Pevensey & Westham	d						19 28			19 17					20 00							20 28			
Pevensey Bay	d																								
Normans Bay	d																								
Cooden Beach	d						19 34								20 06							20 34			
Collington	d						19 37								20 09							20 37			
Bexhill 4	d						19 39			19 25					20 11						20 24	20 40			
St Leonards Warrior Sq 4	d						19 45			19 32					20 18						20 31	20 46			
Hastings 4	a						19 48			19 35					20 21						20 34	20 49			
	d						19 49			19 36					20 22						20 36	20 50			
Ore	d						19a55								20a27							20a55			
Three Oaks	d																				20 44				
Doleham	d																								
Winchelsea	d									19 50															
Rye	a									19 54											20 54				
	d								19 31	19 56											20 56				
Appledore (Kent)	d								19 40	20 05											21 05				
Ham Street	d								19 45	20 10											21 10				
Ashford International	a								19 53	20 18											21 18				

A 🚲 to Lewes

Table 189

Mondays to Fridays

London, Haywards Heath and Brighton - Lewes, Seaford, Eastbourne, Hastings and Ashford

Network Diagram - see first Page of Table 184

		SN ◇1 A 🚲	SN	SN 1	SN	SN ◇1 A 🚲	SN	SN ◇1	SN ◇1	SN	SN	SN 1	SN ◇1	SN ◇1	SN	SN ◇1	SN	SN	SN 1	SN ◇1	SN	SN 1
London Victoria 15 ⊖	d	19 17				19 47			20 17					20 47		21 17				21 47		
Clapham Junction 10	d	19 23				19 53			20 23					20 53		21 23				21 53		
London Bridge 4 ⊖	d																					
East Croydon	d	19 33				20 03			20 33					21 04		21 33				22 03		
Gatwick Airport 10 ✈	d	19 49				20 19			20 49					21 19		21 49				22 19		
Haywards Heath 3	d	20 07				20 36			21 07					21 37		22 08				22 34		
Wivelsfield 4	d	20 11				20 40			21 11					21 41		22 12				22 38		
Plumpton	d					20 46								21 47						22 44		
Cooksbridge	d					20 50														22 48		
Brighton 10	d		20 10		20 30		20 40			21 04	21 30				21 40		22 04	22 28			22 34	23 06
London Road (Brighton)	d		20 13				20 43			21 07					21 43		22 07				22 37	23 09
Moulsecoomb	d		20 15				20 45			21 09					21 45		22 09				22 39	23 11
Falmer	d		20 19				20 49			21 13					21 49		22 13				22 43	23 15
Lewes 4	a	20 22	20 25		20 43	20 55	20 55		21 22	21 19	21 43			21 54	21 55	22 23	22 19	22 39		22 53	22 49	23 21
	d	20 23	20 28		20 44	20 55	21 00		21 23	21 28	21 44			21 55	21 58	22 23	22 28	22 39		22 53	22 57	23 22
Southease	d														22 04						23 03	
Newhaven Town ⛴	d		20 36				21 08			21 36					22 08		22 36				23 07	
Newhaven Harbour	d		20 38				21 10			21 38					22 10		22 38				23 09	
Bishopstone	d		20 41				21 13			21 41					22 13		22 41				23 12	
Seaford	a		20 44				21 16			21 44					22 16		22 44				23 15	
Glynde	d	20 28							21 28							22 29						23 27
Berwick	d	20 34							21 34							22 34						23 33
Polegate	d	20 39			20 57	21 08			21 39		21 57			22 07		22 39		22 52		23 06		23 38
Hampden Park 4	d	20 43		20 51				21 20	21 43				21 55			22 43			22 55	23 10		23 42
Eastbourne 4	a	20 48		20 56	21 04	21 15		21 25	21 48		22 04		22 00	22 15		22 48		23 03	23 00	23 15		23 47
	d			21 04	21 09	21 21					22 09	22 04	22 15	22 21					23 05	23 20		
Hampden Park 4	d			21a08		21 25						22a08	22a19	22 25					23a09	23 24		
Pevensey & Westham	d					21 30								22 30						23 29		
Pevensey Bay	d																					
Normans Bay	d																					
Cooden Beach	d					21 36								22 36						23 35		
Collington	d					21 39								22 39						23 38		
Bexhill 4	d				21 24	21 41					22 23			22 41						23 40		
St Leonards Warrior Sq 4	d				21 31	21 48					22 31			22 48						23 47		
Hastings 4	a				21 34	21 53					22 34			22 51						23 50		
	d				21 35	21 54																
Ore	d				21 37	21a57																
Three Oaks	d				21 43																	
Doleham	d				21 46																	
Winchelsea	d				21 52																	
Rye	a				21 56																	
	d				21 56																	
Appledore (Kent)	d				22 05																	
Ham Street	d				22 10																	
Ashford International	a				22 18																	

A 🚲 to Lewes

London, Haywards Heath and Brighton - Lewes, Seaford, Eastbourne, Hastings and Ashford

Network Diagram - see first Page of Table 184

		SN	SN	SN	SN
		1		◇1	
London Victoria 15 ⊖	d			22 47	
Clapham Junction 10	d			22 53	
London Bridge 4 ⊖	d				
East Croydon	d			23 03	
Gatwick Airport 10 ✈	d			23 19	
Haywards Heath 3	d			23 34	
Wivelsfield 4	d			23 38	
Plumpton	d			23 44	
Cooksbridge	d				
Brighton 10	d		23 28		23 34
London Road (Brighton)	d				23 37
Moulsecoomb	d				23 39
Falmer	d				23 43
Lewes 4	a		23 39	23 51	23 49
	d		23 39	23 53	23 56
Southease	d				
Newhaven Town	d				00 04
Newhaven Harbour	d				00 06
Bishopstone	d				00 09
Seaford	a				00 12
Glynde	d				
Berwick	d			00 02	
Polegate	d		23 52	00 07	
Hampden Park 4	d	23 47		00 11	
Eastbourne 4	a	23 52	23 59	00 16	
	d	23 56		00 22	
Hampden Park 4	d	00a01			
Pevensey & Westham	d			00 29	
Pevensey Bay	d				
Normans Bay	d				
Cooden Beach	d			00 35	
Collington	d			00 38	
Bexhill 4	d			00 41	
St Leonards Warrior Sq 4	d			00 47	
Hastings 4	a			00 50	
	d				
Ore	d				
Three Oaks	d				
Doleham	d				
Winchelsea	d				
Rye	a				
	d				
Appledore (Kent)	d				
Ham Street	d				
Ashford International	a				

Table 189

Saturdays

London, Haywards Heath and Brighton - Lewes, Seaford, Eastbourne, Hastings and Ashford

Network Diagram - see first Page of Table 184

		SN ◇1	SN	SN ◇1	SN 1	SN	SN ◇1	SN 1	SN	SN		SN	SN ◇1	SN	SN ◇1	SN ◇1	SN ◇1	SN ◇1	SN 1	SN		SN 1	SN	SN ◇1	SN 1
London Victoria 15 ⊖	d	22p47		00 05																					
Clapham Junction 10	d	22p53		00 11																					
London Bridge 4 ⊖	d																								
East Croydon	d	23p03		00 24																					
Gatwick Airport 10 ✈	d	23p19		00 42																		06 11			
Haywards Heath 3	d	23p34		01 06																		06 26			
Wivelsfield 4	d	23p38																				06 30			
Plumpton	d	23p44																							
Cooksbridge	d																								
Brighton 10	d		23p34					05 10		05 52				06 10						06 32			06 40		06 52
London Road (Brighton)	d		23p37							05 55				06 13									06 43		06 55
Moulsecoomb	d		23p39							05 57				06 15									06 45		06 57
Falmer	d		23p43							06 01				06 19									06 49		07 01
Lewes 4	a	23p51	23p49	01 20				05 21		06 07				06 25						06 43		06 41	06 55		07 07
	d	23p53	23p56	01 20				05 21		06 08				06 28						06 45		06 53	06 58		07 09
Southease	d																								
Newhaven Town ⛴	d		00 04							06 16				06 36									07 06		
Newhaven Harbour	d		00 06							06 18				06 38									07 08		
Bishopstone	d		00 09											06 41									07 11		
Seaford	a		00 12							06 23				06 44									07 14		
Glynde	d																								07 14
Berwick	d	00 02																				07 02			07 20
Polegate	d	00 07		01s32				05 33												06 58		07 07			07 25
Hampden Park 4	d	00 11		01s36															06 52			07 11		07 20	07 29
Eastbourne 4	a	00 16		01 41				05 41											06 57	07 05		07 17		07 25	07 34
	d	00 22			05 03		05 38		05 48			05 53	06 04		06 18	06 24	06 45	06 58	07 04	07 09		07 21			07 40
Hampden Park 4	d				05a07				05a52						06 22	06a28		07a02	07a08			07 25			07 44
Pevensey & Westham	d	00 29													06 27							07 30			07 49
Pevensey Bay	d																								
Normans Bay	d														06 31										07 53
Cooden Beach	d	00 35													06 35							07 36			07 57
Collington	d	00 38													06 38							07 39			08 00
Bexhill 4	d	00 41					05 52					06 07	06 18		06 40		07 00			07 24		07 42			08 02
St Leonards Warrior Sq 4	d	00 47					06 00					06 14	06 24		06 49		07 06			07 31		07 48			08 09
Hastings 4	a	00 50					06 04					06 17	06 28		06 53		07 10			07 35		07 51			08 12
	d					05 20	06 05					06 18	06 28		06 54		07 11			07 36		07 52			08 13
Ore	d					05 23	06a08						06a32		06a57		07a14					07a55			08a16
Three Oaks	d					05 29						06 26													
Doleham	d					05 32																			
Winchelsea	d					05 38														07 50					
Rye	a					05 41						06 36								07 54					
	d					05 42						06 38								07 56					
Appledore (Kent)	d					05 51						06 47								08 05					
Ham Street	d					05 56						06 52								08 10					
Ashford International	a					06 04						07 00								08 18					

Table 189

Saturdays

London, Haywards Heath and Brighton - Lewes, Seaford, Eastbourne, Hastings and Ashford

Network Diagram - see first Page of Table 184

		SN	SN	SN ◇1	SN 1	SN		SN 1	SN	SN ◇1	SN 1	SN	SN	SN ◇1	SN 1	SN		SN ◇1	SN	SN ◇1	SN 1	SN ◇1	SN	SN	SN ◇1
London Victoria 15 ⊖	d																	07 47				08 17			
Clapham Junction 10	d																	07 53				08 23			
London Bridge 4 ⊖	d																								
East Croydon	d																	08 03				08 33			
Gatwick Airport 10 ✈	d																	08 20				08 50			
Haywards Heath 3	d							07 33										08 35				09 07			
Wivelsfield 4	d							07 37														09 11			
Plumpton	d																								
Cooksbridge	d																								
Brighton 10	d	07 10	07 22			07 32			07 40		07 52	08 10	08 22			08 32			08 40		08 52		09 10	09 22	
London Road (Brighton)	d	07 13	07 25						07 43		07 55	08 13	08 25						08 43		08 55		09 13	09 25	
Moulsecoomb	d	07 15	07 27						07 45		07 57	08 15	08 27						08 45		08 57		09 15	09 27	
Falmer	d	07 19	07 31						07 49		08 01	08 19	08 31						08 49		09 01		09 19	09 31	
Lewes 4	a	07 25	07 37			07 43		07 48	07 55		08 07	08 25	08 37			08 43		08 49	08 55		09 07	09 22	09 25	09 37	
	d	07 28				07 44		07 53	07 58		08 09	08 28				08 44		08 53	08 58		09 09	09 23	09 28		
Southease	d																						09 34		
Newhaven Town ⛴	d	07 36							08 06			08 36							09 06				09 38		
Newhaven Harbour	d	07 38							08 08			08 38							09 08				09 40		
Bishopstone	d	07 41							08 11			08 41							09 11				09 43		
Seaford	a	07 44							08 14			08 44							09 14				09 46		
Glynde	d										08 14										09 14				
Berwick	d										08 20										09 20				
Polegate	d					07 57		08 05			08 25					08 57		09 05			09 25	09 35			
Hampden Park 4	d				07 52					08 20	08 29				08 52					09 20	09 29	09 39			
Eastbourne 4	a				07 57	08 05		08 13		08 25	08 34				08 57	09 04		09 13		09 25	09 34	09 44			
	d			07 58	08 04	08 09		08 18			08 40			08 58	09 04	09 09		09 19			09 40				09 58
Hampden Park 4	d			08a02	08a08			08 22			08 44			09a02	09a08			09 23			09 44				10a02
Pevensey & Westham	d							08 28			08 49							09 28			09 49				
Pevensey Bay	d																								
Normans Bay	d										08 53										09 53				
Cooden Beach	d							08 34			08 57							09 34			09 57				
Collington	d							08 37			09 00							09 37			10 00				
Bexhill 4	d					08 24		08 39			09 02					09 24		09 39			10 02				
St Leonards Warrior Sq 4	d					08 31		08 46			09 09					09 31		09 46			10 09				
Hastings 4	a					08 35		08 50			09 12					09 35		09 49			10 12				
	d					08 36		08 51			09 13					09 36		09 50			10 13				
Ore	d							08a54			09a16							09a53			10a16				
Three Oaks	d					08 44																			
Doleham	d																								
Winchelsea	d															09 50									
Rye	a					08 54										09 54									
	d					08 56										09 56									
Appledore (Kent)	d					09 05										10 05									
Ham Street	d					09 10										10 10									
Ashford International	a					09 18										10 18									

Table 189

Saturdays

London, Haywards Heath and Brighton - Lewes, Seaford, Eastbourne, Hastings and Ashford

Network Diagram - see first Page of Table 184

		SN 1		SN	SN ◇1	SN	SN ◇1	SN 1	SN ◇1	SN	SN	SN ◇1		SN 1	SN	SN ◇1	SN	SN ◇1	SN 1	SN ◇1	SN	SN		SN ◇1	SN 1
London Victoria 15 ⊖	d				08 47				09 17							09 47				10 17					
Clapham Junction 10	d				08 53				09 23							09 53				10 23					
London Bridge 4 ⊖	d																								
East Croydon	d				09 03				09 33							10 03				10 33					
Gatwick Airport 10 ✈	d				09 20				09 50							10 20				10 50					
Haywards Heath 3	d				09 35				10 07							10 35				11 07					
Wivelsfield 4	d								10 11											11 11					
Plumpton	d				09 44											10 44									
Cooksbridge	d																								
Brighton 10	d			09 32		09 40		09 52		10 10	10 22				10 32		10 40		10 52		11 10	11 22			
London Road (Brighton)	d					09 43		09 55		10 13	10 25						10 43		10 55		11 13	11 25			
Moulsecoomb	d					09 45		09 57		10 15	10 27						10 45		10 57		11 15	11 27			
Falmer	d					09 49		10 01		10 19	10 31						10 49		11 01		11 19	11 31			
Lewes 4	a			09 43	09 52	09 55		10 07	10 22	10 25	10 37				10 43	10 52	10 55		11 07	11 22	11 25	11 37			
	d			09 44	09 53	09 58		10 09	10 23	10 28					10 44	10 53	10 58		11 09	11 23	11 28				
Southease	d									10 34											11 34				
Newhaven Town	d					10 06				10 38							11 06				11 38				
Newhaven Harbour	d					10 08				10 40							11 08				11 40				
Bishopstone	d					10 11				10 43							11 11				11 43				
Seaford	a					10 14				10 46							11 14				11 46				
Glynde	d							10 14											11 14						
Berwick	d							10 20											11 20						
Polegate	d			09 57	10 05			10 25	10 35						10 57	11 05			11 25	11 35					
Hampden Park 4	d	09 52					10 20	10 29	10 39					10 52				11 20	11 29	11 39					11 52
Eastbourne 4	a	09 57		10 04	10 13		10 25	10 34	10 44					10 57	11 04	11 13		11 25	11 34	11 44					11 57
	d	10 04		10 09	10 19			10 40				10 58		11 04	11 09	11 19			11 40					11 58	12 04
Hampden Park 4	d	10a08			10 23			10 44				11a02		11a08		11 23			11 44					12a02	12a08
Pevensey & Westham	d				10 28			10 49								11 28			11 49						
Pevensey Bay	d																								
Normans Bay	d							10 53											11 53						
Cooden Beach	d				10 34			10 57								11 34			11 57						
Collington	d				10 37			11 00								11 37			12 00						
Bexhill 4	d			10 24	10 39			11 02							11 24	11 39			12 02						
St Leonards Warrior Sq 4	d			10 31	10 46			11 09							11 31	11 46			12 09						
Hastings 4	a			10 35	10 49			11 12							11 35	11 49			12 12						
	d			10 36	10 50			11 13							11 36	11 50			12 13						
Ore	d				10a53			11a16								11a53			12a16						
Three Oaks	d			10 44																					
Doleham	d																								
Winchelsea	d														11 50										
Rye	a			10 54											11 54										
	d			10 56											11 56										
Appledore (Kent)	d			11 05											12 05										
Ham Street	d			11 10											12 10										
Ashford International	a			11 18											12 18										

Table 189

Saturdays

London, Haywards Heath and Brighton - Lewes, Seaford, Eastbourne, Hastings and Ashford

Network Diagram - see first Page of Table 184

		SN	SN	SN	SN	SN	SN	SN	SN	SN	SN	SN	SN	SN	SN	SN	SN	SN	SN	SN	SN	SN	SN
			◇1		◇1	1	◇1			◇1	1		◇1		◇1	1	◇1			◇1	1		◇1
London Victoria 15 ⊖	d		10 47				11 17						11 47				12 17						12 47
Clapham Junction 10	d		10 53				11 23						11 53				12 23						12 53
London Bridge 4 ⊖	d																						
East Croydon	d		11 03				11 33						12 03				12 33						13 03
Gatwick Airport 10 ✈	d		11 20				11 50						12 20				12 50						13 20
Haywards Heath 3	d		11 35				12 07						12 35				13 07						13 35
Wivelsfield 4	d						12 11										13 11						
Plumpton	d		11 44										12 44										13 44
Cooksbridge	d																						
Brighton 10	d	11 32		11 40		11 52		12 10	12 22			12 32		12 40		12 52		13 10	13 22			13 32	
London Road (Brighton)	d			11 43		11 55		12 13	12 25					12 43		12 55		13 13	13 25				
Moulsecoomb	d			11 45		11 57		12 15	12 27					12 45		12 57		13 15	13 27				
Falmer	d			11 49		12 01		12 19	12 31					12 49		13 01		13 19	13 31				
Lewes 4	a	11 43	11 52	11 55		12 07	12 22	12 25	12 37			12 43	12 52	12 55		13 07	13 22	13 25	13 37			13 43	13 52
	d	11 44	11 53	11 58		12 09	12 23	12 28				12 44	12 53	12 58		13 09	13 23	13 28				13 44	13 53
Southease	d							12 34										13 34					
Newhaven Town ⛴	d			12 06				12 38						13 06				13 38					
Newhaven Harbour	d			12 08				12 40						13 08				13 40					
Bishopstone	d			12 11				12 43						13 11				13 43					
Seaford	a			12 14				12 46						13 14				13 46					
Glynde	d					12 14										13 14							
Berwick	d					12 20										13 20							
Polegate	d	11 57	12 05			12 25	12 35					12 57	13 05			13 25	13 35					13 57	14 05
Hampden Park 4	d				12 20	12 29	12 39				12 52				13 20	13 29	13 39				13 52		
Eastbourne 4	a	12 04	12 13		12 25	12 34	12 44				12 57	13 04	13 13		13 25	13 34	13 44				13 57	14 04	14 13
	d	12 09	12 19			12 40				12 58	13 04	13 09	13 19			13 40				13 58	14 04	14 09	14 19
Hampden Park 4	d		12 23			12 44				13a02	13a08		13 23			13 44				14a02	14a08		14 23
Pevensey & Westham	d		12 28			12 49							13 28			13 49							14 28
Pevensey Bay	d																						
Normans Bay	d					12 53										13 53							
Cooden Beach	d		12 34			12 57							13 34			13 57							14 34
Collington	d		12 37			13 00							13 37			14 00							14 37
Bexhill 4	d	12 24	12 39			13 02						13 24	13 39			14 02						14 24	14 39
St Leonards Warrior Sq 4	d	12 31	12 46			13 09						13 31	13 46			14 09						14 31	14 46
Hastings 4	a	12 35	12 49			13 12						13 35	13 49			14 12						14 35	14 49
	d	12 36	12 50			13 13						13 36	13 50			14 13						14 36	14 50
Ore	d		12a53			13a16							13a53			14a16							14a53
Three Oaks	d	12 44																				14 44	
Doleham	d																						
Winchelsea	d											13 50											
Rye	a	12 54										13 54										14 54	
	d	12 56										13 56										14 56	
Appledore (Kent)	d	13 05										14 05										15 05	
Ham Street	d	13 10										14 10										15 10	
Ashford International	a	13 18										14 18										15 18	

Table 189

Saturdays

London, Haywards Heath and Brighton - Lewes, Seaford, Eastbourne, Hastings and Ashford

Network Diagram - see first Page of Table 184

		SN	SN	SN	SN	SN	SN	SN	SN	SN	SN	SN	SN	SN	SN	SN	SN	SN	SN	SN	SN	SN
			◇1	1	◇1			◇1	1		◇1		◇1	1	◇1			◇1	1		◇1	
London Victoria 15 ⊖	d				13 17						13 47				14 17						14 47	
Clapham Junction 10	d				13 23						13 53				14 23						14 53	
London Bridge 4 ⊖	d																					
East Croydon	d				13 33						14 03				14 33						15 03	
Gatwick Airport 10 ✈	d				13 50						14 20				14 50						15 20	
Haywards Heath 3	d				14 07						14 35				15 07						15 35	
Wivelsfield 4	d				14 11										15 11							
Plumpton	d										14 44										15 44	
Cooksbridge	d																					
Brighton 10	d	13 40		13 52		14 10	14 22			14 32		14 40		14 52		15 10	15 22			15 32		15 40
London Road (Brighton)	d	13 43		13 55		14 13	14 25					14 43		14 55		15 13	15 25					15 43
Moulsecoomb	d	13 45		13 57		14 15	14 27					14 45		14 57		15 15	15 27					15 45
Falmer	d	13 49		14 01		14 19	14 31					14 49		15 01		15 19	15 31					15 49
Lewes 4	a	13 55		14 07	14 22	14 25	14 37			14 43	14 52	14 55		15 07	15 22	15 25	15 37			15 43	15 52	15 55
	d	13 58		14 09	14 23	14 28				14 44	14 53	14 58		15 09	15 23	15 28				15 44	15 53	15 58
Southease	d					14 34										15 34						
Newhaven Town ⛴	d	14 06				14 38						15 06				15 38						16 06
Newhaven Harbour	d	14 08				14 40						15 08				15 40						16 08
Bishopstone	d	14 11				14 43						15 11				15 43						16 11
Seaford	a	14 14				14 46						15 14				15 46						16 14
Glynde	d			14 14										15 14								
Berwick	d			14 20										15 20								
Polegate	d			14 25	14 35					14 57	15 05			15 25	15 35					15 57	16 05	
Hampden Park 4	d		14 20	14 29	14 39				14 52				15 20	15 29	15 39				15 52			
Eastbourne 4	a		14 25	14 34	14 44				14 57	15 04	15 13		15 25	15 34	15 44				15 57	16 04	16 13	
	d			14 40				14 58	15 04	15 09	15 19			15 40				15 58	16 04	16 09	16 19	
Hampden Park 4	d			14 44				15a02	15a08		15 23			15 44				16a02	16a08		16 23	
Pevensey & Westham	d			14 49							15 28			15 49							16 28	
Pevensey Bay	d																					
Normans Bay	d			14 53										15 53								
Cooden Beach	d			14 57							15 34			15 57							16 34	
Collington	d			15 00							15 37			16 00							16 37	
Bexhill 4	d			15 02						15 24	15 39			16 02						16 24	16 39	
St Leonards Warrior Sq 4	d			15 09						15 31	15 46			16 09						16 31	16 46	
Hastings 4	a			15 12						15 35	15 49			16 12						16 35	16 49	
	d			15 13						15 36	15 50			16 13						16 36	16 50	
Ore	d			15a16							15a53			16a16							16a53	
Three Oaks	d																			16 44		
Doleham	d																					
Winchelsea	d									15 50												
Rye	a									15 54										16 54		
	d									15 56										16 56		
Appledore (Kent)	d									16 05										17 05		
Ham Street	d									16 10										17 10		
Ashford International	a									16 18										17 18		

London, Haywards Heath and Brighton - Lewes, Seaford, Eastbourne, Hastings and Ashford

Network Diagram - see first Page of Table 184

		SN	SN	SN	SN	SN	SN	SN	SN	SN		SN	SN	SN	SN	SN	SN	SN	SN	SN		SN	SN	SN	SN
		◇1	1	◇1			◇1	1		◇1			◇1	1	◇1			◇1	1			◇1		◇1	1
London Victoria 15 ⊖	d			15 17						15 47					16 17							16 47			
Clapham Junction 10	d			15 23						15 53					16 23							16 53			
London Bridge 4 ⊖	d																								
East Croydon	d			15 33						16 03					16 33							17 03			
Gatwick Airport 10 ✈	d			15 50						16 20					16 50							17 20			
Haywards Heath 3	d			16 07						16 35					17 07							17 35			
Wivelsfield 4	d			16 11											17 11										
Plumpton	d									16 44												17 44			
Cooksbridge	d																								
Brighton 10	d		15 52		16 10	16 22			16 32			16 40		16 52		17 10	17 22			17 32			17 40		17 52
London Road (Brighton)	d		15 55		16 13	16 25						16 43		16 55		17 13	17 25						17 43		17 55
Moulsecoomb	d		15 57		16 15	16 27						16 45		16 57		17 15	17 27						17 45		17 57
Falmer	d		16 01		16 19	16 31						16 49		17 01		17 19	17 31						17 49		18 01
Lewes 4	a		16 07	16 22	16 25	16 37			16 43	16 52		16 55		17 07	17 22	17 25	17 37			17 43		17 52	17 55		18 07
	d		16 09	16 23	16 28				16 44	16 53		16 58		17 09	17 23	17 28				17 44		17 53	17 58		18 09
Southease	d				16 34											17 34									
Newhaven Town ⛴	d				16 38							17 06				17 38							18 06		
Newhaven Harbour	d				16 40							17 08				17 40							18 08		
Bishopstone	d				16 43							17 11				17 43							18 11		
Seaford	a				16 46							17 14				17 46							18 14		
Glynde	d		16 14											17 14											18 14
Berwick	d		16 20											17 20											18 20
Polegate	d		16 25	16 35					16 57	17 05				17 25	17 35					17 57		18 05			18 25
Hampden Park 4	d	16 20	16 29	16 39				16 52					17 20	17 29	17 39				17 52					18 20	18 29
Eastbourne 4	a	16 25	16 34	16 44				16 57	17 04	17 13			17 25	17 34	17 44				17 57	18 04		18 13		18 25	18 34
	d		16 40				16 58	17 04	17 09	17 19				17 40				17 58	18 04	18 09		18 19			18 40
Hampden Park 4	d		16 44				17a02	17a08		17 23				17 44				18a02	18a08			18 23			18 44
Pevensey & Westham	d		16 49							17 28				17 49								18 28			18 49
Pevensey Bay	d																								
Normans Bay	d		16 53											17 53											18 53
Cooden Beach	d		16 57							17 34				17 57								18 34			18 57
Collington	d		17 00							17 37				18 00								18 37			19 00
Bexhill 4	d		17 02						17 24	17 39				18 02						18 24		18 39			19 02
St Leonards Warrior Sq 4	d		17 09						17 31	17 46				18 09						18 31		18 46			19 09
Hastings 4	a		17 12						17 35	17 49				18 12						18 35		18 49			19 12
	d		17 13						17 36	17 50				18 13						18 36		18 50			19 13
Ore	d		17a16							17a53				18a16								18a53			19a16
Three Oaks	d																			18 44					
Doleham	d																								
Winchelsea	d								17 50																
Rye	a								17 54											18 54					
	d								17 56											18 56					
Appledore (Kent)	d								18 05											19 05					
Ham Street	d								18 10											19 10					
Ashford International	a								18 18											19 18					

Table 189

Saturdays

London, Haywards Heath and Brighton - Lewes, Seaford, Eastbourne, Hastings and Ashford

Network Diagram - see first Page of Table 184

		SN ◇1	SN	SN	SN ◇1	SN 1	SN	SN ◇1	SN	SN ◇1	SN 1	SN ◇1	SN	SN	SN 1	SN	SN ◇1	SN	SN ◇1	SN 1	SN ◇1 A	SN	SN 1
London Victoria 15 ⊖	d	17 17						17 47				18 17					18 47				19 17		
Clapham Junction 10	d	17 23						17 53				18 23					18 53				19 23		
London Bridge 4 ⊖	d																						
East Croydon	d	17 33						18 03				18 33					19 03				19 33		
Gatwick Airport 10 ✈	d	17 50						18 20				18 50					19 20				19 50		
Haywards Heath 3	d	18 07						18 35				19 07					19 35				20 07		
Wivelsfield 4	d	18 11										19 11									20 11		
Plumpton	d							18 44									19 44						
Cooksbridge	d																						
Brighton 10	d		18 10	18 22			18 32		18 40		18 52		19 10	19 22		19 32		19 40		19 52		20 10	
London Road (Brighton)	d		18 13	18 25					18 43		18 55		19 13	19 25				19 43		19 55		20 13	
Moulsecoomb	d		18 15	18 27					18 45		18 57		19 15	19 27				19 45		19 57		20 15	
Falmer	d		18 19	18 31					18 49		19 01		19 19	19 31				19 49		20 01		20 19	
Lewes 4	a	18 22	18 25	18 37			18 43	18 52	18 55		19 07	19 22	19 25	19 37		19 43	19 52	19 55		20 08	20 22	20 25	
	d	18 23	18 28				18 44	18 53	18 58		19 09	19 23	19 28			19 44	19 53	19 58		20 09	20 23	20 28	
Southease	d		18 34										19 34										
Newhaven Town ⛴	d		18 38						19 06				19 38					20 06				20 36	
Newhaven Harbour	d		18 40						19 08				19 40					20 08				20 38	
Bishopstone	d		18 43						19 11				19 43					20 11				20 41	
Seaford	a		18 46						19 14				19 46					20 14				20 44	
Glynde	d										19 14									20 14	20 28		
Berwick	d										19 20									20 20	20 34		
Polegate	d	18 35					18 57	19 05			19 25	19 35				19 57	20 05			20 25	20 39		
Hampden Park 4	d	18 39				18 52				19 20	19 29	19 39			19 52				20 20	20 29	20 43		20 52
Eastbourne 4	a	18 44				18 57	19 04	19 13		19 25	19 34	19 44			19 57	20 04	20 13		20 25	20 34	20 48		20 57
	d				18 58	19 04	19 09	19 19			19 40				20 04	20 09	20 19				20 54		21 04
Hampden Park 4	d				19a02	19a08		19 23			19 44				20a08		20 23						21a08
Pevensey & Westham	d							19 28			19 49						20 28				21 01		
Pevensey Bay	d																						
Normans Bay	d										19 53												
Cooden Beach	d							19 34			19 57						20 34				21 07		
Collington	d							19 37			20 00						20 37						
Bexhill 4	d						19 24	19 39			20 02					20 24	20 39				21 12		
St Leonards Warrior Sq 4	d						19 31	19 46			20 09					20 31	20 46				21 18		
Hastings 4	a						19 35	19 49			20 12					20 35	20 49				21 21		
	d						19 36	19 50			20 13					20 36	20 50						
Ore	d							19a53			20a16						20a53						
Three Oaks	d															20 44							
Doleham	d																						
Winchelsea	d						19 50																
Rye	a						19 54									20 54							
	d						19 56									20 56							
Appledore (Kent)	d						20 05									21 05							
Ham Street	d						20 10									21 10							
Ashford International	a						20 18									21 18							

A ◇ to Haywards Heath

Table 189

Saturdays

London, Haywards Heath and Brighton - Lewes, Seaford, Eastbourne, Hastings and Ashford

Network Diagram - see first Page of Table 184

		SN		SN	SN	SN	SN	SN	SN	SN	SN	SN		SN	SN	SN	SN	SN	SN	SN	SN	SN		SN	SN
				◇1		◇1	◇1		1		◇1	◇1			◇1		1		◇1		1	1			◇1
London Victoria 15 ⊖	d			19 47			20 17					20 47			21 17				21 47						22 47
Clapham Junction 10	d			19 53			20 23					20 53			21 23				21 53						22 53
London Bridge 4 ⊖	d																								
East Croydon	d			20 03			20 33					21 03			21 33				22 03						23 03
Gatwick Airport 10 ✈	d			20 20			20 50					21 20			21 49				22 20						23 20
Haywards Heath 3	d			20 35			21 07					21 34			22 08				22 34						23 34
Wivelsfield 4	d			20 39			21 11					21 38			22 12				22 38						23 38
Plumpton	d			20 45								21 44							22 44						23 44
Cooksbridge	d																								
Brighton 10	d	20 32			20 40			21 04		21 32				21 40		22 04		22 28		22 34	23 06			23 28	
London Road (Brighton)	d				20 43			21 07						21 43		22 07				22 37	23 09				
Moulsecoomb	d				20 45			21 09						21 45		22 09				22 39	23 11				
Falmer	d				20 49			21 13						21 49		22 13				22 43	23 15				
Lewes 4	a	20 43		20 52	20 55		21 22	21 19		21 43		21 51		21 55	22 23	22 19		22 39	22 51	22 49	23 21			23 39	23 51
	d	20 44		20 53	20 58		21 23	21 28		21 44		21 53		21 58	22 23	22 28		22 39	22 53	22 56	23 22			23 39	23 53
Southease	d																								
Newhaven Town	d				21 06			21 36						22 06		22 36				23 04					
Newhaven Harbour	d				21 08			21 38						22 08		22 38				23 06					
Bishopstone	d				21 11			21 41						22 11		22 41				23 09					
Seaford	a				21 14			21 44						22 14		22 44				23 12					
Glynde	d						21 28								22 29						23 27				
Berwick	d						21 34								22 34						23 33				00 02
Polegate	d	20 57		21 05			21 39			21 57		22 05			22 39			22 52	23 05		23 38			23 52	00 07
Hampden Park 4	d					21 20	21 43		21 51		22 07				22 43		22 55		23 09		23 42	23 47			00 11
Eastbourne 4	a	21 04		21 13		21 25	21 48		21 56	22 04	22 12	22 15			22 48		23 00	23 03	23 14		23 47	23 52		23 59	00 16
	d	21 09		21 19					22 04	22 09		22 21					23 05	23 10	23 20			23 56			00 22
Hampden Park 4	d			21 23					22a08			22 25					23a09		23 24			00a01			
Pevensey & Westham	d			21 28								22 30							23 29						00 29
Pevensey Bay	d																								
Normans Bay	d																								
Cooden Beach	d			21 34								22 36							23 35						00 35
Collington	d			21 37								22 39							23 38						00 38
Bexhill 4	d	21 23		21 39						22 23		22 41						23 24	23 40						00 41
St Leonards Warrior Sq 4	d	21 30		21 46						22 30		22 48						23 31	23 47						00 47
Hastings 4	a	21 33		21 49						22 33		22 51						23 34	23 50						00 50
	d	21 35		21 50																					
Ore	d	21 37		21a53																					
Three Oaks	d	21 43																							
Doleham	d	21 46																							
Winchelsea	d	21 52																							
Rye	a	21 56																							
	d	21 56																							
Appledore (Kent)	d	22 05																							
Ham Street	d	22 10																							
Ashford International	a	22 18																							

Table 189

Saturdays

London, Haywards Heath and Brighton - Lewes, Seaford, Eastbourne, Hastings and Ashford

Network Diagram - see first Page of Table 184

Station		SN
London Victoria 15 ⊖	d	
Clapham Junction 10	d	
London Bridge 4 ⊖	d	
East Croydon	d	
Gatwick Airport 10 ✈	d	
Haywards Heath 3	d	
Wivelsfield 4	d	
Plumpton	d	
Cooksbridge	d	
Brighton 10	d	23 34
London Road (Brighton)	d	23 37
Moulsecoomb	d	23 39
Falmer	d	23 43
Lewes 4	a	23 49
	d	23 56
Southease	d	
Newhaven Town	d	00 04
Newhaven Harbour	d	00 06
Bishopstone	d	00 09
Seaford	a	00 12
Glynde	d	
Berwick	d	
Polegate	d	
Hampden Park 4	d	
Eastbourne 4	a	
	d	
Hampden Park 4	d	
Pevensey & Westham	d	
Pevensey Bay	d	
Normans Bay	d	
Cooden Beach	d	
Collington	d	
Bexhill 4	d	
St Leonards Warrior Sq 4	d	
Hastings 4	a	
	d	
Ore	d	
Three Oaks	d	
Doleham	d	
Winchelsea	d	
Rye	a	
	d	
Appledore (Kent)	d	
Ham Street	d	
Ashford International	a	

Table 189

Sundays

London, Haywards Heath and Brighton - Lewes, Seaford, Eastbourne, Hastings and Ashford

Network Diagram - see first Page of Table 184

		SN ◇1 A	SN A	SN ◇1	SN ◇1	SN	SN ◇1	SN	SN 1	SN	SN	SN 1	SN	SN	SN	SN ◇1	SN	SN 1	SN	SN	SN	SN ◇1	SN
London Victoria 15 ⊖	d	22p47		00 05																			
Clapham Junction 10	d	22p53		00 11																			
London Bridge 4 ⊖	d																						
East Croydon	d	23p03		00 24																			
Gatwick Airport 10 ✈	d	23p20		00 43																			
Haywards Heath 3	d	23p34		01 06																			
Wivelsfield 4	d	23p38																					
Plumpton	d	23p44																					
Cooksbridge	d																						
Brighton 10	d		23p34						07 09	07 15		07 43	07 49	08 09			08 20	08 43	08 49	09 09			09 20
London Road (Brighton)	d		23p37						07 12	07 18		07 46	07 52	08 12				08 46	08 52	09 12			
Moulsecoomb	d		23p39						07 14	07 20		07 48	07 54	08 14				08 48	08 54	09 14			
Falmer	d		23p43						07 18	07 24		07 52	07 58	08 18				08 52	08 58	09 18			
Lewes 4	a	23p51	23p49	01 20					07 24	07 31		07 58	08 04	08 24			08 31	08 58	09 04	09 24			09 31
	d	23p53	23p56	01 20					07 25	07 32		07 59	08 05	08 25			08 32	08 59	09 05	09 25			09 32
Southease	d												08 11						09 11				
Newhaven Town ⛴	d		00 04							07 40			08 15	08 33					09 15	09 33			
Newhaven Harbour	d		00 06							07 42			08 17	08 35					09 17	09 35			
Bishopstone	d		00 09							07 45			08 20	08 38					09 20	09 38			
Seaford	a		00 12							07 48			08 23	08 41					09 23	09 41			
Glynde	d								07 30								08 37						09 37
Berwick	d	00 02							07 36								08 43						09 43
Polegate	d	00 07		01s32					07 41			08 11					08 49	09 11					09 49
Hampden Park 4	d	00 11		01s36					07 45							08 43	08 53					09 43	09 53
Eastbourne 4	a	00 16		01 41					07 50			08 19				08 49	08 58	09 19				09 49	09 58
	d	00 22			06 55		07 26	07 30			07 58	08 26			08 34		09 02	09 26			09 34		10 02
Hampden Park 4	d				06a59		07 30	07a34				08 30			08a38			09 30			09a38		
Pevensey & Westham	d	00 29					07 35					08 35						09 35					
Pevensey Bay	d																						
Normans Bay	d																						
Cooden Beach	d	00 35					07 41					08 41						09 41					
Collington	d	00 38					07 44					08 44						09 44					
Bexhill 4	d	00 41					07 47				08 11	08 46					09 16	09 46					10 16
St Leonards Warrior Sq 4	d	00 47					07 53				08 18	08 53					09 23	09 53					10 23
Hastings 4	a	00 50					07 56				08 22	08 56					09 26	09 56					10 26
	d					07 22	07 57				08 22	08 57					09 27	09 57					10 27
Ore	d					07 24	08a00					09a00						10a00					
Three Oaks	d					07 30																	
Doleham	d					07 33																	
Winchelsea	d					07 39																	
Rye	a					07 43					08 39						09 44						10 44
	d					07 43					08 41						09 46						10 46
Appledore (Kent)	d					07 52					08 50						09 55						10 55
Ham Street	d					07 57					08 55						10 00						11 00
Ashford International	a					08 06					09 03						10 08						11 08

A not 11 December

Table 189

Sundays

London, Haywards Heath and Brighton - Lewes, Seaford, Eastbourne, Hastings and Ashford

Network Diagram - see first Page of Table 184

		SN	SN	SN	SN	SN		SN	SN	SN	SN	SN	SN	SN	SN	SN		SN	SN	SN	SN	SN	SN	SN	SN
		◇1				◇1			◇1				◇1		◇1					◇1		◇1			
		A							A						A							A			
		⚯							⚯						⚯							⚯			
London Victoria 15 ⊖	d	08 47							09 47						10 47							11 47			
Clapham Junction 10	d	08 53							09 53						10 53							11 53			
London Bridge 4 ⊖	d																								
East Croydon	d	09 07							10 07						11 07							12 07			
Gatwick Airport 10 ✈	d	09 29							10 29						11 29							12 29			
Haywards Heath 3	d	09 41							10 41						11 41							12 41			
Wivelsfield 4	d	09 45							10 45						11 45							12 45			
Plumpton	d	09 51							10 51						11 51							12 51			
Cooksbridge	d																								
Brighton 10	d		09 39	10 09				10 20		10 39	11 09			11 20		11 39		12 09			12 20		12 39	13 09	
London Road (Brighton)	d		09 42	10 12						10 42	11 12					11 42		12 12					12 42	13 12	
Moulsecoomb	d		09 44	10 14						10 44	11 14					11 44		12 14					12 44	13 14	
Falmer	d		09 48	10 18						10 48	11 18					11 48		12 18					12 48	13 18	
Lewes 4	a	09 58	09 54	10 24				10 31	10 58	10 54	11 24			11 31	11 58	11 54		12 24			12 31	12 58	12 54	13 24	
	d	09 59	10 03	10 25				10 32	10 59	11 03	11 25			11 32	11 59	12 03		12 25			12 32	12 59	13 03	13 25	
Southease	d		10 09							11 09						12 09							13 09		
Newhaven Town ⛴	d		10 13	10 33						11 13	11 33					12 13		12 33					13 13	13 33	
Newhaven Harbour	d		10 15	10 35						11 15	11 35					12 15		12 35					13 15	13 35	
Bishopstone	d		10 18	10 38						11 18	11 38					12 18		12 38					13 18	13 38	
Seaford	a		10 21	10 41						11 21	11 41					12 21		12 41					13 21	13 41	
Glynde	d							10 37						11 37							12 37				
Berwick	d							10 43						11 43							12 43				
Polegate	d	10 11						10 49	11 11					11 49	12 11						12 49	13 11			
Hampden Park 4	d					10 43		10 53					11 43	11 53						12 43	12 53				
Eastbourne 4	a	10 19				10 49		10 58	11 19				11 49	11 58	12 19					12 49	12 58	13 19			
	d	10 26			10 34			11 02	11 26			11 34		12 02	12 26				12 34		13 02	13 26			13 34
Hampden Park 4	d	10 30			10a38				11 30			11a38			12 30				12a38			13 30			13a38
Pevensey & Westham	d	10 35							11 35						12 35							13 35			
Pevensey Bay	d																								
Normans Bay	d																								
Cooden Beach	d	10 41							11 41						12 41							13 41			
Collington	d	10 44							11 44						12 44							13 44			
Bexhill 4	d	10 46						11 16	11 46					12 16	12 46						13 16	13 46			
St Leonards Warrior Sq 4	d	10 53						11 23	11 53					12 23	12 53						13 23	13 53			
Hastings 4	a	10 56						11 26	11 56					12 26	12 56						13 26	13 56			
	d	10 57						11 27	11 57					12 27	12 57						13 27	13 57			
Ore	d	11a00							12a00						13a00							14a00			
Three Oaks	d																								
Doleham	d																								
Winchelsea	d																								
Rye	a							11 44						12 44							13 44				
	d							11 46						12 46							13 46				
Appledore (Kent)	d							11 55						12 55							13 55				
Ham Street	d							12 00						13 00							14 00				
Ashford International	a							12 08						13 08							14 08				

A ⚯ to Lewes

Table 189

Sundays

London, Haywards Heath and Brighton - Lewes, Seaford, Eastbourne, Hastings and Ashford

Network Diagram - see first Page of Table 184

		SN	SN	SN	SN	SN	SN	SN	SN	SN	SN	SN	SN	SN	SN	SN	SN	SN	SN	SN	SN	SN
		◇1		◇1				◇1		◇1				◇1		◇1				◇1		◇1
				A						A						A						A
				⚲						⚲						⚲						⚲
London Victoria 15 ⊖	d			12 47						13 47						14 47						15 47
Clapham Junction 10	d			12 53						13 53						14 53						15 53
London Bridge 4 ⊖	d																					
East Croydon	d			13 07						14 07						15 07						16 07
Gatwick Airport 10 ✈	d			13 29						14 29						15 29						16 29
Haywards Heath 3	d			13 41						14 41						15 41						16 41
Wivelsfield 4	d			13 45						14 45						15 45						16 45
Plumpton	d																					16 51
Cooksbridge	d																					
Brighton 10	d		13 20		13 39	14 09			14 20		14 39	15 09			15 20		15 39	16 09			16 20	
London Road (Brighton)	d				13 42	14 12					14 42	15 12					15 42	16 12				
Moulsecoomb	d				13 44	14 14					14 44	15 14					15 44	16 14				
Falmer	d				13 48	14 18					14 48	15 18					15 48	16 18				
Lewes 4	a		13 31	13 56	13 54	14 24			14 31	14 56	14 54	15 24			15 31	15 56	15 54	16 24			16 31	16 58
	d		13 32	13 59	14 03	14 25			14 32	14 59	15 03	15 25			15 32	15 59	16 03	16 25			16 32	16 59
Southease	d				14 09						15 09						16 09					
Newhaven Town ⛴	d				14 13	14 33					15 13	15 33					16 13	16 33				
Newhaven Harbour	d				14 15	14 35					15 15	15 35					16 15	16 35				
Bishopstone	d				14 18	14 38					15 18	15 38					16 18	16 38				
Seaford	a				14 21	14 41					15 21	15 41					16 21	16 41				
Glynde	d		13 37						14 37						15 37						16 37	
Berwick	d		13 43						14 43						15 43						16 43	
Polegate	d		13 49	14 11					14 49	15 11					15 49	16 11					16 49	17 11
Hampden Park 4	d	13 43	13 53					14 43	14 53					15 43	15 53					16 43	16 53	
Eastbourne 4	a	13 49	13 58	14 19				14 49	14 58	15 19				15 49	15 58	16 19				16 49	16 58	17 19
	d		14 02	14 26			14 34		15 02	15 26			15 34		16 02	16 26			16 34		17 02	17 26
Hampden Park 4	d			14 30			14a38			15 30			15a38			16 30			16a38			17 30
Pevensey & Westham	d			14 35						15 35						16 35						17 35
Pevensey Bay	d																					
Normans Bay	d																					
Cooden Beach	d			14 41						15 41						16 41						17 41
Collington	d			14 44						15 44						16 44						17 44
Bexhill 4	d		14 16	14 46					15 16	15 46					16 16	16 46					17 16	17 46
St Leonards Warrior Sq 4	d		14 23	14 53					15 23	15 53					16 23	16 53					17 23	17 53
Hastings 4	a		14 26	14 56					15 26	15 56					16 26	16 56					17 26	17 56
	d		14 27	14 57					15 27	15 57					16 27	16 57					17 27	17 57
Ore	d			15a00						16a00						17a00						18a00
Three Oaks	d																					
Doleham	d																					
Winchelsea	d																					
Rye	a		14 44						15 44						16 44						17 44	
	d		14 46						15 46						16 46						17 46	
Appledore (Kent)	d		14 55						15 55						16 55						17 55	
Ham Street	d		15 00						16 00						17 00						18 00	
Ashford International	a		15 08						16 08						17 08						18 08	

A ⚲ to Lewes

Table 189

Sundays

London, Haywards Heath and Brighton - Lewes, Seaford, Eastbourne, Hastings and Ashford

Network Diagram - see first Page of Table 184

		SN	SN	SN	SN	SN	SN	SN		SN	SN	SN	SN	SN	SN	SN	SN	SN		SN	SN	SN	SN	SN	SN
					◇1		◇1					◇1		◇1				◇1			◇1				◇1
							A ⚲							A ⚲							A ⚲				
London Victoria 15 ⊖	d						16 47							17 47							18 47				
Clapham Junction 10	d						16 53							17 53							18 53				
London Bridge 4 ⊖	d																								
East Croydon	d						17 07							18 07							19 07				
Gatwick Airport 10 ✈	d						17 29							18 29							19 29				
Haywards Heath 3	d						17 41							18 41							19 41				
Wivelsfield 4	d						17 45							18 45							19 45				
Plumpton	d						17 51							18 51							19 51				
Cooksbridge	d																								
Brighton 10	d	16 39	17 09			17 20		17 39		18 09			18 20		18 39	19 09				19 20		19 39	20 09		
London Road (Brighton)	d	16 42	17 12					17 42		18 12					18 42	19 12						19 42	20 12		
Moulsecoomb	d	16 44	17 14					17 44		18 14					18 44	19 14						19 44	20 14		
Falmer	d	16 48	17 18					17 48		18 18					18 48	19 18						19 48	20 18		
Lewes 4	a	16 54	17 24			17 31	17 58	17 54		18 24			18 31	18 58	18 54	19 24				19 31	19 58	19 54	20 24		
	d	17 03	17 25			17 32	17 59	18 03		18 25			18 32	18 59	19 03	19 25				19 32	19 59	20 03	20 25		
Southease	d	17 09						18 09							19 09							20 09			
Newhaven Town ⛴	d	17 13	17 33					18 13		18 33					19 13	19 33						20 13	20 33		
Newhaven Harbour	d	17 15	17 35					18 15		18 35					19 15	19 35						20 15	20 35		
Bishopstone	d	17 18	17 38					18 18		18 38					19 18	19 38						20 18	20 38		
Seaford	a	17 21	17 41					18 21		18 41					19 21	19 41						20 21	20 41		
Glynde	d					17 37							18 37							19 37					
Berwick	d					17 43							18 43							19 43					
Polegate	d					17 49	18 11						18 49	19 11						19 49	20 11				
Hampden Park 4	d				17 43	17 53						18 43	18 53					19 43		19 53					20 43
Eastbourne 4	a				17 49	17 58	18 19					18 49	18 58	19 19				19 49		19 58	20 19				20 49
	d			17 34		18 02	18 26				18 34		19 02	19 26			19 34			20 02	20 26			20 34	
Hampden Park 4	d			17a38			18 30				18a38			19 30			19a38				20 30			20a38	
Pevensey & Westham	d						18 35							19 35							20 35				
Pevensey Bay	d																								
Normans Bay	d																								
Cooden Beach	d						18 41							19 41							20 41				
Collington	d						18 44							19 44							20 44				
Bexhill 4	d					18 16	18 46						19 16	19 46						20 16	20 46				
St Leonards Warrior Sq 4	d					18 23	18 53						19 23	19 53						20 23	20 53				
Hastings 4	a					18 26	18 56						19 26	19 56						20 26	20 56				
	d					18 27	18 57						19 27	19 57						20 27	20 57				
Ore	d						19a00							20a00							21a00				
Three Oaks	d																								
Doleham	d																								
Winchelsea	d																								
Rye	a					18 44							19 44							20 44					
	d					18 46							19 46							20 46					
Appledore (Kent)	d					18 55							19 55							20 55					
Ham Street	d					19 00							20 00							21 00					
Ashford International	a					19 08							20 08							21 08					

A ⚲ to Lewes

Table 189

Sundays

London, Haywards Heath and Brighton - Lewes, Seaford, Eastbourne, Hastings and Ashford

Network Diagram - see first Page of Table 184

		SN	SN	SN		SN	SN	SN	SN	SN	SN	SN	SN	SN		SN	SN	SN	SN	SN	SN	SN	SN
			◇1					1		◇1				1			◇1			1			◇1
			A																				
			⚲																				
London Victoria 15 ⊖	d		19 47							20 47							21 47						22 47
Clapham Junction 10	d		19 53							20 53							21 53						22 53
London Bridge 4 ⊖	d																						
East Croydon	d		20 07							21 07							22 07						23 07
Gatwick Airport 10 ✈	d		20 29							21 29							22 29						23 29
Haywards Heath 3	d		20 41							21 41							22 41						23 41
Wivelsfield 4	d		20 45							21 45							22 45						23 45
Plumpton	d		20 51							21 51							22 51						23 51
Cooksbridge	d																						
Brighton 10	d	20 20		20 39		21 09			21 20		21 39	22 09				22 20		22 39	23 09		23 20	23 39	
London Road (Brighton)	d			20 42		21 12					21 42	22 12						22 42	23 12			23 42	
Moulsecoomb	d			20 44		21 14					21 44	22 14						22 44	23 14			23 44	
Falmer	d			20 48		21 18					21 48	22 18						22 48	23 18			23 48	
Lewes 4	a	20 31	20 58	20 54		21 24			21 31	21 58	21 54	22 24				22 31	22 58	22 54	23 24		23 31	23 54	23 58
	d	20 32	20 59	21 03		21 25			21 32	21 59	22 03	22 25				22 32	22 59	23 03			23 32		23 59
Southease	d																						
Newhaven Town ⛴	d			21 11		21 33					22 11	22 33						23 11					
Newhaven Harbour	d			21 13		21 35					22 13	22 35						23 13					
Bishopstone	d			21 16		21 38					22 16	22 38						23 16					
Seaford	a			21 19		21 41					22 19	22 41						23 19					
Glynde	d	20 37							21 37							22 37					23 37		
Berwick	d	20 43							21 43							22 43					23 43		
Polegate	d	20 49	21 11						21 49	22 11						22 49	23 11				23 49		00 11
Hampden Park 4	d	20 53						21 43	21 53					22 43		22 53				23 47	23 53		00 15
Eastbourne 4	a	20 58	21 19					21 49	21 58	22 19				22 49		22 58	23 19			23 52	23 58		00 20
	d	21 02	21 26				21 34		22 02	22 26			22 34				23 26						
Hampden Park 4	d		21 30				21a38			22 30			22a38				23 30						
Pevensey & Westham	d		21 35							22 35							23 35						
Pevensey Bay	d																						
Normans Bay	d																						
Cooden Beach	d		21 41							22 41							23 41						
Collington	d		21 44							22 44							23 44						
Bexhill 4	d	21 16	21 46						22 16	22 46							23 46						
St Leonards Warrior Sq 4	d	21 23	21 53						22 23	22 53							23 53						
Hastings 4	a	21 26	21 56						22 26	22 56							23 56						
	d	21 27	21 57																				
Ore	d		22a00																				
Three Oaks	d																						
Doleham	d																						
Winchelsea	d																						
Rye	a	21 44																					
	d	21 46																					
Appledore (Kent)	d	21 55																					
Ham Street	d	22 00																					
Ashford International	a	22 08																					

A ⚲ to Lewes

Ashford, Hastings, Eastbourne, Seaford and Lewes - Brighton, Haywards Heath and London

Network Diagram - see first Page of Table 184

Miles	Miles			SN	SN	SN	SN	SN	SN	SN	SN	SN		SN	SN	SN	SN	SN	SN	SN	SN	SN		SN	SN
				MX	MX	MO	MX																		
				■1	◇■1	◇■1	◇■1	◇■1			■1	■1			■1			■1		■1	◇■1	◇■1		■1	■1
																					A	A			
																					🛒	🛒			
—	0	**Ashford International**	d																						
—	5½	Ham Street	d																						
—	8½	Appledore (Kent)	d																						
—	15¼	Rye	a																						
—	—		d																						
—	17¼	Winchelsea	d																						
—	21½	Doleham	d																						
—	22¾	Three Oaks	d																						
—	25½	Ore	d																						
0	26½	**Hastings ■4**	a																						
—	—		d	23p22							05 07	05 42							05 58		06 15				
0¾	—	**St Leonards Warrior Sq ■4**	d	23p24							05 09	05 45							06 01		06 18				
4½	—	**Bexhill ■4**	d	23p31							05 16	05 52							06 12		06 26				
5¼	—	Collington	d	23p33							05 18	05 54									06 28				
6¾	—	Cooden Beach	d	23p36							05 21	05 57									06 31				
8½	—	Normans Bay	d																						
10½	—	Pevensey Bay	d																						
11¼	—	Pevensey & Westham	d	23p42							05 27	06 03									06 37				
14¼	—	Hampden Park ■4	d	23p47	00 11	00 15					05 32	06 08							06 24		06 42				07 02
16¼	—	**Eastbourne ■4**	a	23p52	00 16	00 20	01 41				05 37	06 13							06 29		06 47				07 07
—	—		d	23p56				05 08		05 32	05 42				06 14			06 24	06 37	06 47	06 57			07 02	
18¼	—	Hampden Park ■4	d	00 01				05 12		05 36	05 46				06a18			06 28		06 51	07 01			07a06	
20¼	—	Polegate	d	00 05				05 16		05 41	05 50							06 33	06 44	06 55	07 05				
24¼	—	Berwick	d								05 55							06 39		07 00					
29	—	Glynde	d															06 45		07 06					
—	0	**Seaford**	d						05 09					05 45			06 30					06 56			
—	1	Bishopstone	d						05 11					05 47			06 32					06 58			
—	2½	Newhaven Harbour	d						05 14					05 50			06 35					07 01			
—	2¾	Newhaven Town ⛴	d						05 16					05 52			06 37					07 03			
—	5½	Southease	d																			07 07			
32	9	**Lewes ■4**	a	00 17				05 28	05 25	05 53	06 04			06 01			06 46	06 50	06 57	07 11	07 18	07 14			
—	—																								
—	—		d	00 18				05 29	05 32	05 54	06 05			06 09		06 26	06 47	06 51	06 59	07 12	07 22				
36½	—	Falmer	d	00 25					05 39	06 01				06 16		06 33	06 54		07 06	07 19					
38¼	—	Moulsecoomb	d	00 28					05 42	06 05				06 19		06 36	06 57		07 10	07 22					
39¼	—	London Road (Brighton)	d	00 30					05 44	06 07				06 21		06 38	06 59		07 12	07 24					
40	—	**Brighton ■10**	a	00 34					05 48	06 11				06 25		06 42	07 03		07 16	07 28					
—	11¾	Cooksbridge	d															06 56			07 27				
—	14½	Plumpton	d					05 37			06 13							07 01			07 32				
—	18¼	Wivelsfield ■4	a															07 07			07 39				
—	21¼	**Haywards Heath ■3**	a					05 46			06 23							07 12			07 44				
—	—	**Gatwick Airport ■10** ✈	a					05 58			06 41							07 29							
—	—	East Croydon 🚋	a					06 14			06 58							07 45			08 13				
—	—	**London Bridge ■4** ⊖	a								07 14							08 01							
—	—	Clapham Junction ■10	a					06 25													08 23				
—	—	**London Victoria ■15** ⊖	a					06 32													08 32				

A 🛒 from Lewes

Ashford, Hastings, Eastbourne, Seaford and Lewes - Brighton, Haywards Heath and London

Network Diagram - see first Page of Table 184

		SN	SN	SN	SN	SN	SN	SN	SN	SN	SN	SN	SN	SN	SN	SN	SN	SN	SN	SN	SN	SN	SN
				1	◇1			◇1	◇1					◇1	1	1	◇1	◇1	◇1	1	1		
								A						A				A	A				
								🚲						🚲				🚲	🚲				
Ashford International	d										06 13	06 38											
Ham Street	d										06 22	06 47											
Appledore (Kent)	d										06 27	06 52											
Rye	a										06 36	07 01											
	d										06 36												
Winchelsea	d										06 40												
Doleham	d										06 46												
Three Oaks	d										06 50												
Ore	d										06 55												
Hastings 4	a										06 58												
	d							06 49			07 12			07 20				07 38					
St Leonards Warrior Sq 4	d							06 52			07 15			07 23				07 40					
Bexhill 4	d							06 59			07 22			07 31				07 47					
Collington	d							07 01						07 33				07 49					
Cooden Beach	d							07 04						07 36				07 52					
Normans Bay	d																	07 55					
Pevensey Bay	d																	07 59					
Pevensey & Westham	d							07 10						07 42				08 01					
Hampden Park 4	d				07 11			07 15						07 46	07 51		08 09	08 06		08 29	08 39		
Eastbourne 4	a				07 16			07 20			07 37			07 51	07 56		08 14	08 11		08 34	08 44		
	d			07 14	07 21			07 32	07 38		07 47			07 57		08 04	08 21	08 18		08 40			
Hampden Park 4	d			07 19	07a25				07a42					08 01		08 08	08a25			08a44			
Polegate	d			07 23				07 39			07 54			08 05		08 12		08 25					
Berwick	d			07 29				07 44						08 11		08 18		08 30					
Glynde	d			07 35										08 16		08 23		08 36					
Seaford	d		07 16				07 33						07 59						08 21				
Bishopstone	d		07 18				07 35						08 01						08 23				
Newhaven Harbour	d		07 21				07 38						08 04						08 26				
Newhaven Town	d		07 23				07 40			07 49			08 06						08 28				
Southease	d		07 27				07 44						08 10						08 32				
Lewes 4	a		07 33	07 41			07 50	07 53		07 57	08 07		08 17	08 22		08 29		08 42	08 39				
	d	07 23	07 34	07 42		07 45	07 51	07 55		07 58	08 07		08 19	08 23		08 30		08 48				08 46	08 58
Falmer	d	07 30	07 41			07 52	07 58			08 05			08 26			08 37						08 53	09 05
Moulsecoomb	d	07 33	07 44			07 55	08 01			08 08			08 29			08 40						08 56	09 08
London Road (Brighton)	d	07 35	07 46			07 57	08 03			08 10			08 32			08 42						08 58	09 10
Brighton 10	a	07 39	07 50			08 01	08 07			08 14	08 20		08 35			08 46						09 02	09 14
Cooksbridge	d			07 48				08 00						08 28									
Plumpton	d			07 53				08 05						08 33									
Wivelsfield 4	a							08 11						08 39				09 00					
Haywards Heath 3	a			08 03				08 16						08 44				09 05					
Gatwick Airport 10	a													08 56				09 22					
East Croydon	a			08 31				08 46						09 14				09 38					
London Bridge 4	a			08 51																			
Clapham Junction 10	a							09 00						09 23				09 48					
London Victoria 15	a							09 09						09 32				09 58					

A 🚲 from Lewes

Table 189

Mondays to Fridays

Ashford, Hastings, Eastbourne, Seaford and Lewes - Brighton, Haywards Heath and London

Network Diagram - see first Page of Table 184

		SN	SN	SN	SN	SN	SN	SN	SN	SN	SN	SN	SN	SN	SN	SN	SN	SN	SN	SN	SN	SN
					◇1	1	◇1		◇1	1	◇1				◇1	1		◇1		◇1	1	◇1
					A 🍴				A 🍴													
Ashford International	d	07 17	07 39										08 32				08 52					
Ham Street	d	07 26	07 48										08 41				09 01					
Appledore (Kent)	d	07 31	07 53										08 46				09 06					
Rye	a	07 40	08 02										08 55				09 15					
	d	07 45											08 55				09 16					
Winchelsea	d	07 48															09 19					
Doleham	d	07 55															09 26					
Three Oaks	d	07 58											09 06				09 29					
Ore	d	08 04				08 22			08 47							09 20	09 35			09 50		
Hastings 4	a	08 07				08 25			08 50				09 13			09 23	09 38			09 53		
	d	08 10				08 26			08 52				09 14			09 24				09 55		
St Leonards Warrior Sq 4	d	08 13				08 28			08 54				09 17			09 26				09 57		
Bexhill 4	d	08 22				08 35			09 01				09 24			09 35				10 04		
Collington	d					08 37			09 03							09 37				10 06		
Cooden Beach	d					08 40			09 06							09 40				10 09		
Normans Bay	d					08 43										09 43						
Pevensey Bay	d																					
Pevensey & Westham	d					08 48			09 13							09 48				10 15		
Hampden Park 4	d					08 52	09 07		09 17	09 29	09 42					09 52				10 20	10 29	10 39
Eastbourne 4	a	08 37				08 57	09 12		09 22	09 34	09 47		09 39			09 58				10 25	10 34	10 44
	d	08 45			08 56	09 04	09 19		09 28	09 40			09 47		09 55	10 04		10 20		10 31	10 40	
Hampden Park 4	d				09 00	09 08	09a23			09a44					09 59	10 08		10a24			10a44	
Polegate	d	08 52			09 04	09 12			09 35				09 54		10 03	10 12				10 37		
Berwick	d					09 18									10 09	10 18						
Glynde	d					09 23										10 23						
Seaford	d			08 57				09 25						09 58					10 25			
Bishopstone	d			08 59				09 27						10 00					10 27			
Newhaven Harbour	d			09 02				09 30						10 03					10 30			
Newhaven Town ⛴	d			09 04				09 32						10 05					10 32			
Southease	d							09 36											10 36			
Lewes 4	a	09 07		09 13	09 16	09 29		09 44	09 47				10 07	10 14	10 18	10 29			10 44	10 49		
	d	09 07		09 14	09 18	09 29		09 44	09 48			09 58	10 07	10 14	10 19	10 29			10 44	10 50		
Falmer	d			09 21		09 36		09 51				10 05		10 21		10 36			10 51			
Moulsecoomb	d			09 24		09 39		09 54				10 08		10 24		10 39			10 54			
London Road (Brighton)	d			09 27		09 42		09 57				10 10		10 27		10 42			10 57			
Brighton 10	a	09 20		09 30		09 45		10 00				10 14	10 20	10 30		10 45			11 00			
Cooksbridge	d				09 23				09 53						10 24							
Plumpton	d				09 28				09 58						10 29							
Wivelsfield 4	a				09 34										10 35							
Haywards Heath 3	a				09 38				10 07						10 40					11 05		
Gatwick Airport 10 ✈	a				09 56				10 25						10 55					11 24		
East Croydon	a				10 11				10 41						11 11					11 40		
London Bridge 4 ⊖	a																					
Clapham Junction 10	a				10 21				10 51						11 21					11 50		
London Victoria 15 ⊖	a				10 28				10 58						11 28					11 57		

A 🍴 from Lewes

Ashford, Hastings, Eastbourne, Seaford and Lewes - Brighton, Haywards Heath and London

Network Diagram - see first Page of Table 184

		SN	SN	SN	SN	SN	SN	SN	SN	SN		SN	SN	SN	SN	SN	SN	SN	SN	SN		SN	SN	SN	SN
					◇1	1	◇1		◇1	1		◇1				◇1	1	◇1		◇1		1	◇1		
Ashford International	d		09 32											10 32											11 32
Ham Street	d		09 41											10 41											11 41
Appledore (Kent)	d		09 46											10 46											11 46
Rye	a		09 55											10 55											11 55
	d		09 55											10 55											11 55
Winchelsea	d		09 59																						11 59
Doleham	d																								
Three Oaks	d													11 06											
Ore	d					10 22			10 50								11 22			11 50					
Hastings 4	a		10 13			10 25			10 53					11 13			11 25			11 53					12 13
	d		10 14			10 26			10 55					11 14			11 26			11 55					12 14
St Leonards Warrior Sq 4	d		10 17			10 28			10 57					11 17			11 28			11 57					12 17
Bexhill 4	d		10 24			10 35			11 04					11 24			11 35			12 04					12 24
Collington	d					10 37			11 06								11 37			12 06					
Cooden Beach	d					10 40			11 09								11 40			12 09					
Normans Bay	d					10 43											11 43								
Pevensey Bay	d																								
Pevensey & Westham	d					10 48			11 15								11 48			12 15					
Hampden Park 4	d					10 52			11 20	11 29		11 39					11 52			12 20		12 29	12 39		
Eastbourne 4	a		10 39			10 57			11 25	11 34		11 44		11 39			11 57			12 25		12 34	12 44		12 39
	d		10 47		10 58	11 04	11 19		11 31	11 40				11 47		11 58	12 04	12 19		12 31		12 40			12 47
Hampden Park 4	d				11 02	11 08	11a23			11a44						12 02	12 08	12a23				12a44			
Polegate	d		10 54		11 06	11 12			11 37					11 54		12 06	12 12			12 37					12 54
Berwick	d					11 18											12 18								
Glynde	d					11 23											12 23								
Seaford	d			10 58				11 25							11 58				12 25						
Bishopstone	d			11 00				11 27							12 00				12 27						
Newhaven Harbour	d			11 03				11 30							12 03				12 30						
Newhaven Town	d			11 05				11 32							12 05				12 32						
Southease	d							11 36											12 36						
Lewes 4	a		11 07	11 14	11 19	11 29		11 44	11 49					12 07	12 14	12 19	12 29		12 44	12 49					13 07
	d	10 58	11 07	11 14	11 20	11 29		11 44	11 50				11 58	12 07	12 14	12 20	12 29		12 44	12 50				12 58	13 07
Falmer	d	11 05		11 21		11 36		11 51					12 05		12 21		12 36		12 51					13 05	
Moulsecoomb	d	11 08		11 24		11 39		11 54					12 08		12 24		12 39		12 54					13 08	
London Road (Brighton)	d	11 10		11 27		11 42		11 57					12 10		12 27		12 42		12 57					13 10	
Brighton 10	a	11 14	11 20	11 30		11 45		12 00					12 14	12 20	12 30		12 45		13 00					13 14	13 20
Cooksbridge	d																								
Plumpton	d				11 28											12 28									
Wivelsfield 4	a				11 35											12 35									
Haywards Heath 3	a				11 40				12 05							12 40				13 05					
Gatwick Airport 10	a				11 55				12 24							12 55				13 24					
East Croydon	a				12 11				12 40							13 11				13 40					
London Bridge 4	a																								
Clapham Junction 10	a				12 21				12 50							13 21				13 50					
London Victoria 15	a				12 28				12 57							13 28				13 57					

Ashford, Hastings, Eastbourne, Seaford and Lewes - Brighton, Haywards Heath and London

Network Diagram - see first Page of Table 184

		SN	SN	SN	SN	SN		SN	SN	SN	SN	SN	SN	SN	SN	SN		SN	SN	SN	SN	SN	SN	SN	SN
			◇1	1	◇1			◇1	1	◇1				◇1	1	◇1			◇1 A 🛒	1	◇1				◇1 A 🛒
Ashford International	d											12 32											13 32		
Ham Street	d											12 41											13 41		
Appledore (Kent)	d											12 46											13 46		
Rye	a											12 55											13 55		
	d											12 55											13 55		
Winchelsea	d																						13 59		
Doleham	d																								
Three Oaks	d											13 06													
Ore	d			12 22				12 50							13 22				13 50						
Hastings 4	a			12 25				12 53				13 13			13 25				13 53				14 13		
	d			12 26				12 55				13 14			13 26				13 55				14 14		
St Leonards Warrior Sq 4	d			12 28				12 57				13 17			13 28				13 57				14 17		
Bexhill 4	d			12 35				13 04				13 24			13 35				14 04				14 24		
Collington	d			12 37				13 06							13 37				14 06						
Cooden Beach	d			12 40				13 09							13 40				14 09						
Normans Bay	d			12 43											13 43										
Pevensey Bay	d																								
Pevensey & Westham	d			12 48				13 15							13 48				14 15						
Hampden Park 4	d			12 52				13 20	13 29	13 39					13 52				14 20	14 29	14 39				
Eastbourne 4	a			12 57				13 25	13 34	13 44		13 39			13 57				14 25	14 34	14 44		14 39		
	d		12 58	13 04	13 19			13 31	13 40			13 47		13 58	14 04	14 19			14 31	14 40			14 47		14 58
Hampden Park 4	d		13 02	13 08	13a23				13a44					14 02	14 08	14a23				14a44					15 02
Polegate	d		13 06	13 12				13 37				13 54		14 06	14 12				14 37				14 54		15 06
Berwick	d			13 18											14 18										
Glynde	d			13 23											14 23										
Seaford	d	12 58				13 25							13 58					14 25						14 58	
Bishopstone	d	13 00				13 27							14 00					14 27						15 00	
Newhaven Harbour	d	13 03				13 30							14 03					14 30						15 03	
Newhaven Town	d	13 05				13 32							14 05					14 32						15 05	
Southease	d					13 36												14 36							
Lewes 4	a	13 14	13 19	13 29		13 44		13 49				14 07	14 14	14 19	14 29			14 44	14 49				15 07	15 14	15 18
	d	13 14	13 20	13 29		13 44		13 50			13 58	14 07	14 14	14 20	14 29			14 44	14 50			14 58	15 07	15 14	15 19
Falmer	d	13 21		13 36		13 51					14 05		14 21		14 36			14 51				15 05		15 21	
Moulsecoomb	d	13 24		13 39		13 54					14 08		14 24		14 39			14 54				15 08		15 24	
London Road (Brighton)	d	13 27		13 42		13 57					14 10		14 27		14 42			14 57				15 10		15 27	
Brighton 10	a	13 30		13 45		14 00					14 14	14 20	14 30		14 45			15 00				15 14	15 20	15 30	
Cooksbridge	d																								15 24
Plumpton	d		13 28											14 28											15 29
Wivelsfield 4	a		13 35											14 35											15 35
Haywards Heath 3	a		13 40					14 05						14 40					15 05						15 40
Gatwick Airport 10	a		13 55					14 24						14 55					15 24						15 55
East Croydon	a		14 11					14 40						15 11					15 40						16 11
London Bridge 4	a																								
Clapham Junction 10	a		14 21					14 50						15 21					15 50						16 21
London Victoria 15	a		14 28					14 57						15 28					15 57						16 28

A 🛒 from Lewes

Ashford, Hastings, Eastbourne, Seaford and Lewes - Brighton, Haywards Heath and London

Network Diagram - see first Page of Table 184

Station		SN 1	SN ◇1	SN	SN ◇1 A	SN 1	SN ◇1	SN	SN	SN	SN ◇1 A	SN 1	SN ◇1	SN	SN ◇1 A	SN 1	SN ◇1	SN	SN	SN	SN ◇1 A	SN 1
Ashford International	d								14 32										15 32			
Ham Street	d								14 41										15 41			
Appledore (Kent)	d								14 46										15 46			
Rye	a								14 55										15 55			
	d								14 55										15 55			
Winchelsea	d																		15 59			
Doleham	d																					
Three Oaks	d								15 06													
Ore	d	14 22			14 50							15 20			15 48							16 22
Hastings 4	a	14 25			14 53				15 13			15 23			15 51				16 13			16 25
	d	14 26			14 55				15 14			15 24			15 52				16 14			16 26
St Leonards Warrior Sq 4	d	14 28			14 57				15 17			15 26			15 54				16 17			16 28
Bexhill 4	d	14 35			15 04				15 24			15 33			16 01				16 24			16 35
Collington	d	14 37			15 06							15 35			16 03							16 37
Cooden Beach	d	14 40			15 09							15 38			16 06							16 40
Normans Bay	d	14 43										15 41			16 09							16 43
Pevensey Bay	d											15 45			16 13							
Pevensey & Westham	d	14 48			15 15							15 47			16 15							16 48
Hampden Park 4	d	14 52			15 20	15 29	15 39					15 52			16 20	16 29	16 39					16 52
Eastbourne 4	a	14 57			15 25	15 34	15 44		15 39			15 57			16 25	16 34	16 44		16 39			16 57
	d	15 04	15 19		15 31	15 40			15 47		15 58	16 04	16 19		16 31	16 40			16 45		16 58	17 04
Hampden Park 4	d	15 08	15a23			15a44					16 02	16 08	16a23			16a44			16 49		17 02	17 08
Polegate	d	15 12			15 37				15 54		16 06	16 12			16 37				16 54		17 06	17 12
Berwick	d	15 18										16 18										17 18
Glynde	d	15 23										16 23										17 23
Seaford	d			15 25						15 58				16 25						16 58		
Bishopstone	d			15 27						16 00				16 27						17 00		
Newhaven Harbour	d			15 30						16 03				16 30						17 03		
Newhaven Town	d			15 32						16 05				16 32						17 05		
Southease	d			15 36										16 36								
Lewes 4	a	15 29		15 44	15 49				16 07	16 14	16 18	16 29		16 44	16 49				17 07	17 14	17 18	17 29
	d	15 29		15 44	15 50			15 58	16 07	16 14	16 20	16 29		16 44	16 50			16 58	17 07	17 14	17 19	17 29
Falmer	d	15 36		15 51				16 05		16 21		16 36		16 51				17 05		17 21		17 36
Moulsecoomb	d	15 39		15 54				16 08		16 24		16 39		16 54				17 08		17 24		17 39
London Road (Brighton)	d	15 42		15 57				16 10		16 27		16 42		16 57				17 10		17 27		17 42
Brighton 10	a	15 45		16 00				16 14	16 20	16 30		16 45		17 00				17 14	17 20	17 30		17 45
Cooksbridge	d										16 25										17 24	
Plumpton	d										16 30										17 29	
Wivelsfield 4	a										16 38										17 35	
Haywards Heath 3	a				16 05						16 42				17 06						17 39	
Gatwick Airport 10	a				16 25						16 57				17 25						17 54	
East Croydon	a				16 40						17 13				17 41						18 11	
London Bridge 4	a																					
Clapham Junction 10	a				16 50						17 22				17 50						18 21	
London Victoria 15	a				16 58						17 29				17 58						18 29	

A — from Lewes

Ashford, Hastings, Eastbourne, Seaford and Lewes - Brighton, Haywards Heath and London

Network Diagram - see first Page of Table 184

		SN	SN	SN	SN	SN	SN	SN		SN	SN	SN	SN	SN	SN	SN	SN	SN		SN	SN	SN	SN	SN	SN
		◇[1]		◇[1]	[1]			◇[1]			◇[1]	[1]		◇[1]		◇[1]	[1]					[1]		◇[1]	[1]
				A 🛒							A 🛒														
Ashford International ⇌	d						16 32													17 32	17 58				
Ham Street	d						16 41													17 41	18 07				
Appledore (Kent)	d						16 46													17 46	18 12				
Rye	a						16 55													17 55	18 21				
	d						16 55													17 55					
Winchelsea	d																			17 59					
Doleham	d																								
Three Oaks	d						17 06																		
Ore	d			16 50								17 22				17 50									18 22
Hastings [4]	a			16 53			17 13					17 25				17 53				18 13					18 25
	d			16 55			17 14					17 26				17 55				18 14					18 26
St Leonards Warrior Sq [4]	d			16 57			17 17					17 28				17 57				18 17					18 28
Bexhill [4]	d			17 04			17 24					17 35				18 04				18 24					18 35
Collington	d			17 06								17 37				18 06									18 37
Cooden Beach	d			17 09								17 40				18 09									18 40
Normans Bay	d											17 43													18 43
Pevensey Bay	d																								
Pevensey & Westham	d			17 15								17 48				18 15									18 48
Hampden Park [4]	d			17 20	17 29			17 40				17 52	17 55	18 13		18 20	18 28					18 42			18 52
Eastbourne [4]	a			17 25	17 34		17 39	17 48				17 57	18 00	18 18		18 25	18 34			18 39		18 49			18 57
	d	17 21		17 31	17 40		17 45				17 57	18 01		18 25		18 31	18 43			18 47				18 58	19 04
Hampden Park [4]	d	17a25			17a44						18 01	18 05		18a29			18a47							19 02	19 08
Polegate	d			17 37			17 52				18 05	18 11				18 37				18 54				19 06	19 12
Berwick	d											18 17													19 18
Glynde	d											18 22													19 23
Seaford	d		17 25							17 58					18 26			18 44					19 02		
Bishopstone	d		17 27							18 00					18 28			18 46					19 04		
Newhaven Harbour	d		17 30							18 03					18 31										
Newhaven Town ⛴	d		17 32							18 05					18 33			18 50					19 08		
Southease	d		17 36												18 37										
Lewes [4]	a		17 44	17 49			18 04			18 14	18 17	18 28			18 44	18 49		18 59		19 07			19 17	19 20	19 29
	d		17 44	17 50		17 55	18 07			18 14	18 18	18 28			18 44	18 50		18 59		19 07			19 18	19 21	19 29
Falmer	d		17 51			18 02				18 21		18 35			18 51			19 06					19 25		19 36
Moulsecoomb	d		17 54			18 05				18 24		18 38			18 54			19 09					19 28		19 39
London Road (Brighton)	d		17 57			18 07				18 27		18 41			18 57			19 12					19 30		19 42
Brighton [10]	a		18 00			18 11	18 20			18 30		18 44			19 00			19 15		19 21			19 34		19 45
Cooksbridge	d										18 23													19 26	
Plumpton	d										18 28					18 58								19 31	
Wivelsfield [4]	a										18 34					19 06									
Haywards Heath [3]	a			18 07							18 38					19 10								19 40	
Gatwick Airport [10] ✈	a			18 26							18 56					19 25								19 55	
East Croydon 🚊	a			18 42							19 12					19 43								20 11	
London Bridge [4] ⊖	a																								
Clapham Junction [10]	a			18 52							19 21					19 52								20 20	
London Victoria [15] ⊖	a			18 59							19 29					19 59								20 28	

A 🛒 from Lewes

Ashford, Hastings, Eastbourne, Seaford and Lewes - Brighton, Haywards Heath and London

Network Diagram - see first Page of Table 184

		SN	SN	SN	SN	SN	SN	SN	SN	SN	SN	SN	SN	SN	SN	SN	SN	SN	SN	SN	SN	SN
		◇1		◇1	◇1				1		1	◇1	◇1		1		◇1		1		◇1	◇1
																						A
Ashford International	d						18 32	18 58								19 32				19 58		
Ham Street	d						18 41	19 07								19 41				20 07		
Appledore (Kent)	d						18 46	19 12								19 46				20 12		
Rye	a						18 55	19 21								19 55				20 21		
	d						18 55									19 55				20 22		
Winchelsea	d															19 59						
Doleham	d																					
Three Oaks	d						19 06															
Ore	d			18 50									19 50						20 22			20 50
Hastings 4	a			18 53			19 13						19 54			20 13			20 25	20 39		20 53
	d			18 55			19 14				19 27		19 55			20 14			20 26			20 55
St Leonards Warrior Sq 4	d			18 57			19 17				19 30		19 57			20 17			20 28			20 57
Bexhill 4	d			19 04			19 24				19 37		20 04			20 24			20 35			21 04
Collington	d			19 06							19 39		20 06						20 37			21 06
Cooden Beach	d			19 09							19 42		20 09						20 40			21 09
Normans Bay	d																					
Pevensey Bay	d																					
Pevensey & Westham	d			19 15							19 48		20 15						20 46			21 15
Hampden Park 4	d	18 55		19 20	19 36				19 50		19 52		20 20		20 29		20 43		20 51			21 20
Eastbourne 4	a	19 01		19 25	19 41		19 44		19 56		19 57		20 25		20 34	20 39	20 48		20 56			21 25
	d	19 19		19 31	19 51		19 48				20 03	20 19	20 31			20 45			21 04		21 21	21 31
Hampden Park 4	d	19a23			19a55						20 07	20a23							21 08		21a25	
Polegate	d			19 37			19 55				20 11		20 37			20 52			21 12			21 37
Berwick	d										20 17								21 18			
Glynde	d										20 22								21 23			
Seaford	d		19 19			19 37				19 58				20 28				20 58				
Bishopstone	d		19 21			19 39				20 00				20 30				21 00				
Newhaven Harbour	d		19 24			19 42				20 03				20 33				21 03				
Newhaven Town	d		19 26			19 44				20 05				20 35				21 05				
Southease	d					19 48								20 39								
Lewes 4	a		19 35	19 49		19 55	20 07			20 14	20 28		20 49	20 46		21 07		21 14	21 29			21 49
	d		19 38	19 50		19 57	20 08			20 14	20 28		20 50	20 53		21 07		21 14	21 29			21 50
Falmer	d		19 45			20 04				20 21	20 35			21 00				21 21	21 36			
Moulsecoomb	d		19 48			20 07				20 24	20 38			21 03				21 24	21 39			
London Road (Brighton)	d		19 50			20 09				20 27	20 41			21 05				21 27	21 42			
Brighton 10	a		19 55			20 13	20 20			20 33	20 44			21 09		21 20		21 33	21 45			
Cooksbridge	d																					
Plumpton	d												20 58									
Wivelsfield 4	a			20 05									21 05									22 02
Haywards Heath 3	a			20 10									21 09									22 06
Gatwick Airport 10	a			20 25									21 25									22 25
East Croydon	a			20 41									21 41									22 41
London Bridge 4	a																					
Clapham Junction 10	a			20 50									21 51									22 50
London Victoria 15	a			20 59									21 58									22 57

A from Lewes

Table 189

Mondays to Fridays

Ashford, Hastings, Eastbourne, Seaford and Lewes - Brighton, Haywards Heath and London

Network Diagram - see first Page of Table 184

		SN	SN	SN	SN	SN	SN	SN	SN	SN		SN	SN	SN	SN	SN	SN	SN	SN						
				◇1		1	◇1		◇1			◇1		1		◇1		1	1						
Ashford International ⇌	d		20 32							21 32					22 32										
Ham Street	d		20 41							21 41					22 41										
Appledore (Kent)	d		20 46							21 46					22 46										
Rye	a		20 55							21 55					22 55										
	d		20 55							21 57					22 55										
Winchelsea	d									22 00					22 58										
Doleham	d														23 05										
Three Oaks	d		21 06												23 08										
Ore	d						21 22							22 22	23 14										
Hastings 4	a		21 13				21 25			22 14				22 25	23 17										
	d		21 14				21 30			22 15				22 26					23 22						
St Leonards Warrior Sq 4	d		21 17				21 32			22 18				22 29					23 24						
Bexhill 4	d		21 24				21 39			22 25				22 38					23 31						
Collington	d						21 41							22 40					23 33						
Cooden Beach	d						21 44							22 43					23 36						
Normans Bay	d													22 46											
Pevensey Bay	d																								
Pevensey & Westham	d						21 50							22 51					23 42						
Hampden Park 4	d			21 43			21 55					22 43		22 55		23 10		23 42	23 47						
Eastbourne 4	a		21 39	21 48			22 00			22 40		22 48		23 00		23 15		23 47	23 52						
	d		21 45			22 04	22 15		22 21	22 45				23 05		23 20			23 56						
Hampden Park 4	d					22 08	22 19		22a25					23 09		23a24			00 01						
Polegate	d		21 52			22 12	22 23			22 52				23 13					00 05						
Berwick	d					22 18	22 29							23 18											
Glynde	d					22 23								23 24											
Seaford	d	21 28			21 58			22 20					22 58				23 25								
Bishopstone	d	21 30			22 00			22 22					23 00				23 27								
Newhaven Harbour	d	21 33			22 03			22 25					23 03				23 30								
Newhaven Town ⛴	d	21 35			22 05			22 27					23 05				23 32								
Southease	d																								
Lewes 4	a	21 44	22 07		22 14	22 29	22 38	22 35		23 07			23 14	23 29			23 40		00 17						
	d	21 53	22 07		22 14	22 29	22 40	22 42		23 07			23 14	23 30			23 40		00 18						
Falmer	d	22 00			22 21	22 36		22 49					23 21	23 37			23 47		00 25						
Moulsecoomb	d	22 03			22 24	22 39		22 52					23 24	23 40			23 50		00 28						
London Road (Brighton)	d	22 05			22 27	22 42		22 54					23 27	23 42			23 53		00 30						
Brighton 10	a	22 09	22 20		22 31	22 45		22 58		23 20			23 31	23 46			23 56		00 34						
Cooksbridge	d																								
Plumpton	d						22 48																		
Wivelsfield 4	a						22 54																		
Haywards Heath 3	a						22 58																		
Gatwick Airport 10 ✈	a						23 12																		
East Croydon 🚋	a						23 30																		
London Bridge 4 ⊖	a																								
Clapham Junction 10	a						23 42																		
London Victoria 15 ⊖	a						23 52																		

Table 189

Saturdays

Ashford, Hastings, Eastbourne, Seaford and Lewes - Brighton, Haywards Heath and London

Network Diagram - see first Page of Table 184

		SN 1	SN ◇1	SN ◇1	SN 1	SN	SN	SN ◇1	SN	SN ◇1		SN	SN	SN ◇1	SN 1	SN 1	SN	SN ◇1	SN 1	SN		SN	SN	SN ◇1	SN 1
Ashford International	d																					06 13			
Ham Street	d																					06 22			
Appledore (Kent)	d																					06 27			
Rye	a																					06 36			
	d																					06 51			
Winchelsea	d																					06 54			
Doleham	d																					07 01			
Three Oaks	d																					07 04			
Ore	d														06 22			06 50				07 10			07 22
Hastings 4	a														06 25			06 53				07 13			07 25
	d	23p22													06 26			06 55				07 14			07 26
St Leonards Warrior Sq 4	d	23p24													06 28			06 57				07 17			07 28
Bexhill 4	d	23p31													06 35			07 04				07 24			07 35
Collington	d	23p33													06 37			07 06							07 37
Cooden Beach	d	23p36													06 40			07 09							07 40
Normans Bay	d														06 43										07 43
Pevensey Bay	d																								
Pevensey & Westham	d	23p42													06 48			07 15							07 48
Hampden Park 4	d	23p47	00 11												06 52	07 11		07 20	07 29						07 52
Eastbourne 4	a	23p52	00 16	01 41											06 57	07 17		07 25	07 34			07 39			07 57
	d	23p56			05 03		05 48	06 18		06 24		06 38		06 58	07 04	07 21		07 31	07 40			07 47		07 58	08 04
Hampden Park 4	d	00 01			05 07		05 52	06a22		06 28				07 02	07 08	07a25			07a44					08 02	08 08
Polegate	d	00 05			05 11		05 57			06 32		06 45		07 06	07 12			07 37				07 54		08 06	08 12
Berwick	d									06 38					07 18										08 18
Glynde	d									06 43					07 23										08 23
Seaford	d					05 05			06 28				06 58				07 28						07 58		
Bishopstone	d					05 07			06 30				07 00				07 30						08 00		
Newhaven Harbour	d					05 10			06 33				07 03				07 33						08 03		
Newhaven Town	d					05 12			06 35				07 05				07 35						08 05		
Southease	d																								
Lewes 4	a	00 17			05 24	05 21	06 10		06 44	06 49		06 57	07 14	07 18	07 29		07 44	07 49				08 07	08 14	08 18	08 29
	d	00 18			05 26	05 28	06 10		06 44	06 50		06 58	07 14	07 20	07 29		07 44	07 50		07 58		08 07	08 14	08 20	08 29
Falmer	d	00 25				05 35	06 18		06 51			07 05	07 21		07 36		07 51			08 05			08 21		08 36
Moulsecoomb	d	00 28				05 38	06 21		06 54			07 09	07 24		07 39		07 54			08 08			08 24		08 39
London Road (Brighton)	d	00 30				05 40	06 24		06 57			07 11	07 27		07 42		07 57			08 10			08 27		08 42
Brighton 10	a	00 34				05 44	06 27		07 00			07 15	07 30		07 45		08 00			08 14		08 20	08 30		08 45
Cooksbridge	d																								
Plumpton	d													07 28										08 28	
Wivelsfield 4	a													07 35										08 35	
Haywards Heath 3	a				05 41					07 05				07 40				08 05						08 40	
Gatwick Airport 10	a				06 03					07 25				07 55				08 24						08 55	
East Croydon	a									07 41				08 11				08 40						09 11	
London Bridge 4	a																								
Clapham Junction 10	a									07 51				08 21				08 50						09 21	
London Victoria 15	a									07 58				08 28				08 57						09 28	

		SN 1	SN	SN ◇1	SN 1	SN		SN	SN	SN ◇1	SN 1	SN ◇1	SN	SN ◇1	SN 1	SN ◇1		SN	SN	SN	SN ◇1	SN 1	SN ◇1	SN	SN ◇1
Ashford International	d							07 32											08 32						
Ham Street	d							07 41											08 41						
Appledore (Kent)	d							07 46											08 46						
Rye	a							07 55											08 55						
	d							07 55											08 55						
Winchelsea	d							07 59																	
Doleham	d																								
Three Oaks	d																		09 06						
Ore	d			07 50							08 22			08 50								09 22			09 50
Hastings 4	a			07 53				08 13			08 25			08 53					09 13			09 25			09 53
	d			07 55				08 14			08 26			08 55					09 14			09 26			09 55
St Leonards Warrior Sq 4	d			07 57				08 17			08 28			08 57					09 17			09 28			09 57
Bexhill 4	d			08 04				08 24			08 35			09 04					09 24			09 35			10 04
Collington	d			08 06							08 37			09 06								09 37			10 06
Cooden Beach	d			08 09							08 40			09 09								09 40			10 09
Normans Bay	d										08 43											09 43			
Pevensey Bay	d																								
Pevensey & Westham	d			08 15							08 48			09 15								09 48			10 15
Hampden Park 4	d			08 20	08 29						08 52			09 20	09 29	09 39						09 52			10 20
Eastbourne 4	a			08 25	08 34			08 39			08 57			09 25	09 34	09 44			09 39			09 57			10 25
	d	08 18		08 31	08 40			08 47		08 58	09 04	09 19		09 31	09 40				09 47		09 58	10 04	10 19		10 31
Hampden Park 4	d	08a22			08a44					09 02	09 08	09a23			09a44						10 02	10 08	10a23		
Polegate	d			08 37				08 54		09 06	09 12			09 37					09 54		10 06	10 12			10 37
Berwick	d										09 18											10 18			
Glynde	d										09 23											10 23			
Seaford	d		08 25						08 58				09 25							09 58				10 25	
Bishopstone	d		08 27						09 00				09 27							10 00				10 27	
Newhaven Harbour	d		08 30						09 03				09 30							10 03				10 30	
Newhaven Town	d		08 32						09 05				09 32							10 05				10 32	
Southease	d		08 36										09 36											10 36	
Lewes 4	a		08 44	08 49				09 07	09 14	09 18	09 29		09 44	09 49					10 07	10 14	10 18	10 29		10 44	10 49
	d		08 44	08 50		08 58		09 07	09 14	09 20	09 29		09 44	09 50				09 58	10 07	10 14	10 20	10 29		10 44	10 50
Falmer	d		08 51			09 05			09 21		09 36		09 51					10 05		10 21		10 36		10 51	
Moulsecoomb	d		08 54			09 08			09 24		09 39		09 54					10 08		10 24		10 39		10 54	
London Road (Brighton)	d		08 57			09 10			09 27		09 42		09 57					10 10		10 27		10 42		10 57	
Brighton 10	a		09 00			09 14		09 20	09 30		09 45		10 00					10 14	10 20	10 30		10 45		11 00	
Cooksbridge	d																								
Plumpton	d									09 28											10 28				
Wivelsfield 4	a									09 35											10 35				
Haywards Heath 3	a			09 05						09 40				10 05							10 40				11 05
Gatwick Airport 10	a			09 24						09 55				10 24							10 55				11 24
East Croydon	a			09 40						10 11				10 40							11 11				11 40
London Bridge 4	a																								
Clapham Junction 10	a			09 50						10 21				10 50							11 21				11 50
London Victoria 15	a			09 57						10 28				10 57							11 28				11 57

Table 189

Saturdays

Ashford, Hastings, Eastbourne, Seaford and Lewes - Brighton, Haywards Heath and London

Network Diagram - see first Page of Table 184

Station		SN 1		SN ◇1	SN	SN	SN	SN ◇1	SN 1	SN ◇1	SN	SN ◇1		SN 1	SN ◇1	SN	SN	SN	SN ◇1	SN 1	SN ◇1	SN		SN ◇1	SN 1
Ashford International	d					09 32											10 32								
Ham Street	d					09 41											10 41								
Appledore (Kent)	d					09 46											10 46								
Rye	a					09 55											10 55								
	d					09 55											10 55								
Winchelsea	d					09 59																			
Doleham	d																								
Three Oaks	d																11 06								
Ore	d								10 22			10 50								11 22				11 50	
Hastings 4	a					10 13			10 25			10 53					11 13			11 25				11 53	
	d					10 14			10 26			10 55					11 14			11 26				11 55	
St Leonards Warrior Sq 4	d					10 17			10 28			10 57					11 17			11 28				11 57	
Bexhill 4	d					10 24			10 35			11 04					11 24			11 35				12 04	
Collington	d								10 37			11 06								11 37				12 06	
Cooden Beach	d								10 40			11 09								11 40				12 09	
Normans Bay	d								10 43											11 43					
Pevensey Bay	d																								
Pevensey & Westham	d								10 48			11 15								11 48				12 15	
Hampden Park 4	d	10 29		10 39					10 52			11 20		11 29	11 39					11 52				12 20	12 29
Eastbourne 4	a	10 34		10 44		10 39			10 57			11 25		11 34	11 44		11 39			11 57				12 25	12 34
	d	10 40				10 47		10 58	11 04	11 19		11 31		11 40			11 47		11 58	12 04	12 19			12 31	12 40
Hampden Park 4	d	10a44						11 02	11 08	11a23				11a44					12 02	12 08	12a23				12a44
Polegate	d					10 54		11 06	11 12			11 37					11 54		12 06	12 12				12 37	
Berwick	d								11 18											12 18					
Glynde	d								11 23											12 23					
Seaford	d						10 58				11 25							11 58				12 25			
Bishopstone	d						11 00				11 27							12 00				12 27			
Newhaven Harbour	d						11 03				11 30							12 03				12 30			
Newhaven Town	d						11 05				11 32							12 05				12 32			
Southease	d										11 36											12 36			
Lewes 4	a					11 07	11 14	11 18	11 29		11 44	11 49					12 07	12 14	12 18	12 29		12 44		12 49	
	d				10 58	11 07	11 14	11 20	11 29		11 44	11 50				11 58	12 07	12 14	12 20	12 29		12 44		12 50	
Falmer	d				11 05		11 21		11 36		11 51					12 05		12 21		12 36		12 51			
Moulsecoomb	d				11 08		11 24		11 39		11 54					12 08		12 24		12 39		12 54			
London Road (Brighton)	d				11 10		11 27		11 42		11 57					12 10		12 27		12 42		12 57			
Brighton 10	a				11 14	11 20	11 30		11 45		12 00					12 14	12 20	12 30		12 45		13 00			
Cooksbridge	d																								
Plumpton	d							11 28											12 28						
Wivelsfield 4	a							11 35											12 35						
Haywards Heath 3	a							11 40				12 05							12 40					13 05	
Gatwick Airport 10	a							11 55				12 24							12 55					13 24	
East Croydon	a							12 11				12 40							13 11					13 40	
London Bridge 4	a																								
Clapham Junction 10	a							12 21				12 50							13 21					13 50	
London Victoria 15	a							12 28				12 57							13 28					13 57	

Station		SN ◇1	SN	SN	SN	SN ◇1	SN 1	SN ◇1		SN	SN ◇1	SN 1	SN ◇1	SN	SN	SN	SN ◇1	SN 1		SN ◇1	SN	SN ◇1	SN 1	SN ◇1	SN
Ashford International	d			11 32											12 32										
Ham Street	d			11 41											12 41										
Appledore (Kent)	d			11 46											12 46										
Rye	a			11 55											12 55										
	d			11 55											12 55										
Winchelsea	d			11 59																					
Doleham	d																								
Three Oaks	d														13 06										
Ore	d						12 22				12 50							13 22				13 50			
Hastings 4	a			12 13			12 25				12 53				13 13			13 25				13 53			
	d			12 14			12 26				12 55				13 14			13 26				13 55			
St Leonards Warrior Sq 4	d			12 17			12 28				12 57				13 17			13 28				13 57			
Bexhill 4	d			12 24			12 35				13 04				13 24			13 35				14 04			
Collington	d						12 37				13 06							13 37				14 06			
Cooden Beach	d						12 40				13 09							13 40				14 09			
Normans Bay	d						12 43											13 43							
Pevensey Bay	d																								
Pevensey & Westham	d						12 48				13 15							13 48				14 15			
Hampden Park 4	d	12 39					12 52				13 20	13 29	13 39					13 52				14 20	14 29	14 39	
Eastbourne 4	a	12 44		12 39			12 57				13 25	13 34	13 44		13 39			13 57				14 25	14 34	14 44	
	d			12 47		12 58	13 04	13 19			13 31	13 40			13 47		13 58	14 04		14 19		14 31	14 40		
Hampden Park 4	d					13 02	13 08	13a23				13a44					14 02	14 08		14a23			14a44		
Polegate	d			12 54		13 06	13 12				13 37				13 54		14 06	14 12				14 37			
Berwick	d						13 18											14 18							
Glynde	d						13 23											14 23							
Seaford	d				12 58					13 25						13 58					14 25				
Bishopstone	d				13 00					13 27						14 00					14 27				
Newhaven Harbour	d				13 03					13 30						14 03					14 30				
Newhaven Town	d				13 05					13 32						14 05					14 32				
Southease	d									13 36											14 36				
Lewes 4	a			13 07	13 14	13 19	13 29			13 44	13 49				14 07	14 14	14 19	14 29			14 44	14 49			
	d		12 58	13 07	13 14	13 20	13 29			13 44	13 50			13 58	14 07	14 14	14 20	14 29			14 44	14 50			14 58
Falmer	d		13 05		13 21		13 36			13 51				14 05		14 21		14 36			14 51				15 05
Moulsecoomb	d		13 08		13 24		13 39			13 54				14 08		14 24		14 39			14 54				15 08
London Road (Brighton)	d		13 10		13 27		13 42			13 57				14 10		14 27		14 42			14 57				15 10
Brighton 10	a		13 14	13 20	13 30		13 45			14 00				14 14	14 20	14 30		14 45			15 00				15 14
Cooksbridge	d																								
Plumpton	d					13 28											14 28								
Wivelsfield 4	a					13 35											14 35								
Haywards Heath 3	a					13 40					14 05						14 40					15 05			
Gatwick Airport 10	a					13 55					14 24						14 55					15 24			
East Croydon	a					14 11					14 40						15 11					15 40			
London Bridge 4	a																								
Clapham Junction 10	a					14 21					14 50						15 21					15 50			
London Victoria 15	a					14 28					14 57						15 28					15 57			

Ashford, Hastings, Eastbourne, Seaford and Lewes - Brighton, Haywards Heath and London

Network Diagram - see first Page of Table 184

		SN	SN	SN ◇1	SN 1	SN ◇1	SN	SN ◇1	SN 1	SN ◇1	SN	SN	SN	SN ◇1	SN 1	SN ◇1	SN	SN ◇1	SN 1	SN ◇1	SN	SN
Ashford International	d	13 32										14 32										15 32
Ham Street	d	13 41										14 41										15 41
Appledore (Kent)	d	13 46										14 46										15 46
Rye	a	13 55										14 55										15 55
	d	13 55										14 55										15 55
Winchelsea	d	13 59																				15 59
Doleham	d																					
Three Oaks	d											15 06										
Ore	d				14 22			14 50							15 22			15 50				
Hastings 4	a	14 13			14 25			14 53				15 13			15 25			15 53				16 13
	d	14 14			14 26			14 55				15 14			15 26			15 55				16 14
St Leonards Warrior Sq 4	d	14 17			14 28			14 57				15 17			15 28			15 57				16 17
Bexhill 4	d	14 24			14 35			15 04				15 24			15 35			16 04				16 24
Collington	d				14 37			15 06							15 37			16 06				
Cooden Beach	d				14 40			15 09							15 40			16 09				
Normans Bay	d				14 43										15 43							
Pevensey Bay	d																					
Pevensey & Westham	d				14 48			15 15							15 48			16 15				
Hampden Park 4	d				14 52			15 20	15 29	15 39					15 52			16 20	16 29	16 39		
Eastbourne 4	a	14 39			14 57			15 25	15 34	15 44		15 39			15 57			16 25	16 34	16 44		16 39
	d	14 47		14 58	15 04	15 19		15 31	15 40			15 47		15 58	16 04	16 19		16 31	16 40			16 47
Hampden Park 4	d			15 02	15 08	15a23			15a44					16 02	16 08	16a23			16a44			
Polegate	d	14 54		15 06	15 12			15 37				15 54		16 06	16 12			16 37				16 54
Berwick	d				15 18										16 18							
Glynde	d				15 23										16 23							
Seaford	d		14 58				15 25						15 58				16 25					
Bishopstone	d		15 00				15 27						16 00				16 27					
Newhaven Harbour	d		15 03				15 30						16 03				16 30					
Newhaven Town	d		15 05				15 32						16 05				16 32					
Southease	d						15 36										16 36					
Lewes 4	a	15 07	15 14	15 19	15 29		15 44	15 49				16 07	16 14	16 18	16 29		16 44	16 49				17 07
	d	15 07	15 14	15 20	15 29		15 44	15 50			15 58	16 07	16 14	16 20	16 29		16 44	16 50			16 58	17 07
Falmer	d		15 21		15 36		15 51				16 05		16 21		16 36		16 51				17 05	
Moulsecoomb	d		15 24		15 39		15 54				16 08		16 24		16 39		16 54				17 08	
London Road (Brighton)	d		15 27		15 42		15 57				16 10		16 27		16 42		16 57				17 10	
Brighton 10	a	15 20	15 30		15 45		16 00				16 14	16 20	16 30		16 45		17 00				17 14	17 20
Cooksbridge	d																					
Plumpton	d			15 28										16 28								
Wivelsfield 4	a			15 35										16 35								
Haywards Heath 3	a			15 40				16 05						16 40				17 05				
Gatwick Airport 10	a			15 55				16 24						16 55				17 24				
East Croydon	a			16 11				16 40						17 11				17 40				
London Bridge 4	a																					
Clapham Junction 10	a			16 21				16 50						17 21				17 50				
London Victoria 15	a			16 28				16 57						17 28				17 57				

		SN	SN ◇1	SN 1	SN ◇1	SN	SN ◇1	SN 1	SN ◇1	SN	SN	SN	SN ◇1	SN 1	SN ◇1	SN	SN ◇1	SN 1	SN ◇1	SN	SN	SN	SN ◇1
Ashford International	d										16 32										17 32		
Ham Street	d										16 41										17 41		
Appledore (Kent)	d										16 46										17 46		
Rye	a										16 55										17 55		
	d										16 55										17 55		
Winchelsea	d																				17 59		
Doleham	d																						
Three Oaks	d										17 06												
Ore	d			16 22			16 50							17 22			17 50						
Hastings 4	a			16 25			16 53				17 13			17 25			17 53				18 13		
	d			16 26			16 55				17 14			17 26			17 55				18 14		
St Leonards Warrior Sq 4	d			16 28			16 57				17 17			17 28			17 57				18 17		
Bexhill 4	d			16 35			17 04				17 24			17 35			18 04				18 24		
Collington	d			16 37			17 06							17 37			18 06						
Cooden Beach	d			16 40			17 09							17 40			18 09						
Normans Bay	d			16 43										17 43									
Pevensey Bay	d																						
Pevensey & Westham	d			16 48			17 15							17 48			18 15						
Hampden Park 4	d			16 52			17 20	17 29	17 39					17 52			18 20	18 29	18 39				
Eastbourne 4	a			16 57			17 25	17 34	17 44		17 39			17 57			18 25	18 34	18 44		18 39		
	d		16 58	17 04	17 19		17 31	17 40			17 47		17 58	18 04	18 19		18 31	18 40			18 47		18 58
Hampden Park 4	d		17 02	17 08	17a23			17a44					18 02	18 08	18a23			18a44					19 02
Polegate	d		17 06	17 12			17 37				17 54		18 06	18 12			18 37				18 54		19 06
Berwick	d			17 18										18 18									
Glynde	d			17 23										18 23									
Seaford	d	16 58				17 25						17 58				18 25						18 58	
Bishopstone	d	17 00				17 27						18 00				18 27						19 00	
Newhaven Harbour	d	17 03				17 30						18 03				18 30						19 03	
Newhaven Town	d	17 05				17 32						18 05				18 32						19 05	
Southease	d					17 36										18 36							
Lewes 4	a	17 14	17 18	17 29		17 44	17 49				18 07	18 14	18 18	18 29		18 44	18 49				19 07	19 14	19 18
	d	17 14	17 20	17 29		17 44	17 50			17 58	18 07	18 14	18 20	18 29		18 44	18 50			18 58	19 07	19 14	19 20
Falmer	d	17 21		17 36		17 51				18 05		18 21		18 36		18 51				19 05		19 21	
Moulsecoomb	d	17 24		17 39		17 54				18 08		18 24		18 39		18 54				19 08		19 24	
London Road (Brighton)	d	17 27		17 42		17 57				18 10		18 27		18 42		18 57				19 10		19 27	
Brighton 10	a	17 30		17 45		18 00				18 14	18 20	18 30		18 45		19 00				19 14	19 20	19 30	
Cooksbridge	d																						
Plumpton	d		17 28										18 28										19 28
Wivelsfield 4	a		17 35										18 35										19 35
Haywards Heath 3	a		17 40				18 05						18 40				19 05						19 40
Gatwick Airport 10	a		17 55				18 24						18 55				19 25						19 55
East Croydon	a		18 11				18 40						19 11				19 41						20 11
London Bridge 4	a																						
Clapham Junction 10	a		18 21				18 50						19 21				19 51						20 21
London Victoria 15	a		18 28				18 57						19 28				19 58						20 28

Table 189

Saturdays

Ashford, Hastings, Eastbourne, Seaford and Lewes - Brighton, Haywards Heath and London

Network Diagram - see first Page of Table 184

		SN 1	SN ◇1	SN	SN ◇1	SN 1	SN ◇1	SN	SN	SN	SN 1	SN ◇1	SN ◇1	SN	SN 1	SN	SN 1	SN	SN 1	SN ◇1	SN ◇1 A 🛒	SN	SN
Ashford International	d								18 32							19 32							20 32
Ham Street	d								18 41							19 41							20 41
Appledore (Kent)	d								18 46							19 46							20 46
Rye	a								18 55							19 55							20 55
	d								18 55							19 55							20 55
Winchelsea	d															19 59							
Doleham	d																						
Three Oaks	d								19 06														21 06
Ore	d	18 22			18 50						19 22		19 50						20 22		20 50		
Hastings 4	a	18 25			18 53				19 13		19 25		19 53			20 13			20 25		20 53		21 13
	d	18 26			18 55				19 14		19 26		19 55			20 14			20 26		20 55		21 14
St Leonards Warrior Sq 4	d	18 28			18 57				19 17		19 28		19 57			20 17			20 28		20 57		21 17
Bexhill 4	d	18 35			19 04				19 24		19 35		20 04			20 24			20 35		21 04		21 24
Collington	d	18 37			19 06						19 37		20 06						20 37		21 06		
Cooden Beach	d	18 40			19 09						19 40		20 09						20 40		21 09		
Normans Bay	d	18 43									19 43								20 43				
Pevensey Bay	d																						
Pevensey & Westham	d	18 48			19 15						19 48		20 15						20 48		21 15		
Hampden Park 4	d	18 52			19 20	19 29	19 39				19 52		20 20		20 29		20 43		20 52		21 20		
Eastbourne 4	a	18 57			19 25	19 34	19 44		19 39		19 57		20 25		20 34	20 39	20 48		20 57		21 25		21 39
	d	19 04	19 19		19 31	19 40			19 47		20 04	20 19	20 31			20 45			21 04	21 19	21 31		21 45
Hampden Park 4	d	19 08	19a23			19a44					20 08	20a23							21 08	21a23			
Polegate	d	19 12			19 37				19 54		20 12		20 37			20 52			21 12		21 37		21 52
Berwick	d	19 18									20 18								21 18				
Glynde	d	19 23									20 23								21 23				
Seaford	d			19 25						19 58				20 28				20 58				21 28	
Bishopstone	d			19 27						20 00				20 30				21 00				21 30	
Newhaven Harbour	d			19 30						20 03				20 33				21 03				21 33	
Newhaven Town ⛴	d			19 32						20 05				20 35				21 05				21 35	
Southease	d			19 36																			
Lewes 4	a	19 29		19 44	19 49				20 07	20 14	20 29		20 49	20 44		21 07		21 14	21 29		21 49	21 44	22 07
	d	19 29		19 44	19 50			19 58	20 07	20 14	20 29		20 50	20 53		21 07		21 14	21 29		21 50	21 53	22 07
Falmer	d	19 36		19 51				20 05		20 21	20 36			21 00				21 21	21 36			22 00	
Moulsecoomb	d	19 39		19 54				20 08		20 24	20 39			21 03				21 24	21 39			22 03	
London Road (Brighton)	d	19 42		19 57				20 10		20 27	20 42			21 05				21 27	21 42			22 05	
Brighton 10	a	19 45		20 00				20 14	20 20	20 30	20 45			21 09		21 20		21 30	21 45			22 10	22 20
Cooksbridge	d																						
Plumpton	d																						
Wivelsfield 4	a				20 02								21 04								22 02		
Haywards Heath 3	a				20 07								21 09								22 06		
Gatwick Airport 10 ✈	a				20 25								21 26								22 24		
East Croydon 🚌	a				20 41								21 41								22 40		
London Bridge 4 ⊖	a																						
Clapham Junction 10	a				20 51								21 51								22 49		
London Victoria 15 ⊖	a				20 58								21 58								22 57		

A 🛒 from Lewes

Table 189

Saturdays

Ashford, Hastings, Eastbourne, Seaford and Lewes - Brighton, Haywards Heath and London

Network Diagram - see first Page of Table 184

		SN		SN	SN	SN	SN	SN	SN	SN	SN	SN		SN	SN	SN	SN	SN
		◇1			1	◇1		◇1		◇1		1			◇1		1	1
Ashford International	d								21 32					22 32				
Ham Street	d								21 41					22 41				
Appledore (Kent)	d								21 46					22 46				
Rye	a								21 55					22 55				
	d								21 57					22 55				
Winchelsea	d								22 00					22 59				
Doleham	d													23 05				
Three Oaks	d													23 09				
Ore	d				21 22							22 22		23 14				
Hastings 4	a				21 25				22 14			22 25		23 17				
	d				21 26	21 42			22 15			22 26						23 22
St Leonards Warrior Sq 4	d				21 28	21 44			22 18			22 29						23 24
Bexhill 4	d				21 35	21 51			22 25			22 38						23 31
Collington	d				21 37	21 53						22 40						23 33
Cooden Beach	d				21 40	21 56						22 43						23 36
Normans Bay	d											22 46						
Pevensey Bay	d																	
Pevensey & Westham	d				21 46	22 02						22 51						23 42
Hampden Park 4	d	21 43			21 51	22 07				22 43		22 55			23 09		23 42	23 47
Eastbourne 4	a	21 48			21 56	22 12			22 40	22 48		23 00			23 14		23 47	23 52
	d				22 04	22 18		22 21	22 45			23 05			23 20			23 56
Hampden Park 4	d				22 08			22a25				23 09			23a24			00 01
Polegate	d				22 12	22 25			22 52			23 13						00 05
Berwick	d				22 18							23 18						
Glynde	d				22 23							23 24						
Seaford	d			21 58			22 20				22 58					23 25		
Bishopstone	d			22 00			22 22				23 00					23 27		
Newhaven Harbour	d			22 03			22 25				23 03					23 30		
Newhaven Town ⛴	d			22 05			22 27				23 05					23 32		
Southease	d																	
Lewes 4	a			22 14	22 29	22 38	22 35		23 07		23 14	23 29				23 40		00 17
	d			22 14	22 29	22 40	22 42		23 07		23 14	23 30				23 40		00 18
Falmer	d			22 21	22 36		22 49				23 21	23 37				23 47		00 25
Moulsecoomb	d			22 24	22 39		22 52				23 24	23 40				23 50		00 28
London Road (Brighton)	d			22 27	22 42		22 54				23 27	23 42				23 53		00 30
Brighton 10	a			22 31	22 45		22 58		23 20		23 31	23 46				23 56		00 34
Cooksbridge	d																	
Plumpton	d					22 48												
Wivelsfield 4	a					22 54												
Haywards Heath 3	a					22 58												
Gatwick Airport 10 ✈	a					23 12												
East Croydon	a					23 29												
London Bridge 4 ⊖	a																	
Clapham Junction 10	a					23 41												
London Victoria 15 ⊖	a					23 52												

Table 189

Sundays

Ashford, Hastings, Eastbourne, Seaford and Lewes - Brighton, Haywards Heath and London

Network Diagram - see first Page of Table 184

		SN	SN	SN	SN	SN	SN	SN	SN	SN	SN	SN	SN	SN	SN	SN	SN	SN	SN	SN	SN	SN	SN
		1	◇1	◇1	◇1		◇1		1	◇1		1			◇1			1			◇1		
		A	A		B ⚲					B ⚲					B ⚲						B ⚲		
Ashford International	d																			08 15			
Ham Street	d																			08 24			
Appledore (Kent)	d																			08 29			
Rye	a																			08 38			
	d																			08 40			
Winchelsea	d																			08 43			
Doleham	d																			08 50			
Three Oaks	d																			08 53			
Ore	d														08 14					08 59	09 14		
Hastings 4	a														08 17					09 02	09 17		
	d	23p22													08 18					09 03	09 18		
St Leonards Warrior Sq 4	d	23p24													08 21					09 06	09 21		
Bexhill 4	d	23p31													08 28					09 13	09 28		
Collington	d	23p33													08 30						09 30		
Cooden Beach	d	23p36													08 33						09 33		
Normans Bay	d																						
Pevensey Bay	d																						
Pevensey & Westham	d	23p42													08 39						09 39		
Hampden Park 4	d	23p47	00 11						07 45						08 43	08 53					09 43	09 53	
Eastbourne 4	a	23p52	00 16	01 41					07 50						08 49	08 58				09 29	09 49	09 58	
	d	23p56			06 55		07 26	07 30		07 55		08 26		08 34	08 55			09 26		09 34	09 55		
Hampden Park 4	d	00 01			06 59		07a30	07 34				08a30		08 38				09a30		09 38			
Polegate	d	00 05			07 04			07 38		08 02				08 42	09 02					09 42	10 02		
Berwick	d							07 44						08 48						09 48			
Glynde	d							07 49						08 53						09 53			
Seaford	d										07 53		08 27				08 53		09 27				09 53
Bishopstone	d										07 55		08 29				08 55		09 29				09 55
Newhaven Harbour	d										07 58		08 32				08 58		09 32				09 58
Newhaven Town	d										08 00		08 34				09 00		09 34				10 00
Southease	d										08 04						09 04						10 04
Lewes 4	a	00 17			07 16			07 55		08 14	08 11		08 43	08 59	09 14		09 11		09 43	09 59	10 14		10 11
	d	00 18			07 20	07 22		07 56		08 16	08 18		08 44	09 00	09 16		09 18		09 44	10 00	10 16		10 18
Falmer	d	00 25				07 29		08 03			08 25		08 51				09 25		09 51				10 25
Moulsecoomb	d	00 28				07 32		08 07			08 28		08 54				09 28		09 54				10 28
London Road (Brighton)	d	00 30				07 34		08 09			08 30		08 56				09 30		09 56				10 30
Brighton 10	a	00 34				07 38		08 13			08 34		09 00	09 12			09 34		10 00	10 12			10 34
Cooksbridge	d																						
Plumpton	d									08 24					09 24						10 24		
Wivelsfield 4	a				07 32					08 31					09 31						10 31		
Haywards Heath 3	a				07 36					08 36					09 35						10 35		
Gatwick Airport 10 ✈	a				07 51					08 51					09 52						10 52		
East Croydon	a				08 10					09 10					10 10						11 10		
London Bridge 4 ⊖	a																						
Clapham Junction 10	a				08 23					09 24					10 24						11 24		
London Victoria 15 ⊖	a				08 30					09 31					10 31						11 31		

A not 11 December

B ⚲ from Lewes

Table 189

Sundays

Ashford, Hastings, Eastbourne, Seaford and Lewes - Brighton, Haywards Heath and London

Network Diagram - see first Page of Table 184

		SN	SN	SN	SN	SN	SN	SN	SN	SN	SN	SN	SN	SN	SN	SN	SN	SN	SN	SN	SN	SN	SN
		◇[1]			◇[1]			◇[1]			◇[1]			◇[1]			◇[1]			◇[1]			◇[1]
					A 🛒						A 🛒						A 🛒						A 🛒
Ashford International	d			09 21						10 21						11 21						12 21	
Ham Street	d			09 30						10 30						11 30						12 30	
Appledore (Kent)	d			09 35						10 35						11 35						12 35	
Rye	a			09 44						10 44						11 44						12 44	
	d			09 45						10 45						11 45						12 45	
Winchelsea	d																						
Doleham	d																						
Three Oaks	d																						
Ore	d				10 14						11 14						12 14						13 14
Hastings [4]	a			10 02	10 17					11 02	11 17					12 02	12 17					13 02	13 17
	d			10 03	10 18					11 03	11 18					12 03	12 18					13 03	13 18
St Leonards Warrior Sq [4]	d			10 06	10 21					11 06	11 21					12 06	12 21					13 06	13 21
Bexhill [4]	d			10 13	10 28					11 13	11 28					12 13	12 28					13 13	13 28
Collington	d				10 30						11 30						12 30						13 30
Cooden Beach	d				10 33						11 33						12 33						13 33
Normans Bay	d																						
Pevensey Bay	d																						
Pevensey & Westham	d				10 39						11 39						12 39						13 39
Hampden Park [4]	d				10 43	10 53					11 43	11 53					12 43	12 53					13 43
Eastbourne [4]	a			10 29	10 49	10 58				11 29	11 49	11 58				12 29	12 49	12 58				13 29	13 49
	d	10 26		10 34	10 55			11 26		11 34	11 55			12 26		12 34	12 55			13 26		13 34	13 55
Hampden Park [4]	d	10a30		10 38				11a30		11 38				12a30		12 38				13a30		13 38	
Polegate	d			10 42	11 02					11 42	12 02					12 42	13 02					13 42	14 02
Berwick	d			10 48						11 48						12 48						13 48	
Glynde	d			10 53						11 53						12 53						13 53	
Seaford	d		10 27				10 53		11 27				11 53		12 27				12 53		13 27		
Bishopstone	d		10 29				10 55		11 29				11 55		12 29				12 55		13 29		
Newhaven Harbour	d		10 32				10 58		11 32				11 58		12 32				12 58		13 32		
Newhaven Town ⛴	d		10 34				11 00		11 34				12 00		12 34				13 00		13 34		
Southease	d						11 04						12 04						13 04				
Lewes [4]	a		10 43	10 59	11 14		11 11		11 43	11 59	12 14		12 11		12 43	12 59	13 14		13 11		13 43	13 59	14 14
	d		10 44	11 00	11 16		11 18		11 44	12 00	12 16		12 18		12 44	13 00	13 16		13 18		13 44	14 00	14 16
Falmer	d		10 51				11 25		11 51				12 25		12 51				13 25		13 51		
Moulsecoomb	d		10 54				11 28		11 54				12 28		12 54				13 28		13 54		
London Road (Brighton)	d		10 56				11 30		11 56				12 30		12 56				13 30		13 56		
Brighton [10]	a		11 00	11 12			11 34		12 00	12 12			12 34		13 00	13 12			13 34		14 00	14 12	
Cooksbridge	d																						
Plumpton	d				11 24						12 24												
Wivelsfield [4]	a				11 31						12 31						13 31						14 31
Haywards Heath [3]	a				11 35						12 35						13 35						14 35
Gatwick Airport [10] ✈	a				11 51						12 51						13 52						14 51
East Croydon 🚋	a				12 09						13 10						14 10						15 10
London Bridge [4] ⊖	a																						
Clapham Junction [10]	a				12 24						13 24						14 24						15 24
London Victoria [15] ⊖	a				12 31						13 31						14 31						15 31

A 🛒 from Lewes

Table 189

Sundays

Ashford, Hastings, Eastbourne, Seaford and Lewes - Brighton, Haywards Heath and London

Network Diagram - see first Page of Table 184

		SN		SN	SN	SN	SN	SN	SN	SN	SN	SN		SN	SN	SN	SN	SN	SN	SN	SN	SN		SN	SN
					◇1			◇1			◇1				◇1			◇1			◇1				◇1
								A ⚯							A ⚯						A ⚯				
Ashford International ✈	d						13 21							14 21						15 21					
Ham Street	d						13 30							14 30						15 30					
Appledore (Kent)	d						13 35							14 35						15 35					
Rye	a						13 44							14 44						15 44					
	d						13 45							14 45						15 45					
Winchelsea	d																								
Doleham	d																								
Three Oaks	d																								
Ore	d							14 14							15 14						16 14				
Hastings 4	a						14 02	14 17						15 02	15 17					16 02	16 17				
	d						14 03	14 18						15 03	15 18					16 03	16 18				
St Leonards Warrior Sq 4	d						14 06	14 21						15 06	15 21					16 06	16 21				
Bexhill 4	d						14 13	14 28						15 13	15 28					16 13	16 28				
Collington	d							14 30							15 30						16 30				
Cooden Beach	d							14 33							15 33						16 33				
Normans Bay	d																								
Pevensey Bay	d																								
Pevensey & Westham	d							14 39							15 39						16 39				
Hampden Park 4	d	13 53						14 43	14 53						15 43	15 53					16 43	16 53			
Eastbourne 4	a	13 58					14 29	14 49	14 58					15 29	15 49	15 58				16 29	16 49	16 58			
	d				14 26		14 34	14 55			15 26			15 34	15 55			16 26		16 34	16 55				17 26
Hampden Park 4	d				14a30		14 38				15a30			15 38				16a30		16 38					17a30
Polegate	d						14 42	15 02						15 42	16 02					16 42	17 02				
Berwick	d						14 48							15 48						16 48					
Glynde	d						14 53							15 53						16 53					
Seaford	d			13 53		14 27				14 53		15 27					15 53		16 27					16 53	
Bishopstone	d			13 55		14 29				14 55		15 29					15 55		16 29					16 55	
Newhaven Harbour	d			13 58		14 32				14 58		15 32					15 58		16 32					16 58	
Newhaven Town ⛴	d			14 00		14 34				15 00		15 34					16 00		16 34					17 00	
Southease	d			14 04						15 04							16 04							17 04	
Lewes 4	a			14 11		14 43	14 59	15 14		15 11		15 43		15 59	16 14		16 11		16 43	16 59	17 14			17 11	
	d			14 18		14 44	15 00	15 16		15 18		15 44		16 00	16 16		16 18		16 44	17 00	17 16			17 18	
Falmer	d			14 25		14 51				15 25		15 51					16 25		16 51					17 25	
Moulsecoomb	d			14 28		14 54				15 28		15 54					16 28		16 54					17 28	
London Road (Brighton)	d			14 30		14 56				15 30		15 56					16 30		16 56					17 30	
Brighton 10	a			14 34		15 00	15 12			15 34		16 00		16 12			16 34		17 00	17 12				17 34	
Cooksbridge	d																								
Plumpton	d														16 24						17 24				
Wivelsfield 4	a							15 31							16 31						17 31				
Haywards Heath 3	a							15 35							16 35						17 35				
Gatwick Airport 10 ✈	a							15 51							16 51						17 51				
East Croydon 🚋	a							16 10							17 10						18 10				
London Bridge 4 ⊖	a																								
Clapham Junction 10	a							16 24							17 24						18 24				
London Victoria 15 ⊖	a							16 31							17 31						18 31				

A ⚯ from Lewes

Table 189

Sundays

Ashford, Hastings, Eastbourne, Seaford and Lewes - Brighton, Haywards Heath and London

Network Diagram - see first Page of Table 184

		SN	SN	SN	SN	SN	SN	SN	SN	SN	SN	SN	SN	SN	SN	SN	SN	SN	SN	SN	SN	SN	SN
				◇1			◇1			◇1			◇1			◇1			◇1			◇1	
				A 🚲																			
Ashford International	d		16 21						17 21						18 21						19 21		
Ham Street	d		16 30						17 30						18 30						19 30		
Appledore (Kent)	d		16 35						17 35						18 35						19 35		
Rye	a		16 44						17 44						18 44						19 44		
	d		16 45						17 45						18 45						19 45		
Winchelsea	d																						
Doleham	d																						
Three Oaks	d																						
Ore	d			17 14						18 14						19 14						20 14	
Hastings 4	a		17 02	17 17					18 02	18 17					19 02	19 17					20 02	20 17	
	d		17 03	17 18					18 03	18 18					19 03	19 18					20 03	20 18	
St Leonards Warrior Sq 4	d		17 06	17 21					18 06	18 21					19 06	19 21					20 06	20 21	
Bexhill 4	d		17 13	17 28					18 13	18 28					19 13	19 28					20 13	20 28	
Collington	d			17 30						18 30						19 30						20 30	
Cooden Beach	d			17 33						18 33						19 33						20 33	
Normans Bay	d																						
Pevensey Bay	d																						
Pevensey & Westham	d			17 39						18 39						19 39						20 39	
Hampden Park 4	d			17 43	17 53					18 43	18 53					19 43	19 53					20 43	20 53
Eastbourne 4	a		17 29	17 49	17 58				18 29	18 49	18 58				19 29	19 49	19 58				20 29	20 49	20 58
	d		17 34	17 55			18 26		18 34	18 55			19 26		19 34	19 55			20 26		20 34	20 55	
Hampden Park 4	d		17 38				18a30		18 38				19a30		19 38				20a30		20 38		
Polegate	d		17 42	18 02					18 42	19 02					19 42	20 02					20 42	21 02	
Berwick	d		17 48						18 48						19 48						20 48		
Glynde	d		17 53						18 53						19 53						20 53		
Seaford	d	17 27				17 53		18 27				18 53		19 27				19 53		20 27			
Bishopstone	d	17 29				17 55		18 29				18 55		19 29				19 55		20 29			
Newhaven Harbour	d	17 32				17 58		18 32				18 58		19 32				19 58		20 32			
Newhaven Town ⛴	d	17 34				18 00		18 34				19 00		19 34				20 00		20 34			
Southease	d					18 04						19 04						20 04					
Lewes 4	a	17 43	17 59	18 14		18 12		18 43	18 59	19 14		19 11		19 43	19 59	20 14		20 11		20 43	20 59	21 14	
	d	17 44	18 00	18 16		18 18		18 44	19 00	19 16		19 18		19 44	20 00	20 16		20 18		20 44	21 00	21 16	
Falmer	d	17 51				18 25		18 51				19 25		19 51				20 25		20 51			
Moulsecoomb	d	17 54				18 28		18 54				19 28		19 54				20 28		20 54			
London Road (Brighton)	d	17 56				18 30		18 56				19 30		19 56				20 30		20 56			
Brighton 10	a	18 00	18 12			18 34		19 00	19 12			19 34		20 00	20 12			20 34		21 00	21 12		
Cooksbridge	d																						
Plumpton	d			18 24						19 24						20 24						21 24	
Wivelsfield 4	a			18 31						19 31						20 31						21 31	
Haywards Heath 3	a			18 35						19 35						20 35						21 35	
Gatwick Airport 10 ✈	a			18 51						19 51						20 51						21 51	
East Croydon 🚋	a			19 10						20 10						21 10						22 10	
London Bridge 4 ⊖	a																						
Clapham Junction 10	a			19 24						20 24						21 24						22 24	
London Victoria 15 ⊖	a			19 31						20 31						21 31						22 31	

A 🚲 from Lewes

Sundays

Ashford, Hastings, Eastbourne, Seaford and Lewes - Brighton, Haywards Heath and London

Network Diagram - see first Page of Table 184

		SN	SN	SN		SN	SN	SN	SN	SN	SN	SN	SN	SN		SN	SN	SN	SN	SN
			◇1					1		◇1				1				◇1	1	
Ashford International	d					20 21						21 21				22 32				
Ham Street	d					20 30						21 30				22 41				
Appledore (Kent)	d					20 35						21 35				22 46				
Rye	a					20 44						21 44				22 55				
	d					20 45						21 45				22 55				
Winchelsea	d															22 58				
Doleham	d															23 05				
Three Oaks	d															23 08				
Ore	d							21 14						22 14		23 14				
Hastings 4	a					21 02		21 17				22 02		22 17		23 17				
	d					21 03		21 18				22 03		22 18					23 22	
St Leonards Warrior Sq 4	d					21 06		21 21				22 06		22 21					23 24	
Bexhill 4	d					21 13		21 28				22 13		22 28					23 31	
Collington	d							21 30						22 30					23 33	
Cooden Beach	d							21 33						22 33					23 36	
Normans Bay	d																			
Pevensey Bay	d																			
Pevensey & Westham	d							21 39						22 39					23 42	
Hampden Park 4	d							21 43	21 53					22 43			22 53		23 47	23 53
Eastbourne 4	a					21 29		21 49	21 58			22 29		22 49			22 58		23 52	23 58
	d		21 26			21 34		21 59		22 26		22 34		22 59				23 26		
Hampden Park 4	d		21a30			21 38				22a30		22 38						23a30		
Polegate	d					21 42		22 06				22 42		23 06						
Berwick	d					21 48						22 48								
Glynde	d					21 53						22 53								
Seaford	d	20 53		21 27			21 53				22 27		22 53							
Bishopstone	d	20 55		21 29			21 55				22 29		22 55							
Newhaven Harbour	d	20 58		21 32			21 58				22 32		22 58							
Newhaven Town ⛴	d	21 00		21 34			22 00				22 34		23 00							
Southease	d																			
Lewes 4	a	21 09		21 43		21 59	22 09	22 18			22 43	22 59	23 09	23 18						
	d	21 18		21 44		22 00	22 10	22 19			22 44	23 00	23 10	23 19						
Falmer	d	21 25		21 51			22 17	22 26			22 51		23 17	23 26						
Moulsecoomb	d	21 28		21 54			22 20	22 29			22 54		23 20	23 29						
London Road (Brighton)	d	21 30		21 56			22 22	22 31			22 56		23 22	23 31						
Brighton 10	a	21 34		22 00		22 12	22 26	22 35			23 00	23 12	23 26	23 35						
Cooksbridge	d																			
Plumpton	d																			
Wivelsfield 4	a																			
Haywards Heath 3	a																			
Gatwick Airport 10 ✈	a																			
East Croydon 🚋	a																			
London Bridge 4 ⊖	a																			
Clapham Junction 10	a																			
London Victoria 15 ⊖	a																			

Route Diagram for Table 194

HIGH SPEED SERVICES

DM-24/11
Design BAJS

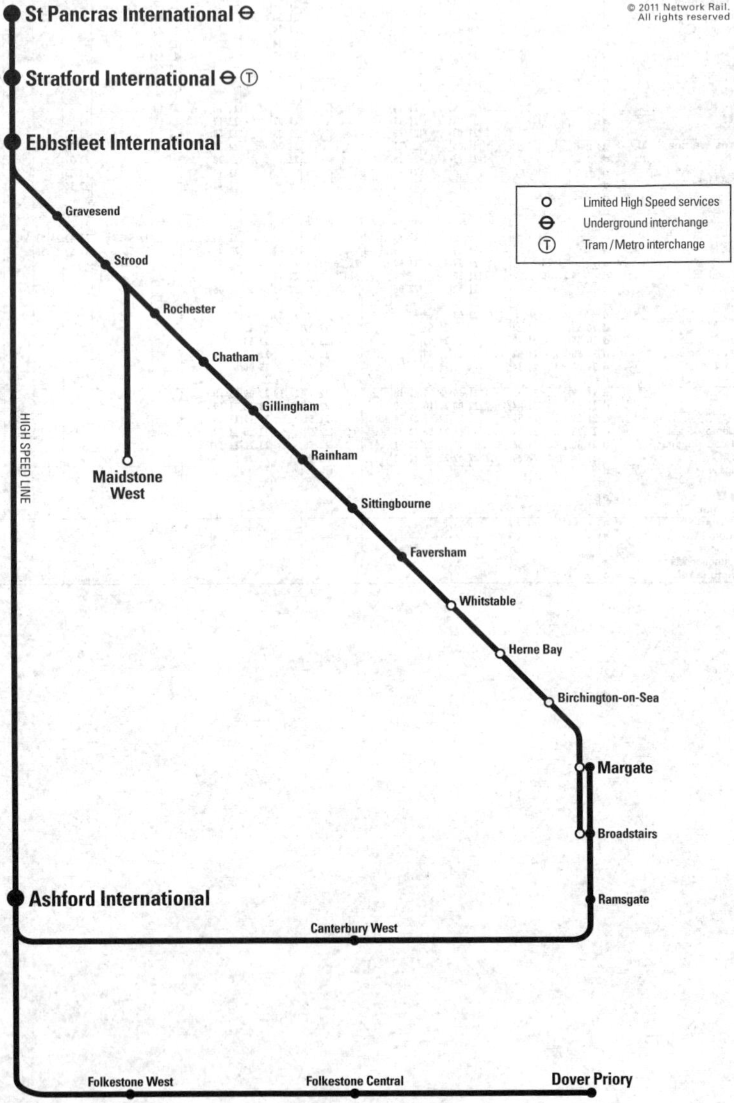

St Pancras International - Kent High Speed Domestic Services

Miles	Miles	Miles			SE	SE	SE	SE MX [1]	SE MO	SE MX	SE MX	SE	SE	SE [1]		SE	SE	SE	SE	SE	SE	SE	SE	SE	SE
—	—	—	**St Pancras International** [15] ⊖	d	22p55	23p12	23p25		23p42	23p55	00 12		06 25				06 40	06 55	07 10	07 25		07 40	07 52	08 10	08 25
6	6	6	**Stratford International** ⊖	d	23p02	23p19	23p32		23p49	00 02	00 19		06 32				06 47	07 02	07 17	07 32		07 47	08 02	08 17	08 32
22¾	22¾	22¾	**Ebbsfleet International**	a	23p12	23p30	23p42		23p59	00 12	00 30		06 42				06 58	07 12	07 28	07 42		07 59	08 12	08 29	08 42
—	—	—		d	23p13	23p31	23p43		00 01	00 13	00 31		06 42				06 59	07 13	07 29	07 43		08 00	08 13	08 30	08 43
24¾	—	—	Gravesend [4]	d	23p18		23p48			00 18			06 46					07 21		07 48			08 18		08 48
32	—	—	Strood [4]	d	23p28		23p58			00 28			06 57					07 31		07 58			08 28		08 58
—	—	—	Maidstone West	d									07a12												
33	—	—	Rochester [4]	d	23p33		00 03			00 33								07 36		08 03			08 33		09 03
33½	—	—	Chatham [4]	d	23p35		00 05			00 35								07 38		08 05			08 35		09 05
35¼	—	—	Gillingham (Kent) [4]	d	23p40		00 10			00 40								07 43		08 10			08 40		09 10
38¼	—	—	Rainham (Kent)	d	23p45		00 15			00 45								07 48		08 15			08 45		09 15
44	—	—	Sittingbourne [4]	d	23p53		00 23			00 53								07 57		08 23			08 53		09 23
51¾	—	—	**Faversham** [2]	a	00 03		00 33			01 03								08 05		08 33			09 03		09 33
58¾	—	—	Whitstable	d																					
62½	—	—	Herne Bay	d																					
70½	—	—	Birchington-on-Sea	d																					
73½	—	—	Margate [4]	d								05 47				06 48					07 49				
76¾	—	—	**Broadstairs**	a								05 52				06 53					07 54				
—	56	56	**Ashford International**	a		23p50			00 20		00 50						07 18		07 48			08 20		08 50	
—	—	—		d		23p52		00 03						06 33			07 22		07 50			08 22		08 52	
—	69¼	—	Folkestone West	d		00 05													08 03					09 05	
—	70	—	Folkestone Central	d		00 08													08 06					09 08	
—	77¼	—	**Dover Priory** [4]	a		00 20													08 18					09 20	
—	—	70¼	**Canterbury West** [4]	a				00 24				06 19		06 54		07 19	07 38				08 24	08 38			
—	—	—		d				00 25						06 55			07 39					08 39			
—	—	—	Deal	a																					
—	—	—	Sandwich	a																					
—	—	87¾	Ramsgate [4]	d				00a47						07a17			08 01					08 59			
—	—	87¾	Broadstairs	d													08 06					09 05			
—	—	91	**Margate** [4]	a													08 11					09 10			

			SE	SE	SE	SE	SE	SE	SE	SE	SE	SE		SE	SE	SE	SE	SE	SE	SE	SE	SE	SE		SE
St Pancras International [15] ⊖	d			08 40	08 55	09 10	09 25		09 37	09 55	10 10	10 28			10 40	10 52	11 12	11 25		11 42	11 55	12 12	12 22		
Stratford International ⊖	d			08 47	09 05	09 17	09 32		09 44	10 02	10 17	10 35			10 47	10 59	11 19	11 32		11 49	12 02	12 19	12 32		
Ebbsfleet International	a			08 59	09 15	09 28	09 42		09 55	10 12	10 28	10 45			10 58	11 09	11 30	11 42		12 00	12 12	12 30	12 42		
	d			09 00	09 17	09 29	09 43		09 56	10 13	10 29	10 46			10 59	11 13	11 31	11 43		12 01	12 13	12 31	12 43		
Gravesend [4]	d				09 22		09 48			10 18		10 51				11 18		11 48			12 18		12 48		
Strood [4]	d				09 32		09 58			10 28		11 01				11 28		11 58			12 28		12 58		
Maidstone West	d																								
Rochester [4]	d				09 37		10 03			10 33		11 06				11 33		12 03			12 33		13 03		
Chatham [4]	d				09 39		10 05			10 35		11 08				11 35		12 05			12 35		13 05		
Gillingham (Kent) [4]	d				09 44		10 10			10 40		11 13				11 40		12 10			12 40		13 10		
Rainham (Kent)	d				09 49		10 15			10 45		11 18				11 45		12 15			12 45		13 15		
Sittingbourne [4]	d				09 56		10 23			10 53		11 25				11 53		12 23			12 53		13 23		
Faversham [2]	a				10 04		10 33			11 03		11 33				12 03		12 33			13 03		13 33		
Whitstable	d																								
Herne Bay	d																								
Birchington-on-Sea	d																								
Margate [4]	d		08 53					09 53						10 53					11 53						12 53
Broadstairs	a		08 58					09 58						10 58					11 58						12 58
Ashford International	a			09 20		09 48			10 15		10 48				11 18		11 50			12 20		12 50			
	d			09 22		09 52			10 22		10 52				11 22		11 52			12 22		12 52			
Folkestone West	d					10 05					11 05						12 05					13 05			
Folkestone Central	d					10 08					11 08						12 08					13 08			
Dover Priory [4]	a					10 20					11 20						12 20					13 20			
Canterbury West [4]	a		09 24	09 38				10 24	10 38					11 24	11 38				12 24	12 38					13 24
	d			09 39					10 39						11 39					12 39					
Deal	a																								
Sandwich	a																								
Ramsgate [4]	d			09 59					10 59						11 59					12 59					
Broadstairs	d			10 05					11 05						12 05					13 05					
Margate [4]	a			10 10					11 10						12 10					13 10					

St Pancras International - Kent High Speed Domestic Services

		SE	SE	SE	SE	SE	SE	SE	SE	SE		SE	SE	SE	SE	SE	SE	SE	SE	SE	SE		SE	SE	SE
St Pancras International 15 ⊖	d	12 42	12 52	13 12	13 25		13 42	13 55	14 12	14 25			14 42	14 55	15 12	15 25		15 42	15 55	16 10	16 25			16 42	16 55
Stratford International ⊖	d	12 49	12 58	13 19	13 32		13 49	14 02	14 19	14 32			14 49	15 02	15 19	15 32		15 49	16 02	16 17	16 32			16 49	17 02
Ebbsfleet International	a	13 00	13 08	13 30	13 42		14 00	14 12	14 30	14 42			15 00	15 12	15 30	15 42		16 00	16 12	16 28	16 42			17 00	17 12
	d	13 01	13 13	13 31	13 43		14 01	14 13	14 31	14 43			15 01	15 13	15 31	15 43		16 01	16 13	16 29	16 43			17 01	17 13
Gravesend 4	d		13 18		13 48			14 18		14 48				15 18		15 48			16 18		16 48				17 18
Strood 4	d		13 28		13 58			14 28		14 58				15 28		15 58			16 28		16 58				17 28
Maidstone West	d																								
Rochester 4	d		13 33		14 03			14 33		15 03				15 33		16 03			16 33		17 03				17 34
Chatham 4	d		13 35		14 05			14 35		15 05				15 35		16 05			16 35		17 05				17 37
Gillingham (Kent) 4	d		13 40		14 10			14 40		15 10				15 40		16 10			16 40		17 10				17 43
Rainham (Kent)	d		13 45		14 15			14 45		15 15				15 45		16 15			16 45		17 15				17 48
Sittingbourne 4	d		13 53		14 23			14 53		15 23				15 53		16 23			16 53		17 23				17 57
Faversham 2	a		14 03		14 33			15 03		15 33				16 03		16 33			17 03		17 33				18 05
Whitstable	d																								
Herne Bay	d																								
Birchington-on-Sea	d																								
Margate 4	d					13 53						14 53					15 53						16 53		
Broadstairs	a					13 58						14 58					15 58						16 58		
Ashford International	a	13 20		13 50			14 20		14 50				15 20		15 50			16 20		16 48				17 20	
	d	13 22		13 52			14 22		14 52				15 22		15 52			16 22		16 52				17 23	
Folkestone West	d			14 05					15 05						16 05					17 05					
Folkestone Central	d			14 08					15 08						16 08					17 08					
Dover Priory 4	a			14 20					15 20						16 20					17 20					
Canterbury West 4	a	13 38				14 24	14 38					15 24	15 38				16 24	16 38					17 24	17 39	
	d	13 39					14 39						15 39					16 39						17 40	
Deal	a																								
Sandwich	a																								
Ramsgate 4	d	13 59					14 59						15 59					16 59						17 59	
Broadstairs	d	14 05					15 05						16 05					17 05						18 05	
Margate 4	a	14 10					15 10						16 10					17 10						18 10	

		SE		SE	SE	SE	SE	SE		SE		SE	SE	SE	SE		SE	SE	SE		SE	SE		SE	SE
St Pancras International 15 ⊖	d	17 10		17 14	17 18			17 25		17 40		17 44	17 48	17 55	18 10		18 14	18 18			18 25	18 40		18 48	18 55
Stratford International ⊖	d	17 17		17 21	17 25			17 32		17 47		17 51	17 55	18 02	18 17		18 21	18 25			18 32	18 47		18 55	19 02
Ebbsfleet International	a				17 35			17 42					18 05	18 12				18 35			18 42			19 05	19 12
	d							17 43						18 13							18 43				19 13
Gravesend 4	d			17 36								18 06					18 38								19 20
Strood 4	d			17 46								18 18					18 49								19 30
Maidstone West	d			18a02								18a32					19a05								
Rochester 4	d							18 02						18 31							19 03				19 35
Chatham 4	d							18 05						18 34							19 06				19 38
Gillingham (Kent) 4	d							18 10						18 39							19 11				19 43
Rainham (Kent)	d							18 15						18 44							19 16				19 48
Sittingbourne 4	d							18 23						18 52							19 24				19 55
Faversham 2	a							18 31						19 00							19 32				20 04
Whitstable	d							18 40						19 09							19 42				
Herne Bay	d							18 46						19 15							19 48				
Birchington-on-Sea	d							18 55						19 24							19 57				
Margate 4	d					17 53	18 53	19 02						19 30					19 53		20 04				
Broadstairs	a					17 58	18 58	19 08						19 36					19 58		20 09				
Ashford International	a	17 46								18 16					18 46							19 16			
	d	17 50	17 53							18 23	18 20				18 50	18 53						19 23	19 20		
Folkestone West	d	18 03									18 33				19 05								19 33		
Folkestone Central	d	18 06									18 36				19 08								19 36		
Dover Priory 4	a	18 18									18 47				19 20								19 47		
Canterbury West 4	a		18 09			18 24	19 24			18 39						19 09			20 24			19 39			
	d		18 10							18 40						19 10						19 40			
Deal	a										19 06												20 06		
Sandwich	a										19 13												20 13		
Ramsgate 4	d		18 29							18 59						19 31						19 59			
Broadstairs	d		18 35							19 05						19 36						20 05			
Margate 4	a		18 40							19 10						19 41						20 10			

		SE	SE	SE	SE	SE		SE	SE	SE	SE	SE	SE	SE	SE	SE	SE		SE	SE	SE	SE	SE	SE	SE
St Pancras International 15 ⊖	d	19 10	19 25		19 42	19 55		20 12	20 25		20 42	20 55	21 12	21 25		21 42	21 55		22 12	22 25	22 42	22 55	23 12	23 25	23 55
Stratford International ⊖	d	19 17	19 32		19 49	20 02		20 19	20 32		20 49	21 02	21 19	21 32		21 49	22 02		22 19	22 32	22 49	23 02	23 19	23 32	00 02
Ebbsfleet International	a	19 28	19 42		20 00	20 12		20 30	20 42		21 00	21 12	21 30	21 42		22 00	22 12		22 30	22 42	23 00	23 12	23 30	23 42	00 12
	d	19 29	19 45		20 01	20 13		20 31	20 43		21 01	21 13	21 31	21 43		22 01	22 13		22 31	22 43	23 01	23 13	23 31	23 43	00 13
Gravesend 4	d		19 51			20 18			20 48			21 18		21 48			22 18			22 48		23 18		23 48	00 18
Strood 4	d		20 01			20 28			20 58			21 28		21 58			22 28			22 58		23 28		23 58	00 28
Maidstone West	d																								
Rochester 4	d		20 08			20 33			21 03			21 33		22 03			22 33			23 03		23 33		00 03	00 33
Chatham 4	d		20 10			20 35			21 05			21 35		22 05			22 35			23 05		23 35		00 05	00 35
Gillingham (Kent) 4	d		20 15			20 40			21 10			21 40		22 10			22 40			23 10		23 40		00 10	00 40
Rainham (Kent)	d		20 20			20 45			21 15			21 45		22 15			22 45			23 15		23 45		00 15	00 45
Sittingbourne 4	d		20 27			20 53			21 23			21 53		22 23			22 53			23 23		23 53		00 23	00 53
Faversham 2	a		20 36			21 03			21 33			22 03		22 33			23 03			23 33		00 03		00 33	01 03
Whitstable	d																								
Herne Bay	d																								
Birchington-on-Sea	d																								
Margate 4	d									20 53					21 53										
Broadstairs	a									20 58					21 58										
Ashford International	a	19 48			20 20			20 50			21 20		21 50			22 20			22 50		23 20		23 50		
	d	19 52		19 55	20 22			20 52			21 22		21 52			22 22			22 52		23 22		23 52		
Folkestone West	d	20 05						21 05					22 05						23 05				00 05		
Folkestone Central	d	20 08						21 08					22 08						23 08				00 08		
Dover Priory 4	a	20 20						21 20					22 20						23 20				00 20		
Canterbury West 4	a			20 11	20 38					21 24	21 38				22 24	22 38					23 38				
	d			20 12	20 39						21 39					22 39					23 39				
Deal	a																								
Sandwich	a																								
Ramsgate 4	d			20 32	21 00						21 59					22 59					23a59				
Broadstairs	d			20 38	21 05						22 05					23 05									
Margate 4	a			20 43	21 11						22 10					23 10									

Table 194

Saturdays

St Pancras International - Kent High Speed Domestic Services

		SE	SE	SE	SE	SE 1	SE	SE	SE	SE 1	SE		SE	SE	SE	SE	SE 1	SE	SE	SE	SE	SE		SE	SE
St Pancras International 15 ⊖	d	22p55	23p12	23p25	23p55		00 12		06 10				06 40	06 52	07 12	07 25			07 42	07 52	08 12	08 28			08 40
Stratford International ⊖	d	23p02	23p19	23p32	00 02		00 19		06 17				06 47	06 59	07 19	07 32			07 49	07 58	08 19	08 35			08 47
Ebbsfleet International	a	23p12	23p30	23p42	00 12		00 30		06 28				06 58	07 09	07 30	07 42			08 00	08 08	08 30	08 45			08 58
	d	23p13	23p31	23p43	00 13		00 31		06 29				06 59	07 13	07 31	07 43			08 01	08 13	08 31	08 46			08 59
Gravesend 4	d	23p18		23p48	00 18									07 17		07 48				08 18		08 51			
Strood 4	d	23p28		23p58	00 28									07 27		07 58				08 28		09 01			
Maidstone West	d																								
Rochester 4	d	23p33		00 03	00 33									07 32		08 03				08 33		09 06			
Chatham 4	d	23p35		00 05	00 35									07 34		08 05				08 35		09 08			
Gillingham (Kent) 4	d	23p40		00 10	00 40									07 39		08 10				08 40		09 13			
Rainham (Kent)	d	23p45		00 15	00 45									07 44		08 15				08 45		09 18			
Sittingbourne 4	d	23p53		00 23	00 53									07 51		08 23				08 53		09 25			
Faversham 2	a	00 03		00 33	01 03									08 00		08 33				09 03		09 34			
Whitstable	d																								
Herne Bay	d																								
Birchington-on-Sea	d																								
Margate 4	d							05 53			06 53							07 53						08 53	
Broadstairs	a							05 58			06 58							07 58						08 58	
Ashford International	a		23p50				00 50		06 48				07 18		07 51				08 20		08 50				09 18
	d		23p52			00 03			06 52	07 03			07 22		07 52		08 03		08 22		08 52				09 22
Folkestone West	d		00 05						07 05						08 05						09 05				
Folkestone Central	d		00 08						07 08						08 08						09 08				
Dover Priory 4	a		00 20						07 20						08 20						09 20				
Canterbury West 4	a					00 24		06 24		07 21	07 24		07 38				08 21	08 24	08 38					09 24	09 38
	d					00 25				07 22			07 39				08 22		08 39						09 39
Deal	a																								
Sandwich	a																								
Ramsgate 4	d					00a47				07a44			07 59				08a44		08 59						09 59
Broadstairs	d												08 05						09 05						10 05
Margate 4	a												08 10						09 10						10 10

		SE	SE	SE	SE	SE	SE	SE	SE		SE	SE	SE	SE	SE	SE	SE	SE	SE	SE		SE	SE	SE	SE
St Pancras International 15 ⊖	d	08 50	09 10	09 25		09 42	09 55	10 12	10 28			10 42	10 52	11 12	11 25		11 42	11 55	12 12	12 28			12 42	12 55	13 12
Stratford International ⊖	d	09 04	09 17	09 32		09 49	10 02	10 19	10 35			10 49	10 58	11 19	11 32		11 49	12 02	12 19	12 35			12 49	13 06	13 19
Ebbsfleet International	a	09 14	09 28	09 42		10 00	10 12	10 30	10 45			11 00	11 08	11 30	11 42		12 00	12 12	12 30	12 45			13 00	13 16	13 30
	d	09 15	09 29	09 43		10 01	10 13	10 31	10 46			11 01	11 13	11 31	11 43		12 01	12 13	12 31	12 46			13 01	13 17	13 31
Gravesend 4	d	09 20		09 48			10 18		10 51				11 18		11 48			12 18		12 51				13 22	
Strood 4	d	09 30		09 58			10 28		11 01				11 28		11 58			12 28		13 01				13 32	
Maidstone West	d																								
Rochester 4	d	09 34		10 03			10 33		11 06				11 33		12 03			12 33		13 06				13 37	
Chatham 4	d	09 37		10 05			10 35		11 08				11 35		12 05			12 35		13 08				13 39	
Gillingham (Kent) 4	d	09 41		10 10			10 40		11 13				11 40		12 10			12 40		13 13				13 44	
Rainham (Kent)	d	09 46		10 15			10 45		11 18				11 45		12 15			12 45		13 18				13 49	
Sittingbourne 4	d	09 54		10 23			10 53		11 25				11 53		12 23			12 53		13 25				13 56	
Faversham 2	a	10 03		10 33			11 03		11 34				12 03		12 33			13 03		13 34				14 04	
Whitstable	d																								
Herne Bay	d																								
Birchington-on-Sea	d																								
Margate 4	d				09 53						10 53					11 53						12 53			
Broadstairs	a				09 58						10 58					11 58						12 58			
Ashford International	a		09 48			10 20		10 50				11 20		11 50			12 20		12 50				13 20		13 50
	d		09 52			10 22		10 52				11 22		11 52			12 22		12 52				13 22		13 52
Folkestone West	d		10 05					11 05						12 05					13 05						14 05
Folkestone Central	d		10 08					11 08						12 08					13 08						14 08
Dover Priory 4	a		10 20					11 20						12 20					13 20						14 20
Canterbury West 4	a				10 24	10 38					11 24	11 38				12 24	12 38					13 24	13 38		
	d					10 39						11 39					12 39						13 39		
Deal	a																								
Sandwich	a																								
Ramsgate 4	d					10 59						11 59					12 59						13 59		
Broadstairs	d					11 05						12 05					13 05						14 05		
Margate 4	a					11 10						12 10					13 10						14 10		

Table 194

Saturdays

St Pancras International - Kent High Speed Domestic Services

		SE	SE	SE	SE	SE	SE		SE	SE	SE	SE	SE	SE	SE	SE	SE	SE		SE	SE	SE	SE	SE	SE
St Pancras International 15 ⊖	d	13 25		13 42	13 55	14 12	14 25			14 42	14 55	15 12	15 25		15 42	15 55	16 10	16 28			16 42	16 55	17 12	17 25	
Stratford International ⊖	d	13 32		13 49	14 02	14 19	14 32			14 49	15 02	15 19	15 32		15 49	16 02	16 17	16 35			16 49	17 02	17 19	17 32	
Ebbsfleet International	a	13 42		14 00	14 12	14 30	14 42			15 00	15 12	15 30	15 42		16 00	16 12	16 28	16 45			17 00	17 12	17 30	17 42	
	d	13 43		14 01	14 13	14 31	14 43			15 01	15 13	15 31	15 43		16 01	16 13	16 29	16 46			17 01	17 13	17 31	17 43	
Gravesend 4	d	13 48			14 18		14 48				15 18		15 48			16 18		16 51				17 18		17 48	
Strood 4	d	13 58			14 28		14 58				15 28		15 58			16 28		17 01				17 28		17 58	
Maidstone West	d																								
Rochester 4	d	14 03			14 33		15 03				15 33		16 03			16 33		17 06				17 33		18 03	
Chatham 4	d	14 05			14 35		15 05				15 35		16 05			16 35		17 08				17 35		18 05	
Gillingham (Kent) 4	d	14 10			14 40		15 10				15 40		16 10			16 40		17 13				17 40		18 10	
Rainham (Kent)	d	14 15			14 45		15 15				15 45		16 15			16 45		17 18				17 45		18 15	
Sittingbourne 4	d	14 23			14 53		15 23				15 53		16 23			16 53		17 25				17 53		18 23	
Faversham 2	a	14 33			15 03		15 33				16 03		16 33			17 03		17 34				18 03		18 33	
Whitstable	d																								
Herne Bay	d																								
Birchington-on-Sea	d																								
Margate 4	d		13 53						14 53					15 53						16 53					17 53
Broadstairs	a		13 58						14 58					15 58						16 58					17 58
Ashford International	a			14 20		14 50				15 20		15 50			16 20		16 48				17 20		17 50		
	d			14 22		14 52				15 22		15 52			16 22		16 52				17 22		17 52		
Folkestone West	d					15 05						16 05					17 05						18 05		
Folkestone Central	d					15 08						16 08					17 08						18 08		
Dover Priory 4	a					15 20						16 20					17 20						18 20		
Canterbury West 4	a		14 24	14 38					15 24	15 38				16 24	16 38					17 24	17 38				18 24
	d			14 39						15 39					16 39						17 39				
Deal	a																								
Sandwich	a																								
Ramsgate 4	d			14 59						15 59					16 59						17 59				
Broadstairs	d			15 05						16 05					17 05						18 05				
Margate 4	a			15 10						16 10					17 10						18 10				

		SE	SE	SE	SE		SE	SE	SE	SE	SE	SE	SE	SE	SE	SE		SE	SE	SE	SE	SE	SE	SE	SE
St Pancras International 15 ⊖	d	17 42	17 55	18 12	18 25			18 42	18 55	19 12	19 25		19 42	19 55	20 12	20 25			20 42	20 55	21 12	21 25		21 42	21 55
Stratford International ⊖	d	17 49	18 02	18 19	18 32			18 49	19 02	19 19	19 32		19 49	20 02	20 19	20 32			20 49	21 02	21 19	21 32		21 49	22 02
Ebbsfleet International	a	18 00	18 12	18 30	18 42			19 00	19 12	19 30	19 42		20 00	20 12	20 30	20 42			21 00	21 12	21 30	21 42		22 00	22 12
	d	18 01	18 13	18 31	18 43			19 01	19 13	19 31	19 43		20 01	20 13	20 31	20 43			21 01	21 13	21 31	21 43		22 01	22 13
Gravesend 4	d		18 18		18 48				19 18		19 48			20 18		20 48				21 18		21 48			22 18
Strood 4	d		18 28		18 58				19 28		19 58			20 28		20 58				21 28		21 58			22 28
Maidstone West	d																								
Rochester 4	d		18 33		19 03				19 33		20 03			20 33		21 03				21 33		22 03			22 33
Chatham 4	d		18 35		19 05				19 35		20 05			20 35		21 05				21 35		22 05			22 35
Gillingham (Kent) 4	d		18 40		19 10				19 40		20 10			20 40		21 10				21 40		22 10			22 40
Rainham (Kent)	d		18 45		19 15				19 45		20 15			20 45		21 15				21 45		22 15			22 45
Sittingbourne 4	d		18 53		19 23				19 53		20 23			20 53		21 23				21 53		22 23			22 53
Faversham 2	a		19 03		19 33				20 03		20 33			21 03		21 33				22 03		22 31			23 01
Whitstable	d																								
Herne Bay	d																								
Birchington-on-Sea	d																								
Margate 4	d						18 53					19 53						20 53					21 53		
Broadstairs	a						18 58					19 58						20 58					21 58		
Ashford International	a	18 20		18 50				19 20		19 50			20 20		20 50				21 20		21 50			22 20	
	d	18 22		18 52				19 22		19 52			20 22		20 52				21 22		21 52			22 22	
Folkestone West	d			19 05						20 05					21 05						22 05				
Folkestone Central	d			19 08						20 08					21 08						22 08				
Dover Priory 4	a			19 20						20 20					21 20						22 20				
Canterbury West 4	a	18 38					19 24	19 38				20 24	20 38					21 24	21 38				22 24	22 38	
	d	18 39						19 39					20 39						21 39					22 39	
Deal	a																								
Sandwich	a																								
Ramsgate 4	d	18 59						19 59					20 59						21 59					22 59	
Broadstairs	d	19 05						20 05					21 05						22 05					23 05	
Margate 4	a	19 10						20 10					21 10						22 10					23 10	

		SE	SE		SE	SE	SE	SE	SE
St Pancras International 15 ⊖	d	22 12	22 25		22 42	22 55	23 12	23 25	23 55
Stratford International ⊖	d	22 19	22 32		22 49	23 02	23 19	23 32	00 02
Ebbsfleet International	a	22 30	22 42		23 00	23 12	23 30	23 42	00 12
	d	22 31	22 43		23 01	23 13	23 31	23 43	00 13
Gravesend 4	d		22 48			23 18		23 48	00 18
Strood 4	d		22 58			23 28		23 58	00 28
Maidstone West	d								
Rochester 4	d		23 03			23 33		00 03	00 33
Chatham 4	d		23 05			23 35		00 05	00 35
Gillingham (Kent) 4	d		23 10			23 40		00 10	00 40
Rainham (Kent)	d		23 15			23 45		00 15	00 45
Sittingbourne 4	d		23 23			23 53		00 23	00 53
Faversham 2	a		23 31			00 01		00 31	01 01
Whitstable	d								
Herne Bay	d								
Birchington-on-Sea	d								
Margate 4	d								
Broadstairs	a								
Ashford International	a	22 50			23 20		23 50		
	d	22 52			23 22		23 52		
Folkestone West	d	23 05					00 05		
Folkestone Central	d	23 08					00 08		
Dover Priory 4	a	23 20					00 20		
Canterbury West 4	a				23 38				
	d				23 39				
Deal	a								
Sandwich	a								
Ramsgate 4	d				23a59				
Broadstairs	d								
Margate 4	a								

Table 194

Sundays

St Pancras International - Kent High Speed Domestic Services

		SE	SE	SE	SE	SE	SE	SE	SE	SE	SE		SE	SE	SE	SE	SE	SE	SE	SE	SE	SE		SE	SE
								1																	
		A	A	A	A																				
St Pancras International 15 ⊖	d	22p55	23p12	23p25	23p55	00 12				08 42	08 52		09 10	09 25		09 42	09 55	10 10	10 28		10 42	10 52		11 12	11 25
Stratford International ⊖	d	23p02	23p19	23p32	00 02	00 19				08 49	08 58		09 17	09 32		09 49	10 02	10 17	10 35		10 49	10 58		11 19	11 32
Ebbsfleet International	a	23p12	23p30	23p42	00 12	00 30				09 00	09 08		09 28	09 42		10 00	10 12	10 28	10 45		11 00	11 09		11 30	11 42
	d	23p13	23p31	23p43	00 13	00 31				09 01	09 13		09 29	09 43		10 01	10 13	10 29	10 46		11 01	11 14		11 31	11 43
Gravesend 4	d	23p18		23p48	00 18						09 18			09 48			10 18		10 51			11 18			11 48
Strood 4	d	23p28		23p58	00 28						09 28			09 58			10 28		11 01			11 28			11 58
Maidstone West	d																								
Rochester 4	d	23p33		00 03	00 33						09 33			10 03			10 33		11 06			11 33			12 03
Chatham 4	d	23p35		00 05	00 35						09 35			10 05			10 35		11 08			11 35			12 05
Gillingham (Kent) 4	d	23p40		00 10	00 40						09 40			10 10			10 40		11 13			11 40			12 10
Rainham (Kent)	d	23p45		00 15	00 45						09 45			10 15			10 45		11 18			11 45			12 15
Sittingbourne 4	d	23p53		00 23	00 53						09 53			10 23			10 53		11 25			11 53			12 23
Faversham 2	a	00 01		00 31	01 01						10 01			10 33			11 03		11 34			12 03			12 33
Whitstable	d																								
Herne Bay	d																								
Birchington-on-Sea	d																								
Margate 4	d						07 53		08 53						09 53					10 53					
Broadstairs	a						07 58		08 58						09 58					10 58					
Ashford International	a		23p50			00 50				09 20			09 48			10 20		10 48			11 20			11 50	
	d		23p52					09 03		09 22			09 52			10 22		10 52			11 22			11 52	
Folkestone West	d		00 05										10 05					11 05						12 05	
Folkestone Central	d		00 08										10 08					11 08						12 08	
Dover Priory 4	a		00 20										10 20					11 20						12 20	
Canterbury West 4	a						08 24	09 21	09 24	09 38					10 24	10 38				11 24	11 38				
	d							09 22		09 39						10 39					11 39				
Deal	a																								
Sandwich	a																								
Ramsgate 4	d							09a44		09 59						10 59					11 59				
Broadstairs	d									10 05						11 05					12 05				
Margate 4	a									10 10						11 10					12 10				

		SE	SE	SE	SE	SE	SE	SE	SE		SE	SE	SE	SE	SE	SE	SE	SE	SE	SE		SE	SE	SE	SE
St Pancras International 15 ⊖	d		11 42	11 55	12 12	12 28		12 42	12 52		13 12	13 25		13 42	13 55	14 12	14 25		14 42	14 55		15 12	15 25		15 42
Stratford International ⊖	d		11 49	12 02	12 19	12 35		12 49	12 58		13 19	13 32		13 49	14 02	14 19	14 32		14 49	15 02		15 19	15 32		15 49
Ebbsfleet International	a		12 00	12 12	12 30	12 45		13 00	13 08		13 30	13 42		14 00	14 12	14 30	14 42		15 00	15 12		15 30	15 42		16 00
	d		12 01	12 13	12 31	12 46		13 01	13 13		13 31	13 43		14 01	14 13	14 31	14 43		15 01	15 13		15 31	15 43		16 01
Gravesend 4	d			12 18		12 51			13 18			13 48			14 18		14 48			15 18			15 48		
Strood 4	d			12 28		13 01			13 28			13 58			14 28		14 58			15 28			15 58		
Maidstone West	d																								
Rochester 4	d			12 33		13 06			13 33			14 03			14 33		15 03			15 33			16 03		
Chatham 4	d			12 35		13 08			13 35			14 05			14 35		15 05			15 35			16 05		
Gillingham (Kent) 4	d			12 40		13 13			13 40			14 10			14 40		15 10			15 40			16 10		
Rainham (Kent)	d			12 45		13 18			13 45			14 15			14 45		15 15			15 45			16 15		
Sittingbourne 4	d			12 53		13 25			13 53			14 23			14 53		15 23			15 53			16 23		
Faversham 2	a			13 03		13 34			14 03			14 33			15 03		15 33			16 03			16 33		
Whitstable	d																								
Herne Bay	d																								
Birchington-on-Sea	d																								
Margate 4	d	11 53					12 53						13 53					14 53						15 53	
Broadstairs	a	11 58					12 58						13 58					14 58						15 58	
Ashford International	a		12 20		12 50			13 20			13 50			14 20		14 50			15 20			15 50			16 20
	d		12 22		12 52			13 22			13 52			14 22		14 52			15 22			15 52			16 22
Folkestone West	d				13 05						14 05					15 05						16 05			
Folkestone Central	d				13 08						14 08					15 08						16 08			
Dover Priory 4	a				13 20						14 20					15 20						16 20			
Canterbury West 4	a	12 24	12 38				13 24	13 38					14 24	14 38				15 24	15 38					16 24	16 38
	d		12 39					13 39						14 39					15 39						16 39
Deal	a																								
Sandwich	a																								
Ramsgate 4	d		12 59					13 59						14 59					15 59						16 59
Broadstairs	d		13 05					14 05						15 05					16 05						17 05
Margate 4	a		13 10					14 10						15 10					16 10						17 10

A not 11 December

Table 194

Sundays

St Pancras International - Kent High Speed Domestic Services

		SE	SE	SE	SE	SE	SE		SE	SE	SE	SE	SE	SE	SE	SE	SE	SE		SE	SE	SE	SE	SE	SE
St Pancras International 15 ⊖	d	15 55	16 10	16 25		16 42	16 55		17 12	17 25		17 42	17 58	18 12	18 25		18 42	18 55		19 12	19 25		19 42	19 55	20 12
Stratford International ⊖	d	16 02	16 17	16 32		16 49	17 02		17 19	17 32		17 49	18 08	18 19	18 32		18 49	19 02		19 19	19 32		19 49	20 02	20 19
Ebbsfleet International	a	16 12	16 28	16 42		17 00	17 12		17 30	17 42		18 00	18 18	18 30	18 42		19 00	19 12		19 30	19 42		20 00	20 12	20 30
	d	16 13	16 29	16 43		17 01	17 13		17 31	17 43		18 01	18 19	18 31	18 43		19 01	19 13		19 31	19 43		20 01	20 13	20 31
Gravesend 4	d	16 18		16 48			17 18			17 48			18 24		18 48			19 18			19 48			20 18	
Strood 4	d	16 28		16 58			17 28			17 58			18 34		18 58			19 28			19 58			20 28	
Maidstone West	d																								
Rochester 4	d	16 33		17 03			17 33			18 03			18 39		19 03			19 33			20 03			20 33	
Chatham 4	d	16 35		17 05			17 35			18 05			18 41		19 05			19 35			20 05			20 35	
Gillingham (Kent) 4	d	16 40		17 10			17 40			18 10			18 46		19 10			19 40			20 10			20 40	
Rainham (Kent)	d	16 45		17 15			17 45			18 15			18 51		19 15			19 45			20 15			20 45	
Sittingbourne 4	d	16 53		17 23			17 53			18 23			18 58		19 23			19 53			20 23			20 53	
Faversham 2	a	17 03		17 33			18 03			18 33			19 07		19 33			20 03			20 33			21 03	
Whitstable	d																								
Herne Bay	d																								
Birchington-on-Sea	d																								
Margate 4	d				16 53						17 53					18 53						19 53			
Broadstairs	a				16 58						17 58					18 58						19 58			
Ashford International	a		16 48			17 20			17 50			18 20		18 50			19 20			19 50			20 20		20 50
	d		16 52			17 22			17 52			18 22		18 52			19 22			19 52			20 22		20 52
Folkestone West	d		17 05						18 05					19 05						20 05					21 05
Folkestone Central	d		17 08						18 08					19 08						20 08					21 08
Dover Priory 4	a		17 20						18 20					19 20						20 20					21 20
Canterbury West 4	a				17 24	17 38					18 24	18 38				19 24	19 38					20 24	20 38		
	d					17 39						18 39					19 39						20 39		
Deal	a																								
Sandwich	a																								
Ramsgate 4	d					17 59						18 59					19 59						20 59		
Broadstairs	d					18 05						19 05					20 05						21 05		
Margate 4	a					18 10						19 10					20 10						21 10		

		SE	SE	SE	SE		SE	SE	SE	SE	SE	SE	SE	SE	SE	SE		SE	SE						
St Pancras International 15 ⊖	d	20 25		20 42	20 55		21 12	21 25		21 42	21 55	22 12	22 25	22 42	22 55	23 12		23 25	23 42						
Stratford International ⊖	d	20 32		20 49	21 02		21 19	21 32		21 49	22 02	22 19	22 32	22 49	23 02	23 19		23 32	23 49						
Ebbsfleet International	a	20 42		21 00	21 12		21 30	21 42		22 00	22 12	22 30	22 42	23 00	23 12	23 30		23 42	23 59						
	d	20 43		21 01	21 13		21 31	21 43		22 01	22 13	22 31	22 43	23 01	23 13	23 31		23 43	00 01						
Gravesend 4	d	20 48			21 18			21 48			22 18		22 48		23 18			23 48							
Strood 4	d	20 58			21 28			21 58			22 28		22 58		23 28			23 58							
Maidstone West	d																								
Rochester 4	d	21 03			21 33			22 03			22 33		23 03		23 33			00 03							
Chatham 4	d	2 1 05			21 35			22 05			22 35		23 05		23 35			00 05							
Gillingham (Kent) 4	d	21 10			21 40			22 10			22 40		23 10		23 40			00 10							
Rainham (Kent)	d	21 15			21 45			22 15			22 45		23 15		23 45			00 15							
Sittingbourne 4	d	21 23			21 53			22 23			22 53		23 23		23 53			00 23							
Faversham 2	a	21 33			22 03			22 33			23 03		23 31		00 03			00 33							
Whitstable	d																								
Herne Bay	d																								
Birchington-on-Sea	d																								
Margate 4	d		20 53						21 53																
Broadstairs	a		20 58						21 58																
Ashford International	a			21 20			21 50			22 20		22 50		23 20		23 50			00 20						
	d			21 22			21 52			22 22		22 52		23 22		23 52									
Folkestone West	d						22 05					23 05				00 05									
Folkestone Central	d						22 08					23 08				00 08									
Dover Priory 4	a						22 20					23 20				00 20									
Canterbury West 4	a		21 24	21 38					22 24	22 38				23 38											
	d			21 39						22 39				23 39											
Deal	a																								
Sandwich	a																								
Ramsgate 4	d			21 59						22 59				23a59											
Broadstairs	d			22 05						23 05															
Margate 4	a			22 10						23 10															

Kent - St Pancras International High Speed Domestic Services

Miles	Miles	Miles			SE	SE	SE	SE	SE	SE	SE	SE	SE	SE		SE	SE	SE	SE	SE	SE	SE	SE	SE	SE
—	—	0	Margate [4]	d							05 47											06 48			
—	—	3¼	Broadstairs	d							05 54											06 54			
—	—	5½	Ramsgate [4]	d			05 00				06 00							06 26				07 00			
—	—	20¾	**Canterbury West**	a			05 23				06 19							06 45				07 19			
—	—	—		d			05 25				06 20							06 50				07 20			
—	—	—	Sandwich	d								05 50					06 18						06 50		
—	—	—	Deal	d								05 56					06 24						06 56		
—	0	—	**Dover Priory**	d					05 44			06 12					06 42						07 12		
—	7¼	—	Folkestone Central	d					05 56			06 23					06 53						07 23		
—	8	—	Folkestone West	d					05 58			06 26					06 56						07 26		
—	21¼	—	**Ashford International**	a			05 41		06 11		06 36	06 39					07 09	07 06				07 36	07 39		
—	—	—																							
—	—	—		d	05 13		05 43		06 13		06 43						07 13					07 43			
0	—	—	**Broadstairs**	d										06 00						06 30					07 00
3¼	—	—	Margate [4]	d										06 05						06 35					07 05
6¼	—	—	Birchington-on-Sea	d										06 10						06 40					07 10
14¼	—	—	Herne Bay	d										06 19						06 49					07 19
18¼	—	—	Whitstable	d										06 25						06 55					07 25
25	—	—	**Faversham [2]**	a										06 33						07 03					07 33
—	—	—		d		04 56		05 28		05 58				06 34						07 04					07 34
32¾	—	—	Sittingbourne [4]	d		05 07		05 37		06 07				06 42						07 13					07 42
38½	—	—	Rainham (Kent)	d		05 15		05 45		06 15				06 50						07 21					07 50
41½	—	—	Gillingham (Kent) [4]	d		05 20		05 50		06 20				06 55						07 26					07 55
43¼	—	—	Chatham [4]	d		05 24		05 54		06 24				07 00						07 30					08 00
43¾	—	—	Rochester [4]	d		05 27		05 57		06 27				07 03						07 33					08 03
—	—	—	Maidstone West	d												06 56					07 26				
44¾	—	—	Strood [4]	d		05 32		06 02		06 32						07 12					07 42				
52	—	—	Gravesend	d		05 43		06 13		06 43						07 22					07 52				
54	54½	68¼	**Ebbsfleet International** ≡	a	05 32	05 47	06 02	06 17	06 32	06 47				07 17		07 26				07 47	07 56				08 17
—	—	—		d	05 33	05 48	06 03	06 18	06 33	06 48			07 06	07 18		07 26			07 34	07 48	07 56			08 04	08 18
70¾	71¼	85	**Stratford International** ⊖	a	05 44	05 59	06 14	06 29	06 44	06 59	07 11		07 18	07 29		07 38	07 41		07 45	07 59	08 07	08 11		08 15	08 29
76¾	77¼	91	**St Pancras International [4]** ⊖	a	05 51	06 06	06 21	06 36	06 51	07 06	07 18		07 25	07 36		07 45	07 48		07 52	08 06	08 14	08 19		08 22	08 36

			SE	SE	SE	SE	SE	SE	SE	SE	SE	SE		SE	SE	SE	SE	SE	SE	SE	SE	SE	SE		SE
Margate [4]	d							07 49						08 53					09 53						10 53
Broadstairs	d							07 55						08 59					09 59						10 59
Ramsgate [4]	d				07 30			08 01						09 05					10 05						11 05
Canterbury West	a				07 49			08 24						09 24					10 24						11 24
	d		07 39		07 50			08 25		08 39				09 25		09 39			10 25		10 39				11 25
Sandwich	d																								
Deal	d																								
Dover Priory	d										08 44						09 44					10 44			
Folkestone Central	d										08 56						09 56					10 56			
Folkestone West	d										08 58						09 58					10 58			
Ashford International	a				08 06			08 41			09 11			09 41			10 11		10 41			11 11			11 41
	d				08 13			08 43			09 13			09 43			10 13		10 43			11 13			11 43
Broadstairs	d		08 06							09 05						10 05					11 05				
Margate [4]	d		08a11							09a10						10a10					11a10				
Birchington-on-Sea	d																								
Herne Bay	d																								
Whitstable	d																								
Faversham [2]	a																								
	d						07 58		08 28			08 58			09 28			09 58		10 28			10 58		
Sittingbourne [4]	d						08 06		08 37			09 07			09 37			10 07		10 37			11 07		
Rainham (Kent)	d						08 14		08 45			09 15			09 45			10 15		10 45			11 15		
Gillingham (Kent) [4]	d						08 19		08 50			09 20			09 50			10 20		10 50			11 20		
Chatham [4]	d						08 24		08 54			09 24			09 54			10 24		10 54			11 24		
Rochester [4]	d						08 26		08 57			09 27			09 57			10 27		10 57			11 27		
Maidstone West	d			07 56																					
Strood [4]	d			08 12			08 32		09 02			09 32			10 02			10 32		11 02			11 32		
Gravesend	d			08 22			08 43		09 13			09 43			10 13			10 43		11 13			11 43		
Ebbsfleet International ≡	a			08 26			08 47	09 02	09 17		09 32	09 47		10 02	10 16		10 32	10 47	11 02	11 17		11 32	11 47		12 02
	d			08 26		08 34	08 48	09 03	09 18		09 33	09 48		10 03	10 17		10 33	10 48	11 03	11 18		11 33	11 48		12 03
Stratford International ⊖	a			08 37	08 41	08 45	08 59	09 14	09 29		09 44	09 59		10 14	10 28		10 44	10 59	11 14	11 29		11 44	11 59		12 14
St Pancras International [4] ⊖	a			08 44	08 48	08 52	09 07	09 21	09 36		09 51	10 06		10 21	10 35		10 51	11 06	11 21	11 36		11 51	12 06		12 21

Kent - St Pancras International High Speed Domestic Services

		SE	SE	SE	SE	SE	SE	SE	SE	SE		SE	SE	SE	SE	SE	SE	SE	SE	SE	SE		SE	SE	SE
Margate 4	d					11 53						12 53					13 53						14 53		
Broadstairs	d					11 59						12 59					13 59						14 59		
Ramsgate 4	d					12 05						13 05					14 05						15 05		
Canterbury West	a					12 24						13 24					14 24						15 24		
	d		11 39			12 25		12 39				13 25		13 39			14 25		14 39				15 25		15 39
Sandwich	d																								
Deal	d																								
Dover Priory	d			11 44					12 44						13 44					14 44					
Folkestone Central	d			11 56					12 56						13 56					14 56					
Folkestone West	d			11 58					12 58						13 58					14 58					
Ashford International	a			12 11		12 41			13 11			13 41			14 11		14 41			15 11			15 41		
	d			12 13		12 43			13 13			13 43			14 13		14 43			15 13			15 43		
Broadstairs	d		12 05					13 05						14 05					15 05						16 05
Margate 4	d		12a10					13a10						14a10					15a10						16a10
Birchington-on-Sea	d																								
Herne Bay	d																								
Whitstable	d																								
Faversham 2	a																								
	d	11 28			11 58		12 28			12 58			13 28			13 58		14 28			14 58			15 28	
Sittingbourne 4	d	11 37			12 07		12 37			13 07			13 37			14 07		14 37			15 07			15 37	
Rainham (Kent)	d	11 45			12 15		12 45			13 15			13 45			14 15		14 45			15 15			15 45	
Gillingham (Kent) 4	d	11 50			12 20		12 50			13 20			13 50			14 20		14 50			15 20			15 50	
Chatham 4	d	11 54			12 24		12 54			13 24			13 54			14 24		14 54			15 24			15 54	
Rochester 4	d	11 57			12 27		12 57			13 27			13 57			14 27		14 57			15 27			15 57	
Maidstone West	d																								
Strood 4	d	12 02			12 32		13 02			13 32			14 02			14 32		15 02			15 32			16 02	
Gravesend	d	12 13			12 43		13 13			13 43			14 13			14 43		15 13			15 43			16 13	
Ebbsfleet International	a	12 17		12 32	12 47	13 02	13 17		13 32	13 47		14 02	14 17		14 32	14 47	15 02	15 17		15 32	15 47		16 02	16 17	
	d	12 18		12 33	12 48	13 03	13 18		13 33	13 51		14 03	14 18		14 33	14 48	15 03	15 18		15 33	15 51		16 03	16 18	
Stratford International ⊖	a	12 29		12 44	12 59	13 14	13 29		13 44	14 01		14 14	14 28		14 44	14 59	15 14	15 29		15 44	16 02		16 14	16 29	
St Pancras International 4 ⊖	a	12 36		12 51	13 06	13 21	13 36		13 51	14 09		14 21	14 39		14 51	15 06	15 21	15 36		15 51	16 09		16 21	16 36	

		SE	SE	SE	SE	SE	SE	SE		SE	SE	SE	SE	SE	SE	SE	SE	SE	SE		SE	SE	SE	SE	SE
Margate 4	d			15 53						16 53						17 53							18 53		
Broadstairs	d			15 59						16 59						17 59							18 59		
Ramsgate 4	d			16 05						17 05						18 05							19 05		
Canterbury West	a			16 24						17 24						18 24							19 24		
	d			16 25		16 39				17 25		17 40			18 10	18 25		18 40			19 10		19 25		19 40
Sandwich	d																								
Deal	d																								
Dover Priory	d	15 44					16 44						17 44						18 44						
Folkestone Central	d	15 56					16 56						17 56						18 56						
Folkestone West	d	15 58					16 58						17 58						18 58						
Ashford International	a	16 11		16 41			17 11			17 41			18 11			18 41			19 11				19 41		
	d	16 13		16 43			17 13			17 43			18 13			18 43			19 13				19 43		
Broadstairs	d					17 05						18 05			18 35			19 05			19 36				20 05
Margate 4	d					17a10						18a10			18a40			19a10			19a41				20a10
Birchington-on-Sea	d																								
Herne Bay	d																								
Whitstable	d																								
Faversham 2	a																								
	d		15 58		16 28			16 58			17 28			17 58			18 28							19 28	
Sittingbourne 4	d		16 07		16 37			17 07			17 37			18 07			18 37							19 37	
Rainham (Kent)	d		16 15		16 45			17 15			17 45			18 15			18 45							19 45	
Gillingham (Kent) 4	d		16 20		16 50			17 20			17 50			18 20			18 50							19 50	
Chatham 4	d		16 24		16 54			17 24			17 54			18 24			18 54							19 54	
Rochester 4	d		16 27		16 57			17 27			17 57			18 27			18 57							19 57	
Maidstone West	d																					19 13			
Strood 4	d		16 32		17 02			17 32			18 02			18 32			19 02					19 32		20 02	
Gravesend	d		16 43		17 13			17 43			18 13			18 43			19 13					19 43		20 13	
Ebbsfleet International	a	16 32	16 47	17 02	17 17		17 32	17 47		18 02	18 17		18 32	18 47		19 02	19 17		19 32			19 47	20 02	20 17	
	d	16 33	16 51	17 03	17 18		17 33	17 48		18 03	18 18		18 33	18 51		19 03	19 18		19 35			19 50	20 03	20 18	
Stratford International ⊖	a	16 44	17 02	17 14	17 28		17 44	17 59		18 14	18 29		18 44	19 02		19 14	19 29		19 46			20 01	20 14	20 29	
St Pancras International 4 ⊖	a	16 51	17 09	17 21	17 36		17 51	18 06		18 21	18 36		18 51	19 09		19 21	19 36		19 53			20 08	20 21	20 36	

Table 194

Mondays to Fridays

Kent - St Pancras International High Speed Domestic Services

		SE	SE	SE	SE	SE		SE	SE	SE	SE	SE	SE	SE	SE	SE	SE		SE [1]	SE
Margate [4]	d				19 53						20 53					21 53				
Broadstairs	d				19 59						20 59					21 59				
Ramsgate [4]	d				20 05						21 05					22 05			22 24	
Canterbury West	a				20 24						21 24					22 24			22 46	
	d			20 12	20 25			20 39			21 25		21 39			22 25	22 39		22 47	
Sandwich	d																			
Deal	d																			
Dover Priory	d	19 44							20 44					21 44						22 44
Folkestone Central	d	19 56							20 56					21 56						22 56
Folkestone West	d	19 58							20 58					21 58						22 58
Ashford International	a	20 12			20 41				21 11		21 41			22 11		22 41			23 08	23 11
	d	20 13			20 43				21 13		21 43			22 13		22 43				23 13
Broadstairs	d			20 38				21 05					22 05				23 05			
Margate [4]	d			20a43				21a11					22a10				23a10			
Birchington-on-Sea	d																			
Herne Bay	d																			
Whitstable	d																			
Faversham [2]	a																			
	d		19 58			20 28				20 58		21 28			21 58					
Sittingbourne [4]	d		20 07			20 37				21 07		21 37			22 07					
Rainham (Kent)	d		20 15			20 45				21 15		21 45			22 15					
Gillingham (Kent) [4]	d		20 20			20 50				21 20		21 50			22 20					
Chatham [4]	d		20 24			20 54				21 24		21 54			22 24					
Rochester [4]	d		20 27			20 57				21 27		21 57			22 27					
Maidstone West	d																			
Strood [4]	d		20 32			21 02				21 32		22 02			22 32					
Gravesend	d		20 43			21 13				21 43		22 13			22 43					
Ebbsfleet International	a	20 32	20 47		21 02	21 17			21 32	21 47	22 02	22 17		22 32	22 47	23 02				23 32
	d	20 33	20 51		21 03	21 18			21 33	21 48	22 03	22 18		22 33	22 48	23 03				23 33
Stratford International ⊖	a	20 44	21 02		21 14	21 29			21 44	21 59	22 14	22 29		22 44	22 59	23 14				23 44
St Pancras International [4] ⊖	a	20 51	21 09		21 21	21 36			21 51	22 06	22 21	22 36		22 51	23 06	23 21				23 52

Saturdays

		SE	SE	SE	SE	SE	SE	SE	SE	SE	SE		SE	SE	SE	SE	SE	SE	SE	SE	SE	SE		SE	SE
Margate [4]	d						05 53				06 53						07 53					08 53			
Broadstairs	d						05 59				06 59						07 59					08 59			
Ramsgate [4]	d		05 05				06 05				07 05						08 05					09 05			
Canterbury West	a		05 24				06 24				07 24						08 24					09 24			
	d		05 25				06 25				07 25			07 39			08 25		08 39			09 25			09 39
Sandwich	d																								
Deal	d																								
Dover Priory	d				05 44				06 44						07 44					08 44					
Folkestone Central	d				05 56				06 56						07 56					08 56					
Folkestone West	d				05 58				06 58						07 58					08 58					
Ashford International	a		05 41		06 11		06 41		07 11		07 41				08 11		08 41			09 11		09 41			
	d	05 13	05 43		06 13		06 43		07 13		07 43				08 13		08 43			09 13		09 43			
Broadstairs	d													08 05					09 05						10 05
Margate [4]	d													08a10					09a10						10a10
Birchington-on-Sea	d																								
Herne Bay	d																								
Whitstable	d																								
Faversham [2]	a																								
	d			05 28		05 58		06 28		06 58			07 28			07 58		08 28			08 58			09 28	
Sittingbourne [4]	d			05 37		06 07		06 37		07 07			07 37			08 07		08 37			09 07			09 37	
Rainham (Kent)	d			05 45		06 15		06 45		07 15			07 45			08 15		08 45			09 15			09 45	
Gillingham (Kent) [4]	d			05 50		06 20		06 50		07 20			07 50			08 20		08 50			09 20			09 50	
Chatham [4]	d			05 54		06 24		06 54		07 24			07 54			08 24		08 54			09 24			09 54	
Rochester [4]	d			05 57		06 27		06 57		07 27			07 57			08 27		08 57			09 27			09 57	
Maidstone West	d																								
Strood [4]	d			06 02		06 32		07 02		07 32			08 02			08 32		09 02			09 32			10 02	
Gravesend	d			06 13		06 43		07 13		07 43			08 13			08 43		09 13			09 43			10 13	
Ebbsfleet International	a	05 32	06 02	06 17	06 32	06 47	07 02	07 17	07 32	07 47	08 02		08 17		08 32	08 47	09 02	09 17		09 32	09 47	10 02		10 17	
	d	05 33	06 03	06 18	06 33	06 48	07 03	07 18	07 33	07 48	08 03		08 18		08 33	08 48	09 03	09 18		09 33	09 48	10 03		10 18	
Stratford International ⊖	a	05 44	06 14	06 29	06 44	06 59	07 14	07 29	07 44	07 59	08 14		08 29		08 44	08 59	09 14	09 29		09 44	09 59	10 14		10 29	
St Pancras International [4] ⊖	a	05 51	06 21	06 36	06 51	07 06	07 21	07 36	07 51	08 06	08 21		08 36		08 51	09 06	09 21	09 36		09 51	10 06	10 21		10 36	

Table 194

Saturdays

Kent - St Pancras International High Speed Domestic Services

		SE	SE	SE	SE	SE	SE	SE	SE		SE	SE	SE	SE	SE	SE	SE	SE	SE	SE		SE	SE	SE	SE
Margate 4	d			09 53					10 53						11 53					12 53					
Broadstairs	d			09 59					10 59						11 59					12 59					
Ramsgate 4	d			10 05					11 05						12 05					13 05					
Canterbury West	a			10 24					11 24						12 24					13 24					
	d			10 25		10 39			11 25			11 39			12 25		12 39			13 25			13 39		
Sandwich	d																								
Deal	d																								
Dover Priory	d	09 44					10 44						11 44					12 44						13 44	
Folkestone Central	d	09 56					10 56						11 56					12 56						13 56	
Folkestone West	d	09 58					10 58						11 58					12 58						13 58	
Ashford International	a	10 11		10 41			11 11		11 41				12 11		12 41			13 11		13 41				14 11	
	d	10 13		10 43			11 13		11 43				12 13		12 43			13 13		13 43				14 13	
Broadstairs	d					11 05						12 05					13 05						14 05		
Margate 4	d					11a10						12a10					13a10						14a10		
Birchington-on-Sea	d																								
Herne Bay	d																								
Whitstable	d																								
Faversham 2	a																								
	d		09 58		10 28			10 58			11 28			11 58		12 28			12 58			13 28			13 58
Sittingbourne 4	d		10 07		10 37			11 07			11 37			12 07		12 37			13 07			13 37			14 07
Rainham (Kent)	d		10 15		10 45			11 15			11 45			12 15		12 45			13 15			13 45			14 15
Gillingham (Kent) 4	d		10 20		10 50			11 20			11 50			12 20		12 50			13 20			13 50			14 20
Chatham 4	d		10 24		10 54			11 24			11 54			12 24		12 54			13 24			13 54			14 24
Rochester 4	d		10 27		10 57			11 27			11 57			12 27		12 57			13 27			13 57			14 27
Maidstone West	d																								
Strood 4	d		10 32		11 02			11 32			12 02			12 32		13 02			13 32			14 02			14 32
Gravesend	d		10 43		11 13			11 43			12 13			12 43		13 13			13 43			14 13			14 43
Ebbsfleet International	a	10 32	10 47	11 02	11 17		11 32	11 47	12 02		12 17		12 32	12 47	13 02	13 17		13 32	13 47	14 02		14 17		14 32	14 47
	d	10 33	10 48	11 03	11 18		11 33	11 48	12 03		12 18		12 33	12 48	13 03	13 18		13 33	13 48	14 03		14 18		14 33	14 51
Stratford International ⊖	a	10 44	10 59	11 14	11 29		11 44	11 59	12 14		12 29		12 44	12 59	13 14	13 29		13 44	13 59	14 14		14 29		14 44	15 02
St Pancras International 4 ⊖	a	10 51	11 06	11 21	11 36		11 51	12 06	12 21		12 36		12 51	13 06	13 21	13 36		13 51	14 06	14 21		14 36		14 51	15 09

		SE	SE	SE	SE	SE	SE		SE	SE	SE	SE	SE	SE	SE	SE	SE	SE		SE	SE	SE	SE	SE	SE
Margate 4	d	13 53					14 53						15 53					16 53						17 53	
Broadstairs	d	13 59					14 59						15 59					16 59						17 59	
Ramsgate 4	d	14 05					15 05						16 05					17 05						18 05	
Canterbury West	a	14 24					15 24						16 24					17 24						18 24	
	d	14 25		14 39			15 25			15 39			16 25		16 39			17 25			17 39			18 25	
Sandwich	d																								
Deal	d																								
Dover Priory	d				14 44						15 44					16 44						17 44			
Folkestone Central	d				14 56						15 56					16 56						17 56			
Folkestone West	d				14 58						15 58					16 58						17 58			
Ashford International	a	14 41			15 11		15 41				16 11		16 41			17 11		17 41				18 11		18 41	
	d	14 43			15 13		15 46				16 13		16 43			17 13		17 43				18 13		18 43	
Broadstairs	d			15 05						16 05					17 05						18 05				
Margate 4	d			15a10						16a10					17a10						18a10				
Birchington-on-Sea	d																								
Herne Bay	d																								
Whitstable	d																								
Faversham 2	a																								
	d		14 28			14 58			15 28			15 58		16 28			16 58			17 28			17 58		18 28
Sittingbourne 4	d		14 37			15 07			15 37			16 07		16 37			17 07			17 37			18 07		18 37
Rainham (Kent)	d		14 45			15 15			15 45			16 15		16 45			17 15			17 45			18 15		18 45
Gillingham (Kent) 4	d		14 50			15 20			15 50			16 20		16 50			17 20			17 50			18 20		18 50
Chatham 4	d		14 54			15 24			15 54			16 24		16 54			17 24			17 54			18 24		18 54
Rochester 4	d		14 57			15 27			15 57			16 27		16 57			17 27			17 57			18 27		18 57
Maidstone West	d																								
Strood 4	d		15 02			15 32			16 02			16 32		17 02			17 32			18 02			18 32		19 02
Gravesend	d		15 13			15 43			16 13			16 43		17 13			17 43			18 13			18 43		19 12
Ebbsfleet International	a	15 02	15 17		15 32	15 47	16 05		16 17		16 32	16 47	17 02	17 17		17 32	17 47	18 02		18 17		18 32	18 47	19 02	19 16
	d	15 03	15 18		15 33	15 51	16 06		16 18		16 33	16 51	17 03	17 18		17 33	17 48	18 03		18 18		18 33	18 51	19 03	19 17
Stratford International ⊖	a	15 14	15 29		15 44	16 02	16 17		16 29		16 44	17 02	17 14	17 29		17 44	17 59	18 14		18 29		18 44	19 02	19 14	19 27
St Pancras International 4 ⊖	a	15 21	15 36		15 51	16 09	16 24		16 36		16 51	17 09	17 21	17 36		17 51	18 09	18 21		18 36		18 51	19 09	19 21	19 38

Table 194

Saturdays

Kent - St Pancras International High Speed Domestic Services

		SE	SE	SE	SE		SE	SE	SE	SE	SE	SE	SE	SE	SE	SE		SE	SE	SE	SE	SE	SE	SE [1]	SE
Margate [4]	d				18 53						19 53					20 53						21 53			
Broadstairs	d				18 59						19 59					20 59						21 59			
Ramsgate [4]	d				19 05						20 05					21 05						22 05		22 24	
Canterbury West	a				19 24						20 24					21 24						22 24		22 46	
	d	18 39			19 25			19 39			20 25		20 39			21 25			21 39			22 25	22 39	22 47	
Sandwich	d																								
Deal	d																								
Dover Priory	d		18 44						19 44					20 44						21 44					22 44
Folkestone Central	d		18 56						19 56					20 56						21 56					22 56
Folkestone West	d		18 58						19 58					20 58						21 58					22 58
Ashford International	a		19 11		19 41				20 11		20 41			21 11		21 41				22 11		22 41		23 08	23 11
	d		19 13		19 43				20 13		20 43			21 13		21 43				22 13		22 43			23 13
Broadstairs	d	19 05						20 05					21 05						22 05				23 05		
Margate [4]	d	19a10						20a10					21a10						22a10				23a10		
Birchington-on-Sea	d																								
Herne Bay	d																								
Whitstable	d																								
Faversham [2]	a																								
	d			18 58			19 28			19 58		20 28			20 58			21 28			21 58				
Sittingbourne [4]	d			19 07			19 37			20 07		20 37			21 07			21 37			22 07				
Rainham (Kent)	d			19 15			19 45			20 15		20 45			21 15			21 45			22 15				
Gillingham (Kent) [4]	d			19 20			19 50			20 20		20 50			21 20			21 50			22 20				
Chatham [4]	d			19 24			19 54			20 24		20 54			21 24			21 54			22 24				
Rochester [4]	d			19 27			19 57			20 27		20 57			21 27			21 57			22 27				
Maidstone West	d																								
Strood [4]	d			19 32			20 02			20 32		21 02			21 32			22 02			22 32				
Gravesend	d			19 43			20 13			20 43		21 13			21 43			22 13			22 43				
Ebbsfleet International	a		19 32	19 47	20 02		20 17		20 32	20 47	21 02	21 17		21 32	21 47	22 02		22 17		22 32	22 47	23 02			23 32
	d		19 35	19 48	20 03		20 18		20 33	20 51	21 03	21 18		21 33	21 48	22 03		22 18		22 33	22 48	23 03			23 33
Stratford International ⊖	a		19 46	19 59	20 14		20 29		20 44	21 02	21 14	21 29		21 44	21 59	22 14		22 29		22 44	22 59	23 14			23 44
St Pancras International [4] ⊖	a		19 53	20 06	20 21		20 36		20 51	21 09	21 21	21 36		21 51	22 06	22 21		22 36		22 51	23 06	23 21			23 51

Sundays

		SE	SE	SE	SE	SE	SE	SE	SE	SE	SE		SE	SE	SE	SE	SE	SE	SE	SE	SE	SE		SE	SE
Margate [4]	d						07 53				08 53						09 53					10 53			
Broadstairs	d						07 59				08 59						09 59					10 59			
Ramsgate [4]	d						08 05				09 05						10 05					11 05			
Canterbury West	a						08 24				09 24						10 24					11 24			
	d						08 25				09 25			09 39			10 25		10 39			11 25			11 39
Sandwich	d																								
Deal	d																								
Dover Priory	d				07 44				08 44						09 44					10 44					
Folkestone Central	d				07 56				08 56						09 56					10 56					
Folkestone West	d				07 58				08 58						09 58					10 58					
Ashford International	a				08 11		08 41		09 11		09 41				10 11		10 41			11 11		11 41			
	d		07 43		08 13		08 43		09 13		09 43				10 13		10 43			11 13		11 43			
Broadstairs	d													10 05					11 05						12 05
Margate [4]	d													10a10					11a10						12a10
Birchington-on-Sea	d																								
Herne Bay	d																								
Whitstable	d																								
Faversham [2]	a																								
	d	06 58		07 28		07 58		08 28		08 58			09 28			09 58		10 28			10 58			11 28	
Sittingbourne [4]	d	07 07		07 37		08 07		08 37		09 07			09 37			10 07		10 37			11 07			11 37	
Rainham (Kent)	d	07 15		07 45		08 15		08 45		09 15			09 45			10 15		10 45			11 15			11 45	
Gillingham (Kent) [4]	d	07 20		07 50		08 20		08 50		09 20			09 50			10 20		10 50			11 20			11 50	
Chatham [4]	d	07 24		07 54		08 24		08 54		09 24			09 54			10 24		10 54			11 24			11 54	
Rochester [4]	d	07 27		07 57		08 27		08 57		09 27			09 57			10 27		10 57			11 27			11 57	
Maidstone West	d																								
Strood [4]	d	07 32		08 02		08 32		09 02		09 32			10 02			10 32		11 02			11 32			12 02	
Gravesend	d	07 43		08 13		08 43		09 13		09 43			10 13			10 43		11 13			11 43			12 13	
Ebbsfleet International	a	07 47	08 02	08 17	08 32	08 47	09 02	09 17	09 32	09 47	10 02		10 17		10 32	10 47	11 02	11 17		11 32	11 47	12 02		12 17	
	d	07 48	08 03	08 18	08 33	08 48	09 03	09 18	09 33	09 48	10 03		10 18		10 33	10 48	11 03	11 18		11 33	11 48	12 03		12 18	
Stratford International ⊖	a	07 59	08 14	08 29	08 44	08 59	09 14	09 29	09 44	09 59	10 14		10 29		10 44	10 59	11 14	11 29		11 44	11 59	12 14		12 29	
St Pancras International [4] ⊖	a	08 06	08 21	08 36	08 51	09 06	09 21	09 36	09 51	10 06	10 21		10 36		10 51	11 06	11 21	11 36		11 51	12 06	12 21		12 36	

Kent - St Pancras International High Speed Domestic Services

		SE	SE	SE	SE	SE	SE	SE	SE		SE	SE	SE	SE	SE	SE	SE	SE	SE	SE		SE	SE	SE	SE
Margate 4	d			11 53					12 53						13 53					14 53					
Broadstairs	d			11 59					12 59						13 59					14 59					
Ramsgate 4	d			12 05					13 05						14 05					15 05					
Canterbury West	a			12 24					13 24						14 24					15 24					
	d			12 25		12 39			13 25			13 39			14 25		14 39			15 25			15 39		
Sandwich	d																								
Deal	d																								
Dover Priory	d	11 44					12 44						13 44					14 44						15 44	
Folkestone Central	d	11 56					12 56						13 56					14 56						15 56	
Folkestone West	d	11 58					12 58						13 58					14 58						15 58	
Ashford International	a	12 11		12 41			13 11		13 41				14 11		14 41			15 11		15 41				16 11	
	d	12 13		12 43			13 13		13 43				14 13		14 43			15 13		15 43				16 13	
Broadstairs	d					13 05						14 05					15 05						16 05		
Margate 4	d					13a10						14a10					15a10						16a10		
Birchington-on-Sea	d																								
Herne Bay	d																								
Whitstable	d																								
Faversham 2	a																								
	d		11 58		12 28			12 58			13 28			13 58		14 28			14 58			15 28			15 58
Sittingbourne 4	d		12 07		12 37			13 07			13 37			14 07		14 37			15 07			15 37			16 07
Rainham (Kent)	d		12 15		12 45			13 15			13 45			14 15		14 45			15 15			15 45			16 15
Gillingham (Kent) 4	d		12 20		12 50			13 20			13 50			14 20		14 50			15 20			15 50			16 20
Chatham 4	d		12 24		12 54			13 24			13 54			14 24		14 54			15 24			15 54			16 24
Rochester 4	d		12 27		12 57			13 27			13 57			14 27		14 57			15 27			15 57			16 27
Maidstone West	d																								
Strood 4	d		12 32		13 02			13 32			14 02			14 32		15 02			15 32			16 02			16 32
Gravesend	d		12 43		13 13			13 43			14 13			14 43		15 13			15 43			16 13			16 43
Ebbsfleet International	a	12 32	12 47	13 02	13 17		13 32	13 47	14 02		14 17		14 32	14 47	15 02	15 17		15 32	15 47	16 02		16 17		16 32	16 47
	d	12 33	12 48	13 03	13 18		13 33	13 51	14 03		14 18		14 33	14 48	15 03	15 18		15 33	15 51	16 03		16 18		16 33	16 51
Stratford International ⊖	a	12 44	12 59	13 14	13 29		13 44	14 02	14 14		14 29		14 44	14 59	15 14	15 29		15 44	16 02	16 14		16 29		16 44	17 02
St Pancras International 4 ⊖	a	12 51	13 06	13 21	13 36		13 51	14 09	14 21		14 36		14 51	15 06	15 21	15 36		15 51	16 09	16 21		16 36		16 51	17 09

		SE	SE	SE	SE	SE	SE		SE	SE	SE	SE	SE	SE	SE	SE	SE	SE		SE	SE	SE	SE	SE	SE
Margate 4	d	15 53					16 53						17 53					18 53						19 53	
Broadstairs	d	15 59					16 59						17 59					18 59						19 59	
Ramsgate 4	d	16 05					17 05						18 05					19 05						20 05	
Canterbury West	a	16 24					17 24						18 24					19 24						20 24	
	d	16 25		16 39			17 25			17 39			18 25		18 39			19 25			19 39			20 25	
Sandwich	d																								
Deal	d																								
Dover Priory	d				16 44						17 44					18 44						19 44			
Folkestone Central	d				16 56						17 56					18 56						19 56			
Folkestone West	d				16 58						17 58					18 58						19 58			
Ashford International	a	16 41			17 11		17 41				18 11		18 41			19 11		19 41				20 11		20 41	
	d	16 43			17 13		17 43				18 13		18 43			19 13		19 43				20 13		20 43	
Broadstairs	d			17 05						18 05					19 05						20 05				
Margate 4	d			17a10						18a10					19a10						20a10				
Birchington-on-Sea	d																								
Herne Bay	d																								
Whitstable	d																								
Faversham 2	a																								
	d		16 28			16 58			17 28			17 58		18 28			18 58			19 28			19 58		20 28
Sittingbourne 4	d		16 37			17 07			17 37			18 07		18 37			19 07			19 37			20 07		20 37
Rainham (Kent)	d		16 45			17 15			17 45			18 15		18 45			19 15			19 45			20 15		20 45
Gillingham (Kent) 4	d		16 50			17 20			17 50			18 20		18 50			19 20			19 50			20 20		20 50
Chatham 4	d		16 54			17 24			17 54			18 24		18 54			19 24			19 54			20 24		20 54
Rochester 4	d		16 57			17 27			17 57			18 27		18 57			19 27			19 57			20 27		20 57
Maidstone West	d																								
Strood 4	d		17 02			17 32			18 02			18 32		19 02			19 32			20 02			20 32		21 02
Gravesend	d		17 13			17 43			18 13			18 43		19 13			19 43			20 13			20 43		21 13
Ebbsfleet International	a	17 02	17 17		17 32	17 47	18 02		18 17		18 32	18 47	19 02	19 17		19 32	19 47	20 02		20 17		20 32	20 47	21 02	21 17
	d	17 03	17 18		17 33	17 48	18 03		18 18		18 33	18 48	19 03	19 18		19 33	19 48	20 03		20 18		20 33	20 51	21 03	21 18
Stratford International ⊖	a	17 14	17 29		17 44	17 59	18 14		18 29		18 44	18 59	19 14	19 29		19 44	19 59	20 14		20 29		20 44	21 02	21 14	21 29
St Pancras International 4 ⊖	a	17 21	17 36		17 51	18 09	18 21		18 36		18 51	19 06	19 21	19 36		19 51	20 06	20 21		20 36		20 51	21 09	21 21	21 36

Table 194

Sundays

Kent - St Pancras International
High Speed Domestic Services

		SE	SE	SE	SE	SE	SE	SE	SE	SE	SE	SE
									[1]			
Margate [4]	d				20 53						21 53	
Broadstairs	d				20 59						21 59	
Ramsgate [4]	d				21 05				21 40		22 05	
Canterbury West	a				21 24				22 02		22 24	
	d	20 39			21 25		21 39		22 04		22 25	22 39
Sandwich	d											
Deal	d											
Dover Priory	d		20 44					21 44				
Folkestone Central	d		20 56					21 56				
Folkestone West	d		20 58					21 58				
Ashford International	a		21 11		21 41			22 11	22 25		22 41	
	d		21 13		21 43			22 13			22 43	
Broadstairs	d	21 05					22 05					23 05
Margate [4]	d	21a10					22a10					23a10
Birchington-on-Sea	d											
Herne Bay	d											
Whitstable	d											
Faversham [2]	a											
	d			20 58		21 28				21 58		
Sittingbourne [4]	d			21 07		21 37				22 07		
Rainham (Kent)	d			21 15		21 45				22 15		
Gillingham (Kent) [4]	d			21 20		21 50				22 20		
Chatham [4]	d			21 24		21 54				22 24		
Rochester [4]	d			21 27		21 57				22 27		
Maidstone West	d											
Strood [4]	d			21 32		22 02				22 32		
Gravesend	d			21 43		22 13				22 43		
Ebbsfleet International	a		21 32	21 47	22 02	22 17		22 32		22 47	23 02	
	d		21 33	21 48	22 03	22 18		22 33		22 48	23 03	
Stratford International ⊖	a		21 44	21 59	22 14	22 29		22 44		22 59	23 14	
St Pancras International [4] ⊖	a		21 51	22 06	22 21	22 36		22 51		23 06	23 21	

Network Diagram for Tables 195, 196 — also 199 ⊙

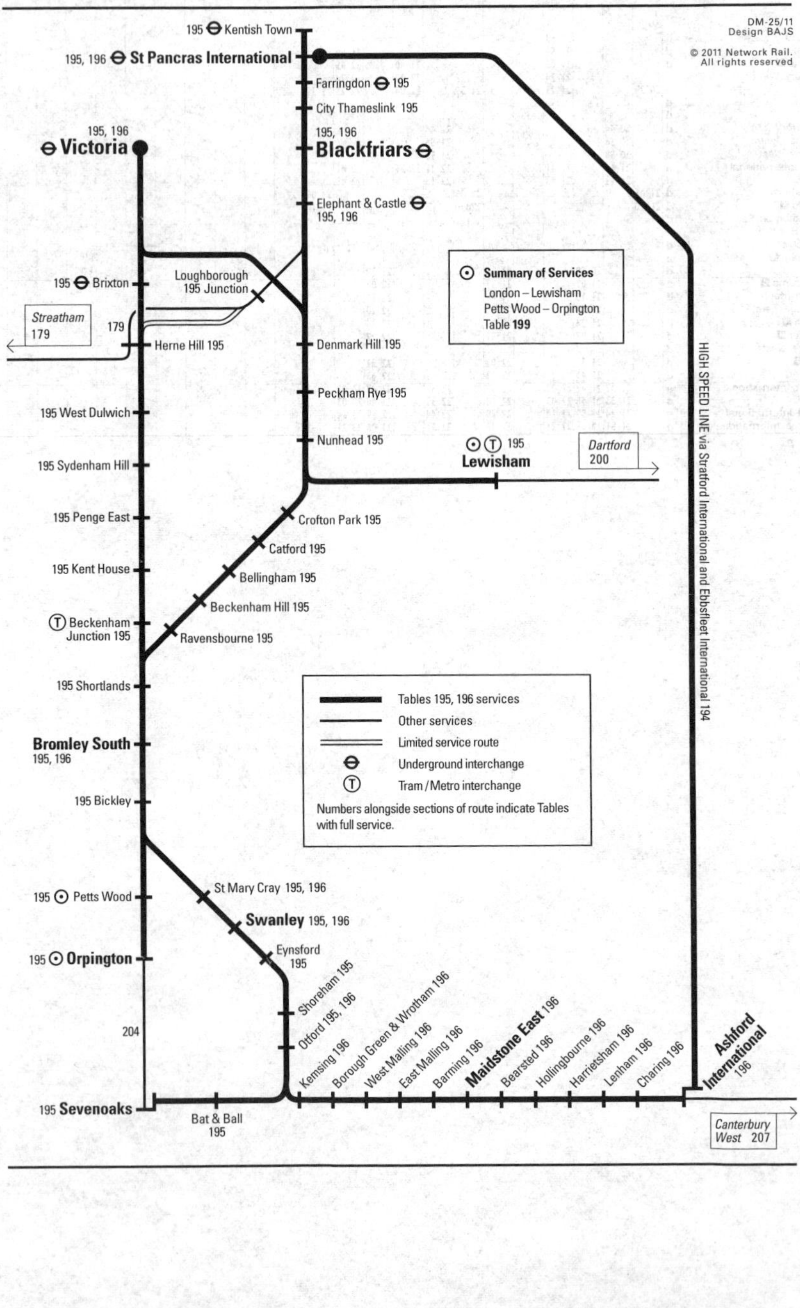

London - Catford, Beckenham Junction, Bromley South, Orpington, Otford and Sevenoaks

Network Diagram - see first Page of Table 195

Miles	Miles	Miles			SE MX	SE MO 1	SE MX 1	SE MX	SE MX 1	SE	SE 1	SE	FC		SE	FC	SE 1	SE	SE 1	SE	SE 1	FC	FC		SE
0	—	0	**London Victoria 15** ⊖	d	23p43	23p45	23p52	23p55	00 07	00 35	05 22				05 40		05 52		06 07	06 10	06 22				06 30
3¼	—	—	Brixton ⊖	d				00 02							05 47					06 17					06 37
—	—	—	Kentish Town ⊖	d												05 50						05 54	06 08		
—	—	—	St Pancras International 15 ⊖	d									05 36			05 54						05 58	06 12		
—	—	—	Farringdon ⊖	d									05 42			06 00						06 04	06 18		
—	—	—	City Thameslink 3	d								05 26	05 44			06 03						06 07	06 21		
—	0	—	**London Blackfriars 3** ⊖	d								05 28	05 47			06 06						06 10	06 24		
—	1¼	—	Elephant & Castle ⊖	d								05 32	05 50			06 09						06 16	06 27		
—	—	—	Loughborough Jn	d												06 13							06 31		
4	—	—	Herne Hill 4	d				00 04		00 43			05a57		05 49	06a17				06 19			06a35		06 39
5	—	—	West Dulwich	d				00 06							05 51					06 21					06 41
5¾	—	—	Sydenham Hill	d				00 08							05 53					06 23					06 43
7¼	—	—	Penge East	d				00 11		00 48					05 56					06 26					06 46
7¾	—	—	Kent House 4	d				00 13							05 58					06 28					06 48
8¾	—	—	**Beckenham Junction 4**	d				00 15		00 50					06 00					06 30					06 50
—	3¾	4¼	Denmark Hill 4	d	23p52							05 39										06 22			
—	4½	5	Peckham Rye 4	d	23p55							05 41										06 25			
—	5¼	5¾	Nunhead 4	d	23p57							05 44										06 27			
—	—	7½	Lewisham 4	a																					
—	6½	—	Crofton Park	d	23p59							05 47										06 30			
—	7½	—	Catford	d	00 03							05 49										06 33			
—	8¼	—	Bellingham	d	00 05							05 52										06 35			
—	9	—	Beckenham Hill	d	00 07							05 54										06 37			
—	9¾	—	Ravensbourne	d	00 09							05 56										06 39			
10	10½	—	Shortlands 4	d	00 11			00 18				05 58			06 03					06 33		06 41			06 54
11	11½	—	**Bromley South 4**	d	00 14	00 02	00 09	00 21	00 25	00 55	05 39	06 01			06 06		06 09	06 16	06 23	06 37	06 39	06 44			06 57
12	12½	—	Bickley 4	d	00 17			00 24				06 03			06 09			06 18		06 39		06 47			07 00
13¾	—	—	Petts Wood 4	d	00 21			00 29							06 14					06 44					07 04
15	—	—	**Orpington 4**	d	00a25			00a32							06a18					06a49					07a08
—	14¾	—	St Mary Cray	d		00 08	00 15		00 31	01 01	05 45	06 08						06 23	06 30		06 45	06 51			
—	17½	—	**Swanley 4**	d		00a12	00a19		00 36	01a05	05a49	06 12					06a19	06 28	06 34		06a49	06 56			
—	20½	—	Eynsford	d					00 40			06 17						06 32				07 00			
—	22¾	—	Shoreham (Kent)	d					00 44			06 20						06 36				07 04			
—	24	—	Otford 4	d					00a47			06 23						06 39	06a42			07 07			
—	25¾	—	Bat & Ball	d								06 26						06 42				07 10			
—	27	—	**Sevenoaks 4**	a								06 29						06 45				07 14			

		SE 1	SE 1	SE	FC	SE	SE 1	SE 1	FC 1		FC	FC 1	SE	SE 1	SE	SE 1	FC	FC 1	FC		FC	SE	SE	SE 1	SE
London Victoria 15 ⊖	d	06 37	06 45			06 50	06 58	07 07					07 10	07 22	07 25	07 36						07 40	07 43	07 52	07 55
Brixton ⊖	d					06 57							07 17		07 32							07 47			08 02
Kentish Town ⊖	d				06 30						06 48						07 08		07 24						
St Pancras International 15 ⊖	d				06 34				06 44		06 52	07 04					07 12	07 16	07 28		07 32				
Farringdon ⊖	d				06 40				06 50		06 58	07 10					07 18	07 22	07 34		07 38				
City Thameslink 3	d			06 39	06 43				06 53		07 01	07 13					07 21	07 25	07 37		07 41				
London Blackfriars 3 ⊖	d			06 42	06 46				06 58		07 04	07 16					07 24	07 28	07 40		07 44				
Elephant & Castle ⊖	d			06 46	06 49				07 02		07 07	07 19					07 28	07 33	07 44		07 47				
Loughborough Jn	d				06 53						07 11	07 23						07 37			07 51				
Herne Hill 4	d				06a57	06 59					07a15	07a27	07 19		07 34			07a40			07a55	07 49			08 04
West Dulwich	d					07 02							07 21		07 36							07 51			08 06
Sydenham Hill	d					07 04							07 23		07 38							07 53			08 08
Penge East	d					07 07							07 26		07 41							07 56			08 11
Kent House 4	d					07 09							07 28		07 43							07 58			08 13
Beckenham Junction 4	d					07 11							07 30		07 45							08 00			08 15
Denmark Hill 4	d			06 52					07 09								07 34		07 50				07 53		
Peckham Rye 4	d			06 55					07 12								07 36		07 53				07 56		
Nunhead 4	d			06 57					07 14								07 39		07 56				07 59		
Lewisham 4	a																						08 07		
Crofton Park	d			07 00					07 17								07 42								
Catford	d			07 03					07 20								07 44		08 00						
Bellingham	d			07 05					07 22								07 47		08 02						
Beckenham Hill	d			07 07					07 24								07 49								
Ravensbourne	d			07 09					07 26								07 51								
Shortlands 4	d			07 11		07 14			07 28				07 33		07 48		07 54					08 03			
Bromley South 4	d	06 58	07 02	07 14		07 17	07 19	07 23	07 31				07 38	07 40	07 51	07 53	07 57		08a10			08 06		08a09	08 22
Bickley 4	d			07 17		07 20			07 34				07 40		07 54		08 00					08 09			08 24
Petts Wood 4	d					07 24							07 49		07 59							08 14			08 29
Orpington 4	d					07a28							07a53		08a02							08a19			08a32
St Mary Cray	d	07 04	07 08	07 21			07 25	07 30	07 38							08 00	08 04								
Swanley 4	d	07 08	07a12	07 26			07a29	07 34	07 44					07a48		08 04	08 10								
Eynsford	d			07 30					07 48								08 15								
Shoreham (Kent)	d			07 34					07 52								08 18								
Otford 4	d	07a16		07 37				07a42	07 55							08a12	08 21								
Bat & Ball	d			07 40					07 58								08 24								
Sevenoaks 4	a			07 43					08 01								08 27								

London - Catford, Beckenham Junction, Bromley South, Orpington, Otford and Sevenoaks

Network Diagram - see first Page of Table 195

		SE 1	SE 1	FC	FC		FC	SE	SE	FC	SE 1	SE	SE 1	FC 1	FC 1		SE	SE	FC	FC 1	FC	FC	FC	SE 1	SE
London Victoria 15	⊖ d	07 58	08 07					08 09	08 10		08 22	08 25	08 37				08 39	08 40						08 52	08 55
Brixton	⊖ d								08 17			08 32						08 47							09 02
Kentish Town	⊖ d				07 44										08 20						08 36		08 52		
St Pancras International 15	⊖ d			07 38	07 48		07 52			08 12				08 16	08 24				08 28	08 32	08 40	08 44	08 56		
Farringdon	⊖ d			07 44	07 54		07 58			08 18				08 22	08 30				08 34	08 38	08 46	08 50	09 02		
City Thameslink 3	d			07 47	07 57		08 01			08 21				08 25	08 33				08 37	08 41	08 49	08 53	09 05		
London Blackfriars 3	⊖ d			07 50	08 00		08 04			08 24				08 28	08 36				08 40	08 44	08 52	08 56	09 08		
Elephant & Castle	⊖ d			07 54	08 04		08 07			08 27				08 32					08 44	08 47	08 56	09 00	09 12		
Loughborough Jn.	d						08 11			08 31										08 51		09 04	09 16		
Herne Hill 4	d						08a15		08 19	08a36		08 34			08a45			08 48		08a57		09a08	09a21		09 04
West Dulwich	d								08 21			08 36						08 51							09 06
Sydenham Hill	d								08 23			08 38						08 53							09 08
Penge East	d								08 26			08 41						08 56							09 11
Kent House 4	d								08 28			08 43						08 58							09 13
Beckenham Junction 4	d								08 30			08 45						09 00							09 15
Denmark Hill 4	d			08 00	08 10			08 18						08 38			08 48		08 52		09 02				
Peckham Rye 4	d			08 03	08 13			08 21						08 41			08 51		08 55						
Nunhead 4	d			08 06	08 15			08 23						08 43			08 53		08 57						
Lewisham 4	a							08 30									09 01								
Crofton Park	d			08 09	08 18									08 46					09 00						
Catford	d			08 12	08 21									08 49					09 03		09 09				
Bellingham	d			08 15	08 23									08 51					09 05						
Beckenham Hill	d			08 17	08 25									08 53					09 07						
Ravensbourne	d			08 19	08 27									08 55					09 09						
Shortlands 4	d			08 22	08 30				08 33			08 48		08 57				09 03	09 11						09 18
Bromley South 4	d	08 28	08 24	08 25	08 33				08 36		08a39	08 51	08 53	09 00				09 07	09 14		09 18			09a08	09 21
Bickley 4	d			08 28	08 35				08 39			08 54		09 03				09 09	09 17		09 20				09 24
Petts Wood 4	d			08 32					08 44			08 59						09 14							09 29
Orpington 4	d			08a35					08a47			09a02						09a17							09a33
St Mary Cray	d	08 34	08 31		08 40								09 00	09 07					09 21		09 25				
Swanley 4	d	08a39	08 35		08 44								09 04	09 12					09 26		0936				
Eynsford	d				08 49									09 16					09 30		09 40				
Shoreham (Kent)	d				08 52									09 20					09 34		09 44				
Otford 4	d		08a43		08 55								09a12	09 23					09 37		09 47				
Bat & Ball	d				08 58									09 26					09 40		09 50				
Sevenoaks 4	a				09 01									09 29					09 45		09 53				

			SE 1	SE 1	SE	SE	FC	FC	SE 1	SE	SE 1		SE	SE	FC	FC	FC	SE 1	SE	SE 1	SE 1		SE	SE	FC
London Victoria 15	⊖ d		08 58	09 07	09 09	09 10			09 22	09 25	09 37		09 39	09 40				09 52	09 55	09 58	10 07		10 09	10 10	
Brixton	⊖ d					09 17				09 32				09 47					10 02					10 17	
Kentish Town	⊖ d							09 12							09 26		09 44								09 54
St Pancras International 15	⊖ d						09 00	09 16							09 30	09 34	09 48								10 00
Farringdon	⊖ d						09 06	09 22							09 36	09 40	09 53								10 05
City Thameslink 3	d						09 09	09 25							09 39	09 43	09 57								10 09
London Blackfriars 3	⊖ d						09 12	09 28							09 42	09 46	10 00								10 12
Elephant & Castle	⊖ d						09 16	09 31							09 46	09 49	10 03								10 16
Loughborough Jn.	d							09 35								09 53	10 07								
Herne Hill 4	d					09 19		09a39		09 34				09 49		09a57	10a11		10 04					10 19	
West Dulwich	d					09 21				09 36				09 51					10 06					10 21	
Sydenham Hill	d					09 23				09 38				09 53					10 08					10 23	
Penge East	d					09 26				09 41				09 56					10 11					10 26	
Kent House 4	d					09 28				09 43				09 58					10 13					10 28	
Beckenham Junction 4	d					09 30				09 45				10 00					10 15					10 30	
Denmark Hill 4	d				09 18		09 22						09 48		09 52								10 18		10 22
Peckham Rye 4	d				09 21		09 25						09 51		09 55								10 21		10 25
Nunhead 4	d				09 23		09 27						09 53		09 57								10 23		10 27
Lewisham 4	a				09 31								10 01										10 31		
Crofton Park	d						09 30								10 00										10 30
Catford	d						09 33								10 03										10 33
Bellingham	d						09 35								10 05										10 35
Beckenham Hill	d						09 37								10 07										10 37
Ravensbourne	d						09 39								10 09										10 39
Shortlands 4	d					09 33	09 41			09 48				10 03	10 11				10 18					10 33	10 41
Bromley South 4	d		09 19	09 23		09 36	09 44		09a38	09 52	09 53			10 07	10 14			10a08	10 21	10 19	10 23			10 36	10 44
Bickley 4	d					09 39	09 47			09 54				10 09	10 17				10 24					10 39	10 47
Petts Wood 4	d					09 44				09 59				10 14					10 29					10 44	
Orpington 4	d					09a47				10a02				10a17					10a32					10a47	
St Mary Cray	d		09 25				09 51				10 00				10 21					10 25					10 51
Swanley 4	d		09a29	09 33			09 56				10 04				10 26					10a29	10 33				10 56
Eynsford	d						10 00								10 30										11 00
Shoreham (Kent)	d						10 04								10 34										11 04
Otford 4	d			09a41			10 07				10a12				10 37						10a41				11 07
Bat & Ball	d						10 10								10 40										11 10
Sevenoaks 4	a						10 13								10 43										11 13

London - Catford, Beckenham Junction, Bromley South, Orpington, Otford and Sevenoaks

Network Diagram - see first Page of Table 195

Station		FC	FC	SE 1	SE	SE 1	SE		SE	FC	FC	FC	SE 1	SE	SE 1	SE 1	SE		SE	FC	FC	FC	SE 1	SE	SE 1
London Victoria 15 ⊖	d			10 22	10 25	10 37	10 39		10 40				10 52	10 55	10 58	11 07	11 09		11 10				11 22	11 25	11 37
Brixton ⊖	d				10 32				10 47					11 02					11 17					11 32	
Kentish Town ⊖	d	10 00	10 14							10 26	10 30	10 44								10 56	11 00	11 14			
St Pancras International 15 ⊖	d	10 04	10 18							10 30	10 34	10 48								11 00	11 04	11 18			
Farringdon ⊖	d	10 09	10 24							10 35	10 39	10 54								11 05	11 09	11 24			
City Thameslink 3	d	10 13	10 27							10 39	10 43	10 57								11 09	11 13	11 27			
London Blackfriars 3 ⊖	d	10 16	10 30							10 42	10 46	11 00								11 12	11 16	11 30			
Elephant & Castle ⊖	d	10 19	10 33							10 46	10 49	11 03								11 16	11 19	11 33			
Loughborough Jn	d	10 23	10 37								10 53	11 07									11 23	11 37			
Herne Hill 4	d	10a27	10a41		10 34				10 49		10a57	11a11		11 04					11 19		11a27	11a41		11 34	
West Dulwich	d				10 36				10 51					11 06					11 21					11 36	
Sydenham Hill	d				10 38				10 53					11 08					11 23					11 38	
Penge East	d				10 41				10 56					11 11					11 26					11 41	
Kent House 4	d				10 43				10 58					11 13					11 28					11 43	
Beckenham Junction 4	d				10 45				11 00					11 15					11 30					11 45	
Denmark Hill 4	d						10 48			10 52							11 18			11 22					
Peckham Rye 4	d						10 51			10 55							11 21			11 25					
Nunhead 4	d						10 53			10 57							11 23			11 27					
Lewisham 4	a						11 01										11 31								
Crofton Park	d									11 00										11 30					
Catford	d									11 03										11 33					
Bellingham	d									11 05										11 35					
Beckenham Hill	d									11 07										11 37					
Ravensbourne	d									11 09										11 39					
Shortlands 4	d				10 48				11 03	11 11				11 18					11 33	11 41				11 48	
Bromley South 4	d			10a38	10 51	10 53			11 06	11 14			11a08	11 21	11 19	11 23			11 36	11 44			11a38	11 51	11 53
Bickley 4	d				10 54				11 09	11 17				11 24					11 39	11 47				11 54	
Petts Wood 4	d				10 59				11 14					11 29					11 44					11 59	
Orpington 4	d				11a02				11a17					11a32					11a47					12a02	
St Mary Cray	d					11 00				11 21					11 25					11 51					12 00
Swanley 4	d					11 04				11 26					11a29	11 33				11 56					12 04
Eynsford	d									11 30										12 00					
Shoreham (Kent)	d									11 34										12 04					
Otford 4	d					11a12				11 37						11a41				12 07					12a12
Bat & Ball	d									11 40										12 10					
Sevenoaks 4	a									11 43										12 13					

Station		SE	SE		FC	FC	FC	SE 1	SE	SE 1	SE 1	SE	SE		FC	FC	FC		FC	SE 1	SE	SE 1		SE
London Victoria 15 ⊖	d	11 39	11 40					11 52	11 55	11 58	12 07	12 09	12 10							15 22	15 25	15 37		15 39
Brixton ⊖	d		11 47						12 02				12 17								15 32			
Kentish Town ⊖	d				11 26	11 30	11 44								11 56	12 00	12 14		15 14					
St Pancras International 15 ⊖	d				11 30	11 34	11 48								12 00	12 04	12 18		15 18					
Farringdon ⊖	d				11 35	11 39	11 53								12 05	12 09	12 23		15 23					
City Thameslink 3	d				11 39	11 43	11 57								12 09	12 13	12 27		15 27					
London Blackfriars 3 ⊖	d				11 42	11 46	12 00								12 12	12 16	12 30		15 30					
Elephant & Castle ⊖	d				11 46	11 49	12 03								12 16	12 19	12 33		15 33					
Loughborough Jn	d					11 53	12 07									12 23	12 37		15 37					
Herne Hill 4	d		11 49			11a57	12a11		12 04				12 19			12a27	12a41		15a41		15 34			
West Dulwich	d		11 51						12 06				12 21								15 36			
Sydenham Hill	d		11 53						12 08				12 23								15 38			
Penge East	d		11 56						12 11				12 26								15 41			
Kent House 4	d		11 58						12 13				12 28								15 43			
Beckenham Junction 4	d		12 00						12 15				12 30					and at the same minutes past each hour until			15 45			
Denmark Hill 4	d	11 48			11 52							12 18			12 22									15 48
Peckham Rye 4	d	11 51			11 55							12 21			12 25									15 51
Nunhead 4	d	11 53			11 57							12 23			12 27									15 53
Lewisham 4	a	12 01										12 31												16 01
Crofton Park	d				12 00										12 30									
Catford	d				12 03										12 33									
Bellingham	d				12 05										12 35									
Beckenham Hill	d				12 07										12 37									
Ravensbourne	d				12 09										12 39									
Shortlands 4	d		12 03		12 11				12 18				12 33		12 41						15 48			
Bromley South 4	d		12 06		12 14			12a08	12 21	12 19	12 23		12 36		12 44					15a38	15 51	15 53		
Bickley 4	d		12 09		12 17				12 24				12 39		12 47						15 54			
Petts Wood 4	d		12 14						12 29				12 44								15 59			
Orpington 4	d		12a17						12a32				12a47								16a02			
St Mary Cray	d				12 21					12 25					12 51							16 00		
Swanley 4	d				12 26					12a29	12 33				12 56							16 04		
Eynsford	d				12 30										13 00									
Shoreham (Kent)	d				12 34										13 04									
Otford 4	d				12 37						12a41				13 07							16a12		
Bat & Ball	d				12 40										13 10									
Sevenoaks 4	a				12 43										13 13									

London - Catford, Beckenham Junction, Bromley South, Orpington, Otford and Sevenoaks

Network Diagram - see first Page of Table 195

		SE	FC	FC	FC	SE [1]	SE	SE	SE [1]		SE [1]	SE	SE	FC	FC	SE [1]	SE	SE [1]	SE [1]		FC	FC	SE	SE	FC
London Victoria [15] ⊖	d	15 40				15 52		15 55	15 58		16 07	16 09	16 10			16 22	16 25	16 28	16 37				16 39	16 40	
Brixton ⊖	d	15 47						16 02					16 17				16 32							16 47	
Kentish Town ⊖	d		15 26	15 30	15 44									15 56	16 00						16 10	16 14			16 24
St Pancras International [15] ⊖	d		15 30	15 34	15 48									16 00	16 04						16 14	16 18			16 28
Farringdon ⊖	d		15 35	15 39	15 53									16 05	16 09						16 19	16 23			16 33
City Thameslink [3]	d		15 39	15 43	15 57									16 09	16 13						16 23	16 27			16 37
London Blackfriars [3] ⊖	d		15 42	15 46	16 00									16 12	16 16						16 26	16 30			16 42
Elephant & Castle ⊖	d		15 46	15 49	16 03									16 16	16 19						16 30	16 33			16 46
Loughborough Jn.	d			15 53	16 07										16 23							16 37			
Herne Hill [4]	d	15 49		15a57	16a11			16 04					16 19		16a27		16 34					16a41		16 49	
West Dulwich	d	15 51						16 06					16 21				16 36							16 51	
Sydenham Hill	d	15 53						16 08					16 23				16 38							16 53	
Penge East	d	15 56						16 11					16 26				16 41							16 56	
Kent House [4]	d	15 58						16 13					16 28				16 43							16 58	
Beckenham Junction [4]	d	16 00					16 12	16 15					16 30				16 45							17 00	
Denmark Hill [4]	d		15 52									16 18		16 22							16 39		16 48		16 52
Peckham Rye [4]	d		15 55									16 21		16 25							16 42		16 51		16 55
Nunhead [4]	d		15 57									16 23		16 27							16 44		16 53		16 57
Lewisham [4]	a											16 31											16 58		
Crofton Park	d		16 00											16 30							16 47				17 00
Catford	d		16 03											16 33							16 50				17 03
Bellingham	d		16 05											16 35							16 52				17 05
Beckenham Hill	d		16 07											16 37							16 54				17 07
Ravensbourne	d		16 09											16 39							16 56				17 09
Shortlands [4]	d	16 03	16 11					16 18					16 33	16 41			16 48				16 58			17 03	17 11
Bromley South [4]	d	16 06	16 14			16a08		16 21	16 19		16 23		16 36	16 44		16a38	16 51	16 49	16 53		17 01			17 06	17 14
Bickley [4]	d	16 09	16 17					16 24					16 39	16 47			16 54				17 04			17 09	17 17
Petts Wood [4]	d	16 14						16 29					16 44				16 59				17 08			17 14	
Orpington [4]	d	16a17						16a32					16a49				17a04				17a15			17a19	
St Mary Cray	d		16 21						16 25					16 51				16 55	17 00						17 21
Swanley [4]	d		16 26						16a29		16 33			16 56				16a59	17 04						17 30
Eynsford	d		16 30											17 00											17 34
Shoreham (Kent)	d		16 34											17 04											17 38
Otford [4]	d		16 37								16a41			17 07					17a12						17 41
Bat & Ball	d		16 40											17 10											17 44
Sevenoaks [4]	a		16 43											17 14											17 49

		FC	FC [1]	FC	SE [1]		SE [1]	SE	SE	SE	SE [1]	SE	FC	FC	FC [1]		FC	SE [1]	SE [1]	SE	SE	SE [1]	FC	FC	FC [1]
London Victoria [15] ⊖	d				16 57		16 58	16 59	17 04	17 04	17 12	17 15						17 27	17 28	17 30	17 34	17 42			
Brixton ⊖	d							17 06				17 22								17 37					
Kentish Town ⊖	d	16 30		16 46										16 58			17 14						17 18	17 28	
St Pancras International [15] ⊖	d	16 34	16 40	16 52									16 58	17 02	17 14		17 18						17 22	17 32	17 36
Farringdon ⊖	d	16 39	16 45	16 57									17 03	17 07	17 19		17 23						17 27	17 37	17 41
City Thameslink [3]	d	16 43	16 49	17 01									17 07	17 11	17 23		17 27						17 31	17 41	17 45
London Blackfriars [3] ⊖	d	16 46	16 52	17 04									17 10	17 14	17 25		17 30						17 36	17 44	17 48
Elephant & Castle ⊖	d	16 49	16 56	17 08									17 14	17 18	17 29		17 34						17 40	17 48	17 52
Loughborough Jn.	d	16 53	17 00	17 12										17 22			17 38							17 52	
Herne Hill [4]	d	16a57	17 06	17a15				17 11				17 24		17a25	17 36		17a42			17 39				17a55	
West Dulwich	d		17 08					17 13				17 27								17 42					
Sydenham Hill	d		17 10					17 15				17 29								17 44					
Penge East	d		17 13					17 18				17 32								17 47					
Kent House [4]	d		17 15					17 20				17 34								17 49					
Beckenham Junction [4]	d		17a20					17 23				17 37								17 51					
Denmark Hill [4]	d								17 13				17 20								17 43		17 47		
Peckham Rye [4]	d								17 16				17 23								17 46		17 50		
Nunhead [4]	d								17 18				17 26								17 49		17 52		
Lewisham [4]	a								17 23												17 55				
Crofton Park	d												17 29										17 55		
Catford	d												17 32										17 58		
Bellingham	d												17 35										18 01		
Beckenham Hill	d												17 37										18 03		
Ravensbourne	d												17 39										18 05		
Shortlands [4]	d							17 26				17 40	17 43							17 55			18 07		
Bromley South [4]	d				17a13		17 19	17 29		17 24	17 31	17 43	17 46		17 48			17a43	17 50	17 58		17 59	18 10		18 11
Bickley [4]	d							17 31				17 45			17 50					18 00			18 12		
Petts Wood [4]	d							17 36				17 50								18 05					
Orpington [4]	d							17a41				17a55								18a10					
St Mary Cray	d									17 30	17 38				17 55				17 57			18 06	18 22		18 18
Swanley [4]	d									17a34	17 42		17 55		17a59				18 01			18 11	18 26		18 22
Eynsford	d												18 00										18 31		
Shoreham (Kent)	d												18 03										18 34		
Otford [4]	d						17a35				17a50		18 06						18a09			18a19	18 38		18a30
Bat & Ball	d												18 14										18 41		
Sevenoaks [4]	a												18 23										18 50		

London - Catford, Beckenham Junction, Bromley South, Orpington, Otford and Sevenoaks

Network Diagram - see first Page of Table 195

Station		SE	FC	SE 1	SE	SE 1	SE	SE 1	FC 1	FC	FC	FC	SE	SE	SE 1	SE 1	SE 1	SE	SE	SE 1	FC	FC
London Victoria 15 ⊖	d	17 45		17 54	17 56	17 57	18 00	18 03					18 15	18 18	18 18	18 24	18 27	18 30	18 39	18 42		
Brixton ⊖	d	17 52					18 07						18 22					18 37				
Kentish Town ⊖	d										17 48										18 08	18 20
St Pancras International 15 ⊖	d		17 44						17 56	17 48	17 52	18 04									18 12	18 24
Farringdon ⊖	d		17 49						18 01	17 53	17 57	18 09									18 17	18 29
City Thameslink 3	d		17 53						18 05	17 57	18 01	18 13									18 21	18 33
London Blackfriars 3 ⊖	d		17 56						18 10	18 00	18 04	18 16									18 24	18 36
Elephant & Castle ⊖	d		18 00						18 14	18 05	18 08	18 20									18 28	18 40
Loughborough Jn	d										18 12	18 24										18 44
Herne Hill 4	d	17 54	18 07				18 10		18 21		18a16	18a27	18 24					18 39				18a47
West Dulwich	d	17 57	18 09				18 12						18 27					18 42				
Sydenham Hill	d	17 59	18 11				18 14						18 29					18 44				
Penge East	d	18 02	18 14				18 17						18 32					18 47				
Kent House 4	d	18 04	18a18				18 20						18 34					18 49				
Beckenham Junction 4	d	18 06					18 22						18 36					18 51				
Denmark Hill 4	d				18 06					18 15				18 28					18 48		18 34	
Peckham Rye 4	d				18 09					18 18				18 32					18 51		18 38	
Nunhead 4	d				18 11					18 20				18 34					18 54		18 40	
Lewisham 4	a				18 17									18 42					19 02			
Crofton Park	d									18 23											18 43	
Catford	d									18 26											18 46	
Bellingham	d									18 29											18 49	
Beckenham Hill	d									18 31											18 51	
Ravensbourne	d									18 33											18 53	
Shortlands 4	d	18 10					18 25			18 35			18 39					18 55			18 57	
Bromley South 4	d	18 15		18 19		18a14	18 28	18 24	18 31	18 38			18 42		18 39	18 46	18a43	18 58		18 59	19 00	
Bickley 4	d	18 18					18 31			18 40			18 45					19 00			19 03	
Petts Wood 4	d	18 26					18 36						18 54					19 07				
Orpington 4	d	18a32					18a41						18a59					19a12				
St Mary Cray	d			18 25					18 38	18 45					18 45	18 52				19 06	19 10	
Swanley 4	d			18a29					18a42	18 53					18 50	18a56				19 11	19 15	
Eynsford	d									18 57											19 19	
Shoreham (Kent)	d									19 01											19 23	
Otford 4	d							18a42		19 04					18a58					19a19	19 26	
Bat & Ball	d									19 07											19 29	
Sevenoaks 4	a									19 12											19 37	

Station		SE	FC 1	FC	FC	SE 1	SE 1	SE	SE 1	SE	SE	FC	FC	FC	SE 1	SE	SE	SE 1	SE	SE	SE	FC	FC
London Victoria 15 ⊖	d	18 45				18 57	18 58	19 00	19 07	19 09	19 10				19 22	19 25	19 28	19 37	19 39	19 40			
Brixton ⊖	d	18 52						19 07			19 17					19 32				19 47			
Kentish Town ⊖	d			18 34								18 54									19 26		
St Pancras International 15 ⊖	d		18 30	18 38	18 48							19 00	19 04	19 18							19 30	19 34	19 48
Farringdon ⊖	d		18 35	18 43	18 53							19 05	19 09	19 23							19 36	19 39	19 53
City Thameslink 3	d		18 39	18 47	18 57							19 09	19 13	19 27							19 39	19 43	19 57
London Blackfriars 3 ⊖	d		18 42	18 50	19 00							19 12	19 16	19 30							19 42	19 46	20 00
Elephant & Castle ⊖	d		18 46	18 54	19 04							19 16	19 19	19 33							19 46	19 49	20 03
Loughborough Jn	d			18 58	19 08								19 23	19 37								19 53	20 07
Herne Hill 4	d	18 54		19a01	19a11			19 09			19 19		19a27	19a41		19 34				19 49		19a57	20a11
West Dulwich	d	18 56						19 12			19 21					19 36				19 51			
Sydenham Hill	d	18 58						19 14			19 23					19 38				19 53			
Penge East	d	19 01						19 17			19 26					19 41				19 56			
Kent House 4	d	19 03						19 19			19 28					19 43				19 58			
Beckenham Junction 4	d	19 06						19 21			19 30					19 45				20 00			
Denmark Hill 4	d		18 52							19 18		19 22							19 48		19 52		
Peckham Rye 4	d		18 55							19 21		19 25							19 51		19 55		
Nunhead 4	d		18 57							19 23		19 27							19 53		19 57		
Lewisham 4	a									19 31									20 01				
Crofton Park	d		19 00									19 30									20 00		
Catford	d		19 03									19 33									20 03		
Bellingham	d		19 05									19 35									20 05		
Beckenham Hill	d		19 07									19 37									20 07		
Ravensbourne	d		19 09									19 39									20 09		
Shortlands 4	d	19 09	19 13					19 25			19 33	19 41				19 48				20 03	20 11		
Bromley South 4	d	19 12	19 16			19a13	19 19	19 28	19 27		19 36	19 44			19a38	19 51	19 49	19 53		20 06	20 14		
Bickley 4	d	19 15	19 19					19 30			19 39	19 47				19 54				20 09	20 17		
Petts Wood 4	d	19 20						19 35			19 44					19 59				20 14			
Orpington 4	d	19a25						19a38			19a48					20a02				20a18			
St Mary Cray	d		19 23				19 25					19 51					19 55	20 00			20 21		
Swanley 4	d		19 29				19a29		19 36			19 56					19a59	20 04			20 26		
Eynsford	d		19 33									20 00									20 30		
Shoreham (Kent)	d		19 37									20 04									20 34		
Otford 4	d		19 40						19a44			20 07						20a12			20 37		
Bat & Ball	d		19 43									20 10									20 40		
Sevenoaks 4	a		19 50									20 13									20 43		

London - Catford, Beckenham Junction, Bromley South, Orpington, Otford and Sevenoaks

Network Diagram - see first Page of Table 195

		SE	SE		SE	SE	SE	FC	FC	FC	SE	SE	SE		FC	FC	SE	SE	SE	SE	FC	FC	SE		SE
		1				1					1		1				1		1	1			1		
London Victoria 15 ⊖	d	19 52	19 55		19 58	20 07	20 10				20 22	20 25	20 37				20 52	20 55	20 58	21 07			21 22		21 25
Brixton ⊖	d		20 02				20 17					20 32						21 02							21 32
Kentish Town ⊖	d							19 56							20 26	20 30					20 56	21 01			
St Pancras International 15 ⊖	d							20 00	20 04	20 18					20 30	20 34					21 00	21 06			
Farringdon ⊖	d							20 05	20 09	20 23					20 35	20 39					21 05	21 10			
City Thameslink 3	d							20 09	20 13	20 27					20 39	20 43					21 09	21 13			
London Blackfriars 3 ⊖	d							20 12	20 16	20 30					20 42	20 46					21 12	21 16			
Elephant & Castle ⊖	d							20 16	20 19	20 33					20 46	20 49					21 16	21 19			
Loughborough Jn.	d								20 23	20 37						20 53						21 23			
Herne Hill 4	d		20 04				20 19		20a27	20a41		20 34				20a57		21 04				21a27			21 34
West Dulwich	d		20 06				20 21					20 36						21 06							21 36
Sydenham Hill	d		20 08				20 23					20 38						21 08							21 38
Penge East	d		20 11				20 26					20 41						21 11							21 41
Kent House 4	d		20 13				20 28					20 43						21 13							21 43
Beckenham Junction 4	d		20 15				20 30					20 45						21 15							21 45
Denmark Hill 4	d							20 22							20 52						21 22				
Peckham Rye 4	d							20 25							20 55						21 25				
Nunhead 4	d							20 27							20 57						21 27				
Lewisham 4	a																								
Crofton Park	d							20 30							21 00						21 30				
Catford	d							20 33							21 03						21 33				
Bellingham	d							20 35							21 05						21 35				
Beckenham Hill	d							20 37							21 07						21 37				
Ravensbourne	d							20 39							21 09						21 39				
Shortlands 4	d		20 18				20 33	20 41				20 48			21 11			21 18			21 41				21 48
Bromley South 4	d	20a08	20 21		20 19	20 23	20 36	20 44			20a38	20 51	20 53		21 14		21a09	21 21	21 19	21 23	21 44		21a38		21 51
Bickley 4	d		20 24				20 39	20 47				20 54			21 17			21 24			21 47				21 54
Petts Wood 4	d		20 29				20 44					20 59						21 29							21 59
Orpington 4	d		20a32				20a47					21a02						21a32							22a02
St Mary Cray	d				20 25			20 51					21 00		21 21				21 25	21 30	21 51				
Swanley 4	d				20a29	20 33		20 56					21 04		21 26				21a29	21 34	21 56				
Eynsford	d							21 00							21 30						22 00				
Shoreham (Kent)	d							21 04							21 34						22 04				
Otford 4	d					20a41		21 07					21a12		21 37					21a42	22 07				
Bat & Ball	d							21 10							21 40						22 10				
Sevenoaks 4	a							21 13							21 43						22 13				

		FC	SE	SE	SE	FC	SE	SE	SE		SE	SE	SE	SE	SE	SE	SE	SE	SE		SE	SE			
				1			1		1				1		1		1				1				
London Victoria 15 ⊖	d		21 43	21 52	21 55		22 07	22 13	22 22		22 25	22 43	22 52	22 55	23 07	23 13	23 22	23 25	23 43		23 52	23 55			
Brixton ⊖	d				22 02						22 32			23 02				23 32				00 02			
Kentish Town ⊖	d	21 31				22 01																			
St Pancras International 15 ⊖	d	21 36				22 06																			
Farringdon ⊖	d	21 40				22 10																			
City Thameslink 3	d	21 43				22 13																			
London Blackfriars 3 ⊖	d	21 46				22 16																			
Elephant & Castle ⊖	d	21 49				22 19																			
Loughborough Jn.	d	21 53				22 23																			
Herne Hill 4	d	21a57			22 04	22a27					22 34			23 04				23 34				00 04			
West Dulwich	d				22 06						22 36			23 06				23 36				00 06			
Sydenham Hill	d				22 08						22 38			23 08				23 38				00 08			
Penge East	d				22 11						22 41			23 11				23 41				00 11			
Kent House 4	d				22 13						22 43			23 13				23 43				00 13			
Beckenham Junction 4	d				22 15						22 45			23 15				23 45				00 15			
Denmark Hill 4	d		21 52					22 22				22 52				23 22			23 52						
Peckham Rye 4	d		21 55					22 25				22 55				23 25			23 55						
Nunhead 4	d		21 57					22 27				22 57				23 27			23 57						
Lewisham 4	a																								
Crofton Park	d		22 00					22 30				23 00				23 30			23 59						
Catford	d		22 03					22 33				23 03				23 33			00 03						
Bellingham	d		22 05					22 35				23 05				23 35			00 05						
Beckenham Hill	d		22 07					22 37				23 07				23 37			00 07						
Ravensbourne	d		22 09					22 39				23 09				23 39			00 09						
Shortlands 4	d		22 11		22 18			22 41			22 48	23 11		23 18		23 41		23 48	00 11			00 18			
Bromley South 4	d		22 14	22 09	22 21		22 23	22 44	22a38		22 51	23 14	23 09	23 21	23 23	23 44	23a38	23 51	00 14		00 09	00 21			
Bickley 4	d		22 17		22 24			22 47			22 54	23 17		23 24		23 47		23 54	00 17			00 24			
Petts Wood 4	d				22 29						22 59	23 21		23 29		23 54		23 59	00 21			00 29			
Orpington 4	d				22a32						23a02	23a25		23a32		23a57		00a02	00a25			00a32			
St Mary Cray	d		22 21	22 15			22 30	22 51					23 15		23 30						00 15				
Swanley 4	d		22 26	22a19			22 34	22 56					23a19		23 34						00a19				
Eynsford	d		22 30					23 00																	
Shoreham (Kent)	d		22 34					23 04																	
Otford 4	d		22 37				22a42	23 07							23a42										
Bat & Ball	d		22 40					23 10																	
Sevenoaks 4	a		22 43					23 13																	

Table 195

Saturdays

London - Catford, Beckenham Junction, Bromley South, Orpington, Otford and Sevenoaks

Network Diagram - see first Page of Table 195

		SE	SE [1]	SE	SE [1]	SE	SE [1]	SE	SE [1]	SE	SE [1]	SE	SE	SE	SE [1]	SE [1]	SE	SE	SE [1]	SE	SE [1]	SE	SE
London Victoria [15] ⊖	d	23p43	23p52	23p55	00 07	00 35	05 22	05 55	06 07	06 13	06 22	06 25	06 43	06 55	06 58	07 07	07 10	07 13	07 22	07 25	07 37	07 39	07 40
Brixton ⊖	d			00 02				06 02				06 32		07 02			07 17			07 32			07 47
Kentish Town ⊖	d																						
St Pancras International [15] ⊖	d																						
Farringdon ⊖	d																						
City Thameslink [3]	d																						
London Blackfriars [3] ⊖	d																						
Elephant & Castle ⊖	d																						
Loughborough Jn.	d																						
Herne Hill [4]	d			00 04		00 43		06 04				06 34		07 04			07 19			07 34			07 49
West Dulwich	d			00 06				06 06				06 36		07 06			07 21			07 36			07 51
Sydenham Hill	d			00 08				06 08				06 38		07 08			07 23			07 38			07 53
Penge East	d			00 11		00 48		06 11				06 41		07 11			07 26			07 41			07 56
Kent House [4]	d			00 13				06 13				06 43		07 13			07 28			07 43			07 58
Beckenham Junction [4]	d			00 15		00 50		06 15				06 45		07 15			07 30			07 45			08 00
Denmark Hill [4]	d	23p52								06 22			06 52					07 22				07 48	
Peckham Rye [4]	d	23p55								06 25			06 55					07 25				07 51	
Nunhead [4]	d	23p57								06 27			06 57					07 27				07 53	
Lewisham [4]	a																					08 02	
Crofton Park	d	23p59								06 30			07 00					07 30					
Catford	d	00 03								06 33			07 03					07 33					
Bellingham	d	00 05								06 35			07 05					07 35					
Beckenham Hill	d	00 07								06 37			07 07					07 37					
Ravensbourne	d	00 09								06 39			07 09					07 39					
Shortlands [4]	d	00 11		00 18				06 18		06 41		06 48	07 11	07 18			07 33	07 41		07 48			08 03
Bromley South [4]	d	00 14	00 09	00 21	00 25	00 55	05 39	06 21	06 23	06 44	06 39	06 51	07 14	07 21	07 19	07 23	07 36	07 44	07a38	07 51	07 53		08 06
Bickley [4]	d	00 17		00 24				06 24		06 47		06 54	07 17	07 24			07 39	07 47		07 54			08 09
Petts Wood [4]	d	00 21		00 29				06 29				06 59		07 29			07 44			07 59			08 14
Orpington [4]	d	00a25		00a32				06a32				07a02		07a32			07a47			08a02			08a17
St Mary Cray	d		00 15		00 31	01 01	05 45		06 30	06 51	06 45		07 21		07 25	07 30		07 51			08 00		
Swanley [4]	d		00a19		00 36	01a05	05a49		06 34	06 56	06a49		07 26		07a29	07 34		07 56			08 04		
Eynsford	d				00 40					07 00			07 30					08 00					
Shoreham (Kent)	d				00 44					07 04			07 34					08 04					
Otford [4]	d				00a47				06a42	07 07			07 37			07a42		08 07			08a12		
Bat & Ball	d									07 10			07 40					08 10					
Sevenoaks [4]	a									07 13			07 43					08 13					

		SE	SE [1]	SE	SE [1]	SE [1]	SE	SE	SE	SE [1]	SE	SE [1]	SE		SE	SE	SE	SE [1]	SE	SE [1]	SE [1]	SE
London Victoria [15] ⊖	d	07 43	07 52	07 55	07 58	08 07	08 09	08 10	08 13	08 22	08 25	08 37	08 39		18 39	18 40	18 43	18 52	18 55	18 58	19 07	19 09
Brixton ⊖	d			08 02				08 17			08 32					18 47			19 02			
Kentish Town ⊖	d																					
St Pancras International [15] ⊖	d																					
Farringdon ⊖	d																					
City Thameslink [3]	d																					
London Blackfriars [3] ⊖	d																					
Elephant & Castle ⊖	d																					
Loughborough Jn.	d																					
Herne Hill [4]	d			08 04				08 19			08 34					18 49			19 04			
West Dulwich	d			08 06				08 21			08 36					18 51			19 06			
Sydenham Hill	d			08 08				08 23			08 38					18 53			19 08			
Penge East	d			08 11				08 26			08 41					18 56			19 11			
Kent House [4]	d			08 13				08 28			08 43			and at		18 58			19 13			
Beckenham Junction [4]	d			08 15				08 30			08 45			the same		19 00			19 15			
Denmark Hill [4]	d	07 52					08 18		08 22				08 48	minutes	18 48		18 52					19 18
Peckham Rye [4]	d	07 55					08 21		08 25				08 51	past	18 51		18 55					19 21
Nunhead [4]	d	07 57					08 23		08 27				08 53	each	18 53		18 57					19 23
Lewisham [4]	a						08 31						09 01	hour until	19 01							19 31
Crofton Park	d	08 00							08 30								19 00					
Catford	d	08 03							08 33								19 03					
Bellingham	d	08 05							08 35								19 05					
Beckenham Hill	d	08 07							08 37								19 07					
Ravensbourne	d	08 09							08 39								19 09					
Shortlands [4]	d	08 11		08 18				08 33	08 41		08 48					19 03	19 11		19 18			
Bromley South [4]	d	08 14	08a08	08 21	08 19	08 23		08 36	08 44	08a38	08 51	08 53				19 06	19 14	19a08	19 21	19 19	19 23	
Bickley [4]	d	08 17		08 24				08 39	08 47		08 54					19 09	19 17		19 24			
Petts Wood [4]	d			08 29				08 44			08 59					19 14			19 29			
Orpington [4]	d			08a32				08a47			09a02					19a17			19a32			
St Mary Cray	d	08 21			08 25				08 51			09 00					19 21			19 25		
Swanley [4]	d	08 26			08a29	08 33			08 56			09 04					19 26			19a29	19 33	
Eynsford	d	08 30							09 00								19 30					
Shoreham (Kent)	d	08 34							09 04								19 34					
Otford [4]	d	08 37				08a41			09 07			09a12					19 37				19a41	
Bat & Ball	d	08 40							09 10								19 40					
Sevenoaks [4]	a	08 43							09 13								19 43					

London - Catford, Beckenham Junction, Bromley South, Orpington, Otford and Sevenoaks

Network Diagram - see first Page of Table 195

		SE	SE		SE 1	SE	SE 1	SE	SE	SE	SE 1	SE	SE 1		SE 1	SE	SE	SE 1	SE	SE	SE 1	SE	SE 1		SE
London Victoria 15 ⊖	d	19 10	19 13		19 22	19 25	19 37	19 39	19 40	19 43	19 52	19 55	19 58		20 07	20 10	20 13	20 22	20 25	20 43	20 52	20 55	21 07		21 13
Brixton ⊖	d	19 17				19 32			19 47			20 02				20 17			20 32			21 02			
Kentish Town ⊖	d																								
St Pancras International 15 ⊖	d																								
Farringdon ⊖	d																								
City Thameslink 3	d																								
London Blackfriars 3 ⊖	d																								
Elephant & Castle ⊖	d																								
Loughborough Jn.	d																								
Herne Hill 4	d	19 19				19 34			19 49			20 04				20 19			20 34			21 04			
West Dulwich	d	19 21				19 36			19 51			20 06				20 21			20 36			21 06			
Sydenham Hill	d	19 23				19 38			19 53			20 08				20 23			20 38			21 08			
Penge East	d	19 26				19 41			19 56			20 11				20 26			20 41			21 11			
Kent House 4	d	19 28				19 43			19 58			20 13				20 28			20 43			21 13			
Beckenham Junction 4	d	19 30				19 45			20 00			20 15				20 30			20 45			21 15			
Denmark Hill 4	d		19 22					19 48		19 52							20 22			20 52					21 22
Peckham Rye 4	d		19 25					19 51		19 55							20 25			20 55					21 25
Nunhead 4	d		19 27					19 53		19 57							20 27			20 57					21 27
Lewisham 4	a							20 01																	
Crofton Park	d		19 30							20 00							20 30			21 00					21 30
Catford	d		19 33							20 03							20 33			21 03					21 33
Bellingham	d		19 35							20 05							20 35			21 05					21 35
Beckenham Hill	d		19 37							20 07							20 37			21 07					21 37
Ravensbourne	d		19 39							20 09							20 39			21 09					21 39
Shortlands 4	d	19 33	19 41			19 48			20 03	20 11		20 18				20 33	20 41		20 48	21 11		21 18			21 41
Bromley South 4	d	19 36	19 44		19a38	19 51	19 53		20 06	20 14	20a08	20 21	20 19		20 23	20 36	20 44	20a38	20 51	21 14	21 09	21 21	21 23		21 44
Bickley 4	d	19 39	19 47			19 54			20 09	20 17		20 24				20 39	20 47		20 54	21 17		21 24			21 47
Petts Wood 4	d	19 44				19 59			20 14			20 29				20 44			20 59			21 29			
Orpington 4	d	19a48				20a02			20a18			20a32				20a47			21a02			21a32			
St Mary Cray	d		19 51				20 00			20 21			20 25		20 30		20 51			21 21	21 15		21 30		21 51
Swanley 4	d		19 56				20 04			20 26			20a29		20 34		20 56			21 26	21a19		21 34		21 56
Eynsford	d		20 00							20 30							21 00			21 30					22 00
Shoreham (Kent)	d		20 04							20 34							21 04			21 34					22 04
Otford 4	d		20 07				20a12			20 37					20a42		21 07			21 37			21a42		22 07
Bat & Ball	d		20 10							20 40							21 10			21 40					22 10
Sevenoaks 4	a		20 13							20 43							21 13			21 43					22 13

		SE 1	SE	SE	SE 1	SE	SE 1	SE	SE 1		SE	SE	SE 1	SE	SE 1	SE	SE 1	SE	SE		SE 1	SE			
London Victoria 15 ⊖	d	21 22	21 25	21 43	21 52	21 55	22 07	22 13	22 22		22 25	22 43	22 52	22 55	23 07	23 13	23 22	23 25	23 43		23 52	23 55			
Brixton ⊖	d		21 32			22 02					22 32			23 02				23 32				00 02			
Kentish Town ⊖	d																								
St Pancras International 15 ⊖	d																								
Farringdon ⊖	d																								
City Thameslink 3	d																								
London Blackfriars 3 ⊖	d																								
Elephant & Castle ⊖	d																								
Loughborough Jn.	d																								
Herne Hill 4	d		21 34			22 04					22 34			23 04				23 34				00 04			
West Dulwich	d		21 36			22 06					22 36			23 06				23 36				00 06			
Sydenham Hill	d		21 38			22 08					22 38			23 08				23 38				00 08			
Penge East	d		21 41			22 11					22 41			23 11				23 41				00 11			
Kent House 4	d		21 43			22 13					22 43			23 13				23 43				00 13			
Beckenham Junction 4	d		21 45			22 15					22 45			23 15				23 45				00 15			
Denmark Hill 4	d			21 52				22 22				22 52				23 22			23 52						
Peckham Rye 4	d			21 55				22 25				22 55				23 25			23 55						
Nunhead 4	d			21 57				22 27				22 57				23 27			23 57						
Lewisham 4	a																								
Crofton Park	d			22 00				22 30				23 00				23 30			23 58						
Catford	d			22 03				22 33				23 03				23 33			00 03						
Bellingham	d			22 05				22 35				23 05				23 35			00 05						
Beckenham Hill	d			22 07				22 37				23 07				23 37			00 07						
Ravensbourne	d			22 09				22 39				23 09				23 39			00 09						
Shortlands 4	d		21 48	22 11		22 18		22 41			22 48	23 11		23 18		23 41		23 48	00 11			00 18			
Bromley South 4	d	21a38	21 51	22 14	22 09	22 21	22 23	22 44	22a38		22 51	23 14	23 09	23 21	23 23	23 44	23a38	23 51	00 14		00 09	00 21			
Bickley 4	d		21 54	22 17		22 24		22 47			22 54	23 17		23 24		23 47		23 54	00 17			00 24			
Petts Wood 4	d		21 59			22 29					22 59	23 22		23 29		23 52		23 59	00 22			00 29			
Orpington 4	d		22a02			22a32					23a02	23a25		23a32		23a55		00a02	00a25			00a32			
St Mary Cray	d			22 21	22 15		22 30	22 51					23 15		23 30						00 15				
Swanley 4	d			22 26	22a19		22 34	22 56					23a19		23 34						00a19				
Eynsford	d			22 30				23 00																	
Shoreham (Kent)	d			22 34				23 04																	
Otford 4	d			22 37			22a42	23 07							23a42										
Bat & Ball	d			22 40				23 10																	
Sevenoaks 4	a			22 43				23 13																	

London - Catford, Beckenham Junction, Bromley South, Orpington, Otford and Sevenoaks

Network Diagram - see first Page of Table 195

		SE	SE	SE	SE	SE	SE	SE	SE	SE	SE	SE	SE		SE	SE	SE	SE	SE	SE	SE	SE
			1		1		1		1		1					1		1		1		
		A	A	A																		
London Victoria 15 ⊖	d	23p43	23p52	23p55	00 07	00 35	07 24	07 39	07 45	07 51	08 05	08 09	08 21	and at the same minutes past each hour until	22 21	22 24	22 39	22 45	22 51	23 05	23 09	23 21
Brixton ⊖	d			00 02						07 58			08 28		22 28				22 58			23 28
Kentish Town ⊖	d																					
St Pancras International 15 ⊖	d																					
Farringdon ⊖	d																					
City Thameslink 3	d																					
London Blackfriars 3 ⊖	d																					
Elephant & Castle ⊖	d																					
Loughborough Jn	d																					
Herne Hill 4	d			00 04		00 43				08 00			08 30		22 30				23 00			23 30
West Dulwich	d			00 06						08 02			08 32		22 32				23 02			23 32
Sydenham Hill	d			00 08						08 04			08 34		22 34				23 04			23 34
Penge East	d			00 11		00 48				08 07			08 37		22 37				23 07			23 37
Kent House 4	d			00 13						08 09			08 39		22 39				23 09			23 39
Beckenham Junction 4	d			00 15		00 50				08 11			08 41		22 41				23 11			23 41
Denmark Hill 4	d	23p52						07 48				08 18					22 48				23 18	
Peckham Rye 4	d	23p55						07 51				08 21					22 51				23 21	
Nunhead 4	d	23p57						07 53				08 23					22 53				23 23	
Lewisham 4	a																					
Crofton Park	d	23p58						07 56				08 26					22 56				23 26	
Catford	d	00 03						07 59				08 29					22 59				23 29	
Bellingham	d	00 05						08 01				08 31					23 01				23 31	
Beckenham Hill	d	00 07						08 03				08 33					23 03				23 33	
Ravensbourne	d	00 09						08 05				08 35					23 05				23 35	
Shortlands 4	d	00 11		00 18				08 07		08 14		08 37	08 44		22 44		23 07		23 14		23 37	23 44
Bromley South 4	d	00 14	00 09	00 21	00 25	00 55	07 44	08 10	08 01	08 18	08a21	08 40	08 48		22 48	22 44	23 10	23 01	23 18	23a21	23 40	23 48
Bickley 4	d	00 17		00 24				08 13		08 20		08 43	08 50		22 50		23 13		23 20		23 43	23 50
Petts Wood 4	d	00 22		00 29						08 25			08 55		22 55		23 22		23 25		23 52	23 55
Orpington 4	d	00a25		00a32						08a28			08a58		22a58		23a26		23a29		23a56	23a59
St Mary Cray	d		00 15		00 31	01 01	07 50	08 17	08 08			08 47				22 50		23 08				
Swanley 4	d		00a19		00 36	01a05	07a54	08 22	08 12			08 52				22a54		23 12				
Eynsford	d				00 40			08 26				08 56										
Shoreham (Kent)	d				00 44			08 30				09 00										
Otford 4	d				00a47			08 33	08a20			09 03						23a20				
Bat & Ball	d							08 36				09 06										
Sevenoaks 4	a							08 39				09 09										

		SE
		1
London Victoria 15 ⊖	d	23 45
Brixton ⊖	d	
Kentish Town ⊖	d	
St Pancras International 15 ⊖	d	
Farringdon ⊖	d	
City Thameslink 3	d	
London Blackfriars 3 ⊖	d	
Elephant & Castle ⊖	d	
Loughborough Jn	d	
Herne Hill 4	d	
West Dulwich	d	
Sydenham Hill	d	
Penge East	d	
Kent House 4	d	
Beckenham Junction 4	d	
Denmark Hill 4	d	
Peckham Rye 4	d	
Nunhead 4	d	
Lewisham 4	a	
Crofton Park	d	
Catford	d	
Bellingham	d	
Beckenham Hill	d	
Ravensbourne	d	
Shortlands 4	d	
Bromley South 4	d	00 02
Bickley 4	d	
Petts Wood 4	d	
Orpington 4	d	
St Mary Cray	d	00 08
Swanley 4	d	00a12
Eynsford	d	
Shoreham (Kent)	d	
Otford 4	d	
Bat & Ball	d	
Sevenoaks 4	a	

A not 11 December

Sevenoaks, Otford, Orpington, Bromley South, Beckenham Junction and Catford - London

Network Diagram - see first Page of Table 195

Miles	Miles	Miles			SE MO 1	SE MX 1	SE MO 1	SE MX 1	SE	SE	SE	SE	FC		SE	SE	FC	SE	SE 1	SE 1	SE	SE 1	FC		SE
—	0	—	**Sevenoaks 4**	d														05 40							
—	1¼	—	Bat & Ball	d														05 43							
—	3	—	Otford 4	d														05 46				06 15			
—	4¼	—	Shoreham (Kent)	d														05 49							
—	6½	—	Eynsford	d														05 53							
—	9½	—	**Swanley 4**	d	23p32			00 10		04 33								05 58		06 02		06 25			
—	12¼	—	St Mary Cray	d	23p36			00 14		04 37								06 02		06 06					
0	—	—	**Orpington 4**	d					04 34		04 55	05 10			05 34	05 40					06 10				
1¼	—	—	Petts Wood 4	d					04 37		04 58	05 13			05 37	05 43					06 13				
3	14½	—	Bickley 4	d					04 41	04 41	05 02	05 17			05 41	05 47		06 06			06 17				
4	15½	—	**Bromley South 4**	d	23p43	23p50	00 13	00 20	04 44	04 50	05 05	05 20			05 44	05 50		06 10	06 12	06 15	06 20	06 33			
5	16½	—	Shortlands 4	d					04 47	04 53	05 08	05 23			05 47	05 53		06 13			06 23				
—	17¼	—	Ravensbourne	d					04 49						05 49			06 15							
—	18	—	Beckenham Hill	d					04 51						05 51			06 17							
—	18¾	—	Bellingham	d					04 53						05 53			06 19							
—	19½	—	Catford	d					04 56						05 56			06 22							
—	20½	—	Crofton Park	d					04 58						05 58			06 25							
—	—	0	Lewisham 4	d																					
—	21¾	1¾	Nunhead 4	d					05 01						06 01			06 27							
—	22½	2½	Peckham Rye 4	d					05 04						06 04			06 30							
—	23¼	3¼	Denmark Hill 4	d					05 07						06 07			06 33							
6¼	—	—	**Beckenham Junction 4**	d						04 56	05 11	05 26				05 56					06 26				06 40
7¼	—	—	Kent House 4	d						04 58	05 13	05 28				05 58					06 28				06 42
7¾	—	—	Penge East	d						05 00	05 15	05 30				06 00					06 30				06 44
9¼	—	—	Sydenham Hill	d						05 03	05 18	05 33				06 03					06 33				06 47
10	—	—	West Dulwich	d						05 05	05 20	05 35				06 05					06 35				06 49
11	—	—	Herne Hill 4	d						05 08	05 23	05 38	05 54			06 08	06 16				06 38	06 43	06 46		06 52
—	—	—	Loughborough Jn	d													06 19						06 49		
—	25¾	—	Elephant & Castle ⊖	d					05 13		05 29		06 00		06 13		06 24	06 40					06 54		
—	27	—	**London Blackfriars 3** ⊖	d					05 17		05 33		06 04		06 17		06 30	06 48					06 58		
—	—	—	City Thameslink 3	a					05 19		05 35		06 06		06 19		06 32	06 50					07 00		
—	—	—	Farringdon ⊖	a							05 38		06 10				06 36	06 54					07 04		
—	—	—	St Pancras International 15 ⊖	a							05 42		06 14				06 40	06 58					07 08		
—	—	—	Kentish Town ⊖	a							05 47		06 18				06 44	07 02							
11	—	—	Brixton ⊖	d						05 10		05 40				06 10					06 40				06 54
15	—	7½	**London Victoria 15** ⊖	a	00 02	00 07	00 29	00 38		05 17		05 47				06 18			06 28	06 31	06 47	06 51			07 03

		SE	FC	SE	SE 1	SE 1	SE	SE 1	SE 1		SE 1	SE	SE	FC	SE	SE	SE 1	SE 1	SE		SE 1	SE	FC 1	FC	SE
Sevenoaks 4	d			06 13												06 42									
Bat & Ball	d			06 16												06 48									
Otford 4	d			06 19				06 38	06 46							06 51		07 01			07 14				
Shoreham (Kent)	d			06 22												06 54									
Eynsford	d			06 26												06 58									
Swanley 4	d			06 31	06 35			06 48	06 54		06 57					07 03		07 10			07 22	07 23			
St Mary Cray	d			06 35	06 39						07 01					07 07						07 27			
Orpington 4	d						06 40								06 58				07 08						
Petts Wood 4	d						06 43								07 01				07 11						
Bickley 4	d			06 39			06 47								07 05	07 11			07 16						
Bromley South 4	d			06 42	06 46	06 50	06 50	06 57	07 02		07 08				07 08	07 14	07 16	07 20	07 20		07 31	07 34			07 34
Shortlands 4	d			06 45			06 53								07 11	07 17			07 23						07 36
Ravensbourne	d			06 47												07 19									
Beckenham Hill	d			06 49												07 21									
Bellingham	d			06 51												07 23									
Catford	d			06 54												07 26									
Crofton Park	d			06 57												07 29									
Lewisham 4	d	06 41											07 15												
Nunhead 4	d			06 59									07 20			07 31									
Peckham Rye 4	d	06 47		07 02									07 23			07 34									
Denmark Hill 4	d	06 50		07 05									07 29			07 37									
Beckenham Junction 4	d						06 56					07 08			07 14				07 26						07 39
Kent House 4	d						06 58					07 11			07 17				07 28						07 42
Penge East	d						07 00					07 14			07 19				07 30						07 44
Sydenham Hill	d						07 03					07 17			07 22				07 33						07 47
West Dulwich	d						07 05					07 19			07 24				07 35						07 49
Herne Hill 4	d		06 57				07 08					07 22		07 24	07 31				07 38				07 41	07 47	07 52
Loughborough Jn	d		07 00											07 27	07 34									07 50	
Elephant & Castle ⊖	d		07 06	07 12				07 16						07 32	07 38	07 44							07 48	07 54	
London Blackfriars 3 ⊖	d		07 12	07 18				07 24						07 36	07 42	07 48							07 54	07 58	
City Thameslink 3	a		07 14	07 20				07 26						07 38	07 44	07 50							07 56	08 00	
Farringdon ⊖	a		07 18	07 24				07 30						07 42	07 48	07 54							08 00	08 03	
St Pancras International 15 ⊖	a		07 22	07 28				07 34						07 46	07 52	07 58							08 04	08 08	
Kentish Town ⊖	a			07 32												08 02								08 14	
Brixton ⊖	d						07 10					07 24							07 40						07 54
London Victoria 15 ⊖	a	07 04			07 07	07 09	07 19		07 22		07 30	07 33	07 42				07 38	07 43	07 49		07 53	07 55			08 03

Sevenoaks, Otford, Orpington, Bromley South, Beckenham Junction and Catford - London

Network Diagram - see first Page of Table 195

		SE	SE	SE	SE [1]		SE [1]	FC	SE	SE [1]	SE [1]	SE [1]	SE	SE	FC		SE	SE	SE [1]	SE [1]	SE [1]	SE [1]	FC	SE	SE
Sevenoaks [4]	d			07 11														07 36							
Bat & Ball	d			07 14														07 39							
Otford [4]	d			07 18	07 23						07 38							07 43			07 56				
Shoreham (Kent)	d			07 21														07 46							
Eynsford	d			07 24														07 49							
Swanley [4]	d			07 30	07 32					07 40	07 47							07 54	07 55	08 02	08 05				
St Mary Cray	d			07 34						07 45								07 59	08 00	08 06					
Orpington [4]	d	07 28							07 38					07 47											
Petts Wood [4]	d	07 31							07 41					07 50											
Bickley [4]	d	07 35		07 39					07 46					07 55				08 03							
Bromley South [4]	d	07 38		07 42	07 40		07 49		07 50	07 53	07 57			07 58			08 04	08 08	08 06	08 12	08 13	08 16			
Shortlands [4]	d	07 41		07 44					07 53					08 00			08 06	08 10							
Ravensbourne	d			07 47														08 13							
Beckenham Hill	d			07 49														08 15							
Bellingham	d			07 51										08 05				08 17							
Catford	d			07 53										08 08				08 20							
Crofton Park	d			07 56										08 10											
Lewisham [4]	d		07 46										08 05												08 25
Nunhead [4]	d		07 51	07 58									08 11	08 14											08 30
Peckham Rye [4]	d		07 54	08 01									08 13	08 16											08 33
Denmark Hill [4]	d		07 59	08 04									08 17	08 19				08 26		08 30					08 36
Beckenham Junction [4]	d	07 44							07 56			07 59					08 10							08 22	
Kent House [4]	d	07 47							07 58			08 02					08 12							08 24	
Penge East	d	07 49							08 00			08 04					08 14							08 26	
Sydenham Hill	d	07 52							08 03			08 07					08 17							08 29	
West Dulwich	d	07 54							08 05			08 09					08 19							08 31	
Herne Hill [4]	d	07 57						08 01	08 08			08 13			08 20		08 23						08 32	08 34	
Loughborough Jn	d	08 00						08 04				08 16			08 23								08 36		
Elephant & Castle	⊖ d	08 05		08 13	08 00			08 09				08 21		08 25	08 28			08 35	08 31				08 40		
London Blackfriars [3]	⊖ d	08 09		08 17	08 04			08 13				08 25		08 29	08 33			08 42	08 37				08 46		
City Thameslink [3]	a	08 11		08 19	08 06			08 15				08 27		08 31	08 35			08 44	08 39				08 48		
Farringdon	⊖ a	08 15		08 23	08 10			08 19				08 30		08 35	08 39			08 48	08 43				08 52		
St Pancras International [15]	⊖ a	08 19		08 27	08 14			08 23				08 35		08 39	08 43			08 52	08 47				08 56		
Kentish Town	⊖ a			08 32				08 29							08 48			08 57					09 00		
Brixton	⊖ d								08 10								08 25							08 36	
London Victoria [15]	⊖ a		08 11				08 09		08 20	08 17	08 23		08 29				08 35			08 42	08 36	08 39		08 45	08 49

			SE [1]	SE	FC [1]	SE	SE [1]	SE [1]	FC	SE [1]	SE		SE	FC [1]	FC	SE	SE [1]	SE	SE [1]	SE	SE		SE [1]	FC	SE
Sevenoaks [4]	d					07 53													08 24						
Bat & Ball	d					07 56													08 27						
Otford [4]	d					08 00	08 09												08 31				08 46		
Shoreham (Kent)	d					08 03													08 34						
Eynsford	d					08 06													08 37						
Swanley [4]	d					08 11		08 22											08 42				08 54		
St Mary Cray	d					08 16		08 27											08 46				08 58		
Orpington [4]	d			08 10							08 26							08 40			08 47				08 55
Petts Wood [4]	d			08 13							08 29							08 43			08 50				08 58
Bickley [4]	d			08 17		08 20					08 33							08 47	08 51		08 55				09 02
Bromley South [4]	d		08 18	08 22		08 26	08 25	08 33			08 36					08 44	08 50	08 50	08 54		08 58		09 05		09 05
Shortlands [4]	d		08 20	08 24		08 29					08 39					08 46		08 53	08 56		09 00				09 08
Ravensbourne	d		08 23													08 49					09 03				
Beckenham Hill	d		08 25													08 51					09 05				
Bellingham	d		08 27			08 33										08 53			09 01		09 07				
Catford	d		08 30			08 36										08 56			09 04		09 09				
Crofton Park	d					08 39										08 58					09 12				
Lewisham [4]	d												08 46							09 06					
Nunhead [4]	d					08 41							08 52			09 01				09 11	09 14				
Peckham Rye [4]	d		08 36			08 44							08 55			09 04			09 09	09 14	09 17				
Denmark Hill [4]	d		08 39			08 47							09 02			09 07			09 12	09 17	09 19				
Beckenham Junction [4]	d			08 28							08 42							08 56							09 11
Kent House [4]	d			08 30						08 42	08 45							08 58							09 13
Penge East	d									08 44	08 47							09 00							09 15
Sydenham Hill	d									08 47	08 50							09 03							09 18
West Dulwich	d			08 35						08 49	08 52							09 05							09 20
Herne Hill [4]	d			08 38	08 41				08 47	08 52	08 54			08 57	09 02			09 08						09 20	09 23
Loughborough Jn	d								08 50	08 55					09 05									09 23	
Elephant & Castle	⊖ d		08 45		08 50	08 54			08 58	09 02				09 06	09 10	09 14			09 20		09 26			09 30	
London Blackfriars [3]	⊖ d		08 50		08 54	08 58			09 02	09 06				09 10	09 14	09 18			09 26		09 30			09 34	
City Thameslink [3]	a		08 52		08 56	09 00			09 04	09 08				09 12	09 16	09 20			09 27		09 32			09 36	
Farringdon	⊖ a		08 56		09 00	09 04			09 08	09 12				09 16	09 20	09 24			09 32		09 36			09 40	
St Pancras International [15]	⊖ a		09 00		09 04	09 08			09 12	09 16				09 20	09 24	09 28			09 36		09 40			09 44	
Kentish Town	⊖ a					09 13			09 16							09 34					09 45			09 48	
Brixton	⊖ d			08 40							08 57							09 10							09 25
London Victoria [15]	⊖ a			08 50			08 53	08 53			09 06		09 11				09 09	09 19		09 29			09 23		09 34

Sevenoaks, Otford, Orpington, Bromley South, Beckenham Junction and Catford - London

Network Diagram - see first Page of Table 195

		SE	SE [1]	SE [1]	FC	SE	SE [1]		SE	FC	SE	FC	SE	SE [1]	SE	SE [1]	SE		FC	SE	FC	SE	SE [1]	SE [1]	SE
Sevenoaks [4]	d	08 43											09 13									09 42			
Bat & Ball	d	08 46											09 16									09 46			
Otford [4]	d	08 49					09 17						09 21			09 46						09 50			
Shoreham (Kent)	d	08 52											09 24									09 53			
Eynsford	d	08 56											09 28									09 56			
Swanley [4]	d	09 01	09 05				09 26						09 33			09 54						10 01	10 05		
St Mary Cray	d	09 05	09 09										09 37			09 58						10 05	10 09		
Orpington [4]	d					09 10					09 25				09 40					09 55					10 10
Petts Wood [4]	d					09 13					09 28				09 43					09 58					10 13
Bickley [4]	d	09 09				09 17					09 32		09 42		09 47					10 02		10 10			10 17
Bromley South [4]	d	09 12	09 15	09 20		09 20	09 34				09 35		09 45	09 50	09 50	10 05				10 05		10 15	10 15	10 20	10 20
Shortlands [4]	d	09 15				09 23					09 38		09 48		09 53					10 08		10 18			10 23
Ravensbourne	d	09 17											09 50									10 20			
Beckenham Hill	d	09 19											09 52									10 22			
Bellingham	d	09 21											09 54									10 24			
Catford	d	09 24											09 57									10 27			
Crofton Park	d	09 26											09 59									10 29			
Lewisham [4]	d								09 38								10 08								
Nunhead [4]	d	09 29							09 43				10 02				10 13					10 32			
Peckham Rye [4]	d	09 31							09 45				10 04				10 15					10 34			
Denmark Hill [4]	d	09 34							09 49				10 07				10 19					10 37			
Beckenham Junction [4]	d					09 26					09 41				09 56					10 11					10 26
Kent House [4]	d					09 28					09 43				09 58					10 13					10 28
Penge East	d					09 30					09 45				10 00					10 15					10 30
Sydenham Hill	d					09 33					09 48				10 03					10 18					10 33
West Dulwich	d					09 35					09 50				10 05					10 20					10 35
Herne Hill [4]	d				09 36	09 38				09 46	09 53	10 01			10 08				10 16	10 23	10 31				10 38
Loughborough Jn	d				09 40					09 50		10 04							10 19		10 34				
Elephant & Castle ⊖	d	09 42			09 45					09 55		10 09	10 14						10 24		10 39	10 44			
London Blackfriars [3] ⊖	d	09 46			09 50					10 00		10 14	10 18						10 30		10 44	10 48			
City Thameslink [3]	a	09 48			09 52					10 02		10 16	10 20						10 32		10 46	10 50			
Farringdon ⊖	a	09 52			09 56					10 06		10 19	10 24						10 35		10 49	10 54			
St Pancras International [15] ⊖	a	09 56			10 00					10 10		10 23	10 28						10 40		10 53	10 58			
Kentish Town ⊖	a	10 00			10 05					10 14		10 27	10 33						10 44		10 57	11 03			
Brixton ⊖	d					09 40					09 55				10 10					10 25					10 40
London Victoria [15] ⊖	a		09 38	09 43		09 49	09 51		10 00		10 02			10 07	10 17	10 21	10 28			10 32			10 41	10 37	10 47

		SE	FC		SE	SE [1]	SE	SE [1]	FC	SE	SE	FC	SE		SE [1]	SE	SE [1]	SE [1]	FC		FC	SE		SE
Sevenoaks [4]	d				10 02								10 32											
Bat & Ball	d				10 05								10 35											
Otford [4]	d				10 08	10 17							10 38		10 46									
Shoreham (Kent)	d				10 11								10 41											
Eynsford	d				10 15								10 45											
Swanley [4]	d				10 20	10 26							10 50		10 54		11 05							
St Mary Cray	d				10 24								10 54		10 58		11 09							
Orpington [4]	d						10 25			10 40						10 55						15 10		
Petts Wood [4]	d						10 28			10 43						10 58						15 13		
Bickley [4]	d				10 28		10 32			10 47			10 58			11 02						15 17		
Bromley South [4]	d				10 31	10 35	10 35	10 50		10 50			11 01		11 05	11 05	11 15	11 20				15 20		
Shortlands [4]	d				10 34		10 38			10 53			11 04			11 08						15 23		
Ravensbourne	d				10 36								11 06											
Beckenham Hill	d				10 38								11 08							and at				
Bellingham	d				10 40								11 10							the same				
Catford	d				10 43								11 13							minutes				
Crofton Park	d				10 45								11 15							past				
Lewisham [4]	d	10 38									11 08									each				15 38
Nunhead [4]	d	10 43			10 48						11 13		11 18							hour until				15 43
Peckham Rye [4]	d	10 45			10 50						11 15		11 20											15 45
Denmark Hill [4]	d	10 49			10 54						11 19		11 24											15 49
Beckenham Junction [4]	d						10 41			10 56						11 11						15 26		
Kent House [4]	d						10 43			10 58						11 13						15 28		
Penge East	d						10 45			11 00						11 15						15 30		
Sydenham Hill	d						10 48			11 03						11 18						15 33		
West Dulwich	d						10 50			11 05						11 20						15 35		
Herne Hill [4]	d		10 46				10 53		11 01	11 08		11 16				11 23			11 31		15 31	15 38		
Loughborough Jn	d		10 49						11 04			11 19							11 34		15 34			
Elephant & Castle ⊖	d		10 54		11 00				11 09			11 24	11 30						11 39		15 39			
London Blackfriars [3] ⊖	d		11 00		11 04				11 14			11 30	11 34						11 44		15 44			
City Thameslink [3]	a		11 02		11 06				11 16			11 32	11 36						11 46		15 46			
Farringdon ⊖	a		11 06		11 10				11 19			11 36	11 40						11 49		15 49			
St Pancras International [15] ⊖	a		11 10		11 14				11 23			11 40	11 44						11 53		15 53			
Kentish Town ⊖	a		11 14		11 19				11 27			11 44	11 49						11 57		15 57			
Brixton ⊖	d						10 55			11 10						11 25						15 40		
London Victoria [15] ⊖	a	10 58				10 51	11 02	11 07		11 17	11 28				11 21	11 32	11 37	11 37				15 47		15 58

Sevenoaks, Otford, Orpington, Bromley South, Beckenham Junction and Catford - London

Network Diagram - see first Page of Table 195

		FC	SE	SE 1	SE	SE 1	FC	SE	SE		FC	SE 1	SE 1	SE	SE	SE 1	FC	SE	SE		FC	SE 1	SE 1	SE	FC 1
Sevenoaks 4	d		15 02									15 32										16 02			
Bat & Ball	d		15 05									15 35										16 05			
Otford 4	d		15 08	15 17								15 38	15 46									16 08	16 17		
Shoreham (Kent)	d		15 11									15 41										16 11			
Eynsford	d		15 15									15 45										16 15			
Swanley 4	d		15 20	15 26								15 50	15 54		16 05							16 20	16 26		
St Mary Cray	d		15 24									15 54	15 58		16 09							16 24			
Orpington 4	d				15 25			15 40						15 55				16 10						16 25	
Petts Wood 4	d				15 28			15 43						15 58				16 13						16 28	
Bickley 4	d		15 28		15 32			15 47				15 58		16 02				16 17				16 28		16 32	
Bromley South 4	d		15 31	15 35	15 35	15 50		15 50				16 01	16 05	16 05	16 15	16 20		16 20				16 31	16 35	16 35	
Shortlands 4	d		15 34		15 38			15 53				16 04		16 08				16 23				16 34		16 38	
Ravensbourne	d		15 36									16 06										16 36			
Beckenham Hill	d		15 38									16 08										16 38			
Bellingham	d		15 40									16 10										16 40			
Catford	d		15 43									16 13										16 43			
Crofton Park	d		15 45									16 15										16 45			
Lewisham 4	d								16 08										16 38						
Nunhead 4	d		15 48						16 13			16 18							16 43			16 48			
Peckham Rye 4	d		15 50						16 15			16 20							16 45			16 50			
Denmark Hill 4	d		15 54						16 19			16 24							16 49			16 54			
Beckenham Junction 4	d				15 41			15 56						16 11				16 26						16 41	
Kent House 4	d				15 43			15 58						16 13				16 28						16 43	
Penge East	d				15 45			16 00						16 15				16 30						16 45	
Sydenham Hill	d				15 48			16 03						16 18				16 33						16 48	
West Dulwich	d				15 50			16 05						16 20				16 35						16 50	
Herne Hill 4	d	15 46			15 53		16 01	16 08			16 16			16 23			16 31	16 38			16 50			16 53	17 01
Loughborough Jn	d	15 49					16 04				16 19						16 34				16 53				
Elephant & Castle ⊖	d	15 54	16 00				16 09				16 24	16 30					16 39				17 00	17 04			17 08
London Blackfriars 3 ⊖	d	16 00	16 04				16 14				16 30	16 38					16 44				17 04	17 08			17 12
City Thameslink 3	a	16 02	16 06				16 16				16 32	16 40					16 46				17 06	17 10			17 14
Farringdon ⊖	a	16 06	16 10				16 19				16 35	16 43					16 49				17 09	17 13			17 17
St Pancras International 15 ⊖	a	16 10	16 14				16 23				16 39	16 47					16 53				17 13	17 17			17 21
Kentish Town ⊖	a	16 14	16 19				16 28				16 44						16 58				17 18				
Brixton ⊖	d				15 55			16 10						16 25				16 40						16 55	
London Victoria 15 ⊖	a			15 51	16 02	16 07		16 17	16 28				16 21	16 32	16 37	16 38		16 47	17 01				16 51	17 04	

		SE	SE 1	SE	SE		FC	SE	SE 1	SE	SE 1	SE 1	FC	SE	SE 1		SE	FC	SE 1	SE 1	SE	SE 1	SE 1	SE 1	FC
Sevenoaks 4	d	16 22						16 32											17 02						
Bat & Ball	d	16 25						16 35											17 05						
Otford 4	d	16 28						16 38	16 46										17 08	17 17					
Shoreham (Kent)	d							16 41											17 11						
Eynsford	d							16 45											17 15						
Swanley 4	d	16 37						16 50	16 54		17 05								17 20	17 26			17 35		
St Mary Cray	d	16 41						16 54	16 58		17 09								17 24				17 39		
Orpington 4	d			16 40						16 55				17 10							17 24	17 34			
Petts Wood 4	d			16 43						16 58				17 13							17 28	17 37			
Bickley 4	d			16 47				16 58		17 02				17 17					17 28		17 32	17 42			
Bromley South 4	d	16 47	16 50	16 50				17 01	17 05	17 05	17 15	17 20		17 20					17 31	17 35	17 35	17 45	17 46	17 50	
Shortlands 4	d			16 53				17 04		17 08				17 23					17 34		17 38				
Ravensbourne	d							17 06											17 36						
Beckenham Hill	d							17 08											17 38						
Bellingham	d	16 52						17 10											17 40						
Catford	d	16 55						17 13											17 43						
Crofton Park	d							17 15											17 45						
Lewisham 4	d				17 08												17 38								
Nunhead 4	d	16 59			17 13			17 18									17 43		17 48						
Peckham Rye 4	d	17 02			17 15			17 20									17 45		17 50						
Denmark Hill 4	d	17 05			17 19			17 24									17 49		17 54						
Beckenham Junction 4	d			16 56						17 11				17 26	17 30						17 41	17 49			
Kent House 4	d			16 58						17 13				17 28	17 33						17 43				
Penge East	d			17 00						17 15				17 30	17 35						17 45				
Sydenham Hill	d			17 03						17 18				17 33	17 38						17 48				
West Dulwich	d			17 05						17 20				17 35	17 40						17 50				
Herne Hill 4	d			17 11			17 21			17 23			17 31	17 38	17 44			17 48			17 53				18 06
Loughborough Jn	d						17 24						17 34		17 47			17 51							18 09
Elephant & Castle ⊖	d	17 12					17 28	17 34					17 39		17 52			17 56	18 00			18 05			18 14
London Blackfriars 3 ⊖	d	17 16					17 32	17 40					17 46		17 56			18 00	18 06			18 10			18 18
City Thameslink 3	a	17 18					17 34	17 42					17 48		17 58			18 02	18 08			18 12			18 20
Farringdon ⊖	a	17 23					17 37	17 45					17 51		18 01			18 05	18 11			18 15			18 23
St Pancras International 15 ⊖	a	17 27					17 41	17 49					17 55		18 05			18 09	18 15			18 19			18 27
Kentish Town ⊖	a	17 32					17 46						18 00					18 14							18 32
Brixton ⊖	d			17 13						17 25				17 40							17 55				
London Victoria 15 ⊖	a		17 07	17 20	17 28				17 23	17 33	17 38	17 37		17 48			17 59			17 53	18 03		18 08	18 07	

Sevenoaks, Otford, Orpington, Bromley South, Beckenham Junction and Catford - London

Network Diagram - see first Page of Table 195

Station			SE	SE	FC	SE 1	SE 1	SE	SE 1	SE 1	FC		SE	SE	FC 1	FC	SE 1	SE 1	SE	SE	SE 1		FC	SE	SE
Sevenoaks 4	d					17 32											18 02			18 18					
Bat & Ball	d					17 35											18 05			18 21					
Otford 4	d					17 38	17 46										18 08	18 17		18 24					
Shoreham (Kent)	d					17 41											18 11			18 27					
Eynsford	d					17 45											18 15			18 31					
Swanley 4	d					17 50	17 54		18 05								18 20	18 26		18 36					
St Mary Cray	d					17 54	17 58		18 09								18 24			18 40					
Orpington 4	d		17 40					17 55					18 09						18 25					18 40	
Petts Wood 4	d		17 43					17 58					18 12						18 28					18 43	
Bickley 4	d		17 47			17 58		18 02					18 17				18 28		18 32					18 47	
Bromley South 4	d		17 50			18 01	18 05	18 05	18 15	18 20			18 20				18 31	18 35	18 35	18 46	18 50			18 50	
Shortlands 4	d		17 53			18 04		18 08					18 23				18 34		18 38					18 53	
Ravensbourne	d					18 06											18 36								
Beckenham Hill	d					18 08											18 38								
Bellingham	d					18 10											18 40								
Catford	d					18 13											18 43								
Crofton Park	d					18 15											18 45								
Lewisham 4	d			18 08										18 38											19 08
Nunhead 4	d			18 13		18 18								18 43			18 48								19 13
Peckham Rye 4	d			18 15		18 20								18 45			18 50								19 15
Denmark Hill 4	d			18 19		18 23								18 49			18 54			18 59					19 19
Beckenham Junction 4	d		17 56					18 11					18 26						18 41					18 56	
Kent House 4	d		17 58					18 13					18 28						18 43					18 58	
Penge East	d		18 00					18 15					18 30						18 45					19 00	
Sydenham Hill	d		18 03					18 18					18 33						18 48					19 03	
West Dulwich	d		18 05					18 20					18 35						18 50					19 05	
Herne Hill 4	d		18 09		18 20			18 24			18 32		18 38		18 41	18 48			18 53				19 02	19 08	
Loughborough Jn	d				18 23						18 35					18 51							19 05		
Elephant & Castle ⊖	d				18 28	18 32					18 40				18 48	18 56	19 00						19 10		
London Blackfriars 3 ⊖	d				18 32	18 36					18 44				18 52	19 00	19 06						19 18		
City Thameslink 3	a				18 34	18 38					18 46				18 54	19 02	19 08						19 20		
Farringdon ⊖	a				18 37	18 41					18 49				18 57	19 05	19 11						19 23		
St Pancras International 15 ⊖	a				18 41	18 45					18 53				19 01	19 09	19 15						19 27		
Kentish Town ⊖	a				18 46											19 14							19 32		
Brixton ⊖	d		18 11					18 26					18 40						18 55					19 10	
London Victoria 15 ⊖	a		18 18	18 29			18 21	18 33	18 37	18 37			18 48	18 58				18 53	19 03	19 13	19 07			19 17	19 28

Station		FC	SE	SE 1	SE	SE	SE		SE 1	SE 1	FC	SE	FC	SE	SE 1	SE	SE 1		FC	SE	FC	SE	SE 1	SE	SE
Sevenoaks 4	d		18 32			18 45								19 02								19 32			19 45
Bat & Ball	d		18 35			18 48								19 05								19 35			19 48
Otford 4	d		18 38	18 46		18 51								19 08	19 17							19 38	19 46		19 51
Shoreham (Kent)	d		18 41			18 54								19 11								19 41			19 54
Eynsford	d		18 45			18 58								19 15								19 45			19 58
Swanley 4	d		18 50	18 54		19 03	19 05							19 20	19 26							19 50	19 54		20 03
St Mary Cray	d		18 54	18 58			19 09							19 24								19 54	19 58		
Orpington 4	d				18 55							19 10				19 25				19 40				19 55	
Petts Wood 4	d				18 58							19 13				19 28				19 43				19 58	
Bickley 4	d		18 58		19 02							19 17		19 28		19 32				19 47		19 58		20 02	
Bromley South 4	d		19 01	19 05	19 05	19 11	19 15		19 17	19 20		19 20		19 31	19 35	19 35	19 50			19 50		20 01	20 05	20 05	20a11
Shortlands 4	d		19 04		19 08							19 23		19 34		19 38				19 53		20 04		20 08	
Ravensbourne	d		19 06											19 36								20 06			
Beckenham Hill	d		19 08											19 38								20 08			
Bellingham	d		19 10											19 40								20 10			
Catford	d		19 13											19 43								20 13			
Crofton Park	d		19 15											19 45								20 15			
Lewisham 4	d																								
Nunhead 4	d		19 18											19 48								20 18			
Peckham Rye 4	d		19 20											19 50								20 20			
Denmark Hill 4	d		19 24			19 28								19 54								20 24			
Beckenham Junction 4	d				19 11							19 26				19 41				19 56				20 11	
Kent House 4	d				19 13							19 28				19 43				19 58				20 13	
Penge East	d				19 15							19 30				19 45				20 00				20 15	
Sydenham Hill	d				19 18							19 33				19 48				20 03				20 18	
West Dulwich	d				19 20							19 35				19 50				20 05				20 20	
Herne Hill 4	d	19 17			19 23						19 31	19 38	19 47			19 53			20 05	20 08	20 16			20 23	
Loughborough Jn	d	19 20									19 34		19 50						20 08		20 19				
Elephant & Castle ⊖	d	19 25	19 30								19 39		19 55	20 00					20 13		20 24	20 30			
London Blackfriars 3 ⊖	d	19 30	19 34								19 46		20 00	20 04					20 18		20 30	20 34			
City Thameslink 3	a	19 32	19 36								19 48		20 02	20 06					20 20		20 32	20 36			
Farringdon ⊖	a	19 36	19 40								19 51		20 06	20 10					20 23		20 36	20 40			
St Pancras International 15 ⊖	a	19 40	19 44								19 55		20 10	20 14					20 27		20 40	20 44			
Kentish Town ⊖	a	19 44	19 49								19 59		20 14	20 19					20 31		20 44	20 49			
Brixton ⊖	d				19 25							19 40				19 55				20 10				20 25	
London Victoria 15 ⊖	a			19 21	19 32	19 43	19 37		19 35	19 37		19 47			19 51	20 02	20 07			20 17			20 21	20 32	

Sevenoaks, Otford, Orpington, Bromley South, Beckenham Junction and Catford - London

Network Diagram - see first Page of Table 195

		SE [1]	SE [1]		FC	SE	FC	SE	SE [1]	SE [1]	FC	SE	SE		SE [1]	FC	FC	SE	SE	SE [1]	SE [1]	FC	SE		SE
Sevenoaks [4]	d							20 02					20 32						21 02						21 32
Bat & Ball	d							20 05					20 35						21 05						21 35
Otford [4]	d							20 08	20 16				20 38						21 08	21 16					21 38
Shoreham (Kent)	d							20 11					20 41						21 11						21 41
Eynsford	d							20 15					20 45						21 15						21 45
Swanley [4]	d	20 05						20 20	20 24				20 50		21 10				21 20	21 24					21 50
St Mary Cray	d	20 09						20 24	20 28				20 54		21 14				21 24	21 28					21 54
Orpington [4]	d					20 10						20 40						21 10					21 40		
Petts Wood [4]	d					20 13						20 43						21 13					21 43		
Bickley [4]	d					20 17		20 28				20 47	20 58					21 17	21 28				21 47		21 58
Bromley South [4]	d	20 15	20 20			20 20		20 31	20 35	20 50		20 50	21 01		21 20			21 20	21 31	21 35	21 50		21 50		22 01
Shortlands [4]	d					20 23		20 34				20 53	21 04					21 23	21 34				21 53		22 04
Ravensbourne	d							20 36					21 06						21 36						22 06
Beckenham Hill	d							20 38					21 08						21 38						22 08
Bellingham	d							20 40					21 10						21 40						22 10
Catford	d							20 43					21 13						21 43						22 13
Crofton Park	d							20 45					21 15						21 45						22 15
Lewisham [4] 🚊	d																								
Nunhead [4]	d							20 48					21 18						21 48						22 18
Peckham Rye [4]	d							20 50					21 20						21 50						22 20
Denmark Hill [4]	d							20 54					21 23						21 53						22 23
Beckenham Junction [4] 🚊	d					20 26						20 56						21 26					21 56		
Kent House [4]	d					20 28						20 58						21 28					21 58		
Penge East	d					20 30						21 00						21 30					22 00		
Sydenham Hill	d					20 33						21 03						21 33					22 03		
West Dulwich	d					20 35						21 05						21 35					22 05		
Herne Hill [4]	d				20 35	20 38	20 46				21 05	21 08				21 16	21 35	21 38				21 57	22 08		
Loughborough Jn	d				20 38		20 49				21 08					21 19	21 38					22 00			
Elephant & Castle ⊖	d				20 43		20 54	21 00			21 13					21 24	21 43					22 04			
London Blackfriars [3] ⊖	d				20 48		21 00	21 04			21 18					21 30	21 48					22 08			
City Thameslink [3]	a				20 50		21 02	21 06			21 20					21 32	21 50					22 10			
Farringdon ⊖	a				20 53		21 06	21 10			21 23					21 36	21 53					22 13			
St Pancras International [15] ⊖	a				20 57		21 10	21 14			21 27					21 40	21 57					22 17			
Kentish Town ⊖	a				21 01		21 14	21 19			21 31					21 44	22 01					22 21			
Brixton ⊖	d					20 40						21 10						21 40					22 10		
London Victoria [15] ⊖	a	20 37	20 38			20 47			20 51	21 07		21 17	21 33		21 37			21 47	22 03	21 51	22 07		22 17		22 33

		SE [1]	SE	SE	SE [1]	SE [1]	SE	SE	SE [1]		SE	SE [1]	SE [1]
Sevenoaks [4]	d			22 02				22 32					
Bat & Ball	d			22 05				22 35					
Otford [4]	d			22 08	22 16			22 38				23 16	
Shoreham (Kent)	d			22 11				22 41					
Eynsford	d			22 15				22 45					
Swanley [4]	d	22 10		22 20	22 24			22 50	23 10			23 24	
St Mary Cray	d	22 14		22 24	22 28			22 54	23 14			23 28	
Orpington [4]	d		22 10				22 40				23 10		
Petts Wood [4]	d		22 13				22 43				23 13		
Bickley [4]	d		22 17	22 28			22 47	22 58			23 17		
Bromley South [4]	d	22 20	22 20	22 31	22 35	22 50	22 50	23 01	23 20		23 20	23 35	23 50
Shortlands [4]	d		22 23	22 34			22 53	23 04			23 23		
Ravensbourne	d			22 36				23 06					
Beckenham Hill	d			22 38				23 08					
Bellingham	d			22 40				23 10					
Catford	d			22 43				23 13					
Crofton Park	d			22 45				23 15					
Lewisham [4] 🚊	d												
Nunhead [4]	d			22 48				23 18					
Peckham Rye [4]	d			22 50				23 20					
Denmark Hill [4]	d			22 53				23 23					
Beckenham Junction [4] 🚊	d		22 26				22 56				23 26		
Kent House [4]	d		22 28				22 58				23 28		
Penge East	d		22 30				23 00				23 30		
Sydenham Hill	d		22 33				23 03				23 33		
West Dulwich	d		22 35				23 05				23 35		
Herne Hill [4]	d		22 38				23 08				23 38		
Loughborough Jn	d												
Elephant & Castle ⊖	d												
London Blackfriars [3] ⊖	d												
City Thameslink [3]	a												
Farringdon ⊖	a												
St Pancras International [15] ⊖	a												
Kentish Town ⊖	a												
Brixton ⊖	d		22 40				23 10				23 40		
London Victoria [15] ⊖	a	22 37	22 47	23 03	22 51	23 07	23 17	23 33	23 37		23 47	23 51	00 07

Sevenoaks, Otford, Orpington, Bromley South, Beckenham Junction and Catford - London

Network Diagram - see first Page of Table 195

		SE 1	SE 1	SE	SE 1	SE	SE	SE 1	SE	SE 1		SE	SE	SE 1	SE	SE	SE 1	SE 1	SE	SE		SE 1	SE	
Sevenoaks 4	d						05 55						06 25							06 55				
Bat & Ball	d						05 58						06 28							06 58				
Otford 4	d						06 01	06 16					06 31	06 46						07 01		07 17		
Shoreham (Kent)	d						06 04						06 34							07 04				
Eynsford	d						06 08						06 38							07 08				
Swanley 4	d		00 10		06 05		06 13	06 24					06 43	06 54			07 05			07 13		07 26		
St Mary Cray	d		00 14		06 09		06 17	06 28					06 47	06 58			07 09			07 17				
Orpington 4	d			05 44		06 10			06 25			06 40				06 55			07 10					
Petts Wood 4	d			05 47		06 13			06 28			06 43				06 58			07 13					
Bickley 4	d			05 51		06 17	06 21		06 32			06 47	06 51			07 02			07 17	07 21				
Bromley South 4	d	23p50	00 20	05 54	06 16	06 20	06 24	06 35	06 35	06 50		06 50	06 54	07 05		07 05	07 15	07 20	07 20	07 24		07 35		
Shortlands 4	d			05 57		06 23	06 27		06 38			06 53	06 57			07 08			07 23	07 27				
Ravensbourne	d			05 59			06 29						06 59							07 29				
Beckenham Hill	d			06 01			06 31						07 01							07 31				and at the same minutes past each hour until
Bellingham	d			06 03			06 33						07 03							07 33				
Catford	d			06 06			06 36						07 06							07 36				
Crofton Park	d			06 08			06 38						07 08							07 38				
Lewisham 4	d														07 08								07 38	
Nunhead 4	d			06 11			06 41						07 11		07 15					07 41			07 45	
Peckham Rye 4	d			06 13			06 43						07 13		07 17					07 43			07 47	
Denmark Hill 4	d			06 17			06 47						07 17		07 21					07 47			07 51	
Beckenham Junction 4	d					06 26			06 41			06 56				07 11			07 26					
Kent House 4	d					06 28			06 43			06 58				07 13			07 28					
Penge East	d					06 30			06 45			07 00				07 15			07 30					
Sydenham Hill	d					06 33			06 48			07 03				07 18			07 33					
West Dulwich	d					06 35			06 50			07 05				07 20			07 35					
Herne Hill 4	d					06 38			06 53			07 08				07 23			07 38					
Loughborough Jn	d																							
Elephant & Castle ⊖	d																							
London Blackfriars 3 ⊖	d																							
City Thameslink 3	a																							
Farringdon ⊖	a																							
St Pancras International 15 ⊖	a																							
Kentish Town ⊖	a																							
Brixton ⊖	d					06 40			06 55			07 10				07 25			07 40					
London Victoria 15 ⊖	a	00 07	00 38	06 26	06 37	06 47	06 56	06 51	07 02	07 07		07 17	07 26	07 21	07 30	07 32	07 37	07 37	07 47	07 56		07 51	08 00	

		SE	SE	SE 1	SE	SE		SE 1	SE	SE	SE 1	SE 1	SE	SE	SE 1	SE		SE 1	SE	SE	SE 1	SE	SE 1	SE 1	SE
Sevenoaks 4	d					18 25								18 55						19 25					
Bat & Ball	d					18 28								18 58						19 28					
Otford 4	d					18 31		18 46						19 01	19 17					19 31	19 46				
Shoreham (Kent)	d					18 34								19 04						19 34					
Eynsford	d					18 38								19 08						19 38					
Swanley 4	d					18 43		18 54			19 05			19 13	19 26					19 43	19 54		20 05		
St Mary Cray	d					18 47		18 58			19 09			19 17						19 47	19 58		20 09		
Orpington 4	d		18 25		18 40					18 55			19 10			19 25			19 40			19 55			20 10
Petts Wood 4	d		18 28		18 43					18 58			19 13			19 28			19 43			19 58			20 13
Bickley 4	d		18 32		18 47	18 51				19 02			19 17	19 21		19 32			19 47	19 51		20 02			20 17
Bromley South 4	d		18 35	18 50	18 50	18 54		19 05		19 05	19 15	19 20	19 20	19 24	19 35	19 35		19 50	19 50	19 54	20 05	20 05	20 15	20 20	20 20
Shortlands 4	d		18 38		18 53	18 57				19 08			19 23	19 27		19 38			19 53	19 57		20 08			20 23
Ravensbourne	d					18 59								19 29						19 59					
Beckenham Hill	d					19 01								19 31						20 01					
Bellingham	d					19 03								19 33						20 03					
Catford	d					19 06								19 36						20 06					
Crofton Park	d					19 08								19 38						20 08					
Lewisham 4	d	18 38							19 08																
Nunhead 4	d	18 45				19 11			19 15					19 41						20 11					
Peckham Rye 4	d	18 47				19 13			19 17					19 43						20 13					
Denmark Hill 4	d	18 51				19 17			19 21					19 47						20 17					
Beckenham Junction 4	d		18 41		18 56					19 11			19 26			19 41			19 56			20 11			20 26
Kent House 4	d		18 43		18 58					19 13			19 28			19 43			19 58			20 13			20 28
Penge East	d		18 45		19 00					19 15			19 30			19 45			20 00			20 15			20 30
Sydenham Hill	d		18 48		19 03					19 18			19 33			19 48			20 03			20 18			20 33
West Dulwich	d		18 50		19 05					19 20			19 35			19 50			20 05			20 20			20 35
Herne Hill 4	d		18 53		19 08					19 23			19 38			19 53			20 08			20 23			20 38
Loughborough Jn	d																								
Elephant & Castle ⊖	d																								
London Blackfriars 3 ⊖	d																								
City Thameslink 3	a																								
Farringdon ⊖	a																								
St Pancras International 15 ⊖	a																								
Kentish Town ⊖	a																								
Brixton ⊖	d		18 55		19 10					19 25			19 40			19 55			20 10			20 25			20 40
London Victoria 15 ⊖	a	19 00	19 02	19 07	19 17	19 26		19 21	19 30	19 32	19 37	19 37	19 47	19 56	19 51	20 02		20 07	20 17	20 26	20 21	20 32	20 37	20 37	20 47

Table 195

Saturdays

Sevenoaks, Otford, Orpington, Bromley South, Beckenham Junction and Catford - London

Network Diagram - see first Page of Table 195

		SE		SE [1]	SE	SE	SE [1]	SE [1]	SE	SE	SE [1]	SE	
Sevenoaks [4]	d	19 55				20 25				20 55			
Bat & Ball	d	19 58				20 28				20 58			
Otford [4]	d	20 01				20 31	20 46			21 01			
Shoreham (Kent)	d	20 04				20 34				21 04			
Eynsford	d	20 08				20 38				21 08			
Swanley [4]	d	20 13				20 43	20 54	21 10		21 13			
St Mary Cray	d	20 17				20 47	20 58	21 14		21 17			
Orpington [4]	d				20 40				21 10			21 40	
Petts Wood [4]	d				20 43				21 13			21 43	
Bickley [4]	d	20 21			20 47	20 51			21 17	21 21		21 47	
Bromley South [4]	d	20 24		20 50	20 50	20 54	21 05	21 20	21 20	21 24	21 50	21 50	
Shortlands [4]	d	20 27			20 53	20 57			21 23	21 27		21 53	
Ravensbourne	d	20 29				20 59				21 29			
Beckenham Hill	d	20 31				21 01				21 31			
Bellingham	d	20 33				21 03				21 33			
Catford	d	20 36				21 06				21 36			
Crofton Park	d	20 38				21 08				21 38			
Lewisham [4]	d												
Nunhead [4]	d	20 41				21 11				21 41			
Peckham Rye [4]	d	20 43				21 13				21 43			
Denmark Hill [4]	d	20 47				21 17				21 47			
Beckenham Junction [4]	d				20 56				21 26			21 56	
Kent House [4]	d				20 58				21 28			21 58	
Penge East	d				21 00				21 30			22 00	
Sydenham Hill	d				21 03				21 33			22 03	
West Dulwich	d				21 05				21 35			22 05	
Herne Hill [4]	d				21 08				21 38			22 08	
Loughborough Jn	d												
Elephant & Castle ⊖	d												
London Blackfriars [3] ⊖	d												
City Thameslink [3]	a												
Farringdon ⊖	a												
St Pancras International [15] ⊖	a												
Kentish Town ⊖	a												
Brixton ⊖	d				21 10				21 40			22 10	
London Victoria [15] ⊖	a	20 56		21 07	21 17	21 26	21 21	21 37	21 47	21 56	22 07	22 17	

		SE	SE [1]	SE [1]	SE	SE	SE [1]	SE	SE	SE [1]		SE	SE [1]
Sevenoaks [4]	d	21 25				21 55			22 25				
Bat & Ball	d	21 28				21 58			22 28				
Otford [4]	d	21 31	21 46			22 01			22 31				23 16
Shoreham (Kent)	d	21 34				22 04			22 34				
Eynsford	d	21 38				22 08			22 38				
Swanley [4]	d	21 43	21 54	22 10		22 13			22 43	23 10			23 24
St Mary Cray	d	21 47	21 58	22 14		22 17			22 47	23 14			23 28
Orpington [4]	d				22 10			22 40				23 10	
Petts Wood [4]	d				22 13			22 43				23 13	
Bickley [4]	d	21 51			22 17	22 21		22 47	22 51			23 17	
Bromley South [4]	d	21 54	22 05	22 20	22 20	22 24	22 50	22 50	22 54	23 20		23 20	23 35
Shortlands [4]	d	21 57			22 23	22 27		22 53	22 57			23 23	
Ravensbourne	d	21 59				22 29			22 59				
Beckenham Hill	d	22 01				22 31			23 01				
Bellingham	d	22 03				22 33			23 03				
Catford	d	22 06				22 36			23 06				
Crofton Park	d	22 08				22 38			23 08				
Lewisham [4]	d												
Nunhead [4]	d	22 11				22 41			23 11				
Peckham Rye [4]	d	22 13				22 43			23 13				
Denmark Hill [4]	d	22 17				22 47			23 17				
Beckenham Junction [4]	d				22 26			22 56				23 26	
Kent House [4]	d				22 28			22 58				23 28	
Penge East	d				22 30			23 00				23 30	
Sydenham Hill	d				22 33			23 03				23 33	
West Dulwich	d				22 35			23 05				23 35	
Herne Hill [4]	d				22 38			23 08				23 38	
Loughborough Jn	d												
Elephant & Castle ⊖	d												
London Blackfriars [3] ⊖	d												
City Thameslink [3]	a												
Farringdon ⊖	a												
St Pancras International [15] ⊖	a												
Kentish Town ⊖	a												
Brixton ⊖	d				22 40			23 10				23 40	
London Victoria [15] ⊖	a	22 26	22 21	22 37	22 47	22 56	23 07	23 17	23 26	23 37		23 47	23 51

		SE [1]
Sevenoaks [4]	d	
Bat & Ball	d	
Otford [4]	d	
Shoreham (Kent)	d	
Eynsford	d	
Swanley [4]	d	
St Mary Cray	d	
Orpington [4]	d	
Petts Wood [4]	d	
Bickley [4]	d	
Bromley South [4]	d	23 50
Shortlands [4]	d	
Ravensbourne	d	
Beckenham Hill	d	
Bellingham	d	
Catford	d	
Crofton Park	d	
Lewisham [4]	d	
Nunhead [4]	d	
Peckham Rye [4]	d	
Denmark Hill [4]	d	
Beckenham Junction [4]	d	
Kent House [4]	d	
Penge East	d	
Sydenham Hill	d	
West Dulwich	d	
Herne Hill [4]	d	
Loughborough Jn	d	
Elephant & Castle ⊖	d	
London Blackfriars [3] ⊖	d	
City Thameslink [3]	a	
Farringdon ⊖	a	
St Pancras International [15] ⊖	a	
Kentish Town ⊖	a	
Brixton ⊖	d	
London Victoria [15] ⊖	a	00 07

Table 195

Sundays

Sevenoaks, Otford, Orpington, Bromley South, Beckenham Junction and Catford - London

Network Diagram - see first Page of Table 195

		SE [1] A	SE	SE	SE	SE [1]	SE	SE	SE [1]	SE [1]		SE	SE	SE [1]	SE	SE		SE	SE [1]		SE [1]	SE	SE [1]	
Sevenoaks [4]	d												07 54			08 24		22 24				22 54		
Bat & Ball	d												07 57			08 27		22 27				22 57		
Otford [4]	d								07 43				08 00			08 30		22 30	22 43			23 00		
Shoreham (Kent)	d												08 03			08 33		22 33				23 03		
Eynsford	d												08 07			08 37		22 37				23 07		
Swanley [4]	d					07 32			07 51				08 12	08 32		08 42		22 42	22 51			23 12	23 32	
St Mary Cray	d					07 36			07 55				08 16	08 36		08 46		22 46	22 55			23 16	23 36	
Orpington [4]	d		06 43	07 06	07 13		07 36	07 43				08 06			08 36									
Petts Wood [4]	d		06 46	07 09	07 16		07 39	07 46				08 09			08 39									
Bickley [4]	d		06 50	07 13	07 20		07 43	07 50				08 13	08 20		08 43	08 50		22 50				23 20		
Bromley South [4]	d	23p50	06 53	07 16	07 23	07 43	07 46	07 53	08 02	08 13		08 16	08 23	08 43	08 46	08 53		22 53	23 02		23 13	23 23	23 43	
Shortlands [4]	d		06 56	07 19	07 26		07 49	07 56				08 19	08 26		08 49	08 56		22 56				23 26		
Ravensbourne	d		06 58		07 28			07 58					08 28			08 58		22 58				23 28		
Beckenham Hill	d		07 00		07 30			08 00					08 30			09 00	and at the same minutes past each hour until	23 00				23 30		
Bellingham	d		07 02		07 32			08 02					08 32			09 02		23 02				23 32		
Catford	d		07 05		07 35			08 05					08 35			09 05		23 05				23 35		
Crofton Park	d		07 07		07 37			08 07					08 37			09 07		23 07				23 37		
Lewisham [4] ⛴	d																							
Nunhead [4]	d		07 10		07 40			08 10					08 40			09 10		23 10				23 40		
Peckham Rye [4]	d		07 12		07 42			08 12					08 42			09 12		23 12				23 42		
Denmark Hill [4]	d		07 16		07 46			08 16					08 46			09 16		23 16				23 46		
Beckenham Junction [4] ⛴	d			07 22			07 52					08 22			08 52									
Kent House [4]	d			07 24			07 54					08 24			08 54									
Penge East	d			07 26			07 56					08 26			08 56									
Sydenham Hill	d			07 29			07 59					08 29			08 59									
West Dulwich	d			07 31			08 01					08 31			09 01									
Herne Hill [4]	d			07 34			08 04					08 34			09 04									
Loughborough Jn	d																							
Elephant & Castle ⊖	d																							
London Blackfriars [3] ⊖	d																							
City Thameslink [3]	a																							
Farringdon ⊖	a																							
St Pancras International [15] ⊖	a																							
Kentish Town ⊖	a																							
Brixton ⊖	d			07 36			08 06					08 36			09 06									
London Victoria [15] ⊖	a	00 07	07 25	07 43	07 55	08 03	08 13	08 25	08 18	08 29		08 43	08 55	09 02	09 13	09 25		23 25	23 18		23 29	23 55	00 02	

A not 11 December

London - Maidstone East and Ashford International

Network Diagram - see first Page of Table 195

Miles	Miles	Miles			SE MO 1	SE MX 1	SE MX 1	SE 1	SE 1	SE 1	SE 1	SE 1	SE 1		SE 1	SE 1	SE 1	SE 1	SE 1	SE 1	SE 1	SE 1	SE 1		SE 1
0	—	—	**London Victoria 15** ⊖	d	22p45	23p07	00 07		06 07	06 37	07 07	07 36	08 07		08 37	09 07	09 37	10 07	10 37	11 07	11 37	12 07	12 37		13 07
—	0	—	**London Blackfriars 3** ⊖195	d																					
—	1¼	—	Elephant & Castle ⊖195	d																					
11	11½	—	Bromley South 4 195	d	23p01	23p23	00 25		06 23	06 58	07 23	07 53	08 24		08 53	09 23	09 53	10 23	10 53	11 23	11 53	12 23	12 53		13 23
14¾	—	—	St Mary Cray 195	d	23p08	23p30	00 31		06 30	07 04	07 30	08 00	08 31		09 00		10 00		11 00		12 00		13 00		
17½	—	—	Swanley 4 195	d	23p12	23p34	00 36		06 34	07 08	07 34	08 04	08 35		09 04	09 33	10 04	10 33	11 04	11 33	12 04	12 33	13 04		13 33
24	—	—	Otford 4 195	d	23p20	23p42	00 47		06 42	07 16	07 42	08 12	08 43		09 12	09 41	10 12	10 41	11 12	11 41	12 12	12 41	13 12		13 41
27	—	—	Kemsing	d		23p47	00 52		06 47	07 21	07 47	08 17	08 48		09 17		10 17		11 17		12 17		13 17		
29½	—	—	Borough Green & Wrotham	d	23p28	23p52	00 56		06 52	07 26	07 52	08 22	08 53		09 22	09 48	10 22	10 48	11 22	11 48	12 22	12 48	13 22		13 48
34¾	—	—	West Malling	d	23p34	23p58	01 03		06 58	07 32	07 58	08 28	08 59		09 28	09 55	10 28	10 55	11 28	11 55	12 28	12 55	13 28		13 55
35¾	—	—	East Malling	d	23p37	00 01	01 06		07 01	07 35	08 01	08 31	09 02		09 31		10 31		11 31		12 31		13 31		
37½	—	—	Barming	d	23p41	00 05	01 09		07 05	07 39	08 05	08 35	09 06		09 35		10 35		11 35		12 35		13 35		
40	—	—	**Maidstone East 4**	a	23p45	00 09	01 13		07 09	07 43	08 09	08 39	09 10		09 39	10 02	10 39	11 02	11 39	12 02	12 39	13 02	13 39		14 02
—	—	—		d	23p46	00 10	01 14	06 34	07 10	07 44	08 10	08 40	09 11		09 40	10 03	10 40	11 03	11 40	12 03	12 40	13 03	13 40		14 03
42¾	—	—	Bearsted	d	23p51	00 15	01 19	06 39	07 15	07 49	08 15	08 45	09 16		09 45	10 08	10 45	11 08	11 45	12 08	12 45	13 08	13 45		14 08
45	—	—	Hollingbourne	d	23p54	00 18	01 22	06 42	07 18	07 52	08 18	08 48	09 19		09 48		10 48		11 48		12 48		13 48		
47½	—	—	Harrietsham	d	23p58	00 22	01 26	06 46	07 22	07 56	08 22	08 52	09 23		09 52		10 52		11 52		12 52		13 52		
49¼	—	—	Lenham	d	00 01	00 25	01 29	06 49	07 25	07 59	08 25	08 55	09 26		09 55		10 55		11 55		12 55		13 55		
53¼	—	—	Charing	d	00 06	00 30	01 34	06 54	07 30	08 04	08 30	09 00	09 31		10 00		11 00		12 00		13 00		14 00		
59¼	—	56	**Ashford International**	a	00 15	00 39	01 43	07 02	07 39	08 13	08 39	09 09	09 40		10 09	10 27	11 09	11 27	12 09	12 27	13 09	13 27	14 09		14 27
—	—	—		d																					

		SE 1	SE 1	SE 1	SE 1	SE 1	SE 1	SE 1	SE 1		SE 1	SE 1	SE 1	FC 1	SE 1	SE 1	SE 1	SE 1	SE 1		SE 1	SE 1	SE 1	SE 1	SE 1
London Victoria 15 ⊖	d	13 37	14 07	14 37	15 07	15 37	16 07	16 37	16 58		17 12	17 28	17 42		18 03	18 18	18 42	19 07	19 37		20 07	20 37	21 07	22 07	23 07
London Blackfriars 3 ⊖195	d													17 48											
Elephant & Castle ⊖195	d													17 52											
Bromley South 4 195	d	13 53	14 23	14 53	15 23	15 53	16 23	16 53	17 19		17 31	17 50	17 59	18 11	18 24	18 39	18 59	19 27	19 53		20 23	20 53	21 23	22 23	23 23
St Mary Cray 195	d	14 00		15 00		16 00		17 00			17 38	17 57	18 06	18 18		18 45	19 06		20 00			21 00	21 30	22 30	23 30
Swanley 4 195	d	14 04	14 33	15 04	15 33	16 04	16 33	17 04			17 42	18 01	18 11	18 22		18 50	19 11	19 36	20 04		20 33	21 04	21 34	22 34	23 34
Otford 4 195	d	14 12	14 41	15 12	15 41	16 12	16 41	17 12	17 35		17 51	18 10	18 19	18 31	18 43	18 58	19 19	19 44	20 12		20 41	21 12	21 42	22 42	23 42
Kemsing	d	14 17		15 17		16 17		17 17			17 56		18 24	18 36		19 03	19 24		20 17			21 17	21 47	22 47	23 47
Borough Green & Wrotham	d	14 22	14 48	15 22	15 48	16 22	16 48	17 22	17 43		18 00	18 17	18 29	18 41	18 51	19 08	19 29	19 51	20 22		20 48	21 22	21 52	22 52	23 52
West Malling	d	14 28	14 55	15 28	15 55	16 28	16 55	17 28	17 49		18 07	18 24	18 35	18 47	18 57	19 14	19 35	19 57	20 28		20 55	21 28	21 58	22 58	23 58
East Malling	d	14 31		15 31		16 31		17 31			18 10		18 38	18 50		19 17	19 38		20 31			21 31	22 01	23 01	00 01
Barming	d	14 35		15 35		16 35		17 35			18 13		18 42	18 54		19 21	19 42		20 35			21 35	22 05	23 05	00 05
Maidstone East 4	a	14 39	15 02	15 39	16 02	16 39	17 02	17 39	17 56		18 17	18 33	18 46	18 58	19 04	19 25	19 46	20 04	20 39		21 02	21 39	22 09	23 09	00 09
	d	14 40	15 03	15 40	16 03	16 40	17 03	17 40	17 57		18 18		18 47	18 59	19 06	19 26	19 47	20 05	20 40		21 03	21 40	22 10	23 10	00 10
Bearsted	d	14 45	15 08	15 45	16 08	16 45	17 08	17 45	18 02		18 23		18 52	19 04	19 11	19 31	19 52	20 10	20 45		21 08	21 45	22 15	23 15	00 15
Hollingbourne	d	14 48		15 48	16 11	16 48	17 11	17 48	18 06		18 27		18 55	19 08	19 15	19 34	19 55	20 13	20 48		21 11	21 48	22 18	23 18	00 18
Harrietsham	d	14 52		15 52	16 15	16 52	17 15	17 52	18 09		18 30		18 59	19 11	19 18	19 38	19 59	20 17	20 52		21 15	21 52	22 22	23 22	00 22
Lenham	d	14 55		15 55	16 18	16 55	17 18	17 55	18 13		18 34		19 02	19 15	19 22	19 41	20 02	20 20	20 55		21 18	21 55	22 25	23 25	00 25
Charing	d	15 00		16 00	16 23	17 00	17 23	18 00	18 18		18 39		19 07	19 20	19 27	19 46	20 07	20 25	21 00		21 23	22 00	22 30	23 30	00 30
Ashford International	a	15 09	15 30	16 09	16 32	17 09	17 34	18 11	18 28		18 50		19 18	19 32	19 40	19 58	20 18	20 34	21 09		21 32	22 09	22 39	23 39	00 39
	d																								

Saturdays

		SE 1	SE 1	SE 1	SE 1	SE 1	SE 1	SE 1	SE 1	SE 1		SE 1	SE 1	SE 1	SE 1	SE 1	SE 1	SE 1	SE 1	SE 1		SE 1	SE 1	SE 1	SE 1
London Victoria 15 ⊖	d	23p07	00 07		06 07	07 07	07 37	08 07	08 37	09 07		09 37	10 07	10 37	11 07	11 37	12 07	12 37	13 07	13 37		14 07	14 37	15 07	15 37
London Blackfriars 3 ⊖195	d																								
Elephant & Castle ⊖195	d																								
Bromley South 4 195	d	23p23	00 25		06 23	07 23	07 53	08 23	08 53	09 23		09 53	10 23	10 53	11 23	11 53	12 23	12 53	13 23	13 53		14 23	14 53	15 23	15 53
St Mary Cray 195	d	23p30	00 31		06 30	07 30	08 00		09 00			10 00		11 00		12 00		13 00		14 00			15 00		16 00
Swanley 4 195	d	23p34	00 36		06 34	07 34	08 04	08 33	09 04	09 33		10 04	10 33	11 04	11 33	12 04	12 33	13 04	13 33	14 04		14 33	15 04	15 33	16 04
Otford 4 195	d	23p42	00 47		06 42	07 42	08 12	08 41	09 12	09 41		10 12	10 41	11 12	11 41	12 12	12 41	13 12	13 41	14 12		14 41	15 12	15 41	16 12
Kemsing	d	23p47	00 52		06 47	07 47	08 17		09 17			10 17		11 17		12 17		13 17		14 17			15 17		16 17
Borough Green & Wrotham	d	23p52	00 56		06 52	07 52	08 22	08 48	09 22	09 48		10 22	10 48	11 22	11 48	12 22	12 48	13 22	13 48	14 22		14 48	15 22	15 48	16 22
West Malling	d	23p58	01 03		06 58	07 58	08 28	08 55	09 28	09 55		10 28	10 55	11 28	11 55	12 28	12 55	13 28	13 55	14 28		14 55	15 28	15 55	16 28
East Malling	d	00 01	01 06		07 01	08 01	08 31		09 31			10 31		11 31		12 31		13 31		14 31			15 31		16 31
Barming	d	00 05	01 09		07 05	08 05	08 35		09 35			10 35		11 35		12 35		13 35		14 35			15 35		16 35
Maidstone East 4	a	00 09	01 13		07 09	08 09	08 39	09 02	09 39	10 02		10 39	11 02	11 39	12 02	12 39	13 02	13 39	14 02	14 39		15 02	15 39	16 02	16 39
	d	00 10	01 14	06 10	07 10	08 10	08 40	09 03	09 40	10 03		10 40	11 03	11 40	12 03	12 40	13 03	13 40	14 03	14 40		15 03	15 40	16 03	16 40
Bearsted	d	00 15	01 19	06 15	07 15	08 15	08 45	09 08	09 45	10 08		10 45	11 08	11 45	12 08	12 45	13 08	13 45	14 08	14 45		15 08	15 45	16 08	16 45
Hollingbourne	d	00 18	01 22	06 18	07 18	08 18	08 48		09 48			10 48		11 48		12 48		13 48		14 48			15 48		16 48
Harrietsham	d	00 22	01 26	06 22	07 22	08 22	08 52		09 52			10 52		11 52		12 52		13 52		14 52			15 52		16 52
Lenham	d	00 25	01 29	06 25	07 25	08 25	08 55		09 55			10 55		11 55		12 55		13 55		14 55			15 55		16 55
Charing	d	00 30	01 34	06 30	07 30	08 30	09 00		10 00			11 00		12 00		13 00		14 00		15 00			16 00		17 00
Ashford International	a	00 39	01 43	06 39	07 39	08 39	09 09	09 27	10 09	10 27		11 09	11 27	12 09	12 27	13 09	13 27	14 09	14 27	15 09		15 27	16 09	16 27	17 09
	d																								

Table 196

Saturdays

London - Maidstone East and Ashford International

Network Diagram - see first Page of Table 195

			SE 1	SE 1	SE 1	SE 1	SE 1	SE 1	SE 1	SE 1	SE 1	SE 1	SE 1	SE 1
London Victoria 15	⊖	d	16 07	16 37	17 07	17 37	18 07	18 37	19 07	19 37	20 07	21 07	22 07	23 07
London Blackfriars 3	⊖195	d												
Elephant & Castle	⊖195	d												
Bromley South 4	195	d	16 23	16 53	17 23	17 53	18 23	18 53	19 23	19 53	20 23	21 23	22 23	23 23
St Mary Cray	195	d		17 00		18 00		19 00		20 00	20 30	21 30	22 30	23 30
Swanley 4	195	d	16 33	17 04	17 33	18 04	18 33	19 04	19 33	20 04	20 34	21 34	22 34	23 34
Otford 4	195	d	16 41	17 12	17 41	18 12	18 41	19 12	19 41	20 12	20 42	21 42	22 42	23 42
Kemsing		d		17 17		18 17		19 17		20 17	20 47	21 47	22 47	23 47
Borough Green & Wrotham		d	16 48	17 22	17 48	18 22	18 48	19 22	19 48	20 22	20 52	21 52	22 52	23 52
West Malling		d	16 55	17 28	17 55	18 28	18 55	19 28	19 55	20 28	20 58	21 58	22 58	23 58
East Malling		d		17 31		18 31		19 31		20 31	21 01	22 01	23 01	00 01
Barming		d		17 35		18 35		19 35		20 35	21 05	22 05	23 05	00 05
Maidstone East 4		a	17 02	17 39	18 02	18 39	19 02	19 39	20 02	20 39	21 09	22 09	23 09	00 09
		d	17 03	17 40	18 03	18 40	19 03	19 40	20 03	20 40	21 10	22 10	23 10	00 10
Bearsted		d	17 08	17 45	18 08	18 45	19 08	19 45	20 08	20 45	21 15	22 15	23 15	00 15
Hollingbourne		d		17 48		18 48		19 48		20 48	21 18	22 18	23 18	00 18
Harrietsham		d		17 52		18 52		19 52		20 52	21 22	22 22	23 22	00 22
Lenham		d		17 55		18 55		19 55		20 55	21 25	22 25	23 25	00 25
Charing		d		18 00		19 00		20 00		21 00	21 30	22 30	23 30	00 30
Ashford International		a	17 27	18 09	18 27	19 09	19 27	20 09	20 27	21 09	21 39	22 39	23 39	00 39
		d												

Sundays

			SE 1 A	SE 1	SE 1	SE 1	SE 1	SE 1	SE 1	SE 1	SE 1	SE 1	SE 1	SE 1	SE 1	SE 1	SE 1	SE 1	SE 1	SE 1
London Victoria 15	⊖	d	23p07	00 07	07 45	08 45	09 45	10 45	11 45	12 45	13 45	14 45	15 45	16 45	17 45	18 45	19 45	20 45	21 45	22 45
London Blackfriars 3	⊖195	d																		
Elephant & Castle	⊖195	d																		
Bromley South 4	195	d	23p23	00 25	08 01	09 01	10 01	11 01	12 01	13 01	14 01	15 01	16 01	17 01	18 01	19 01	20 01	21 01	22 01	23 01
St Mary Cray	195	d	23p30	00 31	08 08	09 08	10 08	11 08	12 08	13 08	14 08	15 08	16 08	17 08	18 08	19 08	20 08	21 08	22 08	23 08
Swanley 4	195	d	23p34	00 36	08 12	09 12	10 12	11 12	12 12	13 12	14 12	15 12	16 12	17 12	18 12	19 12	20 12	21 12	22 12	23 12
Otford 4	195	d	23p42	00 47	08 20	09 20	10 20	11 20	12 20	13 20	14 20	15 20	16 20	17 20	18 20	19 20	20 20	21 20	22 20	23 20
Kemsing		d	23p47	00 52																
Borough Green & Wrotham		d	23p52	00 56	08 28	09 28	10 28	11 28	12 28	13 28	14 28	15 28	16 28	17 28	18 28	19 28	20 28	21 28	22 28	23 28
West Malling		d	23p58	01 03	08 34	09 34	10 34	11 34	12 34	13 34	14 34	15 34	16 34	17 34	18 34	19 34	20 34	21 34	22 34	23 34
East Malling		d	00 01	01 06	08 37	09 37	10 37	11 37	12 37	13 37	14 37	15 37	16 37	17 37	18 37	19 37	20 37	21 37	22 37	23 37
Barming		d	00 05	01 09	08 41	09 41	10 41	11 41	12 41	13 41	14 41	15 41	16 41	17 41	18 41	19 41	20 41	21 41	22 41	23 41
Maidstone East 4		a	00 09	01 13	08 45	09 45	10 45	11 45	12 45	13 45	14 45	15 45	16 45	17 45	18 45	19 45	20 45	21 45	22 45	23 45
		d	00 10	01 14	08 46	09 46	10 46	11 46	12 46	13 46	14 46	15 46	16 46	17 46	18 46	19 46	20 46	21 46	22 46	23 46
Bearsted		d	00 15	01 19	08 51	09 51	10 51	11 51	12 51	13 51	14 51	15 51	16 51	17 51	18 51	19 51	20 51	21 51	22 51	23 51
Hollingbourne		d	00 18	01 22	08 54	09 54	10 54	11 54	12 54	13 54	14 54	15 54	16 54	17 54	18 54	19 54	20 54	21 54	22 54	23 54
Harrietsham		d	00 22	01 26	08 58	09 58	10 58	11 58	12 58	13 58	14 58	15 58	16 58	17 58	18 58	19 58	20 58	21 58	22 58	23 58
Lenham		d	00 25	01 29	09 01	10 01	11 01	12 01	13 01	14 01	15 01	16 01	17 01	18 01	19 01	20 01	21 01	22 01	23 01	00 01
Charing		d	00 30	01 34	09 06	10 06	11 06	12 06	13 06	14 06	15 06	16 06	17 06	18 06	19 06	20 06	21 06	22 06	23 06	00 06
Ashford International		a	00 39	01 43	09 15	10 15	11 15	12 15	13 15	14 15	15 15	16 15	17 15	18 15	19 15	20 15	21 15	22 15	23 15	00 15
		d																		

A not 11 December

Ashford International and Maidstone East to London

Network Diagram - see first Page of Table 195

Miles	Miles	Miles			SE 1	SE 1	SE 1	SE 1	SE 1	SE 1	SE 1	SE 1	SE 1		SE 1	SE 1	SE 1	SE 1	SE 1	SE 1	SE 1	SE 1	SE 1		SE 1
14¼	—	0	**Ashford International** ⇌	a																					
—	—	—		d	05 20	05 44	05 50	06 03	06 16	06 25	06 40	06 58	07 15		07 47	08 26	08 47	09 30	09 47	10 30	10 47	11 30	11 47		12 30
20¼	—	—	Charing	d	05 28	05 53	05 58	06 11	06 24	06 33	06 48	07 06	07 23		07 55	08 34	08 55		09 55		10 55		11 55		
24¼	—	—	Lenham	d	05 33	05 58	06 03	06 16	06 29	06 38	06 53	07 11	07 28		08 00	08 39	09 00		10 00		11 00		12 00		
26	—	—	Harrietsham	d	05 36	06 01	06 06	06 19	06 32	06 41	06 56	07 14	07 31		08 03	08 42	09 03		10 03		11 03		12 03		
28½	—	—	Hollingbourne	d	05 40	06 04	06 10	06 23	06 36	06 45	07 00	07 18	07 35		08 07	08 46	09 07		10 07		11 07		12 07		
30¾	—	—	Bearsted	d	05 43	06 09	06 13	06 26	06 39	06 48	07 03	07 21	07 38		08 11	08 49	09 11	09 48	10 11	10 48	11 11	11 48	12 11		12 48
33½	—	—	**Maidstone East** 4	a	05 48	06 14	06 20	06 31	06 44	06 53	07 08	07 26	07 43		08 17	08 54	09 17	09 53	10 17	10 53	11 17	11 53	12 17		12 53
—	—	—		d	05 49	06 15	06 20	06 32	06 45	06 54	07 09	07 27	07 44		08 18	08 55	09 18	09 55	10 18	10 55	11 18	11 55	12 18		12 55
36	—	—	Barming	d	05 54		06 25	06 37	06 50	06 59	07 14	07 32	07 49		08 23		09 23		10 23		11 23		12 23		
37¾	—	—	East Malling	d	05 57		06 29	06 41	06 54	07 03	07 18	07 36			08 26		09 26		10 26		11 26		12 26		
38¾	—	—	West Malling	d	06 00	06 22	06 31	06 44	06 57	07 06	07 21	07 39	07 54		08 29	09 02	09 29	10 02	10 29	11 02	11 29	12 02	12 29		13 02
44	—	—	Borough Green & Wrotham	d	06 07	06 30	06 38	06 51	07 04	07 13	07 28	07 46	08 01		08 36	09 09	09 36	10 09	10 36	11 09	11 36	12 09	12 36		13 09
46½	—	—	Kemsing	d				06 55	07 08	07 17	07 32	07 50			08 40		09 40		10 40		11 40		12 40		
49½	—	—	Otford 4 195	a	06 15	06 38	06 46	07 00	07 13	07 22	07 37	07 55	08 09		08 46	09 17	09 46	10 17	10 46	11 17	11 46	12 17	12 46		13 17
56	—	—	Swanley 4 195	a	06 24	06 47	06 54	07 09	07 22	07 31	07 46	08 04			08 54	09 25	09 54	10 25	10 54	11 25	11 54	12 25	12 54		13 25
58¾	—	—	St Mary Cray 195	a											08 58		09 58		10 58		11 58		12 58		
62½	0	—	Bromley South 4 195	a	06 33	06 56	07 02	07 19	07 30	07 40	07 57	08 13	08 25		09 04	09 34	10 04	10 34	11 04	11 34	12 04	12 34	13 04		13 34
—	10¼	—	Elephant & Castle ⊖195	a		07 15				07 59															
—	11½	—	**London Blackfriars** 3 ⊖195	a		07 22				08 04															
73½	—	—	**London Victoria** 15 ⊖	a	06 51		07 22	07 43	07 53		08 23	08 36	08 53		09 23	09 51	10 21	10 51	11 21	11 51	12 21	12 51	13 21		13 51

		SE 1	SE 1	SE 1	SE 1	SE 1	SE 1	SE 1	SE 1		SE 1	SE 1	SE 1	SE 1	SE 1	SE 1	SE 1	SE 1	SE 1		SE 1				
Ashford International ⇌	a																								
	d	12 47	13 30	13 47	14 30	14 47	15 24	15 47	16 26		16 47	17 26	17 49		18 26	18 49	19 19	20 17	21 17		22 17				
Charing	d	12 55		13 55		14 55	15 32	15 55	16 34		16 55	17 34	17 57		18 34	18 57	19 27	20 25	21 25		22 25				
Lenham	d	13 00		14 00		15 00	15 37	16 00	16 39		17 00	17 39	18 02		18 39	19 02	19 32	20 30	21 30		22 30				
Harrietsham	d	13 03		14 03		15 03	15 40	16 03	16 42		17 03	17 42	18 05		18 42	19 05	19 35	20 33	21 33		22 33				
Hollingbourne	d	13 07		14 07		15 07	15 44	16 07	16 46		17 07	17 46	18 09		18 46	19 09	19 39	20 37	21 37		22 37				
Bearsted	d	13 11	13 48	14 11	14 48	15 11	15 48	16 11	16 49		17 11	17 49	18 12		18 49	19 12	19 42	20 41	21 41		22 41				
Maidstone East 4	a	13 17	13 53	14 17	14 53	15 17	15 53	16 17	16 54		17 17	17 54	18 17		18 54	19 17	19 47	20 47	21 47		22 47				
	d	13 18	13 55	14 18	14 55	15 18	15 55	16 18	16 55		17 18	17 55	18 18	18 40	18 55	19 18	19 48	20 48	21 48		22 48				
Barming	d	13 23		14 23		15 23		16 23			17 23		18 23			19 23	19 53	20 53	21 53		22 53				
East Malling	d	13 26		14 26		15 26		16 26			17 26		18 26			19 26	19 56	20 56	21 56		22 56				
West Malling	d	13 29	14 02	14 29	15 02	15 29	16 02	16 29	17 02		17 29	18 02	18 29	18 47	19 02	19 29	19 59	20 59	21 59		22 59				
Borough Green & Wrotham	d	13 36	14 09	14 36	15 09	15 36	16 09	16 36	17 09		17 36	18 09	18 36	18 54	19 09	19 36	20 06	21 06	22 06		23 06				
Kemsing	d	13 40		14 40		15 40		16 40			17 40		18 40			19 40	20 10	21 10	22 10		23 10				
Otford 4 195	a	13 46	14 17	14 46	15 17	15 46	16 17	16 46	17 17		17 46	18 17	18 46		19 17	19 46	20 16	21 16	22 16		23 16				
Swanley 4 195	a	13 54	14 25	14 54	15 25	15 54	16 25	16 54	17 25		17 54	18 25	18 54		19 25	19 54	20 24	21 24	22 24		23 24				
St Mary Cray 195	a	13 58		14 58		15 58		16 58			17 58		18 58			19 58	20 28	21 28	22 28		23 28				
Bromley South 4 195	a	14 04	14 34	15 04	15 34	16 04	16 34	17 04	17 34		18 05	18 34	19 04	19 16	19 34	20 04	20 34	21 34	22 34		23 34				
Elephant & Castle ⊖195	a																								
London Blackfriars 3 ⊖195	a																								
London Victoria 15 ⊖	a	14 21	14 51	15 21	15 51	16 21	16 51	17 23	17 53		18 21	18 53	19 21	19 35	19 51	20 21	20 51	21 51	22 51		23 51				

Saturdays

		SE 1	SE 1	SE 1	SE 1	SE 1	SE 1	SE 1	SE 1	SE 1		SE 1	SE 1	SE 1	SE 1	SE 1	SE 1	SE 1	SE 1	SE 1		SE 1	SE 1	SE 1	SE 1
Ashford International ⇌	a																								
	d	05 20	05 47	06 30	06 47	07 30	07 47	08 30	08 47	09 30		09 47	10 30	10 47	11 30	11 47	12 30	12 47	13 30	13 47		14 30	14 47	15 30	15 47
Charing	d	05 28	05 55		06 55		07 55		08 55			09 55		10 55		11 55		12 55		13 55			14 55		15 55
Lenham	d	05 33	06 00		07 00		08 00		09 00			10 00		11 00		12 00		13 00		14 00			15 00		16 00
Harrietsham	d	05 36	06 03		07 03		08 03		09 03			10 03		11 03		12 03		13 03		14 03			15 03		16 03
Hollingbourne	d	05 40	06 07		07 07		08 07		09 07			10 07		11 07		12 07		13 07		14 07			15 07		16 07
Bearsted	d	05 43	06 11	06 48	07 11	07 48	08 11	08 48	09 11	09 48		10 11	10 48	11 11	11 48	12 11	12 48	13 11	13 48	14 11		14 48	15 11	15 48	16 11
Maidstone East 4	a	05 48	06 17	06 53	07 17	07 53	08 17	08 53	09 17	09 53		10 17	10 53	11 17	11 53	12 17	12 53	13 17	13 53	14 17		14 53	15 17	15 53	16 17
	d	05 49	06 18	06 55	07 18	07 55	08 18	08 55	09 18	09 55		10 18	10 55	11 18	11 55	12 18	12 55	13 18	13 55	14 18		14 55	15 18	15 55	16 18
Barming	d	05 54	06 23		07 23		08 23		09 23			10 23		11 23		12 23		13 23		14 23			15 23		16 23
East Malling	d	05 58	06 26		07 26		08 26		09 26			10 26		11 26		12 26		13 26		14 26			15 26		16 26
West Malling	d	06 01	06 29	07 02	07 29	08 02	08 29	09 02	09 29	10 02		10 29	11 02	11 29	12 02	12 29	13 02	13 29	14 02	14 29		15 02	15 29	16 02	16 29
Borough Green & Wrotham	d	06 08	06 36	07 09	07 36	08 09	08 36	09 09	09 36	10 09		10 36	11 09	11 36	12 09	12 36	13 09	13 36	14 09	14 36		15 09	15 36	16 09	16 36
Kemsing	d		06 40		07 40		08 40		09 40			10 40		11 40		12 40		13 40		14 40			15 40		16 40
Otford 4 195	a	06 16	06 46	07 17	07 46	08 17	08 46	09 17	09 46	10 17		10 46	11 17	11 46	12 17	12 46	13 17	13 46	14 17	14 46		15 17	15 46	16 17	16 46
Swanley 4 195	a	06 24	06 54	07 25	07 54	08 25	08 54	09 25	09 54	10 25		10 54	11 25	11 54	12 25	12 54	13 25	13 54	14 25	14 54		15 25	15 54	16 25	16 54
St Mary Cray 195	a	06 28	06 58		07 58		08 58		09 58			10 58		11 58		12 58		13 58		14 58			15 58		16 58
Bromley South 4 195	a	06 34	07 04	07 34	08 04	08 34	09 04	09 34	10 04	10 34		11 04	11 34	12 04	12 34	13 04	13 34	14 04	14 34	15 04		15 34	16 04	16 34	17 04
Elephant & Castle ⊖195	a																								
London Blackfriars 3 ⊖195	a																								
London Victoria 15 ⊖	a	06 51	07 21	07 51	08 21	08 51	09 21	09 51	10 21	10 51		11 21	11 51	12 21	12 51	13 21	13 51	14 21	14 51	15 21		15 51	16 21	16 51	17 21

Saturdays

Ashford International and Maidstone East to London

Network Diagram - see first Page of Table 195

			SE 1	SE 1	SE 1	SE 1	SE 1	SE 1	SE 1	SE 1	SE 1
Ashford International		a									
		d	16 30	16 47	17 30	17 47	18 30	18 47	19 47	20 47	22 17
Charing		d		16 55		17 55		18 55	19 55	20 55	22 25
Lenham		d		17 00		18 00		19 00	20 00	21 00	22 30
Harrietsham		d		17 03		18 03		19 03	20 03	21 03	22 33
Hollingbourne		d		17 07		18 07		19 07	20 07	21 07	22 37
Bearsted		d	16 48	17 11	17 48	18 11	18 48	19 11	20 11	21 11	22 41
Maidstone East 4		a	16 53	17 17	17 53	18 17	18 53	19 17	20 17	21 17	22 47
		d	16 55	17 18	17 55	18 18	18 55	19 18	20 18	21 18	22 48
Barming		d		17 23		18 23		19 23	20 23	21 23	22 53
East Malling		d		17 26		18 26		19 26	20 26	21 26	22 56
West Malling		d	17 02	17 29	18 02	18 29	19 02	19 29	20 29	21 29	22 59
Borough Green & Wrotham		d	17 09	17 36	18 09	18 36	19 09	19 36	20 36	21 36	23 06
Kemsing		d		17 40		18 40		19 40	20 40	21 40	23 10
Otford 4	195	a	17 17	17 46	18 17	18 46	19 17	19 46	20 46	21 46	23 16
Swanley 4	195	a	17 25	17 54	18 25	18 54	19 25	19 54	20 54	21 54	23 24
St Mary Cray	195	a		17 58		18 58		19 58	20 58	21 58	23 28
Bromley South 4	195	a	17 34	18 04	18 34	19 04	19 34	20 04	21 04	22 04	23 34
Elephant & Castle	⊖195	a									
London Blackfriars 3	⊖195	a									
London Victoria 15	⊖	a	17 51	18 21	18 51	19 21	19 51	20 21	21 21	22 21	23 51

Sundays

			SE 1	SE 1	SE 1	SE 1	SE 1	SE 1	SE 1	SE 1	SE 1	SE 1	SE 1	SE 1	SE 1	SE 1	SE 1	SE 1
Ashford International		a																
		d	06 47	07 47	08 47	09 47	10 47	11 47	12 47	13 47	14 47	15 47	16 47	17 47	18 47	19 47	20 47	21 47
Charing		d	06 55	07 55	08 55	09 55	10 55	11 55	12 55	13 55	14 55	15 55	16 55	17 55	18 55	19 55	20 55	21 55
Lenham		d	07 00	08 00	09 00	10 00	11 00	12 00	13 00	14 00	15 00	16 00	17 00	18 00	19 00	20 00	21 00	22 00
Harrietsham		d	07 03	08 03	09 03	10 03	11 03	12 03	13 03	14 03	15 03	16 03	17 03	18 03	19 03	20 03	21 03	22 03
Hollingbourne		d	07 07	08 07	09 07	10 07	11 07	12 07	13 07	14 07	15 07	16 07	17 07	18 07	19 07	20 07	21 07	22 07
Bearsted		d	07 11	08 11	09 11	10 11	11 11	12 11	13 11	14 11	15 11	16 11	17 11	18 11	19 11	20 11	21 11	22 11
Maidstone East 4		a	07 16	08 16	09 16	10 16	11 16	12 16	13 16	14 16	15 16	16 16	17 16	18 16	19 16	20 16	21 16	22 16
		d	07 16	08 16	09 16	10 16	11 16	12 16	13 16	14 16	15 16	16 16	17 16	18 16	19 16	20 16	21 16	22 16
Barming		d	07 21	08 21	09 21	10 21	11 21	12 21	13 21	14 21	15 21	16 21	17 21	18 21	19 21	20 21	21 21	22 21
East Malling		d	07 25	08 25	09 25	10 25	11 25	12 25	13 25	14 25	15 25	16 25	17 25	18 25	19 25	20 25	21 25	22 25
West Malling		d	07 28	08 28	09 28	10 28	11 28	12 28	13 28	14 28	15 28	16 28	17 28	18 28	19 28	20 28	21 28	22 28
Borough Green & Wrotham		d	07 35	08 35	09 35	10 35	11 35	12 35	13 35	14 35	15 35	16 35	17 35	18 35	19 35	20 35	21 35	22 35
Kemsing		d																
Otford 4	195	a	07 43	08 43	09 43	10 43	11 43	12 43	13 43	14 43	15 43	16 43	17 43	18 43	19 43	20 43	21 43	22 43
Swanley 4	195	a	07 51	08 51	09 51	10 51	11 51	12 51	13 51	14 51	15 51	16 51	17 51	18 51	19 51	20 51	21 51	22 51
St Mary Cray	195	a	07 55	08 55	09 55	10 55	11 55	12 55	13 55	14 55	15 55	16 55	17 55	18 55	19 55	20 55	21 55	22 55
Bromley South 4	195	a	08 02	09 02	10 02	11 02	12 02	13 02	14 02	15 02	16 02	17 02	18 02	19 02	20 02	21 02	22 02	23 02
Elephant & Castle	⊖195	a																
London Blackfriars 3	⊖195	a																
London Victoria 15	⊖	a	08 18	09 18	10 18	11 18	12 18	13 18	14 18	15 18	16 18	17 18	18 18	19 18	20 18	21 18	22 18	23 18

London - Lewisham, Hither Green, Petts Wood and Orpington (Summary of Services)

		SE MX	SE MX	SE MO ■1	SE MX ■1	SE MO	SE MX	SE MO	SE MX	SE MX		SE MO	SE MX	SE MX	SE MX	SE MX	SE	SE	SE	SE		SE	SE	FC ■1	SE
London Charing Cross ■4 ⊖	d		23p36	23p38	23p45	23p46		23p50	23p52			23p56	00 02	00 06	00 10	00 15	00 18	00 48	04 50	04 56		05 02	05 20		
London Waterloo (East) ■4 ⊖	d		23p39	23p41	23p48	23p49		23p53	23p55			23p59	00 05	00 09	00 13	00 18	00 21	00 51	04 53	04 59		05 05	05 23		
London Cannon Street ■4 ⊖	d																								
London Blackfriars ■3 ⊖	d																							05 24	
London Bridge ■4 ⊖	d		23p44	23p46	23p53	23p54		23p58	23p59			00 04	00 10	00 14	00 18	00 23	00 26	00 56	04a57	05 04		05 10	05a27	05a30	
London Victoria ■15 ⊖	d	23p25					23p43			23p55															
New Cross ■4 ⊖	d							00 04	00 05				00 15		00 23		00 31	01 01		05 09		05 15			05 31
St Johns	d								00 07																05 33
Lewisham ■4	a		23p51			00 02		00 07	00 10			00 11	00 19	00 21	00 27		00 35	01 05		05 13		05 19			05 35
Hither Green ■4	a		23p56			00 07						00 16		00 26	00 31			01 09		05 17					
Petts Wood ■4	a	23p59	00 08			00 20	00 21			00 29				00 38				01 22							
Orpington ■4	a	00 02	00 12	00 01	00 08	00 23	00 25			00 32				00 42		00 46		01 25							

		SE	SE ■1	SE	SE	SE		SE	FC ■1	SE	SE	SE	SE	SE	SE	SE		SE	FC ■1	SE ■1	SE	SE	SE	SE	SE ■1
London Charing Cross ■4 ⊖	d	05 26	05 30	05 32	05 36	05 39				05 47		05 52	05 56	06 02	06 06			06 09		06 15		06 17		06 26	06 30
London Waterloo (East) ■4 ⊖	d	05 29	05 33	05 35	05 39	05 42				05 50		05 55	05 59	06 05	06 09			06 12		06 18		06 20		06 29	06 33
London Cannon Street ■4 ⊖	d										05 52					06 12							06 27		
London Blackfriars ■3 ⊖	d								05 44										06 14						
London Bridge ■4 ⊖	d	05 34	05 39	05 42	05 44	05 47			05a50	05 55	05a55	05a59	06 04	06 10	06 14	06a15		06 17	06a20	06 24		06 26	06a30	06 34	06 38
London Victoria ■15 ⊖	d							05 40													06 10				
New Cross ■4 ⊖	d	05 39		05 48		05 52				06 01			06 09	06 15								06 32		06 40	
St Johns	d									06 03												06 34			
Lewisham ■4	a	05 43		05 51	05 52	05 56				06 05			06 13	06 19	06 22			06 26				06 37		06 43	
Hither Green ■4	a	05 47			05 56								06 17		06 27									06 48	
Petts Wood ■4	a				06 08			06 14							06 39						06 44				
Orpington ■4	a		05 54		06 11			06 18							06 42					06 40	06 49				06 53

		SE		SE	FC ■1	SE	SE	SE ■1	SE	SE	FC ■1	SE		SE	SE	SE ■1	SE	SE	SE	SE	SE	FC ■1		SE	SE ■1
London Charing Cross ■4 ⊖	d			06 32		06 36	06 39	06 45		06 47		06 52			06 56	07 00		07 02	07 06						07 10
London Waterloo (East) ■4 ⊖	d			06 35		06 39	06 42	06 48		06 50		06 55			06 59	07 03		07 05	07 09						07 13
London Cannon Street ■4 ⊖	d								06 50					07 00							07 10			07 13	
London Blackfriars ■3 ⊖	d				06 34						06 50											07 09			
London Bridge ■4 ⊖	d			06 40	06a41	06 44	06 47	06 53	06 54	06 55	06a56	06a59		07 04	07 05	07 08		07 10	07 14		07 14	07a15		07a16	07a18
London Victoria ■15 ⊖	d	06 30															06 50			07 09					
New Cross ■4 ⊖	d			06 46					06 59	07 02				07 09							07 20				
St Johns	d								07 01	07 04				07 11							07 22				
Lewisham ■4	a			06 49		06 53	06 56		07 04	07 07				07 14				07 18		07 24	07 26				
Hither Green ■4	a					06 58			07 08						07 18				07 23		07 31				
Petts Wood ■4	a	07 04				07 10			07 21								07 24		07 36						
Orpington ■4	a	07 08				07 13		07 09	07 25							07 25	07 28		07 40						

		SE	SE ■1	SE	SE	SE	SE	SE		SE	SE	SE ■1	SE	SE	SE	FC ■1	SE	SE		SE	SE	SE ■1	SE	SE ■1	SE
London Charing Cross ■4 ⊖	d	07 12	07 15	07 17						07 26		07 29					07 36			07 39		07 40	07 44		
London Waterloo (East) ■4 ⊖	d	07 15	07 18	07 20						07 29		07 32					07 39			07 42		07 43	07 47		
London Cannon Street ■4 ⊖	d				07 20		07 24	07 27			07 30			07 32	07 36			07 41			07 44			07 47	
London Blackfriars ■3 ⊖	d															07 32									
London Bridge ■4 ⊖	d	07 21	07 23	07a24	07 24		07 28	07a30		07 34	07 34	07 38		07a36	07 40	07a41	07 44	07 45		07 47	07a47	07a48	07a51	07 51	
London Victoria ■15 ⊖	d					07 10							07 25												07 40
New Cross ■4 ⊖	d						07 33				07 39							07 50							
St Johns	d						07 35				07 41														
Lewisham ■4	a	07 29					07 38				07 44				07 48			07 54		07 56					
Hither Green ■4	a				07 34					07 45							07 53	07 58							
Petts Wood ■4	a					07 49							07 59				08 06								08 14
Orpington ■4	a		07 38		07 48	07 53						07 53	08 02				08 09							08 08	08 19

		SE	SE	SE		SE	SE ■1	SE	SE	SE	SE ■1	SE	FC	SE		SE	SE	SE	FC ■1	SE	SE	SE	SE ■1	SE	
London Charing Cross ■4 ⊖	d			07 48			07 52			07 59	08 00					08 03	08 05			08 11			08 13		
London Waterloo (East) ■4 ⊖	d			07 51			07 55			08 02	08 03					08 06	08 08			08 14			08 16		
London Cannon Street ■4 ⊖	d	07 51				07 54		07 56	08 00					08 05				08 10						08 16	
London Blackfriars ■3 ⊖	d												07 50						08 08						
London Bridge ■4 ⊖	d	07 55		07 56		07 58	08a00	08a00	08 04	08a06	08 09			08a08		08 11	08 13	08 14	08a16	08 19			08a20	08 20	
London Victoria ■15 ⊖	d		07 43									07 55									08 09	08 10			
New Cross ■4 ⊖	d	08 00				08 04			08 09									08 20						09a38	
St Johns	d					08 06			08 11									08 22							
Lewisham ■4	a	08 04	08 07			08 10			08 14							08 18		08 25		08 28	08 30				
Hither Green ■4	a	08 10															08 23	08 29							
Petts Wood ■4	a	08 23										08 29	08 32				08 36					08 44			
Orpington ■4	a	08 26		08 15							08 25	08 32	08 35				08 39					08 47			

London - Lewisham, Hither Green, Petts Wood and Orpington (Summary of Services)

		SE	SE	SE 1	SE	SE	SE	SE	SE 1	SE		SE	SE 1	SE	SE	SE	SE 1	SE	SE	SE		SE	SE	SE	SE
London Charing Cross 4 ⊖	d	08 15		08 17	08 20		08 23		08 27	08 31			08 33			08 37		08 41					08 44		08 49
London Waterloo (East) 4 ⊖	d	08 18		08 20	08 23		08 26		08 30	08 34			08 36			08 40		08 44					08 47		08 52
London Cannon Street 4 ⊖	d		08 19			08 25		08 30				08 36			08 39		08 42					08 47		08 51	
London Blackfriars 3 ⊖	d																								
London Bridge 4 ⊖	d	08a22	08 23	08 25	08 29	08a28	08 31	08 34	08 35	08 39		08a39	08 41		08 43	08 45	08 46	08 49				08 51	08a52	08 55	08 57
London Victoria 15 ⊖	d													08 25					08 39	08 40					
New Cross 4 ⊖	d		08 29				08 38	08 41							08 49							10a08		09 00	
St Johns	d		08 31				08 40	08 43							08 51									09 02	
Lewisham 4	a		08 33				08 43	08 45		08 48					08 54			08 56	09 01					09 05	
Hither Green 4	a		08 38		08 41										08 59	08 55								09 10	
Petts Wood 4	a		08 51											08 59		09 08				09 14				09 23	
Orpington 4	a		08 54	08 41					08 53				08 57	09 02		09 11	09 07			09 17				09 26	09 22

		SE	SE 1	SE	SE	SE		SE	SE 1	SE	SE	SE	FC 1	SE	SE	SE		SE	SE	SE 1	SE 1	SE	SE	SE	FC 1
London Charing Cross 4 ⊖	d		08 53		08 55				09 00		09 02			09 06		09 11				09 13			09 17		
London Waterloo (East) 4 ⊖	d		08 56		08 58				09 03		09 05			09 09		09 14				09 16			09 20		
London Cannon Street 4 ⊖	d	08 54		08 56		09 00		09 03				09 07			09 09				09 15		09 18			09 20	
London Blackfriars 3 ⊖	d												09 00												09 16
London Bridge 4 ⊖	d	08 58	09 01	09a00	09 03	09 04		09a06	09 08		09 10	09a10	09a11	09 14	09 14	09 19			09 19	09a20	09 22		09a24	09 25	09a26
London Victoria 15 ⊖	d									08 55								09 09				09 10			
New Cross 4 ⊖	d	09 04				09 09									09 19				10a38					09 29	
St Johns	d	09 06				09 11									09 21									09 31	
Lewisham 4	a	09 09				09 14					09 18				09 24	09 28		09 31						09 34	
Hither Green 4	a				09 14									09 23	09 28									09 38	
Petts Wood 4	a									09 29				09 36								09 44		09 51	
Orpington 4	a		09 20						09 26	09 33				09 39							09 40	09 47		09 55	

		SE		SE	SE	SE	SE 1	SE	SE	SE	FC 1	SE		SE	SE	SE	SE 1	SE	SE 1	SE	SE	SE		FC 1	SE
London Charing Cross 4 ⊖	d				09 26		09 30		09 32			09 36			09 39		09 40		09 45		09 47				
London Waterloo (East) 4 ⊖	d				09 29		09 33		09 35			09 39			09 42		09 43		09 48		09 50				
London Cannon Street 4 ⊖	d	09 24		09 27		09 30				09 37				09 40				09 47				09 50			09 54
London Blackfriars 3 ⊖	d										09 34													09 50	
London Bridge 4 ⊖	d	09 28		09a30	09 34	09 34	09 39		09 40	09a40	09a41	09 44		09 44	09 47		09a48	09 51	09 53		09a54	09 54		09a56	09 58
London Victoria 15 ⊖	d							09 25								09 39				09 40					
New Cross 4 ⊖	d	09 33				09 39								09 49				11a08				09 59			10 03
St Johns	d	09 35				09 41								09 51								10 01			10 05
Lewisham 4	a	09 38				09 44			09 49					09 54	09 56	10 01						10 04			10 08
Hither Green 4	a				09 43							09 53		09 58								10 08			
Petts Wood 4	a							09 59				10 06								10 14		10 21			
Orpington 4	a						09 55	10 02				10 09							10 08	10 17		10 24			

		SE	SE	SE	SE 1	SE	SE	SE		FC 1	SE	SE	SE	SE	SE 1	SE	SE 1	SE		SE	SE	FC 1	SE	SE	SE
London Charing Cross 4 ⊖	d		09 56		10 00		10 02				10 06		10 09		10 10		10 15			10 17					10 26
London Waterloo (East) 4 ⊖	d		09 59		10 03		10 05				10 09		10 12		10 13		10 18			10 20					10 29
London Cannon Street 4 ⊖	d	09 57		10 00				10 07				10 10				10 17					10 20		10 24	10 27	
London Blackfriars 3 ⊖	d									10 05												10 20			
London Bridge 4 ⊖	d	10a00	10 04	10 04	10 09		10 10	10a10		10a11	10 14	10 14	10 17		10a18	10 21	10 23			10a24	10 24	10a26	10 28	10a30	10 34
London Victoria 15 ⊖	d					09 55								10 09				10 10							
New Cross 4 ⊖	d			10 09								10 19				11a38					10 29		10 33		
St Johns	d			10 11								10 21									10 31		10 35		
Lewisham 4	a			10 14			10 19					10 24	10 26	10 31							10 34		10 38		
Hither Green 4	a		10 13								10 23	10 28									10 38				10 43
Petts Wood 4	a					10 29					10 36							10 44			10 51				
Orpington 4	a				10 25	10 32					10 39						10 38	10 47			10 54				

		SE	SE 1	SE		SE	SE	FC 1	SE	SE	SE	SE	SE 1	SE		SE 1	SE	SE	SE	FC 1	SE	SE	SE	SE	
London Charing Cross 4 ⊖	d		10 30			10 32			10 36		10 39		10 40			10 45		10 47					10 56		
London Waterloo (East) 4 ⊖	d		10 33			10 35			10 39		10 42		10 43			10 48		10 50					10 59		
London Cannon Street 4 ⊖	d	10 30					10 37			10 40				10 47					10 50		10 54	10 57		11 00	
London Blackfriars 3 ⊖	d							10 35												10 50					
London Bridge 4 ⊖	d	10 34	10 39			10 40	10a40	10a41	10 44	10 44	10 47		10a48	10 51		10 53		10a54	10 54	10a56	10 58	11a00	11 04	11 04	
London Victoria 15 ⊖	d			10 25								10 39					10 40								
New Cross 4 ⊖	d	10 39								10 49				12a08					10 59		11 03			11 09	
St Johns	d	10 41								10 51									11 01		11 05			11 11	
Lewisham 4	a	10 44				10 49				10 54	10 56	11 01							11 04		11 08			11 14	
Hither Green 4	a								10 53	10 58									11 08				11 13		
Petts Wood 4	a			10 59					11 06								11 14		11 21						
Orpington 4	a		10 55	11 02					11 09							11 08	11 17		11 24						

		SE 1	SE	SE	SE	FC 1	SE	SE	SE	SE		SE 1	SE	SE 1	SE	SE	SE	FC 1	SE	SE		SE	SE	SE 1	SE
London Charing Cross 4 ⊖	d	11 00		11 02			11 06		11 09			11 10		11 15		11 17						11 26		11 30	
London Waterloo (East) 4 ⊖	d	11 03		11 05			11 09		11 12			11 13		11 18		11 20						11 29		11 33	
London Cannon Street 4 ⊖	d				11 07			11 10					11 17				11 20		11 24	11 27			11 30		
London Blackfriars 3 ⊖	d					11 05												11 20							
London Bridge 4 ⊖	d	11 09		11 10	11a10	11a11	11 14	11 14	11 17			11a18	11 21	11 23		11a24	11 24	11a26	11 28	11a30		11 34	11 34	11 39	
London Victoria 15 ⊖	d		10 55							11 09					11 10										11 25
New Cross 4 ⊖	d							11 19					12a38				11 29		11 33				11 39		
St Johns	d							11 21									11 31		11 35				11 41		
Lewisham 4	a			11 19				11 24	11 26	11 31							11 33		11 38				11 44		
Hither Green 4	a						11 23	11 28									11 38					11 43			
Petts Wood 4	a		11 29				11 36								11 44		11 51								11 59
Orpington 4	a	11 25	11 32				11 39							11 38	11 47		11 54							11 55	12 02

London - Lewisham, Hither Green, Petts Wood and Orpington (Summary of Services)

		SE	SE	FC [1]	SE	SE		SE	SE	SE [1]	SE	SE [1]	SE	SE	SE	FC [1]		SE	SE	SE	SE	SE [1]	SE	SE	SE
London Charing Cross [4] ⊖	d	11 32			11 36			11 39		11 40		11 45		11 47						11 56		12 00		12 02	
London Waterloo (East) [4] ⊖	d	11 35			11 39			11 42		11 43		11 48		11 50						11 59		12 03		12 05	
London Cannon Street [4] ⊖	d		11 37			11 40					11 47				11 50			11 54	11 57		12 00				12 07
London Blackfriars [3] ⊖	d			11 35												11 50									
London Bridge [4] ⊖	d	11 40	11a40	11a41	11 44	11 44		11 47		11a48	11 51	11 53		11a54	11 54	11a56		11 58	12a00	12 04	12 04	12 09		12 10	12a10
London Victoria [15] ⊖	d								11 39				11 40										11 55		
New Cross [4] ⊖	d					11 49					13a08				11 59			12 03			12 09				
St Johns	d					11 51									12 01			12 05			12 11				
Lewisham [4]	a	11 49				11 54		11 56	12 01						12 03			12 08			12 14			12 19	
Hither Green [4]	a				11 53	11 58									12 08					12 13					
Petts Wood [4]	a				12 06								12 14		12 21								12 29		
Orpington [4]	a				12 09							12 08	12 17		12 24							12 25	12 32		

		FC [1]		SE	SE	SE	SE	SE [1]	SE	SE [1]	SE	SE		SE	FC [1]	SE	SE	SE	SE	SE [1]	SE	SE		SE	FC [1]
London Charing Cross [4] ⊖	d			12 06		12 09		12 10		12 15		12 17						12 26		12 30		12 32			
London Waterloo (East) [4] ⊖	d			12 09		12 12		12 13		12 18		12 20						12 29		12 33		12 35			
London Cannon Street [4] ⊖	d				12 10				12 17					12 20		12 24	12 27		12 30					12 37	
London Blackfriars [3] ⊖	d	12 05													12 20										12 35
London Bridge [4] ⊖	d	12a11		12 14	12 14	12 17		12a18	12 21	12 23		12a24		12 24	12a26	12 28	12a30	12 34	12 34	12 39		12 40		12a40	12a41
London Victoria [15] ⊖	d						12 09				12 10										12 25				
New Cross [4] ⊖	d				12 19				13a38					12 29		12 33			12 39						
St Johns	d				12 21									12 31		12 35			12 41						
Lewisham [4]	a				12 24	12 26	12 31							12 34		12 38			12 44			12 49			
Hither Green [4]	a			12 23	12 28									12 38				12 43							
Petts Wood [4]	a			12 36							12 44			12 51							12 59				
Orpington [4]	a			12 39						12 38	12 47			12 54						12 55	13 02				

		SE	SE	SE	SE	SE [1]	SE	SE [1]		SE	SE	SE	FC [1]	SE	SE	SE	SE	SE [1]		SE	SE	SE	FC [1]	SE	SE
London Charing Cross [4] ⊖	d	12 36		12 39		12 40		12 45			12 47					12 56		13 00			13 02			13 06	
London Waterloo (East) [4] ⊖	d	12 39		12 42		12 43		12 48			12 50					12 59		13 03			13 05			13 09	
London Cannon Street [4] ⊖	d		12 40				12 47					12 50		12 54	12 57		13 00					13 07			13 10
London Blackfriars [3] ⊖	d												12 50										13 05		
London Bridge [4] ⊖	d	12 44	12 44	12 47		12a48	12 51	12 53			12a54	12 54	12a56	12 58	13a00	13 04	13 04	13 09			13 10	13a10	13a11	13 14	13 14
London Victoria [15] ⊖	d				12 39					12 40										12 55					
New Cross [4] ⊖	d		12 49				14a08					12 59		13 03			13 09								13 19
St Johns	d		12 51									13 01		13 05			13 11								13 21
Lewisham [4]	a		12 54	12 56	13 01							13 03		13 08			13 14				13 19				13 24
Hither Green [4]	a	12 53	12 58									13 08				13 13								13 23	13 28
Petts Wood [4]	a	13 06								13 14		13 21								13 29				13 36	
Orpington [4]	a	13 09						13 08		13 17		13 24						13 25		13 32				13 39	

		SE	SE	SE [1]		SE	SE [1]	SE	SE	SE	FC [1]	SE	SE	SE		SE	SE [1]	SE	SE	SE	FC [1]	SE	SE	SE	
London Charing Cross [4] ⊖	d	13 09		13 10			13 15		13 17					13 26			13 30		13 32			13 36		13 39	
London Waterloo (East) [4] ⊖	d	13 12		13 13			13 18		13 20					13 29			13 33		13 35			13 39		13 42	
London Cannon Street [4] ⊖	d					13 17				13 20		13 24	13 27			13 30				13 37			13 40		
London Blackfriars [3] ⊖	d										13 20										13 35				
London Bridge [4] ⊖	d	13 17		13a18		13 21	13 23		13a24	13 24	13a26	13 28	13a30	13 34		13 34	13 39		13 40	13a40	13a41	13 44	13 44	13 47	
London Victoria [15] ⊖	d		13 09					13 10										13 25							
New Cross [4] ⊖	d					14a38				13 29		13 33				13 39							13 49		
St Johns	d									13 31		13 35				13 41							13 51		
Lewisham [4]	a	13 26	13 31							13 34		13 38				13 44			13 49				13 54	13 56	
Hither Green [4]	a									13 38				13 43								13 53	13 58		
Petts Wood [4]	a							13 44		13 51								13 59				14 06			
Orpington [4]	a						13 38	13 47		13 54							13 55	14 02				14 09			

		SE	SE [1]	SE	SE [1]	SE	SE	SE	FC [1]	SE		SE	SE	SE	SE [1]	SE	SE	SE	FC [1]	SE		SE	SE	SE	SE [1]
London Charing Cross [4] ⊖	d		13 40		13 45		13 47						13 56		14 00		14 02			14 06			14 09		14 10
London Waterloo (East) [4] ⊖	d		13 43		13 48		13 50						13 59		14 03		14 05			14 09			14 12		14 13
London Cannon Street [4] ⊖	d			13 47				13 50		13 54		13 57		14 00				14 07				14 10			
London Blackfriars [3] ⊖	d								13 50										14 05						
London Bridge [4] ⊖	d		13a48	13 51	13 53		13a54	13 54	13a56	13 58		14a00	14 04	14 04	14 09		14 10	14a10	14a11	14 14		14 14	14 17		14a18
London Victoria [15] ⊖	d	13 39				13 40										13 55								14 09	
New Cross [4] ⊖	d			15a08				13 59		14 03				14 09								14 19			
St Johns	d							14 01		14 05				14 11								14 21			
Lewisham [4]	a	14 01						14 04		14 08				14 14			14 19					14 24	14 26	14 31	
Hither Green [4]	a							14 08					14 13							14 23		14 28			
Petts Wood [4]	a					14 14		14 21								14 29				14 36					
Orpington [4]	a				14 08	14 17		14 24							14 25	14 32				14 39					

		SE	SE [1]	SE	SE	SE		FC [1]	SE	SE	SE	SE	SE [1]	SE	SE	SE		FC [1]	SE	SE	SE	SE	SE [1]	SE	SE [1]
London Charing Cross [4] ⊖	d		14 15		14 17						14 26		14 30		14 32				14 36		14 39		14 40		14 45
London Waterloo (East) [4] ⊖	d		14 18		14 20						14 29		14 33		14 35				14 39		14 42		14 43		14 48
London Cannon Street [4] ⊖	d	14 17				14 20			14 24	14 27		14 30				14 37				14 40				14 47	
London Blackfriars [3] ⊖	d							14 20										14 35							
London Bridge [4] ⊖	d	14 21	14 23		14a24	14 24		14a26	14 28	14a30	14 34	14 34	14 39		14 40	14a40		14a41	14 44	14 44	14 47		14a48	14 51	14 53
London Victoria [15] ⊖	d			14 10										14 25								14 39			
New Cross [4] ⊖	d	15a38				14 29			14 33			14 39								14 49				16a08	
St Johns	d					14 31			14 35			14 41								14 51					
Lewisham [4]	a					14 34			14 38			14 44			14 49					14 54	14 56	15 01			
Hither Green [4]	a					14 38					14 43								14 53	14 58					
Petts Wood [4]	a			14 44		14 51								14 59					15 06						
Orpington [4]	a		14 38	14 47		14 54							14 55	15 02					15 09						15 08

London - Lewisham, Hither Green, Petts Wood and Orpington (Summary of Services)

		SE		SE	SE	FC ■1	SE	SE	SE	SE	SE ■1	SE		SE	SE	FC ■1	SE	SE	SE	SE	SE ■1	SE		SE ■1	SE
London Charing Cross ■4 ⊖	d			14 47					14 56		15 00			15 02			15 06		15 09		15 10			15 15	
London Waterloo (East) ■4 ⊖	d			14 50					14 59		15 03			15 05			15 09		15 12		15 13			15 18	
London Cannon Street ■4 ⊖	d				14 50		14 54	14 57		15 00					15 07			15 10				15 17			
London Blackfriars ■3 ⊖	d					14 50										15 05									
London Bridge ■4 ⊖	d			14a54	14 54	14a56	14 58	15a00	15 04	15 04	15 09			15 10	15a10	15a11	15 14	15 14	15 17		15a18	15 21		15 23	
London Victoria ■15 ⊖	d	14 40										14 55								15 09					15 10
New Cross ■4 ⊖	d				14 59		15 03			15 09								15 19				16a38			
St Johns	d				15 01		15 05			15 11								15 21							
Lewisham ■4	a				15 04		15 08			15 14				15 19				15 24	15 26	15 31					
Hither Green ■4	a				15 08				15 13								15 23	15 28							
Petts Wood ■4	a	15 14			15 21							15 29					15 36								15 44
Orpington ■4	a	15 17			15 24						15 25	15 32					15 39							15 38	15 47

		SE	SE	FC ■1	SE	SE	SE	SE		SE ■1	SE	SE	SE	FC ■1	SE	SE	SE	SE		SE ■1	SE	SE ■1	SE	SE	SE
London Charing Cross ■4 ⊖	d	15 17					15 26			15 30		15 32			15 36		15 39			15 40		15 45		15 47	
London Waterloo (East) ■4 ⊖	d	15 20					15 29			15 33		15 35			15 39		15 42			15 43		15 48		15 50	
London Cannon Street ■4 ⊖	d		15 20		15 24	15 27		15 30					15 37			15 40					15 47				15 50
London Blackfriars ■3 ⊖	d			15 20										15 35											
London Bridge ■4 ⊖	d	15a24	15 24	15a26	15 28	15a30	15 34	15 34		15 39		15 40	15a40	15a41	15 44	15 44	15 47			15a48	15 51	15 53		15a54	15 54
London Victoria ■15 ⊖	d										15 25							15 39					15 40		
New Cross ■4 ⊖	d		15 29		15 33			15 39								15 49					17a11				15 59
St Johns	d		15 31		15 35			15 41								15 51									16 01
Lewisham ■4	a		15 34		15 38			15 44				15 49				15 54	15 56	16 01							16 03
Hither Green ■4	a		15 38				15 43								15 53	15 58									16 08
Petts Wood ■4	a		15 51								15 59				16 06								16 14		16 21
Orpington ■4	a		15 54							15 55	16 02				16 09							16 08	16 17		16 24

		FC ■1	SE	SE		SE	SE	SE ■1	SE	SE	SE	FC ■1	SE	SE		SE	SE	SE	SE ■1	SE	SE ■1	SE	FC ■1	SE	
London Charing Cross ■4 ⊖	d					15 56		16 00		16 02			16 06			16 09			16 10		16 15			16 20	
London Waterloo (East) ■4 ⊖	d					15 59		16 03		16 05			16 09			16 12			16 13		16 18			16 23	
London Cannon Street ■4 ⊖	d		15 54	15 57			16 00				16 07			16 10						16 17		16 20			
London Blackfriars ■3 ⊖	d	15 50										16 05											16 20		
London Bridge ■4 ⊖	d	15a56	15 58	16a00		16 04	16 04	16 09		16 10	16a10	16a11	16 14	16 14		16 17			16a18	16 21	16a22	16 24	16a26	16a28	
London Victoria ■15 ⊖	d								15 55								16 09	16 10							
New Cross ■4 ⊖	d		16 03				16 10							16 20						17a39		16 30			
St Johns	d		16 05				16 12							16 22								16 32			
Lewisham ■4	a		16 08				16 14			16 19				16 24		16 26	16 31					16 34			
Hither Green ■4	a					16 13							16 23	16 29								16 39			
Petts Wood ■4	a								16 29				16 36					16 44				16 51			
Orpington ■4	a							16 25	16 32				16 39					16 49				16 57			

		SE	SE	SE	SE	SE ■1	SE	SE	SE	SE		FC	FC ■1	SE	SE ■1	SE	SE	SE	SE	SE		SE ■1	SE ■1	SE	SE
London Charing Cross ■4 ⊖	d			16 26		16 28		16 30		16 32					16 37	16 39						16 41		16 42	16 45
London Waterloo (East) ■4 ⊖	d			16 29		16 31		16 33		16 35					16 40	16 42						16 44		16 45	16 48
London Cannon Street ■4 ⊖	d	16 24	16 27		16 30				16 35					16 39			16 42			16 44			16 46		
London Blackfriars ■3 ⊖	d											16 26	16 36												
London Bridge ■4 ⊖	d	16 28	16a30	16 34	16 34	16 36		16 38	16a38	16 40			16a42	16 43	16a44	16a46	16 46			16a47		16a48	16a49	16 51	16a52
London Victoria ■15 ⊖	d						16 25											16 39	16 40						
New Cross ■4 ⊖	d	16 34			16 40									16 49			16 52								
St Johns	d	16 36			16 42									16 51											
Lewisham ■4	a	16 38			16 44			16 47						16 53			16 55	16 58						17 00	
Hither Green ■4	a			16 43						16 49				16 58										17 05	
Petts Wood ■4	a						16 59			17 03		17 08							17 14					17 18	
Orpington ■4	a					16 52	17 04			17 06		17 15							17 19					17 24	

		SE	SE	SE	SE	SE		SE	SE ■1	SE	SE	SE ■1	SE	SE ■1	SE	SE		SE	SE	SE ■1	SE	SE	SE	SE	SE
London Charing Cross ■4 ⊖	d		16 49		16 51			16 55	16 57				16 59	17 01				17 03			17 06		17 10		17 12
London Waterloo (East) ■4 ⊖	d		16 52		16 54			16 58	16a59				17 02	17 04				17 06			17 09		17 13		17 15
London Cannon Street ■4 ⊖	d	16 51		16 54		16 56				16 58		17 02			17 04	17 06				17 08		17 12		17 16	
London Blackfriars ■3 ⊖	d																								
London Bridge ■4 ⊖	d	16 55	16 57	16a57	16 59	17 00		17a02		17 02		17a05	17a06	17a08	17 08	17a09		17 11		17a11	17 14	17 16	17 19	17a19	17 21
London Victoria ■15 ⊖	d										16 59								17 04						
New Cross ■4 ⊖	d	17 01								17 08					17 14							17 22			
St Johns	d	17 03								17 10												17 24			
Lewisham ■4	a	17 05			17 07					17 12					17 17			17 20	17 23			17 26			17 30
Hither Green ■4	a		17 07							17 17								17 25			18 21		17 28		
Petts Wood ■4	a					17 24					17 36							17 39							
Orpington ■4	a					17 27					17 41							17 45							

		SE ■1		SE	SE	SE	SE ■1	SE	SE ■1	SE	SE ■1	SE		SE	SE	SE ■1	SE	SE	SE	SE	SE	SE ■1		SE	SE
London Charing Cross ■4 ⊖	d	17 14				17 17	17 19			17 21	17 23						17 26	17 29	17 30		17 32			17 34	
London Waterloo (East) ■4 ⊖	d	17a17				17 20	17a21			17 24	17 26						17 29	17 32	17a32		17 35			17 37	
London Cannon Street ■4 ⊖	d			17 19				17 21	17 24			17 26		17 28		17 30				17 34		17 37			
London Blackfriars ■3 ⊖	d																								
London Bridge ■4 ⊖	d			17 23		17a24		17 25	17a27	17a28	17a30	17 30		17a31		17a33	17 35	17a36		17 39	17 41	17a40		17 43	
London Victoria ■15 ⊖	d				17 15										17 30										17 34
New Cross ■4 ⊖	d							17 31				17 36								17 45					
St Johns	d							17 33												17 47					
Lewisham ■4	a							17 35				17 39					17 43			17 49				17 52	17 55
Hither Green ■4	a							17 40									17 48				17 51				
Petts Wood ■4	a			17 43	17 50										18 05		18 01								
Orpington ■4	a			17 47	17 55										18 10		18 18								

London - Lewisham, Hither Green, Petts Wood and Orpington (Summary of Services)

		SE	SE	SE	SE 1	SE	SE 1	SE		SE	SE 1	SE	SE	SE	SE 1	SE	SE	SE		SE	SE	SE	SE 1	SE	SE
London Charing Cross 4 ⊖	d			17 39	17 41			17 43			17 45		17 47			17 50	17 52			17 54	17 56		17 59		
London Waterloo (East) 4 ⊖	d			17 42	17a43			17 46			17 48		17 50			17 53	17a54			17 57	17 59		18a01		
London Cannon Street 4 ⊖	d	17 39	17 41			17 43	17 45			17 47		17 50			17 52			17 56						18 00	18 02
London Blackfriars 3 ⊖	d																								
London Bridge 4 ⊖	d	17a42	17 45	17a46		17 47	17a48	17a50		17 51	17a52	17a53	17 55		17a55	17a57		18 00		18 02	18 04			18a03	18 06
London Victoria 15 ⊖	d													17 45								17 56			
New Cross 4 ⊖	d					17 53				17 58								18 06							
St Johns	d					17 55												18 08							
Lewisham 4	a					17 58				18 01			18 04					18 10			18 13	18 17			
Hither Green 4	a					18 03							18 09							18 12					
Petts Wood 4	a		18 08										18 23	18 26											18 28
Orpington 4	a		18 11										18 29	18 32											18 32

		SE	SE	SE 1		SE	SE 1	SE	SE 1	SE	SE	SE	SE 1	SE		SE	SE	SE	SE	FC 1	SE 1	SE	SE	SE	
London Charing Cross 4 ⊖	d		18 01	18 03				18 05	18 07			18 09		18 12		18 14			18 18		18 21				
London Waterloo (East) 4 ⊖	d		18 04	18a05				18 08	18 10			18 12		18 15		18 17			18 21		18a23				
London Cannon Street 4 ⊖	d					18 04	18 08			18 10	18 12		18 14				18 18	18 21				18 23		18 25	
London Blackfriars 3 ⊖	d																			18 20					
London Bridge 4 ⊖	d		18a08			18 08	18a11	18a12	18a14	18 14	18a15	18 17	18a17	18a20		18 23	18 23	18a24	18 26	18a27		18 27		18 29	
London Victoria 15 ⊖	d	18 00																					18 15		
New Cross 4 ⊖	d					18 14				18 20							18 28							18 35	
St Johns	d					18 16											18 30							18 37	
Lewisham 4	a					18 19				18 23		18 26					18 33		18 35					18 40	
Hither Green 4	a					18 24						18 31				18 35								18 45	
Petts Wood 4	a	18 35										18 43										18 49	18 53		
Orpington 4	a	18 41										18 49										18 53	18 59		

		SE	SE	SE 1	SE	SE	SE 1	SE	SE	SE 1		SE	SE	SE	SE	SE 1	SE 1	SE	SE	SE		SE 1	SE	SE	FC 1
London Charing Cross 4 ⊖	d		18 23			18 27		18 30		18 32		18 34		18 37	18 39		18 41					18 45			
London Waterloo (East) 4 ⊖	d		18 26			18 30		18 33		18 35		18 37		18 40	18 42		18 44					18 48			
London Cannon Street 4 ⊖	d			18 28	18 30		18 32		18 34				18 40			18 44				18 46			18 48		
London Blackfriars 3 ⊖	d																								18 46
London Bridge 4 ⊖	d		18a31	18a31	18a33	18a34	18a35	18 38	18 38	18a39		18a41	18 44	18 46	18 48	18a47	18 50			18a49		18a52	18 52		18a54
London Victoria 15 ⊖	d	18 18																18 30	18 39					18 45	
New Cross 4 ⊖	d								18 44				18 50		18 55										
St Johns	d								18 46				18 52												
Lewisham 4	a	18 42							18 48				18 54		18 59				19 02						
Hither Green 4	a							18 48						18 55											
Petts Wood 4	a							19 02										19 06					19 13	19 19	
Orpington 4	a							19 06									19 06	19 12					19 19	19 25	

		SE	SE	SE	SE	SE		SE	SE	SE 1	SE	SE 1	SE	SE	FC 1	SE		SE	SE	SE	SE 1	SE	SE 1	SE	SE
London Charing Cross 4 ⊖	d		18 48		18 52			18 56		19 00			19 02			19 06			19 09		19 10		19 15		19 17
London Waterloo (East) 4 ⊖	d		18 51		18 55			18 59		19 03			19 05			19 09			19 12		19 13		19 18		19 20
London Cannon Street 4 ⊖	d	18 50		18 54		18 57			19 00			19 04		19 07				19 10				19 17			
London Blackfriars 3 ⊖	d														19 05										
London Bridge 4 ⊖	d	18 54	18 57	18 58	18a59	19a00		19 04	19 04	19 09		19a07	19 10	19a10	19a11	19 14		19 14	19 17		19a18	19a20	19 23		19a24
London Victoria 15 ⊖	d										19 00									19 09				19 10	
New Cross 4 ⊖	d	19 00		19 05					19 09									19 19							
St Johns	d	19 02		19 07					19 11									19 21							
Lewisham 4	a	19 04	19 06	19 10					19 14				19 19					19 24	19 26	19 31					
Hither Green 4	a	19 09						19 14								19 23		19 28							
Petts Wood 4	a										19 35					19 38								19 44	
Orpington 4	a									19 27	19 38					19 43							19 38	19 48	

		SE		FC 1	SE	SE	SE	SE	SE 1	SE	SE	SE		FC 1	SE	SE	SE	SE	SE 1	SE	SE 1	SE		SE	SE
London Charing Cross 4 ⊖	d						19 26		19 30		19 32				19 36		19 39		19 40		19 45			19 47	
London Waterloo (East) 4 ⊖	d						19 29		19 33		19 35				19 39		19 42		19 43		19 48			19 50	
London Cannon Street 4 ⊖	d	19 20			19 24	19 27		19 30				19 37				19 40				19 47					19 50
London Blackfriars 3 ⊖	d			19 20										19 35											
London Bridge 4 ⊖	d	19 24		19a26	19 28	19a30	19 34	19 34	19 39		19 40	19a40		19a41	19 44	19 44	19 47		19a48	19a50	19 53			19a54	19 54
London Victoria 15 ⊖	d									19 25								19 39				19 40			
New Cross 4 ⊖	d	19 29			19 33			19 39								19 49									19 59
St Johns	d	19 31			19 35			19 41								19 51									20 01
Lewisham 4	a	19 33			19 38			19 44			19 49					19 55	19 56	20 01							20 04
Hither Green 4	a	19 38					19 43								19 53	19 59									20 08
Petts Wood 4	a	19 51								19 59					20 06							20 14			20 21
Orpington 4	a	19 54							19 55	20 02					20 09						20 08	20 18			20 24

		FC 1	SE	SE	SE	SE	SE 1	SE		SE	FC 1	SE	SE	SE	SE 1	SE	SE 1	SE		SE	SE	SE	SE	SE 1	SE
London Charing Cross 4 ⊖	d				19 56		20 00			20 02		20 06		20 09	20 10		20 15				20 17	20 22		20 30	
London Waterloo (East) 4 ⊖	d				19 59		20 03			20 05		20 09		20 12	20 13		20 18				20 20	20 25		20 33	
London Cannon Street 4 ⊖	d		19 54	19 57		20 00							20 10			20 17				20 20			20 27		
London Blackfriars 3 ⊖	d	19 50									20 05														
London Bridge 4 ⊖	d	19a56	19 58	20a00	20 04	20 04	20 09			20 10	20a11	20 14	20 14	20 17	20a18	20a20	20 23			20 24	20 25	20 30	20a30	20 39	
London Victoria 15 ⊖	d							19 55										20 10							20 25
New Cross 4 ⊖	d		20 03			20 09							20 19							20 29	20 32	20 35			
St Johns	d		20 05			20 11							20 21							20 31	20 34				
Lewisham 4	a		20 08			20 14				20 19			20 25	20 26						20 34	20 36	20 38			
Hither Green 4	a				20 13							20 23	20 29							20 38		20 44			
Petts Wood 4	a							20 29				20 36						20 44		20 51					20 59
Orpington 4	a						20 25	20 32				20 39					20 38	20 47		20 54				20 55	21 02

London - Lewisham, Hither Green, Petts Wood and Orpington (Summary of Services)

		SE	FC 1	SE		SE	SE 1	SE	SE 1	SE	SE	SE	SE 1	SE		SE	FC 1	SE	SE	SE 1	SE	SE	SE	SE 1	
London Charing Cross 4 ⊖	d	20 32		20 36		20 39	20 40		20 45	20 47	20 52		21 00			21 02		21 06	21 09	21 10	21 17	21 22	21 26	21 30	
London Waterloo (East) 4 ⊖	d	20 35		20 39		20 42	20 43		20 48	20 50	20 55		21 03			21 05		21 09	21 12	21 13	21 20	21 25	21 29	21 33	
London Cannon Street 4 ⊖	d							20 47				20 57													
London Blackfriars 3 ⊖	d		20 35														21 05								
London Bridge 4 ⊖	d	20 40	20a41	20 44		20 47	20a48	20a50	20 53	20 55	21 00	21a00	21 09			21 10	21a11	21 14	21 17	21 19	21 25	21 30	21a33	21 39	
London Victoria 15 ⊖	d													20 55											
New Cross 4 ⊖	d	20 45								21 00	21 05					21 15					21 30	21 35			
St Johns	d									21 02											21 32				
Lewisham 4	a	20 49				20 56				21 05	21 09					21 19		21 21	21 26		21 35	21 39			
Hither Green 4	a			20 53							21 13							21 26				21 43			
Petts Wood 4	a			21 06										21 29				21 38							
Orpington 4	a			21 09					21 08				21 25	21 32				21 42		21 34				21 55	

		SE	SE	FC 1	SE	SE	SE 1	SE 1	SE	SE		SE	SE 1	SE	SE	FC 1	SE	SE	SE 1	SE		SE	SE	SE 1	SE
London Charing Cross 4 ⊖	d		21 32		21 36	21 39	21 40	21 45	21 47	21 52		21 56	22 00		22 02		22 06	22 09	22 10	22 17		22 22	22 26	22 30	
London Waterloo (East) 4 ⊖	d		21 35		21 39	21 42	21 43	21 48	21 50	21 55		21 59	22 03		22 05		22 09	22 12	22 13	22 20		22 25	22 29	22 33	
London Cannon Street 4 ⊖	d																								
London Blackfriars 3 ⊖	d			21 35												22 05									
London Bridge 4 ⊖	d		21 40	21a41	21 44	21 47	21a48	21 53	21 55	22 00		22a03	22 09		22 10	22a11	22 14	22 17	22 19	22 25		22 30	22a33	22 39	
London Victoria 15 ⊖	d	21 25												21 55											22 25
New Cross 4 ⊖	d		21 45						22 00	22 05					22 15					22 30		22 35			
St Johns	d								22 02											22 32					
Lewisham 4	a		21 49		21 51	21 56			22 05	22 09					22 19		22 21	22 26		22 35		22 39			
Hither Green 4	a				21 56					22 13							22 26					22 43			
Petts Wood 4	a	21 59			22 08									22 29			22 38								22 59
Orpington 4	a	22 02			22 12			22 08					22 25	22 32			22 42		22 34					22 54	23 02

		SE	SE	SE	SE 1	SE 1		SE	SE	SE	SE 1	SE	SE	SE	SE	SE		SE 1	SE	SE	SE	SE 1	SE	SE	SE
London Charing Cross 4 ⊖	d	22 32	22 36	22 39	22 40	22 45		22 47	22 52	22 56	23 00			23 02	23 06	23 09		23 10	23 17	23 22	23 26	23 30			23 32
London Waterloo (East) 4 ⊖	d	22 35	22 39	22 42	22 43	22 48		22 50	22 55	22 59	23 03			23 05	23 09	23 12		23 13	23 20	23 25	23 29	23 33			23 35
London Cannon Street 4 ⊖	d																								
London Blackfriars 3 ⊖	d																								
London Bridge 4 ⊖	d	22 40	22 44	22 47	22a48	22 53		22 55	23 00	23a03	23 09			23 10	23 14	23 17		23 19	23 25	23 30	23a33	23 39			23 40
London Victoria 15 ⊖	d											22 43	22 55										23 13	23 25	
New Cross 4 ⊖	d	22 45						23 00	23 05					23 15					23 30	23 35					23 45
St Johns	d							23 02											23 32						
Lewisham 4	a	22 49	22 51	22 56				23 05	23 09					23 19	23 21	23 26			23 35	23 39					23 49
Hither Green 4	a		22 56						23 13						23 26					23 43					
Petts Wood 4	a		23 08									23 21	23 29		23 38								23 51	23 59	
Orpington 4	a		23 12			23 08					23 24	23 25	23 32		23 42			23 34				23 54	23 57	00 02	

		SE		SE	SE 1	SE 1	SE	SE	SE	SE
London Charing Cross 4 ⊖	d	23 36		23 39	23 40	23 45		23 52		23 56
London Waterloo (East) 4 ⊖	d	23 39		23 42	23 43	23 48		23 55		23 59
London Cannon Street 4 ⊖	d									
London Blackfriars 3 ⊖	d									
London Bridge 4 ⊖	d	23 44		23 47	23a48	23 53		23 59		00a03
London Victoria 15 ⊖	d						23 43		23 55	
New Cross 4 ⊖	d							00 05		
St Johns	d							00 07		
Lewisham 4	a	23 51		23 56				00 10		
Hither Green 4	a	23 56								
Petts Wood 4	a	00 08					00 21		00 29	
Orpington 4	a	00 12				00 08	00 25		00 32	

Saturdays

		SE	SE	SE 1	SE	SE	SE	SE	SE	SE		SE	SE	SE	SE	SE	SE	SE	SE	SE		SE	SE	SE	SE 1
London Charing Cross 4 ⊖	d		23p36	23p45		23p52		00 02	00 06	00 10		00 15	00 18	00 48	04 52	05 22	05 26	05 32	05 36	05 39		05 47	05 52	05 56	06 00
London Waterloo (East) 4 ⊖	d		23p39	23p48		23p55		00 05	00 09	00 13		00 18	00 21	00 51	04 55	05 25	05 29	05 35	05 39	05 42		05 50	05 55	05 59	06 03
London Cannon Street 4 ⊖	d																								
London Blackfriars 3 ⊖	d																								
London Bridge 4 ⊖	d		23p44	23p53		23p59		00 10	00 14	00 18		00 23	00 26	00 56	05 00	05 30	05a33	05 40	05 44	05 47		05 55	06 00	06a03	06 08
London Victoria 15 ⊖	d	23p25			23p43		23p55																		
New Cross 4 ⊖	d					00 05		00 15		00 23			00 31	01 01	05 05	05 35		05 45				06 00	06 05		
St Johns	d					00 07																06 02			
Lewisham 4	a		23p51			00 10		00 19	00 21	00 27			00 35	01 05	05 09	05 39		05 49	05 52	05 56		06 05	06 09		
Hither Green 4	a		23p56						00 26	00 31				01 09	05 13	05 43			05 57				06 13		
Petts Wood 4	a	23p59	00 08		00 21		00 29		00 38					01 22					06 09						
Orpington 4	a	00 02	00 12	00 08	00 25		00 32		00 42			00 46		01 25					06 12						06 23

Table 199

Saturdays

London - Lewisham, Hither Green, Petts Wood and Orpington (Summary of Services)

	SE	SE	SE	SE	SE		SE	SE	SE	SE	SE	SE	SE	SE	SE		SE 1	SE	SE	SE	SE	SE	SE	SE
London Charing Cross 4 ⊖ d		06 02	06 06	06 09	06 17		06 22		06 26	06 32	06 36	06 39	06 47	06 52	06 56		07 00		07 02	07 06	07 09		07 17	07 22
London Waterloo (East) 4 ⊖ d		06 05	06 09	06 12	06 20		06 25		06 29	06 35	06 39	06 42	06 50	06 55	06 59		07 03		07 05	07 09	07 12		07 20	07 25
London Cannon Street 4 ⊖ d																								
London Blackfriars 3 ⊖ d																								
London Bridge 4 ⊖ d		06 10	06 14	06 17	06 25		06 30		06a33	06 40	06 44	06 47	06 55	07 00	07a03		07 08		07 10	07 14	07 17		07 25	07 30
London Victoria 15 ⊖ d	05 55							06 25										06 55				07 10		
New Cross 4 ⊖ d		06 15			06 30		06 35			06 45			07 00	07 05					07 15				07 30	07 35
St Johns d					06 32								07 02										07 32	
Lewisham 4 a		06 19	06 22	06 26	06 35		06 39			06 49	06 52	06 56	07 05	07 08					07 19	07 22	07 26		07 35	07 39
Hither Green 4 a			06 27				06 43				06 57			07 14						07 27				07 44
Petts Wood 4 a	06 29		06 39					06 59			07 09							07 29		07 39		07 44		
Orpington 4 a	06 32		06 42					07 02			07 12						07 23	07 32		07 42		07 47		

	SE		SE 1	SE	SE	SE	SE	SE	SE 1	SE	SE		SE	SE	SE	SE 1	SE	SE	SE	SE	SE		SE	SE
London Charing Cross 4 ⊖ d	07 26		07 30		07 32	07 36	07 39		07 45		07 47		07 52	07 56		08 00		08 02		08 06			08 09	
London Waterloo (East) 4 ⊖ d	07 29		07 33		07 35	07 39	07 42		07 48		07 50		07 55	07 59		08 03		08 05		08 09			08 12	
London Cannon Street 4 ⊖ d															08 00				08 07		08 10			
London Blackfriars 3 ⊖ d																								
London Bridge 4 ⊖ d	07a33		07 38		07 40	07 44	07 47		07 53		07a54		08 00	08a03	08 04	08 08		08 10	08a10	08 14	08 14		08 17	
London Victoria 15 ⊖ d				07 25				07 39		07 40							07 55							08 09
New Cross 4 ⊖ d					07 45								08 05		08 09			08 15			08 19			
St Johns d															08 11						08 21			
Lewisham 4 a					07 49	07 52	07 56	08 02					08 08		08 13			08 19			08 24		08 26	08 31
Hither Green 4 a						07 57							08 14							08 23	08 28			
Petts Wood 4 a				07 59		08 09				08 14							08 29			08 36				
Orpington 4 a			07 54	08 02		08 12			08 08	08 17						08 23	08 32			08 39				

	SE	SE 1	SE	SE	SE	SE	SE		SE	SE	SE 1	SE	SE	SE	SE	SE	SE		SE	SE 1	SE	SE 1	SE	SE
London Charing Cross 4 ⊖ d		08 15		08 17					08 26		08 30		08 32		08 36		08 39			08 40		08 45		08 47
London Waterloo (East) 4 ⊖ d		08 18		08 20					08 29		08 33		08 35		08 39		08 42			08 43		08 48		08 50
London Cannon Street 4 ⊖ d	08 17				08 20	08 24	08 27			08 30				08 37		08 40					08 47			
London Blackfriars 3 ⊖ d																								
London Bridge 4 ⊖ d	08 21	08 23		08a24	08 24	08 28	08a30		08 34	08 34	08 39		08 40	08a40	08 44	08 44	08 47			08a48	08 51	08 53		08a54
London Victoria 15 ⊖ d			08 10									08 25							08 39				08 40	
New Cross 4 ⊖ d	09a38				08 29	08 33				08 39						08 49					10a08			
St Johns d					08 31	08 35				08 41						08 51								
Lewisham 4 a					08 34	08 38				08 44			08 49			08 54	08 56		09 01					
Hither Green 4 a					08 38				08 43						08 53	08 58								
Petts Wood 4 a			08 44		08 51							08 59			09 06								09 14	
Orpington 4 a		08 38	08 47		08 54						08 55	09 02			09 09							09 08	09 17	

	SE	SE	SE		SE	SE	SE 1	SE	SE	SE	SE	SE	SE		SE	SE 1	and at the same minutes past each hour until	SE 1	SE	SE 1	SE	SE	
London Charing Cross 4 ⊖ d					08 56		09 00		09 02		09 06		09 09			09 10		18 10		18 15		18 17	
London Waterloo (East) 4 ⊖ d					08 59		09 03		09 05		09 09		09 12			09 13		18 13		18 18		18 20	
London Cannon Street 4 ⊖ d	08 50	08 54	08 57			09 00				09 07		09 10							18 17				
London Blackfriars 3 ⊖ d																							
London Bridge 4 ⊖ d	08 54	08 58	09a00		09 04	09 04	09 09		09 10	09a10	09 14	09 14	09 17			09a18		18a18	18a20	18 23		18a24	
London Victoria 15 ⊖ d								08 55							09 09						18 10		
New Cross 4 ⊖ d	08 59	09 03				09 09						09 19											
St Johns d	09 01	09 05				09 11						09 21											
Lewisham 4 a	09 04	09 08				09 14			09 19			09 24	09 26		09 31								
Hither Green 4 a	09 08				09 13						09 23	09 28											
Petts Wood 4 a	09 21							09 29			09 36										18 44		
Orpington 4 a	09 24						09 25	09 32			09 39									18 38	18 47		

	SE	SE	SE	SE	SE	SE 1	SE	SE	SE		SE	SE	SE	SE	SE 1	SE	SE 1	SE	SE		SE	SE	SE	SE
London Charing Cross 4 ⊖ d				18 26		18 30		18 32			18 36		18 39		18 40		18 45		18 47					18 56
London Waterloo (East) 4 ⊖ d				18 29		18 33		18 35			18 39		18 42		18 43		18 48		18 50					18 59
London Cannon Street 4 ⊖ d	18 20	18 24	18 27		18 30				18 37			18 40				18 47					18 50	18 54	18 57	
London Blackfriars 3 ⊖ d																								
London Bridge 4 ⊖ d	18 24	18 28	18a30	18 34	18 34	18 39		18 40	18a40		18 44	18 44	18 47		18a48	18a50	18 53		18a54		18 54	18 58	19a00	19 04
London Victoria 15 ⊖ d							18 25							18 39				18 40						
New Cross 4 ⊖ d	18 29	18 33			18 39							18 49									18 59	19 03		
St Johns d	18 31	18 35			18 41							18 51									19 01	19 05		
Lewisham 4 a	18 34	18 38			18 44			18 49				18 54	18 56	19 01							19 04	19 08		
Hither Green 4 a	18 38			18 43							18 53	18 58									19 08			19 13
Petts Wood 4 a	18 51						18 59				19 06							19 14			19 21			
Orpington 4 a	18 54					18 55	19 02				19 09						19 08	19 17			19 24			

	SE	SE 1	SE	SE	SE		SE	SE	SE	SE	SE 1	SE 1	SE	SE	SE		SE	SE	SE	SE 1	SE	SE	SE	SE
London Charing Cross 4 ⊖ d		19 00		19 02			19 06		19 09		19 10	19 15			19 17				19 26	19 30		19 32	19 36	19 39
London Waterloo (East) 4 ⊖ d		19 03		19 05			19 09		19 12		19 13	19 18			19 20				19 29	19 33		19 35	19 39	19 42
London Cannon Street 4 ⊖ d	19 00				19 07			19 10						19 20			19 24	19 27						
London Blackfriars 3 ⊖ d																								
London Bridge 4 ⊖ d	19 04	19 09		19 10	19a10		19 14	19 14	19 17		19a18	19 23		19 24	19 25		19 28	19a30	19 34	19 39		19 40	19 44	19 47
London Victoria 15 ⊖ d			18 55							19 09			19 10								19 25			
New Cross 4 ⊖ d	19 09							19 19						19 29			19 33					19 45		
St Johns d	19 11							19 21						19 31			19 35							
Lewisham 4 a	19 14			19 19				19 24	19 26	19 31				19 34	19 37		19 38					19 49	19 51	19 56
Hither Green 4 a							19 23	19 28						19 38					19 43				19 56	
Petts Wood 4 a			19 29				19 36						19 44	19 51							19 59		20 08	
Orpington 4 a		19 25	19 32				19 39					19 38	19 48	19 54						19 55	20 02		20 12	

Table 199

Saturdays

London - Lewisham, Hither Green, Petts Wood and Orpington (Summary of Services)

	SE		SE	SE	SE	SE	SE	SE	SE	SE	SE		SE	SE	SE	SE	SE	SE	SE	SE	SE		SE	SE
				1			1							1				1						
London Charing Cross 4 ⊖ d				19 40	19 47	19 52	19 55		19 56	20 02	20 06		20 09	20 10		20 17	20 22	20 25		20 26	20 32		20 36	20 39
London Waterloo (East) 4 ⊖ d				19 43	19 50	19 55	19 58		19 59	20 05	20 09		20 12	20 13		20 20	20 25	20 28		20 29	20 35		20 39	20 42
London Cannon Street 4 ⊖ d																								
London Blackfriars 3 ⊖ d																								
London Bridge 4 ⊖ d				19a48	19 55	20 00	20 03		20a04	20 10	20 14		20 17	20 19		20 25	20 30	20 33		20a34	20 40		20 44	20 47
London Victoria 15 ⊖ d	19 39		19 40					19 55							20 10				20 25					
New Cross 4 ⊖ d					20 00	20 05				20 15						20 30	20 35				20 45			
St Johns d					20 02											20 32								
Lewisham 4 a	20 01				20 05	20 09				20 19	20 21		20 26			20 35	20 39				20 49		20 51	20 56
Hither Green 4 a						20 13					20 26						20 43						20 56	
Petts Wood 4 a			20 14					20 29			20 38				20 44				20 59				21 08	
Orpington 4 a			20 18				20 18	20 32			20 42			20 34	20 47			20 48	21 02				21 12	

	SE	SE	SE	SE	SE	SE	SE		SE	SE	SE	SE	SE	SE	SE	SE	SE		SE	SE	SE	SE	SE	SE
	1			1							1			1							1			1
London Charing Cross 4 ⊖ d	20 40	20 47	20 52	20 55		20 56	21 02		21 06	21 09	21 10	21 17	21 22	21 25		21 26	21 32		21 36	21 39	21 40	21 47	21 52	21 55
London Waterloo (East) 4 ⊖ d	20 43	20 50	20 55	20 58		20 59	21 05		21 09	21 12	21 13	21 20	21 25	21 28		21 29	21 35		21 39	21 42	21 43	21 50	21 55	21 58
London Cannon Street 4 ⊖ d																								
London Blackfriars 3 ⊖ d																								
London Bridge 4 ⊖ d	20 49	20 55	21 00	21 03		21a04	21 10		21 14	21 17	21 19	21 25	21 30	21 33		21a34	21 40		21 44	21 47	21 49	21 55	22 00	22 03
London Victoria 15 ⊖ d					20 55										21 25									
New Cross 4 ⊖ d		21 00	21 05				21 15					21 30	21 35				21 45					22 00	22 05	
St Johns d		21 02										21 32										22 02		
Lewisham 4 a		21 05	21 09				21 19		21 21	21 26		21 35	21 39				21 49		21 51	21 56		22 05	22 09	
Hither Green 4 a			21 13						21 26				21 43						21 56				22 13	
Petts Wood 4 a					21 29				21 38						21 59				22 08					
Orpington 4 a	21 04			21 18	21 32				21 42		21 34			21 48	22 02				22 12		22 04			22 18

	SE	SE	SE		SE	SE	SE	SE	SE	SE	SE	SE	SE		SE	SE	SE	SE	SE	SE	SE	SE	SE	
							1			1							1			1				
London Charing Cross 4 ⊖ d		21 56	22 02		22 06	22 09	22 10	22 17	22 22	22 25		22 26	22 32		22 36	22 39	22 40	22 47	22 52	22 55			22 56	
London Waterloo (East) 4 ⊖ d		21 59	22 05		22 09	22 12	22 13	22 20	22 25	22 28		22 29	22 35		22 39	22 42	22 43	22 50	22 55	22 58			22 59	
London Cannon Street 4 ⊖ d																								
London Blackfriars 3 ⊖ d																								
London Bridge 4 ⊖ d		22a04	22 10		22 14	22 17	22 19	22 25	22 30	22 33		22a34	22 40		22 44	22 47	22 49	22 55	23 00	23 03			23a04	
London Victoria 15 ⊖ d	21 55										22 25										22 43	22 55		
New Cross 4 ⊖ d			22 15					22 30	22 35				22 45					23 00	23 05					
St Johns d								22 32										23 02						
Lewisham 4 a			22 19		22 21	22 26		22 35	22 39				22 49		22 51	22 56		23 05	23 09					
Hither Green 4 a					22 26				22 43						22 56				23 13					
Petts Wood 4 a	22 29				22 38						22 59				23 08						23 22	23 29		
Orpington 4 a	22 32				22 42		22 34			22 48	23 02				23 12		23 04			23 18	23 25	23 32		

	SE	SE	SE	SE	SE	SE	SE	SE	SE		SE	SE	SE	SE	SE	SE	SE	SE	SE		SE			
				1			1								1	1								
London Charing Cross 4 ⊖ d	23 02	23 06	23 09	23 10	23 17	23 22	23 25				23 26	23 32	23 36	23 39	23 40	23 45		23 52			23 56			
London Waterloo (East) 4 ⊖ d	23 05	23 09	23 12	23 13	23 20	23 25	23 28				23 29	23 35	23 39	23 42	23 43	23 48		23 55			23 59			
London Cannon Street 4 ⊖ d																								
London Blackfriars 3 ⊖ d																								
London Bridge 4 ⊖ d	23 10	23 14	23 17	23 19	23 25	23 30	23 33				23a34	23 40	23 44	23 47	23 49	23 53		23 59			00a04			
London Victoria 15 ⊖ d								23 13	23 25								23 43		23 55					
New Cross 4 ⊖ d	23 15				23 30	23 35						23 45						00 05						
St Johns d					23 32													00 07						
Lewisham 4 a	23 19	23 21	23 26		23 35	23 39						23 49	23 51	23 55				00 10						
Hither Green 4 a		23 26				23 43							23 56											
Petts Wood 4 a		23 38						23 52	23 59				00 08				00 22		00 29					
Orpington 4 a		23 42		23 34			23 48	23 55	00 02				00 12		00 04	00 08	00 25		00 32					

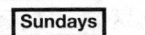

Sundays

	SE	SE	SE	SE	SE	SE	SE	SE	SE		SE	SE	SE	SE	SE	SE	SE	SE	SE		SE	SE	SE	SE
			1	1																				
	A	A	A	A	A	A	A																	
London Charing Cross 4 ⊖ d		23p36	23p40	23p45		23p52		00 02	00 06		00 10	00 10	00 15	00 18	00 48	07 30	07 35	07 46	07 50			07 56	08 00	08 05
London Waterloo (East) 4 ⊖ d		23p39	23p43	23p48		23p55		00 05	00 09		00 13	00 13	00 18	00 21	00 51	07 33	07 38	07 49	07 53			07 59	08 03	08 08
London Cannon Street 4 ⊖ d																								
London Blackfriars 3 ⊖ d																								
London Bridge 4 ⊖ d		23p44	23p49	23p53		23p59		00 10	00 14		00 18	00 18	00 23	00 26	00 56	07a37	07 43	07 54	07 58			08 04	08a07	08 13
London Victoria 15 ⊖ d	23p25				23p43		23p55														07 51			
New Cross 4 ⊖ d						00 05		00 15			00 23			00 31	01 01		07 49		08 04					08 19
St Johns d						00 07											07 51							08 21
Lewisham 4 a		23p51				00 10		00 19	00 21		00 27			00 35	01 05		07 53	08 02	08 07			08 11		08 23
Hither Green 4 a		23p56							00 26		00 31				01 09			08 07				08 16		
Petts Wood 4 a	23p59	00 08			00 22		00 29		00 38			00 38			01 22			08 20			08 25			
Orpington 4 a	00 02	00 12	00 04	00 08	00 25		00 32		00 42			00 41	00 46		01 25			08 23			08 28			

A not 11 December

Table 199

Sundays

London - Lewisham, Hither Green, Petts Wood and Orpington (Summary of Services)

			SE 1	SE	SE	SE	SE 1		SE	SE	SE	SE	SE 1	SE	SE	SE	SE		SE	SE	SE	SE 1	SE	SE	SE	SE 1
London Charing Cross 4	⊖	d	08 08	08 10	08 16	08 20	08 23			08 26	08 30	08 35	08 38	08 40	08 46	08 50			08 56	09 00	09 05	09 08	09 10	09 16	09 20	09 23
London Waterloo (East) 4	⊖	d	08 11	08 13	08 19	08 23	08 26			08 29	08 33	08 38	08 41	08 43	08 49	08 53			08 59	09 03	09 08	09 11	09 13	09 19	09 23	09 26
London Cannon Street 4	⊖	d																								
London Blackfriars 3	⊖	d																								
London Bridge 4	⊖	d	08 16	08 18	08 24	08 28	08 31			08 34	08a37	08 43	08 46	08 48	08 54	08 58			09 04	09a07	09 13	09 16	09 18	09 24	09 28	09 31
London Victoria 15	⊖	d							08 21								08 51									
New Cross 4	⊖	d				08 34						08 49				09 04					09 19				09 34	
St Johns		d										08 51									09 21					
Lewisham 4		a		08 27	08 32	08 37				08 41		08 53		08 57	09 02	09 07			09 11		09 23		09 27	09 32	09 37	
Hither Green 4		a			08 37					08 46					09 07				09 16					09 37		
Petts Wood 4		a			08 50				08 55						09 20		09 25							09 50		
Orpington 4		a	08 31		08 53		08 46		08 58				09 01		09 23		09 28					09 31		09 53		09 46

			SE		SE	SE	SE	SE 1	SE	SE	SE	SE 1		SE 1		SE	SE	SE	SE	SE 1	SE	SE	SE	SE 1	
London Charing Cross 4	⊖	d			09 26	09 30	09 35	09 38	09 40	09 46	09 50	09 53	and at the same minutes past each hour until	19 53			19 56	20 00	20 05	20 08	20 10	20 16	20 20	20 23	
London Waterloo (East) 4	⊖	d			09 29	09 33	09 38	09 41	09 43	09 49	09 53	09 56		19 56			19 59	20 03	20 08	20 11	20 13	20 19	20 23	20 26	
London Cannon Street 4	⊖	d																							
London Blackfriars 3	⊖	d																							
London Bridge 4	⊖	d			09 34	09a37	09 43	09 46	09 48	09 54	09 58	10 01		20 01			20 04	20a07	20 13	20 16	20 18	20 24	20 28	20 31	
London Victoria 15	⊖	d	09 21													19 51									
New Cross 4	⊖	d					09 49				10 04								20 19				20 34		
St Johns		d					09 51												20 21						
Lewisham 4		a			09 41		09 53		09 57	10 02	10 07						20 11		20 23		20 27	20 32	20 37		
Hither Green 4		a			09 46					10 07							20 16					20 37			
Petts Wood 4		a	09 55							10 20						20 25						20 50			
Orpington 4		a	09 58					10 01		10 23		10 16		20 16		20 28				20 31		20 53		20 46	

			SE	SE	SE	SE	SE 1	SE	SE	SE	SE		SE	SE	SE	SE 1	SE	SE	SE	SE 1	SE		SE	SE	SE	SE 1
London Charing Cross 4	⊖	d		20 26	20 30	20 35	20 38	20 40	20 46	20 50			20 56	21 00	21 05	21 08	21 10	21 16	21 20	21 23			21 26	21 30	21 35	21 38
London Waterloo (East) 4	⊖	d		20 29	20 33	20 38	20 41	20 43	20 49	20 53			20 59	21 03	21 08	21 11	21 13	21 19	21 23	21 26			21 29	21 33	21 38	21 41
London Cannon Street 4	⊖	d																								
London Blackfriars 3	⊖	d																								
London Bridge 4	⊖	d		20 34	20a37	20 43	20 46	20 48	20 54	20 58			21 04	21a07	21 13	21 16	21 18	21 24	21 28	21 31			21 34	21a37	21 43	21 46
London Victoria 15	⊖	d	20 21								20 51										21 21					
New Cross 4	⊖	d				20 49				21 04					21 19				21 34						21 49	
St Johns		d				20 51									21 21										21 51	
Lewisham 4		a		20 41		20 53		20 57	21 02	21 07			21 11		21 23		21 27	21 32	21 37				21 41		21 53	
Hither Green 4		a		20 46					21 07				21 16					21 37					21 46			
Petts Wood 4		a	20 55						21 20		21 25							21 50			21 55					
Orpington 4		a	20 58				21 01		21 23		21 28					21 31		21 53		21 46	21 58					22 01

			SE	SE	SE	SE	SE		SE	SE	SE 1	SE	SE	SE	SE 1	SE	SE		SE	SE	SE 1	SE	SE	SE	SE	SE
London Charing Cross 4	⊖	d	21 40	21 46	21 50		21 56		22 00	22 05	22 08	22 10	22 16	22 20	22 23		22 26		22 30	22 35	22 38	22 40	22 46		22 50	
London Waterloo (East) 4	⊖	d	21 43	21 49	21 53		21 59		22 03	22 08	22 11	22 13	22 19	22 23	22 26		22 29		22 33	22 38	22 41	22 43	22 49		22 53	
London Cannon Street 4	⊖	d																								
London Blackfriars 3	⊖	d																								
London Bridge 4	⊖	d	21 48	21 54	21 58		22 04		22a07	22 13	22 16	22 18	22 24	22 28	22 31		22 34		22a37	22 43	22 46	22 48	22 54		22 58	
London Victoria 15	⊖	d				21 51										22 21								22 39		22 51
New Cross 4	⊖	d			22 04					22 19				22 34						22 49					23 04	
St Johns		d								22 21										22 51						
Lewisham 4		a	21 57	22 02	22 07		22 11			22 23		22 27	22 32	22 37			22 41			22 53		22 57	23 02		23 07	
Hither Green 4		a		22 07			22 16						22 37				22 46						23 07			
Petts Wood 4		a		22 20		22 25							22 50			22 55							23 20	23 22		23 25
Orpington 4		a		22 23		22 28					22 31		22 53		22 46	22 58					23 01		23 23	23 26		23 29

			SE		SE	SE	SE 1	SE	SE	SE	SE 1	SE	SE		SE	SE	SE	SE 1	SE	SE	SE					
London Charing Cross 4	⊖	d	22 56		23 00	23 05	23 08	23 10	23 16	23 20	23 23				23 26	23 30	23 35	23 38	23 46	23 50	23 56					
London Waterloo (East) 4	⊖	d	22 59		23 03	23 08	23 11	23 13	23 19	23 23	23 26				23 29	23 33	23 38	23 41	23 49	23 53	23 59					
London Cannon Street 4	⊖	d																								
London Blackfriars 3	⊖	d																								
London Bridge 4	⊖	d	23 04		23a07	23 13	23 16	23 18	23 24	23 28	23 31				23 34	23a37	23 43	23 46	23 54	23 58	00 04					
London Victoria 15	⊖	d										23 09	23 21													
New Cross 4	⊖	d				23 19				23 34							23 49			00 04						
St Johns		d				23 21											23 51									
Lewisham 4		a	23 11			23 23		23 26	23 32	23 37					23 41		23 53		00 02	00 07	00 11					
Hither Green 4		a	23 16						23 37						23 46				00 07		00 16					
Petts Wood 4		a							23 50			23 52	23 55						00 20							
Orpington 4		a					23 31		23 53		23 46	23 56	23 59					00 01	00 23							

Orpington, Petts Wood, Hither Green and Lewisham - London (Summary of Services)

		SE MX	SE MX 1	SE	SE	SE	SE	FC 1	SE	SE		SE	SE	SE	SE	SE	FC 1	SE	SE	SE		SE	SE 1	SE	FC 1
Orpington 4	d	23p21	23p37	04 34	04 55		05 10		05 14				05 15					05 34	05 40				05 54		
Petts Wood 4	d	23p24		04 37	04 58		05 13						05 18					05 37	05 43						
Hither Green 4	d	23p37				05 08				05 23			05 30		05 38										
Lewisham 4	d	23p43				05 13				05 28			05 36	05 39	05 43	05 50						05 56			
St Johns	d													05 41											
New Cross 4	⊖ d					05 16				05 31			05 39	05 43	05 46	05 53									
London Victoria 15	⊖ a						05 47												06 18						
London Bridge 4	⊖ d	23p52	23p55			05 22		05 34	05 37	05 37		05 42	05 46	05 49	05 53	05 59	06 02			06 02		06 06	06 10	06 13	06 16
London Blackfriars 3	⊖ a			05 17	05 32			05 41									06 10	06 17							06 23
London Cannon Street 4	⊖ a									05 41										06 06					
London Waterloo (East) 4	⊖ d	23p57	23p59			05 27			05 42			05 47	05 50	05 53	05 57	06 04						06 10	06 15	06 18	
London Charing Cross 4	⊖ a	00 01	00 03			05 30			05 47			05 50	05 55	05 56	06 01	06 07						06 13	06 18	06 21	

		SE	SE	SE	SE 1	SE		SE	SE	SE	SE	SE	SE 1	SE 1	SE	SE		FC 1	SE	SE	SE	SE	SE 1	SE	FC 1
Orpington 4	d				06 09				06 01	06 10			06 20	06 24							06 22	06 40			
Petts Wood 4	d								06 04	06 13											06 25	06 43			
Hither Green 4	d			06 08					06 16			06 22									06 38				
Lewisham 4	d	06 09		06 13				06 20	06 22		06 25	06 27				06 35			06 39	06 41	06 43				
St Johns	d	06 11										06 29							06 41						
New Cross 4	⊖ d	06 13		06 16					06 25			06 31				06 38			06 43						
London Victoria 15	⊖ a									06 47										07 04		07 19			
London Bridge 4	⊖ d	06 19	06 20	06 22	06 25	06 28		06 29	06 32		06 34	06 37	06 38	06 40	06 43	06 44		06 46	06 49		06 52		06 55	06 57	06 58
London Blackfriars 3	⊖ a																	06 52							07 04
London Cannon Street 4	⊖ a		06 24			06 32							06 42			06 48								07 03	
London Waterloo (East) 4	⊖ d	06 24		06 27	06 30			06 33	06 36		06 40	06 42		06 45	06 49				06 54		06 57		07 00		
London Charing Cross 4	⊖ a	06 27		06 30	06 33			06 36	06 39		06 43	06 45		06 49	06 52				06 57		07 02		07 05		

		SE		SE	SE	SE	SE	SE	SE	SE 1	SE 1	SE		SE	SE	SE	SE	SE	SE	SE	SE 1	SE 1		SE	FC 1
Orpington 4	d								06 43	06 54						06 52	06 58			07 03		07 04		07 08	
Petts Wood 4	d								06 46							06 55	07 01			07 06				07 11	
Hither Green 4	d					06 56	06 51		06 58							07 08				07 19					
Lewisham 4	d	06 48		06 50	06 55		06 57	07 01	07 04					07 08				07 11	07 15	07 25					
St Johns	d	06 50					06 59																		
New Cross 4	⊖ d	06 52					07 01	07 04						07 11											
London Victoria 15	⊖ a																		07 42					07 49	
London Bridge 4	⊖ d	07 00		07 01	07 04	07 07	07 08	07 10		07 10	07 15	07 15		07 18	07 18	07 19		07 21			07 21	07 23			07 24
London Blackfriars 3	⊖ a																07 42								07 30
London Cannon Street 4	⊖ a	07 05					07 14	07 16				07 21		07 23		07 25					07 27	07 28			
London Waterloo (East) 4	⊖ d			07 06	07 10	07 12			07 17	07 15	07 20				07 23			07 26		07 37					
London Charing Cross 4	⊖ a			07 11	07 15	07 17			07 22	07 20	07 25				07 28			07 31		07 42					

		SE	SE	SE	SE 1	SE	SE	SE		SE 1	SE	SE 1	SE	SE	SE	SE	SE	SE		SE 1	SE 1	SE	SE	SE	SE 1
Orpington 4	d				07 14						07 11											07 22	07 28		
Petts Wood 4	d										07 15											07 25	07 31		
Hither Green 4	d	07 11	07 16								07 28						07 32	07 36				07 39			
Lewisham 4	d	07 17		07 20		07 22							07 30	07 35			07 38					07 44		07 46	
St Johns	d	07 19				07 24											07 40								
New Cross 4	⊖ d	07 21		07 23		07 26								07 38			07 42								
London Victoria 15	⊖ a																							08 11	
London Bridge 4	⊖ d	07 27	07 27	07 29	07 30	07 34	07 34	07 36		07 37	07 38		07 42	07 44	07 45	07 46	07 48	07 48		07 51	07 52	07 54			07 54
London Blackfriars 3	⊖ a																						08 08		
London Cannon Street 4	⊖ a	07 33		07 35		07 39		07 41			07 44			07 50		07 52	07 54				07 57				07 59
London Waterloo (East) 4	⊖ d		07 32		07 35		07 39			07 42		07 45	07 47		07 51			07 53		07 56		07 59			
London Charing Cross 4	⊖ a		07 37		07 40		07 44			07 47		07 49	07 52		07 56			07 58		08 01		08 04			

		SE	SE 1	SE		SE	SE	SE	SE 1 ⚲	SE	SE	SE	SE	SE		SE	SE	SE 1	SE	SE	SE	SE 1	SE	SE 1	
Orpington 4	d					07 33	07 38												07 41	07 47					
Petts Wood 4	d					07 36	07 41												07 44	07 50					
Hither Green 4	d					07 49										07 52			07 58				08 02		
Lewisham 4	d							07 48		07 50	07 55					07 57			08 03		08 05				
St Johns	d							07 50								08 00									
New Cross 4	⊖ d							07 53			07 58					08 02									
London Victoria 15	⊖ a						08 20														08 29				
London Bridge 4	⊖ d	07 58		07 58		08 00		08 02		08 02	08 04	08 06		08 06		08 09		08 10				08 11	08 14	08 14	
London Blackfriars 3	⊖ a																			08 29					
London Cannon Street 4	⊖ a	08 04				08 06		08 08			08 10	08 12				08 15						08 17		08 20	
London Waterloo (East) 4	⊖ d		08 01	08 03					08 05	08 07			08 09	08 11			08 13	08 15	08 17				08 19		
London Charing Cross 4	⊖ a		08 06	08 08					08 08	08 12			08 14	08 16			08 18	08 20	08 22				08 24		

Orpington, Petts Wood, Hither Green and Lewisham - London (Summary of Services)

	SE	SE 1	SE	SE	SE	SE	SE	SE 1 ⊥	SE		SE	SE	SE	SE	SE	SE 1	SE	SE	SE		SE 1	SE	SE 1	SE 1
Orpington 4 d				07 52	07 57												08 01		08 10					
Petts Wood 4 d				07 55	08 00												08 04		08 13					
Hither Green 4 d														08 12			08 17					08 22		
Lewisham 4 d						08 08	08 11		08 15					08 17			08 23	08 25						
St Johns d						08 12								08 21										
New Cross 4 ⊖ d						08 14			08 18					08 23										
London Victoria 15 ⊖ a																		08 49	08 50					
London Bridge 4 ⊖ d	08 18		08 18	08 20		08 22	08 22	08 24	08 26			08 26	08 28	08 30		08 30					08 32	08 34	08 34	
London Blackfriars 3 ⊖ a																								
London Cannon Street 4 ⊖ a	08 24			08 26		08 28		08 29	08 32				08 35	08 36							08 38		08 41	
London Waterloo (East) 4 ⊖ d		08 21	08 23		08 25		08 27				08 29	08 31			08 33	08 35	08 37					08 39		08 41
London Charing Cross 4 ⊖ a		08 26	08 28		08 30		08 32				08 34	08 36			08 39	08 40	08 42					08 44		08 46

	SE	SE	SE	SE	SE 1		SE	SE	SE	SE	SE	SE	SE	SE	SE		SE 1	SE 1	SE	SE 1	SE	SE 1	SE	SE
Orpington 4 d			08 13										08 21	08 26										08 32
Petts Wood 4 d			08 16										08 24	08 29										08 35
Hither Green 4 d												08 32	08 37						08 42					
Lewisham 4 d				08 28			08 31	08 35				08 37			08 46						08 48			
St Johns d				08 30								08 40									08 50			
New Cross 4 ⊖ d				08 32				08 38				08 42									08 52			
London Victoria 15 ⊖ a														09 06	09 11									
London Bridge 4 ⊖ d	08 38	08 39	08 40	08 42			08 42	08 44	08 46		08 46	08 50					08 50	08 51	08 54	08 56	08 58		08 58	09 00
London Blackfriars 3 ⊖ a																								
London Cannon Street 4 ⊖ a		08 43	08 46	08 48				08 50	08 52			08 55						08 57		09 02	09 04			09 06
London Waterloo (East) 4 ⊖ d	08 43				08 45		08 47			08 49	08 51		08 53				08 55		08 59			09 01	09 03	
London Charing Cross 4 ⊖ a	08 48				08 50		08 52			08 54	08 56		08 58				09 00		09 04			09 04	09 08	

	SE		SE	SE	SE 1	SE	SE	SE	SE	FC 1	SE		SE 1	SE 1	SE 1	SE	SE	SE	SE	SE	SE		SE 1	SE
Orpington 4 d	08 40															08 43	08 47			08 52	08 55		09 04	
Petts Wood 4 d	08 43															08 46	08 50			08 55	08 58			
Hither Green 4 d						08 50		08 55								08 59				09 08				09 14
Lewisham 4 d			08 52			08 55					08 59					09 04		09 06						
St Johns d						08 57					09 01					09 07								
New Cross 4 ⊖ d						08 59			07 50		09 03					09 09								
London Victoria 15 ⊖ a	09 19																	09 29			09 34			
London Bridge 4 ⊖ d			09 01	09 02	09 04	09 06		09 06	09 08	09 09	09 10		09 12	09 12	09 15	09 18			09 18	09 21			09 23	09 24
London Blackfriars 3 ⊖ a										09 21							09 30							
London Cannon Street 4 ⊖ a				09 08	09 09	09 12			09 14		09 18		09 18			09 23							09 28	
London Waterloo (East) 4 ⊖ d			09 06				09 08	09 11						09 17	09 20				09 23	09 26				09 29
London Charing Cross 4 ⊖ a			09 12				09 13	09 16						09 22	09 25				09 28	09 31				09 34

	SE	SE 1	SE	SE	SE	SE	SE		SE	SE	SE 1	SE	SE 1	SE	SE	FC 1	SE		SE	SE	SE	SE 1	SE	SE
Orpington 4 d		09 09			09 03	09 10					09 24						09 21		09 25			09 39		
Petts Wood 4 d					09 06	09 13											09 24		09 28					
Hither Green 4 d					09 19									09 28			09 37				09 42			
Lewisham 4 d	09 15			09 20	09 24		09 26			09 29				09 34	09 38								09 45	09 50
St Johns d	09 17				09 26					09 31				09 36									09 47	
New Cross 4 ⊖ d	09 19		08 20		09 28					09 33				09 38									09 49	
London Victoria 15 ⊖ a						09 49									10 00				10 02					
London Bridge 4 ⊖ d	09 26	09 27	09 30	09 30	09 34		09 35		09 38	09 39	09 41	09 42	09 44	09 45		09 46	09 49			09 51	09 52	09 55	09 55	09 58
London Blackfriars 3 ⊖ a																09 53								
London Cannon Street 4 ⊖ a	09 32		09 36		09 40					09 45		09 48		09 51						09 57			10 00	
London Waterloo (East) 4 ⊖ d		09 32		09 35			09 40		09 43		09 46		09 49				09 54				09 57	10 00		10 03
London Charing Cross 4 ⊖ a		09 36		09 40			09 45		09 48		09 51		09 54				09 59				10 00	10 03		10 06

	FC 1	SE	SE		SE	SE	SE	SE	SE 1	SE	SE 1	SE	SE		FC 1	SE	SE	SE	SE	SE	SE 1	SE	FC 1	
Orpington 4 d			09 33		09 40				09 54							09 51	09 55				10 09			
Petts Wood 4 d			09 36		09 43											09 54	09 58							
Hither Green 4 d			09 49									09 58				10 07			10 12					
Lewisham 4 d			09 54			09 56		09 59				10 04	10 08							10 14		10 20		
St Johns d			09 56					10 01				10 06								10 16				
New Cross 4 ⊖ d		08 49	09 58					10 03				10 08								10 18				
London Victoria 15 ⊖ a					10 17								10 28				10 32							
London Bridge 4 ⊖ d	10 00	10 01	10 04			10 05	10 08	10 09	10 11	10 11	10 13	10 14			10 16	10 19		10 21	10 22	10 24	10 25	10 28	10 30	
London Blackfriars 3 ⊖ a	10 08														10 23								10 37	
London Cannon Street 4 ⊖ a		10 04	10 08					10 13		10 15		10 19						10 24		10 28				
London Waterloo (East) 4 ⊖ d						10 10	10 13		10 15		10 18					10 24			10 27		10 30	10 33		
London Charing Cross 4 ⊖ a						10 13	10 16		10 19		10 22					10 27			10 30		10 33	10 36		

Orpington, Petts Wood, Hither Green and Lewisham - London (Summary of Services)

		SE	SE	SE	SE	SE	SE	SE 1	SE	SE 1		SE	SE	FC 1	SE	SE	SE	SE	SE	SE 1		SE	FC 1	SE	SE
Orpington 4	d		10 03	10 10				10 24							10 21	10 25				10 39					10 33
Petts Wood 4	d		10 06	10 13											10 24	10 28									10 36
Hither Green 4	d		10 19									10 28			10 37			10 42							10 49
Lewisham 4	d		10 24		10 26		10 29					10 34	10 38						10 44			10 50			10 54
St Johns	d		10 26				10 31					10 36							10 46						10 56
New Cross 4	d	09 19	10 28				10 33					10 38							10 48					09 49	10 58
London Victoria 15	a			10 47									10 58			11 02									
London Bridge 4	d	10 31	10 34		10 35	10 38	10 39	10 41	10 41	10 43		10 45		10 45	10 49		10 51	10 52	10 54	10 55		10 58	11 00	11 01	11 04
London Blackfriars 3	a													10 52									11 07		
London Cannon Street 4	a	10 36	10 38				10 43		10 45			10 50					10 54		10 58					11 06	11 08
London Waterloo (East) 4	d				10 40	10 43		10 45		10 49					10 54			10 57		11 00		11 03			
London Charing Cross 4	a				10 43	10 46		10 49		10 52					10 57			11 00		11 03		11 06			

		SE	SE	SE	SE	SE 1		SE	SE 1	SE	SE	FC 1	SE	SE	SE	SE		SE	SE 1	SE	FC 1	SE	SE	SE	SE
Orpington 4	d	10 40				10 54							10 51	10 55					11 09				11 03	11 10	
Petts Wood 4	d	10 43											10 54	10 58									11 06	11 13	
Hither Green 4	d									10 58			11 07			11 12							11 19		
Lewisham 4	d		10 56		10 59					11 04	11 08							11 14		11 20			11 24		11 26
St Johns	d				11 01					11 06								11 16					11 26		
New Cross 4	d				11 03					11 08								11 18				10 19	11 28		
London Victoria 15	a	11 17									11 28			11 32										11 47	
London Bridge 4	d		11 05	11 08	11 09	11 11		11 11	11 13	11 15		11 15	11 19		11 21	11 22		11 24	11 25	11 28	11 30	11 31	11 34		11 35
London Blackfriars 3	a											11 22									11 37				
London Cannon Street 4	a				11 13			11 15		11 19					11 24			11 28				11 36	11 38		
London Waterloo (East) 4	d		11 10	11 13		11 15			11 19				11 24			11 27			11 30	11 33					11 40
London Charing Cross 4	a		11 13	11 16		11 19			11 22				11 27			11 30			11 33	11 36					11 43

		SE		SE	SE 1	SE	SE 1	SE	SE	FC 1	SE	SE		SE	SE	SE	SE 1	SE	FC 1	SE	SE	SE		SE	SE
Orpington 4	d				11 24						11 21	11 25					11 39				11 33	11 40			
Petts Wood 4	d										11 24	11 28									11 36	11 43			
Hither Green 4	d							11 28			11 37				11 42						11 49				
Lewisham 4	d			11 29				11 34	11 38							11 44		11 50			11 54			11 56	
St Johns	d			11 31				11 36								11 46					11 56				
New Cross 4	d			11 33				11 38								11 48				10 49	11 58				
London Victoria 15	a								11 58			12 02										12 17			
London Bridge 4	d	11 38		11 39	11 41	11 41	11 43	11 45		11 45	11 49			11 51	11 52	11 54	11 55	11 58	12 00	12 01	12 04			12 05	12 08
London Blackfriars 3	a									11 52									12 07						
London Cannon Street 4	a			11 43		11 45		11 49						11 54		11 58				12 04	12 08				
London Waterloo (East) 4	d	11 43			11 45		11 49				11 54				11 57		12 00	12 03						12 10	12 13
London Charing Cross 4	a	11 46			11 49		11 52				11 57				12 00		12 03	12 06						12 13	12 16

		SE	SE 1	SE	SE 1	SE	SE	FC 1		SE	SE	SE	SE	SE	SE 1	SE	FC 1	SE		SE	SE	SE	SE	SE	SE 1
Orpington 4	d		11 54							11 51	11 55				12 09					12 03	12 10				12 24
Petts Wood 4	d									11 54	11 58									12 06	12 13				
Hither Green 4	d					11 58				12 07			12 12							12 19					
Lewisham 4	d	11 59				12 04	12 08							12 14		12 20				12 24		12 26		12 29	
St Johns	d	12 01				12 06								12 16						12 26				12 31	
New Cross 4	d	12 03				12 08								12 18				11 19		12 28				12 33	
London Victoria 15	a						12 28				12 32										12 47				
London Bridge 4	d	12 09	12 11	12 11	12 13	12 15		12 15		12 19		12 21	12 22	12 24	12 25	12 28	12 30	12 31		12 34		12 35	12 38	12 39	12 41
London Blackfriars 3	a							12 22									12 37								
London Cannon Street 4	a	12 13		12 15		12 19						12 24		12 28				12 36		12 38				12 43	
London Waterloo (East) 4	d		12 15		12 19					12 24			12 27		12 30	12 33						12 40	12 43		12 45
London Charing Cross 4	a		12 19		12 22					12 27			12 30		12 33	12 36						12 43	12 46		12 49

		SE	SE 1	SE		SE	FC 1	SE	SE	SE	SE	SE	SE 1	SE		FC 1	SE	SE	SE	SE	SE	SE	SE 1	SE	
Orpington 4	d							12 21	12 25				12 39					12 33	12 40				12 54		
Petts Wood 4	d							12 24	12 28									12 36	12 43						
Hither Green 4	d			12 28				12 37			12 42							12 49							
Lewisham 4	d			12 34		12 38						12 44		12 50				12 54		12 56		12 59			
St Johns	d			12 36								12 46						12 56				13 01			
New Cross 4	d			12 38								12 48					11 49	12 58				13 03			
London Victoria 15	a					12 58			13 02										13 17						
London Bridge 4	d	12 41	12 43	12 45			12 45	12 49		12 51	12 52	12 54	12 55	12 58		13 00	13 01	13 04		13 05	13 08	13 09	13 11	13 11	
London Blackfriars 3	a						12 52									13 07									
London Cannon Street 4	a	12 45		12 49						12 54		12 58					13 06	13 08				13 13		13 15	
London Waterloo (East) 4	d		12 49					12 54			12 57		13 00	13 03						13 10	13 13		13 15		
London Charing Cross 4	a		12 52					12 57			13 00		13 03	13 06						13 13	13 16		13 19		

		SE 1	SE	SE	FC 1	SE	SE	SE	SE	SE		SE 1	SE	FC 1	SE	SE	SE	SE	SE	SE		SE 1	SE	SE 1	SE
Orpington 4	d					12 51	12 55					13 09				13 03	13 10					13 24			
Petts Wood 4	d					12 54	12 58									13 06	13 13								
Hither Green 4	d		12 58			13 07			13 12							13 19									13 28
Lewisham 4	d		13 04	13 08						13 14			13 20			13 24		13 26		13 29					13 34
St Johns	d		13 06							13 16						13 26				13 31					13 36
New Cross 4	d		13 08							13 18					12 19	13 28				13 33					13 38
London Victoria 15	a			13 28			13 32										13 47								
London Bridge 4	d	13 13	13 15		13 15	13 19		13 21	13 22	13 24		13 25	13 28	13 30	13 31	13 34		13 35	13 38	13 39		13 41	13 41	13 43	13 45
London Blackfriars 3	a				13 22									13 37											
London Cannon Street 4	a		13 19					13 24		13 28					13 36	13 38				13 43			13 45		13 49
London Waterloo (East) 4	d	13 19				13 24			13 27			13 30	13 33					13 40	13 43			13 45		13 49	
London Charing Cross 4	a	13 22				13 27			13 30			13 33	13 36					13 43	13 46			13 49		13 52	

Orpington, Petts Wood, Hither Green and Lewisham - London (Summary of Services)

		SE	FC 1	SE	SE	SE		SE	SE	SE 1	SE	FC 1	SE	SE	SE	SE		SE	SE	SE 1	SE	SE 1	SE	SE	FC 1
Orpington 4	d			13 21	13 25					13 39				13 33	13 40					13 54					
Petts Wood 4	d			13 24	13 28									13 36	13 43										
Hither Green 4	d			13 37				13 42						13 49									13 58		
Lewisham 4	d	13 38							13 44		13 50			13 54		13 56			13 59				14 04	14 08	
St Johns	d								13 46					13 56					14 01				14 06		
New Cross 4	⊖ d								13 48				12 49	13 58					14 03				14 08		
London Victoria 15	⊖ a	13 58			14 02										14 17									14 28	
London Bridge 4	⊖ d		13 45	13 49		13 51		13 52	13 54	13 55	13 58	14 00	14 01	14 04		14 05		14 08	14 09	14 11	14 11	14 13	14 15		14 15
London Blackfriars 3	⊖ a		13 52									14 07													14 22
London Cannon Street 4	⊖ a					13 54			13 58				14 06	14 08					14 13		14 15		14 19		
London Waterloo (East) 4	⊖ d			13 54				13 57		14 00	14 03					14 10		14 13		14 15		14 19			
London Charing Cross 4	⊖ a			13 57				14 00		14 03	14 06					14 13		14 16		14 19		14 22			

		SE		SE	SE	SE	SE	SE 1	SE	FC 1	SE	SE		SE	SE	SE	SE	SE 1	SE	SE 1	SE	SE		FC 1	SE
Orpington 4	d	13 51		13 55				14 09				14 03		14 10				14 24							14 21
Petts Wood 4	d	13 54		13 58								14 06		14 13											14 24
Hither Green 4	d	14 07				14 12						14 19									14 28				14 37
Lewisham 4	d						14 14		14 20			14 24			14 26		14 29				14 34	14 38			
St Johns	d						14 16					14 26					14 31				14 36				
New Cross 4	⊖ d						14 18				13 19	14 28					14 33				14 38				
London Victoria 15	⊖ a			14 32										14 47								14 58			
London Bridge 4	⊖ d	14 19			14 21	14 22	14 24	14 25	14 28	14 30	14 31	14 34			14 35	14 38	14 39	14 41	14 41	14 43	14 45			14 45	14 49
London Blackfriars 3	⊖ a									14 37														14 52	
London Cannon Street 4	⊖ a				14 24		14 28				14 36	14 38					14 43		14 45		14 49				
London Waterloo (East) 4	⊖ d	14 24				14 27		14 30	14 33						14 40	14 43		14 45		14 49					14 54
London Charing Cross 4	⊖ a	14 27				14 30		14 33	14 36						14 43	14 46		14 49		14 52					14 57

		SE	SE	SE	SE	SE 1	SE	FC 1		SE	SE	SE	SE	SE	SE	SE 1	SE	SE 1		SE	SE	FC 1	SE	SE	SE
Orpington 4	d	14 25				14 39					14 33	14 40				14 54							14 51	14 55	
Petts Wood 4	d	14 28									14 36	14 43											14 54	14 58	
Hither Green 4	d			14 42							14 49									14 58			15 07		
Lewisham 4	d				14 44		14 50				14 54		14 56		14 59					15 04	15 08				
St Johns	d				14 46						14 56				15 01					15 06					
New Cross 4	⊖ d				14 48					13 49	14 58				15 03					15 08					
London Victoria 15	⊖ a	15 02										15 17									15 28			15 32	
London Bridge 4	⊖ d		14 51	14 52	14 54	14 55	14 58	15 00		15 01	15 04		15 05	15 08	15 09	15 11	15 11	15 13		15 15		15 15	15 19		15 21
London Blackfriars 3	⊖ a							15 07														15 22			
London Cannon Street 4	⊖ a		14 54		14 58					15 06	15 08				15 13		15 15			15 19					15 24
London Waterloo (East) 4	⊖ d			14 57		15 00	15 03						15 10	15 13		15 15		15 19					15 24		
London Charing Cross 4	⊖ a			15 00		15 03	15 06						15 13	15 16		15 19		15 22					15 27		

		SE	SE	SE 1		SE	FC 1	SE	SE	SE	SE	SE	SE	SE 1		SE	SE 1	SE	SE	FC 1	SE	SE	SE	SE	
Orpington 4	d			15 09					15 03	15 10				15 24							15 21	15 25			
Petts Wood 4	d								15 06	15 13											15 24	15 28			
Hither Green 4	d	15 12							15 19									15 28			15 37			15 42	
Lewisham 4	d		15 14			15 20			15 24		15 26		15 29					15 34	15 38						
St Johns	d		15 16						15 26				15 31					15 36							
New Cross 4	⊖ d		15 18					14 19	15 28				15 33					15 38							
London Victoria 15	⊖ a									15 47									15 58			16 02			
London Bridge 4	⊖ d	15 22	15 24	15 25		15 28	15 30	15 31	15 34		15 35	15 38	15 39	15 41		15 41	15 43	15 45		15 45	15 50		15 51	15 53	
London Blackfriars 3	⊖ a						15 37													15 52					
London Cannon Street 4	⊖ a		15 28					15 36	15 38				15 43			15 45		15 49					15 54		
London Waterloo (East) 4	⊖ d	15 27		15 30		15 33					15 40	15 43		15 46			15 49				15 55			15 58	
London Charing Cross 4	⊖ a	15 30		15 33		15 36					15 43	15 46		15 49			15 52				15 58			16 01	

		SE	SE 1	SE	FC 1	SE	SE	SE	SE	SE		SE	SE 1	SE	SE 1	SE	SE	FC 1	SE	SE		SE	SE	SE	SE 1
Orpington 4	d		15 39				15 33	15 40					15 54						15 51	15 55					16 08
Petts Wood 4	d						15 36	15 43											15 54	15 58					
Hither Green 4	d						15 49									15 58			16 07				16 12		
Lewisham 4	d	15 44		15 50			15 54		15 56	15 59						16 04	16 08							16 14	
St Johns	d	15 46					15 56			16 01						16 06								16 16	
New Cross 4	⊖ d	15 48				14 49	15 58			16 03						16 08								16 18	
London Victoria 15	⊖ a							16 17									16 28			16 32					
London Bridge 4	⊖ d	15 54	15 55	15 58	16 00	16 01	16 04		16 05	16 09		16 09	16 12	16 12	16 14	16 15		16 16	16 19			16 21	16 22	16 24	16 25
London Blackfriars 3	⊖ a				16 07													16 25							
London Cannon Street 4	⊖ a	15 58				16 06	16 08			16 13				16 16		16 19						16 24		16 28	
London Waterloo (East) 4	⊖ d		16 00	16 03					16 10			16 14	16 17		16 20				16 25				16 28		16 30
London Charing Cross 4	⊖ a		16 03	16 06					16 13			16 18	16 20		16 24				16 28				16 31		16 33

		SE	SE	SE	SE	SE		SE	SE	SE	SE 1	SE	SE	SE	SE 1	SE		SE	SE	SE	SE	SE 1	SE	SE	SE
Orpington 4	d				16 03	16 10					16 25					16 21		16 25				16 39			16 33
Petts Wood 4	d				16 06	16 13										16 24		16 28							16 36
Hither Green 4	d				16 19								16 28			16 37				16 42					16 50
Lewisham 4	d	16 20			16 24			16 26		16 29			16 34	16 38							16 44		16 50		
St Johns	d				16 26					16 31			16 36								16 46				
New Cross 4	⊖ d		15 19		16 28					16 33			16 38								16 48			15 49	
London Victoria 15	⊖ a					16 47								17 01				17 04							
London Bridge 4	⊖ d	16 29	16 31	16 32	16 34			16 35	16 38	16 39	16 42	16 42	16 45		16 46	16 49			16 51	16 52	16 54	16 56	16 59	17 01	17 02
London Blackfriars 3	⊖ a																								
London Cannon Street 4	⊖ a		16 36		16 38					16 43		16 46	16 49						16 54		16 58			17 05	
London Waterloo (East) 4	⊖ d	16 34		16 38				16 40	16 43		16 49				16 53	16 55				16 57		17 01	17 04		17 07
London Charing Cross 4	⊖ a	16 37		16 42				16 44	16 46		16 52				16 56	16 58				17 00		17 04	17 07		17 10

Orpington, Petts Wood, Hither Green and Lewisham - London (Summary of Services)

		SE		SE	SE	SE	SE	SE	SE	SE [1]	SE	SE [1]		SE	SE	SE	SE	SE	SE	FC [1]	SE [1]	SE		SE	SE
Orpington [4]	d	16 40							16 51	16 54							16 55				17 09				17 03
Petts Wood [4]	d	16 43							16 54								16 58								17 06
Hither Green [4]	d			16 50	16 56				17 09					17 00	17 07										17 19
Lewisham [4]	d					16 56	16 59							17 05		17 08			17 14			17 20			17 24
St Johns	d			16 54			17 01							17 09					17 16						17 26
New Cross [4]	d			16 56			17 03							17 11					17 18					16 20	17 28
London Victoria [15]	a	17 20														17 28	17 33								
London Bridge [4]	d			17 04	17 06	17 07	17 09	17 09		17 12	17 13	17 18		17 19	17 22			17 22	17 25	17 27	17 28	17 30		17 31	17 34
London Blackfriars [3]	a																			17 35					
London Cannon Street [4]	a			17 09		17 11	17 15				17 17			17 24				17 26	17 29		17 32			17 36	17 38
London Waterloo (East) [4]	d				17 11			17 14	17 25	17 16		17 23			17 29							17 35			
London Charing Cross [4]	a				17 15			17 18	17 29	17 20		17 26			17 33							17 38			

		SE	SE	SE	SE	SE	SE [1]	SE		SE	SE	SE [1]	SE	SE	SE [1]	SE	SE	SE		SE [1]	SE	SE	SE	SE	SE
Orpington [4]	d	17 10	17 13				17 24						17 20	17 24	17 34					17 39				17 37	17 40
Petts Wood [4]	d	17 13											17 24	17 28	17 37									17 40	17 43
Hither Green [4]	d									17 28			17 38				17 42							17 53	
Lewisham [4]	d			17 27		17 30				17 35	17 38							17 44			17 50		17 56		
St Johns	d									17 37								17 46						17 57	
New Cross [4]	d					17 33				17 39								17 48				16 49		17 59	
London Victoria [15]	a	17 48									17 59			18 03											18 18
London Bridge [4]	d			17 36	17 38	17 39	17 42	17 42		17 45		17 45	17 49			17 52	17 54	17 55		17 58	18 00	18 03	18 04	18 06	
London Blackfriars [3]	a														18 09										
London Cannon Street [4]	a					17 44		17 46		17 49						17 56		17 59			18 04	18 07		18 11	
London Waterloo (East) [4]	d		17 37	17 41	17 43		17 47					17 50	17 54				17 59			18 03			18 09		
London Charing Cross [4]	a		17 40	17 44	17 46		17 50					17 53	17 57				18 03			18 06			18 12		

		SE	SE	SE [1]		FC [1]	SE	SE	SE	SE [1]	SE	SE	SE	SE		SE	SE [1]	SE	SE	SE	SE	SE	SE	SE	
Orpington [4]	d			17 54							17 50		17 55				18 09				18 03	18 09			
Petts Wood [4]	d										17 54		17 58								18 06	18 12			
Hither Green [4]	d							17 58			18 07			18 12						18 21	18 19				
Lewisham [4]	d		17 59					18 05	18 08							18 14		18 20			18 24		18 26	18 29	
St Johns	d							18 07								18 16					18 26				
New Cross [4]	d		18 02					18 09				17 08				18 18					18 28			18 32	
London Victoria [15]	a								18 29				18 33									18 48			
London Bridge [4]	d	18 07	18 09	18 10		18 13	18 13	18 16		18 16	18 19	18 21		18 23		18 24	18 25	18 28	18 31	18 33	18 34		18 36	18 38	
London Blackfriars [3]	a					18 21																			
London Cannon Street [4]	a		18 13				18 17	18 20				18 24				18 29			18 35		18 38			18 42	
London Waterloo (East) [4]	d	18 13		18 15						18 21	18 24			18 28			18 30	18 33		18 38			18 42		
London Charing Cross [4]	a	18 16		18 18						18 25	18 27			18 31			18 35	18 37		18 41			18 45		

		SE	SE [1]	SE [1]	SE	SE	SE	FC [1]	SE	SE		SE	SE	SE	SE [1]	SE	FC [1]	SE	SE	SE		SE	SE	SE	SE [1]
Orpington [4]	d		18 24						18 21	18 25									18 33	18 40					18 54
Petts Wood [4]	d								18 24	18 28									18 36	18 43					
Hither Green [4]	d					18 28			18 37				18 42						18 49						
Lewisham [4]	d					18 35	18 38							18 45		18 50			18 54			18 56		18 59	
St Johns	d					18 37								18 47					18 56						
New Cross [4]	d					18 39								18 49					18 58					19 03	
London Victoria [15]	a						18 58			19 03										19 17					
London Bridge [4]	d	18 38	18 41	18 43	18 43	18 46		18 46	18 49			18 51	18 53	18 55	18 55	18 58	19 01	19 01	19 05			19 05	19 08	19 09	19 10
London Blackfriars [3]	a							18 55									19 09								
London Cannon Street [4]	a				18 47	18 51						18 54		18 59				19 06	19 10					19 13	
London Waterloo (East) [4]	d	18 45	18 46	18 49					18 54				18 58		19 00	19 03						19 10	19 13		19 15
London Charing Cross [4]	a	18 48	18 49	18 52					18 57				19 01		19 04	19 06						19 13	19 16		19 18

		SE	SE [1]	SE	SE	FC [1]		SE	SE	SE	SE	SE [1]	SE	SE	FC [1]	SE		SE	SE	SE	SE	SE [1]	SE	SE [1]	SE
Orpington [4]	d							18 50	18 55			19 08				19 03		19 10				19 24			
Petts Wood [4]	d							18 54	18 58							19 06		19 13							
Hither Green [4]	d			18 59				19 07		19 12						19 19									19 28
Lewisham [4]	d			19 05	19 08						19 14			19 20		19 24			19 26	19 29					19 34
St Johns	d			19 07							19 16					19 26									19 36
New Cross [4]	d			19 09							19 18		18 14			19 28				19 32					19 38
London Victoria [15]	a				19 28				19 32									19 47							
London Bridge [4]	d	19 12	19 13	19 15		19 17		19 19		19 22	19 24	19 25	19 28	19 28	19 30	19 34			19 35	19 38	19 38	19 41	19 41	19 43	19 45
London Blackfriars [3]	a					19 22									19 37										
London Cannon Street [4]	a	19 16		19 20							19 28		19 33			19 38				19 43			19 45		19 49
London Waterloo (East) [4]	d		19 18					19 24		19 27		19 30		19 33					19 40		19 43	19 46		19 49	
London Charing Cross [4]	a		19 21					19 27		19 30		19 33		19 36					19 43		19 46	19 49		19 52	

		FC [1]		SE	SE	SE	SE [1]	SE	SE	SE	FC [1]	SE		SE	SE [1]	SE	SE [1]	FC [1]	SE	SE	SE	SE [1]		SE	SE
Orpington [4]	d				19 21	19 25	19 39	19 40							19 54					19 51	19 55	20 09			20 10
Petts Wood [4]	d				19 24	19 28		19 43												19 54	19 58				20 13
Hither Green [4]	d				19 37				19 42											20 07					
Lewisham [4]	d			19 38	19 43				19 48			19 52		19 56					20 08	20 13					
St Johns	d			19 40															20 10						
New Cross [4]	d			19 42					19 51	18 35		19 56							20 12					19 00	
London Victoria [15]	a					20 02		20 17													20 32				20 47
London Bridge [4]	d	19 45		19 49	19 52		19 55		19 58	19 59	20 00	20 04		20 06	20 11	20 11	20 13	20 15	20 19	20 22		20 25		20 28	
London Blackfriars [3]	a	19 52									20 07							20 22							
London Cannon Street [4]	a									20 03						20 15								20 31	
London Waterloo (East) [4]	d			19 54	19 57		20 00		20 03			20 09		20 11	20 16		20 19		20 24	20 27		20 30			
London Charing Cross [4]	a			19 57	20 00		20 03		20 06			20 12		20 14	20 19		20 22		20 27	20 30		20 33			

Orpington, Petts Wood, Hither Green and Lewisham - London (Summary of Services)

		SE	FC 1	SE	SE	SE 1	SE	SE 1		FC 1	SE	SE	SE	SE	FC 1	SE	SE	SE 1		SE	SE 1	FC 1	SE	SE	SE 1
Orpington 4	d					20 24						20 21	20 40					20 53						20 51	21 09
Petts Wood 4	d											20 24	20 43											20 54	
Hither Green 4	d	20 12										20 38		20 42										21 07	
Lewisham 4	d	20 18		20 22	20 26						20 38	20 43		20 48		20 53	20 56						21 08	21 13	
St Johns	d										20 40												21 10		
New Cross 4 ⊖	d	20 21		20 26							20 42			20 51		20 56							21 12		
London Victoria 15 ⊖	a												21 17												
London Bridge 4 ⊖	d	20 28	20 30	20 34	20 36	20 40	20 41	20 43		20 45	20 49	20 52		20 58	21 00	21 04	21 06	21 09		21 11	21 14	21 15	21 19	21 22	21 25
London Blackfriars 3 ⊖	a		20 37							20 52					21 07							21 22			
London Cannon Street 4 ⊖	a						20 45																		
London Waterloo (East) 4 ⊖	d	20 33		20 39	20 41	20 45		20 48			20 54	20 57		21 03		21 09	21 11	21 14		21 16	21 19		21 24	21 27	21 30
London Charing Cross 4 ⊖	a	20 36		20 42	20 44	20 48		20 51			20 57	21 00		21 06		21 12	21 14	21 18		21 19	21 22		21 27	21 30	21 33

		SE	SE	FC 1		SE	SE	SE 1	SE	SE 1	FC 1	SE	SE	SE		SE	SE	SE	SE 1	SE	SE 1	SE	SE	SE 1	
Orpington 4	d	21 10						21 23					21 21	21 40					21 53				21 51	22 09	
Petts Wood 4	d	21 13											21 24	21 43									21 54		
Hither Green 4	d		21 12										21 37			21 42							22 07		
Lewisham 4	d		21 18			21 23	21 26					21 38	21 43			21 48	21 53	21 56				22 08	22 13		
St Johns	d											21 40										22 10			
New Cross 4 ⊖	d		21 21			21 26						21 42				21 51	21 56					22 12			
London Victoria 15 ⊖	a	21 47												22 17											
London Bridge 4 ⊖	d		21 28	21 30		21 34	21 36	21 39	21 41	21 44	21 45	21 49	21 52			21 58	22 02	22 05	22 09	22 11	22 14	22 19	22 22	22 25	
London Blackfriars 3 ⊖	a			21 37							21 52														
London Cannon Street 4 ⊖	a																								
London Waterloo (East) 4 ⊖	d		21 33			21 39	21 41	21 44	21 46	21 49		21 54	21 57			22 03	22 07	22 10	22 14	22 16	22 19	22 24	22 27	22 30	
London Charing Cross 4 ⊖	a		21 36			21 42	21 44	21 48	21 49	21 52		21 57	22 00			22 06	22 10	22 13	22 18	22 19	22 22	22 27	22 30	22 33	

		SE	SE	SE	SE	SE 1	SE	SE 1	SE	SE		SE	SE	SE	SE	SE 1	SE	SE 1	SE	SE		SE 1	SE	SE	SE
Orpington 4	d	22 10				22 23				22 21		22 40				22 53				22 51		23 09	23 10		
Petts Wood 4	d	22 13								22 24		22 43								22 54			23 13		
Hither Green 4	d		22 12							22 37			22 42							23 07				23 12	
Lewisham 4	d		22 18	22 23	22 26				22 38	22 43			22 48	22 53	22 56				23 08	23 13				23 18	23 23
St Johns	d								22 40										23 10						
New Cross 4 ⊖	d		22 21	22 26					22 42				22 51	22 56					23 12					23 21	23 26
London Victoria 15 ⊖	a	22 47										23 17											23 47		
London Bridge 4 ⊖	d		22 28	22 32	22 35	22 39	22 41	22 44	22 49	22 52			22 58	23 02	23 05	23 09	23 11	23 14	23 19	23 22		23 25		23 28	23 32
London Blackfriars 3 ⊖	a																								
London Cannon Street 4 ⊖	a																								
London Waterloo (East) 4 ⊖	d		22 33	22 37	22 40	22 44	22 46	22 49	22 54	22 57			23 03	23 07	23 10	23 14	23 16	23 19	23 24	23 27		23 30		23 33	23 37
London Charing Cross 4 ⊖	a		22 36	22 40	22 43	22 48	22 49	22 52	22 57	23 00			23 06	23 10	23 13	23 18	23 19	23 22	23 27	23 30		23 33		23 36	23 40

		SE	SE	SE	SE	SE 1
Orpington 4	d				23 21	23 37
Petts Wood 4	d				23 24	
Hither Green 4	d				23 37	
Lewisham 4	d	23 26		23 38	23 43	
St Johns	d			23 40		
New Cross 4 ⊖	d			23 42		
London Victoria 15 ⊖	a					
London Bridge 4 ⊖	d	23 35	23 41	23 49	23 52	23 55
London Blackfriars 3 ⊖	a					
London Cannon Street 4 ⊖	a					
London Waterloo (East) 4 ⊖	d	23 40	23 46	23 54	23 57	23 59
London Charing Cross 4 ⊖	a	23 43	23 49	23 57	00 01	00 03

Saturdays

		SE	SE 1	SE	SE	SE	SE	SE	SE	SE		SE	SE	SE	SE	SE	SE	SE 1	SE	SE		SE	SE	SE	SE
Orpington 4	d	23p21	23p37	05 44									05 51	06 10				06 24				06 21	06 25	06 40	
Petts Wood 4	d	23p24		05 47									05 54	06 13								06 24	06 28	06 43	
Hither Green 4	d	23p37					05 42						06 07		06 12							06 37			06 42
Lewisham 4	d	23p43				05 39	05 48	05 50	05 56	06 02			06 13		06 18	06 20	06 26		06 32			06 43			06 48
St Johns	d					05 41				06 04									06 34						
New Cross 4 ⊖	d					05 43	05 51			06 06					06 21				06 36						06 51
London Victoria 15 ⊖	a			06 26										06 47									07 02	07 17	
London Bridge 4 ⊖	d	23p52	23p55		05 45	05 49	05 57	05 59	06 05	06 12		06 15	06 21		06 27	06 29	06 35	06 39	06 42	06 45		06 51			06 57
London Blackfriars 3 ⊖	a																								
London Cannon Street 4 ⊖	a																								
London Waterloo (East) 4 ⊖	d	23p57	23p59		05 50	05 53	06 02	06 04	06 10	06 17		06 20	06 26		06 32	06 34	06 40	06 44	06 47	06 50		06 56			07 02
London Charing Cross 4 ⊖	a	00 01	00 03		05 53	05 56	06 05	06 07	06 13	06 20		06 25	06 29		06 35	06 37	06 43	06 47	06 50	06 55		06 59			07 05

Table 199

Saturdays

Orpington, Petts Wood, Hither Green and Lewisham - London (Summary of Services)

		SE	SE	SE 1	SE	SE		SE	SE	SE	SE 1	SE	SE	SE	SE	SE 1		SE	SE	SE	SE	SE	SE	SE 1	SE
Orpington 4	d			06 54					06 51	06 55	07 09	07 10				07 24				07 21		07 25		07 39	
Petts Wood 4	d								06 54	06 58		07 13								07 24		07 28			
Hither Green 4	d								07 07				07 12							07 37			07 42		
Lewisham 4	d	06 50	06 56		07 02	07 08			07 13				07 18	07 20	07 26				07 32		07 38				07 50
St Johns	d				07 04														07 34						
New Cross 4	⊖ d				07 06								07 21						07 36						
London Victoria 15	⊖ a					07 30				07 32		07 47									08 00	08 02			
London Bridge 4	⊖ d	06 59	07 05	07 09	07 12			07 15	07 21		07 24		07 27	07 29	07 35	07 39		07 41	07 42	07 49			07 52	07 55	07 58
London Blackfriars 3	⊖ a																								
London Cannon Street 4	⊖ a																	07 45							
London Waterloo (East) 4	⊖ d	07 04	07 10	07 14	07 17			07 20	07 26		07 29		07 32	07 34	07 40	07 44			07 47	07 54			07 57	08 00	08 03
London Charing Cross 4	⊖ a	07 07	07 13	07 17	07 20			07 25	07 29		07 33		07 35	07 40	07 43	07 48			07 50	07 57			08 00	08 03	08 06

		SE		SE	SE	SE	SE	SE	SE 1	SE	SE 1	SE		SE	SE	SE	SE	SE	SE	SE 1	SE	SE		SE	SE
Orpington 4	d			07 33	07 40				07 54					07 51		07 55				08 09				08 03	08 10
Petts Wood 4	d			07 36	07 43									07 54		07 58								08 06	08 13
Hither Green 4	d			07 49								07 58		08 07				08 12						08 19	
Lewisham 4	d			07 54		07 56	07 59	07 59				08 04			08 08				08 14		08 20			08 24	
St Johns	d			07 56				08 01				08 06							08 16					08 26	
New Cross 4	⊖ d			07 58				08 03				08 08							08 18					08 28	
London Victoria 15	⊖ a				08 17										08 30	08 32									08 47
London Bridge 4	⊖ d	08 01		08 04		08 05	08 08	08 09	08 11	08 11	08 14	08 15		08 19			08 21	08 22	08 24	08 25	08 28	08 31		08 34	
London Blackfriars 3	⊖ a																								
London Cannon Street 4	⊖ a	08 04		08 08				08 13		08 15		08 19					08 24		08 28			08 34		08 38	
London Waterloo (East) 4	⊖ d					08 10	08 13		08 15		08 19			08 24				08 27		08 30	08 33				
London Charing Cross 4	⊖ a					08 13	08 16		08 19		08 22			08 27				08 30		08 33	08 36				

		SE	SE	SE	SE 1	SE	SE 1	SE		SE	SE	SE	SE	SE	SE	SE 1	SE	SE	SE		SE	SE	SE	SE	SE 1
Orpington 4	d				08 24					08 21		08 25				08 39			08 33		08 40				08 54
Petts Wood 4	d									08 24		08 28							08 36		08 43				
Hither Green 4	d							08 28		08 37				08 42					08 49						
Lewisham 4	d	08 26		08 29				08 34			08 38				08 44		08 50		08 54			08 56		08 59	
St Johns	d			08 31				08 36							08 46				08 56					09 01	
New Cross 4	⊖ d			08 33				08 38							08 48				08 58					09 03	
London Victoria 15	⊖ a										09 00	09 02									09 17				
London Bridge 4	⊖ d	08 35	08 38	08 39	08 41	08 41	08 44	08 45		08 49			08 51	08 52	08 54	08 55	08 58	09 01	09 04			09 05	09 08	09 09	09 11
London Blackfriars 3	⊖ a																								
London Cannon Street 4	⊖ a			08 43		08 45		08 49					08 54		08 58			09 04	09 08					09 13	
London Waterloo (East) 4	⊖ d	08 40	08 43		08 45		08 49			08 54				08 57		09 00	09 03					09 10	09 13		09 15
London Charing Cross 4	⊖ a	08 43	08 46		08 49		08 52			08 57				09 00		09 03	09 06					09 13	09 16		09 19

		SE	SE 1	SE	SE		SE	SE	SE	SE	SE	SE 1	SE	SE	SE		SE	SE	SE	SE	SE 1	SE	SE 1	SE	SE
Orpington 4	d				08 51			08 55				09 09			09 03		09 10				09 24				09 21
Petts Wood 4	d				08 54			08 58							09 06		09 13								09 24
Hither Green 4	d			08 58	09 07					09 12					09 19									09 28	09 37
Lewisham 4	d			09 04			09 08				09 14		09 20		09 24			09 26		09 29				09 34	
St Johns	d			09 06							09 16				09 26					09 31				09 36	
New Cross 4	⊖ d			09 08							09 18			08 19	09 28					09 33				09 38	
London Victoria 15	⊖ a						09 30	09 32									09 47								
London Bridge 4	⊖ d	09 11	09 14	09 15	09 19				09 21	09 22	09 24	09 25	09 28	09 31	09 34			09 35	09 38	09 39	09 41	09 41	09 44	09 45	09 49
London Blackfriars 3	⊖ a																								
London Cannon Street 4	⊖ a	09 15		09 19					09 24		09 28			09 34	09 38					09 43		09 45		09 49	
London Waterloo (East) 4	⊖ d		09 19		09 24					09 27		09 30	09 33					09 40	09 43		09 45		09 49		09 54
London Charing Cross 4	⊖ a		09 22		09 27					09 30		09 33	09 36					09 43	09 46		09 49		09 52		09 57

			SE	SE	SE	SE	SE	SE 1	SE	SE		SE		SE	SE	SE	SE	SE	SE	SE	SE 1	SE		SE 1
Orpington 4	d			09 25				09 39			and at the same minutes past each hour until					18 33	18 40				18 54			
Petts Wood 4	d			09 28												18 36	18 43							
Hither Green 4	d					09 42										18 49								
Lewisham 4	d		09 38				09 44		09 50							18 54		18 56		18 59				
St Johns	d						09 46									18 56				19 01				
New Cross 4	⊖ d						09 48			08 49		17 49		18 19	18 49	18 58				19 03				
London Victoria 15	⊖ a		10 00	10 02													19 17							
London Bridge 4	⊖ d				09 51	09 52	09 54	09 55	09 58	10 01		19 01		19a30	20a00	19 04		19 05	19 08	19 09	19 11	19 11		19 14
London Blackfriars 3	⊖ a																							
London Cannon Street 4	⊖ a				09 54		09 58			10 04		19 04				19 08				19 13		19 15		
London Waterloo (East) 4	⊖ d					09 57		10 00	10 03									19 10	19 13		19 15			19 19
London Charing Cross 4	⊖ a					10 00		10 03	10 06									19 13	19 16		19 19			19 22

		SE	SE	SE	SE	SE 1	SE	SE	SE		SE	SE	SE	SE	SE 1	SE	SE	SE	SE 1		SE	SE	SE	SE	SE
Orpington 4	d			18 51	18 55	19 09	19 10								19 28		19 21	19 25	19 39		19 40				
Petts Wood 4	d			18 54	18 58		19 13										19 24	19 28			19 43				
Hither Green 4	d	18 58		19 07					19 12								19 37					19 42			
Lewisham 4	d	19 04	19 08	19 12				19 14	19 18			19 20	19 26			19 38	19 43					19 48	19 53	19 56	
St Johns	d	19 06						19 16								19 40									
New Cross 4	⊖ d	19 08						19 18			19 19	19 23				19 42						19 51	19 56		
London Victoria 15	⊖ a		19 30		19 32		19 47											20 02			20 17				
London Bridge 4	⊖ d	19 15		19 21		19 25		19a24	19 28		20a30	19 34	19 37	19 41	19 44	19 49	19 52		19 55			19 58	20 04	20 06	20 11
London Blackfriars 3	⊖ a																								
London Cannon Street 4	⊖ a	19 19																							
London Waterloo (East) 4	⊖ d			19 26		19 30			19 32			19 39	19 42	19 46	19 48	19 54	19 57		20 00			20 04	20 09	20 11	20 16
London Charing Cross 4	⊖ a			19 29		19 33			19 35			19 42	19 45	19 49	19 51	19 58	20 00		20 03			20 07	20 12	20 14	20 19

Table 199

Saturdays

Orpington, Petts Wood, Hither Green and Lewisham - London (Summary of Services)

Station		SE 1	SE	SE	SE		SE 1	SE	SE	SE	SE	SE	SE 1	SE	SE		SE 1	SE	SE	SE	SE	SE	SE 1	SE	SE
Orpington 4	d	19 58		19 51	19 55		20 09	20 10					20 28		20 21		20 39	20 40					20 58		20 51
Petts Wood 4	d			19 54	19 58			20 13							20 24			20 43							20 54
Hither Green 4	d			20 07					20 12						20 37				20 42						21 07
Lewisham 4	d		20 08	20 13					20 18	20 23	20 26			20 38	20 43				20 48	20 53	20 56			21 08	21 13
St Johns	d		20 10											20 40										21 10	
New Cross 4	⊖ d		20 12						20 21	20 26				20 42					20 51	20 56				21 12	
London Victoria 15	⊖ a				20 32			20 47										21 17							
London Bridge 4	⊖ d	20 14	20 19	20 22			20 25		20 28	20 34	20 36	20 41	20 44	20 49	20 52		20 55		20 58	21 04	21 06	21 11	21 14	21 19	21 22
London Blackfriars 3	⊖ a																								
London Cannon Street 4	⊖ a																								
London Waterloo (East) 4	⊖ d	20 18	20 24	20 27			20 30		20 34	20 39	20 41	20 46	20 48	20 54	20 57		21 00		21 04	21 09	21 11	21 16	21 18	21 24	21 27
London Charing Cross 4	⊖ a	20 21	20 28	20 30			20 33		20 37	20 42	20 44	20 49	20 51	20 58	21 00		21 03		21 07	21 12	21 14	21 19	21 21	21 28	21 30

Station			SE 1	SE	SE	SE	SE	SE	SE 1	SE	SE		SE 1	SE	SE	SE	SE	SE	SE 1	SE	SE		SE 1	SE	SE
Orpington 4	d		21 09	21 10					21 28		21 21		21 39	21 40					21 58		21 51		22 09	22 10	
Petts Wood 4	d			21 13							21 24			21 43							21 54			22 13	
Hither Green 4	d				21 12						21 37				21 42						22 07				22 12
Lewisham 4	d				21 18	21 23	21 26			21 38	21 43				21 48	21 53	21 56			22 08	22 13				22 18
St Johns	d									21 40										22 10					
New Cross 4	⊖ d				21 21	21 26				21 42					21 51	21 56				22 12					22 21
London Victoria 15	⊖ a			21 47										22 17										22 47	
London Bridge 4	⊖ d		21 25		21 28	21 34	21 36	21 41	21 44	21 49	21 52		21 55		21 58	22 02	22 05	22 11	22 14	22 19	22 22		22 25		22 28
London Blackfriars 3	⊖ a																								
London Cannon Street 4	⊖ a																								
London Waterloo (East) 4	⊖ d		21 30		21 34	21 39	21 41	21 46	21 48	21 54	21 57		22 00		22 04	22 07	22 10	22 16	22 18	22 24	22 27		22 30		22 34
London Charing Cross 4	⊖ a		21 33		21 37	21 42	21 44	21 49	21 51	21 58	22 00		22 03		22 07	22 10	22 13	22 19	22 21	22 28	22 30		22 33		22 37

Station		SE	SE	SE	SE 1	SE	SE		SE 1	SE	SE	SE	SE	SE	SE 1	SE	SE		SE 1	SE	SE	SE	SE	SE	SE
Orpington 4	d				22 28		22 21		22 39	22 40					22 58		22 51		23 09	23 10					
Petts Wood 4	d						22 24			22 43							22 54			23 13					
Hither Green 4	d						22 37				22 42						23 07				23 12				
Lewisham 4	d	22 23	22 26			22 38	22 43				22 48	22 53	22 56			23 08	23 13				23 18	23 23	23 26		23 38
St Johns	d					22 40										23 10									23 40
New Cross 4	⊖ d	22 26				22 42					22 51	22 56				23 12					23 21	23 26			23 42
London Victoria 15	⊖ a									23 17										23 47					
London Bridge 4	⊖ d	22 32	22 35	22 41	22 44	22 49	22 52		22 55		22 58	23 02	23 05	23 11	23 14	23 19	23 22		23 25		23 28	23 32	23 35	23 41	23 49
London Blackfriars 3	⊖ a																								
London Cannon Street 4	⊖ a																								
London Waterloo (East) 4	⊖ d	22 37	22 40	22 46	22 48	22 54	22 57		23 00		23 04	23 07	23 10	23 16	23 18	23 24	23 27		23 30		23 34	23 37	23 40	23 46	23 54
London Charing Cross 4	⊖ a	22 40	22 43	22 49	22 51	22 58	23 00		23 03		23 07	23 10	23 13	23 20	23 21	23 27	23 30		23 33		23 37	23 40	23 43	23 49	23 57

Station		SE	SE 1
Orpington 4	d	23 21	23 37
Petts Wood 4	d	23 24	
Hither Green 4	d	23 37	
Lewisham 4	d	23 43	
St Johns	d		
New Cross 4	⊖ d		
London Victoria 15	⊖ a		
London Bridge 4	⊖ d	23 52	23 55
London Blackfriars 3	⊖ a		
London Cannon Street 4	⊖ a		
London Waterloo (East) 4	⊖ d	23 57	23 59
London Charing Cross 4	⊖ a	00 01	00 03

Sundays

Station		SE A	SE 1 A	SE	SE	SE	SE	SE	SE	SE		SE 1	SE	SE	SE	SE	SE 1	SE	SE	SE		SE	SE 1	SE	SE
Orpington 4	d	23p21	23p37	06 43	07 06				07 10	07 13		07 28	07 36				07 43			07 40		07 43	07 58	08 06	
Petts Wood 4	d	23p24		06 46	07 09				07 13	07 16			07 39							07 43		07 46		08 09	
Hither Green 4	d	23p37						07 12	07 26							07 42				07 56					
Lewisham 4	d	23p43				07 08		07 18	07 31					07 38		07 48		07 52	07 56	08 01					08 08
St Johns	d																	07 54							
New Cross 4	⊖ d					07 11								07 41				07 56							08 11
London Victoria 15	⊖ a			07 25	07 43					07 55			08 13									08 25		08 43	
London Bridge 4	⊖ d	23p52	23p55			07 20	07 23	07 26	07 40			07 43		07 50	07 53	07 56	07 59	08 04	08 07	08 10			08 13		08 20
London Blackfriars 3	⊖ a																								
London Cannon Street 4	⊖ a																								
London Waterloo (East) 4	⊖ d	23p57	23p59			07 25	07 28	07 31	07 45			07 48		07 55	07 58	08 01	08 04	08 08	08 11	08 15			08 18		08 25
London Charing Cross 4	⊖ a	00 01	00 03			07 28	07 31	07 34	07 48			07 52		07 58	08 01	08 04	08 07	08 11	08 14	08 18			08 22		08 28

A not 11 December

Orpington, Petts Wood, Hither Green and Lewisham - London (Summary of Services)

		SE	SE	SE	SE	SE		SE 1	SE	SE	SE	SE	SE 1	SE	SE	SE		SE 1	SE	SE	SE	SE	SE 1	
Orpington 4	d					08 10		08 28	08 36				08 43			08 40		08 58	09 06				09 13	
Petts Wood 4	d					08 13			08 39							08 43			09 09					and at the same minutes past each hour until
Hither Green 4	d		08 12			08 26						08 42				08 56						09 12		
Lewisham 4	d		08 18	08 22	08 26	08 31				08 38		08 48		08 52	08 56	09 01				09 08		09 18		
St Johns	d			08 24										08 54										
New Cross 4	d			08 26						08 41				08 56						09 11				
London Victoria 15	a								09 13										09 43					
London Bridge 4	d	08 23	08 26	08 34	08 37	08 40		08 43		08 50	08 53	08 56	08 59	09 04	09 07	09 10		09 13		09 20	09 23	09 26	09 29	
London Blackfriars 3	a																							
London Cannon Street 4	a																							
London Waterloo (East) 4	d	08 28	08 31	08 38	08 41	08 45		08 48		08 55	08 58	09 01	09 04	09 08	09 11	09 15		09 18		09 25	09 28	09 31	09 34	
London Charing Cross 4	a	08 31	08 34	08 41	08 44	08 49		08 52		08 58	09 01	09 04	09 07	09 11	09 14	09 18		09 22		09 28	09 31	09 34	09 37	

		SE 1		SE	SE	SE	SE 1	SE	SE	SE	SE	SE 1		SE	SE	SE	SE 1	SE	SE	SE	SE	SE		SE	SE
Orpington 4	d	19 13				19 10	19 28	19 36				19 43				19 40	19 58	20 06							20 10
Petts Wood 4	d					19 13		19 39								19 43		20 09							20 13
Hither Green 4	d					19 26					19 42					19 56					20 12				20 26
Lewisham 4	d			19 22	19 26	19 31			19 38		19 48			19 52	19 56	20 01			20 08		20 18	20 22		20 26	20 31
St Johns	d			19 24										19 54								20 24			
New Cross 4	d			19 26					19 41					19 56					20 11			20 26			
London Victoria 15	a							20 13										20 43							
London Bridge 4	d	19 29		19 34	19 37	19 40	19 43		19 50	19 53	19 56	19 59		20 04	20 07	20 10	20 13		20 20	20 23	20 26	20 34		20 37	20 40
London Blackfriars 3	a																								
London Cannon Street 4	a																								
London Waterloo (East) 4	d	19 34		19 38	19 41	19 45	19 48		19 55	19 58	20 01	20 04		20 08	20 11	20 15	20 18		20 25	20 28	20 31	20 38		20 41	20 45
London Charing Cross 4	a	19 37		19 41	19 44	19 49	19 52		19 58	20 01	20 04	20 07		20 11	20 14	20 18	20 22		20 28	20 31	20 34	20 41		20 44	20 49

		SE 1	SE	SE	SE	SE	SE 1	SE		SE	SE	SE 1	SE	SE	SE	SE	SE	SE		SE	SE 1	SE	SE	SE	SE
Orpington 4	d	20 28	20 36				20 43				20 40	20 58	21 06							21 10	21 28	21 36			
Petts Wood 4	d		20 39								20 43		21 09							21 13		21 39			
Hither Green 4	d					20 42					20 56					21 12				21 26					21 42
Lewisham 4	d			20 38		20 48		20 52		20 56	21 01			21 08		21 18	21 22	21 26		21 31			21 38		21 48
St Johns	d							20 54									21 24								
New Cross 4	d			20 41				20 56						21 11			21 26						21 41		
London Victoria 15	a		21 13										21 43									22 13			
London Bridge 4	d	20 43		20 50	20 53	20 56	20 59	21 04		21 07	21 10	21 13		21 20	21 23	21 26	21 34	21 37		21 40	21 43		21 50	21 53	21 56
London Blackfriars 3	a																								
London Cannon Street 4	a																								
London Waterloo (East) 4	d	20 48		20 55	20 58	21 01	21 04	21 08		21 11	21 15	21 18		21 25	21 28	21 31	21 38	21 41		21 45	21 48		21 55	21 58	22 01
London Charing Cross 4	a	20 52		20 58	21 01	21 04	21 07	21 11		21 14	21 18	21 22		21 28	21 31	21 34	21 41	21 44		21 49	21 52		21 58	22 01	22 04

		SE 1	SE	SE		SE	SE 1	SE	SE	SE	SE	SE	SE	SE		SE 1	SE	SE	SE	SE	SE 1	SE	SE	SE	
Orpington 4	d	21 43				21 40	21 58	22 06						22 10		22 28	22 36				22 43			22 40	
Petts Wood 4	d					21 43		22 09						22 13			22 39							22 43	
Hither Green 4	d					21 56					22 12			22 26						22 42				22 56	
Lewisham 4	d		21 52	21 56		22 01			22 08		22 18	22 22	22 26	22 31				22 38		22 48		22 52	22 56	23 01	
St Johns	d		21 54									22 24										22 54			
New Cross 4	d		21 56						22 11			22 26						22 41				22 56			
London Victoria 15	a							22 43									23 13								
London Bridge 4	d	21 59	22 04	22 07		22 10	22 13		22 20	22 23	22 26	22 34	22 37	22 40		22 43		22 50	22 53	22 56	22 59	23 04	23 07	23 10	
London Blackfriars 3	a																								
London Cannon Street 4	a																								
London Waterloo (East) 4	d	22 04	22 08	22 11		22 15	22 18		22 25	22 28	22 31	22 38	22 41	22 45		22 48		22 55	22 58	23 01	23 04	23 08	23 11	23 15	
London Charing Cross 4	a	22 07	22 11	22 14		22 18	22 22		22 28	22 31	22 34	22 41	22 44	22 49		22 52		22 58	23 01	23 04	23 07	23 11	23 14	23 18	

		SE 1	SE	SE	SE	SE	SE	SE
Orpington 4	d	22 58						23 10
Petts Wood 4	d							23 13
Hither Green 4	d				23 12			23 26
Lewisham 4	d		23 08		23 18	23 22	23 26	23 31
St Johns	d					23 24		
New Cross 4	d		23 11			23 26		
London Victoria 15	a							
London Bridge 4	d	23 13	23 20	23 23	23 26	23 34	23 37	23 40
London Blackfriars 3	a							
London Cannon Street 4	a							
London Waterloo (East) 4	d	23 18	23 25	23 28	23 31	23 38	23 41	23 45
London Charing Cross 4	a	23 22	23 28	23 31	23 34	23 41	23 44	23 49

Network Diagram for Tables 200, 203, 204 | also 199 ⊙

DM-26/11
Design BAJS

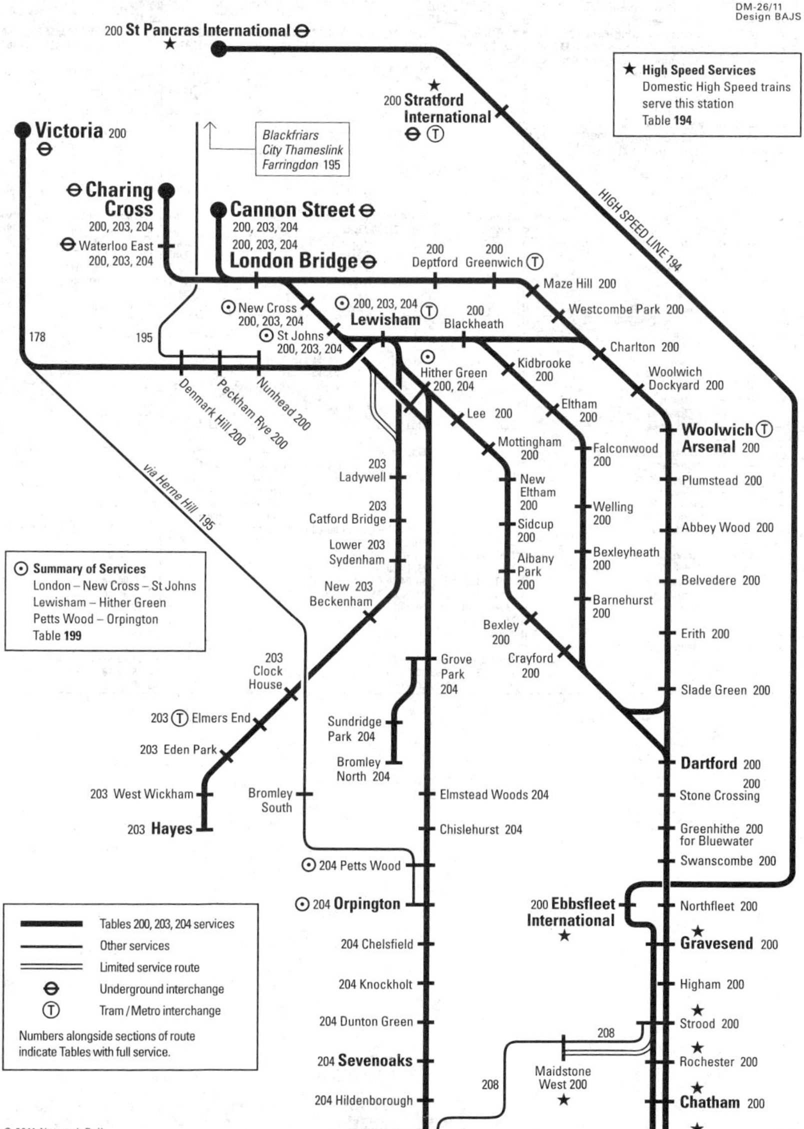

London - Dartford and Gillingham

Network Diagram - see first Page of Table 200

Miles	Miles	Miles	Miles	Miles	Station		SE MX	SE MO	SE	SE MX	SE MO	SE MO	SE MX	SE MO	SE MX		SE MO	SE MX	SE MX	SE MX	SE MO	SE MO	SE MX	SE MX	SE MX
—	—	—	—	0	**St Pancras Int'l** 15 ⊖	d			23p25										23p55						
—	—	—	—	6	**Stratford International** ⊖ ⛴	d			23p32										00 02						
—	—	—	—	22¾	**Ebbsfleet International**	d			23p43										00 13						
0	—	0	0	—	**London Charing Cross** 4 ⊖	d	22p39	22p40		23p09	23p10	23p20	23p22	23p26	23p26		23p30	23p32		23p39	23p50	23p56	23p56	00 02	00 10
0¾	—	0¾	0¾	—	**London Waterloo (East)** 4 ⊖	d	22p42	22p43		23p12	23p13	23p23	23p25	23p29	23p29		23p33	23p35		23p42	23p53	23p59	23p59	00 05	00 13
—	0	—	—	—	**London Cannon Street** 4 ⊖	d																			
1¾	1¾	1¾	1¾	—	**London Bridge** 4 ⊖	d	22p47	22p48		23p17	23p18	23p28	23p30	23p34	23p34		23p38	23p40		23p47	23p58	00 04	00 04	00 10	00 18
—	3¾	—	—	—	Deptford	d									23p40		23p44						00 10		
—	4¼	—	—	—	Greenwich 4 ⛴	d									23p42		23p46						00 12		
—	5¼	—	—	—	Maze Hill	d									23p45		23p49						00 15		
—	5¾	—	—	—	Westcombe Park	d									23p47		23p51						00 17		
—	—	—	—	0	**London Victoria** 15 ⊖	d																			
—	—	—	—	4¼	Denmark Hill 4	d																			
—	—	—	—	5	Peckham Rye 4	d																			
—	—	—	—	5¾	Nunhead 4	d																			
—	—	4¾	4¾	—	New Cross 4 ⊖	d						23p34	23p35					23p45			00 04			00 15	00 23
—	—	5½	5½	—	St Johns	d																			
6	—	6	6	7½	Lewisham 4 ⛴	d	22p56	22p57		23p26	23p27	23p38	23p39	23p42				23p49		23p56	00 08	00 12		00 19	00 27
7	—	7	—	8½	Blackheath 4	d	22p59	23p00		23p29	23p30	23p40						23p52		23p59	00 10			00 22	
—	—	8	—	9½	Kidbrooke	d						23p43						23p55			00 13			00 25	
—	—	9	—	10½	Eltham	d						23p47						23p58			00 17			00 28	
—	—	10¼	—	11¾	Falconwood	d						23p49						00 01			00 19			00 31	
—	—	11¼	—	12¾	Welling	d						23p52						00 03			00 22			00 33	
—	—	12¾	—	14¼	Bexleyheath	d						23p54						00 06			00 24			00 36	
—	—	14	—	15½	Barnehurst 4	d						23p57						00 08			00 27			00 38	
—	—	—	7¼	—	Hither Green 4	d							23p44	23p46								00 16			00 32
—	—	—	8	—	Lee	d							23p46	23p48								00 18			00 34
—	—	—	9½	—	Mottingham	d							23p49	23p51								00 21			00 37
—	—	—	10½	—	New Eltham	d							23p51	23p53								00 23			00 39
—	—	—	12	—	Sidcup 4	d							23p55	23p57								00 27			00 43
—	—	—	13	—	Albany Park	d							23p57	23p59								00 29			00 45
—	—	—	14	—	Bexley	d							23p59	00 01								00 31			00 47
—	—	—	15½	—	Crayford	d							00 03	00 04								00 34			00 51
9	6½	—	—	—	Charlton 4	d	23p03	23p04		23p33	23p34				23p50		23p54			00 03			00 20		
10	7½	—	—	—	Woolwich Dockyard	d									23p53		23p57						00 23		
10¾	8¼	—	—	—	**Woolwich Arsenal** 4 ⛴	d	23p09	23p10		23p39	23p40				23p56		23p59			00 09			00 26		
11¼	8¾	—	—	—	Plumstead	d									23p58		00 02						00 28		
12¾	10¼	—	—	—	Abbey Wood	d	23p13	23p14		23p43	23p44				00 01		00 05			00 13			00 31		
14¼	11¾	—	—	—	Belvedere	d									00 03		00 07						00 33		
15½	13	—	—	—	Erith	d									00 06		00 10						00 36		
16¾	14¼	—	—	—	Slade Green 4	d									00 09		00 14						00 39		
18¾	16¼	17	17¼	18½	**Dartford** 4	a	23p24	23p24		23p54	23p54	00 04	00 08	00 09	00 14		00 19	00 16		00 24	00 33	00 39	00 44	00 46	00 56
—	—	—	—	—		d	23p25	23p25		23p55	23p55									00 25					
20¾	—	—	19¼	—	Stone Crossing	d	23p29	23p29		23p58	23p59									00 29					
21½	—	—	20	—	Greenhithe for Bluewater	d	23p31	23p31		23p59	00 01									00 31					
22¾	—	—	21¼	—	Swanscombe	d	23p34	23p34		00 04	00 04									00 34					
23½	—	—	22	—	Northfleet	d	23p36	23p36		00 06	00 06									00 36					
25½	—	—	24	24¾	**Gravesend** 4	d	23p40	23p40	23p48	00 10	00 10								00 18	00 40					
30	—	—	28½	29¼	Higham	d	23p46	23p46		00 16	00 16									00 46					
32¾	—	—	31¼	32	Strood 4	d	23p52	23p52	23p58	00 22	00 22								00 28	00 52					
—	—	—	—	—	Maidstone West	d																			
33¾	—	—	32¼	33	Rochester 4	d	23p56	23p56	00 03	00 26	00 26								00 33	00 56					
34½	—	—	32¾	33½	**Chatham** 4	d	23p58	23p58	00 05	00 28	00 28								00 35	00 58					
36	—	—	34½	35¼	**Gillingham (Kent)** 4	a	00 03	00 03	00 09	00 33	00 33								00 39	01 03					

London - Dartford and Gillingham

Network Diagram - see first Page of Table 200

		SE	SE	SE	SE	SE	SE	SE	SE	SE	SE	SE	SE	SE	SE	SE	SE	SE	SE	SE	SE	SE
St Pancras Int'l 15 ⊖	d											06 25					06 55					07 25
Stratford International ⊖ ⛴	d											06 32					07 02					07 32
Ebbsfleet International	d											06 42					07 13					07 43
London Charing Cross 4 ⊖	d	00 18		04 50	04 56	05 02	05 20	05 26	05 32	05 39	05 52		05 56	06 02	06 09			06 26	06 32	06 39	06 52	
London Waterloo (East) 4 ⊖	d	00 21		04 53	04 59	05 05	05 23	05 29	05 35	05 42	05 55		05 59	06 05	06 12			06 29	06 35	06 42	06 55	
London Cannon Street 4 ⊖	d															06 27						
London Bridge 4 ⊖	d	00 26		04 58	05 04	05 10	05 28	05 34	05 42	05 47	06 01		06 04	06 10	06 17	06 31		06 34	06 40	06 47	07 00	
Deptford	d			05 04			05 34				06 07					06 37					07 07	
Greenwich 4 ⛴	d			05 06			05 36				06 09					06 39					07 09	
Maze Hill	d			05 09			05 39				06 12					06 42					07 12	
Westcombe Park	d			05 11			05 41				06 14					06 44					07 14	
London Victoria 15 ⊖	d																					
Denmark Hill 4	d																					
Peckham Rye 4	d																					
Nunhead 4	d																					
New Cross 4 ⊖	d	00 31			05 09	05 15		05 39	05 48	05 52			06 09	06 15				06 40	06 46			
St Johns	d																					
Lewisham 4 ⛴	d	00 35			05 13	05 19		05 43	05 52	05 56			06 13	06 19	06 26			06 44	06 50	06 56		
Blackheath 4	d	00 38				05 22			05 54	05 59				06 22	06 29				06 53	06 59		
Kidbrooke	d					05 25			05 57					06 25					06 56			
Eltham	d					05 28			06 00					06 28					06 59			
Falconwood	d					05 31			06 03					06 31					07 01			
Welling	d					05 33			06 05					06 33					07 04			
Bexleyheath	d					05 36			06 08					06 36					07 06			
Barnehurst 4	d					05 38			06 10					06 38					07 11			
Hither Green 4	d				05 18			05 48					06 18					06 48				
Lee	d				05 20			05 50					06 20					06 50				
Mottingham	d				05 23			05 53					06 23					06 53				
New Eltham	d				05 25			05 55					06 25					06 55				
Sidcup 4	d				05 29			05 59					06 29					06 59				
Albany Park	d				05 31			06 01					06 31					07 01				
Bexley	d				05 33			06 03					06 33					07 03				
Crayford	d				05 36			06 06					06 36					07 06				
Charlton 4	d	00 42		05 14			05 44			06 03	06 17				06 33	06 47				07 03	07 17	
Woolwich Dockyard	d			05 17			05 47				06 20					06 50					07 20	
Woolwich Arsenal 4 ⛴	d	00 47		05 20			05 50			06 09	06 23				06 39	06 53				07 09	07 23	
Plumstead	d	00 49		05 22			05 52				06 25					06 55					07 25	
Abbey Wood	d	00 53		05 25			05 55			06 13	06 28				06 43	06 58				07 13	07 28	
Belvedere	d	00 55		05 27			05 57				06 30					07 00					07 30	
Erith	d	00 58		05 30			06 00				06 33					07 03					07 33	
Slade Green 4	d	01 00		05 34			06 04			06 19	06 37					07 07					07 37	
Dartford 4	a	01 05		05 38	05 41	05 45	06 08	06 11	06 17	06 24	06 44		06 41	06 45	06 54	07 12		07 11	07 18	07 23	07 46	
	d	01 06	05 25		05 42	05 55		06 12		06 25			06 42		06 55			07 12		07 25		
Stone Crossing	d				05 46			06 16					06 46					07 16				
Greenhithe for Bluewater	d	01 10	05 30		05 48	06 00		06 18		06 30			06 48		07 00			07 18		07 30		
Swanscombe	d				05 51			06 21					06 51					07 21				
Northfleet	d				05 53			06 23					06 53					07 23				
Gravesend 4	d	01 17	05 37		05a57	06 07		06a27		06 38		06 46	06 59		07a06		07 21	07 27		07 37		07 48
Higham	d	01 23	05 43			06 13				06 44			07 05							07 43		
Strood 4	d	01 29	05 48			06 18				06 49		06 57	07 17				07 31	07a37		07 48		07 58
Maidstone West	d											07a12										
Rochester 4	d	01 33	05 52			06 22				06 53			07 21				07 36			07 52		08 03
Chatham 4	d	01 35	05 55			06 25				06 56			07 24				07 38			07 55		08 05
Gillingham (Kent) 4	a	01 41	05 59			06 29				07 00			07 28				07 42			07 59		08 09

London - Dartford and Gillingham

Network Diagram - see first Page of Table 200

		SE	SE	SE	SE	SE	SE		SE	SE	SE	SE	SE	SE	SE	SE	SE		SE	SE	SE	SE	SE	SE	SE
St Pancras Int'l 15 ⊖	d										07 52											08 25			
Stratford International ⊖ ⛴	d										08 02											08 32			
Ebbsfleet International	d										08 13											08 43			
London Charing Cross 4 ⊖	d	06 56	07 02				07 12					07 26				07 39							07 59		08 03
London Waterloo (East) 4 ⊖	d	06 59	07 05				07 15					07 29				07 42							08 02		08 06
London Cannon Street 4 ⊖	d				07 10	07 13			07 24	07 27			07 32	07 36	07 41				07 44	07 54	07 56			08 05	
London Bridge 4 ⊖	d	07 05	07 10		07 14	07 17	07 21		07 28	07 31		07 34	07 37	07 40	07 45	07 47			07 48	07 58	08 01		08 07	08 09	08 11
Deptford	d					07 23							07 43						07 54		08 07			08 15	
Greenwich 4 ⛴	d					07 25				07 38			07 45						07 59		08 09			08 19	
Maze Hill	d					07 28							07 48						08 02		08 12			08 22	
Westcombe Park	d					07 30							07 50						08 04		08 14			08 24	
London Victoria 15 ⊖	d			07 09													07 43								
Denmark Hill 4	d																07 53								
Peckham Rye 4	d																07 56								
Nunhead 4	d																07 59								
New Cross 4 ⊖	d				07 20				07 33						07 50					08 04					
St Johns	d				07 22				07 35											08 06					
Lewisham 4 ⛴	d		07 18	07 27	07 27		07 30		07 38					07 49	07 54	07 56	08 08			08 11					08 19
Blackheath 4	d		07 21	07 29			07 32		07 41					07 52		07 59	08 10			08 13					08 22
Kidbrooke	d		07 24						07 44					07 55						08 16					08 25
Eltham	d		07 27						07 47					07 58						08 20					08 28
Falconwood	d		07 29						07 50					08 01						08 22					08 31
Welling	d		07 32						07 52					08 03						08 25					08 33
Bexleyheath	d		07 34						07 55					08 06						08 27					08 36
Barnehurst 4	d		07 37	07 40					07 59					08 08						08 30					08 38
Hither Green 4	d	07 18			07 31							07 45			07 59										
Lee	d	07 20			07 33							07 47			08 01										
Mottingham	d	07 23			07 36							07 50			08 04										
New Eltham	d	07 26			07 39							07 53			08 07								08 21		
Sidcup 4	d	07 29			07 42							07 56			08 13								08 25		
Albany Park	d	07 31			07 44							07 58			08 15								08 27		
Bexley	d	07 34			07 47							08 01			08 17								08 29		
Crayford	d	07 37	07a46		07 50				08a08			08 05			08 21								08 33		
Charlton 4	d					07 33	07 37			07 44			07 53		08a50	08 04			08 07		08 17			08 27	
Woolwich Dockyard	d					07 36							07 56						08 10		08 20			08 30	
Woolwich Arsenal 4 ⛴	d					07 39	07 43			07 49			07 59			08 09			08 13		08 23			08 33	
Plumstead	d					07 41							08 01						08 15		08 25			08 35	
Abbey Wood	d					07 44	07 48			07 53			08 04			08 13			08 18		08 28			08 38	
Belvedere	d					07 46							08 06						08 20		08 30			08 40	
Erith	d					07 49							08 09						08 23		08 33			08 43	
Slade Green 4	d				07a57	07 52				07a59			08a12			08 20			08a26	08a35	08 37			08a46	
Dartford 4	a	07 42		07 48		07 57	07 59					08 11		08 15		08 25	08 27				08 42		08 38		08 45
	d	07 43					08 00					08 12				08 25							08 39		
Stone Crossing	d	07 47										08 16											08 43		
Greenhithe for Bluewater	d	07 49					08 05					08 18				08 30							08 45		
Swanscombe	d	07 52										08 21											08 48		
Northfleet	d	07 54										08 23											08 50		
Gravesend 4	d	07a58					08 12				08 18	08a27				08 37						08 48	08a55		
Higham	d						08 18									08 43									
Strood 4	d						08 23				08 28					08 48						08 58			
Maidstone West	d																								
Rochester 4	d						08 27				08 33					08 52						09 03			
Chatham 4	d						08 30				08 35					08 55						09 05			
Gillingham (Kent) 4	a						08 35				08 39					08 59						09 09			

Table 200

Mondays to Fridays

London - Dartford and Gillingham

Network Diagram - see first Page of Table 200

		SE	SE	SE	SE	SE	SE	SE	SE	SE	SE	SE	SE	SE	SE	SE	SE	SE	SE	SE	SE	SE
St Pancras Int'l 15 ⊖	d					08 55												09 25				
Stratford International ⊖ ⛴	d					09 05												09 32				
Ebbsfleet International	d					09 17												09 43				
London Charing Cross 4 ⊖	d		08 11				08 20		08 23	08 31			08 41						08 55	09 02		
London Waterloo (East) 4 ⊖	d		08 14				08 23		08 26	08 34			08 44						08 58	09 05		
London Cannon Street 4 ⊖	d	08 10			08 16			08 25			08 36	08 39			08 47	08 54	08 56				09 07	09 09
London Bridge 4 ⊖	d	08 14	08 19		08 20		08 29	08 29	08 31	08 39	08 40	08 43	08 49		08 51	08 58	09 01		09 03	09 10	09 11	09 14
Deptford	d				08 27			08 35			08 46				08 57		09 07				09 17	
Greenwich 4 ⛴	d				08 29			08 39			08 49				08 59		09 09				09 19	
Maze Hill	d				08 32			08 42			08 52				09 02		09 12				09 22	
Westcombe Park	d				08 34			08 44			08 54				09 04		09 14				09 24	
London Victoria 15 ⊖	d			08 09										08 39								
Denmark Hill 4	d			08 18										08 48								
Peckham Rye 4	d			08 21										08 51								
Nunhead 4	d			08 23										08 53								
New Cross 4 ⊖	d	08 20							08 38			08 49				09 04						09 19
St Johns	d	08 22							08 40			08 51				09 06						09 21
Lewisham 4 ⛴	d	08 25	08 28	08 32					08 43	08 49		08 54	08 56	09 02		09 09				09 19		09 24
Blackheath 4	d		08 31	08 34					08 46	08 52			08 59	09 04		09 12				09 22		
Kidbrooke	d			08 37					08 49	08 55				09 07		09 15				09 25		
Eltham	d			08 41					08 52	08 58				09 11		09 18				09 28		
Falconwood	d			08 43					08 55	09 01				09 13		09 21				09 31		
Welling	d			08 46					08 57	09 03				09 16		09 23				09 33		
Bexleyheath	d			08 48					09 00	09 06				09 18		09 26				09 36		
Barnehurst 4	d			08 51					09 04	09 08				09 21		09 32				09 38		
Hither Green 4	d	08 29					08 44					08 59							09 15			09 29
Lee	d	08 31					08 46					09 01							09 17			09 31
Mottingham	d	08 34					08 49					09 04							09 20			09 34
New Eltham	d	08 37					08 51					09 06							09 22			09 36
Sidcup 4	d	08 40					08 55					09 10							09 26			09 40
Albany Park	d	08 42					08 57					09 12							09 28			09 42
Bexley	d	08 45					08 59					09 14							09 30			09 44
Crayford	d	08 48					09 03					09 18							09 33			09 48
Charlton 4	d	09a13	08 35		08 37			08 47			08 57	09a45	09 03		09 07		09 17				09 27	10a15
Woolwich Dockyard	d				08 40			08 50			09 00				09 10		09 20				09 30	
Woolwich Arsenal 4 ⛴	d		08 40		08 43			08 53			09 03		09 09		09 13		09 23				09 33	
Plumstead	d				08 45			08 55			09 05				09 15		09 25				09 35	
Abbey Wood	d		08 45		08 48			08 58			09 08		09 13		09 18		09 28				09 38	
Belvedere	d				08 50			09 00			09 10				09 20		09 30				09 40	
Erith	d				08 53			09 03			09 13				09 23		09 33				09 43	
Slade Green 4	d				08a57			09 07	09a09		09a16				09a26	09a42	09 37				09a45	
Dartford 4	a		08 54	08 58			09 08	09 12		09 15			09 24	09 28			09 42		09 38	09 45		
	d		08 55				09 09						09 25						09 39			
Stone Crossing	d						09 13												09 43			
Greenhithe for Bluewater	d		09 00				09 15						09 30						09 45			
Swanscombe	d						09 18												09 48			
Northfleet	d						09 20												09 50			
Gravesend 4	d		09 07			09 22	09a25						09 37					09 48	09a55			
Higham	d		09 13										09 43									
Strood 4	d		09 18			09 32							09 48					09 58				
Maidstone West	d																					
Rochester 4	d		09 22			09 37							09 52					10 03				
Chatham 4	d		09 25			09 39							09 55					10 05				
Gillingham (Kent) 4	a		09 29			09 43							09 59					10 09				

London - Dartford and Gillingham

Network Diagram - see first Page of Table 200

		SE	SE	SE	SE	SE	SE	SE	SE		SE	SE	SE	SE	SE	SE	SE	SE	SE		SE	SE	SE	SE	SE
St Pancras Int'l 15 ⊖	d						09 55											10 28							
Stratford International ⊖	d						10 02											10 35							
Ebbsfleet International	d						10 13											10 46							
London Charing Cross 4 ⊖	d	09 11						09 26	09 32				09 39						09 56		10 02			10 09	
London Waterloo (East) 4 ⊖	d	09 14						09 29	09 35				09 42						09 59		10 05			10 12	
London Cannon Street 4 ⊖	d			09 15	09 24	09 27					09 37	09 40			09 47	09 54	09 57					10 07	10 10		
London Bridge 4 ⊖	d	09 19		09 19	09 28	09 31		09 34	09 40		09 41	09 44	09 47		09 51	09 58	10 01		10 04		10 10	10 11	10 14	10 17	
Deptford	d			09 25		09 37					09 47				09 57		10 07					10 17			
Greenwich 4	d			09 29		09 39					09 49				09 59		10 09					10 19			
Maze Hill	d			09 32		09 42					09 52				10 02		10 12					10 22			
Westcombe Park	d			09 34		09 44					09 54				10 04		10 14					10 24			
London Victoria 15 ⊖	d		09 09											09 39											10 09
Denmark Hill 4	d		09 18											09 48											10 18
Peckham Rye 4	d		09 21											09 51											10 21
Nunhead 4	d		09 23											09 53											10 23
New Cross 4 ⊖	d				09 33							09 49				10 03							10 19		
St Johns	d				09 35							09 51				10 05							10 21		
Lewisham 4	d	09 29	09 32		09 38				09 49			09 54	09 56	10 02		10 08					10 19		10 24	10 26	10 32
Blackheath 4	d	09 31	09 34		09 41				09 52				09 59	10 04		10 11					10 22			10 29	10 34
Kidbrooke	d		09 37		09 44				09 55					10 07		10 14					10 25				10 37
Eltham	d		09 41		09 47				09 58					10 11		10 17					10 28				10 41
Falconwood	d		09 43		09 50				10 01					10 13		10 20					10 31				10 43
Welling	d		09 46		09 52				10 03					10 16		10 22					10 33				10 46
Bexleyheath	d		09 48		09 55				10 06					10 18		10 25					10 36				10 48
Barnehurst 4	d		09 51		10 02				10 08					10 21		10 32					10 38				10 51
Hither Green 4	d							09 44				09 59							10 14				10 29		
Lee	d							09 46				10 01							10 16				10 31		
Mottingham	d							09 49				10 04							10 19				10 34		
New Eltham	d							09 51				10 06							10 21				10 36		
Sidcup 4	d							09 55				10 10							10 25				10 40		
Albany Park	d							09 57				10 12							10 27				10 42		
Bexley	d							09 59				10 14							10 29				10 44		
Crayford	d							10 03				10 18							10 33				10 48		
Charlton 4	d	09 37		09 40		09 47					09 57	10a45	10 03		10 07		10 17					10 27	11a15	10 33	
Woolwich Dockyard	d			09 43		09 50					10 00				10 10		10 20					10 30			
Woolwich Arsenal 4	d	09 42		09 46		09 53					10 03		10 09		10 13		10 23					10 33		10 39	
Plumstead	d			09 48		09 55					10 05				10 15		10 25					10 35			
Abbey Wood	d	09 46		09 51		09 58					10 08		10 13		10 18		10 28					10 38		10 43	
Belvedere	d			09 53		10 00					10 10				10 20		10 30					10 40			
Erith	d			09 56		10 03					10 13				10 23		10 33					10 43			
Slade Green 4	d			09a59	10a12	10 07					10a16				10a26	10a42	10 37					10a46			
Dartford 4	a	09 54	09 58			10 12		10 08	10 15				10 24	10 28			10 42		10 38		10 45			10 54	10 58
	d	09 55						10 09					10 25						10 39					10 55	
Stone Crossing	d							10 13											10 43						
Greenhithe for Bluewater	d	10 00						10 15					10 30						10 45					11 00	
Swanscombe	d							10 18											10 48						
Northfleet	d							10 20											10 50						
Gravesend 4	d	10 07					10 18	10a25					10 37					10 51	10a55					11 07	
Higham	d	10 13											10 43											11 13	
Strood 4	d	10 18					10 28						10 48					11 01						11 18	
Maidstone West	d																								
Rochester 4	d	10 22					10 33						10 52					11 06						11 23	
Chatham 4	d	10 25					10 35						10 55					11 08						11 25	
Gillingham (Kent) 4	a	10 29					10 39						10 59					11 12						11 29	

London - Dartford and Gillingham

Network Diagram - see first Page of Table 200

Station		SE	SE	SE	SE	SE	SE	SE	SE	SE	SE	SE	SE	SE	SE	SE	SE	SE	SE	SE	SE	SE	SE
St Pancras Int'l 15 ⊖	d				10 52										11 25								
Stratford International ⊖ ⛴	d				10 59										11 32								
Ebbsfleet International	d				11 13										11 43								
London Charing Cross 4 ⊖	d					10 26	10 32			10 39						10 56	11 02			11 09			
London Waterloo (East) 4 ⊖	d					10 29	10 35			10 42						10 59	11 05			11 12			
London Cannon Street 4 ⊖	d	10 17	10 24	10 27				10 37	10 40			10 47	10 54	10 57				11 07	11 10			11 17	11 24
London Bridge 4 ⊖	d	10 21	10 28	10 31		10 34	10 40	10 41	10 44	10 47		10 51	10 58	11 01		11 04	11 10	11 11	11 14	11 17		11 21	11 28
Deptford	d	10 27		10 37				10 47				10 57		11 07				11 17				11 27	
Greenwich 4 ⛴	d	10 29		10 39				10 49				10 59		11 09				11 19				11 29	
Maze Hill	d	10 32		10 42				10 52				11 02		11 12				11 22				11 32	
Westcombe Park	d	10 34		10 44				10 54				11 04		11 14				11 24				11 34	
London Victoria 15 ⊖	d										10 39										11 09		
Denmark Hill 4	d										10 48										11 18		
Peckham Rye 4	d										10 51										11 21		
Nunhead 4	d										10 53										11 23		
New Cross 4 ⊖	d		10 33						10 49				11 03						11 19				11 33
St Johns	d		10 35						10 51				11 05						11 21				11 35
Lewisham 4 ⛴	d		10 38				10 49		10 54	10 56	11 02		11 08				11 19		11 24	11 26	11 32		11 38
Blackheath 4	d		10 41				10 52			10 59	11 04		11 11				11 22			11 29	11 34		11 41
Kidbrooke	d		10 44				10 55				11 07		11 14				11 25				11 37		11 44
Eltham	d		10 47				10 58				11 11		11 17				11 28				11 41		11 47
Falconwood	d		10 50				11 01				11 13		11 20				11 31				11 43		11 50
Welling	d		10 52				11 03				11 16		11 22				11 33				11 46		11 52
Bexleyheath	d		10 55				11 06				11 18		11 25				11 36				11 48		11 55
Barnehurst 4	d		11 02				11 08				11 21		11 32				11 38				11 51		12 02
Hither Green 4	d					10 44			10 59							11 14			11 29				
Lee	d					10 46			11 01							11 16			11 31				
Mottingham	d					10 49			11 04							11 19			11 34				
New Eltham	d					10 51			11 06							11 21			11 36				
Sidcup 4	d					10 55			11 10							11 25			11 40				
Albany Park	d					10 57			11 12							11 27			11 42				
Bexley	d					10 59			11 14							11 29			11 44				
Crayford	d					11 03			11 18							11 33			11 48				
Charlton 4	d	10 37		10 47				10 57	11a45	11 03		11 07		11 17				11 27	12a15	11 33		11 37	
Woolwich Dockyard	d	10 40		10 50				11 00				11 10		11 20				11 30				11 40	
Woolwich Arsenal 4 ⛴	d	10 43		10 53				11 03		11 09		11 13		11 23				11 33		11 39		11 43	
Plumstead	d	10 45		10 55				11 05				11 15		11 25				11 35				11 45	
Abbey Wood	d	10 48		10 58				11 08		11 13		11 18		11 28				11 38		11 43		11 48	
Belvedere	d	10 50		11 00				11 10				11 20		11 30				11 40				11 50	
Erith	d	10 53		11 03				11 13				11 23		11 33				11 43				11 53	
Slade Green 4	d	10a56	11a12	11 07				11a16				11a26	11a42	11 37				11a45				11a56	12a12
Dartford 4	a			11 12		11 08	11 15			11 24	11 28			11 42		11 38	11 45			11 54	11 58		
	d					11 09				11 25						11 39				11 55			
Stone Crossing	d					11 13										11 43							
Greenhithe for Bluewater	d					11 15				11 30						11 45				12 00			
Swanscombe	d					11 18										11 48							
Northfleet	d					11 20										11 50							
Gravesend 4	d				11 18	11a25				11 37					11 48	11a55				12 07			
Higham	d									11 43										12 13			
Strood 4	d				11 28					11 48					11 58					12 18			
Maidstone West	d																						
Rochester 4	d				11 33					11 52					12 03					12 22			
Chatham 4	d				11 35					11 55					12 05					12 25			
Gillingham (Kent) 4	a				11 39					11 59					12 09					12 29			

London - Dartford and Gillingham

Network Diagram - see first Page of Table 200

		SE	SE	SE	SE	SE	SE	SE	SE	SE	SE	SE	SE	SE	SE	SE	SE	SE	SE	SE	SE	SE
St Pancras Int'l 15 ⊖	d		11 55										12 22									
Stratford International ⊖ ⛴	d		12 02										12 32									
Ebbsfleet International	d		12 13										12 43									
London Charing Cross 4 ⊖	d			11 26	11 32			11 39						11 56	12 02			12 09				
London Waterloo (East) 4 ⊖	d			11 29	11 35			11 42						11 59	12 05			12 12				
London Cannon Street 4 ⊖	d	11 27				11 37	11 40			11 47	11 54	11 57				12 07	12 10			12 17	12 24	12 27
London Bridge 4 ⊖	d	11 31		11 34	11 40	11 41	11 44	11 47		11 51	11 58	12 01		12 04	12 10	12 11	12 14	12 17		12 21	12 28	12 31
Deptford	d	11 37				11 47				11 57		12 07				12 17				12 27		12 37
Greenwich 4 ⛴	d	11 39				11 49				11 59		12 09				12 19				12 29		12 39
Maze Hill	d	11 42				11 52				12 02		12 12				12 22				12 32		12 42
Westcombe Park	d	11 44				11 54				12 04		12 14				12 24				12 34		12 44
London Victoria 15 ⊖	d								11 39										12 09			
Denmark Hill 4	d								11 48										12 18			
Peckham Rye 4	d								11 51										12 21			
Nunhead 4	d								11 53										12 23			
New Cross 4 ⊖	d						11 49				12 03						12 19				12 33	
St Johns	d						11 51				12 05						12 21				12 35	
Lewisham 4 ⛴	d				11 49		11 54	11 56	12 02		12 08				12 19		12 24	12 26	12 32		12 38	
Blackheath 4	d				11 52			11 59	12 04		12 11				12 22			12 29	12 34		12 41	
Kidbrooke	d				11 55				12 07		12 14				12 25				12 37		12 44	
Eltham	d				11 58				12 11		12 17				12 28				12 41		12 47	
Falconwood	d				12 01				12 13		12 20				12 31				12 43		12 50	
Welling	d				12 03				12 16		12 22				12 33				12 46		12 52	
Bexleyheath	d				12 06				12 18		12 25				12 36				12 48		12 55	
Barnehurst 4	d				12 08				12 21		12 32				12 38				12 51		13 02	
Hither Green 4	d			11 44			11 59							12 14			12 29					
Lee	d			11 46			12 01							12 16			12 31					
Mottingham	d			11 49			12 04							12 19			12 34					
New Eltham	d			11 51			12 06							12 21			12 36					
Sidcup 4	d			11 55			12 10							12 25			12 40					
Albany Park	d			11 57			12 12							12 27			12 42					
Bexley	d			11 59			12 14							12 29			12 44					
Crayford	d			12 03			12 18							12 33			12 48					
Charlton 4	d	11 47				11 57	12a45	12 03		12 07		12 17				12 27	13a15	12 33		12 37		12 47
Woolwich Dockyard	d	11 50				12 00				12 10		12 20				12 30				12 40		12 50
Woolwich Arsenal 4 ⛴	d	11 53				12 03		12 09		12 13		12 23				12 33		12 39		12 43		12 53
Plumstead	d	11 55				12 05				12 15		12 25				12 35				12 45		12 55
Abbey Wood	d	11 58				12 08		12 13		12 18		12 28				12 38		12 43		12 48		12 58
Belvedere	d	12 00				12 10				12 20		12 30				12 40				12 50		13 00
Erith	d	12 03				12 13				12 23		12 33				12 43				12 53		13 03
Slade Green 4	d	12 07				12a16				12a26	12a42	12 37				12a46				12a56	13a12	13 07
Dartford 4	a	12 12		12 08	12 15			12 24	12 28			12 42		12 38	12 45			12 54	12 58			13 12
	d			12 09				12 25						12 39				12 55				
Stone Crossing	d			12 13										12 43								
Greenhithe for Bluewater	d			12 15				12 30						12 45				13 00				
Swanscombe	d			12 18										12 48								
Northfleet	d			12 20										12 50								
Gravesend 4	d		12 18	12a25				12 37					12 48	12a55				13 07				
Higham	d							12 43										13 13				
Strood 4	d		12 28					12 48					12 58					13 18				
Maidstone West	d																					
Rochester 4	d		12 33					12 52					13 03					13 22				
Chatham 4	d		12 35					12 55					13 05					13 25				
Gillingham (Kent) 4	a		12 39					12 59					13 09					13 29				

London - Dartford and Gillingham

Network Diagram - see first Page of Table 200

		SE	SE	SE	SE	SE	SE	SE	SE	SE	SE	SE	SE	SE	SE	SE	SE	SE	SE	SE	SE	SE	SE
St Pancras Int'l 15 ⊖	d	12 52										13 25										13 55	
Stratford International ⊖ ⛴	d	12 58										13 32										14 02	
Ebbsfleet International	d	13 13										13 43										14 13	
London Charing Cross 4 ⊖	d		12 26	12 32			12 39						12 56	13 02			13 09						13 26
London Waterloo (East) 4 ⊖	d		12 29	12 35			12 42						12 59	13 05			13 12						13 29
London Cannon Street 4 ⊖	d				12 37	12 40			12 47	12 54	12 57				13 07	13 10			13 17	13 24	13 27		
London Bridge 4 ⊖	d		12 34	12 40	12 41	12 44	12 47		12 51	12 58	13 01		13 04	13 10	13 11	13 14	13 17		13 21	13 28	13 31		13 34
Deptford	d				12 47				12 57		13 07				13 17				13 27		13 37		
Greenwich 4 ⛴	d				12 49				12 59		13 09				13 19				13 29		13 39		
Maze Hill	d				12 52				13 02		13 12				13 22				13 32		13 42		
Westcombe Park	d				12 54				13 04		13 14				13 24				13 34		13 44		
London Victoria 15 ⊖	d							12 39										13 09					
Denmark Hill 4	d							12 48										13 18					
Peckham Rye 4	d							12 51										13 21					
Nunhead 4	d							12 53										13 23					
New Cross 4 ⊖	d					12 49				13 03						13 19				13 33			
St Johns	d					12 51				13 05						13 21				13 35			
Lewisham 4 ⛴	d			12 49		12 54	12 56	13 02		13 08				13 19		13 24	13 26	13 32		13 38			
Blackheath 4	d			12 52			12 59	13 04		13 11				13 22			13 29	13 34		13 41			
Kidbrooke	d			12 55				13 07		13 14				13 25				13 37		13 44			
Eltham	d			12 58				13 11		13 17				13 28				13 41		13 47			
Falconwood	d			13 01				13 13		13 20				13 31				13 43		13 50			
Welling	d			13 03				13 16		13 22				13 33				13 46		13 52			
Bexleyheath	d			13 06				13 18		13 25				13 36				13 48		13 55			
Barnehurst 4	d			13 08				13 21		13 32				13 38				13 51		14 02			
Hither Green 4	d		12 44			12 59							13 14			13 29							13 44
Lee	d		12 46			13 01							13 16			13 31							13 46
Mottingham	d		12 49			13 04							13 19			13 34							13 49
New Eltham	d		12 51			13 06							13 21			13 36							13 51
Sidcup 4	d		12 55			13 10							13 25			13 40							13 55
Albany Park	d		12 57			13 12							13 27			13 42							13 57
Bexley	d		12 59			13 14							13 29			13 44							13 59
Crayford	d		13 03			13 18							13 33			13 48							14 03
Charlton 4	d				12 57	13a45	13 03		13 07		13 17				13 27	14a15	13 33		13 37		13 47		
Woolwich Dockyard	d				13 00				13 10		13 20				13 30				13 40		13 50		
Woolwich Arsenal 4 ⛴	d				13 03		13 09		13 13		13 23				13 33		13 39		13 43		13 53		
Plumstead	d				13 05				13 15		13 25				13 35				13 45		13 55		
Abbey Wood	d				13 08		13 13		13 18		13 28				13 38		13 43		13 48		13 58		
Belvedere	d				13 10				13 20		13 30				13 40				13 50		14 00		
Erith	d				13 13				13 23		13 33				13 43				13 53		14 03		
Slade Green 4	d				13a16				13a26	13a42	13 37				13a46				13a56	14a12	14 07		
Dartford 4	a		13 08	13 15			13 24	13 28			13 42		13 38	13 45			13 54	13 58			14 12		14 08
	d		13 09				13 25						13 39				13 55						14 09
Stone Crossing	d		13 13										13 43										14 13
Greenhithe for Bluewater	d		13 15				13 30						13 45				14 00						14 15
Swanscombe	d		13 18										13 48										14 18
Northfleet	d		13 20										13 50										14 20
Gravesend 4	d	13 18	13a25				13 37					13 48	13a55				14 07					14 18	14a25
Higham	d						13 43										14 13						
Strood 4	d	13 28					13 48					13 58					14 18					14 28	
Maidstone West	d																						
Rochester 4	d	13 33					13 52					14 03					14 22					14 33	
Chatham 4	d	13 35					13 55					14 05					14 25					14 35	
Gillingham (Kent) 4	a	13 39					13 59					14 09					14 29					14 39	

Table 200

Mondays to Fridays

London - Dartford and Gillingham

Network Diagram - see first Page of Table 200

		SE	SE		SE	SE	SE	SE	SE	SE	SE	SE	SE		SE	SE	SE	SE	SE	SE	SE	SE	SE		SE
St Pancras Int'l 15 ⊖	d										14 25											14 55			
Stratford International ⊖ ⛴	d										14 32											15 02			
Ebbsfleet International	d										14 43											15 13			
London Charing Cross 4 ⊖	d	13 32				13 39						13 56	14 02				14 09						14 26		14 32
London Waterloo (East) 4 ⊖	d	13 35				13 42						13 59	14 05				14 12						14 29		14 35
London Cannon Street 4 ⊖	d		13 37		13 40			13 47	13 54	13 57					14 07	14 10			14 17	14 24	14 27				
London Bridge 4 ⊖	d	13 40	13 41		13 44	13 47		13 51	13 58	14 01		14 04	14 10		14 11	14 14	14 17		14 21	14 28	14 31		14 34		14 40
Deptford	d		13 47					13 57		14 07					14 17				14 27		14 37				
Greenwich 4 ⛴	d		13 49					13 59		14 09					14 19				14 29		14 39				
Maze Hill	d		13 52					14 02		14 12					14 22				14 32		14 42				
Westcombe Park	d		13 54					14 04		14 14					14 24				14 34		14 44				
London Victoria 15 ⊖	d						13 39											14 09							
Denmark Hill 4	d						13 48											14 18							
Peckham Rye 4	d						13 51											14 21							
Nunhead 4	d						13 53											14 23							
New Cross 4 ⊖	d				13 49				14 03							14 19				14 33					
St Johns	d				13 51				14 05							14 21				14 35					
Lewisham 4 ⛴	d	13 49			13 54	13 56	14 02		14 08				14 19			14 24	14 26	14 32		14 38					14 49
Blackheath 4	d	13 52				13 59	14 04		14 11				14 22				14 29	14 34		14 41					14 52
Kidbrooke	d	13 55					14 07		14 14				14 25					14 37		14 44					14 55
Eltham	d	13 58					14 11		14 17				14 28					14 41		14 47					14 58
Falconwood	d	14 01					14 13		14 20				14 31					14 43		14 50					15 01
Welling	d	14 03					14 16		14 22				14 33					14 46		14 52					15 03
Bexleyheath	d	14 06					14 18		14 25				14 36					14 48		14 55					15 06
Barnehurst 4	d	14 08					14 21		14 32				14 38					14 51		15 02					15 08
Hither Green 4	d				13 59							14 14				14 29							14 44		
Lee	d				14 01							14 16				14 31							14 46		
Mottingham	d				14 04							14 19				14 34							14 49		
New Eltham	d				14 06							14 21				14 36							14 51		
Sidcup 4	d				14 10							14 25				14 40							14 55		
Albany Park	d				14 12							14 27				14 42							14 57		
Bexley	d				14 14							14 29				14 44							14 59		
Crayford	d				14 18							14 33				14 48							15 03		
Charlton 4	d		13 57		14a45	14 03		14 07		14 17					14 27	15a15	14 33		14 37		14 47				
Woolwich Dockyard	d		14 00					14 10		14 20					14 30				14 40		14 50				
Woolwich Arsenal 4 ⛴	d		14 03			14 09		14 13		14 23					14 33		14 39		14 43		14 53				
Plumstead	d		14 05					14 15		14 25					14 35				14 45		14 55				
Abbey Wood	d		14 08			14 13		14 18		14 28					14 38		14 43		14 48		14 58				
Belvedere	d		14 10					14 20		14 30					14 40				14 50		15 00				
Erith	d		14 13					14 23		14 33					14 43				14 53		15 03				
Slade Green 4	d		14a16					14a26	14a42	14 37					14a46				14a56	15a12	15 07				
Dartford 4	a	14 15				14 24	14 28			14 42		14 38	14 45				14 54	14 58			15 12		15 08		15 15
	d					14 25						14 39					14 55						15 09		
Stone Crossing	d											14 43											15 13		
Greenhithe for Bluewater	d					14 30						14 45					15 00						15 15		
Swanscombe	d											14 48											15 18		
Northfleet	d											14 50											15 20		
Gravesend 4	d					14 37					14 48	14a55					15 07					15 18	15a25		
Higham	d					14 43											15 13								
Strood 4	d					14 48					14 58						15 18					15 28			
Maidstone West	d																								
Rochester 4	d					14 52					15 03						15 22					15 33			
Chatham 4	d					14 55					15 05						15 25					15 35			
Gillingham (Kent) 4	a					14 59					15 09						15 29					15 39			

Table 200

Mondays to Fridays

London - Dartford and Gillingham

Network Diagram - see first Page of Table 200

		SE	SE	SE	SE	SE	SE	SE	SE	SE	SE	SE	SE	SE	SE	SE	SE	SE	SE	SE	SE	SE	SE
St Pancras Int'l 15 ⊖	d								15 25										15 55				
Stratford International ⊖ ⛴	d								15 32										16 02				
Ebbsfleet International	d								15 43										16 13				
London Charing Cross 4 ⊖	d			14 39						14 56	15 02			15 09						15 26	15 32		
London Waterloo (East) 4 ⊖	d			14 42						14 59	15 05			15 12						15 29	15 35		
London Cannon Street 4 ⊖	d	14 37	14 40			14 47	14 54	14 57				15 07	15 10			15 17	15 24	15 27				15 37	15 40
London Bridge 4 ⊖	d	14 41	14 44	14 47		14 51	14 58	15 01		15 04	15 10	15 11	15 14	15 17		15 21	15 28	15 31		15 34	15 40	15 41	15 44
Deptford	d	14 47				14 57		15 07				15 17				15 27		15 37				15 47	
Greenwich 4 ⛴	d	14 49				14 59		15 09				15 19				15 29		15 39				15 49	
Maze Hill	d	14 52				15 02		15 12				15 22				15 32		15 42				15 52	
Westcombe Park	d	14 54				15 04		15 14				15 24				15 34		15 44				15 54	
London Victoria 15 ⊖	d				14 39										15 09								
Denmark Hill 4	d				14 48										15 18								
Peckham Rye 4	d				14 51										15 21								
Nunhead 4	d				14 53										15 23								
New Cross 4 ⊖	d		14 49				15 03						15 19				15 33						15 49
St Johns	d		14 51				15 05						15 21				15 35						15 51
Lewisham 4 ⛴	d		14 54	14 56	15 02		15 08				15 19		15 24	15 26	15 32		15 38				15 49		15 54
Blackheath 4	d			14 59	15 04		15 11				15 22			15 29	15 34		15 41				15 52		
Kidbrooke	d				15 07		15 14				15 25				15 37		15 44				15 55		
Eltham	d				15 11		15 17				15 28				15 41		15 47				15 58		
Falconwood	d				15 13		15 20				15 31				15 43		15 50				16 01		
Welling	d				15 16		15 22				15 33				15 46		15 52				16 03		
Bexleyheath	d				15 18		15 25				15 36				15 48		15 55				16 06		
Barnehurst 4	d				15 21		15 32				15 38				15 51		15a58				16 08		
Hither Green 4	d		14 59							15 14			15 29							15 44			15 59
Lee	d		15 01							15 16			15 31							15 46			16 01
Mottingham	d		15 04							15 19			15 34							15 49			16 04
New Eltham	d		15 06							15 21			15 36							15 51			16 06
Sidcup 4	d		15 10							15 25			15 40							15 55			16 10
Albany Park	d		15 12							15 27			15 42							15 57			16 12
Bexley	d		15 14							15 29			15 44							15 59			16 14
Crayford	d		15 18							15 33			15 48							16 03			16 18
Charlton 4	d	14 57	15a45	15 03		15 07		15 17				15 27	16a15	15 33		15 37		15 47				15 57	16a45
Woolwich Dockyard	d	15 00				15 10		15 20				15 30				15 40		15 50				16 00	
Woolwich Arsenal 4 ⛴	d	15 03		15 09		15 13		15 23				15 33		15 39		15 43		15 53				16 03	
Plumstead	d	15 05				15 15		15 25				15 35				15 45		15 55				16 05	
Abbey Wood	d	15 08		15 13		15 18		15 28				15 38		15 43		15 48		15 58				16 08	
Belvedere	d	15 10				15 20		15 30				15 40				15 50		16 00				16 10	
Erith	d	15 13				15 23		15 33				15 43				15 53		16 03				16 13	
Slade Green 4	d	15a15				15a26	15a42	15 37				15a46				15a56		16 07				16a16	
Dartford 4	a			15 24	15 28			15 42		15 38	15 45			15 54	15 58			16 12		16 08	16 15		
	d			15 25						15 39				15 55						16 09			
Stone Crossing	d									15 43										16 13			
Greenhithe for Bluewater	d			15 30						15 45				16 00						16 15			
Swanscombe	d									15 48										16 18			
Northfleet	d									15 50										16 20			
Gravesend 4	d			15 37					15 48	15a55				16 07					16 18	16a25			
Higham	d			15 43										16 13									
Strood 4	d			15 48					15 58					16 18					16 28				
Maidstone West	d																						
Rochester 4	d			15 52					16 03					16 22					16 33				
Chatham 4	d			15 55					16 05					16 25					16 35				
Gillingham (Kent) 4	a			15 59					16 09					16 29					16 39				

London - Dartford and Gillingham

Network Diagram - see first Page of Table 200

Station		SE	SE	SE	SE	SE	SE	SE	SE	SE	SE	SE	SE	SE	SE	SE	SE	SE	SE	SE	SE	SE	SE
St Pancras Int'l [15] ⊖	d						16 25										16 55						17 14
Stratford International ⊖ ⛴	d						16 32										17 02						17 21
Ebbsfleet International	d						16 43										17 13						
London Charing Cross [4] ⊖	d	15 39						15 56	16 02			16 09						16 26	16 30				
London Waterloo (East) [4] ⊖	d	15 42						15 59	16 05			16 12						16 29	16 33				
London Cannon Street [4] ⊖	d			15 47	15 54	15 57				16 07	16 10			16 17	16 24	16 27				16 35	16 39	16 42	
London Bridge [4] ⊖	d	15 47		15 51	15 58	16 01		16 04	16 10	16 11	16 14	16 17		16 21	16 28	16 31		16 34	16 38	16 39	16 43	16 46	
Deptford	d			15 57		16 07				16 17				16 27		16 37				16 45			
Greenwich [4] ⛴	d			15 59		16 09				16 20				16 30		16 40				16 48			
Maze Hill	d			16 02		16 12				16 23				16 33		16 43				16 51			
Westcombe Park	d			16 04		16 14				16 25				16 35		16 45				16 53			
London Victoria [15] ⊖	d		15 39										16 09										
Denmark Hill [4]	d		15 48										16 18										
Peckham Rye [4]	d		15 51										16 21										
Nunhead [4]	d		15 53										16 23										
New Cross [4] ⊖	d				16 03						16 20				16 34						16 49	16 52	
St Johns	d				16 05						16 22				16 36						16 51		
Lewisham [4] ⛴	d	15 56	16 02		16 08				16 19		16 25	16 27	16 32		16 39				16 49		16 54	16 56	
Blackheath [4]	d	15 59	16 04		16 11				16 22			16 29	16 34		16 42				16 53			16 59	
Kidbrooke	d		16 07		16 14				16 25				16 37		16 45				16 56			17 02	
Eltham	d		16 11		16 17				16 29				16 41		16 48				16 59			17 06	
Falconwood	d		16 13		16 20				16 31				16 43		16 51				17 02			17 08	
Welling	d		16 16		16 22				16 34				16 46		16 53				17 04			17 11	
Bexleyheath	d		16 18		16 25				16 36				16 48		16 56				17 07			17 13	
Barnehurst [4]	d		16 21		16 33				16 39				16 51		17 02				17 11			17 17	
Hither Green [4]	d							16 14			16 29							16 44			16 58		
Lee	d							16 16			16 31							16 46			17 00		
Mottingham	d							16 19			16 34							16 49			17 03		
New Eltham	d							16 21			16 37							16 51			17 06		
Sidcup [4]	d							16 25			16 40							16 55			17 09		
Albany Park	d							16 27			16 42							16 57			17 11		
Bexley	d							16 29			16 45							16 59			17 14		
Crayford	d							16 33			16 48							17 03			17 17	17a32	
Charlton [4]	d	16 03		16 07		16 17				16 27	17a15	16 34		16 37		16 47				16 56	17a45		
Woolwich Dockyard	d			16 10		16 20				16 30				16 40		16 50				16 59			
Woolwich Arsenal [4] ⛴	d	16 09		16 13		16 23				16 33		16 39		16 43		16 53				17 02			
Plumstead	d			16 15		16 25				16 35				16 45		16 55				17 04			
Abbey Wood	d	16 13		16 18		16 28				16 39		16 43		16 48		16 59				17 07			
Belvedere	d			16 20		16 30				16 41				16 51		17 01				17 10			
Erith	d			16 23		16 33				16 44				16 53		17 04				17 12			
Slade Green [4]	d			16a26		16 37				16a48				16a56	17a14	17 07				17 15			
Dartford [4]	a	16 24	16 28		16 42	16 45		16 38	16 48			16 54	17 00			17 14		17 08	17 23	17 22			
	d	16 25						16 39				16 55						17 09					
Stone Crossing	d							16 43										17 13					
Greenhithe for Bluewater	d	16 30						16 45				17 00						17 15					
Swanscombe	d							16 48										17 18					
Northfleet	d							16 50										17 20					
Gravesend [4]	d	16 37					16 48	16a55				17 07					17 18	17a27					17 36
Higham	d	16 43										17 13											
Strood [4]	d	16 48					16 58					17 18					17 28						17 46
Maidstone West	d																						18a02
Rochester [4]	d	16 52					17 03					17 22					17 34						
Chatham [4]	d	16 55					17 05					17 25					17 37						
Gillingham (Kent) [4]	a	16 59					17 09					17 31					17 41						

London - Dartford and Gillingham

Network Diagram - see first Page of Table 200

Station		SE	SE	SE	SE	SE	SE	SE	SE	SE	SE	SE	SE	SE	SE	SE	SE	SE	SE	SE	SE	SE
St Pancras Int'l	d																17 44					
Stratford International	d																17 51					
Ebbsfleet International	d																					
London Charing Cross	d			16 45	16 49		16 51		16 55				17 06	17 10		17 12		17 17				17 29
London Waterloo (East)	d			16 48	16 52		16 54		16 58				17 09	17 13		17 15		17 20				17 32
London Cannon Street	d	16 44				16 54		16 58		17 04	17 06				17 16				17 21	17 26	17 28	
London Bridge	d	16 48		16 53	16 57	16 58	16 59	17 02	17 04	17 08	17 10		17 14	17 19	17 20	17 21		17 26	17 25	17 30	17 32	17 37
Deptford	d			16 59		17 04							17 20		17 26							17 43
Greenwich	d	16 56		17 02		17 07					17 18		17 23		17 29						17 40	17 46
Maze Hill	d			17 05		17 10							17 26		17 32							17 49
Westcombe Park	d			17 07		17 12							17 28		17 34							17 51
London Victoria	d		16 39									17 04										
Denmark Hill	d		16 48									17 13										
Peckham Rye	d		16 51									17 16										
Nunhead	d		16 53									17 18										
New Cross	d							17 08		17 14									17 31	17 36		
St Johns	d							17 10											17 33			
Lewisham	d		17 02				17 08	17 13		17 18		17 25				17 30			17 36	17 40		
Blackheath	d		17 04				17 10			17 22		17 28				17 34				17 43		
Kidbrooke	d		17 07				17 13			17 25		17 31				17 37				17 46		
Eltham	d		17 11				17 17			17 29		17 34				17 40				17 50		
Falconwood	d		17 13				17 19			17 31		17 37				17 43				17 52		
Welling	d		17 16				17 22			17 34		17 39				17 45				17 55		
Bexleyheath	d		17 18				17 24			17 36		17 42				17 48				17 58		
Barnehurst	d		17 21				17 27			17 41		17 45				17 51				18 02		
Hither Green	d				17 07			17 18						17 29					17 41			
Lee	d				17 09			17 20						17 31					17 43			
Mottingham	d				17 12			17 23						17 34					17 46			
New Eltham	d				17 15			17 26	17 20					17 36				17 42	17 48			
Sidcup	d				17a20			17 30	17 26					17a41				17 47	17 52			
Albany Park	d							17 32	17 28									17 49	17 54			
Bexley	d							17 35	17 30									17 52	17 57			
Crayford	d							17 39	17 34									17 55	18a00			
Charlton	d	17 02		17 10		17 15		18a05			17 24		17 30		17 37						17 46	17 53
Woolwich Dockyard	d			17 13		17 18							17 33		17 40							17 56
Woolwich Arsenal	d	17 07		17 16		17 21					17 29		17 36		17 43						17 51	17 59
Plumstead	d			17 18		17 23							17 38		17 45							18 01
Abbey Wood	d	17 11		17 21		17 26					17 33		17 42		17 48						17 55	18 05
Belvedere	d			17 24		17 29							17 44		17 51							18 07
Erith	d			17 26		17 31							17 47		17 53							18 10
Slade Green	d			17a29		17 34				17a52			17a49		17 56					18a12		18a14
Dartford	a	17 26	17 31			17 43	17 38		17 39		17 44	17 54			18 06	18 00		18 00			18 06	
	d	17 28							17 40		17 47							18 02			18 08	
Stone Crossing	d								17 44												18 12	
Greenhithe for Bluewater	d	17 33							17 46		17 52							18 07			18 14	
Swanscombe	d								17 49												18 17	
Northfleet	d								17 51												18 19	
Gravesend	d	17 40							17a57		18 00						18 06	18 19			18a27	
Higham	d	17 46									18 06							18 25				
Strood	d	17 52									18 14						18 18	18a33				
Maidstone West	d																18a32					
Rochester	d	17 57									18 20											
Chatham	d	18 00									18 23											
Gillingham (Kent)	a	18 07									18 30											

London - Dartford and Gillingham

Network Diagram - see first Page of Table 200

		SE	SE	SE	SE	SE	SE		SE	SE	SE	SE	SE	SE	SE	SE	SE		SE	SE	SE	SE	SE	SE	SE
St Pancras Int'l 15 ⊖	d										18 14														
Stratford International ⊖ ⛴	d										18 21														
Ebbsfleet International	d																								
London Charing Cross 4 ⊖	d	17 30	17 32		17 34	17 39							17 50	17 52	17 54	17 56					18 01			18 12	18 14
London Waterloo (East) 4 ⊖	d	17 33	17 35		17 37	17 42							17 53	17 55	17 57	17 59					18 04			18 15	18 17
London Cannon Street 4 ⊖	d			17 39					17 43	17 47		17 50					18 00			18 04		18 10	18 12		
London Bridge 4 ⊖	d		17 41	17 43	17 43	17 48			17 47	17 51		17 54	17 58		18 02	18 04	18 04			18 08	18 10	18 14	18 16	18 21	18 23
Deptford	d			17 49									18 04				18 10							18 27	
Greenwich 4 ⛴	d			17 52								18 02	18 07				18 13						18 24	18 29	
Maze Hill	d			17 55									18 10				18 16							18 32	
Westcombe Park	d			17 57									18 12				18 18							18 34	
London Victoria 15 ⊖	d						17 34												17 56						
Denmark Hill 4	d						17 43												18 06						
Peckham Rye 4	d						17 46												18 09						
Nunhead 4	d						17 49												18 11						
New Cross 4 ⊖	d								17 53	17 58										18 14		18 20			
St Johns	d								17 55											18 16					
Lewisham 4 ⛴	d				17 53		17 56		17 59	18 02						18 14			18 18	18 20		18 24			
Blackheath 4	d	17 49			17 56		18 00			18 05				18 09		18 17			18 23			18 27			
Kidbrooke	d	17 52			17 59		18 03			18 08				18 12		18 20			18 26			18 30			
Eltham	d	17 56			18 02		18 06			18 12				18 16		18 23			18 30			18 34			
Falconwood	d	17 58			18 05		18 09			18 14				18 18		18 26			18 32			18 36			
Welling	d	18 01			18 07		18 11			18 17				18 21		18 28			18 35			18 39			
Bexleyheath	d	18 04			18 10		18 14			18 20				18 24		18 31			18 38			18 42			
Barnehurst 4	d	18 07			18 12		18 16			18 23				18 27		18a36			18 41			18a47			
Hither Green 4	d		17 51						18 03						18 13					18 25					18 35
Lee	d		17 53						18 05						18 15					18 27					18 37
Mottingham	d		17 56						18 08						18 18					18 30					18 40
New Eltham	d		17 59			18 04			18 11						18 21					18 32	18 26				18 43
Sidcup 4	d		18a04			18 08			18 15						18 25					18 36	18 30				18 47
Albany Park	d					18 10			18 17											18 38	18 32				18 49
Bexley	d					18 13			18 20											18 40	18 35				18 51
Crayford	d					18 16			18a23	18a36					18a32					18 44	18 38				18a54
Charlton 4	d			18 00								18 08	18 15				18 21			19a10			18 30	18 37	
Woolwich Dockyard	d			18 03									18 18				18 24							18 40	
Woolwich Arsenal 4 ⛴	d			18 06								18 13	18 21				18 27						18 35	18 43	
Plumstead	d			18 08									18 23				18 29							18 45	
Abbey Wood	d			18 11								18 17	18 26				18 32						18 40	18 48	
Belvedere	d			18 14									18 29				18 35							18 50	
Erith	d			18 16									18 31				18 37							18 53	
Slade Green 4	d			18 19	18a22								18a36				18 41							18a55	
Dartford 4	a	18 16		18 27		18 21	18 25					18 29		18 36			18 48		18 53		18 44		18 52		
	d					18 22						18 31									18 45		18 54		
Stone Crossing	d																				18 49				
Greenhithe for Bluewater	d					18 27						18 36									18 51		18 59		
Swanscombe	d																				18 54				
Northfleet	d																				18 56				
Gravesend 4	d					18 34					18 38	18a45									19 02		19a09		
Higham	d					18 40															19 08				
Strood 4	d					18 45					18 49										19 14				
Maidstone West	d										19a05														
Rochester 4	d					18 51															19 19				
Chatham 4	d					18 54															19 22				
Gillingham (Kent) 4	a					19 02															19 29				

London - Dartford and Gillingham

Network Diagram - see first Page of Table 200

		SE	SE		SE	SE	SE	SE	SE	SE	SE	SE	SE		SE	SE	SE	SE	SE	SE	SE	SE	SE		SE
St Pancras Int'l 15 ⊖	d					18 55															19 25				
Stratford International ⊖ ⛴	d					19 02															19 32				
Ebbsfleet International	d					19 13															19 45				
London Charing Cross 4 ⊖	d		18 18				18 23				18 34	18 37	18 39					18 48				18 56	19 02		
London Waterloo (East) 4 ⊖	d		18 21				18 26				18 37	18 40	18 42					18 51				18 59	19 05		
London Cannon Street 4 ⊖	d	18 21			18 25			18 30		18 34						18 46	18 50		18 54	18 57					19 07
London Bridge 4 ⊖	d	18 25	18 26		18 29		18 32	18 34		18 38	18 42	18 46	18 48			18 50	18 54	18 57	18 58	19 01		19 04	19 10		19 11
Deptford	d	18 31									18 48					18 56				19 07					19 17
Greenwich 4 ⛴	d	18 34						18 42			18 51					18 59				19 10					19 19
Maze Hill	d	18 37									18 54					19 02				19 13					19 22
Westcombe Park	d	18 39									18 56					19 04				19 15					19 24
London Victoria 15 ⊖	d								18 18						18 39										
Denmark Hill 4	d								18 28						18 48										
Peckham Rye 4	d								18 32						18 51										
Nunhead 4	d								18 34						18 54										
New Cross 4 ⊖	d				18 35					18 44			18 55				19 00		19 05						
St Johns	d				18 37					18 46							19 02		19 07						
Lewisham 4 ⛴	d		18 36		18 41				18 43	18 49			18 59		19 03		19 05	19 07	19 11				19 19		
Blackheath 4	d		18 39						18 46	18 52			19 02		19 06			19 10	19 14				19 22		
Kidbrooke	d		18 42						18 49	18 55			19 05		19 09				19 17				19 25		
Eltham	d		18 46						18 53	18 59			19 09		19 13				19 21				19 29		
Falconwood	d		18 48						18 55	19 01			19 11		19 16				19 23				19 31		
Welling	d		18 51						18 58	19 04			19 14		19 18				19 26				19 34		
Bexleyheath	d		18 54						19 01	19 07			19 16		19 21				19 29				19 36		
Barnehurst 4	d		18 57						19 04	19a12			19a21		19 25				19a34				19 39		
Hither Green 4	d				18 46							18 56					19 09					19 14			
Lee	d				18 48							18 58					19 11					19 16			
Mottingham	d				18 51							19 01					19 14					19 19			
New Eltham	d				18 54		18 48					19 04					19 17					19 22			
Sidcup 4	d				18 58		18 51					19 08					19 20					19 25			
Albany Park	d				19 00		18 53					19 10					19 22					19 27			
Bexley	d				19 03		18 56					19 13					19 25					19 30			
Crayford	d				19 10		18 59					19 16					19 29					19 33			
Charlton 4	d	18 41			19a40			18 48			18 59					19 06	20a10	19 15		19 18					19 27
Woolwich Dockyard	d	18 44									19 02					19 09				19 21					19 30
Woolwich Arsenal 4 ⛴	d	18 47						18 53			19 05					19 12		19 20		19 24					19 33
Plumstead	d	18 49									19 07					19 14				19 26					19 35
Abbey Wood	d	18 53						18 57			19 10					19 17		19 24		19 29					19 38
Belvedere	d	18 55									19 13					19 19				19 32					19 40
Erith	d	18 58									19 15					19 22				19 34					19 43
Slade Green 4	d	19 01									19 18					19a26				19 37					19a45
Dartford 4	a	19 09	19 06				19 04	19 09	19 13		19 28	19 21			19 34			19 34		19 44		19 38	19 48		
	d						19 05	19 10				19 22						19 35				19 39			
Stone Crossing	d						19 09	19 14				19 26										19 43			
Greenhithe for Bluewater	d						19 11	19 16				19 29						19 40				19 46			
Swanscombe	d						19 14	19 19				19 32										19 49			
Northfleet	d						19 16	19 21				19 34										19 51			
Gravesend 4	d					19 20	19a24	19 26				19 38						19 47			19 51	19a57			
Higham	d							19 32				19 44						19 53							
Strood 4	d					19 30		19 38				19a53						19 58			20 01				
Maidstone West	d																								
Rochester 4	d					19 35		19 45										20 03			20 08				
Chatham 4	d					19 38		19 48										20 05			20 10				
Gillingham (Kent) 4	a					19 42		19 55										20 13			20 14				

Table 200

Mondays to Fridays

London - Dartford and Gillingham

Network Diagram - see first Page of Table 200

		SE	SE	SE	SE	SE	SE	SE	SE	SE	SE	SE	SE	SE	SE	SE	SE	SE	SE	SE	SE	SE	SE
St Pancras Int'l 15 ⊖	d							19 55										20 25					
Stratford International ⊖ ⛴	d							20 02										20 32					
Ebbsfleet International	d							20 13										20 43					
London Charing Cross 4 ⊖	d		19 09						19 26	19 32			19 39						19 56	20 02		20 09	
London Waterloo (East) 4 ⊖	d		19 12						19 29	19 35			19 42						19 59	20 05		20 12	
London Cannon Street 4 ⊖	d	19 10			19 17	19 24	19 27				19 37	19 40			19 47	19 54	19 57				20 10		20 17
London Bridge 4 ⊖	d	19 14	19 17		19 21	19 28	19 31		19 34	19 40	19 41	19 44	19 47		19 51	19 58	20 01		20 04	20 10	20 14	20 17	20 21
Deptford	d				19 27		19 37				19 47				19 57		20 07						20 27
Greenwich 4 ⛴	d				19 29		19 39				19 49				19 59		20 09						20 29
Maze Hill	d				19 32		19 42				19 52				20 02		20 12						20 32
Westcombe Park	d				19 34		19 44				19 54				20 04		20 14						20 34
London Victoria 15 ⊖	d			19 09										19 39									
Denmark Hill 4	d			19 18										19 48									
Peckham Rye 4	d			19 21										19 51									
Nunhead 4	d			19 23										19 53									
New Cross 4 ⊖	d	19 19				19 33						19 49				20 03					20 19		
St Johns	d	19 21				19 35						19 51				20 05					20 21		
Lewisham 4 ⛴	d	19 24	19 26	19 32		19 38				19 49		19 55	19 56	20 02		20 08				20 19	20 25	20 26	
Blackheath 4	d		19 29	19 34		19 41				19 52			19 59	20 04		20 11				20 22		20 29	
Kidbrooke	d			19 37		19 44				19 55				20 07		20 14				20 25			
Eltham	d			19 41		19 47				19 58				20 11		20 17				20 28			
Falconwood	d			19 43		19 50				20 01				20 13		20 20				20 31			
Welling	d			19 46		19 52				20 03				20 16		20 22				20 33			
Bexleyheath	d			19 48		19 55				20 06				20 18		20 25				20 36			
Barnehurst 4	d			19 51		19a58				20 08				20 21		20a28				20 38			
Hither Green 4	d	19 29							19 44			20 00							20 14		20 30		
Lee	d	19 31							19 46			20 02							20 16		20 32		
Mottingham	d	19 34							19 49			20 05							20 19		20 35		
New Eltham	d	19 36							19 51			20 07							20 21		20 37		
Sidcup 4	d	19 40							19 55			20 11							20 25		20 41		
Albany Park	d	19 42							19 57			20 13							20 27		20 43		
Bexley	d	19 44							19 59			20 15							20 29		20 45		
Crayford	d	19 48							20 03			20 18							20 33		20 48		
Charlton 4	d		19 33		19 37		19 47				19 57		20 03		20 07		20 17					20 33	20 37
Woolwich Dockyard	d				19 40		19 50				20 00				20 10		20 20						20 40
Woolwich Arsenal 4 ⛴	d		19 39		19 43		19 53				20 03		20 09		20 13		20 23					20 39	20 43
Plumstead	d				19 45		19 55				20 05				20 15		20 25						20 45
Abbey Wood	d		19 43		19 48		19 58				20 08		20 13		20 18		20 28					20 43	20 48
Belvedere	d				19 50		20 00				20 10				20 20		20 30						20 50
Erith	d				19 53		20 03				20 13				20 23		20 33						20 53
Slade Green 4	d				19a55		20 07				20a15				20a25		20 37						20 57
Dartford 4	a	19 53	19 55	19 58			20 13		20 08	20 15		20 23	20 25	20 28			20 43		20 38	20 45	20 53	20 54	21 02
	d		19 55						20 09				20 25						20 39			20 55	
Stone Crossing	d								20 13										20 43				
Greenhithe for Bluewater	d		20 00						20 15				20 30						20 45			21 00	
Swanscombe	d								20 18										20 48				
Northfleet	d								20 20										20 50				
Gravesend 4	d		20 07					20 18	20a25				20 37					20 48	20a55			21 07	
Higham	d		20 13										20 43									21 13	
Strood 4	d		20 18					20 28					20 48					20 58				21 18	
Maidstone West	d																						
Rochester 4	d		20 22					20 33					20 52					21 03				21 22	
Chatham 4	d		20 25					20 35					20 55					21 05				21 25	
Gillingham (Kent) 4	a		20 29					20 39					20 59					21 09				21 29	

London - Dartford and Gillingham

Network Diagram - see first Page of Table 200

		SE	SE	SE	SE	SE	SE	SE	SE	SE	SE	SE	SE	SE	SE	SE	SE	SE	SE	SE	SE	SE	SE
St Pancras Int'l 15 ⊖	d	20 55						21 25						21 55						22 25			
Stratford International ⊖ ⛴	d	21 02						21 32						22 02						22 32			
Ebbsfleet International	d	21 13						21 43						22 13						22 43			
London Charing Cross 4 ⊖	d		20 22		20 32	20 39			20 52		21 02	21 09			21 22	21 26	21 32	21 39			21 52	21 56	22 02
London Waterloo (East) 4 ⊖	d		20 25		20 35	20 42			20 55		21 05	21 12			21 25	21 29	21 35	21 42			21 55	21 59	22 05
London Cannon Street 4 ⊖	d			20 27			20 47			20 57													
London Bridge 4 ⊖	d		20 30	20 31	20 40	20 47	20 51		21 00	21 01	21 10	21 17	21 20		21 30	21 34	21 40	21 47	21 50		22 00	22 04	22 10
Deptford	d			20 37			20 57			21 07			21 26			21 40			21 56			22 10	
Greenwich 4 ⛴	d			20 39			20 59			21 09			21 28			21 42			21 58			22 12	
Maze Hill	d			20 42			21 02			21 12			21 31			21 45			22 01			22 15	
Westcombe Park	d			20 44			21 04			21 14			21 33			21 47			22 03			22 17	
London Victoria 15 ⊖	d																						
Denmark Hill 4	d																						
Peckham Rye 4	d																						
Nunhead 4	d																						
New Cross 4 ⊖	d		20 35		20 45				21 05		21 15				21 35		21 45				22 05		22 15
St Johns	d																						
Lewisham 4 ⛴	d		20 39		20 49	20 56			21 09		21 19	21 26			21 39		21 49	21 56			22 09		22 19
Blackheath 4	d				20 52	20 59					21 22	21 29					21 52	21 59					22 22
Kidbrooke	d				20 55						21 25						21 55						22 25
Eltham	d				20 58						21 28						21 58						22 28
Falconwood	d				21 01						21 31						22 01						22 31
Welling	d				21 03						21 33						22 03						22 33
Bexleyheath	d				21 06						21 36						22 06						22 36
Barnehurst 4	d				21 08						21 38						22 08						22 38
Hither Green 4	d		20 44						21 14						21 44						22 14		
Lee	d		20 46						21 16						21 46						22 16		
Mottingham	d		20 49						21 19						21 49						22 19		
New Eltham	d		20 51						21 21						21 51						22 21		
Sidcup 4	d		20 55						21 25						21 55						22 25		
Albany Park	d		20 57						21 27						21 57						22 27		
Bexley	d		20 59						21 29						21 59						22 29		
Crayford	d		21 03						21 33						22 03						22 33		
Charlton 4	d			20 47		21 03	21 07			21 17		21 33	21 36			21 50		22 03	22 06			22 20	
Woolwich Dockyard	d			20 50			21 10			21 20			21 39			21 53			22 09			22 23	
Woolwich Arsenal 4 ⛴	d			20 53		21 09	21 13			21 23		21 39	21 42			21 56		22 09	22 12			22 26	
Plumstead	d			20 55			21 15			21 25			21 44			21 58			22 14			22 28	
Abbey Wood	d			20 58		21 13	21 18			21 28		21 43	21 47			22 01		22 13	22 17			22 31	
Belvedere	d			21 00			21 20			21 30			21 50			22 03			22 20			22 33	
Erith	d			21 03			21 23			21 33			21 52			22 06			22 22			22 36	
Slade Green 4	d			21 07			21 27			21 37			21 56			22 09			22 26			22 39	
Dartford 4	a		21 08	21 12	21 15	21 24	21 32		21 38	21 42	21 45	21 54	22 00		22 08	22 14	22 16	22 24	22 30		22 38	22 44	22 46
	d		21 09			21 25			21 39			21 55			22 09			22 25			22 39		
Stone Crossing	d		21 13						21 43						22 13						22 43		
Greenhithe for Bluewater	d		21 15			21 30			21 45			22 00			22 15			22 30			22 45		
Swanscombe	d		21 18						21 48						22 18						22 48		
Northfleet	d		21 20						21 50						22 20						22 50		
Gravesend 4	d	21 18	21a25			21 37		21 48	21a55			22 07		22 18	22a25			22 37		22 48	22a55		
Higham	d					21 43						22 13						22 43					
Strood 4	d	21 28				21 48		21 58				22 18		22 28				22 48		22 58			
Maidstone West	d																						
Rochester 4	d	21 33				21 52		22 03				22 22		22 33				22 52		23 03			
Chatham 4	d	21 35				21 55		22 05				22 25		22 35				22 55		23 05			
Gillingham (Kent) 4	a	21 39				21 59		22 09				22 29		22 39				22 59		23 09			

London - Dartford and Gillingham

Network Diagram - see first Page of Table 200

Station		SE	SE	SE	SE	SE	SE	SE	SE	SE	SE	SE	SE	SE	SE	SE	SE	SE	SE	SE
St Pancras Int'l 15 ⊖	d			22 55									23 25					23 55		
Stratford International ⊖ ⛴	d			23 02									23 32					00 02		
Ebbsfleet International	d			23 13									23 43					00 13		
London Charing Cross 4 ⊖	d	22 09			22 22	22 26	22 32	22 39		22 52	22 56	23 02		23 09	23 22	23 26	23 32		23 39	23 56
London Waterloo (East) 4 ⊖	d	22 12			22 25	22 29	22 35	22 42		22 55	22 59	23 05		23 12	23 25	23 29	23 35		23 42	23 59
London Cannon Street 4 ⊖	d																			
London Bridge 4 ⊖	d	22 17	22 20		22 30	22 34	22 40	22 47	22 50	23 00	23 04	23 10		23 17	23 30	23 34	23 40		23 47	00 04
Deptford	d		22 26			22 40			22 56		23 10					23 40				00 10
Greenwich 4 ⛴	d		22 28			22 42			22 58		23 12					23 42				00 12
Maze Hill	d		22 31			22 45			23 01		23 15					23 45				00 15
Westcombe Park	d		22 33			22 47			23 03		23 17					23 47				00 17
London Victoria 15 ⊖	d																			
Denmark Hill 4	d																			
Peckham Rye 4	d																			
Nunhead 4	d																			
New Cross 4 ⊖	d				22 35		22 45			23 05		23 15			23 35		23 45			
St Johns	d																			
Lewisham 4 ⛴	d	22 26			22 39		22 49	22 56		23 09		23 19		23 26	23 39		23 49		23 56	
Blackheath 4	d	22 29					22 52	22 59				23 22		23 29			23 52		23 59	
Kidbrooke	d						22 55					23 25					23 55			
Eltham	d						22 58					23 28					23 58			
Falconwood	d						23 01					23 31					00 01			
Welling	d						23 03					23 33					00 03			
Bexleyheath	d						23 06					23 36					00 06			
Barnehurst 4	d						23 08					23 38					00 08			
Hither Green 4	d				22 44					23 14					23 44					
Lee	d				22 46					23 16					23 46					
Mottingham	d				22 49					23 19					23 49					
New Eltham	d				22 51					23 21					23 51					
Sidcup 4	d				22 55					23 25					23 55					
Albany Park	d				22 57					23 27					23 57					
Bexley	d				22 59					23 29					23 59					
Crayford	d				23 03					23 33					00 03					
Charlton 4	d	22 33	22 36			22 50		23 03	23 06		23 20			23 33		23 50			00 03	00 20
Woolwich Dockyard	d		22 39			22 53			23 09		23 23					23 53				00 23
Woolwich Arsenal 4 ⛴	d	22 39	22 42			22 56		23 09	23 12		23 26			23 39		23 56			00 09	00 26
Plumstead	d		22 44			22 58			23 14		23 28					23 58				00 28
Abbey Wood	d	22 43	22 47			23 01		23 13	23 17		23 31			23 43		00 01			00 13	00 31
Belvedere	d		22 50			23 03			23 20		23 33					00 03				00 33
Erith	d		22 52			23 06			23 22		23 36					00 06				00 36
Slade Green 4	d		22 56			23 09			23 26		23 39					00 09				00 39
Dartford 4	a	22 54	23 00		23 08	23 14	23 16	23 24	23 30	23 38	23 44	23 46		23 54	00 08	00 14	00 16		00 24	00 44
	d	22 55			23 09			23 25						23 55					00 25	
Stone Crossing	d				23 13			23 29						23 58					00 29	
Greenhithe for Bluewater	d	23 00			23 15			23 31						23 59					00 31	
Swanscombe	d				23 18			23 34						00 04					00 34	
Northfleet	d				23 20			23 36						00 06					00 36	
Gravesend 4	d	23 07		23 18	23a25			23 40					23 48	00 10				00 18	00 40	
Higham	d	23 13						23 46						00 16					00 46	
Strood 4	d	23 18		23 28				23 52					23 58	00 22				00 28	00 52	
Maidstone West	d																			
Rochester 4	d	23 22		23 33				23 56					00 03	00 26				00 33	00 56	
Chatham 4	d	23 25		23 35				23 58					00 05	00 28				00 35	00 58	
Gillingham (Kent) 4	a	23 29		23 39				00 03					00 09	00 33				00 39	01 03	

Table 200

Saturdays

London - Dartford and Gillingham

Network Diagram - see first Page of Table 200

		SE	SE	SE	SE	SE	SE	SE	SE	SE	SE	SE	SE	SE	SE	SE	SE	SE	SE	SE	SE	SE	SE
St Pancras Int'l 15 ⊖	d		23p25					23p55															
Stratford International ⊖ ⛴	d		23p32					00 02															
Ebbsfleet International	d		23p43					00 13															
London Charing Cross 4 ⊖	d	22p39		23p09	23p22	23p26	23p32		23p39	23p56	00 02	00 10	00 18	04 52		05 22	05 26	05 32	05 39	05 52	05 56	06 02	06 09
London Waterloo (East) 4 ⊖	d	22p42		23p12	23p25	23p29	23p35		23p42	23p59	00 05	00 13	00 21	04 55		05 25	05 29	05 35	05 42	05 55	05 59	06 05	06 12
London Cannon Street 4 ⊖	d																						
London Bridge 4 ⊖	d	22p47		23p17	23p30	23p34	23p40		23p47	00 04	00 10	00 18	00 26	05 00		05 30	05 34	05 40	05 47	06 00	06 04	06 10	06 17
Deptford	d					23p40				00 10							05 40				06 10		
Greenwich 4 ⛴	d					23p42				00 12							05 42				06 12		
Maze Hill	d					23p45				00 15							05 45				06 15		
Westcombe Park	d					23p47				00 17							05 47				06 17		
London Victoria 15 ⊖	d																						
Denmark Hill 4	d																						
Peckham Rye 4	d																						
Nunhead 4	d																						
New Cross 4 ⊖	d				23p35		23p45				00 15	00 23	00 31	05 05		05 35		05 45		06 05		06 15	
St Johns	d																						
Lewisham 4 ⛴	d	22p56		23p26	23p39		23p49		23p56		00 19	00 27	00 35	05 09		05 39		05 49	05 56	06 09		06 19	06 26
Blackheath 4	d	22p59		23p29			23p52		23p59		00 22		00 38					05 52	05 59			06 22	06 29
Kidbrooke	d						23p55				00 25							05 55				06 25	
Eltham	d						23p58				00 28							05 58				06 28	
Falconwood	d						00 01				00 31							06 01				06 31	
Welling	d						00 03				00 33							06 03				06 33	
Bexleyheath	d						00 06				00 36							06 06				06 36	
Barnehurst 4	d						00 08				00 38							06 08				06 38	
Hither Green 4	d				23p44							00 32		05 14		05 44				06 14			
Lee	d				23p46							00 34		05 16		05 46				06 16			
Mottingham	d				23p49							00 37		05 19		05 49				06 19			
New Eltham	d				23p51							00 39		05 21		05 51				06 21			
Sidcup 4	d				23p55							00 43		05 25		05 55				06 25			
Albany Park	d				23p57							00 45		05 27		05 57				06 27			
Bexley	d				23p59							00 47		05 29		05 59				06 29			
Crayford	d				00 03							00 51		05 33		06 03				06 33			
Charlton 4	d	23p03		23p33		23p50			00 03	00 20			00 42				05 50		06 03		06 20		06 33
Woolwich Dockyard	d					23p53				00 23							05 53				06 23		
Woolwich Arsenal 4 ⛴	d	23p09		23p39		23p56			00 09	00 26			00 47				05 56		06 09		06 26		06 39
Plumstead	d					23p58				00 28			00 49				05 58				06 28		
Abbey Wood	d	23p13		23p43		00 01			00 13	00 31			00 53				06 01		06 13		06 31		06 43
Belvedere	d					00 03				00 33			00 55				06 03				06 33		
Erith	d					00 06				00 36			00 58				06 06				06 36		
Slade Green 4	d					00 09				00 39			01 00				06 09				06 39		
Dartford 4	a	23p24		23p54	00 08	00 14	00 16		00 24	00 44	00 46	00 56	01 05	05 38		06 08	06 14	06 16	06 24	06 38	06 44	06 46	06 54
	d	23p25		23p55					00 25				01 06	05 39	05 55	06 09			06 25	06 39			06 55
Stone Crossing	d	23p29		23p58					00 29					05 43		06 13				06 43			
Greenhithe for Bluewater	d	23p31		23p59					00 31				01 10	05 45	06 00	06 15			06 30	06 45			07 00
Swanscombe	d	23p34		00 04					00 34					05 48		06 18				06 48			
Northfleet	d	23p36		00 06					00 36					05 50		06 20				06 50			
Gravesend 4	d	23p40	23p48	00 10				00 18	00 40				01 17	05a55	06 07	06a25			06 37	06a55			07 07
Higham	d	23p46		00 16					00 46				01 23		06 13				06 43				07 13
Strood 4	d	23p52	23p58	00 22				00 28	00 52				01 29		06 18				06 48				07 18
Maidstone West	d																						
Rochester 4	d	23p56	00 03	00 26				00 33	00 56				01 33		06 22				06 52				07 22
Chatham 4	d	23p58	00 05	00 28				00 35	00 58				01 35		06 25				06 55				07 25
Gillingham (Kent) 4	a	00 03	00 09	00 33				00 39	01 03				01 41		06 29				06 59				07 29

Table 200

Saturdays

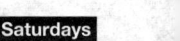

London - Dartford and Gillingham

Network Diagram - see first Page of Table 200

		SE	SE	SE	SE	SE		SE	SE	SE	SE	SE	SE	SE	SE	SE		SE	SE	SE	SE	SE	SE	SE	SE
St Pancras Int'l 15 ⊖	d	06 52						07 25					07 52							08 28					
Stratford International ⊖ ⛴	d	06 59						07 32					07 58							08 35					
Ebbsfleet International	d	07 13						07 43					08 13							08 46					
London Charing Cross 4 ⊖	d		06 22	06 26	06 32	06 39			06 52	06 56	07 02	07 09		07 22	07 26	07 32		07 39			07 52	07 56	08 02		
London Waterloo (East) 4 ⊖	d		06 25	06 29	06 35	06 42			06 55	06 59	07 05	07 12		07 25	07 29	07 35		07 42			07 55	07 59	08 05		
London Cannon Street 4 ⊖	d																							08 07	08 10
London Bridge 4 ⊖	d		06 30	06 34	06 40	06 47			07 00	07 04	07 10	07 17		07 30	07 34	07 40		07 47			08 00	08 04	08 10	08 11	08 14
Deptford	d			06 40						07 10					07 40							08 10		08 17	
Greenwich 4 ⛴	d			06 42						07 12					07 42							08 12		08 19	
Maze Hill	d			06 45						07 15					07 45							08 15		08 22	
Westcombe Park	d			06 47						07 17					07 47							08 17		08 24	
London Victoria 15 ⊖	d																		07 39						
Denmark Hill 4	d																		07 48						
Peckham Rye 4	d																		07 51						
Nunhead 4	d																		07 53						
New Cross 4 ⊖	d		06 35		06 45				07 05		07 15			07 35		07 45					08 05		08 15		08 19
St Johns	d																								08 21
Lewisham 4 ⛴	d		06 39		06 49	06 56			07 09		07 19	07 26		07 39		07 49		07 56	08 02		08 09		08 19		08 24
Blackheath 4	d				06 52	06 59					07 22	07 29				07 52		07 59	08 04				08 22		
Kidbrooke	d				06 55						07 25					07 55			08 07				08 25		
Eltham	d				06 58						07 28					07 58			08 11				08 28		
Falconwood	d				07 01						07 31					08 01			08 13				08 31		
Welling	d				07 03						07 33					08 03			08 16				08 33		
Bexleyheath	d				07 06						07 36					08 06			08 18				08 36		
Barnehurst 4	d				07 08						07 38					08 08			08 21				08 38		
Hither Green 4	d		06 44						07 14					07 44							08 14				08 29
Lee	d		06 46						07 16					07 46							08 16				08 31
Mottingham	d		06 49						07 19					07 49							08 19				08 34
New Eltham	d		06 51						07 21					07 51							08 21				08 36
Sidcup 4	d		06 55						07 25					07 55							08 25				08 40
Albany Park	d		06 57						07 27					07 57							08 27				08 42
Bexley	d		06 59						07 29					07 59							08 29				08 44
Crayford	d		07 03						07 33					08 03							08 33				08 48
Charlton 4	d			06 50		07 03				07 20		07 33			07 50			08 03				08 20		08 27	09a15
Woolwich Dockyard	d			06 53						07 23					07 53							08 23		08 30	
Woolwich Arsenal 4 ⛴	d			06 56		07 09				07 26		07 39			07 56			08 09				08 26		08 33	
Plumstead	d			06 58						07 28					07 58							08 28		08 35	
Abbey Wood	d			07 01		07 13				07 31		07 43			08 01			08 13				08 31		08 38	
Belvedere	d			07 03						07 33					08 03							08 33		08 40	
Erith	d			07 06						07 36					08 06							08 36		08 43	
Slade Green 4	d			07 09						07 39					08 09							08 39		08a46	
Dartford 4	a		07 08	07 14	07 16	07 24			07 38	07 44	07 46	07 54		08 08	08 14	08 16		08 24	08 29		08 38	08 44	08 46		
	d		07 09			07 25			07 39			07 55		08 09				08 25			08 39				
Stone Crossing	d		07 13						07 43					08 13							08 43				
Greenhithe for Bluewater	d		07 15			07 30			07 45			08 00		08 15				08 30			08 45				
Swanscombe	d		07 18						07 48					08 18							08 48				
Northfleet	d		07 20						07 50					08 20							08 50				
Gravesend 4	d	07 17	07a25			07 37		07 48	07a55			08 07	08 18	08a25				08 37		08 51	08a55				
Higham	d					07 43						08 13						08 43							
Strood 4	d	07 27				07 48		07 58				08 18	08 28					08 48		09 01					
Maidstone West	d																								
Rochester 4	d	07 32				07 52		08 03				08 22	08 33					08 52		09 06					
Chatham 4	d	07 34				07 55		08 05				08 25	08 35					08 55		09 08					
Gillingham (Kent) 4	a	07 38				07 59		08 09				08 29	08 39					08 59		09 12					

Table 200

Saturdays

London - Dartford and Gillingham

Network Diagram - see first Page of Table 200

		SE		SE	SE	SE	SE	SE	SE	SE	SE	SE		SE	SE	SE	SE	SE	SE	SE	SE	SE		SE	SE
St Pancras Int'l 15 ⊖	d							08 50											09 25						
Stratford International ⊖ ⛴	d							09 04											09 32						
Ebbsfleet International	d							09 15											09 43						
London Charing Cross 4 ⊖	d	08 09							08 26	08 32				08 39						08 56	09 02				09 09
London Waterloo (East) 4 ⊖	d	08 12							08 29	08 35				08 42						08 59	09 05				09 12
London Cannon Street 4 ⊖	d				08 17	08 24	08 27				08 37	08 40				08 47	08 54	08 57				09 07		09 10	
London Bridge 4 ⊖	d	08 17			08 21	08 28	08 31		08 34	08 40	08 41	08 44		08 47		08 51	08 58	09 01		09 04	09 10	09 11		09 14	09 17
Deptford	d				08 27		08 37				08 47					08 57		09 07				09 17			
Greenwich 4 ⛴	d				08 29		08 39				08 49					08 59		09 09				09 19			
Maze Hill	d				08 32		08 42				08 52					09 02		09 12				09 22			
Westcombe Park	d				08 34		08 44				08 54					09 04		09 14				09 24			
London Victoria 15 ⊖	d			08 09											08 39										
Denmark Hill 4	d			08 18											08 48										
Peckham Rye 4	d			08 21											08 51										
Nunhead 4	d			08 23											08 53										
New Cross 4 ⊖	d					08 33						08 49					09 03							09 19	
St Johns	d					08 35						08 51					09 05							09 21	
Lewisham 4 ⛴	d	08 26		08 32		08 38				08 49		08 54		08 56	09 02		09 08				09 19			09 24	09 26
Blackheath 4	d	08 29		08 34		08 41				08 52				08 59	09 04		09 11				09 22				09 29
Kidbrooke	d			08 37		08 44				08 55					09 07		09 14				09 25				
Eltham	d			08 41		08 47				08 58					09 11		09 17				09 28				
Falconwood	d			08 43		08 50				09 01					09 13		09 20				09 31				
Welling	d			08 46		08 52				09 03					09 16		09 22				09 33				
Bexleyheath	d			08 48		08 55				09 06					09 18		09 25				09 36				
Barnehurst 4	d			08 51		09 02				09 08					09 21		09 32				09 38				
Hither Green 4	d								08 44			08 59								09 14				09 29	
Lee	d								08 46			09 01								09 16				09 31	
Mottingham	d								08 49			09 04								09 19				09 34	
New Eltham	d								08 51			09 06								09 21				09 36	
Sidcup 4	d								08 55			09 10								09 25				09 40	
Albany Park	d								08 57			09 12								09 27				09 42	
Bexley	d								08 59			09 14								09 29				09 44	
Crayford	d								09 03			09 18								09 33				09 48	
Charlton 4	d	08 33			08 37		08 47				08 57	09a45		09 03		09 07		09 17				09 27		10a15	09 33
Woolwich Dockyard	d				08 40		08 50				09 00					09 10		09 20				09 30			
Woolwich Arsenal 4 ⛴	d	08 39			08 43		08 53				09 03			09 09		09 13		09 23				09 33			09 39
Plumstead	d				08 45		08 55				09 05					09 15		09 25				09 35			
Abbey Wood	d	08 43			08 48		08 58				09 08			09 13		09 18		09 28				09 38			09 43
Belvedere	d				08 50		09 00				09 10					09 20		09 30				09 40			
Erith	d				08 53		09 03				09 13					09 23		09 33				09 43			
Slade Green 4	d				08a56	09a12	09 07				09a16					09a26	09a42	09 37				09a46			
Dartford 4	a	08 54		08 58			09 12		09 08	09 15				09 24	09 28			09 42		09 38	09 45				09 54
	d	08 55							09 09					09 25						09 39					09 55
Stone Crossing	d								09 13											09 43					
Greenhithe for Bluewater	d	09 00							09 15					09 30						09 45					10 00
Swanscombe	d								09 18											09 48					
Northfleet	d								09 20											09 50					
Gravesend 4	d	09 07						09 20	09a25					09 37					09 48	09a55					10 07
Higham	d	09 13												09 43											10 13
Strood 4	d	09 18						09 30						09 48					09 58						10 18
Maidstone West	d																								
Rochester 4	d	09 22						09 34						09 52					10 03						10 22
Chatham 4	d	09 25						09 37						09 55					10 05						10 25
Gillingham (Kent) 4	a	09 29						09 41						09 59					10 09						10 29

London - Dartford and Gillingham

Network Diagram - see first Page of Table 200

		SE	SE	SE	SE	SE	SE	SE		SE	SE	SE	SE	SE	SE	SE	SE	SE		SE	SE	SE	SE	SE	SE
St Pancras Int'l 15 ⊖	d					09 55											10 28								
Stratford International ⊖ ⛴	d					10 02											10 35								
Ebbsfleet International	d					10 13											10 46								
London Charing Cross 4 ⊖	d						09 26	09 32				09 39						09 56		10 02			10 09		
London Waterloo (East) 4 ⊖	d						09 29	09 35				09 42						09 59		10 05			10 12		
London Cannon Street 4 ⊖	d		09 17	09 24	09 27					09 37	09 40			09 47	09 54	09 57					10 07	10 10			10 17
London Bridge 4 ⊖	d		09 21	09 28	09 31		09 34	09 40		09 41	09 44	09 47		09 51	09 58	10 01		10 04		10 10	10 11	10 14	10 17		10 21
Deptford	d		09 27		09 37					09 47				09 57		10 07					10 17				10 27
Greenwich 4 ⛴	d		09 29		09 39					09 49				09 59		10 09					10 19				10 29
Maze Hill	d		09 32		09 42					09 52				10 02		10 12					10 22				10 32
Westcombe Park	d		09 34		09 44					09 54				10 04		10 14					10 24				10 34
London Victoria 15 ⊖	d	09 09											09 39											10 09	
Denmark Hill 4	d	09 18											09 48											10 18	
Peckham Rye 4	d	09 21											09 51											10 21	
Nunhead 4	d	09 23											09 53											10 23	
New Cross 4 ⊖	d			09 33							09 49				10 03							10 19			
St Johns	d			09 35							09 51				10 05							10 21			
Lewisham 4 ⛴	d	09 32		09 38				09 49			09 54	09 56	10 02		10 08					10 19		10 24	10 26	10 32	
Blackheath 4	d	09 34		09 41				09 52				09 59	10 04		10 11					10 22			10 29	10 34	
Kidbrooke	d	09 37		09 44				09 55					10 07		10 14					10 25				10 37	
Eltham	d	09 41		09 47				09 58					10 11		10 17					10 28				10 41	
Falconwood	d	09 43		09 50				10 01					10 13		10 20					10 31				10 43	
Welling	d	09 46		09 52				10 03					10 16		10 22					10 33				10 46	
Bexleyheath	d	09 48		09 55				10 06					10 18		10 25					10 36				10 48	
Barnehurst 4	d	09 51		10 02				10 08					10 21		10 32					10 38				10 51	
Hither Green 4	d						09 44				09 59							10 14				10 29			
Lee	d						09 46				10 01							10 16				10 31			
Mottingham	d						09 49				10 04							10 19				10 34			
New Eltham	d						09 51				10 06							10 21				10 36			
Sidcup 4	d						09 55				10 10							10 25				10 40			
Albany Park	d						09 57				10 12							10 27				10 42			
Bexley	d						09 59				10 14							10 29				10 44			
Crayford	d						10 03				10 18							10 33				10 48			
Charlton 4	d		09 37		09 47					09 57	10a45	10 03		10 07		10 17					10 27	11a15	10 33		10 37
Woolwich Dockyard	d		09 40		09 50					10 00				10 10		10 20					10 30				10 40
Woolwich Arsenal 4 ⛴	d		09 43		09 53					10 03		10 09		10 13		10 23					10 33		10 39		10 43
Plumstead	d		09 45		09 55					10 05				10 15		10 25					10 35				10 45
Abbey Wood	d		09 48		09 58					10 08		10 13		10 18		10 28					10 38		10 43		10 48
Belvedere	d		09 50		10 00					10 10				10 20		10 30					10 40				10 50
Erith	d		09 53		10 03					10 13				10 23		10 33					10 43				10 53
Slade Green 4	d		09a56	10a12	10 07					10a16				10a26	10a42	10 37					10a46				10a56
Dartford 4	a	09 58			10 12		10 08	10 15				10 24	10 28			10 42		10 38		10 45			10 54	10 58	
	d						10 09					10 25						10 39					10 55		
Stone Crossing	d						10 13											10 43							
Greenhithe for Bluewater	d						10 15					10 30						10 45					11 00		
Swanscombe	d						10 18											10 48							
Northfleet	d						10 20											10 50							
Gravesend 4	d					10 18	10a25					10 37					10 51	10a55					11 07		
Higham	d											10 43											11 13		
Strood 4	d					10 28						10 48					11 01						11 18		
Maidstone West	d																								
Rochester 4	d					10 33						10 52					11 06						11 22		
Chatham 4	d					10 35						10 55					11 08						11 25		
Gillingham (Kent) 4	a					10 39						10 59					11 12						11 29		

Table 200

Saturdays

London - Dartford and Gillingham

Network Diagram - see first Page of Table 200

		SE	SE	SE	SE	SE	SE	SE	SE	SE	SE	SE	SE	SE	SE	SE	SE	SE	SE	SE	SE	SE
St Pancras Int'l 15 ⊖	d			10 52										11 28								
Stratford International ⊖	d			10 58										11 35								
Ebbsfleet International	d			11 13										11 46								
London Charing Cross 4 ⊖	d				10 26	10 32			10 39						10 56	11 02			11 09			
London Waterloo (East) 4 ⊖	d				10 29	10 35			10 42						10 59	11 05			11 12			
London Cannon Street 4 ⊖	d	10 24	10 27				10 37	10 40			10 47	10 54	10 57				11 07	11 10			11 17	11 24
London Bridge 4 ⊖	d	10 28	10 31		10 34	10 40	10 41	10 44	10 47		10 51	10 58	11 01		11 04	11 10	11 11	11 14	11 17		11 21	11 28
Deptford	d		10 37				10 47				10 57		11 07				11 17				11 27	
Greenwich 4	d		10 39				10 49				10 59		11 09				11 19				11 29	
Maze Hill	d		10 42				10 52				11 02		11 12				11 22				11 32	
Westcombe Park	d		10 44				10 54				11 04		11 14				11 24				11 34	
London Victoria 15 ⊖	d									10 39										11 09		
Denmark Hill 4	d									10 48										11 18		
Peckham Rye 4	d									10 51										11 21		
Nunhead 4	d									10 53										11 23		
New Cross 4 ⊖	d	10 33						10 49				11 03						11 19				11 33
St Johns	d	10 35						10 51				11 05						11 21				11 35
Lewisham 4	d	10 38				10 49		10 54	10 56	11 02		11 08				11 19		11 24	11 26	11 32		11 38
Blackheath 4	d	10 41				10 52			10 59	11 04		11 11				11 22			11 29	11 34		11 41
Kidbrooke	d	10 44				10 55				11 07		11 14				11 25				11 37		11 44
Eltham	d	10 47				10 58				11 11		11 17				11 28				11 41		11 47
Falconwood	d	10 50				11 01				11 13		11 20				11 31				11 43		11 50
Welling	d	10 52				11 03				11 16		11 22				11 33				11 46		11 52
Bexleyheath	d	10 55				11 06				11 18		11 25				11 36				11 48		11 55
Barnehurst 4	d	11 02				11 08				11 21		11 32				11 38				11 51		12 02
Hither Green 4	d				10 44			10 59							11 14			11 29				
Lee	d				10 46			11 01							11 16			11 31				
Mottingham	d				10 49			11 04							11 19			11 34				
New Eltham	d				10 51			11 06							11 21			11 36				
Sidcup 4	d				10 55			11 10							11 25			11 40				
Albany Park	d				10 57			11 12							11 27			11 42				
Bexley	d				10 59			11 14							11 29			11 44				
Crayford	d				11 03			11 18							11 33			11 48				
Charlton 4	d		10 47				10 57	11a45	11 03		11 07		11 17				11 27	12a15	11 33		11 37	
Woolwich Dockyard	d		10 50				11 00				11 10		11 20				11 30				11 40	
Woolwich Arsenal 4	d		10 53				11 03		11 09		11 13		11 23				11 33		11 39		11 43	
Plumstead	d		10 55				11 05				11 15		11 25				11 35				11 45	
Abbey Wood	d		10 58				11 08		11 13		11 18		11 28				11 38		11 43		11 48	
Belvedere	d		11 00				11 10				11 20		11 30				11 40				11 50	
Erith	d		11 03				11 13				11 23		11 33				11 43				11 53	
Slade Green 4	d	11a12	11 07				11a16				11a26	11a42	11 37				11a46				11a56	12a12
Dartford 4	a		11 12		11 08	11 15			11 24	11 28			11 42		11 38	11 45			11 54	11 58		
	d				11 09				11 25						11 39				11 55			
Stone Crossing	d				11 13										11 43							
Greenhithe for Bluewater	d				11 15				11 30						11 45				12 00			
Swanscombe	d				11 18										11 48							
Northfleet	d				11 20										11 50							
Gravesend 4	d			11 18	11a25				11 37					11 51	11a55				12 07			
Higham	d								11 43										12 13			
Strood 4	d			11 28					11 48					12 01					12 18			
Maidstone West	d																					
Rochester 4	d			11 33					11 52					12 06					12 22			
Chatham 4	d			11 35					11 55					12 08					12 25			
Gillingham (Kent) 4	a			11 39					11 59					12 12					12 29			

Table 200

Saturdays

London - Dartford and Gillingham

Network Diagram - see first Page of Table 200

Station		SE	SE	SE	SE	SE	SE	SE	SE	SE		SE	SE	SE	SE	SE	SE	SE	SE	SE		SE	SE	SE	SE
St Pancras Int'l [15] ⊖	d		11 55											12 28											12 55
Stratford International ⊖ ⛴	d		12 02											12 35											13 06
Ebbsfleet International	d		12 13											12 46											13 17
London Charing Cross [4] ⊖	d			11 26	11 32			11 39							11 56	12 02			12 09						
London Waterloo (East) [4] ⊖	d			11 29	11 35			11 42							11 59	12 05			12 12						
London Cannon Street [4] ⊖	d	11 27				11 37	11 40			11 47		11 54	11 57				12 07	12 10				12 17	12 24	12 27	
London Bridge [4] ⊖	d	11 31		11 34	11 40	11 41	11 44	11 47		11 51		11 58	12 01		12 04	12 10	12 11	12 14	12 17			12 21	12 28	12 31	
Deptford	d	11 37				11 47				11 57			12 07				12 17					12 27		12 37	
Greenwich [4] ⛴	d	11 39				11 49				11 59			12 09				12 19					12 29		12 39	
Maze Hill	d	11 42				11 52				12 02			12 12				12 22					12 32		12 42	
Westcombe Park	d	11 44				11 54				12 04			12 14				12 24					12 34		12 44	
London Victoria [15] ⊖	d								11 39											12 09					
Denmark Hill [4]	d								11 48											12 18					
Peckham Rye [4]	d								11 51											12 21					
Nunhead [4]	d								11 53											12 23					
New Cross [4] ⊖	d						11 49					12 03						12 19					12 33		
St Johns	d						11 51					12 05						12 21					12 35		
Lewisham [4] ⛴	d				11 49		11 54	11 56	12 02			12 08				12 19		12 24	12 26	12 32			12 38		
Blackheath [4]	d				11 52			11 59	12 04			12 11				12 22			12 29	12 34			12 41		
Kidbrooke	d				11 55				12 07			12 14				12 25				12 37			12 44		
Eltham	d				11 58				12 11			12 17				12 28				12 41			12 47		
Falconwood	d				12 01				12 13			12 20				12 31				12 43			12 50		
Welling	d				12 03				12 16			12 22				12 33				12 46			12 52		
Bexleyheath	d				12 06				12 18			12 25				12 36				12 48			12 55		
Barnehurst [4]	d				12 08				12 21			12 32				12 38				12 51			13 02		
Hither Green [4]	d			11 44			11 59								12 14			12 29							
Lee	d			11 46			12 01								12 16			12 31							
Mottingham	d			11 49			12 04								12 19			12 34							
New Eltham	d			11 51			12 06								12 21			12 36							
Sidcup [4]	d			11 55			12 10								12 25			12 40							
Albany Park	d			11 57			12 12								12 27			12 42							
Bexley	d			11 59			12 14								12 29			12 44							
Crayford	d			12 03			12 18								12 33			12 48							
Charlton [4]	d	11 47				11 57	12a45	12 03		12 07			12 17				12 27	13a15	12 33			12 37		12 47	
Woolwich Dockyard	d	11 50				12 00				12 10			12 20				12 30					12 40		12 50	
Woolwich Arsenal [4] ⛴	d	11 53				12 03		12 09		12 13			12 23				12 33		12 39			12 43		12 53	
Plumstead	d	11 55				12 05				12 15			12 25				12 35					12 45		12 55	
Abbey Wood	d	11 58				12 08		12 13		12 18			12 28				12 38		12 43			12 48		12 58	
Belvedere	d	12 00				12 10				12 20			12 30				12 40					12 50		13 00	
Erith	d	12 03				12 13				12 23			12 33				12 43					12 53		13 03	
Slade Green [4]	d	12 07				12a16				12a26		12a42	12 37				12a46					12a56	13a12	13 07	
Dartford [4]	a	12 12		12 08	12 15			12 24	12 28				12 42		12 38	12 45			12 54	12 58				13 12	
	d			12 09				12 25							12 39				12 55						
Stone Crossing	d			12 13											12 43										
Greenhithe for Bluewater	d			12 15				12 30							12 45				13 00						
Swanscombe	d			12 18											12 48										
Northfleet	d			12 20											12 50										
Gravesend [4]	d		12 18	12a25				12 37						12 51	12a55				13 07						13 22
Higham	d							12 43											13 13						
Strood [4]	d		12 28					12 48						13 01					13 18						13 32
Maidstone West	d																								
Rochester [4]	d		12 33					12 52						13 06					13 22						13 37
Chatham [4]	d		12 35					12 55						13 08					13 25						13 39
Gillingham (Kent) [4]	a		12 39					12 59						13 12					13 29						13 43

Table 200

Saturdays

London - Dartford and Gillingham

Network Diagram - see first Page of Table 200

		SE	SE	SE	SE	SE	SE	SE	SE	SE	SE	SE	SE	SE	SE	SE	SE	SE	SE	SE	SE	SE	SE
St Pancras Int'l 15 ⊖	d										13 25										13 55		
Stratford International ⊖ ⛴	d										13 32										14 02		
Ebbsfleet International	d										13 43										14 13		
London Charing Cross 4 ⊖	d	12 26	12 32			12 39						12 56	13 02			13 09						13 26	13 32
London Waterloo (East) 4 ⊖	d	12 29	12 35			12 42						12 59	13 05			13 12						13 29	13 35
London Cannon Street 4 ⊖	d			12 37	12 40			12 47	12 54	12 57				13 07	13 10			13 17	13 24	13 27			
London Bridge 4 ⊖	d	12 34	12 40	12 41	12 44	12 47		12 51	12 58	13 01		13 04	13 10	13 11	13 14	13 17		13 21	13 28	13 31		13 34	13 40
Deptford	d			12 47				12 57		13 07				13 17				13 27		13 37			
Greenwich 4 ⛴	d			12 49				12 59		13 09				13 19				13 29		13 39			
Maze Hill	d			12 52				13 02		13 12				13 22				13 32		13 42			
Westcombe Park	d			12 54				13 04		13 14				13 24				13 34		13 44			
London Victoria 15 ⊖	d						12 39										13 09						
Denmark Hill 4	d						12 48										13 18						
Peckham Rye 4	d						12 51										13 21						
Nunhead 4	d						12 53										13 23						
New Cross 4 ⊖	d				12 49				13 03						13 19				13 33				
St Johns	d				12 51				13 05						13 21				13 35				
Lewisham 4 ⛴	d		12 49		12 54	12 56	13 02		13 08				13 19		13 24	13 26	13 32		13 38				13 49
Blackheath 4	d		12 52			12 59	13 04		13 11				13 22			13 29	13 34		13 41				13 52
Kidbrooke	d		12 55				13 07		13 14				13 25				13 37		13 44				13 55
Eltham	d		12 58				13 11		13 17				13 28				13 41		13 47				13 58
Falconwood	d		13 01				13 13		13 20				13 31				13 43		13 50				14 01
Welling	d		13 03				13 16		13 22				13 33				13 46		13 52				14 03
Bexleyheath	d		13 06				13 18		13 25				13 36				13 48		13 55				14 06
Barnehurst 4	d		13 08				13 21		13 32				13 38				13 51		14 02				14 08
Hither Green 4	d	12 44			12 59							13 14			13 29							13 44	
Lee	d	12 46			13 01							13 16			13 31							13 46	
Mottingham	d	12 49			13 04							13 19			13 34							13 49	
New Eltham	d	12 51			13 06							13 21			13 36							13 51	
Sidcup 4	d	12 55			13 10							13 25			13 40							13 55	
Albany Park	d	12 57			13 12							13 27			13 42							13 57	
Bexley	d	12 59			13 14							13 29			13 44							13 59	
Crayford	d	13 03			13 18							13 33			13 48							14 03	
Charlton 4	d			12 57	13a45	13 03		13 07		13 17				13 27	14a15	13 33		13 37		13 47			
Woolwich Dockyard	d			13 00				13 10		13 20				13 30				13 40		13 50			
Woolwich Arsenal 4 ⛴	d			13 03		13 09		13 13		13 23				13 33		13 39		13 43		13 53			
Plumstead	d			13 05				13 15		13 25				13 35				13 45		13 55			
Abbey Wood	d			13 08		13 13		13 18		13 28				13 38		13 43		13 48		13 58			
Belvedere	d			13 10				13 20		13 30				13 40				13 50		14 00			
Erith	d			13 13				13 23		13 33				13 43				13 53		14 03			
Slade Green 4	d			13a16				13a26	13a42	13 37				13a46				13a56	14a12	14 07			
Dartford 4	a	13 08	13 15			13 24	13 28			13 42		13 38	13 45			13 54	13 58			14 12		14 08	14 15
	d	13 09				13 25						13 39				13 55						14 09	
Stone Crossing	d	13 13										13 43										14 13	
Greenhithe for Bluewater	d	13 15				13 30						13 45				14 00						14 15	
Swanscombe	d	13 18										13 48										14 18	
Northfleet	d	13 20										13 50										14 20	
Gravesend 4	d	13a25				13 37					13 48	13a55				14 07					14 18	14a25	
Higham	d					13 43										14 13							
Strood 4	d					13 48					13 58					14 18					14 28		
Maidstone West	d																						
Rochester 4	d					13 52					14 03					14 22					14 33		
Chatham 4	d					13 55					14 05					14 25					14 35		
Gillingham (Kent) 4	a					13 59					14 09					14 29					14 39		

Table 200

Saturdays

London - Dartford and Gillingham

Network Diagram - see first Page of Table 200

		SE		SE	SE	SE	SE	SE	SE	SE	SE	SE		SE	SE	SE	SE	SE	SE	SE	SE	SE		SE	SE
St Pancras Int'l 15 ⊖	d									14 25											14 55				
Stratford International ⊖	d									14 32											15 02				
Ebbsfleet International	d									14 43											15 13				
London Charing Cross 4 ⊖	d				13 39						13 56	14 02				14 09						14 26		14 32	
London Waterloo (East) 4 ⊖	d				13 42						13 59	14 05				14 12						14 29		14 35	
London Cannon Street 4 ⊖	d	13 37		13 40			13 47	13 54	13 57					14 07	14 10			14 17	14 24	14 27					14 37
London Bridge 4 ⊖	d	13 41		13 44	13 47		13 51	13 58	14 01		14 04	14 10		14 11	14 14	14 17		14 21	14 28	14 31		14 34		14 40	14 41
Deptford	d	13 47					13 57		14 07					14 17				14 27		14 37					14 47
Greenwich 4	d	13 49					13 59		14 09					14 19				14 29		14 39					14 49
Maze Hill	d	13 52					14 02		14 12					14 22				14 32		14 42					14 52
Westcombe Park	d	13 54					14 04		14 14					14 24				14 34		14 44					14 54
London Victoria 15 ⊖	d					13 39											14 09								
Denmark Hill 4	d					13 48											14 18								
Peckham Rye 4	d					13 51											14 21								
Nunhead 4	d					13 53											14 23								
New Cross 4 ⊖	d			13 49				14 03							14 19				14 33						
St Johns	d			13 51				14 05							14 21				14 35						
Lewisham 4	d			13 54	13 56	14 02		14 08				14 19			14 24	14 26	14 32		14 38					14 49	
Blackheath 4	d				13 59	14 04		14 11				14 22				14 29	14 34		14 41					14 52	
Kidbrooke	d					14 07		14 14				14 25					14 37		14 44					14 55	
Eltham	d					14 11		14 17				14 28					14 41		14 47					14 58	
Falconwood	d					14 13		14 20				14 31					14 43		14 50					15 01	
Welling	d					14 16		14 22				14 33					14 46		14 52					15 03	
Bexleyheath	d					14 18		14 25				14 36					14 48		14 55					15 06	
Barnehurst 4	d					14 21		14 32				14 38					14 51		15 02					15 08	
Hither Green 4	d			13 59							14 14				14 29							14 44			
Lee	d			14 01							14 16				14 31							14 46			
Mottingham	d			14 04							14 19				14 34							14 49			
New Eltham	d			14 06							14 21				14 36							14 51			
Sidcup 4	d			14 10							14 25				14 40							14 55			
Albany Park	d			14 12							14 27				14 42							14 57			
Bexley	d			14 14							14 29				14 44							14 59			
Crayford	d			14 18							14 33				14 48							15 03			
Charlton 4	d	13 57		14a45	14 03		14 07		14 17					14 27	15a15	14 33		14 37		14 47					14 57
Woolwich Dockyard	d	14 00					14 10		14 20					14 30				14 40		14 50					15 00
Woolwich Arsenal 4	d	14 03			14 09		14 13		14 23					14 33		14 39		14 43		14 53					15 03
Plumstead	d	14 05					14 15		14 25					14 35				14 45		14 55					15 05
Abbey Wood	d	14 08			14 13		14 18		14 28					14 38		14 43		14 48		14 58					15 08
Belvedere	d	14 10					14 20		14 30					14 40				14 50		15 00					15 10
Erith	d	14 13					14 23		14 33					14 43				14 53		15 03					15 13
Slade Green 4	d	14a16					14a26	14a42	14 37					14a46				14a56	15a12	15 07					15a16
Dartford 4	a				14 24	14 28			14 42		14 38	14 45				14 54	14 58			15 12		15 08		15 15	
	d				14 25						14 39					14 55						15 09			
Stone Crossing	d										14 43											15 13			
Greenhithe for Bluewater	d				14 30						14 45					15 00						15 15			
Swanscombe	d										14 48											15 18			
Northfleet	d										14 50											15 20			
Gravesend 4	d				14 37					14 48	14a55					15 07					15 18	15a25			
Higham	d				14 43											15 13									
Strood 4	d				14 48					14 58						15 18					15 28				
Maidstone West	d																								
Rochester 4	d				14 52					15 03						15 22					15 33				
Chatham 4	d				14 55					15 05						15 25					15 35				
Gillingham (Kent) 4	a				14 59					15 09						15 29					15 39				

Table 200

Saturdays

London - Dartford and Gillingham

Network Diagram - see first Page of Table 200

Station		SE	SE	SE	SE	SE	SE	SE	SE	SE	SE	SE	SE	SE	SE	SE	SE	SE	SE	SE	SE	SE	SE
St Pancras Int'l	d							15 25										15 55					
Stratford International	d							15 32										16 02					
Ebbsfleet International	d							15 43										16 13					
London Charing Cross	d		14 39						14 56	15 02			15 09						15 26	15 32			15 39
London Waterloo (East)	d		14 42						14 59	15 05			15 12						15 29	15 35			15 42
London Cannon Street	d	14 40			14 47	14 54	14 57				15 07	15 10			15 17	15 24	15 27				15 37	15 40	
London Bridge	d	14 44	14 47		14 51	14 58	15 01		15 04	15 10	15 11	15 14	15 17		15 21	15 28	15 31		15 34	15 40	15 41	15 44	15 47
Deptford	d				14 57		15 07				15 17				15 27		15 37				15 47		
Greenwich	d				14 59		15 09				15 19				15 29		15 39				15 49		
Maze Hill	d				15 02		15 12				15 22				15 32		15 42				15 52		
Westcombe Park	d				15 04		15 14				15 24				15 34		15 44				15 54		
London Victoria	d			14 39										15 09									
Denmark Hill	d			14 48										15 18									
Peckham Rye	d			14 51										15 21									
Nunhead	d			14 53										15 23									
New Cross	d	14 49				15 03						15 19				15 33						15 49	
St Johns	d	14 51				15 05						15 21				15 35						15 51	
Lewisham	d	14 54	14 56	15 02		15 08				15 19		15 24	15 26	15 32		15 38				15 49		15 54	15 56
Blackheath	d		14 59	15 04		15 11				15 22			15 29	15 34		15 41				15 52			15 59
Kidbrooke	d			15 07		15 14				15 25				15 37		15 44				15 55			
Eltham	d			15 11		15 17				15 28				15 41		15 47				15 58			
Falconwood	d			15 13		15 20				15 31				15 43		15 50				16 01			
Welling	d			15 16		15 22				15 33				15 46		15 52				16 03			
Bexleyheath	d			15 18		15 25				15 36				15 48		15 55				16 06			
Barnehurst	d			15 21		15 32				15 38				15 51		16 02				16 08			
Hither Green	d	14 59							15 14			15 29							15 44			15 59	
Lee	d	15 01							15 16			15 31							15 46			16 01	
Mottingham	d	15 04							15 19			15 34							15 49			16 04	
New Eltham	d	15 06							15 21			15 36							15 51			16 06	
Sidcup	d	15 10							15 25			15 40							15 55			16 10	
Albany Park	d	15 12							15 27			15 42							15 57			16 12	
Bexley	d	15 14							15 29			15 44							15 59			16 14	
Crayford	d	15 18							15 33			15 48							16 03			16 18	
Charlton	d	15a45	15 03		15 07		15 17				15 27	16a15	15 33		15 37		15 47				15 57	16a45	16 03
Woolwich Dockyard	d				15 10		15 20				15 30				15 40		15 50				16 00		
Woolwich Arsenal	d		15 09		15 13		15 23				15 33		15 39		15 43		15 53				16 03		16 09
Plumstead	d				15 15		15 25				15 35				15 45		15 55				16 05		
Abbey Wood	d		15 13		15 18		15 28				15 38		15 43		15 48		15 58				16 08		16 13
Belvedere	d				15 20		15 30				15 40				15 50		16 00				16 10		
Erith	d				15 23		15 33				15 43				15 53		16 03				16 13		
Slade Green	d				15a26	15a42	15 37				15a46				15a56	16a12	16 07				16a16		
Dartford	a		15 24	15 28			15 42		15 38	15 45			15 54	15 58			16 12		16 08	16 15			16 24
	d		15 25						15 39				15 55						16 09				16 25
Stone Crossing	d								15 43										16 13				
Greenhithe for Bluewater	d		15 30						15 45				16 00						16 15				16 30
Swanscombe	d								15 48										16 18				
Northfleet	d								15 50										16 20				
Gravesend	d		15 37					15 48	15a55				16 07					16 18	16a25				16 37
Higham	d		15 43										16 13										16 43
Strood	d		15 48					15 58					16 18					16 28					16 48
Maidstone West	d																						
Rochester	d		15 52					16 03					16 22					16 33					16 52
Chatham	d		15 55					16 05					16 25					16 35					16 55
Gillingham (Kent)	a		15 59					16 09					16 29					16 39					16 59

Table 200

Saturdays

London - Dartford and Gillingham

Network Diagram - see first Page of Table 200

Station		SE	SE	SE		SE	SE	SE	SE	SE	SE	SE	SE	SE		SE	SE	SE	SE	SE	SE	SE	SE	SE	
St Pancras Int'l 15 ⊖	d						16 28											16 55							
Stratford International ⊖ ⛴	d						16 35											17 02							
Ebbsfleet International	d						16 46											17 13							
London Charing Cross 4 ⊖	d							15 56	16 02			16 09							16 26	16 32			16 39		
London Waterloo (East) 4 ⊖	d							15 59	16 05			16 12							16 29	16 35			16 42		
London Cannon Street 4 ⊖	d		15 47	15 54		15 57				16 07	16 10			16 17		16 24	16 27				16 37	16 40			
London Bridge 4 ⊖	d		15 51	15 58		16 01		16 04	16 10	16 11	16 14	16 17		16 21		16 28	16 31		16 34	16 40	16 41	16 44	16 47		
Deptford	d		15 57			16 07				16 17				16 27			16 37				16 47				
Greenwich 4 ⛴	d		15 59			16 09				16 19				16 29			16 39				16 49				
Maze Hill	d		16 02			16 12				16 22				16 32			16 42				16 52				
Westcombe Park	d		16 04			16 14				16 24				16 34			16 44				16 54				
London Victoria 15 ⊖	d	15 39											16 09											16 39	
Denmark Hill 4	d	15 48											16 18											16 48	
Peckham Rye 4	d	15 51											16 21											16 51	
Nunhead 4	d	15 53											16 23											16 53	
New Cross 4 ⊖	d			16 03							16 19					16 33						16 49			
St Johns	d			16 05							16 21					16 35						16 51			
Lewisham 4 ⛴	d	16 02		16 08					16 19		16 24	16 26	16 32			16 38				16 49		16 54	16 56	17 02	
Blackheath 4	d	16 04		16 11					16 22			16 29	16 34			16 41				16 52			16 59	17 04	
Kidbrooke	d	16 07		16 14					16 25				16 37			16 44				16 55				17 07	
Eltham	d	16 11		16 17					16 28				16 41			16 47				16 58				17 11	
Falconwood	d	16 13		16 20					16 31				16 43			16 50				17 01				17 13	
Welling	d	16 16		16 22					16 33				16 46			16 52				17 03				17 16	
Bexleyheath	d	16 18		16 25					16 36				16 48			16 55				17 06				17 18	
Barnehurst 4	d	16 21		16 32					16 38				16 51			17 02				17 08				17 21	
Hither Green 4	d							16 14			16 29								16 44			16 59			
Lee	d							16 16			16 31								16 46			17 01			
Mottingham	d							16 19			16 34								16 49			17 04			
New Eltham	d							16 21			16 36								16 51			17 06			
Sidcup 4	d							16 25			16 40								16 55			17 10			
Albany Park	d							16 27			16 42								16 57			17 12			
Bexley	d							16 29			16 44								16 59			17 14			
Crayford	d							16 33			16 48								17 03			17 18			
Charlton 4	d		16 07			16 17				16 27	17a15	16 33		16 37			16 47				16 57	17a45	17 03		
Woolwich Dockyard	d		16 10			16 20				16 30				16 40			16 50				17 00				
Woolwich Arsenal 4 ⛴	d		16 13			16 23				16 33		16 39		16 43			16 53				17 03		17 09		
Plumstead	d		16 15			16 25				16 35				16 45			16 55				17 05				
Abbey Wood	d		16 18			16 28				16 38		16 43		16 48			16 58				17 08		17 13		
Belvedere	d		16 20			16 30				16 40				16 50			17 00				17 10				
Erith	d		16 23			16 33				16 43				16 53			17 03				17 13				
Slade Green 4	d		16a26	16a42		16 37				16a46				16a56		17a12	17 07				17a16				
Dartford 4	a	16 28				16 42		16 38	16 45			16 54	16 58				17 12		17 08	17 15			17 24	17 28	
	d							16 39				16 55							17 09				17 25		
Stone Crossing	d							16 43											17 13						
Greenhithe for Bluewater	d							16 45				17 00							17 15				17 30		
Swanscombe	d							16 48											17 18						
Northfleet	d							16 50											17 20						
Gravesend 4	d						16 51	16a55				17 07						17 18	17a25				17 37		
Higham	d											17 13											17 43		
Strood 4	d						17 01					17 18						17 28					17 48		
Maidstone West	d																								
Rochester 4	d						17 06					17 22						17 33					17 52		
Chatham 4	d						17 08					17 25						17 35					17 55		
Gillingham (Kent) 4	a						17 12					17 29						17 39					17 59		

London - Dartford and Gillingham

Network Diagram - see first Page of Table 200

		SE	SE	SE	SE	SE	SE	SE	SE	SE		SE	SE	SE	SE	SE	SE	SE	SE	SE		SE	SE	SE	SE
St Pancras Int'l 15 ⊖	d				17 25											17 55									
Stratford International ⊖ ⛴	d				17 32											18 02									
Ebbsfleet International	d				17 43											18 13									
London Charing Cross 4 ⊖	d					16 56	17 02			17 09							17 26	17 32				17 39			
London Waterloo (East) 4 ⊖	d					16 59	17 05			17 12							17 29	17 35				17 42			
London Cannon Street 4 ⊖	d	16 47	16 54	16 57				17 07	17 10				17 17	17 24	17 27				17 37	17 40				17 47	17 54
London Bridge 4 ⊖	d	16 51	16 58	17 01		17 04	17 10	17 11	17 14	17 17			17 21	17 28	17 31		17 34	17 40	17 41	17 44		17 47		17 51	17 58
Deptford	d	16 57		17 07				17 17					17 27		17 37				17 47					17 57	
Greenwich 4 ⛴	d	16 59		17 09				17 19					17 29		17 39				17 49					17 59	
Maze Hill	d	17 02		17 12				17 22					17 32		17 42				17 52					18 02	
Westcombe Park	d	17 04		17 14				17 24					17 34		17 44				17 54					18 04	
London Victoria 15 ⊖	d											17 09											17 39		
Denmark Hill 4	d											17 18											17 48		
Peckham Rye 4	d											17 21											17 51		
Nunhead 4	d											17 23											17 53		
New Cross 4 ⊖	d		17 03						17 19					17 33						17 49					18 03
St Johns	d		17 05						17 21					17 35						17 51					18 05
Lewisham 4 ⛴	d		17 08				17 19		17 24	17 26		17 32		17 38				17 49		17 54		17 56	18 02		18 08
Blackheath 4	d		17 11				17 22			17 29		17 34		17 41				17 52				17 59	18 04		18 11
Kidbrooke	d		17 14				17 25					17 37		17 44				17 55					18 07		18 14
Eltham	d		17 17				17 28					17 41		17 47				17 58					18 11		18 17
Falconwood	d		17 20				17 31					17 43		17 50				18 01					18 13		18 20
Welling	d		17 22				17 33					17 46		17 52				18 03					18 16		18 22
Bexleyheath	d		17 25				17 36					17 48		17 55				18 06					18 18		18 25
Barnehurst 4	d		17 32				17 38					17 51		18 02				18 08					18 21		18a27
Hither Green 4	d					17 14			17 29								17 44			17 59					
Lee	d					17 16			17 31								17 46			18 01					
Mottingham	d					17 19			17 34								17 49			18 04					
New Eltham	d					17 21			17 36								17 51			18 06					
Sidcup 4	d					17 25			17 40								17 55			18 10					
Albany Park	d					17 27			17 42								17 57			18 12					
Bexley	d					17 29			17 44								17 59			18 14					
Crayford	d					17 33			17 48								18 03			18 18					
Charlton 4	d	17 07		17 17				17 27	18a15	17 33			17 37		17 47				17 57	18a45		18 03		18 07	
Woolwich Dockyard	d	17 10		17 20				17 30					17 40		17 50				18 00					18 10	
Woolwich Arsenal 4 ⛴	d	17 13		17 23				17 33		17 39			17 43		17 53				18 03			18 09		18 13	
Plumstead	d	17 15		17 25				17 35					17 45		17 55				18 05					18 15	
Abbey Wood	d	17 18		17 28				17 38		17 43			17 48		17 58				18 08			18 13		18 18	
Belvedere	d	17 20		17 30				17 40					17 50		18 00				18 10					18 20	
Erith	d	17 23		17 33				17 43					17 53		18 03				18 13					18 23	
Slade Green 4	d	17a26	17a42	17 37				17a46					17a56	18a12	18 07				18a16					18a26	
Dartford 4	a			17 42		17 38	17 45			17 54		17 58			18 12		18 08	18 15				18 24	18 28		
	d					17 39				17 55							18 09					18 25			
Stone Crossing	d					17 43											18 13								
Greenhithe for Bluewater	d					17 45				18 00							18 15					18 30			
Swanscombe	d					17 48											18 18								
Northfleet	d					17 50											18 20								
Gravesend 4	d				17 48	17a55				18 07						18 18	18a25					18 37			
Higham	d									18 13												18 43			
Strood 4	d				17 58					18 18						18 28						18 48			
Maidstone West	d																								
Rochester 4	d				18 03					18 22						18 33						18 52			
Chatham 4	d				18 05					18 25						18 35						18 55			
Gillingham (Kent) 4	a				18 09					18 29						18 39						18 59			

Table 200

Saturdays

London - Dartford and Gillingham

Network Diagram - see first Page of Table 200

		SE	SE	SE	SE	SE		SE	SE	SE	SE	SE	SE	SE	SE	SE		SE	SE	SE	SE	SE	SE	SE	SE
St Pancras Int'l 15 ⊖	d		18 25											18 55											19 25
Stratford International ⊖ ⛴	d		18 32											19 02											19 32
Ebbsfleet International	d		18 43											19 13											19 43
London Charing Cross 4 ⊖	d			17 56	18 02				18 09						18 26	18 32				18 39					
London Waterloo (East) 4 ⊖	d			17 59	18 05				18 12						18 29	18 35				18 42					
London Cannon Street 4 ⊖	d	17 57				18 07		18 10			18 17	18 24	18 27					18 37	18 40			18 47	18 54	18 57	
London Bridge 4 ⊖	d	18 01		18 04	18 10	18 11		18 14	18 17		18 21	18 28	18 31		18 34	18 40		18 41	18 44	18 47		18 51	18 58	19 01	
Deptford	d	18 07				18 17					18 27		18 37					18 47				18 57		19 07	
Greenwich 4 ⛴	d	18 09				18 19					18 29		18 39					18 49				18 59		19 09	
Maze Hill	d	18 12				18 22					18 32		18 42					18 52				19 02		19 12	
Westcombe Park	d	18 14				18 24					18 34		18 44					18 54				19 04		19 14	
London Victoria 15 ⊖	d									18 09											18 39				
Denmark Hill 4	d									18 18											18 48				
Peckham Rye 4	d									18 21											18 51				
Nunhead 4	d									18 23											18 53				
New Cross 4 ⊖	d							18 19				18 33							18 49				19 03		
St Johns	d							18 21				18 35							18 51				19 05		
Lewisham 4 ⛴	d				18 19			18 24	18 26	18 32		18 38				18 49			18 54	18 56	19 02		19 08		
Blackheath 4	d				18 22				18 29	18 34		18 41				18 52				18 59	19 04		19 11		
Kidbrooke	d				18 25					18 37		18 44				18 55					19 07		19 14		
Eltham	d				18 28					18 41		18 47				18 58					19 11		19 17		
Falconwood	d				18 31					18 43		18 50				19 01					19 13		19 20		
Welling	d				18 33					18 46		18 52				19 03					19 16		19 22		
Bexleyheath	d				18 36					18 48		18 55				19 06					19 18		19 25		
Barnehurst 4	d				18 38					18 51		18a58				19 08					19 21		19a28		
Hither Green 4	d			18 14				18 29							18 44				18 59						
Lee	d			18 16				18 31							18 46				19 01						
Mottingham	d			18 19				18 34							18 49				19 04						
New Eltham	d			18 21				18 36							18 51				19 06						
Sidcup 4	d			18 25				18 40							18 55				19 10						
Albany Park	d			18 27				18 42							18 57				19 12						
Bexley	d			18 29				18 44							18 59				19 14						
Crayford	d			18 33				18 48							19 03				19 18						
Charlton 4	d	18 17				18 27		19a15	18 33		18 37		18 47					18 57	19a45	19 03		19 07		19 17	
Woolwich Dockyard	d	18 20				18 30					18 40		18 50					19 00				19 10		19 20	
Woolwich Arsenal 4 ⛴	d	18 23				18 33			18 39		18 43		18 53					19 03		19 09		19 13		19 23	
Plumstead	d	18 25				18 35					18 45		18 55					19 05				19 15		19 25	
Abbey Wood	d	18 28				18 38			18 43		18 48		18 58					19 08		19 13		19 18		19 28	
Belvedere	d	18 30				18 40					18 50		19 00					19 10				19 20		19 30	
Erith	d	18 33				18 43					18 53		19 03					19 13				19 23		19 33	
Slade Green 4	d	18 37				18a45					18a56		19 07					19a15				19a26		19 37	
Dartford 4	a	18 42		18 38	18 45				18 54	18 58			19 12		19 08	19 15				19 24	19 28			19 42	
	d			18 39					18 55						19 09					19 25					
Stone Crossing	d			18 43											19 13										
Greenhithe for Bluewater	d			18 45					19 00						19 15					19 30					
Swanscombe	d			18 48											19 18										
Northfleet	d			18 50											19 20										
Gravesend 4	d		18 48	18a55					19 07					19 18	19a25					19 37					19 48
Higham	d								19 13											19 43					
Strood 4	d		18 58						19 18					19 28						19 48					19 58
Maidstone West	d																								
Rochester 4	d		19 03						19 22					19 33						19 52					20 03
Chatham 4	d		19 05						19 25					19 35						19 55					20 05
Gillingham (Kent) 4	a		19 09						19 29					19 39						19 59					20 09

Table 200

Saturdays

London - Dartford and Gillingham

Network Diagram - see first Page of Table 200

	SE		SE	SE	SE	SE	SE	SE	SE	SE	SE		SE	SE	SE	SE	SE	SE	SE	SE	SE		SE	SE
St Pancras Int'l 15 ⊖ d										19 55							20 25							20 55
Stratford International ⊖ ⛴ d										20 02							20 32							21 02
Ebbsfleet International d										20 13							20 43							21 13
London Charing Cross 4 ⊖ d	18 56		19 02			19 09					19 26		19 32	19 39				19 52	19 56	20 02	20 09			
London Waterloo (East) 4 ⊖ d	18 59		19 05			19 12					19 29		19 35	19 42				19 55	19 59	20 05	20 12			
London Cannon Street 4 ⊖ d				19 07	19 10			19 24	19 27															
London Bridge 4 ⊖ d	19 04		19 10	19 11	19 14	19 17		19 28	19 31		19 34		19 40	19 47		19 50		20 00	20 05	20 10	20 17		20 20	
Deptford d				19 17					19 37							19 56			20 11				20 26	
Greenwich 4 ⛴ d				19 19					19 39							19 58			20 13				20 28	
Maze Hill d				19 22					19 42							20 01			20 16				20 31	
Westcombe Park d				19 24					19 44							20 03			20 18				20 33	
London Victoria 15 ⊖ d							19 09								19 39									
Denmark Hill 4 d							19 18								19 48									
Peckham Rye 4 d							19 21								19 51									
Nunhead 4 d							19 23								19 53									
New Cross 4 ⊖ d					19 19			19 33					19 45					20 05		20 15				
St Johns d					19 21			19 35																
Lewisham 4 ⛴ d			19 19		19 24	19 26	19 32	19 38					19 49	19 56	20 02			20 09		20 19	20 26			
Blackheath 4 d			19 22			19 29	19 34	19 41					19 52	19 59	20 04					20 22	20 29			
Kidbrooke d			19 25				19 37	19 44					19 55		20 07					20 25				
Eltham d			19 28				19 41	19 47					19 58		20 11					20 28				
Falconwood d			19 31				19 43	19 50					20 01		20 13					20 31				
Welling d			19 33				19 46	19 52					20 03		20 16					20 33				
Bexleyheath d			19 36				19 48	19 55					20 06		20 18					20 36				
Barnehurst 4 d			19 38				19 51	19a58					20 08		20 21					20 38				
Hither Green 4 d	19 14				19 29						19 44							20 14						
Lee d	19 16				19 31						19 46							20 16						
Mottingham d	19 19				19 34						19 49							20 19						
New Eltham d	19 21				19 36						19 51							20 21						
Sidcup 4 d	19 25				19 40						19 55							20 25						
Albany Park d	19 27				19 42						19 57							20 27						
Bexley d	19 29				19 44						19 59							20 29						
Crayford d	19 33				19 48						20 03							20 33						
Charlton 4 d				19 27	20a15	19 33			19 47					20 03		20 06			20 20		20 33		20 36	
Woolwich Dockyard d				19 30					19 50							20 09			20 23				20 39	
Woolwich Arsenal 4 ⛴ d				19 33		19 39			19 53					20 09		20 12			20 26		20 39		20 42	
Plumstead d				19 35					19 55							20 14			20 28				20 44	
Abbey Wood d				19 38		19 43			19 58					20 13		20 17			20 31		20 43		20 47	
Belvedere d				19 40					20 00							20 20			20 34				20 50	
Erith d				19 43					20 03							20 22			20 36				20 52	
Slade Green 4 d				19 46					20 07							20 26			20 39				20 56	
Dartford 4 a	19 38		19 45	19 52		19 54	19 58		20 12		20 08		20 15	20 24	20 28	20 31		20 38	20 44	20 46	20 54		21 01	
d	19 39					19 55					20 09			20 25				20 39			20 55			
Stone Crossing d	19 43										20 13							20 43						
Greenhithe for Bluewater d	19 45					20 00					20 15			20 30				20 45			21 00			
Swanscombe d	19 48										20 18							20 48						
Northfleet d	19 50										20 20							20 50						
Gravesend 4 d	19a55					20 07				20 18	20a25			20 37			20 48	20a55			21 07			21 18
Higham d						20 13								20 43							21 13			
Strood 4 d						20 18				20 28				20 48			20 58				21 18			21 28
Maidstone West d																								
Rochester 4 d						20 22				20 33				20 52			21 03				21 22			21 33
Chatham 4 d						20 25				20 35				20 55			21 05				21 25			21 35
Gillingham (Kent) 4 a						20 29				20 39				20 59			21 09				21 29			21 39

Table 200

London - Dartford and Gillingham

Network Diagram - see first Page of Table 200

		SE	SE	SE	SE	SE	SE	SE		SE	SE	SE	SE	SE	SE	SE	SE	SE		SE	SE	SE	SE	SE	SE
St Pancras Int'l 15 ⊖	d						21 25						21 55									22 25			
Stratford International ⊖ ⛴	d						21 32						22 02									22 32			
Ebbsfleet International	d						21 43						22 13									22 43			
London Charing Cross 4 ⊖	d	20 22	20 26	20 32	20 39			20 52		20 56	21 02	21 09		21 22	21 26	21 32	21 39	21 52		21 56	22 02		22 09	22 22	22 26
London Waterloo (East) 4 ⊖	d	20 25	20 29	20 35	20 42			20 55		20 59	21 05	21 12		21 25	21 29	21 35	21 42	21 55		21 59	22 05		22 12	22 25	22 29
London Cannon Street 4 ⊖	d																								
London Bridge 4 ⊖	d	20 30	20 35	20 40	20 47	20 50		21 00		21 05	21 10	21 17		21 30	21 35	21 40	21 47	22 00		22 05	22 10		22 17	22 30	22 35
Deptford	d		20 41			20 56				21 11					21 41					22 11					22 41
Greenwich 4 ⛴	d		20 43			20 58				21 13					21 43					22 13					22 43
Maze Hill	d		20 46			21 01				21 16					21 46					22 16					22 46
Westcombe Park	d		20 48			21 03				21 18					21 48					22 18					22 48
London Victoria 15 ⊖	d																								
Denmark Hill 4	d																								
Peckham Rye 4	d																								
Nunhead 4	d																								
New Cross 4 ⊖	d	20 35		20 45				21 05			21 15			21 35		21 45		22 05			22 15			22 35	
St Johns	d																								
Lewisham 4 ⛴	d	20 39		20 49	20 56			21 09			21 19	21 26		21 39		21 49	21 56	22 09			22 19		22 26	22 39	
Blackheath 4	d			20 52	20 59						21 22	21 29				21 52	21 59				22 22		22 29		
Kidbrooke	d			20 55							21 25					21 55					22 25				
Eltham	d			20 58							21 28					21 58					22 28				
Falconwood	d			21 01							21 31					22 01					22 31				
Welling	d			21 03							21 33					22 03					22 33				
Bexleyheath	d			21 06							21 36					22 06					22 36				
Barnehurst 4	d			21 08							21 38					22 08					22 38				
Hither Green 4	d	20 44						21 14						21 44				22 14						22 44	
Lee	d	20 46						21 16						21 46				22 16						22 46	
Mottingham	d	20 49						21 19						21 49				22 19						22 49	
New Eltham	d	20 51						21 21						21 51				22 21						22 51	
Sidcup 4	d	20 55						21 25						21 55				22 25						22 55	
Albany Park	d	20 57						21 27						21 57				22 27						22 57	
Bexley	d	20 59						21 29						21 59				22 29						22 59	
Crayford	d	21 03						21 33						22 03				22 33						23 03	
Charlton 4	d		20 50		21 03	21 06				21 20		21 33			21 50		22 03			22 20			22 33		22 50
Woolwich Dockyard	d		20 53			21 09				21 23					21 53					22 23					22 53
Woolwich Arsenal 4 ⛴	d		20 56		21 09	21 12				21 26		21 39			21 56		22 09			22 26			22 39		22 56
Plumstead	d		20 58			21 14				21 28					21 58					22 28					22 58
Abbey Wood	d		21 01		21 13	21 17				21 31		21 43			22 01		22 13			22 31			22 43		23 01
Belvedere	d		21 04			21 20				21 34					22 04					22 34					23 04
Erith	d		21 06			21 22				21 36					22 06					22 36					23 06
Slade Green 4	d		21 09			21 26				21 39					22 09					22 39					23 09
Dartford 4	a	21 08	21 14	21 16	21 24	21 31		21 38		21 44	21 46	21 54		22 08	22 14	22 16	22 24	22 38		22 44	22 46		22 54	23 08	23 14
	d	21 09			21 25			21 39				21 55		22 09			22 25						22 55		
Stone Crossing	d	21 13						21 43						22 13			22 29						22 59		
Greenhithe for Bluewater	d	21 15			21 30			21 45				22 00		22 15			22 31						23 01		
Swanscombe	d	21 18						21 48						22 18			22 34						23 04		
Northfleet	d	21 20						21 50						22 20			22 36						23 06		
Gravesend 4	d	21a25			21 37		21 48	21a55				22 07	22 18	22a25			22 40					22 48	23 10		
Higham	d				21 43							22 13					22 46						23 16		
Strood 4	d				21 48		21 58					22 18	22 28				22 52					22 58	23 22		
Maidstone West	d																								
Rochester 4	d				21 52		22 03					22 22	22 33				22 56					23 03	23 26		
Chatham 4	d				21 55		22 05					22 25	22 35				22 58					23 05	23 28		
Gillingham (Kent) 4	a				21 59		22 09					22 29	22 39				23 03					23 09	23 33		

Table 200

Saturdays

London - Dartford and Gillingham

Network Diagram - see first Page of Table 200

		SE	SE	SE		SE	SE	SE	SE	SE	SE	SE	SE	SE		SE	SE
St Pancras Int'l 15 ⊖	d		22 55						23 25					23 55			
Stratford International ⊖ ⛴	d		23 02						23 32					00 02			
Ebbsfleet International	d		23 13						23 43					00 13			
London Charing Cross 4 ⊖	d	22 32		22 39		22 52	22 56	23 02		23 09	23 22	23 26	23 32			23 39	23 56
London Waterloo (East) 4 ⊖	d	22 35		22 42		22 55	22 59	23 05		23 12	23 25	23 29	23 35			23 42	23 59
London Cannon Street 4 ⊖	d																
London Bridge 4 ⊖	d	22 40		22 47		23 00	23 05	23 10		23 17	23 30	23 35	23 40			23 47	00 05
Deptford	d						23 11					23 41					00 11
Greenwich 4 ⛴	d						23 13					23 43					00 13
Maze Hill	d						23 16					23 46					00 16
Westcombe Park	d						23 18					23 48					00 18
London Victoria 15 ⊖	d																
Denmark Hill 4	d																
Peckham Rye 4	d																
Nunhead 4	d																
New Cross 4 ⊖	d	22 45				23 05		23 15			23 35		23 45				
St Johns	d																
Lewisham 4 ⛴	d	22 49		22 56		23 09		23 19		23 26	23 39		23 49			23 56	
Blackheath 4	d	22 52		22 59				23 22		23 29			23 52			23 58	
Kidbrooke	d	22 55						23 25					23 55				
Eltham	d	22 58						23 28					23 58				
Falconwood	d	23 01						23 31					00 01				
Welling	d	23 03						23 33					00 03				
Bexleyheath	d	23 06						23 36					00 06				
Barnehurst 4	d	23 08						23 38					00 08				
Hither Green 4	d					23 14					23 44						
Lee	d					23 16					23 46						
Mottingham	d					23 19					23 49						
New Eltham	d					23 21					23 51						
Sidcup 4	d					23 25					23 55						
Albany Park	d					23 27					23 57						
Bexley	d					23 29					23 59						
Crayford	d					23 33					00 03						
Charlton 4	d			23 03			23 20			23 33		23 50				00 03	00 20
Woolwich Dockyard	d						23 23					23 53					00 23
Woolwich Arsenal 4 ⛴	d			23 09			23 26			23 39		23 56				00 09	00 26
Plumstead	d						23 28					23 58					00 28
Abbey Wood	d			23 13			23 31			23 43		00 01				00 13	00 31
Belvedere	d						23 34					00 04					00 34
Erith	d						23 36					00 06					00 36
Slade Green 4	d						23 39					00 09					00 39
Dartford 4	a	23 16		23 24		23 38	23 44	23 46		23 54	00 08	00 14	00 16			00 24	00 44
	d			23 25						23 55						00 25	
Stone Crossing	d			23 29						23 58						00 29	
Greenhithe for Bluewater	d			23 31						23 59						00 31	
Swanscombe	d			23 34						00 04						00 34	
Northfleet	d			23 36						00 06						00 36	
Gravesend 4	d		23 18	23 40					23 48	00 10				00 18		00 40	
Higham	d			23 46						00 16						00 46	
Strood 4	d		23 28	23 52					23 58	00 22				00 28		00 52	
Maidstone West	d																
Rochester 4	d		23 33	23 56					00 03	00 26				00 33		00 56	
Chatham 4	d		23 35	23 58					00 05	00 28				00 35		00 58	
Gillingham (Kent) 4	a		23 39	00 03					00 09	00 33				00 39		01 03	

Table 200

Sundays

London - Dartford and Gillingham

Network Diagram - see first Page of Table 200

		SE A	SE A	SE A	SE A	SE A	SE A	SE A	SE A	SE A
St Pancras Int'l 15 ⊖	d		23p25					23p55		
Stratford International ⊖ ⛴	d		23p32					00 02		
Ebbsfleet International	d		23p43					00 13		
London Charing Cross 4 ⊖	d	22p39		23p09	23p22	23p26	23p32		23p39	23p56
London Waterloo (East) 4 ⊖	d	22p42		23p12	23p25	23p29	23p35		23p42	23p59
London Cannon Street 4 ⊖	d									
London Bridge 4 ⊖	d	22p47		23p17	23p30	23p35	23p40		23p47	00 05
Deptford	d					23p41				00 11
Greenwich 4 ⛴	d					23p43				00 13
Maze Hill	d					23p46				00 16
Westcombe Park	d					23p48				00 18
London Victoria 15 ⊖	d									
Denmark Hill 4	d									
Peckham Rye 4	d									
Nunhead 4	d									
New Cross 4 ⊖	d				23p35		23p45			
St Johns	d									
Lewisham 4 ⛴	d	22p56		23p26	23p39		23p49		23p56	
Blackheath 4	d	22p59		23p29			23p52		23p58	
Kidbrooke	d						23p55			
Eltham	d						23p58			
Falconwood	d						00 01			
Welling	d						00 03			
Bexleyheath	d						00 06			
Barnehurst 4	d						00 08			
Hither Green 4	d				23p44					
Lee	d				23p46					
Mottingham	d				23p49					
New Eltham	d				23p51					
Sidcup 4	d				23p55					
Albany Park	d				23p57					
Bexley	d				23p59					
Crayford	d				00 03					
Charlton 4	d	23p03		23p33		23p50			00 03	00 20
Woolwich Dockyard	d					23p53				00 23
Woolwich Arsenal 4 ⛴	d	23p09		23p39		23p56			00 09	00 26
Plumstead	d					23p58				00 28
Abbey Wood	d	23p13		23p43		00 01			00 13	00 31
Belvedere	d					00 04				00 34
Erith	d					00 06				00 36
Slade Green 4	d					00 09				00 39
Dartford 4	a	23p24		23p54	00 08	00 14	00 16		00 24	00 44
	d	23p25		23p55					00 25	
Stone Crossing	d	23p29		23p58					00 29	
Greenhithe for Bluewater	d	23p31		23p59					00 31	
Swanscombe	d	23p34		00 04					00 34	
Northfleet	d	23p36		00 06					00 36	
Gravesend 4	d	23p40	23p48	00 10				00 18	00 40	
Higham	d	23p46		00 16					00 46	
Strood 4	d	23p52	23p58	00 22				00 28	00 52	
Maidstone West	d									
Rochester 4	d	23p56	00 03	00 26				00 33	00 56	
Chatham 4	d	23p58	00 05	00 28				00 35	00 58	
Gillingham (Kent) 4	a	00 03	00 09	00 33				00 39	01 03	

		SE	SE	SE	SE	SE	SE	SE	SE	SE	SE	SE	SE	SE
St Pancras Int'l 15 ⊖	d												08 52	
Stratford International ⊖ ⛴	d												08 58	
Ebbsfleet International	d												09 13	
London Charing Cross 4 ⊖	d	00 02	00 10	00 18		07 30		07 50	07 56	08 00	08 10	08 20		08 26
London Waterloo (East) 4 ⊖	d	00 05	00 13	00 21		07 33		07 53	07 59	08 03	08 13	08 23		08 29
London Cannon Street 4 ⊖	d													
London Bridge 4 ⊖	d	00 10	00 18	00 26		07 38		07 58	08 04	08 08	08 18	08 28		08 34
Deptford	d					07 44				08 14				
Greenwich 4 ⛴	d					07 46				08 16				
Maze Hill	d					07 49				08 19				
Westcombe Park	d					07 51				08 21				
London Victoria 15 ⊖	d													
Denmark Hill 4	d													
Peckham Rye 4	d													
Nunhead 4	d													
New Cross 4 ⊖	d	00 15	00 23	00 31				08 04				08 34		
St Johns	d													
Lewisham 4 ⛴	d	00 19	00 27	00 35				08 08	08 12		08 27	08 38		08 42
Blackheath 4	d	00 22		00 38				08 10			08 30	08 40		
Kidbrooke	d	00 25						08 13				08 43		
Eltham	d	00 28						08 17				08 47		
Falconwood	d	00 31						08 19				08 49		
Welling	d	00 33						08 22				08 52		
Bexleyheath	d	00 36						08 24				08 54		
Barnehurst 4	d	00 38						08 27				08 57		
Hither Green 4	d		00 32						08 16					08 46
Lee	d		00 34						08 18					08 48
Mottingham	d		00 37						08 21					08 51
New Eltham	d		00 39						08 23					08 53
Sidcup 4	d		00 43						08 27					08 57
Albany Park	d		00 45						08 29					08 59
Bexley	d		00 47						08 31					09 01
Crayford	d		00 51						08 34					09 04
Charlton 4	d			00 42		07 54				08 24	08 34			
Woolwich Dockyard	d					07 57				08 27				
Woolwich Arsenal 4 ⛴	d			00 47		08 00				08 30	08 40			
Plumstead	d			00 49		08 02				08 32				
Abbey Wood	d			00 53		08 05				08 35	08 44			
Belvedere	d			00 55		08 07				08 37				
Erith	d			00 58		08 10				08 40				
Slade Green 4	d			01 00		08 14				08 44				
Dartford 4	a	00 46	00 56	01 05		08 19		08 33	08 39	08 49	08 54	09 03		09 09
	d			01 06	07 55		08 25		08 40		08 55			09 10
Stone Crossing	d				07 59		08 29		08 44					09 14
Greenhithe for Bluewater	d			01 10	08 01		08 31		08 46		09 00			09 16
Swanscombe	d				08 04		08 34		08 49					09 19
Northfleet	d				08 06		08 36		08 51					09 21
Gravesend 4	d			01 17	08 10		08 40		08a55		09 07		09 18	09a25
Higham	d			01 23	08 16		08 46				09 13			
Strood 4	d			01 29	08 22		08 52				09 18		09 28	
Maidstone West	d													
Rochester 4	d			01 33	08 26		08 56				09 23		09 33	
Chatham 4	d			01 35	08 28		08 58				09 26		09 35	
Gillingham (Kent) 4	a			01 41	08 33		09 03				09 30		09 39	

A not 11 December

Table 200

Sundays

London - Dartford and Gillingham

Network Diagram - see first Page of Table 200

Station		SE	SE	SE	SE	SE	SE	SE	SE	SE	SE	SE	SE	SE	SE	SE	SE	SE	SE	SE	SE	SE	SE
St Pancras Int'l 15 ⊖	d				09 25						09 55						10 28						10 52
Stratford International ⊖ ⛴	d				09 32						10 02						10 35						10 58
Ebbsfleet International	d				09 43						10 13						10 46						11 14
London Charing Cross 4 ⊖	d	08 30	08 40	08 50		08 56	09 00	09 10		09 20		09 26	09 30	09 40		09 50		09 56	10 00	10 10		10 20	
London Waterloo (East) 4 ⊖	d	08 33	08 43	08 53		08 59	09 03	09 13		09 23		09 29	09 33	09 43		09 53		09 59	10 03	10 13		10 23	
London Cannon Street 4 ⊖	d																						
London Bridge 4 ⊖	d	08 38	08 48	08 58		09 04	09 08	09 18	09 23	09 28		09 34	09 38	09 48	09 53	09 58		10 04	10 08	10 18	10 23	10 28	
Deptford	d	08 44					09 14		09 29				09 44		09 59				10 14		10 29		
Greenwich 4 ⛴	d	08 46					09 16		09 31				09 46		10 01				10 16		10 31		
Maze Hill	d	08 49					09 19		09 34				09 49		10 04				10 19		10 34		
Westcombe Park	d	08 51					09 21		09 36				09 51		10 06				10 21		10 36		
London Victoria 15 ⊖	d																						
Denmark Hill 4	d																						
Peckham Rye 4	d																						
Nunhead 4	d																						
New Cross 4 ⊖	d			09 04						09 34						10 04						10 34	
St Johns	d																						
Lewisham 4 ⛴	d		08 57	09 08		09 12		09 27		09 38		09 42		09 57		10 08		10 12		10 27		10 38	
Blackheath 4	d		09 00	09 10				09 30		09 40				10 00		10 10				10 30		10 40	
Kidbrooke	d			09 13						09 43						10 13						10 43	
Eltham	d			09 17						09 47						10 17						10 47	
Falconwood	d			09 19						09 49						10 19						10 49	
Welling	d			09 22						09 52						10 22						10 52	
Bexleyheath	d			09 24						09 54						10 24						10 54	
Barnehurst 4	d			09 27						09 57						10 27						10 57	
Hither Green 4	d					09 16						09 46						10 16					
Lee	d					09 18						09 48						10 18					
Mottingham	d					09 21						09 51						10 21					
New Eltham	d					09 23						09 53						10 23					
Sidcup 4	d					09 27						09 57						10 27					
Albany Park	d					09 29						09 59						10 29					
Bexley	d					09 31						10 01						10 31					
Crayford	d					09 34						10 04						10 34					
Charlton 4	d	08 54	09 04				09 24	09 34	09 39				09 54	10 04	10 09				10 24	10 34	10 39		
Woolwich Dockyard	d	08 57					09 27		09 42				09 57		10 12				10 27		10 42		
Woolwich Arsenal 4 ⛴	d	09 00	09 10				09 30	09 40	09 45				10 00	10 10	10 15				10 30	10 40	10 45		
Plumstead	d	09 02					09 32		09a47				10 02		10a17				10 32		10a47		
Abbey Wood	d	09 05	09 14				09 35	09 44					10 05	10 14					10 35	10 44			
Belvedere	d	09 07					09 37						10 07						10 37				
Erith	d	09 10					09 40						10 10						10 40				
Slade Green 4	d	09 14					09 44						10 14						10 44				
Dartford 4	a	09 19	09 24	09 33		09 39	09 49	09 54		10 03		10 09	10 19	10 24		10 33		10 39	10 49	10 54		11 03	
	d		09 25			09 40		09 55				10 10		10 25				10 40		10 55			
Stone Crossing	d					09 44						10 14						10 44					
Greenhithe for Bluewater	d		09 30			09 46		10 00				10 16		10 30				10 46		11 00			
Swanscombe	d					09 49						10 19						10 49					
Northfleet	d					09 51						10 21						10 51					
Gravesend 4	d		09 37		09 48	09a55		10 07			10 18	10a25		10 37			10 51	10a55		11 07			11 18
Higham	d		09 43					10 13						10 43						11 13			
Strood 4	d		09 48		09 58			10 18			10 28			10 48			11 01			11 18			11 28
Maidstone West	d																						
Rochester 4	d		09 52		10 03			10 23			10 33			10 52			11 06			11 23			11 33
Chatham 4	d		09 55		10 05			10 26			10 35			10 55			11 08			11 26			11 35
Gillingham (Kent) 4	a		10 02		10 09			10 30			10 39			11 02			11 12			11 30			11 39

Table 200

Sundays

London - Dartford and Gillingham

Network Diagram - see first Page of Table 200

		SE		SE	SE	SE	SE	SE	SE	SE	SE	SE		SE	SE	SE	SE	SE	SE	SE	SE	SE		SE	SE
St Pancras Int'l 15 ⊖	d							11 25							11 55						12 28				
Stratford International ⊖ ⛴	d							11 32							12 02						12 35				
Ebbsfleet International	d							11 43							12 13						12 46				
London Charing Cross 4 ⊖	d	10 26		10 30	10 40		10 50		10 56	11 00	11 10			11 20		11 26	11 30	11 40		11 50		11 56		12 00	12 10
London Waterloo (East) 4 ⊖	d	10 29		10 33	10 43		10 53		10 59	11 03	11 13			11 23		11 29	11 33	11 43		11 53		11 59		12 03	12 13
London Cannon Street 4 ⊖	d																								
London Bridge 4 ⊖	d	10 34		10 38	10 48	10 53	10 58		11 04	11 08	11 18	11 23		11 28		11 34	11 38	11 48	11 53	11 58		12 04		12 08	12 18
Deptford	d			10 44		10 59				11 14		11 29					11 44		11 59					12 14	
Greenwich 4 ⛴	d			10 46		11 01				11 16		11 31					11 46		12 01					12 16	
Maze Hill	d			10 49		11 04				11 19		11 34					11 49		12 04					12 19	
Westcombe Park	d			10 51		11 06				11 21		11 36					11 51		12 06					12 21	
London Victoria 15 ⊖	d																								
Denmark Hill 4	d																								
Peckham Rye 4	d																								
Nunhead 4	d																								
New Cross 4 ⊖	d						11 04							11 34						12 04					
St Johns	d																								
Lewisham 4 ⛴	d	10 42			10 57		11 08		11 12		11 27			11 38		11 42		11 57		12 08		12 12			12 27
Blackheath 4	d				11 00		11 10				11 30			11 40				12 00		12 10					12 30
Kidbrooke	d						11 13							11 43						12 13					
Eltham	d						11 17							11 47						12 17					
Falconwood	d						11 19							11 49						12 19					
Welling	d						11 22							11 52						12 22					
Bexleyheath	d						11 24							11 54						12 24					
Barnehurst 4	d						11 27							11 57						12 27					
Hither Green 4	d	10 46							11 16							11 46						12 16			
Lee	d	10 48							11 18							11 48						12 18			
Mottingham	d	10 51							11 21							11 51						12 21			
New Eltham	d	10 53							11 23							11 53						12 23			
Sidcup 4	d	10 57							11 27							11 57						12 27			
Albany Park	d	10 59							11 29							11 59						12 29			
Bexley	d	11 01							11 31							12 01						12 31			
Crayford	d	11 04							11 34							12 04						12 34			
Charlton 4	d			10 54	11 04	11 09				11 24	11 34	11 39					11 54	12 04	12 09					12 24	12 34
Woolwich Dockyard	d			10 57		11 12				11 27		11 42					11 57		12 12					12 27	
Woolwich Arsenal 4 ⛴	d			11 00	11 10	11 15				11 30	11 40	11 45					12 00	12 10	12 15					12 30	12 40
Plumstead	d			11 02		11a17				11 32		11a47					12 02		12a17					12 32	
Abbey Wood	d			11 05	11 14					11 35	11 44						12 05	12 14						12 35	12 44
Belvedere	d			11 07						11 37							12 07							12 37	
Erith	d			11 10						11 40							12 10							12 40	
Slade Green 4	d			11 14						11 44							12 14							12 44	
Dartford 4	a	11 09		11 19	11 24		11 33		11 39	11 49	11 54			12 03		12 09	12 19	12 24		12 33		12 39		12 49	12 54
	d	11 10			11 25				11 40		11 55					12 10		12 25				12 40			12 55
Stone Crossing	d	11 14							11 44							12 14						12 44			
Greenhithe for Bluewater	d	11 16			11 30				11 46		12 00					12 16		12 30				12 46			13 00
Swanscombe	d	11 19							11 49							12 19						12 49			
Northfleet	d	11 21							11 51							12 21						12 51			
Gravesend 4	d	11a25			11 37			11 48	11a55		12 07				12 18	12a25		12 37			12 51	12a55			13 07
Higham	d				11 43						12 13							12 43							13 13
Strood 4	d				11 48			11 58			12 18				12 28			12 48			13 01				13 18
Maidstone West	d																								
Rochester 4	d				11 52			12 03			12 23				12 33			12 52			13 06				13 23
Chatham 4	d				11 55			12 05			12 26				12 35			12 55			13 08				13 26
Gillingham (Kent) 4	a				12 02			12 09			12 30				12 39			13 02			13 12				13 30

Table 200

Sundays

London - Dartford and Gillingham

Network Diagram - see first Page of Table 200

		SE	SE	SE	SE	SE	SE	SE		SE	SE	SE	SE	SE	SE	SE	SE	SE		SE	SE	SE	SE	SE	SE
St Pancras Int'l 15 ⊖	d			12 52							13 25						14 02							14 25	
Stratford International ⊖ ⛴	d			12 58							13 32						14 02							14 32	
Ebbsfleet International	d			13 13							13 43						14 13							14 43	
London Charing Cross 4 ⊖	d		12 20		12 26	12 30	12 40			12 50		12 56	13 00	13 10		13 20		13 26		13 30	13 40		13 50		13 56
London Waterloo (East) 4 ⊖	d		12 23		12 29	12 33	12 43			12 53		12 59	13 03	13 13		13 23		13 29		13 33	13 43		13 53		13 59
London Cannon Street 4 ⊖	d																								
London Bridge 4 ⊖	d	12 23	12 28		12 34	12 38	12 48	12 53		12 58		13 04	13 08	13 18	13 23	13 28		13 34		13 38	13 48	13 53	13 58		14 04
Deptford	d	12 29				12 44		12 59					13 14		13 29					13 44		13 59			
Greenwich 4 ⛴	d	12 31				12 46		13 01					13 16		13 31					13 46		14 01			
Maze Hill	d	12 34				12 49		13 04					13 19		13 34					13 49		14 04			
Westcombe Park	d	12 36				12 51		13 06					13 21		13 36					13 51		14 06			
London Victoria 15 ⊖	d																								
Denmark Hill 4	d																								
Peckham Rye 4	d																								
Nunhead 4	d																								
New Cross 4 ⊖	d		12 34							13 04						13 34							14 04		
St Johns	d																								
Lewisham 4 ⛴	d		12 38		12 42		12 57			13 08		13 12		13 27		13 38		13 42			13 57		14 08		14 12
Blackheath 4	d		12 40				13 00			13 10				13 30		13 40					14 00		14 10		
Kidbrooke	d		12 43							13 13						13 43							14 13		
Eltham	d		12 47							13 17						13 47							14 17		
Falconwood	d		12 49							13 19						13 49							14 19		
Welling	d		12 52							13 22						13 52							14 22		
Bexleyheath	d		12 54							13 24						13 54							14 24		
Barnehurst 4	d		12 57							13 27						13 57							14 27		
Hither Green 4	d				12 46							13 16						13 46							14 16
Lee	d				12 48							13 18						13 48							14 18
Mottingham	d				12 51							13 21						13 51							14 21
New Eltham	d				12 53							13 23						13 53							14 23
Sidcup 4	d				12 57							13 27						13 57							14 27
Albany Park	d				12 59							13 29						13 59							14 29
Bexley	d				13 01							13 31						14 01							14 31
Crayford	d				13 04							13 34						14 04							14 34
Charlton 4	d	12 39				12 54	13 04	13 09					13 24	13 34	13 39					13 54	14 04	14 09			
Woolwich Dockyard	d	12 42				12 57		13 12					13 27		13 42					13 57		14 12			
Woolwich Arsenal 4 ⛴	d	12 45				13 00	13 10	13 15					13 30	13 40	13 45					14 00	14 10	14 15			
Plumstead	d	12a47				13 02		13a17					13 32		13a47					14 02		14a17			
Abbey Wood	d					13 05	13 14						13 35	13 44						14 05	14 14				
Belvedere	d					13 07							13 37							14 07					
Erith	d					13 10							13 40							14 10					
Slade Green 4	d					13 14							13 44							14 14					
Dartford 4	a		13 03		13 09	13 19	13 24			13 33		13 39	13 49	13 54		14 03		14 09		14 19	14 24		14 33		14 39
	d				13 10		13 25					13 40		13 55				14 10			14 25				14 40
Stone Crossing	d				13 14							13 44						14 14							14 44
Greenhithe for Bluewater	d				13 16		13 30					13 46		14 00				14 16			14 30				14 46
Swanscombe	d				13 19							13 49						14 19							14 49
Northfleet	d				13 21							13 51						14 21							14 51
Gravesend 4	d			13 18	13a25		13 37				13 48	13a55		14 07			14 18	14a25			14 37			14 48	14a55
Higham	d						13 43							14 13							14 43				
Strood 4	d			13 28			13 48				13 58			14 18			14 28				14 48			14 58	
Maidstone West	d																								
Rochester 4	d			13 33			13 52				14 03			14 23			14 33				14 52			15 03	
Chatham 4	d			13 35			13 55				14 05			14 26			14 35				14 55			15 05	
Gillingham (Kent) 4	a			13 39			14 02				14 09			14 30			14 39				15 02			15 09	

Table 200

Sundays

London - Dartford and Gillingham

Network Diagram - see first Page of Table 200

		SE	SE	SE	SE	SE	SE	SE	SE	SE	SE	SE	SE	SE	SE	SE	SE	SE	SE	SE	SE	SE
St Pancras Int'l 15 ⊖	d					14 55						15 25						15 55				
Stratford International ⊖	d					15 02						15 32						16 02				
Ebbsfleet International	d					15 13						15 43						16 13				
London Charing Cross 4 ⊖	d	14 00	14 10		14 20		14 26	14 30	14 40		14 50		14 56	15 00	15 10		15 20		15 26	15 30	15 40	
London Waterloo (East) 4 ⊖	d	14 03	14 13		14 23		14 29	14 33	14 43		14 53		14 59	15 03	15 13		15 23		15 29	15 33	15 43	
London Cannon Street 4 ⊖	d																					
London Bridge 4 ⊖	d	14 08	14 18	14 23	14 28		14 34	14 38	14 48	14 53	14 58		15 04	15 08	15 18	15 23	15 28		15 34	15 38	15 48	15 53
Deptford	d	14 14		14 29				14 44		14 59				15 14		15 29				15 44		15 59
Greenwich 4	d	14 16		14 31				14 46		15 01				15 16		15 31				15 46		16 01
Maze Hill	d	14 19		14 34				14 49		15 04				15 19		15 34				15 49		16 04
Westcombe Park	d	14 21		14 36				14 51		15 06				15 21		15 36				15 51		16 06
London Victoria 15 ⊖	d																					
Denmark Hill 4	d																					
Peckham Rye 4	d																					
Nunhead 4	d																					
New Cross 4 ⊖	d				14 34						15 04						15 34					
St Johns	d																					
Lewisham 4	d		14 27		14 38		14 42		14 57		15 08		15 12		15 27		15 38		15 42		15 57	
Blackheath 4	d		14 30		14 40				15 00		15 10				15 30		15 40				16 00	
Kidbrooke	d				14 43						15 13						15 43					
Eltham	d				14 47						15 17						15 47					
Falconwood	d				14 49						15 19						15 49					
Welling	d				14 52						15 22						15 52					
Bexleyheath	d				14 54						15 24						15 54					
Barnehurst 4	d				14 57						15 27						15 57					
Hither Green 4	d						14 46						15 16						15 46			
Lee	d						14 48						15 18						15 48			
Mottingham	d						14 51						15 21						15 51			
New Eltham	d						14 53						15 23						15 53			
Sidcup 4	d						14 57						15 27						15 57			
Albany Park	d						14 59						15 29						15 59			
Bexley	d						15 01						15 31						16 01			
Crayford	d						15 04						15 34						16 04			
Charlton 4	d	14 24	14 34	14 39				14 54	15 04	15 09				15 24	15 34	15 39				15 54	16 04	16 09
Woolwich Dockyard	d	14 27		14 42				14 57		15 12				15 27		15 42				15 57		16 12
Woolwich Arsenal 4	d	14 30	14 40	14 45				15 00	15 10	15 15				15 30	15 40	15 45				16 00	16 10	16 15
Plumstead	d	14 32		14a47				15 02		15a17				15 32		15a47				16 02		16a17
Abbey Wood	d	14 35	14 44					15 05	15 14					15 35	15 44					16 05	16 14	
Belvedere	d	14 37						15 07						15 37						16 07		
Erith	d	14 40						15 10						15 40						16 10		
Slade Green 4	d	14 44						15 14						15 44						16 14		
Dartford 4	a	14 49	14 54		15 03		15 09	15 19	15 24		15 33		15 39	15 49	15 54		16 03		16 09	16 19	16 24	
	d		14 55				15 10		15 25				15 40		15 55				16 10		16 25	
Stone Crossing	d						15 14						15 44						16 14			
Greenhithe for Bluewater	d		15 00				15 16		15 30				15 46		16 00				16 16		16 30	
Swanscombe	d						15 19						15 49						16 19			
Northfleet	d						15 21						15 51						16 21			
Gravesend 4	d		15 07			15 18	15a25		15 37			15 48	15a55		16 07			16 18	16a25		16 37	
Higham	d		15 13						15 43						16 13						16 43	
Strood 4	d		15 18			15 28			15 48			15 58			16 18			16 28			16 48	
Maidstone West	d																					
Rochester 4	d		15 23			15 33			15 52			16 03			16 23			16 33			16 52	
Chatham 4	d		15 26			15 35			15 55			16 05			16 26			16 35			16 55	
Gillingham (Kent) 4	a		15 30			15 39			16 02			16 09			16 30			16 39			17 02	

Table 200

Sundays

London - Dartford and Gillingham

Network Diagram - see first Page of Table 200

Station		SE	SE	SE	SE	SE	SE	SE	SE	SE	SE	SE	SE	SE	SE	SE	SE	SE	SE	SE	SE	SE	SE
St Pancras Int'l 15 ⊖	d		16 25						16 55						17 25						17 58		
Stratford International ⊖ ⛴	d		16 32						17 02						17 32						18 08		
Ebbsfleet International	d		16 43						17 13						17 43						18 19		
London Charing Cross 4 ⊖	d	15 50		15 56	16 00	16 10		16 20		16 26	16 30	16 40		16 50		16 56	17 00	17 10		17 20		17 26	17 30
London Waterloo (East) 4 ⊖	d	15 53		15 59	16 03	16 13		16 23		16 29	16 33	16 43		16 53		16 59	17 03	17 13		17 23		17 29	17 33
London Cannon Street 4 ⊖	d																						
London Bridge 4 ⊖	d	15 58		16 04	16 08	16 18	16 23	16 28		16 34	16 38	16 48	16 53	16 58		17 04	17 08	17 18	17 23	17 28		17 34	17 38
Deptford	d				16 14		16 29				16 44		16 59				17 14		17 29				17 44
Greenwich 4 ⛴	d				16 16		16 31				16 46		17 01				17 16		17 31				17 46
Maze Hill	d				16 19		16 34				16 49		17 04				17 19		17 34				17 49
Westcombe Park	d				16 21		16 36				16 51		17 06				17 21		17 36				17 51
London Victoria 15 ⊖	d																						
Denmark Hill 4	d																						
Peckham Rye 4	d																						
Nunhead 4	d																						
New Cross 4 ⊖	d	16 04						16 34						17 04						17 34			
St Johns	d																						
Lewisham 4 ⛴	d	16 08		16 12		16 27		16 38		16 42		16 57		17 08		17 12		17 27		17 38		17 42	
Blackheath 4	d	16 10				16 30		16 40				17 00		17 10				17 30		17 40			
Kidbrooke	d	16 13						16 43						17 13						17 43			
Eltham	d	16 17						16 47						17 17						17 47			
Falconwood	d	16 19						16 49						17 19						17 49			
Welling	d	16 22						16 52						17 22						17 52			
Bexleyheath	d	16 24						16 54						17 24						17 54			
Barnehurst 4	d	16 27						16 57						17 27						17 57			
Hither Green 4	d			16 16						16 46						17 16						17 46	
Lee	d			16 18						16 48						17 18						17 48	
Mottingham	d			16 21						16 51						17 21						17 51	
New Eltham	d			16 23						16 53						17 23						17 53	
Sidcup 4	d			16 27						16 57						17 27						17 57	
Albany Park	d			16 29						16 59						17 29						17 59	
Bexley	d			16 31						17 01						17 31						18 01	
Crayford	d			16 34						17 04						17 34						18 04	
Charlton 4	d				16 24	16 34	16 39				16 54	17 04	17 09				17 24	17 34	17 39				17 54
Woolwich Dockyard	d				16 27		16 42				16 57		17 12				17 27		17 42				17 57
Woolwich Arsenal 4 ⛴	d				16 30	16 40	16 45				17 00	17 10	17 15				17 30	17 40	17 45				18 00
Plumstead	d				16 32		16a47				17 02		17a17				17 32		17a47				18 02
Abbey Wood	d				16 35	16 44					17 05	17 14					17 35	17 44					18 05
Belvedere	d				16 37						17 07						17 37						18 07
Erith	d				16 40						17 10						17 40						18 10
Slade Green 4	d				16 44						17 14						17 44						18 14
Dartford 4	a	16 33		16 39	16 49	16 54		17 03		17 09	17 19	17 24		17 33		17 39	17 49	17 54		18 03		18 09	18 19
	d			16 40		16 55				17 10		17 25				17 40		17 55				18 10	
Stone Crossing	d			16 44						17 14						17 44						18 14	
Greenhithe for Bluewater	d			16 46		17 00				17 16		17 30				17 46		18 00				18 16	
Swanscombe	d			16 49						17 19						17 49						18 19	
Northfleet	d			16 51						17 21						17 51						18 21	
Gravesend 4	d		16 48	16a55		17 07			17 18	17a25		17 37			17 48	17a55		18 07			18 24	18a25	
Higham	d					17 13						17 43						18 13					
Strood 4	d		16 58			17 18			17 28			17 48			17 58			18 18			18 34		
Maidstone West	d																						
Rochester 4	d		17 03			17 23			17 33			17 52			18 03			18 23			18 39		
Chatham 4	d		17 05			17 26			17 35			17 55			18 05			18 26			18 41		
Gillingham (Kent) 4	a		17 09			17 30			17 39			18 02			18 09			18 30			18 45		

Table 200

Sundays

London - Dartford and Gillingham

Network Diagram - see first Page of Table 200

		SE	SE	SE	SE	SE		SE	SE	SE	SE	SE	SE	SE	SE	SE	SE		SE	SE	SE	SE	SE	SE	SE
St Pancras Int'l 15 ⊖	d				18 25							18 55									19 25				
Stratford International ⊖ ⛴	d				18 32							19 02									19 32				
Ebbsfleet International	d				18 43							19 13									19 43				
London Charing Cross 4 ⊖	d	17 40		17 50		17 56		18 00	18 10		18 20		18 26	18 30	18 40		18 50		18 56	19 00		19 10	19 20	19 26	19 30
London Waterloo (East) 4 ⊖	d	17 43		17 53		17 59		18 03	18 13		18 23		18 29	18 33	18 43		18 53		18 59	19 03		19 13	19 23	19 29	19 33
London Cannon Street 4 ⊖	d																								
London Bridge 4 ⊖	d	17 48	17 53	17 58		18 04		18 08	18 18	18 23	18 28		18 34	18 38	18 48	18 53	18 58		19 04	19 08		19 18	19 28	19 34	19 38
Deptford	d		17 59					18 14		18 29				18 44		18 59				19 14					19 44
Greenwich 4 ⛴	d		18 01					18 16		18 31				18 46		19 01				19 16					19 46
Maze Hill	d		18 04					18 19		18 34				18 49		19 04				19 19					19 49
Westcombe Park	d		18 06					18 21		18 36				18 51		19 06				19 21					19 51
London Victoria 15 ⊖	d																								
Denmark Hill 4	d																								
Peckham Rye 4	d																								
Nunhead 4	d																								
New Cross 4 ⊖	d			18 04							18 34						19 04						19 34		
St Johns	d																								
Lewisham 4 ⛴	d	17 57		18 08		18 12			18 27		18 38		18 42		18 57		19 08		19 12			19 27	19 38	19 42	
Blackheath 4	d	18 00		18 10					18 30		18 40				19 00		19 10					19 30	19 40		
Kidbrooke	d			18 13							18 43						19 13						19 43		
Eltham	d			18 17							18 47						19 17						19 47		
Falconwood	d			18 19							18 49						19 19						19 49		
Welling	d			18 22							18 52						19 22						19 52		
Bexleyheath	d			18 24							18 54						19 24						19 54		
Barnehurst 4	d			18 27							18 57						19 27						19 57		
Hither Green 4	d					18 16							18 46						19 16					19 46	
Lee	d					18 18							18 48						19 18					19 48	
Mottingham	d					18 21							18 51						19 21					19 51	
New Eltham	d					18 23							18 53						19 23					19 53	
Sidcup 4	d					18 27							18 57						19 27					19 57	
Albany Park	d					18 29							18 59						19 29					19 59	
Bexley	d					18 31							19 01						19 31					20 01	
Crayford	d					18 34							19 04						19 34					20 04	
Charlton 4	d	18 04	18 09					18 24	18 34	18 39				18 54	19 04	19 09				19 24		19 34			19 54
Woolwich Dockyard	d		18 12					18 27		18 42				18 57		19 12				19 27					19 57
Woolwich Arsenal 4 ⛴	d	18 10	18 15					18 30	18 40	18 45				19 00	19 10	19 15				19 30		19 40			20 00
Plumstead	d		18a17					18 32		18a47				19 02		19a17				19 32					20 02
Abbey Wood	d	18 14						18 35	18 44					19 05	19 14					19 35		19 44			20 05
Belvedere	d							18 37						19 07						19 37					20 07
Erith	d							18 40						19 10						19 40					20 10
Slade Green 4	d							18 44						19 14						19 44					20 14
Dartford 4	a	18 24		18 33		18 39		18 49	18 54		19 03		19 09	19 19	19 24		19 33		19 39	19 49		19 54	20 03	20 09	20 19
	d	18 25				18 40			18 55				19 10		19 25							19 55			
Stone Crossing	d					18 44							19 14		19 29							19 59			
Greenhithe for Bluewater	d	18 30				18 46			19 00				19 16		19 31							20 01			
Swanscombe	d					18 49							19 19		19 34							20 04			
Northfleet	d					18 51							19 21		19 36							20 06			
Gravesend 4	d	18 37			18 48	18a55			19 07			19 18	19a25		19 40						19 48	20 10			
Higham	d	18 43							19 13						19 46							20 16			
Strood 4	d	18 48			18 58				19 18			19 28			19 52						19 58	20 22			
Maidstone West	d																								
Rochester 4	d	18 52			19 03				19 23			19 33			19 56						20 03	20 26			
Chatham 4	d	18 55			19 05				19 26			19 35			19 58						20 05	20 28			
Gillingham (Kent) 4	a	19 02			19 09				19 30			19 39			20 03						20 09	20 33			

Table 200 **Sundays**

London - Dartford and Gillingham

Network Diagram - see first Page of Table 200

		SE	SE		SE	SE	SE	SE	SE	SE	SE	SE	SE	SE	SE
St Pancras Int'l 15 ⊖	d	19 55							23 25						
Stratford International ⊖ ⛴	d	20 02							23 32						
Ebbsfleet International	d	20 13							23 43						
London Charing Cross 4 ⊖	d		19 40		22 40	22 50	22 56	23 00		23 10	23 20	23 26	23 30	23 50	23 56
London Waterloo (East) 4 ⊖	d		19 43		22 43	22 53	22 59	23 03		23 13	23 23	23 29	23 33	23 53	23 59
London Cannon Street 4 ⊖	d														
London Bridge 4 ⊖	d		19 48		22 48	22 58	23 04	23 08		23 18	23 28	23 34	23 38	23 58	00 04
Deptford	d							23 14					23 44		
Greenwich 4 ⛴	d							23 16					23 46		
Maze Hill	d							23 19					23 49		
Westcombe Park	d							23 21					23 51		
London Victoria 15 ⊖	d														
Denmark Hill 4	d														
Peckham Rye 4	d														
Nunhead 4	d														
New Cross 4 ⊖	d					23 04					23 34			00 04	
St Johns	d														
Lewisham 4 ⛴	d		19 57		22 57	23 08	23 12			23 27	23 38	23 42		00 08	00 12
Blackheath 4	d		20 00		23 00	23 10				23 30	23 40			00 10	
Kidbrooke	d					23 13					23 43			00 13	
Eltham	d					23 17					23 47			00 17	
Falconwood	d					23 19					23 49			00 19	
Welling	d					23 22					23 52			00 22	
Bexleyheath	d			and at the same minutes past each hour until		23 24					23 54			00 24	
Barnehurst 4	d					23 27					23 57			00 27	
Hither Green 4	d						23 16					23 46			00 16
Lee	d						23 18					23 48			00 18
Mottingham	d						23 21					23 51			00 21
New Eltham	d						23 23					23 53			00 23
Sidcup 4	d						23 27					23 57			00 27
Albany Park	d						23 29					23 59			00 29
Bexley	d						23 31					00 01			00 31
Crayford	d						23 34					00 04			00 34
Charlton 4	d		20 04		23 04			23 24		23 34			23 54		
Woolwich Dockyard	d							23 27					23 57		
Woolwich Arsenal 4 ⛴	d		20 10		23 10			23 30		23 40			23 59		
Plumstead	d							23 32					00 02		
Abbey Wood	d		20 14		23 14			23 35		23 44			00 05		
Belvedere	d							23 37					00 07		
Erith	d							23 40					00 10		
Slade Green 4	d							23 44					00 14		
Dartford 4	a		20 24		23 24	23 33	23 39	23 49		23 54	00 04	00 09	00 19	00 33	00 39
	d		20 25		23 25					23 55					
Stone Crossing	d		20 29		23 29					23 59					
Greenhithe for Bluewater	d		20 31		23 31					00 01					
Swanscombe	d		20 34		23 34					00 04					
Northfleet	d		20 36		23 36					00 06					
Gravesend 4	d	20 18	20 40		23 40				23 48	00 10					
Higham	d		20 46		23 46					00 16					
Strood 4	d	20 28	20 52		23 52				23 58	00 22					
Maidstone West	d														
Rochester 4	d	20 33	20 56		23 56				00 03	00 26					
Chatham 4	d	20 35	20 58		23 58				00 05	00 28					
Gillingham (Kent) 4	a	20 39	21 03		00 03				00 09	00 33					

Table 200

Mondays to Fridays

Gillingham and Dartford - London

Network Diagram - see first Page of Table 200

Miles	Miles	Miles	Miles	Miles			SE	SE	SE	SE	SE	SE	SE	SE	SE		SE	SE	SE	SE	SE	SE	SE	SE	SE
0	—	—	0	0	**Gillingham (Kent)** [4]	d	04 09			04 34		04 54			05 20				05 24	05 45					
1¾	—	—	1¾	1¾	**Chatham** [4]	d	04 13			04 38		04 58			05 24				05 28	05 49					
2¼	—	—	2¼	2¼	Rochester [4]	d	04 15			04 40		05 00			05 27				05 30	05 51					
—	—	—	—	—	Maidstone West	d																			
3¼	—	—	3¼	3¼	Strood [4]	d	04 20			04 45		05 05			05 32				05 35						
6	—	—	6	6	Higham	d	04 25			04 50		05 10							05 40						
10½	—	—	10½	10½	**Gravesend** [4]	d	04 33			04 58		05 18		05 28	05 43				05 48						
12½	—	—	12½	—	Northfleet	d				05 02				05 32											
13¼	—	—	13¼	—	Swanscombe	d				05 04				05 34											
14½	—	—	14½	—	Greenhithe for Bluewater	d	04 38			05 07		05 23		05 37					05 53						
15¼	—	—	15¼	—	Stone Crossing	d				05 09				05 39											
17¼	0	0	17¼	0	**Dartford** [4]	a	04 43			05 13		05 28		05 43					05 58						
—	—	—	—	—		d	04 44		05 01	05 14	05 22	05 29	05 31	05 44			05 52	05 56	05 59		06 01		06 13	06 16	
19¼	2	—	—	—	Slade Green [4]	d			05 05				05 35								06 05			06 20	
20½	3¼	—	—	—	Erith	d			05 08				05 38								06 08			06 23	
21¾	4½	—	—	—	Belvedere	d			05 10				05 40								06 10			06 25	
23¼	6	—	—	—	Abbey Wood	d			05 13			05 38	05 43						06 08		06 13			06 28	
24¾	7½	—	—	—	Plumstead	d			05 16				05 46								06 16			06 31	
25¼	8	—	—	—	**Woolwich Arsenal** [4] (ferry)	d			05 19			05 43	05 49						06 13		06 19			06 34	
26	8¾	—	—	—	Woolwich Dockyard	d			05 22				05 52								06 22			06 37	
27	9¾	—	—	—	Charlton [4]	d			05 25			05 47	05 55						06 17		06 25			06 40	
—	—	—	19	—	Crayford	d	04 48			05 18				05 48				06 01							
—	—	—	20½	—	Bexley	d	04 51			05 21				05 51				06 04							
—	—	—	21½	—	Albany Park	d	04 54			05 24				05 54				06 07							
—	—	—	22½	—	Sidcup [4]	d	04 57			05 27				05 57				06 10							
—	—	—	24	—	New Eltham	d	05 00			05 30				06 00				06 13							
—	—	—	25	—	Mottingham	d	05 02			05 32				06 02				06 16							
—	—	—	26½	—	Lee	d	05 05			05 35				06 05				06 19							
—	—	—	27¼	—	Hither Green [4]	d	05 08	05 23		05 38				06 08				06 22							
—	—	3	—	3	Barnehurst [4]	d					05 29						05 59					06 14	06 20		
—	—	4¼	—	4¼	Bexleyheath	d					05 31						06 01					06 16	06 22		
—	—	5¾	—	5¾	Welling	d					05 34						06 04					06 19	06 25		
—	—	6¾	—	6¾	Falconwood	d					05 37						06 07					06 22	06 28		
—	—	8	—	8	Eltham	d					05 40						06 10					06 25	06 31		
—	—	9	—	9	Kidbrooke	d					05 43						06 13					06 28	06 34		
29	—	10	—	10	Blackheath [4]	d					05 46	05 52					06 16		06 22			06 31	06 37		
30	—	11	28½	11	Lewisham [4] (ferry)	d	05 13	05 28		05 43	05 50	05 56		06 13			06 20	06 27	06 25			06 35	06 41		06 48
—	—	11½	29	—	St Johns	d												06 29							06 50
—	—	12¼	29¾	—	New Cross [4] (Underground)	d	05 16	05 31		05 46	05 53			06 16				06 31				06 38			06 52
—	—	—	—	12¾	Nunhead [4]	d																			
—	—	—	—	13½	Peckham Rye [4]	d																	06 47		
—	—	—	—	14¼	Denmark Hill [4]	d																	06 50		
—	—	—	—	18½	**London Victoria** [15] (Underground)	a																	07 04		
—	10½	—	—	—	Westcombe Park	d			05 27				05 57								06 27			06 42	
—	11	—	—	—	Maze Hill	d			05 29				05 59								06 29			06 44	
—	12	—	—	—	Greenwich [4] (ferry)	d			05 32				06 02								06 32			06 47	
—	12½	—	—	—	**Deptford**	a			05 34				06 04								06 34			06 49	
34¼	15½	15¼	32¾	—	London Bridge [4] (Underground)	a	05 22	05 36	05 41	05 52	05 58	06 05	06 12	06 22			06 28	06 37	06 34	06 27	06 42	06 43		06 56	06 58
—	16¼	—	—	—	**London Cannon Street** [4] (Underground)	a		05 41												06 32		06 48		07 03	07 05
35¼	—	16¼	33¾	—	**London Waterloo (East)** [4] (Underground)	a	05 26		05 46	05 57	06 03	06 10	06 17	06 26			06 33	06 41	06 39		06 48				
—	—	—	—	—	**London Charing Cross** [4] (Underground)	a	05 30		05 50	06 01	06 07	06 13	06 21	06 30			06 36	06 45	06 43		06 52				
—	—	—	—	12½	**Ebbsfleet International**	a									05 47										
—	—	—	—	29¾	**Stratford International** (Underground) (ferry)	a									05 59										
—	—	—	—	35¼	**St Pancras Int'l** [15] (Underground)	a									06 06										

Table 200

Mondays to Fridays

Gillingham and Dartford - London

Network Diagram - see first Page of Table 200

		SE	SE	SE	SE	SE	SE	SE	SE	SE	SE	SE	SE	SE	SE	SE 1	SE	SE	SE	SE	SE	SE
Gillingham (Kent) 4	d		05 50	05 54						06 07					06 20	06 34						
Chatham 4	d		05 54	05 58						06 11					06 24	06 38						
Rochester 4	d		05 57	06 00						06 13					06 27	06 41						
Maidstone West	d																					
Strood 4	d		06 02	06 05						06 18					06 32							
Higham	d			06 10						06 23												
Gravesend 4	d	06 05	06 13	06 18						06 31				06 34	06 43						06 47	
Northfleet	d	06 09												06 38							06 51	
Swanscombe	d	06 11												06 40							06 53	
Greenhithe for Bluewater	d	06 14		06 23						06 37				06 43							06 56	
Stone Crossing	d	06 16												06 45							06 58	
Dartford 4	a	06 20		06 28						06 41				06 49							07 02	
	d	06 21		06 29		06 31		06 31	06 39	06 42				06 50						07 00	07 03	
Slade Green 4	d							06 36										06 55				
Erith	d							06 39										06 57				
Belvedere	d							06 41										07 00				
Abbey Wood	d			06 38				06 45		06 51								07 03			07 12	
Plumstead	d							06 48										07 06				
Woolwich Arsenal 4	d			06 43				06 51		06 56								07 09			07 17	
Woolwich Dockyard	d							06 53										07 12				
Charlton 4	d			06 47				06 57										07 15			07 22	
Crayford	d				06 30	06 35							06 50	06 55								
Bexley	d				06 33	06 38							06 53	06 58								
Albany Park	d				06 36	06 41							06 56	07 01								
Sidcup 4	d				06 39	06 44							06 59	07 04								
New Eltham	d				06 43	06 47							07 02	07 07								
Mottingham	d				06 45	06 50							07 05	07 10								
Lee	d				06 48	06 53							07 08	07 13								
Hither Green 4	d				06 51	06 56						07 08	07 11	07 16								07 28
Barnehurst 4	d	06 28					06 39		06 49		06 53								07 00	07 08		
Bexleyheath	d	06 31					06 41		06 52		06 56								07 03	07 11		
Welling	d	06 34					06 44		06 55		06 59								07 06	07 14		
Falconwood	d	06 37					06 47		06 57		07 01								07 08	07 16		
Eltham	d	06 40					06 50		07 00		07 04								07 11	07 19		
Kidbrooke	d	06 43					06 53		07 03		07 07								07 14	07 22		
Blackheath 4	d	06 47		06 52			06 57		07 08	07 05	07 11								07 18	07 27		
Lewisham 4	d	06 50		06 55	06 57		07 01		07 11	07 08	07 15		07 17				07 20		07 22	07 30		
St Johns	d				06 59								07 19						07 24			
New Cross 4 ⊖	d				07 01		07 04			07 11			07 21				07 23		07 26			
Nunhead 4	d										07 20											
Peckham Rye 4	d										07 23											
Denmark Hill 4	d										07 29											
London Victoria 15 ⊖	a										07 42											
Westcombe Park	d							06 59										07 17				
Maze Hill	d							07 01										07 19				
Greenwich 4	d							07 05										07 23			07 28	
Deptford	a							07 07										07 25				
London Bridge 4 ⊖	a	07 00		07 03	07 07	07 06	07 09	07 14	07 20	07 17		07 18	07 26	07 26		07 20	07 28	07 33	07 33	07 40	07 35	07 37
London Cannon Street 4 ⊖	a				07 14		07 16	07 21		07 23		07 25	07 33			07 27	07 35		07 39		07 42	07 44
London Waterloo (East) 4 ⊖	a	07 05		07 09		07 11			07 25					07 31				07 38		07 46		
London Charing Cross 4 ⊖	a	07 11		07 15		07 17			07 31					07 37				07 44		07 52		
Ebbsfleet International	a		06 17												06 47							
Stratford International ⊖	a		06 29												06 59							
St Pancras Int'l 15 ⊖	a		06 36												07 06							

Gillingham and Dartford - London

Network Diagram - see first Page of Table 200

		SE	SE	SE	SE	SE [1]	SE		SE	SE	SE	SE	SE	SE	SE	SE	SE		SE	SE	SE	SE	SE	SE	SE
Gillingham (Kent) [4]	d				06 38	07 04																			
Chatham [4]	d				06 42	07 08																			
Rochester [4]	d				06 44	07 11																			
Maidstone West	d																		06 56						
Strood [4]	d				06 49							06 57							07 12						
Higham	d				06 54							07 02													
Gravesend [4]	d				07 02							07 09					07 17		07 22						
Northfleet	d																07 21								
Swanscombe	d																07 23								
Greenhithe for Bluewater	d				07 07							07 16					07 26								
Stone Crossing	d																07 28								
Dartford [4]	a				07 12							07 21					07 33								
	d		07 05		07 12		07 17				07 20	07 23			07 25		07 34				07 36				07 40
Slade Green [4]	d		07 09						07 19						07 29								07 39		
Erith	d		07 12						07 22						07 32								07 42		
Belvedere	d		07 14						07 24						07 34								07 44		
Abbey Wood	d		07 18						07 28			07 34			07 38								07 48		
Plumstead	d		07 21						07 31						07 41								07 51		
Woolwich Arsenal [4] ⛴	d		07 24						07 34			07 39			07 44								07 54		
Woolwich Dockyard	d		07 26						07 36						07 46								07 56		
Charlton [4]	d		07 30						07 40			07 44			07 50								08 00		
Crayford	d			07 10	07 17											07 30	07 38								
Bexley	d			07 13	07 20											07 33	07 41								
Albany Park	d			07 16	07 22											07 36	07 44								
Sidcup [4]	d			07 19	07 25											07 39	07 47					07 51			
New Eltham	d			07 23	07 28											07 43	07 50					07 54			
Mottingham	d			07 25	07 31											07 45						07 56			
Lee	d			07 28	07 34											07 48						07 59			
Hither Green [4]	d			07 32	07 36								07 49			07 52						08 02			
Barnehurst [4]	d	07 13					07 24				07 28			07 33						07 38	07 44				07 48
Bexleyheath	d	07 16					07 26				07 31			07 36						07 41	07 46				07 51
Welling	d	07 19					07 29				07 34			07 39						07 44	07 49				07 54
Falconwood	d	07 21					07 32				07 36			07 41						07 46	07 52				07 56
Eltham	d	07 24					07 35				07 39			07 44						07 49	07 55				07 59
Kidbrooke	d	07 27					07 38				07 42			07 47						07 52	07 58				08 02
Blackheath [4]	d	07 31					07 42				07 47			07 51						07 57	08 02				08 07
Lewisham [4] ⛴	d	07 35		07 38			07 46			07 48	07 50			07 55		07 57					08 05			08 08	08 11
St Johns	d			07 40						07 50						08 00								08 12	
New Cross [4] ⊖	d	07 38		07 42						07 53				07 58		08 02								08 14	
Nunhead [4]	d						07 51														08 11				
Peckham Rye [4]	d						07 54														08 13				
Denmark Hill [4]	d						07 59														08 17				
London Victoria [15] ⊖	a						08 11														08 29				
Westcombe Park	d		07 32						07 42						07 52								08 02		
Maze Hill	d		07 34						07 44						07 54								08 04		
Greenwich [4] ⛴	d		07 37						07 47			07 51			07 57								08 07		
Deptford	a		07 39						07 49						07 59								08 09		
London Bridge [4] ⊖	a	07 43	07 45	07 47	07 47	07 51			07 57	08 01	08 00	07 57	07 59	08 03	08 05	08 08	08 05					08 13	08 16	08 20	08 20
London Cannon Street [4] ⊖	a	07 50	07 52	07 54		07 57				08 08		08 04	08 06	08 10	08 12	08 15								08 28	
London Waterloo (East) [4] ⊖	a				07 52				08 02		08 06						08 10			08 12		08 18	08 22		08 26
London Charing Cross [4] ⊖	a				07 58				08 08		08 12						08 16			08 18		08 24	08 28		08 32
Ebbsfleet International	a																								
Stratford International ⊖ ⛴	a																		07 36						
St Pancras Int'l [15] ⊖	a																		07 43						

Table 200

Mondays to Fridays

Gillingham and Dartford - London

Network Diagram - see first Page of Table 200

		SE	SE	SE	SE	SE	SE	SE	SE	SE	SE	SE	SE	SE	SE	SE	SE	SE	SE	SE	SE	SE
							1														1	1
Gillingham (Kent) 4	d					07 12	07 19													07 38	07 46	08 03
Chatham 4	d					07 16	07 24													07 42	07 50	08 08
Rochester 4	d					07 18														07 44		08 11
Maidstone West	d														07 26							
Strood 4	d	07 18				07 23									07 42					07 49		
Higham	d	07 23				07 28														07 54		
Gravesend 4	d	07 31				07 36								07 48	07 52					08 02		
Northfleet	d					07 40								07 52								
Swanscombe	d					07 42								07 54								
Greenhithe for Bluewater	d	07 37				07 45								07 57						08 08		
Stone Crossing	d					07 47								07 59								
Dartford 4	a	07 42				07 51								08 03						08 12		
	d	07 43		07 45		07 52			07 56				08 02	08 04				08 06		08 13		
Slade Green 4	d			07 50							07 59					08 00		08 10				
Erith	d			07 52							08 02							08 13				
Belvedere	d			07 55							08 04							08 15				
Abbey Wood	d	07 52		07 58							08 08			08 14				08 18				
Plumstead	d			08 01							08 11							08 21				
Woolwich Arsenal 4 ⛴	d	07 57		08 05							08 14			08 19				08 24				
Woolwich Dockyard	d			08 07							08 16							08 27				
Charlton 4	d	08 03		08 11							08 20			08 24				08 30				
Crayford	d				07 50	07 56													08 10	08 17		
Bexley	d				07 53	07 59													08 13	08 20		
Albany Park	d				07 56	08 02													08 16	08 23		
Sidcup 4	d				07 59	08 05				08 11									08 19	08 26		
New Eltham	d				08 03	08 09				08 14									08 23	08 30		
Mottingham	d				08 05					08 16									08 25			
Lee	d				08 08					08 19									08 28			
Hither Green 4	d				08 12					08 22									08 32			
Barnehurst 4	d		07 53					07 58	08 04				08 09			08a12	08 13					
Bexleyheath	d		07 56					08 01	08 06				08 11				08 16					
Welling	d		07 59					08 04	08 09				08 14				08 19					
Falconwood	d		08 01					08 06	08 12				08 17				08 21					
Eltham	d		08 04					08 09	08 15				08 20				08 24					
Kidbrooke	d		08 07					08 12	08 18				08 23				08 27					
Blackheath 4	d		08 11					08 17	08 22				08 27				08 31					
Lewisham 4 ⛴	d		08 15		08 17				08 25			08 28	08 31				08 35		08 37			
St Johns	d				08 21							08 30							08 40			
New Cross 4 ⊖	d		08 18		08 23							08 32					08 38		08 42			
Nunhead 4	d								08 30													
Peckham Rye 4	d								08 33													
Denmark Hill 4	d								08 36													
London Victoria 15 ⊖	a								08 49													
Westcombe Park	d			08 13							08 22							08 32				
Maze Hill	d			08 15							08 24							08 34				
Greenwich 4 ⛴	d	08 11		08 19							08 27			08 31				08 37				
Deptford	a			08 21							08 29							08 39				
London Bridge 4 ⊖	a	08 17	08 25	08 27	08 29	08 25	08 09			08 33	08 37	08 41	08 40	08 38			08 43	08 45	08 49	08 45	08 31	08 49
London Cannon Street 4 ⊖	a	08 24	08 32	08 35	08 36		08 17					08 48		08 44			08 50	08 52	08 55		08 38	08 57
London Waterloo (East) 4 ⊖	a					08 30		08 32		08 38	08 42		08 46							08 50		
London Charing Cross 4 ⊖	a					08 36		08 39		08 44	08 48		08 52							08 56		
Ebbsfleet International	a																					
Stratford International ⊖ ⛴	a														08 06							
St Pancras Int'l 15 ⊖	a														08 13							

Gillingham and Dartford - London

Network Diagram - see first Page of Table 200

		SE	SE	SE	SE	SE	SE	SE	SE	SE	SE	SE	SE	SE	SE	SE	SE	SE	SE 1	SE	SE	SE	SE
Gillingham (Kent) 4	d																08 08	08 19	08 24				
Chatham 4	d																08 12	08 24	08 28				
Rochester 4	d																08 14	08 26	08 31				
Maidstone West	d										07 56												
Strood 4	d									07 58	08 12						08 19	08 32					
Higham	d									08 03							08 24						
Gravesend 4	d							08 06		08 17	08 22						08 33	08 43					
Northfleet	d							08 10									08 37						
Swanscombe	d							08 12									08 39						
Greenhithe for Bluewater	d							08 15		08 23							08 42						
Stone Crossing	d							08 17									08 44						
Dartford 4	a							08 21		08 27							08 49						
	d							08 22	08 24	08 29						08 38	08 49					08 52	
Slade Green 4	d	08 17		08 17				08 27				08 31	08 31							08 39			08 47
Erith	d			08 19								08 33								08 41			
Belvedere	d			08 22								08 36								08 44			
Abbey Wood	d			08 25				08 34				08 39								08 47			
Plumstead	d			08 28								08 42								08 50			
Woolwich Arsenal 4 ⛴	d			08 31				08 40				08 45								08 53			
Woolwich Dockyard	d			08 34								08 47								08 56			
Charlton 4	d			08 37			08 37	08 45				08 50								08 59			
Crayford	d					08 28	09 07			08 34							08 54						
Bexley	d					08 31	09 10			08 37							08 57						
Albany Park	d					08 34	09 13			08 40							09 00						
Sidcup 4	d		08 31			08 37	09 16			08 43							09 03						
New Eltham	d		08 34			08 41	09 19			08 46							09 06						
Mottingham	d		08 36			08 43	09 21			08 49							09 08						
Lee	d		08 39			08 46	09 24			08 52							09 11						
Hither Green 4	d		08 42			08 50	09 28			08 55					08 59		09 14						
Barnehurst 4	d	08 24							08 30				08a36	08 37		08 45						08 59	09a04
Bexleyheath	d	08 27							08 33					08 40		08 47						09 01	
Welling	d	08 30							08 36					08 43		08 50						09 04	
Falconwood	d	08 32							08 38					08 45		08 53						09 07	
Eltham	d	08 35							08 41					08 48		08 56						09 10	
Kidbrooke	d	08 38							08 44					08 51		08 59						09 13	
Blackheath 4	d	08 42							08 48					08 55		09 02						09 16	
Lewisham 4 ⛴	d	08 46			08 48	08 55	09 34		08 52					08 59	09 04	09 06					09 15	09 20	
St Johns	d				08 50	08 57	09 36							09 01	09 07						09 17		
New Cross 4 ⊖	d				08 52	08 59	09 38							09 03	09 09						09 19		
Nunhead 4	d	08 52														09 11							
Peckham Rye 4	d	08 55														09 14							
Denmark Hill 4	d	09 02														09 17							
London Victoria 15 ⊖	a	09 11														09 29							
Westcombe Park	d			08 39								08 52								09 01			
Maze Hill	d			08 41								08 54								09 03			
Greenwich 4 ⛴	d			08 45				08 51				08 58								09 07			
Deptford	a			08 47								09 00								09 09			
London Bridge 4 ⊖	a		08 52	08 56	08 57	09 05	09 44	09 00	09 00	09 05		09 07		09 09	09 17		09 23		09 11	09 17	09 25	09 29	
London Cannon Street 4 ⊖	a				09 04	09 12	09 51	09 08				09 14		09 18	09 23				09 18		09 32		
London Waterloo (East) 4 ⊖	a		08 58	09 02					09 05	09 10							09 28			09 22		09 34	
London Charing Cross 4 ⊖	a		09 04	09 08					09 12	09 16							09 34			09 28		09 40	
Ebbsfleet International	a																	08 47					
Stratford International ⊖ ⛴	a										08 36							08 59					
St Pancras Int'l 15 ⊖	a										08 43							09 07					

Table 200

Mondays to Fridays

Gillingham and Dartford - London

Network Diagram - see first Page of Table 200

		SE	SE	SE	SE		SE	SE	SE	SE	SE	SE	SE	SE	SE		SE	SE	SE	SE	SE	SE	SE	SE	SE
Gillingham (Kent) 4	d											08 50								08 54					
Chatham 4	d											08 54								08 58					
Rochester 4	d											08 57								09 00					
Maidstone West	d																								
Strood 4	d											09 02								09 05					
Higham	d																			09 10					
Gravesend 4	d				08 48						09 02	09 13								09 18					09 32
Northfleet	d										09 06														09 36
Swanscombe	d										09 08														09 38
Greenhithe for Bluewater	d				08 53						09 11									09 23					09 41
Stone Crossing	d										09 13														09 43
Dartford 4	a				08 58						09 17									09 28					09 47
	d				08 58			09 01	09 08		09 18			09 22						09 29		09 31	09 38		09 48
Slade Green 4	d			08 54				09 05		09 15					09 17				09 25			09 35		09 45	
Erith	d			08 56				09 08		09 18									09 28			09 38		09 48	
Belvedere	d			08 59				09 10		09 20									09 30			09 40		09 50	
Abbey Wood	d			09 02	09 07			09 13		09 23									09 33	09 38		09 43		09 53	
Plumstead	d			09 05				09 16		09 26									09 36			09 46		09 56	
Woolwich Arsenal 4	d			09 08	09 12			09 19		09 29									09 39	09 43		09 49		09 59	
Woolwich Dockyard	d			09 10				09 22		09 32									09 42			09 52		10 02	
Charlton 4	d		09 07	09 13	09 17			09 25		09 35								09 40	09 45	09 47		09 55		10 05	
Crayford	d		09 37								09 22							10 07							09 52
Bexley	d		09 40								09 25							10 10							09 55
Albany Park	d		09 43								09 28							10 13							09 58
Sidcup 4	d		09 46								09 31							10 16							10 01
New Eltham	d		09 49								09 34							10 19							10 04
Mottingham	d		09 51								09 36							10 21							10 06
Lee	d		09 54								09 39							10 24							10 09
Hither Green 4	d	09 19	09 58								09 42						09 49	10 28							10 12
Barnehurst 4	d						09 08		09 16					09 29	09a34						09 38		09 46		
Bexleyheath	d						09 10		09 19					09 31							09 40		09 49		
Welling	d						09 13		09 22					09 34							09 43		09 52		
Falconwood	d						09 16		09 24					09 37							09 46		09 54		
Eltham	d						09 19		09 27					09 40							09 49		09 57		
Kidbrooke	d						09 22		09 30					09 43							09 52		10 00		
Blackheath 4	d				09 21		09 25		09 34					09 46						09 52	09 55		10 04		
Lewisham 4	d	09 24	10 04		09 26		09 29		09 38				09 45	09 50			09 54	10 34		09 56	09 59		10 08		
St Johns	d	09 26	10 06				09 31						09 47				09 56	10 36			10 01				
New Cross 4 ⊖	d	09 28	10 08				09 33						09 49				09 58	10 38			10 03				
Nunhead 4	d								09 43														10 13		
Peckham Rye 4	d								09 45														10 15		
Denmark Hill 4	d								09 49														10 19		
London Victoria 15 ⊖	a								10 00														10 28		
Westcombe Park	d			09 15				09 27		09 37									09 47			09 57		10 07	
Maze Hill	d			09 17				09 29		09 39									09 49			09 59		10 09	
Greenwich 4	d			09 21				09 32		09 42									09 52			10 02		10 12	
Deptford	a			09 23				09 34		09 44									09 54			10 04		10 14	
London Bridge 4 ⊖	a	09 33	10 14	09 29	09 34		09 38	09 41		09 50	09 52		09 54	09 58			10 04	10 44	10 00	10 05	10 08	10 11		10 20	10 22
London Cannon Street 4 ⊖	a	09 40	10 19	09 36			09 45	09 48		09 57			10 00				10 08	10 50	10 04		10 13	10 15		10 24	
London Waterloo (East) 4 ⊖	a				09 39						09 56			10 02						10 09					10 26
London Charing Cross 4 ⊖	a				09 45						10 00			10 06						10 13					10 30
Ebbsfleet International	a											09 17													
Stratford International ⊖	a											09 29													
St Pancras Int'l 15 ⊖	a											09 36													

Gillingham and Dartford - London

Network Diagram - see first Page of Table 200

		SE	SE	SE	SE	SE	SE	SE	SE	SE	SE	SE	SE	SE	SE	SE	SE	SE	SE	SE	SE	SE
Gillingham (Kent) [4]	d	09 20						09 24						09 50							09 54	
Chatham [4]	d	09 24						09 28						09 54							09 58	
Rochester [4]	d	09 27						09 30						09 57							10 00	
Maidstone West	d																					
Strood [4]	d	09 32						09 35						10 02							10 05	
Higham	d							09 40													10 10	
Gravesend [4]	d	09 43						09 48					10 02	10 13							10 18	
Northfleet	d												10 06									
Swanscombe	d												10 08									
Greenhithe for Bluewater	d							09 53					10 11								10 23	
Stone Crossing	d												10 13									
Dartford [4]	a							09 58					10 17								10 28	
	d			09 52				09 59		10 01	10 08		10 18			10 22					10 29	
Slade Green [4]	d						09 55			10 05		10 15					10 17			10 25		
Erith	d						09 58			10 08		10 18								10 28		
Belvedere	d						10 00			10 10		10 20								10 30		
Abbey Wood	d						10 03	10 07		10 13		10 23								10 33	10 38	
Plumstead	d						10 06			10 16		10 26								10 36		
Woolwich Arsenal [4]	d						10 09	10 12		10 19		10 29								10 39	10 43	
Woolwich Dockyard	d						10 12			10 22		10 32								10 42		
Charlton [4]	d					10 07	10 15	10 17		10 25		10 35							10 37	10 45	10 47	
Crayford	d					10 37							10 22						11 07			
Bexley	d					10 40							10 25						11 10			
Albany Park	d					10 43							10 28						11 13			
Sidcup [4]	d					10 46							10 31						11 16			
New Eltham	d					10 49							10 34						11 19			
Mottingham	d					10 51							10 36						11 21			
Lee	d					10 54							10 39						11 24			
Hither Green [4]	d				10 19	10 58							10 42					10 49	11 28			
Barnehurst [4]	d			09 59					10 08		10 16					10 29	10a34					10 38
Bexleyheath	d			10 01					10 10		10 19					10 31						10 40
Welling	d			10 04					10 13		10 22					10 34						10 43
Falconwood	d			10 07					10 16		10 24					10 37						10 46
Eltham	d			10 10					10 19		10 27					10 40						10 49
Kidbrooke	d			10 13					10 22		10 30					10 43						10 52
Blackheath [4]	d			10 16				10 21	10 25		10 34					10 46					10 52	10 55
Lewisham [4]	d		10 14	10 20	10 24	11 04		10 26	10 29		10 38				10 44	10 50		10 54	11 34		10 56	10 59
St Johns	d		10 16		10 26	11 06			10 31						10 46			10 56	11 36			11 01
New Cross [4] ⊖	d		10 18		10 28	11 08			10 33						10 48			10 58	11 38			11 03
Nunhead [4]	d										10 43											
Peckham Rye [4]	d										10 45											
Denmark Hill [4]	d										10 49											
London Victoria [15] ⊖	a										10 58											
Westcombe Park	d						10 17			10 27		10 37								10 47		
Maze Hill	d						10 19			10 29		10 39								10 49		
Greenwich [4]	d						10 22			10 32		10 42								10 52		
Deptford	a						10 24			10 34		10 44								10 54		
London Bridge [4] ⊖	a		10 24	10 28	10 34	11 14	10 30	10 35	10 38	10 41		10 50	10 52		10 54	10 58		11 04	11 44	11 00	11 05	11 08
London Cannon Street [4] ⊖	a		10 28		10 38	11 19	10 36		10 43	10 45		10 54			10 58			11 08	11 49	11 06		11 13
London Waterloo (East) [4] ⊖	a			10 32				10 39					10 56			11 02					11 09	
London Charing Cross [4] ⊖	a			10 36				10 43					11 00			11 06					11 13	
Ebbsfleet International	a	09 47												10 16								
Stratford International ⊖	a	09 59												10 28								
St Pancras Int'l [15] ⊖	a	10 06												10 35								

Gillingham and Dartford - London

Network Diagram - see first Page of Table 200

		SE	SE	SE	SE	SE	SE	SE	SE	SE	SE	SE	SE	SE	SE	SE	SE	SE	SE	SE	SE	SE	SE
Gillingham (Kent) 4	d					10 20							10 24						10 50				
Chatham 4	d					10 24							10 28						10 54				
Rochester 4	d					10 27							10 30						10 57				
Maidstone West	d																						
Strood 4	d					10 32							10 35						11 02				
Higham	d												10 40										
Gravesend 4	d				10 32	10 43							10 48					11 02	11 13				
Northfleet	d				10 36													11 06					
Swanscombe	d				10 38													11 08					
Greenhithe for Bluewater	d				10 41								10 53					11 11					
Stone Crossing	d				10 43													11 13					
Dartford 4	a				10 47								10 58					11 17					
	d	10 31	10 38		10 48			10 52					10 59		11 01	11 08		11 18			11 22		
Slade Green 4	d	10 35		10 45					10 47			10 55			11 05		11 15					11 17	
Erith	d	10 38		10 48								10 58			11 08		11 18						
Belvedere	d	10 40		10 50								11 00			11 10		11 20						
Abbey Wood	d	10 43		10 53								11 03	11 08		11 13		11 23						
Plumstead	d	10 46		10 56								11 06			11 16		11 26						
Woolwich Arsenal 4	d	10 49		10 59								11 09	11 13		11 19		11 29						
Woolwich Dockyard	d	10 52		11 02								11 12			11 22		11 32						
Charlton 4	d	10 55		11 05							11 07	11 15	11 17		11 25		11 35						
Crayford	d				10 52						11 37							11 22					
Bexley	d				10 55						11 40							11 25					
Albany Park	d				10 58						11 43							11 28					
Sidcup 4	d				11 01						11 46							11 31					
New Eltham	d				11 04						11 49							11 34					
Mottingham	d				11 06						11 51							11 36					
Lee	d				11 09						11 54							11 39					
Hither Green 4	d				11 12					11 19	11 58							11 42					11 49
Barnehurst 4	d		10 46					10 59	11a04					11 08		11 16					11 29	11a34	
Bexleyheath	d		10 49					11 01						11 10		11 19					11 31		
Welling	d		10 52					11 04						11 13		11 22					11 34		
Falconwood	d		10 54					11 07						11 16		11 24					11 37		
Eltham	d		10 57					11 10						11 19		11 27					11 40		
Kidbrooke	d		11 00					11 13						11 22		11 30					11 43		
Blackheath 4	d		11 04					11 16					11 22	11 25		11 34					11 46		
Lewisham 4	d		11 08				11 14	11 20		11 24	12 04		11 26	11 29		11 38				11 44	11 50		11 54
St Johns	d						11 16			11 26	12 06			11 31						11 46			11 56
New Cross 4 ⊖	d						11 18			11 28	12 08			11 33						11 48			11 58
Nunhead 4	d		11 13													11 43							
Peckham Rye 4	d		11 15													11 45							
Denmark Hill 4	d		11 19													11 49							
London Victoria 15 ⊖	a		11 28													11 58							
Westcombe Park	d	10 57		11 07								11 17			11 27		11 37						
Maze Hill	d	10 59		11 09								11 19			11 29		11 39						
Greenwich 4	d	11 02		11 12								11 22			11 32		11 42						
Deptford	a	11 04		11 14								11 24			11 34		11 44						
London Bridge 4 ⊖	a	11 11		11 20	11 22		11 24	11 28		11 34	12 14	11 30	11 35	11 38	11 41		11 50	11 52		11 54	11 58		12 04
London Cannon Street 4 ⊖	a	11 15		11 24			11 28			11 38	12 19	11 36		11 43	11 45		11 54			11 58			12 08
London Waterloo (East) 4 ⊖	a				11 26			11 32					11 39					11 56			12 02		
London Charing Cross 4 ⊖	a				11 30			11 36					11 43					12 00			12 06		
Ebbsfleet International	a					10 47													11 17				
Stratford International ⊖	a					10 59													11 29				
St Pancras Int'l 15 ⊖	a					11 06													11 36				

Gillingham and Dartford - London

Network Diagram - see first Page of Table 200

		SE	SE		SE	SE	SE	SE	SE	SE	SE	SE	SE		SE	SE	SE	SE	SE	SE	SE	SE	SE		SE
Gillingham (Kent) 4	d				10 54						11 20							11 24							11 50
Chatham 4	d				10 58						11 24							11 28							11 54
Rochester 4	d				11 00						11 27							11 30							11 57
Maidstone West	d																								
Strood 4	d				11 05						11 32							11 35							12 02
Higham	d				11 10													11 40							
Gravesend 4	d				11 18					11 32	11 43							11 48					12 02		12 13
Northfleet	d									11 36													12 06		
Swanscombe	d									11 38													12 08		
Greenhithe for Bluewater	d				11 23					11 41								11 53					12 11		
Stone Crossing	d									11 43													12 13		
Dartford 4	a				11 28					11 47								11 58					12 17		
	d				11 29		11 31	11 38		11 48			11 52					11 59		12 01	12 08		12 18		
Slade Green 4	d		11 25				11 35		11 45								11 55			12 05		12 15			
Erith	d		11 28				11 38		11 48								11 58			12 08		12 18			
Belvedere	d		11 30				11 40		11 50								12 00			12 10		12 20			
Abbey Wood	d		11 33		11 38		11 43		11 53								12 03	12 08		12 13		12 23			
Plumstead	d		11 36				11 46		11 56								12 06			12 16		12 26			
Woolwich Arsenal 4 ⛴	d		11 39		11 43		11 49		11 59								12 09	12 13		12 19		12 29			
Woolwich Dockyard	d		11 42				11 52		12 02								12 12			12 22		12 32			
Charlton 4	d	11 37	11 45		11 47		11 55		12 05							12 07	12 15	12 17		12 25		12 35			
Crayford	d	12 07								11 52						12 37							12 22		
Bexley	d	12 10								11 55						12 40							12 25		
Albany Park	d	12 13								11 58						12 43							12 28		
Sidcup 4	d	12 16								12 01						12 46							12 31		
New Eltham	d	12 19								12 04						12 49							12 34		
Mottingham	d	12 21								12 06						12 51							12 36		
Lee	d	12 24								12 09						12 54							12 39		
Hither Green 4	d	12 28								12 12					12 19	12 58							12 42		
Barnehurst 4	d					11 38		11 46					11 59						12 08		12 16				
Bexleyheath	d					11 40		11 49					12 01						12 10		12 19				
Welling	d					11 43		11 52					12 04						12 13		12 22				
Falconwood	d					11 46		11 54					12 07						12 16		12 24				
Eltham	d					11 49		11 57					12 10						12 19		12 27				
Kidbrooke	d					11 52		12 00					12 13						12 22		12 30				
Blackheath 4	d				11 52	11 55		12 04					12 16					12 22	12 25		12 34				
Lewisham 4 ⛴	d	12 34			11 56	11 59		12 08				12 14	12 20		12 24	13 04		12 26	12 29		12 38				
St Johns	d	12 36				12 01						12 16			12 26	13 06			12 31						
New Cross 4 ⊖	d	12 38				12 03						12 18			12 28	13 08			12 33						
Nunhead 4	d							12 13													12 43				
Peckham Rye 4	d							12 15													12 45				
Denmark Hill 4	d							12 19													12 49				
London Victoria 15 ⊖	a							12 28													12 58				
Westcombe Park	d		11 47				11 57		12 07								12 17			12 27		12 37			
Maze Hill	d		11 49				11 59		12 09								12 19			12 29		12 39			
Greenwich 4 ⛴	d		11 52				12 02		12 12								12 22			12 32		12 42			
Deptford	a		11 54				12 04		12 14								12 24			12 34		12 44			
London Bridge 4 ⊖	a	12 44	12 00		12 05	12 08	12 11		12 20	12 22		12 24	12 28		12 34	13 14	12 30	12 35	12 38	12 41		12 50	12 52		
London Cannon Street 4 ⊖	a	12 49	12 04			12 13	12 15		12 24			12 28			12 38	13 19	12 36		12 43	12 45		12 54			
London Waterloo (East) 4 ⊖	a				12 09					12 26			12 32					12 39					12 56		
London Charing Cross 4 ⊖	a				12 13					12 30			12 36					12 43					13 00		
Ebbsfleet International	a										11 47														12 17
Stratford International ⊖ ⛴	a										11 59														12 29
St Pancras Int'l 15 ⊖	a										12 06														12 36

Gillingham and Dartford - London

Network Diagram - see first Page of Table 200

		SE	SE	SE	SE	SE	SE	SE	SE		SE	SE	SE	SE	SE	SE	SE	SE	SE		SE	SE	SE	SE	SE
Gillingham (Kent) 4	d							11 54							12 20								12 24		
Chatham 4	d							11 58							12 24								12 28		
Rochester 4	d							12 00							12 27								12 30		
Maidstone West	d																								
Strood 4	d							12 05							12 32								12 35		
Higham	d							12 10															12 40		
Gravesend 4	d							12 18						12 32	12 43								12 48		
Northfleet	d													12 36											
Swanscombe	d													12 38											
Greenhithe for Bluewater	d							12 23						12 41									12 53		
Stone Crossing	d													12 43											
Dartford 4	a							12 28						12 47									12 58		
	d		12 22					12 29			12 31	12 38		12 48			12 52						12 59		13 01
Slade Green 4	d			12 17			12 25				12 35		12 45					12 47				12 55			13 05
Erith	d						12 28				12 38		12 48									12 58			13 08
Belvedere	d						12 30				12 40		12 50									13 00			13 10
Abbey Wood	d						12 33	12 38			12 43		12 53									13 03	13 08		13 13
Plumstead	d						12 36				12 46		12 56									13 06			13 16
Woolwich Arsenal 4 ⛴	d						12 39	12 43			12 49		12 59									13 09	13 13		13 19
Woolwich Dockyard	d						12 42				12 52		13 02									13 12			13 22
Charlton 4	d					12 37	12 45	12 47			12 55		13 05								13 07	13 15	13 17		13 25
Crayford	d					13 07								12 52							13 37				
Bexley	d					13 10								12 55							13 40				
Albany Park	d					13 13								12 58							13 43				
Sidcup 4	d					13 16								13 01							13 46				
New Eltham	d					13 19								13 04							13 49				
Mottingham	d					13 21								13 06							13 51				
Lee	d					13 24								13 09							13 54				
Hither Green 4	d				12 49	13 28								13 12					13 19		13 58				
Barnehurst 4	d		12 29	12a34					12 38			12 46					12 59	13a04						13 08	
Bexleyheath	d		12 31						12 40			12 49					13 01							13 10	
Welling	d		12 34						12 43			12 52					13 04							13 13	
Falconwood	d		12 37						12 46			12 54					13 07							13 16	
Eltham	d		12 40						12 49			12 57					13 10							13 19	
Kidbrooke	d		12 43						12 52			13 00					13 13							13 22	
Blackheath 4	d		12 46					12 52	12 55			13 04					13 16						13 22	13 25	
Lewisham 4 ⛴	d	12 44	12 50		12 54	13 34		12 56	12 59			13 08				13 14	13 20		13 24		14 04		13 26	13 29	
St Johns	d	12 46			12 56	13 36			13 01							13 16			13 26		14 06			13 31	
New Cross 4 ⊖	d	12 48			12 58	13 38			13 03							13 18			13 28		14 08			13 33	
Nunhead 4	d											13 13													
Peckham Rye 4	d											13 15													
Denmark Hill 4	d											13 19													
London Victoria 15 ⊖	a											13 28													
Westcombe Park	d						12 47				12 57		13 07									13 17			13 27
Maze Hill	d						12 49				12 59		13 09									13 19			13 29
Greenwich 4 ⛴	d						12 52				13 02		13 12									13 22			13 32
Deptford	a						12 54				13 04		13 14									13 24			13 34
London Bridge 4 ⊖	a	12 54	12 58		13 04	13 44	13 00	13 05	13 08		13 11		13 20	13 22		13 24	13 28		13 34		14 14	13 30	13 35	13 38	13 41
London Cannon Street 4 ⊖	a	12 58			13 08	13 49	13 06		13 13		13 15		13 24			13 28			13 38		14 19	13 36		13 43	13 45
London Waterloo (East) 4 ⊖	a		13 02					13 09						13 26			13 32						13 39		
London Charing Cross 4 ⊖	a		13 06					13 13						13 30			13 36						13 43		
Ebbsfleet International	a														12 47										
Stratford International ⊖ ⛴	a														12 59										
St Pancras Int'l 15 ⊖	a														13 06										

Gillingham and Dartford - London

Network Diagram - see first Page of Table 200

		SE	SE	SE	SE		SE	SE	SE	SE	SE	SE	SE	SE	SE		SE	SE	SE	SE	SE	SE	SE	SE	SE
Gillingham (Kent) 4	d				12 50								12 54							13 20					
Chatham 4	d				12 54								12 58							13 24					
Rochester 4	d				12 57								13 00							13 27					
Maidstone West	d																								
Strood 4	d				13 02								13 05							13 32					
Higham	d												13 10												
Gravesend 4	d			13 02	13 13								13 18						13 32	13 43					
Northfleet	d			13 06															13 36						
Swanscombe	d			13 08															13 38						
Greenhithe for Bluewater	d			13 11									13 23						13 41						
Stone Crossing	d			13 13															13 43						
Dartford 4	a			13 17									13 28						13 47						
	d	13 08		13 18				13 22					13 29		13 31		13 38		13 48			13 52			
Slade Green 4	d		13 15						13 17			13 25			13 35			13 45					13 47		
Erith	d		13 18									13 28			13 38			13 48							
Belvedere	d		13 20									13 30			13 40			13 50							
Abbey Wood	d		13 23									13 33	13 38		13 43			13 53							
Plumstead	d		13 26									13 36			13 46			13 56							
Woolwich Arsenal 4 ⛴	d		13 29									13 39	13 43		13 49			13 59							
Woolwich Dockyard	d		13 32									13 42			13 52			14 02							
Charlton 4	d		13 35								13 37	13 45	13 47		13 55			14 05							14 07
Crayford	d			13 22							14 07								13 52						14 37
Bexley	d			13 25							14 10								13 55						14 40
Albany Park	d			13 28							14 13								13 58						14 43
Sidcup 4	d			13 31							14 16								14 01						14 46
New Eltham	d			13 34							14 19								14 04						14 49
Mottingham	d			13 36							14 21								14 06						14 51
Lee	d			13 39							14 24								14 09						14 54
Hither Green 4	d			13 42						13 49	14 28								14 12					14 19	14 58
Barnehurst 4	d	13 16						13 29	13a34					13 38			13 46					13 59	14a04		
Bexleyheath	d	13 19						13 31						13 40			13 49					14 01			
Welling	d	13 22						13 34						13 43			13 52					14 04			
Falconwood	d	13 24						13 37						13 46			13 54					14 07			
Eltham	d	13 27						13 40						13 49			13 57					14 10			
Kidbrooke	d	13 30						13 43						13 52			14 00					14 13			
Blackheath 4	d	13 34						13 46					13 52	13 55			14 04					14 16			
Lewisham 4 ⛴	d	13 38					13 44	13 50		13 54	14 34		13 56	13 59			14 08				14 14	14 20		14 24	15 04
St Johns	d						13 46			13 56	14 36			14 01							14 16			14 26	15 06
New Cross 4 ⊖	d						13 48			13 58	14 38			14 03							14 18			14 28	15 08
Nunhead 4	d	13 43															14 13								
Peckham Rye 4	d	13 45															14 15								
Denmark Hill 4	d	13 49															14 19								
London Victoria 15 ⊖	a	13 58															14 28								
Westcombe Park	d		13 37									13 47			13 57			14 07							
Maze Hill	d		13 39									13 49			13 59			14 09							
Greenwich 4 ⛴	d		13 42									13 52			14 02			14 12							
Deptford	a		13 44									13 54			14 04			14 14							
London Bridge 4 ⊖	a		13 50	13 52			13 54	13 58		14 04	14 44	14 00	14 05	14 08	14 11			14 20	14 22		14 24	14 28		14 34	15 14
London Cannon Street 4 ⊖	a		13 54				13 58			14 08	14 49	14 06		14 13	14 15			14 24			14 28			14 38	15 19
London Waterloo (East) 4 ⊖	a			13 56				14 02					14 09						14 26			14 32			
London Charing Cross 4 ⊖	a			14 00				14 06					14 13						14 30			14 36			
Ebbsfleet International	a				13 17															13 47					
Stratford International ⊖ ⛴	a				13 29															14 01					
St Pancras Int'l 15 ⊖	a				13 36															14 10					

Gillingham and Dartford - London

Network Diagram - see first Page of Table 200

		SE	SE	SE	SE	SE	SE	SE	SE	SE	SE	SE	SE	SE	SE	SE	SE	SE	SE	SE	SE	SE
Gillingham (Kent) ■4	d		13 24						13 50							13 54						14 20
Chatham ■4	d		13 28						13 54							13 58						14 24
Rochester ■4	d		13 30						13 57							14 00						14 27
Maidstone West	d																					
Strood ■4	d		13 35						14 02							14 05						14 32
Higham	d		13 40													14 10						
Gravesend ■4	d		13 48					14 02	14 13							14 18					14 32	14 43
Northfleet	d							14 06													14 36	
Swanscombe	d							14 08													14 38	
Greenhithe for Bluewater	d		13 53					14 11								14 23					14 41	
Stone Crossing	d							14 13													14 43	
Dartford ■4	a		13 58					14 17								14 28					14 47	
	d		13 59		14 01	14 08		14 18			14 22					14 29		14 31	14 38		14 48	
Slade Green ■4	d	13 55			14 05		14 15					14 17			14 25			14 35		14 45		
Erith	d	13 58			14 08		14 18								14 28			14 38		14 48		
Belvedere	d	14 00			14 10		14 20								14 30			14 40		14 50		
Abbey Wood	d	14 03	14 08		14 13		14 23								14 33	14 38		14 43		14 53		
Plumstead	d	14 06			14 16		14 26								14 36			14 46		14 56		
Woolwich Arsenal ■4 ⛴	d	14 09	14 13		14 19		14 29								14 39	14 43		14 49		14 59		
Woolwich Dockyard	d	14 12			14 22		14 32								14 42			14 52		15 02		
Charlton ■4	d	14 15	14 17		14 25		14 35							14 37	14 45	14 47		14 55		15 05		
Crayford	d							14 22						15 07							14 52	
Bexley	d							14 25						15 10							14 55	
Albany Park	d							14 28						15 13							14 58	
Sidcup ■4	d							14 31						15 16							15 01	
New Eltham	d							14 34						15 19							15 04	
Mottingham	d							14 36						15 21							15 06	
Lee	d							14 39						15 24							15 09	
Hither Green ■4	d							14 42					14 49	15 28							15 12	
Barnehurst ■4	d			14 08		14 16					14 29	14a34					14 38		14 46			
Bexleyheath	d			14 10		14 19					14 31						14 40		14 49			
Welling	d			14 13		14 22					14 34						14 43		14 52			
Falconwood	d			14 16		14 24					14 37						14 46		14 54			
Eltham	d			14 19		14 27					14 40						14 49		14 57			
Kidbrooke	d			14 22		14 30					14 43						14 52		15 00			
Blackheath ■4	d		14 22	14 25		14 34					14 46					14 52	14 55		15 04			
Lewisham ■4 ⛴	d		14 26	14 29		14 38				14 44	14 50		14 54	15 34		14 56	14 59		15 08			
St Johns	d			14 31						14 46			14 56	15 36			15 01					
New Cross ■4 ⊖	d			14 33						14 48			14 58	15 38			15 03					
Nunhead ■4	d					14 43													15 13			
Peckham Rye ■4	d					14 45													15 15			
Denmark Hill ■4	d					14 49													15 19			
London Victoria ■15 ⊖	a					14 58													15 28			
Westcombe Park	d	14 17			14 27		14 37								14 47			14 57		15 07		
Maze Hill	d	14 19			14 29		14 39								14 49			14 59		15 09		
Greenwich ■4 ⛴	d	14 22			14 32		14 42								14 52			15 02		15 12		
Deptford	a	14 24			14 34		14 44								14 54			15 04		15 14		
London Bridge ■4 ⊖	a	14 30	14 35	14 38	14 41		14 50	14 52		14 54	14 58		15 04	15 44	15 00	15 05	15 08	15 11		15 20	15 22	
London Cannon Street ■4 ⊖	a	14 36		14 43	14 45		14 54			14 58			15 08	15 49	15 06		15 13	15 15		15 24		
London Waterloo (East) ■4 ⊖	a		14 39					14 56			15 02					15 09					15 26	
London Charing Cross ■4 ⊖	a		14 43					15 00			15 06					15 13					15 30	
Ebbsfleet International	a								14 17													14 47
Stratford International ⊖ ⛴	a								14 28													14 59
St Pancras Int'l ■15 ⊖	a								14 39													15 06

Gillingham and Dartford - London

Network Diagram - see first Page of Table 200

Station		SE	SE	SE	SE	SE	SE		SE	SE	SE	SE	SE	SE	SE	SE	SE		SE	SE	SE	SE	SE	SE	SE
Gillingham (Kent)	d								14 24						14 50							14 54			
Chatham	d								14 28						14 54							14 58			
Rochester	d								14 30						14 57							15 00			
Maidstone West	d																								
Strood	d								14 35						15 02							15 05			
Higham	d								14 40													15 10			
Gravesend	d								14 48					15 02	15 13							15 18			
Northfleet	d													15 06											
Swanscombe	d													15 08											
Greenhithe for Bluewater	d								14 53					15 11								15 23			
Stone Crossing	d													15 13											
Dartford	a								14 58					15 17								15 28			
	d		14 52						14 59		15 01	15 08		15 18			15 22					15 29		15 31	15 38
Slade Green	d			14 47			14 55				15 05		15 15								15 25			15 35	
Erith	d						14 58				15 08		15 18								15 28			15 38	
Belvedere	d						15 00				15 10		15 20								15 30			15 40	
Abbey Wood	d						15 03		15 08		15 13		15 23								15 33	15 38		15 43	
Plumstead	d						15 06				15 16		15 26								15 36			15 46	
Woolwich Arsenal	d						15 09		15 13		15 19		15 29								15 39	15 43		15 49	
Woolwich Dockyard	d						15 12				15 22		15 32								15 42			15 52	
Charlton	d					15 07	15 15		15 17		15 25		15 35							15 37	15 45	15 47		15 55	
Crayford	d					15 37								15 22						16 07					
Bexley	d					15 40								15 25						16 10					
Albany Park	d					15 43								15 28						16 13					
Sidcup	d					15 46								15 31						16 16					
New Eltham	d					15 49								15 34						16 19					
Mottingham	d					15 51								15 36						16 21					
Lee	d					15 54								15 39						16 24					
Hither Green	d				15 19	15 58								15 42					15 49	16 28					
Barnehurst	d		14 59	15a04						15 08		15 16					15 29						15 38		15 46
Bexleyheath	d		15 01							15 10		15 19					15 31						15 40		15 49
Welling	d		15 04							15 13		15 22					15 34						15 43		15 52
Falconwood	d		15 07							15 16		15 24					15 37						15 46		15 54
Eltham	d		15 10							15 19		15 27					15 40						15 49		15 57
Kidbrooke	d		15 13							15 22		15 30					15 43						15 52		16 00
Blackheath	d		15 16						15 22	15 25		15 34					15 46					15 52	15 55		16 04
Lewisham	d	15 14	15 20		15 24	16 04			15 26	15 29		15 38				15 44	15 50		15 54	16 34		15 56	15 59		16 08
St Johns	d	15 16			15 26	16 06				15 31						15 46			15 56	16 36			16 01		
New Cross	d	15 18			15 28	16 08				15 33						15 48			15 58	16 38			16 03		
Nunhead	d											15 43													16 13
Peckham Rye	d											15 45													16 15
Denmark Hill	d											15 49													16 19
London Victoria	a											15 58													16 28
Westcombe Park	d						15 17				15 27		15 37								15 47			15 57	
Maze Hill	d						15 19				15 29		15 39								15 49			15 59	
Greenwich	d						15 22				15 32		15 42								15 52			16 02	
Deptford	a						15 24				15 34		15 44								15 54			16 04	
London Bridge	a	15 24	15 28		15 34	16 15	15 30		15 35	15 38	15 41		15 50	15 52		15 54	15 58		16 04	16 44	16 00	16 05	16 09	16 12	
London Cannon Street	a	15 28			15 38	16 19	15 36			15 43	15 45		15 54			15 58			16 08	16 49	16 06		16 13	16 16	
London Waterloo (East)	a		15 32						15 39					15 57			16 02					16 09			
London Charing Cross	a		15 36						15 43					16 01			16 06					16 13			
Ebbsfleet International	a														15 17										
Stratford International	a														15 29										
St Pancras Int'l	a														15 36										

Table 200

Mondays to Fridays

Gillingham and Dartford - London

Network Diagram - see first Page of Table 200

		SE	SE		SE	SE	SE	SE	SE	SE	SE	SE	SE		SE	SE	SE	SE	SE	SE	SE	SE	SE		SE
Gillingham (Kent) 4	d				15 20							15 24							15 50						
Chatham 4	d				15 24							15 28							15 54						
Rochester 4	d				15 27							15 30							15 57						
Maidstone West	d																								
Strood 4	d				15 32							15 35							16 02						
Higham	d											15 40													
Gravesend 4	d		15 32		15 43							15 48						16 02	16 13						
Northfleet	d		15 36															16 06							
Swanscombe	d		15 38															16 08							
Greenhithe for Bluewater	d		15 41									15 53						16 11							
Stone Crossing	d		15 43															16 13							
Dartford 4	a		15 47									15 58						16 17							
	d		15 48				15 52					15 59			16 01	16 08		16 18			16 22				
Slade Green 4	d	15 45						15 47			15 55				16 05		16 15					16 17			
Erith	d	15 48									15 58				16 08		16 18								
Belvedere	d	15 50									16 00				16 10		16 20								
Abbey Wood	d	15 53									16 03	16 08			16 13		16 23								
Plumstead	d	15 56									16 06				16 16		16 26								
Woolwich Arsenal 4 ⛴	d	15 59									16 09	16 13			16 19		16 29								
Woolwich Dockyard	d	16 02									16 12				16 22		16 32								
Charlton 4	d	16 05								16 07	16 15	16 17			16 25		16 35								16 37
Crayford	d		15 52							16 37								16 22							17 07
Bexley	d		15 55							16 40								16 25							17 10
Albany Park	d		15 58							16 43								16 28							17 13
Sidcup 4	d		16 01							16 46								16 31					16 38		17 16
New Eltham	d		16 04							16 49								16 34					16 41		17 19
Mottingham	d		16 06							16 51								16 36					16 43		17 21
Lee	d		16 09							16 54								16 39					16 46		17 24
Hither Green 4	d		16 12						16 19	17 00								16 42					16 50		17 28
Barnehurst 4	d						15 59	16a04					16 08			16 16					16 29	16a34			
Bexleyheath	d						16 01						16 10			16 19					16 31				
Welling	d						16 04						16 13			16 22					16 34				
Falconwood	d						16 07						16 16			16 24					16 37				
Eltham	d						16 10						16 19			16 27					16 40				
Kidbrooke	d						16 13						16 22			16 30					16 43				
Blackheath 4	d						16 16					16 22	16 25			16 34					16 46				
Lewisham 4 ⛴	d					16 14	16 20		16 24	17 05		16 26	16 29			16 38				16 44	16 50				17 35
St Johns	d					16 16			16 26	17 09			16 31							16 46			16 54		17 37
New Cross 4 ⊖	d					16 18			16 28	17 11			16 33							16 48			16 56		17 39
Nunhead 4	d															16 43									
Peckham Rye 4	d															16 45									
Denmark Hill 4	d															16 49									
London Victoria 15 ⊖	a															17 01									
Westcombe Park	d	16 07									16 17				16 27		16 37								
Maze Hill	d	16 09									16 19				16 29		16 39								
Greenwich 4 ⛴	d	16 12									16 22				16 32		16 42								
Deptford	a	16 14									16 24				16 34		16 44								
London Bridge 4 ⊖	a	16 20	16 22			16 24	16 29		16 34	17 18	16 30	16 35	16 39		16 42		16 50	16 52		16 54	16 58		17 04		17 45
London Cannon Street 4 ⊖	a	16 24				16 28			16 38	17 24	16 36		16 43		16 46		16 54			16 58			17 09		17 49
London Waterloo (East) 4 ⊖	a		16 27				16 33					16 39						16 56			17 03				
London Charing Cross 4 ⊖	a		16 31				16 37					16 44						17 00			17 07				
Ebbsfleet International	a				15 47														16 17						
Stratford International ⊖ ⛴	a				16 02														16 29						
St Pancras Int'l 15 ⊖	a				16 09														16 36						

Gillingham and Dartford - London

Network Diagram - see first Page of Table 200

Station		SE	SE	SE	SE	SE	SE	SE	SE		SE	SE	SE	SE	SE	SE	SE	SE	SE		SE	SE	SE	SE	SE
Gillingham (Kent) 4	d		15 54									16 20			16 24						16 50				
Chatham 4	d		15 58									16 24			16 28						16 54				
Rochester 4	d		16 00									16 27			16 30						16 57				
Maidstone West	d																								
Strood 4	d		16 05									16 32			16 35						17 02				
Higham	d		16 10												16 40										
Gravesend 4	d		16 18								16 32	16 43			16 48				17 02		17 13				
Northfleet	d										16 36								17 06						
Swanscombe	d										16 38								17 08						
Greenhithe for Bluewater	d		16 23								16 41				16 53				17 11						
Stone Crossing	d										16 43								17 13						
Dartford 4	a		16 28								16 48				16 58				17 17						
	d		16 29		16 31	16 38	16 42				16 52				16 59		17 01	17 08	17 18				17 22		
Slade Green 4	d	16 25			16 35			16 44					16 55				17 05								
Erith	d	16 28			16 38			16 46					16 58				17 08								
Belvedere	d	16 30			16 40			16 49					17 00				17 10								
Abbey Wood	d	16 33	16 38		16 43			16 52					17 03		17 08		17 13								
Plumstead	d	16 36			16 46			16 55					17 06				17 16								
Woolwich Arsenal 4 ⛴	d	16 39	16 43		16 49			16 58					17 09		17 13		17 19								
Woolwich Dockyard	d	16 42			16 52			17 00					17 12				17 22								
Charlton 4	d	16 45	16 47		16 55			17 03					17 15		17 17		17 25								
Crayford	d						16 46												17 22						17 37
Bexley	d						16 49												17 25						17 40
Albany Park	d						16 52												17 28						17 43
Sidcup 4	d						16 55												17 31						17 46
New Eltham	d						16 58												17 34						17 49
Mottingham	d						17 00												17 36						17 51
Lee	d						17 03												17 39						17 54
Hither Green 4	d						17 07							17 19					17 42					17 53	17 58
Barnehurst 4	d			16 38		16 46					16 59					17 08		17 16					17 29		
Bexleyheath	d			16 40		16 49					17 01					17 10		17 19					17 31		
Welling	d			16 43		16 52					17 04					17 13		17 22					17 34		
Falconwood	d			16 46		16 54					17 07					17 16		17 24					17 37		
Eltham	d			16 49		16 57					17 10					17 19		17 27					17 40		
Kidbrooke	d			16 52		17 00					17 13					17 22		17 30					17 43		
Blackheath 4	d		16 52	16 55		17 04					17 16				17 22	17 25		17 34					17 46		
Lewisham 4 ⛴	d		16 56	16 59		17 08			17 14		17 20			17 24	17 27	17 30		17 38				17 44	17 50		18 05
St Johns	d			17 01					17 16					17 26								17 46		17 57	18 07
New Cross 4 ⊖	d			17 03					17 18					17 28		17 33						17 48		17 59	18 09
Nunhead 4	d					17 13												17 43							
Peckham Rye 4	d					17 15												17 45							
Denmark Hill 4	d					17 19												17 49							
London Victoria 15 ⊖	a					17 28												17 59							
Westcombe Park	d	16 47			16 57			17 05					17 17				17 27								
Maze Hill	d	16 49			16 59			17 07					17 19				17 29								
Greenwich 4 ⛴	d	16 52			17 02			17 11					17 22				17 32								
Deptford	a	16 54			17 04			17 13					17 24				17 34								
London Bridge 4 ⊖	a	17 01	17 07	17 09	17 13		17 21	17 21	17 24		17 29		17 31	17 34	17 35	17 39	17 42		17 53			17 55	18 00	18 06	18 16
London Cannon Street 4 ⊖	a	17 05	17 11	17 15	17 17			17 26	17 29				17 36	17 38		17 44	17 46					17 59	18 04	18 11	18 20
London Waterloo (East) 4 ⊖	a						17 28				17 34				17 40				17 58						
London Charing Cross 4 ⊖	a						17 33				17 38				17 44				18 03						
Ebbsfleet International	a											16 47									17 17				
Stratford International ⊖ ⛴	a											17 02									17 28				
St Pancras Int'l 15 ⊖	a											17 09									17 36				

Gillingham and Dartford - London

Network Diagram - see first Page of Table 200

		SE	SE	SE	SE		SE	SE	SE	SE	SE	SE	SE	SE	SE		SE	SE	SE	SE	SE	SE	SE	SE	SE
Gillingham (Kent) 4	d				16 54								17 20						17 24						
Chatham 4	d				16 58								17 24						17 28						
Rochester 4	d				17 00								17 27						17 30						
Maidstone West	d																								
Strood 4	d				17 05								17 32						17 35						
Higham	d				17 10														17 40						
Gravesend 4	d				17 18							17 32	17 43						17 48						
Northfleet	d											17 36													
Swanscombe	d											17 38													
Greenhithe for Bluewater	d				17 23							17 41							17 53						
Stone Crossing	d											17 43													
Dartford 4	a				17 28							17 47							17 58						
	d				17 29				17 31	17 38		17 48			17 52				17 59			18 01		18 08	
Slade Green 4	d		17 15	17 25			17 29		17 35		17 45						17 55					18 05			18 15
Erith	d		17 18	17 28					17 38		17 48						17 57					18 08			18 18
Belvedere	d		17 20	17 30					17 40		17 50						18 00					18 10			18 20
Abbey Wood	d		17 23	17 33	17 38				17 43		17 53						18 03		18 08			18 13			18 23
Plumstead	d		17 26	17 36					17 46		17 56						18 06					18 16			18 26
Woolwich Arsenal 4 ⛴	d		17 29	17 39	17 43				17 49		17 59						18 09		18 13			18 19			18 29
Woolwich Dockyard	d		17 32	17 42					17 52		18 02						18 11					18 22			18 32
Charlton 4	d	17 30	17 35	17 45	17 47				17 55		18 05						18 14		18 17			18 25			18 35
Crayford	d	18 01										17 52									18 01				
Bexley	d	18 04										17 55													
Albany Park	d	18 07										17 58													
Sidcup 4	d	18 10										18 01											18 20		
New Eltham	d	18 13										18 04											18 23		
Mottingham	d	18 15										18 06													
Lee	d	18 18										18 09													
Hither Green 4	d	18 21										18 12						18 19					18 28		
Barnehurst 4	d						17a37	17 38		17 46					17 59					18 10	18a11			18 16	
Bexleyheath	d							17 40		17 49					18 01					18 12				18 19	
Welling	d							17 43		17 52					18 04					18 15				18 22	
Falconwood	d							17 46		17 54					18 07					18 18				18 24	
Eltham	d							17 49		17 57					18 10					18 20				18 27	
Kidbrooke	d							17 52		18 00					18 13					18 23				18 30	
Blackheath 4	d				17 52			17 55		18 04					18 16				18 22					18 34	
Lewisham 4 ⛴	d				17 56			17 59		18 08				18 14	18 20			18 24	18 26	18 29			18 35	18 38	
St Johns	d													18 16				18 26					18 37		
New Cross 4 ⊖	d							18 02						18 18				18 28		18 32			18 39		
Nunhead 4	d									18 13														18 43	
Peckham Rye 4	d									18 15														18 45	
Denmark Hill 4	d									18 19														18 49	
London Victoria 15 ⊖	a									18 29														18 58	
Westcombe Park	d		17 37	17 47					17 57		18 07						18 16					18 27			18 37
Maze Hill	d		17 39	17 49					17 59		18 09						18 18					18 29			18 39
Greenwich 4 ⛴	d		17 42	17 52					18 02		18 12						18 22					18 32			18 42
Deptford	a		17 44	17 54					18 04		18 14						18 24					18 34			18 44
London Bridge 4 ⊖	a	18 33	17 52	18 03	18 04			18 09	18 13		18 20	18 22		18 24	18 28		18 31	18 34	18 35	18 38		18 43	18 46		18 50
London Cannon Street 4 ⊖	a		17 56	18 07				18 13	18 17		18 24			18 29			18 35	18 38		18 42		18 47	18 51		18 54
London Waterloo (East) 4 ⊖	a	18 37			18 08							18 27			18 32				18 41						
London Charing Cross 4 ⊖	a	18 41			18 12							18 31			18 37				18 45						
Ebbsfleet International	a												17 47												
Stratford International ⊖ ⛴	a												17 59												
St Pancras Int'l 15 ⊖	a												18 06												

Gillingham and Dartford - London

Network Diagram - see first Page of Table 200

		SE	SE	SE	SE	SE	SE	SE	SE	SE	SE	SE	SE	SE	SE	SE	SE	SE	SE	SE	SE	SE
Gillingham (Kent) 4	d		17 50						17 54						18 20						18 24	
Chatham 4	d		17 54						17 58						18 24						18 28	
Rochester 4	d		17 57						18 00						18 27						18 30	
Maidstone West	d																					
Strood 4	d		18 02						18 05						18 32						18 35	
Higham	d								18 10												18 40	
Gravesend 4	d	18 02	18 13						18 18					18 32	18 43						18 48	
Northfleet	d	18 06												18 36								
Swanscombe	d	18 08												18 38								
Greenhithe for Bluewater	d	18 11							18 23					18 41							18 53	
Stone Crossing	d	18 13												18 43								
Dartford 4	a	18 17							18 28					18 47							18 58	
	d	18 18			18 22				18 29		18 31		18 38	18 48				18 52			18 59	
Slade Green 4	d						18 25				18 35						18 51					
Erith	d						18 28				18 38						18 53					
Belvedere	d						18 30				18 40						18 56					
Abbey Wood	d						18 33		18 38		18 43						18 59				19 08	
Plumstead	d						18 36				18 46						19 02					
Woolwich Arsenal 4 ⛴	d						18 39		18 43		18 49						19 05				19 13	
Woolwich Dockyard	d						18 42				18 52						19 07					
Charlton 4	d						18 45		18 47		18 55						19 10				19 17	
Crayford	d	18 22				18 25						18 37		18 52					18 55			
Bexley	d	18 25										18 40		18 55								
Albany Park	d	18 28										18 43		18 58								
Sidcup 4	d	18 31										18 46		19 01								
New Eltham	d	18 34										18 49		19 04								
Mottingham	d	18 36										18 51		19 06								
Lee	d	18 39										18 54		19 09								
Hither Green 4	d	18 42						18 49				18 59		19 12						19 19		
Barnehurst 4	d				18 29	18a37				18 38			18 46					18 59	19a07			19 08
Bexleyheath	d				18 31					18 40			18 49					19 01				19 10
Welling	d				18 34					18 43			18 52					19 04				19 13
Falconwood	d				18 37					18 46			18 54					19 07				19 16
Eltham	d				18 40					18 49			18 57					19 10				19 19
Kidbrooke	d				18 43					18 52			19 00					19 13				19 22
Blackheath 4	d				18 46				18 52	18 55			19 04					19 16			19 22	19 25
Lewisham 4 ⛴	d			18 45	18 50			18 54	18 56	18 59		19 05	19 08			19 14		19 20		19 24	19 26	19 29
St Johns	d			18 47				18 56				19 07				19 16				19 26		
New Cross 4 ⊖	d			18 49				18 58		19 03		19 09				19 18				19 28		19 32
Nunhead 4	d												19 13									
Peckham Rye 4	d												19 15									
Denmark Hill 4	d												19 19									
London Victoria 15 ⊖	a												19 28									
Westcombe Park	d						18 47				18 57						19 12					
Maze Hill	d						18 49				18 59						19 14					
Greenwich 4 ⛴	d						18 52				19 02						19 18					
Deptford	a						18 54				19 04						19 20					
London Bridge 4 ⊖	a	18 52		18 55	18 58		19 00	19 04	19 05	19 08	19 11	19 15		19 22		19 24	19 27	19 28		19 34	19 35	19 38
London Cannon Street 4 ⊖	a			18 59			19 06	19 10		19 13	19 16	19 20				19 28	19 33			19 38		19 43
London Waterloo (East) 4 ⊖	a	18 57			19 02				19 09					19 26				19 32			19 39	
London Charing Cross 4 ⊖	a	19 01			19 06				19 13					19 30				19 36			19 43	
Ebbsfleet International	a		18 17												18 47							
Stratford International ⊖ ⛴	a		18 29												19 02							
St Pancras Int'l 15 ⊖	a		18 36												19 09							

Gillingham and Dartford - London

Network Diagram - see first Page of Table 200

		SE	SE	SE	SE	SE	SE		SE	SE	SE	SE	SE	SE	SE	SE	SE		SE	SE	SE	SE	SE	SE	SE
Gillingham (Kent) 4	d					18 50				18 54						19 24					19 50		19 54		
Chatham 4	d					18 54				18 58						19 28					19 54		19 58		
Rochester 4	d					18 57				19 00						19 30					19 57		20 00		
Maidstone West	d												19 13												
Strood 4	d					19 02				19 05			19 32			19 35					20 02		20 05		
Higham	d									19 10						19 40							20 10		
Gravesend 4	d				19 02	19 13				19 18		19 32	19 43			19 48				20 02	20 13		20 18		
Northfleet	d				19 06							19 36								20 06					
Swanscombe	d				19 08							19 38								20 08					
Greenhithe for Bluewater	d				19 11					19 23		19 41				19 53				20 11			20 23		
Stone Crossing	d				19 13							19 43								20 13					
Dartford 4	a				19 17					19 28		19 47				19 58				20 17			20 28		
	d			19 01	19 18				19 22	19 29	19 31	19 48			19 55	19 59	20 01		20 16	20 18		20 25	20 29	20 31	20 46
Slade Green 4	d		18 55	19 05			19 20				19 35			19 50			20 05		20 20					20 35	20 50
Erith	d			19 08			19 23				19 38			19 53			20 08		20 23					20 38	20 53
Belvedere	d			19 10			19 25				19 40			19 55			20 10		20 25					20 40	20 55
Abbey Wood	d			19 13			19 28			19 38	19 43			19 58		20 08	20 13		20 28				20 38	20 43	20 58
Plumstead	d			19 16			19 31				19 46			20 01			20 16		20 31					20 46	21 01
Woolwich Arsenal 4 ⛴	d			19 19			19 34			19 43	19 49			20 04		20 13	20 19		20 34				20 43	20 49	21 04
Woolwich Dockyard	d			19 22			19 37				19 52			20 07			20 22		20 37					20 52	21 07
Charlton 4	d			19 25			19 40			19 47	19 55			20 10		20 17	20 25		20 40				20 47	20 55	21 10
Crayford	d	19 07	19a08		19 22							19 52								20 22					
Bexley	d	19 10			19 25							19 55								20 25					
Albany Park	d	19 13			19 28							19 58								20 28					
Sidcup 4	d	19 16			19 31							20 01								20 31					
New Eltham	d	19 19			19 34							20 04								20 34					
Mottingham	d	19 21			19 36							20 06								20 36					
Lee	d	19 24			19 39							20 09								20 39					
Hither Green 4	d	19 28			19 42							20 12								20 42					
Barnehurst 4	d								19 30						20 02							20 32			
Bexleyheath	d								19 32						20 04							20 34			
Welling	d								19 35						20 07							20 37			
Falconwood	d								19 38						20 10							20 40			
Eltham	d								19 41						20 12							20 42			
Kidbrooke	d								19 44						20 15							20 45			
Blackheath 4	d								19 48	19 52					20 19	20 22						20 49	20 52		
Lewisham 4 ⛴	d	19 34			19 48				19 52	19 56		20 18			20 22	20 26				20 48		20 53	20 56		
St Johns	d	19 36																							
New Cross 4 ⊖	d	19 38			19 51				19 56			20 21			20 26					20 51		20 56			
Nunhead 4	d																								
Peckham Rye 4	d																								
Denmark Hill 4	d																								
London Victoria 15 ⊖	a																								
Westcombe Park	d			19 27			19 42				19 57			20 12			20 27		20 42					20 57	21 12
Maze Hill	d			19 29			19 44				19 59			20 14			20 29		20 44					20 59	21 14
Greenwich 4 ⛴	d			19 32			19 47				20 02			20 17			20 32		20 47					21 02	21 17
Deptford	a			19 34			19 49				20 04			20 19			20 34		20 49					21 04	21 19
London Bridge 4 ⊖	a	19 44		19 41	19 57		19 59		20 03	20 06	20 11	20 27		20 27	20 33	20 36	20 41		20 57	20 57		21 03	21 06	21 11	21 27
London Cannon Street 4 ⊖	a	19 49		19 45			20 03				20 15			20 31			20 45								
London Waterloo (East) 4 ⊖	a				20 02				20 08	20 11		20 32			20 38	20 40				21 02		21 08	21 10	21 15	
London Charing Cross 4 ⊖	a				20 06				20 12	20 14		20 36			20 42	20 44				21 06		21 12	21 14	21 19	
Ebbsfleet International	a					19 17							19 47								20 17				
Stratford International ⊖ ⛴	a					19 29							20 01								20 29				
St Pancras Int'l 15 ⊖	a					19 36							20 08								20 36				

Gillingham and Dartford - London

Network Diagram - see first Page of Table 200

		SE	SE		SE	SE	SE	SE	SE	SE	SE	SE	SE		SE	SE	SE	SE	SE	SE	SE	SE	SE		SE
Gillingham (Kent) 4	d		20 20			20 24				20 50		20 54					21 20		21 24			21 50			21 54
Chatham 4	d		20 24			20 28				20 54		20 58					21 24		21 28			21 54			21 58
Rochester 4	d		20 27			20 30				20 57		21 00					21 27		21 30			21 57			22 00
Maidstone West	d																								
Strood 4	d		20 32			20 35				21 02		21 05					21 32		21 35			22 02			22 05
Higham	d					20 40						21 10							21 40						22 10
Gravesend 4	d	20 32	20 43			20 48			21 02	21 13		21 18				21 32	21 43		21 48		22 02	22 13			22 18
Northfleet	d	20 36							21 06							21 36					22 06				
Swanscombe	d	20 38							21 08							21 38					22 08				
Greenhithe for Bluewater	d	20 41				20 53			21 11			21 23				21 41			21 53		22 11				22 23
Stone Crossing	d	20 43							21 13							21 43					22 13				
Dartford 4	a	20 47				20 58			21 17			21 28				21 47			21 58		22 17				22 28
	d	20 48			20 55	20 59	21 01	21 16	21 18		21 25	21 29	21 31		21 46	21 48		21 55	21 59	22 01	22 18		22 25		22 29
Slade Green 4	d						21 05	21 20					21 35		21 50					22 05					
Erith	d						21 08	21 23					21 38		21 53					22 08					
Belvedere	d						21 10	21 25					21 40		21 55					22 10					
Abbey Wood	d					21 08	21 13	21 28				21 38	21 43		21 58				22 08	22 13					22 38
Plumstead	d						21 16	21 31					21 46		22 01					22 16					
Woolwich Arsenal 4 ⛴	d					21 13	21 19	21 34				21 43	21 49		22 04				22 13	22 19					22 43
Woolwich Dockyard	d						21 22	21 37					21 52		22 07					22 22					
Charlton 4	d					21 17	21 25	21 40				21 47	21 55		22 10				22 17	22 25					22 47
Crayford	d	20 52							21 22							21 52					22 22				
Bexley	d	20 55							21 25							21 55					22 25				
Albany Park	d	20 58							21 28							21 58					22 28				
Sidcup 4	d	21 01							21 31							22 01					22 31				
New Eltham	d	21 04							21 34							22 04					22 34				
Mottingham	d	21 06							21 36							22 06					22 36				
Lee	d	21 09							21 39							22 09					22 39				
Hither Green 4	d	21 12							21 42							22 12					22 42				
Barnehurst 4	d				21 02						21 32							22 02					22 32		
Bexleyheath	d				21 04						21 34							22 04					22 34		
Welling	d				21 07						21 37							22 07					22 37		
Falconwood	d				21 10						21 40							22 10					22 40		
Eltham	d				21 12						21 42							22 12					22 42		
Kidbrooke	d				21 15						21 45							22 15					22 45		
Blackheath 4	d				21 19	21 22					21 49	21 52						22 19	22 22				22 49		22 52
Lewisham 4 ⛴	d	21 18			21 23	21 26			21 48		21 53	21 56				22 18		22 23	22 26		22 48		22 53		22 56
St Johns	d																								
New Cross 4 ⊖	d	21 21			21 26				21 51		21 56					22 21		22 26			22 51		22 56		
Nunhead 4	d																								
Peckham Rye 4	d																								
Denmark Hill 4	d																								
London Victoria 15 ⊖	a																								
Westcombe Park	d						21 27	21 42					21 57		22 12					22 27					
Maze Hill	d						21 29	21 44					21 59		22 14					22 29					
Greenwich 4 ⛴	d						21 32	21 47					22 02		22 17					22 32					
Deptford	a						21 34	21 49					22 04		22 19					22 34					
London Bridge 4 ⊖	a	21 27			21 33	21 36	21 41	21 57	21 57		22 01	22 05	22 11		22 27	22 27		22 31	22 35	22 41	22 57		23 01		23 05
London Cannon Street 4 ⊖	a																								
London Waterloo (East) 4 ⊖	a	21 32			21 38	21 40	21 45		22 02		22 06	22 09	22 15			22 32		22 36	22 39	22 45	23 02		23 06		23 09
London Charing Cross 4 ⊖	a	21 36			21 42	21 44	21 49		22 06		22 10	22 13	22 19			22 36		22 40	22 43	22 49	23 06		23 10		23 13
Ebbsfleet International	a		20 47							21 17							21 47					22 17			
Stratford International ⊖ ⛴	a		21 02							21 29							21 59					22 29			
St Pancras Int'l 15 ⊖	a		21 09							21 36							22 06					22 36			

Gillingham and Dartford - London

Network Diagram - see first Page of Table 200

Station		SE	SE	SE	SE	SE	SE	SE
Gillingham (Kent) 4	d			22 20		22 24		22 54
Chatham 4	d			22 24		22 28		22 58
Rochester 4	d			22 27		22 30		23 00
Maidstone West	d							
Strood 4	d			22 32		22 35		23 05
Higham	d					22 40		23 10
Gravesend 4	d		22 32	22 43		22 48		23 18
Northfleet	d		22 36					
Swanscombe	d		22 38					
Greenhithe for Bluewater	d		22 41			22 53		23 23
Stone Crossing	d		22 43					
Dartford 4	a		22 47			22 58		23 28
	d	22 31	22 48		22 55	22 59	23 01	
Slade Green 4	d	22 35					23 05	
Erith	d	22 38					23 08	
Belvedere	d	22 40					23 10	
Abbey Wood	d	22 43				23 08	23 13	
Plumstead	d	22 46					23 16	
Woolwich Arsenal 4 ⛴	d	22 49				23 13	23 19	
Woolwich Dockyard	d	22 52					23 22	
Charlton 4	d	22 55				23 17	23 25	
Crayford	d		22 52					
Bexley	d		22 55					
Albany Park	d		22 58					
Sidcup 4	d		23 01					
New Eltham	d		23 04					
Mottingham	d		23 06					
Lee	d		23 09					
Hither Green 4	d		23 12					
Barnehurst 4	d				23 02			
Bexleyheath	d				23 04			
Welling	d				23 07			
Falconwood	d				23 10			
Eltham	d				23 12			
Kidbrooke	d				23 15			
Blackheath 4	d				23 19	23 22		
Lewisham 4 ⛴	d		23 18		23 23	23 26		
St Johns	d							
New Cross 4 ⊖	d		23 21		23 26			
Nunhead 4	d							
Peckham Rye 4	d							
Denmark Hill 4	d							
London Victoria 15 ⊖	a							
Westcombe Park	d	22 57					23 27	
Maze Hill	d	22 59					23 29	
Greenwich 4 ⛴	d	23 02					23 32	
Deptford	a	23 04					23 34	
London Bridge 4 ⊖	a	23 11	23 27		23 31	23 35	23 41	
London Cannon Street 4 ⊖	a							
London Waterloo (East) 4 ⊖	a	23 15	23 32		23 36	23 39	23 45	
London Charing Cross 4 ⊖	a	23 19	23 36		23 40	23 43	23 49	
Ebbsfleet International	a			22 47				
Stratford International ⊖ ⛴	a			22 59				
St Pancras Int'l 15 ⊖	a			23 06				

Table 200

Saturdays

Gillingham and Dartford - London

Network Diagram - see first Page of Table 200

		SE	SE	SE	SE	SE	SE	SE	SE	SE	SE	SE	SE	SE	SE	SE	SE	SE	SE	SE	SE	SE	SE
Gillingham (Kent) 4	d				04 48				05 18			05 50		05 54				06 20		06 24			
Chatham 4	d				04 52				05 22			05 54		05 58				06 24		06 28			
Rochester 4	d				04 54				05 24			05 57		06 00				06 27		06 30			
Maidstone West	d																						
Strood 4	d				04 59				05 29			06 02		06 05				06 32		06 35			
Higham	d				05 04				05 34					06 10						06 40			
Gravesend 4	d				05 12				05 42		06 02	06 13		06 18			06 32	06 43		06 48			07 02
Northfleet	d				05 15				05 45		06 06						06 36						07 06
Swanscombe	d				05 17				05 47		06 08						06 38						07 08
Greenhithe for Bluewater	d				05 21				05 51		06 11			06 23			06 41			06 53			07 11
Stone Crossing	d				05 23				05 53		06 13						06 43						07 13
Dartford 4	a				05 27				05 57		06 17			06 28			06 47			06 58			07 17
	d	05 05	05 18	05 22	05 29	05 35	05 48	05 52	05 59	06 05	06 18		06 22	06 29	06 35	06 38	06 48		06 52	06 59	07 01	07 08	07 18
Slade Green 4	d	05 10				05 40				06 10					06 40						07 05		
Erith	d	05 12				05 42				06 12					06 42						07 08		
Belvedere	d	05 15				05 45				06 15					06 45						07 10		
Abbey Wood	d	05 18			05 38	05 48			06 08	06 18				06 38	06 48					07 08	07 13		
Plumstead	d	05 21				05 51				06 21					06 51						07 16		
Woolwich Arsenal 4	d	05 24			05 43	05 54			06 13	06 24				06 43	06 54					07 13	07 19		
Woolwich Dockyard	d	05 26				05 56				06 26					06 56						07 22		
Charlton 4	d	05 29			05 47	05 59			06 17	06 29				06 47	06 59					07 17	07 25		
Crayford	d		05 22				05 52				06 22						06 52						07 22
Bexley	d		05 25				05 55				06 25						06 55						07 25
Albany Park	d		05 28				05 58				06 28						06 58						07 28
Sidcup 4	d		05 31				06 01				06 31						07 01						07 31
New Eltham	d		05 34				06 04				06 34						07 04						07 34
Mottingham	d		05 36				06 06				06 36						07 06						07 36
Lee	d		05 39				06 09				06 39						07 09						07 39
Hither Green 4	d		05 42				06 12				06 42						07 12						07 42
Barnehurst 4	d			05 29				05 59					06 29			06 46			06 59			07 16	
Bexleyheath	d			05 31				06 01					06 31			06 49			07 01			07 19	
Welling	d			05 34				06 04					06 34			06 52			07 04			07 22	
Falconwood	d			05 37				06 07					06 37			06 54			07 07			07 24	
Eltham	d			05 40				06 10					06 40			06 57			07 10			07 27	
Kidbrooke	d			05 43				06 13					06 43			07 00			07 13			07 30	
Blackheath 4	d			05 46	05 52			06 16	06 22				06 46	06 52		07 04			07 16	07 22		07 34	
Lewisham 4	d		05 48	05 50	05 56		06 18	06 20	06 26		06 48		06 50	06 56		07 08	07 18		07 20	07 26		07 38	
St Johns	d																						
New Cross 4 ⊖	d		05 51				06 21				06 51						07 21						
Nunhead 4	d															07 15						07 45	
Peckham Rye 4	d															07 17						07 47	
Denmark Hill 4	d															07 21						07 51	
London Victoria 15 ⊖	a															07 30						08 00	
Westcombe Park	d	05 31				06 01				06 31					07 01						07 27		
Maze Hill	d	05 33				06 03				06 33					07 03						07 29		
Greenwich 4	d	05 37				06 07				06 37					07 07						07 32		
Deptford	a	05 39				06 09				06 39					07 09						07 34		
London Bridge 4 ⊖	a	05 45	05 56	05 59	06 05	06 15	06 26	06 29	06 35	06 45	06 56		06 59	07 05	07 15		07 26		07 29	07 35	07 41		07 52
London Cannon Street 4 ⊖	a																				07 45		
London Waterloo (East) 4 ⊖	a	05 49	06 01	06 03	06 09	06 19	06 31	06 33	06 39	06 49	07 01		07 03	07 09	07 19		07 31		07 33	07 39			07 56
London Charing Cross 4 ⊖	a	05 53	06 05	06 07	06 13	06 25	06 35	06 37	06 43	06 55	07 05		07 07	07 13	07 25		07 35		07 40	07 43			08 00
Ebbsfleet International	a											06 17						06 47					
Stratford International ⊖	a											06 29						06 59					
St Pancras Int'l 15 ⊖	a											06 36						07 06					

Table 200

Saturdays

Gillingham and Dartford - London

Network Diagram - see first Page of Table 200

		SE	SE	SE	SE	SE		SE	SE	SE	SE	SE	SE	SE	SE	SE		SE	SE	SE	SE	SE	SE	SE	SE
Gillingham (Kent) 4	d	06 50				06 54								07 20						07 24					
Chatham 4	d	06 54				06 58								07 24						07 28					
Rochester 4	d	06 57				07 00								07 27						07 30					
Maidstone West	d																								
Strood 4	d	07 02				07 05								07 32						07 35					
Higham	d					07 10														07 40					
Gravesend 4	d	07 13				07 18							07 32	07 43						07 48					
Northfleet	d												07 36												
Swanscombe	d												07 38												
Greenhithe for Bluewater	d					07 23							07 41							07 53					
Stone Crossing	d												07 43												
Dartford 4	a					07 28							07 47							07 58					
	d		07 22			07 29			07 31		07 38		07 48			07 52				07 59		08 01		08 08	
Slade Green 4	d			07 25					07 35			07 45						07 55				08 05			08 15
Erith	d			07 28					07 38			07 48						07 58				08 08			08 18
Belvedere	d			07 30					07 40			07 50						08 00				08 10			08 20
Abbey Wood	d			07 33		07 38			07 43			07 53						08 03		08 08		08 13			08 23
Plumstead	d			07 36					07 46			07 56						08 06				08 16			08 26
Woolwich Arsenal 4 ⛴	d			07 39		07 43			07 49			07 59						08 09		08 13		08 19			08 29
Woolwich Dockyard	d			07 42					07 52			08 02						08 12				08 22			08 32
Charlton 4	d			07 45		07 47			07 55			08 05						08 15		08 17		08 25			08 35
Crayford	d									07 37			07 52										08 07		
Bexley	d									07 40			07 55										08 10		
Albany Park	d									07 43			07 58										08 13		
Sidcup 4	d									07 46			08 01										08 16		
New Eltham	d									07 49			08 04										08 19		
Mottingham	d									07 51			08 06										08 21		
Lee	d									07 54			08 09										08 24		
Hither Green 4	d				07 49					07 58			08 12						08 19				08 28		
Barnehurst 4	d		07 29					07 38			07 46					07 59					08 08			08 16	
Bexleyheath	d		07 31					07 40			07 49					08 01					08 10			08 19	
Welling	d		07 34					07 43			07 52					08 04					08 13			08 22	
Falconwood	d		07 37					07 46			07 54					08 07					08 16			08 24	
Eltham	d		07 40					07 49			07 57					08 10					08 19			08 27	
Kidbrooke	d		07 43					07 52			08 00					08 13					08 22			08 30	
Blackheath 4	d		07 46			07 52		07 55			08 04					08 16				08 22	08 25			08 34	
Lewisham 4 ⛴	d		07 50		07 54	07 56		07 59		08 04	08 08				08 14	08 20			08 24	08 26	08 29		08 34	08 38	
St Johns	d				07 56			08 01		08 06					08 16				08 26		08 31		08 36		
New Cross 4 ⊖	d				07 58			08 03		08 08					08 18				08 28		08 33		08 38		
Nunhead 4	d										08 15													08 45	
Peckham Rye 4	d										08 17													08 47	
Denmark Hill 4	d										08 21													08 51	
London Victoria 15 ⊖	a										08 30													09 00	
Westcombe Park	d			07 47					07 57			08 07						08 17				08 27			08 37
Maze Hill	d			07 49					07 59			08 09						08 19				08 29			08 39
Greenwich 4 ⛴	d			07 52					08 02			08 12						08 22				08 32			08 42
Deptford	a			07 54					08 04			08 14						08 24				08 34			08 44
London Bridge 4 ⊖	a		07 58	08 00	08 04	08 05		08 08	08 11	08 14		08 20	08 22		08 24	08 28		08 30	08 34	08 35	08 38	08 41	08 44		08 50
London Cannon Street 4 ⊖	a			08 04	08 08			08 13	08 15	08 19		08 24			08 28			08 34	08 38		08 43	08 45	08 49		08 54
London Waterloo (East) 4 ⊖	a		08 02			08 09							08 26			08 32				08 39					
London Charing Cross 4 ⊖	a		08 06			08 13							08 30			08 36				08 43					
Ebbsfleet International	a	07 17												07 47											
Stratford International ⊖ ⛴	a	07 29												07 59											
St Pancras Int'l 15 ⊖	a	07 36												08 06											

Gillingham and Dartford - London

Network Diagram - see first Page of Table 200

		SE		SE	SE	SE	SE	SE	SE	SE	SE	SE		SE	SE	SE	SE	SE	SE	SE	SE	SE		SE	SE
Gillingham (Kent) 4	d			07 50							07 54							08 20							
Chatham 4	d			07 54							07 58							08 24							
Rochester 4	d			07 57							08 00							08 27							
Maidstone West	d																								
Strood 4	d			08 02							08 05							08 32							
Higham	d										08 10														
Gravesend 4	d	08 02		08 13							08 18						08 32	08 43							
Northfleet	d	08 06															08 36								
Swanscombe	d	08 08															08 38								
Greenhithe for Bluewater	d	08 11									08 23						08 41								
Stone Crossing	d	08 13															08 43								
Dartford 4	a	08 17									08 28						08 47								
	d	08 18				08 22					08 29			08 31	08 38		08 48			08 52					
Slade Green 4	d									08 25				08 35		08 45					08 47				08 55
Erith	d									08 28				08 38		08 48									08 58
Belvedere	d									08 30				08 40		08 50									09 00
Abbey Wood	d									08 33	08 38			08 43		08 53									09 03
Plumstead	d									08 36				08 46		08 56									09 06
Woolwich Arsenal 4	d									08 39	08 43			08 49		08 59									09 09
Woolwich Dockyard	d									08 42				08 52		09 02									09 12
Charlton 4	d								08 37	08 45	08 47			08 55		09 05								09 07	09 15
Crayford	d	08 22						08 37	09 07								08 52							09 37	
Bexley	d	08 25						08 40	09 10								08 55							09 40	
Albany Park	d	08 28						08 43	09 13								08 58							09 43	
Sidcup 4	d	08 31						08 46	09 16								09 01							09 46	
New Eltham	d	08 34						08 49	09 19								09 04							09 49	
Mottingham	d	08 36						08 51	09 21								09 06							09 51	
Lee	d	08 39						08 54	09 24								09 09							09 54	
Hither Green 4	d	08 42					08 49	08 58	09 28								09 12					09 19		09 58	
Barnehurst 4	d					08 29						08 38			08 46					08 59	09a04				
Bexleyheath	d					08 31						08 40			08 49					09 01					
Welling	d					08 34						08 43			08 52					09 04					
Falconwood	d					08 37						08 46			08 54					09 07					
Eltham	d					08 40						08 49			08 57					09 10					
Kidbrooke	d					08 43						08 52			09 00					09 13					
Blackheath 4	d					08 46					08 52	08 55			09 04					09 16					
Lewisham 4	d				08 44	08 50	08 54	09 04	09 34		08 56	08 59			09 08				09 14	09 20		09 24		10 04	
St Johns	d				08 46		08 56	09 06	09 36			09 01							09 16			09 26		10 06	
New Cross 4 ⊖	d				08 48		08 58	09 08	09 38			09 03							09 18			09 28		10 08	
Nunhead 4	d														09 15										
Peckham Rye 4	d														09 17										
Denmark Hill 4	d														09 21										
London Victoria 15 ⊖	a														09 30										
Westcombe Park	d									08 47				08 57		09 07									09 17
Maze Hill	d									08 49				08 59		09 09									09 19
Greenwich 4	d									08 52				09 02		09 12									09 22
Deptford	a									08 54				09 04		09 14									09 24
London Bridge 4 ⊖	a	08 52			08 54	08 58	09 04	09 14	09 44	09 00	09 05	09 08		09 11		09 20	09 22		09 24	09 28		09 34		10 14	09 30
London Cannon Street 4 ⊖	a				08 58		09 08	09 19	09 49	09 04		09 13		09 15		09 24			09 28			09 38		10 19	09 34
London Waterloo (East) 4 ⊖	a	08 56				09 02					09 09						09 26			09 32					
London Charing Cross 4 ⊖	a	09 00				09 06					09 13						09 30			09 36					
Ebbsfleet International	a			08 17														08 47							
Stratford International ⊖	a			08 29														08 59							
St Pancras Int'l 15 ⊖	a			08 36														09 06							

Table 200

Saturdays

Gillingham and Dartford - London

Network Diagram - see first Page of Table 200

		SE	SE	SE	SE	SE	SE	SE	SE	SE	SE	SE	SE	SE	SE	SE	SE	SE	SE	SE	SE	SE	SE	SE
Gillingham (Kent) 4	d	08 24						08 50							08 54						09 20		
Chatham 4	d	08 28						08 54							08 58						09 24		
Rochester 4	d	08 30						08 57							09 00						09 27		
Maidstone West	d																						
Strood 4	d	08 35						09 02							09 05						09 32		
Higham	d	08 40													09 10								
Gravesend 4	d	08 48					09 02	09 13							09 18					09 32	09 43		
Northfleet	d						09 06													09 36			
Swanscombe	d						09 08													09 38			
Greenhithe for Bluewater	d	08 53					09 11								09 23					09 41			
Stone Crossing	d						09 13													09 43			
Dartford 4	a	08 58					09 17								09 28					09 47			
	d	08 59		09 01	09 08		09 18			09 22					09 29		09 31	09 38		09 48			09 52
Slade Green 4	d			09 05		09 15					09 17			09 25			09 35		09 45				
Erith	d			09 08		09 18								09 28			09 38		09 48				
Belvedere	d			09 10		09 20								09 30			09 40		09 50				
Abbey Wood	d	09 08		09 13		09 23								09 33	09 38		09 43		09 53				
Plumstead	d			09 16		09 26								09 36			09 46		09 56				
Woolwich Arsenal 4	d	09 13		09 19		09 29								09 39	09 43		09 49		09 59				
Woolwich Dockyard	d			09 22		09 32								09 42			09 52		10 02				
Charlton 4	d	09 17		09 25		09 35							09 37	09 45	09 47		09 55		10 05				
Crayford	d						09 22						10 07							09 52			
Bexley	d						09 25						10 10							09 55			
Albany Park	d						09 28						10 13							09 58			
Sidcup 4	d						09 31						10 16							10 01			
New Eltham	d						09 34						10 19							10 04			
Mottingham	d						09 36						10 21							10 06			
Lee	d						09 39						10 24							10 09			
Hither Green 4	d						09 42					09 49	10 28							10 12			
Barnehurst 4	d		09 08		09 16					09 29	09a34					09 38		09 46					09 59
Bexleyheath	d		09 10		09 19					09 31						09 40		09 49					10 01
Welling	d		09 13		09 22					09 34						09 43		09 52					10 04
Falconwood	d		09 16		09 24					09 37						09 46		09 54					10 07
Eltham	d		09 19		09 27					09 40						09 49		09 57					10 10
Kidbrooke	d		09 22		09 30					09 43						09 52		10 00					10 13
Blackheath 4	d	09 22	09 25		09 34					09 46					09 52	09 55		10 04					10 16
Lewisham 4	d	09 26	09 29		09 38				09 44	09 50		09 54	10 34		09 56	09 59		10 08				10 14	10 20
St Johns	d		09 31						09 46			09 56	10 36			10 01						10 16	
New Cross 4 ⊖	d		09 33						09 48			09 58	10 38			10 03						10 18	
Nunhead 4	d				09 45													10 15					
Peckham Rye 4	d				09 47													10 17					
Denmark Hill 4	d				09 51													10 21					
London Victoria 15 ⊖	a				10 00													10 30					
Westcombe Park	d			09 27		09 37								09 47			09 57		10 07				
Maze Hill	d			09 29		09 39								09 49			09 59		10 09				
Greenwich 4	d			09 32		09 42								09 52			10 02		10 12				
Deptford	a			09 34		09 44								09 54			10 04		10 14				
London Bridge 4 ⊖	a	09 35	09 38	09 41		09 50	09 52		09 54	09 58		10 04	10 44	10 00	10 05	10 08	10 11		10 20	10 22		10 24	10 28
London Cannon Street 4 ⊖	a		09 43	09 45		09 54			09 58			10 08	10 49	10 04		10 13	10 15		10 24			10 28	
London Waterloo (East) 4 ⊖	a	09 39					09 56			10 02					10 09					10 26			10 32
London Charing Cross 4 ⊖	a	09 43					10 00			10 06					10 13					10 30			10 36
Ebbsfleet International	a							09 17													09 47		
Stratford International ⊖	a							09 29													09 59		
St Pancras Int'l 15 ⊖	a							09 36													10 06		

Table 200

Saturdays

Gillingham and Dartford - London

Network Diagram - see first Page of Table 200

		SE	SE	SE		SE	SE	SE	SE	SE	SE	SE	SE	SE		SE	SE	SE	SE	SE	SE	SE	SE	SE	
Gillingham (Kent) 4	d						09 24						09 50								09 54				
Chatham 4	d						09 28						09 54								09 58				
Rochester 4	d						09 30						09 57								10 00				
Maidstone West	d																								
Strood 4	d						09 35						10 02								10 05				
Higham	d						09 40														10 10				
Gravesend 4	d						09 48					10 02	10 13								10 18				
Northfleet	d											10 06													
Swanscombe	d											10 08													
Greenhithe for Bluewater	d						09 53					10 11									10 23				
Stone Crossing	d											10 13													
Dartford 4	a						09 58					10 17									10 28				
	d						09 59		10 01	10 08		10 18				10 22					10 29		10 31	10 38	
Slade Green 4	d	09 47				09 55			10 05		10 15						10 17			10 25			10 35		
Erith	d					09 58			10 08		10 18									10 28			10 38		
Belvedere	d					10 00			10 10		10 20									10 30			10 40		
Abbey Wood	d					10 03	10 08		10 13		10 23									10 33	10 38		10 43		
Plumstead	d					10 06			10 16		10 26									10 36			10 46		
Woolwich Arsenal 4 ⛴	d					10 09	10 13		10 19		10 29									10 39	10 43		10 49		
Woolwich Dockyard	d					10 12			10 22		10 32									10 42			10 52		
Charlton 4	d			10 07		10 15	10 17		10 25		10 35								10 37	10 45	10 47		10 55		
Crayford	d			10 37								10 22							11 07						
Bexley	d			10 40								10 25							11 10						
Albany Park	d			10 43								10 28							11 13						
Sidcup 4	d			10 46								10 31							11 16						
New Eltham	d			10 49								10 34							11 19						
Mottingham	d			10 51								10 36							11 21						
Lee	d			10 54								10 39							11 24						
Hither Green 4	d		10 19	10 58								10 42						10 49	11 28						
Barnehurst 4	d	10a04						10 08		10 16						10 29	10a34					10 38		10 46	
Bexleyheath	d							10 10		10 19						10 31						10 40		10 49	
Welling	d							10 13		10 22						10 34						10 43		10 52	
Falconwood	d							10 16		10 24						10 37						10 46		10 54	
Eltham	d							10 19		10 27						10 40						10 49		10 57	
Kidbrooke	d							10 22		10 30						10 43						10 52		11 00	
Blackheath 4	d						10 22	10 25		10 34						10 46					10 52	10 55		11 04	
Lewisham 4 ⛴	d		10 24	11 04			10 26	10 29		10 38				10 44		10 50		10 54	11 34		10 56	10 59		11 08	
St Johns	d		10 26	11 06				10 31						10 46				10 56	11 36			11 01			
New Cross 4 ⊖	d		10 28	11 08				10 33						10 48				10 58	11 38			11 03			
Nunhead 4	d									10 45														11 15	
Peckham Rye 4	d									10 47														11 17	
Denmark Hill 4	d									10 51														11 21	
London Victoria 15 ⊖	a									11 00														11 30	
Westcombe Park	d					10 17			10 27		10 37									10 47			10 57		
Maze Hill	d					10 19			10 29		10 39									10 49			10 59		
Greenwich 4 ⛴	d					10 22			10 32		10 42									10 52			11 02		
Deptford	a					10 24			10 34		10 44									10 54			11 04		
London Bridge 4 ⊖	a		10 34	11 14		10 30	10 35	10 38	10 41		10 50	10 52		10 54		10 58		11 04	11 44	11 00	11 05	11 08	11 11		
London Cannon Street 4 ⊖	a		10 38	11 19		10 34		10 43	10 45		10 54			10 58				11 08	11 49	11 04		11 13	11 15		
London Waterloo (East) 4 ⊖	a						10 39					10 56				11 02					11 09				
London Charing Cross 4 ⊖	a						10 43					11 00				11 06					11 13				
Ebbsfleet International	a												10 17												
Stratford International ⊖ ⛴	a												10 29												
St Pancras Int'l 15 ⊖	a												10 36												

Table 200

Saturdays

Gillingham and Dartford - London

Network Diagram - see first Page of Table 200

		SE	SE	SE	SE	SE	SE	SE	SE	SE		SE	SE	SE	SE	SE	SE	SE	SE	SE		SE	SE	SE	SE
Gillingham (Kent) [4]	d			10 20								10 24						10 50							
Chatham [4]	d			10 24								10 28						10 54							
Rochester [4]	d			10 27								10 30						10 57							
Maidstone West	d																								
Strood [4]	d			10 32								10 35						11 02							
Higham	d											10 40													
Gravesend [4]	d		10 32	10 43								10 48					11 02	11 13							
Northfleet	d		10 36														11 06								
Swanscombe	d		10 38														11 08								
Greenhithe for Bluewater	d		10 41									10 53					11 11								
Stone Crossing	d		10 43														11 13								
Dartford [4]	a		10 47									10 58					11 17								
	d		10 48			10 52						10 59		11 01	11 08		11 18			11 22					
Slade Green [4]	d	10 45					10 47			10 55				11 05		11 15						11 17			11 25
Erith	d	10 48								10 58				11 08		11 18									11 28
Belvedere	d	10 50								11 00				11 10		11 20									11 30
Abbey Wood	d	10 53								11 03		11 08		11 13		11 23									11 33
Plumstead	d	10 56								11 06				11 16		11 26									11 36
Woolwich Arsenal [4]	d	10 59								11 09		11 13		11 19		11 29									11 39
Woolwich Dockyard	d	11 02								11 12				11 22		11 32									11 42
Charlton [4]	d	11 05							11 07	11 15		11 17		11 25		11 35								11 37	11 45
Crayford	d		10 52						11 37								11 22							12 07	
Bexley	d		10 55						11 40								11 25							12 10	
Albany Park	d		10 58						11 43								11 28							12 13	
Sidcup [4]	d		11 01						11 46								11 31							12 16	
New Eltham	d		11 04						11 49								11 34							12 19	
Mottingham	d		11 06						11 51								11 36							12 21	
Lee	d		11 09						11 54								11 39							12 24	
Hither Green [4]	d		11 12					11 19	11 58								11 42						11 49	12 28	
Barnehurst [4]	d					10 59	11a04						11 08		11 16					11 29		11a34			
Bexleyheath	d					11 01							11 10		11 19					11 31					
Welling	d					11 04							11 13		11 22					11 34					
Falconwood	d					11 07							11 16		11 24					11 37					
Eltham	d					11 10							11 19		11 27					11 40					
Kidbrooke	d					11 13							11 22		11 30					11 43					
Blackheath [4]	d					11 16						11 22	11 25		11 34					11 46					
Lewisham [4]	d				11 14	11 20		11 24	12 04			11 26	11 29		11 38				11 44	11 50			11 54	12 34	
St Johns	d				11 16			11 26	12 06				11 31						11 46				11 56	12 36	
New Cross [4] ⊖	d				11 18			11 28	12 08				11 33						11 48				11 58	12 38	
Nunhead [4]	d														11 45										
Peckham Rye [4]	d														11 47										
Denmark Hill [4]	d														11 51										
London Victoria [15] ⊖	a														12 00										
Westcombe Park	d	11 07								11 17				11 27		11 37									11 47
Maze Hill	d	11 09								11 19				11 29		11 39									11 49
Greenwich [4]	d	11 12								11 22				11 32		11 42									11 52
Deptford	a	11 14								11 24				11 34		11 44									11 54
London Bridge [4] ⊖	a	11 20	11 22		11 24	11 28		11 34	12 14	11 30		11 35	11 38	11 41		11 50	11 52		11 54	11 58			12 04	12 44	12 00
London Cannon Street [4] ⊖	a	11 24			11 28			11 38	12 19	11 34			11 43	11 45		11 54			11 58				12 08	12 49	12 04
London Waterloo (East) [4] ⊖	a		11 26			11 32						11 39					11 56			12 02					
London Charing Cross [4] ⊖	a		11 30			11 36						11 43					12 00			12 06					
Ebbsfleet International	a			10 47														11 17							
Stratford International ⊖	a			10 59														11 29							
St Pancras Int'l [15] ⊖	a			11 06														11 36							

Table 200

Saturdays

Gillingham and Dartford - London

Network Diagram - see first Page of Table 200

		SE	SE	SE	SE	SE	SE	SE	SE	SE	SE	SE	SE	SE	SE	SE	SE	SE	SE	SE	SE	SE	SE
Gillingham (Kent) 4	d	10 54						11 20							11 24							11 50	
Chatham 4	d	10 58						11 24							11 28							11 54	
Rochester 4	d	11 00						11 27							11 30							11 57	
Maidstone West	d																						
Strood 4	d	11 05						11 32							11 35							12 02	
Higham	d	11 10													11 40								
Gravesend 4	d	11 18					11 32	11 43							11 48						12 02	12 13	
Northfleet	d						11 36														12 06		
Swanscombe	d						11 38														12 08		
Greenhithe for Bluewater	d	11 23					11 41								11 53						12 11		
Stone Crossing	d						11 43														12 13		
Dartford 4	a	11 28					11 47								11 58						12 17		
	d	11 29		11 31	11 38		11 48			11 52					11 59		12 01	12 08			12 18		12 22
Slade Green 4	d			11 35		11 45					11 47			11 55			12 05		12 15				
Erith	d			11 38		11 48								11 58			12 08		12 18				
Belvedere	d			11 40		11 50								12 00			12 10		12 20				
Abbey Wood	d	11 38		11 43		11 53								12 03	12 08		12 13		12 23				
Plumstead	d			11 46		11 56								12 06			12 16		12 26				
Woolwich Arsenal 4 ⛴	d	11 43		11 49		11 59								12 09	12 13		12 19		12 29				
Woolwich Dockyard	d			11 52		12 02								12 12			12 22		12 32				
Charlton 4	d	11 47		11 55		12 05							12 07	12 15	12 17		12 25		12 35				
Crayford	d						11 52						12 37								12 22		
Bexley	d						11 55						12 40								12 25		
Albany Park	d						11 58						12 43								12 28		
Sidcup 4	d						12 01						12 46								12 31		
New Eltham	d						12 04						12 49								12 34		
Mottingham	d						12 06						12 51								12 36		
Lee	d						12 09						12 54								12 39		
Hither Green 4	d						12 12					12 19	12 58								12 42		
Barnehurst 4	d		11 38		11 46					11 59	12a04					12 08		12 16					12 29
Bexleyheath	d		11 40		11 49					12 01						12 10		12 19					12 31
Welling	d		11 43		11 52					12 04						12 13		12 22					12 34
Falconwood	d		11 46		11 54					12 07						12 16		12 24					12 37
Eltham	d		11 49		11 57					12 10						12 19		12 27					12 40
Kidbrooke	d		11 52		12 00					12 13						12 22		12 30					12 43
Blackheath 4	d	11 52	11 55		12 04					12 16					12 22	12 25		12 34					12 46
Lewisham 4 ⛴	d	11 56	11 59		12 08				12 14	12 20		12 24	13 04		12 26	12 29		12 38				12 44	12 50
St Johns	d		12 01						12 16			12 26	13 06			12 31						12 46	
New Cross 4 ⊖	d		12 03						12 18			12 28	13 08			12 33						12 48	
Nunhead 4	d				12 15													12 45					
Peckham Rye 4	d				12 17													12 47					
Denmark Hill 4	d				12 21													12 51					
London Victoria 15 ⊖	a				12 30													13 00					
Westcombe Park	d			11 57		12 07								12 17			12 27		12 37				
Maze Hill	d			11 59		12 09								12 19			12 29		12 39				
Greenwich 4 ⛴	d			12 02		12 12								12 22			12 32		12 42				
Deptford	a			12 04		12 14								12 24			12 34		12 44				
London Bridge 4 ⊖	a	12 05	12 08	12 11		12 20	12 22		12 24	12 28		12 34	13 14	12 30	12 35	12 38	12 41		12 50	12 52		12 54	12 58
London Cannon Street 4 ⊖	a		12 13	12 15		12 24			12 28			12 38	13 19	12 34		12 43	12 45		12 54			12 58	
London Waterloo (East) 4 ⊖	a	12 09					12 26			12 32					12 39					12 56			13 02
London Charing Cross 4 ⊖	a	12 13					12 30			12 36					12 43					13 00			13 06
Ebbsfleet International	a							11 47														12 17	
Stratford International ⊖ ⛴	a							11 59														12 29	
St Pancras Int'l 15 ⊖	a							12 06														12 36	

Table 200

Saturdays

Gillingham and Dartford - London

Network Diagram - see first Page of Table 200

		SE		SE	SE	SE	SE	SE	SE	SE	SE	SE		SE	SE	SE	SE	SE	SE	SE	SE	SE		SE	SE
Gillingham (Kent) 4	d						11 54							12 20							12 24				
Chatham 4	d						11 58							12 24							12 28				
Rochester 4	d						12 00							12 27							12 30				
Maidstone West	d																								
Strood 4	d						12 05							12 32							12 35				
Higham	d						12 10														12 40				
Gravesend 4	d						12 18					12 32		12 43							12 48				
Northfleet	d											12 36													
Swanscombe	d											12 38													
Greenhithe for Bluewater	d						12 23					12 41									12 53				
Stone Crossing	d											12 43													
Dartford 4	a						12 28					12 47									12 58				
	d						12 29		12 31	12 38		12 48				12 52					12 59			13 01	13 08
Slade Green 4	d	12 17				12 25			12 35		12 45						12 47			12 55				13 05	
Erith	d					12 28			12 38		12 48									12 58				13 08	
Belvedere	d					12 30			12 40		12 50									13 00				13 10	
Abbey Wood	d					12 33	12 38		12 43		12 53									13 03	13 08			13 13	
Plumstead	d					12 36			12 46		12 56									13 06				13 16	
Woolwich Arsenal 4 ⛴	d					12 39	12 43		12 49		12 59									13 09	13 13			13 19	
Woolwich Dockyard	d					12 42			12 52		13 02									13 12				13 22	
Charlton 4	d				12 37	12 45	12 47		12 55		13 05								13 07	13 15	13 17			13 25	
Crayford	d				13 07							12 52							13 37						
Bexley	d				13 10							12 55							13 40						
Albany Park	d				13 13							12 58							13 43						
Sidcup 4	d				13 16							13 01							13 46						
New Eltham	d				13 19							13 04							13 49						
Mottingham	d				13 21							13 06							13 51						
Lee	d				13 24							13 09							13 54						
Hither Green 4	d			12 49	13 28							13 12						13 19	13 58						
Barnehurst 4	d	12a34						12 38		12 46						12 59	13a04					13 08			13 16
Bexleyheath	d							12 40		12 49						13 01						13 10			13 19
Welling	d							12 43		12 52						13 04						13 13			13 22
Falconwood	d							12 46		12 54						13 07						13 16			13 24
Eltham	d							12 49		12 57						13 10						13 19			13 27
Kidbrooke	d							12 52		13 00						13 13						13 22			13 30
Blackheath 4	d						12 52	12 55		13 04						13 16					13 22	13 25			13 34
Lewisham 4 ⛴	d			12 54	13 34		12 56	12 59		13 08					13 14	13 20		13 24	14 04		13 26	13 29			13 38
St Johns	d			12 56	13 36			13 01							13 16			13 26	14 06			13 31			
New Cross 4 ⊖	d			12 58	13 38			13 03							13 18			13 28	14 08			13 33			
Nunhead 4	d									13 15															13 45
Peckham Rye 4	d									13 17															13 47
Denmark Hill 4	d									13 21															13 51
London Victoria 15 ⊖	a									13 30															14 00
Westcombe Park	d					12 47			12 57		13 07									13 17				13 27	
Maze Hill	d					12 49			12 59		13 09									13 19				13 29	
Greenwich 4 ⛴	d					12 52			13 02		13 12									13 22				13 32	
Deptford	a					12 54			13 04		13 14									13 24				13 34	
London Bridge 4 ⊖	a			13 04	13 44	13 00	13 05	13 08	13 11		13 20	13 22			13 24	13 28		13 34	14 14	13 30	13 35	13 38		13 41	
London Cannon Street 4 ⊖	a			13 08	13 49	13 04		13 13	13 15		13 24				13 28			13 38	14 19	13 34		13 43		13 45	
London Waterloo (East) 4 ⊖	a						13 09					13 26				13 33					13 39				
London Charing Cross 4 ⊖	a						13 13					13 30				13 36					13 43				
Ebbsfleet International	a													12 47											
Stratford International ⊖ ⛴	a													12 59											
St Pancras Int'l 15 ⊖	a													13 06											

Table 200

Saturdays

Gillingham and Dartford - London

Network Diagram - see first Page of Table 200

		SE	SE	SE	SE	SE	SE	SE		SE	SE	SE	SE	SE	SE	SE	SE	SE		SE	SE	SE	SE	SE	SE
Gillingham (Kent) 4	d			12 50								12 54						13 20							
Chatham 4	d			12 54								12 58						13 24							
Rochester 4	d			12 57								13 00						13 27							
Maidstone West	d																								
Strood 4	d			13 02								13 05						13 32							
Higham	d											13 10													
Gravesend 4	d		13 02	13 13								13 18					13 32	13 43							
Northfleet	d		13 06														13 36								
Swanscombe	d		13 08														13 38								
Greenhithe for Bluewater	d		13 11									13 23					13 41								
Stone Crossing	d		13 13														13 43								
Dartford 4	a		13 17									13 28					13 47								
	d		13 18			13 22						13 29		13 31	13 38		13 48				13 52				
Slade Green 4	d	13 15					13 17				13 25			13 35		13 45						13 47			13 55
Erith	d	13 18									13 28			13 38		13 48									13 58
Belvedere	d	13 20									13 30			13 40		13 50									14 00
Abbey Wood	d	13 23									13 33	13 38		13 43		13 53									14 03
Plumstead	d	13 26									13 36			13 46		13 56									14 06
Woolwich Arsenal 4 ⛴	d	13 29									13 39	13 43		13 49		13 59									14 09
Woolwich Dockyard	d	13 32									13 42			13 52		14 02									14 12
Charlton 4	d	13 35								13 37	13 45	13 47		13 55		14 05								14 07	14 15
Crayford	d		13 22							14 07							13 52							14 37	
Bexley	d		13 25							14 10							13 55							14 40	
Albany Park	d		13 28							14 13							13 58							14 43	
Sidcup 4	d		13 31							14 16							14 01							14 46	
New Eltham	d		13 34							14 19							14 04							14 49	
Mottingham	d		13 36							14 21							14 06							14 51	
Lee	d		13 39							14 24							14 09							14 54	
Hither Green 4	d		13 42					13 49		14 28							14 12						14 19	14 58	
Barnehurst 4	d					13 29	13a34						13 38		13 46						13 59	14a04			
Bexleyheath	d					13 31							13 40		13 49						14 01				
Welling	d					13 34							13 43		13 52						14 04				
Falconwood	d					13 37							13 46		13 54						14 07				
Eltham	d					13 40							13 49		13 57						14 10				
Kidbrooke	d					13 43							13 52		14 00						14 13				
Blackheath 4	d					13 46						13 52	13 55		14 04						14 16				
Lewisham 4 ⛴	d				13 44	13 50		13 54		14 34		13 56	13 59		14 08					14 14	14 20		14 24	15 04	
St Johns	d				13 46			13 56		14 36			14 01							14 16			14 26	15 06	
New Cross 4 ⊖	d				13 48			13 58		14 38			14 03							14 18			14 28	15 08	
Nunhead 4	d														14 15										
Peckham Rye 4	d														14 17										
Denmark Hill 4	d														14 21										
London Victoria 15 ⊖	a														14 30										
Westcombe Park	d	13 37									13 47			13 57		14 07									14 17
Maze Hill	d	13 39									13 49			13 59		14 09									14 19
Greenwich 4 ⛴	d	13 42									13 52			14 02		14 12									14 22
Deptford	a	13 44									13 54			14 04		14 14									14 24
London Bridge 4 ⊖	a	13 50	13 52		13 54	13 58		14 04		14 44	14 00	14 05	14 08	14 11		14 20	14 22			14 24	14 28		14 34	15 14	14 30
London Cannon Street 4 ⊖	a	13 54			13 58			14 08		14 49	14 04		14 13	14 15		14 24				14 28			14 38	15 19	14 34
London Waterloo (East) 4 ⊖	a		13 56			14 02						14 09					14 26				14 32				
London Charing Cross 4 ⊖	a		14 00			14 06						14 13					14 30				14 36				
Ebbsfleet International	a			13 17														13 47							
Stratford International ⊖ ⛴	a			13 29														13 59							
St Pancras Int'l 15 ⊖	a			13 36														14 06							

Table 200

Saturdays

Gillingham and Dartford - London

Network Diagram - see first Page of Table 200

		SE	SE	SE		SE	SE	SE	SE	SE	SE	SE	SE	SE		SE	SE	SE	SE	SE	SE	SE	SE	SE	
Gillingham (Kent) 4	d	13 24							13 50								13 54						14 20		
Chatham 4	d	13 28							13 54								13 58						14 24		
Rochester 4	d	13 30							13 57								14 00						14 27		
Maidstone West	d																								
Strood 4	d	13 35							14 02								14 05						14 32		
Higham	d	13 40															14 10								
Gravesend 4	d	13 48						14 02	14 13								14 18					14 32	14 43		
Northfleet	d							14 06														14 36			
Swanscombe	d							14 08														14 38			
Greenhithe for Bluewater	d	13 53						14 11									14 23					14 41			
Stone Crossing	d							14 13														14 43			
Dartford 4	a	13 58						14 17									14 28					14 47			
	d	13 59		14 01		14 08		14 18			14 22						14 29		14 31	14 38		14 48			
Slade Green 4	d			14 05			14 15					14 17				14 25			14 35		14 45				
Erith	d			14 08			14 18									14 28			14 38		14 48				
Belvedere	d			14 10			14 20									14 30			14 40		14 50				
Abbey Wood	d	14 08		14 13			14 23									14 33	14 38		14 43		14 53				
Plumstead	d			14 16			14 26									14 36			14 46		14 56				
Woolwich Arsenal 4 ⛴	d	14 13		14 19			14 29									14 39	14 43		14 49		14 59				
Woolwich Dockyard	d			14 22			14 32									14 42			14 52		15 02				
Charlton 4	d	14 17		14 25			14 35							14 37		14 45	14 47		14 55		15 05				
Crayford	d							14 22						15 07								14 52			
Bexley	d							14 25						15 10								14 55			
Albany Park	d							14 28						15 13								14 58			
Sidcup 4	d							14 31						15 16								15 01			
New Eltham	d							14 34						15 19								15 04			
Mottingham	d							14 36						15 21								15 06			
Lee	d							14 39						15 24								15 09			
Hither Green 4	d							14 42					14 49	15 28								15 12			
Barnehurst 4	d		14 08			14 16					14 29	14a34						14 38		14 46					
Bexleyheath	d		14 10			14 19					14 31							14 40		14 49					
Welling	d		14 13			14 22					14 34							14 43		14 52					
Falconwood	d		14 16			14 24					14 37							14 46		14 54					
Eltham	d		14 19			14 27					14 40							14 49		14 57					
Kidbrooke	d		14 22			14 30					14 43							14 52		15 00					
Blackheath 4	d	14 22	14 25			14 34					14 46						14 52	14 55		15 04					
Lewisham 4 ⛴	d	14 26	14 29			14 38				14 44	14 50		14 54	15 34			14 56	14 59		15 08				15 14	
St Johns	d		14 31							14 46			14 56	15 36				15 01						15 16	
New Cross 4 ⊖	d		14 33							14 48			14 58	15 38				15 03						15 18	
Nunhead 4	d					14 45														15 15					
Peckham Rye 4	d					14 47														15 17					
Denmark Hill 4	d					14 51														15 21					
London Victoria 15 ⊖	a					15 00														15 30					
Westcombe Park	d			14 27			14 37									14 47			14 57		15 07				
Maze Hill	d			14 29			14 39									14 49			14 59		15 09				
Greenwich 4 ⛴	d			14 32			14 42									14 52			15 02		15 12				
Deptford	a			14 34			14 44									14 54			15 04		15 14				
London Bridge 4 ⊖	a	14 35	14 38	14 41			14 50	14 52		14 54	14 58		15 04	15 44		15 00	15 05	15 08	15 11		15 20	15 22		15 24	
London Cannon Street 4 ⊖	a		14 43	14 45			14 54			14 58			15 08	15 49		15 04		15 13	15 15		15 24			15 28	
London Waterloo (East) 4 ⊖	a	14 39						14 56			15 02						15 09					15 26			
London Charing Cross 4 ⊖	a	14 43						15 00			15 06						15 13					15 30			
Ebbsfleet International	a								14 17														14 47		
Stratford International ⊖ ⛴	a								14 29														15 02		
St Pancras Int'l 15 ⊖	a								14 36														15 09		

Table 200

Saturdays

Gillingham and Dartford - London

Network Diagram - see first Page of Table 200

		SE	SE	SE	SE	SE	SE	SE	SE	SE	SE	SE	SE	SE	SE	SE	SE	SE	SE	SE	SE	SE	SE
Gillingham (Kent) 4	d						14 24						14 50							14 54			
Chatham 4	d						14 28						14 54							14 58			
Rochester 4	d						14 30						14 57							15 00			
Maidstone West	d																						
Strood 4	d						14 35						15 02							15 05			
Higham	d						14 40													15 10			
Gravesend 4	d						14 48					15 02	15 13							15 18			
Northfleet	d											15 06											
Swanscombe	d											15 08											
Greenhithe for Bluewater	d						14 53					15 11								15 23			
Stone Crossing	d											15 13											
Dartford 4	a						14 58					15 17								15 28			
	d	14 52					14 59		15 01	15 08		15 18			15 22					15 29		15 31	15 38
Slade Green 4	d		14 47			14 55			15 05		15 15					15 17			15 25			15 35	
Erith	d					14 58			15 08		15 18								15 28			15 38	
Belvedere	d					15 00			15 10		15 20								15 30			15 40	
Abbey Wood	d					15 03	15 08		15 13		15 23								15 33	15 38		15 43	
Plumstead	d					15 06			15 16		15 26								15 36			15 46	
Woolwich Arsenal 4 ⛴	d					15 09	15 13		15 19		15 29								15 39	15 43		15 49	
Woolwich Dockyard	d					15 12			15 22		15 32								15 42			15 52	
Charlton 4	d				15 07	15 15	15 17		15 25		15 35							15 37	15 45	15 47		15 55	
Crayford	d				15 37							15 22						16 07					
Bexley	d				15 40							15 25						16 10					
Albany Park	d				15 43							15 28						16 13					
Sidcup 4	d				15 46							15 31						16 16					
New Eltham	d				15 49							15 34						16 19					
Mottingham	d				15 51							15 36						16 21					
Lee	d				15 54							15 39						16 24					
Hither Green 4	d			15 19	15 58							15 42					15 49	16 28					
Barnehurst 4	d	14 59	15a04					15 08		15 16					15 29	15a34					15 38		15 46
Bexleyheath	d	15 01						15 10		15 19					15 31						15 40		15 49
Welling	d	15 04						15 13		15 22					15 34						15 43		15 52
Falconwood	d	15 07						15 16		15 24					15 37						15 46		15 54
Eltham	d	15 10						15 19		15 27					15 40						15 49		15 57
Kidbrooke	d	15 13						15 22		15 30					15 43						15 52		16 00
Blackheath 4	d	15 16					15 22	15 25		15 34					15 46					15 52	15 55		16 04
Lewisham 4 ⛴	d	15 20		15 24	16 04		15 26	15 29		15 38				15 44	15 50		15 54	16 34		15 56	15 59		16 08
St Johns	d			15 26	16 06			15 31						15 46			15 56	16 36			16 01		
New Cross 4 ⊖	d			15 28	16 08			15 33						15 48			15 58	16 38			16 03		
Nunhead 4	d									15 45													16 15
Peckham Rye 4	d									15 47													16 17
Denmark Hill 4	d									15 51													16 21
London Victoria 15 ⊖	a									16 00													16 30
Westcombe Park	d					15 17			15 27		15 37								15 47			15 57	
Maze Hill	d					15 19			15 29		15 39								15 49			15 59	
Greenwich 4 ⛴	d					15 22			15 32		15 42								15 52			16 02	
Deptford	a					15 24			15 34		15 44								15 54			16 04	
London Bridge 4 ⊖	a	15 28		15 34	16 14	15 30	15 35	15 38	15 41		15 50	15 52		15 54	15 58		16 04	16 44	16 00	16 05	16 08	16 11	
London Cannon Street 4 ⊖	a			15 38	16 19	15 34		15 43	15 45		15 54			15 58			16 08	16 49	16 04		16 13	16 15	
London Waterloo (East) 4 ⊖	a	15 32					15 39					15 56			16 02					16 09			
London Charing Cross 4 ⊖	a	15 36					15 43					16 00			16 06					16 13			
Ebbsfleet International	a												15 17										
Stratford International ⊖ ⛴	a												15 29										
St Pancras Int'l 15 ⊖	a												15 36										

Table 200

Saturdays

Gillingham and Dartford - London

Network Diagram - see first Page of Table 200

		SE	SE	SE	SE	SE		SE	SE	SE	SE	SE	SE	SE	SE	SE		SE	SE	SE	SE	SE	SE	SE	SE
Gillingham (Kent) 4	d			15 20								15 24							15 50						
Chatham 4	d			15 24								15 28							15 54						
Rochester 4	d			15 27								15 30							15 57						
Maidstone West	d																								
Strood 4	d			15 32								15 35							16 02						
Higham	d											15 40													
Gravesend 4	d		15 32	15 43								15 48						16 02	16 13						
Northfleet	d		15 36															16 06							
Swanscombe	d		15 38															16 08							
Greenhithe for Bluewater	d		15 41									15 53						16 11							
Stone Crossing	d		15 43															16 13							
Dartford 4	a		15 47									15 58						16 17							
	d		15 48			15 52						15 59		16 01	16 08			16 18			16 22				
Slade Green 4	d	15 45						15 47			15 55			16 05		16 15						16 17			16 25
Erith	d	15 48									15 58			16 08		16 18									16 28
Belvedere	d	15 50									16 00			16 10		16 20									16 30
Abbey Wood	d	15 53									16 03	16 08		16 13		16 23									16 33
Plumstead	d	15 56									16 06			16 16		16 26									16 36
Woolwich Arsenal 4 ⛴	d	15 59									16 09	16 13		16 19		16 29									16 39
Woolwich Dockyard	d	16 02									16 12			16 22		16 32									16 42
Charlton 4	d	16 05								16 07	16 15	16 17		16 25		16 35								16 37	16 45
Crayford	d		15 52							16 37								16 22						17 07	
Bexley	d		15 55							16 40								16 25						17 10	
Albany Park	d		15 58							16 43								16 28						17 13	
Sidcup 4	d		16 01							16 46								16 31						17 16	
New Eltham	d		16 04							16 49								16 34						17 19	
Mottingham	d		16 06							16 51								16 36						17 21	
Lee	d		16 09							16 54								16 39						17 24	
Hither Green 4	d		16 12						16 19	16 58								16 42					16 49	17 28	
Barnehurst 4	d					15 59		16a04					16 08		16 16						16 29	16a34			
Bexleyheath	d					16 01							16 10		16 19						16 31				
Welling	d					16 04							16 13		16 22						16 34				
Falconwood	d					16 07							16 16		16 24						16 37				
Eltham	d					16 10							16 19		16 27						16 40				
Kidbrooke	d					16 13							16 22		16 30						16 43				
Blackheath 4	d					16 16						16 22	16 25		16 34						16 46				
Lewisham 4 ⛴	d				16 14	16 20			16 24	17 04		16 26	16 29		16 38					16 44	16 50		16 54	17 34	
St Johns	d				16 16				16 26	17 06			16 31							16 46			16 56	17 36	
New Cross 4 ⊖	d				16 18				16 28	17 08			16 33							16 48			16 58	17 38	
Nunhead 4	d														16 45										
Peckham Rye 4	d														16 47										
Denmark Hill 4	d														16 51										
London Victoria 15 ⊖	a														17 00										
Westcombe Park	d	16 07									16 17			16 27		16 37									16 47
Maze Hill	d	16 09									16 19			16 29		16 39									16 49
Greenwich 4 ⛴	d	16 12									16 22			16 32		16 42									16 52
Deptford	a	16 14									16 24			16 34		16 44									16 54
London Bridge 4 ⊖	a	16 20	16 22		16 24	16 28			16 34	17 14	16 30	16 35	16 38	16 41		16 50		16 52		16 54	16 58		17 04	17 44	17 00
London Cannon Street 4 ⊖	a	16 24			16 28				16 38	17 19	16 34		16 43	16 45		16 54				16 58			17 08	17 49	17 04
London Waterloo (East) 4 ⊖	a		16 26			16 32						16 39						16 56			17 02				
London Charing Cross 4 ⊖	a		16 30			16 36						16 43						17 00			17 06				
Ebbsfleet International	a			15 47															16 17						
Stratford International ⊖ ⛴	a			16 02															16 29						
St Pancras Int'l 15 ⊖	a			16 09															16 36						

Table 200

Saturdays

Gillingham and Dartford - London

Network Diagram - see first Page of Table 200

		SE		SE	SE	SE	SE	SE	SE	SE	SE	SE		SE	SE	SE	SE	SE	SE	SE	SE	SE		SE	SE
Gillingham (Kent) 4	d	15 54							16 20								16 24							16 50	
Chatham 4	d	15 58							16 24								16 28							16 54	
Rochester 4	d	16 00							16 27								16 30							16 57	
Maidstone West	d																								
Strood 4	d	16 05							16 32								16 35							17 02	
Higham	d	16 10															16 40								
Gravesend 4	d	16 18						16 32	16 43								16 48					17 02		17 13	
Northfleet	d							16 36														17 06			
Swanscombe	d							16 38														17 08			
Greenhithe for Bluewater	d	16 23						16 41									16 53					17 11			
Stone Crossing	d							16 43														17 13			
Dartford 4	a	16 28						16 47									16 58					17 17			
	d	16 29			16 31	16 38		16 48			16 52						16 59		17 01	17 08		17 18			
Slade Green 4	d				16 35		16 45					16 47				16 55			17 05		17 15				
Erith	d				16 38		16 48									16 58			17 08		17 18				
Belvedere	d				16 40		16 50									17 00			17 10		17 20				
Abbey Wood	d	16 38			16 43		16 53									17 03	17 08		17 13		17 23				
Plumstead	d				16 46		16 56									17 06			17 16		17 26				
Woolwich Arsenal 4 ⛴	d	16 43			16 49		16 59									17 09	17 13		17 19		17 29				
Woolwich Dockyard	d				16 52		17 02									17 12			17 22		17 32				
Charlton 4	d	16 47			16 55		17 05								17 07	17 15	17 17		17 25		17 35				
Crayford	d							16 52							17 37							17 22			
Bexley	d							16 55							17 40							17 25			
Albany Park	d							16 58							17 43							17 28			
Sidcup 4	d							17 01							17 46							17 31			
New Eltham	d							17 04							17 49							17 34			
Mottingham	d							17 06							17 51							17 36			
Lee	d							17 09							17 54							17 39			
Hither Green 4	d							17 12						17 19	17 58							17 42			
Barnehurst 4	d			16 38		16 46					16 59	17a04						17 08		17 16					
Bexleyheath	d			16 40		16 49					17 01							17 10		17 19					
Welling	d			16 43		16 52					17 04							17 13		17 22					
Falconwood	d			16 46		16 54					17 07							17 16		17 24					
Eltham	d			16 49		16 57					17 10							17 19		17 27					
Kidbrooke	d			16 52		17 00					17 13							17 22		17 30					
Blackheath 4	d	16 52		16 55		17 04					17 16						17 22	17 25		17 34					
Lewisham 4 ⛴	d	16 56		16 59		17 08				17 14	17 20			17 24	18 04		17 26	17 29		17 38					17 44
St Johns	d			17 01						17 16				17 26	18 06			17 31							17 46
New Cross 4 ⊖	d			17 03						17 18				17 28	18 08			17 33							17 48
Nunhead 4	d					17 15														17 45					
Peckham Rye 4	d					17 17														17 47					
Denmark Hill 4	d					17 21														17 51					
London Victoria 15 ⊖	a					17 30														18 00					
Westcombe Park	d				16 57		17 07									17 17			17 27		17 37				
Maze Hill	d				16 59		17 09									17 19			17 29		17 39				
Greenwich 4 ⛴	d				17 02		17 12									17 22			17 32		17 42				
Deptford	a				17 04		17 14									17 24			17 34		17 44				
London Bridge 4 ⊖	a	17 05		17 08	17 11		17 20	17 22		17 24	17 28			17 34	18 14	17 30	17 35	17 38	17 41		17 50	17 52			17 54
London Cannon Street 4 ⊖	a			17 13	17 15		17 24			17 28				17 38	18 19	17 34		17 43	17 45		17 54				17 58
London Waterloo (East) 4 ⊖	a	17 09						17 26			17 32						17 39					17 56			
London Charing Cross 4 ⊖	a	17 13						17 30			17 36						17 43					18 00			
Ebbsfleet International	a								16 47															17 17	
Stratford International ⊖ ⛴	a								17 02															17 29	
St Pancras Int'l 15 ⊖	a								17 09															17 36	

Table 200

Saturdays

Gillingham and Dartford - London

Network Diagram - see first Page of Table 200

		SE	SE	SE	SE	SE	SE	SE	SE	SE	SE	SE	SE	SE	SE	SE	SE	SE	SE	SE	SE	SE	SE
Gillingham (Kent) 4	d						16 54						17 20							17 24			
Chatham 4	d						16 58						17 24							17 28			
Rochester 4	d						17 00						17 27							17 30			
Maidstone West	d																						
Strood 4	d						17 05						17 32							17 35			
Higham	d						17 10													17 40			
Gravesend 4	d						17 18					17 32	17 43							17 48			
Northfleet	d											17 36											
Swanscombe	d											17 38											
Greenhithe for Bluewater	d						17 23					17 41								17 53			
Stone Crossing	d											17 43											
Dartford 4	a						17 28					17 47								17 58			
	d	17 22					17 29		17 31	17 38		17 48			17 52					17 59		18 01	18 08
Slade Green 4	d		17 17			17 25			17 35		17 45					17 47			17 55			18 05	
Erith	d					17 28			17 38		17 48								17 58			18 08	
Belvedere	d					17 30			17 40		17 50								18 00			18 10	
Abbey Wood	d					17 33	17 38		17 43		17 53								18 03	18 08		18 13	
Plumstead	d					17 36			17 46		17 56								18 06			18 16	
Woolwich Arsenal 4	d					17 39	17 43		17 49		17 59								18 09	18 13		18 19	
Woolwich Dockyard	d					17 42			17 52		18 02								18 12			18 22	
Charlton 4	d				17 37	17 45	17 47		17 55		18 05							18 07	18 15	18 17		18 25	
Crayford	d				18 07							17 52						18 37					
Bexley	d				18 10							17 55						18 40					
Albany Park	d				18 13							17 58						18 43					
Sidcup 4	d				18 16							18 01						18 46					
New Eltham	d				18 19							18 04						18 49					
Mottingham	d				18 21							18 06						18 51					
Lee	d				18 24							18 09						18 54					
Hither Green 4	d			17 49	18 28							18 12					18 19	18 58					
Barnehurst 4	d	17 29	17a34					17 38		17 46					17 59	18a04					18 08		18 16
Bexleyheath	d	17 31						17 40		17 49					18 01						18 10		18 19
Welling	d	17 34						17 43		17 52					18 04						18 13		18 22
Falconwood	d	17 37						17 46		17 54					18 07						18 16		18 24
Eltham	d	17 40						17 49		17 57					18 10						18 19		18 27
Kidbrooke	d	17 43						17 52		18 00					18 13						18 22		18 30
Blackheath 4	d	17 46					17 52	17 55		18 04					18 16					18 22	18 25		18 34
Lewisham 4	d	17 50		17 54	18 34		17 56	17 59		18 08				18 14	18 20		18 24	19 04		18 26	18 29		18 38
St Johns	d			17 56	18 36			18 01						18 16			18 26	19 06			18 31		
New Cross 4	d			17 58	18 38			18 03						18 18			18 28	19 08			18 33		
Nunhead 4	d									18 15													18 45
Peckham Rye 4	d									18 17													18 47
Denmark Hill 4	d									18 21													18 51
London Victoria 15	a									18 30													19 00
Westcombe Park	d					17 47			17 57		18 07								18 17			18 27	
Maze Hill	d					17 49			17 59		18 09								18 19			18 29	
Greenwich 4	d					17 52			18 02		18 12								18 22			18 32	
Deptford	a					17 54			18 04		18 14								18 24			18 34	
London Bridge 4	a	17 58		18 04	18 44	18 00	18 05	18 08	18 11		18 20	18 22		18 24	18 28		18 34	19 14	18 30	18 35	18 38	18 41	
London Cannon Street 4	a			18 08	18 49	18 04		18 13	18 15		18 24			18 28			18 38	19 19	18 34		18 43	18 45	
London Waterloo (East) 4	a	18 02					18 09					18 26			18 32					18 39			
London Charing Cross 4	a	18 06					18 13					18 30			18 36					18 43			
Ebbsfleet International	a												17 47										
Stratford International	a												17 59										
St Pancras Int'l 15	a												18 09										

Table 200

Saturdays

Gillingham and Dartford - London

Network Diagram - see first Page of Table 200

		SE	SE	SE	SE	SE	SE	SE	SE	SE	SE	SE	SE	SE	SE	SE	SE	SE	SE	SE	SE	SE
Gillingham (Kent) 4	d			17 50						17 54					18 20			18 24			18 50	
Chatham 4	d			17 54						17 58					18 24			18 28			18 54	
Rochester 4	d			17 57						18 00					18 27			18 30			18 57	
Maidstone West	d																					
Strood 4	d			18 02						18 05					18 32			18 35			19 02	
Higham	d									18 10								18 40				
Gravesend 4	d		18 02	18 13						18 18				18 32	18 43			18 48		19 02	19 12	
Northfleet	d		18 06											18 36						19 06		
Swanscombe	d		18 08											18 38						19 08		
Greenhithe for Bluewater	d		18 11							18 23				18 41				18 53		19 11		
Stone Crossing	d		18 13											18 43						19 13		
Dartford 4	a		18 17							18 28				18 47				18 58		19 17		
	d		18 18			18 22				18 29		18 31	18 38	18 48			18 52	18 59	19 01	19 18		
Slade Green 4	d	18 15					18 17	18 25				18 35				18 55			19 05			19 25
Erith	d	18 18						18 28				18 38				18 58			19 08			19 28
Belvedere	d	18 20						18 30				18 40				19 00			19 10			19 30
Abbey Wood	d	18 23						18 33		18 38		18 43				19 03		19 08	19 13			19 33
Plumstead	d	18 26						18 36				18 46				19 06			19 16			19 36
Woolwich Arsenal 4 ⛴	d	18 29						18 39		18 43		18 49				19 09		19 13	19 19			19 39
Woolwich Dockyard	d	18 32						18 42				18 52				19 12			19 22			19 42
Charlton 4	d	18 35						18 45		18 47		18 55				19 15		19 17	19 25			19 45
Crayford	d		18 22											18 52						19 22		
Bexley	d		18 25											18 55						19 25		
Albany Park	d		18 28											18 58						19 28		
Sidcup 4	d		18 31											19 01						19 31		
New Eltham	d		18 34											19 04						19 34		
Mottingham	d		18 36											19 06						19 36		
Lee	d		18 39											19 09						19 39		
Hither Green 4	d		18 42						18 49					19 12						19 42		
Barnehurst 4	d					18 29	18a34				18 38		18 46				18 59					
Bexleyheath	d					18 31					18 40		18 49				19 01					
Welling	d					18 34					18 43		18 52				19 04					
Falconwood	d					18 37					18 46		18 54				19 07					
Eltham	d					18 40					18 49		18 57				19 10					
Kidbrooke	d					18 43					18 52		19 00				19 13					
Blackheath 4	d					18 46				18 52	18 55		19 04				19 16	19 22				
Lewisham 4 ⛴	d				18 44	18 50			18 54	18 56	18 59		19 08	19 18			19 20	19 26		19 48		
St Johns	d				18 46				18 56		19 01											
New Cross 4 ⊖	d				18 48				18 58		19 03						19 23			19 51		
Nunhead 4	d												19 15									
Peckham Rye 4	d												19 17									
Denmark Hill 4	d												19 21									
London Victoria 15 ⊖	a												19 30									
Westcombe Park	d	18 37						18 47				18 57				19 17			19 27			19 47
Maze Hill	d	18 39						18 49				18 59				19 19			19 29			19 49
Greenwich 4 ⛴	d	18 42						18 52				19 02				19 22			19 32			19 52
Deptford	a	18 44						18 54				19 04				19 24			19 34			19 54
London Bridge 4 ⊖	a	18 50	18 52		18 54	18 58		19 00	19 04	19 05	19 08	19 11		19 27		19 30	19 33	19 36	19 41	19 57		20 00
London Cannon Street 4 ⊖	a	18 54			18 58			19 04	19 08		19 13	19 15										
London Waterloo (East) 4 ⊖	a		18 56			19 02				19 09				19 32			19 39	19 42	19 45	20 04		
London Charing Cross 4 ⊖	a		19 00			19 06				19 13				19 35			19 42	19 45	19 49	20 07		
Ebbsfleet International	a			18 17											18 47						19 16	
Stratford International ⊖ ⛴	a			18 29											19 02						19 27	
St Pancras Int'l 15 ⊖	a			18 36											19 09						19 38	

Table 200

Saturdays

Gillingham and Dartford - London

Network Diagram - see first Page of Table 200

		SE	SE	SE	SE	SE	SE	SE	SE	SE	SE	SE	SE	SE	SE	SE	SE	SE	SE	SE	SE	SE	SE
Gillingham (Kent) 4	d		18 54			19 20			19 24			19 50		19 54			20 20		20 24			20 50	
Chatham 4	d		18 58			19 24			19 28			19 54		19 58			20 24		20 28			20 54	
Rochester 4	d		19 00			19 27			19 30			19 57		20 00			20 27		20 30			20 57	
Maidstone West	d																						
Strood 4	d		19 05			19 32			19 35			20 02		20 05			20 32		20 35			21 02	
Higham	d		19 10						19 40					20 10					20 40				
Gravesend 4	d		19 18		19 32	19 43			19 48		20 02	20 13		20 18		20 32	20 43		20 48		21 02	21 13	
Northfleet	d				19 36						20 06					20 36					21 06		
Swanscombe	d				19 38						20 08					20 38					21 08		
Greenhithe for Bluewater	d		19 23		19 41				19 53		20 11			20 23		20 41			20 53		21 11		
Stone Crossing	d				19 43						20 13					20 43					21 13		
Dartford 4	a		19 28		19 47				19 58		20 17			20 28		20 47			20 58		21 17		
	d	19 25	19 29	19 31	19 48			19 55	19 59	20 01	20 18		20 25	20 29	20 31	20 48		20 55	20 59	21 01	21 18		21 25
Slade Green 4	d			19 35			19 55			20 05					20 35					21 05			
Erith	d			19 38			19 58			20 08					20 38					21 08			
Belvedere	d			19 40			20 00			20 10					20 40					21 10			
Abbey Wood	d		19 38	19 43			20 03		20 08	20 13				20 38	20 43				21 08	21 13			
Plumstead	d			19 46			20 06			20 16					20 46					21 16			
Woolwich Arsenal 4 ⛴	d		19 43	19 49			20 09		20 13	20 19				20 43	20 49				21 13	21 19			
Woolwich Dockyard	d			19 52			20 12			20 22					20 52					21 22			
Charlton 4	d		19 47	19 55			20 15		20 17	20 25				20 47	20 55				21 17	21 25			
Crayford	d				19 52						20 22					20 52					21 22		
Bexley	d				19 55						20 25					20 55					21 25		
Albany Park	d				19 58						20 28					20 58					21 28		
Sidcup 4	d				20 01						20 31					21 01					21 31		
New Eltham	d				20 04						20 34					21 04					21 34		
Mottingham	d				20 06						20 36					21 06					21 36		
Lee	d				20 09						20 39					21 09					21 39		
Hither Green 4	d				20 12						20 42					21 12					21 42		
Barnehurst 4	d	19 32						20 02					20 32					21 02					21 32
Bexleyheath	d	19 34						20 04					20 34					21 04					21 34
Welling	d	19 37						20 07					20 37					21 07					21 37
Falconwood	d	19 40						20 10					20 40					21 10					21 40
Eltham	d	19 42						20 12					20 42					21 12					21 42
Kidbrooke	d	19 45						20 15					20 45					21 15					21 45
Blackheath 4	d	19 49	19 52					20 19	20 22				20 49	20 52				21 19	21 22				21 49
Lewisham 4 ⛴	d	19 53	19 56		20 18			20 23	20 26		20 48		20 53	20 56		21 18		21 23	21 26		21 48		21 53
St Johns	d																						
New Cross 4 ⊖	d	19 56			20 21			20 26			20 51		20 56			21 21		21 26			21 51		21 56
Nunhead 4	d																						
Peckham Rye 4	d																						
Denmark Hill 4	d																						
London Victoria 15 ⊖	a																						
Westcombe Park	d			19 57			20 17			20 27					20 57					21 27			
Maze Hill	d			19 59			20 19			20 29					20 59					21 29			
Greenwich 4 ⛴	d			20 02			20 22			20 32					21 02					21 32			
Deptford	a			20 04			20 24			20 34					21 04					21 34			
London Bridge 4 ⊖	a	20 03	20 06	20 11	20 27		20 30	20 33	20 36	20 41	20 57		21 03	21 06	21 11	21 27		21 33	21 36	21 41	21 57		22 01
London Cannon Street 4 ⊖	a																						
London Waterloo (East) 4 ⊖	a	20 08	20 10	20 15	20 34			20 38	20 40	20 45	21 04		21 08	21 10	21 15	21 34		21 38	21 40	21 45	22 04		22 06
London Charing Cross 4 ⊖	a	20 12	20 14	20 19	20 37			20 42	20 44	20 49	21 07		21 12	21 14	21 19	21 37		21 42	21 44	21 49	22 07		22 10
Ebbsfleet International	a					19 47						20 17					20 47					21 17	
Stratford International ⊖ ⛴	a					19 59						20 29					21 02					21 29	
St Pancras Int'l 15 ⊖	a					20 06						20 36					21 09					21 36	

Table 200

Saturdays

Gillingham and Dartford - London

Network Diagram - see first Page of Table 200

		SE	SE	SE	SE	SE	SE	SE	SE	SE	SE	SE	SE	SE	SE	SE	SE	SE	SE
Gillingham (Kent) 4	d	20 54			21 20		21 24			21 50		21 54			22 20		22 24		22 54
Chatham 4	d	20 58			21 24		21 28			21 54		21 58			22 24		22 28		22 58
Rochester 4	d	21 00			21 27		21 30			21 57		22 00			22 27		22 30		23 00
Maidstone West	d																		
Strood 4	d	21 05			21 32		21 35			22 02		22 05			22 32		22 35		23 05
Higham	d	21 10					21 40					22 10					22 40		23 10
Gravesend 4	d	21 18		21 32	21 43		21 48		22 02	22 13		22 18		22 32	22 43		22 48		23 18
Northfleet	d			21 36					22 06					22 36					
Swanscombe	d			21 38					22 08					22 38					
Greenhithe for Bluewater	d	21 23		21 41			21 53		22 11			22 23		22 41			22 53		23 23
Stone Crossing	d			21 43					22 13					22 43					
Dartford 4	a	21 28		21 47			21 58		22 17			22 28		22 47			22 58		23 28
	d	21 29	21 31	21 48		21 55	21 59	22 01	22 18		22 25	22 29	22 31	22 48		22 55	22 59	23 01	
Slade Green 4	d		21 35					22 05					22 35					23 05	
Erith	d		21 38					22 08					22 38					23 08	
Belvedere	d		21 40					22 10					22 40					23 10	
Abbey Wood	d	21 38	21 43				22 08	22 13				22 38	22 43				23 08	23 13	
Plumstead	d		21 46					22 16					22 46					23 16	
Woolwich Arsenal 4 ⛴	d	21 43	21 49				22 13	22 19				22 43	22 49				23 13	23 19	
Woolwich Dockyard	d		21 52					22 22					22 52					23 22	
Charlton 4	d	21 47	21 55				22 17	22 25				22 47	22 55				23 17	23 25	
Crayford	d			21 52					22 22					22 52					
Bexley	d			21 55					22 25					22 55					
Albany Park	d			21 58					22 28					22 58					
Sidcup 4	d			22 01					22 31					23 01					
New Eltham	d			22 04					22 34					23 04					
Mottingham	d			22 06					22 36					23 06					
Lee	d			22 09					22 39					23 09					
Hither Green 4	d			22 12					22 42					23 12					
Barnehurst 4	d					22 02					22 32					23 02			
Bexleyheath	d					22 04					22 34					23 04			
Welling	d					22 07					22 37					23 07			
Falconwood	d					22 10					22 40					23 10			
Eltham	d					22 12					22 42					23 12			
Kidbrooke	d					22 15					22 45					23 15			
Blackheath 4	d	21 52				22 19	22 22				22 49	22 52				23 19	23 22		
Lewisham 4 ⛴	d	21 56		22 18		22 23	22 26		22 48		22 53	22 56		23 18		23 23	23 26		
St Johns	d																		
New Cross 4 ⊖	d			22 21		22 26			22 51		22 56			23 21		23 26			
Nunhead 4	d																		
Peckham Rye 4	d																		
Denmark Hill 4	d																		
London Victoria 15 ⊖	a																		
Westcombe Park	d		21 57					22 27					22 57					23 27	
Maze Hill	d		21 59					22 29					22 59					23 29	
Greenwich 4 ⛴	d		22 02					22 32					23 02					23 32	
Deptford	a		22 04					22 34					23 04					23 34	
London Bridge 4 ⊖	a	22 05	22 11	22 27		22 31	22 35	22 41	22 57		23 01	23 05	23 11	23 27		23 31	23 35	23 41	
London Cannon Street 4 ⊖	a																		
London Waterloo (East) 4 ⊖	a	22 09	22 15	22 34		22 36	22 39	22 45	23 04		23 06	23 09	23 15	23 34		23 36	23 39	23 45	
London Charing Cross 4 ⊖	a	22 13	22 19	22 37		22 40	22 43	22 49	23 07		23 10	23 13	23 20	23 37		23 40	23 43	23 49	
Ebbsfleet International	a				21 47					22 17					22 47				
Stratford International ⊖ ⛴	a				21 59					22 29					22 59				
St Pancras Int'l 15 ⊖	a				22 06					22 36					23 06				

Table 200

Sundays

Gillingham and Dartford - London

Network Diagram - see first Page of Table 200

		SE	SE	SE	SE	SE	SE	SE	SE	SE		SE	SE	SE	SE	SE	SE	SE	SE	SE		SE	SE	SE	SE
Gillingham (Kent) [4]	d							06 45					07 15	07 20				07 45	07 50						08 15
Chatham [4]	d							06 49					07 19	07 24				07 49	07 54						08 19
Rochester [4]	d							06 51					07 21	07 27				07 51	07 57						08 21
Maidstone West	d																								
Strood [4]	d							06 56					07 26	07 32				07 56	08 02						08 26
Higham	d							07 01					07 31					08 01							08 31
Gravesend [4]	d							07 09					07 39	07 43				08 09	08 13						08 39
Northfleet	d							07 12					07 42					08 12							08 42
Swanscombe	d							07 14					07 44					08 14							08 44
Greenhithe for Bluewater	d							07 18					07 48					08 18							08 48
Stone Crossing	d							07 20					07 50					08 20							08 50
Dartford [4]	a							07 24					07 54					08 24							08 54
	d	06 40	06 43	06 48	07 10	07 13	07 18	07 29	07 40	07 43		07 48	07 59		08 10	08 13	08 18	08 29				08 40	08 43	08 48	08 59
Slade Green [4]	d		06 48			07 18				07 48						08 18							08 48		
Erith	d		06 50			07 20				07 50						08 20							08 50		
Belvedere	d		06 53			07 23				07 53						08 23							08 53		
Abbey Wood	d		06 56			07 26		07 38		07 56			08 08			08 26		08 38					08 56		09 08
Plumstead	d		06 59			07 29				07 59						08 29				08 47			08 59		
Woolwich Arsenal [4] ⛴	d		07 02			07 32		07 43		08 02			08 13			08 32		08 43		08 50			09 02		09 13
Woolwich Dockyard	d		07 04			07 34				08 04						08 34				08 52			09 04		
Charlton [4]	d		07 07			07 37		07 47		08 07			08 17			08 37		08 47		08 55			09 07		09 17
Crayford	d			06 52			07 22					07 52					08 22							08 52	
Bexley	d			06 55			07 25					07 55					08 25							08 55	
Albany Park	d			06 58			07 28					07 58					08 28							08 58	
Sidcup [4]	d			07 01			07 31					08 01					08 31							09 01	
New Eltham	d			07 04			07 34					08 04					08 34							09 04	
Mottingham	d			07 06			07 36					08 06					08 36							09 06	
Lee	d			07 09			07 39					08 09					08 39							09 09	
Hither Green [4]	d			07 12			07 42					08 12					08 42							09 12	
Barnehurst [4]	d	06 47			07 17				07 47						08 17							08 47			
Bexleyheath	d	06 49			07 19				07 49						08 19							08 49			
Welling	d	06 52			07 22				07 52						08 22							08 52			
Falconwood	d	06 55			07 25				07 55						08 25							08 55			
Eltham	d	06 58			07 28				07 58						08 28							08 58			
Kidbrooke	d	07 01			07 31				08 01						08 31							09 01			
Blackheath [4]	d	07 04			07 34			07 52	08 04				08 22		08 34			08 52				09 04			09 22
Lewisham [4] ⛴	d	07 08		07 18	07 38		07 48	07 56	08 08			08 18	08 26		08 38		08 48	08 56				09 08		09 18	09 26
St Johns	d																								
New Cross [4] ⊖	d	07 11			07 41				08 11						08 41							09 11			
Nunhead [4]	d																								
Peckham Rye [4]	d																								
Denmark Hill [4]	d																								
London Victoria [15] ⊖	a																								
Westcombe Park	d		07 09			07 39				08 09						08 39				08 57			09 09		
Maze Hill	d		07 11			07 41				08 11						08 41				08 59			09 11		
Greenwich [4] ⛴	d		07 15			07 45				08 15						08 45				09 03			09 15		
Deptford	a		07 17			07 47				08 17						08 47				09 05			09 17		
London Bridge [4] ⊖	a	07 19	07 23	07 26	07 49	07 53	07 56	08 06	08 19	08 23		08 26	08 36		08 49	08 53	08 56	09 06		09 11		09 19	09 23	09 26	09 36
London Cannon Street [4] ⊖	a																								
London Waterloo (East) [4] ⊖	a	07 25	07 27	07 30	07 55	07 57	08 00	08 11	08 25	08 27		08 30	08 41		08 55	08 57	09 00	09 11				09 25	09 27	09 30	09 41
London Charing Cross [4] ⊖	a	07 28	07 31	07 34	07 58	08 01	08 04	08 14	08 28	08 31		08 34	08 44		08 58	09 01	09 04	09 14				09 28	09 31	09 34	09 44
Ebbsfleet International	a													07 47					08 17						
Stratford International ⊖ ⛴	a													07 59					08 29						
St Pancras Int'l [15] ⊖	a													08 06					08 36						

Table 200

Sundays

Gillingham and Dartford - London

Network Diagram - see first Page of Table 200

		SE	SE	SE	SE	SE	SE	SE	SE	SE	SE	SE	SE	SE	SE	SE	SE	SE	SE	SE	SE	SE	SE
Gillingham (Kent) [4]	d	08 20					08 50	08 54					09 20	09 24					09 50	09 54			
Chatham [4]	d	08 24					08 54	08 58					09 24	09 28					09 54	09 58			
Rochester [4]	d	08 27					08 57	09 00					09 27	09 30					09 57	10 00			
Maidstone West	d																						
Strood [4]	d	08 32					09 02	09 05					09 32	09 35					10 02	10 05			
Higham	d							09 10						09 40						10 10			
Gravesend [4]	d	08 43				09 02	09 13	09 18				09 32	09 43	09 48				10 02	10 13	10 18			
Northfleet	d					09 06						09 36						10 06					
Swanscombe	d					09 08						09 38						10 08					
Greenhithe for Bluewater	d					09 11		09 23				09 41		09 53				10 11		10 23			
Stone Crossing	d					09 13						09 43						10 13					
Dartford [4]	a					09 17		09 28				09 47		09 58				10 17		10 28			
	d			09 10	09 13	09 18		09 29		09 40	09 43	09 48		09 59		10 10	10 13	10 18		10 29		10 40	10 43
Slade Green [4]	d				09 18						09 48						10 18						10 48
Erith	d				09 20						09 50						10 20						10 50
Belvedere	d				09 23						09 53						10 23						10 53
Abbey Wood	d				09 26			09 38			09 56			10 08			10 26			10 38			10 56
Plumstead	d		09 17		09 29				09 47		09 59				10 17		10 29				10 47		10 59
Woolwich Arsenal [4] ⛴	d		09 20		09 32			09 43	09 50		10 02			10 13	10 20		10 32			10 43	10 50		11 02
Woolwich Dockyard	d		09 22		09 34				09 52		10 04				10 22		10 34				10 52		11 04
Charlton [4]	d		09 25		09 37			09 47	09 55		10 07			10 17	10 25		10 37			10 47	10 55		11 07
Crayford	d					09 22						09 52						10 22					
Bexley	d					09 25						09 55						10 25					
Albany Park	d					09 28						09 58						10 28					
Sidcup [4]	d					09 31						10 01						10 31					
New Eltham	d					09 34						10 04						10 34					
Mottingham	d					09 36						10 06						10 36					
Lee	d					09 39						10 09						10 39					
Hither Green [4]	d					09 42						10 12						10 42					
Barnehurst [4]	d			09 17						09 47						10 17						10 47	
Bexleyheath	d			09 19						09 49						10 19						10 49	
Welling	d			09 22						09 52						10 22						10 52	
Falconwood	d			09 25						09 55						10 25						10 55	
Eltham	d			09 28						09 58						10 28						10 58	
Kidbrooke	d			09 31						10 01						10 31						11 01	
Blackheath [4]	d			09 34				09 52		10 04				10 22		10 34				10 52		11 04	
Lewisham [4] ⛴	d			09 38		09 48		09 56		10 08		10 18		10 26		10 38		10 48		10 56		11 08	
St Johns	d																						
New Cross [4] ⊖	d			09 41						10 11						10 41						11 11	
Nunhead [4]	d																						
Peckham Rye [4]	d																						
Denmark Hill [4]	d																						
London Victoria [15] ⊖	a																						
Westcombe Park	d		09 27		09 39				09 57		10 09				10 27		10 39				10 57		11 09
Maze Hill	d		09 29		09 41				09 59		10 11				10 29		10 41				10 59		11 11
Greenwich [4] ⛴	d		09 33		09 45				10 03		10 15				10 33		10 45				11 03		11 15
Deptford	a		09 35		09 47				10 05		10 17				10 35		10 47				11 05		11 17
London Bridge [4] ⊖	a		09 41	09 49	09 53	09 56		10 06	10 11	10 19	10 23	10 26		10 36	10 41	10 49	10 53	10 56		11 06	11 11	11 19	11 23
London Cannon Street [4] ⊖	a																						
London Waterloo (East) [4] ⊖	a			09 55	09 57	10 00		10 11		10 25	10 27	10 30		10 41		10 55	10 57	11 00		11 11		11 25	11 27
London Charing Cross [4] ⊖	a			09 58	10 01	10 04		10 14		10 28	10 31	10 34		10 44		10 58	11 01	11 04		11 14		11 28	11 31
Ebbsfleet International	a	08 47					09 17						09 47						10 17				
Stratford International ⊖ ⛴	a	08 59					09 29						09 59						10 29				
St Pancras Int'l [15] ⊖	a	09 06					09 36						10 06						10 36				

Table 200

Sundays

Gillingham and Dartford - London

Network Diagram - see first Page of Table 200

		SE	SE	SE	SE	SE	SE	SE	SE	SE	SE	SE	SE	SE	SE	SE	SE	SE	SE	SE	SE	SE
Gillingham (Kent) 4	d		10 20	10 24					10 50	10 54					11 20	11 24					11 50	11 54
Chatham 4	d		10 24	10 28					10 54	10 58					11 24	11 28					11 54	11 58
Rochester 4	d		10 27	10 30					10 57	11 00					11 27	11 30					11 57	12 00
Maidstone West	d																					
Strood 4	d		10 32	10 35					11 02	11 05					11 32	11 35					12 02	12 05
Higham	d			10 40						11 10						11 40						12 10
Gravesend 4	d	10 32	10 43	10 48				11 02	11 13	11 18				11 32	11 43	11 48				12 02	12 13	12 18
Northfleet	d	10 36						11 06						11 36						12 06		
Swanscombe	d	10 38						11 08						11 38						12 08		
Greenhithe for Bluewater	d	10 41		10 53				11 11		11 23				11 41		11 53				12 11		12 23
Stone Crossing	d	10 43						11 13						11 43						12 13		
Dartford 4	a	10 47		10 58				11 17		11 28				11 47		11 58				12 17		12 28
	d	10 48		10 59		11 10	11 13	11 18		11 29		11 40	11 43	11 48		11 59		12 10	12 13	12 18		12 29
Slade Green 4	d						11 18						11 48						12 18			
Erith	d						11 20						11 50						12 20			
Belvedere	d						11 23						11 53						12 23			
Abbey Wood	d			11 08			11 26			11 38			11 56			12 08			12 26			12 38
Plumstead	d				11 17		11 29				11 47		11 59				12 17		12 29			
Woolwich Arsenal 4	d			11 13	11 20		11 32			11 43	11 50		12 02			12 13	12 20		12 32			12 43
Woolwich Dockyard	d				11 22		11 34				11 52		12 04				12 22		12 34			
Charlton 4	d			11 17	11 25		11 37			11 47	11 55		12 07			12 17	12 25		12 37			12 47
Crayford	d	10 52						11 22						11 52						12 22		
Bexley	d	10 55						11 25						11 55						12 25		
Albany Park	d	10 58						11 28						11 58						12 28		
Sidcup 4	d	11 01						11 31						12 01						12 31		
New Eltham	d	11 04						11 34						12 04						12 34		
Mottingham	d	11 06						11 36						12 06						12 36		
Lee	d	11 09						11 39						12 09						12 39		
Hither Green 4	d	11 12						11 42						12 12						12 42		
Barnehurst 4	d					11 17						11 47						12 17				
Bexleyheath	d					11 19						11 49						12 19				
Welling	d					11 22						11 52						12 22				
Falconwood	d					11 25						11 55						12 25				
Eltham	d					11 28						11 58						12 28				
Kidbrooke	d					11 31						12 01						12 31				
Blackheath 4	d			11 22		11 34				11 52		12 04				12 22		12 34				12 52
Lewisham 4 ⛴	d	11 18		11 26		11 38		11 48		11 56		12 08		12 18		12 26		12 38		12 48		12 56
St Johns	d																					
New Cross 4 ⊖	d					11 41						12 11						12 41				
Nunhead 4	d																					
Peckham Rye 4	d																					
Denmark Hill 4	d																					
London Victoria 15 ⊖	a																					
Westcombe Park	d				11 27		11 39				11 57		12 09				12 27		12 39			
Maze Hill	d				11 29		11 41				11 59		12 11				12 29		12 41			
Greenwich 4 ⛴	d				11 33		11 45				12 03		12 15				12 33		12 45			
Deptford	a				11 35		11 47				12 05		12 17				12 35		12 47			
London Bridge 4 ⊖	a	11 26		11 36	11 41	11 49	11 53	11 56		12 06	12 11	12 19	12 23	12 26		12 36	12 41	12 49	12 53	12 56		13 06
London Cannon Street 4 ⊖	a																					
London Waterloo (East) 4 ⊖	a	11 30		11 41		11 55	11 57	12 00		12 11		12 25	12 27	12 30		12 41		12 55	12 57	13 00		13 11
London Charing Cross 4 ⊖	a	11 34		11 44		11 58	12 01	12 04		12 14		12 28	12 31	12 34		12 44		12 58	13 01	13 04		13 14
Ebbsfleet International	a		10 47						11 17						11 47						12 17	
Stratford International ⊖ ⛴	a		10 59						11 29						11 59						12 29	
St Pancras Int'l 15 ⊖	a		11 06						11 36						12 06						12 36	

Table 200

Sundays

Gillingham and Dartford - London

Network Diagram - see first Page of Table 200

		SE	SE	SE	SE	SE	SE	SE	SE	SE	SE	SE	SE	SE	SE	SE	SE	SE	SE	SE	SE	SE	SE
Gillingham (Kent) [4]	d					12 20	12 24					12 50	12 54					13 20	13 24				
Chatham [4]	d					12 24	12 28					12 54	12 58					13 24	13 28				
Rochester [4]	d					12 27	12 30					12 57	13 00					13 27	13 30				
Maidstone West	d																						
Strood [4]	d					12 32	12 35					13 02	13 05					13 32	13 35				
Higham	d						12 40						13 10						13 40				
Gravesend [4]	d				12 32	12 43	12 48				13 02	13 13	13 18				13 32	13 43	13 48				14 02
Northfleet	d				12 36						13 06						13 36						14 06
Swanscombe	d				12 38						13 08						13 38						14 08
Greenhithe for Bluewater	d				12 41		12 53				13 11		13 23				13 41		13 53				14 11
Stone Crossing	d				12 43						13 13						13 43						14 13
Dartford [4]	a				12 47		12 58				13 17		13 28				13 47		13 58				14 17
	d		12 40	12 43	12 48		12 59		13 10	13 13	13 18		13 29		13 40	13 43	13 48		13 59		14 10	14 13	14 18
Slade Green [4]	d			12 48						13 18						13 48						14 18	
Erith	d			12 50						13 20						13 50						14 20	
Belvedere	d			12 53						13 23						13 53						14 23	
Abbey Wood	d			12 56			13 08			13 26			13 38			13 56			14 08			14 26	
Plumstead	d	12 47		12 59				13 17		13 29				13 47		13 59				14 17		14 29	
Woolwich Arsenal [4]	d	12 50		13 02			13 13	13 20		13 32			13 43	13 50		14 02			14 13	14 20		14 32	
Woolwich Dockyard	d	12 52		13 04				13 22		13 34				13 52		14 04				14 22		14 34	
Charlton [4]	d	12 55		13 07			13 17	13 25		13 37			13 47	13 55		14 07			14 17	14 25		14 37	
Crayford	d				12 52						13 22						13 52						14 22
Bexley	d				12 55						13 25						13 55						14 25
Albany Park	d				12 58						13 28						13 58						14 28
Sidcup [4]	d				13 01						13 31						14 01						14 31
New Eltham	d				13 04						13 34						14 04						14 34
Mottingham	d				13 06						13 36						14 06						14 36
Lee	d				13 09						13 39						14 09						14 39
Hither Green [4]	d				13 12						13 42						14 12						14 42
Barnehurst [4]	d		12 47						13 17						13 47						14 17		
Bexleyheath	d		12 49						13 19						13 49						14 19		
Welling	d		12 52						13 22						13 52						14 22		
Falconwood	d		12 55						13 25						13 55						14 25		
Eltham	d		12 58						13 28						13 58						14 28		
Kidbrooke	d		13 01						13 31						14 01						14 31		
Blackheath [4]	d		13 04				13 22		13 34				13 52		14 04				14 22		14 34		
Lewisham [4]	d		13 08		13 18		13 26		13 38		13 48		13 56		14 08		14 18		14 26		14 38		14 48
St Johns	d																						
New Cross [4] ⊖	d		13 11						13 41						14 11						14 41		
Nunhead [4]	d																						
Peckham Rye [4]	d																						
Denmark Hill [4]	d																						
London Victoria [15] ⊖	a																						
Westcombe Park	d	12 57		13 09				13 27		13 39				13 57		14 09				14 27		14 39	
Maze Hill	d	12 59		13 11				13 29		13 41				13 59		14 11				14 29		14 41	
Greenwich [4]	d	13 03		13 15				13 33		13 45				14 03		14 15				14 33		14 45	
Deptford	a	13 05		13 17				13 35		13 47				14 05		14 17				14 35		14 47	
London Bridge [4] ⊖	a	13 11	13 19	13 23	13 26		13 36	13 41	13 49	13 53	13 56		14 06	14 11	14 19	14 23	14 26		14 36	14 41	14 49	14 53	14 56
London Cannon Street [4] ⊖	a																						
London Waterloo (East) [4] ⊖	a		13 25	13 27	13 30		13 41		13 55	13 57	14 00		14 11		14 25	14 27	14 30		14 41		14 55	14 57	15 00
London Charing Cross [4] ⊖	a		13 28	13 31	13 34		13 44		13 58	14 01	14 04		14 14		14 28	14 31	14 34		14 44		14 58	15 01	15 04
Ebbsfleet International	a					12 47						13 17						13 47					
Stratford International ⊖	a					12 59						13 29						14 02					
St Pancras Int'l [15] ⊖	a					13 06						13 36						14 09					

Table 200

Sundays

Gillingham and Dartford - London

Network Diagram - see first Page of Table 200

		SE	SE	SE	SE	SE	SE	SE	SE	SE	SE	SE	SE	SE	SE	SE	SE	SE	SE	SE	SE	SE
Gillingham (Kent) 4	d	13 50	13 54					14 20	14 24					14 50	14 54					15 20	15 24	
Chatham 4	d	13 54	13 58					14 24	14 28					14 54	14 58					15 24	15 28	
Rochester 4	d	13 57	14 00					14 27	14 30					14 57	15 00					15 27	15 30	
Maidstone West	d																					
Strood 4	d	14 02	14 05					14 32	14 35					15 02	15 05					15 32	15 35	
Higham	d		14 10						14 40						15 10						15 40	
Gravesend 4	d	14 13	14 18				14 32	14 43	14 48				15 02	15 13	15 18				15 32	15 43	15 48	
Northfleet	d						14 36						15 06						15 36			
Swanscombe	d						14 38						15 08						15 38			
Greenhithe for Bluewater	d		14 23				14 41		14 53				15 11		15 23				15 41		15 53	
Stone Crossing	d						14 43						15 13						15 43			
Dartford 4	a		14 28				14 47		14 58				15 17		15 28				15 47		15 58	
	d		14 29		14 40	14 43	14 48		14 59		15 10	15 13	15 18		15 29		15 40	15 43	15 48		15 59	
Slade Green 4	d					14 48						15 18						15 48				
Erith	d					14 50						15 20						15 50				
Belvedere	d					14 53						15 23						15 53				
Abbey Wood	d		14 38			14 56			15 08			15 26			15 38			15 56			16 08	
Plumstead	d			14 47		14 59				15 17		15 29				15 47		15 59				16 17
Woolwich Arsenal 4	d		14 43	14 50		15 02			15 13	15 20		15 32			15 43	15 50		16 02			16 13	16 20
Woolwich Dockyard	d			14 52		15 04				15 22		15 34				15 52		16 04				16 22
Charlton 4	d		14 47	14 55		15 07			15 17	15 25		15 37			15 47	15 55		16 07			16 17	16 25
Crayford	d						14 52						15 22						15 52			
Bexley	d						14 55						15 25						15 55			
Albany Park	d						14 58						15 28						15 58			
Sidcup 4	d						15 01						15 31						16 01			
New Eltham	d						15 04						15 34						16 04			
Mottingham	d						15 06						15 36						16 06			
Lee	d						15 09						15 39						16 09			
Hither Green 4	d						15 12						15 42						16 12			
Barnehurst 4	d				14 47						15 17						15 47					
Bexleyheath	d				14 49						15 19						15 49					
Welling	d				14 52						15 22						15 52					
Falconwood	d				14 55						15 25						15 55					
Eltham	d				14 58						15 28						15 58					
Kidbrooke	d				15 01						15 31						16 01					
Blackheath 4	d		14 52		15 04				15 22		15 34				15 52		16 04				16 22	
Lewisham 4	d		14 56		15 08		15 18		15 26		15 38		15 48		15 56		16 08		16 18		16 26	
St Johns	d																					
New Cross 4 ⊖	d				15 11						15 41						16 11					
Nunhead 4	d																					
Peckham Rye 4	d																					
Denmark Hill 4	d																					
London Victoria 15 ⊖	a																					
Westcombe Park	d			14 57		15 09				15 27		15 39				15 57		16 09				16 27
Maze Hill	d			14 59		15 11				15 29		15 41				15 59		16 11				16 29
Greenwich 4	d			15 03		15 15				15 33		15 45				16 03		16 15				16 33
Deptford	a			15 05		15 17				15 35		15 47				16 05		16 17				16 35
London Bridge 4 ⊖	a		15 06	15 11	15 19	15 23	15 26		15 36	15 41	15 49	15 53	15 56		16 06	16 11	16 19	16 23	16 26		16 36	16 41
London Cannon Street 4 ⊖	a																					
London Waterloo (East) 4 ⊖	a		15 11		15 25	15 27	15 30		15 41		15 55	15 57	16 00		16 11		16 25	16 27	16 30		16 41	
London Charing Cross 4 ⊖	a		15 14		15 28	15 31	15 34		15 44		15 58	16 01	16 04		16 14		16 28	16 31	16 34		16 44	
Ebbsfleet International	a	14 17						14 47						15 17						15 47		
Stratford International ⊖	a	14 29						14 59						15 29						16 02		
St Pancras Int'l 15 ⊖	a	14 36						15 06						15 36						16 09		

Table 200

Sundays

Gillingham and Dartford - London

Network Diagram - see first Page of Table 200

		SE	SE	SE	SE	SE	SE	SE	SE	SE		SE	SE	SE	SE	SE	SE	SE	SE	SE		SE	SE	SE	SE
Gillingham (Kent) [4]	d				15 50	15 54						16 20	16 24					16 50	16 54						17 20
Chatham [4]	d				15 54	15 58						16 24	16 28					16 54	16 58						17 24
Rochester [4]	d				15 57	16 00						16 27	16 30					16 57	17 00						17 27
Maidstone West	d																								
Strood [4]	d				16 02	16 05						16 32	16 35					17 02	17 05						17 32
Higham	d					16 10							16 40						17 10						
Gravesend [4]	d			16 02	16 13	16 18				16 32		16 43	16 48				17 02	17 13	17 18					17 32	17 43
Northfleet	d			16 06						16 36							17 06							17 36	
Swanscombe	d			16 08						16 38							17 08							17 38	
Greenhithe for Bluewater	d			16 11		16 23				16 41			16 53				17 11		17 23					17 41	
Stone Crossing	d			16 13						16 43							17 13							17 43	
Dartford [4]	a			16 17		16 28				16 47			16 58				17 17		17 28					17 47	
	d	16 10	16 13	16 18		16 29		16 40	16 43	16 48			16 59		17 10	17 13	17 18		17 29			17 40	17 43	17 48	
Slade Green [4]	d		16 18						16 48							17 18							17 48		
Erith	d		16 20						16 50							17 20							17 50		
Belvedere	d		16 23						16 53							17 23							17 53		
Abbey Wood	d		16 26			16 38			16 56				17 08			17 26			17 38				17 56		
Plumstead	d		16 29				16 47		16 59					17 17		17 29				17 47			17 59		
Woolwich Arsenal [4] ⛴	d		16 32			16 43	16 50		17 02				17 13	17 20		17 32			17 43	17 50			18 02		
Woolwich Dockyard	d		16 34				16 52		17 04					17 22		17 34				17 52			18 04		
Charlton [4]	d		16 37			16 47	16 55		17 07				17 17	17 25		17 37			17 47	17 55			18 07		
Crayford	d			16 22						16 52							17 22							17 52	
Bexley	d			16 25						16 55							17 25							17 55	
Albany Park	d			16 28						16 58							17 28							17 58	
Sidcup [4]	d			16 31						17 01							17 31							18 01	
New Eltham	d			16 34						17 04							17 34							18 04	
Mottingham	d			16 36						17 06							17 36							18 06	
Lee	d			16 39						17 09							17 39							18 09	
Hither Green [4]	d			16 42						17 12							17 42							18 12	
Barnehurst [4]	d	16 17						16 47							17 17							17 47			
Bexleyheath	d	16 19						16 49							17 19							17 49			
Welling	d	16 22						16 52							17 22							17 52			
Falconwood	d	16 25						16 55							17 25							17 55			
Eltham	d	16 28						16 58							17 28							17 58			
Kidbrooke	d	16 31						17 01							17 31							18 01			
Blackheath [4]	d	16 34				16 52		17 04					17 22		17 34				17 52			18 04			
Lewisham [4] ⛴	d	16 38		16 48		16 56		17 08		17 18			17 26		17 38		17 48		17 56			18 08		18 18	
St Johns	d																								
New Cross [4] ⊖	d	16 41						17 11							17 41							18 11			
Nunhead [4]	d																								
Peckham Rye [4]	d																								
Denmark Hill [4]	d																								
London Victoria [15] ⊖	a																								
Westcombe Park	d		16 39				16 57		17 09					17 27		17 39				17 57			18 09		
Maze Hill	d		16 41				16 59		17 11					17 29		17 41				17 59			18 11		
Greenwich [4] ⛴	d		16 45				17 03		17 15					17 33		17 45				18 03			18 15		
Deptford	a		16 47				17 05		17 17					17 35		17 47				18 05			18 17		
London Bridge [4] ⊖	a	16 49	16 53	16 56		17 06	17 11	17 19	17 23	17 26			17 36	17 41	17 49	17 53	17 56		18 06	18 11		18 19	18 23	18 26	
London Cannon Street [4] ⊖	a																								
London Waterloo (East) [4] ⊖	a	16 55	16 57	17 00		17 11		17 25	17 27	17 30			17 41		17 55	17 57	18 00		18 11			18 25	18 27	18 30	
London Charing Cross [4] ⊖	a	16 58	17 01	17 04		17 14		17 28	17 31	17 34			17 44		17 58	18 01	18 04		18 14			18 28	18 31	18 34	
Ebbsfleet International	a				16 17							16 47						17 17							17 47
Stratford International ⊖ ⛴	a				16 29							17 02						17 29							17 59
St Pancras Int'l [15] ⊖	a				16 36							17 09						17 36							18 09

Table 200

Sundays

Gillingham and Dartford - London

Network Diagram - see first Page of Table 200

		SE	SE	SE	SE	SE		SE	SE	SE	SE	SE	SE	SE	SE	SE		SE	SE	SE	SE	SE	SE	SE	SE
Gillingham (Kent) 4	d	17 24						17 50	17 54				18 20	18 24					18 50	18 54				19 20	19 24
Chatham 4	d	17 28						17 54	17 58				18 24	18 28					18 54	18 58				19 24	19 28
Rochester 4	d	17 30						17 57	18 00				18 27	18 30					18 57	19 00				19 27	19 30
Maidstone West	d																								
Strood 4	d	17 35						18 02	18 05				18 32	18 35					19 02	19 05				19 32	19 35
Higham	d	17 40							18 10					18 40						19 10					19 40
Gravesend 4	d	17 48				18 02		18 13	18 18			18 32	18 43	18 48				19 02	19 13	19 18			19 32	19 43	19 48
Northfleet	d					18 06						18 36						19 06					19 36		
Swanscombe	d					18 08						18 38						19 08					19 38		
Greenhithe for Bluewater	d	17 53				18 11			18 23			18 41		18 53				19 11		19 23			19 41		19 53
Stone Crossing	d					18 13						18 43						19 13					19 43		
Dartford 4	a	17 58				18 17			18 28			18 47		18 58				19 17		19 28			19 47		19 58
	d	17 59		18 10	18 13	18 18			18 29	18 40	18 43	18 48		18 59	19 10	19 13		19 18		19 29	19 40	19 43	19 48		19 59
Slade Green 4	d				18 18						18 48					19 18						19 48			
Erith	d				18 20						18 50					19 20						19 50			
Belvedere	d				18 23						18 53					19 23						19 53			
Abbey Wood	d	18 08			18 26				18 38		18 56			19 08		19 26				19 38		19 56			20 08
Plumstead	d		18 17		18 29						18 59					19 29						19 59			
Woolwich Arsenal 4 ⛴	d	18 13	18 20		18 32				18 43		19 02			19 13		19 32				19 43		20 02			20 13
Woolwich Dockyard	d		18 22		18 34						19 04					19 34						20 04			
Charlton 4	d	18 17	18 25		18 37				18 47		19 07			19 17		19 37				19 47		20 07			20 17
Crayford	d					18 22						18 52						19 22					19 52		
Bexley	d					18 25						18 55						19 25					19 55		
Albany Park	d					18 28						18 58						19 28					19 58		
Sidcup 4	d					18 31						19 01						19 31					20 01		
New Eltham	d					18 34						19 04						19 34					20 04		
Mottingham	d					18 36						19 06						19 36					20 06		
Lee	d					18 39						19 09						19 39					20 09		
Hither Green 4	d					18 42						19 12						19 42					20 12		
Barnehurst 4	d			18 17						18 47					19 17						19 47				
Bexleyheath	d			18 19						18 49					19 19						19 49				
Welling	d			18 22						18 52					19 22						19 52				
Falconwood	d			18 25						18 55					19 25						19 55				
Eltham	d			18 28						18 58					19 28						19 58				
Kidbrooke	d			18 31						19 01					19 31						20 01				
Blackheath 4	d	18 22		18 34					18 52	19 04				19 22	19 34					19 52	20 04				20 22
Lewisham 4 ⛴	d	18 26		18 38		18 48			18 56	19 08		19 18		19 26	19 38			19 48		19 56	20 08		20 18		20 26
St Johns	d																								
New Cross 4 ⊖	d			18 41						19 11					19 41						20 11				
Nunhead 4	d																								
Peckham Rye 4	d																								
Denmark Hill 4	d																								
London Victoria 15 ⊖	a																								
Westcombe Park	d		18 27		18 39						19 09					19 39						20 09			
Maze Hill	d		18 29		18 41						19 11					19 41						20 11			
Greenwich 4 ⛴	d		18 33		18 45						19 15					19 45						20 15			
Deptford	a		18 35		18 47						19 17					19 47						20 17			
London Bridge 4 ⊖	a	18 36	18 41	18 49	18 53	18 56			19 06	19 19	19 23	19 26		19 36	19 49	19 53		19 56		20 06	20 19	20 23	20 26		20 36
London Cannon Street 4 ⊖	a																								
London Waterloo (East) 4 ⊖	a	18 41		18 55	18 57	19 00			19 11	19 25	19 27	19 30		19 41	19 55	19 57		20 00		20 11	20 25	20 27	20 30		20 41
London Charing Cross 4 ⊖	a	18 44		18 58	19 01	19 04			19 14	19 28	19 31	19 34		19 44	19 58	20 01		20 04		20 14	20 28	20 31	20 34		20 44
Ebbsfleet International	a							18 17					18 47						19 17					19 47	
Stratford International ⊖ ⛴	a							18 29					18 59						19 29					19 59	
St Pancras Int'l 15 ⊖	a							18 36					19 06						19 36					20 06	

Table 200

Sundays

Gillingham and Dartford - London

Network Diagram - see first Page of Table 200

		SE		SE	SE	SE	SE	SE	SE	SE	SE	SE		SE	SE	SE	SE	SE	SE	SE	SE	SE		SE	SE
Gillingham (Kent) [4]	d					19 45	19 50				20 15	20 20					20 45	20 50				21 15		21 20	
Chatham [4]	d					19 49	19 54				20 19	20 24					20 49	20 54				21 19		21 24	
Rochester [4]	d					19 51	19 57				20 21	20 27					20 51	20 57				21 21		21 27	
Maidstone West	d																								
Strood [4]	d					19 56	20 02				20 26	20 32					20 56	21 02				21 26		21 32	
Higham	d					20 01					20 31						21 01					21 31			
Gravesend [4]	d					20 09	20 13				20 39	20 43					21 09	21 13				21 39		21 43	
Northfleet	d					20 12					20 42						21 12					21 42			
Swanscombe	d					20 14					20 44						21 14					21 44			
Greenhithe for Bluewater	d					20 18					20 48						21 18					21 48			
Stone Crossing	d					20 20					20 50						21 20					21 50			
Dartford [4]	a					20 24					20 54						21 24					21 54			
	d	20 10		20 13	20 18	20 29		20 40	20 43	20 48	20 59			21 10	21 13	21 18	21 29		21 40	21 43	21 48	21 59			22 10
Slade Green [4]	d			20 18					20 48						21 18					21 48					
Erith	d			20 20					20 50						21 20					21 50					
Belvedere	d			20 23					20 53						21 23					21 53					
Abbey Wood	d			20 26		20 38			20 56		21 08				21 26		21 38			21 56		22 08			
Plumstead	d			20 29					20 59						21 29					21 59					
Woolwich Arsenal [4] ⛴	d			20 32		20 43			21 02		21 13				21 32		21 43			22 02		22 13			
Woolwich Dockyard	d			20 34					21 04						21 34					22 04					
Charlton [4]	d			20 37		20 47			21 07		21 17				21 37		21 47			22 07		22 17			
Crayford	d				20 22					20 52						21 22					21 52				
Bexley	d				20 25					20 55						21 25					21 55				
Albany Park	d				20 28					20 58						21 28					21 58				
Sidcup [4]	d				20 31					21 01						21 31					22 01				
New Eltham	d				20 34					21 04						21 34					22 04				
Mottingham	d				20 36					21 06						21 36					22 06				
Lee	d				20 39					21 09						21 39					22 09				
Hither Green [4]	d				20 42					21 12						21 42					22 12				
Barnehurst [4]	d	20 17						20 47						21 17					21 47						22 17
Bexleyheath	d	20 19						20 49						21 19					21 49						22 19
Welling	d	20 22						20 52						21 22					21 52						22 22
Falconwood	d	20 25						20 55						21 25					21 55						22 25
Eltham	d	20 28						20 58						21 28					21 58						22 28
Kidbrooke	d	20 31						21 01						21 31					22 01						22 31
Blackheath [4]	d	20 34				20 52		21 04			21 22			21 34			21 52		22 04			22 22			22 34
Lewisham [4] ⛴	d	20 38			20 48	20 56		21 08		21 18	21 26			21 38		21 48	21 56		22 08		22 18	22 26			22 38
St Johns	d																								
New Cross [4] ⊖	d	20 41						21 11						21 41					22 11						22 41
Nunhead [4]	d																								
Peckham Rye [4]	d																								
Denmark Hill [4]	d																								
London Victoria [15] ⊖	a																								
Westcombe Park	d			20 39					21 09						21 39					22 09					
Maze Hill	d			20 41					21 11						21 41					22 11					
Greenwich [4] ⛴	d			20 45					21 15						21 45					22 15					
Deptford	a			20 47					21 17						21 47					22 17					
London Bridge [4] ⊖	a	20 49		20 53	20 56	21 06		21 19	21 23	21 26	21 36			21 49	21 53	21 56	22 06		22 19	22 23	22 26	22 36			22 49
London Cannon Street [4] ⊖	a																								
London Waterloo (East) [4] ⊖	a	20 55		20 57	21 00	21 11		21 25	21 27	21 30	21 41			21 55	21 57	22 00	22 11		22 25	22 27	22 30	22 41			22 55
London Charing Cross [4] ⊖	a	20 58		21 01	21 04	21 14		21 28	21 31	21 34	21 44			21 58	22 01	22 04	22 14		22 28	22 31	22 34	22 44			22 58
Ebbsfleet International	a						20 17					20 47						21 17						21 47	
Stratford International ⊖ ⛴	a						20 29					21 02						21 29						21 59	
St Pancras Int'l [15] ⊖	a						20 36					21 09						21 36						22 06	

Table 200

Sundays

Gillingham and Dartford - London

Network Diagram - see first Page of Table 200

		SE	SE	SE	SE	SE	SE	SE		SE	SE
Gillingham (Kent) 4	d			21 45	21 50					22 15	22 20
Chatham 4	d			21 49	21 54					22 19	22 24
Rochester 4	d			21 51	21 57					22 21	22 27
Maidstone West	d										
Strood 4	d			21 56	22 02					22 26	22 32
Higham	d			22 01						22 31	
Gravesend 4	d			22 09	22 13					22 39	22 43
Northfleet	d			22 12						22 42	
Swanscombe	d			22 14						22 44	
Greenhithe for Bluewater	d			22 18						22 48	
Stone Crossing	d			22 20						22 50	
Dartford 4	a			22 24						22 54	
	d	22 13	22 18	22 29		22 40	22 43	22 48		22 59	
Slade Green 4	d	22 18					22 48				
Erith	d	22 20					22 50				
Belvedere	d	22 23					22 53				
Abbey Wood	d	22 26		22 38			22 56			23 08	
Plumstead	d	22 29					22 59				
Woolwich Arsenal 4 ⛴	d	22 32		22 43			23 02			23 13	
Woolwich Dockyard	d	22 34					23 04				
Charlton 4	d	22 37		22 47			23 07			23 17	
Crayford	d		22 22					22 52			
Bexley	d		22 25					22 55			
Albany Park	d		22 28					22 58			
Sidcup 4	d		22 31					23 01			
New Eltham	d		22 34					23 04			
Mottingham	d		22 36					23 06			
Lee	d		22 39					23 09			
Hither Green 4	d		22 42					23 12			
Barnehurst 4	d					22 47					
Bexleyheath	d					22 49					
Welling	d					22 52					
Falconwood	d					22 55					
Eltham	d					22 58					
Kidbrooke	d					23 01					
Blackheath 4	d			22 52		23 04				23 22	
Lewisham 4 ⛴	d		22 48	22 56		23 08		23 18		23 26	
St Johns	d										
New Cross 4 ⊖	d					23 11					
Nunhead 4	d										
Peckham Rye 4	d										
Denmark Hill 4	d										
London Victoria 15 ⊖	a										
Westcombe Park	d	22 39					23 09				
Maze Hill	d	22 41					23 11				
Greenwich 4 ⛴	d	22 45					23 15				
Deptford	a	22 47					23 17				
London Bridge 4 ⊖	a	22 53	22 56	23 06		23 19	23 23	23 26		23 36	
London Cannon Street 4 ⊖	a										
London Waterloo (East) 4 ⊖	a	22 57	23 00	23 11		23 25	23 27	23 30		23 41	
London Charing Cross 4 ⊖	a	23 01	23 04	23 14		23 28	23 31	23 34		23 44	
Ebbsfleet International	a				22 17						22 47
Stratford International ⊖ ⛴	a				22 29						22 59
St Pancras Int'l 15 ⊖	a				22 36						23 06

London - Hayes (Kent) via Catford Bridge

Network Diagram - see first Page of Table 200

Miles	Miles			SE MO	SE MX	SE	SE	SE	SE	SE	SE	SE		SE	SE	SE	SE	SE	SE	SE	SE	SE		SE	
0	—	**London Charing Cross** 4	⊖ d	23p35	23p52		05 47	06 17	06 47		07 17			07 44		08 15		08 44			09 17			09 47	
0¾	—	**London Waterloo (East)** 4	⊖ d	23p38	23p55		05 50	06 20	06 50		07 20			07 47		08 18		08 47			09 20			09 50	
—	0	**London Cannon Street** 4	⊖ d							07 00		07 30			08 00		08 30		09 00	09 03		09 30			
1¾	0¾	**London Bridge** 4	⊖ d	23p43	23p59		05 55	06 26	06 55	07 04	07 25	07 34		07 53	08 04	08 23	08 34	08 53	09 04	09 07	09 25	09 34		09 55	
4¾	—	New Cross 4	⊖ d	23p49	00 05	05 31	06 01	06 32	07 02	07 09		07 39			08 09		08 41		09 09			09 39			
5½	—	St Johns	d	23p51	00 07	05 33	06 03	06 34	07 04	07 11		07 41			08 11		08 43		09 11			09 41			
6	—	**Lewisham** 4	d	23p54	00 10	05 36	06 06	06 38	07 08	07 16		07 44			08 17		08 46		09 14			09 44			
6¾	—	Ladywell	d	23p57	00 13	05 39	06 09	06 41	07 11	07 19	07 34	07 47		08 04	08 20	08 34	08 49	09 04	09 17	09 22	09 34	09 47		10 04	
7½	—	**Catford Bridge**	d	23p59	00 15	05 41	06 11	06 43	07 13	07 21	07 36	07 49		08 06	08 22	08 36	08 51	09 06	09 19	09 24	09 36	09 49		10 06	
9	—	Lower Sydenham	d	00 02	00 18	05 44	06 14	06 46	07 16	07 24	07 39	07 52		08 09	08 25	08 39	08 54	09 09	09 22	09 27	09 39	09 52		10 09	
9½	—	New Beckenham 4	d	00 04	00 20	05 46	06 16	06 48	07 18	07 26	07 41	07 54		08 11	08 27	08 41	08 56	09 11	09 24	09a29	09 41	09 54		10 11	
10¼	—	Clock House	d	00 06	00 23	05 48	06 18	06 50	07 20	07 29	07 43	07 57		08 13	08 29	08 43	08 58	09 13	09 27		09 43	09 57		10 13	
11	—	Elmers End 4	d	00 09	00 25	05 51	06 21	06 53	07 23	07 31	07 46	07 59		08 16	08 32	08 46	09 01	09 16	09 29		09 46	09 59		10 16	
12½	—	Eden Park	d	00 12	00 29	05 54	06 24	06 56	07 26	07 35	07 49	08 03		08 19	08 35	08 49	09 04	09 19	09 33		09 49	10 03		10 19	
13¼	—	West Wickham	d	00 15	00 31	05 57	06 27	06 59	07 29	07 37	07 52	08 05		08 22	08 38	08 52	09 07	09 22	09 35		09 52	10 05		10 22	
14½	—	**Hayes (Kent)**	a	00 18	00 34	06 00	06 30	07 02	07 32	07 40	07 56	08 08		08 25	08 41	08 55	09 10	09 25	09 38		09 55	10 08		10 25	

		SE		SE	SE	SE	SE	SE		SE	SE	SE	SE	SE	SE	SE	SE	SE		SE	SE	SE	SE	SE
London Charing Cross 4	⊖ d				15 17		15 47			16 20		16 39		16 59		17 21		17 43			18 05		18 27	
London Waterloo (East) 4	⊖ d				15 20		15 50			16 23		16 42		17 02		17 24		17 46			18 08		18 30	
London Cannon Street 4	⊖ d	10 00		15 00		15 30		16 00			16 30		16 51		17 12		17 34			17 56		18 18		18 40
London Bridge 4	⊖ d	10 04		15 04	15 25	15 34	15 55	16 04		16 29	16 34	16 47	16 55	17 07	17 16	17 29	17 39	17 52		18 00	18 13	18 23	18 35	18 44
New Cross 4	⊖ d	10 09	and at the same minutes past each hour until	15 09		15 39		16 10			16 40		17 01		17 22		17 45			18 06		18 28		18 50
St Johns	d	10 11		15 11		15 41		16 12			16 42		17 03		17 24		17 47			18 08		18 30		18 52
Lewisham 4	d	10 14		15 14		15 44		16 15			16 45		17 06		17 27		17 50			18 11		18 33		18 55
Ladywell	d	10 17		15 17	15 34	15 47	16 04	16 18		16 38	16 48	16 57	17 09	17 17	17 30	17 40	17 53	18 01		18 14	18 23	18 36	18 45	18 58
Catford Bridge	d	10 19		15 19	15 36	15 49	16 06	16 20		16 40	16 50	16 59	17 11	17 19	17 32	17 42	17 55	18 03		18 16	18 25	18 38	18 47	19 00
Lower Sydenham	d	10 22		15 22	15 39	15 52	16 09	16 23		16 43	16 53	17 02	17 14	17 22	17 35	17 45	17 58	18 06		18 19	18 28	18 41	18 50	19 03
New Beckenham 4	d	10 24		15 24	15 41	15 54	16 11	16 25		16 45	16 55	17 04	17 16	17 24	17 37	17 47	18 00	18 08		18 21	18 30	18 43	18 52	19 05
Clock House	d	10 27		15 27	15 43	15 57	16 13	16 27		16 48	16 57	17 07	17 18	17 27	17 39	17 49	18 02	18 11		18 23	18 33	18 46	18 55	19 07
Elmers End 4	d	10 29		15 29	15 46	15 59	16 16	16 30		16 51	17 00	17 10	17 21	17 30	17 42	17 52	18 05	18 14		18 26	18 36	18 49	18 58	19 10
Eden Park	d	10 33		15 33	15 49	16 03	16 19	16 34		16 54	17 04	17 13	17 25	17 33	17 46	17 56	18 09	18 17		18 30	18 39	18 52	19 01	19 14
West Wickham	d	10 35		15 35	15 52	16 05	16 22	16 36		16 57	17 06	17 16	17 27	17 36	17 48	17 58	18 11	18 20		18 32	18 42	18 55	19 04	19 16
Hayes (Kent)	a	10 38		15 38	15 55	16 08	16 25	16 42		17 02	17 12	17 21	17 32	17 42	17 54	18 03	18 16	18 26		18 38	18 47	19 00	19 10	19 22

		SE	SE	SE	SE		SE	SE	SE	SE		SE	SE
London Charing Cross 4	⊖ d	18 52		19 17			19 47		20 17	20 47		23 17	23 52
London Waterloo (East) 4	⊖ d	18 55		19 20			19 50		20 20	20 50		23 20	23 55
London Cannon Street 4	⊖ d		19 00		19 30			20 00					
London Bridge 4	⊖ d	19 00	19 04	19 25	19 34		19 55	20 04	20 25	20 55		23 25	23 59
New Cross 4	⊖ d		19 09		19 39			20 09	20 32	21 00		23 30	00 05
St Johns	d		19 11		19 41			20 11	20 34	21 02	and every 30 minutes until	23 32	00 07
Lewisham 4	d		19 14		19 44			20 14	20 37	21 05		23 35	00 10
Ladywell	d	19 09	19 17	19 34	19 47		20 04	20 17	20 40	21 08		23 38	00 13
Catford Bridge	d	19 11	19 19	19 36	19 49		20 06	20 19	20 42	21 10		23 40	00 15
Lower Sydenham	d	19 14	19 22	19 39	19 52		20 09	20 22	20 45	21 13		23 43	00 18
New Beckenham 4	d	19 16	19 24	19 41	19 54		20 11	20 24	20 47	21 15		23 45	00 20
Clock House	d	19 19	19 27	19 43	19 57		20 13	20 27	20 50	21 18		23 48	00 23
Elmers End 4	d	19 22	19 29	19 46	19 59		20 16	20 29	20 52	21 20		23 50	00 25
Eden Park	d	19 25	19 33	19 49	20 03		20 19	20 33	20 56	21 24		23 54	00 29
West Wickham	d	19 28	19 35	19 52	20 05		20 22	20 35	20 58	21 26		23 56	00 31
Hayes (Kent)	a	19 33	19 39	19 55	20 09		20 25	20 39	21 01	21 29		23 59	00 34

Saturdays

		SE	SE		SE	SE	SE	SE	SE		SE	SE		SE	SE	SE		SE		SE
London Charing Cross 4	⊖ d	23p52	05 47		07 17	07 47		08 17			08 47				19 17	19 47		23 17		23 52
London Waterloo (East) 4	⊖ d	23p55	05 50		07 20	07 50		08 20			08 50				19 20	19 50		23 20		23 55
London Cannon Street 4	⊖ d						08 00		08 30			09 00		19 00						
London Bridge 4	⊖ d	23p59	05 55		07 25	07 55	08 04	08 25	08 34		08 55	09 04		19 04	19 25	19 55		23 25		23 59
New Cross 4	⊖ d	00 05	06 00		07 30		08 09		08 39			09 09	and at the same minutes past each hour until	19 09		20 00		23 30		00 05
St Johns	d	00 07	06 02	and every 30 minutes until	07 32		08 11		08 41			09 11		19 11		20 02	and every 30 minutes until	23 32		00 07
Lewisham 4	d	00 10	06 05		07 35		08 14		08 44			09 14		19 14	19 37	20 05		23 35		00 10
Ladywell	d	00 13	06 08		07 38	08 04	08 17	08 34	08 47		09 04	09 17		19 17	19 40	20 08		23 38		00 13
Catford Bridge	d	00 15	06 10		07 40	08 06	08 19	08 36	08 49		09 06	09 19		19 19	19 42	20 10		23 40		00 15
Lower Sydenham	d	00 18	06 13		07 43	08 09	08 22	08 39	08 52		09 09	09 22		19 22	19 45	20 13		23 43		00 18
New Beckenham 4	d	00 20	06 15		07 45	08 11	08 24	08 41	08 54		09 11	09 24		19 24	19 47	20 15		23 45		00 20
Clock House	d	00 23	06 18		07 48	08 13	08 27	08 43	08 57		09 13	09 27		19 27	19 50	20 18		23 48		00 23
Elmers End 4	d	00 25	06 20		07 50	08 16	08 29	08 46	08 59		09 16	09 29		19 29	19 52	20 20		23 50		00 25
Eden Park	d	00 29	06 24		07 54	08 19	08 33	08 49	09 03		09 19	09 33		19 33	19 56	20 24		23 54		00 29
West Wickham	d	00 31	06 26		07 56	08 22	08 35	08 52	09 05		09 22	09 35		19 35	19 58	20 26		23 56		00 31
Hayes (Kent)	a	00 34	06 29		07 59	08 25	08 41	08 55	09 08		09 25	09 38		19 38	20 01	20 29		23 59		00 34

Table 203

Sundays

London - Hayes (Kent) via Catford Bridge

Network Diagram - see first Page of Table 200

Station			SE A	SE		SE	SE
London Charing Cross 4	⊖	d	23p52	07 35	and every 30 minutes until	23 05	23 35
London Waterloo (East) 4	⊖	d	23p55	07 38		23 08	23 38
London Cannon Street 4	⊖	d					
London Bridge 4	⊖	d	23p59	07 43		23 13	23 43
New Cross 4	⊖	d	00 05	07 49		23 19	23 49
St Johns		d	00 07	07 51		23 21	23 51
Lewisham 4	🚋	d	00 10	07 54		23 24	23 54
Ladywell		d	00 13	07 57		23 27	23 57
Catford Bridge		d	00 15	07 59		23 29	23 59
Lower Sydenham		d	00 18	08 02		23 32	00 02
New Beckenham 4		d	00 20	08 04		23 34	00 04
Clock House		d	00 23	08 06		23 36	00 06
Elmers End 4	🚋	d	00 25	08 09		23 39	00 09
Eden Park		d	00 29	08 12		23 42	00 12
West Wickham		d	00 31	08 15		23 45	00 15
Hayes (Kent)		a	00 34	08 18		23 48	00 18

A not 11 December

Hayes (Kent) - London via Catford Bridge

Network Diagram - see first Page of Table 200

Mondays to Fridays

Miles	Miles	Station		SE	SE	SE	SE	SE	SE	SE	SE	SE	SE	SE	SE	SE	SE	SE	SE	SE	SE	SE	SE
0	—	**Hayes (Kent)**	d	05 15	05 45	06 15	06 23	06 45	06 55	07 13	07 23	07 33	07 43	07 53	08 03	08 13	08 23	08 33	08 50	09 08	09 20	09 38	09 50
1¼	—	West Wickham	d	05 18	05 48	06 18	06 26	06 48	06 58	07 16	07 26	07 36	07 46	07 56	08 06	08 16	08 26	08 36	08 53	09 11	09 23	09 41	09 53
2	—	Eden Park	d	05 20	05 50	06 20	06 28	06 50	07 00	07 18	07 28	07 38	07 48	07 58	08 08	08 18	08 28	08 38	08 55	09 13	09 25	09 43	09 55
3½	—	Elmers End [4]	d	05 24	05 54	06 24	06 32	06 54	07 04	07 22	07 32	07 42	07 52	08 02	08 12	08 22	08 32	08 42	08 59	09 17	09 29	09 47	09 59
4¼	—	Clock House	d	05 26	05 56	06 26	06 34	06 56	07 06	07 24	07 34	07 44	07 54	08 04	08 14	08 24	08 34	08 44	09 01	09 19	09 31	09 49	10 01
5	—	New Beckenham [4]	d	05 28	05 58	06 28	06 37	06 59	07 09	07 27	07 37	07 47	07 57	08 07	08 17	08 27	08 37	08 47	09 04	09 21	09 34	09 51	10 03
5½	—	Lower Sydenham	d	05 30	06 00	06 30	06 39	07 01	07 11	07 29	07 39	07 49	07 59	08 09	08 19	08 29	08 39	08 49	09 06	09 23	09 36	09 53	10 05
7	—	**Catford Bridge**	d	05 33	06 03	06 33	06 42	07 04	07 14	07 32	07 42	07 52	08 02	08 12	08 22	08 32	08 42	08 52	09 09	09 26	09 39	09 56	10 08
7¾	—	Ladywell	d	05 35	06 05	06 35	06 44	07 06	07 16	07 34	07 44	07 54	08 04	08 14	08 24	08 34	08 44	08 54	09 11	09 28	09 41	09 58	10 10
8½	—	**Lewisham [4]**	d	05 39	06 09	06 39	06 48		07 20		07 48		08 08		08 28		08 48		09 15		09 45		10 14
9	—	St Johns	a	05 41	06 11	06 41	06 50				07 50		08 12		08 30		08 50		09 17		09 47		10 16
9¾	—	New Cross [4] ⊖	a	05 43	06 13	06 43	06 52		07 23		07 52		08 14		08 32		08 52		09 19		09 49		10 18
12¾	0	**London Bridge [4]** ⊖	a	05 48	06 18	06 48	06 58	07 17	07 28	07 44	08 01		08 20		08 41		08 57		09 25	09 37	09 54	10 07	10 24
—	0¾	**London Cannon Street [4]** ⊖	a				07 05		07 35		08 08		08 28		08 48		09 04		09 32		10 00		10 28
13¾	—	**London Waterloo (East) [4]** ⊖	a	05 53	06 24	06 53		07 22		07 50		08 08		08 28		08 48		09 07		09 42		10 12	
14½	—	**London Charing Cross [4]** ⊖	a	05 56	06 27	06 57		07 28		07 56		08 14		08 34		08 54		09 13		09 48		10 16	

Station		SE	SE		SE	SE	SE	SE	SE	SE	SE	SE	SE	SE	SE	SE	SE	SE	SE	SE	SE
Hayes (Kent)	d	10 08	10 20	and at the same minutes past each hour until	15 20	15 38	15 50		16 08	16 20	16 38	16 50	17 08	17 20	17 37	17 47	18 08	18 21	18 38	18 50	19 05
West Wickham	d	10 11	10 23		15 23	15 41	15 53		16 11	16 23	16 41	16 53	17 11	17 23	17 40	17 50	18 11	18 24	18 41	18 53	19 08
Eden Park	d	10 13	10 25		15 25	15 43	15 55		16 13	16 25	16 43	16 55	17 13	17 25	17 42	17 52	18 13	18 26	18 43	18 55	19 10
Elmers End [4]	d	10 17	10 29		15 29	15 47	15 59		16 17	16 29	16 47	16 59	17 17	17 29	17 46	17 56	18 17	18 30	18 47	18 59	19 17
Clock House	d	10 19	10 31		15 31	15 49	16 01		16 19	16 31	16 49	17 01	17 19	17 31	17 48	17 58	18 19	18 32	18 49	19 01	19 19
New Beckenham [4]	d	10 21	10 33		15 33	15 51	16 03	16 15	16 21	16 33	16 51	17 03	17 21	17 33	17 50	18 00	18 21	18 34	18 51	19 03	19 21
Lower Sydenham	d	10 23	10 35		15 35	15 53	16 05	16 17	16 23	16 35	16 53	17 05	17 23	17 35	17 52	18 02	18 23	18 36	18 53	19 05	19 23
Catford Bridge	d	10 26	10 38		15 38	15 56	16 08	16 20	16 26	16 38	16 56	17 08	17 26	17 38	17 55	18 05	18 26	18 39	18 56	19 08	19 26
Ladywell	d	10 28	10 40		15 40	15 58	16 10	16 22	16 28	16 40	16 58	17 10	17 28	17 40	17 57	18 07	18 28	18 41	18 58	19 10	19 28
Lewisham [4]	d		10 44		15 44		16 14			16 44		17 14		17 44		18 14		18 45		19 14	
St Johns	a		10 46		15 46		16 16			16 46		17 16		17 46		18 16		18 47		19 16	
New Cross [4] ⊖	a		10 48		15 48		16 18			16 48		17 18		17 48		18 18		18 49		19 18	
London Bridge [4] ⊖	a	10 37	10 54		15 54	16 09	16 24	16 32	16 37	16 54	17 08	17 24	17 38	17 55	18 07	18 24	18 38	18 55	19 07	19 24	19 37
London Cannon Street [4] ⊖	a		10 58		15 58		16 28			16 58		17 29		17 59		18 29		18 59		19 28	
London Waterloo (East) [4] ⊖	a	10 42				16 13		16 37	16 42		17 13		17 42		18 12		18 44		19 12		19 42
London Charing Cross [4] ⊖	a	10 46				16 18		16 42	16 46		17 18		17 46		18 16		18 48		19 16		19 46

Station		SE		SE
Hayes (Kent)	d	19 14	and every 30 minutes until	23 14
West Wickham	d	19 17		23 17
Eden Park	d	19 19		23 19
Elmers End [4]	d	19 23		23 23
Clock House	d	19 25		23 25
New Beckenham [4]	d	19 27		23 27
Lower Sydenham	d	19 29		23 29
Catford Bridge	d	19 32		23 32
Ladywell	d	19 34		23 34
Lewisham [4]	d	19 38		23 38
St Johns	a	19 40		23 40
New Cross [4] ⊖	a	19 42		23 42
London Bridge [4] ⊖	a	19 49		23 49
London Cannon Street [4] ⊖	a			
London Waterloo (East) [4] ⊖	a	19 53		23 53
London Charing Cross [4] ⊖	a	19 57		23 57

Saturdays

Station		SE	SE		SE	SE	SE	SE	SE	SE		SE	SE	SE		SE	SE	SE
Hayes (Kent)	d	05 15	05 38	and every 30 minutes until	07 08	07 36	07 50	08 08	08 20	08 38	and at the same minutes past each hour until	18 38	18 50	19 14	and every 30 minutes until	22 14	22 44	23 14
West Wickham	d	05 18	05 41		07 11	07 39	07 53	08 11	08 23	08 41		18 41	18 53	19 17		22 17	22 47	23 17
Eden Park	d	05 20	05 43		07 13	07 41	07 55	08 13	08 25	08 43		18 43	18 55	19 19		22 19	22 49	23 19
Elmers End [4]	d	05 24	05 47		07 17	07 45	07 59	08 17	08 29	08 47		18 47	18 59	19 23		22 23	22 53	23 23
Clock House	d	05 26	05 49		07 19	07 47	08 01	08 19	08 31	08 49		18 49	19 01	19 25		22 25	22 55	23 25
New Beckenham [4]	d	05 28	05 51		07 21	07 49	08 03	08 21	08 33	08 51		18 51	19 03	19 27		22 27	22 57	23 27
Lower Sydenham	d	05 30	05 53		07 23	07 51	08 05	08 23	08 35	08 53		18 53	19 05	19 29		22 29	22 59	23 29
Catford Bridge	d	05 33	05 56		07 26	07 54	08 08	08 26	08 38	08 56		18 56	19 08	19 32		22 32	23 02	23 32
Ladywell	d	05 35	05 58		07 28	07 56	08 10	08 28	08 40	08 58		18 58	19 10	19 34		22 34	23 04	23 34
Lewisham [4]	d	05 39	06 02		07 32	07 59	08 14		08 44				19 14	19 38		22 38	23 08	23 38
St Johns	a	05 41	06 04		07 34		08 16		08 46				19 16	19 40		22 40	23 10	23 40
New Cross [4] ⊖	a	05 43	06 06		07 36		08 18		08 48				19 18	19 42		22 42	23 12	23 42
London Bridge [4] ⊖	a	05 48	06 12		07 42	08 07	08 24	08 37	08 54	09 07		19 07	19 24	19 49		22 49	23 19	23 49
London Cannon Street [4] ⊖	a						08 28		08 58									
London Waterloo (East) [4] ⊖	a	05 53	06 16		07 46	08 12		08 42		09 12		19 12		19 53		22 53	23 23	23 53
London Charing Cross [4] ⊖	a	05 56	06 20		07 50	08 16		08 46		09 16		19 16		19 58		22 58	23 27	23 57

Sundays

Station		SE		SE
Hayes (Kent)	d	07 28	and every 30 minutes until	22 58
West Wickham	d	07 31		23 01
Eden Park	d	07 33		23 03
Elmers End [4]	d	07 37		23 07
Clock House	d	07 39		23 09
New Beckenham [4]	d	07 41		23 11
Lower Sydenham	d	07 43		23 13
Catford Bridge	d	07 46		23 16
Ladywell	d	07 48		23 18
Lewisham [4]	d	07 52		23 22
St Johns	a	07 54		23 24
New Cross [4] ⊖	a	07 56		23 26
London Bridge [4] ⊖	a	08 03		23 33
London Cannon Street [4] ⊖	a			
London Waterloo (East) [4] ⊖	a	08 08		23 38
London Charing Cross [4] ⊖	a	08 11		23 41

Table 204

Mondays to Fridays

London - Grove Park, Bromley North, Orpington, Sevenoaks and Tonbridge

Network Diagram - see first Page of Table 200

Miles	Miles			SE MO 1	SE MX 1	SE MX	SE MX	SE MO 1	SE MX 1	SE MX 1	SE MX	SE MO		SE MX	SE MX	SE MX	SE MX	SE MX	SE	SE 1	SE	SE		SE	SE
0	—	**London Charing Cross 4** ⊖	d	23p23	23p30		23p36	23p38	23p40	23p45		23p46				00 06	00 15		00 48	05 30	05 36				06 06
0¾	—	**London Waterloo (East) 4** ⊖	d	23p26	23p33		23p39	23p41	23p43	23p48		23p49				00 09	00 18		00 51	05 33	05 39				06 09
—	—	**London Cannon Street 4** ⊖	d																						
1¾	—	**London Bridge 4** ⊖	d	23p31	23p39		23p44	23p46	23p49	23p53		23p54				00 14	00 23		00 56	05 39	05 44				06 14
4¾	—	New Cross 4 ⊖	d																01 01						
5½	—	St Johns	d																						
6	—	**Lewisham 4**	d				23p52					00 03				00 22			01 05		05 52				06 23
7¼	—	Hither Green 4	d				23p56					00 07				00 26			01 09		05 56				06 27
9	0	**Grove Park 4**	d				23p59				00 07	00 11				00 30		00 37	01 13		06 00			06 16	06 30
—	1¼	Sundridge Park	d								00 10							00 40						06 19	
—	1¾	**Bromley North**	a								00 12							00 42						06 21	
10¼	—	Elmstead Woods	d				00 03					00 14				00 33			01 16		06 03				06 33
11¼	—	Chislehurst	d				00 05					00 17				00 35			01 19		06 05				06 36
12¾	—	Petts Wood 4	d			23p59	00 08					00 20		00 21	00 29	00 38			01 22		06 08	06 14			06 39
13¾	—	**Orpington 4**	a	23p46	23p54	00 02	00 12	00 01		00 08		00 23		00 25	00 32	00 42	00 46		01 25	05 54	06 11	06 18			06 42
—	—		d	23p46	23p54			00 02		00 09							00 46			05 55	06 12				06 44
15¼	—	Chelsfield 3	d	23p49	23p57												00 49			05 58	06 15				06 47
16½	—	Knockholt	d																		06 18				06 50
20½	—	Dunton Green	d														00 56				06 23				06 55
22	—	**Sevenoaks 4**	a	23p57	00 05			00 11	00 11	00 18							00 59			06 05	06 26				06 59
—	—		d	23p57	00 05			00 12	00 12	00 19							00 59			06 06					
27	—	Hildenborough	d		00 11												01 05			06 12					
29½	—	**Tonbridge 4**	a	00 05	00 15			00 20	00 20	00 27							01 10			06 16					

		SE 1	SE	SE	SE 1	SE	SE	SE 1		SE	SE	SE 1	SE	SE	SE	SE 1	SE 1	SE		SE 1	SE	SE	SE	SE 1	SE
London Charing Cross 4 ⊖	d	06 15			06 30		06 36	06 45				07 00			07 06	07 10	07 15			07 29					07 36
London Waterloo (East) 4 ⊖	d	06 18			06 33		06 39	06 48				07 03			07 09	07 13	07 18			07 32					07 39
London Cannon Street 4 ⊖	d										06 50							07 20						07 47	
London Bridge 4 ⊖	d	06 24			06 38		06 44	06 53			06 54	07 08			07 14	07 19	07 23	07 24		07 38				07 51	07 44
New Cross 4 ⊖	d										06 59														
St Johns	d										07 01														
Lewisham 4	d						06 53				07 04														
Hither Green 4	d						06 58				07 08				07 23			07 35							07 53
Grove Park 4	d		06 36				07 02			07 06	07 12			07 25	07 27			07 38			07 46				07 57
Sundridge Park	d		06 39							07 09				07 28							07 49				
Bromley North	a		06 41							07 11				07 30							07 51				
Elmstead Woods	d						07 05				07 15				07 30			07 41							08 00
Chislehurst	d						07 07				07 18				07 33			07 44							08 03
Petts Wood 4	d			06 44		07 04	07 10				07 21		07 24		07 36							07 49	07 59		08 06
Orpington 4	a	06 40		06 49	06 53	07 08	07 13	07 09			07 25	07 25	07 28		07 40		07 38	07 48		07 53		07 53	08 02	08 08	08 09
	d	06 40			06 54		07 14	07 10				07 26			07 42		07 39			07 54				08 09	08 12
Chelsfield 3	d						07 17								07 45					07 57					08 15
Knockholt	d						07 20								07 48					08 00					
Dunton Green	d						07 25								07 53										08 21
Sevenoaks 4	a	06 49			07 03		07 28	07 19				07 35			08 00	07 42	07 48			08 06				08 18	08 24
	d	06 50			07 03			07 19				07 35				07 43	07 49			08 07				08 19	
Hildenborough	d				07 09							07 41								08 13					
Tonbridge 4	a	06 58			07 13			07 27				07 45				07 51	07 58			08 17				08 27	

		SE 1	SE	SE		SE	SE	SE 1	SE 1	SE	SE	SE	SE 1	SE 1		SE	SE	SE 1	SE 1	SE	SE	SE 1	SE	SE	
London Charing Cross 4 ⊖	d	07 40	07 48					07 52	08 00			08 05	08 13	08 17				08 27	08 33				08 37		
London Waterloo (East) 4 ⊖	d	07 43	07 51					07 55	08 03			08 08	08 16	08 20				08 30	08 36				08 40		
London Cannon Street 4 ⊖	d						07 51										08 19					08 42			
London Bridge 4 ⊖	d	07 49	07 56				07 55	08 01	08 09			08 13	08 21	08 25			08 23	08 35	08 41			08 46	08 45		
New Cross 4 ⊖	d						08 00										08 29								
St Johns	d																08 31								
Lewisham 4	d						08 05										08 34								
Hither Green 4	d						08 10					08 23					08 38						08 55		
Grove Park 4	d			08 06			08 14			08 26		08 27					08 42			08 46			08 59	09 06	
Sundridge Park	d			08 09						08 29										08 49				09 09	
Bromley North	a			08 11						08 31										08 51				09 11	
Elmstead Woods	d						08 17					08 30					08 45						09 02		
Chislehurst	d						08 20					08 32					08 48						09 05		
Petts Wood 4	d					08 14	08 23				08 29	08 36				08 44	08 51				08 59		09 08		
Orpington 4	a		08 15			08 19	08 26		08 25		08 32	08 39		08 41		08 47	08 54	08 53	08 57		09 02	09 07	09 11		
	d								08 26			08 45		08 42				08 54	08 58			09 07	09 12		
Chelsfield 3	d											08 48											09 15		
Knockholt	d											08 51											09 18		
Dunton Green	d											08 56											09 23		
Sevenoaks 4	a	08 11						08 27	08 35			08 59	08 44	08 51				09 03	09 07			09 17	09 26		
	d	08 12						08 28	08 35				08 45	08 52				09 03	09 07			09 17			
Hildenborough	d								08 41									09 09							
Tonbridge 4	a	08 20						08 36	08 47				08 53	09 00				09 13	09 18			09 25			

London - Grove Park, Bromley North, Orpington, Sevenoaks and Tonbridge

Network Diagram - see first Page of Table 200

		SE	SE	SE [1]	SE	SE [1]	SE	SE	SE [1]	SE [1]		SE	SE	SE	SE [1]	SE	SE	SE	SE [1]	SE [1]		SE	SE	SE [1]	SE
London Charing Cross [4] ⊖	d		08 49	08 53		09 00		09 06	09 13						09 30			09 36	09 40	09 45				10 00	
London Waterloo (East) [4] ⊖	d		08 52	08 56		09 03		09 09	09 16						09 33			09 39	09 43	09 48				10 03	
London Cannon Street [4] ⊖	d				08 51					09 18				09 20									09 50		
London Bridge [4] ⊖	d		08 57	09 01	08 55	09 08		09 14	09 21	09 22				09 25	09 39			09 44	09 49	09 53			09 54	10 09	
New Cross [4] ⊖	d				09 00									09 29									09 59		
St Johns	d				09 02									09 31									10 01		
Lewisham [4]	d				09 06									09 34									10 04		
Hither Green [4]	d				09 10			09 23						09 38				09 53					10 08		
Grove Park [4]	d				09 14			09 27				09 35		09 42		09 55		09 57					10 12		10 15
Sundridge Park	d											09 38				09 58									10 18
Bromley North	a											09 40				10 00									10 20
Elmstead Woods	d				09 17			09 30						09 45				10 00					10 15		
Chislehurst	d				09 20			09 33						09 48				10 03					10 18		
Petts Wood [4]	d	09 14			09 23		09 29	09 36					09 44	09 51			09 59	10 06				10 14	10 21		
Orpington [4]	a	09 17	09 22	09 20	09 26	09 26	09 33	09 39		09 40			09 47	09 55	09 55		10 02	10 09		10 08		10 17	10 24	10 25	
	d			09 21		09 26		09 42		09 41					09 56			10 12		10 09				10 26	
Chelsfield [3]	d							09 45										10 15							
Knockholt	d							09 48										10 18							
Dunton Green	d							09 53										10 23							
Sevenoaks [4]	a			09 30		09 35		09 57	09 43	09 50					10 05			10 26	10 11	10 18				10 35	
	d			09 31		09 35			09 44	09 50					10 05				10 12	10 19				10 35	
Hildenborough	d					09 41									10 11									10 41	
Tonbridge [4]	a			09 40		09 46			09 52	09 58					10 15				10 20	10 27				10 45	

		SE	SE	SE [1]	SE [1]	SE		SE	SE	SE [1]	SE	SE	SE	SE [1]	SE [1]	SE		SE	SE [1]	SE	SE	SE	SE [1]	SE [1]	SE
London Charing Cross [4] ⊖	d		10 06	10 10	10 15					10 30			10 36	10 40	10 45				11 00			11 06	11 10	11 15	
London Waterloo (East) [4] ⊖	d		10 09	10 13	10 18					10 33			10 39	10 43	10 48				11 03			11 09	11 13	11 18	
London Cannon Street [4] ⊖	d								10 20									10 50							
London Bridge [4] ⊖	d		10 14	10 19	10 23				10 24	10 39			10 44	10 49	10 53			10 54	11 09			11 14	11 19	11 23	
New Cross [4] ⊖	d								10 29									10 59							
St Johns	d								10 31									11 01							
Lewisham [4]	d								10 34									11 04							
Hither Green [4]	d		10 23						10 38				10 53					11 08				11 23			
Grove Park [4]	d		10 27			10 35			10 42		10 55		10 57					11 12		11 15		11 27			11 35
Sundridge Park	d					10 38					10 58									11 18					11 38
Bromley North	a					10 40					11 00									11 20					11 40
Elmstead Woods	d		10 30						10 45				11 00					11 15				11 30			
Chislehurst	d		10 33						10 48				11 03					11 18				11 33			
Petts Wood [4]	d	10 29	10 36					10 44	10 51			10 59	11 06			11 14		11 21			11 29	11 36			
Orpington [4]	a	10 32	10 39		10 38			10 47	10 54	10 55		11 02	11 09		11 08	11 17		11 24	11 25		11 32	11 39		11 38	
	d		10 42		10 39					10 56			11 12		11 09				11 26			11 42		11 39	
Chelsfield [3]	d		10 45										11 15									11 45			
Knockholt	d		10 48										11 18									11 48			
Dunton Green	d		10 53										11 23									11 53			
Sevenoaks [4]	a		10 56	10 41	10 48					11 05			11 26	11 11	11 18				11 35			11 56	11 41	11 48	
	d			10 42	10 49					11 05				11 12	11 19				11 35				11 42	11 49	
Hildenborough	d									11 11									11 41						
Tonbridge [4]	a			10 50	10 57					11 15				11 20	11 27				11 45				11 50	11 57	

		SE		SE	SE [1]	SE	SE	SE	SE [1]	SE [1]	SE	SE		SE [1]	SE	SE	SE	SE [1]	SE [1]	SE	SE	SE		SE [1]	SE
London Charing Cross [4] ⊖	d				11 30			11 36	11 40	11 45				12 00			12 06	12 10	12 15					12 30	
London Waterloo (East) [4] ⊖	d				11 33			11 39	11 43	11 48				12 03			12 09	12 13	12 18					12 33	
London Cannon Street [4] ⊖	d			11 20								11 50										12 20			
London Bridge [4] ⊖	d			11 24	11 39			11 44	11 49	11 53		11 54		12 09			12 14	12 19	12 23			12 24		12 39	
New Cross [4] ⊖	d			11 29								11 59										12 29			
St Johns	d			11 31								12 01										12 31			
Lewisham [4]	d			11 34								12 04										12 34			
Hither Green [4]	d			11 38				11 53				12 08					12 23					12 38			
Grove Park [4]	d			11 42		11 55		11 57				12 12			12 15		12 27			12 35		12 42			12 55
Sundridge Park	d					11 58									12 18					12 38					12 58
Bromley North	a					12 00									12 20					12 40					13 00
Elmstead Woods	d			11 45				12 00				12 15					12 30					12 45			
Chislehurst	d			11 48				12 03				12 18					12 33					12 48			
Petts Wood [4]	d	11 44		11 51			11 59	12 06			12 14	12 21				12 29	12 36				12 44	12 51			
Orpington [4]	a	11 47		11 54	11 55		12 02	12 09		12 08	12 17	12 24		12 25		12 32	12 39		12 38		12 47	12 54		12 55	
	d				11 56			12 12		12 09				12 26			12 42		12 39					12 56	
Chelsfield [3]	d							12 15									12 45								
Knockholt	d							12 18									12 48								
Dunton Green	d							12 23									12 53								
Sevenoaks [4]	a				12 05			12 26	12 11	12 18				12 35			12 56	12 41	12 48					13 05	
	d				12 05				12 12	12 19				12 35				12 42	12 49					13 05	
Hildenborough	d				12 11									12 41										13 11	
Tonbridge [4]	a				12 15				12 20	12 27				12 45				12 50	12 57					13 15	

London - Grove Park, Bromley North, Orpington, Sevenoaks and Tonbridge

Network Diagram - see first Page of Table 200

		SE	SE	SE 1	SE 1	SE	SE	SE 1		SE	SE	SE 1	SE 1	SE	SE	SE	SE 1	SE		SE	SE	SE 1	SE 1	SE	SE
London Charing Cross 4 ⊖	d		12 36	12 40	12 45			13 00			13 06	13 10	13 15				13 30				13 36	13 40	13 45		
London Waterloo (East) 4 ⊖	d		12 39	12 43	12 48			13 03			13 09	13 13	13 18				13 33				13 39	13 43	13 48		
London Cannon Street 4 ⊖	d						12 50									13 20									13 50
London Bridge 4 ⊖	d		12 44	12 49	12 53		12 54	13 09			13 14	13 19	13 23			13 24	13 39				13 44	13 49	13 53		13 54
New Cross 4 ⊖	d						12 59									13 29									13 59
St Johns	d						13 01									13 31									14 01
Lewisham 4	d						13 04									13 34									14 04
Hither Green 4	d		12 53				13 08				13 23					13 38					13 53				14 08
Grove Park 4	d		12 57				13 12				13 27			13 35		13 42		13 55			13 57				14 12
Sundridge Park	d													13 38				13 58							
Bromley North	a													13 40				14 00							
Elmstead Woods	d		13 00				13 15				13 30					13 45					14 00				14 15
Chislehurst	d		13 03				13 18				13 33					13 48					14 03				14 18
Petts Wood 4	d	12 59	13 06			13 14	13 21			13 29	13 36				13 44	13 51				13 59	14 06			14 14	14 21
Orpington 4	a	13 02	13 09		13 08	13 17	13 24	13 25		13 32	13 39		13 38		13 47	13 54	13 55			14 02	14 09		14 08	14 17	14 24
	d		13 12		13 09			13 26			13 42		13 39				13 56				14 12		14 09		
Chelsfield 3	d		13 15								13 45										14 15				
Knockholt	d		13 18								13 48										14 18				
Dunton Green	d		13 23								13 53										14 23				
Sevenoaks 4	a		13 26	13 11	13 18			13 35			13 56	13 41	13 48				14 05				14 26	14 11	14 18		
	d			13 12	13 19			13 35				13 42	13 49				14 05					14 12	14 19		
Hildenborough	d							13 41									14 11								
Tonbridge 4	a			13 20	13 27			13 45				13 50	13 57				14 15					14 20	14 27		

		SE 1	SE	SE		SE	SE 1	SE 1	SE	SE	SE	SE 1	SE	SE		SE	SE 1	SE 1	SE	SE	SE 1	SE	SE	SE	
London Charing Cross 4 ⊖	d	14 00				14 06	14 10	14 15				14 30				14 36	14 40	14 45			15 00			15 06	
London Waterloo (East) 4 ⊖	d	14 03				14 09	14 13	14 18				14 33				14 39	14 43	14 48			15 03			15 09	
London Cannon Street 4 ⊖	d										14 20									14 50					
London Bridge 4 ⊖	d	14 09				14 14	14 19	14 23			14 24	14 39				14 44	14 49	14 53		14 54	15 09			15 14	
New Cross 4 ⊖	d										14 29									14 59					
St Johns	d										14 31									15 01					
Lewisham 4	d										14 34									15 04					
Hither Green 4	d					14 23					14 38					14 53				15 08				15 23	
Grove Park 4	d		14 15			14 27			14 35		14 42		14 55			14 57				15 12		15 15		15 27	
Sundridge Park	d		14 18						14 38				14 58									15 18			
Bromley North	a		14 20						14 40				15 00									15 20			
Elmstead Woods	d					14 30					14 45					15 00				15 15				15 30	
Chislehurst	d					14 33					14 48					15 03				15 18				15 33	
Petts Wood 4	d			14 29		14 36				14 44	14 51			14 59		15 06			15 14	15 21			15 29	15 36	
Orpington 4	a	14 25		14 32		14 39		14 38		14 47	14 54	14 55		15 02		15 09		15 08	15 17	15 24	15 25		15 32	15 39	
	d	14 26				14 42		14 39				14 56				15 12		15 09			15 26			15 42	
Chelsfield 3	d					14 45										15 15								15 45	
Knockholt	d					14 48										15 18								15 48	
Dunton Green	d					14 53										15 23								15 53	
Sevenoaks 4	a	14 35				14 56	14 41	14 48				15 05				15 26	15 11	15 18			15 35			15 56	
	d	14 35					14 42	14 49				15 05					15 12	15 19			15 35				
Hildenborough	d	14 41										15 11									15 41				
Tonbridge 4	a	14 45					14 50	14 57				15 16					15 20	15 27			15 45				

		SE 1	SE 1	SE	SE	SE	SE 1	SE	SE	SE		SE 1	SE 1	SE	SE	SE 1	SE	SE	SE	SE 1		SE 1	SE	SE	SE 1
London Charing Cross 4 ⊖	d	15 10	15 15				15 30			15 36		15 40	15 45			16 00			16 06	16 10		16 15			16 28
London Waterloo (East) 4 ⊖	d	15 13	15 18				15 33			15 39		15 43	15 48			16 03			16 09	16 13		16 18			16 31
London Cannon Street 4 ⊖	d					15 20									15 50										
London Bridge 4 ⊖	d	15 19	15 23			15 24	15 39			15 44		15 49	15 53		15 54	16 09			16 14	16 19		16 23			16 36
New Cross 4 ⊖	d					15 29									15 59										
St Johns	d					15 31									16 01										
Lewisham 4	d					15 34									16 04										
Hither Green 4	d					15 38				15 53					16 08				16 23						
Grove Park 4	d			15 35		15 42		15 55		15 57					16 12		16 15		16 27				16 35		
Sundridge Park	d			15 38				15 58									16 18						16 38		
Bromley North	a			15 40				16 00									16 20						16 40		
Elmstead Woods	d					15 45				16 00					16 15				16 30						
Chislehurst	d					15 48				16 03					16 18				16 33						
Petts Wood 4	d				15 44	15 51			15 59	16 06				16 14	16 21			16 29	16 36					16 44	
Orpington 4	a		15 38		15 47	15 54	15 55		16 02	16 09			16 08	16 17	16 24	16 25		16 32	16 39					16 49	16 52
	d		15 39				15 56			16 12			16 09			16 26			16 42						16 53
Chelsfield 3	d									16 15									16 45						
Knockholt	d									16 18									16 48						
Dunton Green	d									16 23									16 53						
Sevenoaks 4	a	15 41	15 48				16 05			16 26		16 11	16 18			16 35			16 58	16 42		16 46			17 02
	d	15 42	15 49				16 05					16 12	16 19			16 35				16 43		16 47			17 03
Hildenborough	d						16 11									16 41									17 09
Tonbridge 4	a	15 50	15 57				16 15					16 20	16 27			16 45				16 51		16 55			17 13

London - Grove Park, Bromley North, Orpington, Sevenoaks and Tonbridge

Network Diagram - see first Page of Table 200

		SE	SE	SE	SE ■1	SE ■1		SE	SE	SE	SE ■1	SE	SE ■1	SE ■1	SE	SE		SE	SE ■1	SE	SE ■1	SE ■1	SE	SE	SE
London Charing Cross [4] ⊖	d			16 32	16 37	16 41				16 42	16 57			17 01				17 03	17 14			17 23			17 26
London Waterloo (East) [4] ⊖	d			16 35	16 40	16 44				16 45	17 00			17 04				17 06	17 18			17 26			17 29
London Cannon Street [4] ⊖	d	16 20										16 56	17 02							17 19	17 24				
London Bridge [4] ⊖	d	16 24		16 40	16 45	16 49				16 51		17 00	17 06	17 09				17 11		17 23	17 28	17 31			17 35
New Cross [4] ⊖	d	16 30																							
St Johns	d	16 32																							
Lewisham [4] 🚊	d	16 35								17 01								17 21							17 44
Hither Green [4]	d	16 39		16 50						17 06								17 26							17 49
Grove Park [4]	d	16 43		16 54				16 57		17 10		17 15			17 17			17 30		17 35			17 40		17 53
Sundridge Park	d							17 00							17 20								17 43		
Bromley North	a							17 02							17 22								17 45		
Elmstead Woods	d	16 46		16 57						17 13		17 18						17 33		17 38					17 56
Chislehurst	d	16 48		17 00						17 15		17 21						17 35		17 40					17 58
Petts Wood [4]	d	16 51	16 59	17 03					17 14	17 19		17 24				17 36		17 40		17 44				17 50	18 02
Orpington [4]	a	16 57	17 04	17 06					17 19	17 24		17 27				17 41		17 45		17 47				17 55	18 07
	d			17 07								17 28								17 50					
Chelsfield [3]	d			17 10								17 31		17 28						17 53		17 50			
Knockholt	d			17 13								17 34								17 56					
Dunton Green	d			17 18								17 39								18 01					
Sevenoaks [4]	a			17 23	17 09	17 13					17 27	17 44	17 31	17 37					17 45	18 07	17 53	17 59			
	d				17 10	17 14					17 27		17 32	17 37					17 46		17 54	17 59			
Hildenborough	d													17 43							18 00	18 05			
Tonbridge [4]	a				17 18	17 22					17 35		17 40	17 48					17 54		18 04	18 09			

		SE ■1		SE	SE	SE ■1	SE ■1	SE	SE	SE ■1	SE	SE		SE ■1	SE ■1	SE	SE	SE	SE ■1	SE	SE ■1	SE		SE	SE
London Charing Cross [4] ⊖	d	17 41					17 45		17 47	18 03					18 07			18 09	18 21						18 30
London Waterloo (East) [4] ⊖	d	17 44					17 48		17 50	18 06					18 10			18 12	18 24						18 33
London Cannon Street [4] ⊖	d				17 41	17 45						18 02		18 08						18 23	18 32				
London Bridge [4] ⊖	d				17 45	17 49	17 53		17 55			18 06		18 12	18 15			18 17		18 27	18 36				18 38
New Cross [4] ⊖	d																								
St Johns	d																								
Lewisham [4] 🚊	d								18 05									18 27							
Hither Green [4]	d								18 10									18 31							18 49
Grove Park [4]	d				17 59			18 03	18 14			18 20				18 23		18 35		18 41		18 45			18 53
Sundridge Park	d							18 06								18 26						18 48			
Bromley North	a							18 08								18 28						18 50			
Elmstead Woods	d				18 02				18 17			18 23						18 38		18 44					18 56
Chislehurst	d				18 05				18 20			18 25						18 40		18 46					18 58
Petts Wood [4]	d			18 05	18 08				18 23		18 26	18 29					18 36	18 44		18 50				18 54	19 03
Orpington [4]	a			18 10	18 11				18 29		18 32	18 32					18 41	18 49		18 53				18 59	19 06
	d				18 12							18 34								18 58					19 12
Chelsfield [3]	d				18 15		18 12					18 37			18 34					19 01					19 15
Knockholt	d				18 18							18 40								19 04					19 18
Dunton Green	d				18 23							18 45								19 09					19 23
Sevenoaks [4]	a	18 11			18 28	18 15	18 21			18 33		18 50		18 37	18 42				18 52	19 14	19 00				19 28
	d	18 11				18 16	18 21			18 34				18 38	18 43				18 52		19 00				
Hildenborough	d						18 27							18 44	18 49										
Tonbridge [4]	a	18 19				18 24	18 32			18 42				18 48	18 54				19 00		19 08				

		SE ■1	SE ■1	SE	SE	SE ■1	SE ■1	SE		SE	SE ■1	SE	SE	SE ■1	SE ■1	SE	SE	SE		SE ■1	SE	SE	SE	SE ■1	SE ■1
London Charing Cross [4] ⊖	d	18 32	18 41			18 45					19 00		19 06	19 10	19 15					19 30			19 36	19 40	19 45
London Waterloo (East) [4] ⊖	d	18 35	18 44			18 48					19 03		19 09	19 13	19 18					19 33			19 39	19 43	19 48
London Cannon Street [4] ⊖	d				18 48		19 04											19 20							
London Bridge [4] ⊖	d	18 40	18 50		18 52	18 53	19 09				19 09		19 14	19 19	19 23			19 24		19 39			19 44	19 49	19 53
New Cross [4] ⊖	d																	19 29							
St Johns	d																	19 31							
Lewisham [4] 🚊	d																	19 34							
Hither Green [4]	d												19 23					19 38					19 53		
Grove Park [4]	d				19 05			19 08					19 27			19 32		19 42			19 52		19 57		
Sundridge Park	d							19 11								19 35					19 55				
Bromley North	a							19 13								19 37					19 57				
Elmstead Woods	d				19 08								19 30					19 45					20 00		
Chislehurst	d				19 10								19 33					19 48					20 03		
Petts Wood [4]	d			19 07	19 14					19 20		19 35	19 38				19 44	19 51				19 59	20 06		
Orpington [4]	a		19 06	19 12	19 19					19 25	19 27	19 38	19 43		19 38		19 48	19 54		19 55		20 02	20 09		20 08
	d		19 07								19 28		19 44		19 39					19 56			20 12		20 09
Chelsfield [3]	d	18 58									19 31		19 47										20 15		
Knockholt	d												19 50										20 18		
Dunton Green	d												19 55										20 23		
Sevenoaks [4]	a	19 06	19 16			19 20	19 32				19 38		19 58	19 41	19 48					20 05			20 26	20 11	20 18
	d	19 06	19 17			19 21	19 33				19 39			19 42	19 49					20 05				20 12	20 19
Hildenborough	d	19 12					19 40				19 45									20 11					
Tonbridge [4]	a	19 17	19 25			19 29	19 44				19 50			19 53	19 57					20 15				20 20	20 27

London - Grove Park, Bromley North, Orpington, Sevenoaks and Tonbridge

Network Diagram - see first Page of Table 200

	SE	SE	SE 1		SE	SE	SE	SE 1	SE 1	SE	SE	SE	SE 1		SE	SE	SE 1	SE 1	SE 1	SE	SE	SE	SE 1	
London Charing Cross 4 ⊖ d			20 00				20 06	20 10	20 15				20 30			20 36	20 40	20 45	21 00			21 06	21 10	
London Waterloo (East) 4 ⊖ d			20 03				20 09	20 13	20 18				20 33			20 39	20 43	20 48	21 03			21 09	21 13	
London Cannon Street 4 ⊖ d		19 50										20 20												
London Bridge 4 ⊖ d		19 54	20 09				20 14	20 19	20 23			20 24	20 39			20 44	20 49	20 53	21 09			21 14	21 19	
New Cross 4 ⊖ d		19 59										20 29												
St Johns d		20 01										20 31												
Lewisham 4 d		20 04										20 34										21 22		
Hither Green 4 d		20 08					20 23					20 38				20 53						21 26		
Grove Park 4 d		20 12			20 17		20 27			20 37		20 42				20 57				21 07		21 30		
Sundridge Park d					20 20					20 40										21 10				
Bromley North a					20 22					20 42										21 12				
Elmstead Woods d		20 15					20 30					20 45				21 00						21 33		
Chislehurst d		20 18					20 33					20 48				21 03						21 35		
Petts Wood 4 d	20 14	20 21				20 29	20 36				20 44	20 51			20 59	21 06					21 29	21 38		
Orpington 4 a	20 18	20 24	20 25			20 32	20 39		20 38		20 47	20 54	20 55		21 02	21 09		21 08	21 25		21 32	21 42	21 34	
d			20 26				20 42		20 39				20 56			21 12		21 09	21 26			21 43	21 35	
Chelsfield 3 d							20 45									21 15						21 46		
Knockholt d							20 48									21 18						21 49		
Dunton Green d							20 53									21 23						21 54		
Sevenoaks 4 a			20 35				20 56	20 41	20 48				21 05			21 26	21 11	21 18	21 35			21 57	21 44	
d			20 35					20 42	20 49				21 05				21 12	21 19	21 35				21 44	
Hildenborough d			20 41										21 11						21 41					
Tonbridge 4 a			20 45					20 50	20 57				21 15				21 20	21 27	21 45				21 52	

	SE 1	SE	SE	SE	SE 1	SE 1	SE 1	SE	SE		SE	SE 1	SE 1	SE	SE	SE	SE 1	SE 1	SE 1		SE	SE	SE	SE
London Charing Cross 4 ⊖ d	21 30			21 36	21 40	21 45	22 00				22 06	22 10	22 30			22 36	22 40	22 45	23 00					23 06
London Waterloo (East) 4 ⊖ d	21 33			21 39	21 43	21 48	22 03				22 09	22 13	22 33			22 39	22 43	22 48	23 03					23 09
London Cannon Street 4 ⊖ d																								
London Bridge 4 ⊖ d	21 39			21 44	21 49	21 53	22 09				22 14	22 19	22 39			22 44	22 49	22 53	23 09					23 14
New Cross 4 ⊖ d																								
St Johns d																								
Lewisham 4 d				21 52							22 22					22 52								23 22
Hither Green 4 d				21 56							22 26					22 56								23 26
Grove Park 4 d		21 37		22 00				22 07			22 30			22 37		23 00					23 07			23 30
Sundridge Park d		21 40						22 10						22 40							23 10			
Bromley North a		21 42						22 12						22 42							23 12			
Elmstead Woods d				22 03							22 33					23 03								23 33
Chislehurst d				22 05							22 35					23 05								23 35
Petts Wood 4 d			21 59	22 08					22 29		22 38				22 59	23 08						23 21	23 29	23 38
Orpington 4 a	21 55		22 02	22 12		22 08	22 25		22 32		22 42	22 34	22 54		23 02	23 12		23 08	23 24			23 25	23 32	23 42
d	21 56					22 09	22 26					22 35	22 54					23 09	23 24					
Chelsfield 3 d	21 59						22 29						22 57						23 27					
Knockholt d																								
Dunton Green d																								
Sevenoaks 4 a	22 06				22 11	22 18	22 36					22 44	23 05				23 11	23 18	23 35					
d	22 07				22 12	22 19	22 37					22 44	23 05				23 12	23 19	23 35					
Hildenborough d	22 13						22 43						23 11						23 41					
Tonbridge 4 a	22 17				22 20	22 27	22 47					22 52	23 15				23 20	23 27	23 45					

	SE 1	SE 1	SE	SE	SE		SE	SE 1	SE 1
London Charing Cross 4 ⊖ d	23 10	23 30					23 36	23 40	23 45
London Waterloo (East) 4 ⊖ d	23 13	23 33					23 39	23 43	23 48
London Cannon Street 4 ⊖ d									
London Bridge 4 ⊖ d	23 19	23 39					23 44	23 49	23 53
New Cross 4 ⊖ d									
St Johns d									
Lewisham 4 d							23 52		
Hither Green 4 d							23 56		
Grove Park 4 d			23 37				23 59		
Sundridge Park d			23 40						
Bromley North a			23 42						
Elmstead Woods d							00 03		
Chislehurst d							00 05		
Petts Wood 4 d				23 54	23 59		00 08		
Orpington 4 a	23 34	23 54		23 57	00 02		00 12		00 08
d	23 35	23 54							00 09
Chelsfield 3 d		23 57							
Knockholt d									
Dunton Green d									
Sevenoaks 4 a	23 44	00 05						00 11	00 18
d	23 44	00 05						00 12	00 19
Hildenborough d		00 11							
Tonbridge 4 a	23 52	00 15						00 20	00 27

London - Grove Park, Bromley North, Orpington, Sevenoaks and Tonbridge

Network Diagram - see first Page of Table 200

		SE 1	SE	SE	SE 1	SE 1	SE	SE	SE	SE		SE	SE	SE	SE	SE 1	SE	SE	SE	SE		SE	SE	SE 1	SE
London Charing Cross 4 ⊖	d	23p30		23p36	23p40	23p45				00 06		00 15		00 48	05 36	06 00			06 06				06 36	07 00	
London Waterloo (East) 4 ⊖	d	23p33		23p39	23p43	23p48				00 09		00 18		00 51	05 39	06 03			06 09				06 39	07 03	
London Cannon Street 4 ⊖	d																								
London Bridge 4 ⊖	d	23p39		23p44	23p49	23p53				00 14		00 23		00 56	05 44	06 08			06 14				06 44	07 08	
New Cross 4 ⊖	d													01 01											
St Johns	d																								
Lewisham 4	d			23p52						00 22				01 05	05 53				06 23				06 53		
Hither Green 4	d			23p56						00 26				01 09	05 57				06 27				06 57		
Grove Park 4	d			23p59			00 07			00 30			00 37	01 13	06 01		06 07		06 31	06 37			07 01		07 07
Sundridge Park	d						00 10						00 40				06 10			06 40					07 10
Bromley North	a						00 12						00 42				06 12			06 42					07 12
Elmstead Woods	d			00 03						00 33				01 16	06 04				06 34				07 04		
Chislehurst	d			00 05						00 35				01 19	06 06				06 36				07 06		
Petts Wood 4	d		23p59	00 08				00 21	00 29	00 38				01 22	06 09			06 29	06 39			06 59	07 09		
Orpington 4	a	23p54	00 02	00 12		00 08		00 25	00 32	00 42		00 46		01 25	06 12	06 23		06 32	06 42			07 02	07 12	07 23	
	d	23p54				00 09						00 46			06 13	06 24			06 43				07 13	07 24	
Chelsfield 3	d	23p57										00 49			06 16				06 46				07 16		
Knockholt	d														06 19				06 49				07 19		
Dunton Green	d											00 56			06 24				06 54				07 24		
Sevenoaks 4	a	00 05			00 11	00 18						00 59			06 27	06 33			06 57				07 27	07 33	
	d	00 05			00 12	00 19						00 59				06 33								07 33	
Hildenborough	d	00 11										01 05				06 39								07 39	
Tonbridge 4	a	00 15			00 20	00 27						01 10				06 43								07 43	

		SE	SE	SE	SE	SE 1		SE	SE	SE	SE 1	SE	SE 1	SE	SE	SE		SE 1	SE	SE	SE	SE 1	SE	SE	SE
London Charing Cross 4 ⊖	d		07 06			07 30				07 36	07 45		08 00			08 06		08 15				08 30			08 36
London Waterloo (East) 4 ⊖	d		07 09			07 33				07 39	07 48		08 03			08 09		08 18				08 33			08 39
London Cannon Street 4 ⊖	d																				08 20				
London Bridge 4 ⊖	d		07 14			07 38				07 44	07 53		08 08			08 14		08 23			08 24	08 39			08 44
New Cross 4 ⊖	d																				08 29				
St Johns	d																				08 31				
Lewisham 4	d		07 23							07 53											08 34				
Hither Green 4	d		07 27							07 57						08 23					08 38				08 53
Grove Park 4	d		07 31	07 35				07 55		08 01				08 15		08 27			08 35		08 42		08 55		08 57
Sundridge Park	d			07 38				07 58						08 18					08 38				08 58		
Bromley North	a			07 40				08 00						08 20					08 40				09 00		
Elmstead Woods	d		07 34							08 04						08 30					08 45				09 00
Chislehurst	d		07 36							08 06						08 33					08 48				09 03
Petts Wood 4	d	07 29	07 39		07 44				07 59	08 09		08 14			08 29	08 36				08 44	08 51			08 59	09 06
Orpington 4	a	07 32	07 42		07 47	07 54			08 02	08 12	08 08	08 17	08 23		08 32	08 39		08 38		08 47	08 54	08 55		09 02	09 09
	d		07 43			07 54				08 13	08 09		08 24			08 42		08 39				08 56			09 12
Chelsfield 3	d		07 46							08 16						08 45									09 15
Knockholt	d		07 49							08 19						08 48									09 18
Dunton Green	d		07 54							08 24						08 53									09 23
Sevenoaks 4	a		07 57			08 02				08 27	08 18		08 33			08 56		08 48				09 05			09 26
	d					08 03					08 19		08 33					08 49				09 05			
Hildenborough	d					08 09							08 39									09 11			
Tonbridge 4	a					08 14					08 27		08 43					08 57				09 15			

		SE 1		SE 1	SE	SE	SE 1	SE	SE	SE	SE 1	SE 1		SE	SE	SE	SE 1	SE	SE	SE	SE 1	SE 1		SE	SE
London Charing Cross 4 ⊖	d	08 40		08 45			09 00			09 06	09 10	09 15					09 30			09 36	09 40	09 45			
London Waterloo (East) 4 ⊖	d	08 43		08 48			09 03			09 09	09 13	09 18					09 33			09 39	09 43	09 48			
London Cannon Street 4 ⊖	d					08 50										09 20									09 50
London Bridge 4 ⊖	d	08 49		08 53		08 54	09 09			09 14	09 19	09 23				09 24	09 39			09 44	09 49	09 53			09 54
New Cross 4 ⊖	d					08 59										09 29									09 59
St Johns	d					09 01										09 31									10 01
Lewisham 4	d					09 04										09 34									10 04
Hither Green 4	d					09 08				09 23						09 38				09 53					10 08
Grove Park 4	d					09 12		09 15		09 27				09 35		09 42		09 55		09 57					10 12
Sundridge Park	d							09 18						09 38				09 58							
Bromley North	a							09 20						09 40				10 00							
Elmstead Woods	d					09 15				09 30						09 45				10 00					10 15
Chislehurst	d					09 18				09 33						09 48				10 03					10 18
Petts Wood 4	d				09 14	09 21			09 29	09 36					09 44	09 51			09 59	10 06				10 14	10 21
Orpington 4	a			09 08	09 17	09 24	09 25		09 32	09 39		09 38			09 47	09 54	09 55		10 02	10 09		10 08		10 17	10 24
	d			09 09			09 26			09 42		09 39					09 56			10 12		10 09			
Chelsfield 3	d									09 45										10 15					
Knockholt	d									09 48										10 18					
Dunton Green	d									09 53										10 23					
Sevenoaks 4	a	09 11		09 18			09 35			09 56	09 41	09 48					10 05			10 26	10 11	10 18			
	d	09 12		09 19			09 35				09 42	09 49					10 05				10 12	10 19			
Hildenborough	d						09 41										10 11								
Tonbridge 4	a	09 20		09 27			09 45				09 50	09 57					10 15				10 20	10 27			

Table 204

Saturdays

London - Grove Park, Bromley North, Orpington, Sevenoaks and Tonbridge

Network Diagram - see first Page of Table 200

		SE ■1	SE	SE	SE	SE ■1	SE ■1	SE		SE	SE	SE ■1	SE	SE	SE	SE ■1	SE ■1	SE		SE	SE ■1	SE	SE	SE	SE ■1
London Charing Cross ■4 ⊖	d	10 00			10 06	10 10	10 15					10 30			10 36	10 40	10 45				11 00			11 06	11 10
London Waterloo (East) ■4 ⊖	d	10 03			10 09	10 13	10 18					10 33			10 39	10 43	10 48				11 03			11 09	11 13
London Cannon Street ■4 ⊖	d										10 20									10 50					
London Bridge ■4 ⊖	d	10 09			10 14	10 19	10 23				10 24	10 39			10 44	10 49	10 53			10 54	11 09			11 14	11 19
New Cross ■4 ⊖	d										10 29									10 59					
St Johns	d										10 31									11 01					
Lewisham ■4	d										10 34									11 04					
Hither Green ■4	d				10 23						10 38				10 53					11 08				11 23	
Grove Park ■4	d		10 15		10 27			10 35			10 42		10 55		10 57					11 12		11 15		11 27	
Sundridge Park	d		10 18					10 38					10 58									11 18			
Bromley North	a		10 20					10 40					11 00									11 20			
Elmstead Woods	d				10 30						10 45				11 00					11 15				11 30	
Chislehurst	d				10 33						10 48				11 03					11 18				11 33	
Petts Wood ■4	d			10 29	10 36					10 44	10 51			10 59	11 06			11 14		11 21			11 29	11 36	
Orpington ■4	a	10 25		10 32	10 39		10 38			10 47	10 54	10 55		11 02	11 09		11 08	11 17		11 24	11 25		11 32	11 39	
	d	10 26			10 42		10 39					10 56			11 12		11 09				11 26			11 42	
Chelsfield ■3	d				10 45										11 15									11 45	
Knockholt	d				10 48										11 18									11 48	
Dunton Green	d				10 53										11 23									11 53	
Sevenoaks ■4	a	10 35			10 56	10 41	10 48					11 05			11 26	11 11	11 18				11 35			11 56	11 41
	d	10 35				10 42	10 49					11 05				11 12	11 19				11 35				11 42
Hildenborough	d	10 41										11 11									11 41				
Tonbridge ■4	a	10 45				10 50	10 57					11 15				11 20	11 27				11 45				11 50

		SE ■1	SE	SE		SE	SE ■1	SE	SE	SE	SE ■1	SE ■1	SE	SE		SE ■1	SE	SE	SE	SE ■1	SE ■1	SE	SE	SE	
London Charing Cross ■4 ⊖	d	11 15					11 30			11 36	11 40	11 45				12 00			12 06	12 10	12 15				
London Waterloo (East) ■4 ⊖	d	11 18					11 33			11 39	11 43	11 48				12 03			12 09	12 13	12 18				
London Cannon Street ■4 ⊖	d					11 20								11 50										12 20	
London Bridge ■4 ⊖	d	11 23				11 24	11 39			11 44	11 49	11 53		11 54		12 09			12 14	12 19	12 23			12 24	
New Cross ■4 ⊖	d					11 29								11 59										12 29	
St Johns	d					11 31								12 01										12 31	
Lewisham ■4	d					11 34								12 04										12 34	
Hither Green ■4	d					11 38				11 53				12 08					12 23					12 38	
Grove Park ■4	d		11 35			11 42		11 55		11 57				12 12			12 15		12 27			12 35		12 42	
Sundridge Park	d		11 38					11 58									12 18					12 38			
Bromley North	a		11 40					12 00									12 20					12 40			
Elmstead Woods	d					11 45				12 00				12 15					12 30					12 45	
Chislehurst	d					11 48				12 03				12 18					12 33					12 48	
Petts Wood ■4	d			11 44		11 51			11 59	12 06			12 14	12 21				12 29	12 36				12 44	12 51	
Orpington ■4	a	11 38		11 47		11 54	11 55		12 02	12 09		12 08	12 17	12 24		12 25		12 32	12 39		12 38		12 47	12 54	
	d	11 39					11 56			12 12		12 09				12 26			12 42		12 39				
Chelsfield ■3	d									12 15									12 45						
Knockholt	d									12 18									12 48						
Dunton Green	d									12 23									12 53						
Sevenoaks ■4	a	11 48					12 05			12 26	12 11	12 18				12 35			12 56	12 41	12 48				
	d	11 49					12 05				12 12	12 19				12 35				12 42	12 49				
Hildenborough	d						12 11									12 41									
Tonbridge ■4	a	11 57					12 15				12 20	12 27				12 45				12 50	12 57				

		SE ■1	SE	SE	SE	SE ■1	SE ■1	SE	SE	SE ■1		SE	SE	SE	SE ■1	SE ■1	SE	SE	SE	SE ■1		SE	SE	SE	SE ■1
London Charing Cross ■4 ⊖	d	12 30			12 36	12 40	12 45			13 00				13 06	13 10	13 15				13 30				13 36	13 40
London Waterloo (East) ■4 ⊖	d	12 33			12 39	12 43	12 48			13 03				13 09	13 13	13 18				13 33				13 39	13 43
London Cannon Street ■4 ⊖	d								12 50										13 20						
London Bridge ■4 ⊖	d	12 39			12 44	12 49	12 53		12 54	13 09				13 14	13 19	13 23			13 24	13 39				13 44	13 49
New Cross ■4 ⊖	d								12 59										13 29						
St Johns	d								13 01										13 31						
Lewisham ■4	d								13 04										13 34						
Hither Green ■4	d				12 53				13 08					13 23					13 38					13 53	
Grove Park ■4	d		12 55		12 57				13 12			13 15		13 27			13 35		13 42			13 55		13 57	
Sundridge Park	d		12 58									13 18					13 38					13 58			
Bromley North	a		13 00									13 20					13 40					14 00			
Elmstead Woods	d				13 00				13 15					13 30					13 45					14 00	
Chislehurst	d				13 03				13 18					13 33					13 48					14 03	
Petts Wood ■4	d			12 59	13 06			13 14	13 21				13 29	13 36				13 44	13 51				13 59	14 06	
Orpington ■4	a	12 55		13 02	13 09		13 08	13 17	13 24	13 25			13 32	13 39		13 38		13 47	13 54	13 55			14 02	14 09	
	d	12 56			13 12		13 09			13 26				13 42		13 39				13 56				14 12	
Chelsfield ■3	d				13 15									13 45										14 15	
Knockholt	d				13 18									13 48										14 18	
Dunton Green	d				13 23									13 53										14 23	
Sevenoaks ■4	a	13 05			13 26	13 11	13 18			13 35				13 56	13 41	13 48				14 05				14 26	14 11
	d	13 05				13 12	13 19			13 35					13 42	13 49				14 05					14 12
Hildenborough	d	13 11								13 41										14 11					
Tonbridge ■4	a	13 15				13 20	13 27			13 45					13 50	13 57				14 15					14 20

Table 204

Saturdays

London - Grove Park, Bromley North, Orpington, Sevenoaks and Tonbridge

Network Diagram - see first Page of Table 200

		SE 1	SE	SE	SE 1	SE		SE	SE	SE 1	SE 1	SE	SE	SE	SE 1	SE		SE	SE	SE 1	SE 1	SE	SE	SE 1	SE
London Charing Cross 4 ⊖	d	13 45			14 00				14 06	14 10	14 15				14 30				14 36	14 40	14 45			15 00	
London Waterloo (East) 4 ⊖	d	13 48			14 03				14 09	14 13	14 18				14 33				14 39	14 43	14 48			15 03	
London Cannon Street 4 ⊖	d			13 50										14 20									14 50		
London Bridge 4 ⊖	d	13 53		13 54	14 09				14 14	14 19	14 23			14 24	14 39				14 44	14 49	14 53		14 54	15 09	
New Cross 4 ⊖	d			13 59										14 29									14 59		
St Johns	d			14 01										14 31									15 01		
Lewisham 4	d			14 04										14 34									15 04		
Hither Green 4	d			14 08					14 23					14 38					14 53				15 08		
Grove Park 4	d			14 12		14 15			14 27			14 35		14 42		14 55			14 57				15 12		15 15
Sundridge Park	d					14 18						14 38				14 58									15 18
Bromley North	a					14 20						14 40				15 00									15 20
Elmstead Woods	d			14 15					14 30					14 45					15 00				15 15		
Chislehurst	d			14 18					14 33					14 48					15 03				15 18		
Petts Wood 4	d		14 14	14 21				14 29	14 36				14 44	14 51				14 59	15 06			15 14	15 21		
Orpington 4	a	14 08	14 17	14 24	14 25			14 32	14 39		14 38		14 47	14 54	14 55			15 02	15 09		15 08	15 17	15 24	15 25	
	d	14 09			14 26				14 42		14 39				14 56				15 12		15 09			15 26	
Chelsfield 3	d								14 45										15 15						
Knockholt	d								14 48										15 18						
Dunton Green	d								14 53										15 23						
Sevenoaks 4	a	14 18			14 35				14 56	14 41	14 48				15 05				15 26	15 11	15 18			15 35	
	d	14 19			14 35					14 42	14 49				15 05					15 12	15 19			15 35	
Hildenborough	d				14 41										15 11									15 41	
Tonbridge 4	a	14 27			14 45					14 50	14 57				15 15					15 20	15 27			15 45	

		SE		SE	SE 1	SE 1	SE	SE	SE	SE 1	SE	SE		SE	SE 1	SE 1	SE	SE	SE 1	SE	SE	SE		SE 1	SE 1
London Charing Cross 4 ⊖	d			15 06	15 10	15 15				15 30				15 36	15 40	15 45			16 00			16 06		16 10	16 15
London Waterloo (East) 4 ⊖	d			15 09	15 13	15 18				15 33				15 39	15 43	15 48			16 03			16 09		16 13	16 18
London Cannon Street 4 ⊖	d								15 20									15 50							
London Bridge 4 ⊖	d			15 14	15 19	15 23			15 24	15 39				15 44	15 49	15 53		15 54	16 09			16 14		16 19	16 23
New Cross 4 ⊖	d								15 29									15 59							
St Johns	d								15 31									16 01							
Lewisham 4	d								15 34									16 04							
Hither Green 4	d			15 23					15 38					15 53				16 08				16 23			
Grove Park 4	d			15 27			15 35		15 42		15 55			15 57				16 12		16 15		16 27			
Sundridge Park	d						15 38				15 58									16 18					
Bromley North	a						15 40				16 00									16 20					
Elmstead Woods	d			15 30					15 45					16 00				16 15				16 30			
Chislehurst	d			15 33					15 48					16 03				16 18				16 33			
Petts Wood 4	d	15 29		15 36				15 44	15 51			15 59		16 06			16 14	16 21			16 29	16 36			
Orpington 4	a	15 32		15 39		15 38		15 47	15 54	15 55		16 02		16 09		16 08	16 17	16 24	16 25		16 32	16 39			16 38
	d			15 42		15 39				15 56				16 12		16 09			16 26			16 42			16 39
Chelsfield 3	d			15 45										16 15								16 45			
Knockholt	d			15 48										16 18								16 48			
Dunton Green	d			15 53										16 23								16 53			
Sevenoaks 4	a			15 56	15 41	15 48				16 05				16 26	16 11	16 18			16 35			16 56		16 41	16 48
	d				15 42	15 49				16 05					16 12	16 19			16 35					16 42	16 49
Hildenborough	d									16 11									16 41						
Tonbridge 4	a				15 50	15 57				16 15					16 20	16 27			16 45					16 50	16 57

		SE	SE	SE	SE 1	SE	SE	SE		SE 1	SE 1	SE	SE	SE 1	SE	SE	SE	SE 1		SE 1	SE	SE	SE	SE 1	SE
London Charing Cross 4 ⊖	d				16 30			16 36		16 40	16 45			17 00			17 06	17 10		17 15				17 30	
London Waterloo (East) 4 ⊖	d				16 33			16 39		16 43	16 48			17 03			17 09	17 13		17 18				17 33	
London Cannon Street 4 ⊖	d			16 20									16 50										17 20		
London Bridge 4 ⊖	d			16 24	16 39			16 44		16 49	16 53		16 54	17 09			17 14	17 19		17 23			17 24	17 39	
New Cross 4 ⊖	d			16 29									16 59										17 29		
St Johns	d			16 31									17 01										17 31		
Lewisham 4	d			16 34									17 04										17 34		
Hither Green 4	d			16 38				16 53					17 08				17 23						17 38		
Grove Park 4	d	16 35		16 42		16 55		16 57					17 12		17 15		17 27				17 35		17 42		17 55
Sundridge Park	d	16 38				16 58									17 18						17 38				17 58
Bromley North	a	16 40				17 00									17 20						17 40				18 00
Elmstead Woods	d			16 45				17 00					17 15				17 30						17 45		
Chislehurst	d			16 48				17 03					17 18				17 33						17 48		
Petts Wood 4	d		16 44	16 51			16 59	17 06				17 14	17 21			17 29	17 36					17 44	17 51		
Orpington 4	a		16 47	16 54	16 55		17 02	17 09			17 08	17 17	17 24	17 25		17 32	17 39			17 38		17 47	17 54	17 55	
	d				16 56			17 12			17 09			17 26			17 42			17 39				17 56	
Chelsfield 3	d							17 15									17 45								
Knockholt	d							17 18									17 48								
Dunton Green	d							17 23									17 53								
Sevenoaks 4	a				17 05			17 26		17 11	17 18			17 35			17 56	17 41		17 48				18 05	
	d				17 05					17 12	17 19			17 35				17 42		17 49				18 05	
Hildenborough	d				17 11									17 41										18 11	
Tonbridge 4	a				17 15					17 20	17 27			17 45				17 50		17 57				18 15	

Table 204

Saturdays

London - Grove Park, Bromley North, Orpington, Sevenoaks and Tonbridge

Network Diagram - see first Page of Table 200

		SE	SE	SE 1		SE 1	SE	SE	SE 1	SE	SE	SE	SE 1	SE 1		SE	SE	SE	SE 1	SE	SE	SE	SE 1	SE 1	
London Charing Cross 4 ⊖	d		17 36	17 40		17 45			18 00			18 06	18 10	18 15					18 30			18 36	18 40	18 45	
London Waterloo (East) 4 ⊖	d		17 39	17 43		17 48			18 03			18 09	18 13	18 18					18 33			18 39	18 43	18 48	
London Cannon Street 4 ⊖	d							17 50										18 20							
London Bridge 4 ⊖	d		17 44	17 49		17 53		17 54	18 09			18 14	18 19	18 23				18 24	18 39			18 44	18 49	18 53	
New Cross 4 ⊖	d							17 59										18 29							
St Johns	d							18 01										18 31							
Lewisham 4	d							18 04										18 34							
Hither Green 4	d		17 53					18 08				18 23						18 38				18 53			
Grove Park 4	d		17 57					18 12		18 15		18 27				18 35		18 42		18 55		18 57			
Sundridge Park	d									18 18						18 38				18 58					
Bromley North	a									18 20						18 40				19 00					
Elmstead Woods	d		18 00					18 15				18 30						18 45				19 00			
Chislehurst	d		18 03					18 18				18 33						18 48				19 03			
Petts Wood 4	d	17 59	18 06				18 14	18 21			18 29	18 36					18 44	18 51			18 59	19 06			
Orpington 4	a	18 02	18 09			18 08	18 17	18 24	18 25		18 32	18 39		18 38			18 47	18 54	18 55		19 02	19 09		19 08	
	d		18 12			18 09			18 26			18 42		18 39					18 56			19 12		19 09	
Chelsfield 3	d		18 15									18 45										19 15			
Knockholt	d		18 18									18 48										19 18			
Dunton Green	d		18 23									18 53										19 23			
Sevenoaks 4	a		18 26	18 11		18 18			18 35			18 56	18 41	18 48					19 05			19 26	19 11	19 18	
	d			18 12		18 19			18 35				18 42	18 49					19 05				19 12	19 19	
Hildenborough	d								18 41										19 11						
Tonbridge 4	a			18 20		18 27			18 45				18 50	18 58					19 15				19 20	19 27	

		SE	SE	SE 1	SE	SE	SE	SE 1	SE 1	SE		SE	SE	SE 1	SE	SE	SE	SE 1	SE 1	SE		SE	SE	SE	SE 1
London Charing Cross 4 ⊖	d			19 00			19 06	19 10	19 15					19 30			19 36	19 40	19 55					20 06	20 10
London Waterloo (East) 4 ⊖	d			19 03			19 09	19 13	19 18					19 33			19 39	19 43	19 58					20 09	20 13
London Cannon Street 4 ⊖	d		18 50										19 20												
London Bridge 4 ⊖	d		18 54	19 09			19 14	19 19	19 23				19 24	19 39			19 44	19 49	20 03					20 14	20 19
New Cross 4 ⊖	d		18 59										19 29												
St Johns	d		19 01										19 31												
Lewisham 4	d		19 04										19 34				19 52							20 22	
Hither Green 4	d		19 09				19 23						19 38				19 56							20 26	
Grove Park 4	d		19 12		19 15		19 27			19 35			19 42		19 55		20 00					20 15		20 30	
Sundridge Park	d				19 18					19 38					19 58							20 18			
Bromley North	a				19 20					19 40					20 00							20 20			
Elmstead Woods	d		19 15				19 30						19 45				20 03							20 33	
Chislehurst	d		19 18				19 33						19 48				20 05							20 35	
Petts Wood 4	d	19 14	19 21			19 29	19 36					19 44	19 51			19 59	20 08			20 14			20 29	20 38	
Orpington 4	a	19 17	19 24	19 25		19 32	19 39		19 38			19 48	19 54	19 55		20 02	20 12		20 18	20 18			20 32	20 42	20 34
	d			19 26			19 42		19 39					19 56			20 13		20 21					20 43	20 35
Chelsfield 3	d						19 45										20 16							20 46	
Knockholt	d						19 48										20 19							20 49	
Dunton Green	d						19 53										20 24							20 54	
Sevenoaks 4	a			19 35			19 56	19 41	19 49					20 05			20 27	20 11	20 30					20 57	20 44
	d			19 35				19 42	19 49					20 05				20 12	20 31						20 44
Hildenborough	d			19 41										20 11											
Tonbridge 4	a			19 45				19 50	19 58					20 15				20 20	20 39						20 52

		SE	SE	SE 1	SE	SE		SE 1	SE 1	SE	SE	SE	SE 1	SE 1	SE	SE		SE	SE 1	SE 1	SE	SE	SE	SE 1	SE 1
London Charing Cross 4 ⊖	d			20 25		20 36		20 40	20 55			21 06	21 10	21 25				21 36	21 40	21 55			22 06	22 10	22 25
London Waterloo (East) 4 ⊖	d			20 28		20 39		20 43	20 58			21 09	21 13	21 28				21 39	21 43	21 58			22 09	22 13	22 28
London Cannon Street 4 ⊖	d																								
London Bridge 4 ⊖	d			20 33		20 44		20 49	21 03			21 14	21 19	21 33				21 44	21 49	22 03			22 14	22 19	22 33
New Cross 4 ⊖	d																								
St Johns	d																								
Lewisham 4	d					20 52						21 22						21 52					22 22		
Hither Green 4	d					20 56						21 26						21 56					22 26		
Grove Park 4	d	20 37				21 00				21 07		21 30			21 37			22 00			22 07		22 30		
Sundridge Park	d	20 40								21 10					21 40						22 10				
Bromley North	a	20 42								21 12					21 42						22 12				
Elmstead Woods	d					21 03						21 33						22 03					22 33		
Chislehurst	d					21 05						21 35						22 05					22 35		
Petts Wood 4	d		20 44		20 59	21 08					21 29	21 38				21 59		22 08				22 29	22 38		
Orpington 4	a		20 47	20 48	21 02	21 12		21 04	21 18		21 32	21 42	21 34	21 48		22 02		22 12	22 04	22 18		22 32	22 42	22 34	22 48
	d			20 51		21 13		21 05	21 21			21 43	21 35	21 51					22 05	22 21				22 35	22 49
Chelsfield 3	d					21 16						21 46													22 52
Knockholt	d					21 19						21 49													
Dunton Green	d					21 24						21 54													
Sevenoaks 4	a			21 00		21 27		21 14	21 30			21 57	21 44	22 00					22 14	22 30				22 44	22 59
	d			21 01				21 14	21 31				21 44	22 01					22 14	22 31				22 44	23 00
Hildenborough	d			21 07										22 07											23 06
Tonbridge 4	a			21 11				21 22	21 39				21 52	22 11					22 22	22 39				22 52	23 10

Table 204

Saturdays

London - Grove Park, Bromley North, Orpington, Sevenoaks and Tonbridge

Network Diagram - see first Page of Table 200

		SE	SE	SE	SE 1	SE 1	SE	SE	SE	SE	SE 1	SE 1	SE	SE	SE	SE	SE 1	SE 1
London Charing Cross 4 ⊖	d			22 36	22 40	22 55				23 06	23 10	23 25				23 36	23 40	23 45
London Waterloo (East) 4 ⊖	d			22 39	22 43	22 58				23 09	23 13	23 28				23 39	23 43	23 48
London Cannon Street 4 ⊖	d																	
London Bridge 4 ⊖	d			22 44	22 49	23 03				23 14	23 19	23 33				23 44	23 49	23 53
New Cross 4 ⊖	d																	
St Johns	d																	
Lewisham 4	d			22 52						23 22						23 52		
Hither Green 4	d			22 56						23 26						23 56		
Grove Park 4	d	22 37		23 00			23 07			23 30			23 37			23 59		
Sundridge Park	d	22 40					23 10						23 40					
Bromley North	a	22 42					23 12						23 42					
Elmstead Woods	d			23 03						23 33						00 03		
Chislehurst	d			23 05						23 35						00 05		
Petts Wood 4	d		22 59	23 08				23 22	23 29	23 38				23 52	23 59	00 08		
Orpington 4	a		23 02	23 12	23 04	23 18		23 25	23 32	23 42	23 34	23 48		23 55	00 02	00 12	00 04	00 08
	d				23 05	23 19					23 35	23 49					00 05	00 09
Chelsfield 3	d											23 52						
Knockholt	d																	
Dunton Green	d																	
Sevenoaks 4	a				23 14	23 28					23 44	23 59					00 14	00 18
	d				23 14	23 28					23 44	23 59					00 14	00 19
Hildenborough	d											00 06						
Tonbridge 4	a				23 22	23 36					23 52	00 10					00 22	00 27

Sundays

		SE 1 A	SE A	SE A	SE 1 A	SE 1 A	SE	SE A	SE A	SE	SE	SE	SE	SE	SE	SE	SE 1	SE	SE 1	SE	SE 1	SE	SE
London Charing Cross 4 ⊖	d	23p25		23p36	23p40	23p45				00 06	00 10	00 15		00 48	07 46		08 08	08 16	08 23		08 38	08 46	
London Waterloo (East) 4 ⊖	d	23p28		23p39	23p43	23p48				00 09	00 13	00 18		00 51	07 49		08 11	08 19	08 26		08 41	08 49	
London Cannon Street 4 ⊖	d																						
London Bridge 4 ⊖	d	23p33		23p44	23p49	23p53				00 14	00 18	00 23		00 56	07 54		08 16	08 24	08 31		08 46	08 54	
New Cross 4 ⊖	d													01 01									
St Johns	d																						
Lewisham 4	d			23p52						00 22				01 05	08 03			08 33				09 03	
Hither Green 4	d			23p56						00 26				01 09	08 07			08 37				09 07	
Grove Park 4	d			23p59			00 07			00 30	00 29		00 37	01 13	08 11			08 41				09 11	
Sundridge Park	d						00 10						00 40										
Bromley North	a						00 12						00 42										
Elmstead Woods	d			00 03						00 33	00 32			01 16	08 14			08 44				09 14	
Chislehurst	d			00 05						00 35	00 35			01 19	08 17			08 47				09 17	
Petts Wood 4	d		23p59	00 08				00 22	00 29	00 38	00 38			01 22	08 20	08 25		08 50		08 55		09 20	09 25
Orpington 4	a	23p48	00 02	00 12	00 04	00 08		00 25	00 32	00 42	00 41	00 46		01 25	08 23	08 28	08 31	08 53	08 46	08 58	09 01	09 23	09 28
	d	23p49			00 05	00 09					00 42	00 46					08 32	08 54	08 46		09 02		
Chelsfield 3	d	23p52									00 45	00 49						08 57					
Knockholt	d																	09 00					
Dunton Green	d											00 56						09 05					
Sevenoaks 4	a	23p59			00 14	00 18					00 52	00 59					08 41	09 08	08 55		09 11		
	d	23p59			00 14	00 19					00 53	00 59					08 42		08 56		09 12		
Hildenborough	d	00 06									00 59	01 05					08 48						
Tonbridge 4	a	00 10			00 22	00 27					01 04	01 10					08 52		09 04		09 20		

		SE 1	SE	SE 1	SE	SE 1	SE	SE 1		SE 1	SE	SE 1	SE	SE 1	SE	SE 1	SE	SE	SE 1	SE	SE 1	SE
London Charing Cross 4 ⊖	d	09 08	09 16	09 23		09 38	09 46	09 53	and at the same minutes past each hour until	19 53		20 08	20 16	20 23		20 38	20 46		21 08	21 16	21 23	
London Waterloo (East) 4 ⊖	d	09 11	09 19	09 26		09 41	09 49	09 56		19 56		20 11	20 19	20 26		20 41	20 49		21 11	21 19	21 26	
London Cannon Street 4 ⊖	d																					
London Bridge 4 ⊖	d	09 16	09 24	09 31		09 46	09 54	10 01		20 01		20 16	20 24	20 31		20 46	20 54		21 16	21 24	21 31	
New Cross 4 ⊖	d																					
St Johns	d																					
Lewisham 4	d		09 33				10 03						20 33				21 03			21 33		
Hither Green 4	d		09 37				10 07						20 37				21 07			21 37		
Grove Park 4	d		09 41				10 11						20 41				21 11			21 41		
Sundridge Park	d																					
Bromley North	a																					
Elmstead Woods	d		09 44				10 14						20 44				21 14			21 44		
Chislehurst	d		09 47				10 17						20 47				21 17			21 47		
Petts Wood 4	d		09 50		09 55		10 20				20 25		20 50		20 55		21 20	21 25		21 50		21 55
Orpington 4	a	09 31	09 53	09 46	09 58	10 01	10 23	10 16		20 16	20 28	20 31	20 53	20 46	20 58	21 01	21 23	21 28	21 31	21 53	21 46	21 58
	d	09 32	09 54	09 46		10 02		10 16		20 16		20 32	20 54	20 46		21 02			21 32	21 54	21 46	
Chelsfield 3	d		09 57										20 57							21 57		
Knockholt	d		10 00										21 00							22 00		
Dunton Green	d		10 05										21 05							22 05		
Sevenoaks 4	a	09 41	10 08	09 55		10 11		10 25		20 25		20 41	21 08	20 55		21 11			21 41	22 08	21 55	
	d	09 42		09 56		10 12		10 26		20 26		20 42		20 56		21 12			21 42		21 56	
Hildenborough	d	09 48										20 48							21 48			
Tonbridge 4	a	09 52		10 04		10 20		10 34		20 34		20 52		21 04		21 20			21 52		22 04	

A not 11 December

Table 204

Sundays

London - Grove Park, Bromley North, Orpington, Sevenoaks and Tonbridge

Network Diagram - see first Page of Table 200

		SE [1]		SE	SE	SE [1]	SE	SE [1]	SE	SE [1]	SE	SE		SE	SE [1]	SE	SE [1]	SE	SE	SE [1]	SE				
London Charing Cross [4] ⊖	d	21 38		21 46		22 08	22 16	22 23		22 38	22 46				23 08	23 16	23 23			23 38	23 46				
London Waterloo (East) [4] ⊖	d	21 41		21 49		22 11	22 19	22 26		22 41	22 49				23 11	23 19	23 26			23 41	23 49				
London Cannon Street [4] ⊖	d																								
London Bridge [4] ⊖	d	21 46		21 54		22 16	22 24	22 31		22 46	22 54				23 16	23 24	23 31			23 46	23 54				
New Cross [4] ⊖	d																								
St Johns	d																								
Lewisham [4] (bus)	d			22 03			22 33				23 03					23 33					00 03				
Hither Green [4]	d			22 07			22 37				23 07					23 37					00 07				
Grove Park [4]	d			22 11			22 41				23 11					23 41					00 11				
Sundridge Park	d																								
Bromley North	a																								
Elmstead Woods	d			22 14			22 44				23 14					23 44					00 14				
Chislehurst	d			22 17			22 47				23 17					23 47					00 17				
Petts Wood [4]	d			22 20	22 25		22 50		22 55		23 20	23 22		23 25		23 50		23 52	23 55		00 20				
Orpington [4]	a	22 01		22 23	22 28	22 31	22 53	22 46	22 58	23 01	23 23	23 26		23 29	23 31	23 53	23 46	23 56	23 59	00 01	00 23				
	d	22 02				22 32		22 46		23 02					23 32		23 46			00 02					
Chelsfield [3]	d							22 49									23 49								
Knockholt	d																								
Dunton Green	d																								
Sevenoaks [4]	a	22 11				22 41		22 57		23 11					23 41		23 57			00 11					
	d	22 12				22 42		22 57		23 12					23 42		23 57			00 12					
Hildenborough	d					22 48									23 48										
Tonbridge [4]	a	22 20				22 52		23 05		23 20					23 52		00 05			00 20					

Tonbridge, Sevenoaks, Orpington, Bromley North, Grove Park - London

Network Diagram - see first Page of Table 200

Miles	Miles			SE MX	SE MX 1	SE MX	SE	SE	SE A	SE	SE 1	SE		SE 1	SE	SE	SE	SE 1	SE 1	SE 1	SE	SE		SE	SE
0	—	**Tonbridge** 4	d		23p14			04 52			05 32			05 50				06 00	06 06	06 19					
2½	—	Hildenborough	d		23p18			04 56			05 36							06 04		06 23					
7½	—	**Sevenoaks** 4	a		23p24			05 02			05 42			05 58				06 10	06 14	06 30					
—	—		d		23p25			05 03			05 43			05 59			06 02	06 11	06 15	06 32					06 36
1½	—	Dunton Green	d														06 05								06 39
5½	—	Knockholt	d														06 10								06 44
6¾	—	Chelsfield 3	d		23p32			05 10			05 50						06 13								06 47
8¼	—	**Orpington** 4	a		23p36			05 13			05 53			06 08			06 16	06 19	06 23						06 50
—	—		d	23p21	23p37		05 10	05 14	05 15	05 40	05 54	06 01		06 09	06 10		06 22	06 20	06 24		06 40			06 43	06 52
9¼	—	Petts Wood 4	d	23p24			05a13		05 18	05a43		06 04			06a13		06 25				06a43			06 46	06 55
10¾	—	Chislehurst	d	23p27					05 21			06 07					06 28							06 49	06 58
11¾	—	Elmstead Woods	d	23p29					05 23			06 09					06 30							06 51	07 00
—	0	**Bromley North**	d			00 23										06 25						06 45			
—	0½	Sundridge Park	d			00 25										06 27						06 47			
13	1¾	**Grove Park** 4	d	23p33		00a28			05 27			06 12				06a30	06 34					06a50		06 54	07 04
14¾	—	Hither Green 4	d	23p37					05 30			06 16					06 38							06 58	07 08
16	—	**Lewisham** 4	d	23p43					05 36			06 22					06 43							07 04	
16½	—	St Johns	a																						
17¼	—	New Cross 4 ⊖	a						05 39			06 25													
20¼	—	**London Bridge** 4 ⊖	a	23p52	23p54			05 37	05 45		06 09	06 31		06 24			06 51	06 38	06 39	06 54					07 18
—	—	**London Cannon Street** 4 ⊖	a															06 42							07 25
21¼	—	**London Waterloo (East)** 4 ⊖	a	23p56	23p59			05 41	05 50		06 14	06 36		06 29			06 56		06 44	06 59				07 16	
22	—	**London Charing Cross** 4 ⊖	a	00 01	00 03			05 47	05 55		06 18	06 39		06 33			07 02		06 49	07 05				07 22	

		SE 1	SE 1	SE 1	SE	SE	SE	SE		SE 1	SE 1	SE	SE	SE	SE 1	SE 1	SE 1	SE		SE	SE	SE	SE 1	SE 1	SE 1
Tonbridge 4	d	06 32	06 40	06 44						06 51	07 02				07 11	07 15	07 23						07 31	07 35	07 42
Hildenborough	d	06 36								06 55					07 15	07 20							07 35	07 40	
Sevenoaks 4	a	06 43	06 48	06 52						07 02	07 10				07 22	07 26	07 31						07 42	07 46	07 50
	d	06 44	06 49	06 53				06 56		07 03	07 11			07 17	07 23	07 27	07 32					07 37	07 43	07 47	07 51
Dunton Green	d							06 59						07 20								07 40			
Knockholt	d							07 04						07 25								07 45			
Chelsfield 3	d							07 07						07 28	07 32							07 48	07 52		
Orpington 4	a	06 53		07 02				07 10		07 13				07 31								07 51			
	d	06 54		07 04	07 03	07 08		07 11		07 14		07 22		07 33				07 38		07 41		07 52			
Petts Wood 4	d				07 06	07a11		07 15				07 25		07 36				07a41		07 44		07 55			
Chislehurst	d				07 09			07 18				07 28		07 39						07 47		07 59			
Elmstead Woods	d				07 11			07 20				07 31		07 41						07 50		08 01			
Bromley North	d						07 15						07 35								07 55				
Sundridge Park	d						07 17						07 37								07 57				
Grove Park 4	d				07 15		07a20	07 24				07 34	07a40	07 45						07 53	08a00	08 05			
Hither Green 4	d				07 19			07 28				07 39		07 49						07 58					
Lewisham 4	d				07 25							07 44								08 03					
St Johns	a																								
New Cross 4 ⊖	a																								
London Bridge 4 ⊖	a	07 09	07 14	07 22				07 37		07 29	07 36	07 53		07 59	07 50	07 53						08 18	08 09	08 13	
London Cannon Street 4 ⊖	a			07 29				07 44						08 06		07 59						08 26		08 20	
London Waterloo (East) 4 ⊖	a	07 14	07 19		07 36					07 34	07 41	07 58			07 55		08 00			08 16			08 14		08 20
London Charing Cross 4 ⊖	a	07 20	07 25		07 42					07 40	07 47	08 04			08 01		08 06			08 22			08 20		08 26

		SE	SE	SE		SE	SE	SE 1	SE 1	SE 1	SE	SE	SE	SE		SE 1	SE 1	SE 1	SE	SE	SE	SE	SE 1	SE 1	
Tonbridge 4	d							07 51	07 59	08 04						08 11	08 15	08 22					08 35	08 40	
Hildenborough	d							07 55								08 15	08 20						08 39		
Sevenoaks 4	a							08 02	08 07	08 12						08 22	08 26	08 30					08 45	08 48	
	d						07 57	08 03	08 08	08 12				08 17		08 23	08 27	08 31				08 37	08 45	08 49	
Dunton Green	d						08 00							08 20								08 40			
Knockholt	d						08 05							08 25								08 45			
Chelsfield 3	d						08 08	08 12						08 28		08 32						08 48	08 53		
Orpington 4	a						08 12							08 31								08 51			
	d	07 57	08 01	08 10			08 13				08 21	08 26		08 32					08 40	08 43		08 52			
Petts Wood 4	d	08 00	08 04	08a13			08 16				08 24	08a29		08 35					08a43	08 46		08 55			
Chislehurst	d	08 03	08 07				08 20				08 27			08 39						08 49		08 58			
Elmstead Woods	d	08 06	08 10				08 22				08 29			08 41						08 51		09 00			
Bromley North	d					08 15							08 35								08 55				
Sundridge Park	d					08 17							08 37								08 57				
Grove Park 4	d	08 09	08 13			08a20	08 26				08 33		08a40	08 45						08 55	09a00	09 04			
Hither Green 4	d		08 17								08 37									08 59		09 08			
Lewisham 4	d		08 23																	09 04					
St Johns	a																			09 07					
New Cross 4 ⊖	a																			09 09					
London Bridge 4 ⊖	a						08 39	08 29	08 33					08 59		08 49	08 55			09 17		09 20	09 11	09 14	
London Cannon Street 4 ⊖	a						08 46		08 41					09 06			09 02			09 23					
London Waterloo (East) 4 ⊖	a	08 24	08 36					08 34		08 40	08 52					08 54		09 00				09 25	09 16	09 19	
London Charing Cross 4 ⊖	a	08 30	08 42					08 40		08 46	08 58					09 00		09 04				09 31	09 22	09 25	

A not 26 December

Tonbridge, Sevenoaks, Orpington, Bromley North, Grove Park - London

Network Diagram - see first Page of Table 200

		SE	SE	SE	SE	SE	SE	SE	SE	SE		SE	SE	SE	SE	SE	SE	SE	SE	SE		SE	SE	SE	SE
			1		1				1	1				1				1	1					1	
Tonbridge 4	d		08 44		08 50				09 02	09 10				09 20				09 32	09 40					09 50	
Hildenborough	d		08 48						09 06									09 36							
Sevenoaks 4	a		08 54		08 58				09 13	09 18				09 28				09 43	09 48					09 58	
	d		08 55		08 59			09 06	09 14	09 19				09 29			09 36	09 44	09 49					09 59	
Dunton Green	d							09 09									09 39								
Knockholt	d							09 14									09 44								
Chelsfield 3	d							09 17									09 47								
Orpington 4	a		09 03		09 08			09 20	09 24					09 38			09 50	09 53						10 08	
	d	08 55	09 04	09 03	09 09	09 10		09 21	09 24			09 25	09 33	09 39	09 40		09 51	09 54		09 55			10 03	10 09	10 10
Petts Wood 4	d	08a58		09 06		09a13		09 24				09a28	09 36		09a43		09 54			09a58			10 06		10a13
Chislehurst	d			09 09				09 27					09 39				09 57						10 09		
Elmstead Woods	d			09 11				09 30					09 41				09 59						10 11		
Bromley North	d						09 25									09 45						10 05			
Sundridge Park	d						09 27									09 47						10 07			
Grove Park 4	d			09 15			09a30	09 33					09 45			09a50	10 03					10a10	10 15		
Hither Green 4	d			09 19				09 37					09 49				10 07						10 19		
Lewisham 4	d			09 24									09 54										10 24		
St Johns	a			09 26									09 56										10 26		
New Cross 4 ⊖	a			09 28									09 58										10 28		
London Bridge 4 ⊖	a		09 22	09 33	09 26			09 49	09 40	09 43			10 04	09 55			10 19	10 10	10 13				10 34	10 25	
London Cannon Street 4 ⊖	a		09 28	09 40									10 08										10 38		
London Waterloo (East) 4 ⊖	a				09 31			09 53	09 45	09 48				09 59			10 23	10 15	10 18					10 29	
London Charing Cross 4 ⊖	a				09 37			09 59	09 51	09 54				10 03			10 27	10 19	10 22					10 33	

		SE	SE	SE	SE	SE		SE	SE	SE	SE	SE	SE	SE	SE	SE		SE	SE	SE	SE	SE	SE	SE	SE
				1	1				1				1	1					1				1	1	
Tonbridge 4	d			10 02	10 10				10 20				10 32	10 40					10 50				11 02	11 10	
Hildenborough	d			10 06									10 36										11 06		
Sevenoaks 4	a			10 13	10 18				10 28				10 43	10 48					10 58				11 13	11 18	
	d		10 06	10 14	10 19				10 29			10 36	10 44	10 49					10 59			11 06	11 14	11 19	
Dunton Green	d		10 09									10 39										11 09			
Knockholt	d		10 14									10 44										11 14			
Chelsfield 3	d		10 17									10 47										11 17			
Orpington 4	a		10 20	10 23					10 38			10 50	10 53						11 08			11 20	11 23		
	d		10 21	10 24		10 25		10 33	10 39	10 40		10 51	10 54		10 55			11 03	11 09	11 10		11 21	11 24		11 25
Petts Wood 4	d		10 24			10a28		10 36		10a43		10 54			10a58			11 06		11a13		11 24			11a28
Chislehurst	d		10 27					10 39				10 57						11 09				11 27			
Elmstead Woods	d		10 29					10 41				10 59						11 11				11 29			
Bromley North	d	10 25									10 45					11 05					11 25				
Sundridge Park	d	10 27									10 47					11 07					11 27				
Grove Park 4	d	10a30	10 33					10 45			10a50	11 03				11a10		11 15			11a30	11 33			
Hither Green 4	d		10 37					10 49				11 07						11 19				11 37			
Lewisham 4	d							10 54										11 24							
St Johns	a							10 56										11 26							
New Cross 4 ⊖	a							10 58										11 28							
London Bridge 4 ⊖	a		10 49	10 40	10 43			11 04	10 55			11 19	11 10	11 13				11 34	11 25			11 49	11 40	11 43	
London Cannon Street 4 ⊖	a							11 08										11 38							
London Waterloo (East) 4 ⊖	a		10 53	10 45	10 48				10 59			11 23	11 15	11 18					11 29			11 53	11 45	11 48	
London Charing Cross 4 ⊖	a		10 57	10 49	10 52				11 03			11 27	11 19	11 22					11 33			11 57	11 49	11 52	

		SE		SE	SE	SE	SE	SE	SE	SE	SE	SE		SE	SE	SE	SE	SE	SE	SE	SE	SE		SE	SE
				1				1	1					1				1	1			1			
Tonbridge 4	d			11 20				11 32	11 40					11 50				12 02	12 10			12 20			
Hildenborough	d							11 36										12 06							
Sevenoaks 4	a			11 28				11 43	11 48					11 58				12 13	12 18			12 28			
	d			11 29			11 36	11 44	11 49					11 59			12 06	12 14	12 19			12 29			
Dunton Green	d						11 39										12 09								
Knockholt	d						11 44										12 14								
Chelsfield 3	d						11 47										12 17								
Orpington 4	a			11 38			11 50	11 53						12 08			12 20	12 23				12 38			
	d	11 33		11 39	11 40		11 51	11 54		11 55		12 03		12 09	12 10		12 21	12 24		12 25	12 33	12 39		12 40	
Petts Wood 4	d	11 36			11a43		11 54			11a58		12 06			12a13		12 24			12a28	12 36			12a43	
Chislehurst	d	11 39					11 57					12 09					12 27				12 39				
Elmstead Woods	d	11 41					11 59					12 11					12 29				12 41				
Bromley North	d					11 45					12 05					12 25									12 45
Sundridge Park	d					11 47					12 07					12 27									12 47
Grove Park 4	d	11 45				11a50	12 03				12a10	12 15				12a30	12 33				12 45				12a50
Hither Green 4	d	11 49					12 07					12 19					12 37				12 49				
Lewisham 4	d	11 54										12 24									12 54				
St Johns	a	11 56										12 26									12 56				
New Cross 4 ⊖	a	11 58										12 28									12 58				
London Bridge 4 ⊖	a	12 04		11 55			12 19	12 10	12 13			12 34		12 25			12 49	12 40	12 43		13 04	12 55			
London Cannon Street 4 ⊖	a	12 08										12 38									13 08				
London Waterloo (East) 4 ⊖	a			11 59			12 23	12 15	12 18					12 29			12 53	12 45	12 48			12 59			
London Charing Cross 4 ⊖	a			12 03			12 27	12 19	12 22					12 33			12 57	12 49	12 52			13 03			

Tonbridge, Sevenoaks, Orpington, Bromley North, Grove Park - London

Network Diagram - see first Page of Table 200

		SE	SE ■1	SE ■1	SE	SE	SE	SE ■1		SE	SE	SE	SE ■1	SE ■1	SE	SE	SE ■1	SE		SE	SE	SE ■1	SE ■1	SE	SE
Tonbridge ■4	d		12 32	12 40				12 50					13 02	13 10			13 20					13 32	13 40		
Hildenborough	d		12 36										13 06									13 36			
Sevenoaks ■4	a		12 43	12 48				12 58					13 13	13 18			13 28					13 43	13 48		
	d	12 36	12 44	12 49				12 59				13 06	13 14	13 19			13 29				13 36	13 44	13 49		
Dunton Green	d	12 39										13 09									13 39				
Knockholt	d	12 44										13 14									13 44				
Chelsfield ■3	d	12 47										13 17									13 47				
Orpington ■4	a	12 50	12 53					13 08				13 20	13 23				13 38				13 50	13 53			
	d	12 51	12 54		12 55		13 03	13 09		13 10		13 21	13 24		13 25	13 33	13 39	13 40			13 51	13 54		13 55	
Petts Wood ■4	d	12 54			12a58		13 06			13a13		13 24			13a28	13 36		13a43			13 54			13a58	
Chislehurst	d	12 57					13 09					13 27				13 39					13 57				
Elmstead Woods	d	12 59					13 11					13 29				13 41					13 59				
Bromley North	d					13 05					13 25									13 45					14 05
Sundridge Park	d					13 07					13 27									13 47					14 07
Grove Park ■4	d	13 03				13a10	13 15				13a30	13 33				13 45				13a50	14 03				14a10
Hither Green ■4	d	13 07					13 19					13 37				13 49					14 07				
Lewisham ■4 ⛴	d						13 24									13 54									
St Johns	a						13 26									13 56									
New Cross ■4 ⊖	a						13 28									13 58									
London Bridge ■4 ⊖	a	13 19	13 10	13 13			13 34	13 25				13 49	13 40	13 43		14 04	13 55				14 19	14 10	14 13		
London Cannon Street ■4 ⊖	a						13 38									14 08									
London Waterloo (East) ■4 ⊖	a	13 23	13 15	13 18				13 29				13 53	13 45	13 48			13 59				14 23	14 15	14 18		
London Charing Cross ■4 ⊖	a	13 27	13 19	13 22				13 33				13 57	13 49	13 52			14 03				14 27	14 19	14 22		

		SE	SE ■1	SE		SE	SE	SE ■1	SE ■1	SE	SE	SE ■1	SE	SE		SE	SE ■1	SE ■1	SE	SE	SE	SE ■1	SE	SE	
Tonbridge ■4	d		13 50					14 02	14 10			14 20					14 32	14 40				14 50			
Hildenborough	d							14 06									14 36								
Sevenoaks ■4	a		13 58					14 13	14 18			14 28					14 43	14 48				14 58			
	d		13 59				14 06	14 14	14 19			14 29				14 36	14 44	14 49				14 59			
Dunton Green	d						14 09									14 39									
Knockholt	d						14 14									14 44									
Chelsfield ■3	d						14 17									14 47									
Orpington ■4	a		14 08				14 20	14 23				14 38				14 50	14 53					15 08			
	d	14 03	14 09	14 10			14 21	14 24		14 25	14 33	14 39	14 40			14 51	14 54		14 55		15 03	15 09	15 10		
Petts Wood ■4	d	14 06		14a13			14 24			14a28	14 36		14a43			14 54			14a58		15 06		15a13		
Chislehurst	d	14 09					14 27				14 39					14 57					15 09				
Elmstead Woods	d	14 11					14 29				14 41					14 59					15 11				
Bromley North	d					14 25								14 45						15 05				15 25	
Sundridge Park	d					14 27								14 47						15 07				15 27	
Grove Park ■4	d	14 15				14a30	14 33				14 45			14a50		15 03				15a10	15 15			15a30	
Hither Green ■4	d	14 19					14 37				14 49					15 07					15 19				
Lewisham ■4 ⛴	d	14 24									14 54										15 24				
St Johns	a	14 26									14 56										15 26				
New Cross ■4 ⊖	a	14 28									14 58										15 28				
London Bridge ■4 ⊖	a	14 34	14 25				14 49	14 40	14 43		15 04	14 55				15 19	15 10	15 13			15 34	15 25			
London Cannon Street ■4 ⊖	a	14 38									15 08										15 38				
London Waterloo (East) ■4 ⊖	a		14 29				14 53	14 45	14 48			14 59				15 23	15 15	15 18				15 29			
London Charing Cross ■4 ⊖	a		14 33				14 57	14 49	14 52			15 03				15 27	15 19	15 22				15 33			

		SE	SE ■1	SE ■1	SE	SE	SE ■1	SE	SE	SE		SE ■1	SE ■1	SE	SE	SE	SE ■1	SE	SE	SE		SE ■1	SE ■1	SE	SE
Tonbridge ■4	d		15 02	15 10			15 20					15 32	15 40				15 50					16 02	16 10		
Hildenborough	d		15 06									15 36										16 06			
Sevenoaks ■4	a		15 13	15 18			15 28					15 43	15 48				15 58					16 13	16 18		
	d	15 06	15 14	15 19			15 29			15 36		15 44	15 49				15 59			16 06		16 14	16 19		
Dunton Green	d	15 09								15 39										16 09					
Knockholt	d	15 14								15 44										16 14					
Chelsfield ■3	d	15 17								15 47										16 17		16 21			
Orpington ■4	a	15 20	15 23				15 38			15 50		15 53					16 07			16 20		16 24			
	d	15 21	15 24		15 25	15 33	15 39	15 40		15 51		15 54		15 55		16 03	16 08	16 10		16 21		16 25		16 25	16 33
Petts Wood ■4	d	15 24			15a28	15 36		15a43		15 54				15a58		16 06		16a13		16 24				16a28	16 36
Chislehurst	d	15 27				15 39				15 57						16 09				16 27					16 39
Elmstead Woods	d	15 29				15 41				15 59						16 11				16 29					16 41
Bromley North	d								15 45						16 05				16 25						
Sundridge Park	d								15 47						16 07				16 27						
Grove Park ■4	d	15 33				15 45			15a50	16 03					16a10	16 15			16a30	16 33					16 45
Hither Green ■4	d	15 37				15 49				16 07						16 19				16 37					16 50
Lewisham ■4 ⛴	d					15 54										16 24									
St Johns	a					15 56										16 26									
New Cross ■4 ⊖	a					15 58										16 28									
London Bridge ■4 ⊖	a	15 49	15 40	15 43		16 04	15 55			16 19		16 11	16 14			16 34	16 25			16 48		16 42	16 46		17 01
London Cannon Street ■4 ⊖	a					16 08										16 38									
London Waterloo (East) ■4 ⊖	a	15 55	15 45	15 48			15 59			16 24		16 16	16 20				16 29			16 54		16 48	16 52		17 06
London Charing Cross ■4 ⊖	a	15 58	15 49	15 52			16 03			16 28		16 20	16 24				16 33			16 58		16 52	16 56		17 10

Tonbridge, Sevenoaks, Orpington, Bromley North, Grove Park - London

Network Diagram - see first Page of Table 200

		SE 1	SE	SE	SE	SE 1		SE 1	SE	SE	SE	SE 1	SE	SE	SE	SE		SE 1	SE 1	SE	SE	SE 1	SE	SE	SE
Tonbridge 4	d	16 20				16 32		16 40				16 50						17 02	17 10			17 20			
Hildenborough	d					16 36												17 06							
Sevenoaks 4	a	16 28				16 43		16 48				16 58						17 13	17 18			17 28			
	d	16 29			16 36	16 44		16 52				16 59				17 05		17 14	17 19			17 29			17 35
Dunton Green	d				16 39											17 08									17 38
Knockholt	d				16 44											17 13									17 43
Chelsfield 3	d				16 47											17 16									17 46
Orpington 4	a	16 38			16 50	16 53						17 08				17 19		17 23				17 38			17 49
	d	16 39	16 40		16 51	16 54			16 55		17 03	17 09	17 10	17 13		17 20		17 24		17 24	17 37	17 39	17 40		17 50
Petts Wood 4	d		16a43		16 54				16a58		17 06		17a13			17 24				17a27	17 40		17a43		17 54
Chislehurst	d				16 57						17 09					17 27					17 43				17 57
Elmstead Woods	d				16 59						17 11					17 29					17 45				17 59
Bromley North	d			16 45						17 07					17 27									17 50	
Sundridge Park	d			16 47						17 09					17 29									17 52	
Grove Park 4	d			16a50	17 03					17a12	17 15				17a32	17 34					17 49			17a55	18 03
Hither Green 4	d				17 09						17 19					17 38					17 53				18 07
Lewisham 4	d										17 24														
St Johns	a										17 26										17 57				
New Cross 4 ⊖	a										17 28										17 59				
London Bridge 4 ⊖	a	16 56				17 11		17 17			17 34	17 27				17 49		17 41	17 44		18 06	17 58			18 18
London Cannon Street 4 ⊖	a										17 38	17 32									18 11				
London Waterloo (East) 4 ⊖	a	17 00			17 24	17 16		17 22						17 36		17 53		17 46	17 50			18 02			18 23
London Charing Cross 4 ⊖	a	17 04			17 29	17 20		17 26						17 40		17 57		17 50	17 53			18 06			18 27

		SE 1		SE 1	SE	SE	SE 1	SE	SE	SE	SE 1	SE 1		SE 1	SE	SE	SE	SE	SE	SE	SE 1	SE 1		SE	SE
Tonbridge 4	d	17 32		17 40			17 50				18 02	18 10		18 23							18 32	18 40			
Hildenborough	d	17 36									18 06										18 36				
Sevenoaks 4	a	17 43		17 48			17 58				18 13	18 18		18 31							18 43	18 48			
	d	17 44		17 49			17 59			18 05	18 14	18 19		18 32						18 35	18 44	18 49			
Dunton Green	d									18 08										18 38					
Knockholt	d									18 13										18 43					
Chelsfield 3	d									18 16										18 46					
Orpington 4	a	17 53					18 08			18 19	18 23									18 49	18 53				
	d	17 54			17 55	18 03	18 09	18 09		18 21	18 24				18 25		18 33	18 40		18 50	18 54			18 55	19 03
Petts Wood 4	d				17a58	18 06		18a12		18 24					18a28		18 36	18a43		18 54				18a58	19 06
Chislehurst	d					18 09				18 27							18 39			18 57					19 09
Elmstead Woods	d					18 11				18 29							18 41			18 59					19 11
Bromley North	d								18 13							18 33			18 55						
Sundridge Park	d								18 15							18 35			18 57						
Grove Park 4	d					18 15			18a18	18 33						18a38	18 45		19a00	19 03					19 15
Hither Green 4	d					18 19				18 37							18 49			19 07					19 19
Lewisham 4	d					18 24											18 54								19 24
St Johns	a					18 26											18 56								19 26
New Cross 4 ⊖	a					18 28											18 58								19 28
London Bridge 4 ⊖	a	18 09		18 16		18 34	18 25			18 48	18 40	18 43		18 55			19 04			19 19	19 10	19 13			19 34
London Cannon Street 4 ⊖	a					18 38											19 10								19 38
London Waterloo (East) 4 ⊖	a	18 14		18 20			18 29			18 53	18 45	18 48		18 59						19 23	19 14	19 17			
London Charing Cross 4 ⊖	a	18 18		18 25			18 35			18 57	18 49	18 52		19 04						19 27	19 18	19 21			

		SE 1	SE	SE	SE	SE 1	SE 1	SE		SE 1	SE	SE	SE	SE 1	SE 1	SE	SE 1	SE		SE	SE	SE 1	SE 1	SE	SE
Tonbridge 4	d	18 50				19 02	19 10			19 20				19 32	19 40		19 51					20 02	20 10		
Hildenborough	d					19 06								19 36								20 06			
Sevenoaks 4	a	18 59				19 13	19 18			19 28				19 43	19 48		19 59					20 13	20 18		
	d	18 59			19 06	19 14	19 19			19 29			19 36	19 44	19 49		20 00				20 06	20 14	20 19		
Dunton Green	d				19 09								19 39								20 09				
Knockholt	d				19 14								19 44								20 14				
Chelsfield 3	d				19 17								19 47								20 17				
Orpington 4	a	19 08			19 20	19 23				19 38			19 50	19 53			20 08				20 20	20 23			
	d	19 08	19 10		19 21	19 24		19 25		19 39	19 40		19 51	19 54		19 55	20 09			20 10	20 21	20 24			20 40
Petts Wood 4	d		19a13		19 24			19a28			19a43		19 54			19a58				20a13	20 24				20a43
Chislehurst	d				19 27								19 57								20 27				
Elmstead Woods	d				19 29								19 59								20 29				
Bromley North	d			19 18								19 42						20 02						20 27	
Sundridge Park	d			19 20								19 44						20 04						20 29	
Grove Park 4	d			19a23	19 33							19a47	20 03					20a07			20 34			20a32	
Hither Green 4	d				19 37								20 07								20 38				
Lewisham 4	d				19 43								20 13								20 43				
St Johns	a																								
New Cross 4 ⊖	a																								
London Bridge 4 ⊖	a	19 25			19 52	19 40	19 43			19 54			20 22	20 10	20 13		20 24				20 52	20 39	20 42		
London Cannon Street 4 ⊖	a																								
London Waterloo (East) 4 ⊖	a	19 29			19 56	19 45	19 48			19 59			20 26	20 15	20 18		20 29				20 56	20 44	20 47		
London Charing Cross 4 ⊖	a	19 33			20 00	19 49	19 52			20 03			20 30	20 19	20 22		20 33				21 00	20 48	20 51		

Tonbridge, Sevenoaks, Orpington, Bromley North, Grove Park - London

Network Diagram - see first Page of Table 200

		SE	SE	SE 1		SE 1	SE 1	SE	SE	SE	SE 1	SE 1	SE	SE		SE	SE 1	SE 1	SE 1	SE	SE	SE	SE 1	SE 1	
Tonbridge 4	d			20 32		20 40	20 50				21 02	21 10					21 32	21 40	21 50				22 02	22 10	
Hildenborough	d			20 36							21 06						21 36						22 06		
Sevenoaks 4	a			20 43		20 48	20 58				21 13	21 18					21 43	21 48	21 58				22 13	22 18	
	d		20 35	20 44		20 49	20 59			21 05	21 14	21 19				21 35	21 44	21 49	21 59			22 05	22 14	22 19	
Dunton Green	d		20 38							21 08						21 38						22 08			
Knockholt	d		20 43							21 13						21 43						22 13			
Chelsfield 3	d		20 46							21 16						21 46						22 16			
Orpington 4	a		20 49	20 52			21 08			21 19	21 22					21 49	21 52		22 08			22 19	22 22		
	d		20 51	20 53			21 09	21 10		21 21	21 23		21 40			21 51	21 53		22 09	22 10		22 21	22 23		
Petts Wood 4	d		20 54					21a13		21 24			21a43			21 54				22a13		22 24			
Chislehurst	d		20 57							21 27						21 57						22 27			
Elmstead Woods	d		20 59							21 29						21 59						22 29			
Bromley North	d	20 53							21 23					21 53							22 23				
Sundridge Park	d	20 55							21 25					21 55							22 25				
Grove Park 4	d	20a58	21 03						21a28	21 33				21a58		22 03					22a28	22 33			
Hither Green 4	d		21 07							21 37						22 07						22 37			
Lewisham 4	d		21 13							21 43						22 13						22 43			
St Johns	a																								
New Cross 4 ⊖	a																								
London Bridge 4 ⊖	a		21 22	21 08		21 13	21 24			21 52	21 38	21 43				22 22	22 08	22 13	22 24			22 52	22 38	22 43	
London Cannon Street 4 ⊖	a																								
London Waterloo (East) 4 ⊖	a		21 26	21 13		21 18	21 29			21 56	21 43	21 48				22 26	22 13	22 18	22 29			22 56	22 43	22 48	
London Charing Cross 4 ⊖	a		21 30	21 18		21 22	21 33			22 00	21 48	21 52				22 30	22 18	22 22	22 33			23 00	22 48	22 52	

		SE	SE	SE	SE 1	SE 1	SE 1	SE	SE	SE		SE 1	SE
Tonbridge 4	d				22 31	22 40	22 50					23 14	
Hildenborough	d				22 35							23 18	
Sevenoaks 4	a				22 41	22 48	22 58					23 24	
	d				22 42	22 49	22 59					23 25	
Dunton Green	d												
Knockholt	d												
Chelsfield 3	d				22 49							23 32	
Orpington 4	a				22 52		23 08					23 36	
	d	22 40		22 51	22 53		23 09	23 10		23 21		23 37	
Petts Wood 4	d	22a43		22 54				23a13		23 24			
Chislehurst	d			22 57						23 27			
Elmstead Woods	d			22 59						23 29			
Bromley North	d		22 53						23 23				23 53
Sundridge Park	d		22 55						23 25				23 55
Grove Park 4	d		22a58	23 03					23a28	23 33			23a58
Hither Green 4	d			23 07						23 37			
Lewisham 4	d			23 13						23 43			
St Johns	a												
New Cross 4 ⊖	a												
London Bridge 4 ⊖	a			23 22	23 08	23 13	23 24			23 52		23 54	
London Cannon Street 4 ⊖	a												
London Waterloo (East) 4 ⊖	a			23 26	23 13	23 18	23 29			23 56		23 59	
London Charing Cross 4 ⊖	a			23 30	23 18	23 22	23 33			00 01		00 03	

Saturdays

		SE	SE 1	SE	SE	SE	SE	SE	SE	SE 1		SE	SE	SE	SE	SE 1	SE	SE 1	SE	SE		SE	SE 1	SE	SE
Tonbridge 4	d		23p14							06 02						06 32		06 50					07 02		
Hildenborough	d		23p18							06 06						06 36							07 06		
Sevenoaks 4	a		23p24							06 13						06 43		06 58					07 13		
	d		23p25			05 36			06 06	06 14					06 36	06 44		06 59				07 06	07 14		
Dunton Green	d					05 39			06 09						06 39							07 09			
Knockholt	d					05 44			06 14						06 44							07 14			
Chelsfield 3	d		23p32			05 47			06 17						06 47							07 17			
Orpington 4	a		23p36			05 50			06 20	06 23					06 50	06 53		07 08				07 20	07 23		
	d	23p21	23p37		05 44	05 51	06 10		06 21	06 24		06 25	06 40		06 51	06 54	06 55	07 09	07 10			07 21	07 24	07 25	07 33
Petts Wood 4	d	23p24			05a47	05 54	06a13		06 24			06a28	06a43		06 54		06a58		07a13			07 24		07a28	07 36
Chislehurst	d	23p27				05 57			06 27						06 57							07 27			07 39
Elmstead Woods	d	23p29				05 59			06 29						06 59							07 29			07 41
Bromley North	d			00 23				06 23						06 53						07 23					
Sundridge Park	d			00 25				06 25						06 55						07 25					
Grove Park 4	d	23p33		00a28		06 03		06a28	06 33					06a58	07 03					07a28		07 33			07 45
Hither Green 4	d	23p37				06 07			06 37						07 07							07 37			07 49
Lewisham 4	d	23p43				06 13			06 43						07 13										07 54
St Johns	a																								07 56
New Cross 4 ⊖	a																								07 58
London Bridge 4 ⊖	a	23p52	23p54			06 21			06 51	06 39					07 21	07 09		07 24				07 49	07 39		08 04
London Cannon Street 4 ⊖	a																								08 08
London Waterloo (East) 4 ⊖	a	23p56	23p59			06 25			06 55	06 43					07 25	07 13		07 29				07 53	07 43		
London Charing Cross 4 ⊖	a	00 01	00 03			06 29			06 59	06 47					07 29	07 17		07 33				07 57	07 48		

Table 204

Saturdays

Tonbridge, Sevenoaks, Orpington, Bromley North, Grove Park - London

Network Diagram - see first Page of Table 200

		SE 1	SE	SE	SE	SE 1		SE 1	SE	SE	SE	SE 1	SE	SE	SE	SE 1		SE 1	SE	SE	SE 1	SE	SE	SE	SE 1
Tonbridge 4	d	07 20				07 32		07 40				07 50				08 02		08 10			08 20				08 32
Hildenborough	d					07 36										08 06									08 36
Sevenoaks 4	a	07 28				07 43		07 48				07 58				08 13		08 18			08 28				08 43
	d	07 29			07 36	07 44		07 49				07 59			08 06	08 14		08 19			08 29			08 36	08 44
Dunton Green	d				07 39										08 09									08 39	
Knockholt	d				07 44										08 14									08 44	
Chelsfield 3	d				07 47										08 17									08 47	
Orpington 4	a	07 38			07 50	07 53						08 08			08 20	08 23					08 38			08 50	08 53
	d	07 39	07 40		07 51	07 54			07 55		08 03	08 09	08 10		08 21	08 24			08 25	08 33	08 39	08 40		08 51	08 54
Petts Wood 4	d		07a43		07 54				07a58		08 06		08a13		08 24				08a28	08 36		08a43		08 54	
Chislehurst	d				07 57						08 09				08 27					08 39				08 57	
Elmstead Woods	d				07 59						08 11				08 29					08 41				08 59	
Bromley North	d			07 45						08 05				08 25									08 45		
Sundridge Park	d			07 47						08 07				08 27									08 47		
Grove Park 4	d			07a50	08 03					08a10	08 15			08a30	08 33					08 45			08a50	09 03	
Hither Green 4	d				08 07						08 19				08 37					08 49				09 07	
Lewisham 4	d										08 24									08 54					
St Johns	a										08 26									08 56					
New Cross 4 ⊖	a										08 28									08 58					
London Bridge 4 ⊖	a	07 55			08 19	08 10		08 13			08 34	08 25			08 49	08 40		08 43		09 04	08 55			09 19	09 10
London Cannon Street 4 ⊖	a										08 38									09 08					
London Waterloo (East) 4 ⊖	a	07 59			08 23	08 15		08 19				08 29			08 53	08 45		08 49			08 59			09 23	09 15
London Charing Cross 4 ⊖	a	08 03			08 27	08 19		08 22				08 33			08 57	08 49		08 52			09 03			09 27	09 19

		SE 1		SE	SE	SE	SE 1	SE	SE	SE	SE 1	SE 1		SE	SE	SE 1	SE	SE	SE	SE 1	SE 1	SE		SE	SE
Tonbridge 4	d	08 40					08 50				09 02	09 10				09 20				09 32	09 40				
Hildenborough	d										09 06									09 36					
Sevenoaks 4	a	08 48					08 58				09 13	09 18				09 28				09 43	09 48				
	d	08 49					08 59			09 06	09 14	09 19				09 29			09 36	09 44	09 49				
Dunton Green	d									09 09									09 39						
Knockholt	d									09 14									09 44						
Chelsfield 3	d									09 17									09 47						
Orpington 4	a						09 08			09 20	09 23					09 38			09 50	09 53					
	d			08 55		09 03	09 09	09 10		09 21	09 24			09 25	09 33	09 39	09 40		09 51	09 54		09 55			10 03
Petts Wood 4	d			08a58		09 06		09a13		09 24				09a28	09 36		09a43		09 54			09a58			10 06
Chislehurst	d					09 09				09 27					09 39				09 57						10 09
Elmstead Woods	d					09 11				09 29					09 41				09 59						10 11
Bromley North	d				09 05				09 25									09 45						10 05	
Sundridge Park	d				09 07				09 27									09 47						10 07	
Grove Park 4	d				09a10	09 15			09a30	09 33					09 45			09a50	10 03					10a10	10 15
Hither Green 4	d					09 19				09 37					09 49				10 07						10 19
Lewisham 4	d					09 24									09 54										10 24
St Johns	a					09 26									09 56										10 26
New Cross 4 ⊖	a					09 28									09 58										10 28
London Bridge 4 ⊖	a	09 13				09 34	09 25			09 49	09 40	09 43			10 04	09 55			10 19	10 10	10 13				10 34
London Cannon Street 4 ⊖	a					09 38									10 08										10 38
London Waterloo (East) 4 ⊖	a	09 19					09 29			09 53	09 45	09 49				09 59			10 23	10 15	10 19				
London Charing Cross 4 ⊖	a	09 22					09 33			09 57	09 49	09 52				10 03			10 27	10 19	10 22				

		SE 1	SE	SE	SE	SE 1	SE 1	SE		SE	SE 1	SE	SE	SE	SE 1	SE 1	SE	SE		SE	SE 1	SE	SE	SE	SE 1
Tonbridge 4	d	09 50				10 02	10 10				10 20				10 32	10 40					10 50				11 02
Hildenborough	d					10 06									10 36										11 06
Sevenoaks 4	a	09 58				10 13	10 18				10 28				10 43	10 48					10 58				11 13
	d	09 59			10 06	10 14	10 19				10 29			10 36	10 44	10 49					10 59			11 06	11 14
Dunton Green	d				10 09									10 39										11 09	
Knockholt	d				10 14									10 44										11 14	
Chelsfield 3	d				10 17									10 47										11 17	
Orpington 4	a	10 08			10 20	10 23					10 38			10 50	10 53						11 08			11 20	11 23
	d	10 09	10 10		10 21	10 24		10 25		10 33	10 39	10 40		10 51	10 54		10 55			11 03	11 09	11 10		11 21	11 24
Petts Wood 4	d		10a13		10 24			10a28		10 36		10a43		10 54			10a58			11 06		11a13		11 24	
Chislehurst	d				10 27					10 39				10 57						11 09				11 27	
Elmstead Woods	d				10 29					10 41				10 59						11 11				11 29	
Bromley North	d			10 25									10 45					11 05					11 25		
Sundridge Park	d			10 27									10 47					11 07					11 27		
Grove Park 4	d			10a30	10 33					10 45			10a50	11 03				11a10		11 15			11a30	11 33	
Hither Green 4	d				10 37					10 49				11 07						11 19				11 37	
Lewisham 4	d									10 54										11 24					
St Johns	a									10 56										11 26					
New Cross 4 ⊖	a									10 58										11 28					
London Bridge 4 ⊖	a	10 25			10 49	10 40	10 43			11 04	10 55			11 19	11 10	11 13				11 34	11 25			11 49	11 40
London Cannon Street 4 ⊖	a									11 08										11 38					
London Waterloo (East) 4 ⊖	a	10 29			10 53	10 45	10 49				10 59			11 23	11 15	11 19					11 29			11 53	11 45
London Charing Cross 4 ⊖	a	10 33			10 57	10 49	10 52				11 03			11 27	11 19	11 22					11 33			11 57	11 49

Table 204

Saturdays

Tonbridge, Sevenoaks, Orpington, Bromley North, Grove Park - London

Network Diagram - see first Page of Table 200

		SE 1	SE	SE		SE 1	SE	SE	SE	SE 1	SE 1	SE	SE	SE		SE 1	SE	SE	SE	SE 1	SE 1	SE	SE	SE 1	
Tonbridge 4	d	11 10				11 20				11 32	11 40					11 50				12 02	12 10			12 20	
Hildenborough	d									11 36										12 06					
Sevenoaks 4	a	11 18				11 28				11 43	11 48					11 58				12 13	12 18			12 28	
	d	11 19				11 29			11 36	11 44	11 49					11 59			12 06	12 14	12 19			12 29	
Dunton Green	d								11 39										12 09						
Knockholt	d								11 44										12 14						
Chelsfield 3	d								11 47										12 17						
Orpington 4	a					11 38			11 50	11 53						12 08			12 20	12 23				12 38	
	d		11 25	11 33		11 39	11 40		11 51	11 54		11 55		12 03		12 09	12 10		12 21	12 24		12 25	12 33	12 39	
Petts Wood 4	d		11a28	11 36			11a43		11 54			11a58		12 06			12a13		12 24			12a28	12 36		
Chislehurst	d			11 39					11 57					12 09					12 27				12 39		
Elmstead Woods	d			11 41					11 59					12 11					12 29				12 41		
Bromley North	d							11 45					12 05					12 25							
Sundridge Park	d							11 47					12 07					12 27							
Grove Park 4	d			11 45				11a50	12 03				12a10	12 15				12a30	12 33				12 45		
Hither Green 4	d			11 49					12 07					12 19					12 37				12 49		
Lewisham 4	d			11 54										12 24									12 54		
St Johns	a			11 56										12 26									12 56		
New Cross 4	a			11 58										12 28									12 58		
London Bridge 4	a	11 43		12 04		11 55			12 19	12 10	12 13			12 34		12 25			12 49	12 40	12 43		13 04	12 55	
London Cannon Street 4	a			12 08										12 38									13 08		
London Waterloo (East) 4	a	11 49				11 59			12 23	12 15	12 19					12 29			12 53	12 45	12 49			12 59	
London Charing Cross 4	a	11 52				12 03			12 27	12 19	12 22					12 33			12 57	12 49	12 52			13 03	

		SE	SE	SE	SE 1	SE 1	SE	SE	SE	SE 1		SE	SE	SE	SE 1	SE 1	SE	SE	SE 1	SE		SE	SE	SE 1	SE 1
Tonbridge 4	d				12 32	12 40				12 50					13 02	13 10			13 20					13 32	13 40
Hildenborough	d				12 36										13 06									13 36	
Sevenoaks 4	a				12 43	12 48				12 58					13 13	13 18			13 28					13 43	13 48
	d			12 36	12 44	12 49				12 59				13 06	13 14	13 19			13 29				13 36	13 44	13 49
Dunton Green	d			12 39										13 09									13 39		
Knockholt	d			12 44										13 14									13 44		
Chelsfield 3	d			12 47										13 17									13 47		
Orpington 4	a			12 50	12 53					13 08				13 20	13 23				13 38				13 50	13 53	
	d	12 40		12 51	12 54		12 55		13 03	13 09		13 10		13 21	13 24		13 25	13 33	13 39	13 40			13 51	13 54	
Petts Wood 4	d	12a43		12 54			12a58		13 06			13a13		13 24			13a28	13 36		13a43			13 54		
Chislehurst	d			12 57					13 09					13 27				13 39					13 57		
Elmstead Woods	d			12 59					13 11					13 29				13 41					13 59		
Bromley North	d		12 45					13 05					13 25									13 45			
Sundridge Park	d		12 47					13 07					13 27									13 47			
Grove Park 4	d		12a50	13 03				13a10	13 15				13a30	13 33				13 45				13a50	14 03		
Hither Green 4	d			13 07					13 19					13 37				13 49					14 07		
Lewisham 4	d								13 24									13 54							
St Johns	a								13 26									13 56							
New Cross 4	a								13 28									13 58							
London Bridge 4	a			13 19	13 10	13 13			13 34	13 25				13 49	13 40	13 43		14 04	13 55				14 19	14 10	14 13
London Cannon Street 4	a								13 38									14 08							
London Waterloo (East) 4	a			13 23	13 15	13 19				13 29				13 53	13 45	13 49			13 59				14 23	14 15	14 19
London Charing Cross 4	a			13 27	13 19	13 22				13 33				13 57	13 49	13 52			14 03				14 27	14 19	14 22

		SE	SE	SE	SE 1	SE		SE	SE	SE 1	SE 1	SE	SE	SE 1	SE	SE		SE	SE 1	SE 1	SE	SE	SE	SE 1	SE
Tonbridge 4	d				13 50					14 02	14 10			14 20					14 32	14 40				14 50	
Hildenborough	d									14 06									14 36						
Sevenoaks 4	a				13 58					14 13	14 18			14 28					14 43	14 48				14 58	
	d				13 59				14 06	14 14	14 19			14 29				14 36	14 44	14 49				14 59	
Dunton Green	d								14 09									14 39							
Knockholt	d								14 14									14 44							
Chelsfield 3	d								14 17									14 47							
Orpington 4	a				14 08				14 20	14 23				14 38				14 50	14 53					15 08	
	d	13 55		14 03	14 09	14 10			14 21	14 24		14 25	14 33	14 39	14 40			14 51	14 54		14 55		15 03	15 09	15 10
Petts Wood 4	d	13a58		14 06		14a13			14 24			14a28	14 36		14a43			14 54			14a58		15 06		15a13
Chislehurst	d			14 09					14 27				14 39					14 57					15 09		
Elmstead Woods	d			14 11					14 29				14 41					14 59					15 11		
Bromley North	d		14 05					14 25								14 45						15 05			
Sundridge Park	d		14 07					14 27								14 47						15 07			
Grove Park 4	d		14a10	14 15				14a30	14 33				14 45			14a50		15 03				15a10	15 15		
Hither Green 4	d			14 19					14 37				14 49					15 07					15 19		
Lewisham 4	d			14 24									14 54										15 24		
St Johns	a			14 26									14 56										15 26		
New Cross 4	a			14 28									14 58										15 28		
London Bridge 4	a			14 34	14 25				14 49	14 40	14 43		15 04	14 55				15 19	15 10	15 13			15 34	15 25	
London Cannon Street 4	a			14 38									15 08										15 38		
London Waterloo (East) 4	a				14 29				14 53	14 45	14 49			14 59				15 23	15 15	15 19				15 29	
London Charing Cross 4	a				14 33				14 57	14 49	14 52			15 03				15 27	15 19	15 22				15 33	

Table 204

Saturdays

Tonbridge, Sevenoaks, Orpington, Bromley North, Grove Park - London

Network Diagram - see first Page of Table 200

		SE		SE	SE 1	SE 1	SE	SE	SE 1	SE	SE	SE		SE 1	SE 1	SE	SE	SE	SE 1	SE	SE	SE		SE 1	SE 1
Tonbridge 4	d				15 02	15 10			15 20					15 32	15 40				15 50					16 02	16 10
Hildenborough	d				15 06									15 36										16 06	
Sevenoaks 4	a				15 13	15 18			15 28					15 43	15 48				15 58					16 13	16 18
	d			15 06	15 14	15 19			15 29			15 36		15 44	15 49				15 59			16 06		16 14	16 19
Dunton Green	d			15 09								15 39										16 09			
Knockholt	d			15 14								15 44										16 14			
Chelsfield 3	d			15 17								15 47										16 17			
Orpington 4	a			15 20	15 23				15 38			15 50		15 53					16 08			16 20		16 23	
	d			15 21	15 24		15 25	15 33	15 39	15 40		15 51		15 54		15 55		16 03	16 09	16 10		16 21		16 24	
Petts Wood 4	d			15 24			15a28	15 36		15a43		15 54				15a58		16 06		16a13		16 24			
Chislehurst	d			15 27				15 39				15 57						16 09				16 27			
Elmstead Woods	d			15 29				15 41				15 59						16 11				16 29			
Bromley North	d	15 25									15 45						16 05				16 25				
Sundridge Park	d	15 27									15 47						16 07				16 27				
Grove Park 4	d	15a30		15 33				15 45			15a50	16 03					16a10	16 15			16a30	16 33			
Hither Green 4	d			15 37				15 49				16 07						16 19				16 37			
Lewisham 4	d							15 54										16 24							
St Johns	a							15 56										16 26							
New Cross 4 ⊖	a							15 58										16 28							
London Bridge 4 ⊖	a			15 49	15 40	15 43		16 04	15 55			16 19		16 10	16 13			16 34	16 25			16 49		16 40	16 43
London Cannon Street 4 ⊖	a							16 08										16 38							
London Waterloo (East) 4 ⊖	a			15 53	15 45	15 49			15 59			16 23		16 15	16 19				16 29			16 53		16 45	16 49
London Charing Cross 4 ⊖	a			15 57	15 49	15 52			16 03			16 27		16 19	16 22				16 33			16 57		16 49	16 52

		SE	SE	SE 1	SE	SE	SE	SE 1		SE 1	SE	SE	SE	SE 1	SE	SE	SE	SE 1		SE 1	SE	SE	SE 1	SE	SE
Tonbridge 4	d			16 20				16 32		16 40				16 50				17 02		17 10			17 20		
Hildenborough	d							16 36										17 06							
Sevenoaks 4	a			16 28				16 43		16 48				16 58				17 13		17 18			17 28		
	d			16 29			16 36	16 44		16 49				16 59			17 06	17 14		17 19			17 29		
Dunton Green	d						16 39										17 09								
Knockholt	d						16 44										17 14								
Chelsfield 3	d						16 47										17 17								
Orpington 4	a			16 38			16 50	16 53						17 08			17 20	17 23					17 38		
	d	16 25	16 33	16 39	16 40		16 51	16 54			16 55		17 03	17 09	17 10		17 21	17 24			17 25	17 33	17 39	17 40	
Petts Wood 4	d	16a28	16 36		16a43		16 54				16a58		17 06		17a13		17 24				17a28	17 36		17a43	
Chislehurst	d		16 39				16 57						17 09				17 27					17 39			
Elmstead Woods	d		16 41				16 59						17 11				17 29					17 41			
Bromley North	d					16 45						17 05				17 25									17 45
Sundridge Park	d					16 47						17 07				17 27									17 47
Grove Park 4	d		16 45			16a50	17 03					17a10	17 15			17a30	17 33					17 45			17a50
Hither Green 4	d		16 49				17 07						17 19				17 37					17 49			
Lewisham 4	d		16 54										17 24									17 54			
St Johns	a		16 56										17 26									17 56			
New Cross 4 ⊖	a		16 58										17 28									17 58			
London Bridge 4 ⊖	a		17 04	16 55			17 19	17 10		17 13			17 34	17 25			17 49	17 40		17 43		18 04	17 55		
London Cannon Street 4 ⊖	a		17 08										17 38									18 08			
London Waterloo (East) 4 ⊖	a			16 59			17 23	17 15		17 19				17 29			17 53	17 45		17 49			17 59		
London Charing Cross 4 ⊖	a			17 03			17 27	17 19		17 22				17 33			17 57	17 49		17 52			18 03		

		SE	SE 1	SE 1		SE	SE	SE	SE 1	SE	SE	SE	SE 1	SE 1		SE	SE	SE 1	SE	SE	SE	SE 1	SE 1	SE	
Tonbridge 4	d		17 32	17 40					17 50				18 02	18 10				18 20				18 32	18 40		
Hildenborough	d		17 36										18 06									18 36			
Sevenoaks 4	a		17 43	17 48					17 58				18 13	18 18				18 28				18 43	18 48		
	d	17 36	17 44	17 49					17 59			18 06	18 14	18 19				18 29			18 36	18 44	18 49		
Dunton Green	d	17 39										18 09									18 39				
Knockholt	d	17 44										18 14									18 44				
Chelsfield 3	d	17 47										18 17									18 47				
Orpington 4	a	17 50	17 53						18 08			18 20	18 23					18 38			18 50	18 53			
	d	17 51	17 54			17 55		18 03	18 09	18 10		18 21	18 24			18 25	18 33	18 39	18 40		18 51	18 54		18 55	
Petts Wood 4	d	17 54				17a58		18 06		18a13		18 24				18a28	18 36		18a43		18 54			18a58	
Chislehurst	d	17 57						18 09				18 27					18 39				18 57				
Elmstead Woods	d	17 59						18 11				18 29					18 41				18 59				
Bromley North	d						18 05				18 25									18 45					
Sundridge Park	d						18 07				18 27									18 47					
Grove Park 4	d	18 03					18a10	18 15			18a30	18 33					18 45			18a50	19 03				
Hither Green 4	d	18 07						18 19				18 37					18 49				19 07				
Lewisham 4	d							18 24									18 54				19 12				
St Johns	a							18 26									18 56								
New Cross 4 ⊖	a							18 28									18 58								
London Bridge 4 ⊖	a	18 19	18 10	18 13				18 34	18 25			18 49	18 40	18 43			19 04	18 55			19 21	19 10	19 13		
London Cannon Street 4 ⊖	a							18 38									19 08								
London Waterloo (East) 4 ⊖	a	18 23	18 15	18 19					18 29			18 53	18 45	18 49				18 59			19 25	19 15	19 19		
London Charing Cross 4 ⊖	a	18 27	18 19	18 22					18 33			18 57	18 49	18 52				19 03			19 29	19 19	19 22		

Tonbridge, Sevenoaks, Orpington, Bromley North, Grove Park - London

Network Diagram - see first Page of Table 200

		SE	SE	SE	SE	SE	SE	SE	SE	SE		SE	SE	SE	SE	SE	SE	SE	SE	SE		SE	SE	SE	SE
		■1						■1	■1						■1	■1						■1	■1		
Tonbridge ■4	d	18 50						19 10	19 18						19 40	19 50						20 10	20 18		
Hildenborough	d								19 22														20 22		
Sevenoaks ■4	a	18 58						19 18	19 28						19 48	19 58						20 18	20 28		
	d	18 59				19 06		19 19	19 29				19 36		19 49	19 59				20 06		20 19	20 29		
Dunton Green	d					19 09							19 39							20 09					
Knockholt	d					19 14							19 44							20 14					
Chelsfield ■3	d					19 17							19 47							20 17					
Orpington ■4	a	19 08				19 20		19 27	19 38				19 50		19 57	20 08				20 20		20 27	20 38		
	d	19 09		19 10		19 21	19 25	19 28	19 39	19 40			19 51	19 55	19 58	20 09		20 10		20 21		20 28	20 39	20 40	
Petts Wood ■4	d			19a13		19 24	19a28			19a43			19 54	19a58				20a13		20 24				20a43	
Chislehurst	d					19 27							19 57							20 27					
Elmstead Woods	d					19 29							19 59							20 29					
Bromley North	d		19 05		19 25							19 45					20 05		20 25						20 53
Sundridge Park	d		19 07		19 27							19 47					20 07		20 27						20 55
Grove Park ■4	d		19a10		19a30	19 33						19a50	20 03				20a10		20a30	20 33					20a58
Hither Green ■4	d					19 37							20 07							20 37					
Lewisham ■4	d					19 43							20 13							20 43					
St Johns	a																								
New Cross ■4 ⊖	a																								
London Bridge ■4 ⊖	a	19 24				19 52		19 43	19 54				20 22		20 13	20 24				20 52		20 43	20 54		
London Cannon Street ■4 ⊖	a																								
London Waterloo (East) ■4 ⊖	a	19 29				19 56		19 48	19 59				20 26		20 18	20 29				20 56		20 48	20 59		
London Charing Cross ■4 ⊖	a	19 33				20 00		19 51	20 03				20 30		20 21	20 33				21 00		20 51	21 03		

		SE	SE	SE	SE	SE		SE	SE	SE	SE	SE	SE	SE	SE	SE		SE	SE	SE	SE	SE	SE	SE	SE
			■1	■1					■1	■1				■1	■1					■1	■1				■1
Tonbridge ■4	d		20 40	20 50					21 10	21 18				21 40	21 50					22 10	22 18				22 40
Hildenborough	d									21 22											22 22				
Sevenoaks ■4	a		20 48	20 58					21 18	21 28				21 48	21 58					22 18	22 28				22 48
	d	20 36	20 49	20 59				21 06	21 19	21 29			21 36	21 49	21 59				22 06	22 19	22 29				22 49
Dunton Green	d	20 39						21 09					21 39						22 09						
Knockholt	d	20 44						21 14					21 44						22 14						
Chelsfield ■3	d	20 47						21 17					21 47						22 17						
Orpington ■4	a	20 50	20 57	21 08				21 20	21 27	21 38			21 50	21 57	22 08				22 20	22 27	22 38				22 57
	d	20 51	20 58	21 09	21 10			21 21	21 28	21 39	21 40		21 51	21 58	22 09	22 10			22 21	22 28	22 39	22 40		22 51	22 58
Petts Wood ■4	d	20 54			21a13			21 24			21a43		21 54			22a13			22 24			22a43		22 54	
Chislehurst	d	20 57						21 27					21 57						22 27					22 57	
Elmstead Woods	d	20 59						21 29					21 59						22 29					22 59	
Bromley North	d					21 23						21 53						22 23					22 53		
Sundridge Park	d					21 25						21 55						22 25					22 55		
Grove Park ■4	d	21 03				21a28		21 33				21a58	22 03					22a28	22 33				22a58	23 03	
Hither Green ■4	d	21 07						21 37					22 07						22 37					23 07	
Lewisham ■4	d	21 13						21 43					22 13						22 43					23 13	
St Johns	a																								
New Cross ■4 ⊖	a																								
London Bridge ■4 ⊖	a	21 22	21 13	21 24				21 52	21 43	21 54			22 22	22 13	22 24				22 52	22 43	22 54			23 22	23 13
London Cannon Street ■4 ⊖	a																								
London Waterloo (East) ■4 ⊖	a	21 26	21 18	21 29				21 56	21 48	21 59			22 26	22 18	22 29				22 56	22 48	22 59			23 26	23 18
London Charing Cross ■4 ⊖	a	21 30	21 21	21 33				22 00	21 51	22 03			22 30	22 21	22 33				23 00	22 51	23 03			23 30	23 21

		SE		SE	SE	SE	SE	SE
		■1					■1	
Tonbridge ■4	d	22 50					23 14	
Hildenborough	d						23 18	
Sevenoaks ■4	a	22 58					23 24	
	d	22 59					23 25	
Dunton Green	d							
Knockholt	d							
Chelsfield ■3	d						23 32	
Orpington ■4	a	23 08					23 36	
	d	23 09		23 10		23 21	23 37	
Petts Wood ■4	d			23a13		23 24		
Chislehurst	d					23 27		
Elmstead Woods	d					23 29		
Bromley North	d				23 23			23 53
Sundridge Park	d				23 25			23 55
Grove Park ■4	d				23a28	23 33		23a58
Hither Green ■4	d					23 37		
Lewisham ■4	d					23 43		
St Johns	a							
New Cross ■4 ⊖	a							
London Bridge ■4 ⊖	a	23 24				23 52	23 54	
London Cannon Street ■4 ⊖	a							
London Waterloo (East) ■4 ⊖	a	23 29				23 56	23 59	
London Charing Cross ■4 ⊖	a	23 33				00 01	00 03	

Table 204

Sundays

Tonbridge, Sevenoaks, Orpington, Bromley North, Grove Park - London

Network Diagram - see first Page of Table 200

		SE A	SE 1 A	SE	SE	SE	SE	SE	SE 1	SE		SE	SE 1	SE	SE 1	SE	SE	SE 1	SE	SE		SE 1	SE 1	SE	SE
Tonbridge 4	d		23p14						07 10				07 23		07 38			08 10				08 25	08 38		
Hildenborough	d		23p18												07 42								08 42		
Sevenoaks 4	a		23p24						07 18				07 31		07 48			08 18				08 33	08 48		
	d		23p25						07 19				07 32		07 49			08 19		08 25		08 33	08 49		
Dunton Green	d																			08 28					
Knockholt	d																			08 33					
Chelsfield 3	d		23p32										07 39							08 36					
Orpington 4	a		23p36						07 27				07 42		07 57			08 27		08 39		08 42	08 57		
	d	23p21	23p37		06 43	07 06	07 10	07 13	07 28	07 36		07 40	07 43	07 43	07 58	08 06	08 10	08 28	08 36	08 40		08 43	08 58	09 06	09 10
Petts Wood 4	d	23p24			06a46	07a09	07 13	07a16		07a39		07 43		07a46		08a09	08 13		08a39	08 43				09a09	09 13
Chislehurst	d	23p27					07 16					07 46					08 16			08 46					09 16
Elmstead Woods	d	23p29					07 18					07 48					08 18			08 48					09 18
Bromley North	d			00 23																					
Sundridge Park	d			00 25																					
Grove Park 4	d	23p33		00a28			07 22					07 52					08 22			08 52					09 22
Hither Green 4	d	23p37					07 26					07 56					08 26			08 56					09 26
Lewisham 4	d	23p43					07 31					08 01					08 31			09 01					09 31
St Johns	a																								
New Cross 4	⊖ a																								
London Bridge 4	⊖ a	23p52	23p54				07 39		07 43			08 09	07 58		08 13		08 39	08 43		09 09		08 58	09 13		09 39
London Cannon Street 4	⊖ a																								
London Waterloo (East) 4	⊖ a	23p56	23p59				07 44		07 48			08 14	08 03		08 18		08 44	08 48		09 14		09 03	09 18		09 44
London Charing Cross 4	⊖ a	00 01	00 03				07 48		07 52			08 18	08 07		08 22		08 49	08 52		09 18		09 07	09 22		09 49

		SE 1		SE 1	SE 1		SE	SE	SE 1	SE 1	SE	SE	SE 1	SE	SE		SE 1	SE 1	SE	SE	SE 1	SE	SE	SE 1
Tonbridge 4	d	08 55		18 55	19 10				19 25	19 38			20 10				20 25	20 38			21 10			21 25
Hildenborough	d									19 42								20 42						
Sevenoaks 4	a	09 03		19 03	19 18				19 33	19 48			20 18				20 33	20 48			21 18			21 33
	d	09 03		19 03	19 19			19 25	19 33	19 49			20 19		20 25		20 33	20 49			21 19		21 25	21 33
Dunton Green	d							19 28							20 28								21 28	
Knockholt	d							19 33							20 33								21 33	
Chelsfield 3	d							19 36							20 36								21 36	
Orpington 4	a	09 12	and at the same minutes past each hour until	19 12	19 27			19 39	19 42	19 57			20 27		20 39		20 42	20 57			21 27		21 39	21 42
	d	09 13		19 13	19 28		19 36	19 40	19 43	19 58	20 06	20 10	20 28	20 36	20 40		20 43	20 58	21 06	21 10	21 28	21 36	21 40	21 43
Petts Wood 4	d						19a39	19 43			20a09	20 13		20a39	20 43				21a09	21 13		21a39	21 43	
Chislehurst	d							19 46				20 16			20 46					21 16			21 46	
Elmstead Woods	d							19 48				20 18			20 48					21 18			21 48	
Bromley North	d																							
Sundridge Park	d																							
Grove Park 4	d							19 52				20 22			20 52					21 22			21 52	
Hither Green 4	d							19 56				20 26			20 56					21 26			21 56	
Lewisham 4	d							20 01				20 31			21 01					21 31			22 01	
St Johns	a																							
New Cross 4	⊖ a																							
London Bridge 4	⊖ a	09 28		19 28	19 43			20 09	19 58	20 13		20 39	20 43		21 09		20 58	21 13		21 39	21 43		22 09	21 58
London Cannon Street 4	⊖ a																							
London Waterloo (East) 4	⊖ a	09 33		19 33	19 48			20 14	20 03	20 18		20 44	20 48		21 14		21 03	21 18		21 44	21 48		22 14	22 03
London Charing Cross 4	⊖ a	09 37		19 37	19 52			20 18	20 07	20 22		20 49	20 52		21 18		21 07	21 22		21 49	21 52		22 18	22 07

		SE 1		SE	SE	SE 1	SE	SE	SE 1	SE 1	SE
Tonbridge 4	d	21 38				22 10			22 25	22 38	
Hildenborough	d	21 42								22 42	
Sevenoaks 4	a	21 48				22 18			22 33	22 48	
	d	21 49				22 19		22 25	22 33	22 49	
Dunton Green	d							22 28			
Knockholt	d							22 33			
Chelsfield 3	d							22 36			
Orpington 4	a	21 57				22 27		22 39	22 42	22 57	
	d	21 58		22 06	22 10	22 28	22 36	22 40	22 43	22 58	23 10
Petts Wood 4	d			22a09	22 13		22a39	22 43			23 13
Chislehurst	d				22 16			22 46			23 16
Elmstead Woods	d				22 18			22 48			23 18
Bromley North	d										
Sundridge Park	d										
Grove Park 4	d				22 22			22 52			23 22
Hither Green 4	d				22 26			22 56			23 26
Lewisham 4	d				22 31			23 01			23 31
St Johns	a										
New Cross 4	⊖ a										
London Bridge 4	⊖ a	22 13			22 39	22 43		23 09	22 58	23 13	23 39
London Cannon Street 4	⊖ a										
London Waterloo (East) 4	⊖ a	22 18			22 44	22 48		23 14	23 03	23 18	23 44
London Charing Cross 4	⊖ a	22 22			22 49	22 52		23 18	23 07	23 22	23 49

A not 11 December

Network Diagram for Tables 206, 207, 208

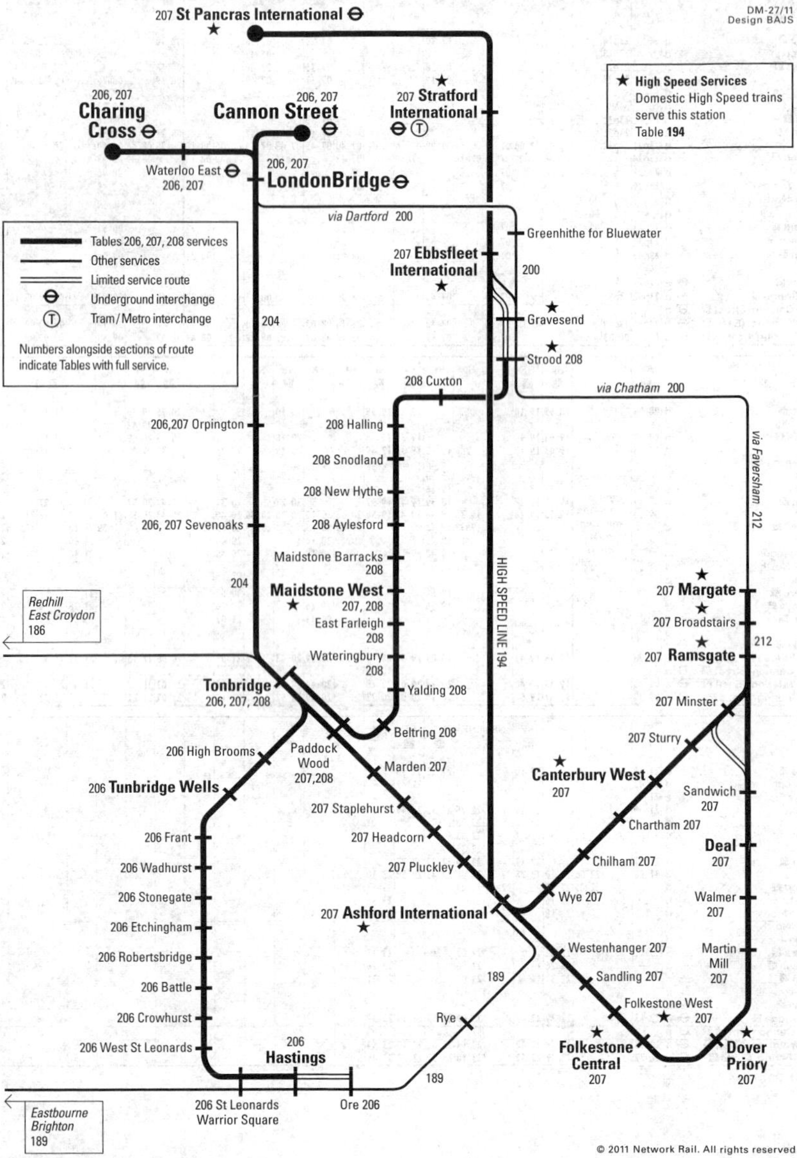

London and Tonbridge - Tunbridge Wells and Hastings

Network Diagram - see first Page of Table 206

Miles	Station		SE MO 1	SE MX 1	SE MO 1	SE MX 1	SE MX 1	SE 1	SE 1	SE 1	SE 1		SE 1	SE 1	SE 1	SE 1	SE 1	SE 1	SE 1	SE 1	SE 1		SE 1	SE 1	SE 1
—	London Charing Cross 4 ⊖	d	22p23	22p45	23p23	23p30	23p45							06 15		06 45	07 00	07 15	07 29		08 00		08 17	08 27	
0¾	London Waterloo (East) 4 ⊖	d	22p26	22p48	23p26	23p33	23p48							06 18		06 48	07 03	07 18	07 32		08 03		08 20	08 30	
—	London Cannon Street 4 ⊖	d																		07 47					08 42
1¾	London Bridge 4 ⊖	d	22p31	22p53	23p31	23p39	23p53							06 24		06 53	07 08	07 23	07 38	07 51	08 09		08 25	08 35	08 46
13¾	Orpington 4	d	22p46	23p09	23p46	23p54	00 09							06 40		07 10	07 26	07 39	07 54	08 09	08 26		08 42	08 54	09 07
22	Sevenoaks 4	d	22p57	23p19	23p57	00 05	00 19							06 50		07 19	07 35	07 49	08 07	08 19	08 35		08 52	09 03	09 17
29½	Tonbridge 4	a	23p05	23p27	00 05	00 15	00 27							06 58		07 27	07 45	07 58	08 17	08 27	08 47		09 00	09 13	09 25
—		d	23p06	23p28	00 06	00 16	00 27	05 00	05 30	06 08	06 20		06 35	06 58	07 18	07 31	07 46	07 59	08 17	08 27	08 48		09 00	09 16	09 26
33	High Brooms	d	23p12	23p35	00 12	00 22	00 34	05 06	05 36	06 14	06 26		06 41	07 04	07 24	07 37	07 55	08 05	08 23	08 34	08 54		09 06	09 23	09 35
34½	Tunbridge Wells 4	a	23p15	23p39	00 15	00 26	00 38	05 10	05 40	06 17	06 30		06 45	07 08	07 28	07 41	08 02	08 08	08 30	08 40	08 58		09 10	09 27	09 39
—		d	23p17	23p40	00 17		00 40			06 18			06 46			07 42		08 13		08 49			09 14		09 42
36¾	Frant	d	23p22	23p45	00 22		00 45			06 23			06 51			07 47		08 18					09 19		
39¼	Wadhurst	d	23p27	23p50	00 27		00 50			06 28			06 57			07 52		08 24		08 57			09 25		09 50
43¼	Stonegate	d	23p33	23p56	00 33		00 56			06 34			07 03			07 58		08 30					09 31		
47½	Etchingham	d	23p38	00 01	00 38		01 00			06 38			07 08			08 02		08 34		09 05			09 36		
49¼	Robertsbridge	d	23p42	00 05	00 42		01 04			06 42			07 13			08 06		08 38		09 09			09 40		
55½	Battle	d	23p50	00 13	00 50		01 12			06 50			07 21			08 15		08 46		09 17			09 48		10 06
57½	Crowhurst	d	23p53	00 16	00 53		01 15			06 54			07 24			08 18		08 49					09 51		
60¾	West St Leonards	d	23p58	00 21	00 58		01 20			06 59			07 31			08 23		08 54					09 57		
—	St Leonards Warrior Sq 4	d	00 01	00 25	01 01		01 23			07 03			07 34			08 26		08 57		09 28			10 00		10 16
62½	Hastings 4	a	00 04	00 28	01 04		01 26			07 07			07 38			08 30		09 01		09 32			10 03		10 20
63½	Ore	a								07 12															

Station		SE 1	SE 1	SE 1	SE 1	SE 1	SE 1		SE 1	SE 1	SE 1	SE 1	SE 1	SE 1	SE 1	SE 1	SE 1		SE 1	SE 1	SE 1	SE 1	SE 1	SE 1	SE 1
London Charing Cross 4 ⊖	d	09 00		09 30	09 45	10 00	10 15		10 30	10 45	11 00	11 15	11 30	11 45	12 00	12 15	12 30		12 45	13 00	13 15	13 30	13 45	14 00	14 15
London Waterloo (East) 4 ⊖	d	09 03		09 33	09 48	10 03	10 18		10 33	10 48	11 03	11 18	11 33	11 48	12 03	12 18	12 33		12 48	13 03	13 18	13 33	13 48	14 03	14 18
London Cannon Street 4 ⊖	d		09 18																						
London Bridge 4 ⊖	d	09 08	09 22	09 39	09 53	10 09	10 23		10 39	10 53	11 09	11 23	11 39	11 53	12 09	12 23	12 39		12 53	13 09	13 23	13 39	13 53	14 09	14 23
Orpington 4	d	09 26	09 41	09 56	10 09	10 26	10 39		10 56	11 09	11 26	11 39	11 56	12 09	12 26	12 39	12 56		13 09	13 26	13 39	13 56	14 09	14 26	14 39
Sevenoaks 4	d	09 35	09 50	10 05	10 19	10 35	10 49		11 05	11 19	11 35	11 49	12 05	12 19	12 35	12 49	13 05		13 19	13 35	13 49	14 05	14 19	14 35	14 49
Tonbridge 4	a	09 46	09 58	10 15	10 27	10 45	10 57		11 15	11 27	11 45	11 57	12 15	12 27	12 45	12 57	13 15		13 27	13 45	13 57	14 15	14 27	14 45	14 57
	d	09 46	09 59	10 16	10 28	10 46	11 01		11 16	11 28	11 46	11 58	12 16	12 28	12 46	12 58	13 16		13 28	13 46	13 58	14 16	14 28	14 46	14 58
High Brooms	d	09 53	10 05	10 23	10 35	10 54	11 07		11 23	11 35	11 53	12 05	12 23	12 35	12 53	13 05	13 23		13 35	13 53	14 05	14 23	14 35	14 53	15 05
Tunbridge Wells 4	a	09 57	10 09	10 27	10 39	10 57	11 11		11 27	11 39	11 57	12 09	12 27	12 39	12 57	13 09	13 27		13 39	13 57	14 09	14 27	14 39	14 57	15 09
	d		10 13		10 40		11 12			11 40		12 10		12 40		13 10			13 40		14 10		14 40		15 10
Frant	d		10 18				11 17					12 15				13 15					14 15				15 15
Wadhurst	d		10 22		10 48		11 22			11 48		12 20		12 48		13 20			13 48		14 20		14 48		15 20
Stonegate	d		10 28				11 28					12 26				13 26					14 26				15 26
Etchingham	d		10 33				11 32					12 31				13 31					14 31				15 31
Robertsbridge	d		10 37				11 36					12 35				13 35					14 35				15 35
Battle	d		10 45		11 04		11 44			12 04		12 43		13 04		13 43			14 04		14 43		15 04		15 43
Crowhurst	d		10 48				11 48					12 46				13 46					14 46				15 46
West St Leonards	d		10 53				11 53					12 51				13 51					14 51				15 51
St Leonards Warrior Sq 4	d		10 57		11 14		11 56			12 15		12 55		13 15		13 55			14 15		14 55		15 15		15 55
Hastings 4	a		11 00		11 17		12 00			12 18		12 59		13 18		13 59			14 18		14 59		15 18		15 59
Ore	a																								

Station		SE 1	SE 1		SE 1	SE 1	SE 1	SE 1	SE 1	SE 1	SE 1	SE 1	SE 1		SE 1	SE 1	SE 1	SE 1		SE 1	SE 1	SE 1	SE 1		SE 1
London Charing Cross 4 ⊖	d	14 30	14 45		15 00	15 15	15 30	15 45	16 00	16 15	16 28	16 41			17 01	17 19	17 23			17 45	17 59	18 07			18 32
London Waterloo (East) 4 ⊖	d	14 33	14 48		15 03	15 18	15 33	15 48	16 03	16 18	16 31	16 44			17 04	17 22	17 26			17 48	18 02	18 10			18 35
London Cannon Street 4 ⊖	d												17 02					17 37					18 28		
London Bridge 4 ⊖	d	14 39	14 53		15 09	15 23	15 39	15 53	16 09	16 23	16 36	16 49	17 06		17 09		17 31	17 42		17 53		18 15	18 32		18 40
Orpington 4	d	14 56	15 09		15 26	15 39	15 56	16 09	16 26		16 53														
Sevenoaks 4	d	15 05	15 19		15 35	15 49	16 05	16 19	16 35	16 47	17 03	17 14	17 32		17 37		17 59			18 21		18 43			19 06
Tonbridge 4	a	15 16	15 27		15 45	15 57	16 15	16 27	16 45	16 55	17 13	17 22	17 40		17 48		18 09			18 32		18 54			19 17
	d	15 16	15 28		15 46	15 58	16 16	16 28	16 46	16 55	17 13	17 22	17 41		17 48		18 11			18 32		18 54			19 17
High Brooms	d	15 23	15 35		15 53	16 05	16 23	16 35	16 53	17 01	17 21	17 28	17 47		17 54	18 04	18 17	18 21		18 38	18 42	19 00	19 09		19 23
Tunbridge Wells 4	a	15 27	15 39		15 57	16 09	16 27	16 39	16 59	17 05	17 26	17 32	17 50		18 00	18 08	18 22	18 24		18 44	18 46	19 06	19 13		19 29
	d		15 40			16 14		16 40		17 05		17 38	17 52			18 08		18 29	18 33		18 49		19 20		
Frant	d					16 19		16 45		17 10			17 57			18 13			18 38		18 54		19 25		
Wadhurst	d		15 48			16 25		16 49		17 15		17 46	18 02			18 18		18 37	18 43		18 59		19 30		
Stonegate	d					16 31		16 55		17 21			18 08			18 24			18 49		19 05		19 36		
Etchingham	d					16 35		17 00		17 25		17 55	18 13			18 28		18 46	18 54		19 10		19 41		
Robertsbridge	d					16 39		17 04		17 29		17 59	18 17			18 32			18 58		19 14		19 45		
Battle	d		16 04			16 47		17 12		17 37		18 07	18 25			18 40		18 56	19 06		19 22		19 53		
Crowhurst	d					16 50		17 15		17 40			18 28			18 43			19 09		19 26		19 56		
West St Leonards	d		16 12			16 55		17 21		17 45			18 34			18 48			19 15		19 34		20 01		
St Leonards Warrior Sq 4	d		16 15			16 58		17 24		17 48		18 17	18 37			18 51		19 06	19 18		19 37		20 05		
Hastings 4	a		16 18			17 01		17 28		17 55		18 24	18 43			18 54		19 12	19 23		19 42		20 08		
Ore	a															19 00							20 15		

London and Tonbridge - Tunbridge Wells and Hastings

Network Diagram - see first Page of Table 206

		SE 1	SE 1	SE 1	SE 1	SE 1	SE 1	SE 1	SE 1		SE 1	SE 1	SE 1	SE 1	SE 1	SE 1	SE 1	SE 1	SE 1		SE 1				
London Charing Cross [4] ⊖	d	18 45		19 15	19 30	19 45	20 00	20 15	20 30		20 45	21 00	21 30	21 45	22 00	22 30	22 45	23 00	23 30		23 45				
London Waterloo (East) [4] ⊖	d	18 48		19 18	19 33	19 48	20 03	20 18	20 33		20 48	21 03	21 33	21 48	22 03	22 33	22 48	23 03	23 33		23 48				
London Cannon Street [4] ⊖	d		19 04																						
London Bridge [4] ⊖	d	18 53	19 09	19 23	19 39	19 53	20 09	20 23	20 39		20 53	21 09	21 39	21 53	22 09	22 39	22 53	23 09	23 39		23 53				
Orpington [4]	d			19 39	19 56	20 09	20 26	20 39	20 56		21 09	21 26	21 56	22 09	22 26	22 54	23 09	23 24	23 54		00 09				
Sevenoaks [4]	d	19 21	19 33	19 49	20 05	20 19	20 35	20 49	21 05		21 19	21 35	22 07	22 19	22 37	23 05	23 19	23 35	00 05		00 19				
Tonbridge [4]	a	19 29	19 44	19 57	20 15	20 27	20 45	20 57	21 15		21 27	21 45	22 17	22 27	22 47	23 15	23 27	23 45	00 15		00 27				
	d	19 30	19 45	19 58	20 16	20 28	20 46	20 58	21 16		21 28	21 46	22 17	22 28	22 47	23 16	23 28	23 46	00 16		00 27				
High Brooms	d	19 36	19 53	20 05	20 23	20 35	20 53	21 05	21 23		21 35	21 53	22 24	22 35	22 54	23 22	23 35	23 52	00 22		00 34				
Tunbridge Wells [4]	a	19 39	19 56	20 09	20 27	20 39	20 57	21 09	21 27		21 39	21 57	22 27	22 39	22 58	23 26	23 39	23 56	00 26		00 38				
	d	19 41	19 57	20 11		20 40		21 10			21 40			22 40			23 40				00 40				
Frant	d	19 46	20 02	20 16		20 45		21 15			21 45			22 45			23 45				00 45				
Wadhurst	d	19 50	20 07	20 21		20 50		21 20			21 50			22 50			23 50				00 50				
Stonegate	d	19 56	20 13	20 27		20 56		21 26			21 56			22 56			23 56				00 56				
Etchingham	d	20 01	20 18	20 32		21 01		21 31			22 01			23 01			00 01				01 00				
Robertsbridge	d	20 05	20 22	20 36		21 05		21 36			22 05			23 05			00 05				01 04				
Battle	d	20 13	20 29	20 44		21 13		21 44			22 13			23 13			00 13				01 12				
Crowhurst	d	20 16		20 47		21 16		21 47			22 16			23 16			00 16				01 15				
West St Leonards	d	20 21		20 53		21 21		21 52			22 21			23 21			00 21				01 20				
St Leonards Warrior Sq [4]	d	20 25	20 39	20 56		21 25		21 56			22 25			23 25			00 25				01 23				
Hastings [4]	a	20 30	20 43	21 00		21 29		21 59			22 29			23 29			00 28				01 26				
Ore	a																								

Saturdays

		SE 1	SE 1	SE 1	SE 1	SE 1	SE 1	SE 1	SE 1	SE 1		SE 1	SE 1	SE 1	SE 1	SE 1	SE 1	SE 1	SE 1	SE 1		SE 1	SE 1	SE 1	SE 1
London Charing Cross [4] ⊖	d	22p45	23p30	23p45				07 45	08 15	08 30		08 45	09 00	09 15	09 30	09 45	10 00	10 15	10 30	10 45		11 00	11 15	11 30	11 45
London Waterloo (East) [4] ⊖	d	22p48	23p33	23p48				07 48	08 18	08 33		08 48	09 03	09 18	09 33	09 48	10 03	10 18	10 33	10 48		11 03	11 18	11 33	11 48
London Cannon Street [4] ⊖	d																								
London Bridge [4] ⊖	d	22p53	23p39	23p53				07 53	08 23	08 39		08 53	09 09	09 23	09 39	09 53	10 09	10 23	10 39	10 53		11 09	11 23	11 39	11 53
Orpington [4]	d	23p09	23p54	00 09				08 09	08 39	08 56		09 09	09 26	09 39	09 56	10 09	10 26	10 39	10 56	11 09		11 26	11 39	11 56	12 09
Sevenoaks [4]	d	23p19	00 05	00 19				08 19	08 49	09 05		09 19	09 35	09 49	10 05	10 19	10 35	10 49	11 05	11 19		11 35	11 49	12 05	12 19
Tonbridge [4]	a	23p27	00 15	00 27				08 27	08 57	09 15		09 27	09 45	09 57	10 15	10 27	10 45	10 57	11 15	11 27		11 45	11 57	12 15	12 27
	d	23p28	00 16	00 27	06 58	07 28	07 58	08 28	08 58	09 16		09 28	09 46	09 58	10 16	10 28	10 46	10 58	11 16	11 28		11 46	11 58	12 16	12 28
High Brooms	d	23p35	00 22	00 34	07 05	07 35	08 05	08 35	09 05	09 23		09 35	09 53	10 05	10 23	10 35	10 53	11 05	11 23	11 35		11 53	12 05	12 23	12 35
Tunbridge Wells [4]	a	23p39	00 26	00 38	07 09	07 39	08 09	08 39	09 09	09 27		09 39	09 57	10 09	10 27	10 39	10 57	11 09	11 27	11 39		11 57	12 09	12 27	12 39
	d	23p40		00 40	07 10		08 10	08 40	09 10			09 40		10 10		10 40		11 10		11 40			12 10		12 40
Frant	d	23p45		00 45	07 15		08 15	08 45	09 15					10 15				11 15					12 15		
Wadhurst	d	23p50		00 50	07 20		08 20	08 50	09 20			09 48		10 20		10 48		11 20		11 48			12 20		12 48
Stonegate	d	23p56		00 56	07 26		08 26	08 56	09 26					10 26				11 26					12 26		
Etchingham	d	00 01		01 00	07 31		08 31	09 01	09 31					10 31				11 31					12 31		
Robertsbridge	d	00 05		01 04	07 35		08 35	09 05	09 35					10 35				11 35					12 35		
Battle	d	00 13		01 12	07 43		08 43	09 13	09 43			10 04		10 43		11 04		11 43		12 04			12 43		13 04
Crowhurst	d	00 16		01 15	07 46		08 46	09 16	09 46					10 46				11 46					12 46		
West St Leonards	d	00 21		01 20	07 51		08 51	09 21	09 51					10 51				11 51					12 51		
St Leonards Warrior Sq [4]	d	00 25		01 23	07 55		08 55	09 25	09 55			10 15		10 55		11 15		11 55		12 15			12 55		13 15
Hastings [4]	a	00 28		01 26	07 59		08 59	09 29	09 59			10 18		10 59		11 18		11 59		12 18			12 59		13 18
Ore	a																								

		SE 1	SE 1	SE 1	SE 1	SE 1		SE 1	SE 1	SE 1	SE 1	SE 1	SE 1	SE 1	SE 1	SE 1		SE 1	SE 1	SE 1	SE 1	SE 1	SE 1	SE 1	SE 1
London Charing Cross [4] ⊖	d	12 00	12 15	12 30	12 45	13 00		13 15	13 30	13 45	14 00	14 15	14 30	14 45	15 00	15 15		15 30	15 45	16 00	16 15	16 30	16 45	17 00	17 15
London Waterloo (East) [4] ⊖	d	12 03	12 18	12 33	12 48	13 03		13 18	13 33	13 48	14 03	14 18	14 33	14 48	15 03	15 18		15 33	15 48	16 03	16 18	16 33	16 48	17 03	17 18
London Cannon Street [4] ⊖	d																								
London Bridge [4] ⊖	d	12 09	12 23	12 39	12 53	13 09		13 23	13 39	13 53	14 09	14 23	14 39	14 53	15 09	15 23		15 39	15 53	16 09	16 23	16 39	16 53	17 09	17 23
Orpington [4]	d	12 26	12 39	12 56	13 09	13 26		13 39	13 56	14 09	14 26	14 39	14 56	15 09	15 26	15 39		15 56	16 09	16 26	16 39	16 56	17 09	17 26	17 39
Sevenoaks [4]	d	12 35	12 49	13 05	13 19	13 35		13 49	14 05	14 19	14 35	14 49	15 05	15 19	15 35	15 49		16 05	16 19	16 35	16 49	17 05	17 19	17 35	17 49
Tonbridge [4]	a	12 45	12 57	13 15	13 27	13 45		13 57	14 15	14 27	14 45	14 57	15 15	15 27	15 45	15 57		16 15	16 27	16 45	16 57	17 15	17 27	17 45	17 57
	d	12 46	12 58	13 16	13 28	13 46		13 58	14 16	14 28	14 46	14 58	15 16	15 28	15 46	15 58		16 16	16 28	16 46	16 58	17 16	17 28	17 46	17 58
High Brooms	d	12 53	13 05	13 23	13 35	13 53		14 05	14 23	14 35	14 53	15 05	15 23	15 35	15 53	16 05		16 23	16 35	16 53	17 05	17 23	17 35	17 53	18 05
Tunbridge Wells [4]	a	12 57	13 09	13 27	13 39	13 57		14 09	14 27	14 39	14 57	15 09	15 27	15 39	15 57	16 09		16 27	16 39	16 57	17 09	17 27	17 39	17 57	18 09
	d		13 10		13 40			14 10		14 40		15 10		15 40		16 10			16 40		17 10		17 40		18 10
Frant	d		13 15					14 15				15 15				16 15					17 15				18 15
Wadhurst	d		13 20		13 48			14 20		14 48		15 20		15 48		16 20			16 48		17 20		17 48		18 20
Stonegate	d		13 26					14 26				15 26				16 26					17 26				18 26
Etchingham	d		13 31					14 31				15 31				16 31					17 31				18 31
Robertsbridge	d		13 35					14 35				15 35				16 35					17 35				18 35
Battle	d		13 43		14 04			14 43		15 04		15 43		16 04		16 43			17 04		17 43		18 04		18 43
Crowhurst	d		13 46					14 46				15 46				16 46					17 46				18 46
West St Leonards	d		13 51					14 51				15 51				16 51					17 51				18 51
St Leonards Warrior Sq [4]	d		13 55		14 15			14 55		15 15		15 55		16 15		16 55			17 15		17 55		18 15		18 55
Hastings [4]	a		13 59		14 18			14 59		15 18		15 59		16 18		16 59			17 18		17 59		18 18		18 59
Ore	a																								

Table 206

Saturdays

London and Tonbridge - Tunbridge Wells and Hastings

Network Diagram - see first Page of Table 206

		SE 1	SE 1	SE 1	SE 1	SE 1	SE 1	SE 1	SE 1	SE 1	SE 1	SE 1	SE 1	SE 1	SE 1	SE 1	SE 1	SE 1	SE 1
London Charing Cross 4 ⊖	d	17 30	17 45	18 00	18 15	18 30	18 45	19 00	19 15	19 30	19 55	20 25	20 55	21 25	21 55	22 25	22 55	23 25	23 45
London Waterloo (East) 4 ⊖	d	17 33	17 48	18 03	18 18	18 33	18 48	19 03	19 18	19 33	19 58	20 28	20 58	21 28	21 58	22 28	22 58	23 28	23 48
London Cannon Street 4 ⊖	d																		
London Bridge 4 ⊖	d	17 39	17 53	18 09	18 23	18 39	18 53	19 09	19 23	19 39	20 03	20 33	21 03	21 33	22 03	22 33	23 03	23 33	23 53
Orpington 4	d	17 56	18 09	18 26	18 39	18 56	19 09	19 26	19 39	19 56	20 21	20 51	21 21	21 51	22 21	22 49	23 19	23 49	00 09
Sevenoaks 4	d	18 05	18 19	18 35	18 49	19 05	19 19	19 35	19 49	20 05	20 31	21 01	21 31	22 01	22 31	23 00	23 28	23 59	00 19
Tonbridge 4	a	18 15	18 27	18 45	18 58	19 15	19 27	19 45	19 58	20 15	20 39	21 11	21 39	22 11	22 39	23 10	23 36	00 10	00 27
	d	18 16	18 28	18 46	18 58	19 16	19 28	19 46	19 58	20 16	20 40	21 11	21 40	22 11	22 40	23 11	23 37	00 11	00 27
High Brooms	d	18 23	18 35	18 53	19 05	19 23	19 35	19 53	20 05	20 23	20 46	21 19	21 46	22 19	22 46	23 17	23 43	00 17	00 34
Tunbridge Wells 4	a	18 27	18 39	18 57	19 09	19 27	19 39	19 57	20 09	20 27	20 50	21 23	21 50	22 23	22 50	23 21	23 47	00 21	00 38
	d		18 40		19 10		19 40		20 10		20 51		21 51		22 51		23 48		00 39
Frant	d				19 15				20 15		20 56		21 56		22 56		23 53		00 44
Wadhurst	d		18 48		19 20		19 48		20 20		21 01		22 01		23 01		23 58		00 49
Stonegate	d				19 26				20 26		21 07		22 07		23 07		00 04		00 55
Etchingham	d				19 31				20 31		21 12		22 12		23 12		00 09		00 59
Robertsbridge	d				19 35				20 35		21 16		22 16		23 16		00 13		01 03
Battle	d		19 04		19 43		20 04		20 43		21 24		22 24		23 24		00 21		01 11
Crowhurst	d				19 46				20 46		21 27		22 27		23 27		00 24		01 15
West St Leonards	d				19 51				20 51		21 32		22 32		23 33		00 29		01 20
St Leonards Warrior Sq 4	d		19 15		19 55		20 15		20 55		21 36		22 36		23 36		00 33		01 23
Hastings 4	a		19 18		19 59		20 18		20 59		21 39		22 39		23 39		00 36		01 26
Ore	a																		

Sundays

		SE 1 A	SE 1 A	SE 1 A	SE 1	SE 1	SE 1	SE 1	SE 1	SE 1
London Charing Cross 4 ⊖	d	22p55	23p25	23p45		08 23		09 23	09 53	10 23
London Waterloo (East) 4 ⊖	d	22p58	23p28	23p48		08 26		09 26	09 56	10 26
London Cannon Street 4 ⊖	d									
London Bridge 4 ⊖	d	23p03	23p33	23p53		08 31		09 31	10 01	10 31
Orpington 4	d	23p19	23p49	00 09		08 46		09 46	10 16	10 46
Sevenoaks 4	d	23p28	23p59	00 19		08 56		09 56	10 26	10 56
Tonbridge 4	a	23p36	00 10	00 27		09 04		10 04	10 34	11 04
	d	23p37	00 11	00 27	08 25	09 04	09 34	10 04	10 34	11 04
High Brooms	d	23p43	00 17	00 34	08 31	09 10	09 40	10 10	10 40	11 10
Tunbridge Wells 4	a	23p47	00 21	00 38	08 35	09 14	09 44	10 14	10 44	11 14
	d	23p48		00 39		09 15	09 45	10 15	10 45	11 15
Frant	d	23p53		00 44		09 20		10 20		11 20
Wadhurst	d	23p58		00 49		09 25	09 52	10 25	10 52	11 25
Stonegate	d	00 04		00 55		09 31		10 31		11 31
Etchingham	d	00 09		00 59		09 36		10 36		11 36
Robertsbridge	d	00 13		01 03		09 40		10 40		11 40
Battle	d	00 21		01 11		09 48	10 08	10 48	11 08	11 48
Crowhurst	d	00 24		01 15		09 51		10 51		11 51
West St Leonards	d	00 29		01 20		09 56		10 56		11 56
St Leonards Warrior Sq 4	d	00 33		01 23		10 00	10 18	11 00	11 18	12 00
Hastings 4	a	00 36		01 26		10 03	10 21	11 03	11 21	12 03
Ore	a									

		SE 1	SE 1	SE 1	SE 1	SE 1	SE 1	SE 1	SE 1	SE 1	SE 1	SE 1	SE 1	SE 1
London Charing Cross 4 ⊖	d	10 53	11 23	11 53	12 23	12 53	13 23	13 53	14 23	14 53	15 23	15 53	16 23	16 53
London Waterloo (East) 4 ⊖	d	10 56	11 26	11 56	12 26	12 56	13 26	13 56	14 26	14 56	15 26	15 56	16 26	16 56
London Cannon Street 4 ⊖	d													
London Bridge 4 ⊖	d	11 01	11 31	12 01	12 31	13 01	13 31	14 01	14 31	15 01	15 31	16 01	16 31	17 01
Orpington 4	d	11 16	11 46	12 16	12 46	13 16	13 46	14 16	14 46	15 16	15 46	16 16	16 46	17 16
Sevenoaks 4	d	11 26	11 56	12 26	12 56	13 26	13 56	14 26	14 56	15 26	15 56	16 26	16 56	17 26
Tonbridge 4	a	11 34	12 04	12 34	13 04	13 34	14 04	14 34	15 04	15 34	16 04	16 34	17 04	17 34
	d	11 34	12 04	12 34	13 04	13 34	14 04	14 34	15 04	15 34	16 04	16 34	17 04	17 34
High Brooms	d	11 40	12 10	12 40	13 10	13 40	14 10	14 40	15 10	15 40	16 10	16 40	17 10	17 40
Tunbridge Wells 4	a	11 44	12 14	12 44	13 14	13 44	14 14	14 44	15 14	15 44	16 14	16 44	17 14	17 44
	d	11 45	12 15	12 45	13 15	13 45	14 15	14 45	15 15	15 45	16 15	16 45	17 15	17 45
Frant	d		12 20		13 20		14 20		15 20		16 20		17 20	
Wadhurst	d	11 52	12 25	12 52	13 25	13 52	14 25	14 52	15 25	15 52	16 25	16 52	17 25	17 52
Stonegate	d		12 31		13 31		14 31		15 31		16 31		17 31	
Etchingham	d		12 36		13 36		14 36		15 36		16 36		17 36	
Robertsbridge	d		12 40		13 40		14 40		15 40		16 40		17 40	
Battle	d	12 08	12 48	13 08	13 48	14 08	14 48	15 08	15 48	16 08	16 48	17 08	17 48	18 08
Crowhurst	d		12 51		13 51		14 51		15 51		16 51		17 51	
West St Leonards	d		12 56		13 56		14 56		15 56		16 56		17 56	
St Leonards Warrior Sq 4	d	12 18	13 00	13 18	14 00	14 18	15 00	15 18	16 00	16 18	17 00	17 18	18 00	18 18
Hastings 4	a	12 21	13 03	13 21	14 03	14 21	15 03	15 21	16 03	16 21	17 03	17 21	18 03	18 21
Ore	a													

		SE 1	SE 1	SE 1	SE 1	SE 1	SE 1	SE 1	SE 1	SE 1	SE 1
London Charing Cross 4 ⊖	d	17 23	17 53	18 23	18 53	19 23	19 53	20 23	21 23	22 23	23 23
London Waterloo (East) 4 ⊖	d	17 26	17 56	18 26	18 56	19 26	19 56	20 26	21 26	22 26	23 26
London Cannon Street 4 ⊖	d										
London Bridge 4 ⊖	d	17 31	18 01	18 31	19 01	19 31	20 01	20 31	21 31	22 31	23 31
Orpington 4	d	17 46	18 16	18 46	19 16	19 46	20 16	20 46	21 46	22 46	23 46
Sevenoaks 4	d	17 56	18 26	18 56	19 26	19 56	20 26	20 56	21 56	22 57	23 57
Tonbridge 4	a	18 04	18 34	19 04	19 34	20 04	20 34	21 04	22 04	23 05	00 05
	d	18 04	18 34	19 04	19 34	20 04	20 34	21 04	22 04	23 06	00 06
High Brooms	d	18 10	18 40	19 10	19 40	20 10	20 40	21 10	22 10	23 12	00 12
Tunbridge Wells 4	a	18 14	18 44	19 14	19 44	20 14	20 44	21 14	22 14	23 15	00 15
	d	18 15	18 45	19 15	19 45	20 15		21 15	22 15	23 17	00 17
Frant	d	18 20		19 20		20 20		21 20	22 20	23 22	00 22
Wadhurst	d	18 25	18 52	19 25	19 52	20 25		21 25	22 25	23 27	00 27
Stonegate	d	18 31		19 31		20 31		21 31	22 31	23 33	00 33
Etchingham	d	18 36		19 36		20 36		21 36	22 36	23 38	00 38
Robertsbridge	d	18 40		19 40		20 40		21 40	22 40	23 42	00 42
Battle	d	18 48	19 08	19 48	20 08	20 48		21 48	22 48	23 50	00 50
Crowhurst	d	18 51		19 51		20 51		21 51	22 51	23 53	00 53
West St Leonards	d	18 56		19 56		20 56		21 56	22 56	23 58	00 58
St Leonards Warrior Sq 4	d	19 00	19 18	20 00	20 18	21 00		22 00	23 00	00 01	01 01
Hastings 4	a	19 03	19 21	20 03	20 21	21 03		22 03	23 03	00 04	01 04
Ore	a										

A not 11 December

Table 206

Mondays to Fridays

Hastings and Tunbridge Wells - Tonbridge and London

Network Diagram - see first Page of Table 206

Miles			SE MX	SE	SE	SE	SE	SE	SE	SE	SE		SE	SE	SE	SE	SE	SE	SE	SE	SE		SE	SE	SE
			1	1	1	1	1	1	1	1	1		1	1 A	1 B	1	1 A	1	1	1	1		1	1	1
0	Ore	d												06 12			06 37							07 40	
1	**Hastings 4**	d	22p10			05 17		05 37	05 48		06 03			06 20	06 28		06 41		07 01		07 25			07 44	
1¾	St Leonards Warrior Sq 4	d	22p13			05 20		05 40	05 51		06 06			06 23	06 31		06 44		07 04		07 28			07 47	
2¾	West St Leonards	d	22p16			05 23		05 43			06 09				06 34		06 47		07 07		07 31			07 50	
6	Crowhurst	d	22p22			05 29		05 49			06 15				06 40		06 53		07 13		07 37			07 56	
8	Battle	d	22p26			05 33		05 53	06 01		06 19			06 33	06 44		06 57		07 17		07 41			08 00	
14¼	Robertsbridge	d	22p33			05 40		06 00			06 27			06 40			07 05		07 25		07 48			08 07	
16	Etchingham	d	22p37			05 44		06 04	06 10		06 31			06 44	06 53		07 09		07 29		07 52			08 11	
19¾	Stonegate	d	22p42			05 49		06 09			06 36			06 50			07 14		07 34		07 57			08 17	
24¼	Wadhurst	d	22p49			05 56		06 16	06 21		06 43			06 57	07 04		07 21		07 41		08 04			08 24	
26¾	Frant	d	22p53			06 00		06 20			06 47			07 01			07 25		07 45		08 08			08 28	
29	**Tunbridge Wells 4**	a	22p58			06 06		06 25	06 29		06 53			07 06	07 11		07 31		07 51		08 13			08 33	
—																									
—		d	22p59	05 21	05 50	06 09	06 21	06 34		06 40	06 56		07 00	07 16		07 20	07 36	07 40	07 56	08 00	08 18		08 25	08 40	08 51
30½	High Brooms	d	23p02	05 24	05 53	06 12	06 24	06 37		06 44	07 00		07 04	07 20		07 24	07 40	07 44	08 00	08 04	08 22		08 28	08 43	08 54
34	**Tonbridge 4**	a	23p08	05 30	05 59	06 18	06 30	06 44		06 50			07 10			07 30		07 50		08 10			08 34	08 49	09 00
41½	Sevenoaks 4	a	23p24	05 42	06 10	06 30	06 43	06 52		07 02			07 22			07 42		08 02		08 22			08 45	08 58	09 13
49¾	Orpington 4	a	23p36	05 53	06 19		06 53	07 02		07 13														09 08	09 24
61¾	**London Bridge 4** ⊖	a	23p54	06 09	06 38	06 54	07 09	07 22		07 29			07 50			08 09	08 24	08 29		08 49	09 03		09 11	09 26	09 40
—	**London Cannon Street 4** ⊖	a			06 42			07 29									08 30				09 10				
62¾	**London Waterloo (East) 4** ⊖	a	23p59	06 14		06 59	07 14			07 34	07 44		07 55	08 04		08 14		08 34	08 44	08 54			09 16	09 31	09 45
63½	**London Charing Cross 4** ⊖	a	00 03	06 18		07 05	07 20			07 40	07 50		08 01	08 08		08 20		08 40	08 50	09 00			09 22	09 37	09 51

		SE	SE	SE	SE	SE	SE		SE	SE	SE	SE	SE	SE	SE	SE	SE		SE	SE	SE	SE	SE	SE	SE
		1	1	1	1	1	1		1	1	1	1	1	1	1	1	1		1	1	1	1	1	1	1
Ore	d																								
Hastings 4	d	08 15		08 47		09 29			09 50		10 31		10 50		11 31		11 50			12 31		12 50		13 31	
St Leonards Warrior Sq 4	d	08 18		08 50		09 32			09 53		10 34		10 53		11 34		11 53			12 34		12 53		13 34	
West St Leonards	d	08 21		08 53					09 56				10 56				11 56					12 56			
Crowhurst	d	08 27		08 58					10 02				11 02				12 02					13 02			
Battle	d	08 31		09 02		09 42			10 06		10 44		11 06		11 44		12 06			12 44		13 06		13 44	
Robertsbridge	d	08 38		09 09					10 13				11 13				12 13					13 13			
Etchingham	d	08 42		09 13					10 17				11 17				12 17					13 17			
Stonegate	d	08 47		09 18					10 23				11 23				12 23					13 23			
Wadhurst	d	08 54		09 25		09 58			10 30		11 00		11 29		12 00		12 29			13 00		13 29		14 00	
Frant	d	08 58		09 29					10 34				11 33				12 33					13 33			
Tunbridge Wells 4	a	09 03		09 34		10 05			10 39		11 07		11 38		12 07		12 38			13 07		13 38		14 07	
	d	09 09	09 21	09 39	09 51	10 09	10 21		10 39	10 51	11 09	11 21	11 39	11 51	12 09	12 21	12 39		12 51	13 09	13 21	13 39	13 51	14 09	14 21
High Brooms	d	09 12	09 24	09 42	09 54	10 12	10 24		10 43	10 54	11 12	11 24	11 42	11 54	12 12	12 24	12 42		12 54	13 12	13 24	13 42	13 54	14 12	14 24
Tonbridge 4	a	09 18	09 30	09 48	10 00	10 18	10 30		10 49	11 00	11 18	11 30	11 48	12 00	12 18	12 30	12 48		13 00	13 18	13 30	13 48	14 00	14 18	14 30
Sevenoaks 4	a	09 28	09 43	09 58	10 13	10 28	10 43		10 58	11 13	11 28	11 43	11 58	12 13	12 28	12 43	12 58		13 13	13 28	13 43	13 58	14 13	14 28	14 43
Orpington 4	a	09 38	09 53	10 08	10 23	10 38	10 53		11 08	11 23	11 38	11 53	12 08	12 23	12 38	12 53	13 08		13 23	13 38	13 53	14 08	14 23	14 38	14 53
London Bridge 4 ⊖	a	09 55	10 10	10 25	10 40	10 55	11 10		11 25	11 40	11 55	12 10	12 25	12 40	12 55	13 10	13 25		13 40	13 55	14 10	14 25	14 40	14 55	15 10
London Cannon Street 4 ⊖	a																								
London Waterloo (East) 4 ⊖	a	09 59	10 15	10 29	10 45	10 59	11 15		11 29	11 45	11 59	12 15	12 29	12 45	12 59	13 15	13 29		13 45	13 59	14 15	14 29	14 45	14 59	15 15
London Charing Cross 4 ⊖	a	10 03	10 19	10 33	10 49	11 03	11 19		11 33	11 49	12 03	12 19	12 33	12 49	13 03	13 19	13 33		13 49	14 03	14 19	14 33	14 49	15 03	15 19

		SE	SE		SE	SE	SE	SE	SE	SE	SE	SE	SE		SE	SE	SE	SE	SE	SE	SE	SE	SE		SE
		1	1		1	1	1	1	1	1	1	1	1		1	1	1	1	1	1	1	1	1		1
Ore	d																								
Hastings 4	d	13 50			14 31		14 50		15 31		15 45		16 19			16 50		17 19		17 50		18 19			18 46
St Leonards Warrior Sq 4	d	13 53			14 34		14 53		15 34		15 48		16 21			16 53		17 22		17 53		18 22			18 49
West St Leonards	d	13 56					14 56				15 51		16 25			16 56		17 25		17 56		18 25			18 52
Crowhurst	d	14 02					15 02				15 57		16 30			17 02		17 31		18 02		18 31			18 58
Battle	d	14 06			14 44		15 06		15 44		16 01		16 34			17 06		17 35		18 06		18 35			19 02
Robertsbridge	d	14 13					15 13				16 08		16 41			17 13		17 42		18 13		18 42			19 09
Etchingham	d	14 17					15 17				16 12		16 45			17 17		17 46		18 17		18 46			19 12
Stonegate	d	14 23					15 23				16 17		16 50			17 23		17 52		18 23		18 51			19 18
Wadhurst	d	14 29			15 00		15 29		16 00		16 24		16 57			17 29		17 59		18 29		18 58			19 24
Frant	d	14 33					15 33				16 28		17 01			17 33		18 03		18 33		19 02			19 28
Tunbridge Wells 4	a	14 38			15 07		15 38		16 07		16 33		17 06			17 38		18 08		18 39		19 07			19 33
	d	14 39	14 51		15 09	15 21	15 39	15 51	16 09	16 21	16 36	16 51	17 06		17 21	17 39	17 49	18 13	18 19	18 39	18 51	19 09	19 21		19 38
High Brooms	d	14 42	14 54		15 12	15 24	15 42	15 54	16 12	16 24	16 39	16 55	17 10		17 24	17 42	17 52	18 16	18 22	18 42	18 54	19 12	19 24		19 41
Tonbridge 4	a	14 48	15 00		15 18	15 30	15 48	16 00	16 18	16 30	16 46	17 01	17 16		17 30	17 49	17 59	18 22	18 28	18 50	19 00	19 18	19 30		19 47
Sevenoaks 4	a	14 58	15 13		15 28	15 43	15 58	16 13	16 28	16 43	16 58	17 13	17 28		17 43	17 58	18 13	18 31	18 43	18 59	19 13	19 28	19 43		19 59
Orpington 4	a	15 08	15 23		15 38	15 53	16 07	16 24	16 38	16 53	17 08	17 23	17 38		17 53	18 08	18 23		18 53	19 08	19 23	19 38	19 53		20 08
London Bridge 4 ⊖	a	15 25	15 40		15 55	16 11	16 25	16 42	16 56	17 11	17 27	17 41	17 58		18 09	18 25	18 40	18 55	19 10	19 25	19 40	19 54	20 10		20 24
London Cannon Street 4 ⊖	a										17 32														
London Waterloo (East) 4 ⊖	a	15 29	15 45		15 59	16 16	16 29	16 48	17 00	17 16		17 46	18 02		18 14	18 29	18 45	18 59	19 14	19 29	19 45	19 59	20 15		20 29
London Charing Cross 4 ⊖	a	15 33	15 49		16 03	16 20	16 33	16 52	17 04	17 20		17 50	18 06		18 18	18 35	18 49	19 04	19 18	19 33	19 49	20 03	20 19		20 33

A from Hastings

B from Tunbridge Wells

Hastings and Tunbridge Wells - Tonbridge and London

Network Diagram - see first Page of Table 206

		SE	SE	SE	SE	SE	SE	SE	SE		SE	SE	SE
Ore	d												
Hastings	d			19 50			20 50				21 50	22 10	
St Leonards Warrior Sq	d			19 53			20 53				21 53	22 13	
West St Leonards	d			19 56			20 56				21 56	22 16	
Crowhurst	d			20 02			21 02				22 02	22 22	
Battle	d			20 06			21 06				22 06	22 26	
Robertsbridge	d			20 14			21 14				22 14	22 33	
Etchingham	d			20 17			21 17				22 17	22 37	
Stonegate	d			20 23			21 23				22 23	22 42	
Wadhurst	d			20 29			21 29				22 29	22 49	
Frant	d			20 33			21 33				22 33	22 53	
Tunbridge Wells	a			20 38			21 38				22 38	22 58	
	d	19 51	20 21	20 39	20 51	21 21	21 39	21 51	22 21		22 39	22 59	23 33
High Brooms	d	19 54	20 24	20 42	20 54	21 24	21 42	21 54	22 24		22 42	23 02	23 36
Tonbridge	a	20 00	20 30	20 48	21 00	21 30	21 48	22 00	22 30		22 48	23 08	23 42
Sevenoaks	a	20 13	20 43	20 58	21 13	21 43	21 58	22 13	22 41		22 58	23 24	
Orpington	a	20 23	20 52	21 08	21 22	21 52	22 08	22 22	22 52		23 08	23 36	
London Bridge ⊖	a	20 39	21 08	21 24	21 38	22 08	22 24	22 38	23 08		23 24	23 54	
London Cannon Street ⊖	a												
London Waterloo (East) ⊖	a	20 44	21 13	21 29	21 43	22 13	22 29	22 43	23 13		23 29	23 59	
London Charing Cross ⊖	a	20 48	21 18	21 33	21 48	22 18	22 33	22 48	23 18		23 33	00 03	

Saturdays

		SE	SE	SE	SE	SE	SE	SE	SE	SE		SE	SE	SE	SE	SE	SE	SE	SE	SE		SE	SE	SE	SE
Ore	d																								
Hastings	d	22p10		05 50	06 20		06 50		07 20			07 50		08 20		08 50		09 31		09 50			10 31		10 50
St Leonards Warrior Sq	d	22p13		05 53	06 23		06 53		07 23			07 53		08 23		08 53		09 34		09 53			10 34		10 53
West St Leonards	d	22p16		05 56	06 26		06 56		07 26			07 56		08 26		08 56				09 56					10 56
Crowhurst	d	22p22		06 02	06 32		07 02		07 32			08 02		08 32		09 02				10 02					11 02
Battle	d	22p26		06 06	06 36		07 06		07 36			08 06		08 36		09 06		09 44		10 06			10 44		11 06
Robertsbridge	d	22p33		06 13	06 43		07 13		07 44			08 13		08 44		09 14				10 13					11 13
Etchingham	d	22p37		06 17	06 47		07 17		07 47			08 17		08 47		09 17				10 17					11 17
Stonegate	d	22p42		06 23	06 53		07 23		07 53			08 23		08 53		09 23				10 23					11 23
Wadhurst	d	22p49		06 29	06 59		07 29		07 59			08 29		08 59		09 29		10 00		10 29			11 00		11 29
Frant	d	22p53		06 33	07 03		07 33		08 03			08 33		09 03		09 33				10 33					11 33
Tunbridge Wells	a	22p58		06 38	07 08		07 38		08 08			08 38		09 08		09 38		10 07		10 38			11 07		11 38
	d	22p59	05 48	06 39	07 09	07 21	07 39	07 51	08 09	08 21		08 39	08 51	09 09	09 21	09 39	09 51	10 09	10 21	10 39		10 51	11 09	11 21	11 39
High Brooms	d	23p02	05 51	06 42	07 12	07 24	07 42	07 54	08 12	08 24		08 42	08 54	09 12	09 24	09 42	09 54	10 12	10 24	10 42		10 54	11 12	11 24	11 42
Tonbridge	a	23p08	05 57	06 48	07 18	07 30	07 48	08 00	08 18	08 30		08 48	09 00	09 18	09 30	09 48	10 00	10 18	10 30	10 48		11 00	11 18	11 30	11 48
Sevenoaks	a	23p24		06 58	07 28	07 43	07 58	08 13	08 28	08 43		08 58	09 13	09 28	09 43	09 58	10 13	10 28	10 43	10 58		11 13	11 28	11 43	11 58
Orpington	a	23p36		07 08	07 38	07 53	08 08	08 23	08 38	08 53		09 08	09 23	09 38	09 53	10 08	10 23	10 38	10 53	11 08		11 23	11 38	11 53	12 08
London Bridge ⊖	a	23p54		07 24	07 55	08 10	08 25	08 40	08 55	09 10		09 25	09 40	09 55	10 10	10 25	10 40	10 55	11 10	11 25		11 40	11 55	12 10	12 25
London Cannon Street ⊖	a																								
London Waterloo (East) ⊖	a	23p59		07 29	07 59	08 15	08 29	08 45	08 59	09 15		09 29	09 45	09 59	10 15	10 29	10 45	10 59	11 15	11 29		11 45	11 59	12 15	12 29
London Charing Cross ⊖	a	00 03		07 33	08 03	08 19	08 33	08 49	09 03	09 19		09 33	09 49	10 03	10 19	10 33	10 49	11 03	11 19	11 33		11 49	12 03	12 19	12 33

		SE	SE	SE	SE	SE		SE	SE	SE	SE	SE	SE	SE	SE	SE		SE	SE	SE	SE	SE	SE	SE	SE
Ore	d																								
Hastings	d		11 31		11 50			12 31		12 50		13 31		13 50		14 31			14 50		15 31		15 50		16 31
St Leonards Warrior Sq	d		11 34		11 53			12 34		12 53		13 34		13 53		14 34			14 53		15 34		15 53		16 34
West St Leonards	d				11 56					12 56				13 56					14 56				15 56		
Crowhurst	d				12 02					13 02				14 02					15 02				16 02		
Battle	d		11 44		12 06			12 44		13 06		13 44		14 06		14 44			15 06		15 44		16 06		16 44
Robertsbridge	d				12 13					13 13				14 13					15 13				16 13		
Etchingham	d				12 17					13 17				14 17					15 17				16 17		
Stonegate	d				12 23					13 23				14 23					15 23				16 23		
Wadhurst	d		12 00		12 29			13 00		13 29		14 00		14 29		15 00			15 29		16 00		16 29		17 00
Frant	d				12 33					13 33				14 33					15 33				16 33		
Tunbridge Wells	a		12 07		12 38			13 07		13 38		14 07		14 38		15 07			15 38		16 07		16 38		17 07
	d	11 51	12 09	12 21	12 39	12 51		13 09	13 21	13 39	13 51	14 09	14 21	14 39	14 51	15 09		15 21	15 39	15 51	16 09	16 21	16 39	16 51	17 09
High Brooms	d	11 54	12 12	12 24	12 42	12 54		13 12	13 24	13 42	13 54	14 12	14 24	14 42	14 54	15 12		15 24	15 42	15 54	16 12	16 24	16 42	16 54	17 12
Tonbridge	a	12 00	12 18	12 30	12 48	13 00		13 18	13 30	13 48	14 00	14 18	14 30	14 48	15 00	15 18		15 30	15 48	16 00	16 18	16 30	16 48	17 00	17 18
Sevenoaks	a	12 13	12 28	12 43	12 58	13 13		13 28	13 43	13 58	14 13	14 28	14 43	14 58	15 13	15 28		15 43	15 58	16 13	16 28	16 43	16 58	17 13	17 28
Orpington	a	12 23	12 38	12 53	13 08	13 23		13 38	13 53	14 08	14 23	14 38	14 53	15 08	15 23	15 38		15 53	16 08	16 23	16 38	16 53	17 08	17 23	17 38
London Bridge ⊖	a	12 40	12 55	13 10	13 25	13 40		13 55	14 10	14 25	14 40	14 55	15 10	15 25	15 40	15 55		16 10	16 25	16 40	16 55	17 10	17 25	17 40	17 55
London Cannon Street ⊖	a																								
London Waterloo (East) ⊖	a	12 45	12 59	13 15	13 29	13 45		13 59	14 15	14 29	14 45	14 59	15 15	15 29	15 45	15 59		16 15	16 29	16 45	16 59	17 15	17 29	17 45	17 59
London Charing Cross ⊖	a	12 49	13 03	13 19	13 33	13 49		14 03	14 19	14 33	14 49	15 03	15 19	15 33	15 49	16 03		16 19	16 33	16 49	17 03	17 19	17 33	17 49	18 03

Table 206

Saturdays

Hastings and Tunbridge Wells - Tonbridge and London

Network Diagram - see first Page of Table 206

		SE 1		SE 1	SE 1	SE 1	SE 1	SE 1	SE 1	SE 1	SE 1	SE 1		SE 1	SE 1	SE 1	SE 1	SE 1	SE 1
Ore	d																		
Hastings 4	d			16 50		17 20		17 50		18 50		19 50			20 50		21 50	22 10	
St Leonards Warrior Sq 4	d			16 53		17 23		17 53		18 53		19 53			20 53		21 53	22 13	
West St Leonards	d			16 56		17 26		17 56		18 56		19 56			20 56		21 56	22 16	
Crowhurst	d			17 02		17 32		18 02		19 02		20 02			21 02		22 02	22 22	
Battle	d			17 06		17 36		18 06		19 06		20 06			21 06		22 06	22 26	
Robertsbridge	d			17 13		17 44		18 13		19 13		20 13			21 13		22 13	22 33	
Etchingham	d			17 17		17 47		18 17		19 17		20 17			21 17		22 17	22 37	
Stonegate	d			17 23		17 53		18 23		19 23		20 23			21 23		22 23	22 42	
Wadhurst	d			17 29		17 59		18 29		19 29		20 29			21 29		22 29	22 49	
Frant	d			17 33		18 03		18 33		19 33		20 33			21 33		22 33	22 53	
Tunbridge Wells 4	a			17 38		18 08		18 38		19 38		20 38			21 38		22 38	22 58	
	d	17 21		17 39	17 51	18 09	18 21	18 39	19 08	19 39	20 08	20 39		21 05	21 39	22 05	22 39	22 59	23 33
High Brooms	d	17 24		17 42	17 54	18 12	18 24	18 42	19 11	19 42	20 11	20 42		21 08	21 42	22 08	22 42	23 02	23 36
Tonbridge 4	a	17 30		17 48	18 00	18 18	18 30	18 48	19 17	19 48	20 17	20 48		21 14	21 48	22 14	22 48	23 08	23 45
Sevenoaks 4	a	17 43		17 58	18 13	18 28	18 43	18 58	19 28	19 58	20 28	20 58		21 28	21 58	22 28	22 58	23 24	
Orpington 4	a	17 53		18 08	18 23	18 38	18 53	19 08	19 38	20 08	20 38	21 08		21 38	22 08	22 38	23 08	23 36	
London Bridge 4 ⊖	a	18 10		18 25	18 40	18 55	19 10	19 24	19 54	20 24	20 54	21 24		21 54	22 24	22 54	23 24	23 54	
London Cannon Street 4 ⊖	a																		
London Waterloo (East) 4 ⊖	a	18 15		18 29	18 45	18 59	19 15	19 29	19 59	20 29	20 59	21 29		21 59	22 29	22 59	23 29	23 59	
London Charing Cross 4 ⊖	a	18 19		18 33	18 49	19 03	19 19	19 33	20 03	20 33	21 03	21 33		22 03	22 33	23 03	23 33	00 03	

Sundays

		SE 1 A	SE 1	SE 1	SE 1	SE 1	SE 1	SE 1	SE 1	SE 1		SE 1	SE 1	SE 1	SE 1	SE 1	SE 1	SE 1	SE 1	SE 1		SE 1	SE 1	SE 1	SE 1
Ore	d																								
Hastings 4	d	22p10	07 27		08 27	09 08	09 27	10 08	10 27	11 08		11 27	12 08	12 27	13 08	13 27	14 08	14 27	15 08	15 27		16 08	16 27	17 08	17 27
St Leonards Warrior Sq 4	d	22p13	07 29		08 29	09 11	09 29	10 11	10 29	11 11		11 29	12 11	12 29	13 11	13 29	14 11	14 29	15 11	15 29		16 11	16 29	17 11	17 29
West St Leonards	d	22p16	07 33		08 33		09 33		10 33			11 33		12 33		13 33		14 33		15 33			16 33		17 33
Crowhurst	d	22p22	07 38		08 38		09 38		10 38			11 38		12 38		13 38		14 38		15 38			16 38		17 38
Battle	d	22p26	07 43		08 43	09 21	09 43	10 21	10 43	11 21		11 43	12 21	12 43	13 21	13 43	14 21	14 43	15 21	15 43		16 21	16 43	17 21	17 43
Robertsbridge	d	22p33	07 50		08 50		09 50		10 50			11 50		12 50		13 50		14 50		15 50			16 50		17 50
Etchingham	d	22p37	07 53		08 53		09 53		10 53			11 53		12 53		13 53		14 53		15 53			16 53		17 53
Stonegate	d	22p42	07 59		08 59		09 59		10 59			11 59		12 59		13 59		14 59		15 59			16 59		17 59
Wadhurst	d	22p49	08 05		09 05	09 37	10 05	10 37	11 05	11 37		12 05	12 37	13 05	13 37	14 05	14 37	15 05	15 37	16 05		16 37	17 05	17 37	18 05
Frant	d	22p53	08 09		09 09		10 09		11 09			12 09		13 09		14 09		15 09		16 09			17 09		18 09
Tunbridge Wells 4	a	22p58	08 14		09 14	09 44	10 14	10 44	11 14	11 44		12 14	12 44	13 14	13 44	14 14	14 44	15 14	15 44	16 14		16 44	17 14	17 44	18 14
	d	22p59	08 15	08 45	09 15	09 45	10 15	10 45	11 15	11 45		12 15	12 45	13 15	13 45	14 15	14 45	15 15	15 45	16 15		16 45	17 15	17 45	18 15
High Brooms	d	23p02	08 18	08 48	09 18	09 48	10 18	10 48	11 18	11 48		12 18	12 48	13 18	13 48	14 18	14 48	15 18	15 48	16 18		16 48	17 18	17 48	18 18
Tonbridge 4	a	23p08	08 24	08 54	09 24	09 54	10 24	10 54	11 24	11 54		12 24	12 54	13 24	13 54	14 24	14 54	15 24	15 54	16 24		16 54	17 24	17 54	18 24
Sevenoaks 4	a	23p24	08 33	09 03	09 33	10 03	10 33	11 03	11 33	12 03		12 33	13 03	13 33	14 03	14 33	15 03	15 33	16 03	16 33		17 03	17 33	18 03	18 33
Orpington 4	a	23p36	08 42	09 12	09 42	10 12	10 42	11 12	11 42	12 12		12 42	13 12	13 42	14 12	14 42	15 12	15 42	16 12	16 42		17 12	17 42	18 12	18 42
London Bridge 4 ⊖	a	23p54	08 58	09 28	09 58	10 28	10 58	11 28	11 58	12 28		12 58	13 28	13 58	14 28	14 58	15 28	15 58	16 28	16 58		17 28	17 58	18 28	18 58
London Cannon Street 4 ⊖	a																								
London Waterloo (East) 4 ⊖	a	23p59	09 03	09 33	10 03	10 33	11 03	11 33	12 03	12 33		13 03	13 33	14 03	14 33	15 03	15 33	16 03	16 33	17 03		17 33	18 03	18 33	19 03
London Charing Cross 4 ⊖	a	00 03	09 07	09 37	10 07	10 37	11 07	11 37	12 07	12 37		13 07	13 37	14 07	14 37	15 07	15 37	16 07	16 37	17 07		17 37	18 07	18 37	19 07

		SE 1	SE 1	SE 1	SE 1	SE 1		SE 1	SE 1
Ore	d								
Hastings 4	d	18 08	18 27	19 27		20 27		21 27	22 27
St Leonards Warrior Sq 4	d	18 11	18 29	19 29		20 29		21 29	22 29
West St Leonards	d		18 33	19 33		20 33		21 33	22 33
Crowhurst	d		18 38	19 38		20 38		21 38	22 38
Battle	d	18 21	18 43	19 43		20 43		21 43	22 43
Robertsbridge	d		18 50	19 50		20 50		21 50	22 50
Etchingham	d		18 53	19 53		20 53		21 53	22 53
Stonegate	d		18 59	19 59		20 59		21 59	22 59
Wadhurst	d	18 37	19 05	20 05		21 05		22 05	23 05
Frant	d		19 09	20 09		21 09		22 09	23 09
Tunbridge Wells 4	a	18 44	19 14	20 14		21 14		22 14	23 14
	d	18 45	19 15	20 15	20 53	21 15		22 15	23 15
High Brooms	d	18 48	19 18	20 18	20 56	21 18		22 18	23 18
Tonbridge 4	a	18 54	19 24	20 24	21 02	21 24		22 24	23 24
Sevenoaks 4	a	19 03	19 33	20 33		21 33		22 33	
Orpington 4	a	19 12	19 42	20 42		21 42		22 42	
London Bridge 4 ⊖	a	19 28	19 58	20 58		21 58		22 58	
London Cannon Street 4 ⊖	a								
London Waterloo (East) 4 ⊖	a	19 33	20 03	21 03		22 03		23 03	
London Charing Cross 4 ⊖	a	19 37	20 07	21 07		22 07		23 07	

A not 11 December

London and Tonbridge - Ashford International, Folkestone, Dover, Canterbury West, Ramsgate and Margate

Network Diagram - see first Page of Table 206

Miles	Miles	Miles	Miles			SE MX 1	SE MO 1	SE MX 1	SE	SE MO 1	SE MX 1		SE MO 1	SE MO		SE MX 1	SE MX 1	SE MO 1	SE MX 1		SE MX		SE 1	SE	
—	—	—	0	St Pancras Intl. 15 ⊖	d				23p12					23p42							00 12				
—	—	—	6	Stratford International ⊖	d				23p19					23p49							00 19				
—	—	—	22¾	Ebbsfleet International	d				23p31					00 01							00 31				
0	—	—	—	London Charing Cross 4 ⊖	d	21p40	22p08	22p10		22p38	22p40		23p08				23p10	23p38	23p40						
0¾	—	—	—	London Waterloo (East) 4 ⊖	d	21p43	22p11	22p13		22p41	22p43		23p11				23p13	23p41	23p43						
—	—	—	—	London Cannon Street 4 ⊖	d																				
1¾	—	—	—	London Bridge 4 ⊖	d	21p49	22p16	22p19		22p46	22p49		23p16				23p19	23p46	23p49						
13¾	—	—	—	Orpington 4	d		22p32	22p35		23p02			23p32				23p35	00 02							
22	—	—	—	Sevenoaks 4	d	22p12	22p42	22p44		23p12	23p12		23p42				23p44	00 12	00 12						
29½	—	—	—	Tonbridge 4	a	22p20	22p52	22p52		23p20	23p20		23p52				23p52	00 20	00 20						
—	—	—	—		d	22p20	22p52	22p53		23p20	23p20		23p52				23p53	00 20	00 20				04 50		
34¾	—	—	—	Paddock Wood 4	d	22p28	23p00	23p00		23p28	23p28		23p59				23p59	00 28	00 28				04 58	05 42	
—	—	—	—	Maidstone West 4 194	a																			06 01	
39½	—	—	—	Marden	d	22p33	23p05	23p06		23p33	23p33		00 05				00 06	00 33	00 33				05 03		
41¾	—	—	—	Staplehurst	d	22p37	23p09	23p10		23p37	23p37		00 09				00 10	00 37	00 37				05 07		
45¼	—	—	—	Headcorn	d	22p43	23p15	23p15		23p43	23p43		00 15				00 15	00 43	00 43				05 13		
50½	—	—	—	Pluckley	d	22p49		23p21		23p49	23p49						00 21	00 49	00 49				05 19		
56	0	—	56	Ashford International	a	22p56	23p26	23p29	23p50	23p56	23p56		00 26	00 20			00 29	00 56	00 56		00 50		05 27		
—	—	—	—																						
—	—	—	—		d	23p00	23p30	23p32	23p52	00 01	00 01	00 03				00 03	00 32		01 00	01 03			05 30		
—	4¼	—	—	Wye	d							00 09				00 09				01 09					
—	9	—	—	Chilham	d							00 15				00 15				01 15					
—	11	—	—	Chartham	d							00 19				00 19				01 19					
—	14¼	—	—	Canterbury West 4	d							00 25				00 25				01a24					
—	16½	—	—	Sturry	d							00 29				00 29									
64¼	—	—	—	Westenhanger	d	23p08	23p38	23p41			00 09						00 41		01 08				05 38		
65½	—	—	—	Sandling	d	23p11	23p41	23p43		00 11	00 12						00 43		01 11				05 41		
69¼	—	—	—	Folkestone West	d	23p17	23p47	23p49	00 05	00 17	00 18						00 49		01 17				05 47		
70	—	—	—	Folkestone Central	d	23p20	23p50	23p52	00 08	00 19	00 21						00 52		01 20				05 50		
77¼	—	—	—	Dover Priory 4	a	23p31	00 01	00 05	00 20	00 30	00 32						01 03		01 31				06 01		
—	—	—	—		d	23p32	00 02	00 06															06 02		
82¼	—	—	—	Martin Mill	d	23p41	00 11	00 15															06 11		
85	—	—	—	Walmer	d	23p45	00 15	00 19															06 15		
86½	—	—	—	Deal	d	23p49	00 19	00 23															06 19		
90¾	—	—	—	Sandwich	d	23p56	00 26	00 30															06 26		
—	25½	4¾	—	Minster 4	d							00 41				00 41									
99	29½	—	—	Ramsgate 4	a	00 08	00 38	00 42				00 47				00 47							06 38		
101¼	31¾	—	—	Broadstairs	a																				
104½	35	—	—	Margate 4	a																				

		SE 1	SE	SE 1	SE 1	SE 1	SE	SE	SE 1	SE		SE	SE 1	SE	SE 1	SE	SE 1		SE	SE		SE 1		SE	
St Pancras Intl. 15 ⊖	d							06 25		06 40		07 10				07 40				08 10				08 40	
Stratford International ⊖	d							06 32		06 47		07 17				07 47				08 17				08 47	
Ebbsfleet International	d							06 42		06 59		07 29				08 00				08 30				09 00	
London Charing Cross 4 ⊖	d					05 30							06 30				07 10					07 40			
London Waterloo (East) 4 ⊖	d					05 33							06 33				07 13					07 43			
London Cannon Street 4 ⊖	d																								
London Bridge 4 ⊖	d					05 39							06 38				07 19					07 49			
Orpington 4	d					05 55							06 54												
Sevenoaks 4	d					06 06							07 03				07 43					08 12			
Tonbridge 4	a					06 16							07 13				07 51					08 20			
	d					06 20							07 14				07 51					08 20			
Paddock Wood 4	d		06 20			06 28	06 50						07 22	07 40			07 59		08 10			08 28			
Maidstone West 4 194	a		06 39				07 09	07 12						07 59					08 29						
Marden	d					06 33							07 27				08 04					08 33			
Staplehurst	d					06 37							07 31				08 08					08 37			
Headcorn	d					06 43							07 37				08 14					08 43			
Pluckley	d					06 49							07 43				08 20					08 49			
Ashford International	a					06 58				07 18		07 48	07 51			08 20	08 27			08 50		08 57		09 20	
	d	06 02		06 30	06 33	07 00			07 03	07 22		07 50	07 52		07 58	08 22	08 31	08 34		08 52		09 00	09 03	09 22	
Wye	d				06 39				07 09				07 58					08 40					09 09		
Chilham	d				06 45				07 15				08 04					08 46							
Chartham	d				06 49				07 19				08 08					08 50							
Canterbury West 4	d				06 55				07a24	07 39			08 15			08 39		08a55					09 22	09 39	
Sturry	d				06 59					07 44			08 19										09 26		
Westenhanger	d	06 10		06 38		07 08									08 08		08 39					09 08			
Sandling	d	06 13		06 41		07 11									08 11		08 42					09 11			
Folkestone West	d	06 19		06 47		07 17						08 03			08 17		08 47			09 05		09 17			
Folkestone Central	d	06 22		06 50		07 20						08 06			08 20		08 50			09 08		09 20			
Dover Priory 4	a	06 33		07 00		07 31						08 18			08 31		09 01			09 20		09 31			
	d			07 07		07 50									08 32							09 32			
Martin Mill	d			07 16		07 59									08 41							09 41			
Walmer	d			07 20		08 04									08 45							09 45			
Deal	d			07 25		08 08									08 49							09 49			
Sandwich	d			07 32		08 16									08 56							09 56			
Minster 4	d				07 11					07 55			08 31										09 38		
Ramsgate 4	a			07 44	07 17	08 29				08 00			08 38		09 08	08 59						10 08	09 44	09 59	
Broadstairs	a									08 06						09 04								10 04	
Margate 4	a									08 11						09 10								10 10	

London and Tonbridge - Ashford International, Folkestone, Dover, Canterbury West, Ramsgate and Margate

Network Diagram - see first Page of Table 206

		SE 1		SE	SE	SE 1			SE 1	SE	SE 1		SE	SE	SE 1		SE		SE 1		SE	SE	SE 1		SE
St Pancras Intl. 15 ⊖	d				09 10					09 42				10 10			10 40					11 12			11 42
Stratford International ⊖	d				09 17					09 49				10 17			10 47					11 19			11 49
Ebbsfleet International	d				09 29					10 01				10 29			10 59					11 31			12 01
London Charing Cross 4 ⊖	d	08 13				08 33			08 53		09 13				09 40				10 10				10 40		
London Waterloo (East) 4 ⊖	d	08 16				08 36			08 56		09 16				09 43				10 13				10 43		
London Cannon Street 4 ⊖	d																								
London Bridge 4 ⊖	d	08 21				08 41			09 01		09 21				09 49				10 19				10 49		
Orpington 4	d					08 58			09 21																
Sevenoaks 4	d	08 45				09 07			09 31		09 44				10 12				10 42				11 12		
Tonbridge 4	a	08 53				09 18			09 40		09 52				10 20				10 50				11 20		
	d	08 53		09 03		09 20			09 42		09 52		10 03		10 20				10 50		11 04		11 20		
Paddock Wood 4	d	09 01		09 10		09 28					10 00		10 10		10 28				10 58		11 11		11 28		
Maidstone West 4 194	a			09 29									10 29								11 30				
Marden	d	09 06				09 33					10 05				10 33				11 03				11 33		
Staplehurst	d	09 10				09 37					10 09				10 37				11 07				11 37		
Headcorn	d	09 16				09 43					10 15				10 43				11 13				11 43		
Pluckley	d	09 22				09 49					10 21				10 49				11 19				11 49		
Ashford International	a	09 29			09 50	09 56			10 12	10 20	10 28			10 48	10 56		11 18		11 26			11 50	11 56		12 20
	d	09 33	09 36		09 52	10 00	10 03			10 22	10 32	10 34		10 52	11 00	11 03	11 22		11 30	11 33		11 52	12 00	12 03	12 22
Wye	d		09 42				10 09					10 40				11 09				11 39				12 09	
Chilham	d		09 48									10 46								11 45					
Chartham	d		09 52									10 50								11 49					
Canterbury West 4	d		09a57				10 22			10 39		10a55				11 22	11 39			11a54				12 22	12 39
Sturry	d						10 26									11 26								12 26	
Westenhanger	d	09 41				10 08					10 40				11 08				11 38				12 08		
Sandling	d	09 44				10 11					10 43				11 11				11 41				12 11		
Folkestone West	d	09 49			10 05	10 17					10 48			11 05	11 17				11 47			12 05	12 17		
Folkestone Central	d	09 52			10 08	10 20					10 51			11 08	11 20				11 50			12 08	12 20		
Dover Priory 4	a	10 03			10 20	10 31					11 02			11 20	11 31				12 01			12 20	12 31		
	d					10 32									11 32								12 32		
Martin Mill	d					10 41									11 41								12 41		
Walmer	d					10 45									11 45								12 45		
Deal	d					10 49									11 49								12 49		
Sandwich	d					10 56									11 56								12 56		
Minster 4	d						10 38									11 38								12 38	
Ramsgate 4	a					11 08	10 44			10 59					12 08	11 44	11 59						13 08	12 44	12 59
Broadstairs	a									11 04							12 04								13 04
Margate 4	a									11 10							12 10								13 10

		SE 1			SE	SE	SE 1		SE	SE 1		SE	SE		SE 1		SE	SE 1		SE	SE	SE 1			SE
St Pancras Intl. 15 ⊖	d					12 12			12 42				13 12				13 42				14 12				14 42
Stratford International ⊖	d					12 19			12 49				13 19				13 49				14 19				14 49
Ebbsfleet International	d					12 31			13 01				13 31				14 01				14 31				15 01
London Charing Cross 4 ⊖	d	11 10					11 40			12 10					12 40			13 10				13 40			
London Waterloo (East) 4 ⊖	d	11 13					11 43			12 13					12 43			13 13				13 43			
London Cannon Street 4 ⊖	d																								
London Bridge 4 ⊖	d	11 19					11 49			12 19					12 49			13 19				13 49			
Orpington 4	d																								
Sevenoaks 4	d	11 42					12 12			12 42					13 12			13 42				14 12			
Tonbridge 4	a	11 50					12 20			12 50					13 20			13 50				14 20			
	d	11 50			12 03		12 20			12 50		13 03			13 20			13 50		14 03		14 20			
Paddock Wood 4	d	11 58			12 10		12 28			12 58		13 10			13 28			13 58		14 10		14 28			
Maidstone West 4 194	a				12 29							13 29								14 29					
Marden	d	12 03					12 33			13 03					13 33			14 03				14 33			
Staplehurst	d	12 07					12 37			13 07					13 37			14 07				14 37			
Headcorn	d	12 13					12 43			13 13					13 43			14 13				14 43			
Pluckley	d	12 19					12 49			13 19					13 49			14 19				14 49			
Ashford International	a	12 26				12 50	12 56		13 20	13 26			13 50		13 56		14 20	14 26			14 50	14 56			15 20
	d	12 30	12 33			12 52	13 00	13 03	13 22	13 30	13 33		13 52		14 00	14 03	14 22	14 30	14 33		14 52	15 00	15 03		15 22
Wye	d		12 39					13 09			13 39					14 09			14 39				15 09		
Chilham	d		12 45								13 45								14 45						
Chartham	d		12 49								13 49								14 49						
Canterbury West 4	d		12a54					13 22	13 39		13a54					14 22	14 39		14a54				15 22		15 39
Sturry	d							13 26								14 26							15 26		
Westenhanger	d	12 38					13 08			13 38					14 08			14 38				15 08			
Sandling	d	12 41					13 11			13 41					14 11			14 41				15 11			
Folkestone West	d	12 47				13 05	13 17			13 47			14 05		14 17			14 47			15 05	15 17			
Folkestone Central	d	12 50				13 08	13 20			13 50			14 08		14 20			14 50			15 08	15 20			
Dover Priory 4	a	13 01				13 20	13 31			14 01			14 20		14 31			15 01			15 20	15 31			
	d						13 32								14 32							15 32			
Martin Mill	d						13 41								14 41							15 41			
Walmer	d						13 45								14 45							15 45			
Deal	d						13 49								14 49							15 49			
Sandwich	d						13 56								14 56							15 56			
Minster 4	d							13 38								14 38						16 08	15 38		
Ramsgate 4	a						14 08	13 44	13 59						15 08	14 44	14 59					16 14	15 44		15 59
Broadstairs	a								14 04								15 04								16 04
Margate 4	a								14 10								15 10								16 10

London and Tonbridge - Ashford International, Folkestone, Dover, Canterbury West, Ramsgate and Margate

Network Diagram - see first Page of Table 206

Station		SE 1		SE	SE	SE 1		SE	SE 1			SE	SE	SE 1		SE	SE 1		SE	SE			SE 1		SE 1
St Pancras Intl. 15 ⊖	d				15 12			15 42					16 10			16 42				17 10					
Stratford International ⊖	d				15 19			15 49					16 17			16 49				17 17					
Ebbsfleet International	d				15 31			16 01					16 29			17 01									
London Charing Cross 4 ⊖	d	14 10				14 40			15 10					15 40			16 10						16 37		
London Waterloo (East) 4 ⊖	d	14 13				14 43			15 13					15 43			16 13						16 40		
London Cannon Street 4 ⊖	d																								16 46
London Bridge 4 ⊖	d	14 19				14 49			15 19					15 49			16 19						16 45		16 50
Orpington 4	d																								
Sevenoaks 4	d	14 42				15 12			15 42					16 12			16 43						17 10		
Tonbridge 4	a	14 50				15 20			15 50					16 20			16 51						17 18		
	d	14 50		15 03		15 20			15 50			16 03		16 20			16 51						17 18		
Paddock Wood 4	d	14 58		15 10		15 28			15 58			16 10		16 28			16 59		17 02				17 26		
Maidstone West 4 194	a			15 29								16 29							17 21						
Marden	d	15 03				15 33			16 03					16 33			17 04						17 32		
Staplehurst	d	15 07				15 37			16 07					16 37			17 08						17 36		
Headcorn	d	15 13				15 43			16 13					16 43			17 14						17 42		
Pluckley	d	15 19				15 49			16 19					16 49			17 20						17 48		
Ashford International	a	15 26			15 50	15 56		16 20	16 26				16 48	16 56		17 20	17 27			17 46			17 56		
	d	15 30	15 33		15 52	16 00	16 03	16 22	16 30	16 35			16 52	17 00	17 03	17 23	17 31	17 35		17 50	17 53		18 00	18 03	
Wye	d		15 39				16 09			16 41					17 09			17 41						18 09	
Chilham	d		15 45							16 47					17 15			17 47						18 15	
Chartham	d		15 49							16 51					17 19			17 51						18 19	
Canterbury West 4	d		15a54				16 22	16 39		16a56					17 25	17 40		17a58			18 10			18 25	
Sturry	d						16 26								17 29									18 29	
Westenhanger	d	15 38				16 08			16 38					17 08			17 39						18 08		
Sandling	d	15 41				16 11			16 41					17 11			17 42						18 11		
Folkestone West	d	15 47			16 05	16 17			16 47				17 05	17 17			17 47			18 03			18 17		
Folkestone Central	d	15 50			16 08	16 20			16 50				17 08	17 20			17 50			18 06			18 20		
Dover Priory 4	a	16 01			16 20	16 31			17 01				17 20	17 31			18 01			18 18			18 31		
	d	16 02				16 32			17 02					17 32			18 02						18 32		
Martin Mill	d	16 11				16 41			17 11					17 41			18 11						18 41		
Walmer	d	16 15				16 45			17 15					17 45			18 15						18 45		
Deal	d	16 19				16 49			17 19					17 49			18 19						18 49		
Sandwich	d	16 26				16 56			17 26					17 56			18 26						18 56		
Minster 4	d					17 08	16 38								17 41									18 41	
Ramsgate 4	a	16 38				17 14	16 44	16 59	17 38					18 08	17 47	17 59	18 40				18 29		19 10	18 49	
Broadstairs	a							17 04								18 04					18 34				
Margate 4	a							17 10								18 10					18 40				18 28

Station		SE 1	SE	SE 1	SE	SE	SE			SE	SE 1	SE 1	SE 1	SE	SE	SE		SE 1		SE 1	SE 1	SE	SE	SE	SE 1
St Pancras Intl. 15 ⊖	d				17 14	17 25	17 40							17 44	17 55	18 10							18 14	18 25	
Stratford International ⊖	d				17 21	17 32	17 47							17 51	18 02	18 17							18 21	18 32	
Ebbsfleet International	d					17 43									18 13									18 43	
London Charing Cross 4 ⊖	d			16 57							17 14									17 41					18 03
London Waterloo (East) 4 ⊖	d			17 00							17 18									17 44					18 06
London Cannon Street 4 ⊖	d	17 08										17 24	17 30					17 45			17 52				
London Bridge 4 ⊖	d	17 12										17 28	17 34					17 49			17 56				
Orpington 4	d																								
Sevenoaks 4	d			17 27							17 46	17 54						18 16		18 11					18 34
Tonbridge 4	a			17 35							17 54	18 04						18 24		18 19					18 42
	d			17 36							17 54	18 05						18 25		18 20					18 43
Paddock Wood 4	d		17 30	17 43						17 52	18 02	18 12						18 32		18 28		18 42			18 50
Maidstone West 4 194	a		17 49		18 02					18 11				18 32								19 01	19 05		
Marden	d			17 49							18 08	18 18						18 38		18 33					18 56
Staplehurst	d			17 53							18 12	18 22						18 42		18 37					19 00
Headcorn	d			17 59							18 18	18 28						18 48		18 43					19 06
Pluckley	d			18 05								18 34						18 54		18 49					
Ashford International	a			18 15			18 16				18 30	18 42				18 46		19 01		18 58					19 18
	d						18 20	18 23			18 32	18 44				18 50	18 53	19 03		19 04					19 23
Wye	d										18 38							19 09							
Chilham	d										18 44							19 15							
Chartham	d										18 48							19 19							
Canterbury West 4	d							18 40			18 54						19 10	19 25							
Sturry	d										18 59							19 29							
Westenhanger	d											18 53								19 12					19 31
Sandling	d											18 56								19 15					19 34
Folkestone West	d						18 33					19 01				19 05				19 20					19 40
Folkestone Central	d						18 36					19 04				19 08				19 23					19a44
Dover Priory 4	a						18 47					19 15				19 20				19 34					
	d						18 50					19 16								19 35					
Martin Mill	d											19 26								19 44					
Walmer	d											19 30								19 48					
Deal	d						19 07					19 35								19 53					
Sandwich	d						19a13					19 41								19 59					
Minster 4	d										19 10							19 41							
Ramsgate 4	a							18 59			19 19	19 56					19 30	19 49		20 14					
Broadstairs	a							19 04									19 36								
Margate 4	a	18 55				19 01		19 10					19 19		19 29		19 41				19 36			20 03	

London and Tonbridge - Ashford International, Folkestone, Dover, Canterbury West, Ramsgate and Margate

Network Diagram - see first Page of Table 206

		SE		SE 1		SE 1	SE 1	SE	SE 1	SE 1	SE		SE 1			SE	SE	SE 1		SE	SE 1		SE	SE	
St Pancras Intl. 15 ⊖	d	18 40									19 10						19 42			20 12				20 42	
Stratford International ⊖	d	18 47									19 17						19 49			20 19				20 49	
Ebbsfleet International	d										19 29						20 01			20 31				21 01	
London Charing Cross 4 ⊖	d						18 21						18 41					19 10			19 40				
London Waterloo (East) 4 ⊖	d						18 24						18 44					19 13			19 43				
London Cannon Street 4 ⊖	d			18 08		18 14			18 32	18 44															
London Bridge 4 ⊖	d			18 12		18 18			18 36	18 48			18 50					19 19			19 49				
Orpington 4	d												19 07												
Sevenoaks 4	d			18 38			18 52		19 00				19 17					19 42			20 12				
Tonbridge 4	a			18 48			19 00		19 08				19 25					19 53			20 20				
	d			18 49			19 01		19 09				19 25					19 54			20 20		20 33		
Paddock Wood 4	d			18 56			19 09	19 12	19 17				19 33			19 42		20 01			20 28		20 40		
Maidstone West 4 194	a							19 31								20 01							20 59		
Marden	d			19 02					19 23				19 38					20 07			20 33				
Staplehurst	d			19 06			19 17		19 27				19 42					20 11			20 37				
Headcorn	d			19 12			19 23		19 33				19 48					20 17			20 43				
Pluckley	d			19 18					19 39				19 54					20 23			20 49				
Ashford International	a	19 16		19 27			19 35		19 49		19 48		20 02				20 20	20 31		20 50	20 56			21 20	
	d	19 20	19 23	19 29			19 37				19 52	19 55	20 06	20 08			20 22	20 37	20 40	20 52	21 00	21 03		21 22	
Wye	d			19 36										20 14					20 46			21 09			
Chilham	d			19 42															20 52			21 15			
Chartham	d			19 45															20 56			21 19			
Canterbury West 4	d		19 40	19 52								20 12		20 27			20 39		21a02			21 25		21 39	
Sturry	d			19 56										20 31								21 29			
Westenhanger	d						19 45						20 14					20 45			21 08				
Sandling	d						19 48						20 17					20 48			21 11				
Folkestone West	d	19 33					19 54				20 05		20 23					20 54		21 05	21 17				
Folkestone Central	d	19 36					19 57				20 08		20 26					20 57		21 08	21 20				
Dover Priory 4	a	19 47					20 08				20 20		20 37					21 08		21 20	21 31				
	d	19 50					20 09						20 38								21 32				
Martin Mill	d						20 18						20 47								21 41				
Walmer	d						20 23						20 51								21 45				
Deal	d	20 07					20 27						20 55								21 49				
Sandwich	d	20a13					20 34						21 02								21 56				
Minster 4	d			20 08										20 43								21 41			
Ramsgate 4	a		19 59	20 18			20 48					20 32	21 16	20 52			20 59				22 08	21 47		21 59	
Broadstairs	a		20 04									20 37					21 05							22 04	
Margate 4	a		20 10			19 59				20 31		20 43					21 11							22 10	

		SE 1	SE	SE 1		SE	SE	SE 1	SE	SE 1			SE	SE	SE 1	SE	SE 1		SE 1	SE 1					
St Pancras Intl. 15 ⊖	d		21 12				21 42		22 12					22 42		23 12									
Stratford International ⊖	d		21 19				21 49		22 19					22 49		23 19									
Ebbsfleet International	d		21 31				22 01		22 31					23 01		23 31									
London Charing Cross 4 ⊖	d	20 10		20 40				21 10		21 40					22 10		22 40		23 10	23 40					
London Waterloo (East) 4 ⊖	d	20 13		20 43				21 13		21 43					22 13		22 43		23 13	23 43					
London Cannon Street 4 ⊖	d																								
London Bridge 4 ⊖	d	20 19		20 49				21 19		21 49					22 19		22 49		23 19	23 49					
Orpington 4	d							21 35							22 35				23 35						
Sevenoaks 4	d	20 42		21 12				21 44		22 12					22 44		23 12		23 44	00 12					
Tonbridge 4	a	20 50		21 20				21 52		22 20					22 52		23 20		23 52	00 20					
	d	20 50		21 20		21 33		21 53		22 20			22 33		22 53		23 20		23 53	00 20					
Paddock Wood 4	d	20 58		21 28		21 40		22 00		22 28			22 40		23 00		23 28		23 59	00 28					
Maidstone West 4 194	a					21 59							22 59												
Marden	d	21 03		21 33				22 06		22 33					23 06		23 33		00 06	00 33					
Staplehurst	d	21 07		21 37				22 10		22 37					23 10		23 37		00 10	00 37					
Headcorn	d	21 13		21 43				22 15		22 43					23 15		23 43		00 15	00 43					
Pluckley	d	21 19		21 49				22 21		22 49					23 21		23 49		00 21	00 49					
Ashford International	a	21 26	21 50	21 56			22 20	22 29	22 50	22 56				23 20	23 29	23 50	23 56		00 29	00 56					
	d	21 30	21 52	22 00	22 03		22 22	22 32	22 52	23 00	23 03			23 22	23 32	23 52	00 01	00 03	00 32	01 00	01 03				
Wye	d				22 09						23 09							00 09			01 09				
Chilham	d				22 15						23 15							00 15			01 15				
Chartham	d				22 19						23 19							00 19			01 19				
Canterbury West 4	d				22 25		22 39				23 25			23 39				00 25			01a24				
Sturry	d				22 29						23 29							00 29							
Westenhanger	d	21 38		22 08				22 41		23 08					23 41		00 09		00 41	01 08					
Sandling	d	21 41		22 11				22 43		23 11					23 43		00 12		00 43	01 11					
Folkestone West	d	21 47	22 05	22 17				22 49	23 05	23 17					23 49	00 05	00 18		00 49	01 17					
Folkestone Central	d	21 50	22 08	22 20				22 52	23 08	23 20					23 52	00 08	00 21		00 52	01 20					
Dover Priory 4	a	22 01	22 20	22 31				23 03	23 20	23 31					00 05	00 20	00 32		01 03	01 31					
	d			22 32						23 32					00 06										
Martin Mill	d			22 41						23 41					00 15										
Walmer	d			22 45						23 45					00 19										
Deal	d			22 49						23 49					00 23										
Sandwich	d			22 56						23 56					00 30										
Minster 4	d				22 41						23 41							00 41							
Ramsgate 4	a			23 08	22 47		22 59			00 08	23 47			23 59	00 42			00 47							
Broadstairs	a						23 04																		
Margate 4	a						23 10																		

Table 207

Saturdays

London and Tonbridge - Ashford International, Folkestone, Dover, Canterbury West, Ramsgate and Margate

Network Diagram - see first Page of Table 206

		SE 1	SE 1	SE	SE 1	SE 1	SE 1	SE 1	SE	SE 1		SE	SE 1	SE 1	SE	SE 1	SE	SE 1	SE	SE 1		SE	SE 1	SE	
St Pancras Intl. 15 ⊖	d			23p12					00 12						06 10		06 40					07 12		07 42	
Stratford International ⊖	d			23p19					00 19						06 17		06 47					07 19		07 49	
Ebbsfleet International	d			23p31					00 31						06 29		06 59					07 31		08 01	
London Charing Cross 4 ⊖	d	21p40	22p10		22p40		23p10	23p40										06 00							
London Waterloo (East) 4 ⊖	d	21p43	22p13		22p43		23p13	23p43										06 03							
London Cannon Street 4 ⊖	d																								
London Bridge 4 ⊖	d	21p49	22p19		22p49		23p19	23p49										06 08							
Orpington 4	d		22p35				23p35											06 24							
Sevenoaks 4	d	22p12	22p44		23p12		23p44	00 12										06 33							
Tonbridge 4	a	22p20	22p52		23p20		23p52	00 20										06 43							
	d	22p20	22p53		23p20		23p53	00 20				06 03				06 20		06 50	07 03						
Paddock Wood 4	d	22p28	23p00		23p28		23p59	00 28				06 10				06 28		06 58	07 10						
Maidstone West 4 194	a											06 29							07 29						
Marden	d	22p33	23p06		23p33		00 06	00 33								06 33		07 03							
Staplehurst	d	22p37	23p10		23p37		00 10	00 37								06 37		07 07							
Headcorn	d	22p43	23p15		23p43		00 15	00 43								06 43		07 13							
Pluckley	d	22p49	23p21		23p49		00 21	00 49								06 49		07 19							
Ashford International	a	22p56	23p29	23p50	23p56		00 29	00 56	00 50						06 48	06 56	07 18	07 26				07 51		08 20	
	d	23p00	23p32	23p52	00 01	00 03	00 32	01 00		01 03			06 30	06 33	06 52	07 03	07 22	07 30		07 33		07 52	08 03	08 22	
Wye	d					00 09				01 09				06 39		07 09				07 39			08 09		
Chilham	d					00 15				01 15				06 45						07 45					
Chartham	d					00 19				01 19				06 49						07 49					
Canterbury West 4	d					00 25				01a24				06a54		07 22	07 39			07a54			08 22	08 39	
Sturry	d					00 29										07 26							08 26		
Westenhanger	d	23p08	23p41		00 09		00 41	01 08					06 38					07 38							
Sandling	d	23p11	23p43		00 12		00 43	01 11					06 41					07 41							
Folkestone West	d	23p17	23p49	00 05	00 18		00 49	01 17					06 47		07 05			07 47				08 05			
Folkestone Central	d	23p20	23p52	00 08	00 21		00 52	01 20					06 50		07 08			07 50				08 08			
Dover Priory 4	a	23p31	00 05	00 20	00 32		01 03	01 31					07 01		07 20			08 01				08 20			
	d	23p32	00 06										07 02					08 02							
Martin Mill	d	23p41	00 15										07 11					08 11							
Walmer	d	23p45	00 19										07 15					08 15							
Deal	d	23p49	00 23										07 19					08 19							
Sandwich	d	23p56	00 30										07 26					08 26							
Minster 4	d					00 41										07 38							08 38		
Ramsgate 4	a	00 08	00 42			00 47							07 38			07 44	07 59	08 38					08 44	08 59	
Broadstairs	a																08 04							09 04	
Margate 4	a																08 10							09 10	

		SE 1		SE	SE	SE 1	SE		SE 1		SE	SE	SE 1	SE	SE 1		SE		SE	SE 1	SE	SE 1		SE	SE
St Pancras Intl. 15 ⊖	d				08 12		08 40					09 10		09 42					10 12		10 42				11 12
Stratford International ⊖	d				08 19		08 47					09 17		09 49					10 19		10 49				11 19
Ebbsfleet International	d				08 31		08 59					09 29		10 01					10 31		11 01				11 31
London Charing Cross 4 ⊖	d	07 00				07 30			08 00				08 40		09 10					09 40		10 10			
London Waterloo (East) 4 ⊖	d	07 03				07 33			08 03				08 43		09 13					09 43		10 13			
London Cannon Street 4 ⊖	d																								
London Bridge 4 ⊖	d	07 08				07 38			08 08				08 49		09 19					09 49		10 19			
Orpington 4	d	07 24				07 54			08 24																
Sevenoaks 4	d	07 33				08 03			08 33				09 12		09 42					10 12		10 42			
Tonbridge 4	a	07 43				08 14			08 43				09 20		09 50					10 20		10 50			
	d	07 50		08 03		08 20			08 50		09 03		09 20		09 50		10 03			10 20		10 50		11 03	
Paddock Wood 4	d	07 58		08 10		08 28			08 58		09 10		09 28		09 58		10 10			10 28		10 58		11 10	
Maidstone West 4 194	a			08 29							09 29						10 29							11 29	
Marden	d	08 03				08 33			09 03				09 33		10 03					10 33		11 03			
Staplehurst	d	08 07				08 37			09 07				09 37		10 07					10 37		11 07			
Headcorn	d	08 13				08 43			09 13				09 43		10 13					10 43		11 13			
Pluckley	d	08 19				08 49			09 19				09 49		10 19					10 49		11 19			
Ashford International	a	08 27			08 50	08 56	09 18		09 26			09 48	09 56	10 20	10 26				10 50	10 56	11 20	11 26			11 50
	d	08 31	08 34		08 52	09 03	09 22		09 30	09 33		09 52	10 03	10 22	10 30	10 33			10 52	11 03	11 22	11 30	11 33		11 52
Wye	d		08 40			09 09				09 39			10 09			10 39				11 09			11 39		
Chilham	d		08 46							09 45						10 45							11 45		
Chartham	d		08 50							09 49						10 49							11 49		
Canterbury West 4	d		08a55			09 22	09 39			09a54			10 22	10 39		10a54				11 22	11 39		11a54		
Sturry	d					09 26							10 26							11 26					
Westenhanger	d	08 39							09 38						10 38							11 38			
Sandling	d	08 42							09 41						10 41							11 41			
Folkestone West	d	08 47			09 05				09 47			10 05			10 47				11 05			11 47			12 05
Folkestone Central	d	08 50			09 08				09 50			10 08			10 50				11 08			11 50			12 08
Dover Priory 4	a	09 01			09 20				10 01			10 20			11 01				11 20			12 01			12 20
	d	09 02							10 02						11 02							12 02			
Martin Mill	d	09 11							10 11						11 11							12 11			
Walmer	d	09 15							10 15						11 15							12 15			
Deal	d	09 19							10 19						11 19							12 19			
Sandwich	d	09 26							10 26						11 26							12 26			
Minster 4	d					09 38							10 38							11 38					
Ramsgate 4	a	09 38				09 48	09 59		10 38				10 44	10 59	11 38					11 44	11 59	12 38			
Broadstairs	a						10 04							11 04							12 04				
Margate 4	a						10 10							11 10							12 10				

Table 207

Saturdays

London and Tonbridge - Ashford International, Folkestone, Dover, Canterbury West, Ramsgate and Margate

Network Diagram - see first Page of Table 206

		SE 1	SE		SE 1		SE	SE	SE 1	SE	SE 1		SE		SE	SE 1	SE	SE 1		SE	SE	SE 1	SE		
St Pancras Intl. 15 ⊖	d		11 42					12 12		12 42					13 12		13 42				14 12		14 42		
Stratford International ⊖	d		11 49					12 19		12 49					13 19		13 49				14 19		14 49		
Ebbsfleet International	d		12 01					12 31		13 01					13 31		14 01				14 31		15 01		
London Charing Cross 4 ⊖	d	10 40			11 10				11 40		12 10					12 40		13 10				13 40			
London Waterloo (East) 4 ⊖	d	10 43			11 13				11 43		12 13					12 43		13 13				13 43			
London Cannon Street 4 ⊖	d																								
London Bridge 4 ⊖	d	10 49			11 19				11 49		12 19					12 49		13 19				13 49			
Orpington 4	d																								
Sevenoaks 4	d	11 12			11 42				12 12		12 42					13 12		13 42				14 12			
Tonbridge 4	a	11 20			11 50				12 20		12 50					13 20		13 50				14 20			
	d	11 20			11 50		12 03		12 20		12 50		13 03			13 20		13 50		14 03		14 20			
Paddock Wood 4	d	11 28			11 58		12 10		12 28		12 58		13 10			13 28		13 58		14 10		14 28			
Maidstone West 4 194	a						12 29						13 29							14 29					
Marden	d	11 33			12 03				12 33		13 03					13 33		14 03				14 33			
Staplehurst	d	11 37			12 07				12 37		13 07					13 37		14 07				14 37			
Headcorn	d	11 43			12 13				12 43		13 13					13 43		14 13				14 43			
Pluckley	d	11 49			12 19				12 49		13 19					13 49		14 19				14 49			
Ashford International	a	11 56	12 20		12 26			12 50	12 56	13 20	13 26				13 50	13 56	14 20	14 26			14 50	14 56	15 20		
	d	12 03	12 22		12 30	12 33		12 52	13 03	13 22	13 30	13 33			13 52	14 03	14 22	14 30	14 33		14 52	15 03	15 22		
Wye	d	12 09				12 39			13 09			13 39				14 09			14 39			15 09			
Chilham	d					12 45						13 45							14 45						
Chartham	d					12 49						13 49							14 49						
Canterbury West 4	d	12 22	12 39			12a54			13 22	13 39		13a54				14 22	14 39		14a54			15 22	15 39		
Sturry	d	12 26							13 26							14 26						15 26			
Westenhanger	d				12 38						13 38							14 38							
Sandling	d				12 41						13 41							14 41							
Folkestone West	d				12 47			13 05			13 47				14 05			14 47			15 05				
Folkestone Central	d				12 50			13 08			13 50				14 08			14 50			15 08				
Dover Priory 4	a				13 01			13 20			14 01				14 20			15 01			15 20				
	d				13 02						14 02							15 02							
Martin Mill	d				13 11						14 11							15 11							
Walmer	d				13 15						14 15							15 15							
Deal	d				13 19						14 19							15 19							
Sandwich	d				13 26						14 26							15 26							
Minster 4	d	12 38							13 38							14 38						15 38			
Ramsgate 4	a	12 44	12 59		13 38				13 44	13 59	14 38					14 44	14 59	15 38				15 44	15 59		
Broadstairs	a		13 04							14 04							15 04						16 04		
Margate 4	a		13 10							14 10							15 10						16 10		

		SE 1		SE	SE	SE 1	SE	SE 1		SE		SE	SE 1	SE	SE 1		SE	SE	SE 1	SE		SE 1		SE	SE
St Pancras Intl. 15 ⊖	d				15 12		15 42					16 10		16 42				17 12		17 42					18 12
Stratford International ⊖	d				15 19		15 49					16 17		16 49				17 19		17 49					18 19
Ebbsfleet International	d				15 31		16 01					16 29		17 01				17 31		18 01					18 31
London Charing Cross 4 ⊖	d	14 10				14 40		15 10					15 40		16 10				16 40			17 10			
London Waterloo (East) 4 ⊖	d	14 13				14 43		15 13					15 43		16 13				16 43			17 13			
London Cannon Street 4 ⊖	d																								
London Bridge 4 ⊖	d	14 19				14 49		15 19					15 49		16 19				16 49			17 19			
Orpington 4	d																								
Sevenoaks 4	d	14 42				15 12		15 42					16 12		16 42				17 12			17 42			
Tonbridge 4	a	14 50				15 20		15 50					16 20		16 50				17 20			17 50			
	d	14 50		15 03		15 20		15 50		16 03			16 20		16 50		17 03		17 20			17 50		18 03	
Paddock Wood 4	d	14 58		15 10		15 28		15 58		16 10			16 28		16 58		17 10		17 28			17 58		18 10	
Maidstone West 4 194	a			15 29						16 29							17 29							18 29	
Marden	d	15 03				15 33		16 03					16 33		17 03				17 33			18 03			
Staplehurst	d	15 07				15 37		16 07					16 37		17 07				17 37			18 07			
Headcorn	d	15 13				15 43		16 13					16 43		17 13				17 43			18 13			
Pluckley	d	15 19				15 49		16 19					16 49		17 19				17 49			18 19			
Ashford International	a	15 26			15 50	15 56	16 20	16 26				16 48	16 56	17 20	17 26			17 50	17 56	18 20		18 26			18 50
	d	15 30	15 33		15 52	16 03	16 22	16 30	16 33			16 52	17 03	17 22	17 30	17 33		17 52	18 03	18 22		18 30	18 33		18 52
Wye	d		15 39			16 09			16 39				17 09			17 39			18 09				18 39		
Chilham	d		15 45						16 45							17 45							18 45		
Chartham	d		15 49						16 49							17 49							18 49		
Canterbury West 4	d		15a54			16 22	16 39		16a54				17 22	17 39		17a54			18 22	18 39			18a54		
Sturry	d					16 26							17 26						18 26						
Westenhanger	d	15 38						16 38							17 38							18 38			
Sandling	d	15 41						16 41							17 41							18 41			
Folkestone West	d	15 47			16 05			16 47				17 05			17 47			18 05				18 47			19 05
Folkestone Central	d	15 50			16 08			16 50				17 08			17 50			18 08				18 50			19 08
Dover Priory 4	a	16 01			16 20			17 01				17 20			18 01			18 20				19 01			19 20
	d	16 02						17 02							18 02							19 02			
Martin Mill	d	16 11						17 11							18 11							19 11			
Walmer	d	16 15						17 15							18 15							19 15			
Deal	d	16 19						17 19							18 19							19 19			
Sandwich	d	16 26						17 26							18 26							19 26			
Minster 4	d					16 38							17 38						18 38						
Ramsgate 4	a	16 38				16 44	16 59	17 38					17 44	17 59	18 38				18 44	18 59		19 38			
Broadstairs	a						17 04							18 04						19 04					
Margate 4	a						17 10							18 10						19 10					

Table 207

Saturdays

London and Tonbridge - Ashford International, Folkestone, Dover, Canterbury West, Ramsgate and Margate

Network Diagram - see first Page of Table 206

		SE	SE	SE	SE	SE		SE	SE	SE	SE	SE	SE	SE	SE	SE		SE	SE	SE	SE	SE	SE	SE	SE
		[1]		[1]				[1]		[1]			[1]		[1]				[1]		[1]			[1]	
St Pancras Intl. [15] ⊖	d		18 42			19 12			19 42			20 12		20 42				21 12		21 42			22 12		22 42
Stratford International ⊖	d		18 49			19 19			19 49			20 19		20 49				21 19		21 49			22 19		22 49
Ebbsfleet International	d		19 01			19 31			20 01			20 31		21 01				21 31		22 01			22 31		23 01
London Charing Cross [4] ⊖	d	17 40		18 10				18 40		19 10			19 40		20 10				20 40		21 10			21 40	
London Waterloo (East) [4] ⊖	d	17 43		18 13				18 43		19 13			19 43		20 13				20 43		21 13			21 43	
London Cannon Street [4] ⊖	d																								
London Bridge [4] ⊖	d	17 49		18 19				18 49		19 19			19 49		20 19				20 49		21 19			21 49	
Orpington [4]	d														20 35				21 05		21 35			22 05	
Sevenoaks [4]	d	18 12		18 42				19 12		19 42			20 12		20 44				21 14		21 44			22 14	
Tonbridge [4]	a	18 20		18 50				19 20		19 50			20 20		20 52				21 22		21 52			22 22	
	d	18 20		18 50	19 03			19 20		19 50	20 03		20 20		20 53	21 03			21 23		21 53	22 03		22 23	
Paddock Wood [4]	d	18 28		18 58	19 10			19 28		19 58	20 10		20 28		21 00	21 10			21 30		22 00	22 10		22 30	
Maidstone West [4] 194	a				19 29						20 29					21 29						22 29			
Marden	d	18 33		19 03				19 33		20 03			20 33		21 05				21 35		22 05			22 35	
Staplehurst	d	18 37		19 07				19 37		20 07			20 37		21 09				21 39		22 09			22 39	
Headcorn	d	18 43		19 13				19 43		20 13			20 43		21 14				21 44		22 14			22 44	
Pluckley	d	18 49		19 19				19 49		20 19			20 49		21 20				21 50		22 20			22 50	
Ashford International	a	18 56	19 20	19 26		19 50		19 56	20 20	20 26		20 50	20 56	21 20	21 28			21 50	21 58	22 20	22 28		22 50	22 58	23 20
	d	19 03	19 22	19 30		19 52		20 03	20 22	20 30		20 52	21 03	21 22	21 31			21 52	22 03	22 22	22 31		22 52	23 03	23 22
Wye	d	19 09						20 09					21 09						22 09					23 09	
Chilham	d	19 15						20 15					21 15						22 15					23 15	
Chartham	d	19 19						20 19					21 19						22 19					23 19	
Canterbury West [4]	d	19 25	19 39					20 25	20 39				21 25	21 39					22 25	22 39				23 25	23 39
Sturry	d	19 29						20 29					21 29						22 29					23 29	
Westenhanger	d			19 38						20 38					21 40						22 40				
Sandling	d			19 41						20 41					21 42						22 42				
Folkestone West	d			19 47		20 05				20 47		21 05			21 47			22 05			22 47		23 05		
Folkestone Central	d			19 50		20 08				20 50		21 08			21 50			22 08			22 50		23 08		
Dover Priory [4]	a			20 01		20 20				21 01		21 20			22 01			22 20			23 01		23 20		
	d			20 02						21 02					22 02						23 02				
Martin Mill	d			20 11						21 11					22 11						23 11				
Walmer	d			20 15						21 15					22 15						23 15				
Deal	d			20 19						21 19					22 19						23 19				
Sandwich	d			20 26						21 26					22 26						23 26				
Minster [4]	d	19 41						20 41					21 41						22 41					23 41	
Ramsgate [4]	a	19 47	19 59	20 38				20 47	20 59	21 38			21 47	21 59	22 38				22 48	22 59	23 38			23 47	23 59
Broadstairs	a		20 04						21 04					22 04						23 04					
Margate [4]	a		20 10						21 10					22 10						23 10					

		SE		SE	SE	SE	SE
		[1]			[1]	[1]	[1]
St Pancras Intl. [15] ⊖	d			23 12			
Stratford International ⊖	d			23 19			
Ebbsfleet International	d			23 31			
London Charing Cross [4] ⊖	d	22 10			22 40	23 10	23 40
London Waterloo (East) [4] ⊖	d	22 13			22 43	23 13	23 43
London Cannon Street [4] ⊖	d						
London Bridge [4] ⊖	d	22 19			22 49	23 19	23 49
Orpington [4]	d	22 35			23 05	23 35	00 05
Sevenoaks [4]	d	22 44			23 14	23 44	00 14
Tonbridge [4]	a	22 52			23 22	23 52	00 22
	d	22 53			23 23	23 53	00 23
Paddock Wood [4]	d	23 00			23 30	23 59	00 30
Maidstone West [4] 194	a						
Marden	d	23 05			23 35	00 05	00 35
Staplehurst	d	23 09			23 39	00 09	00 39
Headcorn	d	23 14			23 44	00 14	00 44
Pluckley	d	23 20			23 50	00 20	00 50
Ashford International	a	23 28		23 50	23 58	00 28	00 58
	d	23 31		23 52	00 03	00 31	01 01
Wye	d				00 09		
Chilham	d				00 15		
Chartham	d				00 19		
Canterbury West [4]	d				00 25		
Sturry	d				00 29		
Westenhanger	d	23 40				00 40	01 10
Sandling	d	23 42				00 42	01 12
Folkestone West	d	23 47		00 05		00 47	01 17
Folkestone Central	d	23 50		00 08		00 50	01 20
Dover Priory [4]	a	00 01		00 20		01 01	01 31
	d	00 02					
Martin Mill	d	00 11					
Walmer	d	00 15					
Deal	d	00 19					
Sandwich	d	00 26					
Minster [4]	d				00 41		
Ramsgate [4]	a	00 38			00 47		
Broadstairs	a						
Margate [4]	a						

Table 207

Sundays

London and Tonbridge - Ashford International, Folkestone, Dover, Canterbury West, Ramsgate and Margate

Network Diagram - see first Page of Table 206

		SE ■ A	SE A	SE ■ A	SE ■ A	SE ■ A	SE	SE ■	SE	SE		SE ■	SE ■	SE ■	SE	SE	SE ■		SE	SE ■		SE	SE	SE ■	
St Pancras Intl. 15 ⊖	d		23p12				00 12									08 42			09 10				09 42		
Stratford International ⊖	d		23p19				00 19									08 49			09 17				09 49		
Ebbsfleet International	d		23p31				00 31									09 01			09 29				10 01		
London Charing Cross 4 ⊖	d	22p10		22p40	23p10	23p40											08 08			08 38				09 08	
London Waterloo (East) 4 ⊖	d	22p13		22p43	23p13	23p43											08 11			08 41				09 11	
London Cannon Street 4 ⊖	d																								
London Bridge 4 ⊖	d	22p19		22p49	23p19	23p49											08 16			08 46				09 16	
Orpington 4	d	22p35		23p05	23p35	00 05											08 32			09 02				09 32	
Sevenoaks 4	d	22p44		23p14	23p44	00 14											08 42			09 12				09 42	
Tonbridge 4	a	22p52		23p22	23p52	00 22											08 52			09 20				09 52	
	d	22p53		23p23	23p53	00 23			06 26					08 20			08 52			09 20				09 52	
Paddock Wood 4	d	23p00		23p30	23p59	00 30			06 34	07 34				08 28	08 34		09 00			09 28		09 34		10 00	
Maidstone West 4 194	a								06 53	07 53					08 53							09 53			
Marden	d	23p05		23p35	00 05	00 35								08 33			09 05			09 33				10 05	
Staplehurst	d	23p09		23p39	00 09	00 39								08 37			09 09			09 37				10 09	
Headcorn	d	23p14		23p44	00 14	00 44								08 43			09 15			09 43				10 15	
Pluckley	d	23p20		23p50	00 20	00 50								08 49						09 49					
Ashford International	a	23p28	23p50	23p58	00 28	00 58	00 50							08 56		09 20	09 26		09 48	09 56			10 20	10 26	
	d	23p31	23p52	00 03	00 31	01 01		01 04				08 30	08 33	09 03		09 22	09 30	09 33	09 52	10 03			10 22	10 30	10 33
Wye	d			00 09				01 10					08 39	09 09				09 39		10 09					10 39
Chilham	d			00 15				01 16					08 45					09 45							10 45
Chartham	d			00 19				01 20					08 49					09 49							10 49
Canterbury West 4	d			00 25				01a25					08a54	09 22		09 39		09a54		10 22			10 39		10a54
Sturry	d			00 29										09 26						10 26					
Westenhanger	d	23p40			00 40	01 10						08 38					09 38							10 38	
Sandling	d	23p42			00 42	01 12						08 41					09 41							10 41	
Folkestone West	d	23p47	00 05		00 47	01 17						08 47					09 47		10 05					10 47	
Folkestone Central	d	23p50	00 08		00 50	01 20						08 50					09 50		10 08					10 50	
Dover Priory 4	a	00 01	00 20		01 01	01 31						09 01					10 01		10 20					11 01	
	d	00 02										09 02					10 02							11 02	
Martin Mill	d	00 11										09 11					10 11							11 11	
Walmer	d	00 15										09 15					10 15							11 15	
Deal	d	00 19										09 19					10 19							11 19	
Sandwich	d	00 26										09 26					10 26							11 26	
Minster 4	d			00 41										09 38						10 38					
Ramsgate 4	a	00 38		00 47								09 38		09 44		09 59	10 38			10 44			10 59	11 38	
Broadstairs	a															10 04							11 04		
Margate 4	a															10 10							11 10		

		SE	SE ■	SE	SE	SE ■			SE	SE ■	SE	SE	SE ■		SE	SE ■	SE		SE	SE ■		SE	SE ■	SE	SE
St Pancras Intl. 15 ⊖	d	10 10			10 42				11 12			11 42			12 12				12 42			13 12			13 42
Stratford International ⊖	d	10 17			10 49				11 19			11 49			12 19				12 49			13 19			13 49
Ebbsfleet International	d	10 29			11 01				11 31			12 01			12 31				13 01			13 31			14 01
London Charing Cross 4 ⊖	d		09 38			10 08				10 38			11 08			11 38				12 08			12 38		
London Waterloo (East) 4 ⊖	d		09 41			10 11				10 41			11 11			11 41				12 11			12 41		
London Cannon Street 4 ⊖	d																								
London Bridge 4 ⊖	d		09 46			10 16				10 46			11 16			11 46				12 16			12 46		
Orpington 4	d		10 02			10 32				11 02			11 32			12 02				12 32			13 02		
Sevenoaks 4	d		10 12			10 42				11 12			11 42			12 12				12 42			13 12		
Tonbridge 4	a		10 20			10 52				11 20			11 52			12 20				12 52			13 20		
	d		10 20			10 52				11 20			11 52			12 20				12 52			13 20		
Paddock Wood 4	d		10 28	10 34		11 00				11 28	11 34		12 00			12 28	12 34			13 00			13 28	13 34	
Maidstone West 4 194	a			10 53							11 53						12 53							13 53	
Marden	d		10 33			11 05				11 33			12 05			12 33				13 05			13 33		
Staplehurst	d		10 37			11 09				11 37			12 09			12 37				13 09			13 37		
Headcorn	d		10 43			11 15				11 43			12 15			12 43				13 15			13 43		
Pluckley	d		10 49							11 49						12 49							13 49		
Ashford International	a	10 48	10 56		11 20	11 26			11 50	11 56		12 20	12 26		12 50	12 56			13 20	13 26		13 50	13 56		14 20
	d	10 52	11 03		11 22	11 30	11 33		11 52	12 03		12 22	12 30	12 33	12 52	13 03			13 22	13 30	13 33	13 52	14 03		14 22
Wye	d		11 09				11 39			12 09				12 39		13 09					13 39		14 09		
Chilham	d						11 45							12 45							13 45				
Chartham	d						11 49							12 49							13 49				
Canterbury West 4	d		11 22		11 39		11a54			12 22		12 39		12a54		13 22			13 39		13a54		14 22		14 39
Sturry	d		11 26							12 26						13 26							14 26		
Westenhanger	d					11 38							12 38							13 38					
Sandling	d					11 41							12 41							13 41					
Folkestone West	d	11 05				11 47			12 05				12 47		13 05					13 47		14 05			
Folkestone Central	d	11 08				11 50			12 08				12 50		13 08					13 50		14 08			
Dover Priory 4	a	11 20				12 01			12 20				13 01		13 20					14 01		14 20			
	d					12 02							13 02							14 02					
Martin Mill	d					12 11							13 11							14 11					
Walmer	d					12 15							13 15							14 15					
Deal	d					12 19							13 19							14 19					
Sandwich	d					12 26							13 26							14 26					
Minster 4	d		11 38							12 38						13 38							14 38		
Ramsgate 4	a		11 44		11 59	12 38				12 44		12 59	13 38			13 44			13 59	14 38			14 44		14 59
Broadstairs	a				12 04							13 04							14 04						15 04
Margate 4	a				12 10							13 10							14 10						15 10

A not 11 December

Table 207

Sundays

London and Tonbridge - Ashford International, Folkestone, Dover, Canterbury West, Ramsgate and Margate

Network Diagram - see first Page of Table 206

		SE 1			SE	SE 1	SE	SE	SE 1		SE	SE 1	SE		SE	SE 1		SE	SE 1	SE	SE	SE 1			SE
St Pancras Intl. 15 ⊖	d				14 12			14 42			15 12				15 42			16 10			16 42				17 12
Stratford International ⊖	d				14 19			14 49			15 19				15 49			16 17			16 49				17 19
Ebbsfleet International	d				14 31			15 01			15 31				16 01			16 29			17 01				17 31
London Charing Cross 4 ⊖	d	13 08				13 38			14 08			14 38				15 08			15 38			16 08			
London Waterloo (East) 4 ⊖	d	13 11				13 41			14 11			14 41				15 11			15 41			16 11			
London Cannon Street 4 ⊖	d																								
London Bridge 4 ⊖	d	13 16				13 46			14 16			14 46				15 16			15 46			16 16			
Orpington 4	d	13 32				14 02			14 32			15 02				15 32			16 02			16 32			
Sevenoaks 4	d	13 42				14 12			14 42			15 12				15 42			16 12			16 42			
Tonbridge 4	a	13 52				14 20			14 52			15 20				15 52			16 20			16 52			
	d	13 52				14 20			14 52			15 20				15 52			16 20			16 52			
Paddock Wood 4	d	14 00				14 28	14 34		15 00			15 28	15 34			16 00			16 28	16 34		17 00			
Maidstone West 4 194	a						14 53						15 53							16 53					
Marden	d	14 05				14 33			15 05			15 33				16 05			16 33			17 05			
Staplehurst	d	14 09				14 37			15 09			15 37				16 09			16 37			17 09			
Headcorn	d	14 15				14 43			15 15			15 43				16 15			16 43			17 15			
Pluckley	d					14 49						15 49							16 49						
Ashford International	a	14 26			14 50	14 56		15 20	15 26		15 50	15 56			16 20	16 26		16 48	16 56		17 20	17 26			17 50
	d	14 30	14 33		14 52	15 03		15 22	15 30	15 33	15 52	16 03			16 22	16 30	16 33	16 52	17 03		17 22	17 30	17 33		17 52
Wye	d		14 39			15 09				15 39		16 09					16 39		17 09				17 39		
Chilham	d		14 45							15 45							16 45						17 45		
Chartham	d		14 49							15 49							16 49						17 49		
Canterbury West 4	d		14a54			15 22		15 39		15a54		16 22			16 39		16a54		17 22		17 39		17a54		
Sturry	d					15 26						16 26							17 26						
Westenhanger	d	14 38							15 38							16 38						17 38			
Sandling	d	14 41							15 41							16 41						17 41			
Folkestone West	d	14 47			15 05				15 47		16 05					16 47		17 05				17 47			18 05
Folkestone Central	d	14 50			15 08				15 50		16 08					16 50		17 08				17 50			18 08
Dover Priory 4	a	15 01			15 20				16 01		16 20					17 01		17 20				18 01			18 20
	d	15 02							16 02							17 02						18 02			
Martin Mill	d	15 11							16 11							17 11						18 11			
Walmer	d	15 15							16 15							17 15						18 15			
Deal	d	15 19							16 19							17 19						18 19			
Sandwich	d	15 26							16 26							17 26						18 26			
Minster 4	d					15 38						16 38							17 38						
Ramsgate 4	a	15 38				15 44		15 59	16 38			16 44			16 59	17 38			17 44		17 59	18 38			
Broadstairs	a							16 04							17 04						18 04				
Margate 4	a							16 10							17 10						18 10				

		SE 1	SE	SE	SE 1	SE	SE 1	SE	SE		SE 1	SE	SE 1	SE	SE	SE 1	SE	SE 1	SE		SE	SE 1	SE	SE 1	SE
St Pancras Intl. 15 ⊖	d			17 42		18 12			18 42			19 12			19 42		20 12				20 42		21 12		
Stratford International ⊖	d			17 49		18 19			18 49			19 19			19 49		20 19				20 49		21 19		
Ebbsfleet International	d			18 01		18 31			19 01			19 31			20 01		20 31				21 01		21 31		
London Charing Cross 4 ⊖	d	16 38			17 08		17 38				18 08		18 38			19 08		19 38				20 08		20 38	
London Waterloo (East) 4 ⊖	d	16 41			17 11		17 41				18 11		18 41			19 11		19 41				20 11		20 41	
London Cannon Street 4 ⊖	d																								
London Bridge 4 ⊖	d	16 46			17 16		17 46				18 16		18 46			19 16		19 46				20 16		20 46	
Orpington 4	d	17 02			17 32		18 02				18 32		19 02			19 32		20 02				20 32		21 02	
Sevenoaks 4	d	17 12			17 42		18 12				18 42		19 12			19 42		20 12				20 42		21 12	
Tonbridge 4	a	17 20			17 52		18 20				18 52		19 20			19 52		20 20				20 52		21 20	
	d	17 20			17 52		18 20				18 52		19 20			19 52		20 20				20 52		21 20	
Paddock Wood 4	d	17 28	17 34		18 00		18 28	18 34			19 00		19 28	19 34		20 00		20 28	20 34			21 00		21 28	21 34
Maidstone West 4 194	a		17 53					18 53						19 53					20 53						21 53
Marden	d	17 33			18 05		18 33				19 05		19 33			20 05		20 33				21 05		21 33	
Staplehurst	d	17 37			18 09		18 37				19 09		19 37			20 09		20 37				21 09		21 37	
Headcorn	d	17 43			18 15		18 43				19 15		19 43			20 15		20 43				21 15		21 43	
Pluckley	d	17 49					18 49						19 49					20 49						21 49	
Ashford International	a	17 56		18 20	18 26	18 50	18 56		19 20		19 26	19 50	19 56		20 20	20 26	20 50	20 56			21 20	21 26	21 50	21 56	
	d	18 03		18 22	18 30	18 52	19 03		19 22		19 30	19 52	20 03		20 22	20 30	20 52	21 03			21 22	21 30	21 52	22 03	
Wye	d	18 09					19 09						20 09					21 09						22 09	
Chilham	d	18 15					19 15						20 15					21 15						22 15	
Chartham	d	18 19					19 19						20 19					21 19						22 19	
Canterbury West 4	d	18 25		18 39			19 25		19 39				20 25		20 39			21 25			21 39			22 25	
Sturry	d	18 29					19 29						20 29					21 29						22 29	
Westenhanger	d				18 38						19 38					20 38						21 38			
Sandling	d				18 41						19 41					20 41						21 41			
Folkestone West	d				18 47	19 05					19 47	20 05				20 47	21 05					21 47	22 05		
Folkestone Central	d				18 50	19 08					19 50	20 08				20 50	21 08					21 50	22 08		
Dover Priory 4	a				19 01	19 20					20 01	20 20				21 01	21 20					22 01	22 20		
	d				19 02						20 02					21 02						22 02			
Martin Mill	d				19 11						20 11					21 11						22 11			
Walmer	d				19 15						20 15					21 15						22 15			
Deal	d				19 19						20 19					21 19						22 19			
Sandwich	d				19 26						20 26					21 26						22 26			
Minster 4	d	18 41					19 41						20 41					21 41						22 41	
Ramsgate 4	a	18 47		18 59	19 38		19 47		19 59		20 38		20 47		20 59	21 38		21 47			21 59	22 38		22 47	
Broadstairs	a			19 04					20 04						21 04						22 04				
Margate 4	a			19 10					20 10						21 10						22 10				

Table 207

Sundays

London and Tonbridge - Ashford International, Folkestone, Dover, Canterbury West, Ramsgate and Margate

Network Diagram - see first Page of Table 206

		SE	SE [1]	SE	SE [1]		SE	SE [1]	SE	SE [1]	SE [1]	SE [1]	SE
St Pancras Intl. [15] ⊖	d	21 42		22 12			22 42		23 12				23 42
Stratford International ⊖	d	21 49		22 19			22 49		23 19				23 49
Ebbsfleet International	d	22 01		22 31			23 01		23 31				00 01
London Charing Cross [4] ⊖	d		21 08		21 38			22 08		22 38	23 08	23 38	
London Waterloo (East) [4] ⊖	d		21 11		21 41			22 11		22 41	23 11	23 41	
London Cannon Street [4] ⊖	d												
London Bridge [4] ⊖	d		21 16		21 46			22 16		22 46	23 16	23 46	
Orpington [4]	d		21 32		22 02			22 32		23 02	23 32	00 02	
Sevenoaks [4]	d		21 42		22 12			22 42		23 12	23 42	00 12	
Tonbridge [4]	a		21 52		22 20			22 52		23 20	23 52	00 20	
	d		21 52		22 20			22 52		23 20	23 52	00 20	
Paddock Wood [4]	d		22 00		22 28			23 00		23 28	23 59	00 28	
Maidstone West [4] 194	a												
Marden	d		22 05		22 33			23 05		23 33	00 05	00 33	
Staplehurst	d		22 09		22 37			23 09		23 37	00 09	00 37	
Headcorn	d		22 15		22 43			23 15		23 43	00 15	00 43	
Pluckley	d				22 49					23 49		00 49	
Ashford International	a	22 20	22 26	22 50	22 56		23 20	23 26	23 50	23 56	00 26	00 56	00 20
	d	22 22	22 30	22 52	23 03		23 22	23 30	23 52	00 01			
Wye	d				23 09								
Chilham	d				23 15								
Chartham	d				23 19								
Canterbury West [4]	d	22 39			23 25		23 39						
Sturry	d				23 29								
Westenhanger	d		22 38					23 38					
Sandling	d		22 41					23 41		00 11			
Folkestone West	d		22 47	23 05				23 47	00 05	00 17			
Folkestone Central	d		22 50	23 08				23 50	00 08	00 19			
Dover Priory [4]	a		23 01	23 20				00 01	00 20	00 30			
	d		23 02					00 02					
Martin Mill	d		23 11					00 11					
Walmer	d		23 15					00 15					
Deal	d		23 19					00 19					
Sandwich	d		23 26					00 26					
Minster [4]	d				23 41								
Ramsgate [4]	a	22 59	23 39		23 47		23 59	00 38					
Broadstairs	a	23 04											
Margate [4]	a	23 10											

Margate, Ramsgate, Canterbury West, Dover, Folkestone, Ashford International - Tonbridge and London

Network Diagram - see first Page of Table 206

Miles	Miles	Miles	Miles			SE MX 1	SE	SE	SE 1	SE 1	SE	SE 1	SE	SE 1		SE	SE	SE 1	SE 1	SE 1	SE	SE	SE 1	SE	
0	0	—	—	**Margate 4**	d																05 47				
3¼	3¼	—	—	Broadstairs	d																05 54				
5½	5½	—	—	**Ramsgate 4**	d	21p22					05 00			04 50				05 36		05 26	06 00				
—	9½	0	—	Minster 4	d						05 06							05 42							
13¾	—	4¾	—	Sandwich	d	21p34								05 04						05 40		05 50			
18	—	—	—	**Deal**	d	21p40								05 10						05 46		05 56			
19½	—	—	—	Walmer	d	21p43								05 13						05 49					
22¼	—	—	—	Martin Mill	d	21p48								05 17						05 53					
27¼	—	—	—	**Dover Priory 4**	a	21p56								05 26						06 02		06 10			
—	—	—	—		d	21p57			04 37					05 27		05 44			05 45	06 04		06 12			
34½	—	—	—	**Folkestone Central**	d	22p09			04 49					05 39		05 56				06 15		06 23			
35¼	—	—	—	Folkestone West	d	22p11			04 51					05 42		05 58				06 18		06 26			
39	—	—	—	Sandling	d	22p16			04 56					05 47						06 23					
40¼	—	—	—	Westenhanger	d	22p19			04 59					05 49						06 26					
—	18½	—	—	Sturry	d						05 18							05 54							
—	20¾	—	—	**Canterbury West 4**	d						05 25	05 36						06 00			06 20				
—	24	—	—	Chartham	d							05 41						06 05							
—	26	—	—	Chilham	d							05 44						06 08							
—	30¾	—	—	Wye	d							05 51						06 15							
48½	35	—	0	**Ashford International**	a	22p28			05 08		05 41	05 57		05 59		06 11		06 21		06 35	06 36	06 39			
—	—	—	—																						
—	—	—	—		d	22p33	05 13		05 13	05 29	05 43			06 03		06 13		06 24		06 38	06 43		06 45		
54	—	—	—	Pluckley	d	22p39			05 19	05 35				06 09				06 30		06 44			06 51		
59¼	—	—	—	Headcorn	d	22p46			05 26	05 42				06 16				06 37		06 51			06 58		
62¾	—	—	—	Staplehurst	d	22p51			05 31	05 47				06 21				06 42		06 56			07 03		
65	—	—	—	Marden	d	22p55			05 35	05 51				06 25				06 46		07 00			07 07		
—	—	—	—	Maidstone West 4 194	d			05 18					05 56				06 26							06 56	
69¾	—	—	—	Paddock Wood 4	d	23p01		05a37	05 42	05 58			06a15	06 32			06a45	06 53		07 07			07 14		
75	—	—	—	**Tonbridge 4**	a	23p10			05 49	06 05				06 39				07 01		07 14			07 21		
—	—	—	—		d	23p14			05 50	06 06				06 40				07 02		07 15			07 23		
82¼	—	—	—	Sevenoaks 4	a	23p24			05 58	06 14				06 48				07 10		07 26			07 31		
90¾	—	—	—	Orpington 4	a	23p36			06 08	06 23															
102¾	—	—	—	**London Bridge 4** ⊖	a	23p54			06 24	06 39				07 14				07 36	07 51	07 53					
—	—	—	—	**London Cannon Street 4** ⊖	a														07 57	07 59					
103¾	—	—	—	**London Waterloo (East) 4** ⊖	a	23p59			06 29	06 44				07 19				07 41					08 00		
104½	—	—	—	**London Charing Cross 4** ⊖	a	00 03			06 33	06 49				07 25				07 47					08 06		
—	—	—	33¼	**Ebbsfleet International**	a		05 32				06 02					06 32									
—	—	—	50	**Stratford International** ⊖	a		05 44				06 14					06 44					07 11			07 36	
—	—	—	56	**St Pancras Intl. 15** ⊖	a		05 51				06 21					06 51					07 18			07 43	

		SE	SE 1	SE 1	SE	SE	SE 1	SE 1	SE	SE		SE 1	SE	SE	SE 1	SE 1	SE 1	SE 1	SE 1	SE		SE	SE	SE	
Margate 4	d												06 48												
Broadstairs	d												06 54												
Ramsgate 4	d		06 08			06 26	06 12	06 42					07 00			06 59	06 49	07 10	07 19			07 30			
Minster 4	d		06 17					06 48										07 16							
Sandwich	d				06 18		06 26							06 50			07 01								
Deal	d				06 24		06 32							06 56			07 07								
Walmer	d						06 35										07 10								
Martin Mill	d						06 39										07 15								
Dover Priory 4	a				06 38		06 48							07 10			07 23								
	d			06 24	06 42		06 49							07 12			07 24						07 42		
Folkestone Central	d			06 36	06 53		07 00					07 14		07 23			07 36						07 53		
Folkestone West	d			06 38	06 56		07 03					07 17		07 26			07 38						07 56		
Sandling	d			06 43			07 08					07 22					07 43								
Westenhanger	d			06 46			07 11					07 25					07 46								
Sturry	d		06 29					07 00										07 28							
Canterbury West 4	d		06 34			06 50		07 06					07 20					07 36				07 50			
Chartham	d		06 39					07 11										07 41							
Chilham	d		06 42					07 14										07 44							
Wye	d		06 49					07 21										07 51							
Ashford International	a		06 55	06 55	07 09	07 06	07 20	07 27				07 34	07 36	07 39			07 55	07 58				08 06	08 09		
	d		06 57	07 03	07 13		07 22	07 29				07 38	07 43		07 45		08 03					08 13			
Pluckley	d		07 04	07 09			07 28					07 44			07 51		08 09								
Headcorn	d		07 11	07 16			07 35	07 40				07 51			07 58		08 16								
Staplehurst	d		07 16	07 22			07 40	07 45				07 56			08 03		08 21								
Marden	d		07 20	07 26			07 44	07 49				08 00			08 07		08 25								
Maidstone West 4 194	d	07 01							07 26	07 41										07 56				08 18	
Paddock Wood 4	d	07a20	07 27	07 33			07 51	07 55		08a00		08 07			08 14		08 31							08 37	
Tonbridge 4	a		07 34	07 41			07 58	08 03				08 14			08 21		08 39							08 45	
	d		07 35	07 42			07 59	08 04				08 15			08 22		08 40								
Sevenoaks 4	a		07 46	07 50			08 07	08 12				08 26			08 30		08 48								
Orpington 4	a																								
London Bridge 4 ⊖	a		08 13				08 33					08 55				08 49	09 14		09 11						
London Cannon Street 4 ⊖	a		08 20				08 41					09 02				08 57			09 18						
London Waterloo (East) 4 ⊖	a			08 20				08 40							09 00		09 19								
London Charing Cross 4 ⊖	a			08 26				08 46							09 04		09 25								
Ebbsfleet International	a																								
Stratford International ⊖	a				07 41				08 06				08 11							08 36		08 41			
St Pancras Intl. 15 ⊖	a				07 48				08 13				08 19							08 43		08 48			

Margate, Ramsgate, Canterbury West, Dover, Folkestone, Ashford International - Tonbridge and London

Network Diagram - see first Page of Table 206

		SE 1	SE 1	SE	SE 1	SE 1	SE		SE	SE 1	SE 1	SE	SE 1	SE 1	SE	SE	SE 1	SE 1		SE	SE 1	SE 1	SE	SE
Margate 4	d			07 49								08 53								09 53				
Broadstairs	d			07 55								08 59								09 59				
Ramsgate 4	d	07 22		08 01	07 40	08 16				08 05	08 40	09 05					09 22	09 40		10 05				
Minster 4	d			08 07	07 53					08 16	08 46							09 46						
Sandwich	d	07 34			08 01					08 25							09 34							
Deal	d	07 40			08 07					08 31							09 40							
Walmer	d	07 43			08 10					08 34							09 43							
Martin Mill	d	07 48			08 15					08 38							09 48							
Dover Priory 4	a	07 56			08 23					08 47							09 56							
	d	07 57			08 24		08 44			08 57			09 24		09 44		09 57				10 24		10 44	
Folkestone Central	d	08 09			08 36		08 56			09 09			09 36		09 56		10 09				10 36		10 56	
Folkestone West	d	08 11			08 38		08 58			09 11			09 38		09 58		10 11				10 38		10 58	
Sandling	d	08 16			08 43					09 16			09 43				10 16				10 43			
Westenhanger	d	08 19			08 46					09 19			09 46				10 19				10 46			
Sturry	d			08 19							08 58							09 58						
Canterbury West 4	d		08 00	08 25		08 36					09 07	09 25		09 36				10 07		10 25		10 36		
Chartham	d		08 05			08 41								09 41								10 41		
Chilham	d		08 08			08 44								09 44								10 44		
Wye	d		08 15			08 51					09 19			09 51				10 19				10 51		
Ashford International	a	08 28	08 21	08 41	08 55	08 58	09 11			09 28	09 25	09 41	09 55	09 58	10 11		10 28	10 25		10 41	10 55	10 58	11 11	
	d	08 33		08 43	09 03		09 13			09 33		09 43	10 03		10 13		10 33			10 43	11 03		11 13	
Pluckley	d	08 39			09 09					09 39			10 09				10 39				11 09			
Headcorn	d	08 46			09 16					09 46			10 16				10 46				11 16			
Staplehurst	d	08 51			09 21					09 51			10 21				10 51				11 21			
Marden	d	08 55			09 25					09 55			10 25				10 55				11 25			
Maidstone West 4 194	d								09 28							10 28								11 28
Paddock Wood 4	d	09 01			09 31				09 47	10 01			10 31			10 47	11 01				11 31			11 47
Tonbridge 4	a	09 09			09 39				09 57	10 09			10 39			10 55	11 09				11 39			11 55
	d	09 10			09 40					10 10			10 40				11 10				11 40			
Sevenoaks 4	a	09 18			09 48					10 18			10 48				11 18				11 48			
Orpington 4	a																							
London Bridge 4 ⊖	a	09 43			10 13					10 43			11 13				11 43				12 13			
London Cannon Street 4 ⊖	a																							
London Waterloo (East) 4 ⊖	a	09 48			10 18					10 48			11 18				11 48				12 18			
London Charing Cross 4 ⊖	a	09 54			10 22					10 52			11 22				11 52				12 22			
Ebbsfleet International	a			09 02			09 32					10 02			10 32					11 02			11 32	
Stratford International ⊖	a			09 14			09 44					10 14			10 44					11 14			11 44	
St Pancras Intl. 15 ⊖	a			09 21			09 51					10 21			10 51					11 21			11 51	

		SE 1	SE 1	SE	SE 1	SE 1		SE	SE	SE 1	SE 1	SE	SE 1	SE 1	SE	SE		SE 1	SE 1	SE	SE 1	SE 1	SE	SE
Margate 4	d			10 53								11 53								12 53				
Broadstairs	d			10 59								11 59								12 59				
Ramsgate 4	d	10 22	10 40	11 05						11 22	11 40	12 05						12 22	12 40	13 05				
Minster 4	d		10 46								11 46								12 46					
Sandwich	d	10 34								11 34								12 34						
Deal	d	10 40								11 40								12 40						
Walmer	d	10 43								11 43								12 43						
Martin Mill	d	10 48								11 48								12 48						
Dover Priory 4	a	10 56								11 56								12 56						
	d	10 57			11 24			11 44		11 57			12 24		12 44			12 57			13 24		13 44	
Folkestone Central	d	11 09			11 36			11 56		12 09			12 36		12 56			13 09			13 36		13 56	
Folkestone West	d	11 11			11 38			11 58		12 11			12 38		12 58			13 11			13 38		13 58	
Sandling	d	11 16			11 43					12 16			12 43					13 16			13 43			
Westenhanger	d	11 19			11 46					12 19			12 46					13 19			13 46			
Sturry	d		10 58								11 58								12 58					
Canterbury West 4	d		11 07	11 25		11 36					12 07	12 25		12 36					13 07	13 25		13 36		
Chartham	d					11 41								12 41								13 41		
Chilham	d					11 44								12 44								13 44		
Wye	d		11 19			11 51					12 19			12 51					13 19			13 51		
Ashford International	a	11 28	11 25	11 41	11 55	11 58		12 11		12 28	12 25	12 41	12 55	12 58	13 11			13 28	13 25	13 41	13 55	13 58	14 11	
	d	11 33		11 43	12 03			12 13		12 33		12 43	13 03		13 13			13 33		13 43	14 03		14 13	
Pluckley	d	11 39			12 09					12 39			13 09					13 39			14 09			
Headcorn	d	11 46			12 16					12 46			13 16					13 46			14 16			
Staplehurst	d	11 51			12 21					12 51			13 21					13 51			14 21			
Marden	d	11 55			12 25					12 55			13 25					13 55			14 25			
Maidstone West 4 194	d								12 28							13 28								14 28
Paddock Wood 4	d	12 01			12 31				12 47	13 01			13 31			13 47		14 01			14 31			14 47
Tonbridge 4	a	12 09			12 39				12 58	13 09			13 39			13 55		14 09			14 39			14 55
	d	12 10			12 40					13 10			13 40					14 10			14 40			
Sevenoaks 4	a	12 18			12 48					13 18			13 48					14 18			14 48			
Orpington 4	a																							
London Bridge 4 ⊖	a	12 43			13 13					13 43			14 13					14 43			15 13			
London Cannon Street 4 ⊖	a																							
London Waterloo (East) 4 ⊖	a	12 48			13 18					13 48			14 18					14 48			15 18			
London Charing Cross 4 ⊖	a	12 52			13 22					13 52			14 22					14 52			15 22			
Ebbsfleet International	a			12 02				12 32				13 02			13 32					14 02			14 32	
Stratford International ⊖	a			12 14				12 44				13 14			13 44					14 14			14 44	
St Pancras Intl. 15 ⊖	a			12 21				12 51				13 21			13 51					14 21			14 51	

Margate, Ramsgate, Canterbury West, Dover, Folkestone, Ashford International - Tonbridge and London

Network Diagram - see first Page of Table 206

		SE 1	SE 1		SE	SE 1	SE 1	SE	SE	SE 1	SE 1	SE	SE 1	SE 1		SE	SE	SE 1	SE 1	SE	SE	SE 1	SE 1	SE	
Margate 4	d				13 53							14 53								15 53					
Broadstairs	d				13 59							14 59								15 59					
Ramsgate 4	d	13 22	13 40		14 05					14 22	14 40	15 05						15 22	15 40	16 05		15 50			
Minster 4	d		13 46								14 46								15 46						
Sandwich	d	13 34								14 34								15 34				16 02			
Deal	d	13 40								14 40								15 40				16 08			
Walmer	d	13 43								14 43								15 43				16 11			
Martin Mill	d	13 48								14 48								15 48				16 16			
Dover Priory 4	a	13 56								14 56								15 56				16 24			
	d	13 57				14 24		14 44		14 57			15 24			15 44		15 57				16 24		16 44	
Folkestone Central	d	14 09				14 36		14 56		15 09			15 36			15 56		16 09				16 36		16 56	
Folkestone West	d	14 11				14 38		14 58		15 11			15 38			15 58		16 11				16 38		16 58	
Sandling	d	14 16				14 43				15 16			15 43					16 16				16 43			
Westenhanger	d	14 19				14 46				15 19			15 46					16 19				16 46			
Sturry	d		13 58								14 58								15 58						
Canterbury West 4	d		14 07		14 25		14 36				15 04	15 25		15 36					16 04	16 25			16 36		
Chartham	d						14 41							15 41									16 41		
Chilham	d						14 44							15 44									16 44		
Wye	d		14 19				14 51				15 16			15 51					16 16				16 51		
Ashford International	a	14 28	14 25		14 41	14 55	14 58	15 11		15 28	15 22	15 41	15 55	15 58		16 11		16 28	16 22	16 41		16 55	16 58	17 11	
	d	14 33			14 43	15 03		15 13		15 33		15 43	16 03			16 13		16 33		16 43		17 03		17 13	
Pluckley	d	14 39				15 09				15 39			16 09					16 39				17 09			
Headcorn	d	14 46				15 16				15 46			16 16					16 46				17 16			
Staplehurst	d	14 51				15 21				15 51			16 21					16 51				17 21			
Marden	d	14 55				15 25				15 55			16 25					16 55				17 25			
Maidstone West 4 194	d								15 28								16 33				16 58				
Paddock Wood 4	d	15 01				15 31			15 47	16 01			16 31				16a52	17 01			17a17	17 31			
Tonbridge 4	a	15 09				15 39			15 55	16 09			16 39					17 09				17 39			
	d	15 10				15 40				16 10			16 40					17 10				17 40			
Sevenoaks 4	a	15 18				15 48				16 18			16 48					17 18				17 48			
Orpington 4	a																								
London Bridge 4 ⊖	a	15 43				16 14				16 46			17 17					17 44				18 16			
London Cannon Street 4 ⊖	a																								
London Waterloo (East) 4 ⊖	a	15 48				16 20				16 52			17 22					17 50				18 20			
London Charing Cross 4 ⊖	a	15 52				16 24				16 56			17 26					17 53				18 25			
Ebbsfleet International	a				15 02			15 32				16 02				16 32				17 02				17 32	
Stratford International ⊖	a				15 14			15 44				16 14				16 44				17 14				17 44	
St Pancras Intl. 15 ⊖	a				15 21			15 51				16 21				16 51				17 21				17 51	

		SE	SE 1	SE 1	SE	SE 1	SE 1	SE	SE	SE 1	SE 1		SE	SE	SE 1	SE 1	SE	SE	SE	SE 1	SE 1		SE	SE	
Margate 4	d				16 53								17 53										18 53		
Broadstairs	d				16 59								17 59										18 59		
Ramsgate 4	d		16 22	16 40	17 05	16 50				17 22	17 40		18 05		17 50					18 22	18 40		19 05		
Minster 4	d			16 46							17 46										18 46				
Sandwich	d		16 34			17 02				17 34					18 02					18 34					
Deal	d		16 40			17 08				17 40					18 08					18 40					
Walmer	d		16 43			17 11				17 43					18 11					18 43					
Martin Mill	d		16 48			17 16				17 48					18 16					18 48					
Dover Priory 4	a		16 56			17 24				17 56					18 24					18 56					
	d		16 57			17 24		17 44		17 57					18 24		18 44			18 57					
Folkestone Central	d		17 09			17 36		17 56		18 09					18 36		18 56			19 09					
Folkestone West	d		17 11			17 38		17 58		18 11					18 38		18 58			19 11					
Sandling	d		17 16			17 43				18 16					18 43					19 16					
Westenhanger	d		17 19			17 46				18 19					18 46					19 19					
Sturry	d			16 58							17 58										18 58				
Canterbury West 4	d			17 04	17 25		17 36				18 04		18 25			18 36					19 07		19 25		
Chartham	d						17 41									18 41									
Chilham	d						17 44									18 44									
Wye	d			17 16			17 51				18 16					18 51					19 19				
Ashford International	a		17 28	17 22	17 41	17 55	17 58	18 11		18 28	18 23		18 41		18 55	18 58	19 11			19 29	19 26		19 41		
	d		17 33		17 43	18 03		18 13		18 33			18 43		19 03		19 13			19 33			19 43		
Pluckley	d		17 39			18 09				18 39					19 09					19 39					
Headcorn	d		17 46			18 16				18 46					19 16					19 46					
Staplehurst	d		17 51			18 21				18 51					19 21					19 51					
Marden	d		17 55			18 25				18 55					19 25					19 55					
Maidstone West 4 194	d	17 28							18 18					18 48				19 13	19 18					19 58	
Paddock Wood 4	d	17a47	18 01			18 31			18a37	19 01				19a07	19 31				19a37	20 01				20 17	
Tonbridge 4	a		18 09			18 39				19 09					19 39					20 09				20 25	
	d		18 10			18 40				19 10					19 40					20 10					
Sevenoaks 4	a		18 18			18 48				19 18					19 48					20 18					
Orpington 4	a																								
London Bridge 4 ⊖	a		18 43			19 13				19 43					20 13					20 42					
London Cannon Street 4 ⊖	a																								
London Waterloo (East) 4 ⊖	a		18 48			19 17				19 48					20 18					20 47					
London Charing Cross 4 ⊖	a		18 52			19 21				19 52					20 22					20 51					
Ebbsfleet International	a				18 02			18 32					19 02				19 32	19 47					20 02		
Stratford International ⊖	a				18 14			18 44					19 14				19 46	20 01					20 14		
St Pancras Intl. 15 ⊖	a				18 21			18 51					19 21				19 53	20 08					20 21		

Margate, Ramsgate, Canterbury West, Dover, Folkestone, Ashford International - Tonbridge and London

Network Diagram - see first Page of Table 206

Mondays to Fridays

		SE 1	SE 1	SE	SE 1	SE 1	SE	SE		SE 1	SE 1	SE	SE 1	SE 1	SE	SE	SE 1	SE 1		SE	SE 1	SE	SE 1	SE	SE 1
Margate 4	d						19 53								20 53							21 53			
Broadstairs	d						19 59								20 59							21 59			
Ramsgate 4	d				19 22	19 40	20 05						20 22	20 40	21 05						21 22	22 05	22 24		22 45
Minster 4	d					19 46								20 46									22 30		
Sandwich	d				19 34								20 34								21 34				22 57
Deal	d				19 40								20 40								21 40				23 03
Walmer	d				19 43								20 43								21 43				23 06
Martin Mill	d				19 48								20 48								21 48				23 11
Dover Priory 4	a				19 56								20 56								21 56				23 19
	d	19 24		19 44	19 57					20 24		20 44	20 57				21 24			21 44	21 57			22 44	23 24
Folkestone Central	d	19 36		19 56	20 09					20 36		20 56	21 09				21 36			21 56	22 09			22 56	23 36
Folkestone West	d	19 38		19 58	20 11					20 38		20 58	21 11				21 38			21 58	22 11			22 58	23 38
Sandling	d	19 43			20 16					20 43			21 16				21 43				22 16				23 43
Westenhanger	d	19 46			20 19					20 46			21 19				21 46				22 19				23 46
Sturry	d					19 58								20 58									22 42		
Canterbury West 4	d		19 36			20 07	20 25				20 36			21 07	21 25			21 36				22 25	22 47		
Chartham	d		19 41								20 41							21 41					22 52		
Chilham	d		19 44								20 44							21 44					22 55		
Wye	d		19 51			20 19					20 51			21 19				21 51					23 02		
Ashford International	a	19 55	19 58	20 12	20 28	20 25	20 41			20 55	20 58	21 11	21 28	21 25	21 41		21 55	21 58		22 11	22 28	22 41	23 08	23 11	23 55
	d	20 03		20 13	20 33		20 43			21 03		21 13	21 33		21 43		22 03			22 13	22 33	22 43		23 13	
Pluckley	d	20 09			20 39					21 09			21 39				22 09				22 39				
Headcorn	d	20 16			20 46					21 16			21 46				22 16				22 46				
Staplehurst	d	20 21			20 51					21 21			21 51				22 21				22 51				
Marden	d	20 25			20 55					21 25			21 55				22 25				22 55				
Maidstone West 4 194	d							20 58								21 58									
Paddock Wood 4	d	20 31			21 01			21 17		21 31			22 01			22 17	22 31				23 01				
Tonbridge 4	a	20 39			21 09			21 25		21 39			22 09			22 25	22 39				23 10				
	d	20 40			21 10					21 40			22 10				22 40				23 14				
Sevenoaks 4	a	20 48			21 18					21 48			22 18				22 48				23 24				
Orpington 4	a																				23 36				
London Bridge 4 ⊖	a	21 13			21 43					22 13			22 43				23 13				23 54				
London Cannon Street 4 ⊖	a																								
London Waterloo (East) 4 ⊖	a	21 18			21 48					22 18			22 48				23 18				23 59				
London Charing Cross 4 ⊖	a	21 22			21 52					22 22			22 52				23 22				00 03				
Ebbsfleet International	a			20 32			21 02					21 32			22 02					22 32		23 02		23 32	
Stratford International ⊖	a			20 44			21 14					21 44			22 14					22 44		23 14		23 44	
St Pancras Intl. 15 ⊖	a			20 51			21 21					21 51			22 21					22 51		23 21		23 52	

Saturdays

		SE 1	SE	SE 1	SE	SE	SE	SE 1	SE 1	SE		SE 1	SE	SE	SE 1	SE	SE 1	SE 1	SE	SE		SE 1	SE	SE 1	SE 1
Margate 4	d									05 53						06 53							07 53		
Broadstairs	d									05 59						06 59							07 59		
Ramsgate 4	d	21p22			05 05			05 32		06 05		05 50			06 40	07 05	06 50					07 40	08 05	07 50	
Minster 4	d							05 38							06 46							07 46			
Sandwich	d	21p34										06 02					07 02							08 02	
Deal	d	21p40										06 08					07 08							08 08	
Walmer	d	21p43										06 11					07 11							08 11	
Martin Mill	d	21p48										06 16					07 16							08 16	
Dover Priory 4	a	21p56										06 24					07 24							08 24	
	d	21p57		04 50		05 44			05 50			06 24	06 44				07 24		07 44					08 24	
Folkestone Central	d	22p09		05 02		05 56			06 02			06 36	06 56				07 36		07 56					08 36	
Folkestone West	d	22p11		05 04		05 58			06 04			06 38	06 58				07 38		07 58					08 38	
Sandling	d	22p16		05 09					06 09			06 43					07 43							08 43	
Westenhanger	d	22p19		05 12					06 12			06 46					07 46							08 46	
Sturry	d							05 50							06 58							07 58			
Canterbury West 4	d				05 25			05 56		06 25					07 04	07 25		07 36				08 07	08 25		08 36
Chartham	d							06 01							07 09			07 41							08 41
Chilham	d							06 04							07 12			07 44							08 44
Wye	d							06 11							07 19			07 51				08 19			08 51
Ashford International	a	22p28		05 21	05 41	06 11		06 17	06 21	06 41		06 55	07 11		07 26	07 41	07 55	07 58	08 11			08 25	08 41	08 55	08 58
	d	22p33	05 13	05 25	05 43	06 13		06 25		06 43		07 03	07 13		07 33	07 43	08 03		08 13			08 33	08 43	09 03	
Pluckley	d	22p39		05 31				06 31				07 09			07 39		08 09					08 39		09 09	
Headcorn	d	22p46		05 38				06 38				07 16			07 46		08 16					08 46		09 16	
Staplehurst	d	22p51		05 43				06 43				07 21			07 51		08 21					08 51		09 21	
Marden	d	22p55		05 47				06 47				07 25			07 55		08 25					08 55		09 25	
Maidstone West 4 194	d						06 28							07 28						08 28					
Paddock Wood 4	d	23p01		05 53			06 47	06 53				07 31		07 47	08 01		08 31			08 47		09 01		09 31	
Tonbridge 4	a	23p10		06 01			06 55	07 01				07 39		07 55	08 09		08 39			08 55		09 09		09 39	
	d	23p14		06 02				07 02				07 40			08 10		08 40					09 10		09 40	
Sevenoaks 4	a	23p24		06 13				07 13				07 48			08 18		08 48					09 18		09 48	
Orpington 4	a	23p36		06 23				07 23																	
London Bridge 4 ⊖	a	23p54		06 39				07 39				08 13			08 43		09 13					09 43		10 13	
London Cannon Street 4 ⊖	a																								
London Waterloo (East) 4 ⊖	a	23p59		06 43				07 43				08 19			08 49		09 19					09 49		10 19	
London Charing Cross 4 ⊖	a	00 03		06 47				07 48				08 22			08 52		09 22					09 52		10 22	
Ebbsfleet International	a		05 32		06 02	06 32				07 02			07 32			08 02			08 32				09 02		
Stratford International ⊖	a		05 44		06 14	06 44				07 14			07 44			08 14			08 44				09 14		
St Pancras Intl. 15 ⊖	a		05 51		06 21	06 51				07 21			07 51			08 21			08 51				09 21		

Table 207

Saturdays

Margate, Ramsgate, Canterbury West, Dover, Folkestone, Ashford International - Tonbridge and London

Network Diagram - see first Page of Table 206

		SE	SE	SE [1]	SE	SE [1]	SE [1]		SE	SE	SE [1]	SE	SE [1]	SE [1]	SE	SE	SE [1]		SE	SE [1]	SE [1]	SE	SE	SE [1]	SE
Margate [4]	d				08 53							09 53							10 53						11 53
Broadstairs	d				08 59							09 59							10 59						11 59
Ramsgate [4]	d			08 40	09 05	08 50					09 40	10 05	09 50				10 40		11 05	10 50				11 40	12 05
Minster [4]	d			08 46							09 46						10 46							11 46	
Sandwich	d					09 02							10 02							11 02					
Deal	d					09 08							10 08							11 08					
Walmer	d					09 11							10 11							11 11					
Martin Mill	d					09 16							10 16							11 16					
Dover Priory [4]	a					09 24							10 24							11 24					
	d	08 44				09 24			09 44				10 24		10 44					11 24		11 44			
Folkestone Central	d	08 56				09 36			09 56				10 36		10 56					11 36		11 56			
Folkestone West	d	08 58				09 38			09 58				10 38		10 58					11 38		11 58			
Sandling	d					09 43							10 43							11 43					
Westenhanger	d					09 46							10 46							11 46					
Sturry	d			08 58							09 58						10 58							11 58	
Canterbury West [4]	d			09 07	09 25		09 36				10 07	10 25		10 36			11 07		11 25		11 36			12 07	12 25
Chartham	d						09 41							10 41							11 41				
Chilham	d						09 44							10 44							11 44				
Wye	d			09 19			09 51				10 19			10 51			11 19				11 51			12 19	
Ashford International	a	09 11		09 25	09 41	09 55	09 58		10 11		10 25	10 41	10 55	10 58	11 11		11 25		11 41	11 55	11 58	12 11		12 25	12 41
	d	09 13		09 33	09 43	10 03			10 13		10 33	10 43	11 03		11 13		11 33		11 43	12 03		12 13		12 33	12 43
Pluckley	d			09 39		10 09					10 39		11 09				11 39			12 09				12 39	
Headcorn	d			09 46		10 16					10 46		11 16				11 46			12 16				12 46	
Staplehurst	d			09 51		10 21					10 51		11 21				11 51			12 21				12 51	
Marden	d			09 55		10 25					10 55		11 25				11 55			12 25				12 55	
Maidstone West [4] 194	d		09 28							10 28						11 28							12 28		
Paddock Wood [4]	d		09 47	10 01		10 31				10 47	11 01		11 31			11 47	12 01			12 31			12 47	13 01	
Tonbridge [4]	a		09 55	10 09		10 39				10 55	11 09		11 39			11 55	12 09			12 39			12 55	13 09	
	d			10 10		10 40					11 10		11 40				12 10			12 40				13 10	
Sevenoaks [4]	a			10 18		10 48					11 18		11 48				12 18			12 48				13 18	
Orpington [4]	a																								
London Bridge [4] ⊖	a			10 43		11 13					11 43		12 13				12 43			13 13				13 43	
London Cannon Street [4] ⊖	a																								
London Waterloo (East) [4] ⊖	a			10 49		11 19					11 49		12 19				12 49			13 19				13 49	
London Charing Cross [4] ⊖	a			10 52		11 22					11 52		12 22				12 52			13 22				13 52	
Ebbsfleet International	a	09 32			10 02				10 32			11 02			11 32				12 02			12 32			13 02
Stratford International ⊖	a	09 44			10 14				10 44			11 14			11 44				12 14			12 44			13 14
St Pancras Intl. [15] ⊖	a	09 51			10 21				10 51			11 21			11 51				12 21			12 51			13 21

		SE [1]	SE [1]		SE	SE	SE [1]	SE	SE [1]	SE [1]	SE	SE	SE [1]		SE	SE [1]	SE [1]	SE	SE	SE [1]	SE	SE [1]	SE [1]		SE
Margate [4]	d							12 53							13 53						14 53				
Broadstairs	d							12 59							13 59						14 59				
Ramsgate [4]	d	11 50					12 40	13 05	12 50				13 40		14 05	13 50				14 40	15 05	14 50			
Minster [4]	d						12 46						13 46							14 46					
Sandwich	d	12 02							13 02							14 02						15 02			
Deal	d	12 08							13 08							14 08						15 08			
Walmer	d	12 11							13 11							14 11						15 11			
Martin Mill	d	12 16							13 16							14 16						15 16			
Dover Priory [4]	a	12 24							13 24							14 24						15 24			
	d	12 24			12 44				13 24		13 44					14 24		14 44				15 24			15 44
Folkestone Central	d	12 36			12 56				13 36		13 56					14 36		14 56				15 36			15 56
Folkestone West	d	12 38			12 58				13 38		13 58					14 38		14 58				15 38			15 58
Sandling	d	12 43							13 43							14 43						15 43			
Westenhanger	d	12 46							13 46							14 46						15 46			
Sturry	d						12 58						13 58							14 58					
Canterbury West [4]	d		12 36				13 07	13 25		13 36			14 07		14 25		14 36			15 07	15 25		15 36		
Chartham	d		12 41							13 41							14 41						15 41		
Chilham	d		12 44							13 44							14 44						15 44		
Wye	d		12 51				13 19			13 51			14 19				14 51			15 19			15 51		
Ashford International	a	12 55	12 58		13 11		13 25	13 41	13 55	13 58	14 11		14 25		14 41	14 55	14 58	15 11		15 25	15 41	15 55	15 58		16 11
	d	13 03			13 13		13 33	13 43	14 03		14 13		14 33		14 43	15 03		15 13		15 33	15 46	16 03			16 13
Pluckley	d	13 09					13 39		14 09				14 39			15 09				15 39		16 09			
Headcorn	d	13 16					13 46		14 16				14 46			15 16				15 46		16 16			
Staplehurst	d	13 21					13 51		14 21				14 51			15 21				15 51		16 21			
Marden	d	13 25					13 55		14 25				14 55			15 25				15 55		16 25			
Maidstone West [4] 194	d					13 28						14 28							15 28						
Paddock Wood [4]	d	13 31				13 47	14 01		14 31			14 47	15 01			15 31			15 47	16 01		16 31			
Tonbridge [4]	a	13 39				13 55	14 09		14 39			14 55	15 09			15 39			15 55	16 09		16 39			
	d	13 40					14 10		14 40				15 10			15 40				16 10		16 40			
Sevenoaks [4]	a	13 48					14 18		14 48				15 18			15 48				16 18		16 48			
Orpington [4]	a																								
London Bridge [4] ⊖	a	14 13					14 43		15 13				15 43			16 13				16 43		17 13			
London Cannon Street [4] ⊖	a																								
London Waterloo (East) [4] ⊖	a	14 19					14 49		15 19				15 49			16 19				16 49		17 19			
London Charing Cross [4] ⊖	a	14 22					14 52		15 22				15 52			16 22				16 52		17 22			
Ebbsfleet International	a				13 32			14 02			14 32				15 02			15 32			16 05				16 32
Stratford International ⊖	a				13 44			14 14			14 44				15 14			15 44			16 17				16 44
St Pancras Intl. [15] ⊖	a				13 51			14 21			14 51				15 21			15 51			16 24				16 51

Table 207

Margate, Ramsgate, Canterbury West, Dover, Folkestone, Ashford International - Tonbridge and London

Network Diagram - see first Page of Table 206

		SE	SE 1	SE	SE 1	SE 1	SE	SE	SE 1		SE	SE 1	SE 1	SE	SE	SE 1	SE	SE 1	SE 1		SE	SE	SE 1	SE	
Margate 4	d			15 53							16 53						17 53							18 53	
Broadstairs	d			15 59							16 59						17 59							18 59	
Ramsgate 4	d		15 40	16 05	15 50				16 40		17 05	16 50				17 40	18 05	17 50					18 40	19 05	
Minster 4	d		15 46						16 46							17 46							18 46		
Sandwich	d				16 02							17 02						18 02							
Deal	d				16 08							17 08						18 08							
Walmer	d				16 11							17 11						18 11							
Martin Mill	d				16 16							17 16						18 16							
Dover Priory 4	a				16 24							17 24						18 24							
	d				16 24		16 44					17 24		17 44				18 24			18 44				
Folkestone Central	d				16 36		16 56					17 36		17 56				18 36			18 56				
Folkestone West	d				16 38		16 58					17 38		17 58				18 38			18 58				
Sandling	d				16 43							17 43						18 43							
Westenhanger	d				16 46							17 46						18 46							
Sturry	d		15 58						16 58							17 58							18 58		
Canterbury West 4	d		16 07	16 25		16 36			17 07		17 25		17 36			18 07	18 25		18 36				19 07	19 25	
Chartham	d					16 41							17 41						18 41						
Chilham	d					16 44							17 44						18 44						
Wye	d		16 19			16 51			17 19				17 51			18 19			18 51				19 19		
Ashford International	a		16 25	16 41	16 55	16 58	17 11		17 25		17 41	17 55	17 58	18 11		18 25	18 41	18 55	18 58		19 11		19 25	19 41	
	d		16 33	16 43	17 03		17 13		17 33		17 43	18 03		18 13		18 33	18 43	19 03			19 13		19 33	19 43	
Pluckley	d		16 39		17 09				17 39			18 09				18 39		19 09					19 39		
Headcorn	d		16 46		17 16				17 46			18 16				18 46		19 16					19 46		
Staplehurst	d		16 51		17 21				17 51			18 21				18 51		19 21					19 51		
Marden	d		16 55		17 25				17 55			18 25				18 55		19 25					19 55		
Maidstone West 4 194	d	16 28						17 28							18 28							19 28			
Paddock Wood 4	d	16 47	17 01		17 31			17 47	18 01			18 31			18 47	19 01		19 31				19 47	20 01		
Tonbridge 4	a	16 55	17 09		17 39			17 55	18 09			18 39			18 55	19 09		19 39				19 55	20 09		
	d		17 10		17 40				18 10			18 40				19 10		19 40					20 10		
Sevenoaks 4	a		17 18		17 48				18 18			18 48				19 18		19 48					20 18		
Orpington 4	a															19 27		19 57					20 27		
London Bridge 4 ⊖	a		17 43		18 13				18 43			19 13				19 43		20 13					20 43		
London Cannon Street 4 ⊖	a																								
London Waterloo (East) 4 ⊖	a		17 49		18 19				18 49			19 19				19 48		20 18					20 48		
London Charing Cross 4 ⊖	a		17 52		18 22				18 52			19 22				19 51		20 21					20 51		
Ebbsfleet International	a			17 02			17 32				18 02			18 32			19 02				19 32			20 02	
Stratford International ⊖	a			17 14			17 44				18 14			18 44			19 14				19 46			20 14	
St Pancras Intl. 15 ⊖	a			17 21			17 51				18 21			18 51			19 21				19 53			20 21	

		SE 1	SE 1	SE	SE	SE 1		SE	SE 1	SE	SE	SE 1	SE	SE 1	SE	SE		SE 1	SE	SE 1	SE	SE 1			
Margate 4	d							19 53					20 53						21 53						
Broadstairs	d							19 59					20 59						21 59						
Ramsgate 4	d	18 50				19 40		20 05	19 50			20 40	21 05	20 50				21 22	22 05	22 24		22 45			
Minster 4	d					19 46						20 46								22 30					
Sandwich	d	19 02							20 02					21 02				21 34				22 57			
Deal	d	19 08							20 08					21 08				21 40				23 03			
Walmer	d	19 11							20 11					21 11				21 43				23 06			
Martin Mill	d	19 16							20 16					21 16				21 48				23 11			
Dover Priory 4	a	19 24							20 24					21 24				21 56				23 19			
	d	19 24		19 44					20 24	20 44				21 24	21 44			21 57			22 44	23 24			
Folkestone Central	d	19 36		19 56					20 36	20 56				21 36	21 56			22 09			22 56	23 36			
Folkestone West	d	19 38		19 58					20 38	20 58				21 38	21 58			22 11			22 58	23 38			
Sandling	d	19 43							20 43					21 43				22 16				23 43			
Westenhanger	d	19 46							20 46					21 46				22 19				23 46			
Sturry	d					19 58						20 58								22 42					
Canterbury West 4	d		19 36			20 04		20 25				21 04	21 25						22 25	22 47					
Chartham	d		19 41			20 09						21 09								22 52					
Chilham	d		19 44			20 12						21 12								22 55					
Wye	d		19 51			20 19						21 19								23 02					
Ashford International	a	19 55	19 58	20 11		20 25		20 41	20 55	21 11		21 25	21 41	21 55	22 11			22 28	22 41	23 08	23 11	23 55			
	d	20 03		20 13		20 33		20 43	21 03	21 13		21 33	21 43	22 03	22 13			22 33	22 43		23 13				
Pluckley	d	20 09				20 39			21 09			21 39		22 09				22 39							
Headcorn	d	20 16				20 46			21 16			21 46		22 16				22 46							
Staplehurst	d	20 21				20 51			21 21			21 51		22 21				22 51							
Marden	d	20 25				20 55			21 25			21 55		22 25				22 55							
Maidstone West 4 194	d				20 28						21 28					22 28									
Paddock Wood 4	d	20 31			20 47	21 01			21 31		21 47	22 01		22 31		22 47		23 01							
Tonbridge 4	a	20 39			20 55	21 09			21 39		21 55	22 09		22 39		22 55		23 10							
	d	20 40				21 10			21 40			22 10		22 40				23 14							
Sevenoaks 4	a	20 48				21 18			21 48			22 18		22 48				23 24							
Orpington 4	a	20 57				21 27			21 57			22 27		22 57				23 36							
London Bridge 4 ⊖	a	21 13				21 43			22 13			22 43		23 13				23 54							
London Cannon Street 4 ⊖	a																								
London Waterloo (East) 4 ⊖	a	21 18				21 48			22 18			22 48		23 18				23 59							
London Charing Cross 4 ⊖	a	21 21				21 51			22 21			22 51		23 21				00 03							
Ebbsfleet International	a			20 32				21 02		21 32			22 02		22 32				23 02		23 32				
Stratford International ⊖	a			20 44				21 14		21 44			22 14		22 44				23 14		23 44				
St Pancras Intl. 15 ⊖	a			20 51				21 21		21 51			22 21		22 51				23 21		23 51				

Table 207

Sundays

Margate, Ramsgate, Canterbury West, Dover, Folkestone, Ashford International - Tonbridge and London

Network Diagram - see first Page of Table 206

		SE 1 A	SE 1	SE	SE 1	SE 1	SE	SE	SE 1	SE		SE 1	SE	SE	SE 1	SE	SE 1	SE	SE	SE 1	SE 1		SE	SE 1	SE
Margate 4	d												07 53					08 53							09 53
Broadstairs	d												07 59					08 59							09 59
Ramsgate 4	d	21p22							06 50			07 40	08 05		07 50		08 40	09 05		08 50				09 40	10 05
Minster 4	d											07 46					08 46							09 46	
Sandwich	d	21p34							07 02						08 02					09 02					
Deal	d	21p40							07 08						08 08					09 08					
Walmer	d	21p43							07 11						08 11					09 11					
Martin Mill	d	21p48							07 16						08 16					09 16					
Dover Priory 4	a	21p56							07 24						08 24					09 24					
	d	21p57							07 24	07 44					08 24	08 44				09 24			09 44		
Folkestone Central	d	22p09							07 36	07 56					08 36	08 56				09 36			09 56		
Folkestone West	d	22p11							07 38	07 58					08 38	08 58				09 38			09 58		
Sandling	d	22p16							07 43						08 43					09 43					
Westenhanger	d	22p19							07 46						08 46					09 46					
Sturry	d											07 58					08 58							09 58	
Canterbury West 4	d											08 04	08 25				09 04	09 25			09 36			10 07	10 25
Chartham	d											08 09					09 09				09 41				
Chilham	d											08 12					09 12				09 44				
Wye	d											08 19					09 19				09 51			10 19	
Ashford International	a	22p28							07 55	08 11		08 25	08 41		08 55	09 11	09 25	09 41		09 55	09 58		10 11	10 25	10 41
	d	22p33	06 33		07 03	07 33	07 43		08 03	08 13		08 33	08 43		09 03	09 13	09 33	09 43		10 03			10 13	10 33	10 43
Pluckley	d	22p39	06 39			07 39						08 39					09 39							10 39	
Headcorn	d	22p46	06 46		07 14	07 46			08 14			08 46			09 14		09 46			10 14				10 46	
Staplehurst	d	22p51	06 51		07 19	07 51			08 19			08 51			09 19		09 51			10 19				10 51	
Marden	d	22p55	06 55		07 23	07 55			08 23			08 55			09 23		09 55			10 23				10 55	
Maidstone West 4 194	d			07 03				08 03						09 03					10 03						
Paddock Wood 4	d	23p01	07 01	07a22	07 29	08 01		08a22	08 29			09 01		09a22	09 29		10 01		10a22	10 29				11 01	
Tonbridge 4	a	23p10	07 09		07 38	08 09			08 38			09 09			09 38		10 09			10 38				11 09	
	d	23p14	07 10		07 38	08 10			08 38			09 10			09 38		10 10			10 38				11 10	
Sevenoaks 4	a	23p24	07 18		07 48	08 18			08 48			09 18			09 48		10 18			10 48				11 18	
Orpington 4	a	23p36	07 27		07 57	08 27			08 57			09 27			09 57		10 27			10 57				11 27	
London Bridge 4 ⊖	a	23p54	07 43		08 13	08 43			09 13			09 43			10 13		10 43			11 13				11 43	
London Cannon Street 4 ⊖	a																								
London Waterloo (East) 4 ⊖	a	23p59	07 48		08 18	08 48			09 18			09 48			10 18		10 48			11 18				11 48	
London Charing Cross 4 ⊖	a	00 03	07 52		08 22	08 52			09 22			09 52			10 22		10 52			11 22				11 52	
Ebbsfleet International	a						08 02			08 32			09 02			09 32		10 02					10 32		11 02
Stratford International ⊖	a						08 14			08 44			09 14			09 44		10 14					10 44		11 14
St Pancras Intl. 15 ⊖	a						08 21			08 51			09 21			09 51		10 21					10 51		11 21

		SE	SE 1	SE 1	SE	SE 1	SE		SE	SE 1	SE 1	SE	SE 1	SE	SE	SE 1	SE 1		SE	SE 1	SE	SE	SE 1	SE 1	SE
Margate 4	d						10 53							11 53							12 53				
Broadstairs	d						10 59							11 59							12 59				
Ramsgate 4	d		09 50			10 40	11 05			10 50			11 40	12 05		11 50				12 40	13 05		12 50		
Minster 4	d					10 46							11 46							12 46					
Sandwich	d		10 02							11 02						12 02							13 02		
Deal	d		10 08							11 08						12 08							13 08		
Walmer	d		10 11							11 11						12 11							13 11		
Martin Mill	d		10 16							11 16						12 16							13 16		
Dover Priory 4	a		10 24							11 24						12 24							13 24		
	d		10 24		10 44					11 24		11 44				12 24			12 44				13 24		13 44
Folkestone Central	d		10 36		10 56					11 36		11 56				12 36			12 56				13 36		13 56
Folkestone West	d		10 38		10 58					11 38		11 58				12 38			12 58				13 38		13 58
Sandling	d		10 43							11 43						12 43							13 43		
Westenhanger	d		10 46							11 46						12 46							13 46		
Sturry	d					10 58							11 58							12 58					
Canterbury West 4	d			10 36		11 07	11 25				11 36		12 07	12 25			12 36			13 07	13 25			13 36	
Chartham	d			10 41							11 41						12 41							13 41	
Chilham	d			10 44							11 44						12 44							13 44	
Wye	d			10 51		11 19					11 51		12 19				12 51			13 19				13 51	
Ashford International	a		10 55	10 58	11 11	11 25	11 41			11 55	11 58	12 11	12 25	12 41		12 55	12 58		13 11	13 25	13 41		13 55	13 58	14 11
	d		11 03		11 13	11 33	11 43			12 03		12 13	12 33	12 43		13 03			13 13	13 33	13 43		14 03		14 13
Pluckley	d					11 39							12 39							13 39					
Headcorn	d		11 14			11 46				12 14			12 46			13 14				13 46			14 14		
Staplehurst	d		11 19			11 51				12 19			12 51			13 19				13 51			14 19		
Marden	d		11 23			11 55				12 23			12 55			13 23				13 55			14 23		
Maidstone West 4 194	d	11 03							12 03						13 03							14 03			
Paddock Wood 4	d	11a22	11 29			12 01			12a22	12 29			13 01		13a22	13 29				14 01		14a22	14 29		
Tonbridge 4	a		11 38			12 09				12 38			13 09			13 38				14 09			14 38		
	d		11 38			12 10				12 38			13 10			13 38				14 10			14 38		
Sevenoaks 4	a		11 48			12 18				12 48			13 18			13 48				14 18			14 48		
Orpington 4	a		11 57			12 27				12 57			13 27			13 57				14 27			14 57		
London Bridge 4 ⊖	a		12 13			12 43				13 13			13 43			14 13				14 43			15 13		
London Cannon Street 4 ⊖	a																								
London Waterloo (East) 4 ⊖	a		12 18			12 48				13 18			13 48			14 18				14 48			15 18		
London Charing Cross 4 ⊖	a		12 22			12 52				13 22			13 52			14 22				14 52			15 22		
Ebbsfleet International	a				11 32		12 02					12 32		13 02					13 32		14 02				14 32
Stratford International ⊖	a				11 44		12 14					12 44		13 14					13 44		14 14				14 44
St Pancras Intl. 15 ⊖	a				11 51		12 21					12 51		13 21					13 51		14 21				14 51

A not 11 December

Table 207

Sundays

Margate, Ramsgate, Canterbury West, Dover, Folkestone, Ashford International - Tonbridge and London

Network Diagram - see first Page of Table 206

		SE	SE		SE	SE	SE	SE	SE	SE	SE	SE	SE		SE	SE	SE	SE	SE	SE	SE	SE	SE		SE
		1 A 🚲				1	1		1			1	1			1			1	1		1			
Margate 4	d		13 53							14 53							15 53						16 53		
Broadstairs	d		13 59							14 59							15 59						16 59		
Ramsgate 4	d	13 40	14 05			13 50			14 40	15 05		14 50				15 40	16 05		15 50			16 40	17 05		
Minster 4	d	13 46							14 46							15 46						16 46			
Sandwich	d					14 02						15 02							16 02						
Deal	d					14 08						15 08							16 08						
Walmer	d					14 11						15 11							16 11						
Martin Mill	d					14 16						15 16							16 16						
Dover Priory 4	a					14 24						15 24							16 24						
	d					14 24		14 44				15 24			15 44				16 24		16 44				
Folkestone Central	d					14 36		14 56				15 36			15 56				16 36		16 56				
Folkestone West	d					14 38		14 58				15 38			15 58				16 38		16 58				
Sandling	d					14 43						15 43							16 43						
Westenhanger	d					14 46						15 46							16 46						
Sturry	d	13 58							14 58							15 58						16 58			
Canterbury West 4	d	14 07	14 25				14 36		15 07	15 25			15 36			16 07	16 25			16 36		17 07	17 25		
Chartham	d						14 41						15 41							16 41					
Chilham	d						14 44						15 44							16 44					
Wye	d	14 19					14 51		15 19				15 51			16 19				16 51		17 19			
Ashford International	a	14 25	14 41			14 55	14 58	15 11	15 25	15 41		15 55	15 58		16 11	16 25	16 41		16 55	16 58	17 11	17 25	17 41		
	d	14 33	14 43			15 03		15 13	15 33	15 43		16 03			16 13	16 33	16 43		17 03		17 13	17 33	17 43		
Pluckley	d	14 39							15 39							16 39						17 39			
Headcorn	d	14 46				15 14			15 46			16 14				16 46			17 14			17 46			
Staplehurst	d	14 51				15 19			15 51			16 19				16 51			17 19			17 51			
Marden	d	14 55				15 23			15 55			16 23				16 55			17 23			17 55			
Maidstone West 4 194	d				15 03						16 03							17 03							18 03
Paddock Wood 4	d	15 01			15a22	15 29			16 01		16a22	16 29				17 01		17a22	17 29			18 01			18a22
Tonbridge 4	a	15 09				15 38			16 09			16 38				17 09			17 38			18 09			
	d	15 10				15 38			16 10			16 38				17 10			17 38			18 10			
Sevenoaks 4	a	15 18				15 48			16 18			16 48				17 18			17 48			18 18			
Orpington 4	a	15 27				15 57			16 27			16 57				17 27			17 57			18 27			
London Bridge 4 ⊖	a	15 43				16 13			16 43			17 13				17 43			18 13			18 43			
London Cannon Street 4 ⊖	a																								
London Waterloo (East) 4 ⊖	a	15 48				16 18			16 48			17 18				17 48			18 18			18 48			
London Charing Cross 4 ⊖	a	15 52				16 22			16 52			17 22				17 52			18 22			18 52			
Ebbsfleet International	a		15 02					15 32		16 02					16 32		17 02				17 32		18 02		
Stratford International ⊖	a		15 14					15 44		16 14					16 44		17 14				17 44		18 14		
St Pancras Intl. 15 ⊖	a		15 21					15 51		16 21					16 51		17 21				17 51		18 21		

		SE	SE	SE	SE	SE	SE	SE	SE		SE	SE	SE	SE	SE	SE	SE	SE	SE		SE	SE	SE	SE	SE
		1	1		1			1	1			1			1		1				1		1		
Margate 4	d					17 53							18 53					19 53						20 53	
Broadstairs	d					17 59							18 59					19 59						20 59	
Ramsgate 4	d	16 50			17 40	18 05		17 50				18 40	19 05		18 50		19 40	20 05			19 50		20 40	21 05	
Minster 4	d				17 46							18 46					19 46						20 46		
Sandwich	d	17 02						18 02							19 02						20 02				
Deal	d	17 08						18 08							19 08						20 08				
Walmer	d	17 11						18 11							19 11						20 11				
Martin Mill	d	17 16						18 16							19 16						20 16				
Dover Priory 4	a	17 24						18 24							19 24						20 24				
	d	17 24		17 44				18 24			18 44				19 24	19 44					20 24	20 44			
Folkestone Central	d	17 36		17 56				18 36			18 56				19 36	19 56					20 36	20 56			
Folkestone West	d	17 38		17 58				18 38			18 58				19 38	19 58					20 38	20 58			
Sandling	d	17 43						18 43							19 43						20 43				
Westenhanger	d	17 46						18 46							19 46						20 46				
Sturry	d				17 58							18 58					19 58						20 58		
Canterbury West 4	d		17 36		18 07	18 25			18 36			19 04	19 25				20 04	20 25					21 04	21 25	
Chartham	d		17 41						18 41			19 09					20 09						21 09		
Chilham	d		17 44						18 44			19 12					20 12						21 12		
Wye	d		17 51		18 19				18 51			19 19					20 19						21 19		
Ashford International	a	17 55	17 58	18 11	18 25	18 41		18 55	18 58		19 11	19 25	19 41		19 55	20 11	20 25	20 41			20 55	21 11	21 25	21 41	
	d	18 03		18 13	18 33	18 43		19 03			19 13	19 33	19 43		20 03	20 13	20 33	20 43			21 03	21 13	21 33	21 43	
Pluckley	d				18 39							19 39					20 39						21 39		
Headcorn	d	18 14			18 46			19 14				19 46			20 14		20 46				21 14		21 46		
Staplehurst	d	18 19			18 51			19 19				19 51			20 19		20 51				21 19		21 51		
Marden	d	18 23			18 55			19 23				19 55			20 23		20 55				21 23		21 55		
Maidstone West 4 194	d						19 03							20 03					21 03						22 03
Paddock Wood 4	d	18 29			19 01		19a22	19 29				20 01		20a22	20 29		21 01		21a22		21 29		22 01		22 23
Tonbridge 4	a	18 38			19 09			19 38				20 09			20 38		21 09				21 38		22 09		22 32
	d	18 38			19 10			19 38				20 10			20 38		21 10				21 38		22 10		
Sevenoaks 4	a	18 48			19 18			19 48				20 18			20 48		21 18				21 48		22 18		
Orpington 4	a	18 57			19 27			19 57				20 27			20 57		21 27				21 57		22 27		
London Bridge 4 ⊖	a	19 13			19 43			20 13				20 43			21 13		21 43				22 13		22 43		
London Cannon Street 4 ⊖	a																								
London Waterloo (East) 4 ⊖	a	19 18			19 48			20 18				20 48			21 18		21 48				22 18		22 48		
London Charing Cross 4 ⊖	a	19 22			19 52			20 22				20 52			21 22		21 52				22 22		22 52		
Ebbsfleet International	a			18 32		19 02					19 32		20 02			20 32		21 02				21 32		22 02	
Stratford International ⊖	a			18 44		19 14					19 44		20 14			20 44		21 14				21 44		22 14	
St Pancras Intl. 15 ⊖	a			18 51		19 21					19 51		20 21			20 51		21 21				21 51		22 21	

A 🚲 from Ashford International

Table 207

Sundays

Margate, Ramsgate, Canterbury West, Dover, Folkestone, Ashford International - Tonbridge and London

Network Diagram - see first Page of Table 206

		SE 1	SE	SE 1	SE	SE 1
Margate 4	d				21 53	
Broadstairs	d				21 59	
Ramsgate 4	d	20 50		21 40	22 05	21 50
Minster 4	d			21 46		
Sandwich	d	21 02				22 02
Deal	d	21 08				22 08
Walmer	d	21 11				22 11
Martin Mill	d	21 16				22 16
Dover Priory 4	a	21 24				22 24
	d	21 24	21 44			22 24
Folkestone Central	d	21 36	21 56			22 36
Folkestone West	d	21 38	21 58			22 38
Sandling	d	21 43				22 43
Westenhanger	d	21 46				22 46
Sturry	d			21 58		
Canterbury West 4	d			22 04	22 25	
Chartham	d			22 09		
Chilham	d			22 12		
Wye	d			22 19		
Ashford International	a	21 55	22 11	22 25	22 41	22 55
	d	22 03	22 13		22 43	
Pluckley	d					
Headcorn	d	22 14				
Staplehurst	d	22 19				
Marden	d	22 23				
Maidstone West 4 194	d					
Paddock Wood 4	d	22 29				
Tonbridge 4	a	22 38				
	d	22 38				
Sevenoaks 4	a	22 48				
Orpington 4	a	22 57				
London Bridge 4 ⊖	a	23 13				
London Cannon Street 4 ⊖	a					
London Waterloo (East) 4 ⊖	a	23 18				
London Charing Cross 4 ⊖	a	23 22				
Ebbsfleet International	a		22 32		23 02	
Stratford International ⊖	a		22 44		23 14	
St Pancras Intl. 15 ⊖	a		22 51		23 21	

Strood - Maidstone West and Paddock Wood

Network Diagram - see first Page of Table 206

Miles			SE	SE	SE	SE	SE	SE	SE	SE	SE		SE	SE	SE	SE	SE	SE	SE	SE	SE		SE	SE	SE
0	St Pancras International	d					06 25																		
5¼	Stratford International	d					06 32																		
22	Ebbsfleet International	d					06 42																		
25	Gravesend	d					06 46																		
33	**Strood** 4	d	04 55	05 33	06 03	06 35	06 57	07 18	07 55	08 35	09 05		09 35	10 05	10 35	11 05	11 35	12 05	12 35	13 05	13 35		14 05	14 35	15 05
35¼	Cuxton	d	04 59	05 37	06 07	06 39		07 22	07 59	08 39	09 09		09 39	10 09	10 39	11 09	11 39	12 09	12 39	13 09	13 39		14 09	14 39	15 09
37	Halling	d	05 02	05 40	06 10	06 42		07 25	08 02	08 42	09 12		09 42	10 12	10 42	11 12	11 42	12 12	12 42	13 12	13 42		14 12	14 42	15 12
38½	Snodland	d	05 05	05 43	06 13	06 45		07 28	08 05	08 45	09 15		09 45	10 15	10 45	11 15	11 45	12 15	12 45	13 15	13 45		14 15	14 45	15 15
39¾	New Hythe	d	05 08	05 46	06 16	06 48		07 31	08 08	08 48	09 18		09 48	10 18	10 48	11 18	11 48	12 18	12 48	13 18	13 48		14 18	14 48	15 18
40¾	Aylesford	d	05 10	05 48	06 18	06 50		07 33	08 10	08 50	09 20		09 50	10 20	10 50	11 20	11 50	12 20	12 50	13 20	13 50		14 20	14 50	15 20
43¾	Maidstone Barracks	d	05 15	05 53	06 23	06 55		07 38	08 15	08 55	09 25		09 55	10 25	10 55	11 25	11 55	12 25	12 55	13 25	13 55		14 25	14 55	15 25
44¼	**Maidstone West** 4 194	a	05 17	05 55	06 25	07 00	07 12	07 40	08 17	08 57	09 27		09 57	10 27	10 57	11 27	11 57	12 27	12 57	13 27	13 57		14 27	14 57	15 27
—		d	05 18	05 56	06 26	07 01		07 41	08 18		09 28			10 28		11 28		12 28		13 28			14 28		15 28
46	East Farleigh	d	05 21	05 59	06 29	07 04		07 44	08 21		09 31			10 31		11 31		12 31		13 31			14 31		15 31
49	Wateringbury	d	05 26	06 04	06 34	07 09		07 49	08 26		09 36			10 36		11 36		12 36		13 36			14 36		15 36
50¾	Yalding	d	05 30	06 08	06 38	07 13		07 53	08 30		09 40			10 40		11 40		12 40		13 40			14 40		15 40
52¼	Beltring	d	05 33	06 11	06 41	07 16		07 56	08 33		09 43			10 43		11 43		12 43		13 43			14 43		15 43
54¼	**Paddock Wood** 4	a	05 37	06 15	06 45	07 20		08 00	08 37		09 47			10 47		11 47		12 47		13 47			14 47		15 47
59½	Tonbridge 4	a							08 45		09 57			10 55		11 55		12 58		13 55			14 55		15 55

		SE	SE	SE	SE	SE	SE		SE	SE	SE	SE	SE	SE	SE	SE	SE		SE	SE					
St Pancras International	d					17 14			17 44		18 14														
Stratford International	d					17 21			17 51		18 21														
Ebbsfleet International	d																								
Gravesend	d					17 36			18 06		18 38														
Strood 4	d	15 35	16 10	16 35	17 05	17 46	17 55		18 18	18 25	18 49	18 55	19 35	20 05	20 35	21 05	21 35		22 05	22 35					
Cuxton	d	15 39	16 14	16 39	17 09		17 59			18 29		18 59	19 39	20 09	20 39	21 09	21 39		22 09	22 39					
Halling	d	15 42	16 17	16 42	17 12		18 02			18 32		19 02	19 42	20 12	20 42	21 12	21 42		22 12	22 42					
Snodland	d	15 45	16 20	16 45	17 15		18 05			18 35		19 05	19 45	20 15	20 45	21 15	21 45		22 15	22 45					
New Hythe	d	15 48	16 23	16 48	17 18		18 08			18 38		19 08	19 48	20 18	20 48	21 18	21 48		22 18	22 48					
Aylesford	d	15 50	16 25	16 50	17 20		18 10			18 40		19 10	19 50	20 20	20 50	21 20	21 50		22 20	22 50					
Maidstone Barracks	d	15 55	16 30	16 55	17 25		18 15			18 45		19 15	19 55	20 25	20 55	21 25	21 55		22 25	22 55					
Maidstone West 4 194	a	15 57	16 32	16 57	17 27	18 02	18 17		18 32	18 47	19 05	19 17	19 57	20 27	20 57	21 27	21 57		22 27	22 57					
	d		16 33	16 58	17 28		18 18			18 48		19 18	19 58		20 58		21 58								
East Farleigh	d		16 36	17 01	17 31		18 21			18 51		19 21	20 01		21 01		22 01								
Wateringbury	d		16 41	17 06	17 36		18 26			18 56		19 26	20 06		21 06		22 06								
Yalding	d		16 45	17 10	17 40		18 30			19 00		19 30	20 10		21 10		22 10								
Beltring	d		16 48	17 13	17 43		18 33			19 03		19 33	20 13		21 13		22 13								
Paddock Wood 4	a		16 52	17 17	17 47		18 37			19 07		19 37	20 17		21 17		22 17								
Tonbridge 4	a												20 25		21 25		22 25								

Saturdays

		SE	SE	SE	SE	SE	SE	SE	SE	SE		SE	SE	SE	SE	SE	SE	SE	SE	SE		SE	SE	SE	SE
St Pancras International	d																								
Stratford International	d																								
Ebbsfleet International	d																								
Gravesend	d																								
Strood 4	d	06 05	06 35	07 05	07 35	08 05	08 35	09 05	09 35	10 05		10 35	11 05	11 35	12 05	12 35	13 05	13 35	14 05	14 35		15 05	15 35	16 05	16 35
Cuxton	d	06 09	06 39	07 09	07 39	08 09	08 39	09 09	09 39	10 09		10 39	11 09	11 39	12 09	12 39	13 09	13 39	14 09	14 39		15 09	15 39	16 09	16 39
Halling	d	06 12	06 42	07 12	07 42	08 12	08 42	09 12	09 42	10 12		10 42	11 12	11 42	12 12	12 42	13 12	13 42	14 12	14 42		15 12	15 42	16 12	16 42
Snodland	d	06 15	06 45	07 15	07 45	08 15	08 45	09 15	09 45	10 15		10 45	11 15	11 45	12 15	12 45	13 15	13 45	14 15	14 45		15 15	15 45	16 15	16 45
New Hythe	d	06 18	06 48	07 18	07 48	08 18	08 48	09 18	09 48	10 18		10 48	11 18	11 48	12 18	12 48	13 18	13 48	14 18	14 48		15 18	15 48	16 18	16 48
Aylesford	d	06 20	06 50	07 20	07 50	08 20	08 50	09 20	09 50	10 20		10 50	11 20	11 50	12 20	12 50	13 20	13 50	14 20	14 50		15 20	15 50	16 20	16 50
Maidstone Barracks	d	06 25	06 55	07 25	07 55	08 25	08 55	09 25	09 55	10 25		10 55	11 25	11 55	12 25	12 55	13 25	13 55	14 25	14 55		15 25	15 55	16 25	16 55
Maidstone West 4 194	a	06 27	06 57	07 27	07 57	08 27	08 57	09 27	09 57	10 27		10 57	11 27	11 57	12 27	12 57	13 27	13 57	14 27	14 57		15 27	15 57	16 27	16 57
	d	06 28		07 28		08 28		09 28		10 28			11 28		12 28		13 28		14 28			15 28		16 28	
East Farleigh	d	06 31		07 31		08 31		09 31		10 31			11 31		12 31		13 31		14 31			15 31		16 31	
Wateringbury	d	06 36		07 36		08 36		09 36		10 36			11 36		12 36		13 36		14 36			15 36		16 36	
Yalding	d	06 40		07 40		08 40		09 40		10 40			11 40		12 40		13 40		14 40			15 40		16 40	
Beltring	d	06 43		07 43		08 43		09 43		10 43			11 43		12 43		13 43		14 43			15 43		16 43	
Paddock Wood 4	a	06 47		07 47		08 47		09 47		10 47			11 47		12 47		13 47		14 47			15 47		16 47	
Tonbridge 4	a	06 55		07 55		08 55		09 55		10 55			11 55		12 55		13 55		14 55			15 55		16 55	

		SE	SE	SE	SE	SE		SE	SE	SE	SE	SE	SE	SE											
St Pancras International	d																								
Stratford International	d																								
Ebbsfleet International	d																								
Gravesend	d																								
Strood 4	d	17 05	17 35	18 05	18 35	19 05		19 35	20 05	20 35	21 05	21 35	22 05	22 35											
Cuxton	d	17 09	17 39	18 09	18 39	19 09		19 39	20 09	20 39	21 09	21 39	22 09	22 39											
Halling	d	17 12	17 42	18 12	18 42	19 12		19 42	20 12	20 42	21 12	21 42	22 12	22 42											
Snodland	d	17 15	17 45	18 15	18 45	19 15		19 45	20 15	20 45	21 15	21 45	22 15	22 45											
New Hythe	d	17 18	17 48	18 18	18 48	19 18		19 48	20 18	20 48	21 18	21 48	22 18	22 48											
Aylesford	d	17 20	17 50	18 20	18 50	19 20		19 50	20 20	20 50	21 20	21 50	22 20	22 50											
Maidstone Barracks	d	17 25	17 55	18 25	18 55	19 25		19 55	20 25	20 55	21 25	21 55	22 25	22 55											
Maidstone West 4 194	a	17 27	17 57	18 27	18 57	19 27		19 57	20 27	20 57	21 27	21 57	22 27	22 57											
	d	17 28		18 28		19 28			20 28		21 28		22 28												
East Farleigh	d	17 31		18 31		19 31			20 31		21 31		22 31												
Wateringbury	d	17 36		18 36		19 36			20 36		21 36		22 36												
Yalding	d	17 40		18 40		19 40			20 40		21 40		22 40												
Beltring	d	17 43		18 43		19 43			20 43		21 43		22 43												
Paddock Wood 4	a	17 47		18 47		19 47			20 47		21 47		22 47												
Tonbridge 4	a	17 55		18 55		19 55			20 55		21 55		22 55												

Table 208

Sundays

Strood - Maidstone West and Paddock Wood

Network Diagram - see first Page of Table 206

		SE	SE	SE	SE	SE	SE	SE	SE	SE		SE	SE	SE	SE	SE	SE	SE							
St Pancras International	d																								
Stratford International	d																								
Ebbsfleet International	d																								
Gravesend	d																								
Strood ■	d	06 35	07 35	08 35	09 35	10 35	11 35	12 35	13 35	14 35		15 35	16 35	17 35	18 35	19 35	20 35	21 35							
Cuxton	d	06 39	07 39	08 39	09 39	10 39	11 39	12 39	13 39	14 39		15 39	16 39	17 39	18 39	19 39	20 39	21 39							
Halling	d	06 42	07 42	08 42	09 42	10 42	11 42	12 42	13 42	14 42		15 42	16 42	17 42	18 42	19 42	20 42	21 42							
Snodland	d	06 45	07 45	08 45	09 45	10 45	11 45	12 45	13 45	14 45		15 45	16 45	17 45	18 45	19 45	20 45	21 45							
New Hythe	d	06 48	07 48	08 48	09 48	10 48	11 48	12 48	13 48	14 48		15 48	16 48	17 48	18 48	19 48	20 48	21 48							
Aylesford	d	06 50	07 50	08 50	09 50	10 50	11 50	12 50	13 50	14 50		15 50	16 50	17 50	18 50	19 50	20 50	21 50							
Maidstone Barracks	d	06 55	07 55	08 55	09 55	10 55	11 55	12 55	13 55	14 55		15 55	16 55	17 55	18 55	19 55	20 55	21 55							
Maidstone West ■ 194	a	06 57	07 57	08 57	09 57	10 57	11 57	12 57	13 57	14 57		15 57	16 57	17 57	18 57	19 57	20 57	21 57							
	d	07 03	08 03	09 03	10 03	11 03	12 03	13 03	14 03	15 03		16 03	17 03	18 03	19 03	20 03	21 03	22 03							
East Farleigh	d	07 07	08 07	09 07	10 07	11 07	12 07	13 07	14 07	15 07		16 07	17 07	18 07	19 07	20 07	21 07	22 07							
Wateringbury	d	07 12	08 12	09 12	10 12	11 12	12 12	13 12	14 12	15 12		16 12	17 12	18 12	19 12	20 12	21 12	22 12							
Yalding	d	07 15	08 15	09 15	10 15	11 15	12 15	13 15	14 15	15 15		16 15	17 15	18 15	19 15	20 15	21 15	22 15							
Beltring	d	07 18	08 18	09 18	10 18	11 18	12 18	13 18	14 18	15 18		16 18	17 18	18 18	19 18	20 18	21 18	22 18							
Paddock Wood ■	a	07 22	08 22	09 22	10 22	11 22	12 22	13 22	14 22	15 22		16 22	17 22	18 22	19 22	20 22	21 22	22 22							
Tonbridge ■	a																	22 32							

Paddock Wood and Maidstone West - Strood

Network Diagram - see first Page of Table 206

Miles			SE	SE	SE	SE	SE	SE	SE	SE	SE		SE	SE	SE	SE	SE	SE	SE	SE	SE		SE	SE	SE
0	Tonbridge 4	d											09 03		10 03		11 04		12 03		13 03			14 03	
5¼	**Paddock Wood 4**	d	05 42	06 20		06 50			07 40	08 10			09 10		10 10		11 11		12 10		13 10			14 10	
7	Beltring	d	05 46	06 24		06 54			07 44	08 14			09 14		10 14		11 15		12 14		13 14			14 14	
8¾	Yalding	d	05 49	06 27		06 57			07 48	08 18			09 18		10 18		11 19		12 18		13 18			14 18	
10½	Wateringbury	d	05 52	06 30		07 00			07 51	08 21			09 21		10 21		11 22		12 21		13 21			14 21	
13½	East Farleigh	d	05 56	06 34		07 04			07 55	08 25			09 25		10 25		11 26		12 25		13 25			14 25	
15¼	**Maidstone West 4** 194	a	06 01	06 39		07 09			07 59	08 29			09 29		10 29		11 30		12 29		13 29			14 29	
—		d	06 02	06 40	06 56	07 10	07 26	07 56	08 02	08 32	09 02		09 32	10 02	10 32	11 02	11 32	12 02	12 32	13 02	13 32		14 02	14 32	15 02
15½	Maidstone Barracks	d	06 04	06 42		07 12			08 04	08 34	09 04		09 34	10 04	10 34	11 04	11 34	12 04	12 34	13 04	13 34		14 04	14 34	15 04
18¾	Aylesford	d	06 09	06 47		07 17			08 09	08 39	09 09		09 39	10 09	10 39	11 09	11 39	12 09	12 39	13 09	13 39		14 09	14 39	15 09
19½	New Hythe	d	06 11	06 49		07 19			08 11	08 41	09 11		09 41	10 11	10 41	11 11	11 41	12 11	12 41	13 11	13 41		14 11	14 41	15 11
21	Snodland	d	06 14	06 52		07 22			08 14	08 44	09 14		09 44	10 14	10 44	11 14	11 44	12 14	12 44	13 14	13 44		14 14	14 44	15 14
22½	Halling	d	06 17	06 55		07 25			08 17	08 47	09 17		09 47	10 17	10 47	11 17	11 47	12 17	12 47	13 17	13 47		14 17	14 47	15 17
24¼	Cuxton	d	06 20	06 58		07 28			08 20	08 50	09 20		09 50	10 20	10 50	11 20	11 50	12 20	12 50	13 20	13 50		14 20	14 50	15 20
26½	**Strood 4**	a	06 24	07 02	07 11	07 32	07 41	08 11	08 24	08 54	09 24		09 54	10 24	10 54	11 24	11 54	12 24	12 54	13 24	13 54		14 24	14 54	15 24
34½	Gravesend	d			07 22		07 52	08 22																	
37½	Ebbsfleet International	d																							
54¼	Stratford International	d			07 37		08 07	08 37																	
59½	St Pancras International	a			07 43		08 13	08 43																	

		SE	SE	SE	SE	SE	SE		SE	SE	SE	SE	SE	SE	SE	SE	SE		SE
Tonbridge 4	d	15 03		16 03									20 33		21 33				22 33
Paddock Wood 4	d	15 10		16 10	17 02	17 30	17 52		18 42		19 12	19 42		20 40		21 40			22 40
Beltring	d	15 14		16 14	17 06	17 34	17 56		18 46		19 16	19 46		20 44		21 44			22 44
Yalding	d	15 18		16 18	17 09	17 37	17 59		18 50		19 20	19 49		20 48		21 48			22 48
Wateringbury	d	15 21		16 21	17 12	17 40	18 02		18 53		19 23	19 52		20 51		21 51			22 51
East Farleigh	d	15 25		16 25	17 16	17 44	18 06		18 57		19 27	19 56		20 55		21 55			22 55
Maidstone West 4 194	a	15 29		16 29	17 21	17 49	18 11		19 01		19 31	20 01		20 59		21 59			22 59
	d	15 44	16 02	16 32	17 22	17 50	18 18		19 02	19 13	19 32	20 02	20 32	21 02	21 32	22 02	22 32		23 02
Maidstone Barracks	d	15 46	16 04	16 34	17 24	17 52	18 20		19 04		19 34	20 04	20 34	21 04	21 34	22 04	22 34		23 04
Aylesford	d	15 51	16 09	16 39	17 29	17 57	18 25		19 09		19 39	20 09	20 39	21 09	21 39	22 09	22 39		23 09
New Hythe	d	15 53	16 11	16 41	17 31	17 59	18 27		19 11		19 41	20 11	20 41	21 11	21 41	22 11	22 41		23 11
Snodland	d	15 56	16 14	16 44	17 34	18 02	18 30		19 14		19 44	20 14	20 44	21 14	21 44	22 14	22 44		23 14
Halling	d	15 59	16 17	16 47	17 37	18 05	18 33		19 17		19 47	20 17	20 47	21 17	21 47	22 17	22 47		23 17
Cuxton	d	16 02	16 20	16 50	17 40	18 08	18 36		19 20		19 50	20 20	20 50	21 20	21 50	22 20	22 50		23 20
Strood 4	a	16 06	16 24	16 54	17 44	18 12	18 40		19 24	19 30	19 54	20 24	20 54	21 24	21 54	22 24	22 54		23 24
Gravesend	d									19 43									
Ebbsfleet International	d									19 50									
Stratford International	d									20 02									
St Pancras International	a									20 08									

Saturdays

		SE	SE	SE	SE	SE	SE	SE	SE	SE		SE	SE	SE	SE	SE	SE	SE	SE	SE		SE	SE	SE	SE
Tonbridge 4	d	06 03		07 03		08 03		09 03		10 03			11 03		12 03		13 03		14 03			15 03		16 03	
Paddock Wood 4	d	06 10		07 10		08 10		09 10		10 10			11 10		12 10		13 10		14 10			15 10		16 10	
Beltring	d	06 14		07 14		08 14		09 14		10 14			11 14		12 14		13 14		14 14			15 14		16 14	
Yalding	d	06 18		07 18		08 18		09 18		10 18			11 18		12 18		13 18		14 18			15 18		16 18	
Wateringbury	d	06 21		07 21		08 21		09 21		10 21			11 21		12 21		13 21		14 21			15 21		16 21	
East Farleigh	d	06 25		07 25		08 25		09 25		10 25			11 25		12 25		13 25		14 25			15 25		16 25	
Maidstone West 4 194	a	06 29		07 29		08 29		09 29		10 29			11 29		12 29		13 29		14 29			15 29		16 29	
	d	06 32	07 02	07 32	08 02	08 32	09 02	09 32	10 02	10 32		11 02	11 32	12 02	12 32	13 02	13 32	14 02	14 32	15 02		15 32	16 02	16 32	17 02
Maidstone Barracks	d	06 34	07 04	07 34	08 04	08 34	09 04	09 34	10 04	10 34		11 04	11 34	12 04	12 34	13 04	13 34	14 04	14 34	15 04		15 34	16 04	16 34	17 04
Aylesford	d	06 39	07 09	07 39	08 09	08 39	09 09	09 39	10 09	10 39		11 09	11 39	12 09	12 39	13 09	13 39	14 09	14 39	15 09		15 39	16 09	16 39	17 09
New Hythe	d	06 41	07 11	07 41	08 11	08 41	09 11	09 41	10 11	10 41		11 11	11 41	12 11	12 41	13 11	13 41	14 11	14 41	15 11		15 41	16 11	16 41	17 11
Snodland	d	06 44	07 14	07 44	08 14	08 44	09 14	09 44	10 14	10 44		11 14	11 44	12 14	12 44	13 14	13 44	14 14	14 44	15 14		15 44	16 14	16 44	17 14
Halling	d	06 47	07 17	07 47	08 17	08 47	09 17	09 47	10 17	10 47		11 17	11 47	12 17	12 47	13 17	13 47	14 17	14 47	15 17		15 47	16 17	16 47	17 17
Cuxton	d	06 50	07 20	07 50	08 20	08 50	09 20	09 50	10 20	10 50		11 20	11 50	12 20	12 50	13 20	13 50	14 20	14 50	15 20		15 50	16 20	16 50	17 20
Strood 4	a	06 54	07 24	07 54	08 24	08 54	09 24	09 54	10 24	10 54		11 24	11 54	12 24	12 54	13 24	13 54	14 24	14 54	15 24		15 54	16 24	16 54	17 24
Gravesend	d																								
Ebbsfleet International	d																								
Stratford International	d																								
St Pancras International	a																								

		SE	SE	SE	SE	SE		SE	SE	SE	SE	SE	SE	SE
Tonbridge 4	d	17 03		18 03		19 03			20 03		21 03		22 03	
Paddock Wood 4	d	17 10		18 10		19 10			20 10		21 10		22 10	
Beltring	d	17 14		18 14		19 14			20 14		21 14		22 14	
Yalding	d	17 18		18 18		19 18			20 18		21 18		22 18	
Wateringbury	d	17 21		18 21		19 21			20 21		21 21		22 21	
East Farleigh	d	17 25		18 25		19 25			20 25		21 25		22 25	
Maidstone West 4 194	a	17 29		18 29		19 29			20 29		21 29		22 29	
	d	17 32	18 02	18 32	19 02	19 32		20 02	20 32	21 02	21 32	22 02	22 32	23 02
Maidstone Barracks	d	17 34	18 04	18 34	19 04	19 34		20 04	20 34	21 04	21 34	22 04	22 34	23 04
Aylesford	d	17 39	18 09	18 39	19 09	19 39		20 09	20 39	21 09	21 39	22 09	22 39	23 09
New Hythe	d	17 41	18 11	18 41	19 11	19 41		20 11	20 41	21 11	21 41	22 11	22 41	23 11
Snodland	d	17 44	18 14	18 44	19 14	19 44		20 14	20 44	21 14	21 44	22 14	22 44	23 14
Halling	d	17 47	18 17	18 47	19 17	19 47		20 17	20 47	21 17	21 47	22 17	22 47	23 17
Cuxton	d	17 50	18 20	18 50	19 20	19 50		20 20	20 50	21 20	21 50	22 20	22 50	23 20
Strood 4	a	17 54	18 24	18 54	19 24	19 54		20 24	20 54	21 24	21 54	22 24	22 54	23 24
Gravesend	d													
Ebbsfleet International	d													
Stratford International	d													
St Pancras International	a													

Table 208

Sundays

Paddock Wood and Maidstone West - Strood

Network Diagram - see first Page of Table 206

			SE	SE	SE	SE	SE	SE	SE	SE	SE		SE	SE	SE	SE	SE	SE	SE
Tonbridge ■4		d	06 26																
Paddock Wood ■4		d	06 34	07 34	08 34	09 34	10 34	11 34	12 34	13 34	14 34		15 34	16 34	17 34	18 34	19 34	20 34	21 34
Beltring		d	06 38	07 38	08 38	09 38	10 38	11 38	12 38	13 38	14 38		15 38	16 38	17 38	18 38	19 38	20 38	21 38
Yalding		d	06 41	07 41	08 41	09 41	10 41	11 41	12 41	13 41	14 41		15 41	16 41	17 41	18 41	19 41	20 41	21 41
Wateringbury		d	06 44	07 44	08 44	09 44	10 44	11 44	12 44	13 44	14 44		15 44	16 44	17 44	18 44	19 44	20 44	21 44
East Farleigh		d	06 48	07 48	08 48	09 48	10 48	11 48	12 48	13 48	14 48		15 48	16 48	17 48	18 48	19 48	20 48	21 48
Maidstone West ■4	194	a	06 53	07 53	08 53	09 53	10 53	11 53	12 53	13 53	14 53		15 53	16 53	17 53	18 53	19 53	20 53	21 53
		d	07 00	08 00	09 02	10 02	11 02	12 02	13 02	14 02	15 02		16 02	17 02	18 02	19 02	20 00	21 00	22 00
Maidstone Barracks		d	07 02	08 02	09 04	10 04	11 04	12 04	13 04	14 04	15 04		16 04	17 04	18 04	19 04	20 02	21 02	22 02
Aylesford		d	07 07	08 07	09 09	10 09	11 09	12 09	13 09	14 09	15 09		16 09	17 09	18 09	19 09	20 07	21 07	22 07
New Hythe		d	07 09	08 09	09 11	10 11	11 11	12 11	13 11	14 11	15 11		16 11	17 11	18 11	19 11	20 09	21 09	22 09
Snodland		d	07 12	08 12	09 14	10 14	11 14	12 14	13 14	14 14	15 14		16 14	17 14	18 14	19 14	20 12	21 12	22 12
Halling		d	07 15	08 15	09 17	10 17	11 17	12 17	13 17	14 17	15 17		16 17	17 17	18 17	19 17	20 15	21 15	22 15
Cuxton		d	07 18	08 18	09 20	10 20	11 20	12 20	13 20	14 20	15 20		16 20	17 20	18 20	19 20	20 18	21 18	22 18
Strood ■4		a	07 22	08 22	09 24	10 24	11 24	12 24	13 24	14 24	15 24		16 24	17 24	18 24	19 24	20 22	21 22	22 22
Gravesend		d																	
Ebbsfleet International		d																	
Stratford International		d																	
St Pancras International		a																	

Network Diagram for Table 212

DM-28/11
Design BAJS

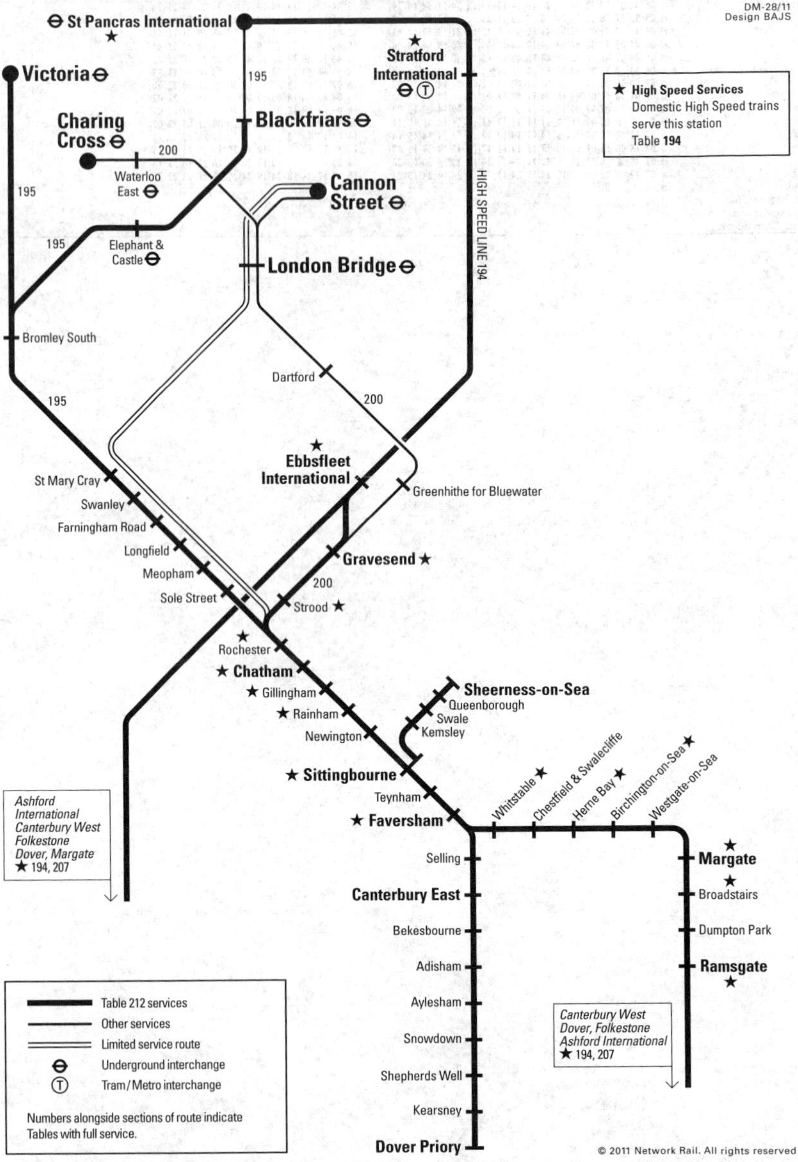

London - Medway, Sheerness-on-Sea, Dover and Ramsgate

Network Diagram - see first Page of Table 212

Miles	Miles	Miles	Miles	Miles			SE MO 1		SE MX 1	SE	SE MX 1	SE MX 1	SE MO 1	SE MX	SE	SE MX 1	SE MX	SE MO	SE MO	SE MX	SE MO 1	SE MX 1	SE MX 1	SE MX
—	—	—	—	0	**St Pancras Internatnl 15 ⊖**	d				22p55					23p25				23p42	23p55				
—	—	—	—	6	**Stratford International ⊖**	d				23p02					23p32				23p49	00 02				
—	—	—	—	22¾	**Ebbsfleet International**	d				23p13					23p43				00 01	00 13				
0	0	—	—	—	**London Victoria 15 ⊖**	d	22p05		22p22		22p52		23p05			23p22					23p45	23p52	00 10	
—	—	—	—	—	**London Blackfriars 3 ⊖**	d																		
—	—	—	—	—	Elephant & Castle ⊖	d																		
11	11	—	—	—	Bromley South 4	d	22p22		22p39		23p09		23p22			23p39					00 02	00 09		
14¾	14¾	—	—	—	St Mary Cray	d					23p15										00 08	00 15		
17½	17½	—	—	—	Swanley 4	d					23p19										00 12	00 19		
20½	20½	—	—	—	Farningham Road	d					23p24										00 17	00 24		
23½	23½	—	—	—	Longfield	d			22p52		23p28					23p52					00 21	00 28		
26	26	—	—	—	Meopham	d			22p57		23p32					23p57					00 25	00 32		
27	27	—	—	—	Sole Street	d					23p35										00 28	00 35		
—	—	—	0	—	**London Charing Cross 4 ⊖**	d											23p09	23p10						23p39
—	—	—	0¾	—	**London Waterloo (East) 4 ⊖**	d											23p12	23p13						23p42
—	—	—	—	—	**London Cannon Street 4 ⊖**	d																		
—	—	—	1¾	—	**London Bridge 4 ⊖**	d											23p17	23p18						23p47
—	—	—	18¾	—	Dartford 4	d											23p55	23p55						00 25
—	—	—	21½	—	Greenhithe for Bluewater	d											23p59	00 01						00 31
—	—	—	25½	24¾	Gravesend 4	d				23p18					23p48		00 10	00 10		00 18				00 40
—	—	—	32¾	32	Strood 4	d				23p28					23p58		00 22	00 22		00 28				00 52
33¾	33¾	—	33¾	33	Rochester 4	d	22p46		23p09	23p33	23p45		23p46		00 03	00 09	00 26	00 26		00 33	00 37	00 45	00 49	00 56
34¼	34¼	—	34¼	33½	**Chatham 4**	d	22p48		23p12	23p35	23p47		23p48		00 05	00 12	00 28	00 28		00 35	00 40	00 47	00 52	00 58
36	36	—	36	35¼	**Gillingham (Kent) 4**	d	22p53		23p17	23p40	23p52		23p53		00 10	00 17	00a33	00a33		00 40	00 44	00a52	00 57	01a03
39	39	—	—	38¼	Rainham (Kent)	d	22p57		23p21	23p45	23p56		23p57		00 15	00 21				00 45	00 49		01 01	
41½	41½	—	—	40¾	Newington	d					00 01										00 53		01 05	
44¾	44¾	0	—	44	**Sittingbourne 4**	a	23p04		23p28	23p52	00 06		00 04		00 22	00 28				00 52	00 58		01 10	
—	—	—	—	—		d	23p05		23p29	23p53	00 07		00 05	00 15	00 23	00 29				00 53	00 58		01 11	
—	—	2	—	—	Kemsley	d								00 20										
—	—	4	—	—	Swale	d								00 23										
—	—	6	—	—	Queenborough	d								00 27										
—	—	8	—	—	**Sheerness-on-Sea**	a								00 32										
47½	47½	—	—	46¾	Teynham	d			23p33							00 33					01 03		01 15	
52	52	—	—	51¾	**Faversham 2**	a	23p13		23p39	00 03	00 15		00 13		00 33	00 39				01 03	01 09		01 23	
—	—	—	—	—																				
—	—	—	—	—		d	23p17	23p19	23p43			23p45	00 17			00 43							01 24	
—	55¼	—	—	—	Selling	d		23p24				23p50												
—	61¾	—	—	—	**Canterbury East 4**	d		23p33				23p59												
—	64¾	—	—	—	Bekesbourne	d		23p37																
—	67¾	—	—	—	Adisham	d		23p42																
—	68¾	—	—	—	Aylesham	d		23p44				00 07												
—	69¾	—	—	—	Snowdown	d		23p47																
—	71¾	—	—	—	Shepherds Well	d		23p51																
—	75	—	—	—	Kearsney	d		23p55																
—	77¼	—	—	—	**Dover Priory 4**	a		00 01				00 18												
59	—	—	—	—	Whitstable	d	23p25		23p51				00 25			00 51							01 32	
60½	—	—	—	—	Chestfield & Swalecliffe	d	23p28		23p54				00 28			00 54							01 35	
62¾	—	—	—	—	**Herne Bay**	d	23p32		23p58				00 32			00 58							01 39	
70¾	—	—	—	—	Birchington-on-Sea	d	23p41		00 07				00 41			01 07							01 48	
72½	—	—	—	—	Westgate-on-Sea	d	23p44		00 10				00 44			01 10							01 51	
73¾	—	—	—	—	**Margate 4**	d	23p48		00 14				00 48			01 14							01 55	
77	—	—	—	—	Broadstairs	d	23p54		00 20				00 54			01 20							02 01	
78¼	—	—	—	—	Dumpton Park	d	23p57		00 23				00 57			01 23							02 04	
79¼	—	—	—	—	**Ramsgate 4**	a	00 01		00 26				01 00			01 26							02 07	

London - Medway, Sheerness-on-Sea, Dover and Ramsgate

Network Diagram - see first Page of Table 212

		SE MX	SE	SE	SE	SE 1	SE	SE 1	SE	SE		SE	SE	SE	SE 1	SE 1	SE	SE 1	SE 1	SE		SE	SE	SE
St Pancras Internatnl 15 ⊖	d	00 12																				06 25		
Stratford International ⊖	d	00 19																				06 32		
Ebbsfleet International	d	00 31																				06 42		
London Victoria 15 ⊖	d		00 35													05 22			05 52					
London Blackfriars 3 ⊖	d																							
Elephant & Castle ⊖	d																							
Bromley South 4	d		00 55													05 39			06 09					
St Mary Cray	d		01 01													05 45								
Swanley 4	d		01 05													05 49			06 20					
Farningham Road	d		01 10													05 54								
Longfield	d		01 14													05 58			06 26					
Meopham	d		01 18													06 02			06 30					
Sole Street	d															06 05								
London Charing Cross 4 ⊖	d			00 18																05 39				
London Waterloo (East) 4 ⊖	d			00 21																05 42				
London Cannon Street 4 ⊖	d																							
London Bridge 4 ⊖	d			00 26																05 47				
Dartford 4	d			01 06					05 25											06 25				
Greenhithe for Bluewater	d			01 10					05 30											06 30				
Gravesend 4	d			01 17					05 37											06 38		06 46		
Strood 4	d			01 29					05 48											06 49		06a56		
Rochester 4	d		01 29	01 33					05 52							06 15			06 41	06 53				
Chatham 4	d		01 31	01 35					05 55							06 17			06 44	06 56				
Gillingham (Kent) 4	d		01a35	01a41	05 00			05 47	05a59							06 22			06 48	07a00				
Rainham (Kent)	d				05 04			05 51								06 26			06 53					
Newington	d				05 08			05 55								06 30			06 57					
Sittingbourne 4	a							06 00								06 35			07 02					
	d						05 33	06 01				06 03	06 22			06 36	06 53		07 02				07 09	
Kemsley	d				05 15		05 38					06 08	06 27				06 58						07 14	
Swale	d				05 18		05 43					06 11	06 30				07 01						07 17	
Queenborough	d				05 22		05 47					06 15	06 35				07 05						07 22	
Sheerness-on-Sea	a				05 27		05 51					06 20	06 40				07 10						07 27	
Teynham	d							06 05								06 40			07 07					
Faversham 2	a							06 11								06 46			07 13					
	d					05 15		06 12							06 15	06 47		07 05	07 13					
Selling	d					05 20		06 17										07 09						
Canterbury East 4	d					05 29		06 26										07 18						
Bekesbourne	d					05 33		06 30										07 23						
Adisham	d					05 38		06 35										07 27						
Aylesham	d					05 40		06 37										07 29						
Snowdown	d					05 43		06 40										07 32						
Shepherds Well	d					05 47		06 44										07 35						
Kearsney	d					05 51		06 48										07 40						
Dover Priory 4	a					05 56		06 53										07 45						
Whitstable	d														06 23	06 55			07 21					
Chestfield & Swalecliffe	d														06 26	06 58			07 24					
Herne Bay	d														06 30	07 02			07 28					
Birchington-on-Sea	d														06 39	07 11			07 37					
Westgate-on-Sea	d														06 42	07 14			07 41					
Margate 4	d									05 47				06 48	06b52	07 18			07 45					07 49
Broadstairs	d									05 54				06 54	06 58	07 24			07 50					07 55
Dumpton Park	d														07 01	07 27			07 53					
Ramsgate 4	a									05 59				06 59	07 04	07 30			07 56					08 00

b Arr. 0646

London - Medway, Sheerness-on-Sea, Dover and Ramsgate

Network Diagram - see first Page of Table 212

		SE 1	SE	SE	SE	SE	SE 1	SE 1	SE	SE 1	SE	SE	SE	SE 1	SE	SE 1		SE	SE	SE	SE	SE 1	
St Pancras Internatnl 15 ⊖	d				06 55								07 25								07 52		
Stratford International ⊖	d				07 02								07 32								08 02		
Ebbsfleet International	d				07 13								07 43								08 13		
London Victoria 15 ⊖	d	06 22						06 45		06 58	07 09					07 22			07 43			07 52	
London Blackfriars 3 ⊖	d																						
Elephant & Castle ⊖	d																						
Bromley South 4	d	06 39						07 02		07 19						07 40						08 09	
St Mary Cray	d	06 45						07 08		07 25													
Swanley 4	d	06 49						07 13		07 29						07 49							
Farningham Road	d	06 54						07 18		07 34													
Longfield	d	06 58						07 22		07 38						07 55						08 22	
Meopham	d	07 02						07 26		07 42						07 59						08 27	
Sole Street	d	07 05						07 28		07 45													
London Charing Cross 4 ⊖	d		05 56			06 26			06 39									07 12					
London Waterloo (East) 4 ⊖	d		05 59			06 29			06 42									07 15					
London Cannon Street 4 ⊖	d																						
London Bridge 4 ⊖	d		06 04			06 34			06 47									07 21					
Dartford 4	d		06 42			07 12			07 25		07a48							08 00	08a27				
Greenhithe for Bluewater	d		06 48			07 18			07 30									08 05					
Gravesend 4	d		06 59		07 21	07 27			07 37				07 48					08 12			08 18		
Strood 4	d		07b17		07 31	07a37			07 48				07 58					08 23			08 28		
Rochester 4	d	07 15	07 21		07 36			07 40	07 52	07 56			08 03			08 11		08 27			08 33	08 39	
Chatham 4	d	07 17	07 24		07 38			07 43	07 55	07 59			08 05			08 13		08 30			08 35	08 42	
Gillingham (Kent) 4	d	07 22	07a28		07 43			07 48	07a59	08a03			08 10			08 18		08a35			08 40	08 47	
Rainham (Kent)	d	07 26			07 48			07 52					08 15			08 22					08 45	08 51	
Newington	d	07 30						07 56								08 26						08 55	
Sittingbourne 4	a	07 37			07 56			08 01					08 22			08 31					08 52	09 00	
	d	07 38		07 45	07 57			08 02				08 13	08 23			08 32				08 40	08 53	09 01	
Kemsley	d			07 50								08 18								08 45			
Swale	d			07 53								08 21								08 48			
Queenborough	d			07 57								08 25								08 52			
Sheerness-on-Sea	a			08 02								08 30								08 57			
Teynham	d	07 42						08 06								08 36							
Faversham 2	a	07 48			08 05			08 12					08 33			08 42					09 03	09 09	
	d	07 49					07 51	08 13						08 16		08 46	08 49					09 13	09 15
Selling	d						07 55	08 18									08 53						
Canterbury East 4	d						08 05	08 27									09 02						09 29
Bekesbourne	d						08 10	08 31									09 07						
Adisham	d						08 14	08 36									09 11						
Aylesham	d						08 17	08 38									09 13						
Snowdown	d						08 19	08 41									09 16						
Shepherds Well	d						08 23	08 45									09 20						
Kearsney	d						08 28	08 49									09 24						
Dover Priory 4	a						08 35	08 54									09 29						09 50
Whitstable	d	07 57												08 24		08 54						09 21	
Chestfield & Swalecliffe	d	08 00												08 27		08 57							
Herne Bay	d	08 04												08 31		09 01						09 26	
Birchington-on-Sea	d	08 13												08 40		09 10						09 35	
Westgate-on-Sea	d	08 17												08 43		09 13							
Margate 4	d	08 21												08 47	08 53	09 17						09 41	
Broadstairs	d	08 26												08 53	08 59	09 23						09 46	
Dumpton Park	d	08 29												08 56		09 26							
Ramsgate 4	a	08 32												08 59	09 04	09 29						09 51	

b Arr. 0710

London - Medway, Sheerness-on-Sea, Dover and Ramsgate

Network Diagram - see first Page of Table 212

		SE	SE 1	SE	SE	SE	SE 1		SE	SE	SE	SE 1		SE	SE 1	SE	SE	SE	SE 1		SE	SE
St Pancras Internatnl 15 ⊖	d				08 25						08 55						09 25					
Stratford International ⊖	d				08 32						09 05						09 32					
Ebbsfleet International	d				08 43						09 17						09 43					
London Victoria 15 ⊖	d		07 58				08 22					08 52			08 58				09 22			
London Blackfriars 3 ⊖	d																					
Elephant & Castle ⊖	d																					
Bromley South 4	d		08 28				08 39					09 09			09 19				09 39			
St Mary Cray	d		08 34												09 25							
Swanley 4	d		08 39												09 29							
Farningham Road	d		08 44												09 34							
Longfield	d		08 49				08 52					09 22			09 38				09 52			
Meopham	d		08 53				08 57					09 27			09 42				09 57			
Sole Street	d		08 56												09 45							
London Charing Cross 4 ⊖	d	07 39							08 11					08 41							09 11	
London Waterloo (East) 4 ⊖	d	07 42							08 14					08 44							09 14	
London Cannon Street 4 ⊖	d																					
London Bridge 4 ⊖	d	07 47							08 19					08 49							09 19	
Dartford 4	d	08 25							08 55					09 25							09 55	
Greenhithe for Bluewater	d	08 30							09 00					09 30							10 00	
Gravesend 4	d	08 37			08 48				09 07		09 22			09 37			09 48				10 07	
Strood 4	d	08 48			08 58				09 18		09 32			09 48			09 58				10 18	
Rochester 4	d	08 52	09a07		09 03		09 09		09 22		09 37	09 39		09 52	09 56		10 03		10 09		10 22	
Chatham 4	d	08 55			09 05		09 12		09 25		09 39	09 42		09 55	09 59		10 05		10 12		10 25	
Gillingham (Kent) 4	d	08a59			09 10		09 17		09a29		09 44	09 47		09a59	10a03		10 10		10 17		10a29	
Rainham (Kent)	d				09 15		09 21				09 49	09 51					10 15		10 21			
Newington	d											09 55										
Sittingbourne 4	a				09 22		09 28				09 56	10 01					10 22		10 28			
	d			09 10	09 23		09 29			09 40	09 56	10 01				10 10	10 23		10 29			10 40
Kemsley	d			09 15						09 45						10 15						10 45
Swale	d			09 18						09 48						10 18						10 48
Queenborough	d			09 22						09 52						10 22						10 52
Sheerness-on-Sea	a			09 27						09 57						10 27						10 57
Teynham	d						09 33												10 33			
Faversham 2	a				09 33		09 39				10 04	10 09					10 33		10 39			
	d						09 43	09 45				10 13	10 15						10 43	10 45		
Selling	d							09 50												10 50		
Canterbury East 4	d							09 59					10 29							10 59		
Bekesbourne	d							10 03												11 03		
Adisham	d							10 08												11 08		
Aylesham	d							10 10												11 10		
Snowdown	d							10 13												11 13		
Shepherds Well	d							10 17												11 17		
Kearsney	d							10 21												11 21		
Dover Priory 4	a							10 26					10 50							11 26		
Whitstable	d						09 51					10 21							10 51			
Chestfield & Swalecliffe	d						09 54												10 54			
Herne Bay	d						09 58					10 26							10 58			
Birchington-on-Sea	d						10 07					10 35							11 07			
Westgate-on-Sea	d						10 10												11 10			
Margate 4	d					09 53	10 14					10 41						10 53	11 14			
Broadstairs	d					09 59	10 20					10 46						10 59	11 20			
Dumpton Park	d						10 23												11 23			
Ramsgate 4	a					10 04	10 26					10 51						11 04	11 26			

London - Medway, Sheerness-on-Sea, Dover and Ramsgate

Network Diagram - see first Page of Table 212

		SE	SE [1]		SE	SE [1]	SE	SE	SE	SE [1]			SE	SE	SE	SE [1]		SE	SE [1]	SE	SE		SE	SE [1]	
St Pancras Internatnl [15] ⊖	d	09 55						10 28							10 52						11 25				
Stratford International ⊖	d	10 02						10 35							10 59						11 32				
Ebbsfleet International	d	10 13						10 46							11 13						11 43				
London Victoria [15] ⊖	d		09 52			09 58				10 22						10 52			10 58					11 22	
London Blackfriars [3] ⊖	d																								
Elephant & Castle ⊖	d																								
Bromley South [4]	d		10 09			10 19				10 39						11 09			11 19					11 39	
St Mary Cray	d					10 25													11 25						
Swanley [4]	d					10 29													11 29						
Farningham Road	d					10 34													11 34						
Longfield	d		10 22			10 38				10 52						11 22			11 38					11 52	
Meopham	d		10 27			10 42				10 57						11 27			11 42					11 57	
Sole Street	d					10 45													11 45						
London Charing Cross [4] ⊖	d				09 39								10 09					10 39							
London Waterloo (East) [4] ⊖	d				09 42								10 12					10 42							
London Cannon Street [4] ⊖	d																								
London Bridge [4] ⊖	d				09 47								10 17					10 47							
Dartford [4]	d				10 25								10 55					11 25							
Greenhithe for Bluewater	d				10 30								11 00					11 30							
Gravesend [4]	d	10 18			10 37			10 51					11 07		11 18			11 37			11 48				
Strood [4]	d	10 28			10 48			11 01					11 18		11 28			11 48			11 58				
Rochester [4]	d	10 33	10 39		10 52	10 56		11 06		11 09			11 23		11 33	11 39		11 52	11 56		12 03			12 09	
Chatham [4]	d	10 35	10 42		10 55	10 59		11 08		11 12			11 25		11 35	11 42		11 55	11 59		12 05			12 12	
Gillingham (Kent) [4]	d	10 40	10 47		10a59	11a03		11 13		11 17			11a29		11 40	11 47		11a59	12a03		12 10			12 17	
Rainham (Kent)	d	10 45	10 51					11 18		11 21					11 45	11 51					12 15			12 21	
Newington	d		10 55													11 55									
Sittingbourne [4]	a	10 52	11 00					11 25		11 29					11 52	12 00					12 22			12 28	
	d	10 53	11 01				11 10	11 25		11 29				11 40	11 53	12 01				12 10	12 23			12 29	
Kemsley	d						11 15							11 45						12 15					
Swale	d						11 18							11 48						12 18					
Queenborough	d						11 22							11 52						12 22					
Sheerness-on-Sea	a						11 27							11 57						12 27					
Teynham	d									11 33														12 33	
Faversham [2]	a	11 03	11 09					11 33		11 39					12 03	12 09					12 33			12 39	
	d		11 13	11 15						11 43	11 45					12 13	12 15							12 43	12 45
Selling	d										11 50														12 50
Canterbury East [4]	d			11 29							11 59						12 29								12 59
Bekesbourne	d										12 03														13 03
Adisham	d										12 08														13 08
Aylesham	d										12 10														13 10
Snowdown	d										12 13														13 13
Shepherds Well	d										12 17														13 17
Kearsney	d										12 21														13 21
Dover Priory [4]	a			11 50							12 26						12 50								13 26
Whitstable	d		11 21							11 51						12 21								12 51	
Chestfield & Swalecliffe	d									11 54														12 54	
Herne Bay	d		11 26							11 58						12 26								12 58	
Birchington-on-Sea	d		11 35							12 07						12 35								13 07	
Westgate-on-Sea	d									12 10														13 10	
Margate [4]	d		11 41						11 53	12 14						12 41							12 53	13 14	
Broadstairs	d		11 46						11 59	12 20						12 46							12 59	13 20	
Dumpton Park	d									12 23														13 23	
Ramsgate [4]	a		11 51						12 04	12 26						12 51							13 04	13 26	

London - Medway, Sheerness-on-Sea, Dover and Ramsgate

Network Diagram - see first Page of Table 212

		SE	SE	SE	SE 1	SE		SE 1	SE	SE	SE	SE 1	SE	SE	SE		SE 1	SE	SE 1	SE	SE	SE
St Pancras Internatnl 15 ⊖	d			11 55						12 22					12 52						13 25	
Stratford International ⊖	d			12 02						12 32					12 58						13 32	
Ebbsfleet International	d			12 13						12 43					13 13						13 43	
London Victoria 15 ⊖	d				11 52			11 58				12 22					12 52		12 58			
London Blackfriars 3 ⊖	d																					
Elephant & Castle ⊖	d																					
Bromley South 4	d				12 09			12 19				12 39					13 09		13 19			
St Mary Cray	d							12 25											13 25			
Swanley 4	d							12 29											13 29			
Farningham Road	d							12 34											13 34			
Longfield	d				12 22			12 38				12 52					13 22		13 38			
Meopham	d				12 27			12 42				12 57					13 27		13 42			
Sole Street	d							12 45											13 45			
London Charing Cross 4 ⊖	d	11 09				11 39							12 09					12 39				
London Waterloo (East) 4 ⊖	d	11 12				11 42							12 12					12 42				
London Cannon Street 4 ⊖	d																					
London Bridge 4 ⊖	d	11 17				11 47							12 17					12 47				
Dartford 4	d	11 55				12 25							12 55					13 25				
Greenhithe for Bluewater	d	12 00				12 30							13 00					13 30				
Gravesend 4	d	12 07		12 18		12 37				12 48			13 07		13 18			13 37			13 48	
Strood 4	d	12 18		12 28		12 48				12 58			13 18		13 28			13 48			13 58	
Rochester 4	d	12 22		12 33	12 39	12 52		12 56		13 03		13 09	13 22		13 33		13 39	13 52	13 56		14 03	
Chatham 4	d	12 25		12 35	12 42	12 55		12 59		13 05		13 12	13 25		13 35		13 42	13 55	13 59		14 05	
Gillingham (Kent) 4	d	12a29		12 40	12 47	12a59		13a03		13 10		13 17	13a29		13 40		13 47	13a59	14a03		14 10	
Rainham (Kent)	d			12 45	12 51					13 15		13 21			13 45		13 51				14 15	
Newington	d				12 55												13 55					
Sittingbourne 4	a			12 52	13 00					13 22		13 29			13 52		14 00				14 22	
	d		12 40	12 53	13 01				13 10	13 23		13 29		13 40	13 53		14 01			14 10	14 23	
Kemsley	d		12 45						13 15					13 45						14 15		
Swale	d		12 48						13 18					13 48						14 18		
Queenborough	d		12 52						13 22					13 52						14 22		
Sheerness-on-Sea	a		12 57						13 27					13 57						14 27		
Teynham	d											13 33										
Faversham 2	a			13 03	13 09					13 33		13 39			14 03		14 09				14 33	
	d				13 13 13 15							13 43 13 45					14 13 14 15					
Selling	d											13 50										
Canterbury East 4	d				13 29							13 59					14 29					
Bekesbourne	d											14 03										
Adisham	d											14 08										
Aylesham	d											14 10										
Snowdown	d											14 13										
Shepherds Well	d											14 17										
Kearsney	d											14 21										
Dover Priory 4	a				13 50							14 26					14 50					
Whitstable	d				13 21							13 51					14 21					
Chestfield & Swalecliffe	d											13 54										
Herne Bay	d				13 26							13 58					14 26					
Birchington-on-Sea	d				13 35							14 07					14 35					
Westgate-on-Sea	d											14 10										
Margate 4	d				13 41						13 53	14 14					14 41					14 53
Broadstairs	d				13 46						13 59	14 20					14 46					14 59
Dumpton Park	d											14 23										
Ramsgate 4	a				13 51						14 04	14 26					14 51					15 04

London - Medway, Sheerness-on-Sea, Dover and Ramsgate

Network Diagram - see first Page of Table 212

		SE 1	SE	SE	SE	SE 1	SE	SE 1	SE	SE	SE	SE 1	SE	SE	SE	SE 1	SE	SE 1
St Pancras Internatnl 15 ⊖	d				13 55					14 25					14 55			
Stratford International ⊖	d				14 02					14 32					15 02			
Ebbsfleet International	d				14 13					14 43					15 13			
London Victoria 15 ⊖	d	13 22				13 52		13 58				14 22				14 52		14 58
London Blackfriars 3 ⊖	d																	
Elephant & Castle ⊖	d																	
Bromley South 4	d	13 39				14 09		14 19				14 39				15 09		15 19
St Mary Cray	d							14 25										15 25
Swanley 4	d							14 29										15 29
Farningham Road	d							14 34										15 34
Longfield	d	13 52				14 22		14 38				14 52				15 22		15 38
Meopham	d	13 57				14 27		14 42				14 57				15 27		15 42
Sole Street	d							14 45										15 45
London Charing Cross 4 ⊖	d		13 09				13 39						14 09				14 39	
London Waterloo (East) 4 ⊖	d		13 12				13 42						14 12				14 42	
London Cannon Street 4 ⊖	d																	
London Bridge 4 ⊖	d		13 17				13 47						14 17				14 47	
Dartford 4	d		13 55				14 25						14 55				15 25	
Greenhithe for Bluewater	d		14 00				14 30						15 00				15 30	
Gravesend 4	d		14 07		14 18		14 37			14 48			15 07		15 18		15 37	
Strood 4	d		14 18		14 28		14 48			14 58			15 18		15 28		15 48	
Rochester 4	d	14 09	14 22		14 33	14 39	14 52	14 56		15 03		15 09	15 22		15 33	15 39	15 52	15 56
Chatham 4	d	14 12	14 25		14 35	14 42	14 55	14 59		15 05		15 12	15 25		15 35	15 42	15 55	15 59
Gillingham (Kent) 4	d	14 17	14a29		14 40	14 47	14a59	15a03		15 10		15 17	15a29		15 40	15 47	15a59	16a03
Rainham (Kent)	d	14 21			14 45	14 51				15 15		15 20			15 45	15 51		
Newington	d					14 55										15 55		
Sittingbourne 4	a	14 28			14 52	15 00				15 22		15 28			15 52	16 00		
	d	14 29		14 40	14 53	15 01			15 10	15 23		15 29		15 40	15 53	16 01		
Kemsley	d			14 45					15 15					15 45				
Swale	d			14 48					15 18					15 48				
Queenborough	d			14 52					15 22					15 52				
Sheerness-on-Sea	a			14 57					15 27					15 57				
Teynham	d	14 33										15 33						
Faversham 2	a	14 39			15 03	15 09				15 33		15 39			16 03	16 09		
	d	14 43 / 14 45				15 13 / 15 15						15 43 / 15 45				16 13 / 16 15		
Selling	d	14 50										15 50				16 19		
Canterbury East 4	d	14 59				15 29						15 59				16 28		
Bekesbourne	d	15 03										16 03				16 33		
Adisham	d	15 08										16 08				16 37		
Aylesham	d	15 10										16 10				16 39		
Snowdown	d	15 13										16 13						
Shepherds Well	d	15 17				15 39						16 17				16 44		
Kearsney	d	15 21										16 21						
Dover Priory 4	a	15 26				15 48						16 27				16 52		
Whitstable	d	14 51				15 21						15 51				16 21		
Chestfield & Swalecliffe	d	14 54										15 54				16 24		
Herne Bay	d	14 58				15 26						15 58				16 28		
Birchington-on-Sea	d	15 07				15 35						16 07				16 37		
Westgate-on-Sea	d	15 10										16 10				16 40		
Margate 4	d	15 14				15 41					15 53	16 14				16 44		
Broadstairs	d	15 20				15 46					15 59	16 20				16 50		
Dumpton Park	d	15 23										16 23				16 53		
Ramsgate 4	a	15 26				15 51					16 04	16 26				16 56		

London - Medway, Sheerness-on-Sea, Dover and Ramsgate

Network Diagram - see first Page of Table 212

		SE	SE	SE	SE 1		SE	SE	SE	SE 1		SE	SE 1	SE	SE	SE	SE 1		SE	SE 1	SE	SE 1	SE
St Pancras Internatnl 15 ⊖	d		15 25						16 55						16 25								16 55
Stratford International ⊖	d		15 32						16 02						16 32								17 02
Ebbsfleet International	d		15 43						16 13						16 43								17 13
London Victoria 15 ⊖	d				15 22					15 52			15 58				16 22			16 28			
London Blackfriars 3 ⊖	d																						
Elephant & Castle ⊖	d																						
Bromley South 4	d				15 39					16 09			16 19				16 39			16 49			
St Mary Cray	d												16 25							16 55			
Swanley 4	d												16 29							16 59			
Farningham Road	d												16 34							17 04			
Longfield	d				15 52					16 22			16 38				16 52			17 08			
Meopham	d				15 57					16 27			16 42				16 57			17 12			
Sole Street	d												16 45							17 15			
London Charing Cross 4 ⊖	d						15 09					15 39							16 09				
London Waterloo (East) 4 ⊖	d						15 12					15 42							16 12				
London Cannon Street 4 ⊖	d																					16 46	
London Bridge 4 ⊖	d						15 17					15 47							16 17			16 50	
Dartford 4	d						15 55					16 25							16 55				
Greenhithe for Bluewater	d						16 00					16 30							17 00				
Gravesend 4	d		15 48				16 07		16 18			16 37			16 48				17 07				17 18
Strood 4	d		15 58				16 18		16 28			16 48			16 58				17 18				17 28
Rochester 4	d		16 03		16 09		16 22		16 33	16 39		16 52	16 56		17 03		17 10		17 22	17a27		17 29	17 34
Chatham 4	d		16 05		16 12		16 25		16 35	16 42		16 55	16 59		17 05		17 13		17 25			17 31	17 37
Gillingham (Kent) 4	d		16 10		16 17		16a29		16 40	16 47		16a59	17a03		17 10		17 18		17a31			17 36	17 43
Rainham (Kent)	d		16 15		16 21				16 45	16 51					17 15		17 23					17 41	17 48
Newington	d									16 55							17 27						
Sittingbourne 4	a		16 22		16 28				16 52	17 00					17 22		17 32					17 48	17 56
	d	16 10	16 23		16 29			16 40	16 53	17 01				17 10	17 23		17 33				17 40	17 48	17 57
Kemsley	d	16 15						16 45						17 15							17 45		
Swale	d	16 18						16 48						17 18							17 48		
Queenborough	d	16 22						16 52						17 22							17 52		
Sheerness-on-Sea	a	16 27						16 57						17 27							17 57		
Teynham	d				16 33					17 05							17 37						
Faversham 2	a		16 33		16 39				17 03	17 11					17 33		17 43					17 56	18 05
	d				16 43	16 45				17 15	17 19						17 47	17 49				17 57	
Selling	d					16 50					17 23							17 54					
Canterbury East 4	d					16 59					17 32							18 03					
Bekesbourne	d					17 03												18 07					
Adisham	d					17 08												18 12					
Aylesham	d					17 10					17 40							18 14					
Snowdown	d					17 13												18 17					
Shepherds Well	d					17 17					17 45							18 21					
Kearsney	d					17 21												18 25					
Dover Priory 4	a					17 27					17 53							18 32					
Whitstable	d				16 51					17 23							17 55					18 05	
Chestfield & Swalecliffe	d				16 54					17 26							17 58					18 08	
Herne Bay	d				16 58					17 30							18 02					18 12	
Birchington-on-Sea	d				17 07					17 39							18 11					18 21	
Westgate-on-Sea	d				17 10					17 42							18 15					18 25	
Margate 4	d			16 53	17 14					17 46						17 53	18 19					18 29	
Broadstairs	d			16 59	17 20					17 52						17 59	18 24					18 34	
Dumpton Park	d				17 23					17 55							18 27					18 37	
Ramsgate 4	a			17 04	17 26					17 58						18 04	18 32					18 43	

Table 212

London - Medway, Sheerness-on-Sea, Dover and Ramsgate

Network Diagram - see first Page of Table 212

		SE 1		SE	SE		SE	SE	SE 1	SE	SE	SE	SE 1		SE 1		SE	SE	SE	SE	SE 1	SE	SE	SE 1	SE
St Pancras Internatnl 15 ⊖	d				17 14		17 18					17 25						17 44		17 48			17 55		
Stratford International ⊖	d				17 21		17 25					17 32						17 51		17 55			18 02		
Ebbsfleet International	d						17a35					17 43								18a05			18 13		
London Victoria 15 ⊖	d	16 57		17 04									17 27								17 54				
London Blackfriars 3 ⊖	d																								
Elephant & Castle ⊖	d																								
Bromley South 4	d	17 13		17 24									17 44								18 19				
St Mary Cray	d			17 30																	18 25				
Swanley 4	d			17 34																	18 30				
Farningham Road	d			17 39																	18 35				
Longfield	d			17 44																					
Meopham	d			17 48																	18 41				
Sole Street	d			17 51																	18 44				
London Charing Cross 4 ⊖	d																		17 17						
London Waterloo (East) 4 ⊖	d																		17 20						
London Cannon Street 4 ⊖	d								17 08	16 44					17 30		17 06							17 52	
London Bridge 4 ⊖	d								17 12	16 48					17 34		17 10		17 26					17 56	
Dartford 4	d									17 28							17 47		18 02						
Greenhithe for Bluewater	d									17 33							17 52		18 07						
Gravesend 4	d				17 36					17 40							18 00	18 06	18b19						
Strood 4	d				17a46					17 52							18 14	18a17	18a33						
Rochester 4	d	17 40		18a04					17 49	17 57		18 02	18 10		18 15		18 20				18a56		18 31	18 38	
Chatham 4	d	17 43							17 52	18 00		18 05	18 13		18 18		18 23						18 34	18 41	
Gillingham (Kent) 4	d	17 48							17 57	18a07		18 10	18 18		18 24		18a30						18 39	18 46	
Rainham (Kent)	d	17 53							18 02			18 15	18 23		18 29								18 44	18 51	
Newington	d	17 57							18 06						18 33										
Sittingbourne 4	a	18 02							18 11			18 22	18 30		18 38								18 51	18 58	
	d	18 03							18 12		18 15	18 23	18 30		18 38							18 44	18 52	18 59	
Kemsley	d										18 20											18 49			
Swale	d										18 23											18 54			
Queenborough	d										18 27											18 58			
Sheerness-on-Sea	a										18 32											19 02			
Teynham	d	18 07							18 16				18 35												
Faversham 2	a	18 13							18 22			18 31	18 41		18 47								19 00	19 07	
	d	18 17	18 19						18 24			18 32	18 44	18 50	18 49								19 01	19 08	
Selling	d		18 23											18 54											
Canterbury East 4	d		18 32											19 04											
Bekesbourne	d													19 08											
Adisham	d													19 12											
Aylesham	d		18 40											19 15											
Snowdown	d													19 17											
Shepherds Well	d		18 45											19 21											
Kearsney	d													19 25											
Dover Priory 4	a		18 55											19 32											
Whitstable	d	18 25							18 32			18 40	18 52		18 57								19 09	19 16	
Chestfield & Swalecliffe	d	18 28							18 35				18 55		19 00										
Herne Bay	d	18 32							18 39			18 46	18 59		19 04								19 15	19 22	
Birchington-on-Sea	d	18 41							18 48			18 55	19 08		19 12								19 24	19 31	
Westgate-on-Sea	d	18 45							18 52				19 11		19 16										
Margate 4	d	18 49						18 53	18 57			19 02	19 15		19 20								19 30	19 37	19 53
Broadstairs	d	18 54						18 59	19 01			19a08	19 21		19 26								19a36	19a45	19 59
Dumpton Park	d	18 57							19 04				19 24		19 29										
Ramsgate 4	a	19 02						19 04	19 10				19 30		19 34										20 04

b Arr. 1813

London - Medway, Sheerness-on-Sea, Dover and Ramsgate

Network Diagram - see first Page of Table 212

		SE ■1		SE	SE	SE	SE	SE ■1	SE	SE ■1	SE ■1		SE	SE	SE	SE ■1	SE	SE ■1		SE	SE	SE ■1
St Pancras Internatnl ■15 ⊖	d				18 14	18 18			18 25					18 48			18 55					
Stratford International ⊖	d				18 21	18 25			18 32					18 55			19 02					
Ebbsfleet International	d					18a35			18 43					19a05			19 13					
London Victoria ■15 ⊖	d	17 57								18 24	18 27							18 57				18 58
London Blackfriars ■3 ⊖	d																					
Elephant & Castle ⊖	d																					
Bromley South ■4	d	18 15								18 46	18 44							19 14				19 19
St Mary Cray	d									18 52												19 25
Swanley ■4	d									18 57												19 29
Farningham Road	d									19 02												19 34
Longfield	d	18 28								19 06												19 39
Meopham	d									19 11												19 43
Sole Street	d									19 13												19 46
London Charing Cross ■4 ⊖	d			17 39									18 01								18 37	
London Waterloo (East) ■4 ⊖	d			17 42									18 04								18 40	
London Cannon Street ■4 ⊖	d							18 14								18 44				18 30		
London Bridge ■4 ⊖	d			17 48				18 18					18 10			18 48				18 34	18 46	
Dartford ■4	d			18 22									18 45							19 10	19 22	
Greenhithe for Bluewater	d			18 27									18 51							19 16	19 29	
Gravesend ■4	d			18 34	18 38								19 02				19 20			19 26	19 38	
Strood ■4	d			18 45	18a49								19 14				19 30			19 38	19a53	
Rochester ■4	d	18 43		18 51					19 03	19 23	19 12		19 19			19 27	19 35	19 40		19 45		19 56
Chatham ■4	d	18 46		18 54				19 00	19 06	19 26	19 15		19 22			19 30	19 38	19 43		19 48		19 59
Gillingham (Kent) ■4	d	18 51		19a02				19 05	19 11	19a32	19 20		19a29			19 34	19 43	19 49		19a55		20a06
Rainham (Kent)	d	18 56						19 10	19 16		19 25					19 39	19 48	19 54				
Newington	d	19 00						19 14								19 43		19 58				
Sittingbourne ■4	a	19 05						19 19	19 24		19 32					19 48	19 55	20 03				
	d	19 06					19 10	19 19	19 24		19 33				19 40	19 49	19 55	20 03				
Kemsley	d						19 15								19 45							
Swale	d						19 18								19 48							
Queenborough	d						19 22								19 52							
Sheerness-on-Sea	a						19 27								19 57							
Teynham	d	19 10									19 37					19 53						
Faversham ■2	a	19 16						19 27	19 32		19 43					19 59	20 04	20 11				
	d	19 20	19 22					19 28	19 33		19 47	19 49				20 00		20 15	20 17			
Selling	d		19 26									19 54							20 21			
Canterbury East ■4	d		19 36									20 03							20 30			
Bekesbourne	d											20 07							20 35			
Adisham	d											20 12							20 39			
Aylesham	d											20 14							20 41			
Snowdown	d											20 17										
Shepherds Well	d											20 21							20 46			
Kearsney	d											20 25										
Dover Priory ■4	a		19 54									20 32							20 56			
Whitstable	d	19 28						19 36	19 42		19 55					20 08		20 23				
Chestfield & Swalecliffe	d	19 31						19 39			19 58					20 11		20 26				
Herne Bay	d	19 35						19 43	19 48		20 02					20 15		20 30				
Birchington-on-Sea	d	19 44						19 52	19 57		20 11					20 24		20 39				
Westgate-on-Sea	d	19 48						19 55			20 15					20 27		20 43				
Margate ■4	d	19a54						19 59	20 04		20 19					20 31		20 47				
Broadstairs	d							20 05	20a09		20 25					20 37		20 52				
Dumpton Park	d							20 08			20 28					20 40		20 55				
Ramsgate ■4	a							20 13			20 33					20 49		21 00				

London - Medway, Sheerness-on-Sea, Dover and Ramsgate

Network Diagram - see first Page of Table 212

		SE	SE	SE	SE	SE 1			SE	SE	SE	SE	SE 1		SE	SE	SE		SE	SE	SE 1		SE	SE	SE
St Pancras Internatnl 15 ⊖	d			19 25								19 55							20 25						20 55
Stratford International ⊖	d			19 32								20 02							20 32						21 02
Ebbsfleet International	d			19 45								20 13							20 43						21 13
London Victoria 15 ⊖	d					19 22				19 28			19 52			19 58					20 22				
London Blackfriars 3 ⊖	d																								
Elephant & Castle ⊖	d																								
Bromley South 4	d					19 39				19 49			20 09			20 19					20 39				
St Mary Cray	d									19 55						20 25									
Swanley 4	d									19 59						20 29									
Farningham Road	d									20 04						20 34									
Longfield	d					19 52				20 08			20 22			20 38					20 52				
Meopham	d					19 57				20 12			20 27			20 42					20 57				
Sole Street	d									20 15						20 45									
London Charing Cross 4 ⊖	d	18 48							19 09						19 39								20 09		
London Waterloo (East) 4 ⊖	d	18 51							19 12						19 42								20 12		
London Cannon Street 4 ⊖	d																								
London Bridge 4 ⊖	d	18 57							19 17						19 47								20 17		
Dartford 4	d	19 35							19 55						20 25								20 55		
Greenhithe for Bluewater	d	19 40							20 00						20 30								21 00		
Gravesend 4	d	19 47		19 51					20 07			20 18			20 37				20 48				21 07		21 18
Strood 4	d	19 58		20 01					20 18			20 28			20 48				20 58				21 18		21 28
Rochester 4	d	20 03		20 08		20 13			20 22	20 26		20 33	20 39		20 52	20 56			21 03		21 09		21 22		21 33
Chatham 4	d	20 05		20 10		20 16			20 25	20 29		20 35	20 42		20 55	20 59			21 05		21 12		21 25		21 35
Gillingham (Kent) 4	d	20a13		20 15		20 21			20a29	20a33		20 40	20 47		20a59	21a03			21 10		21 17		21a29		21 40
Rainham (Kent)	d			20 20		20 25						20 45	20 51						21 15		21 21				21 45
Newington	d												20 55												
Sittingbourne 4	a			20 27		20 32						20 52	21 00						21 22		21 28				21 53
	d		20 10	20 27		20 33					20 40	20 53	21 01				21 10		21 23		21 29			21 40	21 53
Kemsley	d		20 15								20 45						21 15							21 45	
Swale	d		20 18								20 48						21 18							21 48	
Queenborough	d		20 22								20 52						21 22							21 52	
Sheerness-on-Sea	a		20 27								20 57						21 27							21 57	
Teynham	d					20 37															21 33				
Faversham 2	a			20 36		20 43						21 03	21 09						21 33		21 39				22 03
	d					20 47	20 49						21 13	21 15							21 43	21 45			
Selling	d						20 54							21 19								21 50			
Canterbury East 4	d						21 03							21 28								21 59			
Bekesbourne	d						21 07							21 33								22 03			
Adisham	d						21 12							21 37								22 08			
Aylesham	d						21 14							21 39								22 10			
Snowdown	d						21 17															22 13			
Shepherds Well	d						21 21							21 44								22 17			
Kearsney	d						21 25															22 21			
Dover Priory 4	a						21 32							21 52								22 26			
Whitstable	d					20 55							21 21								21 51				
Chestfield & Swalecliffe	d					20 58							21 24								21 54				
Herne Bay	d					21 02							21 28								21 58				
Birchington-on-Sea	d					21 11							21 37								22 07				
Westgate-on-Sea	d					21 15							21 40								22 10				
Margate 4	d				20 53	21 19							21 44							21 53	22 14				
Broadstairs	d				20 59	21 24							21 50							21 59	22 20				
Dumpton Park	d					21 27							21 53								22 23				
Ramsgate 4	a				21 04	21 32							21 56							22 04	22 26				

London - Medway, Sheerness-on-Sea, Dover and Ramsgate

Network Diagram - see first Page of Table 212

		SE 1			SE	SE 1	SE	SE 1		SE	SE	SE	SE 1		SE	SE	SE 1	SE	SE	SE	SE 1	SE	SE		SE 1
St Pancras Internatnl 15 ⊖	d						21 25					21 55				22 25				22 55			23 25		
Stratford International ⊖	d						21 32					22 02				22 32				23 02			23 32		
Ebbsfleet International	d						21 43					22 13				22 43				23 13			23 43		
London Victoria 15 ⊖	d	20 52				20 58		21 22					21 52				22 22				22 52				
London Blackfriars 3 ⊖	d																								
Elephant & Castle ⊖	d																								
Bromley South 4	d	21 09				21 19		21 39					22 09				22 39				23 09				
St Mary Cray	d					21 25							22 15								23 15				
Swanley 4	d					21 29							22 19								23 19				
Farningham Road	d					21 34							22 24								23 24				
Longfield	d	21 22				21 38		21 52					22 28				22 52				23 28				
Meopham	d	21 27				21 42		21 57					22 32				22 57				23 32				
Sole Street	d					21 45							22 35								23 35				
London Charing Cross 4 ⊖	d				20 39					21 09					21 39			22 09				22 39			
London Waterloo (East) 4 ⊖	d				20 42					21 12					21 42			22 12				22 42			
London Cannon Street 4 ⊖	d																								
London Bridge 4 ⊖	d				20 47					21 17					21 47			22 17				22 47			
Dartford 4	d				21 25					21 55					22 25			22 55				23 25			
Greenhithe for Bluewater	d				21 30					22 00					22 30			23 00				23 31			
Gravesend 4	d				21 37		21 48			22 07		22 18			22 37	22 48		23 07		23 18		23 40	23 48		
Strood 4	d				21 48		21 58			22 18		22 28			22 48	22 58		23 18		23 28		23 52	23 58		
Rochester 4	d	21 39			21 52	21 56	22 03	22 09		22 22		22 33	22 45		22 52	23 03	23 09	23 22		23 33	23 45	23 56	00 03		
Chatham 4	d	21 42			21 55	21 59	22 05	22 12		22 25		22 35	22 47		22 55	23 05	23 12	23 25		23 35	23 47	23 58	00 05		
Gillingham (Kent) 4	d	21 47			21a59	22a03	22 10	22 17		22a29		22 40	22 52		22a59	23 10	23 17	23a29		23 40	23 52	00a03	00 10		
Rainham (Kent)	d	21 51					22 15	22 21				22 45	22 56			23 15	23 21			23 45	23 56		00 15		
Newington	d	21 55											23 00								00 01				
Sittingbourne 4	a	22 00					22 22	22 28				22 52	23 05			23 22	23 28			23 52	00 06		00 22		
	d	22 01					22 23	22 29			22 40	22 53	23 06			23 23	23 29		23 32	23 53	00 07		00 23		
Kemsley	d										22 45								23 37						
Swale	d										22 48								23 40						
Queenborough	d										22 52								23 44						
Sheerness-on-Sea	a										22 57								23 49						
Teynham	d							22 33									23 33								
Faversham 2	a	22 09					22 33	22 39				23 03	23 17			23 33	23 39			00 03	00 15		00 33		
	d	22 13	22 15					22 43	22 45								23 43								23 45
Selling	d		22 19						22 50																23 50
Canterbury East 4	d		22 28						22 59																23 59
Bekesbourne	d		22 33						23 03																
Adisham	d		22 37						23 08																
Aylesham	d		22 39						23 10																00 07
Snowdown	d								23 13																
Shepherds Well	d		22 44						23 17																
Kearsney	d								23 21																
Dover Priory 4	a		22 52						23 26																00 18
Whitstable	d	22 21						22 51									23 51								
Chestfield & Swalecliffe	d	22 24						22 54									23 54								
Herne Bay	d	22 28						22 58									23 58								
Birchington-on-Sea	d	22 37						23 07									00 07								
Westgate-on-Sea	d	22 40						23 10									00 10								
Margate 4	d	22 44						23 14									00 14								
Broadstairs	d	22 50						23 20									00 20								
Dumpton Park	d	22 53						23 23									00 23								
Ramsgate 4	a	22 56						23 26									00 26								

London - Medway, Sheerness-on-Sea, Dover and Ramsgate

Network Diagram - see first Page of Table 212

Station		SE 1	SE	SE	SE 1	SE
St Pancras Internatnl 15 ⊖	d			23 55		
Stratford International ⊖	d			00 02		
Ebbsfleet International	d			00 13		
London Victoria 15 ⊖	d	23 22			23 52	
London Blackfriars 3 ⊖	d					
Elephant & Castle ⊖	d					
Bromley South 4	d	23 39			00 09	
St Mary Cray	d				00 15	
Swanley 4	d				00 19	
Farningham Road	d				00 24	
Longfield	d	23 52			00 28	
Meopham	d	23 57			00 32	
Sole Street	d				00 35	
London Charing Cross 4 ⊖	d		23 09			23 39
London Waterloo (East) 4 ⊖	d		23 12			23 42
London Cannon Street 4 ⊖	d					
London Bridge 4 ⊖	d		23 17			23 47
Dartford 4	d		23 55			00 25
Greenhithe for Bluewater	d		23 59			00 31
Gravesend 4	d		00 10	00 18		00 40
Strood 4	d		00 22	00 28		00 52
Rochester 4	d	00 09	00 26	00 33	00 45	00 56
Chatham 4	d	00 12	00 28	00 35	00 47	00 58
Gillingham (Kent) 4	d	00 17	00a33	00 40	00a52	01a03
Rainham (Kent)	d	00 21		00 45		
Newington	d					
Sittingbourne 4	a	00 28		00 52		
	d	00 29		00 53		
Kemsley	d					
Swale	d					
Queenborough	d					
Sheerness-on-Sea	a					
Teynham	d	00 33				
Faversham 2	a	00 39		01 03		
	d	00 43				
Selling	d					
Canterbury East 4	d					
Bekesbourne	d					
Adisham	d					
Aylesham	d					
Snowdown	d					
Shepherds Well	d					
Kearsney	d					
Dover Priory 4	a					
Whitstable	d	00 51				
Chestfield & Swalecliffe	d	00 54				
Herne Bay	d	00 58				
Birchington-on-Sea	d	01 07				
Westgate-on-Sea	d	01 10				
Margate 4	d	01 14				
Broadstairs	d	01 20				
Dumpton Park	d	01 23				
Ramsgate 4	a	01 26				

Table 212

Saturdays

London - Medway, Sheerness-on-Sea, Dover and Ramsgate

Network Diagram - see first Page of Table 212

	SE 1	SE	SE 1	SE 1	SE	SE	SE 1	SE	SE		SE 1	SE 1	SE	SE	SE	SE	SE 1	SE	SE		SE 1	SE	SE 1	SE
St Pancras Internatnl 15 ⊖ d		22p55				23p25			23p55					00 12										
Stratford International ⊖ d		23p02				23p32			00 02					00 19										
Ebbsfleet International d		23p13				23p43			00 13					00 31										
London Victoria 15 ⊖ d	22p22		22p52				23p22				23p52	00 10			00 35								05 22	
London Blackfriars 3 ⊖ d																								
Elephant & Castle ⊖ d																								
Bromley South 4 d	22p39		23p09				23p39				00 09				00 55								05 39	
St Mary Cray d			23p15								00 15				01 01								05 45	
Swanley 4 d			23p19								00 19				01 05								05 49	
Farningham Road d			23p24								00 24				01 10								05 54	
Longfield d	22p52		23p28				23p52				00 28				01 14								05 58	
Meopham d	22p57		23p32				23p57				00 32				01 18								06 02	
Sole Street d			23p35								00 35												06 05	
London Charing Cross 4 ⊖ d								23p09					23p39			00 18								
London Waterloo (East) 4 ⊖ d								23p12					23p42			00 21								
London Cannon Street 4 ⊖ d																								
London Bridge 4 ⊖ d								23p17					23p47			00 26								
Dartford 4 d								23p55					00 25			01 06								05 55
Greenhithe for Bluewater d								23p59					00 31			01 10								06 00
Gravesend 4 d		23p18				23p48		00 10	00 18				00 40			01 17								06 07
Strood 4 d		23p28				23p58		00 22	00 28				00 52			01 29								06 18
Rochester 4 d	23p09	23p33	23p45			00 03	00 09	00 26	00 33		00 45	00 49	00 56		01 29	01 33							06 15	06 22
Chatham 4 d	23p12	23p35	23p47			00 05	00 12	00 28	00 35		00 47	00 52	00 58		01 31	01 35							06 17	06 25
Gillingham (Kent) 4 d	23p17	23p40	23p52			00 10	00 17	00a33	00 40		00a52	00 57	01a03		01a35	01a41	05 47						06 22	06a29
Rainham (Kent) d	23p21	23p45	23p56			00 15	00 21		00 45			01 01					05 51						06 26	
Newington d			00 01									01 05					05 55						06 30	
Sittingbourne 4 a	23p28	23p52	00 06			00 22	00 28		00 52			01 10					06 00						06 35	
d	23p29	23p53	00 07		00 15	00 23	00 29		00 53			01 11					06 01		06 10				06 36	
Kemsley d					00 20														06 15					
Swale d					00 23														06 18					
Queenborough d					00 27														06 22					
Sheerness-on-Sea a					00 32														06 27					
Teynham d	23p33						00 33					01 15					06 05						06 40	
Faversham 2 a	23p39	00 03	00 15			00 33	00 39		01 03			01 23					06 11						06 46	
d	23p43			23p45			00 43					01 24					06 12				06 17		06 47	
Selling d				23p50													06 17							
Canterbury East 4 d				23p59													06 26							
Bekesbourne d																	06 30							
Adisham d																	06 35							
Aylesham d				00 07													06 37							
Snowdown d																	06 40							
Shepherds Well d																	06 44							
Kearsney d																	06 48							
Dover Priory 4 a				00 18													06 53							
Whitstable d	23p51						00 51					01 32									06 25		06 55	
Chestfield & Swalecliffe d	23p54						00 54					01 35									06 28		06 58	
Herne Bay d	23p58						00 58					01 39									06 32		07 02	
Birchington-on-Sea d	00 07						01 07					01 48									06 41		07 11	
Westgate-on-Sea d	00 10						01 10					01 51									06 44		07 14	
Margate 4 d	00 14						01 14					01 55						05 53			06 48	06 53	07 18	
Broadstairs d	00 20						01 20					02 01						05 59			06 54	06 59	07 24	
Dumpton Park d	00 23						01 23					02 04									06 57		07 27	
Ramsgate 4 a	00 26						01 26					02 07						06 04			07 00	07 04	07 30	

Table 212

Saturdays

London - Medway, Sheerness-on-Sea, Dover and Ramsgate

Network Diagram - see first Page of Table 212

	SE	SE	SE	SE	SE		SE	SE	SE	SE	SE	SE	SE	SE	SE		SE	SE	SE	SE		SE	SE	SE
			1				1					1	1				1	1		1				
St Pancras Internatnl 15 ⊖ d										06 52					07 25									07 52
Stratford International ⊖ d										06 59					07 32									07 58
Ebbsfleet International d										07 13					07 43									08 13
London Victoria 15 ⊖ d							06 22					06 58								07 22				
London Blackfriars 3 ⊖ d																								
Elephant & Castle ⊖ d																								
Bromley South 4 d							06 39					07 19								07 39				
St Mary Cray d							06 45					07 25												
Swanley 4 d							06 49					07 29												
Farningham Road d							06 54					07 34												
Longfield d							06 58					07 38								07 52				
Meopham d							07 02					07 42								07 57				
Sole Street d							07 05					07 45												
London Charing Cross 4 ⊖ d	05 39							06 09			06 39											07 09		
London Waterloo (East) 4 ⊖ d	05 42							06 12			06 42											07 12		
London Cannon Street 4 ⊖ d																								
London Bridge 4 ⊖ d	05 47							06 17			06 47											07 17		
Dartford 4 d	06 25							06 55			07 25											07 55		
Greenhithe for Bluewater d	06 30							07 00			07 30											08 00		
Gravesend 4 d	06 37							07 07		07 17	07 37				07 48							08 07		08 18
Strood 4 d	06 48							07 18		07 27	07 48				07 58							08 18		08 28
Rochester 4 d	06 52						07 15	07 22		07 32	07 52	07 56			08 03					08 09		08 22		08 33
Chatham 4 d	06 55						07 17	07 25		07 34	07 55	07 59			08 05					08 12		08 25		08 35
Gillingham (Kent) 4 d	06a59						07 22	07a29		07 39	07a59	08a03			08 10					08 17		08a29		08 40
Rainham (Kent) d							07 26			07 44					08 15					08 21				08 45
Newington d							07 30													08 25				
Sittingbourne 4 a							07 35			07 51					08 22					08 30				08 52
d		06 40		07 10			07 36		07 40	07 51				08 10	08 23					08 31			08 40	08 53
Kemsley d		06 45		07 15					07 45					08 15									08 45	
Swale d		06 48		07 18					07 48					08 18									08 48	
Queenborough d		06 52		07 22					07 52					08 22									08 52	
Sheerness-on-Sea a		06 57		07 27					07 57					08 27									08 57	
Teynham d							07 40													08 35				
Faversham 2 a							07 46			08 03					08 33					08 41				09 03
d			06 50				07 47						07 50				08 13	08 15		08 45	08 50			
Selling d			06 55										07 55								08 55			
Canterbury East 4 d			07 04										08 04					08 29			09 04			
Bekesbourne d			07 08										08 08								09 08			
Adisham d			07 13										08 13								09 13			
Aylesham d			07 15										08 15								09 15			
Snowdown d			07 18										08 18								09 18			
Shepherds Well d			07 22										08 22								09 22			
Kearsney d			07 26										08 26								09 26			
Dover Priory 4 a			07 31										08 31					08 48			09 31			
Whitstable d							07 55										08 21			08 53				
Chestfield & Swalecliffe d							07 58													08 56				
Herne Bay d							08 02										08 26			09 00				
Birchington-on-Sea d							08 11										08 35			09 09				
Westgate-on-Sea d							08 14													09 12				
Margate 4 d					07 53		08 18										08 41		08 53	09 16				
Broadstairs d					07 59		08 24										08 46		08 59	09 22				
Dumpton Park d							08 27													09 25				
Ramsgate 4 a					08 04		08 30										08 51		09 04	09 28				

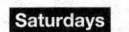

London - Medway, Sheerness-on-Sea, Dover and Ramsgate

Network Diagram - see first Page of Table 212

		SE [1]		SE	SE [1]	SE	SE	SE	SE [1]		SE	SE	SE	SE [1]		SE	SE [1]	SE	SE	SE	SE [1]	
St Pancras Internatnl [15] ⊖	d						08 28						08 50						09 25			
Stratford International ⊖	d						08 35						09b04						09 32			
Ebbsfleet International	d						08 46						09 15						09 43			
London Victoria [15] ⊖	d	07 52			07 58				08 22					08 52			08 58				09 22	
London Blackfriars [3] ⊖	d																					
Elephant & Castle ⊖	d																					
Bromley South [4]	d	08 09			08 19				08 39					09 09			09 19				09 39	
St Mary Cray	d				08 25												09 25					
Swanley [4]	d				08 29												09 29					
Farningham Road	d				08 34												09 34					
Longfield	d	08 22			08 38				08 52					09 22			09 38				09 52	
Meopham	d	08 27			08 42				08 57					09 27			09 42				09 57	
Sole Street	d				08 45												09 45					
London Charing Cross [4] ⊖	d			07 39							08 09					08 39						
London Waterloo (East) [4] ⊖	d			07 42							08 12					08 42						
London Cannon Street [4] ⊖	d																					
London Bridge [4] ⊖	d			07 47							08 17					08 47						
Dartford [4]	d			08 25							08 55					09 25						
Greenhithe for Bluewater	d			08 30							09 00					09 30						
Gravesend [4]	d			08 37			08 51				09 07		09 20			09 37			09 48			
Strood [4]	d			08 48			09 01				09 18		09 30			09 48			09 58			
Rochester [4]	d	08 39		08 52	08 56		09 06		09 09		09 22		09 34	09 39		09 52	09 56		10 03		10 09	
Chatham [4]	d	08 42		08 55	08 59		09 08		09 12		09 25		09 37	09 42		09 55	09 59		10 05		10 12	
Gillingham (Kent) [4]	d	08 47		08a59	09a03		09 13		09 17		09a29		09 41	09 47		09a59	10a03		10 10		10 17	
Rainham (Kent)	d	08 51					09 18		09 21				09 46	09 51					10 15		10 21	
Newington	d	08 55												09 55								
Sittingbourne [4]	a	09 00					09 25		09 28				09 54	10 00					10 22		10 28	
	d	09 01				09 10	09 25		09 29			09 40	09 54	10 01				10 10	10 23		10 29	
Kemsley	d					09 15						09 45						10 15				
Swale	d					09 18						09 48						10 18				
Queenborough	d					09 22						09 52						10 22				
Sheerness-on-Sea	a					09 27						09 57						10 27				
Teynham	d								09 33												10 33	
Faversham [2]	a	09 09					09 34		09 39				10 03	10 09					10 33		10 39	
	d	09 13	09 15						09 43	09 45				10 13	10 15						10 43	10 45
Selling	d									09 50												10 50
Canterbury East [4]	d		09 29							09 59					10 29							10 59
Bekesbourne	d									10 03												11 03
Adisham	d									10 08												11 08
Aylesham	d									10 10												11 10
Snowdown	d									10 13												11 13
Shepherds Well	d									10 17												11 17
Kearsney	d									10 21												11 21
Dover Priory [4]	a		09 48							10 27					10 48							11 27
Whitstable	d	09 21							09 51					10 21							10 51	
Chestfield & Swalecliffe	d								09 54												10 54	
Herne Bay	d	09 26							09 58					10 26							10 58	
Birchington-on-Sea	d	09 35							10 07					10 35							11 07	
Westgate-on-Sea	d								10 10												11 10	
Margate [4]	d	09 41						09 53	10 14					10 41						10 53	11 14	
Broadstairs	d	09 46						09 59	10 20					10 46						10 59	11 20	
Dumpton Park	d								10 23												11 23	
Ramsgate [4]	a	09 51						10 04	10 26					10 51						11 04	11 26	

b Arr. 0856

Table 212

Saturdays

London - Medway, Sheerness-on-Sea, Dover and Ramsgate

Network Diagram - see first Page of Table 212

		SE	SE	SE	SE [1]		SE	SE [1]	SE	SE		SE	SE [1]		SE	SE	SE	SE [1]		SE		SE [1]	SE	SE	SE
St Pancras Internatnl [15] ⊖	d			09 55						10 28							10 52							11 28	
Stratford International ⊖	d			10 02						10 35							10 58							11 35	
Ebbsfleet International	d			10 13						10 46							11 13							11 46	
London Victoria [15] ⊖	d				09 52			09 58					10 22					10 52				10 58			
London Blackfriars [3] ⊖	d																								
Elephant & Castle ⊖	d																								
Bromley South [4]	d				10 09			10 19					10 39					11 09				11 19			
St Mary Cray	d							10 25														11 25			
Swanley [4]	d							10 29														11 29			
Farningham Road	d							10 34														11 34			
Longfield	d				10 22			10 38					10 52					11 22				11 38			
Meopham	d				10 27			10 42					10 57					11 27				11 42			
Sole Street	d							10 45														11 45			
London Charing Cross [4] ⊖	d	09 09					09 39								10 09					10 39					
London Waterloo (East) [4] ⊖	d	09 12					09 42								10 12					10 42					
London Cannon Street [4] ⊖	d																								
London Bridge [4] ⊖	d	09 17					09 47								10 17					10 47					
Dartford [4]	d	09 55					10 25								10 55					11 25					
Greenhithe for Bluewater	d	10 00					10 30								11 00					11 30					
Gravesend [4]	d	10 07		10 18			10 37			10 51					11 07		11 18			11 37				11 51	
Strood [4]	d	10 18		10 28			10 48			11 01					11 18		11 28			11 48				12 01	
Rochester [4]	d	10 22		10 33	10 39		10 52	10 56		11 06			11 09		11 22		11 33	11 39		11 52		11 56		12 06	
Chatham [4]	d	10 25		10 35	10 42		10 55	10 59		11 08			11 12		11 25		11 35	11 42		11 55		11 59		12 08	
Gillingham (Kent) [4]	d	10a29		10 40	10 47		10a59	11a03		11 13			11 17		11a29		11 40	11 47		11a59		12a03		12 13	
Rainham (Kent)	d			10 45	10 51					11 18			11 21				11 45	11 51						12 18	
Newington	d				10 55													11 55							
Sittingbourne [4]	a			10 52	11 00					11 25			11 28				11 52	12 00						12 25	
	d		10 40	10 53	11 01				11 10	11 25			11 29			11 40	11 53	12 01					12 10	12 25	
Kemsley	d		10 45						11 15							11 45							12 15		
Swale	d		10 48						11 18							11 48							12 18		
Queenborough	d		10 52						11 22							11 52							12 22		
Sheerness-on-Sea	a		10 57						11 27							11 57							12 27		
Teynham	d												11 33												
Faversham [2]	a			11 03	11 09					11 34			11 39				12 03	12 09						12 34	
	d				11 13	11 15							11 43	11 45				12 13	12 15						
Selling	d													11 50											
Canterbury East [4]	d					11 29								11 59					12 29						
Bekesbourne	d													12 03											
Adisham	d													12 08											
Aylesham	d													12 10											
Snowdown	d													12 13											
Shepherds Well	d													12 17											
Kearsney	d													12 21											
Dover Priory [4]	a					11 48								12 27					12 48						
Whitstable	d				11 21								11 51					12 21							
Chestfield & Swalecliffe	d												11 54												
Herne Bay	d				11 26								11 58					12 26							
Birchington-on-Sea	d				11 35								12 07					12 35							
Westgate-on-Sea	d												12 10												
Margate [4]	d				11 41							11 53	12 14					12 41							12 53
Broadstairs	d				11 46							11 59	12 20					12 46							12 59
Dumpton Park	d												12 23												
Ramsgate [4]	a				11 51							12 04	12 26					12 51							13 04

London - Medway, Sheerness-on-Sea, Dover and Ramsgate

Network Diagram - see first Page of Table 212

		SE ■1		SE	SE	SE		SE ■1		SE	SE ■1	SE	SE	SE	SE ■1			SE	SE	SE	SE ■1		SE	SE ■1	SE
St Pancras Internatnl ■15 ⊖	d					11 55							12 28							12 55					
Stratford International ⊖	d					12 02							12 35							13 06					
Ebbsfleet International	d					12 13							12 46							13 17					
London Victoria ■15 ⊖	d	11 22						11 52			11 58				12 22						12 52			12 58	
London Blackfriars ■3 ⊖	d																								
Elephant & Castle ⊖	d																								
Bromley South ■4	d	11 39						12 09			12 19				12 39						13 09			13 19	
St Mary Cray	d										12 25													13 25	
Swanley ■4	d										12 29													13 29	
Farningham Road	d										12 34													13 34	
Longfield	d	11 52						12 22			12 38				12 52						13 22			13 38	
Meopham	d	11 57						12 27			12 42				12 57						13 27			13 42	
Sole Street	d										12 45													13 45	
London Charing Cross ■4 ⊖	d			11 09						11 39								12 09					12 39		
London Waterloo (East) ■4 ⊖	d			11 12						11 42								12 12					12 42		
London Cannon Street ■4 ⊖	d																								
London Bridge ■4 ⊖	d			11 17						11 47								12 17					12 47		
Dartford ■4	d			11 55						12 25								12 55					13 25		
Greenhithe for Bluewater	d			12 00						12 30								13 00					13 30		
Gravesend ■4	d			12 07		12 18				12 37			12 51					13 07		13 22			13 37		
Strood ■4	d			12 18		12 28				12 48			13 01					13 18		13 32			13 48		
Rochester ■4	d	12 09		12 22		12 33		12 39		12 52	12 56		13 06		13 09			13 22		13 37	13 39		13 52	13 56	
Chatham ■4	d	12 12		12 25		12 35		12 42		12 55	12 59		13 08		13 12			13 25		13 39	13 42		13 55	13 59	
Gillingham (Kent) ■4	d	12 17		12a29		12 40		12 47		12a59	13a03		13 13		13 17			13a29		13 44	13 47		13a59	14a03	
Rainham (Kent)	d	12 21				12 45		12 51					13 18		13 21					13 49	13 51				
Newington	d							12 55													13 55				
Sittingbourne ■4	a	12 28				12 52		13 00					13 25		13 29					13 56	14 00				
	d	12 29			12 40	12 53		13 01				13 10	13 25		13 29				13 40	13 56	14 01				14 10
Kemsley	d				12 45							13 15							13 45						14 15
Swale	d				12 48							13 18							13 48						14 18
Queenborough	d				12 52							13 22							13 52						14 22
Sheerness-on-Sea	a				12 57							13 27							13 57						14 27
Teynham	d	12 33													13 33										
Faversham ■2	a	12 39				13 03		13 09					13 34		13 39					14 04	14 09				
	d	12 43	12 45					13 13	13 15						13 43	13 45					14 13	14 15			
Selling	d		12 50													13 50									
Canterbury East ■4	d		12 59						13 29							13 59						14 29			
Bekesbourne	d		13 03													14 03									
Adisham	d		13 08													14 08									
Aylesham	d		13 10													14 10									
Snowdown	d		13 13													14 13									
Shepherds Well	d		13 17													14 17									
Kearsney	d		13 21													14 21									
Dover Priory ■4	a		13 27						13 48							14 27						14 48			
Whitstable	d	12 51						13 21							13 51						14 21				
Chestfield & Swalecliffe	d	12 54													13 54										
Herne Bay	d	12 58						13 26							13 58						14 26				
Birchington-on-Sea	d	13 07						13 35							14 07						14 35				
Westgate-on-Sea	d	13 10													14 10										
Margate ■4	d	13 14						13 41						13 53	14 14						14 41				
Broadstairs	d	13 20						13 46						13 59	14 20						14 46				
Dumpton Park	d	13 23													14 23										
Ramsgate ■4	a	13 26						13 51						14 04	14 26						14 51				

Table 212

Saturdays

London - Medway, Sheerness-on-Sea, Dover and Ramsgate

Network Diagram - see first Page of Table 212

		SE		SE	SE 1		SE	SE	SE	SE 1		SE		SE 1	SE	SE	SE	SE 1		SE	SE	SE		SE 1	
St Pancras Internatnl 15 ⊖	d	13 25							13 55							14 25						14 55			
Stratford International ⊖	d	13 32							14 02							14 32						15 02			
Ebbsfleet International	d	13 43							14 13							14 43						15 13			
London Victoria 15 ⊖	d				13 22					13 52				13 58				14 22						14 52	
London Blackfriars 3 ⊖	d																								
Elephant & Castle ⊖	d																								
Bromley South 4	d				13 39					14 09				14 19				14 39						15 09	
St Mary Cray	d													14 25											
Swanley 4	d													14 29											
Farningham Road	d													14 34											
Longfield	d				13 52					14 22				14 38				14 52						15 22	
Meopham	d				13 57					14 27				14 42				14 57						15 27	
Sole Street	d													14 45											
London Charing Cross 4 ⊖	d						13 09					13 39								14 09					
London Waterloo (East) 4 ⊖	d						13 12					13 42								14 12					
London Cannon Street 4 ⊖	d																								
London Bridge 4 ⊖	d						13 17					13 47								14 17					
Dartford 4	d						13 55					14 25								14 55					
Greenhithe for Bluewater	d						14 00					14 30								15 00					
Gravesend 4	d	13 48					14 07		14 18			14 37				14 48				15 07		15 18			
Strood 4	d	13 58					14 18		14 28			14 48				14 58				15 18		15 28			
Rochester 4	d	14 03			14 09		14 22		14 33	14 39		14 52		14 56		15 03		15 09		15 22		15 33		15 39	
Chatham 4	d	14 05			14 12		14 25		14 35	14 42		14 55		14 59		15 05		15 12		15 25		15 35		15 42	
Gillingham (Kent) 4	d	14 10			14 17		14a29		14 40	14 47		14a59		15a03		15 10		15 17		15a29		15 40		15 47	
Rainham (Kent)	d	14 15			14 21				14 45	14 51						15 15		15 21				15 45		15 51	
Newington	d									14 55														15 55	
Sittingbourne 4	a	14 22			14 28				14 52	15 00						15 22		15 28				15 52		16 00	
	d	14 23			14 29			14 40	14 53	15 01					15 10	15 23		15 29			15 40	15 53		16 01	
Kemsley	d							14 45							15 15						15 45				
Swale	d							14 48							15 18						15 48				
Queenborough	d							14 52							15 22						15 52				
Sheerness-on-Sea	a							14 57							15 27						15 57				
Teynham	d				14 33													15 33							
Faversham 2	a	14 33			14 39				15 03	15 09						15 33		15 39				16 03		16 09	
	d				14 43	14 45				15 13	15 15							15 43	15 45					16 13	16 15
Selling	d					14 50													15 50						
Canterbury East 4	d					14 59					15 29								15 59						16 29
Bekesbourne	d					15 03													16 03						
Adisham	d					15 08													16 08						
Aylesham	d					15 10													16 10						
Snowdown	d					15 13													16 13						
Shepherds Well	d					15 17													16 17						
Kearsney	d					15 21													16 21						
Dover Priory 4	a					15 27					15 48								16 27						16 48
Whitstable	d				14 51					15 21								15 51						16 21	
Chestfield & Swalecliffe	d				14 54													15 54							
Herne Bay	d				14 58					15 26								15 58						16 26	
Birchington-on-Sea	d				15 07					15 35								16 07						16 35	
Westgate-on-Sea	d				15 10													16 10							
Margate 4	d			14 53	15 14					15 41							15 53	16 14						16 41	
Broadstairs	d			14 59	15 20					15 46							15 59	16 20						16 46	
Dumpton Park	d				15 23													16 23							
Ramsgate 4	a			15 04	15 26					15 51							16 04	16 26						16 51	

London - Medway, Sheerness-on-Sea, Dover and Ramsgate

Network Diagram - see first Page of Table 212

		SE	SE 1	SE	SE	SE	SE 1			SE	SE	SE	SE 1		SE	SE 1	SE	SE		SE	SE 1		SE	SE	SE
St Pancras Internatnl 15 ⊖	d				15 25							15 55						16 28							16 55
Stratford International ⊖	d				15 32							16 02						16 35							17 02
Ebbsfleet International	d				15 43							16 13						16 46							17 13
London Victoria 15 ⊖	d		14 58				15 22						15 52			15 58					16 22				
London Blackfriars 3 ⊖	d																								
Elephant & Castle ⊖	d																								
Bromley South 4	d		15 19				15 39						16 09			16 19					16 39				
St Mary Cray	d		15 25													16 25									
Swanley 4	d		15 29													16 29									
Farningham Road	d		15 34													16 34									
Longfield	d		15 38				15 52						16 22			16 38					16 52				
Meopham	d		15 42				15 57						16 27			16 42					16 57				
Sole Street	d		15 45													16 45									
London Charing Cross 4 ⊖	d	14 39								15 09					15 39								16 09		
London Waterloo (East) 4 ⊖	d	14 42								15 12					15 42								16 12		
London Cannon Street 4 ⊖	d																								
London Bridge 4 ⊖	d	14 47								15 17					15 47								16 17		
Dartford 4	d	15 25								15 55					16 25								16 55		
Greenhithe for Bluewater	d	15 30								16 00					16 30								17 00		
Gravesend 4	d	15 37			15 48					16 07		16 18			16 37			16 51					17 07		17 18
Strood 4	d	15 48			15 58					16 18		16 28			16 48			17 01					17 18		17 28
Rochester 4	d	15 52	15 56		16 03		16 09			16 22		16 33	16 39		16 52	16 56		17 06			17 09		17 22		17 33
Chatham 4	d	15 55	15 59		16 05		16 12			16 25		16 35	16 42		16 55	16 59		17 08			17 12		17 25		17 35
Gillingham (Kent) 4	d	15a59	16a03		16 10		16 17			16a29		16 40	16 47		16a59	17a03		17 13			17 17		17a29		17 40
Rainham (Kent)	d				16 15		16 21					16 45	16 51					17 18			17 21				17 45
Newington	d												16 55												
Sittingbourne 4	a				16 22		16 28					16 52	17 00					17 25			17 28				17 52
	d			16 10	16 23		16 29				16 40	16 53	17 01				17 10	17 25			17 29			17 40	17 53
Kemsley	d			16 15							16 45						17 15							17 45	
Swale	d			16 18							16 48						17 18							17 48	
Queenborough	d			16 22							16 52						17 22							17 52	
Sheerness-on-Sea	a			16 27							16 57						17 27							17 57	
Teynham	d						16 33														17 33				
Faversham 2	a				16 33		16 39					17 03	17 09					17 34			17 39				18 03
	d						16 43	16 45					17 13	17 15							17 43	17 45			
Selling	d							16 50														17 50			
Canterbury East 4	d							16 59						17 29								17 59			
Bekesbourne	d							17 03														18 03			
Adisham	d							17 08														18 08			
Aylesham	d							17 10														18 10			
Snowdown	d							17 13														18 13			
Shepherds Well	d							17 17														18 17			
Kearsney	d							17 21														18 21			
Dover Priory 4	a							17 27						17 48								18 27			
Whitstable	d						16 51						17 21								17 51				
Chestfield & Swalecliffe	d						16 54														17 54				
Herne Bay	d						16 58						17 26								17 58				
Birchington-on-Sea	d						17 07						17 35								18 07				
Westgate-on-Sea	d						17 10														18 10				
Margate 4	d					16 53	17 14						17 41							17 53	18 14				
Broadstairs	d					16 59	17 20						17 46							17 59	18 20				
Dumpton Park	d						17 23														18 23				
Ramsgate 4	a					17 04	17 26						17 51							18 04	18 26				

Table 212

Saturdays

London - Medway, Sheerness-on-Sea, Dover and Ramsgate

Network Diagram - see first Page of Table 212

		SE 1		SE		SE 1	SE	SE	SE	SE 1		SE	SE	SE		SE 1		SE	SE 1	SE	SE	SE	SE 1		
St Pancras Internatnl 15 ⊖	d							17 25						17 55							18 25				
Stratford International ⊖	d							17 32						18 02							18 32				
Ebbsfleet International	d							17 43						18 13							18 43				
London Victoria 15 ⊖	d	16 52				16 58				17 22						17 52			17 58				18 22		
London Blackfriars 3 ⊖	d																								
Elephant & Castle ⊖	d																								
Bromley South 4	d	17 09				17 19				17 39						18 09			18 19				18 39		
St Mary Cray	d					17 25													18 25						
Swanley 4	d					17 29													18 29						
Farningham Road	d					17 34													18 34						
Longfield	d	17 22				17 38				17 52						18 22			18 38				18 52		
Meopham	d	17 27				17 42				17 57						18 27			18 42				18 57		
Sole Street	d					17 45													18 45						
London Charing Cross 4 ⊖	d			16 39								17 09						17 39							
London Waterloo (East) 4 ⊖	d			16 42								17 12						17 42							
London Cannon Street 4 ⊖	d																								
London Bridge 4 ⊖	d			16 47								17 17						17 47							
Dartford 4	d			17 25								17 55						18 25							
Greenhithe for Bluewater	d			17 30								18 00						18 30							
Gravesend 4	d			17 37				17 48				18 07		18 18				18 37			18 48				
Strood 4	d			17 48				17 58				18 18		18 28				18 48			18 58				
Rochester 4	d	17 39		17 52		17 56		18 03		18 09		18 22		18 33		18 39		18 52	18 56		19 03		19 09		
Chatham 4	d	17 42		17 55		17 59		18 05		18 12		18 25		18 35		18 42		18 55	18 59		19 05		19 12		
Gillingham (Kent) 4	d	17 47		17a59		18a03		18 10		18 17		18a29		18 40		18 47		18a59	19a03		19 10		19 17		
Rainham (Kent)	d	17 51						18 15		18 21				18 45		18 51					19 15		19 21		
Newington	d	17 55														18 55									
Sittingbourne 4	a	18 00						18 22		18 28				18 52		19 00					19 22		19 28		
	d	18 01					18 10	18 23		18 29			18 40	18 53		19 01				19 10	19 23		19 29		
Kemsley	d						18 15						18 45							19 15					
Swale	d						18 18						18 48							19 18					
Queenborough	d						18 22						18 52							19 22					
Sheerness-on-Sea	a						18 27						18 57							19 27					
Teynham	d									18 33													19 33		
Faversham 2	a	18 09						18 33		18 39				19 03		19 09					19 33		19 39		
	d	18 13	18 15							18 43	18 45					19 13	19 15						19 43	19 45	
Selling	d										18 50													19 50	
Canterbury East 4	d		18 29								18 59						19 29							19 59	
Bekesbourne	d										19 03													20 03	
Adisham	d										19 08													20 08	
Aylesham	d										19 10													20 10	
Snowdown	d										19 13													20 13	
Shepherds Well	d										19 17													20 17	
Kearsney	d										19 21													20 21	
Dover Priory 4	a		18 48								19 27						19 48							20 27	
Whitstable	d	18 21								18 51						19 21							19 51		
Chestfield & Swalecliffe	d									18 54													19 54		
Herne Bay	d	18 26								18 58						19 26							19 58		
Birchington-on-Sea	d	18 35								19 07						19 35							20 07		
Westgate-on-Sea	d									19 10													20 10		
Margate 4	d	18 41							18 53	19 14						19 41						19 53	20 14		
Broadstairs	d	18 46							18 59	19 20						19 46						19 59	20 20		
Dumpton Park	d									19 23													20 23		
Ramsgate 4	a	18 51							19 04	19 26						19 51						20 04	20 26		

Table 212

Saturdays

London - Medway, Sheerness-on-Sea, Dover and Ramsgate

Network Diagram - see first Page of Table 212

		SE	SE	SE	SE 1		SE	SE 1	SE	SE	SE	SE 1		SE	SE	SE	SE 1		SE	SE 1	SE	SE
St Pancras Internatnl 15 ⊖	d			18 55						19 25						19 55					20 25	
Stratford International ⊖	d			19 02						19 32						20 02					20 32	
Ebbsfleet International	d			19 13						19 43						20 13					20 43	
London Victoria 15 ⊖	d				18 52			18 58				19 22					19 52			19 58		
London Blackfriars 3 ⊖	d																					
Elephant & Castle ⊖	d																					
Bromley South 4	d				19 09			19 19				19 39					20 09			20 19		
St Mary Cray	d							19 25												20 25		
Swanley 4	d							19 29												20 29		
Farningham Road	d							19 34												20 34		
Longfield	d				19 22			19 38				19 52					20 22			20 38		
Meopham	d				19 27			19 42				19 57					20 27			20 42		
Sole Street	d							19 45												20 45		
London Charing Cross 4 ⊖	d	18 09					18 39							19 09					19 39			
London Waterloo (East) 4 ⊖	d	18 12					18 42							19 12					19 42			
London Cannon Street 4 ⊖	d																					
London Bridge 4 ⊖	d	18 17					18 47							19 17					19 47			
Dartford 4	d	18 55					19 25							19 55					20 25			
Greenhithe for Bluewater	d	19 00					19 30							20 00					20 30			
Gravesend 4	d	19 07		19 18			19 37			19 48				20 07		20 18			20 37		20 48	
Strood 4	d	19 18		19 28			19 48			19 58				20 18		20 28			20 48		20 58	
Rochester 4	d	19 22		19 33	19 39		19 52	19 56		20 03		20 09		20 22		20 33	20 39		20 52	20 56	21 03	
Chatham 4	d	19 25		19 35	19 42		19 55	19 59		20 05		20 12		20 25		20 35	20 42		20 55	20 59	21 05	
Gillingham (Kent) 4	d	19a29		19 40	19 47		19a59	20a03		20 10		20 17		20a29		20 40	20 47		20a59	21a03	21 10	
Rainham (Kent)	d			19 45	19 51					20 15		20 21				20 45	20 51				21 15	
Newington	d				19 55												20 55					
Sittingbourne 4	a			19 52	20 00					20 22		20 28				20 52	21 00				21 22	
	d		19 40	19 53	20 01				20 10	20 23		20 29			20 40	20 53	21 01				21 23	
Kemsley	d		19 45						20 15						20 45							
Swale	d		19 48						20 18						20 48							
Queenborough	d		19 52						20 22						20 52							
Sheerness-on-Sea	a		19 57						20 27						20 57							
Teynham	d											20 33										
Faversham 2	a			20 03	20 09					20 33		20 39				21 03	21 09				21 33	
	d				20 13	20 15						20 43	20 45				21 13	21 15				
Selling	d												20 50									
Canterbury East 4	d					20 29							20 59					21a27				
Bekesbourne	d												21 03									
Adisham	d												21 08									
Aylesham	d												21 10									
Snowdown	d												21 13									
Shepherds Well	d												21 17									
Kearsney	d												21 21									
Dover Priory 4	a					20 48							21 27									
Whitstable	d				20 21							20 51					21 21					
Chestfield & Swalecliffe	d											20 54										
Herne Bay	d				20 26							20 58					21 26					
Birchington-on-Sea	d				20 35							21 07					21 35					
Westgate-on-Sea	d											21 10										
Margate 4	d				20 41						20 53	21 14					21 41					21 53
Broadstairs	d				20 46						20 59	21 20					21 46					21 59
Dumpton Park	d											21 23										
Ramsgate 4	a				20 51						21 04	21 26					21 51					22 04

London - Medway, Sheerness-on-Sea, Dover and Ramsgate

Network Diagram - see first Page of Table 212

		SE 1	SE	SE	SE	SE 1	SE	SE	SE 1	SE	SE	SE	SE 1	SE	SE	SE 1	SE	SE	SE	SE 1
St Pancras Internatnl 15 ⊖	d				20 55			21 25				21 55			22 25				22 55	
Stratford International ⊖	d				21 02			21 32				22 02			22 32				23 02	
Ebbsfleet International	d				21 13			21 43				22 13			22 43				23 13	
London Victoria 15 ⊖	d	20 22				20 52			21 22				21 52			22 22				22 52
London Blackfriars 3 ⊖	d																			
Elephant & Castle ⊖	d																			
Bromley South 4	d	20 39				21 09			21 39				22 09			22 39				23 09
St Mary Cray	d					21 15							22 15							23 15
Swanley 4	d					21 19							22 19							23 19
Farningham Road	d					21 24							22 24							23 24
Longfield	d	20 52				21 28			21 52				22 28			22 52				23 28
Meopham	d	20 57				21 32			21 57				22 32			22 57				23 32
Sole Street	d					21 35							22 35							23 35
London Charing Cross 4 ⊖	d		20 09				20 39			21 09				21 39			22 09			
London Waterloo (East) 4 ⊖	d		20 12				20 42			21 12				21 42			22 12			
London Cannon Street 4 ⊖	d																			
London Bridge 4 ⊖	d		20 17				20 47			21 17				21 47			22 17			
Dartford 4	d		20 55				21 25			21 55				22 25			22 55			
Greenhithe for Bluewater	d		21 00				21 30			22 00				22 31			23 01			
Gravesend 4	d		21 07		21 18		21 37	21 48		22 07		22 18		22 40	22 48		23 10		23 18	
Strood 4	d		21 18		21 28		21 48	21 58		22 18		22 28		22 52	22 58		23 22		23 28	
Rochester 4	d	21 09	21 22		21 33	21 45	21 52	22 03	22 09	22 22		22 33	22 45	22 56	23 03	23 09	23 26		23 33	23 45
Chatham 4	d	21 12	21 25		21 35	21 47	21 55	22 05	22 12	22 25		22 35	22 47	22 58	23 05	23 12	23 28		23 35	23 47
Gillingham (Kent) 4	d	21 17	21a29		21 40	21 52	21a59	22 10	22 17	22a29		22 40	22 52	23a03	23 10	23 17	23a33		23 40	23 52
Rainham (Kent)	d	21 21			21 45	21 56		22 15	22 21			22 45	22 56		23 15	23 21			23 45	23 56
Newington	d					22 00							23 00							00 01
Sittingbourne 4	a	21 28			21 52	22 05		22 22	22 28			22 52	23 05		23 22	23 28			23 52	00 06
	d	21 29		21 40	21 53	22 06		22 23	22 29		22 40	22 53	23 06		23 23	23 29		23 32	23 53	00 07
Kemsley	d			21 45							22 45							23 37		
Swale	d			21 48							22 48							23 40		
Queenborough	d			21 52							22 52							23 44		
Sheerness-on-Sea	a			21 57							22 57							23 49		
Teynham	d	21 33							22 33							23 33				
Faversham 2	a	21 39			22 03	22 14		22 31	22 39			23 01	23 14		23 31	23 39			00 01	00 16
	d	21 43 / 21 45				22 15			22 43 / 22 45							23 43 / 23 45				
Selling	d	21 50							22 50							23 50				
Canterbury East 4	d	21 59				22a26			22 59							23 59				
Bekesbourne	d	22 03							23 03											
Adisham	d	22 08							23 08											
Aylesham	d	22 10							23 10							00 07				
Snowdown	d	22 13							23 13											
Shepherds Well	d	22 17							23 17											
Kearsney	d	22 21							23 21											
Dover Priory 4	a	22 27							23 27							00 18				
Whitstable	d	21 51							22 51							23 51				
Chestfield & Swalecliffe	d	21 54							22 54							23 54				
Herne Bay	d	21 58							22 58							23 58				
Birchington-on-Sea	d	22 07							23 07							00 07				
Westgate-on-Sea	d	22 10							23 10							00 10				
Margate 4	d	22 14							23 14							00 14				
Broadstairs	d	22 20							23 20							00 20				
Dumpton Park	d	22 23							23 23							00 23				
Ramsgate 4	a	22 26							23 26							00 26				

London - Medway, Sheerness-on-Sea, Dover and Ramsgate

Network Diagram - see first Page of Table 212

		SE	SE		SE [1]	SE	SE	SE [1]	SE
St Pancras Internatnl [15] ⊖	d		23 25				23 55		
Stratford International ⊖	d		23 32				00 02		
Ebbsfleet International	d		23 43				00 13		
London Victoria [15] ⊖	d				23 22			23 52	
London Blackfriars [3] ⊖	d								
Elephant & Castle ⊖	d								
Bromley South [4]	d				23 39			00 09	
St Mary Cray	d							00 15	
Swanley [4]	d							00 19	
Farningham Road	d							00 24	
Longfield	d				23 52			00 28	
Meopham	d				23 57			00 32	
Sole Street	d							00 35	
London Charing Cross [4] ⊖	d	22 39				23 09			23 39
London Waterloo (East) [4] ⊖	d	22 42				23 12			23 42
London Cannon Street [4] ⊖	d								
London Bridge [4] ⊖	d	22 47				23 17			23 47
Dartford [4]	d	23 25				23 55			00 25
Greenhithe for Bluewater	d	23 31				23 59			00 31
Gravesend [4]	d	23 40	23 48			00 10	00 18		00 40
Strood [4]	d	23 52	23 58			00 22	00 28		00 52
Rochester [4]	d	23 56	00 03		00 09	00 26	00 33	00 45	00 56
Chatham [4]	d	23 58	00 05		00 12	00 28	00 35	00 47	00 58
Gillingham (Kent) [4]	d	00a03	00 10		00 17	00a33	00 40	00a52	01a03
Rainham (Kent)	d		00 15		00 21		00 45		
Newington	d								
Sittingbourne [4]	a		00 22		00 28		00 52		
	d		00 23		00 29		00 53		
Kemsley	d								
Swale	d								
Queenborough	d								
Sheerness-on-Sea	a								
Teynham	d				00 33				
Faversham [2]	a		00 31		00 39		01 01		
	d				00 43				
Selling	d								
Canterbury East [4]	d								
Bekesbourne	d								
Adisham	d								
Aylesham	d								
Snowdown	d								
Shepherds Well	d								
Kearsney	d								
Dover Priory [4]	a								
Whitstable	d				00 51				
Chestfield & Swalecliffe	d				00 54				
Herne Bay	d				00 58				
Birchington-on-Sea	d				01 07				
Westgate-on-Sea	d				01 10				
Margate [4]	d				01 14				
Broadstairs	d				01 20				
Dumpton Park	d				01 23				
Ramsgate [4]	a				01 26				

Table 212

Sundays

London - Medway, Sheerness-on-Sea, Dover and Ramsgate

Network Diagram - see first Page of Table 212

		SE		SE	SE	SE	SE	SE	SE	SE		SE	SE	SE	SE	SE	SE	SE	SE	SE		SE	SE	SE	
		1			1			1				1	1							1				1	
		A		A	A		A	A	A	A		A		A											
St Pancras Internatnl 15 ⊖	d			22p55			23p25			23p55					00 12										
Stratford International ⊖	d			23p02			23p32			00 02					00 19										
Ebbsfleet International	d			23p13			23p43			00 13					00 31										
London Victoria 15 ⊖	d	22p22			22p52			23p22				23p52	00 10			00 35				07 24				08 05	
London Blackfriars 3 ⊖	d																								
Elephant & Castle ⊖	d																								
Bromley South 4	d	22p39			23p09			23p39				00 09				00 55				07 44				08 22	
St Mary Cray	d				23p15							00 15				01 01				07 50					
Swanley 4	d				23p19							00 19				01 05				07 54					
Farningham Road	d				23p24							00 24				01 10				07 59					
Longfield	d	22p52			23p28			23p52				00 28				01 14				08 03					
Meopham	d	22p57			23p32			23p57				00 32				01 18				08 07					
Sole Street	d				23p35							00 35								08 10					
London Charing Cross 4 ⊖	d								23p09					23p39			00 18								
London Waterloo (East) 4 ⊖	d								23p12					23p42			00 21								
London Cannon Street 4 ⊖	d																								
London Bridge 4 ⊖	d								23p17					23p47			00 26								
Dartford 4	d								23p55					00 25			01 06					07 55			
Greenhithe for Bluewater	d								23p59					00 31			01 10					08 01			
Gravesend 4	d			23p18			23p48		00 10	00 18				00 40			01 17					08 10			
Strood 4	d			23p28			23p58		00 22	00 28				00 52			01 29					08 22			
Rochester 4	d	23p09		23p33	23p45		00 03	00 09	00 26	00 33		00 45	00 49	00 56		01 29	01 33			08 20		08 26		08 46	
Chatham 4	d	23p12		23p35	23p47		00 05	00 12	00 28	00 35		00 47	00 52	00 58		01 31	01 35			08 22		08 28		08 48	
Gillingham (Kent) 4	d	23p17		23p40	23p52		00 10	00 17	00a33	00 40		00a52	00 57	01a03		01a35	01a41			08 27		08a33		08 53	
Rainham (Kent)	d	23p21		23p45	23p56		00 15	00 21		00 45			01 01							08 31				08 57	
Newington	d				00 01								01 05							08 35					
Sittingbourne 4	a	23p28		23p52	00 06		00 22	00 28		00 52			01 10							08 40				09 04	
	d	23p29		23p53	00 07	00 15	00 23	00 29		00 53			01 11						08 10	08 41				09 05	
Kemsley	d					00 20													08 15						
Swale	d					00 23													08 18						
Queenborough	d					00 27													08 22						
Sheerness-on-Sea	a					00 32													08 27						
Teynham	d	23p33						00 33					01 15							08 45					
Faversham 2	a	23p39		00 01	00 16		00 31	00 39		01 01			01 23							08 51				09 13	
	d	23p43	23p45					00 43					01 24							08 52				09 17	09 19
Selling	d		23p50																						09 24
Canterbury East 4	d		23p59																	09a04					09 33
Bekesbourne	d																								09 37
Adisham	d																								09 42
Aylesham	d		00 07																						09 44
Snowdown	d																								09 47
Shepherds Well	d																								09 51
Kearsney	d																								09 55
Dover Priory 4	a		00 18																						10 00
Whitstable	d	23p51						00 51					01 32											09 25	
Chestfield & Swalecliffe	d	23p54						00 54					01 35											09 28	
Herne Bay	d	23p58						00 58					01 39											09 32	
Birchington-on-Sea	d	00 07						01 07					01 48											09 41	
Westgate-on-Sea	d	00 10						01 10					01 51											09 44	
Margate 4	d	00 14						01 14					01 55					07 53					08 53	09 48	
Broadstairs	d	00 20						01 20					02 01					07 59					08 59	09 54	
Dumpton Park	d	00 23						01 23					02 04											09 57	
Ramsgate 4	a	00 26						01 26					02 07					08 04					09 04	10 00	

A not 11 December

Table 212

Sundays

London - Medway, Sheerness-on-Sea, Dover and Ramsgate

Network Diagram - see first Page of Table 212

		SE	SE	SE 1	SE 1	SE		SE	SE	SE 1		SE	SE	SE	SE 1	SE		SE	SE	SE 1		SE	SE	SE	SE 1
St Pancras Internatnl 15 ⊖	d							08 52						09 25				09 55						10 28	
Stratford International ⊖	d							08 58						09 32				10 02						10 35	
Ebbsfleet International	d							09 13						09 43				10 13						10 46	
London Victoria 15 ⊖	d				08 24					09 05					09 24					10 05					10 24
London Blackfriars 3 ⊖	d																								
Elephant & Castle ⊖	d																								
Bromley South 4	d				08 44					09 22					09 44					10 22					10 44
St Mary Cray	d				08 50										09 50										10 50
Swanley 4	d				08 54										09 54										10 54
Farningham Road	d				08 59										09 59										10 59
Longfield	d				09 03										10 03										11 03
Meopham	d				09 07										10 07										11 07
Sole Street	d				09 10										10 10										11 10
London Charing Cross 4 ⊖	d					08 10						08 40				09 10						09 40			
London Waterloo (East) 4 ⊖	d					08 13						08 43				09 13						09 43			
London Cannon Street 4 ⊖	d																								
London Bridge 4 ⊖	d					08 18						08 48				09 18						09 48			
Dartford 4	d	08 25				08 55						09 25				09 55						10 25			
Greenhithe for Bluewater	d	08 31				09 00						09 30				10 00						10 30			
Gravesend 4	d	08 40				09 07		09 18				09 37		09 48		10 07		10 18				10 37		10 51	
Strood 4	d	08 52				09 18		09 28				09 48		09 58		10 18		10 28				10 48		11 01	
Rochester 4	d	08 56			09 20	09 23		09 33		09 46		09 52		10 03	10 20	10 23		10 33		10 46		10 52		11 06	11 20
Chatham 4	d	08 58			09 22	09 26		09 35		09 48		09 55		10 05	10 22	10 26		10 35		10 48		10 55		11 08	11 22
Gillingham (Kent) 4	d	09a03			09 27	09a30		09 40		09 53		10a02		10 10	10 27	10a30		10 40		10 53		11a02		11 13	11 27
Rainham (Kent)	d				09 31			09 45		09 57				10 15	10 31			10 45		10 57				11 18	11 31
Newington	d				09 35										10 35										11 35
Sittingbourne 4	a				09 40			09 52		10 04				10 22	10 40			10 52		11 04				11 25	11 40
	d		09 10		09 41			09 53		10 05			10 10	10 23	10 41			10 53		11 05			11 10	11 25	11 41
Kemsley	d		09 15										10 15										11 15		
Swale	d		09 18										10 18										11 18		
Queenborough	d		09 22										10 22										11 22		
Sheerness-on-Sea	a		09 27										10 27										11 27		
Teynham	d				09 45										10 45										11 45
Faversham 2	a				09 51			10 01		10 13				10 33	10 51			11 03		11 13				11 34	11 51
	d			09 19	09 52					10 17	10 19				10 52					11 17	11 19				11 52
Selling	d			09 24							10 24										11 24				
Canterbury East 4	d			09 33	10a04						10 33				11a04						11 33				12a04
Bekesbourne	d			09 37							10 37										11 37				
Adisham	d			09 42							10 42										11 42				
Aylesham	d			09 44							10 44										11 44				
Snowdown	d			09 47							10 47										11 47				
Shepherds Well	d			09 51							10 51										11 51				
Kearsney	d			09 55							10 55										11 55				
Dover Priory 4	a			10 00							11 00										12 00				
Whitstable	d									10 25										11 25					
Chestfield & Swalecliffe	d									10 28										11 28					
Herne Bay	d									10 32										11 32					
Birchington-on-Sea	d									10 41										11 41					
Westgate-on-Sea	d									10 44										11 44					
Margate 4	d								09 53	10 48									10 53	11 48					
Broadstairs	d								09 59	10 54									10 59	11 54					
Dumpton Park	d									10 57										11 57					
Ramsgate 4	a								10 04	11 00									11 04	12 00					

Table 212

Sundays

London - Medway, Sheerness-on-Sea, Dover and Ramsgate

Network Diagram - see first Page of Table 212

		SE		SE	SE	SE 1		SE	SE	SE	SE 1	SE		SE	SE	SE 1		SE	SE	SE	SE 1	SE		SE	SE
St Pancras Internatnl 15 ⊖	d			10 52						11 25				11 55						12 28				12 52	
Stratford International ⊖	d			10 58						11 32				12 02						12 35				12 58	
Ebbsfleet International	d			11 14						11 43				12 13						12 46				13 13	
London Victoria 15 ⊖	d					11 05					11 24					12 05					12 24				
London Blackfriars 3 ⊖	d																								
Elephant & Castle ⊖	d																								
Bromley South 4	d					11 22					11 44					12 22					12 44				
St Mary Cray	d										11 50										12 50				
Swanley 4	d										11 54										12 54				
Farningham Road	d										11 59										12 59				
Longfield	d										12 03										13 03				
Meopham	d										12 07										13 07				
Sole Street	d										12 10										13 10				
London Charing Cross 4 ⊖	d	10 10						10 40				11 10						11 40				12 10			
London Waterloo (East) 4 ⊖	d	10 13						10 43				11 13						11 43				12 13			
London Cannon Street 4 ⊖	d																								
London Bridge 4 ⊖	d	10 18						10 48				11 18						11 48				12 18			
Dartford 4	d	10 55						11 25				11 55						12 25				12 55			
Greenhithe for Bluewater	d	11 00						11 30				12 00						12 30				13 00			
Gravesend 4	d	11 07		11 18				11 37		11 48		12 07		12 18				12 37		12 51		13 07		13 18	
Strood 4	d	11 18		11 28				11 48		11 58		12 18		12 28				12 48		13 01		13 18		13 28	
Rochester 4	d	11 23		11 33		11 46		11 52		12 03	12 20	12 23		12 33		12 46		12 52		13 06	13 20	13 23		13 33	
Chatham 4	d	11 26		11 35		11 48		11 55		12 05	12 22	12 26		12 35		12 48		12 55		13 08	13 22	13 26		13 35	
Gillingham (Kent) 4	d	11a30		11 40		11 53		12a02		12 10	12 27	12a30		12 40		12 53		13a02		13 13	13 27	13a30		13 40	
Rainham (Kent)	d			11 45		11 57				12 15	12 31			12 45		12 57				13 18	13 31			13 45	
Newington	d										12 35										13 35				
Sittingbourne 4	a			11 52		12 04				12 22	12 40			12 52		13 04				13 25	13 40			13 52	
	d			11 53		12 05			12 10	12 23	12 41			12 53		13 05			13 10	13 25	13 41			13 53	
Kemsley	d								12 15										13 15						
Swale	d								12 18										13 18						
Queenborough	d								12 22										13 22						
Sheerness-on-Sea	a								12 27										13 27						
Teynham	d										12 45										13 45				
Faversham 2	a			12 03		12 13				12 33	12 51			13 03		13 13				13 34	13 51			14 03	
	d					12 17	12 19				12 52					13 17	13 19				13 52				
Selling	d						12 24										13 24								
Canterbury East 4	d						12 33				13a04						13 33				14a04				
Bekesbourne	d						12 37										13 37								
Adisham	d						12 42										13 42								
Aylesham	d						12 44										13 44								
Snowdown	d						12 47										13 47								
Shepherds Well	d						12 51										13 51								
Kearsney	d						12 55										13 55								
Dover Priory 4	a						13 00										14 00								
Whitstable	d					12 25										13 25									
Chestfield & Swalecliffe	d					12 28										13 28									
Herne Bay	d					12 32										13 32									
Birchington-on-Sea	d					12 41										13 41									
Westgate-on-Sea	d					12 44										13 44									
Margate 4	d				11 53	12 48									12 53	13 48									13 53
Broadstairs	d				11 59	12 54									12 59	13 54									13 59
Dumpton Park	d					12 57										13 57									
Ramsgate 4	a				12 04	13 00									13 04	14 00									14 04

Table 212

Sundays

London - Medway, Sheerness-on-Sea, Dover and Ramsgate

Network Diagram - see first Page of Table 212

		SE 1		SE	SE	SE	SE 1	SE		SE	SE	SE 1		SE	SE	SE	SE 1	SE		SE	SE	SE 1		SE	SE
St Pancras Internatnl 15 ⊖	d					13 25				13 55						14 25				14 55					
Stratford International ⊖	d					13 32				14 02						14 32				15 02					
Ebbsfleet International	d					13 43				14 13						14 43				15 13					
London Victoria 15 ⊖	d	13 05					13 24					14 05					14 24					15 05			
London Blackfriars 3 ⊖	d																								
Elephant & Castle ⊖	d																								
Bromley South 4	d	13 22					13 44					14 22					14 44					15 22			
St Mary Cray	d						13 50										14 50								
Swanley 4	d						13 54										14 54								
Farningham Road	d						13 59										14 59								
Longfield	d						14 03										15 03								
Meopham	d						14 07										15 07								
Sole Street	d						14 10										15 10								
London Charing Cross 4 ⊖	d			12 40				13 10						13 40				14 10						14 40	
London Waterloo (East) 4 ⊖	d			12 43				13 13						13 43				14 13						14 43	
London Cannon Street 4 ⊖	d																								
London Bridge 4 ⊖	d			12 48				13 18						13 48				14 18						14 48	
Dartford 4	d			13 25				13 55						14 25				14 55						15 25	
Greenhithe for Bluewater	d			13 30				14 00						14 30				15 00						15 30	
Gravesend 4	d			13 37		13 48		14 07		14 18				14 37		14 48		15 07		15 18				15 37	
Strood 4	d			13 48		13 58		14 18		14 28				14 48		14 58		15 18		15 28				15 48	
Rochester 4	d	13 46		13 52		14 03	14 20	14 23		14 33		14 46		14 52		15 03	15 20	15 23		15 33		15 46		15 52	
Chatham 4	d	13 48		13 55		14 05	14 22	14 26		14 35		14 48		14 55		15 05	15 22	15 26		15 35		15 48		15 55	
Gillingham (Kent) 4	d	13 53		14a02		14 10	14 27	14a30		14 40		14 53		15a02		15 10	15 27	15a30		15 40		15 53		16a02	
Rainham (Kent)	d	13 57				14 15	14 31			14 45		14 57				15 15	15 31			15 45		15 57			
Newington	d						14 35										15 35								
Sittingbourne 4	a	14 04				14 22	14 40			14 52		15 04				15 22	15 40			15 52		16 04			
	d	14 05			14 10	14 23	14 41			14 53		15 05			15 10	15 23	15 41			15 53		16 05			16 10
Kemsley	d				14 15										15 15										16 15
Swale	d				14 18										15 18										16 18
Queenborough	d				14 22										15 22										16 22
Sheerness-on-Sea	a				14 27										15 27										16 27
Teynham	d						14 45										15 45								
Faversham 2	a	14 13				14 33	14 51			15 03		15 13				15 33	15 51			16 03		16 13			
	d	14 17	14 19				14 52					15 17	15 19				15 52					16 17	16 19		
Selling	d		14 24										15 24										16 24		
Canterbury East 4	d		14 33				15a04						15 33				16a04						16 33		
Bekesbourne	d		14 37										15 37										16 37		
Adisham	d		14 42										15 42										16 42		
Aylesham	d		14 44										15 44										16 44		
Snowdown	d		14 47										15 47										16 47		
Shepherds Well	d		14 51										15 51										16 51		
Kearsney	d		14 55										15 55										16 55		
Dover Priory 4	a		15 00										16 00										17 00		
Whitstable	d	14 25										15 25										16 25			
Chestfield & Swalecliffe	d	14 28										15 28										16 28			
Herne Bay	d	14 32										15 32										16 32			
Birchington-on-Sea	d	14 41										15 41										16 41			
Westgate-on-Sea	d	14 44										15 44										16 44			
Margate 4	d	14 48									14 53	15 48									15 53	16 48			
Broadstairs	d	14 54									14 59	15 54									15 59	16 54			
Dumpton Park	d	14 57										15 57										16 57			
Ramsgate 4	a	15 00									15 04	16 00									16 04	17 00			

Table 212

Sundays

London - Medway, Sheerness-on-Sea, Dover and Ramsgate

Network Diagram - see first Page of Table 212

		SE	SE 1	SE	SE	SE	SE 1		SE	SE	SE	SE 1	SE	SE	SE	SE 1		SE	SE	SE	SE 1	SE
St Pancras Internatnl 15 ⊖	d	15 25			15 55						16 25			16 55						17 25		
Stratford International ⊖	d	15 32			16 02						16 32			17 02						17 32		
Ebbsfleet International	d	15 43			16 13						16 43			17 13						17 43		
London Victoria 15 ⊖	d		15 24				16 05					16 24				17 05					17 24	
London Blackfriars 3 ⊖	d																					
Elephant & Castle ⊖	d																					
Bromley South 4	d		15 44				16 22					16 44				17 22					17 44	
St Mary Cray	d		15 50									16 50									17 50	
Swanley 4	d		15 54									16 54									17 54	
Farningham Road	d		15 59									16 59									17 59	
Longfield	d		16 03									17 03									18 03	
Meopham	d		16 07									17 07									18 07	
Sole Street	d		16 10									17 10									18 10	
London Charing Cross 4 ⊖	d			15 10					15 40				16 10					16 40				17 10
London Waterloo (East) 4 ⊖	d			15 13					15 43				16 13					16 43				17 13
London Cannon Street 4 ⊖	d																					
London Bridge 4 ⊖	d			15 18					15 48				16 18					16 48				17 18
Dartford 4	d			15 55					16 25				16 55					17 25				17 55
Greenhithe for Bluewater	d			16 00					16 30				17 00					17 30				18 00
Gravesend 4	d	15 48		16 07	16 18				16 37		16 48		17 07	17 18				17 37		17 48		18 07
Strood 4	d	15 58		16 18	16 28				16 48		16 58		17 18	17 28				17 48		17 58		18 18
Rochester 4	d	16 03	16 20	16 23	16 33		16 46		16 52		17 03	17 20	17 23	17 33		17 46		17 52		18 03	18 20	18 23
Chatham 4	d	16 05	16 22	16 26	16 35		16 48		16 55		17 05	17 22	17 26	17 35		17 48		17 55		18 05	18 22	18 26
Gillingham (Kent) 4	d	16 10	16 27	16a30	16 40		16 53		17a02		17 10	17 27	17a30	17 40		17 53		18a02		18 10	18 27	18a30
Rainham (Kent)	d	16 15	16 31		16 45		16 57				17 15	17 31		17 45		17 57				18 15	18 31	
Newington	d		16 35									17 35									18 35	
Sittingbourne 4	a	16 22	16 40		16 52		17 04				17 22	17 40		17 52		18 04				18 22	18 40	
	d	16 23	16 41		16 53		17 05			17 10	17 23	17 41		17 53		18 05			18 10	18 23	18 41	
Kemsley	d									17 15									18 15			
Swale	d									17 18									18 18			
Queenborough	d									17 22									18 22			
Sheerness-on-Sea	a									17 27									18 27			
Teynham	d		16 45									17 45									18 45	
Faversham 2	a	16 33	16 51		17 03		17 13				17 33	17 51		18 03		18 13				18 33	18 51	
	d		16 52				17 17	17 19				17 52				18 17	18 19				18 52	
Selling	d							17 24									18 24					
Canterbury East 4	d		17a04					17 33				18a04					18 33				19a04	
Bekesbourne	d							17 37									18 37					
Adisham	d							17 42									18 42					
Aylesham	d							17 44									18 44					
Snowdown	d							17 47									18 47					
Shepherds Well	d							17 51									18 51					
Kearsney	d							17 55									18 55					
Dover Priory 4	a							18 00									19 00					
Whitstable	d						17 25									18 25						
Chestfield & Swalecliffe	d						17 28									18 28						
Herne Bay	d						17 32									18 32						
Birchington-on-Sea	d						17 41									18 41						
Westgate-on-Sea	d						17 44									18 44						
Margate 4	d					16 53	17 48								17 53	18 48						
Broadstairs	d					16 59	17 54								17 59	18 54						
Dumpton Park	d						17 57									18 57						
Ramsgate 4	a					17 04	18 00								18 04	19 00						

Table 212

Sundays

London - Medway, Sheerness-on-Sea, Dover and Ramsgate

Network Diagram - see first Page of Table 212

		SE	SE	SE 1		SE	SE	SE	SE 1	SE	SE	SE	SE 1		SE	SE	SE	SE 1	SE	SE	SE	SE 1	
St Pancras Internatnl 15 ⊖	d	17 58						18 25			18 55						19 25			19 55			
Stratford International ⊖	d	18 08						18 32			19 02						19 32			20 02			
Ebbsfleet International	d	18 19						18 43			19 13						19 43			20 13			
London Victoria 15 ⊖	d			18 05					18 24				19 05					19 24				20 05	
London Blackfriars 3 ⊖	d																						
Elephant & Castle ⊖	d																						
Bromley South 4	d			18 22					18 44				19 22					19 44				20 22	
St Mary Cray	d								18 50									19 50					
Swanley 4	d								18 54									19 54					
Farningham Road	d								18 59									19 59					
Longfield	d								19 03									20 03					
Meopham	d								19 07									20 07					
Sole Street	d								19 10									20 10					
London Charing Cross 4 ⊖	d					17 40				18 10					18 40				19 10				
London Waterloo (East) 4 ⊖	d					17 43				18 13					18 43				19 13				
London Cannon Street 4 ⊖	d																						
London Bridge 4 ⊖	d					17 48				18 18					18 48				19 18				
Dartford 4	d					18 25				18 55					19 25				19 55				
Greenhithe for Bluewater	d					18 30				19 00					19 31				20 01				
Gravesend 4	d	18 24				18 37		18 48		19 07	19 18				19 40		19 48		20 10	20 18			
Strood 4	d	18 34				18 48		18 58		19 18	19 28				19 52		19 58		20 22	20 28			
Rochester 4	d	18 39		18 46		18 52		19 03	19 20	19 23	19 33		19 46		19 56		20 03	20 20	20 26	20 33		20 46	
Chatham 4	d	18 41		18 48		18 55		19 05	19 22	19 26	19 35		19 48		19 58		20 05	20 22	20 28	20 35		20 48	
Gillingham (Kent) 4	d	18 46		18 53		19a02		19 10	19 27	19a30	19 40		19 53		20a03		20 10	20 27	20a33	20 40		20 53	
Rainham (Kent)	d	18 51		18 57				19 15	19 31		19 45		19 57				20 15	20 31		20 45		20 57	
Newington	d								19 35									20 35					
Sittingbourne 4	a	18 58		19 04				19 22	19 40		19 52		20 04				20 22	20 40		20 52		21 04	
	d	18 58		19 05			19 10	19 23	19 41		19 53		20 05			20 10	20 23	20 41		20 53		21 05	
Kemsley	d						19 15									20 15							
Swale	d						19 18									20 18							
Queenborough	d						19 22									20 22							
Sheerness-on-Sea	a						19 27									20 27							
Teynham	d								19 45									20 45					
Faversham 2	a	19 07		19 13				19 33	19 51		20 03		20 13				20 33	20 51		21 03		21 13	
	d			19 17	19 19								20 17	20 19								21 17	21 19
Selling	d				19 24									20 24									21 24
Canterbury East 4	d				19 33									20 33									21 33
Bekesbourne	d				19 37									20 37									21 37
Adisham	d				19 42									20 42									21 42
Aylesham	d				19 44									20 44									21 44
Snowdown	d				19 47									20 47									21 47
Shepherds Well	d				19 51									20 51									21 51
Kearsney	d				19 55									20 55									21 55
Dover Priory 4	a				20 00									21 00									22 00
Whitstable	d			19 25									20 25									21 25	
Chestfield & Swalecliffe	d			19 28									20 28									21 28	
Herne Bay	d			19 32									20 32									21 32	
Birchington-on-Sea	d			19 41									20 41									21 41	
Westgate-on-Sea	d			19 44									20 44									21 44	
Margate 4	d		18 53	19 48								19 53	20 48								20 53	21 48	
Broadstairs	d		18 59	19 54								19 59	20 54								20 59	21 54	
Dumpton Park	d			19 57									20 57									21 57	
Ramsgate 4	a		19 04	20 00								20 04	21 00								21 04	22 00	

Table 212

Sundays

London - Medway, Sheerness-on-Sea, Dover and Ramsgate

Network Diagram - see first Page of Table 212

	SE	SE	SE	SE 1	SE		SE	SE	SE 1		SE	SE	SE	SE 1	SE		SE	SE 1		SE	SE	SE	SE 1	SE
St Pancras Internatnl 15 ⊖ d			20 25				20 55						21 25				21 55					22 25		
Stratford International ⊖ d			20 32				21 02						21 32				22 02					22 32		
Ebbsfleet International d			20 43				21 13						21 43				22 13					22 43		
London Victoria 15 ⊖ d				20 24					21 05					21 24				22 05					22 24	
London Blackfriars 3 ⊖ d																								
Elephant & Castle ⊖ d																								
Bromley South 4 d				20 44					21 22					21 44				22 22					22 44	
St Mary Cray d				20 50										21 50									22 50	
Swanley 4 d				20 54										21 54									22 54	
Farningham Road d				20 59										21 59									22 59	
Longfield d				21 03										22 03									23 03	
Meopham d				21 07										22 07									23 07	
Sole Street d				21 10										22 10									23 10	
London Charing Cross 4 ⊖ d	19 40				20 10						20 40				21 10					21 40				22 10
London Waterloo (East) 4 ⊖ d	19 43				20 13						20 43				21 13					21 43				22 13
London Cannon Street 4 ⊖ d																								
London Bridge 4 ⊖ d	19 48				20 18						20 48				21 18					21 48				22 18
Dartford 4 d	20 25				20 55						21 25				21 55					22 25				22 55
Greenhithe for Bluewater d	20 31				21 01						21 31				22 01					22 31				23 01
Gravesend 4 d	20 40		20 48		21 10		21 18				21 40		21 48		22 10		22 18			22 40		22 48		23 10
Strood 4 d	20 52		20 58		21 22		21 28				21 52		21 58		22 22		22 28			22 52		22 58		23 22
Rochester 4 d	20 56		21 03	21 20	21 26		21 33		21 46		21 56		22 03	22 20	22 26		22 33	22 46		22 56		23 03	23 20	23 26
Chatham 4 d	20 58		21 05	21 22	21 28		21 35		21 48		21 58		22 05	22 22	22 28		22 35	22 48		22 58		23 05	23 22	23 28
Gillingham (Kent) 4 d	21a03		21 10	21 27	21a33		21 40		21 53		22a03		22 10	22 27	22a33		22 40	22 53		23a03		23 10	23 27	23a33
Rainham (Kent) d			21 15	21 31			21 45		21 57				22 15	22 31			22 45	22 57				23 15	23 31	
Newington d				21 35										22 35									23 35	
Sittingbourne 4 a			21 22	21 40			21 52		22 04				22 22	22 40			22 52	23 04				23 22	23 40	
d		21 10	21 23	21 41			21 53		22 05			22 10	22 23	22 41			22 53	23 05			23 10	23 23	23 41	
Kemsley d		21 15										22 15									23 15			
Swale d		21 18										22 18									23 18			
Queenborough d		21 22										22 22									23 22			
Sheerness-on-Sea a		21 27										22 27									23 27			
Teynham d				21 45										22 45									23 45	
Faversham 2 a			21 33	21 51			22 03		22 13				22 33	22 51			23 03	23 13				23 31	23 51	
d									22 17	22 19								23 17	23 19					
Selling d										22 24									23 24					
Canterbury East 4 d										22 33									23 33					
Bekesbourne d										22 37									23 37					
Adisham d										22 42									23 42					
Aylesham d										22 44									23 44					
Snowdown d										22 47									23 47					
Shepherds Well d										22 51									23 51					
Kearsney d										22 55									23 55					
Dover Priory 4 a										23 00									00 01					
Whitstable d									22 25									23 25						
Chestfield & Swalecliffe d									22 28									23 28						
Herne Bay d									22 32									23 32						
Birchington-on-Sea d									22 41									23 41						
Westgate-on-Sea d									22 44									23 44						
Margate 4 d								21 53	22 48									23 48						
Broadstairs d								21 59	22 54									23 54						
Dumpton Park d									22 57									23 57						
Ramsgate 4 a								22 04	23 00									00 01						

Table 212

Sundays

London - Medway, Sheerness-on-Sea, Dover and Ramsgate

Network Diagram - see first Page of Table 212

		SE		SE [1]	SE	SE	SE	SE	SE [1]
St Pancras Internatnl [15] ⊖	d	22 55				23 25		23 42	
Stratford International ⊖	d	23 02				23 32		23 49	
Ebbsfleet International	d	23 13				23 43		00 01	
London Victoria [15] ⊖	d			23 05					23 45
London Blackfriars [3] ⊖	d								
Elephant & Castle ⊖	d								
Bromley South [4]	d			23 22					00 02
St Mary Cray	d								00 08
Swanley [4]	d								00 12
Farningham Road	d								00 17
Longfield	d								00 21
Meopham	d								00 25
Sole Street	d								00 28
London Charing Cross [4] ⊖	d				22 40		23 10		
London Waterloo (East) [4] ⊖	d				22 43		23 13		
London Cannon Street [4] ⊖	d								
London Bridge [4] ⊖	d				22 48		23 18		
Dartford [4]	d				23 25		23 55		
Greenhithe for Bluewater	d				23 31		00 01		
Gravesend [4]	d	23 18			23 40	23 48	00 10		
Strood [4]	d	23 28			23 52	23 58	00 22		
Rochester [4]	d	23 33		23 46	23 56	00 03	00 26		00 37
Chatham [4]	d	23 35		23 48	23 58	00 05	00 28		00 40
Gillingham (Kent) [4]	d	23 40		23 53	00a03	00 10	00a33		00 44
Rainham (Kent)	d	23 45		23 57		00 15			00 49
Newington	d								00 53
Sittingbourne [4]	a	23 52		00 04		00 22			00 58
	d	23 53		00 05		00 23			00 58
Kemsley	d								
Swale	d								
Queenborough	d								
Sheerness-on-Sea	a								
Teynham	d								01 03
Faversham [2]	a	00 03		00 13		00 33			01 09
	d			00 17					
Selling	d								
Canterbury East [4]	d								
Bekesbourne	d								
Adisham	d								
Aylesham	d								
Snowdown	d								
Shepherds Well	d								
Kearsney	d								
Dover Priory [4]	a								
Whitstable	d			00 25					
Chestfield & Swalecliffe	d			00 28					
Herne Bay	d			00 32					
Birchington-on-Sea	d			00 41					
Westgate-on-Sea	d			00 44					
Margate [4]	d			00 48					
Broadstairs	d			00 54					
Dumpton Park	d			00 57					
Ramsgate [4]	a			01 00					

Ramsgate, Dover, Sheerness-on-Sea and Medway - London

Network Diagram - see first Page of Table 212

Miles	Miles	Miles	Miles	Miles			SE MO 1	SE MX 1	SE MX 1	SE MO 1	SE MX 1	SE MX	SE	SE	SE	SE	SE	SE	SE 1	SE 1	SE	SE	SE	SE 1
0	—	—	—	—	**Ramsgate** [4]	d		22p05		22p34	23p05									04 36				
1	—	—	—	—	Dumpton Park	d		22p08		22p37	23p08									04 39				
2¼	—	—	—	—	Broadstairs	d		22p11		22p40	23p11									04 42				
5½	—	—	—	—	**Margate** [4]	d		22p16		22p45	23p16									04 47				
6¾	—	—	—	—	Westgate-on-Sea	d		22p20		22p49	23p20									04 50				
8½	—	—	—	—	Birchington-on-Sea	d		22p24		22p53	23p24									04 54				
16¼	—	—	—	—	**Herne Bay**	d		22p33		23p02	23p33									05 03				
18½	—	—	—	—	Chestfield & Swalecliffe	d		22p36		23p05	23p36									05 06				
20½	—	—	—	—	Whitstable	d		22p39		23p08	23p39									05 10				
—	0	—	—	—	**Dover Priory** [4]	d			22p45															04 42
—	2¼	—	—	—	Kearsney	d																		04 46
—	5½	—	—	—	Shepherds Well	d																		04 51
—	7½	—	—	—	Snowdown	d																		04 55
—	8½	—	—	—	Aylesham	d																		04 57
—	9½	—	—	—	Adisham	d																		05 00
—	12½	—	—	—	Bekesbourne	d																		05 04
—	15½	—	—	—	**Canterbury East** [4]	d			23p02															05 09
—	22	—	—	—	Selling	d																		05 18
27¼	25¼	—	—	0	**Faversham** [2]	a		22p48	23p13	23p17	23p48									05 18				05 23
—	—	—	—	—		d	22p34	22p52	23p14	23p21	23p52						04 56			05 19		05 28		05 34
31¾	29¾	—	—	4½	Teynham	d	22p40	22p58			23p58													05 40
—	—	0	—	—	**Sheerness-on-Sea**	d						23p53												
—	—	2	—	—	Queenborough	d						23p57												
—	—	4	—	—	Swale	d						00 01												
—	—	6	—	—	Kemsley	d						00 05												
34½	32½	8	—	7¼	**Sittingbourne** [4]	a	22p44	23p02	23p21	23p28	00 02	00 10					05 06			05 26		05 36		05 44
—	—	—	—	—		d	22p45	23p03	23p22	23p29	00 03						05 07			05 27		05 37		05 45
37¾	35¾	—	—	10½	Newington	d	22p50		23p27		00 08													05 50
40¼	38¼	—	—	13	Rainham (Kent)	d	22p54	23p10	23p31	23p36	00 12						05 15			05 35		05 45		05 55
43¼	41¼	—	0	16	**Gillingham (Kent)** [4]	d	22p59	23p15	23p36	23p41	00a17		04 09	04 34	04 54		05 20	05 24	05 30	05 40	05 45	05 50	05 54	06 02
45	43	—	1¾	17¾	**Chatham** [4]	d	23p04	23p20	23p41	23p46			04 13	04 38	04 58		05 24	05 28	05 34	05 44	05 49	05 54	05 58	06 06
45½	43½	—	2¼	18¼	Rochester [4]	d	23p06	23p22	23p43	23p48			04 15	04 40	05 00		05 27	05 30	05 36	05 47	05 51	05 57	06 00	06 09
—	—	—	3¼	19¼	Strood [4]	a							04 20	04 45	05 05		05 31	05 35				06 01	06 05	
—	—	—	10½	26½	Gravesend [4]	a							04 32	04 57	05 17		05 42	05 47				06 12	06 17	
—	—	—	14½	—	Greenhithe for Bluewater	a							04 38	05 07	05 23			05 53					06 23	
—	—	—	17¼	—	Dartford [4]	a							04 43	05 13	05 28			05 58					06 28	
—	—	—	34¼	—	**London Bridge** [4] ⊖	a							05 22	05 52	06 05			06 34			06 27		07 03	
—	—	—	—	—	**London Cannon Street** [4] ⊖	a															06 32			
—	—	—	35¼	—	**London Waterloo (East)** [4] ⊖	a							05 26	05 57	06 10			06 39					07 09	
—	—	—	36	—	**London Charing Cross** [4] ⊖	a							05 30	06 01	06 13			06 43					07 15	
52¼	50¼	—	—	—	Sole Street	d	23p17		23p54										05 47					06 19
53¼	51¼	—	—	—	Meopham	d	23p19	23p33	23p56										05 49					06 22
55¾	53¾	—	—	—	Longfield	d	23p23	23p37	23p59										05 53					06 26
58¾	56¾	—	—	—	Farningham Road	d	23p27		00 04										05 57					06 29
61¾	59¾	—	—	—	Swanley [4]	a	23p32		00 09										06 02					06 34
64½	62½	—	—	—	St Mary Cray	a	23p36		00 14										06 06					06 39
68¼	66¼	—	—	—	Bromley South [4]	a	23p42	23p50	00 20	00 13									06 14	06 12				06 45
—	—	—	—	—	Elephant & Castle ⊖	a																		
—	—	—	—	—	**London Blackfriars** [3] ⊖	a																		
79¼	77¼	—	—	—	**London Victoria** [15] ⊖	a	00 02	00 07	00 38	00 29									06 31	06 28				07 07
—	—	—	—	28½	**Ebbsfleet International**	a										05 32	05 47					06 17		
—	—	—	—	45¼	**Stratford International** ⊖	a										05 44	05 59					06 29		
—	—	—	—	51¼	**St Pancras Internatnl** [15] ⊖	a										05 51	06 06					06 36		

Ramsgate, Dover, Sheerness-on-Sea and Medway - London

Network Diagram - see first Page of Table 212

		SE 1	SE	SE	SE 1	SE	SE	SE 1	SE 1	SE	SE 1	SE	SE 1	SE	SE	SE 1	SE	SE 1	SE 1	SE 1	SE	SE
Ramsgate 4	d				05 06						05 40							06 09				
Dumpton Park	d				05 09						05 43							06 12				
Broadstairs	d				05 12						05 46			06 00				06 15		06 25		06 30
Margate 4	d				05 17						05 51			06 05				06 20		06 30		06 35
Westgate-on-Sea	d				05 20						05 54							06 23				
Birchington-on-Sea	d				05 24						05 58			06 10				06 27		06 35		06 40
Herne Bay	d				05 33						06 07			06 19				06 36		06 44		06 49
Chestfield & Swalecliffe	d				05 36						06 10							06 39				
Whitstable	d				05 40						06 14			06 25				06 43		06 49		06 55
Dover Priory 4	d	05 05											05 45						06 13			
Kearsney	d	05 09											05 50						06 17			
Shepherds Well	d	05 14											05 55						06 22			
Snowdown	d	05 18											05 59						06 26			
Aylesham	d	05 20											06 02						06 28			
Adisham	d	05 23											06 04						06 31			
Bekesbourne	d	05 27											06 09						06 35			
Canterbury East 4	d	05 32											06 15						06 40			
Selling	d	05 41											06 24						06 49			
Faversham 2	a	05 46			05 48						06 22		06 29	06 33				06 51	06 55	06 57		07 03
	d				05 49	05 58			06 08		06 23		06 37	06 34				06 52		06 58		07 04
Teynham	d				05 55				06 14				06 43									
Sheerness-on-Sea	d		05 31				05 57								06 29						06 46	
Queenborough	d		05 35				06 01								06 35						06 50	
Swale	d		05 39				06 05								06 39						06 54	
Kemsley	d		05 43				06 09								06 42						06 58	
Sittingbourne 4	a		05 48		05 59	06 06	06 14		06 18		06 30		06 47	06 41	06 47			07 00		07 05	07 05	07 12
	d				06 00	06 07			06 19		06 31		06 48	06 42				07 01		07 06		07 13
Newington	d				06 05				06 24				06 54									
Rainham (Kent)	d				06 10	06 15			06 29		06 39		06 59	06 50				07 09		07 14		07 21
Gillingham (Kent) 4	d			06 07	06 15	06 20		06 24	06 34	06 38	06 44	06 50	07 04	06 55		07 08	07 12	07 15		07 19		07 26
Chatham 4	d			06 11	06 19	06 24		06 28	06 38	06 42	06 48	06 54	07 08	07 00		07 12	07 16	07 20		07 24		07 30
Rochester 4	d			06 13	06 22	06 27		06 31	06 41	06 44		06 57	07 11	07 03		07 15	07 18					07 33
Strood 4	a			06 18		06 31				06 49							07 23					
Gravesend 4	a			06 30		06 42				07 01							07 35					
Greenhithe for Bluewater	a			06 36						07 07							07 45					
Dartford 4	a			06 41						07 12							07 51					
London Bridge 4 ⊖	a			07 17					07 20	07 47			07 51				08 25			08 09		
London Cannon Street 4 ⊖	a			07 23					07 27				07 57							08 17		
London Waterloo (East) 4 ⊖	a									07 52							08 30					
London Charing Cross 4 ⊖	a									07 58							08 36					
Sole Street	d							06 41				07 07				07 25						
Meopham	d							06 44				07 10				07 28						
Longfield	d							06 48				07 14						07 35				
Farningham Road	d							06 51				07 17				07 33						
Swanley 4	a							06 56				07 22				07 38						
St Mary Cray	a							07 01				07 27				07 44						
Bromley South 4	a				06 49			07 07			07 15	07 33				07 52		07 49				
Elephant & Castle ⊖	a																					
London Blackfriars 3 ⊖	a																					
London Victoria 15 ⊖	a				07 09			07 30			07 38	07 55				08 17		08 09				
Ebbsfleet International	a					06 47								07 17								07 47
Stratford International ⊖	a					06 59								07 29								07 59
St Pancras Internatnl 15 ⊖	a					07 06								07 36								08 06

Ramsgate, Dover, Sheerness-on-Sea and Medway - London

Network Diagram - see first Page of Table 212

		SE	SE	SE	SE	SE	SE		SE	SE	SE	SE	SE	SE	SE	SE	SE		SE	SE	SE	SE	SE	SE	SE
		[1]		[1]	[1]	[1]			[1]		[1]	[1]			[1]		[1]			[1]	[1]	[1]			
Ramsgate [4]	d			06 32							06 59				07 05		07 19					07 35	08 01		
Dumpton Park	d			06 35							07 02				07 08		07 22					07 38			
Broadstairs	d			06 38		06 48				07 00	07 05				07 11		07 25					07 41	08 06		
Margate [4]	d			06 43		06 53				07 05	07 10				07 16		07 30					07 46	08a11		
Westgate-on-Sea	d			06 46		06 56					07 13				07 20		07 33					07 50			
Birchington-on-Sea	d			06 50		07 00				07 10	07 17				07 24		07 37					07 54			
Herne Bay	d			06 59		07 09				07 19	07 26				07 33		07 46					08 03			
Chestfield & Swalecliffe	d			07 02		07 12					07 30				07 36		07 49					08 06			
Whitstable	d			07 06		07 16				07 25	07 33				07 39		07 53					08 09			
Dover Priory [4]	d				06 39							07 04									07 35				
Kearsney	d				06 43							07 08									07 39				
Shepherds Well	d				06 48							07 13									07 44				
Snowdown	d				06 52							07 17									07 48				
Aylesham	d				06 54							07 19									07 50				
Adisham	d				06 57							07 22									07 53				
Bekesbourne	d				07 01							07 26									07 57				
Canterbury East [4]	d				07 06							07 31									08 02				
Selling	d				07 15							07 40									08 11				
Faversham [2]	a			07 14	07 20	07 24				07 33	07 41	07 45			07 48		08 01				08 16	08 18			
	d			07 16		07 25				07 34	07 42				07 49	07 58	08 02				08 22			08 28	
Teynham	d			07 22											07 55										
Sheerness-on-Sea	d						07 16						07 35						08 07						08 36
Queenborough	d						07 22						07 39						08 11						08 40
Swale	d						07 26						07 43						08 15						08 44
Kemsley	d						07 29						07 47						08 19						08 48
Sittingbourne [4]	a			07 26		07 32	07 34			07 41	07 49		07 52		07 59	08 05	08 09		08 25		08 29			08 36	08 56
	d			07 27		07 33				07 42	07 50				08 00	08 06	08 10				08 30			08 37	
Newington	d			07 32											08 05						08 35				
Rainham (Kent)	d			07 37		07 41				07 50	07 58				08 10	08 14	08 18				08 40			08 45	
Gillingham (Kent) [4]	d	07 33	07 38	07 42		07 46			07 50	07 55	08 03			08 08	08 15	08 19	08 24			08 32	08 45			08 50	
Chatham [4]	d	07 37	07 42	07 46		07 50			07 54	08 00	08 08			08 12	08 19	08 24	08 28			08 36	08 50			08 54	
Rochester [4]	d	07 40	07 44						07 56	08 03	08 11			08 14	08 22	08 26	08 31			08 39	08 52			08 57	
Strood [4]	a		07 49											08 19		08 31								09 01	
Gravesend [4]	a		08 01											08 31		08 42								09 12	
Greenhithe for Bluewater	a		08 07											08 42											
Dartford [4]	a		08 12											08 49											
London Bridge [4] ⊖	a		08 45			08 31					08 49			09 23			09 11								
London Cannon Street [4] ⊖	a					08 38					08 57						09 18								
London Waterloo (East) [4] ⊖	a		08 50											09 28											
London Charing Cross [4] ⊖	a		08 56											09 34											
Sole Street	d								08 07											08 49					
Meopham	d	07 51							08 09						08 33					08 52	09 03				
Longfield	d	07 55							08 13						08 37					08 56	09 07				
Farningham Road	d								08 17											08 59					
Swanley [4]	a	08 01							08 22											09 04					
St Mary Cray	a	08 06							08 26											09 09					
Bromley South [4]	a	08-12		08 15					08 33						08 50					09 15	09 20				
Elephant & Castle ⊖	a																								
London Blackfriars [3] ⊖	a																								
London Victoria [15] ⊖	a	08 42		08 39					08 53						09 09					09 38	09 43				
Ebbsfleet International	a									08 17						08 47								09 17	
Stratford International ⊖	a									08 29						08 59								09 29	
St Pancras Internatnl [15] ⊖	a									08 36						09 07								09 36	

Ramsgate, Dover, Sheerness-on-Sea and Medway - London

Network Diagram - see first Page of Table 212

		SE	SE 1	SE 1	SE	SE	SE	SE 1	SE 1	SE 1	SE	SE	SE	SE	SE 1	SE 1	SE	SE	SE	SE 1	SE 1	SE 1
Ramsgate 4	d			08 05						08 40	08 59					09 05						09 40
Dumpton Park	d			08 08												09 08						
Broadstairs	d			08 11						08 45	09 05					09 11						09 45
Margate 4	d			08 16						08 50	09a10					09 16						09 50
Westgate-on-Sea	d			08 20												09 20						
Birchington-on-Sea	d			08 24						08 55						09 24						09 55
Herne Bay	d			08 33						09 04						09 33						10 04
Chestfield & Swalecliffe	d			08 36												09 36						
Whitstable	d			08 39						09 09						09 39						10 09
Dover Priory 4	d		08 05						08 45						09 05						09 45	
Kearsney	d		08 09												09 09							
Shepherds Well	d		08 14												09 14							
Snowdown	d		08 18												09 18							
Aylesham	d		08 20												09 20							
Adisham	d		08 23												09 23							
Bekesbourne	d		08 27												09 27							
Canterbury East 4	d		08 32						09 02						09 32						10 02	
Selling	d		08 41												09 41							
Faversham 2	a		08 46	08 48					09 14	09 18					09 46	09 48					10 14	10 18
	d			08 52	08 58					09 22		09 28				09 52	09 58					10 22
Teynham	d			08 58												09 58						
Sheerness-on-Sea	d					09 02							09 32					10 02				
Queenborough	d					09 06							09 36					10 06				
Swale	d					09 10							09 40					10 10				
Kemsley	d					09 14							09 44					10 14				
Sittingbourne 4	a			09 02	09 06	09 19				09 29		09 36	09 49			10 02	10 06	10 19				10 29
	d			09 03	09 07					09 30		09 37				10 03	10 07					10 30
Newington	d									09 35												10 35
Rainham (Kent)	d			09 10	09 15					09 40		09 45				10 10	10 15					10 40
Gillingham (Kent) 4	d	08 54		09 15	09 20		09 24	09 32		09 45		09 50		09 54		10 15	10 20		10 24	10 32		10 45
Chatham 4	d	08 58		09 20	09 24		09 28	09 36		09 50		09 54		09 58		10 20	10 24		10 28	10 36		10 50
Rochester 4	d	09 00		09 22	09 27		09 30	09 39		09 52		09 57		10 00		10 22	10 27		10 30	10 39		10 52
Strood 4	a	09 05			09 31		09 35					10 01		10 05			10 31		10 35			
Gravesend 4	a	09 17			09 42		09 47					10 12		10 17			10 42		10 47			
Greenhithe for Bluewater	a	09 23					09 53							10 23					10 53			
Dartford 4	a	09 28					09 58							10 28					10 58			
London Bridge 4 ⊖	a	10 05					10 35							11 05					11 35			
London Cannon Street 4 ⊖	a																					
London Waterloo (East) 4 ⊖	a	10 09					10 39							11 09					11 39			
London Charing Cross 4 ⊖	a	10 13					10 43							11 13					11 43			
Sole Street	d							09 49												10 49		
Meopham	d			09 33				09 52		10 03						10 33				10 52		11 03
Longfield	d			09 37				09 56		10 07						10 37				10 56		11 07
Farningham Road	d							09 59												10 59		
Swanley 4	a							10 04												11 04		
St Mary Cray	a							10 09												11 09		
Bromley South 4	a			09 50				10 15		10 20						10 50				11 15		11 20
Elephant & Castle ⊖	a																					
London Blackfriars 3 ⊖	a																					
London Victoria 15 ⊖	a			10 07				10 41		10 37						11 07				11 37		11 37
Ebbsfleet International	a				09 47							10 16					10 47					
Stratford International ⊖	a				09 59							10 28					10 59					
St Pancras Internatnl 15 ⊖	a				10 06							10 35					11 06					

Table 212

Mondays to Fridays

Ramsgate, Dover, Sheerness-on-Sea and Medway - London

Network Diagram - see first Page of Table 212

		SE	SE	SE	SE	SE 1	SE 1	SE	SE	SE	SE 1	SE 1	SE 1	SE	SE	SE	SE	SE 1	SE 1	SE	SE	SE	SE 1
Ramsgate 4	d	09 59					10 05						10 40	10 59					11 05				
Dumpton Park	d						10 08												11 08				
Broadstairs	d	10 05					10 11						10 45	11 05					11 11				
Margate 4	d	10a10					10 16						10 50	11a10					11 16				
Westgate-on-Sea	d						10 20												11 20				
Birchington-on-Sea	d						10 24						10 55						11 24				
Herne Bay	d						10 33						11 04						11 33				
Chestfield & Swalecliffe	d						10 36												11 36				
Whitstable	d						10 39						11 09						11 39				
Dover Priory 4	d					10 05						10 45						11 05					
Kearsney	d					10 09												11 09					
Shepherds Well	d					10 14												11 14					
Snowdown	d					10 18												11 18					
Aylesham	d					10 20												11 20					
Adisham	d					10 23												11 23					
Bekesbourne	d					10 27												11 27					
Canterbury East 4	d					10 32						11 02						11 32					
Selling	d					10 41												11 41					
Faversham 2	a					10 46	10 48					11 14	11 18					11 46	11 48				
	d		10 28			10 52		10 58				11 22			11 28			11 52		11 58			
Teynham	d					10 58												11 58					
Sheerness-on-Sea	d			10 32					11 02							11 32					12 02		
Queenborough	d			10 36					11 06							11 36					12 06		
Swale	d			10 40					11 10							11 40					12 10		
Kemsley	d			10 44					11 14							11 44					12 14		
Sittingbourne 4	a		10 36	10 49		11 02		11 06	11 19			11 29			11 36	11 49		12 02		12 06	12 19		
	d		10 37			11 03		11 07				11 30			11 37			12 03		12 07			
Newington	d											11 35											
Rainham (Kent)	d		10 45			11 10		11 15				11 40			11 45			12 10		12 15			
Gillingham (Kent) 4	d		10 50		10 54	11 15		11 20		11 24	11 32	11 45			11 50		11 54	12 15		12 20		12 24	12 32
Chatham 4	d		10 54		10 58	11 20		11 24		11 28	11 36	11 50			11 54		11 58	12 20		12 24		12 28	12 36
Rochester 4	d		10 57		11 00	11 22		11 27		11 30	11 39	11 52			11 57		12 00	12 22		12 27		12 30	12 39
Strood 4	a		11 01		11 05			11 31		11 35					12 01		12 05			12 31		12 35	
Gravesend 4	a		11 12		11 17			11 42		11 47					12 12		12 17			12 42		12 47	
Greenhithe for Bluewater	a				11 23					11 53							12 23					12 53	
Dartford 4	a				11 28					11 58							12 28					12 58	
London Bridge 4 ⊖	a				12 05					12 35							13 05					13 35	
London Cannon Street 4 ⊖	a																						
London Waterloo (East) 4 ⊖	a				12 09					12 39							13 09					13 39	
London Charing Cross 4 ⊖	a				12 13					12 43							13 13					13 43	
Sole Street	d										11 49												12 49
Meopham	d					11 33					11 52	12 03						12 33					12 52
Longfield	d					11 37					11 56	12 07						12 37					12 56
Farningham Road	d										11 59												12 59
Swanley 4	a										12 04												13 04
St Mary Cray	a										12 09												13 09
Bromley South 4	a					11 50					12 15	12 20						12 50					13 15
Elephant & Castle ⊖	a																						
London Blackfriars 3 ⊖	a																						
London Victoria 15 ⊖	a					12 07					12 37	12 37						13 07					13 37
Ebbsfleet International	a		11 17					11 47							12 17					12 47			
Stratford International ⊖	a		11 29					11 59							12 29					12 59			
St Pancras Internatnl 15 ⊖	a		11 36					12 06							12 36					13 06			

Ramsgate, Dover, Sheerness-on-Sea and Medway - London

Network Diagram - see first Page of Table 212

		SE 1	SE 1	SE	SE	SE	SE	SE 1	SE 1	SE	SE	SE	SE 1	SE 1	SE 1	SE	SE	SE	SE	SE 1	SE 1	SE	SE
Ramsgate 4	d		11 40	11 59					12 05						12 40	12 59					13 05		
Dumpton Park	d								12 08												13 08		
Broadstairs	d		11 45	12 05					12 11						12 45	13 05					13 11		
Margate 4	d		11 50	12a10					12 16						12 50	13a10					13 16		
Westgate-on-Sea	d								12 20												13 20		
Birchington-on-Sea	d		11 55						12 24						12 55						13 24		
Herne Bay	d		12 04						12 33						13 04						13 33		
Chestfield & Swalecliffe	d								12 36												13 36		
Whitstable	d		12 09						12 39						13 09						13 39		
Dover Priory 4	d	11 45						12 05						12 45						13 05			
Kearsney	d							12 09												13 09			
Shepherds Well	d							12 14												13 14			
Snowdown	d							12 18												13 18			
Aylesham	d							12 20												13 20			
Adisham	d							12 23												13 23			
Bekesbourne	d							12 27												13 27			
Canterbury East 4	d	12 02						12 32						13 02						13 32			
Selling	d							12 41												13 41			
Faversham 2	a	12 14	12 18					12 46	12 48					13 14	13 18					13 46	13 48		
	d	12 22			12 28			12 52		12 58				13 22			13 28			13 52		13 58	
Teynham	d							12 58												13 58			
Sheerness-on-Sea	d					12 32					13 02							13 32					14 02
Queenborough	d					12 36					13 06							13 36					14 06
Swale	d					12 40					13 10							13 40					14 10
Kemsley	d					12 44					13 14							13 44					14 14
Sittingbourne 4	a	12 29			12 36	12 49		13 02		13 06	13 19			13 29			13 36	13 49		14 02		14 06	14 19
	d	12 30			12 37			13 03		13 07				13 30			13 37			14 03		14 07	
Newington	d	12 35												13 35									
Rainham (Kent)	d	12 40			12 45			13 10		13 15				13 40			13 45			14 10		14 15	
Gillingham (Kent) 4	d	12 45			12 50		12 54	13 15		13 20		13 24	13 32	13 45			13 50		13 54	14 15		14 20	
Chatham 4	d	12 50			12 54		12 58	13 20		13 24		13 28	13 36	13 50			13 54		13 58	14 20		14 24	
Rochester 4	d	12 52			12 57		13 00	13 22		13 27		13 30	13 39	13 52			13 57		14 00	14 22		14 27	
Strood 4	a				13 01		13 05			13 31		13 35					14 01		14 05			14 31	
Gravesend 4	a				13 12		13 17			13 42		13 47					14 12		14 17			14 42	
Greenhithe for Bluewater	a						13 23					13 53							14 23				
Dartford 4	a						13 28					13 58							14 28				
London Bridge 4 ⊖	a						14 05					14 35							15 05				
London Cannon Street 4 ⊖	a																						
London Waterloo (East) 4 ⊖	a						14 09					14 39							15 09				
London Charing Cross 4 ⊖	a						14 13					14 43							15 13				
Sole Street	d												13 49										
Meopham	d	13 03						13 33					13 52	14 03						14 33			
Longfield	d	13 07						13 37					13 56	14 07						14 37			
Farningham Road	d												13 59										
Swanley 4	a												14 04										
St Mary Cray	a												14 09										
Bromley South 4	a	13 20						13 50					14 15	14 20						14 50			
Elephant & Castle ⊖	a																						
London Blackfriars 3 ⊖	a																						
London Victoria 15 ⊖	a	13 37						14 07					14 37	14 37						15 07			
Ebbsfleet International	a				13 17					13 47							14 17					14 47	
Stratford International ⊖	a				13 29					14 01							14 28					14 59	
St Pancras Internatnl 15 ⊖	a				13 36					14 10							14 39					15 06	

Ramsgate, Dover, Sheerness-on-Sea and Medway - London

Network Diagram - see first Page of Table 212

Station		SE		SE [1]	SE [1]	SE [1]	SE	SE	SE	SE	SE [1]	SE [1]		SE	SE	SE	SE	SE [1]	SE [1]	SE	SE	SE		SE	
Ramsgate [4]	d					13 40	13 59					14 05							14 40	14 59					
Dumpton Park	d											14 08													
Broadstairs	d					13 45	14 05					14 11							14 45	15 05					
Margate [4]	d					13 50	14a10					14 16							14 50	15a10					
Westgate-on-Sea	d											14 20													
Birchington-on-Sea	d					13 55						14 24							14 55						
Herne Bay	d					14 04						14 33							15 04						
Chestfield & Swalecliffe	d											14 36													
Whitstable	d					14 09						14 39							15 09						
Dover Priory [4]	d				13 45						14 05							14 45							
Kearsney	d										14 09														
Shepherds Well	d										14 14														
Snowdown	d										14 18														
Aylesham	d										14 20														
Adisham	d										14 23														
Bekesbourne	d										14 27														
Canterbury East [4]	d				14 02						14 32							15 02							
Selling	d										14 41														
Faversham [2]	a				14 14	14 18					14 46	14 48						15 14	15 18						
	d					14 22		14 28				14 52		14 58					15 22		15 28				
Teynham	d											14 58													
Sheerness-on-Sea	d								14 32						15 02							15 32			
Queenborough	d								14 36						15 06							15 36			
Swale	d								14 40						15 10							15 40			
Kemsley	d								14 44						15 14							15 44			
Sittingbourne [4]	a					14 29		14 36	14 49			15 02		15 06	15 19				15 29		15 36	15 55			
	d					14 30		14 37				15 03		15 07					15 30		15 37				
Newington	d					14 35													15 35						
Rainham (Kent)	d					14 40		14 45				15 10		15 15					15 40		15 45				
Gillingham (Kent) [4]	d	14 24		14 32		14 45		14 50		14 54		15 15		15 20		15 24	15 32		15 45		15 50			15 54	
Chatham [4]	d	14 28		14 36		14 50		14 54		14 58		15 20		15 24		15 28	15 36		15 50		15 54			15 58	
Rochester [4]	d	14 30		14 39		14 52		14 57		15 00		15 22		15 27		15 30	15 39		15 52		15 57			16 00	
Strood [4]	a	14 35						15 01		15 05				15 31		15 35					16 01			16 05	
Gravesend [4]	a	14 47						15 12		15 17				15 42		15 47					16 12			16 17	
Greenhithe for Bluewater	a	14 53								15 23						15 53								16 23	
Dartford [4]	a	14 58								15 28						15 58								16 28	
London Bridge [4] ⊖	a	15 35								16 05						16 35								17 07	
London Cannon Street [4] ⊖	a																							17 11	
London Waterloo (East) [4] ⊖	a	15 39								16 09						16 39									
London Charing Cross [4] ⊖	a	15 43								16 13						16 44									
Sole Street	d			14 49													15 49								
Meopham	d			14 52		15 03						15 33					15 52		16 03						
Longfield	d			14 56		15 07						15 37					15 56		16 07						
Farningham Road	d			14 59													15 59								
Swanley [4]	a			15 04													16 04								
St Mary Cray	a			15 09													16 09								
Bromley South [4]	a			15 15		15 20						15 50					16 15		16 20						
Elephant & Castle ⊖	a																								
London Blackfriars [3] ⊖	a																								
London Victoria [15] ⊖	a			15 37		15 37						16 07					16 37		16 38						
Ebbsfleet International	a							15 17						15 47							16 17				
Stratford International ⊖	a							15 29						16 02							16 29				
St Pancras Internatnl [15] ⊖	a							15 36						16 09							16 36				

Ramsgate, Dover, Sheerness-on-Sea and Medway - London

Network Diagram - see first Page of Table 212

		SE [1]	SE [1]	SE	SE	SE	SE [1]	SE [1]	SE [1]		SE	SE	SE	SE	SE [1]	SE [1]	SE [1]	SE	SE		SE	SE [1]	SE [1]	SE [1]	SE
Ramsgate [4]	d		15 05						15 35		15 59						16 05							16 35	16 59
Dumpton Park	d		15 08						15 38								16 08							16 38	
Broadstairs	d		15 11						15 41		16 05						16 11							16 41	17 05
Margate [4]	d		15 16						15 46		16a10						16 16							16 46	17a10
Westgate-on-Sea	d		15 20						15 50								16 20							16 50	
Birchington-on-Sea	d		15 24						15 54								16 24							16 54	
Herne Bay	d		15 33						16 03								16 33							17 03	
Chestfield & Swalecliffe	d		15 36						16 06								16 36							17 06	
Whitstable	d		15 39						16 09								16 39							17 09	
Dover Priory [4]	d	15 05						15 39								16 05							16 39		
Kearsney	d	15 09						15 43								16 09							16 43		
Shepherds Well	d	15 14						15 48								16 14							16 48		
Snowdown	d	15 18														16 18									
Aylesham	d	15 20						15 52								16 20							16 52		
Adisham	d	15 23						15 55								16 23							16 55		
Bekesbourne	d	15 27														16 27									
Canterbury East [4]	d	15 32						16 02								16 32							17 02		
Selling	d	15 41						16 11								16 41							17 11		
Faversham [2]	a	15 46	15 48					16 16	16 18							16 46	16 48						17 16	17 18	
	d		15 52	15 58					16 22			16 28					16 52	16 58						17 22	
Teynham	d		15 58														16 58								
Sheerness-on-Sea	d				16 02								16 32						17 02						
Queenborough	d				16 06								16 36						17 06						
Swale	d				16 10								16 40						17 10						
Kemsley	d				16 14								16 44						17 14						
Sittingbourne [4]	a		16 02	16 06	16 19				16 29			16 36	16 49				17 02	17 06	17 19					17 29	
	d		16 03	16 07					16 30			16 37					17 03	17 07						17 30	
Newington	d								16 35															17 35	
Rainham (Kent)	d		16 10	16 15					16 40			16 45					17 10	17 15						17 40	
Gillingham (Kent) [4]	d		16 15	16 20		16 24	16 32		16 45			16 50		16 54	17 02		17 15	17 20			17 24	17 32		17 45	
Chatham [4]	d		16 20	16 24		16 28	16 36		16 50			16 54		16 58	17 06		17 20	17 24			17 28	17 36		17 50	
Rochester [4]	d		16 22	16 27		16 30	16 39		16 52			16 57		17 00	17 09		17 22	17 27			17 30	17 39		17 52	
Strood [4]	a			16 31		16 35						17 01		17 05				17 31			17 35				
Gravesend [4]	a			16 42		16 47						17 12		17 17				17 42			17 47				
Greenhithe for Bluewater	a					16 53								17 23							17 53				
Dartford [4]	a					16 58								17 28							17 58				
London Bridge [4] ⊖	a					17 35								18 04							18 35				
London Cannon Street [4] ⊖	a																								
London Waterloo (East) [4] ⊖	a					17 40								18 08							18 41				
London Charing Cross [4] ⊖	a					17 44								18 12							18 45				
Sole Street	d						16 49								17 19							17 49			
Meopham	d		16 33				16 52		17 03						17 22		17 33					17 52		18 03	
Longfield	d		16 37				16 56		17 07						17 26		17 37					17 56		18 07	
Farningham Road	d						16 59								17 29							17 59			
Swanley [4]	a						17 04								17 34							18 04			
St Mary Cray	a						17 09								17 39							18 09			
Bromley South [4]	a		16 50				17 15		17 20						17 45		17 50					18 15		18 20	
Elephant & Castle ⊖	a																								
London Blackfriars [3] ⊖	a																								
London Victoria [15] ⊖	a		17 07				17 38		17 37						18 08		18 07					18 37		18 37	
Ebbsfleet International	a			16 47								17 17						17 47							
Stratford International ⊖	a			17 02								17 28						17 59							
St Pancras Internatnl [15] ⊖	a			17 09								17 36						18 06							

Ramsgate, Dover, Sheerness-on-Sea and Medway - London

Network Diagram - see first Page of Table 212

		SE	SE	SE	SE ■1	SE ■1		SE	SE	SE	SE	SE ■1	SE ■1	SE	SE	SE		SE	SE ■1	SE ■1	SE	SE	SE ■1	SE ■1	SE ■1
Ramsgate ■4	d					17 05							17 35	17 59						18 05	18 29				18 35
Dumpton Park	d					17 08							17 38							18 08					18 38
Broadstairs	d					17 11							17 41	18 05						18 11	18 35				18 41
Margate ■4	d					17 16							17 46	18a10						18 16	18a40				18 46
Westgate-on-Sea	d					17 20							17 50							18 20					18 50
Birchington-on-Sea	d					17 24							17 54							18 24					18 54
Herne Bay	d					17 33							18 03							18 33					19 03
Chestfield & Swalecliffe	d					17 36							18 06							18 36					19 06
Whitstable	d					17 39							18 09							18 39					19 09
Dover Priory ■4	d				17 05							17 39							18 05					18 39	
Kearsney	d				17 09							17 43							18 09					18 43	
Shepherds Well	d				17 14							17 48							18 14					18 48	
Snowdown	d				17 18														18 18						
Aylesham	d				17 20							17 52							18 20					18 52	
Adisham	d				17 23							17 55							18 23					18 55	
Bekesbourne	d				17 27														18 27						
Canterbury East ■4	d				17 32							18 02							18 32					19 02	
Selling	d				17 41							18 11							18 41					19 11	
Faversham ■2	a				17 46	17 48						18 16	18 18						18 46	18 48				19 16	19 18
	d	17 28			17 52			17 58				18 22			18 28				18 52					19 22	
Teynham	d				17 58														18 58						
Sheerness-on-Sea	d		17 32						18 02							18 37									
Queenborough	d		17 36						18 06							18 41									
Swale	d		17 40						18 10							18 45									
Kemsley	d		17 44						18 14							18 49									
Sittingbourne ■4	a	17 36	17 52		18 02			18 06	18 19			18 29			18 36	18 54			19 02					19 29	
	d	17 37			18 03			18 07				18 30			18 37				19 03					19 30	
Newington	d											18 35												19 35	
Rainham (Kent)	d	17 45			18 10			18 15				18 40			18 45				19 10					19 40	
Gillingham (Kent) ■4	d	17 50		17 54	18 15			18 20		18 24	18 32	18 45			18 50			18 54	19 15			19 24		19 45	
Chatham ■4	d	17 54		17 58	18 20			18 24		18 28	18 36	18 50			18 54			18 58	19 20			19 28		19 50	
Rochester ■4	d	17 57		18 00	18 22			18 27		18 30	18 39	18 52			18 57			19 00	19 22			19 30	19 39	19 52	
Strood ■4	a	18 02		18 05				18 31		18 35					19 01			19 05				19 35			
Gravesend ■4	a	18 13		18 17				18 42		18 47					19 12			19 17				19 47			
Greenhithe for Bluewater	a			18 23						18 53								19 23				19 53			
Dartford ■4	a			18 28						18 58								19 28				19 58			
London Bridge ■4 ⊖	a			19 05						19 35								20 06				20 36			
London Cannon Street ■4 ⊖	a																								
London Waterloo (East) ■4 ⊖	a			19 09						19 39								20 11				20 40			
London Charing Cross ■4 ⊖	a			19 13						19 43								20 14				20 44			
Sole Street	d										18 49												19 49		
Meopham	d				18 33						18 52	19 03							19 33				19 52	20 03	
Longfield	d				18 37						18 56	19 07							19 37				19 56	20 07	
Farningham Road	d										18 59												19 59		
Swanley ■4	a										19 04												20 04		
St Mary Cray	a										19 09												20 09		
Bromley South ■4	a				18 50						19 15	19 20							19 50				20 15	20 20	
Elephant & Castle ⊖	a																								
London Blackfriars ■3 ⊖	a																								
London Victoria ■15 ⊖	a				19 07						19 37	19 37							20 07				20 37	20 38	
Ebbsfleet International	a	18 17						18 47							19 17										
Stratford International ⊖	a	18 29						19 02							19 29										
St Pancras Internatnl ■15 ⊖	a	18 36						19 09							19 36										

Ramsgate, Dover, Sheerness-on-Sea and Medway - London

Network Diagram - see first Page of Table 212

		SE	SE	SE	SE	SE 1	SE 1	SE	SE	SE	SE	SE 1	SE 1	SE	SE	SE	SE	SE	SE 1	SE 1	SE	SE
Ramsgate 4	d	18 59					19 05						19 25	19 31	19 59					20 05	20 32	
Dumpton Park	d						19 08						19 28							20 08		
Broadstairs	d	19 05					19 11						19 31	19 36	20 05					20 11	20 38	
Margate 4	d	19a10					19 16						19 38	19a41	20a10					20 16	20a43	
Westgate-on-Sea	d						19 20						19 41							20 20		
Birchington-on-Sea	d						19 24						19 45							20 24		
Herne Bay	d						19 33						19 54							20 33		
Chestfield & Swalecliffe	d						19 36						19 58							20 36		
Whitstable	d						19 39						20 01							20 39		
Dover Priory 4	d					19 05						19 40							20 05			
Kearsney	d					19 09													20 09			
Shepherds Well	d					19 14													20 14			
Snowdown	d					19 18													20 18			
Aylesham	d					19 20													20 20			
Adisham	d					19 23													20 23			
Bekesbourne	d					19 27													20 27			
Canterbury East 4	d					19 32						19 57							20 32			
Selling	d					19 41													20 41			
Faversham 2	a					19 46	19 48					20 08	20 10						20 46	20 48		
	d			19 28		19 52			19 58			20 14				20 28			20 52			20 58
Teynham	d					19 58													20 58			
Sheerness-on-Sea	d		19 16					19 46		20 02							20 32					
Queenborough	d		19 23					19 53		20 06							20 36					
Swale	d		19 27					19 57		20 10							20 40					
Kemsley	d		19 31					20 01		20 14							20 44					
Sittingbourne 4	a		19 36	19 36		20 02		20 06	20 06	20 19		20 21				20 36	20 49		21 02			21 06
	d			19 37		20 03			20 07			20 22				20 37			21 03			21 07
Newington	d											20 27										
Rainham (Kent)	d			19 45		20 10			20 15			20 31				20 45			21 10			21 15
Gillingham (Kent) 4	d			19 50	19 54	20 15			20 20		20 24	20 36				20 50		20 54	21 15			21 20
Chatham 4	d			19 54	19 58	20 20			20 24		20 28	20 41				20 54		20 58	21 20			21 24
Rochester 4	d			19 57	20 00	20 22			20 27		20 30	20 43				20 57		21 00	21 22			21 27
Strood 4	a			20 01	20 05				20 31		20 35					21 01		21 05				21 31
Gravesend 4	a			20 12	20 17				20 42		20 47					21 12		21 17				21 42
Greenhithe for Bluewater	a				20 23						20 53							21 23				
Dartford 4	a				20 28						20 58							21 28				
London Bridge 4 ⊖	a				21 06						21 36							22 05				
London Cannon Street 4 ⊖	a																					
London Waterloo (East) 4 ⊖	a				21 10						21 40							22 09				
London Charing Cross 4 ⊖	a				21 14						21 44							22 13				
Sole Street	d											20 54										
Meopham	d					20 33						20 56							21 33			
Longfield	d					20 37						21 00							21 37			
Farningham Road	d											21 04										
Swanley 4	a											21 09										
St Mary Cray	a											21 14										
Bromley South 4	a					20 50						21 20							21 50			
Elephant & Castle ⊖	a																					
London Blackfriars 3 ⊖	a																					
London Victoria 15 ⊖	a					21 07						21 37							22 07			
Ebbsfleet International	a			20 17					20 47							21 17						21 47
Stratford International ⊖	a			20 29					21 02							21 29						21 59
St Pancras Internatnl 15 ⊖	a			20 36					21 09							21 36						22 06

Table 212

Mondays to Fridays

Ramsgate, Dover, Sheerness-on-Sea and Medway - London

Network Diagram - see first Page of Table 212

		SE	SE	SE	SE	SE	SE	SE	SE	SE	SE	SE	SE	SE	SE	SE	SE	SE	SE	SE	SE	SE	SE
					1				1	1					1	1		1			1	1	1
Ramsgate 4	d	21 00								21 05		21 59						22 05	22 59				23 05
Dumpton Park	d									21 08								22 08					23 08
Broadstairs	d	21 05								21 11		22 05						22 11	23 05				23 11
Margate 4	d	21a11								21 16		22a10						22 16	23a10				23 16
Westgate-on-Sea	d									21 20								22 20					23 20
Birchington-on-Sea	d									21 24								22 24					23 24
Herne Bay	d									21 33								22 33					23 33
Chestfield & Swalecliffe	d									21 36								22 36					23 36
Whitstable	d									21 39								22 39					23 39
Dover Priory 4	d				20 45				21 05						21 45	22 05					22 45	23 05	
Kearsney	d								21 09							22 09						23 09	
Shepherds Well	d								21 14							22 14						23 14	
Snowdown	d								21 18							22 18						23 18	
Aylesham	d								21 20							22 20						23 20	
Adisham	d								21 23							22 23						23 23	
Bekesbourne	d								21 27							22 27						23 27	
Canterbury East 4	d				21 02				21 32						22 02	22 32					23 02	23 32	
Selling	d								21 41							22 41						23 41	
Faversham 2	a				21 13				21 46	21 48					22 13	22 46		22 48			23 13	23 46	23 48
	d				21 14	21 28			21 52		21 58				22 14			22 52			23 14		23 52
Teynham	d								21 58									22 58					23 58
Sheerness-on-Sea	d		21 02					21 32					22 02							23 02			
Queenborough	d		21 06					21 36					22 06							23 06			
Swale	d		21 10					21 40					22 10							23 10			
Kemsley	d		21 14					21 44					22 14							23 14			
Sittingbourne 4	a		21 19		21 21	21 36			22 02		22 06		22 19		22 21			23 02		23 19	23 21		00 02
	d				21 22	21 37			22 03		22 07				22 22			23 03			23 22		00 03
Newington	d				21 27			21 51							22 27						23 27		00 08
Rainham (Kent)	d				21 31	21 45		21 55	22 10		22 15				22 31			23 10			23 31		00 12
Gillingham (Kent) 4	d			21 24	21 36	21 50	21 54	22a02	22 15		22 20			22 24	22 36		22 54	23 15			23 36		00a17
Chatham 4	d			21 28	21 41	21 54	21 58		22 20		22 24			22 28	22 41		22 58	23 20			23 41		
Rochester 4	d			21 30	21 43	21 57	22 00		22 22		22 27			22 30	22 43		23 00	23 22			23 43		
Strood 4	a			21 35		22 01	22 05				22 31			22 35			23 05						
Gravesend 4	a			21 47		22 12	22 17				22 42			22 47			23 17						
Greenhithe for Bluewater	a			21 53			22 23							22 53			23 23						
Dartford 4	a			21 58			22 28							22 58			23 28						
London Bridge 4 ⊖	a			22 35			23 05							23 35									
London Cannon Street 4 ⊖	a																						
London Waterloo (East) 4 ⊖	a			22 39			23 09							23 39									
London Charing Cross 4 ⊖	a			22 43			23 13							23 43									
Sole Street	d				21 54										22 54						23 54		
Meopham	d				21 56				22 33						22 56			23 33			23 56		
Longfield	d				22 00				22 37						23 00			23 37			23 59		
Farningham Road	d				22 04										23 04						00 04		
Swanley 4	a				22 09										23 09						00 09		
St Mary Cray	a				22 14										23 14						00 14		
Bromley South 4	a				22 20				22 50						23 20			23 50			00 20		
Elephant & Castle ⊖	a																						
London Blackfriars 3 ⊖	a																						
London Victoria 15 ⊖	a				22 37				23 07						23 37			00 07			00 38		
Ebbsfleet International	a					22 17					22 47												
Stratford International ⊖	a					22 29					22 59												
St Pancras Internatnl 15 ⊖	a					22 36					23 06												

Ramsgate, Dover, Sheerness-on-Sea and Medway - London

Network Diagram - see first Page of Table 212

Station		SE
Ramsgate 4	d	
Dumpton Park	d	
Broadstairs	d	
Margate 4	d	
Westgate-on-Sea	d	
Birchington-on-Sea	d	
Herne Bay	d	
Chestfield & Swalecliffe	d	
Whitstable	d	
Dover Priory 4	d	
Kearsney	d	
Shepherds Well	d	
Snowdown	d	
Aylesham	d	
Adisham	d	
Bekesbourne	d	
Canterbury East 4	d	
Selling	d	
Faversham 2	a	
	d	
Teynham	d	
Sheerness-on-Sea	d	23 53
Queenborough	d	23 57
Swale	d	00 01
Kemsley	d	00 05
Sittingbourne 4	a	00 10
	d	
Newington	d	
Rainham (Kent)	d	
Gillingham (Kent) 4	d	
Chatham 4	d	
Rochester 4	d	
Strood 4	a	
Gravesend 4	a	
Greenhithe for Bluewater	a	
Dartford 4	a	
London Bridge 4 ⊖	a	
London Cannon Street 4 ⊖	a	
London Waterloo (East) 4 ⊖	a	
London Charing Cross 4 ⊖	a	
Sole Street	d	
Meopham	d	
Longfield	d	
Farningham Road	d	
Swanley 4	a	
St Mary Cray	a	
Bromley South 4	a	
Elephant & Castle ⊖	a	
London Blackfriars 3 ⊖	a	
London Victoria 15 ⊖	a	
Ebbsfleet International	a	
Stratford International ⊖	a	
St Pancras Internatnl 15 ⊖	a	

Table 212

Saturdays

Ramsgate, Dover, Sheerness-on-Sea and Medway - London

Network Diagram - see first Page of Table 212

		SE 1	SE 1	SE 1	SE	SE	SE	SE 1	SE	SE		SE	SE 1	SE 1	SE	SE	SE 1	SE 1	SE 1	SE		SE	SE	SE 1	SE 1
Ramsgate 4	d	22p05		23p05				04 32						05 05					05 40						06 05
Dumpton Park	d	22p08		23p08										05 08											06 08
Broadstairs	d	22p11		23p11				04 37						05 11					05 45						06 11
Margate 4	d	22p16		23p16				04 42						05 16					05 50						06 16
Westgate-on-Sea	d	22p20		23p20										05 20											06 20
Birchington-on-Sea	d	22p24		23p24				04 47						05 24					05 55						06 24
Herne Bay	d	22p33		23p33				04 56						05 33					06 04						06 33
Chestfield & Swalecliffe	d	22p36		23p36										05 36											06 36
Whitstable	d	22p39		23p39				05 01						05 39					06 09						06 39
Dover Priory 4	d		22p45										05 05					05 45						06 05	
Kearsney	d												05 09											06 09	
Shepherds Well	d												05 14											06 14	
Snowdown	d												05 18											06 18	
Aylesham	d												05 20											06 20	
Adisham	d												05 23											06 23	
Bekesbourne	d												05 27											06 27	
Canterbury East 4	d		23p02										05 32					06 02						06 32	
Selling	d												05 41											06 41	
Faversham 2	a	22p48	23p13	23p48				05 09					05 46	05 48				06 14	06 18					06 46	06 48
	d	22p52	23p14	23p52				05 09		05 28			05 52		05 58			06 22		06 28				06 52	
Teynham	d	22p58		23p58									05 58											06 58	
Sheerness-on-Sea	d				23p53																	06 32			
Queenborough	d				23p57																	06 36			
Swale	d				00 01																	06 40			
Kemsley	d				00 05																	06 44			
Sittingbourne 4	a	23p02	23p21	00 02	00 10			05 17		05 36			06 02		06 06			06 29		06 36		06 49		07 02	
	d	23p03	23p22	00 03				05 17		05 37			06 03		06 07			06 30		06 37				07 03	
Newington	d		23p27	00 08				05 23										06 35							
Rainham (Kent)	d	23p10	23p31	00 12				05 27		05 45			06 10		06 15			06 40		06 45				07 10	
Gillingham (Kent) 4	d	23p15	23p36	00a17		04 48	05 18	05 32		05 50		05 54	06 15		06 20	06 24	06 32	06 45		06 50			06 54	07 15	
Chatham 4	d	23p20	23p41			04 52	05 22	05 36		05 54		05 58	06 20		06 24	06 28	06 36	06 50		06 54			06 58	07 20	
Rochester 4	d	23p22	23p43			04 54	05 24	05 39		05 57		06 00	06 22		06 27	06 30	06 39	06 52		06 57			07 00	07 22	
Strood 4	a					04 59	05 29			06 01		06 05			06 31	06 35				07 01			07 05		
Gravesend 4	a					05 11	05 41			06 12		06 17			06 42	06 47				07 12			07 17		
Greenhithe for Bluewater	a					05 20	05 50					06 23				06 53							07 23		
Dartford 4	a					05 27	05 57					06 28				06 58							07 28		
London Bridge 4 ⊖	a					06 05	06 35					07 05				07 35							08 05		
London Cannon Street 4 ⊖	a																								
London Waterloo (East) 4 ⊖	a					06 09	06 39					07 09				07 39							08 09		
London Charing Cross 4 ⊖	a					06 13	06 43					07 13				07 43							08 13		
Sole Street	d		23p54					05 49									06 49								
Meopham	d	23p33	23p56					05 52					06 33				06 52	07 03						07 33	
Longfield	d	23p37	23p59					05 56					06 37				06 56	07 07						07 37	
Farningham Road	d		00 04					06 00									06 59								
Swanley 4	a		00 09					06 05									07 04								
St Mary Cray	a		00 14					06 09									07 09								
Bromley South 4	a	23p50	00 20					06 15					06 50				07 15	07 20						07 50	
Elephant & Castle ⊖	a																								
London Blackfriars 3 ⊖	a																								
London Victoria 15 ⊖	a	00 07	00 38					06 37					07 07				07 37	07 37						08 07	
Ebbsfleet International	a								05 32	06 17					06 47					07 17					
Stratford International ⊖	a								05 44	06 29					06 59					07 29					
St Pancras Internatnl 15 ⊖	a								05 51	06 36					07 06					07 36					

Table 212

Saturdays

Ramsgate, Dover, Sheerness-on-Sea and Medway - London

Network Diagram - see first Page of Table 212

		SE	SE	SE	SE	SE	SE		SE	SE	SE	SE	SE	SE	SE	SE	SE		SE	SE	SE	SE	SE	SE	
					1	1	1					1	1				1		1	1					
Ramsgate 4	d						06 40						07 05							07 40	07 59				
Dumpton Park	d												07 08												
Broadstairs	d						06 45						07 11							07 45	08 05				
Margate 4	d						06 50						07 16							07 50	08a10				
Westgate-on-Sea	d												07 20												
Birchington-on-Sea	d						06 55						07 24							07 55					
Herne Bay	d						07 04						07 33							08 04					
Chestfield & Swalecliffe	d												07 36												
Whitstable	d						07 09						07 39							08 09					
Dover Priory 4	d					06 45						07 05							07 45						
Kearsney	d											07 09													
Shepherds Well	d											07 14													
Snowdown	d											07 18													
Aylesham	d											07 20													
Adisham	d											07 23													
Bekesbourne	d											07 27													
Canterbury East 4	d					07 02						07 32							08 02						
Selling	d											07 41													
Faversham 2	a					07 14	07 18					07 46	07 48						08 14	08 18					
	d	06 58					07 22		07 28				07 52	07 58						08 22		08 28			
Teynham	d												07 58												
Sheerness-on-Sea	d		07 02							07 32					08 02								08 32		
Queenborough	d		07 06							07 36					08 06								08 36		
Swale	d		07 10							07 40					08 10								08 40		
Kemsley	d		07 14							07 44					08 14								08 44		
Sittingbourne 4	a	07 06	07 19				07 29		07 36	07 49			08 02	08 06	08 19					08 29		08 36	08 49		
	d	07 07					07 30		07 37				08 03	08 07						08 30		08 37			
Newington	d						07 35													08 35					
Rainham (Kent)	d	07 15					07 40		07 45				08 10	08 15						08 40		08 45			
Gillingham (Kent) 4	d	07 20		07 24	07 32		07 45		07 50		07 54		08 15	08 20		08 24	08 32			08 45		08 50		08 54	
Chatham 4	d	07 24		07 28	07 36		07 50		07 54		07 58		08 20	08 24		08 28	08 36			08 50		08 54		08 58	
Rochester 4	d	07 27		07 30	07 39		07 52		07 57		08 00		08 22	08 27		08 30	08 39			08 52		08 57		09 00	
Strood 4	a	07 31		07 35					08 01		08 05			08 31		08 35						09 01		09 05	
Gravesend 4	a	07 42		07 47					08 12		08 17			08 42		08 47						09 12		09 17	
Greenhithe for Bluewater	a			07 53							08 23					08 53								09 23	
Dartford 4	a			07 58							08 28					08 58								09 28	
London Bridge 4 ⊖	a			08 35							09 05					09 35								10 05	
London Cannon Street 4 ⊖	a																								
London Waterloo (East) 4 ⊖	a			08 39							09 09					09 39								10 09	
London Charing Cross 4 ⊖	a			08 43							09 13					09 43								10 13	
Sole Street	d				07 49												08 49								
Meopham	d				07 52		08 03						08 33				08 52			09 03					
Longfield	d				07 56		08 07						08 37				08 56			09 07					
Farningham Road	d				07 59												08 59								
Swanley 4	a				08 04												09 04								
St Mary Cray	a				08 09												09 09								
Bromley South 4	a				08 15		08 20						08 50				09 15			09 20					
Elephant & Castle ⊖	a																								
London Blackfriars 3 ⊖	a																								
London Victoria 15 ⊖	a				08 37		08 37						09 07				09 37			09 37					
Ebbsfleet International	a	07 47							08 17					08 47								09 17			
Stratford International ⊖	a	07 59							08 29					08 59								09 29			
St Pancras Internatnl 15 ⊖	a	08 06							08 36					09 06								09 36			

Table 212

Saturdays

Ramsgate, Dover, Sheerness-on-Sea and Medway - London

Network Diagram - see first Page of Table 212

		SE 1	SE 1	SE		SE	SE	SE 1	SE 1	SE 1	SE	SE	SE	SE		SE 1	SE 1	SE	SE	SE	SE 1	SE 1	SE 1	SE	
Ramsgate 4	d		08 05							08 40	08 59						09 05						09 40	09 59	
Dumpton Park	d		08 08														09 08								
Broadstairs	d		08 11							08 45	09 05						09 11						09 45	10 05	
Margate 4	d		08 16							08 50	09a10						09 16						09 50	10a10	
Westgate-on-Sea	d		08 20														09 20								
Birchington-on-Sea	d		08 24							08 55							09 24						09 55		
Herne Bay	d		08 33							09 04							09 33						10 04		
Chestfield & Swalecliffe	d		08 36														09 36								
Whitstable	d		08 39							09 09							09 39						10 09		
Dover Priory 4	d	08 05							08 45							09 05						09 45			
Kearsney	d	08 09														09 09									
Shepherds Well	d	08 14														09 14									
Snowdown	d	08 18														09 18									
Aylesham	d	08 20														09 20									
Adisham	d	08 23														09 23									
Bekesbourne	d	08 27														09 27									
Canterbury East 4	d	08 32							09 02							09 32						10 02			
Selling	d	08 41														09 41									
Faversham 2	a	08 46	08 48						09 14	09 18						09 46	09 48					10 14	10 18		
	d	08 52		08 58					09 22			09 28				09 52		09 58				10 22			
Teynham	d	08 58														09 58									
Sheerness-on-Sea	d					09 02							09 32						10 02						
Queenborough	d					09 06							09 36						10 06						
Swale	d					09 10							09 40						10 10						
Kemsley	d					09 14							09 44						10 14						
Sittingbourne 4	a	09 02		09 06		09 19			09 29			09 36	09 49			10 02		10 06	10 19			10 29			
	d	09 03		09 07					09 30			09 37				10 03		10 07				10 30			
Newington	d								09 35													10 35			
Rainham (Kent)	d	09 10		09 15					09 40			09 45				10 10		10 15				10 40			
Gillingham (Kent) 4	d	09 15		09 20			09 24	09 32	09 45			09 50		09 54		10 15		10 20		10 24	10 32	10 45			
Chatham 4	d	09 20		09 24			09 28	09 36	09 50			09 54		09 58		10 20		10 24		10 28	10 36	10 50			
Rochester 4	d	09 22		09 27			09 30	09 39	09 52			09 57		10 00		10 22		10 27		10 30	10 39	10 52			
Strood 4	a			09 31			09 35					10 01		10 05				10 31		10 35					
Gravesend 4	a			09 42			09 47					10 12		10 17				10 42		10 47					
Greenhithe for Bluewater	a						09 53							10 23						10 53					
Dartford 4	a						09 58							10 28						10 58					
London Bridge 4 ⊖	a						10 35							11 05						11 35					
London Cannon Street 4 ⊖	a																								
London Waterloo (East) 4 ⊖	a						10 39							11 09						11 39					
London Charing Cross 4 ⊖	a						10 43							11 13						11 43					
Sole Street	d							09 49													10 49				
Meopham	d	09 33						09 52	10 03							10 33					10 52	11 03			
Longfield	d	09 37						09 56	10 07							10 37					10 56	11 07			
Farningham Road	d							09 59													10 59				
Swanley 4	a							10 04													11 04				
St Mary Cray	a							10 09													11 09				
Bromley South 4	a	09 50						10 15	10 20							10 50					11 15	11 20			
Elephant & Castle ⊖	a																								
London Blackfriars 3 ⊖	a																								
London Victoria 15 ⊖	a	10 07						10 37	10 37							11 07					11 37	11 37			
Ebbsfleet International	a			09 47								10 17						10 47							
Stratford International ⊖	a			09 59								10 29						10 59							
St Pancras Internatnl 15 ⊖	a			10 06								10 36						11 06							

Table 212

Saturdays

Ramsgate, Dover, Sheerness-on-Sea and Medway - London

Network Diagram - see first Page of Table 212

		SE	SE	SE	SE 1	SE 1	SE	SE	SE	SE 1		SE 1	SE 1	SE	SE	SE	SE	SE 1	SE 1	SE		SE	SE	SE 1	
Ramsgate 4	d					10 05							10 40	10 59					11 05						
Dumpton Park	d					10 08													11 08						
Broadstairs	d					10 11							10 45	11 05					11 11						
Margate 4	d					10 16							10 50	11a10					11 16						
Westgate-on-Sea	d					10 20													11 20						
Birchington-on-Sea	d					10 24							10 55						11 24						
Herne Bay	d					10 33							11 04						11 33						
Chestfield & Swalecliffe	d					10 36													11 36						
Whitstable	d					10 39							11 09						11 39						
Dover Priory 4	d				10 05							10 45						11 05							
Kearsney	d				10 09													11 09							
Shepherds Well	d				10 14													11 14							
Snowdown	d				10 18													11 18							
Aylesham	d				10 20													11 20							
Adisham	d				10 23													11 23							
Bekesbourne	d				10 27													11 27							
Canterbury East 4	d				10 32							11 02						11 32							
Selling	d				10 41													11 41							
Faversham 2	a				10 46	10 48						11 14	11 18					11 46	11 48						
	d	10 28				10 52	10 58						11 22		11 28				11 52	11 58					
Teynham	d					10 58													11 58						
Sheerness-on-Sea	d		10 32					11 02								11 32						12 02			
Queenborough	d		10 36					11 06								11 36						12 06			
Swale	d		10 40					11 10								11 40						12 10			
Kemsley	d		10 44					11 14								11 44						12 14			
Sittingbourne 4	a	10 36	10 49			11 02	11 06	11 19					11 29		11 36	11 49			12 02	12 06		12 19			
	d	10 37				11 03	11 07						11 30		11 37				12 03	12 07					
Newington	d												11 35												
Rainham (Kent)	d	10 45				11 10	11 15						11 40		11 45				12 10	12 15					
Gillingham (Kent) 4	d	10 50		10 54		11 15	11 20		11 24	11 32			11 45		11 50		11 54		12 15	12 20			12 24	12 32	
Chatham 4	d	10 54		10 58		11 20	11 24		11 28	11 36			11 50		11 54		11 58		12 20	12 24			12 28	12 36	
Rochester 4	d	10 57		11 00		11 22	11 27		11 30	11 39			11 52		11 57		12 00		12 22	12 27			12 30	12 39	
Strood 4	a	11 01		11 05			11 31		11 35						12 01		12 05			12 31			12 35		
Gravesend 4	a	11 12		11 17			11 42		11 47						12 12		12 17			12 42			12 47		
Greenhithe for Bluewater	a			11 23					11 53								12 23						12 53		
Dartford 4	a			11 28					11 58								12 28						12 58		
London Bridge 4 ⊖	a			12 05					12 35								13 05						13 35		
London Cannon Street 4 ⊖	a																								
London Waterloo (East) 4 ⊖	a			12 09					12 39								13 09						13 39		
London Charing Cross 4 ⊖	a			12 13					12 43								13 13						13 43		
Sole Street	d									11 49														12 49	
Meopham	d					11 33				11 52			12 03						12 33					12 52	
Longfield	d					11 37				11 56			12 07						12 37					12 56	
Farningham Road	d									11 59														12 59	
Swanley 4	a									12 04														13 04	
St Mary Cray	a									12 09														13 09	
Bromley South 4	a					11 50				12 15			12 20						12 50					13 15	
Elephant & Castle ⊖	a																								
London Blackfriars 3 ⊖	a																								
London Victoria 15 ⊖	a					12 07				12 37			12 37						13 07					13 37	
Ebbsfleet International	a	11 17					11 47								12 17					12 47					
Stratford International ⊖	a	11 29					11 59								12 29					12 59					
St Pancras Internatnl 15 ⊖	a	11 36					12 06								12 36					13 06					

Table 212

Saturdays

Ramsgate, Dover, Sheerness-on-Sea and Medway - London

Network Diagram - see first Page of Table 212

		SE 1	SE 1	SE	SE	SE	SE	SE 1	SE 1	SE	SE	SE	SE 1	SE 1	SE 1	SE	SE	SE	SE	SE 1	SE 1	SE	SE
Ramsgate 4	d		11 40	11 59					12 05						12 40	12 59					13 05		
Dumpton Park	d								12 08												13 08		
Broadstairs	d		11 45	12 05					12 11						12 45	13 05					13 11		
Margate 4	d		11 50	12a10					12 16						12 50	13a10					13 16		
Westgate-on-Sea	d								12 20												13 20		
Birchington-on-Sea	d		11 55						12 24						12 55						13 24		
Herne Bay	d		12 04						12 33						13 04						13 33		
Chestfield & Swalecliffe	d								12 36												13 36		
Whitstable	d		12 09						12 39						13 09						13 39		
Dover Priory 4	d	11 45						12 05						12 45						13 05			
Kearsney	d							12 09												13 09			
Shepherds Well	d							12 14												13 14			
Snowdown	d							12 18												13 18			
Aylesham	d							12 20												13 20			
Adisham	d							12 23												13 23			
Bekesbourne	d							12 27												13 27			
Canterbury East 4	d	12 02						12 32						13 02						13 32			
Selling	d							12 41												13 41			
Faversham 2	a	12 14	12 18					12 46	12 48					13 14	13 18					13 46	13 48		
	d	12 22			12 28			12 52		12 58				13 22			13 28			13 52		13 58	
Teynham	d							12 58												13 58			
Sheerness-on-Sea	d					12 32					13 02							13 32					14 02
Queenborough	d					12 36					13 06							13 36					14 06
Swale	d					12 40					13 10							13 40					14 10
Kemsley	d					12 44					13 14							13 44					14 14
Sittingbourne 4	a	12 29			12 36	12 49		13 02		13 06	13 19			13 29			13 36	13 49		14 02		14 06	14 19
	d	12 30			12 37			13 03		13 07				13 30			13 37			14 03		14 07	
Newington	d	12 35												13 35									
Rainham (Kent)	d	12 40			12 45			13 10		13 15				13 40			13 45			14 10		14 15	
Gillingham (Kent) 4	d	12 45			12 50		12 54	13 15		13 20		13 24	13 32	13 45			13 50		13 54	14 15		14 20	
Chatham 4	d	12 50			12 54		12 58	13 20		13 24		13 28	13 36	13 50			13 54		13 58	14 20		14 24	
Rochester 4	d	12 52			12 57		13 00	13 22		13 27		13 30	13 39	13 52			13 57		14 00	14 22		14 27	
Strood 4	a				13 01		13 05			13 31		13 35					14 01		14 05			14 31	
Gravesend 4	a				13 12		13 17			13 42		13 47					14 12		14 17			14 42	
Greenhithe for Bluewater	a						13 23					13 53							14 23				
Dartford 4	a						13 28					13 58							14 28				
London Bridge 4 ⊖	a						14 05					14 35							15 05				
London Cannon Street 4 ⊖	a																						
London Waterloo (East) 4 ⊖	a						14 09					14 39							15 09				
London Charing Cross 4 ⊖	a						14 13					14 43							15 13				
Sole Street	d												13 49										
Meopham	d	13 03						13 33					13 52	14 03						14 33			
Longfield	d	13 07						13 37					13 56	14 07						14 37			
Farningham Road	d												13 59										
Swanley 4	a												14 04										
St Mary Cray	a												14 09										
Bromley South 4	a	13 20						13 50					14 15	14 20						14 50			
Elephant & Castle ⊖	a																						
London Blackfriars 3 ⊖	a																						
London Victoria 15 ⊖	a	13 37						14 07					14 37	14 37						15 07			
Ebbsfleet International	a				13 17					13 47							14 17					14 47	
Stratford International ⊖	a				13 29					13 59							14 29					15 02	
St Pancras Internatnl 15 ⊖	a				13 36					14 06							14 36					15 09	

Table 212

Saturdays

Ramsgate, Dover, Sheerness-on-Sea and Medway - London

Network Diagram - see first Page of Table 212

		SE	SE ■1	SE ■1	SE ■1	SE	SE	SE	SE	SE ■1	SE ■1	SE	SE	SE	SE ■1	SE ■1	SE ■1	SE	SE	SE	SE
Ramsgate ■4	d				13 40	13 59					14 05						14 40	14 59			
Dumpton Park	d										14 08										
Broadstairs	d				13 45	14 05					14 11						14 45	15 05			
Margate ■4	d				13 50	14a10					14 16						14 50	15a10			
Westgate-on-Sea	d										14 20										
Birchington-on-Sea	d				13 55						14 24						14 55				
Herne Bay	d				14 04						14 33						15 04				
Chestfield & Swalecliffe	d										14 36										
Whitstable	d				14 09						14 39						15 09				
Dover Priory ■4	d			13 45						14 05						14 45					
Kearsney	d									14 09											
Shepherds Well	d									14 14											
Snowdown	d									14 18											
Aylesham	d									14 20											
Adisham	d									14 23											
Bekesbourne	d									14 27											
Canterbury East ■4	d			14 02						14 32						15 02					
Selling	d									14 41											
Faversham ■2	a			14 14	14 18					14 46	14 48					15 14	15 18				
	d			14 22			14 28			14 52		14 58				15 22			15 28		
Teynham	d									14 58											
Sheerness-on-Sea	d							14 32					15 02							15 32	
Queenborough	d							14 36					15 06							15 36	
Swale	d							14 40					15 10							15 40	
Kemsley	d							14 44					15 14							15 44	
Sittingbourne ■4	a			14 29			14 36	14 49		15 02		15 06	15 19			15 29			15 36	15 49	
	d			14 30			14 37			15 03		15 07				15 30			15 37		
Newington	d			14 35												15 35					
Rainham (Kent)	d			14 40			14 45			15 10		15 15				15 40			15 45		
Gillingham (Kent) ■4	d	14 24	14 32	14 45			14 50		14 54	15 15		15 20		15 24	15 32	15 45			15 50		15 54
Chatham ■4	d	14 28	14 36	14 50			14 54		14 58	15 20		15 24		15 28	15 36	15 50			15 54		15 58
Rochester ■4	d	14 30	14 39	14 52			14 57		15 00	15 22		15 27		15 30	15 39	15 52			15 57		16 00
Strood ■4	a	14 35					15 01		15 05			15 31		15 35					16 01		16 05
Gravesend ■4	a	14 47					15 12		15 17			15 42		15 47					16 12		16 17
Greenhithe for Bluewater	a	14 53							15 23					15 53							16 23
Dartford ■4	a	14 58							15 28					15 58							16 28
London Bridge ■4 ⊖	a	15 35							16 05					16 35							17 05
London Cannon Street ■4 ⊖	a																				
London Waterloo (East) ■4 ⊖	a	15 39							16 09					16 39							17 09
London Charing Cross ■4 ⊖	a	15 43							16 13					16 43							17 13
Sole Street	d		14 49												15 49						
Meopham	d		14 52	15 03						15 33					15 52	16 03					
Longfield	d		14 56	15 07						15 37					15 56	16 07					
Farningham Road	d		14 59												15 59						
Swanley ■4	a		15 04												16 04						
St Mary Cray	a		15 09												16 09						
Bromley South ■4	a		15 15	15 20						15 50					16 15	16 20					
Elephant & Castle ⊖	a																				
London Blackfriars ■3 ⊖	a																				
London Victoria ■15 ⊖	a		15 37	15 37						16 07					16 37	16 37					
Ebbsfleet International	a						15 17					15 47							16 17		
Stratford International ⊖	a						15 29					16 02							16 29		
St Pancras Internatnl ■15 ⊖	a						15 36					16 09							16 36		

Table 212

Saturdays

Ramsgate, Dover, Sheerness-on-Sea and Medway - London

Network Diagram - see first Page of Table 212

		SE 1	SE 1	SE	SE	SE	SE 1	SE 1	SE 1	SE	SE	SE	SE	SE 1	SE 1	SE	SE	SE	SE 1	SE 1	SE 1	SE	SE
Ramsgate 4	d		15 05						15 40	15 59					16 05						16 40	16 59	
Dumpton Park	d		15 08												16 08								
Broadstairs	d		15 11						15 45	16 05					16 11						16 45	17 05	
Margate 4	d		15 16						15 50	16a10					16 16						16 50	17a10	
Westgate-on-Sea	d		15 20												16 20								
Birchington-on-Sea	d		15 24						15 55						16 24						16 55		
Herne Bay	d		15 33						16 04						16 33						17 04		
Chestfield & Swalecliffe	d		15 36												16 36								
Whitstable	d		15 39						16 09						16 39						17 09		
Dover Priory 4	d	15 05						15 45						16 05						16 45			
Kearsney	d	15 09												16 09									
Shepherds Well	d	15 14												16 14									
Snowdown	d	15 18												16 18									
Aylesham	d	15 20												16 20									
Adisham	d	15 23												16 23									
Bekesbourne	d	15 27												16 27									
Canterbury East 4	d	15 32						16 02						16 32						17 02			
Selling	d	15 41												16 41									
Faversham 2	a	15 46	15 48					16 14	16 18					16 46	16 48					17 14	17 18		
	d	15 52		15 58				16 22			16 28			16 52		16 58				17 22			17 28
Teynham	d	15 58												16 58									
Sheerness-on-Sea	d				16 02							16 32					17 02						
Queenborough	d				16 06							16 36					17 06						
Swale	d				16 10							16 40					17 10						
Kemsley	d				16 14							16 44					17 14						
Sittingbourne 4	a	16 02		16 06	16 19			16 29			16 36	16 49		17 02		17 06	17 19			17 29			17 36
	d	16 03		16 07				16 30			16 37			17 03		17 07				17 30			17 37
Newington	d							16 35												17 35			
Rainham (Kent)	d	16 10		16 15				16 40			16 45			17 10		17 15				17 40			17 45
Gillingham (Kent) 4	d	16 15		16 20		16 24	16 32	16 45			16 50		16 54	17 15		17 20		17 24	17 32	17 45			17 50
Chatham 4	d	16 20		16 24		16 28	16 36	16 50			16 54		16 58	17 20		17 24		17 28	17 36	17 50			17 54
Rochester 4	d	16 22		16 27		16 30	16 39	16 52			16 57		17 00	17 22		17 27		17 30	17 39	17 52			17 57
Strood 4	a			16 31		16 35					17 01		17 05			17 31		17 35					18 01
Gravesend 4	a			16 42		16 47					17 12		17 17			17 42		17 47					18 12
Greenhithe for Bluewater	a					16 53							17 23					17 53					
Dartford 4	a					16 58							17 28					17 58					
London Bridge 4 ⊖	a					17 35							18 05					18 35					
London Cannon Street 4 ⊖	a																						
London Waterloo (East) 4 ⊖	a					17 39							18 09					18 39					
London Charing Cross 4 ⊖	a					17 43							18 13					18 43					
Sole Street	d						16 49												17 49				
Meopham	d	16 33					16 52	17 03						17 33					17 52	18 03			
Longfield	d	16 37					16 56	17 07						17 37					17 56	18 07			
Farningham Road	d						16 59												17 59				
Swanley 4	a						17 04												18 04				
St Mary Cray	a						17 09												18 09				
Bromley South 4	a	16 50					17 15	17 20						17 50					18 15	18 20			
Elephant & Castle ⊖	a																						
London Blackfriars 3 ⊖	a																						
London Victoria 15 ⊖	a	17 07					17 37	17 37						18 07					18 37	18 37			
Ebbsfleet International	a			16 47							17 17					17 47							18 17
Stratford International ⊖	a			17 02							17 29					17 59							18 29
St Pancras Internatnl 15 ⊖	a			17 09							17 36					18 09							18 36

Table 212

Saturdays

Ramsgate, Dover, Sheerness-on-Sea and Medway - London

Network Diagram - see first Page of Table 212

		SE	SE	SE 1	SE 1	SE	SE	SE	SE 1	SE 1	SE 1	SE	SE	SE	SE	SE 1	SE 1	SE	SE	SE	SE 1	SE 1	SE 1
Ramsgate 4	d				17 05						17 40	17 59					18 05						18 40
Dumpton Park	d				17 08												18 08						
Broadstairs	d				17 11						17 45	18 05					18 11						18 45
Margate 4	d				17 16						17 50	18a10					18 16						18 50
Westgate-on-Sea	d				17 20												18 20						
Birchington-on-Sea	d				17 24						17 55						18 24						18 55
Herne Bay	d				17 33						18 04						18 33						19 04
Chestfield & Swalecliffe	d				17 36												18 36						
Whitstable	d				17 39						18 09						18 39						19 09
Dover Priory 4	d			17 05						17 45						18 05						18 45	
Kearsney	d			17 09												18 09							
Shepherds Well	d			17 14												18 14							
Snowdown	d			17 18												18 18							
Aylesham	d			17 20												18 20							
Adisham	d			17 23												18 23							
Bekesbourne	d			17 27												18 27							
Canterbury East 4	d			17 32						18 02						18 32						19 02	
Selling	d			17 41												18 41							
Faversham 2	a			17 46	17 48					18 14	18 18					18 46	18 48					19 14	19 18
	d				17 52	17 58					18 22		18 28				18 52	18 58					19 22
Teynham	d				17 58												18 58						
Sheerness-on-Sea	d	17 32					18 02							18 32					19 02				
Queenborough	d	17 36					18 06							18 36					19 06				
Swale	d	17 40					18 10							18 40					19 10				
Kemsley	d	17 44					18 14							18 44					19 14				
Sittingbourne 4	a	17 49			18 02	18 06	18 19				18 29		18 36	18 49			19 02	19 06	19 19				19 29
	d				18 03	18 07					18 30		18 37				19 03	19 07					19 30
Newington	d										18 35												19 35
Rainham (Kent)	d				18 10	18 15					18 40		18 45				19 10	19 15					19 40
Gillingham (Kent) 4	d		17 54		18 15	18 20		18 24	18 32		18 45		18 50		18 54		19 15	19 20		19 24	19 32		19 45
Chatham 4	d		17 58		18 20	18 24		18 28	18 36		18 50		18 54		18 58		19 20	19 24		19 28	19 36		19 50
Rochester 4	d		18 00		18 22	18 27		18 30	18 39		18 52		18 57		19 00		19 22	19 27		19 30	19 39		19 52
Strood 4	a		18 05			18 31		18 35					19 01		19 05			19 31		19 35			
Gravesend 4	a		18 17			18 42		18 47					19 12		19 17			19 42		19 47			
Greenhithe for Bluewater	a		18 23					18 53							19 23					19 53			
Dartford 4	a		18 28					18 58							19 28					19 58			
London Bridge 4 ⊖	a		19 05					19 36							20 06					20 36			
London Cannon Street 4 ⊖	a																						
London Waterloo (East) 4 ⊖	a		19 09					19 42							20 10					20 40			
London Charing Cross 4 ⊖	a		19 13					19 45							20 14					20 44			
Sole Street	d								18 49												19 49		
Meopham	d				18 33				18 52		19 03						19 33				19 52		20 03
Longfield	d				18 37				18 56		19 07						19 37				19 56		20 07
Farningham Road	d								18 59												19 59		
Swanley 4	a								19 04												20 04		
St Mary Cray	a								19 09												20 09		
Bromley South 4	a				18 50				19 15		19 20						19 50				20 15		20 20
Elephant & Castle ⊖	a																						
London Blackfriars 3 ⊖	a																						
London Victoria 15 ⊖	a				19 07				19 37		19 37						20 07				20 37		20 37
Ebbsfleet International	a					18 47							19 16					19 47					
Stratford International ⊖	a					19 02							19 27					19 59					
St Pancras Internatnl 15 ⊖	a					19 09							19 38					20 06					

Table 212

Saturdays

Ramsgate, Dover, Sheerness-on-Sea and Medway - London

Network Diagram - see first Page of Table 212

		SE		SE	SE	SE	SE 1	SE 1	SE	SE	SE	SE		SE 1	SE	SE	SE	SE 1	SE 1	SE	SE	SE		SE	SE 1
Ramsgate 4	d	18 59						19 05		19 59									20 05		20 59				
Dumpton Park	d							19 08											20 08						
Broadstairs	d	19 05						19 11		20 05									20 11		21 05				
Margate 4	d	19a10						19 16		20a10									20 16		21a10				
Westgate-on-Sea	d							19 20											20 20						
Birchington-on-Sea	d							19 24											20 24						
Herne Bay	d							19 33											20 33						
Chestfield & Swalecliffe	d							19 36											20 36						
Whitstable	d							19 39											20 39						
Dover Priory 4	d						19 05											20 05							
Kearsney	d						19 09											20 09							
Shepherds Well	d						19 14											20 14							
Snowdown	d						19 18											20 18							
Aylesham	d						19 20											20 20							
Adisham	d						19 23											20 23							
Bekesbourne	d						19 27											20 27							
Canterbury East 4	d						19 32											20 32							
Selling	d						19 41											20 41							
Faversham 2	a						19 46	19 48										20 46	20 48						
	d			19 28			19 52		19 58					20 14	20 28			20 52		20 58					21 14
Teynham	d						19 58											20 58							
Sheerness-on-Sea	d				19 32						20 02					20 32						21 02			
Queenborough	d				19 36						20 06					20 36						21 06			
Swale	d				19 40						20 10					20 40						21 10			
Kemsley	d				19 44						20 14					20 44						21 14			
Sittingbourne 4	a			19 36	19 49		20 02		20 06		20 19			20 21	20 36	20 49		21 02		21 06		21 19			21 21
	d			19 37			20 03		20 07					20 22	20 37			21 03		21 07					21 22
Newington	d													20 27											21 27
Rainham (Kent)	d			19 45			20 10		20 15					20 31	20 45			21 10		21 15					21 31
Gillingham (Kent) 4	d			19 50		19 54	20 15		20 20			20 24		20 36	20 50		20 54	21 15		21 20				21 24	21 36
Chatham 4	d			19 54		19 58	20 20		20 24			20 28		20 41	20 54		20 58	21 20		21 24				21 28	21 41
Rochester 4	d			19 57		20 00	20 22		20 27			20 30		20 43	20 57		21 00	21 22		21 27				21 30	21 43
Strood 4	a			20 01		20 05			20 31			20 35			21 01		21 05			21 31				21 35	
Gravesend 4	a			20 12		20 17			20 42			20 47			21 12		21 17			21 42				21 47	
Greenhithe for Bluewater	a					20 23						20 53					21 23							21 53	
Dartford 4	a					20 28						20 58					21 28							21 58	
London Bridge 4 ⊖	a					21 06						21 36					22 05							22 35	
London Cannon Street 4 ⊖	a																								
London Waterloo (East) 4 ⊖	a					21 10						21 40					22 09							22 39	
London Charing Cross 4 ⊖	a					21 14						21 44					22 13							22 43	
Sole Street	d													20 54											21 54
Meopham	d						20 33							20 56				21 33							21 56
Longfield	d						20 37							21 00				21 37							22 00
Farningham Road	d													21 04											22 04
Swanley 4	a													21 09											22 09
St Mary Cray	a													21 14											22 14
Bromley South 4	a						20 50							21 20				21 50							22 20
Elephant & Castle ⊖	a																								
London Blackfriars 3 ⊖	a																								
London Victoria 15 ⊖	a						21 07							21 37				22 07							22 37
Ebbsfleet International	a			20 17					20 47						21 17					21 47					
Stratford International ⊖	a			20 29					21 02						21 29					21 59					
St Pancras Internatnl 15 ⊖	a			20 36					21 09						21 36					22 06					

Table 212

Saturdays

Ramsgate, Dover, Sheerness-on-Sea and Medway - London

Network Diagram - see first Page of Table 212

		SE	SE	SE	SE	SE	SE	SE		SE	SE	SE	SE	SE	SE	SE	SE	SE		SE					
				1	1						1	1		1			1	1							
Ramsgate 4	d				21 05		21 59							22 05	22 59			23 05							
Dumpton Park	d				21 08									22 08				23 08							
Broadstairs	d				21 11		22 05							22 11	23 05			23 11							
Margate 4	d				21 16		22a10							22 16	23a10			23 16							
Westgate-on-Sea	d				21 20									22 20				23 20							
Birchington-on-Sea	d				21 24									22 24				23 24							
Herne Bay	d				21 33									22 33				23 33							
Chestfield & Swalecliffe	d				21 36									22 36				23 36							
Whitstable	d				21 39									22 39				23 39							
Dover Priory 4	d			21 05								22 05					23 05								
Kearsney	d			21 09								22 09					23 09								
Shepherds Well	d			21 14								22 14					23 14								
Snowdown	d			21 18								22 18					23 18								
Aylesham	d			21 20								22 20					23 20								
Adisham	d			21 23								22 23					23 23								
Bekesbourne	d			21 27								22 27					23 27								
Canterbury East 4	d			21 32							22 02	22 32					23 32								
Selling	d			21 41								22 41					23 41								
Faversham 2	a			21 46	21 48						22 13	22 46		22 48			23 46	23 49							
	d	21 28		21 52		21 58					22 14			22 52				23 52							
Teynham	d			21 58										22 58				23 58							
Sheerness-on-Sea	d							22 02								23 02				23 53					
Queenborough	d							22 06								23 06				23 57					
Swale	d							22 10								23 10				00 01					
Kemsley	d							22 14								23 14				00 05					
Sittingbourne 4	a	21 36		22 02		22 06		22 19			22 21			23 02		23 19		00 02		00 10					
	d	21 37		22 03		22 07					22 22			23 03				00 03							
Newington	d										22 27							00 08							
Rainham (Kent)	d	21 45		22 10		22 15					22 31			23 10				00 12							
Gillingham (Kent) 4	d	21 50	21 54	22 15		22 20				22 24	22 36		22 54	23 15				00a17							
Chatham 4	d	21 54	21 58	22 20		22 24				22 28	22 41		22 58	23 20											
Rochester 4	d	21 57	22 00	22 22		22 27				22 30	22 43		23 00	23 22											
Strood 4	a	22 01	22 05			22 31				22 35			23 05												
Gravesend 4	a	22 12	22 17			22 42				22 47			23 17												
Greenhithe for Bluewater	a		22 23							22 53			23 23												
Dartford 4	a		22 28							22 58			23 28												
London Bridge 4 ⊖	a		23 05							23 35															
London Cannon Street 4 ⊖	a																								
London Waterloo (East) 4 ⊖	a		23 09							23 39															
London Charing Cross 4 ⊖	a		23 13							23 43															
Sole Street	d										22 54														
Meopham	d			22 33							22 56			23 33											
Longfield	d			22 37							23 00			23 37											
Farningham Road	d										23 04														
Swanley 4	a										23 09														
St Mary Cray	a										23 14														
Bromley South 4	a			22 50							23 20			23 50											
Elephant & Castle ⊖	a																								
London Blackfriars 3 ⊖	a																								
London Victoria 15 ⊖	a			23 07							23 37			00 07											
Ebbsfleet International	a	22 17				22 47																			
Stratford International ⊖	a	22 29				22 59																			
St Pancras Internatnl 15 ⊖	a	22 36				23 06																			

Table 212

Sundays

Ramsgate, Dover, Sheerness-on-Sea and Medway - London

Network Diagram - see first Page of Table 212

		SE	SE	SE	SE	SE	SE	SE	SE	SE		SE	SE	SE	SE	SE	SE	SE	SE	SE		SE	SE	SE	SE
		1	1			1			1					1			1	1				1			
		A	A	A																					
Ramsgate 4	d	22p05	23p05						06 34									07 34							
Dumpton Park	d	22p08	23p08						06 37									07 37							
Broadstairs	d	22p11	23p11						06 40									07 40							
Margate 4	d	22p16	23p16						06 45									07 45							
Westgate-on-Sea	d	22p20	23p20						06 49									07 49							
Birchington-on-Sea	d	22p24	23p24						06 53									07 53							
Herne Bay	d	22p33	23p33						07 02									08 02							
Chestfield & Swalecliffe	d	22p36	23p36						07 05									08 05							
Whitstable	d	22p39	23p39						07 08									08 08							
Dover Priory 4	d																07 34								
Kearsney	d																07 38								
Shepherds Well	d																07 43								
Snowdown	d																07 47								
Aylesham	d																07 49								
Adisham	d																07 52								
Bekesbourne	d																07 56								
Canterbury East 4	d																08 01								
Selling	d																08 10								
Faversham 2	a	22p48	23p49						07 17								08 15	08 17							
	d	22p52	23p52			06 34		06 58	07 21				07 28	07 34		07 58	08 21		08 28			08 34		08 58	
Teynham	d	22p58	23p58			06 40								07 40								08 40			
Sheerness-on-Sea	d			23p53																			08 42		
Queenborough	d			23p57																			08 46		
Swale	d			00 01																			08 50		
Kemsley	d			00 05																			08 54		
Sittingbourne 4	a	23p02	00 02	00 10		06 44		07 06	07 28				07 36	07 44		08 06	08 28		08 36			08 44	08 59	09 06	
	d	23p03	00 03			06 45		07 07	07 29				07 37	07 45		08 07	08 29		08 37			08 45		09 07	
Newington	d		00 08			06 50								07 50								08 50			
Rainham (Kent)	d	23p10	00 12			06 54		07 15	07 36				07 45	07 54		08 15	08 36		08 45			08 54		09 15	
Gillingham (Kent) 4	d	23p15	00a17		06 45	06 59	07 15	07 20	07 41	07 45			07 50	07 59	08 15	08 20	08 41		08 50	08 54		08 59		09 20	09 24
Chatham 4	d	23p20			06 49	07 04	07 19	07 24	07 46	07 49			07 54	08 04	08 19	08 24	08 46		08 54	08 58		09 04		09 24	09 28
Rochester 4	d	23p22			06 51	07 06	07 21	07 27	07 48	07 51			07 57	08 06	08 21	08 27	08 48		08 57	09 00		09 06		09 27	09 30
Strood 4	a				06 56		07 26	07 31		07 56			08 01		08 26	08 31			09 01	09 05				09 31	09 35
Gravesend 4	a				07 08		07 38	07 42		08 08			08 12		08 38	08 42			09 12	09 17				09 42	09 47
Greenhithe for Bluewater	a				07 17		07 47			08 17					08 47					09 23					09 53
Dartford 4	a				07 24		07 54			08 24					08 54					09 28					09 58
London Bridge 4 ⊖	a				08 06		08 36			09 06					09 36					10 06					10 36
London Cannon Street 4 ⊖	a																								
London Waterloo (East) 4 ⊖	a				08 11		08 41			09 11					09 41					10 11					10 41
London Charing Cross 4 ⊖	a				08 14		08 44			09 14					09 44					10 14					10 44
Sole Street	d					07 17								08 17								09 17			
Meopham	d	23p33				07 19								08 19								09 19			
Longfield	d	23p37				07 23								08 23								09 23			
Farningham Road	d					07 27								08 27								09 27			
Swanley 4	a					07 32								08 32								09 32			
St Mary Cray	a					07 36								08 36								09 36			
Bromley South 4	a	23p50				07 42			08 13					08 42			09 13					09 42			
Elephant & Castle ⊖	a																								
London Blackfriars 3 ⊖	a																								
London Victoria 15 ⊖	a	00 07				08 03			08 29					09 02			09 29					10 02			
Ebbsfleet International	a							07 47				08 02	08 17			08 47			09 17					09 47	
Stratford International ⊖	a							07 59				08 14	08 29			08 59			09 29					09 59	
St Pancras Internatnl 15 ⊖	a							08 06				08 21	08 36			09 06			09 36					10 06	

A not 11 December

Table 212

Sundays

Ramsgate, Dover, Sheerness-on-Sea and Medway - London

Network Diagram - see first Page of Table 212

		SE 1	SE 1	SE	SE	SE 1		SE	SE	SE	SE 1	SE 1	SE	SE	SE	SE 1		SE	SE	SE	SE 1	SE 1	SE	SE	SE
Ramsgate 4	d		08 34									09 34	09 59									10 34	10 59		
Dumpton Park	d		08 37									09 37										10 37			
Broadstairs	d		08 40									09 40	10 05									10 40	11 05		
Margate 4	d		08 45									09 45	10a10									10 45	11a10		
Westgate-on-Sea	d		08 49									09 49										10 49			
Birchington-on-Sea	d		08 53									09 53										10 53			
Herne Bay	d		09 02									10 02										11 02			
Chestfield & Swalecliffe	d		09 05									10 05										11 05			
Whitstable	d		09 08									10 08										11 08			
Dover Priory 4	d	08 34									09 34										10 34				
Kearsney	d	08 38									09 38										10 38				
Shepherds Well	d	08 43									09 43										10 43				
Snowdown	d	08 47									09 47										10 47				
Aylesham	d	08 49									09 49										10 49				
Adisham	d	08 52									09 52										10 52				
Bekesbourne	d	08 56									09 56										10 56				
Canterbury East 4	d	09 01				09 22					10 01					10 22					11 01				
Selling	d	09 10									10 10										11 10				
Faversham 2	a	09 15	09 17			09 33					10 15	10 17				10 33					11 15	11 17			
	d		09 21	09 28		09 34			09 58			10 21		10 28		10 34			10 58			11 21		11 28	
Teynham	d					09 40										10 40									
Sheerness-on-Sea	d							09 42										10 42							
Queenborough	d							09 46										10 46							
Swale	d							09 50										10 50							
Kemsley	d							09 54										10 54							
Sittingbourne 4	a		09 28	09 36		09 44		09 59	10 06			10 28		10 36		10 44		10 59	11 06			11 28		11 36	
	d		09 29	09 37		09 45			10 07			10 29		10 37		10 45			11 07			11 29		11 37	
Newington	d					09 50										10 50									
Rainham (Kent)	d		09 36	09 45		09 54			10 15			10 36		10 45		10 54			11 15			11 36		11 45	
Gillingham (Kent) 4	d		09 41	09 50	09 54	09 59			10 20	10 24		10 41		10 50	10 54	10 59			11 20	11 24		11 41		11 50	11 54
Chatham 4	d		09 46	09 54	09 58	10 04			10 24	10 28		10 46		10 54	10 58	11 04			11 24	11 28		11 46		11 54	11 58
Rochester 4	d		09 48	09 57	10 00	10 06			10 27	10 30		10 48		10 57	11 00	11 06			11 27	11 30		11 48		11 57	12 00
Strood 4	a			10 01	10 05				10 31	10 35				11 01	11 05				11 31	11 35				12 01	12 05
Gravesend 4	a			10 12	10 17				10 42	10 47				11 12	11 17				11 42	11 47				12 12	12 17
Greenhithe for Bluewater	a				10 23					10 53					11 23					11 53					12 23
Dartford 4	a				10 28					10 58					11 28					11 58					12 28
London Bridge 4 ⊖	a				11 06					11 36					12 06					12 36					13 06
London Cannon Street 4 ⊖	a																								
London Waterloo (East) 4 ⊖	a				11 11					11 41					12 11					12 41					13 11
London Charing Cross 4 ⊖	a				11 14					11 44					12 14					12 44					13 14
Sole Street	d					10 17										11 17									
Meopham	d					10 19										11 19									
Longfield	d					10 23										11 23									
Farningham Road	d					10 27										11 27									
Swanley 4	a					10 32										11 32									
St Mary Cray	a					10 36										11 36									
Bromley South 4	a		10 13			10 42						11 13				11 42						12 13			
Elephant & Castle ⊖	a																								
London Blackfriars 3 ⊖	a																								
London Victoria 15 ⊖	a		10 29			11 02						11 29				12 02						12 29			
Ebbsfleet International	a			10 17					10 47					11 17					11 47					12 17	
Stratford International ⊖	a			10 29					10 59					11 29					11 59					12 29	
St Pancras Internatnl 15 ⊖	a			10 36					11 06					11 36					12 06					12 36	

Table 212

Sundays

Ramsgate, Dover, Sheerness-on-Sea and Medway - London

Network Diagram - see first Page of Table 212

		SE 1		SE	SE	SE	SE 1	SE 1	SE	SE	SE	SE 1		SE	SE	SE	SE 1	SE 1	SE	SE	SE	SE 1		SE	SE
Ramsgate 4	d							11 34	11 59									12 34	12 59						
Dumpton Park	d							11 37										12 37							
Broadstairs	d							11 40	12 05									12 40	13 05						
Margate 4	d							11 45	12a10									12 45	13a10						
Westgate-on-Sea	d							11 49										12 49							
Birchington-on-Sea	d							11 53										12 53							
Herne Bay	d							12 02										13 02							
Chestfield & Swalecliffe	d							12 05										13 05							
Whitstable	d							12 08										13 08							
Dover Priory 4	d						11 34										12 34								
Kearsney	d						11 38										12 38								
Shepherds Well	d						11 43										12 43								
Snowdown	d						11 47										12 47								
Aylesham	d						11 49										12 49								
Adisham	d						11 52										12 52								
Bekesbourne	d						11 56										12 56								
Canterbury East 4	d	11 22					12 01					12 22					13 01					13 22			
Selling	d						12 10										13 10								
Faversham 2	a	11 33					12 15	12 17				12 33					13 15	13 17				13 33			
	d	11 34			11 58		12 21			12 28		12 34			12 58		13 21			13 28		13 34			13 58
Teynham	d	11 40										12 40										13 40			
Sheerness-on-Sea	d			11 42										12 42										13 42	
Queenborough	d			11 46										12 46										13 46	
Swale	d			11 50										12 50										13 50	
Kemsley	d			11 54										12 54										13 54	
Sittingbourne 4	a	11 44		11 59	12 06		12 28			12 36		12 44		12 59	13 06		13 28			13 36		13 44		13 59	14 06
	d	11 45			12 07		12 29			12 37		12 45			13 07		13 29			13 37		13 45			14 07
Newington	d	11 50										12 50										13 50			
Rainham (Kent)	d	11 54			12 15		12 36			12 45		12 54			13 15		13 36			13 45		13 54			14 15
Gillingham (Kent) 4	d	11 59			12 20	12 24	12 41			12 50	12 54	12 59			13 20	13 24	13 41			13 50	13 54	13 59			14 20
Chatham 4	d	12 04			12 24	12 28	12 46			12 54	12 58	13 04			13 24	13 28	13 46			13 54	13 58	14 04			14 24
Rochester 4	d	12 06			12 27	12 30	12 48			12 57	13 00	13 06			13 27	13 30	13 48			13 57	14 00	14 06			14 27
Strood 4	a				12 31	12 35				13 01	13 05				13 31	13 35				14 01	14 05				14 31
Gravesend 4	a				12 42	12 47				13 12	13 17				13 42	13 47				14 12	14 17				14 42
Greenhithe for Bluewater	a					12 53					13 23					13 53					14 23				
Dartford 4	a					12 58					13 28					13 58					14 28				
London Bridge 4 ⊖	a					13 36					14 06					14 36					15 06				
London Cannon Street 4 ⊖	a																								
London Waterloo (East) 4 ⊖	a					13 41					14 11					14 41					15 11				
London Charing Cross 4 ⊖	a					13 44					14 14					14 44					15 14				
Sole Street	d	12 17										13 17										14 17			
Meopham	d	12 19										13 19										14 19			
Longfield	d	12 23										13 23										14 23			
Farningham Road	d	12 27										13 27										14 27			
Swanley 4	a	12 32										13 32										14 32			
St Mary Cray	a	12 36										13 36										14 36			
Bromley South 4	a	12 42					13 13					13 42					14 13					14 42			
Elephant & Castle ⊖	a																								
London Blackfriars 3 ⊖	a																								
London Victoria 15 ⊖	a	13 02					13 29					14 02					14 29					15 02			
Ebbsfleet International	a				12 47					13 17					13 47					14 17					14 47
Stratford International ⊖	a				12 59					13 29					14 02					14 29					14 59
St Pancras Internatnl 15 ⊖	a				13 06					13 36					14 09					14 36					15 06

Ramsgate, Dover, Sheerness-on-Sea and Medway - London

Network Diagram - see first Page of Table 212

		SE	SE 1	SE 1	SE	SE	SE	SE 1		SE	SE	SE	SE 1	SE 1	SE	SE	SE	SE 1		SE	SE	SE	SE 1	SE 1	SE
Ramsgate 4	d			13 34	13 59									14 34	14 59									15 34	15 59
Dumpton Park	d			13 37										14 37										15 37	
Broadstairs	d			13 40	14 05									14 40	15 05									15 40	16 05
Margate 4	d			13 45	14a10									14 45	15a10									15 45	16a10
Westgate-on-Sea	d			13 49										14 49										15 49	
Birchington-on-Sea	d			13 53										14 53										15 53	
Herne Bay	d			14 02										15 02										16 02	
Chestfield & Swalecliffe	d			14 05										15 05										16 05	
Whitstable	d			14 08										15 08										16 08	
Dover Priory 4	d		13 34										14 34										15 34		
Kearsney	d		13 38										14 38										15 38		
Shepherds Well	d		13 43										14 43										15 43		
Snowdown	d		13 47										14 47										15 47		
Aylesham	d		13 49										14 49										15 49		
Adisham	d		13 52										14 52										15 52		
Bekesbourne	d		13 56										14 56										15 56		
Canterbury East 4	d		14 01					14 22					15 01					15 22					16 01		
Selling	d		14 10										15 10										16 10		
Faversham 2	a		14 15	14 17				14 33					15 15	15 17				15 33					16 15	16 17	
	d		14 21			14 28		14 34			14 58		15 21			15 28		15 34			15 58		16 21		
Teynham	d							14 40										15 40							
Sheerness-on-Sea	d									14 42										15 42					
Queenborough	d									14 46										15 46					
Swale	d									14 50										15 50					
Kemsley	d									14 54										15 54					
Sittingbourne 4	a		14 28			14 36		14 44		14 59	15 06		15 28			15 36		15 44		15 59	16 06		16 28		
	d		14 29			14 37		14 45			15 07		15 29			15 37		15 45			16 07		16 29		
Newington	d							14 50										15 50							
Rainham (Kent)	d		14 36			14 45		14 54			15 15		15 36			15 45		15 54			16 15		16 36		
Gillingham (Kent) 4	d	14 24	14 41			14 50	14 54	14 59			15 20	15 24	15 41			15 50	15 54	15 59			16 20	16 24	16 41		
Chatham 4	d	14 28	14 46			14 54	14 58	15 04			15 24	15 28	15 46			15 54	15 58	16 04			16 24	16 28	16 46		
Rochester 4	d	14 30	14 48			14 57	15 00	15 06			15 27	15 30	15 48			15 57	16 00	16 06			16 27	16 30	16 48		
Strood 4	a	14 35				15 01	15 05				15 31	15 35				16 01	16 05				16 31	16 35			
Gravesend 4	a	14 47				15 12	15 17				15 42	15 47				16 12	16 17				16 42	16 47			
Greenhithe for Bluewater	a	14 53					15 23					15 53					16 23					16 53			
Dartford 4	a	14 58					15 28					15 58					16 28					16 58			
London Bridge 4 ⊖	a	15 36					16 06					16 36					17 06					17 36			
London Cannon Street 4 ⊖	a																								
London Waterloo (East) 4 ⊖	a	15 41					16 11					16 41					17 11					17 41			
London Charing Cross 4 ⊖	a	15 44					16 14					16 44					17 14					17 44			
Sole Street	d							15 17										16 17							
Meopham	d							15 19										16 19							
Longfield	d							15 23										16 23							
Farningham Road	d							15 27										16 27							
Swanley 4	a							15 32										16 32							
St Mary Cray	a							15 36										16 36							
Bromley South 4	a		15 13					15 42					16 13					16 42					17 13		
Elephant & Castle ⊖	a																								
London Blackfriars 3 ⊖	a																								
London Victoria 15 ⊖	a		15 29					16 02					16 29					17 02					17 29		
Ebbsfleet International	a					15 17					15 47					16 17					16 47				
Stratford International ⊖	a					15 29					16 02					16 29					17 02				
St Pancras Internatnl 15 ⊖	a					15 36					16 09					16 36					17 09				

Table 212

Sundays

Ramsgate, Dover, Sheerness-on-Sea and Medway - London

Network Diagram - see first Page of Table 212

Station		SE	SE	SE 1		SE	SE	SE	SE 1	SE 1	SE	SE	SE	SE 1		SE	SE	SE	SE 1	SE 1	SE	SE	SE	SE 1	
Ramsgate 4	d									16 34	16 59									17 34	17 59				
Dumpton Park	d									16 37										17 37					
Broadstairs	d									16 40	17 05									17 40	18 05				
Margate 4	d									16 45	17a10									17 45	18a10				
Westgate-on-Sea	d									16 49										17 49					
Birchington-on-Sea	d									16 53										17 53					
Herne Bay	d									17 02										18 02					
Chestfield & Swalecliffe	d									17 05										18 05					
Whitstable	d									17 08										18 08					
Dover Priory 4	d								16 34										17 34						
Kearsney	d								16 38										17 38						
Shepherds Well	d								16 43										17 43						
Snowdown	d								16 47										17 47						
Aylesham	d								16 49										17 49						
Adisham	d								16 52										17 52						
Bekesbourne	d								16 56										17 56						
Canterbury East 4	d			16 22					17 01					17 22					18 01					18 22	
Selling	d								17 10										18 10						
Faversham 2	a			16 33					17 15	17 17				17 33					18 15	18 17				18 33	
	d	16 28		16 34			16 58		17 21			17 28		17 34			17 58		18 21			18 28		18 34	
Teynham	d			16 40										17 40										18 40	
Sheerness-on-Sea	d					16 42										17 42									
Queenborough	d					16 46										17 46									
Swale	d					16 50										17 50									
Kemsley	d					16 54										17 54									
Sittingbourne 4	a	16 36		16 44		16 59	17 06		17 28			17 36		17 44		17 59	18 06		18 28			18 36		18 44	
	d	16 37		16 45			17 07		17 29			17 37		17 45			18 07		18 29			18 37		18 45	
Newington	d			16 50										17 50										18 50	
Rainham (Kent)	d	16 45		16 54			17 15		17 36			17 45		17 54			18 15		18 36			18 45		18 54	
Gillingham (Kent) 4	d	16 50	16 54	16 59			17 20	17 24	17 41			17 50	17 54	17 59			18 20	18 24	18 41			18 50	18 54	18 59	
Chatham 4	d	16 54	16 58	17 04			17 24	17 28	17 46			17 54	17 58	18 04			18 24	18 28	18 46			18 54	18 58	19 04	
Rochester 4	d	16 57	17 00	17 06			17 27	17 30	17 48			17 57	18 00	18 06			18 27	18 30	18 48			18 57	19 00	19 06	
Strood 4	a	17 01	17 05				17 31	17 35				18 01	18 05				18 31	18 35				19 01	19 05		
Gravesend 4	a	17 12	17 17				17 42	17 47				18 12	18 17				18 42	18 47				19 12	19 17		
Greenhithe for Bluewater	a		17 23					17 53					18 23					18 53					19 23		
Dartford 4	a		17 28					17 58					18 28					18 58					19 28		
London Bridge 4 ⊖	a		18 06					18 36					19 06					19 36					20 06		
London Cannon Street 4 ⊖	a																								
London Waterloo (East) 4 ⊖	a		18 11					18 41					19 11					19 41					20 11		
London Charing Cross 4 ⊖	a		18 14					18 44					19 14					19 44					20 14		
Sole Street	d			17 17										18 17										19 17	
Meopham	d			17 19										18 19										19 19	
Longfield	d			17 23										18 23										19 23	
Farningham Road	d			17 27										18 27										19 27	
Swanley 4	a			17 32										18 32										19 32	
St Mary Cray	a			17 36										18 36										19 36	
Bromley South 4	a			17 42					18 13					18 42					19 13					19 42	
Elephant & Castle ⊖	a																								
London Blackfriars 3 ⊖	a																								
London Victoria 15 ⊖	a			18 02					18 29					19 02					19 29					20 02	
Ebbsfleet International	a	17 17					17 47					18 17					18 47					19 17			
Stratford International ⊖	a	17 29					17 59					18 29					18 59					19 29			
St Pancras Internatnl 15 ⊖	a	17 36					18 09					18 36					19 06					19 36			

Table 212

Sundays

Ramsgate, Dover, Sheerness-on-Sea and Medway - London

Network Diagram - see first Page of Table 212

		SE	SE	SE	SE [1]	SE [1]	SE	SE	SE	SE [1]		SE	SE	SE	SE [1]	SE [1]	SE	SE	SE	SE [1]		SE	SE	SE	
Ramsgate [4]	d					18 34	18 59									19 34	19 59								
Dumpton Park	d					18 37										19 37									
Broadstairs	d					18 40	19 05									19 40	20 05								
Margate [4]	d					18 45	19a10									19 45	20a10								
Westgate-on-Sea	d					18 49										19 49									
Birchington-on-Sea	d					18 53										19 53									
Herne Bay	d					19 02										20 02									
Chestfield & Swalecliffe	d					19 05										20 05									
Whitstable	d					19 08										20 08									
Dover Priory [4]	d				18 34										19 34										
Kearsney	d				18 38										19 38										
Shepherds Well	d				18 43										19 43										
Snowdown	d				18 47										19 47										
Aylesham	d				18 49										19 49										
Adisham	d				18 52										19 52										
Bekesbourne	d				18 56										19 56										
Canterbury East [4]	d				19 01					19 22					20 01										
Selling	d				19 10										20 10										
Faversham [2]	a				19 15	19 17				19 33					20 15	20 17									
	d		18 58		19 21				19 28	19 34				19 58	20 21				20 28	20 34				20 58	
Teynham	d									19 40										20 40					
Sheerness-on-Sea	d	18 42										19 42										20 42			
Queenborough	d	18 46										19 46										20 46			
Swale	d	18 50										19 50										20 50			
Kemsley	d	18 54										19 54										20 54			
Sittingbourne [4]	a	19 01	19 06		19 28				19 36	19 44		19 59		20 06	20 28				20 36	20 44		20 59		21 06	
	d		19 07		19 29				19 37	19 45				20 07	20 29				20 37	20 45				21 07	
Newington	d									19 50										20 50					
Rainham (Kent)	d		19 15		19 36				19 45	19 54				20 15	20 36				20 45	20 54				21 15	
Gillingham (Kent) [4]	d		19 20	19 24	19 41			19 45	19 50	19 59			20 15	20 20	20 41			20 45	20 50	20 59			21 15	21 20	
Chatham [4]	d		19 24	19 28	19 46			19 49	19 54	20 04			20 19	20 24	20 46			20 49	20 54	21 04			21 19	21 24	
Rochester [4]	d		19 27	19 30	19 48			19 51	19 57	20 06			20 21	20 27	20 48			20 51	20 57	21 06			21 21	21 27	
Strood [4]	a		19 31	19 35				19 56	20 01				20 26	20 31				20 56	21 01				21 26	21 31	
Gravesend [4]	a		19 42	19 47				20 08	20 12				20 38	20 42				21 08	21 12				21 38	21 42	
Greenhithe for Bluewater	a			19 53				20 17					20 47					21 17					21 47		
Dartford [4]	a			19 58				20 24					20 54					21 24					21 54		
London Bridge [4] ⊖	a			20 36				21 06					21 36					22 06					22 36		
London Cannon Street [4] ⊖	a																								
London Waterloo (East) [4] ⊖	a			20 41				21 11					21 41					22 11					22 41		
London Charing Cross [4] ⊖	a			20 44				21 14					21 44					22 14					22 44		
Sole Street	d									20 17										21 17					
Meopham	d									20 19										21 19					
Longfield	d									20 23										21 23					
Farningham Road	d									20 27										21 27					
Swanley [4]	a									20 32										21 32					
St Mary Cray	a									20 36										21 36					
Bromley South [4]	a				20 13					20 42					21 13					21 42					
Elephant & Castle ⊖	a																								
London Blackfriars [3] ⊖	a																								
London Victoria [15] ⊖	a				20 29					21 02					21 29					22 02					
Ebbsfleet International	a		19 47						20 17					20 47					21 17					21 47	
Stratford International ⊖	a		19 59						20 29					21 02					21 29					21 59	
St Pancras Internatnl [15] ⊖	a		20 06						20 36					21 09					21 36					22 06	

Table 212

Sundays

Ramsgate, Dover, Sheerness-on-Sea and Medway - London

Network Diagram - see first Page of Table 212

		SE 1	SE 1	SE	SE	SE	SE 1		SE	SE	SE	SE 1	SE 1	SE	SE 1	SE 1	SE		SE 1	SE	SE				
Ramsgate 4	d		20 34	20 59									21 34	21 59					22 34	22 59					
Dumpton Park	d		20 37										21 37						22 37						
Broadstairs	d		20 40	21 05									21 40	22 05					22 40	23 05					
Margate 4	d		20 45	21a10									21 45	22a10					22 45	23a10					
Westgate-on-Sea	d		20 49										21 49						22 49						
Birchington-on-Sea	d		20 53										21 53						22 53						
Herne Bay	d		21 02										22 02						23 02						
Chestfield & Swalecliffe	d		21 05										22 05						23 05						
Whitstable	d		21 08										22 08						23 08						
Dover Priory 4	d	20 34										21 34				22 34									
Kearsney	d	20 38										21 38				22 38									
Shepherds Well	d	20 43										21 43				22 43									
Snowdown	d	20 47										21 47				22 47									
Aylesham	d	20 49										21 49				22 49									
Adisham	d	20 52										21 52				22 52									
Bekesbourne	d	20 56										21 56				22 56									
Canterbury East 4	d	21 01										22 01				23 01									
Selling	d	21 10										22 10				23 10									
Faversham 2	a	21 15	21 17									22 15	22 17			23 15			23 17						
	d	21 21				21 28	21 34				21 58	22 21			22 34				23 21						
Teynham	d						21 40								22 40										
Sheerness-on-Sea	d								21 42								22 42				23 42				
Queenborough	d								21 46								22 46				23 46				
Swale	d								21 50								22 50				23 50				
Kemsley	d								21 54								22 54				23 54				
Sittingbourne 4	a	21 28				21 36	21 44		21 59		22 06	22 28			22 44		22 59		23 28		23 59				
	d	21 29				21 37	21 45				22 07	22 29			22 45				23 29						
Newington	d						21 50								22 50										
Rainham (Kent)	d	21 36				21 45	21 54				22 15	22 36			22 54				23 36						
Gillingham (Kent) 4	d	21 41			21 45	21 50	21 59			22 15	22 20	22 41			22 59				23 41						
Chatham 4	d	21 46			21 49	21 54	22 04			22 19	22 24	22 46			23 04				23 46						
Rochester 4	d	21 48			21 51	21 57	22 06			22 21	22 27	22 48			23 06				23 48						
Strood 4	a				21 56	22 01				22 26	22 31														
Gravesend 4	a				22 08	22 12				22 38	22 42														
Greenhithe for Bluewater	a				22 17					22 47															
Dartford 4	a				22 24					22 54															
London Bridge 4 ⊖	a				23 06					23 36															
London Cannon Street 4 ⊖	a																								
London Waterloo (East) 4 ⊖	a				23 11					23 41															
London Charing Cross 4 ⊖	a				23 14					23 44															
Sole Street	d						22 17								23 17										
Meopham	d						22 19								23 19										
Longfield	d						22 23								23 23										
Farningham Road	d						22 27								23 27										
Swanley 4	a						22 32								23 32										
St Mary Cray	a						22 36								23 36										
Bromley South 4	a	22 13					22 42					23 13			23 42				00 13						
Elephant & Castle ⊖	a																								
London Blackfriars 3 ⊖	a																								
London Victoria 15 ⊖	a	22 29					23 02					23 29			00 02				00 29						
Ebbsfleet International	a					22 17					22 47														
Stratford International ⊖	a					22 29					22 59														
St Pancras Internatnl 15 ⊖	a					22 36					23 06														

Network Diagram for Tables 216, 217, 218, 219, 221, 222

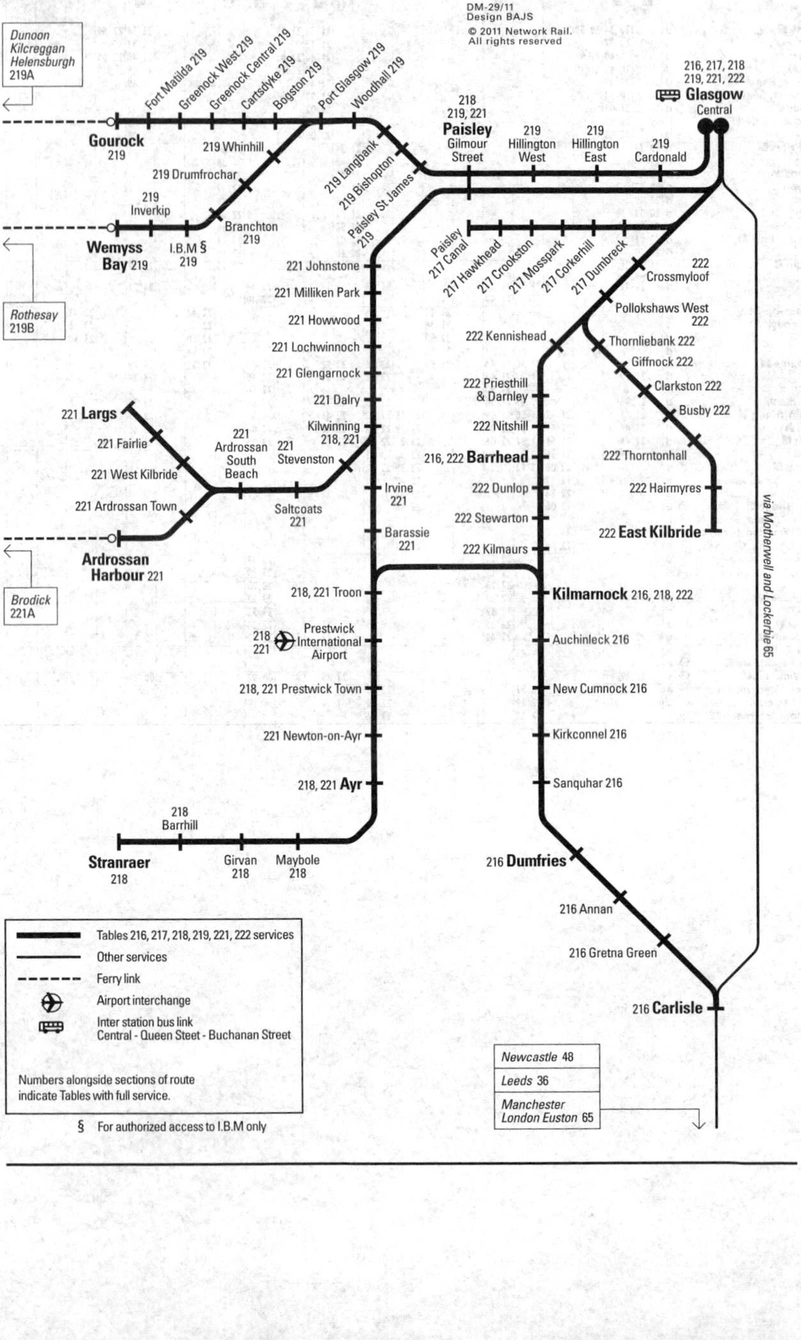

Glasgow Central and Kilmarnock - Dumfries and Carlisle

Network Diagram - see first Page of Table 216

Miles	Miles				SR MO	SR MX	SR	SR	SR SO	SR SX	SR	SR	SR SO		SR	SR SO	SR	SR	SR SO	SR	SR	SR SO	SR		SR	SR SO
0	—	**Glasgow Central** 15	65,222	d	22p12	23p12					07 07	08 37			10 12		12 12	13 12			16 12		17 42		19 12	
7½	—	Barrhead	222	d	22p23	23p33					07 22	08 49									16 23		17 53		19 23	
24¼	74½	**Kilmarnock** 3	218,222	a	22p48	23p59					07 48	09 18			10 51		12 48	13 50			16 49		18 22		19 51	
—	—			d	22p49	23p59					07 48	09 18			10 51		12 48	13 50			16 49		18 26		19 51	
38	89¼	Auchinleck		d	23p06	00 18					08 05	09 35			11 08		13 05	14 07			17 06		18 42		20 08	
45½	96¾	New Cumnock		d	23p14	00 28					08 13	09 43			11 16		13 13	14 15			17 14		18 51		20 16	
52¾	104½	Kirkconnel		d	23p23	00 39					08 22	09 52			11 25		13 22	14 24			17 23		18 59		20 25	
56	107¾	Sanquhar		d	23p28	00 44					08 26	09 57			11 30		13 27	14 29			17 28		19 04		20 30	
82¼	135	**Dumfries**		d	23p56	01a17	04 56	06 17	07 43	07 45	08 57	10 23	11 02		11 58	13 10	13 55	14 57	16 02	17 07	17 56	18 41	19 33		20 57	22 13
97¾	150½	Annan		d	00 11		05 11	06 32	07 58	08 00	09 12	10 38	11 17		12 13	13 25	14 10	15 12	16 17	17 22	18 11	18 56	19 48		21 12	22 28
105½	158	Gretna Green		d	00 20		05 20	06 41	08 07	08 09	09 22	10 47	11 26		12 22	13 34	14 19	15 21	16 26	17 31	18 20	19 05	19 57		21 21	22 37
115½	168	**Carlisle** 8	65	a	00 34		05 33	06 54	08 20	08 22	09 37	11 02	11 39		12 35	13 52	14 32	15 34	16 39	17 44	18 35	19 18	20 11		21 43	22 50
—	—	Newcastle 8	48	a				08 57		10 00	11 07						15 54				20 15					

			SR SX	SR SO	SR SX
Glasgow Central 15	65,222	d	21 12	22 12	23 12
Barrhead	222	d	21 26	22 23	23 33
Kilmarnock 3	218,222	a	21 53	22 50	23 59
		d	21 53	22 51	23 59
Auchinleck		d	22 10	23 07	00 18
New Cumnock		d	22 18	23 16	00 28
Kirkconnel		d	22 27	23 24	00 39
Sanquhar		d	22 32	23 29	00 44
Dumfries		d	23 00	23 57	01a17
Annan		d	23 15	00 12	
Gretna Green		d	23 24	00 21	
Carlisle 8	65	a	23 37	00 34	
Newcastle 8	48	a			

Sundays

			SR A	SR	SR	SR	SR	SR
Glasgow Central 15	65,222	d	22p12			15 12		22 12
Barrhead	222	d	22p23			15 26		22 23
Kilmarnock 3	218,222	a	22p50			15 52		22 48
		d	22p51			15 53		22 49
Auchinleck		d	23p07			16 10		23 06
New Cumnock		d	23p16			16 18		23 14
Kirkconnel		d	23p24			16 27		23 23
Sanquhar		d	23p29			16 32		23 28
Dumfries		d	23p57	13 00	15 01	17 00	19 01	23 56
Annan		d	00 12	13 15	15 16	17 15	19 16	00 11
Gretna Green		d	00 21	13 24	15 25	17 24	19 25	00 20
Carlisle 8	65	a	00 34	13 37	15 38	17 37	19 38	00 34
Newcastle 8	48	a						

A not 11 December

For connections to London Euston please refer to Table 65

Carlisle and Dumfries - Kilmarnock and Glasgow Central

Network Diagram - see first Page of Table 216

Miles	Miles			SR	SR	SR	SR	SR SX	SR SO	SR	SR SO	SR	SR SO	SR	SR	SR SO	SR	SR	SR SO	SR	SR
—	—	Newcastle 8	48 d				06 30	06 47						13 22				17 16			
0	0	**Carlisle 8**	65 d		05 27	06 08	08 15	08 15	09 55	11 15	12 20	13 12	14 22	15 12	16 17	17 12	17 55	19 17	20 22	21 12	23 10
9¾	9¾	Gretna Green	d		05 38	06 19	08 26	08 26	10 06	11 26	12 31	13 23	14 33	15 23	16 28	17 23	18 06	19 28	20 33	21 23	23 21
17½	17½	Annan	d		05 47	06 27	08 34	08 34	10 14	11 34	12 40	13 31	14 41	15 31	16 36	17 31	18 14	19 37	20 41	21 31	23 29
33	33	**Dumfries**	d	05 46	06a04	06 46	08 53	08 53	10a32	11 53	12a57	13 48	14a59	15 50	16a54	17a49	18 31	19 55	20a59	21 50	23a47
59¼	59¼	Sanquhar	d	06 12		07 12	09 19	09 19		12 19		14 16		16 16			18 57	20 21		22 16	
62½	62½	Kirkconnel	d	06 17		07 17	09 24	09 24		12 24		14 21		16 21			19 02	20 26		22 21	
69¾	69¾	New Cumnock	d	06 26		07 26	09 33	09 33		12 33		14 30		16 30			19 13	20 35		22 30	
77¼	77¼	Auchinleck	d	06 34		07 34	09 41	09 41		12 41		14 38		16 38			19 21	20 44		22 38	
91	91	**Kilmarnock 3**	218,222 a	06 51		07 51	09 57	09 57		12 57		14 55		16 55			19 38	21 00		22 55	
—	—		d	06 52		07 53	09 57	09 57		12 57		14 57		16 57			19 57	21 00		22 57	
107¾	—	Barrhead	222 d	07 18		08 20	10 22	10 22						17 22			20 22	21 25		23 22	
115¼	—	**Glasgow Central 15**	65,222 a	07 31		08 37	10 37	10 37		13 35		15 33		17 36			20 36	21 39		23 35	

Sundays

		SR	SR	SR	SR
Newcastle 8	48 d				
Carlisle 8	65 d	13 12	15 12	19 12	21 22
Gretna Green	d	13 23	15 23	19 23	21 33
Annan	d	13 31	15 31	19 31	21 41
Dumfries	d	13 50	15a49	19 50	21a59
Sanquhar	d	14 16		20 16	
Kirkconnel	d	14 21		20 21	
New Cumnock	d	14 30		20 30	
Auchinleck	d	14 38		20 38	
Kilmarnock 3	218,222 a	14 55		20 55	
	d	14 57		20 57	
Barrhead	222 d	15 21		21 21	
Glasgow Central 15	65,222 a	15 36		21 35	

For connections to London Euston please refer to Table 65

Table 217

Mondays to Saturdays

Glasgow Central - Paisley Canal

Network Diagram - see first Page of Table 216

Miles			SR SO	SR	SR	SR	SR	SR	SR	SR	SR	SR	SR	SR	SR	SR	SR	SR	SR	SR	SR	SR	SR
0	**Glasgow Central** 15	d	00 08	06 08	06 38	07 08	07 38	08 08	08 37	09 08	09 38	10 08	10 38	11 08	11 38	12 08	12 38	13 08	13 38	14 08	14 38	15 08	15 38
1¾	Dumbreck	d	00 14	06 14	06 44	07 14	07 44	08 14	08 43	09 14	09 44	10 14	10 44	11 14	11 44	12 14	12 44	13 14	13 44	14 14	14 44	15 14	15 44
3¼	Corkerhill	d	00 16	06 16	06 46	07 16	07 46	08 16	08 45	09 16	09 46	10 16	10 46	11 16	11 46	12 16	12 46	13 16	13 46	14 16	14 46	15 16	15 46
3¾	Mosspark	d	00 18	06 18	06 48	07 18	07 48	08 18	08 47	09 18	09 48	10 18	10 48	11 18	11 48	12 18	12 48	13 18	13 48	14 18	14 48	15 18	15 48
4½	Crookston	d	00 20	06 20	06 50	07 20	07 50	08 20	08 49	09 20	09 50	10 20	10 50	11 20	11 50	12 20	12 50	13 20	13 50	14 20	14 50	15 20	15 50
6½	Hawkhead	d	00 23	06 23	06 53	07 23	07 53	08 23	08 53	09 23	09 53	10 23	10 53	11 23	11 53	12 23	12 53	13 23	13 53	14 23	14 53	15 23	15 53
7	**Paisley Canal**	a	00 26	06 26	06 56	07 26	07 56	08 26	08 56	09 26	09 56	10 26	10 56	11 26	11 56	12 26	12 56	13 26	13 56	14 26	14 56	15 26	15 56

		SR	SR	SR	SR	SR	SR	SR	SR	SR	SR	SR	SR	SR	SR	SR
Glasgow Central 15	d	16 08	16 38	17 08	17 38	18 08	18 38	19 08	19 38	20 08	20 38	21 08	21 38	22 08	22 38	23 08
Dumbreck	d	16 14	16 44	17 14	17 44	18 14	18 44	19 14	19 44	20 14	20 44	21 14	21 44	22 14	22 44	23 14
Corkerhill	d	16 16	16 46	17 16	17 46	18 16	18 46	19 16	19 46	20 16	20 46	21 16	21 46	22 16	22 45	23 16
Mosspark	d	16 18	16 48	17 18	17 48	18 18	18 48	19 18	19 48	20 18	20 48	21 18	21 48	22 18	22 47	23 18
Crookston	d	16 20	16 50	17 20	17 50	18 20	18 50	19 20	19 50	20 20	20 50	21 20	21 50	22 20	22 49	23 20
Hawkhead	d	16 23	16 53	17 23	17 53	18 23	18 53	19 23	19 53	20 23	20 53	21 23	21 53	22 23	22 53	23 23
Paisley Canal	a	16 26	16 56	17 26	17 56	18 26	18 56	19 26	19 56	20 26	20 56	21 26	21 56	22 26	22 56	23 26

Table 217

Mondays to Saturdays

Paisley Canal - Glasgow Central

Network Diagram - see first Page of Table 216

Miles			SR	SR	SR	SR	SR	SR	SR	SR	SR	SR	SR	SR	SR	SR	SR	SR	SR	SR	SR	SR	SR
0	**Paisley Canal**	d	06 30	07 00	07 30	08 00	08 30	09 00	09 30	10 00	10 30	11 00	11 30	12 00	12 30	13 00	13 30	14 00	14 30	15 00	15 30	16 00	16 30
0½	Hawkhead	d	06 33	07 03	07 33	08 03	08 33	09 03	09 33	10 03	10 33	11 03	11 33	12 03	12 33	13 03	13 33	14 03	14 33	15 03	15 33	16 03	16 33
2½	Crookston	d	06 36	07 06	07 36	08 06	08 36	09 06	09 36	10 06	10 36	11 06	11 36	12 06	12 36	13 06	13 36	14 06	14 36	15 06	15 36	16 06	16 36
3¼	Mosspark	d	06 38	07 08	07 38	08 08	08 38	09 08	09 38	10 08	10 38	11 08	11 38	12 08	12 38	13 08	13 38	14 08	14 38	15 08	15 38	16 08	16 38
3¾	Corkerhill	d	06 40	07 10	07 40	08 10	08 40	09 10	09 40	10 10	10 40	11 10	11 40	12 10	12 40	13 10	13 40	14 10	14 40	15 10	15 40	16 10	16 40
5¼	Dumbreck	d	06 43	07 13	07 44	08 13	08 43	09 13	09 43	10 13	10 43	11 13	11 43	12 13	12 43	13 13	13 43	14 13	14 43	15 13	15 43	16 13	16 43
7	**Glasgow Central** 15	a	06 49	07 20	07 52	08 21	08 53	09 19	09 49	10 19	10 49	11 19	11 49	12 19	12 49	13 19	13 49	14 19	14 49	15 19	15 49	16 19	16 49

		SR	SR	SR	SR	SR	SR	SR	SR	SR	SR	SR	SR	SR
Paisley Canal	d	17 00	17 30	18 00	18 30	19 00	19 30	20 00	20 30	21 00	21 30	22 00	22 30	23 00
Hawkhead	d	17 03	17 33	18 03	18 33	19 03	19 33	20 03	20 33	21 03	21 33	22 03	22 33	23 03
Crookston	d	17 06	17 36	18 06	18 36	19 06	19 36	20 06	20 36	21 06	21 36	22 06	22 36	23 06
Mosspark	d	17 08	17 38	18 08	18 38	19 08	19 38	20 08	20 38	21 08	21 38	22 08	22 38	23 08
Corkerhill	d	17 10	17 40	18 10	18 40	19 10	19 40	20 10	20 40	21 10	21 40	22 10	22 40	23 10
Dumbreck	d	17 13	17 43	18 13	18 43	19 13	19 43	20 13	20 43	21 13	21 43	22 13	22 43	23 13
Glasgow Central 15	a	17 19	17 53	18 19	18 49	19 19	19 50	20 19	20 49	21 19	21 49	22 19	22 50	23 22

No Sunday Service

Table 218

Mondays to Saturdays

Glasgow Central and Kilmarnock - Girvan, Stranraer

Network Diagram - see first Page of Table 216

Miles	Miles			SR	SR	SR	SR	SR	SR	SR	SR	SR	SR	SR	SR	SR	SR	SR	SR	SR	SR
				MX							SO	SX								SX	SO
									◇		◇	◇									
0	—	**Glasgow Cen.** 15 219,221,222	d	22p12			*07c30*	*08c00*	09 41	*10c30*	11 40	11 42	*12c30*	*13c30*	15e12	*16c30*	*17e12*	*18c30*	*20c30*	*22e12*	*22c30*
7¼	—	Paisley Gilmour St. 219,221 ✈	d						09 54		11 53	11 53									
—	—	Kilwinning 4 221	d						10 14		12 11	12 11									
—	0	**Kilmarnock** 3 222	a	22p50											15 50		17 51			22 50	
—	—		d	23p06				08 37		11 05			13 04	14 04	16 03	17 04	18 09	19 05	21 10	23 06	23 06
35	10¾	Troon 221	d	23p18				08 49		11 18			13 16	14 16	16 16	17 16	18 21	19 17	21 22	23 18	23 18
37¾	11¾	Prestwick Int. Airport 221 ✈	d	23p23				08 54		11 23			13 21	14 21	16 20	17 21	18 26	19 21	21 27	23 23	23 23
38¼	12½	Prestwick Town 221	d	23p25				08 56		11 25			13 23	14 23	16 22	17 23	18 28	19 23	21 29	23 25	23 25
41½	15½	**Ayr** 221	a	23p30				09 03	10 35	11 32	12 29	12 29	13 30	14 30	16 30	17 30	18 36	19 30	21 34	23 30	23 30
—	—		d	23p31	05 30	06 35	08 37	09 05	10 35	11 33	12 30	12 30	13 32	14 31	16 30	17 31	18 37	19 31	21 35	23 31	23 31
50½	24½	Maybole	d	23p42	05 41	06 46	08 48	09 16	10 47	11 44	12 41	12 41	13 43	14 42	16 42	17 42	18 48	19 42	21 46	23 42	23 42
62¾	36½	**Girvan**	d	23p57	05a57	07a02	09 03	09a32	11 07	12a00	12 56	12 56	13a59	14a58	16a58	17 57	19a04	20 03	22a02	23 57	23 57
75	51¼	Barrhill	d	00 16			09 22		11 26		13 16	13 16				18 16		20 22		00 16	00 16
101	77¼	**Stranraer**	a	00 52			09 58		12 02		13 52	13 52				18 52		20 58		00 52	00 52

Sundays

		SR	SR	SR	SR
			◇	◇	
		A			
Glasgow Cen. 15 219,221,222	d		11 42	16 25	*17c00*
Paisley Gilmour St. 219,221 ✈	d		11 53	16 39	
Kilwinning 4 221	d		12 11	16 56	
Kilmarnock 3 222	a				
	d	23p06			
Troon 221	d	23p18			
Prestwick Int. Airport 221 ✈	d	23p23			
Prestwick Town 221	d	23p25			
Ayr 221	a	23p30	12 29	17 17	
	d	23p31	12 30	17 19	18 40
Maybole	d	23p42	12 41	17 30	18 51
Girvan	d	23p57	12 56	17 47	19 06
Barrhill	d	00 16	13 16	18 06	19 25
Stranraer	a	00 52	13 52	18 42	20 07

A not 11 December

c Change at Ayr (Table 221)

e Passengers may leave 18 min later by changing at Ayr (Table 221)

Table 218

Mondays to Saturdays

Stranraer and Girvan - Kilmarnock and Glasgow Central

Network Diagram - see first Page of Table 216

Miles	Miles			SR	SR	SR	SR	SR	SR	SR	SR	SR	SR	SR	SR	SR	SR	SR
					◇			◇		◇			◇			◇	◇	
0	—	**Stranraer**	d			07 11		10 12		12 36			14 43			19 08	21 13	
26	—	Barrhill	d			07 45		10 46		13 17			15 17			19 43	21 48	
38¼	—	**Girvan**	d	06 02	07 07	08 03	09 37	11 04	12 31	13 35	14 32	15 03	15 35	17 32	19 09	20 01	22 06	22 27
50½	—	Maybole	d	06 18	07 23	08 19	09 53	11 20	12 55	13 57	14 56	15 19	15 51	17 56	19 25	20 17	22 22	22 43
59¼	—	**Ayr**	a	06 30	07 36	08 31	10 05	11 36	13 07	14 09	15 08	15 31	16 04	18 08	19 37	20 29	22 34	22 55
—	—		d		07 36		10 06	11 37	13 08	14 10	15 18	15 32	16 06	18 18	19 38	20 30	22 35	
62½	—	Prestwick Town 221	a		07 41		10 11	11 42	13 13		15 23		16 11	18 23	19 43		22 40	
63	—	Prestwick Int. Airport 221 ✈	a		07 44		10 13	11 44	13 15		15 25		16 14	18 25	19 45			
63¼	0	Troon 221	a		07 49		10 18	11 49	13 20		15 30		16 19	18 30	19 50		22 45	
—	10¾	**Kilmarnock** 3	a		08 07		10 34	12 05	13 36		15 47		16 34	18 46	20 06			
—	—		d								15 57							
—	—	Glengarnock	d															
74¼	—	Kilwinning 4 221	a							14 27		15 47					22 55	
93¾	—	Paisley Gilmour St. 219,221 ✈	a							14 46		16 15				21 11	23 14	
101	—	**Glasgow Cen.** 15 219,221,222	a	*07c38*	*08c35*	*09c36*	*11c07*	*12c36*	*14c07*	15 01	16e33	16 31	*17c09*	*19c08*	*20c36*	21 27	23 25	*23c58*

Sundays

		SR	SR	SR
		◇	◇	◇
Stranraer	d	10 40	14 40	19 45
Barrhill	d	11 14	15 14	20 19
Girvan	d	11 32	15 32	20 37
Maybole	d	11 48	15 48	20 53
Ayr	a	12 00	15 59	21 04
	d	12 00	15 59	21 04
Prestwick Town 221	a			
Prestwick Int. Airport 221 ✈	a			
Troon 221	a			
Kilmarnock 3	a			21 26
	d			21 31
Glengarnock	d			
Kilwinning 4 221	a	12 15	16 14	
Paisley Gilmour St. 219,221 ✈	a	12 36	16 38	
Glasgow Cen. 15 219,221,222	a	12 51	16 49	22 05

c Change at Ayr (Table 221)

e Passengers may arrive 16 09 by changing at Ayr (Table 221)

Glasgow Central - Wemyss Bay and Gourock

Network Diagram - see first Page of Table 216

Miles	Miles			SR	SR MX	SR	SR	SR	SR	SR	SR	SR	SR	SR	SR	SR	SR	SR	SR	SR	SR	SR	SR
0	0	**Glasgow Central** 15 221	d	23p20	23p50	05 55	06 05	06 25	06 32	06 55	07 04	07 25	07 35	07 50	08 05	08 28	08 36	08 50	09 05	09 25	09 35	09 50	10 05
3¾	3¾	Cardonald	d	23p27	23p57				06 39		07 12	07 32	07 42		08 12		08 42		09 12		09 42		10 12
4½	4½	Hillington East	d	23p29	23p59		06 13		06 41		07 14	07 34	07 44		08 14		08 44		09 14		09 44		10 14
5	5	Hillington West	d	23p31	00 01	06 03	06 15		06 43	07 03	07 16	07 36	07 46	07 58	08 16		08 46		09 16		09 46		10 16
7¼	7¼	Paisley Gilmour Street 221 ⇐	a	23p35	00 05	06 07	06 19	06 35	06 47	07 07	07 20	07 40	07 50	08 02	08 20	08 38	08 50	09 00	09 19	09 35	09 50	10 01	10 20
—	—		d	23p35	00 05	06 07	06 19	06 36	06 47	07 07	07 20	07 40	07 51	08 02	08 20	08 38	08 50	09 01	09 20	09 36	09 50	10 01	10 20
8	8	Paisley St James	d	23p37	00 07			06 38			07 22		07 53		08 22		08 52		09 22		09 52		10 22
12¼	12¼	Bishopton	d	23p43	00 13	06 13	06 25	06 44	06 53	07 13	07 28	07 46	07 59	08 08	08 28	08 44	08 58	09 07	09 28	09 42	09 58	10 07	10 28
16¼	16¼	Langbank	d	23p49	00 19			06 49			07 34		08 04		08 34		09 04		09 34		10 04		10 34
19	19	Woodhall	d	23p53	00 23		06 33	06 53	07 01		07 38	07 54	08 08		08 38		09 08		09 38		10 08		10 38
20¼	20¼	Port Glasgow	d	23p56	00 26	06 23	06 36	06 56	07 04	07 23	07 41	07 57	08 11	08 18	08 41	08 53	09 11	09 16	09 41	09 51	10 11	10 16	10 41
—	22½	Whinhill	d				06 40		07 08					08 22				09 21				10 21	
—	23	Drumfrochar	d				06 43		07 11					08 25				09 23				10 23	
—	24¾	Branchton	d				06 46		07 14					08 28				09 26				10 26	
—	25½	I.B.M. §	d				06 48		07 16					08 30				09 29				10 29	
—	28¾	Inverkip	d				06 53		07 25					08 35				09 34				10 34	
—	31	**Wemyss Bay**	a				06 58		07 30					08 40				09 40				10 40	
21¼	—	Bogston	d	23p58	00 28			06 58		07 25	07 43	07 59	08 13		08 43		09 13		09 43		10 13		10 43
22	—	Cartsdyke	d	00 01	00 30	06 26		07 01		07 27	07 45	08 01	08 16		08 45		09 15		09 45		10 15		10 45
23	—	Greenock Central	d	00 02	00 32	06 28		07 03		07 29	07 47	08 03	08 18		08 47	08 58	09 17		09 47	09 56	10 17		10 47
23¾	—	Greenock West	d	00 05	00 35	06 31		07 05		07 32	07 50	08 06	08 20		08 50	09 01	09 20		09 50	09 59	10 20		10 50
25	—	Fort Matilda	d	00 08	00 38			07 08		07 35	07 53	08 09	08 23		08 53	09 04	09 23		09 53	10 02	10 23		10 53
26¼	—	**Gourock**	a	00 12	00 42	06 36		07 13		07 39	07 57	08 13	08 28		08 57	09 09	09 27		09 58	10 06	10 27		10 57

		SR	SR	SR	SR	SR	SR	SR	SR	SR	SR	SR	SR	SR	SR	SR	SR	SR	SR	SR	SR	SR	SR
Glasgow Central 15 221	d	10 25	10 35	10 50	11 05	11 25	11 35	11 50	12 05	12 25	12 35	12 50	13 05	13 25	13 35	13 50	14 05	14 25	14 35	14 50	15 05	15 25	15 35
Cardonald	d		10 42		11 12		11 42		12 12		12 42		13 12		13 42		14 12		14 42		15 12		15 42
Hillington East	d		10 44		11 14		11 44		12 14		12 44		13 14		13 44		14 14		14 44		15 14		15 44
Hillington West	d		10 46		11 16		11 46		12 16		12 46		13 16		13 46		14 16		14 46		15 16		15 46
Paisley Gilmour Street 221 ⇐	a	10 35	10 50	11 00	11 19	11 35	11 50	12 00	12 20	12 35	12 50	13 00	13 20	13 35	13 50	14 00	14 20	14 35	14 50	15 00	15 19	15 35	15 50
	d	10 36	10 50	11 01	11 20	11 36	11 50	12 01	12 20	12 36	12 50	13 01	13 20	13 36	13 50	14 01	14 20	14 36	14 50	15 01	15 20	15 36	15 50
Paisley St James	d		10 52		11 22		11 52		12 22		12 52		13 22		13 52		14 22		14 52		15 22		15 52
Bishopton	d	10 42	10 58	11 07	11 28	11 42	11 58	12 07	12 28	12 42	12 58	13 07	13 28	13 42	13 58	14 07	14 28	14 42	14 58	15 07	15 28	15 42	15 58
Langbank	d		11 04		11 34		12 04		12 34		13 04		13 34		14 04		14 34		15 04		15 34		16 04
Woodhall	d		11 08		11 38		12 08		12 38		13 08		13 38		14 08		14 38		15 08		15 38		16 08
Port Glasgow	d	10 51	11 11	11 16	11 41	11 51	12 11	12 16	12 41	12 51	13 11	13 16	13 41	13 51	14 11	14 16	14 41	14 51	15 11	15 16	15 41	15 51	16 11
Whinhill	d			11 21				12 21				13 21				14 21				15 21			
Drumfrochar	d			11 23				12 23				13 23				14 23				15 23			
Branchton	d			11 26				12 26				13 26				14 26				15 26			
I.B.M. §	d			11 29				12 29				13 29				14 29				15 29			
Inverkip	d			11 34				12 34				13 34				14 34				15 34			
Wemyss Bay	a			11 40				12 40				13 40				14 40				15 40			
Bogston	d		11 13		11 43		12 13		12 43		13 13		13 43		14 13		14 43		15 13		15 43		16 13
Cartsdyke	d		11 15		11 45		12 15		12 45		13 15		13 45		14 15		14 45		15 15		15 45		16 15
Greenock Central	d	10 56	11 17		11 47	11 56	12 17		12 47	12 56	13 17		13 47	13 56	14 17		14 47	14 56	15 17		15 47	15 56	16 17
Greenock West	d	10 59	11 20		11 50	11 59	12 20		12 50	12 59	13 20		13 50	13 59	14 20		14 50	14 59	15 20		15 50	15 59	16 20
Fort Matilda	d	11 02	11 23		11 53	12 02	12 23		12 53	13 02	13 23		13 53	14 02	14 23		14 53	15 02	15 23		15 53	16 02	16 23
Gourock	a	11 06	11 27		11 57	12 06	12 27		12 57	13 06	13 27		13 57	14 06	14 27		14 57	15 06	15 27		15 57	16 06	16 27

		SR	SR	SR	SR	SR	SR	SR	SR	SR	SR	SR	SR	SR	SR	SR	SR	SR	SR	SR	SR	SR
Glasgow Central 15 221	d	15 50	16 05	16 23	16 33	16 55	17 05	17 15	17 25	17 40	17 55	18 05	18 25	18 35	18 50	19 05	19 25	19 40	19 50	20 05	20 35	20 50
Cardonald	d		16 12	16 30	16 41		17 12	17 22		17 47		18 12		18 42		19 12		19 47		20 12	20 42	
Hillington East	d		16 14	16 32	16 43		17 14	17 24		17 49		18 14		18 44		19 14		19 49		20 14	20 44	
Hillington West	d	15 58	16 16	16 34	16 45	17 02	17 16			17 51		18 16		18 46		19 15		19 51		20 15	20 46	
Paisley Gilmour Street 221 ⇐	a	16 02	16 20	16 38	16 48	17 06	17 20	17 29	17 37	17 55	18 05	18 20	18 35	18 50	19 01	19 19	19 35	19 55	20 00	20 21	20 50	21 00
	d	16 02	16 20	16 38	16 48	17 06	17 21	17 29	17 37	17 55	18 06	18 20	18 36	18 50	19 01	19 20	19 36	19 55	20 01	20 21	20 50	21 01
Paisley St James	d		16 22	16 40			17 23			17 57		18 22		18 52		19 22		19 57		20 23	20 52	
Bishopton	d	16 08	16 28	16 46	16 54	17 13	17 29	17 35		18 03	18 10	18 28	18 42	18 58	19 07	19 28	19 42	20 03	20 07	20 29	20 58	21 07
Langbank	d		16 34	16 52			17 34			18 09		18 34		19 04		19 34		20 09		20 35	21 04	
Woodhall	d		16 38	16 56			17 38			18 12		18 38		19 08		19 38		20 13		20 39	21 08	
Port Glasgow	d	16 18	16 41	16 59	17 04	17 23	17 41	17 45	17 51	18 14	18 21	18 41	18 51	19 11	19 16	19 41	19 51	20 16	20 17	20 42	21 11	21 16
Whinhill	d	16 22			17 08			17 49			18 25				19 21			20 20			21 15	
Drumfrochar	d	16 25			17 11			17 52			18 28				19 23			20 23			21 18	
Branchton	d	16 28			17 14			17 55			18 31				19 26			20 26			21 21	
I.B.M. §	d	16 30						17 57			18 33				19 29			20 28			21 23	
Inverkip	d	16 35			17 19			18 02			18 38				19 34			20 33			21 28	
Wemyss Bay	a	16 40			17 25			18 08			18 44				19 40			20 38			21 34	
Bogston	d		16 43	17 01		17 25	17 43			18 18		18 43		19 13		19 43				20 44		
Cartsdyke	d		16 45	17 03		17 27	17 46			18 20		18 45		19 15		19 45			20 20	20 46		21 20
Greenock Central	d		16 47	17 05		17 29	17 48		17 56	18 22		18 47	18 56	19 17		19 47	19 56		20 22	20 48		21 22
Greenock West	d		16 50	17 08		17 32	17 50		17 58	18 25		18 50	18 59	19 20		19 50	19 59		20 25	20 51		21 24
Fort Matilda	d		16 53	17 11		17 35	17 53		18 01	18 28		18 53	19 02	19 23		19 53	20 02		20 28	20 54		21 27
Gourock	a		16 57	17 15		17 39	17 57		18 06	18 32		18 57	19 06	19 27		19 57	20 06		20 34	20 58		21 32

§ For authorised access to and from I.B.M. only

Glasgow Central - Wemyss Bay and Gourock

Network Diagram - see first Page of Table 216

		SR	SR	SR	SR	SR	SR	SR	SR
Glasgow Central 15 221	d	21 05	21 35	21 50	22 05	22 35	22 50	23 20	23 50
Cardonald	d	21 12	21 42		22 12	22 42		23 27	23 57
Hillington East	d	21 14	21 44		22 14	22 44		23 29	23 59
Hillington West	d	21 16	21 46		22 16	22 46		23 31	00 01
Paisley Gilmour Street 221 ✈	a	21 21	21 50	22 00	22 20	22 50	23 00	23 35	00 05
	d	21 21	21 50	22 01	22 20	22 50	23 01	23 35	00 05
Paisley St James	d	21 22	21 52		22 22	22 52		23 37	00 07
Bishopton	d	21 28	21 58	22 07	22 28	22 58	23 07	23 43	00 13
Langbank	d	21 34	22 04		22 34	23 04		23 49	00 19
Woodhall	d	21 38	22 08		22 38	23 08		23 53	00 23
Port Glasgow	d	21 41	22 11	22 16	22 41	23 11	23 16	23 56	00 26
Whinhill	d		22 15			23 15			
Drumfrochar	d		22 18			23 18			
Branchton	d		22 21			23 21			
I.B.M. §	d		22 23			23 23			
Inverkip	d		22 28			23 28			
Wemyss Bay	a		22 34			23 34			
Bogston	d	21 43			22 43			23 58	00 28
Cartsdyke	d	21 45		22 20	22 45		23 20	00 01	00 30
Greenock Central	d	21 47		22 22	22 47		23 22	00 02	00 32
Greenock West	d	21 50		22 24	22 50		23 24	00 05	00 35
Fort Matilda	d	21 53		22 27	22 53		23 29	00 08	00 38
Gourock	a	21 58		22 33	22 57		23 33	00 12	00 42

Sundays

		SR A	SR A	SR	SR	SR	SR	SR	SR	SR	SR	SR	SR	SR	SR	SR	SR	SR
Glasgow Central 15 221	d	23p20	23p50	07 20	07 50	08 20	08 50	09 20	09 50	10 20	10 50	11 20	11 50	12 20	12 50	13 20	13 50	14 20
Cardonald	d	23p27	23p57	07 27		08 27		09 27		10 27		11 27		12 27		13 27		14 27
Hillington East	d	23p29	23p59	07 29	07 58	08 29	08 58	09 29	09 58	10 29	10 58	11 29	11 58	12 29	12 58	13 29	13 58	14 29
Hillington West	d	23p31	00 01	07 31		08 31		09 31		10 31		11 31		12 31	13 00	13 31		14 31
Paisley Gilmour Street 221 ✈	a	23p35	00 05	07 35	08 03	08 35	09 03	09 35	10 03	10 35	11 03	11 35	12 03	12 35	13 03	13 35	14 03	14 35
	d	23p35	00 05	07 35	08 03	08 35	09 03	09 35	10 03	10 35	11 03	11 35	12 03	12 35	13 03	13 35	14 03	14 35
Paisley St James	d	23p37	00 07			08 37		09 37		10 37		11 37		12 37		13 37		14 37
Bishopton	d	23p43	00 13	07 41	08 09	08 43	09 09	09 43	10 09	10 43	11 09	11 43	12 09	12 43	13 09	13 43	14 09	14 43
Langbank	d	23p49	00 19			08 49		09 49		10 49		11 49		12 49		13 49		14 49
Woodhall	d	23p53	00 23	07 49		08 53		09 53		10 53		11 53		12 53		13 53		14 53
Port Glasgow	d	23p56	00 26	07 52	08 19	08 56	09 19	09 56	10 19	10 56	11 19	11 56	12 19	12 56	13 19	13 56	14 19	14 56
Whinhill	d				08 23		09 23		10 23		11 23		12 22		13 23		14 23	
Drumfrochar	d				08 26		09 26		10 26		11 26		12 25		13 26		14 26	
Branchton	d				08 29		09 29		10 29		11 29		12 28		13 29		14 29	
I.B.M. §	d				08 31		09 31		10 31		11 31		12 30		13 31		14 31	
Inverkip	d				08 36		09 36		10 36		11 36		12 35		13 36		14 36	
Wemyss Bay	a				08 42		09 42		10 42		11 42		12 42		13 42		14 42	
Bogston	d	23p58	00 28	07 54		08 58		09 58		10 58		11 58		12 58		13 58		14 58
Cartsdyke	d	00 01	00 30	07 56		09 00		10 00		11 00		12 00		13 00		14 00		15 00
Greenock Central	d	00 02	00 32	07 58		09 02		10 02		11 02		12 02		13 02		14 02		15 02
Greenock West	d	00 05	00 35	08 01		09 05		10 05		11 05		12 05		13 05		14 05		15 05
Fort Matilda	d	00 08	00 38			09 08		10 08		11 08		12 08		13 08		14 08		15 08
Gourock	a	00 12	00 42	08 06		09 12		10 12		11 12		12 12		13 12		14 12		15 12

		SR	SR	SR	SR	SR	SR	SR	SR	SR	SR	SR	SR	SR	SR	SR
Glasgow Central 15 221	d	14 50	15 20	15 50	16 20	16 50	17 20	17 50	18 20	18 50	19 20	19 50	20 20	21 20	22 20	23 20
Cardonald	d		15 27		16 27		17 27		18 27		19 27		20 27	21 27	22 27	23 27
Hillington East	d	14 58	15 29	15 58	16 29	16 58	17 29	17 58	18 29	18 58	19 29	19 58	20 29	21 29	22 29	23 29
Hillington West	d		15 31		16 31		17 31		18 31		19 31		20 31	21 31	22 31	23 31
Paisley Gilmour Street 221 ✈	a	15 03	15 35	16 03	16 35	17 03	17 35	18 03	18 35	19 03	19 35	20 03	20 35	21 35	22 35	23 35
	d	15 03	15 35	16 03	16 35	17 03	17 35	18 03	18 35	19 03	19 35	20 03	20 35	21 35	22 35	23 35
Paisley St James	d		15 37		16 37		17 37		18 37		19 37		20 37	21 37	22 37	23 37
Bishopton	d	15 09	15 43	16 09	16 43	17 09	17 43	18 09	18 43	19 09	19 43	20 09	20 43	21 43	22 43	23 43
Langbank	d		15 49		16 49		17 49		18 49		19 49		20 49	21 49	22 49	23 49
Woodhall	d		15 53		16 53		17 53		18 53		19 53		20 53	21 53	22 53	23 53
Port Glasgow	d	15 19	15 56	16 19	16 56	17 19	17 56	18 19	18 56	19 19	19 56	20 19	20 56	21 56	22 56	23 56
Whinhill	d	15 23		16 23		17 23		18 23		19 23		20 23				
Drumfrochar	d	15 26		16 26		17 26		18 26		19 26		20 26				
Branchton	d	15 29		16 29		17 29		18 29		19 29		20 29				
I.B.M. §	d	15 31		16 31		17 31		18 31		19 31		20 31				
Inverkip	d	15 36		16 36		17 36		18 36		19 36		20 36				
Wemyss Bay	a	15 42		16 42		17 42		18 42		19 42		20 42				
Bogston	d		15 58		16 58		17 58		18 58		19 58		20 58	21 58	22 58	23 58
Cartsdyke	d		16 00		17 00		18 00		19 00		20 00		21 00	22 00	23 00	00 01
Greenock Central	d		16 02		17 02		18 02		19 02		20 02		21 02	22 02	23 02	00 02
Greenock West	d		16 05		17 05		18 05		19 05		20 05		21 05	22 05	23 05	00 05
Fort Matilda	d		16 08		17 08		18 08		19 08		20 08		21 08	22 08	23 08	00 08
Gourock	a		16 12		17 12		18 12		19 12		20 12		21 12	22 12	23 12	00 12

§ For authorised access to and from I.B.M. only

A not 11 December

Gourock and Wemyss Bay - Glasgow Central

Network Diagram - see first Page of Table 216

Miles	Miles			SR MX	SR	SR	SR SX	SR SO	SR SX	SR SX	SR SO	SR		SR SX	SR SO	SR SX	SR	SR	SR SX	SR	SR	SR		SR	SR
0	—	**Gourock**	d	23p20	05 20	06 05	06 22	06 35	06 44	07 06	07 06			07 22	07 36	07 47	07 52		08 09	08 24	08 36			09 06	09 23
1¼	—	Fort Matilda	d	23p23	05 23	06 08	06 25	06 38	06 47	07 09	07 09			07 25	07 39		07 55		08 12	08 27	08 39			09 09	09 26
2½	—	Greenock West	d	23p26	05 26	06 11	06 28	06 41	06 50	07 12	07 12			07 28	07 42	07 52	07 58		08 15	08 30	08 42			09 12	09 29
3¼	—	Greenock Central	d	23p29	05 29	06 14	06 31	06 44	06 53	07 15	07 15			07 31	07 45	07 55	08 01		08 18	08 33	08 45			09 15	09 32
4¼	—	Cartsdyke	d	23p31	05 31	06 16	06 33	06 46	06 55	07 17	07 17			07 33	07 47		08 03			08 35	08 47			09 17	
5	—	Bogston	d	23p33	05 33		06 35	06 48	06 57	07 19	07 19			07 35	07 49		08 05			08 37	08 49			09 19	
—	0	**Wemyss Bay**	d									07 13						07 50				08 50			
—	2¼	Inverkip	d									07 18						07 54				08 54			
—	4¾	I.B.M. §	d									07 23						07 59				08 59			
—	6¼	Branchton	d									07 25						08 02				09 02			
—	8	Drumfrochar	d									07 28						08 04				09 04			
—	8½	Whinhill	d									07 30						08 07				09 07			
6	10¾	Port Glasgow	d	23p36	05 36	06 19	06 38	06 51	07 00	07 22	07 22	07 35		07 38	07 52	07 59	08 08	08 12	08 22	08 40	08 52	09 11		09 22	09 36
7¼	12	Woodhall	d	23p38	05 38		06 40	06 53	07 02		07 24	07 37		07 40	07 54		08 10	08 14		08 42	08 54			09 24	
10	14¾	Langbank	d	23p43	05 43		06 45	06 58	07 07		07 29			07 45	07 59			08 19		08 47	08 59			09 29	
14	18	Bishopton	d	23p48	05 48	06 28	06 50	07 03	07 12	07 31	07 34	07 45		07 50	08 04	08 08	08 19	08 24	08 31	08 52	09 04	09 20		09 34	09 45
18¼	22¼	Paisley St James	d	23p54	05 54	06 34	06 56	07 09	07 18		07 40			07 56	08 10			08 30		08 58	09 10			09 40	
19	23	Paisley Gilmour Street 221 ⇐	a	23p56	05 55	06 36	06 58	07 11	07 20	07 37	07 42	07 51		07 58	08 12	08 14	08 25	08 32	08 37	09 00	09 11	09 26		09 42	09 51
—	—		d	23p57	05 56	06 37	06 59	07 12	07 21	07 38	07 43	07 52		07 59	08 13	08 14	08 26	08 33	08 38	09 01	09 12	09 27		09 43	09 52
21¼	25¼	Hillington West	d	00 01	05 59	06 40	07 02	07 15	07 24	07 41	07 46	07 55		08 02	08 16	08 18	08 29			09 04	09 15			09 46	
21¾	25¾	Hillington East	d	00 02	06 01	06 42	07 04	07 17	07 26	07 43	07 48	07 57		08 04	08 18	08 20	08 31			09 06	09 17			09 48	
22½	26½	Cardonald	d	00 04	06 03	06 44	07 06	07 19	07 28	07 45	07 50	07 59		08 06	08 20	08 22	08 33			09 08	09 19			09 50	
26½	31	**Glasgow Central** 15 221	a	00 12	06 12	06 52	07 14	07 27	07 36	07 54	07 58	08 07		08 14	08 30	08 33	08 42	08 44	08 49	09 16	09 29	09 39		09 58	10 03

		SR	SR	SR	SR	SR	SR	SR		SR	SR	SR	SR	SR	SR	SR	SR	SR		SR	SR	SR	SR	SR	SR
Gourock	d	09 36		10 06	10 23	10 36		11 06		11 23	11 36		12 06	12 23	12 36		13 06	13 23		13 36		14 06	14 23	14 36	
Fort Matilda	d	09 39		10 09	10 26	10 39		11 09		11 26	11 39		12 09	12 26	12 39		13 09	13 26		13 39		14 09	14 26	14 39	
Greenock West	d	09 42		10 12	10 29	10 42		11 12		11 29	11 42		12 12	12 29	12 42		13 12	13 29		13 42		14 12	14 29	14 42	
Greenock Central	d	09 45		10 15	10 32	10 45		11 15		11 32	11 45		12 15	12 32	12 45		13 15	13 32		13 45		14 15	14 32	14 45	
Cartsdyke	d	09 47		10 17		10 47		11 17			11 47		12 17		12 47		13 17			13 47		14 17		14 47	
Bogston	d	09 49		10 19		10 49		11 19			11 49		12 19		12 49		13 19			13 49		14 19		14 49	
Wemyss Bay	d		09 50				10 55					11 50				12 50					13 50				14 50
Inverkip	d		09 54				10 59					11 54				12 54					13 54				14 54
I.B.M. §	d		09 59				11 04					11 59				12 59					13 59				14 59
Branchton	d		10 02				11 07					12 02				13 02					14 02				15 02
Drumfrochar	d		10 04				11 09					12 04				13 04					14 04				15 04
Whinhill	d		10 07				11 12					12 07				13 07					14 07				15 07
Port Glasgow	d	09 52	10 11	10 22	10 36	10 52	11 16	11 22		11 36	11 52	12 11	12 22	12 36	12 52	13 11	13 22	13 36		13 52	14 11	14 22	14 36	14 52	15 11
Woodhall	d	09 54		10 24		10 54		11 24			11 54		12 24		12 54		13 24			13 54		14 24		14 54	
Langbank	d	09 59		10 29		10 59		11 29			11 59		12 29		12 59		13 29			13 59		14 29		14 59	
Bishopton	d	10 04	10 20	10 34	10 45	11 04	11 25	11 34		11 45	12 04	12 20	12 34	12 45	13 04	13 20	13 34	13 45		14 04	14 20	14 34	14 45	15 04	15 20
Paisley St James	d	10 10		10 40		11 10		11 40			12 10		12 40		13 10		13 40			14 10		14 40		15 10	
Paisley Gilmour Street 221 ⇐	a	10 12	10 26	10 42	10 51	11 12	11 31	11 42		11 51	12 12	12 26	12 42	12 51	13 12	13 26	13 43	13 51		14 12	14 26	14 42	14 51	15 12	15 26
	d	10 13	10 27	10 43	10 52	11 13	11 32	11 43		11 52	12 13	12 27	12 43	12 52	13 13	13 27	13 43	13 52		14 13	14 27	14 43	14 52	15 13	15 27
Hillington West	d	10 16		10 46		11 16		11 46			12 16		12 46		13 16		13 46			14 16		14 46		15 16	
Hillington East	d	10 18		10 48		11 18		11 48			12 18		12 48		13 18		13 48			14 18		14 48		15 18	
Cardonald	d	10 20		10 50		11 20		11 50			12 20		12 50		13 20		13 50			14 20		14 50		15 20	
Glasgow Central 15 221	a	10 28	10 38	10 58	11 03	11 28	11 43	11 58		12 03	12 29	12 38	12 58	13 03	13 28	13 38	13 58	14 03		14 28	14 38	14 58	15 03	15 29	15 38

		SR	SR	SR		SR	SR	SR	SR	SR	SR	SR	SR	SR		SR	SR	SR	SR	SR	SR	SR	SR	SR	
Gourock	d	15 06	15 23	15 36			16 06	16 23	16 36		17 06	17 23	17 48			18 06	18 23		18 40		19 06	19 22	19 45		
Fort Matilda	d	15 09	15 26	15 39			16 09	16 26	16 39		17 09	17 26	17 51			18 09	18 26		18 43		19 09	19 25	19 48		
Greenock West	d	15 12	15 29	15 42			16 12	16 29	16 42		17 12	17 29	17 54			18 12	18 29		18 46		19 12	19 28	19 51		
Greenock Central	d	15 15	15 32	15 45			16 15	16 32	16 45		17 15	17 32	17 57			18 15	18 32		18 49		19 15	19 31	19 54		
Cartsdyke	d	15 17		15 47			16 17		16 47		17 17		17 59			18 17			18 51		19 17	19 33	19 56		
Bogston	d	15 19		15 49			16 19		16 49		17 19		18 01			18 19			18 53		19 19	19 35			
Wemyss Bay	d					15 55				16 45				17 49				18 26		18 55				19 44	
Inverkip	d					15 59				16 49				17 53				18 30		18 59				19 48	
I.B.M. §	d					16 04				16 54				18 02				18 39		19 04				19 53	
Branchton	d					16 07				16 57				18 05				18 41		19 07				19 56	
Drumfrochar	d					16 09				16 59				18 07				18 44		19 09				19 58	
Whinhill	d					16 12				17 02				18 10				18 46		19 12				20 01	
Port Glasgow	d	15 22	15 36	15 52		16 16	16 22	16 36	16 52	17 06	17 22	17 36	18 04	18 14		18 22	18 36	18 51	18 56	19 16	19 22	19 38	19 59	20 06	
Woodhall	d	15 24		15 54			16 24		16 54		17 24		18 06			18 24			18 58		19 24	19 40		20 08	
Langbank	d	15 29		15 59			16 29		16 59		17 29		18 11			18 29			19 03		19 29	19 45		20 13	
Bishopton	d	15 34	15 45	16 04		16 25	16 34	16 45	17 04	17 15	17 34	17 45	18 16	18 23		18 34	18 45	19 00	19 08	19 25	19 34	19 50	20 08	20 18	
Paisley St James	d	15 40		16 10			16 40		17 10		17 40		18 22			18 40			19 14		19 40	19 56		20 24	
Paisley Gilmour Street 221 ⇐	a	15 42	15 51	16 12		16 31	16 42	16 51	17 11	17 21	17 42	17 51	18 24	18 30		18 42	18 51	19 06	19 16	19 31	19 42	19 58	20 14	20 26	
	d	15 43	15 52	16 13		16 32	16 43	16 52	17 12	17 22	17 43	17 52	18 25	18 31		18 43	18 52	19 06	19 17	19 32	19 43	19 59	20 15	20 27	
Hillington West	d	15 46	15 55	16 16			16 46	16 56	17 15		17 46		18 28			18 46			19 20		19 46	20 02		20 30	
Hillington East	d	15 48		16 18			16 48		17 17		17 48		18 30			18 48			19 22		19 48	20 04		20 32	
Cardonald	d	15 50		16 20			16 50		17 19		17 50		18 32			18 50			19 24		19 50	20 06		20 34	
Glasgow Central 15 221	a	15 58	16 06	16 28		16 45	16 59	17 05	17 31	17 34	17 58	18 05	18 40	18 44		18 58	19 04	19 17	19 32	19 44	19 59	20 14	20 26	20 43	

§ For authorised access to and from I.B.M. only

Gourock and Wemyss Bay - Glasgow Central

Network Diagram - see first Page of Table 216

		SR	SR	SR	SR	SR	SR SX	SR SO	SR	SR	SR	SR SO
Gourock	d	20 20	20 44		21 24	21 45			22 20		23 20	
Fort Matilda	d	20 23	20 47		21 27	21 48			22 23		23 23	
Greenock West	d	20 26	20 50		21 30	21 51			22 26		23 26	
Greenock Central	d	20 29	20 53		21 33	21 54			22 29		23 29	
Cartsdyke	d	20 31	20 55		21 35	21 56			22 31		23 31	
Bogston	d	20 33			21 37				22 33		23 33	
Wemyss Bay	d			20 44			21 44	21 50		22 44		23 40
Inverkip	d			20 48			21 48	21 54		22 48		23 44
I.B.M. §	d			20 53			21 53	21 59		22 53		23 49
Branchton	d			20 56			21 56	22 02		22 56		23 52
Drumfrochar	d			20 58			21 58	22 04		22 58		23 54
Whinhill	d			21 01			22 01	22 07		23 01		23 57
Port Glasgow	d	20 36	20 58	21 06	21 40	21 59	22 06	22 11	22 36	23 06	23 36	00 01
Woodhall	d	20 38		21 08	21 42		22 08	22 14	22 38	23 08	23 38	
Langbank	d	20 43		21 13	21 47		22 13	22 18	22 43	23 13	23 43	
Bishopton	d	20 48	21 07	21 18	21 52	22 08	22 18	22 24	22 48	23 18	23 48	00 10
Paisley St James	d	20 54		21 24	21 58		22 24	22 29	22 54	23 24	23 54	
Paisley Gilmour Street 221 ⇜	a	20 56	21 13	21 26	22 00	22 14	22 26	22 32	22 56	23 26	23 56	00 16
	d	20 56	21 14	21 27	22 01	22 15	22 27	22 32	22 57	23 27	23 57	00 17
Hillington West	d	21 00		21 30	22 04		22 30	22 35	23 00	23 30	00 01	
Hillington East	d	21 02		21 32	22 06		22 32	22 37	23 02	23 32	00 02	
Cardonald	d	21 04		21 34	22 08		22 34	22 39	23 04	23 34	00 04	
Glasgow Central 15 221	a	21 12	21 30	21 42	22 15	22 26	22 42	22 46	23 14	23 42	00 12	00 28

Sundays

		SR A	SR A	SR	SR	SR	SR	SR	SR	SR	SR	SR	SR	SR	SR	SR	SR
Gourock	d	23p20		08 23		09 23		10 23		11 23		12 23		13 23		14 23	
Fort Matilda	d	23p23		08 26		09 26		10 26		11 26		12 26		13 26		14 26	
Greenock West	d	23p26		08 29		09 29		10 29		11 29		12 29		13 29		14 29	
Greenock Central	d	23p29		08 32		09 32		10 32		11 32		12 32		13 32		14 32	
Cartsdyke	d	23p31		08 34		09 34		10 34		11 34		12 34		13 34		14 34	
Bogston	d	23p33		08 36		09 36		10 36		11 36		12 36		13 36		14 36	
Wemyss Bay	d		23p40		08 50		09 50		10 57		11 50		12 50		13 50		14 50
Inverkip	d		23p44		08 54		09 54		11 01		11 54		12 54		13 54		14 54
I.B.M. §	d		23p49		08 59		09 59		11 06		11 59		12 59		13 59		14 59
Branchton	d		23p52		09 02		10 02		11 09		12 02		13 02		14 02		15 02
Drumfrochar	d		23p54		09 04		10 04		11 11		12 04		13 04		14 04		15 04
Whinhill	d		23p57		09 07		10 07		11 13		12 07		13 07		14 07		15 07
Port Glasgow	d	23p36	00 01	08 39	09 11	09 39	10 11	10 39	11 17	11 39	12 11	12 39	13 11	13 39	14 11	14 39	15 11
Woodhall	d	23p38		08 41		09 41		10 41		11 41		12 41		13 41		14 41	
Langbank	d	23p43		08 46		09 46		10 46		11 46		12 46		13 46		14 46	
Bishopton	d	23p48	00 10	08 51	09 20	09 51	10 20	10 51	11 27	11 51	12 20	12 51	13 20	13 51	14 20	14 51	15 20
Paisley St James	d	23p54		08 57		09 57		10 57		11 57		12 57		13 57		14 57	
Paisley Gilmour Street 221 ⇜	a	23p56	00 16	08 59	09 26	09 59	10 26	10 59	11 31	11 58	12 26	12 59	13 26	13 59	14 26	14 59	15 26
	d	23p57	00 17	09 00	09 27	10 00	10 27	11 00	11 32	11 59	12 27	13 00	13 27	14 00	14 27	15 00	15 27
Hillington West	d	00 01		09 03		10 03		11 03		12 03		13 03		14 03		15 03	
Hillington East	d	00 02		09 05	09 31	10 05	10 31	11 05	11 36	12 05	12 31	13 05	13 31	14 05	14 31	15 05	15 31
Cardonald	d	00 04		09 07		10 07		11 07		12 07		13 07		14 07		15 07	
Glasgow Central 15 221	a	00 12	00 28	09 15	09 40	10 15	10 40	11 15	11 46	12 15	12 40	13 15	13 40	14 15	14 40	15 15	15 40

		SR	SR	SR	SR	SR	SR	SR	SR	SR	SR	SR	SR	SR	SR
Gourock	d	15 23		16 23		17 23		18 23		19 23		20 23		21 23	22 23
Fort Matilda	d	15 26		16 26		17 26		18 26		19 26		20 26		21 26	22 26
Greenock West	d	15 29		16 29		17 29		18 29		19 29		20 29		21 29	22 29
Greenock Central	d	15 32		16 32		17 32		18 32		19 32		20 32		21 32	22 32
Cartsdyke	d	15 34		16 34		17 34		18 34		19 34		20 34		21 34	22 34
Bogston	d	15 36		16 36		17 36		18 36		19 36		20 36		21 36	22 36
Wemyss Bay	d		15 55		16 50		17 50		18 55		19 50		20 50		
Inverkip	d		15 59		16 54		17 54		18 59		19 54		20 54		
I.B.M. §	d		16 04		16 59		17 59		19 04		19 59		20 59		
Branchton	d		16 07		17 02		18 02		19 07		20 02		21 02		
Drumfrochar	d		16 09		17 04		18 04		19 09		20 04		21 04		
Whinhill	d		16 12		17 07		18 07		19 12		20 07		21 07		
Port Glasgow	d	15 39	16 16	16 39	17 11	17 39	18 11	18 39	19 16	19 39	20 11	20 39	21 11	21 39	22 39
Woodhall	d	15 41		16 41		17 41		18 41		19 41		20 41		21 41	22 41
Langbank	d	15 46		16 46		17 46		18 46		19 46		20 46		21 46	22 46
Bishopton	d	15 51	16 25	16 51	17 20	17 51	18 20	18 51	19 25	19 51	20 20	20 51	21 20	21 51	22 51
Paisley St James	d	15 57		16 57		17 57		18 57		19 57		20 57		21 57	22 57
Paisley Gilmour Street 221 ⇜	a	15 59	16 31	16 59	17 26	17 59	18 26	18 59	19 31	19 59	20 26	20 59	21 26	21 59	22 59
	d	16 00	16 32	17 00	17 27	18 00	18 27	19 00	19 32	20 00	20 27	21 00	21 27	22 00	23 00
Hillington West	d	16 03		17 03		18 03		19 03		20 03		21 03		22 03	23 03
Hillington East	d	16 05	16 36	17 05	17 31	18 05	18 31	19 05	19 36	20 05	20 31	21 05	21 31	22 05	23 05
Cardonald	d	16 07		17 07		18 07		19 07		20 07		21 07		22 07	23 07
Glasgow Central 15 221	a	16 15	16 45	17 15	17 40	18 15	18 40	19 15	19 44	20 15	20 40	21 15	21 40	22 15	23 15

§ For authorised access to and from I.B.M. only

A not 11 December

Table 219A SHIPPING SERVICES

Mondays to Saturdays

until 29 March 2012

Glasgow and Gourock - Dunoon, Kilcreggan and Helensburgh Pier

Argyll Ferries Ltd in association with ScotRail

All Kilcreggan and Helensburgh Pier sailings operated by Clyde Marine Transport Ltd
Tel. 0871 200 22 33

			SX		SX																				
Glasgow Central 15	219 d	05 55	05 55	06 25	06 25	06 55	.	07 04	07 25	07 35	07 35	.	08 28	08 36	09 05	09 25	09 35	.	10 25	10 35	10 35	11 25	11 25	.	12 25
Paisley Gilmour Street	219 d	06 07	06 07	06 36	06 36	07 07	.	07 20	07 40	07 51	07 51	.	08 38	08 50	09 20	09 36	09 50	.	10 36	10 50	10 50	11 36	11 36	.	12 36
Gourock	219 a	06 36	06 36	07 13	07 13	07 39	.	07 57	08 13	08 28	08 28	.	09 09	09 27	09 58	10 06	10 27	.	11 06	11 27	11 27	12 06	12 06	.	13 06
Gourock	d	06 45	07 00	07 20	07 30	07 50	.	08 05	08 20	08 50	08 50	.	09 20	09 50	10 05	10 20	10 50	.	11 20	11 35	11 50	12 20	12 25	.	13 20
Dunoon	a	07 10	.	07 45	.	08 15	.	.	08 45	09 15	.	.	09 45	10 15	.	10 45	11 15	.	11 45	.	12 15	12 45	.	.	13 45
Kilcreggan	a	.	07 12	.	07 42	.	.	08 17	.	.	09 02	.	.	.	10 20	.	.	.	.	11 47	.	.	12 37	.	.
Helensburgh Pier	a	.	.	.	.	.	.	.	.	.	.	.	.	.	10 45	.	.	.	.	.	.	.	.	.	.

														B										FSO	A
Glasgow Central 15	219 d	13 25	13 25	14 25	14 35	14 35	15 25	15 25	15 35	15 35	16 05	16 23	16 55	17 25	17 25	17 40	.	18 25	18 35	19 25	20 05	20 50	21 50	22 50	23 50
Paisley Gilmour Street	219 d	13 36	13 36	14 36	14 50	14 50	15 36	15 36	15 50	15 50	16 20	16 38	17 06	17 37	17 37	17 55	.	18 36	18 50	19 36	20 21	21 01	22 01	23 01	00 05
Gourock	219 a	14 06	14 06	15 06	15 27	15 27	16 06	16 06	16 27	16 27	16 57	17 15	17 39	18 06	18 06	18 32	.	19 06	19 27	20 06	20 58	21 32	22 33	23 33	00 42
Gourock	d	14 15	14 20	15 20	15 45	15 50	16 15	16 20	16 50	16 50	17 20	17 25	17 50	18 10	18 20	18 50	.	19 20	19 50	20 20	21 20	21 40	22 40	23 40	01 00
Dunoon	a	.	14 45	15 45	.	16 15	.	16 45	17 15	.	17 45	.	18 15	.	18 45	19 15	.	19 45	20 15	20 45	21 45	22 05	23 05	00 05	01 20
Kilcreggan	a	14 30	.	.	15 57	.	16 27	.	.	17 03	.	17 37	.	18 25	.	.	.	.	.	.	.	.	.	.	.
Helensburgh Pier	a	14 55	.	.	.	.	.	.	.	.	.	.	.	.	.	.	.	.	.	.	.	.	.	.	.

Sundays

until 25 March 2012

Glasgow Central 15	219 d	07 20	.	08 20	09 20	.	10 20	11 20	.	12 20	13 20	.	14 20	15 20	.	16 20	17 20	.	18 20	19 20	.	20 20	.	.	21 20
Paisley Gilmour Street	219 d	07 35	.	08 35	09 35	.	10 35	11 35	.	12 35	13 35	.	14 35	15 35	.	16 35	17 35	.	18 35	19 35	.	20 35	.	.	21 35
Gourock	219 a	08 06	.	09 12	10 12	.	11 12	12 12	.	13 12	14 12	.	15 12	16 12	.	17 12	18 12	.	19 12	20 12	.	21 12	.	.	22 12
Gourock	d	08 20	.	09 20	10 20	.	11 20	12 20	.	13 20	14 20	.	15 20	16 20	.	17 20	18 20	.	19 20	20 20	.	21 20	.	.	22 20
Dunoon	a	08 45	.	09 45	10 45	.	11 45	12 45	.	13 45	14 45	.	15 45	16 45	.	17 45	18 45	.	19 45	20 45	.	21 45	.	.	22 45
Kilcreggan	a	.	.	.	.	.	.	.	.	.	.	.	.	.	.	.	.	.	.	.	.	.	.	.	.
Helensburgh Pier	a	.	.	.	.	.	.	.	.	.	.	.	.	.	.	.	.	.	.	.	.	.	.	.	.

A Saturday and Sunday mornings only
B The ferry will be held for a maximum of 15 minutes in the event of a late-running train

Mondays to Saturdays

until 29 March 2012

Helensburgh Pier, Kilcreggan and Dunoon - Gourock and Glasgow

Argyll Ferries Ltd in association with ScotRail

All Helensburgh Pier and Kilcreggan sailings operated by Clyde Marine Transport Ltd
Tel. 0871 200 22 33

		SX	SO	SX		SX																			
Helensburgh Pier	d	.	.	.	.	.	.	.	.	.	.	.	.	.	.	.	.	.	10 50		.	.	.	.	.
Kilcreggan	d	.	.	07 15	.	07 50	.	.	08 20	.	.	.	09 10	.	.	.	.	.	11 15		11 50	.	.	12 45	.
Dunoon	d	06 45	06 45	.	07 15	.	.	07 50	.	08 20	08 50	.	.	09 20	09 50	.	10 20	10 50	.	11 20	.	11 50	12 20	.	12 50
Gourock	a	07 15	07 15	07 27	07 40	08 02	.	08 15	08 32	08 45	09 15	.	09 22	09 45	10 15	.	10 45	11 15	11 27	11 45	12 02	12 15	12 45	12 57	13 15
Gourock	219 d	07 22	07 36	07 47	07 52	08 09	.	08 24	09 06	09 06	09 23	.	09 36	10 06	10 23	.	11 06	11 23	11 36	12 06	12 23	12 23	13 06	13 06	13 23
Paisley Gilmour Street	219 a	07 58	08 12	08 14	08 25	08 37	.	09 00	09 42	09 42	09 51	.	10 12	10 42	10 51	.	11 42	11 51	12 12	12 42	12 51	12 51	13 43	13 43	13 51
Glasgow Central 15	219 a	08 14	08 30	08 33	08 42	08 49	.	09 16	09 58	09 58	10 03	.	10 28	10 58	11 03	.	11 58	12 03	12 29	12 58	13 03	13 03	13 58	13 58	14 03

																								A	
Helensburgh Pier	d	.	.	15 00	.	.	.	.	.	.	.	.	.	.	.	.	.	.	.	.	.	.	.	.	.
Kilcreggan	d	.	.	15 30	.	16 00	.	16 30	.	.	.	17 05	.	.	17 40	.	.	18 30	.	.	.	.	.	.	.
Dunoon	d	13 50	14 50	.	.	.	15 50	.	.	16 20	16 50	.	.	17 20	.	17 50	.	.	18 20	18 50	19 20	19 50	20 50	21 45	22 10
Gourock	a	14 15	15 15	15 42	.	16 12	16 15	16 42	.	16 45	17 15	17 17	.	17 45	17 52	18 15	.	18 42	18 45	19 15	19 45	20 15	21 15	22 15	22 35
Gourock	219 d	14 23	15 23	16 06	.	16 23	16 23	17 06	.	17 06	17 23	17 23	.	18 06	18 06	18 23	.	19 06	19 06	19 22	20 20	20 44	21 24	22 20	23 20
Paisley Gilmour Street	219 a	14 51	15 51	16 42	.	16 51	16 51	17 42	.	17 42	17 51	17 51	.	18 42	18 42	18 51	.	19 42	19 42	19 58	20 56	21 13	22 00	22 56	23 56
Glasgow Central 15	219 a	15 03	16 06	16 59	.	17 05	17 05	17 58	.	17 58	18 05	18 05	.	18 58	18 58	19 04	.	19 59	19 59	20 14	21 12	21 30	22 15	23 14	00 12

Sundays

until 25 March 2012

Helensburgh Pier	d	.	.	.	.	.	.	.	.	.	.	.	.	.	.	.	.	.	.	.		.	.	.	.
Kilcreggan	d	.	.	.	.	.	.	.	.	.	.	.	.	.	.	.	.	.	.	.		.	.	.	.
Dunoon	d	08 50	09 50	10 50	.	11 50	12 50	.	13 50	14 50	.	15 50	16 50	.	17 50	.	18 50	19 50	.	20 50	21 50	.	.	.	.
Gourock	a	09 15	10 15	11 15	.	12 15	13 15	.	14 15	15 15	.	16 15	17 15	.	18 15	.	19 15	20 15	.	21 15	22 15	.	.	.	.
Gourock	219 d	09 23	10 23	11 23	.	12 23	13 23	.	14 23	15 23	.	16 23	17 23	.	18 23	.	19 23	20 23	.	21 23	22 23	.	.	.	.
Paisley Gilmour Street	219 a	09 59	10 59	11 58	.	12 59	13 59	.	14 59	15 59	.	16 59	17 59	.	18 59	.	19 59	20 59	.	21 59	22 59	.	.	.	.
Glasgow Central 15	219 a	10 15	11 15	12 15	.	13 15	14 15	.	15 15	16 15	.	17 15	18 15	.	19 15	.	20 15	21 15	.	22 15	23 15	.	.	.	.

A Connection is not guaranteed

For details of Gourock/Dunoon sailings from 30 March 2012
please telephone 08000 66 5000
or visit www.argyllferries.co.uk

For details of Kilcreggan/Helensburgh Pier sailings
please telephone 0871 200 22 33

Table 219B SHIPPING SERVICES

Glasgow and Wemyss Bay - Rothesay (Bute)

Caledonian MacBrayne Ltd in association with ScotRail

Mondays to Saturdays
until 29 March 2012

			SX	SX													
Glasgow Central 15	219	d	06 05	06 32	07 50	08 50	09 50	10 50	11 50	12 50	13 50	14 50	15 50	16 33	17 15	17 55	18 50
Paisley Gilmour Street	219	d	06 19	06 47	08 02	09 01	10 01	11 01	12 01	13 01	14 01	15 01	16 02	16 48	17 29	18 06	19 01
Wemyss Bay	219	a	06 58	07 30	08 40	09 40	10 40	11 40	12 40	13 40	14 40	15 40	16 40	17 25	18 08	18 44	19 40
Wemyss Bay	⛴	d	**07 15**	**08 00**	**08 45**	**10 15**	**11 00**	**12 00**	**13 05**	**14 05**	**15 00**	**16 00**	**16 45**	**17 30**	**18 15**	**19 00**	**19 45**
Rothesay	⛴	a	**07 50**	**08 35**	**09 20**	**10 50**	**11 35**	**12 35**	**13 40**	**14 40**	**15 35**	**16 35**	**17 20**	**18 05**	**18 50**	**19 35**	**20 20**

Sundays
until 25 March 2012

Glasgow Central 15	219	d	07 50	08 50	10 50	11 50	12 50	13 50	14 50	15 50	16 50	17 50	18 50
Paisley Gilmour Street	219	d	08 03	09 03	11 03	12 03	13 03	14 03	15 03	16 03	17 03	18 03	19 03
Wemyss Bay	219	a	08 42	09 42	11 42	12 42	13 42	14 42	15 42	16 42	17 42	18 42	19 42
Wemyss Bay	⛴	d	**08 45**	**10 15**	**12 00**	**13 00**	**14 00**	**15 00**	**16 00**	**17 00**	**18 00**	**19 00**	**19 45**
Rothesay	⛴	a	**09 20**	**10 50**	**12 35**	**13 35**	**14 35**	**15 35**	**16 35**	**17 35**	**18 35**	**19 35**	**20 20**

Mondays to Saturdays
until 29 March 2012

			SX	SX													
Rothesay	⛴	d	**06 25**	**07 00**	**08 00**	**08 45**	**10 10**	**11 00**	**12 00**	**13 00**	**14 00**	**15 00**	**16 00**	**16 45**	**17 30**	**18 15**	**19 00**
Wemyss Bay	⛴	a	**07 00**	**07 35**	**08 35**	**09 20**	**10 45**	**11 35**	**12 35**	**13 35**	**14 35**	**15 35**	**16 35**	**17 20**	**18 05**	**18 50**	**19 35**
Wemyss Bay	219	d	07 13	07 50	08 50	09 50	10 55	11 50	12 50	13 50	14 50	15 55	16 45	17 49	18 26	18 55	19 44
Paisley Gilmour Street	219	a	07 51	08 32	09 26	10 26	11 32	12 26	13 26	14 26	15 26	16 31	17 21	18 30	19 06	19 31	20 26
Glasgow Central 15	219	a	08 07	08 44	09 39	10 38	11 43	12 38	13 38	14 38	15 38	16 45	17 34	18 44	19 17	19 44	20 43

Sundays
until 25 March 2012

Rothesay	⛴	d	**08 00**	**09 30**	**10 45**	**12 00**	**13 00**	**14 00**	**15 00**	**16 00**	**17 00**	**18 00**	**19 00**
Wemyss Bay	⛴	a	**08 35**	**10 05**	**11 20**	**12 35**	**13 35**	**14 35**	**15 35**	**16 35**	**17 35**	**18 35**	**19 35**
Wemyss Bay	219	d	08 50	10 57	11 50	12 50	13 50	14 50	15 55	16 50	17 50	18 55	19 50
Paisley Gilmour Street	219	a	09 26	11 31	12 26	13 26	14 26	15 26	16 31	17 26	18 26	19 31	20 26
Glasgow Central 15	219	a	09 40	11 46	12 40	13 40	14 40	15 40	16 45	17 40	18 40	19 44	20 40

For details of sailings from 30 March 2012
please telephone 08000 66 5000
or visit www.calmac.co.uk

Network Diagram for Tables 220, 223, 224, 226, 232

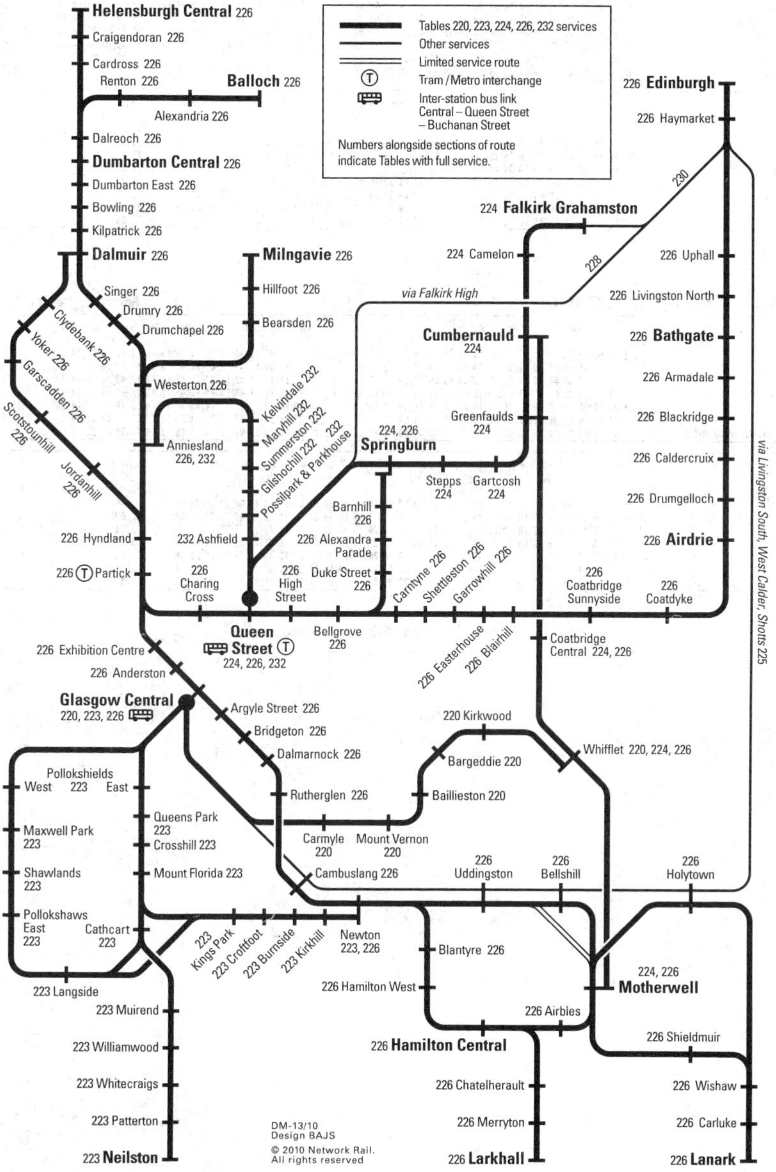

Glasgow Central - Whifflet

Network Diagram - see first Page of Table 220

Miles			SR SO	SR	SR	SR	SR	SR	SR	SR	SR		SR	SR	SR	SR	SR	SR	SR	SR	SR		SR	SR	SR
0	**Glasgow Central** 15	d	00 16	06 17	06 46	07 16	07 46	08 16	08 43	09 16	09 46		10 16	10 46	11 16	11 46	12 16	12 46	13 16	13 46	14 16		14 46	15 16	15 46
5½	Carmyle	d	00 26	06 26	06 56	07 26	07 56	08 26	08 56	09 26	09 56		10 26	10 56	11 26	11 56	12 26	12 56	13 26	13 56	14 26		14 56	15 26	15 56
6¾	Mount Vernon	d	00 29	06 29	06 59	07 29	07 59	08 29	08 59	09 29	09 59		10 29	10 59	11 29	11 59	12 29	12 59	13 29	13 59	14 29		14 59	15 29	15 59
8	Baillieston	d	00 32	06 32	07 02	07 32	08 02	08 32	09 02	09 32	10 02		10 32	11 02	11 32	12 02	12 32	13 02	13 32	14 02	14 32		15 02	15 32	16 02
9¼	Bargeddie	d	00 35	06 35	07 05	07 35	08 05	08 35	09 05	09 35	10 05		10 35	11 05	11 35	12 05	12 35	13 05	13 35	14 05	14 35		15 05	15 35	16 05
10	Kirkwood	d	00 39	06 39	07 09	07 39	08 09	08 39	09 09	09 39	10 09		10 39	11 09	11 39	12 09	12 39	13 09	13 39	14 09	14 39		15 09	15 39	16 09
12½	**Whifflet**	a	00 45	06 47	07 15	07 47	08 15	08 48	09 15	09 45	10 15		10 45	11 15	11 45	12 15	12 45	13 15	13 45	14 16	14 45		15 15	15 45	16 15

		SR	SR	SR	SR	SR	SR		SR SX	SR SO	SR	SR	SR	SR	SR	SR	SR		SR						
Glasgow Central 15	d	16 16	16 46	17 16	17 46	18 16	18 46		19 13	19 16	19 46	20 16	20 46	21 16	21 46	22 16	22 46		23 16						
Carmyle	d	16 26	16 56	17 26	17 56	18 26	18 56		19 26	19 26	19 56	20 26	20 56	21 26	21 56	22 26	22 56		23 26						
Mount Vernon	d	16 29	16 59	17 29	17 59	18 29	18 59		19 29	19 29	19 59	20 29	20 59	21 29	21 59	22 29	22 59		23 29						
Baillieston	d	16 32	17 02	17 32	18 02	18 32	19 02		19 32	19 32	20 02	20 32	21 02	21 32	22 02	22 32	23 02		23 32						
Bargeddie	d	16 35	17 05	17 35	18 05	18 35	19 05		19 35	19 35	20 05	20 35	21 05	21 35	22 05	22 35	23 05		23 35						
Kirkwood	d	16 39	17 09	17 39	18 09	18 39	19 09		19 39	19 39	20 09	20 39	21 09	21 39	22 09	22 39	23 09		23 39						
Whifflet	a	16 45	17 15	17 45	18 15	18 45	19 15		19 45	19 45	20 15	20 45	21 15	21 45	22 15	22 45	23 15		23 45						

Whifflet - Glasgow Central

Mondays to Saturdays

Miles			SR	SR	SR	SR	SR	SR	SR	SR	SR		SR	SR	SR	SR	SR	SR	SR	SR	SR		SR	SR	SR
0	**Whifflet**	d	06 06	06 36	07 06	07 36	08 06	08 36	09 06	09 36	10 06		10 36	11 06	11 36	12 06	12 36	13 06	13 36	14 06	14 36		15 06	15 36	16 06
2½	Kirkwood	d	06 09	06 39	07 09	07 39	08 09	08 39	09 09	09 39	10 09		10 39	11 09	11 39	12 09	12 39	13 09	13 39	14 09	14 39		15 09	15 39	16 09
3¼	Bargeddie	d	06 12	06 42	07 12	07 42	08 12	08 42	09 12	09 42	10 12		10 42	11 12	11 42	12 12	12 42	13 12	13 42	14 12	14 42		15 12	15 42	16 12
4½	Baillieston	d	06 15	06 45	07 15	07 45	08 15	08 45	09 15	09 45	10 15		10 45	11 15	11 45	12 15	12 45	13 15	13 45	14 15	14 45		15 15	15 45	16 15
5¾	Mount Vernon	d	06 18	06 48	07 18	07 48	08 18	08 48	09 18	09 48	10 18		10 48	11 18	11 48	12 18	12 48	13 18	13 48	14 18	14 48		15 18	15 48	16 18
7	Carmyle	d	06 21	06 51	07 21	07 51	08 21	08 51	09 21	09 51	10 21		10 51	11 21	11 51	12 21	12 51	13 21	13 51	14 21	14 51		15 21	15 51	16 21
12½	**Glasgow Central** 15	a	06 35	07 05	07 35	08 05	08 36	09 07	09 37	10 05	10 35		11 05	11 35	12 05	12 35	13 05	13 35	14 05	14 35	15 05		15 35	16 05	16 35

		SR	SR	SR	SR SO	SR SX	SR		SR	SR	SR	SR	SR	SR	SR	SR	SR SX		SR SO						
Whifflet	d	16 36	17 06	17 36	18 06	18 12	18 36		19 06	19 36	20 06	20 36	21 06	21 36	22 06	22 36	23 06		23 06						
Kirkwood	d	16 39	17 09	17 39	18 09	18 14	18 39		19 09	19 39	20 09	20 39	21 09	21 39	22 09	22 39	23 09		23 09						
Bargeddie	d	16 42	17 12	17 42	18 12	18 17	18 42		19 12	19 42	20 12	20 42	21 12	21 42	22 12	22 42	23 12		23 12						
Baillieston	d	16 45	17 15	17 45	18 15	18 20	18 45		19 15	19 45	20 15	20 45	21 15	21 45	22 15	22 45	23 15		23 15						
Mount Vernon	d	16 48	17 18	17 48	18 18	18 23	18 48		19 18	19 48	20 18	20 48	21 18	21 48	22 18	22 48	23 18		23 18						
Carmyle	d	16 51	17 21	17 51	18 21	18 26	18 51		19 21	19 51	20 21	20 51	21 21	21 51	22 21	22 51	23 21		23 21						
Glasgow Central 15	a	17 05	17 35	18 05	18 35	18 40	19 05		19 35	20 05	20 35	21 05	21 35	22 05	22 38	23 05	23 35		23 37						

No Sunday Service

Table 221

Mondays to Saturdays

Glasgow Central - Ardrossan, Largs and Ayr

Network Diagram - see first Page of Table 216

Miles	Miles	Miles	Station			SR SO	SR MSX	SR MX	SR SO	SR MSX	SR MX	SR	SR	SR	SR	SR	SR
0	0	—	**Glasgow Central** 15	219	d	23p15	23p15	23p30	23p45	23p45	00 15	06 00	06 15	06 30	06 45	07 00	07 15
7¼	7¼	—	Paisley Gilmour Street	219	a	23p25	23p25	23p40	23p55	23p55	00 25	06 11	06 25	06 40	06 55	07 10	07 25
—	—	—			d	23p26	23p26	23p41	23p56	23p56	00 26	06 12	06 26	06 41	06 56	07 11	07 26
10¾	10¾	—	Johnstone		d	23p30	23p30	23p45	23p59	23p59	00 30	06 14	06 30	06 45	07 00	07 15	07 31
11½	11½	—	Milliken Park		d	23p33	23p33		00 03	00 03			06 33		07 03		07 34
13	13	—	Howwood		d	23p36	23p36		00 06	00 06			06 36		07 06		07 37
16½	16½	—	Lochwinnoch		d	23p40	23p40		00 10	00 10			06 40				07 41
20½	20½	—	Glengarnock		d	23p45	23p45		00 15	00 15			06 45		07 13		07 46
23¼	23¼	—	Dalry		d	23p49	23p49		00 19	00 19			06 49		07 17		07 50
26¾	26¾	—	Kilwinning 4		d	23p54	23p54	23p59	00 23	00 23	00 42	06 28	06 54	06 59	07 23	07 29	07 54
—	29	—	Stevenston		d	23p57	23p57		00 27	00 27			06 57		07 27		07 58
—	30¼	—	Saltcoats		d	23p59	23p59		00 29	00 29			07 00		07 29		08 00
—	31¼	—	Ardrossan South Beach		d	00 02	00 02		00 31	00a32			07 02		07 31		08 02
—	—	31¾	Ardrossan Town		d	00a06									07 35		
—	—	32¼	**Ardrossan Harbour**		a										07 37		
—	35¾	—	West Kilbride		d		00 08		00 37				07 08				08 08
—	39¾	—	Fairlie		d		00 14		00 43				07 13				08 14
—	42¾	—	**Largs**		a		00 19		00 49				07 20				08 20
30	—	—	Irvine		d			00 03			00 47	06 32		07 03		07 33	
33¾	—	—	Barassie		d			00 08			00 51			07 07			
35	—	—	Troon		d			00 11			00 54	06 38		07 10		07 39	
37¾	—	—	Prestwick Int. Airport ✈		d			00 15			00 58	06 42		07 14		07 43	
38¼	—	—	Prestwick Town		d			00 17			01 00	06 44		07 16		07 45	
40¼	—	—	Newton-on-Ayr		d			00 20			01 04			07 19			
41½	—	—	**Ayr**		a			00 25			01 11	06 52		07 24		07 52	

Station			SR	SR	SR SX	SR C	SR	SR	SR	SR	SR	SR	SR ◇ D	SR
Glasgow Central 15	219	d	07 30	08 00	08 15		08 30	08 34	08 45	09 00	09 15	09 30	09 41	09 45
Paisley Gilmour Street	219	a	07 40	08 10	08 25		08 40	08 44	08 55	09 10	09 25	09 40	09 53	09 56
		d	07 41	08 11	08 26		08 41	08 45	08 56	09 11	09 26	09 41	09 54	09 57
Johnstone		d	07 45	08 15	08 30		08 45	08 49	09 00	09 17	09 30	09 45		10 00
Milliken Park		d			08 33			08 52	09 03		09 33			10 04
Howwood		d			08 36			08 55			09 36			
Lochwinnoch		d			08 40			08 59			09 40			
Glengarnock		d		08 24	08 45		08 54	09 04	09 11		09 45	09 54		10 12
Dalry		d		08 28	08 49		08 58	09 08			09 49			10 16
Kilwinning 4		d	08 00	08 33	08 54		09 03	09 12	09 18	09 31	09 54	10 01	10 14	10 21
Stevenston		d			08 57			09 16	09 21		09 57			10 23
Saltcoats		d			09 00			09 18	09 24		10 00			10 26
Ardrossan South Beach		d			09a02			09 20	09 26		10 02			10 28
Ardrossan Town		d						09 24			10 06			
Ardrossan Harbour		a						09 26			10 08			
West Kilbride		d							09 31					10 33
Fairlie		d							09 35					10 39
Largs		a							09 44					10 46
Irvine		d	08 04	08 37			09 07			09 35		10 05		
Barassie		d	08 09	08 42			09 11					10 10		
Troon		d	08 12	08 45		08 49	09 14			09 41		10 13		
Prestwick Int. Airport ✈		d	08 16	08 49		08 54	09 18			09 45		10 17		
Prestwick Town		d	08 18	08 51		08 56	09 20			09 47		10 19		
Newton-on-Ayr		d	08 21	08 54			09 24					10 22		
Ayr		a	08 26	08 58		09 03	09 27			09 53		10 26	10 35	

Station			SR	SR	SR	SR	SR C	SR	SR	SR	SR SO ◇ D	SR SX ◇ D	SR	SR
Glasgow Central 15	219	d	10 00	10 15	10 30	10 45		11 00	11 15	11 30	11 40	11 42	11 45	12 00
Paisley Gilmour Street	219	a	10 10	10 25	10 40	10 55		11 10	11 25	11 40	11 52	11 52	11 55	12 09
		d	10 11	10 26	10 41	10 56		11 11	11 26	11 41	11 53	11 53	11 56	12 10
Johnstone		d	10 15	10 30	10 45	11 00		11 15	11 30	11 45			12 01	12 14
Milliken Park		d		10 33		11 03			11 33				12 03	
Howwood		d		10 36					11 36					
Lochwinnoch		d		10 40					11 40					
Glengarnock		d		10 45	10 55	11 11			11 45				12 11	
Dalry		d	10 26	10 49					11 49					
Kilwinning 4		d	10 31	10 54	11 01	11 18		11 29	11 54	11 59	12 11	12 11	12 18	12 27
Stevenston		d		10 57		11 21			11 57				12 22	
Saltcoats		d		11 00		11 24			12 00				12 24	
Ardrossan South Beach		d		11 02		11 26			12 02				12 26	
Ardrossan Town		d		11 06					12 06					
Ardrossan Harbour		a		11 08					12 09					
West Kilbride		d				11 32							12 32	
Fairlie		d				11 37							12 38	
Largs		a				11 44							12 44	
Irvine		d	10 35		11 05			11 33		12 03				12 33
Barassie		d			11 10					12 08				
Troon		d	10 43		11 13		11 18	11 39		12 11				12 39
Prestwick Int. Airport ✈		d	10 47		11 17		11 23	11 43		12 15				12 43
Prestwick Town		d	10 49		11 19		11 25	11 45		12 17				12 45
Newton-on-Ayr		d			11 22					12 20				
Ayr		a	10 54		11 26		11 32	11 52		12 24	12 29	12 29		12 52

C From Kilmarnock to Girvan

D To Stranraer

Glasgow Central - Ardrossan, Largs and Ayr

Network Diagram - see first Page of Table 216

Station			SR	SR	SR	SR C	SR	SR	SR	SR	SR C	SR	SR	SR
Glasgow Central 15	219	d	12 15	12 30	12 45		13 00	13 15	13 30	13 45		14 00	14 15	14 30
Paisley Gilmour Street	219	a	12 25	12 40	12 55		13 10	13 25	13 40	13 55		14 10	14 25	14 40
		d	12 26	12 41	12 56		13 11	13 26	13 41	13 56		14 11	14 26	14 41
Johnstone		d	12 30	12 45	13 00		13 15	13 30	13 45	14 00		14 15	14 30	14 45
Milliken Park		d	12 33		13 03			13 33		14 03			14 33	
Howwood		d	12 36					13 36					14 36	
Lochwinnoch		d	12 40					13 40					14 40	
Glengarnock		d	12 45		13 11			13 45		14 11			14 45	
Dalry		d	12 49		13 15			13 49				14 26	14 49	
Kilwinning 4		d	12 54	12 59	13 20		13 29	13 54	13 59	14 18		14 31	14 54	14 59
Stevenston		d	12 57		13 23			13 57		14 21			14 57	
Saltcoats		d	13 00		13 26			14 00		14 24			15 00	
Ardrossan South Beach		d	13 02		13 28			14 02		14 26			15 01	
Ardrossan Town		d	13 06					14 06					15 06	
Ardrossan Harbour		a	13 09					14 09					15 09	
West Kilbride		d			13 34					14 32				
Fairlie		d			13 39					14 37				
Largs		a			13 46					14 44				
Irvine		d		13 03			13 33		14 03			14 35		15 03
Barassie		d		13 08					14 08					15 08
Troon		d		13 11		13 16	13 39		14 11		14 16	14 41		15 11
Prestwick Int. Airport ✈		d		13 15		13 21	13 43		14 15		14 21	14 45		15 15
Prestwick Town		d		13 17		13 23	13 45		14 17		14 23	14 47		15 17
Newton-on-Ayr		d		13 20					14 20					15 20
Ayr		a		13 24		13 30	13 52		14 24		14 30	14 54		15 24

Station			SR	SR	SR D	SR	SR	SR	SR	SR	SR	SR E	SR	SR F
Glasgow Central 15	219	d	14 45	15 00	15 12	15 15	15 30	15 45	16 00	16 18	16 30	16 41	16 50	
Paisley Gilmour Street	219	a	14 55	15 10		15 25	15 40	15 55	16 10	16 27	16 40	16 53	17 00	
		d	14 56	15 11		15 26	15 41	15 56	16 11	16 28	16 41	16 54	17 01	
Johnstone		d	15 00	15 15		15 30	15 45	16 00	16 15	16 32	16 45	16 58	17 05	
Milliken Park		d	15 03			15 33		16 03		16 35		17 01	17 08	
Howwood		d				15 36				16 38			17 11	
Lochwinnoch		d				15 40				16 42		17 06		
Glengarnock		d	15 11			15 45		16 11		16 47		17 11	17 18	
Dalry		d				15 49				16 51		17 15	17 22	
Kilwinning 4		d	15 18	15 29		15 54	15 59	16 18	16 29	16 56	17 00	17 20	17 26	
Stevenston		d	15 21			15 57		16 21		17 01		17 24	17 30	
Saltcoats		d	15 24			16 00		16 24		17 09		17 27	17 32	
Ardrossan South Beach		d	15 26			16 02		16 26		17 11		17a29	17 35	
Ardrossan Town		d				16 06							17 38	
Ardrossan Harbour		a				16 09							17 44	
West Kilbride		d	15 32					16 32		17 17				
Fairlie		d	15 37					16 37		17 22				
Largs		a	15 44					16 44		17 28				
Irvine		d		15 33			16 03		16 33		17 04			
Barassie		d					16 08				17 08			
Troon		d		15 39	16 16		16 11		16 39		17 11			17 16
Prestwick Int. Airport ✈		d		15 43	16 20		16 15		16 43		17 15			17 21
Prestwick Town		d		15 45	16 22		16 17		16 45		17 17			17 23
Newton-on-Ayr		d					16 20				17 21			
Ayr		a		15 52	16 30		16 24		16 52		17 25			17 30

Station			SR	SR D	SR SX	SR	SR SX	SR SO	SR	SR	SR	SR	SR	SR
Glasgow Central 15	219	d	17 00	17 12	17 13	17 20	17 30	17 30	17 35	17 45	18 00	18 15	18 30	18 45
Paisley Gilmour Street	219	a	17 10			17 31		17 40	17 47	17 55	18 10	18 25	18 40	18 55
		d	17 11		17u24	17 32	17u41	17 41	17 47	17 56	18 11	18 26	18 41	18 56
Johnstone		d	17 15			17 36		17 45	17 53	18 00	18 15	18 30	18 45	19 00
Milliken Park		d				17 39			17 56	18 03		18 33		19 03
Howwood		d							17 59			18 36		
Lochwinnoch		d	17 21						18 03			18 40		
Glengarnock		d	17 26		17 35				18 08	18 11		18 45		19 11
Dalry		d	17 30			17 49			18 12	18 15	18 26	18 49	18 57	
Kilwinning 4		d	17 35		17 42	17 54		17 59	18 16	18 20	18 31	18 54	19 02	19 18
Stevenston		d				17 57			18 20	18 23		18 57		19 21
Saltcoats		d				18 00			18 22	18 26		19 00		19 24
Ardrossan South Beach		d				18 02			18 24	18 28		19 02		19 26
Ardrossan Town		d							18a27			19 06		
Ardrossan Harbour		a										19 09		
West Kilbride		d				18 08				18 34				19 32
Fairlie		d				18 13				18 39				19 37
Largs		a				18 20				18 48				19 44
Irvine		d	17 39		17 46		18 00	18 03			18 35		19 06	
Barassie		d	17 44				18 04	18 08			18 40		19 11	
Troon		d	17 47	18 21	17 52		18 07	18 11			18 43		19 14	
Prestwick Int. Airport ✈		d	17 51	18 26	17 56		18 11	18 15			18 47		19 18	
Prestwick Town		d	17 53	18 28	17 58		18 13	18 17			18 49		19 20	
Newton-on-Ayr		d	17 56				18 17	18 20			18 52		19 23	
Ayr		a	18 00	18 36	18 05		18 21	18 24			18 56		19 26	

C From Kilmarnock to Girvan
D To Girvan
E from 27 February
F From Kilmarnock to Stranraer

Table 221

Mondays to Saturdays

Glasgow Central - Ardrossan, Largs and Ayr

Network Diagram - see first Page of Table 216

		SR A	SR	SR	SR	SR	SR	SR	SR	SR	SR D	SR	SR	SR
Glasgow Central 15 219	d		19 00	19 15	19 30	19 45	20 00	20 15	20 30	20 45		21 00	21 15	21 30
Paisley Gilmour Street 219	a		19 10	19 25	19 40	19 55	20 10	20 25	20 40	20 55		21 10	21 25	21 40
	d		19 11	19 26	19 41	19 56	20 11	20 26	20 41	20 56		21 11	21 26	21 41
Johnstone	d		19 15	19 30	19 45	20 00	20 15	20 30	20 45	21 00		21 15	21 30	21 45
Milliken Park	d			19 33		20 03		20 33		21 03			21 33	
Howwood	d			19 36				20 36					21 36	
Lochwinnoch	d			19 40				20 40					21 40	
Glengarnock	d			19 45		20 11		20 45		21 11			21 45	
Dalry	d			19 49				20 49					21 49	
Kilwinning 4	d		19 29	19 54	20 00	20 18	20 29	20 54	20 59	21 18		21 29	21 53	21 59
Stevenston	d			19 57		20 22		20 57		21 21			21 57	
Saltcoats	d			20 00		20 24		21 00		21 24			22 00	
Ardrossan South Beach	d			20 02		20 26		21 02		21 26			22 02	
Ardrossan Town	d			20 06				21 06					22 06	
Ardrossan Harbour	a			20 09				21 09					22 09	
West Kilbride	d					20 32				21 32				
Fairlie	d					20 37				21 37				
Largs	a					20 44				21 44				
Irvine	d		19 33		20 04		20 33		21 03			21 33		22 03
Barassie	d				20 09				21 08					22 08
Troon	d	19 17	19 39		20 12		20 39		21 11		21 22	21 39		22 11
Prestwick Int. Airport ✈	d	19 21	19 43		20 16		20 43		21 15		21 27	21 43		22 15
Prestwick Town	d	19 23	19 45		20 18		20 45		21 17		21 29	21 45		22 17
Newton-on-Ayr	d				20 21				21 20					22 20
Ayr	a	19 30	19 52		20 25		20 52		21 24		21 34	21 52		22 24

		SR	SR	SR SX E	SR	SR	SR	SR SO A	SR	SR FO	SR FX	SR	SR FO	SR FSX
Glasgow Central 15 219	d	21 45	22 00	22 12	22 15	22 30	22 45		23 00	23 15	23 15	23 30	23 45	23 45
Paisley Gilmour Street 219	a	21 55	22 10		22 25	22 40	22 55		23 10	23 25	23 25	23 40	23 55	23 55
	d	21 56	22 11		22 26	22 41	22 56		23 11	23 26	23 26	23 41	23 56	23 56
Johnstone	d	22 02	22 15		22 30	22 45	23 00		23 15	23 30	23 30	23 45	23 59	23 59
Milliken Park	d	22 04			22 33		23 03			23 33	23 33		00 03	00 03
Howwood	d				22 36					23 36	23 36		00 06	00 06
Lochwinnoch	d				22 40					23 40	23 40		00 10	00 10
Glengarnock	d	22 12			22 45		23 11			23 45	23 45		00 15	00 15
Dalry	d				22 49					23 49	23 49		00 19	00 19
Kilwinning 4	d	22 19	22 29		22 56	22 59	23 18		23 27	23 54	23 54	23 59	00 23	00 23
Stevenston	d	22 21			23 00		23 21			23 57	23 57		00 27	00 27
Saltcoats	d	22 24			23 02		23 24			23 59	23 59		00 29	00 29
Ardrossan South Beach	d	22 26			23 04		23 26			00 02	00 02		00 31	00a32
Ardrossan Town	d				23a07					00a06				
Ardrossan Harbour	a													
West Kilbride	d	22 32					23 32				00 08		00 37	
Fairlie	d	22 37					23 37				00 14		00 43	
Largs	a	22 44					23 44				00 19		00 49	
Irvine	d		22 33			23 03			23 33			00 03		
Barassie	d					23 08						00 08		
Troon	d		22 39	23 18		23 11		23 18	23 39			00 11		
Prestwick Int. Airport ✈	d		22 43	23 23		23 15		23 23	23 43			00 15		
Prestwick Town	d		22 45	23 25		23 17		23 25	23 45			00 17		
Newton-on-Ayr	d					23 20						00 20		
Ayr	a		22 52	23 30		23 24		23 30	23 52			00 25		

Sundays

		SR F	SR F	SR	SR	SR	SR	SR	SR	SR
Glasgow Central 15 219	d	23p15	23p30	08 40	09 00	09 42	10 00	10 42	11 00	11 15
Paisley Gilmour Street 219	a	23p25	23p40	08 50	09 10	09 52	10 10	10 54	11 10	11 25
	d	23p26	23p41	08 51	09 11	09 53	10 11	10 54	11 11	11 26
Johnstone	d	23p30	23p45	08 55	09 15	09 57	10 15	10 59	11 15	11 30
Milliken Park	d	23p33		08 58		10 00		11 01		11 33
Howwood	d	23p36				10 03		11 04		
Lochwinnoch	d	23p40				10 07		11 08		
Glengarnock	d	23p45		09 06		10 12		11 13		
Dalry	d	23p49		09 10		10 16		11 17		
Kilwinning 4	d	23p54	23p59	09 15	09 29	10 21	10 29	11 22	11 29	11 46
Stevenston	d	23p57		09 18		10 24		11 26		11 49
Saltcoats	d	23p59		09 21		10 27		11 28		11 52
Ardrossan South Beach	d	00 02		09 23		10 28		11 30		11 54
Ardrossan Town	d			09 27						11 59
Ardrossan Harbour	a			09 30						12 02
West Kilbride	d	00 08				10 34		11 36		
Fairlie	d	00 14				10 41		11 42		
Largs	a	00 19				10 47		11 47		
Irvine	d		00 03		09 33		10 33		11 33	
Barassie	d		00 08		09 38		10 38		11 38	
Troon	d		00 11		09 41		10 41		11 41	
Prestwick Int. Airport ✈	d		00 15		09 45		10 45		11 45	
Prestwick Town	d		00 17		09 47		10 47		11 47	
Newton-on-Ayr	d		00 20							
Ayr	a		00 25		09 54		10 54		11 54	

A From Kilmarnock to Stranraer
D From Kilmarnock to Girvan
E To Stranraer
F not 11 December

Table 221

Sundays

Glasgow Central - Ardrossan, Largs and Ayr

Network Diagram - see first Page of Table 216

Station		SR	SR	SR	SR	SR	SR	SR	SR
		◇ D							
Glasgow Central 15 219	d	11 42	11 45	12 00	12 42	13 00	13 42	14 00	14 05
Paisley Gilmour Street 219	a	11 52	11 57	12 10	12 55	13 10	13 54	14 10	14 15
	d	11 53	11 57	12 11	12 56	13 11	13 54	14 11	14 16
Johnstone	d		12 03	12 15	13 00	13 15	13 59	14 15	14 20
Milliken Park	d		12 05		13 03		14 01		14 23
Howwood	d		12 08		13 06		14 04		
Lochwinnoch	d		12 12		13 10		14 08		
Glengarnock	d		12 17		13 15		14 13		
Dalry	d		12 21		13 19		14 17		
Kilwinning 4	d	12 11	12 26	12 30	13 23	13 29	14 22	14 29	14 36
Stevenston	d		12 30		13 27		14 26		14 39
Saltcoats	d		12 32		13 29		14 28		14 42
Ardrossan South Beach	d		12 34		13 31		14 30		14 44
Ardrossan Town	d								14 49
Ardrossan Harbour	a								14 52
West Kilbride	d		12 40		13 37		14 36		
Fairlie	d		12 46		13 43		14 42		
Largs	a		12 51		13 48		14 47		
Irvine	d			12 34		13 33		14 33	
Barassie	d			12 39		13 38		14 38	
Troon	d			12 42		13 41		14 41	
Prestwick Int. Airport ✈	d			12 46		13 45		14 45	
Prestwick Town	d			12 48		13 47		14 47	
Newton-on-Ayr	d								
Ayr	a	12 29		12 54		13 54		14 54	

Station		SR	SR	SR	SR	SR	SR	SR	SR
						◇ D			
Glasgow Central 15 219	d	14 42	15 00	15 42	16 00	16 25	16 42	16 54	17 00
Paisley Gilmour Street 219	a	14 54	15 10	15 53	16 10	16 38	16 55	17 06	17 10
	d	14 54	15 11	15 53	16 11	16 39	16 55	17 07	17 12
Johnstone	d	14 59	15 15	15 58	16 15		17 00	17 11	17 17
Milliken Park	d	15 01		16 00			17 02	17 14	
Howwood	d	15 04		16 03			17 05		
Lochwinnoch	d	15 08		16 07			17 09		
Glengarnock	d	15 13		16 12			17 14		
Dalry	d	15 17		16 16			17 18		
Kilwinning 4	d	15 22	15 29	16 20	16 29	16 56	17 23	17 28	17 31
Stevenston	d	15 26		16 24			17 27	17 31	
Saltcoats	d	15 28		16 26			17 29	17 34	
Ardrossan South Beach	d	15 30		16 28			17 31	17 36	
Ardrossan Town	d							17 40	
Ardrossan Harbour	a							17 43	
West Kilbride	d	15 36		16 34			17 37		
Fairlie	d	15 42		16 40			17 43		
Largs	a	15 47		16 47			17 48		
Irvine	d		15 33		16 33				17 35
Barassie	d		15 38		16 38				17 40
Troon	d		15 41		16 41				17 43
Prestwick Int. Airport ✈	d		15 45		16 45				17 47
Prestwick Town	d		15 47		16 47				17 49
Newton-on-Ayr	d								
Ayr	a		15 54		16 54	17 17			17 54

Station		SR	SR	SR	SR	SR	SR	SR	SR	SR	SR	SR	SR
Glasgow Central 15 219	d	17 42	18 00	18 42	19 00	19 42	20 00	20 42	21 00	21 42	22 00	22 42	23 00
Paisley Gilmour Street 219	a	17 54	18 10	18 52	19 10	19 52	20 10	20 52	21 10	21 51	22 10	22 52	23 10
	d	17 54	18 11	18 53	19 11	19 53	20 11	20 53	21 11	21 52	22 11	22 53	23 11
Johnstone	d	17 59	18 15	18 58	19 15	19 58	20 15	20 58	21 15	21 57	22 15	22 58	23 15
Milliken Park	d	18 01		19 00		20 00		21 00		21 59		23 00	
Howwood	d	18 04		19 03		20 03		21 03		22 02		23 03	
Lochwinnoch	d	18 08		19 07		20 07		21 07		22 06		23 07	
Glengarnock	d	18 13		19 12		20 12		21 12		22 11		23 12	
Dalry	d	18 17		19 16		20 16		21 16		22 15		23 16	
Kilwinning 4	d	18 22	18 29	19 21	19 29	20 21	20 29	21 21	21 29	22 20	22 29	23 26	23 29
Stevenston	d	18 26		19 25		20 25		21 25		22 24		23 29	
Saltcoats	d	18 28		19 27		20 27		21 27		22 26		23 32	
Ardrossan South Beach	d	18 30		19 29		20 29		21 29		22 28		23 34	
Ardrossan Town	d												
Ardrossan Harbour	a												
West Kilbride	d	18 36		19 35		20 35		21 35		22 33		23 40	
Fairlie	d	18 42		19 41		20 41		21 41		22 39		23 45	
Largs	a	18 47		19 47		20 47		21 47		22 47		23 51	
Irvine	d		18 33		19 33		20 33		21 33		22 33		23 33
Barassie	d		18 38		19 38		20 38		21 38		22 38		23 38
Troon	d		18 41		19 41		20 41		21 41		22 41		23 41
Prestwick Int. Airport ✈	d		18 45		19 45		20 45		21 45		22 45		23 45
Prestwick Town	d		18 47		19 47		20 47		21 47		22 47		23 47
Newton-on-Ayr	d												
Ayr	a		18 54		19 54		20 54		21 54		22 54		23 54

D To Stranraer

Table 221

Mondays to Saturdays

Ayr, Largs and Ardrossan - Glasgow Central

Network Diagram - see first Page of Table 216

Miles	Miles	Miles			SR MO			SR	SR		SR		SR				SR	SR			SR SX		SR SX		
0	—	—	**Ayr**	d				05 12	05 40		06 13						06 43				06 57		07 13		
1¼	—	—	Newton-on-Ayr	d				05 15	05 43		06 16						06 46						07 16		
3¼	—	—	Prestwick Town	d				05 18	05 46		06 19						06 49				07 02		07 19		
3¾	—	—	Prestwick Int. Airport ✈	d				05 20	05 48		06 21						06 51				07 04		07 21		
6½	—	—	Troon	d				05 24	05 52		06 25						06 55				07 08		07 25		
7¾	—	—	Barassie	d				05 26	05 54		06 27						06 57				07 10		07 27		
11½	—	—	Irvine	d				05 31	05 59		06 32						07 02				07 15		07 32		
—	0	—	**Largs**	d	23p01													06 41							
—	3	—	Fairlie	d	23p06													06 46							
—	7	—	West Kilbride	d	23p11													06 51							
—	—	0	**Ardrossan Harbour**	d																					
—	—	0½	Ardrossan Town	d									06 30												
—	11½	1	Ardrossan South Beach	d	23p17								06 33					06 57							
—	12½	2	Saltcoats	d	23p19								06 35					07 02							
—	13¾	3¼	Stevenston	d	23p22								06 38					07 05							
14¾	16	5½	Kilwinning 4	d	23p28			05 36	06 04		06 37		06 42				07 07	07 10			07 20		07 37		
18½	19¾	9¼	Dalry	d	23p32			05 40	06 08				06 46					07 14			07 24		07 41		
21	22¼	11¾	Glengarnock	d	23p36			05 44	06 12				06 50					07 18			07 28				
25	26¼	15¾	Lochwinnoch	d	23p41			05 49	06 17				06 55								07 33				
28½	29¾	19¼	Howwood	d	23p45			05 53	06 21				06 59								07 37				
30	31¼	20¾	Milliken Park	d	23p48			05 56	06 24				07 02					07 26			07 40				
30¾	32	21½	Johnstone	d	23p51			05 59	06 27		06 50		07 05				07 20	07 29			07 43		07 52		
34¼	35½	25	Paisley Gilmour Street 219	a	23p55			06 03	06 31		06 55		07 09				07 25	07 34			07 47		07 57		
—	—	—		d	23p56			06 04	06 32		06 55		07 10				07 25	07 34			07 48		07 57		
41½	42¾	32¼	**Glasgow Central 15** 219	a	00 07			06 15	06 43		07 07		07 22				07 38	07 47			07 59		08 09		

		SR SO	SR SX	SR SX	SR ◇ C			SR				SR		SR SX	SR SX	SR		SR SO			SR SX	SR		SR SO	SR SX
Ayr	d	07 13	07 25		07 36			07 43						07 58		08 13						08 43			
Newton-on-Ayr	d	07 16												08 01		08 16									
Prestwick Town	d	07 19	07 30		07 41			07 48						08 03		08 19						08 48			
Prestwick Int. Airport ✈	d	07 21	07 32		07 44			07 50						08 05		08 21						08 50			
Troon	d	07 25	07 36		07a49			07 54						08 09		08 25						08 54			
Barassie	d	07 27	07 38											08 11		08 27									
Irvine	d	07 32	07 43					08 00						08 16		08 32						08 59			
Largs	d			07 25								07 42									08 28			08 51	
Fairlie	d			07 30								07 47									08 33			08 56	
West Kilbride	d			07 35								07 52									08 38			09 01	
Ardrossan Harbour	d														08 11			08 29							
Ardrossan Town	d														08 14			08 31							
Ardrossan South Beach	d			07 41								07 58			08 16			08 33			08 44			09 07	09 07
Saltcoats	d			07 43								08 00			08 18			08 35			08 46			09 09	09 09
Stevenston	d			07 46								08 03			08 21			08 37			08 49			09 12	09 12
Kilwinning 4	d	07 37		07 50				08 04				08 08		08 20	08 25	08 34		08 41			08 53	09 04		09 16	09 16
Dalry	d	07 41		07 55								08 12			08 30			08 46			08 57				
Glengarnock	d	07 45	07 52									08 16			08 34			08 50			09 01			09 22	09 22
Lochwinnoch	d	07 50		08 01								08 21			08 39			08 55						09 27	09 27
Howwood	d	07 54	07 59												08 43			08 59						09 31	09 31
Milliken Park	d	07 57		08 06								08 26			08 46			09 02			09 09			09 32	09 32
Johnstone	d	08 00	08 03	08 09				08 18				08 29		08 34	08 48	08 50		09 05			09 12	09 18		09 35	09 35
Paisley Gilmour Street 219	a	08 04	08 07	08 13				08 22				08 34		08 42	08 53	08 56		09 09			09 16	09 23		09 39	09 39
	d	08 05	08 08	08 13				08 23				08 35		08 43	08 53	08 56		09 10			09 17	09 24		09 40	09 40
Glasgow Central 15 219	a	08 16	08 19	08 24				08 35				08 46		08 55	09 04	09 08		09 23			09 33	09 36		09 54	09 54

				SR	SR			SR	SR C		SR			SR	SR			SR		SR			SR D	SR SO E	SR
Ayr	d			09 13				09 43	10 06					10 13				10 43					11 13	11 13	
Newton-on-Ayr	d			09 16										10 16									11 16	11 16	
Prestwick Town	d			09 19				09 48	10 11					10 19				10 48					11 19	11 19	
Prestwick Int. Airport ✈	d			09 21				09 50	10 13					10 21				10 50					11 21	11 21	
Troon	d			09 25				09 54	10a18					10 25				10 54					11 25	11 25	
Barassie	d			09 27										10 27									11 27	11 27	
Irvine	d			09 32				09 59						10 32				10 59					11 32	11 32	
Largs	d										09 53									10 53					
Fairlie	d										09 58									10 58					
West Kilbride	d										10 03									11 03					
Ardrossan Harbour	d				09 31										10 28										11 28
Ardrossan Town	d				09 33										10 31										11 31
Ardrossan South Beach	d				09 35						10 09				10 33					11 09					11 33
Saltcoats	d				09 37						10 11				10 35					11 11					11 35
Stevenston	d				09 40						10 14				10 38					11 14					11 38
Kilwinning 4	d			09 37	09 45			10 04			10 18			10 37	10 42			11 04		11 18			11 37	11 37	11 42
Dalry	d			09 41	09 49										10 47										11 47
Glengarnock	d				09 53						10 25				10 51					11 25					11 51
Lochwinnoch	d				09 58										10 56										11 56
Howwood	d							10 16							11 00										12 00
Milliken Park	d				10 03						10 33				11 03					11 33					12 03
Johnstone	d			09 52	10 06			10 20			10 35			10 50	11 06			11 18		11 35			11 50	11 50	12 06
Paisley Gilmour Street 219	a			09 57	10 10			10 24			10 40			10 55	11 10			11 23		11 39			11 55	11 55	12 10
	d			09 57	10 11			10 25			10 41			10 55	11 11			11 23		11 39			11 55	11 56	12 11
Glasgow Central 15 219	a			10 09	10 22			10 36			10 52			11 07	11 22			11 36		11 52			12 07	12 07	12 22

C From Girvan to Kilmarnock

D until 17 February, SX from 20 February

E from 18 February

Ayr, Largs and Ardrossan - Glasgow Central

Network Diagram - see first Page of Table 216

		SR	SR	SR	SR	SR	SR	SR	SR	SR	SR	SR	SR
				SX	SO			SX					
		◇ A		D	E			F	G	H			
Ayr	d	11 37	11 43			12 13		12 43	12 43	13 08		13 13	
Newton-on-Ayr	d					12 16						13 16	
Prestwick Town	d	11 42	11 48			12 19		12 47	12 47	13 13		13 19	
Prestwick Int. Airport ✈	d	11 44	11 50			12 21		12 49	12 49	13 15		13 21	
Troon	d	11a49	11 54			12 25		12 53	12 53	13a20		13 25	
Barassie	d					12 27						13 27	
Irvine	d		11 59			12 32		12 58	12 58			13 32	
Largs	d			11 53	11 53						12 53		
Fairlie	d			11 58	11 58						12 58		
West Kilbride	d			12 05	12 05						13 05		
Ardrossan Harbour	d						12 28						13 28
Ardrossan Town	d						12 31						13 31
Ardrossan South Beach	d			12 11	12 11		12 33				13 11		13 33
Saltcoats	d			12 13	12 13		12 35				13 13		13 35
Stevenston	d			12 16	12 16		12 38				13 16		13 38
Kilwinning 4	d		12 04	12 20	12 20	12 37	12 42	13 03	13 03		13 20	13 37	13 42
Dalry	d						12 47						13 47
Glengarnock	d			12 26	12 26		12 51				13 26		13 51
Lochwinnoch	d						12 56						13 56
Howwood	d						13 00						14 00
Milliken Park	d			12 34	12 34		13 03				13 34		14 03
Johnstone	d		12 18	12 37	12 37	12 50	13 06	13 18	13 18		13 37	13 50	14 06
Paisley Gilmour Street 219	a		12 23	12 41	12 41	12 55	13 10	13 23	13 23		13 41	13 55	14 10
	d		12 24	12 42	12 42	12 55	13 11	13 24	13 24		13 42	13 55	14 11
Glasgow Central 15 219	a		12 36	12 52	12 53	13 07	13 22	13 35	13 36		13 52	14 07	14 24

		SR	SR	SR	SR	SR	SR	SR	SR	SR	SR	SR	SR	SR	SR
					SO										
				◇ I	J	K						L	L		◇ A
Ayr	d	13 43		14 10	14 13	14 13		14 43		15 13		15 32	15 18	15 43	16 06
Newton-on-Ayr	d				14 16	14 16				15 16					
Prestwick Town	d	13 48			14 19	14 19		14 48		15 19			15 23	15 48	16 11
Prestwick Int. Airport ✈	d	13 50			14 21	14 21		14 50		15 21			15 25	15 50	16 14
Troon	d	13 54			14 25	14 25		14 54		15 25			15 30	15 54	16a19
Barassie	d				14 27	14 27				15 27					
Irvine	d	13 59			14 32	14 32		14 59		15 32				15 59	
Largs	d		13 53						14 53						
Fairlie	d		13 58						14 58						
West Kilbride	d		14 03						15 03						
Ardrossan Harbour	d						14 28				15 28				
Ardrossan Town	d						14 31				15 31				
Ardrossan South Beach	d		14 09				14 33		15 09		15 33				
Saltcoats	d		14 11				14 35		15 11		15 35				
Stevenston	d		14 14				14 38		15 14		15 38				
Kilwinning 4	d	14 04	14 18	14 27	14 37	14 37	14 42	15 04	15 18	15 37	15 43	15 48		16 04	
Dalry	d						14 47				15 47				
Glengarnock	d		14 25				14 51		15 25	15 43	15 51				
Lochwinnoch	d						14 56				15 56				
Howwood	d						15 00				16 00				
Milliken Park	d		14 33				15 03		15 33		16 03				
Johnstone	d	14 18	14 35		14 50	14 50	15 05	15 18	15 35	15 52	16 06			16 18	
Paisley Gilmour Street 219	a	14 22	14 40	14 46	14 55	14 55	15 10	15 24	15 40	15 57	16 10	16 15		16 22	
	d	14 23	14 40	14 46	14 55	14 55	15 10	15 25	15 40	15 57	16 11	16 16		16 23	
Glasgow Central 15 219	a	14 35	14 52	15 01	15 06	15 07	15 22	15 36	15 52	16 09	16 25	16 31	16 33	16 34	

		SR	SR	SR	SR	SR	SR	SR	SR	SR	SR
Ayr	d		16 13		16 43		17 13			17 43	
Newton-on-Ayr	d		16 16		16 46		17 16				
Prestwick Town	d		16 19		16 49		17 19			17 48	
Prestwick Int. Airport ✈	d		16 21		16 51		17 21			17 50	
Troon	d		16 25		16 55		17 25			17 54	
Barassie	d		16 27				17 27				
Irvine	d		16 32		17 00		17 32			17 59	
Largs	d	15 53				16 50			17 35		
Fairlie	d	15 58				16 55			17 40		
West Kilbride	d	16 03				17 00			17 45		
Ardrossan Harbour	d			16 28							18 00
Ardrossan Town	d			16 31							18 03
Ardrossan South Beach	d	16 09		16 33		17 06		17 42	17 51		18 06
Saltcoats	d	16 11		16 35		17 08		17 44	17 53		18 08
Stevenston	d	16 14		16 38		17 11		17 47	17 56		18 11
Kilwinning 4	d	16 18	16 37	16 42	17 05	17 15	17 36	17 50	18 00	18 04	18 16
Dalry	d			16 47		17 20	17 41	17 55	18 05	18 09	
Glengarnock	d	16 25	16 43	16 51		17 24		17 59		18 13	18 23
Lochwinnoch	d			16 56		17 29				18 18	
Howwood	d			17 00					18 14		18 30
Milliken Park	d	16 33		17 03		17 34		18 07			18 33
Johnstone	d	16 35	16 52	17 06	17 19	17 36	17 52	18 09	18 18	18 24	18 35
Paisley Gilmour Street 219	a	16 40	16 57	17 10	17 23	17 41	17 58	18 14	18 22	18 28	18 40
	d	16 41	16 57	17 11	17 24	17 41	17 58	18 14	18 23	18 29	18 40
Glasgow Central 15 219	a	16 52	17 09	17 24	17 36	17 55	18 09	18 25	18 34	18 42	18 52

A From Stranraer to Kilmarnock
D until 10 February, from 26 March
E until 4 February, from 11 February until 24 March, from 31 March
F from 13 February until 23 March
G until 11 February, SO from 18 February until 17 March, from 24 March
H From Girvan to Kilmarnock
I From Stranraer
J from 31 March
K until 30 March, SX from 2 April
L From Girvan

Ayr, Largs and Ardrossan - Glasgow Central

Network Diagram - see first Page of Table 216

		SR	SR	SR	SR	SR	SR	SR	SR	SR	SR	SR	SR	SR
			A					A					◇ D	
Ayr	d	18 13	18 18		18 43		19 13	19 38		19 43		20 13	20 30	
Newton-on-Ayr	d	18 16					19 16					20 16		
Prestwick Town	d	18 19	18 23		18 48		19 19	19 43		19 48		20 19		
Prestwick Int. Airport ✈	d	18 21	18 25		18 50		19 21	19 45		19 50		20 21		
Troon	d	18 25	18a30		18 54		19 25	19a50		19 54		20 25		
Barassie	d	18 27					19 27					20 27		
Irvine	d	18 32			18 59		19 32			19 59		20 32		
Largs	d					18 53					19 53			
Fairlie	d					18 58					19 58			
West Kilbride	d					19 03					20 03			
Ardrossan Harbour	d								19 28					20 33
Ardrossan Town	d			18 32					19 30					20 35
Ardrossan South Beach	d			18 34		19 09			19 34		20 09			20 38
Saltcoats	d			18 36		19 11			19 36		20 11			20 40
Stevenston	d			18 39		19 14			19 39		20 14			20 43
Kilwinning 4	d	18 37		18 43	19 04	19 18	19 37		19 43	20 04	20 18	20 36		20 48
Dalry	d	18 41		18 47					19 47					20 54
Glengarnock	d			18 51		19 25			19 51		20 25			20 58
Lochwinnoch	d			18 56					19 56					21 04
Howwood	d			19 00					20 00					21 08
Milliken Park	d			19 03		19 33			20 03		20 33			21 11
Johnstone	d	18 52		19 06	19 18	19 35	19 50		20 06	20 18	20 35	20 50		21 13
Paisley Gilmour Street 219	a	18 57		19 10	19 23	19 40	19 57		20 10	20 25	20 40	20 55	21 11	21 18
	d	18 57		19 11	19 23	19 40	19 57		20 11	20 25	20 40	20 55	21 12	21 18
Glasgow Central 15 219	a	19 08		19 22	19 34	19 53	20 08		20 22	20 36	20 52	21 07	21 27	21 32

		SR	SR	SR	SR	SR	SR	SR	SR	SR	SR
									◇ D		
Ayr	d	20 43		21 13		21 43		22 13	22 35		23 00
Newton-on-Ayr	d			21 16				22 16			23 03
Prestwick Town	d	20 48		21 19		21 48		22 19	22 40		23 06
Prestwick Int. Airport ✈	d	20 50		21 21		21 50		22 21			23 08
Troon	d	20 54		21 25		21 54		22 25	22 45		23 12
Barassie	d			21 27				22 27			23 14
Irvine	d	20 59		21 32		21 59		22 32			23 19
Largs	d		20 53				21 53			22 53	
Fairlie	d		20 58				21 58			22 58	
West Kilbride	d		21 03				22 03			23 03	
Ardrossan Harbour	d				21 28						
Ardrossan Town	d				21 31						
Ardrossan South Beach	d		21 09		21 34		22 09			23 09	
Saltcoats	d		21 11		21 36		22 11			23 11	
Stevenston	d		21 14		21 39		22 14			23 14	
Kilwinning 4	d	21 04	21 18	21 37	21 43	22 04	22 18	22 37	22 55	23 18	23 24
Dalry	d			21 41	21 47	22 09	22 23	22 41			23 28
Glengarnock	d		21 25		21 51		22 27			23 24	23 32
Lochwinnoch	d				21 56					23 29	
Howwood	d				22 00					23 33	
Milliken Park	d		21 33		22 03		22 35			23 36	
Johnstone	d	21 18	21 35	21 52	22 06	22 20	22 37	22 52		23 39	23 43
Paisley Gilmour Street 219	a	21 22	21 40	21 57	22 10	22 24	22 42	22 57	23 14	23 43	23 47
	d	21 23	21 40	21 57	22 11	22 25	22 42	22 57	23 15	23 44	23 48
Glasgow Central 15 219	a	21 34	21 52	22 09	22 22	22 36	22 54	23 09	23 25	23 54	23 58

Sundays

		SR	SR	SR	SR	SR	SR
							◇ D
Ayr	d	09 43		10 43		11 43	12 00
Newton-on-Ayr	d						
Prestwick Town	d	09 48		10 48		11 48	
Prestwick Int. Airport ✈	d	09 50		10 50		11 50	
Troon	d	09 54		10 54		11 54	
Barassie	d	09 56		10 56		11 56	
Irvine	d	10 01		11 01		12 01	
Largs	d		09 53		10 53		
Fairlie	d		09 58		10 58		
West Kilbride	d		10 03		11 03		
Ardrossan Harbour	d						
Ardrossan Town	d						
Ardrossan South Beach	d		10 09		11 09		
Saltcoats	d		10 11		11 11		
Stevenston	d		10 14		11 14		
Kilwinning 4	d	10 06	10 18	11 06	11 18	12 06	12 15
Dalry	d		10 23		11 23		
Glengarnock	d		10 27		11 27		
Lochwinnoch	d		10 32		11 32		
Howwood	d		10 36		11 36		
Milliken Park	d		10 39		11 39		
Johnstone	d	10 19	10 41	11 19	11 41	12 19	
Paisley Gilmour Street 219	a	10 24	10 46	11 24	11 46	12 24	12 36
	d	10 24	10 46	11 24	11 46	12 24	12 36
Glasgow Central 15 219	a	10 36	10 58	11 36	11 58	12 36	12 51

A From Girvan to Kilmarnock

D From Stranraer

Ayr, Largs and Ardrossan - Glasgow Central

Network Diagram - see first Page of Table 216

		SR	SR	SR	SR	SR	SR	SR	SR	SR
Ayr	d			12 43		13 43		14 43		
Newton-on-Ayr	d									
Prestwick Town	d			12 48		13 48		14 48		
Prestwick Int. Airport ✈	d			12 50		13 50		14 50		
Troon	d			12 54		13 54		14 54		
Barassie	d			12 56		13 56		14 56		
Irvine	d			13 01		14 01		15 01		
Largs	d	11 53			12 56		13 53			14 58
Fairlie	d	11 58			13 01		13 58			15 03
West Kilbride	d	12 03			13 06		14 03			15 08
Ardrossan Harbour	d		12 35						15 04	
Ardrossan Town	d									
Ardrossan South Beach	d	12 09	12 40		13 12		14 09		15 09	15 14
Saltcoats	d	12 11	12 42		13 14		14 11		15 11	15 16
Stevenston	d	12 14	12 45		13 17		14 14		15 14	15 19
Kilwinning 4	d	12 18	12 49	13 06	13 21	14 06	14 18	15 06	15 18	15 23
Dalry	d	12 23			13 25		14 23			15 27
Glengarnock	d	12 27			13 29		14 27			15 31
Lochwinnoch	d	12 32			13 34		14 32			15 36
Howwood	d	12 36			13 38		14 36			15 40
Milliken Park	d	12 39	13 02		13 41		14 39		15 31	15 43
Johnstone	d	12 42	13 04	13 19	13 44	14 19	14 41	15 19	15 33	15 46
Paisley Gilmour Street 219	a	12 46	13 09	13 24	13 48	14 24	14 46	15 24	15 38	15 50
	d	12 47	13 10	13 24	13 48	14 24	14 46	15 24	15 39	15 51
Glasgow Central 15 219	a	12 58	13 22	13 36	14 02	14 36	14 58	15 36	15 50	16 01

		SR	SR ◇ E	SR	SR	SR	SR	SR	SR	SR
Ayr	d	15 43	15 59		16 43		17 43			18 43
Newton-on-Ayr	d									
Prestwick Town	d	15 48			16 48		17 48			18 48
Prestwick Int. Airport ✈	d	15 50			16 50		17 50			18 50
Troon	d	15 54			16 54		17 54			18 54
Barassie	d	15 56			16 56		17 56			18 56
Irvine	d	16 01			17 01		18 01			19 01
Largs	d			15 53		16 53			17 53	
Fairlie	d			15 58		16 58			18 00	
West Kilbride	d			16 03		17 03			18 05	
Ardrossan Harbour	d							18 00		
Ardrossan Town	d									
Ardrossan South Beach	d			16 09		17 09		18 05	18 11	
Saltcoats	d			16 11		17 11		18 07	18 13	
Stevenston	d			16 14		17 14		18 10	18 16	
Kilwinning 4	d	16 06	16 14	16 19	17 06	17 18	18 06	18 14	18 20	19 06
Dalry	d			16 23		17 23			18 24	
Glengarnock	d			16 27		17 27			18 28	
Lochwinnoch	d			16 32		17 32			18 33	
Howwood	d			16 36		17 36			18 37	
Milliken Park	d			16 39		17 39		18 27	18 40	
Johnstone	d	16 19		16 42	17 19	17 41	18 19	18 29	18 43	19 19
Paisley Gilmour Street 219	a	16 24	16 38	16 46	17 24	17 46	18 24	18 37	18 47	19 24
	d	16 24	16 38	16 47	17 24	17 46	18 24	18 38	18 48	19 24
Glasgow Central 15 219	a	16 36	16 49	16 58	17 36	17 58	18 36	18 48	18 58	19 36

		SR	SR	SR	SR	SR	SR	SR ◇ E	SR	SR	SR	SR
Ayr	d		19 43			20 43		21 04	21 43		23 00	
Newton-on-Ayr	d											
Prestwick Town	d		19 48			20 48			21 48		23 05	
Prestwick Int. Airport ✈	d		19 50			20 50			21 50		23 07	
Troon	d		19 54			20 54			21 54		23 11	
Barassie	d		19 56			20 56			21 56		23 13	
Irvine	d		20 01			21 01			22 01		23 18	
Largs	d	18 53		19 53			20 53			21 53		23 01
Fairlie	d	18 58		19 58			20 58			21 58		23 06
West Kilbride	d	19 03		20 03			21 03			22 03		23 11
Ardrossan Harbour	d				20 31							
Ardrossan Town	d											
Ardrossan South Beach	d	19 09		20 09	20 36		21 09			22 09		23 17
Saltcoats	d	19 11		20 11	20 38		21 11			22 11		23 19
Stevenston	d	19 14		20 14	20 41		21 14			22 14		23 22
Kilwinning 4	d	19 18	20 06	20 18	20 45	21 06	21 18		22 06	22 18	23 22	23 28
Dalry	d	19 23		20 23			21 23			22 23		23 32
Glengarnock	d	19 27		20 27			21 27			22 27		23 36
Lochwinnoch	d	19 32		20 32			21 32			22 32		23 41
Howwood	d	19 36		20 36			21 36			22 36		23 45
Milliken Park	d	19 39		20 39	20 58		21 39			22 39		23 48
Johnstone	d	19 41	20 19	20 41	21 00	21 19	21 41		22 19	22 41	23 37	23 51
Paisley Gilmour Street 219	a	19 46	20 24	20 46	21 05	21 24	21 46		22 24	22 46	23 42	23 55
	d	19 47	20 24	20 47	21 06	21 24	21 47		22 24	22 47	23 42	23 56
Glasgow Central 15 219	a	19 58	20 36	20 58	21 17	21 36	21 58	22 05	22 36	22 58	23 54	00 07

E From Stranraer

Table 221A SHIPPING SERVICES

Glasgow and Ardrossan - Brodick (Arran)

Caledonian MacBrayne Ltd in association with ScotRail

Mondays to Saturdays

until 29 March 2012

Glasgow Central 15	221	d	08 34	11 15	14 15	16 50
Paisley Gilmour Street	221	d	08 45	11 26	14 26	17 01
Ardrossan Harbour	221	a	09 26	12 09	15 09	17 45
Ardrossan Harbour	⛴	d	09 45	12 30	15 15	18 00
Brodick	⛴	a	10 40	13 25	16 10	18 55

Sundays

until 25 March 2012

Glasgow Central 15	221	d	08 40	11 15	14 05	16 54
Paisley Gilmour Street	221	d	08 51	11 26	14 16	17 07
Ardrossan Harbour	221	a	09 30	12 02	14 52	17 43
Ardrossan Harbour	⛴	d	09 45	12 30	15 15	18 00
Brodick	⛴	a	10 40	13 25	16 10	18 55

Mondays to Saturdays

until 29 March 2012

Brodick	⛴	d	08 20	11 05	13 50	16 40	19 20
Ardrossan Harbour	⛴	a	09 15	12 00	14 45	17 35	20 15
Ardrossan Harbour	221	d	09 31	12 28	15 28	18 00	20 33
Paisley Gilmour Street	221	a	10 10	13 10	16 10	18 40	21 18
Glasgow Central 15	221	a	10 22	13 22	16 25	18 52	21 32

Sundays

until 25 March 2012

Brodick	⛴	d	11 05	13 50	16 40	19 20
Ardrossan Harbour	⛴	a	12 00	14 45	17 35	20 15
Ardrossan Harbour	221	d	12 35	15 04	18 00	20 31
Paisley Gilmour Street	221	a	13 09	15 38	18 37	21 05
Glasgow Central 15	221	a	13 22	15 50	18 48	21 17

For details of sailings from 30 March 2012
please telephone 08000 66 5000 or visit www.calmac.co.uk

Table 221B

Mondays to Saturdays

Cairnryan (Loch Ryan Port) - Belfast Port

		SR MX	SR	SR	SR	SR	SR	SR	SR	SR	SR
Ayr	d				08 45		12 45		16 45		
Cairnryan (Loch Ryan Port)	a				09 55		13 55		17 55		
Cairnryan (Loch Ryan Port)	d	23p30	03 45	07 30		11 30		15 30		19 30	23 30
Belfast Port	a	01 45	06 00	09 45		13 45		17 45		21 45	01 45

Sundays

		SR A	SR	SR	SR	SR	SR	SR	SR
Ayr	d			08 45		12 45		16 30	
Cairnryan (Loch Ryan Port)	a			09 55		13 55		17 40	
Cairnryan (Loch Ryan Port)	d	23p30	05 30		11 30		15 30		19 30
Belfast Port	a	01 45	07 45		13 45		17 45		21 45

A not 11 December

Ferry service operated by Stena Line.
Please telephone 08705 70 70 70 or visit www.stenaline.co.uk for details

Table 221B

Mondays to Saturdays

Belfast Port - Cairnryan (Loch Ryan Port)

		SR MX	SR	SR	SR	SR	SR	SR	SR	SR	SR
Belfast Port	d	23p30	03 30	07 30		11 30		15 30		19 30	23 30
Cairnryan (Loch Ryan Port)	a	01 45	05 45	09 45		13 45		17 45		21 45	01 45
Cairnryan (Loch Ryan Port)	d				10 15		14 15		18 15		
Ayr	a				11 25		15 25		19 25		

Sundays

		SR A	SR	SR	SR	SR	SR	SR	SR
Belfast Port	d	23p30	07 30		11 30		15 30		21 00
Cairnryan (Loch Ryan Port)	a	01 45	09 45		13 45		17 45		23 15
Cairnryan (Loch Ryan Port)	d			10 15		14 15		18 15	
Ayr	a			11 25		15 25		19 25	

A not 11 December

Ferry service operated by Stena Line.
Please telephone 08705 70 70 70 or visit www.stenaline.co.uk for details

Glasgow Central - East Kilbride, Barrhead and Kilmarnock

Network Diagram - see first Page of Table 216

Miles	Miles			SR SO	SR SO	SR	SR	SR	SR	SR A	SR SX	SR SO		SR SX	SR	SR SX	SR SO	SR	SR	SR SX	SR SO	SR		SR B	SR
0	0	**Glasgow Central 15**	d	00 12	00 18	06 12	06 30	06 48	06 52	07 07	07 12	07 18		07 23	07 37	07 43	07 48	07 52	08 07	08 17	08 18	08 23		08 37	08 48
2¼	2¼	Crossmyloof	d	00 18	00 24	06 18	06 36	06 54	06 58		07 18	07 24		07 29		07 49	07 54	07 58		08 24	08 24	08 29			08 54
3¼	3¼	Pollokshaws West	d	00 21	00 27	06 21	06 39	06 57	07 01		07 21	07 27		07 32		07 52	07 57	08 01		08 27	08 27	08 32			08 57
—	4¼	Thornliebank	d		00 30	06 24		07 00			07 24	07 30				07 55	08 00			08 30	08 30				09 00
—	5¼	Giffnock	d		00 33	06 27		07 03			07 27	07 33				07 58	08 03			08 33	08 33				09 03
—	6½	Clarkston	d		00 37	06 31		07 07			07 31	07 37				08 02	08 07			08 37	08 37				09 07
—	7¼	Busby	d		00 40	06 34		07 10			07 35	07 40				08 08	08 10			08 40	08 40				09 10
—	8½	Thorntonhall	d		00 43	06 37											08 13			08 43					09 13
—	10	Hairmyres	d		00 47	06 41		07 15			07 41	07 45				08 14	08 16			08 46	08 46				09 16
—	11½	**East Kilbride**	a		00 51	06 45		07 19			07 50	07 50				08 18	08 21			08 51	08 51				09 21
4½	—	Kennishead	d	00 24			06 42		07 04					07 35				08 04				08 35			
5	—	Priesthill & Darnley	d	00 26			06 44		07 06					07 37				08 06				08 37			
5¾	—	Nitshill	d	00 29			06 47		07 09					07 40				08 09				08 40			
7½	—	**Barrhead**	d	00 33			06 51		07a14	07 22				07a44	07 50			08a15	08 21			08a46		08 49	
16½	—	Dunlop	d	00 45			07 03			07 34					08 02				08 33					09 01	
18¾	—	Stewarton	d	00 49			07 07			07 38					08 06				08 37					09 05	
22	—	Kilmaurs	d	00 53			07 11			07 44					08 10				08 41					09 10	
24¼	—	**Kilmarnock 3**	a	00 59			07 17			07 48					08 16				08 47					09 18	

		SR	SR	SR	SR	SR	SR	SR		SR B	SR	SR	SR	SR	SR	SR	SR	SR		SR	SR	SR	SR A	SR	SR
Glasgow Central 15	d	08 57	09 12	09 18	09 27	09 42	09 48	09 57		10 12	10 18	10 27	10 42	10 48	10 57	11 12	11 18	11 27		11 42	11 48	11 57	12 12	12 18	12 27
Crossmyloof	d	09 03		09 24	09 33		09 54	10 03			10 24	10 33		10 54	11 03		11 24	11 33			11 54	12 03		12 24	12 33
Pollokshaws West	d	09 06		09 27	09 36		09 57	10 06			10 27	10 36		10 57	11 06		11 27	11 36			11 57	12 06		12 27	12 36
Thornliebank	d			09 30			10 00				10 30			11 00			11 30				12 00			12 30	
Giffnock	d			09 33			10 03				10 33			11 03			11 33				12 03			12 33	
Clarkston	d			09 37			10 07				10 37			11 07			11 37				12 07			12 37	
Busby	d			09 40			10 10				10 40			11 10			11 40				12 10			12 40	
Thorntonhall	d						10 13							11 13							12 13				
Hairmyres	d			09 45			10 16				10 45			11 16			11 45				12 16			12 45	
East Kilbride	a			09 50			10 21				10 50			11 21			11 50				12 21			12 50	
Kennishead	d	09 09			09 39			10 09				10 39			11 09			11 39				12 09			12 39
Priesthill & Darnley	d	09 11			09 41			10 11				10 41			11 11			11 41				12 11			12 41
Nitshill	d	09 14			09 44			10 14				10 44			11 14			11 44				12 14			12 44
Barrhead	d	09a18			09a49	09 53		10a19				10a48	10 53		11a18			11a48		11 53		12a18			12a48
Dunlop	d					10 05							11 05			11 35				12 05					
Stewarton	d		09 39			10 09				10 39			11 09			11 39				12 09			12 37		
Kilmaurs	d					10 13							11 13			11 43				12 13					
Kilmarnock 3	a		09 49			10 21				10 51			11 21			11 50				12 21			12 48		

		SR	SR	SR		SR B	SR	SR	SR	SR	SR	SR	SR	SR		SR	SR	SR	SR C	SR	SR	SR	SR	SR	
Glasgow Central 15	d	12 42	12 48	12 57		13 12	13 18	13 27	13 42	13 48	13 57	14 12	14 18	14 27		14 42	14 48	14 57	15 12	15 18	15 27	15 42	15 48	15 57	
Crossmyloof	d		12 54	13 03			13 24	13 33		13 54	14 03		14 24	14 33			14 54	15 03		15 24	15 33		15 54	16 03	
Pollokshaws West	d		12 57	13 06			13 27	13 36		13 57	14 06		14 27	14 36			14 57	15 06		15 27	15 36		15 57	16 06	
Thornliebank	d		13 00				13 30			14 00			14 30				15 00			15 30			16 00		
Giffnock	d		13 03				13 33			14 03			14 33				15 03			15 33			16 03		
Clarkston	d		13 07				13 37			14 07			14 37				15 07			15 37			16 07		
Busby	d		13 10				13 40			14 10			14 40				15 10			15 40			16 10		
Thorntonhall	d		13 13							14 13							15 13						16 13		
Hairmyres	d		13 16				13 45			14 16			14 45				15 16			15 45			16 16		
East Kilbride	a		13 21				13 50			14 21			14 50				15 21			15 50			16 21		
Kennishead	d			13 09				13 39			14 09			14 39				15 09			15 39			16 09	
Priesthill & Darnley	d			13 11				13 41			14 11			14 41				15 11			15 41			16 11	
Nitshill	d			13 14				13 44			14 14			14 44				15 14			15 44			16 14	
Barrhead	d	12 53		13a18				13a48	13 53		14a18			14a48		14 53		15a18			15a48	15 53		16a18	
Dunlop	d	13 05							14 05			14 33				15 05			15 33			16 05			
Stewarton	d	13 09				13 39			14 09			14 37				15 09			15 37			16 09			
Kilmaurs	d	13 13							14 13			14 42				15 13			15 42			16 13			
Kilmarnock 3	a	13 20				13 50			14 21			14 49				15 21			15 50			16 21			

		SR A	SR	SR	SR	SR	SR	SR SX	SR C	SR SO		SR SX	SR	SR SX	SR B	SR SX	SR SO	SR	SR SX	SR		SR	SR	SR	SR
Glasgow Central 15	d	16 12	16 18	16 27	16 42	16 48	16 57	17 01	17 12	17 18		17 21	17 27	17 32	17 42	17 48	17 48	17 57	18 03	18 12		18 18	18 27	18 42	18 48
Crossmyloof	d		16 24	16 33		16 54	17 03	17 07		17 24			17 33	17 38		17 54	17 54	18 03	18 09			18 24	18 33		18 54
Pollokshaws West	d		16 27	16 36		16 57	17 06	17 10		17 27			17 36	17 41		17 57	17 57	18 06	18 12			18 27	18 36		18 57
Thornliebank	d		16 30			17 00		17 13		17 30				17 44		18 00	18 00		18 15			18 30			19 00
Giffnock	d		16 33			17 03		17 16		17 33				17 47		18 03	18 03		18 18			18 33			19 03
Clarkston	d		16 37			17 07		17 20		17 37		17 34		17 51		18 07	18 07		18 22			18 37			19 07
Busby	d		16 40			17 10		17 23		17 40				17 54		18 10	18 10		18 25			18 40			19 10
Thorntonhall	d		16 43			17 13				17 43				17 57			18 13		18 28						19 13
Hairmyres	d		16 46			17 16		17 28		17 46		17 44		18 00		18 15	18 16		18 31			18 45			19 16
East Kilbride	a		16 51			17 21		17 34		17 51		17 48		18 05		18 21	18 21		18 36			18 51			19 21
Kennishead	d			16 39			17 09						17 39					18 09					18 39		
Priesthill & Darnley	d			16 41			17 11						17 41					18 11					18 41		
Nitshill	d			16 44			17 14						17 44					18 14					18 44		
Barrhead	d	16 23		16a48	16 53		17a18		17 23				17a48		17 53			18a19		18 23			18a49	18 53	
Dunlop	d	16 35			17 05				17 35						18 05					18 35				19 05	
Stewarton	d	16 39			17 09				17 39						18 09					18 39				19 09	
Kilmaurs	d	16 43			17 13				17 43						18 13					18 43				19 13	
Kilmarnock 3	a	16 49			17 21				17 51						18 22					18 51				19 22	

A To Newcastle **B** To Carlisle **C** To Girvan

Table 222

Glasgow Central - East Kilbride, Barrhead and Kilmarnock

Network Diagram - see first Page of Table 216

		SR	SR A	SR	SR	SR		SR	SR	SR	SR	SR	SR	SR	SR	SR A		SR	SR	SR	SR B	SR
Glasgow Central 15	d	18 57	19 12	19 18	19 33	19 48		20 12	20 18	20 33	20 48	21 12	21 18	21 33	21 48	22 12		22 18	22 33	22 48	23 12	23 18
Crossmyloof	d	19 03		19 24	19 39	19 54			20 24	20 39	20 54		21 24	21 39	21 54			22 24	22 39	22 54	23 18	23 24
Pollokshaws West	d	19 06		19 27	19 42	19 57			20 27	20 42	20 57		21 27	21 42	21 57			22 27	22 42	22 57	23 21	23 27
Thornliebank	d			19 30		20 00			20 30		21 00		21 30		22 00			22 30		23 00		23 30
Giffnock	d			19 33		20 03			20 33		21 03		21 33		22 03			22 33		23 03		23 33
Clarkston	d			19 37		20 07			20 37		21 07		21 37		22 07			22 37		23 07		23 37
Busby	d			19 40		20 10			20 40		21 10		21 40		22 10			22 40		23 10		23 40
Thorntonhall	d					20 13					21 13				22 13					23 13		23 43
Hairmyres	d			19 45		20 16			20 45		21 16		21 45		22 16			22 45		23 16		23 46
East Kilbride	a			19 50		20 21			20 50		21 21		21 50		22 21			22 50		23 21		23 51
Kennishead	d	19 09			19 45					20 45				21 45					22 45		23 24	
Priesthill & Darnley	d	19 11			19 47					20 47				21 47					22 47		23 26	
Nitshill	d	19 14			19 50					20 50				21 50					22 50		23 29	
Barrhead	d	19a18	19 23		19 53			20 23		20 53		21 26		21 53		22 23			22 53		23 33	
Dunlop	d		19 35		20 05					21 05		21 37		22 05		22 35			23 05		23 45	
Stewarton	d		19 39		20 09			20 39		21 09		21 41		22 09		22 39			23 09		23 49	
Kilmaurs	d		19 43		20 13					21 14		21 46		22 13		22 43			23 13		23 53	
Kilmarnock 3	a		19 51		20 20			20 51		21 21		21 53		22 20		22 50			23 20		23 59	

Sundays

		SR	SR	SR	SR	SR	SR	SR	SR	SR		SR	SR	SR	SR	SR	SR	SR	SR	SR		SR	SR	SR	SR A
Glasgow Central 15	d	08 12	08 18	08 48	09 12	09 18	09 48	10 12	10 18	10 48		11 12	11 18	11 48	12 12	12 18	12 48	13 12	13 18	13 48		14 12	14 18	14 48	15 12
Crossmyloof	d		08 24	08 54		09 24	09 54		10 24	10 54			11 24	11 54		12 24	12 54		13 24	13 54			14 24	14 54	
Pollokshaws West	d	08 20	08 27	08 57	09 20	09 27	09 57	10 20	10 27	10 57		11 20	11 27	11 57	12 20	12 27	12 57	13 20	13 27	13 57		14 20	14 27	14 57	15 20
Thornliebank	d		08 30	09 00		09 30	10 00		10 30	11 00			11 30	12 00		12 30	13 00		13 30	14 00			14 30	15 00	
Giffnock	d		08 33	09 03		09 33	10 03		10 33	11 03			11 33	12 03		12 33	13 03		13 33	14 03			14 33	15 03	
Clarkston	d		08 37	09 07		09 37	10 07		10 37	11 07			11 37	12 07		12 37	13 07		13 37	14 07			14 37	15 07	
Busby	d		08 40	09 10		09 40	10 10		10 40	11 10			11 40	12 10		12 40	13 10		13 40	14 10			14 40	15 10	
Thorntonhall	d			09 13			10 13			11 13				12 13			13 13			14 13				15 13	
Hairmyres	d		08 46	09 17		09 46	10 17		10 46	11 17			11 46	12 17		12 46	13 17		13 46	14 17			14 46	15 17	
East Kilbride	a		08 50	09 21		09 50	10 21		10 50	11 21			11 50	12 21		12 50	13 21		13 50	14 21			14 50	15 21	
Kennishead	d																								
Priesthill & Darnley	d																								
Nitshill	d																								
Barrhead	d	08 26			09 26			10 26				11 26			12 26			13 26				14 26			15 26
Dunlop	d	08 38			09 38			10 38				11 38			12 38			13 38				14 38			15 38
Stewarton	d	08 42			09 42			10 42				11 42			12 42			13 42				14 42			15 42
Kilmaurs	d	08 46			09 46			10 46				11 46			12 46			13 46				14 46			15 46
Kilmarnock 3	a	08 52			09 52			10 52				11 52			12 52			13 52				14 52			15 52

		SR	SR	SR	SR	SR		SR	SR	SR	SR	SR	SR	SR	SR	SR		SR	SR	SR	SR	SR A	SR	SR	SR
Glasgow Central 15	d	15 18	15 48	16 12	16 18	16 48		17 12	17 18	17 48	18 12	18 18	18 48	19 12	19 18	19 48		20 18	20 48	21 18	21 48	22 12	22 18	22 48	23 18
Crossmyloof	d	15 24	15 54		16 24	16 54			17 24	17 54		18 24	18 54		19 24	19 54		20 24	20 54	21 24	21 54		22 24	22 54	23 24
Pollokshaws West	d	15 27	15 57	16 20	16 27	16 57		17 20	17 27	17 57	18 20	18 27	18 57	19 20	19 27	19 57		20 27	20 57	21 27	21 57		22 27	22 57	23 27
Thornliebank	d	15 30	16 00		16 30	17 00			17 30	18 00		18 30	19 00		19 30	20 00		20 30	21 00	21 30	22 00		22 30	23 00	23 30
Giffnock	d	15 33	16 03		16 33	17 03			17 33	18 03		18 33	19 03		19 33	20 03		20 33	21 03	21 33	22 03		22 33	23 03	23 33
Clarkston	d	15 37	16 07		16 37	17 07			17 37	18 07		18 37	19 07		19 37	20 07		20 37	21 07	21 37	22 07		22 37	23 07	23 37
Busby	d	15 40	16 10		16 40	17 10			17 40	18 10		18 40	19 10		19 40	20 10		20 40	21 10	21 40	22 10		22 40	23 10	23 40
Thorntonhall	d		16 13			17 13				18 13			19 13			20 13			21 13		22 13			23 13	23 43
Hairmyres	d	15 46	16 17		16 46	17 17			17 46	18 17		18 46	19 17		19 46	20 17		20 46	21 17	21 46	22 17		22 46	23 17	23 47
East Kilbride	a	15 50	16 21		16 50	17 21			17 50	18 21		18 50	19 21		19 50	20 21		20 50	21 21	21 50	22 21		22 50	23 21	23 51
Kennishead	d																								
Priesthill & Darnley	d																								
Nitshill	d																								
Barrhead	d			16 26				17 26			18 26			19 26								22 23			
Dunlop	d			16 38				17 38			18 38			19 38								22 35			
Stewarton	d			16 42				17 42			18 42			19 42								22 39			
Kilmaurs	d			16 46				17 46			18 46			19 46								22 44			
Kilmarnock 3	a			16 52				17 52			18 52			19 52								22 48			

A To Carlisle

B To Dumfries

Kilmarnock, Barrhead and East Kilbride - Glasgow Central

Network Diagram - see first Page of Table 216

Miles	Miles			SR MX	SR MO	SR	SR SX	SR	SR	SR A	SR SX	SR SO		SR	SR SX	SR SO	SR SX	SR SX	SR	SR B	SR SX	SR		SR	SR
0	—	**Kilmarnock** 3	d			05 22		06 22		06 52					07 22	07 22				07 53					08 23
2¼	—	Kilmaurs	d			05 26		06 26		06 56					07 26	07 26				07 57					08 27
5½	—	Stewarton	d			05 31		06 31		07 02					07 31	07 31				08 03					08 32
7¾	—	Dunlop	d			05 36		06 36		07 06					07 36	07 36				08 08					08 37
16¾	—	**Barrhead**	d			05 46		06 46		07 18	07 24	07 27			07 48	07 48		07 56		08 20		08 27			08 49
18½	—	Nitshill	d			05 49		06 49			07 27	07 30				07 51		07 59				08 30			
19½	—	Priesthill & Darnley	d			05 52		06 52			07 29	07 32				07 53		08 01				08 32			
20	—	Kennishead	d			05 54		06 54			07 31	07 34				07 55		08 03				08 34			
—	0	**East Kilbride**	d	23p56	23p56		06 17		06 54					07 24			07 42		07 58		08 10			08 25	
—	1½	Hairmyres	d	23p59	23p59		06 21		06 58					07 28			07 45		08 01		08 18			08 29	
—	3	Thorntonhall	d	00 02	00 03		06 24		07 01					07 31					08 05					08 32	
—	4¼	Busby	d	00 05	00 06		06 27		07 04					07 35					08 09		08 23			08 35	
—	5	Clarkston	d	00 08	00 09		06 30		07 07					07 38			07 52		08 12		08 26			08 38	
—	6¼	Giffnock	d	00 11	00 12		06 34		07 11					07 41					08 15		08 29			08 41	
—	7¼	Thornliebank	d	00 14	00 14		06 36		07 13					07 44					08 18		08 31			08 44	
21¼	8¼	Pollokshaws West	d	00 17	00 17	05 57	06 40	06 57	07 17		07 35	07 38		07 48		07 58		08 07	08 21		08 35	08 38		08 47	
22¼	9¼	Crossmyloof	d	00 21	00 21	06 00	06 43	07 00	07 20		07 38	07 41		07 51		08 01		08 10	08 24		08 38	08 41		08 51	
24¼	11½	**Glasgow Central** 15	a	00 27	00 27	06 08	06 49	07 08	07 27	07 31	07 45	07 47		07 57	08 00	08 09	08 09	08 16	08 31	08 37	08 45	08 49		08 58	09 03

		SR	SR	SR	SR	SR	SR	SR		SR	SR C	SR SO D	SR	SR	SR	SR	SR	SR		SR	SR	SR	SR	SR	SR
Kilmarnock 3	d			08 57			09 27				09 57	09 59			10 27			10 57				11 27			11 57
Kilmaurs	d			09 01			09 31				10 01	10 02			10 31			11 01				11 31			12 01
Stewarton	d			09 06			09 36				10 06	10 07			10 36			11 06				11 36			12 06
Dunlop	d			09 11			09 41				10 11	10 12			10 41			11 11				11 41			12 11
Barrhead	d	08 57		09 22	09 27		09 52	09 57			10 22	10 22	10 27		10 52	10 57				11 27		11 52	11 57		
Nitshill	d	09 00			09 30			10 00					10 30			11 00				11 30			12 00		
Priesthill & Darnley	d	09 02			09 32			10 02					10 32			11 02				11 32			12 02		
Kennishead	d	09 04			09 34			10 04					10 34			11 04				11 34			12 04		
East Kilbride	d		08 55			09 26				09 55				10 26			10 55				11 26			11 55	
Hairmyres	d		08 59			09 30				09 59				10 30			10 59				11 30			11 59	
Thorntonhall	d		09 02							10 02							11 02							12 02	
Busby	d		09 05			09 35				10 05				10 35			11 05				11 35			12 05	
Clarkston	d		09 08			09 38				10 08				10 38			11 08				11 38			12 08	
Giffnock	d		09 11			09 41				10 11				10 41			11 11				11 41			12 11	
Thornliebank	d		09 14			09 44				10 14				10 44			11 14				11 44			12 14	
Pollokshaws West	d	09 07	09 17		09 37	09 47		10 07		10 17			10 37	10 47		11 07	11 17			11 37	11 47		12 07	12 17	
Crossmyloof	d	09 11	09 21		09 41	09 51		10 11		10 21			10 41	10 51		11 11	11 21			11 41	11 51		12 11	12 21	
Glasgow Central 15	a	09 17	09 27	09 36	09 47	09 57	10 07	10 17		10 27	10 37	10 37	10 47	10 57	11 06	11 17	11 27	11 35		11 47	11 57	12 05	12 17	12 27	12 34

		SR	SR	SR		SR	SR	SR B	SR	SR	SR	SR	SR	SR		SR	SR	SR	SR	SR	SR B	SR	SR	SR	
Kilmarnock 3	d			12 27				12 57			13 27			13 57				14 27			14 57			15 27	
Kilmaurs	d			12 31							13 31			14 01				14 31						15 31	
Stewarton	d			12 36				13 06			13 36			14 06				14 36			15 06			15 36	
Dunlop	d			12 41							13 41			14 11				14 41						15 41	
Barrhead	d	12 27		12 52		12 57			13 27		13 52	13 57				14 27		14 52	14 57			15 27		15 52	
Nitshill	d	12 30				13 00			13 30			14 00				14 30			15 00			15 30			
Priesthill & Darnley	d	12 32				13 02			13 32			14 02				14 32			15 02			15 32			
Kennishead	d	12 34				13 04			13 34			14 04				14 34			15 04			15 34			
East Kilbride	d		12 26				12 55			13 26			13 55				14 26			14 55			15 26		
Hairmyres	d		12 30				12 59			13 30			13 59				14 30			14 59			15 30		
Thorntonhall	d						13 02						14 02							15 02					
Busby	d		12 35				13 05			13 35			14 05				14 35			15 05			15 35		
Clarkston	d		12 38				13 08			13 38			14 08				14 38			15 08			15 38		
Giffnock	d		12 41				13 11			13 41			14 11				14 41			15 11			15 41		
Thornliebank	d		12 44				13 14			13 44			14 14				14 44			15 14			15 44		
Pollokshaws West	d	12 37	12 47			13 07	13 17		13 37	13 47		14 07	14 17			14 37	14 47		15 07	15 17		15 37	15 47		
Crossmyloof	d	12 41	12 51			13 11	13 21		13 41	13 51		14 11	14 21			14 41	14 51		15 11	15 21		15 41	15 51		
Glasgow Central 15	a	12 47	12 57	13 05		13 17	13 27	13 35	13 47	13 57	14 05	14 17	14 27	14 33		14 47	14 57	15 05	15 19	15 27	15 33	15 47	15 57	16 06	

		SR	SR	SR E	SR	SR	SR	SR	SR	SR F		SR	SR	SR	SR	SR SO	SR SX	SR	SR	SR SO		SR SX	SR	SR	SR
Kilmarnock 3	d			15 57			16 27			16 57				17 27				17 57					18 27		
Kilmaurs	d			16 01			16 31			17 01				17 31				18 01					18 31		
Stewarton	d			16 06			16 36			17 06				17 36				18 06					18 36		
Dunlop	d			16 11			16 41			17 11				17 41				18 11					18 41		
Barrhead	d	15 57			16 27		16 52	16 57		17 22		17 27		17 52	17 57			18 22	18 27				18 52	18 57	
Nitshill	d	16 00			16 30			17 00				17 30			18 00				18 30					19 00	
Priesthill & Darnley	d	16 02			16 32			17 02				17 32			18 02				18 32					19 02	
Kennishead	d	16 04			16 34			17 04				17 34			18 04				18 34					19 04	
East Kilbride	d		15 55			16 26			16 55				17 26			17 55	17 55			18 26		18 26			18 55
Hairmyres	d		15 59			16 30			16 59				17 30			17 59	18 05			18 30		18 36			18 59
Thorntonhall	d		16 02						17 02							18 02	18 08								19 02
Busby	d		16 05			16 35			17 05				17 35			18 05	18 11			18 35		18 41			19 05
Clarkston	d		16 08			16 38			17 08				17 38			18 08	18 14			18 38		18 44			19 08
Giffnock	d		16 11			16 41			17 11				17 41			18 11	18 18			18 41		18 47			19 11
Thornliebank	d		16 14			16 44			17 14				17 44			18 14	18 20			18 44		18 50			19 14
Pollokshaws West	d	16 07	16 17		16 37	16 47		17 07	17 17			17 37	17 47		18 07	18 17	18 23		18 37	18 47		18 53		19 07	19 17
Crossmyloof	d	16 11	16 21		16 41	16 51		17 11	17 21			17 41	17 51		18 11	18 21	18 26		18 41	18 51		18 56		19 11	19 21
Glasgow Central 15	a	16 17	16 27	16 33	16 47	16 57	17 05	17 18	17 27	17 36		17 49	17 58	18 05	18 17	18 27	18 32	18 37	18 47	18 57		19 03	19 07	19 19	19 27

A From Dumfries
B From Carlisle
C until 17 February, SX from 20 February. From Newcastle
D from 18 February. From Newcastle
E From Girvan
F From Newcastle

Kilmarnock, Barrhead and East Kilbride - Glasgow Central

Network Diagram - see first Page of Table 216

		SR	SR	SR	SR	SR		SR A	SR	SR	SR	SR B	SR	SR	SR	SR		SR	SR	SR	SR A	SR	SR		
Kilmarnock 3	d	18 57			19 27			19 57		20 27		21 00		21 27		21 57			22 27		22 57				
Kilmaurs	d	19 01			19 31					20 31				21 31					22 31		23 01				
Stewarton	d	19 06			19 36			20 06		20 36		21 10		21 36		22 06			22 36		23 06				
Dunlop	d	19 11			19 41					20 41				21 41					22 41		23 11				
Barrhead	d	19 22	19 27		19 51			20 22		20 51		21 25		21 51		22 22			22 51		23 22				
Nitshill	d		19 30		19 54					20 54				21 54					22 54						
Priesthill & Darnley	d		19 32		19 57					20 57				21 57					22 57						
Kennishead	d		19 34		19 59					20 59				21 59					22 59						
East Kilbride	d			19 26		19 55			20 26		20 55		21 26		21 55			22 26		22 55		23 26	23 56		
Hairmyres	d			19 30		19 59			20 30		20 59		21 30		21 59			22 30		22 59		23 30	23 59		
Thorntonhall	d					20 02					21 02				22 02					23 02			00 02		
Busby	d			19 35		20 05			20 35		21 05		21 35		22 05			22 35		23 05		23 35	00 05		
Clarkston	d			19 38		20 08			20 38		21 08		21 38		22 08			22 38		23 08		23 38	00 08		
Giffnock	d			19 41		20 11			20 41		21 11		21 41		22 11			22 41		23 11		23 41	00 11		
Thornliebank	d			19 44		20 14			20 44		21 14		21 44		22 14			22 44		23 14		23 44	00 14		
Pollokshaws West	d		19 37	19 47	20 02	20 17			20 47	21 02	21 17		21 47	22 02	22 17			22 47	23 02	23 17		23 47	00 17		
Crossmyloof	d		19 41	19 51	20 05	20 21			20 51	21 05	21 21		21 51	22 05	22 21			22 51	23 05	23 21		23 50	00 21		
Glasgow Central 15	a	19 37	19 47	19 57	20 13	20 27		20 36	20 57	21 13	21 27	21 39	21 57	22 13	22 27	22 37		22 57	23 13	23 27	23 35	23 56	00 27		

Sundays

		SR C	SR	SR	SR	SR	SR	SR	SR	SR		SR	SR	SR	SR	SR	SR	SR	SR	SR		SR	SR	SR	SR A
Kilmarnock 3	d				08 57			09 57				10 57			11 57			12 57				13 57			14 57
Kilmaurs	d				09 01			10 01				11 01			12 01			13 01				14 01			15 01
Stewarton	d				09 06			10 06				11 06			12 06			13 06				14 06			15 06
Dunlop	d				09 11			10 11				11 11			12 11			13 11				14 11			15 11
Barrhead	d				09 21			10 21				11 21			12 21			13 21				14 21			15 21
Nitshill	d																								
Priesthill & Darnley	d																								
Kennishead	d																								
East Kilbride	d	23p56	08 26	08 55		09 26	09 55		10 26	10 55			11 26	11 55		12 26	12 55		13 26	13 55			14 26	14 55	
Hairmyres	d	23p59	08 30	08 59		09 30	09 59		10 30	10 59			11 30	11 59		12 30	12 59		13 30	13 59			14 30	14 59	
Thorntonhall	d	00 02		09 02			10 02			11 02				12 02			13 02			14 02				15 02	
Busby	d	00 05	08 35	09 05		09 35	10 05		10 35	11 05			11 35	12 05		12 35	13 05		13 35	14 05			14 35	15 05	
Clarkston	d	00 08	08 38	09 08		09 38	10 08		10 38	11 08			11 38	12 08		12 38	13 08		13 38	14 08			14 38	15 08	
Giffnock	d	00 11	08 41	09 12		09 41	10 12		10 41	11 12			11 41	12 12		12 41	13 12		13 41	14 12			14 41	15 12	
Thornliebank	d	00 14	08 44	09 14		09 44	10 14		10 44	11 14			11 44	12 14		12 44	13 14		13 44	14 14			14 44	15 14	
Pollokshaws West	d	00 17	08 47	09 17	09 27	09 47	10 17	10 27	10 47	11 17		11 27	11 47	12 17	12 27	12 47	13 17	13 27	13 47	14 17		14 27	14 47	15 17	15 27
Crossmyloof	d	00 21	08 50	09 20		09 50	10 20		10 50	11 20			11 50	12 20		12 50	13 20		13 50	14 20			14 50	15 20	
Glasgow Central 15	a	00 27	08 56	09 26	09 36	09 56	10 26	10 40	10 56	11 26		11 36	11 56	12 26	12 36	12 56	13 26	13 36	13 56	14 26		14 36	14 56	15 26	15 36

		SR	SR	SR	SR	SR		SR	SR	SR	SR	SR	SR	SR	SR	SR		SR	SR	SR	SR A	SR	SR ◇ D	SR	SR
Kilmarnock 3	d			15 57				16 57			17 57			18 57				19 57			20 57		21 31		
Kilmaurs	d			16 01				17 01			18 01			19 01				20 01			21 01				
Stewarton	d			16 06				17 06			18 06			19 06				20 06			21 06				
Dunlop	d			16 11				17 11			18 11			19 11				20 11			21 11				
Barrhead	d			16 21				17 21			18 21			19 21				20 21			21 21				
Nitshill	d																								
Priesthill & Darnley	d																								
Kennishead	d																								
East Kilbride	d	15 26	15 55		16 26	16 55			17 26	17 55		18 26	18 55		19 26	19 55			20 26	20 55		21 26		21 55	22 26
Hairmyres	d	15 30	15 59		16 30	16 59			17 30	17 59		18 30	18 59		19 30	19 59			20 30	20 59		21 30		21 59	22 30
Thorntonhall	d		16 02			17 02				18 02			19 02			20 02				21 02				22 02	
Busby	d	15 35	16 05		16 35	17 05			17 35	18 05		18 35	19 05		19 35	20 05			20 35	21 05		21 35		22 05	22 35
Clarkston	d	15 38	16 08		16 38	17 08			17 38	18 08		18 38	19 08		19 38	20 08			20 38	21 08		21 38		22 08	22 38
Giffnock	d	15 41	16 12		16 41	17 12			17 41	18 12		18 41	19 12		19 41	20 12			20 41	21 12		21 41		22 12	22 41
Thornliebank	d	15 44	16 14		16 44	17 14			17 44	18 14		18 44	19 14		19 44	20 14			20 44	21 14		21 44		22 14	22 44
Pollokshaws West	d	15 47	16 17	16 27	16 47	17 17		17 27	17 47	18 17	18 27	18 47	19 17	19 27	19 47	20 17		20 27	20 47	21 17		21 47		22 17	22 47
Crossmyloof	d	15 50	16 20		16 50	17 20			17 50	18 20		18 50	19 20		19 50	20 20			20 50	21 20		21 50		22 20	22 50
Glasgow Central 15	a	15 56	16 26	16 36	16 56	17 26		17 36	17 56	18 26	18 36	18 56	19 26	19 36	19 56	20 26		20 36	20 56	21 26	21 35	21 56	22 05	22 26	22 56

		SR		SR	SR
Kilmarnock 3	d				
Kilmaurs	d				
Stewarton	d				
Dunlop	d				
Barrhead	d				
Nitshill	d				
Priesthill & Darnley	d				
Kennishead	d				
East Kilbride	d	22 55		23 26	23 56
Hairmyres	d	22 59		23 30	23 59
Thorntonhall	d	23 02			00 03
Busby	d	23 05		23 35	00 06
Clarkston	d	23 08		23 38	00 09
Giffnock	d	23 12		23 41	00 12
Thornliebank	d	23 14		23 44	00 14
Pollokshaws West	d	23 17		23 47	00 17
Crossmyloof	d	23 20		23 50	00 21
Glasgow Central 15	a	23 26		23 56	00 27

A From Carlisle
B From Newcastle
C not 11 December
D From Stranraer

Glasgow Central, Cathcart Circle, Neilston and Newton

Network Diagram - see first Page of Table 220

Miles	Miles	Miles			SR SO	SR SO	SR SO	SR	SR	SR	SR	SR SX	SR SO		SR SX	SR SX	SR SX	SR	SR SX	SR	SR SX	SR SO	SR SX		SR
0	0	0	**Glasgow Central** 15 226	d	23p50	00 05	00 20	06 14	06 17	06 20	06 34	06 36	06 45		06 50	07 00	07 03	07 06	07 14	07 20	07 29	07 35	07 35		07 45
2¼	—	—	Pollokshields West	d			00 27	06 20				06 42	06 51				07 09		07 20						07 51
2¾	—	—	Maxwell Park	d			00 29	06 22				06 44	06 53				07 11		07 22						07 53
3½	—	—	Shawlands	d			00 31	06 24				06 46	06 55				07 13		07 24						07 55
3¾	—	—	Pollokshaws East	d			00 32	06 25				06 48	06 56				07 14		07 25						07 56
4¼	—	—	Langside	d			00 34	06 27				06 50	06 58				07 16		07 27						07 58
—	1¾	1¾	Pollokshields East	d	23p55	00 10			06 22	06 25	06 39				06 55	07 05		07 11		07 25	07 34	07 40	07 40		
—	2¼	2¼	Queens Park	d	23p56	00 11			06 23	06 26	06 40				06 56	07 06		07 12		07 26	07 35	07 41	07 41		
—	2½	2½	Crosshill	d	23p58	00 13			06 25	06 28	06 42				06 58	07 08		07 14		07 28	07 37	07 43	07 43		
—	3¼	3¼	Mount Florida	d	23p59	00 15			06 27	06 30	06 44				07 00	07 10		07 16		07 30	07 39	07 45	07 45		
5¼	—	4	Cathcart	d		00 17	00a37	06a30	06 29		06 46				07a03	07 12		07 20	07a30		07 41	07 47	07a47		
—	—	4¾	Muirend	d		00 20			06 32		06 49					07 15		07 23			07 44	07 50			
—	—	6	Williamwood	d		00 23			06 35		06 52					07 18		07 26			07 47	07 53			
—	—	6¾	Whitecraigs	d		00 25			06 37		06 54					07 20		07 28			07 49	07 55			
—	—	7¾	Patterton	d		00 28			06 40		06 57					07 23		07 31			07 52	07 58			
—	—	11¾	**Neilston**	a		00 34			06 46		07 03					07 29		07 37			07 58	08 04			
5¾	4½	—	Kings Park	d	00 03					06 33		06 54	07 03				07 20			07 33					08 03
6	4¾	—	Croftfoot	d	00 05					06 35		06 56	07 05				07 22			07 35					08 05
7	5¾	—	Burnside	d	00 08					06 38		06 58	07 08				07 25			07 38					08 08
8½	7¼	—	Kirkhill	a	00 11					06 41		07 01	07 11				07 28			07 41					08 11
10	8¾	—	**Newton** 226	a	00 14					06 45		07 04	07 14				07 31			07 44					08 14

		SR SX	SR SX	SR SX	SR SX	SR SO	SR SX	SR SX	SR SX		SR	SR SX	SR SX	SR SO	SR SX	SR	SR	SR SO	SR SX		SR	SR	SR	SR	SR
Glasgow Central 15 226	d	07 48	07 54	07 56	08 01	08 05	08 10	08 12	08 15		08 20	08 26	08 33	08 35	08 39	08 45	08 50	09 05	09 08		09 14	09 20	09 35	09 45	09 50
Pollokshields West	d		08 00				08 16						08 39			08 51					09 20			09 51	
Maxwell Park	d		08 02				08 18						08 41			08 53					09 22			09 53	
Shawlands	d		08 04				08 20						08 43			08 55					09 24			09 55	
Pollokshaws East	d		08 05				08 21						08 44			08 56					09 25			09 56	
Langside	d		08 07				08 23						08 46			08 58					09 27			09 58	
Pollokshields East	d			08 01	08 06	08 10		08 17	08 21		08 25	08 31		08 40	08 44		08 55	09 10	09 13			09 25	09 40		09 55
Queens Park	d			08 02	08 07	08 11		08 18	08 22		08 26	08 32		08 41	08 45		08 57	09 11	09 14			09 26	09 41		09 56
Crosshill	d			08 04	08 09	08 13		08 20	08 24		08 28	08 34		08 43	08 47		08 59	09 13	09 16			09 28	09 43		09 58
Mount Florida	d			08 06	08 11	08 15		08 22	08 26		08 30	08 36		08 45	08 49		09 01	09 15	09 18			09 30	09 45		10 00
Cathcart	d		08a10		08 13	08 17	08a26	08a24	08a28			08 38	08a49	08 47	08 51		09a03	09 17	09 20		09a30		09 47		10a03
Muirend	d	07 58			08 16	08 20						08 41		08 50	08 54			09 20	09 23				09 50		
Williamwood	d	08 01			08 19	08 23						08 44		08 53	08 57			09 23	09 26				09 53		
Whitecraigs	d	08 03			08 21	08 25						08 46		08 55	08 59			09 25	09 28				09 55		
Patterton	d	08 06			08 24	08 28						08 49		08 58	09 02			09 28	09 31				09 58		
Neilston	a	08 12			08 30	08 34						08 55		09 04	09 08			09 34	09 37				10 04		
Kings Park	d			08 09							08 33					09 03						09 33		10 03	
Croftfoot	d			08 11							08 35					09 05						09 35		10 05	
Burnside	d			08 14							08 38					09 08						09 38		10 08	
Kirkhill	a			08 17							08 41					09 11						09 41		10 11	
Newton 226	a			08 20							08 44					09 15						09 45		10 14	

		SR	SR	SR		SR		SR	SR	SR	SR	SR	SR	SR	SR	SR SO		SR SX	SR SO	SR SX	SR	SR	SR	SR
Glasgow Central 15 226	d	10 05	10 15	10 20	and at the same minutes past each hour until	14 20		14 35	14 45	14 50	15 05	15 15	15 20	15 35	15 45	15 50		15 50	16 05	16 05	16 15	16 20	16 35	16 45
Pollokshields West	d		10 21						14 51			15 21			15 51						16 21			16 51
Maxwell Park	d		10 23						14 53			15 23			15 53						16 23			16 53
Shawlands	d		10 25						14 55			15 25			15 55						16 25			16 55
Pollokshaws East	d		10 26						14 56			15 26			15 56						16 26			16 56
Langside	d		10 28						14 58			15 28			15 58						16 28			16 58
Pollokshields East	d	10 10		10 25		14 25		14 40		14 55	15 10		15 25	15 40		15 55		15 55	16 10	16 10		16 25	16 40	
Queens Park	d	10 11		10 26		14 26		14 41		14 56	15 11		15 26	15 41		15 57		15 57	16 11	16 11		16 27	16 41	
Crosshill	d	10 13		10 28		14 28		14 43		14 58	15 13		15 28	15 43		15 59		16 03	16 13	16 13		16 29	16 43	
Mount Florida	d	10 15		10 30		14 30		14 45		15 00	15 15		15 30	15 45		16 02		16 05	16 15	16 15		16 31	16 45	
Cathcart	d	10 17	10a31					14 47		15a03	15 17	15a31		15 47		16a04		16a06	16 17	16 17	16a31		16 47	
Muirend	d	10 20						14 50			15 20			15 50					16 20	16 20			16 50	
Williamwood	d	10 23						14 53			15 23			15 53					16 23	16 23			16 53	
Whitecraigs	d	10 25						14 55			15 25			15 55					16 25	16 25			16 55	
Patterton	d	10 28						14 58			15 28			15 58					16 28	16 28			16 58	
Neilston	a	10 34						15 04			15 34			16 04					16 36	16 38			17 04	
Kings Park	d			10 33		14 33			15 03				15 33		16 03							16 34		17 03
Croftfoot	d			10 35		14 35			15 05				15 35		16 05							16 36		17 05
Burnside	d			10 38		14 38			15 08				15 38		16 08							16 38		17 08
Kirkhill	a			10 41		14 41			15 11				15 41		16 11							16 41		17 11
Newton 226	a			10 44		14 44			15 14				15 45		16 15							16 45		17 14

Glasgow Central, Cathcart Circle, Neilston and Newton

Network Diagram - see first Page of Table 220

		SR	SR SX		SR SX	SR SO	SR SX	SR SX	SR SO	SR SX	SR SO	SR SX	SR SX		SR SO	SR SX	SR	SR	SR	SR	SR	SR	SR		SR
Glasgow Central 15 226	d	16 50	16 59		17 05	17 07	17 08	17 14	17 15	17 18	17 20	17 23	17 29		17 35	17 38	17 45	17 50	18 07	18 15	18 20	18 35	18 45		18 50
Pollokshields West	d				17 11				17 21			17 29					17 51			18 21			18 51		
Maxwell Park	d				17 13				17 23			17 32					17 53			18 23			18 53		
Shawlands	d				17 15				17 25			17 34					17 55			18 25			18 55		
Pollokshaws East	d				17 16				17 26			17 35					17 56			18 26			18 56		
Langside	d				17 18				17 28			17 37					17 58			18 28			18 58		
Pollokshields East	d	16 55	17 04			17 12	17 13			17 23	17 25		17 34		17 40	17 43		17 55	18 12		18 25	18 40			18 55
Queens Park	d	16 56	17 05			17 13	17 14			17 24	17 26		17 35		17 41	17 44		17 56	18 13		18 26	18 41			18 56
Crosshill	d	16 58	17 07			17 15	17 16			17 26	17 28		17 37		17 43	17 46		17 58	18 15		18 28	18 43			18 58
Mount Florida	d	17 00	17 09			17 17	17 18			17 28	17 30		17 39		17 45	17 48		18 00	18 17		18 30	18 45			19 00
Cathcart	d	17a03	17 11		17a21	17 19			17a31	17 30		17a40			17 47	17 50		18a03	18 19	18a31		18 47			19a03
Muirend	d		17 14			17 22		17 25		17 33					17 50	17 53			18 22			18 50			
Williamwood	d		17 17			17 25		17 28		17 36					17 53	17 56			18 25			18 53			
Whitecraigs	d		17 19			17 27		17 30		17 38					17 55	17 58			18 27			18 55			
Patterton	d		17 22			17 30		17 33		17 41					17 58	18 01			18 30			18 58			
Neilston	a		17 28			17 36		17 39		17 47					18 04	18 07			18 36			19 04			
Kings Park	d						17 21				17 33		17 42				18 03				18 33		19 03		
Croftfoot	d						17 23				17 35		17 44				18 05				18 35		19 05		
Burnside	d						17 26				17 38		17 47				18 08				18 38		19 08		
Kirkhill	a						17 29				17 41		17 50				18 11				18 41		19 11		
Newton 226	a						17 32				17 44		17 53				18 14				18 45		19 14		

		SR	SR	SR	SR	SR	SR	SR	SR		SR	SR	SR	SR	SR	SR	SR	SR	SR		SR	SR	SR	SR	SR
Glasgow Central 15 226	d	19 05	19 15	19 20	19 35	19 45	19 50	20 05	20 15		20 20	20 35	20 45	20 50	21 05	21 15	21 20	21 35	21 45		21 50	22 05	22 15	22 20	22 35
Pollokshields West	d		19 21			19 51			20 21				20 51			21 21			21 51				22 21		
Maxwell Park	d		19 23			19 53			20 23				20 53			21 23			21 53				22 23		
Shawlands	d		19 25			19 55			20 25				20 55			21 25			21 55				22 25		
Pollokshaws East	d		19 26			19 56			20 26				20 56			21 26			21 56				22 26		
Langside	d		19 28			19 58			20 28				20 58			21 28			21 58				22 28		
Pollokshields East	d	19 10		19 25	19 40		19 55	20 10			20 25	20 40		20 55	21 10		21 25	21 40			21 55	22 10		22 25	22 40
Queens Park	d	19 11		19 26	19 41		19 56	20 11			20 26	20 41		20 56	21 11		21 26	21 41			21 56	22 11		22 26	22 41
Crosshill	d	19 13		19 28	19 43		19 58	20 13			20 28	20 43		20 58	21 13		21 28	21 43			21 58	22 13		22 28	22 43
Mount Florida	d	19 15		19 30	19 45		20 00	20 15			20 30	20 45		21 00	21 15		21 30	21 45			22 00	22 15		22 30	22 45
Cathcart	d	19 17	19a31		19 47		20a03	20 17	20a31			20 47		21a03	21 17	21a31		21 47			22a03	22 17	22a31		22 47
Muirend	d	19 20			19 50			20 20				20 50			21 20			21 50				22 20			22 50
Williamwood	d	19 23			19 53			20 23				20 53			21 23			21 53				22 23			22 53
Whitecraigs	d	19 25			19 55			20 25				20 55			21 25			21 55				22 25			22 55
Patterton	d	19 28			19 58			20 28				20 58			21 28			21 58				22 28			22 58
Neilston	a	19 34			20 04			20 34				21 04			21 34			22 04				22 34			23 04
Kings Park	d			19 33		20 03					20 33		21 03				21 33		22 03					22 33	
Croftfoot	d			19 35		20 05					20 35		21 05				21 35		22 05					22 35	
Burnside	d			19 38		20 08					20 38		21 08				21 38		22 08					22 38	
Kirkhill	a			19 41		20 11					20 41		21 11				21 41		22 11					22 41	
Newton 226	a			19 45		20 14					20 44		21 14				21 44		22 14					22 44	

		SR	SR	SR	SR		SR	SR FO
Glasgow Central 15 226	d	22 45	22 50	23 05	23 15		23 20	23 50
Pollokshields West	d	22 51			23 21			
Maxwell Park	d	22 53			23 23			
Shawlands	d	22 55			23 25			
Pollokshaws East	d	22 56			23 26			
Langside	d	22 58			23 28			
Pollokshields East	d		22 55	23 10			23 25	23 55
Queens Park	d		22 56	23 11			23 26	23 56
Crosshill	d		22 58	23 13			23 28	23 58
Mount Florida	d		23 00	23 15			23 30	23 59
Cathcart	d		23a03	23 17	23a31			
Muirend	d			23 20				
Williamwood	d			23 23				
Whitecraigs	d			23 25				
Patterton	d			23 28				
Neilston	a			23 34				
Kings Park	d	23 03					23 33	00 03
Croftfoot	d	23 05					23 35	00 05
Burnside	d	23 08					23 38	00 08
Kirkhill	a	23 11					23 41	00 11
Newton 226	a	23 14					23 45	00 14

Table 223

Sundays

Glasgow Central, Cathcart Circle, Neilston and Newton

Network Diagram - see first Page of Table 220

	SR	SR	SR	SR	SR	SR		SR		SR	SR	SR	SR	SR		SR	SR					
Glasgow Central 15 226 d	08 23	08 34	08 53	09 08	09 23	09 34	and at the same minutes past each hour until	12 34		12 59	13 08	13 23	13 34	13 53	and at the same minutes past each hour until	22 53	23 08					
Pollokshields West d		08 40				09 40		12 40					13 40									
Maxwell Park d		08 42				09 42		12 42					13 42									
Shawlands d		08 44				09 44		12 44					13 44									
Pollokshaws East d		08 45				09 45		12 45					13 45									
Langside d		08 47				09 47		12 47					13 47									
Pollokshields East d	08 28		08 58	09 13	09 28					13 04	13 13	13 28		13 58		22 58	23 13					
Queens Park d	08 29		08 59	09 14	09 29					13 05	13 14	13 29		13 59		22 59	23 14					
Crosshill d	08 31		09 01	09 16	09 31					13 07	13 16	13 31		14 01		23 01	23 16					
Mount Florida d	08 33		09 03	09 18	09 33					13 09	13 18	13 33		14 03		23 03	23 18					
Cathcart d	08 35		09 05		09 35					13 11		13 35		14 05		23 05						
Muirend d	08 38		09 08		09 38					13 14		13 38		14 08		23 08						
Williamwood d	08 41		09 11		09 41					13 17		13 41		14 11		23 11						
Whitecraigs d	08 43		09 13		09 43					13 19		13 43		14 13		23 13						
Patterton d	08 46		09 16		09 46					13 22		13 46		14 16		23 16						
Neilston a	08 52		09 22		09 52					13 28		13 52		14 22		23 22						
Kings Park d		08 51		09 21		09 52		12 52			13 21		13 52				23 21					
Croftfoot d		08 53		09 23		09 54		12 54			13 23		13 54				23 23					
Burnside d		08 56		09 26		09 57		12 57			13 26		13 57				23 26					
Kirkhill a		08 59		09 29		10 00		13 00			13 29		14 00				23 29					
Newton 226 a		09 02		09 32		10 03		13 03			13 32		14 03				23 32					

Newton, Neilston, Cathcart Circle and Glasgow Central

Network Diagram - see first Page of Table 220

Miles	Miles	Miles		SR SO	SR	SR	SR	SR	SR SX	SR	SR SX	SR SX		SR SO	SR SX	SR SO	SR SX	SR SX	SR SX	SR SO	SR SX	SR SX		SR
0	0	—	**Newton** 226 d			06 20		06 50			07 15			07 20				07 41		07 50	07 51			
1½	1½	—	Kirkhill d			06 23		06 53			07 18			07 23				07 44		07 53	07 54			
2¾	2¾	—	Burnside d			06 26		06 56			07 21			07 26				07 47		07 56	07 57			
3¾	3¾	—	Croftfoot d			06 30		06 58			07 23			07 28				07 49		07 58	07 59			
4¼	4¼	—	Kings Park d			06 32		07 00			07 25			07 30				07 51		08 00	08 02			
—	—	—	**Neilston** d				06 30			07 00					07 24	07 30			07 41					07 56
—	—	3¾	Patterton d				06 36			07 06					07 30	07 36			07 47					08 02
—	—	4¾	Whitecraigs d				06 39			07 09					07 33	07 39			07 50					08 05
—	—	5½	Williamwood d				06 41			07 11					07 35	07 41			07 52					08 08
—	—	7	Muirend d				06 44			07 14					07 38	07 44			07 55					08 11
4¾	—	7¾	Cathcart d	00 37	06 30		06 47		07 03	07 17		07 32			07 41	07 47	07 47		07 58			08 10		08 14
—	5½	8½	Mount Florida d	00 39	06 32		06 49	07 04		07 19		07 34			07 43	07 49		07 55	08 01	08 04		08 12		08 17
—	6	9	Crosshill d	00 41	06 34		06 51	07 06		07 21		07 36			07 45	07 51		07 57	08 03	08 06		08 14		08 19
—	6½	9½	Queens Park d	00 43	06 36		06 53	07 08		07 23		07 38			07 47	07 53		07 59	08 05	08 08		08 16		08 21
—	6¾	9¾	Pollokshields East d	00 44	06 37		06 54	07 09		07 24		07 39			07 48	07 54		08 00	08 07	08 09		08 18		08 23
5¾	—	—	Langside d			06 37			07 05		07 29			07 35			07 50				08 06			
6¼	—	—	Pollokshaws East d			06 39			07 07		07 31			07 37			07 52				08 08			
6¾	—	—	Shawlands d			06 42			07 09		07 33			07 39			07 54				08 10			
7½	—	—	Maxwell Park d			06 44			07 11		07 35			07 41			07 56				08 12			
8	—	—	Pollokshields West d			06 48			07 13		07 37			07 43			07 58				08 13			
10	8¾	11¾	**Glasgow Central** 15 226 a	00 49	06 43	06 54	06 59	07 14	07 20	07 29	07 43	07 47		07 50	07 55	07 59	08 05	08 07	08 12	08 14	08 21	08 23		08 28

	SR SX	SR SX	SR SX	SR SX	SR SO	SR SX	SR SX	SR SO		SR SX	SR SX	SR SX	SR SO	SR	SR SX	SR SO	SR SX	SR		SR	SR	SR	SR	
Newton 226 d				08 21	08 20						08 33		08 50		09 00					09 20		09 50		
Kirkhill d				08 24	08 23						08 36		08 53		09 02					09 23		09 53		
Burnside d				08 27	08 26						08 39		08 56		09 05					09 26		09 56		
Croftfoot d				08 29	08 28						08 42		08 58		09 07					09 28		09 58		
Kings Park d				08 31	08 30						08 44		09 00		09 10					09 30		10 00		
Neilston d	08 07						08 21	08 30				08 43				09 00	09 04				09 30			
Patterton d	08 13						08 27	08 36				08 49				09 06	09 10				09 36			
Whitecraigs d	08 16						08 30	08 39				08 52				09 09	09 13				09 39			
Williamwood d	08 18						08 32	08 41				08 54				09 11	09 15				09 41			
Muirend d	08 21						08 36	08 44				08 57				09 14	09 18				09 44			
Cathcart d		08 26	08 24			08 33	08 39	08 47		08 49		09 00		09 03		09 17	09 21	09 32			09 47		10 03	
Mount Florida d		08 28		08 35			08 42	08 49		08 52		09 02	09 04		09 14	09 19	09 23	09 34			09 49	10 04		
Crosshill d		08 30		08 37			08 44	08 51		08 54		09 04	09 06		09 16	09 21	09 25	09 36			09 51	10 06		
Queens Park d		08 32		08 39			08 46	08 53		08 56		09 06	09 08		09 18	09 23	09 27	09 38			09 53	10 08		
Pollokshields East d	08 29	08 33		08 40			08 48	08 54		08 58		09 07	09 09		09 19	09 24	09 28	09 39			09 54	10 09		
Langside d			08 27		08 35	08 35					08 49			09 05						09 35			10 05	
Pollokshaws East d			08 29		08 37	08 37					08 51			09 07						09 37			10 07	
Shawlands d			08 31		08 39	08 39					08 54			09 09						09 39			10 09	
Maxwell Park d			08 33		08 41	08 41					08 56			09 11						09 41			10 11	
Pollokshields West d			08 35		08 43	08 43					09 00			09 13						09 43			10 13	
Glasgow Central 15 226 a	08 34	08 39	08 43	08 47	08 50	08 52	08 54	08 59		09 03	09 06	09 12	09 14	09 22	09 24	09 29	09 33	09 44		09 50	09 59	10 14	10 20	

	SR		SR	SR		SR	SR	SR	SR	SR	SR	SR	SR	SR		SR SO	SR SX	SR	SR	SR	SR	SR SO	SR SX
Newton 226 d						14 20		14 50				15 20		15 50						16 20		16 50	16 50
Kirkhill d						14 23		14 53				15 23		15 53						16 23		16 53	16 53
Burnside d						14 26		14 56				15 26		15 56						16 26		16 56	16 56
Croftfoot d						14 28		14 58				15 28		15 58						16 28		16 58	16 58
Kings Park d						14 30		15 00				15 30		16 00						16 30		17 00	17 00
Neilston d	10 00		14 00				14 30			15 00			15 30					16 00			16 30		
Patterton d	10 06	and at	14 06				14 36			15 06			15 36					16 06			16 36		
Whitecraigs d	10 09	the same	14 09				14 39			15 09			15 39					16 09			16 39		
Williamwood d	10 11	minutes	14 11				14 41			15 11			15 41					16 11			16 41		
Muirend d	10 14	past	14 14				14 44			15 14			15 44					16 14			16 44		
Cathcart d	10 17	each	14 17	14 32			14 47		15 03	15 17	15 32		15 47			16 04	16 06	16 17	16 32		16 47		
Mount Florida d	10 19	hour until	14 19	14 34			14 49	15 04		15 19	15 34		15 49	16 04				16 19	16 34		16 49	17 04	17 04
Crosshill d	10 21		14 21	14 36			14 51	15 06		15 21	15 36		15 51	16 06				16 21	16 36		16 51	17 06	17 06
Queens Park d	10 23		14 23	14 38			14 53	15 08		15 23	15 38		15 53	16 08				16 23	16 38		16 53	17 08	17 08
Pollokshields East d	10 24		14 24	14 39			14 54	15 09		15 24	15 39		15 54	16 09				16 24	16 39		16 54	17 09	17 09
Langside d						14 35			15 05			15 35				16 07	16 09			16 35			
Pollokshaws East d						14 37			15 07			15 37				16 09	16 11			16 37			
Shawlands d						14 39			15 09			15 39				16 11	16 13			16 39			
Maxwell Park d						14 41			15 11			15 41				16 13	16 15			16 41			
Pollokshields West d						14 43			15 13			15 43				16 16	16 18			16 43			
Glasgow Central 15 226 a	10 29		14 29	14 44		14 50	14 59	15 14	15 21	15 29	15 44	15 50	15 59	16 14		16 22	16 24	16 29	16 44	16 50	16 59	17 14	17 17

Table 223

Mondays to Saturdays

Newton, Neilston, Cathcart Circle and Glasgow Central

Network Diagram - see first Page of Table 220

		SR		SR SX	SR SO	SR SX	SR SX	SR SO	SR	SR SX	SR SO	SR SX		SR	SR	SR SX	SR SO	SR SX	SR	SR	SR	SR		SR	SR
Newton 226	d								17 20					17 50						18 20		18 50			
Kirkhill	d								17 23					17 53						18 23		18 53			
Burnside	d								17 26					17 56						18 26		18 56			
Croftfoot	d								17 28					17 58						18 28		18 58			
Kings Park	d								17 30					18 00						18 30		19 00			
Neilston	d			16 53	17 00		17 14				17 30	17 39				17 54	18 00	18 04			18 30				19 00
Patterton	d			16 59	17 06		17 20				17 36	17 45				18 00	18 06	18 10			18 36				19 06
Whitecraigs	d			17 02	17 09		17 23				17 39	17 48				18 03	18 09	18 13			18 39				19 09
Williamwood	d			17 04	17 11		17 25				17 41	17 50				18 05	18 11	18 15			18 41				19 11
Muirend	d			17 07	17 14		17 28				17 44	17 53				18 08	18 14	18 18			18 44				19 14
Cathcart	d	17 03		17 10	17 17	17 21	17 31	17 32		17 41	17 47	17 56			18 03	18 11	18 17	18 21	18 32		18 47			19 03	19 17
Mount Florida	d			17 12	17 19	17 23	17 33	17 34		17 43	17 49	17 58		18 04		18 13	18 19	18 23	18 34		18 49	19 04			19 19
Crosshill	d			17 14	17 21	17 25	17 35	17 36		17 45	17 51	18 00		18 06		18 15	18 21	18 25	18 36		18 51	19 06			19 21
Queens Park	d			17 16	17 23	17 27	17 37	17 38		17 47	17 53	18 02		18 08		18 17	18 23	18 27	18 38		18 53	19 08			19 23
Pollokshields East	d			17 17	17 24	17 29	17 38	17 39		17 48	17 54	18 03		18 09		18 18	18 24	18 28	18 39		18 54	19 09			19 24
Langside	d	17 05							17 35						18 05					18 35				19 05	
Pollokshaws East	d	17 07							17 37						18 07					18 37				19 07	
Shawlands	d	17 09							17 39						18 09					18 39				19 09	
Maxwell Park	d	17 11							17 41						18 11					18 41				19 11	
Pollokshields West	d	17 13							17 43						18 13					18 43				19 13	
Glasgow Central 15 226	a	17 20		17 22	17 29	17 38	17 43	17 44	17 50	17 55	17 59	18 08		18 14	18 20	18 25	18 29	18 34	18 44	18 50	18 59	19 14		19 21	19 29

		SR	SR	SR	SR	SR	SR	SR		SR	SR	SR	SR	SR	SR	SR	SR	SR		SR	SR	SR	SR	SR	SR
Newton 226	d		19 20		19 50					20 20		20 50				21 20		21 50					22 20		22 50
Kirkhill	d		19 23		19 53					20 23		20 53				21 23		21 53					22 23		22 53
Burnside	d		19 26		19 56					20 26		20 56				21 26		21 56					22 26		22 56
Croftfoot	d		19 28		19 58					20 28		20 58				21 28		21 58					22 28		22 58
Kings Park	d		19 30		20 00					20 30		21 00				21 30		22 00					22 30		23 00
Neilston	d			19 30			20 00				20 30			21 00			21 30				22 00			22 30	
Patterton	d			19 36			20 06				20 36			21 06			21 36				22 06			22 36	
Whitecraigs	d			19 39			20 09				20 39			21 09			21 39				22 09			22 39	
Williamwood	d			19 41			20 11				20 41			21 11			21 41				22 11			22 41	
Muirend	d			19 44			20 14				20 44			21 14			21 44				22 14			22 44	
Cathcart	d	19 32		19 47		20 03	20 17	20 32			20 47		21 03	21 17	21 32		21 47			22 03	22 17	22 32		22 47	
Mount Florida	d	19 34		19 49	20 04		20 19	20 34			20 49	21 04		21 19	21 34		21 49	22 04			22 19	22 34		22 49	23 04
Crosshill	d	19 36		19 51	20 06		20 21	20 36			20 51	21 06		21 21	21 36		21 51	22 06			22 21	22 36		22 51	23 06
Queens Park	d	19 38		19 53	20 08		20 23	20 38			20 53	21 08		21 23	21 38		21 53	22 08			22 23	22 38		22 53	23 08
Pollokshields East	d	19 39		19 54	20 09		20 24	20 39			20 54	21 09		21 24	21 39		21 54	22 09			22 24	22 39		22 54	23 09
Langside	d		19 35			20 05				20 35			21 05			21 35				22 05			22 35		
Pollokshaws East	d		19 37			20 07				20 37			21 07			21 37				22 07			22 37		
Shawlands	d		19 39			20 09				20 39			21 09			21 39				22 09			22 39		
Maxwell Park	d		19 41			20 11				20 41			21 11			21 41				22 11			22 41		
Pollokshields West	d		19 43			20 13				20 43			21 13			21 43				22 14			22 43		
Glasgow Central 15 226	a	19 44	19 52	19 59	20 15	20 20	20 29	20 44		20 50	20 59	21 15	21 20	21 29	21 44	21 50	21 59	22 15		22 20	22 29	22 44	22 50	22 59	23 15

		SR	SR	SR		SR	SR
Newton 226	d					23 20	
Kirkhill	d					23 23	
Burnside	d					23 26	
Croftfoot	d					23 28	
Kings Park	d					23 30	
Neilston	d		23 00				23 30
Patterton	d		23 06				23 36
Whitecraigs	d		23 09				23 39
Williamwood	d		23 11				23 41
Muirend	d		23 14				23 44
Cathcart	d	23 03	23 17	23 32			23 47
Mount Florida	d		23 19	23 34			23 49
Crosshill	d		23 21	23 36			23 51
Queens Park	d		23 23	23 38			23 53
Pollokshields East	d		23 24	23 39			23 54
Langside	d	23 05				23 35	
Pollokshaws East	d	23 07				23 37	
Shawlands	d	23 09				23 39	
Maxwell Park	d	23 11				23 41	
Pollokshields West	d	23 13				23 43	
Glasgow Central 15 226	a	23 20	23 29	23 44		23 50	23 59

Newton, Neilston, Cathcart Circle and Glasgow Central

Network Diagram - see first Page of Table 220

			SR	SR	SR	SR		SR	SR	SR		SR	SR	SR	SR	SR
Newton	226	d		09 09		09 39		21 39		22 09			22 39		23 09	
Kirkhill		d		09 12		09 42		21 42		22 12			22 42		23 12	
Burnside		d		09 15		09 45		21 45		22 15			22 45		23 15	
Croftfoot		d		09 17		09 47		21 47		22 17			22 47		23 17	
Kings Park		d		09 19		09 49		21 49		22 19			22 49		23 19	
Neilston		d	08 48		09 19				21 48			22 19		22 48		23 19
Patterton		d	08 54		09 25		and at the same minutes past each hour until		21 54			22 25		22 54		23 25
Whitecraigs		d	08 57		09 28				21 57			22 28		22 57		23 28
Williamwood		d	08 59		09 30				21 59			22 30		22 59		23 30
Muirend		d	09 02		09 33				22 02			22 33		23 02		23 33
Cathcart		d	09 05		09 36				22 05			22 36		23 05		23 36
Mount Florida		d	09 07		09 38	09 53		21 53	22 07			22 38	22 53	23 07		23 38
Crosshill		d	09 09		09 40	09 55		21 55	22 09			22 40	22 55	23 09		23 40
Queens Park		d	09 11		09 42	09 57		21 57	22 11			22 42	22 57	23 11		23 42
Pollokshields East		d	09 12		09 43	09 58		21 58	22 12			22 43	22 58	23 12		23 43
Langside		d		09 23						22 23					23 23	
Pollokshaws East		d		09 25						22 25					23 25	
Shawlands		d		09 27						22 27					23 27	
Maxwell Park		d		09 29						22 29					23 29	
Pollokshields West		d		09 31						22 31					23 31	
Glasgow Central 15	226	a	09 17	09 38	09 48	10 03		22 03	22 17	22 37		22 48	23 03	23 17	23 37	23 48

Table 224

Mondays to Saturdays

Motherwell and Glasgow Queen Street - Cumbernauld and Falkirk Grahamston

Network Diagram - see first Page of Table 220

Miles	Miles																								
				SR MX		SR		SR	SR	SR				SR	SR	SR			SR	SR	SR				SR
—	0	**Motherwell** 226	d												07 35					08 37					
—	4½	Whifflet	d												07 43					08 45					
—	5¼	**Coatbridge Central**	d						06 45						07 46					08 48					
0	—	**Glasgow Queen Street** 10	d	23p51		05 51		06 21		06 51				07 21		07 52			08 24		08 51				09 21
1¼	—	Springburn	d	23p55		05 55		06 25		06 55				07 26		07 55			08 29		08 55				09 25
5¼	—	Stepps	d	00 02		06 02		06 32		07 02				07 33		08 02			08 36		09 02				09 32
7¾	—	Gartcosh	d	00 06		06 06		06 36		07 06				07 37		08 06			08 40		09 06				09 36
13¼	11	Greenfaulds	d	00 14		06 14		06 44	06 51	07 14				07 45	07 52	08 14			08 48	08 55	09 14				09 44
14	11¾	**Cumbernauld**	d	00a18		06a18		06 46	06a57	07a18				07 47	07a57	08a19			08 50	09a01	09a20				09 48
22½	—	Camelon 4	d					06 57						08 04					09 04						10 04
24	—	**Falkirk Grahamston**	a					07 03						08 11					09 07						10 07

		SR	SR			SR	SR	SR				SR	SR	SR			SR	SR		SR			SR	SR	SR
Motherwell 226	d	09 37					10 37						11 37					12 37						13 37	
Whifflet	d	09 45					10 45						11 45					12 45						13 45	
Coatbridge Central	d	09 48					10 48						11 48					12 48						13 48	
Glasgow Queen Street 10	d		09 52			10 21		10 51				11 22		11 51			12 24			12 51			13 23		13 51
Springburn	d		09 55			10 25		10 55				11 29		11 55			12 29			12 55			13 28		13 55
Stepps	d		10 02			10 32		11 02				11 36		12 02			12 36			13 02			13 35		14 02
Gartcosh	d		10 06			10 36		11 06				11 39		12 06			12 40			13 06			13 39		14 06
Greenfaulds	d	09 55	10 14			10 44	10 55	11 14				11 47	11 55	12 14			12 48	12 55		13 14			13 47	13 55	14 14
Cumbernauld	d	10a01	10a19			10 47	11a01	11a18				11 50	12a01	12a18			12 50	13a01		13a18			13 48	14a01	14a18
Camelon 4	d					11 04						12 04					13 04						14 04		
Falkirk Grahamston	a					11 07						12 07					13 07						14 07		

				SR		SR	SR			SR	SR	SR				SR	SR	SR		SR SX		SR SX	SR	SR	
Motherwell 226	d					14 37					15 37						16 37							17 37	
Whifflet	d					14 45					15 45						16 45							17 45	
Coatbridge Central	d					14 48					15 48						16 48							17 48	
Glasgow Queen Street 10	d			14 21			14 51			15 21		15 54				16 22		16 51		17 03		17 33	17 22		
Springburn	d			14 25			14 55			15 29		15 56				16 25		16 55					17 28		
Stepps	d			14 32			15 02			15 36		16 02				16 32		17 02					17 35		
Gartcosh	d			14 36			15 06			15 39		16 06				16 36		17 06					17 39		
Greenfaulds	d			14 44		14 55	15 14			15 47	15 55	16 14				16 44	16 55	17 15					17 45	17 55	
Cumbernauld	d			14 48		15a01	15a19			15 48	16a01	16a21				16 46	17a01	17a20					17 47	18a01	
Camelon 4	d			15 04						16 04						17 01				17 30		18 02	18 04		
Falkirk Grahamston	a			15 07						16 07						17 07				17 32		18 04	18 07		

		SR			SR	SR	SR		SR	SR				SR	SR	SR			SR	SR		SR		SR	SR
Motherwell 226	d					18 37				19 37						20 37						21 37			
Whifflet	d					18 45				19 45						20 45						21 45			
Coatbridge Central	d					18 48				19 48						20 48						21 48			
Glasgow Queen Street 10	d	17 51			18 24		18 51		19 21					19 51	20 21				20 51	21 21				21 51	22 21
Springburn	d	17 55			18 29		18 55		19 27					19 56	20 25				20 55	21 25				21 55	22 26
Stepps	d	18 02			18 36		19 02		19 34					20 03	20 32				21 02	21 32				22 02	22 33
Gartcosh	d	18 06			18 40		19 06		19 37					20 07	20 36				21 06	21 36				22 05	22 37
Greenfaulds	d	18 14			18 48	18 55	19 14		19 45	19 55				20 15	20 44	20 55			21 14	21 44		21 55		22 15	22 45
Cumbernauld	d	18a19			18 50	19a01	19a18		19a50	20a01				20 17	20a48	21a01			21 16	21a48		22a01		22 16	22a49
Camelon 4	d				19 04									20 31					21 27					22 27	
Falkirk Grahamston	a				19 07									20 34					21 33					22 34	

			SR	SR	SR																				
Motherwell 226	d																								
Whifflet	d																								
Coatbridge Central	d																								
Glasgow Queen Street 10	d		22 51	23 21	23 51																				
Springburn	d		22 55	23 25	23 55																				
Stepps	d		23 02	23 32	00 02																				
Gartcosh	d		23 06	23 36	00 06																				
Greenfaulds	d		23 14	23 44	00 14																				
Cumbernauld	d		23 16	23a48	00a18																				
Camelon 4	d		23 29																						
Falkirk Grahamston	a		23 36																						

Sundays

		SR A	SR	SR	SR		SR	SR	SR	SR		SR	SR	SR	SR		SR	SR	SR	SR					
Motherwell 226	d																								
Whifflet	d																								
Coatbridge Central	d																								
Glasgow Queen Street 10	d	23p51	08 19	09 22	10 21		11 21	12 23	13 21	14 21		15 21	16 21	17 21	18 23		19 22	20 21	21 21	22 21					
Springburn	d	23p55	08 24	09 25	10 25		11 25	12 25	13 25	14 25		15 25	16 25	17 25	18 25		19 25	20 25	21 25	22 25					
Stepps	d	00 02	08 30	09 32	10 32		11 32	12 32	13 32	14 32		15 32	16 32	17 32	18 32		19 32	20 32	21 32	22 32					
Gartcosh	d	00 06	08 34	09 36	10 36		11 36	12 36	13 36	14 36		15 36	16 36	17 36	18 36		19 36	20 36	21 36	22 36					
Greenfaulds	d	00 14	08 42	09 44	10 44		11 44	12 43	13 44	14 44		15 44	16 44	17 44	18 44		19 44	20 44	21 44	22 44					
Cumbernauld	d	00a18	08a46	09a49	10a48		11a48	12a50	13a48	14a48		15a48	16a48	17a48	18a50		19a49	20a48	21a48	22a48					
Camelon 4	d																								
Falkirk Grahamston	a																								

A not 11 December

Falkirk Grahamston and Cumbernauld - Glasgow Queen Street and Motherwell

Network Diagram - see first Page of Table 220

Miles	Miles		SR	SR	SR	SR	SR	SR	SR SX	SR	SR		SR	SR	SR	SR	SR	SR	SR	SR	SR		SR	SR
0	—	**Falkirk Grahamston** d	05 43			06 44				07 44				08 43			09 43			10 43				11 43
1½	—	Camelon 4 d	05 45			06 46				07 46				08 45			09 45			10 45				11 45
10	—	**Cumbernauld** d	05 58	06 28		06 58	07 08	07 28		07 59	08 10		08 30	08 58	09 10	09 28	09 58	10 10	10 28	10 58	11 10		11 28	11 58
10¾	0¾	Greenfaulds d	05 59	06 29		06 59	07 10	07 29		08 02	08 12		08 31	08 59	09 12	09 29	09 59	10 12	10 29	10 59	11 12		11 29	11 59
16¼	—	Gartcosh d	06 06	06 36		07 06		07 36		08 09			08 38	09 06		09 36	10 06		10 36	11 06			11 36	12 06
18¾	—	Stepps d	06 10	06 40		07 10		07 40		08 13			08 42	09 10		09 40	10 10		10 40	11 10			11 40	12 10
22¾	—	Springburn d	06 16	06 46		07 16		07 46		08 20			08 48	09 16		09 46	10 16		10 46	11 16			11 46	12 16
24	—	**Glasgow Queen Street 10** a	06 25	06 55		07 29		07 55		08 29			08 59	09 25		09 56	10 26		10 55	11 25			11 55	12 25
—	6¼	**Coatbridge Central** d			06 40		07 20		07 40		08 20				09 20			10 20			11 20			
—	7¼	Whifflet d			06 42		07 22		07 42		08 22				09 22			10 22			11 22			
—	11¾	**Motherwell** 226 a			06 51		07 30		07 49		08 32				09 32			10 32			11 32			

	SR	SR	SR	SR	SR	SR	SR		SR	SR	SR	SR	SR	SR	SR	SR	SR		SR	SR SX	SR	SR SX	SR	SR
Falkirk Grahamston d			12 43			13 43				14 43			15 43			16 43					17 43			
Camelon 4 d			12 45			13 45				14 45			15 45			16 45					17 45			
Cumbernauld d	12 10	12 28	12 58	13 10	13 28	13 58	14 10		14 28	14 58	15 10	15 28	15 58	16 10	16 28	16 58	17 10		17 28		17 58		18 10	18 28
Greenfaulds d	12 12	12 29	12 59	13 12	13 29	13 59	14 12		14 29	14 59	15 12	15 29	15 59	16 12	16 29	16 59	17 12		17 29		17 59		18 12	18 29
Gartcosh d		12 36	13 06		13 36	14 06			14 36	15 06		15 36	16 06		16 36	17 06			17 36		18 06			18 36
Stepps d		12 40	13 10		13 40	14 10			14 40	15 10		15 40	16 10		16 40	17 10			17 40		18 10			18 40
Springburn d		12 46	13 16		13 46	14 16			14 46	15 16		15 46	16 16		16 46	17 16			17 46		18 16			18 46
Glasgow Queen Street 10 a		12 55	13 25		13 55	14 25			14 55	15 25		15 55	16 25		16 59	17 27			17 56		18 27			18 55
Coatbridge Central d	12 20			13 20			14 20				15 20			16 20			17 20			17 32		17 56	18 20	
Whifflet d	12 22			13 22			14 22				15 22			16 22			17 22			17 34		18 00	18 22	
Motherwell 226 a	12 32			13 32			14 32				15 32			16 32			17 32			17 40		18 08	18 32	

	SR SX	SR	SR		SR	SR	SR	SR	SR	SR	SR	SR	SR		SR	SR	SR
Falkirk Grahamston d		18 45				19 43					21 13				22 13		23 13
Camelon 4 d		18 47				19 45					21 15				22 15		23 15
Cumbernauld d		19 01	19 10		19 28	19 58	20 10	20 28	20 58	21 10	21 28	21 58	22 10		22 28	22 58	23 28
Greenfaulds d		19 02	19 12		19 29	19 59	20 12	20 29	20 59	21 12	21 29	21 59	22 12		22 29	22 59	23 29
Gartcosh d		19 09			19 36	20 06		20 36	21 06		21 36	22 06			22 36	23 06	23 36
Stepps d		19 13			19 40	20 10		20 40	21 10		21 40	22 10			22 40	23 10	23 40
Springburn d		19 19			19 46	20 16		20 46	21 16		21 46	22 16			22 46	23 16	23 46
Glasgow Queen Street 10 a		19 29			19 55	20 26		20 55	21 25		21 55	22 26			22 55	23 26	23 55
Coatbridge Central d	18 39		19 20				20 20			21 20			22 20				
Whifflet d	18 41		19 22				20 22			21 22			22 22				
Motherwell 226 a	18 49		19 32				20 32			21 32			22 32				

Sundays

	SR	SR	SR	SR		SR	SR	SR	SR		SR	SR	SR	SR		SR	SR	SR
Falkirk Grahamston d																		
Camelon 4 d																		
Cumbernauld d	08 55	09 58	10 58	11 58		12 58	13 58	14 58	15 58		16 58	17 58	18 58	19 58		20 58	21 58	22 58
Greenfaulds d	08 56	09 59	10 59	11 59		12 59	13 59	14 59	15 59		16 59	17 59	18 59	19 59		20 59	21 59	22 59
Gartcosh d	09 03	10 06	11 06	12 06		13 06	14 06	15 06	16 06		17 06	18 06	19 06	20 06		21 06	22 06	23 06
Stepps d	09 07	10 10	11 10	12 10		13 10	14 10	15 10	16 10		17 10	18 10	19 10	20 10		21 10	22 10	23 10
Springburn d	09 13	10 16	11 16	12 16		13 16	14 16	15 16	16 16		17 16	18 16	19 16	20 16		21 16	22 16	23 16
Glasgow Queen Street 10 a	09 22	10 25	11 25	12 25		13 26	14 26	15 25	16 25		17 25	18 26	19 26	20 26		21 26	22 25	23 25
Coatbridge Central d																		
Whifflet d																		
Motherwell 226 a																		

Network Diagram for Tables 225, 228, 229, 230, 238, 240, 242

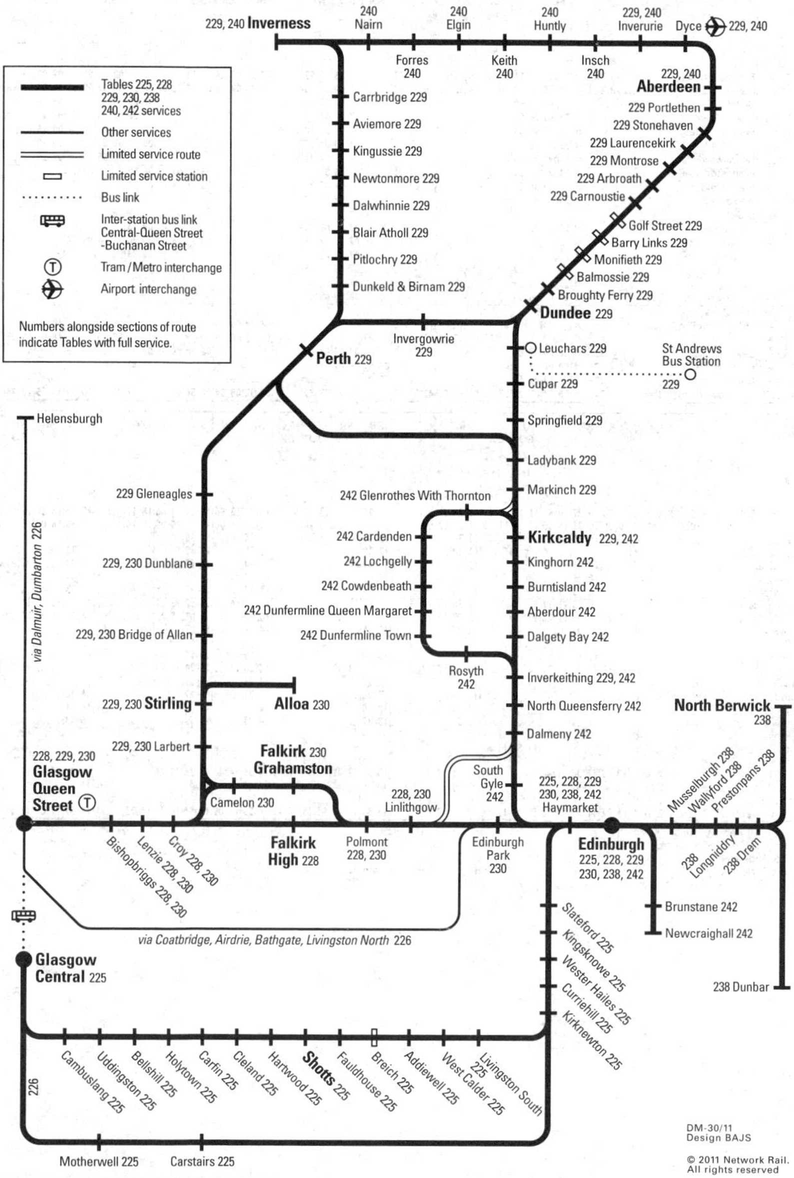

Edinburgh - Shotts, Carstairs, Motherwell and Glasgow Central

Network Diagram - see first page of Table 225

Miles	Miles			SR MX	SR	XC SX ◇1 trolley	XC SO ◇1 A	XC SO ◇1 B trolley	SR	SR SX C	SR SO D	SR SX D	XC SO ◇1	XC SX ◇1 E	SR SO	SR SX	SR	SR SX F	SR	SR SO F	XC SX ◇1 G trolley	XC SO ◇1 G trolley	SR
0	0	**Edinburgh** 10 230,238,242	d	22p56	05 51	06 24	06 26	06 26	06 40		06 55	06 55	07 26	07 26	07 51	07 57	08 25	08 33	08 57	09 03	09 11	09 11	09 26
1¼	1¼	Haymarket 230,238,242	d	23p00	05 55		06 30	06 30	06 45		07 00	07 00	07 30	07 31	07 55	08 02	08 31	08 37	09 01	09 07	09 16	09 16	09 30
3	3	Slateford	d	23p04	05 59						07 04	07 04					08 35	08 41		09 08			09 34
3¾	3¾	Kingsknowe	d	23p07	06 03						07 07	07 07					08 38	08 44		09 11			09 38
4¾	4¾	Wester Hailes	d	23p10	06 05						07 10	07 10					08 41	08 47		09 16			09 40
7½	7½	Curriehill	d	23p14	06 09						07 13	07 13					08 44	08 51		09 20			09 44
11	11	Kirknewton	d	23p21	06 16						07 21	07 21					08 52	08 55		09 25			09 52
14	—	Livingston South	d	23p26	06 21				07 01		07 26	07 26			08 10	08 19	08 58		09 17				09 58
16¾	—	West Calder	d	23p31	06 27				07 07		07 31	07 31			08 15	08 25	09 03		09 22				10 03
18½	—	Addiewell	d	23p34	06 31						07 34	07 34					09 07						10 07
21	—	Breich	d																				
23¼	—	Fauldhouse	d	23p42	06 39						07 43	07 43					09 15						10 15
26¾	—	**Shotts**	d	23p47	06 44				07 19		07 47	07 47			08 27	08 37	09 20		09 34				10 20
28¼	—	Hartwood	d	23p50	06 47						07 50	07 50					09 23						10 23
31½	—	Cleland	d	23p54	06 52						07 55	07 55					09 27						10 27
33¼	—	Carfin	d	23p58	06 56						07 58	07 58					09 31						10 31
34¼	—	Holytown	d	00 01	06 58						08 00	08 00					09 33						10 33
—	28½	Carstairs	d															09 13		09 44			
—	44½	**Motherwell**	a			07 04	07 12	07 12					08 14	08 08				09 32		10 00	10 04	10 05	
—	—		d			07 05	07 13	07 13		07 47			08 15	08 09				09 33		10 00	10 05	10 06	
36	—	Bellshill 226	d	00 04	07 04				07 30	07 53	08 03	08 03			08 38	08 48	09 36		09 46				10 36
38¾	—	Uddingston 226	d	00 08	07 10					07 57	08 07						09 41						10 41
42	—	Cambuslang 226	d	00 13	07 16					08a03													
47¼	57¼	**Glasgow Central** 15 226	a	00 24	07 29	07 27	07 42	07 42	07 52		08 24	08 29	08 32	08 24	08 56	09 08	09 57	09 59	10 09	10 15	10 26	10 25	10 55

		SR	SR	SR	XC SO ◇1 H	XC SX ◇1 H	SR	SR	SR	SR	XC SO ◇1 I trolley	XC SX ◇1 J trolley	SR	SR	SR	SR	XC ◇1 K	SR	SR SX	SR SO	SR	SR SX	SR SO
Edinburgh 10 230,238,242	d	09 56	10 27	10 56	11 11	11 11	11 26	11 56	12 26	12 56	13 11	13 12	13 26	13 56	14 27	14 56	15 11	15 26	15 56	15 56	16 27	16 57	16 57
Haymarket 230,238,242	d	10 00	10 31	11 00	11 16	11 16	11 31	12 00	12 31	13 00	13 16	13 16	13 30	14 00	14 31	15 00	15 16	15 30	16 00	16 00	16 31	17 01	17 01
Slateford	d		10 35				11 35		12 35				13 34		14 35			15 34			16 35		
Kingsknowe	d		10 39				11 38		12 39				13 38		14 39			15 38			16 39		
Wester Hailes	d		10 41				11 41		12 41				13 40		14 41			15 40			16 41		
Curriehill	d		10 45				11 44		12 45				13 44		14 45			15 44			16 45		
Kirknewton	d		10 53				11 53		12 53				13 53		14 53			15 53			16 53		
Livingston South	d	10 15	10 58	11 17			11 58	12 16	12 57	13 16			13 58	14 16	14 58	15 17		15 58	16 15	16 15	16 57	17 16	17 16
West Calder	d	10 20	11 03	11 22			12 03	12 21	13 02	13 21			14 03	14 21	15 03	15 22		16 03	16 20	16 20	17 02	17 21	17 21
Addiewell	d		11 07				12 07		13 06				14 07		15 07			16 07			17 06		
Breich	d																						
Fauldhouse	d		11 15				12 15		13 14				14 15		15 15			16 15			17 14		
Shotts	d	10 33	11 20	11 34			12 20	12 33	13 19	13 33			14 20	14 33	15 20	15 34		16 20	16 32	16 32	17 18	17 33	17 33
Hartwood	d		11 23				12 23		13 22				14 23		15 23			16 23			17 21		
Cleland	d		11 27				12 27		13 26				14 27		15 27			16 28			17 26		
Carfin	d		11 31				12 31		13 30				14 31		15 31			16 31			17 29		
Holytown	d		11 33				12 33		13 32				14 33		15 33			16 33			17 31		
Carstairs	d																						
Motherwell	a				11 52	11 52					13 52	13 52					15 52						
	d				11 53	11 53					13 53	13 53					15 54						
Bellshill 226	d	10 45	11 36	11 46			12 36	12 46	13 35	13 47			14 36	14 46	15 36	15 46		16 36	16 42	16 46	17 34	17 43	17 43
Uddingston 226	d		11 41				12 41		13 40				14 41		15 41			16 41			17 38		
Cambuslang 226	d																				17 44		
Glasgow Central 15 226	a	11 02	11 57	12 10	12 13	12 14	12 55	13 09	13 55	14 09	14 13	14 12	14 55	15 09	15 56	16 12	16 23	16 57	17 00	17 09	17 57	18 02	18 09

A from 18 February until 24 March
B until 11 February, SO from 31 March
C To Anderston
D From Newcraighall
E From Dunbar
F From North Berwick
G From Newcastle
H From Birmingham New Street
I From Bristol Temple Meads
J From Bath Spa
K From Plymouth

Edinburgh - Shotts, Carstairs, Motherwell and Glasgow Central

Network Diagram - see first page of Table 225

		XC SX ◇1 A	XC SO ◇1 A	SR	SR SX	SR SO	SR SX	SR	SR SX	SR B	SR	XC SO ◇1 A	XC SX ◇1 A	SR SO	SR SX	GR SX R 1 D	XC SO ◇1 E	XC SX ◇1 E	SR	SR
Edinburgh 10 230,238,242	d	17 11	17 11	17 18	17 42	17 48	17 48	17 56		18 24	18 56	19 11	19 11	19 18	19 27	20 16	21 13	21 14	21 26	22 56
Haymarket 230,238,242	d	17 15	17 16	17 23	17 46	17 53	17 53	18 00		18 28	19 00	19 16	19 16	19 23	19 31	20 21	21 18	21 19	21 30	23 00
Slateford	d			17 28		17 57	17 57			18 31				19 27	19 36				21 34	23 04
Kingsknowe	d			17 32		18 00	18 00			18 34				19 31	19 39				21 38	23 07
Wester Hailes	d			17 34		18 03	18 03	18 09		18 37				19 33	19 42				21 40	23 10
Curriehill	d			17 38				18 12		18 40				19 37	19 45				21 44	23 14
Kirknewton	d			17 45				18 20		18 47				19 45	19 54				21 51	23 21
Livingston South	d			17 50		18 14	18 14	18 25			19 17			19 49	19 58				21 56	23 26
West Calder	d			17 56		18 19	18 19	18 30			19 22			19 54	20 03				22 02	23 31
Addiewell	d			18 00				18 33						19 58	20 07				22 05	23 34
Breich	d							18 38												
Fauldhouse	d			18 08				18 42						20 06	20 15				22 13	23 42
Shotts	d			18 13		18 31	18 31	18 46			19 34			20 11	20 20				22 20	23 47
Hartwood	d			18 16				18 49						20 14	20 23				22 23	23 50
Cleland	d			18 21				18 54						20 18	20 27				22 27	23 54
Carfin	d			18 24				18 57						20 22	20 31				22 31	23 58
Holytown	d			18 26				18 59						20 24	20 33				22 33	00 01
Carstairs	d				18 17				18 30	19 10										
Motherwell	a	17 52	17 52	18 35	18 38				18 52	19 32		19 52	19 54			21 03	22 00	22 01		
	d	17 53	17 53		18 39					19 32		19 53	19 55			21 03	22 02	22 03		
Bellshill 226	d					18 41	18 41	19 04			19 46			20 28	20 36				22 36	00 04
Uddingston 226	d							19 07						20 32	20 41				22 41	00 08
Cambuslang 226	d						18 51	19 16												00 13
Glasgow Central 15 226	a	18 16	18 11		18 53	18 57	19 04	19 31		19 53	20 03	20 11	20 15	20 47	20 57	21 28	22 22	22 27	22 55	00 24

Sundays

		SR F	XC ◇1 G	SR	XC ◇1 H	SR	XC ◇1 I	SR	XC ◇1 J	SR	XC ◇1 E	SR	XC ◇1 E	GR R 1 D	VT R 1 I
Edinburgh 10 230,238,242	d	22p56	12 17	12 24	13 10	14 23	15 10	16 23	17 11	18 24	19 18	20 23	21 12	21 21	
Haymarket 230,238,242	d	23p00	12 21	12 28	13 15	14 27	15 15	16 27	17 15	18 27	19 23	20 27	21 16	21 26	
Slateford	d	23p04		12 32		14 31		16 31		18 31		20 31			
Kingsknowe	d	23p07		12 35		14 34		16 34		18 34		20 34			
Wester Hailes	d	23p10		12 38		14 37		16 37		18 37		20 37			
Curriehill	d	23p14		12 41		14 40		16 40		18 40		20 40			
Kirknewton	d	23p21		12 48		14 47		16 47		18 47		20 47			
Livingston South	d	23p26		12 53		14 52		16 52		18 52		20 52			
West Calder	d	23p31		13a00		14a59		16a59		18a59		20a59			
Addiewell	d	23p34													
Breich	d														
Fauldhouse	d	23p42													
Shotts	d	23p47													
Hartwood	d	23p50													
Cleland	d	23p54													
Carfin	d	23p58													
Holytown	d	00 01													
Carstairs	d														
Motherwell	a		12 55		13 50		15 51		17 52		20 00		21 53	22 06	
	d		12 56		13 51		15 52		17 53		20 02		21 54	22 06	23 08
Bellshill 226	d	00 04													
Uddingston 226	d	00 08													
Cambuslang 226	d	00 13													
Glasgow Central 15 226	a	00 24	13 12		14 14		16 13		18 12		20 20		22 14	22 29	23 22

A From Penzance
B From North Berwick
C From Manchester Airport
D From London Kings Cross
E From Plymouth
F not 11 December
G From Leeds
H From Sheffield
I From Birmingham New Street
J From Bristol Temple Meads

Glasgow Central, Motherwell, Carstairs and Shotts - Edinburgh

Network Diagram - see first page of Table 225

Miles	Miles				SR MX	SR SO	XC ◇1 A	XC SX ◇1 B	SR	SR SX C	SR SX D	SR SX	GR SX R 1 E		GR SO R 1 E	SR	SR F	SR	XC SO ◇1 G	XC SX ◇1 G	SR	SR	XC SO ◇1 H		XC SX ◇1 H	SR
0	0	**Glasgow Central** 15	226	d	23p06	00 06	06 01	06 01	06 16				06 50		06 50	07 00	07 05	07 13	07 50	07 50	08 03	08 20	09 00		09 00	09 02
5¼	—	Cambuslang	226	d	23p15	00 15			06 25		06 45							07 23								
8½	—	Uddingston	226	d	23p20	00 20			06 30									07 29				08 32				
11¼	—	Bellshill	226	d	23p25	00 25			06 35							07 15		07 34			08 19	08 36				09 20
—	12¼	**Motherwell**		a			06 15	06 15			07 06		07 04		07 04		07 26		08 04	08 04			09 14		09 14	
—	—			d			06 16	06 16		06 37		06 57	07 04		07 04		07 27		08 05	08 05			09 15		09 15	
—	28½	Carstairs		d								07a25					07 47									
13¼	—	Holytown		d	23p29	00 29			06 39	06a43								07 38				08 40				
14	—	Carfin		d	23p32	00 32			06 42									07 41				08 43				
15¾	—	Cleland		d	23p36	00 36			06 46									07 45				08 47				
19	—	Hartwood		d	23p41	00 41			06 51									07 50				08 52				
20½	—	**Shotts**		d	23p45	00 45			06 55							07 28		07 54			08 31	08 56				09 32
24	—	Fauldhouse		d	23p51	00 51			07 01									08 00				09 02				
26¼	—	Breich		d														08 04								
28¾	—	Addiewell		d	23p58	00 58			07 08									08 08				09 09				
30½	—	West Calder		d	00 01	01 01			07 11							07 40		08 11			08 43	09 12				09 44
33¼	—	Livingston South		d	00 05	01 05			07 15							07 44		08 16			08 48	09 17				09 48
36¼	46¼	Kirknewton		d	00 10				07 20							07 50	08 04	08 21				09 22				
40¾	49¾	Curriehill		d	00 15				07 26							07 55	08 09	08 27				09 27				
42½	52½	Wester Hailes		d	00 19				07 30								08 12	08 30				09 31				
43½	53½	Kingsknowe		d	00 21				07 33								08 15	08 33				09 33				
44¼	54¼	Slateford		d	00 24				07 36								08 17	08 36				09 36				
46	56	Haymarket	230,238,242	d	00 30	01 18	06 57	06 57	07 42				07 45		07 46	08 03	08 26	08 42	08 50	08 50	09 02	09 42	09 57		09 58	10 03
47¼	57¼	**Edinburgh** 10	230,238,242	a	00 34	01 23	07 02	07 02	07 49				07 52		07 52	08 12	08 33	08 46	08 54	08 55	09 10	09 48	10 02		10 02	10 10

			SR	SR	SR	XC SX ◇1 H	XC SO ◇1 H	SR	SR		SR	SR	XC ◇1 G	SR	SR	SR	SR	XC SO ◇1 I	XC SX ◇1 I		SR	SR F	SR	SR SO	SR SX	SR
Glasgow Central 15	226	d	09 18	10 05	10 18	10 59	10 59	11 05	11 18		12 05	12 18	12 51	13 05	13 18	14 05	14 18	15 00	15 00		15 03	15 14	15 18	16 05	16 06	16 18
Cambuslang	226	d																								
Uddingston	226	d	09 30		10 30				11 30			12 30			13 30		14 30						15 31			16 30
Bellshill	226	d	09 34	10 20	10 35			11 20	11 35		12 20	12 35		13 20	13 35	14 20	14 36				15 19		15 35	16 20	16 22	16 35
Motherwell		a				11 13	11 13						13 05					15 13	15 13			15 33				
		d				11 14	11 14						13 06					15 14	15 14			15 34				
Carstairs		d																				16 00				
Holytown		d	09 38		10 39				11 39			12 39			13 39		14 40						15 39			16 39
Carfin		d	09 41		10 41				11 42			12 41			13 41		14 42						15 41			16 41
Cleland		d	09 45		10 45				11 46			12 45			13 45		14 46						15 45			16 45
Hartwood		d	09 50		10 51				11 51			12 51			13 51		14 52						15 51			16 51
Shotts		d	09 54	10 32	10 54			11 32	11 55		12 32	12 55		13 32	13 55	14 32	14 56				15 32		15 57	16 32	16 35	16 55
Fauldhouse		d	10 00		11 00				12 01			13 01			14 01		15 02						16 03			17 01
Breich		d																								
Addiewell		d	10 07		11 07				12 08			13 08			14 08		15 09						16 10			17 08
West Calder		d	10 11	10 44	11 10			11 44	12 12		12 44	13 11		13 44	14 11	14 44	15 12				15 44		16 14	16 44	16 47	17 11
Livingston South		d	10 16	10 49	11 15			11 49	12 17		12 49	13 16		13 49	14 16	14 49	15 17				15 49		16 19	16 49	16 51	17 16
Kirknewton		d	10 20		11 20				12 21			13 22			14 21		15 23					16 16	16 23			17 22
Curriehill		d	10 26		11 26				12 27			13 28			14 26		15 28					16 21	16 29			17 28
Wester Hailes		d	10 29		11 29				12 30			13 31			14 30		15 32					16 24	16 32			17 31
Kingsknowe		d	10 32		11 32				12 33			13 34			14 32		15 34					16 26	16 35			17 34
Slateford		d	10 34		11 35				12 36			13 36			14 35		15 37					16 29	16 38			17 36
Haymarket	230,238,242	d	10 41	11 02	11 42	11 57	11 56	12 03	12 42		13 03	13 42		14 03	14 42	15 02	15 46	15 56	15 56		16 04	16 33	16 46	17 03	17 10	17 42
Edinburgh 10	230,238,242	a	10 46	11 09	11 46	12 02	12 02	12 10	12 46		13 10	13 47	13 54	14 10	14 47	15 09	15 51	16 01	16 01		16 11	16 39	16 52	17 11	17 14	17 47

A until 11 February, SO from 18 February. To Plymouth
B from 13 February. To Plymouth
C To Lanark
D From Garscadden to Coatbridge Central
E To London Kings Cross
F To North Berwick
G To Plymouth
H To Penzance
I To Bristol Temple Meads

Glasgow Central, Motherwell, Carstairs and Shotts - Edinburgh

Network Diagram - see first page of Table 225

			XC	XC	SR		SR	SR	SR	SR	SR	SR	XC	XC	SR		SR	SR	SR	XC	SR	SR
			SX	SO	SO		SX	SO	SX		SX	SO	SO	SX			SX	SO	SX	SX		
			◇1	◇1									◇1	◇1						◇1		
			A	A										B								
Glasgow Central 15	226	d	16 52	16 52	17 04		17 13	17 18	17 20	18 05	18 14	18 18	18 52	18 59	19 05		19 15	19 18	19 49	21 05	21 18	23 06
Cambuslang	226	d									18 23	18 27										23 15
Uddingston	226	d						17 30			18 29	18 29					19 30	19 30			21 30	23 20
Bellshill	226	d			17 19		17 29	17 34	17 34	18 20	18 34	18 34			19 20		19 35	19 35			21 36	23 25
Motherwell		a	17 13	17 13									19 13	19 14					20 05	21 22		
		d	17 14	17 14									19 14	19 15					20 06	21 23		
Carstairs		d																	20 27			
Holytown		d						17 39	17 39		18 38	18 38					19 39	19 39			21 40	23 29
Carfin		d						17 42	17 42		18 43	18 43					19 42	19 42			21 42	23 32
Cleland		d						17 46	17 46		18 47	18 47					19 46	19 46			21 46	23 36
Hartwood		d						17 51	17 51		18 52	18 52					19 51	19 51			21 52	23 41
Shotts		d			17 32		17 44	17 55	17 55	18 32	18 56	18 56			19 33		19 55	19 55			21 56	23 45
Fauldhouse		d						18 01	18 01		19 02	19 02					20 01	20 01			22 02	23 51
Breich		d																				
Addiewell		d						18 08	18 08		19 09	19 09					20 08	20 08			22 09	23 58
West Calder		d			17 44		17 59	18 11	18 11	18 44	19 13	19 13			19 45		20 12	20 12			22 12	00 01
Livingston South		d			17 49		18 03	18 15	18 15	18 49	19 18	19 18			19 50		20 17	20 17			22 16	00 05
Kirknewton		d						18 21	18 21		19 23	19 23					20 21	20 21			22 21	00 10
Curriehill		d						18 26	18 26		19 29	19 29					20 27	20 27			22 26	00 15
Wester Hailes		d						18 30	18 30		19 32	19 32					20 30	20 30			22 30	00 19
Kingsknowe		d						18 32	18 32		19 35	19 35					20 33	20 33			22 32	00 21
Slateford		d						18 35	18 35		19 37	19 37					20 35	20 35			22 35	00 24
Haymarket	230,238,242	d	17 54	17 56	18 09		18 21	18 40	18 40	19 03	19 42	19 42	19 52	19 53	20 02		20 43	20 43	20 53		22 43	00 30
Edinburgh 10	230,238,242	a	17 59	18 01	18 15		18 28	18 46	18 46	19 11	19 48	19 48	19 57	19 58	20 10		20 47	20 47	20 58	22 25	22 48	00 34

Sundays

			SR	XC	XC	SR	XC	SR	XC	SR	XC		SR	XC	SR	XC
				◇1	◇1		◇1		◇1		◇1			◇1		◇1
			C	D	D		D		E		A			B		
Glasgow Central 15	226	d	23p06	10 55	11 51		13 49		14 55		16 55			18 57		20 58
Cambuslang	226	d	23p15													
Uddingston	226	d	23p20													
Bellshill	226	d	23p25													
Motherwell		a		11 09	12 06		14 03		15 10		17 10			19 10		21 17
		d		11 10	12 07		14 04		15 11		17 11			19 11		21 18
Carstairs		d														
Holytown		d	23p29													
Carfin		d	23p32													
Cleland		d	23p36													
Hartwood		d	23p41													
Shotts		d	23p45													
Fauldhouse		d	23p51													
Breich		d														
Addiewell		d	23p58													
West Calder		d	00 01			13 09		15 14		17 14			19 14		21 14	
Livingston South		d	00 05			13 13		15 16		17 16			19 16		21 16	
Kirknewton		d	00 10			13 18		15 21		17 21			19 21		21 21	
Curriehill		d	00 15			13 22		15 27		17 27			19 27		21 27	
Wester Hailes		d	00 19			13 27		15 30		17 30			19 30		21 30	
Kingsknowe		d	00 21			13 28		15 33		17 33			19 33		21 33	
Slateford		d	00 24			13 32		15 35		17 35			19 35		21 35	
Haymarket	230,238,242	d	00 30	11 51	12 49	13 38	14 42	15 41	15 51	17 44	17 51		19 41	19 51	21 41	22 04
Edinburgh 10	230,238,242	a	00 34	11 55	12 54	13 42	14 47	15 48	15 56	17 48	17 56		19 48	19 56	21 48	22 08

A To Birmingham New Street
B To Newcastle
C not 11 December
D To Exeter St Davids
E To Bristol Temple Meads

Lanark, Coatbridge, Motherwell, Larkhall, Hamilton, Edinburgh and Bathgate, Airdrie and Springburn - Glasgow - Milngavie, Dalmuir, Balloch and Helensburgh

Network Diagram - see first Page of Table 220

Miles	Miles	Miles	Miles	Miles			SR MO	SR MX	SR MO	SR MX	SR MSX	SR SO	SR MO	SR SO	SR MX	SR MX	SR SO	SR MX	SR MX A	SR B	SR	SR	SR	SR
0	—	—	—	—	**Lanark**	d																		
8½	—	—	—	—	Carluke	d																		
13	—	—	—	—	Wishaw	d																		
16½	—	—	—	—	Holytown	d													00 01					
15	—	—	—	—	Shieldmuir	d																		
—	—	—	—	0	**Coatbridge Central**	d																		
—	—	—	—	1	Whifflet	d																		
16¼	0	0	—	5½	**Motherwell**	a																		
—	—	—	—	—		d	22p40							23p20										
—	3	—	—	—	Bellshill	d													00 04					
20½	5½	—	—	—	Uddingston	d													00 08					
—	—	0¾	—	—	Airbles	d	22p42							23p22										
—	—	—	—	0	**Larkhall**	d											23p37							06 07
—	—	—	—	1½	Merryton	d											23p39							06 09
—	—	—	—	2¾	Chatelherault	d											23p42							06 12
—	—	3	—	5¼	**Hamilton Central**	d	22p47							23p27			23p46							06 16
—	—	3¾	—	0	Hamilton West	d	22p50							23p30			23p48							06 18
—	—	5¾	—	—	Blantyre	d	22p53							23p33			23p52							06 22
22½	—	8¼	—	—	Newton	d	22p57							23p39										
24	9	—	—	—	Cambuslang	d	23p01							23p43					00 13					
25¾	10¾	—	—	—	Rutherglen	d	23p04							23p47			00 01							06 28
26½	11½	—	—	—	Dalmarnock	d								23p49										
27	12	—	—	—	Bridgeton	d	23p07							23p51										
—	—	—	0	—	**Edinburgh**	d				22p19			22p40		22p51	23p37		23p51		04 50				
—	—	—	1¼	—	Haymarket	d				22p23			22p44		22p55	23p42		23p55						
—	—	—	3¾	—	Edinburgh Park	d				22p30			22p49		23p00	23p47		23p59						
—	—	—	12½	—	Uphall	d				22p38			22p57		23p08	23p55		00 08						
—	—	—	15½	—	Livingston North	d				22p41			23p00		23p11	23p59		00 11						
—	—	—	18½	—	**Bathgate**	a				22p46			23p05		23p16	00 04		00 16						
—	—	—	—	—		d				22p47			23p06		23p17								05 36	
—	—	—	21	—	Armadale	d				22p51			23p10		23p21								05 40	
—	—	—	23¼	—	Blackridge	d				22p55			23p14		23p25								05 43	
—	—	—	28¾	—	Caldercruix	d				23p01			23p20		23p31								05 50	
—	—	—	31¾	—	Drumgelloch	d				23p05			23p24		23p35								05 53	
—	—	—	33¼	—	**Airdrie**	d			22p58	23p12			23p28		23p38						05 35		05 57	
—	—	—	34¼	—	Coatdyke	d			23p00	23p14			23p30		23p40						05 37		05 59	
—	—	—	35¼	—	Coatbridge Sunnyside	d			23p02	23p16			23p32		23p43						05 39		06 01	
—	—	—	35¾	—	Blairhill	d			23p05	23p19			23p35		23p45						05 42		06 04	
—	—	—	38½	—	Easterhouse	d			23p09	23p23			23p39		23p49						05 46		06 08	
—	—	—	39½	—	Garrowhill	d			23p11	23p25			23p41		23p52						05 48		06 10	
—	—	—	40¾	—	Shettleston	d			23p14	23p28			23p44		23p54						05 51		06 13	
—	—	—	41½	—	Carntyne	d			23p16	23p30			23p46		23p56						05 53		06 15	
—	—	—	—	0	**Springburn**	d		23p09			23p39	23p39												
—	—	—	—	0¼	Barnhill	d		23p10			23p40	23p40												
—	—	—	—	1½	Alexandra Parade	d		23p13			23p43	23p43												
—	—	—	—	1¾	Duke Street	d		23p15			23p45	23p45												
—	—	—	43¼	2¼	Bellgrove	d		23p17	23p19	23p33	23p47	23p47	23p49		23p59						05 56		06 18	
—	—	—	43¾	2¾	High Street	d		23p19	23p21	23p35	23p49	23p49	23p51		00 02						05 58		06 20	
—	—	—	44¼	3¼	**Glasgow Queen St LL** 10	a		23p21	23p23	23p37	23p51	23p51	23p53		00 04						06 00		06 22	
—	—	—	—	—		d		23p23	23p24	23p45	23p53	23p53	23p54		00 04						06 01		06 23	
—	—	—	45	4	Charing Cross	d		23p25	23p27	23p47	23p55	23p55	23p57		00 06						06 03		06 25	
28¼	13¼	—	—	—	Argyle Street	d								23p55			00 06							06 34
28¾	13¾	—	—	—	**Glasgow Central LL** 15	a	23p14							23p57			00 07		00b24					06 37
—	—	—	—	—		d	23p14							23p58			00 07							06 37
29¼	14¼	—	—	—	Anderston	d								23p59			00 09							06 39
29¾	14¾	—	—	—	Exhibition Centre	d	23p18							00 01			00 11							06 41
31	16	—	47	6	**Partick**	d	23p22	23p29	23p32	23p51	23p59	23p59	00 01	00 05	00 11		00 14				06 07		06 29	06 44
31½	16½	0	47½	6½	Hyndland 3	d	23p24	23p32	23p34	23p53	00 02	00 02	00 03	00 08	00 13		00 17				06 10		06 32	06 47
—	—	0½	—	—	Jordanhill	d	23p26			23p55	00 04		00 05		00 15						06 12			
—	—	1½	—	—	Scotstounhill	d	23p28			23p58	00 06		00 07		00 17						06 14			
—	—	2	—	—	Garscadden	d	23p30			23p59	00a08		00 09		00a19						06 16			
—	—	3	—	—	Yoker	d	23p33			00 02			00 12								06 19			
—	—	4	—	—	Clydebank	d	23p35			00 04											06 21			
32½	17½	—	48½	7½	Anniesland	d		23p35	23p37			00 05		00 12			00 20						06 35	06 50
33¾	18¾	—	49¾	8¾	Westerton	d		23p38	23p40			00 08		00 15			00 23			05 56			06 38	06 53
35	—	—	—	—	Bearsden	d								00 17										
35¾	—	—	—	—	Hillfoot	d								00 18										
37¼	—	—	—	—	**Milngavie**	a								00 23										
—	20	—	51	10	Drumchapel	d		23p40	23p42			00 10					00 25						06 40	06 55
—	20¾	—	51¾	10¾	Drumry	d		23p42	23p44			00 12					00 27						06 42	06 57
—	21¾	—	52¾	11¾	Singer	d		23p45	23p47			00 15					00 30						06 45	07 00
—	22¼	5¼	53½	12½	**Dalmuir**	a	23p39	23p47	23p49	00 08		00 17	00 16				00 32			06 03	06 24		06 47	07 02
—	—	—	—	—		d	23p39	23p48	23p50	00 08		00 18								06 04	06 24	06 30	06 48	
—	—	—	54¾	13¾	Kilpatrick	d	23p41	23p51				00 21										06 32	06 51	
—	—	—	56½	15½	Bowling	d	23p44	23p54				00 24										06 35	06 54	
—	—	—	59¼	18¼	Dumbarton East	d	23p49	23p58	23p58	00 15		00 28									06 32	06 40	06 58	
—	—	—	60	19	Dumbarton Central	d	23p51	23p59	23p59	00 18		00 30									06 34	06 42	07 00	
—	—	—	60¼	19¼	Dalreoch	d	23p52	00 02	00 01	00 19		00 32									06 35	06 43	07 02	
—	—	—	—	20¾	Renton	d	23p55	00 05				00 35									06 38		07 05	
—	—	—	—	22	Alexandria	d	23p58	00 07				00 37									06 41		07 07	
—	—	—	—	23	**Balloch**	a	00 01	00 11				00 41									06 44		07 11	
—	—	—	63½	—	Cardross	d			00 06	00 24												06 48		
—	—	—	67¼	—	Craigendoran	d			00 11	00 29												06 53		
—	—	—	68¼	—	**Helensburgh Central**	a			00 14	00 32										06c26		06 56		

A From Edinburgh
B To Fort William
b Glasgow Central High Level
c Helensburgh Upper

Table 226

Mondays to Saturdays

Lanark, Coatbridge, Motherwell, Larkhall, Hamilton, Edinburgh and Bathgate, Airdrie and Springburn - Glasgow - Milngavie, Dalmuir, Balloch and Helensburgh

Network Diagram - see first Page of Table 220

		SR	SR	SR SO	SR SX	SR	SR SX	SR	SR	SR SX	SR	SR SO	SR SX	SR	SR A	SR SX	SR SX	SR	SR	SR SX	SR	SR SO
Lanark	d										06 23					06 53						
Carluke	d										06 33					07 03						
Wishaw	d										06 38					07 08						
Holytown	d														06 58							
Shieldmuir	d										06 42					07 12						
Coatbridge Central	d													06 40								
Whifflet	d													06 42								
Motherwell	a										06 46			06 51		07 15						
	d		06 16			06 21					06 46			06 51		07 15					07 18	
Bellshill	d		06 22								06 52				07 04						07 24	
Uddingston	d		06 26								06 56				07 10						07 28	
Airbles	d					06 23								06 54								
Larkhall	d							06 37										07 07				
Merryton	d							06 39										07 09				
Chatelherault	d							06 42										07 12				
Hamilton Central	d					06 28		06 46						06 59				07 16				
Hamilton West	d					06 31		06 48						07 01				07 18				
Blantyre	d					06 34		06 52						07 05				07 22				
Newton	d					06 38								07 09								
Cambuslang	d		06 31			06 42					07 01			07 12	07 16						07 33	
Rutherglen	d		06 34			06 45		06 57			07 04			07 16		07 25		07 30			07 37	
Dalmarnock	d		06 36			06 47					07 06			07 18							07 39	
Bridgeton	d		06 38			06 49					07 08			07 20							07 41	
Edinburgh	d									06 07									06 21	06 37		
Haymarket	d									06 11									06 25	06 41		
Edinburgh Park	d									06 16									06 30	06 46		
Uphall	d									06 24									06 38	06 54		
Livingston North	d									06 27									06 41	06 57		
Bathgate	a									06 33									06 46	07 03		
	d	05 51							06 21	06 34									06 47	07 04		
Armadale	d	05 55							06 25										06 51			
Blackridge	d	05 58							06 28										06 55			
Caldercruix	d	06 05							06 35										07 01			
Drumgelloch	d	06 08							06 38	06 46									07 05	07 16		
Airdrie	d	06 12			06 27				06 42	06 50			06 57						07 12	07 20		
Coatdyke	d	06 14			06 29				06 44				06 59						07 14	07 22		
Coatbridge Sunnyside	d	06 16			06 31				06 46	06 53			07 01						07 16	07 24		
Blairhill	d	06 19			06 34				06 49				07 04						07 19	07 27		
Easterhouse	d	06 23			06 38				06 53				07 08						07 23			
Garrowhill	d	06 25			06 40				06 55				07 10						07 25			
Shettleston	d	06 28			06 43				06 58				07 13						07 28			
Carntyne	d	06 30			06 45				07 00				07 15						07 30			
Springburn	d			06 39			06 49					07 09					07 19					07 39
Barnhill	d			06 40			06 50					07 10					07 20					07 40
Alexandra Parade	d			06 43			06 53					07 13					07 23					07 43
Duke Street	d			06 45			06 55					07 15					07 25					07 45
Bellgrove	d	06 33		06 47	06 48		06 57		07 03			07 17	07 18				07 27		07 33			07 47
High Street	d	06 35		06 49	06 50		06 59		07 05	07 10		07 19	07 20				07 29		07 35	07 40		07 49
Glasgow Queen St LL 10	a	06 37		06 51	06 52		07 01		07 08	07 12		07 21	07 22				07 31		07 37	07 42		07 51
	d	06 40		06 53	06 53		07 02		07 10	07 13		07 23	07 23				07 32		07 40	07 43		07 53
Charing Cross	d	06 42		06 55	06 55		07 04		07 12	07 15		07 25	07 25				07 34		07 42	07 45		07 55
Argyle Street	d		06 42			06 53		07 02			07 12			07 23		07 30		07 35			07 44	
Glasgow Central LL 15	a		06 46			06 55		07 06			07 15			07 26	07b29	07 31		07 37			07 46	
	d		06 46			06 58		07 07			07 16			07 28		07 32		07 38			07 46	
Anderston	d		06 48			06 59		07 09			07 18			07 29		07a33		07 39			07 48	
Exhibition Centre	d		06 50			07 01		07 11			07 20			07 31				07 41			07 50	
Partick	d	06 47	06 54	06 59	06 59	07 05	07 08	07 14	07 17	07 20	07 24	07 29	07 29	07 35			07 38	07 45	07 47	07 50	07 53	07 59
Hyndland 3	d	06 49	06 56	07 02	07 02	07 08	07 10	07 16	07 19	07 22	07 26	07 32	07 32	07 38			07 40	07 47	07 49	07 52	07 55	08 02
Jordanhill	d		06 58				07 12				07 28						07 42				07 57	
Scotstounhill	d		07 00				07 15				07 30						07 45				08 00	
Garscadden	d	06 53	07 02				07 17				07 32						07 47				08 02	
Yoker	d		07 05				07 19				07 35						07 49				08 05	
Clydebank	d		07 07				07 21				07 37						07 51				08 07	
Anniesland	d			07 05	07 05	07 11		07 19		07 25		07 35	07 35	07 41				07 50		07 55		08 05
Westerton	d			07 08	07 08	07 14		07 22		07 28		07 38	07 38	07 44				07 53		07 58		08 08
Bearsden	d					07 16				07 31				07 46						08 01		
Hillfoot	d					07 17				07 33				07 48						08 03		
Milngavie	a					07 22				07 37				07 52						08 07		
Drumchapel	d			07 10	07 10			07 25				07 40	07 40					07 56				08 10
Drumry	d			07 12	07 12			07 27				07 42	07 42					07 58				08 12
Singer	d			07 15	07 15			07 29				07 45	07 45					08 00				08 15
Dalmuir	a	06 59	07 11	07 17	07 17		07 26	07 32	07 29		07 41	07 47	07 47				07 56	08 03	07 59		08 11	08 17
	d	06 59		07 18	07 18				07 29			07 48	07 48						07 59			08 18
Kilpatrick	d			07 21	07 21							07 51	07 51									08 21
Bowling	d			07 24	07 24							07 54	07 54									08 24
Dumbarton East	d	07 06		07 28	07 28				07 36			07 58	07 58						08 06			08 28
Dumbarton Central	d	07 09		07 30	07 30				07 39			08 00	08 00						08 09			08 30
Dalreoch	d	07 10		07 32	07 32				07 40			08 02	08 02						08 10			08 32
Renton	d			07 35	07 35							08 05	08 05									08 35
Alexandria	d			07 37	07 37							08 07	08 07									08 37
Balloch	a			07 41	07 41							08 11	08 11									08 41
Cardross	d	07 15							07 45										08 15			
Craigendoran	d	07 20							07 50										08 20			
Helensburgh Central	a	07 24							07 54										08 24			

A From Edinburgh

b Glasgow Central High Level

Table 226

Mondays to Saturdays

Lanark, Coatbridge, Motherwell, Larkhall, Hamilton, Edinburgh and Bathgate, Airdrie and Springburn - Glasgow - Milngavie, Dalmuir, Balloch and Helensburgh

Network Diagram - see first Page of Table 220

		SR SX	SR SO	SR SX	SR SX	SR SO	SR SX	SR	SR SX	SR ◇ A	SR SO	SR SX	SR SX	SR SX	SR SO B	SR SO	SR SX	SR SO	SR SX	SR SX	SR SO	SR	SR SX
Lanark	d						07 22				07 23									07 47			
Carluke	d						07 32				07 33									07 57			
Wishaw	d						07 37				07 38									08 04			
Holytown	d														08 00								
Shieldmuir	d						07 41				07 42									08 07			
Coatbridge Central	d																07 40						
Whifflet	d																07 42						
Motherwell	a						07 44				07 46						07 49			08 13			
	d		07 19	07 19			07 44				07 47		07 47				07 50	07 50		08 13			
Bellshill	d										07 53		07 53		08 03								
Uddingston	d										07 57		07 57		08 07					08 19			
Airbles	d		07 21	07 21													07 52	07 52					
Larkhall	d					07 37						07 37									08 07		
Merryton	d					07 39						07 39									08 09		
Chatelherault	d					07 42						07 42									08 12		
Hamilton Central	d		07 26	07 26		07 46						07 46					07 57	07 57			08 15		
Hamilton West	d		07 29	07 29		07 48						07 48					08 00	08 00			08 18		
Blantyre	d		07 32	07 32		07 52						07 52					08 03	08 03			08 21		
Newton	d		07 37	07 37								07 56					08 07	08 07					
Cambuslang	d		07 41	07 41							08 02	08 00	08 05				08 11	08 11					
Rutherglen	d		07 46	07 46		07 59	07 56				08 05	08 05	08 10				08 14	08 14		08 26	08 30		
Dalmarnock	d		07 48	07 48							08 06	08 07	08 12				08 17	08 17					
Bridgeton	d		07 50	07 50							08 08	08 09	08 14				08 19	08 19					
Edinburgh	d							06 48	07 07													07 21	07 37
Haymarket	d							06 52	07 11													07 25	07 41
Edinburgh Park	d							06 57	07 16													07 30	07 46
Uphall	d							07 05	07 24													07 38	07 54
Livingston North	d							07 08	07 27													07 41	07 57
Bathgate	a							07 13	07 33													07 46	08 03
	d							07 17	07 34													07 47	08 04
Armadale	d							07 21														07 51	
Blackridge	d							07 25														07 55	
Caldercruix	d							07 31														08 01	
Drumgelloch	d							07 35	07 46													08 05	08 16
Airdrie	d	07 27						07 42	07 50					07 57								08 12	08 20
Coatdyke	d	07 29						07 44	07 52					07 59								08 14	08 22
Coatbridge Sunnyside	d	07 31						07 46	07 54					08 01								08 16	08 24
Blairhill	d	07 34						07 49	07 57					08 04								08 19	08 27
Easterhouse	d	07 38						07 53						08 08								08 23	
Garrowhill	d	07 40						07 55						08 10								08 25	
Shettleston	d	07 43						07 58						08 13								08 28	
Carntyne	d	07 45						08 00						08 15								08 30	
Springburn	d				07 49											08 09			08 19				
Barnhill	d				07 50											08 10			08 20				
Alexandra Parade	d				07 53											08 13			08 23				
Duke Street	d				07 55											08 15			08 25				
Bellgrove	d	07 48			07 57			08 03						08 18		08 18			08 27			08 33	
High Street	d	07 50			07 59			08 05	08 10					08 20		08 20			08 29			08 35	08 40
Glasgow Queen St LL 10	a	07 52			08 01			08 07	08 12					08 22		08 22			08 31			08 37	08 42
	d	07 53			08 02			08 10	08 13	08b21				08 23		08 23			08 32			08 40	08 43
Charing Cross	d	07 55			08 04			08 12	08 15					08 25		08 25			08 34			08 42	08 45
Argyle Street	d		07 54	07 54		08 04	08 02				08 13	08 13	08 18				08 23	08 23		08 32	08 36		
Glasgow Central LL 15	a		07 56	07 56		08 07	08 03				08 15	08 15	08 21		08e24		08 25	08 25		08 33	08 37		
	d		07 58	08 00		08 07	08 07				08 16	08 18	08 22				08 28	08 28		08 37	08 37		
Anderston	d		07 59	08 01		08 09	08 09				08 18	08 19	08a23				08 30	08 30		08 39	08 39		
Exhibition Centre	d		08 01	08 03		08 11	08 11				08 20	08 21					08 32	08 32		08 41	08 41		
Partick	d	07 59	08 05	08 07	08 09	08 14	08 14	08 17	08 20		08 23	08 24		08 29		08 29	08 36	08 36	08 39	08 44	08 44	08 47	08 50
Hyndland 3	d	08 02	08 08	08 09	08 11	08 17	08 17	08 19	08 22		08 25	08 27		08 32		08 32	08 38	08 38	08 41	08 47	08 47	08 49	08 52
Jordanhill	d				08 13						08 27	08 28							08 43				
Scotstounhill	d				08 15						08 30	08 30							08 45				
Garscadden	d				08 17						08 32	08 32							08 47				
Yoker	d				08 20						08 35	08 35							08 50				
Clydebank	d				08 22						08 37	08 37							08 52				
Anniesland	d	08 05	08 11	08 14		08 20	08 20		08 25					08 35		08 35	08 41	08 41		08 50	08 50		08 55
Westerton	d	08 08	08 14	08 21		08 23	08 25		08 28					08 38		08 38	08 44	08 44		08 53	08 53		08 58
Bearsden	d		08 16	08 24					08 31								08 46	08 46					09 01
Hillfoot	d		08 17	08 26					08 33								08 48	08 48					09 03
Milngavie	a		08 22	08 29					08 39								08 52	08 52					09 07
Drumchapel	d	08 10				08 25	08 27							08 40		08 40				08 55	08 55		
Drumry	d	08 12				08 27	08 29							08 42		08 42				08 57	08 57		
Singer	d	08 15				08 30	08 32							08 45		08 45				09 00	09 00		
Dalmuir	a	08 17			08 28	08 32	08 34	08 29		08 39	08 41	08 43		08 47		08 47			08 56	09 02	09 02	08 59	
	d	08 18						08 29		08 39				08 48		08 48						08 59	
Kilpatrick	d	08 21												08 51		08 51							
Bowling	d	08 24												08 54		08 54							
Dumbarton East	d	08 28						08 36						08 58		08 58						09 06	
Dumbarton Central	d	08 30						08 39		08 48				09 00		09 00						09 09	
Dalreoch	d	08 32						08 40						09 02		09 02						09 10	
Renton	d	08 35												09 05		09 05							
Alexandria	d	08 37												09 07		09 07							
Balloch	a	08 41												09 11		09 11							
Cardross	d							08 45														09 15	
Craigendoran	d							08 50														09 20	
Helensburgh Central	a							08 55		09c03												09 24	

A To Oban
B From Newcraighall
b Glasgow Queen St High Level
c Helensburgh Upper
e Glasgow Central High Level

Table 226

Mondays to Saturdays

Lanark, Coatbridge, Motherwell, Larkhall, Hamilton, Edinburgh and Bathgate, Airdrie and Springburn - Glasgow - Milngavie, Dalmuir, Balloch and Helensburgh

Network Diagram - see first Page of Table 220

		SR SX	SR	SR SX A	SR SX	SR SO	SR SO	SR SX	SR SX	SR SX	SR	SR	SR SX	SR SO	SR SO	SR SX	SR SO	SR SX	SR	SR	SR	SR
Lanark	d						07 53			08 23					08 23							
Carluke	d			08 13			08 03			08 33					08 33							
Wishaw	d			08 21			08 08			08 38					08 38							
Holytown	d						08 13															
Shieldmuir	d			08 23						08 42					08 42							
Coatbridge Central	d																					
Whifflet	d																					
Motherwell	a			08 26			08 19			08 46					08 45							
	d		08 17	08 27			08 20	08 20		08 46					08 46	08 46			08 50			
Bellshill	d		08 22												08 52	08 52						
Uddingston	d		08 26	08 33											08 58	08 58						
Airbles	d						08 22	08 22											08 52			
Larkhall	d	08 07									08 37										09 07	
Merryton	d	08 09									08 39										09 09	
Chatelherault	d	08 12									08 42										09 12	
Hamilton Central	d	08 15					08 27	08 27			08 46								08 57		09 16	
Hamilton West	d	08 18					08 30	08 30			08 48								09 00		09 18	
Blantyre	d	08 21					08 33	08 33			08 52								09 03		09 22	
Newton	d						08 37	08 37											09 07			
Cambuslang	d	08 30	08 31				08 41	08 41							09 03	09 03			09 11			
Rutherglen	d		08 34				08 46	08 46		08 56	09 00				09 07	09 07			09 16		09 29	
Dalmarnock	d		08 36				08 48	08 48							09 09	09 09			09 17			
Bridgeton	d		08 38				08 51	08 51							09 11	09 11			09 19			
Edinburgh	d											07 54	08 07									08 21
Haymarket	d											07 57	08 11									08 25
Edinburgh Park	d											08 02	08 16									08 30
Uphall	d											08 09	08 24									08 38
Livingston North	d											08 13	08 27									08 41
Bathgate	a											08 17	08 33									08 46
	d											08 18	08 34	08 34								08 47
Armadale	d											08 22										08 51
Blackridge	d											08 25										08 55
Caldercruix	d											08 32										09 01
Drumgelloch	d											08 35	08 46	08 46								09 05
Airdrie	d				08 27							08 42	08 50	08 50				08 57				09 12
Coatdyke	d				08 29							08 44						08 59				09 14
Coatbridge Sunnyside	d				08 31							08 46	08 53	08 53				09 01				09 16
Blairhill	d				08 34							08 49						09 04				09 19
Easterhouse	d				08 38							08 53						09 08				09 23
Garrowhill	d				08 40							08 55						09 10				09 25
Shettleston	d				08 43							08 58						09 13				09 28
Carntyne	d				08 45							09 00						09 15				09 30
Springburn	d					08 39			08 49								09 09			09 19		
Barnhill	d					08 40			08 50								09 10			09 20		
Alexandra Parade	d					08 43			08 53								09 13			09 23		
Duke Street	d					08 45			08 55								09 15			09 25		
Bellgrove	d				08 48	08 48			08 57			09 03					09 17	09 18		09 27		09 33
High Street	d				08 50	08 50			08 59			09 05	09 10	09 10			09 19	09 20		09 29		09 35
Glasgow Queen St LL 10 ⛴	a				08 52	08 52			09 01			09 07	09 12	09 12			09 23	09 22		09 31		09 37
	d				08 53	08 53			09 02			09 10	09 13	09 13			09 23	09 23		09 32		09 40
Charing Cross	d				08 55	08 55			09 04			09 12	09 15	09 15			09 25	09 25		09 34		09 42
Argyle Street	d	08 36	08 42	08 47			08 55	08 55		09 01	09 05				09 15	09 15			09 24		09 34	
Glasgow Central LL 15	a	08 37	08 46	08 48			08 56	08 56		09 03	09 07				09 16	09 16			09 26		09 37	
	d	08 39	08 46	08 48			08 59	08 59		09 03	09 07				09 18	09 18			09 28		09 37	
Anderston	d	08a42	08 48	08 51			09 00	09 00		09 05	09 09				09 20	09 20			09 29		09 39	
Exhibition Centre	d		08 50	08 54			09 02	09 02		09 07	09 11				09 22	09 22			09 31		09 41	
Partick ⛴	d		08 54	08 57	08 59	08 59	09 06	09 06	09 09	09 12	09 14	09 17	09 20	09 20	09 25	09 25	09 29	09 29	09 35	09 39	09 44	09 47
Hyndland 3	d		08 56	08 59	09 02	09 02	09 09	09 09	09 11	09 14	09 17	09 20	09 22	09 22	09 27	09 27	09 32	09 32	09 38	09 41	09 47	09 49
Jordanhill	d		08 58	09 01					09 12	09 17					09 29	09 29				09 43		
Scotstounhill	d		09 00	09 03					09 15	09 19					09 32	09 32				09 45		
Garscadden	d		09 02	09a06					09 18	09a21					09 34	09 34				09 47		
Yoker	d		09 05						09 20						09 36	09 36				09 50		
Clydebank	d		09 07						09 22						09 38	09 38				09 52		
Anniesland	d				09 05	09 05	09 12	09 12			09 20		09 25	09 25			09 35	09 35	09 41		09 50	
Westerton	d				09 08	09 08	09 15	09 15			09 23		09 28	09 28			09 38	09 38	09 44		09 53	
Bearsden	d						09 17	09 17					09 31	09 31					09 46			
Hillfoot	d						09 20	09 20					09 33	09 33					09 47			
Milngavie	a						09 23	09 23					09 37	09 37					09 52			
Drumchapel	d				09 10	09 10					09 25						09 40	09 40			09 55	
Drumry	d				09 12	09 12					09 27						09 42	09 42			09 57	
Singer	d				09 15	09 15					09 30						09 45	09 45			10 00	
Dalmuir	a		09 11		09 17	09 17			09 26		09 32	09 29			09 42	09 42	09 47	09 47		09 56	10 02	09 59
	d				09 18	09 18						09 29					09 48	09 48				09 59
Kilpatrick	d				09 21	09 21											09 51	09 51				
Bowling	d				09 24	09 24											09 54	09 54				
Dumbarton East	d				09 28	09 28						09 36					09 58	09 58				10 06
Dumbarton Central	d				09 30	09 30						09 39					10 00	10 00				10 09
Dalreoch	d				09 32	09 32						09 40					10 02	10 02				10 10
Renton	d				09 35	09 35											10 05	10 05				
Alexandria	d				09 37	09 37											10 07	10 07				
Balloch	a				09 41	09 41											10 11	10 11				
Cardross	d											09 45										10 15
Craigendoran	d											09 49										10 20
Helensburgh Central	a											09 54										10 24

A From Carstairs

Table 226

Mondays to Saturdays

Lanark, Coatbridge, Motherwell, Larkhall, Hamilton, Edinburgh and Bathgate, Airdrie and Springburn - Glasgow - Milngavie, Dalmuir, Balloch and Helensburgh

Network Diagram - see first Page of Table 220

		SR	SR	SR	SR	SR	SR	SR	SR	SR	SR	SR	SR	SR	SR	SR	SR	SR	SR	SR	SR	SR	SR
					SO	SX									SO								
							A								◇ B								A
Lanark	d				08 53							09 23										09 53	
Carluke	d				09 03							09 33										10 04	
Wishaw	d				09 08							09 38										10 08	
Holytown	d				09 13		09 33															10 13	10 33
Shieldmuir	d											09 42											
Coatbridge Central	d																						
Whifflet	d																						
Motherwell	a				09 22							09 46										10 20	
	d		09 16		09 22	09 22						09 47		09 50						10 16		10 20	
Bellshill	d		09 22				09 36					09 52								10 22			10 36
Uddingston	d		09 26				09 41					09 56								10 26			10 41
Airbles	d				09 25	09 25								09 52								10 23	
Larkhall	d								09 37								10 07						
Merryton	d								09 39								10 09						
Chatelherault	d								09 42								10 12						
Hamilton Central	d				09 30	09 30			09 46					09 57			10 16					10 28	
Hamilton West	d				09 32	09 32			09 48					10 00			10 18					10 30	
Blantyre	d				09 36	09 36			09 52					10 03			10 22					10 34	
Newton	d				09 40	09 40								10 08								10 38	
Cambuslang	d		09 31		09 43	09 43						10 01		10 11						10 31		10 41	
Rutherglen	d		09 34		09 47	09 47			09 59			10 08		10 15			10 30			10 34		10 48	
Dalmarnock	d		09 36		09 49	09 49						10 10		10 17						10 36		10 50	
Bridgeton	d		09 38		09 51	09 51						10 12		10 19						10 38		10 52	
Edinburgh	d	08 37								08 48	09 07							09 21	09 37				
Haymarket	d	08 41								08 52	09 11							09 25	09 41				
Edinburgh Park	d	08 46								08 57	09 16							09 30	09 46				
Uphall	d	08 54								09 05	09 24							09 38	09 54				
Livingston North	d	08 57								09 08	09 27							09 41	09 57				
Bathgate	a	09 03								09 13	09 33							09 46	10 03				
	d	09 04								09 17	09 34							09 47	10 04				
Armadale	d									09 21								09 51					
Blackridge	d									09 25								09 55					
Caldercruix	d									09 31								10 01					
Drumgelloch	d	09 16								09 35	09 46							10 05	10 16				
Airdrie	d	09 20		09 27						09 42	09 50		09 57					10 12	10 20		10 27		
Coatdyke	d			09 29						09 44			09 59					10 14			10 29		
Coatbridge Sunnyside	d	09 23		09 31						09 46	09 53		10 01					10 16	10 23		10 31		
Blairhill	d			09 34						09 49			10 04					10 19			10 34		
Easterhouse	d			09 38						09 53			10 08					10 23			10 38		
Garrowhill	d			09 40						09 55			10 10					10 25			10 40		
Shettleston	d			09 43						09 58			10 13					10 28			10 43		
Carntyne	d			09 45						10 00			10 15					10 30			10 45		
Springburn	d							09 49								10 19							
Barnhill	d							09 50								10 20							
Alexandra Parade	d							09 53								10 23							
Duke Street	d							09 55								10 25							
Bellgrove	d			09 48				09 57		10 03			10 18			10 27		10 33			10 48		
High Street	d	09 40		09 50				09 59		10 05	10 10		10 20			10 29		10 35	10 40		10 50		
Glasgow Queen St LL 10	a	09 42		09 52				10 01		10 07	10 12		10 22			10 31		10 37	10 42		10 52		
	d	09 43		09 53				10 02		10 10	10 13		10 23		10c37	10 32		10 40	10 43		10 53		
Charing Cross	d	09 45		09 55				10 04		10 12	10 15		10 25			10 34		10 42	10 45		10 55		
Argyle Street	d		09 42		09 54	09 54			10 04			10 14		10 24			10 36			10 42		10 56	
Glasgow Central LL 15	a		09 46		09 56	09 56	09b57		10 07			10 16		10 26			10 37			10 46		10 57	10b55
	d		09 46		09 58	09 58			10 07			10 16		10 28			10 38			10 46		10 58	
Anderston	d		09 48		09 59	09 59			10 09			10 18		10 29			10 39			10 48		10 59	
Exhibition Centre	d		09 50		10 01	10 01			10 11			10 20		10 31			10 41			10 50		11 01	
Partick	d	09 50	09 54	09 59	10 05	10 05		10 09	10 14	10 17	10 20	10 24	10 29	10 35		10 39	10 45	10 47	10 50	10 54	10 59	11 05	
Hyndland 3	d	09 52	09 56	10 02	10 08	10 08		10 11	10 17	10 19	10 22	10 26	10 32	10 38		10 41	10 47	10 49	10 52	10 56	11 02	11 08	
Jordanhill	d		09 58					10 13				10 28				10 43				10 58			
Scotstounhill	d		10 00					10 15				10 30				10 45				11 00			
Garscadden	d		10 02					10 17				10 32				10 47				11 02			
Yoker	d		10 05					10 20				10 35				10 50				11 05			
Clydebank	d		10 07					10 22				10 37				10 52				11 07			
Anniesland	d	09 55		10 05	10 11	10 11			10 20		10 25		10 35	10 41			10 50		10 55		11 05	11 11	
Westerton	d	09 58		10 08	10 14	10 14			10 23		10 28		10 38	10 44			10 53		10 58		11 08	11 15	
Bearsden	d	10 01			10 16	10 16					10 31			10 46					11 01			11 17	
Hillfoot	d	10 03			10 18	10 18					10 33			10 47					11 03			11 19	
Milngavie	a	10 07			10 22	10 22					10 37			10 52					11 07			11 25	
Drumchapel	d			10 10					10 25				10 40				10 55				11 10		
Drumry	d			10 12					10 27				10 42				10 57				11 12		
Singer	d			10 15					10 30				10 45				11 00				11 15		
Dalmuir	a		10 11	10 17				10 26	10 32	10 29		10 41	10 47		10 52	10 56	11 02	10 59		11 11	11 17		
	d			10 18						10 29			10 48		10 52			10 59			11 18		
Kilpatrick	d			10 21									10 51								11 21		
Bowling	d			10 24									10 54								11 24		
Dumbarton East	d			10 28						10 36			10 58					11 06			11 28		
Dumbarton Central	d			10 30						10 39			11 00		11 05			11 09			11 30		
Dalreoch	d			10 32						10 40			11 02					11 10			11 32		
Renton	d			10 35									11 05								11 35		
Alexandria	d			10 37									11 07								11 37		
Balloch	a			10 41									11 11								11 41		
Cardross	d									10 45								11 15					
Craigendoran	d									10 50								11 20					
Helensburgh Central	a									10 54					11e20			11 24					

A From Edinburgh
B from 24 March. To Oban
b Glasgow Central High Level
c Glasgow Queen St High Level
e Helensburgh Upper

Table 226

Mondays to Saturdays

Lanark, Coatbridge, Motherwell, Larkhall, Hamilton, Edinburgh and Bathgate, Airdrie and Springburn - Glasgow - Milngavie, Dalmuir, Balloch and Helensburgh

Network Diagram - see first Page of Table 220

		SR	SR	SR	SR	SR	SR	SR	SR	SR	SR	SR	SR	SR	SR	SR	SR	SR	SR	SR	SR	SR	SR
																A					◇ B		
Lanark	d					10 21									10 53							11 23	
Carluke	d					10 31									11 03							11 33	
Wishaw	d					10 37									11 08							11 41	
Holytown	d														11 13	11 33							
Shieldmuir	d					10 41																11 44	
Coatbridge Central	d																						
Whifflet	d																						
Motherwell	a					10 45									11 20							11 48	
	d					10 46		10 50					11 16		11 20							11 49	
Bellshill	d					10 52							11 22			11 36						11 55	
Uddingston	d					10 56							11 26			11 41						12 01	
Airbles	d							10 52							11 22								
Larkhall	d		10 37							11 07								11 37					
Merryton	d		10 39							11 09								11 39					
Chatelherault	d		10 42							11 12								11 42					
Hamilton Central	d		10 46					10 57		11 16					11 27			11 46					
Hamilton West	d		10 48					11 00		11 18					11 30			11 48					
Blantyre	d		10 52					11 03		11 22					11 33			11 52					
Newton	d							11 07							11 37								
Cambuslang	d					11 01		11 11					11 31		11 41							12 06	
Rutherglen	d		10 59			11 05		11 15		11 29			11 34		11 46			11 59				12 09	
Dalmarnock	d					11 07		11 17					11 36		11 48							12 11	
Bridgeton	d					11 09		11 19					11 38		11 50							12 13	
Edinburgh	d			09 48	10 07						10 21	10 37							10 48	11 07			
Haymarket	d			09 52	10 11						10 25	10 41							10 52	11 11			
Edinburgh Park	d			09 57	10 16						10 30	10 46							10 57	11 16			
Uphall	d			10 05	10 24						10 38	10 54							11 05	11 24			
Livingston North	d			10 08	10 27						10 41	10 57							11 08	11 27			
Bathgate	a			10 13	10 33						10 46	11 03							11 13	11 33			
	d			10 17	10 34						10 47	11 04							11 17	11 34			
Armadale	d			10 21							10 51								11 21				
Blackridge	d			10 25							10 55								11 25				
Caldercruix	d			10 31							11 01								11 31				
Drumgelloch	d			10 35	10 46						11 05	11 16							11 35	11 46			
Airdrie	d			10 42	10 50		10 57				11 12	11 20		11 27					11 42	11 50			11 57
Coatdyke	d			10 44			10 59				11 14			11 29					11 44				11 59
Coatbridge Sunnyside	d			10 46	10 53		11 01				11 16	11 23		11 31					11 46	11 53			12 01
Blairhill	d			10 49			11 04				11 19			11 34					11 49				12 04
Easterhouse	d			10 53			11 08				11 23			11 38					11 53				12 08
Garrowhill	d			10 55			11 10				11 25			11 40					11 55				12 10
Shettleston	d			10 58			11 13				11 28			11 43					11 58				12 13
Carntyne	d			11 00			11 15				11 30			11 45					12 00				12 15
Springburn	d	10 49							11 19								11 49						
Barnhill	d	10 50							11 20								11 50						
Alexandra Parade	d	10 53							11 23								11 53						
Duke Street	d	10 55							11 25								11 55						
Bellgrove	d	10 57		11 03			11 18		11 27		11 33			11 48			11 57		12 03				12 18
High Street	d	10 59		11 05	11 10		11 20		11 29		11 35	11 40		11 50			11 59		12 05	12 10			12 20
Glasgow Queen St LL 10	a	11 01		11 07	11 12		11 22		11 31		11 37	11 42		11 52			12 01		12 07	12 12			12 22
	d	11 02		11 10	11 13		11 23		11 32		11 40	11 43		11 53			12 02		12 10	12 13	12c21		12 23
Charing Cross	d	11 04		11 12	11 15		11 25		11 34		11 42	11 45		11 55			12 04		12 12	12 15			12 25
Argyle Street	d		11 04			11 15		11 23		11 34			11 42		11 53			12 05				12 17	
Glasgow Central LL 15	a		11 07			11 16		11 26		11 37			11 46		11 57	11b57		12 07				12 18	
	d		11 07			11 17		11 28		11 37			11 46		11 58			12 07				12 19	
Anderston	d		11 09			11 19		11 29		11 39			11 48		12 00			12 09				12 20	
Exhibition Centre	d		11 11			11 21		11 31		11 41			11 50		12 02			12 11				12 22	
Partick	d	11 09	11 15	11 17	11 20	11 24	11 29	11 35	11 39	11 44	11 47	11 50	11 54	11 59	12 05		12 08	12 14	12 17	12 20		12 26	12 29
Hyndland 3	d	11 11	11 17	11 19	11 22	11 26	11 32	11 38	11 41	11 47	11 49	11 52	11 56	12 02	12 08		12 10	12 17	12 19	12 22		12 28	12 32
Jordanhill	d	11 13				11 28			11 43				11 58				12 12					12 30	
Scotstounhill	d	11 15				11 31			11 45				12 00				12 15					12 32	
Garscadden	d	11 17				11 33			11 47				12 02				12 17					12 35	
Yoker	d	11 20				11 35			11 50				12 05				12 19					12 37	
Clydebank	d	11 22				11 37			11 52				12 07				12 21					12 39	
Anniesland	d		11 20		11 25		11 35	11 41		11 50		11 55		12 05	12 11			12 20		12 25			12 35
Westerton	d		11 23		11 28		11 38	11 44		11 53		11 58		12 08	12 14			12 23		12 28			12 38
Bearsden	d				11 31			11 46				12 01			12 16					12 31			
Hillfoot	d				11 33			11 47				12 03			12 18					12 33			
Milngavie	a				11 37			11 52				12 07			12 22					12 37			
Drumchapel	d		11 25				11 40			11 55				12 10				12 25					12 40
Drumry	d		11 27				11 42			11 57				12 12				12 27					12 42
Singer	d		11 30				11 45			12 00				12 15				12 30					12 45
Dalmuir	a	11 26	11 32	11 29		11 42	11 47		11 56	12 02	11 59		12 11	12 17			12 26	12 32	12 29		12 38	12 43	12 47
	d			11 29			11 48				11 59			12 18					12 29		12 42		12 48
Kilpatrick	d						11 51							12 21									12 51
Bowling	d						11 54							12 24									12 54
Dumbarton East	d			11 36			11 58				12 06			12 28					12 36				12 58
Dumbarton Central	d			11 39			12 00				12 09			12 30					12 39		12 48		13 00
Dalreoch	d			11 40			12 02				12 10			12 32					12 40				13 02
Renton	d						12 05							12 35									13 05
Alexandria	d						12 07							12 37									13 07
Balloch	a						12 11							12 41									13 11
Cardross	d			11 45							12 15								12 45				
Craigendoran	d			11 50							12 20								12 50				
Helensburgh Central	a			11 54							12 24								12 54		13e03		

A From Edinburgh
B To Oban
b Glasgow Central High Level
c Glasgow Queen St High Level
e Helensburgh Upper

Lanark, Coatbridge, Motherwell, Larkhall, Hamilton, Edinburgh and Bathgate, Airdrie and Springburn - Glasgow - Milngavie, Dalmuir, Balloch and Helensburgh

Network Diagram - see first Page of Table 220

		SR	SR	SR	SR	SR	SR	SR	SR	SR	SR	SR	SR	SR	SR	SR	SR	SR	SR	SR	SR	SR
														SX	SO							
										A												
Lanark	d								11 53							12 23						
Carluke	d								12 03							12 33						
Wishaw	d								12 08							12 41						
Holytown	d								12 13	12 33												
Shieldmuir	d															12 45						
Coatbridge Central	d																					
Whifflet	d																					
Motherwell	a								12 19							12 48						
	d	11 50					12 16		12 20							12 48		12 50				
Bellshill	d						12 22			12 36						12 54						
Uddingston	d						12 26			12 41						12 58						
Airbles	d	11 52							12 22									12 52				
Larkhall	d			12 07								12 37								13 07		
Merryton	d			12 09								12 39								13 09		
Chatelherault	d			12 12								12 42								13 12		
Hamilton Central	d	11 57		12 16					12 28			12 46						12 57		13 16		
Hamilton West	d	12 00		12 18					12 30			12 48						13 00		13 18		
Blantyre	d	12 03		12 22					12 34			12 52						13 03		13 22		
Newton	d	12 07							12 38									13 07				
Cambuslang	d	12 11					12 31		12 41							13 03		13 11				
Rutherglen	d	12 17		12 29			12 34		12 45			12 59				13 06		13 16		13 29		
Dalmarnock	d	12 19					12 36		12 48							13 08		13 18				
Bridgeton	d	12 21					12 38		12 50							13 10		13 20				
Edinburgh	d				11 21	11 37							11 48	12 07	12 10						12 21	12 37
Haymarket	d				11 25	11 41							11 52	12 11	12 14						12 25	12 41
Edinburgh Park	d				11 30	11 46							11 57	12 16	12 19						12 30	12 46
Uphall	d				11 38	11 54							12 05	12 24	12 27						12 38	12 54
Livingston North	d				11 41	11 57							12 08	12 27	12 30						12 41	12 57
Bathgate	a				11 46	12 03							12 13	12 33	12 33						12 47	13 03
	d				11 47	12 04							12 17	12 34	12 34						12 47	13 04
Armadale	d				11 51								12 21								12 51	
Blackridge	d				11 55								12 25								12 55	
Caldercruix	d				12 01								12 31								13 01	
Drumgelloch	d				12 05	12 16							12 35	12 46	12 46						13 05	13 16
Airdrie	d				12 12	12 20		12 27					12 42	12 50	12 50		12 57				13 12	13 20
Coatdyke	d				12 14			12 29					12 44				12 59				13 14	
Coatbridge Sunnyside	d				12 16	12 23		12 31					12 46	12 53	12 53		13 01				13 16	13 23
Blairhill	d				12 19			12 34					12 49				13 04				13 19	
Easterhouse	d				12 23			12 38					12 53				13 08				13 23	
Garrowhill	d				12 25			12 40					12 55				13 10				13 25	
Shettleston	d				12 28			12 43					12 58				13 13				13 28	
Carntyne	d				12 30			12 45					13 00				13 15				13 30	
Springburn	d		12 19								12 49								13 19			
Barnhill	d		12 20								12 50								13 20			
Alexandra Parade	d		12 23								12 53								13 23			
Duke Street	d		12 25								12 55								13 25			
Bellgrove	d		12 27		12 33			12 48			12 57		13 03				13 18		13 27		13 33	
High Street	d		12 29		12 35	12 40		12 50			12 59		13 05	13 10	13 10		13 20		13 29		13 35	13 40
Glasgow Queen St LL 10 ⛴	a		12 31		12 38	12 42		12 52			13 01		13 08	13 12	13 12		13 22		13 31		13 37	13 42
	d		12 32		12 40	12 43		12 53			13 02		13 10	13 13	13 13		13 23		13 32		13 41	13 43
Charing Cross	d		12 34		12 42	12 45		12 55			13 04		13 12	13 15	13 15		13 25		13 34		13 43	13 45
Argyle Street	d	12 24		12 35			12 42		12 54			13 05				13 14		13 24		13 34		
Glasgow Central LL 15	a	12 26		12 37			12 46		12 56	12b55		13 07				13 17		13 27		13 37		
	d	12 28		12 37			12 46		12 58			13 07				13 18		13 28		13 37		
Anderston	d	12 30		12 39			12 48		12 59			13 09				13 19		13 29		13 39		
Exhibition Centre	d	12 32		12 41			12 50		13 01			13 11				13 21		13 31		13 41		
Partick ⛴	d	12 35	12 39	12 44	12 47	12 50	12 54	12 59	13 05		13 08	13 14	13 17	13 20	13 20	13 25	13 29	13 35	13 38	13 44	13 47	13 50
Hyndland 3	d	12 38	12 41	12 47	12 49	12 52	12 56	13 02	13 08		13 10	13 17	13 19	13 22	13 22	13 27	13 32	13 38	13 40	13 47	13 49	13 52
Jordanhill	d		12 43				12 58				13 12					13 29			13 42			
Scotstounhill	d		12 45				13 00				13 15					13 31			13 45			
Garscadden	d		12 47				13 02				13 17					13 33			13 47			
Yoker	d		12 50				13 05				13 19					13 35			13 49			
Clydebank	d		12 52				13 07				13 21					13 37			13 51			
Anniesland	d	12 41		12 50		12 55		13 05	13 11			13 20		13 25	13 25		13 35	13 41		13 50		13 55
Westerton	d	12 44		12 53		12 58		13 08	13 14			13 23		13 28	13 28		13 38	13 44		13 53		13 58
Bearsden	d	12 46				13 01			13 16					13 31	13 31			13 46				14 01
Hillfoot	d	12 48				13 03			13 18					13 33	13 33			13 47				14 03
Milngavie	a	12 52				13 07			13 22					13 37	13 37			13 52				14 07
Drumchapel	d			12 55				13 10				13 25					13 40			13 55		
Drumry	d			12 57				13 12				13 27					13 42			13 57		
Singer	d			13 00				13 15				13 30					13 45			14 00		
Dalmuir	a		12 56	13 02	12 59		13 13	13 17			13 26	13 32	13 29			13 42	13 47		13 56	14 02	13 59	
	d				12 59			13 18					13 29				13 48				13 59	
Kilpatrick	d							13 21									13 51					
Bowling	d							13 24									13 54					
Dumbarton East	d				13 06			13 28					13 36				13 58				14 06	
Dumbarton Central	d				13 09			13 30					13 39				14 00				14 09	
Dalreoch	d				13 10			13 32					13 40				14 02				14 10	
Renton	d							13 35									14 05					
Alexandria	d							13 37									14 07					
Balloch	a							13 41									14 11					
Cardross	d				13 15								13 45								14 15	
Craigendoran	d				13 20								13 50								14 20	
Helensburgh Central	a				13 24								13 54								14 24	

A From Edinburgh

b Glasgow Central High Level

Table 226

Mondays to Saturdays

Lanark, Coatbridge, Motherwell, Larkhall, Hamilton, Edinburgh and Bathgate, Airdrie and Springburn - Glasgow - Milngavie, Dalmuir, Balloch and Helensburgh

Network Diagram - see first Page of Table 220

		SR	SR	SR	SR	SR	SR	SR	SR	SR	SR	SR	SR	SR	SR	SR	SR	SR	SR	SR	SR	SR	SR
					A															A			SO
Lanark	d			12 53						13 23									13 53				
Carluke	d			13 03						13 33									14 03				
Wishaw	d			13 08						13 40									14 08				
Holytown	d			13 13	13 32														14 13	14 33			
Shieldmuir	d									13 43													
Coatbridge Central	d																						
Whifflet	d																						
Motherwell	a			13 19						13 47									14 19				
	d	13 16		13 20						13 48		13 50					14 16		14 20				
Bellshill	d	13 22			13 35					13 54							14 22			14 36			
Uddingston	d	13 26			13 40					13 59							14 26			14 41			
Airbles	d			13 22								13 52							14 22				
Larkhall	d						13 37							14 07								14 37	
Merryton	d						13 39							14 09								14 39	
Chatelherault	d						13 42							14 12								14 42	
Hamilton Central	d			13 27			13 46					13 57		14 16					14 27			14 46	
Hamilton West	d			13 30			13 48					14 00		14 18					14 30			14 48	
Blantyre	d			13 33			13 52					14 03		14 22					14 33			14 52	
Newton	d			13 37								14 07							14 37				
Cambuslang	d	13 31		13 41						14 04		14 11					14 31		14 41				
Rutherglen	d	13 34		13 45			13 59			14 06		14 15		14 29			14 36		14 45			14 59	
Dalmarnock	d	13 36		13 47						14 08		14 17					14 38		14 47				
Bridgeton	d	13 38		13 49						14 10		14 19					14 40		14 49				
Edinburgh	d							12 48	13 07						13 21	13 37							13 48
Haymarket	d							12 52	13 11						13 25	13 41							13 52
Edinburgh Park	d							12 57	13 16						13 30	13 46							13 57
Uphall	d							13 05	13 24						13 38	13 54							14 05
Livingston North	d							13 08	13 27						13 41	13 57							14 08
Bathgate	a							13 13	13 33						13 46	14 03							14 13
	d							13 17	13 34						13 47	14 04							14 17
Armadale	d							13 21							13 51								14 21
Blackridge	d							13 25							13 55								14 25
Caldercruix	d							13 31							14 01								14 31
Drumgelloch	d							13 35	13 46						14 05	14 16							14 35
Airdrie	d		13 27					13 42	13 50		13 57				14 12	14 20		14 27					14 42
Coatdyke	d		13 29					13 44			13 59				14 14			14 29					14 44
Coatbridge Sunnyside	d		13 31					13 46	13 53		14 01				14 16	14 23		14 31					14 46
Blairhill	d		13 34					13 49			14 04				14 19			14 34					14 49
Easterhouse	d		13 38					13 53			14 08				14 23			14 38					14 53
Garrowhill	d		13 40					13 55			14 10				14 25			14 40					14 55
Shettleston	d		13 43					13 58			14 13				14 28			14 43					14 58
Carntyne	d		13 45					14 00			14 15				14 30			14 45					15 00
Springburn	d					13 49							14 19								14 49		
Barnhill	d					13 50							14 20								14 50		
Alexandra Parade	d					13 53							14 23								14 53		
Duke Street	d					13 55							14 25								14 55		
Bellgrove	d		13 48			13 57		14 03			14 18		14 27		14 33			14 48			14 57		15 03
High Street	d		13 50			13 59		14 05	14 10		14 20		14 29		14 35	14 40		14 50			15 00		15 05
Glasgow Queen St LL 10	a		13 52			14 01		14 07	14 12		14 22		14 31		14 37	14 42		14 52			15 02		15 07
	d		13 53			14 02		14 10	14 13		14 23		14 32		14 40	14 43		14 53			15 03		15 10
Charing Cross	d		13 55			14 04		14 12	14 15		14 25		14 34		14 42	14 45		14 55			15 05		15 12
Argyle Street	d	13 42		13 53			14 04			14 14		14 23		14 35			14 43		14 53			15 04	
Glasgow Central LL 15	a	13 46		13 56	13b55		14 07			14 16		14 26		14 37			14 45		14 56	14b55		15 07	
	d	13 46		13 58			14 07			14 16		14 28		14 37			14 48		15 00			15 07	
Anderston	d	13 48		13 59			14 09			14 18		14 29		14 39			14 49		15 01			15 09	
Exhibition Centre	d	13 50		14 01			14 11			14 20		14 31		14 41			14 51		15 03			15 11	
Partick	d	13 54	13 59	14 05		14 09	14 14	14 17	14 20	14 24	14 29	14 35	14 38	14 44	14 47	14 50	14 55	14 59	15 07		15 09	15 14	15 17
Hyndland 3	d	13 56	14 02	14 08		14 11	14 17	14 19	14 22	14 26	14 32	14 38	14 40	14 47	14 49	14 52	14 58	15 02	15 09		15 11	15 17	15 19
Jordanhill	d	13 58				14 13				14 28			14 42				15 00				15 13		
Scotstounhill	d	14 00				14 15				14 30			14 45				15 02				15 16		
Garscadden	d	14 02				14 17				14 32			14 47				15 05				15 18		
Yoker	d	14 05				14 20				14 34			14 49				15 07				15 20		
Clydebank	d	14 07				14 22				14 36			14 51				15 09				15 22		
Anniesland	d		14 05	14 11			14 20		14 25		14 35	14 41		14 50		14 55		15 05	15 12			15 20	
Westerton	d		14 08	14 14			14 23		14 28		14 38	14 44		14 53		14 58		15 08	15 16			15 23	
Bearsden	d			14 16					14 31			14 46				15 01			15 19				
Hillfoot	d			14 17					14 33			14 47				15 03			15 21				
Milngavie	a			14 22					14 37			14 52				15 07			15 24				
Drumchapel	d		14 10				14 25				14 40			14 55				15 10				15 25	
Drumry	d		14 12				14 27				14 42			14 57				15 12				15 27	
Singer	d		14 15				14 30				14 45			15 00				15 15				15 30	
Dalmuir	a	14 11	14 17			14 26	14 32	14 29		14 42	14 47		14 56	15 02	14 59		15 13	15 17			15 26	15 32	15 29
	d		14 18					14 29			14 48				14 59			15 18					15 29
Kilpatrick	d		14 21								14 51							15 21					
Bowling	d		14 24								14 54							15 24					
Dumbarton East	d		14 28					14 36			14 58				15 06			15 28					15 36
Dumbarton Central	d		14 30					14 39			15 00				15 09			15 30					15 39
Dalreoch	d		14 32					14 40			15 02				15 10			15 32					15 40
Renton	d		14 35								15 05							15 35					
Alexandria	d		14 37								15 07							15 37					
Balloch	a		14 41								15 11							15 41					
Cardross	d							14 45							15 15								15 45
Craigendoran	d							14 50							15 20								15 50
Helensburgh Central	a							14 54							15 26								15 54

A From Edinburgh

b Glasgow Central High Level

Table 226

Mondays to Saturdays

Lanark, Coatbridge, Motherwell, Larkhall, Hamilton, Edinburgh and Bathgate, Airdrie and Springburn - Glasgow - Milngavie, Dalmuir, Balloch and Helensburgh

Network Diagram - see first Page of Table 220

		SR SX	SR		SR SX	SR SO	SR	SR	SR	SR	SR	SR	SR		SR	SR	SR A	SR	SR	SR	SR	SR	SR		SR
Lanark	d				14 23	14 23										14 53						15 23			
Carluke	d				14 33	14 32										15 03						15 33			
Wishaw	d				14 38	14 41										15 08						15 38			
Holytown	d															15 13	15 33								
Shieldmuir	d				14 42	14 45																15 42			
Coatbridge Central	d																								
Whifflet	d																								
Motherwell	a				14 46	14 48										15 18						15 47			
	d				14 46	14 49		14 50					15 16			15 20						15 48			15 50
Bellshill	d				14 52	14 55							15 22				15 36					15 52			
Uddingston	d				14 56	14 59							15 26				15 41					15 56			
Airbles	d							14 52								15 22									15 52
Larkhall	d									15 07									15 37						
Merryton	d									15 09									15 39						
Chatelherault	d									15 12									15 42						
Hamilton Central	d							14 57		15 16						15 27			15 46						15 57
Hamilton West	d							15 00		15 18						15 30			15 48						16 00
Blantyre	d							15 03		15 22						15 33			15 52						16 03
Newton	d							15 07								15 37									16 07
Cambuslang	d				15 01	15 04		15 11					15 31			15 41						16 01			16 11
Rutherglen	d				15 04	15 06		15 16		15 29			15 34			15 45			15 59			16 07			16 16
Dalmarnock	d				15 06	15 08		15 18					15 36			15 47						16 09			16 18
Bridgeton	d				15 08	15 10		15 20					15 38			15 49						16 11			16 21
Edinburgh	d	13 48	14 10								14 21	14 37								14 48	15 07				
Haymarket	d	13 52	14 14								14 25	14 41								14 52	15 11				
Edinburgh Park	d	13 57	14 19								14 30	14 46								14 57	15 16				
Uphall	d	14 05	14 27								14 38	14 54								15 05	15 24				
Livingston North	d	14 08	14 30								14 41	14 57								15 08	15 27				
Bathgate	a	14 13	14 33								14 46	15 03								15 13	15 33				
	d	14 17	14 34								14 47	15 04								15 17	15 34				
Armadale	d	14 21									14 51									15 21					
Blackridge	d	14 25									14 55									15 25					
Caldercruix	d	14 31									15 01									15 31					
Drumgelloch	d	14 35	14 46								15 05	15 16								15 35	15 46				
Airdrie	d	14 42	14 50				14 57				15 12	15 20			15 27					15 42	15 50		15 57		
Coatdyke	d	14 44					14 59				15 14				15 29					15 44			15 59		
Coatbridge Sunnyside	d	14 46	14 53				15 01				15 16	15 23			15 31					15 46	15 53		16 01		
Blairhill	d	14 49					15 04				15 19				15 34					15 49			16 04		
Easterhouse	d	14 53					15 08				15 23				15 38					15 53			16 08		
Garrowhill	d	14 55					15 10				15 25				15 40					15 55			16 10		
Shettleston	d	14 58					15 13				15 28				15 43					15 58			16 13		
Carntyne	d	15 00					15 15				15 30				15 45					16 00			16 15		
Springburn	d								15 19									15 49							
Barnhill	d								15 20									15 50							
Alexandra Parade	d								15 23									15 53							
Duke Street	d								15 25									15 55							
Bellgrove	d	15 03					15 18		15 27		15 33				15 48			15 57		16 03			16 18		
High Street	d	15 05	15 10				15 20		15 29		15 35	15 40			15 50			15 59		16 05	16 10		16 20		
Glasgow Queen St LL 10 ⛴	a	15 07	15 12				15 22		15 31		15 37	15 42			15 52			16 01		16 07	16 12		16 22		
	d	15 10	15 13				15 23		15 32		15 40	15 43			15 53			16 02		16 10	16 13		16 23		
Charing Cross	d	15 12	15 15				15 25		15 34		15 42	15 45			15 55			16 04		16 12	16 15		16 25		
Argyle Street	d				15 12	15 15		15 24		15 36			15 42			15 53			16 04			16 14			16 24
Glasgow Central LL 15	a				15 16	15 19		15 25		15 37			15 46			15 56	15b56		16 07			16 16			16 26
	d				15 16	15 19		15 28		15 38			15 46			15 58			16 07			16 18			16 28
Anderston	d				15 18	15 21		15 29		15 39			15 48			15 59			16 09			16 20			16 29
Exhibition Centre	d				15 20	15 23		15 31		15 41			15 50			16 01			16 11			16 22			16 31
Partick ⛴	d	15 17	15 20		15 24	15 27	15 29	15 35	15 39	15 45	15 47	15 50	15 54		15 59	16 05		16 08	16 14	16 17	16 20	16 25	16 29		16 35
Hyndland 3	d	15 19	15 22		15 26	15 29	15 32	15 38	15 41	15 47	15 49	15 52	15 56		16 02	16 07		16 10	16 17	16 19	16 22	16 27	16 32		16 38
Jordanhill	d				15 28	15 31			15 43				15 58					16 12				16 29			
Scotstounhill	d				15 31	15 33			15 45				16 00					16 15				16 32			
Garscadden	d				15 33	15 35			15 47				16 03					16 17				16 34			
Yoker	d				15 35	15 38			15 50				16 05					16 19				16 36			
Clydebank	d				15 38	15 40			15 52				16 07					16 21				16 38			
Anniesland	d		15 25				15 35	15 43		15 50		15 55			16 05	16 10			16 20		16 25		16 35		16 41
Westerton	d		15 28				15 38	15 47		15 53		15 58			16 08	16 13			16 23		16 28		16 38		16 44
Bearsden	d		15 31					15 50				16 01				16 16					16 31				16 46
Hillfoot	d		15 33					15 52				16 03				16 18					16 33				16 47
Milngavie	a		15 37					15 55				16 07				16 22					16 37				16 52
Drumchapel	d						15 40			15 55					16 10				16 25				16 40		
Drumry	d						15 42			15 57					16 12				16 27				16 42		
Singer	d						15 45			16 00					16 15				16 30				16 45		
Dalmuir	a	15 29			15 42	15 44	15 47		15 56	16 02	15 59		16 12		16 17			16 26	16 32	16 29		16 43	16 47		
	d	15 29					15 48				15 59				16 18					16 29			16 48		
Kilpatrick	d						15 51								16 21								16 51		
Bowling	d						15 54								16 24								16 54		
Dumbarton East	d	15 36					15 58				16 06				16 28					16 36			16 58		
Dumbarton Central	d	15 39					16 00				16 09				16 30					16 39			17 00		
Dalreoch	d	15 45					16 02				16 10				16 32					16 40			17 02		
Renton	d						16 05								16 35								17 05		
Alexandria	d						16 07								16 37								17 07		
Balloch	a						16 11								16 41								17 11		
Cardross	d	15 49									16 15									16 45					
Craigendoran	d	15 54									16 20									16 50					
Helensburgh Central	a	15 58									16 24									16 54					

A From Edinburgh

b Glasgow Central High Level

Table 226

Mondays to Saturdays

Lanark, Coatbridge, Motherwell, Larkhall, Hamilton, Edinburgh and Bathgate, Airdrie and Springburn - Glasgow - Milngavie, Dalmuir, Balloch and Helensburgh

Network Diagram - see first Page of Table 220

		SR	SR	SR	SR	SR	SR	SR	SR A	SR	SR	SR	SR	SR SX	SR SO	SR SX	SR SO	SR SX	SR	SR SX	SR	SR	SR
Lanark	d							15 53						16 20	16 23								
Carluke	d							16 03						16 30	16 33								
Wishaw	d							16 08						16 35	16 38								
Holytown	d							16 13	16 33														
Shieldmuir	d													16 39	16 42								
Coatbridge Central	d																						
Whifflet	d																						
Motherwell	a							16 19						16 42	16 48								
	d					16 16		16 20						16 42	16 49				16 50				
Bellshill	d					16 22			16 36					16 51	16 55								
Uddingston	d					16 26			16 41					16 55	16 59								
Airbles	d							16 22											16 52				
Larkhall	d		16 07								16 37											17 07	
Merryton	d		16 09								16 39											17 09	
Chatelherault	d		16 12								16 42											17 12	
Hamilton Central	d		16 16					16 28			16 46								16 58			17 16	
Hamilton West	d		16 18					16 30			16 48								17 00			17 18	
Blantyre	d		16 22					16 34			16 52								17 04			17 22	
Newton	d							16 38											17 08				
Cambuslang	d					16 31		16 41						17 00	17 04				17 11				
Rutherglen	d		16 30			16 34		16 46			16 59			17 06	17 06				17 16			17 31	
Dalmarnock	d					16 36		16 48						17 08	17 08				17 18				
Bridgeton	d					16 38		16 50						17 10	17 10				17 20				
Edinburgh	d			15 21	15 37							15 51	16 07										16 19
Haymarket	d			15 25	15 41							15 55	16 11										16 25
Edinburgh Park	d			15 30	15 46							16 00	16 16										16 30
Uphall	d			15 38	15 54							16 08	16 24										16 38
Livingston North	d			15 41	15 57							16 11	16 27										16 41
Bathgate	a			15 46	16 03							16 16	16 33										16 46
	d			15 47	16 04							16 17	16 34										16 47
Armadale	d			15 51								16 21											16 51
Blackridge	d			15 55								16 25											16 55
Caldercruix	d			16 01								16 31											17 01
Drumgelloch	d			16 05	16 16							16 35	16 46										17 05
Airdrie	d			16 12	16 20		16 27					16 42	16 50				16 57	16 57					17 12
Coatdyke	d			16 14			16 29					16 44					16 59	16 59					17 14
Coatbridge Sunnyside	d			16 16	16 23		16 31					16 46	16 53				17 01	17 01					17 16
Blairhill	d			16 19			16 34					16 49					17 04	17 04					17 19
Easterhouse	d			16 23			16 38					16 53					17 08	17 08					17 23
Garrowhill	d			16 25			16 40					16 55					17 10	17 10					17 25
Shettleston	d			16 28			16 43					16 58					17 13	17 13					17 28
Carntyne	d			16 30			16 45					17 00					17 15	17 15					17 30
Springburn	d	16 19								16 49											17 22		
Barnhill	d	16 20								16 50											17 23		
Alexandra Parade	d	16 23								16 53											17 26		
Duke Street	d	16 25								16 55											17 28		
Bellgrove	d	16 27		16 33			16 48			16 57		17 03				17 15	17 18	17 18		17 27	17 30		17 33
High Street	d	16 29		16 35	16 40		16 50			16 59		17 05	17 10			17 17	17 20	17 20		17 29	17 32		17 35
Glasgow Queen St LL 10	a	16 31		16 37	16 42		16 52			17 01		17 07	17 13			17 19	17 22	17 22		17 31	17 34		17 37
	d	16 32		16 40	16 43		16 53			17 02		17 11	17 13			17 20	17 23	17 23		17 31	17 35		17 40
Charing Cross	d	16 34		16 42	16 45		16 55			17 04		17 13	17 15			17 22	17 25	17 25		17 34	17 37		17 42
Argyle Street	d		16 35			16 42		16 54			17 05			17 14	17 14				17 24			17 36	
Glasgow Central LL 15	a		16 37			16 46		16 56	16b57		17 07			17 16	17 16				17 26			17 37	
	d		16 38			16 47		16 58			17 07			17 16	17 16				17 28			17 38	
Anderston	d		16 39			16 48		16 59			17 09			17 18	17 18				17 29			17 39	
Exhibition Centre	d		16 41			16 50		17 01			17 11			17 20	17 20				17 31			17 41	
Partick	d	16 39	16 45	16 47	16 50	16 54	16 59	17 05		17 08	17 14	17 18	17 20	17 23	17 23	17 27	17 29	17 29	17 35	17 38	17 41	17 45	17 47
Hyndland 3	d	16 41	16 47	16 49	16 52	16 56	17 02	17 08		17 10	17 17	17 20	17 22	17 25	17 25		17 32	17 32	17 38		17 43	17 47	17 49
Jordanhill	d	16 43				16 58				17 12				17 27	17 27						17 45		
Scotstounhill	d	16 45				17 01				17 15				17 30	17 30						17 48		
Garscadden	d	16 48				17 03				17 17				17 32	17 32						17 50		
Yoker	d	16 50				17 06				17 19				17 34	17 34						17 52		
Clydebank	d	16 52				17 08				17 21				17 36	17 36						17 54		
Anniesland	d		16 50		16 55		17 05	17 12			17 20		17 25				17 35	17 35	17 41			17 50	
Westerton	d		16 53		16 58		17 08	17 15			17 23		17 28				17 38	17 38	17 44			17 53	
Bearsden	d				17 01			17 17					17 31						17 46				
Hillfoot	d				17 03			17 18					17 33						17 47				
Milngavie	a				17 07			17 23					17 37						17 52				
Drumchapel	d		16 55				17 10				17 25						17 40	17 40				17 55	
Drumry	d		16 57				17 12				17 27						17 42	17 42				17 57	
Singer	d		17 00				17 15				17 30						17 45	17 45				18 00	
Dalmuir	a	16 56	17 02	16 59		17 12	17 17			17 26	17 32	17 30		17 41	17 41		17 47	17 47			17 58	18 02	17 59
	d			16 59			17 18					17 30					17 48	17 51					17 59
Kilpatrick	d						17 21										17 51	17 53					
Bowling	d						17 24										17 54	17 56					
Dumbarton East	d			17 06			17 28					17 37					17 58	18 01					18 06
Dumbarton Central	d			17 09			17 30					17 40				17 46	18 00	18 04		18 00			18 09
Dalreoch	d			17 10			17 32					17 41				17 48	18 02	18 05		18 02			18 10
Renton	d						17 35										18 05			18 05			
Alexandria	d						17 37										18 07			18 07			
Balloch	a						17 41										18 11			18 11			
Cardross	d			17 15								17 46				17 53		18 09					18 15
Craigendoran	d			17 20								17 51				17 58		18 17					18 20
Helensburgh Central	a			17 24								17 54				18 01		18 20					18 26

A From Edinburgh

b Glasgow Central High Level

Lanark, Coatbridge, Motherwell, Larkhall, Hamilton, Edinburgh and Bathgate, Airdrie and Springburn - Glasgow - Milngavie, Dalmuir, Balloch and Helensburgh

Network Diagram - see first Page of Table 220

		SR	SR	SR	SR	SR	SR	SR	SR	SR	SR	SR	SR	SR	SR	SR	SR	SR	SR	SR	SR	SR	SR
			SX	SO		SO	SX				SO	SX					SX	SO		SX	SO		
								A						◇ B									
Lanark	d		16 53			16 53									17 23								
Carluke	d		17 03			17 03									17 33								
Wishaw	d		17 08			17 08									17 38								
Holytown	d					17 13		17 31															
Shieldmuir	d		17 12												17 42								
Coatbridge Central	d											17 32								17 56			
Whifflet	d											17 34								18 00			
Motherwell	a		17 16			17 19						17 40			17 47					18 08			
	d		17 16	17 16		17 20	17 20					17 40			17 48			17 50		18 11			
Bellshill	d		17 23	17 23				17 34							17 55					18 17			
Uddingston	d		17 27	17 27				17 38							17 59					18 21			
Airbles	d					17 22	17 22					17 43						17 52					
Larkhall	d										17 37						17 49				18 07		
Merryton	d										17 39						17 51				18 09		
Chatelherault	d										17 42						17 54				18 12		
Hamilton Central	d					17 27	17 27				17 46	17 48					17 57	17 57			18 16		
Hamilton West	d					17 30	17 30				17 48	17 50					18 00	18 00			18 18		
Blantyre	d					17 33	17 33				17 52	17 54					18 03	18 03			18 22		
Newton	d					17 37	17 37										18 07	18 07					
Cambuslang	d		17 31	17 31		17 41	17 41	17 44							18 04		18 11	18 11					
Rutherglen	d		17 34	17 34		17 45	17 45				17 59	18 02			18 06		18 15	18 15		18 29	18 30		
Dalmarnock	d		17 36	17 36		17 47	17 47								18 08		18 17	18 17					
Bridgeton	d		17 38	17 38		17 49	17 49								18 10		18 19	18 19					
Edinburgh	d	16 41								16 48			17 07									17 22	17 37
Haymarket	d	16 46								16 52			17 11									17 26	17 42
Edinburgh Park	d	16 50								16 57			17 16									17 31	17 48
Uphall	d	16 58								17 06			17 27									17 39	17 56
Livingston North	d	17 02								17 09			17 30									17 42	17 59
Bathgate	a	17 06								17 14			17 35									17 46	18 04
	d	17 07								17 17			17 35									17 47	18 05
Armadale	d									17 21												17 51	
Blackridge	d									17 25												17 55	
Caldercruix	d									17 31												18 01	
Drumgelloch	d	17 19								17 35			17 48									18 05	18 17
Airdrie	d	17 23			17 27					17 42			17 51			17 57						18 12	18 21
Coatdyke	d				17 29					17 44						17 59						18 14	
Coatbridge Sunnyside	d	17 26			17 31					17 46			17 55			18 01						18 16	18 24
Blairhill	d				17 34					17 49						18 04						18 19	
Easterhouse	d				17 38					17 53						18 08						18 23	
Garrowhill	d				17 40					17 55						18 10						18 25	
Shettleston	d				17 43					17 58						18 13						18 28	
Carntyne	d				17 45					18 00						18 15						18 30	
Springburn	d								17 49										18 19				
Barnhill	d								17 50										18 20				
Alexandra Parade	d								17 53										18 23				
Duke Street	d								17 55										18 25				
Bellgrove	d				17 48				17 57	18 03						18 18			18 27			18 33	
High Street	d	17 42			17 50				17 59	18 05			18 10			18 20			18 29			18 35	18 40
Glasgow Queen St LL 10 ⛴	a	17 44			17 53				18 01	18 07			18 12			18 22			18 31			18 37	18 42
	d	17 45			17 53				18 02	18 10			18 14	18c21		18 23			18 32			18 40	18 43
Charing Cross	d	17 47			17 55				18 04	18 12			18 17			18 25			18 34			18 42	18 46
Argyle Street	d		17 42	17 42		17 53	17 53				18 04	18 07			18 14		18 23	18 23		18 34	18 35		
Glasgow Central LL 15	a		17 46	17 46		17 54	17 54	17b57			18 07	18 08			18 16		18 26	18 26		18 37	18 37		
	d		17 47	17 47		17 58	17 58				18 11	18 11			18 19		18 28	18 28		18 37	18 37		
Anderston	d		17 48	17 48		17 59	17 59				18 13	18 13			18 20		18 29	18 29		18 39	18 39		
Exhibition Centre	d		17 50	17 50		18 01	18 01				18 15	18 15			18 22		18 31	18 31		18 41	18 41		
Partick ⛴	d	17 51	17 54	17 54	17 59	18 05	18 05		18 09	18 16	18 18	18 18	18 21		18 26	18 29	18 35	18 35	18 39	18 44	18 44	18 47	18 50
Hyndland 3	d	17 53	17 56	17 56	18 02	18 07	18 07		18 11	18 18	18 20	18 20	18 24		18 28	18 32	18 37	18 37	18 41	18 47	18 47	18 49	18 53
Jordanhill	d		17 58	17 58					18 13						18 30				18 43			18 51	
Scotstounhill	d		18 00	18 00					18 15						18 32				18 45			18 54	
Garscadden	d		18 02	18 02					18 17						18 35				18a47			18 56	
Yoker	d		18 04	18 04					18 20						18 37							18 58	
Clydebank	d		18 06	18 06					18 22						18 39							19 00	
Anniesland	d	17 56			18 05	18 10	18 10				18 23	18 23	18 27			18 35	18 40	18 40		18 50	18 50		18 56
Westerton	d	17 59			18 08	18 13	18 13				18 26	18 26	18 30			18 38	18 43	18 43		18 53	18 53		18 59
Bearsden	d	18 02				18 16	18 16						18 32				18 46	18 46					19 02
Hillfoot	d	18 04				18 17	18 17						18 34				18 47	18 47					19 03
Milngavie	a	18 07				18 22	18 22						18 38				18 52	18 52					19 07
Drumchapel	d				18 10						18 29	18 29				18 40				18 55	18 55		
Drumry	d				18 12						18 31	18 31				18 42				18 57	18 57		
Singer	d				18 15						18 33	18 33				18 45				19 00	19 00		
Dalmuir	a		18 11	18 11	18 17				18 26	18 29	18 36	18 36		18 38	18 43	18 47				19 02	19 02	19 04	
	d				18 18					18 29				18 38		18 48						19 04	
Kilpatrick	d				18 21											18 51							
Bowling	d				18 24											18 54							
Dumbarton East	d				18 28					18 36						18 58						19 12	
Dumbarton Central	d				18 30					18 39				18 47		19 00						19 14	
Dalreoch	d				18 32					18 40						19 02						19 15	
Renton	d				18 35											19 05							
Alexandria	d				18 37											19 07							
Balloch	a				18 41											19 11							
Cardross	d									18 45												19 20	
Craigendoran	d									18 50												19 25	
Helensburgh Central	a									18 53				19e02								19 28	

A From Edinburgh
B To Oban

b Glasgow Central High Level
c Glasgow Queen St High Level

e Helensburgh Upper

Lanark, Coatbridge, Motherwell, Larkhall, Hamilton, Edinburgh and Bathgate, Airdrie and Springburn - Glasgow - Milngavie, Dalmuir, Balloch and Helensburgh

Network Diagram - see first Page of Table 220

		SR SX	SR SO	SR	SR SO	SR SX	SR SX A	SR	SR	SR	SR	SR	SR	SR SX	SR SO	SR A	SR	SR	SR	SR	SR	SR
Lanark	d				17 53							18 23										18 53
Carluke	d				18 03							18 33										19 03
Wishaw	d				18 08							18 38										19 08
Holytown	d				18 13											18 59						19 13
Shieldmuir	d											18 42										
Coatbridge Central	d													18 39								
Whifflet	d													18 41								
Motherwell	a				18 19							18 45		18 49								19 19
	d		18 16		18 20	18 20						18 45		18 50	18 50					19 16		19 20
Bellshill	d		18 22				18 41					18 52				19 04				19 22		
Uddingston	d		18 26									18 56				19 07				19 26		
Airbles	d				18 22	18 22								18 52	18 52							19 23
Larkhall	d	18 05							18 37								19 07					
Merryton	d	18 07							18 39								19 09					
Chatelherault	d	18 14							18 42								19 12					
Hamilton Central	d	18 18			18 27	18 27			18 46					18 57	18 57		19 16					19 28
Hamilton West	d	18 21			18 30	18 30			18 48					19 00	19 00		19 18					19 30
Blantyre	d	18 24			18 33	18 33			18 52					19 03	19 03		19 22					19 34
Newton	d				18 37	18 37								19 07	19 07							19 38
Cambuslang	d	18 31	18 31		18 41	18 41	18 51					19 01		19 11	19 11	19 16				19 31		19 41
Rutherglen	d	18 34	18 34		18 45	18 45			18 59			19 06		19 16	19 16		19 29			19 34		19 45
Dalmarnock	d	18 36	18 36		18 47	18 47						19 08		19 18	19 18					19 36		19 47
Bridgeton	d	18 38	18 38		18 49	18 49						19 10		19 20	19 20					19 38		19 49
Edinburgh	d									17 51	18 05							18 20	18 37			
Haymarket	d									17 56	18 10							18 24	18 42			
Edinburgh Park	d									18 01	18 16							18 30	18 46			
Uphall	d									18 09	18 24							18 38	18 55			
Livingston North	d									18 12	18 28							18 41	18 57			
Bathgate	a									18 17	18 34							18 46	19 03			
	d									18 17	18 35							18 47	19 03			
Armadale	d									18 21								18 51				
Blackridge	d									18 25								18 55				
Caldercruix	d									18 31								19 01				
Drumgelloch	d									18 35	18 46							19 05	19 17			
Airdrie	d			18 27						18 42	18 51							19 12	19 20			
Coatdyke	d			18 29						18 44								19 14				
Coatbridge Sunnyside	d			18 31						18 46	18 53							19 16	19 23			
Blairhill	d			18 34						18 49								19 19				
Easterhouse	d			18 38						18 53								19 23				
Garrowhill	d			18 40						18 55								19 25				
Shettleston	d			18 43						18 58								19 28				
Carntyne	d			18 45						19 00								19 30				
Springburn	d							18 49					19 09								19 39	
Barnhill	d							18 50					19 10								19 40	
Alexandra Parade	d							18 53					19 13								19 43	
Duke Street	d							18 55					19 15								19 45	
Bellgrove	d			18 48				18 57		19 03			19 17					19 33			19 47	
High Street	d			18 50				18 59		19 05	19 12		19 19					19 35	19 40		19 49	
Glasgow Queen St LL 10	a			18 52				19 01		19 07	19 14		19 21					19 37	19 42		19 51	
	d			18 53				19 02		19 10	19 14		19 23					19 40	19 43		19 53	
Charing Cross	d			18 55				19 04		19 12	19 17		19 25					19 42	19 45		19 55	
Argyle Street	d	18 42	18 42		18 53	18 53			19 04			19 13		19 24	19 24		19 35			19 42		19 53
Glasgow Central LL 15	a	18 46	18 46		18 56	18 56	19b04		19 07			19 15		19 25	19 25	19b31	19 37			19 46		19 56
	d	18 46	18 46		18 58	18 58			19 07			19 17		19 28	19 28		19 37			19 46		19 58
Anderston	d	18 48	18 48		18 59	18 59			19 09			19 19		19 29	19 29		19 39			19 48		19 59
Exhibition Centre	d	18 50	18 50		19 01	19 01			19 11			19 21		19 31	19 31		19 41			19 50		20 01
Partick	d	18a53	18a53	19 00	19 05	19 05		19 09	19 14	19 17	19 21	19a24	19 29	19 35	19 35		19 44	19 47	19 50	19a53	19 59	20 05
Hyndland 3	d			19 03	19 08	19 08		19 11	19 17	19 19	19 23		19 32	19 38	19 38		19 47	19 49	19 52		20 03	20 08
Jordanhill	d							19 13		19 21	19 25							19 51	19 54			
Scotstounhill	d							19 15		19 24	19 27							19 54	19 57			
Garscadden	d							19a17		19 26	19a30							19 56	19a59			
Yoker	d									19 28								19 58				
Clydebank	d									19 30								20 00				
Anniesland	d			19 06	19 11	19 11			19 20				19 35	19 41	19 41		19 50				20 06	20 11
Westerton	d			19 09	19 14	19 14			19 23				19 38	19 44	19 44		19 53				20 09	20 14
Bearsden	d				19 17	19 17								19 46	19 46							20 17
Hillfoot	d				19 18	19 18								19 48	19 48							20 18
Milngavie	a				19 22	19 22								19 52	19 52							20 22
Drumchapel	d			19 11					19 25				19 40				19 55				20 11	
Drumry	d			19 13					19 27				19 42				19 57				20 13	
Singer	d			19 16					19 30				19 45				20 00				20 16	
Dalmuir	a			19 18					19 32	19 34			19 47				20 02	20 04			20 18	
	d			19 18						19 34			19 48					20 04			20 18	
Kilpatrick	d			19 21									19 51								20 21	
Bowling	d			19 24									19 54								20 24	
Dumbarton East	d			19 28						19 42			19 58					20 12			20 28	
Dumbarton Central	d			19 30						19 44			20 00					20 14			20 30	
Dalreoch	d			19 32						19 45			20 02					20 15			20 32	
Renton	d			19 35									20 05								20 35	
Alexandria	d			19 37									20 07								20 37	
Balloch	a			19 41									20 11								20 41	
Cardross	d									19 50								20 20				
Craigendoran	d									19 55								20 25				
Helensburgh Central	a									19 58								20 28				

A From Edinburgh

b Glasgow Central High Level

Lanark, Coatbridge, Motherwell, Larkhall, Hamilton, Edinburgh and Bathgate, Airdrie and Springburn - Glasgow - Milngavie, Dalmuir, Balloch and Helensburgh

Network Diagram - see first Page of Table 220

		SR	SR	SR	SR	SR	SR	SR	SR	SR	SR	SR	SR	SR SO A	SR SX A	SR	SR	SR	SR	SR	SR	SR	SR
Lanark	d				19 23								19 53					20 23					
Carluke	d				19 33								20 03					20 33					
Wishaw	d				19 40								20 08					20 38					
Holytown	d												20 13	20 24	20 33								
Shieldmuir	d				19 43													20 42					
Coatbridge Central	d																						
Whifflet	d																						
Motherwell	a				19 47								20 19					20 46					
	d				19 48		19 50				20 18		20 20					20 47		20 50			21 15
Bellshill	d				19 54						20 24			20 28	20 36			20 53					21 22
Uddingston	d				19 58						20 28			20 32	20 41			20 57					21 26
Airbles	d						19 52						20 22							20 52			
Larkhall	d	19 37						20 07								20 37					21 07		
Merryton	d	19 39						20 09								20 39					21 09		
Chatelherault	d	19 42						20 12								20 42					21 12		
Hamilton Central	d	19 46					19 57	20 16					20 27			20 46				20 57	21 16		
Hamilton West	d	19 48					20 00	20 18					20 30			20 48				21 00	21 18		
Blantyre	d	19 52					20 03	20 22					20 33			20 52				21 03	21 22		
Newton	d						20 07						20 37							21 07			
Cambuslang	d				20 03		20 11				20 33		20 41					21 02		21 11			21 32
Rutherglen	d	19 59			20 07		20 14	20 29			20 39		20 44			20 59		21 05		21 14	21 29		21 36
Dalmarnock	d				20 09		20 16				20 41		20 46					21 07		21 16			21 38
Bridgeton	d				20 11		20 18				20 43		20 48					21 09		21 18			21 40
Edinburgh	d		18 48	19 07					19 21	19 39							19 51					20 21	
Haymarket	d		18 52	19 12					19 24	19 41							19 55					20 25	
Edinburgh Park	d		18 57	19 18					19 30	19 47							20 00					20 30	
Uphall	d		19 05	19 26					19 38	19 54							20 08					20 38	
Livingston North	d		19 08	19 29					19 44	19 58							20 17					20 41	
Bathgate	a		19 13	19 34					19 48	20 04							20 21					20 46	
	d		19 17						19 49								20 22					20 47	
Armadale	d		19 21						19 53								20 26					20 51	
Blackridge	d		19 25						19 56								20 29					20 55	
Caldercruix	d		19 31						20 03								20 36					21 01	
Drumgelloch	d		19 35						20 06								20 39					21 05	
Airdrie	d		19 42						20 13								20 43					21 12	
Coatdyke	d		19 44						20 15								20 45					21 14	
Coatbridge Sunnyside	d		19 46						20 17								20 47					21 16	
Blairhill	d		19 49						20 20								20 50					21 19	
Easterhouse	d		19 53						20 24								20 54					21 23	
Garrowhill	d		19 55						20 26								20 56					21 25	
Shettleston	d		19 58						20 29								20 59					21 28	
Carntyne	d		20 00						20 31								21 01					21 30	
Springburn	d					20 09						20 39							21 09				
Barnhill	d					20 10						20 40							21 10				
Alexandra Parade	d					20 13						20 43							21 13				
Duke Street	d					20 15						20 45							21 15				
Bellgrove	d		20 03			20 17			20 34			20 47					21 04		21 17			21 33	
High Street	d		20 05			20 19			20 36			20 49					21 06		21 19			21 35	
Glasgow Queen St LL 10 ⛴	a		20 07			20 21			20 38			20 51					21 08		21 21			21 37	
	d		20 10			20 23			20 40			20 53					21 10		21 23			21 40	
Charing Cross	d		20 12			20 25			20 42			20 55					21 12		21 25			21 42	
Argyle Street	d	20 04			20 15		20 23	20 34			20 46		20 52			21 04		21 15		21 22	21 34		21 44
Glasgow Central LL 15	a	20 07			20 18		20 26	20 37			20 48		20 56	20b47	20b57	21 07		21 16		21 26	21 37		21 46
	d	20 08			20 18		20 28	20 37			20 49		20 58			21 07		21 17		21 28	21 37		21 46
Anderston	d	20 09			20 20		20 29	20 39			20 51		20 59			21 09		21 18		21 29	21 39		21 48
Exhibition Centre	d	20 11			20 22		20 31	20 41			20 53		21 01			21 11		21 20		21 31	21 41		21 50
Partick ⛴	d	20 15	20 17		20a25	20 30	20 35	20 44	20 48		20a56	20 59	21 05			21 14	21 17	21a24	21 29	21 35	21 44	21 47	21a53
Hyndland 3	d	20 17	20 19			20 33	20 38	20 47	20 50			21 02	21 08			21 17	21 19		21 32	21 38	21 47	21 49	
Jordanhill	d		20 21						20 52								21 21					21 51	
Scotstounhill	d		20 24						20 54								21 24					21 54	
Garscadden	d		20 26						20 56								21 26					21 56	
Yoker	d		20 28						20 58								21 28					21 58	
Clydebank	d		20 30						21 00								21 30					22 00	
Anniesland	d	20 20				20 36	20 41	20 50				21 05	21 11			21 20			21 35	21 41	21 50		
Westerton	d	20 23				20 39	20 44	20 53				21 08	21 14			21 23			21 38	21 44	21 53		
Bearsden	d						20 46						21 16							21 46			
Hillfoot	d						20 47						21 17							21 47			
Milngavie	a						20 52						21 22							21 52			
Drumchapel	d	20 25				20 41		20 55				21 10				21 25			21 40		21 55		
Drumry	d	20 27				20 43		20 57				21 12				21 27			21 42		21 57		
Singer	d	20 30				20 46		21 00				21 15				21 30			21 45		22 00		
Dalmuir	a	20 32	20 34			20 48		21 02	21 04			21 18				21 32	21 34		21 47		22 02	22 03	
	d		20 34			20 48			21 04			21 18					21 34		21 48			22 04	
Kilpatrick	d					20 51						21 21							21 51				
Bowling	d					20 54						21 24							21 54				
Dumbarton East	d		20 42			20 58			21 11			21 28					21 42		21 58			22 11	
Dumbarton Central	d		20 44			21 00			21 14			21 30					21 44		22 00			22 13	
Dalreoch	d		20 45			21 02			21 15			21 32					21 45		22 02			22 15	
Renton	d					21 05						21 35							22 05				
Alexandria	d					21 07						21 37							22 07				
Balloch	a					21 11						21 41							22 11				
Cardross	d		20 50						21 20								21 50					22 20	
Craigendoran	d		20 55						21 25								21 55					22 25	
Helensburgh Central	a		20 58						21 28								21 58					22 28	

A From Edinburgh

b Glasgow Central High Level

Table 226

Mondays to Saturdays

Lanark, Coatbridge, Motherwell, Larkhall, Hamilton, Edinburgh and Bathgate, Airdrie and Springburn - Glasgow - Milngavie, Dalmuir, Balloch and Helensburgh

Network Diagram - see first Page of Table 220

		SR	SR	SR	SR	SR	SR	SR	SR	SR	SR	SR	SR	SR A	SR	SR	SR	SR	SR	SR	SR	SR FX
Lanark	d		20 53			21 23							21 53				22 23					
Carluke	d		21 03			21 33							22 03				22 33					
Wishaw	d		21 08			21 40							22 08				22 42					
Holytown	d		21 13										22 13	22 33								
Shieldmuir	d					21 43											22 45					
Coatbridge Central	d																					
Whifflet	d																					
Motherwell	a		21 19			21 47							22 19				22 49					
	d		21 20			21 48		21 50			22 16		22 20				22 49		22 50			
Bellshill	d					21 54					22 22			22 36			22 56					
Uddingston	d					21 58					22 26			22 41			23 00					
Airbles	d		21 22					21 52					22 22						22 52			
Larkhall	d			21 37					22 07						22 37					23 07		
Merryton	d			21 39					22 09						22 39					23 09		
Chatelherault	d			21 42					22 12						22 42					23 12		
Hamilton Central	d		21 27	21 46				21 57	22 16				22 27		22 46				22 57	23 16		
Hamilton West	d		21 30	21 48				22 00	22 18				22 30		22 48				23 00	23 18		
Blantyre	d		21 33	21 52				22 03	22 22				22 33		22 52				23 03	23 22		
Newton	d		21 37					22 07					22 37						23 07			
Cambuslang	d		21 41			22 03		22 11			22 31		22 41				23 05		23 11			
Rutherglen	d		21 45	22 01		22 06		22 14	22 30		22 34		22 45		22 59		23 08		23 15	23 29		
Dalmarnock	d		21 47			22 08		22 16			22 36		22 47				23 10		23 17			
Bridgeton	d		21 49			22 10		22 18			22 38		22 49				23 12		23 19			
Edinburgh	d				20 50					21 21						21 51					22 19	
Haymarket	d				20 54					21 25						21 55					22 23	
Edinburgh Park	d				21 00					21 30						22 00					22 30	
Uphall	d				21 08					21 38						22 08					22 38	
Livingston North	d				21 11					21 41						22 11					22 41	
Bathgate	a				21 16					21 46						22 16					22 46	
	d				21 17					21 47						22 17					22 47	
Armadale	d				21 21					21 51						22 21					22 51	
Blackridge	d				21 25					21 55						22 25					22 55	
Caldercruix	d				21 31					22 01						22 31					23 01	
Drumgelloch	d				21 35					22 05						22 35					23 05	
Airdrie	d				21 42					22 12						22 42					23 12	
Coatdyke	d				21 44					22 14						22 44					23 14	
Coatbridge Sunnyside	d				21 46					22 16						22 46					23 16	
Blairhill	d				21 49					22 19						22 49					23 19	
Easterhouse	d				21 53					22 23						22 53					23 23	
Garrowhill	d				21 55					22 25						22 55					23 25	
Shettleston	d				21 58					22 28						22 58					23 28	
Carntyne	d				22 00					22 30						23 00					23 30	
Springburn	d	21 39					22 09					22 39						23 09				23 39
Barnhill	d	21 40					22 10					22 40						23 10				23 40
Alexandra Parade	d	21 43					22 13					22 43						23 13				23 43
Duke Street	d	21 45					22 15					22 45						23 15				23 45
Bellgrove	d	21 47			22 03		22 17			22 33		22 47				23 03		23 17			23 33	23 47
High Street	d	21 49			22 05		22 19			22 35		22 49				23 05		23 19			23 35	23 49
Glasgow Queen St LL 10 ⛴	a	21 51			22 07		22 21			22 37		22 51				23 07		23 21			23 37	23 51
	d	21 53			22 10		22 23			22 40		22 53				23 10		23 23			23 45	23 53
Charing Cross	d	21 55			22 12		22 25			22 42		22 55				23 12		23 25			23 47	23 55
Argyle Street	d		21 53	22 06		22 14		22 22	22 35		22 42		22 53		23 04		23 16		23 23	23 34		
Glasgow Central LL 15	a		21 56	22 07		22 16		22 26	22 37		22 46		22 56	22b55	23 07		23 17		23 26	23 37		
	d		21 58	22 07		22 17		22 28	22 37		22 47		22 58		23 07		23 18		23 28	23 37		
Anderston	d		21 59	22 09		22 19		22 29	22 39		22 49		22 59		23 09		23 19		23 29	23 39		
Exhibition Centre	d		22 01	22 11		22 21		22 31	22 41		22 51		23 01		23 11		23 21		23 31	23 41		
Partick ⛴	d	21 59	22 05	22 14	22 17	22a24	22 30	22 35	22 44	22 47	22a54	22 59	23 05		23 14	23 17	23 25	23 29	23 35	23 44	23 51	23 59
Hyndland 3	d	22 03	22 08	22 17	22 19		22 33	22 38	22 47	22 49		23 03	23 08		23 17	23 19	23 27	23 32	23 38	23 47	23 53	00 02
Jordanhill	d				22 21					22 51						23 21	23 29			23 49	23 55	00 04
Scotstounhill	d				22 24					22 54						23 24	23 31			23 51	23 58	00 06
Garscadden	d				22 26					22 56						23 25	23a33			23a53	23 59	00a08
Yoker	d				22 28					22 58						23 27					00 02	
Clydebank	d				22 30					23 00						23 29					00 04	
Anniesland	d	22 06	22 11	22 20			22 36	22 41	22 50			23 06	23 11		23 20			23 35	23 41			
Westerton	d	22 09	22 14	22 23			22 39	22 44	22 53			23 09	23 14		23 23			23 38	23 44			
Bearsden	d		22 17					22 46					23 17						23 46			
Hillfoot	d		22 18					22 47					23 18						23 47			
Milngavie	a		22 22					22 52					23 22						23 52			
Drumchapel	d	22 11		22 25			22 41		22 55			23 11			23 25			23 40				
Drumry	d	22 13		22 27			22 43		22 57			23 13			23 27			23 42				
Singer	d	22 16		22 30			22 46		23 00			23 16			23 30			23 45				
Dalmuir	a	22 18		22 32	22 34		22 48		23 02	23 04		23 18			23 32	23 33		23 47			00 08	
	d	22 18			22 34		22 48			23 04		23 18				23 33		23 48			00 08	
Kilpatrick	d	22 21					22 51					23 21						23 51				
Bowling	d	22 24					22 54					23 24						23 54				
Dumbarton East	d	22 28			22 42		22 58			23 12		23 28				23 41		23 58			00 15	
Dumbarton Central	d	22 30			22 44		23 00			23 14		23 30				23 43		23 59			00 18	
Dalreoch	d	22 32			22 45		23 02			23 15		23 32				23 44		00 02			00 19	
Renton	d	22 35					23 05					23 35						00 05				
Alexandria	d	22 37					23 07					23 37						00 07				
Balloch	a	22 41					23 11					23 41						00 11				
Cardross	d				22 50					23 20						23 49					00 24	
Craigendoran	d				22 55					23 25						23 54					00 29	
Helensburgh Central	a				22 58					23 28						23 58					00 32	

A From Edinburgh

b Glasgow Central High Level

Lanark, Coatbridge, Motherwell, Larkhall, Hamilton, Edinburgh and Bathgate, Airdrie and Springburn - Glasgow - Milngavie, Dalmuir, Balloch and Helensburgh

Network Diagram - see first Page of Table 220

		SR FO	SR FO	SR	SR	SR	SR FO	SR
Lanark	d							
Carluke	d							
Wishaw	d							
Holytown	d							
Shieldmuir	d							
Coatbridge Central	d							
Whifflet	d							
Motherwell	a							
	d		23 20					
Bellshill	d							
Uddingston	d							
Airbles	d		23 22					
Larkhall	d						23 37	
Merryton	d						23 39	
Chatelherault	d						23 42	
Hamilton Central	d		23 27				23 46	
Hamilton West	d		23 30				23 48	
Blantyre	d		23 33				23 52	
Newton	d		23 39					
Cambuslang	d		23 43					
Rutherglen	d		23 47				00 01	
Dalmarnock	d		23 49					
Bridgeton	d		23 51					
Edinburgh	d			22 51	23 07	23 37		23 51
Haymarket	d			22 55	23 11	23 42		23 55
Edinburgh Park	d			23 00	23 16	23 47		23 59
Uphall	d			23 08	23 24	23 55		00 08
Livingston North	d			23 11	23 27	23 59		00 11
Bathgate	a			23 16	23 32	00 04		00 16
	d			23 17	23 33			
Armadale	d			23 21	23 37			
Blackridge	d			23 25	23 41			
Caldercruix	d			23 31	23 47			
Drumgelloch	d			23 35	23 51			
Airdrie	d			23 38	23a54			
Coatdyke	d			23 40				
Coatbridge Sunnyside	d			23 43				
Blairhill	d			23 45				
Easterhouse	d			23 49				
Garrowhill	d			23 52				
Shettleston	d			23 54				
Carntyne	d			23 56				
Springburn	d	23 39						
Barnhill	d	23 40						
Alexandra Parade	d	23 43						
Duke Street	d	23 45						
Bellgrove	d	23 47		23 59				
High Street	d	23 49		00 02				
Glasgow Queen St LL 10 ⛴	a	23 51		00 04				
	d	23 53		00 04				
Charing Cross	d	23 55		00 06				
Argyle Street	d		23 55				00 06	
Glasgow Central LL 15	a		23 57				00 07	
	d		23 58				00 07	
Anderston	d		23 59				00 09	
Exhibition Centre	d		00 01				00 11	
Partick ⛴	d	23 59	00 05	00 11			00 14	
Hyndland 3	d	00 02	00 08	00 13			00 17	
Jordanhill	d			00 15				
Scotstounhill	d			00 17				
Garscadden	d			00a19				
Yoker	d							
Clydebank	d							
Anniesland	d	00 05	00 12				00 20	
Westerton	d	00 08	00 15				00 23	
Bearsden	d		00 17					
Hillfoot	d		00 18					
Milngavie	a		00 23					
Drumchapel	d	00 10					00 25	
Drumry	d	00 12					00 27	
Singer	d	00 15					00 30	
Dalmuir	a	00 17					00 32	
	d	00 18						
Kilpatrick	d	00 21						
Bowling	d	00 24						
Dumbarton East	d	00 28						
Dumbarton Central	d	00 30						
Dalreoch	d	00 32						
Renton	d	00 35						
Alexandria	d	00 37						
Balloch	a	00 41						
Cardross	d							
Craigendoran	d							
Helensburgh Central	a							

Table 226

Sundays

Lanark, Coatbridge, Motherwell, Larkhall, Hamilton, Edinburgh and Bathgate, Airdrie and Springburn - Glasgow - Milngavie, Dalmuir, Balloch and Helensburgh

Network Diagram - see first Page of Table 220

		SR A	SR A	SR A	SR A	SR A	SR A	SR B	SR	SR	SR	SR	SR	SR	SR	SR	SR	SR	SR
Lanark	d																		
Carluke	d																		
Wishaw	d																		
Holytown	d							00 01											
Shieldmuir	d																		
Coatbridge Central	d																		
Whifflet	d																		
Motherwell	a																		
	d												08 34	08 40		09 10			09 34
Bellshill	d							00 04					08 40						09 40
Uddingston	d							00 08					08 44						09 44
Airbles	d													08 42		09 12			
Larkhall	d																	09 25	
Merryton	d																	09 27	
Chatelherault	d																	09 30	
Hamilton Central	d													08 47		09 17		09 34	
Hamilton West	d													08 50		09 20		09 36	
Blantyre	d													08 53		09 23		09 40	
Newton	d													08 57		09 27			
Cambuslang	d							00 13					08 49	09 01		09 31			09 49
Rutherglen	d												08 53	09 04		09 34		09 48	09 53
Dalmarnock	d																		
Bridgeton	d												08 57	09 07		09 37			09 57
Edinburgh	d		22p19		22p51	23p37	23p51										08 37		
Haymarket	d		22p23		22p55	23p42	23p55										08 41		
Edinburgh Park	d		22p30		23p00	23p47	23p59										08 46		
Uphall	d		22p38		23p08	23p55	00 08										08 57		
Livingston North	d		22p41		23p11	23p59	00 11										09 00		
Bathgate	a		22p46		23p16	00 04	00 16										09 05		
	d		22p47		23p17							08 06					09 06		
Armadale	d		22p51		23p21							08 10					09 10		
Blackridge	d		22p55		23p25							08 14					09 14		
Caldercruix	d		23p01		23p31							08 20					09 20		
Drumgelloch	d		23p05		23p35							08 24					09 24		
Airdrie	d		23p12		23p38					07 58		08 28			08 58		09 28		
Coatdyke	d		23p14		23p40					08 00		08 30			09 00		09 30		
Coatbridge Sunnyside	d		23p16		23p43					08 02		08 32			09 02		09 32		
Blairhill	d		23p19		23p45					08 05		08 35			09 05		09 35		
Easterhouse	d		23p23		23p49					08 09		08 39			09 09		09 39		
Garrowhill	d		23p25		23p52					08 11		08 41			09 11		09 41		
Shettleston	d		23p28		23p54					08 14		08 44			09 14		09 44		
Carntyne	d		23p30		23p56					08 16		08 46			09 16		09 46		
Springburn	d	23p09		23p39															
Barnhill	d	23p10		23p40															
Alexandra Parade	d	23p13		23p43															
Duke Street	d	23p15		23p45															
Bellgrove	d	23p17	23p33	23p47	23p59					08 19		08 49			09 19		09 49		
High Street	d	23p19	23p35	23p49	00 02					08 21		08 51			09 21		09 51		
Glasgow Queen St LL 10	a	23p21	23p37	23p51	00 04					08 23		08 53			09 23		09 53		
	d	23p23	23p45	23p53	00 04					08 24		08 54			09 24		09 54		
Charing Cross	d	23p25	23p47	23p55	00 06					08 27		08 57			09 27		09 57		
Argyle Street	d																		10 01
Glasgow Central LL 15	a							00b24					09 00	09 14		09 44		09 57	10 04
	d												09 04	09 14		09 44		09 57	10 04
Anderston	d																		
Exhibition Centre	d												09 08	09 18		09 48		10 01	10 08
Partick	d	23p29	23p51	23p59	00 11					08 32		09 02	09 12	09 22	09 32	09 52	10 02	10a04	10 12
Hyndland 3	d	23p32	23p53	00 02	00 13					08 34		09 04	09 15	09 24	09 34	09 54	10 04		10 15
Jordanhill	d		23p55	00 04	00 15									09 26		09 56			
Scotstounhill	d		23p58	00 06	00 17									09 28		09 58			
Garscadden	d		23p59	00a08	00a19									09 30		10 00			
Yoker	d		00 02						08 33		09 03			09 33		10 03			
Clydebank	d		00 04						08 35		09 05			09 35		10 05			
Anniesland	d	23p35								08 37		09 07	09 18		09 37		10 07		10 18
Westerton	d	23p38								08 40		09 10	09 21		09 40		10 10		10 21
Bearsden	d												09 25						10 25
Hillfoot	d												09 27						10 27
Milngavie	a												09 30						10 30
Drumchapel	d	23p40								08 42		09 12			09 42		10 12		
Drumry	d	23p42								08 44		09 14			09 44		10 14		
Singer	d	23p45								08 47		09 17			09 47		10 17		
Dalmuir	a	23p47	00 08						08 38	08 49	09 08	09 19		09 39	09 49	10 09	10 19		
	d	23p48	00 08						08 39	08 50	09 09	09 20		09 39	09 50	10 09	10 20		
Kilpatrick	d	23p51							08 41		09 11			09 41		10 11			
Bowling	d	23p54							08 44		09 14			09 44		10 14			
Dumbarton East	d	23p58	00 15						08 49	08 58	09 19	09 28		09 49	09 58	10 19	10 28		
Dumbarton Central	d	23p59	00 18						08 51	09 00	09 21	09 30		09 51	10 00	10 21	10 30		
Dalreoch	d	00 02	00 19						08 52	09 01	09 22	09 31		09 52	10 01	10 22	10 31		
Renton	d	00 05							08 55		09 25			09 55		10 25			
Alexandria	d	00 07							08 58		09 28			09 58		10 28			
Balloch	a	00 11							09 01		09 31			10 01		10 31			
Cardross	d		00 24							09 06		09 36			10 06		10 36		
Craigendoran	d		00 29							09 11		09 41			10 11		10 41		
Helensburgh Central	a		00 32							09 14		09 44			10 14		10 44		

A not 11 December

B not 11 December. From Edinburgh

b Glasgow Central High Level

Table 226

Sundays

Lanark, Coatbridge, Motherwell, Larkhall, Hamilton, Edinburgh and Bathgate, Airdrie and Springburn - Glasgow - Milngavie, Dalmuir, Balloch and Helensburgh

Network Diagram - see first Page of Table 220

		SR	SR		SR			SR	SR	SR		SR		SR	SR			SR		SR	SR	SR	SR	SR	
Lanark	d											10 12												11 12	
Carluke	d											10 22												11 22	
Wishaw	d											10 27												11 27	
Holytown	d																								
Shieldmuir	d											10 31												11 31	
Coatbridge Central	d																								
Whifflet	d																								
Motherwell	a											10 34												11 34	
	d	09 40			10 06			10 10				10 34		10 40				11 06		11 10				11 34	
Bellshill	d				10 12							10 40						11 12						11 40	
Uddingston	d				10 16							10 44						11 16						11 44	
Airbles	d	09 42						10 12						10 42						11 12					
Larkhall	d									10 25												11 25			
Merryton	d									10 27												11 27			
Chatelherault	d									10 30												11 30			
Hamilton Central	d	09 47						10 17		10 34				10 47						11 17		11 34			
Hamilton West	d	09 50						10 20		10 36				10 50						11 20		11 36			
Blantyre	d	09 53						10 23		10 40				10 53						11 23		11 40			
Newton	d	09 57						10 27						10 57						11 27					
Cambuslang	d	10 01			10 21			10 31				10 49		11 01				11 21		11 31				11 49	
Rutherglen	d	10 04			10 24			10 34		10 48		10 53		11 04				11 24		11 34		11 48		11 53	
Dalmarnock	d																								
Bridgeton	d	10 07			10 27			10 37				10 57		11 07				11 27		11 37				11 57	
Edinburgh	d								09 37												10 40				
Haymarket	d								09 41												10 44				
Edinburgh Park	d								09 46												10 49				
Uphall	d								09 57												10 57				
Livingston North	d								10 00												11 00				
Bathgate	a								10 05												11 05				
	d								10 06												11 06				
Armadale	d								10 10												11 10				
Blackridge	d								10 14												11 14				
Caldercruix	d								10 20												11 20				
Drumgelloch	d								10 24												11 24				
Airdrie	d		09 58						10 28						10 58						11 28				
Coatdyke	d		10 00						10 30						11 00						11 30				
Coatbridge Sunnyside	d		10 02						10 32						11 02						11 32				
Blairhill	d		10 05						10 35						11 05						11 35				
Easterhouse	d		10 09						10 39						11 09						11 39				
Garrowhill	d		10 11						10 41						11 11						11 41				
Shettleston	d		10 14						10 44						11 14						11 44				
Carntyne	d		10 16						10 46						11 16						11 46				
Springburn	d																								
Barnhill	d																								
Alexandra Parade	d																								
Duke Street	d																								
Bellgrove	d		10 19						10 49						11 19						11 49				
High Street	d		10 21						10 51						11 21						11 51				
Glasgow Queen St LL 10 ⛴	a		10 23						10 53						11 23						11 53				
	d		10 24						10 54						11 24						11 54				
Charing Cross	d		10 27						10 57						11 27						11 57				
Argyle Street	d	10 11			10 31			10 41		10 53		11 01		11 11				11 31		11 41		11 53		12 01	
Glasgow Central LL 15	a	10 14			10 34			10 44		10 57		11 04		11 14				11 34		11 44		11 57		12 04	
	d	10 14			10 34			10 44		10 57		11 04		11 14				11 34		11 44		11 57		12 04	
Anderston	d																								
Exhibition Centre	d	10 18			10 38			10 48		11 01		11 08		11 18				11 38		11 48		12 01		12 08	
Partick ⛴	d	10 22	10 32		10 42			10 52	11 02	11a04		11 12		11 22	11 32			11 42		11 52	12 02	12a04		12 12	
Hyndland 3	d	10 24	10 34		10 45			10 54	11 04			11 15		11 24	11 34			11 45		11 54	12 04			12 15	
Jordanhill	d	10 26						10 56						11 26						11 56					
Scotstounhill	d	10 28						10 58						11 28						11 58					
Garscadden	d	10 30						11 00						11 30						12 00					
Yoker	d	10 33						11 03						11 33						12 03					
Clydebank	d	10 35						11 05						11 35						12 05					
Anniesland	d		10 37		10 48				11 07			11 18			11 37			11 48			12 07			12 18	
Westerton	d		10 40		10 51				11 10			11 21			11 40			11 51			12 10			12 21	
Bearsden	d				10 55							11 25						11 55						12 25	
Hillfoot	d				10 57							11 27						11 57						12 27	
Milngavie	a				11 00							11 30						12 00						12 30	
Drumchapel	d		10 42						11 12						11 42						12 12				
Drumry	d		10 44						11 14						11 44						12 14				
Singer	d		10 47						11 17						11 47						12 17				
Dalmuir	a	10 39	10 49					11 09	11 19					11 39	11 49					12 09	12 19				
	d	10 39	10 50					11 09	11 20					11 39	11 50					12 09	12 20				
Kilpatrick	d	10 41						11 11						11 41						12 11					
Bowling	d	10 44						11 14						11 44						12 14					
Dumbarton East	d	10 49	10 58					11 19	11 28					11 49	11 58					12 19	12 28				
Dumbarton Central	d	10 51	11 00					11 21	11 30					11 51	12 00					12 21	12 30				
Dalreoch	d	10 52	11 01					11 22	11 31					11 52	12 01					12 22	12 31				
Renton	d	10 55						11 25						11 55						12 25					
Alexandria	d	10 58						11 28						11 58						12 28					
Balloch	a	11 01						11 31						12 01						12 31					
Cardross	d		11 06						11 36						12 06						12 36				
Craigendoran	d		11 11						11 41						12 11						12 41				
Helensburgh Central	a		11 14						11 44						12 14						12 44				

Table 226

Sundays

Lanark, Coatbridge, Motherwell, Larkhall, Hamilton, Edinburgh and Bathgate, Airdrie and Springburn - Glasgow - Milngavie, Dalmuir, Balloch and Helensburgh

Network Diagram - see first Page of Table 220

		SR ◇ A	SR	SR	SR	SR	SR	SR	SR	SR	SR	SR	SR	SR	SR
Lanark	d								12 12						
Carluke	d								12 22						
Wishaw	d								12 27						
Holytown	d														
Shieldmuir	d								12 31						
Coatbridge Central	d														
Whifflet	d														
Motherwell	a								12 34						
	d		11 40		12 06	12 10			12 34	12 40		13 06	13 10		
Bellshill	d				12 12				12 40			13 12			
Uddingston	d				12 16				12 44			13 16			
Airbles	d		11 42			12 12				12 42			13 12		
Larkhall	d							12 25							13 25
Merryton	d							12 27							13 27
Chatelherault	d							12 30							13 30
Hamilton Central	d		11 47			12 17		12 34		12 47			13 17		13 34
Hamilton West	d		11 50			12 20		12 36		12 50			13 20		13 36
Blantyre	d		11 53			12 23		12 40		12 53			13 23		13 40
Newton	d		11 57			12 27				12 57			13 27		
Cambuslang	d		12 01		12 21	12 31			12 49	13 01		13 21	13 31		
Rutherglen	d		12 04		12 24	12 34		12 48	12 53	13 04		13 24	13 34		13 48
Dalmarnock	d														
Bridgeton	d		12 07		12 27	12 37			12 57	13 07		13 27	13 37		
Edinburgh	d						11 40				12 10			12 40	
Haymarket	d						11 44				12 14			12 44	
Edinburgh Park	d						11 49				12 19			12 49	
Uphall	d						11 57				12 27			12 57	
Livingston North	d						12 00				12 30			13 00	
Bathgate	a						12 05				12 35			13 05	
	d						12 06				12 36			13 06	
Armadale	d						12 10				12 40			13 10	
Blackridge	d						12 14				12 44			13 14	
Caldercruix	d						12 20				12 50			13 20	
Drumgelloch	d						12 24				12 54			13 24	
Airdrie	d			11 58			12 28				12 58			13 28	
Coatdyke	d			12 00			12 30				13 00			13 30	
Coatbridge Sunnyside	d			12 02			12 32				13 02			13 32	
Blairhill	d			12 05			12 35				13 05			13 35	
Easterhouse	d			12 09			12 39				13 09			13 39	
Garrowhill	d			12 11			12 41				13 11			13 41	
Shettleston	d			12 14			12 44				13 14			13 44	
Carntyne	d			12 16			12 46				13 16			13 46	
Springburn	d														
Barnhill	d														
Alexandra Parade	d														
Duke Street	d														
Bellgrove	d			12 19			12 49				13 19			13 49	
High Street	d			12 21			12 51				13 21			13 51	
Glasgow Queen St LL 10	a			12 23			12 53				13 23			13 53	
	d	12b20		12 24			12 54				13 24			13 54	
Charing Cross	d			12 27			12 57				13 27			13 57	
Argyle Street	d		12 11		12 31	12 41		12 53	13 01	13 11		13 31	13 41		13 53
Glasgow Central LL 15	a		12 14		12 34	12 44		12 57	13 04	13 14		13 34	13 44		13 57
	d		12 14		12 34	12 44		12 57	13 04	13 14		13 34	13 44		13 57
Anderston	d														
Exhibition Centre	d		12 18		12 38	12 48		13 01	13 08	13 18		13 38	13 48		14 01
Partick	d		12 22	12 32	12 42	12 52	13 02	13a04	13 12	13 22	13 32	13 42	13 52	14 02	14a04
Hyndland 3	d		12 24	12 34	12 45	12 54	13 04		13 15	13 24	13 34	13 45	13 54	14 04	
Jordanhill	d		12 26			12 56				13 26			13 56		
Scotstounhill	d		12 28			12 58				13 28			13 58		
Garscadden	d		12 30			13 00				13 30			14 00		
Yoker	d		12 33			13 03				13 33			14 03		
Clydebank	d		12 35			13 05				13 35			14 05		
Anniesland	d			12 37	12 48		13 07		13 18		13 37	13 48		14 07	
Westerton	d			12 40	12 51		13 10		13 21		13 40	13 51		14 10	
Bearsden	d				12 55				13 25			13 55			
Hillfoot	d				12 57				13 27			13 57			
Milngavie	a				13 00				13 30			14 00			
Drumchapel	d			12 42			13 12				13 42			14 12	
Drumry	d			12 44			13 14				13 44			14 14	
Singer	d			12 47			13 17				13 47			14 17	
Dalmuir	a	12 34	12 39	12 49		13 09	13 19			13 39	13 49		14 09	14 19	
	d	12 34	12 39	12 50		13 09	13 20			13 39	13 50		14 09	14 20	
Kilpatrick	d		12 41			13 11				13 41			14 11		
Bowling	d		12 44			13 14				13 44			14 14		
Dumbarton East	d		12 49	12 58		13 19	13 28			13 49	13 58		14 19	14 28	
Dumbarton Central	d	12 44	12 51	13 00		13 21	13 30			13 51	14 00		14 21	14 30	
Dalreoch	d		12 52	13 01		13 22	13 31			13 52	14 01		14 22	14 31	
Renton	d		12 55			13 25				13 55			14 25		
Alexandria	d		12 58			13 28				13 58			14 28		
Balloch	a		13 01			13 31				14 01			14 31		
Cardross	d			13 06			13 36				14 06			14 36	
Craigendoran	d			13 11			13 41				14 11			14 41	
Helensburgh Central	a	12c59		13 14			13 44				14 14			14 44	

A from 25 March. To Oban

b Glasgow Queen St High Level

c Helensburgh Upper

Table 226

Sundays

Lanark, Coatbridge, Motherwell, Larkhall, Hamilton, Edinburgh and Bathgate, Airdrie and Springburn - Glasgow - Milngavie, Dalmuir, Balloch and Helensburgh

Network Diagram - see first Page of Table 220

		SR	SR	SR	SR	SR	SR	SR	SR	SR	SR	SR	SR	SR	SR
Lanark	d	13 12							14 12						
Carluke	d	13 22							14 22						
Wishaw	d	13 27							14 27						
Holytown	d														
Shieldmuir	d	13 31							14 31						
Coatbridge Central	d														
Whifflet	d														
Motherwell	a	13 34							14 34						
	d	13 34	13 40		14 06	14 10			14 34	14 40		15 06	15 10		
Bellshill	d	13 40			14 12				14 40			15 12			
Uddingston	d	13 44			14 16				14 44			15 16			
Airbles	d		13 42			14 12				14 42			15 12		
Larkhall	d							14 25							15 25
Merryton	d							14 27							15 27
Chatelherault	d							14 30							15 30
Hamilton Central	d		13 47			14 17		14 34		14 47			15 17		15 34
Hamilton West	d		13 50			14 20		14 36		14 50			15 20		15 36
Blantyre	d		13 53			14 23		14 40		14 53			15 23		15 40
Newton	d		13 57			14 27				14 57			15 27		
Cambuslang	d	13 49	14 01		14 21	14 31			14 49	15 01		15 21	15 31		
Rutherglen	d	13 53	14 04		14 24	14 34		14 48	14 53	15 04		15 24	15 34		15 48
Dalmarnock	d														
Bridgeton	d	13 57	14 07		14 27	14 37			14 57	15 07		15 27	15 37		
Edinburgh	d			13 10			13 40				14 10			14 40	
Haymarket	d			13 14			13 44				14 14			14 44	
Edinburgh Park	d			13 19			13 49				14 19			14 49	
Uphall	d			13 27			13 57				14 27			14 57	
Livingston North	d			13 30			14 00				14 30			15 00	
Bathgate	a			13 35			14 05				14 35			15 05	
	d			13 36			14 06				14 36			15 06	
Armadale	d			13 40			14 10				14 40			15 10	
Blackridge	d			13 44			14 14				14 44			15 14	
Caldercruix	d			13 50			14 20				14 50			15 20	
Drumgelloch	d			13 54			14 24				14 54			15 24	
Airdrie	d			13 58			14 28				14 58			15 28	
Coatdyke	d			14 00			14 30				15 00			15 30	
Coatbridge Sunnyside	d			14 02			14 32				15 02			15 32	
Blairhill	d			14 05			14 35				15 05			15 35	
Easterhouse	d			14 09			14 39				15 09			15 39	
Garrowhill	d			14 11			14 41				15 11			15 41	
Shettleston	d			14 14			14 44				15 14			15 44	
Carntyne	d			14 16			14 46				15 16			15 46	
Springburn	d														
Barnhill	d														
Alexandra Parade	d														
Duke Street	d														
Bellgrove	d			14 19			14 49				15 19			15 49	
High Street	d			14 21			14 51				15 21			15 51	
Glasgow Queen St LL 10	a			14 23			14 53				15 23			15 53	
	d			14 24			14 54				15 24			15 54	
Charing Cross	d			14 27			14 57				15 27			15 57	
Argyle Street	d	14 01	14 11		14 31	14 41		14 53	15 01	15 11		15 31	15 41		15 53
Glasgow Central LL 15	a	14 04	14 14		14 34	14 44		14 57	15 04	15 14		15 34	15 44		15 57
	d	14 04	14 14		14 34	14 44		14 57	15 04	15 14		15 34	15 44		15 57
Anderston	d														
Exhibition Centre	d	14 08	14 18		14 38	14 48		15 01	15 08	15 18		15 38	15 48		16 01
Partick	d	14 12	14 22	14 32	14 42	14 52	15 02	15a04	15 12	15 22	15 32	15 42	15 52	16 02	16a04
Hyndland 3	d	14 15	14 24	14 34	14 45	14 54	15 04		15 15	15 24	15 34	15 45	15 54	16 04	
Jordanhill	d		14 26			14 56				15 26			15 56		
Scotstounhill	d		14 28			14 58				15 28			15 58		
Garscadden	d		14 30			15 00				15 30			16 00		
Yoker	d		14 33			15 03				15 33			16 03		
Clydebank	d		14 35			15 05				15 35			16 05		
Anniesland	d	14 18		14 37	14 48		15 07		15 18		15 37	15 48		16 07	
Westerton	d	14 21		14 40	14 51		15 10		15 21		15 40	15 51		16 10	
Bearsden	d	14 25			14 55				15 25			15 55			
Hillfoot	d	14 27			14 57				15 27			15 57			
Milngavie	a	14 30			15 00				15 30			16 00			
Drumchapel	d			14 42			15 12				15 42			16 12	
Drumry	d			14 44			15 14				15 44			16 14	
Singer	d			14 47			15 17				15 47			16 17	
Dalmuir	a		14 39	14 49		15 09	15 19			15 39	15 49		16 09	16 19	
	d		14 39	14 50		15 09	15 20			15 39	15 50		16 09	16 20	
Kilpatrick	d		14 41			15 11				15 41			16 11		
Bowling	d		14 44			15 14				15 44			16 14		
Dumbarton East	d		14 49	14 58		15 19	15 28			15 49	15 58		16 19	16 28	
Dumbarton Central	d		14 51	15 00		15 21	15 30			15 51	16 00		16 21	16 30	
Dalreoch	d		14 52	15 01		15 22	15 31			15 52	16 01		16 22	16 31	
Renton	d		14 55			15 25				15 55			16 25		
Alexandria	d		14 58			15 28				15 58			16 28		
Balloch	a		15 01			15 31				16 01			16 31		
Cardross	d			15 06			15 36				16 06			16 36	
Craigendoran	d			15 11			15 41				16 11			16 41	
Helensburgh Central	a			15 14			15 44				16 14			16 44	

Table 226

Sundays

Lanark, Coatbridge, Motherwell, Larkhall, Hamilton, Edinburgh and Bathgate, Airdrie and Springburn - Glasgow - Milngavie, Dalmuir, Balloch and Helensburgh

Network Diagram - see first Page of Table 220

		SR	SR	SR	SR	SR	SR	SR	SR	SR	SR	SR	SR	SR	SR
Lanark	d	15 12							16 12						
Carluke	d	15 22							16 22						
Wishaw	d	15 27							16 27						
Holytown	d														
Shieldmuir	d	15 31							16 31						
Coatbridge Central	d														
Whifflet	d														
Motherwell	a	15 34							16 34						
	d	15 34	15 40		16 06	16 10			16 34	16 40		17 06	17 10		
Bellshill	d	15 40			16 12				16 40			17 12			
Uddingston	d	15 44			16 16				16 44			17 16			
Airbles	d		15 42			16 12				16 42			17 12		
Larkhall	d							16 25							17 25
Merryton	d							16 27							17 27
Chatelherault	d							16 30							17 30
Hamilton Central	d		15 47			16 17		16 34		16 47			17 17		17 34
Hamilton West	d		15 50			16 20		16 36		16 50			17 20		17 36
Blantyre	d		15 53			16 23		16 40		16 53			17 23		17 40
Newton	d		15 57			16 27				16 57			17 27		
Cambuslang	d	15 49	16 01		16 21	16 31			16 49	17 01		17 21	17 31		
Rutherglen	d	15 53	16 04		16 24	16 34		16 48	16 53	17 04		17 24	17 34		17 48
Dalmarnock	d														
Bridgeton	d	15 57	16 07		16 27	16 37			16 57	17 07		17 27	17 37		
Edinburgh	d			15 10			15 40				16 10			16 40	
Haymarket	d			15 14			15 44				16 14			16 44	
Edinburgh Park	d			15 19			15 49				16 19			16 49	
Uphall	d			15 27			15 57				16 27			16 57	
Livingston North	d			15 30			16 00				16 30			17 00	
Bathgate	a			15 35			16 05				16 35			17 05	
	d			15 36			16 06				16 36			17 06	
Armadale	d			15 40			16 10				16 40			17 10	
Blackridge	d			15 44			16 14				16 44			17 14	
Caldercruix	d			15 50			16 20				16 50			17 20	
Drumgelloch	d			15 54			16 24				16 54			17 24	
Airdrie	d			15 58			16 28				16 58			17 28	
Coatdyke	d			16 00			16 30				17 00			17 30	
Coatbridge Sunnyside	d			16 02			16 32				17 02			17 32	
Blairhill	d			16 05			16 35				17 05			17 35	
Easterhouse	d			16 09			16 39				17 09			17 39	
Garrowhill	d			16 11			16 41				17 11			17 41	
Shettleston	d			16 14			16 44				17 14			17 44	
Carntyne	d			16 16			16 46				17 16			17 46	
Springburn	d														
Barnhill	d														
Alexandra Parade	d														
Duke Street	d														
Bellgrove	d			16 19			16 49				17 19			17 49	
High Street	d			16 21			16 51				17 21			17 51	
Glasgow Queen St LL 10	a			16 23			16 53				17 23			17 53	
	d			16 24			16 54				17 24			17 54	
Charing Cross	d			16 27			16 57				17 27			17 57	
Argyle Street	d	16 01	16 11		16 31	16 41		16 53	17 01	17 11		17 31	17 41		17 53
Glasgow Central LL 15	a	16 04	16 14		16 34	16 44		16 57	17 04	17 14		17 34	17 44		17 57
	d	16 04	16 14		16 34	16 44		16 57	17 04	17 14		17 34	17 44		17 57
Anderston	d														
Exhibition Centre	d	16 08	16 18		16 38	16 48		17 01	17 08	17 18		17 38	17 48		18 01
Partick	d	16 12	16 22	16 32	16 42	16 52	17 02	17a04	17 12	17 22	17 32	17 42	17 52	18 02	18a04
Hyndland 3	d	16 15	16 24	16 34	16 45	16 54	17 04		17 15	17 24	17 34	17 45	17 54	18 04	
Jordanhill	d		16 26			16 56				17 26			17 56		
Scotstounhill	d		16 28			16 58				17 28			17 58		
Garscadden	d		16 30			17 00				17 30			18 00		
Yoker	d		16 33			17 03				17 33			18 03		
Clydebank	d		16 35			17 05				17 35			18 05		
Anniesland	d	16 18		16 37	16 48		17 07		17 18		17 37	17 48		18 07	
Westerton	d	16 21		16 40	16 51		17 10		17 21		17 40	17 51		18 10	
Bearsden	d	16 25			16 55				17 25			17 55			
Hillfoot	d	16 27			16 57				17 27			17 57			
Milngavie	a	16 30			17 00				17 30			18 00			
Drumchapel	d			16 42			17 12				17 42			18 12	
Drumry	d			16 44			17 14				17 44			18 14	
Singer	d			16 47			17 17				17 47			18 17	
Dalmuir	a		16 39	16 49		17 09	17 19			17 39	17 49		18 09	18 19	
	d		16 39	16 50		17 09	17 20			17 39	17 50		18 09	18 20	
Kilpatrick	d		16 41			17 11				17 41			18 11		
Bowling	d		16 44			17 14				17 44			18 14		
Dumbarton East	d		16 49	16 58		17 19	17 28			17 49	17 58		18 19	18 28	
Dumbarton Central	d		16 51	17 00		17 21	17 30			17 51	18 00		18 21	18 30	
Dalreoch	d		16 52	17 01		17 22	17 31			17 52	18 01		18 22	18 31	
Renton	d		16 55			17 25				17 55			18 25		
Alexandria	d		16 58			17 28				17 58			18 28		
Balloch	a		17 01			17 31				18 01			18 31		
Cardross	d			17 06			17 36				18 06			18 36	
Craigendoran	d			17 11			17 41				18 11			18 41	
Helensburgh Central	a			17 14			17 44				18 14			18 44	

Table 226

Sundays

Lanark, Coatbridge, Motherwell, Larkhall, Hamilton, Edinburgh and Bathgate, Airdrie and Springburn - Glasgow - Milngavie, Dalmuir, Balloch and Helensburgh

Network Diagram - see first Page of Table 220

		SR	SR ◇ B	SR	SR	SR	SR	SR	SR	SR	SR	SR	SR	SR	SR	SR	SR	SR	SR	SR	SR
Lanark	d	17 12								18 12								19 12			
Carluke	d	17 22								18 22								19 22			
Wishaw	d	17 27								18 27								19 27			
Holytown	d																				
Shieldmuir	d	17 31								18 31								19 31			
Coatbridge Central	d																				
Whifflet	d																				
Motherwell	a	17 34								18 34								19 34			
	d	17 34		17 40		18 06	18 10			18 34	18 40		19 06	19 10				19 34	19 40		20 06
Bellshill	d	17 40				18 12				18 40			19 12					19 40			20 12
Uddingston	d	17 44				18 16				18 44			19 16					19 44			20 16
Airbles	d			17 42			18 12				18 42			19 12					19 42		
Larkhall	d								18 25								19 25				
Merryton	d								18 27								19 27				
Chatelherault	d								18 30								19 30				
Hamilton Central	d			17 47			18 17		18 34		18 47			19 17			19 34		19 47		
Hamilton West	d			17 50			18 20		18 36		18 50			19 20			19 36		19 50		
Blantyre	d			17 53			18 23		18 40		18 53			19 23			19 40		19 53		
Newton	d			17 57			18 27				18 57			19 27					19 57		
Cambuslang	d	17 49		18 01		18 21	18 31			18 49	19 01		19 21	19 31				19 49	20 01		20 21
Rutherglen	d	17 53		18 04		18 24	18 34		18 48	18 53	19 04		19 24	19 34			19 48	19 53	20 04		20 24
Dalmarnock	d																				
Bridgeton	d	17 57		18 07		18 27	18 37			18 57	19 07		19 27	19 37				19 57	20 07		20 27
Edinburgh	d				17 10			17 40				18 10			18 40	19 10					
Haymarket	d				17 14			17 44				18 14			18 44	19 14					
Edinburgh Park	d				17 19			17 49				18 19			18 49	19 19					
Uphall	d				17 27			17 57				18 27			18 57	19 27					
Livingston North	d				17 30			18 00				18 30			19 00	19 30					
Bathgate	a				17 35			18 05				18 35			19 05	19 35					
	d				17 36			18 06				18 36			19 06						
Armadale	d				17 40			18 10				18 40			19 10						
Blackridge	d				17 44			18 14				18 44			19 14						
Caldercruix	d				17 50			18 20				18 50			19 20						
Drumgelloch	d				17 54			18 24				18 54			19 24						
Airdrie	d				17 58			18 28				18 58			19 28					19 58	
Coatdyke	d				18 00			18 30				19 00			19 30					20 00	
Coatbridge Sunnyside	d				18 02			18 32				19 02			19 32					20 02	
Blairhill	d				18 05			18 35				19 05			19 35					20 05	
Easterhouse	d				18 09			18 39				19 09			19 39					20 09	
Garrowhill	d				18 11			18 41				19 11			19 41					20 11	
Shettleston	d				18 14			18 44				19 14			19 44					20 14	
Carntyne	d				18 16			18 46				19 16			19 46					20 16	
Springburn	d																				
Barnhill	d																				
Alexandra Parade	d																				
Duke Street	d																				
Bellgrove	d				18 19			18 49				19 19			19 49					20 19	
High Street	d				18 21			18 51				19 21			19 51					20 21	
Glasgow Queen St LL 10	a				18 23			18 53				19 23			19 53					20 23	
	d		18b20		18 24			18 54				19 24			19 54					20 24	
Charing Cross	d				18 27			18 57				19 27			19 57					20 27	
Argyle Street	d	18 01		18 11																	
Glasgow Central LL 15	a	18 04		18 14		18 34	18 44		18 57	19 04	19 14		19 34	19 44			19 57	20 04	20 14		20 34
	d	18 04		18 14		18 34	18 44		18 57	19 04	19 14		19 34	19 44			19 57	20 04	20 14		20 34
Anderston	d																				
Exhibition Centre	d	18 08		18 18		18 38	18 48		19 01	19 08	19 18		19 38	19 48			20 01	20 08	20 18		20 38
Partick	d	18 12		18 22	18 32	18 42	18 52	19 02	19a04	19 12	19 22	19 32	19 42	19 52	20 02		20a04	20 12	20 22	20 32	20 42
Hyndland 3	d	18 15		18 24	18 34	18 45	18 54	19 04		19 15	19 24	19 34	19 45	19 54	20 04			20 15	20 24	20 34	20 45
Jordanhill	d			18 26			18 56				19 26			19 56					20 26		
Scotstounhill	d			18 28			18 58				19 28			19 58					20 28		
Garscadden	d			18 30			19 00				19 30			20 00					20 30		
Yoker	d			18 33			19 03				19 33			20 03					20 33		
Clydebank	d			18 35			19 05				19 35			20 05					20 35		
Anniesland	d	18 18			18 37	18 48		19 07		19 18		19 37	19 48		20 07			20 18		20 37	20 48
Westerton	d	18 21			18 40	18 51		19 10		19 21		19 40	19 51		20 10			20 21		20 40	20 51
Bearsden	d	18 25				18 55				19 25			19 55					20 25			20 55
Hillfoot	d	18 27				18 57				19 27			19 57					20 27			20 57
Milngavie	a	18 30				19 00				19 30			20 00					20 30			21 00
Drumchapel	d				18 42			19 12				19 42			20 12					20 42	
Drumry	d				18 44			19 14				19 44			20 14					20 44	
Singer	d				18 47			19 17				19 47			20 17					20 47	
Dalmuir	a		18 34	18 39	18 49		19 09	19 19			19 39	19 49		20 09	20 19				20 39	20 49	
	d		18 34	18 39	18 50		19 09	19 20			19 39	19 50		20 09	20 20				20 39	20 50	
Kilpatrick	d			18 41			19 11				19 41			20 11					20 41		
Bowling	d			18 44			19 14				19 44			20 14					20 44		
Dumbarton East	d			18 49	18 58		19 19	19 28			19 49	19 58		20 19	20 28				20 49	20 58	
Dumbarton Central	d		18 44	18 51	19 00		19 21	19 30			19 51	20 00		20 21	20 30				20 51	21 00	
Dalreoch	d			18 52	19 01		19 22	19 31			19 52	20 01		20 22	20 31				20 52	21 01	
Renton	d			18 55			19 25				19 55			20 25					20 55		
Alexandria	d			18 58			19 28				19 58			20 28					20 58		
Balloch	a			19 01			19 31				20 01			20 31					21 01		
Cardross	d				19 06			19 36				20 06			20 36					21 06	
Craigendoran	d				19 11			19 41				20 11			20 41					21 11	
Helensburgh Central	a		18c59		19 14			19 44				20 14			20 44					21 14	

B To Oban

b Glasgow Queen St High Level

c Helensburgh Upper

Table 226

Sundays

Lanark, Coatbridge, Motherwell, Larkhall, Hamilton, Edinburgh and Bathgate, Airdrie and Springburn - Glasgow - Milngavie, Dalmuir, Balloch and Helensburgh

Network Diagram - see first Page of Table 220

		SR	SR	SR	SR	SR	SR	SR	SR	SR	SR	SR	SR	SR	SR	SR	SR	SR	SR	SR	SR	SR	SR
Lanark	d					20 12							21 12							22 12			
Carluke	d					20 22							21 22							22 22			
Wishaw	d					20 27							21 27							22 27			
Holytown	d																						
Shieldmuir	d					20 31							21 31							22 31			
Coatbridge Central	d																						
Whifflet	d																						
Motherwell	a					20 34							21 34							22 34			
	d	20 10				20 34	20 40		21 06	21 10			21 34	21 40		22 06	22 10			22 34	22 40		23 06
Bellshill	d					20 40			21 12				21 40			22 12				22 40			23 12
Uddingston	d					20 44			21 16				21 44			22 16				22 44			23 16
Airbles	d	20 12					20 42			21 12				21 42			22 12				22 42		
Larkhall	d				20 25							21 25							22 25				
Merryton	d				20 27							21 27							22 27				
Chatelherault	d				20 30							21 30							22 30				
Hamilton Central	d	20 17			20 34		20 47			21 17		21 34		21 47			22 17		22 34		22 47		
Hamilton West	d	20 20			20 36		20 50			21 20		21 36		21 50			22 20		22 36		22 50		
Blantyre	d	20 23			20 40		20 53			21 23		21 40		21 53			22 23		22 40		22 53		
Newton	d	20 27					20 57			21 27				21 57			22 27				22 57		
Cambuslang	d	20 31				20 49	21 01		21 21	21 31			21 49	22 01		22 21	22 31			22 49	23 01		23 21
Rutherglen	d	20 34			20 48	20 53	21 04		21 24	21 34		21 48	21 53	22 04		22 24	22 34		22 48	22 53	23 04		23 24
Dalmarnock	d																						
Bridgeton	d	20 37				20 57	21 07		21 27	21 37			21 57	22 07		22 27	22 37			22 57	23 07		23 27
Edinburgh	d		19 40	20 10							20 40							21 40					
Haymarket	d		19 44	20 14							20 44							21 44					
Edinburgh Park	d		19 49	20 19							20 49							21 49					
Uphall	d		19 57	20 27							20 57							21 57					
Livingston North	d		20 00	20 30							21 00							22 00					
Bathgate	a		20 05	20 35							21 05							22 05					
	d		20 06								21 06							22 06					
Armadale	d		20 10								21 10							22 10					
Blackridge	d		20 14								21 14							22 14					
Caldercruix	d		20 20								21 20							22 20					
Drumgelloch	d		20 24								21 24							22 24					
Airdrie	d		20 28					20 58			21 28				21 58			22 28				22 58	
Coatdyke	d		20 30					21 00			21 30				22 00			22 30				23 00	
Coatbridge Sunnyside	d		20 32					21 02			21 32				22 02			22 32				23 02	
Blairhill	d		20 35					21 05			21 35				22 05			22 35				23 05	
Easterhouse	d		20 39					21 09			21 39				22 09			22 39				23 09	
Garrowhill	d		20 41					21 11			21 41				22 11			22 41				23 11	
Shettleston	d		20 44					21 14			21 44				22 14			22 44				23 14	
Carntyne	d		20 46					21 16			21 46				22 16			22 46				23 16	
Springburn	d																						
Barnhill	d																						
Alexandra Parade	d																						
Duke Street	d																						
Bellgrove	d		20 49					21 19			21 49				22 19			22 49				23 19	
High Street	d		20 51					21 21			21 51				22 21			22 51				23 21	
Glasgow Queen St LL 10	a		20 53					21 23			21 53				22 23			22 53				23 23	
	d		20 54					21 24			21 54				22 24			22 54				23 24	
Charing Cross	d		20 57					21 27			21 57				22 27			22 57				23 27	
Argyle Street	d																						
Glasgow Central LL 15	a	20 44			20 57	21 04	21 14		21 34	21 44		21 57	22 04	22 14		22 34	22 44		22 57	23 04	23 14		23 34
	d	20 44			20 57	21 04	21 14		21 34	21 44		21 57	22 04	22 14		22 34	22 44		22 57	23 04	23 14		23 34
Anderston	d																						
Exhibition Centre	d	20 48			21 01	21 08	21 18		21 38	21 48		22 01	22 08	22 18		22 38	22 48		23 01	23 08	23 18		23 38
Partick	d	20 52	21 02		21a04	21 12	21 22	21 32	21 42	21 52	22 02	22a04	22 12	22 22	22 32	22 42	22 52	23 02	23a04	23 12	23 22	23 32	23 42
Hyndland 3	d	20 54	21 04			21 15	21 24	21 34	21 45	21 54	22 04		22 15	22 24	22 34	22 45	22 54	23 04		23 15	23 24	23 34	23 44
Jordanhill	d	20 56					21 26			21 56				22 26			22 56				23 26		23 46
Scotstounhill	d	20 58					21 28			21 58				22 28			22 58				23 28		23 48
Garscadden	d	21 00					21 30			22 00				22 30			23 00				23 30		23a50
Yoker	d	21 03					21 33			22 03				22 33			23 03				23 33		
Clydebank	d	21 05					21 35			22 05				22 35			23 05				23 35		
Anniesland	d		21 07			21 18		21 37	21 48		22 07		22 18		22 37	22 48		23 07		23 18		23 37	
Westerton	d		21 10			21 21		21 40	21 51		22 10		22 21		22 40	22 51		23 10		23 21		23 40	
Bearsden	d					21 25			21 55				22 25			22 55				23 25			
Hillfoot	d					21 27			21 57				22 27			22 57				23 27			
Milngavie	a					21 30			22 00				22 30			23 00				23 30			
Drumchapel	d		21 12					21 42			22 12				22 42			23 12				23 42	
Drumry	d		21 14					21 44			22 14				22 44			23 14				23 44	
Singer	d		21 17					21 47			22 17				22 47			23 17				23 47	
Dalmuir	a	21 09	21 19				21 39	21 49		22 09	22 19			22 39	22 49		23 09	23 19			23 39	23 49	
	d	21 09	21 20				21 39	21 50		22 09	22 20			22 39	22 50		23 09	23 20			23 39	23 50	
Kilpatrick	d	21 11					21 41			22 11				22 41			23 11				23 41		
Bowling	d	21 14					21 44			22 14				22 44			23 14				23 44		
Dumbarton East	d	21 19	21 28				21 49	21 58		22 19	22 28			22 49	22 58		23 19	23 28			23 49	23 58	
Dumbarton Central	d	21 21	21 30				21 51	22 00		22 21	22 30			22 51	23 00		23 21	23 30			23 51	23 59	
Dalreoch	d	21 22	21 31				21 52	22 01		22 22	22 31			22 52	23 01		23 22	23 31			23 52	00 01	
Renton	d	21 25					21 55			22 25				22 55			23 25				23 55		
Alexandria	d	21 28					21 58			22 28				22 58			23 28				23 58		
Balloch	a	21 31					22 01			22 31				23 01			23 31				00 01		
Cardross	d		21 36					22 06			22 36				23 06			23 36				00 06	
Craigendoran	d		21 41					22 11			22 41				23 11			23 41				00 11	
Helensburgh Central	a		21 45					22 14			22 44				23 14			23 44				00 14	

Table 226

Sundays

Lanark, Coatbridge, Motherwell, Larkhall, Hamilton, Edinburgh and Bathgate, Airdrie and Springburn - Glasgow - Milngavie, Dalmuir, Balloch and Helensburgh

Network Diagram - see first Page of Table 220

		SR	SR	SR
Lanark	d			
Carluke	d			
Wishaw	d			
Holytown	d			
Shieldmuir	d			
Coatbridge Central	d			
Whifflet	d			
Motherwell	a			
	d	23 10		
Bellshill	d			
Uddingston	d			
Airbles	d	23 12		
Larkhall	d			
Merryton	d			
Chatelherault	d			
Hamilton Central	d	23 17		
Hamilton West	d	23 20		
Blantyre	d	23 23		
Newton	d	23 27		
Cambuslang	d	23 31		
Rutherglen	d	23 34		
Dalmarnock	d			
Bridgeton	d	23 37		
Edinburgh	d		22 40	23 18
Haymarket	d		22 44	23 22
Edinburgh Park	d		22 49	23 27
Uphall	d		22 57	23 35
Livingston North	d		23 00	23 38
Bathgate	a		23 05	23 43
	d		23 06	
Armadale	d		23 10	
Blackridge	d		23 14	
Caldercruix	d		23 20	
Drumgelloch	d		23 24	
Airdrie	d		23 28	
Coatdyke	d		23 30	
Coatbridge Sunnyside	d		23 32	
Blairhill	d		23 35	
Easterhouse	d		23 39	
Garrowhill	d		23 41	
Shettleston	d		23 44	
Carntyne	d		23 46	
Springburn	d			
Barnhill	d			
Alexandra Parade	d			
Duke Street	d			
Bellgrove	d		23 49	
High Street	d		23 51	
Glasgow Queen St LL 10	a		23 53	
	d		23 54	
Charing Cross	d		23 57	
Argyle Street	d			
Glasgow Central LL 15	a	23 44		
	d	23 44		
Anderston	d			
Exhibition Centre	d	23 48		
Partick	d	23 52	00 01	
Hyndland 3	d	23 54	00 03	
Jordanhill	d	23 56	00 05	
Scotstounhill	d	23 58	00 07	
Garscadden	d	00a01	00 09	
Yoker	d		00 12	
Clydebank	d			
Anniesland	d			
Westerton	d			
Bearsden	d			
Hillfoot	d			
Milngavie	a			
Drumchapel	d			
Drumry	d			
Singer	d			
Dalmuir	a		00 16	
	d			
Kilpatrick	d			
Bowling	d			
Dumbarton East	d			
Dumbarton Central	d			
Dalreoch	d			
Renton	d			
Alexandria	d			
Balloch	a			
Cardross	d			
Craigendoran	d			
Helensburgh Central	a			

Helensburgh, Balloch, Dalmuir and Milngavie - Glasgow - Springburn, Airdrie, Bathgate and Edinburgh, Hamilton, Larkhall, Motherwell, Coatbridge and Lanark

Network Diagram - see first Page of Table 220

Miles	Miles	Miles	Miles	Miles			SR MO	SR MX	SR MSX	SR SO	SR SO	SR MX	SR SO	SR SO	SR MX		SR	SR	SR	SR	SR SX	SR SO			SR
							A						B		A										
0	—	—	—	—	**Helensburgh Central**	d	22b37	22p40				23p10			23b24										
1¼	—	—	—	—	Craigendoran	d		22p43				23p13													
4¼	—	—	—	—	Cardross	d		22p48				23p18													
—	0	—	—	—	**Balloch**	d			22p53																
—	1	—	—	—	Alexandria	d			22p55																
—	2¼	—	—	—	Renton	d			22p58																
8	3¾	—	—	—	Dalreoch	d		22p53	23p01			23p23													
8¼	4	—	—	—	Dumbarton Central	d		22p55	23p02			23p25													
9	4¾	—	—	—	Dumbarton East	d		22p57	23p04			23p27													
11¾	7½	—	—	—	Bowling	d			23p09																
13½	9¼	—	—	—	Kilpatrick	d			23p12																
14¾	10½	0	0	—	**Dalmuir**	a	23p02	23p05	23p15			23p35			23p49										
—	—	—	—	—		d	23p04	23p05	23p16		23p31	23p35			23p51						05 47	05 47			
15½	11¼	—	0¾	—	Singer	d			23p18		23p33														
16½	12¼	—	1¾	—	Drumry	d			23p20		23p35														
17¼	13	—	2½	—	Drumchapel	d			23p23		23p38														
—	—	—	—	0	**Milngavie**	d								23p42											
—	—	—	—	1½	Hillfoot	d								23p45											
—	—	—	—	2¼	Bearsden	d								23p47											
18½	14¼	—	3¾	3½	Westerton	d	23p13		23p25		23p40			23p50	23p56										
19¾	15½	—	5	4¾	Anniesland	d			23p28		23p44			23p53											
—	—	1¼	—	—	Clydebank	d		23p07				23p37									05 49	05 49			
—	—	2¼	—	—	Yoker	d		23p09				23p39									05 51	05 51			
—	—	3¼	—	—	Garscadden	d		23p13				23p43								05 42	05 54	05 54			
—	—	3¾	—	—	Scotstounhill	d		23p15				23p45								05 44	05 57	05 57			
—	—	4¾	—	—	Jordanhill	d		23p17				23p47								05 46	05 59	05 59			
20¾	16½	5¼	6	5¾	Hyndland 8	d		23p21	23p31		23p47	23p49		23p56						05 48	06 01	06 01			
21¼	17	—	6½	6¼	**Partick**	d		23p23	23p34	23p40	23p50	23p52		23p59						05 51	06 04	06 04			
—	—	—	8¼	7½	Exhibition Centre	d				23p43	23p53			00 02											
—	—	—	8¼	8	Anderston	d				23p45	23p55			00 04											
—	—	—	8¾	8½	**Glasgow Central LL** 15	a				23p46	23p56			00 05											
—	—	—	—	—		d				23p47	23p57		00c06	00 07											
—	—	—	9¼	9	Argyle Street	d				23p49	23p59			00 09											
23¼	19	—	—	—	Charing Cross	d		23p27	23p38			23p56								05 55	06 08	06 08			
24	19¾	—	—	—	**Glasgow Queen St LL** 10	a		23p29	23p40			23p59								05 57	06 10	06 10			
—	—	—	—	—		d		23p30	23p44			23p59								05 58	06 12	06 15			
24½	20¼	—	—	—	High Street	d		23p32	23p46			00 02								06 00	06 14	06 17			
25	20¾	—	—	—	Bellgrove	d		23p34	23p49			00 04								06 02	06 16	06 19			
—	21¼	—	—	—	Duke Street	d																06 21			
—	21½	—	—	—	Alexandra Parade	d																06 22			
—	22¼	—	—	—	Barnhill	d																06 25			
—	23	—	—	—	**Springburn**	a																06 27			
26¾	—	—	—	—	Carntyne	d		23p37	23p52			00 07								06 05	06 19				
27½	—	—	—	—	Shettleston	d		23p40	23p55			00 10								06 08	06 22				
28¾	—	—	—	—	Garrowhill	d		23p42	23p57			00 12								06 10	06 24				
29¼	—	—	—	—	Easterhouse	d		23p45	23p59			00 15								06 13	06 27				
32½	—	—	—	—	Blairhill	d		23p49	00 04			00 19								06 17	06 31				
33	—	—	—	—	Coatbridge Sunnyside	d		23p51	00 06			00 21								06 19	06 33				
34	—	—	—	—	Coatdyke	d		23p54	00 09			00 24								06 22	06 36				
35	—	—	—	—	**Airdrie**	d		23p57	00a12			00a27								06 25	06 45				
36½	—	—	—	—	Drumgelloch	d		23p59												06 28	06 48				
39½	—	—	—	—	Caldercruix	d		00 03												06 32					
45	—	—	—	—	Blackridge	d		00 09												06 38					
47¼	—	—	—	—	Armadale	d		00 13												06 41					
49¾	—	—	—	—	**Bathgate**	a		00 17												06 45	07 00				
—	—	—	—	—		d											05 45		06 18	06 47	07 02				
52¾	—	—	—	—	Livingston North	d											05 49		06 22	06 50	07 06				
55¾	—	—	—	—	Uphall	d											05 52		06 25	06 53	07 09				
64½	—	—	—	—	Edinburgh Park	a											06 00		06 36	07 02	07 19				
67	—	—	—	—	Haymarket	a											06 05		06 41	07 07	07 24				
68¾	—	—	—	—	**Edinburgh**	a	00 13								00 50		06 10		06 46	07 13	07 29				
—	—	—	10½	10¼	Bridgeton	d				23p52				00 12											
—	—	—	11	10¾	Dalmarnock	d				23p54				00 14											
—	—	—	11¾	11½	Rutherglen	d				23p57	00 04			00 16											
—	—	—	13½	13¼	Cambuslang	d				00 01			00 15	00 20											
—	—	0	—	14¾	Newton	d								00 24											
—	—	2½	—	—	Blantyre	d					00 15			00 28											
—	—	4½	—	—	Hamilton West	d					00 18			00 31											
0	—	5¼	—	—	**Hamilton Central**	d					00 21			00 33											
2¼	—	—	—	—	Chatelherault	d					00 24														
3¾	—	—	—	—	Merryton	d					00 27														
5¼	—	—	—	—	**Larkhall**	a					00 30														
0	—	7½	—	—	Airbles	d								00 38											
—	—	—	17	16¾	Uddingston	d				00 05			00 20												
—	—	—	19½	—	Bellshill	d				00 10			00 25												
—	0	8¼	22½	21	**Motherwell**	a				00 16				00 41											
—	—	—	—	—		d				00 16								05 47							06 10
—	4½	—	—	—	Whifflet	a																			06 17
—	5¼	—	—	—	**Coatbridge Central**	a																			06 20
—	—	—	—	22½	Shieldmuir	d				00 20								05 50							
—	—	—	—	—	Holytown	d							00a29												
—	—	—	—	24¼	Wishaw	d				00 23								05 55							
—	—	—	—	28¾	Carluke	d				00 30								06 01							
—	—	—	—	37¼	**Lanark**	a				00 42								06 12							

A From Fort William
B To Edinburgh
C To Birmingham New Street
b Helensburgh Upper, previous night
c Glasgow Central High Level

Helensburgh, Balloch, Dalmuir and Milngavie - Glasgow - Springburn, Airdrie, Bathgate and Edinburgh, Hamilton, Larkhall, Motherwell, Coatbridge and Lanark

Network Diagram - see first Page of Table 220

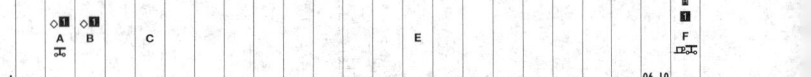

		XC SX ◇1 A	XC ◇1 B	SR SX	SR C	SR SX	SR	SR SX	SR	SR	SR SX E	SR SX	SR SO	SR SX	SR SO	SR	SR SX	SR	GR R 1 F	SR
Helensburgh Central	d																	06 10		
Craigendoran	d																	06 13		
Cardross	d																	06 18		
Balloch	d																			
Alexandria	d																			
Renton	d																			
Dalreoch	d																	06 23		
Dumbarton Central	d																	06 25		
Dumbarton East	d																	06 27		
Bowling	d																			
Kilpatrick	d																			
Dalmuir	a																	06 34		
	d								06 01					06 16	06 16	06 23		06 35		06 31
Singer	d								06 03					06 18	06 18					06 33
Drumry	d								06 05					06 20	06 20					06 35
Drumchapel	d								06 08					06 23	06 23					06 38
Milngavie	d																			
Hillfoot	d																			
Bearsden	d																			
Westerton	d								06 10					06 25	06 25					06 40
Anniesland	d								06 14					06 28	06 28					06 44
Clydebank	d															06 25				
Yoker	d															06 27				
Garscadden	d						06 00	06 08		06 13		06 17	06 20			06 31				
Scotstounhill	d						06 01	06 10		06 15		06 19	06 22			06 33				
Jordanhill	d						06 03	06 12		06 18		06 21	06 24			06 35				
Hyndland 3	d						06 05	06 14	06 17	06 20		06 22	06 26	06 31	06 31	06 37	06 41	06 44		06 48
Partick	d						06 10	06 17	06 20	06 22		06 25	06 29	06 34	06 34	06 40	06 43	06 46		06 50
Exhibition Centre	d						06 13		06 23			06 28	06 32			06 43				06 53
Anderston	d						06 15		06 25			06 30	06 34			06 45				06 55
Glasgow Central LL 15	a						06 17		06 26			06 32	06 35			06 46				06 56
	d	06b01	06b01		06b16		06 17		06 27			06 32	06 36			06 49			06b50	06 57
Argyle Street	d						06 19		06 29			06 34	06 37			06 51				06 58
Charing Cross	d							06 21		06 26				06 38	06 38		06 49	06 54		
Glasgow Queen St LL 10	a							06 23		06 28				06 40	06 40		06 51	06 56		
	d							06 24		06 29				06 42	06 44		06 54	06 57		
High Street	d							06 26		06 31				06 44	06 46		06 56	07 00		
Bellgrove	d							06 28		06 33				06 46	06 49			07 01		
Duke Street	d							06 30							06 51					
Alexandra Parade	d							06 31							06 52					
Barnhill	d							06 34							06 55					
Springburn	a							06 36							06 57					
Carntyne	d									06 36				06 49				07 05		
Shettleston	d									06 39				06 52				07 07		
Garrowhill	d									06 41				06 54				07 10		
Easterhouse	d									06 44				06 57				07 12		
Blairhill	d									06 48				07 01				07 16		
Coatbridge Sunnyside	d									06 50				07 03			07 09	07 19		
Coatdyke	d									06 53				07 06				07 21		
Airdrie	d									06 56				07a09			07 15	07 24		
Drumgelloch	d									06 59							07 18	07 27		
Caldercruix	d									07 03								07 31		
Blackridge	d									07 09								07 37		
Armadale	d									07 12								07 41		
Bathgate	a									07 16							07 29	07 46		
	d									07 17							07 31	07 46		
Livingston North	d									07 21							07 36	07 50		
Uphall	d									07 24							07 39	07 53		
Edinburgh Park	a									07 32							07 53	08 01		
Haymarket	a									07 37							07 57	08 08		
Edinburgh	a									07 43							08 02	08 14		
Bridgeton	d						06 22					06 37	06 40			06 54				
Dalmarnock	d						06 24					06 39	06 42			06 56				
Rutherglen	d						06 25		06 34			06 41	06 45			06 58				07 03
Cambuslang	d				06 25		06 30					06 45	06 49			07 02				
Newton	d											06 49	06 52							
Blantyre	d								06 45			06 53	06 56							07 11
Hamilton West	d								06 48			06 56	06 59							07 14
Hamilton Central	d								06 50			06 59	07 02							07 17
Chatelherault	d								06 54											07 20
Merryton	d								06 57											07 23
Larkhall	a								07 00											07 27
Airbles	d											07 04	07 07							
Uddingston	d				06 30		06 35									07 07				
Bellshill	d				06 35		06 40									07 11				
Motherwell	a	06 15	06 15				06 45					07 06	07 09			07 18			07 04	
	d			06 23		06 37	06 47				06 57	07 07								
Whifflet	a											07 15								
Coatbridge Central	a											07 21								
Shieldmuir	d			06 27			06 49				07 01									
Holytown	d				06a39	06 43														
Wishaw	d			06 30		06 49	06 53				07 09									
Carluke	d			06 37		06 55	06 59				07a15									
Lanark	a			06 47		07 07	07 14													

A from 13 February. To Plymouth
B until 11 February, SO from 18 February. To Plymouth
C To Edinburgh
D To London Euston
E To Carstairs
F To London Kings Cross
b Glasgow Central High Level

Helensburgh, Balloch, Dalmuir and Milngavie - Glasgow - Springburn, Airdrie, Bathgate and Edinburgh, Hamilton, Larkhall, Motherwell, Coatbridge and Lanark

Network Diagram - see first Page of Table 220

		SR	SR	SR	SR	SR	SR		SR	SR	SR	SR	SR	SR	SR	SR	SR		SR			SR	SR	SR	SR
		SX	SO			SX	SO		SX	SO		SO	SX	SX	SO				SX				SX	SO	SO
				A	B						C														
Helensburgh Central	d															06 40									
Craigendoran	d															06 43									
Cardross	d															06 48									
Balloch	d								06 23	06 23													06 53	06 53	
Alexandria	d								06 25	06 25													06 55	06 55	
Renton	d								06 28	06 28													06 58	06 58	
Dalreoch	d								06 31	06 31						06 53							07 01	07 01	
Dumbarton Central	d								06 32	06 32						06 55							07 02	07 02	
Dumbarton East	d								06 34	06 34						06 57							07 04	07 04	
Bowling	d								06 39	06 39													07 09	07 09	
Kilpatrick	d								06 42	06 42													07 12	07 12	
Dalmuir	a								06 45	06 45						07 04							07 15	07 15	
	d								06 46	06 46		06 53	06 53			07 05	07 01						07 16	07 16	07 23
Singer	d								06 48	06 48							07 03						07 18	07 18	
Drumry	d								06 50	06 50							07 05						07 20	07 20	
Drumchapel	d								06 53	06 53							07 08						07 23	07 23	
Milngavie	d					06 42	06 42							06 57								07 12			
Hillfoot	d					06 45	06 45							07 00								07 15			
Bearsden	d					06 47	06 47							07 02								07 17			
Westerton	d					06 50	06 50		06 55	06 55				07 05			07 10					07 20	07 25	07 25	
Anniesland	d					06 53	06 53		06 58	06 58				07 08			07 14					07 23	07 28	07 28	
Clydebank	d											06 55	06 55												07 25
Yoker	d											06 57	06 57												07 27
Garscadden	d	06 46										07 01	07 01						07 16						07 31
Scotstounhill	d	06 48										07 03	07 03						07 18						07 33
Jordanhill	d	06 50										07 05	07 05						07 20						07 35
Hyndland 3	d	06 52				06 56	06 56		07 01	07 01		07 07	07 07	07 11		07 14	07 18		07 22			07 26	07 31	07 31	07 37
Partick ⛴	d	06 55				06 59	06 59		07 04	07 04		07 10	07 10	07 14	07 14	07 17	07 20		07 25			07 29	07 34	07 34	07 40
Exhibition Centre	d					07 02	07 02					07 13	07 13				07 23					07 32			07 43
Anderston	d					07 04	07 04					07 15	07 15				07 25					07 34			07 45
Glasgow Central LL 15	a					07 05	07 05					07 16	07 16				07 27					07 35			07 46
	d			07b05		07 07	07 07				07b13	07 17	07 17				07 27					07 37			07 47
Argyle Street	d					07 09	07 09					07 19	07 19				07 29					07 38			07 49
Charing Cross	d	06 59							07 08	07 08				07 19	07 19	07 24			07 29				07 38	07 38	
Glasgow Queen St LL 10 ⛴	a	07 01							07 10	07 10				07 21	07 21	07 26			07 31				07 40	07 40	
	d	07 02							07 12	07 15				07 24	07 24	07 28			07 32				07 42	07 44	
High Street	d	07 04							07 14	07 17				07 26	07 26	07 30			07 34				07 44	07 46	
Bellgrove	d	07 06							07 16	07 19						07 32			07 36				07 46	07 49	
Duke Street	d	07 08								07 21									07 38					07 51	
Alexandra Parade	d	07 09								07 22									07 39					07 52	
Barnhill	d	07 12								07 25									07 42					07 55	
Springburn	a	07 14								07 27									07 44					07 57	
Carntyne	d								07 19							07 36							07 49		
Shettleston	d								07 22							07 38							07 52		
Garrowhill	d								07 24							07 41							07 54		
Easterhouse	d								07 27							07 43							07 57		
Blairhill	d								07 31							07 47							08 01		
Coatbridge Sunnyside	d								07 33					07 38	07 38	07 50							08 03		
Coatdyke	d								07 36							07 52							08 06		
Airdrie	d								07a39					07 45	07 45	07 55							08a09		
Drumgelloch	d													07 48	07 48	07 58									
Caldercruix	d															08 02									
Blackridge	d															08 08									
Armadale	d															08 12									
Bathgate	a													08 00	08 00	08 16									
	d													08 02	08 02	08 17									
Livingston North	d													08 06	08 06	08 21									
Uphall	d													08 09	08 09	08 24									
Edinburgh Park	a													08 16	08 16	08 33									
Haymarket	a													08 23	08 23	08 38									
Edinburgh	a													08 29	08 29	08 43									
Bridgeton	d					07 12	07 12					07 22	07 22									07 41			07 52
Dalmarnock	d					07 14	07 14					07 24	07 24									07 43			07 54
Rutherglen	d					07 17	07 17					07 26	07 26				07 34					07 46			07 56
Cambuslang	d					07 21	07 21				07 23	07 31	07 31									07 50			08 00
Newton	d					07 24	07 24															07 53			
Blantyre	d					07 28	07 28										07 44					07 58			
Hamilton West	d					07 31	07 31										07 47					08 01			
Hamilton Central	d					07 34	07 34										07 50					08 03			
Chatelherault	d																07 53								
Merryton	d																07 56								
Larkhall	a																08 00								
Airbles	d					07 39	07 39															08 07			
Uddingston	d										07 29	07 35	07 35												08 05
Bellshill	d										07 34	07 40	07 40												08 10
Motherwell	a			07 26		07 41	07 41					07 46	07 46									08 11			08 16
	d		07 10	07 27	07 35		07 42						07 46												08 16
Whifflet	a				07 43																				
Coatbridge Central	a				07 45																				
Shieldmuir	d		07 13										07 50												08 20
Holytown	d						07 48				07a38														
Wishaw	d		07 17	07 32			07 53						07 53												08 23
Carluke	d		07 23	07a38			08 00						08 00												08 30
Lanark	a		07 34				08 13						08 15												08 42

A To North Berwick
B To Cumbernauld
C To Edinburgh
D To London Euston
b Glasgow Central High Level

Table 226

Mondays to Saturdays

Helensburgh, Balloch, Dalmuir and Milngavie - Glasgow - Springburn, Airdrie, Bathgate and Edinburgh, Hamilton, Larkhall, Motherwell, Coatbridge and Lanark

Network Diagram - see first Page of Table 220

		SR	SR	SR	SR	XC	SR	SR	SR	SR	SR	SR	SR	SR	SR	SR	SR	SR	SR	SR	SR
		SX	SX	SO				SX		SO	SX	SX	SO		SO	SX	SO	SX	SX	SO	
						◇1 A ⚲			B					C							
Helensburgh Central	d				07 10													07 34		07 40	
Craigendoran	d				07 13													07 37		07 43	
Cardross	d				07 18													07 42		07 48	
Balloch	d											07 23	07 23								
Alexandria	d											07 25	07 25								
Renton	d											07 28	07 28								
Dalreoch	d				07 23							07 31	07 31					07 47		07 53	
Dumbarton Central	d				07 25							07 32	07 32					07 49		07 55	
Dumbarton East	d				07 27							07 34	07 34					07 51		07 57	
Bowling	d											07 39	07 39					07 56			
Kilpatrick	d											07 42	07 42					07 59			
Dalmuir	a				07 34							07 45	07 45					08 02		08 04	
	d	07 23			07 35		07 31	07 38				07 46	07 46		07 53	07 53		08 02		08 05	08 00
Singer	d						07 33					07 48	07 48								08 02
Drumry	d						07 35					07 50	07 50								08 04
Drumchapel	d						07 38					07 53	07 53								08 07
Milngavie	d		07 27							07 42	07 42								07 58		
Hillfoot	d		07 30							07 45	07 45								08 01		
Bearsden	d		07 32							07 47	07 49								08 02		
Westerton	d		07 35				07 40			07 50	07 52	07 55	07 55						08 05		08 09
Anniesland	d		07 38				07 44			07 53	07 55	07 58	07 58						08 10		08 14
Clydebank	d	07 25						07 40							07 55	07 55		08 05			
Yoker	d	07 27						07 42							07 57	07 57					
Garscadden	d	07 31						07 46							08 01	08 01					
Scotstounhill	d	07 33						07 48							08 03	08 03					
Jordanhill	d	07 35						07 50							08 05	08 05					
Hyndland 3	d	07 37	07 41		07 44		07 47	07 52		07 56	07 58	08 01	08 01		08 07	08 07		08 11	08 13	08 14	08 17
Partick ⛴	d	07 40	07 44	07 44	07 47		07 50	07 55		07 59	08 00	08 04	08 04		08 10	08 10	08 14	08 14	08 16	08 17	08 20
Exhibition Centre	d	07 43					07 53			08 02	08 03				08 13	08 13			08 19		08 23
Anderston	d	07 45					07 55			08 04	08 05				08 15	08 15			08 21		08 25
Glasgow Central LL 15	a	07 46					07 56			08 05	08 07				08 16	08 16			08 23		08 26
	d	07 47				07b50	07 57			08 07	08 09			08b20	08 18	08 18			08 23		08 27
Argyle Street	d	07 49					07 59			08 09	08 11				08 20	08 20			08 24		08 29
Charing Cross	d		07 49	07 49	07 54			07 59				08 08	08 08				08 19	08 19		08 24	
Glasgow Queen St LL 10 ⛴	a		07 51	07 51	07 56			08 01				08 10	08 10				08 21	08 21		08 26	
	d		07 54	07 54	07 58			08 02				08 12	08 15				08 24	08 24		08 28	
High Street	d		07 56	07 56	08 00			08 04				08 14	08 17				08 27	08 27		08 30	
Bellgrove	d				08 01			08 06				08 16	08 19					08 29		08 32	
Duke Street	d							08 08					08 21								
Alexandra Parade	d							08 09					08 22								
Barnhill	d							08 12					08 25								
Springburn	a							08 14					08 27								
Carntyne	d				08 05							08 19						08 32		08 36	
Shettleston	d				08 07							08 22						08 35		08 38	
Garrowhill	d				08 10							08 24						08 37		08 41	
Easterhouse	d				08 12							08 27						08 40		08 43	
Blairhill	d				08 16							08 31						08 44		08 47	
Coatbridge Sunnyside	d		08 09	08 09	08 19							08 33					08 39	08 46		08 50	
Coatdyke	d				08 21							08 36						08 49		08 52	
Airdrie	d		08 15	08 15	08 24							08 44					08 44	08a52		08 55	
Drumgelloch	d		08 18	08 18	08 27							08 47					08 47			08 58	
Caldercruix	d				08 31															09 02	
Blackridge	d				08 37															09 08	
Armadale	d				08 41															09 12	
Bathgate	a		08 30	08 30	08 45							09 00					09 00			09 16	
	d		08 31	08 31	08 46							09 01					09 01			09 17	
Livingston North	d		08 36	08 36	08 51							09 06					09 06			09 20	
Uphall	d		08 39	08 39	08 54							09 09					09 09			09 23	
Edinburgh Park	a		08 47	08 47	09 03							09 18					09 18			09 31	
Haymarket	a		08 52	08 52	09 08							09 22					09 22			09 37	
Edinburgh	a		08 58	08 58	09 13							09 27					09 27			09 43	
Bridgeton	d	07 52								08 12	08 14				08 23	08 23			08 26		
Dalmarnock	d	07 54								08 14	08 16				08 25	08 25			08 28		
Rutherglen	d	07 56					08 05			08 16	08 18				08 27	08 27			08 31		08 34
Cambuslang	d	08 00								08 20	08 22				08 31	08 31					
Newton	d									08 24	08 26										
Blantyre	d						08 14			08 28	08 30										08 44
Hamilton West	d						08 17			08 31	08 33										08 47
Hamilton Central	d						08 20			08 33	08 35										08 49
Chatelherault	d						08 23														08 53
Merryton	d						08 26														08 56
Larkhall	a						08 30														09 00
Airbles	d									08 38	08 40										
Uddingston	d	08 05												08 32	08 36	08 36					
Bellshill	d	08 10												08 36	08 40	08 40					
Motherwell	a	08 17				08 04				08 41	08 43				08 47	08 47			08 46		
	d								08 37	08 41						08 47					
Whifflet	a								08 45												
Coatbridge Central	a								08 48												
Shieldmuir	d															08 50					
Holytown	d									08 47				08a40							
Wishaw	d									08 53						08 53					
Carluke	d									09 00						09 00					
Lanark	a									09 12						09 12					

A To Plymouth
B To Cumbernauld
C To Edinburgh
b Glasgow Central High Level

Table 226

Mondays to Saturdays

Helensburgh, Balloch, Dalmuir and Milngavie - Glasgow - Springburn, Airdrie, Bathgate and Edinburgh, Hamilton, Larkhall, Motherwell, Coatbridge and Lanark

Network Diagram - see first Page of Table 220

		SR	SR	SR	SR	SR	SR	SR	SR		SR	SR	SR	SR	SR	SR	SR	SR	XC		SR	SR	SR	SR	SR
		SX	SX	SX		SX	SO	SX	SX		SX		SX	SO			SX	SO							
																			◇1						
		A																	B		C			D	
Helensburgh Central	d	07b42						08 00	07 54						08 10										
Craigendoran	d							08 03	07 57						08 13										
Cardross	d	07 50						08 08	08 02						08 18										
Balloch	d		07 53				07 53																08 23		
Alexandria	d		07 55				07 55																08 25		
Renton	d		07 58				07 58																08 28		
Dalreoch	d		08 01				08 01		08 07						08 23								08 31		
Dumbarton Central	d	07 56	08 03				08 02	08 14	08 09						08 25								08 32		
Dumbarton East	d						08 04		08 11						08 27								08 34		
Bowling	d						08 09								08 30								08 39		
Kilpatrick	d						08 12								08 32								08 42		
Dalmuir	a						08 15		08 18						08 34								08 45		
	d			08 08			08 16		08 18			08 25			08 35	08 31	08 39						08 46		08 53
Singer	d	08 07					08 18		08 21							08 33							08 48		
Drumry	d						08 20		08 24							08 35							08 50		
Drumchapel	d						08 23		08 26							08 38							08 53		
Milngavie	d				08 12	08 18							08 30									08 42			
Hillfoot	d				08 15	08 21							08 33									08 45			
Bearsden	d				08 17	08 24							08 35									08 47			
Westerton	d				08 20		08 25		08 29				08 38			08 42						08 50	08 55		
Anniesland	d				08 23		08 28		08 32				08 41			08 46						08 53	08 58		
Clydebank	d			08 10								08 27					08 40								08 55
Yoker	d			08 12								08 29					08 42								08 57
Garscadden	d			08 16								08 32					08 46	08 46							09 01
Scotstounhill	d			08 18				08 27				08 34					08 48	08 48							09 03
Jordanhill	d			08 20								08 36					08 50	08 50							09 05
Hyndland 3	d			08 22	08 26		08 31	08 33	08 35			08 38	08 44		08 44	08 49	08 52	08 52				08 56	09 01		09 08
Partick ⛴	d		08 22	08 25	08 29		08 34	08 35	08 37			08 40	08 46	08 46	08 47	08 51	08 55	08 55				08 59	09 04		09 10
Exhibition Centre	d				08 32							08 43				08 54						09 02			09 13
Anderston	d				08 34						08 38	08 45				08 56						09 04			09 15
Glasgow Central LL 15	a				08 35						08 39	08 47				08 58						09 06			09 16
	d				08 37						08 40	08 47				08 58			09e00			09 07		09e18	09 17
Argyle Street	d				08 38						08 42	08 49				09 00						09 08			09 19
Charing Cross	d		08 27	08 30		08 35	08 38	08 40	08 42				08 50	08 50	08 54		08 59	08 59					09 08		
Glasgow Queen St LL 10 ⛴	a	08c37	08 29	08 32		08 37	08 40	08 42	08 44				08 52	08 52	08 56		09 01	09 01					09 10		
	d		08 29	08 33		08 38	08 44	08 42	08 44				08 54	08 54	08 58		09 02	09 02					09 12		
High Street	d		08 31	08 35		08 40	08 46	08 44	08a47				08 56	08 56	09 00		09 04	09 04					09 14		
Bellgrove	d		08 33	08 37			08 49	08 46							09 02		09 06	09 06					09 16		
Duke Street	d		08 35	08 42			08 51										09 08	09 08							
Alexandra Parade	d		08 37	08 43			08 52										09 09	09 09							
Barnhill	d		08 40	08 46			08 55										09 12	09 12							
Springburn	a		08 42	08 48			08 57										09 14	09 14							
Carntyne	d							08 49							09 06								09 19		
Shettleston	d							08 52							09 09								09 22		
Garrowhill	d							08 54							09 11								09 24		
Easterhouse	d							08 57							09 14								09 27		
Blairhill	d							09 01							09 18								09 31		
Coatbridge Sunnyside	d					08 52		09 03					09 12	09 12	09 20								09 33		
Coatdyke	d							09 06							09 23								09 36		
Airdrie	d					08 57		09a09					09 16	09 16	09 26								09a39		
Drumgelloch	d					09 00							09 19	09 19	09 29										
Caldercruix	d					09 04									09 33										
Blackridge	d					09 10									09 39										
Armadale	d					09 14									09 42										
Bathgate	a					09 18							09 32	09 32	09 46										
	d					09 18							09 32	09 32	09 47										
Livingston North	d					09 22							09 37	09 37	09 49										
Uphall	d					09 25							09 40	09 40	09 52										
Edinburgh Park	a					09 33							09 48	09 48	10 01										
Haymarket	a					09 38							09 52	09 52	10 08										
Edinburgh	a					09 43							09 57	09 57	10 14										
Bridgeton	d				08 41						08 45	08 52										09 11			09 22
Dalmarnock	d				08 43						08 47	08 54										09 13			09 24
Rutherglen	d				08 46						08 51	08 57				09 05						09 16			09 27
Cambuslang	d				08 50						08 55	09 01										09 20			09 31
Newton	d				08 54																	09 24			
Blantyre	d				08 58											09 14						09 28			
Hamilton West	d				09 01											09 17						09 31			
Hamilton Central	d				09 04											09 20						09 33			
Chatelherault	d															09 23									
Merryton	d															09 26									
Larkhall	a															09 30									
Airbles	d				09 09																	09 38			
Uddingston	d										09 00	09 05												09 30	09 35
Bellshill	d											09 10												09 34	09 40
Motherwell	a				09 12						09 07	09 18							09 14			09 41			09 47
	d											09 19									09 37	09 41			
Whifflet	a																				09 45				
Coatbridge Central	a																				09 48				
Shieldmuir	d											09 22													
Holytown	d																					09 48		09a38	
Wishaw	d											09 26										09 53			
Carluke	d											09 32										10 00			
Lanark	a											09 43										10 14			

A From Arrochar & Tarbet
B To Penzance
C To Cumbernauld
D To Edinburgh
b Helensburgh Upper
c Glasgow Queen St High Level
e Glasgow Central High Level

Helensburgh, Balloch, Dalmuir and Milngavie - Glasgow - Springburn, Airdrie, Bathgate and Edinburgh, Hamilton, Larkhall, Motherwell, Coatbridge and Lanark

Network Diagram - see first Page of Table 220

		SR	SR SO	SR SX	SR	SR	SR	SR	SR	SR	SR	SR	SR	SR A	SR	SR	SR B	SR	SR	SR	SR	SR	SR
Helensburgh Central	d		08 40	08 40							09 10									09 40			
Craigendoran	d		08 43	08 43							09 13									09 43			
Cardross	d		08 48	08 48							09 18									09 48			
Balloch	d							08 53								09 23							
Alexandria	d							08 55								09 25							
Renton	d							08 58								09 28							
Dalreoch	d		08 53	08 53				09 01			09 23					09 31				09 53			
Dumbarton Central	d		08 55	08 55				09 02			09 25					09 32				09 55			
Dumbarton East	d		08 57	08 57				09 04			09 27					09 34				09 57			
Bowling	d							09 09								09 39							
Kilpatrick	d							09 12								09 42							
Dalmuir	a		09 04	09 04				09 15			09 34					09 45				10 04			
	d		09 05	09 05	09 01	09 08		09 16	09 23		09 35	09 31	09 38			09 46		09 53		10 05	10 01	10 08	
Singer	d				09 03			09 18				09 33				09 48					10 03		
Drumry	d				09 05			09 20				09 35				09 50					10 05		
Drumchapel	d				09 08			09 23				09 38				09 53					10 08		
Milngavie	d	08 57					09 12			09 28					09 42				09 57				10 12
Hillfoot	d	09 00					09 15			09 31					09 45				10 00				10 15
Bearsden	d	09 02					09 18			09 33					09 47				10 02				10 17
Westerton	d	09 05			09 10		09 21	09 25		09 36		09 40			09 50	09 55			10 05		10 10		10 20
Anniesland	d	09 08			09 14		09 24	09 28		09 39		09 44			09 53	09 58			10 08		10 14		10 23
Clydebank	d					09 10			09 25				09 40					09 55				10 10	
Yoker	d					09 12			09 27				09 42					09 57				10 12	
Garscadden	d					09 16			09 31				09 46					10 01				10 16	
Scotstounhill	d					09 18			09 33				09 48					10 03				10 18	
Jordanhill	d					09 20			09 35				09 50					10 05				10 20	
Hyndland 3	d	09 12	09 14	09 14	09 17	09 22	09 28	09 31	09 37	09 42	09 44	09 47	09 52		09 56	10 01		10 07	10 12	10 14	10 17	10 22	10 26
Partick ⛴	d	09 14	09 17	09 17	09 20	09 25	09 30	09 34	09 40	09 44	09 47	09 50	09 55		09 59	10 04		10 10	10 14	10 17	10 20	10 25	10 29
Exhibition Centre	d				09 23		09 33		09 43			09 53			10 02			10 13			10 23		10 32
Anderston	d				09 25		09 35		09 45			09 55			10 04			10 15			10 25		10 34
Glasgow Central LL 15	a				09 26		09 36		09 46			09 56			10 05			10 16			10 26		10 36
	d				09 27		09 37		09 47			09 57			10 07		10b18	10 17			10 27		10 37
Argyle Street	d				09 29		09 38		09 49			09 59			10 08			10 19			10 29		10 39
Charing Cross	d	09 19	09 24	09 24		09 29		09 38		09 49	09 54		09 59			10 08			10 19	10 24		10 29	
Glasgow Queen St LL 10 ⛴	a	09 21	09 26	09 26		09 31		09 40		09 51	09 56		10 01			10 10			10 21	10 26		10 31	
	d	09 24	09 28	09 28		09 32		09 42		09 54	09 58		10 02			10 12			10 24	10 27		10 32	
High Street	d	09 26	09 30	09 30		09 34		09 44		09 57	10 00		10 04			10 14			10 26	10 30		10 34	
Bellgrove	d		09 32	09 32		09 36		09 46			10 02		10 06			10 16				10 32		10 36	
Duke Street	d					09 38							10 08									10 38	
Alexandra Parade	d					09 39							10 09									10 39	
Barnhill	d					09 42							10 12									10 42	
Springburn	a					09 44							10 14									10 44	
Carntyne	d		09 35	09 35				09 49			10 05					10 19				10 36			
Shettleston	d		09 38	09 38				09 52			10 08					10 22				10 38			
Garrowhill	d		09 40	09 40				09 54			10 10					10 24				10 41			
Easterhouse	d		09 43	09 43				09 57			10 13					10 27				10 43			
Blairhill	d		09 47	09 47				10 01			10 17					10 31				10 47			
Coatbridge Sunnyside	d	09 39	09 49	09 49				10 03		10 09	10 19					10 33			10 39	10 50			
Coatdyke	d		09 52	09 52				10 06			10 22					10 36				10 52			
Airdrie	d	09 44	09 55	09 55				10a09		10 15	10 25					10a39			10 44	10 55			
Drumgelloch	d	09 47	09 58	09 58						10 18	10 28								10 47	10 58			
Caldercruix	d		10 02	10 02							10 32									11 02			
Blackridge	d		10 08	10 08							10 38									11 08			
Armadale	d		10 11	10 11							10 41									11 12			
Bathgate	a	10 00	10 15	10 15						10 29	10 45								11 00	11 16			
	d	10 01	10 17	10 17						10 32	10 47								11 01	11 17			
Livingston North	d	10 06	10 20	10 20						10 35	10 50								11 06	11 21			
Uphall	d	10 09	10 23	10 24						10 38	10 53								11 09	11 24			
Edinburgh Park	a	10 17	10 31	10 32						10 47	11 01								11 17	11 32			
Haymarket	a	10 22	10 37	10 38						10 52	11 06								11 22	11 37			
Edinburgh	a	10 28	10 43	10 44						10 57	11 14								11 28	11 43			
Bridgeton	d						09 41		09 52						10 11			10 22					10 42
Dalmarnock	d						09 43		09 54						10 13			10 24					10 44
Rutherglen	d				09 34		09 46		09 56			10 04			10 16			10 26			10 34		10 46
Cambuslang	d						09 50		10 00						10 20			10 31					10 50
Newton	d						09 54								10 23								10 54
Blantyre	d				09 44		09 58					10 14			10 28						10 44		10 58
Hamilton West	d				09 47		10 01					10 17			10 31						10 47		11 01
Hamilton Central	d				09 50		10 03					10 20			10 33						10 50		11 03
Chatelherault	d				09 53							10 23									10 53		
Merryton	d				09 56							10 26									10 56		
Larkhall	a				10 00							10 30									11 00		
Airbles	d						10 08								10 37								11 08
Uddingston	d								10 05								10 30	10 35					
Bellshill	d								10 10								10 35	10 40					
Motherwell	a						10 11		10 16						10 42			10 47					11 11
	d								10 16					10 37	10 43								
Whifflet	a													10 45									
Coatbridge Central	a													10 48									
Shieldmuir	d								10 20														
Holytown	d														10 48		10a39						
Wishaw	d								10 26						10 53								
Carluke	d								10 32						11 00								
Lanark	a								10 44						11 13								

A To Cumbernauld

B To Edinburgh

b Glasgow Central High Level

Helensburgh, Balloch, Dalmuir and Milngavie - Glasgow - Springburn, Airdrie, Bathgate and Edinburgh, Hamilton, Larkhall, Motherwell, Coatbridge and Lanark

Network Diagram - see first Page of Table 220

		SR	SR	SR	SR	SR	SR	XC	SR	SR	SR	SR	SR	SR	SR	SR	SR	SR	SR	SR	SR	SR
								◇1 A	B			C					◇ D					
Helensburgh Central	d				10 10										10 40		10c44					
Craigendoran	d				10 13										10 43							
Cardross	d				10 18										10 48							
Balloch	d	09 53									10 23									10 53		
Alexandria	d	09 55									10 25									10 55		
Renton	d	09 58									10 28									10 58		
Dalreoch	d	10 01			10 23						10 31				10 53					11 01		
Dumbarton Central	d	10 02			10 25						10 32				10 55		10 59			11 02		
Dumbarton East	d	10 04			10 27						10 34				10 57					11 04		
Bowling	d	10 09									10 39									11 09		
Kilpatrick	d	10 12									10 42									11 12		
Dalmuir	a	10 15			10 34						10 45				11 04		11 08			11 15		
	d	10 16	10 23		10 35	10 31	10 38				10 46		10 53		11 05	11 00	11 08	11 08		11 16	11 23	
Singer	d	10 18				10 33					10 48					11 02				11 18		
Drumry	d	10 20				10 35					10 50					11 04				11 20		
Drumchapel	d	10 23				10 38					10 53					11 07				11 23		
Milngavie	d			10 27						10 42				10 57					11 12			11 27
Hillfoot	d			10 30						10 45				11 00					11 15			11 30
Bearsden	d			10 32						10 47				11 02					11 18			11 32
Westerton	d	10 25		10 35		10 40				10 50	10 55			11 05		11 10			11 21	11 25		11 35
Anniesland	d	10 28		10 38		10 44				10 53	10 58			11 08		11 14			11 24	11 28		11 38
Clydebank	d		10 25				10 40						10 55					11 10			11 25	
Yoker	d		10 27				10 42						10 57					11 12			11 27	
Garscadden	d		10 31				10 46						11 01					11 16			11 31	
Scotstounhill	d		10 33				10 48						11 03					11 18			11 33	
Jordanhill	d		10 35				10 50						11 07					11 20			11 35	
Hyndland 3	d	10 31	10 37	10 41	10 44	10 47	10 52			10 56	11 01		11 09	11 11	11 14	11 17		11 22	11 27	11 31	11 37	11 41
Partick	d	10 34	10 40	10 44	10 47	10 50	10 55			10 59	11 04		11 11	11 14	11 17	11 20		11 25	11 30	11 34	11 40	11 44
Exhibition Centre	d		10 43			10 53				11 02			11 14			11 23			11 33		11 43	
Anderston	d		10 45			10 55				11 04			11 16			11 25			11 35		11 45	
Glasgow Central LL 15	a		10 46			10 56				11 05			11 17			11 26			11 38		11 46	
	d		10 47			10 57		10b59		11 07		11b18	11 18			11 27			11 38		11 47	
Argyle Street	d		10 48			10 59				11 08			11 19			11 29			11 39		11 49	
Charing Cross	d	10 38		10 49	10 54		10 59				11 08			11 19	11 24			11 29		11 38		11 49
Glasgow Queen St LL 10	a	10 40		10 51	10 56		11 01				11 11			11 21	11 26		11e30	11 31		11 41		11 51
	d	10 42		10 54	10 58		11 02				11 12			11 24	11 28			11 32		11 42		11 54
High Street	d	10 44		10 56	11 00		11 04				11 14			11 26	11 30			11 34		11 44		11 56
Bellgrove	d	10 46			11 02		11 06				11 16				11 32			11 36		11 46		
Duke Street	d						11 08											11 38				
Alexandra Parade	d						11 09											11 39				
Barnhill	d						11 12											11 42				
Springburn	a						11 14											11 44				
Carntyne	d	10 49			11 05						11 19				11 35					11 49		
Shettleston	d	10 52			11 08						11 22				11 38					11 52		
Garrowhill	d	10 54			11 10						11 24				11 40					11 54		
Easterhouse	d	10 57			11 13						11 27				11 43					11 57		
Blairhill	d	11 01			11 17						11 31				11 47					12 01		
Coatbridge Sunnyside	d	11 03		11 09	11 19						11 33			11 39	11 49					12 03		12 09
Coatdyke	d	11 06			11 22						11 36				11 52					12 06		
Airdrie	d	11a09		11 14	11 25						11a39			11 44	11 55					12a09		12 14
Drumgelloch	d			11 17	11 28									11 47	11 58							12 17
Caldercruix	d				11 32										12 02							
Blackridge	d				11 38										12 08							
Armadale	d				11 41										12 11							
Bathgate	a			11 30	11 45									12 00	12 15							12 30
	d			11 31	11 47									12 01	12 17							12 31
Livingston North	d			11 35	11 51									12 05	12 21							12 35
Uphall	d			11 38	11 54									12 08	12 24							12 38
Edinburgh Park	a			11 47	12 02									12 17	12 32							12 47
Haymarket	a			11 52	12 07									12 22	12 37							12 52
Edinburgh	a			11 58	12 13									12 28	12 43							12 58
Bridgeton	d		10 51							11 11			11 22						11 42		11 52	
Dalmarnock	d		10 53							11 13			11 24						11 44		11 54	
Rutherglen	d		10 56			11 05				11 16			11 27			11 34			11 47		11 56	
Cambuslang	d		11 00							11 20			11 31						11 51		12 00	
Newton	d									11 23									11 54			
Blantyre	d					11 14				11 27						11 45			11 58			
Hamilton West	d					11 17				11 30						11 48			12 01			
Hamilton Central	d					11 20				11 33						11 50			12 04			
Chatelherault	d					11 23										11 54						
Merryton	d					11 26										11 57						
Larkhall	a					11 30										12 00						
Airbles	d									11 38									12 09			
Uddingston	d		11 04									11 30	11 35								12 05	
Bellshill	d		11 09									11 35	11 40								12 09	
Motherwell	a		11 17					11 13		11 40			11 47						12 11		12 16	
	d		11 17						11 37	11 41											12 16	
Whifflet	a								11 45													
Coatbridge Central	a								11 48													
Shieldmuir	d		11 20																		12 20	
Holytown	d									11 48		11a39										
Wishaw	d		11 23							11 53											12 22	
Carluke	d		11 30							12 00											12 30	
Lanark	a		11 42							12 12											12 42	

A To Penzance
B To Cumbernauld
C To Edinburgh
D From Mallaig
b Glasgow Central High Level
c Helensburgh Upper
e Glasgow Queen St High Level

Helensburgh, Balloch, Dalmuir and Milngavie - Glasgow - Springburn, Airdrie, Bathgate and Edinburgh, Hamilton, Larkhall, Motherwell, Coatbridge and Lanark

Network Diagram - see first Page of Table 220

		SR	SR	SR	SR	SR	SR	SR	SR	SR	SR	SR	SR	SR	SR	SR	SR	SR	XC	SR	SR	SR	SR
					A			B											◇■1 C			A	
Helensburgh Central	d	11 10									11 40							12 10					
Craigendoran	d	11 13									11 43							12 13					
Cardross	d	11 18									11 48							12 18					
Balloch	d						11 23								11 53								
Alexandria	d						11 25								11 55								
Renton	d						11 28								11 58								
Dalreoch	d	11 23					11 31				11 53				12 01			12 23					
Dumbarton Central	d	11 25					11 32				11 55				12 02			12 25					
Dumbarton East	d	11 27					11 34				11 57				12 04			12 27					
Bowling	d						11 39								12 09								
Kilpatrick	d						11 42								12 12								
Dalmuir	a	11 34					11 45				12 04				12 15			12 34					
	d	11 35	11 31	11 38			11 46		11 53		12 05	12 01	12 08		12 16	12 23		12 35		12 31	12 38		
Singer	d		11 33				11 48					12 03			12 18					12 33			
Drumry	d		11 35				11 50					12 05			12 20					12 35			
Drumchapel	d		11 38				11 53					12 08			12 23					12 38			
Milngavie	d					11 42				11 57				12 12			12 27						12 42
Hillfoot	d					11 45				12 00				12 15			12 30						12 45
Bearsden	d					11 47				12 02				12 17			12 32						12 47
Westerton	d		11 40			11 50	11 55			12 05		12 10		12 20	12 25		12 35			12 40			12 50
Anniesland	d		11 44			11 53	11 58			12 08		12 14		12 23	12 28		12 38			12 44			12 53
Clydebank	d			11 40					11 55				12 10			12 25					12 40		
Yoker	d			11 42					11 57				12 12			12 27					12 42		
Garscadden	d			11 46					12 01				12 16			12 31					12 46		
Scotstounhill	d			11 48					12 03				12 18			12 33					12 48		
Jordanhill	d			11 50					12 05				12 20			12 35					12 50		
Hyndland ■3	d	11 44	11 47	11 52		11 56	12 01		12 07	12 11	12 14	12 17	12 22	12 26	12 31	12 37	12 41	12 44		12 47	12 52		12 56
Partick	d	11 47	11 50	11 55		11 59	12 04		12 10	12 14	12 17	12 20	12 25	12 29	12 34	12 40	12 44	12 47		12 50	12 55		12 59
Exhibition Centre	d		11 53			12 02			12 13			12 23		12 32		12 43				12 53			13 02
Anderston	d		11 55			12 04			12 15			12 25		12 34		12 45				12 55			13 04
Glasgow Central LL ■15	a		11 56			12 05			12 16			12 26		12 35		12 46				12 56			13 05
	d		11 58			12 07		12b18	12 17			12 27		12 37		12 47			12b51	12 57			13 07
Argyle Street	d		11 59			12 08			12 19			12 29		12 38		12 48				12 59			13 08
Charing Cross	d	11 54		11 59			12 08			12 19	12 24		12 29		12 38		12 49	12 54			12 59		
Glasgow Queen St LL ■10	a	11 56		12 01			12 10			12 21	12 26		12 31		12 40		12 51	12 56			13 01		
	d	11 58		12 02			12 12			12 24	12 28		12 32		12 42		12 54	12 58			13 02		
High Street	d	12 00		12 04			12 14			12 26	12 30		12 34		12 44		12 56	13 00			13 04		
Bellgrove	d	12 02		12 06			12 16				12 32		12 36		12 46			13 02			13 06		
Duke Street	d			12 08									12 38								13 08		
Alexandra Parade	d			12 09									12 39								13 09		
Barnhill	d			12 12									12 42								13 12		
Springburn	a			12 14									12 44								13 14		
Carntyne	d	12 05					12 19				12 35				12 49			13 05					
Shettleston	d	12 08					12 22				12 38				12 52			13 08					
Garrowhill	d	12 10					12 24				12 40				12 54			13 10					
Easterhouse	d	12 13					12 27				12 43				12 57			13 13					
Blairhill	d	12 17					12 31				12 47				13 01			13 17					
Coatbridge Sunnyside	d	12 19					12 33			12 39	12 49				13 03		13 09	13 19					
Coatdyke	d	12 22					12 36				12 52				13 06			13 22					
Airdrie	d	12 25					12a39			12 44	12 55				13a09		13 14	13 25					
Drumgelloch	d	12 28								12 47	12 58						13 17	13 28					
Caldercruix	d	12 32									13 02							13 32					
Blackridge	d	12 38									13 08							13 38					
Armadale	d	12 41									13 11							13 41					
Bathgate	a	12 45								13 00	13 15						13 30	13 45					
	d	12 47								13 01	13 17						13 31	13 47					
Livingston North	d	12 51								13 05	13 21						13 35	13 51					
Uphall	d	12 54								13 08	13 24						13 38	13 54					
Edinburgh Park	a	13 02								13 17	13 32						13 47	14 02					
Haymarket	a	13 07								13 22	13 37						13 52	14 07					
Edinburgh	a	13 13								13 28	13 43						13 58	14 13					
Bridgeton	d					12 11			12 22					12 41		12 51							13 11
Dalmarnock	d					12 13			12 24					12 43		12 53							13 13
Rutherglen	d		12 06			12 16			12 26			12 34		12 46		12 56				13 04			13 16
Cambuslang	d					12 20			12 31					12 50		13 01							13 20
Newton	d					12 23								12 53									13 24
Blantyre	d		12 14			12 27						12 45		12 58						13 14			13 28
Hamilton West	d		12 17			12 30						12 48		13 01						13 17			13 31
Hamilton Central	d		12 20			12 33						12 50		13 03						13 20			13 33
Chatelherault	d		12 23									12 54								13 23			
Merryton	d		12 26									12 57								13 26			
Larkhall	a		12 30									13 00								13 30			
Airbles	d					12 37								13 07									13 38
Uddingston	d							12 30	12 35							13 05							
Bellshill	d							12 35	12 40							13 10							
Motherwell	a					12 40			12 48					13 11		13 16			13 05				13 41
	d				12 37	12 41										13 16						13 37	13 41
Whifflet	a				12 45																	13 45	
Coatbridge Central	a				12 48																	13 48	
Shieldmuir	d															13 20							
Holytown	d					12 48		12a39															13 48
Wishaw	d					12 53										13 23							13 53
Carluke	d					13 00										13 32							14 00
Lanark	a					13 12										13 42							14 12

A To Cumbernauld
B To Edinburgh
C To Plymouth
b Glasgow Central High Level

Helensburgh, Balloch, Dalmuir and Milngavie - Glasgow - Springburn, Airdrie, Bathgate and Edinburgh, Hamilton, Larkhall, Motherwell, Coatbridge and Lanark

Network Diagram - see first Page of Table 220

		SR	SR A	SR	SR	SR	SR	SR	SR	SR	SR	SR	SR	SR	SR	SR B	SR	SR	SR A	SR	SR	SR
Helensburgh Central	d					12 40							13 10									13 40
Craigendoran	d					12 43							13 13									13 43
Cardross	d					12 48							13 18									13 48
Balloch	d	12 23								12 53								13 23				
Alexandria	d	12 25								12 55								13 25				
Renton	d	12 28								12 58								13 28				
Dalreoch	d	12 31				12 53				13 01			13 23					13 31				13 53
Dumbarton Central	d	12 32				12 55				13 02			13 25					13 32				13 55
Dumbarton East	d	12 34				12 57				13 04			13 27					13 34				13 57
Bowling	d	12 39								13 09								13 39				
Kilpatrick	d	12 42								13 12								13 42				
Dalmuir	a	12 45				13 04				13 15			13 34					13 45				14 04
	d	12 46		12 53		13 05	13 01	13 08		13 16	13 23		13 35	13 31	13 38			13 46		13 53		14 05
Singer	d	12 48					13 03			13 18				13 33				13 48				
Drumry	d	12 50					13 05			13 20				13 35				13 50				
Drumchapel	d	12 53					13 08			13 23				13 38				13 53				
Milngavie	d				12 57				13 12			13 27					13 42				13 57	
Hillfoot	d				13 00				13 15			13 30					13 45				14 00	
Bearsden	d				13 02				13 17			13 32					13 47				14 02	
Westerton	d	12 55			13 05		13 10		13 20	13 25		13 35		13 40			13 50	13 55			14 05	
Anniesland	d	12 58			13 08		13 14		13 23	13 28		13 38		13 44			13 53	13 58			14 08	
Clydebank	d			12 55				13 10			13 25				13 40					13 55		
Yoker	d			12 57				13 12			13 27				13 42					13 57		
Garscadden	d			13 01				13 16			13 31				13 46					14 01		
Scotstounhill	d			13 03				13 18			13 33				13 48					14 03		
Jordanhill	d			13 05				13 20			13 35				13 50					14 05		
Hyndland 3	d	13 01		13 07	13 11	13 14	13 17	13 22	13 26	13 31	13 37	13 41	13 44	13 47	13 52		13 56	14 01		14 07	14 11	14 14
Partick	d	13 04		13 10	13 14	13 17	13 20	13 25	13 29	13 34	13 40	13 44	13 47	13 50	13 55		13 59	14 04		14 10	14 14	14 17
Exhibition Centre	d			13 13			13 23		13 32		13 43			13 53			14 02			14 13		
Anderston	d			13 15			13 25		13 34		13 45			13 55			14 04			14 15		
Glasgow Central LL 15	a			13 16			13 26		13 35		13 46			13 56			14 05			14 16		
	d		13b18	13 17			13 27		13 37		13 47			13 57			14 07		14b18	14 17		
Argyle Street	d			13 19			13 29		13 38		13 48			13 59			14 08			14 19		
Charing Cross	d	13 08			13 19	13 24		13 29		13 38		13 49	13 54		13 59			14 08			14 19	14 24
Glasgow Queen St LL 10	a	13 10			13 21	13 26		13 31		13 40		13 51	13 56		14 01			14 10			14 21	14 26
	d	13 12			13 24	13 28		13 32		13 42		13 54	13 58		14 02			14 12			14 24	14 28
High Street	d	13 14			13 26	13 30		13 34		13 44		13 56	14 00		14 04			14 14			14 26	14 30
Bellgrove	d	13 16				13 32		13 36		13 46			14 02		14 06			14 16				14 32
Duke Street	d							13 38							14 08							
Alexandra Parade	d							13 39							14 09							
Barnhill	d							13 42							14 12							
Springburn	a							13 44							14 14							
Carntyne	d	13 19				13 35				13 49			14 05					14 19				14 35
Shettleston	d	13 22				13 38				13 52			14 08					14 22				14 38
Garrowhill	d	13 24				13 40				13 54			14 10					14 24				14 40
Easterhouse	d	13 27				13 43				13 57			14 13					14 27				14 43
Blairhill	d	13 31				13 47				14 01			14 17					14 31				14 47
Coatbridge Sunnyside	d	13 33			13 39	13 49				14 03		14 09	14 19					14 33			14 39	14 49
Coatdyke	d	13 36				13 52				14 06			14 22					14 36				14 52
Airdrie	d	13a39			13 44	13 55				14a09		14 14	14 25					14a39			14 44	14 55
Drumgelloch	d				13 47	13 58						14 17	14 28								14 47	14 58
Caldercruix	d					14 02							14 32									15 02
Blackridge	d					14 08							14 38									15 08
Armadale	d					14 11							14 41									15 11
Bathgate	a				14 00	14 15						14 30	14 45								14 59	15 15
	d				14 01	14 17						14 31	14 47								15 01	15 17
Livingston North	d				14 05	14 21						14 35	14 51								15 05	15 21
Uphall	d				14 08	14 24						14 38	14 54								15 08	15 24
Edinburgh Park	a				14 17	14 32						14 47	15 02								15 17	15 32
Haymarket	a				14 22	14 37						14 52	15 07								15 22	15 37
Edinburgh	a				14 28	14 43						14 58	15 14								15 28	15 44
Bridgeton	d			13 22					13 41		13 51						14 11			14 22		
Dalmarnock	d			13 24					13 43		13 53						14 13			14 24		
Rutherglen	d			13 26			13 34		13 46		13 56			14 04			14 16			14 26		
Cambuslang	d			13 31					13 50		14 00						14 20			14 31		
Newton	d								13 53								14 23					
Blantyre	d						13 44		13 57					14 14			14 27					
Hamilton West	d						13 47		14 00					14 17			14 30					
Hamilton Central	d						13 50		14 03					14 20			14 33					
Chatelherault	d						13 53							14 23								
Merryton	d						13 56							14 26								
Larkhall	a						14 00							14 30								
Airbles	d								14 08								14 37					
Uddingston	d		13 30	13 35							14 04								14 30	14 35		
Bellshill	d		13 35	13 40							14 09								14 36	14 40		
Motherwell	a			13 48					14 11		14 16						14 40			14 48		
	d										14 16					14 37	14 41					
Whifflet	a															14 45						
Coatbridge Central	a															14 48						
Shieldmuir	d										14 20											
Holytown	d		13a39														14 48		14a40			
Wishaw	d										14 23						14 53					
Carluke	d										14 30						15 00					
Lanark	a										14 42						15 12					

A To Edinburgh

B To Cumbernauld

b Glasgow Central High Level

Table 226

Helensburgh, Balloch, Dalmuir and Milngavie - Glasgow - Springburn, Airdrie, Bathgate and Edinburgh, Hamilton, Larkhall, Motherwell, Coatbridge and Lanark

Network Diagram - see first Page of Table 220

		SR	SR	SR	SR	SR	SR	SR	SR		SR	XC	XC	SR	SR	SR	SR	SR	SR		SR	SR	SR	SR	SR
												SO	SX												
												◇1	◇1									◇			
												A	A			B	C	D				E			
												🍴										🍴			
Helensburgh Central	d							14 10														14c39	14 40		
Craigendoran	d							14 13															14 43		
Cardross	d							14 18															14 48		
Balloch	d				13 53										14 23										
Alexandria	d				13 55										14 25										
Renton	d				13 58										14 28										
Dalreoch	d				14 01			14 23							14 31								14 53		
Dumbarton Central	d				14 02			14 25							14 32							14 51	14 55		
Dumbarton East	d				14 04			14 27							14 34								14 57		
Bowling	d				14 09										14 39										
Kilpatrick	d				14 12										14 42										
Dalmuir	a				14 15			14 34							14 45							15 03	15 05		
	d	14 01	14 08		14 16	14 23		14 35	14 31		14 38				14 46				14 53			15 03	15 05	15 00	15 10
Singer	d	14 03			14 18				14 33						14 48									15 02	
Drumry	d	14 05			14 20				14 35						14 50									15 04	
Drumchapel	d	14 08			14 23				14 38						14 53									15 07	
Milngavie	d			14 12			14 27							14 42							14 57				
Hillfoot	d			14 15			14 30							14 45							15 00				
Bearsden	d			14 17			14 32							14 47							15 02				
Westerton	d	14 10		14 20	14 25		14 35		14 40					14 50	14 55						15 05			15 09	
Anniesland	d	14 14		14 23	14 28		14 38		14 44					14 53	14 58						15 08			15 15	
Clydebank	d		14 10			14 25					14 40								14 55						15 12
Yoker	d		14 12			14 27					14 42								14 57						15 14
Garscadden	d		14 16			14 31					14 46								15 01						15 17
Scotstounhill	d		14 18			14 33					14 48								15 03						15 19
Jordanhill	d		14 20			14 35					14 50								15 05						15 21
Hyndland 3	d	14 17	14 22	14 26	14 31	14 37	14 41	14 44	14 47		14 52			14 56	15 01				15 07		15 11		15 14	15 18	15 23
Partick ⛴	d	14 20	14 25	14 29	14 34	14 40	14 44	14 47	14 50		14 55			14 58	15 04				15 10		15 14		15 17	15 20	15 25
Exhibition Centre	d	14 23		14 32		14 43			14 53					15 01					15 13					15 23	
Anderston	d	14 25		14 34		14 45			14 55					15 03					15 15					15 25	
Glasgow Central LL 15	a	14 26		14 35		14 46			14 56					15 04					15 16					15 26	
	d	14 27		14 37		14 47			14 57			15b00	15b00	15 07		15b14		15b18	15 17					15 27	
Argyle Street	d	14 29		14 38		14 48			14 59					15 09					15 19					15 29	
Charing Cross	d		14 29		14 38		14 49	14 54			14 59				15 08						15 19		15 24		15 29
Glasgow Queen St LL 10 ⛴	a		14 31		14 40		14 51	14 56			15 01				15 10						15 21	15e30	15 26		15 31
	d		14 32		14 42		14 54	14 58			15 02				15 12						15 24		15 28		15 32
High Street	d		14 34		14 44		14 56	15 00			15 04				15 14						15 26		15 30		15 34
Bellgrove	d		14 36		14 46			15 02			15 06				15 16								15 32		15 36
Duke Street	d		14 38								15 08														15 38
Alexandra Parade	d		14 39								15 09														15 39
Barnhill	d		14 42								15 12														15 42
Springburn	a		14 44								15 14														15 44
Carntyne	d				14 49			15 05							15 19								15 35		
Shettleston	d				14 52			15 08							15 22								15 38		
Garrowhill	d				14 54			15 10							15 24								15 40		
Easterhouse	d				14 57			15 13							15 27								15 43		
Blairhill	d				15 01			15 17							15 31								15 47		
Coatbridge Sunnyside	d				15 03		15 09	15 19							15 33						15 39		15 49		
Coatdyke	d				15 06			15 22							15 36								15 52		
Airdrie	d				15a09		15 14	15 25							15a39						15 44		15 55		
Drumgelloch	d						15 17	15 28													15 47		15 58		
Caldercruix	d							15 32															16 02		
Blackridge	d							15 38															16 08		
Armadale	d							15 41															16 11		
Bathgate	a						15 30	15 45													16 00		16 15		
	d						15 31	15 47													16 01		16 17		
Livingston North	d						15 35	15 51													16 05		16 21		
Uphall	d						15 38	15 54													16 08		16 24		
Edinburgh Park	a						15 47	16 02													16 17		16 32		
Haymarket	a						15 52	16 07													16 22		16 37		
Edinburgh	a						15 58	16 14													16 28		16 44		
Bridgeton	d			14 41		14 51								15 12					15 22						
Dalmarnock	d			14 43		14 53								15 14					15 24						
Rutherglen	d	14 34		14 46		14 56			15 06					15 16					15 26					15 34	
Cambuslang	d			14 50		15 00								15 20					15 31						
Newton	d			14 53										15 24											
Blantyre	d	14 44		14 57					15 14					15 28										15 44	
Hamilton West	d	14 47		15 00					15 17					15 31										15 47	
Hamilton Central	d	14 50		15 03					15 20					15 33										15 50	
Chatelherault	d	14 53							15 23															15 54	
Merryton	d	14 56							15 26															15 57	
Larkhall	a	15 00							15 30															16 00	
Airbles	d			15 08										15 38											
Uddingston	d					15 04												15 31	15 35						
Bellshill	d					15 09												15 35	15 40						
Motherwell	a			15 11		15 15						15 13	15 13	15 41		15 33			15 48						
	d					15 16								15 41		15 34	15 37								
Whifflet	a																15 45								
Coatbridge Central	a																15 48								
Shieldmuir	d					15 20																			
Holytown	d													15 48				15a39							
Wishaw	d					15 23								15 53											
Carluke	d					15 30								16 00		15a42									
Lanark	a					15 42								16 13											

A To Bristol Temple Meads
B To North Berwick
C To Cumbernauld
D To Edinburgh
E From Mallaig
b Glasgow Central High Level
c Helensburgh Upper
e Glasgow Queen St High Level

Table 226

Mondays to Saturdays

Helensburgh, Balloch, Dalmuir and Milngavie - Glasgow - Springburn, Airdrie, Bathgate and Edinburgh, Hamilton, Larkhall, Motherwell, Coatbridge and Lanark

Network Diagram - see first Page of Table 220

		SR	SR	SR	SR		SR SO	SR SX	SR	SR	SR A	SR SX	SR SO	SR	SR B		SR	SR	SR SX	SR	SR	SR	SR SO	SR SX	SR
Helensburgh Central	d						15 10	15 10													15 40				
Craigendoran	d						15 13	15 13													15 45				
Cardross	d						15 18	15 18													15 50				
Balloch	d		14 53											15 23											15 53
Alexandria	d		14 55											15 25											15 55
Renton	d		14 58											15 28											15 58
Dalreoch	d		15 01				15 23	15 23						15 31							15 55				16 01
Dumbarton Central	d		15 02				15 25	15 25						15 32							15 57				16 02
Dumbarton East	d		15 04				15 27	15 27						15 34							15 59				16 04
Bowling	d		15 09											15 39											16 09
Kilpatrick	d		15 12											15 42											16 12
Dalmuir	a		15 15				15 34	15 34						15 45							16 06				16 15
	d		15 16	15 23			15 35	15 35	15 30	15 38				15 46			15 53			16 01	16 07	16 08			16 16
Singer	d		15 18						15 32					15 48						16 03					16 18
Drumry	d		15 20						15 34					15 50						16 05					16 20
Drumchapel	d		15 23						15 37					15 53						16 08					16 23
Milngavie	d	15 12			15 27							15 42	15 42					15 57					16 12	16 12	
Hillfoot	d	15 15			15 30							15 45	15 45					16 00					16 15	16 15	
Bearsden	d	15 17			15 33							15 49	15 49					16 02					16 17	16 17	
Westerton	d	15 20	15 25		15 36				15 39			15 52	15 52	15 55				16 05		16 10			16 20	16 20	16 25
Anniesland	d	15 23	15 28		15 39				15 43			15 55	15 55	15 58				16 08		16 14			16 23	16 23	16 28
Clydebank	d			15 25						15 40							15 55					16 10			
Yoker	d			15 27						15 42							15 57					16 12			
Garscadden	d			15 31						15 46							16 00					16 16			
Scotstounhill	d			15 33						15 48							16 02					16 18			
Jordanhill	d			15 35						15 50							16 04					16 21			
Hyndland ■3	d	15 26	15 31	15 37	15 42		15 44	15 44	15 47	15 52		15 57	15 57	16 01			16 07	16 11		16 17	16 20	16 23	16 26	16 26	16 32
Partick ⛴	d	15 29	15 34	15 40	15 44		15 47	15 47	15 50	15 55		16 00	16 00	16 04			16 09	16 14		16 20	16 22	16 25	16 29	16 29	16 35
Exhibition Centre	d	15 32		15 43					15 53			16 03	16 03				16 12			16 24			16 32	16 32	
Anderston	d	15 34		15 45					15 55			16 05	16 05				16 15		16 23	16 26			16 34	16 34	
Glasgow Central LL ■15	a	15 37		15 46					15 56			16 07	16 07				16 16		16 24	16 27			16 35	16 35	
	d	15 37		15 47					15 57			16 08	16 08		16b18		16 17		16 25	16 28			16 37	16 37	
Argyle Street	d	15 39		15 48					15 59			16 10	16 10				16 18		16 26	16 30			16 38	16 38	
Charing Cross	d		15 38		15 48		15 54	15 54		15 59				16 08				16 19			16 26	16 29			16 39
Glasgow Queen St LL ■10 ⛴	a		15 40		15 50		15 56	15 56		16 01				16 12				16 21			16 28	16 31			16 41
	d		15 42		15 54		15 58	15 58		16 02				16 12				16 24			16 29	16 32			16 42
High Street	d		15 44		15 56		16 00	16 00		16 04				16 14				16 26			16 31	16 34			16 44
Bellgrove	d		15 46				16 02	16 02		16 06				16 16							16 33	16 36			16 46
Duke Street	d									16 08												16 38			
Alexandra Parade	d									16 09												16 39			
Barnhill	d									16 12												16 42			
Springburn	a									16 14												16 44			
Carntyne	d		15 49				16 05	16 05						16 19							16 36				16 49
Shettleston	d		15 52				16 08	16 08						16 22							16 39				16 52
Garrowhill	d		15 54				16 10	16 10						16 24							16 41				16 54
Easterhouse	d		15 57				16 13	16 13						16 27							16 44				16 57
Blairhill	d		16 01				16 17	16 17						16 31				16 38			16 48				17 01
Coatbridge Sunnyside	d		16 03		16 09		16 19	16 19						16 33				16 40			16 50				17 03
Coatdyke	d		16 06				16 22	16 22						16 36				16 43			16 53				17 06
Airdrie	d		16a09		16 14		16 25	16 25						16a39				16 46			16 56				17a09
Drumgelloch	d				16 17		16 28	16 28										16 49			16 59				
Caldercruix	d						16 32	16 32													17 03				
Blackridge	d						16 38	16 38													17 09				
Armadale	d						16 41	16 41													17 12				
Bathgate	a				16 29		16 45	16 45										17 02			17 16				
	d				16 30		16 47	16 47										17 02			17 17				
Livingston North	d				16 34		16 50	16 50										17 07			17 21				
Uphall	d				16 37		16 53	16 53										17 10			17 24				
Edinburgh Park	a				16 46		17 03	17 03										17 18			17 32				
Haymarket	a				16 51		17 07	17 13										17 22			17 37				
Edinburgh	a				16 58		17 14	17 19										17 28			17 43				
Bridgeton	d	15 42		15 51								16 13	16 13				16 21						16 41	16 41	
Dalmarnock	d	15 44		15 53								16 15	16 15				16 23						16 43	16 43	
Rutherglen	d	15 46		15 55					16 06			16 17	16 17				16 26		16 31	16 35			16 46	16 46	
Cambuslang	d	15 50		16 00								16 21	16 21				16 30						16 50	16 50	
Newton	d	15 54										16 25	16 25										16 54	16 54	
Blantyre	d	15 58							16 15			16 29	16 29							16 45			16 58	16 58	
Hamilton West	d	16 01							16 18			16 32	16 32							16 48			17 01	17 01	
Hamilton Central	d	16 03							16 20			16 34	16 34							16 50			17 03	17 03	
Chatelherault	d								16 24											16 54					
Merryton	d								16 27											16 57					
Larkhall	a								16 30											17 01					
Airbles	d	16 08										16 39	16 39										17 08	17 08	
Uddingston	d			16 04											16 30		16 34								
Bellshill	d			16 09											16 35		16 39								
Motherwell	a	16 11		16 15								16 42	16 42				16 49		16 46				17 11	17 11	
	d			16 16							16 37	16 46	16 42						16 46					17 13	
Whifflet	a										16 45	16 53												17 20	
Coatbridge Central	a										16 48	16 58												17 22	
Shieldmuir	d			16 20															16 50						
Holytown	d												16 48		16a39										
Wishaw	d			16 23									16 53						16 54						
Carluke	d			16 30									17 01						17 01						
Lanark	a			16 42									17 15						17 15						

A To Cumbernauld

B To Edinburgh

b Glasgow Central High Level

Helensburgh, Balloch, Dalmuir and Milngavie - Glasgow - Springburn, Airdrie, Bathgate and Edinburgh, Hamilton, Larkhall, Motherwell, Coatbridge and Lanark

Network Diagram - see first Page of Table 220

Station		SR SX	SR SO	SR SO	SR SX	SR	XC SO ◇1 B	XC SX ◇1 B	SR	SR	SR SO	SR SX	SR SX	SR	SR C	SR SO D	SR SX D	SR SO	SR SX	SR
Helensburgh Central	d					16 10														
Craigendoran	d					16 13														
Cardross	d					16 18														
Balloch	d													16 23						
Alexandria	d													16 25						
Renton	d													16 28						
Dalreoch	d					16 23								16 31						
Dumbarton Central	d					16 25								16 32						
Dumbarton East	d					16 27								16 34						
Bowling	d													16 39						
Kilpatrick	d													16 42						
Dalmuir	a					16 34								16 45						
	d	16 23	16 23			16 35			16 31	16 38				16 46				16 53	16 53	
Singer	d								16 33					16 48						
Drumry	d								16 35					16 50						
Drumchapel	d								16 38					16 53						
Milngavie	d			16 27	16 27						16 42		16 42							16 57
Hillfoot	d			16 30	16 30						16 45		16 45							17 00
Bearsden	d			16 32	16 32						16 47		16 47							17 02
Westerton	d			16 35	16 35				16 40		16 50		16 50	16 55						17 05
Anniesland	d			16 38	16 38				16 44		16 53		16 53	16 58						17 08
Clydebank	d	16 25	16 25							16 40								16 55	16 55	
Yoker	d	16 27	16 27							16 42								16 57	16 57	
Garscadden	d	16 31	16 31							16 46								17 01	17 01	
Scotstounhill	d	16 33	16 33							16 48								17 03	17 03	
Jordanhill	d	16 35	16 35							16 51								17 05	17 05	
Hyndland 3	d	16 37	16 37	16 41	16 41	16 44			16 47	16 53	16 56		16 56	17 01				17 07	17 07	17 11
Partick ⛴	d	16 40	16 40	16 44	16 44	16 47			16 50	16 55	16 59		16 59	17 04				17 10	17 10	17 14
Exhibition Centre	d	16 43	16 43						16 53		17 02		17 04					17 13	17 13	
Anderston	d	16 45	16 45						16 55		17 04	17 04	17 07					17 15	17 15	
Glasgow Central LL 15	a	16 46	16 46						16 56		17 05	17 05	17 09					17 16	17 17	
	d	16 47	16 47				16b52	16b52	16 57		17 07	17 07	17 11			17b18	17b20	17 17	17 18	
Argyle Street	d	16 48	16 48						16 59		17 08	17 09	17 13					17 19	17 21	
Charing Cross	d			16 49	16 49	16 54				16 59				17 08						17 19
Glasgow Queen St LL 10 ⛴	a			16 51	16 51	16 56				17 01				17 10						17 21
	d			16 54	16 54	16 58				17 02				17 12						17 24
High Street	d			16 56	16 56	17 00				17 04				17 14						17 26
Bellgrove	d					17 02				17 06				17 16						
Duke Street	d									17 08										
Alexandra Parade	d									17 09										
Barnhill	d									17 12										
Springburn	a									17 14										
Carntyne	d					17 06								17 19						
Shettleston	d					17 08								17 22						
Garrowhill	d					17 11								17 24						
Easterhouse	d					17 13								17 27						
Blairhill	d			17 08	17 08	17 17								17 31						17 39
Coatbridge Sunnyside	d			17 10	17 10	17 20								17 33						17 41
Coatdyke	d			17 13	17 13	17 22								17 36						17 44
Airdrie	d			17 16	17 16	17 25								17a39						17 47
Drumgelloch	d			17 19	17 19	17 28														17 50
Caldercruix	d					17 32														
Blackridge	d					17 38														
Armadale	d					17 42														
Bathgate	a			17 31	17 31	17 46														18 02
	d			17 32	17 32	17 46														18 04
Livingston North	d			17 36	17 36	17 50														18 08
Uphall	d			17 39	17 39	17 53														18 11
Edinburgh Park	a			17 47	17 47	18 01														18 17
Haymarket	a			17 52	17 56	18 06														18 25
Edinburgh	a			17 57	18 04	18 12														18 32
Bridgeton	d	16 51	16 51								17 11	17 12	17 16					17 22	17 24	
Dalmarnock	d	16 53	16 53								17 13		17 18					17 24	17 26	
Rutherglen	d	16 56	16 56						17 04		17 16		17 21					17 26	17 28	
Cambuslang	d	17 00	17 00						17 08		17 20		17 25					17 31	17 32	
Newton	d										17 23		17 29						17 36	
Blantyre	d								17 14		17 27		17 33						17 40	
Hamilton West	d								17 17		17 30		17 36						17 43	
Hamilton Central	d								17 20		17 33		17 38						17 50	
Chatelherault	d								17 23				17 42							
Merryton	d								17 26				17 45							
Larkhall	a								17 30				17 48							
Airbles	d										17 38								17 55	
Uddingston	d	17 04	17 04									17 20				17 30		17 35		
Bellshill	d	17 09	17 09													17 34	17 34	17 40		
Motherwell	a	17 16	17 16				17 13	17 13			17 40	17 25						17 48	17 57	
	d		17 17								17 41	17 26			17 37				17 58	
Whifflet	a														17 45				18 05	
Coatbridge Central	a														17 48				18 07	
Shieldmuir	d		17 20									17 29								
Holytown	d										17 48					17a39	17a39			
Wishaw	d		17 24								17 53	17 34								
Carluke	d		17 30								18 00	17 41								
Lanark	a		17 42								18 12	17 54								

A To London Euston
B To Birmingham New Street
C To Cumbernauld
D To Edinburgh
b Glasgow Central High Level

Table 226

Mondays to Saturdays

Helensburgh, Balloch, Dalmuir and Milngavie - Glasgow - Springburn, Airdrie, Bathgate and Edinburgh, Hamilton, Larkhall, Motherwell, Coatbridge and Lanark

Network Diagram - see first Page of Table 220

		SR	SR SO	SR SX A	SR	SR SX	SR SO	SR SX	SR	SR SX	SR SO	SR	SR	SR	SR	SR B	SR	SR	SR SX C	SR SO C	SR SX	SR SO	SR
Helensburgh Central	d	16 40											17 10										
Craigendoran	d	16 43											17 13										
Cardross	d	16 48											17 18										
Balloch	d								16 53									17 23					
Alexandria	d								16 55									17 25					
Renton	d								16 58									17 28					
Dalreoch	d	16 53							17 01				17 23					17 31					
Dumbarton Central	d	16 55							17 02				17 25					17 32					
Dumbarton East	d	16 57							17 04				17 27					17 34					
Bowling	d								17 09									17 39					
Kilpatrick	d								17 12									17 42					
Dalmuir	a	17 06							17 15				17 34					17 45					
	d	17 06	17 01	17 01	17 08				17 16	17 23	17 23		17 35	17 31	17 38			17 46			17 53	17 53	
Singer	d		17 03	17 03					17 18					17 33				17 48					
Drumry	d		17 05	17 05					17 20					17 35				17 50					
Drumchapel	d		17 08	17 08					17 23					17 38				17 53					
Milngavie	d						17 13	17 13				17 28					17 42						17 57
Hillfoot	d						17 16	17 16				17 31					17 45						18 00
Bearsden	d						17 18	17 18				17 33					17 47						18 02
Westerton	d		17 10	17 10			17 21	17 21	17 25			17 36		17 40			17 50	17 55					18 05
Anniesland	d		17 13	17 14			17 24	17 24	17 28			17 39		17 44			17 53	17 58					18 08
Clydebank	d				17 10					17 25	17 25				17 40						17 55	17 55	
Yoker	d				17 12					17 27	17 27				17 42						17 57	17 57	
Garscadden	d				17 16					17 31	17 31				17 46						18 00	18 00	
Scotstounhill	d				17 18					17 33	17 33				17 48						18 02	18 02	
Jordanhill	d				17 20					17 35	17 35				17 50						18 04	18 04	
Hyndland 3	d	17 14	17 17	17 17	17 22		17 26	17 26	17 31	17 37	17 37	17 41	17 44	17 47	17 52		17 56	18 01			18 06	18 06	18 11
Partick ⛴	d	17 17	17 20	17 20	17 25		17 29	17 29	17 34	17 40	17 40	17 44	17 47	17 50	17 55		17 59	18 04			18 08	18 08	18 14
Exhibition Centre	d		17 23	17 23			17 32	17 34		17 43	17 43			17 53			18 02				18 11	18 11	
Anderston	d		17 25	17 25		17 34	17 34	17 37		17 45	17 45			17 55			18 04				18 13	18 13	
Glasgow Central LL 15	a		17 26	17 26		17 35	17 35	17 39		17 46	17 46			17 56			18 05				18 15	18 15	
	d		17 27	17 27		17 36	17 37	17 39		17 47	17 47			17 57			18 07		18b14	18b18	18 15	18 15	
Argyle Street	d		17 28	17 28		17 38	17 38	17 40		17 48	17 48			17 59			18 08				18 17	18 17	
Charing Cross	d	17 24			17 29				17 38			17 49	17 54		17 59			18 08					18 18
Glasgow Queen St LL 10 ⛴	a	17 26			17 31				17 40			17 51	17 56		18 01			18 10					18 20
	d	17 28			17 32				17 42			17 54	17 58		18 02			18 12					18 23
High Street	d	17 30			17 34				17 44			17 56	18 00		18 04			18 14					18 26
Bellgrove	d	17 32			17 36				17 46				18 02		18 06			18 16					18 28
Duke Street	d				17 38										18 08								
Alexandra Parade	d				17 39										18 09								
Barnhill	d				17 42										18 12								
Springburn	a				17 44										18 14								
Carntyne	d	17 36							17 49				18 06					18 19					
Shettleston	d	17 38							17 52				18 08					18 22					
Garrowhill	d	17 41							17 54				18 11					18 24					
Easterhouse	d	17 43							17 57				18 13					18 27					
Blairhill	d	17 47							18 01				18 17					18 31					
Coatbridge Sunnyside	d	17 50							18 03			18 09	18 20					18 33					18 39
Coatdyke	d	17 52							18 06				18 22					18 36					
Airdrie	d	17 55							18a09			18 14	18 25					18a39					18 44
Drumgelloch	d	17 58										18 17	18 28										18 47
Caldercruix	d	18 02											18 32										
Blackridge	d	18 08											18 38										
Armadale	d	18 12											18 42										
Bathgate	a	18 16										18 30	18 46										19 00
	d	18 17										18 31	18 47										19 01
Livingston North	d	18 20										18 35	18 50										19 06
Uphall	d	18 23										18 38	18 53										19 09
Edinburgh Park	a	18 32										18 47	19 02										19 17
Haymarket	a	18 37										18 52	19 07										19 22
Edinburgh	a	18 43										18 58	19 14										19 28
Bridgeton	d			17 31			17 41	17 44		17 51	17 51						18 11				18 20	18 20	
Dalmarnock	d			17 33			17 43	17 46		17 53	17 53						18 13				18 22	18 22	
Rutherglen	d		17 34	17 37		17 43	17 46	17 49		17 56	17 56			18 04			18 16				18 23	18 25	
Cambuslang	d			17 41			17 50	17 53		18 00	18 00						18 20		18 23	18 27	18 28	18 30	
Newton	d						17 54	17 56									18 23						
Blantyre	d		17 44				17 58	18 00						18 14			18 27						
Hamilton West	d		17 47				18 01	18 03						18 17			18 30						
Hamilton Central	d		17 49				18 03	18 06						18 20			18 33						
Chatelherault	d		17 53					18 09						18 23									
Merryton	d		17 56					18 12						18 26									
Larkhall	a		18 00					18 15						18 30									
Airbles	d						18 08										18 38						
Uddingston	d			17 45						18 04	18 04								18 29	18 29	18 33	18 34	
Bellshill	d			17 50						18 09	18 09								18 34	18 34	18 37	18 39	
Motherwell	a			18 01		17 57	18 11			18 16	18 16						18 40				18 44	18 48	
	d			18 02		17 58					18 16					18 37	18 41						
Whifflet	a															18 45							
Coatbridge Central	a															18 48							
Shieldmuir	d			18 05		18 01					18 20												
Holytown	d																18 48		18a38	18a38			
Wishaw	d			18 09		18 05					18 23						18 54						
Carluke	d			18a15		18 11					18 30						19 01						
Lanark	a					18 22					18 42						19 14						

A To Carstairs
B To Cumbernauld
C To Edinburgh
b Glasgow Central High Level

Helensburgh, Balloch, Dalmuir and Milngavie - Glasgow - Springburn, Airdrie, Bathgate and Edinburgh, Hamilton, Larkhall, Motherwell, Coatbridge and Lanark

Network Diagram - see first Page of Table 220

		SR	SR		SR	SR	SR	SR	XC SO ◇1 A	SR	SR	XC SX ◇1 B	SR C		SR	SR	SR SO ◇ D 🚌	SR SX A	SR SO A	SR	SR	SR	SR		SR
Helensburgh Central	d	17 40									18 10						18c34					18 40			
Craigendoran	d	17 43									18 13											18 43			
Cardross	d	17 48									18 18											18 48			
Balloch	d						17 53									18 23									18 53
Alexandria	d						17 55									18 25									18 55
Renton	d						17 58									18 29									18 58
Dalreoch	d	17 53					18 01				18 23					18 32						18 53			19 01
Dumbarton Central	d	17 55					18 02				18 25					18 33	18 45					18 55			19 02
Dumbarton East	d	17 57					18 04				18 27					18 35						18 57			19 04
Bowling	d						18 09									18 40									19 09
Kilpatrick	d						18 12									18 43									19 12
Dalmuir	a	18 04					18 15				18 34					18 46	18 56					19 05			19 15
	d	18 05	18 01		18 07		18 16	18 23		18 31	18 35					18 47	18 56				19 01	19 05			19 16
Singer	d		18 03				18 18			18 33						18 49					19 03				19 18
Drumry	d		18 05				18 20			18 35						18 51					19 05				19 20
Drumchapel	d		18 08				18 23			18 38						18 54					19 08				19 23
Milngavie	d					18 12									18 42								19 12		
Hillfoot	d					18 15									18 45								19 15		
Bearsden	d					18 17									18 47								19 17		
Westerton	d		18 10			18 20	18 25			18 40					18 50	18 56					19 10		19 20		19 25
Anniesland	d		18 14			18 23	18 28			18 44					18 53	19 00					19 14		19 23		19 30
Clydebank	d				18 09			18 25			18 37											19 07			
Yoker	d				18 11			18 27			18 39											19 09			
Garscadden	d				18 14			18 31			18 43											19 13			
Scotstounhill	d				18 16			18 33			18 45											19 15			
Jordanhill	d				18 18			18 35			18 47											19 17			
Hyndland 3	d	18 14	18 17		18 22	18 26	18 31	18 37		18 47	18 51				18 56	19 03					19 17	19 21	19 25		19 33
Partick ⛴	d	18 17	18 20		18 25	18 29	18 34	18 40		18 50	18 53				18 59	19 05				19 11	19 20	19 23	19 29		19 35
Exhibition Centre	d		18 23			18 32		18 43		18 53					19 02					19 14	19 23		19 32		
Anderston	d		18 25			18 34		18 45		18 55					19 04					19 16	19 25		19 34		
Glasgow Central LL 15	a		18 26			18 35		18 46		18 56					19 05					19 17	19 26		19 35		
	d		18 27			18 37		18 47	18b52	18 57		18b59			19 07			19b15	19b18	19 18	19 27		19 37		
Argyle Street	d		18 29			18 38		18 48		18 59					19 08					19 19	19 29		19 39		
Charing Cross	d	18 24			18 29		18 38				18 57					19 09						19 27			19 39
Glasgow Queen St LL 10 ⛴	a	18 26			18 31		18 40				18 59					19 11	19e20					19 29			19 41
	d	18 28			18 32		18 45				19 00					19 14						19 30			19 44
High Street	d	18 30			18 34		18 47				19 02					19 16						19 32			19 46
Bellgrove	d	18 32			18 36		18 49				19 04					19 19						19 34			19 49
Duke Street	d				18 38		18 51									19 21									19 51
Alexandra Parade	d				18 39		18 52									19 22									19 52
Barnhill	d				18 42		18 55									19 25									19 55
Springburn	a				18 44		18 57									19 27									19 57
Carntyne	d	18 36									19 07											19 37			
Shettleston	d	18 38									19 10											19 40			
Garrowhill	d	18 41									19 12											19 42			
Easterhouse	d	18 43									19 15											19 45			
Blairhill	d	18 47									19 19											19 49			
Coatbridge Sunnyside	d	18 50									19 21											19 51			
Coatdyke	d	18 52									19 24											19 54			
Airdrie	d	18 55									19 27											19 57			
Drumgelloch	d	18 58									19 30											20 00			
Caldercruix	d	19 02									19 34											20 04			
Blackridge	d	19 08									19 40											20 10			
Armadale	d	19 12									19 43											20 13			
Bathgate	a	19 16									19 47											20 17			
	d	19 17									19 49											20 18			
Livingston North	d	19 20									19 53											20 23			
Uphall	d	19 23									19 56											20 26			
Edinburgh Park	a	19 32									20 04											20 34			
Haymarket	a	19 37									20 09											20 38			
Edinburgh	a	19 45									20 14											20 43			
Bridgeton	d					18 41		18 51							19 11					19 22			19 42		
Dalmarnock	d					18 43		18 53							19 13					19 24			19 44		
Rutherglen	d		18 36			18 46		18 56		19 06					19 16					19 26	19 34		19 46		
Cambuslang	d					18 50		19 00							19 20					19 31			19 50		
Newton	d					18 53									19 23								19 54		
Blantyre	d		18 44			18 58				19 15					19 27						19 44		19 58		
Hamilton West	d		18 47			19 01				19 18					19 30						19 47		20 01		
Hamilton Central	d		18 50			19 03				19 20					19 33						19 49		20 04		
Chatelherault	d		18 53							19 24											19 53				
Merryton	d		18 56							19 27											19 56				
Larkhall	a		19 00							19 30											20 00				
Airbles	d					19 08									19 38								20 09		
Uddingston	d							19 04										19 30	19 30	19 35					
Bellshill	d							19 09										19 35	19 35	19 40					
Motherwell	a					19 11		19 18	19 13			19 14			19 39					19 48			20 12		
	d							19 18					19 37		19 40										
Whifflet	a												19 45												
Coatbridge Central	a												19 48												
Shieldmuir	d							19 20																	
Holytown	d														19 50			19a39	19a39						
Wishaw	d							19 23							19 55										
Carluke	d							19 30							20 03										
Lanark	a							19 42							20 15										

A To Edinburgh
B To Newcastle
C To Cumbernauld
D from 24 March. From Oban
b Glasgow Central High Level
c Helensburgh Upper
e Glasgow Queen St High Level

Table 226

Mondays to Saturdays

Helensburgh, Balloch, Dalmuir and Milngavie - Glasgow - Springburn, Airdrie, Bathgate and Edinburgh, Hamilton, Larkhall, Motherwell, Coatbridge and Lanark

Network Diagram - see first Page of Table 220

		SR	SR SX	SR	SR	SR	SR	SR	SR	SR	SR	SR	SR	SR	SR	SR	XC SX ◇1	SR	SR	SR	SR	SR	SR
			A			B											A	B			A		
Helensburgh Central	d				19 10						19 40					20 10							
Craigendoran	d				19 13						19 43					20 13							
Cardross	d				19 18						19 48					20 18							
Balloch	d							19 23					19 53							20 23			
Alexandria	d							19 25					19 55							20 25			
Renton	d							19 28					19 58							20 28			
Dalreoch	d				19 23			19 31			19 53		20 01			20 23				20 31			
Dumbarton Central	d				19 25			19 32			19 55		20 02			20 25				20 32			
Dumbarton East	d				19 27			19 34			19 57		20 04			20 27				20 34			
Bowling	d							19 39					20 09							20 39			
Kilpatrick	d							19 42					20 12							20 42			
Dalmuir	a				19 35			19 45			20 05		20 15			20 35				20 45			
	d			19 31	19 35			19 46		20 01	20 05		20 16		20 31	20 35				20 46			21 00
Singer	d			19 33				19 48		20 03			20 18		20 33					20 48			21 02
Drumry	d			19 35				19 50		20 05			20 20		20 35					20 50			21 04
Drumchapel	d			19 38				19 53		20 08			20 23		20 38					20 53			21 07
Milngavie	d						19 42					20 12							20 42				
Hillfoot	d						19 45					20 15							20 45				
Bearsden	d						19 47					20 17							20 47				
Westerton	d			19 40			19 50	19 55		20 10		20 20	20 25		20 40				20 50	20 55			21 09
Anniesland	d			19 44			19 54	19 59		20 14		20 22	20 30		20 44				20 53	20 59			21 14
Clydebank	d				19 37						20 07					20 37							
Yoker	d				19 39						20 09					20 39							
Garscadden	d				19 43						20 13					20 43							
Scotstounhill	d				19 45						20 15					20 45							
Jordanhill	d				19 47						20 17					20 47							
Hyndland 3	d			19 47	19 51		19 56	20 02		20 17	20 21	20 25	20 33		20 47	20 51			20 56	21 02			21 17
Partick	d	19 40		19 50	19 53		19 59	20 04	20 10	20 20	20 23	20 28	20 35	20 40	20 50	20 53			20 59	21 04		21 10	21 20
Exhibition Centre	d	19 43		19 53			20 02		20 13	20 23		20 32		20 43	20 53				21 02			21 13	21 23
Anderston	d	19 45		19 55			20 04		20 15	20 25		20 34		20 45	20 55				21 04			21 15	21 25
Glasgow Central LL 15	a	19 46		19 56			20 05		20 16	20 26		20 35		20 46	20 56				21 05			21 16	21 26
	d	19 47	19b49	19 57			20 07		20 17	20 27		20 37		20 47	20 57		21b05		21 07		21b18	21 17	21 27
Argyle Street	d	19 49		19 59			20 08		20 19	20 29		20 38		20 49	20 59				21 08			21 18	21 29
Charing Cross	d				19 57			20 08			20 27		20 40			20 57				21 08			
Glasgow Queen St LL 10	a				19 59			20 10			20 29		20 42			20 59				21 11			
	d				20 00			20 14			20 30		20 44			21 00				21 14			
High Street	d				20 02			20 16			20 32		20 46			21 02				21 16			
Bellgrove	d				20 04			20 19			20 34		20 49			21 04				21 19			
Duke Street	d							20 21					20 51							21 21			
Alexandra Parade	d							20 22					20 52							21 22			
Barnhill	d							20 25					20 55							21 25			
Springburn	a							20 27					20 57							21 27			
Carntyne	d				20 07						20 37					21 07							
Shettleston	d				20 10						20 40					21 10							
Garrowhill	d				20 12						20 42					21 12							
Easterhouse	d				20 15						20 45					21 15							
Blairhill	d				20 19						20 49					21 19							
Coatbridge Sunnyside	d				20 21						20 51					21 21							
Coatdyke	d				20 24						20 54					21 24							
Airdrie	d				20 27						20 57					21 27							
Drumgelloch	d				20 30						21 00					21 30							
Caldercruix	d				20 34						21 04					21 34							
Blackridge	d				20 40						21 10					21 40							
Armadale	d				20 43						21 13					21 43							
Bathgate	a				20 47						21 17					21 47							
	d				20 49						21 19					21 49							
Livingston North	d				20 53						21 23					21 53							
Uphall	d				20 56						21 26					21 56							
Edinburgh Park	a				21 04						21 34					22 04							
Haymarket	a				21 09						21 39					22 09							
Edinburgh	a				21 14						21 44					22 14							
Bridgeton	d	19 52					20 11		20 22			20 41		20 52					21 11			21 21	
Dalmarnock	d	19 54					20 13		20 24			20 43		20 54					21 13			21 23	
Rutherglen	d	19 56		20 04			20 16		20 26	20 34		20 46		20 55	21 04				21 16			21 26	21 34
Cambuslang	d	20 01					20 20		20 31			20 50		21 00					21 20			21 30	
Newton	d						20 23					20 54							21 23				
Blantyre	d			20 14			20 27			20 44		20 58			21 14				21 27				21 44
Hamilton West	d			20 17			20 30			20 47		21 01			21 17				21 30				21 47
Hamilton Central	d			20 20			20 33			20 49		21 03			21 20				21 33				21 50
Chatelherault	d			20 23						20 53					21 23								21 53
Merryton	d			20 26						20 56					21 26								21 56
Larkhall	a			20 30						21 00					21 30								22 00
Airbles	d						20 37					21 08							21 37				
Uddingston	d	20 05							20 35					21 05							21 30	21 34	
Bellshill	d	20 10							20 40					21 09							21 36	21 39	
Motherwell	a	20 16	20 05				20 41		20 48			21 11		21 15			21 22		21 41			21 48	
	d	20 16	20 06			20 37	20 41							21 16				21 37	21 41				
Whifflet	a					20 45												21 45					
Coatbridge Central	a					20 48												21 48					
Shieldmuir	d	20 20												21 19									
Holytown	d						20 48												21 48		21a40		
Wishaw	d	20 23	20 12				20 53							21 23					21 53				
Carluke	d	20 31	20a18				21 00							21 29					22 00				
Lanark	a	20 42					21 12							21 43					22 13				

A To Edinburgh

B To Cumbernauld

b Glasgow Central High Level

Table 226

Mondays to Saturdays

Helensburgh, Balloch, Dalmuir and Milngavie - Glasgow - Springburn, Airdrie, Bathgate and Edinburgh, Hamilton, Larkhall, Motherwell, Coatbridge and Lanark

Network Diagram - see first Page of Table 220

		SR	SR ◇ A	SR	SR	SR	SR	SR	SR	SR	SR	SR	SR	SR	SR	SR	SR	SR	SR B	SR	SR	SR	SR
Helensburgh Central	d	20 40	20b40					21 10					21 40					22 10					
Craigendoran	d	20 43						21 13					21 43					22 13					
Cardross	d	20 48						21 18					21 48					22 18					
Balloch	d				20 53					21 23					21 53						22 23		
Alexandria	d				20 55					21 25					21 55						22 25		
Renton	d				20 59					21 28					21 58						22 28		
Dalreoch	d	20 53			21 01			21 23		21 31			21 53		22 01			22 23			22 31		
Dumbarton Central	d	20 55	21 00		21 02			21 25		21 32			21 55		22 02			22 25			22 32		
Dumbarton East	d	20 57			21 04			21 27		21 34			21 57		22 04			22 27			22 34		
Bowling	d				21 09					21 39					22 09						22 39		
Kilpatrick	d				21 12					21 42					22 12						22 42		
Dalmuir	a	21 04	21 09		21 15			21 35		21 45			22 05		22 15			22 35			22 45		
	d	21 05	21 09		21 16		21 31	21 35		21 46		22 01	22 05		22 16		22 31	22 35			22 46		23 01
Singer	d				21 18		21 33			21 48		22 03			22 18		22 33				22 48		23 03
Drumry	d				21 20		21 35			21 50		22 05			22 20		22 35				22 50		23 05
Drumchapel	d				21 23		21 38			21 53		22 08			22 23		22 38				22 53		23 08
Milngavie	d			21 12					21 42					22 12						22 42			
Hillfoot	d			21 15					21 45					22 15						22 45			
Bearsden	d			21 17					21 47					22 17						22 47			
Westerton	d			21 20	21 26		21 40		21 50	21 55		22 10		22 20	22 25		22 40			22 50	22 55		23 10
Anniesland	d			21 23	21 29		21 44		21 53	22 00		22 14		22 23	22 30		22 44			22 53	23 00		23 14
Clydebank	d	21 07						21 37					22 07					22 37					
Yoker	d	21 09						21 39					22 09					22 39					
Garscadden	d	21 13						21 43					22 13					22 43					
Scotstounhill	d	21 15						21 45					22 15					22 45					
Jordanhill	d	21 17						21 47					22 17					22 47					
Hyndland 3	d	21 21		21 27	21 32		21 47	21 51	21 57	22 03		22 17	22 21	22 26	22 33		22 47	22 51		22 56	23 03		23 17
Partick ⛴	d	21 23		21 30	21 34	21 40	21 50	21 53	21 59	22 05	22 10	22 20	22 23	22 29	22 35	22 40	22 50	22 53		22 59	23 05	23 10	23 20
Exhibition Centre	d			21 33		21 43	21 53		22 02		22 13	22 23		22 32		22 43	22 53			23 02		23 13	23 23
Anderston	d			21 35		21 45	21 55		22 04		22 15	22 25		22 34		22 45	22 55			23 04		23 15	23 25
Glasgow Central LL 15	a			21 37		21 46	21 56		22 05		22 16	22 26		22 35		22 46	22 56			23 05		23 16	23 26
	d			21 37		21 47	21 57		22 07		22 17	22 29		22 37		22 47	22 57		23e06	23 07		23 17	23 27
Argyle Street	d			21 39		21 49	21 59		22 08		22 19	22 31		22 39		22 49	22 59			23 09		23 19	23 29
Charing Cross	d	21 27			21 39			21 57		22 10			22 27		22 40			22 57			23 10		
Glasgow Queen St LL 10 ⛴	a	21 29	21c31		21 42			21 59		22 12			22 29		22 42			22 59			23 12		
	d	21 30			21 44			22 00		22 14			22 30		22 44			23 00			23 14		
High Street	d	21 32			21 46			22 02		22 16			22 32		22 46			23 02			23 16		
Bellgrove	d	21 34			21 49			22 04		22 19			22 34		22 49			23 04			23 19		
Duke Street	d				21 51					22 21					22 51						23 21		
Alexandra Parade	d				21 52					22 22					22 52						23 22		
Barnhill	d				21 55					22 25					22 55						23 25		
Springburn	a				21 57					22 27					22 57						23 27		
Carntyne	d	21 37						22 07					22 37					23 07					
Shettleston	d	21 40						22 10					22 40					23 10					
Garrowhill	d	21 42						22 12					22 42					23 12					
Easterhouse	d	21 45						22 15					22 45					23 15					
Blairhill	d	21 49						22 19					22 49					23 19					
Coatbridge Sunnyside	d	21 51						22 21					22 51					23 21					
Coatdyke	d	21 54						22 24					22 54					23 24					
Airdrie	d	21 57						22 27					22 57					23 27					
Drumgelloch	d	22 00						22 30					23 00					23 30					
Caldercruix	d	22 04						22 34					23 04					23 34					
Blackridge	d	22 10						22 40					23 10					23 40					
Armadale	d	22 13						22 43					23 13					23 43					
Bathgate	a	22 17						22 47					23 17					23 47					
	d	22 19						22 49					23 17										
Livingston North	d	22 23						22 53					23 22										
Uphall	d	22 26						22 56					23 25										
Edinburgh Park	a	22 34						23 05					23 33										
Haymarket	a	22 39						23 09					23 38										
Edinburgh	a	22 44						23 14					23 43										
Bridgeton	d			21 42		21 52			22 11		22 22			22 42		22 52				23 12		23 22	
Dalmarnock	d			21 44		21 54			22 13		22 24			22 44		22 54				23 14		23 24	
Rutherglen	d			21 47		21 56	22 04		22 16		22 26	22 34		22 46		22 56	23 04			23 16		23 26	23 34
Cambuslang	d			21 51		22 01			22 20		22 31			22 50		23 01			23 15	23 20		23 31	
Newton	d			21 54					22 23					22 54						23 24			
Blantyre	d			21 58			22 14		22 28			22 44		22 58			23 14			23 28			23 44
Hamilton West	d			22 01			22 17		22 31			22 47		23 01			23 17			23 31			23 47
Hamilton Central	d			22 04			22 20		22 33			22 49		23 03			23 20			23 33			23 50
Chatelherault	d						22 23					22 53					23 23						23 53
Merryton	d						22 26					22 56					23 26						23 56
Larkhall	a						22 30					23 00					23 29						23 59
Airbles	d			22 09					22 38					23 08						23 38			
Uddingston	d					22 05					22 35					23 05			23 20			23 35	
Bellshill	d					22 10					22 40					23 10			23 25			23 40	
Motherwell	a			22 11		22 16			22 41		22 49			23 11		23 16				23 41		23 46	
	d					22 16			22 41							23 16							
Whifflet	a								22 49														
Coatbridge Central	a								22 51														
Shieldmuir	d					22 20										23 20							
Holytown	d																		23a29				
Wishaw	d					22 23										23 23							
Carluke	d					22 30										23 30							
Lanark	a					22 42										23 42							

A From Mallaig
B To Edinburgh
b Helensburgh Upper
c Glasgow Queen St High Level
e Glasgow Central High Level

Table 226

Mondays to Saturdays

Helensburgh, Balloch, Dalmuir and Milngavie - Glasgow - Springburn, Airdrie, Bathgate and Edinburgh, Hamilton, Larkhall, Motherwell, Coatbridge and Lanark

Network Diagram - see first Page of Table 220

		SR	SR FX	SR FO	SR R A	SR FO	SR FO	SR	SR	SR FO	SR SX R B
Helensburgh Central	d	22 40						23 10			23c24
Craigendoran	d	22 43						23 13			
Cardross	d	22 48						23 18			
Balloch	d		22 53	22 53					23 23		
Alexandria	d		22 55	22 55					23 25		
Renton	d		22 58	22 58					23 28		
Dalreoch	d	22 53	23 01	23 01				23 23	23 31		
Dumbarton Central	d	22 55	23 02	23 02				23 25	23 32		
Dumbarton East	d	22 57	23 04	23 04				23 27	23 34		
Bowling	d		23 09	23 09					23 39		
Kilpatrick	d		23 12	23 12					23 42		
Dalmuir	a	23 05	23 15	23 15				23 35	23 45		23 49
	d	23 05	23 16	23 16			23 31	23 35			23 51
Singer	d		23 18	23 18			23 33				
Drumry	d		23 20	23 20			23 35				
Drumchapel	d		23 23	23 23			23 38				
Milngavie	d									23 42	
Hillfoot	d									23 45	
Bearsden	d									23 47	
Westerton	d		23 25	23 25			23 40			23 50	23 56
Anniesland	d		23 28	23 28			23 44			23 53	
Clydebank	d	23 07						23 37			
Yoker	d	23 09						23 39			
Garscadden	d	23 13						23 43			
Scotstounhill	d	23 15						23 45			
Jordanhill	d	23 17						23 47			
Hyndland 3	d	23 21	23 31	23 31			23 47	23 49		23 56	
Partick	d	23 23	23 34	23 34		23 40	23 50	23 52		23 59	
Exhibition Centre	d					23 43	23 53			00 02	
Anderston	d					23 45	23 55			00 04	
Glasgow Central LL 15	a					23 46	23 56			00 05	
	d				23b40	23 47	23 57			00 07	
Argyle Street	d					23 49	23 59			00 09	
Charing Cross	d	23 27	23 38	23 38				23 56			
Glasgow Queen St LL 10	a	23 29	23 40	23 40				23 59			
	d	23 30	23 44	23 44				23 59			
High Street	d	23 32	23 46	23 46				00 02			
Bellgrove	d	23 34	23 49	23 49				00 04			
Duke Street	d			23 51							
Alexandra Parade	d			23 52							
Barnhill	d			23 55							
Springburn	a			23 57							
Carntyne	d	23 37	23 52					00 07			
Shettleston	d	23 40	23 55					00 10			
Garrowhill	d	23 42	23 57					00 12			
Easterhouse	d	23 45	23 59					00 15			
Blairhill	d	23 49	00 04					00 19			
Coatbridge Sunnyside	d	23 51	00 06					00 21			
Coatdyke	d	23 54	00 09					00 24			
Airdrie	d	23 57	00a12					00a27			
Drumgelloch	d	23 59									
Caldercruix	d	00 03									
Blackridge	d	00 09									
Armadale	d	00 13									
Bathgate	a	00 17									
	d										
Livingston North	d										
Uphall	d										
Edinburgh Park	a										
Haymarket	a										
Edinburgh	a										00 50
Bridgeton	d					23 52				00 12	
Dalmarnock	d					23 54				00 14	
Rutherglen	d					23 57	00 04			00 16	
Cambuslang	d					00 01				00 20	
Newton	d									00 24	
Blantyre	d						00 15			00 28	
Hamilton West	d						00 18			00 31	
Hamilton Central	d						00 21			00 33	
Chatelherault	d						00 24				
Merryton	d						00 27				
Larkhall	a						00 30				
Airbles	d									00 38	
Uddingston	d					00 05					
Bellshill	d					00 10					
Motherwell	a					00 16				00 41	
	d					00 16					
Whifflet	a										
Coatbridge Central	a										
Shieldmuir	d					00 20					
Holytown	d										
Wishaw	d					00 23					
Carluke	d					00 30					
Lanark	a					00 42					

A To London Euston
B From Fort William
b Glasgow Central High Level
c Helensburgh Upper

Table 226

Sundays

Helensburgh, Balloch, Dalmuir and Milngavie - Glasgow - Springburn, Airdrie, Bathgate and Edinburgh, Hamilton, Larkhall, Motherwell, Coatbridge and Lanark

Network Diagram - see first Page of Table 220

		SR A	SR A	SR A	SR	SR	SR	SR	SR	SR		SR		SR		SR		SR	SR	SR			SR		SR
Helensburgh Central	d	22p40		23p10				07 55				08 25							08 55						09 25
Craigendoran	d	22p43		23p13				07 58				08 28							08 58						09 28
Cardross	d	22p48		23p18				08 03				08 33							09 03						09 33
Balloch	d		22p53						08 09					08 39						09 09					
Alexandria	d		22p55						08 11					08 41						09 11					
Renton	d		22p58						08 14					08 44						09 14					
Dalreoch	d	22p53	23p01	23p23				08 08	08 17			08 38		08 47					09 08	09 17					09 38
Dumbarton Central	d	22p55	23p02	23p25				08 10	08 18			08 40		08 48					09 10	09 18					09 40
Dumbarton East	d	22p57	23p04	23p27				08 12	08 20			08 42		08 50					09 12	09 20					09 42
Bowling	d		23p09						08 25					08 55						09 25					
Kilpatrick	d		23p12						08 28					08 58						09 28					
Dalmuir	a	23p05	23p15	23p35				08 19	08 31			08 49		09 01					09 19	09 31					09 49
	d	23p05	23p16	23p35		07 40	08 01	08 20	08 31			08 50		09 01					09 20	09 31					09 50
Singer	d		23p18			07 42		08 22				08 52							09 22						09 52
Drumry	d		23p20			07 45		08 25				08 55							09 25						09 55
Drumchapel	d		23p23			07 47		08 27				08 57							09 27						09 57
Milngavie	d															09 11							09 41		
Hillfoot	d															09 14							09 44		
Bearsden	d															09 16							09 46		
Westerton	d		23p25			07 50		08 30				09 00				09 19			09 30				09 49		10 00
Anniesland	d		23p28			07 53		08 33				09 03				09 22			09 33				09 52		10 03
Clydebank	d	23p07		23p37			08 03		08 33					09 03						09 33					
Yoker	d	23p09		23p39			08 05		08 35					09 05						09 35					
Garscadden	d	23p13		23p43			08 09		08 39					09 09						09 39					
Scotstounhill	d	23p15		23p45			08 11		08 41					09 11						09 41					
Jordanhill	d	23p17		23p47			08 13		08 43					09 13						09 43					
Hyndland 8	d	23p21	23p31	23p49		07 55	08 15	08 35	08 45	08 55		09 05		09 15		09 25			09 35	09 45			09 55		10 05
Partick	d	23p23	23p34	23p52		07 58	08 18	08 38	08 48	08 58		09 08		09 18		09 28		09 36	09 38	09 48			09 58		10 08
Exhibition Centre	d						08 21		08 51	09 01				09 21		09 31		09 39		09 51			10 01		
Anderston	d																								
Glasgow Central LL 15	a						08 23		08 53	09 03				09 23		09 33		09 41		09 53			10 03		
	d						08 24		08 54	09 04				09 24		09 34		09 43		09 54			10 04		
Argyle Street	d																			09 56			10 06		
Charing Cross	d	23p27	23p38	23p56		08 03		08 43				09 13							09 43						10 13
Glasgow Queen St LL 10	a	23p29	23p40	23p59		08 05		08 45				09 15							09 45						10 15
	d	23p30	23p44	23p59		08 05		08 45				09 15							09 45						10 15
High Street	d	23p32	23p46	00 02		08 07		08 47				09 17							09 47						10 17
Bellgrove	d	23p34	23p49	00 04		08 09		08 49				09 19							09 49						10 19
Duke Street	d																								
Alexandra Parade	d																								
Barnhill	d																								
Springburn	a																								
Carntyne	d	23p37	23p52	00 07		08 13		08 53				09 23							09 53						10 23
Shettleston	d	23p40	23p55	00 10		08 15		08 55				09 25							09 55						10 25
Garrowhill	d	23p42	23p57	00 12		08 18		08 58				09 28							09 58						10 28
Easterhouse	d	23p45	23p59	00 15		08 20		09 00				09 30							10 00						10 30
Blairhill	d	23p49	00 04	00 19		08 24		09 04				09 34							10 04						10 34
Coatbridge Sunnyside	d	23p51	00 06	00 21		08 27		09 07				09 37							10 07						10 37
Coatdyke	d	23p54	00 09	00 24		08 29		09 09				09 39							10 09						10 39
Airdrie	d	23p57	00a12	00a27		08 32		09 12				09a42							10 12						10a42
Drumgelloch	d	23p59				08 35		09 15											10 15						
Caldercruix	d	00 03				08 39		09 19											10 19						
Blackridge	d	00 09				08 45		09 25											10 25						
Armadale	d	00 13				08 49		09 29											10 29						
Bathgate	a	00 17				08 53		09 33											10 33						
	d				07 55	08 54		09 34											10 34						
Livingston North	d				07 59	08 59		09 38											10 38						
Uphall	d				08 02	09 02		09 41											10 41						
Edinburgh Park	a				08 10	09 10		09 52											10 49						
Haymarket	a				08 20	09 20		10 02											10 54						
Edinburgh	a				08 25	09 25		10 07											10 59						
Bridgeton	d						08 29		08 59	09 09				09 29		09 39				09 59			10 09		
Dalmarnock	d																								
Rutherglen	d						08 32		09 02	09 12				09 32		09 42		09 49		10 02			10 12		
Cambuslang	d						08 36		09 06	09 16				09 36		09 46				10 06			10 16		
Newton	d								09 09					09 39						10 09					
Blantyre	d								09 13					09 43				09 58		10 13					
Hamilton West	d								09 16					09 46				10 01		10 16					
Hamilton Central	d								09 20					09 50				10 03		10 20					
Chatelherault	d																	10 07							
Merryton	d																	10 10							
Larkhall	a																	10 13							
Airbles	d								09 25					09 55						10 25					
Uddingston	d						08 40			09 20						09 50							10 20		
Bellshill	d						08 45			09 25						09 55							10 25		
Motherwell	a						08 51		09 27	09 33				09 57		10 03				10 27			10 33		
	d									09 33													10 33		
Whifflet	a																								
Coatbridge Central	a																								
Shieldmuir	d									09 37													10 37		
Holytown	d																								
Wishaw	d									09 40													10 40		
Carluke	d									09 47													10 47		
Lanark	a									09 59													10 59		

A not 11 December

b Glasgow Central High Level

Table 226

Sundays

Helensburgh, Balloch, Dalmuir and Milngavie - Glasgow - Springburn, Airdrie, Bathgate and Edinburgh, Hamilton, Larkhall, Motherwell, Coatbridge and Lanark

Network Diagram - see first Page of Table 220

		SR		SR				SR		SR	SR	SR		SR	XC ◇1 D	SR			SR	SR			SR		SR
Helensburgh Central	d										09 55								10 25						
Craigendoran	d										09 58								10 28						
Cardross	d										10 03								10 33						
Balloch	d			09 39								10 09								10 39					
Alexandria	d			09 41								10 11								10 41					
Renton	d			09 44								10 14								10 44					
Dalreoch	d			09 47							10 08	10 17							10 38	10 47					
Dumbarton Central	d			09 48							10 10	10 18							10 40	10 48					
Dumbarton East	d			09 50							10 12	10 20							10 42	10 50					
Bowling	d			09 55								10 25								10 55					
Kilpatrick	d			09 58								10 28								10 58					
Dalmuir	a			10 01							10 19	10 31							10 49	11 01					
	d			10 01							10 20	10 31							10 50	11 01					
Singer	d										10 22								10 52						
Drumry	d										10 25								10 55						
Drumchapel	d										10 27								10 57						
Milngavie	d							10 11								10 41							11 11		
Hillfoot	d							10 14								10 44							11 14		
Bearsden	d							10 16								10 46							11 16		
Westerton	d							10 19			10 30					10 49			11 00				11 19		
Anniesland	d							10 22			10 33					10 52			11 03				11 22		
Clydebank	d			10 03								10 33								11 03					
Yoker	d			10 05								10 35								11 05					
Garscadden	d			10 09								10 39								11 09					
Scotstounhill	d			10 11								10 41								11 11					
Jordanhill	d			10 13								10 43								11 13					
Hyndland 3	d			10 15				10 25			10 35	10 45				10 55			11 05	11 15			11 25		
Partick	d			10 18				10 28		10 36	10 38	10 48				10 58			11 08	11 18			11 28		11 36
Exhibition Centre	d			10 21				10 31		10 39		10 51				11 01				11 21			11 31		11 39
Anderston	d																								
Glasgow Central LL 15	a			10 23				10 33		10 41		10 53				11 03				11 23			11 33		11 41
	d			10 24				10 34		10 43		10 54	10b34		10b55	11 04				11 24			11 34		11 43
Argyle Street	d			10 26				10 36		10 45		10 56				11 06				11 26			11 36		11 45
Charing Cross	d										10 43								11 13						
Glasgow Queen St LL 10	a										10 45								11 15						
	d										10 45								11 15						
High Street	d										10 47								11 17						
Bellgrove	d										10 49								11 19						
Duke Street	d																								
Alexandra Parade	d																								
Barnhill	d																								
Springburn	a																								
Carntyne	d										10 53								11 23						
Shettleston	d										10 55								11 25						
Garrowhill	d										10 58								11 28						
Easterhouse	d										11 00								11 30						
Blairhill	d										11 04								11 34						
Coatbridge Sunnyside	d										11 07								11 37						
Coatdyke	d										11 09								11 39						
Airdrie	d										11 12								11a42						
Drumgelloch	d										11 15														
Caldercruix	d										11 19														
Blackridge	d										11 25														
Armadale	d										11 29														
Bathgate	a										11 33														
	d	11 04									11 34			12 04											
Livingston North	d	11 08									11 38			12 08											
Uphall	d	11 11									11 41			12 11											
Edinburgh Park	a	11 19									11 49			12 19											
Haymarket	a	11 24									11 54			12 24											
Edinburgh	a	11 29									11 59			12 29											
Bridgeton	d			10 29				10 39				10 59				11 09				11 29			11 39		
Dalmarnock	d																								
Rutherglen	d			10 32				10 42		10 49		11 02				11 12				11 32			11 42		11 49
Cambuslang	d			10 36				10 46				11 06				11 16				11 36			11 46		
Newton	d			10 39								11 09								11 39					
Blantyre	d			10 43						10 58		11 13								11 43					11 58
Hamilton West	d			10 46						11 01		11 16								11 46					12 01
Hamilton Central	d			10 50						11 03		11 20								11 50					12 03
Chatelherault	d									11 07															12 07
Merryton	d									11 10															12 10
Larkhall	a									11 13															12 13
Airbles	d			10 55								11 25								11 55					
Uddingston	d							10 50								11 20							11 50		
Bellshill	d							10 55								11 25							11 55		
Motherwell	a			10 57				11 03				11 27			11 09	11 33				11 57			12 03		
	d															11 33									
Whifflet	a																								
Coatbridge Central	a																								
Shieldmuir	d															11 37									
Holytown	d																								
Wishaw	d															11 40									
Carluke	d															11 47									
Lanark	a															11 59									

C To London Euston

D To Exeter St Davids

b Glasgow Central High Level

Table 226

Sundays

Helensburgh, Balloch, Dalmuir and Milngavie - Glasgow - Springburn, Airdrie, Bathgate and Edinburgh, Hamilton, Larkhall, Motherwell, Coatbridge and Lanark

Network Diagram - see first Page of Table 220

		SR	XC ◇1 A	SR	SR	SR	SR	SR	SR	SR	SR	SR	SR	SR
Helensburgh Central	d	10 55				11 25				11 55			12 25	
Craigendoran	d	10 58				11 28				11 58			12 28	
Cardross	d	11 03				11 33				12 03			12 33	
Balloch	d			11 09			11 39				12 09			12 39
Alexandria	d			11 11			11 41				12 11			12 41
Renton	d			11 14			11 44				12 14			12 44
Dalreoch	d	11 08		11 17		11 38	11 47			12 08	12 17		12 38	12 47
Dumbarton Central	d	11 10		11 18		11 40	11 48			12 10	12 18		12 40	12 48
Dumbarton East	d	11 12		11 20		11 42	11 50			12 12	12 20		12 42	12 50
Bowling	d			11 25			11 55				12 25			12 55
Kilpatrick	d			11 28			11 58				12 28			12 58
Dalmuir	a	11 19		11 31		11 49	12 01			12 19	12 31		12 49	13 01
	d	11 20		11 31		11 50	12 01			12 20	12 31		12 50	13 01
Singer	d	11 22				11 52				12 22			12 52	
Drumry	d	11 25				11 55				12 25			12 55	
Drumchapel	d	11 27				11 57				12 27			12 57	
Milngavie	d				11 41			12 11				12 41		
Hillfoot	d				11 44			12 14				12 44		
Bearsden	d				11 46			12 16				12 46		
Westerton	d	11 30			11 49	12 00		12 19		12 30		12 49	13 00	
Anniesland	d	11 33			11 52	12 03		12 22		12 33		12 52	13 03	
Clydebank	d			11 33			12 03				12 33			13 03
Yoker	d			11 35			12 05				12 35			13 05
Garscadden	d			11 39			12 09				12 39			13 09
Scotstounhill	d			11 41			12 11				12 41			13 11
Jordanhill	d			11 43			12 13				12 43			13 13
Hyndland 3	d	11 35		11 45	11 55	12 05	12 15	12 25		12 35	12 45	12 55	13 05	13 15
Partick	d	11 38		11 48	11 58	12 08	12 18	12 28	12 36	12 38	12 48	12 58	13 08	13 18
Exhibition Centre	d			11 51	12 01		12 21	12 31	12 39		12 51	13 01		13 21
Anderston	d													
Glasgow Central LL 15	a			11 53	12 03		12 23	12 33	12 41		12 53	13 03		13 23
	d		11b51	11 54	12 04		12 24	12 34	12 43		12 54	13 04		13 24
Argyle Street	d			11 56	12 06		12 26	12 36	12 45		12 56	13 06		13 26
Charing Cross	d	11 43				12 13				12 43			13 13	
Glasgow Queen St LL 10	a	11 45				12 15				12 45			13 15	
	d	11 45				12 15				12 45			13 15	
High Street	d	11 47				12 17				12 47			13 17	
Bellgrove	d	11 49				12 19				12 49			13 19	
Duke Street	d													
Alexandra Parade	d													
Barnhill	d													
Springburn	a													
Carntyne	d	11 53				12 23				12 53			13 23	
Shettleston	d	11 55				12 25				12 55			13 25	
Garrowhill	d	11 58				12 28				12 58			13 28	
Easterhouse	d	12 00				12 30				13 00			13 30	
Blairhill	d	12 04				12 34				13 04			13 34	
Coatbridge Sunnyside	d	12 07				12 37				13 07			13 37	
Coatdyke	d	12 09				12 39				13 09			13 39	
Airdrie	d	12 12				12 42				13 12			13 42	
Drumgelloch	d	12 15				12 45				13 15			13 45	
Caldercruix	d	12 19				12 49				13 19			13 49	
Blackridge	d	12 25				12 55				13 25			13 55	
Armadale	d	12 29				12 59				13 29			13 59	
Bathgate	a	12 33				13 03				13 33			14 03	
	d	12 34				13 04				13 34			14 04	
Livingston North	d	12 38				13 08				13 38			14 08	
Uphall	d	12 41				13 11				13 41			14 11	
Edinburgh Park	a	12 49				13 19				13 49			14 19	
Haymarket	a	12 54				13 24				13 54			14 24	
Edinburgh	a	12 59				13 30				13 59			14 29	
Bridgeton	d			11 59	12 09		12 29	12 39			12 59	13 09		13 29
Dalmarnock	d													
Rutherglen	d			12 02	12 12		12 32	12 42	12 49		13 02	13 12		13 32
Cambuslang	d			12 06	12 16		12 36	12 46			13 06	13 16		13 36
Newton	d			12 09			12 39				13 09			13 39
Blantyre	d			12 13			12 43		12 58		13 13			13 43
Hamilton West	d			12 16			12 46		13 01		13 16			13 46
Hamilton Central	d			12 20			12 50		13 03		13 20			13 50
Chatelherault	d								13 07					
Merryton	d								13 10					
Larkhall	a								13 13					
Airbles	d			12 25			12 55				13 25			13 55
Uddingston	d				12 20			12 50				13 20		
Bellshill	d				12 25			12 55				13 25		
Motherwell	a		12 06	12 28	12 33		12 57	13 03			13 27	13 33		13 57
	d				12 33							13 33		
Whifflet	a													
Coatbridge Central	a													
Shieldmuir	d				12 37							13 37		
Holytown	d													
Wishaw	d				12 40							13 40		
Carluke	d				12 47							13 47		
Lanark	a				12 59							13 59		

A To Plymouth

b Glasgow Central High Level

Table 226

Sundays

Helensburgh, Balloch, Dalmuir and Milngavie - Glasgow - Springburn, Airdrie, Bathgate and Edinburgh, Hamilton, Larkhall, Motherwell, Coatbridge and Lanark

Network Diagram - see first Page of Table 220

		SR	SR	SR	XC ◇1 B	SR	SR	SR	SR	SR	SR	SR	SR	XC ◇1 D	SR
Helensburgh Central	d			12 55				13 25				13 55			
Craigendoran	d			12 58				13 28				13 58			
Cardross	d			13 03				13 33				14 03			
Balloch	d					13 09			13 39				14 09		
Alexandria	d					13 11			13 41				14 11		
Renton	d					13 14			13 44				14 14		
Dalreoch	d			13 08		13 17		13 38	13 47			14 08	14 17		
Dumbarton Central	d			13 10		13 18		13 40	13 48			14 10	14 18		
Dumbarton East	d			13 12		13 20		13 42	13 50			14 12	14 20		
Bowling	d					13 25			13 55				14 25		
Kilpatrick	d					13 28			13 58				14 28		
Dalmuir	a			13 19		13 31		13 49	14 01			14 19	14 31		
	d			13 20		13 31		13 50	14 01			14 20	14 31		
Singer	d			13 22				13 52				14 22			
Drumry	d			13 25				13 55				14 25			
Drumchapel	d			13 27				13 57				14 27			
Milngavie	d	13 11					13 41			14 11					14 41
Hillfoot	d	13 14					13 44			14 14					14 44
Bearsden	d	13 16					13 46			14 16					14 46
Westerton	d	13 19		13 30			13 49	14 00		14 19		14 30			14 49
Anniesland	d	13 22		13 33			13 52	14 03		14 22		14 33			14 52
Clydebank	d					13 33			14 03				14 33		
Yoker	d					13 35			14 05				14 35		
Garscadden	d					13 39			14 09				14 39		
Scotstounhill	d					13 41			14 11				14 41		
Jordanhill	d					13 43			14 13				14 43		
Hyndland 3	d	13 25		13 35		13 45	13 55	14 05	14 15	14 25		14 35	14 45		14 55
Partick ⛴	d	13 28	13 36	13 38		13 48	13 58	14 08	14 18	14 28	14 36	14 38	14 48		14 58
Exhibition Centre	d	13 31	13 39			13 51	14 01		14 21	14 31	14 39		14 51		15 01
Anderston	d														
Glasgow Central LL 15	a	13 33	13 41			13 53	14 03		14 23	14 33	14 41		14 53		15 03
	d	13 34	13 43		13b49	13 54	14 04		14 24	14 34	14 43		14 54	14b55	15 04
Argyle Street	d	13 36	13 45			13 56	14 06		14 26	14 36	14 45		14 56		15 06
Charing Cross	d			13 43				14 13				14 43			
Glasgow Queen St LL 10 ⛴	a			13 45				14 15				14 45			
	d			13 45				14 15				14 45			
High Street	d			13 47				14 17				14 47			
Bellgrove	d			13 49				14 19				14 49			
Duke Street	d														
Alexandra Parade	d														
Barnhill	d														
Springburn	a														
Carntyne	d			13 53				14 23				14 53			
Shettleston	d			13 55				14 25				14 55			
Garrowhill	d			13 58				14 28				14 58			
Easterhouse	d			14 00				14 30				15 00			
Blairhill	d			14 04				14 34				15 04			
Coatbridge Sunnyside	d			14 07				14 37				15 07			
Coatdyke	d			14 09				14 39				15 09			
Airdrie	d			14 12				14 42				15 12			
Drumgelloch	d			14 15				14 45				15 15			
Caldercruix	d			14 19				14 49				15 19			
Blackridge	d			14 25				14 55				15 25			
Armadale	d			14 29				14 59				15 29			
Bathgate	a			14 33				15 03				15 33			
	d			14 34				15 04				15 34			
Livingston North	d			14 38				15 08				15 38			
Uphall	d			14 41				15 11				15 41			
Edinburgh Park	a			14 49				15 19				15 49			
Haymarket	a			14 54				15 24				15 54			
Edinburgh	a			14 59				15 29				15 59			
Bridgeton	d	13 39				13 59	14 09		14 29	14 39			14 59		15 09
Dalmarnock	d														
Rutherglen	d	13 42	13 49			14 02	14 12		14 32	14 42	14 49		15 02		15 12
Cambuslang	d	13 46				14 06	14 16		14 36	14 46			15 06		15 16
Newton	d					14 09			14 39				15 09		
Blantyre	d		13 58			14 13			14 43		14 58		15 13		
Hamilton West	d		14 01			14 16			14 46		15 01		15 16		
Hamilton Central	d		14 03			14 20			14 50		15 03		15 20		
Chatelherault	d		14 07								15 07				
Merryton	d		14 10								15 10				
Larkhall	a		14 13								15 13				
Airbles	d					14 25			14 55				15 25		
Uddingston	d	13 50					14 20			14 50					15 20
Bellshill	d	13 55					14 25			14 55					15 25
Motherwell	a	14 06			14 03	14 27	14 33		14 57	15 03			15 27	15 10	15 33
	d						14 33								15 33
Whifflet	a														
Coatbridge Central	a														
Shieldmuir	d						14 37								15 37
Holytown	d														
Wishaw	d						14 40								15 40
Carluke	d						14 47								15 47
Lanark	a						14 59								15 59

B To Exeter St Davids

D To Bristol Temple Meads

b Glasgow Central High Level

Table 226

Sundays

Helensburgh, Balloch, Dalmuir and Milngavie - Glasgow - Springburn, Airdrie, Bathgate and Edinburgh, Hamilton, Larkhall, Motherwell, Coatbridge and Lanark

Network Diagram - see first Page of Table 220

Station		SR	SR	SR ◇ C	SR	SR	SR	SR	SR	SR	SR	SR
Helensburgh Central	d	14 25		14c39			14 55			15 25		
Craigendoran	d	14 28					14 58			15 28		
Cardross	d	14 33					15 03			15 33		
Balloch	d		14 39					15 09			15 39	
Alexandria	d		14 41					15 11			15 41	
Renton	d		14 44					15 14			15 44	
Dalreoch	d	14 38	14 47				15 08	15 17		15 38	15 47	
Dumbarton Central	d	14 40	14 48	14 56			15 10	15 18		15 40	15 48	
Dumbarton East	d	14 42	14 50				15 12	15 20		15 42	15 50	
Bowling	d		14 55					15 25			15 55	
Kilpatrick	d		14 58					15 28			15 58	
Dalmuir	a	14 49	15 01	15 05			15 19	15 31		15 49	16 01	
	d	14 50	15 01	15 05			15 20	15 31		15 50	16 01	
Singer	d	14 52					15 22			15 52		
Drumry	d	14 55					15 25			15 55		
Drumchapel	d	14 57					15 27			15 57		
Milngavie	d				15 11				15 41			16 11
Hillfoot	d				15 14				15 44			16 14
Bearsden	d				15 16				15 46			16 16
Westerton	d	15 00			15 19		15 30		15 49	16 00		16 19
Anniesland	d	15 03			15 22		15 33		15 52	16 03		16 22
Clydebank	d		15 03					15 33			16 03	
Yoker	d		15 05					15 35			16 05	
Garscadden	d		15 09					15 39			16 09	
Scotstounhill	d		15 11					15 41			16 11	
Jordanhill	d		15 13					15 43			16 13	
Hyndland 3	d	15 05	15 15		15 25		15 35	15 45	15 55	16 05	16 15	16 25
Partick	d	15 08	15 18		15 28	15 36	15 38	15 48	15 58	16 08	16 18	16 28
Exhibition Centre	d		15 21		15 31	15 39		15 51	16 01		16 21	16 31
Anderston	d											
Glasgow Central LL 15	a		15 23		15 33	15 41		15 53	16 03		16 23	16 33
	d		15 24		15 34	15 43		15 54	16 04		16 24	16 34
Argyle Street	d		15 26		15 36	15 45		15 56	16 06		16 26	16 36
Charing Cross	d	15 13					15 43			16 13		
Glasgow Queen St LL 10	a	15 15		15e31			15 45			16 15		
	d	15 15					15 45			16 15		
High Street	d	15 17					15 47			16 17		
Bellgrove	d	15 19					15 49			16 19		
Duke Street	d											
Alexandra Parade	d											
Barnhill	d											
Springburn	a											
Carntyne	d	15 23					15 53			16 23		
Shettleston	d	15 25					15 55			16 25		
Garrowhill	d	15 28					15 58			16 28		
Easterhouse	d	15 30					16 00			16 30		
Blairhill	d	15 34					16 04			16 34		
Coatbridge Sunnyside	d	15 37					16 07			16 37		
Coatdyke	d	15 39					16 09			16 39		
Airdrie	d	15 42					16 12			16 42		
Drumgelloch	d	15 45					16 15			16 45		
Caldercruix	d	15 49					16 19			16 49		
Blackridge	d	15 55					16 25			16 55		
Armadale	d	15 59					16 29			16 59		
Bathgate	a	16 03					16 33			17 03		
	d	16 04					16 34			17 04		
Livingston North	d	16 08					16 38			17 08		
Uphall	d	16 11					16 41			17 11		
Edinburgh Park	a	16 19					16 49			17 19		
Haymarket	a	16 24					16 54			17 24		
Edinburgh	a	16 29					16 59			17 29		
Bridgeton	d		15 29		15 39			15 59	16 09		16 29	16 39
Dalmarnock	d											
Rutherglen	d		15 32		15 42	15 49		16 02	16 12		16 32	16 42
Cambuslang	d		15 36		15 46			16 06	16 16		16 36	16 46
Newton	d		15 39					16 09			16 39	
Blantyre	d		15 43			15 58		16 13			16 43	
Hamilton West	d		15 46			16 01		16 16			16 46	
Hamilton Central	d		15 50			16 03		16 20			16 50	
Chatelherault	d					16 07						
Merryton	d					16 10						
Larkhall	a					16 13						
Airbles	d		15 55					16 25			16 55	
Uddingston	d				15 50				16 20			16 50
Bellshill	d				15 55				16 25			16 55
Motherwell	a		15 57		16 03			16 27	16 33		16 57	17 05
	d								16 33			
Whifflet	a											
Coatbridge Central	a											
Shieldmuir	d								16 37			
Holytown	d											
Wishaw	d								16 40			
Carluke	d								16 47			
Lanark	a								16 59			

C from 25 March. From Mallaig
D To London Euston
b Glasgow Central High Level
c Helensburgh Upper
e Glasgow Queen St High Level

Table 226

Sundays

Helensburgh, Balloch, Dalmuir and Milngavie - Glasgow - Springburn, Airdrie, Bathgate and Edinburgh, Hamilton, Larkhall, Motherwell, Coatbridge and Lanark

Network Diagram - see first Page of Table 220

		SR	SR	SR	XC ◇1 B	SR	SR	SR	SR	SR	SR	SR	SR	SR	SR
Helensburgh Central	d		15 55				16 25				16 55			17 25	
Craigendoran	d		15 58				16 28				16 58			17 28	
Cardross	d		16 03				16 33				17 03			17 33	
Balloch	d			16 09				16 39				17 09			17 39
Alexandria	d			16 11				16 41				17 11			17 41
Renton	d			16 14				16 44				17 14			17 44
Dalreoch	d		16 08	16 17			16 38	16 47			17 08	17 17		17 38	17 47
Dumbarton Central	d		16 10	16 18			16 40	16 48			17 10	17 18		17 40	17 48
Dumbarton East	d		16 12	16 20			16 42	16 50			17 12	17 20		17 42	17 50
Bowling	d			16 25				16 55				17 25			17 55
Kilpatrick	d			16 28				16 58				17 28			17 58
Dalmuir	a		16 19	16 31			16 49	17 01			17 19	17 31		17 49	18 01
	d		16 20	16 31			16 50	17 01			17 20	17 31		17 50	18 01
Singer	d		16 22				16 52				17 22			17 52	
Drumry	d		16 25				16 55				17 25			17 55	
Drumchapel	d		16 27				16 57				17 27			17 57	
Milngavie	d					16 41			17 11				17 41		
Hillfoot	d					16 44			17 14				17 44		
Bearsden	d					16 46			17 16				17 46		
Westerton	d		16 30			16 49	17 00		17 19		17 30		17 49	18 00	
Anniesland	d		16 33			16 52	17 03		17 22		17 33		17 52	18 03	
Clydebank	d			16 33				17 03				17 33			18 03
Yoker	d			16 35				17 05				17 35			18 05
Garscadden	d			16 39				17 09				17 39			18 09
Scotstounhill	d			16 41				17 11				17 41			18 11
Jordanhill	d			16 43				17 13				17 43			18 13
Hyndland 3	d		16 35	16 45		16 55	17 05	17 15	17 25		17 35	17 45	17 55	18 05	18 15
Partick	d	16 36	16 38	16 48		16 58	17 08	17 18	17 28	17 36	17 38	17 48	17 58	18 08	18 18
Exhibition Centre	d	16 39		16 51		17 01		17 21	17 31	17 39		17 51	18 01		18 21
Anderston	d														
Glasgow Central LL 15	a	16 41		16 53		17 03		17 23	17 33	17 41		17 53	18 03		18 23
	d	16 43		16 54	16b55	17 04		17 24	17 34	17 43		17 54	18 04		18 24
Argyle Street	d	16 45		16 56		17 06		17 26	17 36	17 45		17 56	18 06		
Charing Cross	d		16 43				17 13				17 43			18 13	
Glasgow Queen St LL 10	a		16 45				17 15				17 45			18 15	
	d		16 45				17 15				17 45			18 15	
High Street	d		16 47				17 17				17 47			18 17	
Bellgrove	d		16 49				17 19				17 49			18 19	
Duke Street	d														
Alexandra Parade	d														
Barnhill	d														
Springburn	a														
Carntyne	d		16 53				17 23				17 53			18 23	
Shettleston	d		16 55				17 25				17 55			18 25	
Garrowhill	d		16 58				17 28				17 58			18 28	
Easterhouse	d		17 00				17 30				18 00			18 30	
Blairhill	d		17 04				17 34				18 04			18 34	
Coatbridge Sunnyside	d		17 07				17 37				18 07			18 37	
Coatdyke	d		17 09				17 39				18 09			18 39	
Airdrie	d		17 12				17 42				18 12			18 42	
Drumgelloch	d		17 15				17 45				18 15			18 45	
Caldercruix	d		17 19				17 49				18 19			18 49	
Blackridge	d		17 25				17 55				18 25			18 55	
Armadale	d		17 29				17 59				18 29			18 59	
Bathgate	a		17 33				18 03				18 33			19 03	
	d		17 34				18 04				18 34			19 04	
Livingston North	d		17 38				18 08				18 38			19 08	
Uphall	d		17 41				18 11				18 41			19 11	
Edinburgh Park	a		17 49				18 19				18 49			19 19	
Haymarket	a		17 54				18 24				18 54			19 24	
Edinburgh	a		17 59				18 29				18 59			19 29	
Bridgeton	d			16 59		17 09		17 29	17 39			17 59	18 09		18 29
Dalmarnock	d														
Rutherglen	d	16 49		17 02		17 12		17 32	17 42	17 49		18 02	18 12		18 32
Cambuslang	d			17 06		17 16		17 36	17 46			18 06	18 16		18 36
Newton	d			17 09				17 39				18 09			18 39
Blantyre	d	16 58		17 13				17 43		17 58		18 13			18 43
Hamilton West	d	17 01		17 16				17 46		18 01		18 16			18 46
Hamilton Central	d	17 03		17 20				17 50		18 03		18 20			18 50
Chatelherault	d	17 07								18 07					
Merryton	d	17 10								18 10					
Larkhall	a	17 13								18 13					
Airbles	d			17 25				17 55				18 25			18 55
Uddingston	d					17 20			17 50				18 20		
Bellshill	d					17 25			17 55				18 25		
Motherwell	a			17 27	17 10	17 33		17 57	18 03			18 27	18 33		18 57
	d					17 33							18 33		
Whifflet	a														
Coatbridge Central	a														
Shieldmuir	d					17 37							18 37		
Holytown	d														
Wishaw	d					17 40							18 40		
Carluke	d					17 47							18 47		
Lanark	a					17 59							18 59		

B To Birmingham New Street

b Glasgow Central High Level

Table 226

Sundays

Helensburgh, Balloch, Dalmuir and Milngavie - Glasgow - Springburn, Airdrie, Bathgate and Edinburgh, Hamilton, Larkhall, Motherwell, Coatbridge and Lanark

Network Diagram - see first Page of Table 220

		SR	SR	SR	SR	XC ◇1 A		SR	SR	SR	SR	SR	SR	SR	SR	SR		SR	SR	SR	SR	SR	XC ◇1 B	SR	SR
Helensburgh Central	d			17 55					18 25				18 55			19 25					19 55				20 25
Craigendoran	d			17 58					18 28				18 58			19 28					19 58				20 28
Cardross	d			18 03					18 33				19 03			19 33					20 03				20 33
Balloch	d				18 09					18 39				19 09				19 39				20 09			
Alexandria	d				18 11					18 41				19 11				19 41				20 11			
Renton	d				18 14					18 44				19 14				19 44				20 14			
Dalreoch	d			18 08	18 17				18 38	18 47			19 08	19 17		19 38		19 47			20 08	20 17			20 38
Dumbarton Central	d			18 10	18 18				18 40	18 48			19 10	19 18		19 40		19 48			20 10	20 18			20 40
Dumbarton East	d			18 12	18 20				18 42	18 50			19 12	19 20		19 42		19 50			20 12	20 20			20 42
Bowling	d				18 25					18 55				19 25				19 55				20 25			
Kilpatrick	d				18 28					18 58				19 28				19 58				20 28			
Dalmuir	a			18 19	18 31				18 49	19 01			19 19	19 31		19 49		20 01			20 19	20 31			20 49
	d			18 20	18 31				18 50	19 01			19 20	19 31		19 50		20 01			20 20	20 31			20 50
Singer	d			18 22					18 52				19 22			19 52					20 22				20 52
Drumry	d			18 25					18 55				19 25			19 55					20 25				20 55
Drumchapel	d			18 27					18 57				19 27			19 57					20 27				20 57
Milngavie	d	18 11						18 41			19 11				19 41				20 11					20 41	
Hillfoot	d	18 14						18 44			19 14				19 44				20 14					20 44	
Bearsden	d	18 16						18 46			19 16				19 46				20 16					20 46	
Westerton	d	18 19		18 30				18 49	19 00		19 19		19 30		19 49	20 00			20 19		20 30			20 49	21 00
Anniesland	d	18 22		18 33				18 52	19 03		19 22		19 33		19 52	20 03			20 22		20 33			20 52	21 03
Clydebank	d				18 33					19 03				19 33				20 03				20 33			
Yoker	d				18 35					19 05				19 35				20 05				20 35			
Garscadden	d				18 39					19 09				19 39				20 09				20 39			
Scotstounhill	d				18 41					19 11				19 41				20 11				20 41			
Jordanhill	d				18 43					19 13				19 43				20 13				20 43			
Hyndland 3	d	18 25		18 35	18 45			18 55	19 05	19 15	19 25		19 35	19 45	19 55	20 05		20 15	20 25		20 35	20 45		20 55	21 05
Partick ⛴	d	18 28	18 36	18 38	18 48			18 58	19 08	19 18	19 28	19 36	19 38	19 48	19 58	20 08		20 18	20 28	20 36	20 38	20 48		20 58	21 08
Exhibition Centre	d	18 31	18 39		18 51			19 01		19 21	19 31	19 39		19 51	20 01			20 21	20 31	20 39		20 51		21 01	
Anderston	d																								
Glasgow Central LL 15	a	18 33	18 41		18 53			19 03		19 23	19 33	19 41		19 53	20 03			20 23	20 33	20 41		20 53		21 03	
	d	18 34	18 43		18 54	18b57		19 04		19 24	19 34	19 43		19 54	20 04			20 24	20 34	20 43		20 54	20b58	21 04	
Argyle Street	d																								
Charing Cross	d			18 43					19 13				19 43			20 13					20 43				21 13
Glasgow Queen St LL 10 ⛴	a			18 45					19 15				19 45			20 15					20 45				21 15
	d			18 45					19 15				19 45			20 15					20 45				21 15
High Street	d			18 47					19 17				19 47			20 17					20 47				21 17
Bellgrove	d			18 49					19 19				19 49			20 19					20 49				21 19
Duke Street	d																								
Alexandra Parade	d																								
Barnhill	d																								
Springburn	a																								
Carntyne	d			18 53					19 23				19 53			20 23					20 53				21 23
Shettleston	d			18 55					19 25				19 55			20 25					20 55				21 25
Garrowhill	d			18 58					19 28				19 58			20 28					20 58				21 28
Easterhouse	d			19 00					19 30				20 00			20 30					21 00				21 30
Blairhill	d			19 04					19 34				20 04			20 34					21 04				21 34
Coatbridge Sunnyside	d			19 07					19 37				20 07			20 37					21 07				21 37
Coatdyke	d			19 09					19 39				20 09			20 39					21 09				21 39
Airdrie	d			19 12					19a42				20 12			20a42					21 12				21a42
Drumgelloch	d			19 15									20 15								21 15				
Caldercruix	d			19 19									20 19								21 19				
Blackridge	d			19 25									20 25								21 25				
Armadale	d			19 29									20 29								21 29				
Bathgate	a			19 33									20 33								21 33				
	d			19 34									20 34								21 34				
Livingston North	d			19 38									20 38								21 38				
Uphall	d			19 41									20 41								21 41				
Edinburgh Park	a			19 49									20 49								21 49				
Haymarket	a			19 54									20 54								21 54				
Edinburgh	a			19 59									20 59								21 59				
Bridgeton	d	18 39			18 59			19 09		19 29	19 39			19 59	20 09			20 29	20 39			20 59		21 09	
Dalmarnock	d																								
Rutherglen	d	18 42	18 49		19 02			19 12		19 32	19 42	19 49		20 02	20 12			20 32	20 42	20 49		21 02		21 12	
Cambuslang	d	18 46			19 06			19 16		19 36	19 46			20 06	20 16			20 36	20 46			21 06		21 16	
Newton	d				19 09					19 39				20 09				20 39				21 09			
Blantyre	d		18 58		19 13					19 43		19 58		20 13				20 43		20 58		21 13			
Hamilton West	d		19 01		19 16					19 46		20 01		20 16				20 46		21 01		21 16			
Hamilton Central	d		19 03		19 20					19 50		20 03		20 20				20 50		21 03		21 20			
Chatelherault	d		19 07									20 07								21 07					
Merryton	d		19 10									20 10								21 10					
Larkhall	a		19 13									20 13								21 13					
Airbles	d				19 25					19 55				20 25				20 55				21 25			
Uddingston	d	18 50						19 20			19 50				20 20				20 50					21 20	
Bellshill	d	18 55						19 25			19 55				20 25				20 55					21 25	
Motherwell	a	19 03			19 27	19 10		19 33		19 57	20 03			20 27	20 33			20 57	21 03			21 27	21 17	21 33	
	d							19 33							20 33									21 33	
Whifflet	a																								
Coatbridge Central	a																								
Shieldmuir	d							19 37							20 37									21 37	
Holytown	d																								
Wishaw	d							19 40							20 40									21 40	
Carluke	d							19 47							20 47									21 47	
Lanark	a							19 59							20 59									21 59	

A To Newcastle

B To Edinburgh

b Glasgow Central High Level

Table 226

Sundays

Helensburgh, Balloch, Dalmuir and Milngavie - Glasgow - Springburn, Airdrie, Bathgate and Edinburgh, Hamilton, Larkhall, Motherwell, Coatbridge and Lanark

Network Diagram - see first Page of Table 220

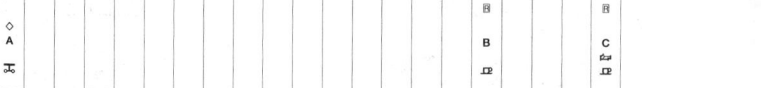

		SR		SR	SR	SR	SR	SR	SR	SR	SR	SR		SR	SR	SR	SR	SR	SR	SR	SR	SR		SR
				◇ A																R B				R C
Helensburgh Central	d			20b40			20 55			21 25					21 55			22 25		22b37	22 55			
Craigendoran	d						20 58			21 28					21 58			22 28			22 58			
Cardross	d						21 03			21 33					22 03			22 33			23 03			
Balloch	d	20 38						21 09			21 39					22 09			22 39			23 09		
Alexandria	d	20 40						21 11			21 41					22 11			22 41			23 11		
Renton	d	20 43						21 14			21 44					22 14			22 44			23 14		
Dalreoch	d	20 46					21 08	21 17		21 38	21 47				22 08	22 17		22 38	22 47		23 08	23 17		
Dumbarton Central	d	20 47		20 53			21 10	21 18		21 40	21 48				22 10	22 18		22 40	22 48		23 10	23 18		
Dumbarton East	d	20 49					21 12	21 20		21 42	21 50				22 12	22 20		22 42	22 50		23 12	23 20		
Bowling	d	20 54						21 25			21 55					22 25			22 55			23 25		
Kilpatrick	d	20 57						21 28			21 58					22 28			22 58			23 28		
Dalmuir	a	21 00		21 03			21 19	21 31		21 49	22 01				22 19	22 31		22 49	23 01	23 02	23 19	23 31		
	d	21 01		21 03			21 20	21 31		21 50	22 01				22 20	22 31		22 50	23 01	23 04		23 31		
Singer	d						21 22			21 52					22 22			22 52						
Drumry	d						21 25			21 55					22 25			22 55						
Drumchapel	d						21 27			21 57					22 27			22 57						
Milngavie	d				21 11				21 41			22 11					22 41							
Hillfoot	d				21 14				21 44			22 14					22 44							
Bearsden	d				21 16				21 46			22 16					22 46							
Westerton	d				21 19		21 30		21 49	22 00		22 19			22 30		22 49	23 00		23 13				
Anniesland	d				21 22		21 33		21 52	22 03		22 22			22 33		22 52	23 03						
Clydebank	d	21 03						21 33			22 03					22 33			23 03			23 33		
Yoker	d	21 05						21 35			22 05					22 35			23a05			23a35		
Garscadden	d	21 09						21 39			22 09					22 39								
Scotstounhill	d	21 11						21 41			22 11					22 41								
Jordanhill	d	21 13						21 43			22 13					22 43								
Hyndland 3	d	21 15			21 25		21 35	21 45	21 55	22 05	22 15	22 25			22 35	22 45	22 55	23 05						
Partick	d	21 18			21 28	21 36	21 38	21 48	21 58	22 08	22 18	22 28		22 36	22 38	22 48	22 58	23 08						
Exhibition Centre	d	21 21			21 31	21 39		21 51	22 01		22 21	22 31		22 39		22 51	23 01							
Anderston	d																							
Glasgow Central LL 15	a	21 23			21 33	21 41		21 53	22 03		22 23	22 33		22 41		22 53	23 03							
	d	21 24			21 34	21 43		21 54	22 04		22 24	22 34		22 43		22 54	23 04							23e15
Argyle Street	d																							
Charing Cross	d						21 43			22 13					22 43			23 13						
Glasgow Queen St LL 10	a			21c19			21 45			22 15					22 45			23 15						
	d						21 45			22 15					22 45			23 15						
High Street	d						21 47			22 17					22 47			23 17						
Bellgrove	d						21 49			22 19					22 49			23 19						
Duke Street	d																							
Alexandra Parade	d																							
Barnhill	d																							
Springburn	a																							
Carntyne	d						21 53			22 23					22 53			23 23						
Shettleston	d						21 55			22 25					22 55			23 25						
Garrowhill	d						21 58			22 28					22 58			23 28						
Easterhouse	d						22 00			22 30					23 00			23 30						
Blairhill	d						22 04			22 34					23 04			23 34						
Coatbridge Sunnyside	d						22 07			22 37					23 07			23 37						
Coatdyke	d						22 09			22 39					23 09			23 39						
Airdrie	d						22 12			22a42					23 12			23a42						
Drumgelloch	d						22 15								23 15									
Caldercruix	d						22 19								23 19									
Blackridge	d						22 25								23 25									
Armadale	d						22 29								23 29									
Bathgate	a						22 33								23 33									
	d						22 34																	
Livingston North	d						22 38																	
Uphall	d						22 41																	
Edinburgh Park	a						22 49																	
Haymarket	a						22 54																	
Edinburgh	a						22 59													00 13				
Bridgeton	d	21 29			21 39			21 59	22 09		22 29	22 39				22 59	23 09							
Dalmarnock	d																							
Rutherglen	d	21 32			21 42	21 49		22 02	22 12		22 32	22 42		22 49		23 02	23 12							
Cambuslang	d	21 36			21 46			22 06	22 16		22 36	22 46				23 06	23 16							
Newton	d	21 39						22 09			22 39					23 09								
Blantyre	d	21 43				21 58		22 13			22 43			22 58		23 13								
Hamilton West	d	21 46				22 01		22 16			22 46			23 01		23 16								
Hamilton Central	d	21 50				22 03		22 20			22 50			23 03		23 20								
Chatelherault	d					22 07								23 07										
Merryton	d					22 10								23 10										
Larkhall	a					22 13								23 15										
Airbles	d	21 55						22 25			22 55					23 25								
Uddingston	d				21 50				22 20			22 50					23 20							
Bellshill	d				21 55				22 25			22 55					23 25							
Motherwell	a	21 57			22 03			22 27	22 33		22 57	23 03				23 27	23 33							
	d								22 33															
Whifflet	a																							
Coatbridge Central	a																							
Shieldmuir	d								22 37															
Holytown	d																							
Wishaw	d								22 40															
Carluke	d								22 47															
Lanark	a								22 59															

A From Mallaig
B From Fort William
C To London Euston
b Helensburgh Upper
c Glasgow Queen St High Level
e Glasgow Central High Level

Network Diagram for Tables 227, 239

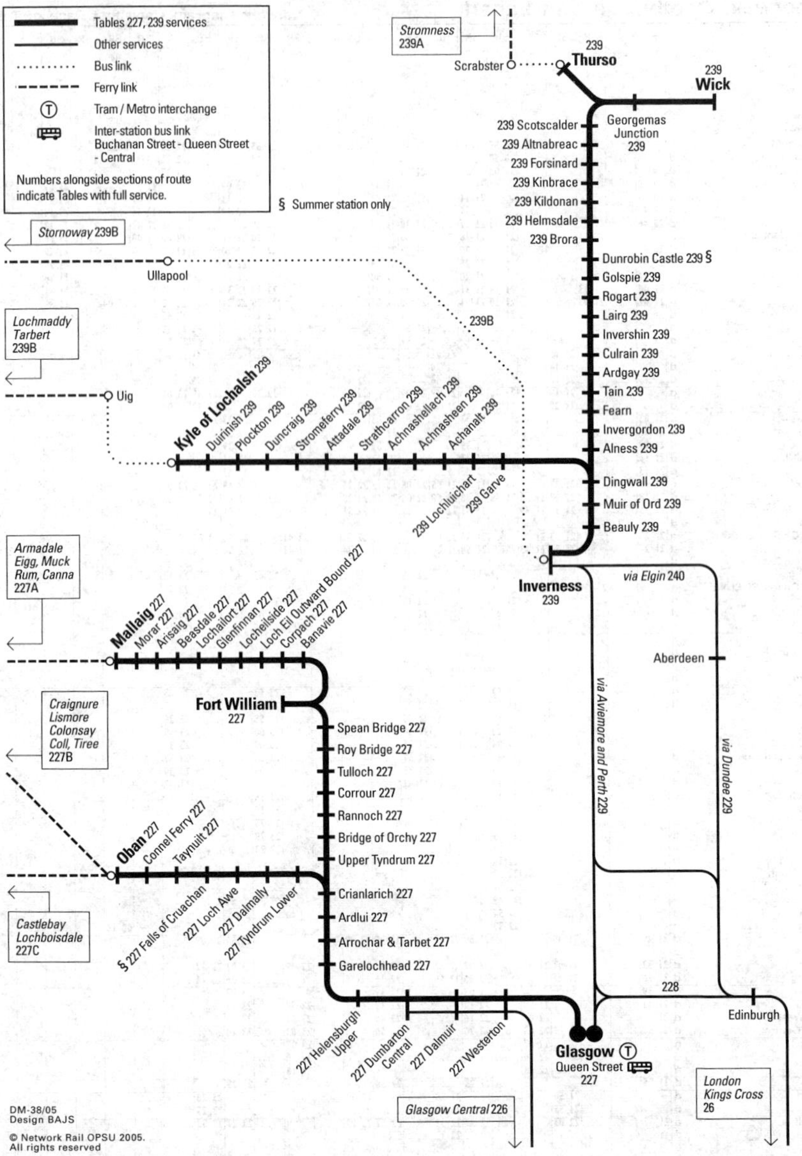

DM-38/05
Design BAJS

Glasgow Queen Street - Oban, Fort William and Mallaig

Network Diagram - see first Page of Table 227

Miles	Miles			SR	SR	SR		SR	SR		SR	
				R				SO				
					◇	◇		◇	◇		◇	
								A				
				🛏		🛒		🛒	🛒		🛒	
—	—	Edinburgh 228	d	04 50								
0	0	**Glasgow Queen St.** 10 226 ⛴	d			08 21		10 37	12 21		18 21	
5½	5½	Westerton 226	d	05 56								
10	10	Dalmuir 226	d	06 04		08 39		10 52	12 42		18 38	
16½	16½	Dumbarton Central 226	d			08 48		11 05	12 48		18 47	
25½	25½	Helensburgh Upper	a	06 26		09 03		11 20	13 03		19 02	
—	—		d	06 29		09 06		11 22	13 06		19 04	
32¼	32¼	Garelochhead	d	06 42		09 17		11 34	13 17		19 16	
43	43	Arrochar & Tarbet	d	07 08		09 37		11 54	13 37		19 36	
51	51	Ardlui	d	07x22		09 53		12 08	13 53		19 52	
59¾	59¾	**Crianlarich**	a	07 43		10 09		12 24	14 09		20 08	
—	—		d	07 44		10 15	10 21	12 26	14 15	14 21	20 14	20 17
64¾	—	Tyndrum Lower	d			10 24		12 35	14 24		20 23	
76¾	—	Dalmally	d			10 42		12 57	14 42		20 41	
79½	—	Loch Awe	d			10 47		13 02	14 47		20 46	
83½	—	Falls of Cruachan §	d									
88½	—	Taynuilt	d			11 03		13 18	15 03		21 02	
95¼	—	Connel Ferry	d			11 14		13 29	15 14		21 13	
101½	—	**Oban**	a			11 27		13 42	15 27		21 26	
—	64½	Upper Tyndrum	d	07 57			10 32			14 32		20 28
—	72¼	Bridge of Orchy	d	08 14			10 46			14 46		20 42
—	87¾	Rannoch	d	08 45			11 08			15 09		21 07
—	95	Corrour	d	08x58			11 20			15 21		21 19
—	105	Tulloch	d	09 18			11 36			15 38		21 35
—	110¾	Roy Bridge	d	09x29			11 46			15 48		21 45
—	114	Spean Bridge	d	09 37			11 54			15 56		21 52
—	122¾	**Fort William**	a	09 54			12 07			16 09		22 05
—	—		d		08 30		12 12			16 19		22 14
—	125	Banavie	d		08 36		12 18			16 25		22 20
—	126	Corpach	d		08 42		12 23			16 30		22 25
—	129	Loch Eil Outward Bound	d		08 49		12 29			16 36		22 31
—	132¾	Locheilside	d		08x54		12x34			16x41		22x36
—	139¼	Glenfinnan	d		09 05		12 46			16 55		22 47
—	148½	Lochailort	d		09x20		13x01			17x10		23x03
—	153¼	Beasdale	d		09x29		13x10			17x19		23x12
—	156¾	Arisaig	d		09 38		13 18			17 27		23 20
—	161¼	Morar	d		09 46		13 26			17 36		23 28
—	164¼	**Mallaig**	a		09 53		13 34			17 43		23 35

Sundays

		SR	SR		SR	
		◇	◇		◇	
		B	B			
		🛒	🛒		🛒	
Edinburgh 228	d					
Glasgow Queen St. 10 226 ⛴	d		12 20		18 20	
Westerton 226	d					
Dalmuir 226	d		12 34		18 34	
Dumbarton Central 226	d		12 44		18 44	
Helensburgh Upper	a		12 59		18 59	
	d		13 06		19 04	
Garelochhead	d		13 17		19 16	
Arrochar & Tarbet	d		13 37		19 36	
Ardlui	d		13 53		19 52	
Crianlarich	a		14 09		20 08	
	d		14 15	14 21	20 14	20 17
Tyndrum Lower	d		14 24		20 23	
Dalmally	d		14 42		20 41	
Loch Awe	d		14 47		20 46	
Falls of Cruachan §	d					
Taynuilt	d		15 03		21 02	
Connel Ferry	d		15 14		21 13	
Oban	a		15 27		21 26	
Upper Tyndrum	d			14 32		20 28
Bridge of Orchy	d			14 46		20 42
Rannoch	d			15 09		21 07
Corrour	d			15 21		21 19
Tulloch	d			15 38		21 35
Roy Bridge	d			15 48		21 45
Spean Bridge	d			15 56		21 52
Fort William	a			16 09		22 05
	d	12 12		16 19		22 14
Banavie	d	12 18		16 25		22 20
Corpach	d	12 23		16 30		22 25
Loch Eil Outward Bound	d	12 29		16 36		22 31
Locheilside	d	12x34		16x41		22x36
Glenfinnan	d	12 46		16 55		22 47
Lochailort	d	13x01		17x10		23x03
Beasdale	d	13x10		17x19		23x12
Arisaig	d	13 18		17 27		23 20
Morar	d	13 26		17 36		23 28
Mallaig	a	13 34		17 43		23 35

§ Summer station only A from 24 March B from 25 March

Mallaig, Fort William and Oban - Glasgow Queen Street

Network Diagram - see first Page of Table 227

Miles	Miles			SR MO	SR MX	SR SX		SR	SR	SR	SR	WR		SR SO	SR	SR	SR	SR SX
				▣	▣													▣
								◇	◇	◇	◇			◇	◇	◇	◇	
									A					B	A			
				⊏	⊏			⊥	⊥	⊥	⊥			⊥	⊥	⊥	⊥	⊏
—	0	**Mallaig**	d						06 03		10 10	14 09			16 05		18 15	
—	3	Morar	d						06 09		10 17	14 23			16 12		18 22	
—	7½	Arisaig	d						06 19		10 26	14 39			16 21		18 31	
—	11	Beasdale	d						06x25		10x33				16x28		18x38	
—	15¾	Lochailort	d						06x34		10x42				16x37		18x47	
—	25	Glenfinnan	d						06 51		10 59	15 20			16 54		19 04	
—	31½	Locheilside	d						07x01		11x09				17x03		19x13	
—	35¼	Loch Eil Outward Bound	d						07 07		11 15	15 40			17 10		19 20	
—	38¼	Corpach	d						07 13		11 21				17 16		19 26	
—	39¼	Banavie	d						07 17		11 25				17 20		19 30	
—	41½	**Fort William**	a						07 25		11 32	16 03			17 28		19 37	
—	—		d	19p00	19p50				07 42		11 40				17 37			19 50
—	50¼	Spean Bridge	d	19p20	20p10				07 55		11 55				17 51			20 10
—	53½	Roy Bridge	d	19b27	20b17				08 02		12 02				17 57			20x17
—	59¼	Tulloch	d	19p40	20p30				08 13		12 14				18 09			20 30
—	69¼	Corrour	d	20b01	20b51				08 30		12 31				18 25			20x51
—	76½	Rannoch	d	20p15	21p06				08 43		12 42				18 37			21 06
—	92	Bridge of Orchy	d	20c47	21p34				09 03		13 03				18 57			21 34
—	99¾	Upper Tyndrum	d	21p05	21p52				09 19		13 19				19 13			21 52
0	—	**Oban**	d					08 11		12 11				16 11		18 11		
6¼	—	Connel Ferry	d					08 23		12 23				16 23		18 23		
13	—	Taynuilt	d					08 35		12 35				16 35		18 35		
18½	—	Falls of Cruachan §	d															
22	—	Loch Awe	d					08 50		12 50				16 50		18 50		
24¾	—	Dalmally	d					08 55		12 55				16 55		18 55		
36¾	—	Tyndrum Lower	d					09 14		13 14				17 14		19 14		
42	104½	**Crianlarich**	a	21p16	22p04			09 29	09 30	13 29	13 30			17 25	19 25	19 26		22 04
—	—																	
—	—		d	21p18	22p05			09 36		13 36	13 36			17 31	19 33			22 05
50¾	113¾	Ardlui	d	21b39	22b26			09 52		13 52	13 52			17 47	19 53			22x26
58¾	121¼	Arrochar & Tarbet	d	21p57	22p44	07 10		10 07		14 07	14 07			18 02	20 08			22 44
69½	132	Garelochhead	d	22p23	23p10	07 30		10 32		14 27	14 27			18 22	20 28			23 10
76¼	138¾	Helensburgh Upper	a	22p35	23p23	07 41		10 42		14 38	14 38			18 33	20 39			23 23
—	—		d	22p37	23p24	07 42		10 44		14 39	14 39			18 34	20 40			23 24
85¼	147¾	Dumbarton Central 226	a			07 56		10 59		14 51	14 51			18 45	20 59			
92½	154¼	Dalmuir 226	a	23p02	23p49			11 08		15 03	15 03			18 56	21 09			23 49
96	157¾	Westerton 226	a	23p11	23p54													23 54
101½	164¼	**Glasgow Queen St.** 10 226 ⛴	a			08 37		11 30		15 30	15 30			19 20	21 31			
—	—	Edinburgh 228	a	00 13	00 50													00 50

§ Summer station only
A ⊥ from Fort William
B from 24 March
b Previous night, stops on request
c Previous night, arr. 2041

Table 227

Sundays

Mallaig, Fort William and Oban - Glasgow Queen Street

Network Diagram - see first Page of Table 227

		SR	SR		SR	SR	SR	SR
							R	
		◇	◇		◇	◇		◇
		A	A					A
Mallaig	d		10 10		16 05			18 15
Morar	d		10 17		16 12			18 22
Arisaig	d		10 26		16 21			18 31
Beasdale	d		10x33		16x28			18x38
Lochailort	d		10x42		16x37			18x47
Glenfinnan	d		10 59		16 54			19 04
Locheilside	d		11x09		17x03			19x13
Loch Eil Outward Bound	d		11 15		17 10			19 20
Corpach	d		11 21		17 16			19 26
Banavie	d		11 25		17 20			19 30
Fort William	a		11 32		17 28			19 37
	d		11 40		17 37		19 00	
Spean Bridge	d		11 55		17 51		19 20	
Roy Bridge	d		12 02		17 57		19x27	
Tulloch	d		12 14		18 09		19 40	
Corrour	d		12 31		18 25		20x01	
Rannoch	d		12 42		18 37		20 15	
Bridge of Orchy	d		13 03		18 57		20 47	
Upper Tyndrum	d		13 19		19 13		21 05	
Oban	d	12 11				18 11		
Connel Ferry	d	12 23				18 23		
Taynuilt	d	12 35				18 35		
Falls of Cruachan §	d							
Loch Awe	d	12 50				18 50		
Dalmally	d	12 55				18 55		
Tyndrum Lower	d	13 14				19 14		
Crianlarich	a	13 29	13 30		19 25	19 26	21 16	
	d	13 36			19 33		21 18	
Ardlui	d	13 52			19 53		21x39	
Arrochar & Tarbet	d	14 07			20 08		21 57	
Garelochhead	d	14 27			20 28		22 23	
Helensburgh Upper	a	14 38			20 39		22 35	
	d	14 39			20 40		22 37	
Dumbarton Central 226	a	14 53			20 53			
Dalmuir 226	a	15 05			21 03		23 02	
Westerton 226	a						23 11	
Glasgow Queen St. 10 226	a	15 31			21 19			
Edinburgh 228	a						00 13	

§ Summer station only

A from 25 March

Table 227A **SHIPPING SERVICES**

Mallaig - Armadale (Skye) and Small Isles

Operated by Caledonian MacBrayne Ltd.

These routes are currently under consultation for

Scottish Government approval.

Please telephone 08000 66 5000

or visit www.calmac.co.uk for information.

Table 227B SHIPPING SERVICES

Oban - Craignure (Mull), Lismore, Colonsay, Coll and Tiree

Operated by Caledonian MacBrayne Ltd

Mondays to Saturdays
until 29 March 2012

		SO H	TTh SO D	TTh SO G	TTh SO	SX	SO C	SO B		SO	SX	FSO
Glasgow Queen St 10 227	d	*18b21*	*18b21*	*18b21*	*08 21*	*08 21*	*08 21*	*10 37*	*12 21*	*12 21*	*12 21*	*18 21*
Oban 227	a	*21 26*	*21 26*	*21 26*	*11 27*	*11 27*	*11 27*	*13 42*	*15 27*	*15 27*	*15 27*	*21 26*
Oban	d	05 30	06 45	06 45	12 00	14 00	14 15	14 15	16 00	17 00	17 15	21 45
Craignure	a	.	.	.	12 46	.	.	.	16 46	.	.	22 31
Lismore	a					14 50	15 05	15 05		17 50	18 05	
Colonsay	a	.	.	.	.	.	.	.	.	.	.	.
Coll	a	08 25	09 25	09 40								
Tiree	a	09 30	10 30	10 45	.	.	.	.	.	.	.	.

Sundays
until 25 March 2012

		Q	E	A
Glasgow Queen St 10 227	d	*18b21*	*18b21*	*12 20*
Oban 227	a	*21 26*	*21 26*	*15 27*
Oban	d	06 30	06 45	16 00
Craignure	a	.	.	16 46
Lismore	a			
Colonsay	a	.	.	.
Coll	a	11 25	11 20	
Tiree	a	10 10	10 05	.

Mondays to Saturdays
until 29 March 2012

		SO	FO	SO	SX	FX	SO B	SO H	TTh SO D	TTH O K	SO B	SO L	SX	SO	
Tiree	d							10 00	10 50	11 00	11 00	11 00			
Coll	d	.	.	.	.	.	.	11 05	11 55	12 05	12 05	12 05	.	.	.
Colonsay	d														
Lismore	d	.	.	09 00	10 00	.	.	.	.	.	.	.	15 00	15 15	.
Craignure	d	06 45	09 00			11 00	13 00								17 00
Oban	a	07 31	09 46	09 50	10 50	11 46	13 46	14 00	14 35	15 00	15 00	15 00	15 50	16 05	17 46
Oban 227	d	*08 11*	*12 11*	*12 11*	*12 11*	*12 11*	*16 11*	*18 11*	*18 11*	*18 11*	*16 11*	*18 11*	*18 11*	*18 11*	*18 11*
Glasgow Queen St 10 227	a	*11 30*	*15 30*	*15 30*	*15 30*	*15 30*	*19 20*	*21 31*	*21 31*	*21 31*	*19 20*	*21 31*	*21 29*	*21 29*	*21 31*

Sundays
until 25 March 2012

		A	A	N	J		
Tiree	d			10 25	10 25		
Coll	d	.	.	11 30	11 30	.	.
Colonsay	d						
Lismore	d	.	11 00	.	.	16 00	.
Craignure	d	11 00					17 00
Oban	a	11 46	11 50	14 10	14 25	16 50	17 46
Oban 227	d	*12 11*	*12 11*	*18 11*	*18 11*	*18 11*	*18 11*
Glasgow Queen St 10 227	a	*15 31*	*15 31*	*21 19*	*21 19*	*21 19*	*21 19*

A 25 March only
B 24 March only
C Not 24 March
D Until 21 January
b Previous night
E Until 15 January. Sails via Tiree
G From 24 January (except Saturday 11 February)
H 11 February only
J From 22 January
K From 24 January
L From 28 January (except 11 Feb & 24 March)
N Until 15 January
Q From 22 January. Sails via Tiree

For details of sailings from 30 March 2012
please telephone 08000 66 5000
or visit www.calmac.co.uk

Oban - Colonsay
This route is currently under consultation for Scottish Government approval.
Please telephone 08000 66 5000 or visit www.calmac.co.uk for information.

Table 227C **SHIPPING SERVICE** **Mondays to Saturdays**

until 29 March 2012

Oban - Castlebay (Barra) and Lochboisdale (South Uist)

Operated by Caledonian MacBrayne Ltd

		TThO A	TThO B	ThO C
Glasgow Queen St 10 227	d	12 21	12 21	12 21
Oban 227	a	15 27	15 27	15 27
Oban	d	**15 40**	**15 40**	**15 40**
Castlebay	a	**20 30**	**20 50**	**22 40**
Lochboisdale	a	**22 10**	**22 40**	**20 50**

Mondays to Saturdays

until 29 March 2012

		MWO D	MWO H	FO G	FO J	ThO E
Lochboisdale	d	**07 00**	**07 00**	**07 00**	**07 00**	**23 00**
Castlebay	d	**08 45**	**08 45**	**08 45**	**08 45**	.
Oban	a	**13 35**	**13 55**	**13 35**	**13 55**	**06 00**
Oban 227	d	18 11	18 11	18 11	18 11	08 11
Glasgow Queen St 10 227	a	21 31	21 31	21 31	21 31	11 30

A Until 19 January
B From 24 January until 27 March
C 29 March only. Sails via Lochboisdale
D Until 18 January
E Until 29 December
G From 6 to 20 January
H 23 January
J 27 January

No Sunday Service

For details of sailings from 30 March 2012
please telephone 08000 66 5000
or visit www.calmac.co.uk

Edinburgh - Falkirk High - Glasgow Queen Street

Network Diagram - see first page of Table 225

Miles	Station		SR	SR	SR	SR	SR	SR	SR	SR	SR		SR	SR	SR	SR	SR	SR	SR	SR	SR		SR	SR	SR
			MX	MO	MX			SX					SX	SX	SO	SX									
			1	1	1	1	1	1	1	1	1			1	1		1	1	1	1	1		1	1	1
									🛒	🛒	🛒			🛒	🛒		🛒	🛒	🛒	🛒	🛒		🛒	🛒	🛒
0	**Edinburgh** 10 225,230,242	d	23p00	23p30	23p30	05 55	06 30	06 45	07 00	07 15	07 30			07 45	07 45		08 00	08 15	08 30	08 45	09 00		09 15	09 30	09 45
1¼	Haymarket 225,230,242	d	23p04	23p34	23p34	05 59	06 34	06 49	07 04	07 19	07 34			07 49	07 49		08 04	08 19	08 34	08 49	09 04		09 19	09 34	09 49
17½	Linlithgow 230	d	23p18	23p48	23p48	06 13	06 48	07 04		07 33	07 48		07 59	08 04	08 04			08 33		09 03			09 33		10 03
22¼	Polmont 3 230	d	23p24	23p54	23p54	06 19	06 55		07 21		07 55						08 22	08 39		09 09			09 39		10 09
25½	**Falkirk High** 3	d	23p29	23p59	23p59	06 24	07 00	07 13	07 26	07 42	08 00		08b11	08 13	08 13		08 26	08 44	08 54	09 14	09 24		09 44	09 54	10 14
35¾	Croy 3 230	a	23p39	00 09	00 09	06 34	07 10	07 23		07 52	08 10					←	08 36		09 03		09 33			10 03	
41	Lenzie 3 230	a	23p44		00 14								08 32	08 25	08 25	08 32									
44	Bishopbriggs 230	a	23p50										↪		08 29	08 36									
47¼	**Glasgow Queen Street** 10 230	a	00 01	00 25	00 26	06 49	07 25	07 38	07 50	08 07	08 25			08 40	08 40	08 48	08 55	09 07	09 19	09 36	09 50		10 06	10 19	10 36

Station		SR	SR	SR	SR	SR	SR		SR	SR	SR	SR	SR	SR	SR	SR	SR		SR	SR	SR	SR	SR	SR	SR
		1	1	1	1	1	1		1	1	1	1	1	1	1	1	1		1	1	1	1	1	1	1
		🛒	🛒	🛒	🛒	🛒	🛒		🛒	🛒	🛒	🛒	🛒	🛒	🛒	🛒	🛒		🛒	🛒	🛒	🛒	🛒	🛒	🛒
Edinburgh 10 225,230,242	d	10 00	10 15	10 30	10 45	11 00	11 15		11 30	11 45	12 00	12 15	12 30	12 45	13 00	13 15	13 30		13 45	14 00	14 15	14 30	14 45	15 00	15 15
Haymarket 225,230,242	d	10 04	10 19	10 34	10 49	11 04	11 19		11 34	11 49	12 04	12 19	12 34	12 49	13 04	13 19	13 34		13 49	14 04	14 19	14 34	14 49	15 04	15 19
Linlithgow 230	d		10 33		11 03		11 33			12 03		12 33		13 03		13 33			14 03		14 33		15 03		15 34
Polmont 3 230	d		10 39		11 09		11 39			12 09		12 39		13 09		13 39			14 09		14 39		15 09		15 40
Falkirk High 3	d	10 24	10 44	10 54	11 14	11 24	11 44		11 54	12 14	12 25	12 44	12 54	13 14	13 24	13 44	13 54		14 14	14 24	14 44	14 54	15 14	15 24	15 45
Croy 3 230	a	10 33		11 03		11 33			12 03		12 34		13 03		13 33		14 03			14 33		15 03		15 33	
Lenzie 3 230	a																								
Bishopbriggs 230	a																								
Glasgow Queen Street 10 230	a	10 49	11 06	11 19	11 37	11 50	12 06		12 20	12 37	12 49	13 06	13 19	13 36	13 51	14 06	14 19		14 36	14 48	15 07	15 22	15 37	15 51	16 07

Station		SR	SR		SR	SR	SR	SR	SR	SR	SR		SR		SR	SR	SR	SR	SR	SR	SR	SR	SR		SR
		1	1		1	1	1	1	1	1	1		1		1	1	1	1	1	1	1	1	1		1
		🛒	🛒		🛒	🛒	🛒	🛒	🛒	🛒	🛒		🛒		🛒	🛒	🛒	🛒	🛒	🛒					
Edinburgh 10 225,230,242	d	15 30	15 45		16 00	16 15	16 30	16 45	17 00	17 15	17 30		17 45		18 00	18 15	18 30	18 45	19 00	19 15	19 30	20 00	20 30		21 00
Haymarket 225,230,242	d	15 34	15 49		16 04	16 19	16 34	16 49	17 04	17 19	17 34		17 49		18 04	18 19	18 34	18 49	19 04	19 19	19 34	20 04	20 34		21 04
Linlithgow 230	d		16 04			16 33		17 06		17 33			18 04			18 33		19 03		19 33	19 48	20 18	20 48		21 19
Polmont 3 230	d		16 10			16 39		17 13		17 39			18 09			18 39		19 09		19 39		20 24			21 25
Falkirk High 3	d	15 54	16 14		16 24	16 44	16 53	17 18	17 24	17 44	17 55		18 14		18 25	18 44	18 55	19 14	19 25	19 44	19 57	20 29	20 57		21 30
Croy 3 230	a	16 03			16 33		17 02		17 34		18 05				18 34		19 05		19 34		20 07		21 07		
Lenzie 3 230	a										18 11														
Bishopbriggs 230	a																								
Glasgow Queen Street 10 230	a	16 19	16 36		16 51	17 07	17 21	17 40	17 51	18 06	18 23		18 37		18 50	19 08	19 23	19 36	19 49	20 07	20 22	20 51	21 21		21 51

Station		SR	SR	SR	SR		SR
		1	1	1	1		1
Edinburgh 10 225,230,242	d	21 30	22 00	22 30	23 00		23 30
Haymarket 225,230,242	d	21 34	22 04	22 34	23 04		23 34
Linlithgow 230	d	21 48	22 18	22 48	23 18		23 48
Polmont 3 230	d		22 24		23 24		23 54
Falkirk High 3	d	21 57	22 29	22 57	23 29		23 59
Croy 3 230	a	22 07		23 07	23 39		00 09
Lenzie 3 230	a				23 44		00 14
Bishopbriggs 230	a				23 50		
Glasgow Queen Street 10 230	a	22 23	22 50	23 22	00 01		00 26

Sundays

Station		SR	SR	SR	SR	SR	SR	SR	SR	SR		SR	SR	SR	SR	SR	SR	SR	SR	SR		SR	SR	SR	SR
		1	1	1	1	1	1	1	1	1		1	1	1	1	1	1	1	1	1		1	1	1	1
		A	A																						
				🛒		🛒	🛒	🛒	🛒	🛒		🛒	🛒		🛒	🛒	🛒	🛒	🛒			🛒	🛒	🛒	🛒
Edinburgh 10 225,230,242	d	23p00	23p30	08 00	09 00	10 00	11 00	12 00	12 30	13 00		13 30	14 00	14 30	15 00	15 30	16 00	16 30	17 00	17 30		18 00	18 30	19 00	19 30
Haymarket 225,230,242	d	23p04	23p34	08 04	09 04	10 04	11 04	12 04	12 33	13 04		13 34	14 04	14 34	15 04	15 34	16 04	16 34	17 04	17 34		18 04	18 34	19 04	19 34
Linlithgow 230	d	23p18	23p48	08 18	09 18	10 18	11 18	12 18	12 48	13 18		13 48	14 18	14 48	15 18	15 48	16 18	16 48	17 18	17 48		18 18	18 48	19 18	19 48
Polmont 3 230	d	23p24	23p54	08 24	09 24	10 24	11 24	12 24		13 24			14 24		15 24		16 24		17 24			18 24		19 24	
Falkirk High 3	d	23p29	23p59	08 29	09 29	10 29	11 29	12 29	12 57	13 29		13 57	14 29	14 57	15 29	15 57	16 29	16 57	17 29	17 57		18 29	18 57	19 29	19 57
Croy 3 230	a	23p39	00 09	08 39	09 39	10 39	11 39	12 39	13 07			14 07		15 07		16 07		17 07		18 07			19 07		20 07
Lenzie 3 230	a	23p44	00 14																						
Bishopbriggs 230	a	23p50																							
Glasgow Queen Street 10 230	a	00 01	00 26	08 59	10 00	11 01	11 56	12 54	13 23	13 51		14 23	14 51	15 22	15 51	16 22	16 51	17 22	17 52	18 22		18 51	19 22	19 51	20 22

Station		SR	SR	SR	SR	SR		SR
		1	1	1	1	1		1
Edinburgh 10 225,230,242	d	20 00	20 30	21 00	22 00	23 00		23 30
Haymarket 225,230,242	d	20 04	20 34	21 04	22 04	23 04		23 34
Linlithgow 230	d	20 18	20 48	21 18	22 18	23 18		23 48
Polmont 3 230	d	20 24		21 24	22 24	23 24		23 54
Falkirk High 3	d	20 29	20 57	21 29	22 29	23 29		23 59
Croy 3 230	a		21 07	21 39	22 39	23 39		00 09
Lenzie 3 230	a							
Bishopbriggs 230	a							
Glasgow Queen Street 10 230	a	20 51	21 22	21 55	22 55	23 55		00 25

A not 11 December

b Falkirk Grahamston

c Falkirk Grahamston, arrival time

Glasgow Queen Street - Falkirk High - Edinburgh

Network Diagram - see first page of Table 225

Miles	Station			SR	SR	SR	SR	SR	SR	SR	SR	SR	SR	SR	SR	SR	SR	SR	SR	SR	SR	SR	SR	SR
				MO	MX		SX	SO	SX												SX	SO		
				1	1	1	1	1	1	1	1	1	1	1	1	1	1	1	1	1	1	1	1	1
										trolley	trolley	trolley		trolley	trolley	trolley	trolley	trolley	trolley	trolley	trolley		trolley	trolley
0	**Glasgow Queen Street 10**	230	d	23p30	23p30	06 00	06 30	06 30	06 45	07 00	07 15	07 30	07 45	08 00	08 15	08 30	08 45	09 00	09 15	09 30	09 45	09 45	10 00	10 15
3¼	Bishopbriggs	230	d																					
6¼	Lenzie 3	230	d				06 38	06 38		07 08														
11½	Croy 3	230	d	23p42	23p42			06 43	06 57			07 41		08 11		08 42		09 12		09 42			10 12	
21¾	**Falkirk High 3**		d	23p52	23p52	06 18	06 51	06 51	07 07	07 21	07 33	07 51	08 04	08 21	08 33	08 52	09 03	09 22	09 33	09 52	10 03	10 03	10 22	10 33
25	Polmont 3	230	a	23p56	23p56	06 23	06 56	06 56		07 26	07 38		08 09	08 26			09 08		09 38		10 08	10 08		10 38
29¾	Linlithgow	230	a	00 03	00 03	06 29	07 02	07 02	07 14	07 32	07 44	07 59	08 15		08 43		09 14		09 43		10 14	10 14		10 44
46	Haymarket	225,230,242	a	00s19	00s20	06s45	07s19	07s19	07s31	07s49	08s01	08s17	08s31	08s45	09s01	09s14	09s30	09s45	10s02	10s12	10s30	10s30	10s44	11s00
47¼	**Edinburgh 10**	225,230,242	a	00 24	00 25	06 50	07 25	07 25	07 37	07 55	08 06	08 25	08 37	08 52	09 07	09 19	09 37	09 52	10 07	10 17	10 37	10 37	10 49	11 05

Station			SR	SR	SR	SR	SR	SR	SR	SR	SR	SR	SR	SR	SR	SR	SR	SR	SR	SR	SR	SR	SR	SR
			1	1	1	1	1	1	1	1	1	1	1	1	1	1	1	1	1	1	1	1	1	1
			trolley	trolley	trolley	trolley	trolley	trolley	trolley	trolley	trolley	trolley	trolley	trolley	trolley	trolley	trolley	trolley	trolley	trolley	trolley	trolley	trolley	trolley
Glasgow Queen Street 10	230	d	10 30	10 45	11 00	11 15	11 30	11 45	12 00	12 15	12 30	12 45	13 00	13 15	13 30	13 45	14 00	14 15	14 30	14 45	15 00	15 15	15 30	15 45
Bishopbriggs	230	d																						
Lenzie 3	230	d																						
Croy 3	230	d	10 42		11 12		11 42		12 12		12 42		13 12		13 42		14 12		14 42		15 12		15 42	
Falkirk High 3		d	10 52	11 03	11 22	11 33	11 52	12 03	12 22	12 33	12 52	13 03	13 22	13 33	13 52	14 03	14 22	14 33	14 52	15 03	15 22	15 33	15 52	16 03
Polmont 3	230	a		11 08		11 38		12 07		12 38		13 08		13 38		14 08		14 38		15 08		15 38		16 08
Linlithgow	230	a		11 14		11 44		12 14		12 44		13 14		13 44		14 14		14 44		15 14		15 44		16 14
Haymarket	225,230,242	a	11s14	11s30	11s45	12s00	12s12	12s30	12s45	13s00	13s14	13s30	13s45	14s00	14s11	14s30	14s45	15s00	15s13	15s30	15s42	16s00	16s12	16s30
Edinburgh 10	225,230,242	a	11 20	11 35	11 50	12 07	12 19	12 36	12 52	13 07	13 19	13 35	13 51	14 05	14 17	14 37	14 50	15 05	15 19	15 37	15 47	16 06	16 19	16 35

Station			SR	SR	SR	SR	SR	SR	SR	SR	SR	SR	SR	SR	SR	SR	SR	SR	SR	SR	SR	SR
					SO	SX									SX	SO						
			1	1	1	1	1	1	1	1	1	1	1	1	1	1	1	1	1	1	1	1
			trolley	trolley	trolley	trolley	trolley	trolley	trolley	trolley	trolley	trolley	trolley	trolley	trolley	trolley	trolley	trolley				
Glasgow Queen Street 10	230	d	16 00	16 15	16 30	16 30	16 45	17 00	17 15	17 30	17 45	18 00	18 15	18 30	18 45	18 45	19 00	19 15	19 30	20 00	20 30	21 00
Bishopbriggs	230	d																				
Lenzie 3	230	d																				
Croy 3	230	d	16 12		16 42	16 42		17 12		17 42		18 12		18 42			19 12			20 12		21 12
Falkirk High 3		d	16 22	16 33	16 52	16 52	17 03	17 22	17 33	17 52	18 03	18 22	18 33	18 52	19 03	19 03	19 22	19 33	19 48	20 22	20 48	21 22
Polmont 3	230	a		16 38			17 08	17 26		17 56	18 08		18 38		19 08	19 08		19 38	19 53		20 53	
Linlithgow	230	a		16 43			17 14		17 41	18 03	18 14		18 44		19 14	19 14		19 44	19 59	20 29	20 59	21 29
Haymarket	225,230,242	a	16s43	17s01	17s13	17s16	17s34	17s45	18s02	18s19	18s33	18s45	19s01	19s13	19s30	19s33	19s46	20s00	20s16	20s45	21s15	21s45
Edinburgh 10	225,230,242	a	16 49	17 07	17 19	17 22	17 40	17 52	18 07	18 24	18 40	18 50	19 07	19 19	19 36	19 39	19 51	20 06	20 21	20 51	21 20	21 50

Station			SR	SR	SR	SR	SR
			1	1	1	1	1
Glasgow Queen Street 10	230	d	21 30	22 00	22 30	23 00	23 30
Bishopbriggs	230	d					
Lenzie 3	230	d					
Croy 3	230	d		22 12		23 12	23 42
Falkirk High 3		d	21 48	22 22	22 48	23 22	23 52
Polmont 3	230	a	21 53		22 53	23 26	23 56
Linlithgow	230	a	21 59	22 29	22 59	23 33	00 03
Haymarket	225,230,242	a	22s18	22s46	23s15	23s49	00s20
Edinburgh 10	225,230,242	a	22 23	22 51	23 20	23 55	00 25

Sundays

Station			SR	SR	SR	SR	SR	SR	SR	SR	SR	SR	SR	SR	SR	SR	SR	SR	SR	SR	SR	SR	SR	SR
			1	1	1	1	1	1	1	1	1	1	1	1	1	1	1	1	1	1	1	1	1	1
			A																					
					trolley	trolley	trolley	trolley	trolley	trolley		trolley	trolley			trolley	trolley	trolley	trolley	trolley	trolley	trolley	trolley	
Glasgow Queen Street 10	230	d	23p30	07 50	08 30	09 30	10 30	11 30	12 30	13 00	13 30	14 00	14 30	15 00	15 30	16 00	16 30	17 00	17 30	18 00	18 30	19 00	19 30	20 00
Bishopbriggs	230	d	}																					
Lenzie 3	230	d	}																					
Croy 3	230	d	23p42	08 02	08 42	09 42	10 42	11 42	12 42	13 12		14 12		15 12		16 12		17 12		18 12		19 12		20 12
Falkirk High 3		d	23p52	08 12	08 52	09 52	10 52	11 52	12 52	13 22	13 48	14 22	14 48	15 22	15 48	16 22	16 48	17 22	17 48	18 22	18 48	19 22	19 48	20 22
Polmont 3	230	a	23p56	08 16	08 56	09 56	10 56	11 56	12 56		13 53		14 53		15 53		16 53		17 53		18 53		19 53	
Linlithgow	230	a	00}03	08 23	09 03	10 03	11 03	12 03	13 02	13 29	13 59	14 29	14 59	15 29	15 59	16 29	16 58	17 29	17 58	18 29	18 59	19 29	19 59	20 29
Haymarket	225,230,242	a	00s20	08 38	09s24	10s23	11s19	12s20	13s21	13s46	14s17	14s47	15s15	15 46	16s18	16s47	17s15	17 47	18s17	18s47	19s16	19s47	20s16	20s46
Edinburgh 10	225,230,242	a	00}25	08 49	09 29	10 28	11 24	12 25	13 26	13 51	14 22	14 52	15 20	15 51	16 23	16 52	17 20	17 52	18 22	18 52	19 21	19 52	20 21	20 51

Station			SR	SR	SR	SR	SR
			1	1	1	1	1
Glasgow Queen Street 10	230	d	20 30	21 00	21 30	22 30	23 30
Bishopbriggs	230	d					
Lenzie 3	230	d					
Croy 3	230	d		21 12	21 42	22 42	23 42
Falkirk High 3		d	20 48	21 22	21 52	22 52	23 52
Polmont 3	230	a	20 53		21 56	22 56	23 56
Linlithgow	230	a	20 59	21 29	22 03	23 03	00 03
Haymarket	225,230,242	a	21s17	21s46	22s19	23s19	00s19
Edinburgh 10	225,230,242	a	21 22	21 53	22 24	23 24	00 24

A not 11 December

Edinburgh and Glasgow Queen Street - Perth, Inverness, Dundee, Aberdeen, Dyce and Inverurie

Network Diagram - see first page of Table 225

Miles	Miles	Miles	Miles	Miles	Station		SR MX ◇1 A 🍴	SR MX ◇1	SR MX ◇1	SR MO ◇1 🍴	SR MX	SR MX	SR R B 🛏	SR ◇1	SR R B 🛏		SR 1	XC ◇1	SR ◇1	SR ◇1 A 🍴	SR 1	SR 1	SR ◇1	SR ◇1 B 🍴	SR ◇1 🍴
—	0	—	0	0	**Edinburgh** 10 242	d	19p28	21p40			22p39	23p09							05 30		06 29	07 00		07 28	
—	1¼	—	1¼	1¼	Haymarket 242	d	19p31	21p44			22p43	23p13							05 33		06 33	07 04		07 31	
—	13¼	—	13¼	—	Inverkeithing 242	d					23p02	23p32			04s58				05 46		06 47	07 20			
—	26	—	26	—	Kirkcaldy 242	d		22p12			23p24	23p54			05s18				06 02		07 03	07 36		08 02	
—	33¼	—	33¼	—	Markinch	d					23p33	00 03							06 11		07 12	07 45			
—	39¼	—	39¼	—	Ladybank	d					23p40	00 10							06 19		07 19	07 53			
—	42¼	—	—	—	Springfield	d																			
—	44½	—	—	—	Cupar	d	20p21					00 17							06 25			07 59			
—	—	—	—	—	Leuchars 5	a	20p28	22p34				00 23			05s47				06 32			08 06		08 25	
—	—	—	—	—	St Andrews Bus Station 🚌	a													07c04			08e24		08g45	
—	—	—	—	—	St Andrews Bus Station 🚌	d													06d00			07f28		07h55	
—	51	—	—	—	Leuchars 5	d	20p28	22p35				00 24							06 32			08 06		08 25	
0	—	0	—	—	**Glasgow Queen St.** 10 230 ⛴	d			21p42	21p45										05 56			07 06		07 41
21	—	21	—	28¼	Larbert 230	d														06 16					
29	—	29	—	36½	Stirling 230	d			22p08	22p11			04s55							06 25			07 33		08u09
—	—	—	—	—	Bridge of Allan 230	d																			
34½	—	34½	—	42	Dunblane 230	d				22p17			05s04							06 31			07 39		08 15
46¾	—	46¾	—	54¼	Gleneagles	d				22p28			05s19							06 43					
62½	—	62½	57	70¾	**Perth**	a			22p37	22p46	00 07		05s39							06 59	07 47		08 04		08 41
—	—	—	—	—		d			22p38	22p46							06 00			07 00	07 47		08 04		08 42
79¾	—	—	—	—	Invergowrie	d															08 05				
83¾	59¼	—	—	—	**Dundee**	a	20p40	22p48	23p02	23p09		00 39			06s08		06 23		06 45	07 22	08 13	08 21		08 40	09 03
—	—	—	—	—		d	20p41	22p49	23p03	23p09							06 24	06 40	06 51	07 23				08 41	09 04
87¼	63¼	—	—	—	Broughty Ferry	d			23p10								06 31								
89	65	—	—	—	Balmossie	d																			
89¾	65¾	—	—	—	Monifieth	d																			
92¾	68¾	—	—	—	Barry Links	d																			
93½	69½	—	—	—	Golf Street	d																			
94	70	—	—	—	Carnoustie	d			23p17	23p21					06s23		06 39		07 03	07 35					09 16
100¼	76¼	—	—	—	Arbroath	d	20p58	23p05	23p24	23p26					06s31		06 46	06 58	07 10	07 42				08 57	09 23
114	90	—	—	—	Montrose	d	21p12	23p19	23p39	23p41				06 25	06s48		07 01	07 13	07 23	07 58				09 13	09 38
124	100	—	—	—	Laurencekirk	d			23p49					06 35					07 35	08 09					
138¼	114¼	—	—	—	Stonehaven	d	21p34	23p40	00 03	00 02				06 49	07s14		07 23	07 34	07 48	08 22				09 34	
146½	122½	—	—	—	Portlethen	d		23p49						06 58					07 59	08 31					
154½	130½	—	—	—	**Aberdeen**	a	21p53	00 03	00 22	00 25				07 13	07 36		07 44	07 55	08 13	08 44				09 52	10 16
—	—	—	—	—		d	21p55							07 14			07 50			08 50				10 00	
160¾	136¾	—	—	—	Dyce 240 ✈	a	22p04							07 24			08 00			08 59				10 08	
171½	147½	—	—	—	**Inverurie** 240	a	22p16							07 44			08 17							10 22	
—	—	78	72½	86¼	Dunkeld & Birnam	d							06s00										08 32		
—	—	91	85½	99¼	Pitlochry	d							06s16										08 45		
—	—	97¾	92¼	106	Blair Atholl	d							06s28										08 55		
—	—	121	116¼	130¼	Dalwhinnie	d							07s00										09 20		
—	—	131¼	126¾	140½	Newtonmore	d							07s12										09 30		
—	—	134	129½	143¼	Kingussie	d							07 19										09 36		
—	—	145¾	141¼	155	Aviemore	d							07 41										09 48		
—	—	152¾	148¼	162	Carrbridge	d							07 54										09 57		
—	—	180	175	188¾	**Inverness**	a	00 05						08 38	09 40									10 28		

A 🍴 to Aberdeen
B From London Euston
c Bus Service. arrives 0713 SO
d Bus Service. departs 0610 SO
e Bus Service. arrives 0830 SO
f Bus Service. departs 0740 SX
g Bus Service. arrives 0900 SO
h Bus Service. departs 0759 SO

Table 229

Edinburgh and Glasgow Queen Street - Perth, Inverness, Dundee, Aberdeen, Dyce and Inverurie

Network Diagram - see first page of Table 225

		SR	SR	SR	SR	SR	SR	SR	SR SX	SR SO	SR	SR SO	SR SX	SR	SR	SR	GR	SR	SR	SR	SR	SR	SR
			■1	◇■1 B 🍴	■1 🍴	◇■1 🍴	◇■1 🍴	■1	◇■1 🍴	◇■1 🍴	■1 🍴	◇■1 🍴	◇■1 🍴		■1	◇■1 🍴	■ ■1 D 🍴	◇■1	◇■1 🍴	■1	◇■1 🍴	◇■1 🍴	■1 🍴
Edinburgh ■10	242 d	07 34	08 00	08 28			08 34	09 00	09 28	09 28				09 35	10 00		10 27		10 35	11 00	11 28		11 35
Haymarket	242 d	07 40	08 04	08 32			08 39	09 04	09 33	09 33				09 40	10 03		10 32		10u40	11 04	11 32		11 40
Inverkeithing	242 d	07 53	08 18					09 17						09 54	10 19		10 47		10u53	11 17			
Kirkcaldy	242 d	08 09	08 34				09 08	09 33						10 10	10 35		11 04		11u10	11 33			12 09
Markinch	d	08 19	08 43				09 17	09 42						10 19	10 44				11 20	11 42			12 18
Ladybank	d		08 51					09 50						10 28	10 51				11 27	11 50			
Springfield	d		08 56																				
Cupar	d		09 00					09 56							10 58					11 56			
Leuchars ■5	a		09 07	09 23				10 03		10 23					11 04		11 28			12 03	12 25		
St Andrews Bus Station 🚌	a		*09b30*	*09b45*				*10b30*		*10b45*					*11b30*		*11b45*			*12b30*	*12b45*		
St Andrews Bus Station 🚌	d		*08e40*	*08b55*				*09b40*		*09b55*					*10b40*		*11b10*			*11b40*	*12b10*		
Leuchars ■5	d		09 07	09 23				10 03		10 23					11 05		11 29			12 03	12 26		
Glasgow Queen St. ■10	230 🚌 d				08 06	08 41					09 08	09 41	09 41			10 10		10 41				11 41	
Larbert	230 d																						
Stirling	230 d				08 36	09 07					09 34	10 07	10 07			10 35		11 08				12 07	
Bridge of Allan	230 d				08 40											10 41							
Dunblane	230 d				08 44						09 41					10 44							
Gleneagles	d				08 56						09 53					10 56							
Perth	a	08 53			09 13	09 38	09 50				10 09	10 36	10 36	10 54		11 14		11 38	11 54			12 36	12 53
	d				09 16	09 38	09 51				10 15	10 38	10 38			11 15		11 39	11 56			12 37	
Invergowrie	d																						
Dundee	a		09 22	09 36	09 41	10 02		10 18	10 32	10 32	10 39	10 59	10 59		11 20		11 43	12 01		12 18	12 38	12 59	
	d			09 37		10 03			10 33	10 33		11 00	11 00				11 43	12 01			12 39	13 00	
Broughty Ferry	d			09 45								11 07	11 07										
Balmossie	d																						
Monifieth	d																						
Barry Links	d																						
Golf Street	d																						
Carnoustie	d											11 15	11 15									13 12	
Arbroath	d			09 56		10 19			10 50	10 50		11 22	11 22				12 01	12 18			12 55	13 19	
Montrose	d					10 39			11 04	11 04		11 36	11 36				12 17	12 33				13 33	
Laurencekirk	d			10 18								11 48	11 48					12 44					
Stonehaven	d			10 31		11 01			11 26	11 26		12 02	12 02				12 40				13 29		
Portlethen	d					11 10																	
Aberdeen	a			10 54		11 25			11 48	11 48		12 21	12 33				13 05	13 14			13 48	14 12	
	d			11 03																			
Dyce	240 ✈ a			11 12																			
Inverurie	240 a			11 27																			
Dunkeld & Birnam	d															11 40							
Pitlochry	d						10 25									11 53			12 25				
Blair Atholl	d																		12 35				
Dalwhinnie	d																		13 03				
Newtonmore	d																		13 14				
Kingussie	d						11 10									12 37			13 19				
Aviemore	d						11 25									12 48			13 34				
Carrbridge	d																		13 43				
Inverness	a						12 03									13 25			14 13				

B 🍴 to Aberdeen

D From Leeds

e Bus Service, arrives 0830 SO

b Bus Service

Table 229

Edinburgh and Glasgow Queen Street - Perth, Inverness, Dundee, Aberdeen, Dyce and Inverurie

Network Diagram - see first page of Table 225

			SR	SR	SR	SR	SR	SR	SR	SR	SR		SR	GR	SR	SR	SR	SR	SR	SR	SR	SR	SR	SR	SR SX	SR SO
			1	◇1	◇1	◇1		1	◇1	◇1	◇1		1	R 1	◇1		1	◇1	◇1	◇1		1	◇1	1	◇1	◇1
					A				A					E					A				A			
				⚲	⚲	⚲			⚲	⚲	⚲			⊏⚲	⚲			⚲	⚲	⚲			⚲	⚲	⚲	⚲
Edinburgh 10	242	d	12 00		12 28		12 35	13 00	13 28		13 35		14 00	14 27		14 35	15 00		15 28		15 35	15 58	16 29			
Haymarket	242	d	12 04		12 32		12 40	13 04	13 32		13u40		14 04	14 32		14 40	15 04		15 32		15 40	16 03	16u33			
Inverkeithing	242	d	12 18				12 54	13 17					14 18	14 47		14 53	15 18				15 54	16 17				
Kirkcaldy	242	d	12 34				13 10	13 33			14u08		14 34	15 04		15 09	15 34				16 10	16 33				
Markinch		d	12 43				13 19	13 42			14 17		14 43			15 19	15 43				16 19	16 42				
Ladybank		d	12 51					13 50					14 51			15 27	15 53				16 27	16 50				
Springfield		d																								
Cupar		d	12 57					13 56					14 57				15 59					16 56	17 17			
Leuchars 5		a	13 04		13 23			14 03	14 23				15 04	15 28			16 06		16 24			17 03	17 24			
St Andrews Bus Station 🚌		a	*13b30*		*13b45*			*14b30*	*14b45*				*15b30*	*15b45*			*16b30*		*16b45*			*17f34*	*17g49*			
St Andrews Bus Station 🚌		d	*12b40*		*12b55*			*13b40*	*13b55*				*14b40*	*15b10*			*15e40*		*15b55*			*16b40*	*16b55*			
Leuchars 5		d	13 04		13 23			14 03	14 23				15 04	15 28			16 06		16 25			17 03	17 24			
Glasgow Queen St. 10	230	d		12 10		12 41				13 41					14 41			15 10		15 41				16 10	16 41	16 41
Larbert	230	d																								
Stirling	230	d		12 35		13 07				14 07					15 07			15 36						16 39		17 07
Bridge of Allan	230	d		12 41														15 41						16 44		
Dunblane	230	d		12 44														15 45						16 49		
Gleneagles		d																						17 02		
Perth		a		13 12		13 35	13 53			14 36	14 54				15 36	15 56		16 12		16 36	16 54			17 18	17 36	17 36
		d		13 12		13 36				14 37	14 55				15 36			16 13		16 36				17 19	17 37	17 37
Invergowrie		d																						17 38		
Dundee		a	13 19		13 35	14 00		14 18	14 35	15 01			15 19	15 46	15 59		16 21		16 37	17 00		17 18	17 38	17 44	17 59	17 59
		d			13 36	14 00			14 36	15 02				15 47	16 00				16 38	17 00			17 39		18 00	18 00
Broughty Ferry		d								15 09													17 47			
Balmossie		d																								
Monifieth		d																								
Barry Links		d																								
Golf Street		d																								
Carnoustie		d								15 16										17 13			17 55		18 13	18 13
Arbroath		d			13 53	14 18			14 53	15 23				16 05	16 20				16 54	17 20			18 02		18 20	18 20
Montrose		d			14 07	14 32				15 39				16 21	16 33				17 09	17 33			18 16			
Laurencekirk		d								15 50									17 20				18 27			
Stonehaven		d			14 29	14 54			15 26					16 44					17 33	17 56			18 41		18 53	18 53
Portlethen		d																								
Aberdeen		a			14 48	15 13			15 46	16 20				17 09	17 13				17 53	18 15			19 00		19 13	19 13
		d			14 56				15 55										17 56				19 07			
Dyce	240 ✈	a			15 04				16 03										18 04				19 16			
Inverurie	240	a			15 19				16 18										18 19				19 35			
Dunkeld & Birnam		d		13 31							15 13							16 36								
Pitlochry		d		13 44							15 26							16 49								
Blair Atholl		d		13 54							15 36							16 59								
Dalwhinnie		d									16 01															
Newtonmore		d																17 32								
Kingussie		d		14 28							16 14							17 37								
Aviemore		d		14 40							16 28							17 49								
Carrbridge		d																17 58								
Inverness		a		15 23							17 04							18 28								

A ⚲ to Aberdeen
E From London Kings Cross. The Northern Lights
e Bus Service. departs 1550 SX
f Bus Service. arrives 1730 SO
g Bus Service. arrives 1745 SO
b Bus Service

Edinburgh and Glasgow Queen Street - Perth, Inverness, Dundee, Aberdeen, Dyce and Inverurie

Network Diagram - see first page of Table 225

		GR SO R 1 D 🍽🛒	SR	GR SX R 1 D 🍽🛒	SR	SR SX E	SR ◇1 🛒	SR SX	SR SO	SR SO ◇1 🛒	SR SX ◇1 🛒		SR ◇1 🛒	SR SX	XC SO ◇1 B	XC SX ◇1 B	SR SO ◇1 🛒	SR SX ◇1 🛒	GR SO R 1 C 🍽🛒	GR SX R 1 C 🍽🛒	SR ◇1 🛒	SR	SR 1	SR 1 🛒	SR ◇1 F 🛒
Edinburgh 10	242 d	16 32	16 33	16 33	17 00	17 27	17 37						17 42	17 58	18 11	18 11			18 30	18 30		18 40	19 00		19 28
Haymarket	242 d	16 38	16 37	16 38	17 04	17 32	17 41						17u46	18 03	18 15	18 15			18 35	18 34		18 45	19 04		19 31
Inverkeithing	242 d		16 53		17 22									18 22	18 29	18 29			18 54	18 54		19 00	19 18		
Kirkcaldy	242 d		17 09		17 39								18 15	18 39	18 47	18 47			19 11	19 11		19 18	19 34		
Markinch	d		17 18		17 48								18 24	18 50	18 57	18 57						19 28	19 43		
Ladybank	d		17 26		17 56								18 31	18 57	19 04	19 04						19 35	19 50		
Springfield	d				18 01																				
Cupar	d				18 05		18 27							19 04	19 11	19 16							19 57		20 21
Leuchars 5	a				18 12		18 33							19 10	19 17	19 22			19 38	19 39			20 03		20 28
St Andrews Bus Station 🚌	a				*18b35*		*18b55*							*19b29*	*19b37*	*19b37*			*19b59*	*19b59*			*20b29*		*20b51*
St Andrews Bus Station 🚌	d				*17b45*		*18b05*							*18b55*	*18b55*	*18b55*			*19b10*	*19b10*			*19b40*		*20b00*
Leuchars 5	d				18 12		18 34							19 11	19 18	19 23			19 38	19 39			20 04		20 28
Glasgow Queen St. 10 230 ⛴	d							17 11		17 41	17 41						18 11	18 11			18 41			19 10	
Larbert	230 d					17 57		17 31									18 30	18 30							
Stirling	230 d	17 18		17 19		18 06		17 45		18 08	18 15						18 41	18 41			19u07			19 37	
Bridge of Allan	230 d					18 13		17 49									18 46	18 46						19 41	
Dunblane	230 d					18a18		17 54		18 15	18 22						18 50	18 50			19 14			19 46	
Gleneagles	d	17 39		17 39				18 06		18 27	18 35						19 02	19 02			19 26			19 58	
Perth	a	17 59	17 54	17 59				18 23		18 43	18 51		18 58				19 19	19 19			19 42	20 02		20 14	
	d	18 00		18 00				18 25		18 44	18 52		18 59				19 22	19 22			19 43			20 15	
Invergowrie	d																				20 00				
Dundee	a				18 34		18 48	18 52		19 06	19 15			19 27	19 32	19 35			19 52	19 53	20 07		20 19	20 36	20 40
	d						18 49	18 54	18 54	19 16	19 16				19 34	19 36			19 53	19 54	20 08				20 41
Broughty Ferry	d							19 00	19 00																
Balmossie	d							19 03	19 03																
Monifieth	d							19 06	19 06																
Barry Links	d							19 10	19 10																
Golf Street	d							19 13	19 13																
Carnoustie	d							19a17	19a17	19 28	19 28														
Arbroath	d						19 05			19 35	19 35				19 50	19 52			20 10	20 11	20 24				20 58
Montrose	d						19 22			19 50	19 50				20 04	20 06			20 26	20 28	20 39				21 12
Laurencekirk	d																								
Stonehaven	d						19 43			20 13	20 13				20 24	20 27			20 49	20 51					21 34
Portlethen	d						19 52																		
Aberdeen	a						20 06			20 33	20 33				20 43	20 45			21 15	21 16	21 19				21 53
	d																								21 55
Dyce	240 ✈ a																								22 04
Inverurie	240 a																								22 16
Dunkeld & Birnam	d												19 18												
Pitlochry	d	18 32		18 32									19 31				19 52	19 52							
Blair Atholl	d																20 01	20 01							
Dalwhinnie	d																20 26	20 26							
Newtonmore	d																20 36	20 36							
Kingussie	d	19 16		19 16									20 14				20 41	20 41							
Aviemore	d	19 29		19 29									20 25				21 00	21 00							
Carrbridge	d																								
Inverness	a	20 11		20 11									21 02				21 37	21 43							00 05

D From London Kings Cross. The Highland Chieftain
E From Newcraighall
B From Plymouth
C From London Kings Cross
F 🛒 to Aberdeen
b Bus Service

Table 229

Mondays to Saturdays

Edinburgh and Glasgow Queen Street - Perth, Inverness, Dundee, Aberdeen, Dyce and Inverurie

Network Diagram - see first page of Table 225

		SR	SR	SR	SR	XC	XC	GR	SR	SR	SR	SR	SR	SR	SR	SR	SR	SR	SR
			SO	SX		SX	SO	SX											
		◇1	◇1	◇1		◇1	◇1	R 1	◇1			◇1	◇1						
						B	B	D						C					
Edinburgh 10 242	d		19 36	19 36	20 00	20 14	20 14	20 29		20 45	21 07	21 40		21 49		22 09	22 39	23 09	
Haymarket 242	d		19 41	19 41	20 04	20 17	20 18	20 34		20 49	21 11	21 44		21 53		22 13	22 43	23 13	
Inverkeithing 242	d		19 54	19 54	20 23	20 31	20 35	20 51		21 03	21 30			22 12		22 32	23 02	23 32	
Kirkcaldy 242	d		20 10	20 10	20 45		20 52	21 08		21 19	21 52	22 12				22 54	23 24	23 54	
Markinch	d		20 19	20 19	20 54	21 03	21 02			21 28	22 01			22 56		23 03	23 33	00 03	
Ladybank	d		20 27	20 27	21 01	21 11	21 10			21 36	22 08			23 03		23 13	23 40	00 10	
Springfield	d															23 18			
Cupar	d				21 07	21 19	21 19				22 15					23 22		00 17	
Leuchars 5	a				21 14	21 25	21 25	21 37			22 22	22 34				23 28		00 23	
St Andrews Bus Station	a				21b59	21b59	21b59	21b59			22b59	22b59				23b59			
St Andrews Bus Station	d				20b40	21b00	21b00	21b00			22b00	22b00				23b00		23b50	
Leuchars 5	d				21 14	21 26	21 27	21 38			22 22	22 35				23 29		00 24	
Glasgow Queen St. 10 230	d	19 41							20 41				21 42		22 48				23 36
Larbert 230	d														23 18				
Stirling 230	d	20 07							21 07				22 08		23 33				00 05
Bridge of Allan 230	d														23 37				00 10
Dunblane 230	d								21 14						23 42				00 15
Gleneagles	d								21 26						23 55				00 27
Perth	a	20 36	20 54	20 54					21 42	22 02			22 37	23 34	00 14		00 07		00 44
	d	20 36	20 55	20 55					21 43				22 38						
Invergowrie	d								22 01										
Dundee	a	20 59			21 30	21 41	21 43	21 52	22 07		22 37	22 48	23 02			23 44		00 39	
	d	20 59						21 52	22 08			22 49	23 03						
Broughty Ferry	d												23 10						
Balmossie	d																		
Monifieth	d																		
Barry Links	d																		
Golf Street	d																		
Carnoustie	d												23 17						
Arbroath	d	21 17						22 10	22 25			23 05	23 24						
Montrose	d	21 31						22 26	22 39			23 19	23 39						
Laurencekirk	d	21 42											23 49						
Stonehaven	d	21 56						22 49	23 01			23 40	00 03						
Portlethen	d											23 49							
Aberdeen	a	22 15						23 14	23 20			00 03	00 22						
	d																		
Dyce 240	a																		
Inverurie 240	a																		
Dunkeld & Birnam	d		21 13	21 13															
Pitlochry	d		21 26	21 26															
Blair Atholl	d		21 35	21 35															
Dalwhinnie	d		22 01	22 03															
Newtonmore	d		22 11	22 14															
Kingussie	d		22 16	22 24															
Aviemore	d		22 28	22 35															
Carrbridge	d		22 36	22 43															
Inverness	a		23 07	23 15															

B From Plymouth
C From Newcraighall
D From London Kings Cross
b Bus Service

Table 229

Sundays

Edinburgh and Glasgow Queen Street - Perth, Inverness, Dundee, Aberdeen, Dyce and Inverurie

Network Diagram - see first page of Table 225

		SR	SR	SR	SR	SR	XC	GR	SR	SR		SR	SR	SR	SR	SR	SR		SR	SR		SR	SR		GR
								R																	R
		◇1	◇1	◇1			◇	1		◇1		◇1		◇1	◇1		◇1		◇1			◇1	◇1		1
		A	B	B	B	B							C												D
		⫪						▭⫪		⫪		⫪		⫪	⫪				⫪			⫪	⫪		▭⫪
Edinburgh 10	242 d	19p28	21p40		22p39	23p09	08 04	09 10	09 15			09 36	09 55	10 55		11 15			12 40	13 15			13 50		14 33
Haymarket	242 d	19p31	21p44		22p43	23p13	08 08	09 14	09 19			09 40	09 59	10 59		11 19			12 44	13 19			13 54		14 38
Inverkeithing	242 d	⌇	⌇		23p02	23p32	08 25	09 32	09 38			09 56	10 18	11 15		11 38			13 00	13 40			14 12		14 56
Kirkcaldy	242 d	⌇	22p12		23p24	23p54	08 40	09 49	10 03			10 12	11a08	11 31		12 03			13 16	14 05			14 28		15 13
Markinch	d	⌇	⌇		23p33	00⌇03			10 12							12 12				14 14					
Ladybank	d	⌇	⌇		23p40	00⌇10			10 18							12 19				14 21					
Springfield	d	⌇	⌇		⌇	⌇																			
Cupar	d	20p21	⌇		⌇	00⌇17	08 57		10 26							12 26				14 28					
Leuchars 5	a	20p28	22p34		⌇	00⌇23	09 05	10 13	10 33					11 54		12 33			13 39	14 35					15 37
St Andrews Bus Station	a	⌇	⌇		⌇	⌇	*09b37*	*10b29*	*10b58*					*12b17*		*12b57*			*13b55*	*14b55*					*15b55*
St Andrews Bus Station	d	⌇	⌇		⌇	⌇	*07b55*	*09b50*	*10b15*					*11b35*		*12b15*			*13b15*	*14b15*					*15b15*
Leuchars 5	d	20p28	22p35		⌇	00⌇24	09 06	10 13	10 33					11 55		12 33			13 40	14 35					15 38
Glasgow Queen St. 10	230 d	⌇	⌇	21p42	⌇	⌇				09 38					11 09		11 45					13 45			
Larbert	230 d	⌇	⌇	⌇	⌇	⌇				10 02					11 29										
Stirling	230 d	⌇	⌇	22p08	⌇	⌇				10 12					11 39		12 12					14 12			
Bridge of Allan	230 d	⌇	⌇	⌇	⌇	⌇																			
Dunblane	230 d	⌇	⌇	⌇	⌇	⌇				10 18					11 45		12 18					14 17			
Gleneagles	d	⌇	⌇	⌇	⌇	⌇				10 30					11 57		12 29					14 29			
Perth	a	⌇	⌇	22p37	00⌇07	⌇				10 47		10 52			12 15		12 46					14 46	15 12		
	d	⌇	⌇	22p38		⌇				10 48		10 53			12 15		12 47					14 48	15 14		
Invergowrie	d	⌇	⌇	⌇		⌇																			
Dundee	a	20p40	22p48	23p02		00⌇39	09 18	10 27	10 50	11 12				12 07		12 48	13 10		13 52	14 50		15 09			15 52
	d	20p41	22p49	23p03			09 20	10 28		11 13				12 08			13 11		13 53			15 11			15 52
Broughty Ferry	d	⌇	⌇	23p10																					
Balmossie	d	⌇	⌇	⌇																					
Monifieth	d	⌇	⌇	⌇																					
Barry Links	d	⌇	⌇	⌇																					
Golf Street	d	⌇	⌇	⌇																					
Carnoustie	d	⌇	⌇	23p17						11 25															
Arbroath	d	20p58	23p05	23p24			09 36	10 45		11 29				12 25			13 27		14 10			15 27			16 10
Montrose	d	21p12	23p19	23p39			09 50	11 01		11 46				12 37			13 42		14 24			15 42			16 26
Laurencekirk	d	⌇	⌇	23p49						12 01												15 53			
Stonehaven	d	21p34	23p40	00⌇03			10 10	11 24		12 10				12 59			14 03		14 46			16 06			16 49
Portlethen	d	⌇	23p49	⌇										13 07											
Aberdeen	a	21p53	00⌇03	00⌇22			10 29	11 52		12 35				13 23			14 23		15 05			16 26			17 14
	d	21p55																							
Dyce	240 ⇆ a	22p04																							
Inverurie	240 a	22p16																							
Dunkeld & Birnam	d	⌇										11 11			12 36								15 31		
Pitlochry	d	⌇										11 24			12 50								15 44		
Blair Atholl	d	⌇										11 34											15 54		
Dalwhinnie	d	⌇										12 01											16 25		
Newtonmore	d	⌇										12 12											16 35		
Kingussie	d	⌇										12 17			13 32								16 40		
Aviemore	d	⌇										12 29			13 44								16 56		
Carrbridge	d	⌇										12 38			13 57								17 06		
Inverness	a	00⌇05										13 15			14 26								17 37		

A not 11 December. ⫪ to Aberdeen
B not 11 December
D From London Kings Cross. The Northern Lights
b Bus Service

Table 229

Sundays

Edinburgh and Glasgow Queen Street - Perth, Inverness, Dundee, Aberdeen, Dyce and Inverurie

Network Diagram - see first page of Table 225

	SR	SR	SR	SR	GR	SR	SR	SR	SR	SR	XC	GR	SR	SR	SR	SR	SR
	◇1		◇1	◇1	R 1	◇1		◇1	1	◇1	◇1	R 1		◇1	◇1	◇1	
	A				C					A	D	F					
	⊤		⊤	⊤	⊡⊤			⊤		⊤		⊡⊤		⊤		⊤	
Edinburgh 10 242 d		15 15		15 50	16 30	17 05	17 15		17 50		18 13	18 42	19 15		21 00		22 25
Haymarket 242 d		15 19		15 54	16 35	17 09	17 19		17 54		18 16	18 47	19 19		21 05		22 29
Inverkeithing 242 d		15 38		16 10		17 22	17 38		18 07		18 30	19 02	19 38		21 19		22 48
Kirkcaldy 242 d		16 03		16 26		17 38	18 00		18 23		18 45	19 19	20 00		21 35		23 10
Markinch d		16 12					18 09				18 54		20 09		21 44		23 19
Ladybank d		16 19					18 16				19 02		20 16		21 50		23 26
Springfield d																	
Cupar d		16 26					18 23				19 08		20 23		21 58		23 33
Leuchars 5 a		16 33				18 01	18 30				19 14	19 43	20 30		22 05		23 40
St Andrews Bus Station a		*16b55*				*18b17*	*18b55*				*19b37*	*19b59*	*20b55*		*22b29*		
St Andrews Bus Station d		*16b15*				*17b35*	*18b00*				*18b30*	*19b15*	*20b00*		*21b30*		
Leuchars 5 d		16 33				18 02	18 30				19 15	19 43	20 30		22 05		23 40
Glasgow Queen St. 10 230 d	14 40		15 45					17 45		18 10				19 45		21 45	
Larbert 230 d	15 00									18 30							
Stirling 230 d	15 09		16 12		17 17			18 12		18 40				20 12		22 11	
Bridge of Allan 230 d																	
Dunblane 230 d	15 16		16 18							18 47				20 17		22 17	
Gleneagles d	15 28		16 29		17 35					18 59				20 29		22 28	
Perth a	15 45		16 45	17 05	17 53			18 44	19 02	19 16				20 46		22 46	
d	15 46		16 47	17 09	17 54			18 45		19 17				20 47		22 46	
Invergowrie d																	
Dundee a		16 48	17 09			18 14	18 46	19 08			19 29	19 57	20 45	21 10	22 18	23 09	23 56
d			17 11			18 15		19 09			19 31	19 58		21 11	22 21	23 09	
Broughty Ferry d																	
Balmossie d																	
Monifieth d																	
Barry Links d																	
Golf Street d																	
Carnoustie d								19 21								23 21	
Arbroath d			17 27			18 32		19 27			19 47	20 15		21 27	22 38	23 26	
Montrose d			17 42			18 46		19 42			20 01	20 31		21 42	22 52	23 41	
Laurencekirk d								19 55									
Stonehaven d			18 03			19 08		20 06			20 24	20 54		22 03	23 14	00 02	
Portlethen d						19 16									23 23		
Aberdeen a			18 23			19 30		20 29			20 43	21 20		22 24	23 36	00 25	
d																	
Dyce 240 a																	
Inverurie 240 a																	
Dunkeld & Birnam d				17 26						19 35							
Pitlochry d	16 16			17 40	18 27					19 48							
Blair Atholl d										19 58							
Dalwhinnie d										20 23							
Newtonmore d										20 33							
Kingussie d	17 00			18 22	19 23					20 38							
Aviemore d	17 13			18 35	19 35					20 50							
Carrbridge d										21 02							
Inverness a	17 49			19 21	20 19					21 33							

A To Elgin
C From London Kings Cross. The Highland Chieftain
D From Plymouth
F From London Kings Cross
b Bus Service

Inverurie, Dyce, Aberdeen, Dundee, Inverness and Perth - Glasgow Queen Street and Edinburgh

Network Diagram - see first page of Table 225

Miles	Miles	Miles	Miles	Miles			XC MX ◇1	SR MSX 1	SR MO 1	SR MO R D	SR MX R D	SR SO 1	SR SX	SR	SR SO A	SR	SR	SR	XC SO ◇1 C	XC SX ◇1 C	SR A	SR
—	—	0	0	0	**Inverness**	d				20p25	20p47											
—	—	28	28	28	Carrbridge	d																
—	—	34¾	34¾	34¾	Aviemore	d				21b08	21b29											
—	—	46½	46½	46½	Kingussie	d				21b22	21b42											
—	—	49¼	49¼	49¼	Newtonmore	d				21b29	21b50											
—	—	59½	59½	59½	Dalwhinnie	d				21b43	22b06											
—	—	82¾	82¾	82¾	Blair Atholl	d				22b09	22b32											
—	—	89½	89½	89½	Pitlochry	d				22b22	22b45											
—	—	102½	102½	102½	Dunkeld & Birnam	d				22b37	23b00											
0	0	—	—	—	**Inverurie**	240 d																
10¾	10¾	—	—	—	Dyce	240 ✈ d																
6¼	6¼	—	—	—	**Aberdeen**	240 a																
—	—	—	—	—		d	21p31	22p27	22p30			23p22										
14¼	14¼	—	—	—	Portlethen	d		22p37				23p32										
22½	22½	—	—	—	Stonehaven	d	21p49	22p46	22p48			23p41										
36¾	36¾	—	—	—	Laurencekirk	d		22p59				23p54										
46¾	46¾	—	—	—	Montrose	d	22p10	23p10	23p11			00 05										
60½	60½	—	—	—	Arbroath	d	22p26	23p24	23p25			00 19										
66¾	66¾	—	—	—	Carnoustie	d		23p31	23p32			00 26						06 00				
67¼	67¼	—	—	—	Golf Street	d												06 02				
68	68	—	—	—	Barry Links	d												06 04				
71	71	—	—	—	Monifieth	d												06 09				
71¾	71¾	—	—	—	Balmossie	d												06 11				
73¼	73¼	—	—	—	Broughty Ferry	d		23p38				00 33						06 15				
77½	77½	—	—	—	**Dundee**	a	22p42	23p48	23p46			00 43						06 26				
—	—	—	—	—		d	22p43	23p49	23p47			00 44				05 56	06 05		06 32	06 32		
81	—	—	—	—	Invergowrie	d		23p54				00 49				06 02						
98¼	—	118	118	118	**Perth**	a		00 12	00 09			01 07				06 19						
—	—	—	—	—		d				23b00	23b21		05 10	05 16	05 35	06 21					06 39	06 55
114	—	133¾	—	133¾	Gleneagles	d				23b18	23b39			05 33		06 36					06 54	
121¼	—	146	—	146	Dunblane	230 d				23b34	23b55			05 46		06 47					07 08	
—	—	—	—	—	Bridge of Allan	230 d								05 49		06 51					07 10	
131¾	—	151½	—	151½	Stirling	230 d				23b45	00u06			05 54		06 55					07 16	
139¾	—	159½	—	159½	Larbert	230 d								06 03		07 04					07 25	
160¾	—	180½	—	—	**Glasgow Queen St.** 10	230 ⛴ a								06 34		07 35						
—	85¾	—	—	—	Leuchars 5	a	22p55										06 16		06 44	06 44		
—	—	—	—	—	St Andrews Bus Station	🚌 a											*07b04*		*07b13*	*07b04*		
—	—	—	—	—	St Andrews Bus Station	🚌 d													*06b10*	*06b14*		
—	—	—	—	—	Leuchars 5	d	22p56										06 17		06 46	06 46		
—	92¼	—	—	—	Cupar	d	23p03										06 25		06 54	06 54		
—	94½	—	—	—	Springfield	d																
—	97½	—	135¾	—	Ladybank	d	23p10						05 36		05 59		06 32		07 03	07 03		07 19
—	103½	—	141	—	Markinch	d	23p18						05 44		06 07		06 40		07 11	07 11		07 26
—	110¾	—	149	—	Kirkcaldy	242 d	23p26						05 53		06 16		06 49		07 21	07 21		07 40
—	123½	—	161¾	—	Inverkeithing	242 d	23p42						06 16		06 40		07 12		07 38	07 43		07 57
—	135½	—	173¾	186½	Haymarket	242 a	23p57						06 39		07 02		07 33		07 55	08 00	08 11	08 17
—	136¾	—	175	187¾	**Edinburgh** 10	242 a	00 05			00 47	01 00		06 46		07 09		07 38		08 01	08 06	08 17	08 22

A To Newcraighall
C To Plymouth
D To London Euston
b Bus Service

Inverurie, Dyce, Aberdeen, Dundee, Inverness and Perth - Glasgow Queen Street and Edinburgh

Network Diagram - see first page of Table 225

		SR	SR	SR	SR	SR	SR	SR	SR		SR	SR	SR	SR	SR	SR	GR	GR	XC	XC	SR	GR	SR	SR	SR
		SX				SX											SX	SO	SO	SX					
																	R	R				R			
			◇1	◇1			1	◇1	1		◇1			◇1		◇1	1	1	◇1	◇1	1	1		◇1	◇1
						B					D					D	E	E	C	C		F			
			🍴					🍴			🍴			🍴		🍴	🍽🍴	🍽🍴				🍽🍴		🍴	🍴
Inverness	d										04 51			06 47								07 55			
Carrbridge	d																								
Aviemore	d													07 25								08 29			
Kingussie	d													07 37								08 42			
Newtonmore	d																								
Dalwhinnie	d																								
Blair Atholl	d						07 12																		
Pitlochry	d						07 25							08 16								09 23			
Dunkeld & Birnam	d						07 38							08 29											
Inverurie 240	d										06 39					07 14									
Dyce 240 ✈	d										06 52					07 26									
Aberdeen 240	a										07 04					07 37									
	d		05 33	05 56				06 33			07 06					07 40	07 52	07 52	08 20	08 20				08 42	09 07
Portlethen	d		05 44					06 43																	
Stonehaven	d		05 52	06 13				06 52			07 22					07 56	08 09	08 09	08 38	08 38					
Laurencekirk	d		06 06								07 36														09 35
Montrose	d		06 17	06 34				07 13			07 47					08 18	08 32	08 32	08 59	08 59				09 18	09 46
Arbroath	d		06 31	06 49				07 27			08 01					08 32	08 48	08 48	09 15	09 15				09 32	10 00
Carnoustie	d			06 56				07 34			08 08					08 39								09 39	
Golf Street	d																								
Barry Links	d																								
Monifieth	d																								
Balmossie	d																								
Broughty Ferry	d							07 41																	
Dundee	a		06 51	07 08				07 51			08 18					08 53	09 05	09 05	09 31	09 31				09 52	10 15
	d		06 52	07 09	07 20	07 38		07 52	08 18		08 20		08 28			08 53	09 06	09 06	09 32	09 32	09 41			09 52	10 17
Invergowrie	d								08 23																
Perth	a		07 14				07 58	08 12	08 40					08 47		09 15						09 54		10 14	
	d	07 03	07 15				08 00	08 12	08 40					08 48		09 15						09 56	10 01	10 14	
Gleneagles	d	07 18	07 30					08 26	08 55													10 13			
Dunblane 230	d	07 31	07 44						09 07			08 28			09 03										
Bridge of Allan 230	d	07 34	07 48						09 11			08 31													
Stirling 230	d	07 39	07 53					08 43	09 15			08 36			09 09	09 44						10 30		10 43	
Larbert 230	d	07 47	08 02									08 45			09 18										
Glasgow Queen St. 10 230 🚢	a	08 20	08 34					09 15	09 46							10 14								11 14	
Leuchars 5	a			07 20	07 31	07 49							08 40				09 20	09 20	09 46	09 46	09 52				10 28
St Andrews Bus Station 🚌	a			*08h05*	*08h05*	*08b12*							*09b00*				*09b45*	*09b45*	*10b12*	*10b12*	*10b12*				*10b45*
St Andrews Bus Station 🚌	d			*07i00*	*07i00*	*07b28*							*08j10*				*08b55*	*08b55*	*09b25*	*09b25*	*09b25*				*10b10*
Leuchars 5	d			07 21	07 32	07 50							08 40				09 20	09 20	09 47	09 47	09 53				10 29
Cupar	d			07 29	07 39	07 58							08 48						09 54	09 54	10 01				
Springfield	d				07 44																				
Ladybank	d				07 48		08 22						08 55						10 01	10 01	10 09		10 24		
Markinch	d				07 56		08 31						09 03						10 08	10 09	10 17		10 32		
Kirkcaldy 242	d			07 49	08 06	08 18	08 41						09 12	09 25			09 44	09 44	10 17	10 17	10 26		10 42		
Inverkeithing 242	d				08 28	08 35	08 57						09 34				10 01	10 01	10 32	10 32	10 42		10 59		
Haymarket 242	a			08 19	08 51	08 54	09 15				09 24	09 27	09 49	09 55	09 59		10 17	10 18	10 51	10 52	11 05	11 11	11 19		11 23
Edinburgh 10 242	a			08 25	08 56	08 59	09 21				09 29	09 32	09 55	10 00	10 06		10 25	10 26	10 58	10 58	11 14	11 17	11 25		11 28

B To Newcraighall
C To Penzance
D 🍴 from Aberdeen
E To London Kings Cross
F To London Kings Cross. The Highland Chieftain
h Bus Service. arrives 0800 SO
i Bus Service. departs 0655 SO
j Bus Service. departs 0814 SO
b Bus Service

Table 229

Mondays to Saturdays

Inverurie, Dyce, Aberdeen, Dundee, Inverness and Perth - Glasgow Queen Street and Edinburgh

Network Diagram - see first page of Table 225

	SR	SR	SR	SR	GR		SR	SR	SR	SR	SR	SR	SR	SR	SR	SR		SR	SR	SR	SR	SR	SR	SR
																				SO	SX		
	1	◇1		◇1	R 1		1	◇1	◇1	1	◇1	1	◇1	◇1	◇1	1			◇1	◇1	1	1	◇1	◇1
				H	I						C				C									
		🛒		🛒	🛏 🛒			🛒	🛒		🛒		🛒	🛒	🛒				🛒	🛒			🛒	🛒
Inverness d		08 43						09 41					10 45										12 46	
Carrbridge d		09 15																					13 26	
Aviemore d		09 23						10 25					11 26										13 34	
Kingussie d		09 39						10 37					11 38										13 47	
Newtonmore d		09 44																					13 51	
Dalwhinnie d								10 51																
Blair Atholl d								11 14															14 21	
Pitlochry d		10 23						11 24					12 27										14 32	
Dunkeld & Birnam d								11 38					12 40										14 44	
Inverurie 240 d											10 38				11 35									
Dyce 240 ✈ d				09 08							10 50				11 47									
Aberdeen 240 a				09 19							11 01				11 58									
d				09 37	09 52				10 38		11 05			11 42	12 07				12 42	13 09				13 42
Portlethen d															12 17									
Stonehaven d				09 53	10 09						11 21				12 26				12 58	13 25				
Laurencekirk d											11 35													
Montrose d				10 15	10 32				11 14		11 46			12 17					13 20	13 44				14 17
Arbroath d				10 29	10 49				11 28		12 00			12 31	13 00				13 34	13 58				14 31
Carnoustie d				10 36					11 35					12 38										14 38
Golf Street d																								
Barry Links d																								
Monifieth d																								
Balmossie d																								
Broughty Ferry d				10 43																				
Dundee a				10 52	11 06				11 49		12 15			12 52	13 15				13 52	14 15				14 52
d	10 35			10 52	11 06		11 30		11 49	12 13	12 16	12 34		12 52	13 16	13 34			13 54	14 17	14 34	14 34		14 52
Invergowrie d																								
Perth a		10 52		11 14				11 57	12 11	12 35			12 58	13 14					14 14				15 01	15 14
d		10 53	11 00	11 14				12 00	12 11	12 38			13 00	13 14				14 01	14 15				15 02	15 14
Gleneagles d		11 08								12 53														
Dunblane 230 d		11 20								13 04														
Bridge of Allan 230 d		11 23								13 08														
Stirling 230 d		11 28		11 43					12 43	13 13				13 43					14 44					15 43
Larbert 230 d																								
Glasgow Queen St. 10 230 ⛴ a		12 09		12 15					13 14	13 47				14 14					15 18					16 14
Leuchars 5 a	10 46				11 20		11 41				12 28	12 46			13 28	13 45				14 29	14 45	14 45		
St Andrews Bus Station 🚌 a	*11b12*				*11b45*		*12b00*				*12b45*	*13b12*			*13b45*	*14b12*				*14b45*	*15b12*	*15b12*		
St Andrews Bus Station 🚌 d	*10b25*				*10b55*		*11b25*				*12b10*	*12b25*			*13b10*	*13b25*				*14b10*	*14b25*	*14b25*		
Leuchars 5 d	10 47				11 20		11 45				12 28	12 46			13 28	13 46				14 29	14 46	14 46		
Cupar d	10 54						11 53					12 53				13 53					14 53	14 53		
Springfield d																								
Ladybank d	11 02		11 23				12 00	12 21				13 01				14 01		14 22			15 01	15 01		
Markinch d	11 09		11 31				12 08	12 29				13 08	13 30			14 08		14 30			15 08	15 08	15 32	
Kirkcaldy 242 d	11 19		11 41		11 44		12 17	12 38				13 18	13 40			14 18		14 39			15 18	15 18	15 41	
Inverkeithing 242 d	11 35		11 57		12 01		12 33	12 54				13 34				14 34		14 55			15 34	15 34	15 57	
Haymarket 242 a	11 50		12 13		12 17		12 49	13 15			13 21	13 51	14 13		14 21	14 49		15 15		15 22	15 49	15 53	16 13	
Edinburgh 10 242 a	11 56		12 18		12 25		12 55	13 20			13 26	13 57	14 19		14 27	14 54		15 20		15 29	15 54	16 00	16 21	

C 🛒 from Aberdeen
H 🛒 from Aberdeen

I To London Kings Cross. The Northern Lights

b Bus Service

Inverurie, Dyce, Aberdeen, Dundee, Inverness and Perth - Glasgow Queen Street and Edinburgh

Network Diagram - see first page of Table 225

		SR	SR	SR	SR	SR	GR	GR	SR	SR	SR	SR	SR	SR	SR	SR	SR	SR	SR	SR	SR	SR
							SO	SX													SO	
		[1]	◇[1]	[1]		◇[1]	R [1]	R [1]		◇[1]		◇[1]			◇[1]	[1]	◇[1]	◇[1]	◇[1]	[1]		[1]
							A	A						D	E				E			
			bike			bike	sleeper/bike	sleeper/bike		bike		bike			bike		bike	bike	bike			
Inverness	d									14 48							15 50					
Carrbridge	d																					
Aviemore	d									15 26							16 29					
Kingussie	d									15 39							16 42					
Newtonmore	d																16 46					
Dalwhinnie	d									15 52												
Blair Atholl	d																17 17					
Pitlochry	d									16 21							17 27					
Dunkeld & Birnam	d									16 34							17 42					
Inverurie 240	d														15 26				16 38			
Dyce 240 (air)	d														15 40				16 54	17 05		
Aberdeen 240	a														15 51				17 05	17 14		
	d		14 04			14 39	14 50	14 50				15 33			16 03			16 37	17 07	17 16		
Portlethen	d																			17 27		
Stonehaven	d		14 20				15 07	15 07				15 49			16 20			16 53		17a37		
Laurencekirk	d		14 34												16 34				17 38			
Montrose	d					15 12	15 30	15 30				16 11						17 15	17 49			
Arbroath	d		14 57			15 26	15 46	15 46				16 25			16 57			17 29	18 03			
Carnoustie	d					15 33									17 04							
Golf Street	d																					
Barry Links	d																					
Monifieth	d																					
Balmossie	d																					
Broughty Ferry	d		15 09												17 11							
Dundee	a		15 15			15 49	16 03	16 03				16 46			17 17			17 49	18 18			
	d	15 13	15 17	15 34		15 49	16 04	16 04				16 47	16 49		17 17	17 26		17 50	18 19			18 42
Invergowrie	d											16 53										
Perth	a	15 35				16 11				16 51		17 10					17 59	18 13				
	d	15 37			16 01	16 11				16 53	17 00	17 11					18 00	18 14			18 28	
Gleneagles	d	15 52								17 08		17 26										
Dunblane 230	d	16 05							16 58	17 20		17 36						18 37			18 49	
Bridge of Allan 230	d	16 09							17 01	17 23											18 52	
Stirling 230	d	16 14				16s41			17 06	17 29		17 42						18 43			18a59	
Larbert 230	d								17 15													
Glasgow Queen St. [10] 230 (connection)	a	16 44				17 18				18 09		18 15						19 16				
Leuchars [5]	a		15 28	15 47			16 17	16 17					17 00		17 29	17 38			18 31			18 53
St Andrews Bus Station (bus)	a		*15b45*	*16d15*			*16b34*	*16b34*					*17g34*		*17e49*	*18f02*			*18b55*			*19b14*
St Andrews Bus Station (bus)	d		*15b10*	*15b25*			*15b55*	*15b55*					*16b40*		*17b10*	*17b17*			*18b05*			*18b25*
Leuchars [5]	d		15 29	15 48			16 18	16 18					17 01		17 29	17 39			18 31			18 54
Cupar	d			15 55									17 08			17 46						19 02
Springfield	d													←		17 51						
Ladybank	d			16 03							17 27		17 15	17 27		17 56	18 23					19 09
Markinch	d			16 10	16 31						→		17 22	17 39		18 03	18 34					19 17
Kirkcaldy 242	d			16 19	16 41		16 45	16 45					17 32	17 48		18 13	18 43					19 26
Inverkeithing 242	d			16 35	16 57		17 01	17 03					17 55	18 04		18 29	18 59					19 42
Haymarket 242	a		16 22	16 51	17 15		17 17	17 19	17 58				18 16	18 18	18 25	18 43	19 14		19 27			20 04
Edinburgh [10] 242	a		16 27	16 58	17 23		17 26	17 27	18 05				18 22	18 25	18 32	18 49	19 22		19 34			20 09

A To London Kings Cross
D From Perth
E (bike) from Aberdeen
g Bus Service. arrives 1730 SO
b Bus Service

Inverurie, Dyce, Aberdeen, Dundee, Inverness and Perth - Glasgow Queen Street and Edinburgh

Network Diagram - see first page of Table 225

		SR	SR	GR	SR	SR	SR	SR	SR	SR	SR		SR	SR	SR	SR	SR	XC	XC	SR	SR		SR	SR	
				SX	SO													SO	SX	SX	FSX		SX	FO	
				[R]																[R]			[R]		
		1	◇1	1	◇1	◇1		◇1	◇1		◇1		◇1	◇	◇1	◇1	◇1	◇1	◇1		1			1	
				B					A					A						C			C		
		[trolley]	[trolley]	[restaurant]	[trolley]	[trolley]		[trolley]	[trolley]		[trolley]		[trolley]	[trolley]		[trolley]				[sleeper] [restaurant]			[sleeper] [restaurant]		
Inverness	d					17 22					18 44					20 15							20 47		
Carrbridge	d					17 59					19 16														
Aviemore	d					18 07					19 30					21 01							21u29		
Kingussie	d					18 19					19 42					21 13							21u42		
Newtonmore	d										19 47					21 18							21u50		
Dalwhinnie	d										19 59					21 31							22u06		
Blair Atholl	d										20 21					21 53							22u32		
Pitlochry	d					19 00					20 31					22 03							22u45		
Dunkeld & Birnam	d					19 16					20 44					22 16							23u00		
Inverurie 240	d								18 43					19 40											
Dyce 240 ✈	d								18 55					19 52											
Aberdeen 240	a								19 06					20 03											
	d		17 36	18 16	18 16			18 30	19 09				19 47	20 05	20 42		21 05	21 17	21 31	21 42	22 27			23 22	
Portlethen	d							18 40					19 57								22 37			23 32	
Stonehaven	d		17 52	18 33	18 33			18 49	19 26				20 06	20 21	20 58		21 21	21 35	21 49	22u00	22 46			23 41	
Laurencekirk	d		18 06						19 40								21 35				22 59			23 54	
Montrose	d		18 17	18 56	18 56			19 10	19 51				20 24	20 43	21 20		21 45	21 56	22 10	22u25	23 10			00 05	
Arbroath	d		18 31	19 12	19 12			19 24	20 05				20 38	20 57	21 34		21 58	22 12	22 26	22u43	23 24			00 19	
Carnoustie	d		18 38					19 31						21 04						22u52	23 31			00 26	
Golf Street	d																								
Barry Links	d																								
Monifieth	d																								
Balmossie	d																								
Broughty Ferry	d																				23 38			00 33	
Dundee	a		18 52	19 29	19 29			19 46	20 20				20 57	21 15	21 52		22 15	22 28	22 42		23 48			00 43	
	d		18 52	19 30	19 30			19 46	20 21	20 42			20 57	21 16	21 52		22 15	22 29	22 43	23u06	23 49			00 44	
Invergowrie	d																				23 54			00 49	
Perth	a		19 14			19 35		20 07			21 00		21 18		22 14	22 30					00 12			01 07	
	d	19 09	19 14			19 37	20 00	20 11			21 02		21 18		22 14	22 30							23u21		
Gleneagles	d					19 52		20 25								22 47							23u39		
Dunblane 230	d					20 05										22 59							23u55		
Bridge of Allan 230	d					20 09										23 02									
Stirling 230	d		19 43			20 14		20 40					21 46		22 43	23 05							00u06		
Larbert 230	d																								
Glasgow Queen St. 10 230 ⛴	a		20 15			20 45		21 14					22 20		23 15	23 39									
Leuchars 5	a			19 43	19 43				20 33	20 53				21 28			22 27	22 41	22 55						
St Andrews Bus Station 🚌	a			*19b59*	*19b59*				*20b59*	*21b15*				*21b49*			*22b59*	*22b59*	*23e29*						
St Andrews Bus Station 🚌	d			*19b10*	*19b10*				*20b00*	*20b30*				*21b00*			*22b00*	*22b00*	*22b30*						
Leuchars 5	d			19 44	19 44				20 33	20 54				21 28			22 27	22 42	22 56	23u25					
Cupar	d									21 01				21 36			22 34	22 49	23 03						
Springfield	d																								
Ladybank	d						20 24			21 09				21 43			22 42	22 57	23 10						
Markinch	d	19 44					20 32			21 16	21 32			21 51			22 49	23 05	23 18						
Kirkcaldy 242	d	19 54		20 08	20 08		20 41			21 26	21 42			21 59			22 59	23 14	23 26	23u53					
Inverkeithing 242	d			20 24	20 24		20 59			21 49				22 23			23 23	23 31	23 42	00u12					
Haymarket 242	a	20 24		20 42	20 42		21 15		21 26	22 10	22 13			22 45			23 43	23 50	23 57						
Edinburgh 10 242	a	20 29		20 48	20 48		21 20		21 31	22 16	22 19			22 50			23 50	23 55	00 05						

A [trolley] from Aberdeen
B To Leeds
C To London Euston
b Bus Service

Table 229

Sundays

Inverurie, Dyce, Aberdeen, Dundee, Inverness and Perth - Glasgow Queen Street and Edinburgh

Network Diagram - see first page of Table 225

		SR	SR	SR	SR	SR	SR	SR	GR	SR	GR	XC	SR	SR	GR	SR	SR	SR	GR	SR	SR	SR	SR
					1			◇1	R 1		R 1	◇1	◇1	◇1	R 1		◇1	◇1	R 1	◇1		◇1	◇1
		A							C		D	E			F				B				
Inverness	d										09 40		10 44				12 33			13 25			
Carrbridge	d										10 10						13 05						
Aviemore	d										10 18		11 22				13 14			14 03			
Kingussie	d										10 31		11 34				13 34			14 16			
Newtonmore	d										10 36						13 39						
Dalwhinnie	d																13 50						
Blair Atholl	d										11 08						14 12						
Pitlochry	d										11 24		12 15				14 21			14 56			
Dunkeld & Birnam	d										11 37		12 34				14 34						
Inverurie 240	d																						
Dyce 240 ✈	d																						
Aberdeen 240	a																						
	d							09 27	09 47			11 12		11 29	11 47			13 27	13 50			15 10	15 30
Portlethen	d																					15 20	
Stonehaven	d							09 43	10 04			11 29		11 45	12 04			13 43	14 07			15 26	15 46
Laurencekirk	d							09 57										13 57					
Montrose	d							10 08	10 27			11 50		12 07	12 27			14 07	14 30			15 48	16 08
Arbroath	d							10 22	10 43			12 06		12 21	12 43			14 22	14 46			16 02	16 22
Carnoustie	d							10 29														16 09	
Golf Street	d																						
Barry Links	d																						
Monifieth	d																						
Balmossie	d																						
Broughty Ferry	d																						
Dundee	a							10 43	11 00			12 24		12 39	13 00			14 43	15 03			16 23	16 41
	d		07 25		08 44	09 25		10 43	11 02	11 25		12 25		12 43	13 01	13 25		14 45	15 04		15 25	16 25	16 43
Invergowrie	d																						
Perth	a				09 03			11 05			11 58		12 51	13 03			14 51	15 06		15 24			17 03
	d				09 03			11 05			11 58		12 52	13 05			14 52	15 08		15 25			17 05
Gleneagles	d				09 20			11 20			12 14			13 20			15 07	15 21					17 20
Dunblane 230	d	23p06			09 31		11 01	11 31			12 27			13 31			15 18	15 33					17 31
Bridge of Allan 230	d	23p09					11 04																
Stirling 230	d	23p14		09 05	09 38		11 10	11 38			12 34			13 38			15 24	15 45					17 38
Larbert 230	d	23p23		09 13	09 47		11 19										15 33						
Glasgow Queen St. 10 230	a				10 15			12 11						14 11			15 56	16 31					18 12
Leuchars 5	a		07 36			09 36			11 15	11 36		12 37			13 14	13 37			15 17		15 36	16 36	
St Andrews Bus Station	a		*09b37*			*09b55*			*11b37*	*11b57*		*12b57*			*13b37*	*13b57*			*15b37*		*15b57*	*16b55*	
St Andrews Bus Station	d					*09b15*			*10b55*	*11b15*		*12b15*			*12b55*	*13b15*			*14b55*		*15b15*	*16b15*	
Leuchars 5	d		07 37			09 37			11 16	11 37		12 38			13 15	13 37			15 18		15 37	16 37	
Cupar	d		07 44			09 44				11 44		12 45				13 44					15 44		
Springfield	d																						
Ladybank	d		07 52			09 52				11 52						13 52					15 52		
Markinch	d		07 59			09 59				11 59						13 59					15 59		
Kirkcaldy 242	d		08 08			10 08			11 40	12 08		13 03	13 29		13 39	14 08			15 42	16 03	16 08	17 02	
Inverkeithing 242	d		08 30			10 30			11 56	12 30		13 18	13 45		13 58	14 30			15 58	16 19	16 30	17 18	
Haymarket 242	a	00 04	08 52	09 59		10 58	11 59		12 15	12 58	13 13	13 36	14 07		14 17	14 56			16 17	16 35	16 54	17 34	
Edinburgh 10	242 a	00 09	09 00	10 04		11 06	12 04		12 23	13 06	13 19	13 42	14 12		14 25	15 03			16 25	16 42	16 59	17 41	

A not 11 December
B To London Kings Cross
C To London Kings Cross. The Northern Lights
D To London Kings Cross. The Highland Chieftain
E To Exeter St Davids
F To London Kings Cross
b Bus Service

Table 229

Sundays

Inverurie, Dyce, Aberdeen, Dundee, Inverness and Perth - Glasgow Queen Street and Edinburgh

Network Diagram - see first page of Table 225

		SR	SR	SR	SR	SR	SR	SR		SR	SR	SR	XC	SR	SR	SR
														R	R	
		◇1		◇1	◇1	◇1		◇1		◇1	◇1	◇1	◇1			1
														B	B	
		☕		☕	☕	☕		☕		☕	☕	☕		🛏 ☕	🛏 ☕	
Inverness	d	15 20		16 15		15 27				18 30				20 25		
Carrbridge	d			16 46						19 02						
Aviemore	d	15 57		16 55						19 11				21u08		
Kingussie	d	16 10		17 14						19 26				21u22		
Newtonmore	d									19 30				21u29		
Dalwhinnie	d									19 42				21u43		
Blair Atholl	d			17 49						20 03				22u09		
Pitlochry	d	16 51		17 58						20 13				22u22		
Dunkeld & Birnam	d	17 04		18 15						20 26				22u37		
Inverurie 240	d					17 14										
Dyce 240 ✈	d					17 30										
Aberdeen 240	a					17 41										
	d				17 10	17 47		19 10			19 35	20 10	21 28		21 42	22 30
Portlethen	d											20 20				
Stonehaven	d				17 26	18 04		19 26			19 51	20 26	21 45		22u00	22 48
Laurencekirk	d					18 18										
Montrose	d				17 48	18 28		19 48			20 13	20 48	22 06		22u25	23 11
Arbroath	d				18 02	18 43		20 02			20 27	21 02	22 22		22u43	23 25
Carnoustie	d							20 09							22u52	23 32
Golf Street	d															
Barry Links	d															
Monifieth	d															
Balmossie	d															
Broughty Ferry	d															
Dundee	a				18 17	19 02		20 18			20 42	21 19	22 38			23 46
	d		17 25		18 19	19 04	19 27	20 20			20 43	21 21	22 39		23u06	23 47
Invergowrie	d															
Perth	a	17 20		18 30		19 25				20 42	21 04					00 09
	d	17 21		18 31		19 27				20 46	21 05			23u00		
Gleneagles	d			18 48							21 20			23u18		
Dunblane 230	d			18 59							21 31			23u34		
Bridge of Allan 230	d															
Stirling 230	d			19 05		19 55					21 38			23u45		
Larbert 230	d			19 13							21 49					
Glasgow Queen St. 10 230 ⛴	a			19 39		20 31					22 15					
Leuchars 5	a		17 36		18 30		19 38	20 31				21 32	22 51			
St Andrews Bus Station 🚌	a		*17b57*		*18b55*		*19b59*	*20b55*				*21b55*	*23b29*			
St Andrews Bus Station 🚌	d		*17b15*		*18b00*		*19b15*	*20b15*				*21b15*	*22b30*			
Leuchars 5	d		17 37		18 31		19 39	20 32				21 33	22 52		23u25	
Cupar	d		17 44				19 46					21 39	22 59			
Springfield	d															
Ladybank	d		17 52				19 54					21 48	23 06			
Markinch	d		17 59				20 01					21 54	23 14			
Kirkcaldy 242	d	17 58	18 07		18 56		20 10	20 59		21 25		22 05	23 22		23u53	
Inverkeithing 242	d	18 14	18 29		19 12		20 31	21 15		21 41		22 21	23 38		00u12	
Haymarket 242	a	18 30	18 52		19 27		20 54	21 31		21 56		22 36	23 53			
Edinburgh 10 242	a	18 35	19 00		19 35		21 01	21 36		22 01		22 43	23 58			

B To London Euston

b Bus Service

Edinburgh, Glasgow Queen Street and Falkirk Grahamston - Stirling, Alloa and Dunblane

Miles	Miles	Miles	Miles			SR	SR	SR	SR	SR	SR	SR	SR	SR		SR	SR	SR	SR	SR	SR	SR	SR	SR
						MX	MO	MX	MX	MX										SX	SO	SX	SO	
													■1	◇■1			■1			■1	■1	■1		
							A	A			B		B	C			B	B	D	E	E	E		
														🛒										
0	0	—	—	**Edinburgh** 10	d				23p33			05 18	05 55				06 30							06 32
1¼	—	—	—	Haymarket	d				23p37			05 22	05 59				06 34							06 36
3¾	—	—	—	Edinburgh Park	d				23p43			05 27												06 42
—	17½	—	—	Linlithgow	d				23p55			05 39	06 13				06 48							06 54
—	22¼	—	—	Polmont 3	d				23p59			05 44	06 19				06 55							07 00
—	—	0	0	**Glasgow Queen Street** 10 ⛴	d	23p18	23p35	23p36		23p48				05 56		06 14			06 21	06 30	06 30	06 45		
—	—	3¼	3¼	Bishopbriggs	d	23p24	23p41			23p53						06 20								
—	—	6¼	6¼	Lenzie 3	d	23p30	23p47			23p59						06 25				06a38	06 38			
—	—	11½	11½	Croy 3	d	23p35	23p53			00 05			06a34			06 32	07a10				06a43	06a57		
—	25½	—	—	**Falkirk Grahamston**	d				00 07		05 43	05 51						06 44						07 07
—	27	—	—	Camelon 4	d				00 10		05a45	05 54						06a46	06a57					07 10
—	28¼	21	21	Larbert	d	23p49	00 05		00 16	00 18		06 00		06 16		06 43								07 15
—	36½	29	29	**Stirling**	d	00 01	00 14	00 05	00 25	00a32		06 09		06 25		06 51							07 01	07 24
—	—	—	35¾	**Alloa**	a	00 12										07 05								
—	40	32½	—	Bridge of Allan	d		00 18	00 10	00 29			06 13											07 05	07 29
—	42	34½	—	**Dunblane**	a		00 22	00 14	00 36			06 20		06 31									07 12	07 35

		SR	SR	SR	SR	SR	SR	SR	SR	SR		SR	SR	SR	SR	SR	SR	SR	SR	SR		SR	SR	SR	SR
		SX																SX							
		■1		■1	■1	◇■1		■1		■1				■1	◇■1				■1	■1		■1	■1		■1
		B			E	F		B		B		B	D	E	G			H	B	E		B	I		
				🛒	🛒			🛒		🛒				🛒	🛒				🛒	🛒		🛒	🛒		🛒
Edinburgh 10	d	06 45		07 00			07 03	07 15		07 30						07 33			07 45			08 00		08 04	08 15
Haymarket	d	06 49		07 04			07 07	07 19		07 34						07 38			07 49			08 04		08 08	08 19
Edinburgh Park	d						07 12									07 42								08 13	
Linlithgow	d	07 04					07 24	07 33		07 48						07 54		07 59	08 04					08 25	08 33
Polmont 3	d			07 21			07 30			07 55						08 00						08 22		08 30	08 39
Glasgow Queen Street 10 ⛴	d		06 48	07a50	07 00	07 06			07 18				07 21	07 30	07 41		07 48			08 00			08 06		09a07
Bishopbriggs	d		06 53						07 23								07 54								
Lenzie 3	d		06 59		07a08				07 29								08 00		08a25						
Croy 3	d	07a23	07 05					07a52	07 35	08a10				07a41			08 06			08a11		08a36			
Falkirk Grahamston	d						07 36					07 44				08 07		08 11						08 37	
Camelon 4	d						07 40					07a46	08a04			08 10		08a14						08 40	
Larbert	d		07 18				07 46		07 50							08 16	08 19							08 46	
Stirling	d		07 40			07 33	07 55		08 06						08u09	08 25	08a31						08 36	08 55	
Alloa	a								08 18																
Bridge of Allan	d		07 44				07 59									08 29							08 40	09 00	
Dunblane	a		07 52			07 39	08 08								08 15	08 36							08 44	09 08	

		SR	SR	SR	SR	SR		SR	SR	SR	SR	SR	SR	SR	SR	SR		SR	SR	SR	SR	SR	SR	SR	SR
			■1			■1		◇■1		■1		■1	■1	■1		■1			■1			■1	◇■1		■1
			B	B	D	E		G				E	B	I					B	B	D	E	G		
			🛒			🛒		🛒		🛒		🛒	🛒	🛒		🛒			🛒			🛒	🛒		🛒
Edinburgh 10	d		08 30						08 31	08 45			09 00		09 03	09 15			09 30					09 33	09 45
Haymarket	d		08 34						08 36	08 49			09 04		09 07	09 19			09 34					09 38	09 49
Edinburgh Park	d								08 43						09 14									09 43	
Linlithgow	d								08 55	09 03					09 26	09 33								09 55	10 03
Polmont 3	d								09 00	09 09					09 31	09 39								10 00	10 09
Glasgow Queen Street 10 ⛴	d	08 18			08 24	08 30		08 41		09a36	08 48	09 00		09 08		10a06		09 18			09 21	09 30	09 41		10a36
Bishopbriggs	d	08 23									08 53							09 23							
Lenzie 3	d	08 29									08 59							09 29							
Croy 3	d	08 35	09a03			08a42					09 05	09a12	09a33					09 35	10a03			09a42			
Falkirk Grahamston	d			08 43					09 07						09 38					09 43				10 08	
Camelon 4	d			08a45	09a04				09 10						09 41					09a45	10a04			10 11	
Larbert	d	08 49							09 16		09 18				09 47			09 52						10 15	
Stirling	d	09 00						09a07	09 25		09 39			09 34	09 56			10 03					10a07	10 24	
Alloa	a	09 13																10 16							
Bridge of Allan	d								09 30		09 42				10 00									10 30	
Dunblane	a								09 36		09 51			09 40	10 07									10 36	

		SR		SR	SR	SR	SR	SR	SR	SR	SR	SR		SR	SR	SR	SR	SR	SR	SR	SR	SR		SR	SR
				■1	■1	◇■1		■1		■1				■1	◇■1		■1		■1	■1		■1			■1
				E	B	F				B	B	D		E	G				E	B					B
				🛒	🛒	🛒		🛒		🛒				🛒	🛒		🛒		🛒	🛒		🛒			🛒
Edinburgh 10	d				10 00		10 02	10 15		10 30						10 32	10 45			11 00	11 03	11 15			11 30
Haymarket	d				10 04		10 07	10 19		10 34						10 36	10 49			11 04	11 08	11 19			11 34
Edinburgh Park	d						10 13									10 43					11 13				
Linlithgow	d						10 25	10 33								10 55	11 03				11 25	11 33			
Polmont 3	d						10 30	10 39								11 00	11 09				11 31	11 39			
Glasgow Queen Street 10 ⛴	d	09 49		10 00		10 10		11a06	10 18			10 21		10 30	10 41		11a37	10 48	11 00			12a06		11 19	
Bishopbriggs	d	09 54							10 23									10 53						11 23	
Lenzie 3	d	10 00							10 29									10 59						11 29	
Croy 3	d	10 06		10a12	10a33				10 35	11a03				10a42				11 05	11a12	11a33				11 35	12a03
Falkirk Grahamston	d						10 36				10 43					11 08					11 38				
Camelon 4	d						10 40				10a45	11a04				11 11					11 41				
Larbert	d	10 18					10 46		10 48							11 15		11 18			11 46			11 48	
Stirling	d	10a31				10 35	10 55		11 00						11a08	11 24		11 30			11 55			12 00	
Alloa	a								11 13															12 13	
Bridge of Allan	d					10 41	11 00									11 30		11 35			12 00				
Dunblane	a					10 44	11 07									11 36		11 43			12 07				

A To Perth
B To Glasgow Queen Street
C To Dyce
D To Falkirk Grahamston
E To Edinburgh
F To Inverness
G To Aberdeen
H From Kirkcaldy to Glasgow Queen Street
I To Dundee

Edinburgh, Glasgow Queen Street and Falkirk Grahamston - Stirling, Alloa and Dunblane

		SR A	SR B	SR [1] C ⚲	SR ◇[1] D ⚲	SR	SR [1] ⚲	SR		SR [1] C ⚲	SR [1] A ⚲	SR ◇[1] E ⚲	SR	SR [1] ⚲	SR	SR [1] A ⚲	SR A	SR B		SR [1] C ⚲	SR ◇[1] D ⚲	SR	SR [1] ⚲	SR	SR [1] A ⚲
Edinburgh [10]	d					11 32	11 45				12 00		12 03	12 15		12 30						12 31	12 45		13 00
Haymarket	d					11 36	11 49				12 04		12 08	12 19		12 34						12 36	12 49		13 04
Edinburgh Park	d					11 43							12 13									12 43			
Linlithgow	d					11 55	12 03						12 26	12 33								12 55	13 03		
Polmont [3]	d					12 01	12 09						12 31	12 39								13 01	13 09		
Glasgow Queen Street [10] ⛴	d		11 22	11 30	11 41		12a37	11 48		12 00		12 10		13a06	12 18			12 24		12 30	12 41		13a36	12 48	
Bishopbriggs	d							11 53							12 23									12 53	
Lenzie [3]	d							11 59							12 29									12 59	
Croy [3]	d			11a42				12 05		12a12	12a34				12 35	13a03				12a42				13 05	13a33
Falkirk Grahamston	d	11 43				12 07							12 37				12 43					13 07			
Camelon [4]	d	11a45	12a04			12 10							12 40				12a45	13a04				13 10			
Larbert	d					12 16		12 18					12 47		12 48							13 16		13 18	
Stirling	d				12a07	12 25		12a31				12 35	12 56		13 00						13a07	13 25		13 31	
Alloa	a														13 13										
Bridge of Allan	d					12 30						12 41	13 00									13 30		13 35	
Dunblane	a					12 36						12 44	13 07									13 36		13 43	

		SR [1] C ⚲	SR	SR [1] ⚲		SR	SR [1] A ⚲	SR A	SR B	SR [1] C ⚲	SR ◇[1] D ⚲	SR	SR [1] ⚲	SR		SR [1] A ⚲	SR [1] C ⚲	SR	SR [1] ⚲	SR	SR [1] A ⚲	SR A	SR B	SR [1] C ⚲	
Edinburgh [10]	d		13 03	13 15			13 30					13 32	13 45			14 00		14 04	14 15		14 30				
Haymarket	d		13 07	13 19			13 34					13 36	13 49			14 04		14 07	14 19		14 34				
Edinburgh Park	d		13 14									13 43						14 13							
Linlithgow	d		13 26	13 33								13 55	14 03					14 25	14 33						
Polmont [3]	d		13 30	13 39								14 00	14 09					14 30	14 39						
Glasgow Queen Street [10] ⛴	d	13 00		14a06		13 19			13 23	13 30	13 41		14a36	13 48			14 00		15a07	14 18			14 21	14 30	
Bishopbriggs	d					13 25								13 53						14 23					
Lenzie [3]	d					13 31								13 59						14 29					
Croy [3]	d	13a12				13 37	14a03			13a42				14 05		14a33	14a12			14 35	15a03			14a42	
Falkirk Grahamston	d		13 37					13 43				14 07						14 37				14 43			
Camelon [4]	d		13 40					13a45	14a04			14 10						14 40				14a45	15a04		
Larbert	d		13 46			13 48						14 15		14 16				14 47		14 48					
Stirling	d		13 55			14 00					14a07	14 24		14 31				14 56		15 00					
Alloa	a					14 13														15 13					
Bridge of Allan	d		14 00									14 28		14 36				15 00							
Dunblane	a		14 07									14 35		14 43				15 07							

		SR ◇[1] D ⚲	SR	SR [1] ⚲	SR	SR [1] C ⚲	SR [1] A ⚲	SR ◇[1] E ⚲	SR	SR [1] ⚲		SR	SR [1] A ⚲	SR A	SR B	SR [1] C ⚲	SR	SR [1] ⚲	SR	SR [1] C ⚲		SR [1] A ⚲	SR [1] F ⚲	SR	SR [1] ⚲
Edinburgh [10]	d		14 33	14 45			15 00		15 03	15 15			15 30				15 33	15 45				16 00		16 03	16 15
Haymarket	d		14 36	14 49			15 04		15 08	15 19			15 34				15 38	15 49				16 04		16 07	16 19
Edinburgh Park	d		14 43						15 14								15 43							16 13	
Linlithgow	d		14 55	15 03					15 25	15 34							15 55	16 04						16 25	16 33
Polmont [3]	d		15 00	15 09					15 30	15 40							16 00	16 10						16 31	16 39
Glasgow Queen Street [10] ⛴	d	14 41		15a37	14 49	15 00		15 10		16a07		15 18			15 21	15 30		16a36	15 48	16 00			16 10		17a07
Bishopbriggs	d				14 54							15 25							15 54						
Lenzie [3]	d				15 00							15 30							15 59						
Croy [3]	d				15 06	15a12	15a33					15 37	16a03			15a42			16 06	16a12		16a33			
Falkirk Grahamston	d		15 08						15 37					15 43			16 07							16 37	
Camelon [4]	d		15 11						15 40					15a45	16a04		16 10							16 40	
Larbert	d		15 15		15 17				15 44			15 50					16 16		16 18					16 46	
Stirling	d	15a07	15 24		15a28			15 36	15 53			16 01					16 25		16a31				16 39	16 55	
Alloa	a											16 15													
Bridge of Allan	d		15 30					15 41	15 57								16 29						16 44	17 00	
Dunblane	a		15 36					15 45	16 07								16 36						16 49	17 07	

A To Glasgow Queen Street
B To Falkirk Grahamston
C To Edinburgh
D To Aberdeen
E To Inverness
F To Dundee

Edinburgh, Glasgow Queen Street and Falkirk Grahamston - Stirling, Alloa and Dunblane

		SR	SR	SR	SR	SR		SR	SR	GR	GR	SR	SR	SR	SR	SR		SR	SR	SR	SR	SR	SR	SR	SR
								SX	SO	SO	SX							SO	SX	SX					
			1			1			◇1	R 1	R 1		1		1	1						1			
			A	A	B	C			D	E	E				C	A		F		G				A	B
			trolley			trolley			trolley	restaurant, trolley	restaurant, trolley		trolley		trolley	trolley						trolley			
Edinburgh 10	d		16 30							16 32	16 33	16 36	16 45			17 00					17 03	17 15			
Haymarket	d		16 34							16 38	16 38	16 41	16 49			17 04					17 07	17 19			
Edinburgh Park	d											16 46									17 13				
Linlithgow	d											16 58	17 06								17 26	17 33			
Polmont 3	d											17 04	17 13								17 32	17 39			
Glasgow Queen Street 10	d	16 19			16 22	16 30		16 33	16 41				17a40	16 48	17 00			17 03	17 03	17 11		18a06	17 18		17 22
Bishopbriggs	d	16 24						16 39						16 53				17 08	17 08				17 23		
Lenzie 3	d	16 30						16a44						16 59				17 14	17 14				17 29		
Croy 3	d	16 36	17a02			16a42								17 05	17a12	17a34		17 19					17 35		
Falkirk Grahamston	d			16 43						17 03	17 04	17 09							17a32		17 38			17 43	
Camelon 4	d			16a45	17a01							17 12									17 41			17a45	18a04
Larbert	d	16 49										17 20		17 23				17 31		17 31	17 47		17 52		
Stirling	d	17 08							17a07	17a18	17a19	17 29		17 35				17 45		17 45	17 56		18 02		
Alloa	a	17 20																					18 14		
Bridge of Allan	d											17 32		17 40				17 49		17 49	18 01				
Dunblane	a											17 40		17 47				17 54		17 54	18 08				

		SR		SR	SR	SR	SR	SR	SR	SR	SR	SR		SR	SR	SR	SR	SR	SR	SR	SR	SR		SR	SR
				SX	SO	SX		SX																	
		1			◇1		1	◇1		1		1		1	◇1		1		1			1		◇1	
		C		H	D	I	A	D				C		A	J				A	A	B	C		D	
		trolley			trolley		trolley	trolley		trolley		trolley		trolley	trolley		trolley		trolley			trolley		trolley	
Edinburgh 10	d					17 27	17 30		17 32	17 45				18 00		18 01	18 15		18 30						18 34
Haymarket	d					17 32	17 34		17 36	17 49				18 04		18 07	18 19		18 34						18 38
Edinburgh Park	d								17 44							18 13									18 43
Linlithgow	d								17 56	18 04						18 25	18 33								18 55
Polmont 3	d								18 01	18 09						18 30	18 39								19 00
Glasgow Queen Street 10	d	17 30		17 33	17 41			17 41		18a37	17 48	18 00			18 11		19a08	18 18			18 24	18 30		18 41	
Bishopbriggs	d			17 38							17 53							18 23							
Lenzie 3	d			17 43							17 59							18 29							
Croy 3	d	17a42					18a05				18 05	18a12		18a34				18 35	19a05			18a42			
Falkirk Grahamston	d			18a04					18 08							18 37				18 45					19 07
Camelon 4	d								18 11							18 40				18a47	19a04				19 10
Larbert	d					17 57			18 17		18 19				18 30	18 46		18 51							19 16
Stirling	d				18 08	18 06		18 15	18 30		18 32				18 41	18 55		19 00						19u07	19 25
Alloa	a								18 42									19 15							
Bridge of Allan	d					18 13					18 37				18 46	18 59									19 29
Dunblane	a				18 14	18 18		18 22			18 44				18 50	19 09								19 13	19 38

		SR	SR	SR	SR	SR	SR	SR		SR	SR	SR	SR	SR	SR	SR	SR	SR		SR	SR	SR	SR	SR	SR
		1		1	1	1		1			1	◇1					1	1			1	◇1			1
				A	C	K					A	D	A			B		C			A	D			
		trolley		trolley	trolley	trolley		trolley				trolley													
Edinburgh 10	d	18 45		19 00			19 03	19 15			19 30			19 33			20 00				20 30		20 33		21 00
Haymarket	d	18 49		19 04			19 07	19 19			19 34			19 37			20 04				20 34		20 38		21 04
Edinburgh Park	d						19 13							19 42									20 42		
Linlithgow	d	19 03					19 25	19 33			19 48			19 55			20 18				20 48		20 54		21 19
Polmont 3	d	19 09					19 30	19 39						20 01			20 24						21 00		21 25
Glasgow Queen Street 10	d	19a36	18 48		19 00	19 10		20a07		19 18		19 41			19 48	19 51	20a51	20 00		20 18		20 41		20 48	21a51
Bishopbriggs	d		18 53							19 23					19 54					20 23				20 53	
Lenzie 3	d		18 59							19 29					20 00					20 29				20 59	
Croy 3	d		19 05	19a34	19a12					19 35	20a07				20 06			20a12		20 35	21a07			21 05	
Falkirk Grahamston	d						19 36						19 43	20 07									21 06		
Camelon 4	d						19 39						19a45	20 10		20a31							21 09		
Larbert	d		19 21				19 44			19 47				20 16	20 18					20 48			21 16	21 18	
Stirling	d		19a32			19 37	19 53			20 00		20a07		20 25	20 30					21 00		21 07	21 25	21a32	
Alloa	a									20 13										21 13					
Bridge of Allan	d					19 41	19 59							20 30	20 35								21 29		
Dunblane	a					19 45	20 07							20 36	20 43							21 14	21 37		

A To Glasgow Queen Street
B To Falkirk Grahamston
C To Edinburgh
D To Aberdeen
E From London Kings Cross to Inverness. **The Highland Chieftain**
F To Perth
G To Carnoustie
H To Markinch
I From Newcraighall
J To Inverness
K To Dundee

Edinburgh, Glasgow Queen Street and Falkirk Grahamston - Stirling, Alloa and Dunblane

		SR A	SR B	SR ■1 C		SR	SR ■1 A	SR ◇■1 D	SR E	SR	SR ■1	SR A	SR B	SR ■1 C		SR	SR ■1 A	SR	SR E	SR ■1 A	SR A	SR B	SR ■1 C	SR	
Edinburgh ■10	d						21 30		21 33		22 00						22 30	22 33		23 00				23 02	
Haymarket	d						21 34		21 37		22 04						22 34	22 37		23 04				23 07	
Edinburgh Park	d								21 43									22 43						23 12	
Linlithgow	d						21 48		21 55		22 18						22 48	22 55		23 18				23 24	
Polmont ■3	d								22 00		22 24							23 00		23 24				23 30	
Glasgow Queen Street ■10 ⛴	d		20 51	21 00		21 18		21 42		21 48	22a50		21 51	22 00		22 18			22 48			22 51	23 00		
Bishopbriggs	d					21 21				21 53						22 23			22 53						
Lenzie ■3	d					21 27				21 59						22 29			22 59						
Croy ■3	d			21a12		21 33	22a07			22 05				22a12		22 35	23a07		23 05	23a39			23a12		
Falkirk Grahamston	d	21 13							22 07			22 13						23 07			23 13			23 37	
Camelon ■4	d	21a15	21a27						22 10			22a15	22a27					23 10			23a15	23a29		23 40	
Larbert	d					21 48			22 16	22 18						22 47		23 16	23 18					23 46	
Stirling	d					22 00		22a08	22 25	22 30						23 01		23 25	23 33					23a56	
Alloa	a					22 13										23 13									
Bridge of Allan	d								22 30	22 35								23 29	23 37						
Dunblane	a								22 34	22 43								23 36	23 42						

		SR	SR ■1 C	SR ■1 A	SR E	SR	SR
Edinburgh ■10	d			23 30		23 33	
Haymarket	d			23 34		23 37	
Edinburgh Park	d					23 43	
Linlithgow	d			23 48		23 55	
Polmont ■3	d			23 54		23 59	
Glasgow Queen Street ■10 ⛴	d	23 18	23 30		23 36		23 48
Bishopbriggs	d	23 24					23 53
Lenzie ■3	d	23 30					23 59
Croy ■3	d	23 35	23a42	00a09			00 05
Falkirk Grahamston	d					00 07	
Camelon ■4	d					00 10	
Larbert	d	23 49				00 16	00 18
Stirling	d	00 01			00 05	00 25	00a32
Alloa	a	00 12					
Bridge of Allan	d				00 10	00 29	
Dunblane	a				00 14	00 36	

Sundays

		SR F	SR G	SR F	SR F	SR ■1 C	SR ■1 A (trolley)		SR ■1 C (trolley)			SR ■1 A		SR ■1 C (trolley)	SR ◇■1 D (trolley)	SR		SR ■1 A (trolley)	SR	SR ■1 C (trolley)		SR		SR ■1 A (trolley)	SR ◇■1 I (trolley)
Edinburgh ■10	d			23p33			08 00					09 00				09 33		10 00				10 32		11 00	
Haymarket	d			23p37			08 04					09 04				09 36		10 04				10 35		11 04	
Edinburgh Park	d			23p43												09 40						10 41			
Linlithgow	d			23p55			08 18					09 18				09 59		10 18				10 54		11 18	
Polmont ■3	d			23p59			08 24					09 24				10 05		10 24				11 00		11 24	
Glasgow Queen Street ■10 ⛴	d	23p18	23p36		23p48	07 50			08 30					09 30	09 38				10 15	10 30					11 09
Bishopbriggs	d	23p24			23p53														10 21						
Lenzie ■3	d	23p30			23p59										09 47				10 27						
Croy ■3	d	23p35			00 05	08a02	08a39		08a42			09a39		09a42				10a39	10 33	10a42				11a39	
Falkirk Grahamston	d			00 07												10 11						11 06			
Camelon ■4	d			00 10												10 14						11 09			
Larbert	d	23p49		00 16	00 18										10 02	10 21			10 45			11 13			11 29
Stirling	d	00 01	00 05	00 25	00a32										10 12	10 30			10 55			11 23			11 39
Alloa	a	00 12																	11 07						
Bridge of Allan	d		00 10	00 29												10 34						11 28			
Dunblane	a		00 14	00 36											10 17	10 41						11 37			11 45

		SR	SR ■1 C (trolley)	SR ◇■1 D	SR			SR ■1 A (trolley)	SR	SR ■1 A (trolley)	SR ■1 C (trolley)	SR		SR ■1 C (trolley)	SR ■1 (trolley)	SR		SR ■1 A (trolley)	SR ◇■1 D (trolley)	SR		SR ■1 (trolley)	SR ■1 C (trolley)	SR	SR ■1 A
Edinburgh ■10	d				11 35			12 00		12 30		12 35			13 00			13 30		13 36		14 00			14 30
Haymarket	d				11 39			12 04		12 33		12 40			13 04			13 34		13 41		14 04			14 34
Edinburgh Park	d				11 43							12 43								13 45					
Linlithgow	d				11 55			12 18		12 48		12 55			13 18			13 48		13 57		14 18			14 48
Polmont ■3	d				12 01			12 24				13 01			13 24					14 03		14 24			
Glasgow Queen Street ■10 ⛴	d	11 15	11 30	11 45					12 15		12 30			13 00	13a51	13 15			13 45			14a51	14 00	14 15	
Bishopbriggs	d	11 21							12 21							13 21								14 21	
Lenzie ■3	d	11 27							12 27							13 27								14 27	
Croy ■3	d	11 33	11a42					12a39	12 33	13a07	12a42			13a12		13 33		14a07					14a12	14 33	15a07
Falkirk Grahamston	d				12 08							13 08								14 09					
Camelon ■4	d				12 10							13 10								14 12					
Larbert	d	11 45			12 15				12 45			13 15				13 45				14 18				14 45	
Stirling	d	11 55		12 12	12 25				12 55			13 25				13 55			14 12	14 26				14 55	
Alloa	a	12 07							13 07							14 07								15 07	
Bridge of Allan	d				12 30							13 30								14 32					
Dunblane	a			12 17	12 38							13 38							14 17	14 38					

A To Glasgow Queen Street
B To Falkirk Grahamston
C To Edinburgh
D To Aberdeen
E To Perth
F not 11 December
G not 11 December. To Perth
I To Inverness

Table 230

Sundays

Edinburgh, Glasgow Queen Street and Falkirk Grahamston - Stirling, Alloa and Dunblane

		SR		SR		SR	SR	SR	SR	SR	SR			SR	SR	SR	SR	GR	SR		SR	SR		SR	SR
																		R							
		◇1				1	1		1	◇1				1	1		1	1			1	1			1
		A				C			D	E					C		D	F			C				D
		⚒					⚒		⚒	⚒				⚒	⚒		⚒	🍽			⚒	⚒			
Edinburgh 10	d			14 36			15 00		15 30		15 35			16 00			16 30	16 30	16 35			17 00			17 30
Haymarket	d			14 39			15 04		15 34		15 39			16 04			16 34	16 35	16 39			17 04			17 34
Edinburgh Park	d			14 43							15 43								16 43						
Linlithgow	d			14 55			15 18		15 48		15 55			16 18			16 48		16 55			17 18			17 48
Polmont 3	d			15 01			15 24				16 01			16 24					17 01			17 24			
Glasgow Queen Street 10 🚢	d	14 40				15 00	15a51	15 15		15 45				16a51	16 00	16 15					17 00	17a52		17 15	
Bishopbriggs	d							15 21								16 21								17 21	
Lenzie 3	d							15 27								16 27								17 27	
Croy 3	d					15a12		15 33	16a07						16a12	16 33	17a07				17a12			17 33	18a07
Falkirk Grahamston	d			15 07							16 07							17 02	17 07						
Camelon 4	d			15 10							16 10								17 10						
Larbert	d	15 00		15 15				15 45			16 15					16 45			17 15					17 48	
Stirling	d	15 09		15 25				15 55		16 12	16 25					16 55		17a17	17 25					17 57	
Alloa	a							16 07								17 07								18 12	
Bridge of Allan	d			15 30							16 30								17 30						
Dunblane	a	15 15		15 38						16 17	16 38								17 38						

		SR	SR	SR	SR	SR	SR	SR		SR	SR	SR	SR	SR	SR	SR	SR	SR		SR	SR	SR	SR	SR	SR
		◇1			1	1	◇1			1		1	1		1	◇1		1		1		1		1	1
		E		B		C	A			D			C		D	E		C				D		C	D
		⚒			⚒	⚒	⚒			⚒		⚒	⚒		⚒	⚒									
Edinburgh 10	d		17 34		18 00					18 30	18 35	19 00			19 30		19 35			20 00		20 30	20 35		21 00
Haymarket	d		17 38		18 04					18 34	18 39	19 04			19 34		19 39			20 04		20 34	20 39		21 04
Edinburgh Park	d		17 43								18 43						19 43						20 43		
Linlithgow	d		17 55		18 18					18 48	18 55	19 18			19 48		19 55			20 18		20 48	20 55		21 18
Polmont 3	d		18 01		18 24						19 01	19 24					20 01			20 24			21 01		21 24
Glasgow Queen Street 10 🚢	d	17 45		17 48	18a51	18 00	18 10	18 16				19a51	19 00	19 15		19 45		20 00		20a51	20 15			21 00	
Bishopbriggs	d			17 54				18 21						19 21							20 21				
Lenzie 3	d			18 00				18 26						19 27							20 27				
Croy 3	d			18a06		18a12		18 33		19a07			19a12	19 33	20a07			20a12			20 33	21a07		21a12	21a39
Falkirk Grahamston	d		18 07								19 07						20 07						21 07		
Camelon 4	d		18 10								19 10						20 10						21 10		
Larbert	d		18 15				18 30	18 45			19 16			19 45			20 14				20 45		21 15		
Stirling	d	18a12	18 25				18 40	18 55			19 26			19 55		20 12	20 24				20 55		21 25		
Alloa	a							19 07						20 07							21 07				
Bridge of Allan	d		18 30								19 30						20 29						21 30		
Dunblane	a		18 37				18 46				19 40					20 17	20 38						21 38		

		SR	SR	SR		SR	SR	SR	SR	SR	SR	SR	SR	SR
			1	◇1			1		1		1	1	1	
			C	E			D		C	G	D	C	D	G
				⚒										
Edinburgh 10	d					21 36	22 00			22 34	23 00		23 30	
Haymarket	d					21 41	22 04			22 39	23 04		23 34	
Edinburgh Park	d					21 45				22 45				
Linlithgow	d					21 57	22 18			22 58	23 18		23 48	
Polmont 3	d					22 03	22 24			23 03	23 24		23 54	
Glasgow Queen Street 10 🚢	d	21 15	21 30	21 45				22 15	22 30			23 30		23 35
Bishopbriggs	d	21 21						22 21						23 41
Lenzie 3	d	21 27						22 27						23 47
Croy 3	d	21 33	21a42				22a39	22 33	22a42		23a39	23a42	00a09	23 53
Falkirk Grahamston	d					22 09				23 10				
Camelon 4	d					22 12				23 14				
Larbert	d	21 45				22 18		22 45		23 19				00 05
Stirling	d	21 55		22 11		22 27		22 55		23 28				00 14
Alloa	a	22 07						23 07						
Bridge of Allan	d					22 32				23 33				00 18
Dunblane	a			22 17		22 38				23 37				00 22

A To Elgin
C To Edinburgh
D To Glasgow Queen Street
E To Aberdeen
F From London Kings Cross to Inverness. **The Highland Chieftain**
G To Perth

Dunblane, Alloa and Stirling - Falkirk Grahamston, Glasgow Queen Street and Edinburgh

Miles	Miles	Miles	Miles		SR MX	SR MX [1] A	SR MX B	SR MO [1] C	SR MX [1] C	SR MO [1] A	SR MX [1] A	SR	SR D		SR B	SR [1] C	SR [1] A	SR SX [1] C	SR	SR SO [1] C	SR [1] A	SR D	SR	
0	0	—	—	**Dunblane** d	23p06							05 21			05 46								06 28	
2	2	—	—	Bridge of Allan d	23p09							05 24			05 49								06 31	
—	—	—	0	**Alloa** d															06 11					
5½	5½	—	6¾	**Stirling** d	23p14							05 30			05 54				06 23				06 36	
13½	13½	—	14¾	Larbert d	23p23							05 38			06 03				06 32				06 45	
—	15	—	—	Camelon [4] d	23p29							05 44	05 45									06 46	06 51	
—	16½	—	—	**Falkirk Grahamston** d	23p32							05 47											06 54	
24	—	—	25¼	Croy [3] d		23p39		23p42	23p42	00 09	00 09				06 14		06 34		06 43	06 43	07 10			
29¼	—	—	30½	Lenzie [3] d		23p44					00 14				06 21			06 38	06 50					
32¼	—	—	33½	Bishopbriggs d		23p50									06 25				06 54					
34½	—	—	35¾	**Glasgow Queen Street** [10] ⛴ a		00 01				00 25	00 26		06 25		06 34		06 49		07 03		07 25	07 29		
—	19½	—	—	Polmont [3] d	23p38			23p56	23p56			05 53				06 23		06 56		06 56			07 02	
—	24¼	—	—	Linlithgow d	23p45			00 03	00 03			06 00				06 29		07 03		07 03			07 09	
—	38	14¾	—	Edinburgh Park d	23p58							06 12											07 23	
—	40½	17¼	—	Haymarket d	00 04		00 12	00s19	00s20			06 20				06s45		07s19		07s19			07 28	
—	41¾	18½	—	**Edinburgh** [10] 225,242 a	00 09		00 18	00 24	00 25			06 24				06 50		07 25		07 25			07 34	

	SR SX [1] C		SR [1] C 🛒	SR F	SR SX [1] A	SR SX	SR	SR SX B	SR [1] C 🛒		SR SX	SR [1] C 🛒	SR [1] A 🛒	SR B	SR [1] C	SR [1] A 🛒	SR D		SR SX		SR ◇[1] H 🛒	SR [1] C 🛒	SR SO [1] A 🛒	SR SX [1] A 🛒
Dunblane d				06 47							07 23			07 31							07 44			
Bridge of Allan d				06 51							07 26			07 34							07 48			
Alloa d							07 11												07 39					
Stirling d				06 55			07 22				07 31			07 39					07 49		07 53			
Larbert d				07 04			07 30				07 39			07 47					07 58		08 02			
Camelon [4] d																	07 46		08 02					
Falkirk Grahamston d																			08 07					
Croy [3] d	06 57			07 15	07 23		07 43					07 41	07 52	07 59		08 10						08 11		
Lenzie [3] d			07 08	07 21		07 34	07 50							08 05							08 18		08 25	08 25
Bishopbriggs d				07 26		07 38	07 55							08 10									08 29	
Glasgow Queen Street [10] ⛴ a				07 35	07 38	07 47	08 04						08 07	08 20		08 25	08 29				08 34		08 40	08 40
Polmont [3] d			07 26						07 38						08 09				08 16			08 26		
Linlithgow d	07 14		07 32						07 44			07 59			08 15				08 23					
Edinburgh Park d																			08 37					
Haymarket d	07s31		07s49					07 52	08s01		08 15	08s17			08s31				08 44			08s45		
Edinburgh [10] 225,242 a	07 37		07 55					07 57	08 06		08 22	08 25			08 37				08 48			08 52		

	SR SX I	SR	SR	SR [1] A 🛒	SR [1] C 🛒		SR [1] C 🛒	SR		SR	SR ◇[1] H 🛒	SR [1] A 🛒	SR D	SR [1] C 🛒	SR [1] C 🛒		SR	SR	SR [1] F	SR [1] A 🛒	SR [1] C 🛒	SR [1] C 🛒	SR	SR
Dunblane d		07 58						08 13		08 28								09 03	09 07					09 28
Bridge of Allan d		08 01						08 16		08 31									09 11					09 31
Alloa d			07 57														08 36							
Stirling d		08 07	08 11					08 23		08 36	08 43						08 53	09 09	09 15				09 23	09 36
Larbert d		08 16	08 19					08 32		08 45							09 02	09 18					09 32	09 45
Camelon [4] d		08 20								08 49			08 45					09 24						09 49
Falkirk Grahamston d	08 11	08 24								08 54								09 27						09 54
Croy [3] d			08 32	08 36			08 42	08 43				09 03			09 12		09 13			09 34		09 42	09 43	
Lenzie [3] d	08 32		08 37					08 50									09 20						09 50	
Bishopbriggs d	08 37		08 42					08 54									09 24						09 54	
Glasgow Queen Street [10] ⛴ a	08 48		08 52	08 55				09 03			09 15	09 19	09 25				09 33		09 46	09 50			10 03	
Polmont [3] d		08 31								09 00				09 08				09 32			09 38			10 00
Linlithgow d		08 38			08 44					09 07				09 14				09 39			09 44			10 07
Edinburgh Park d		08 51								09 21								09 53						10 21
Haymarket d		08 58			09s01		09s14			09 27				09s30	09s45			10 00			10s02	10s12		10 27
Edinburgh [10] 225,242 a		09 04			09 07		09 19			09 32				09 37	09 52			10 06			10 07	10 17		10 34

A From Edinburgh
B From Perth
C From Glasgow Queen Street
D From Falkirk Grahamston
F From Dundeen
H From Aberdeen
I From Kirkcaldy

Table 230

Mondays to Saturdays

Dunblane, Alloa and Stirling - Falkirk Grahamston, Glasgow Queen Street and Edinburgh

		SR		SR	SR	SR	SR	SR	SR	SR	SR	SR		SR	GR	SR		SR	SR	SR	SR	SR		SR	SR
						SX	SO																		
		◇1		1		1	1	1			1			1	R 1	1			◇1	1		1		1	
		A		B	C	D	D	D			B			D	E	D			F	B	C	D		D	
Dunblane	d									09 58		10 13						10 28							
Bridge of Allan	d									10 01		10 16						10 31							
Alloa	d								09 41																10 36
Stirling	d	09 44							09 53	10 06		10 23			10 30			10 36	10 43						10 53
Larbert	d								10 02	10 15		10 32						10 45							11 02
Camelon 4	d				09 45					10 19								10 49			10 45				
Falkirk Grahamston	d									10 24					10 46			10 54							
Croy 3	d			10 03				10 12	10 13		10 33	10 43				10 42				11 03				11 12	11 13
Lenzie 3	d								10 20			10 50													11 20
Bishopbriggs	d								10 24			10 54													11 25
Glasgow Queen Street 10	a	10 14		10 19	10 26				10 33		10 49	11 03							11 14	11 19	11 25				11 34
Polmont 3	d					10 08	10 08			10 30				10 38				11 00				11 08			
Linlithgow	d					10 14	10 14			10 37				10 44				11 07				11 14			
Edinburgh Park	d									10 51								11 21							
Haymarket	d					10s30	10s30	10s44		10 58				11s00	11 11	11s14		11 27				11s30		11s45	
Edinburgh 10 225,242	a					10 37	10 37	10 49		11 04				11 05	11 17	11 20		11 32				11 35		11 50	

		SR	SR	SR		SR	SR	SR		SR	SR	SR	SR	SR	SR	SR	SR	SR		SR		SR	SR	SR	SR
			1	1		1		◇1			◇1	1		1	1			1		1		1		◇1	
			B	D		D		H			I	B	C	D	D			B		D		D		A	
Dunblane	d	10 58						11 20		11 28							11 58						12 13		12 28
Bridge of Allan	d	11 01						11 23		11 31							12 01						12 16		12 31
Alloa	d															11 43									
Stirling	d	11 06					11 23	11 28		11 36	11 43					11 53	12 06						12 23		12 36
Larbert	d	11 15					11 32			11 45						12 02	12 15						12 32		12 45
Camelon 4	d	11 19								11 49			11 45				12 19								12 49
Falkirk Grahamston	d	11 24								11 54							12 24								12 54
Croy 3	d		11 33			11 42	11 43					12 03			12 12	12 13		12 34				12 42	12 43		
Lenzie 3	d						11 50									12 20							12 50		
Bishopbriggs	d						11 54									12 24							12 54		
Glasgow Queen Street 10	a		11 50				12 03	12 09			12 15	12 20	12 25			12 34		12 49					13 03		
Polmont 3	d	11 30		11 38						12 00				12 08			12 30			12 38					13 00
Linlithgow	d	11 37		11 44						12 07				12 14			12 37			12 44					13 07
Edinburgh Park	d	11 51								12 22							12 51								13 21
Haymarket	d	11 58		12s00		12s12				12 27				12s30	12s45		12 57			13s00		13s14		13 22	13 27
Edinburgh 10 225,242	a	12 04		12 07		12 19				12 34				12 36	12 52		13 03			13 07		13 19		13 26	13 32

		SR	SR	SR		SR	SR	SR	SR	SR	SR	SR		SR		SR		SR	SR	SR	SR	SR	SR	SR	
		◇1	1			1	1			1	1	1		1					◇1	1		1	1		
		F	B	C		D	D			J	B	D		D					F	B	C	D	D		
Dunblane	d								12 58	13 04								13 28							
Bridge of Allan	d								13 01	13 08								13 31							
Alloa	d							12 36																13 41	
Stirling	d	12 43						12 53	13 06	13 13						13 23		13 36	13 43					13 53	
Larbert	d							13 02	13 15							13 32		13 45						14 02	
Camelon 4	d			12 45					13 19									13 49			13 45				
Falkirk Grahamston	d								13 24									13 54							
Croy 3	d		13 03				13 12	13 13			13 33			13 42		13 43				14 03			14 12	14 13	
Lenzie 3	d							13 20								13 50								14 20	
Bishopbriggs	d							13 24								13 54								14 24	
Glasgow Queen Street 10	a	13 14	13 19	13 25				13 33		13 47	13 51					14 03			14 14	14 19	14 25			14 33	
Polmont 3	d					13 08			13 30			13 38						14 00				14 08			
Linlithgow	d					13 14			13 37			13 44						14 07				14 14			
Edinburgh Park	d								13 51									14 21							
Haymarket	d					13s30	13s45		13 57			14s00		14s11				14 27				14s30	14s45		
Edinburgh 10 225,242	a					13 35	13 51		14 03			14 05		14 17				14 34				14 37	14 50		

A From Inverurie
B From Edinburgh
C From Falkirk Grahamston
D From Glasgow Queen Street
E From Inverness to London Kings Cross. The Highland Chieftain
F From Aberdeen
H From Inverness
I From Dyce
J From Dundee

Dunblane, Alloa and Stirling - Falkirk Grahamston, Glasgow Queen Street and Edinburgh

		SR	SR	SR		SR	SR		SR	SR		SR	SR	SR	SR	SR	SR	SR	SR			SR	SR		SR
			1	1		1				◇1		1		1	1			1	1			1			
			A	B		B				D		A	E	B	B			A	B			B			
			⚲	⚲		⚲				⚲		⚲		⚲	⚲			⚲	⚲			⚲			
Dunblane	d	13 58					14 13		14 28								14 58						15 13		15 28
Bridge of Allan	d	14 01					14 16		14 31								15 01						15 16		15 31
Alloa	d															14 36									
Stirling	d	14 06					14 23		14 36	14 44						14 53	15 06						15 23		15 36
Larbert	d	14 15					14 32		14 45							15 02	15 15						15 32		15 45
Camelon [4]	d	14 19							14 49				14 45				15 19								15 49
Falkirk Grahamston	d	14 22							14 54								15 24								15 54
Croy [3]	d		14 33			14 42	14 43					15 03			15 12	15 13		15 33				15 42	15 43		
Lenzie [3]	d						14 50									15 20							15 50		
Bishopbriggs	d						14 54									15 24							15 54		
Glasgow Queen Street [10] ⛴	a		14 48				15 03			15 18		15 22	15 25			15 34		15 51					16 03		
Polmont [3]	d	14 30		14 38					15 00					15 08			15 30		15 38						16 00
Linlithgow	d	14 37		14 44					15 07					15 14			15 37		15 44						16 07
Edinburgh Park	d	14 51							15 21								15 51								16 21
Haymarket	d	14 57		15s00		15s13			15 27					15s30	15s42		15 58		16s00			16s12			16 27
Edinburgh [10] 225,242	a	15 02		15 05		15 19			15 32					15 37	15 47		16 04		16 06			16 19			16 33

		SR	SR	SR	SR	SR		SR	SR	SR	SR	SR	SR			SR		SR		SR	SR	SR	SR	SR	
																SO		SX					SO	SX	
		◇1	1		1	1				1	1		1			1		1		1			1	1	
		D	A	E	B	B				F	A		B			B		B		A	E		B	B	
		⚲	⚲		⚲	⚲					⚲		⚲			⚲		⚲		⚲				⚲	
Dunblane	d								15 58	16 05												16 28			
Bridge of Allan	d								16 01	16 09												16 31			
Alloa	d							15 41																	
Stirling	d	15 43						15 53	16 06	16 14		16 21										16 36			
Larbert	d							16 02	16 15			16 29										16 45			
Camelon [4]	d			15 45					16 19												16 45	16 49			
Falkirk Grahamston	d								16 24													16 54			
Croy [3]	d		16 03			16 12		16 13			16 33	16 41				16 42		16 42		17 03					
Lenzie [3]	d							16 20				16 48													
Bishopbriggs	d							16 24				16 52													
Glasgow Queen Street [10] ⛴	a	16 14	16 19	16 25				16 33		16 44	16 51	17 03								17 21	17 27				
Polmont [3]	d				16 08				16 30				16 38									17 00	17 09	17 09	
Linlithgow	d				16 14				16 37				16 44									17 07	17 14	17 14	
Edinburgh Park	d								16 51													17 21			
Haymarket	d				16s30	16s43			16 57				17s01			17s13		17s16				17 27	17s34	17s34	
Edinburgh [10] 225,242	a				16 35	16 49			17 03				17 07			17 19		17 22				17 35	17 40	17 40	

		SR		SR	SR	SR	SR	SR	SR	SR		SR		SR	SR	SR	SR		SR	SR	SR	SR		SR	SR
		1				1	1	1		◇1				◇1	1		1		1		1	1		1	
		B				A	B	B		H				D	A	E	B		B		A	B		B	
		⚲				⚲	⚲	⚲		⚲				⚲	⚲		⚲		⚲		⚲	⚲		⚲	
Dunblane	d				16 58					17 20		17 28		17 36											18 11
Bridge of Allan	d				17 01					17 23		17 31													18 14
Alloa	d			16 34																17 41					
Stirling	d			16 53	17 06				17 23	17 29		17 36		17 42						17 53					18 19
Larbert	d			17 02	17 15				17 32			17 45								18 01					18 28
Camelon [4]	d				17 19							17 49				17 45									
Falkirk Grahamston	d				17 24							17 54													
Croy [3]	d	17 12		17 13		17 34		17 42	17 43						18 05				18 12	18 14	18 35			18 42	18 43
Lenzie [3]	d			17 20					17 50						18 11					18 20					18 50
Bishopbriggs	d			17 24					17 54											18 25					18 54
Glasgow Queen Street [10] ⛴	a			17 34		17 51			18 03	18 09				18 15	18 23	18 27				18 34	18 50				19 05
Polmont [3]	d	17 26			17 30			17 56				18 00					18 08					18 38			
Linlithgow	d				17 37		17 41	18 03				18 07					18 14					18 44			
Edinburgh Park	d				17 50							18 21													
Haymarket	d	17s45			17 58		18s02	18s19				18 28					18s33		18s45			19s01		19s13	
Edinburgh [10] 225,242	a	17 52			18 05		18 07	18 24				18 36					18 40		18 50			19 07		19 19	

A From Edinburgh
B From Glasgow Queen Street
D From Aberdeen
E From Falkirk Grahamston
F From Dundee
H From Inverness

Dunblane, Alloa and Stirling - Falkirk Grahamston, Glasgow Queen Street and Edinburgh

		SR	SR ◇1 A 🛒	SR 1 B 🛒	SR C		SR SX 1 E 🛒	SR SO 1 E 🛒		SR 1 E 🛒	SR	SR	SR 1 B 🛒	SR	SR 1 E 🛒	SR 1 E	SR	SR ◇1 A 🛒		SR 1 B	SR C	SR 1 E	SR	SR	SR ◇1 F 🛒
Dunblane	d	18 28	18 37											19 14			19 28							19 58	20 05
Bridge of Allan	d	18 31												19 17			19 31							20 01	20 09
Alloa	d										18 28	18 54											19 43		
Stirling	d	18 36	18 43								18 53	19 06		19 23			19 36	19 43					19 53	20 06	20 14
Larbert	d	18 45									19 02	19 15		19 32			19 45						20 02	20 15	
Camelon 4	d	18 49			18 47							19 19					19 49				19 45			20 19	
Falkirk Grahamston	d	18 54										19 24					19 54							20 24	
Croy 3	d			19 05						19 12	19 13		19 34	19 43						20 07		20 12	20 13		
Lenzie 3	d										19 20			19 50									20 20		
Bishopbriggs	d										19 24			19 54									20 24		
Glasgow Queen Street 10 ⛴	a		19 16	19 23	19 29						19 33		19 49	20 03				20 15		20 22	20 26		20 34		20 45
Polmont 3	d	19 00					19 08	19 08				19 30			19 38	19 53	20 00							20 32	
Linlithgow	d	19 07					19 14	19 14				19 37			19 44	19 59	20 07					20 29		20 39	
Edinburgh Park	d	19 21										19 51					20 21							20 51	
Haymarket	d	19 27					19s30	19s33		19s46		19 57			20s00	20s16	20 27					20s45		20 58	
Edinburgh 10 225,242	a	19 33					19 36	19 39		19 51		20 01			20 06	20 21	20 34					20 51		21 03	

		SR	SR 1 E	SR		SR ◇1 A 🛒	SR 1 B		SR 1 E	SR	SR C	SR	SR	SR ◇1 A 🛒		SR 1 E	SR 1 B	SR 1 E	SR	SR C	SR	SR	SR ◇1 A	SR 1 E	
Dunblane	d			20 28								20 58	21 13								21 58				
Bridge of Allan	d			20 31								21 01	21 16								22 01				
Alloa	d									20 41									21 42						
Stirling	d	20 21		20 36		20 40				20 53		21 06	21 23	21 46					21 53		22 06	22 23	22 43		
Larbert	d	20 29		20 45						21 02		21 15	21 32						22 02		22 15	22 32			
Camelon 4	d			20 49							21 15	21 19								22 15	22 19				
Falkirk Grahamston	d			20 54								21 24									22 24				
Croy 3	d	20 43					21 07		21 12	21 13			21 43				22 07	22 12	22 13			22 43			
Lenzie 3	d	20 50								21 20			21 50						22 20			22 50			
Bishopbriggs	d	20 54								21 24			21 54						22 24			22 54			
Glasgow Queen Street 10 ⛴	a	21 04				21 14	21 21			21 34	21 55		22 03	22 20			22 23		22 34	22 55		23 03	23 15		
Polmont 3	d		20 53	21 00								21 30				21 53					22 30			22 53	
Linlithgow	d		20 59	21 07					21 29			21 37				21 59		22 29			22 37			22 59	
Edinburgh Park	d			21 21								21 51									22 51				
Haymarket	d		21s15	21 27					21s45			21 57				22s18		22s46			22 57			23s15	
Edinburgh 10 225,242	a		21 20	21 31					21 50			22 02				22 23		22 51			23 01			23 20	

		SR 1 B	SR 1 E	SR	SR ◇1 F 🛒	SR C	SR	SR	SR 1 B	SR 1 E
Dunblane	d				22 59		23 06			
Bridge of Allan	d				23 02		23 09			
Alloa	d			22 41				23 18		
Stirling	d			22 53	23 05		23 14	23a27		
Larbert	d			23 02			23 23			
Camelon 4	d					23 15	23 29			
Falkirk Grahamston	d						23 32			
Croy 3	d	23 07	23 12	23 13					23 39	23 42
Lenzie 3	d			23 20					23 44	
Bishopbriggs	d			23 24					23 50	
Glasgow Queen Street 10 ⛴	a	23 22		23 34	23 39	23 55			00 01	
Polmont 3	d		23 26				23 38			23 56
Linlithgow	d		23 33				23 45			00 03
Edinburgh Park	d						23 58			
Haymarket	d		23s49				00 04			00s20
Edinburgh 10 225,242	a		23 55				00 09			00 25

A From Aberdeen
B From Edinburgh
C From Falkirk Grahamston
E From Glasgow Queen Street
F From Inverness

Table 230

Sundays

Dunblane, Alloa and Stirling - Falkirk Grahamston, Glasgow Queen Street and Edinburgh

	SR A	SR 1 B	SR C	SR 1 D	SR 1 B	SR 1 E	SR 1 F 🚲	SR 1 E 🚲	SR	SR 1 F	SR 1 E 🚲	SR	SR 1 H	SR I	SR 1 F 🚲	SR 1 E 🚲	SR	SR
Dunblane d	23p06												09 31	09 54				11 01
Bridge of Allan d	23p09													09 58				11 04
Alloa d												09 18					10 18	
Stirling d	23p14								09 05			09 28	09 38	10 02			10 28	11 10
Larbert d	23p23								09 13			09 37	09 47	10 11			10 37	11 19
Camelon 4 d	23p29								09 19					10 16				11 24
Falkirk Grahamston d	23p32								09 22					10 19				11 27
Croy 3 d		23p39		23p42	00 09	08 02	08 39	08 42		09 39	09 42	09 48			10 39	10 42	10 48	
Lenzie 3 d		23p44			00 14							09 55	10 02				10 55	
Bishopbriggs d		23p50										09 59					10 59	
Glasgow Queen Street 10 a		00 01			00 26		08 59			10 00		10 08	10 15		11 01		11 08	
Polmont 3 d	23p38			23p56		08 16		08 56	09 28		09 56			10 25		10 56		11 33
Linlithgow d	23p45			00 03		08 23		09 03	09 35		10 03			10 32		11 03		11 40
Edinburgh Park d	23p58								09 47					10 44				11 54
Haymarket d	00 04		00 12	00s20		08 39		09s24	09 59		10s23			10 51		11s19		12 00
Edinburgh 10 225,242 a	00 09		00 18	00 25		08 49		09 29	10 04		10 28			10 56		11 24		12 04

	SR 1 F 🚲	SR 1 E 🚲	SR	SR ◇1 J 🚲	SR	SR 1 F 🚲	SR	GR R 1 K 🚲	SR 1 E 🚲	SR 1 F 🚲	SR L	SR 1 E 🚲	SR	SR	SR ◇1 J 🚲	SR 1 E	SR 1 F 🚲	SR 1 E 🚲	SR
Dunblane d				11 31	12 01			12 27					13 01		13 31				14 01
Bridge of Allan d					12 04								13 04						14 04
Alloa d			11 14				12 14							13 14					
Stirling d			11 25	11 38	12 10		12 25	12 34					13 10	13 25	13 38				14 10
Larbert d			11 34		12 19		12 34						13 19	13 34					14 19
Camelon 4 d					12 24								13 24						14 24
Falkirk Grahamston d					12 27			12 50					13 27						14 27
Croy 3 d	11 39	11 42	11 45			12 39	12 45		12 42	13 07		13 12		13 45			14 07	14 12	
Lenzie 3 d			11 52				12 52							13 52					
Bishopbriggs d			11 56				12 56							13 56					
Glasgow Queen Street 10 a	11 56		12 05	12 11		12 54	13 05			13 23				14 05	14 11		14 23		
Polmont 3 d		11 56			12 33				12 56				13 33			13 53			14 33
Linlithgow d		12 03			12 40				13 02			13 29	13 40			13 59		14 29	14 40
Edinburgh Park d					12 54								13 54						14 54
Haymarket d		12s20			13 00			13 14	13s21		13 38	13s46	14 00			14s17		14s47	15 00
Edinburgh 10 225,242 a		12 25			13 04			13 19	13 26		13 42	13 51	14 04			14 22		14 52	15 04

	SR	SR 1 E 🚲	SR 1 F	SR 1 E	SR	SR ◇1 M 🚲	SR	SR 1 E	SR 1 F 🚲	SR ◇1 J 🚲	SR 1 E 🚲	SR	SR	SR 1 E 🚲	SR 1 F 🚲	SR 1 E 🚲	SR
Dunblane d					15 01	15 18				15 33		16 01					17 01
Bridge of Allan d					15 04							16 04					17 04
Alloa d	14 14						15 16						16 14				
Stirling d	14 25				15 10	15 24	15 28			15 45		16 10	16 25				17 10
Larbert d	14 34				15 19	15 33	15 36					16 19	16 34				17 19
Camelon 4 d					15 24							16 24					17 24
Falkirk Grahamston d					15 27							16 27					17 27
Croy 3 d	14 45		15 07	15 12			15 49		16 07		16 12		16 45		17 07	17 12	
Lenzie 3 d	14 52						15 55						16 52				
Bishopbriggs d	14 56						16 00						16 56				
Glasgow Queen Street 10 a	15 05		15 22			15 56	16 09		16 22	16 31			17 05		17 22		
Polmont 3 d		14 53			15 33			15 53				16 33		16 53			17 33
Linlithgow d		14 59		15 29	15 40			15 59			16 29	16 40		16 58		17 29	17 40
Edinburgh Park d					15 54							16 54					17 54
Haymarket d		15s15		15 46	16 00			16s18			16s47	17 00		17s15		17 47	18 00
Edinburgh 10 225,242 a		15 20		15 51	16 04			16 23			16 52	17 04		17 20		17 52	18 04

A not 11 December
B not 11 December. From Edinburgh
C not 11 December. From Perth
D not 11 December. From Glasgow Queen Street
E From Glasgow Queen Street
F From Edinburgh
H From Dundee
I From Perth
J From Aberdeen
K From Inverness to London Kings Cross. The Highland Chieftain
L From West Calder
M From Inverness

Table 230

Sundays

Dunblane, Alloa and Stirling - Falkirk Grahamston, Glasgow Queen Street and Edinburgh

			SR	SR ◇1 B (trolley)	SR 1 C (trolley)	SR 1 D	SR 1 C (trolley)	SR			SR	SR 1 C (trolley)	SR 1 D (trolley)	SR E	SR 1 C (trolley)		SR ◇1 F (trolley)	SR		SR	SR 1 C (trolley)	SR 1 D (trolley)	SR ◇1 F (trolley)	SR 1 C	SR
Dunblane	d			17 31				18 01									18 59	19 08							20 01
Bridge of Allan	d							18 04										19 11							20 04
Alloa	d		17 14								18 17									19 14					
Stirling	d		17 25	17 38				18 10			18 27						19 05	19 17		19 24			19 55		20 10
Larbert	d		17 34					18 19			18 34						19 13	19 26		19 33					20 19
Camelon 4	d							18 24										19 31							20 24
Falkirk Grahamston	d							18 27										19 34							20 27
Croy 3	d		17 45			18 07	18 12				18 47		19 07		19 12					19 44		20 07		20 12	
Lenzie 3	d		17 52								18 54									19 51					
Bishopbriggs	d		17 56								18 58									19 55					
Glasgow Queen Street 10	a		18 05	18 12		18 22					19 08		19 22				19 39			20 04		20 22	20 31		
Polmont 3	d				17 53			18 33				18 53						19 40			19 53				20 33
Linlithgow	d				17 58		18 29	18 40				18 59			19 29			19 47			19 59			20 29	20 40
Edinburgh Park	d							18 54										20 01							20 54
Haymarket	d				18s17		18s47	19 00				19s16		19 41	19s47			20 07			20s16			20s46	21 00
Edinburgh 10 225,242	a				18 22		18 52	19 04				19 21		19 48	19 52			20 11			20 21			20 51	21 04

		SR	SR 1 C	SR 1 D		SR E	SR 1 C	SR	SR 1 D	SR 1 C	SR	SR ◇1 B (trolley)	SR	SR 1 D		SR 1 C	SR 1 D	SR 1 C							
Dunblane	d							21 01				21 31	22 01											
Bridge of Allan	d							21 04					22 04											
Alloa	d	20 14									21 14													
Stirling	d	20 25						21 10			21 25	21 38	22 10											
Larbert	d	20 34						21 19			21 34	21 49	22 19											
Camelon 4	d							21 24					22 24											
Falkirk Grahamston	d							21 27					22 27											
Croy 3	d	20 45		21 07			21 12		21 39	21 42	21 45			22 39		22 42	23 39	23 42						
Lenzie 3	d	20 52									21 52	22 02												
Bishopbriggs	d	20 56									21 56													
Glasgow Queen Street 10	a	21 05		21 22					21 55		22 05	22 15		22 55			23 55							
Polmont 3	d		20 53					21 33		21 56			22 33			22 56		23 56						
Linlithgow	d		20 59				21 29	21 40		22 03			22 40			23 03		00 03						
Edinburgh Park	d							21 54					22 54											
Haymarket	d		21s17			21 41	21s46	22 00		22s19			23 00			23s19		00s19						
Edinburgh 10 225,242	a		21 22			21 48	21 53	22 04		22 24			23 04			23 24		00 24						

B From Aberdeen
C From Glasgow Queen Street
D From Edinburgh
E From West Calder
F From Inverness

Table 232

Mondays to Saturdays

Glasgow Queen Street - Maryhill and Annieslad

Network Diagram - see first Page of Table 220

Miles			SR SO	SR	SR	SR	SR	SR	SR	SR	SR	SR	SR	SR	SR	SR	SR	SR	SR	SR	SR
0	**Glasgow Queen Street** 10	d	23p54	06 26	06 56	07 26	07 56	08 27	08 56	09 26	09 56	10 26	10 56	11 26	11 56	12 26	12 56	13 26	13 56	14 26	14 56	15 26
2¼	Ashfield	d	23p58	06 30	07 00	07 30	08 00	08 30	09 00	09 30	10 00	10 30	11 00	11 30	12 00	12 30	13 00	13 30	14 00	14 30	15 00	15 30
3	Possilpark & Parkhouse	d	00 01	06 33	07 03	07 33	08 03	08 33	09 03	09 33	10 03	10 33	11 03	11 33	12 03	12 33	13 03	13 33	14 03	14 33	15 03	15 33
3¼	Gilshochill	d	00 03	06 35	07 05	07 35	08 05	08 35	09 05	09 35	10 05	10 35	11 05	11 35	12 05	12 35	13 05	13 35	14 05	14 35	15 05	15 35
4¼	Summerston	d	00 06	06 37	07 07	07 37	08 07	08 37	09 07	09 37	10 07	10 37	11 07	11 37	12 07	12 37	13 07	13 37	14 07	14 37	15 07	15 37
4¾	**Maryhill**	d	00 07	06 39	07 09	07 39	08 09	08 39	09 09	09 39	10 09	10 39	11 09	11 39	12 09	12 39	13 09	13 39	14 09	14 39	15 09	15 39
5½	Kelvindale	d	00 10	06 41	07 11	07 41	08 11	08 41	09 11	09 41	10 11	10 41	11 11	11 41	12 11	12 41	13 11	13 41	14 11	14 41	15 11	15 41
6¼	**Anniesland** 226	a	00 14	06 45	07 15	07 46	08 15	08 47	09 15	09 45	10 16	10 45	11 15	11 46	12 15	12 46	13 15	13 45	14 15	14 45	15 15	15 46

		SR	SR	SR	SR	SR	SR	SR	SR	SR	SR	SR	SR	SR	SR	SR	SR	SR FO
Glasgow Queen Street 10	d	15 56	16 26	16 56	17 26	17 56	18 26	18 56	19 26	19 56	20 26	20 56	21 26	21 56	22 27	22 56	23 26	23 54
Ashfield	d	16 00	16 30	17 00	17 30	18 00	18 30	19 00	19 30	20 00	20 30	21 00	21 30	22 00	22 30	23 00	23 30	23 58
Possilpark & Parkhouse	d	16 03	16 33	17 03	17 33	18 03	18 33	19 03	19 33	20 03	20 33	21 03	21 33	22 03	22 33	23 03	23 33	00 01
Gilshochill	d	16 05	16 35	17 05	17 35	18 05	18 35	19 05	19 35	20 05	20 35	21 05	21 35	22 05	22 35	23 05	23 35	00 03
Summerston	d	16 07	16 37	17 07	17 37	18 07	18 37	19 07	19 37	20 07	20 37	21 07	21 37	22 07	22 37	23 07	23 37	00 06
Maryhill	d	16 09	16 39	17 09	17 39	18 09	18 39	19 09	19 39	20 09	20 39	21 09	21 39	22 09	22 39	23 09	23 39	00 07
Kelvindale	d	16 11	16 41	17 11	17 41	18 11	18 41	19 11	19 41	20 11	20 41	21 11	21 41	22 11	22 41	23 11	23 41	00 10
Anniesland 226	a	16 16	16 45	17 15	17 45	18 16	18 46	19 15	19 45	20 15	20 46	21 15	21 46	22 15	22 46	23 15	23 45	00 14

Table 232

Mondays to Saturdays

Anniesland and Maryhill - Glasgow Queen Street

Network Diagram - see first Page of Table 220

Miles			SR	SR	SR	SR	SR SX	SR	SR	SR	SR	SR	SR	SR	SR	SR	SR	SR	SR	SR	SR	SR	SR
0	**Anniesland** 226	d	06 22	06 52	07 22	07 52		08 24	08 52	09 22	09 52	10 22	10 52	11 22	11 52	12 22	12 52	13 22	13 52	14 22	14 52	15 22	15 52
0¾	Kelvindale	d	06 24	06 54	07 24	07 54		08 26	08 54	09 24	09 54	10 24	10 54	11 24	11 54	12 24	12 54	13 24	13 54	14 24	14 54	15 24	15 54
1½	**Maryhill**	d	06 26	06 56	07 26	07 56	08 17	08 28	08 56	09 26	09 56	10 26	10 56	11 26	11 56	12 26	12 56	13 26	13 56	14 26	14 56	15 26	15 56
2	Summerston	d	06 28	06 58	07 28	07 58		08 30	08 58	09 28	09 58	10 28	10 58	11 28	11 58	12 28	12 58	13 28	13 58	14 28	14 58	15 28	15 58
3	Gilshochill	d	06 30	07 00	07 30	08 00		08 32	09 00	09 30	10 00	10 30	11 00	11 30	12 00	12 30	13 00	13 30	14 00	14 30	15 00	15 30	16 00
3¼	Possilpark & Parkhouse	d	06 32	07 02	07 32	08 02	08 22	08 34	09 02	09 32	10 02	10 32	11 02	11 32	12 02	12 32	13 02	13 32	14 02	14 32	15 02	15 32	16 02
4	Ashfield	d	06 34	07 04	07 34	08 04		08 36	09 04	09 34	10 04	10 34	11 04	11 34	12 04	12 34	13 04	13 34	14 04	14 34	15 04	15 34	16 04
6¼	**Glasgow Queen Street** 10	a	06 42	07 13	07 41	08 11	08 37	08 44	09 11	09 41	10 11	10 41	11 11	11 41	12 12	12 41	13 11	13 41	14 11	14 41	15 13	15 44	16 11

		SR SO	SR SX	SR	SR	SR	SR	SR	SR	SR	SR	SR	SR	SR	SR
Anniesland 226	d	16 22	16 25	16 52	17 24	17 52	18 22	18 52	19 22	19 52	20 22	20 52	21 22	21 52	22 22
Kelvindale	d	16 24	16 27	16 54	17 26	17 54	18 24	18 54	19 24	19 54	20 24	20 54	21 24	21 54	22 24
Maryhill	d	16 26	16 29	16 56	17 28	17 56	18 26	18 56	19 26	19 56	20 26	20 56	21 26	21 56	22 26
Summerston	d	16 28	16 31	16 58	17 30	17 58	18 28	18 58	19 28	19 58	20 28	20 58	21 28	21 58	22 28
Gilshochill	d	16 30	16 33	17 00	17 32	18 00	18 30	19 00	19 30	20 00	20 30	21 00	21 30	22 00	22 30
Possilpark & Parkhouse	d	16 32	16 35	17 02	17 34	18 02	18 32	19 02	19 32	20 02	20 32	21 02	21 32	22 02	22 32
Ashfield	d	16 35	16 38	17 04	17 36	18 04	18 34	19 04	19 34	20 04	20 34	21 04	21 34	22 04	22 34
Glasgow Queen Street 10	a	16 41	16 48	17 14	17 45	18 12	18 44	19 13	19 44	20 11	20 41	21 11	21 41	22 11	22 41

		SR	SR
Anniesland 226	d	22 52	23 22
Kelvindale	d	22 54	23 24
Maryhill	d	22 56	23 26
Summerston	d	22 58	23 28
Gilshochill	d	23 00	23 30
Possilpark & Parkhouse	d	23 02	23 32
Ashfield	d	23 04	23 34
Glasgow Queen Street 10	a	23 11	23 42

No Sunday Service

Haymarket and Edinburgh - North Berwick and Dunbar

Network Diagram - see first page of Table 225

Miles	Miles			GR	XC	XC	SR	SR	SR	XC	SR	SR		SR	XC	SR	SR	SR	XC	SR	SR	SR		XC	SR
				R 1 A	◇1 B	◇1 C			D	◇1 E					◇1 F				◇1 G					◇1 G	
0	0	Haymarket 225,230,242	d		06 57	06 57			08 26	08 50					10 54										
1¼	1¼	Edinburgh 10 225,230,242	a		07 02	07 02			08 33	08 55					10 58										
—	—		d	05 48	07 07	07 07	07 14	08 14	08 45	09 08	09 43	10 13		10 43	11 05	11 43	12 11	12 43	13 06	13 43	14 11	14 43		15 08	15 43
6½	6½	Musselburgh	d				07 20	08 20	08 49		09 47	10 19		10 47		11 47	12 17	12 47		13 47	14 17	14 47			15 47
8¾	8¾	Wallyford	d				07 24		08 53		09 51			10 51		11 51		12 51		13 51		14 51			15 51
11	11	Prestonpans	d				07 27		08 56		09 54			10 54		11 54		12 54		13 54		14 54			15 54
14½	14½	Longniddry	d				07 32		09 01		09 59			10 59		11 59		12 59		13 59		14 59			15 59
19	19	Drem	d				07 37		09 07		10 05			11 05		12 05		13 05		14 05		15 06			16 05
—	29¼	Dunbar	a	06 08	07 26	07 26				09 27		10 38			11 24		12 36		13 26		14 36			15 27	
23½	—	North Berwick	a				07 47	08 38	09 18		10 16			11 16		12 17		13 16		14 16		15 16			16 16

		SR	SR	XC	SR	GR	SR	XC		SR	GR	SR	SR	XC	SR	GR	SR	SR FX		SR FO	SR
			D	◇1 H		R 1 I		◇1 J			R 1 A			◇1 K		R 1 L					
Haymarket 225,230,242	d		16 33		17 05	17 19	17 42	17 54				18 40		19 53		20 43					
Edinburgh 10 225,230,242	a		16 39		17 10	17 27	17 46	17 59				18 44		19 58		20 48					
	d	16 33	16 41	17 08	17 13	17 30	17 48	18 04		18 14	18 30	18 45	19 42	20 05	20 43	21 00	21 44	22 06		23 01	23 12
Musselburgh	d	16 39	16 45		17 18		17 54			18 19		18 51	19 46		20 46		21 49	22 12		23 07	23 18
Wallyford	d		16 49		17 22		17 58			18 23		18 56	19 50		20 50		21 53				23 22
Prestonpans	d		16 52		17 26		18 01			18 25		19 00	19 53		20 53		21 56				23 25
Longniddry	d		16 57		17 31		18 06			18 31		19 06	19 58		20 58		22 01				23 30
Drem	d		17 03		17 37		18 11			18 35		19 12	20 03		21 03		22 07				23 35
Dunbar	a	16 58		17 27		17 51		18 23			18 50			20 24		21 20		22 41		23 33	
North Berwick	a		17 14		17 48		18 21			18 47		19 20	20 15		21 16		22 17				23 54

Saturdays

		GR	XC	SR	SR	XC	SR	SR	SR	SR		XC	SR	SR	SR	SR	XC	SR	SR	SR		SR	XC	SR	SR
		R 1 A	◇1 E		D	◇1 M						◇1 F					◇1 G						◇1 N		
Haymarket 225,230,242	d		06 57		08 26	08 50						10 52													
Edinburgh 10 225,230,242	a		07 02		08 33	08 54						10 58													
	d	06 20	07 07	07 43	08 45	09 06	09 12	09 43	10 12	10 43		11 05	11 12	11 43	12 12	12 43	13 08	13 12	13 43	14 12		14 43	15 08	15 12	15 43
Musselburgh	d			07 47	08 49		09 15	09 47	10 15	10 47			11 15	11 47	12 15	12 47		13 15	13 47	14 15		14 47		15 15	15 47
Wallyford	d			07 51	08 53		09 19	09 51	10 19	10 51			11 19	11 51	12 19	12 51		13 19	13 51	14 19		14 51		15 19	15 51
Prestonpans	d			07 54	08 56		09 22	09 54	10 22	10 54			11 22	11 54	12 22	12 54		13 22	13 54	14 22		14 54		15 22	15 54
Longniddry	d			07 59	09 01		09 27	09 59	10 27	10 59			11 27	11 59	12 27	12 59		13 27	13 59	14 27		14 59		15 27	15 59
Drem	d			08 05	09 07		09 33	10 05	10 33	11 05			11 33	12 05	12 33	13 05		13 33	14 05	14 33		15 05		15 33	16 05
Dunbar	a	06 40	07 26			09 25						11 24					13 28						15 27		
North Berwick	a			08 16	09 18		09 45	10 16	10 45	11 16			11 45	12 17	12 45	13 16		13 45	14 16	14 45		15 16		15 45	16 16

		SR	SR	XC	SR	GR		SR	XC	SR	SR	GR	SR	SR	SR	SR		SR
			D	◇1 O		R 1 I			◇1 P			R 1 Q						
Haymarket 225,230,242	d		16 33			17 18			17 56									
Edinburgh 10 225,230,242	a		16 39			17 26			18 01									
	d	16 12	16 41	17 08	17 12	17 30		17 43	18 05	18 12	18 40	19 00	19 43	20 43	21 43	22 06		23 07
Musselburgh	d	16 15	16 45		17 15			17 47		18 15	18 47		19 47	20 47	21 49	22 12		23 13
Wallyford	d	16 19	16 49		17 19			17 51		18 19	18 51		19 51	20 51	21 53			23 17
Prestonpans	d	16 22	16 52		17 22			17 54		18 22	18 54		19 54	20 54	21 56			23 20
Longniddry	d	16 27	16 57		17 27			17 59		18 27	18 59		19 59	20 59	22 01			23 25
Drem	d	16 33	17 03		17 33			18 05		18 33	19 05		20 05	21 05	22 07			23 31
Dunbar	a			17 27		17 50			18 24			19 20				22 31		
North Berwick	a	16 45	17 14		17 45			18 16		18 45	19 16		20 16	21 16	22 16			23 50

A To London Kings Cross
B until 10 February. From Glasgow Central to Plymouth. from Edinburgh
C from 13 February. From Glasgow Central to Plymouth
D From Glasgow Central
E From Glasgow Central to Plymouth. from Edinburgh
F From Aberdeen to Penzance. from Edinburgh
G To Plymouth
H To Bristol Temple Meads
I From Aberdeen to London Kings Cross
J From Glasgow Central to Birmingham New Street
K From Glasgow Central to Newcastle
L From Aberdeen to Leeds
M From Glasgow Central to Plymouth
N To Exeter St Davids
O To Birmingham New Street
P From Glasgow Central to Birmingham New Street. from Edinburgh
Q To Doncaster

Table 238

Sundays

Haymarket and Edinburgh - North Berwick and Dunbar

Network Diagram - see first page of Table 225

		SR	XC	SR	SR	XC	SR	SR	XC	SR	SR	XC
			◇1			◇1			◇1			◇1
			A			B			B			C
			[trolley]			[trolley]			[trolley]			[trolley]
Haymarket 225,230,242	d					12 49			14 42			
Edinburgh 10 225,230,242	a					12 54			14 47			
	d	10 33	11 05	11 33	12 33	13 06	13 36	14 33	15 07	15 33	16 33	17 07
Musselburgh	d	10 39		11 39	12 39		13 39	14 39		15 39	16 39	
Wallyford	d	10 43		11 43	12 43		13 43	14 43		15 43	16 43	
Prestonpans	d	10 46		11 46	12 46		13 46	14 46		15 46	16 46	
Longniddry	d	10 51		11 51	12 51		13 51	14 51		15 51	16 51	
Drem	d	10 56		11 56	12 56		13 57	14 56		15 56	16 56	
Dunbar	a		11 24			13 25			15 26			17 26
North Berwick	a	11 06		12 06	13 06		14 09	15 06		16 06	17 06	

		GR	SR	XC	SR	GR	SR	GR	XC	SR	GR	SR
		R 1		◇1		R 1		R 1	◇1		R 1	
		D		E		D		F	G		H	
		[restaurant][trolley]		[trolley]		[restaurant][trolley]		[restaurant][trolley]			[restaurant][trolley]	
Haymarket 225,230,242	d			17 51					19 51			
Edinburgh 10 225,230,242	a			17 56					19 56			
	d	17 30	17 33	18 07	18 33	19 00	19 33	20 00	20 05	20 33	21 00	21 33
Musselburgh	d		17 39		18 39		19 39			20 39		21 39
Wallyford	d		17 43		18 43		19 43			20 43		21 43
Prestonpans	d		17 46		18 46		19 46			20 46		21 46
Longniddry	d		17 51		18 51		19 51			20 51		21 51
Drem	d		17 56		18 56		19 56			20 56		21 56
Dunbar	a	17 50		18 26		19 20		20 20	20 29		21 20	
North Berwick	a		18 06		19 06		20 06			21 06		22 06

- **A** To Newton Abbot
- **B** From Glasgow Central to Exeter St Davids. [trolley] from Edinburgh
- **C** To Bristol Temple Meads
- **D** To London Kings Cross
- **E** From Glasgow Central to Birmingham New Street
- **F** To Leeds
- **G** From Glasgow Central to Newcastle
- **H** To Newcastle

Dunbar and North Berwick - Edinburgh and Haymarket

Network Diagram - see first page of Table 225

Mondays to Fridays

Miles	Miles				SR	SR	XC	SR	GR	SR	SR	SR	GR		SR	GR	SR	SR	SR	XC	SR	SR	SR		XC	SR
							◇1 A		R 1 B ☕		A		R 1 C ☕			R 1 D ☕🛒				◇1 E 🛒					◇1 F 🛒	
0	—	**North Berwick**		d	06 07	06 44		07 20			07 56	08 43			09 27		10 27		11 27		12 27		13 27			14 27
—	0	**Dunbar**		d			07 00		07 42				08 54			09 56		10 49		11 37		12 50			13 41	
4½	10¼	Drem		d	06 15	06 51		07 27			08 04	08 51			09 34		10 34		11 34		12 34		13 34			14 34
9	14¾	Longniddry		d	06 21	06 57		07 33			08 10	08 56			09 40		10 40		11 40		12 40		13 40			14 40
12½	18¼	Prestonpans		d	06 26	07 02		07 38		08 07	08 14	09 01			09 45		10 45		11 45		12 45		13 45			14 45
14¾	20½	Wallyford		d	06 29	07 05		07 41		08 10	08 17	09 04			09 48		10 48		11 48		12 48		13 48			14 48
17	22¾	Musselburgh		d	06 33	07 09		07 45		08 13	08 22	09 09			09 52		10 52	11 09	11 52		12 52	13 09	13 52			14 52
22¼	28	**Edinburgh** 10	225,230,242	a	06 40	07 15	07 22	07 55	08 10	08 22	08 32	09 16	09 24		10 00	10 20	11 00	11 15	12 00	12 03	13 00	13 16	14 00		14 10	15 00
—	—			d		07 18	07 26				08 33					10 27										
23½	29¼	**Haymarket**	225,230,242	a		07 22	07 30				08 37					10 31										

			SR	SR	XC	SR	SR	SR	XC		SR	SR	SR	SR	XC	SR	SR	XC	GR		SR
					◇1 F 🛒				◇1 G 🛒		A				◇1 H 🛒			◇1 F	R 1 I ☕🛒		
North Berwick		d		15 26		16 27		17 27			17 53	18 27	19 01	19 26		20 26	21 27				22 27
Dunbar		d	15 05		15 41		17 02		17 43						19 45			21 51	21 57		
Drem		d		15 33		16 34		17 34				18 34	19 06	19 33		20 32	21 34				22 34
Longniddry		d		15 39		16 40		17 40				18 40	19 12	19 40		20 38	21 40				22 40
Prestonpans		d		15 44		16 45		17 45				18 45	19 17	19 45		20 43	21 45				22 45
Wallyford		d		15 47		16 48		17 48				18 48	19 20	19 49		20 46	21 48				22 48
Musselburgh		d	15 24	15 51		16 52	17 22	17 52			18 08	18 52	19 24	19 53		20 49	21 52				22 52
Edinburgh 10	225,230,242	a	15 36	16 00	16 05	17 00	17 28	18 00	18 07		18 18	19 00	19 34	20 00	20 09	20 59	21 59	22 16	22 25		23 00
		d					17 28		18 11		18 24				20 14						
Haymarket	225,230,242	a					17 32		18 14		18 27				20 16						

Saturdays

			SR	SR	GR	SR	GR	SR	SR	GR	SR		SR	SR	XC	SR	SR	SR	SR	XC	SR		SR	SR	SR	XC
					R 1 B ☕🛒	A	R 1 C ☕🛒			R 1 D ☕🛒					◇1 E 🛒					◇1 F 🛒						◇1 F 🛒
North Berwick		d	06 07	07 21		08 21		09 21	09 50		10 21		10 50	11 21		11 50	12 21	12 50	13 21		13 50		14 21	14 50	15 21	
Dunbar		d			07 48		08 55			09 56					11 38					13 38						15 40
Drem		d	06 15	07 28		08 28		09 29	09 57		10 28		10 58	11 28		11 57	12 28	12 57	13 28		13 58		14 28	14 58	15 28	
Longniddry		d	06 21	07 34		08 34		09 34	10 03		10 34		11 03	11 34		12 03	12 34	13 03	13 34		14 03		14 34	15 03	15 34	
Prestonpans		d	06 26	07 39		08 39		09 39	10 08		10 39		11 08	11 39		12 08	12 39	13 08	13 39		14 08		14 39	15 08	15 39	
Wallyford		d	06 29	07 42		08 42		09 42	10 11		10 42		11 11	11 42		12 11	12 42	13 11	13 42		14 11		14 42	15 11	15 42	
Musselburgh		d	06 33	07 46		08 46		09 46	10 15		10 46		11 15	11 46		12 15	12 46	13 15	13 46		14 15		14 46	15 15	15 46	
Edinburgh 10	225,230,242	a	06 40	07 54	08 17	08 53	09 24	09 54	10 23	10 24	10 54		11 23	11 54	12 07	12 23	12 54	13 23	13 54	14 07	14 23		14 54	15 23	15 54	16 04
		d				09 03				10 27																
Haymarket	225,230,242	a				09 06				10 31																

			SR	SR	SR	SR	XC		SR	SR	SR	SR	XC	SR	SR	XC	GR		SR
							◇1 G 🛒		A				◇1 H 🛒			◇1 F 🛒	R 1 I ☕🛒		
North Berwick		d	15 50	16 21	16 50	17 21			17 50	18 21	18 50	19 21		20 21	21 21				22 21
Dunbar		d					17 39						19 41			21 50	22 13		
Drem		d	15 58	16 28	16 58	17 28			17 57	18 28	18 58	19 28		20 28	21 28				22 28
Longniddry		d	16 03	16 34	17 03	17 34			18 03	18 34	19 03	19 34		20 34	21 34				22 34
Prestonpans		d	16 08	16 39	17 08	17 39			18 08	18 39	19 08	19 39		20 39	21 39				22 39
Wallyford		d	16 11	16 42	17 11	17 42			18 11	18 42	19 11	19 42		20 42	21 42				22 42
Musselburgh		d	16 15	16 46	17 15	17 46			18 15	18 46	19 15	19 46		20 46	21 46				22 46
Edinburgh 10	225,230,242	a	16 23	16 54	17 23	17 54	18 05		18 23	18 54	19 23	19 54	20 06	20 54	21 54	22 14	22 41		22 54
		d					18 11		18 24				20 14						
Haymarket	225,230,242	a					18 14		18 27				20 17						

A To Glasgow Central
B From Newcastle
C From Doncaster
D From Leeds to Aberdeen
E From Birmingham New Street
F From Plymouth
G From Plymouth to Aberdeen. 🛒 to Edinburgh
H From Plymouth to Dundee. 🛒 to Edinburgh
I From London Kings Cross

Table 238

Sundays

Dunbar and North Berwick - Edinburgh and Haymarket

Network Diagram - see first page of Table 225

		SR	GR	SR	SR	XC	GR	SR	SR	XC		SR	SR
			R 1			◇1	R 1			◇1			
			A			B	C			D			
			⊏⊥			⊥	⊏⊥			⊥			
North Berwick	d	11 20		12 20	13 24			14 20	15 20			16 20	17 20
Dunbar	d		11 33			13 40	13 54			15 41			
Drem	d	11 27		12 27	13 28			14 24	15 27			16 27	17 27
Longniddry	d	11 33		12 33	13 34			14 30	15 33			16 33	17 33
Prestonpans	d	11 38		12 38	13 39			14 35	15 38			16 38	17 38
Wallyford	d	11 41		12 41	13 42			14 38	15 41			16 41	17 41
Musselburgh	d	11 45		12 45	13 46			14 42	15 45			16 45	17 45
Edinburgh 10 225,230,242	a	11 53	12 01	12 53	13 57	14 07	14 22	14 53	15 53	16 06		16 53	17 53
	d												
Haymarket 225,230,242	a												

		XC	SR	SR	XC	SR	GR	SR		XC	SR	GR	
		◇1			◇1		R 1			◇1		R 1	
		E			F		G			H		C	
		⊥			⊥		⊏⊥			⊥		⊏⊥	
North Berwick	d		18 20	19 20		20 20		21 20			22 20		
Dunbar	d	17 40			19 41		20 54			21 51		23 12	
Drem	d		18 27	19 27		20 27		21 27			22 27		
Longniddry	d		18 33	19 33		20 33		21 33			22 33		
Prestonpans	d		18 38	19 38		20 38		21 38			22 38		
Wallyford	d		18 41	19 41		20 41		21 41			22 41		
Musselburgh	d		18 45	19 45		20 45		21 45			22 45		
Edinburgh 10 225,230,242	a	18 07	18 53	19 53	20 05	20 53	21 17	21 53		22 16	22 53	23 41	
	d	18 13					21 21						
Haymarket 225,230,242	a	18 16					21 26						

- **A** From York
- **B** From Birmingham New Street
- **C** From London Kings Cross
- **D** From Bristol Temple Meads
- **E** From Plymouth to Aberdeen. ⊥ to Edinburgh
- **F** From Penzance
- **G** From London Kings Cross to Glasgow Central
- **H** From Plymouth

Inverness - Kyle of Lochalsh, Thurso and Wick

Network Diagram - see first Page of Table 227

Miles	Miles			SR SO 1	SR ◇1 A	SR ◇1	SR ◇1 A 🚲	SR ◇1	SR 1	SR ◇1	SR ◇1 A 🚲	SR 1	SR 1	SR ◇1 🚲		SR 1	SR FSO 1
—	—	Aberdeen 240	d														
0	0	**Inverness**	d	23p30	07 06	09 00	10 38	11 01	12 16	13 34	13 59	14 39	17 15	17 54		21 09	23 30
10	10	Beauly	d	23p44	07 20	09 14	10 52	11 15	12 30	13 48		14 53	17 29	18 08		21 23	23 44
13	13	Muir of Ord	d	23p50	07 29	09 20	10 58	11 21	12 36	13 54	14 16	14 59	17 35	18 14		21 29	23 50
—	—																
18¾	18¾	Dingwall	d	00 02	07 43	09 31	11 07	11 30	12a47	14 03	14 28	15 11	17 46	18 26	18 29	21 40	00 02
—	30½	Garve	d			09 53		11 51		14 25					18 50		
—	36	Lochluichart	d			10x02		12x00		14x33					18x59		
—	40¼	Achanalt	d			10x08		12x06		14x39					19x05		
—	46½	Achnasheen	d			10 19		12 17		14 50					19 16		
—	59¼	Achnashellach	d			10x36		12x34		15x08					19x33		
—	64½	Strathcarron	d			10 46		12 43		15 17					19 43		
—	67	Attadale	d			10x51		12x48		15x23					19x48		
—	72	Stromeferry	d			11 04		13 01		15 35					20 01		
—	75¾	Duncraig	d			11x12		13x09		15x43					20x09		
—	77	Plockton	d			11 16		13 13		15 46					20 13		
—	78½	Duirinish	d			11x19		13x16		15x49					20x16		
—	82¼	**Kyle of Lochalsh**	a			11 28		13 26		15 59					20 26		
28½	—	Alness	d	00x13	07 55		11 20				14 41	15 24	17 59	18 41		21 53	00x13
31½	—	Invergordon	d	00 18	08 00		11 26				14 46	15a29	18 04	18 46		21 58	00 18
40¾	—	Fearn	d	00x29	08 12		11 38				14 58		18 16	18 57		22x09	00x29
44¼	—	Tain	d	00a35	08 18		11 45				15 04		18 22	19 03		22a15	00a35
57¾	—	Ardgay	d		08 33		12 00				15 21		18a38	19 19			
61	—	Culrain	d		08 37		12 06				15x26			19 24			
61½	—	Invershin	d		08x38		12x07							19x25			
67	—	Lairg	d		08 52		12 19				15 44			19 38			
77	—	Rogart	d		09x05		12x32				15x58			19 52			
84½	—	Golspie	d		09 16		12 43				16 08			20 05			
87	—	Dunrobin Castle §	d		09x19		12x45				16x11						
90½	—	Brora	d		09 30		12 54				16 19			20 15			
101½	—	Helmsdale	d		09 46		13 09				16 34			20 30			
111	—	Kildonan	d		09x59		13x22				16 45			20x42			
118¼	—	Kinbrace	d		10x08		13x31				16x55			20x52			
125¾	—	Forsinard	d		10 22		13 42				17 06			21 03			
134	—	Altnabreac	d		10x32		13x52							21x13			
143	—	Scotscalder	d		10x41		14x01							21x22			
147¼	—	Georgemas Junction	a		10 50		14 12				17 34			21 30			
—	—		d		10 52		14 14				17 36			21 32			
154	—	**Thurso**	a		11 02		14 24				17 46			21 42			
—	—		d		11 04		14 26				17 48			21 44			
160¾	—	Georgemas Junction	d		11 14		14 37				17 58			21 54			
175	—	**Wick**	a		11 32		14 55				18 15			22 14			

Sundays

Inverness - Kyle of Lochalsh, Thurso and Wick

Network Diagram - see first Page of Table 227

		SR 1 A	SR 1	SR ◇1	SR 1	SR 1	SR ◇1 🚲	SR 1
Aberdeen 240	d							
Inverness	d	23p30	10 00	11 11	12 22	15 21	18 00	21 09
Beauly	d	23p44	10 14	11 25	12 36	15 35	18 14	21 23
Muir of Ord	d	23p50	10 20	11 31	12 44	15 43	18 20	21 29
Dingwall	d	00 02	10 32	11 45	12 57	15 54	18 26	21 40
Garve	d			12 10				
Lochluichart	d			12x19				
Achanalt	d			12x25				
Achnasheen	d			12 36				
Achnashellach	d			12x53				
Strathcarron	d			13 03				
Attadale	d			13x08				
Stromeferry	d			13 21				
Duncraig	d			13x29				
Plockton	d			13 33				
Duirinish	d			13x36				
Kyle of Lochalsh	a			13 45				
Alness	d	00x13	10 44		13x08	16x06	18 41	21 53
Invergordon	d	00 18	10 49		13 13	16a12	18 46	21 58
Fearn	d	00x29	11x00		13x24		18 57	22x09
Tain	d	00a35	11a06		13a30		19 03	22a15
Ardgay	d						19 19	
Culrain	d						19 24	
Invershin	d						19x25	
Lairg	d						19 38	
Rogart	d						19 52	
Golspie	d						20 05	
Dunrobin Castle §	d							
Brora	d						20 15	
Helmsdale	d						20 30	
Kildonan	d						20x42	
Kinbrace	d						20x52	
Forsinard	d						21 03	
Altnabreac	d						21x13	
Scotscalder	d						21x22	
Georgemas Junction	a						21 30	
	d						21 32	
Thurso	a						21 42	
	d						21 44	
Georgemas Junction	d						21 54	
Wick	a						22 14	

§ Summer station only from 24 March 2012

A not 11 December

Wick, Thurso and Kyle of Lochalsh - Inverness

Network Diagram - see first Page of Table 227

Miles	Miles			SR	SR	SR	SR	SR	SR	SR	SR	SR	SR	SR	SR	SR	SR
				1	1	◇1	◇1	◇1	1	◇1	1	◇1	◇1	◇1	◇1	1	1
								A				A			A		
0	—	**Wick**	d				06 20	08 12				12 36			16 00		
14¼	—	Georgemas Junction	d				06 37	08 29				12 53			16 17		
21	—	**Thurso**	a				06 46	08 38				13 02			16 26		
—	—		d				06 48	08 41				13 05			16 29		
27¾	—	Georgemas Junction	a				06 59	08 50				13 14			16 37		
—	—		d				07 00	08 53				13 17			16 40		
32	—	Scotscalder	d				07x06					13x23			16x46		
41	—	Altnabreac	d				07x15					13x32			16x55		
49¼	—	Forsinard	d				07 27	0915				13 43			17 07		
56¾	—	Kinbrace	d				07x37					13x53			17x17		
64	—	Kildonan	d				07x48	09 33				14x03			17x26		
73½	—	Helmsdale	d				08 01	09 47				14 18			17 40		
84½	—	Brora	d				08 16	10 03				14 33			17 55		
88	—	Dunrobin Castle §	d					10x08				14x38			18x01		
90½	—	Golspie	d				08 26	10 11				14 42			18 04		
98	—	Rogart	d				08x35	10x19				14x51			18x13		
108	—	Lairg	d		06 34		08 53	10 38				15 08			18 30		
113½	—	Invershin	d		06 43		09x01					15x17			18x39		
114	—	Culrain	d		06 44		09 03					15 20			18 40		
117¼	—	Ardgay	d	06 25	06 51		09 11	10 51				15 25			18 46	19 26	
130¾	—	Tain	d	06 40	07 06		09 26	11 07				15 41			19 03	19 42	22 20
134¼	—	Fearn	d	06 45	07 12		09 31					15 47			19x08	19x47	22x25
143½	—	Invergordon	d	06 58	07 24		09 44	11 26			15 38	15 58			19 20	19 58	22 36
146½	—	Alness	d	07 02	07 28		09 48	11 31			15 43	16x03			19x24	20x03	22x41
—	0	**Kyle of Lochalsh**	d			06 21				12 03			14 35	17 15			
—	3¾	Duirinish	d			06x28				12x10			14x42	17x25			
—	5¼	Plockton	d			06 33				12 14			14 47	17 26			
—	6½	Duncraig	d			06x35				12x17			14x49	17x32			
—	10¼	Stromeferry	d			06 44				12 26			14 58	17 38			
—	15¼	Attadale	d			06x56				12x37			15x09	17x52			
—	17¾	Strathcarron	d			07 02				12 45			15 20	17 55			
—	23	Achnashellach	d			07x11				12x54			15x29	18x07			
—	35¾	Achnasheen	d			07 29				13 13			15 48	18 22			
—	42	Achanalt	d			07x39				13x23			15x58	18x35			
—	46¼	Lochluichart	d			07x45				13x29			16x04	18x42			
—	51¾	Garve	d			07 55				13 39			16 14	18 50			
156¼	63½	Dingwall	d	07 16	07 42	08 16	10 04	11 45	12 54	14 04	15 56	16 19	16 37	19 12	19 38	20 16	22 54
162	69¼	Muir of Ord	d	07 28	07 52	08 28	10 13	11 55	13 05	14 16	16 08	16 29	16 46	19 25	19 48	20 25	23 05
164¾	72¼	Beauly	d	07 33	07 57	08 35	10 19		13 11	14 21	16 13	16x34		19 30	19 54	20x29	23x09
175	82¼	**Inverness**	a	07 48	08 12	08 53	10 35	12 13	13 25	14 37	16 28	16 48	17 06	19 49	20 09	20 44	23 24
—	—	Aberdeen 240	a														

Sundays

Wick, Thurso and Kyle of Lochalsh - Inverness

Network Diagram - see first Page of Table 227

		SR	SR	SR	SR	SR	SR
		1	1	◇1	1	◇1	1
				A			
Wick	d			11 53			
Georgemas Junction	d			12 10			
Thurso	a			12 19			
	d			12 22			
Georgemas Junction	a			12 31			
	d			12 34			
Scotscalder	d			12x40			
Altnabreac	d			12x49			
Forsinard	d			13 00			
Kinbrace	d			13x10			
Kildonan	d			13x20			
Helmsdale	d			13 33			
Brora	d			13 48			
Dunrobin Castle §	d			13x53			
Golspie	d			13 58			
Rogart	d			14x07			
Lairg	d			14 24			
Invershin	d			14x33			
Culrain	d			14x34			
Ardgay	d			14 40			
Tain	d	11 10	14 00	14 55			22 20
Fearn	d	11x15	14x05	15x00			22x25
Invergordon	d	11 26	14 16	15 12	16 19		22 36
Alness	d	11x31	14x21	15x16	16x23		22x41
Kyle of Lochalsh	d					15 22	
Duirinish	d					15x29	
Plockton	d					15 34	
Duncraig	d					15x36	
Stromeferry	d					15 45	
Attadale	d					15x57	
Strathcarron	d					16 03	
Achnashellach	d					16x12	
Achnasheen	d					16 30	
Achanalt	d					16x40	
Lochluichart	d					16x47	
Garve	d					16 56	
Dingwall	d	11 44	14 36	15 30	16 36	17 18	22 54
Muir of Ord	d	11 55	14 47	15 42	16 47	17 29	23 05
Beauly	d	12 00	14x52	15 47	16 52	17 34	23x09
Inverness	a	12 16	15 07	16 02	17 07	17 49	23 24
Aberdeen 240	a						

§ Summer station only from 24 March 2012

Table 239A **SHIPPING SERVICES** **Mondays to Saturdays**

Scrabster - Stromness (Orkney Isles)

Operated by NorthLink Orkney & Shetland Ferries Ltd

		SO	SX	
Inverness	239 d	*07 06*	*07 06*	*13 59*
Thurso	239 a	*11 02*	*11 02*	*17 46*
Scrabster	d	12 00	13 15	19 00
Stromness	a	13 30	14 45	20 30

No Sunday rail connected sailings in this direction

Mondays to Saturdays

		SX	SO	SX
Stromness	d	06 30	09 00	11 00
Scrabster	a	08 00	10 30	12 30
Thurso	239 d	*08 41*	*13 05*	*13 05*
Inverness	239 a	*12 13*	*16 48*	*16 48*

Sundays

Stromness	d	09 00
Scrabster	a	10 30
Thurso	239 d	*12 22*
Inverness	239 a	*16 02*

Customers holding Rail & Sail tickets to/from Stomness should note that a connecting taxi service between Thurso Railway Station and Scrabster is included.
Taxis can be booked by calling 01847 893 434 as soon as possible after ticket purchase, but no later than Helmsdale on northbound journeys and prior to departing Stromness on southbound journeys. Staff will assist if you do not have a mobile phone.

Taxis are also available for hire by other passengers. Normal fares will apply.

Please note that NorthLink Ferries requires all passengers aged 16 and over to be in possession of photographic ID at check-in.

Schedules may alter during the months of February, March and April 2012 to accommodate the NorthLink dry dock refit arrangements.
Please telephone 0845 6000 449 for details

Table 239B SHIPPING SERVICES

Mondays to Saturdays
until 29 March 2012

Ullapool - Stornoway (Lewis), Uig (Skye), Tarbert (Harris) and Lochmaddy (North Uist)

Operated by Caledonian MacBrayne Ltd

		MWFO	SX	SO
Edinburgh	229 d	09b35	10 35	10 35
Glasgow Queen St	229 d	10 10	10b41	10b41
Inverness	229 a	13 25	14c13	14c13
Inverness	239 d	13 34		
Kyle of Lochalsh #	239 a	15f59		
Inverness +	d		15 00	15 40
Ullapool	a		16 20	17 00
Ullapool	d		17 35	18 15
Stornoway	a		20 20	21 00
Uig	d	18 00		
Tarbert	a			
Lochmaddy	a	19 45		

Sundays
until 25 March 2012

Edinburgh	229 d	09 36	
Glasgow Queen St	229 d		11 09
Inverness	229 a	13c15	14c26
Inverness	239 d		
Kyle of Lochalsh #	239 a		
Inverness +	d	15 40	15 40
Ullapool	a	17 00	17 00
Ullapool	d	18 15	18 15
Stornoway	a	21 00	21 00
Uig	d		
Tarbert	a		
Lochmaddy	a		

Mondays to Saturdays
until 29 March 2012

			TTh-SO	MWFO	ThO	SX	SO
Lochmaddy	d		07 30	11 50	12 00		
Tarbert	d						
Uig #	a		09g15	13h35	13h45		
Stornoway	d	07 00				13 50	14 30
Ullapool	a	09 45				16 35	17 15
Ullapool	d	09 50				16 40	17 20
Inverness +	a	11j10				18j00	18j40
Kyle of Lochalsh #	239 d		12 03	17 15	17 15		
Inverness	239 a		14 37	19 49	19 49		
Inverness	229 d	12 46	14 48	20 15	20 15	18 44	20 15
Glasgow Queen St	229 a	16b14	18 09	23 39	23 39	22b20	23 39
Edinburgh	229 a	16 21	18b25	00m09	00m09	22 19	00m09

No Sunday rail connected sailings in this direction

- b Change at Perth
- c Passengers make their own way between rail station and bus station
- f Bus connection dep. Kyle of Lochalsh 1605, Uig arr. 1745
- g Bus connection dep. Uig 0930, Kyle of Lochalsh arr. 1114
- h Bus connection dep. Uig 1445, Kyle of Lochalsh arr. 1619
- j Passengers make their own way between bus station and rail station
- m Change at Stirling
- # Connecting bus service between Uig and Kyle of Lochalsh operated by Scottish Citylink Coaches (Tel. 0871 266 33 33).
- + Bus station. Connecting bus service between Inverness Bus Station and Ullapool operated by Scottish Citylink Coaches (Tel. 0871 266 33 33).

For details of sailings from 30 March 2012
please telephone 08000 66 5000
or visit www.calmac.co.uk

UIG - TARBERT
This route is currently under consultation for Scottish Government approval.
Please telephone 08000 66 5000 or visit www.calmac.co.uk for information.

Aberdeen and Elgin - Inverness

Network Diagram - see first page of Table 225

Miles			SR	SR	SR	SR	SR	SR	SR	SR	SR	SR	SR	SR	SR	SR	SR	SR	SR	SR	SR	SR	SR
			MX																				
			◇1	◇1	◇1	◇1	◇1	1	◇1	◇1	◇1	◇1	◇1	◇1	1	◇1	◇1	◇1	◇1	1	◇1	◇1	◇1
			A				B	C		D	A		A				A		A			A	
									🚲			🚲		🚲		🚲		🚲			🚲		🚲
0	**Aberdeen**	d	21p55			06 14	07 14	07 50	08 23	08 50	10 00	10 14	11 03	11 59	12 50	13 39	14 56	15 30	15 55	16 43	17 18	17 56	18 20
6¼	Dyce ✈	d	22p05			06 24	07 31	08 03	08 36	08a59	10 09	10 23	11 14	12 08	13 01	13 53	15 05	15 39	16 04	16a52	17 29	18 05	18 29
17	**Inverurie**	a	22p16			06 37	07 44	08 17	08 48		10 22	10 35	11 27	12 20	13 15	14 05	15 19	15 51	16 18		17 40	18 19	18 41
—		d	22p17			06 46	07 49		08 48			10 35		12 20		14 05		15 51			17 41		18 41
27½	Insch	d	22p29			06 58	08 01		09 03			10 47		12 33		14 17		16 03			17 53		18 53
40¾	Huntly	d	22p46			07 19	08 17		09 19			11 03		12 49		14 33		16 19			18 09		19 09
53¼	Keith	d	23p00			07 33	08 31		09 33			11 18		13 03		14 47		16 34			18 26		19 24
71¼	**Elgin**	d	23p22	07 03	07 26	07 58	08 53		09 55			11 42		13 27		15 11		16 56			18 54		19 46
83½	Forres	d	23p36	07 17	07 43	08 12	09 07		10 11			11 56		13 41		15 25		17 10			19 08		20 00
93¼	Nairn	d	23p47	07 28	07 54	08 23	09 22		10 22			12 07		13 52		15 41		17 29			19 19		20 15
108¼	**Inverness**	a	00 05	07 46	08 14	08 41	09 40		10 40			12 25		14 10		15 59		17 47			19 38		20 33

		SR	SR	SR	SR	SR
		◇1	◇1	1	◇1	1
		A			A	
			🚲			
Aberdeen	d	19 07	20 11	20 56	21 55	22 50
Dyce ✈	d	19 22	20 20	21 05	22 05	22 59
Inverurie	a	19 35	20 32	21 19	22 16	23 13
	d		20 32		22 17	
Insch	d		20 44		22 29	
Huntly	d		21 00		22 46	
Keith	d		21 14		23 00	
Elgin	d		21 36		23 22	
Forres	d		21 55		23 36	
Nairn	d		22 06		23 47	
Inverness	a		22 24		00 05	

Sundays

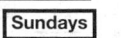

		SR	SR	SR	SR	SR	SR
		◇1	◇1	◇1	◇1	◇1	◇1
		E					
			🚲	🚲	🚲	🚲	🚲
Aberdeen	d	21p55	10 00	13 00	15 25	17 19	21 00
Dyce ✈	d	22p05	10 09	13 09	15 34	17 29	21 09
Inverurie	a	22p16	10 21	13 21	15 46	17 41	21 21
	d	22p17	10 21	13 21	15 47	17 41	21 21
Insch	d	22p29	10 33	13 33	15 59	17 53	21 33
Huntly	d	22p46	10 49	13 51	16 15	18 09	21 49
Keith	d	23p00	11 05	14 04	16 35	18 24	22 09
Elgin	d	23p22	11 27	14 26	16 58	18 45	22 31
Forres	d	23p36	11 41	14 40	17 12	19 00	22 45
Nairn	d	23p47	11 52	14 51	17 31	19 11	22 56
Inverness	a	00 05	12 10	15 10	17 49	19 29	23 14

A From Edinburgh
B From Montrose
C From Perth
D From Glasgow Queen Street
E not 11 December. From Edinburgh

Table 240

Mondays to Saturdays

Inverness and Elgin - Aberdeen

Network Diagram - see first page of Table 225

Miles			SR	SR	SR	SR	SR	SR	SR	SR	SR
			◇1	◇1	◇1	1	◇1	◇1	◇1	◇1	◇1
			A	B			B		A		A
					trolley			trolley		trolley	
0	**Inverness**	d	04 51		05 57			07 07		09 03	
15	Nairn	d	05 08		06 14			07 29		09 21	
24¾	Forres	d	05 19		06 25			07 40		09 37	
37	**Elgin**	d	05 34		06 42			08 00		09 55	
55	Keith	d	05 56		07 03			08 21		10 14	
67½	Huntly	d	06 10		07 19			08 45		10 30	
80¾	Insch	d	06 26		07 35			09 03		10 49	
91¼	**Inverurie**	a	06 38		07 48			09 14		11 01	
—		d	06 39	07 14	07 49	08 22		09 15	10 38	11 01	11 35
102	Dyce ✈	d	06 52	07 26	08 03	08 35	09 08	09 27	10 50	11 13	11 47
108¼	**Aberdeen**	a	07 04	07 37	08 14	08 46	09 19	09 38	11 01	11 24	11 58

Miles			SR	SR	SR	SR	SR	SR	SR	SR	SR	SR	SR	SR
			◇1	1	◇1	◇1	◇1	◇1	1	◇1	1	◇1	◇1	◇
						A		A	C			A		A
			trolley		trolley		trolley			trolley			trolley	
0	**Inverness**	d	10 58		12 42		14 27			15 21			17 11	
15	Nairn	d	11 15		12 59		14 44			15 40			17 28	
24¾	Forres	d	11 26		13 10		14 55			15 51			17 39	
37	**Elgin**	d	11 42		13 28		15 12			16 07			17 58	
55	Keith	d	12 03		13 47		15 32			16 28			18 19	
67½	Huntly	d	12 17		14 01		15 46			16 47			18 40	
80¾	Insch	d	12 35		14 19		16 04			17 04			18 56	
91¼	**Inverurie**	a	12 47		14 31		16 18			17 15			19 09	
—		d	12 47	13 34	14 31	15 26	16 18	16 38		17 16	17 52	18 43	19 09	19 40
102	Dyce ✈	d	13 02	13 48	14 43	15 40	16 31	16 54	17 05	17 30	18 06	18 55	19 21	19 52
108¼	**Aberdeen**	a	13 13	13 59	14 54	15 51	16 41	17 05	17 14	17 41	18 17	19 06	19 32	20 03

		SR	SR	SR	SR
		◇1	◇1	1	◇1
			D		
		trolley			trolley
Inverness	d	18 10	19 57		21 20
Nairn	d	18 27	20 14		21 37
Forres	d	18 38	20 25		21 48
Elgin	d	18 55	20a41		22 06
Keith	d	19 16			22 27
Huntly	d	19 37			22 47
Insch	d	19 53			23 03
Inverurie	a	20 05			23 16
	d	20 05		21 24	23 16
Dyce ✈	d	20 21		21 36	23 28
Aberdeen	a	20 32		21 47	23 39

Sundays

		SR	SR	SR	SR	SR	SR	SR
		◇1	◇1	◇1	◇1	◇1	◇1	◇1
				B		E		E
		trolley	trolley	trolley	trolley	trolley	trolley	trolley
Inverness	d	09 55	12 30	15 27	17 12	18 00	21 00	21 42
Nairn	d	10 12	12 47	15 44	17 30	18 17	21 17	21 59
Forres	d	10 23	12 58	15 55	17 41	18 28	21 28	22 10
Elgin	d	10 38	13 13	16 10	17 56	18a44	21 44	22a26
Keith	d	10 59	13 35	16 32	18 18		22 05	
Huntly	d	11 18	13 52	16 46	18 37		22 19	
Insch	d	11 34	14 08	17 02	18 53		22 35	
Inverurie	a	11 47	14 20	17 14	19 05		22 47	
	d	11 47	14 20	17 14	19 05		22 47	
Dyce ✈	d	11 59	14 32	17 30	19 17		22 59	
Aberdeen	a	12 10	14 43	17 41	19 28		23 10	

A To Edinburgh
B To Glasgow Queen Street
C To Stonehaven
D From Kyle of Lochalsh
E From Glasgow Queen Street

Newcraighall and Edinburgh - Dunfermline, Kirkcaldy and Glenrothes with Thornton

Network Diagram - see first page of Table 225

Miles	Miles			SR	SR	SR	SR	SR	SR	SR	SR	SR	SR	SR	SR	SR	SR	SR	SR
				MX		SX			SX	SO			SO	SX					
					◇1			1			1				◇1			1	
					B		C	D	C	E	D	C	E	E	G	H	E	D	E
0	—	**Newcraighall**	d				06 03						06 57	06 57			07 27		
0¾	—	Brunstane	d				06 06						07 00	07 00			07 30		
4¾	0	**Edinburgh** 10	a				06 16						07 14	07 07			07 37		
—	—		d	23p19	05 30	06 09	06 18	06 29	06 33	06 39	07 00	07 10	07 18	07 18	07 28	07 34	07 39	08 00	08 08
6	1¼	Haymarket	d	23p23	05 33	06 13	06 22	06 33	06 37	06 43	07 04	07 13	07 22	07 22	07 31	07 40	07 43	08 04	08 12
9¼	4½	South Gyle	d	23p28		06 18	06 27		06 43	06 48		07 18	07 27	07 27			07 48		08 17
14¼	9½	Dalmeny	d	23p34		06 24	06 33		06 50	06 54		07 25	07 34	07 34			07 54		
16	11¼	North Queensferry	d	23p38		06 28	06 37		06 54	06 58		07 28	07 37	07 37			07 58		
18	13¼	Inverkeithing	d	23p42	05 46	06 32	06 41	06 47	06 59	07 02	07 20	07 32	07 41	07 41		07 53	08 02	08 18	08 28
—	14¾	Rosyth	d	23p45			06 44						07 45	07 45					
—	17	**Dunfermline Town**	d	23p50			06 49						07 50	07 50					
—	18½	Dunfermline Queen Margaret	d	23p54			06 53						07 53	07 53					
—	22½	Cowdenbeath	d	23p59			06 59						08 00	08 00					
—	24¾	Lochgelly	d	00 06			07 05						08 05	08 05					
—	27	Cardenden	d	00 10			07 09						08 09	08 09					
19½	—	Dalgety Bay	d			06 35			07 03	07 05		07 35					08 05		08 31
22¼	—	Aberdour	d			06 40			07 09	07 10		07 40					08 10		08 36
25	—	Burntisland	d			06 44			07 14	07 14		07 44					08 14		08 40
27½	—	Kinghorn	d			06 49			07 19	07 19		07 49					08 19		08 45
30¾	—	Kirkcaldy	d		06a02	06a56		07a02	07 25	07 24	07a36	07 54			08a02	08a09	08 24	08a33	08 50
39¾	31¾	Glenrothes With Thornton 2	a	00 19			07 15		07 33	07 32		08 04	08 16	08 16			08 32		08 58

		SR	SR	SR	SR	SR	SR	SR	SR	SR	SR	SR	SR	SR	GR	SR	SR	SR	SR	SR
															R					
			◇1			1						1			1			1		
		C	I	E	C	D			H	E	C	D			J	C	E	D		
Newcraighall	d	07 59			08 34					09 17			09 47			10 17			10 47	
Brunstane	d	08 02			08 37					09 21			09 50			10 20			10 50	
Edinburgh 10	a	08 09			08 45					09 28			09 57			10 29			10 57	
	d	08 11	08 34	08 39	08 47	09 00	09 06	09 18	09 35	09 41	09 50	10 00	10 07	10 19	10 27	10 38	10 48	11 00	11 08	11 21
Haymarket	d	08 14	08 39	08 43	08 51	09 04	09 11	09 23	09 40	09 43	09 54	10 03	10 11	10 23	10 32	10 42	10 53	11 04	11 12	11 26
South Gyle	d	08 22		08 48	08 56		09 16	09 28		09 48	10 00		10 16	10 28		10 48	10 57		11 17	11 31
Dalmeny	d	08 28		08 54	09 02		09 22	09 34		09 54	10 06		10 22	10 34		10 54	11 04		11 23	11 37
North Queensferry	d	08 32		08 58	09 06		09 26	09 38		09 58	10 10		10 26	10 38		10 58	11 07		11 27	11 41
Inverkeithing	d	08 36		09 02	09 10	09 17	09 30	09 42	09 54	10 02	10 14	10 19	10 30	10 42	10 47	11 02	11 11	11 17	11 31	11 45
Rosyth	d	08 39			09 13			09 45			10 17			10 45			11 15			11 48
Dunfermline Town	d	08 44			09 18			09 50			10 22			10 50			11 20			11 53
Dunfermline Queen Margaret	d	08 48			09 22			09 54			10 26			10 54			11 23			11 57
Cowdenbeath	d	08 54			09 28			10a03			10 32			11a03			11 30			12a06
Lochgelly	d	09 00			09 34						10 38						11 35			
Cardenden	d	09 04			09 38						10 42						11 39			
Dalgety Bay	d			09 05			09 33			10 05			10 33			11 05			11 34	
Aberdour	d			09 10			09 38			10 10			10 38			11 10			11 39	
Burntisland	d			09 14			09 42			10 14			10 42			11 14			11 43	
Kinghorn	d			09 19			09 47			10 19			10 47			11 19			11 48	
Kirkcaldy	d		09a08	09 24		09a33	09 52		10a09	10 24		10a34	10 52		11a04	11 24		11a33	11 53	
Glenrothes With Thornton 2	a	09 12		09 32	09 44		10 03			10 32	10 48		11 03			11 32	11 46		12 04	

		SR	SR	SR	SR	SR	SR	SR	SR	SR	SR	SR	SR	SR	SR	SR	SR	SR	GR	SR
																			R	
		1			1						1					1			1	
		H	C	E	D			H	C	E	D			C	E	D			K	H
Newcraighall	d		11 17			11 47			12 17			12 47		13 17			13 47			
Brunstane	d		11 21			11 50			12 21			12 50		13 21			13 50			
Edinburgh 10	a		11 29			11 57			12 29			12 57		13 29			13 57			
	d	11 35	11 39	11 49	12 00	12 08	12 18	12 35	12 39	12 49	13 00	13 08	13 19	13 39	13 48	14 00	14 08	14 19	14 27	14 35
Haymarket	d	11 40	11 43	11 53	12 04	12 12	12 23	12 40	12 43	12 53	13 04	13 12	13 23	13 43	13 52	14 04	14 12	14 23	14 32	14 40
South Gyle	d		11 48	11 58		12 17	12 27		12 48	12 58		13 17	13 28	13 48	13 59		14 17	14 28		
Dalmeny	d		11 54	12 03		12 23	12 34		12 54	13 04		13 23	13 34	13 54	14 06		14 23	14 34		
North Queensferry	d		11 58	12 07		12 27	12 37		12 58	13 08		13 27	13 38	13 58	14 09		14 27	14 38		
Inverkeithing	d		12 02	12 11	12 18	12 31	12 41	12 54	13 02	13 12	13 17	13 31	13 42	14 02	14 13	14 18	14 31	14 42	14 47	14 53
Rosyth	d			12 14			12 45			13 15			13 45		14 17			14 45		
Dunfermline Town	d			12 19			12 50			13 20			13 50		14 22			14 50		
Dunfermline Queen Margaret	d			12 23			12 53			13 24			13 54		14 25			14 54		
Cowdenbeath	d			12 29			13a03			13 30			14a03		14 32			15a04		
Lochgelly	d			12 35						13 36					14 37					
Cardenden	d			12 39						13 40					14 41					
Dalgety Bay	d		12 05			12 34			13 05			13 34		14 05			14 34			
Aberdour	d		12 10			12 39			13 10			13 39		14 10			14 39			
Burntisland	d		12 14			12 43			13 14			13 43		14 14			14 43			
Kinghorn	d		12 19			12 48			13 19			13 48		14 19			14 48			
Kirkcaldy	d	12a08	12 24		12a34	12 53		13a09	13 24		13a33	13 53		14 24		14a34	14 53		15a03	15a09
Glenrothes With Thornton 2	a		12 33	12 46		13 04			13 32	13 46		14 04		14 32	14 48		15 04			

A From Edinburgh to Aberdeen
B To Aberdeen
C To Edinburgh
D To Dundee
E To Newcraighall
G To Inverurie
H To Perth
I To Inverness
J From Leeds to Aberdeen
K From London Kings Cross to Aberdeen. The Northern Lights

Newcraighall and Edinburgh - Dunfermline, Kirkcaldy and Glenrothes with Thornton

Network Diagram - see first page of Table 225

		SR	SR	SR	SR	SR		SR	SR	SR		SR	SR	SR			SR	SR	SR	SR		SR	SR		SR SO
				1								1													
		A	B	C				E	B	A		C	B				E	B		C		A			
Newcraighall	d	14 17			14 47				15 17				15 47					16 17					16 47		17 09
Brunstane	d	14 21			14 50				15 20				15 50					16 21					16 50		17 12
Edinburgh 10	a	14 29			14 57				15 29				15 57					16 29					16 57		17 19
	d	14 39	14 49	15 00	15 08	15 20		15 35	15 40	15 48		15 58	16 08	16 19			16 33	16 42	16 49	17 00		17 08	17 13		17 21
Haymarket	d	14 44	14 53	15 04	15 13	15 24		15 40	15 44	15 52		16 03	16 12	16 23			16 37	16 46	16 54	17 04		17 12	17 17		17 25
South Gyle	d	14 49	14 58		15 18	15 29			15 49	15 57			16 17	16 28				16 51	16 59			17 18	17 22		17 31
Dalmeny	d	14 55	15 04		15 24	15 35			15 55	16 03			16 23	16 34				16 58	17 05				17 29		17 38
North Queensferry	d	14 59	15 08		15 28	15 39			15 59	16 07			16 27	16 38				17 02	17 09				17 33		17 41
Inverkeithing	d	15 03	15 12	15 18	15 32	15 43		15 54	16 03	16 11		16 17	16 31	16 42			16 53	17 06	17 13	17 22		17 28	17 37		17 47
Rosyth	d		15 15			15 46				16 14				16 45					17 17			17 33			17 50
Dunfermline Town	d		15 20			15 51				16 19				16 50					17 22			17 38			17 55
Dunfermline Queen Margaret	d		15 24			15 55				16 23				16 54					17 25			17 42			17 59
Cowdenbeath	d		15 30			16a04				16 29				17a04					17a34			17 49			18 05
Lochgelly	d		15 36							16 35												17 55			18 11
Cardenden	d		15 40							16 39												17 59			18 15
Dalgety Bay	d	15 06			15 35				16 06				16 34					17 09					17 40		
Aberdour	d	15 11			15 40				16 11				16 39					17 14					17 45		
Burntisland	d	15 15			15 44				16 15				16 43					17 18					17 49		
Kinghorn	d	15 20			15 49				16 20				16 48					17 23					17 54		
Kirkcaldy	d	15 25		15a34	15 54			16a09	16 25			16a33	16 53				17a08	17 28		17a37			18a03		
Glenrothes With Thornton 2	a	15 33	15 46		16 05				16 33	16 45			17 01					17 36				18 08			18 24

		SR SX				SR		SR SO	SR SX	SR SX	SR SX	XC	SR	SR SX	SR SX	SR SO		GR SX	GR SO	SR	SR	SR		SR	SR
						◇1						◇1						R 1	R 1			1			
						K		B	B	A	C	L	B	M	A	A		N	N	E		C			
Newcraighall	d							17 37		17 37					18 03	18 08					18 34				19 06
Brunstane	d							17 41		17 40					18 06	18 12					18 37				19 09
Edinburgh 10	a							17 48		17 53					18 13	18 20					18 46				19 16
	d	17 21				17 42		17 49	17 49	17 55	17 58	18 11	18 15		18 25	18 25		18 30	18 30	18 40	18 50	19 00		19 09	19 21
Haymarket	d	17 25				17u46		17 53	17 53	17 59	18 03	18 15	18 19		18 30	18 30		18 34	18 35	18 45	18 54	19 04		19 13	19 26
South Gyle	d	17 31						17 58	17 58	18 04			18 24		18 35	18 35					18 59			19 18	19 30
Dalmeny	d	17 38						18 05	18 05	18 10			18 30	18 36	18 41	18 41					19 05			19 24	19 37
North Queensferry	d	17 41						18 09	18 09	18 14			18 34		18 45	18 45					19 09			19 28	19 40
Inverkeithing	d	17 47						18 13	18 13	18 18	18 22	18 29	18 38	18 43	18 49	18 49		18 54	18 54	19 00	19 13	19 18		19 32	19 44
Rosyth	d	17 50								18 21					18 52	18 52					19 16				19 48
Dunfermline Town	d	17 55								18 26					18 57	18 57					19 21				19 53
Dunfermline Queen Margaret	d	17 59								18 30					19 01	19 01					19 25				19 56
Cowdenbeath	d	18 05								18 36					19 07	19 07					19 31				20 03
Lochgelly	d	18 11								18 42					19 13	19 13					19 37				20 08
Cardenden	d	18a23								18 46					19 17	19 17					19 41				20 12
Dalgety Bay	d							18 16	18 16				18 41	18 46										19 35	
Aberdour	d							18 21	18 21				18 46	18 51										19 40	
Burntisland	d							18 25	18 25				18 50	18 55										19 44	
Kinghorn	d							18 30	18 30				18 55	19 00										19 49	
Kirkcaldy	d					18a14		18 35	18 35		18a39	18a46	19 00	19a04				19a11	19a11	19a18		19a33		19a56	
Glenrothes With Thornton 2	a							18 43	18 43	18 52			19 08		19 23	19 23					19 50				20 22

				SR		SR	SR	XC SX	XC SO	SR	GR SX	SR		SR	SR	SR	SR	SR	SR	SR SX	SR SO			SR	SR
				◇1				◇1	◇1		R 1					◇1									
				K			C	P	P		N	E			C	J	E	C	E					C	
Newcraighall	d					19 38				20 08				20 39			21 33			22 37	22 47				
Brunstane	d					19 41				20 10				20 42			21 36			22 40	22 51				
Edinburgh 10	a					19 48				20 19				20 49			21 43			22 49	22 58				
	d			19 36		19 50	20 00	20 14	20 14	20 22	20 29	20 45		20 52	21 07	21 40	21 49	22 09	22 39	22 55	22 59			23 09	23 19
Haymarket	d			19 41		19 54	20 04	20 17	20 18	20a28	20 34	20 49		20 56	21 11	21 44	21 53	22 13	22 43	22a59	23a03			23 13	23 23
South Gyle	d					19 59	20 09							21 00	21 16		21 58	22 18	22 48					23 18	23 28
Dalmeny	d					20 05	20 15							21 07	21 22		22 04	22 24	22 54					23 24	23 34
North Queensferry	d					20 09	20 19							21 10	21 26		22 08	22 28	22 58					23 28	23 38
Inverkeithing	d			19 54		20 13	20 23	20a30	20 35		20 51	21 03		21 14	21 30		22 12	22 32	23 02					23 32	23 42
Rosyth	d					20 16								21 17			22 15								23 45
Dunfermline Town	d					20 21								21 23			22 20								23 50
Dunfermline Queen Margaret	d					20 25								21 26			22 24								23 54
Cowdenbeath	d					20 31								21 33			22 30								23 59
Lochgelly	d					20 37								21 38			22 36								00 06
Cardenden	d					20 41								21 42			22 40								00 10
Dalgety Bay	d						20 26								21 33			22 35	23 05					23 35	
Aberdour	d						20 31								21 38			22 40	23 10					23 40	
Burntisland	d						20 35								21 42			22 44	23 14					23 44	
Kinghorn	d						20 40								21 47			22 49	23 19					23 49	
Kirkcaldy	d			20a10			20a44		20a50		21a08	21a18			21a51	22a12		22a53	23a23					23a53	
Glenrothes With Thornton 2	a					20 50								21 52			22 46								00 19

A To Edinburgh
B To Newcraighall
C To Dundee
E To Perth
J To Aberdeen
K To Inverness
L From Plymouth to Aberdeen
M From Glasgow Queen Street to Markinch
N From London Kings Cross to Aberdeen
P From Plymouth to Dundee

Newcraighall and Edinburgh - Dunfermline, Kirkcaldy and Glenrothes with Thornton

Network Diagram - see first page of Table 225

		SR
Newcraighall	d	23 36
Brunstane	d	23 39
Edinburgh 10	a	23 48
	d	23 48
Haymarket	d	23a52
South Gyle	d	
Dalmeny	d	
North Queensferry	d	
Inverkeithing	d	
Rosyth	d	
Dunfermline Town	d	
Dunfermline Queen Margaret	d	
Cowdenbeath	d	
Lochgelly	d	
Cardenden	d	
Dalgety Bay	d	
Aberdour	d	
Burntisland	d	
Kinghorn	d	
Kirkcaldy	d	
Glenrothes With Thornton 2	a	

Sundays

		SR	XC	GR	SR	SR	SR	SR	SR	SR	SR	SR	SR	SR	SR	SR	SR	GR	SR	SR	SR
		B	◇ C	R 1 C	D	◇1 E	F	F	◇1 C	D	F	F	◇1 C	D	◇1 E	F	F	R 1 H	D	◇1 E	F
Newcraighall	d																				
Brunstane	d																				
Edinburgh 10	a																				
	d	23p19	08 04	09 10	09 15	09 36	09 55	10 15	10 55	11 15	11 55	12 15	12 40	13 15	13 50	14 00	14 15	14 33	15 15	15 50	15 55
Haymarket	d	23p23	08 08	09 14	09 19	09 40	09 59	10 19	10 59	11 19	11 59	12 19	12 44	13 19	13 54	14 04	14 19	14 38	15 19	15 54	15 59
South Gyle	d	23p28			09 24		10 04	10 24		11 24	12 04	12 24		13 24		14 08	14 24		15 24		16 04
Dalmeny	d	23p34			09 30		10 10	10 30		11 30	12 12	12 30		13 32		14 11	14 30		15 30		16 10
North Queensferry	d	23p38			09 34		10 14	10 34		11 34	12 19	12 34		13 36		14 15	14 34		15 34		16 14
Inverkeithing	d	23p42	08 25	09 32	09 38	09 56	10 18	10 38	11 15	11 38	12 23	12 38	13 00	13 40	14 12	14 22	14 41	14 56	15 38	16 10	16 18
Rosyth	d	23p45					10 23				12 26					14 27					16 21
Dunfermline Town	d	23p50					10 28				12 31					14 33					16 26
Dunfermline Queen Margaret	d	23p54					10 33				12 35					14 36					16 30
Cowdenbeath	d	23p59					10 38				12 41					14 43					16 36
Lochgelly	d	00 06					10 45				12 47					14 48					16 42
Cardenden	d	00 10					10 49				12 51					14 52					16 46
Dalgety Bay	d				09 44			10 44		11 44		12 44		13 46			14 44		15 44		
Aberdour	d				09 49			10 49		11 49		12 49		13 51			14 49		15 49		
Burntisland	d				09 53			10 53		11 53		12 53		13 55			14 53		15 53		
Kinghorn	d				09 58			10 58		11 58		12 58		14 00			14 58		15 58		
Kirkcaldy	d		08a39	09a48	10a03	10a12		11 03	11a31	12a02		13 03	13a16	14a04	14a28		15 03	15a13	16a02	16a26	
Glenrothes With Thornton 2	a	00 19					10 55	11 11			12 57	13 11				15 00	15 14				16 52

		SR	SR	SR	SR	SR	XC	SR	GR	SR	SR	SR	SR	SR	SR	SR	SR	SR
		F	◇1 C	D	1 J	F	◇1 K	F	R 1 M	D	F	A	F	◇1 C		F	D	
Newcraighall	d																	
Brunstane	d																	
Edinburgh 10	a																	
	d	16 15	17 05	17 15	17 50	17 55	18 13	18 15	18 42	19 15	19 55		20 15	21 00	21 15	21 55	22 25	23 36
Haymarket	d	16 19	17 09	17 19	17 54	17 59	18 16	18 20	18 47	19 19	19 59		20 19	21 05	21 19	21 59	22 29	23 40
South Gyle	d	16 24		17 24		18 04		18 25		19 24	20 04		20 24		21 24	22 04	22 34	23 45
Dalmeny	d	16 30		17 30		18 10		18 32		19 30	20 10		20 30		21 30	22 10	22 40	23 51
North Queensferry	d	16 34		17 34		18 14		18 35		19 34	20 14		20 34		21 34	22 14	22 44	23 55
Inverkeithing	d	16 38	17 22	17 38	18 07	18 18	18 30	18 39	19 02	19 38	20 18		20 38	21 19	21 38	22 18	22 48	23a58
Rosyth	d					18 21					20 21					22 21		
Dunfermline Town	d					18 26					20 26					22 26		
Dunfermline Queen Margaret	d					18 30					20 30					22 30		
Cowdenbeath	d					18 36					20 36					22 36		
Lochgelly	d					18 42					20 42					22 42		
Cardenden	d					18 46					20 46					22 46		
Dalgety Bay	d	16 41		17 41				18 42		19 41			20 41		21 41		22 51	
Aberdour	d	16 46		17 46				18 47		19 46			20 46		21 46		22 56	
Burntisland	d	16 50		17 50				18 51		19 50			20 50		21 50		23 00	
Kinghorn	d	16 55		17 55				18 56		19 55			20 55		21 55		23 05	
Kirkcaldy	d	17 00	17a38	17a59	18a23		18a44	19 01	19a18	19a59			21 00	21a34	22a02		23a09	
Glenrothes With Thornton 2	a	17 08				18 52		19 09			20 52		21 09			22 54		

B not 11 December
C To Aberdeen
D To Dundee
E To Inverness
F To Edinburgh
H From London Kings Cross to Aberdeen. **The Northern Lights**
J To Perth
K From Plymouth to Aberdeen
M From London Kings Cross to Aberdeen

Glenrothes with Thornton, Kirkcaldy and Dunfermline - Edinburgh and Newcraighall

Network Diagram - see first page of Table 225

Miles	Miles			XC MX ◇1 A	SR MX C	SR SX R A	SR	SR	SR SX C	SR SX E	SR SO C	SR SX	SR E	SR F	SR SX	SR SX C	SR SX G	XC SO ◇1 H	XC SX ◇1 H
0	0	Glenrothes With Thornton 2	d		23p15					06 03			06 30			06 54			
7¼	—	**Kirkcaldy**	d	23p26		23u54			05 53		06 16	06 27		06 49			07 13	07 21	07 21
10	—	Kinghorn	d						05 58		06 21	06 32		06 54			07 18		
12¾	—	Burntisland	d						06 02		06 26	06 36		06 59			07 23		
17½	—	Aberdour	d						06 07		06 31	06 41		07 04			07 28		
20¼	—	Dalgety Bay	d						06 12		06 36	06 46		07 09			07 33		
—	4¾	Cardenden	d		23p23					06 10			06 37			07 01			
—	7	Lochgelly	d		23p27					06 14			06 41			07 05			
—	9½	Cowdenbeath	d		23p33					06 20			06 47			07 11			
—	13½	Dunfermline Queen Margaret	d		23p38					06 26			06 53		07 08	07 17			
—	14¾	**Dunfermline Town**	d		23p44					06 30			06 56		07 11	07 20			
—	17	Rosyth	d		23p47					06 34			07 00		07 15	07 24			
21¾	18½	Inverkeithing	d	23p42	23p51	00u12			06 16	06 40	06 40	06 49	07 06	07 12	07 19	07 30	07 37	07 38	07 43
23¾	20½	North Queensferry	d		23p55				06 20	06 44	06 44	06 53	07 10		07 24	07 34			
25½	22¼	Dalmeny	d		23p58				06 23	06 48	06 48	06 57	07 13	07 19		07 38	07a42		
30½	27¼	South Gyle	d		00 05				06 29	06 54	06 54	07 03	07 20	07 25	07 32	07 44			
33¾	30½	Haymarket	d	23p58	00 12		06 14	06 33	06 40	07 02	07 02	07 12	07 28	07 34	07 40	07 52		07 56	08 01
35	31¾	**Edinburgh 10**	a	00 05	00 18		06 18	06 39	06 46	07 09	07 09	07 16	07 34	07 38	07 46	07 57		08 01	08 06
—	—		d				06 20	06 41		07 10	07 10		07 38						
39	—	Brunstane	d				06 27	06 49		07 17	07 17		07 45						
39¾	—	**Newcraighall**	a				06 34	06 53		07 21	07 21		07 49						

		SR I	SR C	SR C	SR ◇1 A	SR SO J	SR SX	SR SX J	SR F	SR SX F	SR J	SR I	SR 1 L	SR I	SR F	SR ◇1 M	SR J
Glenrothes With Thornton 2	d	07 15				07 32		07 34			08 04	08 16		08 37			09 08
Kirkcaldy	d	07 27		07 40	07 49				08 06	08 18		08 28	08 41		09 12	09 25	
Kinghorn	d	07 32							08 10			08 32			09 17		
Burntisland	d	07 37							08 15			08 37			09 22		
Aberdour	d	07 42							08 20			08 42			09 26		
Dalgety Bay	d	07 46							08 25			08 47			09 31		
Cardenden	d					07 37	07 36	07 42			08 11			08 45			09 16
Lochgelly	d					07 42	07 42	07 47			08 15			08 49			09 20
Cowdenbeath	d					07 48	07 51	07 57			08 24			08 58			09 29
Dunfermline Queen Margaret	d					07 55	07 57	08 03			08 30			09 03			09 34
Dunfermline Town	d					07 59	08 02	08 07			08 33			09 07			09 38
Rosyth	d					08 02	08 03	08 12			08 37			09 10			09 41
Inverkeithing	d	07 50		07 57		08 08	08 10	08 20	08 28	08 35	08 41	08 50	08 57	09 14	09 34		09 46
North Queensferry	d	07 54				08 12		08 26			08 45	08 54		09 18			
Dalmeny	d	07 58				08 16	08 19		08 35		08 49	08 58		09 22			
South Gyle	d	08 04				08 22	08 25	08 34	08 41	08 46	08 55	09 04		09 28			
Haymarket	d	08 12	08 12	08 17	08 19	08 28	08 32	08 45	08 51	08 55	09 03	09 12	09 15	09 36	09 50	09 56	10 04
Edinburgh 10	a	08 17	08 17	08 22	08 25	08 37	08 40	08 53	08 56	08 59	09 12	09 17	09 21	09 42	09 55	10 00	10 13
	d		08 18			08 51				09 01		09 21		09 51			10 21
Brunstane	d		08 26			08 58				09 10		09 29		10 00			10 28
Newcraighall	a		08 31			09 04				09 14		09 34		10 04			10 35

		SR I	GR SX R 1 N	GR SO R 1 N	SR J	SR I	XC SO ◇1 O	XC SX ◇1 O	SR	SR 1 F	SR	SR C	SR I	SR J	SR 1 F	SR
Glenrothes With Thornton 2	d	09 17			09 32	09 49					10 23		10 32	10 51		
Kirkcaldy	d	09 30	09 44	09 44		10 01	10 17	10 17		10 26	10 31	10 42		11 02	11 19	
Kinghorn	d	09 34				10 05					10 36			11 07		
Burntisland	d	09 39				10 10					10 41			11 12		
Aberdour	d	09 44				10 15					10 45			11 16		
Dalgety Bay	d	09 49				10 20					10 50			11 21		
Cardenden	d				09 39								10 40			
Lochgelly	d				09 43								10 44			
Cowdenbeath	d				09 52				10 21				10 53			11 23
Dunfermline Queen Margaret	d				09 58				10 26				10 58			11 28
Dunfermline Town	d				10 01				10 30				11 02			11 32
Rosyth	d				10 05				10 33				11 05			11 35
Inverkeithing	d	09 52	10 01	10 01	10 09	10 23	10 32	10 32	10 37	10 42	10 54	10 59	11 10	11 25	11 35	11 40
North Queensferry	d	09 56			10 13				10 41		10 58		11 14	11 29		11 44
Dalmeny	d	10 00			10 17				10 45		11 02		11 18	11 33		11 48
South Gyle	d	10 06			10 23	10 34			10 51		11 08		11 24	11 39		11 54
Haymarket	d	10 13	10 17	10 19	10 30	10 43	10 52	10 54	11 02	11 06	11 16	11 19	11 34	11 47	11 51	12 02
Edinburgh 10	a	10 19	10 25	10 26	10 36	10 47	10 58	10 58	11 07	11 14	11 21	11 25	11 38	11 52	11 56	12 07
	d				10 51				11 21				11 51			
Brunstane	d				11 01				11 29				12 00			
Newcraighall	a				11 06				11 32				12 03			

A From Aberdeen to London Euston
C From Perth
E From Markinch
F From Dundee
G To Glasgow Queen Street
H From Dundee to Plymouth
I From Newcraighall
J From Edinburgh
L From Blair Atholl
M From Inverness
N From Aberdeen to London Kings Cross
O From Aberdeen to Penzance

Glenrothes with Thornton, Kirkcaldy and Dunfermline - Edinburgh and Newcraighall

Network Diagram - see first page of Table 225

		SR	SR	GR		SR	SR	SR		SR		SR	SR	SR	SR	SR	SR	SR		SR		SR	SR	SR	
																						SO	SX		
				R 1				1					◇1					1						◇1	
			A	B		D	E	F					G			D	E	F						G	
Glenrothes With Thornton 2	d	11 18				11 34	11 48					12 18				12 33	12 47					13 18	13 18		
Kirkcaldy	d	11 27	11 41	11 44			12 00	12 17				12 27	12 38				12 59	13 18				13 26	13 26	13 40	
Kinghorn	d	11 31					12 04					12 31					13 03					13 31	13 31		
Burntisland	d	11 36					12 09					12 36					13 08					13 36	13 36		
Aberdour	d	11 41					12 13					12 41					13 13					13 40	13 40		
Dalgety Bay	d	11 46					12 18					12 46					13 18					13 45	13 45		
Cardenden	d					11 41										12 40									
Lochgelly	d					11 45										12 44									
Cowdenbeath	d					11 54				12 23						12 53				13 23					
Dunfermline Queen Margaret	d					12 00				12 28						12 58				13 28					
Dunfermline Town	d					12 03				12 32						13 02				13 32					
Rosyth	d					12 07				12 35						13 05				13 35					
Inverkeithing	d	11 49	11 57	12 01		12 11	12 21	12 33		12 39		12 49	12 54			13 10	13 21	13 34		13 39		13 49	13 49		
North Queensferry	d					12 15	12 25			12 43		12 53				13 14	13 25			13 43		13 53	13 53		
Dalmeny	d					12 19	12 29			12 47		12 57				13 18	13 29			13 47		13 57	13 57		
South Gyle	d	12 00				12 25	12 35			12 53		13 03				13 24	13 35			13 53		14 03	14 03		
Haymarket	d	12 08	12 13	12 17		12 31	12 43	12 49		13 02		13 11	13 15			13 34	13 43	13 51		14 02		14 10	14 10	14 14	
Edinburgh 10	a	12 14	12 18	12 25		12 37	12 48	12 55		13 07		13 17	13 20			13 38	13 48	13 57		14 06		14 16	14 16	14 19	
	d	12 20					12 51					13 21					13 51					14 18	14 21		
Brunstane	d	12 28					12 59					13 29					13 58					14 28	14 28		
Newcraighall	a	12 32					13 05					13 33					14 04					14 33	14 33		

			SR	SR	SR			SR	SR	SR			SR	SR	SR	SR			SR	SR	SR			SR	SR
															SO	SX									
					1										1	1					◇1				
			D	E	F					A			D	E	F	F					G			D	E
Glenrothes With Thornton 2	d		13 32	13 47					14 18				14 32	14 48						15 18				15 34	15 47
Kirkcaldy	d			13 59	14 18				14 27	14 39				15 00	15 18	15 18				15 26	15 41				15 59
Kinghorn	d			14 03					14 31					15 05						15 31					16 03
Burntisland	d			14 08					14 36					15 10						15 36					16 08
Aberdour	d			14 13					14 41					15 14						15 40					16 13
Dalgety Bay	d			14 18					14 46					15 19						15 45					16 18
Cardenden	d		13 40										14 40											15 42	
Lochgelly	d		13 44										14 44											15 46	
Cowdenbeath	d		13 53					14 22					14 53						15 23					15 55	
Dunfermline Queen Margaret	d		13 58					14 27					14 58						15 28					16 00	
Dunfermline Town	d		14 02					14 31					15 02						15 32					16 04	
Rosyth	d		14 05					14 34					15 05						15 35					16 07	
Inverkeithing	d		14 11	14 21	14 34			14 39	14 49	14 55			15 12	15 23	15 34	15 34			15 39	15 49	15 57			16 11	16 21
North Queensferry	d		14 15	14 25				14 43	14 53				15 16	15 27					15 43	15 53				16 14	16 25
Dalmeny	d		14 19	14 29				14 47	14 57				15 20	15 31					15 47	15 57				16 19	16 29
South Gyle	d		14 25	14 35				14 53	15 03				15 26	15 37					15 53	16 03				16 24	16 35
Haymarket	d		14 33	14 43	14 49			14 59	15 11	15 15			15 34	15 44	15 50	15 53			16 01	16 11	16 14			16 34	16 43
Edinburgh 10	a		14 40	14 48	14 54			15 07	15 16	15 20			15 41	15 50	15 54	16 00			16 07	16 15	16 21			16 38	16 48
	d			14 51					15 20					15 51						16 21					16 51
Brunstane	d			14 58					15 28					16 00						16 28					16 58
Newcraighall	a			15 04					15 32					16 03						16 33					17 04

		SR			SR		SR	SR	GR	GR		SR		SR		SR		SR	SR	SR	SR				SR
									SO	SX		SX		SO				SX	SO						
		1							R 1	R 1															
		F						A	K	K		D		D		E		D	D	F	A				D
Glenrothes With Thornton 2	d						16 20					16 33		16 33		16 48		17 01	17 01						17 37
Kirkcaldy	d	16 19					16 29	16 41	16 45	16 45						17 00				17 32	17 48				
Kinghorn	d						16 34									17 05				17 36					
Burntisland	d						16 39									17 10				17 42					
Aberdour	d						16 43									17 14				17 46					
Dalgety Bay	d						16 48									17 19				17 51					
Cardenden	d											16 40		16 40				17 09	17 09						17 44
Lochgelly	d											16 47		16 47				17 13	17 13						17 48
Cowdenbeath	d				16 23							16 53		16 53				17 22	17 22						17 57
Dunfermline Queen Margaret	d				16 28							16 59		16 59				17 27	17 27						18 03
Dunfermline Town	d				16 32							17 02		17 02				17 31	17 31						18 06
Rosyth	d				16 35							17 06		17 06				17 34	17 34						18 10
Inverkeithing	d	16 35			16 40		16 52	16 57	17 01	17 03		17 10		17 10		17 23		17 38	17 38	17 55	18 04				18 14
North Queensferry	d				16 44							17 14		17 14		17 27		17 42	17 42	17 59					18 18
Dalmeny	d				16 48							17 18		17 18		17 31		17 46	17 46	18 03					18 22
South Gyle	d				16 54		17 03					17 24		17 24		17 37		17 52	17 52	18 09					18 28
Haymarket	d	16 52			17 02		17 11	17 16	17 18	17 19		17 32		17 32		17 45		18 03	18 03	18 16	18 19				18 35
Edinburgh 10	a	16 58			17 07		17 19	17 23	17 26	17 27		17 38		17 38		17 50		18 08	18 08	18 22	18 25				18 41
	d						17 21					17 41		17 51				18 17	18 21						18 48
Brunstane	d						17 28					17 49		17 59				18 26	18 26						18 56
Newcraighall	a						17 32					17 52		18 03				18 32	18 32						18 59

A From Perth
B From Aberdeen to London Kings Cross. The Northern Lights
D From Newcraighall
E From Edinburgh
F From Dundee
G From Inverness
K From Aberdeen to London Kings Cross

Glenrothes with Thornton, Kirkcaldy and Dunfermline - Edinburgh and Newcraighall

Network Diagram - see first page of Table 225

		SR	SR	SR SO	SR SX	SR	SR	SR SX	SR SO	SR SX	SR	SR	SR	SR SO	GR SX	SR	SR
		1				◇1				1			1	◇1	R 1		
		B	C	D	D	E	G	G	B	B	D	G	I	J	K		
Glenrothes With Thornton 2	d			18 11	18 11		18 44	18 52			19 10	19 23				20 02	
Kirkcaldy	d	18 13		18 23	18 23	18 43		19 04	19 26	19 26		19 36	19 54	20 08	20 08		20 27
Kinghorn	d			18 27	18 27			19 08				19 40					20 32
Burntisland	d			18 32	18 32			19 13				19 45					20 37
Aberdour	d			18 37	18 37			19 18				19 50					20 41
Dalgety Bay	d			18 42	18 42			19 23				19 55					20 46
Cardenden	d						18 52				19 18					20 09	
Lochgelly	d						18 56				19 22					20 13	
Cowdenbeath	d						19 05				19 31					20 22	
Dunfermline Queen Margaret	d						19 10				19 36					20 27	
Dunfermline Town	d						19 14				19 40					20 31	
Rosyth	d						19 17				19 43					20 34	
Inverkeithing	d	18 29		18 45	18 46	18 59	19 21	19 27	19 42	19 42	19 47	19 58		20 24	20 24	20 39	20 50
North Queensferry	d			18 49			19 25	19 31			19 51	20 02				20 43	20 54
Dalmeny	d			18 53	18 53		19 29	19 35			19 55	20 06				20 47	20 58
South Gyle	d			18 59	19 12		19 35	19 41			20 01	20 12				20 53	21 04
Haymarket	d	18 44	18 58	19 08	19 22	19 14	19 43	19 49	20 04	20 04	20 10	20 20	20 24	20 42	20 43	21 00	21 11
Edinburgh 10	a	18 49	19 03	19 13	19 31	19 22	19 48	19 54	20 09	20 09	20 14	20 25	20 29	20 48	20 48	21 06	21 17
	d		19 21				19 51				20 16					21 16	
Brunstane	d		19 28				20 00				20 24					21 24	
Newcraighall	a		19 33				20 04				20 27					21 27	

		SR	SR	SR	SR	SR	SR	SR	XC SO	XC SX	SR	SR SX
					◇1	◇		◇1	◇1	◇1		R
		I		B	E	F		J	J	J	I	L
Glenrothes With Thornton 2	d		21 02				22 02				23 15	
Kirkcaldy	d	20 41		21 26	21 42	21 59		22 59	23 14	23 26		23u54
Kinghorn	d			21 30		22 04		23 03				
Burntisland	d			21 36		22 09		23 09				
Aberdour	d			21 40		22 13		23 13				
Dalgety Bay	d			21 45		22 18		23 18				
Cardenden	d		21 09				22 09				23 23	
Lochgelly	d		21 13				22 13				23 27	
Cowdenbeath	d		21 22				22 19				23 33	
Dunfermline Queen Margaret	d		21 27				22 24				23 38	
Dunfermline Town	d		21 31				22 28				23 44	
Rosyth	d		21 34				22 31				23 47	
Inverkeithing	d	20 59	21 39	21 49		22 23	22 39	23 23	23 31	23 42	23 51	00u12
North Queensferry	d		21 43	21 53		22 27	22 43	23 27			23 55	
Dalmeny	d		21 47	21 57		22 31	22 47	23 31			23 58	
South Gyle	d		21 53	22 03		22 37	22 53	23 37			00 05	
Haymarket	d	21 16	22 00	22 10	22 14	22 46	23 00	23 43	23 51	23 58	00 12	
Edinburgh 10	a	21 20	22 07	22 16	22 19	22 50	23 06	23 50	23 55	00 05	00 18	
	d		22 17				23 15					
Brunstane	d		22 25				23 22					
Newcraighall	a		22 28				23 26					

Sundays

		SR	SR	SR	SR	SR	GR	SR	XC	SR	SR	SR
							R 1		◇1		◇1	
		M	B	B	D	D	P	B	R	D	E	D
Glenrothes With Thornton 2	d	23p15			10 56	11 11				12 58		13 11
Kirkcaldy	d		08 08	10 08	11 08		11 40	12 08	13 03	13 10	13 29	
Kinghorn	d		08 13	10 13	11 13			12 13		13 15		
Burntisland	d		08 17	10 17	11 17			12 17		13 19		
Aberdour	d		08 22	10 22	11 22			12 22		13 24		
Dalgety Bay	d		08 27	10 27	11 27			12 27		13 29		
Cardenden	d	23p23				11 18						13 19
Lochgelly	d	23p27				11 22						13 23
Cowdenbeath	d	23p33				11 30						13 30
Dunfermline Queen Margaret	d	23p38				11 36						13 36
Dunfermline Town	d	23p44				11 39						13 39
Rosyth	d	23p47				11 43						13 43
Inverkeithing	d	23p51	08 30	10 30	11 30	11 47	11 56	12 30	13 18	13 32	13 45	13 49
North Queensferry	d	23p55	08 34	10 34	11 34	11 51		12 36		13 42		13 53
Dalmeny	d	23p58	08 38	10 38	11 38	11 56		12 40		13 49		13 58
South Gyle	d	00 05	08 44	10 44	11 44	12 02		12 46		13 55		14 04
Haymarket	d	00 12	08 53	10 58	11 58	12 10	12 16	12 58	13 37	14 04	14 08	14 13
Edinburgh 10	a	00 18	09 00	11 06	12 06	12 18	12 23	13 06	13 42	14 08	14 12	14 20
	d											
Brunstane	d											
Newcraighall	a											

B From Dundee
C From Dunblane
D From Edinburgh
E From Inverness
F From Inverurie
G From Newcraighall
I From Perth
J From Aberdeen
K From Aberdeen to Leeds
L From Aberdeen to London Euston
M not 11 December. From Perth
P From Aberdeen to London Kings Cross. **The Northern Lights**
R From Aberdeen to Exeter St Davids

Table 242

Sundays

Glenrothes with Thornton, Kirkcaldy and Dunfermline - Edinburgh and Newcraighall

Network Diagram - see first page of Table 225

		GR	SR	SR	SR	GR	SR	SR	SR	SR	SR	SR	SR	SR	SR
		◇1 A	B	E	E	◇1 A	◇1 F	B	◇1 G	E	E	◇1 F	B	◇1 G	E
Glenrothes With Thornton 2	d			15 04	15 14					16 53	17 08				18 53
Kirkcaldy	d	13 39	14 08	15 15		15 42	16 03	16 08	17 02	17 07		17 58	18 07	18 56	19 07
Kinghorn	d		14 13	15 20				16 13		17 12			18 12		19 12
Burntisland	d		14 17	15 24				16 17		17 16			18 16		19 16
Aberdour	d		14 22	15 29				16 22		17 21			18 21		19 21
Dalgety Bay	d		14 27	15 34				16 27		17 26			18 26		19 26
Cardenden	d				15 21						17 14				
Lochgelly	d				15 25						17 18				
Cowdenbeath	d				15 33						17 26				
Dunfermline Queen Margaret	d				15 39						17 32				
Dunfermline Town	d				15 42						17 35				
Rosyth	d				15 46						17 39				
Inverkeithing	d	13 58	14 30	15 37	15 50	15 58	16 19	16 30	17 18	17 29	17 43	18 14	18 29	19 12	19 29
North Queensferry	d		14 34	15 41	15 54			16 34		17 33	17 47		18 33		19 33
Dalmeny	d		14 38	15 45	16 00			16 38		17 37	17 51		18 37		19 37
South Gyle	d		14 44	15 51	16 06			16 44		17 43	17 58		18 43		19 43
Haymarket	d	14 18	14 56	15 58	16 16	16 18	16 35	16 55	17 34	17 49	18 07	18 30	18 52	19 27	19 52
Edinburgh 10	a	14 25	15 03	16 07	16 21	16 25	16 42	16 59	17 41	17 56	18 12	18 35	19 00	19 35	19 56
	d														
Brunstane	d														
Newcraighall	a														

		SR	SR	SR	SR	SR	SR	SR	SR	SR	XC	SR
		E	B	◇1 G	E	◇1 F	E	◇1 G		E	◇1 G	H
Glenrothes With Thornton 2	d	19 09			20 54		21 09			22 54		
Kirkcaldy	d		20 10	20 59	21 07	21 25		22 05	22 13	23 06	23 22	23u54
Kinghorn	d		20 15		21 11				22 17	23 10		
Burntisland	d		20 20		21 16				22 22	23 15		
Aberdour	d		20 24		21 20				22 26	23 19		
Dalgety Bay	d		20 29		21 25				22 31	23 24		
Cardenden	d	19 17					21 16					
Lochgelly	d	19 21					21 20					
Cowdenbeath	d	19 29					21 28					
Dunfermline Queen Margaret	d	19 34					21 34					
Dunfermline Town	d	19 38					21 37					
Rosyth	d	19 41					21 41					
Inverkeithing	d	19 45	20 31	21 15	21 28	21 41	21 45	22 21	22 34	23 27	23 38	00u16
North Queensferry	d	19 49	20 36		21 32		21 49		22 38	23 31		
Dalmeny	d	19 53	20 40		21 36		21 53		22 42	23 35		
South Gyle	d	20 00	20 46		21 40		22 00		22 48	23 41		
Haymarket	d	20 09	20 55	21 31	21 51	21 57	22 09	22 37	22 57	23 50	23 54	
Edinburgh 10	a	20 15	21 01	21 36	21 55	22 01	22 13	22 43	23 01	23 56	23 58	
	d											
Brunstane	d											
Newcraighall	a											

A From Aberdeen to London Kings Cross
B From Dundee
E From Edinburgh
F From Inverness
G From Aberdeen
H From Aberdeen to London Euston

Sleeper Services

Sleepers enable you to make long distance journeys while having a relaxing night's sleep. You arrive early at your destination, saving a day's travel — or the early morning dash to the airport. Five Sleeper routes link London Euston direct with over 40 stations in Scotland including most principal business and holiday locations. Direct Sleeper services also link Southwest England with London. Customers joining at the starting point of the train may occupy cabins well before departure. At terminating stations customers may vacate cabins up to approximately 0800 on trains which arrive at an earlier time.

Full details of all Sleeper services are given in Tables 400–406.

First Great Western ("Night Riviera Sleeper")

Both single and twin berth cabins are available and feature locking doors, comfortable beds with sheets and blankets, air conditioning, bedside lighting, complimentary toiletries, wash basin with a shaver point and a soft hand towel. Room service facilities, a wake up call, a light breakfast and newspaper are all complimentary.

The trains recently underwent a complete refurbishment to maximise customer comfort. Improvements include a refurbishment of seating areas and berths and the introduction of a hot breakfast offer to set our customers up for the day. All single and twin cabins are available to holders of standard class tickets and large reclining seats are provided throughout seated accommodation, again available to holders of standard class tickets. Customers in most single berths benefit from Volo TV, a new and innovative on-train entertainment service. Customers can choose from 40 different programmes including comedy, drama, documentaries, children's programmes and sport.

There are a number of inclusive Advance fares available that combine travel and accommodation on one ticket. These can be purchased until 1800 hours the day before departure. Holders of Anytime, Off-Peak and Super Off-Peak tickets may upgrade to sleeping accommodation on payment of the applicable single or twin berth supplement. The Lounge Car is provided for the use of customers with a berth. Here you can sit back and relax with a complimentary hot drink, tempt yourself with one of our delicious hot snacks or unwind with something stronger from our well stocked bar - all served at seat by our on-board team. Customers in seated accommodation can purchase refreshments and snacks from the Express Cafe, which is situated in the Lounge Car.

Dogs and pets are not normally allowed in Sleeper cabins. There are special arrangements for guide dogs. Animals may be conveyed if properly labelled and muzzled, and in suitable containers, in the guards van.

ScotRail Caledonian Sleepers

First Class customers receive a toiletry pack and will be woken with a light breakfast accompanied by tea or coffee and a complimentary newspaper. Standard Class customers are served a light morning snack with tea or coffee. Breakfast is available for an additional small supplement and can be ordered after boarding. Customer lounges are available at the following locations - London Euston, Inverness, Carlisle (Lakes Court Hotel) and Edinburgh Waverley. At Glasgow Central customers may use the on-train Lounge Car which is available prior to departure. Full details of the Caledonian Sleeper on-train and station facilities can be found inside the Caledonian Sleeper Guide which is available from principal sleeper departure points.

There are a number of berth inclusive fares available that include travel and accommodation at one all inclusive price. First class travel is in single berth cabins while Standard Class is in twin berth cabins.

The Lounge Car offers a pleasant relaxing atmosphere in which to unwind before a night's rest. Customers can choose from a wide selection of food and drinks including sandwiches, baguettes, snacks and a well stocked bar. At busy times, use of the Lounge Car may be restricted to First Class ticket holders.

Accompanying dogs are only permitted in Sleeper Cabins providing the owner(s) has exclusive use of the cabin and pays the appropriate charge. There are special arrangements for guide dogs. Dogs and pets cannot be conveyed in the guards van. A virtual tour is available via the ScotRail website. Visit www.scotrail.co.uk for details.

Please note that as a result of on-going engineering work some sleeper services may be subject to diversion causing an extension in journey times between Scotland and London. For full details telephone National Rail Enquiries on 08457 48 49 50 (calls may be recorded).

Sleeper Reservations

To book rail tickets and reserve Sleepers, simply visit any main rail station or rail appointed travel agent. Alternatively you can book by phone using most credit/debit cards.

First Great Western Telesales (www.firstgreatwestern.co.uk)	08457 00 01 25
ScotRail Telesales (www.scotrail.co.uk)	08457 55 00 33

For further information about rail tickets or services, call National Rail Enquiries on 08457 48 49 50 (calls may be recorded for training purposes).

Sleeper Services (continued)

ScotRail Sleeper Services – The Caledonian Sleepers

Operated by ScotRail

Table 400 London and Edinburgh

		Mon–Thu	Fri	Sun
Cabins available from		2300	2300	2230
Edinburgh	d	2340	2340	2315
Carstairs	d	0016*	0016*	2347
Carlisle	d	0141	0141	0112*
Watford Junction	a	0619	0627	0623
London Euston	a	0643	0650	0646
Vacate cabins by		0800	0800	0800

		Mon–Thu	Fri	Sun
Cabins available from		2300	2300	2245
London Euston	d	2350	2350	2327
Watford Junction	d	0010*	0010*	2347
Carlisle	a	0516	0515	0504*
Carstairs	a	0620	0620	0620
Edinburgh	a	0716	0715	0716
Vacate cabins by		0800	0800	0800

a Arrival time
d Departure time
R Reservations Compulsory
* Following morning
Services in this table do not run on Saturday nights.
For details of overnight seated services, please refer to Table 65

Table 401 London and Glasgow

		Mon–Thu	Fri	Sun
Cabins available from		2200	2200	2200
Glasgow Central	d	2340	2340	2315
Motherwell	d	2356	2356	2331
Carstairs	d	0016*	0016*	2347
Carlisle	d	0141	0141	0112*
Watford Junction	a	0619	0627	0623
London Euston	a	0643	0650	0646
Vacate cabins by		0800	0800	0800

		Mon–Thu	Fri	Sun
Cabins available from		2300	2300	2245
London Euston	d	2350	2350	2327
Watford Junction	d	0010*	0010*	2347
Carlisle	a	0516	0515	0504*
Carstairs	a	0620	0620	0620
Motherwell	a	0656	0656	0656
Glasgow Central	a	0720	0720	0720
Vacate cabins by		0745b	0800	0745b

a Arrival time
d Departure time
b From 12 Feb 2012 Cabins to be vacated by 0800
R Reservations Compulsory
* Following morning
Services in this table do not run on Saturday nights.
For details of overnight seated services, please refer to Table 65

Table 402 London and Aberdeen

		Mon–Thu	Fri	Sun
Cabins available from		2110	2110	2050
Aberdeen	dep	2142	2142	2142
Stonehaven	dep	2200	2200	2200
Montrose	dep	2225	2225	2225
Arbroath	dep	2243	2243	2243
Carnoustie	dep	2252	2252	2252
Dundee	dep	2306	2306	2306
Leuchars for St Andrews•	dep	2325	2325	2325
Kirkcaldy•	dep	2353	2353	2353
Inverkeithing•	dep	0012*	0012*	0012*
Preston	arr	0432	0432	0441
Crewe	arr	0534	0534	0537
London Euston	arr	0747	0747	0747
Vacate cabins by		0800	0800	0800

		Mon–Thu	Fri	Sun
Cabins available from		2030	2030	2000
London Euston	dep	2115	2115	2055
Watford Junction	dep	2133	2133	2117
Crewe	dep	2354	2354	2339
Preston	dep	0052*	0052*	0030*
Inverkeithing•	arr	0458	0458	0458
Kirkcaldy•	arr	0518	0518	0518
Leuchars for St Andrews•	arr	0547	0547	0547
Dundee	arr	0608	0608	0608
Carnoustie	arr	0623	0623	0623
Arbroath	arr	0631	0631	0631
Montrose	arr	0648	0648	0648
Stonehaven	arr	0714	0714	0714
Aberdeen	arr	0736	0736	0736
Vacate cabins by		0800	0800	0800

a Arrival time
d Departure time
R Reservations Compulsory
* Following morning
• Customers may depart from London or Watford later, and vacate cabins later, by travelling on the London Euston to Edinburgh Sleeper; then by local connecting service from Edinburgh
Services in this table do not run on Saturday nights
For details of overnight seated services, please refer to Table 65

Sleeper Services (continued)

ScotRail Sleeper Services – The Caledonian Sleepers

Operated by ScotRail

Table 403 London and Inverness

			Mon–Thu	Fri	Sun
Cabins available from			*2000*	*2000*	*1945*
Inverness	... ...	dep	2047	2047	2025
Aviemore	... ...	dep	2129	2129	2108
Kingussie	... ...	dep	2142	2142	2122
Newtonmore	... ...	dep	2150	2150	2129
Dalwhinnie	... ...	dep	2206	2206	2143
Blair Atholl	... ...	dep	2232	2232	2209
Pitlochry	... ...	dep	2245	2245	2222
Dunkeld & Birnam	... ...	dep	2300	2300	2237
Perth	... ...	dep	2321	2321	2300
Gleneagles	... ...	dep	2339	2339	2318
Dunblane	... ...	dep	2355	2355	2334
Stirling•	... ...	dep	0006*	0006*	2345
Falkirk Grahamston	...	dep	0023	0023	0002*
Preston	... ...	arr	0432	0432	0441
Crewe	... ...	arr	0534	0534	0537
London Euston	... ...	arr	0747	0747	0747
Vacate cabins by			*0800*	*0800*	*0800*

			Mon-Thu	Fri	Sun
Cabins available from			*2030*	*2030*	*2000*
London Euston	... ...	dep	2115	2115	2055
Watford Junction	... ...	dep	2133	2133	2117
Crewe	... ...	dep	2354	2354	2339
Preston	... ...	dep	0052*	0052*	0030*
Stirling•	... ...	arr	0455	0455	0455
Dunblane	... ...	arr	0504	0504	0504
Gleneagles	... ...	arr	0519	0519	0519
Perth•	... ...	arr	0539	0539	0539
Dunkeld & Birnam	... ...	arr	0600	0600	0600
Pitlochry	... ...	arr	0616	0616	0616
Blair Atholl	... ...	arr	0628	0628	0628
Dalwhinnie	... ...	arr	0700	0700	0700
Newtonmore	... ...	arr	0712	0712	0712
Kingussie	... ...	arr	0718	0718	0718
Aviemore	... ...	arr	0739	0739	0739
Aviemore	... ...	dep	0741	0741	0741
Carridge	... ...	arr	0752	0752	0752
Carridge	... ...	dep	0754	0754	0754
Inverness	... ...	arr	0838	0838	0838
Vacate cabins by			*0845*	*0845*	*0845*

a Arrival time
d Departure time
R Reservations Compulsory
* Following morning
• Customers may depart from London or Watford later, and vacate cabins later, by travelling on the London Euston to Edinburgh Sleeper; then by local connecting service from Edinburgh.

Services in this table do not run on Saturday nights.
For details of overnight seated services, please refer to Table 65

Table 404 London and Fort William

			Mon–Thu	Fri	Sun
Cabins available from			*1920*	*1920*	*1830*
Fort William	... ...	dep	1950	1950	1900
Spean Bridge	... ...	dep	2010	2010	1920
Roy Bridge	... ...	dep	2017x	2017x	1927x
Tulloch	... ...	dep	2030	2030	1940
Corrour	... ...	dep	2051x	2051x	2001x
Rannoch	... ...	dep	2106	2106	2015
Bridge of Orchy	... ...	dep	2134	2134	2047
Upper Tyndrum	... ...	dep	2152	2152	2105
Crianlarich	... ...	dep	2205	2205	2118
Ardlui	... ...	dep	2226x	2226x	2139x
Arrochar & Tarbet	... ...	dep	2244	2244	2157
Garelochhead	... ...	dep	2310	2310	2223
Helensburgh Upper	...	dep	2324	2324	2237
Dalmuir	... ...	dep	2351	2351	2304
Westerton	... ...	dep	2356	2356	2313
Preston	... ...	arr	0432	0432	0441
Crewe	... ...	arr	0534	0534	0537
London Euston	... ...	arr	0747	0747	0747
Vacate cabins by			*0800*	*0800*	*0800*

			Mon-Thu	Fri	Sun
Cabins available from			*2030*	*2030*	*2000*
London Euston	... ...	dep	2115	2115	2055
Watford Junction	... ...	dep	2133	2133	2117
Crewe	... ...	dep	2354	2354	2339
Preston	... ...	dep	0052*	0052*	0030*
Westerton	... ...	arr	0555	0555	0555
Dalmuir	... ...	arr	0603	0603	0603
Helensburgh Upper	...	arr	0626	0626	0626
Garelochhead	... ...	arr	0641	0641	0641
Arrochar & Tarbet	... ...	arr	0707	0707	0707
Ardlui	... ...	arr	0722x	0722x	0722x
Crianlarich	... ...	arr	0743	0743	0743
Upper Tyndrum	... ...	arr	0755	0755	0755
Bridge of Orchy	... ...	arr	0813	0813	0813
Rannoch	... ...	arr	0841	0841	0841
Corrour	... ...	arr	0858x	0858x	0858x
Tulloch	... ...	arr	0917	0917	0917
Roy Bridge	... ...	arr	0929x	0929x	0929x
Spean Bridge	... ...	arr	0936	0936	0936
Fort William	... ...	arr	0954	0954	0954
Vacate cabins by			*0956*	*0956*	*0956*

a Arrival time
d Departure time
x Stops on request
R Reservations Compulsory
* Following morning

Services in this table do not run on Saturday nights.
For details of overnight seated services, please refer to Tables 65 and 227.

Sleeper Services (continued)

"Night Riviera" Sleeper

Operated by First Great Western

Table 406 London and Penzance

			Mon-Fri Ⓛ	Sun Ⓛ
Occupy cabins at Paddington:			*2230*	*2230*
London Paddington	...	dep	2345	2350
Reading	...	dep	0037*	0037*
Taunton	...	arr	0232	-
Exeter St Davids	...	arr	0306	0404
Newton Abbot	...	arr	0331	0455
Plymouth	...	arr	0412	0535
Liskeard	...	arr	0608	0709
Bodmin Parkway	...	arr	0622	0723
Lostwithiel	...	arr	0628	0729
Par	...	arr	0637	0738
St Austell	...	arr	0646	0746
Truro	...	arr	0706	0806
Redruth	...	arr	0718	0820
Camborne	...	arr	0726	0827
Hayle	...	arr	0735	0838
St Erth	...	arr	0741	0845
Penzance	...	arr	0753	0859
Vacate cabins at Penzance by			*on arival*	*on arrival*

			Mon-Fri Ⓛ	A Sun Ⓛ	B Sun Ⓛ
Occupy cabins at Penzance:			*2105*	*2045*	*2045*
Penzance	...	dep	2145	2115	2115
St Erth	...	dep	2155	2125	2125
Camborne	...	dep	2207	2138	2138
Redruth	...	dep	2214	2145	2145
Truro	...	dep	2227	2200	2200
St Austell	...	dep	2245	2218	2218
Par	...	dep	2254	-	-
Bodmin Parkway	...	dep	2306	2235	2235
Liskeard	...	dep	2321	2250	2250
Plymouth	...	dep	2351	2320	0150*
Totnes	...	dep	0020*	2348	0218
Newton Abbot	...	dep	0033	0001*	0231
Exeter St Davids	...	dep	0106	0057	0259
Taunton	...	dep	0136	-	-
Reading	...	arr	0400	0402s	0511
London Paddington	...	arr	0525	0505	0609
Vacate cabins at Paddington by			*0700*	*0700*	*0700*

Ⓛ Sleeper Lounge Car
* Following morning
A Runs until 12 February 2012 and from 1 April 2012
B Runs from 19 February 2012 until 25 March 2012
s Stops to set down only
Services in this table do not run on Saturday nights.
For details of seated services on this route, please refer to Table 135.

Passenger Representation
Passenger Focus

What is Passenger Focus?

Passenger Focus is the official, independent consumer organisation representing the interests of rail users nationally and bus, coach and tram users across England outside London.

With a strong emphasis on evidence-based campaigning and research, we ensure that we know what is happening on the ground. We use our knowledge to influence decisions on behalf of passengers and we work with the industry, other passenger groups and government to secure journey improvements.

What can Passenger Focus do for me?

We are here to put the interests of rail, bus and coach passengers first. We do this by:

Campaigning for improvements

- we gather research and information, like the National Passenger Survey, where 50,000 passengers give us their views about their rail journeys, so we understand the issues that matter to you
- we work with Government and the industry to ensure that the passenger voice is heard when making decisions about the future
- we focus on a number of key issues:
  - fares and tickets
  - quality and level of services
  - investment in the railway

Providing practical advice

- we provide passengers with advice on how to get the best from the network, explain their rights and help them when things go wrong
- we work with other passenger groups to support them in their work

Resolving complaints

- if you make a complaint and you are unhappy with the response we can take up your complaint with the company involved

Making a complaint

If you have a complaint or comment about any aspect of your rail service, either on the train or at the station, please contact the railway company managing director concerned (contact details are shown on the TOC pages of this timetable).

What should you include in your complaint?

Depending on the nature of your complaint you should include:

- the reason for your complaint
- a description of the inconvenience caused
- which train and which day you travelled on, or which station you used and when
- how many people travelled with you
- your ticket(s) as evidence
- an explanation of the action you would like the company to take to rectify the problem

What next?

If you are not satisfied with the company's response you can contact Passenger Focus or, in the London area, London TravelWatch.

How to get in touch:

Telephone:	0300 123 2350 0800 - 2000 Monday - Friday 0800 - 1600 at weekends
Address:	Passenger Focus FREEPOST (RRRE-ETTC-LEET) PO BOX 4257 MANCHESTER M60 3AR
Fax:	0161 236 1574
Email:	advice@passengerfocus.org.uk
Website:	www.passengerfocus.org.uk

London TravelWatch

London TravelWatch is the independent, statutory watchdog for transport users in and around London, including all services provided by Transport for London, and represents rail passengers in and around London. We investigate suggestions and complaints from passengers who are dissatisfied with responses received from transport operators.

If your journey is within, or began in, London, please contact:

Telephone:	020 7505 9000 (0900-1700 Monday- Friday)
Address:	London TravelWatch 6 Middle Street LONDON EC1A 7JA
E-mail:	info@londontravelwatch.org.uk
Website:	www.londontravelwatch.org.uk

Compensation

Compensation may be payable under each rail company's Passenger's Charter scheme for poor performance (delays or cancellations). For daily tickets and weekly season tickets a fixed rate usually applies depending on the level of delay which you experience. Compensation is made in National Rail vouchers, as a rule, with a minimum of 20% of the fare for the affected journey leg.

Monthly or longer season tickets compensation can differ between companies. On some it is triggered if performance falls below agreed levels and is paid as discount on renewal. Others offer compensation on a journey-by journey basis like for daily tickets. Always check with the train company which issued your ticket or on which you travel for details of the relevant scheme.

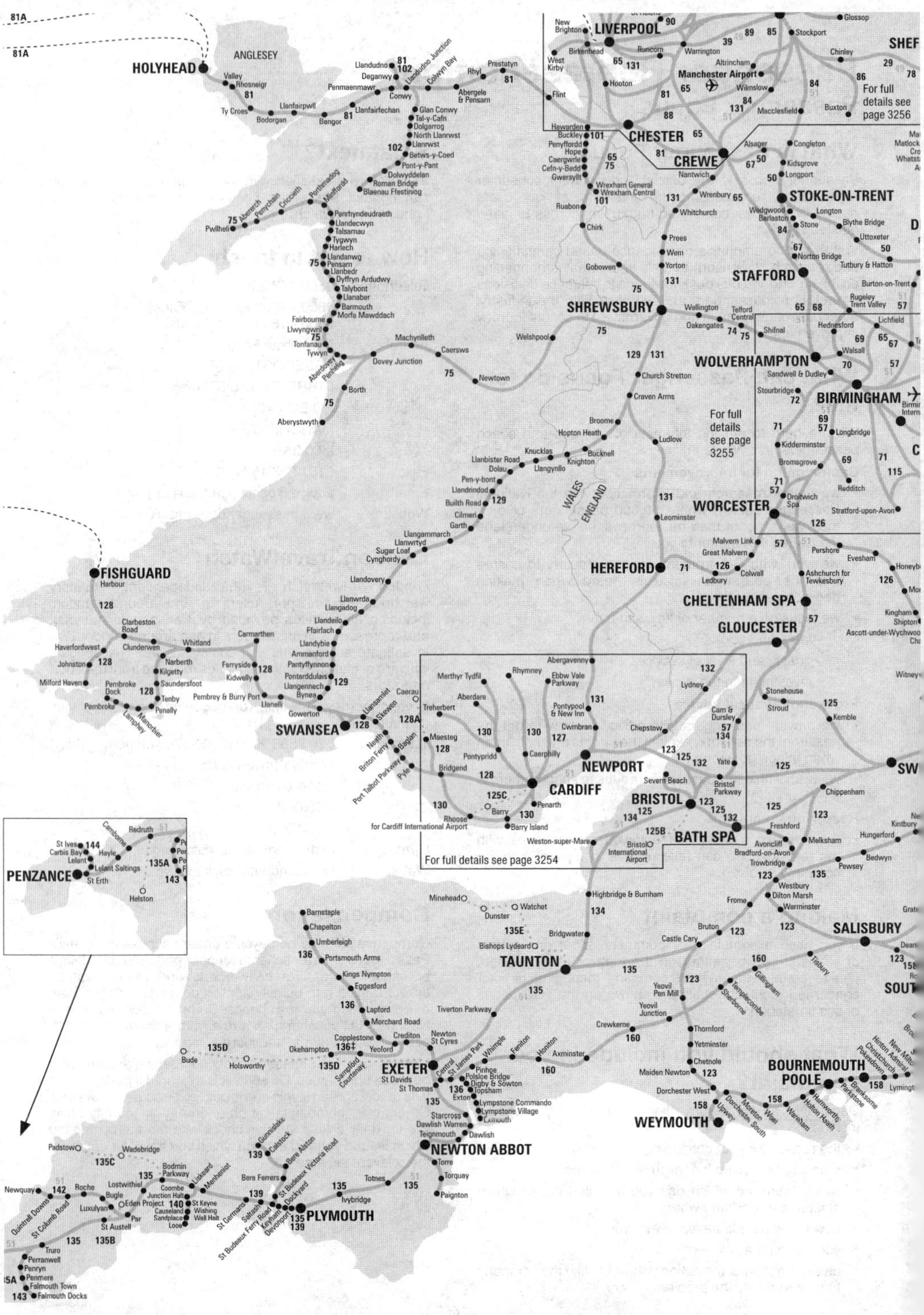
81A
81A
HOLYHEAD
ANGLESEY
Valley
Rhosneigr
81
Ty Croes
Bodorgan
Llanfairpwll
Bangor
81
Llanfairfechan
Penmaenmawr
Llandudno
81
102
Deganwy
Conwy
Llandudno Junction
Colwyn Bay
Rhyl
Prestatyn
81
Abergele & Pensarn
Glan Conwy
Tal-y-Cafn
Dolgarrog
North Llanrwst
Llanrwst
102
Betws-y-Coed
Pont-y-Pant
Dolwyddelan
Roman Bridge
Blaenau Ffestiniog
Pwllheli
75
Abererch
Penychain
Criccieth
Porthmadog
Minffordd
Penrhyndeudraeth
Llandecwyn
Talsarnau
Tygwyn
Harlech
Llandanwg
75
Pensarn
Llanbedr
Dyffryn Ardudwy
Talybont
Llanaber
Barmouth
Morfa Mawddach
Fairbourne
Llwyngwril
75
Tonfanau
Tywyn
Aberdovey
Penhelig
Dovey Junction
Machynlleth
Caersws
75
Newtown
Borth
75
Aberystwyth
New Brighton
LIVERPOOL
90
West Kirby
Birkenhead
65
131
Runcorn
Warrington
39
89
85
Stockport
Glossop
SHEF
Chinley
29
78
Altrincham
Manchester Airport
Wilmslow
65
84
86
For full details see page 3256
Flint
Hooton
81
88
131
84
Macclesfield
Buxton
Hawarden
Buckley
101
Penyffordd
Hope
Caergwrle
Cefn-y-Bedd
Gwersyllt
CHESTER
81
65
75
65
CREWE
Alsager
50
67
Congleton
Kidsgrove
50
Longport
Nantwich
Wrexham General
Wrexham Central
101
Ruabon
Chirk
Gobowen
131
Wrenbury
65
Whitchurch
STOKE-ON-TRENT
Wedgwood
Barlaston
84
Stone
Longton
Blythe Bridge
Uttoxeter
50
67
Norton Bridge
Tutbury & Hatton
Prees
Wem
Yorton
131
STAFFORD
75
SHREWSBURY
Wellington
Telford Central
Oakengates
74
75
Shifnal
Burton-on-Trent
Rugeley Trent Valley
65
68
57
Hednesford
Lichfield
69
65
67
Walsall
70
WOLVERHAMPTON
57
Sandwell & Dudley
Welshpool
75
129
131
Church Stretton
Craven Arms
Stourbridge
72
BIRMINGHAM
71
69
57
Longbridge
Kidderminster
Bromsgrove
69
71
115
Redditch
71
57
Droitwich Spa
Stratford-upon-Avon
For full details see page 3255
Broome
Hopton Heath
Bucknell
Ludlow
Knucklas
Knighton
Llangynllo
Llanbister Road
Dolau
Pen-y-bont
Llandrindod
129
Builth Road
Cilmeri
Garth
WALES
ENGLAND
131
Leominster
WORCESTER
126
Llangammarch
Llanwrtyd
Sugar Loaf
Cynghordy
Llandovery
Malvern Link
Great Malvern
126
57
Pershore
Evesham
Honeyb
126
HEREFORD
71
Ledbury
Colwall
Ashchurch for Tewkesbury
CHELTENHAM SPA
57
Kingham
Shipton
Ascott-under-Wychwood
GLOUCESTER
FISHGUARD
Harbour
128
Llanwrda
Llangadog
Llandeilo
Ffairfach
Llandybie
Ammanford
Pantyffynnon
Pontarddulais
Llangennech
129
Bynea
Clarbeston Road
Haverfordwest
Clunderwen
Whitland
Carmarthen
Johnston
128
Narberth
Kilgetty
Saundersfoot
Ferryside
Kidwelly
128
Milford Haven
Pembroke Dock
128
Tenby
Penally
Pembroke
Lamphey
Manorbier
Pembrey & Burry Port
Llanelli
Gowerton
SWANSEA
128
Llansamlet
Skewen
Neath
Briton Ferry
Baglan
Port Talbot Parkway
Pyle
Caerau
128A
Merthyr Tydfil
Rhymney
Abergavenny
Ebbw Vale Parkway
Aberdare
Treherbert
131
Pontypool & New Inn
Cwmbran
130
130
127
Maesteg
128
Pontypridd
Caerphilly
NEWPORT
Bridgend
128
CARDIFF
125C
Penarth
130
Barry
130
Rhoose for Cardiff International Airport
Barry Island
For full details see page 3254
132
Lydney
Chepstow
Cam & Dursley
57
134
123
125
132
Yate
Severn Beach
Bristol Parkway
BRISTOL
123
125
132
134
125
125B
BATH SPA
Weston-super-Mare
Bristol International Airport
Stonehouse
Stroud
125
Kemble
125
SW
Chippenham
125
123
Freshford
Avoncliff
Bradford-on-Avon
Trowbridge
Melksham
Hungerford
Kintbury
Bedwyn
Pewsey
123
135
Westbury
Dilton Marsh
Warminster
Frome
123
SALISBURY
Witney
PENZANCE
St Ives
144
Carbis Bay
Lelant
Hayle
Lelant Saltings
St Erth
Camborne
Redruth
135A
143
Helston
Highbridge & Burnham
134
Minehead
Watchet
Dunster
135E
Bishops Lydeard
Bridgwater
TAUNTON
135
135
Tiverton Parkway
Barnstaple
Chapelton
Umberleigh
136
Portsmouth Arms
Kings Nympton
Eggesford
136
Lapford
Morchard Road
Copplestone
Crediton
136‡
Yeoford
Newton St Cyres
Okehampton
135D
Bude
Holsworthy
135D
Sampford Courtenay
EXETER
St Davids
Central
St James Park
Whimple
Feniton
Honiton
Axminster
160
Pinhoe
Polsloe Bridge
Digby & Sowton
Topsham
Exton
St Thomas
136
135
Lympstone Commando
Lympstone Village
Exmouth
Starcross
Dawlish Warren
Dawlish
Teignmouth
NEWTON ABBOT
Torre
Torquay
Paignton
Castle Cary
Bruton
123
123
160
Gillingham
Tisbury
Templecombe
Sherborne
Yeovil Pen Mill
Yeovil Junction
Crewkerne
160
Thornford
Yetminster
Chetnole
Maiden Newton
123
Dorchester West
158
Upwey
Dorchester South
Moreton
Wool
158
Wareham
Holton Heath
Hamworthy
Parkstone
Branksome
BOURNEMOUTH
POOLE
158
Pokesdown
Christchurch
Hinton Admiral
New Milton
Lymingt
WEYMOUTH
123
SOUT
Padstow
Wadebridge
135C
Bodmin Parkway
Lostwithiel
135
Liskeard
Menheniot
Coombe Junction Halt
140
St Keyne Wishing Well Halt
Causeland
Sandplace
Looe
Gunnislake
Calstock
139
Bere Alston
Bere Ferrers
St Budeaux Victoria Road
139
St Germans
Saltash
Dockyard
Keyham
Devonport
St Budeaux Ferry Road
135
139
PLYMOUTH
Ivybridge
Totnes
135
135
Newquay
142
Roche
Bugle
Luxulyan
Eden Project
Par
St Austell
Quintrell Downs
St Columb Road
135
135B
Truro
Perranwell
Penryn
Penmere
Falmouth Town
Falmouth Docks
143

SHEFFIELD
Rotherham
Gainsborough Central
Gainsborough Lea Road
Market Rasen
Worksop
RETFORD
Chesterfield
Creswell
Whitwell
Shirebrook
Langwith-Whaley Thorns
Mansfield
Mansfield Woodhouse
Saxilby
LINCOLN
Hykeham
Swinderby
Collingham
Metheringham
Ruskington
Matlock
Matlock Bath
Cromford
Whatstandwell
Ambergate
Sutton Parkway
Kirkby-in-Ashfield
Alfreton
Newstead
Hucknall
Bulwell
Langley Mill
Belper
Duffield
NOTTINGHAM
DERBY
Newark Castle
Rolleston
Fiskerton
Bleasby
Thurgarton
Lowdham
Burton Joyce
Carlton
NEWARK
North Gate
Rauceby
Sleaford
Ancaster
Thorpe Culvert
Wainfleet
Havenhouse
Skegness
Boston
Heckington
Swineshead
Hubberts Bridge
Beeston
Attenborough
Netherfield
Radcliffe
Bingham
Aslockton
Elton & Orston
Bottesford
GRANTHAM
Peartree
Spondon
Long Eaton
Willington
East Midlands Parkway
Loughborough
Barrow-on-Soar
Sileby
Syston
Melton Mowbray
Oakham
Stamford
Spalding
LEICESTER
South Wigston
Narborough
Hinckley
Nuneaton
Tamworth
Birmingham International
COVENTRY
RUGBY
Leamington Spa
Market Harborough
Corby
Oundle
KETTERING
Wellingborough
PETERBOROUGH
Whittlesea
March
Manea
Wisbech
Hunstanton
Sandringham
KINGS LYNN
Watlington
Downham Market
Swaffham
Dereham
Littleport
Brandon
Lakenheath
Shippea Hill
Thetford
Harling Road
Ely
Waterbeach
Sheringham
West Runton
Cromer
Roughton Road
Gunton
North Walsham
Worstead
Hoveton & Wroxham
Salhouse
NORWICH
Brundall Gardens
Brundall
Lingwood
Acle
Great Yarmouth
Berney Arms
Haddiscoe
Buckenham
Cantley
Reedham
Somerleyton
Oulton Broad North
Lowestoft
Oulton Broad South
Wymondham
Spooner Row
Attleborough
Eccles Road
Diss
Beccles
Brampton
Halesworth
Darsham
Saxmundham
Long Buckby
NORTHAMPTON
Huntingdon
St Neots
Bedford
CAMBRIDGE
Newmarket
Bury St Edmunds
Stowmarket
Westerfield
IPSWICH
Felixstowe
Honeybourne
Moreton-in-Marsh
Kingham
Shipton
Chipping Norton
Charlbury
Finstock
Combe
Hanborough
Witney
Abingdon
Banbury
Buckingham
Bicester
OXFORD
MILTON KEYNES
Bletchley
Letchworth
Hitchin
Royston
Stevenage
Luton
Dunstable
Aylesbury Parkway
Aylesbury
Welwyn Garden City
Hertford
STANSTED Airport
Bishops Stortford
Sudbury
COLCHESTER
Braintree
Marks Tey
Manningtree
HARWICH
Walton-on-the-Naze
Clacton-on-Sea
Witham
Chelmsford
Harlow
Hemel Hempstead
St Albans
Watford
Amersham
Princes Risborough
Chinnor
High Wycombe
Henley-on-Thames
Marlow
Didcot Parkway
SWINDON
Maidenhead
Twyford
Slough
Windsor
Heathrow Airport
READING
LONDON
Shenfield
Wickford
Southminster
Southend Airport
Romford
Basildon
Upminster
SOUTHEND
Shoeburyness
Tilbury
Newbury
Thatcham
Theale
Aldermaston
Kintbury
Newbury Racecourse
Midgham
Ascot
Staines
Surbiton
Woking
East Croydon
Oxted
Dartford
Ebbsfleet International
Chatham
Gillingham
Sheerness-on-Sea
Sittingbourne
Faversham
Herne Bay
MARGATE
RAMSGATE
Maidstone
CANTERBURY
Deal
DOVER
Whitchurch
Overton
Basingstoke
Aldershot
Guildford
Dorking
Redhill
Sevenoaks
Tonbridge
Tunbridge Wells
ASHFORD
FOLKESTONE
CHANNEL TUNNEL
Andover
Grateley
Micheldever
Winchester
Shawford
Eastleigh
Alton
Haslemere
GATWICK Airport
Crawley
East Grinstead
Dean
Mottisfont & Dunbridge
Chandlers Ford
Romsey
SOUTHAMPTON
Totton
Southampton Airport Parkway
Horsham
Haywards Heath
Uckfield
Rye
Ashurst New Forest
Beaulieu Road
Brockenhurst
Sway
Fareham
Havant
For full details within this box see other side of sheet
See page 3254
PORTSMOUTH
CHICHESTER
Littlehampton
Bognor Regis
WORTHING
Hove
BRIGHTON
LEWES
Newhaven
Seaford
Bexhill
HASTINGS
EASTBOURNE
For full details see pages 3250-3251
Lymington Town
Lymington Pier
Pier Head
Ryde
Esplanade
St Johns Road
Brading
Sandown
Lake
Shanklin
Ventnor
ISLE OF WIGHT

Passenger Rail Routes
Principal places
Other places
Ferry links
Bus links
65 Black figures indicate timetable numbers*
51 Blue figures indicate summary timetable numbers*
Railair link coach to/from Heathrow Airport
Railair interchange with airport
Airport interchange
National Exhibition Centre
‡ Summer service only
(* National Rail Timetable)
© 2011 Network Rail. All rights reserved.
Designed and drawn by Pindar Creative 01296 390100
PERTH
Leuchars
St Andrews
Gleneagles
Cupar
Springfield
Ladybank
Markinch
Alloa
Cardenden
Dunfermline
Kirkcaldy
Inverkeithing
North Berwick
Falkirk
EDINBURGH
Drem
Dunbar
Bathgate
Wallyford
Musselburgh
Prestonpans
Longniddry
Newcraighall
Shotts
Carstairs
For full details see page 3258
Duns
BERWICK-UPON-TWEED
Earlston
Galashiels
Melrose
Selkirk
Hawick
Chathill
Alnmouth for Alnwick
Acklington
Widdrington
Pegswood
Morpeth
SCOTLAND
ENGLAND
Langholm
Lockerbie
Dumfries
Annan
Gretna Green
Cramlington
Manors
For full details see page 3258
NEWCASTLE
Heworth
Brampton
Haltwhistle
Bardon Mill
Haydon Bridge
Hexham
Corbridge
Riding Mill
Stocksfield
Prudhoe
Wylam
Blaydon
CARLISLE
Wetheral
Dalston
Wigton
Aspatria
Maryport
Flimby
Workington
Harrington
Parton
Whitehaven
Corkickle
St Bees
Nethertown
Braystones
Sellafield
Seascale
Drigg
Ravenglass for Eskdale
Bootle
Silecroft
Millom
Askam
Armathwaite
Lazonby & Kirkoswald
Langwathby
Penrith North Lakes
SUNDERLAND
Chester-le-Street
Seaham
Durham
HARTLEPOOL
Seaton Carew
Bishop Auckland
Shildon
Newton Aycliffe
Heighington
North Road
Billingham
Stockton
Thornaby
South Bank
British Steel Redcar
Redcar Central
Redcar East
Longbeck
Marske
Saltburn
MIDDLESBROUGH
DARLINGTON
Eaglescliffe
Marton
Gypsy Lane
Nunthorpe
Great Ayton
Battersby
Castleton Moor
Danby
Lealholm
Glaisdale
Egton
Grosmont
Sleights
Ruswarp
Whitby
Kildale
Commondale
Goathland
Levisham
Dinsdale
Allens West
Yarm
Richmond
Catterick Camp Centre
Appleby
Kirkby Stephen
Garsdale
Dent
Ribblehead
Horton-in-Ribblesdale
Settle
WINDERMERE
Windermere
Staveley
Burneside
Kendal
Oxenholme Lake District
Green Road
Foxfield
Kirkby-in-Furness
Ulverston
Cark
Kents Bank
Grange-over-Sands
Arnside
Silverdale
Dalton
Roose
BARROW
Carnforth
Wennington
Bentham
Clapham
Giggleswick
Bare Lane
Morecambe
Lancaster
Heysham Port
Long Preston
Hellifield
Northallerton
Thirsk
Pickering
SCARBOROUGH
Seamer
Filey
Hunmanby
Bempton
Bridlington
Malton
Nafferton
Driffield
Hutton Cranswick
Arram
Beverley
Cottingham
HULL
HARROGATE
Knaresborough
YORK
Ilkley
Skipton
Clitheroe
Colne
Keighley
LEEDS
For full details see pages 3256-3257
BLACKPOOL
Kirkham
Lytham
PRESTON
Burnley
Blackburn
BRADFORD
HALIFAX
WAKEFIELD
Selby
Gilberdyke
Broomfleet
Brough
Ferriby
Hessle
Goole
Barton-on-Humber
Barrow Haven
New Holland
Goxhill
Thornton Abbey
Ulceby
Southport
HUDDERSFIELD
Ormskirk
BOLTON
Rochdale
Wigan
Barnsley
DONCASTER
Robin Hood Airport
Scunthorpe
Barnetby
Brigg
Habrough
Stallingborough
Healing
Great Coates
Town
Docks
New Clee
Cleethorpes
GRIMSBY
MANCHESTER
Glossop
St Helens
New Brighton
LIVERPOOL
Birkenhead
Runcorn
Warrington
Stockport
Altrincham
Manchester Airport
Wilmslow
Chinley
Rotherham
SHEFFIELD
Kirton Lindsey
Gainsborough Central
Gainsborough Lea Road
Market Rasen
West Kirby
Hooton
Llandudno Junction
Colwyn Bay
Rhyl
Prestatyn
Abergele & Pensarn
Flint
Glan Conwy
Tal-y-Cafn
Dolgarrog
North Llanrwst
Llanrwst
Betws-y-Coed
Pont-y-Pant
Macclesfield
Buxton
Chesterfield
Worksop
Creswell
Whitwell
Shirebrook
Langwith-Whaley Thorns
Mansfield
Mansfield Woodhouse
RETFORD
Saxilby
LINCOLN
Hykeham
Swinderby
Collingham
Metheringham
Ruskington
Thorpe Culvert
Hawarden
Buckley
Penyffordd
Hope
Caergwrle
Cefn-y-Bedd
CHESTER
CREWE
Alsager
Kidsgrove
Congleton
Matlock
Matlock Bath
Cromford
Whatstandwell
Ambergate
Alfreton
Sutton Parkway
Kirkby-in-Ashfield
Newstead
Newark Castle
Rolleston
Fiskerton
NEWARK

TO STROMNESS
Scrabster
239A
Thurso
239
Georgemas
239
Wick
Scotscalder
Altnabreac
Forsinard
Kinbrace
Kildonan
239
Helmsdale
Brora
Dunrobin Castle ‡
Golspie
Rogart
Lairg
Invershin
Culrain
Ardgay
239
Tain
Fearn
Alness
Invergordon
239B
Ullapool
239B
Lochluichart
Garve
Achanalt
Achnasheen
239
Achnashellach
Dingwall
239B
239
Muir of Ord
Beauly
Strathcarron
Attadale
Stromeferry
239
Duncraig
Plockton
Duirinish
Kyle of Lochalsh
INVERNESS
240
Nairn
Forres
Elgin
Keith
Huntly
Insch
Inverurie
229
240
Dyce
ABERDEEN
Portlethen
Stonehaven
229
Laurencekirk
Montrose
229
Arbroath
Carnoustie
Golf Street
Barry Links
Monifieth
Balmossie
Broughty Ferry
DUNDEE
Invergowrie
229
229
Carrbridge
Aviemore
Kingussie
Newtonmore
Dalwhinnie
Blair Atholl
Pitlochry
229
Dunkeld & Birnam
PERTH
229
Leuchars
229
St Andrews
Cupar
Springfield
Ladybank
229
Markinch
Gleneagles
229
Dunblane
230
STIRLING
Alloa
Cardenden
242
229
Kirkcaldy
Dunfermline
Inverkeithing
Armadale
227A
227A
227A
Mallaig
Morar
Arisaig
Beasdale
227
Lochailort
Glenfinnan
Locheilside
Loch Eil Outward Bound
Corpach
Banavie
Spean Bridge
Roy Bridge
Tulloch
227
Fort William
Corrour
Rannoch
227B
227C
Lismore
227
227B
Connel Ferry
Taynuilt
Falls of Cruachan ‡
MULL
Craignure
227B
Oban
Loch Awe
Dalmally
227
Tyndrum Lower
Upper Tyndrum
Bridge of Orchy
Crianlarich
Ardlui
Arrochar & Tarbet
227B
LOCH LOMOND
Garelochhead
227
JURA
Helensburgh
Balloch
Dunoon
219A
Gourock
Dumbarton
226
Milngavie
228
Falkirk
228
EDINBURGH
219
Rothesay
219B
Wemyss Bay
BUTE
GLASGOW
224
Bathgate
Cumbernauld
Drumgelloch
226
Shotts
Newcraighall
242
Wallyford
Musselburgh
Prestonpans
Longniddry
Drem
238
North Berwick
Dunbar
26
GIGHA
Largs
221
221
Neilston
East Kilbride
26
Motherwell
26
65
225
Carstairs
65
225
Lanark
222
Ardrossan
Irvine
Kilmarnock
Brodick
221A
KINTYRE
ARRAN
Troon
Prestwick
Ayr
Auchinleck
For full details see page 3258
218
New Cumnock
Maybole
Kirkconnel
65
65G
Duns
BERW
26K
Earlston
Galashiels
Melrose
Selkirk
Hawick
Alnmou

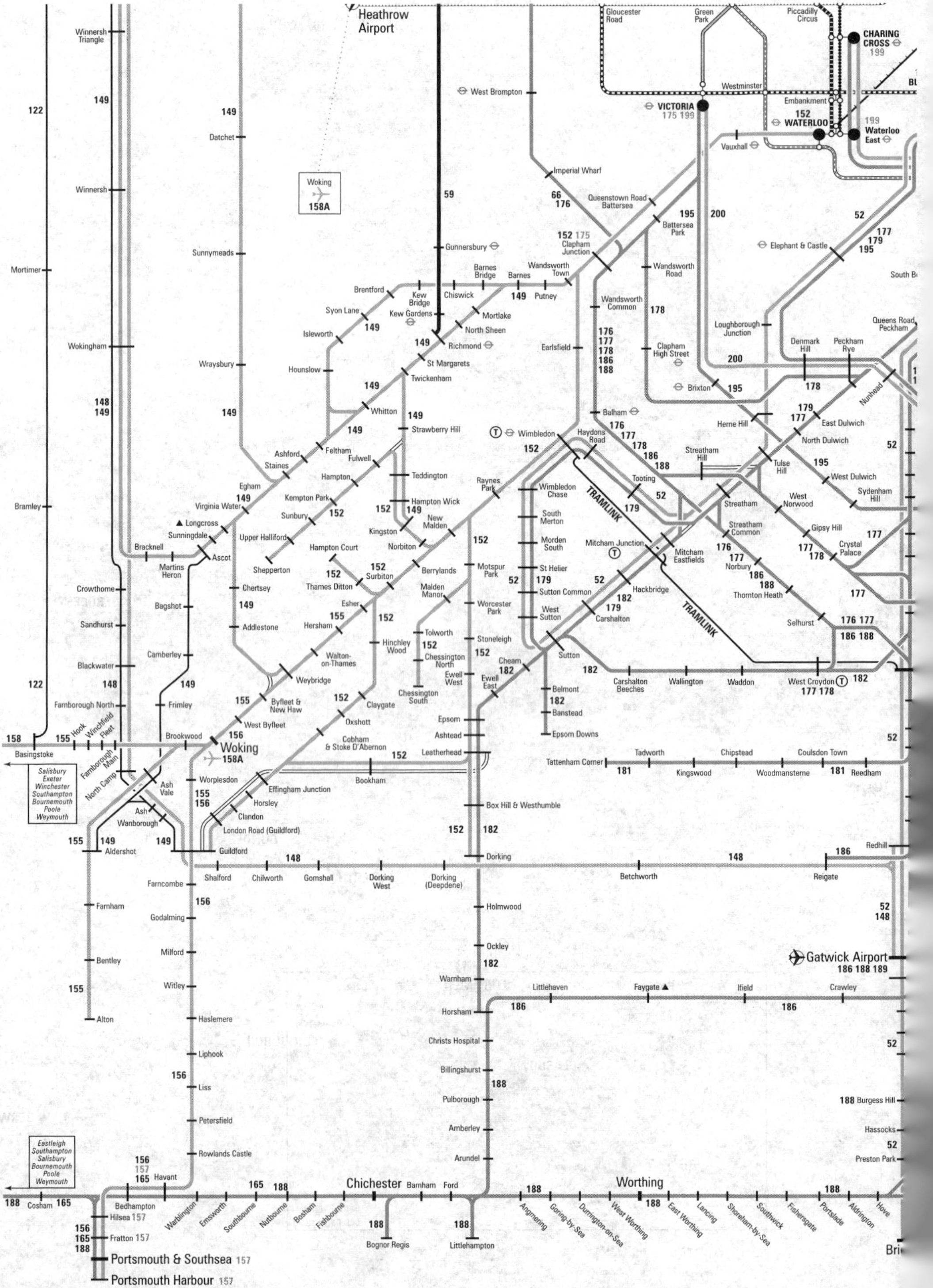
Heathrow Airport
Gloucester Road
Green Park
Piccadilly Circus
CHARING CROSS 199
Westminster
Embankment
VICTORIA 175 199
152 WATERLOO
199 Waterloo East
Vauxhall
West Brompton
Imperial Wharf
Queenstown Road Battersea
Battersea Park
Clapham Junction
Elephant & Castle
Wandsworth Road
Wandsworth Town
Wandsworth Common
Clapham High Street
Loughborough Junction
Denmark Hill
Peckham Rye
Queens Road Peckham
South B
Brixton
Earlsfield
Balham
Herne Hill
Nunhead
East Dulwich
North Dulwich
Tulse Hill
West Dulwich
Sydenham Hill
Streatham Hill
Streatham
West Norwood
Streatham Common
Gipsy Hill
Crystal Palace
Norbury
Thornton Heath
Selhurst
West Croydon
Tooting
Haydons Road
Wimbledon
Wimbledon Chase
South Merton
Morden South
St Helier
Sutton Common
West Sutton
Sutton
Mitcham Junction
Mitcham Eastfields
Hackbridge
Carshalton
TRAMLINK
Carshalton Beeches
Wallington
Waddon
Belmont
Banstead
Epsom Downs
Tattenham Corner
Tadworth
Kingswood
Chipstead
Woodmansterne
Coulsdon Town
Reedham
Redhill
Reigate
Betchworth
Gatwick Airport 186 188 189
Crawley
Ifield
Faygate
Littlehaven
Horsham
Burgess Hill
Hassocks
Preston Park
Gunnersbury
Brentford
Kew Bridge
Chiswick
Barnes Bridge
Barnes
Putney
Syon Lane
Kew Gardens
Mortlake
North Sheen
Richmond
Isleworth
St Margarets
Twickenham
Hounslow
Whitton
Strawberry Hill
Feltham
Fulwell
Teddington
Hampton Wick
Hampton
Kempton Park
Sunbury
Upper Halliford
Shepperton
Kingston
Norbiton
New Malden
Raynes Park
Motspur Park
Worcester Park
Stoneleigh
Ewell East
Ewell West
Cheam
Epsom
Ashtead
Leatherhead
Box Hill & Westhumble
Dorking
Holmwood
Ockley
Warnham
Berrylands
Malden Manor
Tolworth
Chessington North
Chessington South
Hampton Court
Thames Ditton
Surbiton
Esher
Hersham
Hinchley Wood
Walton-on-Thames
Weybridge
Claygate
Oxshott
Cobham & Stoke D'Abernon
Bookham
Byfleet & New Haw
West Byfleet
Woking 158A
Effingham Junction
Horsley
Clandon
London Road (Guildford)
Guildford
Worplesdon
Shalford
Chilworth
Gomshall
Dorking West
Dorking (Deepdene)
Farncombe
Godalming
Milford
Witley
Haslemere
Liphook
Liss
Petersfield
Rowlands Castle
Havant
Datchet
Sunnymeads
Wraysbury
Egham
Staines
Ashford
Virginia Water
Longcross
Sunningdale
Ascot
Chertsey
Addlestone
Bracknell
Martins Heron
Bagshot
Camberley
Frimley
Brookwood
Winnersh Triangle
Winnersh
Wokingham
Crowthorne
Sandhurst
Blackwater
Farnborough North
Mortimer
Bramley
Basingstoke
Hook
Winchfield
Fleet
Farnborough Main
North Camp
Ash Vale
Ash
Wanborough
Aldershot
Farnham
Bentley
Alton
Salisbury Exeter Winchester Southampton Bournemouth Poole Weymouth
Eastleigh Southampton Salisbury Bournemouth Poole Weymouth
Cosham
Bedhampton
Hilsea 157
Fratton 157
Portsmouth & Southsea 157
Portsmouth Harbour 157
Warblington
Emsworth
Southbourne
Nutbourne
Bosham
Fishbourne
Chichester
Barnham
Ford
Bognor Regis
Littlehampton
Arundel
Amberley
Pulborough
Billingshurst
Christs Hospital
Worthing
Angmering
Goring-by-Sea
Durrington-on-Sea
West Worthing
East Worthing
Lancing
Shoreham-by-Sea
Southwick
Fishersgate
Portslade
Aldrington
Hove
Woking 158A
59
122
149
148
155
156
157
158
165
152
176
177
178
179
181
182
186
188
195
200
52
66

Continued on pages 3252-3253

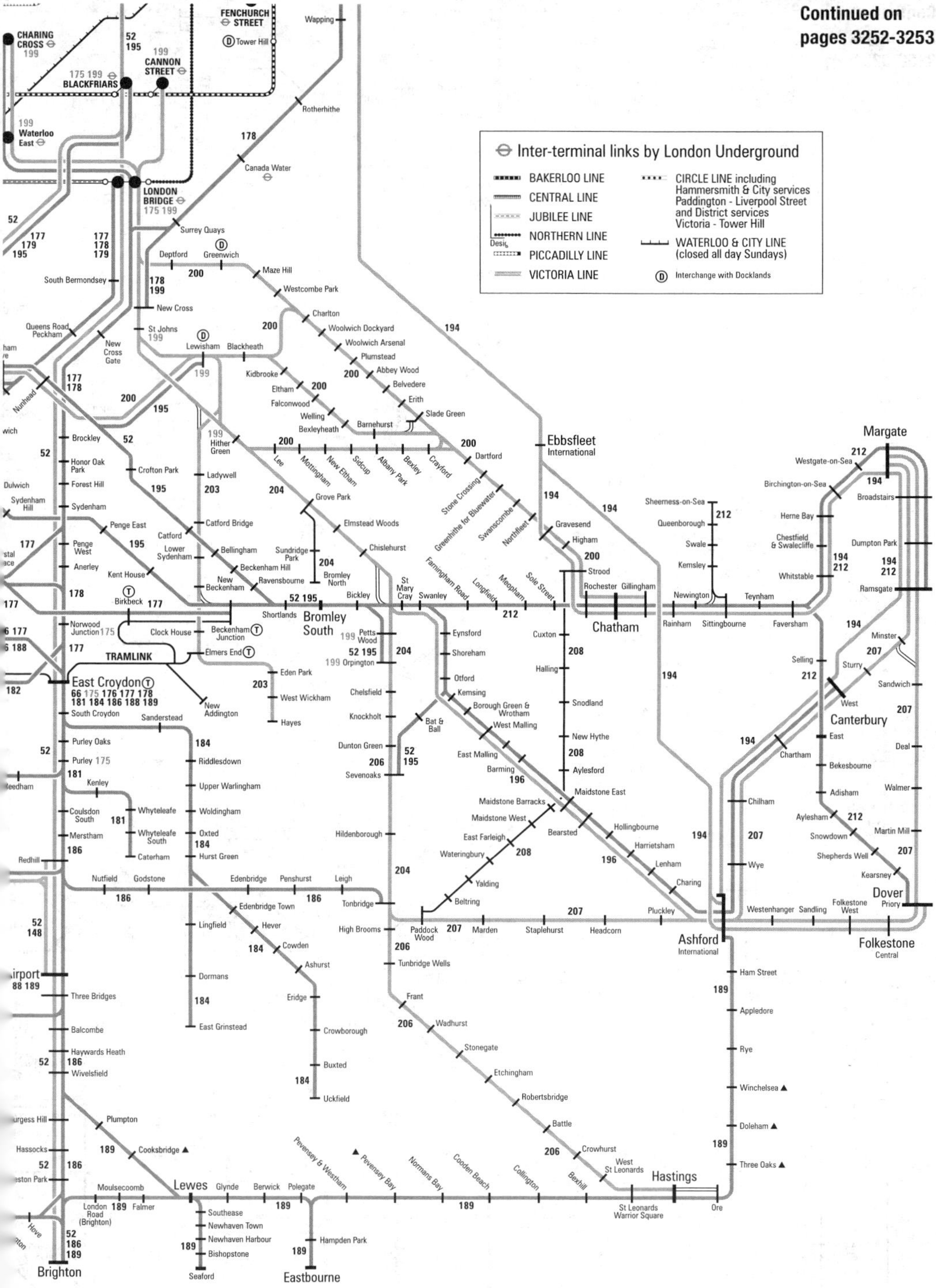

Continued from pages 3250-3251

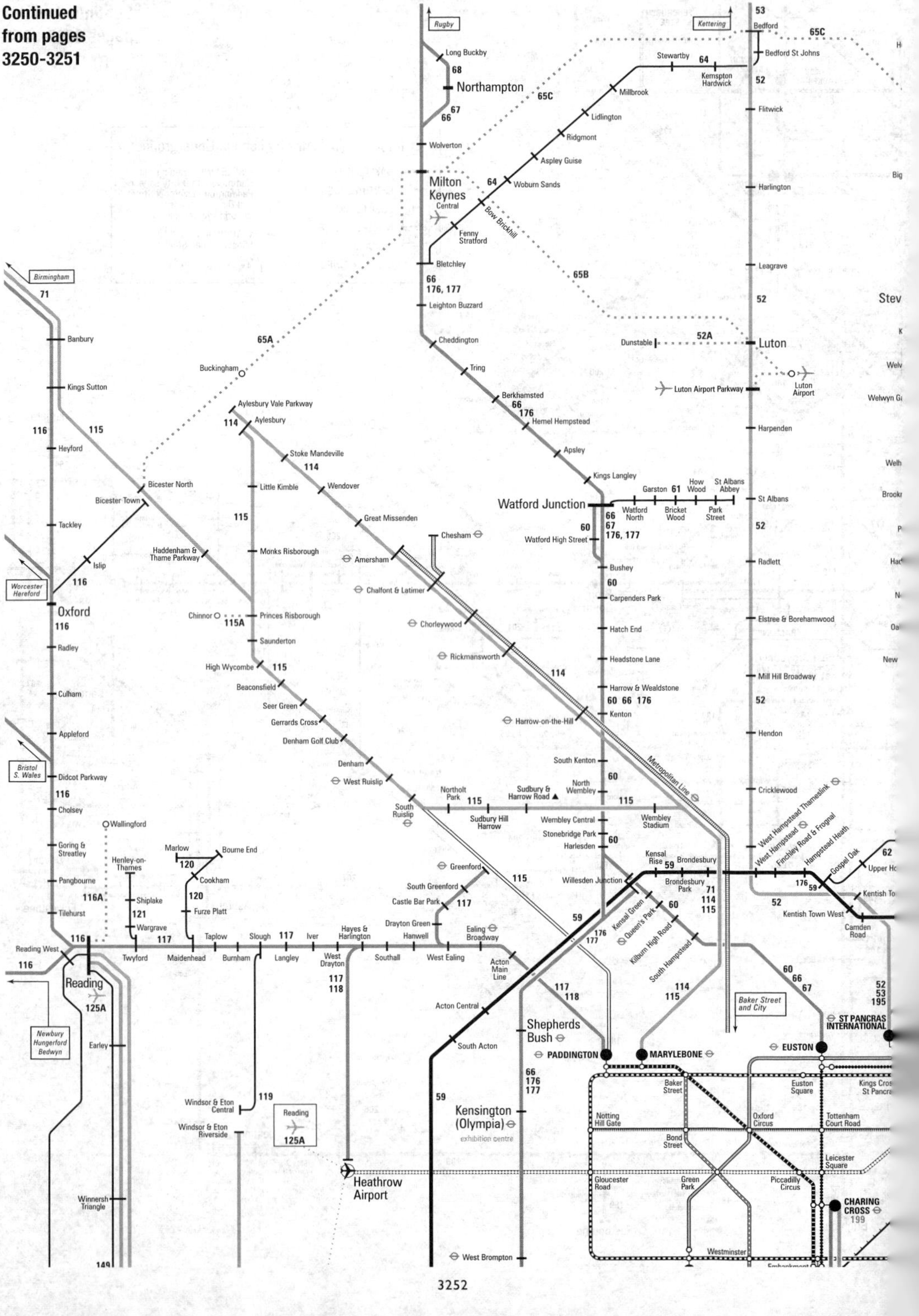

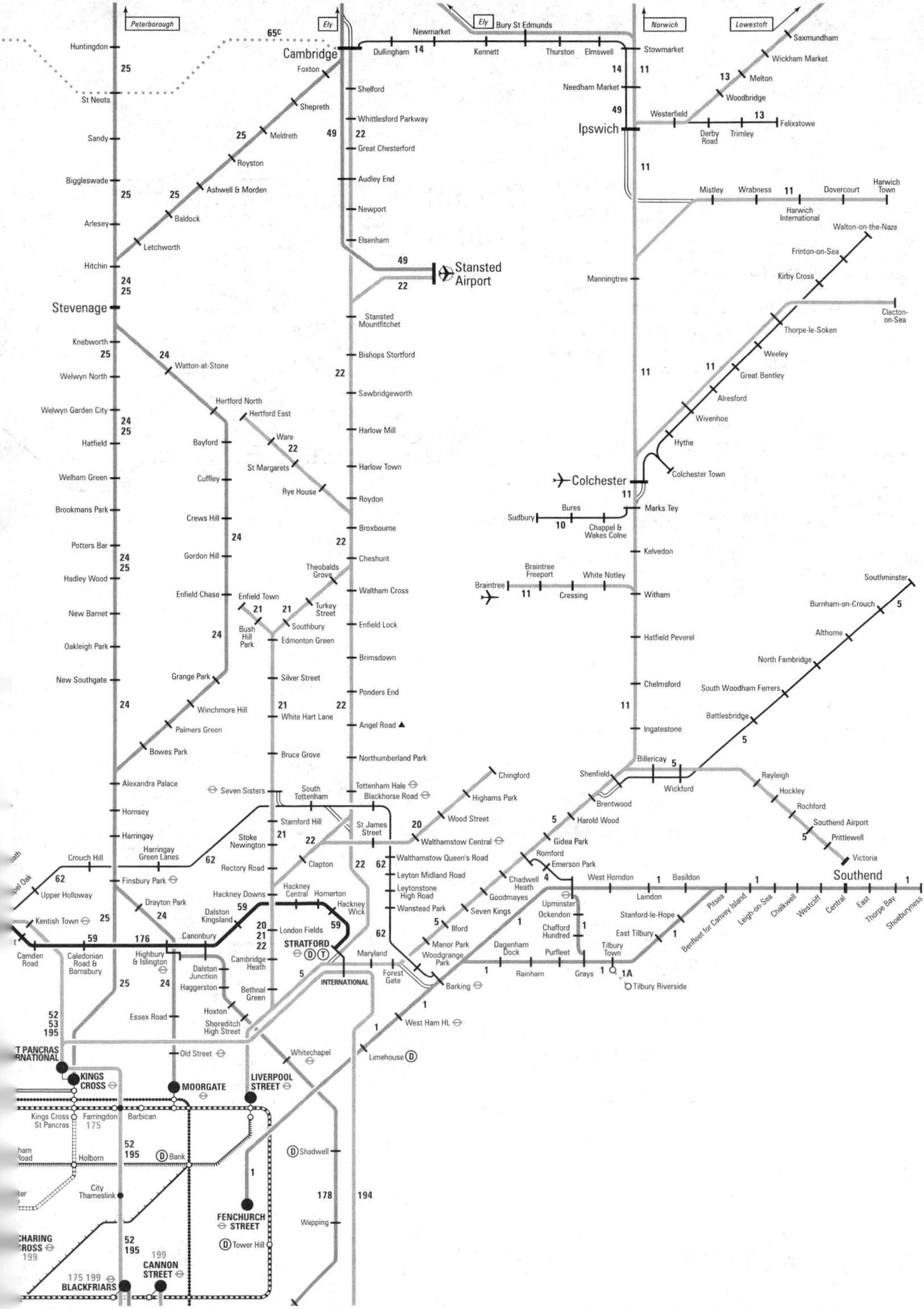
Peterborough
Ely
Ely
Norwich
Lowestoft
65C
Huntingdon
St Neots
Sandy
Biggleswade
Arlesey
Hitchin
Stevenage
Knebworth
Welwyn North
Welwyn Garden City
Hatfield
Welham Green
Brookmans Park
Potters Bar
Hadley Wood
New Barnet
Oakleigh Park
New Southgate
Alexandra Palace
Hornsey
Harringay
Finsbury Park
Drayton Park
Cambridge
Foxton
Shepreth
Meldreth
Royston
Ashwell & Morden
Baldock
Letchworth
Watton-at-Stone
Hertford North
Bayford
Cuffley
Crews Hill
Gordon Hill
Enfield Chase
Grange Park
Winchmore Hill
Palmers Green
Bowes Park
Hertford East
Ware
St Margarets
Rye House
Shelford
Whittlesford Parkway
Great Chesterford
Audley End
Newport
Elsenham
Stansted Airport
Stansted Mountfitchet
Bishops Stortford
Sawbridgeworth
Harlow Mill
Harlow Town
Roydon
Broxbourne
Cheshunt
Theobalds Grove
Waltham Cross
Turkey Street
Enfield Town
Southbury
Bush Hill Park
Edmonton Green
Enfield Lock
Brimsdown
Silver Street
Ponders End
White Hart Lane
Angel Road
Bruce Grove
Northumberland Park
Seven Sisters
South Tottenham
Tottenham Hale
Blackhorse Road
Stamford Hill
St James Street
Stoke Newington
Rectory Road
Clapton
Chingford
Highams Park
Wood Street
Walthamstow Central
Walthamstow Queen's Road
Leyton Midland Road
Leytonstone High Road
Wanstead Park
Crouch Hill
Harringay Green Lanes
Upper Holloway
Kentish Town
Camden Road
Caledonian Road & Barnsbury
Highbury & Islington
Canonbury
Dalston Kingsland
Dalston Junction
Haggerston
Hackney Downs
Hackney Central
Homerton
Hackney Wick
London Fields
Cambridge Heath
Bethnal Green
STRATFORD
INTERNATIONAL
Maryland
Forest Gate
Essex Road
Old Street
Hoxton
Shoreditch High Street
Whitechapel
Limehouse
West Ham HL
Shadwell
Wapping
ST PANCRAS INTERNATIONAL
KINGS CROSS
MOORGATE
LIVERPOOL STREET
Kings Cross St Pancras
Farringdon
Barbican
Holborn
City Thameslink
Bank
FENCHURCH STREET
Tower Hill
CHARING CROSS
CANNON STREET
BLACKFRIARS
Newmarket
Bury St Edmunds
Dullingham
Kennett
Thurston
Elmswell
Stowmarket
Needham Market
Ipswich
Westerfield
Derby Road
Trimley
Felixstowe
Saxmundham
Wickham Market
Melton
Woodbridge
Mistley
Wrabness
Dovercourt
Harwich Town
Harwich International
Manningtree
Walton-on-the-Naze
Frinton-on-Sea
Kirby Cross
Clacton-on-Sea
Thorpe-le-Soken
Weeley
Great Bentley
Alresford
Wivenhoe
Hythe
Colchester Town
Colchester
Marks Tey
Sudbury
Bures
Chappel & Wakes Colne
Kelvedon
Braintree
Braintree Freeport
Cressing
White Notley
Witham
Hatfield Peverel
Chelmsford
Ingatestone
Southminster
Burnham-on-Crouch
Althorne
North Fambridge
South Woodham Ferrers
Battlesbridge
Billericay
Wickford
Shenfield
Brentwood
Harold Wood
Gidea Park
Romford
Emerson Park
Chadwell Heath
Goodmayes
Seven Kings
Ilford
Manor Park
Woodgrange Park
Barking
Upminster
Ockendon
Chafford Hundred
Dagenham Dock
Rainham
Purfleet
Grays
Tilbury Town
Tilbury Riverside
West Horndon
Laindon
Basildon
Stanford-le-Hope
East Tilbury
Pitsea
Benfleet for Canvey Island
Leigh-on-Sea
Chalkwell
Westcliff
Central
East
Thorpe Bay
Shoeburyness
Southend
Rayleigh
Hockley
Rochford
Southend Airport
Prittlewell
Victoria

Cardiff Bristol

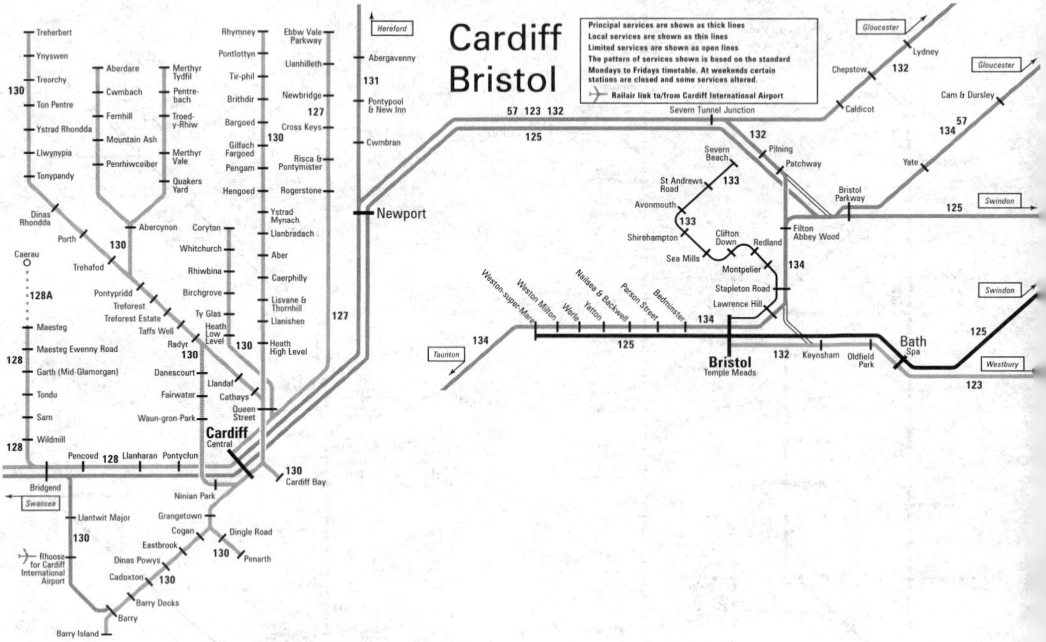

Southampton Portsmouth

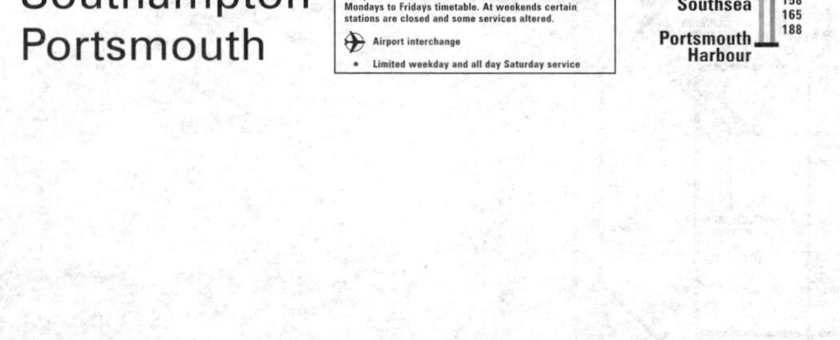

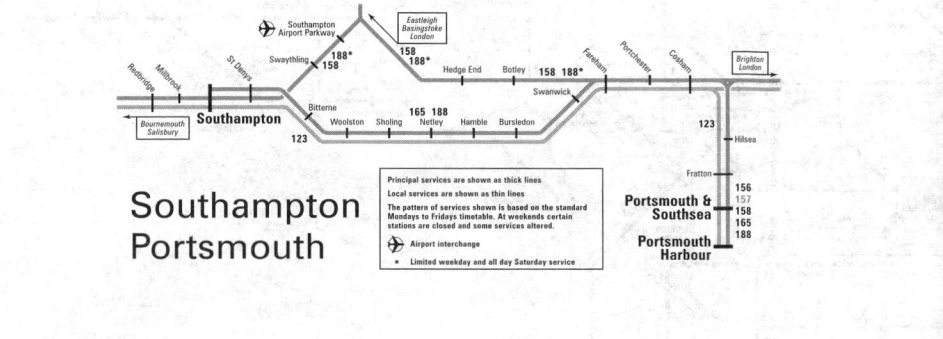

Birmingham
West Midlands
Shrewsbury
Stafford
Stafford
Stafford
Derby
Shifnal
Cosford
Albrighton
Codsall
Bilbrook
74
75
68
Penkridge
70 Wolverhampton
Coseley
Tipton
66
68
75
Dudley Port
Sandwell & Dudley
Smethwick Galton Bridge
METRO
70
The Hawthorns
Jewellery Quarter
Snow Hill
71
Smethwick Rolfe Street
New Street
Rugeley Town
Hednesford
Cannock
Landywood
Bloxwich North
Bloxwich
Walsall
Bescot Stadium
Tame Bridge
Hamstead
Perry Barr
Witton
Aston
Duddeston
70
Lichfield Trent Valley
Lichfield City
Shenstone
69
Blake Street
Butlers Lane
Four Oaks
Sutton Coldfield
Wylde Green
Chester Road
Erdington
Gravelly Hill
67
57
Tamworth
Wilnecote
Polesworth
Atherstone
Water Orton
49 57
Coleshill Parkway
Nuneaton
Leicester
57
Adderley Park
Stechford
Lea Hall
Marston Green
Birmingham International for National Exhibition Centre
66 68
Birmingham
Hampton-in-Arden
Berkswell
Tile Hill
Canley
Bedworth
Rugby
Coventry
Rugby
Langley Green
Rowley Regis
Old Hill
Cradley Heath
Stourbridge Town
72
Lye
Stourbridge Junction
Hagley
Blakedown
Kidderminster
Hartlebury
Droitwich Spa
Hereford
Five Ways
University
69
Selly Oak
Bournville
Kings Norton
Northfield
Longbridge
Barnt Green
Bromsgrove
Alvechurch
Redditch
Moor Street
71
Bordesley
Small Heath
Tyseley
Acocks Green
Olton
Solihull
Widney Manor
Dorridge
Lapworth
115
Spring Road
Hall Green
Yardley Wood
Shirley
Whitlocks End
Wythall
Earlswood
The Lakes
Wood End
Danzey
Henley-in-Arden
Wootton Wawen
Wilmcote
Stratford-upon-Avon
Claverdon
Bearley
Hatton
Warwick Parkway
Warwick
Leamington Spa
71
116
Banbury
Shrub Hill
Foregate Street
126 Worcester
Great Malvern
Cheltenham Spa
Evesham
126
57
Principal services are shown as thick lines
Local services are shown as thin lines
Limited services are shown as open lines
The pattern of services shown is based on the standard Mondays to Fridays timetable. At weekends certain stations are closed and some services altered.
Railair link to/from Birmingham Airport
Tram/Metro Interchange

Liverpool Leeds Manchester Sheffield

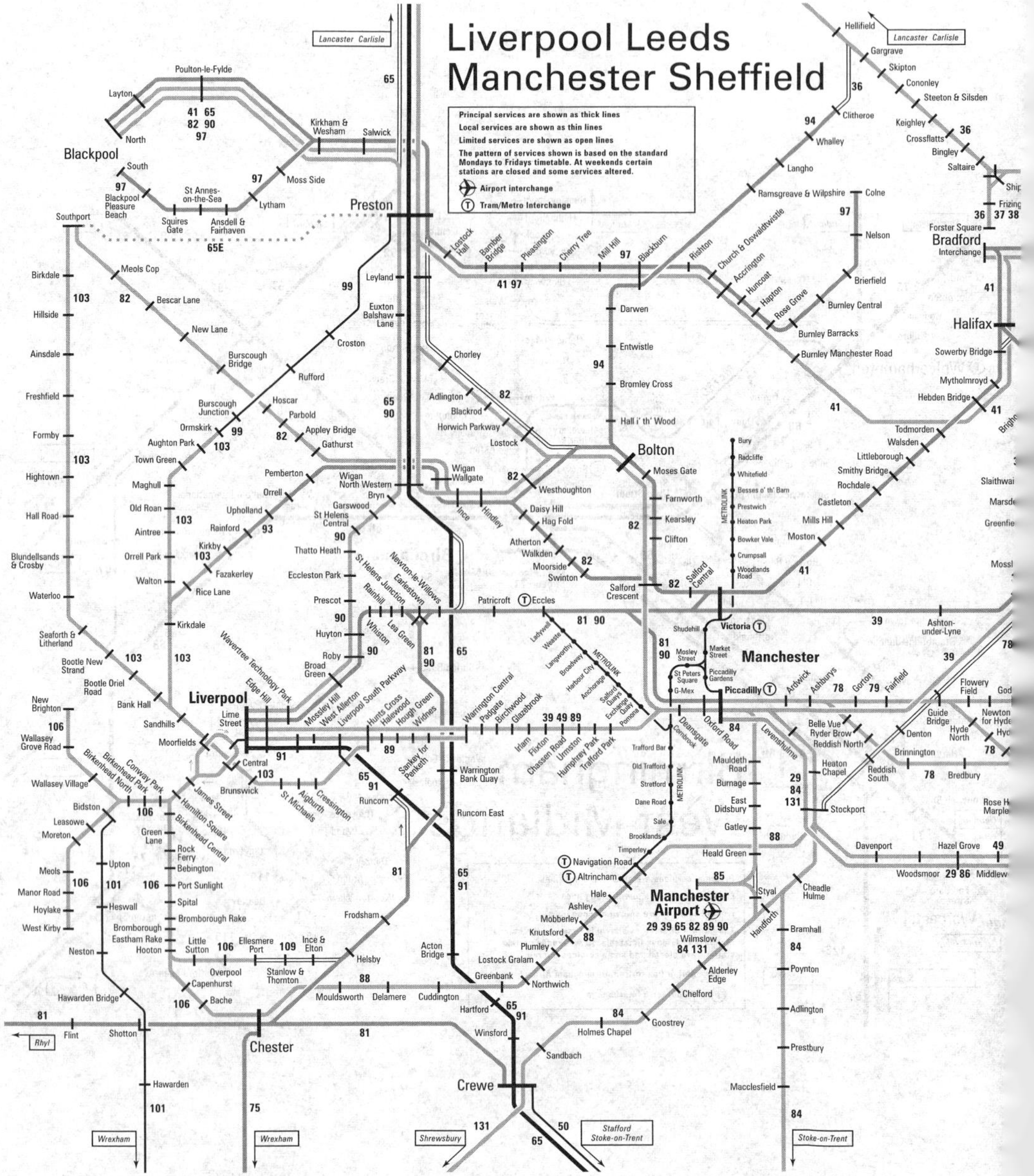

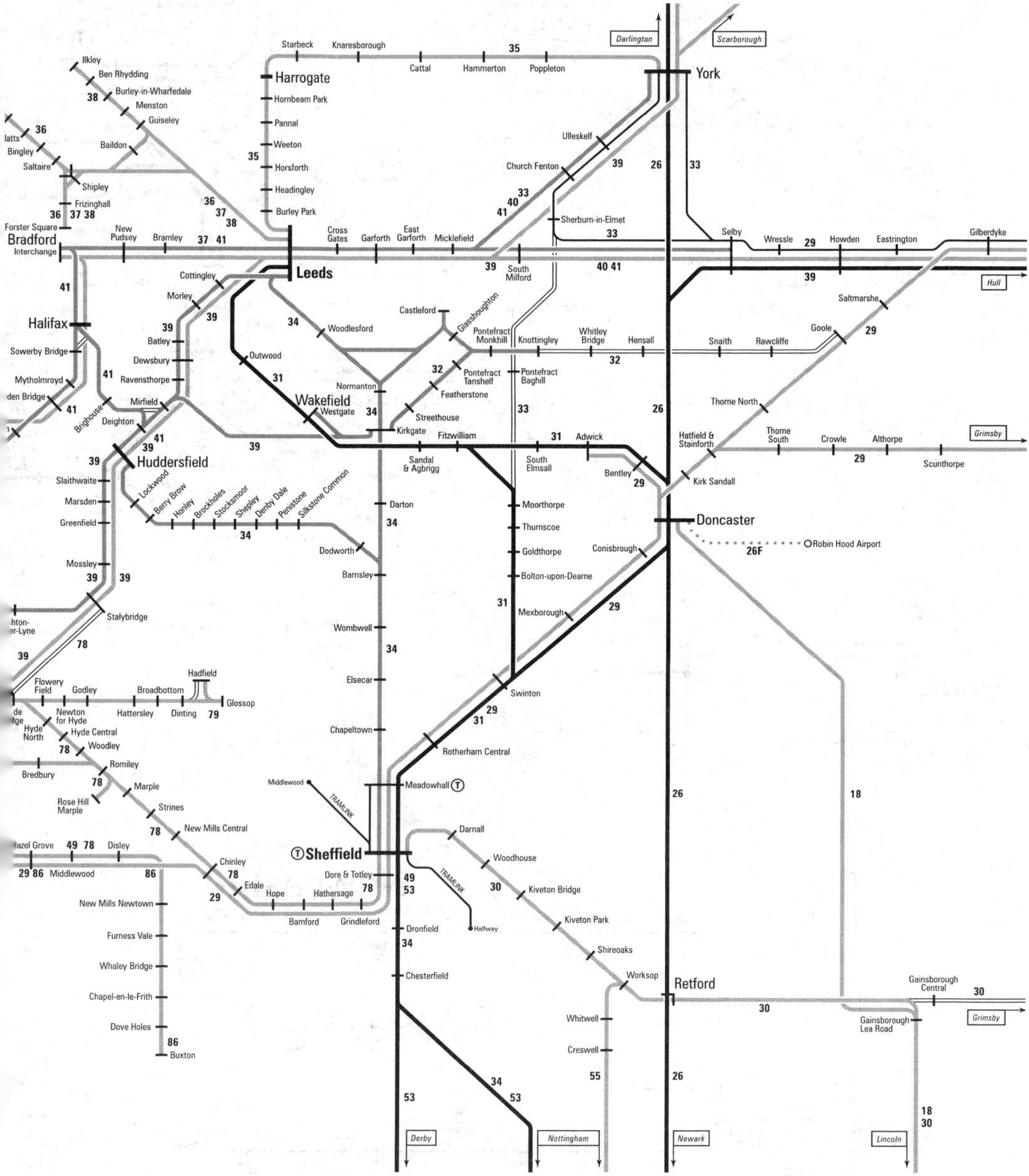
Darlington
Scarborough
York
Starbeck
Knaresborough
Cattal
Hammerton
Poppleton
35
Harrogate
Hornbeam Park
Pannal
Weeton
Horsforth
Headingley
Burley Park
Ilkley
Ben Rhydding
Burley-in-Wharfedale
Menston
Guiseley
Baildon
Bingley
Saltaire
Shipley
Frizinghall
Forster Square
Bradford
Interchange
New Pudsey
Bramley
Cross Gates
Garforth
East Garforth
Micklefield
Leeds
Ulleskelf
Church Fenton
Sherburn-in-Elmet
South Milford
Selby
Wressle
Howden
Eastrington
Gilberdyke
Hull
Cottingley
Morley
Batley
Dewsbury
Ravensthorpe
Mirfield
Deighton
Halifax
Sowerby Bridge
Mytholmroyd
Brighouse
Huddersfield
Slaithwaite
Marsden
Greenfield
Mossley
Stalybridge
Lockwood
Berry Brow
Honley
Brockholes
Stocksmoor
Shepley
Denby Dale
Penistone
Silkstone Common
Dodworth
Barnsley
Wombwell
Elsecar
Chapeltown
Meadowhall
Middlewood
TRAMLINK
Sheffield
Woodlesford
Castleford
Glasshoughton
Outwood
Wakefield
Westgate
Kirkgate
Normanton
Pontefract Monkhill
Pontefract Tanshelf
Featherstone
Streethouse
Knottingley
Pontefract Baghill
Whitley Bridge
Hensall
Snaith
Rawcliffe
Goole
Saltmarshe
Thorne North
Fitzwilliam
Sandal & Agbrigg
South Elmsall
Adwick
Bentley
Hatfield & Stainforth
Thorne South
Crowle
Althorpe
Scunthorpe
Grimsby
Kirk Sandall
Doncaster
Robin Hood Airport
26F
Conisbrough
Darton
Moorthorpe
Thurnscoe
Goldthorpe
Bolton-upon-Dearne
Mexborough
Swinton
Rotherham Central
Hadfield
Flowery Field
Godley
Broadbottom
Glossop
Newton for Hyde
Hattersley
Dinting
Hyde North
Hyde Central
Woodley
Bredbury
Romiley
Marple
Rose Hill Marple
Strines
New Mills Central
Disley
Middlewood
Chinley
Edale
Hope
Hathersage
Bamford
Grindleford
Dore & Totley
New Mills Newtown
Furness Vale
Whaley Bridge
Chapel-en-le-Frith
Dove Holes
Buxton
Darnall
Woodhouse
Kiveton Bridge
Kiveton Park
Shireoaks
Worksop
Halfway
Dronfield
Chesterfield
Whitwell
Creswell
Retford
Gainsborough Central
Gainsborough Lea Road
Derby
Nottingham
Newark
Lincoln

Glasgow Edinburgh

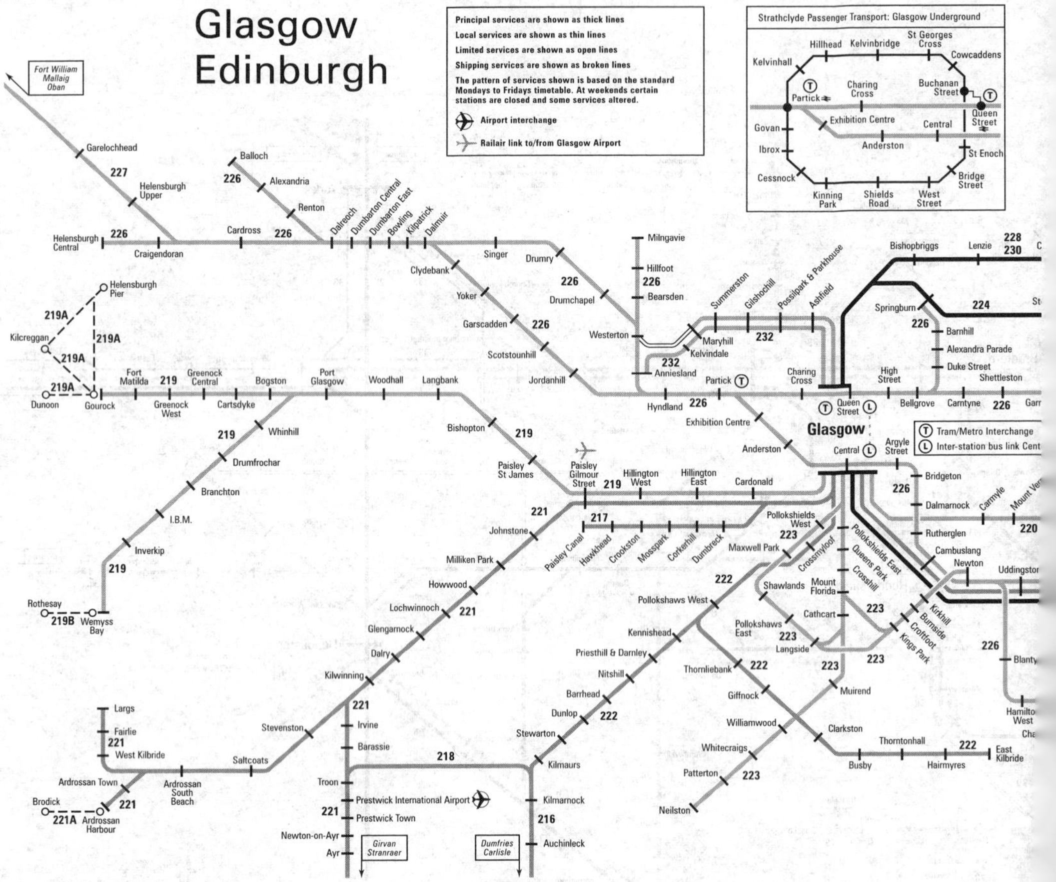

Newcastle

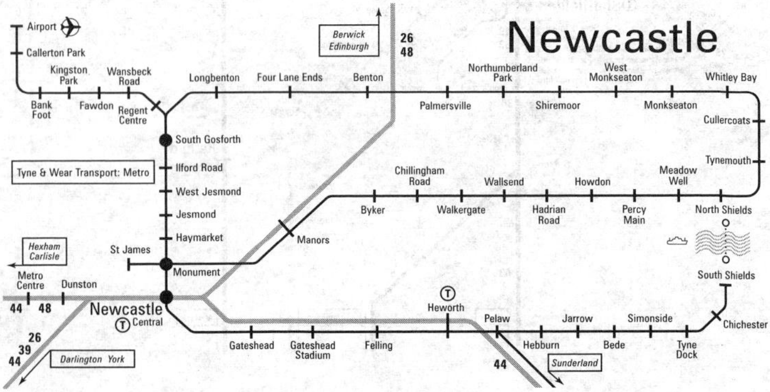

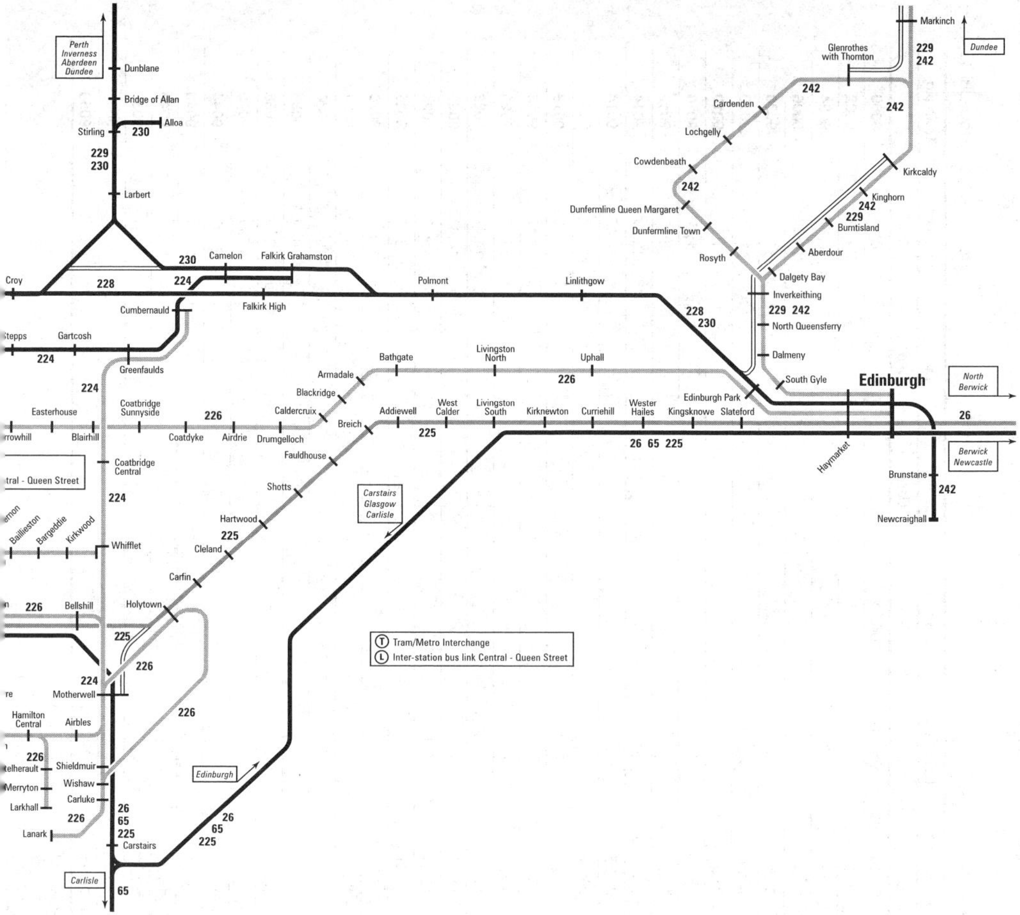
Perth Inverness Aberdeen Dundee
Dunblane
Bridge of Allan
Stirling
Alloa
230
229
230
Larbert
230
Camelon
Falkirk Grahamston
Croy
228
224
Falkirk High
Polmont
Linlithgow
228
230
Cumbernauld
Stepps
Gartcosh
224
Greenfaulds
224
Markinch
Dundee
229
242
Glenrothes with Thornton
242
Cardenden
242
Lochgelly
Cowdenbeath
242
Kirkcaldy
Kinghorn
242
229
Burntisland
Dunfermline Queen Margaret
Dunfermline Town
Aberdour
Rosyth
Dalgety Bay
Inverkeithing
229 242
North Queensferry
Dalmeny
South Gyle
Edinburgh
North Berwick
Edinburgh Park
26
Bathgate
Livingston North
Uphall
226
Armadale
Blackridge
Easterhouse
Coatbridge Sunnyside
226
Caldercruix
Blairhill
Coatdyke
Airdrie
Drumgelloch
Addiewell
West Calder
Livingston South
Kirknewton
Curriehill
Wester Hailes
Kingsknowe
Slateford
Breich
225
26 65 225
Haymarket
Berwick Newcastle
Brunstane
242
Newcraighall
Fauldhouse
Coatbridge Central
Central - Queen Street
224
Shotts
Carstairs Glasgow Carlisle
Hartwood
225
Baillieston
Bargeddie
Kirkwood
Whifflet
Cleland
Carfin
226
Bellshill
Holytown
225
226
Tram/Metro Interchange
Inter-station bus link Central - Queen Street
224
Motherwell
226
Hamilton Central
Airbles
226
Shieldmuir
Wishaw
Merryton
Carluke
Larkhall
226
26
65
225
Lanark
Carstairs
Edinburgh
26
65
225
Carlisle
65

Eurostar™ London St Pancras International → Paris

From 11-Dec-11 to 7-Jul-12

Notes	Mon	Tue	Wed	Thu	Fri	Sat	Sun	London	Ebbsfleet	Ashford	Calais	Lille	Paris	Train No
								Dep	Dep	Dep	Dep	Dep	Arr	
	●	●	●	●	●			05:40	05:58	06:24			09:17	**9080**
						●		06:18		06:55			09:47	**9002**
	●	●	●	●	●			07:01					10:17	**9004**
	●					●		07:31					10:47	**9006**
	●	●	●	●	●			07:54	08:12				11:17	**9008**
						●	●	08:24	08:42				11:47	**9010**
	●				●			08:31					11:47	**9010**
1		●	●	●				08:31					11:47	**9010**
						●		08:54		09:25			12:17	**9012**
	●	●	●	●	●			09:12	09:31	09:55			12:47	**9014**
							●	09:23		09:55			12:47	**9014**
						●		09:31					12:47	**9014**
	●	●	●	●	●		●	10:24	10:42				13:47	**9018**
2						●		10:24	10:42				13:47	**9018**
3						●		11:01					14:17	**9020**
						●		11:24	11:42				14:47	**9022**
		●	●	●	●			11:31					14:47	**9022**
	●	●	●	●	●	●	●	12:24	12:42				15:47	**9024**
							●	13:01					16:17	**9026**
	●	●	●	●	●	●	●	14:01					17:17	**9030**
	●	●	●	●	●		●	15:01					18:17	**9034**
					●		●	15:31					18:47	**9036**
1						●		15:31					18:47	**9036**
	●	●	●	●	●			16:01					19:17	**9038**
	●	●	●	●	●	●	●	16:22		16:55			19:47	**9040**
	●	●	●	●	●	●	●	17:31					20:47	**9044**
	●	●	●	●	●		●	18:01					21:17	**9046**
					●			18:31					21:47	**9048**
	●	●	●	●	●	●	●	19:01					22:17	**9050**
	●	●	●	●	●	●	●	20:01					23:17	**9054**
							●	20:31					23:47	**9056**

Notes 1 Runs until 2 January and from 6 February until 7 July 2 Runs from 21 April until 7 July 3 Runs until 14 April

Eurostar™ Paris → London St Pancras International

From 11-Dec-11 to 7-Jul-12

Notes								Paris	Lille	Calais	Ashford	Ebbsfleet	London	Train No
	Mon	Tue	Wed	Thu	Fri	Sat	Sun	*Dep*	*Dep*	*Dep*	*Arr*	*Arr*	*Arr*	
	●							06:43					08:00	**9005**
	●	●	●	●	●	●		07:13					08:30	**9007**
	●	●	●	●	●			07:43					09:00	**9009**
						●	●	08:13			09:06		09:39	**9011**
	●	●	●	●	●			08:43					10:00	**9013**
	●	●	●	●	●	●	●	09:13				10:18	10:36	**9015**
	●	●	●	●	●			10:13			11:06		11:39	**9019**
						●		10:13					11:30	**9019**
1							●	10:13					11:30	**9019**
	●	●	●	●	●	●	●	11:13					12:30	**9023**
	●				●		●	12:13					13:30	**9027**
1		●	●	●				12:13					13:30	**9027**
	●	●	●	●	●	●	●	13:13				14:18	14:36	**9031**
						●	●	14:13					15:30	**9035**
					●			14:43					16:00	**9037**
	●	●	●	●	●	●	●	15:13			16:06		16:39	**9039**
	●	●	●	●	●	●	●	16:13				17:18	17:36	**9043**
							●	16:43					18:00	**9045**
	●	●	●	●	●	●		17:13					18:30	**9047**
							●	17:13				18:18	18:36	**9047**
					●			17:43					19:00	**9049**
1		●	●	●				17:43					19:00	**9049**
	●	●	●	●	●			18:13				19:18	19:36	**9051**
							●	18:13					19:30	**9051**
							●	18:43					20:00	**9053**
4	●	●	●	●	●	●	●	19:13				20:18	20:36	**9055**
5	●	●	●	●	●	●	●	19:13			20:09		20:41	**9055**
4	●	●	●	●	●	●	●	20:13			21:06		21:39	**9059**
5	●	●	●	●	●	●	●	20:13				21:18	21:39	**9059**
							●	20:43					22:00	**9061**
	●	●	●	●	●			21:13				22:18	22:36	**9063**
							●	21:13					22:30	**9063**

Notes 1 Runs until 2 January and from 6 February until 7 July 2 Runs from 21 April until 7 July 3 Runs until 14 April 4 Runs until 5 February 5 Runs from 6 February

Eurostar™ London St Pancras International → Brussels

From 11-Dec-11 to 7-Jul-12

Notes	Mon	Tue	Wed	Thu	Fri	Sat	Sun	London	Ebbsfleet	Ashford	Calais	Lille	Brussels	Train No
								Dep	*Dep*	*Dep*	*Arr*	*Arr*	*Arr*	
	●	●	●	●	●			06:50	07:04	07:24	08:59	09:30	10:08	**9110**
						●		07:57		08:24		10:26	11:05	**9114**
1	●	●						08:04				10:26	11:05	**9114**
2			●	●	●			08:04				10:26	11:05	**9114**
	●	●	●	●	●			08:57	09:15			11:26	12:05	**9116**
						●	●	08:57	09:15		10:59	11:30	12:08	**9116**
	●	●	●	●	●	●		10:57	11:15			13:26	14:05	**9126**
	●	●	●	●	●	●	●	12:57	13:15		14:59	15:30	16:08	**9132**
	●	●	●	●	●		●	15:04				17:26	18:05	**9140**
	●	●	●	●	●	●	●	16:04				18:26	19:05	**9144**
	●	●	●	●	●		●	17:04				19:26	20:05	**9148**
							●	17:56		18:28		20:26	21:05	**9152**
2	●	●						18:04				20:26	21:05	**9152**
1			●	●	●			18:04				20:26	21:05	**9152**
	●	●	●	●	●	●	●	19:04			20:59	21:30	22:08	**9156**

Notes 1 Runs until 2 January and from 16 February until 7 July 2 Runs until 2 January and from 1 April until 7 July

Eurostar™ Brussels → London St Pancras International

From 11-Dec-11 to 7-Jul-12

Notes	Mon	Tue	Wed	Thu	Fri	Sat	Sun	Brussels	Lille	Calais	Ashford	Ebbsfleet	London	Train No
								Dep	*Dep*	*Dep*	*Arr*	*Arr*	*Arr*	
	●	●	●					06:56	07:36				07:57	**9109**
	●	●	●	●	●	●		07:56	08:34				08:57	**9113**
	●	●	●	●	●	●	●	08:52	09:30	10:01			09:57	**9117**
1	●	●						10:56	11:34				11:57	**9125**
2			●	●	●			10:56	11:34				11:57	**9125**
						●		10:56	11:34				11:57	**9125**
	●	●	●	●	●		●	12:56	13:34			13:45	14:03	**9133**
						●	●	14:52	15:30	16:01		15:45	16:03	**9141**
	●	●	●	●	●			14:56	15:34			15:45	16:03	**9141**
				●	●			15:56	16:34			16:45	17:03	**9145**
							●	15:56	16:34				16:57	**9145**
	●	●	●	●	●	●	●	16:56	17:34		17:33		18:12	**9149**
	●	●	●	●	●			17:56	18:34			18:46	19:05	**9153**
2	●	●						18:56	19:34				19:57	**9157**
1			●	●	●			18:56	19:34				19:57	**9157**
							●	18:56	19:34				19:57	**9157**
	●	●	●	●	●	●	●	19:52	20:30	21:01		20:45	21:03	**9161**

Notes 1 Runs until 2 January and from 16 February until 7 July 2 Runs until 2 January and from 1 April until 7 July

Eurostar™ London St Pancras International → Disneyland™ Paris Route

From 11-Dec-11 to 01-Jul-12

Notes	Mon	Tue	Wed	Thu	Fri	Sat	Sun	London	Ebbsfleet	Ashford	Lille	Marne La Vallée	Train No
								Dep	*Dep*	*Dep*	*Arr*	*Arr*	
1, 2	●		●	●	●		●	10:17	10:35	10:58	12:54	13:57	**9074**
3						●		09:17	09:35	09:58	11:54	13:04	**9074**
4		●	●	●	●			10:17	10:35	10:58		13:57	**9074**

Notes	Mon	Tue	Wed	Thu	Fri	Sat	Sun	Marne La Vallée	Lille	Ashford	Ebbsfleet	London	Train No
								Dep	*Dep*	*Arr*	*Arr*	*Arr*	
5, 6	●		●	●	●		●	18:02		19:03	19:28	19:47	**9057**
7						●		15:40		16:36	16:59	17:24	**9071**

Notes

1 Does not run on Tuesdays except on 20 and 27 December, 3 and 10 April, 29 May, 5 June
2 Does not run on Saturdays except on 9 June
3 Runs on the following Saturdays only – 17, 24 and 31 December, 11 and 18 February, 31 March, 7 and 14 April, 5 and 26 May, 2 June
4 Runs Tuesday–Friday from 14–17 February only
5 Does not run on Saturdays except on 17 December, 11 and 18 February, 31 March, 7 and 14 April, 5 and 26 May, 2 and 9 June
6 Does not run on Tuesdays except on 20 and 27 December, 14 February, 3 and 10 April, 29 May, 5 June
7 Runs on 31 December only

Station key

London	St Pancras International
Ebbsfleet	Ebsfleet International, Kent
Ashford	Ashford International, Kent
Calais	Calais Fréthun
Lille	Lille Europe
Brussels	Brussels-Mid/Zuid
Paris	Gare du Nord
Disneyland® Paris	Marne-la-Vallée

Variations

Amended Eurostar services may run on and around Public Holidays and for engineering works. For up to date information, please refer to the Eurostar website – eurostar.com